2019 County and City Extra
Annual Metro, City, and County Data Book
27th Edition

2019 County and City Extra

Annual Metro, City, and County Data Book

27th Edition

Edited by Deirdre A. Gaquin
and Mary Meghan Ryan

Lanham, MD

Published by Bernan Press
An imprint of The Rowman & Littlefield Publishing Group, Inc.
4501 Forbes Boulevard, Suite 200, Lanham, Maryland 20706
www.rowman.com
800-462-6420

Unit A, Whitacre Mews, 26-34 Stannary Street, London SE11 4AB

ISBN: 978-1-64143-332-7
E-ISBN: 978-1-64143-333-4

∞™ The paper used in this publication meets the minimum requirements of American National Standard for Information Sciences—Permanence of Paper for Printed Library Materials, ANSI/NISO Z39.48-1992.

Printed in the United States of America.

Contents

Page

vii **Introduction**
New and Updated Information for the 2019 Edition
Rankings
Subjects Covered and Volume Organization
Symbols
Sources

xi **Subjects Covered, by Geography Type**

xiv **National Data Maps**

1 **Part A. States**
3 State Highlights and Rankings
17 State Column Headings
24 Table A

51 **Part B. States and Counties**
53 County Highlights and Rankings
69 State and County Column Headings
73 Table B

773 **Part C. Metropolitan Areas**
775 Metropolitan Area Highlights and Rankings
793 Metropolitan Area Column Headings
797 Table C

895 **Part D. Cities of 25,000 or More**
897 City Highlights and Rankings
907 City Column Headings
910 Table D

1175 **Part E. Congressional Districts of the 116th Congress**
1177 Congressional District Highlights and Rankings
1184 Congressional District Column Headings
1186 Table E

Appendices
A-1 A. Geographic Concepts and Codes
B-1 B. Metropolitan Statistical Areas, Metropolitan Divisions, and Components (as defined July 2015)
C-1 C. Core Based Statistical Areas (Metropolitan and Micropolitan), Metropolitan Divisions, and Components (as defined August, 2017)
D-1 D. Maps of Congressional Districts and States
E-1 E. Cities by County
F-1 F. Source Notes and Explanations

INTRODUCTION

County and City Extra is an annual publication that provides the most up-to-date statistical information available for every state, county, metropolitan area, and congressional district, as well as all cities in the United States with a 2010 census population of 25,000 or more. Data for places, including towns and cities with populations of fewer than 25,000 people are published by Bernan Press in a separate companion volume, *Places, Towns and Townships*, now in its sixth edition. These two volumes are designed to meet the needs of libraries, businesses, and other organizations or individuals who desire convenient and timely sources of the most frequently sought information about geographic entities within the United States. The annual updating of *County and City Extra* for 27 years ensures its stature as a reliable and authoritative source for statistical information.

Bernan Press also publishes a companion volume, the *State and Metropolitan Area Data Book*, previously published by the Census Bureau. The recently published second edition provides an expanded collection of data about states and metropolitan areas, including micropolitan areas and their component counties. Another recent addition is the *County and City Extra: Special Historical Edition, 1790-2010* with data from the earliest days of the nation, and states, counties, and cities from their beginnings.

County and City Extra, Places, Towns and Townships, and *State and Metropolitan Area Data Book* are large volumes, but are not big enough to accommodate the wealth of information from the decennial census and the American Community Survey. Two additional volumes in the *County and City Extra* series include this information. *County and City Extra—Special Decennial Census Edition* provides detailed population and housing data from the 2010 census and was published by Bernan Press in December 2011. *The Who, What, and Where of America—Understanding the American Community Survey*, recently released in its seventh edition, includes social and economic details from the ongoing American Community Survey, and the *County and City Extra* Series includes additional books on special topics, such as the recently published *Education and the American Workforce*.

The American Community Survey (ACS) is a national survey that has replaced the census long form as the key source of detailed social and economic data. *County and City Extra* includes data from both the 2010 census and the ACS.

New and Updated Information for the 2019 Edition

This edition includes recently released information from the 2017 Census of Agriculture. In addition, it also includes voting and registration information from November 2018.

Updated data include 2018 population estimates for states, counties, metropolitan areas, and cities. Also included are the latest available data for education, vital statistics, income and poverty, employment and unemployment, residential construction, production by industry, health resources, crime, land use, city government finances, and many other topics.

Table E (Congressional Districts) includes a wide selection of 2017 American Community Survey data, Business Patterns, and Social Security data for the 116th Congress, as well as recently released data from the 2017 Census of Agriculture for the congressional districts of the 116th Congress, along with the 116th Congressional representatives.

In August 2017, the Office of Management and Budget released an updated list of Core Based Statistical Areas (metropolitan and micropolitan areas) based on the 2010 census and some changes in the way these areas are defined. Only one new metropolitan area was delineated, as the Twin Falls Idaho micropolitan area gained enough population to be designated metropolitan. Because most data sources in this book still followed the 2015 metropolitan area delineations, those are used in Table C. Appendixes B and C provide details about the component counties of these metropolitan and micropolitan areas and their 2010 census and 2017 estimated populations. Appendix D has a map for each state showing the metropolitan and micropolitan areas.

This edition includes data from the 2010 census, 2018 population estimates, and the ACS. Annual ACS data are available for all states and all metropolitan areas (all geographic areas with populations of 65,000 or more), but five years are needed to build a sample large enough for reliable estimates for all counties The Census Bureau no longer releases 3-year data which were previously available for areas with populations of 20,000 or more. These have now been replaced with 1-year Supplemental Estimates which are used in this book for Table D, cities with populations of 25,000 or more.

With the now annual release of 1-year and 5-year estimates, *County and City Extra* uses ACS data for all geographic areas. ACS 1-year data for 2017 are included in Table A (States), Table C (metropolitan areas) and Table E (Congressional Districts)—all areas with populations of 65,000 or more. Table D (cities) uses the 1-year supplemental estimates which are less detailed than the regular 1-year estimates. Table B (Counties) includes 5-year data (2013–2017). The release of 5-year data for even the smallest geographic areas means that annual social and economic characteristics are available for all counties and cities.

Although some of the state data are also included in Table B (States and Counties), the separate state data table offers several important features:

- Additional data not available at the county level are provided. Examples include population projections, health insurance coverage, number of immigrants, personal tax payments, information about health service firms not subject to federal tax, and exports by state of origin.

- Additional data that exceeds the space limitations for counties can be found for states. Examples are age of householder, more detailed information about employment in retail trade and services, and detailed government employment and finance data.

- State totals can be found more quickly and compared more readily.

Appendix F, **Source Notes and Explanations**, includes internet references for all data sources. This is especially helpful in today's environment where the data sources are updated at a faster pace. The sources referenced here can be used to track down additional information too cumbersome for this book. Some of the data can be directly found in data tables on the websites; some can be assembled through online access tools; others can be obtained by downloading files and processing them with statistical software; and some need to be ordered from the agencies.

Rankings

The rankings present the geography types by various subjects, including population, land area, population density, population change, age, immigration, birth rate, housing characteristics, race, Hispanic origin, educational attainment, income, unemployment rate, per capita local taxes, poverty rate, value of agricultural products, and violent crime rate.

Subjects Covered and Volume Organization

A summary of the **subjects covered** in each of the five tables appears on **page xi**. The **colored map** portfolio begins on **page xv**.

The main body of this volume contains five basic parts. Each part includes a table that is preceded by highlights and rankings, as well as the complete column headings for the table. **Part A**, which begins on **page 1**, contains data for states. **Part B**, beginning on **page 51**, contains information for states and counties. The county geography codes include county typology codes from the Economic Research Service of the Department of Agriculture. These codes characterize counties by size of the largest place as well as by other criteria for nonmetropolitan counties. (See Appendix A for the definition of each code.) **Part C**, beginning on **page 773**, contains information for metropolitan areas. Statistics for cities with a 2010 census population of 25,000 or more can be found in **Part D**, which begins on **page 895**. **Part E**, beginning on **page 1175**, contains data for the congressional districts of the

116th Congress.

A contents page preceding tables B through E lists the page number on which the data for a given geographic area begin. Counties and cities are listed alphabetically by state. Metropolitan areas are listed alphabetically, except that metropolitan divisions are listed alphabetically within the metropolitan statistical area of which they are components. Congressional districts are listed in numeric order within states.

The appendixes include definitions of geographic concepts (**Appendix A**), sources and definitions of each data item included in this volume (**Appendix F**), an alphabetical listing of metropolitan areas with their component counties delineated as of July 2015, with 2010 census populations (**Appendix B**), a listing of metropolitan and micropolitan areas and their component counties as of August 2017, with 2010 census populations and 2018 estimated populations (**Appendix C**), a list of cities by county (**Appendix E**), and maps showing congressional districts in the United States; and metropolitan areas, counties and selected places within each state (**Appendix D**).

Symbols

D   Indicates that the number has been withheld to avoid disclosure of information pertaining to a specific organization or individual, or because the number does not meet statistical standards for publication.

NA   Indicates that data are not available.

X   Indicates that data are not applicable or are not meaningful for this geographic unit.

In this volume, a figure that is less than half the unit of measure shown will appear as zero.

Sources

All of the data in this volume have been obtained from federal government sources. For a complete list of these sources, see **Appendix F**.

Data included in this volume meet the publication standards established by the U.S. Census Bureau and the other federal statistical agencies from which they were obtained. Every effort has been made to select data that are accurate, meaningful, and useful. All data from censuses, surveys, and administrative records are subject to errors arising from factors such as sampling variability, reporting errors, incomplete coverage, nonresponse, imputations, and processing error. Responsibility of the editors and publishers of this volume is limited to reasonable care in the reproduction and presentation of data obtained from sources believed to be reliable.

County and City Extra: Annual Metro, City, and County Data

Book is part of Bernan Press's *County and City Extra* series. The editors of *County and City Extra* acknowledge the contributions of the late Courtenay Slater and George Hall, the originators of this publication. Their initial contributions continue to enrich the *County and City Extra* series. As always, we are especially grateful to the many federal agency personnel who assisted us in obtaining the data, provided excellent resources on their websites, and patiently answered questions.

Deirdre A. Gaquin has been a data use consultant to private organizations, government agencies, and universities for over 30 years. Prior to that, she was Director of Data Access Services at Data Use & Access Laboratories, a pioneer in private sector distribution of federal statistical data. A former President of the Association of Public Data Users, Ms. Gaquin has served on numerous boards, panels, and task forces concerned with federal statistical data and has worked on five decennial censuses. She holds a Master of Urban Planning (MUP) degree from Hunter College. Ms. Gaquin is also an editor of Bernan Press's *The Who, What, and Where of America: Understanding the American Community Survey*; *Places, Towns and Townships*; *The Congressional District Atlas*, *The Almanac of American Education, Race and Employment in America,* and *the State and Metropolitan Area Data Book.*

Mary Meghan Ryan is the senior research editor for Bernan Press. She is also the editor for the *Handbook of U.S. Labor Statistics, State Profiles,* and the associate editor for *Business Statistics of the United States.*

SUBJECTS COVERED, BY GEOGRAPHY TYPE

State data begin on page 1
County data begin on page 51
Metropolitan area data begin on page 773
City data begin on page 895
Congressional district data begin on page 1175

Subject	Column number				
	Table A. States	Table B. States and Counties	Table C. Metropolitan Areas	Table D. Cities	Table E. Congressional Districts
Land area	1	1	1	1	1
Population					
Total persons, 1990	31				
Total persons, 2000	32	20	20	23	
Total persons, 2010	33	21	21	24	
Total persons, 2017					2
Total persons, 2018	2	2	2	2	
Rank, 2018	3	3	3	3	
Persons per square mile	4	4	4	4	
Race and Hispanic or Latino origin, 2010	45-50				
Race and Hispanic or Latino origin, 2017				5-10	4-11
Race and Hispanic or Latino origin, 2018	5–9	5-9	5-9		
Percent female	21	19	19	22	12
Foreign-born population	22			11	13
Percent born in state of residence	23				14
Immigrants	24				
Age distribution, 2010	52-61				
Age distribution, 2017				12-20	15-23
Age distribution, 2018	10-19	10-18	10-18		
Median age	20, 62			21	24
Percent population change, 1990–2000	34				
Percent population change, 2000–2010	35	22	22	25	
Percent population change, 2010–2018	36	23	23	26	
Components of population change	37-41	24-26	24-26		
Daytime population		33-34	33-34		
Population projections	42-44				
Households					
Total households, 2010	64				
Total households, 2017	25	27	27	27	28
Total households, 2013–2017		27-31			
Percent change in number of households	26, 65				
Household type	28-30, 67-68	29-31	29-31	29-33	30-33
Persons per household	27, 66	28	28	28	29
Persons in group quarters		32	32	34	34-39
Housing					
Housing units in 2010	69-78			47-49	
Housing units in 2017	79-92		89-96	50-58	40-45
Housing units in 2018		87-88	87-88		
Housing units in 2013–2017		89-96			
Percent change in number of housing units	70, 80	88	88	48	
Housing costs	73-77, 83-90	91-95	91-95	52	43-45
Substandard housing units	78, 91	96			
Percent with computer and internet access			96	57-58	
Commuting patterns				55-56	
Percent who lived in same house one year ago	92			59	
Percent who lived in different place one year ago				60	
New residential construction	93-95	169-170	169-170	69-71	
Manufactured housing	96				

SUBJECTS COVERED, BY GEOGRAPHY TYPE — Continued

State data begin on page 1
County data begin on page 51
Metropolitan area data begin on page 773
City data begin on page 895
Congressional district data begin on page 1175

Subject	Column number				
	Table A. States	Table B. States and Counties	Table C. Metropolitan Areas	Table D. Cities	Table E. Congressional Districts
Vital statistics					
Births	97-98	35-36	35-36		
Deaths	99-103	37-38	37-38		
Health					
Persons in nursing facilities				33	37
Medicare enrollees	106	41-43	41-43		
Persons lacking health insurance	104-105	39-40	39-40		59
Crime	107-110	44-47	44-47	35-38	
Education					
School enrollment	111-112	48-49	48-49		25
Educational attainment	113-116	50-51	50-51	39-41	26-27
Expenditures for education	117-118	52-53	52-53		
Income					
Personal income	134-149	62-71	62-71		
Per capita income	122, 136, 149	54, 64	54, 64		46
Household income	123-126	55-58	55-58	42-44	47-48
Family and non-family income				45-46	
Earnings by gender				47-49	
Poverty	127-133	59-61	59-61		49-50
Food stamps					51
Personal income by type	138-140	66-70	66-70		
Earnings by industry	150-158	72-83	72-83		
Transfer payments	141-146	71	71		
Gross state product	159				
Personal tax payments	147				
Disposable personal income	148-149				
Social Security	160-162	84-86	84-86		60-62
Individual income taxes		197-199	197-199		
Labor Force and Employment					
Labor force and unemployment	167-171	97-100	97-100	61-68	52-54
Employment in selected occupations	163-166	101-103	101-103		55-58
Employment by industry	172-183, 207-216	104-112	104-112		73-84
Exports of goods produced	119-121				
Establishments, employment, sales, and payroll					
Manufacturing	207-216	151-154	151-154	88-91	
Construction	217-221				
Wholesale trade	222-226	135-138	135-138	72-75	
Retail trade	227-235	139-142	139-142	76-79	
Information	236-246				
Utilities	247-251				
Transportation and warehousing	252-256				
Finance and insurance	257-261				
Real estate and rental and leasing	262-266	143-146	143-146	80-83	
Professional, scientific, and technical services	267-275	147-150	147-150	84-87	
Health care and social assistance	276-289	159-162	159-162	100-103	

SUBJECTS COVERED, BY GEOGRAPHY TYPE — Continued

State data begin on page 1
County data begin on page 51
Metropolitan area data begin on page 773
City data begin on page 895
Congressional district data begin on page 1175

Subject	Column number				
	Table A. States	Table B. States and Counties	Table C. Metropolitan Areas	Table D. Cities	Table E. Congressional Districts
Arts, entertainment and recreation	290-294			96-99	
Accommodation and food services	295-300	155-158	155-158	92-95	
Other services, except public administration	301-308	163-166	163-166	104-108	
Nonemployer businesses		167-168	167-168		
Government employment	309-314	171, 194-196	171, 194-196	108	
Government payroll	315-330	172-179	172-179	109-116	
Government finances	331-350	180-193	180-193	117-139	
Agriculture	184-202	113-132	113-132		63-72
Land and water	203-206	133-134	133-134		
Voting and elections	351-355				
Climate				140-146	

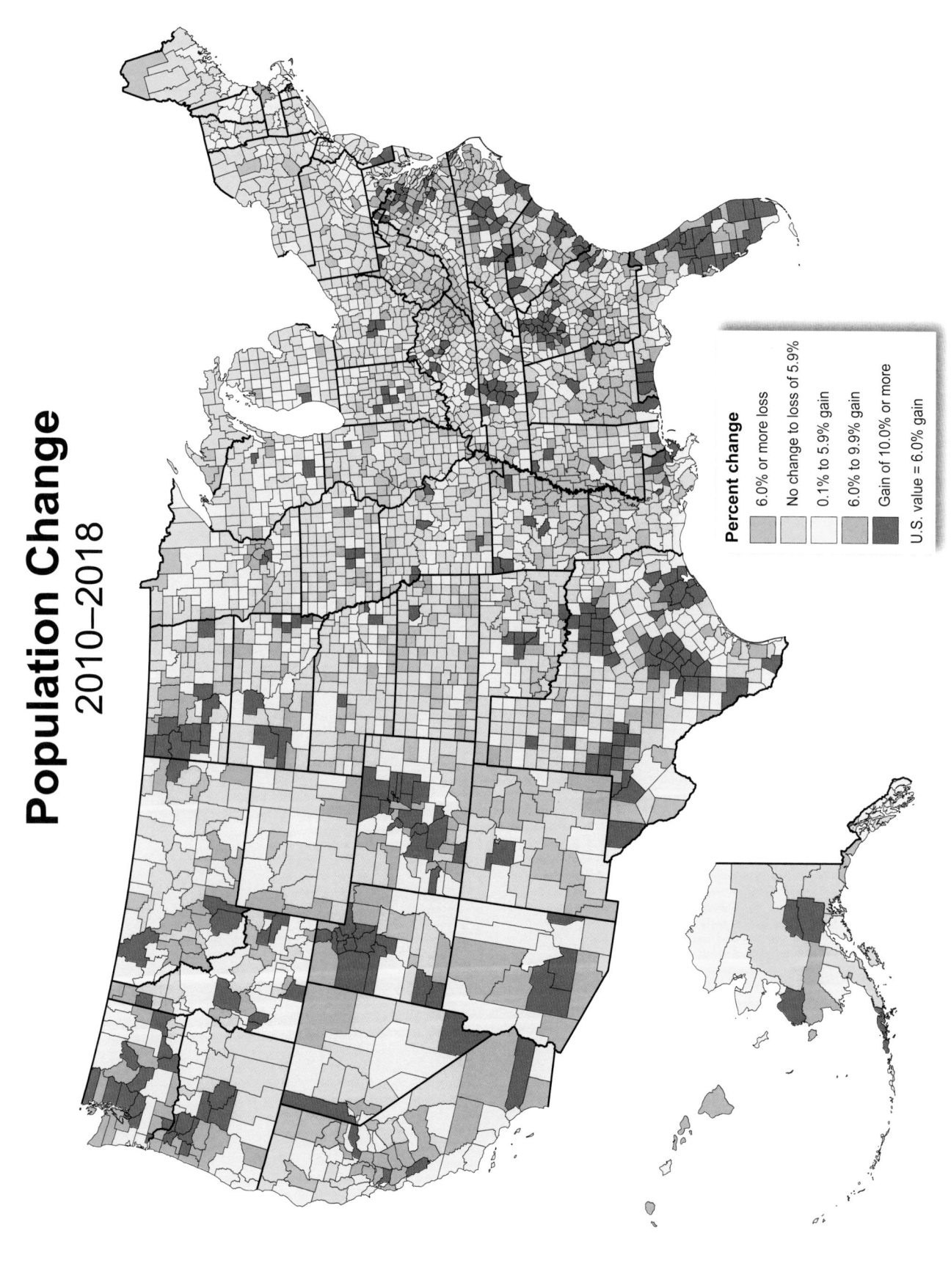

Population Change
2010–2018

Percent change

- 6.0% or more loss
- No change to loss of 5.9%
- 0.1% to 5.9% gain
- 6.0% to 9.9% gain
- Gain of 10.0% or more

U.S. value = 6.0% gain

Black, Not Hispanic or Latino, Population
2018

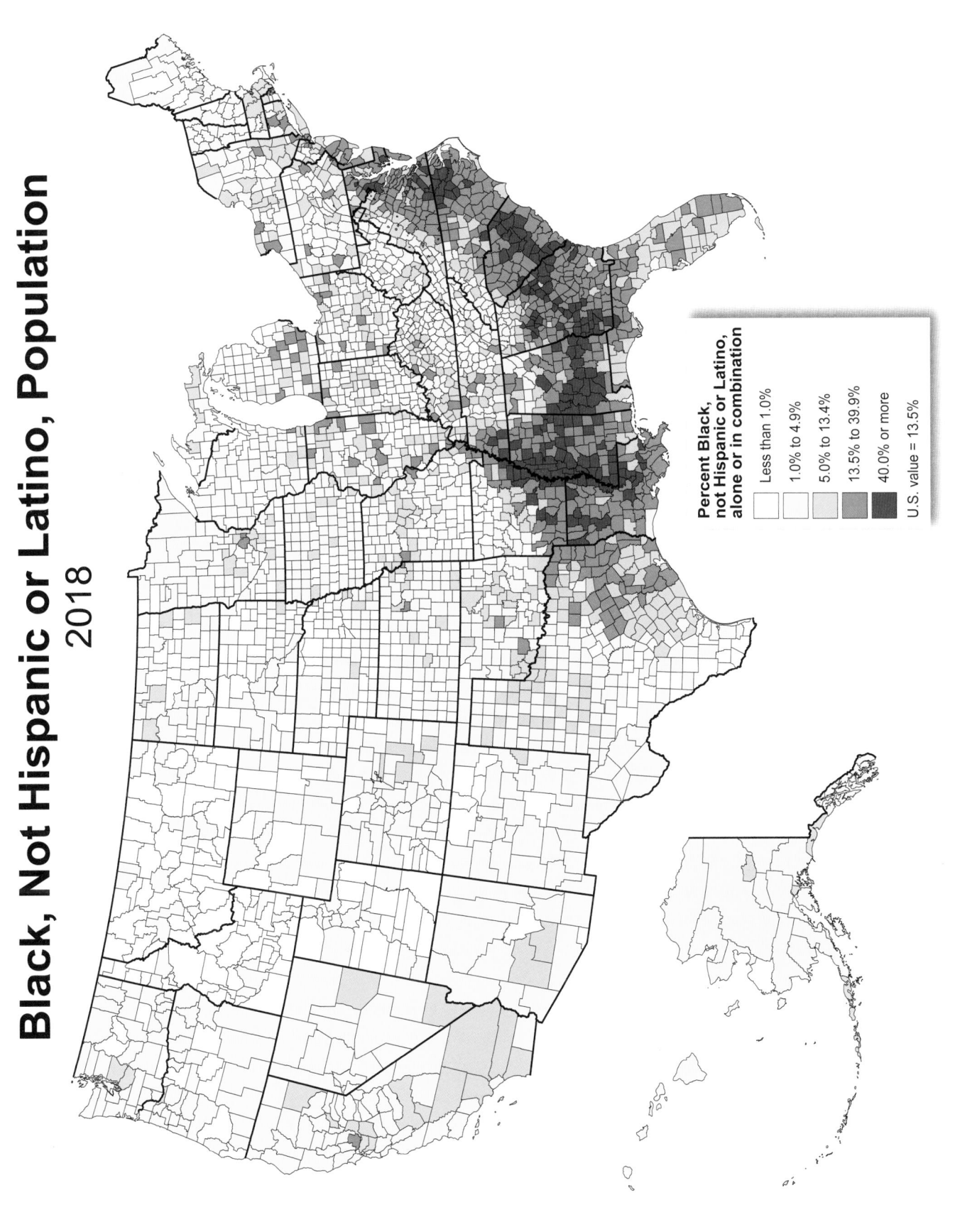

**Percent Black,
not Hispanic or Latino,
alone or in combination**

- Less than 1.0%
- 1.0% to 4.9%
- 5.0% to 13.4%
- 13.5% to 39.9%
- 40.0% or more

U.S. value = 13.5%

Hispanic or Latino Population
2018

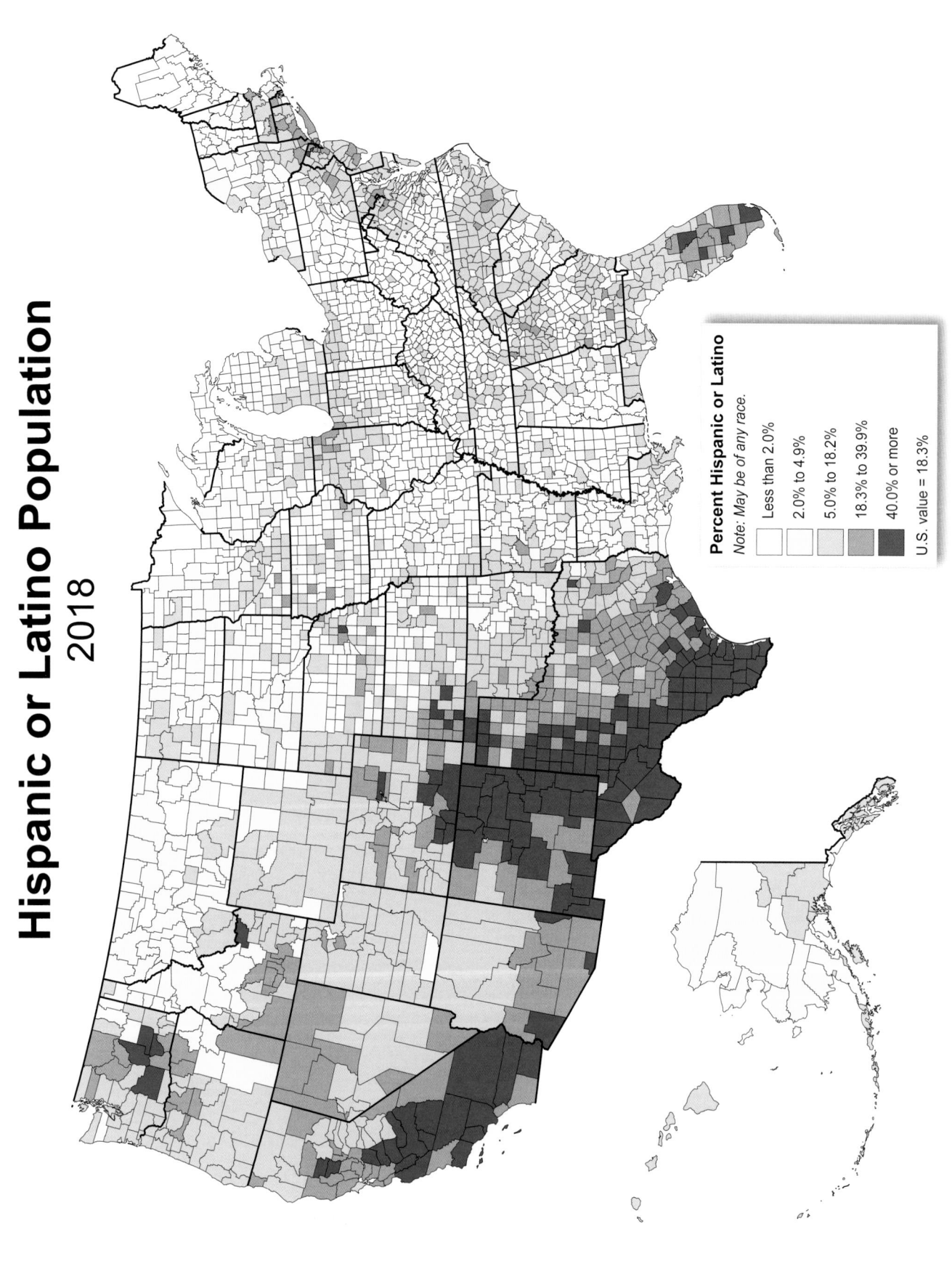

Percent Hispanic or Latino

Note: May be of any race.

Less than 2.0%
2.0% to 4.9%
5.0% to 18.2%
18.3% to 39.9%
40.0% or more

U.S. value = 18.3%

Population Under 18 Years Old
2018

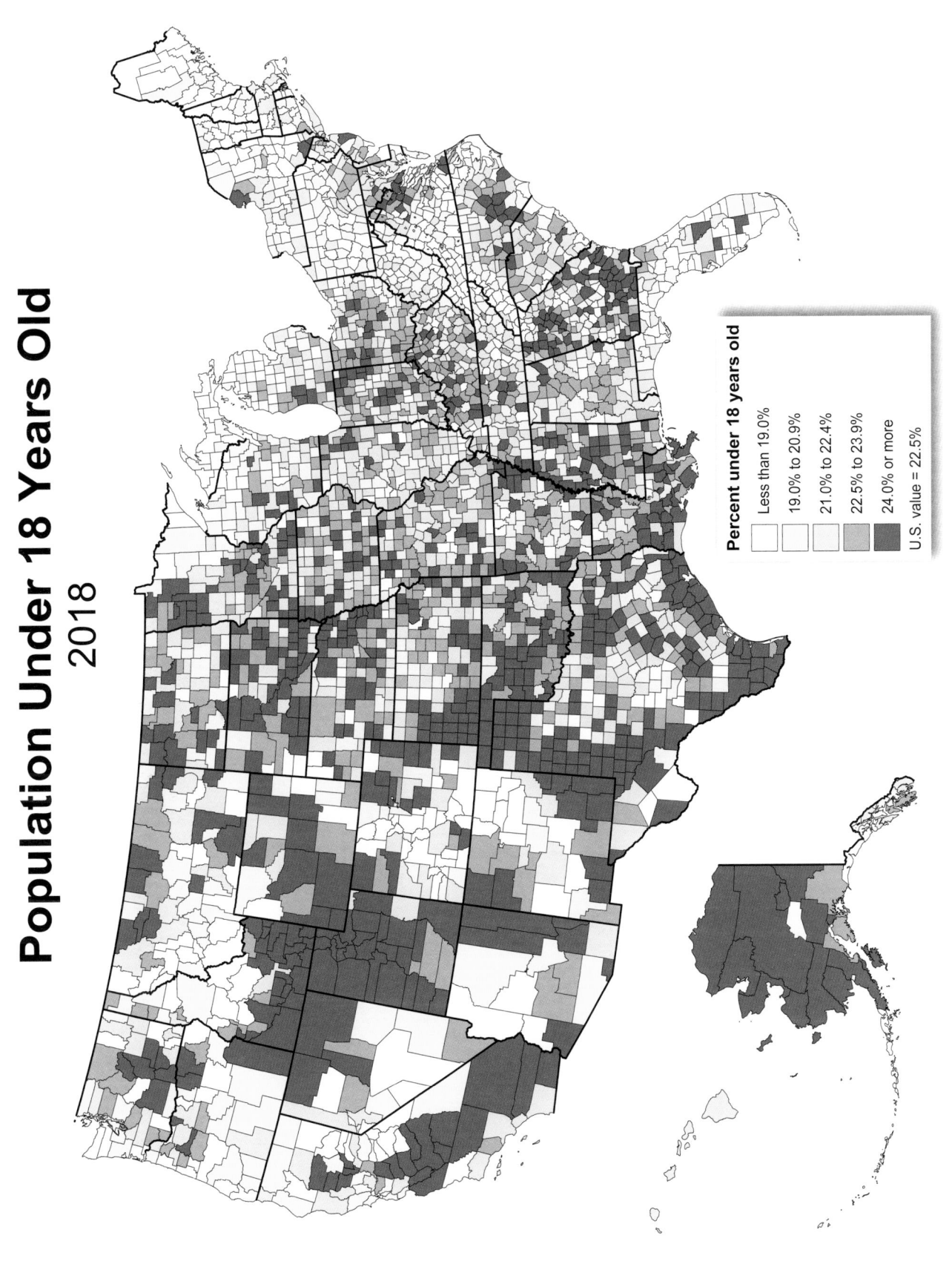

Percent under 18 years old

- Less than 19.0%
- 19.0% to 20.9%
- 21.0% to 22.4%
- 22.5% to 23.9%
- 24.0% or more

U.S. value = 22.5%

Population 65 Years Old and Over
2018

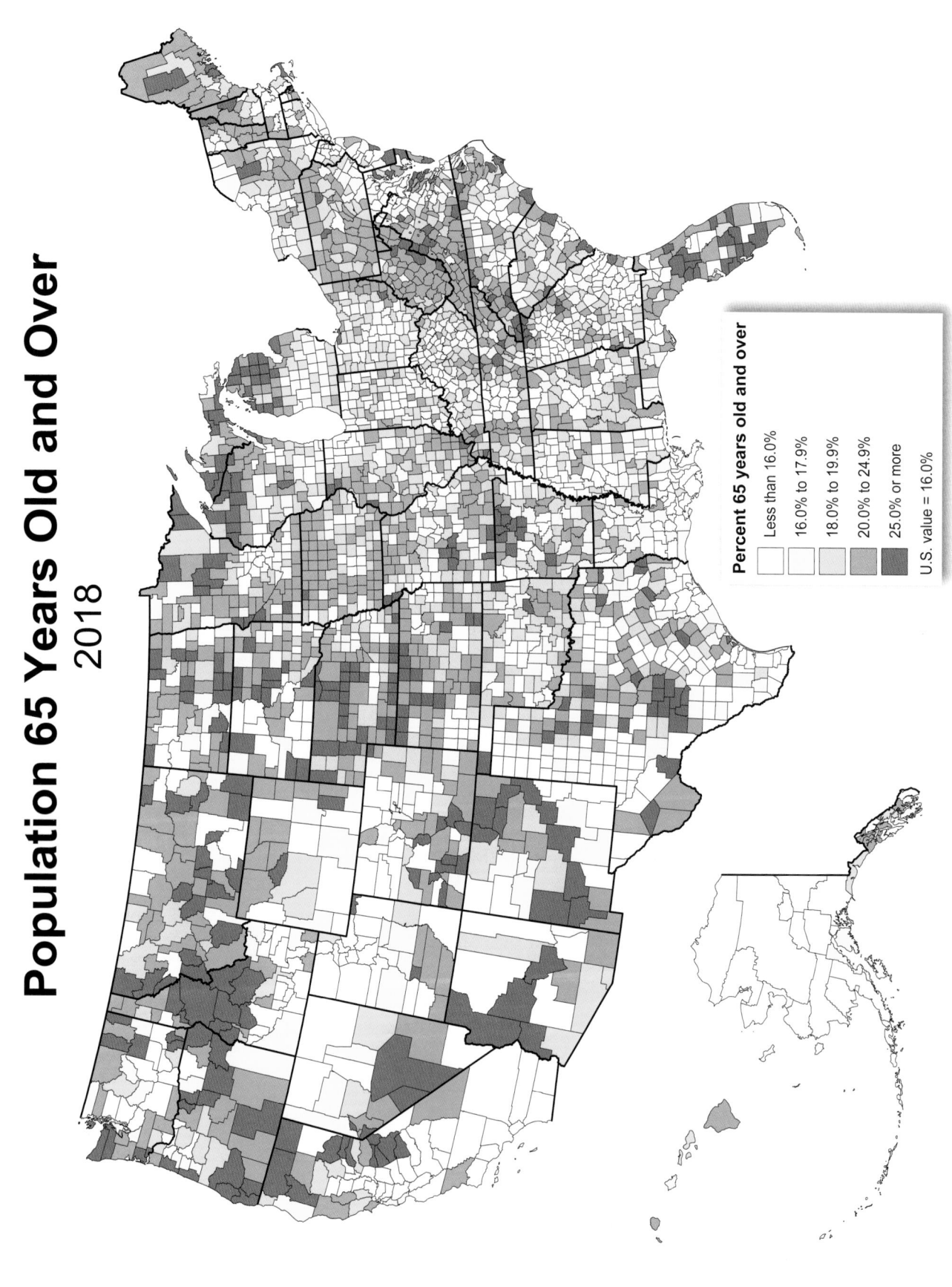

Percent 65 years old and over

Less than 16.0%
16.0% to 17.9%
18.0% to 19.9%
20.0% to 24.9%
25.0% or more

U.S. value = 16.0%

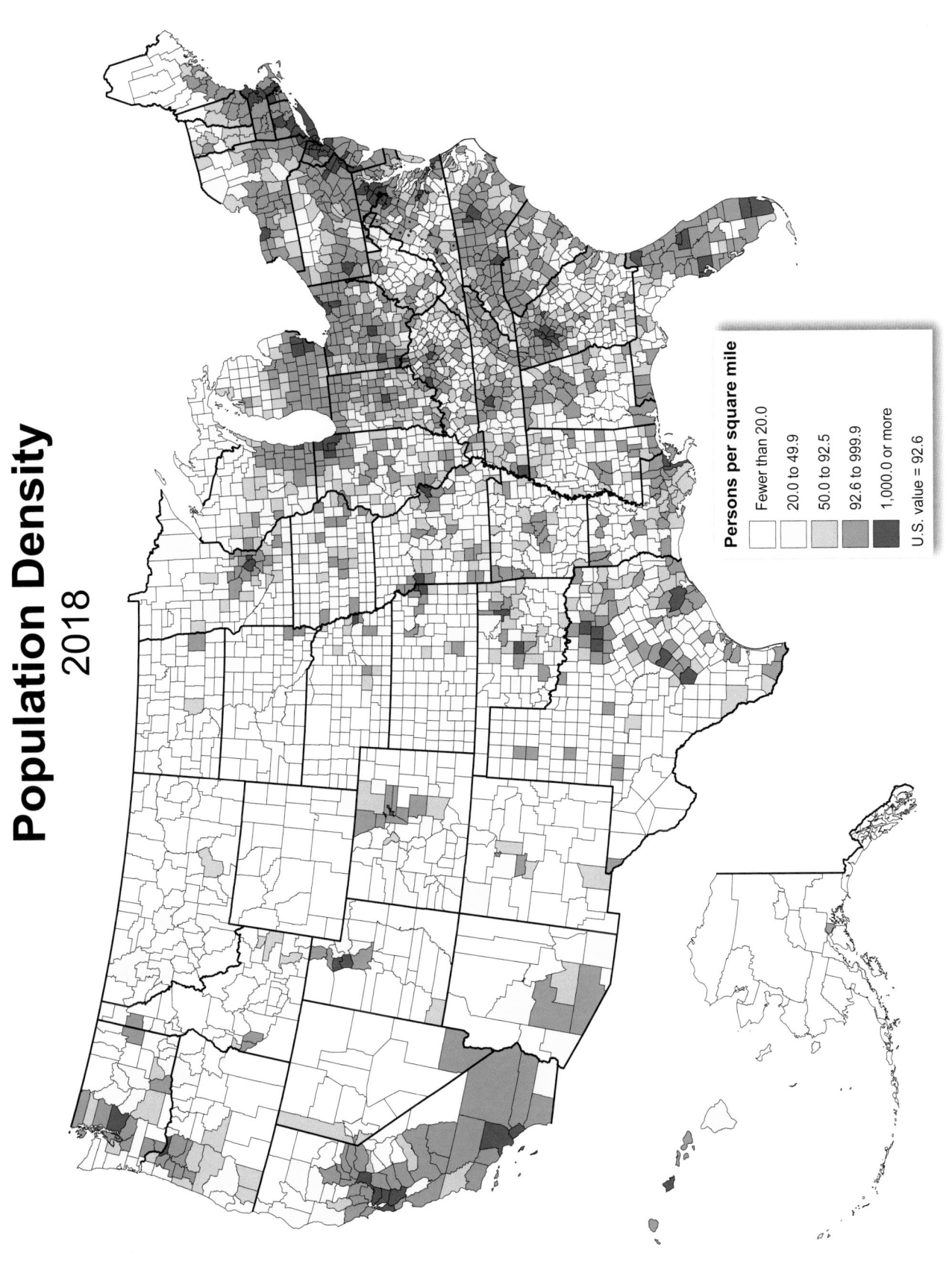

Population Density
2018

Persons per square mile

Fewer than 20.0
20.0 to 49.9
50.0 to 92.5
92.6 to 999.9
1,000.0 or more

U.S. value = 92.6

Unemployment Rate
2018

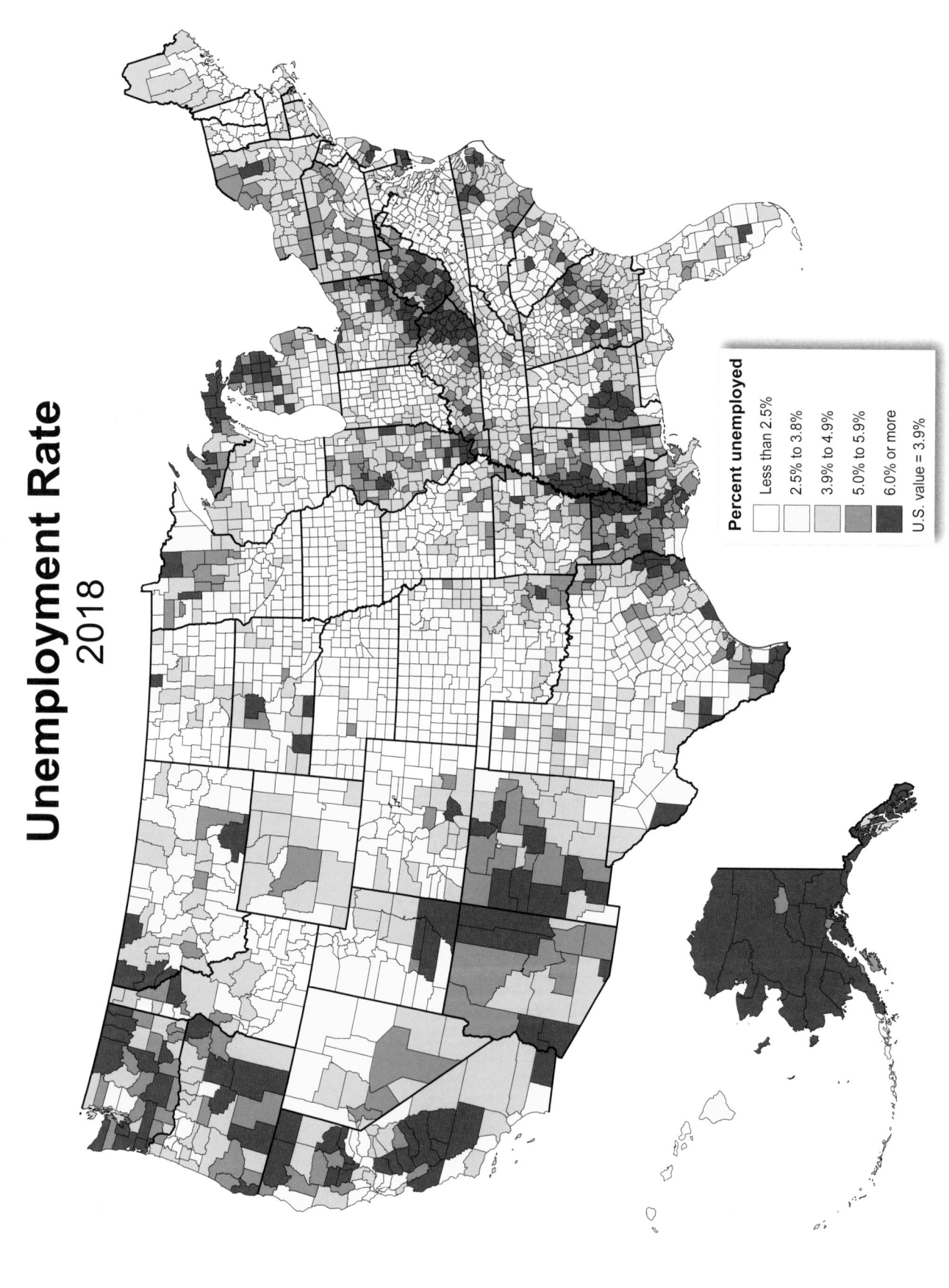

Percent unemployed

- Less than 2.5%
- 2.5% to 3.8%
- 3.9% to 4.9%
- 5.0% to 5.9%
- 6.0% or more

U.S. value = 3.9%

Earnings from Manufacturing

2017

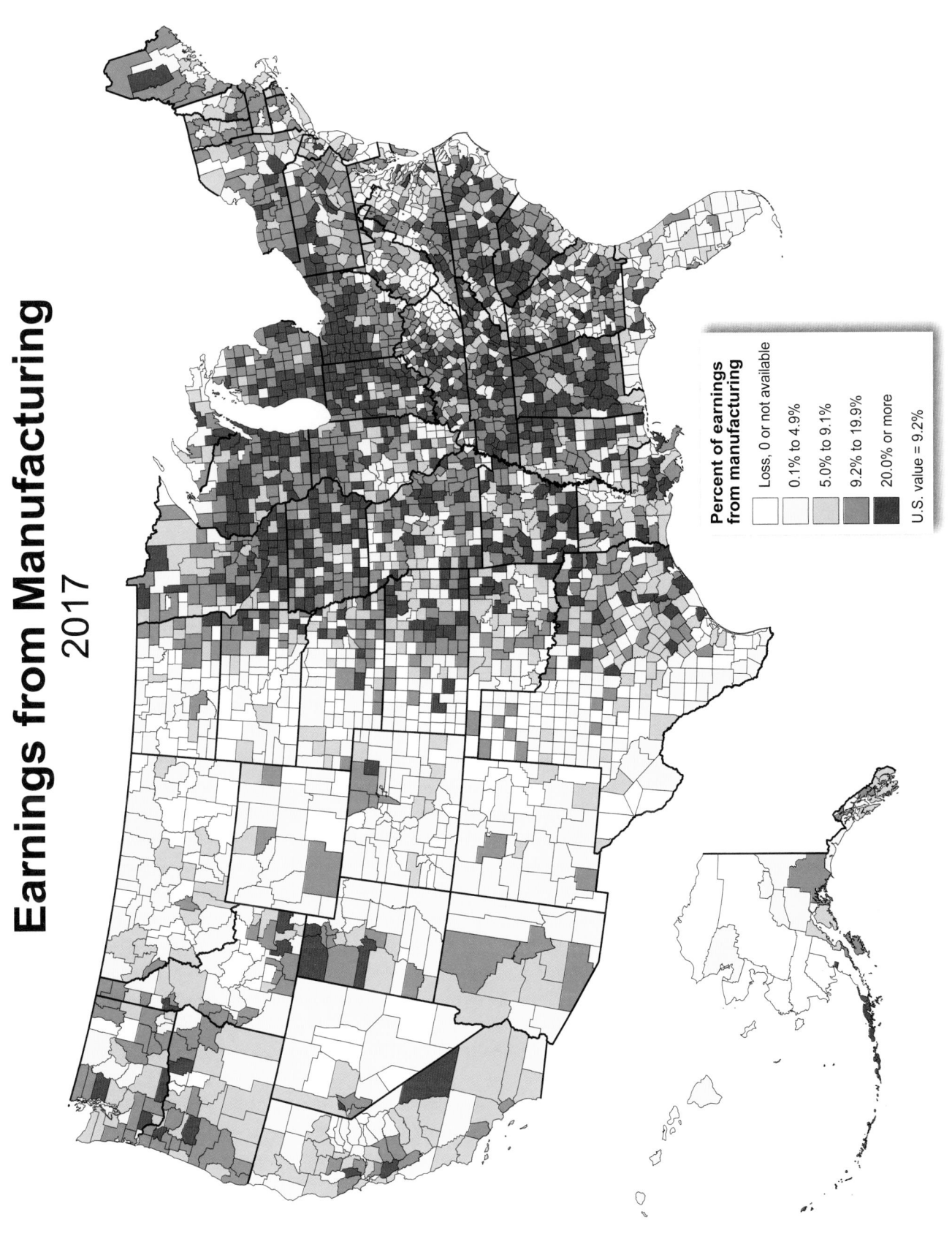

Percent of earnings from manufacturing

- Loss, 0 or not available
- 0.1% to 4.9%
- 5.0% to 9.1%
- 9.2% to 19.9%
- 20.0% or more

U.S. value = 9.2%

PART A.

States

(For explanation of symbols, see page viii)

Page

3   State Highlights and Rankings
17   State Column Headings
24   Table A

Part A—States

1

State Highlights and Rankings

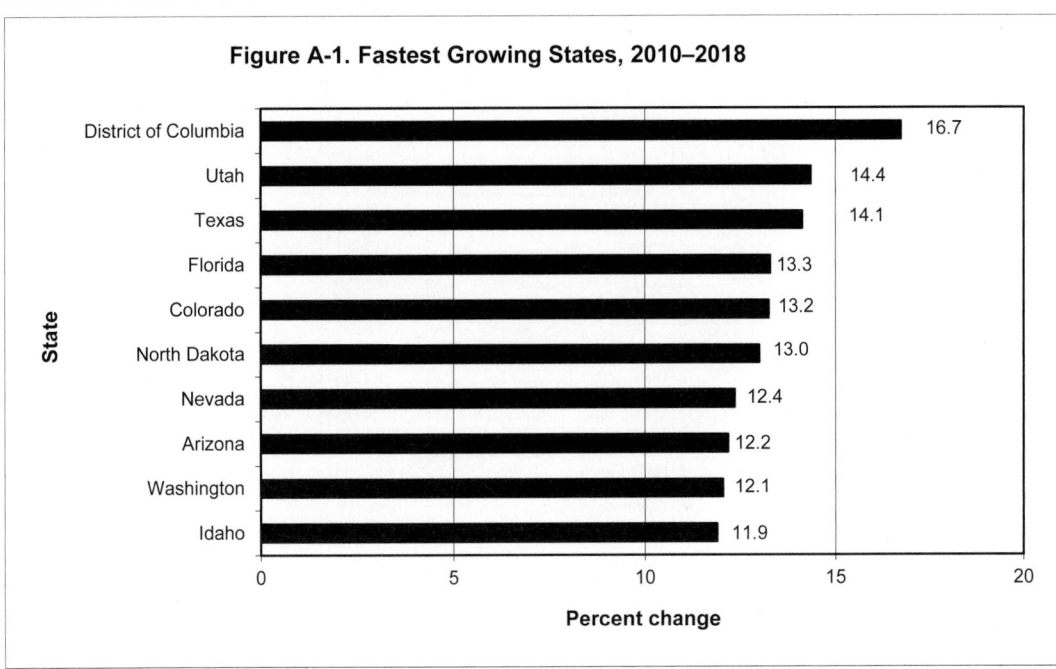

Figure A-1. Fastest Growing States, 2010–2018

State	Percent change
District of Columbia	16.7
Utah	14.4
Texas	14.1
Florida	13.3
Colorado	13.2
North Dakota	13.0
Nevada	12.4
Arizona	12.2
Washington	12.1
Idaho	11.9

There is no simple relationship between population size and land area for most of the geographic entities included in this publication. According to the Census Bureau's 2018 estimates, state populations ranged from a high of over 39 million in California to a low of 577,737 in Wyoming. (The median population for states—with half having a larger population and half having a smaller population—was over 4.4 million people.) California was also one of the largest states in land area (ranking third). Alaska was by far the largest state in area; it was more than twice the size of Texas, the second-largest state, even though its population rank was close to the bottom (ranked 48th). Texas was also the second-largest state in terms of total population with 28.7 million residents. At the other end of the geographic size spectrum were many of the New England states (with Rhode Island ranking as the smallest), plus Delaware, Hawaii, and New Jersey. As a consequence of differing area size and population rank, New Jersey was the most densely settled state, with 1,211.3 persons per square mile while Alaska was the least densely settled, with about 1.3 persons per square mile. California, which had the largest population and third-largest land area, ranked 12th in terms of population density (253.9 persons per square mile). The 15 most populous states remained almost unchanged between 2010 and 2018—Arizona moved into the top 15 while Indiana dropped out—but there were changes within their ranks. Florida became the 3rd most populous state, pushing ahead of New York while Georgia became the 8th most populous state. North Carolina moved up to 9th place while Michigan dropped to 10th.

Not surprisingly, states with higher population density also had higher proportions of developed land. According to the Department of Agriculture's most recent National Resources Inventory, 35.7 percent of New Jersey's land was developed. Connecticut had the second highest proportion with 34.1 percent, followed by Massachusetts at 33.0 percent. Among the reporting states, Nevada had the lowest proportion of developed land, at just 0.8 percent, followed by Wyoming and Montana, with 1.1 percent and 1.2 percent of their land developed. Nearly 85 percent of Nevada's land was owned by the federal government. This was by far the highest percentage in the nation. Federal land accounted for almost 21 percent of the United States' total land area. (Estimates are not available for Alaska, and the District of Columbia. See Appendix F for definitions and additional information.)

The total population of the United States increased 6.0 percent between 2010 and 2018, with 20 states matching or exceeding this rate of growth and the remainder growing more slowly. The District of Columbia experienced a higher growth rate than any of the states (16.7 percent). Texas, North Dakota, Utah, Florida, and Colorado all had growth rates above 13 percent. The District of Columbia ranked 49th by population size—more than either Vermont or Wyoming--and gained more than 100,000 residents in the 8-year period. Texas has the second largest population among all the states and gained more than 3.5 million residents. Despite its growth, North Dakota ranked 47th for total population and 48th for density, with only 11.0 persons per square mile. Texas and Florida ranked among the top five states for total population and for population growth from 2010 to 2018. Florida, with the third-largest population, grew by 13.3 percent, increasing its population by nearly 2.5 million people. Rhode Island and Vermont both ranked among the 10 least populous states, as well as among the 10 states with the lowest population growth between 2010 and 2018. While most states have increased their populations in the eight years, the populations of West Virginia, Illinois, and Connecticut declined by a small amount. Six other states experienced increases below one percent. Louisiana's population has rebounded from a loss of about 250,000 residents after Hurricane Katrina hit the state in August 2005. Its 2018 population of over 4.6 million is slightly higher than its 2005 estimated population on July 1 of that year.

States and the District of Columbia, Selected Rankings

Population, 2018			Land Area, 2018				Population density, 2018			
Population rank	State	Population [col 2]	Population rank	Land area	State	Land area (square miles) [col 1]	Population rank	Density rank	State	Density (per square mile) [col 4]
	United States	327,167,434			United States	3,532,614			United States	92.6
1	California	39,557,045	48	1	Alaska	570,983	49	1	District of Columbia	11,496.8
2	Texas	28,701,845	2	2	Texas	261,257	11	2	New Jersey	1,211.3
3	Florida	21,299,325	1	3	California	155,794	44	3	Rhode Island	1,022.6
4	New York	19,542,209	43	4	Montana	145,546	15	4	Massachusetts	884.8
5	Pennsylvania	12,807,060	36	5	New Mexico	121,312	29	5	Connecticut	737.7
6	Illinois	12,741,080	14	6	Arizona	113,591	19	6	Maryland	622.3
7	Ohio	11,689,442	32	7	Nevada	109,780	45	7	Delaware	496.4
8	Georgia	10,519,475	21	8	Colorado	103,639	4	8	New York	414.7
9	North Carolina	10,383,620	51	9	Wyoming	97,089	3	9	Florida	397.0
10	Michigan	9,995,915	27	10	Oregon	95,988	5	10	Pennsylvania	286.2
11	New Jersey	8,908,520	39	11	Idaho	82,645	7	11	Ohio	286.1
12	Virginia	8,517,685	30	12	Utah	82,196	1	12	California	253.9
13	Washington	7,535,591	35	13	Kansas	81,759	6	13	Illinois	229.5
14	Arizona	7,171,646	22	14	Minnesota	79,625	40	14	Hawaii	221.2
15	Massachusetts	6,902,149	37	15	Nebraska	76,818	12	15	Virginia	215.7
16	Tennessee	6,770,010	46	16	South Dakota	75,810	9	16	North Carolina	213.6
17	Indiana	6,691,878	47	17	North Dakota	68,999	17	17	Indiana	186.8
18	Missouri	6,126,452	18	18	Missouri	68,746	8	18	Georgia	182.3
19	Maryland	6,042,718	28	19	Oklahoma	68,596	10	19	Michigan	176.6
20	Wisconsin	5,813,568	13	20	Washington	66,453	23	20	South Carolina	169.1
21	Colorado	5,695,564	8	21	Georgia	57,715	16	21	Tennessee	164.2
22	Minnesota	5,611,179	10	22	Michigan	56,603	41	22	New Hampshire	151.5
23	South Carolina	5,084,127	31	23	Iowa	55,854	13	23	Washington	113.4
24	Alabama	4,887,871	6	24	Illinois	55,514	26	24	Kentucky	113.2
25	Louisiana	4,659,978	20	25	Wisconsin	54,166	2	25	Texas	109.9
26	Kentucky	4,468,402	3	26	Florida	53,649	25	26	Louisiana	107.9
27	Oregon	4,190,713	33	27	Arkansas	52,035	20	27	Wisconsin	107.3
28	Oklahoma	3,943,079	24	28	Alabama	50,647	24	28	Alabama	96.5
29	Connecticut	3,572,665	9	29	North Carolina	48,619	18	29	Missouri	89.1
30	Utah	3,161,105	4	30	New York	47,123	38	30	West Virginia	75.1
31	Iowa	3,156,145	34	31	Mississippi	46,924	22	31	Minnesota	70.5
32	Nevada	3,034,392	5	32	Pennsylvania	44,743	50	32	Vermont	67.9
33	Arkansas	3,013,825	25	33	Louisiana	43,204	34	33	Mississippi	63.6
34	Mississippi	2,986,530	16	34	Tennessee	41,237	14	34	Arizona	63.1
35	Kansas	2,911,505	7	35	Ohio	40,861	33	35	Arkansas	57.9
36	New Mexico	2,095,428	26	36	Kentucky	39,490	28	36	Oklahoma	57.5
37	Nebraska	1,929,268	12	37	Virginia	39,482	31	37	Iowa	56.5
38	West Virginia	1,805,832	17	38	Indiana	35,826	21	38	Colorado	55.0
39	Idaho	1,754,208	42	39	Maine	30,845	27	39	Oregon	43.7
40	Hawaii	1,420,491	23	40	South Carolina	30,064	42	40	Maine	43.4
41	New Hampshire	1,356,458	38	41	West Virginia	24,041	30	41	Utah	38.5
42	Maine	1,338,404	19	42	Maryland	9,711	35	42	Kansas	35.6
43	Montana	1,062,305	50	43	Vermont	9,218	32	43	Nevada	27.6
44	Rhode Island	1,057,315	41	44	New Hampshire	8,954	37	44	Nebraska	25.1
45	Delaware	967,171	15	45	Massachusetts	7,801	39	45	Idaho	21.2
46	South Dakota	882,235	11	46	New Jersey	7,354	36	46	New Mexico	17.3
47	North Dakota	760,077	40	47	Hawaii	6,422	46	47	South Dakota	11.6
48	Alaska	737,438	29	48	Connecticut	4,843	47	48	North Dakota	11.0
49	District of Columbia	702,455	45	49	Delaware	1,948	43	49	Montana	7.3
50	Vermont	626,299	44	50	Rhode Island	1,034	51	50	Wyoming	6.0
51	Wyoming	577,737	49	51	District of Columbia	61	48	51	Alaska	1.3

States and the District of Columbia, Selected Rankings

Percent population change, 2010–2018				Percent Under 18 years old, 2018				Percent 65 years old and over, 2018			
Population rank	Percent change rank	State	Percent change [col 36]	Population rank	Under 18 years old rank	State	Percent under 18 years old [cols 10 + 11]	Population rank	65 years old and over rank	State	Percent 65 years old and over [cols 17 + 18 + 19]
		United States	6.0			United States	22.5			United States	16.0
49	1	District of Columbia	16.7	30	1	Utah	29.5	42	1	Maine	20.6
30	2	Utah	14.4	2	2	Texas	25.8	3	2	Florida	20.5
2	3	Texas	14.1	39	3	Idaho	25.4	38	3	West Virginia	19.9
3	4	Florida	13.3	48	4	Alaska	24.9	50	4	Vermont	19.3
21	5	Colorado	13.2	37	5	Nebraska	24.7	45	5	Delaware	18.8
47	6	North Dakota	13.0	46	6	South Dakota	24.6	43	6	Montana	18.7
32	7	Nevada	12.4	28	7	Oklahoma	24.3	40	7	Hawaii	18.4
14	8	Arizona	12.2	35	8	Kansas	24.2	5	8	Pennsylvania	18.2
13	9	Washington	12.1	8	9	Georgia	23.8	41	9	New Hampshire	18.0
39	10	Idaho	11.9	34	10	Mississippi	23.6	23	10	South Carolina	17.7
23	11	South Carolina	9.9	17	11	Indiana	23.5	27	11	Oregon	17.6
27	12	Oregon	9.4	25	11	Louisiana	23.5	14	12	Arizona	17.5
9	13	North Carolina	8.9	47	11	North Dakota	23.5	36	12	New Mexico	17.5
8	14	Georgia	8.6	33	14	Arkansas	23.3	29	14	Connecticut	17.2
46	15	South Dakota	8.4	51	14	Wyoming	23.3	10	14	Michigan	17.2
45	16	Delaware	7.7	31	16	Iowa	23.2	44	14	Rhode Island	17.2
43	17	Montana	7.4	22	16	Minnesota	23.2	31	17	Iowa	17.1
16	18	Tennessee	6.7	36	18	New Mexico	23.0	33	18	Arkansas	17.0
12	19	Virginia	6.5	14	19	Arizona	22.9	18	18	Missouri	17.0
1	20	California	6.2	1	20	California	22.8	7	18	Ohio	17.0
22	21	Minnesota	5.8	32	21	Nevada	22.7	24	21	Alabama	16.9
37	22	Nebraska	5.6	26	22	Kentucky	22.6	20	21	Wisconsin	16.9
15	23	Massachusetts	5.4	6	23	Illinois	22.5	46	23	South Dakota	16.6
28	24	Oklahoma	5.1	18	23	Missouri	22.5	15	24	Massachusetts	16.5
19	25	Maryland	4.7	24	25	Alabama	22.3	4	24	New York	16.5
40	26	Hawaii	4.4	21	26	Colorado	22.2	51	24	Wyoming	16.5
48	27	Alaska	3.8	9	26	North Carolina	22.2	16	27	Tennessee	16.4
31	28	Iowa	3.6	16	26	Tennessee	22.2	26	28	Kentucky	16.3
33	29	Arkansas	3.4	19	29	Maryland	22.1	11	29	New Jersey	16.2
17	30	Indiana	3.2	7	29	Ohio	22.1	9	29	North Carolina	16.2
26	31	Kentucky	3.0	12	31	Virginia	22.0	39	31	Idaho	15.9
41	31	New Hampshire	3.0	13	31	Washington	22.0	35	31	Kansas	15.9
25	33	Louisiana	2.8	20	31	Wisconsin	22.0	22	31	Minnesota	15.9
51	34	Wyoming	2.5	11	34	New Jersey	21.9	34	31	Mississippi	15.9
24	35	Alabama	2.3	23	35	South Carolina	21.8	17	35	Indiana	15.8
18	35	Missouri	2.3	10	36	Michigan	21.6	28	35	Oklahoma	15.8
20	37	Wisconsin	2.2	43	36	Montana	21.6	6	37	Illinois	15.7
35	38	Kansas	2.0	40	38	Hawaii	21.4	37	37	Nebraska	15.7
36	39	New Mexico	1.8	45	39	Delaware	21.1	32	37	Nevada	15.7
11	40	New Jersey	1.3	27	40	Oregon	20.9	13	40	Washington	15.5
7	40	Ohio	1.3	4	41	New York	20.8	25	41	Louisiana	15.4
10	42	Michigan	1.1	5	42	Pennsylvania	20.7	19	41	Maryland	15.4
42	43	Maine	0.8	29	43	Connecticut	20.6	12	41	Virginia	15.4
4	43	New York	0.8	38	44	West Virginia	20.2	47	44	North Dakota	15.3
5	43	Pennsylvania	0.8	3	45	Florida	19.9	1	45	California	14.3
34	46	Mississippi	0.6	15	46	Massachusetts	19.8	21	46	Colorado	14.2
44	47	Rhode Island	0.5	44	47	Rhode Island	19.4	8	47	Georgia	13.9
50	48	Vermont	0.1	41	48	New Hampshire	19.0	2	48	Texas	12.5
29	49	Connecticut	0.0	42	49	Maine	18.7	49	49	District of Columbia	12.1
6	50	Illinois	-0.7	50	50	Vermont	18.5	48	50	Alaska	11.7
38	51	West Virginia	-2.5	49	51	District of Columbia	18.2	30	51	Utah	11.1

States and the District of Columbia, Selected Rankings

Percent born in state of residence, 2017

Population rank	Born in state of residence rank	State	Percent born in state of residence [col 23]
		United States	58.2
25	1	Louisiana	78.3
10	2	Michigan	76.1
7	3	Ohio	74.8
5	4	Pennsylvania	72.2
34	5	Mississippi	72.0
20	6	Wisconsin	71.4
31	7	Iowa	70.2
38	8	West Virginia	70.0
24	9	Alabama	69.9
26	10	Kentucky	69.2
17	11	Indiana	68.0
22	12	Minnesota	67.4
6	13	Illinois	66.9
18	14	Missouri	66.0
46	15	South Dakota	64.9
37	16	Nebraska	64.5
42	17	Maine	63.5
4	18	New York	62.9
47	19	North Dakota	62.1
30	20	Utah	61.9
28	21	Oklahoma	61.2
33	22	Arkansas	60.6
15	23	Massachusetts	60.1
16	24	Tennessee	59.7
2	25	Texas	59.7
35	26	Kansas	59.6
9	27	North Carolina	56.4
23	28	South Carolina	56.2
1	29	California	55.6
44	30	Rhode Island	55.5
8	31	Georgia	55.1
36	32	New Mexico	54.3
29	33	Connecticut	54.2
43	34	Montana	53.1
40	35	Hawaii	53.0
11	36	New Jersey	51.9
50	37	Vermont	51.6
12	38	Virginia	49.2
39	39	Idaho	47.6
19	40	Maryland	47.2
13	41	Washington	46.9
27	42	Oregon	46.0
45	43	Delaware	43.2
51	44	Wyoming	43.0
48	45	Alaska	42.5
21	46	Colorado	42.1
41	47	New Hampshire	41.8
14	48	Arizona	39.7
49	49	District of Columbia	37.4
3	50	Florida	36.0
32	51	Nevada	25.9

Number of immigrants, 2017

Population rank	Immigrant rank	State	Number of immigrants [col 24]
		United States	1,127,167
1	1	California	214,243
4	2	New York	139,409
3	3	Florida	127,609
2	4	Texas	110,126
11	5	New Jersey	54,440
6	6	Illinois	40,530
15	7	Massachusetts	37,010
12	8	Virginia	29,466
5	9	Pennsylvania	27,762
13	10	Washington	27,363
8	11	Georgia	26,242
19	12	Maryland	25,095
9	13	North Carolina	21,184
14	14	Arizona	19,344
10	15	Michigan	18,927
7	16	Ohio	16,894
22	17	Minnesota	16,009
21	18	Colorado	14,520
32	19	Nevada	12,733
29	20	Connecticut	11,938
17	21	Indiana	10,052
16	22	Tennessee	9,793
27	23	Oregon	9,221
18	24	Missouri	7,707
26	25	Kentucky	7,537
20	26	Wisconsin	6,681
30	27	Utah	6,390
35	28	Kansas	5,703
31	29	Iowa	5,577
28	30	Oklahoma	5,535
40	31	Hawaii	5,396
37	32	Nebraska	5,327
23	33	South Carolina	5,027
25	34	Louisiana	4,688
44	35	Rhode Island	4,102
36	36	New Mexico	4,002
24	37	Alabama	3,801
33	38	Arkansas	3,071
49	39	District of Columbia	2,885
39	40	Idaho	2,709
41	41	New Hampshire	2,279
45	42	Delaware	2,244
34	43	Mississippi	1,793
42	44	Maine	1,594
48	45	Alaska	1,547
47	46	North Dakota	1,471
46	47	South Dakota	1,017
50	48	Vermont	787
38	49	West Virginia	776
43	50	Montana	529
51	51	Wyoming	444

Birth rate, 2017

Population rank	Birth rate rank	State	Birth rate (per 1,000 population) [col 98]
		United States	11.8
30	1	Utah	15.7
47	2	North Dakota	14.2
48	3	Alaska	14.1
46	4	South Dakota	14.0
49	5	District of Columbia	13.8
2	6	Texas	13.5
37	7	Nebraska	13.4
25	8	Louisiana	13.0
39	9	Idaho	12.9
28	10	Oklahoma	12.8
33	11	Arkansas	12.5
35	11	Kansas	12.5
34	11	Mississippi	12.5
8	14	Georgia	12.4
40	15	Hawaii	12.3
17	15	Indiana	12.3
26	15	Kentucky	12.3
22	15	Minnesota	12.3
31	19	Iowa	12.2
24	20	Alabama	12.1
16	20	Tennessee	12.1
1	22	California	11.9
18	22	Missouri	11.9
32	22	Nevada	11.9
12	22	Virginia	11.9
51	22	Wyoming	11.9
19	27	Maryland	11.8
13	27	Washington	11.8
14	29	Arizona	11.7
6	29	Illinois	11.7
9	29	North Carolina	11.7
7	29	Ohio	11.7
4	33	New York	11.6
21	34	Colorado	11.5
36	35	New Mexico	11.4
23	35	South Carolina	11.4
45	37	Delaware	11.3
10	38	Michigan	11.2
43	38	Montana	11.2
11	38	New Jersey	11.2
20	38	Wisconsin	11.2
5	42	Pennsylvania	10.8
3	43	Florida	10.7
27	44	Oregon	10.5
15	45	Massachusetts	10.3
38	45	West Virginia	10.3
44	47	Rhode Island	10.0
29	48	Connecticut	9.8
42	49	Maine	9.2
50	50	Vermont	9.1
41	51	New Hampshire	9.0

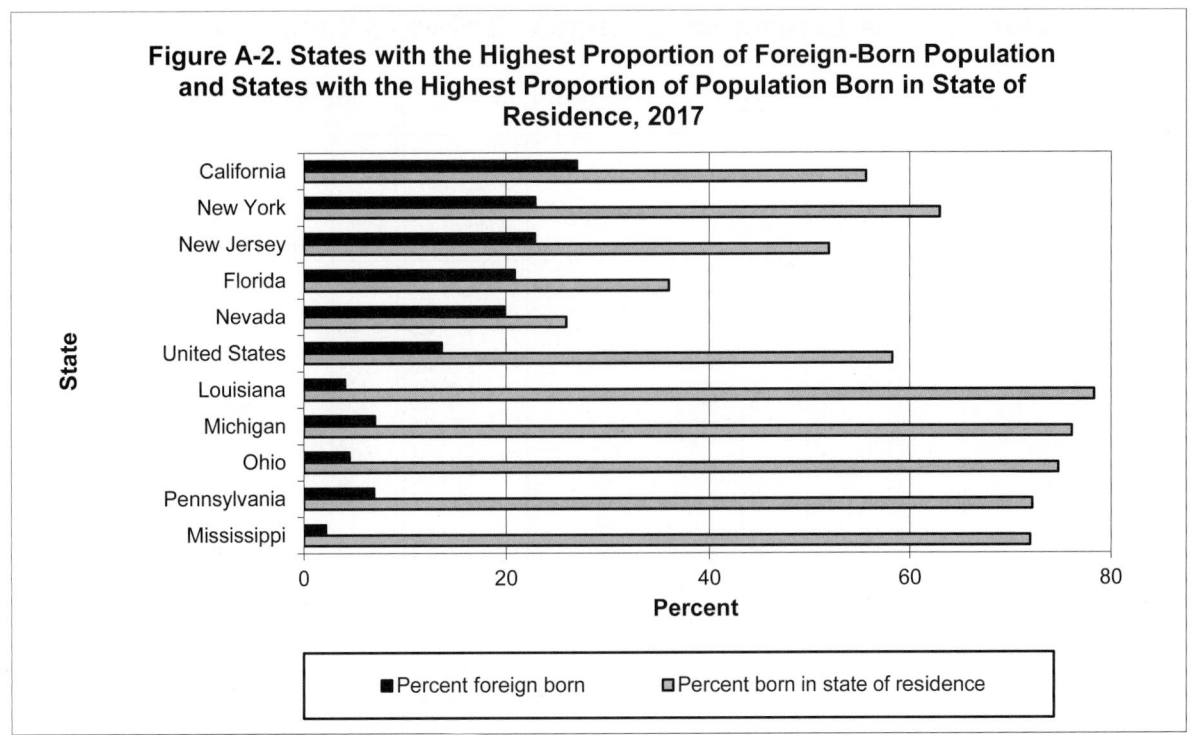

Figure A-2. States with the Highest Proportion of Foreign-Born Population and States with the Highest Proportion of Population Born in State of Residence, 2017

Percent foreign born
Percent born in state of residence

The U.S. median age increased slightly from 37.2 years in 2010 to 38.2 years in 2018, primarily caused by the aging Baby Boomer population. This increase was much less than the jump from 32.1 years to 35.3 years between 1990 and 2000. From 2010 to 2018, the population between 65 and 74 years showed the largest proportional increase, while the proportion between 45 and 54 years showed the largest decrease. The 25 to 34 Millennial group increased by over 11 percent and they outnumber the peak Baby Boomers in the 55 to 64 age group. The median age by state ranged from 29.2 years in Utah to 42.7 years in Maine. Utah had the highest proportion of young residents; in 2018, 29.5 percent of the state's population was younger than 18 years old. The population age 65 years and over ranged from 11.1 percent in Utah to 20.6 percent in Maine. Alaska and North Dakota had the lowest proportions of female residents, and were among just ten states in which men outnumbered women. The District of Columbia had the highest proportion of female residents with 52.6 percent, followed by Alabama and Delaware at 51.6 percent.

Natural growth is the difference between the number of births and the number of deaths. New Hampshire had the fewest births between 2010 and 2018. Maine and West Virginia were the only states to have more deaths than births. A net migration of more than 18,000 people prevented Maine from having a population loss from 2010 to 2018 but West Virginia, with a net outmigration of 27,508, did experience a population decline. California, the largest state in the nation, had nearly 2.0 million more births than deaths and 333,168 new residents through net migration. From 2010 to 2018, California gained 1,043,561 residents from foreign countries and lost 710,393 residents to other states. Florida had a net gain of more than 2 million new residents during this period, about half from other states and half from other countries. Texas gained 1.8 million new residents, 55.6 percent of them from other states. Twenty eight states had a net loss of residents due to migration including New York which lost over 1.1 million residents to other states but gained nearly 675,000 new residents from other countries.

In eight states, 70 percent or more of the residents were born in that same state. Louisiana ranked highest with 78.3 percent. The ten highest rates were mainly in the Midwest and the South. Thirteen states and the District of Columbia had proportions less than 50 percent. Nevada had the lowest proportion by far, with just 25.9 percent of its residents having been born in the state. Nationally, 58.2 percent of Americans lived in the state of their birth.

The U.S. birth rate in 2017 was 11.8 per 1,000 population, a slight decrease from 2016. Utah had the highest birth rate in the nation, with 15.7 births per 1,000 population. North Dakota had the second highest birth rate at 14.2 followed by Alaska with a birth rate of 14.1. Connecticut, Maine, Vermont, and New Hampshire had the lowest birth rates in the nation, all below 10 births per 1,000 population. Utah had the lowest crude death rate with 5.8 deaths per 1,000 population followed by Alaska with a crude death rate of 6.0. However, both states had relatively young populations (In Utah, 40.8 percent of the population was under 25 years old while 34.4 percent of the population was under 25 in Alaska). Once adjusted for age, Alaska's death rate increased to 7.1, and Utah's to 7.0, just under the U.S. rate of 7.3. West Virginia, Alabama, and Kentucky had the highest crude death rates in the nation. Mississippi had the highest age-adjusted death rate followed by West Virginia, both with a mix of younger and older residents. Maine had the highest proportion of senior citizens followed by Florida. However, Florida also had a high proportion of younger people, which helped give the state a crude death rate of 9.7 per 1,000 population, ranking it 16th tied with Iowa and Montana. When Florida's death rate was age-adjusted, it dropped to 6.7, which was well below the national age-adjusted rate of 7.3 and among the lowest ten states. Hawaii had the lowest age-adjusted death rate at 5.8, one of 13 states with rates below 7.0. Mississippi, Arkansas, and the District of Columbia had the highest infant mortality rates, while Massachusetts and Washington had the lowest infant death rates.

States and the District of Columbia, Selected Rankings

Percent of owners with a mortgage paying 30 percent or more of income for housing expenses, 2017				Median value of owner-occupied housing units, 2017				Median gross rent of renter-occupied housing units, 2017			
Population rank	Percent of income for housing rank	State	Percent paying 30% or more of income for housing	Population rank	Median value rank	State	Median value (dollars) [col 88]	Population rank	Median rent rank	State	Median rent (dollars) [col 90]
		United States	27.4			United States	$217,600			United States	$1,012
40	1	Hawaii	38.8	40	1	Hawaii	$617,400	40	1	Hawaii	$1,573
1	2	California	38.2	49	2	District of Columbia	$607,200	49	2	District of Columbia	$1,499
11	3	New Jersey	34.2	1	3	California	$509,400	1	3	California	$1,447
4	4	New York	33.1	15	4	Massachusetts	$385,400	19	4	Maryland	$1,337
3	5	Florida	32.7	21	5	Colorado	$348,900	11	5	New Jersey	$1,284
50	6	Vermont	32.1	13	6	Washington	$339,000	21	6	Colorado	$1,240
27	7	Oregon	31.6	11	7	New Jersey	$334,900	4	7	New York	$1,226
44	8	Rhode Island	31.5	27	8	Oregon	$319,200	13	8	Washington	$1,216
29	9	Connecticut	30.8	4	9	New York	$314,500	15	9	Massachusetts	$1,208
32	10	Nevada	29.9	19	10	Maryland	$312,500	48	10	Alaska	$1,201
36	11	New Mexico	29.4	30	11	Utah	$275,100	12	11	Virginia	$1,179
15	12	Massachusetts	29.3	12	12	Virginia	$273,400	3	12	Florida	$1,128
48	13	Alaska	29.2	48	13	Alaska	$273,100	29	13	Connecticut	$1,125
13	14	Washington	28.8	29	13	Connecticut	$273,100	45	14	Delaware	$1,086
14	15	Arizona	27.9	41	15	New Hampshire	$263,600	27	15	Oregon	$1,079
45	16	Delaware	27.5	32	16	Nevada	$258,200	41	16	New Hampshire	$1,072
43	17	Montana	27.3	44	17	Rhode Island	$257,800	32	17	Nevada	$1,051
21	18	Colorado	27.1	45	18	Delaware	$252,800	14	18	Arizona	$1,020
6	18	Illinois	27.1	43	19	Montana	$231,300	2	19	Texas	$987
19	20	Maryland	27.0	50	20	Vermont	$226,300	30	20	Utah	$986
41	21	New Hampshire	26.8	22	21	Minnesota	$224,000	6	21	Illinois	$974
49	22	District of Columbia	26.6	14	22	Arizona	$223,400	8	22	Georgia	$958
42	23	Maine	26.1	51	23	Wyoming	$214,300	50	23	Vermont	$950
12	24	Virginia	26.0	3	24	Florida	$214,000	44	24	Rhode Island	$941
39	25	Idaho	25.9	39	25	Idaho	$207,100	22	25	Minnesota	$939
2	26	Texas	25.6	6	26	Illinois	$195,300	5	26	Pennsylvania	$893
34	27	Mississippi	25.4	47	27	North Dakota	$194,700	9	27	North Carolina	$861
25	28	Louisiana	25.2	42	28	Maine	$191,200	23	28	South Carolina	$848
8	29	Georgia	25.0	5	29	Pennsylvania	$181,200	25	29	Louisiana	$836
23	29	South Carolina	25.0	20	30	Wisconsin	$178,900	10	30	Michigan	$835
5	31	Pennsylvania	24.3	8	31	Georgia	$173,700	16	31	Tennessee	$833
9	32	North Carolina	24.0	2	32	Texas	$172,200	51	32	Wyoming	$832
30	33	Utah	23.9	36	33	New Mexico	$171,300	39	33	Idaho	$822
51	33	Wyoming	23.9	9	34	North Carolina	$171,200	20	34	Wisconsin	$819
28	35	Oklahoma	23.8	46	35	South Dakota	$167,600	35	35	Kansas	$815
16	36	Tennessee	23.7	16	36	Tennessee	$167,500	36	36	New Mexico	$813
24	37	Alabama	23.0	25	37	Louisiana	$162,500	42	37	Maine	$806
10	38	Michigan	22.7	23	38	South Carolina	$161,800	37	38	Nebraska	$801
20	39	Wisconsin	22.3	18	39	Missouri	$156,700	18	39	Missouri	$800
38	40	West Virginia	22.0	37	40	Nebraska	$155,800	17	40	Indiana	$793
26	41	Kentucky	21.8	10	41	Michigan	$155,700	47	41	North Dakota	$785
22	42	Minnesota	21.7	35	42	Kansas	$150,600	28	42	Oklahoma	$780
18	43	Missouri	21.5	31	43	Iowa	$149,100	7	43	Ohio	$772
33	44	Arkansas	21.1	7	44	Ohio	$144,200	31	44	Iowa	$760
37	45	Nebraska	20.9	24	45	Alabama	$141,300	43	45	Montana	$759
7	46	Ohio	20.5	17	46	Indiana	$141,100	24	46	Alabama	$750
35	47	Kansas	19.8	26	47	Kentucky	$141,000	34	47	Mississippi	$742
46	48	South Dakota	19.0	28	48	Oklahoma	$137,400	26	48	Kentucky	$724
17	49	Indiana	18.9	33	49	Arkansas	$128,500	46	49	South Dakota	$722
31	49	Iowa	18.9	34	50	Mississippi	$120,200	33	50	Arkansas	$711
47	51	North Dakota	16.8	38	51	West Virginia	$119,800	38	51	West Virginia	$690

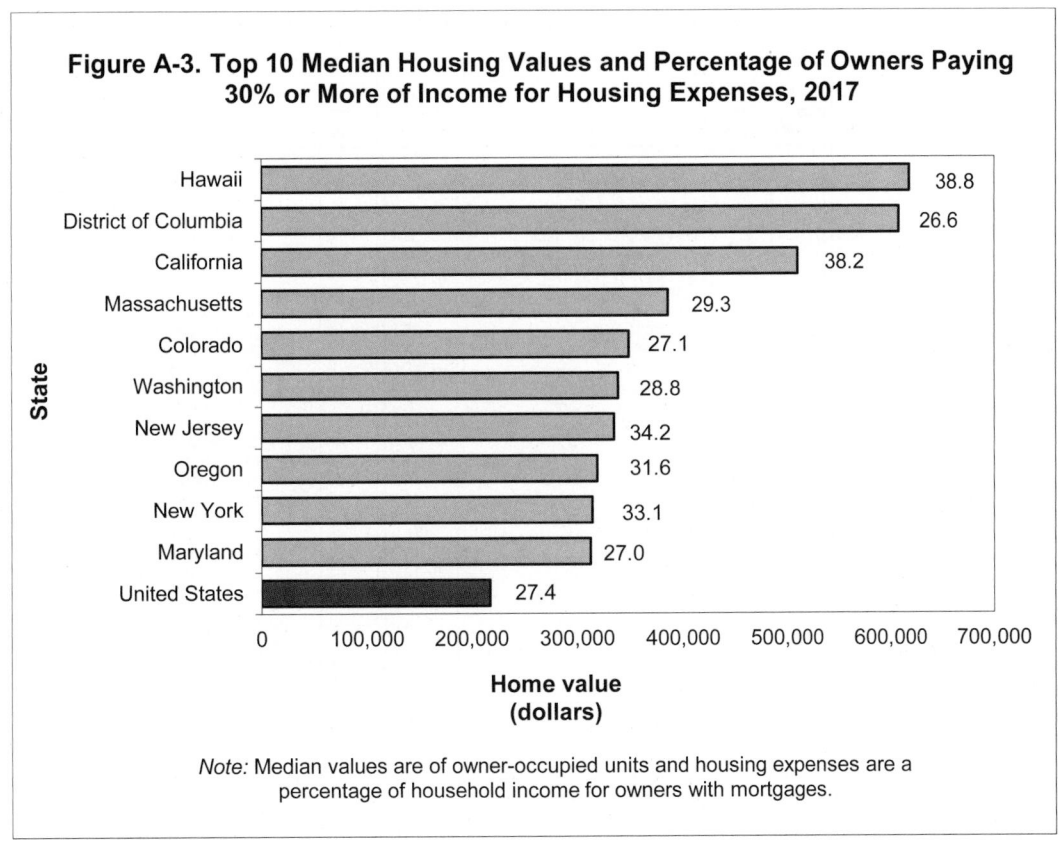

Figure A-3. Top 10 Median Housing Values and Percentage of Owners Paying 30% or More of Income for Housing Expenses, 2017

State	Percentage
Hawaii	38.8
District of Columbia	26.6
California	38.2
Massachusetts	29.3
Colorado	27.1
Washington	28.8
New Jersey	34.2
Oregon	31.6
New York	33.1
Maryland	27.0
United States	27.4

Home value
(dollars)

Note: Median values are of owner-occupied units and housing expenses are a percentage of household income for owners with mortgages.

In 2017, homeowners with mortgages paid a median of 21.2 percent of their incomes for monthly owner costs (mortgage, insurance, taxes, utilities, fuel, etc.). This ranged from a high of 25.5 percent in Hawaii to 18.1 percent in Indiana. Nationally, 27.4 percent of owners with a mortgage paid 30 percent or more of income for housing expenses in 2017. Hawaii and California had the highest proportion of mortgage holders paying 30 percent or more of their income with 38.8 and 38.2 percent respectively, followed by New Jersey at 34.2 percent, New York at 33.1 percent and Florida at 32.7 percent. In 34 states and the District of Columbia, the proportion of mortgaged owners who paid more than 30 percent for housing was lower than the national average. North Dakota had the lowest proportion in the nation with 16.8 percent. Nine states and the District of Columbia had median home values exceeding $300,000 in 2017, led by Hawaii with a median home value of $617,400 Nationally, the median value of owner-occupied housing units was $217,600. Hawaii also had the highest median gross rent, at $1,573. The District of Columbia, California and Maryland all had median gross monthly rents exceeding $1,300.

Many minority groups had above average growth rates since 2000. Currently, in four states and the District of Columbia, the minority population outnumbers the non-Hispanic White population. Nationally, 62.3 percent of the U.S. population was non-Hispanic White alone or in combination, but the racial and ethnic compositions of the states varied widely. In Hawaii, the state with the highest proportion of minorities, Asian and Pacific Islander alone or in combination was the largest race group, representing 75.3 percent of the state's population. Hispanic or Latino residents made up over 49 percent of New Mexico's population and over 39 percent of residents in both California and Texas. The District of Columbia had the highest proportion of Black residents at 46.3 percent, down from 60.5 percent in 2000. Among the states, Mississippi and Louisiana ranked first and second, with Black populations of 38.1 and 33.1 percent, respectively. Alaska had the highest proportion of American Indians and Alaska Natives, who made up 18.9 percent of the population. Oklahoma, New Mexico, and South Dakota all had high proportions of American Indian populations. As might be expected, the states with the largest number of minorities were among the states with the highest total populations. New York was home to over 3.0 million Black residents, and California had the largest number of Hispanics, Asian and Pacific Islanders, and American Indians and Alaska Natives. California had over 395,000 non-Hispanic American Indian and Alaska Native residents, though they made up just 1.0 percent of the state's population. Despite having only about 83,000 Native American residents, South Dakota had the second highest proportion in the nation.

States and the District of Columbia, Selected Rankings

Percent White, not Hispanic or Latino, alone or in combination, 2018				Percent Black, not Hispanic or Latino, alone or in combination, 2018				Percent Hispanic or Latino,[1] 2018			
Population rank	Percent White rank	State	Percent White [col 5]	Population rank	Percent Black rank	State	Percent Black [col 6]	Population rank	Hispanic or Latino rank	State	Percent Hispanic or Latino [col 9]
		United States	62.3			United States	13.5			United States	18.3
42	1	Maine	94.8	49	1	District of Columbia	46.3	36	1	New Mexico	49.1
50	2	Vermont	94.3	34	2	Mississippi	38.1	2	2	Texas	39.6
38	3	West Virginia	93.7	25	3	Louisiana	33.1	1	3	California	39.3
41	4	New Hampshire	91.5	8	4	Georgia	32.6	14	4	Arizona	31.6
43	5	Montana	88.3	19	5	Maryland	31.3	32	5	Nevada	29.0
31	6	Iowa	86.9	23	6	South Carolina	27.7	3	6	Florida	26.1
26	7	Kentucky	86.0	24	7	Alabama	27.3	21	7	Colorado	21.7
47	8	North Dakota	85.9	45	8	Delaware	23.4	11	8	New Jersey	20.6
51	9	Wyoming	85.5	9	9	North Carolina	22.5	4	9	New York	19.2
39	10	Idaho	83.7	12	10	Virginia	20.5	6	10	Illinois	17.4
46	11	South Dakota	83.4	16	11	Tennessee	17.7	29	11	Connecticut	16.5
20	12	Wisconsin	82.7	3	12	Florida	16.5	44	12	Rhode Island	15.9
22	13	Minnesota	81.6	33	13	Arkansas	16.2	30	13	Utah	14.2
18	14	Missouri	81.3	4	14	New York	15.5	27	14	Oregon	13.3
17	15	Indiana	80.6	6	15	Illinois	14.9	13	15	Washington	12.9
7	15	Ohio	80.6	10	15	Michigan	14.9	39	16	Idaho	12.7
37	17	Nebraska	80.3	7	17	Ohio	14.0	15	17	Massachusetts	12.3
30	18	Utah	80.0	11	18	New Jersey	13.7	35	18	Kansas	12.1
27	19	Oregon	78.4	18	19	Missouri	12.7	49	19	District of Columbia	11.3
35	20	Kansas	78.1	2	19	Texas	12.7	37	20	Nebraska	11.2
5	21	Pennsylvania	77.6	5	21	Pennsylvania	11.9	28	21	Oklahoma	10.9
10	22	Michigan	76.9	29	22	Connecticut	11.2	40	22	Hawaii	10.7
16	23	Tennessee	75.3	17	23	Indiana	10.6	19	23	Maryland	10.4
33	24	Arkansas	74.0	32	24	Nevada	10.4	51	24	Wyoming	10.1
44	25	Rhode Island	73.8	26	25	Kentucky	9.3	8	25	Georgia	9.8
15	26	Massachusetts	73.1	28	26	Oklahoma	8.9	9	26	North Carolina	9.6
13	27	Washington	71.7	15	27	Massachusetts	8.2	12	26	Virginia	9.6
28	28	Oklahoma	70.5	22	28	Minnesota	7.7	45	28	Delaware	9.5
21	29	Colorado	70.0	20	29	Wisconsin	7.3	33	29	Arkansas	7.7
29	30	Connecticut	68.1	44	30	Rhode Island	7.2	5	30	Pennsylvania	7.6
24	31	Alabama	66.8	35	31	Kansas	7.0	48	31	Alaska	7.2
48	32	Alaska	66.3	1	32	California	6.5	17	32	Indiana	7.1
23	33	South Carolina	65.2	37	33	Nebraska	5.8	20	33	Wisconsin	6.9
9	34	North Carolina	64.5	14	34	Arizona	5.2	31	34	Iowa	6.2
45	35	Delaware	63.9	13	34	Washington	5.2	23	35	South Carolina	5.8
12	36	Virginia	63.8	21	36	Colorado	4.9	16	36	Tennessee	5.6
6	37	Illinois	62.5	48	37	Alaska	4.8	22	37	Minnesota	5.5
25	38	Louisiana	59.9	31	38	Iowa	4.7	25	38	Louisiana	5.2
34	39	Mississippi	57.5	38	39	West Virginia	4.5	10	38	Michigan	5.2
4	40	New York	56.9	47	40	North Dakota	3.9	24	40	Alabama	4.4
14	41	Arizona	56.3	40	41	Hawaii	3.0	18	41	Missouri	4.3
11	42	New Jersey	56.2	46	41	South Dakota	3.0	46	42	South Dakota	4.1
3	43	Florida	54.9	27	43	Oregon	2.8	43	43	Montana	4.0
8	44	Georgia	54.0	36	44	New Mexico	2.4	41	44	New Hampshire	3.9
19	45	Maryland	52.5	42	45	Maine	2.1	47	44	North Dakota	3.9
32	46	Nevada	51.6	41	46	New Hampshire	2.0	7	44	Ohio	3.9
2	47	Texas	42.8	50	47	Vermont	1.9	26	47	Kentucky	3.8
1	48	California	39.3	30	48	Utah	1.7	34	48	Mississippi	3.4
49	49	District of Columbia	38.8	51	48	Wyoming	1.7	50	49	Vermont	2.0
36	50	New Mexico	38.5	39	50	Idaho	1.2	42	50	Maine	1.7
40	51	Hawaii	36.2	43	51	Montana	1.0	38	50	West Virginia	1.7

1. May be of any race.

States and the District of Columbia, Selected Rankings

Percent high school graduates or more,[1] 2017				Percent college graduates (bachelor's degree or more),[1] 2017				Median household income, 2017			
Popu-lation rank	Percent high school graduates rank	State	Percent high school graduates [col 115]	Popu-lation rank	Percent college graduates rank	State	Percent college graduates [col 116]	Popu-lation rank	Median income rank	State	Median income (dollars) [col 123]
		United States	88.0			United States	32.0			United States	60,336
22	1	Minnesota...........................	93.1	49	1	District of Columbia	57.3	49	1	District of Columbia	82,372
41	1	New Hampshire.......................	93.1	15	2	Massachusetts	43.4	19	2	Maryland............................	80,776
43	3	Montana.............................	93.0	21	3	Colorado....................................	41.2	11	3	New Jersey.........................	80,088
47	4	North Dakota........................	92.9	19	4	Maryland....................................	39.7	40	4	Hawaii...............................	77,765
51	4	Wyoming	92.9	11	4	New Jersey................................	39.7	15	5	Massachusetts	77,385
50	6	Vermont..............................	92.6	29	6	Connecticut...............................	38.7	29	6	Connecticut	74,168
20	7	Wisconsin............................	92.4	12	6	Virginia.....................................	38.7	41	7	New Hampshire....................	73,381
40	8	Hawaii...............................	92.3	50	8	Vermont.....................................	38.3	48	8	Alaska...............................	73,181
42	8	Maine................................	92.3	41	9	New Hampshire............................	36.9	1	9	California	71,805
31	10	Iowa.................................	92.1	22	10	Minnesota..................................	36.1	12	10	Virginia	71,535
30	10	Utah.................................	92.1	4	11	New York	36.0	13	11	Washington	70,979
48	12	Alaska...............................	91.7	13	12	Washington	35.5	21	12	Colorado............................	69,117
46	12	South Dakota........................	91.7	30	13	Utah...	34.6	22	13	Minnesota	68,388
21	14	Colorado............................	91.6	6	14	Illinois......................................	34.4	30	14	Utah.................................	68,358
37	15	Nebraska............................	91.3	35	15	Kansas.....................................	33.7	4	15	New York	64,894
13	15	Washington	91.3	27	15	Oregon.....................................	33.7	44	16	Rhode Island	63,870
35	17	Kansas..............................	91.0	1	17	California	33.6	6	17	Illinois	62,992
27	17	Oregon..............................	91.0	44	18	Rhode Island	33.5	45	18	Delaware	62,852
10	19	Michigan.............................	90.9	40	19	Hawaii......................................	32.9	47	19	North Dakota	61,843
39	20	Idaho	90.8	43	20	Montana....................................	32.3	51	20	Wyoming	60,434
15	20	Massachusetts	90.8	42	21	Maine.......................................	32.1	27	21	Oregon..............................	60,212
45	22	Delaware	90.6	37	22	Nebraska...................................	31.7	37	22	Nebraska	59,970
5	22	Pennsylvania	90.6	45	23	Delaware	31.5	20	23	Wisconsin	59,305
29	24	Connecticut	90.4	5	24	Pennsylvania..............................	31.4	2	24	Texas	59,206
7	25	Ohio.................................	90.3	9	25	North Carolina............................	31.3	5	25	Pennsylvania	59,195
49	26	District of Columbia	90.2	8	26	Georgia.....................................	30.9	31	26	Iowa.................................	58,570
19	27	Maryland............................	89.9	47	27	North Dakota	30.7	32	27	Nevada..............................	58,003
11	27	New Jersey.........................	89.9	20	28	Wisconsin..................................	30.4	50	28	Vermont.............................	57,513
18	29	Missouri.............................	89.7	3	29	Florida......................................	29.7	14	29	Arizona.............................	56,581
12	29	Virginia	89.7	2	30	Texas	29.6	46	30	South Dakota	56,521
6	31	Illinois	89.1	14	31	Arizona.....................................	29.4	35	31	Kansas	56,422
17	32	Indiana..............................	88.6	10	32	Michigan....................................	29.1	42	32	Maine...............................	56,277
3	33	Florida	88.4	18	32	Missouri....................................	29.1	8	33	Georgia.............................	56,183
44	34	Rhode Island	88.3	31	34	Iowa..	28.9	10	34	Michigan............................	54,909
28	35	Oklahoma...........................	88.1	48	35	Alaska......................................	28.8	17	35	Indiana..............................	54,181
9	36	North Carolina......................	87.8	46	36	South Dakota..............................	28.1	7	36	Ohio.................................	54,021
16	36	Tennessee..........................	87.8	7	37	Ohio..	28.0	18	37	Missouri.............................	53,578
23	38	South Carolina......................	87.4	23	37	South Carolina............................	28.0	43	38	Montana............................	53,386
14	39	Arizona	87.2	51	39	Wyoming	27.6	9	39	North Carolina	52,752
38	40	West Virginia	87.1	16	40	Tennessee.................................	27.3	3	40	Florida	52,594
8	41	Georgia.............................	87.0	36	41	New Mexico................................	27.1	39	41	Idaho	52,225
32	42	Nevada..............................	86.8	39	42	Idaho	26.8	16	42	Tennessee..........................	51,340
33	43	Arkansas	86.7	17	42	Indiana.....................................	26.8	23	43	South Carolina.....................	50,570
4	44	New York	86.6	24	44	Alabama....................................	25.5	28	44	Oklahoma...........................	50,051
24	45	Alabama.............................	86.5	28	44	Oklahoma..................................	25.5	26	45	Kentucky............................	48,375
26	46	Kentucky............................	86.3	32	46	Nevada.....................................	24.9	24	46	Alabama............................	48,123
36	47	New Mexico.........................	86.1	26	47	Kentucky...................................	24.0	36	47	New Mexico	46,744
25	48	Louisiana............................	85.1	25	48	Louisiana...................................	23.8	25	48	Louisiana	46,145
34	49	Mississippi..........................	84.4	33	49	Arkansas...................................	23.4	33	49	Arkansas	45,869
2	50	Texas	83.6	34	50	Mississippi.................................	21.9	34	50	Mississippi	43,529
1	51	California	83.3	38	51	West Virginia	20.2	38	51	West Virginia	43,469

1. Population 25 years and older.

States and the District of Columbia, Selected Rankings

Unemployment rate, 2018

Population rank	Unemployment rate rank	State	Unemployment rate [col 171]
		United States	3.9
48	1	Alaska	6.6
49	2	District of Columbia	5.6
38	3	West Virginia	5.3
25	4	Louisiana	4.9
36	4	New Mexico	4.9
14	6	Arizona	4.8
34	6	Mississippi	4.8
32	8	Nevada	4.6
7	8	Ohio	4.6
13	10	Washington	4.5
6	11	Illinois	4.3
26	11	Kentucky	4.3
5	11	Pennsylvania	4.3
1	14	California	4.2
27	14	Oregon	4.2
29	16	Connecticut	4.1
10	16	Michigan	4.1
11	16	New Jersey	4.1
4	16	New York	4.1
44	16	Rhode Island	4.1
51	16	Wyoming	4.1
24	22	Alabama	3.9
8	22	Georgia	3.9
19	22	Maryland	3.9
9	22	North Carolina	3.9
2	22	Texas	3.9
45	27	Delaware	3.8
33	28	Arkansas	3.7
43	28	Montana	3.7
3	30	Florida	3.6
16	31	Tennessee	3.5
17	32	Indiana	3.4
35	32	Kansas	3.4
42	32	Maine	3.4
28	32	Oklahoma	3.4
23	32	South Carolina	3.4
21	37	Colorado	3.3
15	37	Massachusetts	3.3
18	39	Missouri	3.2
30	40	Utah	3.1
46	41	South Dakota	3.0
12	41	Virginia	3.0
20	41	Wisconsin	3.0
22	44	Minnesota	2.9
39	45	Idaho	2.8
37	45	Nebraska	2.8
50	47	Vermont	2.7
47	48	North Dakota	2.6
31	49	Iowa	2.5
41	49	New Hampshire	2.5
40	51	Hawaii	2.4

Per capita state taxes, 2017

Population rank	State taxes rank	State	State taxes per capita (dollars) [col 337]
		United States	X
50	1	Vermont	$5,015
40	2	Hawaii	$4,924
22	3	Minnesota	$4,590
47	4	North Dakota	$4,587
29	5	Connecticut	$4,555
4	6	New York	$4,014
15	7	Massachusetts	$4,012
1	8	California	$3,936
45	9	Delaware	$3,731
11	10	New Jersey	$3,590
19	11	Maryland	$3,569
13	12	Washington	$3,240
42	13	Maine	$3,168
33	14	Arkansas	$3,168
20	15	Wisconsin	$3,129
31	16	Iowa	$3,101
44	17	Rhode Island	$3,083
6	18	Illinois	$2,967
5	19	Pennsylvania	$2,956
32	20	Nevada	$2,877
27	21	Oregon	$2,876
10	22	Michigan	$2,874
51	23	Wyoming	$2,847
35	24	Kansas	$2,806
38	25	West Virginia	$2,804
36	26	New Mexico	$2,766
17	27	Indiana	$2,708
26	28	Kentucky	$2,673
37	29	Nebraska	$2,658
39	30	Idaho	$2,628
12	31	Virginia	$2,623
9	32	North Carolina	$2,614
34	33	Mississippi	$2,608
7	34	Ohio	$2,600
43	35	Montana	$2,527
30	36	Utah	$2,525
25	37	Louisiana	$2,371
21	38	Colorado	$2,354
28	39	Oklahoma	$2,180
8	40	Georgia	$2,150
24	41	Alabama	$2,137
46	42	South Dakota	$2,103
16	43	Tennessee	$2,069
18	44	Missouri	$2,044
14	45	Arizona	$1,980
23	46	South Carolina	$1,956
3	47	Florida	$1,917
2	48	Texas	$1,894
41	49	New Hampshire	$1,859
48	50	Alaska	$1,608
49		District of Columbia	NA

Exports of goods by state of origin, 2018

Population rank	Exports rank	State	Exports (millions of dollars) [col 119]
		United States	1,664,085
2	1	Texas	315,448
1	2	California	178,405
4	3	New York	81,487
13	4	Washington	77,700
25	5	Louisiana	66,237
6	6	Illinois	65,415
10	7	Michigan	57,940
3	8	Florida	57,241
7	9	Ohio	54,293
5	10	Pennsylvania	41,050
8	11	Georgia	40,551
17	12	Indiana	39,339
11	13	New Jersey	35,663
23	14	South Carolina	34,637
9	15	North Carolina	32,730
16	16	Tennessee	32,703
26	17	Kentucky	31,757
15	18	Massachusetts	27,140
20	19	Wisconsin	22,709
22	20	Minnesota	22,685
14	21	Arizona	22,388
27	22	Oregon	22,293
24	23	Alabama	21,349
12	24	Virginia	18,358
29	25	Connecticut	17,400
18	26	Missouri	14,500
30	27	Utah	14,373
31	28	Iowa	14,324
19	29	Maryland	12,076
34	30	Mississippi	11,808
35	31	Kansas	11,604
32	32	Nevada	11,085
21	33	Colorado	8,317
38	34	West Virginia	8,124
37	35	Nebraska	7,945
47	36	North Dakota	6,778
33	37	Arkansas	6,466
28	38	Oklahoma	6,102
41	39	New Hampshire	5,286
48	40	Alaska	4,773
45	41	Delaware	4,703
39	42	Idaho	4,022
36	43	New Mexico	3,655
50	44	Vermont	2,920
42	45	Maine	2,825
49	46	District of Columbia	2,726
44	47	Rhode Island	2,400
43	48	Montana	1,654
46	49	South Dakota	1,437
51	50	Wyoming	1,356
40	51	Hawaii	647

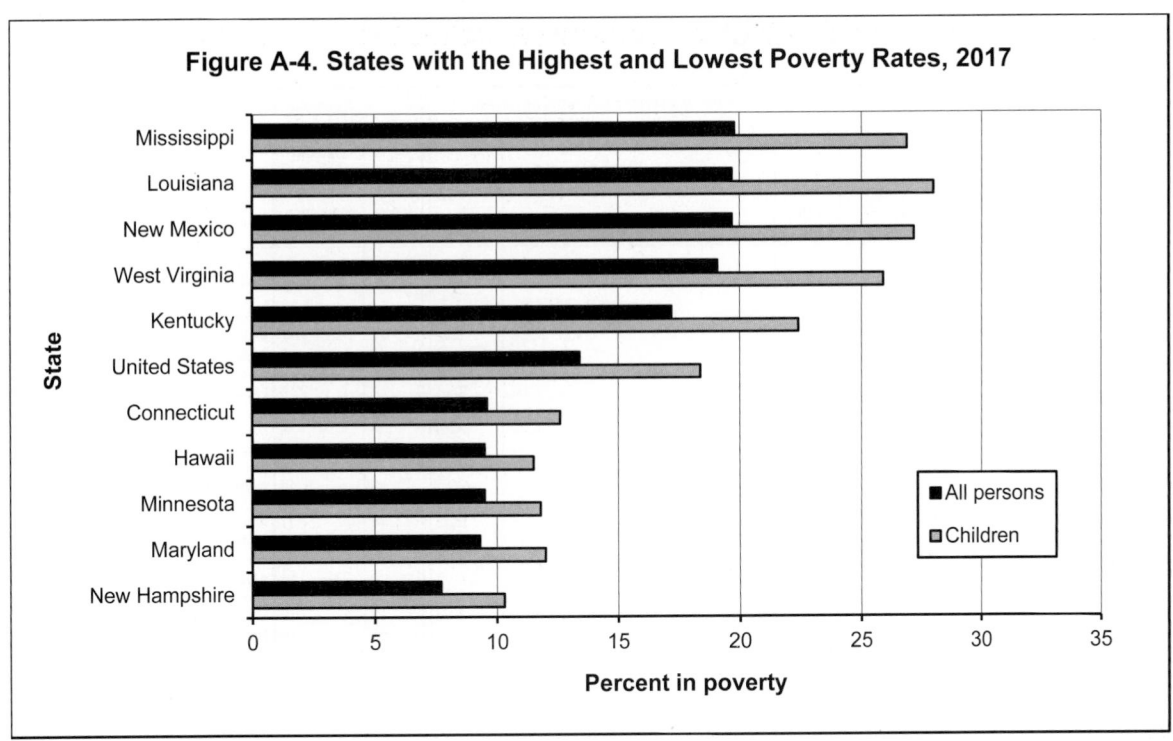

Figure A-4. States with the Highest and Lowest Poverty Rates, 2017

Nationally, 88 percent of the population 25 years old and over had graduated from high school. Twenty-six states and the District of Columbia had high school attainment levels of 90 percent or more, led by Minnesota with 93.1 percent. States in the Midwest and the West tended to have above average high school attainment rates although California had the lowest rate at 83.3 percent, followed by Texas at 83.6 percent. States with above average high school attainment levels do not necessarily have high proportions of college graduates. Nationally, 32.0 percent of the population held bachelor's degrees. In the District of Columbia, 57.3 percent of the population had graduated from college. Even when compared with other large cities, the District of Columbia had among the 10 highest proportions of college graduates in the nation. Of the 50 states, Massachusetts, Colorado, Maryland, Connecticut, New Jersey, Virginia, New Hampshire, Vermont, Minnesota, New York, and Washington each had 35 percent or more of their populations holding bachelor's degrees or more. States in the Northeast tended to have above average college attainment levels, while states in the South had below average rates.

Median household income ranged from $43,469 in West Virginia to $80,776 in Maryland. Nationally, the median household income was $60,336. In Mississippi, 30.5 percent of households had incomes below $25,000. The District of Columbia and New Jersey had the highest proportions of households earning $100,000 or more, at 42.6 percent and 40.3 percent respectively, followed by Maryland at 40.2 percent.

The poverty threshold for an individual was $12,488 in 2017. Mississippi had the highest poverty rate in the nation, with 19.8 percent of its population living in poverty. Mississippi, Louisiana, New Mexico, and West Virginia all had poverty rates of 19 percent or higher. The poverty threshold for a four-person family was $25,094. Among children under 18 years old, 18.4 percent were living in poverty. Over 27 percent of children in New Mexico lived in poverty. New Hampshire had the lowest proportion of children in poverty, at 10.3 percent. The District of Columbia had the highest proportion of residents 65 years and over living in poverty at 14.2 percent, followed by Mississippi at 13.7 percent.

The United States labor force increased by 0.9 percent between 2017 and 2018. From 2000 to 2008, it grew about an average of 1 percent a year but then declined from 2009 to 2011 followed by small increases in recent years. Ten states experienced a decline in their labor force between 2017 and 2018. North Dakota experienced the largest decline, dropping 1.5 percent. Meanwhile, the labor force in Colorado grew by 3.5 percent in the same period. In 2018, the unemployment rate was 3.9 percent, down from 4.4 percent in 2017. Two states and the District of Columbia had an unemployment rate at 5.0 percent or higher. Alaska had the highest unemployment rate in the nation at 6.6 percent followed by the District of Columbia at 5.6 percent and West Virginia at 5.3 percent. Hawaii had the lowest unemployment rate in 2018, at 2.4 percent followed by Iowa and New Hampshire at 2.5 percent. Minnesota, Idaho, Nebraska, Vermont, and North Dakota each also had an unemployment rate below three percent.

States and the District of Columbia, Selected Rankings

Percent of persons below the poverty level, 2017				Percent of children under 18 years old below the poverty level, 2017				Percent of persons lacking health insurance, 2017			
Population rank	Poverty rate rank	State	Poverty rate [col 127]	Population rank	Poverty rate rank	State	Poverty rate [col 128]	Population rank	Percent lacking health insurance rank	State	Percent lacking health insurance [col 104]
		United States	13.4			United States	18.4			United States	8.7
34	1	Mississippi	19.8	25	1	Louisiana	28.0	2	1	Texas	17.3
25	2	Louisiana	19.7	36	2	New Mexico	27.2	28	2	Oklahoma	14.2
36	2	New Mexico	19.7	34	3	Mississippi	26.9	48	3	Alaska	13.7
38	4	West Virginia	19.1	38	4	West Virginia	25.9	8	4	Georgia	13.4
26	5	Kentucky	17.2	49	5	District of Columbia	25.6	3	5	Florida	12.9
24	6	Alabama	16.9	24	6	Alabama	24.6	51	6	Wyoming	12.3
49	7	District of Columbia	16.6	23	7	South Carolina	22.6	34	7	Mississippi	12.0
33	8	Arkansas	16.4	33	8	Arkansas	22.5	32	8	Nevada	11.2
28	9	Oklahoma	15.8	26	9	Kentucky	22.4	23	9	South Carolina	11.0
23	10	South Carolina	15.4	28	10	Oklahoma	21.5	9	10	North Carolina	10.7
16	11	Tennessee	15.0	9	11	North Carolina	21.2	14	11	Arizona	10.1
14	12	Arizona	14.9	16	11	Tennessee	21.2	39	11	Idaho	10.1
8	12	Georgia	14.9	8	13	Georgia	21.0	16	13	Tennessee	9.5
9	14	North Carolina	14.7	2	14	Texas	20.9	24	14	Alabama	9.4
2	14	Texas	14.7	14	15	Arizona	20.8	30	15	Utah	9.2
10	16	Michigan	14.2	3	16	Florida	20.3	18	16	Missouri	9.1
4	17	New York	14.1	7	17	Ohio	20.1	36	16	New Mexico	9.1
3	18	Florida	14.0	10	18	Michigan	19.7	46	16	South Dakota	9.1
7	18	Ohio	14.0	4	18	New York	19.7	12	19	Virginia	8.8
45	20	Delaware	13.6	18	20	Missouri	18.6	35	20	Kansas	8.7
17	21	Indiana	13.5	45	21	Delaware	18.5	43	21	Montana	8.5
18	22	Missouri	13.4	32	21	Nevada	18.5	25	22	Louisiana	8.4
1	23	California	13.3	17	23	Indiana	18.4	37	23	Nebraska	8.3
27	24	Oregon	13.2	1	24	California	18.1	17	24	Indiana	8.2
32	25	Nevada	13.0	6	25	Illinois	17.0	42	25	Maine	8.1
46	25	South Dakota	13.0	5	25	Pennsylvania	17.0	33	26	Arkansas	7.9
39	27	Idaho	12.8	44	27	Rhode Island	16.6	11	27	New Jersey	7.7
6	28	Illinois	12.6	46	27	South Dakota	16.6	21	28	Colorado	7.5
43	29	Montana	12.5	27	29	Oregon	16.5	47	28	North Dakota	7.5
5	29	Pennsylvania	12.5	39	30	Idaho	15.3	1	30	California	7.2
35	31	Kansas	11.9	48	31	Alaska	14.9	6	31	Illinois	6.8
44	32	Rhode Island	11.6	35	32	Kansas	14.8	27	31	Oregon	6.8
50	33	Vermont	11.3	43	33	Montana	14.7	19	33	Maryland	6.1
20	33	Wisconsin	11.3	20	34	Wisconsin	14.5	13	33	Washington	6.1
51	33	Wyoming	11.3	13	35	Washington	14.3	38	33	West Virginia	6.1
48	36	Alaska	11.1	37	36	Nebraska	14.1	7	36	Ohio	6.0
42	36	Maine	11.1	12	37	Virginia	14.0	41	37	New Hampshire	5.8
13	38	Washington	11.0	11	38	New Jersey	13.9	4	38	New York	5.7
37	39	Nebraska	10.8	50	39	Vermont	13.8	29	39	Connecticut	5.5
31	40	Iowa	10.7	15	40	Massachusetts	13.5	5	39	Pennsylvania	5.5
12	41	Virginia	10.6	51	41	Wyoming	13.3	45	41	Delaware	5.4
15	42	Massachusetts	10.5	42	42	Maine	13.1	26	41	Kentucky	5.4
21	43	Colorado	10.3	29	43	Connecticut	12.6	20	41	Wisconsin	5.4
47	43	North Dakota	10.3	31	44	Iowa	12.3	10	44	Michigan	5.2
11	45	New Jersey	10.0	21	45	Colorado	12.0	31	45	Iowa	4.7
30	46	Utah	9.7	19	45	Maryland	12.0	44	46	Rhode Island	4.6
29	47	Connecticut	9.6	22	47	Minnesota	11.8	50	46	Vermont	4.6
40	48	Hawaii	9.5	40	48	Hawaii	11.5	22	48	Minnesota	4.4
22	48	Minnesota	9.5	47	49	North Dakota	10.9	49	49	District of Columbia	3.8
19	50	Maryland	9.3	30	50	Utah	10.7	40	49	Hawaii	3.8
41	51	New Hampshire	7.7	41	51	New Hampshire	10.3	15	51	Massachusetts	2.8

States and the District of Columbia, Selected Rankings

State government employment, 2017				Value of agricultural products sold, 2017				Violent crime rate, 2017			
Popu-rank	State government employment rank	State	State government employment [col 312]	Popu-lation rank	Agricultural sales rank	State	Value of sales (millions of dollars) [col 197]	Popu-lation rank	Violent crime rate rank	State	Violent crime rate (per 100,000 population) [col 108]
		United States	4,381,768			United States	388,523			United States	394
1	1	California	424,359	1	1	California	45,154	49	1	District of Columbia	1,004.9
2	2	Texas	313,065	31	2	Iowa	28,957	48	2	Alaska	829.0
4	3	New York	247,580	2	3	Texas	24,924	36	3	New Mexico	783.5
3	4	Florida	179,738	37	4	Nebraska	21,983	16	4	Tennessee	651.5
5	5	Pennsylvania	164,285	35	5	Kansas	18,783	25	5	Louisiana	557.0
10	6	Michigan	146,697	22	6	Minnesota	18,395	32	6	Nevada	555.9
9	7	North Carolina	144,993	6	7	Illinois	17,010	33	7	Arkansas	554.9
11	8	New Jersey	139,048	9	8	North Carolina	12,901	18	8	Missouri	530.3
7	9	Ohio	137,560	20	9	Wisconsin	11,427	24	9	Alabama	524.2
8	10	Georgia	129,828	17	10	Indiana	11,107	14	10	Arizona	508.0
13	11	Washington	127,234	18	11	Missouri	10,526	23	11	South Carolina	506.2
12	12	Virginia	125,605	46	12	South Dakota	9,722	19	12	Maryland	500.2
6	13	Illinois	121,795	33	13	Arkansas	9,651	28	13	Oklahoma	456.2
15	14	Massachusetts	98,206	13	14	Washington	9,635	45	14	Delaware	453.4
24	15	Alabama	90,729	8	15	Georgia	9,573	10	15	Michigan	450.0
17	16	Indiana	90,341	7	16	Ohio	9,341	1	16	California	449.3
21	17	Colorado	88,130	47	17	North Dakota	8,234	2	17	Texas	438.9
18	18	Missouri	86,498	10	18	Michigan	8,221	6	18	Illinois	438.8
19	19	Maryland	85,163	5	19	Pennsylvania	7,759	46	19	South Dakota	433.6
26	20	Kentucky	84,042	39	20	Idaho	7,567	35	20	Kansas	413.0
22	21	Minnesota	83,359	21	21	Colorado	7,492	3	21	Florida	408.0
23	22	South Carolina	79,834	28	22	Oklahoma	7,466	17	22	Indiana	399.0
16	23	Tennessee	78,746	3	23	Florida	7,357	43	23	Montana	377.1
25	24	Louisiana	73,488	34	24	Mississippi	6,196	21	24	Colorado	368.1
20	25	Wisconsin	72,899	24	25	Alabama	5,981	9	25	North Carolina	363.7
14	26	Arizona	72,850	26	26	Kentucky	5,738	15	26	Massachusetts	358.0
27	27	Oregon	70,153	4	27	New York	5,369	8	27	Georgia	357.2
28	28	Oklahoma	66,128	27	28	Oregon	5,007	4	28	New York	356.7
33	29	Arkansas	62,066	12	29	Virginia	3,961	38	29	West Virginia	350.7
30	30	Utah	60,507	14	30	Arizona	3,852	20	30	Wisconsin	319.9
40	31	Hawaii	58,966	16	31	Tennessee	3,799	5	31	Pennsylvania	313.3
29	32	Connecticut	58,803	43	32	Montana	3,521	37	32	Nebraska	305.9
34	33	Mississippi	55,539	25	33	Louisiana	3,173	13	33	Washington	304.5
35	34	Kansas	53,820	23	34	South Carolina	3,009	7	34	Ohio	297.5
31	35	Iowa	51,176	36	35	New Mexico	2,582	31	35	Iowa	293.4
36	36	New Mexico	45,194	19	36	Maryland	2,473	34	36	Mississippi	285.7
38	37	West Virginia	39,394	30	37	Utah	1,839	27	37	Oregon	281.8
37	38	Nebraska	31,655	51	38	Wyoming	1,472	47	38	North Dakota	281.3
32	39	Nevada	28,936	45	39	Delaware	1,466	40	39	Hawaii	250.6
45	40	Delaware	25,872	11	40	New Jersey	1,098	30	40	Utah	238.9
48	41	Alaska	24,357	50	41	Vermont	781	22	41	Minnesota	238.3
39	42	Idaho	24,176	38	42	West Virginia	754	51	42	Wyoming	237.5
43	43	Montana	20,870	42	43	Maine	667	44	43	Rhode Island	232.2
42	44	Maine	20,172	32	44	Nevada	666	11	44	New Jersey	228.8
47	45	North Dakota	19,026	29	45	Connecticut	580	29	45	Connecticut	228.0
41	46	New Hampshire	18,931	40	46	Hawaii	564	39	46	Idaho	226.4
44	47	Rhode Island	18,151	15	47	Massachusetts	475	26	47	Kentucky	225.8
46	48	South Dakota	14,449	41	48	New Hampshire	188	12	48	Virginia	208.2
50	49	Vermont	14,267	48	49	Alaska	71	41	49	New Hampshire	198.7
51	50	Wyoming	13,088	44	50	Rhode Island	58	50	50	Vermont	165.8
49		District of Columbia	NA	49		District of Columbia	NA	42	51	Maine	121.0

Table A. States — Land Area and Population Characteristics

State code	STATE	Land area,[1] 2018 (sq mi)	Population, 2018			Race alone or in combination, not Hispanic or Latino (percent)				Population characteristics, 2018	Age (percent)					
			Total persons, 2018	Rank	Per square mile	White	Black	American Indian, Alaska Native	Asian and Pacific Islander	Hispanic or Latino[2] (percent)	Under 5 years	5 to 17 years	18 to 24 years	25 to 34 years	35 to 44 years	45 to 54 years
		1	2	3	4	5	6	7	8	9	10	11	12	13	14	15

1. Dry land or land partially or temporarily covered by water.   2. May be of any race.

Table A. States — Population Characteristics, Immigration, and Households

STATE	Population characteristics, 2018 (cont.)									Households, 2017					
	Age (percent) (cont.)				Median age	Percent female	Percent foreign born 2017	Percent born in state of residence 2017	Immigrants admitted to legal status, 2017	Number	Percent change, 2016–2017	Persons per house-hold	Household type		
	55 to 64 years	65 to 74 years	75 to 84 years	85 years and over									Married Couple family	Female house-holder family	House-holder living alone
	16	17	18	19	20	21	22	23	24	25	26	27	28	29	30

Table A. States — Population Change

STATE	Population, 1990–2010			Population change, 1990–2018								Population, 2020–2030		
	Census counts			Percent change			Components of change, 2010–2018					Projections		
									Migration					
	1990	2000	2010	1990–2000	2000–2010	2010–2018	Births	Deaths	Net migration	Inter-national	Net internal	2020	2025	2030
	31	32	33	34	35	36	37	38	39	40	41	42	43	44

Table A. States — Population Characteristics

STATE	Population characteristics, 2010																		
	Race (percent)							Age (percent)										
	White alone	Black alone	American Indian, Alaska Native alone	Asian and Pacific Islander alone	Some other race or two or more races	Percent Hispanic or Latino[1]	Percent foreign born	Under 5 years	5 to 17 years	18 to 24 years	25 to 34 years	35 to 44 years	45 to 54 years	55 to 64 years	65 to 74 years	75 to 84 years	85 years and over	Median age	Percent female
	45	46	47	48	49	50	51	52	53	54	55	56	57	58	59	60	61	62	63

1. May be of any race.

Table A. States — **Households and Housing Units**

STATE	Households, 2010					Housing units, 2010									
				Percent				Occupied units							
								Owner-occupied					Renter-occupied		
											Median owner cost as a percent of income				
	Number	Percent change, 2000-2010	Persons per house-hold	Female family house-holder[1]	One-person house-holds	Total	Percent change, 2000–2010	Total	Percent	Median value[2] (dollars)	With a mort-gage	Without a mort-gage[3]	Median gross rent[4] (dollars)	Median rent as a percent of income	Sub-standard units[5] (percent)
	64	65	66	67	68	69	70	71	72	73	74	75	76	77	78

1. No spouse present.   2. Specified owner-occupied units.   3. Median monthly costs is often in the minimum category—10.0 percent or less, which is indicated as 10.0 percent.   4. Speci-fied renter-occupied units.   5. Overcrowded or lacking complete plumbing facilities.

Table A. States — **Housing Units**

STATE	Housing units, 2017													
			Occupied units											
					Percent who pay 30 percent or more of income for housing expenses[1]		Median owner cost as a percent of income							
	Total	Percent change, 2016-2017	Total	Percent owner-occupied	Owners with a mortgage	Renter	With a mort-gage	Without a mort-gage[2]	Median monthly housing costs (dollars)	Median value of units[3] (dollars)	Percent valued over $500,000	Median gross rent[4] (dollars)	Sub-standard units[5] (percent)	Percent living in a different house than 1 year ago
	79	80	81	82	83	84	85	86	87	88	89	90	91	92

1. Excludes units where owner costs or gross rent as a percentage of houshold income cannot be calculated.   2. Median monthly costs is often in the minimum category—10.0 percent or less, which is indicated as 10.0 percent.   3. Specified owner-occupied units.   4. Specified renter-occupied units.   5. Overcrowded or lacking complete plumbing facilities.

Table A. States — **Residential Contruction, Vital Statistics, and Health**

STATE	Value of residential construction authorized by building permits, 2018			New manufactured homes placed, 2018	Births, 2017		Deaths, 2017					Percent lacking health insurance, 2017		Medicare beneficiaries, 65 years and older 2018
							Number		Rate					
									Total					
	New construction ($1,000)	Number of housing units	Percent single family		Total	Rate[1]	Total	Infant[2]	Crude[1]	Age-adjusted[1]	Infant[3]	All persons	Children under 19 years	
	93	94	95	96	97	98	99	100	101	102	103	104	105	106

1. Per 1,000 resident population.   2. Deaths of infants under 1 year old.   3. Deaths of infants under 1 year old per 1,000 live births.

Table A. States — **Crime and Education**

STATE	Serious crime known to police,[1] 2017				Public elementary and secondary school enrollment, 2016–2017		Educational attainment[3] (percent)				Local government expenditures for education, 2015-2016	
	Violent crime		Property crime				2010		2017			
	Number	Rate[2]	Number	Rate[2]	Total	Student/ teacher ratio	High school graduate or more	Bach-elor's degree or more	High school graduate or more	Bach-elor's degree or more	Total current expen-ditures (mil dol)	Current expen-ditures per student (dollars)
	107	108	109	110	111	112	113	114	115	116	117	118

1. Data for serious crimes have not been adjusted for underreporting; this may affect comparability between geographic areas and over time.   2. Per 100,000 population estimated by the FBI.
3. Persons age 25 and over.

Table A. States — Exports, Income, and Poverty

STATE	Exports of goods by state of origin, 2018 (mil dol)			Income, 2017					Percent below poverty level, 2017						
				Per capita income (dollars)	Households								Families with related children under 18 years		
	Total	Manu-factured	Non-manu-factured		Median income (dollars)	Percent with income of $24,999 or less	Percent with income of $100,000 or more	Median income of family of four	All persons	Children under 18 years	Persons 65 years and over	All families	Married-couple families	Male house-holder[1] families	Female house-holder[1] families
	119	120	121	122	123	124	125	126	127	128	129	130	131	132	133

1. No spouse present.

Table A. States — Personal Income

STATE	Personal income												
	Total, 2018 (mil dol)	Percent change, 2017–2018	Per capita[1], 2018		Sources of personal income (mil dol)								
			Dollars	Rank	Wages and salaries[2], 2018	Proprietors' income, 2018	Divi-dends, interest, and rent, 2018	Transfer payments, 2017					
								Total	Government payments to individuals				
									Total	Social Security	Medical payments	Income main-tenance	Unemploy-ment insurance
	134	135	136	137	138	139	140	141	142	143	144	145	146

1. Based on the resident population estimated as of July 1 of the year shown.   2. Includes supplements to wages and salaries.

Table A. States — Personal Income and Earnings

STATE	Personal tax payments, 2017 (mil dol)	Disposable personal income, 2017		Earnings, 2018									Gross state product, 2018 (mil dol)
		Total (mil dol)	Per capita[1] (dollars)	Percent by selected industries									
				Total (mil dol)	Farm	Goods-related[2]		Service-related and other[3]					
						Total	Manu-facturing	Total	Retail trade	Finance, insurance, real estate, rental and leasing	Health care and social assistance	Govern-ment	
	147	148	149	150	151	152	153	154	155	156	157	158	159

1. Based on the resident population estimated as of July 1 of the year shown.   2. Includes mining, construction, and manufacturing.   3. Includes private sector earnings in forestry, fishing, related activities, and other; utilities; wholesale trade; transportation and warehousing; and information.

Table A. States — Social Security, Employment, and Labor Force

STATE	Social Security beneficiaries, December 2017		Supple-mental Security Income recipients, December 2017	Civilian employment and selected occupations,[2] 2015					Civilian labor force (annual average), 2018				
	Number	Rate[1]		Total	Percent				Total (1,000)	Percent change, 2017–2018	Employed (1,000)	Unemployed	
					Management, business, science, and arts occupations	Services, sales, and office	Construction and production					Total (1,000)	Rate[3]
	160	161	162	163	164	165	166		167	168	169	170	171

1. Per 1,000 resident population estimated as of July 1 of the year shown.   2. Persons 16 years old and over.   3. Percent of civilian labor force.

Table A. States — **Nonfarm Employment and Earnings**

STATE	Nonfarm employment and earnings, 2016											
	Employed		Manufacturing			Employment (1,000)						
	Total (1,000)	Percent change, 2017–2018	Employ-ment (1,000)	Average earnings of production workers		Con-struction	Trans-portation and public utilities	Whole-sale trade	Retail trade	Informa-tion	Financial activities	Services[1]
				Hourly	Weekly							
	172	173	174	175	176	177	178	179	180	181	182	183

1. Includes professional and business services, educational and health services, leisure and hospitality, and other services.

Table A. States — **Agriculture**

STATE	Agriculture, 2017											
	Farms			Farm producers whose primary occupation is farming (percent)	Government payments, average per farm that recieves payments (dollars)	Land in farms					Value of land and buildings (dollars)	
		Percent with:						Acres				
	Number	Fewer than 50 acres	1,000 acres or more			Acreage (1,000)	Percent change, 2012–2017	Average size of farm	Total irrigated (1,000)	Total cropland (1,000)	Average per farm	Average per acre
	184	185	186	187	188	189	190	191	192	193	194	195

Table A. States — **Agriculture, Land, and Water**

STATE	Agriculture, 2017 (cont.)							Land, 2015			
	Value of machinery and equip-ment, average per farm (dollars)	Value of products sold				Organic Farms (number)	Farms with Internet access (percent)	Owned by the federal government (percent)	Developed land (percent)	Rural land (percent)	Public water supply withdrawn, 2015 (mil gal per day)
		Total (mil dol)	Average per farm (dollars)	Percent from:							
				Crops	Livestock and poultry products						
	196	197	198	199	200	201	202	203	204	205	206

Table A. States — **Manufactures and Construction**

STATE	Manufactures, 2016											Construction, 2012			
	All employees			Production workers				Value added by manu-facture (mil dol)	Value of ship-ments (mil dol)	Total cost of materials (mil dol)	Number of estab-lishments	Employees		Value (mil dol)	Annual payroll (mil dol)
	Number (1,000)	Percent change, 2015–2016	Annual payroll (mil dol)	Number (1,000)	Work hours (millions)	Wages						Number	Percent change, 2007–2012		
						Total (mil dol)	Average per worker (dollars)								
	207	208	209	210	211	212	213	214	215	216	217	218	219	220	221

20

Table A. States — **Wholesale Trade and Retail Trade**

STATE	Wholesale trade, 2012					Retail trade,[1] 2012								
	Number of establishments	Employees		Sales (mil dol)	Annual payroll (mil dol)	Number of establishments	Employees		Motor vehicle and parts dealers	Food and beverage stores	Clothing and clothing accessory stores	General merchandise stores	Sales (mil dol)	Annual payroll (mil dol)
		Number	Percent change, 2007–2012				Total	Percent change, 2007–2012						
	222	223	224	225	226	227	228	229	230	231	232	233	234	235

1. Establishments with payroll.

Table A. States — **Information**

STATE	Information, 2012										
	Number of establishments	Employees		Publishing, except Internet	Motion picture and sound recording	Broadcasting, except Internet	Internet publishing and broadcasting and web search portals	Tele-communications	Data processing, hosting, and related services	Receipts (mil dol)	Annual payroll (mil dol)
		Number	Percent change, 2007–2012								
	236	237	238	239	240	241	242	243	244	245	246

Table A. States — **Utilities, Transportation and Warehousing, and Finance and Insurance**

STATE	Utilities, 2012					Transportation and warehousing, 2012					Finance and insurance, 2012				
	Number of establishments	Employees		Receipts (mil dol)	Annual payroll (mil dol)	Number of establishments	Employees		Receipts (mil dol)	Annual payroll (mil dol)	Number of establishments	Employees		Receipts (mil dol)	Annual payroll (mil dol)
		Number	Percent change, 2007–2012				Number	Percent change, 2007–2012				Number	Percent change, 2007–2012		
	247	248	249	250	251	252	253	254	255	256	257	258	259	260	261

Table A. States — **Real Estate and Rental and Leasing and Professional, Scientific, and Technical Services**

STATE	Real estate and rental and leasing, 2012					Professional, scientific, and technical services, 2012							
	Number of establishments	Employees		Receipts (mil dol)	Annual payroll (mil dol)	Number of establishments	Employees		Legal services	Accounting, tax preparation, bookkeeping, and payroll services	Architectural, engineering, and related services	Computer systems design and related services	Receipts (mil dol)	Annual payroll (mil dol)
		Number	Percent change, 2007–2012				Total	Percent change, 2007–2012						
	262	263	264	265	266	267	268	269	270	271	272	273	274	275

Table A. States — Health Care and Social Assistance

STATE	Health care and social assistance, 2012													
	Subject to federal tax						Tax-exempt						
			Employees						Employees				
	Number of estab-lishments	Total	Percent change, 2007–2012	Ambulatory health care services	Hospitals	Receipts (mil dol)	Annual payroll (mil dol)	Number of estab-lishments	Total	Percent change, 2007–2012	Ambulatory health care services	Hospitals	Receipts (mil dol)	Annual payroll (mil dol)
	276	277	278	279	280	281	282	283	284	285	286	287	288	289

Table A. States — Arts, Entertainment, and Recreation and Accommodation and Food Services

| STATE | Arts, entertainment, and recreation, 2012 | | | | | Accommodation and food services, 2012 | | | | |
| | | Employees | | | | | Employees | | | |
	Number of estab-lishments	Number	Percent change, 2007–2012	Receipts (mil dol)	Annual payroll (mil dol)	Number of estab-lishments	Total	Percent change, 2007–2012	Food services and drinking places	Receipts (mil dol)	Annual payroll (mil dol)
	290	291	292	293	294	295	296	297	298	299	300

Table A. States — Other Services, Except Public Administration and Government Employment

| STATE | Other services, except public administration, 2012 | | | | | | | | Government employment, 2017 | | |
| | | Employees | | | | | | | | | |
	Number of estab-lishments	Total	Percent change, 2007–2012	Repair and mainte-nance	Personal and laundry services	Religious, civic, and similar services	Receipts (mil dol)	Annual payroll (mil dol)	Federal civilian	Federal military	State and local
	301	302	303	304	305	306	307	308	309	310	311

Table A. States — State Government Employment and Payroll

STATE	State government employment and payroll, 2017											
	State government employment, 2017			State government payroll, 2017		Full-time equivalent payroll (1000 dollars)						
							Percent of total for:					
	Full-time equivalent employees	Full-time employees	Part-time employees	Full-time March payroll (1000 dollars)	Part-time March payroll (1000 dollars)	Total March payroll (1000 dollars)[1]	Administration	Judicial and legal	Police	Corrections	Highways and transporta-tion	Welfare
	312	313	314	315	316	317	318	319	320	321	322	323

1. Includes program categories not shown separately.

STATE	State government employment and payroll, 2017 (cont.)							State government finances, 2017							
	Full-time equivalent payroll (1000 dollars) (cont.)							General revenue (mil dol)							
	Percent of total for:								From federal government		From own sources				
												Taxes		Taxes per capita[2] (dollars)	
	Health	Hospitals	Social Insurance administration	Natural resources and parks	Utilities, sewerge, and waste management	Elementary and secondary education and libraries	Higher education	Total	Total	Per capita[2] (dollars)	Total	Total	Sales and gross receipts	Total	Sales and gross receipts
	324	325	326	327	328	329	330	331	332	333	334	335	336	337	338

1. Based on resident population estimated as of July 1 of the year shown.

STATE	State government finances, 2017 (cont.)										Voting and registration, November 2018		Presidential election, 2016 (percent of vote cast)		
	General expenditures (mil dol) (cont.)									Debt outstanding					
		Direct expenditures			By selected function										
	Total	To local governments	Total	Per capita[1] (dollars)	Education	Health and hospitals	Highways	Public safety	Public welfare	Natural resources, parks, and recreation	Total (mil dol)	Per capita[1]	Percent registered	Percent voted	Demo-cratic	Repub-lican	All other
	339	340	341	342	343	344	345	346	347	348	349	350	351	352	353	354	355

1. Based on resident population estimated as of July 1 of the year shown.

Table A. States — Land Area and Population Characteristics

State code	STATE	Land area,[1] 2018 (sq mi)	Population, 2018			Race alone or in combination, not Hispanic or Latino (percent)				Population characteristics, 2,018	Age (percent)					
			Total persons, 2018	Rank	Per square mile	White	Black	American Indian, Alaska Native	Asian and Pacific Islander	Hispanic or Latino[2] (percent)	Under 5 years	5 to 17 years	18 to 24 years	25 to 34 years	35 to 44 years	45 to 54 years
		1	2	3	4	5	6	7	8	9	10	11	12	13	14	15
0	United States	3,532,614.3	327,167,434	X	92.6	62.3	13.5	1.3	6.9	18.3	6.1	16.4	9.3	14.0	12.6	12.7
1	Alabama..........................	50,646.6	4,887,871	24	96.5	66.8	27.3	1.2	1.9	4.4	6.0	16.3	9.3	13.2	12.1	12.8
2	Alaska............................	570,983.2	737,438	48	1.3	66.3	4.8	18.9	10.2	7.2	7.2	17.7	9.5	16.1	12.8	11.9
4	Arizona...........................	113,590.7	7,171,646	14	63.1	56.3	5.2	4.5	4.6	31.6	6.1	16.8	9.6	13.7	12.3	11.9
5	Arkansas.........................	52,034.6	3,013,825	33	57.9	74.0	16.2	1.6	2.4	7.7	6.3	17.0	9.3	13.2	12.2	12.2
6	California.........................	155,793.7	39,557,045	1	253.9	39.3	6.5	1.0	17.0	39.3	6.2	16.6	9.5	15.3	13.3	12.8
8	Colorado	103,638.7	5,695,564	21	55.0	70.0	4.9	1.3	4.5	21.7	5.9	16.3	9.2	15.7	13.7	12.5
9	Connecticut......................	4,842.7	3,572,665	29	737.7	68.1	11.2	0.6	5.5	16.5	5.1	15.5	9.7	12.5	11.8	13.9
10	Delaware.........................	1,948.2	967,171	45	496.4	63.9	23.4	0.9	4.7	9.5	5.7	15.4	8.7	13.3	11.5	12.7
11	District of Columbia...........	61.1	702,455	49	11,496.8	38.8	46.3	0.8	5.4	11.3	6.5	11.7	10.6	23.4	15.0	10.7
12	Florida............................	53,648.6	21,299,325	3	397.0	54.9	16.5	0.6	3.7	26.1	5.4	14.5	8.2	13.1	12.1	12.9
13	Georgia	57,715.3	10,519,475	8	182.3	54.0	32.6	0.7	4.9	9.8	6.2	17.6	9.6	14.0	13.0	13.4
15	Hawaii............................	6,422.4	1,420,491	40	221.2	36.2	3.0	1.7	75.3	10.7	6.2	15.2	8.5	14.3	12.7	12.0
16	Idaho.............................	82,645.1	1,754,208	39	21.2	83.7	1.2	1.9	2.6	12.7	6.6	18.8	9.3	13.2	12.5	11.4
17	Illinois............................	55,514.0	12,741,080	6	229.5	62.5	14.9	0.5	6.5	17.4	6.0	16.5	9.2	13.9	12.9	12.9
18	Indiana...........................	35,826.2	6,691,878	17	186.8	80.6	10.6	0.7	3.0	7.1	6.3	17.2	9.8	13.1	12.3	12.5
19	Iowa..............................	55,854.0	3,156,145	31	56.5	86.9	4.7	0.7	3.3	6.2	6.3	16.9	10.1	12.6	12.0	11.8
20	Kansas...........................	81,759.2	2,911,505	35	35.6	78.1	7.0	1.8	3.8	12.1	6.5	17.7	10.1	13.2	12.2	11.5
21	Kentucky.........................	39,490.3	4,468,402	26	113.2	86.0	9.3	0.7	2.1	3.8	6.2	16.4	9.3	13.1	12.4	12.9
22	Louisiana.........................	43,203.9	4,659,978	25	107.9	59.9	33.1	1.2	2.2	5.2	6.6	16.9	9.1	14.3	12.5	12.1
23	Maine.............................	30,844.7	1,338,404	42	43.4	94.8	2.1	1.4	1.8	1.7	4.8	13.9	8.0	12.0	11.4	13.5
24	Maryland.........................	9,710.9	6,042,718	19	622.3	52.5	31.3	0.8	7.7	10.4	6.0	16.1	8.8	13.8	12.8	13.6
25	Massachusetts..................	7,801.2	6,902,149	15	884.8	73.1	8.2	0.6	7.9	12.3	5.2	14.6	10.2	14.4	12.2	13.4
26	Michigan..........................	56,602.9	9,995,915	10	176.6	76.9	14.9	1.3	4.0	5.2	5.7	15.9	9.6	13.0	11.6	12.9
27	Minnesota........................	79,625.4	5,611,179	22	70.5	81.6	7.7	1.8	5.9	5.5	6.3	16.9	8.9	13.6	12.7	12.3
28	Mississippi.......................	46,924.4	2,986,530	34	63.6	57.5	38.1	0.9	1.4	3.4	6.2	17.4	9.8	13.2	12.2	12.3
29	Missouri..........................	68,745.8	6,126,452	18	89.1	81.3	12.7	1.2	2.8	4.3	6.1	16.4	9.2	13.4	12.2	12.3
30	Montana..........................	145,546.1	1,062,305	43	7.3	88.3	1.0	7.7	1.6	4.0	5.9	15.7	9.3	12.9	11.9	11.3
31	Nebraska.........................	76,817.6	1,929,268	37	25.1	80.3	5.8	1.4	3.3	11.2	6.9	17.8	9.9	13.3	12.4	11.4
32	Nevada...........................	109,780.2	3,034,392	32	27.6	51.6	10.4	1.5	11.2	29.0	6.1	16.6	8.2	14.7	13.3	13.0
33	New Hampshire	8,953.5	1,356,458	41	151.5	91.5	2.0	0.8	3.6	3.9	4.7	14.3	9.3	12.5	11.4	14.0
34	New Jersey	7,354.4	8,908,520	11	1,211.3	56.2	13.7	0.5	10.6	20.6	5.8	16.1	8.6	13.0	12.8	13.9
35	New Mexico	121,311.9	2,095,428	36	17.3	38.5	2.4	9.5	2.2	49.1	5.9	17.1	9.4	13.5	12.0	11.5
36	New York.........................	47,123.4	19,542,209	4	414.7	56.9	15.5	0.7	9.7	19.2	5.8	15.0	9.2	14.7	12.4	13.1
37	North Carolina...................	48,619.4	10,383,620	9	213.6	64.5	22.5	1.7	3.7	9.6	5.9	16.3	9.5	13.4	12.5	13.3
38	North Dakota....................	68,999.4	760,077	47	11.0	85.9	3.9	6.2	2.3	3.9	7.2	16.3	11.1	15.1	11.9	10.5
39	Ohio..............................	40,860.8	11,689,442	7	286.1	80.6	14.0	0.7	3.0	3.9	5.9	16.2	9.1	13.2	11.9	12.7
40	Oklahoma........................	68,596.0	3,943,079	28	57.5	70.5	8.9	12.5	3.1	10.9	6.6	17.7	9.6	13.8	12.4	11.7
41	Oregon...........................	95,987.7	4,190,713	27	43.7	78.4	2.8	2.4	6.7	13.3	5.6	15.3	8.7	14.2	13.4	12.2
42	Pennsylvania....................	44,743.2	12,807,060	5	286.2	77.6	11.9	0.5	4.2	7.6	5.5	15.2	9.1	13.3	11.7	12.9
44	Rhode Island....................	1,033.9	1,057,315	44	1,022.6	73.8	7.2	1.0	4.3	15.9	5.1	14.3	10.5	13.8	11.7	13.2
45	South Carolina	30,063.8	5,084,127	23	169.1	65.2	27.7	0.9	2.3	5.8	5.8	16.0	9.2	13.3	12.0	12.7
46	South Dakota....................	75,810.0	882,235	46	11.6	83.4	3.0	9.5	2.2	4.1	7.0	17.6	9.5	13.2	11.8	11.0
47	Tennessee.......................	41,236.8	6,770,010	16	164.2	75.3	17.7	0.8	2.4	5.6	6.0	16.2	9.1	13.8	12.4	13.0
48	Texas.............................	261,257.3	28,701,845	2	109.9	42.8	12.7	0.7	5.7	39.6	7.1	18.7	9.7	14.8	13.5	12.4
49	Utah..............................	82,195.8	3,161,105	30	38.5	80.0	1.7	1.4	5.0	14.2	8.0	21.5	11.3	14.7	13.7	10.2
50	Vermont..........................	9,217.9	626,299	50	67.9	94.3	1.9	1.2	2.6	2.0	4.7	13.8	10.7	11.8	11.3	12.9
51	Virginia...........................	39,481.9	8,517,685	12	215.7	63.8	20.5	0.8	8.1	9.6	6.0	16.0	9.5	14.0	13.0	13.2
53	Washington......................	66,453.0	7,535,591	13	113.4	71.7	5.2	2.5	12.2	12.9	6.1	15.9	8.7	15.3	13.3	12.4
54	West Virginia....................	24,041.2	1,805,832	38	75.1	93.7	4.5	0.8	1.2	1.7	5.3	14.9	8.7	11.9	12.0	13.0
55	Wisconsin........................	54,166.3	5,813,568	20	107.3	82.7	7.3	1.4	3.5	6.9	5.8	16.2	9.5	12.7	12.1	12.7
56	Wyoming.........................	97,088.7	577,737	51	6.0	85.5	1.7	2.9	1.7	10.1	6.2	17.1	9.1	13.5	12.6	11.2

1. Dry land or land partially or temporarily covered by water.   2. May be of any race.

Table A. States — Population Characteristics, Immigration, and Households

STATE	Population characteristics, 2018 (cont.)									Households, 2017					
	Age (percent) (cont.)												Household type		
	55 to 64 years	65 to 74 years	75 to 84 years	85 years and over	Median age	Percent female	Percent foreign born 2017	Percent born in state of residence 2017	Immigrants admitted to legal status, 2017	Number	Percent change, 2016–2017	Persons per house-hold	Married Couple family	Female house-holder family	House-holder living alone
	16	17	18	19	20	21	22	23	24	25	26	27	28	29	30
United States	12.9	9.3	4.7	2	38.2	50.8	13.7	58.2	1,127,167	120,062,818	1.0	2.65	48.2	12.4	27.9
Alabama.........................	13.4	10.0	5.1	1.8	39.2	51.6	3.5	69.9	3,801	1,841,665	-0.6	2.58	46.5	14.6	29.9
Alaska	12.8	7.9	2.9	0.9	34.6	47.9	7.9	42.5	1,547	250,741	0.9	2.84	49.4	11.4	25.3
Arizona..........................	12.1	10.1	5.4	2	37.9	50.3	13.2	39.7	19,344	2,552,972	1.3	2.69	47.3	12.1	27.8
Arkansas.......................	12.8	9.8	5.2	2	38.3	50.9	4.7	60.6	3,071	1,153,082	0.9	2.53	47.9	12.8	29.1
California.......................	12.1	8.3	4.1	1.9	36.8	50.3	26.9	55.6	214,243	13,005,097	0.5	2.98	49.6	13.0	24.0
Colorado........................	12.5	8.8	3.8	1.6	36.9	49.6	9.8	42.1	14,520	2,139,207	1.4	2.57	49.7	9.5	27.1
Connecticut....................	14.3	9.6	5	2.6	41.0	51.2	14.8	54.2	11,938	1,356,762	-0.0	2.56	47.9	12.3	29.0
Delaware........................	14.0	11.2	5.5	2.1	40.7	51.6	10.2	43.2	2,244	357,937	2.0	2.62	49.4	11.8	27.7
District of Columbia...........	10.0	7.0	3.4	1.7	34.0	52.6	14.7	37.4	2,885	281,475	0.1	2.32	25.1	13.8	45.2
Florida...........................	13.4	11.3	6.5	2.7	42.2	51.1	20.9	36.0	127,609	7,689,964	1.5	2.67	46.7	12.7	28.8
Georgia	12.2	8.5	4	1.4	36.9	51.4	10.2	55.1	26,242	3,745,074	1.6	2.72	47.8	14.9	26.7
Hawaii	12.7	10.5	5	2.9	39.2	49.9	18.6	53.0	5,396	458,078	0.5	3.02	50.9	12.8	24.4
Idaho.............................	12.2	9.6	4.6	1.7	36.6	49.9	5.9	47.6	2,709	625,135	2.3	2.70	54.1	8.7	27.5
Illinois...........................	13.1	9.0	4.6	2.1	38.3	50.9	14.3	66.9	40,530	4,808,672	-0.3	2.60	47.4	12.1	29.7
Indiana..........................	13.0	9.2	4.6	2	37.9	50.7	5.3	68.0	10,052	2,557,299	0.9	2.53	48.2	11.8	28.9
Iowa..............................	13.2	9.5	5.1	2.5	38.2	50.2	5.3	70.2	5,577	1,257,505	0.8	2.42	50.5	8.6	29.2
Kansas..........................	12.8	9.0	4.6	2.3	36.9	50.2	6.9	59.6	5,703	1,128,983	1.7	2.51	50.7	9.9	29.0
Kentucky........................	13.4	9.7	4.8	1.8	38.9	50.7	3.8	69.2	7,537	1,725,034	0.4	2.51	48.6	12.2	28.6
Louisiana.......................	13.0	9.2	4.5	1.7	37.2	51.2	4.1	78.3	4,688	1,737,123	0.9	2.62	42.8	15.9	30.7
Maine	15.8	12.2	5.9	2.5	44.9	51.0	3.4	63.5	1,594	540,959	1.7	2.40	48.8	8.3	30.5
Maryland	13.4	9.0	4.4	2	38.8	51.5	15.3	47.2	25,095	2,207,343	0.6	2.68	47.7	14.2	27.4
Massachusetts................	13.6	9.5	4.7	2.3	39.4	51.5	16.9	60.1	37,010	2,604,954	1.0	2.54	47.0	12.2	28.6
Michigan........................	14.0	10.1	5	2.1	39.8	50.8	7.1	76.1	18,927	3,930,017	1.2	2.48	47.2	12.0	29.6
Minnesota......................	13.4	9.1	4.6	2.2	38.1	50.2	8.7	67.4	16,009	2,162,211	0.6	2.52	51.2	8.9	28.4
Mississippi.....................	12.9	9.4	4.7	1.8	37.7	51.5	2.2	72.0	1,793	1,091,980	0.1	2.65	44.2	16.4	30.0
Missouri.........................	13.5	9.7	5.1	2.2	38.7	50.9	4.2	66.0	7,707	2,385,135	0.5	2.49	47.7	11.7	29.5
Montana.........................	14.3	11.3	5.3	2.1	39.9	49.7	2.2	53.1	529	423,091	1.7	2.41	50.4	7.7	30.4
Nebraska........................	12.6	8.9	4.6	2.2	36.6	50.1	7.5	64.5	5,327	754,490	0.9	2.48	50.9	8.9	29.2
Nevada...........................	12.4	9.7	4.6	1.4	38.1	49.9	19.9	25.9	12,733	1,094,613	3.7	2.70	44.9	13.0	28.1
New Hampshire	15.7	10.8	5	2.2	43.0	50.4	6.2	41.8	2,279	528,700	1.5	2.46	52.1	8.5	26.2
New Jersey	13.7	9.1	4.8	2.3	40.0	51.1	22.8	51.9	54,440	3,218,798	0.8	2.74	51.4	13.0	25.4
New Mexico	13.1	10.4	5.1	2	38.1	50.5	9.4	54.3	4,002	767,705	1.2	2.66	42.9	13.4	32.0
New York........................	13.3	9.3	4.9	2.3	39.0	51.4	22.9	62.9	139,409	7,304,332	1.3	2.64	44.0	14.2	29.7
North Carolina.................	12.9	9.7	4.7	1.8	38.9	51.4	8.1	56.4	21,184	3,955,069	1.9	2.53	48.2	12.7	28.6
North Dakota...................	12.5	8.4	4.4	2.5	35.2	48.8	4.1	62.1	1,471	316,306	0.4	2.31	48.3	7.4	31.7
Ohio..............................	13.8	9.8	5	2.2	39.4	51.0	4.5	74.8	16,894	4,667,192	0.9	2.43	45.8	12.5	30.3
Oklahoma.......................	12.5	9.1	4.8	1.9	36.7	50.5	5.7	61.2	5,535	1,470,364	0.1	2.60	48.0	12.5	28.5
Oregon..........................	13.0	10.7	4.9	2	39.4	50.4	9.9	46.0	9,221	1,603,635	2.0	2.53	48.7	9.9	27.7
Pennsylvania...................	14.1	10.2	5.4	2.6	40.8	51.0	7.0	72.2	27,762	5,008,751	1.4	2.47	47.5	11.4	30.4
Rhode Island...................	14.1	9.7	4.9	2.6	40.1	51.4	13.9	55.5	4,102	408,748	0.1	2.49	45.5	12.1	32.3
South Carolina	13.3	10.8	5.1	1.8	39.6	51.5	4.9	56.2	5,027	1,905,100	1.4	2.57	47.3	14.3	28.9
South Dakota..................	13.3	9.6	4.6	2.4	37.1	49.5	3.4	64.9	1,017	344,260	3.1	2.43	48.7	8.8	31.5
Tennessee......................	13.1	9.8	4.8	1.8	38.8	51.2	5.2	59.7	9,793	2,588,655	1.3	2.53	48.5	12.8	28.3
Texas.............................	11.3	7.5	3.6	1.4	34.8	50.3	17.1	59.7	110,126	9,623,874	0.9	2.88	50.7	13.7	25.0
Utah..............................	9.5	6.6	3.3	1.2	31.0	49.6	8.7	61.9	6,390	975,448	3.4	3.13	60.7	9.0	19.6
Vermont..........................	15.4	11.6	5.4	2.3	42.8	50.6	4.5	51.6	787	256,629	0.7	2.33	46.7	9.2	31.0
Virginia..........................	13.0	9.1	4.5	1.8	38.4	50.8	12.5	49.2	29,466	3,120,880	0.0	2.64	50.9	11.8	26.6
Washington	12.8	9.4	4.3	1.8	37.7	50.0	14.3	46.9	27,363	2,840,377	2.6	2.56	49.9	9.8	26.5
West Virginia..................	14.3	11.8	5.9	2.2	42.7	50.5	1.6	70.0	776	715,308	-0.9	2.47	48.4	10.9	29.9
Wisconsin.......................	14.1	9.8	4.9	2.2	39.6	50.2	5.0	71.4	6,681	2,350,293	1.0	2.40	48.5	9.9	29.5
Wyoming.........................	13.8	10.1	4.6	1.8	38.0	49.0	3.5	43.0	444	225,796	1.0	2.50	51.6	8.5	28.5

Table A. States — Population Change

STATE	Population, 1990–2010 Census counts			Population change, 1990–2018 Percent change			Components of change, 2010–2018		Migration			Population, 2020–2030 Projections		
	1990	2000	2010	1990–2000	2000–2010	2010–2018	Births	Deaths	Net migration	Inter-national	Net internal	2020	2025	2030
	31	32	33	34	35	36	37	38	39	40	41	42	43	44
United States	248,709,873	281,421,906	308,745,538	13.2	9.7	6.0	32,514,580	21,799,621	7,694,370	7,694,370	(X)	335,804,546	349,439,199	363,584,435
Alabama........................	4,040,587	4,447,100	4,779,736	10.1	7.5	2.3	484,329	418,734	42,748	37,551	5,197	4,728,915	4,800,092	4,874,243
Alaska...........................	550,043	626,932	710,231	14.0	13.3	3.8	92,762	34,995	-31,287	17,792	-49,079	774,421	820,881	867,674
Arizona.........................	3,665,228	5,130,632	6,392,017	40.0	24.6	12.2	703,872	434,572	508,013	145,998	362,015	8,456,448	9,531,537	10,712,397
Arkansas.......................	2,350,725	2,673,400	2,915,918	13.7	9.1	3.4	314,960	251,951	34,163	25,253	8,910	3,060,219	3,151,005	3,240,208
California......................	29,760,021	33,871,648	37,253,956	13.8	10.0	6.2	4,078,895	2,094,459	333,168	1,043,561	-710,393	42,206,743	44,305,177	46,444,861
Colorado.......................	3,294,394	4,301,261	5,029,196	30.6	16.9	13.2	543,471	289,139	406,752	84,970	321,782	5,278,867	5,522,803	5,792,357
Connecticut...................	3,287,116	3,405,565	3,574,097	3.6	4.9	-0.0	298,938	247,536	-52,931	122,999	-175,930	3,675,650	3,691,016	3,688,630
Delaware.......................	666,168	783,600	897,934	17.6	14.6	7.7	90,864	69,108	47,568	14,957	32,611	963,209	990,694	1,012,658
District of Columbia........	606,900	572,059	601,723	-5.7	5.2	16.7	78,391	40,740	61,805	32,265	29,540	480,540	455,108	433,414
Florida..........................	12,937,926	15,982,378	18,801,310	23.5	17.6	13.3	1,801,326	1,549,217	2,232,735	1,072,348	1,160,387	23,406,525	25,912,458	28,685,769
Georgia	6,478,216	8,186,453	9,687,653	26.4	18.3	8.6	1,074,297	634,603	387,595	182,190	205,405	10,843,753	11,438,622	12,017,838
Hawaii..........................	1,108,229	1,211,537	1,360,301	9.3	12.3	4.4	152,292	90,763	-549	55,050	-55,599	1,412,373	1,438,720	1,466,046
Idaho...........................	1,006,749	1,293,953	1,567,582	28.5	21.1	11.9	186,921	103,264	102,127	16,562	85,565	1,741,333	1,852,627	1,969,624
Illinois..........................	11,430,602	12,419,293	12,830,632	8.6	3.3	-0.7	1,294,578	866,111	-519,943	241,894	-761,837	13,236,720	13,340,507	13,432,892
Indiana.........................	5,544,159	6,080,485	6,483,802	9.7	6.6	3.2	685,293	500,513	25,243	80,287	-55,044	6,627,008	6,721,322	6,810,108
Iowa............................	2,776,755	2,926,324	3,046,355	5.4	4.1	3.6	320,992	237,810	26,463	48,288	-21,825	3,020,496	2,993,222	2,955,172
Kansas.........................	2,477,574	2,688,418	2,853,118	8.5	6.1	2.0	320,372	210,809	-50,988	45,473	-96,461	2,890,566	2,919,002	2,940,084
Kentucky......................	3,685,296	4,041,769	4,339,367	9.7	7.4	3.0	456,319	369,344	42,993	54,633	-11,640	4,424,431	4,489,662	4,554,998
Louisiana......................	4,219,973	4,468,976	4,533,372	5.9	1.4	2.8	516,732	357,057	-34,167	41,559	-75,726	4,719,160	4,762,398	4,802,633
Maine...........................	1,227,928	1,274,923	1,328,361	3.8	4.2	0.8	104,761	112,173	18,302	10,343	7,959	1,408,665	1,414,402	1,411,097
Maryland.......................	4,781,468	5,296,486	5,773,552	10.8	9.0	4.7	600,546	384,372	55,763	192,345	-136,582	6,497,626	6,762,732	7,022,251
Massachusetts...............	6,016,425	6,349,097	6,547,629	5.5	3.1	5.4	592,466	458,279	224,482	351,069	-126,587	6,855,546	6,938,636	7,012,009
Michigan.......................	9,295,297	9,938,444	9,883,640	6.9	-0.6	1.1	933,558	767,504	-53,152	189,665	-242,817	10,695,993	10,713,730	10,694,172
Minnesota.....................	4,375,099	4,919,479	5,303,925	12.4	7.8	5.8	570,171	341,882	81,671	107,830	-26,159	5,900,769	6,108,787	6,306,130
Mississippi....................	2,573,216	2,844,658	2,967,297	10.5	4.3	0.6	316,072	251,454	-46,825	18,614	-65,439	3,044,812	3,069,420	3,092,410
Missouri........................	5,117,073	5,595,211	5,988,927	9.3	7.0	2.3	617,794	478,044	-331	59,677	-60,008	6,199,882	6,315,366	6,430,173
Montana........................	799,065	902,195	989,415	12.9	9.7	7.4	100,933	78,277	49,992	6,640	43,352	1,022,735	1,037,387	1,044,898
Nebraska.......................	1,578,385	1,711,263	1,826,341	8.4	6.7	5.6	216,048	130,333	17,767	33,765	-15,998	1,802,678	1,812,787	1,820,247
Nevada.........................	1,201,833	1,998,257	2,700,551	66.3	35.1	12.4	294,505	183,602	221,704	30,103	191,601	3,452,283	3,863,298	4,282,157
New Hampshire	1,109,252	1,235,786	1,316,470	11.4	6.5	3.0	102,554	93,479	31,684	24,869	6,815	1,524,751	1,586,348	1,646,471
New Jersey	7,730,188	8,414,350	8,791,894	8.9	4.5	1.3	852,207	595,714	-140,088	302,522	-442,610	9,461,635	9,636,644	9,802,440
New Mexico....................	1,515,069	1,819,046	2,059,179	20.1	13.2	1.8	213,795	142,845	-34,628	27,423	-62,051	2,084,341	2,106,584	2,099,708
New York.......................	17,990,455	18,976,457	19,378,102	5.5	2.1	0.8	1,954,011	1,264,995	-523,216	674,384	-1,197,600	19,576,920	19,540,179	19,477,429
North Carolina...............	6,628,637	8,049,313	9,535,483	21.4	18.5	8.9	990,630	708,132	560,003	157,614	402,389	10,709,289	11,449,153	12,227,739
North Dakota.................	638,800	642,200	672,591	0.5	4.7	13.0	87,442	50,698	49,192	13,264	35,928	630,112	620,777	606,566
Ohio.............................	10,847,115	11,353,140	11,536,504	4.7	1.6	1.3	1,138,227	946,276	-35,269	169,396	-204,665	11,644,058	11,605,738	11,550,528
Oklahoma......................	3,145,585	3,450,654	3,751,351	9.7	8.7	5.1	433,393	318,855	76,774	52,615	24,159	3,735,690	3,820,994	3,913,251
Oregon.........................	2,842,321	3,421,399	3,831,074	20.4	12.0	9.4	374,486	283,146	267,949	61,237	206,712	4,260,393	4,536,418	4,833,918
Pennsylvania.................	11,881,643	12,281,054	12,702,379	3.4	3.4	0.8	1,160,725	1,071,084	22,862	259,739	-236,877	12,787,354	12,801,945	12,768,184
Rhode Island.................	1,003,464	1,048,319	1,052,567	4.5	0.4	0.5	89,601	80,297	-4,624	31,873	-36,497	1,154,230	1,157,855	1,152,941
South Carolina	3,486,703	4,012,012	4,625,364	15.1	15.3	9.9	471,964	375,950	359,822	45,047	314,775	4,822,577	4,989,550	5,148,569
South Dakota................	696,004	754,844	814,180	8.5	7.9	8.4	99,830	61,308	29,312	16,801	12,511	801,939	801,845	800,462
Tennessee....................	4,877,185	5,689,283	6,346,105	16.7	11.5	6.7	662,136	529,573	290,164	70,779	219,385	6,780,670	7,073,125	7,380,634
Texas...........................	16,986,510	20,851,820	25,145,561	22.8	20.6	14.1	3,221,263	1,511,232	1,832,775	813,341	1,019,434	28,634,896	30,865,134	33,317,744
Utah............................	1,722,850	2,233,169	2,763,885	29.6	23.8	14.4	420,885	136,102	113,137	46,555	66,582	2,990,094	3,225,680	3,485,367
Vermont........................	562,758	608,827	625,741	8.2	2.8	0.1	48,976	46,463	-1,566	8,548	-10,114	690,686	703,288	711,867
Virginia.........................	6,187,358	7,078,515	8,001,024	14.4	13.0	6.5	843,184	528,521	200,978	263,741	-62,763	8,917,395	9,364,304	9,825,019
Washington...................	4,866,604	5,894,121	6,724,540	21.1	14.1	12.1	729,978	435,888	516,914	221,434	295,480	7,432,136	7,996,400	8,624,801
West Virginia.................	1,793,477	1,808,344	1,852,994	0.8	2.5	-2.5	163,804	182,973	-27,508	7,492	-35,000	1,801,112	1,766,435	1,719,959
Wisconsin......................	4,891,769	5,363,675	5,686,986	9.6	6.0	2.2	551,536	410,971	-11,715	58,966	-70,681	6,004,954	6,088,374	6,150,764
Wyoming.......................	453,588	493,782	563,626	8.9	14.1	2.5	61,495	38,474	-9,463	3,049	-12,512	530,948	529,031	522,979

Table A. States — **Population Characteristics**

STATE	Population characteristics, 2010																		
	Race (percent)					Percent Hispanic or Latino[1]	Percent foreign born	Age (percent)										Median age	Percent female
	White alone	Black alone	American Indian, Alaska Native alone	Asian and Pacific Islander alone	Some other race or two or more races			Under 5 years	5 to 17 years	18 to 24 years	25 to 34 years	35 to 44 years	45 to 54 years	55 to 64 years	65 to 74 years	75 to 84 years	85 years and over		
	45	46	47	48	49	50	51	52	53	54	55	56	57	58	59	60	61	62	63
United States	72.4	12.6	0.9	5.0	9.1	16.3	12.9	6.5	17.5	9.9	13.3	13.3	14.6	11.8	7.0	4.2	1.8	37.2	50.8
Alabama..........................	68.5	26.2	0.6	1.2	3.5	3.9	3.5	6.4	17.3	10.0	12.6	13.0	14.5	12.3	7.8	4.4	1.6	37.9	51.5
Alaska............................	66.7	3.3	14.8	6.4	8.9	5.5	6.9	7.6	18.8	10.5	14.5	13.1	15.6	12.1	5.0	2.1	0.6	33.8	48.0
Arizona...........................	73.0	4.1	4.6	3.0	15.3	29.6	13.4	7.1	18.4	9.9	13.4	12.9	13.2	11.4	7.8	4.4	1.6	35.9	50.3
Arkansas........................	77.0	15.4	0.8	1.4	5.4	6.4	4.5	6.8	17.6	9.7	12.6	12.6	14.0	12.0	8.0	4.6	1.8	37.4	50.9
California........................	57.6	6.2	1.0	13.4	21.9	37.6	27.2	6.8	18.2	10.5	14.2	13.9	14.1	10.8	6.1	3.7	1.6	35.2	50.3
Colorado........................	81.3	4.0	1.1	2.9	10.6	20.7	9.8	6.8	17.5	9.7	14.4	13.9	14.8	11.9	6.2	3.4	1.4	36.1	49.9
Connecticut....................	77.6	10.1	0.3	3.8	8.2	13.4	13.6	5.7	17.2	9.1	11.8	13.6	16.1	12.4	7.1	4.6	2.4	40.0	51.3
Delaware........................	68.9	21.4	0.5	3.2	6.1	8.2	8.0	6.2	16.7	10.1	12.3	12.9	14.9	12.4	8.1	4.5	1.8	38.8	51.6
District of Columbia.........	38.5	50.7	0.3	3.6	7.0	9.1	13.5	5.4	11.3	14.5	20.9	13.4	12.6	10.6	6.1	3.5	1.8	33.8	52.8
Florida...........................	75.0	16.0	0.4	2.5	6.1	22.5	19.4	5.7	15.6	9.3	12.1	12.9	14.6	12.4	9.2	5.7	2.4	40.7	51.1
Georgia..........................	59.7	30.5	0.3	3.3	6.1	8.8	9.7	7.1	18.6	10.0	13.6	14.4	14.4	11.0	6.3	3.1	1.2	35.3	51.2
Hawaii...........................	24.7	1.6	0.3	48.6	24.8	8.9	18.2	6.4	15.9	9.6	13.3	13.0	14.2	12.9	7.4	4.7	2.3	38.6	49.9
Idaho............................	89.1	0.6	1.4	1.3	7.6	11.2	5.5	7.8	19.6	9.9	13.3	12.2	13.3	11.5	7.0	3.8	1.7	34.6	49.9
Illinois..........................	71.5	14.5	0.3	4.6	9.0	15.8	13.7	6.5	17.9	9.7	13.9	13.5	14.6	11.5	6.6	4.0	1.9	36.6	50.8
Indiana..........................	84.3	9.1	0.3	1.6	4.7	6.0	4.6	6.7	18.1	10.0	12.7	13.0	14.6	11.9	7.0	4.3	1.7	37.0	50.8
Iowa.............................	91.3	2.9	0.4	1.8	3.6	5.0	4.6	6.6	17.3	10.0	12.6	12.0	14.4	12.2	7.4	5.0	2.5	38.1	50.5
Kansas..........................	83.8	5.9	1.0	2.5	6.9	10.5	6.5	7.2	18.3	10.1	13.0	12.2	14.2	11.6	6.7	4.3	2.1	36.0	50.4
Kentucky........................	87.8	7.8	0.2	1.2	3.0	3.1	3.2	6.5	17.1	9.5	13.0	13.3	14.8	12.4	7.5	4.2	1.6	38.1	50.8
Louisiana.......................	62.6	32.0	0.7	1.5	3.1	4.2	3.8	6.9	17.7	10.5	13.7	12.5	14.4	11.8	6.9	3.9	1.5	35.8	51.0
Maine............................	95.2	1.2	0.6	1.0	1.9	1.3	3.4	5.2	15.4	8.7	10.9	12.9	16.5	14.5	8.5	5.3	2.1	42.7	51.1
Maryland........................	58.2	29.4	0.4	5.6	6.5	8.2	13.9	6.3	17.1	9.7	13.2	13.8	15.6	12.1	6.7	3.9	1.7	38.0	51.6
Massachusetts.................	80.4	6.6	0.3	5.3	7.3	9.6	15.0	5.6	16.1	10.4	12.9	13.5	15.5	12.3	7.0	4.6	2.2	39.1	51.6
Michigan........................	78.9	14.2	0.6	2.4	3.8	4.4	6.0	6.0	17.7	9.9	11.7	12.9	15.3	12.7	7.3	4.5	1.9	38.9	50.9
Minnesota......................	85.3	5.2	1.1	4.0	4.3	4.7	7.1	6.7	17.5	9.5	13.5	12.8	15.2	11.9	6.7	4.2	2.0	37.4	50.4
Mississippi......................	59.1	37.0	0.5	0.9	2.4	2.7	2.1	7.1	18.4	10.3	12.6	12.6	14.1	11.7	7.2	4.1	1.5	36.0	51.0
Missouri.........................	82.8	11.6	0.5	1.7	3.4	3.5	3.9	6.5	17.3	9.8	12.9	12.5	14.8	12.1	7.5	4.5	2.0	37.9	51.0
Montana.........................	89.4	0.4	6.3	0.7	3.1	2.9	2.0	6.3	16.3	9.6	12.3	11.4	15.1	14.0	8.2	4.7	2.0	39.8	49.8
Nebraska........................	86.1	4.5	1.0	1.9	6.5	9.2	6.1	7.2	17.9	10.0	13.2	12.1	14.2	11.7	6.7	4.7	2.2	36.2	50.4
Nevada..........................	66.2	8.1	1.2	7.8	16.7	26.5	18.8	6.9	17.7	9.2	14.3	14.2	13.9	11.7	7.3	3.6	1.1	36.3	49.5
New Hampshire	93.9	1.1	0.2	2.2	2.5	2.8	5.3	5.3	16.5	9.4	11.0	13.6	17.2	13.5	7.4	4.4	1.8	41.1	50.7
New Jersey	68.6	13.7	0.3	8.3	9.1	17.7	21.0	6.2	17.3	8.7	12.6	14.1	15.7	11.9	7.0	4.5	2.0	39.0	51.3
New Mexico	68.4	2.1	9.4	1.5	18.7	46.3	9.9	7.0	18.1	9.9	12.8	12.1	14.2	12.5	7.5	4.3	1.5	36.7	50.6
New York........................	65.7	15.9	0.6	7.3	10.4	17.6	22.2	6.0	16.4	10.2	13.7	13.5	14.9	11.9	7.0	4.5	2.0	38.0	51.6
North Carolina.................	68.5	21.5	1.3	2.3	6.5	8.4	7.5	6.6	17.3	9.8	13.0	13.9	14.4	11.9	7.3	4.1	1.6	37.4	51.3
North Dakota...................	90.0	1.2	5.4	1.0	2.3	2.0	2.5	6.6	15.7	12.0	13.1	11.2	14.4	12.2	7.0	5.1	2.5	37.0	49.5
Ohio.............................	82.7	12.2	0.2	1.7	3.2	3.1	4.1	6.2	17.4	9.5	12.4	12.8	15.1	12.6	7.4	4.7	2.0	38.8	51.2
Oklahoma.......................	72.2	7.4	8.6	1.8	10.0	8.9	5.5	7.0	17.7	10.2	13.5	12.3	14.0	11.7	7.5	4.4	1.6	36.2	50.5
Oregon..........................	83.6	1.8	1.4	4.0	9.1	11.7	9.8	6.2	16.4	9.4	13.7	13.0	14.1	13.3	7.6	4.3	2.0	38.4	50.5
Pennsylvania...................	81.9	10.8	0.2	2.7	4.3	5.7	5.8	5.7	16.2	9.9	11.9	12.7	15.3	12.8	7.7	5.3	2.5	40.1	51.3
Rhode Island...................	81.4	5.7	0.6	3.0	9.3	12.4	12.8	5.5	15.8	11.4	12.0	13.0	15.4	12.4	7.0	4.9	2.5	39.4	51.7
South Carolina.................	66.2	27.9	0.4	1.4	4.2	5.1	4.7	6.5	16.8	10.3	12.7	13.0	14.3	12.6	8.0	4.1	1.6	37.9	51.4
South Dakota..................	85.9	1.3	8.8	0.9	3.0	2.7	2.7	7.3	17.6	10.0	12.8	11.4	14.4	12.0	7.1	4.8	2.4	36.9	50.0
Tennessee......................	77.6	16.7	0.3	1.5	3.9	4.6	4.5	6.4	17.1	9.6	12.8	13.5	14.6	12.4	7.7	4.2	1.6	38.0	51.3
Texas............................	70.4	11.8	0.7	3.9	13.2	37.6	16.4	7.7	19.6	10.2	14.3	13.8	13.7	10.3	5.9	3.3	1.2	33.6	50.4
Utah.............................	86.1	1.1	1.2	2.9	8.7	13.0	8.0	9.5	22.0	11.5	16.2	12.0	11.1	8.7	5.0	2.9	1.1	29.2	49.8
Vermont.........................	95.3	1.0	0.4	1.3	2.0	1.5	4.4	5.1	15.5	10.4	11.2	12.5	16.4	14.4	7.9	4.5	2.1	41.5	50.7
Virginia..........................	68.6	19.4	0.4	5.6	6.1	7.9	11.4	6.4	16.8	10.0	13.8	13.9	15.2	11.9	6.9	3.8	1.5	37.5	50.9
Washington.....................	77.3	3.6	1.5	7.8	9.9	11.2	13.1	6.5	17.0	9.7	13.9	13.5	14.7	12.4	6.8	3.7	1.8	37.3	50.2
West Virginia...................	93.9	3.4	0.2	0.7	1.8	1.2	1.2	5.6	15.3	9.1	11.7	12.8	14.9	14.3	8.8	5.2	2.0	41.3	50.7
Wisconsin.......................	86.2	6.3	1.0	2.3	4.2	5.9	4.5	6.3	17.3	9.7	12.6	12.8	15.4	12.3	7.0	4.6	2.1	38.5	50.4
Wyoming........................	90.7	0.8	2.4	0.9	5.2	8.9	2.8	7.1	16.9	10.0	13.6	11.9	14.8	13.0	7.0	3.8	1.6	36.8	49.0

1. May be of any race.

Table A. States — Households and Housing Units

STATE	Households, 2010			Percent		Housing units, 2010		Occupied units	Owner-occupied		Median owner cost as a percent of income		Renter-occupied		
	Number	Percent change, 2000-2010	Persons per house-hold	Female family house-holder[1]	One-person house-holds	Total	Percent change, 2000-2010	Total	Percent	Median value[2] (dollars)	With a mort-gage	Without a mort-gage[3]	Median gross rent[4] (dollars)	Median rent as a percent of income	Sub-standard units[5] (percent)
	64	65	66	67	68	69	70	71	72	73	74	75	76	77	78
United States	116,716,292	10.7	2.58	13.1	26.7	131,791,065	13.7	114,567,419	65.4	179,900	25.1	12.8	855	31.6	3.9
Alabama	1,883,791	8.4	2.48	15.3	27.4	2,174,428	10.7	1,815,152	70.1	123,900	23.0	12.3	667	32.2	2.4
Alaska	258,058	16.5	2.65	10.7	25.6	307,065	17.7	254,610	63.9	241,400	23.3	10.8	981	29.0	10.2
Arizona	2,380,990	25.2	2.63	12.4	26.1	2,846,738	30.0	2,334,050	65.2	168,800	26.5	11.3	844	31.6	5.1
Arkansas	1,147,084	10.0	2.47	13.4	27.1	1,317,818	12.3	1,114,902	67.4	106,300	21.5	10.9	638	29.9	3.2
California	12,577,498	9.3	2.90	13.3	23.3	13,682,976	12.0	12,406,475	55.6	370,900	30.6	11.4	1,163	33.8	9.1
Colorado	1,972,868	19.0	2.49	10.1	27.9	2,214,262	22.5	1,960,585	65.9	236,600	25.2	10.7	863	31.2	3.2
Connecticut	1,371,087	5.3	2.52	12.9	27.3	1,488,215	7.4	1,358,809	68.0	288,800	26.8	17.6	992	32.1	2.4
Delaware	342,297	14.6	2.55	14.2	25.6	406,489	18.5	328,765	73.0	243,600	24.8	11.8	952	32.3	2.9
District of Columbia	266,707	7.4	2.11	16.4	44.0	296,836	8.0	252,388	42.5	426,900	24.8	11.0	1,198	30.4	3.5
Florida	7,420,802	17.1	2.48	13.5	27.2	8,994,091	23.2	7,035,068	68.1	164,200	29.5	14.4	947	35.5	3.1
Georgia	3,585,584	19.3	2.63	15.8	25.4	4,091,482	24.7	3,482,420	66.2	156,200	25.2	12.3	819	32.4	3.2
Hawaii	455,338	12.9	2.89	12.6	23.3	519,992	12.9	445,812	58.0	525,400	30.1	10.1	1,291	33.5	9.1
Idaho	579,408	23.4	2.66	9.6	23.8	668,634	26.7	576,709	69.6	165,100	24.7	10.6	683	30.5	3.6
Illinois	4,836,972	5.3	2.59	12.9	27.8	5,297,077	8.4	4,752,857	67.7	191,800	25.9	13.8	848	31.5	3.1
Indiana	2,502,154	7.1	2.52	12.4	26.9	2,797,172	10.5	2,470,905	70.3	123,300	21.6	11.0	683	30.8	2.2
Iowa	1,221,576	6.3	2.41	9.3	28.4	1,337,563	8.5	1,223,439	72.4	123,400	21.3	11.5	629	28.1	1.7
Kansas	1,112,096	7.1	2.49	10.4	27.8	1,234,037	9.1	1,101,658	68.1	127,300	21.8	11.8	682	28.1	2.2
Kentucky	1,719,965	8.1	2.45	12.7	27.5	1,928,617	10.1	1,684,348	68.6	121,600	22.2	11.3	613	29.8	2.5
Louisiana	1,728,360	4.4	2.55	17.2	26.9	1,967,947	6.5	1,689,822	67.6	137,500	21.6	10.5	736	31.7	3.7
Maine	557,219	7.5	2.32	10.0	28.6	722,217	10.8	545,417	72.7	179,100	24.1	13.9	707	29.8	2.5
Maryland	2,156,411	8.9	2.61	14.6	26.1	2,380,605	11.0	2,127,439	67.0	301,400	25.4	12.9	1,131	30.8	2.4
Massachusetts	2,547,075	4.2	2.48	12.5	28.7	2,808,727	7.1	2,520,419	62.2	334,100	26.1	15.3	1,009	30.4	2.0
Michigan	3,872,508	2.3	2.49	13.2	27.9	4,531,231	7.0	3,806,621	72.8	123,300	24.6	13.9	730	33.3	2.1
Minnesota	2,087,227	10.1	2.48	9.5	28.0	2,348,242	13.7	2,091,548	73.0	194,300	24.1	11.9	764	30.2	2.3
Mississippi	1,115,768	6.6	2.58	18.5	26.3	1,276,441	9.9	1,079,999	69.8	100,100	23.5	12.0	672	33.2	4.0
Missouri	2,375,611	8.2	2.45	12.3	28.3	2,714,017	11.1	2,350,628	69.0	139,000	22.6	11.7	682	30.1	2.2
Montana	409,607	14.2	2.35	9.0	29.7	483,006	17.1	402,747	69.7	181,200	24.1	11.3	642	28.3	2.8
Nebraska	721,130	8.2	2.46	9.8	28.7	797,677	10.4	719,304	67.4	127,600	21.4	12.6	669	27.7	2.2
Nevada	1,006,250	34.0	2.65	12.7	25.7	1,175,070	42.0	989,811	57.2	174,800	28.1	12.2	952	31.6	5.0
New Hampshire	518,973	9.3	2.46	9.7	25.6	614,996	12.4	515,431	71.7	243,000	26.5	16.5	951	30.3	1.9
New Jersey	3,214,360	4.9	2.68	13.3	25.2	3,554,909	7.4	3,172,421	66.4	339,200	28.7	18.9	1,114	32.4	4.1
New Mexico	791,395	16.7	2.55	14.0	28.0	902,242	15.6	765,183	67.9	161,200	24.3	10.0	699	29.3	4.7
New York	7,317,755	3.7	2.57	14.9	29.1	8,108,211	5.6	7,196,427	54.3	296,500	26.3	15.5	1,020	31.7	5.5
North Carolina	3,745,155	19.6	2.48	13.7	27.0	4,333,479	23.0	3,670,859	67.2	154,200	24.0	12.5	731	31.3	2.8
North Dakota	281,192	9.3	2.30	8.2	31.5	318,099	9.8	280,412	66.9	123,000	19.6	10.0	583	25.8	1.3
Ohio	4,603,435	3.5	2.44	13.1	28.9	5,128,113	7.2	4,525,066	68.4	134,400	23.4	13.1	685	31.1	1.8
Oklahoma	1,460,450	8.8	2.49	12.3	27.5	1,666,205	10.0	1,432,950	67.8	111,400	21.9	11.2	659	28.9	3.0
Oregon	1,518,938	13.9	2.47	10.5	27.4	1,676,476	15.4	1,507,137	62.5	244,500	27.3	12.9	816	32.7	3.4
Pennsylvania	5,018,904	5.1	2.45	12.2	28.6	5,568,820	6.1	4,936,030	70.1	165,500	23.8	13.7	763	30.4	1.6
Rhode Island	413,600	1.3	2.44	13.5	29.6	463,416	5.4	402,295	60.8	254,500	27.7	15.4	868	30.9	2.6
South Carolina	1,801,181	17.4	2.49	15.6	26.5	2,140,337	22.0	1,761,393	68.7	138,100	23.5	12.0	728	32.2	2.7
South Dakota	322,282	11.0	2.42	9.7	29.4	364,031	12.6	318,955	68.0	129,700	21.9	10.9	591	26.9	2.7
Tennessee	2,493,552	11.7	2.48	13.9	26.9	2,815,087	15.4	2,440,663	68.1	139,000	23.7	11.4	697	31.4	2.5
Texas	8,922,933	20.7	2.75	14.1	24.2	9,996,209	22.5	8,738,664	63.6	128,100	23.4	12.5	801	30.2	5.8
Utah	877,692	25.2	3.10	9.7	18.7	981,821	27.7	880,025	69.9	217,200	24.8	10.0	796	29.5	4.6
Vermont	256,442	6.6	2.34	9.6	28.2	322,698	9.6	256,922	70.4	216,800	26.0	16.3	823	31.8	2.2
Virginia	3,056,058	13.2	2.54	12.4	26.0	3,368,674	16.0	2,992,732	67.7	249,100	24.7	11.4	1,019	30.2	2.6
Washington	2,620,076	15.4	2.51	10.5	27.2	2,888,594	17.9	2,606,863	63.1	271,800	26.7	12.1	908	30.6	3.4
West Virginia	763,831	3.7	2.36	11.2	28.4	882,213	4.5	741,940	74.6	95,100	20.1	10.0	571	29.7	1.8
Wisconsin	2,279,768	9.4	2.43	10.3	28.2	2,625,477	13.1	2,279,532	68.7	169,400	24.5	14.0	715	29.8	2.2
Wyoming	226,879	17.2	2.42	8.9	28.0	262,286	17.2	222,803	69.7	180,100	22.0	10.0	693	25.3	2.8

1. No spouse present. 2. Specified owner-occupied units. 3. Median monthly costs is often in the minimum category—10.0 percent or less, which is indicated as 10.0 percent. 4. Specified renter-occupied units. 5. Overcrowded or lacking complete plumbing facilities.

Table A. States — Housing Units

STATE	Housing units, 2017												
			Occupied units										Percent living in a different house than 1 year ago
					Percent who pay 30 percent or more of income for housing expenses[1]		Median owner cost as a percent of income		Median monthly housing costs (dollars)	Median value of units[3] (dollars)	Percent valued over $500000	Median gross rent[4] (dollars)	Sub-standard units[5] (percent)	
	Total	Percent change, 2016-2017	Total	Percent owner-occupied	Owners with a mortgage	Renter	With a mortgage	Without a mortgage[2]						
	79	80	81	82	83	84	85	86	87	88	89	90	91	92
United States	137,407,308	1.3	120,062,818	63.9	27.4	46.0	21.2	11.3	1,048	217,600	14.8	1,012	3.7	14.3
Alabama	2,258,669	1.3	1,841,665	68.0	23.0	40.8	19.1	10.0	734	141,300	4.2	750	2.2	13.7
Alaska	316,968	2.0	250,741	63.5	29.2	42.0	21.9	11.2	1,285	273,100	9.2	1,201	10.1	18.5
Arizona	2,999,185	1.3	2,552,972	64.7	27.9	44.8	21.2	10.0	1,015	223,400	9.8	1,020	4.9	17.6
Arkansas	1,370,109	1.1	1,153,082	65.3	21.1	39.5	18.5	10.0	691	128,500	3.0	711	.3	15.5
California	14,177,270	0.8	13,005,097	54.8	38.2	52.5	25.3	11.2	1,567	509,400	50.9	1,447	8.6	13.0
Colorado	2,385,495	2.0	2,139,207	65.2	27.1	49.2	21.4	10.0	1,300	348,900	23.2	1,240	.3	18.0
Connecticut	1,517,495	1.2	1,356,762	66.2	30.8	48.3	22.7	14.6	1,390	273,100	16.8	1,125	2.3	11.8
Delaware	432,853	1.6	357,937	70.9	27.5	43.6	21.3	10.0	1,126	252,800	9.2	1,086	1.5	12.8
District of Columbia	314,843	0.4	281,475	42.2	26.6	44.9	21.0	10.0	1,641	607,200	60.3	1,499	4.2	19.1
Florida	9,441,585	1.5	7,689,964	65.2	32.7	52.4	22.9	12.0	1,047	214,000	10.4	1,128	3.3	15.5
Georgia	4,282,254	1.5	3,745,074	62.9	25.0	44.4	19.8	10.0	980	173,700	8.0	958	2.5	14.9
Hawaii	542,955	1.1	458,078	58.5	38.8	51.7	25.5	10.0	1,585	617,400	64.4	1,573	9.6	12.7
Idaho	721,818	3.0	625,135	69.7	25.9	41.7	21.3	10.0	880	207,100	6.3	822	.3	17.0
Illinois	5,359,416	0.6	4,808,672	66.2	27.1	45.2	21.3	12.9	1,081	195,300	9.1	974	2.8	12.9
Indiana	2,885,342	1.1	2,557,299	69.0	18.9	41.7	18.1	10.0	815	141,100	3.4	793	1.9	14.5
Iowa	1,397,739	1.3	1,257,505	71.6	18.9	38.8	18.7	11.0	825	149,100	3.2	760	.2	14.6
Kansas	1,273,776	1.1	1,128,983	65.9	19.8	41.0	19.3	11.4	858	150,600	3.9	815	2.9	16.1
Kentucky	1,984,205	0.9	1,725,034	66.5	21.8	38.4	18.8	10.3	743	141,000	3.7	724	2.4	15.5
Louisiana	2,061,582	1.2	1,737,123	65.2	25.2	47.5	19.7	10.0	781	162,500	4.8	836	2.8	12.9
Maine	742,644	1.6	540,959	73.2	26.1	40.4	20.7	12.2	884	191,200	6.4	806	2.2	13.8
Maryland	2,449,123	0.1	2,207,343	66.7	27.0	47.5	21.5	10.7	1,456	312,500	19.9	1,337	2.4	13.7
Massachusetts	2,894,590	1.3	2,604,954	62.3	29.3	46.5	22.1	14.0	1,464	385,400	31.7	1,208	2.2	13.3
Michigan	4,595,274	0.8	3,930,017	71.3	22.7	44.6	19.3	11.9	862	155,700	4.5	835	.2	14.2
Minnesota	2,437,726	1.2	2,162,211	71.6	21.7	43.7	19.7	10.4	1,070	224,000	7.9	939	2.4	14.2
Mississippi	1,323,754	1.2	1,091,980	68.5	25.4	40.2	20.1	10.0	672	120,200	2.8	742	.3	13.4
Missouri	2,792,445	1.2	2,385,135	67.0	21.5	41.0	19.0	10.8	837	156,700	4.4	800	2.2	15.4
Montana	510,408	2.5	423,091	69.2	27.3	40.2	21.5	11.2	816	231,300	9.6	759	2.7	15.0
Nebraska	837,540	1.3	754,490	66.3	20.9	36.8	19.5	11.3	887	155,800	3.5	801	2.6	16.2
Nevada	1,249,733	2.3	1,094,613	56.6	29.9	45.5	22.0	10.0	1,089	258,200	10.4	1,051	4.6	18.0
New Hampshire	634,689	1.5	528,700	69.8	26.8	44.5	22.2	14.1	1,280	263,600	9.7	1,072	.2	14.8
New Jersey	3,615,891	0.3	3,218,798	63.8	34.2	49.0	24.1	16.1	1,545	334,900	23.6	1,284	3.7	10.6
New Mexico	937,976	2.2	767,705	67.9	29.4	43.3	21.6	10.0	782	171,300	6.0	813	3.6	12.7
New York	8,327,621	1.2	7,304,332	53.8	33.1	49.7	22.9	13.4	1,291	314,500	28.8	1,226	5.4	10.6
North Carolina	4,622,656	1.8	3,955,069	65.4	24.0	44.5	19.6	10.1	878	171,200	7.1	861	2.4	14.9
North Dakota	374,591	1.6	316,306	63.4	16.8	36.6	18.8	10.0	799	194,700	5.5	785	2.2	18.2
Ohio	5,201,701	0.7	4,667,192	65.8	20.5	41.1	19.0	11.3	833	144,200	3.4	772	1.7	14.7
Oklahoma	1,734,074	0.8	1,470,364	65.5	23.8	40.5	19.8	10.2	770	137,400	3.5	780	3.2	17.0
Oregon	1,768,582	2.1	1,603,635	62.8	31.6	48.6	23.0	12.5	1,164	319,200	19.6	1,079	3.5	17.0
Pennsylvania	5,694,402	1.5	5,008,751	68.3	24.3	42.5	20.1	12.4	947	181,200	6.9	893	1.9	12.6
Rhode Island	468,266	1.2	408,748	60.8	31.5	43.0	23.1	13.7	1,190	257,800	11.3	941	2.1	12.0
South Carolina	2,284,820	2.2	1,905,100	68.7	25.0	44.8	19.7	10.0	820	161,800	7.1	848	2.2	14.5
South Dakota	392,650	2.3	344,260	67.7	19.0	37.8	19.5	10.2	774	167,600	4.2	722	3.1	15.5
Tennessee	2,958,799	1.3	2,588,655	65.4	23.7	40.9	19.7	10.0	820	172,200	6.7	833	2.2	14.5
Texas	10,933,375	1.7	9,623,874	62.0	25.6	44.5	20.7	11.2	1,009	172,200	7.3	987	5.2	15.7
Utah	1,084,685	2.9	975,448	69.9	23.9	41.7	21.0	10.0	1,122	275,100	12.2	986	3.8	17.1
Vermont	335,248	1.7	256,629	69.5	32.1	46.9	23.2	15.0	1,088	226,300	8.0	950	1.8	13.4
Virginia	3,512,917	0.6	3,120,880	66.6	26.0	43.7	21.2	10.0	1,237	273,400	20.1	1,179	2.3	15.3
Washington	3,103,263	2.6	2,840,377	62.8	28.8	45.2	22.5	11.3	1,319	339,000	26.3	1,216	3.6	17.8
West Virginia	892,240	0.6	715,308	72.5	22.0	39.6	18.6	10.0	585	119,800	2.6	690	1.7	11.6
Wisconsin	2,695,303	1.0	2,350,293	66.6	22.3	41.0	19.9	12.2	913	178,900	4.8	819	.2	14.4
Wyoming	276,733	2.3	225,796	70.8	23.9	38.0	21.0	10.0	890	214,300	8.9	832	3.3	16.1

1. Excludes units where owner costs or gross rent as a percentage of houshold income cannot be calculated. 2. Median monthly costs is often in the minimum category—10.0 percent or less, which is indicated as 10.0 percent. 3. Specified owner-occupied units. 4. Specified renter-occupied units. 5. Overcrowded or lacking complete plumbing facilities.

Table A. States — Residential Contruction, Vital Statistics, and Health

| STATE | Value of residential construction authorized by building permits, 2018 | | | New manufactured homes placed, 2018 | Births, 2017 | | Deaths, 2017 | | | | | Percent lacking health insurance, 2017 | | Medicare beneficiaries, 65 years and older 2018 |
| | New construction ($1000) | Number of housing units | Percent single family | | Total | Rate[1] | Number Total | Infant[2] | Rate Crude[1] | Age-adjusted[1] | Infant[3] | All persons | Children under 19 years | |
	93	94	95	96	97	98	99	100	101	102	103	104	105	106
United States	271,119,545	1,328,827	64.4	96,555	3,855,500	11.8	2,813,503	22,335	8.6	7.3	5.8	8.7	5.0	58,703,170
Alabama	3,046,657	14,824	87.5	4,807	58,941	12.1	53,238	434	10.9	9.2	7.4	9.4	3.1	1,026,964
Alaska	429,020	1,677	73.2	51	10,445	14.1	4,411	59	6.0	7.1	5.7	13.7	9.6	96,128
Arizona	9,727,722	41,664	77.1	1,967	81,872	11.7	57,758	469	8.2	6.8	5.7	10.1	7.7	1,270,464
Arkansas	1,829,441	10,179	72.2	1,805	37,520	12.5	32,588	307	10.8	9.0	8.2	7.9	4.4	627,298
California	27,844,627	113,502	51.8	3,988	471,658	11.9	268,189	1,973	6.8	6.2	4.2	7.2	3.1	6,118,721
Colorado	10,230,540	42,627	61.3	1,000	64,382	11.5	38,063	291	6.8	6.6	4.5	7.5	4.3	880,478
Connecticut	1,112,212	4,815	53.0	105	35,221	9.8	31,312	160	8.7	6.5	4.5	5.5	3.1	667,292
Delaware	788,602	6,003	91.2	390	10,855	11.3	9,178	72	9.5	7.5	6.6	5.4	3.5	200,970
District of Columbia	518,239	4,615	2.4	0	9,560	13.8	4,965	77	7.2	7.3	8.1	3.8	1.2	92,429
Florida	31,543,714	144,427	67.2	7,322	223,630	10.7	203,636	1,358	9.7	6.7	6.1	12.9	7.3	4,410,311
Georgia	11,146,199	59,315	71.3	3,503	129,243	12.4	83,098	932	8.0	7.9	7.2	13.4	7.5	1,674,828
Hawaii	1,359,881	4,659	55.6	8	17,517	12.3	11,390	92	8.0	5.8	5.3	3.8	2.2	266,717
Idaho	3,099,095	15,824	76.9	468	22,181	12.9	14,011	102	8.2	7.4	4.6	10.1	4.6	320,099
Illinois	4,036,281	21,510	46.7	1,159	149,390	11.7	109,721	912	8.6	7.2	6.1	6.8	2.9	2,192,385
Indiana	4,879,857	21,480	76.4	1,833	82,170	12.3	65,597	600	9.8	8.5	7.3	8.2	6.3	1,232,868
Iowa	2,249,100	11,518	63.5	464	38,430	12.2	30,530	203	9.7	7.4	5.3	4.7	3.1	612,111
Kansas	1,888,570	9,478	56.7	472	36,519	12.5	27,063	221	9.3	7.7	6.1	8.7	5.2	522,921
Kentucky	2,267,765	13,826	56.2	2,819	54,752	12.3	48,212	355	10.8	9.3	6.5	5.4	3.8	911,928
Louisiana	3,108,408	15,835	86.7	4,876	61,018	13.0	45,804	431	9.8	8.8	7.1	8.4	3.1	848,502
Maine	959,299	4,697	77.9	591	12,298	9.2	14,676	70	11.0	7.7	5.7	8.1	4.9	331,086
Maryland	3,701,849	18,647	69.6	125	71,641	11.8	49,926	460	8.2	7.2	6.4	6.1	3.8	1,010,800
Massachusetts	4,157,964	17,044	42.1	200	70,702	10.3	58,803	262	8.6	6.8	3.7	2.8	1.5	1,303,797
Michigan	4,569,368	19,580	79.8	4,467	111,426	11.2	97,602	755	9.8	7.8	6.8	5.2	3.0	2,023,274
Minnesota	5,720,813	25,673	52.9	732	68,595	12.3	44,371	328	8.0	6.6	4.8	4.4	3.4	995,561
Mississippi	1,193,505	6,883	89.1	3,557	37,357	12.5	32,280	322	10.8	9.5	8.6	12.0	4.8	590,782
Missouri	3,167,067	16,875	67.4	1,251	73,034	11.9	61,876	456	10.1	8.2	6.2	9.1	5.1	1,204,203
Montana	869,896	5,099	63.0	296	11,799	11.2	10,200	64	9.7	7.6	5.4	8.5	5.8	222,949
Nebraska	1,309,845	7,866	62.3	160	25,821	13.4	16,878	144	8.8	7.3	5.6	8.3	5.1	337,817
Nevada	3,400,610	17,645	73.7	586	35,756	11.9	24,657	208	8.2	7.7	5.8	11.2	8.0	511,342
New Hampshire	875,243	4,445	61.0	430	12,116	9.0	12,504	51	9.3	7.2	4.2	5.8	2.3	290,038
New Jersey	4,220,431	27,942	37.0	641	101,250	11.2	74,846	453	8.3	6.7	4.5	7.7	3.7	1,583,575
New Mexico	1,037,554	4,813	91.3	1,376	23,767	11.4	18,673	140	8.9	7.5	5.9	9.1	5.1	409,451
New York	6,692,382	37,778	26.6	1,604	229,737	11.6	155,358	1,047	7.8	6.2	4.6	5.7	2.7	3,555,595
North Carolina	13,581,958	71,691	71.5	4,439	120,125	11.7	93,157	847	9.1	7.9	7.1	10.7	4.8	1,930,529
North Dakota	607,898	3,211	59.3	279	10,737	14.2	6,415	46	8.5	6.9	4.3	7.5	7.5	127,621
Ohio	5,189,339	24,221	67.4	1,932	136,832	11.7	123,648	983	10.6	8.5	7.2	6.0	4.5	2,293,632
Oklahoma	2,181,297	10,502	89.1	2,016	50,214	12.8	40,452	387	10.3	9.0	7.7	14.2	8.1	721,972
Oregon	4,180,894	20,132	55.7	1,676	43,631	10.5	36,624	236	8.8	7.2	5.4	6.8	3.6	836,419
Pennsylvania	4,684,321	23,325	65.7	1,695	137,745	10.8	135,656	841	10.6	7.8	6.1	5.5	4.4	2,681,839
Rhode Island	260,274	1,294	72.3	28	10,638	10.0	10,157	66	9.6	7.1	6.2	4.6	2.1	216,219
South Carolina	8,143,578	35,487	86.2	4,035	57,029	11.4	49,441	371	9.8	8.3	6.5	11.0	5.1	1,039,803
South Dakota	854,338	4,963	60.1	243	12,134	14.0	7,996	94	9.2	7.4	7.8	9.1	6.2	170,864
Tennessee	7,048,088	37,169	75.4	2,710	81,016	12.1	70,096	597	10.4	9.0	7.4	9.5	4.4	1,324,333
Texas	34,689,871	192,878	65.4	18,632	382,050	13.5	198,106	2,237	7.0	7.4	5.9	17.3	10.7	4,016,438
Utah	5,610,557	25,574	72.5	271	48,585	15.7	18,035	285	5.8	7.0	5.9	9.2	7.3	385,977
Vermont	365,383	2,080	54.4	121	5,655	9.1	6,007	27	9.6	7.1	4.8	4.6	1.6	143,440
Virginia	5,830,512	31,977	67.0	1,179	100,391	11.9	68,579	592	8.1	7.2	5.9	8.8	5.1	1,469,195
Washington	9,807,980	47,746	49.6	1,600	87,562	11.8	56,995	341	7.7	6.9	3.9	6.1	2.6	1,319,645
West Virginia	500,078	2,887	81.1	1,119	18,675	10.3	23,276	131	12.8	9.6	7.0	6.1	2.6	433,710
Wisconsin	4,008,219	19,113	63.0	776	64,975	11.2	52,681	414	9.1	7.2	6.4	5.4	3.9	1,141,746
Wyoming	593,197	1,812	84.6	108	6,903	11.9	4,768	32	8.2	7.1	4.6	12.3	9.5	106,077

1. Per 1,000 resident population.　　2. Deaths of infants under 1 year old.　　3. Deaths of infants under 1 year old per 1,000 live births.

Table A. States — Crime and Education

STATE	Violent crime		Property crime		Public elementary and secondary school enrollment, 2016–2017		Educational attainment[3] (percent)				Local government expenditures for education, 2015-2016	
							2010		2017		Total current expenditures (mil dol)	Current expenditures per student (dollars)
	Number	Rate[2]	Number	Rate[2]	Total	Student/ teacher ratio	High school graduate or more	Bachelor's degree or more	High school graduate or more	Bachelor's degree or more		
	107	108	109	110	111	112	113	114	115	116	117	118
United States	1,283,220	394.0	7,694,086	2,362.2	50,587,859	16.0	85.6	28.2	88.0	32.0	596,136	11,841
Alabama	25,551	524.2	144,160	2,957.3	744,930	17.5	82.1	21.9	86.5	25.5	6,886	9,258
Alaska	6,133	829.0	26,204	3,542.1	132,737	17.0	91.0	27.9	91.7	28.8	2,320	17,510
Arizona	35,644	508.0	204,515	2,914.9	1,123,137	23.3	85.6	25.9	87.2	29.4	8,552	7,772
Arkansas	16,671	554.9	92,489	3,078.6	493,447	13.8	82.9	19.5	86.7	23.4	4,872	9,900
California	177,627	449.3	987,114	2,496.7	6,309,138	23.3	80.7	30.1	83.3	33.6	72,003	11,420
Colorado	20,638	368.1	151,483	2,701.6	905,019	17.4	89.7	36.4	91.6	41.2	8,648	9,619
Connecticut	8,180	228.0	63,509	1,769.9	535,118	12.6	88.6	35.5	90.4	38.7	10,551	19,615
Delaware	4,361	453.4	23,477	2,440.6	136,264	14.8	87.7	27.8	90.6	31.5	1,941	14,397
District of Columbia	6,974	1,004.9	29,729	4,283.9	85,850	12.8	87.4	50.1	90.2	57.3	1,776	21,135
Florida	85,625	408.0	527,220	2,512.4	2,816,791	15.1	85.5	25.8	88.4	29.7	25,621	9,176
Georgia	37,258	357.2	298,298	2,860.2	1,764,346	15.4	84.3	27.3	87.0	30.9	17,283	9,835
Hawaii	3,577	250.6	40,392	2,829.5	181,550	15.4	89.9	29.5	92.3	32.9	2,502	13,748
Idaho	3,888	226.4	28,079	1,635.4	297,200	18.3	88.3	24.4	90.8	26.8	2,098	7,178
Illinois	56,180	438.8	257,497	2,011.4	2,026,718	15.7	86.9	30.8	89.1	34.4	29,253	14,327
Indiana	26,598	399.0	161,132	2,416.9	1,049,547	17.5	87.0	22.7	88.6	26.8	10,144	9,691
Iowa	9,230	293.4	66,855	2,125.3	509,831	14.2	90.6	24.9	92.1	28.9	5,663	11,148
Kansas	12,030	413.0	81,593	2,800.9	494,347	13.7	89.2	29.8	91.0	33.7	5,066	10,216
Kentucky	10,056	225.8	94,833	2,129.1	684,017	16.3	81.9	20.5	86.3	24.0	6,750	9,831
Louisiana	26,092	557.0	157,712	3,366.8	716,293	14.8	81.9	21.4	85.1	23.8	8,027	11,169
Maine	1,617	121.0	20,133	1,507.1	180,512	12.2	90.3	26.8	92.3	32.1	2,579	14,202
Maryland	30,273	500.2	134,496	2,222.3	886,221	14.8	88.1	36.1	89.9	39.7	12,774	14,523
Massachusetts	24,560	358.0	98,575	1,437.0	964,514	13.3	89.1	39.0	90.8	43.4	16,375	16,986
Michigan	44,826	450.0	179,318	1,800.0	1,528,666	18.3	88.7	25.2	90.9	29.1	16,977	11,051
Minnesota	13,291	238.3	122,212	2,191.5	875,021	15.4	91.8	31.8	93.1	36.1	10,687	12,364
Mississippi	8,526	285.7	81,581	2,733.9	483,150	15.1	81.0	19.5	84.4	21.9	4,235	8,692
Missouri	32,420	530.3	173,253	2,833.9	915,040	13.5	86.9	25.6	89.7	29.1	9,546	10,385
Montana	3,961	377.1	27,225	2,591.6	146,375	13.9	91.7	28.8	93.0	32.3	1,653	11,374
Nebraska	5,873	305.9	43,663	2,274.0	319,194	13.5	90.4	28.6	91.3	31.7	3,912	12,379
Nevada	16,667	555.9	78,322	2,612.4	473,744	20.0	84.7	21.7	86.8	24.9	4,092	8,753
New Hampshire	2,668	198.7	18,555	1,381.8	180,888	12.3	91.5	32.8	93.1	36.9	2,834	15,535
New Jersey	20,604	228.8	140,086	1,555.5	1,410,421	12.2	88.0	35.4	89.9	39.7	26,825	19,041
New Mexico	16,359	783.5	82,306	3,941.7	336,263	15.8	83.3	25.0	86.1	27.1	3,343	9,959
New York	70,799	356.7	300,555	1,514.2	2,729,776	13.1	84.9	32.5	86.6	36.0	59,161	22,231
North Carolina	37,364	363.7	261,486	2,545.3	1,550,062	15.5	84.7	26.5	87.8	31.3	13,467	8,717
North Dakota	2,125	281.3	16,602	2,197.8	109,706	11.8	90.3	27.6	92.9	30.7	1,451	13,358
Ohio	34,683	297.5	282,034	2,419.1	1,710,143	16.7	88.1	24.6	90.3	28.0	20,484	11,933
Oklahoma	17,934	456.2	113,066	2,876.4	693,903	16.9	86.2	22.9	88.1	25.5	5,606	8,091
Oregon	11,674	281.8	123,722	2,986.5	578,947	19.5	88.8	28.8	91.0	33.7	6,239	10,823
Pennsylvania	40,120	313.3	211,220	1,649.4	1,727,497	14.1	88.4	27.1	90.6	31.4	26,045	15,165
Rhode Island	2,460	232.2	18,561	1,751.6	142,150	13.3	83.5	30.2	88.3	33.5	2,284	16,082
South Carolina	25,432	506.2	160,575	3,195.9	771,250	15.2	84.1	24.5	87.4	28.0	7,670	10,045
South Dakota	3,771	433.6	16,317	1,876.2	136,302	13.9	89.6	26.3	91.7	28.1	1,253	9,335
Tennessee	43,755	651.5	197,488	2,940.6	1,001,562	15.6	83.6	23.1	87.8	27.3	8,887	8,876
Texas	124,238	438.9	725,328	2,562.6	5,360,849	15.2	80.7	25.9	83.6	29.6	49,578	9,352
Utah	7,410	238.9	86,238	2,780.2	659,801	22.9	90.6	29.3	92.1	34.6	4,539	7,006
Vermont	1,034	165.8	8,960	1,436.7	88,428	10.8	91.0	33.6	92.6	38.3	1,671	19,023
Virginia	17,632	208.2	151,855	1,792.9	1,287,026	14.1	86.5	34.2	89.7	38.7	14,678	11,435
Washington	22,548	304.5	235,027	3,173.6	1,101,711	18.7	89.8	31.1	91.3	35.5	12,484	11,484
West Virginia	6,368	350.7	33,630	1,852.0	273,855	14.2	83.2	17.5	87.1	20.2	3,170	11,424
Wisconsin	18,539	319.9	104,802	1,808.3	864,432	14.7	90.1	26.3	92.4	30.4	10,122	11,664
Wyoming	1,376	237.5	10,604	1,830.4	94,170	12.6	92.3	24.1	92.9	27.6	1,556	16,431

1. Data for serious crimes have not been adjusted for underreporting; this may affect comparability between geographic areas and over time.   2. Per 100,000 population estimated by the FBI.
3. Persons 25 years old and over.

Table A. States — Exports, Income, and Poverty

STATE	Exports of goods by state of origin, 2018 (mil dol)			Income, 2017					Percent below poverty level, 2017						
				Households									Families with related children under 18 years		
	Total	Manu-factured	Non-manu-factured	Per capita income (dollars)	Median income (dollars)	Percent with income of $24999 or less	Percent with income of $100000 or more	Median income of family of four	All persons	Children under 18 years	Persons 65 years and over	All families	Married-couple families	Male house-holder[1] families	Female house-holder[1] families
	119	120	121	122	123	124	125	126	127	128	129	130	131	132	133
United States	1,664,085	1,156,549	225,668	32,397	60,336	20.3	27.8	90,748	13.4	18.4	9.3	9.5	6.6	18.3	35.7
Alabama	21,349	18,298	2,217	26,498	48,123	27.3	19.7	76,585	16.9	24.6	9.9	12.8	7.8	21.7	45.6
Alaska	4,773	283	4,432	34,222	73,181	14.0	35.4	97,465	11.1	14.9	7.4	7.4	5.8	19.4	23.5
Arizona	22,388	13,482	2,699	29,420	56,581	20.6	24.4	79,026	14.9	20.8	9.0	10.7	8.9	20.2	34.6
Arkansas	6,466	4,704	590	25,316	45,869	27.1	17.2	66,712	16.4	22.5	10.2	11.6	8.6	19.6	41.8
California	178,405	112,610	22,485	35,046	71,805	17.3	35.9	94,505	13.3	18.1	10.2	9.6	8.1	17.2	32.7
Colorado	8,317	6,862	515	36,345	69,117	15.5	32.7	102,233	10.3	12.0	7.8	6.7	4.9	11.3	28.6
Connecticut	17,400	14,062	1,269	42,029	74,168	15.7	37.0	114,110	9.6	12.6	7.1	6.4	3.6	13.3	27.5
Delaware	4,703	3,896	98	33,887	62,852	19.1	28.7	97,540	13.6	18.5	8.5	9.2	7.6	17.2	30.1
District of Columbia	2,726	2,162	341	52,500	82,372	20.6	42.6	129,135	16.6	25.6	14.2	13.3	5.0	23.5	41.6
Florida	57,241	42,119	3,954	29,838	52,594	22.2	22.4	76,953	14.0	20.3	10.2	10.1	8.0	18.2	34.0
Georgia	40,551	31,357	3,647	29,668	56,183	21.6	24.8	80,510	14.9	21.0	10.1	11.1	7.2	20.4	36.0
Hawaii	647	452	153	33,882	77,765	15.2	37.0	102,125	9.5	11.5	9.3	7.4	3.6	13.1	29.5
Idaho	4,022	2,350	443	26,386	52,225	20.6	19.9	72,381	12.8	15.3	8.1	8.6	6.7	16.3	40.0
Illinois	65,415	49,802	3,928	34,196	62,992	19.7	29.8	96,252	12.6	17.0	8.6	9.0	5.6	17.8	35.2
Indiana	39,339	35,104	1,172	28,323	54,181	21.5	21.7	85,368	13.5	18.4	7.7	9.2	5.4	17.5	38.0
Iowa	14,324	11,538	2,374	30,865	58,570	19.3	24.0	92,135	10.7	12.3	6.6	6.7	4.2	13.3	31.7
Kansas	11,604	8,736	2,106	30,146	56,422	19.6	23.6	83,114	11.9	14.8	7.3	7.9	5.4	14.1	34.7
Kentucky	31,757	24,464	493	26,779	48,375	26.5	19.5	77,069	17.2	22.4	10.3	12.9	9.3	25.0	42.9
Louisiana	66,237	40,219	25,395	25,885	46,145	29.3	20.2	76,618	19.7	28.0	12.0	14.7	8.2	28.0	47.3
Maine	2,825	1,587	1,092	31,088	56,277	21.4	22.5	94,215	11.1	13.1	8.1	6.3	4.1	18.6	31.4
Maryland	12,076	8,024	2,280	39,960	80,776	13.8	40.2	115,771	9.3	12.0	7.9	6.2	2.8	11.6	24.5
Massachusetts	27,140	21,592	1,544	41,821	77,385	17.6	39.4	127,579	10.5	13.5	9.0	7.2	3.5	11.4	32.8
Michigan	57,940	48,597	2,447	30,488	54,909	21.4	23.4	90,531	14.2	19.7	8.5	9.7	6.4	22.6	37.7
Minnesota	22,685	18,838	1,460	36,156	68,388	15.7	31.6	109,211	9.5	11.8	7.0	5.8	3.9	15.1	27.2
Mississippi	11,808	8,967	743	23,121	43,529	30.5	15.9	65,138	19.8	26.9	13.7	14.9	7.6	25.0	46.1
Missouri	14,500	12,170	1,293	29,438	53,578	21.9	21.8	83,609	13.4	18.6	8.7	9.2	5.6	19.9	36.5
Montana	1,654	878	441	29,428	53,386	21.9	21.5	92,646	12.5	14.7	7.2	7.7	7.4	17.4	34.6
Nebraska	7,945	6,176	1,454	30,915	59,970	18.2	24.3	91,136	10.8	14.1	7.2	7.2	4.8	14.8	34.3
Nevada	11,085	8,260	643	30,166	58,003	18.9	24.3	82,970	13.0	18.5	8.5	9.1	6.5	13.8	31.0
New Hampshire	5,286	4,171	233	38,237	73,381	14.9	35.1	113,991	7.7	10.3	5.8	4.9	2.4	14.9	27.7
New Jersey	35,663	23,487	4,093	40,567	80,088	15.7	40.3	122,474	10.0	13.9	8.4	7.3	4.8	15.6	29.6
New Mexico	3,655	2,033	181	25,311	46,744	27.1	19.2	67,924	19.7	27.2	12.2	15.2	11.0	30.5	42.8
New York	81,487	39,327	12,700	37,156	64,894	20.9	32.5	99,943	14.1	19.7	11.4	10.4	7.4	18.7	35.8
North Carolina	32,730	28,213	1,621	29,860	52,752	22.8	22.4	82,994	14.7	21.2	9.1	10.6	7.4	23.1	38.3
North Dakota	6,778	4,099	2,550	34,041	61,843	19.1	26.3	102,402	10.3	10.9	9.9	6.1	2.8	12.8	32.4
Ohio	54,293	43,705	3,825	30,038	54,021	22.2	22.5	87,321	14.0	20.1	7.7	9.8	5.7	18.7	39.7
Oklahoma	6,102	4,483	435	26,472	50,051	24.4	19.5	72,569	15.8	21.5	9.1	11.6	8.3	23.4	39.9
Oregon	22,293	16,444	2,487	31,950	60,212	19.7	26.3	88,440	13.2	16.5	8.7	8.8	6.7	19.1	34.4
Pennsylvania	41,050	31,391	5,079	32,711	59,195	21.3	26.3	97,692	12.5	17.0	8.5	8.1	4.7	16.7	35.0
Rhode Island	2,400	1,581	632	34,511	63,870	21.5	30.0	101,338	11.6	16.6	9.0	7.9	4.5	14.0	37.5
South Carolina	34,637	32,198	727	27,909	50,570	24.5	20.4	75,646	15.4	22.6	9.2	11.3	6.9	23.3	41.1
South Dakota	1,437	1,278	111	29,611	56,521	20.6	22.4	86,627	13.0	16.6	8.0	8.4	4.2	17.1	38.2
Tennessee	32,703	24,044	1,636	28,764	51,340	23.6	20.6	77,260	15.0	21.2	9.2	10.9	7.8	19.5	40.7
Texas	315,448	192,538	66,465	29,525	59,206	20.3	27.2	81,958	14.7	20.9	10.8	11.3	8.3	19.3	37.6
Utah	14,373	13,103	777	28,085	68,358	14.1	30.1	86,717	9.7	10.7	6.4	6.7	5.4	10.3	30.0
Vermont	2,920	2,243	82	32,443	57,513	20.5	24.0	86,315	11.3	13.8	7.1	7.0	5.9	15.5	31.3
Virginia	18,358	13,608	3,125	37,442	71,535	16.4	34.8	102,751	10.6	14.0	7.1	7.1	4.3	13.4	30.9
Washington	77,700	59,590	14,392	36,975	70,979	15.9	33.7	105,074	11.0	14.3	8.0	7.1	4.7	17.1	31.2
West Virginia	8,124	3,354	4,488	24,478	43,469	30.3	16.0	73,337	19.1	25.9	10.2	14.1	11.1	29.3	52.1
Wisconsin	22,709	19,294	1,418	31,998	59,305	19.2	24.6	96,972	11.3	14.5	7.8	7.1	4.0	15.1	31.7
Wyoming	1,356	1,262	72	30,883	60,434	19.2	25.1	89,527	11.3	13.3	8.4	7.6	6.3	8.3	32.9

1. No spouse present.

Table A. States — **Personal Income**

STATE	Personal income												
		Per capita[1], 2018			Sources of personal income (mil dol)								
									Transfer payments, 2017				
										Government payments to individuals			
	Total, 2018 (mil dol)	Percent change, 2017–2018	Dollars	Rank	Wages and salaries[2], 2018	Proprietors' income, 2018	Dividends, interest, and rent, 2018	Total	Total	Social Security	Medical payments	Income maintenance	Unemployment insurance
	134	135	136	137	138	139	140	141	142	143	144	145	146
United States	17,572,929	4.5	53,712	X	8,828,520	1,584,843	3,520,984	2,859,632	2,781,115	926,072	1,298,866	268,123	29,514
Alabama..........................	206,924	4.0	42,334	47	97,380	14,938	36,733	45,594	44,417	16,790	18,017	4,503	185
Alaska............................	44,015	4.1	59,687	11	20,899	3,858	8,103	6,958	6,782	1,421	3,040	872	91
Arizona...........................	313,040	5.5	43,650	43	156,737	23,299	60,340	58,882	57,186	20,322	26,602	4,780	309
Arkansas.........................	128,286	4.0	42,566	46	57,553	8,517	29,260	29,062	28,341	9,927	13,098	2,497	158
California........................	2,475,728	4.7	62,586	7	1,250,685	249,672	538,325	331,432	321,862	87,900	159,715	34,081	5,181
Colorado	323,767	5.7	56,846	14	168,828	31,033	71,880	39,530	38,174	13,052	17,492	2,896	426
Connecticut......................	266,382	3.4	74,561	2	116,890	29,319	60,116	33,288	32,430	11,306	15,919	2,497	635
Delaware.........................	49,760	4.1	51,449	22	26,513	3,777	9,191	9,941	9,709	3,401	4,676	685	71
District of Columbia............	57,518	3.6	81,882	1	75,411	9,211	10,422	6,659	6,497	1,179	4,003	900	55
Florida............................	1,052,550	5.2	49,417	27	469,413	62,631	285,971	197,602	192,516	68,844	84,211	18,181	481
Georgia	481,213	4.5	45,745	40	256,425	40,405	84,204	78,432	75,919	26,758	30,323	9,015	354
Hawaii............................	77,509	2.9	54,565	17	37,993	6,006	17,029	11,749	11,407	4,049	4,975	1,224	161
Idaho..............................	75,703	5.4	43,155	44	33,393	8,152	16,767	12,932	12,515	4,959	4,950	977	110
Illinois............................	725,394	4.5	56,933	13	382,433	52,975	148,573	103,970	100,880	34,885	46,025	11,253	1,785
Indiana...........................	312,151	3.7	46,646	36	154,549	29,441	49,240	57,689	56,087	21,175	25,435	4,883	259
Iowa..............................	154,091	4.1	48,823	29	76,180	12,935	30,286	25,221	24,468	9,821	10,329	1,931	399
Kansas...........................	146,028	3.2	50,155	24	71,214	15,603	28,813	22,499	21,799	8,535	9,246	1,829	197
Kentucky.........................	186,685	3.2	41,779	48	92,547	12,430	30,599	43,740	42,672	14,233	20,444	3,860	322
Louisiana.........................	212,223	3.8	45,542	41	100,980	17,482	37,169	45,659	44,531	12,750	22,463	4,679	226
Maine.............................	64,566	4.0	48,241	31	29,849	4,991	12,051	13,633	13,311	4,829	6,078	972	102
Maryland.........................	380,172	3.2	62,914	6	178,101	36,781	72,691	50,568	49,107	15,832	24,316	4,351	572
Massachusetts...................	483,657	4.3	70,073	3	265,850	43,597	96,446	67,100	65,467	19,628	34,229	6,130	1,390
Michigan	475,626	3.3	47,582	33	239,478	32,037	85,946	94,679	92,274	35,305	41,460	8,416	823
Minnesota	316,327	4.3	56,374	15	171,721	23,266	61,128	47,380	46,035	15,961	21,911	4,153	754
Mississippi.......................	113,469	3.8	37,994	51	49,721	8,650	18,672	28,632	27,916	9,394	12,949	3,069	110
Missouri..........................	285,704	3.9	46,635	37	148,382	22,588	53,676	54,381	52,913	19,285	24,284	4,104	330
Montana..........................	50,055	5.0	47,120	35	21,295	4,958	12,229	9,336	9,084	3,324	3,937	627	112
Nebraska.........................	100,534	3.1	52,110	21	49,906	12,079	20,599	14,550	14,088	5,199	5,878	1,157	83
Nevada...........................	146,334	5.7	48,225	32	71,818	9,048	35,615	22,929	22,197	7,883	9,616	2,188	321
New Hampshire	83,293	4.0	61,405	8	38,411	8,350	14,953	11,844	11,522	4,794	5,121	588	71
New Jersey	602,297	3.6	67,609	5	273,599	60,962	111,623	81,905	79,724	27,289	36,624	7,501	1,900
New Mexico	86,328	3.9	41,198	49	40,282	5,245	16,961	19,547	19,041	6,058	8,925	2,140	158
New York	1,341,915	4.7	68,667	4	703,059	137,103	283,754	226,704	221,941	56,554	129,058	22,109	2,118
North Carolina...................	475,927	4.8	45,834	39	243,144	36,575	89,327	88,932	86,459	31,305	35,964	8,343	227
North Dakota.....................	41,277	4.5	54,306	19	23,053	3,298	9,467	5,642	5,462	1,925	2,241	459	109
Ohio..............................	563,926	3.5	48,242	30	290,695	42,998	97,239	106,869	104,066	35,402	50,891	9,124	908
Oklahoma........................	181,886	4.3	46,128	38	81,411	25,588	33,506	33,295	32,351	11,551	13,418	3,066	258
Oregon...........................	209,148	4.9	49,908	26	106,091	18,921	42,609	37,700	36,698	13,107	16,774	3,060	510
Pennsylvania.....................	708,862	3.9	55,349	16	337,700	75,004	122,977	129,731	126,671	44,283	60,726	11,465	1,922
Rhode Island.....................	57,648	3.1	54,523	18	27,438	3,820	10,951	11,206	10,954	3,434	5,288	1,144	152
South Carolina	217,276	3.9	42,736	45	102,043	15,527	40,061	45,646	44,438	17,047	17,906	3,906	186
South Dakota	44,236	4.2	50,141	25	19,697	5,645	10,768	6,536	6,330	2,547	2,571	527	33
Tennessee........................	319,401	4.5	47,179	34	155,873	45,911	47,077	60,246	58,624	21,476	25,361	5,936	236
Texas.............................	1,411,021	5.3	49,161	28	738,782	161,459	250,924	206,050	199,204	60,891	91,179	23,424	2,493
Utah..............................	143,324	6.3	45,340	42	77,442	11,339	30,044	17,392	16,637	6,093	6,332	1,721	163
Vermont..........................	33,569	3.1	53,598	20	15,288	2,779	7,023	6,562	6,415	2,235	3,049	584	64
Virginia...........................	485,098	3.9	56,952	12	249,319	29,153	99,350	64,529	62,496	23,378	25,440	5,234	341
Washington	458,017	6.8	60,781	9	236,733	37,355	101,924	61,992	60,197	20,954	25,453	5,382	1,021
West Virginia.....................	73,278	4.9	40,578	50	33,020	4,451	11,219	20,081	19,644	7,117	8,812	1,714	159
Wisconsin........................	295,073	4.0	50,756	23	149,052	20,096	56,106	48,659	47,263	18,981	20,445	3,756	418
Wyoming.........................	34,719	4.5	60,095	10	14,246	3,582	11,046	4,533	4,393	1,703	1,665	231	65

1. Based on the resident population estimated as of July 1 of the year shown.   2. Includes supplements to wages and salaries.

Table A. States — **Personal Income and Earnings**

STATE	Personal tax payments, 2017 (mil dol)	Disposable personal income, 2017		Earnings, 2018									Gross state product, 2,018 (mil dol)
						Percent by selected industries							
						Goods-related[2]		Service-related and other[3]					
		Total (mil dol)	Per capita[1] (dollars)	Total (mil dol)	Farm	Total	Manu-facturing	Total	Retail trade	Finance, insurance, real estate, rental and leasing	Health care and social assistance	Govern-ment	
	147	148	149	150	151	152	153	154	155	156	157	158	159
United States	2,032,672	14,787,578	45,480	12,427,227	0.6	16.4	9.2	67.2	5.7	9.5	11.1	15.8	20,494,079
Alabama...........................	19,361	179,555	36,831	136,193	1.3	20.8	14.2	57.8	6.3	6.9	11.0	20.1	221,126
Alaska.............................	3,548	38,753	52,384	31,691	0.0	17.4	3.0	51.4	5.3	4.3	12.6	31.2	54,011
Arizona............................	30,175	266,474	37,804	214,050	0.8	15.0	7.6	68.8	6.9	10.8	12.5	15.4	346,792
Arkansas..........................	12,204	111,110	37,000	79,024	2.8	19.0	12.5	61.4	6.6	5.4	12.9	16.8	128,082
California.........................	335,794	2,028,336	51,481	1,778,305	1.1	14.7	9.0	68.4	5.2	8.9	9.5	15.7	2,968,118
Colorado..........................	39,524	266,887	47,524	233,470	0.6	17.9	5.6	66.0	5.2	8.9	9.1	15.5	368,795
Connecticut......................	38,751	218,963	61,267	172,189	0.1	17.2	11.5	69.7	5.4	16.2	11.4	12.9	274,180
Delaware..........................	5,506	42,276	44,172	36,689	1.3	12.5	6.0	70.7	5.7	16.7	13.8	15.2	74,973
District of Columbia...........	8,308	47,203	67,850	104,230	0.0	0.0	D	61.6	1.0	5.4	5.6	36.8	140,280
Florida.............................	101,368	899,256	42,869	628,137	0.4	12.1	4.8	73.5	7.5	9.6	12.6	14.1	1,036,323
Georgia............................	50,975	409,428	39,319	354,567	0.7	15.2	9.0	68.3	5.8	8.4	9.7	15.7	588,172
Hawaii..............................	8,111	67,244	47,215	54,604	0.5	9.9	1.8	61.1	6.1	6.2	10.3	28.5	92,027
Idaho...............................	7,401	64,412	37,473	49,865	3.7	20.7	12.1	59.6	8.0	6.3	11.8	15.9	77,004
Illinois.............................	86,163	607,751	47,532	523,797	0.3	15.8	10.8	70.3	4.8	11.1	10.4	13.7	864,587
Indiana............................	31,693	269,315	40,437	220,937	0.5	26.9	20.4	60.9	6.0	9.1	12.9	11.7	366,707
Iowa................................	15,948	132,094	42,200	108,632	2.4	24.3	16.8	57.3	5.9	10.3	10.5	16.0	190,150
Kansas............................	14,509	126,950	43,615	104,073	1.2	19.6	12.5	62.2	5.4	9.3	11.2	17.1	167,042
Kentucky..........................	19,512	161,315	36,219	127,804	0.8	21.1	14.7	60.1	6.0	7.2	12.6	18.0	208,340
Louisiana.........................	18,924	185,592	39,734	143,220	0.5	22.9	9.5	59.6	6.3	6.3	12.3	17.0	252,117
Maine..............................	6,600	55,460	41,541	42,154	0.3	16.4	9.0	65.9	7.6	7.2	16.1	17.3	64,351
Maryland..........................	49,305	318,953	52,939	258,422	0.2	10.9	4.3	66.0	4.9	10.8	10.8	22.9	412,921
Massachusetts..................	71,194	392,737	57,223	365,189	0.0	13.9	7.5	74.5	4.5	11.6	12.7	11.6	567,255
Michigan...........................	53,928	406,342	40,730	328,234	0.1	22.6	16.7	63.5	5.8	7.3	12.3	13.8	528,008
Minnesota........................	42,021	261,120	46,895	233,194	0.5	18.4	12.1	68.1	5.3	10.1	13.4	13.0	368,317
Mississippi.......................	9,160	100,164	33,504	70,450	2.3	20.0	13.4	55.5	7.5	5.0	11.9	22.3	114,107
Missouri...........................	30,857	244,118	39,963	204,031	0.7	17.2	10.9	67.2	5.9	9.1	12.4	14.9	317,749
Montana...........................	5,082	42,595	40,448	31,378	1.8	16.9	4.4	62.1	8.2	7.2	14.4	19.2	48,970
Nebraska..........................	10,132	87,424	45,591	74,069	4.2	15.4	9.5	64.5	5.5	9.2	11.3	15.9	122,966
Nevada............................	15,275	123,111	41,418	97,385	0.1	13.9	4.3	70.4	6.7	5.8	9.4	15.7	165,803
New Hampshire	8,518	71,604	53,049	55,142	0.1	19.6	11.8	68.5	7.8	8.4	12.5	11.9	84,712
New Jersey	79,332	501,867	56,462	393,657	0.1	13.4	7.6	72.4	6.0	10.7	11.5	14.1	624,852
New Mexico	7,373	75,755	36,187	55,875	1.5	15.1	3.0	57.7	6.5	5.2	12.3	25.6	99,435
New York	201,368	1,079,715	55,114	1,002,876	0.1	9.1	4.1	75.3	4.6	18.2	11.1	15.5	1,676,350
North Carolina..................	51,887	402,420	39,181	333,549	1.0	17.7	11.1	63.5	5.9	9.0	10.1	17.8	565,801
North Dakota....................	3,986	35,497	47,006	32,067	0.8	22.7	5.7	59.0	6.0	8.1	12.3	17.5	54,714
Ohio................................	60,286	484,543	41,541	404,065	0.1	20.8	14.3	64.5	5.7	7.8	13.1	14.7	676,193
Oklahoma.........................	16,090	158,345	40,264	127,087	0.7	24.4	8.8	56.6	5.6	5.4	10.3	18.4	199,976
Oregon............................	26,565	172,857	41,687	150,829	1.0	19.1	11.7	63.8	6.3	7.1	12.3	16.2	238,684
Pennsylvania....................	80,495	602,039	47,069	497,284	0.2	16.4	9.6	71.0	5.1	7.7	14.0	12.4	788,538
Rhode Island....................	6,415	49,519	46,872	37,745	0.0	8.4	8.4	68.6	6.1	9.7	13.8	16.6	61,021
South Carolina..................	21,682	187,498	37,341	142,043	0.2	20.4	13.8	59.7	6.7	7.5	9.4	19.6	230,354
South Dakota	3,916	38,539	44,131	30,042	3.5	17.7	10.3	62.4	7.2	11.0	15.3	16.4	51,581
Tennessee........................	26,731	278,959	41,581	236,702	0.1	18.6	11.6	68.7	6.7	7.9	15.8	12.6	365,602
Texas..............................	126,114	1,214,454	42,879	1,055,611	0.4	21.4	8.2	63.9	5.7	8.8	9.4	14.2	1,775,797
Utah	15,429	119,375	38,469	107,492	0.3	18.7	9.5	65.1	7.7	9.6	8.5	15.8	177,336
Vermont...........................	3,395	29,175	46,716	22,198	0.6	18.4	10.5	62.4	7.3	5.7	15.0	18.6	33,725
Virginia............................	60,007	406,736	48,048	335,513	0.1	11.4	5.6	65.5	4.8	7.4	9.2	23.0	534,449
Washington......................	48,419	380,346	51,222	325,771	1.1	16.0	8.8	65.6	8.8	6.0	10.0	17.2	563,151
West Virginia	6,588	63,285	34,829	45,942	-0.1	22.5	8.2	57.7	6.4	4.6	16.1	19.9	77,477
Wisconsin........................	33,600	250,036	43,169	207,845	0.8	24.3	17.6	60.8	5.8	7.9	12.6	14.1	336,972
Wyoming..........................	3,149	30,072	51,944	21,908	0.8	19.9	D	50.3	5.4	5.3	7.4	24.4	39,371

1. Based on the resident population estimated as of July 1 of the year shown.   2. Includes mining, construction, and manufacturing.   3. Includes private sector earnings in forestry, fishing, related activities, and other; utilities; wholesale trade; transportation and warehousing; and information.

Table A. States — Social Security, Employment, and Labor Force

STATE	Social Security beneficiaries, December 2017 Number	Rate[1]	Supplemental Security Income recipients, December 2017	Civilian employment and selected occupations,[2] 2015 Total	Percent Management, business, science, and arts occupations	Services, sales, and office	Construction and production	Civilian labor force (annual average), 2018 Total (1000)	Percent change, 2017–2018	Employed (1000)	Unemployed Total (1000)	Rate[3]
	160	161	162	163	164	165	166	167	168	169	170	171
United States	60,376,114	185.4	8,226,649	155,058,331	38.2	40.8	21.0	161,640,240	0.9	155,343,944	6,296,296	3.9
Alabama........................	1,131,359	232.1	165,007	2,065,885	34.8	40.0	25.2	2,198,837	0.9	2,112,347	86,490	3.9
Alaska	98,359	133.0	12,564	344,982	37.4	40.6	22.0	356,886	-1.1	333,375	23,511	6.6
Arizona	1,310,666	186.8	119,571	3,125,954	36.1	45.3	18.6	3,439,755	3.4	3,273,550	166,205	4.8
Arkansas	692,178	230.4	107,548	1,296,881	34.0	39.8	26.2	1,351,496	0.3	1,301,459	50,037	3.7
California	5,858,780	148.2	1,261,217	18,757,501	38.7	41.1	20.1	19,398,212	1.0	18,582,802	815,410	4.2
Colorado	852,635	152.1	73,285	2,899,926	41.9	39.4	18.7	3,096,358	3.5	2,994,752	101,606	3.3
Connecticut...................	673,359	187.7	65,812	1,805,023	43.6	39.9	16.5	1,905,312	0.4	1,827,070	78,242	4.1
Delaware	206,939	215.1	16,927	436,376	40.7	39.3	20.0	482,465	1.2	464,337	18,128	3.8
District of Columbia...........	82,253	118.5	26,573	378,780	63.3	30.3	6.4	404,610	0.8	382,140	22,470	5.6
Florida	4,531,636	216.0	578,891	9,488,742	35.2	46.0	18.8	10,234,770	1.4	9,869,673	365,097	3.6
Georgia	1,790,398	171.7	259,792	4,841,845	37.2	40.2	22.6	5,107,656	1.0	4,906,411	201,245	3.9
Hawaii	266,523	186.7	23,930	680,505	34.1	48.5	17.4	678,734	-0.7	662,128	16,606	2.4
Idaho	335,551	195.4	30,908	786,913	34.6	39.5	25.9	857,049	2.7	832,732	24,317	2.8
Illinois	2,220,171	173.4	270,883	6,234,854	37.8	40.8	21.4	6,469,668	-0.3	6,191,319	278,349	4.3
Indiana	1,335,288	200.3	128,575	3,184,244	34.4	38.5	27.1	3,381,713	1.4	3,265,580	116,133	3.4
Iowa	638,322	202.9	51,138	1,619,600	35.5	38.9	25.6	1,686,840	0.5	1,644,280	42,560	2.5
Kansas	544,486	186.9	48,233	1,436,801	38.9	38.5	22.6	1,482,220	0.2	1,432,387	49,833	3.4
Kentucky.......................	980,991	220.2	177,858	1,976,688	33.5	40.2	26.3	2,061,622	0.4	1,972,312	89,310	4.3
Louisiana......................	895,826	191.2	177,338	2,022,766	33.4	42.8	23.8	2,103,495	-0.0	2,000,791	102,704	4.9
Maine	338,770	253.6	37,309	671,486	36.7	41.1	22.1	698,745	0.0	675,221	23,524	3.4
Maryland	983,736	162.5	122,312	3,098,182	45.9	38.0	16.1	3,197,137	0.1	3,071,652	125,485	3.9
Massachusetts...............	1,260,786	183.8	186,405	3,599,534	46.1	38.4	15.5	3,805,450	3.0	3,678,402	127,048	3.3
Michigan.......................	2,186,709	219.5	274,877	4,654,612	36.7	39.5	23.8	4,902,069	0.3	4,698,845	203,224	4.1
Minnesota.....................	1,012,620	181.6	93,892	2,960,124	40.8	38.4	20.8	3,070,224	0.4	2,980,885	89,339	2.9
Mississippi....................	661,656	221.7	119,553	1,226,975	32.5	40.3	27.2	1,275,721	-0.4	1,214,992	60,729	4.8
Missouri........................	1,281,534	209.6	137,796	2,920,301	36.9	40.6	22.5	3,052,386	-0.3	2,954,808	97,578	3.2
Montana	228,685	217.7	18,215	519,277	35.4	42.2	22.4	528,244	0.6	508,588	19,656	3.7
Nebraska......................	340,251	177.2	28,272	1,008,952	37.7	39.0	23.4	1,020,197	0.8	991,688	28,509	2.8
Nevada.........................	521,297	173.9	56,143	1,424,856	28.9	51.5	19.6	1,500,377	2.9	1,431,959	68,418	4.6
New Hampshire	300,267	223.6	19,032	728,045	41.7	38.7	19.7	761,752	1.0	742,512	19,240	2.5
New Jersey....................	1,613,096	179.1	181,512	4,493,519	42.9	39.4	17.7	4,422,942	-0.7	4,239,567	183,375	4.1
New Mexico...................	427,426	204.7	63,706	870,092	37.4	43.9	18.7	940,359	0.4	893,823	46,536	4.9
New York......................	3,586,883	180.7	637,595	9,634,437	40.9	42.7	16.4	9,574,706	0.1	9,181,058	393,648	4.1
North Carolina.................	2,059,436	200.5	232,386	4,783,062	37.6	39.8	22.7	4,981,834	0.9	4,787,320	194,514	3.9
North Dakota.................	130,831	173.2	8,453	406,875	37.3	39.4	23.3	404,299	-1.5	393,755	10,544	2.6
Ohio	2,337,114	200.5	310,489	5,582,008	36.7	39.9	23.4	5,754,931	-0.3	5,491,585	263,346	4.6
Oklahoma......................	778,970	198.2	96,804	1,758,402	35.1	40.8	24.1	1,841,872	0.3	1,779,370	62,502	3.4
Oregon.........................	853,498	206.0	88,659	1,992,899	38.9	40.0	21.1	2,104,516	0.7	2,017,155	87,361	4.2
Pennsylvania..................	2,795,950	218.3	361,250	6,173,143	38.6	39.9	21.5	6,424,421	-0.0	6,148,635	275,786	4.3
Rhode Island..................	222,851	210.3	33,124	537,914	38.4	43.0	18.6	555,807	0.4	533,171	22,636	4.1
South Carolina	1,115,313	222.0	116,683	2,272,475	34.0	42.1	24.0	2,323,209	0.7	2,243,656	79,553	3.4
South Dakota.................	175,389	201.7	14,888	442,470	35.0	41.4	23.6	459,459	0.7	445,599	13,860	3.0
Tennessee.....................	1,431,690	213.2	179,147	3,130,088	34.9	40.8	24.3	3,244,921	1.7	3,131,660	113,261	3.5
Texas...........................	4,126,055	145.8	657,999	13,201,891	36.4	41.0	22.6	13,848,080	1.9	13,314,203	533,877	3.9
Utah	395,718	127.6	31,756	1,505,003	39.1	39.5	21.4	1,572,136	1.5	1,523,158	48,978	3.1
Vermont........................	147,683	236.8	15,374	326,155	41.1	38.0	21.0	346,061	-0.0	336,838	9,223	2.7
Virginia	1,501,543	177.3	157,658	4,164,930	44.1	38.3	17.6	4,331,380	0.5	4,202,801	128,579	3.0
Washington	1,319,176	178.1	150,504	3,599,753	41.4	37.9	20.7	3,793,095	2.0	3,622,299	170,796	4.5
West Virginia	473,398	260.7	73,879	725,200	33.2	42.8	24.0	783,344	0.5	742,179	41,165	5.3
Wisconsin......................	1,212,439	209.2	118,112	2,979,203	36.8	38.6	24.6	3,133,294	-0.2	3,039,295	93,999	3.0
Wyoming.......................	109,624	189.2	6,815	282,202	34.5	37.8	27.7	289,574	-1.1	277,820	11,754	4.1

1. Per 1,000 resident population estimated as of July 1 of the year shown.　　2. Persons 16 years old and over.　　3. Percent of civilian labor force.

Table A. States — Nonfarm Employment and Earnings

STATE	Employed		Manufacturing			Employment (1000)						
	Total (1000)	Percent change, 2017–2018	Employ-ment (1000)	Average earnings of production workers		Con-struction	Trans-portation and public utilities	Whole-sale trade	Retail trade	Informa-tion	Financial activities	Services[1]
				Hourly	Weekly							
	172	173	174	175	176	177	178	179	180	181	182	183
United States	149,074	1.7	12,689	20.43	908.08	7,313	5,750	5,913.6	15,833	2,828	8,569	66,859
Alabama...........................	2,042.0	1.2	267.1	20.11	878.81	89.1	75.9	74.1	230.7	21.1	96.4	791.9
Alaska..............................	327.3	-0.6	12.5	20.18	799.13	15.9	22.2	6.4	35.7	5.6	11.8	124.1
Arizona............................	2,856.0	2.8	170.1	19.49	791.29	158.8	111.0	97.2	326.3	47.4	220.8	1,296.1
Arkansas..........................	1,261.9	1.1	160.5	17.44	730.74	50.6	65.1	47.5	138.9	11.2	60.5	509.4
California..........................	17,175.2	2.0	1,325.4	23.45	968.49	859.6	664.0	698.9	1,688.3	543.7	836.3	7,948.4
Colorado	2,725.3	2.4	147.6	26.90	1,073.31	172.3	89.0	108.0	272.7	74.9	170.5	1,216.9
Connecticut......................	1,689.0	0.1	160.3	26.60	1,103.90	58.6	54.3	61.5	180.7	31.9	126.1	778.5
Delaware..........................	461.5	1.0	27.1	19.14	823.02	22.3	16.5	10.8	52.9	4.1	47.5	213.8
District of Columbia..........	792.2	1.0	1.3	NA	NA	15.7	5.4	4.9	22.9	19.3	29.7	454.5
Florida..............................	8,781.9	2.4	372.0	21.76	950.91	540.9	303.5	345.8	1,131.6	139.7	576.7	4,253.6
Georgia	4,540.0	1.9	408.0	18.90	816.48	196.2	232.4	215.0	495.6	114.6	248.2	1,926.8
Hawaii	656.6	0.5	14.2	20.63	765.37	36.1	33.3	17.9	71.4	9.1	28.8	320.2
Idaho	737.3	3.1	68.2	18.86	782.69	49.1	25.4	29.6	87.5	8.9	36.4	303.8
Illinois..............................	6,117.4	0.9	588.3	21.30	915.90	225.8	316.5	296.3	603.3	94.4	401.8	2,757.1
Indiana.............................	3,144.0	1.0	542.0	21.09	887.89	141.3	155.3	120.3	321.6	29.4	138.7	1,259.2
Iowa.................................	1,584.2	0.7	223.0	19.68	818.69	77.5	67.8	66.1	178.7	22.0	109.1	576.8
Kansas.............................	1,415.8	0.9	165.1	19.95	863.84	61.1	64.1	59.0	145.6	18.7	77.1	560.1
Kentucky..........................	1,931.6	0.5	252.1	20.44	872.79	78.1	114.3	75.1	214.5	22.0	93.0	758.9
Louisiana.........................	1,981.5	0.5	134.9	22.01	964.04	151.1	83.6	69.4	226.5	22.9	91.1	838.5
Maine...............................	628.5	0.7	52.0	22.48	912.69	28.9	18.6	19.5	81.1	7.3	31.9	287.0
Maryland	2,744.3	0.7	108.3	21.13	914.93	163.1	97.4	85.3	284.8	36.5	144.4	1,318.7
Massachusetts.................	3,642.9	0.9	244.1	24.56	1,026.61	157.2	102.2	123.9	353.3	91.5	221.5	1,893.7
Michigan...........................	4,418.6	1.1	629.8	21.31	924.85	169.2	148.9	172.1	470.4	55.8	219.0	1,939.8
Minnesota	2,954.4	0.8	321.4	21.71	885.77	122.5	107.7	130.7	298.6	49.3	184.1	1,307.9
Mississippi.......................	1,154.8	0.3	144.9	20.54	846.25	43.7	58.6	34.2	138.3	11.0	44.4	431.6
Missouri............................	2,887.4	0.5	272.8	22.04	923.48	122.5	111.8	121.0	310.9	50.5	173.3	1,286.7
Montana	477.6	1.1	20.5	20.80	796.64	28.6	18.5	17.3	59.0	6.3	24.9	204.8
Nebraska..........................	1,023.1	0.4	99.7	19.47	782.69	52.3	53.4	40.2	107.7	17.7	73.9	403.8
Nevada.............................	1,386.5	3.4	55.5	19.75	827.53	89.7	70.7	36.9	147.8	15.6	68.2	726.6
New Hampshire	681.0	0.8	70.5	21.64	937.01	26.9	16.7	28.2	94.5	12.4	34.4	306.5
New Jersey.......................	4,154.8	0.9	247.4	22.29	904.97	157.9	214.3	215.8	458.1	69.7	250.5	1,939.2
New Mexico	842.2	1.3	27.0	17.89	678.03	47.2	25.5	21.0	91.2	11.9	34.2	373.0
New York..........................	9,669.9	1.1	443.1	22.04	908.05	398.4	299.2	329.5	934.3	275.2	719.1	4,776.7
North Carolina..................	4,488.2	1.7	474.2	18.27	763.69	219.5	150.7	182.1	500.6	80.0	239.6	1,903.0
North Dakota....................	433.4	0.6	25.9	19.97	756.86	25.9	23.4	23.9	46.9	6.2	24.3	153.7
Ohio.................................	5,559.9	0.6	698.9	21.49	911.18	219.3	226.1	235.0	563.2	70.8	307.9	2,447.4
Oklahoma.........................	1,687.4	1.5	137.7	19.00	811.30	80.3	63.8	57.4	178.1	19.9	79.2	670.1
Oregon.............................	1,909.5	1.8	194.9	21.73	856.16	104.8	65.2	75.5	211.6	34.2	102.0	819.3
Pennsylvania....................	6,006.0	1.1	569.4	20.78	858.21	255.8	291.2	216.8	618.9	85.8	325.5	2,911.3
Rhode Island....................	496.1	0.5	40.3	19.15	779.41	19.2	12.2	16.5	48.7	5.9	35.4	256.8
South Carolina	2,145.3	2.4	247.8	19.29	839.12	102.5	82.4	71.9	252.0	28.2	104.2	882.9
South Dakota	438.9	1.1	44.4	18.80	780.20	22.9	13.4	21.0	52.4	5.6	29.2	169.5
Tennessee........................	3,060.3	1.6	350.7	19.83	848.72	124.8	169.9	119.7	337.6	45.5	162.5	1,309.7
Texas...............................	12,503.4	2.3	881.1	23.54	1,016.93	739.1	559.5	596.7	1,329.1	204.1	776.9	5,218.8
Utah.................................	1,516.5	3.2	133.1	20.81	824.08	104.1	62.4	51.0	172.4	38.6	87.7	609.9
Vermont............................	315.5	0.2	29.8	21.17	855.27	15.1	62.4	9.1	37.2	4.3	12.1	142.7
Virginia.............................	4,000.6	1.1	240.1	19.64	795.42	197.4	135.4	110.2	414.1	67.2	207.4	1,898.6
Washington	3,406.0	2.6	287.9	28.43	1,202.59	213.6	115.3	136.2	386.2	133.9	158.0	1,381.8
West Virginia....................	726.0	1.5	47.1	21.38	893.68	41.1	27.0	20.2	82.8	8.2	29.1	295.4
Wisconsin.........................	2,971.5	0.8	475.5	20.56	857.35	122.2	110.5	127.5	305.3	47.3	152.9	1,217.8
Wyoming...........................	285.5	0.7	9.8	23.95	986.74	20.3	14.5	8.2	29.4	3.6	11.0	99.4

1. Includes professional and business services, educational and health services, leisure and hospitality, and other services.

Table A. States — **Agriculture**

STATE	Farms Number	Farms % Fewer than 50 acres	Farms % 1000 acres or more	Farm producers whose primary occupation is farming (percent)	Government payments, average per farm that recieves payments (dollars)	Land in farms Acreage (1000)	Land in farms Percent change, 2012–2017	Acres Average size of farm	Acres Total irrigated (1000)	Acres Total cropland (1000)	Value of land and buildings Average per farm	Value of land and buildings Average per acre
	184	185	186	187	188	189	190	191	192	193	194	195
United States	2,042,220	41.9	8.5	41.1	$13,906	900,218	-1.6	441	58,013.9	396,433.8	$1,311,808	$2,976
Alabama	40,592	40.1	4.2	37.4	$8,892	8,581	-3.6	211	142.0	2,818.8	$630,736	$2,984
Alaska	990	67.0	4.3	41.9	$9,293	850	1.9	858	2.4	83.7	$616,112	$718
Arizona	19,086	69.1	11.0	53.3	$29,735	26,126	-0.5	1,369	910.9	1,286.6	$1,110,303	$811
Arkansas	42,625	30.3	7.2	41.7	$38,624	13,889	0.6	326	4,855.1	7,825.9	$1,030,741	$3,163
California	70,521	64.0	6.3	46.6	$24,112	24,523	-4.1	348	7,833.6	9,597.4	$3,252,414	$9,353
Colorado	38,893	46.2	14.9	38.2	$22,206	31,821	-0.2	818	2,761.2	11,056.3	$1,315,440	$1,608
Connecticut	5,521	70.9	0.7	39.0	$7,551	382	-12.6	69	7.4	148.6	$862,636	$12,483
Delaware	2,302	55.7	6.9	52.8	$18,604	525	3.3	228	163.3	452.2	$1,920,109	$8,414
District of Columbia	NA	NA	NA	NA	NA	NA	NA	NA	NA	NA	NA	NA
Florida	47,590	71.0	3.2	41.3	$14,795	9,732	1.9	204	1,519.4	2,825.8	$1,206,788	$5,901
Georgia	42,439	42.3	5.3	39.4	$18,310	9,954	3.5	235	1,287.5	4,372.1	$822,958	$3,509
Hawaii	7,328	89.5	1.7	46.7	$12,631	1,135	0.5	155	45.5	191.2	$1,445,188	$9,328
Idaho	24,996	56.0	9.7	40.8	$21,306	11,692	-0.6	468	3,398.3	5,894.7	$1,340,738	$2,866
Illinois	72,651	35.6	10.8	43.4	$10,727	27,006	0.3	372	612.5	24,003.1	$2,705,291	$7,278
Indiana	56,649	46.4	7.1	38.1	$12,628	14,970	1.7	264	555.4	12,909.7	$1,737,741	$6,576
Iowa	86,104	31.7	9.8	45.0	$11,146	30,564	-0.2	355	222.0	26,546.0	$2,506,812	$7,062
Kansas	58,569	21.8	20.2	41.9	$14,089	45,759	-0.8	781	2,503.4	29,125.5	$1,443,891	$1,848
Kentucky	75,966	40.1	2.5	36.4	$7,502	12,962	-0.7	171	83.9	6,630.4	$643,019	$3,769
Louisiana	27,386	46.5	7.6	37.7	$22,822	7,998	1.2	292	1,235.8	4,345.8	$889,146	$3,045
Maine	7,600	47.2	2.4	43.2	$10,806	1,308	-10.1	172	32.3	472.5	$446,614	$2,596
Maryland	12,429	54.7	3.2	42.1	$12,471	1,990	-2.0	160	124.8	1,426.7	$1,258,691	$7,861
Massachusetts	7,241	67.8	0.3	42.8	$7,583	492	-6.1	68	23.9	171.5	$739,711	$10,894
Michigan	47,641	46.3	4.5	43.1	$10,892	9,764	-1.9	205	670.2	7,924.5	$1,015,631	$4,955
Minnesota	68,822	28.8	9.3	45.5	$9,568	25,517	-2.0	371	611.6	21,786.8	$1,799,201	$4,853
Mississippi	34,988	31.6	6.4	37.8	$14,986	10,415	-4.7	298	1,814.5	4,960.6	$817,041	$2,745
Missouri	95,320	29.6	6.2	38.8	$10,366	27,782	-1.7	291	1,529.2	15,599.4	$986,481	$3,385
Montana	27,048	30.9	31.7	48.5	$27,014	58,123	-2.7	2,149	2,061.2	16,406.3	$1,968,381	$916
Nebraska	46,332	23.8	23.8	51.6	$20,745	44,987	-0.8	971	8,588.4	22,242.6	$2,674,492	$2,754
Nevada	3,423	51.7	13.7	50.4	$16,183	6,128	3.6	1,790	790.4	794.7	$1,627,858	$909
New Hampshire	4,123	57.1	0.8	38.6	$11,344	425	-10.3	103	2.2	108.0	$539,732	$5,231
New Jersey	9,883	75.2	1.1	39.6	$10,071	734	2.7	74	86.8	463.0	$1,000,464	$13,469
New Mexico	25,044	52.2	18.2	42.1	$18,436	40,660	-5.9	1,624	626.0	1,825.8	$845,740	$521
New York	33,438	36.7	3.3	48.1	$9,162	6,866	-4.4	205	53.3	4,291.4	$663,082	$3,229
North Carolina	46,418	47.9	3.8	42.7	$10,746	8,431	0.2	182	143.4	5,000.7	$843,154	$4,642
North Dakota	26,364	11.7	40.0	54.3	$22,770	39,342	0.2	1,492	263.9	27,951.7	$2,546,783	$1,707
Ohio	77,805	47.4	3.5	37.3	$12,301	13,965	0.0	179	50.7	10,960.7	$1,112,700	$6,199
Oklahoma	78,531	29.6	10.3	37.5	$11,248	34,156	-0.6	435	573.8	11,715.7	$754,099	$1,734
Oregon	37,616	67.1	6.2	40.3	$22,918	15,962	-2.1	424	1,664.9	4,726.1	$1,032,545	$2,433
Pennsylvania	53,157	42.1	1.4	45.7	$6,823	7,279	-5.5	137	32.1	4,651.2	$897,125	$6,552
Rhode Island	1,043	72.5	0.4	38.6	$14,205	57	-18.3	55	3.0	17.7	$897,835	$16,468
South Carolina	24,791	49.8	3.8	36.1	$10,400	4,745	-4.6	191	210.4	2,035.3	$683,873	$3,573
South Dakota	29,968	19.3	32.0	52.4	$19,416	43,244	0.0	1,443	492.5	19,813.5	$2,984,426	$2,068
Tennessee	69,983	45.2	2.3	35.8	$6,254	10,874	0.1	155	184.9	5,286.3	$608,739	$3,918
Texas	248,416	44.1	8.3	35.8	$20,984	127,036	-2.4	511	4,363.3	29,360.2	$980,409	$1,917
Utah	18,409	62.1	6.9	32.1	$12,633	10,812	-1.5	587	1,097.2	1,654.4	$1,067,323	$1,817
Vermont	6,808	41.1	2.3	42.1	$8,355	1,193	-4.7	175	3.0	479.7	$620,691	$3,541
Virginia	43,225	42.2	3.1	40.1	$10,122	7,798	-6.1	180	63.4	3,084.1	$834,254	$4,624
Washington	35,793	66.6	7.2	39.9	$30,692	14,680	-0.5	410	1,689.4	7,488.6	$1,143,889	$2,789
West Virginia	23,622	34.7	1.5	36.7	$4,853	3,662	1.5	155	1.7	947.3	$411,482	$2,654
Wisconsin	64,793	35.3	3.6	45.6	$4,609	14,319	-1.7	221	454.4	10,085.0	$1,083,640	$4,904
Wyoming	11,938	32.7	25.0	43.0	$14,410	29,005	-4.5	2,430	1,567.6	2,587.5	$1,892,340	$779

Table A. States — Agriculture, Land, and Water

STATE	Value of machinery and equipment, average per farm (dollars)	Value of products sold				Organic Farms (number)	Farms with Internet access (percent)	Owned by the federal government (percent)	Developed land (percent)	Rural land (percent)	Public water supply withdrawn, 2015 (mil gal per day)
		Total (mil dol)	Average per farm (dollars)	Crops	Livestock and poultry products						
	196	197	198	199	200	201	202	203	204	205	206
United States	133,363	$388,522.7	$190,245	49.8	50.2	20,806	75.4	20.8	5.9	70.6	38,595.83
Alabama	88,528	$5,980.6	$147,334	20.3	79.7	57	72.6	2.8	8.7	84.5	761.53
Alaska	91,623	$70.5	$71,171	42.1	57.9	18	87.9	NA	NA	NA	99.18
Arizona	77,604	$3,852.0	$201,824	54.4	45.6	84	57.4	41.5	2.9	55.4	1,195.15
Arkansas	126,667	$9,651.2	$226,420	37.6	62.4	81	73.6	9.6	5.5	82.3	363.06
California	165,070	$45,154.4	$640,297	73.9	26.1	3,794	82.0	46.7	6.2	45.4	5,147.74
Colorado	117,337	$7,491.7	$192,623	29.9	70.1	323	81.4	36.1	3.0	60.4	843.95
Connecticut	62,250	$580.1	$105,074	72.4	27.6	113	82.4	0.5	34.1	61.4	239.93
Delaware	198,096	$1,466.0	$636,826	22.2	77.8	13	78.7	1.6	19.4	59.2	86.35
District of Columbia	NA	NA	NA	NA	NA	NA	NA	NA	NA	NA	0.00
Florida	72,754	$7,357.3	$154,599	77.5	22.5	251	76.3	10.3	14.7	66.5	2,384.85
Georgia	115,773	$9,573.3	$225,577	34.2	65.8	139	76.0	5.5	12.3	79.3	1,069.91
Hawaii	50,701	$563.8	$76,938	74.0	26.0	167	76.1	14.8	6.0	78.6	266.92
Idaho	$175,951	$7,567.4	$302,746	42.4	57.6	295	83.9	62.5	1.7	34.7	275.79
Illinois	$220,485	$17,010.0	$234,133	81.4	18.6	328	76.9	1.4	9.6	87.0	1,475.66
Indiana	$163,136	$11,107.3	$196,073	64.1	35.9	657	71.9	2.1	11.0	85.3	627.84
Iowa	$230,716	$28,956.5	$336,296	47.8	52.2	785	79.6	0.6	5.4	92.6	390.38
Kansas	$180,725	$18,782.7	$320,694	34.4	65.6	117	76.5	0.9	4.0	94.0	351.15
Kentucky	$82,740	$5,737.9	$75,533	44.3	55.7	227	72.4	4.9	8.2	84.4	552.83
Louisiana	$121,758	$3,173.0	$115,861	65.0	35.0	29	69.9	4.0	6.3	75.2	708.92
Maine	$81,792	$667.0	$87,758	61.3	38.7	621	83.6	1.0	4.1	88.7	84.97
Maryland	$124,871	$2,472.8	$198,955	38.3	61.7	134	76.9	2.1	19.4	57.1	749.52
Massachusetts	$65,382	$475.2	$65,624	76.5	23.5	208	84.1	1.4	33.0	58.6	648.06
Michigan	$154,740	$8,220.9	$172,560	56.5	43.5	764	77.2	8.6	11.2	77.1	1,030.44
Minnesota	$223,666	$18,395.4	$267,289	55.4	44.6	735	79.0	6.4	4.5	83.2	515.24
Mississippi	$109,875	$6,196.0	$177,088	37.0	63.0	37	66.0	5.5	6.3	85.5	400.36
Missouri	$104,066	$10,525.9	$110,427	52.0	48.0	415	72.5	4.5	6.7	86.8	797.09
Montana	$164,524	$3,520.6	$130,162	45.0	55.0	221	81.4	28.7	1.2	69.0	153.19
Nebraska	$268,968	$21,983.4	$474,476	42.4	57.6	292	81.3	1.2	2.6	95.3	275.18
Nevada	$155,033	$665.8	$194,495	41.5	58.5	51	82.9	84.1	0.8	14.6	558.26
New Hampshire	$68,629	$187.8	$45,548	57.4	42.6	156	87.2	13.5	12.3	70.2	95.52
New Jersey	$86,532	$1,098.0	$111,095	89.7	10.3	122	80.9	3.4	35.7	50.1	1,175.42
New Mexico	$63,619	$2,582.3	$103,112	25.2	74.8	183	60.5	33.9	1.7	64.2	254.10
New York	$135,626	$5,369.2	$160,572	39.3	60.7	1,497	77.1	0.7	12.3	82.5	2,424.65
North Carolina	$112,477	$12,900.7	$277,924	29.0	71.0	465	75.2	7.1	14.4	70.2	938.01
North Dakota	$375,872	$8,234.1	$312,324	81.1	18.9	129	78.9	3.9	2.3	91.0	84.18
Ohio	$129,614	$9,341.2	$120,059	58.1	41.9	872	74.6	1.4	15.9	81.1	1,306.28
Oklahoma	$90,442	$7,465.5	$95,065	20.3	79.7	54	72.9	2.7	4.9	90.0	611.24
Oregon	$100,328	$5,006.8	$133,103	65.6	34.4	659	85.7	51.7	2.2	44.7	567.04
Pennsylvania	$109,024	$7,758.9	$145,962	35.8	64.2	1,142	69.3	2.3	15.4	80.6	1,391.70
Rhode Island	$62,786	$58.0	$55,607	70.5	29.5	22	84.1	0.5	28.7	52.1	97.46
South Carolina	$83,077	$3,008.7	$121,364	36.4	63.6	75	72.6	5.3	13.5	77.1	633.39
South Dakota	$282,162	$9,721.5	$324,397	53.1	46.9	87	81.0	5.6	2.0	90.6	71.95
Tennessee	$80,447	$3,798.9	$54,284	57.4	42.6	122	72.7	5.2	11.6	80.3	849.69
Texas	$83,627	$24,924.0	$100,332	27.7	72.3	466	72.6	1.8	5.4	90.3	2,885.33
Utah	$97,789	$1,838.6	$99,876	30.5	69.5	95	77.7	64.1	1.6	31.4	785.91
Vermont	$100,672	$781.0	$114,713	24.0	76.0	679	86.4	7.4	6.5	81.7	42.66
Virginia	$86,136	$3,960.5	$91,625	34.4	65.6	252	74.0	8.7	11.9	72.4	695.63
Washington	$121,662	$9,634.5	$269,172	72.5	27.5	933	84.1	28.5	5.7	62.2	866.53
West Virginia	$56,120	$754.3	$31,931	20.3	79.7	63	70.0	8.2	7.5	83.2	184.96
Wisconsin	$156,689	$11,427.4	$176,368	35.6	64.4	1,708	76.1	5.1	7.8	83.6	479.38
Wyoming	$126,844	$1,472.1	$123,313	21.6	78.4	69	80.5	47.2	1.1	50.9	101.35

Agriculture, 2017 (cont.) spans columns 196–202. *Land, 2015* spans columns 203–205.

Table A. States — Manufactures and Construction

STATE	Manufactures, 2016										Construction, 2012				
	All employees			Production workers				Value added by manufacture (mil dol)	Value of shipments (mil dol)	Total cost of materials (mil dol)	Number of establishments	Employees		Value (mil dol)	Annual payroll (mil dol)
	Number (1000)	Percent change, 2015–2016	Annual payroll (mil dol)	Number (1000)	Work hours (millions)	Wages Total (mil dol)	Wages Average per worker (dollars)					Number	Percent change, 2007–2012		
	207	208	209	210	211	212	213	214	215	216	217	218	219	220	221
United States	11,113	-0.5	643,406	7,733	15,681	364,985	47,197	2,408,996	5,354,694	2,942,556	598,065	5,669,623	-22.5	1,366,427	272,546
Alabama	235	0.0	12,256	177	367	7,884	44,623	46,264	131,012	84,504	6,865	78,615	-26.6	17,914	3,312
Alaska	12	-6.5	590	10	21	442	43,467	2,212	6,003	3,933	2,156	23,219	5.1	6,431	1,539
Arizona	137	2.4	9,142	82	166	3,990	48,416	29,122	55,065	25,860	10,540	123,478	-44.3	26,211	5,560
Arkansas	146	-2.4	6,657	117	239	4,721	40,431	25,096	55,731	30,512	4,739	42,539	-15.6	8,874	1,666
California	1,120	-0.7	73,011	706	1,422	34,022	48,163	255,636	493,165	238,271	60,222	597,083	-31.7	148,808	30,402
Colorado	121	0.6	7,373	79	160	3,713	46,973	26,020	50,853	24,694	13,976	123,296	-29.0	29,762	5,868
Connecticut	155	-0.6	10,968	88	178	4,730	53,774	32,663	56,376	23,599	7,173	54,595	-23.8	14,952	2,949
Delaware	25	2.1	1,455	18	36	816	45,582	5,870	16,558	10,640	1,997	17,708	-31.0	3,821	868
District of Columbia	1	6.8	58	1	2	34	42,375	213	330	116	390	8,986	14.7	2,643	476
Florida	270	0.4	15,473	180	360	7,959	44,225	57,038	104,865	48,622	39,536	294,308	-37.9	66,489	11,621
Georgia	352	0.9	18,119	266	539	11,282	42,456	71,133	166,678	95,931	13,790	144,936	-35.2	36,691	6,376
Hawaii	12	1.3	568	7	14	312	43,626	2,093	5,686	3,543	2,378	27,541	-22.5	7,939	1,564
Idaho	56	3.9	3,186	41	83	1,945	47,192	9,195	20,968	11,665	5,165	32,033	-36.4	6,573	1,116
Illinois	538	-0.5	30,952	371	749	17,266	46,545	111,573	252,503	141,331	25,046	204,819	-24.9	54,281	11,446
Indiana	476	0.5	26,341	358	737	17,133	47,923	102,353	241,539	139,185	12,195	123,888	-16.0	27,325	6,178
Iowa	204	-1.9	10,913	148	298	6,563	44,355	43,511	105,663	61,724	7,703	65,860	-6.4	15,586	2,939
Kansas	155	-3.0	8,626	111	221	5,318	47,953	33,892	83,920	49,927	6,070	58,461	-13.7	13,644	2,681
Kentucky	231	0.8	12,487	179	369	8,550	47,873	45,084	128,159	82,825	6,675	63,974	-23.1	13,949	2,760
Louisiana	114	-5.8	8,008	80	169	4,925	61,462	47,821	156,874	109,723	7,318	136,439	0.5	26,212	7,317
Maine	50	3.8	2,657	36	72	1,734	48,178	8,093	15,169	7,240	4,547	25,178	-15.8	4,546	1,011
Maryland	92	-2.6	6,051	56	114	2,754	48,952	22,769	41,214	18,301	12,987	144,715	-24.3	37,372	7,421
Massachusetts	224	-0.6	15,416	131	267	6,678	50,966	46,717	84,735	37,891	15,689	120,685	-10.9	34,227	6,857
Michigan	555	1.3	32,361	399	815	19,868	49,801	103,771	261,293	157,767	16,123	131,609	-17.8	32,535	6,370
Minnesota	298	1.6	16,961	197	396	8,984	45,582	56,929	117,397	60,798	14,615	113,633	-15.6	32,923	6,061
Mississippi	131	0.0	6,329	103	209	4,324	41,947	21,760	56,801	34,820	3,736	41,520	-25.8	8,858	1,703
Missouri	245	-0.7	#VALUE	183	362	9,029	49,373	50,314	118,828	68,337	12,435	110,274	-32.9	25,678	5,306
Montana	17	3.5	888	11	22	522	46,437	3,175	9,396	6,311	4,307	23,981	-21.0	5,149	970
Nebraska	93	-0.1	4,496	71	142	2,986	42,222	19,005	53,112	34,006	5,676	40,562	-9.1	8,728	1,683
Nevada	41	3.0	2,311	28	57	1,312	47,260	8,702	16,682	7,958	4,335	54,321	-55.8	12,254	2,463
New Hampshire	66	0.1	4,137	39	79	1,845	46,760	11,562	20,658	9,183	3,710	24,409	-18.8	5,202	1,210
New Jersey	210	-2.3	13,237	140	286	6,818	48,743	45,823	90,605	44,907	18,806	146,521	-18.7	39,872	8,053
New Mexico	22	-6.8	1,253	15	30	707	48,099	4,936	12,674	7,699	4,084	37,806	-31.3	6,997	1,520
New York	395	-1.0	23,105	261	523	12,404	47,486	79,496	148,469	69,074	41,016	333,187	-4.6	87,292	18,169
North Carolina	411	0.5	20,701	304	617	12,424	40,898	109,824	210,018	100,157	18,294	180,433	-25.6	35,964	6,683
North Dakota	23	-8.2	1,181	17	34	752	44,479	4,923	13,050	8,229	2,729	25,882	33.6	6,557	1,240
Ohio	643	-1.1	36,033	461	945	22,047	47,846	129,554	312,532	182,566	18,439	180,735	-19.4	42,772	8,582
Oklahoma	121	-6.0	6,469	89	175	4,024	45,184	22,705	56,775	34,119	7,541	69,691	-0.2	16,229	3,004
Oregon	160	1.8	9,543	109	217	5,222	47,930	27,846	57,315	29,664	10,051	69,771	-32.2	16,562	3,296
Pennsylvania	522	-0.8	29,380	362	733	17,290	47,761	105,636	217,753	112,161	24,874	237,969	-10.5	55,120	11,763
Rhode Island	36	-4.0	2,148	24	47	1,145	48,202	5,607	11,344	5,793	2,868	17,418	-19.6	4,760	850
South Carolina	213	-3.1	11,641	160	326	7,513	47,018	44,029	109,000	65,011	8,136	68,679	-36.5	15,219	2,669
South Dakota	44	0.5	2,040	32	63	1,263	38,873	7,882	17,441	9,552	2,916	19,737	-4.2	4,189	757
Tennessee	309	2.3	16,329	229	468	10,236	44,797	66,937	149,126	81,964	8,627	103,474	-16.9	23,078	4,505
Texas	725	-2.7	44,620	494	1,016	24,678	49,987	216,626	523,118	307,617	34,641	572,922	-4.0	146,299	27,831
Utah	115	3.4	6,541	76	151	3,562	47,015	23,250	48,428	25,172	7,294	64,534	-27.4	16,329	2,716
Vermont	27	-0.9	1,542	19	37	864	46,376	4,205	8,788	4,479	2,596	15,667	-10.3	3,012	648
Virginia	223	-3.1	12,504	157	318	7,374	46,996	57,359	99,131	41,874	17,108	177,074	-24.7	42,371	8,067
Washington	253	1.4	16,567	166	326	9,067	54,769	60,007	142,700	76,768	17,741	138,649	-30.3	33,760	7,086
West Virginia	45	0.9	2,594	32	66	1,623	50,744	11,341	23,851	12,377	3,017	26,670	-16.6	4,975	1,116
Wisconsin	436	0.1	23,662	310	628	13,931	44,924	78,972	168,601	89,896	12,207	102,542	-18.8	25,625	5,063
Wyoming	8	-6.7	603	6	13	403	66,423	2,452	6,742	4,261	2,610	20,067	-10.9	3,966	877

Table A. States — Wholesale Trade and Retail Trade

STATE	Wholesale trade, 2012					Retail trade,[1] 2012								
	Number of establishments	Employees Number	Percent change, 2007–2012	Sales (mil dol)	Annual payroll (mil dol)	Number of establishments	Employees Total	Percent change, 2007–2012	Motor vehicle and parts dealers	Food and beverage stores	Clothing and clothing accessory stores	General merchandise stores	Sales (mil dol)	Annual payroll (mil dol)
	222	223	224	225	226	227	228	229	230	231	232	233	234	235
United States	419,464	5,881,913	-5.5	7,899,979	362,121	1,062,083	14,703,529	-5.2	1,709,998	2,864,650	1,664,114	2,772,612	4,219,822	369,001
Alabama	5,408	73,312	-9.6	75,845	3,669	18,211	218,531	-8.5	28,975	29,631	21,550	53,855	58,565	5,123
Alaska	743	8,740	-3.6	9,615	517	2,508	33,721	-3.6	3,772	7,386	2,228	8,225	10,474	977
Arizona	6,647	88,916	-13.0	96,619	5,159	17,479	286,184	-15.2	37,592	50,041	29,030	60,429	84,717	7,368
Arkansas	3,462	41,577	-13.3	61,692	2,068	10,923	135,448	-3.3	17,615	18,725	10,562	37,096	36,815	3,062
California	59,293	842,343	-5.1	969,250	58,755	106,419	1,540,055	-8.5	165,764	332,177	215,230	250,267	481,800	43,361
Colorado	7,224	92,714	-12.0	118,605	6,155	18,474	245,704	-6.2	29,189	47,396	24,058	45,245	67,815	6,509
Connecticut	4,324	75,460	-0.7	216,166	5,321	12,597	182,528	-6.9	20,097	43,566	24,279	23,858	51,632	4,975
Delaware	1,029	14,465	-25.6	20,474	1,106	3,616	51,711	-6.7	6,594	9,121	6,215	9,474	14,456	1,270
District of Columbia	430	4,259	-17.8	4,103	341	1,710	19,780	3.5	D	6,619	3,916	D	4,440	525
Florida	31,657	296,207	-9.4	342,238	15,394	71,189	947,877	-6.7	109,996	180,849	133,935	173,836	273,867	24,034
Georgia	13,151	184,561	-13.4	246,067	11,191	33,426	433,840	-8.7	D	83,727	48,250	D	119,801	10,290
Hawaii	1,751	18,761	-7.4	13,466	845	4,643	68,360	-3.3	5,981	13,474	13,170	12,784	18,902	1,835
Idaho	2,012	26,221	-1.1	24,397	1,233	5,815	72,980	-9.3	10,373	11,524	5,115	16,057	20,444	1,794
Illinois	19,302	314,389	-2.0	549,200	20,596	39,947	592,942	-7.2	65,978	111,600	68,011	118,814	166,635	14,576
Indiana	7,823	110,761	-4.4	127,024	5,791	21,601	309,552	-7.1	39,062	48,662	25,910	69,169	85,858	7,079
Iowa	4,992	67,124	3.4	76,728	3,263	12,046	174,556	-1.5	21,506	36,192	12,346	33,369	44,906	3,865
Kansas	4,565	65,118	13.1	103,968	3,701	10,548	145,480	-2.8	17,830	27,677	12,656	29,608	38,276	3,325
Kentucky	4,324	67,581	-4.7	100,077	3,679	15,224	202,615	-5.7	24,909	34,136	16,129	47,191	54,870	4,619
Louisiana	5,610	76,773	1.6	86,301	4,008	16,743	220,257	-4.8	27,024	33,458	21,780	50,414	61,396	5,335
Maine	1,550	16,759	-10.5	16,370	818	6,351	80,155	-3.8	9,746	18,108	5,918	11,905	21,522	1,885
Maryland	5,698	85,955	-13.7	84,734	5,379	18,179	281,678	-4.5	35,373	63,344	34,220	48,063	76,380	7,168
Massachusetts	8,061	139,520	-8.5	182,173	10,304	24,311	351,598	-2.4	32,685	99,593	45,747	40,988	92,915	9,162
Michigan	11,489	166,238	-3.5	254,319	9,800	34,858	441,190	-6.3	52,989	72,592	42,860	101,906	119,302	10,527
Minnesota	8,298	134,596	-3.0	167,376	9,335	19,109	288,888	-5.9	30,830	52,671	25,578	58,637	78,898	6,858
Mississippu	2,858	34,757	-6.6	35,523	1,583	11,594	136,032	-3.8	15,581	18,984	12,603	36,906	37,053	2,968
Missouri	7,955	126,328	-2.2	135,013	6,203	21,456	302,568	-4.6	37,602	47,881	26,145	64,255	90,547	7,278
Montana	1,530	14,443	1.8	15,764	650	4,831	55,418	-5.9	7,496	9,917	3,205	10,123	15,624	1,347
Nebraska	3,160	40,832	5.4	58,624	2,111	7,279	105,953	-2.1	12,622	19,100	7,872	19,657	30,471	2,440
Nevada	2,970	33,250	-20.2	28,436	1,890	8,135	129,977	-7.0	13,417	21,310	23,568	24,118	38,234	3,454
New Hampshire	1,865	24,558	-1.6	22,683	1,588	6,127	95,660	-2.7	11,462	23,302	8,438	14,559	26,018	2,404
New Jersey	14,661	263,316	-7.1	406,845	21,240	31,722	436,299	-5.3	42,776	104,425	63,756	61,632	133,666	12,676
New Mexico	1,937	21,929	-4.4	17,405	1,211	6,590	90,792	-6.8	12,096	13,431	7,112	21,333	25,179	2,215
New York	32,704	368,966	-10.7	434,354	23,106	77,463	905,325	1.4	71,441	211,095	149,390	124,135	251,168	23,641
North Carolina	11,830	172,760	-4.4	175,657	10,376	34,288	446,373	-4.3	57,916	83,490	44,074	91,034	120,691	10,421
North Dakota	1,618	21,533	22.4	32,269	1,223	3,185	47,186	7.1	6,651	7,231	3,332	8,654	15,520	1,204
Ohio	14,266	229,244	-5.9	252,195	12,812	36,531	549,152	-7.1	69,278	100,346	48,156	110,859	153,554	13,099
Oklahoma	4,660	60,195	-1.7	102,935	3,251	13,051	168,839	-1.3	23,146	21,534	14,904	40,799	50,256	4,055
Oregon	5,395 (r)	72,446 (r)	-6.6	70,111	4,163	13,879	187,402	-8.5	21,349	38,829	17,457	38,684	49,481	4,832
Pennsylvania	15,053	242,365	-1.6	295,599	14,996	43,952	643,903	-4.2	75,264	144,969	66,135	106,485	178,795	15,331
Rhode Island	1,367	20,235	-5.9	27,840	1,322	3,795	47,688	-6.2	4,992	12,033	5,213	6,112	12,064	1,207
South Carolina	5,027	64,418	-5.6	59,732	3,368	17,586	220,438	-4.9	26,447	42,487	23,822	45,385	58,094	4,955
South Dakota	1,487	17,702	13.1	25,292	827	3,843	49,867	-1.9	6,834	9,249	2,958	9,057	13,792	1,127
Tennessee	6,902	112,664	-8.8	169,781	6,170	22,615	306,078	-4.6	36,861	50,721	29,518	65,515	91,642	7,420
Texas	32,656	496,603	0.3	1,129,151	31,454	78,281	1,150,148	1.0	147,197	209,508	138,335	228,562	356,116	28,835
Utah	3,664	50,741	-4.1	43,854	2,791	9,095	133,535	-6.1	16,109	21,609	13,300	26,428	38,024	3,335
Vermont	809	10,742	1.1	12,850	566	3,509	38,910	-3.7	4,793	10,689	2,739	2,555	9,934	967
Virginia	7,381	106,428	-11.4	120,174	6,064	27,415	410,918	-4.8	51,166	78,937	44,208	78,638	110,002	10,008
Washington	9,361	121,805	-7.8	143,082	7,084	21,588	307,089	-6.4	37,871	60,125	30,279	60,723	118,924	8,723
West Virginia	1,553	19,901	-3.6	19,749	918	6,393	85,305	-7.5	11,506	13,183	5,563	19,982	22,638	1,908
Wisconsin	7,113	113,112	-3.9	111,021	6,250	19,272	296,956	-7.2	36,012	52,527	21,622	59,092	78,202	6,835
Wyoming	839	8,290	8.4	7,238	477	2,681	30,088	-6.1	4,324	5,469	1,717	5,745	9,446	796

1. Establishments with payroll.

Table A. States — **Information**

STATE	Information, 2012										
	Employees									Receipts (mil dol)	Annual payroll (mil dol)
	Number of estab-lishments	Number	Percent change, 2007–2012	Publishing, except Internet	Motion picture and sound recording	Broad-casting, except Internet	Internet publishing and broad-casting and web search portals	Tele-communi-cations	Data processing, hosting, and related services		
	236	237	238	239	240	241	242	243	244	245	246
United States	138,341	3,321,226	-5.0	876,286	304,497	278,168	183,436	1,134,466	497,300	1,238,463	269,070
Alabama............................	1,574	35,102	-12.4	9,500	1,978	D	224	16,043	3,940	NA	1,898
Alaska	399	6,523	-3.4	680	637	839	29	4,025	D	NA	395
Arizona.............................	2,117	48,994	-6.8	12,950	4,561	D	684	16,008	11,055	NA	2,983
Arkansas..........................	1,020	23,729	-9.0	5,710	D	D	61	7,958	6,554	NA	1,362
California..........................	21,925	561,399	0.9	140,978	113,899	48,593	63,536	112,158	78,236	NA	70,662
Colorado...........................	3,023	81,953	-3.1	16,527	4,294	3,720	2,938	39,441	14,723	NA	5,851
Connecticut.......................	1,675	37,338	-7.5	8,690	2,609	4,887	2,386	12,652	4,534	NA	2,712
Delaware...........................	417	6,964	-18.7	1,390	365	252	183	3,535	1,077	NA	403
District of Columbia............	741	22,144	-9.6	7,781	1,035	4,712	2,189	4,136	1,084	NA	2,215
Florida..............................	8,030	152,775	-12.9	36,131	11,716	14,729	3,032	67,240	18,959	NA	10,280
Georgia.............................	4,155	123,145	0.5	20,111	6,875	12,686	5,706	58,004	19,011	NA	9,197
Hawaii..............................	543	8,329	-17.4	1,510	1,034	D	99	4,051	771	NA	495
Idaho	654	12,264	-19.1	2,654	793	1,055	D	6,084	1,040	NA	557
Illinois..............................	5,404	124,859	-8.6	35,176	9,134	8,037	9,424	42,171	19,375	NA	8,942
Indiana.............................	2,183	42,361	-7.5	10,541	D	D	1,475	15,471	7,241	NA	2,299
Iowa	1,545	30,342	-11.8	9,799	D	D	405	9,876	5,668	NA	1,400
Kansas.............................	1,406	34,052	-35.4	6,968	1,792	2,219	D	17,537	4,665	NA	2,026
Kentucky	1,552	33,009	-2.9	6,069	1,974	2,813	625	11,151	9,665	NA	1,393
Louisiana..........................	1,426	24,743	-19.0	4,191	1,957	3,079	170	12,950	2,235	NA	1,274
Maine	845	11,952	-11.6	3,040	705	977	100	4,735	1,711	NA	538
Maryland	2,381	56,781	-10.0	12,898	3,321	5,392	1,057	22,691	9,865	NA	4,256
Massachusetts..................	3,673	115,614	5.1	46,869	4,771	4,691	8,714	26,157	22,905	NA	10,521
Michigan...........................	3,294	67,232	-13.4	22,993	D	D	1,619	23,596	D	NA	4,349
Minnesota	2,655	63,187	-10.1	23,085	4,282	4,234	D	15,939	9,328	NA	4,534
Mississippu	926	13,879	-12.7	2,504	742	D	64	8,017	809	NA	605
Missouri............................	2,422	59,607	-18.4	15,435	D	D	1,318	22,894	11,355	NA	3,805
Montana............................	615	9,160	-3.6	2,657	653	D	116	3,897	879	NA	427
Nebraska...........................	954	20,647	2.1	7,278	D	D	1,052	5,882	3,361	NA	1,180
Nevada.............................	1,234	17,216	-3.9	3,444	D	D	568	7,165	2,095	NA	931
New Hampshire	802	13,731	-11.3	5,780	768	596	98	4,947	1,300	NA	1,050
New Jersey	3,705	119,179	-11.3	24,725	5,521	3,545	18,231	50,376	15,450	NA	9,815
New Mexico	764	12,516	-10.5	2,155	1,175	1,270	109	7,057	601	NA	536
New York	11,335	286,744	-4.8	71,481	32,463	43,156	20,452	73,996	32,436	NA	25,032
North Carolina...................	3,570	79,833	4.5	20,995	4,995	5,165	1,085	32,220	14,630	NA	5,181
North Dakota.....................	361	7,052	-1.0	2,788	358	D	32	2,134	413	NA	391
Ohio.................................	3,956	90,083	-7.5	29,098	5,242	6,759	4,857	32,372	11,193	NA	5,607
Oklahoma..........................	1,497	28,890	-11.1	4,770	2,001	2,628	130	15,990	2,903	NA	1,377
Oregon.............................	2,010	38,799	-1.2	12,409	3,040	2,874	1,459	11,826	7,031	NA	2,312
Pennsylvania.....................	5,109	130,606	-4.7	38,947	6,549	8,123	2,309	51,934	17,445	NA	8,997
Rhode Island.....................	435	7,236	-10.2	1,918	D	D	D	3,154	508	NA	445
South Carolina	1,436	34,056	3.0	8,022	D	D	214	17,331	3,208	NA	1,796
South Dakota	446	6,750	-7.5	1,829	D	1,108	D	2,577	600	NA	286
Tennessee........................	2,489	48,231	-5.0	9,733	5,219	5,435	653	20,647	6,336	NA	2,674
Texas...............................	9,221	230,781	-7.8	42,166	17,247	16,362	4,957	99,015	48,907	NA	16,243
Utah	1,414	37,498	12.6	11,709	3,447	1,556	2,276	8,780	9,481	NA	2,241
Vermont............................	507	6,775	12.0	2,188	433	576	285	1,483	1,510	NA	370
Virginia.............................	3,916	101,402	-2.6	24,116	5,102	6,648	4,123	41,053	19,447	NA	8,080
Washington	3,281	128,014	14.5	62,052	6,497	3,911	5,719	32,449	15,415	NA	15,482
West Virginia.....................	673	10,945	6.4	2,082	592	1,385	D	5,914	843	NA	509
Wisconsin.........................	2,295	52,807	-2.5	18,801	3,544	5,519	1,088	15,998	7,721	NA	2,982
Wyoming...........................	331	3,998	-3.9	963	386	453	D	1,749	320	NA	173

Table A. States — Utilities, Transportation and Warehousing, and Finance and Insurance

STATE	Utilities, 2012					Transportation and warehousing, 2012					Finance and insurance, 2012				
	Number of establishments	Employees		Receipts (mil dol)	Annual payroll (mil dol)	Number of establishments	Employees		Receipts (mil dol)	Annual payroll (mil dol)	Number of establishments	Employees		Receipts (mil dol)	Annual payroll (mil dol)
		Number	Percent change, 2007–2012				Number	Percent change, 2007–2012				Number	Percent change, 2007–2012		
	247	248	249	250	251	252	253	254	255	256	257	258	259	260	261
United States	17,595	651,234	2.2	531,891	58,922,951	213,809	4,305,464	-3.3	730,541	183,841	468,183	6,040,880	-8.6	3,636,114	523,553
Alabama	424	15,454	7.3	NA	1,361,953	2,836	57,835	-6.4	8,422	2,460	7,294	72,763	1.0	NA	4,466
Alaska	86	2,025	17.0	NA	184,291	1,091	18,957	-5.9	5,176	1,183	740	7,215	-7.2	NA	433
Arizona	265	12,185	1.9	NA	1,096,751	3,110	80,725	-3.6	13,864	3,442	9,196	128,762	-12.9	NA	7,847
Arkansas	320	7,065	-0.9	NA	528,383	2,356	50,798	-15.5	7,945	2,047	4,319	35,504	-6.1	NA	1,924
California	1,143	66,836	4.5	NA	7,009,835	21,218	441,734	-2.3	78,926	19,716	48,523	601,858	-16.4	NA	57,898
Colorado	365	8,498	0.4	NA	736,022	3,443	61,976	-4.3	13,963	2,851	9,828	98,761	-7.8	NA	7,418
Connecticut	153	10,545	3.3	NA	922,836	1,595	44,003	-0.3	5,114	1,681	6,108	119,326	-13.1	NA	16,627
Delaware	48	2,622	0.3	NA	246,949	612	11,938	2.6	1,056	418	1,920	36,438	-14.1	NA	3,034
District of Columbia	47	D	NA	NA	D	193	8,483	-3.7	1,968	342	999	18,080	-7.2	NA	2,666
Florida	699	27,343	-11.6	NA	2,356,891	13,280	209,381	-4.0	49,159	8,958	30,653	338,872	-8.8	NA	22,758
Georgia	599	22,615	-7.7	NA	1,991,441	5,972	154,248	-9.0	26,825	6,840	14,434	164,422	-8.2	NA	12,272
Hawaii	54	3,379	14.4	NA	289,114	847	26,839	-17.1	4,599	1,150	1,401	18,686	-9.9	NA	1,145
Idaho	204	3,709	11.4	NA	287,206	1,736	17,195	1.2	2,390	588	2,793	21,698	-3.9	NA	1,035
Illinois	492	29,968	8.4	NA	3,044,699	13,251	230,695	-3.0	39,888	10,023	22,230	296,035	-15.0	NA	28,201
Indiana	538	15,558	3.8	NA	1,293,728	5,096	118,242	0.1	16,995	4,438	9,692	96,927	-12.0	NA	5,866
Iowa	272	7,656	-0.8	NA	570,315	3,499	55,762	2.4	7,641	2,111	6,071	91,750	0.7	NA	5,780
Kansas	230	7,263	-20.7	NA	607,926	2,510	50,019	6.7	6,561	1,968	5,976	59,099	-4.1	NA	3,717
Kentucky	340	8,685	4.9	NA	699,968	2,910	84,757	7.4	12,816	3,859	6,346	67,888	1.6	NA	3,838
Louisiana	517	11,132	2.5	NA	884,069	3,764	70,059	-2.8	15,110	3,779	7,716	64,813	0.8	NA	3,643
Maine	99	2,363	-6.0	NA	169,783	1,175	14,908	-2.0	1,729	557	1,899	25,688	-4.8	NA	1,574
Maryland	130	9,484	-5.7	NA	1,049,972	3,348	64,906	-3.6	8,719	2,701	7,583	100,204	-20.0	NA	8,630
Massachusetts	274	13,305	0.6	NA	1,324,451	3,558	77,843	-2.1	10,653	3,173,044	9,384	202,811	-8.8	NA	22,940
Michigan	389	23,036	3.7	NA	2,030,234	5,699	106,324	-0.5	20,033	4,525,164	13,181	151,712	-13.5	NA	9,757
Minnesota	320	12,802	8.7	NA	1,218,248	4,617	82,311	2.5	14,948	3,334,532	9,266	157,494	0.6	NA	13,450
Mississippu	592	8,803	1.5	NA	607,227	2,019	33,100	-9.1	4,273	1,303,347	4,692	34,472	-4.0	NA	1,634
Missouri	361	16,131	0.6	NA	1,381,461	4,543	82,336	-7.5	13,788	3,202,496	10,876	132,479	-3.5	NA	8,884
Montana	204	2,925	5.9	NA	232,408	1,475	11,861	1.7	1,972	449,841	1,944	16,206	-4.7	NA	800
Nebraska	115	930	-28.2	NA	77,087	2,283	26,879	-43.8	5,980	1,071,756	4,201	62,434	-3.2	NA	3,811
Nevada	123	4,991	-6.3	NA	466,381	1,409	43,720	-9.6	5,570	1,631,242	4,053	34,396	-18.2	NA	1,982
New Hampshire	120	3,329	4.8	NA	294,495	804	13,787	8.5	1,244	441,785	1,889	24,252	-13.7	NA	1,760
New Jersey	406	20,304	10.7	NA	2,131,755	7,004	160,321	-11.7	26,485	7,078,122	11,927	198,724	-6.9	NA	20,350
New Mexico	234	4,880	-2.6	NA	376,693	1,384	17,510	1.8	2,678	703,942	2,674	22,709	-10.9	NA	1,228
New York	616	42,612	11.2	NA	3,882,982	12,312	240,587	-0.6	43,409	9,676,996	27,518	539,761	-8.6	NA	98,776
North Carolina	478	20,114	-1.8	NA	1,849,812	5,393	108,760	-7.0	14,744	4,277,276	13,088	168,278	-12.5	NA	13,115
North Dakota	124	D	NA	NA	D	1,641	18,847	83.7	4,639	962,681	1,755	17,199	6.0	NA	919
Ohio	627	26,222	-1.1	NA	2,370,045	6,966	158,891	-10.5	23,709	6,649,313	17,443	241,719	-9.2	NA	16,209
Oklahoma	345	8,202	-16.5	NA	617,887	2,641	44,502	-7.4	9,571	2,144,251	6,691	57,760	-4.4	NA	3,078
Oregon	286	8,069	1.1	NA	697,565	2,991	52,351	-8.6	7,897	2,156,783	5,812	57,422	-13.9	NA	3,638
Pennsylvania	757	30,687	5.2	NA	3,061,256	8,175	209,798	1.5	25,255	7,843,461	17,733	266,764	-4.5	NA	20,439
Rhode Island	39	1,217	-5.1	NA	108,147	610	11,271	5.5	1,153	363,060	1,311	25,216	-19.7	NA	2,006
South Carolina	333	11,956	-1.5	NA	955,667	2,497	48,696	-13.1	5,443	1,859,027	7,204	66,331	-0.2	NA	3,510
South Dakota	158	2,216	4.4	NA	162,748	1,146	9,549	4.2	1,526	370,640	1,958	26,472	-11.2	NA	1,254
Tennessee	144	3,256	0.2	NA	201,896	4,047	132,825	0.6	18,040	5,168,090	9,726	112,241	-3.5	NA	7,171
Texas	1,953	52,894	14.6	NA	4,467,197	16,998	386,767	3.6	79,794	19,206,695	39,037	481,749	3.5	NA	33,436
Utah	214	4,319	-6.9	NA	374,644	2,177	45,945	-6.9	8,848	1,957,105	4,865	52,959	-9.7	NA	3,344
Vermont	65	D	NA	NA	D	486	5,731	-8.2	677	200,358	990	9,039	-4.1	NA	570
Virginia	314	15,065	-9.4	NA	1,398,172	4,779	90,068	-5.2	14,858	3,926,070	11,190	153,274	-9.0	NA	11,430
Washington	297	9,213	58.3	NA	759,825	4,840	87,862	0.9	16,791	4,274,033	9,737	97,245	-18.4	NA	7,005
West Virginia	221	5,849	-9.3	NA	453,649	1,234	15,705	-5.3	2,797	602,177	2,148	17,875	-10.5	NA	807
Wisconsin	323	14,046	-10.7	NA	1,247,335	5,251	97,724	-6.7	13,100	3,707,470	9,177	140,391	-2.9	NA	9,149
Wyoming	138	2,435	8.9	NA	203,277	988	10,133	16.9	1,801	466,688	992	6,707	-2.1	NA	330

Table A. States — Real Estate and Rental and Leasing and Professional, Scientific, and Technical Services

STATE	Real estate and rental and leasing, 2012					Professional, scientific, and technical services, 2012								
	Number of establishments	Employees Number	Employees Percent change, 2007–2012	Receipts (mil dol)	Annual payroll (mil dol)	Number of establishments	Employees Total	Percent change, 2007–2012	Legal services	Accounting, tax preparation, bookkeeping, and payroll services	Architectural, engineering, and related services	Computer systems design and related services	Receipts (mil dol)	Annual payroll (mil dol)
	262	263	264	265	266	267	268	269	270	271	272	273	274	275
United States	354,106	1,923,770	-12.1	487,655	85,326	856,463	8,203,735	4.2	1,148,683	1,443,462	1,354,603	1,473,241	1,480,277	581,406
Alabama	3,858	22,852	-15.7	3,919	820	9,109	89,988	-4.3	13,755	12,456	24,527	18,294	16,320	5,725
Alaska	872	4,212	-3.6	1,023	188	1,898	17,648	37.4	D	1,917	8,171	1,253	3,175	1,178
Arizona	8,089	40,479	-23.1	9,330	1,693	16,198	121,381	-6.2	17,690	20,352	21,731	22,873	19,268	7,379
Arkansas	2,802	12,867	-8.8	1,923	410	5,678	32,210	-0.5	D	6,889	5,762	2,813	4,528	1,567
California	49,276	273,511	-12.5	78,740	13,467	114,321	1,303,232	3.4	141,018	384,308	162,594	200,809	234,371	90,437
Colorado	9,295	38,706	-18.6	8,482	1,570	23,872	180,064	12.1	19,729	20,420	39,432	41,352	33,741	12,932
Connecticut	3,219	19,778	-11.9	5,349	958	9,220	97,578	-4.4	12,910	14,369	12,982	16,920	17,994	8,364
Delaware	1,111	5,402	-7.0	5,471	265	2,543	D	D	D	3,109	2,585	5,393	D	D
District of Columbia	1,112	10,103	4.6	3,214	674	5,061	97,555	9.6	31,675	4,829	8,003	14,685	31,866	11,196
Florida	29,845	139,955	-18.1	30,560	5,337	70,785	440,858	2.5	93,530	73,188	60,374	76,034	70,176	27,100
Georgia	10,484	55,551	-15.7	14,232	2,704	28,112	D	D	31,571	42,729	33,823	56,588	D	D
Hawaii	1,919	11,369	-32.2	3,411	484	3,226	21,629	-3.7	D	3,385	5,251	2,847	3,334	1,266
Idaho	2,033	6,268	-25.1	1,040	184	4,198	32,076	1.3	D	3,702	7,951	2,623	4,274	1,728
Illinois	12,035	76,794	-12.2	23,649	3,816	38,673	364,336	-1.3	57,212	62,779	44,413	62,613	70,263	28,315
Indiana	5,729	31,715	-7.5	6,548	1,172	12,829	99,962	3.9	14,668	19,194	18,906	12,437	14,702	5,491
Iowa	2,742	12,031	-18.0	2,268	426	6,204	48,521	14.5	7,489	9,878	5,908	7,957	6,421	2,467
Kansas	2,999	14,256	-6.0	2,743	508	7,110	60,989	8.3	7,462	12,290	12,765	8,129	8,716	3,596
Kentucky	3,534	18,250	-9.4	4,846	637	8,101	62,851	1.5	10,848	15,446	9,866	8,447	7,782	2,817
Louisiana	4,500	31,298	1.2	7,486	1,461	11,728	88,093	3.1	19,363	16,839	26,874	6,092	13,546	5,023
Maine	1,580	6,242	-10.1	1,100	221	3,492	22,943	3.2	4,025	3,317	4,866	2,813	3,353	1,238
Maryland	6,001	42,838	-13.9	13,410	2,253	19,714	244,710	-2.8	D	20,872	44,204	67,825	50,025	20,161
Massachusetts	6,485	42,788	-11.9	13,628	2,358	21,422	255,022	0.8	29,271	25,343	38,428	51,240	60,370	23,827
Michigan	7,826	48,706	-11.2	11,974	1,807	21,650	D	D	26,862	38,730	59,343	32,723	D	D
Minnesota	6,300	34,499	-12.5	7,828	1,396	16,348	140,927	-0.6	D	18,988	17,814	24,040	23,449	9,739
Mississippu	2,374	10,235	0.6	1,709	334	4,747	30,205	-2.6	D	6,904	5,529	3,438	4,023	1,450
Missouri	6,165	33,447	-15.6	6,730	1,298	13,279	137,981	4.3	21,063	22,228	18,976	30,349	24,293	8,615
Montana	1,726	5,207	-18.8	835	162	3,545	16,660	-1.4	2,972	3,236	4,129	1,185	2,192	799
Nebraska	2,001	10,068	0.9	1,732	389	4,448	74,514	82.5	D	42,825	5,660	8,215	5,727	3,639
Nevada	3,866	22,412	-29.1	4,981	815	8,102	47,934	-17.5	9,894	7,385	8,885	4,681	7,759	2,832
New Hampshire	1,338	7,044	-3.1	1,593	310	3,825	30,159	2.4	D	6,571	4,357	5,756	3,948	1,697
New Jersey	8,749	53,751	-16.0	17,328	2,813	29,390	307,549	-7.3	38,055	44,203	39,728	88,570	58,738	24,013
New Mexico	2,369	9,754	-16.5	1,960	369	4,687	44,175	-0.3	5,449	4,647	8,101	4,058	7,619	2,772
New York	32,033	166,315	-3.1	56,410	8,654	59,302	588,820	4.2	121,085	97,246	59,318	77,105	133,639	49,200
North Carolina	10,140	47,155	-12.0	9,302	1,943	22,855	196,287	6.1	23,399	29,415	28,778	36,677	31,948	12,940
North Dakota	912	5,157	37.6	1,445	248	1,722	13,715	40.0	1,902	1,821	3,213	2,586	1,847	736
Ohio	9,932	60,966	-9.1	16,133	2,442	23,961	233,876	2.3	34,707	36,624	40,381	39,420	35,971	14,220
Oklahoma	4,000	21,261	-14.6	4,270	898	9,470	71,997	9.3	12,250	11,842	21,414	7,113	10,991	4,115
Oregon	5,644	26,016	-16.0	4,650	903	11,663	84,493	-0.9	11,773	11,963	12,941	11,952	11,386	5,841
Pennsylvania	9,438	58,585	-15.0	13,364	2,618	29,297	316,658	6.0	51,348	50,126	58,713	42,585	54,834	22,622
Rhode Island	1,058	5,615	-13.5	1,120	219	2,997	21,165	-7.5	4,086	3,091	3,470	4,696	3,338	1,310
South Carolina	4,692	23,189	-23.8	4,334	826	9,721	79,824	6.5	13,690	11,165	20,796	10,923	12,722	4,817
South Dakota	962	3,526	-8.3	583	106	1,822	11,144	9.3	1,820	2,570	2,277	1,305	1,315	482
Tennessee	5,470	30,593	-18.9	6,178	1,220	10,863	104,552	3.7	D	22,269	18,445	11,327	14,200	6,129
Texas	26,639	169,941	-2.2	38,757	7,752	62,322	639,561	18.3	81,308	90,410	171,740	110,640	122,086	47,256
Utah	4,446	16,197	-20.7	3,226	605	9,009	76,345	11.5	9,137	16,734	11,239	10,085	10,555	3,909
Vermont	741	3,092	-8.9	510	104	2,113	15,948	-3.5	D	5,838	2,056	1,874	1,782	740
Virginia	8,862	54,246	-10.3	11,759	2,378	29,368	429,690	11.0	27,122	35,371	73,172	162,320	92,776	36,365
Washington	9,913	45,209	-11.7	9,695	1,895	20,047	167,512	4.9	D	20,084	30,768	32,431	28,284	11,977
West Virginia	1,405	6,011	-14.8	1,256	204	2,974	24,816	11.6	6,084	4,068	4,320	2,733	3,105	1,143
Wisconsin	4,509	23,762	-12.7	4,359	801	11,301	99,162	1.1	14,704	18,173	17,021	13,998	15,135	5,738
Wyoming	1,076	4,546	-2.3	1,259	216	2,141	9,134	3.5	D	1,324	2,603	419	1,297	467

Table A. States — Health Care and Social Assistance

STATE	Health care and social assistance, 2012													
	Subject to federal tax							Tax-exempt						
				Employees							Employees			
	Number of establishments	Total	Percent change, 2007-2012	Ambulatory health care services	Hospitals	Receipts (mil dol)	Annual payroll (mil dol)	Number of establishments	Total	Percent change, 2007-2012	Ambulatory health care services	Hospitals	Receipts (mil dol)	Annual payroll (mil dol)
	276	277	278	279	280	281	282	283	284	285	286	287	288	289
United States	690,525	9,542,138	14.7	5,687,621	677,114	1,008,745	409,812	140,778	8,872,619	4.8	787,378	5,074,227	1,031,697	391,428
Alabama	8,489	142,386	5.5	76,205	20,349	14,628	5,995	1,816	100,808	-2.3	8,624	67,461	11,412	4,244
Alaska	1,851	21,389	38.7	12,315	1,849	2,810	1,098	581	27,312	8.4	4,359	12,617	3,565	1,336
Arizona	15,041	184,186	19.6	106,247	15,871	20,221	7,975	1,831	130,921	4.9	13,850	79,719	16,835	6,261
Arkansas	5,936	86,999	12.7	42,556	12,408	8,541	3,496	1,549	79,456	5.0	6,689	42,744	7,252	2,823
California	89,999	1,005,201	13.8	630,526	66,982	127,356	48,373	13,208	771,239	8.8	72,024	466,701	121,598	42,767
Colorado	12,701	140,738	10.8	82,675	7,852	14,693	6,167	2,168	117,160	4.7	18,826	64,999	14,795	5,710
Connecticut	7,876	131,732	7.6	73,550	D	13,333	6,059	2,420	139,540	6.6	13,781	D	16,240	6,475
Delaware	1,964	30,400	20.1	18,888	D	3,174	1,435	560	31,497	7.1	2,618	D	3,830	1,561
District of Columbia	1,353	24,356	23.6	13,997	3,244	2,871	1,203	712	43,386	4.9	2,717	23,473	6,093	2,393
Florida	51,567	614,004	14.1	360,507	77,106	76,786	27,914	5,092	377,250	3.1	34,574	224,905	47,276	16,521
Georgia	20,166	256,945	12.2	158,607	D	28,196	11,171	2,568	191,515	0.7	11,486	134,809	23,604	8,344
Hawaii	2,794	26,788	-7.7	20,436	D	3,180	1,347	765	39,984	15.5	4,777	21,720	4,957	1,943
Idaho	4,271	49,613	11.5	26,127	2,924	4,281	1,636	594	33,892	15.1	1,393	25,236	3,614	1,535
Illinois	27,624	383,980	18.1	240,920	15,441	39,270	16,151	5,431	386,504	1.3	22,524	230,249	44,161	16,423
Indiana	12,360	206,531	13.8	113,641	15,020	21,191	8,626	2,796	190,392	1.0	12,842	119,354	17,028	5,804
Iowa	5,582	78,961	12.4	43,888	D	7,151	3,357	2,549	127,945	-0.1	7,799	D	D	D
Kansas	5,977	93,121	11.5	52,953	6,761	9,678	3,955	1,957	99,151	4.4	6,359	51,968	6,152	2,429
Kentucky	9,449	127,446	10.2	69,066	8,611	11,985	5,178	1,976	124,432	4.0	11,499	80,486	11,418	3,868
Louisiana	10,240	167,792	15.6	88,911	19,565	15,870	6,157	1,759	117,187	5.7	4,258	77,104	9,939	3,613
Maine	3,071	41,700	4.9	23,055	D	3,487	1,613	1,659	67,531	4.9	7,036	D	D	D
Maryland	13,217	168,241	17.1	105,879	D	18,823	7,785	2,783	191,493	11.3	9,804	D	D	D
Massachusetts	13,136	237,631	17.2	138,145	18,506	26,639	12,209	5,250	349,854	13.5	32,003	169,964	25,847	10,415
Michigan	21,447	270,655	18.4	173,860	14,278	27,435	11,944	4,784	314,875	-1.8	31,655	191,187	27,028	10,346
Minnesota	11,233	189,308	20.6	108,030	D	15,774	7,259	3,874	250,887	9.5	23,077	D	D	D
Mississippi	5,149	84,441	16.3	43,908	11,822	8,731	3,451	1,062	73,179	-1.5	3,226	54,427	6,833	2,684
Missouri	14,644	184,918	15.9	95,013	14,471	17,917	7,525	3,122	215,022	6.0	18,417	129,225	17,263	6,202
Montana	2,545	24,420	12.2	15,400	D	2,508	1,041	967	41,237	14.2	2,978	D	D	D
Nebraska	4,282	57,239	16.0	31,302	2,328	5,707	2,398	1,128	68,230	4.0	3,575	40,591	5,495	1,806
Nevada	5,766	77,665	6.8	42,411	14,806	9,937	3,598	542	30,920	29.3	2,120	20,737	3,216	1,223
New Hampshire	2,775	35,400	8.2	21,181	2,347	444	1,770	803	51,699	1.4	9,014	25,218	5,615	2,317
New Jersey	23,088	297,847	17.7	198,143	10,677	1,468	13,028	3,847	243,028	-2.9	20,746	136,380	27,740	11,297
New Mexico	3,970	67,477	17.5	34,002	8,324	1,176	2,450	997	49,080	2.1	5,093	26,723	5,166	2,138
New York	43,548	540,067	17.4	397,708	3,366	237	22,401	13,186	928,920	7.3	102,840	443,108	100,067	42,779
North Carolina	19,152	292,709	2.0	168,931	7,693	1,090	11,432	3,825	236,861	0.2	16,895	151,084	27,922	10,325
North Dakota	1,235	15,038	6.4	9,934	D	D	776	621	41,601	9.3	1,630	D	3,609	1,638
Ohio	22,945	393,909	13.7	231,564	12,043	1,530	15,471	5,292	404,861	2.5	32,022	254,046	46,278	17,670
Oklahoma	8,868	128,437	6.0	63,736	19,773	3,626	4,996	1,786	84,789	6.5	5,726	49,730	9,413	3,293
Oregon	9,829	105,341	14.7	65,396	D	D	4,534	2,646	112,243	11.8	11,445	D	13,940	5,156
Pennsylvania	27,983	433,818	17.7	266,329	28,531	3,968	19,364	8,569	521,661	3.1	48,929	245,857	52,550	19,962
Rhode Island	2,470	35,597	2.4	20,571	D	D	1,536	766	48,470	2.7	4,687	D	4,756	2,020
South Carolina	8,346	132,360	14.4	70,689	16,924	2,886	5,385	1,502	80,084	-5.3	3,855	51,861	9,119	3,302
South Dakota	1,544	20,514	17.9	11,889	D	D	830	754	42,980	10.0	3,975	D	4,189	1,729
Tennessee	12,286	220,313	18.7	123,165	30,315	4,700	9,564	2,611	160,140	5.2	13,454	100,602	17,842	6,664
Texas	55,176	945,659	21.2	552,817	118,155	20,879	36,493	6,166	400,005	3.6	30,342	268,014	51,047	18,077
Utah	6,601	77,036	14.9	44,035	7,957	8,254	3,017	684	49,139	7.8	5,381	32,987	5,109	1,573
Vermont	1,370	14,976	-2.6	8,847	D	1,297	578	726	29,222	10.1	6,615	D	D	D
Virginia	16,070	236,459	15.9	139,138	17,223	25,556	10,868	2,704	174,649	4.5	13,334	102,848	15,825	5,535
Washington	16,888	194,136	12.9	115,714	D	20,414	8,703	2,945	180,091	4.0	23,965	D	D	D
West Virginia	3,734	57,400	10.8	27,271	5,215	5,125	2,108	1,205	71,675	14.0	8,152	43,463	5,810	2,094
Wisconsin	11,460	175,153	6.1	99,434	1,679	16,357	7,785	3,199	210,988	3.3	23,362	112,126	17,578	5,514
Wyoming	1,457	13,706	17.3	8,109	1,159	1,486	608	441	17,634	0.4	1,026	9,743	1,408	561

Table A. States — Arts, Entertainment, and Recreation and Accommodation and Food Services

STATE	Arts, entertainment, and recreation, 2012					Accommodation and food services, 2012					
	Number of estab-lishments	Employees		Receipts (mil dol)	Annual payroll (mil dol)	Number of estab-lishments	Employees		Food services and drinking places	Receipts (mil dol)	Annual payroll (mil dol)
		Number	Percent change, 2007–2012				Total	Percent change, 2007–2012			
	290	291	292	293	294	295	296	297	298	299	300
United States	124,591	2,081,668	1.0	201,193	64,052	662,489	12,007,689	3.5	10,057,608	708,139	196,103
Alabama..........................	1,086	17,170	-4.5	1,194	297	8,339	157,337	4.3	142,339	7,576	2,071
Alaska.............................	545	5,055	13.4	407	91	2,126	26,836	4.7	20,057	2,221	626
Arizona...........................	1,764	42,407	-8.8	3,810	1,263	11,669	251,455	0.3	203,083	13,997	4,030
Arkansas.........................	781	8,881	-3.6	704	160	5,473	95,854	6.6	85,388	4,307	1,183
California........................	21,191	303,838	0.6	39,179	13,419	78,560	1,394,984	2.1	1,160,464	90,830	25,148
Colorado.........................	2,433	51,235	3.1	3,783	1,323	12,744	240,484	3.8	194,749	13,618	3,995
Connecticut.....................	1,610	26,476	5.2	2,298	715	8,263	134,546	1.9	107,171	9,542	2,591
Delaware.........................	409	8,102	18.2	651	208	1,987	35,609	10.6	31,519	2,148	567
District of Columbia..........	301	7,510	2.6	1,021	412	2,371	60,370	13.9	45,949	5,102	1,505
Florida............................	7,562	169,796	1.8	16,453	4,904	37,118	786,082	5.3	621,439	49,818	13,598
Georgia...........................	2,733	42,851	-4.9	3,780	1,262	18,815	353,638	-0.5	313,419	18,977	5,173
Hawaii............................	495	10,623	-11.4	844	249	3,518	98,364	0.0	59,938	9,537	2,536
Idaho..............................	712	8,944	-0.8	455	138	3,564	54,257	-4.2	43,787	2,680	726
Illinois............................	4,520	77,153	-3.1	7,401	2,348	27,117	469,870	0.2	415,659	27,937	7,707
Indiana	2,069	33,726	-6.0	3,652	941	13,057	255,223	0.4	224,519	13,077	3,433
Iowa...............................	1,466	21,233	-2.0	1,626	364	7,047	115,134	-1.5	96,648	5,469	1,467
Kansas............................	1,000	14,341	-8.3	884	252	5,943	106,850	2.0	95,624	4,873	1,343
Kentucky	1,242	17,360	-6.4	1,207	349	7,678	156,965	3.6	143,432	7,500	2,084
Louisiana.........................	1,376	23,386	-5.6	2,661	720	9,019	193,928	7.6	157,059	11,698	3,111
Maine.............................	849	7,305	-6.3	527	155	3,958	49,672	0.6	40,538	2,901	851
Maryland	1,960	35,932	-4.2	3,391	1,062	11,344	204,222	6.0	181,041	12,517	3,411
Massachusetts..................	3,130	55,585	5.4	5,012	1,788	16,898	273,185	6.2	243,840	17,509	5,020
Michigan..........................	3,369	46,255	-16.1	3,709	1,416	19,491	347,337	2.4	302,053	17,962	4,872
Minnesota	2,714	42,320	0.6	3,127	1,191	11,345	221,859	0.4	184,868	11,723	3,238
Mississippu	656	8,840	8.1	587	161	5,177	116,238	-2.8	82,085	6,999	1,765
Missouri..........................	2,095	38,190	1.8	3,716	1,341	12,459	239,264	-0.9	206,309	12,430	3,409
Montana..........................	1,126	10,903	5.9	785	170	3,458	46,251	0.2	35,921	2,420	650
Nebraska.........................	842	13,090	15.2	780	206	4,326	70,128	1.4	62,732	3,094	855
Nevada...........................	1,290	26,705	-11.8	3,645	772	5,815	296,762	-8.8	102,621	27,482	8,556
New Hampshire	724	12,946	11.7	793	235	3,606	54,047	-2.2	44,957	2,942	891
New Jersey	3,421	56,427	10.5	4,632	1,606	20,127	291,933	0.2	233,932	19,674	5,387
New Mexico	652	12,259	-14.5	1,353	268	4,177	82,601	2.7	64,280	4,350	1,250
New York.........................	11,615	162,729	2.8	21,929	6,900	49,731	679,146	14.8	584,408	49,286	13,734
North Carolina..................	3,471	58,185	5.2	4,774	1,535	19,496	358,602	4.5	318,217	18,622	5,041
North Dakota....................	421	4,901	7.0	242	64	1,935	35,698	17.8	26,990	2,045	521
Ohio...............................	3,810	60,704	-7.1	5,432	1,977	23,432	437,293	0.2	403,421	20,653	5,743
Oklahoma........................	1,052	26,375	0.5	2,791	672	7,403	143,561	11.2	125,756	7,121	1,908
Oregon............................	1,636	24,031	-1.2	1,607	570	10,610	150,482	0.0	126,327	8,467	2,438
Pennsylvania....................	4,402	99,568	19.1	8,748	2,742	27,646	439,159	4.5	386,349	23,504	6,377
Rhode Island....................	537	8,798	-0.4	780	216	2,973	44,063	-0.8	40,040	2,481	706
South Carolina	1,525	24,918	-1.5	1,813	432	9,828	185,282	1.3	158,300	9,764	2,650
South Dakota....................	668	6,204	-3.6	437	103	2,363	37,974	3.4	29,328	1,874	514
Tennessee.......................	2,326	32,490	0.2	3,355	1,150	12,004	241,348	0.8	211,928	12,499	3,546
Texas..............................	6,304	119,132	8.6	10,287	3,309	48,721	976,390	12.7	868,360	54,481	14,744
Utah	923	20,749	12.2	1,181	401	5,108	95,933	4.5	78,587	4,789	1,363
Vermont..........................	451	7,147	-10.8	352	116	1,920	31,365	0.6	18,803	1,564	494
Virginia...........................	2,744	54,248	6.0	4,244	1,268	16,832	320,514	6.0	273,558	17,796	4,909
Washington	2,744	58,770	2.0	5,093	1,553	16,333	234,145	0.4	198,551	14,297	4,160
West Virginia....................	756	8,349	-22.7	632	128	3,629	66,302	7.4	52,982	4,036	976
Wisconsin........................	2,655	43,555	1.8	3,182	1,053	14,137	221,567	-2.6	189,520	10,303	2,764
Wyoming..........................	428	3,971	-1.8	248	79	1,799	27,580	2.2	18,763	1,645	469

Table A. States — Other Services, Except Public Administration and Government Employment

STATE	Other services, except public administration, 2012								Government employment, 2017		
	Number of establishments	Employees					Receipts (mil dol)	Annual payroll (mil dol)	Federal civilian	Federal military	State and local
		Total	Percent change, 2007–2012	Repair and maintenance	Personal and laundry services	Religious, civic, and similar services					
	301	302	303	304	305	306	307	308	309	310	311
United States	529,691	3,430,711	-1.4	1,194,122	1,349,371	887,218	426,694	108,186	2,857,000	1,929,000	19,619,000
Alabama	6,087	37,291	-7.9	17,145	14,117	6,029	4,378	1,117	53,233	28,859	321,082
Alaska	1,355	7,238	-4.3	2,579	2,228	2,431	905	236	15,110	25,473	62,517
Arizona	8,503	62,073	-9.2	23,444	23,403	15,226	6,232	1,736	55,861	33,902	358,887
Arkansas	3,961	21,830	-5.9	8,514	8,577	4,739	2,339	586	20,099	15,117	191,038
California	57,009	395,836	-0.9	143,971	155,062	96,803	50,439	12,251	248,950	206,431	2,325,520
Colorado	10,246	64,398	2.6	22,061	23,944	18,393	8,519	2,100	53,607	52,203	386,937
Connecticut	7,282	43,384	-9.6	13,274	20,799	9,311	4,904	1,382	18,089	13,526	222,540
Delaware	1,513	9,841	-1.7	2,963	4,705	2,173	975	290	5,754	8,566	59,882
District of Columbia	3,357	58,982	18.3	638	7,081	51,263	19,773	4,239	195,159	13,834	41,159
Florida	34,843	195,176	-3.2	60,133	84,877	50,166	20,799	5,415	139,250	91,582	955,564
Georgia	13,828	89,302	-8.9	35,769	36,220	17,313	10,617	2,703	101,246	90,626	584,317
Hawaii	2,808	19,348	-3.8	3,202	7,812	8,334	2,005	539	33,426	55,415	93,533
Idaho	2,553	12,188	-10.9	5,569	4,257	2,362	1,118	311	13,026	8,905	111,207
Illinois	23,334	165,366	-1.4	58,058	59,330	47,978	21,356	5,827	80,111	42,947	748,859
Indiana	10,777	72,937	-3.1	28,900	25,835	18,202	8,910	2,107	38,067	20,609	385,992
Iowa	5,866	30,672	-3.8	11,925	11,612	7,135	3,343	848	17,782	11,476	240,696
Kansas	5,147	29,521	-6.8	10,781	10,367	8,373	3,433	849	25,039	32,223	233,076
Kentucky	5,849	38,364	-6.3	16,863	14,589	6,912	4,071	1,090	36,245	44,911	272,287
Louisiana	6,293	43,500	3.0	21,958	14,140	7,402	5,409	1,479	31,067	33,652	292,812
Maine	2,786	13,755	3.4	4,907	4,517	4,331	1,463	376	15,257	6,800	85,265
Maryland	9,978	79,391	2.6	25,219	31,858	22,314	10,880	2,929	175,887	50,172	342,854
Massachusetts	14,008	93,489	3.6	25,127	42,404	25,958	10,455	2,931	46,592	19,257	396,903
Michigan	15,919	96,150	-5.3	37,715	37,999	20,436	10,408	2,720	52,685	17,849	542,757
Minnesota	10,832	72,715	-11.1	22,221	29,525	20,969	7,877	2,017	32,314	19,975	376,550
Mississippu	3,540	19,232	-5.8	8,304	6,723	4,205	1,952	549	25,354	27,218	219,283
Missouri	10,357	62,825	-6.9	25,284	24,124	13,417	6,980	1,835	58,416	35,716	377,249
Montana	2,278	10,917	5.8	4,644	2,731	3,542	1,222	303	13,214	7,810	75,130
Nebraska	3,989	21,832	-3.2	9,171	7,747	4,914	2,841	612	16,867	12,630	146,317
Nevada	3,538	25,386	-6.8	8,561	12,023	4,802	2,609	706	19,208	18,220	137,834
New Hampshire	2,879	16,603	2.8	5,699	6,736	4,168	1,555	473	7,631	4,679	82,069
New Jersey	18,327	108,216	2.4	32,991	56,552	18,673	11,608	3,150	49,435	25,011	536,221
New Mexico	2,962	17,464	-3.3	7,474	5,336	4,654	1,799	501	29,288	17,348	159,649
New York	45,646	271,689	8.9	56,633	111,369	103,687	39,709	9,395	116,538	55,540	1,286,867
North Carolina	13,716	80,710	-5.4	32,784	31,859	16,067	9,141	2,321	72,433	129,581	658,361
North Dakota	1,716	9,232	-0.3	3,515	3,137	2,580	1,064	254	9,429	11,679	67,481
Ohio	18,851	127,366	-5.8	44,260	55,364	27,742	13,221	3,491	78,517	35,792	691,621
Oklahoma	5,411	32,388	2.3	13,280	12,874	6,234	4,037	940	48,620	33,461	287,440
Oregon	6,894	37,941	-3.0	14,717	13,486	9,738	4,435	1,149	28,273	11,427	248,389
Pennsylvania	25,231	154,319	0.0	51,110	63,740	39,469	17,737	4,367	97,388	35,191	640,542
Rhode Island	2,276	13,046	-9.3	4,172	5,690	3,184	1,445	391	10,910	6,752	54,770
South Carolina	6,666	44,374	-2.5	19,017	15,909	9,448	4,465	1,302	33,770	52,804	323,013
South Dakota	1,805	8,371	-1.7	3,569	2,586	2,216	939	214	11,380	8,112	66,292
Tennessee	8,117	55,990	-10.3	20,581	23,773	11,636	6,526	1,711	49,579	20,615	375,577
Texas	34,116	259,128	2.2	120,606	95,613	42,909	30,172	8,454	200,710	172,334	1,685,472
Utah	4,259	26,026	-0.8	11,864	9,841	4,321	2,544	723	36,130	16,396	202,758
Vermont	1,588	7,211	-0.8	2,223	2,032	2,956	755	199	6,969	3,989	46,928
Virginia	14,726	112,430	1.2	34,521	41,520	36,389	17,079	4,471	197,619	137,423	543,882
Washington	12,425	69,976	-1.7	24,072	29,997	15,907	13,185	2,203	74,962	74,266	498,971
West Virginia	2,661	16,583	0.3	6,969	5,759	3,855	1,773	444	23,862	8,662	122,343
Wisconsin	10,210	62,054	-6.5	21,698	25,964	14,392	6,407	1,732	29,093	15,960	390,612
Wyoming	1,373	6,655	2.0	3,467	1,628	1,560	885	215	7,549	6,074	61,695

Table A. States — State Government Employment and Payroll

STATE	State government employment, 2017			State government payroll, 2017		Full-time equivalent payroll (1000 dollars)						
									Percent of total for:			
	Full-time equivalent employees	Full-time employees	Part-time employees	Full-time March payroll (1000 dollars)	Part-time March payroll (1000 dollars)	Total March payroll (1000 dollars)[1]	Administration	Judicial and legal	Police	Corrections	Highways and transporta-tion	Welfare
	312	313	314	315	316	317	318	319	320	321	322	323
United States	4,381,768	3,790,363	1,609,484	20,545,637	2,374,412	22,920,049	5.3	4.8	3.1	10.0	4.9	4.8
Alabama	90,729	79,167	32,884	372,818	37,392	410,209	3.5	3.6	1.5	4.5	4.3	3.9
Alaska	24,357	22,455	5,288	135,317	6,835	142,152	7.7	6.3	3.7	9.6	13.7	5.9
Arizona	72,850	60,548	32,773	304,476	36,403	340,879	4.2	4.0	3.4	11.3	3.8	6.9
Arkansas	62,066	56,478	16,207	236,527	15,252	251,780	5.2	2.6	2.0	7.5	5.9	5.5
California	424,359	352,883	180,132	2,561,129	416,336	2,977,465	6.2	1.7	3.8	16.6	5.8	0.8
Colorado	88,130	61,866	49,226	361,024	98,094	459,118	3.7	7.6	2.1	8.7	4.0	2.8
Connecticut	58,803	49,853	25,271	333,598	44,350	377,948	6.1	7.7	4.2	10.1	5.9	10.1
Delaware	25,872	22,576	8,028	106,468	12,278	118,746	4.2	8.1	7.3	11.3	4.9	4.7
District of Columbia	X	X	X	X	X	X	X	X	X	X	X	X
Florida	179,738	160,856	50,263	712,657	63,965	776,622	4.4	11.3	2.3	10.0	4.0	3.9
Georgia	129,828	113,412	51,358	505,228	51,473	556,701	3.5	3.3	2.4	9.6	2.8	4.4
Hawaii	58,966	53,067	19,752	257,991	21,430	279,421	2.6	5.2	0.0	4.8	1.7	0.7
Idaho	24,176	20,903	10,611	111,109	11,462	122,571	7.5	4.9	2.4	11.6	5.1	6.6
Illinois	121,795	100,814	51,188	592,534	90,750	683,284	6.1	4.0	3.9	12.6	6.0	8.7
Indiana	90,341	75,983	43,287	345,128	36,454	381,582	3.3	2.9	2.4	5.1	3.9	5.3
Iowa	51,176	41,465	29,300	272,806	24,986	297,792	3.4	4.7	2.1	5.1	4.2	5.1
Kansas	53,820	48,098	18,591	225,768	20,214	245,981	4.0	4.0	2.2	4.8	4.1	4.7
Kentucky	84,042	72,618	25,100	336,144	28,331	364,475	3.9	5.7	2.4	4.2	4.7	6.7
Louisiana	73,488	66,332	20,019	316,195	21,299	337,495	6.4	2.4	3.8	7.0	5.8	6.2
Maine	20,172	17,818	8,549	80,550	8,547	89,097	8.3	5.1	3.8	6.6	10.5	10.3
Maryland	85,163	76,293	13,945	415,911	42,040	457,951	5.5	7.4	3.5	13.7	5.7	6.5
Massachusetts	98,206	88,610	33,753	541,696	48,655	590,350	5.9	10.7	4.9	12.6	3.2	8.0
Michigan	146,697	116,884	73,684	695,759	129,296	825,055	4.5	1.5	2.3	9.1	2.0	7.6
Minnesota	83,359	69,628	33,807	420,506	52,753	473,259	8.9	5.4	1.2	5.0	5.9	2.3
Mississippu	55,539	50,571	13,587	202,152	14,444	216,596	4.0	1.3	2.4	3.4	4.9	6.2
Missouri	86,498	76,891	28,816	308,155	27,433	335,588	4.5	5.4	3.6	10.6	6.0	6.0
Montana	20,870	17,580	9,732	84,557	11,261	95,818	7.9	4.4	2.9	5.9	12.1	8.3
Nebraska	31,655	26,189	10,406	118,756	12,849	131,604	3.7	3.7	3.1	9.2	6.2	6.9
Nevada	28,936	25,807	9,848	132,956	11,800	144,755	9.9	3.7	4.3	13.7	6.2	7.3
New Hampshire	18,931	15,301	10,751	83,309	13,051	96,360	6.7	4.4	3.5	6.7	9.1	10.1
New Jersey	139,048	126,977	30,804	798,700	49,737	848,437	4.2	9.9	3.7	6.2	4.0	6.4
New Mexico	45,194	40,638	13,514	193,484	17,199	210,684	3.0	7.9	1.6	7.3	4.4	3.1
New York	247,580	230,450	46,266	1,455,498	80,455	1,535,954	8.0	9.9	4.0	13.2	3.8	1.6
North Carolina	144,993	129,935	41,302	630,846	50,911	681,756	3.4	5.3	2.4	11.3	5.6	0.7
North Dakota	19,026	16,063	9,538	79,920	11,560	91,480	5.3	4.6	1.6	4.9	6.8	2.0
Ohio	137,560	108,527	76,492	603,331	88,464	691,794	6.8	3.0	2.5	10.5	4.9	2.6
Oklahoma	66,128	58,071	25,111	252,376	22,700	275,076	4.8	4.8	3.9	6.7	4.3	9.4
Oregon	70,153	62,625	27,601	354,130	52,770	406,901	7.8	4.9	2.6	8.1	5.9	10.1
Pennsylvania	164,285	143,060	63,324	758,005	116,169	874,174	5.4	4.0	5.6	11.9	6.9	5.7
Rhode Island	18,151	16,934	6,971	104,006	6,450	110,457	9.1	7.1	2.8	11.1	4.0	7.6
South Carolina	79,834	71,868	21,540	312,418	23,561	335,980	4.8	1.6	2.7	7.7	5.2	5.4
South Dakota	14,449	12,626	6,621	59,950	5,763	65,713	6.6	5.5	2.8	4.9	8.0	11.9
Tennessee	78,746	70,601	26,919	316,440	25,231	341,671	6.1	4.7	2.8	7.0	4.2	8.7
Texas	313,065	276,529	90,782	1,439,559	142,674	1,582,233	3.4	2.2	3.1	9.5	3.8	6.2
Utah	60,507	50,727	29,523	261,713	34,995	296,708	5.3	3.1	1.5	4.8	2.8	3.9
Vermont	14,267	12,879	4,365	71,982	7,959	79,942	7.6	5.0	5.5	7.5	8.3	11.1
Virginia	125,605	106,653	60,110	572,619	73,340	645,959	4.1	3.3	2.9	8.0	6.4	2.4
Washington	127,234	109,285	46,470	604,301	87,538	691,839	3.4	2.2	2.0	6.4	5.9	7.9
West Virginia	39,394	35,825	12,449	139,360	12,016	151,376	4.5	5.5	3.0	6.8	10.6	6.5
Wisconsin	72,899	57,321	50,047	310,637	51,996	362,633	4.7	4.6	1.6	12.7	2.7	2.9
Wyoming	13,088	11,823	3,579	55,140	3,491	58,631	8.1	5.4	2.7	8.0	13.5	4.1

1. Includes program categories not shown separately.

Table A. States — State Government Employment and Payroll and State Government Finances

	State government employment and payroll, 2017 (cont.)							State government finances, 2017							
	Full-time equivalent payroll (1000 dollars) (cont.)							General revenue (mil dol)							
	Percent of total for:							Total	From federal government		From own sources			Taxes per capita[2] (dollars)	
STATE	Health	Hospitals	Social Insurance administration	Natural resources and parks	Utilities, sewerge, and waste management	Elementary and secondary education and libraries	Higher education		Total	Per capita[2] (dollars)	Total	Taxes Total	Taxes Sales and gross receipts	Total	Sales and gross receipts
	324	325	326	327	328	329	330	331	332	333	334	335	336	337	338
United States	4.2	9.0	1.6	3.4	0.1	1.1	39.9	X	X	X	X	X	X	X	X
Alabama	4.7	14.7	1.0	2.2	-	-	49.2	26,772	9,949	2,041	16,822,850	10,418	5,247	2,137	1,076
Alaska	3.0	0.9	1.1	9.1	-	8.5	17.4	8,345	3,287	4,443	5,058,528	1,190	263	1,608	356
Arizona	3.3	0.8	2.1	2.4	-	-	49.7	34,731	15,248	2,173	19,482,769	13,889	8,540	1,979	1,217
Arkansas	5.1	10.4	1.8	3.6	-	-	45.3	21,149	7,916	2,635	13,232,671	9,516	4,702	3,168	1,565
California	3.9	11.1	2.7	4.2	0.2	-	37.1	288,584	93,014	2,353	195,569,881	155,632	47,940	3,936	1,213
Colorado	2.2	6.8	1.6	2.8	-	-	52.2	27,870	8,463	1,509	19,406,670	13,198	5,129	2,354	915
Connecticut	6.5	9.9	1.1	1.5	0.1	-	27.5	27,798	7,535	2,100	20,262,870	16,346	6,650	4,555	1,853
Delaware	7.3	4.1	1.0	2.4	0.4	-	30.8	8,340	2,416	2,512	5,924,509	3,589	556	3,731	579
District of Columbia	X	X	X	X	X	X	X	X	X	X	X	X	X	X	X
Florida	7.4	1.9	1.3	4.2	-	-	44.6	84,010	27,852	1,327	56,158,246	40,218	33,340	1,917	1,589
Georgia	3.2	6.0	0.9	4.8	-	-	53.3	44,066	15,184	1,456	28,882,254	22,419	8,808	2,150	845
Hawaii	4.1	8.6	0.3	1.9	-	39.2	20.4	13,452	2,787	1,953	10,664,224	7,029	4,366	4,924	3,058
Idaho	8.2	1.8	2.7	9.1	-	-	30.6	8,477	2,623	1,528	5,853,974	4,511	2,245	2,627	1,308
Illinois	2.4	8.7	1.4	1.9	-	-	36.6	67,992	19,737	1,542	48,255,626	37,979	18,630	2,967	1,455
Indiana	1.8	1.5	1.0	2.5	-	-	66.4	38,492	14,713	2,207	23,778,836	18,052	10,894	2,708	1,634
Iowa	0.9	17.5	0.9	3.2	-	-	45.6	21,134	6,246	1,986	14,888,387	9,755	4,613	3,101	1,466
Kansas	1.8	21.1	0.2	2.2	-	-	45.8	17,686	4,161	1,428	13,524,708	8,174	4,302	2,806	1,477
Kentucky	4.5	9.6	1.0	3.6	-	-	48.4	27,714	10,830	2,431	16,884,063	11,908	5,650	2,673	1,268
Louisiana	5.6	13.0	1.1	6.1	-	0.2	34.5	27,796	12,637	2,698	15,158,666	11,105	7,014	2,371	1,497
Maine	5.1	2.7	1.6	6.4	-	0.2	30.3	8,579	3,021	2,261	5,558,846	4,233	2,165	3,168	1,621
Maryland	6.7	3.8	0.9	2.9	-	-	31.4	41,021	13,204	2,182	27,817,519	21,600	9,243	3,569	1,527
Massachusetts	6.9	4.7	1.1	2.3	1.1	2.0	26.7	54,787	16,331	2,381	38,455,695	27,518	8,818	4,012	1,286
Michigan	4.1	10.1	0.5	2.5	-	-	51.9	63,999	21,351	2,143	42,647,999	28,629	13,697	2,874	1,375
Minnesota	4.3	4.7	1.1	4.4	1.0	-	43.1	41,354	10,939	1,962	30,414,777	25,595	10,608	4,590	1,902
Mississippu	5.1	17.7	1.0	5.0	-	-	41.6	18,717	8,211	2,752	10,505,315	7,783	4,988	2,608	1,672
Missouri	3.4	11.0	0.4	2.9	-	-	40.3	29,530	11,322	1,852	18,208,192	12,496	5,404	2,044	884
Montana	4.1	3.0	4.0	8.3	-	-	29.6	6,618	3,055	2,908	3,563,234	2,654	576	2,527	549
Nebraska	2.3	11.0	0.8	5.8	-	-	38.8	10,026	3,180	1,656	6,845,781	5,103	2,408	2,658	1,254
Nevada	5.1	4.8	1.4	3.8	-	-	30.9	15,342	5,235	1,746	10,107,580	8,625	6,923	2,877	2,309
New Hampshire	4.9	3.0	1.2	3.2	-	-	35.9	7,012	2,720	2,026	4,291,814	2,497	959	1,859	714
New Jersey	2.8	7.9	0.9	1.8	0.4	11.9	25.3	62,624	18,616	2,067	44,008,401	32,326	13,389	3,590	1,487
New Mexico	4.9	17.9	0.6	3.3	-	-	39.7	17,215	7,227	3,461	9,988,182	5,776	3,070	2,766	1,470
New York	3.6	15.7	2.9	2.0	-	-	19.0	164,594	60,371	3,041	104,223,148	79,678	25,363	4,014	1,278
North Carolina	1.5	15.9	0.9	3.3	0.3	-	43.6	53,199	16,412	1,598	36,786,989	26,855	11,699	2,614	1,139
North Dakota	8.5	3.4	1.5	6.3	-	-	42.9	6,648	1,826	2,417	4,822,067	3,465	1,349	4,587	1,786
Ohio	2.8	10.3	1.3	2.1	-	-	47.5	69,776	24,306	2,085	45,470,057	30,306	19,573	2,599	1,679
Oklahoma	8.3	1.3	1.2	3.1	0.2	-	44.3	21,102	7,280	1,852	13,822,030	8,569	3,765	2,180	958
Oregon	3.1	9.6	3.9	4.5	-	-	35.9	30,351	9,988	2,411	20,362,710	11,915	1,599	2,876	386
Pennsylvania	1.1	5.6	2.2	4.2	-	-	39.2	83,570	29,475	2,302	54,094,855	37,853	19,629	2,956	1,533
Rhode Island	5.4	3.9	1.9	2.4	2.0	2.0	22.5	7,506	2,519	2,377	4,987,180	3,267	1,692	3,083	1,597
South Carolina	6.2	7.1	1.2	2.9	-	-	43.6	26,188	9,008	1,793	17,180,662	9,829	4,637	1,956	923
South Dakota	4.9	1.9	1.4	6.6	-	-	36.4	4,400	1,567	1,802	2,832,741	1,829	1,518	2,103	1,745
Tennessee	6.1	4.2	1.3	5.6	-	-	43.4	29,406	11,162	1,662	18,244,035	13,894	10,011	2,069	1,491
Texas	6.1	6.8	1.2	3.6	-	0.0	50.6	128,757	44,658	1,578	84,099,040	53,613	46,897	1,894	1,657
Utah	3.4	17.9	1.5	2.2	-	-	48.3	18,700	4,524	1,459	14,175,556	7,833	3,531	2,525	1,138
Vermont	3.8	1.8	1.7	5.6	-	-	29.8	6,026	1,992	3,193	4,034,218	3,128	1,059	5,015	1,697
Virginia	5.4	8.9	0.8	2.6	-	-	49.0	47,186	10,700	1,263	36,486,487	22,213	6,916	2,623	817
Washington	5.3	9.8	2.7	4.4	0.5	-	44.2	47,201	14,228	1,921	32,973,197	23,998	19,171	3,240	2,589
West Virginia	1.9	3.0	1.3	4.8	0.0	-	42.2	13,183	5,109	2,814	8,073,261	5,092	2,673	2,804	1,472
Wisconsin	2.3	4.5	1.0	3.3	-	-	50.4	35,546	9,583	1,654	25,962,345	18,133	7,973	3,129	1,376
Wyoming	7.4	4.4	0.9	9.6	-	-	26.3	5,519	2,567	4,431	2,952,282	1,650	763	2,847	1,316

1. Based on resident population estimated as of July 1 of the year shown.

Table A. States — State Government Finances and Voting

STATE	State government finances, 2017 (cont.) General expenditures (mil dol) (cont.)										Debt outstanding		Voting and registration, November 2018		Presidential election, 2016 (percent of vote cast)		
	Direct expenditures				By selected function												
	Total	To local govern- ments	Total	Per capita[1] (dollars)	Educa- tion	Health and hospitals	Highways	Public safety	Public welfare	Natural resources, parks, and recreation	Total (mil dol)	Per capita[1]	Percent registered	Percent voted	Demo- cratic	Repub- lican	All other
	339	340	341	342	343	344	345	346	347	348	349	350	351	352	353	354	355
United States	X	X	X	X	X	X	X	X	X	X	X	X	66.9	53.4	48.0	45.8	6.2
Alabama	28,680	6,932	21,749	4,461	11,472	3,427	1,660	726	8,547	318	8,773	1,800	69.0	50.7	34.4	62.1	3.6
Alaska	9,779	1,830	7,949	10,745	2,524	258	1,144	459	2,725	420	5,922	8,005	67.7	52.8	36.6	51.3	12.2
Arizona	34,888	8,095	26,793	3,819	11,825	591	2,217	1,362	14,686	390	14,291	2,037	68.6	58.9	45.1	48.7	6.2
Arkansas	21,079	5,373	15,706	5,228	7,844	1,405	1,744	546	7,482	352	4,802	1,598	58.5	42.6	33.7	60.6	5.8
California	296,780	107,877	188,902	4,778	97,240	20,930	10,826	10,435	124,082	6,361	152,772	3,864	61.5	51.9	61.7	31.6	6.7
Colorado	29,332	7,604	21,728	3,875	12,011	1,598	1,990	1,271	8,465	519	16,981	3,028	65.6	58.1	48.2	43.3	8.6
Connecticut	26,217	9,190	17,027	4,745	11,398	2,500	1,695	873	4,261	274	38,756	10,801	68.0	54.0	54.6	40.9	4.5
Delaware	9,159	1,583	7,576	7,875	3,315	458	833	473	2,551	163	4,562	4,742	66.3	51.8	53.4	41.9	4.7
District of Columbia	X	X	X	X	X	X	X	X	X	X	X	X	77.6	61.1	90.5	4.1	5.4
Florida	83,042	21,485	61,557	2,933	27,072	5,169	8,748	2,962	27,112	1,655	28,824	1,374	62.7	52.6	47.8	49.0	3.2
Georgia	42,924	12,325	30,599	2,934	18,962	2,848	2,969	1,843	12,476	803	13,051	1,251	66.2	55.9	45.6	50.8	3.6
Hawaii	11,192	328	10,864	7,610	3,410	1,169	318	274	2,984	246	9,656	6,764	53.9	44.0	61.0	29.4	9.6
Idaho	8,298	2,409	5,889	3,430	3,115	204	705	346	2,496	282	3,369	1,962	60.6	47.9	27.5	59.3	13.2
Illinois	70,222	19,193	51,030	3,986	18,521	3,643	6,763	1,798	23,290	510	61,821	4,829	67.8	53.0	55.8	38.8	5.4
Indiana	37,915	9,988	27,927	4,189	15,743	712	2,499	976	13,967	432	21,843	3,276	65.3	49.3	37.8	56.9	5.3
Iowa	20,409	5,506	14,904	4,738	7,283	2,162	2,304	394	6,010	326	6,150	1,955	74.0	59.6	41.8	51.2	7.1
Kansas	17,685	4,860	12,825	4,402	7,403	3,079	1,239	462	4,102	264	7,538	2,588	71.5	56.9	36.1	56.7	7.3
Kentucky	31,724	5,730	25,994	5,836	11,263	2,395	1,997	941	11,508	524	14,404	3,234	73.5	53.8	32.7	62.5	4.8
Louisiana	29,144	6,415	22,728	4,852	9,299	778	1,493	1,026	11,227	1,144	18,093	3,862	68.0	49.8	38.4	58.1	3.5
Maine	9,096	2,429	6,668	4,991	3,251	209	778	253	3,257	145	4,750	3,556	78.4	65.6	46.3	43.5	10.2
Maryland	39,693	9,632	30,061	4,967	12,664	2,770	2,557	2,124	12,930	749	28,027	4,631	72.3	54.2	60.3	33.9	5.8
Massachusetts	55,702	9,129	46,572	6,789	13,179	2,203	3,120	1,877	22,403	460	77,043	11,231	68.0	55.5	59.1	32.3	8.7
Michigan	63,187	21,279	41,908	4,207	25,890	6,026	3,013	2,397	18,792	524	33,464	3,359	73.4	59.5	47.3	47.5	5.2
Minnesota	41,304	13,547	27,757	4,977	16,095	840	2,789	1,122	14,507	975	16,363	2,934	74.9	63.0	46.4	44.9	8.6
Mississippi	18,598	4,527	14,071	4,715	5,541	1,939	1,164	471	6,658	340	7,470	2,503	73.4	54.2	40.1	57.9	1.9
Missouri	28,964	6,298	22,666	3,708	9,976	4,201	1,392	1,063	8,996	440	18,420	3,013	72.3	55.0	38.1	56.8	5.1
Montana	6,581	1,129	5,453	5,191	1,917	272	613	251	2,170	302	2,796	2,661	71.3	63.8	35.9	56.5	7.6
Nebraska	9,849	2,457	7,392	3,850	3,826	496	824	440	2,772	278	2,015	1,049	66.3	50.8	33.7	58.7	7.6
Nevada	13,571	4,773	8,798	2,935	5,150	566	1,000	408	3,893	163	3,249	1,084	61.8	48.7	47.9	45.5	6.6
New Hampshire	6,530	832	5,699	4,244	1,441	159	529	218	2,584	86	7,739	5,764	70.8	56.2	46.8	46.5	6.7
New Jersey	55,739	11,663	44,076	4,894	18,498	3,677	3,126	2,095	18,558	669	65,874	7,315	68.6	54.0	55.5	41.4	3.2
New Mexico	18,380	4,879	13,501	6,466	5,899	1,564	652	636	5,925	313	7,058	3,380	61.7	48.1	48.3	40.0	11.7
New York	165,472	62,034	103,438	5,211	45,767	14,325	5,871	4,421	67,311	1,298	139,235	7,015	62.5	49.5	56.1	32.4	11.5
North Carolina	49,254	13,438	35,816	3,486	21,224	3,444	4,490	2,082	13,031	743	16,310	1,588	69.3	52.4	46.2	49.8	4.0
North Dakota	6,791	1,979	4,813	6,371	2,356	403	970	137	1,288	183	2,886	3,820	73.4	61.9	27.2	63.0	9.8
Ohio	70,095	18,796	51,299	4,400	23,188	6,812	4,044	2,206	25,824	634	33,493	2,873	70.2	52.5	43.6	51.7	4.8
Oklahoma	21,342	4,447	16,896	4,298	8,323	1,300	2,169	806	6,747	244	8,457	2,152	65.1	49.4	28.9	65.3	5.7
Oregon	30,971	5,732	25,239	6,092	9,744	3,235	1,196	1,099	10,591	525	12,657	3,055	72.5	61.1	50.1	39.1	10.8
Pennsylvania	88,869	22,256	66,612	5,202	27,913	8,561	8,159	3,276	31,373	1,073	47,520	3,711	68.3	54.6	47.9	48.6	3.6
Rhode Island	7,319	1,277	6,042	5,702	2,168	253	321	286	2,770	110	8,932	8,430	68.0	51.6	54.4	38.9	6.7
South Carolina	28,580	6,735	21,845	4,348	10,275	3,137	2,069	726	7,812	430	15,745	3,134	64.5	48.7	40.7	54.9	4.4
South Dakota	4,693	863	3,830	4,404	1,520	189	664	168	1,154	230	3,528	4,056	67.3	51.9	31.7	61.5	6.7
Tennessee	30,563	7,883	22,680	3,377	10,574	1,148	1,642	1,251	12,448	462	6,127	912	63.5	49.6	34.7	60.7	4.6
Texas	129,694	30,620	99,074	3,500	55,467	10,078	10,039	5,403	38,496	1,093	50,963	1,801	63.3	48.4	43.2	52.2	4.5
Utah	18,449	3,768	14,681	4,733	8,444	2,306	1,211	523	3,769	267	7,453	2,403	68.4	57.6	27.5	45.5	27.0
Vermont	6,550	1,801	4,750	7,616	2,845	389	438	265	1,843	133	3,503	5,617	69.0	54.9	55.7	29.8	14.5
Virginia	47,654	11,928	35,726	4,218	16,599	6,502	4,838	2,209	11,120	481	27,826	3,285	72.0	57.5	49.8	44.4	5.8
Washington	47,718	12,691	35,027	4,730	19,541	6,309	2,826	1,428	12,291	1,045	33,428	4,514	73.7	61.9	52.5	36.8	10.6
West Virginia	13,029	2,457	10,572	5,822	4,285	448	1,149	382	4,733	327	7,547	4,156	64.5	44.1	26.5	68.6	4.9
Wisconsin	34,333	8,826	25,507	4,401	12,364	2,919	3,845	1,121	10,692	548	23,252	4,012	72.8	64.6	46.5	47.2	6.3
Wyoming	7,215	3,083	4,132	7,132	2,279	421	738	165	824	267	770	1,329	63.5	52.1	21.6	67.4	11.0

1. Based on resident population estimated as of July 1 of the year shown.

States and Counties

(For explanation of symbols, see page viii)

Page

53	County Highlights and Rankings
69	State and County Column Headings
73	Table B
73	**AL**(Autauga)—**AL**(Walker)
87	**AL**(Washington)—**AR**(Cleburne)
101	**AR**(Cleveland)—**AR**(Yell)
115	**CA**(Alameda)—**CO**(Bent)
129	**CO**(Boulder)—**CT**(New London)
143	**CT**(Tolland)—**FL**(Polk)
157	**FL**(Putnam)—**GA**(Echols)
171	**GA**(Effingham)—**GA**(Pulaski)
185	**GA**(Putnam)—**ID**(Canyon)
199	**ID**(Caribou)—**IL**(Hancock)
213	**IL**(Hardin)—**IL**(Williamson)
227	**IL**(Winnebago)—**IN**(Perry)
241	**IN**(Pike)—**IA**(Floyd)
255	**IA**(Franklin)—**IA**(Wright)
269	**KS**(Allen)—**KS**(Nemaha)
283	**KS**(Neosho)—**KY**(Clark)
297	**KY**(Clay)—**KY**(Nicholas)
311	**KY**(Ohio)—**LA**(Natchitoches)
325	**LA**(Orleans)—**MD**(Queen Anne's)
339	**MD**(St. Mary's)—**MI**(Kent)
353	**MI**(Keweenaw)—**MN**(Faribault)
367	**MN**(Fillmore)—**MN**(Yellow Medicine)
381	**MS**(Adams)—**MS**(Stone)
395	**MS**(Sunflower)—**MO**(Jackson)
409	**MO**(Jasper)—**MO**(Wright)
423	**MO**(St. Louis city)—**NE**(Banner)
437	**NE**(Blaine)—**NE**(Pierce)
451	**NE**(Platte)—**NJ**(Hunterdon)
465	**NJ**(Mercer)—**NY**(Fulton)
479	**NY**(Genesee)—**NC**(Cherokee)
493	**NC**(Chowan)—**NC**(Surry)
507	**NC**(Swain)—**ND**(Walsh)
521	**ND**(Ward)—**OH**(Noble)
535	**OH**(Ottawa)—**OK**(Kingfisher)
549	**OK**(Kiowa)—**OR**(Marion)
563	**OR**(Morrow)—**PA**(Pike)
577	**PA**(Potter)—**SC**(Spartanburg)
591	**SC**(Sumter)—**SD**(Todd)
605	**SD**(Tripp)—**TN**(Marion)
619	**TN**(Marshall)—**TX**(Burnet)
633	**TX**(Caldwell)—**TX**(Grimes)
647	**TX**(Guadalupe)—**TX**(Martin)
661	**TX**(Mason)—**TX**(Titus)
675	**TX**(Tom Green)—**VT**(Caledonia)
689	**VT**(Chittenden)—**VA**(Loudoun)
703	**VA**(Louisa)—**VA**(Manassas Park city)
717	**VA**(Martinsville city)—**WV**(Cabell)
731	**WV**(Calhoun)—**WI**(Door)
745	**WI**(Douglas)—**WY**(Fremont)
759	**WY**(Goshen)—**WY**(Weston)

County Highlights and Rankings

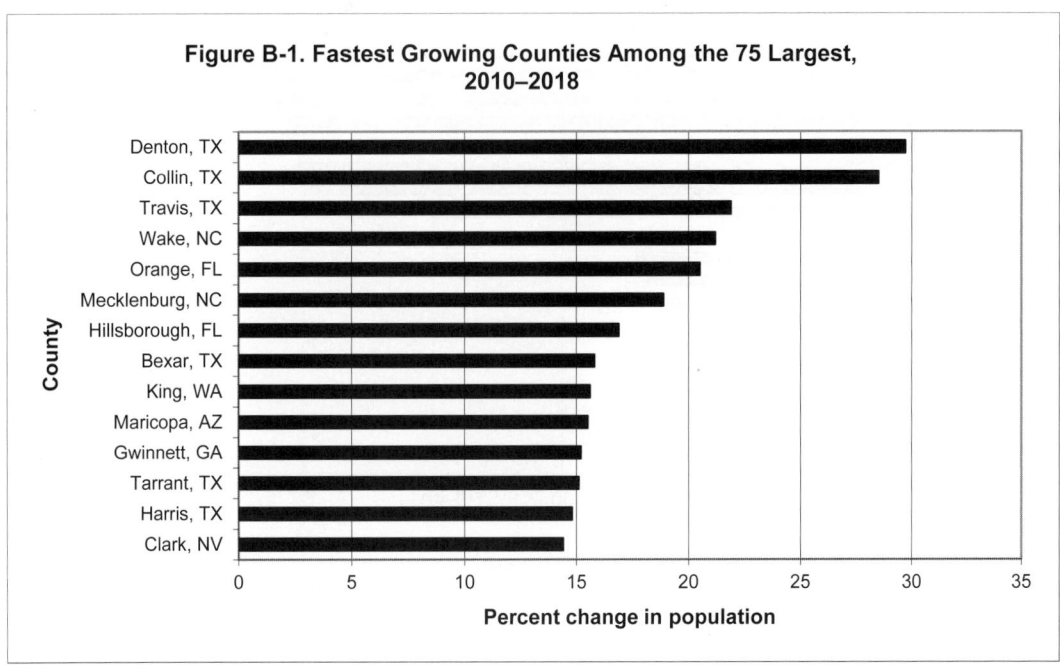

Figure B-1. Fastest Growing Counties Among the 75 Largest, 2010–2018

Eight years after the 2010 census, the 2018 population estimates show that Los Angeles County, CA, remains, by far, the most populous county, with more than 10 million residents. Next is Cook County, IL, which includes Chicago, with nearly 5.2 million people. Its population declined 3.4 percent from 2000 to 2010 and 0.3 percent from 2010 to 2018. New York City consists of five counties (the five boroughs), with Kings (Brooklyn) and Queens each with over 2 million residents, New York (Manhattan) and the Bronx each with about 1.5 million. Queens county moved out of the top 10 in 2014 but Brooklyn's 3 percent growth keeps Kings the 9th most populous county in the nation.

Among the 75 most populous counties, the highest growth rates from 2010 to 2018 were found in the South, with four of the ten top growth rates in Texas. From 2010 to 2018, the fastest-growing of these large counties was Denton, TX, in the Dallas-Fort Worth metropolitan area. During the past eight years, Denton County's population increased by 29.7 percent followed by Collin County, TX (also Dallas) at 28.5 percent. In 2018, Denton County ranked 67th among the most populous counties. Six other counties in Texas also had growth rates over 10 percent: Travis (Austin), Bexar (San Antonio), Harris (Houston), Tarrant (Fort Worth.), Hidalgo (McAllen) and Dallas. Other large counties that experienced more than 10 percent growth in the eight-year period were found mainly in the South and the West. Nearly 1,700 counties lost population during this period. The largest proportional losses were in counties with very small populations. Among the largest counties, St. Louis, MO; Cook, IL; Allegany, IL; New Haven, CT; Suffolk, NY;

Cuyahoga, OH (Cleveland); and Wayne, MI (Detroit), declined in population between 2010 and 2018. Three hundred thirty seven had population growth rates at or above 10 percent from 2010 to 2018. Forty-seven of these fast-growing counties had more than 50,000 residents and twenty-one counties had more than 100,000 residents.

Within states, the number and physical size of counties varied considerably: Delaware had three counties while Texas had 254 counties. For the 3,142 counties (and county equivalents—see Appendix A) in the United States, population in 2018 ranged from nearly 10.2 million in Los Angeles, CA, to 88 in Kalawao County, HI. Other particularly large counties in terms of population are Cook County, IL (nearly 5.2 million people), encompassing Chicago and its suburbs, Harris County, TX (containing Houston) with 4.7 million people, and Maricopa County, AZ (containing Phoenix), with over 4.4 million people. There were 45 counties with a population of 1,000,000 or more; these counties combined contain more than one-fourth of the U.S. population. Over half of the U.S. population lived in the 155 largest counties, those with a population of 450,000 or more. At the other extreme, there were 36 counties with fewer than 1,000 people in 2018. The median county population size was 25,759.

In terms of land area, counties range from the nearly 145,573 square miles of Yukon-Koyukuk Census Area, AK; to Kalawao County, HI, with 12 square miles; New York County, NY (Manhattan), with 22.7 square miles; Bristol County, RI, with 24.1 square miles; and Arlington County, VA, with 26 square miles.[1] Counties tend to be larger in the western United States

---

[1] Several independent cities in Virginia, which are treated as counties for tabulation purposes, were excluded here.

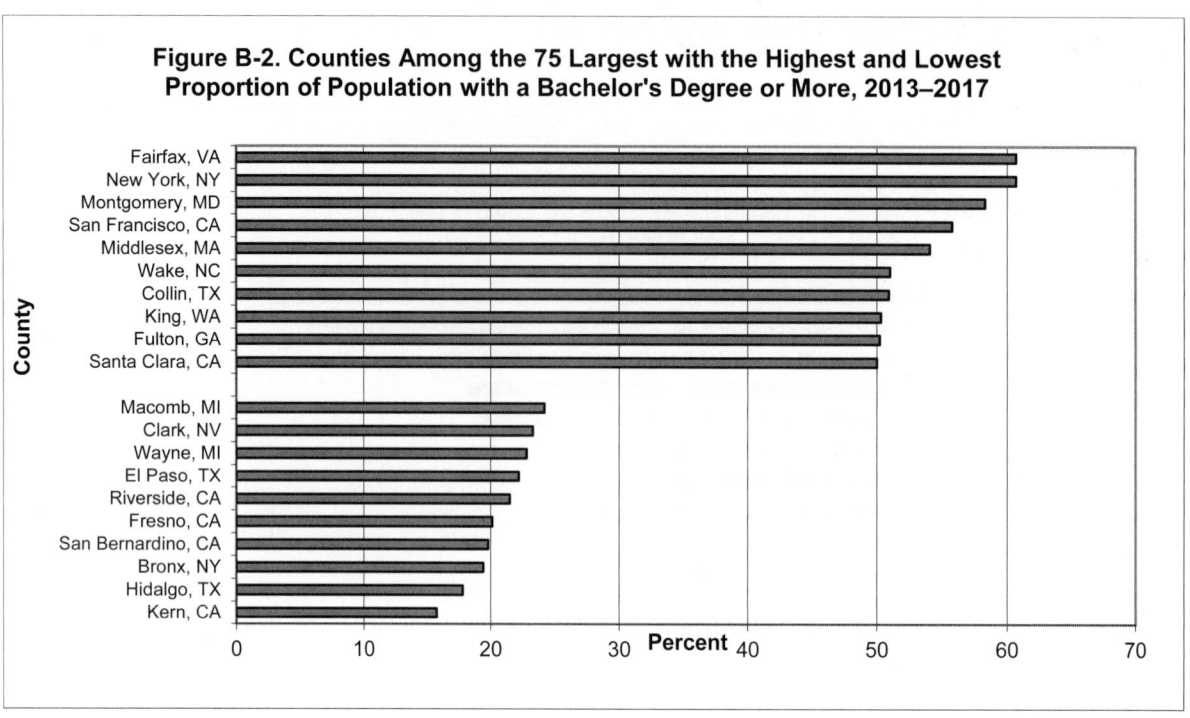

Figure B-2. Counties Among the 75 Largest with the Highest and Lowest Proportion of Population with a Bachelor's Degree or More, 2013–2017

(most of the largest 50 in size are in that region). The median land area for all U.S. counties was about 617 square miles in 2018.

While New York County, NY, had one of the smallest land areas, it had by far the highest population density among U.S. counties in 2018, with nearly 72,000 persons per square mile. No other county approached that density (although three other New York City boroughs were among the top five counties in population density). San Francisco had the highest population density outside of New York City, with Suffolk County, MA (Boston); Philadelphia County, PA; and Washington, DC, also among the top 10 counties. The median county had nearly 45 persons per square mile, with 267 counties having more than 500 persons per square mile. The nation's largest county in terms of population (Los Angeles) had a population density of 2,490 persons per square mile. This density ranked 20th among the 75 most populous U.S. counties.

Proportionally large year-to-year labor force changes are not unusual for counties with small populations. The 2018 annual averages reflect a national labor force that increased by 1.1 percent. Among the 75 most populous counties, 3 counties' labor forces grew by 3.0 percent or more between 2017 and 2018. Maricopa, AZ and Middlesex, MA experienced the largest increase among the 75 most populous counties, at 3.9 percent and 3.3 percent respectively. Travis County, TX followed with an increase of 3.2 percent. Nearly 1,400 counties experienced declines in their labor forces from 2017 to 2018, with 40 counties losing 5 percent or more. Among the most populous 75 counties, 14 counties had decreases

in their labor forces, led by Cook County, IL (Chicago) and Honolulu County, HI at -0.9 percent each.

The national annual average unemployment rate was 3.9 percent in 2018, continuing a steady drop since 2010. The unemployment rate was down from 4.4 percent in 2017, 4.9 percent in 2016, and 5.3 percent in 2015. Nearly 1,500 counties had unemployment rates above the national average of 3.9 percent in 2018 and 20 counties had unemployment rates greater than 10 percent, down from 1,100 counties in 2010, 62 counties in 2016 and 35 counties in 2017. Of the 10 counties with the highest unemployment rates, only Imperial County, CA, and Yuma County, AZ had populations over 100,000. Among the 75 most populous counties, 29 exceeded the national unemployment rate of 3.9 percent and three counties equaled it, with the highest in two California counties—8.0 percent in Kern county and 7.5 percent in Fresno county. Honolulu, HI had the lowest unemployment rate at 2.3 percent, followed by San Francisco, CA and Fairfax, VA at 2.4 percent. Among all smaller counties in 2018, twelve counties in Iowa, nine counties in North Dakota, four counties in Colorado, two counties each in Oklahoma, Texas, and Montana and one county each in Nebraska and Idaho had unemployment rates of less than 2 percent.

Among the 75 largest counties, the two counties with the highest unemployment rates, Fresno and Kern counties in CA, ranked among the top counties for agricultural sales. Meanwhile, Wayne County, MI which ranked second highest in manufacturing employment was tied for the sixth highest unemployment rate among the 75 most populous counties. Fairfax, VA and San Francisco, CA were tied for the second lowest unemployment rate and had the highest percentage of people employed in in professional, scientific, and technical occupations These two counties were also among the top counties for median household income and educational attainment, with more than 55 percent of residents holding bachelor's, master's, doctoral or professional degrees. Four large counties had college-educated proportions of less than 20 percent and three out of the four had the highest unemployment rates among the large counties. Nationally, 32.0 percent of the population held bachelor's degrees or higher in 2017.

75 Largest Counties by 2018 Population
Selected Rankings

Population, 2018			Land area, 2018				Population density, 2018			
Popu-lation rank		Population [col 2]	Popu-lation rank	Land area rank	County	Land area (Square miles) [col 1]	Popu-lation rank	Density rank	County	Density (per square mile) [col 4]
1	Los Angeles, CA	10,105,518	14	1	San Bernardino, CA	20,060	21	1	New York, NY	71,748.9
2	Cook, IL	5,180,493	4	2	Maricopa, AZ	9,199	9	2	Kings, NY	37,216.6
3	Harris, TX	4,698,619	44	3	Pima, AZ	9,187	28	3	Bronx, NY	34,017.4
4	Maricopa, AZ	4,410,824	61	4	Kern, CA	8,132	11	4	Queens, NY	20,945.8
5	San Diego, CA	3,343,364	13	5	Clark, NV	7,892	64	5	San Francisco, CA	18,833.8
6	Orange, CA	3,185,968	10	6	Riverside, CA	7,207	23	6	Philadelphia, PA	11,804.3
7	Miami-Dade, FL	2,761,581	47	7	Fresno, CA	5,958	2	7	Cook, IL	5,482.6
8	Dallas, TX	2,637,772	5	8	San Diego, CA	4,209	30	8	Nassau, NY	4,772.8
9	Kings, NY	2,582,830	1	9	Los Angeles, CA	4,058	55	9	Bergen, NJ	4,023.6
10	Riverside, CA	2,450,758	12	10	King, WA	2,115	6	10	Orange, CA	4,018.6
11	Queens, NY	2,278,906	25	11	Palm Beach, FL	1,966	53	11	Milwaukee, WI	3,926.4
12	King, WA	2,233,163	7	12	Miami-Dade, FL	1,899	49	12	Pinellas, FL	3,563.3
13	Clark, NV	2,231,647	69	13	Ventura, CA	1,843	8	13	Dallas, TX	3,024.6
14	San Bernardino, CA	2,171,603	3	14	Harris, TX	1,705	38	14	Fairfax, VA	2,943.2
15	Tarrant, TX	2,084,931	63	15	Pierce, WA	1,668	19	15	Wayne, MI	2,865.8
16	Bexar, TX	1,986,049	66	16	Hidalgo, TX	1,571	57	16	Du Page, IL	2,833.7
17	Broward, FL	1,951,260	71	17	Worcester, MA	1,511	3	17	Harris, TX	2,755.5
18	Santa Clara, CA	1,937,570	18	18	Santa Clara, CA	1,291	35	18	Cuyahoga, OH	2,720.6
19	Wayne, MI	1,753,893	16	19	Bexar, TX	1,240	72	19	Middlesex, NJ	2,683.3
20	Alameda, CA	1,666,753	17	20	Broward, FL	1,203	1	20	Los Angeles, CA	2,490.1
21	New York, NY	1,628,701	59	21	Erie, NY	1,043	31	21	Franklin, OH	2,461.1
22	Middlesex, MA	1,614,714	27	22	Hillsborough, FL	1,022	15	22	Tarrant, TX	2,414.2
23	Philadelphia, PA	1,584,138	70	23	El Paso, TX	1,013	51	23	Marion, IN	2,408.4
24	Sacramento, CA	1,540,975	34	24	Travis, TX	992	32	24	Hennepin, MN	2,274.2
25	Palm Beach, FL	1,485,941	24	25	Sacramento, CA	965	20	25	Alameda, CA	2,260.6
26	Suffolk, NY	1,481,093	2	26	Cook, IL	945	50	26	Westchester, NY	2,247.1
27	Hillsborough, FL	1,436,888	26	27	Suffolk, NY	912	58	27	Gwinnett, GA	2,154.6
28	Bronx, NY	1,432,132	29	28	Orange, FL	903	42	28	Montgomery, MD	2,134.6
29	Orange, FL	1,380,645	67	29	Denton, TX	879	40	29	Mecklenburg, NC	2,089.2
30	Nassau, NY	1,358,343	8	30	Dallas, TX	872	75	30	Hamilton, OH	2,012.0
31	Franklin, OH	1,310,300	33	31	Oakland, MI	867	43	31	Fulton, GA	1,993.8
32	Hennepin, MN	1,259,428	15	32	Tarrant, TX	864	22	32	Middlesex, MA	1,974.5
33	Oakland, MI	1,259,201	45	33	Collin, TX	841	46	33	St. Louis, MO	1,964.8
34	Travis, TX	1,248,743	41	34	Wake, NC	835	60	34	Prince George's, MD	1,883.8
35	Cuyahoga, OH	1,243,857	22	35	Middlesex, MA	818	65	35	Macomb, MI	1,825.5
36	Allegheny, PA	1,218,452	6	36	Orange, CA	793	73	36	Montgomery, PA	1,715.5
37	Salt Lake, UT	1,152,633	56	37	Shelby, TN	764	36	37	Allegheny, PA	1,668.9
38	Fairfax, VA	1,150,795	52	38	Duval, FL	763	48	38	Honolulu, HI	1,631.8
39	Contra Costa, CA	1,150,215	37	39	Salt Lake, UT	742	26	39	Suffolk, NY	1,624.4
40	Mecklenburg, NC	1,093,901	20	40	Alameda, CA	737	17	40	Broward, FL	1,621.9
41	Wake, NC	1,092,305	62	41	Hartford, CT	735	39	41	Contra Costa, CA	1,604.0
42	Montgomery, MD	1,052,567	36	42	Allegheny, PA	730	16	42	Bexar, TX	1,601.4
43	Fulton, GA	1,050,114	39	43	Contra Costa, CA	717	24	43	Sacramento, CA	1,596.2
44	Pima, AZ	1,039,073	54	44	Fairfield, CT	625	37	44	Salt Lake, UT	1,553.2
45	Collin, TX	1,005,146	19	45	Wayne, MI	612	29	45	Orange, FL	1,529.8
46	St. Louis, MO	996,945	68	46	New Haven, CT	605	54	46	Fairfield, CT	1,510.1
47	Fresno, CA	994,400	48	47	Honolulu, HI	601	18	47	Santa Clara, CA	1,500.7
48	Honolulu, HI	980,080	74	48	Baltimore, MD	598	7	48	Miami-Dade, FL	1,454.4
49	Pinellas, FL	975,280	32	49	Hennepin, MN	554	33	49	Oakland, MI	1,451.7
50	Westchester, NY	967,612	31	50	Franklin, OH	532	68	50	New Haven, CT	1,418.7
51	Marion, IN	954,670	43	51	Fulton, GA	527	27	51	Hillsborough, FL	1,406.2
52	Duval, FL	950,181	40	52	Mecklenburg, NC	524	74	52	Baltimore, MD	1,384.4
53	Milwaukee, WI	948,201	46	53	St. Louis, MO	507	41	53	Wake, NC	1,308.5
54	Fairfield, CT	943,823	42	54	Montgomery, MD	493	34	54	Travis, TX	1,259.1
55	Bergen, NJ	936,692	73	55	Montgomery, PA	483	52	55	Duval, FL	1,245.5
56	Shelby, TN	935,764	60	56	Prince George's, MD	483	56	56	Shelby, TN	1,225.5
57	Du Page, IL	928,589	65	57	Macomb, MI	479	62	57	Hartford, CT	1,214.6
58	Gwinnett, GA	927,781	35	58	Cuyahoga, OH	457	45	58	Collin, TX	1,194.8
59	Erie, NY	919,719	50	59	Westchester, NY	431	12	59	King, WA	1,055.7
60	Prince George's, MD	909,308	58	59	Gwinnett, GA	431	67	60	Denton, TX	977.8
61	Kern, CA	896,764	75	61	Hamilton, OH	406	59	61	Erie, NY	882.1
62	Hartford, CT	892,697	51	62	Marion, IN	396	70	62	El Paso, TX	829.8
63	Pierce, WA	891,299	38	63	Fairfax, VA	391	5	63	San Diego, CA	794.4
64	San Francisco, CA	883,305	57	64	Du Page, IL	328	25	64	Palm Beach, FL	756.0
65	Macomb, MI	874,759	72	65	Middlesex, NJ	309	66	65	Hidalgo, TX	551.2
66	Hidalgo, TX	865,939	30	66	Nassau, NY	285	71	66	Worcester, MA	550.0
67	Denton, TX	859,064	49	67	Pinellas, FL	274	63	67	Pierce, WA	534.4
68	New Haven, CT	857,620	53	68	Milwaukee, WI	242	4	68	Maricopa, AZ	479.5
69	Ventura, CA	850,967	55	69	Bergen, NJ	233	69	69	Ventura, CA	461.9
70	El Paso, TX	840,758	23	70	Philadelphia, PA	134	10	70	Riverside, CA	340.1
71	Worcester, MA	830,839	11	71	Queens, NY	109	13	71	Clark, NV	282.8
72	Middlesex, NJ	829,685	9	72	Kings, NY	69	47	72	Fresno, CA	166.9
73	Montgomery, PA	828,604	64	73	San Francisco, CA	47	44	73	Pima, AZ	113.1
74	Baltimore, MD	828,431	28	74	Bronx, NY	42	61	74	Kern, CA	110.3
75	Hamilton, OH	816,684	21	75	New York, NY	23	14	75	San Bernardino, CA	108.3

75 Largest Counties by 2018 Population
Selected Rankings

Percent population change, 2010–2018				Employment/residence ratio, 2013–2017				Percent White, not Hispanic or Latino, alone or in combination, 2018			
Population rank	Percent change rank	County	Percent change [col 23]	Population rank	Number of employees per resident rank	County	Number of employees per resident [col 34]	Population rank	White rank	County	Percent white [col 5]
67	1	Denton, TX	29.7	21	1	New York, NY	2.88	65	1	Macomb, MI	81.8
45	2	Collin, TX	28.5	43	2	Fulton, GA	1.80	36	2	Allegheny, PA	80.7
34	3	Travis, TX	21.9	64	3	San Francisco, CA	1.45	71	3	Worcester, MA	79.3
41	4	Wake, NC	21.2	32	4	Hennepin, MN	1.34	73	4	Montgomery, PA	78.0
29	5	Orange, FL	20.5	75	5	Hamilton, OH	1.33	59	5	Erie, NY	77.3
40	6	Mecklenburg, NC	18.9	51	6	Marion, IN	1.28	49	6	Pinellas, FL	76.5
27	7	Hillsborough, FL	16.9	40	7	Mecklenburg, NC	1.27	22	7	Middlesex, MA	75.0
16	8	Bexar, TX	15.8	8	8	Dallas, TX	1.26	33	8	Oakland, MI	74.5
12	9	King, WA	15.6	29	9	Orange, FL	1.25	37	9	Salt Lake, UT	73.8
4	10	Maricopa, AZ	15.5	35	10	Cuyahoga, OH	1.23	63	10	Pierce, WA	72.9
58	11	Gwinnett, GA	15.2	57	11	Du Page, IL	1.22	32	11	Hennepin, MN	72.1
15	12	Tarrant, TX	15.1	46	12	St. Louis, MO	1.21	26	12	Suffolk, NY	69.3
3	13	Harris, TX	14.8	34	13	Travis, TX	1.19	57	13	Du Page, IL	68.9
13	14	Clark, NV	14.4	52	13	Duval, FL	1.19	46	14	St. Louis, MO	68.4
43	14	Fulton, GA	14.1	56	15	Shelby, TN	1.18	75	15	Hamilton, OH	67.9
25	16	Palm Beach, FL	12.6	12	16	King, WA	1.17	31	16	Franklin, OH	66.8
31	16	Franklin, OH	12.6	31	16	Franklin, OH	1.17	68	17	New Haven, CT	65.2
63	18	Pierce, WA	12.1	73	16	Montgomery, PA	1.17	12	18	King, WA	65.0
37	19	Salt Lake, UT	12.0	23	19	Philadelphia, PA	1.16	54	19	Fairfield, CT	63.8
10	20	Riverside, CA	11.9	62	19	Hartford, CT	1.16	62	20	Hartford, CT	63.6
66	21	Hidalgo, TX	11.8	3	21	Harris, TX	1.15	41	21	Wake, NC	62.3
17	22	Broward, FL	11.6	37	21	Salt Lake, UT	1.15	67	22	Denton, TX	62.2
8	23	Dallas, TX	11.5	18	23	Santa Clara, CA	1.14	30	23	Nassau, NY	61.8
7	24	Miami-Dade, FL	10.6	36	23	Allegheny, PA	1.14	35	24	Cuyahoga, OH	61.1
20	25	Alameda, CA	10.4	33	25	Oakland, MI	1.13	45	25	Collin, TX	60.6
52	26	Duval, FL	9.9	19	26	Wayne, MI	1.09	74	26	Baltimore, MD	59.9
64	27	San Francisco, CA	9.7	27	26	Hillsborough, FL	1.09	51	27	Marion, IN	58.5
39	28	Contra Costa, CA	9.6	22	28	Middlesex, MA	1.08	55	28	Bergen, NJ	58.3
32	29	Hennepin, MN	9.3	2	29	Cook, IL	1.07	4	29	Maricopa, AZ	58.0
18	30	Santa Clara, CA	8.8	53	29	Milwaukee, WI	1.07	25	30	Palm Beach, FL	57.0
24	31	Sacramento, CA	8.6	59	29	Erie, NY	1.07	52	31	Duval, FL	56.0
42	32	Montgomery, MD	8.3	6	32	Orange, CA	1.06	50	32	Westchester, NY	55.3
5	33	San Diego, CA	8.0	7	32	Miami-Dade, FL	1.06	38	33	Fairfax, VA	54.3
22	34	Middlesex, MA	7.4	41	32	Wake, NC	1.06	44	34	Pima, AZ	54.2
47	35	Fresno, CA	6.9	16	35	Bexar, TX	1.05	53	35	Milwaukee, WI	53.9
61	36	Kern, CA	6.8	25	36	Palm Beach, FL	1.04	27	36	Hillsborough, FL	52.0
14	37	San Bernardino, CA	6.7	38	36	Fairfax, VA	1.04	19	37	Wayne, MI	51.6
38	38	Fairfax, VA	6.4	1	38	Los Angeles, CA	1.03	34	38	Travis, TX	51.1
49	38	Pinellas, FL	6.4	49	38	Pinellas, FL	1.03	15	39	Tarrant, TX	49.5
44	40	Pima, AZ	6.0	4	40	Maricopa, AZ	1.02	24	40	Sacramento, CA	49.3
6	41	Orange, CA	5.8	5	40	San Diego, CA	1.02	40	40	Mecklenburg, NC	49.3
51	42	Marion, IN	5.7	54	40	Fairfield, CT	1.02	5	42	San Diego, CA	48.9
60	43	Prince George's, MD	5.3	13	43	Clark, NV	1.01	21	43	New York, NY	48.6
70	44	El Paso, TX	5.0	61	43	Kern, CA	1.01	39	44	Contra Costa, CA	48.0
33	45	Oakland, MI	4.7	24	45	Sacramento, CA	1.00	69	45	Ventura, CA	47.9
71	46	Worcester, MA	4.1	44	45	Pima, AZ	1.00	42	46	Montgomery, MD	47.0
65	47	Macomb, MI	4.0	47	45	Fresno, CA	1.00	13	47	Clark, NV	46.5
23	48	Philadelphia, PA	3.8	48	45	Honolulu, HI	1.00	72	48	Middlesex, NJ	44.8
73	49	Montgomery, PA	3.6	70	45	El Paso, TX	1.00	64	49	San Francisco, CA	43.8
55	50	Bergen, NJ	3.5	15	50	Tarrant, TX	0.99	2	50	Cook, IL	43.7
28	51	Bronx, NY	3.4	72	51	Middlesex, NJ	0.97	6	51	Orange, CA	43.5
69	52	Ventura, CA	3.3	20	52	Alameda, CA	0.96	29	52	Orange, FL	43.1
9	53	Kings, NY	3.1	66	52	Hidalgo, TX	0.96	43	53	Fulton, GA	41.5
1	54	Los Angeles, CA	2.9	50	54	Westchester, NY	0.95	58	54	Gwinnett, GA	40.3
54	54	Fairfield, CT	2.9	42	55	Montgomery, MD	0.94	17	55	Broward, FL	38.9
74	54	Baltimore, MD	2.9	55	55	Bergen, NJ	0.94	10	56	Riverside, CA	38.2
48	57	Honolulu, HI	2.8	68	55	New Haven, CT	0.94	9	57	Kings, NY	37.3
21	58	New York, NY	2.7	14	58	San Bernardino, CA	0.92	56	57	Shelby, TN	37.3
72	59	Middlesex, NJ	2.4	45	58	Collin, TX	0.92	61	59	Kern, CA	36.5
11	60	Queens, NY	2.2	17	60	Broward, FL	0.91	23	60	Philadelphia, PA	36.4
50	61	Westchester, NY	1.9	69	61	Ventura, CA	0.89	20	61	Alameda, CA	35.4
75	62	Hamilton, OH	1.8	26	62	Suffolk, NY	0.88	18	62	Santa Clara, CA	35.0
30	63	Nassau, NY	1.4	71	62	Worcester, MA	0.88	48	63	Honolulu, HI	32.1
57	64	Du Page, IL	1.3	74	62	Baltimore, MD	0.88	47	64	Fresno, CA	31.6
56	65	Shelby, TN	0.9	58	65	Gwinnett, GA	0.87	3	65	Harris, TX	31.5
59	66	Erie, NY	0.1	30	66	Nassau, NY	0.86	14	66	San Bernardino, CA	31.2
53	67	Milwaukee, WI	0.0	63	66	Pierce, WA	0.86	8	67	Dallas, TX	30.9
62	68	Hartford, CT	-0.1	65	68	Macomb, MI	0.85	16	68	Bexar, TX	29.5
46	69	St. Louis, MO	-0.2	10	69	Riverside, CA	0.82	1	69	Los Angeles, CA	28.2
2	70	Cook, IL	-0.3	39	70	Contra Costa, CA	0.75	11	70	Queens, NY	26.5
36	71	Allegheny, PA	-0.4	60	71	Prince George's, MD	0.74	60	71	Prince George's, MD	14.5
68	72	New Haven, CT	-0.6	9	72	Kings, NY	0.73	7	72	Miami-Dade, FL	14.3
26	73	Suffolk, NY	-0.8	11	73	Queens, NY	0.66	70	73	El Paso, TX	13.1
35	74	Cuyahoga, OH	-2.8	28	73	Bronx, NY	0.66	28	74	Bronx, NY	9.9
19	75	Wayne, MI	-3.7	67	73	Denton, TX	0.66	66	75	Hidalgo, TX	6.7

75 Largest Counties by 2018 Population
Selected Rankings

	Percent Black, not Hispanic or Latino, alone or in combination, 2018				Percent American Indian, Alaska Native, alone or in combination, 2018				Percent Asian or Pacific Islander, alone or in combination, 2018		
Population rank	Black rank	County	Percent black [col 6]	Population rank	American Indian Alaska native rank	County	Percent American Indian, Alaska native [col 7]	Population rank	Asian or Pacific Islander rank	County	Percent Asian or Pacific Islander [col 8]
60	1	Prince George's, MD	64.0	44	1	Pima, AZ	3.1	48	1	Honolulu, HI	78.2
56	2	Shelby, TN	54.4	63	2	Pierce, WA	2.7	18	2	Santa Clara, CA	38.7
43	3	Fulton, GA	44.8	4	3	Maricopa, AZ	2.2	64	3	San Francisco, CA	37.9
23	4	Philadelphia, PA	42.6	12	4	King, WA	1.7	20	4	Alameda, CA	33.6
19	5	Wayne, MI	40.0	24	5	Sacramento, CA	1.5	11	5	Queens, NY	27.9
40	6	Mecklenburg, NC	32.6	32	5	Hennepin, MN	1.5	72	6	Middlesex, NJ	25.4
9	7	Kings, NY	31.4	48	5	Honolulu, HI	1.5	6	7	Orange, CA	22.3
35	8	Cuyahoga, OH	30.9	61	8	Kern, CA	1.3	38	8	Fairfax, VA	21.8
52	9	Duval, FL	30.6	53	9	Milwaukee, WI	1.2	12	9	King, WA	20.9
28	10	Bronx, NY	30.3	13	10	Clark, NV	1.1	39	10	Contra Costa, CA	19.9
51	11	Marion, IN	29.5	19	10	Wayne, MI	1.1	24	11	Sacramento, CA	19.5
74	12	Baltimore, MD	29.4	37	10	Salt Lake, UT	1.1	55	12	Bergen, NJ	17.5
17	13	Broward, FL	29.1	47	10	Fresno, CA	1.1	42	13	Montgomery, MD	16.8
58	14	Gwinnett, GA	27.8	5	14	San Diego, CA	1.0	1	14	Los Angeles, CA	16.1
53	15	Milwaukee, WI	27.7	10	14	Riverside, CA	1.0	45	15	Collin, TX	15.4
75	16	Hamilton, OH	27.6	39	14	Contra Costa, CA	1.0	5	16	San Diego, CA	14.5
46	17	St. Louis, MO	25.3	67	14	Denton, TX	1.0	21	17	New York, NY	13.6
31	18	Franklin, OH	24.2	14	18	San Bernardino, CA	0.9	9	18	Kings, NY	13.4
2	19	Cook, IL	24.1	15	18	Tarrant, TX	0.9	13	19	Clark, NV	13.0
8	20	Dallas, TX	23.2	31	18	Franklin, OH	0.9	22	19	Middlesex, MA	13.0
29	21	Orange, FL	21.4	40	18	Mecklenburg, NC	0.9	57	21	Du Page, IL	12.7
41	22	Wake, NC	21.3	45	18	Collin, TX	0.9	58	21	Gwinnett, GA	12.7
42	23	Montgomery, MD	19.4	59	18	Erie, NY	0.9	47	23	Fresno, CA	11.2
3	24	Harris, TX	19.2	60	18	Prince George's, MD	0.9	63	23	Pierce, WA	11.2
25	25	Palm Beach, FL	19.1	65	18	Macomb, MI	0.9	30	25	Nassau, NY	10.4
11	26	Queens, NY	19.0	11	26	Queens, NY	0.8	67	26	Denton, TX	9.5
27	27	Hillsborough, FL	17.0	20	26	Alameda, CA	0.8	69	27	Ventura, CA	9.0
15	28	Tarrant, TX	16.9	23	26	Philadelphia, PA	0.8	14	28	San Bernardino, CA	8.3
7	29	Miami-Dade, FL	16.6	33	26	Oakland, MI	0.8	32	28	Hennepin, MN	8.3
33	30	Oakland, MI	15.0	41	26	Wake, NC	0.8	73	28	Montgomery, PA	8.3
36	31	Allegheny, PA	14.5	51	26	Marion, IN	0.8	2	31	Cook, IL	8.0
50	31	Westchester, NY	14.5	52	26	Duval, FL	0.8	23	31	Philadelphia, PA	8.0
32	33	Hennepin, MN	14.3	64	26	San Francisco, CA	0.8	33	31	Oakland, MI	8.0
62	34	Hartford, CT	14.1	69	26	Ventura, CA	0.8	10	34	Riverside, CA	7.9
59	35	Erie, NY	14.0	74	26	Baltimore, MD	0.8	41	35	Wake, NC	7.8
68	36	New Haven, CT	13.6	8	36	Dallas, TX	0.7	43	35	Fulton, GA	7.8
21	37	New York, NY	13.4	18	36	Santa Clara, CA	0.7	3	37	Harris, TX	7.7
13	38	Clark, NV	12.5	34	36	Travis, TX	0.7	34	37	Travis, TX	7.7
65	38	Macomb, MI	12.5	43	36	Fulton, GA	0.7	37	39	Salt Lake, UT	7.1
20	40	Alameda, CA	12.0	46	36	St. Louis, MO	0.7	50	40	Westchester, NY	7.0
30	40	Nassau, NY	12.0	49	36	Pinellas, FL	0.7	74	40	Baltimore, MD	7.0
24	42	Sacramento, CA	11.7	58	36	Gwinnett, GA	0.7	8	42	Dallas, TX	6.7
54	43	Fairfield, CT	11.6	75	36	Hamilton, OH	0.7	40	43	Mecklenburg, NC	6.5
49	44	Pinellas, FL	11.3	1	44	Los Angeles, CA	0.6	29	44	Orange, FL	6.4
38	45	Fairfax, VA	10.5	6	44	Orange, CA	0.6	15	45	Tarrant, TX	6.3
67	46	Denton, TX	10.4	9	44	Kings, NY	0.6	54	45	Fairfield, CT	6.3
45	47	Collin, TX	10.3	16	44	Bexar, TX	0.6	52	47	Duval, FL	6.0
73	48	Montgomery, PA	10.2	27	44	Hillsborough, FL	0.6	31	48	Franklin, OH	5.9
72	49	Middlesex, NJ	10.1	28	44	Bronx, NY	0.6	62	48	Hartford, CT	5.9
39	50	Contra Costa, CA	10.0	29	44	Orange, FL	0.6	61	50	Kern, CA	5.6
63	51	Pierce, WA	9.4	35	44	Cuyahoga, OH	0.6	71	51	Worcester, MA	5.5
14	52	San Bernardino, CA	9.1	38	44	Fairfax, VA	0.6	4	52	Maricopa, AZ	5.2
1	53	Los Angeles, CA	8.7	42	44	Montgomery, MD	0.6	60	53	Prince George's, MD	5.1
34	53	Travis, TX	8.7	56	44	Shelby, TN	0.6	46	54	St. Louis, MO	5.0
16	55	Bexar, TX	7.9	62	44	Hartford, CT	0.6	27	55	Hillsborough, FL	4.9
26	55	Suffolk, NY	7.9	68	44	New Haven, CT	0.6	53	56	Milwaukee, WI	4.8
12	57	King, WA	7.8	71	44	Worcester, MA	0.6	68	56	New Haven, CT	4.8
10	58	Riverside, CA	7.0	2	58	Cook, IL	0.5	17	58	Broward, FL	4.6
4	59	Maricopa, AZ	6.2	3	58	Harris, TX	0.5	26	58	Suffolk, NY	4.6
55	60	Bergen, NJ	6.0	17	58	Broward, FL	0.5	65	58	Macomb, MI	4.6
64	60	San Francisco, CA	6.0	21	58	New York, NY	0.5	28	61	Bronx, NY	4.3
61	62	Kern, CA	5.9	26	58	Suffolk, NY	0.5	36	61	Allegheny, PA	4.3
22	63	Middlesex, MA	5.8	36	58	Allegheny, PA	0.5	49	63	Pinellas, FL	4.2
5	64	San Diego, CA	5.7	70	58	El Paso, TX	0.5	59	63	Erie, NY	4.2
57	65	Du Page, IL	5.5	72	58	Middlesex, NJ	0.5	19	65	Wayne, MI	4.0
47	66	Fresno, CA	5.3	22	66	Middlesex, MA	0.4	44	66	Pima, AZ	3.9
71	66	Worcester, MA	5.3	25	66	Palm Beach, FL	0.4	35	67	Cuyahoga, OH	3.7
44	68	Pima, AZ	4.1	30	66	Nassau, NY	0.4	51	67	Marion, IN	3.7
48	69	Honolulu, HI	3.6	50	66	Westchester, NY	0.4	16	69	Bexar, TX	3.6
70	70	El Paso, TX	3.5	54	66	Fairfield, CT	0.4	25	70	Palm Beach, FL	3.4
18	71	Santa Clara, CA	3.0	57	66	Du Page, IL	0.4	75	71	Hamilton, OH	3.2
37	72	Salt Lake, UT	2.2	73	66	Montgomery, PA	0.4	56	72	Shelby, TN	3.1
69	72	Ventura, CA	2.2	55	73	Bergen, NJ	0.3	7	73	Miami-Dade, FL	1.9
6	74	Orange, CA	2.1	7	74	Miami-Dade, FL	0.2	70	74	El Paso, TX	1.7
66	75	Hidalgo, TX	0.5	66	75	Hidalgo, TX	0.1	66	75	Hidalgo, TX	1.0

75 Largest Counties by 2018 Population
Selected Rankings

Percent Hispanic or Latino,[1] 2018				Percent under 18 years old, 2018				Percent 65 years old and over, 2018			
Popu-lation rank	Hispanic or Latino rank	County	Percent Hispanic or Latino [col 9]	Popu-lation rank	Under 18 years old rank	County	Percent under 18 years old [cols 10 and 11]	Popu-lation rank	65 years old and over rank	County	Percent 65 years old and over [cols 17 and 18]
66	1	Hidalgo, TX	91.8	66	1	Hidalgo, TX	33.3	49	1	Pinellas, FL	23.8
70	2	El Paso, TX	82.2	61	2	Kern, CA	29.2	25	2	Palm Beach, FL	23.3
7	3	Miami-Dade, FL	67.7	47	3	Fresno, CA	28.7	44	3	Pima, AZ	19.1
16	4	Bexar, TX	59.9	37	4	Salt Lake, UT	27.9	36	4	Allegheny, PA	18.0
28	5	Bronx, NY	56.0	70	5	El Paso, TX	27.7	46	5	St. Louis, MO	17.3
14	6	San Bernardino, CA	52.8	58	6	Gwinnett, GA	27.4	73	6	Montgomery, PA	17.2
47	6	Fresno, CA	52.8	3	7	Harris, TX	27.0	30	7	Nassau, NY	17.1
61	6	Kern, CA	52.8	14	8	San Bernardino, CA	26.8	35	7	Cuyahoga, OH	17.1
1	9	Los Angeles, CA	48.5	8	8	Dallas, TX	26.7	59	7	Erie, NY	17.1
10	10	Riverside, CA	48.4	15	9	Tarrant, TX	26.7	48	10	Honolulu, HI	16.6
69	11	Ventura, CA	42.5	45	9	Collin, TX	26.7	55	11	Bergen, NJ	16.5
3	12	Harris, TX	42.4	16	12	Bexar, TX	26.0	74	11	Baltimore, MD	16.5
8	13	Dallas, TX	39.9	10	13	Riverside, CA	25.7	62	13	Hartford, CT	16.3
44	14	Pima, AZ	36.8	67	14	Denton, TX	25.5	65	14	Macomb, MI	16.2
6	15	Orange, CA	34.3	28	15	Bronx, NY	25.3	68	14	New Haven, CT	16.2
34	16	Travis, TX	33.8	56	16	Shelby, TN	25.2	50	16	Westchester, NY	16.1
5	17	San Diego, CA	33.5	51	17	Marion, IN	24.9	17	17	Broward, FL	16.0
13	18	Clark, NV	30.9	4	18	Maricopa, AZ	24.5	26	17	Suffolk, NY	16.0
4	19	Maricopa, AZ	30.7	41	18	Wake, NC	24.5	7	19	Miami-Dade, FL	15.9
29	20	Orange, FL	30.5	53	20	Milwaukee, WI	24.3	33	19	Oakland, MI	15.9
17	21	Broward, FL	28.7	40	21	Mecklenburg, NC	24.2	39	21	Contra Costa, CA	15.0
15	22	Tarrant, TX	28.4	19	22	Wayne, MI	24.0	21	22	New York, NY	14.9
11	23	Queens, NY	28.0	24	22	Sacramento, CA	24.0	71	22	Worcester, MA	14.9
27	24	Hillsborough, FL	27.6	38	24	Fairfax, VA	23.8	54	24	Fairfield, CT	14.8
21	25	New York, NY	26.0	63	25	Pierce, WA	23.7	64	24	San Francisco, CA	14.8
18	26	Santa Clara, CA	25.9	31	26	Franklin, OH	23.6	75	26	Hamilton, OH	14.7
39	27	Contra Costa, CA	25.4	13	27	Clark, NV	23.5	4	27	Maricopa, AZ	14.6
2	28	Cook, IL	25.3	69	27	Ventura, CA	23.5	22	27	Middlesex, MA	14.6
50	29	Westchester, NY	24.4	42	29	Montgomery, MD	23.4	42	27	Montgomery, MD	14.6
24	30	Sacramento, CA	23.0	75	30	Hamilton, OH	23.3	69	27	Ventura, CA	14.6
20	31	Alameda, CA	22.5	9	31	Kings, NY	23.2	19	31	Wayne, MI	14.4
25	32	Palm Beach, FL	21.5	39	32	Contra Costa, CA	23.1	57	31	Du Page, IL	14.4
58	33	Gwinnett, GA	20.8	54	32	Fairfield, CT	23.1	11	33	Queens, NY	14.2
72	34	Middlesex, NJ	20.7	27	34	Hillsborough, FL	23.0	72	33	Middlesex, NJ	14.2
54	35	Fairfield, CT	19.4	57	34	Du Page, IL	23.0	13	35	Clark, NV	14.1
55	35	Bergen, NJ	19.4	43	36	Fulton, GA	22.7	6	36	Orange, CA	13.9
9	37	Kings, NY	19.2	18	37	Santa Clara, CA	22.6	10	36	Riverside, CA	13.9
67	37	Denton, TX	19.2	52	37	Duval, FL	22.6	27	38	Hillsborough, FL	13.7
42	39	Montgomery, MD	19.1	6	39	Orange, CA	22.5	24	39	Sacramento, CA	13.6
26	40	Suffolk, NY	19.0	29	39	Orange, FL	22.5	2	40	Cook, IL	13.5
37	41	Salt Lake, UT	18.1	34	39	Travis, TX	22.5	52	40	Duval, FL	13.5
60	42	Prince George's, MD	17.8	50	39	Westchester, NY	22.5	5	42	San Diego, CA	13.4
62	43	Hartford, CT	17.6	60	39	Prince George's, MD	22.5	63	43	Pierce, WA	13.3
68	43	New Haven, CT	17.6	2	45	Cook, IL	22.3	32	44	Hennepin, MN	13.2
30	45	Nassau, NY	16.8	1	45	Los Angeles, CA	22.2	20	45	Alameda, CA	13.0
38	46	Fairfax, VA	16.1	32	45	Hennepin, MN	22.2	1	46	Los Angeles, CA	12.9
64	47	San Francisco, CA	15.2	46	45	St. Louis, MO	22.2	18	47	Santa Clara, CA	12.8
45	48	Collin, TX	15.1	23	48	Philadelphia, PA	22.0	23	47	Philadelphia, PA	12.8
53	49	Milwaukee, WI	14.8	5	49	San Diego, CA	21.9	9	49	Kings, NY	12.7
23	50	Philadelphia, PA	14.4	72	50	Middlesex, NJ	21.8	12	49	King, WA	12.7
57	51	Du Page, IL	14.3	26	51	Suffolk, NY	21.7	53	49	Milwaukee, WI	12.7
40	52	Mecklenburg, NC	13.0	30	51	Nassau, NY	21.7	56	52	Shelby, TN	12.5
71	53	Worcester, MA	11.0	73	51	Montgomery, PA	21.7	38	53	Fairfax, VA	12.4
63	54	Pierce, WA	10.6	74	54	Baltimore, MD	21.6	60	54	Prince George's, MD	12.3
51	55	Marion, IN	10.2	33	55	Oakland, MI	21.5	47	55	Fresno, CA	11.9
41	56	Wake, NC	10.0	55	55	Bergen, NJ	21.5	70	55	El Paso, TX	11.9
48	57	Honolulu, HI	9.7	65	55	Macomb, MI	21.5	28	57	Bronx, NY	11.8
12	58	King, WA	9.5	71	55	Worcester, MA	21.5	51	57	Marion, IN	11.8
49	59	Pinellas, FL	9.3	44	59	Pima, AZ	21.4	16	59	Bexar, TX	11.7
52	60	Duval, FL	9.2	48	59	Honolulu, HI	21.4	29	60	Orange, FL	11.3
22	61	Middlesex, MA	7.9	62	59	Hartford, CT	21.4	31	60	Franklin, OH	11.3
43	62	Fulton, GA	7.3	17	62	Broward, FL	21.3	14	62	San Bernardino, CA	11.1
32	63	Hennepin, MN	6.9	35	63	Cuyahoga, OH	21.2	43	63	Fulton, GA	11.0
56	64	Shelby, TN	6.1	20	64	Alameda, CA	20.9	66	63	Hidalgo, TX	11.0
19	65	Wayne, MI	5.8	12	65	King, WA	20.6	15	65	Tarrant, TX	10.8
35	66	Cuyahoga, OH	5.7	68	65	New Haven, CT	20.6	40	66	Mecklenburg, NC	10.6
31	67	Franklin, OH	5.3	59	67	Erie, NY	20.5	41	66	Wake, NC	10.6
59	67	Erie, NY	5.3	11	68	Queens, NY	20.4	45	68	Collin, TX	10.5
74	67	Baltimore, MD	5.3	7	69	Miami-Dade, FL	20.3	61	69	Kern, CA	10.4
73	70	Montgomery, PA	5.0	22	69	Middlesex, MA	20.3	8	70	Dallas, TX	10.1
33	71	Oakland, MI	3.9	25	71	Palm Beach, FL	19.4	37	70	Salt Lake, UT	10.1
75	72	Hamilton, OH	3.1	36	72	Allegheny, PA	18.9	3	72	Harris, TX	9.8
46	73	St. Louis, MO	2.8	49	73	Pinellas, FL	16.7	67	73	Denton, TX	9.4
65	74	Macomb, MI	2.5	21	74	New York, NY	14.6	58	74	Gwinnett, GA	9.3
36	75	Allegheny, PA	2.0	64	75	San Francisco, CA	13.6	34	75	Travis, TX	9.0

75 Largest Counties by 2018 Population
Selected Rankings

Percent female-headed family households, 2013–2017				Birth rate, 2018				Percent under 65 who have no health insurance, 2017			
Popu-lation rank	Female households rank	County	Percent female households [col 30]	Popu-lation rank	Live birth rate rank	County	Birth rate [col 36]	Popu-lation rank	No health insurance rank	County	Percent with no health insurance [col 40]
28	1	Bronx, NY	30.4	66	1	Hidalgo, TX	16.8	66	1	Hidalgo, TX	29.7
66	2	Hidalgo, TX	21.8	8	2	Dallas, TX	15.2	8	2	Dallas, TX	21.6
56	3	Shelby, TN	20.3	9	2	Kings, NY	15.2	70	3	El Paso, TX	21.2
23	4	Philadelphia, PA	19.7	37	4	Salt Lake, UT	15.0	3	4	Harris, TX	20.7
60	4	Prince George's, MD	19.7	61	4	Kern, CA	15.0	7	5	Miami-Dade, FL	19.4
70	6	El Paso, TX	19.2	3	6	Harris, TX	14.9	15	6	Tarrant, TX	17.0
19	7	Wayne, MI	19.0	47	6	Fresno, CA	14.9	58	7	Gwinnett, GA	16.7
9	8	Kings, NY	18.6	70	8	El Paso, TX	14.8	16	8	Bexar, TX	16.6
7	9	Miami-Dade, FL	18.2	51	9	Marion, IN	14.7	25	9	Palm Beach, FL	16.3
47	10	Fresno, CA	17.7	31	10	Franklin, OH	14.3	17	10	Broward, FL	15.3
14	11	San Bernardino, CA	17.1	28	11	Bronx, NY	14.2	34	11	Travis, TX	15.2
53	12	Milwaukee, WI	16.6	14	12	San Bernardino, CA	14.0	29	12	Orange, FL	14.9
61	13	Kern, CA	16.5	16	13	Bexar, TX	13.9	27	13	Hillsborough, FL	14.0
16	14	Bexar, TX	16.2	53	13	Milwaukee, WI	13.9	49	14	Pinellas, FL	13.9
8	15	Dallas, TX	16.0	52	15	Duval, FL	13.8	13	15	Clark, NV	13.5
11	16	Queens, NY	15.9	15	16	Tarrant, TX	13.7	43	16	Fulton, GA	13.0
35	17	Cuyahoga, OH	15.8	56	16	Shelby, TN	13.7	52	17	Duval, FL	12.8
51	18	Marion, IN	15.7	40	18	Mecklenburg, NC	13.5	40	18	Mecklenburg, NC	12.1
3	19	Harris, TX	15.6	23	19	Philadelphia, PA	13.3	4	19	Maricopa, AZ	11.7
17	19	Broward, FL	15.6	60	20	Prince George's, MD	13.2	56	20	Shelby, TN	11.6
52	19	Duval, FL	15.6	63	20	Pierce, WA	13.2	67	20	Denton, TX	11.6
29	22	Orange, FL	15.3	32	22	Hennepin, MN	13.0	11	22	Queens, NY	11.3
1	23	Los Angeles, CA	15.2	75	22	Pima, AZ	13.0	44	23	Pima, AZ	11.0
75	24	Hamilton, OH	14.9	11	24	Queens, NY	12.8	37	24	Salt Lake, UT	10.9
24	25	Sacramento, CA	14.6	19	24	Wayne, MI	12.8	45	25	Collin, TX	10.8
2	26	Cook, IL	14.5	34	26	Travis, TX	12.6	60	25	Prince George's, MD	10.8
74	26	Baltimore, MD	14.5	48	26	Honolulu, HI	12.6	1	27	Los Angeles, CA	10.7
15	28	Tarrant, TX	14.1	5	28	San Diego, CA	12.5	51	28	Marion, IN	10.6
31	28	Franklin, OH	14.1	24	28	Sacramento, CA	12.5	10	29	Riverside, CA	9.8
62	28	Hartford, CT	14.1	10	30	Riverside, CA	12.4	23	30	Philadelphia, PA	9.7
27	31	Hillsborough, FL	14.0	2	31	Cook, IL	12.3	69	30	Ventura, CA	9.7
43	31	Fulton, GA	14.0	58	31	Gwinnett, GA	12.3	2	32	Cook, IL	9.4
58	31	Gwinnett, GA	14.0	4	33	Maricopa, AZ	12.2	28	32	Bronx, NY	9.4
46	34	St. Louis, MO	13.9	13	33	Clark, NV	12.2	47	32	Fresno, CA	9.4
13	35	Clark, NV	13.8	38	35	Fairfax, VA	12.1	38	35	Fairfax, VA	9.3
68	35	New Haven, CT	13.8	43	35	Fulton, GA	12.1	41	36	Wake, NC	9.2
40	37	Mecklenburg, NC	13.7	27	37	Hillsborough, FL	12.0	14	37	San Bernardino, CA	9.1
65	38	Macomb, MI	13.4	29	37	Orange, FL	12.0	9	38	Kings, NY	8.8
59	39	Erie, NY	13.3	42	37	Montgomery, MD	12.0	72	39	Middlesex, NJ	8.7
10	40	Riverside, CA	13.2	67	40	Denton, TX	11.9	55	40	Bergen, NJ	8.5
44	41	Pima, AZ	12.9	1	41	Los Angeles, CA	11.8	6	41	Orange, CA	8.2
50	42	Westchester, NY	12.4	12	42	King, WA	11.7	5	42	San Diego, CA	8.1
4	43	Maricopa, AZ	12.3	41	42	Wake, NC	11.7	46	42	St. Louis, MO	8.1
39	43	Contra Costa, CA	12.3	6	44	Orange, CA	11.6	61	42	Kern, CA	8.1
48	43	Honolulu, HI	12.3	74	44	Baltimore, MD	11.6	31	45	Franklin, OH	7.9
69	46	Ventura, CA	12.2	18	46	Santa Clara, CA	11.5	54	45	Fairfield, CT	7.9
54	47	Fairfield, CT	12.1	20	46	Alameda, CA	11.5	53	47	Milwaukee, WI	7.8
71	47	Worcester, MA	12.1	35	46	Cuyahoga, OH	11.5	50	48	Westchester, NY	7.7
5	49	San Diego, CA	12.0	7	49	Miami-Dade, FL	11.3	42	49	Montgomery, MD	7.4
				46	49	St. Louis, MO	11.3	19	50	Wayne, MI	7.1
6	50	Orange, CA	11.9	57	49	Du Page, IL	11.3	63	51	Pierce, WA	6.5
20	50	Alameda, CA	11.9	17	52	Broward, FL	11.2	74	51	Baltimore, MD	6.5
25	52	Palm Beach, FL	11.8	45	53	Collin, TX	11.1	21	53	New York, NY	6.3
72	52	Middlesex, NJ	11.8	69	54	Ventura, CA	11.0	35	53	Cuyahoga, OH	6.3
63	54	Pierce, WA	11.6	72	55	Middlesex, NJ	10.9	65	55	Macomb, MI	6.2
30	55	Nassau, NY	11.4	44	56	Pima, AZ	10.8	75	55	Hamilton, OH	6.2
26	56	Suffolk, NY	11.3	33	57	Oakland, MI	10.6	26	57	Suffolk, NY	6.0
42	56	Montgomery, MD	11.3	59	57	Erie, NY	10.6	39	58	Contra Costa, CA	5.9
21	58	New York, NY	11.2	65	57	Macomb, MI	10.6	24	59	Sacramento, CA	5.8
41	58	Wake, NC	11.2	36	60	Allegheny, PA	10.5	57	59	Du Page, IL	5.8
36	60	Allegheny, PA	11.1								
55	61	Bergen, NJ	11.0	39	60	Contra Costa, CA	10.5	12	61	King, WA	5.6
67	61	Denton, TX	11.0	21	62	New York, NY	10.4	68	61	New Haven, CT	5.6
49	63	Pinellas, FL	10.7	22	62	Middlesex, MA	10.4	20	63	Alameda, CA	5.3
37	64	Salt Lake, UT	10.5	30	62	Nassau, NY	10.4	33	64	Oakland, MI	5.2
18	65	Santa Clara, CA	10.2	50	62	Westchester, NY	10.4	18	65	Santa Clara, CA	5.1
34	65	Travis, TX	10.2	26	66	Suffolk, NY	10.3	30	66	Nassau, NY	5.0
33	67	Oakland, MI	10.1	54	66	Fairfield, CT	10.3	32	66	Hennepin, MN	5.0
45	67	Collin, TX	10.1	62	66	Hartford, CT	10.3	62	66	Hartford, CT	5.0
22	69	Middlesex, MA	9.7	71	66	Worcester, MA	10.3	36	69	Allegheny, PA	4.9
				73	66	Montgomery, PA	10.3	64	70	San Francisco, CA	4.7
73	70	Montgomery, PA	9.5								
32	71	Hennepin, MN	9.4	64	71	San Francisco, CA	10.1	73	71	Montgomery, PA	4.6
38	72	Fairfax, VA	9.2	68	71	New Haven, CT	10.1	59	72	Erie, NY	4.5
57	73	Du Page, IL	9.1	25	73	Palm Beach, FL	9.9	48	73	Honolulu, HI	3.8
12	74	King, WA	8.6	55	73	Bergen, NJ	9.9	71	74	Worcester, MA	2.8
64	75	San Francisco, CA	8.1	49	75	Pinellas, FL	8.4	22	75	Middlesex, MA	2.7

75 Largest Counties by 2018 Population
Selected Rankings

Percent college graduates (bachelor's degree or more), 2013–2017				Expenditures per student, 2014–2015				Per capita personal income, 2017			
Population rank	College graduates rank	County	Percent college graduates [col 51]	Population rank	Expenditures rank	County	Expenditures per student (dollars) [col 53]	Population rank	Per capita income rank	County	Per capita income (dollars) [col 64]
21	1	New York, NY	60.7	30	1	Nassau, NY	25,265	21	1	New York, NY	175,960
38	1	Fairfax, VA	60.7	50	2	Westchester, NY	24,510	64	2	San Francisco, CA	119,868
42	3	Montgomery, MD	58.3	26	3	Suffolk, NY	23,116	54	3	Fairfield, CT	110,104
64	4	San Francisco, CA	55.8	21	4	New York, NY	21,491	50	4	Westchester, NY	101,542
22	5	Middlesex, MA	54.1	9	4	Kings, NY	21,491	18	5	Santa Clara, CA	98,032
41	6	Wake, NC	51.0	11	4	Queens, NY	21,491	42	6	Montgomery, MD	86,136
45	7	Collin, TX	50.9	28	4	Bronx, NY	21,491	30	7	Nassau, NY	84,763
12	8	King, WA	50.3	55	8	Bergen, NJ	18,915	12	8	King, WA	83,383
43	9	Fulton, GA	50.2	54	9	Fairfield, CT	18,477	55	9	Bergen, NJ	81,203
18	10	Santa Clara, CA	50.0	62	10	Hartford, CT	18,418	22	10	Middlesex, MA	79,214
32	11	Hennepin, MN	48.2	68	11	New Haven, CT	17,877	43	11	Fulton, GA	78,794
73	11	Montgomery, PA	48.2	73	12	Montgomery, PA	17,363	38	12	Fairfax, VA	78,376
57	13	Du Page, IL	48.0	72	13	Middlesex, NJ	16,718	73	13	Montgomery, PA	77,207
55	14	Bergen, NJ	47.9	36	14	Allegheny, PA	16,405	39	14	Contra Costa, CA	76,527
50	15	Westchester, NY	47.7	22	15	Middlesex, MA	16,365	25	15	Palm Beach, FL	74,754
34	16	Travis, TX	47.5	59	16	Erie, NY	15,999	20	16	Alameda, CA	71,282
54	17	Fairfield, CT	46.5	57	17	Du Page, IL	15,987	32	17	Hennepin, MN	71,067
33	18	Oakland, MI	45.7	2	18	Cook, IL	15,259	57	18	Du Page, IL	69,323
20	19	Alameda, CA	44.7	42	19	Montgomery, MD	15,152	33	19	Oakland, MI	68,971
30	20	Nassau, NY	44.4	60	20	Prince George's, MD	14,531	46	20	St. Louis, MO	67,029
40	21	Mecklenburg, NC	44.1	71	21	Worcester, MA	14,137	26	21	Suffolk, NY	65,758
67	22	Denton, TX	43.4	35	22	Cuyahoga, OH	13,888	6	22	Orange, CA	65,400
46	23	St. Louis, MO	42.8	38	23	Fairfax, VA	13,752	45	23	Collin, TX	64,025
72	24	Middlesex, NJ	42.0	46	24	St. Louis, MO	13,495	34	24	Travis, TX	62,205
39	25	Contra Costa, CA	40.7	74	25	Baltimore, MD	13,424	62	25	Hartford, CT	61,664
36	26	Allegheny, PA	40.0	64	26	San Francisco, CA	13,154	2	26	Cook, IL	59,238
6	27	Orange, CA	39.1	23	27	Philadelphia, PA	13,148	69	27	Ventura, CA	59,178
31	28	Franklin, OH	38.7	32	28	Hennepin, MN	13,096	74	28	Baltimore, MD	59,130
74	29	Baltimore, MD	37.8	48	29	Honolulu, HI	12,855	1	29	Los Angeles, CA	58,419
5	30	San Diego, CA	37.4	75	30	Hamilton, OH	12,492	36	30	Allegheny, PA	58,146
62	30	Hartford, CT	37.4	31	31	Franklin, OH	11,890	5	31	San Diego, CA	57,913
2	32	Cook, IL	37.2	33	32	Oakland, MI	11,787	72	32	Middlesex, NJ	57,598
75	33	Hamilton, OH	36.3	53	33	Milwaukee, WI	11,237	40	33	Mecklenburg, NC	57,368
58	34	Gwinnett, GA	35.3	19	34	Wayne, MI	11,190	75	34	Hamilton, OH	56,931
71	34	Worcester, MA	35.3	12	35	King, WA	11,167	48	35	Honolulu, HI	56,728
9	36	Kings, NY	35.2	1	36	Los Angeles, CA	11,138	41	36	Wake, NC	56,162
26	37	Suffolk, NY	35.0	43	37	Fulton, GA	10,922	8	37	Dallas, TX	55,859
25	38	Palm Beach, FL	34.8	65	37	Macomb, MI	10,922	23	38	Philadelphia, PA	55,718
68	39	New Haven, CT	34.6	47	39	Fresno, CA	10,858	71	39	Worcester, MA	54,891
48	40	Honolulu, HI	34.0	18	40	Santa Clara, CA	10,659	68	40	New Haven, CT	54,543
37	41	Salt Lake, UT	33.6	63	41	Pierce, WA	10,609	67	41	Denton, TX	53,948
59	42	Erie, NY	32.9	61	42	Kern, CA	10,493	3	42	Harris, TX	53,188
29	43	Orange, FL	32.7	51	43	Marion, IN	10,297	35	43	Cuyahoga, OH	52,783
69	44	Ventura, CA	32.6	24	44	Sacramento, CA	10,043	51	44	Marion, IN	50,957
27	45	Hillsborough, FL	32.0	10	45	Riverside, CA	10,012	49	45	Pinellas, FL	50,630
60	46	Prince George's, MD	31.9	5	46	San Diego, CA	9,905	24	46	Sacramento, CA	50,197
44	47	Pima, AZ	31.6	69	47	Ventura, CA	9,881	31	47	Franklin, OH	49,448
17	48	Broward, FL	31.5	39	48	Contra Costa, CA	9,861	37	48	Salt Lake, UT	49,445
35	48	Cuyahoga, OH	31.5	20	49	Alameda, CA	9,819	59	49	Erie, NY	49,330
4	50	Maricopa, AZ	31.4	14	50	San Bernardino, CA	9,801	63	50	Pierce, WA	49,214
1	51	Los Angeles, CA	31.2	6	51	Orange, CA	9,691	9	51	Kings, NY	48,758
15	52	Tarrant, TX	31.1	56	52	Shelby, TN	9,610	17	52	Broward, FL	48,680
11	53	Queens, NY	30.8	66	53	Hidalgo, TX	9,531	56	53	Shelby, TN	47,655
56	54	Shelby, TN	30.6	34	54	Travis, TX	9,390	15	54	Tarrant, TX	47,525
3	55	Harris, TX	30.5	25	55	Palm Beach, FL	9,283	60	55	Prince George's, MD	47,365
8	56	Dallas, TX	30.1	27	56	Hillsborough, FL	9,201	11	56	Queens, NY	46,829
49	56	Pinellas, FL	30.1	58	57	Gwinnett, GA	9,148	7	57	Miami-Dade, FL	46,048
53	56	Milwaukee, WI	30.1	70	58	El Paso, TX	9,134	4	58	Maricopa, AZ	45,573
24	59	Sacramento, CA	29.9	49	59	Pinellas, FL	9,065	53	59	Milwaukee, WI	45,099
51	60	Marion, IN	29.7	16	60	Bexar, TX	9,064	65	60	Macomb, MI	44,850
52	61	Duval, FL	28.7	29	61	Orange, FL	8,972	27	61	Hillsborough, FL	44,709
7	62	Miami-Dade, FL	27.8	8	62	Dallas, TX	8,876	52	62	Duval, FL	44,347
16	63	Bexar, TX	27.3	7	63	Miami-Dade, FL	8,871	13	63	Clark, NV	44,217
23	64	Philadelphia, PA	27.1	17	64	Broward, FL	8,704	16	64	Bexar, TX	43,798
63	65	Pierce, WA	26.0	52	65	Duval, FL	8,657	29	65	Orange, FL	42,541
65	66	Macomb, MI	24.2	3	66	Harris, TX	8,654	19	66	Wayne, MI	41,704
13	67	Clark, NV	23.3	40	67	Mecklenburg, NC	8,582	44	67	Pima, AZ	41,637
19	68	Wayne, MI	22.8	15	68	Tarrant, TX	8,491	47	68	Fresno, CA	41,470
70	69	El Paso, TX	22.2	67	69	Denton, TX	8,397	58	69	Gwinnett, GA	39,856
10	70	Riverside, CA	21.5	45	70	Collin, TX	8,259	10	70	Riverside, CA	39,261
47	71	Fresno, CA	20.1	13	71	Clark, NV	8,254	14	71	San Bernardino, CA	38,816
14	72	San Bernardino, CA	19.8	41	72	Wake, NC	8,145	61	72	Kern, CA	38,560
28	73	Bronx, NY	19.4	44	73	Pima, AZ	7,581	28	73	Bronx, NY	35,564
66	74	Hidalgo, TX	17.8	4	74	Maricopa, AZ	7,291	70	74	El Paso, TX	34,582
61	75	Kern, CA	15.8	37	75	Salt Lake, UT	6,696	66	75	Hidalgo, TX	25,617

75 Largest Counties by 2018 Population
Selected Rankings

Median household income, 2017				Median value of owner-occupied housing units, 2013–2017				Median gross rent of renter-occupied housing units, 2013–2017			
Population rank	Median income rank	County	Median income (dollars) [col 58]	Population rank	Median value rank	County	Median value (dollars) [col 91]	Population rank	Median rent rank	County	Median rent (dollars) [col 94]
18	1	Santa Clara, CA	118,468	64	1	San Francisco, CA	927,400	18	1	Santa Clara, CA	1,955
38	2	Fairfax, VA	117,989	21	2	New York, NY	915,300	38	2	Fairfax, VA	1,823
64	3	San Francisco, CA	109,601	18	3	Santa Clara, CA	829,600	64	3	San Francisco, CA	1,709
30	4	Nassau, NY	107,465	20	4	Alameda, CA	649,100	6	4	Orange, CA	1,693
42	5	Montgomery, MD	102,944	48	5	Honolulu, HI	626,400	42	5	Montgomery, MD	1,693
22	6	Middlesex, MA	97,851	9	6	Kings, NY	623,900	30	6	Nassau, NY	1,663
20	7	Alameda, CA	95,550	6	7	Orange, CA	620,500	48	7	Honolulu, HI	1,653
45	8	Collin, TX	95,394	38	8	Fairfax, VA	534,800	26	8	Suffolk, NY	1,646
39	9	Contra Costa, CA	95,062	39	9	Contra Costa, CA	522,300	69	9	Ventura, CA	1,643
26	10	Suffolk, NY	94,108	69	10	Ventura, CA	520,300	21	10	New York, NY	1,615
55	11	Bergen, NJ	93,805	50	11	Westchester, NY	513,300	39	11	Contra Costa, CA	1,600
54	12	Fairfield, CT	91,170	1	12	Los Angeles, CA	495,800	20	12	Alameda, CA	1,547
50	13	Westchester, NY	90,483	5	13	San Diego, CA	484,900	5	13	San Diego, CA	1,467
57	14	Du Page, IL	89,536	11	14	Queens, NY	481,300	11	14	Queens, NY	1,456
12	15	King, WA	89,519	42	15	Montgomery, MD	467,500	22	15	Middlesex, MA	1,455
73	16	Montgomery, PA	87,338	30	16	Nassau, NY	460,700	50	16	Westchester, NY	1,444
67	17	Denton, TX	86,462	22	17	Middlesex, MA	453,300	54	17	Fairfield, CT	1,439
6	18	Orange, CA	86,031	55	18	Bergen, NJ	451,200	55	18	Bergen, NJ	1,419
72	19	Middlesex, NJ	85,187	12	19	King, WA	446,600	60	19	Prince George's, MD	1,385
21	20	New York, NY	84,133	54	20	Fairfield, CT	417,800	72	20	Middlesex, NJ	1,384
69	21	Ventura, CA	82,436	26	21	Suffolk, NY	379,400	12	21	King, WA	1,379
48	22	Honolulu, HI	80,947	28	22	Bronx, NY	371,800	1	22	Los Angeles, CA	1,322
60	23	Prince George's, MD	80,858	72	23	Middlesex, NJ	329,000	9	23	Kings, NY	1,314
41	24	Wake, NC	77,641	10	24	Riverside, CA	304,500	17	24	Broward, FL	1,271
33	25	Oakland, MI	77,558	24	25	Sacramento, CA	299,900	25	25	Palm Beach, FL	1,264
5	26	San Diego, CA	76,048	73	26	Montgomery, PA	299,300	10	26	Riverside, CA	1,251
32	27	Hennepin, MN	74,568	57	27	Du Page, IL	289,900	45	27	Collin, TX	1,225
74	28	Baltimore, MD	73,309	14	28	San Bernardino, CA	280,200	57	28	Du Page, IL	1,224
34	29	Travis, TX	72,785	34	29	Travis, TX	275,800	74	28	Baltimore, MD	1,224
37	30	Salt Lake, UT	71,396	60	30	Prince George's, MD	272,900	73	30	Montgomery, PA	1,211
62	31	Hartford, CT	70,433	43	31	Fulton, GA	268,900	7	31	Miami-Dade, FL	1,195
71	32	Worcester, MA	70,222	45	32	Collin, TX	265,300	14	32	San Bernardino, CA	1,182
63	33	Pierce, WA	69,027	71	33	Worcester, MA	260,800	34	33	Travis, TX	1,172
58	34	Gwinnett, GA	68,957	37	34	Salt Lake, UT	260,700	58	34	Gwinnett, GA	1,142
68	35	New Haven, CT	66,764	63	35	Pierce, WA	255,800	28	35	Bronx, NY	1,133
40	36	Mecklenburg, NC	65,750	41	36	Wake, NC	250,700	24	36	Sacramento, CA	1,122
15	37	Tarrant, TX	65,021	74	37	Baltimore, MD	249,600	63	37	Pierce, WA	1,116
46	38	St. Louis, MO	64,926	32	38	Hennepin, MN	245,400	29	38	Orange, FL	1,109
1	39	Los Angeles, CA	64,912	68	39	New Haven, CT	244,400	67	38	Denton, TX	1,109
43	40	Fulton, GA	64,901	7	40	Miami-Dade, FL	242,800	68	40	New Haven, CT	1,100
11	41	Queens, NY	64,046	25	41	Palm Beach, FL	242,500	43	41	Fulton, GA	1,089
10	42	Riverside, CA	63,776	62	42	Hartford, CT	235,300	13	42	Clark, NV	1,048
24	43	Sacramento, CA	62,959	67	43	Denton, TX	232,000	2	43	Cook, IL	1,044
4	44	Maricopa, AZ	62,221	2	44	Cook, IL	227,400	62	43	Hartford, CT	1,044
2	45	Cook, IL	61,401	4	45	Maricopa, AZ	225,000	41	45	Wake, NC	1,043
65	46	Macomb, MI	60,475	17	46	Broward, FL	223,400	27	46	Hillsborough, FL	1,040
14	47	San Bernardino, CA	60,270	47	47	Fresno, CA	220,600	4	47	Maricopa, AZ	1,033
25	48	Palm Beach, FL	60,059	13	48	Clark, NV	212,300	40	48	Mecklenburg, NC	1,032
31	49	Franklin, OH	59,214	33	49	Oakland, MI	209,800	32	49	Hennepin, MN	1,031
3	50	Harris, TX	58,664	40	50	Mecklenburg, NC	203,900	37	50	Salt Lake, UT	1,015
36	51	Allegheny, PA	58,547	29	51	Orange, FL	192,400	49	51	Pinellas, FL	1,007
13	52	Clark, NV	57,217	61	52	Kern, CA	190,600	33	52	Oakland, MI	1,003
8	53	Dallas, TX	56,732	58	53	Gwinnett, GA	185,200	52	53	Duval, FL	991
17	54	Broward, FL	56,702	46	54	St. Louis, MO	181,100	15	54	Tarrant, TX	987
9	55	Kings, NY	56,548	27	55	Hillsborough, FL	179,500	71	54	Worcester, MA	987
59	56	Erie, NY	55,581	49	56	Pinellas, FL	167,100	8	56	Dallas, TX	984
75	57	Hamilton, OH	55,178	44	57	Pima, AZ	166,300	3	57	Harris, TX	976
27	58	Hillsborough, FL	54,741	31	58	Franklin, OH	158,400	23	58	Philadelphia, PA	970
16	59	Bexar, TX	54,163	15	59	Tarrant, TX	158,200	16	59	Bexar, TX	942
29	60	Orange, FL	54,021	52	60	Duval, FL	156,200	46	60	St. Louis, MO	937
52	61	Duval, FL	52,105	3	61	Harris, TX	154,100	61	61	Kern, CA	933
49	62	Pinellas, FL	51,488	23	62	Philadelphia, PA	151,500	47	62	Fresno, CA	931
47	63	Fresno, CA	51,452	53	63	Milwaukee, WI	150,300	65	63	Macomb, MI	916
44	64	Pima, AZ	51,392	8	64	Dallas, TX	148,300	31	64	Franklin, OH	903
61	65	Kern, CA	49,904	65	65	Macomb, MI	146,700	56	65	Shelby, TN	894
7	66	Miami-Dade, FL	49,758	75	66	Hamilton, OH	145,800	44	66	Pima, AZ	861
56	67	Shelby, TN	49,563	16	67	Bexar, TX	142,300	53	67	Milwaukee, WI	844
53	68	Milwaukee, WI	47,795	36	68	Allegheny, PA	140,600	51	68	Marion, IN	836
51	69	Marion, IN	47,642	59	69	Erie, NY	139,900	36	69	Allegheny, PA	835
35	70	Cuyahoga, OH	46,918	56	70	Shelby, TN	135,700	19	70	Wayne, MI	826
19	71	Wayne, MI	45,182	35	71	Cuyahoga, OH	123,900	70	71	El Paso, TX	790
70	72	El Paso, TX	44,120	51	72	Marion, IN	123,500	59	72	Erie, NY	778
23	73	Philadelphia, PA	40,193	70	73	El Paso, TX	116,600	35	73	Cuyahoga, OH	766
28	74	Bronx, NY	37,377	19	74	Wayne, MI	92,400	75	74	Hamilton, OH	749
66	75	Hidalgo, TX	36,978	66	75	Hidalgo, TX	82,400	66	75	Hidalgo, TX	699

75 Largest Counties by 2018 Population
Selected Rankings

Percent of population below the poverty level, 2017				Percent under 18 years old below the poverty level, 2017				Unemployment rate, 2018			
Population rank	Poverty rate rank	County	Poverty rate [col 59]	Population rank	Poverty rate for children rank	County	Poverty rate for children under 18 years [col 60]	Population rank	Unemployment rate rank	County	Unemployment rate [col 100]
66	1	Hidalgo, TX	29.5	66	1	Hidalgo, TX	41.3	61	1	Kern, CA	8.0
28	2	Bronx, NY	27.9	28	2	Bronx, NY	39.3	47	2	Fresno, CA	7.5
23	3	Philadelphia, PA	25.3	19	3	Wayne, MI	33.4	66	3	Hidalgo, TX	6.6
19	4	Wayne, MI	22.6	23	4	Philadelphia, PA	31.9	28	4	Bronx, NY	5.7
61	5	Kern, CA	21.2	70	5	El Paso, TX	29.6	23	5	Philadelphia, PA	5.5
47	6	Fresno, CA	21.1	56	6	Shelby, TN	29.2	19	6	Wayne, MI	5.2
70	7	El Paso, TX	21.0	61	7	Kern, CA	29.0	35	6	Cuyahoga, OH	5.2
9	8	Kings, NY	19.8	47	8	Fresno, CA	28.3	63	6	Pierce, WA	5.2
53	9	Milwaukee, WI	19.1	35	9	Cuyahoga, OH	27.1	13	9	Clark, NV	4.8
56	10	Shelby, TN	18.9	9	10	Kings, NY	26.7	1	10	Los Angeles, CA	4.7
35	11	Cuyahoga, OH	18.1	53	11	Milwaukee, WI	26.0	44	11	Pima, AZ	4.5
51	12	Marion, IN	17.6	75	12	Hamilton, OH	25.4	3	12	Harris, TX	4.4
7	13	Miami-Dade, FL	16.7	51	13	Marion, IN	25.0	10	12	Riverside, CA	4.4
44	14	Pima, AZ	16.6	21	14	New York, NY	23.4	59	12	Erie, NY	4.4
21	15	New York, NY	16.3	3	15	Harris, TX	23.2	68	12	New Haven, CT	4.4
75	16	Hamilton, OH	16.2	14	16	San Bernardino, CA	23.0	9	16	Kings, NY	4.2
14	17	San Bernardino, CA	16.0	52	16	Duval, FL	23.0	56	16	Shelby, TN	4.2
31	17	Franklin, OH	16.0	31	18	Franklin, OH	22.5	62	16	Hartford, CT	4.2
3	19	Harris, TX	15.9	44	18	Pima, AZ	22.5	70	16	El Paso, TX	4.2
16	20	Bexar, TX	15.6	16	20	Bexar, TX	22.2	4	20	Maricopa, AZ	4.1
27	21	Hillsborough, FL	15.5	8	21	Dallas, TX	22.1	60	20	Prince George's, MD	4.1
29	22	Orange, FL	15.3	7	22	Miami-Dade, FL	22.0	75	20	Hamilton, OH	4.1
52	23	Duval, FL	15.1	29	23	Orange, FL	21.9	2	23	Cook, IL	4.0
1	24	Los Angeles, CA	14.9	27	24	Hillsborough, FL	21.4	14	23	San Bernardino, CA	4.0
8	25	Dallas, TX	14.8	59	24	Erie, NY	21.4	36	23	Allegheny, PA	4.0
43	25	Fulton, GA	14.8	43	26	Fulton, GA	21.1	43	23	Fulton, GA	4.0
2	27	Cook, IL	14.6	1	27	Los Angeles, CA	20.9	54	23	Fairfield, CT	4.0
59	28	Erie, NY	14.5	2	28	Cook, IL	20.5	65	23	Macomb, MI	4.0
24	29	Sacramento, CA	14.1	13	28	Clark, NV	20.5	74	23	Baltimore, MD	4.0
13	30	Clark, NV	14.0	4	30	Maricopa, AZ	19.1	7	30	Miami-Dade, FL	3.9
4	31	Maricopa, AZ	13.5	24	31	Sacramento, CA	18.2	26	30	Suffolk, NY	3.9
17	32	Broward, FL	13.1	17	32	Broward, FL	18.0	50	30	Westchester, NY	3.9
10	33	Riverside, CA	12.9	49	33	Pinellas, FL	17.2	24	33	Sacramento, CA	3.8
11	34	Queens, NY	12.2	15	34	Tarrant, TX	17.1	31	33	Franklin, OH	3.8
49	34	Pinellas, FL	12.2	25	35	Palm Beach, FL	16.8	69	33	Ventura, CA	3.8
5	36	San Diego, CA	11.9	40	35	Mecklenburg, NC	16.8	8	36	Dallas, TX	3.7
25	37	Palm Beach, FL	11.8	11	37	Queens, NY	16.3	21	36	New York, NY	3.7
15	38	Tarrant, TX	11.6	10	38	Riverside, CA	16.2	40	36	Mecklenburg, NC	3.7
6	39	Orange, CA	11.5	5	39	San Diego, CA	15.7	11	39	Queens, NY	3.6
34	39	Travis, TX	11.5	6	39	Orange, CA	15.7	25	39	Palm Beach, FL	3.6
40	41	Mecklenburg, NC	11.4	65	39	Macomb, MI	15.7	52	39	Duval, FL	3.6
36	42	Allegheny, PA	11.2	62	42	Hartford, CT	15.3	53	39	Milwaukee, WI	3.6
65	42	Macomb, MI	11.2	68	42	New Haven, CT	15.3	72	39	Middlesex, NJ	3.6
62	44	Hartford, CT	11.0	58	44	Gwinnett, GA	15.2	12	44	King, WA	3.5
68	44	New Haven, CT	11.0	36	45	Allegheny, PA	15.1	15	44	Tarrant, TX	3.5
58	46	Gwinnett, GA	10.7	34	46	Travis, TX	14.7	30	44	Nassau, NY	3.5
32	47	Hennepin, MN	10.5	32	47	Hennepin, MN	13.7	51	44	Marion, IN	3.5
71	48	Worcester, MA	10.4	69	48	Ventura, CA	13.2	58	44	Gwinnett, GA	3.5
63	49	Pierce, WA	10.2	46	49	St. Louis, MO	13.1	71	44	Worcester, MA	3.5
64	50	San Francisco, CA	10.1	71	50	Worcester, MA	12.6	17	50	Broward, FL	3.4
46	51	St. Louis, MO	10.0	64	51	San Francisco, CA	12.3	27	50	Hillsborough, FL	3.4
69	52	Ventura, CA	9.5	63	52	Pierce, WA	12.1	41	50	Wake, NC	3.4
12	53	King, WA	9.3	60	53	Prince George's, MD	11.8	55	50	Bergen, NJ	3.4
20	53	Alameda, CA	9.3	12	54	King, WA	11.6	73	50	Montgomery, PA	3.4
37	55	Salt Lake, UT	9.2	41	54	Wake, NC	11.6	5	55	San Diego, CA	3.3
39	56	Contra Costa, CA	9.1	54	56	Fairfield, CT	11.3	16	55	Bexar, TX	3.3
41	57	Wake, NC	8.9	39	57	Contra Costa, CA	11.2	33	55	Oakland, MI	3.3
54	58	Fairfield, CT	8.8	72	58	Middlesex, NJ	11.0	45	55	Collin, TX	3.3
60	59	Prince George's, MD	8.6	37	59	Salt Lake, UT	10.8	49	55	Pinellas, FL	3.3
50	60	Westchester, NY	8.5	50	60	Westchester, NY	10.6	29	60	Orange, FL	3.2
72	60	Middlesex, NJ	8.5	20	61	Alameda, CA	10.5	39	60	Contra Costa, CA	3.2
48	62	Honolulu, HI	8.3	74	62	Baltimore, MD	10.4	42	60	Montgomery, MD	3.2
74	62	Baltimore, MD	8.3	48	63	Honolulu, HI	9.9	67	60	Denton, TX	3.2
22	64	Middlesex, MA	8.0	33	64	Oakland, MI	9.3	57	64	Du Page, IL	3.1
33	65	Oakland, MI	7.8	42	64	Montgomery, MD	9.3	20	65	Alameda, CA	3.0
18	66	Santa Clara, CA	7.5	22	66	Middlesex, MA	8.9	37	65	Salt Lake, UT	3.0
67	67	Denton, TX	7.1	26	66	Suffolk, NY	8.9	46	65	St. Louis, MO	3.0
26	68	Suffolk, NY	7.0	38	68	Fairfax, VA	8.6	6	68	Orange, CA	2.9
42	68	Montgomery, MD	7.0	18	69	Santa Clara, CA	8.1	34	69	Travis, TX	2.8
38	70	Fairfax, VA	6.7	67	70	Denton, TX	7.8	22	70	Middlesex, MA	2.7
55	71	Bergen, NJ	6.6	30	71	Nassau, NY	7.7	18	71	Santa Clara, CA	2.6
30	72	Nassau, NY	6.2	57	72	Du Page, IL	7.6	32	72	Hennepin, MN	2.5
57	72	Du Page, IL	6.2	55	73	Bergen, NJ	6.8	38	73	Fairfax, VA	2.4
45	74	Collin, TX	5.9	73	73	Montgomery, PA	6.8	64	73	San Francisco, CA	2.4
73	75	Montgomery, PA	5.8	45	75	Collin, TX	6.2	48	75	Honolulu, HI	2.3

75 Largest Counties by 2018 Population
Selected Rankings

Manufacturing employment as a percent of total nonfarm employment, 2016				Professional, scientific and technical employment as a percent of total nonfarm employment, 2016				Per capita local government taxes, 2012			
Population rank	Manufacturing rank	County	Percent employed in manufacturing [col 107/col 105]	Population rank	Professional services rank	County	Percent employed in professional services [col 110/col 105]	Population rank	Local taxes rank	County	Per capita local taxes (dollars) [col 183]
65	1	Macomb, MI	23.3	38	1	Fairfax, VA	33.2	30	1	Nassau, NY	5,254
19	2	Wayne, MI	13.2	64	2	San Francisco, CA	17.2	50	2	Westchester, NY	5,135
71	3	Worcester, MA	11.2	42	3	Montgomery, MD	16.8	21	3	New York, NY	5,096
62	4	Hartford, CT	11.1	72	4	Middlesex, NJ	15.0	9	3	Kings, NY	5,096
20	5	Alameda, CA	10.7	21	5	New York, NY	14.6	11	3	Queens, NY	5,096
59	6	Erie, NY	10.4	33	6	Oakland, MI	14.5	28	3	Bronx, NY	5,096
53	7	Milwaukee, WI	10.2	34	7	Travis, TX	13.7	26	7	Suffolk, NY	4,295
6	8	Orange, CA	10.1	18	8	Santa Clara, CA	13.6	64	8	San Francisco, CA	4,001
35	9	Cuyahoga, OH	10.0	22	9	Middlesex, MA	13.2	55	9	Bergen, NJ	3,788
15	10	Tarrant, TX	9.9	43	10	Fulton, GA	12.7	54	10	Fairfield, CT	3,419
69	11	Ventura, CA	9.6	60	11	Prince George's, MD	12.2	42	11	Montgomery, MD	3,168
47	12	Fresno, CA	9.3	41	12	Wake, NC	11.8	57	12	Du Page, IL	3,002
57	13	Du Page, IL	9.2	27	13	Hillsborough, FL	10.5	38	13	Fairfax, VA	2,810
68	13	New Haven, CT	9.2	45	14	Collin, TX	10.1	43	14	Fulton, GA	2,802
14	15	San Bernardino, CA	9.0	5	15	San Diego, CA	10.0	2	15	Cook, IL	2,765
26	15	Suffolk, NY	9.0	20	15	Alameda, CA	10.0	35	15	Cuyahoga, OH	2,765
1	17	Los Angeles, CA	8.7	65	17	Macomb, MI	9.9	72	17	Middlesex, NJ	2,730
37	17	Salt Lake, UT	8.7	8	18	Dallas, TX	9.6	31	18	Franklin, OH	2,717
32	19	Hennepin, MN	8.4	32	18	Hennepin, MN	9.6	23	19	Philadelphia, PA	2,636
75	19	Hamilton, OH	8.4	2	20	Cook, IL	9.4	18	20	Santa Clara, CA	2,621
18	21	Santa Clara, CA	8.2	12	20	King, WA	9.4	62	21	Hartford, CT	2,571
73	21	Montgomery, PA	8.2	54	22	Fairfield, CT	9.2	12	22	King, WA	2,543
5	23	San Diego, CA	8.1	6	23	Orange, CA	9.1	25	23	Palm Beach, FL	2,542
51	23	Marion, IN	8.1	73	23	Montgomery, PA	9.1	73	24	Montgomery, PA	2,541
10	25	Riverside, CA	7.9	69	25	Ventura, CA	8.7	22	25	Middlesex, MA	2,471
49	26	Pinellas, FL	7.8	74	25	Baltimore, MD	8.7	34	26	Travis, TX	2,455
54	27	Fairfield, CT	7.7	3	27	Harris, TX	8.5	75	27	Hamilton, OH	2,403
2	28	Cook, IL	7.5	75	27	Hamilton, OH	8.5	45	28	Collin, TX	2,390
12	28	King, WA	7.5	36	29	Allegheny, PA	8.4	59	29	Erie, NY	2,368
33	28	Oakland, MI	7.5	40	29	Mecklenburg, NC	8.4	20	30	Alameda, CA	2,358
3	31	Harris, TX	7.4	58	29	Gwinnett, GA	8.4	68	30	New Haven, CT	2,358
44	32	Pima, AZ	7.2	25	32	Palm Beach, FL	8.2	8	32	Dallas, TX	2,338
46	33	St. Louis, MO	7.1	37	33	Salt Lake, UT	8.1	36	33	Allegheny, PA	2,228
58	33	Gwinnett, GA	7.1	51	34	Marion, IN	8.0	3	34	Harris, TX	2,171
63	33	Pierce, WA	7.1	55	34	Bergen, NJ	8.0	46	35	St. Louis, MO	2,133
67	36	Denton, TX	6.9	26	36	Suffolk, NY	7.9	7	36	Miami-Dade, FL	2,132
72	37	Middlesex, NJ	6.8	46	36	St. Louis, MO	7.9	15	37	Tarrant, TX	2,029
55	38	Bergen, NJ	6.7	49	36	Pinellas, FL	7.9	40	38	Mecklenburg, NC	1,923
8	39	Dallas, TX	6.6	24	39	Sacramento, CA	7.8	74	39	Baltimore, MD	1,917
4	40	Maricopa, AZ	6.2	17	40	Broward, FL	7.7	32	40	Hennepin, MN	1,910
61	40	Kern, CA	6.2	23	40	Philadelphia, PA	7.7	1	41	Los Angeles, CA	1,891
56	42	Shelby, TN	6.1	39	42	Contra Costa, CA	7.6	53	42	Milwaukee, WI	1,888
22	43	Middlesex, MA	6.0	30	43	Nassau, NY	7.5	39	43	Contra Costa, CA	1,861
70	44	El Paso, TX	5.8	57	43	Du Page, IL	7.5	56	44	Shelby, TN	1,828
31	45	Franklin, OH	5.1	1	45	Los Angeles, CA	7.3	29	45	Orange, FL	1,815
52	46	Duval, FL	5.0	7	46	Miami-Dade, FL	7.2	6	46	Orange, CA	1,806
36	47	Allegheny, PA	4.9	29	46	Orange, FL	7.2	5	47	San Diego, CA	1,791
45	48	Collin, TX	4.7	4	48	Maricopa, AZ	7.1	67	48	Denton, TX	1,790
39	49	Contra Costa, CA	4.6	59	49	Erie, NY	7.0	60	49	Prince George's, MD	1,761
34	50	Travis, TX	4.5	31	50	Franklin, OH	6.7	17	50	Broward, FL	1,742
16	51	Bexar, TX	4.4	50	51	Westchester, NY	6.6	16	51	Bexar, TX	1,675
24	51	Sacramento, CA	4.4	62	51	Hartford, CT	6.6	69	52	Ventura, CA	1,650
40	51	Mecklenburg, NC	4.4	19	53	Wayne, MI	6.5	71	53	Worcester, MA	1,630
74	51	Baltimore, MD	4.4	35	53	Cuyahoga, OH	6.5	49	54	Pinellas, FL	1,597
7	55	Miami-Dade, FL	3.7	52	55	Duval, FL	6.4	52	55	Duval, FL	1,536
11	56	Queens, NY	3.6	71	56	Worcester, MA	6.0	58	56	Gwinnett, GA	1,529
27	56	Hillsborough, FL	3.6	16	57	Bexar, TX	5.9	63	57	Pierce, WA	1,521
29	56	Orange, FL	3.6	61	58	Kern, CA	5.6	33	58	Oakland, MI	1,515
17	59	Broward, FL	3.5	44	59	Pima, AZ	5.4	4	59	Maricopa, AZ	1,506
9	60	Kings, NY	3.4	13	60	Clark, NV	5.2	19	60	Wayne, MI	1,499
23	60	Philadelphia, PA	3.4	48	61	Honolulu, HI	5.1	51	61	Marion, IN	1,447
66	62	Hidalgo, TX	3.2	53	62	Milwaukee, WI	5.0	44	62	Pima, AZ	1,438
50	63	Westchester, NY	3.1	15	63	Tarrant, TX	4.9	41	63	Wake, NC	1,436
41	64	Wake, NC	3.0	67	64	Denton, TX	4.6	37	64	Salt Lake, UT	1,428
30	65	Nassau, NY	2.9	70	64	El Paso, TX	4.6	13	65	Clark, NV	1,367
48	66	Honolulu, HI	2.8	68	66	New Haven, CT	4.5	61	66	Kern, CA	1,365
60	67	Prince George's, MD	2.7	56	67	Shelby, TN	4.2	10	67	Riverside, CA	1,362
25	68	Palm Beach, FL	2.5	47	68	Fresno, CA	4.0	27	68	Hillsborough, FL	1,359
43	69	Fulton, GA	2.4	63	69	Pierce, WA	3.8	24	69	Sacramento, CA	1,357
13	70	Clark, NV	2.3	10	70	Riverside, CA	3.6	48	70	Honolulu, HI	1,348
28	70	Bronx, NY	2.3	9	71	Kings, NY	3.5	70	71	El Paso, TX	1,318
42	72	Montgomery, MD	1.8	66	72	Hidalgo, TX	3.2	14	72	San Bernardino, CA	1,287
64	73	San Francisco, CA	1.3	14	73	San Bernardino, CA	3.1	47	73	Fresno, CA	1,131
38	74	Fairfax, VA	1.0	11	74	Queens, NY	3.0	65	74	Macomb, MI	1,112
21	75	New York, NY	0.8	28	75	Bronx, NY	1.6	66	75	Hidalgo, TX	1,071

75 Largest Counties by 2018 Population
Selected Rankings

Violent crime rate, 2016 (violent crime known to police)				Military as a percent of all federal employment, 2017				Mean federal individual Income Tax, 2016			
Population rank	Violent crime rate rank	County	Violent crime rate per 100,000 population [col 46]	Population rank	Military employment rank	County	Percent military federal employment [col 195/ col 194+195]	Population rank	Mean income tax rank	County	Mean income tax (dollars) [col 199]
56	1	Shelby, TN	1,384	63	1	Pierce, WA	72.4	21	1	New York, NY	44,131
51	2	Marion, IN	1,274	5	2	San Diego, CA	68.1	54	2	Fairfield, CT	31,256
53	3	Milwaukee, WI	1,037	70	2	El Paso, TX	68.1	50	3	Westchester, NY	29,230
19	4	Wayne, MI	1,036	48	4	Honolulu, HI	63.0	18	4	Santa Clara, CA	28,468
23	5	Philadelphia, PA	981	14	5	San Bernardino, CA	59.3	64	5	San Francisco, CA	27,482
13	6	Clark, NV	770	13	6	Clark, NV	54.2	30	6	Nassau, NY	20,437
3	7	Harris, TX	742	45	7	Collin, TX	51.5	55	7	Bergen, NJ	20,424
43	8	Fulton, GA	736	16	8	Bexar, TX	50.7	38	8	Fairfax, VA	20,088
35	9	Cuyahoga, OH	721	58	9	Gwinnett, GA	50.3	12	9	King, WA	20,038
64	10	San Francisco, CA	720	73	10	Montgomery, PA	47.3	22	10	Middlesex, MA	19,878
2	11	Cook, IL	677	67	11	Denton, TX	46.9	43	11	Fulton, GA	18,593
40	12	Mecklenburg, NC	642	52	12	Duval, FL	42.7	73	12	Montgomery, PA	18,332
52	13	Duval, FL	622	55	13	Bergen, NJ	42.0	42	13	Montgomery, MD	18,028
29	14	Orange, FL	616	72	14	Middlesex, NJ	41.9	39	14	Contra Costa, CA	18,016
20	15	Alameda, CA	613	69	15	Ventura, CA	40.3	25	15	Palm Beach, FL	16,338
47	16	Fresno, CA	612	54	16	Fairfield, CT	40.0	45	16	Collin, TX	16,071
16	17	Bexar, TX	609	4	17	Maricopa, AZ	39.5	33	17	Oakland, MI	15,452
61	18	Kern, CA	580	44	18	Pima, AZ	38.7	57	18	Du Page, IL	15,302
21	19	New York, NY	575	71	19	Worcester, MA	38.6	34	19	Travis, TX	15,294
9	19	Kings, NY	575	46	20	St. Louis, MO	37.0	32	20	Hennepin, MN	14,979
11	19	Queens, NY	575	28	21	Bronx, NY	36.6	20	21	Alameda, CA	14,725
28	19	Bronx, NY	575	17	22	Broward, FL	36.2	46	22	St. Louis, MO	14,265
41	19	Wake, NC	575	10	23	Riverside, CA	35.3	6	23	Orange, CA	13,775
7	24	Miami-Dade, FL	571	41	24	Wake, NC	35.1	26	24	Suffolk, NY	13,609
1	25	Los Angeles, CA	554	9	25	Kings, NY	34.7	40	25	Mecklenburg, NC	12,587
74	26	Baltimore, MD	531	27	26	Hillsborough, FL	34.6	67	26	Denton, TX	12,525
8	27	Dallas, TX	515	30	27	Nassau, NY	32.6	41	27	Wake, NC	12,015
24	28	Sacramento, CA	513	6	28	Orange, CA	31.0	8	28	Dallas, TX	11,700
44	29	Pima, AZ	495	33	29	Oakland, MI	29.8	2	29	Cook, IL	11,628
14	30	San Bernardino, CA	491	20	30	Alameda, CA	29.7	1	30	Los Angeles, CA	11,203
63	31	Pierce, WA	483	37	31	Salt Lake, UT	29.5	69	31	Ventura, CA	11,168
75	32	Hamilton, OH	471	40	31	Mecklenburg, NC	29.5	75	32	Hamilton, OH	10,721
32	33	Hennepin, MN	470	22	33	Middlesex, MA	29.2	62	33	Hartford, CT	10,698
25	34	Palm Beach, FL	452	3	34	Harris, TX	28.9	74	34	Baltimore, MD	10,510
71	35	Worcester, MA	438	25	35	Palm Beach, FL	28.6	72	35	Middlesex, NJ	10,459
4	36	Maricopa, AZ	432	66	36	Hidalgo, TX	28.5	5	36	San Diego, CA	10,382
49	37	Pinellas, FL	425	57	37	Du Page, IL	28.1	36	37	Allegheny, PA	10,230
31	38	Franklin, OH	416	49	38	Pinellas, FL	27.7	68	38	New Haven, CT	9,930
59	39	Erie, NY	413	61	39	Kern, CA	27.2	3	39	Harris, TX	9,873
37	40	Salt Lake, UT	412	7	40	Miami-Dade, FL	26.7	71	40	Worcester, MA	9,755
15	41	Tarrant, TX	405	15	41	Tarrant, TX	26.6	15	41	Tarrant, TX	9,540
36	42	Allegheny, PA	388	39	42	Contra Costa, CA	26.5	49	42	Pinellas, FL	9,343
17	43	Broward, FL	387	12	43	King, WA	26.4	13	43	Clark, NV	9,281
34	44	Travis, TX	384	1	44	Los Angeles, CA	26.2	4	44	Maricopa, AZ	9,182
46	45	St. Louis, MO	380	32	45	Hennepin, MN	25.9	17	45	Broward, FL	9,142
70	46	El Paso, TX	364	68	46	New Haven, CT	25.9	27	46	Hillsborough, FL	8,820
60	47	Prince George's, MD	360	50	47	Westchester, NY	25.4	37	47	Salt Lake, UT	8,702
12	48	King, WA	347	18	48	Santa Clara, CA	24.6	35	48	Cuyahoga, OH	8,570
39	49	Contra Costa, CA	343	62	48	Hartford, CT	24.6	56	49	Shelby, TN	8,348
5	50	San Diego, CA	330	24	50	Sacramento, CA	24.3	31	50	Franklin, OH	8,170
68	51	New Haven, CT	324	53	51	Milwaukee, WI	22.7	7	51	Miami-Dade, FL	8,131
10	52	Riverside, CA	313	2	52	Cook, IL	21.9	9	52	Kings, NY	8,128
27	53	Hillsborough, FL	298	60	52	Prince George's, MD	21.9	48	53	Honolulu, HI	8,105
65	54	Macomb, MI	297	31	54	Franklin, OH	21.6	63	54	Pierce, WA	7,944
66	55	Hidalgo, TX	294	36	55	Allegheny, PA	21.3	59	55	Erie, NY	7,721
18	56	Santa Clara, CA	281	11	56	Queens, NY	20.9	29	56	Orange, FL	7,650
62	57	Hartford, CT	264	56	57	Shelby, TN	20.7	24	57	Sacramento, CA	7,287
69	58	Ventura, CA	258	75	58	Hamilton, OH	20.3	16	58	Bexar, TX	7,176
58	59	Gwinnett, GA	247	19	59	Wayne, MI	18.9	52	59	Duval, FL	7,005
48	60	Honolulu, HI	238	8	60	Dallas, TX	18.6	19	60	Wayne, MI	6,806
54	61	Fairfield, CT	230	26	61	Suffolk, NY	18.5	53	61	Milwaukee, WI	6,790
6	62	Orange, CA	229	34	62	Travis, TX	18.4	58	62	Gwinnett, GA	6,625
50	63	Westchester, NY	215	38	63	Fairfax, VA	18.2	44	63	Pima, AZ	6,565
33	64	Oakland, MI	181	65	64	Macomb, MI	17.8	51	64	Marion, IN	6,536
22	65	Middlesex, MA	180	35	65	Cuyahoga, OH	17.6	65	65	Macomb, MI	6,512
42	66	Montgomery, MD	175	29	66	Orange, FL	17.3	23	66	Philadelphia, PA	6,210
67	67	Denton, TX	173	51	67	Marion, IN	17.0	10	67	Riverside, CA	5,875
45	68	Collin, TX	154	59	68	Erie, NY	16.0	47	68	Fresno, CA	5,767
72	69	Middlesex, NJ	140	74	69	Baltimore, MD	15.6	11	69	Queens, NY	5,567
30	70	Nassau, NY	133	23	70	Philadelphia, PA	14.5	60	70	Prince George's, MD	5,553
73	71	Montgomery, PA	123	47	71	Fresno, CA	14.1	14	71	San Bernardino, CA	5,158
26	72	Suffolk, NY	121	42	72	Montgomery, MD	13.6	61	72	Kern, CA	5,147
38	73	Fairfax, VA	100	43	73	Fulton, GA	10.6	70	73	El Paso, TX	4,032
57	74	Du Page, IL	92	21	74	New York, NY	10.5	66	74	Hidalgo, TX	3,300
55	75	Bergen, NJ	86	64	75	San Francisco, CA	10.4	28	75	Bronx, NY	3,148

75 Largest Counties by 2018 Population
Selected Rankings

Nonemployer businesses, 2016				Value of residential construction authorized by building permits, 2018				Full-time equivalent government employees, 2012			
Population rank	Nonemployer Businesses rank	County	Nonemployer businesses [col 167]	Population rank	Value ($1,000) rank	County	Value ($1,000) rank [col 169]	Population rank	Government employees rank	County	Government employees rank [col 171]
1	1	Los Angeles, CA	1,046,426	4	1	Maricopa, AZ	5,797,176	21	1	New York, NY	411,393
2	2	Cook, IL	483,757	1	2	Los Angeles, CA	5,547,221	9	1	Kings, NY	Included in
7	3	Miami-Dade, FL	469,992	12	3	King, WA	3,909,651	11	1	Queens, NY	New York, NY
3	4	Harris, TX	390,881	3	4	Harris, TX	3,879,179	28	1	Bronx, NY	
4	5	Maricopa, AZ	310,913	45	5	Collin, TX	3,684,200	1	2	Los Angeles, CA	386,456
6	6	Orange, CA	307,052	8	6	Dallas, TX	3,411,378	2	3	Cook, IL	198,590
5	7	San Diego, CA	277,207	27	7	Hillsborough, FL	2,780,950	3	4	Harris, TX	166,045
9	8	Kings, NY	269,471	29	8	Orange, FL	2,451,659	4	5	Maricopa, AZ	129,919
17	9	Broward, FL	252,396	34	9	Travis, TX	2,436,028	8	6	Dallas, TX	105,090
11	10	Queens, NY	250,998	5	10	San Diego, CA	2,432,915	7	7	Miami-Dade, FL	102,308
8	11	Dallas, TX	233,530	15	11	Tarrant, TX	2,382,333	5	8	San Diego, CA	97,178
21	12	New York, NY	226,631	20	12	Alameda, CA	2,335,441	6	9	Orange, CA	85,251
12	13	King, WA	172,297	6	13	Orange, CA	2,300,253	16	10	Bexar, TX	76,821
25	14	Palm Beach, FL	170,587	7	14	Miami-Dade, FL	2,258,626	15	11	Tarrant, TX	76,274
15	15	Tarrant, TX	170,222	67	15	Denton, TX	2,183,953	17	12	Broward, FL	73,864
13	16	Clark, NV	167,624	41	16	Wake, NC	2,147,746	10	13	Riverside, CA	68,997
10	17	Riverside, CA	165,022	10	17	Riverside, CA	1,899,242	14	14	San Bernardino, CA	68,989
20	18	Alameda, CA	143,612	2	18	Cook, IL	1,866,748	12	15	King, WA	65,821
18	19	Santa Clara, CA	143,480	13	19	Clark, NV	1,844,987	26	16	Suffolk, NY	63,444
14	20	San Bernardino, CA	143,379	18	20	Santa Clara, CA	1,734,780	35	17	Cuyahoga, OH	62,490
30	21	Nassau, NY	139,758	43	21	Fulton, GA	1,733,436	23	18	Philadelphia, PA	60,937
22	22	Middlesex, MA	139,021	40	22	Mecklenburg, NC	1,657,154	40	19	Mecklenburg, NC	60,489
16	23	Bexar, TX	137,240	37	23	Salt Lake, UT	1,362,405	30	20	Nassau, NY	60,368
29	24	Orange, FL	129,056	25	24	Palm Beach, FL	1,316,857	18	21	Santa Clara, CA	59,919
26	25	Suffolk, NY	128,110	32	25	Hennepin, MN	1,290,595	20	22	Alameda, CA	56,184
19	26	Wayne, MI	126,180	14	26	San Bernardino, CA	1,271,338	19	23	Wayne, MI	52,078
34	27	Travis, TX	118,984	64	27	San Francisco, CA	1,214,058	13	24	Clark, NV	51,796
27	28	Hillsborough, FL	118,525	63	28	Pierce, WA	1,159,171	22	25	Middlesex, MA	51,015
28	29	Bronx, NY	115,123	16	29	Bexar, TX	1,126,679	24	26	Sacramento, CA	50,509
33	30	Oakland, MI	114,295	24	30	Sacramento, CA	1,115,115	25	27	Palm Beach, FL	46,198
42	31	Montgomery, MD	112,683	52	31	Duval, FL	1,077,732	27	28	Hillsborough, FL	45,811
38	32	Fairfax, VA	108,810	31	32	Franklin, OH	1,054,351	29	29	Orange, FL	45,111
43	33	Fulton, GA	107,036	44	33	Pima, AZ	1,025,886	34	30	Travis, TX	45,034
32	34	Hennepin, MN	106,061	17	34	Broward, FL	991,062	36	31	Allegheny, PA	43,945
24	35	Sacramento, CA	104,811	33	35	Oakland, MI	902,670	31	32	Franklin, OH	43,936
58	36	Gwinnett, GA	102,719	58	36	Gwinnett, GA	880,117	43	33	Fulton, GA	43,801
64	37	San Francisco, CA	99,307	22	37	Middlesex, MA	835,505	38	34	Fairfax, VA	43,275
50	38	Westchester, NY	97,354	9	38	Kings, NY	822,800	50	35	Westchester, NY	42,725
31	39	Franklin, OH	95,968	28	39	Bronx, NY	714,972	56	36	Shelby, TN	39,378
55	40	Bergen, NJ	95,446	11	40	Queens, NY	690,157	66	37	Hidalgo, TX	39,042
23	41	Philadelphia, PA	95,065	54	41	Fairfield, CT	667,495	64	38	San Francisco, CA	38,712
40	42	Mecklenburg, NC	94,780	26	42	Suffolk, NY	639,240	42	39	Montgomery, MD	38,590
39	43	Contra Costa, CA	94,711	21	43	New York, NY	632,871	70	40	El Paso, TX	38,262
54	44	Fairfield, CT	94,038	47	44	Fresno, CA	627,312	32	41	Hennepin, MN	35,312
35	45	Cuyahoga, OH	92,595	39	45	Contra Costa, CA	620,207	59	42	Erie, NY	35,259
45	46	Collin, TX	89,459	66	46	Hidalgo, TX	609,699	46	43	St. Louis, MO	35,141
41	47	Wake, NC	87,890	70	47	El Paso, TX	601,524	47	44	Fresno, CA	34,954
37	48	Salt Lake, UT	85,158	65	48	Macomb, MI	571,144	57	45	Du Page, IL	34,627
57	49	Du Page, IL	83,927	57	49	Du Page, IL	566,406	37	46	Salt Lake, UT	34,230
36	50	Allegheny, PA	82,344	61	50	Kern, CA	565,821	51	47	Marion, IN	34,223
56	51	Shelby, TN	81,318	23	51	Philadelphia, PA	564,782	53	48	Milwaukee, WI	34,086
49	52	Pinellas, FL	81,112	60	52	Prince George's, MD	507,945	55	49	Bergen, NJ	32,531
60	53	Prince George's, MD	76,805	48	53	Honolulu, HI	504,266	61	50	Kern, CA	32,191
46	54	St. Louis, MO	76,527	55	54	Bergen, NJ	489,329	49	51	Pinellas, FL	32,162
73	55	Montgomery, PA	71,522	19	55	Wayne, MI	487,983	33	52	Oakland, MI	32,137
67	56	Denton, TX	71,031	46	56	St. Louis, MO	479,346	54	53	Fairfield, CT	32,029
66	57	Hidalgo, TX	70,258	30	57	Nassau, NY	468,220	62	54	Hartford, CT	31,675
69	58	Ventura, CA	69,019	69	58	Ventura, CA	461,558	44	55	Pima, AZ	31,664
52	59	Duval, FL	67,845	36	59	Allegheny, PA	407,660	41	56	Wake, NC	31,235
48	60	Honolulu, HI	66,902	49	60	Pinellas, FL	405,934	39	57	Contra Costa, CA	31,030
74	61	Baltimore, MD	66,764	42	61	Montgomery, MD	385,024	75	58	Hamilton, OH	30,330
44	62	Pima, AZ	65,734	51	62	Marion, IN	361,223	68	59	New Haven, CT	28,448
65	63	Macomb, MI	63,638	73	63	Montgomery, PA	354,320	45	60	Collin, TX	28,433
51	64	Marion, IN	61,939	56	64	Shelby, TN	341,147	71	61	Worcester, MA	28,380
68	65	New Haven, CT	61,104	59	65	Erie, NY	330,737	58	62	Gwinnett, GA	27,778
70	66	El Paso, TX	59,033	50	66	Westchester, NY	327,888	69	63	Ventura, CA	27,714
62	67	Hartford, CT	58,805	72	67	Middlesex, NJ	326,119	60	64	Prince George's, MD	27,062
75	68	Hamilton, OH	57,758	71	68	Worcester, MA	302,360	52	65	Duval, FL	26,681
72	69	Middlesex, NJ	57,590	74	69	Baltimore, MD	289,120	72	66	Middlesex, NJ	26,592
71	70	Worcester, MA	52,792	75	70	Hamilton, OH	280,935	74	67	Baltimore, MD	26,532
47	71	Fresno, CA	51,942	38	71	Fairfax, VA	271,501	63	68	Pierce, WA	23,934
53	72	Milwaukee, WI	48,001	35	72	Cuyahoga, OH	221,135	73	69	Montgomery, PA	23,690
59	73	Erie, NY	47,797	62	73	Hartford, CT	157,760	67	70	Denton, TX	21,018
61	74	Kern, CA	45,491	53	74	Milwaukee, WI	153,741	65	71	Macomb, MI	20,477
63	75	Pierce, WA	43,855	68	75	New Haven, CT	124,211	48	72	Honolulu, HI	9,304

75 Largest Counties by Value of Agricultural Sales
Selected Rankings

Value of agricultural sales, 2017			Average agricultural sales per farm, 2017				Number of farms, 2017			
Value of sales rank	County	Value of sales (millions of dollars) [col 125]	Value of sales rank	Average sales rank	County	Average sales per farm (dollars) [col 126]	Value of sales rank	Number of farms rank	County	Number of farms [col 113]
1	Fresno, CA	5,743	21	1	Hartley, TX	5,930,437	17	1	Lancaster, PA	5,108
2	Tulare, CA	4,475	23	2	Haskell, KS	5,599,502	41	2	San Diego, CA	5,082
3	Monterey, CA	4,116	25	3	Scott, KS	4,809,487	1	3	Fresno, CA	4,774
4	Kern, CA	4,077	11	4	Imperial, CA	4,696,157	2	4	Tulare, CA	4,187
5	Merced, CA	2,938	51	5	Hansford, TX	4,074,127	8	5	Weld, CO	4,062
6	Stanislaus, CA	2,526	3	6	Monterey, CA	3,728,396	6	6	Stanislaus, CA	3,621
7	San Joaquin, CA	2,176	39	7	Sherman, TX	3,420,641	34	7	Sonoma, CA	3,594
8	Weld, CO	2,047	14	8	Deaf Smith, TX	2,916,004	7	8	San Joaquin, CA	3,430
9	Yakima, WA	1,988	27	9	Castro, TX	2,728,944	9	9	Yakima, WA	2,952
10	Grant, WA	1,939	43	10	Grant, KS	2,584,575	49	10	Stearns, MN	2,951
11	Imperial, CA	1,860	4	11	Kern, CA	2,355,161	11	11	Marion, OR	2,761
12	Sioux, IA	1,696	30	12	Gray, KS	2,347,519	40	12	Miami-Dade, FL	2,752
13	Kings, CA	1,649	37	13	Parmer, TX	1,925,302	31	13	Riverside, CA	2,667
14	Deaf Smith, TX	1,639	60	14	Dallam, TX	1,867,426	53	14	San Luis Obispo, CA	2,349
15	Ventura, CA	1,633	42	15	Finney, KS	1,829,091	5	15	Merced, CA	2,337
16	Santa Barbara, CA	1,520	13	16	Kings, CA	1,712,640	15	16	Ventura, CA	2,135
17	Lancaster, PA	1,507	69	17	Morrow, OR	1,590,632	44	17	Rockingham, VA	2,026
18	Madera, CA	1,493	32	18	Cassia, ID	1,584,137	70	18	Benton, AR	1,936
19	Duplin, NC	1,262	75	19	Phelps, NE	1,558,601	22	19	Maricopa, AZ	1,874
20	Sampson, NC	1,249	19	20	Duplin, NC	1,538,648	4	20	Kern, CA	1,731
21	Hartley, TX	1,222	45	21	Gooding, ID	1,456,113	12	21	Sioux, IA	1,724
22	Maricopa, AZ	1,209	64	22	Swisher, TX	1,444,259	52	22	Chester, PA	1,646
23	Haskell, KS	1,159	26	23	Cuming, NE	1,407,956	29	23	Benton, WA	1,520
24	Texas, OK	1,136	10	24	Grant, WA	1,400,936	16	24	Santa Barbara, CA	1,467
25	Scott, KS	1,135	24	25	Texas, OK	1,371,593	18	25	Madera, CA	1,386
26	Cuming, NE	1,132	58	26	Jerome, ID	1,316,016	10	26	Grant, WA	1,384
27	Castro, TX	1,122	20	27	Sampson, NC	1,301,188	72	27	Kossuth, IA	1,347
28	Sussex, DE	1,013	5	28	Merced, CA	1,257,337	36	28	Palm Beach, FL	1,298
29	Benton, WA	1,005	1	29	Fresno, CA	1,202,926	61	29	Mercer, OH	1,231
30	Gray, KS	991	35	30	Yuma, CO	1,186,972	50	30	Plymouth, IA	1,219
31	Riverside, CA	932	38	31	Pinal, AZ	1,131,154	56	31	Twin Falls, ID	1,211
32	Cassia, ID	927	48	32	Dawson, NE	1,091,000	63	32	Glenn, CA	1,173
33	Lyon, IA	924	18	33	Madera, CA	1,076,903	74	33	Allegan, MI	1,172
34	Sonoma, CA	919	71	34	Wayne, NC	1,074,539	66	34	Huron, MI	1,153
35	Yuma, CO	919	2	35	Tulare, CA	1,068,739	57	35	Washington, IA	1,129
36	Palm Beach, FL	902	16	36	Santa Barbara, CA	1,036,090	33	36	Lyon, IA	1,122
37	Parmer, TX	893	12	37	Sioux, IA	983,814	28	37	Sussex, DE	1,119
38	Pinal, AZ	862	68	38	Santa Cruz, CA	970,464	46	38	Custer, NE	1,108
39	Sherman, TX	838	28	39	Sussex, DE	904,900	3	39	Monterey, CA	1,104
40	Miami-Dade, FL	838	55	40	Platte, NE	823,639	47	40	Lincoln, NE	1,040
41	San Diego, CA	831	33	41	Lyon, IA	823,148	67	41	Renville, MN	1,026
42	Finney, KS	823	61	42	Franklin, WA	818,132	13	42	Kings, CA	963
43	Grant, KS	814	73	43	Hamilton, IA	801,623	20	43	Sampson, NC	960
44	Rockingham, VA	796	15	44	Ventura, CA	765,008	59	44	Martin, MN	911
45	Gooding, ID	783	47	45	Lincoln, NE	726,188	65	45	Logan, CO	861
46	Custer, NE	781	65	46	Logan, CO	717,686	55	46	Platte, NE	836
47	Lincoln, NE	755	46	47	Custer, NE	705,014	24	47	Texas, OK	828
48	Dawson, NE	748	6	48	Stanislaus, CA	697,690	19	48	Duplin, NC	820
49	Stearns, MN	748	59	49	Martin, MN	697,610	26	49	Cuming, NE	804
50	Plymouth, IA	738	36	50	Palm Beach, FL	694,699	35	50	Yuma, CO	774
51	Hansford, TX	737	9	51	Yakima, WA	673,451	61	51	Franklin, WA	772
52	Chester, PA	713	29	52	Benton, WA	661,374	38	52	Pinal, AZ	762
53	San Luis Obispo, CA	702	22	53	Maricopa, AZ	645,215	73	53	Hamilton, IA	732
53	Marion, OR	702	7	54	San Joaquin, CA	634,404	48	54	Dawson, NE	686
55	Platte, NE	689	50	55	Plymouth, IA	605,578	68	55	Santa Cruz, CA	625
56	Twin Falls, ID	680	57	56	Washington, IA	595,126	32	56	Cassia, ID	585
57	Washington, IA	672	67	57	Renville, MN	593,752	14	57	Deaf Smith, TX	562
58	Jerome, ID	640	56	58	Twin Falls, ID	561,716	71	58	Wayne, NC	551
59	Martin, MN	636	63	59	Glenn, CA	536,012	45	59	Gooding, ID	538
60	Dallam, TX	635	66	60	Huron, MI	529,729	58	60	Jerome, ID	486
61	Mercer, OH	632	61	61	Mercer, OH	513,089	37	61	Parmer, TX	464
61	Franklin, WA	632	8	62	Weld, CO	503,982	42	62	Finney, KS	450
63	Glenn, CA	629	74	63	Allegan, MI	498,612	64	63	Swisher, TX	432
64	Swisher, TX	624	72	64	Kossuth, IA	436,566	30	64	Gray, KS	422
65	Logan, CO	618	52	65	Chester, PA	432,848	27	65	Castro, TX	411
66	Huron, MI	611	44	66	Rockingham, VA	392,852	11	66	Imperial, CA	396
67	Renville, MN	609	31	67	Riverside, CA	349,450	69	67	Morrow, OR	375
68	Santa Cruz, CA	607	70	68	Benton, AR	306,494	75	68	Phelps, NE	371
69	Morrow, OR	597	40	69	Miami-Dade, FL	304,409	60	69	Dallam, TX	340
70	Benton, AR	593	53	70	San Luis Obispo, CA	298,676	43	70	Grant, KS	315
71	Wayne, NC	592	17	71	Lancaster, PA	295,068	39	71	Sherman, TX	245
72	Kossuth, IA	588	34	72	Sonoma, CA	255,719	25	72	Scott, KS	236
73	Hamilton, IA	587	53	73	Marion, OR	254,104	23	73	Haskell, KS	207
74	Allegan, MI	584	49	74	Stearns, MN	253,466	21	74	Hartley, TX	206
75	Phelps, NE	578	41	75	San Diego, CA	163,601	51	75	Hansford, TX	181

75 Largest Counties by Value of Agricultural Sales
Selected Rankings

Average size of farm, 2017

Value of sales rank	Size of farm rank	County	Average size of farm (acres) [col 119]
21	1	Hartley, TX	4,052
51	2	Hansford, TX	3,243
69	3	Morrow, OR	3,003
60	4	Dallam, TX	2,633
39	5	Sherman, TX	2,409
25	6	Scott, KS	1,951
35	7	Yuma, CO	1,809
23	8	Haskell, KS	1,757
42	8	Finney, KS	1,757
14	10	Deaf Smith, TX	1,722
24	11	Texas, OK	1,544
38	12	Pinal, AZ	1,471
46	13	Custer, NE	1,358
27	14	Castro, TX	1,350
4	15	Kern, CA	1,326
65	16	Logan, CO	1,322
30	17	Gray, KS	1,318
11	18	Imperial, CA	1,317
47	19	Lincoln, NE	1,305
64	20	Swisher, TX	1,304
3	21	Monterey, CA	1,214
37	22	Parmer, TX	1,183
43	23	Grant, KS	1,139
32	24	Cassia, ID	1,100
75	25	Phelps, NE	921
48	26	Dawson, NE	889
61	27	Franklin, WA	797
10	28	Grant, WA	753
13	29	Kings, CA	640
67	30	Renville, MN	608
9	31	Yakima, WA	603
8	32	Weld, CO	517
59	33	Martin, MN	493
16	34	Santa Barbara, CA	487
18	35	Madera, CA	466
55	36	Platte, NE	459
26	37	Cuming, NE	452
72	38	Kossuth, IA	441
73	39	Hamilton, IA	431
66	40	Huron, MI	430
50	41	Plymouth, IA	413
5	42	Merced, CA	405
29	43	Benton, WA	404
63	44	Glenn, CA	398
53	45	San Luis Obispo, CA	396
56	46	Twin Falls, ID	387
36	47	Palm Beach, FL	376
58	48	Jerome, ID	353
45	49	Gooding, ID	350
1	50	Fresno, CA	345
20	51	Sampson, NC	314
33	52	Lyon, IA	309
71	53	Wayne, NC	300
2	54	Tulare, CA	299
19	55	Duplin, NC	296
12	56	Sioux, IA	280
57	57	Washington, IA	275
22	58	Maricopa, AZ	253
28	59	Sussex, DE	246
7	60	San Joaquin, CA	225
49	61	Stearns, MN	221
61	62	Mercer, OH	218
6	63	Stanislaus, CA	200
74	64	Allegan, MI	196
34	65	Sonoma, CA	158
70	66	Benton, AR	126
15	67	Ventura, CA	122
44	68	Rockingham, VA	113
53	69	Marion, OR	105
68	70	Santa Cruz, CA	102
31	71	Riverside, CA	99
52	72	Chester, PA	91
17	73	Lancaster, PA	77
41	74	San Diego, CA	44
40	75	Miami-Dade, FL	29

Average value of land and buildings per farm, 2017

Value of sales rank	Value of land and buildings per farm rank	County	Average value per farm (dollars) [col 122]
11	1	Imperial, CA	14,670,312
4	2	Kern, CA	9,787,244
3	3	Monterey, CA	8,944,364
13	4	Kings, CA	6,917,469
5	5	Merced, CA	5,299,308
18	6	Madera, CA	5,102,429
16	7	Santa Barbara, CA	5,060,150
21	8	Hartley, TX	5,028,050
75	9	Phelps, NE	4,707,223
51	10	Hansford, TX	4,353,971
38	11	Pinal, AZ	4,065,306
67	12	Renville, MN	3,990,664
1	13	Fresno, CA	3,917,829
61	14	Franklin, WA	3,662,394
63	15	Glenn, CA	3,547,184
50	16	Plymouth, IA	3,535,476
32	17	Cassia, ID	3,508,509
34	18	Sonoma, CA	3,501,852
2	19	Tulare, CA	3,501,053
73	20	Hamilton, IA	3,495,669
72	21	Kossuth, IA	3,480,288
39	22	Sherman, TX	3,446,896
69	23	Morrow, OR	3,385,469
7	24	San Joaquin, CA	3,384,002
46	25	Custer, NE	3,361,912
59	26	Martin, MN	3,308,478
36	27	Palm Beach, FL	3,149,296
6	28	Stanislaus, CA	3,116,617
15	29	Ventura, CA	3,106,351
33	30	Lyon, IA	3,082,560
48	31	Dawson, NE	3,034,516
53	32	San Luis Obispo, CA	2,991,939
60	33	Dallam, TX	2,986,690
25	34	Scott, KS	2,955,605
35	35	Yuma, CO	2,953,997
12	36	Sioux, IA	2,918,016
55	37	Platte, NE	2,903,960
26	38	Cuming, NE	2,752,249
42	39	Finney, KS	2,749,764
23	40	Haskell, KS	2,682,671
66	41	Huron, MI	2,597,983
10	42	Grant, WA	2,574,272
22	43	Maricopa, AZ	2,338,321
47	44	Lincoln, NE	2,184,451
68	45	Santa Cruz, CA	2,183,024
58	46	Jerome, ID	2,132,761
61	47	Mercer, OH	2,113,330
45	48	Gooding, ID	2,106,203
30	49	Gray, KS	2,103,461
28	50	Sussex, DE	2,085,980
14	51	Deaf Smith, TX	1,942,201
57	52	Washington, IA	1,894,242
27	53	Castro, TX	1,863,235
43	54	Grant, KS	1,794,738
31	55	Riverside, CA	1,794,629
56	56	Twin Falls, ID	1,718,569
9	57	Yakima, WA	1,662,430
29	58	Benton, WA	1,573,284
65	59	Logan, CO	1,570,536
24	60	Texas, OK	1,563,361
20	61	Sampson, NC	1,534,742
71	62	Wayne, NC	1,497,288
19	63	Duplin, NC	1,422,426
17	64	Lancaster, PA	1,410,238
64	65	Swisher, TX	1,364,672
8	66	Weld, CO	1,335,953
37	67	Parmer, TX	1,330,531
53	68	Marion, OR	1,292,998
74	69	Allegan, MI	1,172,374
49	70	Stearns, MN	1,135,611
52	71	Chester, PA	1,110,075
40	72	Miami-Dade, FL	1,068,826
41	73	San Diego, CA	1,014,281
44	74	Rockingham, VA	997,634
70	75	Benton, AR	815,643

Average value of land and buildings per acre, 2017

Value of sales rank	Value of land and buildings per acre rank	County	Average value per acre (dollars) [col 123]
40	1	Miami-Dade, FL	37,450
15	2	Ventura, CA	25,498
41	3	San Diego, CA	23,209
34	4	Sonoma, CA	22,186
68	5	Santa Cruz, CA	21,352
17	6	Lancaster, PA	18,285
31	7	Riverside, CA	18,144
6	8	Stanislaus, CA	15,619
7	9	San Joaquin, CA	15,020
5	10	Merced, CA	13,086
53	11	Marion, OR	12,367
52	12	Chester, PA	12,140
2	13	Tulare, CA	11,726
1	14	Fresno, CA	11,359
11	15	Imperial, CA	11,135
18	16	Madera, CA	10,958
13	17	Kings, CA	10,815
12	18	Sioux, IA	10,405
16	19	Santa Barbara, CA	10,381
33	20	Lyon, IA	9,988
61	21	Mercer, OH	9,673
22	22	Maricopa, AZ	9,236
63	23	Glenn, CA	8,915
44	24	Rockingham, VA	8,844
50	25	Plymouth, IA	8,561
28	26	Sussex, DE	8,473
36	27	Palm Beach, FL	8,379
73	28	Hamilton, IA	8,115
72	29	Kossuth, IA	7,892
53	30	San Luis Obispo, CA	7,547
4	31	Kern, CA	7,380
3	32	Monterey, CA	7,368
57	33	Washington, IA	6,889
59	34	Martin, MN	6,712
67	35	Renville, MN	6,560
70	36	Benton, AR	6,478
55	37	Platte, NE	6,328
26	38	Cuming, NE	6,087
66	39	Huron, MI	6,048
58	40	Jerome, ID	6,039
45	41	Gooding, ID	6,016
74	42	Allegan, MI	5,981
49	43	Stearns, MN	5,149
75	44	Phelps, NE	5,114
71	45	Wayne, NC	4,990
20	46	Sampson, NC	4,891
19	47	Duplin, NC	4,798
61	48	Franklin, WA	4,595
56	49	Twin Falls, ID	4,439
29	50	Benton, WA	3,898
10	51	Grant, WA	3,421
48	52	Dawson, NE	3,412
32	53	Cassia, ID	3,190
38	54	Pinal, AZ	2,764
9	55	Yakima, WA	2,755
8	56	Weld, CO	2,586
46	57	Custer, NE	2,475
47	58	Lincoln, NE	1,674
35	59	Yuma, CO	1,633
30	60	Gray, KS	1,596
43	61	Grant, KS	1,576
42	62	Finney, KS	1,565
23	63	Haskell, KS	1,527
25	64	Scott, KS	1,515
39	65	Sherman, TX	1,431
27	66	Castro, TX	1,380
51	67	Hansford, TX	1,342
21	68	Hartley, TX	1,241
65	69	Logan, CO	1,188
60	70	Dallam, TX	1,134
14	71	Deaf Smith, TX	1,128
69	72	Morrow, OR	1,127
37	73	Parmer, TX	1,125
64	74	Swisher, TX	1,046
24	75	Texas, OK	1,013

Table B. States and Counties — Land Area and Population

State / county code	CBSA code[1]	County code[2]	STATE County	Population, 2018				Population and population characteristics, 2018										
								Race alone or in combination, not Hispanic or Latino (percent)					Age (percent)					
				Land area[3] (sq. mi)	Total persons 2018	Rank	Per square mile	White	Black	American Indian, Alaska Native	Asian and Pacific Islander	Percent Hispanic or Latino[4]	Under 5 years	5 to 17 years	18 to 24 years	25 to 34 years	35 to 44 years	45 to 54 years
				1	2	3	4	5	6	7	8	9	10	11	12	13	14	15

1. CBSA = Core Based Statistical Area. See Appendix A for explanation. See Appendix B for list of metropolitan areas with component counties.   2. County type code from the Economic Research Service of USDA Rural-Urban Continuum Codes. See Appendix A for definition.   3. Dry land or land partially or temporarily covered by water.   4. May be of any race.

Table B. States and Counties — Population and Households

STATE County	Population, 2018 (cont.)				Population change, 2000-2018							Households, 2013-2017				
	Age (percent) (cont.)				Total persons		Percent change		Components of change, 2010-2018						Percent	
	55 to 64 years	65 to 74 years	75 years and over	Percent female	2000	2010	2000-2010	2010-2018	Births	Deaths	Net Migration	Number	Persons per household	Family house-holds	Female family house-holder[1]	One person
	16	17	18	19	20	21	22	23	24	25	26	27	28	29	30	31

1. No spouse present.

Table B. States and Counties — Population, Vital Statistics, Health, and Crime

STATE County	Persons in group quarters, 2018	Daytime Population, 2013-2017		Births, 2018		Deaths, 2018		Persons under 65 with no health insurance, 2016		Medicare, 2018			Serious crimes known to police[2], 2016	
													Total	
		Number	Employment/ residence ratio	Total	Rate[1]	Number	Rate[1]	Number	Percent	Total beneficiaries	Enrolled in Original Medicare	Enrolled in Medicare Advantage	Number	Rate[3]
	32	33	34	35	36	37	38	39	40	41	42	43	44	45

1. Per 1,000 estimated resident population.   2. Data for serious crimes have not been adjusted for underreporting; this may affect comparability between geographic areas and over time.   3. Per 100,000 population estimated by the FBI.

Table B. States and Counties — Crime, Education, Money Income, and Poverty

STATE County	Serious crimes known to police[2], 2016 (cont.)[1]		Education						Local government expenditures,[5] 2014-2015		Money income, 2013-2017				Income and poverty, 2017			
	Rate		School enrollment and attainment, 2013-2017									Households			Percent below poverty level			
			Enrollment[3]		Attainment[4] (percent)								Percent					
	Violent	Property	Total	Percent private	High school graduate or less	Bachelor's degree or more	Total current spending (mil dol)	Current spending per student (dollars)	Per capita income[6]	Median income (dollars)	with income of less than $50,000	with income of $200,000 or more	Median household income (dollars)	All persons	Children under 18 years	Children 5 to 17 years in families
	46	47	48	49	50	51	52	53	54	55	56	57	58	59	60	61

1. Data for serious crimes have not been adjusted for underreporting; this may affect comparability between geographic areas and over time.   2. Per 100,000 population estimated by the FBI.   3. All persons 3 years old and over enrolled in nursery school through college.   4. Persons 25 years old and over.   5. Elementary and secondary education expenditures.   6. Based on population estimated by the American Community Survey, 2013–2017.

Table B. States and Counties — **Personal Income and Earnings**

STATE County	Personal income, 2017										Earnings, 2017		
			Per capita[1]			Supplements to wages and salaries, employer contributions (mil dol)						Contributions for government social insurance (mil dol)	
	Total (mil dol)	Percent change 2016-2017	Dollars	Rank	Wages and salaries (mil dol)	Pension and insurance	Government social insurance	Proprietors' income (mil dol)	Dividends, interest, and rent (mil dol)	Personal transfer reecipts (mil dol)	Total (mil dol)	From employee and self-employed	From employer
	62	63	64	65	66	67	68	69	70	71	72	73	74

1. Based on the resident population estimated as of July 1 of the year shown.

Table B. States and Counties — **Earnings, Social Security, and Housing**

STATE County	Earnings, 2017 (cont.)									Social Security beneficiaries, December 2017		Supplemental Security Income recipients, 2017	Housing units, 2018	
	Percent by selected industries													
	Farm	Mining, quarrying, and extractions	Construction	Manu-facturing	Information; professional, scientific, technical services	Retail trade	Finance, insurance, real estate, and leasing	Health care and social assistance	Govern-ment	Number	Rate[1]		Total	Percent change, 2010-2018
	75	76	77	78	79	80	81	82	83	84	85	86	87	88

1. Per 1,000 resident population estimated as of July 1 of the year shown.

Table B. States and Counties — **Housing, Labor Force, and Employment**

STATE County	Housing units, 2013-2017									Civilian labor force, 2018				Civilian employment[6], 2013-2017		
		Occupied units										Unemployment			Percent	
			Owner-occupied				Renter-occupied									
					Median owner cost as a percent of income			Median rent as a percent of income[2]	Sub-standard units[4] (percent)		Percent change, 2017-2018				Management, business, science, and arts	Construction, production, and maintenance occupations
	Total	Percent	Median value[1]	With a mort-gage	Without a mort-gage[2]	Median rent[3]				Total		Total	Rate[5]	Total		
	89	90	91	92	93	94	95	96		97	98	99	100	101	102	103

1. Specified owner-occupied units.   2. A value of 10.0 represents 10 percent or less; a value of 50.0 represents 50 percent or more.   3. Specified renter-occupied units.   4. Overcrowded or lacking complete plumbing facilities.   5. Percent of civilian labor force.   6. Civilian employed persons 16 years old and over.

Table B. States and Counties — **Nonfarm Employment and Agriculture**

STATE County	Private nonfarm establishments, employment and payroll, 2016									Agriculture, 2017				
		Employment						Annual payroll		Farms				Farm producers whose primary occupation is farming (percent)
												Percent with:		
	Number of establish-ments	Total	Health care and social assistance	Manufac-turing	Retail trade	Finance and insurance	Professional, scientific, and technical services	Total (mil dol)	Average per employee (dollars)	Number		Fewer than 50 acres	1000 acres or more	
	104	105	106	107	108	109	110	111	112	113		114	115	116

Table B. States and Counties — **Agriculture**

STATE County	Agriculture, 2017 (cont.)															
	Land in farms					Value of land and buildings (dollars)		Value of machinery and equiopmnet, average per farm (dollars)	Value of products sold:				Organic farms (number)	Farms with internet access (percent)	Government payments	
			Acres								Percent from:						
	Acreage (1,000)	Percent change, 2012-2017	Average size of farm	Total irrigated (1,000)	Total cropland (1,000)	Average per farm	Average per acre		Total (mil dol)	Average per farm (acres)	Crops	Livestock and poultry products			Total ($1,000)	Percent of farms
	117	118	119	120	121	122	123	124	125	126	127	128	129	130	131	132

Table B. States and Counties — **Water Use, Wholesale Trade, Retail Trade, and Real Estate**

STATE County	Water use, 2015		Wholesale Trade[1], 2012				Retail Trade[2], 2012				Real estate and rental and leasing,[2] 2012			
	Public supply water withdrawn (mil gal/ day)	Public supply gallons withdrawn per person per day	Number of establish-ments	Number of employees	Sales (mil dol)	Average payroll (mil dol)	Number of establish-ments	Number of employees	Sales (mil dol)	Average payroll (mil dol)	Number of establish-ments	Number of employees	Sales (mil dol)	Average payroll (mil dol)
	133	134	135	136	137	138	139	140	141	142	143	144	145	146

1   Merchant wholesalers, except manufacturers' sales branches and offices.   2. Employer establishments.

Table B. States and Counties — **Professional Services, Manufacturing, and Accommodation and Food Services**

STATE County	Professional, scientific, and technical services, 2012				Manufacturing, 2012				Accommodation and food services, 2012			
	Number of establish-ments	Number of employees	Sales (mil dol)	Average payroll (mil dol)	Number of establish-ments	Number of employees	Receipts (mil dol)	Annual payroll (mil dol)	Number of establis-hments	Number of employees	Receipts (mil dol)	Annual payroll (mil dol)
	147	148	149	150	151	152	153	154	155	156	157	158

Table B. States and Counties — **Health Care and Social Assistance, Other Services, Nonemployer Businesses, and Residential Construction**

STATE County	Health care and social assistance, 2012				Other services, 2012				Nonemployer businesses, 2016		Value of residential construction authorized by building permits, 2018	
	Number of establish-ments	Number of employees	Receipts (mil dol)	Annual payroll (mil dol)	Number of establish-ments	Number of employees	Receipts (mil dol)	Annual payroll (mil dol)	Number	Receipts (mil dol)	New construction ($1,000)	Number of housing units
	159	160	161	162	163	164	165	166	167	168	169	170

Table B. States and Counties — **Government Employment and Payroll, and Local Government Finances**

STATE County	Government employment and payroll, 2012									Local government finances, 2012				
	Full-time equivalent employees	March payroll (dollars)	March payroll (percent of total)							Total (mil dol)	General revenue			
			Adminis-tration, judicial, and legal	Police and corrections	Fire protection	Highways and transpor-tation	Health and welfare	Natural resources and utilities	Education and libraries		Inter-govern-mental (mil dol)	Taxes		
												Total (mil dol)	Per capita[1] (dollars)	
													Total	Property
	171	172	173	174	175	176	177	178	179	180	181	182	183	184

1. Based on the resident population estimated as of July 1 of the year shown.

Table B. States and Counties — **Local Government Finances, Government Employment, and Income Taxes**

STATE County	Local government finances, 2012 (cont.)							Debt outstanding		Government employment, 2017			Individual income tax returns, 2016		
	Direct general expenditure							Total (mil dol)	Per capita[1] (dollars)	Federal civilian	Federal military	State and local	Number of returns	Mean adjusted gross income	Mean income tax
	Total (mil dol)	Per capita[1] (dollars)	Percent of total for:												
			Education	Health and hospitals	Police protection	Public welfare	Highways								
	185	186	187	188	189	190	191	192	193	194	195	196	197	198	199

1. Based on the resident population estimated as of July 1 of the year shown.

State / county code	CBSA code[1]	County code[2]	STATE County	Land area[3] (sq. mi)	Total persons 2018	Rank	Per square mile	White	Black	American Indian, Alaska Native	Asian and Pacific Islancer	Percent Hispanic or Latino[4]	Under 5 years	5 to 17 years	18 to 24 years	25 to 34 years	35 to 44 years	45 to 54 years
				1	2	3	4	5	6	7	8	9	10	11	12	13	14	15
00000		0	UNITED STATES	3,532,614.3	327,167,434	X	92.6	62.3	13.5	1.3	6.9	18.3	6.1	16.4	9.3	14.0	12.6	12.7
01000		0	ALABAMA	50,646.6	4,887,871	X	96.5	66.8	27.3	1.2	1.9	4.4	6.0	16.3	9.3	13.2	12.1	12.8
01001	33,860	2	Autauga....................	594.4	55,601	921	93.5	75.8	20.2	0.9	1.8	3.0	6.1	17.6	8.0	12.9	13.0	14.0
01003	19,300	3	Baldwin	1,589.8	218,022	310	137.1	84.6	9.5	1.4	1.6	4.6	5.5	16.1	7.2	11.3	11.9	13.2
01005	21,640	6	Barbour	885.0	24,881	1,611	28.1	46.5	48.9	0.8	0.7	4.3	5.2	15.7	7.9	13.9	12.0	13.0
01007	13,820	1	Bibb..........................	622.5	22,400	1,707	36.0	75.5	21.7	0.8	0.5	2.6	5.7	14.7	7.9	14.9	13.2	14.2
01009	13,820	1	Blount........................	644.8	57,840	892	89.7	88.1	1.9	1.2	0.5	9.6	6.0	17.2	7.7	12.0	12.2	13.5
01011		6	Bullock	622.8	10,138	2,418	16.3	22.0	70.0	0.6	0.4	8.0	5.9	15.2	8.1	15.1	12.9	12.4
01013		6	Butler........................	776.8	19,680	1,844	25.3	52.2	45.1	0.7	1.6	1.5	5.7	16.6	7.7	11.6	12.1	11.8
01015	11,500	3	Calhoun......................	605.9	114,277	539	188.6	73.7	21.8	1.0	1.5	3.9	5.8	15.9	9.1	13.2	11.9	12.5
01017	46,740	6	Chambers	596.6	33,615	1,339	56.3	56.3	40.3	0.6	1.5	2.6	5.7	15.1	8.0	12.6	11.2	13.1
01019		6	Cherokee	553.5	26,032	1,567	47.0	93.2	4.9	1.4	0.5	1.6	4.6	14.5	7.1	10.6	10.6	13.8
01021	13,820	1	Chilton......................	692.9	44,153	1,093	63.7	81.2	10.6	0.8	0.7	7.9	6.2	17.6	8.0	12.6	12.4	13.2
01023		9	Choctaw	913.5	12,841	2,234	14.1	57.0	41.9	0.5	0.3	1.0	5.2	14.7	7.3	10.2	10.8	13.1
01025		7	Clarke.......................	1,238.4	23,920	1,647	19.3	53.3	44.8	0.8	0.7	1.4	5.8	15.9	8.3	11.0	11.7	13.0
01027		9	Clay..........................	604.0	13,275	2,214	22.0	82.3	15.0	1.1	0.5	3.0	5.2	15.1	8.1	10.9	11.3	13.9
01029		8	Cleburne	560.1	14,987	2,097	26.8	93.9	3.5	0.9	0.4	2.5	6.0	16.8	7.1	11.7	11.7	13.9
01031	21,460	4	Coffee	679.0	51,909	962	76.4	72.2	18.3	2.1	2.5	7.6	6.2	17.5	8.0	12.7	12.8	13.3
01033	22,520	3	Colbert	592.7	54,762	933	92.4	80.0	16.9	1.3	0.9	2.7	5.7	15.1	7.9	12.7	11.5	13.1
01035		7	Conecuh.....................	850.2	12,277	2,272	14.4	51.3	46.2	1.0	0.4	2.2	5.3	15.5	7.6	11.1	10.3	12.1
01037	45,180	8	Coosa........................	650.9	10,715	2,377	16.5	66.4	30.9	1.0	0.3	2.5	4.6	12.0	6.8	10.3	10.6	14.6
01039		6	Covington...................	1,030.6	36,986	1,247	35.9	84.7	13.3	1.2	0.6	1.7	6.0	15.9	7.1	11.7	10.9	12.5
01041		8	Crenshaw	608.9	13,824	2,174	22.7	72.7	24.3	1.2	1.3	2.3	5.8	17.1	7.5	11.9	11.5	12.8
01043	18,980	4	Cullman.....................	734.8	83,442	684	113.6	93.1	1.6	1.3	0.9	4.4	6.2	16.3	7.6	12.9	12.0	12.8
01045	37,120	4	Dale..........................	561.1	48,956	1,006	87.3	70.5	21.6	1.4	2.3	6.6	6.7	16.3	8.7	14.7	11.6	12.1
01047	42,820	4	Dallas	978.7	38,310	1,219	39.1	27.9	70.6	0.5	0.7	1.1	6.1	17.7	8.8	11.7	11.1	11.8
01049	22,840	6	DeKalb	777.1	71,385	757	91.9	82.0	1.9	2.6	0.6	14.8	5.9	18.1	8.1	11.9	12.3	13.3
01051	33,860	2	Elmore.......................	618.4	81,887	694	132.4	74.5	22.0	1.0	1.2	3.0	5.8	16.5	8.3	14.1	13.2	13.8
01053	12,120	6	Escambia	945.2	36,748	1,259	38.9	61.9	32.4	4.6	0.6	2.5	6.0	16.4	7.6	13.5	12.4	13.0
01055	23,460	3	Etowah	535.3	102,501	595	191.5	79.2	16.3	1.1	1.0	4.0	5.8	15.7	8.2	12.1	12.0	13.5
01057		6	Fayette	627.7	16,433	2,013	26.2	85.5	12.8	0.8	0.5	1.8	5.6	15.5	7.9	11.5	11.0	12.9
01059		6	Franklin	633.9	31,363	1,395	49.5	77.4	4.5	1.1	0.5	17.8	6.6	17.9	8.1	12.4	12.4	13.2
01061	20,020	3	Geneva	574.5	26,314	1,555	45.8	85.3	10.2	1.6	0.6	4.0	5.4	16.5	7.1	11.3	11.5	13.5
01063		8	Greene	647.0	8,233	2,574	12.7	18.2	80.0	0.5	0.4	1.7	5.8	16.4	7.7	11.6	10.1	10.9
01065	46,220	3	Hale..........................	644.0	14,726	2,113	22.9	40.3	58.1	0.5	0.4	1.4	6.6	16.4	8.8	11.8	11.1	11.7
01067	20,020	3	Henry	561.8	17,209	1,965	30.6	70.6	26.6	0.9	0.5	2.7	5.3	15.3	6.9	10.8	11.9	13.2
01069	20,020	3	Houston.....................	579.9	104,722	576	180.6	67.9	27.9	1.0	1.5	3.4	6.1	17.0	7.7	13.0	12.3	12.9
01071	42,460	6	Jackson	1,078.0	51,736	966	48.0	91.6	4.1	3.2	0.7	3.0	5.4	15.5	7.4	11.3	12.0	13.5
01073	13,820	1	Jefferson	1,111.4	659,300	101	593.2	50.7	43.8	0.6	2.2	4.0	6.4	16.4	8.8	14.5	12.7	12.2
01075		8	Lamar........................	604.8	13,844	2,170	22.9	87.5	11.3	0.8	0.4	1.7	5.4	16.0	7.1	10.8	11.3	13.1
01077	22,520	3	Lauderdale..................	668.0	92,387	638	138.3	86.0	10.7	0.9	1.0	2.9	5.1	14.5	11.3	11.9	10.7	12.6
01079	19,460	3	Lawrence	690.7	32,957	1,359	47.7	80.9	11.7	9.3	0.6	2.2	5.5	16.1	7.4	12.0	11.2	14.3
01081	12,220	3	Lee...........................	607.6	163,941	400	269.8	68.9	23.5	0.7	4.8	3.8	5.9	15.4	18.0	14.2	12.0	11.8
01083	26,620	2	Limestone..................	560.0	96,174	619	171.7	78.0	14.4	1.4	2.1	6.1	5.6	17.0	7.5	13.0	13.6	14.6
01085	33,860	2	Lowndes.....................	715.9	9,974	2,429	13.9	25.6	72.2	0.6	0.4	1.7	6.2	16.5	7.6	12.5	10.7	12.7
01087		6	Macon........................	608.8	18,439	1,903	30.3	17.0	80.7	0.7	1.0	1.8	4.6	12.3	17.8	11.3	9.0	11.2
01089	26,620	2	Madison	801.6	366,519	194	457.2	66.8	25.6	1.6	3.6	5.1	5.8	16.0	9.5	14.0	12.2	13.5
01091		7	Marengo.....................	976.9	19,066	1,870	19.5	45.7	51.6	0.6	0.5	2.6	6.3	16.4	7.9	12.0	10.9	12.7
01093		7	Marion	742.3	29,763	1,438	40.1	92.9	4.3	0.9	0.5	2.6	5.4	15.4	7.4	11.4	11.2	13.9
01095	10,700	4	Marshall	565.8	96,109	620	169.9	81.8	3.1	1.3	0.9	14.3	7.0	17.9	8.0	12.5	11.7	12.8
01097	33,660	2	Mobile.......................	1,229.4	413,757	172	336.6	58.0	36.6	1.5	2.5	3.1	6.5	16.9	9.0	14.0	12.0	12.2
01099		7	Monroe	1,025.7	21,067	1,772	20.5	55.5	41.9	2.0	0.7	1.6	5.2	16.3	8.4	10.7	11.0	13.2
01101	33,860	2	Montgomery	785.3	225,763	301	287.5	34.3	59.3	0.6	3.7	3.5	6.7	16.6	9.8	14.5	12.4	12.1
01103	19,460	3	Morgan.......................	579.4	119,089	523	205.5	77.2	13.6	1.7	1.0	8.5	6.0	16.8	7.9	12.2	12.1	13.7
01105		8	Perry	719.7	9,140	2,489	12.7	30.1	67.8	0.5	0.8	1.4	5.5	15.8	15.0	10.5	10.0	10.9
01107	46,220	3	Pickens	881.4	19,938	1,831	22.6	54.8	40.5	0.5	0.5	4.8	5.3	14.4	8.3	13.5	11.4	13.7
01109	45,980	6	Pike	672.1	33,338	1,348	49.6	57.3	38.2	1.3	2.6	2.4	5.4	13.6	22.6	12.2	9.9	10.1
01111		6	Randolph....................	580.5	22,725	1,693	39.1	76.8	20.3	0.9	0.7	2.9	5.8	15.7	8.5	10.8	10.8	13.4
01113	17,980	2	Russell......................	641.2	57,781	894	90.1	47.9	46.0	1.1	1.8	5.6	6.9	17.3	8.3	15.2	12.5	12.7
01115	13,820	1	St. Clair	631.6	88,690	656	140.4	86.9	10.0	0.9	1.2	2.5	6.0	16.7	7.1	13.3	12.7	13.8
01117	13,820	1	Shelby	785.4	215,707	313	274.6	78.7	13.5	0.7	2.7	5.8	5.8	17.7	8.2	12.1	13.7	14.2
01119		8	Sumter	903.8	12,691	2,243	14.0	25.2	71.8	0.4	2.2	1.2	5.7	13.2	19.5	10.8	8.3	10.4
01121	45,180	4	Talladega...................	736.8	79,828	703	108.3	64.0	33.5	0.9	1.0	2.4	5.4	15.8	8.3	12.9	11.9	13.6
01123	10,760	6	Tallapoosa..................	716.5	40,497	1,169	56.5	69.8	27.5	0.8	0.8	2.4	5.5	15.1	7.6	11.4	10.2	13.3
01125	46,220	3	Tuscaloosa.................	1,320.9	208,911	321	158.2	62.3	32.5	0.6	2.0	3.9	6.0	14.9	16.4	14.7	12.0	11.2
01127	13,820	1	Walker.......................	791.0	63,711	837	80.5	90.3	6.9	1.0	0.8	2.6	6.0	16.2	7.7	11.8	11.5	13.3

1. CBSA = Core Based Statistical Area. See Appendix A for explanation. See Appendix B for list of metropolitan areas with component counties.   2. County type code from the Economic Research Service of USDA Rural-Urban Continuum Codes. See Appendix A for definition.   3. Dry land or land partially or temporarily covered by water.   4. May be of any race.

Table B. States and Counties — Population and Households

STATE County	Age (percent) (cont.)			Percent female	Population change, 2000-2018				Components of change, 2010-2018			Households, 2013-2017				
	55 to 64 years	65 to 74 years	75 years and over		Total persons 2000	Total persons 2010	Percent change 2000-2010	Percent change 2010-2018	Births	Deaths	Net Migration	Number	Persons per household	Family households	Female family householder[1]	One person
	16	17	18	19	20	21	22	23	24	25	26	27	28	29	30	31
UNITED STATES	12.9	9.3	6.7	50.8	281,421,906	308,758,105	9.7	6.0	32,514,580	21,799,621	7,694,370	118,825,921	2.63	65.9	12.7	27.7
ALABAMA	13.4	10.0	6.9	51.6	4,447,100	4,780,138	7.5	2.3	484,329	418,734	42,748	1,856,695	2.55	66.5	14.8	29.3
Autauga	12.9	8.8	6.7	51.4	43,671	54,574	25.0	1.9	5,247	4,556	338	21,054	2.59	70.8	11.4	26.0
Baldwin	14.4	12.3	8.2	51.5	140,415	182,264	29.8	19.6	18,267	16,586	33,655	76,133	2.63	65.7	9.4	30.4
Barbour	12.9	11.6	7.9	47.2	29,038	27,457	-5.4	-9.4	2,333	2,579	-2,342	9,191	2.54	65.7	19.4	31.9
Bibb	12.9	9.7	6.8	46.8	20,826	22,920	10.1	-2.3	2,113	2,060	-566	6,916	2.97	76.7	14.9	21.4
Blount	13.2	10.8	7.4	50.7	51,024	57,321	12.3	0.9	5,661	5,119	28	20,690	2.76	74.0	9.8	24.0
Bullock	14.1	9.4	7.0	45.5	11,714	10,911	-6.9	-7.1	1,093	1,035	-846	3,670	2.74	66.0	27.2	30.2
Butler	14.2	11.2	9.1	53.4	21,399	20,943	-2.1	-6.0	1,998	2,172	-1,084	7,050	2.81	64.8	17.3	30.8
Calhoun	14.0	10.6	7.2	51.9	112,249	118,594	5.7	-3.6	11,052	11,657	-3,673	45,099	2.49	68.1	16.7	27.3
Chambers	14.7	11.4	8.1	52.1	36,583	34,171	-6.6	-1.6	3,242	3,713	-65	13,694	2.44	63.5	16.0	32.3
Cherokee	15.7	13.6	9.4	50.5	23,988	25,989	8.3	0.2	1,916	2,821	968	10,795	2.37	70.1	10.4	27.9
Chilton	13.3	10.1	6.7	50.9	39,593	43,630	10.2	1.2	4,504	4,080	130	16,768	2.59	71.1	14.3	25.2
Choctaw	15.7	13.0	10.0	52.7	15,922	13,858	-13.0	-7.3	1,099	1,405	-710	5,463	2.38	65.8	16.7	31.6
Clarke	14.4	10.9	9.0	52.6	27,867	25,833	-7.3	-7.4	2,253	2,394	-1,788	9,602	2.53	62.9	12.2	34.2
Clay	14.8	11.5	9.2	51.1	14,254	13,930	-2.3	-4.7	1,135	1,489	-301	5,338	2.46	70.1	13.6	27.2
Cleburne	13.5	11.3	8.2	50.5	14,123	14,972	6.0	0.1	1,436	1,527	112	5,773	2.56	67.2	9.4	30.1
Coffee	12.5	10.0	7.0	50.8	43,615	49,952	14.5	3.9	5,278	4,139	808	19,620	2.57	68.5	12.9	28.1
Colbert	14.1	11.2	8.7	52.0	54,984	54,428	-1.0	0.6	5,047	5,759	1,096	21,983	2.46	68.1	13.7	28.9
Conecuh	15.6	12.6	9.8	52.1	14,089	13,233	-6.1	-7.2	1,160	1,416	-701	4,716	2.67	65.9	18.2	33.7
Coosa	18.0	13.5	9.7	49.6	12,202	11,758	-3.6	-8.9	774	1,114	-705	4,204	2.51	60.6	11.1	36.1
Covington	14.9	11.7	9.4	51.6	37,631	37,766	0.4	-2.1	3,660	4,218	-188	15,285	2.41	67.5	12.5	28.5
Crenshaw	14.5	11.6	7.4	51.7	13,665	13,898	1.7	-0.5	1,251	1,444	125	5,358	2.56	67.2	15.8	29.7
Cullman	13.6	10.9	7.6	50.6	77,483	80,406	3.8	3.8	8,106	8,050	3,037	31,097	2.59	69.3	10.8	27.5
Dale	13.1	9.8	7.1	50.9	49,129	50,249	2.3	-2.6	5,486	4,088	-2,696	18,825	2.56	67.6	14.5	27.8
Dallas	14.8	10.8	7.3	53.8	46,365	43,818	-5.5	-12.6	4,310	4,372	-5,490	16,487	2.44	62.6	24.5	34.0
DeKalb	13.1	10.3	6.9	50.4	64,452	71,116	10.3	0.4	6,953	6,353	-280	25,482	2.76	70.6	11.6	26.9
Elmore	13.2	9.2	5.9	51.7	65,874	79,293	20.4	3.3	7,743	6,228	1,121	29,115	2.62	71.9	13.3	25.4
Escambia	13.1	10.3	7.6	49.3	38,440	38,320	-0.3	-4.1	3,684	3,878	-1,365	13,226	2.63	64.4	14.6	33.1
Etowah	13.7	11.3	7.7	51.6	103,459	104,427	0.9	-1.8	9,766	11,440	-157	39,061	2.61	67.6	13.2	29.0
Fayette	14.4	12.1	9.0	51.2	18,495	17,232	-6.8	-4.6	1,449	1,926	-309	6,955	2.35	70.5	10.3	27.1
Franklin	12.5	9.6	7.3	49.5	31,223	31,709	1.6	-1.1	3,470	3,157	-650	11,533	2.71	69.4	14.2	27.3
Geneva	14.3	11.8	8.5	51.2	25,764	26,787	4.0	-1.8	2,445	2,930	26	10,693	2.46	70.5	13.6	25.1
Greene	15.4	13.0	9.3	52.8	9,974	9,043	-9.3	-9.0	845	905	-760	3,025	2.80	60.9	22.0	36.9
Hale	14.4	11.1	8.1	52.4	17,185	15,762	-8.3	-6.6	1,618	1,514	-1,157	5,664	2.61	64.6	20.6	32.3
Henry	13.9	13.7	9.0	51.8	16,310	17,300	6.1	-0.5	1,470	1,797	249	6,727	2.50	67.6	10.8	29.9
Houston	13.2	10.4	7.4	52.0	88,787	101,554	14.4	3.1	10,674	8,819	1,393	39,560	2.61	65.5	15.9	30.2
Jackson	14.9	11.8	8.3	50.9	53,926	53,224	-1.3	-2.8	4,663	5,640	-466	20,368	2.54	69.4	10.1	28.1
Jefferson	13.1	9.3	6.5	52.7	662,047	658,506	-0.5	0.1	72,097	57,977	-12,880	261,390	2.46	63.3	17.9	31.7
Lamar	14.6	11.9	9.8	51.1	15,904	14,564	-8.4	-4.9	1,189	1,636	-263	6,019	2.30	67.3	10.0	30.9
Lauderdale	13.7	11.5	8.6	52.0	87,966	92,709	5.4	-0.3	7,589	9,036	1,198	38,634	2.34	63.5	12.1	31.0
Lawrence	14.8	11.1	7.5	51.3	34,803	34,339	-1.3	-4.0	2,999	3,272	-1,101	13,056	2.53	71.4	11.9	26.6
Lee	10.8	7.4	4.5	50.8	115,092	140,300	21.9	16.9	14,978	8,361	16,848	59,001	2.55	63.0	14.3	27.4
Limestone	13.4	9.2	6.0	49.9	65,676	82,782	26.0	16.2	8,266	6,112	11,098	32,386	2.74	71.3	11.1	26.2
Lowndes	15.0	10.7	8.1	53.2	13,473	11,296	-16.2	-11.7	1,086	1,086	-1,340	4,309	2.38	69.6	29.4	28.3
Macon	13.5	12.3	8.0	54.5	24,105	21,448	-11.0	-14.0	1,600	1,933	-2,724	7,852	2.17	58.8	22.3	36.4
Madison	14.1	8.7	6.4	51.1	276,700	334,811	21.0	9.5	34,173	24,128	21,733	142,253	2.42	64.5	12.5	30.5
Marengo	14.1	10.9	8.7	53.1	22,539	21,038	-6.7	-9.4	1,981	2,166	-1,804	7,975	2.45	57.9	13.9	39.3
Marion	14.1	11.7	9.5	50.7	31,214	30,776	-1.4	-3.3	2,492	3,334	-146	12,453	2.37	70.5	12.7	27.0
Marshall	13.1	9.8	7.2	50.6	82,231	93,019	13.1	3.3	10,873	9,042	1,350	34,588	2.71	70.0	11.8	26.6
Mobile	13.3	9.7	6.5	52.4	399,843	413,145	3.3	0.1	45,785	35,223	-9,729	153,794	2.63	64.5	18.0	29.1
Monroe	14.9	11.3	9.0	52.5	24,324	23,067	-5.2	-8.7	1,867	2,162	-1,725	8,207	2.62	62.2	14.3	35.7
Montgomery	12.6	8.9	6.2	52.8	223,510	229,378	2.6	-1.6	25,789	17,198	-12,263	89,776	2.45	62.6	20.3	32.6
Morgan	13.7	10.1	7.3	50.7	111,064	119,486	7.6	-0.3	11,722	10,502	-1,543	45,904	2.55	68.8	13.3	27.8
Perry	12.9	10.3	9.1	53.2	11,861	10,591	-10.8	-13.6	974	1,093	-1,335	3,039	2.92	59.6	26.7	39.6
Pickens	14.4	10.7	8.3	50.1	20,949	19,746	-5.7	1.0	1,820	2,001	309	7,620	2.48	64.7	13.9	34.0
Pike	11.2	8.6	6.3	51.7	29,605	32,895	11.1	1.3	3,106	2,658	-28	12,284	2.55	59.6	17.3	32.4
Randolph	14.8	11.7	8.7	51.3	22,380	22,916	2.4	-0.8	2,036	2,412	188	8,867	2.49	68.4	12.1	27.7
Russell	12.8	8.7	5.7	52.0	49,756	52,947	6.4	9.1	7,012	4,795	2,431	22,690	2.55	63.8	18.2	31.2
St. Clair	13.7	10.1	6.5	50.4	64,742	83,345	28.7	6.4	8,600	7,371	4,148	32,486	2.61	72.3	11.7	24.1
Shelby	13.0	9.4	5.9	51.7	143,293	195,313	36.3	10.4	19,644	11,345	12,152	76,868	2.68	71.7	9.2	24.4
Sumter	14.0	9.9	8.1	54.3	14,798	13,763	-7.0	-7.8	1,162	1,291	-949	5,073	2.41	54.0	19.4	41.1
Talladega	14.1	10.9	7.1	51.7	80,321	82,283	2.4	-3.0	7,092	8,147	-1,361	31,651	2.45	67.0	16.9	29.1
Tallapoosa	15.3	12.9	8.7	51.5	41,475	41,618	0.3	-2.7	3,765	4,396	-475	16,369	2.45	66.0	15.2	27.5
Tuscaloosa	11.4	8.1	5.2	51.9	164,875	194,668	18.1	7.3	20,392	13,974	7,857	71,507	2.72	66.0	15.7	27.5
Walker	14.1	11.4	7.9	51.3	70,713	67,023	-5.2	-4.9	6,541	8,265	-1,546	25,143	2.55	70.2	14.6	25.2

1. No spouse present.

Table B. States and Counties — Population, Vital Statistics, Health, and Crime

STATE County	Persons in group quarters, 2018	Daytime Population, 2013-2017		Births, 2018		Deaths, 2018		Persons under 65 with no health insurance, 2016		Medicare, 2018			Serious crimes known to police[2], 2016 Total	
		Number	Employment/residence ratio	Total	Rate[1]	Number	Rate[1]	Number	Percent	Total beneficiaries	Enrolled in Original Medicare	Enrolled in Medicare Advantage	Number	Rate[3]
	32	33	34	35	36	37	38	39	40	41	42	43	44	45
UNITED STATES	8,091,609	321,004,407	1.00	3,855,500	11.8	2,814,013	8.6	26,749,668	10.0	58,703,170	37,955,674	20,747,496	9,167,220	2,837
ALABAMA........................	117,443	4,802,090	0.98	57,216	11.7	53,425	10.9	427,972	10.8	1,026,964	623,978	402,986	169,248	3,480
Autauga............................	455	44,104	0.55	655	11.8	532	9.6	4,002	8.5	10,641	5,696	4,945	1,875	3,440
Baldwin	2,190	188,856	0.83	2,254	10.3	2,228	10.2	17,733	10.7	50,999	28,779	22,220	4,456	2,147
Barbour	2,820	26,387	1.02	261	10.5	324	13.0	2,252	12.5	6,327	3,855	2,472	714	2,770
Bibb..................................	2,151	18,991	0.55	250	11.2	256	11.4	1,646	9.7	4,846	2,348	2,498	216	961
Blount...............................	489	45,270	0.42	681	11.8	662	11.4	5,704	12.1	12,434	5,921	6,513	1,649	2,865
Bullock	1,661	9,493	0.77	115	11.3	120	11.8	937	13.2	2,029	1,119	910	193	1,815
Butler...............................	333	19,693	0.94	221	11.2	239	12.1	1,703	10.7	4,849	3,737	1,112	672	3,368
Calhoun............................	2,739	115,526	1.00	1,293	11.3	1,494	13.1	10,386	11.2	27,130	19,623	7,507	4,766	4,180
Chambers	458	28,221	0.60	357	10.6	461	13.7	2,876	10.7	8,810	6,276	2,534	1,362	4,000
Cherokee	290	22,442	0.65	219	8.4	340	13.1	2,366	11.9	7,054	4,633	2,421	719	2,790
Chilton..............................	393	36,499	0.58	526	11.9	506	11.5	5,181	14.2	9,258	4,013	5,245	1,473	3,356
Choctaw............................	129	12,385	0.81	134	10.4	176	13.7	1,136	11.3	3,819	3,043	776	68	523
Clarke...............................	280	24,583	0.99	267	11.2	307	12.8	2,219	11.4	6,388	3,648	2,740	589	2,413
Clay..................................	255	12,473	0.83	128	9.6	177	13.3	1,416	13.4	3,647	2,416	1,231	155	1,152
Cleburne	178	12,179	0.50	167	11.1	198	13.2	1,427	11.9	3,503	2,706	797	191	1,274
Coffee	518	47,145	0.82	652	12.6	541	10.4	4,583	10.8	10,482	7,775	2,707	1,209	2,357
Colbert..............................	474	56,763	1.11	610	11.1	685	12.5	4,221	9.7	13,855	10,265	3,590	1,489	2,748
Conecuh............................	45	11,854	0.80	126	10.3	183	14.9	1,225	12.8	3,487	2,636	851	217	1,731
Coosa...............................	248	8,444	0.33	90	8.4	122	11.4	1,097	13.3	2,632	1,715	917	223	2,123
Covington..........................	575	36,083	0.90	426	11.5	537	14.5	3,635	12.3	9,707	7,716	1,991	934	2,474
Crenshaw..........................	132	12,350	0.73	141	10.2	181	13.1	1,293	11.5	3,516	2,216	1,300	183	1,344
Cullman............................	1,049	77,580	0.87	977	11.7	1,039	12.5	8,562	12.8	19,548	12,316	7,232	1,691	2,059
Dale..................................	922	50,686	1.06	651	13.3	552	11.3	4,460	11.0	10,388	7,807	2,581	1,501	3,129
Dallas...............................	852	40,808	1.00	460	12.0	533	13.9	3,369	10.4	9,687	5,946	3,741	2,344	5,785
DeKalb..............................	782	67,296	0.86	817	11.4	807	11.3	9,705	16.6	15,454	10,804	4,650	1,713	2,496
Elmore..............................	5,021	66,597	0.56	896	10.9	818	10.0	5,531	8.5	16,806	9,599	7,207	1,992	2,439
Escambia	2,685	38,343	1.06	435	11.8	485	13.2	3,680	13.2	8,713	5,592	3,121	944	2,511
Etowah	2,086	98,915	0.90	1,175	11.5	1,473	14.4	9,476	11.5	25,656	15,386	10,270	4,367	4,325
Fayette.............................	291	14,985	0.73	167	10.2	225	13.7	1,401	10.8	4,832	3,562	1,270	151	908
Franklin	272	29,997	0.88	426	13.6	364	11.6	3,419	13.1	6,698	5,294	1,404	760	2,426
Geneva	229	22,340	0.59	272	10.3	357	13.6	2,978	14.1	6,765	4,973	1,792	669	2,505
Greene..............................	45	7,919	0.74	99	12.0	98	11.9	738	11.1	2,267	1,762	505	184	2,201
Hale..................................	221	12,653	0.55	186	12.6	207	14.1	1,341	11.2	4,031	3,065	966	243	1,631
Henry	199	14,535	0.62	182	10.6	218	12.7	1,559	11.7	4,709	2,908	1,801	268	1,561
Houston............................	1,416	111,072	1.16	1,272	12.1	1,180	11.3	9,498	11.1	23,301	15,493	7,808	4,108	3,947
Jackson	597	49,096	0.84	570	11.0	679	13.1	5,240	12.6	12,973	9,337	3,636	NA	NA
Jefferson	16,694	723,030	1.21	8,412	12.8	7,306	11.1	53,889	9.9	130,617	61,599	69,018	30,102	4,566
Lamar...............................	217	12,524	0.72	135	9.8	195	14.1	1,204	11.1	3,815	3,178	637	105	765
Lauderdale........................	2,086	87,583	0.87	866	9.4	1,116	12.1	7,267	9.9	21,630	15,601	6,029	2,044	2,220
Lawrence	229	26,954	0.49	358	10.9	411	12.5	3,804	14.0	7,775	5,396	2,379	485	1,502
Lee...................................	4,958	145,734	0.85	1,865	11.4	1,114	6.8	14,359	10.5	23,185	15,272	7,913	5,053	3,157
Limestone	2,696	79,310	0.68	995	10.3	842	8.8	8,497	11.1	17,335	11,809	5,526	1,860	1,995
Lowndes............................	96	9,012	0.61	119	11.9	138	13.8	937	11.4	2,775	1,228	1,547	282	3,268
Macon...............................	1,723	17,825	0.79	172	9.3	243	13.2	1,435	10.4	4,568	2,636	1,932	695	3,822
Madison	8,320	385,887	1.19	4,149	11.3	3,207	8.7	26,207	8.8	64,152	46,165	17,987	14,967	4,207
Marengo............................	254	19,593	0.98	230	12.1	276	14.5	1,571	10.1	5,343	4,204	1,139	535	2,735
Marion	750	29,200	0.93	287	9.6	404	13.6	2,644	11.4	7,041	5,479	1,562	746	2,489
Marshall	1,046	95,579	1.02	1,363	14.2	1,132	11.8	10,702	13.7	20,341	14,844	5,497	2,940	3,101
Mobile	7,277	423,045	1.05	5,337	12.9	4,500	10.9	42,679	12.4	82,690	37,469	45,221	19,105	4,606
Monroe	230	21,650	0.98	204	9.7	283	13.4	2,128	12.3	5,276	3,827	1,449	528	2,471
Montgomery......................	9,120	261,868	1.35	3,047	13.5	2,190	9.7	20,575	11.1	42,515	22,753	19,762	10,690	4,744
Morgan.............................	1,998	119,791	1.01	1,410	11.8	1,333	11.2	10,877	11.2	25,883	18,534	7,349	3,672	3,079
Perry	783	9,225	0.81	107	11.7	131	14.3	786	11.3	2,439	1,955	484	NA	NA
Pickens	1,776	17,436	0.60	214	10.7	221	11.1	1,734	11.7	4,951	3,920	1,031	109	518
Pike..................................	2,241	35,403	1.15	344	10.3	344	10.3	3,347	12.8	6,284	3,848	2,436	1,457	4,417
Randolph...........................	400	19,805	0.68	248	10.9	312	13.7	2,121	12.0	5,686	4,210	1,476	470	2,079
Russell..............................	574	49,326	0.61	755	13.1	654	11.3	5,370	10.8	11,333	7,374	3,959	2,303	3,821
St. Clair............................	1,562	70,481	0.57	1,019	11.5	960	10.8	6,805	9.4	17,859	8,586	9,273	2,018	2,305
Shelby	2,512	191,437	0.83	2,282	10.6	1,571	7.3	13,311	7.4	36,261	19,053	17,208	3,678	1,744
Sumter..............................	939	12,372	0.83	128	10.1	148	11.7	1,276	12.9	3,057	2,461	596	127	981
Talladega...........................	2,942	82,530	1.05	833	10.4	1,063	13.3	6,266	9.8	19,295	11,038	8,257	3,394	4,220
Tallapoosa........................	576	38,775	0.87	409	10.1	556	13.7	3,417	10.7	11,246	7,406	3,840	1,380	3,466
Tuscaloosa........................	10,557	213,039	1.10	2,488	11.9	1,808	8.7	15,705	9.2	35,622	21,663	13,959	7,236	3,524
Walker..............................	851	61,372	0.85	745	11.7	998	15.7	5,959	11.5	17,467	8,834	8,633	2,422	3,738

1. Per 1,000 estimated resident population. 2. Data for serious crimes have not been adjusted for underreporting; this may affect comparability between geographic areas and over time. 3. Per 100,000 population estimated by the FBI.

Table B. States and Counties — Crime, Education, Money Income, and Poverty

STATE County	Serious crimes known to police[2], 2016 (cont.)[1] Rate Violent	Property	Education — Enrollment[3] Total	Percent private	High school graduate or less	Bachelor's degree or more	Local government expenditures,[5] 2014-2015 Total current spending (mil dol)	Current spending per student (dollars)	Per capita income[6]	Median income (dollars)	Households Percent with income of less than $50,000	with income of $200,000 or more	Median household income (dollars)	All persons	Children under 18 years	Children 5 to 17 years in families
	46	47	48	49	50	51	52	53	54	55	56	57	58	59	60	61
UNITED STATES	386	2,451	81,751,797	16.2	40.0	30.9	575,809.9	12,261	31,177	57,652	43.8	6.3	60,336	13.4	18.4	17.3
ALABAMA......................	532	2,948	1,188,682	13.8	45.6	24.5	6,806.5	9,146	25,746	46,472	52.8	3.3	48,193	16.9	24.4	22.8
Autauga........................	281	3,160	13,438	17.1	45.9	25.0	72.9	7,541	27,824	55,317	45.2	2.2	58,343	13.4	19.3	18.6
Baldwin.........................	211	1,936	44,265	17.6	37.6	30.7	269.9	8,822	29,364	52,562	46.8	4.7	56,607	10.1	14.7	14.3
Barbour.........................	407	2,362	5,317	9.1	62.4	12.0	34.2	9,107	17,561	33,368	67.0	0.8	32,490	33.4	50.3	48.8
Bibb...............................	67	894	4,626	9.1	61.7	13.2	29.0	8,624	20,911	43,404	56.1	1.3	45,795	20.2	27.3	26.8
Blount...........................	752	2,112	12,428	8.4	52.5	13.1	76.2	7,969	22,021	47,412	52.3	1.9	48,253	12.8	18.5	17.7
Bullock.........................	320	1,495	2,122	11.5	65.2	13.4	16.6	10,918	20,856	29,655	67.8	1.7	29,113	34.4	48.3	49.0
Butler...........................	586	2,782	4,156	12.8	59.3	16.1	29.1	9,134	19,004	36,326	63.9	0.8	36,842	21.3	33.0	31.8
Calhoun........................	897	3,283	27,798	9.6	49.0	17.9	168.7	9,199	23,638	43,686	55.3	1.9	45,937	17.7	24.2	22.2
Chambers.....................	552	3,448	7,081	11.6	57.6	13.3	41.9	8,949	22,002	37,342	62.5	1.0	36,883	18.2	29.6	30.1
Cherokee......................	369	2,421	5,109	5.8	58.7	12.5	36.7	9,072	23,010	40,041	59.2	1.8	44,842	17.2	25.0	23.3
Chilton..........................	688	2,668	9,659	7.2	61.6	15.1	62.1	8,144	23,368	43,501	55.8	1.4	46,405	16.8	22.6	21.5
Choctaw........................	115	407	2,718	29.4	59.8	11.6	14.9	9,451	20,994	32,122	64.8	1.8	36,711	23.7	34.8	34.1
Clarke...........................	471	1,942	5,232	16.1	62.9	13.0	40.5	9,450	20,765	33,827	63.8	1.9	36,719	23.3	31.9	32.4
Clay..............................	305	847	2,835	10.9	60.4	10.3	17.1	8,438	21,330	37,287	62.8	1.8	39,642	18.1	25.5	24.2
Cleburne.......................	100	1,174	3,175	9.0	61.6	12.4	23.6	8,735	20,873	37,396	60.2	1.0	45,480	16.1	22.4	21.2
Coffee..........................	263	2,094	11,864	9.3	43.9	22.7	83.1	8,883	26,216	49,821	50.1	2.6	51,998	15.5	24.8	21.8
Colbert..........................	328	2,419	11,445	7.6	49.8	18.8	80.9	9,806	23,675	45,477	54.0	1.6	46,100	15.4	22.2	21.9
Conecuh........................	287	1,444	2,619	11.4	69.0	8.8	18.5	12,111	16,337	30,434	71.8	0.6	30,796	23.7	42.9	41.6
Coosa...........................	276	1,847	1,899	3.9	61.7	11.0	10.3	9,766	20,342	34,792	66.4	1.6	42,442	17.4	27.6	26.3
Covington.....................	400	2,074	7,867	5.9	53.5	15.5	54.1	8,707	22,431	39,467	59.2	1.5	39,093	17.7	25.9	25.9
Crenshaw.....................	154	1,190	3,055	11.0	58.5	16.3	19.4	8,547	21,580	38,937	61.6	1.9	38,419	19.9	29.3	25.9
Cullman........................	113	1,946	17,023	8.7	53.7	14.9	115.5	9,005	21,857	40,997	58.5	1.9	45,925	13.8	18.7	18.3
Dale..............................	559	2,570	11,997	8.9	46.6	16.8	56.4	8,867	23,194	44,711	55.6	1.8	42,572	17.7	25.9	24.0
Dallas...........................	1,046	4,738	10,463	14.3	55.3	14.2	70.1	9,944	18,248	30,065	69.8	1.6	31,329	27.9	43.2	39.4
DeKalb..........................	329	2,167	16,508	9.8	60.3	13.0	102.7	8,473	20,020	38,842	60.5	1.9	39,906	19.5	27.8	26.5
Elmore..........................	249	2,190	18,985	20.9	47.7	22.8	103.6	7,876	26,251	54,981	45.2	3.3	59,652	12.0	16.5	15.9
Escambia......................	471	2,040	7,875	10.7	62.8	12.1	52.9	9,433	18,164	35,026	64.7	1.5	37,870	23.3	33.7	32.3
Etowah.........................	709	3,616	23,061	7.5	49.4	16.9	135.8	8,502	22,278	42,064	57.0	2.0	41,791	18.1	29.3	27.3
Fayette.........................	72	836	3,604	8.6	58.3	14.6	21.1	8,702	21,191	36,541	62.5	1.6	39,394	19.4	27.6	25.8
Franklin........................	281	2,145	7,426	6.4	61.1	13.4	54.2	9,135	19,314	39,501	61.6	1.4	41,025	20.5	29.8	27.6
Geneva.........................	431	2,074	5,667	4.8	56.7	11.1	34.2	8,530	21,084	39,293	60.5	1.4	38,561	21.7	34.3	33.9
Greene..........................	610	1,591	1,837	11.4	60.4	11.4	12.8	10,227	14,197	20,954	76.5	0.7	28,108	33.2	49.4	47.8
Hale..............................	255	1,376	3,490	13.6	61.7	14.4	25.8	9,282	20,269	34,679	63.9	2.3	34,905	25.1	35.5	33.6
Henry............................	204	1,357	3,517	17.5	53.2	17.1	21.3	8,344	23,983	45,569	55.5	2.2	48,094	17.0	27.5	25.8
Houston........................	649	3,297	24,833	14.7	46.5	20.9	137.5	8,760	24,781	42,803	56.3	3.3	44,753	16.6	26.5	23.8
Jackson........................	NA	NA	10,509	8.3	59.4	13.4	77.6	9,492	20,946	39,281	61.7	1.5	42,658	16.6	23.3	21.2
Jefferson......................	874	3,692	165,739	16.3	37.4	31.9	1,024.1	9,837	29,456	49,321	50.5	4.9	50,731	16.7	23.1	20.8
Lamar...........................	80	684	3,016	6.6	58.1	13.3	19.9	8,406	21,152	36,016	63.4	1.3	39,796	18.7	26.1	24.4
Lauderdale....................	261	1,959	22,423	10.6	49.4	22.5	119.5	9,206	25,803	44,888	55.4	2.5	46,646	13.7	18.8	17.4
Lawrence......................	257	1,245	7,198	6.3	62.8	10.2	45.1	9,000	22,419	43,779	55.2	0.8	42,912	16.8	24.4	23.7
Lee...............................	572	2,584	54,453	9.2	34.6	34.9	201.5	9,040	26,170	47,564	52.1	3.6	51,372	17.8	19.2	19.1
Limestone....................	190	1,805	21,605	13.1	47.0	24.6	119.1	9,681	26,685	52,831	47.3	4.0	57,342	11.9	16.5	15.5
Lowndes.......................	591	2,677	2,253	13.5	60.1	13.7	21.8	13,761	18,976	29,785	69.9	1.5	33,130	25.9	40.0	38.6
Macon...........................	759	3,063	5,804	47.7	50.7	20.1	24.4	11,332	19,564	32,308	66.8	0.9	30,849	30.6	44.7	42.5
Madison........................	653	3,554	93,979	16.2	30.3	40.6	499.4	9,420	34,232	61,318	41.6	6.2	62,750	12.8	18.1	15.4
Marengo.......................	440	2,296	4,829	11.0	56.5	15.4	35.4	9,033	22,996	32,255	65.1	1.3	37,469	22.8	32.5	32.0
Marion..........................	280	2,209	6,246	7.2	54.6	13.4	41.1	8,696	21,835	35,719	64.3	2.3	38,049	19.3	27.5	25.8
Marshall........................	354	2,746	22,374	4.9	51.3	17.7	155.5	8,936	22,710	41,104	58.6	2.9	42,751	20.1	31.4	30.5
Mobile...........................	585	4,021	103,046	18.7	46.3	23.0	563.8	8,947	24,347	45,802	53.3	2.9	45,615	19.7	34.2	29.5
Monroe..........................	416	2,054	4,397	8.7	63.7	12.5	32.3	8,809	17,264	26,036	70.7	1.3	36,432	23.8	34.2	31.8
Montgomery..................	592	4,152	59,592	23.4	39.9	32.3	270.5	8,528	26,712	46,545	53.0	3.6	45,833	21.3	33.7	31.8
Morgan..........................	221	2,858	26,942	10.4	47.3	20.9	184.3	9,497	25,013	47,529	52.2	2.4	49,274	14.8	20.7	19.0
Perry.............................	NA	NA	2,677	17.7	61.9	16.9	15.5	9,461	13,449	22,973	79.3	0.4	26,703	37.2	51.3	49.9
Pickens.........................	147	370	4,416	20.6	58.0	11.8	24.6	9,329	20,089	36,220	63.7	1.8	38,379	22.3	31.2	30.3
Pike..............................	676	3,741	11,213	6.2	52.0	24.7	40.4	9,461	20,808	35,684	63.5	1.2	40,680	27.7	37.7	37.0
Randolph.......................	288	1,792	4,851	11.5	58.1	14.6	33.0	8,770	20,983	39,485	60.6	1.7	41,112	17.0	27.9	27.0
Russell..........................	582	3,238	14,957	12.2	49.5	16.9	90.1	8,477	21,279	38,988	59.9	1.1	36,186	23.2	34.9	34.8
St. Clair........................	448	1,858	18,668	11.3	52.0	16.0	106.5	8,213	24,686	53,483	45.8	1.9	52,755	13.5	17.6	16.7
Shelby..........................	297	1,447	55,814	19.5	28.9	42.2	276.5	9,496	35,330	74,063	32.9	7.1	74,098	7.4	9.1	9.0
Sumter..........................	263	718	4,106	5.7	57.1	18.2	17.8	10,576	14,739	21,663	74.7	0.4	26,495	35.9	46.1	44.7
Talladega.......................	533	3,686	18,212	9.8	54.6	13.6	112.9	9,190	21,382	39,219	61.2	1.3	41,733	18.3	27.5	26.0
Tallapoosa....................	881	2,584	8,799	8.0	53.2	18.2	52.3	8,748	22,430	42,181	56.6	1.6	44,469	18.3	28.0	27.3
Tuscaloosa...................	395	3,129	60,712	9.2	41.2	30.2	264.1	9,342	24,895	50,513	49.4	3.2	51,644	15.9	19.7	19.9
Walker..........................	491	3,247	13,441	7.4	57.3	11.1	98.6	9,201	21,217	38,872	60.1	1.8	41,925	17.4	22.7	20.4

1. Data for serious crimes have not been adjusted for underreporting; this may affect comparability between geographic areas and over time.   2. Per 100,000 population estimated by the FBI.   3. All persons 3 years old and over enrolled in nursery school through college.   4. Persons 25 years old and over.   5. Elementary and secondary education expenditures.   6. Based on population estimated by the American Community Survey, 2013–2017.

STATE County	Personal income, 2017										Earnings, 2017		
	Total (mil dol)	Percent change 2016-2017	Per capita[1] Dollars	Per capita[1] Rank	Wages and salaries (mil dol)	Supplements to wages and salaries, employer contributions (mil dol) Pension and insurance	Supplements to wages and salaries, employer contributions (mil dol) Government social insurance	Proprietors' income (mil dol)	Dividends, interest, and rent (mil dol)	Personal transfer reecipts (mil dol)	Total (mil dol)	Contributions for government social insurance (mil dol) From employee and self-employed	Contributions for government social insurance (mil dol) From employer
	62	63	64	65	66	67	68	69	70	71	72	73	74
UNITED STATES	16,820,250	4.4	51,731	X	8,447,954	1,342,095	604,277	1,503,084	3,356,872	2,859,632	11,897,410	692,322	604,277
ALABAMA	198,916	4.1	40,802	X	93,889	16,417	6,826	13,658	35,489	45,594	130,790	8,567	6,826
Autauga............................	2,247	2.9	40,484	1,475	458	83	33	97	344	477	671	52	33
Baldwin	9,372	5.0	44,079	1,012	2,817	444	206	672	1,856	1,938	4,140	300	206
Barbour............................	845	3.3	33,453	2,560	308	64	23	66	138	283	461	32	23
Bibb..................................	681	3.7	30,022	2,928	184	35	13	26	74	213	259	21	13
Blount..............................	1,955	5.3	33,707	2,527	329	64	24	128	244	495	544	46	24
Bullock............................	283	2.7	27,500	3,048	98	22	7	34	42	94	161	10	7
Butler..............................	698	3.1	35,196	2,313	244	48	18	43	109	224	354	25	18
Calhoun...........................	4,159	3.7	36,255	2,157	1,853	402	138	201	752	1,212	2,594	176	138
Chambers	1,138	3.7	33,758	2,515	333	66	24	33	166	369	456	37	24
Cherokee	889	5.3	34,371	2,432	188	40	14	58	135	284	300	25	14
Chilton............................	1,470	3.9	33,350	2,576	377	72	27	67	183	409	543	43	27
Choctaw..........................	482	2.0	37,253	1,993	181	30	12	32	60	174	256	20	12
Clarke..............................	854	1.7	35,448	2,281	336	63	24	49	133	272	473	35	24
Clay.................................	444	5.8	33,230	2,589	146	30	11	42	69	144	228	17	11
Cleburne	526	4.3	35,298	2,297	105	20	7	47	60	148	179	14	7
Coffee	2,183	5.7	42,076	1,255	580	110	43	186	414	504	920	62	43
Colbert	2,049	3.5	37,602	1,933	1,120	213	85	117	333	591	1,535	104	85
Conecuh	394	3.2	31,616	2,795	133	28	10	27	60	157	198	15	10
Coosa..............................	326	3.1	30,332	2,903	58	12	4	11	47	107	85	8	4
Covington........................	1,290	4.7	34,785	2,375	478	97	37	82	195	419	695	50	37
Crenshaw.........................	511	6.2	36,832	2,073	142	29	10	71	67	154	253	16	10
Cullman...........................	3,196	5.7	38,615	1,788	1,173	206	85	305	437	824	1,769	121	85
Dale.................................	1,764	3.7	35,834	2,220	1,280	303	109	75	312	491	1,767	99	109
Dallas..............................	1,371	1.5	34,955	2,356	505	96	38	69	204	530	709	52	38
DeKalb............................	2,219	6.0	30,982	2,852	822	158	61	174	320	663	1,215	85	61
Elmore.............................	3,316	3.1	40,601	1,457	755	147	56	153	537	734	1,111	84	56
Escambia	1,192	3.4	31,842	2,775	534	106	38	53	199	394	732	53	38
Etowah............................	3,706	3.7	36,069	2,192	1,412	249	105	234	560	1,156	1,999	147	105
Fayette............................	560	4.5	33,996	2,483	144	34	11	17	78	207	206	18	11
Franklin	1,039	5.6	32,985	2,619	393	84	30	64	147	305	571	40	30
Geneva............................	897	3.7	33,958	2,488	176	38	13	79	134	288	306	24	13
Greene.............................	268	1.5	32,156	2,732	67	16	5	14	46	106	102	8	5
Hale.................................	534	3.7	36,043	2,195	107	23	8	31	79	177	169	14	8
Henry	677	5.2	39,459	1,648	150	26	10	49	110	188	236	19	10
Houston...........................	4,265	3.6	40,878	1,421	2,112	371	153	244	775	1,041	2,881	191	153
Jackson............................	1,857	4.3	35,774	2,232	609	118	46	116	330	525	890	66	46
Jefferson..........................	34,280	4.6	52,003	374	20,436	3,157	1,436	3,733	7,216	6,112	28,762	1,790	1,436
Lamar..............................	457	3.1	32,803	2,646	143	28	10	20	66	161	202	17	10
Lauderdale.......................	3,373	3.2	36,448	2,124	1,117	206	82	181	679	880	1,587	119	82
Lawrence	1,091	5.5	33,003	2,615	182	38	14	55	128	328	289	27	14
Lee..................................	5,970	5.0	36,941	2,049	2,465	492	176	303	1,133	1,042	3,436	215	176
Limestone........................	3,812	5.0	40,381	1,491	1,197	234	90	209	547	756	1,731	117	90
Lowndes..........................	398	4.4	39,483	1,643	117	25	9	44	53	125	195	13	9
Macon.............................	599	2.5	31,938	2,759	216	63	16	10	101	202	305	22	16
Madison...........................	17,926	4.6	49,650	486	12,208	2,031	914	866	3,567	2,776	16,018	967	914
Marengo..........................	738	2.9	38,086	1,873	301	57	21	41	119	240	421	30	21
Marion.............................	964	5.4	32,315	2,711	365	70	27	71	155	303	534	38	27
Marshall..........................	3,345	4.2	35,005	2,348	1,374	265	101	218	556	889	1,958	133	101
Mobile.............................	15,353	2.4	37,089	2,017	8,674	1,425	631	1,028	2,512	3,879	11,757	765	631
Monroe............................	699	3.3	32,754	2,652	282	51	20	27	125	231	380	29	20
Montgomery.....................	9,763	3.8	43,074	1,134	6,658	1,290	495	749	2,053	2,118	9,192	547	495
Morgan............................	4,588	3.8	38,617	1,787	2,207	395	161	262	772	1,109	3,025	201	161
Perry	286	3.3	30,607	2,881	75	17	6	26	38	121	124	10	6
Pickens	642	3.4	31,799	2,781	152	36	11	34	91	216	232	19	11
Pike.................................	1,205	3.2	36,225	2,167	614	123	44	119	202	296	900	56	44
Randolph..........................	723	4.9	31,900	2,764	174	36	13	49	111	247	272	22	13
Russell............................	1,872	4.6	32,818	2,643	563	104	41	67	301	583	775	58	41
St. Clair	3,258	4.5	36,941	2,049	810	141	59	150	391	736	1,160	88	59
Shelby.............................	11,194	4.7	52,406	361	4,984	694	342	744	1,925	1,457	6,764	430	342
Sumter............................	412	2.0	32,437	2,697	129	29	9	41	60	147	208	14	9
Talladega.........................	2,715	3.6	33,909	2,492	1,406	250	103	95	364	837	1,854	129	103
Tallapoosa.......................	1,616	4.2	39,724	1,603	501	93	37	97	294	484	728	56	37
Tuscaloosa.......................	7,774	4.1	37,407	1,968	4,439	850	317	390	1,472	1,658	5,995	373	317
Walker.............................	2,474	3.3	38,614	1,789	731	137	54	124	455	789	1,046	83	54

1. Based on the resident population estimated as of July 1 of the year shown.

Table B. States and Counties — Earnings, Social Security, and Housing

STATE County	Earnings, 2017 (cont.)									Social Security beneficiaries, December 2017		Supplemental Security Income recipients, 2017	Housing units, 2018	
	Percent by selected industries													
	Farm	Mining, quarrying, and extractions	Construction	Manufacturing	Information; professional, scientific, technical services	Retail trade	Finance, insurance, real estate, and leasing	Health care and social assistance	Government	Number	Rate[1]		Total	Percent change, 2010-2018
	75	76	77	78	79	80	81	82	83	84	85	86	87	88
UNITED STATES	0.6	0.9	6.1	9.2	13.8	5.8	9.6	11.2	16.1	60,376,114	185	8,226,649	138,537,078	5.2
ALABAMA	0.9	0.3	6.0	14.2	9.8	6.4	7.0	11.1	20.7	1,131,359	232	165,007	2,274,565	4.7
Autauga	0.7	D	7.9	18.0	D	8.2	4.9	9.8	19.2	11,910	215	1,458	23,734	7.2
Baldwin	0.4	0.2	10.3	6.4	5.9	11.9	7.9	12.5	13.9	53,970	254	3,531	116,631	12.1
Barbour	7.8	3.0	3.3	25.6	D	6.7	2.6	D	19.5	7,110	281	1,396	12,005	1.5
Bibb	0.9	D	24.4	7.8	D	6.5	2.1	D	26.9	5,545	245	935	9,239	2.8
Blount	6.0	D	12.3	11.6	4.6	7.4	3.6	D	20.1	13,780	238	1,252	24,429	2.3
Bullock	15.9	0.0	D	18.7	D	3.2	1.6	12.2	22.5	2,120	206	580	4,552	1.3
Butler	5.8	0.0	5.1	22.0	D	8.1	2.9	D	14.3	5,445	275	1,077	10,087	1.3
Calhoun	0.8	D	3.3	16.1	4.6	7.6	3.5	9.6	32.9	30,330	264	4,628	53,888	1.1
Chambers	3.3	D	4.7	28.5	3.4	7.1	2.1	D	22.4	9,900	294	1,484	17,023	0.2
Cherokee	7.7	0.0	4.1	17.6	2.8	10.1	3.3	D	23	7,890	305	851	16,661	2.4
Chilton	0.2	D	10.6	21.5	D	8.9	3.4	D	18.4	10,440	237	1,386	19,791	2.7
Choctaw	1.1	D	D	D	2.3	6.2	2.1	D	9.8	4,310	333	824	7,394	1.7
Clarke	0.8	0.5	3.7	26.3	D	8.6	5.5	8.1	20.9	7,270	302	1,395	12,808	1.3
Clay	6.9	0.0	3.5	40.6	1.2	4.4	D	D	20.3	3,995	299	513	6,835	0.9
Cleburne	12.2	0.0	23.2	12.6	D	7.7	2.1	1.7	23.2	3,965	266	522	6,850	2.0
Coffee	6.8	D	3.6	16.2	D	9.6	4.1	10.8	16.8	11,580	223	1,371	23,273	4.2
Colbert	0.2	0.6	7.8	29.5	2.4	7.9	4.1	7.8	20.6	15,310	281	1,977	26,731	3.8
Conecuh	6.7	D	1.5	12.6	1.6	3.8	1.3	D	20.7	3,970	318	714	7,177	1.2
Coosa	0.7	0.0	2.9	37.2	D	3.3	D	D	19.8	2,950	274	442	6,594	1.6
Covington	3.7	D	5.6	17.8	3.2	9.2	4.3	D	16.3	10,770	290	1,453	18,975	0.8
Crenshaw	18.7	-0.1	3.5	20.8	1.6	2.9	2.7	D	13	3,995	288	627	6,829	1.5
Cullman	5.6	D	6.9	20.5	3.5	7.9	4.7	12.3	13.3	21,930	265	2,606	38,023	2.6
Dale	1.3	D	2.7	21.5	3.5	2.2	1.4	2.7	48.5	11,565	235	1,870	23,149	2.1
Dallas	2.7	D	4.9	26.2	2.6	7.6	3.5	14.2	19.2	11,015	281	4,041	20,361	0.8
DeKalb	5.4	D	5.9	29.1	3.1	7.1	2.2	9.9	15.1	17,520	245	2,107	31,660	1.8
Elmore	0.1	D	8.5	16.1	5.1	10.9	4.7	9.1	22.9	18,670	229	2,295	34,418	5.4
Escambia	-0.6	2.9	6.3	19.7	1.9	7.6	4.0	8.7	30.9	9,975	266	1,437	16,676	1.1
Etowah	0.6	D	5.5	15.8	3.7	8.3	5.4	D	15	28,885	281	4,557	47,846	0.8
Fayette	1.9	0.8	3.7	23.0	2.0	9.2	3.4	D	29.7	5,400	328	727	8,507	0.9
Franklin	2.9	0.8	3.9	40.4	1.8	4.7	3.9	D	19	7,555	240	1,142	14,229	1.5
Geneva	12.4	D	5.6	10.3	D	6.8	4.8	4.4	22.8	7,585	287	1,180	12,850	1.3
Greene	9.4	0.0	2.5	25.1	D	5.0	D	D	30.6	2,605	313	747	5,111	2.1
Hale	13.4	D	6.4	19.5	1.6	5.2	3.5	5.6	26.5	4,585	310	1,067	7,845	2.5
Henry	4.2	0.0	6.9	11.8	D	4.4	2.8	D	16.1	5,150	300	621	9,183	3.3
Houston	-0.1	D	4.4	7.8	5.2	10.4	4.8	18.1	19.1	25,480	244	4,004	47,784	5.4
Jackson	2.5	D	5.7	31.8	2.6	8.0	3.7	D	20.1	14,475	279	1,636	25,253	1.9
Jefferson	0.0	0.3	6.1	6.4	11.3	4.9	11.5	16.3	15.9	142,080	216	23,428	309,560	3.0
Lamar	1.1	D	4.6	37.1	2.0	5.3	3.5	6.6	15.6	4,310	309	622	7,435	1.1
Lauderdale	0.2	D	8.1	10.1	5.3	10.5	5.3	16.9	19.2	24,025	260	2,598	45,463	3.8
Lawrence	5.4	D	9.8	2.9	2.2	9.0	5.4	D	25.3	9,035	273	1,292	15,475	1.6
Lee	0.3	0.2	7.5	12.0	5.6	6.7	4.2	5.9	33.3	25,475	158	3,271	70,369	12.8
Limestone	1.3	D	15.8	13.8	4.9	8.2	2.9	4.3	31.7	19,070	202	2,072	36,529	4.4
Lowndes	18.1	D	4.3	36.4	D	2.5	D	D	14.9	3,170	315	766	5,224	1.7
Macon	1.3	D	D	D	D	3.8	0.7	D	65.8	4,855	259	1,051	10,283	0.3
Madison	0.1	D	3.0	12.0	26.1	5.0	3.6	7.4	28.2	66,130	183	6,841	164,272	12.2
Marengo	3.8	-0.3	5.5	23.7	2.5	6.5	4.7	D	19.5	6,075	314	1,482	10,379	1.3
Marion	5.1	D	3.5	31.2	1.1	6.5	4.9	D	15.5	8,005	268	1,043	14,939	1.4
Marshall	2.2	D	6.1	28.6	4.1	8.5	3.2	7.0	18	22,650	237	2,987	40,816	1.2
Mobile	0.3	0.4	6.1	15.5	9.8	6.4	8.0	12.6	15	91,400	221	15,112	184,688	3.6
Monroe	0.0	D	3.9	25.8	D	6.1	3.6	D	19.6	6,040	283	942	11,455	1.1
Montgomery	0.6	0.0	5.7	10.1	9.6	5.3	6.1	11.5	29.9	46,445	205	9,647	105,162	3.5
Morgan	0.6	0.1	8.1	32.6	4.9	6.2	4.1	7.3	13.8	28,720	242	3,404	52,273	2.1
Perry	8.7	0.0	2.1	18.3	D	3.8	2.8	8.1	21.7	2,750	294	1,004	4,778	1.0
Pickens	8.1	D	3.9	18.4	D	5.1	D	D	35	5,605	278	1,147	9,623	1.5
Pike	3.9	0.1	2.8	22.8	5.9	5.6	4.3	6.5	22	6,915	208	1,522	16,226	6.3
Randolph	8.6	D	5.3	19.2	2.6	8.2	4.4	D	22.5	6,345	280	853	12,109	1.0
Russell	1.3	0.2	6.2	25.6	D	8.0	5.5	11.3	20.5	12,820	225	1,963	27,855	13.3
St. Clair	1.6	D	10.3	19.6	4.5	8.6	3.9	8.3	15	19,850	225	2,015	37,179	4.9
Shelby	0.0	0.5	7.5	6.0	11.3	7.4	18.5	7.6	8.1	38,160	179	2,525	88,388	9.1
Sumter	15.4	0.0	2.7	11.2	D	3.4	2.1	D	34.7	3,370	266	1,061	6,909	1.8
Talladega	0.3	D	4.0	41.1	2.4	4.6	2.1	D	15.2	21,610	270	3,909	37,910	2.2
Tallapoosa	0.2	D	9.6	16.7	5.7	7.2	3.8	D	15.9	12,550	308	1,561	22,520	1.8
Tuscaloosa	0.1	2.2	5.4	20.7	6.0	5.9	5.0	7.4	28.5	39,565	190	6,131	93,004	9.6
Walker	0.7	1.6	5.4	10.9	4.0	12.0	4.7	D	16.8	20,010	312	3,235	31,241	1.4

1. Per 1,000 resident population estimated as of July 1 of the year shown.

Table B. States and Counties — **Housing, Labor Force, and Employment**

STATE County	Housing units, 2013-2017								Civilian labor force, 2018				Civilian employment[6], 2013-2017		
			Occupied units								Unemployment			Percent	
			Owner-occupied			Renter-occupied									
				Median owner cost as a percent of income			Median rent as a percent of income[2]	Sub-standard units[4] (percent)		Percent change, 2017-2018				Management, business, science, and arts	Construction, production, and maintenance occupations
			Median value[1]	With a mort-gage	Without a mort-gage[2]	Median rent[3]			Total		Total	Rate[5]	Total		
	Total	Percent													
	89	90	91	92	93	94	95	96	97	98	99	100	101	102	103
UNITED STATES	118,825,921	63.8	193,500	22.0	11.6	982.0	30.3	3.7	161,640,240	0.9	6,296,296	3.9	150,599,165	37.4	21.1
ALABAMA	1,856,695	68.6	132,100	19.9	10.3	747.0	29.7	2.0	2,198,837	0.9	86,490	3.9	2,055,509	34.1	25.6
Autauga	21,054	73.3	143,000	19.7	10.0	932.0	32.6	1.6	25,957	-0.1	942.0	3.6	24,112	35.3	23.5
Baldwin	76,133	72.9	182,000	21.4	10.0	904.0	29.6	1.2	93,849	1.9	3,393	3.6	89,527	35.7	20.5
Barbour	9,191	62.5	89,300	20.4	12.3	569.0	29.0	2.2	8,373	0.7	433.0	5.2	8,878	25.0	35.5
Bibb	6,916	75.4	105,500	19.6	10.0	710.0	29.8	0.6	8,661	1.3	344.0	4.0	8,171	24.4	38.3
Blount	20,690	78.5	122,200	19.6	10.0	649.0	26.8	2.3	25,006	1.1	878.0	3.5	21,380	28.5	35.3
Bullock	3,670	70.0	66,800	23.3	11.4	611.0	34.1	0.9	4,776	-1.2	224.0	4.7	4,290	19.7	44.6
Butler	7,050	70.1	88,800	23.0	12.3	585.0	27.6	1.7	8,914	-0.3	427.0	4.8	7,727	26.9	37.3
Calhoun	45,099	69.4	110,100	19.5	10.2	645.0	29.0	1.9	45,972	0.4	2,139	4.7	47,392	29.0	29.9
Chambers	13,694	66.5	86,400	22.5	11.7	684.0	26.9	4.0	15,276	0.5	597.0	3.9	14,527	24.3	39.2
Cherokee	10,795	78.1	116,300	20.9	12.3	596.0	32.7	2.3	11,622	2.5	415.0	3.6	9,879	28.8	38.4
Chilton	16,768	75.3	98,600	20.2	10.0	678.0	31.4	3.4	19,476	1.1	703.0	3.6	17,675	25.3	36.4
Choctaw	5,463	80.2	69,000	19.4	12.6	521.0	34.5	2.5	4,694	6.5	260.0	5.5	4,301	23.6	39.1
Clarke	9,602	66.0	93,500	20.1	12.7	546.0	30.6	2.4	7,627	-1.4	570.0	7.5	7,933	21.6	39.3
Clay	5,338	76.5	89,300	22.6	10.0	482.0	23.1	1.3	5,963	2.9	233.0	3.9	5,509	22.2	44.8
Cleburne	5,773	74.4	111,800	21.6	12.2	549.0	24.3	2.3	5,743	0.3	244.0	4.2	5,743	25.7	39.7
Coffee	19,620	65.4	147,800	18.8	10.0	731.0	27.6	1.4	20,817	-0.3	822.0	3.9	21,639	31.6	29.8
Colbert	21,983	72.8	108,500	19.5	10.8	655.0	31.8	0.7	23,258	0.0	1,074	4.6	22,180	27.1	31.6
Conecuh	4,716	77.6	76,100	20.3	11.2	566.0	29.1	2.8	4,494	0.2	235.0	5.2	3,945	15.9	40.2
Coosa	4,204	80.3	87,300	22.6	12.0	547.0	21.3	2.4	4,376	-0.1	183.0	4.2	3,897	17.6	35.5
Covington	15,285	75.1	96,200	20.6	10.6	589.0	25.6	2.7	15,617	-0.6	715.0	4.6	14,686	29.2	34.3
Crenshaw	5,358	71.0	76,800	18.3	11.5	532.0	25.0	0.9	6,298	-1.6	257.0	4.1	5,700	26.4	36.4
Cullman	31,097	74.8	121,900	21.9	11.9	644.0	29.0	2.2	37,830	0.0	1,241	3.3	32,072	29.3	32.7
Dale	18,825	59.7	108,000	19.0	10.0	672.0	29.8	1.4	20,120	0.9	846.0	4.2	17,988	28.2	29.8
Dallas	16,487	59.2	80,800	21.0	12.9	599.0	34.3	4.8	14,860	-1.1	973.0	6.5	14,461	26.7	34.1
DeKalb	25,482	71.2	102,900	19.4	11.5	579.0	24.3	3.0	30,129	1.9	1,150	3.8	28,416	23.7	40.4
Elmore	29,115	73.0	155,300	19.4	10.0	825.0	28.8	1.7	37,215	0.0	1,283	3.4	33,054	34.8	25.7
Escambia	13,226	71.8	94,500	18.9	11.5	580.0	31.8	2.6	14,352	-0.6	656.0	4.6	12,134	24.6	29.6
Etowah	39,061	71.9	105,100	20.5	11.3	634.0	28.4	1.7	43,096	0.1	1,768	4.1	41,412	29.7	30.0
Fayette	6,955	76.9	83,200	20.2	10.6	523.0	31.0	1.9	6,482	-1.1	267.0	4.1	6,307	29.0	34.3
Franklin	11,533	68.9	87,600	18.8	11.9	596.0	26.4	4.2	14,203	1.6	530.0	3.7	12,534	24.4	40.7
Geneva	10,693	73.6	87,800	19.7	11.3	589.0	24.5	1.7	10,851	0.6	426.0	3.9	10,306	22.9	38.3
Greene	3,025	68.0	67,700	32.9	20.0	533.0	35.0	4.7	2,838	-0.5	191.0	6.7	2,411	22.3	33.8
Hale	5,664	74.9	88,800	25.1	12.4	483.0	40.0	3.8	5,991	0.8	305.0	5.1	5,252	27.6	31.2
Henry	6,727	82.2	112,600	20.1	10.0	603.0	26.0	1.0	6,766	0.8	300.0	4.4	6,949	32.8	28.8
Houston	39,560	64.6	127,100	19.5	10.0	725.0	28.8	1.4	45,150	1.0	1,825	4.0	44,108	31.1	24.5
Jackson	20,368	73.6	105,000	19.5	10.0	607.0	28.6	2.6	23,241	0.6	955.0	4.1	20,261	26.1	39.5
Jefferson	261,390	62.8	149,000	20.7	10.7	847.0	30.9	1.7	314,014	1.2	11,655	3.7	300,739	38.8	18.9
Lamar	6,019	75.8	71,500	17.8	10.4	409.0	28.9	2.0	5,721	-0.3	218.0	3.8	5,376	28.8	37.8
Lauderdale	38,634	68.4	126,800	19.3	10.0	633.0	26.8	1.5	42,141	0.2	1,766	4.2	39,857	31.2	25.7
Lawrence	13,056	80.0	98,700	20.2	10.6	531.0	25.0	1.3	13,919	2.1	583.0	4.2	12,476	23.6	42.5
Lee	59,001	59.2	157,100	19.3	10.0	818.0	34.3	3.1	74,654	1.6	2,703	3.6	71,677	41.0	19.7
Limestone	32,386	77.1	146,300	18.9	10.0	622.0	28.4	2.4	42,393	2.1	1,503	3.5	38,944	36.1	27.0
Lowndes	4,309	73.4	63,000	26.5	15.8	624.0	35.5	2.3	3,625	-0.9	265.0	7.3	3,533	23.0	38.0
Macon	7,852	64.7	77,100	23.2	13.3	603.0	32.2	2.1	7,816	-0.9	427.0	5.5	7,348	29.4	27.2
Madison	142,253	67.5	173,400	17.9	10.0	801.0	28.5	1.6	179,752	2.2	6,220	3.5	169,756	46.3	16.9
Marengo	7,975	71.3	88,100	23.2	13.7	552.0	29.9	2.7	7,589	-1.4	380.0	5.0	6,645	29.6	32.3
Marion	12,453	75.7	87,200	19.1	11.1	517.0	28.7	1.8	12,549	0.2	513.0	4.1	11,899	25.6	34.4
Marshall	34,588	70.7	118,500	20.8	10.1	615.0	28.5	3.7	42,598	1.3	1,441	3.4	38,456	28.3	34.1
Mobile	153,794	66.4	124,500	20.8	10.7	828.0	32.3	2.3	187,406	0.3	8,798	4.7	173,195	32.3	24.6
Monroe	8,207	61.0	88,000	22.4	12.0	499.0	30.6	1.3	7,158	-0.8	442.0	6.2	6,154	28.7	32.7
Montgomery	89,776	59.1	124,100	19.9	10.0	846.0	31.4	2.2	105,579	-0.1	4,219	4.0	100,874	36.8	20.0
Morgan	45,904	71.6	128,200	19.8	10.0	622.0	27.8	2.2	56,339	2.4	1,983	3.5	50,611	30.3	30.0
Perry	3,039	75.3	69,100	44.7	16.7	512.0	37.1	3.1	3,397	-1.2	222.0	6.5	2,478	23.4	27.4
Pickens	7,620	73.7	91,800	21.1	11.8	429.0	29.6	1.8	7,805	1.1	356.0	4.6	6,903	22.6	37.6
Pike	12,284	59.2	109,200	19.7	10.0	637.0	34.3	2.1	15,230	-0.4	686.0	4.5	14,352	31.5	27.8
Randolph	8,867	72.7	85,200	21.1	10.0	588.0	27.1	3.5	9,538	0.6	383.0	4.0	8,565	23.4	42.1
Russell	22,690	58.9	114,700	22.6	12.0	759.0	29.4	4.1	23,753	1.6	955.0	4.0	22,959	28.7	25.8
St. Clair	32,486	80.4	142,800	19.6	10.6	723.0	26.8	1.3	39,683	1.3	1,387	3.5	38,522	28.9	29.6
Shelby	76,868	79.6	199,500	19.3	10.0	975.0	26.6	1.3	112,891	1.4	3,219	2.9	104,093	44.3	15.1
Sumter	5,073	64.5	69,500	23.4	14.2	534.0	37.2	1.9	4,768	-3.7	281.0	5.9	4,353	25.5	25.0
Talladega	31,651	72.2	95,200	20.4	11.2	598.0	28.4	2.0	34,978	1.0	1,497	4.3	30,937	28.6	32.9
Tallapoosa	16,369	71.9	107,000	19.0	10.1	614.0	31.7	4.3	17,772	-2.4	744.0	4.2	15,317	28.3	35.6
Tuscaloosa	71,507	62.8	161,700	20.3	10.0	816.0	30.9	2.1	101,569	1.7	3,714	3.7	90,941	35.8	25.9
Walker	25,143	75.6	87,300	20.4	10.7	609.0	32.2	2.0	25,132	0.9	1,068	4.2	24,280	26.3	32.6

1. Specified owner-occupied units.   2. A value of 10.0 represents 10 percent or less; a value of 50.0 represents 50 percent or more.   3. Specified renter-occupied units.   4. Overcrowded or lacking complete plumbing facilities.   5. Percent of civilian labor force.   6. Civilian employed persons 16 years old and over.

Table B. States and Counties — **Nonfarm Employment and Agriculture**

STATE County	Private nonfarm establishments, employment and payroll, 2016									Agriculture, 2017			
	Number of establishments	Employment						Annual payroll		Farms			Farm producers whose primary occupation is farming (percent)
		Total	Health care and social assistance	Manufacturing	Retail trade	Finance and insurance	Professional, scientific, and technical services	Total (mil dol)	Average per employee (dollars)	Number	Percent with:		
											Fewer than 50 acres	1000 acres or more	
	104	105	106	107	108	109	110	111	112	113	114	115	116
UNITED STATES	7,757,807	126,752,238	19,735,708	11,590,420	15,967,893	6,336,795	8,799,893	6,435,142	50,769	2,042,220	41.9	8.5	41.1
ALABAMA	99,584	1,673,249	245,766	250,252	237,123	70,109	100,476	68,971	41,220	40,592	40.1	4.2	37.4
Autauga	851	10,790	1,639	984	2,715	392	266	332	30,815	371	31.5	6.7	37.1
Baldwin	5,235	61,341	7,858	4,120	13,738	1,607	2,120	1,960	31,955	842	53.8	4.5	45.0
Barbour	452	6,857	679	2,355	877	145	116	233	34,044	498	20.3	5.2	41.4
Bibb	290	3,387	628	313	484	74	99	135	39,891	205	35.6	5.9	32.3
Blount	675	6,286	838	1,093	1,308	201	231	199	31,609	1,146	40.8	1.4	43.1
Bullock	107	2,097	399	D	207	54	17	65	31,207	255	18.4	9.4	33.6
Butler	409	6,157	921	1,413	977	145	56	195	31,619	420	30.0	2.4	37.7
Calhoun	2,326	35,843	6,020	5,985	6,561	977	926	1,188	33,139	643	43.4	1.4	34.5
Chambers	547	6,276	620	1,939	1,158	146	178	208	33,188	331	25.4	11.5	28.5
Cherokee	361	3,905	434	1,088	933	113	58	124	31,636	530	40.4	4.7	38.0
Chilton	738	7,609	767	1,812	1,445	206	112	252	33,172	463	41.9	1.3	42.3
Choctaw	252	2,835	404	D	360	64	55	140	49,376	188	30.9	7.4	35.1
Clarke	595	6,821	922	1,638	1,634	361	70	222	32,591	320	41.3	5.0	24.4
Clay	190	3,277	508	1,786	294	84	59	102	31,227	381	24.7	2.4	46.5
Cleburne	160	1,703	65	303	289	55	11	71	41,695	319	31.0	0.9	44.7
Coffee	986	13,388	1,933	3,417	2,399	488	785	436	32,541	788	31.5	4.3	41.8
Colbert	1,229	22,474	2,658	7,039	2,942	654	292	855	38,066	591	39.9	8.5	43.1
Conecuh	188	2,441	441	437	275	40	29	81	33,143	344	27.9	6.7	40.7
Coosa	93	944	110	385	110	12	20	35	36,630	215	17.2	2.8	32.7
Covington	808	10,187	1,687	2,123	1,861	343	297	336	33,006	907	34.5	3.0	34.4
Crenshaw	214	3,355	458	1,331	276	101	33	113	33,830	543	28.2	4.1	39.7
Cullman	1,729	25,274	3,709	5,451	4,124	768	437	882	34,881	1,781	46.7	0.2	40.4
Dale	739	11,146	1,248	560	1,277	351	896	536	48,119	469	27.7	6.6	38.1
Dallas	738	10,487	1,772	2,858	1,627	305	223	356	33,930	528	28.0	16.7	33.8
DeKalb	1,091	17,745	2,433	7,025	2,449	423	375	611	34,460	1,939	44.8	1.5	43.2
Elmore	1,167	14,359	2,058	2,764	2,836	396	394	485	33,809	538	47.2	4.5	33.8
Escambia	732	10,055	1,193	1,975	1,838	404	157	349	34,698	437	46.7	8.0	37.2
Etowah	1,974	30,834	7,349	5,344	4,951	1,039	580	1,018	33,028	817	55.2	0.5	38.2
Fayette	314	3,175	664	862	628	76	40	101	31,952	324	28.4	3.4	37.2
Franklin	523	9,646	1,029	5,420	910	381	130	322	33,385	729	26.3	2.6	41.1
Geneva	407	3,934	584	714	825	131	106	119	30,130	820	33.7	4.9	42.5
Greene	111	1,379	285	456	175	31	D	48	34,539	325	24.9	16.9	47.6
Hale	180	1,854	388	496	260	64	21	70	37,538	393	27.7	9.4	37.6
Henry	298	2,513	176	308	358	96	151	92	36,508	455	25.5	9.7	36.9
Houston	2,704	43,799	9,656	4,360	8,031	1,185	1,142	1,696	38,722	698	42.8	5.0	34.4
Jackson	846	13,259	1,782	5,546	1,960	314	198	428	32,298	1,355	44.8	2.4	31.8
Jefferson	16,484	314,992	54,315	22,626	40,644	22,620	15,623	15,783	50,105	387	63.3	1.0	29.1
Lamar	240	3,141	328	1,503	366	107	47	115	36,709	269	29.0	2.6	24.7
Lauderdale	2,031	25,563	4,830	2,460	5,641	984	834	762	29,807	1,309	48.1	3.4	33.7
Lawrence	387	3,138	798	150	762	113	73	86	27,492	1,252	46.5	2.4	39.1
Lee	2,726	43,945	6,191	6,940	7,084	1,100	1,608	1,395	31,746	314	43.9	5.7	35.5
Limestone	1,372	16,958	2,551	3,448	2,840	383	738	609	35,887	1,156	52.2	3.5	35.5
Lowndes	103	1,969	D	975	194	27	10	80	40,666	512	35.0	9.2	38.1
Macon	200	5,244	1,655	653	470	36	27	213	40,611	373	26.5	7.5	34.0
Madison	8,325	158,629	24,786	16,258	20,392	3,721	36,754	7,895	49,772	1,021	56.4	4.4	36.3
Marengo	467	6,045	1,009	1,408	952	228	75	226	37,382	471	29.9	5.5	31.5
Marion	531	7,656	1,123	2,828	1,106	403	73	243	31,729	582	30.6	0.9	33.4
Marshall	1,805	30,833	3,723	10,569	5,037	789	636	1,003	32,533	1,444	51.7	0.6	38.7
Mobile	8,736	151,652	21,180	16,379	21,503	5,636	9,969	6,435	42,432	653	60.9	3.1	39.3
Monroe	392	5,400	671	1,298	914	164	45	217	40,094	477	41.5	7.1	34.0
Montgomery	5,592	103,893	17,353	13,125	13,066	4,161	5,661	4,341	41,783	575	27.0	9.7	41.3
Morgan	2,573	42,737	5,844	11,942	5,610	1,377	1,529	1,800	42,110	1,164	51.6	1.1	32.7
Perry	117	1,561	137	434	197	63	17	45	28,775	349	32.1	14.3	41.3
Pickens	266	2,639	526	600	449	126	90	86	32,599	377	31.0	6.9	37.5
Pike	647	11,135	1,095	2,250	1,546	352	481	426	38,229	594	26.4	5.2	35.5
Randolph	329	3,809	435	1,215	727	156	45	104	27,176	597	33.3	3.2	38.0
Russell	781	11,156	1,389	3,005	2,245	347	199	374	33,490	296	31.1	10.1	29.6
St. Clair	1,281	16,848	1,859	3,621	2,920	489	786	586	34,764	490	42.0	1.0	34.4
Shelby	5,132	83,416	7,145	5,705	9,198	9,926	5,438	4,111	49,284	447	50.6	1.8	26.3
Sumter	196	2,991	392	191	252	56	D	117	39,043	367	20.2	12.5	39.3
Talladega	1,229	24,080	2,709	9,007	2,835	498	431	1,058	43,926	566	42.2	1.1	40.2
Tallapoosa	740	10,844	2,271	2,626	1,590	251	236	329	30,372	347	25.9	3.2	33.9
Tuscaloosa	4,085	78,617	12,223	14,983	10,572	1,667	2,316	3,093	39,347	557	43.8	3.1	31.9
Walker	1,221	14,913	3,422	2,088	3,427	475	442	509	34,161	501	49.9	2.0	43.2

	Agriculture, 2017 (cont.)														
	Land in farms				Value of land and buildings (dollars)		Value of machinery and equipmnet, average per farm (dollars)	Value of products sold:				Organic farms (number)	Farms with internet access (percent)	Government payments	
		Acres								Percent from:					
STATE County	Acreage (1,000)	Percent change, 2012-2017	Average size of farm	Total irrigated (1,000)	Total cropland (1,000)	Average per farm	Average per acre		Total (mil dol)	Average per farm (acres)	Crops	Livestock and poultry products			Total ($1,000)	Percent of farms
	117	118	119	120	121	122	123	124	125	126	127	128	129	130	131	132
UNITED STATES	900,218	-1.6	441	58,013.9	396,433.8	1,311,808	2,976	133,363	388,522.7	190,245	49.8	50.2	20,806	75.4	8,943,574	31.5
ALABAMA	8,581	-3.6	211	142.0	2,818.8	630,736	2,984	88,528	5,980.6	147,334	20.3	79.7	57	72.6	134,654	37.3
Autauga	113	1.6	305	1.4	36.9	672,902	2,205	96,682	21.5	57,844	58.4	41.6	NA	76.8	1,069	37.5
Baldwin	175	-9.1	208	7.4	110.4	1,208,662	5,822	136,496	120.4	142,973	84.4	15.6	NA	78.1	6,316	27.3
Barbour	153	-25.2	307	3.6	37.3	684,780	2,233	87,026	105.6	211,978	11.5	88.5	2	60.6	3,003	62.9
Bibb	56	-0.6	273	0.1	15.8	766,325	2,807	68,656	4.2	20,483	53.5	46.5	NA	73.2	395	26.3
Blount	148	1.4	129	0.9	43.8	465,684	3,602	87,452	242.9	211,915	5.5	94.5	3	74.6	3,166	32.3
Bullock	115	-30.0	452	0.1	20.0	968,327	2,142	83,263	D	D	D	D	NA	69.0	1,277	47.1
Butler	84	-4.5	201	0.6	17.7	492,971	2,454	83,737	132.0	314,355	3.5	96.5	NA	73.8	1,160	40.2
Calhoun	89	9.5	138	1.1	28.5	587,727	4,246	74,079	86.8	135,003	15.0	85.0	NA	77.1	913	28.8
Chambers	129	33.5	389	0.2	12.5	976,835	2,513	61,548	9.1	27,369	18.6	81.4	NA	71.9	822	38.4
Cherokee	121	-2.3	229	0.8	72.8	725,287	3,167	125,506	152.1	286,940	25.9	74.1	1	73.2	2,145	38.1
Chilton	76	-16.5	165	0.9	22.0	581,653	3,529	76,741	14.5	31,298	46.2	53.8	NA	73.9	761	19.7
Choctaw	82	20.4	439	0.0	6.6	899,167	2,050	68,483	8.3	43,941	9.6	90.4	NA	66.5	275	41.0
Clarke	65	36.0	202	0.0	11.2	460,092	2,279	61,402	2.9	8,994	42.7	57.3	NA	56.6	264	27.5
Clay	71	-8.5	187	0.0	12.2	525,095	2,807	85,885	81.3	213,462	1.2	98.8	NA	71.7	1,328	42.5
Cleburne	48	-3.6	152	0.4	8.9	524,930	3,460	71,623	117.5	368,197	2.6	97.4	7	76.8	366	21.0
Coffee	177	-12.4	225	4.0	64.3	592,097	2,633	89,163	199.5	253,216	8.6	91.4	4	70.9	5,525	56.9
Colbert	150	-1.6	254	D	85.8	677,872	2,665	105,238	60.2	101,846	62.9	37.1	NA	73.8	3,500	39.6
Conecuh	104	11.0	302	0.1	26.7	647,835	2,142	75,294	21.0	61,125	41.5	58.5	NA	56.7	693	44.2
Coosa	46	27.7	214	0.0	5.2	489,452	2,292	62,564	1.7	7,940	17.6	82.4	NA	72.6	270	27.9
Covington	161	-22.6	178	1.3	54.3	477,739	2,684	79,394	126.5	139,485	16.6	83.4	6	71.6	4,147	47.0
Crenshaw	114	-12.0	211	0.0	23.6	525,225	2,494	97,983	164.9	303,591	2.3	97.7	NA	67.6	1,603	49.7
Cullman	209	7.7	117	1.9	60.9	466,918	3,977	77,508	470.7	264,303	4.0	96.0	NA	75.5	3,139	31.3
Dale	137	5.6	292	2.4	52.5	879,051	3,009	103,692	172.0	366,825	9.9	90.1	NA	77.2	2,946	47.3
Dallas	263	3.1	498	6.4	76.7	934,297	1,875	124,270	64.0	121,212	43.6	56.4	NA	69.3	3,427	51.1
DeKalb	247	7.9	128	1.1	91.5	502,086	3,935	88,244	573.3	295,658	4.4	95.6	2	75.8	4,176	34.6
Elmore	94	3.7	174	2.6	34.9	521,814	2,996	75,563	27.6	51,290	63.0	37.0	3	74.3	855	24.7
Escambia	106	-1.5	242	3.1	55.3	594,861	2,458	92,069	31.0	70,886	88.5	11.5	NA	72.5	3,842	40.7
Etowah	89	3.7	109	0.6	24.8	419,478	3,836	78,981	93.4	114,356	6.7	93.3	NA	73.8	804	21.5
Fayette	68	-15.9	211	0.2	21.0	464,587	2,206	79,352	24.6	75,957	31.9	68.1	NA	75.9	660	48.1
Franklin	130	-13.9	178	D	32.4	435,546	2,451	84,184	139.4	191,202	4.5	95.5	NA	65.8	1,531	40.5
Geneva	183	-16.2	224	5.5	81.7	553,557	2,476	99,070	137.6	167,778	25.0	75.0	1	71.8	4,527	51.7
Greene	153	27.4	472	0.1	20.4	920,549	1,951	95,162	25.9	79,828	4.5	95.5	NA	67.7	1,127	49.2
Hale	158	-1.7	402	1.1	20.7	907,427	2,260	101,638	63.5	161,539	6.6	93.4	2	66.7	1,946	51.1
Henry	174	2.5	382	12.8	74.2	986,630	2,580	147,514	122.9	270,119	22.9	77.1	NA	76.3	3,937	60.2
Houston	149	-25.0	213	10.0	85.9	751,866	3,533	102,777	69.7	99,887	68.1	31.9	NA	71.8	7,557	50.4
Jackson	219	-5.7	161	1.4	95.5	490,606	3,042	86,387	153.5	113,276	19.9	80.1	3	72.5	3,198	36.0
Jefferson	38	-2.8	98	0.2	7.0	432,444	4,413	53,634	4.9	12,770	27.6	72.4	NA	80.1	220	11.1
Lamar	74	-10.5	274	0.3	12.0	508,777	1,859	63,797	10.4	38,509	30.5	69.5	NA	68.4	394	32.7
Lauderdale	211	-0.5	161	0.9	109.0	583,196	3,626	85,411	72.3	55,264	55.7	44.3	NA	69.4	3,934	41.5
Lawrence	214	-12.3	171	6.4	120.8	648,125	3,796	112,499	212.9	170,043	27.7	72.3	NA	70.0	4,147	39.1
Lee	68	14.8	216	0.2	9.0	895,686	4,150	95,632	D	D	D	D	4	79.9	432	26.8
Limestone	225	-8.9	194	10.4	151.1	803,618	4,132	109,978	131.4	113,669	59.8	40.2	NA	75.3	3,378	32.4
Lowndes	203	-6.8	396	6.2	46.5	752,311	1,898	105,508	80.9	157,920	15.7	84.3	NA	60.4	2,573	53.3
Macon	120	16.3	322	2.6	40.8	756,523	2,347	98,817	19.6	52,458	84.2	15.8	NA	66.8	1,238	37.0
Madison	185	-11.7	181	10.7	131.5	961,058	5,306	110,872	70.4	68,913	91.8	8.2	2	77.7	2,670	29.3
Marengo	147	-10.9	313	0.8	28.0	627,909	2,007	79,112	15.9	33,735	32.9	67.1	NA	68.4	1,680	58.2
Marion	83	-27.4	142	D	20.3	331,932	2,339	62,866	105.3	181,003	3.1	96.9	NA	69.9	881	45.2
Marshall	145	-11.0	101	0.3	44.9	445,314	4,431	86,970	283.6	196,403	2.9	97.1	3	78.3	1,729	24.9
Mobile	95	6.9	145	3.1	37.7	688,889	4,738	83,715	90.6	138,712	88.8	11.2	NA	77.0	1,537	15.8
Monroe	141	0.6	297	1.3	42.1	710,642	2,396	90,050	35.4	74,298	59.3	40.7	NA	58.5	2,156	51.4
Montgomery	233	5.9	405	0.1	57.0	1,078,207	2,660	81,751	46.9	81,496	30.8	69.2	NA	73.0	2,808	38.1
Morgan	135	-11.6	116	0.4	45.9	510,162	4,403	65,751	99.7	85,684	10.8	89.2	2	78.4	1,622	26.1
Perry	163	3.8	468	3.0	41.2	1,032,601	2,208	96,333	37.2	106,536	29.9	70.1	1	60.2	1,415	57.3
Pickens	105	2.1	278	2.4	27.1	702,898	2,528	96,970	88.8	235,520	8.9	91.1	NA	68.2	1,346	41.6
Pike	166	-1.0	279	2.9	40.6	730,910	2,620	87,152	138.8	233,722	7.2	92.8	NA	70.9	3,305	54.4
Randolph	120	5.6	202	0.2	19.7	636,356	3,157	97,755	152.7	255,797	1.8	98.2	3	77.2	1,680	36.2
Russell	99	-15.9	333	3.7	31.2	847,048	2,541	90,179	26.1	88,118	47.3	52.7	NA	66.9	2,666	44.9
St. Clair	59	-12.6	120	0.8	14.4	514,787	4,277	77,055	58.3	118,880	13.3	86.7	NA	83.1	565	21.6
Shelby	67	15.0	150	2.0	26.2	597,813	3,976	69,175	16.5	37,007	84.0	16.0	6	77.0	399	17.7
Sumter	180	-24.8	491	1.1	31.1	919,441	1,872	81,695	21.9	59,594	22.1	77.9	NA	75.7	1,987	55.0
Talladega	80	-20.4	140	4.4	30.0	464,811	3,309	89,072	40.4	71,350	29.0	71.0	NA	75.4	1,080	38.0
Tallapoosa	66	8.0	190	D	8.5	541,614	2,855	60,191	16.5	47,640	12.1	87.9	NA	75.5	494	23.6
Tuscaloosa	95	10.4	170	0.4	23.5	573,374	3,364	62,210	38.6	69,284	17.9	82.1	2	77.2	919	30.9
Walker	65	19.2	130	0.1	16.0	391,595	3,019	87,298	55.1	109,928	7.9	92.1	NA	67.5	431	15.8

— **Water Use, Wholesale Trade, Retail Trade, and Real Estate**

STATE County	Water use, 2015		Wholesale Trade[1], 2012				Retail Trade[2], 2012				Real estate and rental and leasing,[2] 2012			
	Public supply water withdrawn (mil gal/day)	Public supply gallons withdrawn per person per day	Number of establishments	Number of employees	Sales (mil dol)	Average payroll (mil dol)	Number of establishments	Number of employees	Sales (mil dol)	Average payroll (mil dol)	Number of establishments	Number of employees	Sales (mil dol)	Average payroll (mil dol)
	133	134	135	136	137	138	139	140	141	142	143	144	145	146
UNITED STATES	38,595.83	120.1	355,983	4,880,666	5,208,023.5	287,549.6	1,062,083	14,703,529	4,219,821.9	369,001.4	354,106	1,923,770	487,655.2	85,326.0
ALABAMA	761.53	156.7	4,600	60,332	57,746.6	2,894.7	18,211	218,531	58,565.0	5,123.1	3,858	22,852	3,919.4	819.6
Autauga...................	3.64	65.8	22	D	D	D	166	2,385	607.9	54.6	31	D	D	D
Baldwin	23.67	116.2	175	1,868	1,118.2	84.1	950	12,072	3,145.8	280.0	292	1,760	250.3	53.8
Barbour	3.23	121.9	16	181	114.0	4.0	94	868	206.5	18.2	15	20	3.3	0.6
Bibb.......................	5.18	229.4	14	52	41.0	2.3	58	474	118.9	11.3	6	8	1.9	0.3
Blount.....................	56.86	985.9	36	290	153.7	10.5	135	1,255	298.7	28.6	11	19	3.3	0.5
Bullock	2.11	197.3	5	D	D	D	23	244	92.6	5.3	4	12	0.9	0.1
Butler.....................	2.28	113.1	13	44	63.5	2.0	97	914	209.0	19.5	13	18	2.8	0.5
Calhoun...................	25.25	218.4	97	1,792	1,808.8	73.6	477	5,954	1,463.5	134.1	73	299	48.9	8.0
Chambers	4.20	123.1	13	104	32.6	4.2	120	1,172	282.0	23.6	14	50	5.1	0.9
Cherokee	3.20	123.7	12	48	55.2	2.0	88	859	200.2	17.9	12	49	5.7	1.8
Chilton....................	4.40	100.1	20	320	260.5	12.6	152	1,397	442.8	32.0	19	52	6.4	1.2
Choctaw	1.21	91.9	9	D	D	D	54	337	100.0	7.1	6	D	D	D
Clarke.....................	2.58	104.6	13	126	75.2	3.8	138	1,311	341.0	28.4	13	48	6.6	1.2
Clay........................	1.78	131.3	6	D	D	D	34	291	67.7	5.4	6	9	0.6	0.1
Cleburne	0.48	32.0	5	49	6.6	0.8	36	275	64.0	6.9	3	4	0.5	0.2
Coffee	6.34	123.8	29	250	213.2	10.5	195	2,129	610.1	55.5	47	212	21.5	4.4
Colbert	8.26	152.0	78	853	657.4	32.1	228	2,829	1,011.3	76.5	31	144	17.8	3.5
Conecuh	1.32	104.2	5	236	103.9	8.8	41	280	136.4	5.6	3	3	0.2	0.1
Coosa......................	0.27	25.2	5	D	D	D	22	161	37.9	3.5	3	1	0.6	0.1
Covington	4.09	108.1	34	445	470.5	17.9	202	1,834	452.0	40.3	27	97	12.3	3.1
Crenshaw.................	1.93	138.2	12	405	309.0	15.2	38	301	72.7	5.9	6	20	1.6	0.4
Cullman...................	23.24	283.4	93	896	1,068.8	37.9	332	3,264	896.4	76.1	47	195	21.6	5.6
Dale........................	5.90	119.0	18	169	41.0	4.3	138	1,170	323.5	26.4	30	199	33.7	7.4
Dallas.....................	5.91	143.7	28	215	107.1	8.5	179	1,630	413.1	37.0	30	88	13.5	2.2
DeKalb....................	5.91	83.1	37	415	161.0	13.7	246	2,173	579.7	53.2	24	140	9.3	3.3
Elmore.....................	12.19	149.6	37	282	136.1	9.7	224	2,649	711.6	61.0	48	D	D	D
Escambia	5.00	132.3	22	129	134.1	6.1	176	1,542	374.0	30.3	15	63	6.2	1.2
Etowah	16.85	163.5	82	837	549.9	31.2	392	4,675	1,236.5	96.1	62	367	57.2	10.5
Fayette	1.70	101.4	7	24	34.8	0.6	62	562	131.2	12.2	4	D	D	D
Franklin	5.94	187.4	19	92	44.3	3.5	100	1,116	277.7	28.0	13	33	4.7	0.6
Geneva	1.78	66.5	20	D	D	D	91	713	160.8	14.6	7	14	1.4	0.4
Greene.....................	1.39	163.9	2	D	D	D	23	164	40.3	2.8	1	D	D	D
Hale........................	3.10	205.7	7	24	29.4	0.9	43	317	76.5	6.4	8	D	D	D
Henry	1.66	96.4	8	101	40.6	3.9	55	364	100.3	7.9	3	3	0.3	0.0
Houston...................	18.94	181.8	168	D	D	D	570	7,598	2,164.9	182.5	100	423	73.0	16.0
Jackson...................	11.79	224.9	27	D	D	D	185	1,873	454.9	40.1	25	D	D	D
Jefferson.................	48.98	74.2	977	15,345	15,668.5	816.2	2,806	38,691	10,154.0	961.4	681	6,526	1,138.7	283.7
Lamar......................	1.42	102.3	7	D	D	D	51	344	80.9	7.1	3	D	D	D
Lauderdale...............	12.39	133.8	76	1,244	577.6	39.2	419	4,920	1,190.8	104.5	96	378	52.2	10.5
Lawrence	7.73	233.4	12	64	38.9	2.2	85	793	218.0	17.0	5	11	2.6	0.3
Lee.........................	15.83	100.8	75	613	504.3	28.3	477	6,450	1,632.1	141.6	113	544	81.0	16.0
Limestone	11.52	125.7	45	447	332.7	17.3	261	2,804	777.1	64.3	52	166	30.7	5.5
Lowndes..................	0.95	90.8	2	D	D	D	21	177	100.8	3.2	2	D	D	D
Macon	3.31	173.3	6	D	D	D	45	392	93.2	7.1	5	18	1.1	0.3
Madison...................	67.15	190.2	331	4,111	3,768.8	222.9	1,316	18,653	4,958.0	450.2	409	1,706	339.9	60.9
Marengo	2.77	138.3	19	151	105.9	5.3	102	883	199.7	17.8	10	72	20.9	2.9
Marion	6.06	200.9	23	176	222.1	8.0	102	976	229.0	19.9	14	28	4.7	0.7
Marshall	23.76	250.8	81	1,253	1,177.7	47.8	419	4,559	1,280.0	102.0	58	591	34.1	9.6
Mobile	66.10	159.1	499	6,116	3,680.0	283.8	1,454	19,204	5,102.6	454.7	410	2,125	419.1	83.2
Monroe....................	2.31	106.6	16	151	101.0	7.0	89	863	211.0	17.6	13	39	4.8	1.2
Montgomery.............	28.00	123.6	299	5,401	4,140.8	257.0	911	12,148	3,258.7	302.9	228	1,907	342.5	65.5
Morgan....................	25.60	214.1	152	2,080	1,417.0	89.2	498	5,507	1,673.5	127.6	82	340	76.2	12.4
Perry	2.02	209.3	5	59	14.7	1.5	32	174	34.7	3.6	4	D	D	D
Pickens	3.00	143.8	10	69	29.8	2.2	59	427	100.6	9.0	2	D	D	D
Pike........................	4.58	138.6	29	D	D	D	143	1,465	373.6	31.3	26	91	17.8	2.0
Randolph..................	1.22	53.8	5	D	D	D	70	704	158.3	15.0	10	27	3.2	0.6
Russell	8.45	141.6	13	D	D	D	155	1,810	499.7	40.7	39	D	D	D
St. Clair...................	8.93	102.6	69	1,160	476.4	49.2	223	2,613	704.4	56.9	36	101	22.6	3.3
Shelby.....................	14.21	68.1	353	4,260	4,651.3	272.0	610	8,195	2,567.4	210.9	205	1,318	396.0	59.9
Sumter....................	2.06	157.2	11	105	60.2	3.5	46	283	62.1	4.4	7	16	1.9	0.3
Talladega.................	16.00	197.9	52	D	D	D	275	2,748	743.4	60.8	37	210	22.2	4.6
Tallapoosa...............	11.87	290.6	20	D	D	D	169	1,503	361.8	32.3	27	92	20.9	3.6
Tuscaloosa...............	31.43	154.1	143	1,681	1,180.8	83.5	733	9,622	2,619.3	218.3	182	1,485	164.6	44.3
Walker.....................	43.88	672.0	44	406	279.4	18.2	297	3,216	963.5	78.7	38	158	28.5	5.5

1   Merchant wholesalers, except manufacturers' sales branches and offices.   2. Employer establishments.

Table B. States and Counties — Professional Services, Manufacturing, and Accommodation and Food Services

STATE County	Professional, scientific, and technical services, 2012				Manufacturing, 2012				Accommodation and food services, 2012			
	Number of establishments	Number of employees	Sales (mil dol)	Average payroll (mil dol)	Number of establishments	Number of employees	Receipts (mil dol)	Annual payroll (mil dol)	Number of establishments	Number of employees	Receipts (mil dol)	Annual payroll (mil dol)
	147	148	149	150	151	152	153	154	155	156	157	158
UNITED STATES	856,463	8,203,735	1,480,277.1	581,406.1	297,191	11,214,165	5,696,729.6	593,397.0	662,489	12,007,689	708,138.6	196,103.3
ALABAMA	9,109	89,988	16,319.9	5,724.6	4,283	232,650	124,809.8	11,099.5	8,339	157,337	7,576.5	2,071.1
Autauga	58	D	D	D	24	941	665.9	57.5	84	1,954	93.4	24.8
Baldwin	450	1,899	211.5	86.2	146	3,780	1,438.8	166.8	462	10,726	560.6	161.1
Barbour	39	105	16.6	3.9	25	2,837	735.1	103.3	49	596	26.2	6.4
Bibb	16	44	3.6	1.1	15	283	117.5	10.8	11	170	10.1	2.2
Blount	48	223	20.1	7.5	40	1,247	343.0	40.9	43	576	27.1	7.1
Bullock	5	D	D	D	4	D	D	D	7	D	D	D
Butler	20	58	4.8	1.7	19	1,029	811.3	42.2	40	754	32.2	8.5
Calhoun	167	1,140	137.1	43.1	114	5,957	2,713.2	256.9	212	4,673	199.1	53.0
Chambers	32	134	15.4	4.3	21	1,513	474.0	58.3	49	566	30.3	7.5
Cherokee	18	52	7.1	1.7	16	949	368.0	33.0	36	369	17.2	4.5
Chilton	38	94	9.6	2.9	40	1,884	287.2	56.7	52	767	35.4	9.3
Choctaw	21	50	3.4	1.2	5	D	D	D	22	139	7.6	1.7
Clarke	29	88	12.0	2.3	31	1,724	681.3	88.5	45	641	28.0	6.6
Clay	11	56	3.5	1.6	10	1,161	D	40.9	10	117	4.8	1.2
Cleburne	8	25	1.5	0.5	12	608	269.2	23.2	12	D	D	D
Coffee	64	459	77.8	21.7	36	3,344	1,089.9	93.2	87	1,281	61.3	15.2
Colbert	87	305	34.9	11.5	98	4,638	2,547.0	220.1	101	1,624	72.8	19.1
Conecuh	12	28	4.6	1.4	11	357	79.7	11.5	11	156	6.2	1.6
Coosa	5	17	2.2	0.7	6	430	D	17.4	4	D	D	D
Covington	72	279	24.1	8.8	32	2,141	671.9	74.9	55	836	33.1	7.8
Crenshaw	12	32	2.9	0.8	9	1,082	D	38.7	12	D	D	D
Cullman	110	455	40.2	13.4	105	4,041	1,880.8	175.9	131	2,298	111.2	29.7
Dale	98	783	126.5	46.0	31	412	110.2	14.0	83	1,131	54.6	13.5
Dallas	49	193	14.1	5.4	41	3,065	1,309.9	131.0	52	873	36.1	8.7
DeKalb	72	361	32.6	11.2	106	6,814	1,551.9	243.9	98	1,545	79.0	20.9
Elmore	85	440	82.4	18.2	55	2,610	800.2	140.1	93	1,517	66.9	18.7
Escambia	39	157	18.6	5.8	36	2,097	758.9	102.1	59	816	37.2	8.9
Etowah	130	1,250	82.2	35.5	96	4,715	1,355.8	194.1	172	3,231	153.0	40.0
Fayette	13	36	2.9	1.0	20	675	143.3	23.9	20	D	D	D
Franklin	27	158	15.0	6.1	47	3,830	981.2	135.9	41	470	23.8	5.9
Geneva	31	123	8.3	2.5	20	581	D	19.6	24	D	D	D
Greene	3	D	D	D	7	379	102.2	12.5	2	D	D	D
Hale	6	21	2.0	0.5	14	537	D	20.9	11	D	D	D
Henry	22	106	13.6	4.4	14	268	D	11.3	22	D	D	D
Houston	208	1,130	140.6	52.7	98	3,985	1,390.8	151.8	234	4,602	213.0	57.0
Jackson	60	243	23.4	8.7	69	5,196	1,540.4	196.5	75	1,151	49.0	12.7
Jefferson	1,833	16,087	2,933.8	1,064.3	582	23,463	10,951.8	1,260.0	1,352	27,207	1,461.1	422.6
Lamar	15	50	3.7	1.7	16	1,035	334.2	48.5	18	D	D	47.0
Lauderdale	159	766	75.5	29.0	83	3,123	778.2	102.7	167	3,831	159.1	47.0
Lawrence	32	122	15.7	6.6	20	1,039	D	D	41	D	D	D
Lee	202	1,474	138.0	55.1	111	5,903	2,386.1	248.4	323	5,947	271.6	70.4
Limestone	114	706	114.5	42.7	61	3,537	841.4	161.6	108	1,691	81.4	21.9
Lowndes	7	D	D	D	11	1,231	2,375.0	83.6	3	46	1.7	0.6
Macon	13	D	D	D	9	728	D	25.3	29	509	29.0	8.0
Madison	1,328	32,575	7,651.1	2,648.8	283	16,571	7,992.2	959.7	720	14,659	728.7	202.7
Marengo	17	80	10.0	2.9	23	1,356	557.0	63.5	41	466	20.3	5.1
Marion	30	82	4.9	1.8	40	2,594	686.6	92.7	48	561	25.4	6.6
Marshall	124	558	50.7	18.8	107	10,666	3,234.5	327.5	180	2,936	124.4	33.9
Mobile	850	9,039	1,175.1	474.0	343	16,063	10,562.7	886.3	671	13,684	617.9	167.9
Monroe	17	41	4.8	1.3	17	975	423.0	67.1	30	361	15.3	3.8
Montgomery	606	6,178	1,307.8	403.9	197	12,585	10,786.6	615.4	491	9,986	474.5	130.9
Morgan	198	1,361	152.1	62.7	182	11,009	D	D	202	D	D	D
Perry	8	14	1.0	0.3	7	D	166.0	17.8	11	D	D	D
Pickens	14	75	3.9	2.1	22	552	D	17.0	17	D	D	D
Pike	30	645	60.9	28.4	24	1,303	611.7	57.5	72	1,349	57.8	14.8
Randolph	17	46	3.9	1.1	21	690	251.6	27.7	24	316	15.6	3.6
Russell	51	215	17.5	5.1	42	2,697	1,209.2	130.6	77	1,440	70.2	16.7
St. Clair	98	648	63.4	17.4	77	2,884	931.3	134.8	120	1,969	89.8	24.7
Shelby	564	4,724	845.2	269.3	152	5,062	1,700.0	259.0	337	6,640	334.4	93.6
Sumter	8	D	D	D	7	156	D	D	25	262	10.7	2.8
Talladega	76	455	34.0	15.5	88	8,419	D	473.1	110	D	D	D
Tallapoosa	52	216	26.2	9.2	30	2,239	456.3	79.3	57	863	37.0	10.6
Tuscaloosa	337	2,167	322.9	99.7	136	11,487	14,291.1	707.2	390	D	D	D
Walker	93	445	39.1	20.9	44	1,710	505.7	65.0	95	1,468	75.3	18.9

Table B. States and Counties — Health Care and Social Assistance, Other Services, Nonemployer Businesses, and Residential Construction

STATE County	Health care and social assistance, 2012				Other services, 2012				Nonemployer businesses, 2016		Value of residential construction authorized by building permits, 2018	
	Number of establish-ments	Number of employees	Receipts (mil dol)	Annual payroll (mil dol)	Number of establish-ments	Number of employees	Receipts (mil dol)	Annual payroll (mil dol)	Number	Receipts (mil dol)	New construction ($1,000)	Number of housing units
	159	160	161	162	163	164	165	166	167	168	169	170
UNITED STATES	831,303	18,414,757	2,040,441.2	801,239.5	529,691	3,430,711	426,693.7	108,185.7	24,813,048	1,165,668.3	271,119,545	1,328,827
ALABAMA	10,305	243,194	26,039.6	10,238.9	6,087	37,291	4,378.0	1,117.1	324,994	13,580.5	3,046,657	14,824
Autauga	95	1,580	119.4	46.2	58	D	D	D	3,153	115.5	56,148	185
Baldwin	444	7,029	622.5	265.3	269	1,203	110.5	31.9	18,470	898.2	615,245	3,047
Barbour	45	791	66.7	24.1	21	72	6.5	1.6	1,439	47.3	1,537	6
Bibb	29	D	D	D	20	D	D	D	1,232	49.6	2,423	13
Blount	48	D	D	D	64	D	D	D	3,663	142.7	1,504	11
Bullock	14	413	30.3	11.2	6	D	D	D	508	17.2	0	0
Butler	40	948	89.0	32.4	17	71	6.7	2.0	1,023	38.4	1,652	7
Calhoun	273	5,785	573.5	221.0	177	785	80.2	23.3	6,412	239.6	10,958	70
Chambers	59	1,247	99.1	40.9	33	141	12.2	3.7	2,289	58.9	1,704	15
Cherokee	41	406	35.7	14.7	19	73	5.9	1.7	1,536	71.4	1,033	8
Chilton	56	822	66.4	25.4	36	D	D	D	2,955	106.2	10,303	95
Choctaw	28	356	30.9	12.0	22	D	D	D	854	23.4	0	0
Clarke	53	882	68.2	29.3	36	126	11.5	3.0	1,530	52.1	1,431	7
Clay	21	D	D	D	11	D	D	D	799	34.5	211	3
Cleburne	10	D	D	D	9	45	4.8	1.3	957	35.9	170	1
Coffee	101	1,798	174.3	68.3	67	310	26.6	8.2	2,661	95.1	17,693	112
Colbert	128	2,620	281.6	110.9	71	D	D	D	3,513	134.2	19,333	160
Conecuh	16	336	31.6	12.9	14	D	D	D	687	21.2	0	0
Coosa	5	D	D	D	8	D	D	D	403	12.9	0	0
Covington	93	1,727	139.0	55.2	49	229	21.7	6.1	2,284	80.6	2,006	15
Crenshaw	14	489	28.7	14.4	13	D	D	D	856	26.8	877	4
Cullman	182	2,533	242.2	101.0	101	499	56.3	15.0	5,678	257.1	15,967	135
Dale	60	1,134	86.7	35.8	50	217	13.1	3.9	2,429	84.5	3,001	24
Dallas	102	2,011	173.5	65.6	51	375	30.0	8.3	2,307	68.3	3,858	28
DeKalb	123	2,294	189.2	73.9	51	181	16.8	5.0	4,710	214.7	13,377	85
Elmore	109	1,981	156.9	59.2	78	392	38.7	9.0	5,189	226.1	12,865	74
Escambia	67	1,265	105.7	42.7	46	198	17.7	4.3	2,120	67.5	1,588	11
Etowah	316	7,433	701.9	303.4	125	632	98.9	19.0	7,267	316.1	16,901	104
Fayette	50	801	54.1	23.5	22	D	D	D	1,071	39.3	390	2
Franklin	63	1,112	96.4	36.0	36	D	D	D	1,868	76.0	1,583	20
Geneva	33	632	42.9	19.4	20	D	D	D	1,521	62.9	1,698	13
Greene	13	290	16.8	7.9	5	D	D	D	452	12.5	626	6
Hale	17	445	28.1	11.0	7	10	1.2	0.2	798	27.8	2,047	23
Henry	28	466	22.4	10.9	16	D	D	D	1,058	38.5	4,967	24
Houston	314	9,145	1,061.9	455.9	185	1,056	115.5	27.6	7,150	320.3	87,200	377
Jackson	116	D	D	D	42	175	15.8	5.0	3,121	127.0	6,001	37
Jefferson	1,688	57,068	7,766.2	2,830.6	1,042	9,351	1,262.3	306.0	47,895	2,153.2	471,455	1,657
Lamar	22	346	18.6	8.5	11	D	D	D	946	39.0	0	0
Lauderdale	254	4,337	449.8	158.9	115	D	D	D	6,424	302.7	14,773	175
Lawrence	36	736	44.1	20.3	30	80	9.0	2.3	1,947	67.3	649	3
Lee	235	5,923	541.5	218.4	172	787	72.8	18.6	10,154	435.4	296,764	1,131
Limestone	121	2,163	170.1	74.9	82	512	46.6	13.8	5,810	226.1	31,270	159
Lowndes	5	90	5.5	2.3	4	D	D	D	655	20.3	0	0
Macon	24	D	D	D	15	D	D	D	967	25.9	511	2
Madison	932	21,762	2,475.1	985.4	474	3,503	570.6	126.8	24,256	989.8	427,069	2,782
Marengo	61	984	75.7	30.7	30	89	6.3	1.7	975	31.4	715	5
Marion	79	1,355	125.9	46.5	27	D	D	D	1,808	81.9	0	0
Marshall	191	3,727	336.0	124.7	84	370	26.4	7.4	7,146	338.9	12,609	77
Mobile	734	21,863	2,397.2	927.8	570	3,577	334.8	96.2	30,532	1,104.7	177,668	783
Monroe	30	709	50.6	21.3	18	D	D	D	1,366	48.2	781	4
Montgomery	666	16,589	1,780.7	762.2	429	3,172	404.6	113.9	15,399	667.9	69,574	395
Morgan	340	5,733	497.1	187.4	150	980	94.0	27.2	7,567	310.8	26,957	149
Perry	8	142	7.1	3.2	7	9	0.7	0.2	488	15.7	0	0
Pickens	25	705	44.7	20.6	17	D	D	D	1,106	36.3	870	7
Pike	63	1,156	91.7	39.4	39	139	10.2	2.8	1,734	73.2	7,137	49
Randolph	35	634	49.3	21.1	23	D	D	D	1,352	50.8	0	0
Russell	65	D	D	D	61	275	22.2	7.3	3,261	93.5	38,189	261
St. Clair	93	1,907	133.5	54.5	81	265	26.8	7.0	5,547	223.9	37,381	200
Shelby	439	6,297	583.4	240.5	281	1,792	215.0	56.1	17,166	880.4	241,691	1,045
Sumter	24	415	26.9	10.7	5	21	2.0	0.5	710	25.8	780	9
Talladega	160	D	D	D	66	D	D	D	3,992	158.2	6,907	43
Tallapoosa	88	2,181	186.3	78.2	44	169	14.8	3.9	2,568	111.7	34,951	137
Tuscaloosa	437	13,201	1,413.0	613.0	235	D	D	D	12,164	562.9	229,546	1,017
Walker	171	3,178	311.7	114.6	83	D	D	D	3,750	138.7	946	4

Table B. States and Counties — Government Employment and Payroll, and Local Government Finances

STATE County	Government employment and payroll, 2012									Local government finances, 2012				
			March payroll (percent of total)							General revenue				
												Taxes		
											Inter-govern-mental (mil dol)	Total (mil dol)	Per capita[1] (dollars)	
	Full-time equivalent employees	March payroll (dollars)	Adminis-tration, judicial, and legal	Police and corrections	Fire protection	Highways and transpor-tation	Health and welfare	Natural resources and utilities	Education and libraries	Total (mil dol)			Total	Property
	171	172	173	174	175	176	177	178	179	180	181	182	183	184
UNITED STATES	X	X	X	X	X	X	X	X	X	X	X	X	X	X
ALABAMA	X	X	X	X	X	X	X	X	X	X	X	X	X	X
Autauga	1,582	5,202,816	4.0	9.6	6.8	2.7	1.7	5.0	67.1	125.4	65.8	41.7	751	262
Baldwin	7,374	22,581,577	7.4	8.0	2.9	4.3	20.7	5.6	47.7	640.7	189.9	231.1	1,211	537
Barbour	1,162	3,226,895	2.8	6.5	3.7	2.8	22.4	6.2	54.3	79.4	44.6	19.5	719	241
Bibb	837	2,413,468	3.7	5.9	0.0	3.6	26.0	2.1	58.0	59.5	31.7	7.9	351	147
Blount	1,539	4,659,233	4.8	7.3	1.6	3.1	0.9	5.3	75.6	107.3	70.3	23.0	398	220
Bullock	552	1,468,315	4.4	5.2	0.0	4.7	37.7	0.1	46.6	28.4	20.9	4.8	454	337
Butler	934	2,423,650	4.8	7.9	2.9	6.4	14.6	5.7	55.8	65.7	35.4	23.2	1,142	306
Calhoun	5,708	17,129,463	3.6	6.8	2.8	2.8	32.2	7.0	43.2	507.7	169.3	112.4	958	366
Chambers	1,193	3,265,131	6.9	10.3	3.6	6.5	3.3	9.0	58.5	79.2	43.1	21.6	634	304
Cherokee	997	3,526,515	5.0	5.1	0.1	2.9	16.9	6.0	63.4	50.9	29.6	16.6	640	293
Chilton	1,218	3,862,506	5.9	8.9	0.5	4.3	1.4	6.0	72.4	95.1	55.9	25.1	572	321
Choctaw	383	970,992	9.1	5.8	0.0	6.4	0.0	1.9	74.4	27.8	15.9	7.3	536	470
Clarke	1,107	3,358,366	4.7	9.6	0.0	3.2	12.7	8.4	59.5	70.9	38.1	25.5	1,015	336
Clay	699	1,916,771	2.1	5.9	0.1	5.2	39.3	5.7	40.5	52.0	20.5	9.5	704	493
Cleburne	633	2,123,561	3.8	6.3	0.1	3.4	9.9	5.1	70.2	36.9	24.6	7.3	490	274
Coffee	2,026	5,912,313	3.1	6.9	2.2	3.8	13.7	5.8	63.9	136.4	72.2	40.1	782	349
Colbert	3,178	10,303,212	2.2	5.5	2.5	2.4	36.7	11.6	37.7	258.1	88.3	46.3	850	424
Conecuh	486	1,319,565	6.8	10.8	0.0	6.5	1.3	10.9	62.6	33.3	20.8	7.6	588	279
Coosa	265	695,770	2.4	13.6	0.0	6.3	0.6	1.2	75.2	21.9	15.4	4.4	397	290
Covington	1,587	4,552,054	7.2	6.3	1.6	5.3	1.1	22.2	53.7	120.6	57.2	30.6	805	249
Crenshaw	472	1,600,404	4.4	5.5	0.0	6.3	0.9	7.4	75.5	27.8	16.6	6.6	471	206
Cullman	3,911	11,764,023	3.0	6.7	1.9	3.3	31.4	8.4	43.9	194.4	96.2	54.4	676	276
Dale	1,600	4,956,908	3.8	7.4	2.7	2.6	26.4	5.1	50.9	131.8	55.8	34.7	688	250
Dallas	1,746	4,733,521	4.8	9.2	3.2	2.5	1.5	6.4	67.0	113.7	68.6	33.9	791	371
DeKalb	2,193	6,908,865	4.2	8.4	2.2	3.5	4.3	10.3	66.0	169.1	97.9	42.8	602	293
Elmore	2,265	6,703,799	3.5	10.3	1.2	3.1	0.8	4.6	75.0	153.6	86.5	43.7	541	251
Escambia	1,604	4,378,782	4.5	9.0	2.3	4.4	15.2	2.8	58.4	116.3	47.9	27.6	726	330
Etowah	3,980	11,900,349	4.3	10.5	6.2	3.7	6.9	8.4	56.6	284.1	137.1	99.7	955	293
Fayette	541	1,471,267	6.2	6.8	1.8	7.2	2.2	10.0	65.4	50.8	33.7	12.6	742	260
Franklin	1,331	3,838,038	4.8	7.1	2.1	3.7	3.3	12.5	65.2	84.8	50.1	15.5	488	176
Geneva	1,102	3,351,087	3.2	5.0	0.1	3.9	27.3	3.4	56.6	106.8	34.4	20.2	751	302
Greene	456	1,298,955	3.6	6.0	0.0	5.0	31.6	4.7	48.5	30.5	13.4	5.5	620	359
Hale	605	1,537,609	4.7	7.4	0.0	3.8	23.7	1.0	59.3	51.7	27.1	9.4	613	301
Henry	549	1,493,829	6.9	8.0	2.0	5.6	2.8	4.3	68.4	33.3	19.9	9.4	546	269
Houston	5,714	19,682,365	3.7	6.6	3.6	2.3	45.1	5.9	30.9	590.6	124.8	126.4	1,222	429
Jackson	2,490	8,016,220	3.3	6.6	1.8	3.9	29.0	8.0	46.4	205.9	91.7	40.1	756	359
Jefferson	27,700	103,543,070	5.4	12.8	7.2	3.5	7.3	9.3	49.8	2,895.7	935.7	1,334.8	2,022	856
Lamar	454	1,337,464	7.1	9.0	0.8	4.9	2.6	9.6	64.8	31.4	20.5	6.5	457	274
Lauderdale	2,704	9,293,198	4.1	8.4	4.2	4.1	2.8	16.3	57.5	230.1	103.9	91.1	984	414
Lawrence	1,156	3,399,543	4.4	7.8	0.4	3.4	14.2	4.4	64.8	74.9	46.2	11.0	324	217
Lee	6,506	23,295,526	2.9	5.8	2.5	1.6	40.7	4.1	41.4	640.1	158.1	164.2	1,115	594
Limestone	2,694	10,450,795	2.4	6.2	1.4	1.9	21.8	7.7	57.3	213.7	86.7	39.0	445	236
Lowndes	502	1,360,565	8.1	8.4	0.0	4.3	0.5	2.4	75.6	38.0	25.6	9.0	830	443
Macon	731	2,048,937	7.8	7.7	2.4	4.5	1.6	16.0	58.1	49.6	28.9	15.3	746	268
Madison	17,330	64,421,407	3.9	6.3	3.3	2.9	40.3	7.4	32.3	1,978.9	813.4	389.2	1,134	579
Marengo	1,007	2,884,299	5.2	7.8	3.8	5.1	8.0	6.1	61.8	87.7	38.7	15.2	746	331
Marion	992	2,975,248	4.1	7.5	1.3	5.2	1.2	15.9	64.8	75.9	39.2	22.6	745	282
Marshall	4,582	15,491,666	2.4	5.3	2.4	1.7	30.3	11.3	46.0	395.1	144.9	75.8	799	378
Mobile	15,334	47,151,677	5.5	11.5	5.1	4.9	9.2	7.3	53.7	1,405.0	626.1	561.4	1,356	491
Monroe	1,069	3,209,902	3.2	6.5	1.2	3.7	34.3	2.7	48.2	82.1	40.2	13.0	573	337
Montgomery	8,484	27,145,960	5.0	15.4	6.4	3.3	4.4	9.5	49.6	1,098.6	290.3	265.5	1,154	360
Morgan	4,927	17,209,848	3.0	7.3	3.3	2.5	22.7	9.2	50.8	514.7	208.9	123.2	1,023	501
Perry	634	1,533,195	4.2	5.7	0.1	9.3	22.6	2.7	54.6	35.7	28.0	5.6	546	240
Pickens	699	1,770,074	5.4	8.5	0.0	6.6	2.9	6.6	68.1	65.0	32.5	7.6	389	243
Pike	1,061	3,438,644	6.1	11.4	3.5	4.1	4.1	13.7	55.5	103.3	44.5	21.4	644	263
Randolph	771	2,493,832	3.6	8.3	0.1	4.4	13.3	1.8	67.8	67.1	30.1	11.3	500	257
Russell	2,491	7,257,682	19.9	8.4	3.1	2.7	1.7	7.6	53.3	148.3	81.2	49.2	851	413
St. Clair	2,191	7,157,617	7.3	9.7	4.9	3.2	0.1	3.1	71.1	184.8	107.5	55.3	649	287
Shelby	5,778	16,879,679	6.7	14.3	5.9	3.1	2.9	4.8	60.5	441.4	172.8	191.6	954	567
Sumter	560	1,553,057	5.4	7.7	1.9	5.9	1.9	7.7	67.6	34.6	20.5	8.9	664	293
Talladega	3,476	9,539,423	3.6	6.8	2.5	2.7	19.3	8.7	54.0	201.6	106.6	60.5	740	379
Tallapoosa	1,698	5,118,158	4.4	8.1	3.8	2.6	22.1	9.3	47.3	118.2	65.1	34.0	826	434
Tuscaloosa	10,215	37,068,838	3.6	7.2	3.6	3.5	48.2	3.7	29.3	991.4	234.1	212.4	1,070	420
Walker	2,414	6,546,224	3.1	8.7	1.3	3.2	3.4	7.9	70.5	157.6	87.1	48.0	726	246

1. Based on the resident population estimated as of July 1 of the year shown.

Table B. States and Counties — Local Government Finances, Government Employment, and Income Taxes

STATE County	Local government finances, 2012 (cont.) Direct general expenditure — Total (mil dol) [185]	Per capita¹ (dollars) [186]	Percent of total for: Education [187]	Health and hospitals [188]	Police protection [189]	Public welfare [190]	Highways [191]	Debt outstanding Total (mil dol) [192]	Per capita¹ (dollars) [193]	Government employment, 2017 Federal civilian [194]	Federal military [195]	State and local [196]	Individual income tax returns, 2016 Number of returns [197]	Mean adjusted gross income [198]	Mean income tax [199]
UNITED STATES	X	X	X	X	X	X	X	X	X	2,857,000	1,929,000	19,619,000	149,076,410	67,996	9,590
ALABAMA	X	X	X	X	X	X	X	X	X	53,233	28,859	321,082	2,043,540	55,469	6,620
Autauga	119.9	2,161	60.8	0.1	7.0	0.5	2.9	149.8	2,699	86	266	2,165	24,090	55,124	5,567
Baldwin	700.0	3,669	34.5	19.2	6.1	0.1	7.7	911.0	4,775	350	971	9,262	95,900	61,610	7,919
Barbour	74.3	2,732	47.4	18.7	6.4	0.0	3.9	37.2	1,369	54	106	1,556	9,210	39,606	3,502
Bibb	57.9	2,564	51.4	26.2	4.4	0.0	4.1	55.2	2,445	72	87	1,209	7,940	46,788	4,000
Blount	108.1	1,870	72.0	0.8	5.8	0.3	6.1	48.6	841	92	246	1,843	22,110	48,770	4,525
Bullock	30.6	2,921	53.3	22.5	3.6	0.7	8.6	14.8	1,416	35	37	641	3,820	32,630	2,324
Butler	60.7	2,987	47.3	9.6	5.4	0.5	9.3	65.0	3,202	41	83	888	8,090	39,970	3,245
Calhoun	517.7	4,414	32.7	36.2	5.9	0.0	3.9	358.0	3,052	3,613	536	8,631	47,590	46,197	4,383
Chambers	78.6	2,308	50.4	1.2	8.3	0.3	7.0	72.0	2,112	54	142	1,774	14,260	37,272	2,908
Cherokee	48.3	1,856	75.1	0.1	4.8	0.0	4.5	60.1	2,309	48	109	1,253	9,480	44,768	4,099
Chilton	96.3	2,198	62.9	0.6	7.0	0.4	5.7	23.3	533	62	192	1,765	17,190	45,879	4,198
Choctaw	28.4	2,080	53.7	0.0	6.0	0.1	13.4	22.9	1,681	25	55	473	5,040	46,357	4,341
Clarke	67.0	2,664	60.9	0.3	7.8	0.2	6.2	111.3	4,422	68	102	1,744	9,970	48,521	4,928
Clay	70.4	5,240	51.0	26.2	4.1	0.1	4.4	26.5	1,971	57	56	911	5,660	44,349	4,269
Cleburne	41.7	2,813	52.6	0.1	4.4	17.0	6.0	35.4	2,387	43	64	730	5,640	47,357	4,000
Coffee	144.1	2,812	62.6	0.4	4.8	0.2	4.8	136.0	2,654	243	219	2,405	21,150	55,561	6,194
Colbert	259.3	4,762	32.1	37.0	3.6	0.2	3.5	178.7	3,282	605	231	4,073	23,700	52,680	5,946
Conecuh	37.1	2,859	59.4	0.0	8.0	0.6	6.4	64.7	4,982	28	53	725	4,790	36,771	3,028
Coosa	22.3	2,029	59.1	0.1	7.7	0.2	19.6	8.9	810	17	45	337	3,890	42,238	3,642
Covington	141.5	3,727	42.0	0.3	6.6	0.1	12.6	930.5	24,517	115	156	2,046	14,660	46,402	4,424
Crenshaw	29.8	2,119	65.1	6.8	9.7	0.0	3.3	16.9	1,199	40	59	592	5,710	41,488	3,624
Cullman	206.4	2,566	52.3	2.1	7.2	1.1	7.3	191.6	2,381	203	349	4,298	33,760	49,009	5,079
Dale	146.4	2,902	56.7	19.7	4.5	0.2	2.5	62.7	1,242	2,995	3,774	2,113	19,990	44,664	4,054
Dallas	143.5	3,347	61.4	0.1	8.3	0.4	3.2	105.2	2,455	155	164	2,483	15,710	36,829	3,084
DeKalb	174.9	2,461	64.2	3.0	8.3	0.4	7.1	113.8	1,602	166	302	3,280	26,760	41,081	3,667
Elmore	159.9	1,983	65.0	0.8	7.4	0.0	7.2	169.3	2,100	161	326	4,440	35,310	55,829	5,845
Escambia	124.2	3,269	45.2	24.5	6.3	0.4	4.3	40.7	1,071	62	146	4,064	14,190	43,307	4,003
Etowah	278.9	2,672	46.7	1.9	11.2	0.2	4.8	218.9	2,097	301	430	5,065	41,770	45,540	4,425
Fayette	33.4	1,968	66.1	1.2	2.5	0.0	10.0	12.4	731	39	72	1,219	6,250	41,627	3,389
Franklin	94.1	2,961	58.5	0.1	4.4	0.0	6.5	55.6	1,752	88	133	1,895	12,160	40,986	3,728
Geneva	79.5	2,953	44.2	28.4	5.0	0.2	5.9	34.0	1,262	55	112	1,362	9,980	42,862	3,697
Greene	31.5	3,551	49.2	28.3	3.2	0.5	3.8	17.4	1,960	27	35	612	3,260	32,521	2,212
Hale	48.8	3,170	51.5	17.8	6.3	0.0	12.3	13.5	876	45	62	840	6,290	38,844	3,195
Henry	34.2	1,979	64.6	0.0	6.7	0.7	13.2	44.3	2,565	44	72	677	7,010	46,179	4,710
Houston	591.0	5,716	25.3	46.6	3.9	0.1	3.3	407.2	3,938	315	480	8,319	44,380	53,117	6,847
Jackson	209.8	3,957	51.6	23.7	4.0	0.3	4.2	118.1	2,227	154	219	2,982	21,050	45,419	4,370
Jefferson	2,885.7	4,372	40.1	5.3	6.6	0.0	4.0	7,596.1	11,509	8,212	3,111	52,409	291,420	67,948	9,855
Lamar	32.3	2,262	61.7	0.0	6.4	0.4	4.7	29.7	2,081	37	59	559	5,240	41,780	3,211
Lauderdale	225.0	2,431	58.9	0.1	6.2	0.1	6.7	265.7	2,871	281	389	4,808	38,240	54,610	6,350
Lawrence	78.1	2,309	60.0	13.5	6.3	0.5	6.4	41.6	1,229	83	140	1,260	13,490	44,173	3,788
Lee	638.8	4,338	33.9	39.7	4.1	0.0	2.6	782.4	5,313	298	727	17,243	63,090	57,114	6,654
Limestone	276.5	3,155	51.2	23.1	4.8	0.2	3.7	282.8	3,227	1,450	391	5,431	38,940	60,795	6,886
Lowndes	39.8	3,667	69.6	0.0	5.6	0.0	9.7	34.2	3,148	28	43	503	4,800	39,451	3,621
Macon	52.1	2,539	58.2	0.3	5.4	0.0	2.5	68.8	3,349	942	79	1,922	7,630	34,644	2,720
Madison	1,830.4	5,335	30.6	39.1	3.7	0.0	2.5	1,931.7	5,631	17,985	2,241	25,417	167,930	68,525	9,198
Marengo	94.5	4,633	40.6	31.0	3.2	0.0	2.7	33.7	1,651	65	100	1,516	8,230	45,237	4,391
Marion	72.1	2,379	61.7	0.0	6.4	0.0	5.4	62.6	2,065	75	124	1,475	10,830	42,118	3,712
Marshall	395.8	4,177	40.0	33.4	5.5	0.2	1.9	306.5	3,234	281	403	5,957	39,200	47,203	5,118
Mobile	1,433.8	3,464	41.2	6.0	6.8	0.5	8.3	1,386.2	3,349	2,583	2,571	22,829	172,670	50,832	5,953
Monroe	83.9	3,713	40.0	33.9	5.1	0.1	8.3	7.6	334	51	90	1,392	7,990	44,248	4,181
Montgomery	1,084.1	4,711	25.4	43.2	5.2	0.3	2.1	1,050.3	4,564	6,315	3,613	26,511	97,760	53,976	6,824
Morgan	592.0	4,917	54.2	17.4	4.2	0.3	2.9	883.2	7,336	307	501	6,504	51,940	52,227	5,582
Perry	37.4	3,675	46.2	24.5	3.6	0.4	7.2	37.3	3,663	24	75	464	3,560	30,237	1,854
Pickens	72.8	3,752	37.4	29.1	3.2	0.1	5.3	52.7	2,716	350	78	925	7,310	41,317	3,471
Pike	119.3	3,594	39.5	22.5	7.4	0.0	3.2	140.0	4,218	95	135	3,277	12,460	47,742	4,751
Randolph	70.0	3,087	46.0	32.1	4.6	0.0	1.9	57.2	2,521	60	95	1,129	8,930	42,297	3,648
Russell	149.9	2,593	59.3	0.1	5.7	0.1	3.0	302.5	5,233	102	241	2,809	23,230	38,295	3,062
St. Clair	188.6	2,213	57.2	6.9	10.0	0.1	4.2	290.2	3,404	117	370	2,817	36,330	53,217	5,345
Shelby	463.8	2,308	61.2	1.7	10.9	0.2	3.8	773.4	3,849	385	901	8,384	93,860	78,687	11,090
Sumter	37.0	2,754	54.6	0.8	7.3	0.1	13.6	25.2	1,879	36	50	1,260	4,790	33,132	2,638
Talladega	213.4	2,610	55.2	4.8	7.5	0.4	5.6	225.8	2,762	469	329	4,377	32,470	44,474	4,020
Tallapoosa	123.8	3,008	45.4	17.8	6.1	0.0	4.1	118.8	2,886	93	171	1,984	17,220	47,421	4,843
Tuscaloosa	994.6	5,008	29.0	43.5	4.8	0.0	4.7	615.9	3,101	1,588	855	23,485	81,870	56,135	6,860
Walker	158.5	2,394	61.5	0.1	5.4	0.0	8.0	116.9	1,765	194	271	3,050	24,780	47,219	4,502

1. Based on the resident population estimated as of July 1 of the year shown.

State / county code	CBSA code[1]	County code[2]	STATE County	Land area[3] (sq. mi)	Total persons 2018	Rank	Per square mile	White	Black	American Indian, Alaska Native	Asian and Pacific Islander	Percent Hispanic or Latino[4]	Under 5 years	5 to 17 years	18 to 24 years	25 to 34 years	35 to 44 years	45 to 54 years
				1	2	3	4	5	6	7	8	9	10	11	12	13	14	15
			ALABAMA—Cont'd															
01129		8	Washington	1,080.2	16,378	2,018	15.2	66.3	23.9	8.4	1.3	1.6	5.3	16.7	8.2	11.1	11.1	13.7
01131		9	Wilcox	888.5	10,627	2,385	12.0	27.3	71.2	0.5	0.4	1.4	6.4	17.4	9.3	10.9	10.9	12.0
01133		6	Winston	613.0	23,660	1,657	38.6	94.9	1.3	1.5	0.5	3.2	5.4	15.0	7.5	10.5	11.1	14.1
02000		0	ALASKA	570,983.2	737,438	X	1.3	66.3	4.8	18.9	10.2	7.2	7.2	17.7	9.5	16.1	12.8	11.9
02013		9	Aleutians East	6,985.1	3,515	2,937	0.5	11.0	11.1	20.9	45.5	14.7	2.4	5.5	9.6	16.0	21.2	22.1
02016		9	Aleutians West	4,392.1	5,723	2,778	1.3	26.2	7.3	12.5	44.2	13.8	3.1	8.0	9.1	18.5	18.1	20.1
02020	11,260	2	Anchorage	1,706.4	291,538	238	170.8	63.8	7.6	12.0	15.6	9.3	7.2	17.3	9.8	17.3	13.1	12.0
02050		7	Bethel	40,569.1	18,216	1,916	0.4	12.7	1.3	85.3	1.9	2.4	11.2	24.7	10.5	15.5	10.2	10.0
02060		9	Bristol Bay	482.0	877	3,112	1.8	58.7	2.7	42.3	5.1	7.5	6.4	12.7	8.7	15.7	10.9	12.3
02068		8	Denali	12,637.0	2,059	3,042	0.2	83.8	3.0	8.0	6.2	3.2	5.5	13.1	6.3	15.7	14.1	17.6
02070		9	Dillingham	18,331.4	5,000	2,831	0.3	23.4	1.5	77.7	2.5	3.8	10.0	21.6	10.1	15.6	10.4	10.5
02090	21,820	3	Fairbanks North Star	7,329.5	98,971	604	13.5	75.0	6.4	10.9	6.0	8.4	7.6	16.5	13.2	18.7	12.5	10.2
02100		9	Haines	2,339.6	2,474	3,007	1.1	84.7	1.7	15.8	2.3	3.2	3.6	13.5	6.3	9.8	12.0	13.1
02105		9	Hoonah-Angoon	6,556.6	2,151	3,034	0.3	54.7	2.9	42.5	2.9	6.4	4.7	13.7	5.6	9.9	10.5	14.9
02110	27,940	5	Juneau	2,703.9	32,113	1,378	11.9	71.5	2.1	17.6	11.7	6.8	5.7	15.5	8.6	15.1	13.8	13.4
02122		7	Kenai Peninsula	16,023.3	58,533	883	3.7	85.1	1.2	11.8	3.5	4.3	6.1	16.5	7.5	12.6	11.8	12.2
02130	28,540	7	Ketchikan Gateway	4,856.9	13,918	2,168	2.9	70.8	1.6	19.8	10.8	5.8	5.9	16.4	7.9	13.9	12.7	12.4
02150		7	Kodiak Island	6,615.4	13,345	2,204	2.0	55.1	1.6	16.8	24.9	8.8	7.8	17.8	9.3	16.2	13.6	11.4
02158		0	Kusilvak	17,073.9	8,303	2,561	0.5	5.7	0.7	92.5	1.1	2.6	13.1	27.7	10.9	15.9	9.0	8.8
02164		9	Lake and Peninsula	23,897.4	1,587	3,075	0.1	31.6	2.4	67.4	5.3	3.5	10.1	18.4	7.9	14.7	13.0	12.0
02170	11,260	2	Matanuska-Susitna	24,713.8	107,610	563	4.4	85.0	2.1	10.9	4.0	5.1	7.1	19.7	8.1	14.3	13.4	12.2
02180		7	Nome	22,992.0	10,008	2,427	0.4	20.5	1.3	79.4	2.5	2.5	10.1	24.6	9.9	15.7	11.7	9.9
02185		7	North Slope	88,824.4	9,872	2,438	0.1	35.0	2.2	54.4	9.5	4.3	8.0	18.5	7.7	16.7	12.8	15.8
02188		7	Northwest Arctic	35,648.5	7,671	2,618	0.2	15.9	1.6	82.3	2.2	3.8	10.2	25.1	10.1	16.3	10.3	10.8
02195		9	Petersburg	2,900.6	3,221	2,955	1.1	76.7	3.2	14.8	6.1	6.0	6.0	14.8	7.6	12.0	11.6	12.9
02198		9	Prince of Wales-Hyder	5,262.8	6,422	2,717	1.2	52.2	1.5	47.3	3.5	3.7	6.1	16.8	7.1	12.1	11.2	13.5
02220		7	Sitka	2,870.0	8,647	2,536	3.0	68.4	2.0	20.8	10.8	7.0	5.1	16.4	8.2	14.5	13.6	12.0
02230		9	Skagway	433.9	1,148	3,102	2.6	85.6	1.7	7.5	5.0	5.5	5.3	10.5	4.2	18.7	19.5	13.9
02240		9	Southeast Fairbanks	24,822.8	6,918	2,681	0.3	77.0	2.3	15.4	3.8	6.4	7.4	17.9	6.5	14.6	12.4	12.5
02261		9	Valdez-Cordova	34,221.9	9,164	2,488	0.3	74.8	1.4	18.5	6.5	5.3	6.8	16.6	7.2	13.4	12.2	12.8
02275		9	Wrangell	2,556.0	2,503	3,005	1.0	76.0	1.8	24.0	5.8	3.0	4.6	15.4	7.2	10.2	8.8	11.9
02282		9	Yakutat	7,623.3	604	3,134	0.1	44.5	5.3	48.3	11.9	4.6	5.5	13.1	6.1	13.2	11.6	16.9
02290		9	Yukon-Koyukuk	145,573.9	5,327	2,806	0.0	27.1	1.5	73.1	1.4	2.8	7.0	20.3	8.1	13.5	11.9	10.2
04000		0	ARIZONA	113,590.7	7,171,646	X	63.1	56.3	5.2	4.5	4.6	31.6	6.1	16.8	9.6	13.7	12.3	11.9
04001		6	Apache	11,197.5	71,818	754	6.4	19.2	1.1	74.0	0.8	6.4	6.7	20.5	9.5	13.1	10.8	11.3
04003	43,420	3	Cochise	6,164.6	126,770	505	20.6	57.0	4.8	1.6	3.6	35.6	5.8	15.7	8.9	12.5	11.0	10.6
04005	22,380	3	Coconino	18,618.7	142,854	457	7.7	56.2	2.0	27.1	3.2	14.3	5.5	15.1	20.1	14.2	11.0	10.1
04007	37,740	4	Gila	4,758.0	53,889	941	11.3	63.1	0.9	17.2	1.2	18.7	5.6	14.5	6.4	9.9	8.7	10.4
04009	40,940	7	Graham	4,622.7	38,072	1,224	8.2	52.2	2.0	12.9	1.2	33.1	7.2	19.8	10.5	14.7	12.9	10.6
04011		7	Greenlee	1,842.0	9,483	2,464	5.1	44.7	2.2	3.6	1.2	47.3	8.0	19.3	8.8	14.8	13.4	11.2
04012		6	La Paz	4,499.6	21,098	1,770	4.7	58.5	1.4	12.9	1.2	28.1	4.7	12.0	5.7	9.3	8.0	8.4
04013	38,060	1	Maricopa	9,199.3	4,410,824	4	479.5	56.9	6.4	2.2	5.6	31.3	6.3	17.5	9.3	14.6	13.0	12.5
04015	29,420	3	Mohave	13,311.1	209,550	320	15.7	78.6	1.5	2.9	2.0	16.8	4.4	12.7	6.2	10.2	9.0	10.9
04017	43,320	4	Navajo	9,949.9	110,445	549	11.1	43.1	1.4	44.7	1.1	11.5	6.9	19.7	8.3	12.1	10.7	10.9
04019	46,060	2	Pima	9,187.2	1,039,073	44	113.1	53.2	4.2	3.0	4.2	37.6	5.6	15.2	11.8	12.8	11.4	11.0
04021	38,060	1	Pinal	5,365.8	447,138	157	83.3	58.3	5.4	5.2	2.8	30.4	5.6	16.9	7.9	13.1	13.0	11.2
04023	35,700	4	Santa Cruz	1,236.9	46,511	1,041	37.6	15.2	0.5	0.5	0.7	83.4	6.9	19.8	9.5	11.2	10.9	11.3
04025	39,140	3	Yavapai	8,123.5	231,993	288	28.6	81.9	1.1	2.3	1.8	14.7	4.2	12.1	6.5	9.1	8.8	10.6
04027	49,740	3	Yuma	5,514.0	212,128	315	38.5	31.4	2.3	1.3	1.9	64.3	7.2	18.0	11.2	13.9	11.0	10.1
05000		0	ARKANSAS	52,034.6	3,013,825	X	57.9	74.0	16.2	1.6	2.4	7.7	6.3	17.0	9.3	13.2	12.2	12.2
05001		6	Arkansas	988.8	17,769	1,936	18.0	71.1	25.5	0.8	1.1	3.3	6.6	16.3	7.5	11.5	11.7	12.4
05003		7	Ashley	925.4	20,046	1,824	21.7	69.4	25.1	0.8	0.4	5.5	6.1	16.7	7.5	11.2	11.1	13.1
05005	34,260	7	Baxter	554.2	41,619	1,140	75.1	95.8	0.6	1.7	0.8	2.5	4.6	13.1	5.8	9.4	9.2	11.2
05007	22,220	2	Benton	847.6	272,608	252	321.6	75.2	2.3	2.7	5.3	16.9	7.0	19.3	8.1	14.7	14.3	12.5
05009	25,460	7	Boone	590.0	37,480	1,239	63.5	95.4	0.7	2.1	1.1	2.6	6.4	16.6	7.3	11.7	11.4	12.5
05011		7	Bradley	649.2	10,897	2,359	16.8	56.4	27.9	0.8	0.5	15.7	6.1	17.9	7.0	12.1	12.0	12.5
05013	15,780	9	Calhoun	628.6	5,277	2,810	8.4	73.9	22.2	1.0	0.8	4.1	4.5	14.4	7.8	11.8	10.6	13.5
05015		6	Carroll	630.0	28,223	1,492	44.8	80.9	1.0	2.2	2.5	15.2	5.9	15.6	7.5	10.6	10.5	11.9
05017		6	Chicot	644.3	10,438	2,395	16.2	39.9	54.0	0.7	0.8	5.8	5.7	16.6	8.3	11.1	10.6	12.0
05019	11,660	7	Clark	866.1	22,061	1,719	25.5	69.8	25.0	1.0	0.9	4.9	5.3	13.7	21.5	11.1	9.6	10.5
05021		7	Clay	639.5	14,847	2,107	23.2	96.4	1.3	1.2	0.4	2.1	6.2	15.5	7.5	11.4	11.1	12.9
05023		6	Cleburne	553.7	24,965	1,606	45.1	96.1	0.7	1.6	0.7	2.4	4.4	14.6	6.2	9.7	10.6	12.1

1. CBSA = Core Based Statistical Area. See Appendix A for explanation. See Appendix B for list of metropolitan areas with component counties. 2. County type code from the Economic Research Service of USDA Rural-Urban Continuum Codes. See Appendix A for definition. 3. Dry land or land partially or temporarily covered by water. 4. May be of any race.

Table B. States and Counties — **Population and Households**

STATE County	Population, 2018 (cont.) Age (percent) (cont.) 55 to 64 years	65 to 74 years	75 years and over	Percent female	Population change, 2000-2018 Total persons 2000	2010	Percent change 2000-2010	2010-2018	Components of change, 2010-2018 Births	Deaths	Net Migration	Households, 2013-2017 Number	Persons per household	Percent Family house-holds	Female family house-holder[1]	One person
	16	17	18	19	20	21	22	23	24	25	26	27	28	29	30	31
ALABAMA—Cont'd																
Washington	14.7	11.3	7.8	50.8	18,097	17,581	-2.9	-6.8	1,383	1,650	-945	6,001	2.77	72.0	14.4	25.4
Wilcox	13.7	11.5	7.9	52.4	13,183	11,667	-11.5	-8.9	1,112	1,217	-952	3,841	2.77	61.1	21.6	35.7
Winston	14.9	12.4	9.1	50.7	24,843	24,488	-1.4	-3.4	2,003	2,571	-242	9,439	2.50	66.8	11.0	29.9
ALASKA	12.8	7.9	3.9	47.9	626,932	710,249	13.3	3.8	92,762	34,995	-31,287	252,536	2.81	66.6	10.7	25.5
Aleutians East	14.0	6.4	2.8	32.5	2,697	3,141	16.5	11.9	131	69	307	812	2.53	63.7	14.8	25.4
Aleutians West	16.2	5.7	1.2	34.5	5,465	5,561	1.8	2.9	265	113	-2	1,218	3.57	58.0	7.7	30.8
Anchorage	12.1	7.3	3.8	49.1	260,283	291,829	12.1	-0.1	37,867	13,462	-24,916	106,012	2.74	66.7	11.7	24.6
Bethel	10.2	5.2	2.5	48.5	16,006	17,013	6.3	7.1	3,605	964	-1,449	4,524	3.81	75.3	19.5	18.1
Bristol Bay	18.8	9.5	5.0	46.6	1,258	997	-20.7	-12.0	84	65	-140	358	2.39	65.1	9.8	26.5
Denali	15.7	8.9	3.0	44.3	1,893	1,822	-3.8	13.0	181	54	107	678	2.31	55.0	5.5	37.9
Dillingham	12.5	6.3	3.1	49.6	4,922	4,847	-1.5	3.2	848	311	-387	1,405	3.32	71.5	20.4	23.9
Fairbanks North Star	11.0	7.2	3.1	46.1	82,840	97,585	17.8	1.4	13,888	3,957	-8,736	36,396	2.63	64.1	7.9	26.8
Haines	19.6	15.8	6.3	50.6	2,392	2,508	4.8	-1.4	155	146	-42	1,087	2.27	55.2	6.5	29.3
Hoonah-Angoon	18.3	15.0	7.4	47.3	NA	2,109	NA	2.0	167	132	4	802	2.48	67.5	11.7	26.8
Juneau	14.5	9.3	4.1	49.2	30,711	31,275	1.8	2.7	3,110	1,522	-761	12,273	2.59	64.2	9.3	26.8
Kenai Peninsula	15.9	11.8	5.6	47.9	49,691	55,400	11.5	5.7	5,914	3,547	772	21,779	2.58	63.9	7.6	29.5
Ketchikan Gateway	15.2	10.1	5.5	49.0	14,070	13,519	-3.9	3.0	1,410	760	-256	5,270	2.55	64.7	10.6	27.3
Kodiak Island	13.6	6.9	3.5	46.8	13,913	13,606	-2.2	-1.9	1,828	480	-1,638	4,538	2.96	70.0	11.9	24.7
Kusilvak	8.6	4.1	1.8	47.3	7,028	7,459	6.1	11.3	1,936	552	-544	1,752	4.52	83.1	27.3	13.2
Lake and Peninsula	13.5	7.1	3.2	48.8	1,823	1,635	-10.3	-2.9	274	121	-206	408	2.96	68.4	19.1	25.0
Matanuska-Susitna	13.3	8.1	3.8	48.1	59,322	88,992	50.0	20.9	11,730	4,602	11,350	30,613	3.24	70.4	7.9	23.4
Nome	10.4	5.4	2.3	47.4	9,196	9,492	3.2	5.4	1,841	664	-670	2,897	3.25	75.9	20.2	19.7
North Slope	13.8	4.9	1.9	37.8	7,385	9,430	27.7	4.7	1,384	419	-528	2,041	3.28	78.0	22.9	17.7
Northwest Arctic	9.9	4.3	3.0	46.0	7,208	7,523	4.4	2.0	1,491	424	-927	1,849	4.01	76.5	22.6	17.4
Petersburg	16.0	12.9	6.1	47.2	NA	3,207	NA	0.4	292	177	-101	1,255	2.53	64.6	12.5	30.6
Prince of Wales-Hyder	16.3	12.4	4.7	45.2	NA	6,170	NA	4.1	648	354	-43	2,315	2.75	64.9	11.7	29.2
Sitka	14.6	9.7	6.0	49.1	8,835	8,881	0.5	-2.6	785	496	-529	3,545	2.40	59.6	10.9	33.4
Skagway	13.2	9.4	5.1	48.0	NA	968	NA	18.6	90	46	131	423	2.13	47.8	6.1	35.0
Southeast Fairbanks	14.0	9.8	4.7	44.9	6,174	7,029	13.8	-1.6	895	379	-640	2,139	3.04	66.0	9.3	29.8
Valdez-Cordova	17.3	10.0	3.7	47.6	10,195	9,636	-5.5	-4.9	1,005	470	-1,027	2,849	3.22	64.0	5.3	30.0
Wrangell	19.9	14.3	7.6	48.2	NA	2,365	NA	5.8	195	204	151	1,084	2.24	64.5	9.1	26.4
Yakutat	14.1	12.4	7.1	44.5	808	662	-18.1	-8.8	62	22	-102	255	2.40	57.3	11.8	37.6
Yukon-Koyukuk	13.8	10.2	5.0	47.0	6,551	5,588	-14.7	-4.7	681	483	-465	1,959	2.66	62.8	17.3	31.4
ARIZONA	12.1	10.1	7.4	50.3	5,130,632	6,392,288	24.6	12.2	703,872	434,572	508,013	2,482,311	2.68	65.4	12.4	27.4
Apache	12.9	9.0	6.3	50.8	69,423	71,517	3.0	0.4	8,244	4,999	-2,962	19,530	3.59	68.6	21.4	27.8
Cochise	13.2	12.7	9.6	49.2	117,755	131,357	11.6	-3.5	13,150	10,460	-7,484	49,160	2.36	66.4	11.8	28.8
Coconino	11.5	8.0	4.5	50.6	116,320	134,431	15.6	6.3	13,703	6,476	1,169	47,588	2.65	61.9	13.1	25.0
Gila	15.8	16.6	12.1	50.6	51,335	53,594	4.4	0.6	4,994	6,200	1,538	21,585	2.42	65.9	12.8	28.7
Graham	10.4	7.9	6.0	46.7	33,489	37,219	11.1	2.3	4,659	2,303	-1,527	10,976	3.04	69.9	12.7	26.4
Greenlee	11.2	7.4	5.7	48.6	8,547	8,437	-1.3	12.4	1,105	475	390	3,364	2.76	72.2	13.9	23.9
La Paz	12.5	18.3	21.0	48.7	19,715	20,489	3.9	3.0	1,673	2,057	1,007	8,798	2.30	64.4	10.1	30.4
Maricopa	11.6	8.8	6.4	50.5	3,072,149	3,817,359	24.3	15.5	447,550	234,806	379,528	1,489,533	2.75	65.5	12.3	26.9
Mohave	16.3	17.2	13.1	49.4	155,032	200,182	29.1	4.7	15,133	23,119	17,225	83,902	2.39	63.3	10.3	29.1
Navajo	13.2	11.0	7.2	49.9	97,470	107,488	10.3	2.8	13,087	7,937	-2,170	34,251	3.07	71.2	19.0	24.3
Pima	12.5	11.2	8.5	50.8	843,746	980,263	16.2	6.0	96,599	75,418	38,490	398,530	2.45	61.5	12.9	30.5
Pinal	11.9	12.3	8.1	47.9	179,727	375,768	109.1	19.0	37,834	22,784	55,586	133,513	2.85	69.6	11.3	25.6
Santa Cruz	12.3	10.6	7.5	51.7	38,381	47,420	23.6	-1.9	5,386	2,393	-3,971	15,568	2.95	75.7	17.2	20.5
Yavapai	17.2	18.8	12.8	51.2	167,517	211,014	26.0	9.9	15,284	23,317	28,757	94,343	2.29	63.4	8.3	29.8
Yuma	9.8	9.2	9.5	48.5	160,026	195,750	22.3	8.4	25,471	11,828	2,437	71,670	2.77	74.9	12.9	20.4
ARKANSAS	12.8	9.8	7.2	50.9	2,673,400	2,916,028	9.1	3.4	314,960	251,951	34,163	1,147,291	2.52	66.3	13.1	28.5
Arkansas	14.3	11.3	8.3	51.6	20,749	19,007	-8.4	-6.5	2,036	1,943	-1,336	7,692	2.35	62.8	14.2	31.7
Ashley	13.8	11.8	8.6	51.3	24,209	21,845	-9.8	-8.2	2,122	2,098	-1,834	8,182	2.52	68.0	12.7	28.4
Baxter	15.7	16.2	14.7	51.7	38,386	41,513	8.1	0.3	2,888	5,577	2,808	18,398	2.21	65.5	8.2	29.7
Benton	10.8	7.8	5.6	50.3	153,406	221,351	44.3	23.2	28,683	14,020	36,225	90,906	2.74	73.6	10.1	21.2
Boone	13.6	11.6	9.1	50.8	33,948	36,910	8.7	1.5	3,807	3,635	423	14,887	2.47	68.4	9.1	27.8
Bradley	13.5	10.4	8.6	51.3	12,600	11,505	-8.7	-5.3	1,107	1,215	-502	4,566	2.36	64.1	15.0	32.2
Calhoun	15.9	12.6	8.9	49.6	5,744	5,368	-6.5	-1.7	390	475	-7	2,061	2.45	72.2	11.4	26.9
Carroll	14.8	14.2	9.0	50.2	25,357	27,448	8.2	2.8	2,628	2,499	657	10,832	2.54	65.0	8.4	30.5
Chicot	15.4	10.8	9.5	49.5	14,117	11,800	-16.4	-11.5	1,136	1,273	-1,232	4,323	2.38	64.5	19.9	33.4
Clark	11.6	9.3	7.4	52.6	23,546	22,993	-2.3	-4.1	1,968	2,088	-812	8,820	2.23	62.5	13.2	31.5
Clay	13.9	11.7	9.7	51.1	17,609	16,083	-8.7	-7.7	1,432	1,952	-714	6,428	2.34	62.6	11.9	33.2
Cleburne	15.6	14.3	12.5	50.8	24,046	25,981	8.0	-3.9	1,957	3,059	110	10,646	2.35	66.8	10.2	29.5

1. No spouse present.

Table B. States and Counties — Population, Vital Statistics, Health, and Crime

STATE County	Persons in group quarters, 2018	Daytime Population, 2013-2017 Number	Employment/ residence ratio	Births, 2018 Total	Rate[1]	Deaths, 2018 Number	Rate[1]	Persons under 65 with no health insurance, 2016 Number	Percent	Medicare, 2018 Total beneficiaries	Enrolled in Original Medicare	Enrolled in Medicare Advantage	Serious crimes known to police[2], 2016 Total Number	Rate[3]
	32	33	34	35	36	37	38	39	40	41	42	43	44	45
ALABAMA—Cont'd														
Washington	147	15,796	0.83	160	9.8	186	11.4	1,783	13.1	4,088	2,902	1,186	244	1,469
Wilcox	108	10,898	0.99	135	12.7	139	13.1	919	10.5	3,184	2,494	690	257	2,350
Winston	301	23,047	0.89	242	10.2	340	14.4	2,403	12.9	6,013	4,260	1,753	296	1,248
ALASKA	26,772	746,092	1.02	10,693	14.5	4,738	6.4	100,787	15.5	96,128	94,613	1,515	30,842	4,157
Aleutians East	1,729	3,454	1.05	19	5.4	11	3.1	1,019	33.5	163	D	D	NA	NA
Aleutians West	2,528	6,607	1.21	31	5.4	11	1.9	1,134	22.3	221	D	D	NA	NA
Anchorage	7,605	307,417	1.06	4,252	14.6	1,789	6.1	33,891	12.9	36,552	35,919	633	18,071	6,042
Bethel	294	18,126	1.03	435	23.9	137	7.5	3,931	23.9	1,437	D	D	NA	NA
Bristol Bay	16	1,051	1.26	6	6.8	9	10.3	178	22.9	141	D	D	NA	NA
Denali	106	2,811	1.33	28	13.6	1	0.5	255	14.5	250	D	D	NA	NA
Dillingham	52	5,042	1.03	103	20.6	43	8.6	943	20.9	493	D	D	NA	NA
Fairbanks North Star	4,816	99,181	0.98	1,580	16.0	505	5.1	11,887	13.6	11,598	11,497	101	NA	NA
Haines	0	2,491	0.97	16	6.5	10	4.0	413	20.5	582	D	D	NA	NA
Hoonah-Angoon	0	2,131	0.98	18	8.4	31	14.4	430	25.3	350	D	D	NA	NA
Juneau	973	32,870	1.02	331	10.3	169	5.3	3,658	13.1	4,868	4,823	45	1,877	5,694
Kenai Peninsula	1,654	57,040	0.96	702	12.0	523	8.9	8,646	17.9	11,338	11,025	313	NA	NA
Ketchikan Gateway	252	13,941	1.03	160	11.5	94	6.8	1,937	16.6	2,451	2,427	24	NA	NA
Kodiak Island	386	14,185	1.06	207	15.5	57	4.3	2,639	21.7	1,587	1,568	19	NA	NA
Kusilvak	9	8,293	1.08	249	30.0	106	12.8	1,683	22.2	535	D	D	NA	NA
Lake and Peninsula	37	1,468	1.30	38	23.9	19	12.0	397	28.0	181	181	0	NA	NA
Matanuska-Susitna	2,082	88,125	0.69	1,495	13.9	608	5.7	14,355	15.7	13,878	13,611	267	NA	NA
Nome	174	9,963	1.03	210	21.0	111	11.1	1,938	21.5	850	D	D	NA	NA
North Slope	2,652	17,754	2.51	156	15.8	69	7.0	1,774	19.6	513	D	D	NA	NA
Northwest Arctic	396	8,119	1.16	166	21.6	79	10.3	1,694	24.0	567	567	0	NA	NA
Petersburg	44	3,293	1.01	22	6.8	42	13.0	575	21.4	783	771	12	NA	NA
Prince of Wales-Hyder	50	6,411	0.98	74	11.5	37	5.8	1,346	24.3	967	D	D	NA	NA
Sitka	256	8,830	1.00	88	10.2	39	4.5	1,471	19.7	1,397	1,384	13	NA	NA
Skagway	32	1,048	1.01	11	9.6	23	20.0	142	14.7	298	D	D	NA	NA
Southeast Fairbanks	374	7,205	1.11	92	13.3	43	6.2	1,271	21.4	1,228	1,207	21	NA	NA
Valdez-Cordova	187	10,457	1.21	113	12.3	50	5.5	1,408	17.0	1,413	1,395	18	NA	NA
Wrangell	19	2,482	1.01	22	8.8	55	22.0	372	19.0	501	D	D	NA	NA
Yakutat	18	722	1.11	4	6.6	0	0.0	119	23.2	120	120	0	NA	NA
Yukon-Koyukuk	31	5,575	1.06	65	12.2	67	12.6	1,281	27.6	863	D	D	NA	NA
ARIZONA	159,442	6,780,803	0.99	83,550	11.7	58,806	8.2	669,819	11.9	1,270,464	774,266	496,198	239,015	3,448
Apache	931	70,200	0.92	972	13.5	702	9.8	12,002	19.5	12,386	11,406	980	334	467
Cochise	5,699	126,323	1.00	1,395	11.0	1,294	10.2	9,801	10.5	31,351	21,793	9,558	2,939	2,609
Coconino	12,364	137,884	0.99	1,567	11.0	879	6.2	15,639	13.8	19,462	17,022	2,440	4,716	3,361
Gila	935	54,106	1.05	567	10.5	795	14.8	5,448	14.4	16,295	13,972	2,323	682	1,802
Graham	2,710	36,516	0.90	527	13.8	300	7.9	3,025	10.2	5,621	3,627	1,994	557	2,766
Greenlee	34	11,247	1.51	147	15.5	50	5.3	703	8.4	1,250	1,060	190	105	1,071
La Paz	388	21,413	1.15	208	9.9	306	14.5	2,420	19.6	5,425	4,252	1,173	557	2,766
Maricopa	65,225	4,198,031	1.02	53,688	12.2	32,044	7.3	418,740	11.7	673,120	390,629	282,491	144,667	3,405
Mohave	4,635	193,903	0.84	1,754	8.4	3,230	15.4	17,171	12.1	64,238	43,880	20,358	6,743	3,351
Navajo	2,010	108,379	1.01	1,484	13.4	1,070	9.7	12,345	13.9	23,082	18,587	4,495	2,339	2,153
Pima	25,279	1,006,153	1.00	11,251	10.8	9,977	9.6	88,068	11.0	219,585	116,876	102,709	48,215	4,737
Pinal	25,313	352,205	0.63	4,539	10.2	3,207	7.2	35,200	11.3	76,167	43,777	32,390	7,086	1,727
Santa Cruz	437	45,933	0.98	640	13.8	320	6.9	5,598	14.9	9,487	4,449	5,038	768	1,656
Yavapai	4,199	216,705	0.95	1,830	7.9	3,011	13.0	19,797	12.8	78,478	56,162	22,316	4,926	2,189
Yuma	9,283	201,805	0.97	2,981	14.1	1,621	7.6	23,862	15.1	34,508	26,766	7,742	4,418	2,143
ARKANSAS	84,227	2,977,354	1.00	37,191	12.3	31,093	10.3	228,342	9.4	627,298	475,876	151,422	114,134	3,819
Arkansas	247	20,195	1.24	236	13.3	226	12.7	1,300	8.9	4,271	3,642	629	783	4,278
Ashley	191	20,549	0.97	239	11.9	256	12.8	1,321	8.1	5,124	4,455	669	573	2,778
Baxter	595	42,189	1.07	345	8.3	698	16.8	2,408	8.5	15,088	10,636	4,452	1,378	3,367
Benton	2,146	259,475	1.06	3,685	13.5	1,790	6.6	22,490	10.0	41,589	27,374	14,215	5,738	2,313
Boone	465	37,726	1.03	479	12.8	452	12.1	2,501	8.5	10,046	7,532	2,514	1,089	2,923
Bradley	226	10,716	0.93	122	11.2	130	11.9	1,010	11.6	2,543	2,176	367	207	1,880
Calhoun	175	4,981	0.90	49	9.3	44	8.3	335	8.6	1,208	956	252	80	1,537
Carroll	230	27,590	0.98	327	11.6	302	10.7	2,967	14.0	7,269	4,892	2,377	546	1,970
Chicot	764	11,193	1.05	121	11.6	155	14.8	757	9.5	2,645	2,103	542	324	2,980
Clark	2,758	21,782	0.93	224	10.2	241	10.9	1,371	8.5	4,596	3,546	1,050	725	3,215
Clay	125	13,572	0.74	183	12.3	196	13.2	1,030	9.0	4,097	3,428	669	204	1,368
Cleburne	339	24,293	0.89	219	8.8	385	15.4	1,774	9.6	7,912	6,543	1,369	730	2,881

1. Per 1,000 estimated resident population.   2. Data for serious crimes have not been adjusted for underreporting; this may affect comparability between geographic areas and over time.   3. Per 100,000 population estimated by the FBI.

Table B. States and Counties — Crime, Education, Money Income, and Poverty

STATE County	Serious crimes known to police[2], 2016 (cont.)[1] Rate Violent	Property	Education School enrollment and attainment, 2013-2017 Enrollment[3] Total	Percent private	High school graduate or less	Bachelor's degree or more	Local government expenditures,[5] 2014-2015 Total current spending (mil dol)	Current spending per student (dollars)	Money income, 2013-2017 Per capita income[6]	Median income (dollars)	Households Percent with income of less than $50,000	with income of $200,000 or more	Income and poverty, 2017 Median household income (dollars)	Percent below poverty level All persons	Children under 18 years	Children 5 to 17 years in families
	46	47	48	49	50	51	52	53	54	55	56	57	58	59	60	61
ALABAMA—Cont'd																
Washington	289	1,180	3,971	9.2	62.4	10.7	26.8	8,877	23,239	42,185	60.3	1.2	44,249	20.2	28.2	27.2
Wilcox	640	1,710	2,703	16.9	64.1	12.0	18.7	10,293	15,774	27,012	73.4	1.4	25,700	32	47.0	46.4
Winston	101	1,147	4,743	4.0	58.9	12.9	42.3	10,032	20,580	35,362	63.6	1.1	38,562	21.3	30.1	27.1
ALASKA	804	3,353	189,481	12.0	35.2	29.0	2,648.7	20,197	35,065	76,114	31.4	7.2	74,058	11	14.5	13.3
Aleutians East	NA	NA	451	1.8	55.9	11.5	10.1	40,862	31,254	66,607	36.8	5.3	69,375	14.6	11.5	10.9
Aleutians West	NA	NA	1,022	7.2	50.8	16.2	13.1	26,640	35,998	85,192	23.3	9.8	80,290	8.1	7.6	7.0
Anchorage	1,144	4,898	77,720	12.4	30.4	34.6	828.4	17,117	38,977	82,271	27.3	9.3	78,579	9.6	12.2	11.4
Bethel	NA	NA	5,422	0.6	64.5	12.6	170.4	33,273	18,654	53,853	46.8	2.4	45,582	28.7	35.5	34.4
Bristol Bay	NA	NA	214	10.7	42.3	20.3	21.8	46,607	42,002	79,500	29.1	5.3	70,094	10.9	19.1	20.4
Denali	NA	NA	371	12.9	29.8	44.5	10.7	12,235	33,084	83,295	28.9	3.5	73,220	8	9.0	8.6
Dillingham	NA	NA	1,333	3.0	52.3	17.4	36.3	33,896	24,647	58,708	43.6	3.5	52,641	20.8	31.4	30.0
Fairbanks North Star	NA	NA	27,757	14.3	27.1	33.1	297.7	19,439	35,328	76,250	31.0	6.2	74,241	7.4	9.0	8.5
Haines	NA	NA	425	4.5	31.8	34.7	6.4	23,458	35,907	70,640	39.5	9.7	53,413	11.4	19.6	17.1
Hoonah-Angoon	NA	NA	334	16.2	47.0	21.9	10.8	35,629	33,704	57,900	41.4	2.1	50,573	17.6	32.2	29.0
Juneau	855	4,838	7,960	8.1	24.5	40.3	92.8	19,309	41,904	90,749	22.3	8.8	90,436	8.3	10.7	8.8
Kenai Peninsula	NA	NA	12,766	14.6	38.6	24.1	182.0	20,177	33,336	65,279	37.4	4.8	63,559	10.2	13.9	12.4
Ketchikan Gateway	NA	NA	3,047	11.5	38.4	24.1	46.8	20,145	33,771	67,321	36.2	6.2	71,298	9.9	12.8	11.7
Kodiak Island	NA	NA	3,515	13.8	40.4	24.1	55.9	22,587	32,625	74,167	30.5	5.3	71,118	7.5	10.0	9.4
Kusilvak	NA	NA	2,642	1.1	74.1	4.9	NA	NA	11,693	36,468	65.9	0.6	31,250	37.5	45.3	44.3
Lake and Peninsula	NA	NA	345	0.9	57.4	16.0	NA	NA	23,434	45,208	54.9	2.7	47,644	15.7	22.3	23.0
Matanuska-Susitna	NA	NA	26,854	15.8	40.1	20.6	305.8	16,965	30,409	74,887	33.6	5.8	72,296	11.3	12.7	10.9
Nome	NA	NA	2,877	1.4	58.6	14.0	87.8	34,538	20,952	53,821	46.6	4.1	53,877	23.2	28.8	26.5
North Slope	NA	NA	2,164	3.1	51.6	15.3	82.3	40,833	48,777	77,266	33.4	9.3	82,736	12.2	16.5	15.0
Northwest Arctic	NA	NA	2,219	2.3	65.7	10.8	76.2	35,863	21,879	61,533	41.9	5.5	53,060	26	33.1	30.7
Petersburg	NA	NA	678	12.2	40.4	26.5	10.7	24,721	35,044	63,490	38.4	4.1	59,176	7.4	9.7	9.1
Prince of Wales-Hyder	NA	NA	1,401	9.6	47.8	16.8	39.1	26,711	26,695	52,114	47.5	2.0	46,488	18.5	24.0	19.5
Sitka	NA	NA	2,019	8.3	33.0	32.9	39.7	22,562	36,617	70,765	31.0	4.9	69,501	8.1	10.0	8.2
Skagway	NA	NA	158	7.0	31.0	32.2	3.1	30,600	39,376	70,673	29.3	2.8	66,991	4.3	8.6	9.3
Southeast Fairbanks	NA	NA	1,644	20.3	41.6	19.5	28.1	23,568	31,051	63,866	37.6	3.1	59,382	12.8	18.0	17.2
Valdez-Cordova	NA	NA	2,137	11.6	32.1	32.7	34.5	24,950	37,935	86,019	26.6	8.7	86,196	9.2	11.9	11.3
Wrangell	NA	NA	477	5.7	47.7	19.4	6.8	24,726	29,943	56,094	43.0	1.8	55,696	12.4	18.8	16.5
Yakutat	NA	NA	131	13.7	48.8	19.6	3.0	29,859	32,393	64,583	38.0	2.0	59,955	15.3	30.7	33.8
Yukon-Koyukuk	NA	NA	1,398	4.6	57.0	12.4	66.0	11,056	21,057	37,819	60.4	1.3	37,907	23.2	29.3	26.0
ARIZONA	470	2,978	1,751,835	11.1	37.7	28.4	8,244.5	7,477	27,964	53,510	46.7	4.7	56,508	14.9	21.0	19.7
Apache	87	380	20,626	3.9	54.4	11.5	135.2	12,357	13,865	32,360	65.8	0.5	33,053	33.1	43.3	42.0
Cochise	348	2,261	29,774	10.6	35.9	23.6	157.7	8,117	24,896	47,847	52.1	2.9	48,966	16.1	25.0	23.5
Coconino	367	2,994	48,585	6.8	31.7	35.4	171.8	9,069	25,722	53,523	47.5	4.5	54,399	18.4	21.5	21.5
Gila	773	3,151	10,147	10.9	42.5	19.0	71.1	9,149	22,433	41,179	59.7	1.8	38,897	24.1	39.0	33.1
Graham	103	1,699	10,103	7.0	45.5	14.1	57.5	8,435	17,874	48,173	51.6	0.7	46,378	20.9	26.4	25.7
Greenlee	20	1,050	2,371	8.4	47.4	12.1	15.4	8,509	24,935	56,298	46.0	1.5	63,557	10.1	11.7	10.9
La Paz	273	2,493	3,368	5.3	59.8	11.2	23.8	9,889	21,707	36,479	63.6	0.6	36,389	20.9	32.5	33.4
Maricopa	432	2,973	1,093,894	11.6	35.7	31.4	5,264.2	7,291	30,186	58,580	42.7	5.9	62,221	13.5	19.1	18.0
Mohave	239	3,112	36,874	15.9	50.9	12.3	171.2	7,119	23,527	41,567	58.9	1.7	42,210	17.3	28.7	25.1
Navajo	248	1,906	28,636	6.0	47.4	15.5	172.9	9,673	17,685	38,798	59.8	1.5	40,883	26.4	36.9	31.9
Pima	495	4,242	262,652	10.4	34.3	31.6	1,090.0	7,581	27,323	48,676	51.1	3.8	51,392	16.6	22.5	20.7
Pinal	214	1,513	95,128	12.1	44.7	18.6	394.3	7,185	22,944	52,628	47.6	2.3	53,114	13	17.0	15.1
Santa Cruz	147	1,509	12,810	8.2	51.0	22.1	75.0	7,458	19,482	39,630	60.7	2.2	39,265	23.6	35.2	35.1
Yavapai	288	1,901	43,585	16.6	35.7	25.0	186.2	7,720	27,504	48,259	51.7	2.6	49,860	13.9	20.7	19.6
Yuma	290	1,853	53,282	5.9	54.3	14.3	254.9	6,851	20,600	43,253	56.4	1.9	46,013	19	26.1	27.5
ARKANSAS	551	3,269	741,993	11.2	48.7	22.0	4,737.1	9,650	24,426	43,813	55.5	2.9	45,916	16.3	22.5	21.2
Arkansas	486	3,791	3,861	10.3	56.4	14.1	26.6	8,914	23,766	38,532	63.4	2.6	43,752	19.9	26.3	24.5
Ashley	315	2,463	5,037	5.1	58.5	13.4	35.1	8,857	20,703	36,407	62.7	1.5	40,495	19.8	28.5	26.9
Baxter	225	3,142	7,374	7.3	47.8	18.4	46.1	8,903	24,737	40,072	62.2	1.5	43,011	13.9	21.0	19.7
Benton	312	2,001	63,285	12.6	42.2	31.7	388.5	9,213	30,611	61,271	40.6	6.3	64,728	9.1	11.6	10.9
Boone	690	2,233	8,169	8.2	47.2	16.2	54.5	8,742	22,288	40,727	61.0	2.4	41,770	14.9	21.6	19.5
Bradley	309	1,572	2,579	5.5	60.8	14.4	22.0	10,533	21,575	36,310	62.2	1.7	35,950	20.9	29.1	27.0
Calhoun	250	1,287	1,064	9.4	63.5	12.3	5.9	10,709	22,866	37,225	61.8	0.7	42,484	15.2	21.4	19.9
Carroll	361	1,609	5,785	13.0	50.2	19.3	37.7	9,484	21,754	39,686	60.3	2.2	38,297	16.4	25.8	24.1
Chicot	340	2,640	2,710	13.3	60.6	13.2	17.8	11,355	20,560	32,412	67.3	2.2	31,810	30.1	42.2	38.9
Clark	399	2,816	7,474	15.1	43.6	26.4	37.8	13,794	20,382	37,144	60.4	1.4	40,536	21.4	25.9	23.1
Clay	221	1,146	3,159	7.5	62.8	10.7	21.3	8,305	19,171	32,219	69.4	0.6	35,164	18.1	25.4	23.9
Cleburne	462	2,419	4,531	9.7	54.8	15.9	33.2	9,771	26,189	42,312	56.9	2.6	43,170	15.6	23.9	21.7

1. Data for serious crimes have not been adjusted for underreporting; this may affect comparability between geographic areas and over time.　2. Per 100,000 population estimated by the FBI.　3. All persons 3 years old and over enrolled in nursery school through college.　4. Persons 25 years old and over.　5. Elementary and secondary education expenditures.　6. Based on population estimated by the American Community Survey, 2013–2017.

Table B. States and Counties — Personal Income and Earnings

STATE County	Personal income, 2017										Earnings, 2017		
			Per capita[1]		Wages and salaries (mil dol)	Supplements to wages and salaries, employer contributions (mil dol)		Proprietors' income (mil dol)	Dividends, interest, and rent (mil dol)	Personal transfer receipts (mil dol)		Contributions for government social insurance (mil dol)	
	Total (mil dol)	Percent change 2016-2017	Dollars	Rank		Pension and insurance	Government social insurance				Total (mil dol)	From employee and self-employed	From employer
	62	63	64	65	66	67	68	69	70	71	72	73	74
ALABAMA—Cont'd													
Washington	587	3.0	35,512	2,274	234	50	16	28	70	170	328	23	16
Wilcox	336	2.2	31,328	2,828	134	27	9	23	55	144	192	15	9
Winston	810	5.3	34,145	2,468	292	55	22	88	130	261	457	33	22
ALASKA	42,301	2.0	57,180	X	20,346	5,280	1,511	3,644	7,839	6,958	30,781	1,582	1,511
Aleutians East	199	2.8	59,084	182	142	30	10	15	15	12	197	11	10
Aleutians West	305	-3.2	53,010	343	220	48	16	18	29	22	302	16	16
Anchorage	18,701	1.5	63,532	122	9,850	2,266	756	1,911	3,660	2,801	14,783	780	756
Bethel	775	2.9	42,863	1,157	323	128	21	21	80	246	493	21	21
Bristol Bay	110	1.3	126,725	4	66	17	5	13	15	9	100	5	5
Denali	162	4.2	78,138	41	115	24	9	9	23	39	157	9	9
Dillingham	293	5.9	59,340	173	127	39	10	32	52	52	208	10	10
Fairbanks North Star	5,434	2.2	54,497	298	2,636	749	213	246	1,054	865	3,843	185	213
Haines	151	5.7	59,951	159	41	11	3	24	39	29	79	5	3
Hoonah-Angoon	118	2.8	55,045	277	32	13	2	9	26	29	56	3	2
Juneau	2,130	2.2	66,367	90	1,024	347	66	184	442	249	1,621	72	66
Kenai Peninsula	2,919	1.9	49,800	472	1,042	309	72	239	640	601	1,662	90	72
Ketchikan Gateway	901	2.7	65,034	102	393	116	28	128	162	155	666	33	28
Kodiak Island	819	3.1	60,891	146	363	105	29	120	155	117	616	30	29
Kusilvak	253	1.5	30,872	2,860	73	44	4	5	25	116	126	5	4
Lake and Peninsula	97	10.5	59,760	160	43	17	3	5	20	19	67	3	3
Matanuska-Susitna	4,773	3.1	44,803	928	1,099	310	81	380	696	760	1,870	104	81
Nome	496	3.2	49,983	466	209	74	14	22	60	150	319	14	14
North Slope	847	-2.8	86,588	25	1,310	242	84	10	101	64	1,646	89	84
Northwest Arctic	354	3.7	46,033	790	208	56	15	11	33	123	290	14	15
Petersburg	209	0.9	63,637	117	61	22	4	39	53	43	126	6	4
Prince of Wales-Hyder	267	4.4	41,420	1,346	99	39	6	22	53	63	166	8	6
Sitka	571	5.2	65,745	96	218	66	16	84	133	79	384	19	16
Skagway	89	6.6	76,710	47	39	10	3	15	18	10	68	3	3
Southeast Fairbanks	329	2.4	47,802	641	176	45	12	22	55	78	255	14	12
Valdez-Cordova	553	4.0	59,622	165	304	86	21	43	114	81	454	23	21
Wrangell	112	-0.3	44,286	987	36	14	2	8	24	30	60	3	2
Yakutat	32	-3.1	52,812	347	11	5	1	3	7	7	19	1	1
Yukon-Koyukuk	302	2.4	56,357	238	87	48	5	6	55	110	146	6	5
ARIZONA	296,649	5.6	42,085	X	147,391	21,926	10,560	22,138	57,465	58,882	202,016	12,746	10,560
Apache	2,352	5.0	32,845	2,640	820	208	63	51	347	997	1,142	75	63
Cochise	4,902	3.7	39,294	1,673	1,883	428	154	291	982	1,564	2,757	177	154
Coconino	6,513	5.0	46,266	770	2,872	591	213	494	1,481	1,160	4,170	246	213
Gila	2,047	5.8	38,257	1,835	647	130	47	79	439	834	903	72	47
Graham	1,139	2.5	30,391	2,898	387	85	29	55	154	413	555	35	29
Greenlee	347	6.4	36,664	2,096	310	52	20	17	34	91	399	23	20
La Paz	646	6.1	31,335	2,827	226	45	18	46	125	246	335	24	18
Maricopa	196,286	5.7	45,573	841	109,634	14,864	7,714	14,872	37,363	31,663	147,084	9,052	7,714
Mohave	6,395	3.7	30,865	2,861	1,987	330	149	365	1,132	2,277	2,831	248	149
Navajo	3,401	4.3	31,213	2,837	1,219	243	99	170	559	1,378	1,731	126	99
Pima	42,585	5.4	41,637	1,313	18,459	3,262	1,352	2,933	9,507	10,033	26,006	1,697	1,352
Pinal	12,610	6.6	29,309	2,965	2,733	533	203	662	1,720	3,555	4,131	319	203
Santa Cruz	1,682	4.5	36,392	2,136	641	134	51	239	321	414	1,065	70	51
Yavapai	8,533	4.9	37,398	1,971	2,636	444	194	634	2,255	2,626	3,908	322	194
Yuma	7,212	5.5	34,752	2,379	2,937	578	255	1,229	1,047	1,631	4,998	261	255
ARKANSAS	123,313	3.8	41,063	X	55,941	8,526	4,175	7,301	27,787	29,062	75,943	5,057	4,175
Arkansas	779	-1.1	43,376	1,094	424	67	34	103	103	193	628	38	34
Ashley	680	0.9	33,543	2,550	312	47	25	24	84	249	408	30	25
Baxter	1,460	3.8	35,293	2,298	576	97	45	72	278	554	790	66	45
Benton	21,712	5.1	81,533	33	7,610	852	519	266	11,818	1,743	9,247	604	519
Boone	1,283	3.8	34,333	2,439	579	97	43	80	211	403	799	58	43
Bradley	417	5.1	38,378	1,812	141	24	11	45	48	145	221	15	11
Calhoun	173	3.9	32,907	2,627	153	22	11	4	20	51	191	12	11
Carroll	922	7.4	32,990	2,618	361	62	29	87	168	268	539	37	29
Chicot	371	-1.2	34,860	2,367	116	20	10	22	53	149	167	12	10
Clark	774	3.4	34,713	2,386	355	66	27	37	113	237	484	32	27
Clay	501	5.2	33,559	2,546	115	21	10	50	71	181	195	15	10
Cleburne	911	3.3	36,358	2,141	240	44	19	54	182	296	357	31	19

1. Based on the resident population estimated as of July 1 of the year shown.

Table B. States and Counties — Earnings, Social Security, and Housing

	Earnings, 2017 (cont.)									Social Security beneficiaries, December 2017		Supplemental Security Income recipients, 2017	Housing units, 2018	
	Percent by selected industries													
STATE County	Farm	Mining, quarrying, and extractions	Construction	Manufacturing	Information; professional, scientific, technical services	Retail trade	Finance, insurance, real estate, and leasing	Health care and social assistance	Government	Number	Rate[1]		Total	Percent change, 2010-2018
	75	76	77	78	79	80	81	82	83	84	85	86	87	88

ALABAMA—Cont'd														
Washington	3	D	4.1	40.4	D	2.5	D	D	13.7	4,790	290	694	8,573	2
Wilcox	5.2	0	3.4	37.9	D	4.7	2.6	D	19.9	3,795	354	1,386	5,780	2.3
Winston	3.8	D	5	39	D	5.9	3.1	7.5	13	6,790	286	990	13,747	2
ALASKA	0	7.3	6.7	3.1	7.1	5.4	4.3	12.3	31.6	98,359	133	12,564	318,336	3.7
Aleutians East	0	0	D	75.7	D	0.8	D	D	10.6	165	49	14	752	0.7
Aleutians West	-0.1	D	3.3	39.9	D	4.9	D	2.5	15.6	235	41	11	1,963	1.8
Anchorage	0	4.6	6.3	0.9	10.3	5.6	5.9	14.7	27.2	36,920	125	5,978	118,236	4.6
Bethel	0	D	D	D	D	4.8	5	D	45.5	1,790	99	404	6,038	2
Bristol Bay	0	0	D	41.9	D	D	D	D	21.6	135	156	11	976	0.8
Denali	0	D	D	0.4	D	1.2	D	0.6	23.2	260	125	14	1,764	-0.3
Dillingham	0	D	1.8	D	D	3.4	D	25.4	27	550	112	114	2,453	1.1
Fairbanks North Star	0.1	3	7.9	1.1	4.2	5.5	3.1	10.6	48.7	11,215	112	1,124	44,300	6
Haines	0	D	11.1	9.5	4.3	8.1	D	9.5	19.8	600	238	41	1,678	2.9
Hoonah-Angoon	0	0	D	3.1	D	4.9	D	D	50.6	475	221	38	1,770	1.3
Juneau	-0.1	7.4	5.9	1.6	5.2	5.2	3.7	7.6	47.3	4,525	141	469	13,791	5.6
Kenai Peninsula	0	7.4	6.8	5.4	4.3	6.3	3.4	13.7	30.4	11,780	201	1,007	31,341	2.5
Ketchikan Gateway	0	D	6.8	5.5	2.5	8.5	4.5	10.7	32.1	2,400	173	250	6,414	3.7
Kodiak Island	0	0.4	5.5	14.5	1.9	3.3	2.8	9.5	33.6	1,685	125	143	5,455	2.9
Kusilvak	0	0	D	D	0.2	6.6	D	D	67.2	805	98	201	2,238	2.5
Lake and Peninsula	0	0	3.5	D	D	2.5	D	D	39.2	195	120	17	1,512	0.4
Matanuska-Susitna	0.3	0.6	18.2	1.4	6.4	9	4.4	14.9	26	14,520	136	1,658	41,990	1.6
Nome	0	D	2.7	D	1.4	4.3	3.4	19.8	44.4	1,120	113	216	4,102	2.3
North Slope	0	59.2	2.8	0	D	0.7	D	D	13.4	660	67	32	2,630	5.2
Northwest Arctic	0	D	D	0.1	D	D	D	D	30.1	755	98	96	2,746	1.4
Petersburg	0	D	5.6	9.7	2.2	6.5	2.2	D	38.2	745	227	43	1,701	3.5
Prince of Wales-Hyder	0	D	2.5	5.2	D	7.6	3.2	5.4	50.3	1,035	161	102	3,447	2.7
Sitka	0	0.3	7.4	8.8	2.5	7.1	2.6	12.3	33.8	1,375	158	82	4,237	3.3
Skagway	0	0	6.1	4.6	D	13.9	D	0.7	25.5	125	108	0	697	9.6
Southeast Fairbanks	0	D	4.8	1	4.9	4.9	0.9	D	32.5	1,275	185	141	3,905	-0.3
Valdez-Cordova	0	D	6.8	9.2	3.9	4	D	5.2	29.2	1,465	158	124	6,196	1.5
Wrangell	0	0.1	3.4	8.8	D	7.5	1.8	10.9	45.6	510	202	24	1,454	2.4
Yakutat	0	0	D	0.6	D	5.9	0.5	D	57.2	115	190	0	459	2
Yukon-Koyukuk	0	1.9	2.2	D	D	3.9	D	7.8	68	925	172	200	4,091	1.3
ARIZONA	0.9	0.7	6.1	7.5	10.2	7.1	10.7	12.6	16	1,310,666	187	119,571	3,035,669	6.7
Apache	0.3	1.2	2.1	0.7	2.1	2.9	2	12.7	60.1	13,090	183	4,160	32,934	1.3
Cochise	3.5	0.2	3.6	1.2	8.5	6.2	3.4	9	47.5	32,540	261	3,122	61,328	3.9
Coconino	0.2	D	4	10.1	4.9	6.8	4.1	15.1	31.1	20,370	145	2,493	66,840	5.6
Gila	-0.1	9.8	6.6	11.7	D	7.4	2.1	9	34.5	17,335	324	1,423	33,731	3.2
Graham	7.1	D	3	2	2	9.3	D	10.8	34.8	6,310	168	784	13,567	4.5
Greenlee	1.1	D	2	0.1	D	1.6	D	D	8.1	1,470	155	119	4,470	2.2
La Paz	7.2	0.9	1.8	2.4	4.7	12.3	D	D	38.9	5,715	277	477	16,291	1.5
Maricopa	0.3	0.4	6.6	7.5	11.2	7	12.9	12.4	11.7	689,850	160	61,104	1,762,834	7.5
Mohave	0.2	D	6.9	6.5	5.6	12.8	5	19.1	17.5	67,710	327	4,702	115,269	3.9
Navajo	0.8	2.7	5	1	7.7	9	2.4	14.1	34.2	24,275	223	4,579	58,154	2.1
Pima	0.3	0.7	5	10	10	6.6	6.4	14.3	24.3	221,130	216	20,644	462,749	5
Pinal	5.8	2.3	5	6	4	8.1	3.2	7.4	34	84,425	196	6,231	177,159	11.3
Santa Cruz	0.5	D	2.4	2.5	2.5	8.7	1.9	4.4	33.9	9,850	213	1,415	18,384	2.1
Yavapai	0.3	2.4	8.2	6.1	7.1	9.7	5.3	15.5	19.2	79,400	348	3,689	118,394	7.2
Yuma	17.3	D	3.4	3.6	5	8.2	3.3	9.9	27.1	37,195	179	4,629	93,565	6.5
ARKANSAS	1.7	0.7	6	12.5	6.4	6.8	5.3	13	17.3	692,178	230	107,548	1,380,504	4.9
Arkansas	7.3	0.6	3.2	33.7	3.8	6.9	3.6	D	9.5	4,620	257	730	9,460	0.3
Ashley	1.2	0	9.4	34.2	D	5.4	2.7	D	12.5	5,805	286	906	10,171	0.4
Baxter	-0.2	D	5.3	16.6	4.8	9.2	7.6	27.2	11	16,000	387	1,026	22,981	1.8
Benton	1.1	0.6	5.3	7	8.9	4.8	-0.7	6.1	6.7	44,670	168	3,524	108,486	16.5
Boone	0.8	0	D	12.2	3.9	8.5	3.7	9.1	21.9	11,135	298	1,178	17,022	1.1
Bradley	6.7	D	5.7	21.1	1.8	4.3	3.5	15.9	17.5	2,855	263	515	5,789	-1.2
Calhoun	0.4	D	2.9	74.5	D	D	D	1.7	7	1,360	259	166	2,917	0.7
Carroll	8.5	D	6.4	28.2	2.7	6.1	4.5	9.1	11.4	8,040	288	593	13,774	1.6
Chicot	10.2	0.1	8.3	1.4	D	6.2	7.4	16.4	27.7	2,965	279	906	5,432	0.2
Clark	1	D	1.8	20.7	3.6	9.1	3.9	D	24.5	5,020	225	779	10,542	1.5
Clay	14	0	6.3	2.7	D	6.9	3.3	10.8	21.7	4,650	312	648	8,010	-0.3
Cleburne	1.9	4.3	8.5	17.1	3.6	8.8	5.6	D	14.3	8,545	341	741	16,100	1.7

1. Per 1,000 resident population estimated as of July 1 of the year shown.

Table B. States and Counties — Housing, Labor Force, and Employment

STATE County	Housing units, 2013-2017								Civilian labor force, 2018				Civilian employment[6], 2013-2017		
	Occupied units										Unemployment			Percent	
			Owner-occupied			Renter-occupied									
				Median owner cost as a percent of income			Median rent as a percent of income[2]	Sub-standard units[4] (percent)		Percent change, 2017-2018				Management, business, science, and arts	Construction, production, and maintenance occupations
	Total	Percent	Median value[1]	With a mort-gage	Without a mort-gage[2]	Median rent[3]			Total		Total	Rate[5]	Total		
	89	90	91	92	93	94	95	96	97	98	99	100	101	102	103
ALABAMA—Cont'd															
Washington	6,001	82.4	83,900	19.0	11.0	657	24	3.5	6,667	-0.4	389	5.8	5,710	20.6	41.8
Wilcox	3,841	62.2	81,600	21.7	16.1	494	26.7	0.4	2,734	-2.4	262	9.6	2,901	24.4	35.7
Winston	9,439	77.3	82,900	21.7	12.7	528	26.6	1.3	9,781	0.9	410	4.2	8,902	23.3	39.5
ALASKA	252,536	63.7	261,900	22.0	10.3	1,200	28.1	9.6	356,886	-1.1	23,511	6.6	354,045	36.7	23.2
Aleutians East	812	59.4	124,700	17.8	10.0	989	19.9	4.2	2,321	-8.6	69	3	2,405	16.3	60.5
Aleutians West	1,218	30.1	238,800	20.7	13.5	1,277	16.9	11.7	3,615	-3.3	128	3.5	3,961	17.4	50.6
Anchorage	106,012	60.1	304,500	22.1	11.0	1,261	28.6	4.8	151,950	-1.2	8,348	5.5	152,751	40.0	18.3
Bethel	4,524	63.2	152,600	19.5	11.6	1,253	22	53.8	7,400	0.6	945	12.8	6,075	36.2	20.2
Bristol Bay	358	57.3	186,700	19.2	10.3	1,051	18.7	6.1	441	4.8	28	6.3	508	30.5	29.9
Denali	678	78.6	224,200	20.2	10.0	871	13.7	16.7	1,088	-5.3	85	7.8	1,529	23.1	20.9
Dillingham	1,405	62.0	189,500	20.5	11.8	1,039	24.1	31.7	2,027	-1.2	166	8.2	1,989	42.8	20.7
Fairbanks North Star	36,396	59.0	230,600	22.6	10.3	1,272	30.2	11.1	46,101	-0.7	2,675	5.8	46,725	37.6	23.5
Haines	1,087	70.7	243,100	27.2	10.0	1,016	18.8	11.6	1,092	0.9	104	9.5	1,437	36.6	23.7
Hoonah-Angoon	802	73.6	226,800	22.6	10.0	850	22.8	11.2	1,158	1.4	146	12.6	1,039	32.5	28.7
Juneau	12,273	65.5	343,100	22.1	10.0	1,181	25	4.6	17,232	-0.3	762	4.4	17,970	46.3	18.4
Kenai Peninsula	21,779	71.2	234,600	22.0	10.0	994	25.7	7.6	26,497	-1.3	2,044	7.7	25,564	32.9	27.2
Ketchikan Gateway	5,270	61.9	265,700	21.7	11.2	1,139	31.6	5.4	7,026		422	6	6,899	29.7	25.6
Kodiak Island	4,538	59.0	267,700	23.6	11.3	1,294	29.8	9.9	6,210	-1.7	362	5.8	7,010	27.7	36.9
Kusilvak	1,752	74.0	88,600	17.5	14.5	625	17	64.7	2,708	-1.9	539	19.9	2,125	30.7	24.0
Lake and Peninsula	408	68.1	118,500	22.2	11.0	746	15.5	26	739	2.9	86	11.6	581	37.5	31.2
Matanuska-Susitna	30,613	76.5	235,600	22.1	10.0	1,098	29.8	8.5	47,654	-1.4	3,640	7.6	42,695	32.1	28.6
Nome	2,897	60.6	143,000	19.0	12.7	1,343	27	43.1	4,113	0.1	477	11.6	3,639	34.3	19.8
North Slope	2,041	51.9	153,900	13.1	10.0	1,029	17.5	38.1	3,413	-5.2	240	7	5,412	31.9	35.3
Northwest Arctic	1,849	57.1	145,800	18.7	14.2	1,229	19.4	45.6	2,924	-1.4	416	14.2	2,654	35.9	23.6
Petersburg	1,255	68.2	205,000	19.9	10.0	885	25.2	4	1,404	-0.9	122	8.7	1,644	22.9	42.2
Prince of Wales-Hyder	2,315	73.0	169,100	19.6	10.0	840	24.4	10.9	2,899	1.7	315	10.9	2,780	29.2	34.6
Sitka	3,545	56.6	350,900	24.6	10.0	1,104	27.6	3.9	4,408	-0.8	183	4.2	4,702	39.5	22.6
Skagway	423	52.0	293,800	23.0	10.1	1,069	20.8	5.9	2,940	0.7	82	9.8	701	29.7	23.8
Southeast Fairbanks	2,139	71.7	191,700	19.6	10.0	1,088	25	13.6	2,940	0	282	9.6	2,941	31.3	31.8
Valdez-Cordova	2,849	73.4	252,200	19.4	10.0	974	19.4	7.1	4,849	-0.6	361	7.4	4,755	27.0	34.0
Wrangell	1,084	66.6	194,000	23.1	10.4	793	27.3	5.5	1,051	0.1	74	7	1,095	34.0	26.4
Yakutat	255	60.4	185,000	22.7	11.6	1,030	25.6	7.1	245	4.7	20	8.2	377	24.9	32.9
Yukon-Koyukuk	1,959	70.4	80,600	18.3	11.6	653	24.6	47.1	2,545	2.7	389	15.3	2,082	33.7	25.7
ARIZONA	2,482,311	63.1	193,200	21.7	10.0	972	29.5	5	3,439,755	3.4	166,205	4.8	2,953,891	35.7	18.8
Apache	19,530	77.6	72,800	19.7	10.0	487	18	25	20,665	1.3	2,080	10.1	18,197	29.7	24.3
Cochise	49,160	68.9	144,400	20.0	10.0	805	28.6	3.3	49,774	0.7	2,789	5.6	43,404	34.4	17.3
Coconino	47,588	59.3	241,400	22.0	10.0	1,079	32.4	9.6	77,083	2	4,233	5.5	65,283	36.5	18.3
Gila	21,585	72.9	153,600	23.1	11.5	767	27.1	5.8	21,518	0.8	1,267	5.9	18,216	31.6	24.2
Graham	10,976	68.0	123,500	19.9	10.0	793	25.8	6.9	14,878	3.4	764	5.1	12,412	28.3	26.9
Greenlee	3,364	47.1	87,500	17.2	10.0	429	10	4.8	4,280	7.2	182	4.3	3,675	24.0	45.6
La Paz	8,798	74.3	77,400	21.0	10.0	570	26.5	6.2	8,938	2.7	557	6.2	6,474	26.4	28.3
Maricopa	1,489,533	61.0	225,000	21.3	10.0	1,033	29.3	4.7	2,229,526	3.9	92,307	4.1	1,929,015	37.4	17.9
Mohave	83,902	68.3	138,700	23.8	10.0	786	28.6	4.7	85,442	3.5	4,934	5.8	69,774	24.3	23.6
Navajo	34,251	68.9	115,100	20.9	10.0	690	27.8	13.5	40,598	-0.4	3,151	7.8	33,186	29.3	23.2
Pima	398,530	61.9	166,300	21.8	10.5	861	31.6	4.2	486,261	2	21,828	4.5	433,478	36.4	17.1
Pinal	133,513	72.6	157,200	21.7	10.5	1,014	29.3	4.1	178,216	3.7	8,952	5	144,930	29.4	22.3
Santa Cruz	15,568	67.2	138,400	23.4	11.4	627	30.6	6.4	19,325	1.2	1,803	9.3	17,421	25.6	23.9
Yavapai	94,343	70.7	215,000	25.5	10.9	919	30.3	2.7	105,618	3.5	4,719	4.5	83,535	31.9	20.9
Yuma	71,670	67.5	117,000	23.0	10.0	830	28.2	6.9	97,636	2	16,639	17	74,891	24.9	29.4
ARKANSAS	1,147,291	65.6	118,500	19.3	10.0	709	28.4	3.1	1,351,496	0.3	50,037	3.7	1,276,536	33.0	26.6
Arkansas	7,692	62.7	80,300	20.3	10.2	660	28.4	0.9	9,070	1.1	308	3.4	7,920	27.7	33.2
Ashley	8,182	74.0	68,200	18.3	10.2	608	34.2	2.2	7,683	0.7	420	5.5	7,905	27.5	36.8
Baxter	18,398	75.4	124,400	22.2	10.5	667	27.4	2.4	16,463	0.6	678	4.1	15,926	30.1	28.1
Benton	90,906	66.3	163,000	18.4	10.0	845	23	3.2	134,404	1.4	3,872	2.9	119,813	37.6	23.1
Boone	14,887	72.1	116,600	20.0	10.0	631	27.1	3	15,856	0.3	561	3.5	15,773	29.8	25.9
Bradley	4,566	61.9	74,300	17.8	10.3	567	29.2	3.9	4,362	1.5	196	4.5	4,112	25.9	43.7
Calhoun	2,061	83.2	71,000	18.0	10.0	611	44.5	1.3	2,404	0.3	94	3.9	2,215	24.5	46.0
Carroll	10,832	77.5	121,100	23.3	10.0	592	25.7	6.6	12,639	-2.8	406	3.2	11,400	27.5	33.9
Chicot	4,323	66.3	63,000	24.4	13.4	564	31.6	2.9	3,340	-3.7	230	6.9	3,659	30.1	26.1
Clark	8,820	62.0	95,000	17.4	10.1	594	29.3	2.4	9,580	2.1	366	3.8	10,291	33.6	22.1
Clay	6,428	70.2	70,000	20.4	12.0	557	30.6	3.3	5,835	-0.8	256	4.4	6,234	22.3	35.4
Cleburne	10,646	75.0	127,000	20.2	10.5	676	28.9	1.9	9,174	-1.2	416	4.5	10,142	27.7	33.0

1. Specified owner-occupied units lacking complete plumbing facilities.   2. A value of 10.0 represents 10 percent or less; a value of 50.0 represents 50 percent or more.   3. Specified renter-occupied units.   4. Overcrowded or
5. Percent of civilian labor force.   6. Civilian employed persons 16 years old and over.

Table B. States and Counties — Nonfarm Employment and Agriculture

	Private nonfarm establishments, employment and payroll, 2016									Agriculture, 2017			
		Employment						Annual payroll		Farms			Farm producers whose primary occupation is farming (percent)
STATE County	Number of establish-ments	Total	Health care and social assistance	Manufac-turing	Retail trade	Finance and insurance	Professional, scientific, and technical services	Total (mil dol)	Average per employee (dollars)	Number	Fewer than 50 acres	1000 acres or more	
	104	105	106	107	108	109	110	111	112	113	114	115	116
ALABAMA—Cont'd													
Washington	210	4,979	283	3,417	264	55	32	377	75,753	435	36.6	5.3	34.1
Wilcox	180	1,918	268	D	233	86	19	88	45,973	318	25.8	19.8	39.1
Winston	448	6,393	731	2,765	884	174	90	195	30,454	484	40.3	1.0	37.1
ALASKA	21,077	266,072	49,799	12,701	35,101	7,602	19,498	15,239	57,275	990	67.0	4.3	41.9
Aleutians East	55	2,265	D	D	57	D	NA	92	40,677	(1)46	(1)65.2	(1)28.3	(1)31.2
Aleutians West	115	3,720	103	2,600	154	D	11	154	41,447	(1)	(1)	(1)	(1)
Anchorage	8,798	147,302	25,839	1,845	16,111	5,015	15,488	8,950	60,759	(2) 350	(2)64.3	(2) 0.9	(2)44.4
Bethel	261	3,189	1,129	48	768	32	18	142	44,457	(1)	(1)	(1)	(1)
Bristol Bay	77	392	D	98	44	D	D	48	123,000	(1)	(1)	(1)	(1)
Denali	104	459	13	NA	32	D	4	48	105,303	(3)	(3)	(3)	(3)
Dillingham	89	1,182	670	42	187	10	D	69	58,485	(1)	(1)	(1)	(1)
Fairbanks North Star	2,466	27,962	6,101	616	5,205	760	1,201	1,430	51,124	(3) 274	(3)49.6	(3) 8.0	(3)45.0
Haines	141	589	127	33	113	D	12	28	47,195	(4)	(4)	(4)	(4)
Hoonah-Angoon	74	212	30	D	59	NA	D	11	50,396	(4)	(4)	(4)	(4)
Juneau	1,151	11,456	2,335	297	1,904	329	562	571	49,830	(4)60	(4)96.7	(4) 0.0	(4)41.1
Kenai Peninsula	2,104	15,364	3,880	748	2,736	280	571	790	51,408	260	82.7	1.9	37.9
Ketchikan Gateway	602	5,102	821	294	803	210	117	287	56,230	(4)	(4)	(4)	(4)
Kodiak Island	482	5,634	717	2,622	453	72	58	201	35,737	(1)	(1)	(1)	(1)
Kusilvak	76	674	D	D	308	D	NA	18	26,932	(1)	(1)	(1)	(1)
Lake and Peninsula	58	240	NA	63	24	D	NA	15	63,154	(1)	(1)	(1)	(1)
Matanuska-Susitna	2,204	18,400	4,078	286	3,632	500	790	927	50,383	(2)	(2)	(2)	(2)
Nome	174	2,080	949	D	357	50	7	105	50,509	(1)	(1)	(1)	(1)
North Slope	157	4,698	326	D	236	D	41	415	88,233	(1)	(1)	(1)	(1)
Northwest Arctic	81	1,917	D	NA	146	D	D	157	81,696	(1)	(1)	(1)	(1)
Petersburg	172	994	177	195	227	22	13	46	45,997	(4)	(4)	(4)	(4)
Prince of Wales-Hyder	148	982	184	153	233	28	D	39	39,732	(4)	(4)	(4)	(4)
Sitka	375	2,920	796	413	415	60	52	141	48,337	(4)	(4)	(4)	(4)
Skagway	117	375	9	1	94	D	NA	30	79,288	(4)	(4)	(4)	(4)
Southeast Fairbanks	167	1,215	110	16	202	15	45	85	69,640	(3)	(3)	(3)	(3)
Valdez-Cordova	496	2,806	447	162	311	D	94	196	69,708	(2)	(2)	(2)	(2)
Wrangell	91	594	D	D	129	D	14	22	37,439	(4)	(4)	(4)	(4)
Yakutat	28	143	17	D	39	NA	NA	6	40,084	(4)	(4)	(4)	(4)
Yukon-Koyukuk	96	338	32	NA	121	NA	D	14	42,849	(3)	(3)	(3)	(3)
ARIZONA	139,134	2,379,409	359,183	144,208	320,561	147,682	148,267	106,431	44,730	19,086	69.1	11.0	53.3
Apache	442	6,722	2,692	84	1,268	74	102	252	37,461	5,551	72.3	10.5	55.1
Cochise	2,150	25,795	4,892	391	5,343	469	3,563	928	35,983	1,083	39.6	17.7	47.4
Coconino	3,650	51,713	8,356	5,590	8,259	905	1,713	2,002	38,720	2,142	77.8	11.6	55.7
Gila	994	11,611	2,421	159	2,112	163	268	481	41,443	298	67.1	5.0	43.8
Graham	476	6,814	1,712	212	1,629	112	502	246	36,120	448	64.3	10.0	34.8
Greenlee	86	3,848	122	NA	176	17	19	237	61,471	123	52.0	8.1	55.4
La Paz	341	4,077	611	198	944	65	44	116	28,504	97	28.9	26.8	54.5
Maricopa	91,270	1,623,299	233,035	100,313	207,576	122,111	114,799	78,086	48,103	1,874	81.7	4.7	44.0
Mohave	3,697	41,954	8,666	2,965	9,654	1,002	947	1,362	32,464	317	60.6	17.4	40.7
Navajo	1,734	19,173	4,355	372	4,191	355	387	687	35,823	4,205	67.0	11.8	61.4
Pima	20,180	316,661	61,442	22,850	48,632	12,820	17,161	12,446	39,305	661	79.7	7.9	42.9
Pinal	3,488	48,859	8,582	4,079	8,931	963	969	1,695	34,692	762	56.2	15.9	55.9
Santa Cruz	1,163	11,420	1,240	363	2,420	205	265	383	33,519	219	47.9	16.4	49.6
Yavapai	5,825	60,153	13,238	3,508	10,771	1,234	1,768	2,052	34,110	850	73.2	8.5	46.2
Yuma	2,963	42,536	7,324	3,124	8,262	1,014	1,250	1,379	32,412	456	60.7	13.2	50.4
ARKANSAS	65,611	1,023,854	170,777	153,952	147,616	36,831	37,811	40,969	40,015	42,625	30.3	7.2	41.7
Arkansas	510	8,786	964	3,790	1,115	248	72	339	38,541	488	16.2	32.2	43.6
Ashley	383	5,844	952	1,854	748	153	75	250	42,735	353	43.3	11.6	35.8
Baxter	1,033	13,145	3,812	2,275	2,275	555	533	452	34,402	479	35.5	3.8	36.9
Benton	6,063	115,639	9,403	11,315	13,112	2,875	7,645	6,779	58,619	1,936	48.2	1.4	38.7
Boone	878	12,035	2,277	1,711	2,115	345	224	428	35,575	1,313	33.0	4.3	41.9
Bradley	254	2,848	521	739	293	113	29	80	27,925	181	36.5	1.7	32.3
Calhoun	59	421	D	D	59	14	D	16	38,941	101	25.7	4.0	35.1
Carroll	695	9,000	816	3,016	1,206	195	D	309	34,329	1,169	25.7	4.0	41.1
Chicot	207	2,029	653	9	355	92	33	65	32,019	291	19.9	36.1	51.3
Clark	499	6,919	1,129	1,310	1,251	217	176	216	31,260	377	27.6	5.8	32.1
Clay	288	2,473	715	113	505	91	43	72	29,061	542	27.1	15.7	42.9
Cleburne	563	5,649	865	1,326	1,084	184	155	164	29,045	676	27.1	1.8	41.6

1. Aleutians West, Bethel, Bristol Bay, Dillingham, Kodiak Island, Kusilvak, Lake and Peninsula, Nome, North Slope, and Northwest Arctic are included with Aleutians East.   2. Matanuska-Susitna and Valdez-Cordova are included with Anchorage   3. Denali, Southeast Fairbanks, and Yukon-Koyukuk are included with Fairbanks North Star   4. Haines, Hoonah-Angoon, Ketchican Gateway, Petersburg, Prince of Wales-Hyder, Sitka, Skagway, Wrangell, and Yakutat are included with Juneau

Table B. States and Counties — **Agriculture**

STATE County	Acreage (1,000) [117]	Percent change, 2012-2017 [118]	Average size of farm [119]	Total irrigated (1,000) [120]	Total cropland (1,000) [121]	Value of land and buildings — Average per farm [122]	Average per acre [123]	Value of machinery and equipment, average per farm (dollars) [124]	Total (mil dol) [125]	Average per farm (acres) [126]	Crops [127]	Livestock and poultry products [128]	Organic farms (number) [129]	Farms with internet access (percent) [130]	Total ($1,000) [131]	Percent of farms [132]
ALABAMA—Cont'd																
Washington	120	25.1	275	0.1	22.3	556,827	2,026	72,905	31.3	71,885	23.1	76.9	NA	65.1	1,739	33.8
Wilcox	165	38.2	520	D	26.9	945,109	1,818	66,889	9.1	28,736	26.7	73.3	NA	64.2	1,920	57.5
Winston	57	-1.4	118	0.6	11.9	326,386	2,765	59,645	27.7	57,295	3.5	96.5	NA	70.5	631	43.2
ALASKA	850	1.9	858	2.4	83.7	616,112	718	91,623	70.5	71,171	42.1	57.9	18	87.9	2,091	22.7
Aleutians East	(1)681	(1)2.0	(1)14,811	(1)0.0	(1)1.1	(1)573,623	(1)39	(1)90,364	(1)3.0	(1)64,774	(1)13.1	(1)86.9	(1)1	(1)89.1	(1)193	(1)28.3
Aleutians West	(1)	(1)	(1)	(1)	(1)	(1)	(1)	(1)	(1)	(1)	(1)	(1)	(1)	(1)	(1)	(1)
Anchorage	(2)34	(2)-5.5	(2)98	(2)1.1	(2)15.6	(2)809,796	(2)8,242	(2)106,917	(2)37.5	(2)107,245	(2)45.6	(2)54.4	(2)4	(2)87.7	(2)262	(2)20.6
Bethel	(1)	(1)	(1)	(1)	(1)	(1)	(1)	(1)	(1)	(1)	(1)	(1)	(1)	(1)	(1)	(1)
Bristol Bay	(3)	(3)	(3)	(3)	(3)	(3)	(3)	(3)	(3)	(3)	(3)	(3)	(3)	(3)	(3)	(3)
Denali	(1)	(1)	(1)	(1)	(1)	(1)	(1)	(1)	(1)	(1)	(1)	(1)	(1)	NA	NA	NA
Dillingham	(1)	(1)	(1)	(1)	(1)	(1)	(1)	(1)	(1)	(1)	(1)	(1)	(1)	(1)	(1)	(1)
Fairbanks North Star	(3)102	(3)2.4	(3)372	(3)1.1	(3)63.2	(3)610,607	(3)1,640	(3)82,638	(3)10.4	(3)37,927	(3)81.6	(3)18.4	(3)5	(3)86.9	(3)1,124	(3)21.9
Haines	(4)	(4)	(4)	(4)	(4)	(4)	(4)	(4)	(4)	(4)	(4)	(4)	(4)	(4)	(4)	(4)
Hoonah-Angoon																
Juneau	(4)1	(4)-0.3	(4)9	(4)0.0	(4)0.0	(4)881,816	(4)100,397	(4)225,293	(4)14.1	(4)235,489	(4)6.5	(4)93.5	(4)1	(4)85.0	(4)11	(4)11.7
Kenai Peninsula	32	8.1	121	0.1	0.2	307,385	2,537	49,878	5.4	20,856	50.0	50.0	6	89.6	502	28.1
Ketchikan Gateway	(4)	(4)	(4)	(4)	(4)	(4)	(4)	(4)	(4)	(4)	(4)	(4)	(4)	(4)	(4)	(4)
Kodiak Island	(1)	(1)	(1)	(1)	(1)	(1)	(1)	(1)	(1)	(1)	(1)	(1)	(1)	(1)	(1)	(1)
Kusilvak	(1)	(1)	(1)	(1)	(1)	(1)	(1)	(1)	(1)	(1)	(1)	(1)	(1)	(1)	(1)	(1)
Lake and Peninsula	(2)	(2)	(2)	(2)	(2)	(2)	(2)	(2)	(2)	(2)	(2)	(2)	(2)	(2)	(2)	(2)
Matanuska-Susitna	(1)	(1)	(1)	(1)	(1)	(1)	(1)	(1)	(1)	(1)	(1)	(1)	(1)	(1)	(1)	(1)
Nome	(1)	(1)	(1)	(1)	(1)	(1)	(1)	(1)	(1)	(1)	(1)	(1)	(1)	(1)	(1)	(1)
North Slope	(1)	(1)	(1)	(1)	(1)	(1)	(1)	(1)	(1)	(1)	(1)	(1)	(1)	(1)	(1)	(1)
Northwest Arctic	(1)	(1)	(1)	(1)	(1)	(1)	(1)	(1)	(1)	(1)	(1)	(1)	(1)	(1)	(1)	(1)
Petersburg	(4)	(4)	(4)	(4)	(4)	(4)	(4)	(4)	(4)	(4)	(4)	(4)	(4)	(4)	(4)	(4)
Prince of Wales-Hyder	(4)	(4)	(4)	(4)	(4)	(4)	(4)	(4)	(4)	(4)	(4)	(4)	(4)	(4)	(4)	(4)
Sitka	(4)	(4)	(4)	(4)	(4)	(4)	(4)	(4)	(4)	(4)	(4)	(4)	(4)	(4)	(4)	(4)
Skagway	(4)	(4)	(4)	(4)	(4)	(4)	(3)	(3)	(3)	(3)	(3)	(3)	(3)	(3)	(3)	(3)
Southeast Fairbanks	(3)	(3)	(3)	(3)	(3)	(4)	(3)	(3)	(3)	(3)	(3)	(3)	(3)	(3)	(3)	(3)
Valdez-Cordova	(2)	(2)	(2)	(2)	(2)	(2)	(2)	(2)	(2)	(2)	(2)	(2)	(2)	(2)	(2)	(2)
Wrangell	(4)	(4)	(4)	(4)	(4)	(4)	(4)	(4)	(4)	(4)	(4)	(4)	(4)	(4)	(4)	(4)
Yakutat	(4)	(4)	(4)	(4)	(4)	(4)	(4)	(4)	(4)	(4)	(4)	(4)	(4)	(4)	(4)	(4)
Yukon-Koyukuk	(3)	(3)	(3)	(3)	(3)	(3)	(3)	(3)	(3)	(3)	(3)	(3)	(3)	(3)	(3)	(3)
ARIZONA	26,126	-0.5	1,369	910.9	1,286.6	1,110,303	811	77,604	3,852.0	201,824	54.4	45.6	84	57.4	22,331	3.9
Apache	5,555	-0.8	1,001	11.9	30.4	275,085	275	30,785	18.0	3,243	20.1	79.9	4	43.6	278	0.6
Cochise	973	6.2	899	86.0	152.9	1,802,553	2,005	99,038	144.7	133,648	56.9	43.1	4	78.9	3,119	10.6
Coconino	6,139	5.6	2,866	1.3	6.9	607,821	212	34,544	23.9	11,162	4.1	95.9	2	43.9	807	0.8
Gila	1,214	2.1	4,074	1.3	2.3	1,583,528	389	51,499	7.3	24,362	7.7	92.3	NA	75.5	143	1.7
Graham	1,290	3.1	2,880	46.7	52.4	1,866,459	648	107,676	62.1	138,558	88.2	11.8	9	73.0	1,083	12.7
Greenlee	66	25.9	536	5.1	5.0	835,412	1,559	76,520	8.7	70,650	24.9	75.1	NA	84.6	87	5.7
La Paz	250	D	2,574	97.1	102.6	5,190,405	2,016	484,196	D	D	D	D	1	71.1	1,280	34.0
Maricopa	474	-0.3	253	180.2	257.2	2,338,321	9,236	171,562	1,209.1	645,215	39.3	60.7	18	85.0	5,310	9.4
Mohave	745	-40.1	2,351	20.9	30.7	1,972,873	839	96,071	32.3	101,871	71.1	28.9	NA	87.4	390	2.8
Navajo	4,413	2.1	1,049	6.7	66.0	231,932	221	26,006	49.9	11,871	8.6	91.4	NA	40.4	340	0.3
Pima	2,618	D	3,960	30.0	40.7	2,088,810	527	79,142	75.5	114,174	84.3	15.7	3	72.0	1,234	5.4
Pinal	1,121	-4.6	1,471	232.2	294.1	4,065,306	2,764	282,808	861.9	1,131,154	35.7	64.3	4	85.4	3,943	20.9
Santa Cruz	198	-8.0	903	2.6	3.2	1,800,767	1,994	62,799	19.6	89,639	48.8	51.2	1	88.1	413	5.0
Yavapai	822	-0.3	967	7.5	8.0	1,596,867	1,651	63,905	35.7	42,036	40.1	59.9	4	86.4	115	1.5
Yuma	247	15.2	542	181.4	234.3	5,006,516	9,235	468,849	D	D	D	D	34	84.4	3,789	14.9
ARKANSAS	13,889	0.6	326	4,855.1	7,825.9	1,030,741	3,163	126,667	9,651.2	226,420	37.6	62.4	81	73.6	321,742	19.5
Arkansas	414	3.0	849	314.3	359.0	2,675,627	3,151	312,157	214.3	439,098	99.6	0.4	NA	68.6	22,110	85.9
Ashley	132	18.3	374	88.9	103.9	1,081,824	2,894	201,843	70.2	198,856	90.4	9.6	NA	64.9	5,447	32.9
Baxter	101	10.4	212	0.0	13.3	569,724	2,690	58,020	31.8	66,309	2.7	97.3	NA	80.6	259	9.6
Benton	244	-20.0	126	0.2	72.9	815,643	6,478	77,246	593.4	306,494	1.3	98.7	8	74.5	456	3.0
Boone	306	19.0	233	0.3	42.3	614,116	2,636	69,650	164.0	124,918	1.9	98.1	NA	76.6	1,492	7.6
Bradley	30	50.4	164	0.5	6.2	539,607	3,287	82,166	42.1	232,503	15.8	84.2	NA	74.0	21	7.2
Calhoun	19	35.1	186	D	3.1	480,703	2,591	61,897	5.5	54,683	6.3	93.7	NA	74.3	48	16.8
Carroll	290	13.3	248	0.0	54.6	683,129	2,750	83,790	363.6	311,050	0.9	99.1	9	76.5	878	8.2
Chicot	307	6.2	1,057	221.3	273.3	3,139,169	2,971	320,397	148.3	509,519	96.6	3.4	NA	72.5	11,746	76.6
Clark	103	14.1	273	2.3	29.6	661,236	2,421	94,828	17.5	46,414	32.4	67.6	NA	70.3	1,237	15.4
Clay	286	-13.6	529	208.8	258.2	2,278,119	4,310	271,792	197.6	364,603	83.2	16.8	NA	70.3	12,965	59.8
Cleburne	129	-17.8	192	0.2	29.2	562,588	2,938	64,986	57.6	85,138	2.6	97.4	NA	73.7	292	8.9

1. Aleutians West, Bethel, Bristol Bay, Dillingham, Kodiak Island, Kusilvak, Lake and Peninsula, Nome, North Slope, and Northwest Arctic are included with Aleutians East.   2. Matanuska-Susitna and Valdez-Cordova are included with Anchorage.   3. Denali, Southeast Fairbanks, and Yukon-Koyukuk are included with Fairbanks North Star.   4. Haines, Hoonah-Angoon, Ketchican Gateway, Petersburg, Prince of Wales-Hyder, Sitka, Skagway, Wrangell, and Yakutat are included with Juneau.

Water Use, Wholesale Trade, Retail Trade, and Real Estate

STATE County	Water use, 2015		Wholesale Trade[1], 2012				Retail Trade[2], 2012				Real estate and rental and leasing,[2] 2012			
	Public supply water withdrawn (mil gal/day)	Public supply gallons withdrawn per person per day	Number of establishments	Number of employees	Sales (mil dol)	Average payroll (mil dol)	Number of establishments	Number of employees	Sales (mil dol)	Average payroll (mil dol)	Number of establishments	Number of employees	Sales (mil dol)	Average payroll (mil dol)
	133	134	135	136	137	138	139	140	141	142	143	144	145	146
ALABAMA—Cont'd														
Washington	2.81	167.2	3	D	D	D	34	232	75.7	5.5	1	D	D	D
Wilcox	2.80	253.2	7	D	D	D	47	269	72.8	5.5	3	D	D	D
Winston	0.81	33.9	22	171	207.7	6.8	98	754	165.0	16.3	8	22	3.5	0.6
ALASKA	99.18	134.3	638	7,734	5,216.3	440.9	2,508	33,721	10,474.3	977.4	872	4,212	1,022.7	187.6
Aleutians East	1.22	365.2	1	D	D	D	8	D	D	D	3	7	1.3	0.2
Aleutians West	2.27	398.1	13	111	145.9	7.8	11	148	53.4	4.7	4	34	11.9	1.9
Anchorage	44.49	148.9	336	5,228	3,147.7	296.6	860	15,253	4,966.8	462.2	383	2,403	631.3	112.1
Bethel	0.30	16.7	5	28	6.9	0.6	54	855	162.8	15.4	7	D	D	D
Bristol Bay	0.07	78.5	4	D	D	D	9	52	15.8	1.6	1	D	D	D
Denali	0.04	20.8	NA	NA	NA	NA	13	99	13.4	1.1	NA	NA	NA	NA
Dillingham	0.25	50.0	2	D	D	D	18	214	58.4	4.6	6	D	D	D
Fairbanks North Star	14.12	141.7	(3)69	666	413.5	36.5	301	4,758	1,732.5	153.1	144	661	159.6	33.2
Haines	0.29	114.4	1	D	D	D	19	115	21.6	3.5	5	3	0.8	0.1
Hoonah-Angoon	0.53	248.5	NA	NA	NA	NA	14	48	11.4	1.0	2	D	D	D
Juneau	4.80	146.5	36	265	196.9	12.8	142	1,821	491.4	53.0	61	249	42.2	7.0
Kenai Peninsula	3.63	62.5	44	383	262.4	18.2	266	2,482	804.2	69.7	66	238	68.9	12.7
Ketchikan Gateway	5.70	415.8	10	D	D	D	121	856	235.9	28.1	28	103	17.5	3.3
Kodiak Island	7.64	550.1	22	93	78.1	4.1	41	463	115.9	12.2	13	71	6.2	1.6
Kusilvak	0.48	59.1	2	D	D	D	25	339	46.6	4.6	2	D	D	D
Lake and Peninsula	0.12	76.8	1	D	D	D	4	D	D	D	4	8	1.0	0.1
Matanuska-Susitna	2.69	26.6	40	298	134.9	14.8	244	3,415	1,039.1	89.3	75	181	38.3	6.2
Nome	0.68	69.1	4	D	D	D	34	360	78.7	7.9	5	18	4.0	0.5
North Slope	0.38	39.2	9	234	354.0	19.2	20	240	94.9	6.8	8	49	10.9	2.5
Northwest Arctic	0.57	73.5	1	D	D	D	12	D	D	D	4	6	0.7	0.0
Petersburg	0.65	204.6	8	33	22.2	1.8	28	231	44.2	6.0	5	D	D	D
Prince of Wales-Hyder	0.34	53.6	2	D	D	D	25	204	48.2	5.1	3	D	D	D
Sitka	1.22	137.7	9	48	38.3	1.9	57	424	98.5	12.4	16	47	4.3	1.2
Skagway	0.24	227.1	2	D	D	D	38	118	32.2	4.3	2	D	D	D
Southeast Fairbanks	0.24	35.1	4	D	D	D	34	248	78.6	6.3	8	11	0.7	0.1
Valdez-Cordova	4.83	515.9	8	44	62.7	4.9	52	372	114.0	9.5	10	21	3.0	0.9
Wrangell	0.64	268.7	2	D	D	D	20	180	27.7	4.7	3	2	0.5	0.0
Yakutat	0.51	832.0	1	D	D	D	5	41	5.2	0.9	1	D	D	D
Yukon-Koyukuk	0.24	43.4	2	D	D	D	33	130	32.9	2.4	3	3	1.1	0.1
ARIZONA	1,195.15	175.0	5,570	73,496	69,437.3	4,144.3	17,479	286,184	84,716.5	7,367.8	8,089	40,479	9,329.7	1,693.2
Apache	5.77	80.7	15	D	D	D	105	1,133	324.3	22.2	12	D	D	D
Cochise	16.15	127.7	47	269	133.9	10.1	408	5,266	1,267.3	115.2	113	424	57.1	11.4
Coconino	19.87	142.8	95	738	439.3	33.8	590	7,337	1,896.5	164.8	188	667	137.3	28.1
Gila	4.83	90.9	23	169	68.5	8.6	169	2,005	486.0	46.0	61	149	27.0	4.1
Graham	3.80	100.9	15	D	D	D	93	1,524	381.8	33.6	25	80	17.4	2.6
Greenlee	1.70	178.4	3	D	D	D	16	143	44.2	3.1	3	D	D	D
La Paz	2.89	143.4	11	94	64.2	4.2	81	924	436.0	19.8	21	72	10.7	1.5
Maricopa	776.54	186.3	3,957	57,945	60,841.1	3,426.0	10,415	183,609	57,296.7	4,930.7	5,398	29,825	7,607.5	1,352.0
Mohave	47.86	233.8	114	816	391.1	30.5	593	8,918	2,712.7	211.4	199	628	83.2	15.6
Navajo	14.50	133.9	36	291	170.0	12.1	300	3,935	1,120.3	89.1	94	211	36.0	7.0
Pima	175.40	173.7	703	6,172	3,099.3	269.6	2,770	43,642	11,377.2	1,094.8	1,250	6,042	973.5	205.5
Pinal	63.24	155.5	101	1,633	785.6	123.5	484	8,142	2,375.2	184.3	180	574	105.4	15.6
Santa Cruz	5.17	111.3	150	D	D	D	219	2,344	498.3	47.8	45	192	23.9	3.2
Yavapai	21.14	95.1	163	1,385	880.4	59.1	787	9,854	2,504.3	233.3	341	941	153.0	27.7
Yuma	36.29	177.7	137	2,433	1,439.8	102.5	449	7,408	1,996.0	171.9	159	639	91.9	18.0
ARKANSAS	363.06	121.9	2,884	34,492	31,256.1	1,630.8	10,923	135,448	36,815.3	3,061.5	2,802	12,867	1,922.7	409.8
Arkansas	1.18	64.0	36	428	300.4	19.8	99	1,066	336.0	26.0	22	67	10.0	1.7
Ashley	1.20	57.6	12	136	198.7	6.8	85	863	185.2	17.2	12	26	3.1	0.8
Baxter	3.46	84.3	21	D	D	D	210	2,105	476.6	43.4	36	150	43.7	13.8
Benton	64.74	259.3	237	2,550	2,366.0	150.5	660	10,143	2,906.0	241.3	245	897	173.2	35.7
Boone	0.99	26.6	36	D	D	D	143	1,739	493.3	42.2	37	D	D	D
Bradley	0.21	18.9	10	96	54.9	3.0	39	338	98.9	7.6	7	14	0.8	0.2
Calhoun	0.24	45.9	2	D	D	D	17	78	17.8	1.5	1	D	D	D
Carroll	8.60	310.4	9	94	33.5	3.9	147	1,142	230.2	24.0	26	72	4.3	1.0
Chicot	0.62	56.2	12	109	169.1	6.4	49	379	75.9	7.6	11	D	D	D
Clark	1.84	81.3	10	D	D	D	96	1,158	273.7	27.0	29	94	10.9	1.5
Clay	0.91	60.2	15	258	192.9	8.3	55	485	179.4	11.4	6	D	D	D
Cleburne	11.15	437.8	21	D	D	D	108	1,052	313.1	23.4	21	D	D	D

1 Merchant wholesalers, except manufacturers' sales branches and offices.   2. Employer establishments.

Professional Services, Manufacturing, and Accommodation and Food Services

STATE County	Professional, scientific, and technical services, 2012				Manufacturing, 2012				Accommodation and food services, 2012			
	Number of establish-ments	Number of employees	Sales (mil dol)	Average payroll (mil dol)	Number of establish-ments	Number of employees	Receipts (mil dol)	Annual payroll (mil dol)	Number of establis-hments	Number of employees	Receipts (mil dol)	Annual payroll (mil dol)
	147	148	149	150	151	152	153	154	155	156	157	158
ALABAMA—Cont'd												
Washington	13	50	6.4	3.5	14	3,022	D	236.0	11	D	D	D
Wilcox	10	D	D	D	8	471	D	32.9	12	D	D	D
Winston	28	78	8.5	2.4	53	2,624	608.2	79.4	36	D	D	D
ALASKA	1,898	17,648	3,175.2	1,178.3	527	12,450	D	514.5	2,126	26,836	2,221.3	626.0
Aleutians East	NA	NA	NA	NA	5	D	D	D	11	D	D	D
Aleutians West	1	D	D	D	15	2,120	598.5	81.6	7	118	14.2	4.1
Anchorage	1,141	13,516	2,523.8	958.8	182	2,049	479.8	95.7	788	14,957	1,106.2	338.1
Bethel	6	D	D	D	4	10	D	0.4	18	D	D	D
Bristol Bay	1	D	D	D	6	509	D	17.1	19	57	15.7	4.0
Denali	6	5	1.2	0.3	NA	NA	NA	NA	34	106	63.9	17.3
Dillingham	3	D	D	D	4	267	D	8.5	12	49	4.7	0.9
Fairbanks North Star	237	1,683	293.4	86.5	67	641	1,941.2	36.2	213	3,092	255.3	66.4
Haines	5	8	0.9	0.2	8	44	26.3	3.3	20	94	5.7	1.6
Hoonah-Angoon	NA	NA	NA	NA	NA	NA	NA	NA	16	48	8.4	1.8
Juneau	89	514	79.7	31.4	26	236	75.4	11.7	119	1,329	81.5	24.1
Kenai Peninsula	122	541	65.0	27.6	63	758	D	49.6	265	1,646	149.4	37.4
Ketchikan Gateway	28	93	12.7	4.6	11	648	152.4	27.0	66	560	45.7	11.8
Kodiak Island	24	72	26.5	5.7	22	1,744	D	59.6	47	453	31.5	8.7
Kusilvak	NA	NA	NA	NA	NA	NA	NA	NA	NA	NA	NA	NA
Lake and Peninsula	NA	NA	NA	NA	4	237	57.1	6.7	11	11	9.8	2.6
Matanuska-Susitna	165	915	122.7	45.4	45	222	53.8	9.1	200	1,782	135.5	35.3
Nome	6	7	1.4	0.5	3	D	D	D	18	176	14.8	3.4
North Slope	6	46	12.7	5.9	NA	NA	NA	NA	33	783	132.9	31.7
Northwest Arctic	3	D	D	D	NA	NA	NA	NA	7	99	6.1	2.1
Petersburg	5	10	0.5	0.2	8	D	104.9	9.8	16	63	5.2	1.1
Prince of Wales-Hyder	1	D	D	D	8	161	D	5.6	26	108	10.6	2.6
Sitka	18	74	5.5	2.0	14	325	D	11.8	39	358	30.3	7.9
Skagway	2	D	D	D	3	6	D	D	22	69	13.0	3.7
Southeast Fairbanks	8	25	4.0	2.0	6	23	D	0.8	24	212	16.5	4.8
Valdez-Cordova	17	90	17.6	5.0	14	385	D	14.7	72	462	41.4	10.1
Wrangell	3	D	D	D	4	59	D	D	6	31	2.9	0.7
Yakutat	NA	NA	NA	NA	NA	NA	NA	NA	6	14	3.7	0.9
Yukon-Koyukuk	1	D	D	D	NA	NA	NA	NA	11	54	5.1	1.1
ARIZONA	16,198	121,381	19,268.1	7,378.7	4,269	131,941	51,243.5	8,193.2	11,669	251,455	13,996.6	4,030.3
Apache	27	D	D	D	10	86	D	D	70	816	47.1	12.6
Cochise	217	4,592	586.7	254.7	43	279	141.0	14.2	277	3,875	173.4	48.4
Coconino	331	1,584	178.5	65.3	90	4,025	2,181.3	312.0	545	11,436	765.7	191.8
Gila	81	354	44.5	15.4	18	723	D	32.2	130	1,673	94.6	26.5
Graham	24	227	7.3	16.4	13	167	D	5.4	57	866	36.2	9.0
Greenlee	3	D	D	D	NA	NA	NA	NA	16	D	D	D
La Paz	13	D	D	D	12	199	D	D	79	D	D	D
Maricopa	11,557	90,488	15,557.1	5,822.6	2,889	91,348	34,583.4	5,426.8	6,776	159,029	9,105.9	2,655.2
Mohave	239	931	72.4	30.8	133	2,566	D	109.5	382	5,787	256.7	74.3
Navajo	113	364	30.7	9.8	31	402	179.8	22.1	225	3,197	186.6	48.1
Pima	2,531	16,514	2,241.1	940.0	640	24,297	8,686.6	1,906.7	1,787	42,311	2,154.7	637.4
Pinal	255	1,430	101.7	42.7	111	2,713	2,244.1	133.8	345	6,125	350.5	90.1
Santa Cruz	64	167	20.6	6.8	27	289	211.0	10.2	103	1,413	58.6	17.4
Yavapai	522	1,748	190.9	74.3	184	2,765	706.9	130.8	548	8,223	407.5	130.8
Yuma	221	1,364	132.3	68.0	68	2,084	884.3	79.8	329	5,736	307.5	76.2
ARKANSAS	5,678	32,210	4,528.0	1,567.0	2,688	153,706	62,712.9	6,290.8	5,473	95,854	4,307.3	1,182.5
Arkansas	23	78	9.6	2.4	27	3,628	1,927.2	126.1	39	D	D	D
Ashley	27	71	10.0	2.4	29	2,172	1,339.9	135.4	27	425	17.3	4.4
Baxter	75	401	30.1	12.1	50	2,201	574.4	86.7	99	1,372	61.6	16.1
Benton	619	6,232	1,062.7	402.1	160	9,219	D	363.0	401	8,290	366.8	105.1
Boone	61	D	D	D	54	1,700	493.7	69.0	68	D	D	D
Bradley	11	31	2.7	0.8	8	459	127.9	18.9	11	D	D	D
Calhoun	2	D	D	D	NA	NA	NA	NA	6	17	1.0	0.2
Carroll	36	130	9.7	3.4	32	3,546	741.9	102.5	133	1,185	56.7	17.0
Chicot	13	35	3.6	1.4	6	81	D	1.7	17	187	7.5	1.9
Clark	28	463	74.8	23.9	23	1,186	392.7	53.9	55	1,025	41.5	12.1
Clay	17	39	3.0	0.9	16	341	D	12.0	19	D	D	D
Cleburne	43	167	13.8	4.9	31	1,183	190.3	42.6	59	766	33.9	8.6

Table B. States and Counties — Health Care and Social Assistance, Other Services, Nonemployer Businesses, and Residential Construction

STATE County	Health care and social assistance, 2012				Other services, 2012				Nonemployer businesses, 2016		Value of residential construction authorized by building permits, 2018	
	Number of establishments	Number of employees	Receipts (mil dol)	Annual payroll (mil dol)	Number of establishments	Number of employees	Receipts (mil dol)	Annual payroll (mil dol)	Number	Receipts (mil dol)	New construction ($1,000)	Number of housing units
	159	160	161	162	163	164	165	166	167	168	169	170
ALABAMA—Cont'd												
Washington	19	D	D	D	9	D	D	D	1,065	31.2	0	0
Wilcox	18	262	16.0	6.7	8	31	3.1	0.8	617	19.7	580	3
Winston	36	684	57.9	21.4	20	D	D	D	1,664	74.7	588	5
ALASKA	2,432	48,701	6,375.5	2,434.2	1,355	7,238	904.6	235.8	56,946	2,566.2	429,020	1,677
Aleutians East	10	D	D	D	4	D	D	D	236	20.0	0	2
Aleutians West	14	D	D	D	6	D	D	D	236	12.2	589	6
Anchorage	1,165	25,616	3,656.2	1,347.8	580	3,863	514.2	136.0	21,131	1,044.4	306,813	1,083
Bethel	47	D	D	D	14	56	8.4	1.1	714	18.9	270	1
Bristol Bay	2	D	D	D	2	D	D	D	194	8.0	310	2
Denali	3	12	1.0	0.6	3	D	D	D	169	6.5	NA	NA
Dillingham	8	D	D	D	6	17	1.5	0.6	793	25.7	592	3
Fairbanks North Star	290	5,748	746.9	305.5	185	842	88.8	25.6	5,802	227.7	3,483	13
Haines	10	134	9.2	4.0	7	D	D	D	423	16.5	1,608	10
Hoonah-Angoon	7	44	3.6	1.5	3	D	D	D	300	11.9	285	1
Juneau	144	2,458	275.5	112.4	82	406	46.5	12.9	2,894	133.6	13,642	68
Kenai Peninsula	226	3,651	352.9	144.4	138	648	78.5	19.9	6,763	271.9	21,414	114
Ketchikan Gateway	36	799	90.1	39.3	42	142	14.1	3.8	1,326	79.1	11,779	47
Kodiak Island	39	733	79.7	35.4	30	150	19.1	4.4	1,457	72.3	10,697	50
Kusilvak	19	D	D	D	4	D	D	D	NA	NA	0	0
Lake and Peninsula	NA	NA	NA	NA	1	D	D	D	268	10.6	NA	NA
Matanuska-Susitna	267	3,621	411.5	161.6	123	572	64.4	16.7	7,299	316.8	35,198	176
Nome	27	D	D	D	13	D	D	D	525	13.9	30	1
North Slope	9	D	D	D	7	D	D	D	290	7.3	628	3
Northwest Arctic	4	D	D	D	9	D	D	D	256	8.3	5,541	11
											1,995	11
Petersburg	11	176	17.5	6.4	13	D	D	D	752	51.2		
Prince of Wales-Hyder	10	197	13.4	6.4	7	D	D	D	578	27.7	630	3
Sitka	25	937	111.5	47.7	25	100	8.3	2.3	1,319	73.0	3,790	16
Skagway	4	4	0.3	0.1	5	22	1.3	0.4	139	7.3	3,228	22
Southeast Fairbanks	11	D	D	D	7	D	D	D	537	19.3	NA	NA
Valdez-Cordova	24	455	46.1	18.7	28	109	10.7	3.4	1,213	48.3	3,358	13
Wrangell	7	D	D	D	7	D	D	D	312	11.9	970	8
Yakutat	3	D	D	D	NA	NA	NA	NA	103	4.7	2,170	13
Yukon-Koyukuk	10	32	2.3	1.2	4	D	D	D	374	11.2	0	0
ARIZONA	16,872	315,107	37,055.9	14,236.1	8,503	62,073	6,231.7	1,736.0	467,815	21,329.4	9,727,722	41,664
Apache	64	3,300	412.8	148.1	19	75	7.7	1.6	2,764	61.6	13,213	58
Cochise	273	4,896	408.9	167.4	150	684	53.1	16.1	6,703	203.1	39,907	227
Coconino	381	6,995	1,040.7	354.3	230	1,307	105.8	32.7	9,228	383.5	129,939	665
Gila	133	2,479	259.1	97.6	57	225	18.2	5.3	3,306	121.3	41,557	169
Graham	78	822	61.3	25.1	33	219	31.2	8.0	1,498	53.6	27,222	138
Greenlee	7	D	D	D	2	D	D	D	248	5.5	467	22
La Paz	21	D	D	D	15	D	D	D	818	34.0	2,092	10
Maricopa	10,811	199,139	23,736.9	9,260.4	5,265	42,665	4,489.1	1,246.0	310,913	15,241.9	6,577,381	26,724
Mohave	478	8,222	995.0	364.2	290	1,394	110.3	29.4	10,781	480.1	203,858	1,018
Navajo	241	3,832	439.1	177.5	117	525	46.0	11.4	5,456	179.8	69,308	368
Pima	2,777	56,539	6,617.5	2,441.8	1,483	10,691	1,008.6	281.2	65,734	2,585.0	1,065,132	4,404
Pinal	420	8,118	786.3	313.8	240	1,249	120.5	33.1	18,402	672.5	872,761	4,619
Santa Cruz	70	1,135	146.0	41.0	44	154	13.4	3.7	4,275	184.1	35,028	148
Yavapai	759	11,555	1,245.1	517.8	364	1,717	142.9	41.0	18,667	773.2	489,306	2,079
Yuma	359	7,092	794.1	282.4	194	1,099	77.8	25.0	9,022	350.4	160,550	1,015
ARKANSAS	7,485	166,455	15,792.6	6,318.7	3,961	21,830	2,339.4	586.3	201,227	8,553.7	1,829,441	10,179
Arkansas	46	988	63.6	27.6	30	112	7.6	3.0	1,360	62.0	1,683	18
Ashley	46	931	64.3	26.8	25	100	9.3	2.6	1,083	35.8	85	1
Baxter	170	3,490	337.5	133.3	80	326	25.4	6.5	3,031	129.5	4,742	41
Benton	472	8,091	751.6	281.5	256	1,613	145.1	44.1	17,972	810.1	759,045	3,996
Boone	126	2,336	195.6	74.3	48	227	24.5	6.5	2,824	115.0	6,483	56
Bradley	25	530	38.6	14.9	21	69	6.7	1.8	543	27.0	75	1
Calhoun	4	D	D	D	2	D	D	D	188	6.0	0	0
Carroll	50	752	57.9	24.0	39	114	10.7	2.8	2,567	87.4	2,212	28
Chicot	36	900	51.2	26.7	10	58	6.5	1.6	563	20.4	170	2
Clark	59	934	65.9	26.4	27	92	10.7	2.4	1,289	46.7	2,351	41
Clay	33	695	42.1	19.8	29	D	D	D	785	32.6	71	2
Cleburne	45	828	54.1	21.5	33	121	10.7	2.4	2,174	89.4	1,844	8

Table B. States and Counties — Government Employment and Payroll, and Local Government Finances

	Government employment and payroll, 2012									Local government finances, 2012				
			March payroll (percent of total)							General revenue				
												Taxes		
STATE County	Full-time equivalent employees	March payroll (dollars)	Adminis-tration, judicial, and legal	Police and corrections	Fire protection	Highways and transpor-tation	Health and welfare	Natural resources and utilities	Education and libraries	Total (mil dol)	Inter-govern-mental (mil dol)	Total (mil dol)	Per capita[1] (dollars) Total	Property
	171	172	173	174	175	176	177	178	179	180	181	182	183	184
ALABAMA—Cont'd														
Washington	673	2,075,254	4.0	4.1	0.0	2.0	21.7	3.3	64.7	40.9	25.0	11.8	691	514
Wilcox	583	1,459,476	6.1	7.4	0.0	6.3	11.1	6.3	60.3	29.0	18.4	7.7	674	358
Winston	1,387	3,355,200	3.1	5.2	0.8	2.7	29.1	3.2	54.4	62.5	36.3	16.1	667	283
ALASKA	X	X	X	X	X	X	X	X	X	X	X	X	X	X
Aleutians East	184	728,454	19.1	7.1	0.2	11.9	2.3	7.0	41.2	34.8	17.1	10.2	3,215	0
Aleutians West	278	1,422,298	17.8	11.2	3.2	9.9	3.0	15.4	24.7	56.1	18.9	21.5	3,872	853
Anchorage	10,003	52,917,485	4.5	7.7	6.5	5.4	2.3	9.8	62.6	1,313.0	582.8	546.6	1,831	1,623
Bethel	302	1,160,315	19.0	13.8	3.3	7.0	2.2	43.9	0.1	65.9	43.9	9.6	543	0
Bristol Bay	78	333,504	12.5	13.6	0.7	18.6	2.8	5.7	46.1	16.8	7.9	5.5	5,590	3,083
Denali	82	322,133	9.4	0.0	0.0	0.0	4.0	0.0	85.9	11.0	7.8	2.8	1,472	0
Dillingham	293	1,115,865	13.8	10.5	0.7	3.7	2.6	29.8	35.5	40.8	28.5	5.7	1,140	460
Fairbanks North Star	2,949	14,833,210	7.9	3.4	2.6	2.4	1.8	5.3	75.9	380.0	201.2	148.5	1,481	1,335
Haines	105	554,027	8.6	6.3	0.8	5.6	0.6	5.8	68.5	20.5	12.5	5.3	2,089	1,020
Hoonah-Angoon	90	310,388	14.5	8.3	2.0	8.6	2.0	9.8	54.0	12.4	8.3	1.7	814	39
Juneau	2,061	10,714,562	5.3	5.1	2.9	7.0	24.9	13.7	41.0	338.0	110.1	83.0	2,549	1,125
Kenai Peninsula	2,080	9,477,210	10.6	5.1	7.7	3.9	1.5	4.4	61.5	445.9	125.4	111.8	1,965	1,014
Ketchikan Gateway	699	3,359,138	10.3	7.2	4.6	11.2	1.5	15.2	47.8	123.4	42.9	28.8	2,087	994
Kodiak Island	637	2,986,849	7.4	6.7	2.5	6.1	0.9	9.3	64.9	102.4	55.1	27.0	1,893	1,004
Kusilvak	286	832,391	24.5	17.3	0.7	6.1	0.8	19.3	17.7	58.3	48.1	1.6	208	0
Lake and Peninsula	163	640,681	11.6	0.0	0.1	1.6	1.2	2.7	78.9	24.1	18.4	2.8	1,706	0
Matanuska-Susitna	2,847	12,057,275	8.3	3.7	1.6	2.4	3.8	2.2	76.5	386.7	229.3	136.9	1,458	1,165
Nome	378	1,484,923	12.5	9.6	0.1	4.9	2.6	23.5	37.5	50.2	28.5	9.5	963	231
North Slope	1,749	8,359,644	27.7	5.0	3.3	11.1	11.6	11.4	26.8	503.2	75.9	366.0	37,957	37,888
Northwest Arctic	630	2,686,215	7.5	8.0	1.7	3.7	1.1	9.5	61.6	100.8	72.5	4.2	541	0
Petersburg	512	2,386,453	4.4	6.0	0.8	10.0	32.9	10.6	32.3	82.3	42.5	9.6	2,490	1,229
Prince of Wales-Hyder	289	1,128,652	6.7	2.6	1.0	2.1	2.2	19.6	61.2	30.3	21.8	3.3	576	89
Sitka	525	2,686,315	6.2	5.6	2.0	2.6	30.9	12.2	35.9	89.4	30.2	15.4	1,705	671
Skagway	66	277,303	9.2	10.8	6.1	7.0	16.4	6.9	36.1	19.8	9.1	8.4	8,710	2,132
Southeast Fairbanks	12	40,359	51.1	0.0	0.0	7.5	18.3	0.0	17.1	1.8	1.3	0.0	0	0
Valdez-Cordova	506	2,285,718	8.9	9.3	3.5	9.2	14.4	12.9	38.6	103.7	27.4	50.7	5,213	4,747
Wrangell	NA	NA	NA	NA	NA	NA	NA	NA	NA	NA	NA	NA	NA	NA
Yakutat	56	174,101	20.5	10.7	0.0	9.9	2.5	2.0	50.3	6.3	4.3	1.3	1,936	647
Yukon-Koyukuk	365	1,481,198	10.8	1.7	0.6	2.6	1.1	7.6	73.3	41.9	35.8	0.9	148	52
ARIZONA	X	X	X	X	X	X	X	X	X	X	X	X	X	X
Apache	2,657	8,600,597	5.6	5.3	1.9	2.9	2.7	1.1	79.6	168.2	116.4	31.5	431	379
Cochise	4,879	16,984,358	11.7	10.2	5.2	2.9	3.0	3.3	61.1	397.9	175.5	144.2	1,092	821
Coconino	4,575	17,536,070	11.8	13.5	9.2	3.5	4.5	6.4	48.1	469.7	159.1	223.4	1,643	979
Gila	2,222	7,331,024	14.5	15.3	7.8	3.9	2.3	5.8	48.1	194.4	80.9	87.8	1,652	1,207
Graham	2,165	7,913,958	6.9	8.1	0.2	2.5	26.5	4.9	50.0	137.7	81.5	29.0	774	382
Greenlee	376	1,216,974	14.2	15.2	0.0	7.6	5.4	1.1	53.9	32.1	12.7	13.6	1,545	1,283
La Paz	799	2,443,896	12.2	19.6	6.3	4.6	4.4	6.2	44.6	60.9	26.7	21.8	1,075	779
Maricopa	129,919	553,767,788	8.2	13.2	5.3	2.8	6.3	12.4	50.5	14,121.0	4,763.7	5,936.1	1,506	958
Mohave	5,613	20,393,845	13.0	13.4	11.7	4.5	2.0	5.6	47.4	538.5	183.2	229.9	1,131	849
Navajo	4,056	13,281,721	8.7	9.6	5.1	2.8	1.5	3.5	67.5	523.9	174.9	109.2	1,020	745
Pima	31,634	115,785,276	10.5	14.5	6.6	3.5	2.2	7.1	52.9	3,257.1	1,214.5	1,427.3	1,438	1,057
Pinal	9,793	33,904,548	13.3	15.5	5.5	3.5	3.8	5.1	52.2	961.4	426.5	329.1	850	624
Santa Cruz	2,004	6,229,659	10.5	13.1	10.4	3.9	2.5	1.8	56.6	161.7	83.6	52.4	1,108	737
Yavapai	6,155	23,081,009	10.4	13.4	9.4	4.0	2.1	5.5	45.2	648.3	201.2	335.8	1,579	1,029
Yuma	7,924	25,609,990	12.0	12.1	3.1	2.2	2.4	7.3	59.9	638.9	314.0	221.6	1,108	716
ARKANSAS	X	X	X	X	X	X	X	X	X	X	X	X	X	X
Arkansas	988	2,636,492	5.7	8.3	2.3	3.4	19.7	5.4	51.8	59.0	32.8	17.1	906	316
Ashley	866	2,414,339	4.8	9.8	2.9	4.1	2.0	4.2	71.6	63.9	38.0	15.5	719	291
Baxter	1,228	3,503,816	4.6	8.5	3.2	6.2	1.3	7.6	68.0	81.3	46.3	22.7	553	251
Benton	7,214	24,863,912	5.8	8.5	5.2	2.0	0.5	6.6	70.3	624.9	346.9	196.3	845	405
Boone	1,391	3,599,052	4.9	7.8	2.9	3.4	0.3	7.1	72.7	96.8	61.2	19.7	527	210
Bradley	467	1,184,067	4.0	5.4	0.9	4.3	3.1	2.7	79.4	35.7	24.9	6.9	603	215
Calhoun	169	422,712	9.1	11.0	0.0	8.6	4.4	3.4	61.8	17.3	7.1	2.7	511	302
Carroll	1,012	2,598,555	4.9	8.8	2.4	5.9	2.4	9.3	64.4	71.0	38.3	16.2	585	295
Chicot	716	2,139,884	6.2	8.0	0.0	2.0	31.0	4.0	48.8	35.1	21.3	8.7	762	307
Clark	763	2,247,437	7.0	17.2	2.0	3.9	2.5	9.0	58.1	67.1	41.9	13.1	572	219
Clay	859	3,044,204	5.9	15.6	0.0	4.6	23.1	14.3	35.5	49.8	25.0	7.5	478	259
Cleburne	801	2,107,158	6.7	9.2	0.5	4.7	1.5	7.6	69.0	57.0	31.3	15.0	583	313

1. Based on the resident population estimated as of July 1 of the year shown.

Local Government Finances, Government Employment, and Income Taxes

STATE County	Local government finances, 2012 (cont.)							Debt outstanding		Government employment, 2017			Individual income tax returns, 2016		
	Direct general expenditure														
			Percent of total for:												
	Total (mil dol)	Per capita[1] (dollars)	Education	Health and hospitals	Police protection	Public welfare	Highways	Total (mil dol)	Per capita[1] (dollars)	Federal civilian	Federal military	State and local	Number of returns	Mean adjusted gross income	Mean income tax
	185	186	187	188	189	190	191	192	193	194	195	196	197	198	199
ALABAMA—Cont'd															
Washington	42.8	2,504	67.0	3.3	3.6	0.1	11.2	186.5	10,900	33	70	920	6,480	50,342	4,568
Wilcox	31.8	2,786	61.3	2.7	5.4	0.0	7.4	45.1	3,945	66	45	716	4,340	35,347	2,799
Winston	67.7	2,809	62.8	0.9	3.3	0.0	6.0	53.1	2,204	70	100	1,077	8,940	46,631	4,863
ALASKA	X	X	X	X	X	X	X	X	X	15,110	25,473	62,517	348,070	67,556	9,362
Aleutians East	35.1	11,095	24.9	0.3	3.1	0.0	6.3	40.2	12,717	18	11	240	890	48,128	4,982
Aleutians West	55.3	9,975	16.7	0.1	7.8	0.0	12.5	41.9	7,550	15	30	462	2,110	60,145	6,718
Anchorage	1,268.0	4,246	52.5	2.1	9.8	0.0	5.8	1,857.9	6,222	8,509	11,607	19,463	146,640	75,397	11,418
Bethel	70.7	3,986	0.0	0.1	6.7	0.0	3.2	8.4	476	76	120	2,909	6,760	37,464	3,732
Bristol Bay	15.8	15,960	28.3	4.7	6.6	0.0	2.4	1.0	993	50	6	167	500	56,336	6,758
Denali	10.7	5,696	75.8	0.1	0.0	0.0	0.0	0.0	0	200	42	157	1,150	62,783	8,118
Dillingham	39.6	7,872	29.2	2.5	8.2	2.1	5.2	15.1	2,990	45	33	676	2,290	44,460	4,558
Fairbanks North Star	342.4	3,415	63.0	1.6	2.3	0.0	6.2	170.2	1,698	3,041	9,791	7,512	46,040	65,853	8,618
Haines	15.3	5,980	38.0	1.6	3.3	0.0	6.3	16.4	6,424	10	17	167	1,310	57,027	5,921
Hoonah-Angoon	11.8	5,536	49.2	1.1	4.3	0.0	4.8	3.0	1,396	100	14	268	970	44,114	4,684
Juneau	318.0	9,768	26.7	30.7	5.4	0.0	4.2	225.5	6,927	704	453	5,954	16,760	73,302	9,977
Kenai Peninsula	437.7	7,692	32.5	38.4	2.0	0.0	2.4	171.8	3,019	371	478	4,564	28,390	65,030	8,724
Ketchikan Gateway	133.0	9,654	26.9	0.8	3.6	0.0	4.1	145.8	10,581	223	286	1,686	7,160	61,359	7,904
Kodiak Island	95.8	6,729	46.7	0.6	5.3	0.0	3.3	62.8	4,413	292	1,002	1,118	6,710	56,519	6,433
Kusilvak	70.2	8,985	80.8	0.2	1.6	0.0	1.3	3.8	489	19	55	1,560	2,970	22,510	1,280
Lake and Peninsula	20.2	12,184	72.3	0.1	0.5	0.0	0.8	3.8	2,267	44	11	365	720	38,553	3,481
Matanuska-Susitna	393.6	4,190	61.3	2.3	2.6	0.0	6.9	404.7	4,309	220	702	4,906	44,990	67,231	8,618
Nome	44.7	4,511	29.0	1.0	4.3	0.0	6.8	12.3	1,244	49	66	1,579	3,670	47,331	5,130
North Slope	459.1	47,609	17.7	2.7	3.1	1.5	3.7	510.2	52,913	20	48	2,011	3,830	51,469	6,393
Northwest Arctic	89.1	11,410	62.5	0.1	1.7	0.0	2.2	72.5	9,289	40	49	982	2,460	50,653	5,633
Petersburg	85.2	22,155	24.0	26.0	3.2	1.2	7.1	28.2	7,342	92	48	387	1,900	49,715	6,194
Prince of Wales-Hyder	28.0	4,867	53.2	1.1	4.5	0.0	2.7	4.0	704	96	43	962	2,340	50,544	5,676
Sitka	79.2	8,752	28.6	27.3	5.4	0.0	1.8	117.1	12,949	121	243	1,003	4,540	62,965	8,711
Skagway	17.6	18,327	12.7	9.9	7.3	0.1	9.4	6.5	6,776	58	8	122	780	56,879	7,263
Southeast Fairbanks	1.9	262	0.2	0.1	0.0	0.0	8.6	0.9	119	399	44	432	3,240	53,904	6,118
Valdez-Cordova	84.7	8,716	25.8	23.7	2.1	0.0	3.8	37.8	3,895	143	209	1,117	4,920	61,116	7,638
Wrangell	NA	NA	NA	NA	NA	NA	NA	NA	NA	46	17	275	1,100	47,432	4,773
Yakutat	6.6	9,847	45.8	2.9	9.1	0.0	7.6	1.0	1,548	23	4	103	240	47,933	5,129
Yukon-Koyukuk	46.4	8,035	79.2	0.3	1.0	0.0	1.2	6.9	1,200	86	36	1,370	2,760	33,900	3,004
ARIZONA	X	X	X	X	X	X	X	X	X	55,861	33,902	358,887	2,943,300	60,362	7,795
Apache	161.6	2,208	65.6	3.6	3.3	0.0	6.5	280.9	3,837	2,632	160	8,055	24,720	36,792	2,736
Cochise	407.1	3,082	44.0	3.5	12.3	4.9	7.3	161.6	1,223	4,834	4,071	6,230	51,680	47,084	4,575
Coconino	457.2	3,361	35.9	3.4	6.5	1.6	7.6	377.9	2,779	2,773	306	16,181	59,500	56,172	6,803
Gila	163.2	3,071	37.4	1.4	11.8	2.5	6.1	46.8	881	314	119	5,157	21,670	45,417	4,446
Graham	132.6	3,543	64.5	0.4	8.6	1.6	4.9	28.1	752	395	78	2,492	11,200	46,437	4,082
Greenlee	31.0	3,517	44.5	5.9	11.6	0.0	6.8	16.8	1,911	35	21	512	3,390	55,090	4,953
La Paz	82.5	4,069	27.8	3.1	9.7	0.6	7.2	44.7	2,204	328	46	1,900	6,490	36,862	3,097
Maricopa	13,916.1	3,530	41.6	5.1	8.2	1.5	4.1	27,988.0	7,100	21,124	13,786	196,038	1,846,890	66,056	9,182
Mohave	555.1	2,730	33.9	2.7	6.9	0.1	8.7	627.7	3,087	461	459	7,139	81,660	42,857	4,178
Navajo	397.5	3,712	44.4	24.0	5.0	0.8	4.3	156.9	1,465	1,802	241	7,550	39,320	41,105	3,428
Pima	3,531.8	3,559	37.0	3.1	9.1	2.7	5.3	5,788.9	5,833	12,845	8,121	67,186	441,640	56,276	6,565
Pinal	1,130.4	2,918	46.7	4.4	9.1	1.6	3.8	1,030.3	2,660	1,626	914	18,312	145,670	49,216	4,627
Santa Cruz	148.9	3,149	48.5	3.1	10.0	0.0	3.8	161.3	3,410	1,586	103	2,091	20,320	42,166	4,153
Yavapai	653.7	3,074	36.5	2.1	7.2	1.8	9.0	725.7	3,413	1,603	516	9,301	104,930	52,696	6,074
Yuma	616.3	3,081	47.8	2.1	6.0	2.5	4.6	668.5	3,342	3,503	4,961	10,743	84,260	41,809	3,859
ARKANSAS	X	X	X	X	X	X	X	X	X	20,099	15,117	191,038	1,221,420	55,640	6,669
Arkansas	54.5	2,887	54.8	0.8	6.7	0.0	6.5	53.2	2,814	189	70	921	7,620	49,596	6,010
Ashley	63.4	2,945	60.9	0.2	5.8	0.0	6.5	95.2	4,425	68	79	962	7,920	46,047	4,249
Baxter	82.1	2,001	58.9	0.0	7.5	0.1	8.6	143.9	3,507	133	161	1,478	17,580	47,434	5,187
Benton	620.5	2,672	61.2	0.2	5.6	0.0	5.6	1,204.1	5,184	471	1,042	9,690	113,120	103,959	15,978
Boone	94.8	2,540	65.0	0.1	4.7	0.0	4.2	59.7	1,600	150	146	3,035	15,560	48,002	4,904
Bradley	34.0	2,985	65.5	0.0	5.4	0.1	7.3	14.7	1,294	29	42	789	4,240	40,071	3,579
Calhoun	20.8	3,913	57.2	1.1	3.3	0.5	6.0	106.6	20,089	10	20	263	1,900	46,913	4,087
Carroll	75.8	2,746	55.7	0.1	5.3	0.0	7.5	76.9	2,784	88	109	1,117	11,990	38,709	3,396
Chicot	34.4	3,008	57.3	2.8	6.4	0.1	7.0	15.4	1,344	43	39	886	3,870	40,799	4,535
Clark	65.6	2,861	64.3	0.1	4.3	0.0	5.6	101.8	4,437	90	78	2,506	8,200	44,228	4,056
Clay	49.7	3,171	48.6	25.1	4.0	0.0	5.7	31.5	2,010	53	58	849	5,800	37,871	3,575
Cleburne	54.0	2,093	60.3	0.2	4.9	0.1	9.9	57.4	2,225	90	97	913	10,400	45,671	4,564

1. Based on the resident population estimated as of July 1 of the year shown.

State / county code	CBSA code[1]	County code[2]	STATE County	Land area[3] (sq. mi)	Total persons 2018	Rank	Per square mile	White	Black	American Indian, Alaska Native	Asian and Pacific Islancer	Percent Hispanic or Latino[4]	Under 5 years	5 to 17 years	18 to 24 years	25 to 34 years	35 to 44 years	45 to 54 years
				1	2	3	4	5	6	7	8	9	10	11	12	13	14	15
			ARKANSAS—Cont'd															
05025	38,220	3	Cleveland	597.8	8,018	2,591	13.4	85.6	12.2	0.9	0.3	2.4	5.1	16.7	7.3	10.7	11.5	13.0
05027	31,620	7	Columbia	766.0	23,537	1,662	30.7	60.2	36.0	0.8	1.4	2.9	5.8	14.9	17.4	11.2	10.1	10.9
05029		6	Conway	552.3	20,891	1,780	37.8	83.4	12.3	1.6	0.9	4.0	5.8	16.7	6.9	12.0	11.5	12.8
05031	27,860	3	Craighead	707.3	108,558	560	153.5	77.1	17.0	0.8	1.6	5.2	7.0	18.0	10.5	15.4	12.8	11.5
05033	22,900	2	Crawford	591.2	63,406	839	107.2	86.6	2.2	3.9	2.1	8.0	6.3	18.2	7.9	12.6	12.2	12.9
05035	32,820	1	Crittenden	610.3	48,342	1,016	79.2	42.6	54.4	0.6	1.0	2.6	7.6	19.4	8.9	13.3	11.8	12.2
05037		6	Cross	616.4	16,676	2,000	27.1	74.0	23.5	0.9	1.0	2.0	6.3	17.1	8.0	11.4	12.2	12.5
05039		6	Dallas	667.4	7,182	2,646	10.8	54.6	42.2	1.1	0.4	3.4	5.2	16.1	7.0	10.7	10.4	11.7
05041		6	Desha	768.1	11,512	2,326	15.0	45.7	47.6	0.8	0.8	6.4	6.7	18.9	7.5	11.2	10.9	11.3
05043		6	Drew	828.4	18,328	1,910	22.1	67.2	28.5	0.7	0.8	3.9	6.0	15.5	13.7	12.3	11.0	11.4
05045	30,780	2	Faulkner	647.9	124,806	510	192.6	81.8	13.0	1.3	2.0	4.1	6.1	17.0	15.0	14.4	12.4	11.7
05047		6	Franklin	608.9	17,810	1,933	29.2	93.1	1.5	2.3	1.4	3.4	5.6	17.3	8.1	11.3	11.9	12.5
05049		9	Fulton	618.2	12,269	2,274	19.8	96.8	1.2	1.8	0.5	1.5	4.9	15.6	6.8	9.0	9.7	12.4
05051	26,300	3	Garland	677.7	99,154	601	146.3	84.0	9.6	1.5	1.3	5.9	5.4	14.7	7.2	11.4	11.0	12.0
05053	30,780	2	Grant	631.8	18,188	1,917	28.8	93.5	3.1	1.2	0.6	2.9	5.4	17.0	7.5	12.1	12.7	13.5
05055	37,500	4	Greene	577.7	45,325	1,068	78.5	94.0	2.4	1.2	0.9	2.9	6.5	17.9	8.2	13.3	12.8	13.3
05057	26,260	6	Hempstead	727.5	21,741	1,738	29.9	56.1	30.8	1.1	0.8	13.2	7.2	18.6	8.0	11.1	11.4	11.8
05059	31,680	6	Hot Spring	615.2	33,701	1,335	54.8	84.2	12.0	1.5	0.8	3.5	5.1	15.4	8.0	13.0	12.4	13.2
05061		6	Howard	588.6	13,341	2,206	22.7	65.1	21.3	1.7	0.8	12.6	7.0	19.0	7.7	11.7	11.4	12.4
05063	12,900	7	Independence	764.0	37,678	1,232	49.3	89.9	2.9	1.2	1.1	6.5	6.4	17.8	8.7	11.9	12.1	12.4
05065		9	Izard	580.6	13,593	2,191	23.4	93.9	2.5	1.7	0.7	2.6	4.3	13.7	6.8	10.5	10.6	13.2
05067		6	Jackson	633.9	16,811	1,988	26.5	78.2	18.4	1.3	0.9	2.9	5.8	14.3	7.8	14.5	13.0	12.9
05069	38,220	3	Jefferson	870.0	68,114	785	78.3	39.7	57.5	0.8	1.2	2.1	6.1	16.0	10.2	13.0	11.5	12.1
05071		7	Johnson	659.9	26,742	1,539	40.5	80.8	2.3	2.0	2.8	14.1	6.8	18.0	9.4	12.4	11.8	12.2
05073		8	Lafayette	528.3	6,682	2,696	12.6	60.4	36.5	0.9	0.7	2.8	5.1	13.3	7.5	10.4	10.5	12.9
05075		6	Lawrence	587.6	16,434	2,012	28.0	96.1	1.6	1.4	0.6	1.7	5.8	16.1	9.4	11.7	11.2	12.6
05077		7	Lee	602.6	8,985	2,503	14.9	42.4	54.5	1.1	0.8	2.5	5.0	13.3	7.9	15.3	12.5	13.4
05079	38,220	3	Lincoln	561.6	13,383	2,200	23.8	65.2	30.8	0.9	0.4	3.9	4.0	12.8	10.1	17.2	14.6	14.2
05081	45,500	3	Little River	532.2	12,326	2,264	23.2	74.6	20.6	2.4	0.8	3.7	6.0	16.3	7.4	11.3	11.5	12.8
05083		6	Logan	708.1	21,737	1,740	30.7	92.0	2.0	2.0	2.7	3.1	6.0	15.6	7.7	11.3	11.2	14.0
05085	30,780	2	Lonoke	770.9	73,657	746	95.5	87.4	7.0	1.2	1.6	4.8	6.8	19.0	8.1	14.1	13.7	12.9
05087	22,220	2	Madison	834.3	16,481	2,011	19.8	90.9	0.9	2.4	1.5	6.0	6.7	16.9	7.4	11.6	11.1	12.7
05089		9	Marion	597.0	16,722	1,997	28.0	95.7	0.9	2.2	1.0	2.3	5.0	13.6	5.5	9.0	8.8	11.7
05091	45,500	3	Miller	625.7	43,592	1,103	69.7	70.3	25.9	1.4	0.8	3.6	6.6	17.0	8.1	13.2	12.6	12.6
05093	14,180	4	Mississippi	900.6	41,239	1,146	45.8	59.5	36.3	0.7	0.7	4.2	7.2	18.9	8.9	13.1	11.9	12.1
05095		7	Monroe	607.1	6,900	2,684	11.4	56.1	40.6	1.2	1.0	3.0	6.5	14.5	7.0	10.6	9.7	12.3
05097		8	Montgomery	779.9	8,924	2,507	11.4	92.2	1.0	2.5	1.8	4.6	4.7	13.7	6.8	8.7	9.0	13.7
05099	26,260	7	Nevada	617.8	8,326	2,557	13.5	64.2	31.6	0.8	0.7	4.2	5.8	16.8	6.7	11.5	10.6	13.0
05101	25,460	9	Newton	820.9	7,805	2,608	9.5	95.8	1.0	3.0	0.6	2.0	4.9	14.4	6.5	9.8	10.3	11.8
05103	15,780	7	Ouachita	732.8	23,606	1,659	32.2	56.7	41.0	1.0	0.7	2.5	5.6	16.8	7.2	11.2	10.7	12.2
05105	30,780	2	Perry	551.6	10,352	2,397	18.8	93.6	2.7	2.0	0.7	3.1	6.0	16.4	7.5	10.5	11.3	13.8
05107	25,760	6	Phillips	695.6	18,029	1,921	25.9	35.7	62.1	0.7	0.7	2.1	7.7	18.1	8.0	10.1	10.1	11.1
05109		9	Pike	600.6	10,673	2,382	17.8	89.0	3.9	1.6	0.8	6.4	5.2	16.2	7.9	10.8	11.4	14.0
05111	27,860	3	Poinsett	758.4	23,974	1,643	31.6	87.9	9.1	0.9	0.5	3.2	6.8	17.3	8.0	12.7	11.2	13.1
05113		7	Polk	857.7	20,049	1,823	23.4	89.9	0.9	3.7	1.3	6.6	6.0	16.8	7.2	10.2	10.5	12.0
05115	40,780	5	Pope	812.5	64,000	833	78.8	85.5	3.8	1.7	1.6	9.4	6.3	16.3	12.9	13.5	11.1	11.9
05117		8	Prairie	647.9	8,074	2,583	12.5	85.9	12.2	0.9	0.3	1.8	5.3	14.7	7.2	10.5	9.7	13.8
05119	30,780	2	Pulaski	758.9	392,680	180	517.4	53.6	38.4	1.0	2.9	6.2	6.6	16.6	8.7	14.8	12.8	12.1
05121		7	Randolph	652.2	17,948	1,924	27.5	94.6	1.6	1.4	2.0	2.1	6.3	17.4	7.3	12.5	11.6	12.0
05123	22,620	6	St. Francis	634.8	25,439	1,585	40.1	40.9	53.0	1.0	1.0	5.4	6.2	15.0	7.9	14.9	14.4	12.4
05125	30,780	2	Saline	723.5	121,421	518	167.8	85.3	8.5	1.1	1.7	5.0	5.8	17.4	7.2	12.8	13.5	12.9
05127		6	Scott	892.3	10,319	2,399	11.6	86.3	1.2	3.4	3.5	7.7	5.6	17.6	7.0	11.4	10.5	13.0
05129		9	Searcy	666.1	7,958	2,598	11.9	94.9	0.8	3.2	0.6	2.7	5.3	15.2	6.6	9.8	10.0	12.6
05131	22,900	2	Sebastian	531.9	127,753	500	240.2	72.1	8.0	3.4	5.4	14.6	6.6	17.3	8.9	13.6	12.1	12.7
05133		6	Sevier	565.1	17,139	1,973	30.3	58.7	4.6	3.2	1.8	34.0	7.9	20.5	9.1	12.6	11.4	12.7
05135		7	Sharp	604.4	17,366	1,953	28.7	95.2	1.3	2.3	0.8	2.3	5.4	15.2	9.3	10.1	12.2	12.2
05137		9	Stone	606.4	12,457	2,251	20.5	96.1	0.8	2.2	0.7	2.0	4.8	14.4	6.2	9.4	10.2	11.0
05139	20,980	7	Union	1,039.2	39,126	1,201	37.7	62.1	33.4	1.1	0.9	4.1	6.6	17.5	7.7	11.8	11.8	12.4
05141		8	Van Buren	709.7	16,603	2,005	23.4	95.0	1.0	2.0	0.6	3.1	4.8	15.2	6.3	9.1	10.3	12.5
05143	22,220	2	Washington	942.0	236,961	283	251.6	73.2	4.3	2.3	5.8	17.1	6.8	17.6	14.6	15.1	13.2	10.9
05145	42,620	4	White	1,035.1	78,727	713	76.1	89.7	5.4	1.3	1.2	4.4	5.9	17.1	11.4	12.3	11.6	12.7
05147		9	Woodruff	586.8	6,490	2,710	11.1	71.1	27.0	1.0	0.6	2.1	5.9	16.0	7.3	10.2	10.5	12.6
05149	40,780	6	Yell	930.1	21,535	1,750	23.2	76.0	2.0	1.3	1.4	20.5	6.4	18.3	7.8	11.4	11.8	12.8

1. CBSA = Core Based Statistical Area. See Appendix A for explanation. See Appendix B for list of metropolitan areas with component counties. Service of USDA Rural-Urban Continuum Codes. See Appendix A for definition. 3. Dry land or land partially or temporarily covered by water. 2. County type code from the Economic Research 4. May be of any race.

Table B. States and Counties — **Population and Households**

STATE County	Age (percent) (cont.) 55 to 64 years	65 to 74 years	75 years and over	Percent female	Total persons 2000	2010	Percent change 2000-2010	2010-2018	Components of change 2010-2018 Births	Deaths	Net Migration	Households 2013-2017 Number	Persons per household	Family house-holds	Female family house-holder[1]	One person
	16	17	18	19	20	21	22	23	24	25	26	27	28	29	30	31
ARKANSAS—Cont'd																
Cleveland	14.6	12.3	8.7	50.4	8,571	8,692	1.4	-7.8	695	818	-553	3,292	2.50	71.9	13.1	25.8
Columbia	12.3	9.4	8.0	51.8	25,603	24,552	-4.1	-4.1	2,367	2,536	-872	9,337	2.38	66.4	17.4	27.5
Conway	14.6	10.8	8.8	50.9	20,336	21,270	4.6	-1.8	2,036	2,081	-319	8,185	2.53	67.5	14.8	29.5
Craighead	11.0	8.0	5.9	51.4	82,148	96,443	17.4	12.6	11,966	7,451	7,569	39,838	2.52	65.8	13.9	26.9
Crawford	13.3	9.7	7.0	50.7	53,247	61,948	16.3	2.4	6,217	5,132	405	23,870	2.58	73.7	11.4	23.1
Crittenden	12.6	8.4	5.7	52.4	50,866	50,906	0.1	-5.0	6,422	4,040	-4,998	18,659	2.60	64.8	21.8	29.1
Cross	13.7	10.8	8.0	51.8	19,526	17,878	-8.4	-6.7	1,831	1,809	-1,236	6,726	2.52	70.9	15.9	24.6
Dallas	15.6	12.9	10.2	50.6	9,210	8,122	-11.8	-11.6	658	883	-716	3,144	2.21	63.7	14.8	35.1
Desha	14.5	11.0	8.1	52.8	15,341	13,001	-15.3	-11.5	1,364	1,310	-1,564	5,230	2.30	64.3	19.6	33.1
Drew	12.7	9.4	8.1	51.1	18,723	18,517	-1.1	-1.0	1,920	1,649	-473	7,038	2.50	63.6	13.9	28.0
Faulkner	10.9	7.6	4.9	51.1	86,014	113,242	31.7	10.2	12,726	7,339	6,112	43,835	2.66	65.5	11.7	26.7
Franklin	14.0	10.7	8.7	50.0	17,771	18,129	2.0	-1.8	1,591	1,864	-42	6,862	2.55	67.5	10.8	28.0
Fulton	15.3	14.5	11.7	50.9	11,642	12,236	5.1	0.3	884	1,429	584	5,117	2.33	72.0	12.8	22.4
Garland	14.5	13.4	10.4	51.9	88,068	96,000	9.0	3.3	9,095	11,248	5,326	40,062	2.39	62.9	13.1	30.2
Grant	13.8	10.4	7.6	50.6	16,464	17,842	8.4	1.9	1,581	1,561	334	6,851	2.62	73.8	10.8	24.3
Greene	12.0	9.3	6.7	50.8	37,331	42,090	12.7	7.7	4,679	3,928	2,479	16,821	2.59	72.2	13.2	22.9
Hempstead	13.9	9.8	8.2	51.8	23,587	22,593	-4.2	-3.8	2,686	1,963	-1,579	7,930	2.75	68.8	14.0	28.6
Hot Spring	14.0	11.2	7.7	47.6	30,353	33,011	8.8	2.1	2,898	3,194	970	12,291	2.56	69.8	11.4	25.9
Howard	12.9	10.0	8.0	51.9	14,300	13,775	-3.7	-3.2	1,508	1,340	-605	5,042	2.63	69.1	17.3	29.4
Independence	13.1	9.8	7.7	51.2	34,233	36,641	7.0	2.8	3,829	3,460	684	14,288	2.52	69.2	11.3	26.3
Izard	15.1	13.7	12.1	48.1	13,249	13,701	3.4	-0.8	949	1,538	483	5,189	2.43	65.5	6.6	31.3
Jackson	13.5	10.6	7.5	50.3	18,418	17,998	-2.3	-6.6	1,643	1,861	-979	6,179	2.31	60.1	14.2	37.1
Jefferson	13.8	10.3	7.0	50.6	84,278	77,456	-8.1	-12.1	7,614	6,957	-10,135	27,377	2.39	61.3	18.3	34.4
Johnson	12.9	9.5	6.9	50.4	22,781	25,540	12.1	4.7	2,927	2,145	438	9,900	2.56	68.9	11.0	26.8
Lafayette	16.3	12.8	11.2	50.9	8,559	7,643	-10.7	-12.6	606	813	-755	2,860	2.42	63.9	16.0	31.9
Lawrence	13.5	10.6	9.1	50.6	17,774	17,410	-2.0	-5.6	1,562	1,977	-573	6,584	2.46	68.5	10.7	28.4
Lee	12.9	10.9	8.7	43.8	12,580	10,428	-17.1	-13.8	819	982	-1,291	3,541	2.25	61.6	16.6	34.1
Lincoln	11.8	8.5	6.8	38.2	14,492	14,142	-2.4	-5.4	965	1,070	-672	3,928	2.31	72.4	15.2	23.7
Little River	13.8	12.4	8.6	51.8	13,628	13,168	-3.4	-6.4	1,168	1,354	-663	5,300	2.33	62.2	14.6	33.2
Logan	14.3	11.3	8.5	50.1	22,486	22,361	-0.6	-2.8	2,191	2,330	-481	8,269	2.56	70.3	11.9	25.3
Lonoke	12.1	8.0	5.3	50.7	52,828	68,355	29.4	7.8	7,886	5,241	2,692	26,281	2.70	75.3	13.1	20.9
Madison	14.3	11.2	7.8	50.1	14,243	15,722	10.4	4.8	1,715	1,403	454	6,190	2.56	73.7	9.4	23.9
Marion	17.9	17.5	11.1	50.9	16,140	16,646	3.1	0.5	1,314	2,061	831	6,663	2.43	68.1	9.4	28.1
Miller	13.0	9.8	7.1	50.9	40,443	43,462	7.5	0.3	4,968	3,703	-1,108	17,020	2.49	67.3	16.9	27.5
Mississippi	13.1	8.8	6.0	51.3	51,979	46,480	-10.6	-11.3	5,301	4,172	-6,435	17,238	2.48	65.0	19.3	29.9
Monroe	16.1	12.8	10.4	53.5	10,254	8,155	-20.5	-15.4	778	931	-1,117	3,328	2.21	58.1	17.5	37.8
Montgomery	16.4	14.9	12.2	50.5	9,245	9,493	2.7	-6.0	699	1,086	-176	3,855	2.31	68.7	7.5	27.9
Nevada	14.9	11.5	9.2	50.4	9,955	9,020	-9.4	-7.7	881	953	-624	3,452	2.42	65.6	13.3	32.1
Newton	15.9	15.9	10.6	49.3	8,608	8,327	-3.3	-6.3	613	788	-349	3,152	2.49	68.1	6.2	28.4
Ouachita	15.8	11.7	8.7	52.6	28,790	26,128	-9.2	-9.7	2,322	2,931	-1,925	10,016	2.40	63.3	17.6	34.3
Perry	14.3	11.8	8.4	50.6	10,209	10,441	2.3	-0.9	917	1,050	50	3,692	2.74	74.5	9.2	21.3
Phillips	14.6	11.2	7.8	53.0	26,445	21,755	-17.7	-17.1	2,486	2,217	-4,050	7,823	2.47	61.4	22.9	35.3
Pike	14.1	11.5	8.9	50.0	11,303	11,287	-0.1	-5.4	932	1,141	-400	4,313	2.48	67.9	9.9	29.0
Poinsett	13.0	10.3	7.6	51.4	25,614	24,577	-4.0	-2.5	2,586	2,809	-368	9,483	2.50	70.9	16.1	26.5
Polk	14.3	13.2	9.8	51.3	20,229	20,658	2.1	-2.9	1,962	2,218	-340	8,058	2.49	67.7	12.5	28.7
Pope	12.2	9.0	6.7	50.4	54,469	61,754	13.4	3.6	6,569	4,781	466	23,147	2.59	64.3	10.6	29.4
Prairie	15.0	12.3	11.5	49.7	9,539	8,716	-8.6	-7.4	707	867	-483	3,920	2.09	65.1	14.0	31.4
Pulaski	13.0	9.4	6.2	52.2	361,474	382,786	5.9	2.6	45,402	29,651	-5,602	155,435	2.49	60.4	16.0	34.1
Randolph	13.0	10.9	9.1	50.6	18,195	17,970	-1.2	-0.1	1,755	1,988	221	7,339	2.33	68.7	12.7	28.4
St. Francis	12.9	9.8	6.4	44.9	29,329	28,254	-3.7	-10.0	2,830	2,330	-3,353	9,325	2.49	61.9	18.4	34.5
Saline	12.5	10.4	7.4	51.0	83,529	107,130	28.3	13.3	11,015	8,512	11,687	43,314	2.65	71.0	11.6	24.9
Scott	14.1	11.7	9.2	49.3	10,996	11,218	2.0	-8.0	1,019	1,028	-901	3,972	2.65	67.7	12.4	27.5
Searcy	15.7	14.1	10.8	49.9	8,261	8,189	-0.9	-2.8	675	958	55	3,336	2.35	67.6	7.6	28.4
Sebastian	12.8	9.3	6.7	51.1	115,071	125,761	9.3	1.6	14,079	10,315	-1,715	50,301	2.50	64.5	12.8	30.3
Sevier	11.4	8.3	6.2	49.7	15,757	17,059	8.3	0.5	2,257	1,297	-879	5,984	2.85	70.5	13.5	25.9
Sharp	15.0	14.4	11.7	50.7	17,119	17,264	0.8	0.6	1,476	2,137	763	7,296	2.31	62.8	10.3	32.1
Stone	16.6	15.1	12.4	50.8	11,499	12,396	7.8	0.5	1,002	1,409	470	4,910	2.51	67.7	7.1	28.9
Union	14.2	10.4	7.5	51.3	45,629	41,639	-8.7	-6.0	4,258	4,337	-2,449	16,189	2.44	66.5	16.1	30.5
Van Buren	15.8	14.2	11.9	50.3	16,192	17,274	6.7	-3.9	1,353	1,898	-109	6,867	2.41	68.7	10.4	27.4
Washington	10.1	7.0	4.8	50.1	157,715	203,046	28.7	16.7	26,691	12,208	19,281	84,460	2.56	61.8	9.3	27.9
White	12.5	9.5	7.0	50.8	67,165	77,078	14.8	2.1	7,972	6,722	412	29,217	2.56	70.2	12.1	25.3
Woodruff	14.4	13.5	9.6	51.9	8,741	7,264	-16.9	-10.7	642	829	-591	2,874	2.31	60.0	16.8	35.9
Yell	13.6	9.8	8.0	49.8	21,139	22,185	4.9	-2.9	2,347	2,084	-909	7,555	2.81	70.7	13.4	26.3

1. No spouse present.

Table B. States and Counties — Population, Vital Statistics, Health, and Crime

STATE County	Persons in group quarters, 2018	Daytime Population, 2013-2017		Births, 2018		Deaths, 2018		Persons under 65 with no health insurance, 2016		Medicare, 2018			Serious crimes known to police[2], 2016 Total	
		Number	Employment/ residence ratio	Total	Rate[1]	Number	Rate[1]	Number	Percent	Total beneficiaries	Enrolled in Original Medicare	Enrolled in Medicare Advantage	Number	Rate[3]
	32	33	34	35	36	37	38	39	40	41	42	43	44	45
ARKANSAS—Cont'd														
Cleveland	52	6,150	0.33	84	10.5	85	10.6	509	7.7	1,966	1,636	330	116	1,409
Columbia	2,064	23,763	0.98	256	10.9	284	12.1	1,627	9.0	5,116	4,286	830	519	2,165
Conway	286	20,015	0.89	216	10.3	212	10.1	1,470	8.8	5,044	3,986	1,058	747	3,564
Craighead	3,754	109,127	1.10	1,446	13.3	1,005	9.3	8,402	9.5	18,463	14,640	3,823	4,502	4,252
Crawford	540	55,602	0.75	703	11.1	652	10.3	5,088	9.8	13,480	8,202	5,278	2,004	3,253
Crittenden	1,038	46,673	0.87	700	14.5	541	11.2	3,019	7.3	9,015	6,939	2,076	2,810	5,789
Cross	225	16,193	0.86	212	12.7	208	12.5	1,169	8.5	3,888	3,049	839	573	3,338
Dallas	401	7,556	0.99	76	10.6	82	11.4	442	8.1	1,910	1,388	522	235	3,130
Desha	56	12,513	1.10	150	13.0	174	15.1	903	9.5	2,824	2,280	544	NA	NA
Drew	904	17,979	0.92	221	12.1	204	11.1	1,371	9.4	3,749	3,118	631	541	2,879
Faulkner	4,199	111,619	0.83	1,513	12.1	896	7.2	8,558	8.2	19,278	16,408	2,870	4,780	3,886
Franklin	447	16,681	0.83	178	10.0	192	10.8	1,367	9.6	4,198	2,891	1,307	540	3,067
Fulton	165	11,057	0.75	92	7.5	197	16.1	809	9.2	3,566	2,675	891	145	1,189
Garland	2,167	98,994	1.03	1,070	10.8	1,354	13.7	7,596	10.2	28,329	20,970	7,359	5,257	5,402
Grant	143	15,041	0.59	181	10.0	183	10.1	1,005	6.7	3,880	3,172	708	492	2,714
Greene	602	43,113	0.94	570	12.6	503	11.1	2,970	7.9	9,437	7,339	2,098	1,809	4,058
Hempstead	301	22,369	1.02	315	14.5	233	10.7	1,951	10.9	4,639	3,537	1,102	854	3,888
Hot Spring	2,347	30,511	0.77	344	10.2	377	11.2	1,962	7.8	7,695	5,952	1,743	711	2,125
Howard	181	15,698	1.41	168	12.6	164	12.3	1,301	12.0	3,079	2,525	554	247	1,872
Independence	954	38,601	1.10	456	12.1	424	11.3	2,818	9.4	8,451	7,249	1,202	970	2,628
Izard	993	12,981	0.88	115	8.5	193	14.2	1,040	11.4	3,871	2,994	877	281	2,099
Jackson	2,218	17,449	1.00	203	12.1	211	12.6	1,089	9.1	3,787	3,137	650	795	4,626
Jefferson	5,400	73,341	1.07	851	12.5	834	12.2	4,002	7.5	15,336	11,359	3,977	4,146	5,888
Johnson	620	25,949	0.98	357	13.3	248	9.3	2,575	12.1	5,656	4,116	1,540	720	2,744
Lafayette	96	6,331	0.71	78	11.7	97	14.5	522	10.1	1,775	1,506	269	77	1,121
Lawrence	652	15,685	0.83	190	11.6	253	15.4	1,066	8.3	4,315	3,314	1,001	248	1,492
Lee	1,753	9,137	0.83	82	9.1	117	13.0	514	8.8	2,033	1,428	605	258	2,715
Lincoln	3,737	13,171	0.77	104	7.8	154	11.5	849	10.6	2,387	1,947	440	178	1,294
Little River	123	11,833	0.85	156	12.7	170	13.8	862	8.8	3,153	2,517	636	236	1,914
Logan	580	20,517	0.84	274	12.6	292	13.4	1,485	8.7	5,665	4,072	1,593	681	3,156
Lonoke	572	54,972	0.50	936	12.7	682	9.3	4,793	7.6	12,903	10,247	2,656	1,724	2,388
Madison	79	13,119	0.57	243	14.7	141	8.6	1,685	13.0	3,862	2,506	1,356	97	615
Marion	141	15,694	0.87	170	10.2	276	16.5	1,115	9.6	5,285	3,658	1,627	444	2,761
Miller	1,474	39,888	0.78	568	13.0	470	10.8	2,992	8.4	8,648	6,749	1,899	2,221	5,054
Mississippi	813	47,107	1.21	587	14.2	512	12.4	3,061	8.6	8,401	6,236	2,165	2,198	5,089
Monroe	84	7,214	0.93	86	12.5	119	17.2	518	9.5	2,012	1,575	437	232	3,197
Montgomery	121	7,779	0.59	84	9.4	146	16.4	722	11.2	2,613	2,073	540	23	260
Nevada	157	7,796	0.77	104	12.5	101	12.1	543	8.3	2,089	1,626	463	NA	NA
Newton	51	6,769	0.62	72	9.2	102	13.1	580	10.0	2,400	1,813	587	118	1,508
Ouachita	352	23,691	0.93	235	10.0	342	14.5	1,382	7.3	6,163	4,402	1,761	669	2,786
Perry	152	8,190	0.45	115	11.1	135	13.0	802	9.8	2,672	2,082	590	272	2,685
Phillips	246	19,068	0.93	279	15.5	263	14.6	1,260	8.3	4,302	3,205	1,097	NA	NA
Pike	196	9,731	0.73	106	9.9	129	12.1	1,097	12.8	2,723	2,198	525	120	1,118
Poinsett	341	21,144	0.68	329	13.7	337	14.1	1,822	9.4	5,747	4,173	1,574	664	2,775
Polk	155	20,138	0.99	237	11.8	284	14.2	1,878	12.1	5,448	4,552	896	378	1,880
Pope	3,568	64,885	1.06	800	12.5	583	9.1	5,014	9.9	12,445	9,389	3,056	2,284	3,591
Prairie	131	7,013	0.61	76	9.4	109	13.5	670	10.7	2,099	1,737	362	91	1,109
Pulaski	8,776	463,360	1.39	5,112	13.0	3,774	9.6	26,186	7.9	76,239	58,838	17,401	26,117	6,625
Randolph	349	16,412	0.83	226	12.6	257	14.3	1,230	9.1	4,536	3,295	1,241	524	3,019
St. Francis	4,098	26,701	1.00	308	12.1	315	12.4	1,652	9.2	4,941	3,656	1,285	1,380	5,255
Saline	1,430	89,826	0.52	1,318	10.9	1,048	8.6	6,225	6.4	24,778	19,643	5,135	3,770	3,157
Scott	79	10,379	0.95	110	10.7	121	11.7	908	11.1	2,566	1,832	734	234	2,345
Searcy	71	7,208	0.76	92	11.6	111	13.9	589	10.0	2,502	1,867	635	67	859
Sebastian	2,275	141,685	1.26	1,687	13.2	1,265	9.9	12,637	11.9	25,801	17,447	8,354	6,557	5,148
Sevier	173	15,882	0.81	280	16.3	148	8.6	2,690	18.8	2,934	2,482	452	305	1,762
Sharp	189	15,771	0.78	180	10.4	239	13.8	1,286	10.2	5,937	4,617	1,320	NA	NA
Stone	151	12,001	0.90	118	9.5	166	13.3	1,016	11.2	4,162	3,511	651	228	1,830
Union	524	42,600	1.17	480	12.3	547	14.0	2,807	8.6	9,475	7,672	1,803	1,578	3,961
Van Buren	189	15,941	0.85	143	8.6	255	15.4	1,301	10.6	5,082	3,892	1,190	367	2,204
Washington	8,268	225,005	1.01	3,255	13.7	1,558	6.6	23,998	12.3	33,266	24,634	8,632	NA	NA
White	3,334	74,537	0.87	901	11.4	812	10.3	5,486	8.6	16,490	13,352	3,138	NA	NA
Woodruff	106	6,459	0.88	82	12.6	98	15.1	542	10.8	1,831	1,482	349	102	1,536
Yell	323	19,479	0.75	282	13.1	234	10.9	2,250	12.9	4,585	3,524	1,061	437	2,022

1. Per 1,000 estimated resident population.   2. Data for serious crimes have not been adjusted for underreporting; this may affect comparability between geographic areas and over time.   3. Per 100,000 population estimated by the FBI.

Table B. States and Counties — Crime, Education, Money Income, and Poverty

STATE County	Serious crimes known to police[2], 2016 (cont.)[1] Rate Violent	Property	School enrollment and attainment, 2013-2017 Enrollment[3] Total	Percent private	Attainment[4] (percent) High school graduate or less	Bachelor's degree or more	Local government expenditures,[5] 2014-2015 Total current spending (mil dol)	Current spending per student (dollars)	Per capita income[6]	Median income (dollars)	Households Percent with income of less than $50,000	with income of $200,000 or more	Median household income (dollars)	Percent below poverty level All persons	Children under 18 years	Children 5 to 17 years in families
	46	47	48	49	50	51	52	53	54	55	56	57	58	59	60	61
ARKANSAS—Cont'd																
Cleveland	158	1,251	2,011	7.6	57.8	17.0	12.7	8,415	23,171	44,840	55.6	1.6	47,812	14.3	21.1	18.7
Columbia	342	1,823	6,712	5.9	55.6	21.5	35.5	8,787	20,296	37,072	61.5	1.6	38,488	25.5	32.5	34.0
Conway	196	3,369	4,429	9.6	58.5	15.8	44.8	13,605	22,365	39,638	57.7	2.3	43,519	17.2	26.8	25.8
Craighead	434	3,819	29,700	6.1	44.9	26.5	159.4	8,625	25,594	45,672	54.4	3.3	49,355	14.9	19.5	18.8
Crawford	471	2,782	15,206	6.0	53.4	14.5	99.8	9,023	22,104	43,504	56.8	1.5	44,850	17.5	28.1	27.4
Crittenden	1,479	4,310	13,040	7.0	54.3	16.9	94.7	9,141	20,721	38,558	58.7	1.8	39,272	21.1	31.9	30.3
Cross	553	2,785	4,031	4.9	63.2	13.8	31.8	9,180	22,894	41,081	58.9	2.1	41,661	18.4	29.4	28.8
Dallas	626	2,504	1,749	21.3	59.2	14.1	7.4	8,661	18,309	35,794	69.8	0.3	33,739	21	33.5	31.3
Desha	NA	NA	3,033	2.9	63.7	12.6	26.5	9,815	18,187	27,036	70.2	1.7	33,228	29	40.5	37.5
Drew	335	2,544	5,192	10.9	54.9	18.5	39.9	12,635	20,300	36,092	58.6	1.5	41,339	20.3	25.5	23.2
Faulkner	392	3,494	37,129	13.7	39.3	29.7	167.7	8,859	25,240	50,316	49.8	3.0	51,535	13.4	14.8	13.8
Franklin	494	2,573	4,064	9.1	59.1	11.3	28.2	10,052	19,988	39,472	61.0	0.6	41,140	18	25.5	23.8
Fulton	172	1,017	2,424	9.2	54.9	12.1	15.5	9,450	19,674	36,051	64.4	0.4	35,723	20.6	28.9	26.1
Garland	654	4,749	20,522	7.4	42.7	20.1	148.3	9,801	25,690	41,672	57.0	2.7	44,662	15.9	25.2	24.1
Grant	342	2,372	4,099	9.1	52.4	19.0	38.1	7,935	25,814	49,968	50.0	1.1	54,819	12.2	16.4	14.8
Greene	428	3,630	10,964	7.5	55.8	16.1	66.3	8,508	22,094	45,566	53.7	1.8	46,029	14.8	20.3	19.6
Hempstead	692	3,196	5,604	10.2	58.9	13.1	38.8	10,426	18,817	38,701	61.7	1.0	39,505	24.2	37.2	32.6
Hot Spring	230	1,895	7,663	9.0	55.8	13.8	49.1	9,203	20,868	40,626	59.5	1.3	42,329	16.8	23.4	21.4
Howard	205	1,668	3,285	7.5	53.6	15.3	28.6	9,880	23,627	34,851	64.0	2.8	36,744	19.1	28.4	27.9
Independence	496	2,132	8,990	10.4	52.5	18.0	59.1	9,175	23,056	39,945	58.1	2.6	42,332	15.9	21.6	21.5
Izard	254	1,845	2,399	4.4	55.0	12.9	21.2	12,059	19,737	39,135	63.1	1.2	37,958	19.3	28.0	25.8
Jackson	628	3,997	3,530	2.2	65.7	9.2	22.1	9,641	19,458	32,783	67.6	2.5	36,235	22.2	30.5	28.8
Jefferson	1,139	4,749	18,713	12.4	52.9	16.8	122.9	10,306	20,371	37,630	62.0	1.7	38,677	23.5	34.4	33.2
Johnson	267	2,477	5,979	14.1	63.8	15.7	41.5	8,893	18,757	35,758	66.8	0.9	39,798	18.4	24.3	22.5
Lafayette	131	990	1,334	15.7	61.1	15.0	7.0	10,499	25,140	32,500	65.5	2.9	33,378	24.1	35.9	34.0
Lawrence	241	1,251	4,144	12.8	55.7	15.5	33.3	10,446	19,422	37,603	63.0	0.5	40,777	16.9	26.7	24.7
Lee	358	2,357	1,716	12.5	69.3	8.4	10.6	12,289	15,610	27,901	69.7	1.1	28,875	37.3	44.9	40.9
Lincoln	182	1,112	2,327	21.7	71.9	7.9	15.4	9,361	13,142	38,873	59.5	1.1	43,821	23.4	26.1	24.3
Little River	146	1,768	2,536	3.4	55.3	10.3	19.0	9,757	23,412	36,963	59.3	1.5	42,063	17	23.9	21.7
Logan	380	2,776	4,872	8.9	60.6	12.0	36.6	9,219	19,708	37,982	63.6	1.7	37,676	20.5	29.7	29.3
Lonoke	368	2,020	18,814	11.2	45.8	20.1	120.5	8,761	25,184	57,290	43.5	1.8	54,378	11.1	14.9	14.1
Madison	140	476	3,297	10.2	66.2	11.6	20.9	8,911	23,203	42,894	56.3	2.3	40,568	17	25.2	24.2
Marion	348	2,413	2,683	3.4	51.4	16.0	21.3	13,288	19,200	36,113	67.2	0.5	39,539	18.3	31.6	29.2
Miller	476	4,578	9,966	11.1	51.7	15.8	66.4	9,690	22,227	41,862	57.8	1.6	44,325	18.8	28.6	28.7
Mississippi	993	4,096	10,882	4.9	56.9	12.2	77.7	9,841	20,378	36,417	64.7	1.6	39,678	24.3	33.0	30.6
Monroe	482	2,715	1,576	7.4	65.1	9.3	12.4	11,108	20,486	31,584	68.9	2.0	32,427	27.3	41.5	41.6
Montgomery	45	214	1,588	1.3	58.1	12.3	10.5	9,688	21,480	35,252	62.7	1.2	35,500	21.1	35.6	34.3
Nevada	NA	NA	1,908	3.7	59.0	17.0	13.5	9,506	18,644	36,995	64.5	0.4	46,687	19.5	29.4	27.5
Newton	332	1,175	1,680	4.3	59.7	15.7	15.0	11,569	18,053	38,134	65.7	0.7	34,036	19.8	33.0	30.9
Ouachita	621	2,166	5,184	4.6	56.9	15.3	46.1	10,977	19,780	32,136	65.6	1.4	39,576	19.9	27.9	25.9
Perry	523	2,162	2,378	7.8	56.9	12.9	14.2	8,815	21,781	46,168	53.8	1.3	44,118	15.1	23.0	21.7
Phillips	NA	NA	5,198	6.3	55.3	11.3	51.6	12,263	17,287	26,652	72.6	2.1	27,663	39.8	59.4	60.2
Pike	103	1,016	2,347	10.9	53.1	14.9	18.7	9,175	20,180	36,893	63.0	0.5	37,493	18.5	26.5	24.2
Poinsett	322	2,454	5,254	5.0	63.5	9.8	44.9	10,445	18,361	37,487	64.8	0.4	39,778	21	31.9	30.1
Polk	313	1,566	4,335	8.1	54.5	12.5	33.8	9,415	18,735	33,870	69.4	1.1	35,678	22.3	33.4	33.1
Pope	469	3,123	18,101	7.1	50.1	22.2	94.2	9,332	21,650	40,668	58.7	2.6	45,803	16.7	21.5	19.6
Prairie	110	1,000	1,572	6.8	59.5	13.8	11.6	9,223	22,653	41,244	62.9	0.8	43,139	16.1	24.2	23.0
Pulaski	1,109	5,516	97,496	19.3	36.1	33.7	646.9	10,959	29,855	48,850	51.0	4.9	52,361	15	20.3	18.8
Randolph	323	2,696	4,194	6.6	53.8	14.5	20.2	8,334	20,932	35,930	66.0	0.8	35,989	19.4	26.7	24.2
St. Francis	773	4,482	6,122	7.6	60.7	9.5	44.5	10,964	16,518	33,102	67.7	1.4	31,561	33.7	42.0	40.9
Saline	321	2,836	28,159	9.5	42.0	25.5	132.8	7,856	28,410	58,985	41.5	3.3	61,384	7.9	10.6	10.2
Scott	301	2,044	2,180	1.9	62.7	10.2	23.2	9,326	18,077	37,396	68.2	1.1	33,354	20.6	31.3	27.8
Searcy	141	718	1,544	6.7	60.1	13.1	17.2	11,445	21,475	36,716	66.7	1.9	30,640	21.6	35.2	33.6
Sebastian	646	4,502	32,068	9.8	49.2	19.0	192.0	9,486	23,916	40,932	57.8	2.6	44,058	18.6	25.9	23.2
Sevier	295	1,468	4,631	2.9	63.1	10.6	38.7	11,697	18,388	43,675	56.6	0.5	41,649	19.5	29.5	27.8
Sharp	NA	NA	3,408	6.4	59.3	10.5	25.2	8,564	20,078	31,792	69.4	1.1	34,266	23.9	37.0	35.4
Stone	329	1,501	2,476	9.8	56.9	13.4	15.5	8,954	19,881	33,091	67.5	1.1	32,778	21.2	33.3	31.9
Union	610	3,351	10,032	9.9	52.4	20.1	69.9	8,931	23,463	41,106	57.0	2.6	43,827	17.5	24.9	24.9
Van Buren	270	1,934	3,103	8.9	60.7	12.9	26.1	11,429	20,568	34,428	66.9	0.9	36,244	19.8	28.2	25.6
Washington	NA	NA	69,296	9.2	42.4	31.9	390.9	9,656	26,371	47,452	52.6	4.2	50,400	13.8	16.8	15.7
White	NA	NA	21,663	30.1	53.8	20.8	120.4	9,242	23,120	44,074	54.9	2.8	44,088	15.2	21.0	20.0
Woodruff	136	1,400	1,257	3.3	65.2	11.4	12.0	11,137	19,987	30,097	68.3	1.4	32,271	26.8	39.3	35.1
Yell	338	1,684	5,176	3.8	63.9	13.7	41.4	9,582	20,209	39,696	59.9	1.3	40,325	18.8	27.8	25.6

1. Data for serious crimes have not been adjusted for underreporting; this may affect comparability between geographic areas and over time.   2. Per 100,000 population estimated by the FBI.   3. All persons 3 years old and over enrolled in nursery school through college.   4. Persons 25 years old and over.   5. Elementary and secondary education expenditures.   6. Based on population estimated by the American Community Survey, 2013–2017.

Table B. States and Counties — Personal Income and Earnings

| STATE County | Personal income, 2017 | | | | | | | | | | Earnings, 2017 | | |
| | | | Per capita[1] | | | Supplements to wages and salaries, employer contributions (mil dol) | | | | | | | Contributions for government social insurance (mil dol) | |
	Total (mil dol)	Percent change 2016-2017	Dollars	Rank	Wages and salaries (mil dol)	Pension and insurance	Government social insurance	Proprietors' income (mil dol)	Dividends, interest, and rent (mil dol)	Personal transfer receipts (mil dol)	Total (mil dol)	From employee and self-employed	From employer
	62	63	64	65	66	67	68	69	70	71	72	73	74
ARKANSAS—Cont'd													
Cleveland	313	5.3	38,144	1,857	35	7	3	37	34	90	82	6	3
Columbia	877	6.7	37,104	2,014	354	64	27	58	145	258	503	34	27
Conway	774	3.1	37,012	2,031	265	44	20	75	110	234	404	27	20
Craighead	3,852	3.2	35,963	2,206	2,134	335	164	297	516	948	2,929	187	164
Crawford	2,021	3.8	32,076	2,744	779	118	60	97	241	594	1,054	77	60
Crittenden	1,784	4.9	36,589	2,105	666	110	52	157	205	508	985	65	52
Cross	575	3.1	34,106	2,473	186	31	15	30	77	188	262	20	15
Dallas	243	2.3	32,911	2,625	99	15	8	4	32	100	127	10	8
Desha	416	-1.9	35,361	2,292	182	29	15	46	61	152	271	17	15
Drew	650	2.8	35,057	2,343	255	46	19	71	90	194	391	25	19
Faulkner	4,441	3.0	35,918	2,210	1,817	268	136	168	565	1,013	2,389	160	136
Franklin	592	5.4	33,102	2,602	184	39	14	39	85	179	276	19	14
Fulton	333	3.4	27,598	3,043	67	14	5	20	51	146	106	11	5
Garland	3,775	4.3	38,259	1,834	1,477	214	113	283	731	1,189	2,087	157	113
Grant	672	2.7	36,975	2,040	174	27	13	28	80	169	241	19	13
Greene	1,505	4.9	33,405	2,569	621	105	49	125	190	440	900	61	49
Hempstead	687	5.9	31,407	2,818	304	54	24	57	84	231	438	29	24
Hot Spring	995	3.9	29,628	2,951	348	60	26	45	134	347	479	38	26
Howard	463	6.1	34,352	2,434	253	45	20	59	56	142	377	23	20
Independence	1,259	3.9	33,558	2,547	639	106	50	100	184	391	895	60	50
Izard	395	2.3	28,838	2,993	113	22	9	29	60	159	172	15	9
Jackson	559	-2.7	32,623	2,672	210	36	16	78	69	188	341	24	16
Jefferson	2,336	0.3	33,796	2,507	1,280	236	103	109	334	784	1,728	114	103
Johnson	762	4.6	28,716	3,002	308	53	24	61	89	244	446	31	24
Lafayette	241	1.7	35,108	2,335	46	9	4	25	38	80	84	6	4
Lawrence	554	5.6	33,534	2,551	150	27	12	61	79	201	250	18	12
Lee	249	-0.7	27,174	3,057	72	14	6	14	39	104	105	8	6
Lincoln	348	-0.8	25,489	3,086	110	23	9	32	39	116	174	12	9
Little River	427	3.7	34,547	2,407	183	26	13	26	54	140	248	18	13
Logan	725	4.4	33,395	2,570	199	37	15	75	91	268	326	23	15
Lonoke	2,747	3.8	37,686	1,925	551	84	42	104	379	630	781	60	42
Madison	587	9.5	35,934	2,208	133	23	10	77	70	147	243	16	10
Marion	486	3.9	29,581	2,953	126	28	10	21	85	204	184	18	10
Miller	1,433	2.5	32,577	2,680	553	84	41	85	213	410	763	55	41
Mississippi	1,102	-8.3	26,139	3,077	905	133	70	-232	189	455	875	77	70
Monroe	225	-0.3	31,816	2,778	76	12	6	11	35	96	106	9	6
Montgomery	262	4.5	29,336	2,964	45	9	4	28	41	102	86	8	4
Nevada	276	4.1	33,148	2,600	98	16	7	23	36	105	144	10	7
Newton	222	3.7	28,297	3,020	33	7	3	15	38	89	58	7	3
Ouachita	840	2.4	35,209	2,310	273	52	20	21	111	283	366	29	20
Perry	349	4.3	33,750	2,518	46	8	4	24	45	108	82	8	4
Phillips	553	1.6	29,762	2,944	201	37	16	0	84	246	255	21	16
Pike	343	5.6	31,975	2,754	90	16	7	28	57	117	141	11	7
Poinsett	743	5.7	30,758	2,870	214	35	17	46	84	283	312	25	17
Polk	597	5.6	29,674	2,948	199	38	16	73	89	222	326	24	16
Pope	2,162	3.0	33,875	2,499	1,174	191	93	112	291	585	1,569	102	93
Prairie	274	3.0	33,271	2,584	61	10	5	19	41	90	95	8	5
Pulaski	19,240	2.8	48,838	553	13,871	2,151	1,038	1,453	3,857	3,814	18,512	1,120	1,038
Randolph	569	8.9	32,433	2,700	183	34	15	43	76	211	274	21	15
St. Francis	714	4.9	27,538	3,046	301	59	24	62	91	273	446	30	24
Saline	4,801	3.5	40,232	1,513	969	139	73	214	592	1,123	1,395	113	73
Scott	316	7.4	30,278	2,905	101	20	8	43	42	110	171	12	8
Searcy	213	0.9	26,884	3,061	48	9	4	12	36	97	73	8	4
Sebastian	5,160	3.0	40,280	1,505	3,017	456	228	541	891	1,204	4,241	268	228
Sevier	523	4.8	30,532	2,884	187	33	16	56	60	144	291	18	16
Sharp	550	4.5	31,610	2,797	131	22	10	43	79	250	206	19	10
Stone	369	4.6	29,452	2,958	86	16	7	28	75	163	136	13	7
Union	1,729	11.0	43,836	1,038	901	151	65	163	328	439	1,280	84	65
Van Buren	502	2.3	30,426	2,893	149	26	11	17	94	205	203	19	11
Washington	9,021	5.8	38,883	1,740	5,457	793	383	796	1,448	1,529	7,429	452	383
White	2,677	3.0	33,881	2,496	974	148	75	141	399	757	1,337	98	75
Woodruff	230	5.3	34,945	2,358	72	13	6	20	32	88	111	8	6
Yell	693	5.7	32,189	2,728	226	42	18	68	90	218	353	24	18

1. Based on the resident population estimated as of July 1 of the year shown.

Table B. States and Counties — Earnings, Social Security, and Housing

STATE County	Earnings, 2017 (cont.) Percent by selected industries									Social Security beneficiaries, December 2017		Supplemental Security Income recipients, 2017	Housing units, 2018	
	Farm	Mining, quarrying, and extractions	Construction	Manufacturing	Information; professional, scientific, technical services	Retail trade	Finance, insurance, real estate, and leasing	Health care and social assistance	Government	Number	Rate[1]		Total	Percent change, 2010-2018
	75	76	77	78	79	80	81	82	83	84	85	86	87	88
ARKANSAS—Cont'd														
Cleveland	37.1	0	D	4.9	D	1.8	D	6	20	2,135	260	276	4,105	1
Columbia	2.5	9.7	2.9	27.6	D	5.8	4.3	D	21.5	5,770	244	1,206	11,660	0.6
Conway	11	1.4	11.2	15.9	1.4	6.9	2.9	D	18.4	5,710	273	905	9,850	1.4
Craighead	0.2	D	6.4	14.3	4.4	7.9	4.7	23.5	15.7	20,715	193	4,013	46,255	14.2
Crawford	2.2	0.7	7.9	22.5	D	6.6	3.2	6.9	12	15,415	245	2,032	26,977	3.3
Crittenden	2.5	D	6.1	14.6	2.4	6.9	3.5	10.2	15.1	10,355	212	3,286	21,822	1.5
Cross	0.3	0	2.7	6.7	3	14	6.2	D	23.4	4,380	260	784	8,001	1.9
Dallas	0.4	0	3	24.4	1.5	8.6	3.5	D	12.5	2,185	296	406	4,318	0.3
Desha	13.1	0.1	3.2	24.2	1.7	5.3	3.6	D	17.3	3,245	276	729	6,304	0.7
Drew	5.6	0.1	7.1	11.5	D	7.4	4	D	26.6	4,255	229	719	8,624	2.5
Faulkner	-0.1	1.5	9.4	8	13.6	8.5	4.4	13.9	18.3	21,225	172	2,756	50,522	8.4
Franklin	8.3	5.2	4	18.3	D	7	1.7	D	21.5	4,750	266	544	8,086	0.8
Fulton	3.2	D	8.7	3.8	3.1	5.6	4.3	D	28.4	4,095	340	443	6,843	1
Garland	0.3	0.3	10.2	6.9	4.7	10.5	6	22	13.3	30,465	309	3,994	51,026	1
Grant	2.1	D	8	31.7	D	7.1	D	D	18.1	4,175	230	401	8,046	3.8
Greene	3.3	D	5.4	33.5	D	7.8	4.4	12.2	13.2	10,730	238	1,750	19,166	7.1
Hempstead	8.5	D	3.7	28.8	2.1	6.1	2.5	D	20.6	5,230	239	1,029	10,539	1.2
Hot Spring	0	D	6.7	19.4	D	5.8	3	D	21	8,745	260	1,169	14,462	0.6
Howard	10.8	D	4.1	40	D	5.6	D	9.8	11.4	3,415	253	518	6,274	0.7
Independence	2.5	D	5.4	19	D	7	4.6	22.4	12.3	9,590	256	1,177	16,591	2.5
Izard	4.5	D	6.8	7.6	D	6.9	6.4	16.9	27.6	4,585	335	524	7,297	0.9
Jackson	4.3	1.6	2.6	23.8	4.1	7.3	2.4	D	20.8	4,250	248	733	7,587	-0.2
Jefferson	2.1	0.1	2.8	19.4	2.1	5.9	3.7	14.7	29.1	16,535	239	4,369	33,387	1.1
Johnson	5.7	D	5.4	26.8	1.6	6.1	3	D	14.8	6,415	242	961	11,542	2
Lafayette	26	1.4	10.8	4.4	D	D	2.9	7.7	23.6	2,010	293	426	4,390	0.9
Lawrence	14.9	1	5.5	9	D	8.1	2.6	D	23	4,880	295	889	8,009	0.2
Lee	3.7	0.1	D	D	D	6.2	D	D	31.8	2,225	242	709	4,365	0.2
Lincoln	12.7	D	6.8	6.5	D	3.1	2.1	D	37.1	2,650	194	519	4,944	1.7
Little River	6.1	D	5	47.9	D	5.6	1.4	3.2	16	3,460	280	411	6,527	1.1
Logan	15.2	1.7	6.2	19	2.4	7.5	3.8	9.3	20.1	6,370	293	912	10,191	0.8
Lonoke	2	D	12.1	13.1	5.2	8.5	6.7	9.5	19.6	14,215	195	1,888	29,755	9.2
Madison	20.3	0.1	6	22.8	4.3	7	2.1	4.6	14.8	4,365	267	467	7,586	1.4
Marion	0.3	D	7	41.3	D	7.3	5.4	6.8	14.3	5,840	355	531	9,531	1.9
Miller	-0.2	1.3	8.3	23.2	D	5.1	3.6	D	15.3	9,615	219	2,073	19,597	1.6
Mississippi	-8.1	D	7.8	38.9	1.6	5.9	3.5	D	15.3	9,955	236	3,040	20,612	0.7
Monroe	5	0	2.5	5.5	D	7.6	5.4	D	19.6	2,175	307	531	4,452	-0.2
Montgomery	15.3	D	10.2	2.4	1.4	5	3.8	3.6	28.3	2,870	322	319	5,860	1.7
Nevada	9	0.1	D	D	D	6.1	2.3	9.5	14	2,385	286	453	4,582	0.2
Newton	1.4	0.1	12.3	3.2	D	D	D	D	35.1	2,770	354	353	4,707	1
Ouachita	0.8	1.2	3.9	12.1	3	7.8	3.6	D	25.1	6,865	288	1,313	13,085	-0.3
Perry	12.8	D	14.5	2.4	D	3.8	D	D	23.2	2,845	275	420	4,990	1.7
Phillips	-8	0	3	9.2	D	8.5	5	17.9	24.2	4,935	266	1,733	10,257	1.3
Pike	7.5	D	8.4	11.5	D	7.8	8.8	D	20	3,105	289	352	5,653	1.3
Poinsett	3.2	0.6	5.7	13.3	2	6.4	3.6	11.5	20.2	6,480	268	1,446	11,013	0.8
Polk	9.3	0.8	6.1	18.3	2.5	7.1	4.5	D	16	6,085	302	677	10,131	1.3
Pope	2.3	0.8	8.4	15.4	4	6.5	4.1	9.7	15.6	14,100	221	1,987	26,437	3.5
Prairie	12.6	0.1	4.8	2.2	D	6.4	3.4	10.3	19.7	2,425	294	309	4,545	0.9
Pulaski	0.1	0.2	4.6	5.1	10.8	6.5	9.6	13.9	23.7	81,045	206	16,348	185,966	5.9
Randolph	2.3	D	7.1	21.2	D	6.9	4.1	D	20	5,165	294	704	8,608	1.1
St. Francis	5.8	0	D	D	2	7.8	3.1	D	31.6	5,625	217	1,838	10,970	0.6
Saline	0	D	13.5	6.3	5	12.8	4.7	16.8	16.3	26,900	225	2,746	49,317	10
Scott	16.8	0	3.6	27.1	D	4.3	1.4	D	18.6	3,010	288	410	5,276	1.7
Searcy	-6.5	0	D	10.1	D	7.4	3.3	17	25.4	2,855	360	422	4,933	0.7
Sebastian	0.6	1.4	4.1	17.7	4.7	6.5	9.1	17.9	11.6	28,500	222	4,247	57,218	4.7
Sevier	13.5	D	5.8	D	D	7.1	3.9	8.2	20.1	3,245	190	452	6,959	1
Sharp	5.3	D	8.7	3.6	D	10.6	4.9	D	17.8	6,440	370	913	9,882	0.6
Stone	4.7	0	7.1	5.6	D	13.5	7.2	D	20.8	4,570	365	573	6,882	2.5
Union	0.3	8.7	8.3	20.7	2.2	5.5	3.2	9.8	10.2	10,665	270	1,792	20,081	2.2
Van Buren	-1.5	D	4.7	2.9	D	8.8	D	D	17	5,580	338	617	10,463	1.2
Washington	1.1	D	6.9	10.5	5.6	6.5	5.4	12.8	17.6	36,075	155	4,451	95,013	8.2
White	0.1	0.8	7.4	9.3	3.4	9	5.1	18.2	13.7	18,510	234	2,655	33,942	4.5
Woodruff	19.3	D	2.9	11.2	D	4.3	2.8	9.4	20.8	1,995	304	398	3,888	-0.2
Yell	12.1	D	6	27.5	D	4.4	D	D	19.9	5,340	248	788	9,919	1.7

1. Per 1,000 resident population estimated as of July 1 of the year shown.

Table B. States and Counties — Housing, Labor Force, and Employment

STATE County	Housing units, 2013-2017 Occupied units Owner-occupied Total	Percent	Median value[1]	Median owner cost as a percent of income With a mortgage	Without a mortgage[2]	Renter-occupied Median rent[3]	Median rent as a percent of income[2]	Sub-standard units[4] (percent)	Civilian labor force, 2018 Total	Percent change, 2017-2018	Unemployment Total	Rate[5]	Civilian employment[6], 2013-2017 Total	Percent Management, business, science, and arts	Construction, production, and maintenance occupations
	89	90	91	92	93	94	95	96	97	98	99	100	101	102	103
ARKANSAS—Cont'd															
Cleveland	3,292	74.0	87,200	18.4	10.5	621	23.1	1	3,302	-0.8	129	3.9	3,362	30.1	35.5
Columbia	9,337	65.7	76,200	19.1	11.0	664	27.9	4.2	8,991	-0.8	429	4.8	9,877	28.9	29.5
Conway	8,185	70.9	98,700	20.6	10.0	627	32.1	2.7	8,198	-0.4	358	4.4	8,377	26.3	32.5
Craighead	39,838	58.3	134,600	17.6	10.0	731	28.8	2.6	54,120	0.9	1,658	3.1	48,216	34.3	26.2
Crawford	23,870	75.7	112,500	19.3	11.5	667	28	3.2	26,861	-0.3	962	3.6	25,751	29.7	30.2
Crittenden	18,659	56.7	106,300	19.5	10.5	713	32.3	4.2	21,467	0.3	925	4.3	20,282	29.4	29.1
Cross	6,726	67.5	79,400	17.9	11.6	663	26.8	1.8	7,441	-2.8	310	4.2	7,242	26.0	32.5
Dallas	3,144	68.6	64,500	20.6	11.4	655	24.5	0.9	2,811	-0.6	124	4.4	2,910	18.6	39.6
Desha	5,230	58.1	56,700	19.5	12.4	533	29.6	2	5,443	-0.1	247	4.5	4,440	27.4	31.5
Drew	7,038	65.7	93,200	17.3	10.4	647	33.7	1.5	7,757	-0.5	388	5	7,629	34.2	22.7
Faulkner	43,835	62.3	153,500	19.4	10.0	777	29.8	3.1	61,476	0.1	2,016	3.3	57,306	36.0	21.4
Franklin	6,862	73.6	90,600	16.9	10.0	598	29.8	3	7,406	0	266	3.6	6,598	27.5	32.9
Fulton	5,117	78.1	91,300	21.5	10.5	504	31.9	5.6	4,805	1.8	192	4	4,132	29.7	30.0
Garland	40,062	67.0	131,500	19.6	10.1	721	33.2	2.7	40,797	1.1	1,651	4	39,800	31.8	22.2
Grant	6,851	79.8	123,500	17.6	10.6	727	25.4	2.5	8,321	-0.1	259	3.1	7,561	31.4	31.6
Greene	16,821	67.3	110,400	18.0	11.6	717	27.3	2	19,755	0.1	691	3.5	19,093	27.8	34.3
Hempstead	7,930	68.9	76,200	18.9	10.5	624	32.2	3.5	9,908	0.8	353	3.6	8,819	26.9	36.6
Hot Spring	12,291	74.8	88,900	19.3	10.5	655	29.5	2.6	13,993	-0.7	527	3.8	13,378	30.4	29.5
Howard	5,042	66.2	94,100	20.7	10.5	555	28.1	3.3	5,922	-0.8	205	3.5	5,560	27.1	42.1
Independence	14,288	70.7	104,400	20.2	10.0	618	29.5	3.3	16,222	0.5	662	4.1	15,305	29.6	33.5
Izard	5,189	78.7	79,400	21.8	10.7	576	27	1.5	4,869	-0.2	270	5.5	4,615	30.3	28.1
Jackson	6,179	70.6	61,300	18.3	11.3	576	28.9	3.5	5,786	-1.7	356	6.2	5,700	22.3	38.7
Jefferson	27,377	63.5	81,800	20.5	10.1	702	29.4	2.2	28,066	0.2	1,484	5.3	26,874	27.9	29.3
Johnson	9,900	70.8	95,400	21.0	10.3	605	29.3	5.2	10,445	-1.2	473	4.5	10,427	25.9	38.2
Lafayette	2,860	72.6	65,900	20.6	10.0	406	32.1	1.8	2,497	-0.4	131	5.2	2,580	26.9	36.4
Lawrence	6,584	67.2	77,100	18.6	10.7	529	25.8	1.5	6,858	0	269	3.9	6,448	27.9	30.8
Lee	3,541	55.4	67,100	20.8	13.5	542	31.8	2.5	2,917	-1.8	141	4.8	2,842	20.8	36.9
Lincoln	3,928	75.0	66,100	19.2	10.0	539	28.3	4.8	4,041	-0.3	174	4.3	3,359	25.6	32.6
Little River	5,300	69.6	72,400	17.4	10.0	543	29	1.8	5,485	-0.3	289	5.3	4,623	26.3	42.4
Logan	8,269	73.3	90,400	18.8	10.5	562	23.8	2.9	8,749	-1.7	353	4	8,339	27.5	34.2
Lonoke	26,281	68.5	135,100	19.0	10.0	764	26.9	3	33,853	-0.1	1,087	3.2	32,577	34.6	25.4
Madison	6,190	76.5	108,500	19.1	10.0	644	26.6	4	7,426	0.7	213	2.9	6,557	29.3	35.9
Marion	6,663	78.4	117,300	22.7	10.0	586	28.8	2.9	6,506	0.4	269	4.1	5,353	26.0	31.1
Miller	17,020	63.5	108,500	18.3	10.5	710	31.4	3	19,722	-0.3	950	4.8	18,399	30.3	27.4
Mississippi	17,238	56.4	81,400	18.8	10.5	619	28.4	3.6	17,510	-1.6	995	5.7	17,270	22.8	36.5
Monroe	3,328	61.7	54,500	18.8	10.0	492	29.8	2.8	2,746	-1.9	119	4.3	2,954	20.5	29.8
Montgomery	3,855	81.6	96,900	21.9	11.6	551	24	3.6	3,036	-1.1	146	4.8	3,248	29.1	33.1
Nevada	3,452	74.5	62,700	22.5	10.0	661	32.1	5.1	3,613	1	128	3.5	3,294	28.9	35.4
Newton	3,152	85.1	91,600	21.7	10.0	474	25.7	5.6	3,312	-0.4	112	3.4	3,114	27.8	32.6
Ouachita	10,016	67.2	67,900	18.1	11.7	542	29.4	3.6	9,755	0.9	454	4.7	9,290	30.5	32.5
Perry	3,692	81.4	99,100	20.3	10.0	663	23.4	3.2	4,248	0	177	4.2	3,943	28.7	28.8
Phillips	7,823	47.6	67,100	21.4	11.1	571	31	2.4	6,608	1.1	406	6.1	6,718	25.9	28.5
Pike	4,313	77.2	78,600	20.3	10.0	512	26.2	2.9	4,255	0.3	177	4.2	4,466	26.9	36.5
Poinsett	9,483	64.7	78,200	19.8	10.6	564	26.8	5.7	10,269	0	395	3.8	9,492	24.3	35.5
Polk	8,058	76.3	87,100	26.2	10.0	539	26.8	5.4	8,003	0	333	4.2	7,222	28.4	33.5
Pope	23,147	67.0	126,100	19.3	10.5	660	29.3	2.8	28,998	-0.2	1,296	4.5	27,026	30.2	29.5
Prairie	3,920	70.8	65,300	19.1	11.1	539	23.9	4.5	3,568	-3.5	139	3.9	3,454	28.1	36.7
Pulaski	155,435	58.9	148,300	19.8	10.0	825	29.4	2.2	189,210	0.3	6,598	3.5	182,512	41.2	16.7
Randolph	7,339	72.0	81,500	19.1	10.0	578	31.1	3.5	7,175	3.6	285	4	6,549	29.7	35.2
St. Francis	9,325	58.6	61,900	21.7	10.8	593	31.3	2.6	8,320	-0.4	429	5.2	8,677	23.2	37.0
Saline	43,341	77.2	147,400	18.8	10.0	812	24.7	2.5	57,716	0.3	1,793	3.1	55,741	35.4	21.5
Scott	3,972	73.8	69,800	19.0	10.0	492	33.6	3.9	4,380	-0.3	161	3.7	4,069	23.7	41.7
Searcy	3,336	79.4	89,700	19.5	10.0	500	34.4	3.5	2,957	0.7	128	4.3	3,082	25.0	41.8
Sebastian	50,301	59.8	116,800	19.8	10.0	655	27.9	3.1	57,075	-0.3	2,043	3.6	55,376	29.4	28.9
Sevier	5,984	75.3	75,400	19.1	10.0	547	24.3	8.5	5,549	-0.9	259	4.7	7,225	21.2	45.0
Sharp	7,296	73.5	79,900	21.1	10.0	578	32.4	4.5	5,798	-2.8	276	4.8	5,867	26.6	30.8
Stone	4,910	77.2	107,300	26.7	10.2	585	30.4	3.2	4,801	0.1	218	4.5	4,345	31.4	35.9
Union	16,189	73.5	79,900	17.9	11.3	650	29.7	5.1	15,960	-0.6	886	5.6	15,544	33.4	28.2
Van Buren	6,867	77.0	98,900	23.4	11.8	616	34	2.8	5,921	-2	311	5.3	5,646	26.9	32.4
Washington	84,460	53.3	162,900	18.5	10.0	743	27.5	4.6	122,569	1.5	3,191	2.6	106,905	37.5	23.7
White	29,217	67.2	116,400	18.1	11.0	686	28.2	2.2	33,786	0.4	1,478	4.4	32,331	33.4	27.9
Woodruff	2,874	65.8	63,700	18.1	12.9	484	31.4	1.7	2,829	-3.3	134	4.7	2,603	35.4	27.0
Yell	7,555	70.9	100,300	21.0	10.0	595	23.4	4.7	8,505	-0.5	357	4.2	8,852	23.5	39.5

1. Specified owner-occupied units.　2. A value of 10.0 represents 10 percent or less; a value of 50.0 represents 50 percent or more.　3. Specified renter-occupied units.　4. Overcrowded or lacking complete plumbing facilities.　5. Percent of civilian labor force.　6. Civilian employed persons 16 years old and over.

Table B. States and Counties — Nonfarm Employment and Agriculture

STATE County	Private nonfarm establishments, employment and payroll, 2016									Agriculture, 2017			
	Number of establish-ments	Employment						Annual payroll		Farms			Farm producers whose primary occupation is farming (percent)
		Total	Health care and social assistance	Manufac-turing	Retail trade	Finance and insurance	Professional, scientific, and technical services	Total (mil dol)	Average per employee (dollars)	Number	Percent with:		
											Fewer than 50 acres	1000 acres or more	
	104	105	106	107	108	109	110	111	112	113	114	115	116

STATE County	104	105	106	107	108	109	110	111	112	113	114	115	116
ARKANSAS—Cont'd													
Cleveland	74	488	115	64	65	D	D	16	32,270	205	28.8	1.0	53.8
Columbia	558	7,176	1,159	2,016	989	260	313	267	37,224	297	32.3	2.0	33.3
Conway	412	4,682	520	811	865	126	73	170	36,227	768	28.9	3.4	43.2
Craighead	2,480	43,051	10,872	6,071	7,455	1,077	1,011	1,575	36,582	523	32.3	20.8	43.1
Crawford	1,061	17,759	1,676	3,973	1,972	402	276	581	32,702	799	44.2	2.1	35.4
Crittenden	825	13,964	1,981	1,610	2,255	218	237	441	31,579	262	26.7	34.7	53.6
Cross	343	3,732	791	535	792	177	77	116	31,157	300	18.3	28.0	57.8
Dallas	189	2,397	727	574	366	61	36	67	28,024	126	19.8	3.2	42.2
Desha	301	3,564	494	885	652	130	55	117	32,800	275	19.6	34.9	45.0
Drew	409	4,770	1,008	706	986	181	88	154	32,235	318	23.6	10.1	32.7
Faulkner	2,522	35,065	5,340	3,739	6,052	1,018	1,080	1,321	37,684	1,191	43.7	2.9	35.9
Franklin	278	3,411	532	839	591	278	80	117	34,431	752	25.5	5.5	40.9
Fulton	160	1,421	590	101	213	71	30	36	25,574	795	19.2	4.2	40.2
Garland	2,712	33,063	7,261	2,375	6,152	1,011	1,529	1,060	32,070	357	47.6	0.3	38.5
Grant	270	3,358	227	1,231	484	79	98	107	31,926	281	44.1	0.7	31.1
Greene	778	14,289	1,647	4,690	2,051	590	357	510	35,686	631	37.6	10.3	36.5
Hempstead	377	6,221	1,019	2,338	888	165	123	195	31,339	613	19.7	6.0	47.7
Hot Spring	481	5,741	1,168	1,253	900	206	75	202	35,191	563	44.2	1.4	36.7
Howard	285	5,846	784	2,964	574	101	33	189	32,359	586	27.8	1.9	44.2
Independence	786	14,012	2,904	3,534	1,916	381	194	507	36,219	890	23.6	4.7	37.4
Izard	227	1,998	577	221	401	94	28	60	30,211	632	19.1	6.6	44.3
Jackson	316	4,043	809	1,145	831	100	83	137	33,799	424	22.9	18.9	54.5
Jefferson	1,330	20,658	3,889	5,227	3,415	768	276	739	35,779	436	36.0	17.4	43.8
Johnson	393	7,519	958	2,683	969	139	79	219	29,063	577	26.7	1.9	46.8
Lafayette	103	706	125	46	129	53	23	24	33,865	287	17.4	10.8	43.0
Lawrence	284	3,007	645	455	637	82	36	86	28,519	535	24.3	12.5	43.2
Lee	118	899	271	D	169	41	29	31	34,478	221	14.5	27.1	60.2
Lincoln	162	1,414	277	307	236	55	17	47	33,211	369	33.6	16.3	46.6
Little River	169	2,676	300	1,264	418	63	55	132	49,227	414	17.9	6.5	39.2
Logan	373	4,070	663	1,117	755	215	53	131	32,121	873	24.6	3.2	42.7
Lonoke	1,044	11,507	1,629	1,839	2,076	533	422	354	30,789	702	35.6	13.8	42.7
Madison	187	2,479	227	891	511	80	44	76	30,841	1,229	21.2	3.3	45.9
Marion	206	2,827	275	1,386	494	130	69	81	28,518	587	25.4	6.5	43.6
Miller	735	11,331	1,056	2,468	1,417	362	145	436	38,471	513	37.2	6.0	36.9
Mississippi	790	17,271	1,750	4,644	1,833	252	81	653	37,795	284	16.5	48.6	73.2
Monroe	188	1,647	298	112	298	63	19	48	28,985	186	20.4	35.5	38.3
Montgomery	131	820	71	40	129	47	11	26	31,513	428	30.4	1.2	46.8
Nevada	120	2,094	448	D	274	41	26	73	34,817	355	26.5	3.1	36.6
Newton	89	942	259	70	103	D	D	25	26,203	537	19.4	1.5	38.5
Ouachita	500	7,469	1,230	2,622	945	196	143	285	38,174	205	42.9	0.5	26.9
Perry	102	906	196	D	159	20	13	25	27,975	397	29.2	1.3	42.7
Phillips	395	4,017	959	277	918	105	86	121	30,164	231	10.8	45.5	68.2
Pike	206	1,942	264	254	320	84	50	52	27,022	394	19.5	2.5	44.0
Poinsett	361	3,506	690	648	712	113	41	115	32,716	363	23.1	30.9	59.7
Polk	436	4,939	1,025	1,259	868	143	72	146	29,629	793	32.4	1.1	44.6
Pope	1,574	23,014	3,278	4,624	3,475	1,403	718	856	37,201	919	39.0	1.7	39.6
Prairie	148	907	165	D	204	39	28	25	27,791	350	13.7	26.3	49.9
Pulaski	12,079	206,244	41,794	12,679	27,174	12,955	11,746	9,254	44,868	411	56.4	5.4	37.7
Randolph	319	3,394	827	606	726	114	57	95	28,126	657	21.0	7.8	44.3
St. Francis	435	5,538	1,284	777	1,026	179	112	166	29,962	278	28.1	29.1	55.4
Saline	1,887	21,703	4,706	1,410	4,233	518	647	669	30,833	371	52.3	0.5	32.0
Scott	136	1,890	242	859	304	43	10	57	30,152	528	23.9	1.3	45.0
Searcy	110	1,037	306	180	205	39	8	23	21,805	631	15.1	7.3	44.2
Sebastian	3,368	62,998	11,096	13,510	8,542	1,536	1,356	2,512	39,882	706	43.9	2.3	35.8
Sevier	255	4,030	550	D	740	136	69	124	30,890	540	27.0	3.0	44.2
Sharp	313	2,579	637	110	723	161	32	64	24,665	622	18.6	2.9	43.8
Stone	222	1,908	459	160	495	107	37	52	27,029	526	19.0	3.4	40.6
Union	1,087	16,620	2,201	3,373	2,171	425	448	782	47,046	268	39.6	0.4	32.3
Van Buren	326	3,626	733	72	601	82	43	126	34,827	611	22.3	2.1	36.1
Washington	5,312	88,197	14,671	13,010	12,962	2,316	3,908	3,589	40,691	2,279	42.7	1.1	37.6
White	1,540	22,615	4,614	1,894	3,821	640	497	730	32,298	1,613	34.2	3.7	37.7
Woodruff	130	1,229	129	225	277	50	7	46	37,693	187	16.0	36.9	52.5
Yell	300	4,788	999	1,725	560	180	92	152	31,811	718	21.2	4.3	46.7

Table B. States and Counties — **Agriculture**

STATE County	Land in farms					Value of land and buildings (dollars)		Value of machinery and equipment, average per farm (dollars)	Value of products sold:				Organic farms (number)	Farms with internet access (percent)	Government payments	
	Acreage (1,000)	Percent change, 2012-2017	Acres: Average size of farm	Acres: Total irrigated (1,000)	Total cropland (1,000)	Average per farm	Average per acre		Total (mil dol)	Average per farm (acres)	Percent from: Crops	Percent from: Livestock and poultry products			Total ($1,000)	Percent of farms
	117	118	119	120	121	122	123	124	125	126	127	128	129	130	131	132

STATE County	117	118	119	120	121	122	123	124	125	126	127	128	129	130	131	132
ARKANSAS—Cont'd																
Cleveland	32	16.2	154	0.1	6.7	652,384	4,232	161,950	128.9	628,927	0.4	99.6	NA	69.3	228	10.7
Columbia	54	19.2	183	0.3	12.1	425,028	2,323	83,478	49.0	164,848	8.0	92.0	NA	66.0	45	4.7
Conway	172	-4.1	224	18.7	79.9	568,722	2,541	89,668	172.3	224,285	8.7	91.3	NA	68.1	838	11.8
Craighead	321	-4.8	615	253.9	293.5	2,835,272	4,613	347,738	195.2	373,256	98.3	1.7	NA	78.4	14,200	54.9
Crawford	122	-2.4	153	2.9	52.2	469,607	3,068	69,950	53.9	67,469	32.7	67.3	3	69.0	416	5.3
Crittenden	315	-6.9	1,201	187.2	292.5	4,625,254	3,851	408,836	165.3	630,737	99.5	0.5	1	69.8	12,248	81.3
Cross	272	-2.4	908	208.6	251.8	3,058,715	3,370	390,962	149.8	499,310	99.6	0.4	1	73.3	17,873	76.7
Dallas	29	38.4	233	0.0	4.2	454,901	1,949	49,777	1.7	13,825	67.5	32.5	NA	66.7	44	10.3
Desha	311	16.6	1,133	249.4	279.1	3,685,791	3,254	552,926	168.1	611,418	95.8	4.2	NA	75.6	9,994	79.3
Drew	134	3.1	421	57.2	77.0	1,217,911	2,893	194,702	60.1	188,858	67.1	32.9	NA	71.4	3,310	34.0
Faulkner	201	8.4	168	7.0	70.0	646,522	3,840	72,429	27.0	22,665	44.0	56.0	1	76.7	2,565	9.2
Franklin	184	15.0	244	1.2	56.5	626,738	2,564	86,566	181.2	240,979	2.8	97.2	2	76.3	520	5.9
Fulton	224	9.6	282	1.4	27.5	526,315	1,867	60,535	29.0	36,434	8.1	91.9	NA	73.2	672	10.9
Garland	34	-4.9	95	0.1	8.2	496,951	5,226	46,231	10.0	27,972	30.5	69.5	NA	74.5	93	5.9
Grant	49	-23.9	175	0.3	7.6	632,688	3,612	70,223	6.3	22,438	15.1	84.9	NA	82.2	36	4.3
Greene	261	0.3	414	164.8	214.7	1,754,440	4,239	169,942	139.3	220,792	91.9	8.1	NA	73.1	10,936	42.6
Hempstead	186	-5.2	304	D	51.5	760,967	2,504	111,077	216.0	352,426	2.4	97.6	NA	70.3	512	10.9
Hot Spring	77	12.5	137	0.4	20.4	382,205	2,783	59,745	29.1	51,675	4.1	95.9	NA	75.0	180	4.3
Howard	150	2.2	256	0.4	34.5	731,438	2,855	98,674	262.1	447,229	0.7	99.3	NA	69.1	83	3.9
Independence	268	7.9	301	27.5	83.4	691,058	2,299	104,678	172.9	194,303	12.2	87.8	NA	73.3	2,947	16.3
Izard	190	9.8	300	0.3	31.7	613,810	2,047	74,547	65.9	104,286	2.0	98.0	1	75.6	438	11.1
Jackson	271	-11.8	639	187.9	243.4	2,151,881	3,369	220,281	125.7	296,552	92.9	7.1	1	71.5	14,540	66.7
Jefferson	292	0.2	671	212.8	253.4	2,190,461	3,267	283,777	169.6	389,021	84.9	15.1	NA	70.0	14,205	60.1
Johnson	104	-12.5	179	1.4	38.8	501,184	2,792	70,205	139.0	240,931	3.0	97.0	2	74.4	116	2.1
Lafayette	133	15.6	464	24.3	67.7	1,182,237	2,547	136,321	119.2	415,411	15.6	84.4	NA	80.5	3,646	33.4
Lawrence	270	6.7	504	147.2	204.1	1,807,457	3,586	203,207	150.6	281,490	66.3	33.7	1	76.4	13,714	40.6
Lee	258	-1.1	1,167	169.5	246.7	3,702,289	3,173	414,909	130.1	588,670	99.8	0.2	NA	69.7	6,534	72.4
Lincoln	209	4.5	566	135.5	161.5	1,743,946	3,082	282,169	179.0	485,000	52.5	47.5	NA	62.6	7,490	51.8
Little River	159	-7.1	385	10.3	58.2	929,079	2,414	114,187	85.5	206,606	19.4	80.6	NA	69.3	1,229	15.5
Logan	187	-5.4	214	D	63.0	535,423	2,499	88,687	225.5	258,293	2.8	97.2	1	73.4	420	6.1
Lonoke	367	8.3	523	224.3	284.9	1,925,684	3,683	222,351	184.2	262,422	85.5	14.5	1	73.9	14,638	40.6
Madison	278	3.1	226	0.7	60.7	707,947	3,133	81,624	279.3	227,291	2.2	97.8	1	74.4	830	19.4
Marion	179	31.1	305	0.4	23.2	744,565	2,438	80,728	52.0	88,608	1.9	98.1	2	78.5	210	9.0
Miller	127	-22.8	247	6.7	58.2	636,224	2,578	93,153	34.9	67,973	45.2	54.8	NA	73.5	1,786	9.7
Mississippi	477	0.2	1,678	350.2	469.3	5,765,623	3,436	743,149	300.9	1,059,602	100.0	0.0	NA	78.2	12,422	78.2
Monroe	203	-24.4	1,091	159.9	189.0	3,078,477	2,823	366,858	D	D	D	D	NA	63.4	8,684	85.5
Montgomery	77	3.8	181	0.3	22.4	469,348	2,599	77,836	27.8	64,895	3.3	96.7	NA	64.3	9	2.1
Nevada	78	16.3	218	0.0	21.5	516,831	2,366	76,092	55.7	156,955	2.8	97.2	NA	67.3	158	9.3
Newton	101	-11.6	188	0.0	14.6	458,102	2,436	55,239	24.0	44,665	3.6	96.4	6	76.0	92	6.9
Ouachita	28	8.8	138	NA	5.4	308,205	2,231	49,231	11.3	55,312	3.1	96.9	NA	63.9	22	3.4
Perry	78	10.3	195	6.6	31.7	539,122	2,758	96,815	56.1	141,340	21.8	78.2	2	75.6	1,013	18.6
Phillips	363	3.1	1,573	273.8	355.3	5,012,409	3,186	499,656	189.7	821,251	99.8	0.2	NA	68.8	11,787	90.0
Pike	82	17.8	209	0.5	23.1	545,769	2,608	79,626	106.5	270,330	0.9	99.1	NA	80.2	177	11.4
Poinsett	317	-17.8	872	256.1	298.8	3,331,838	3,821	442,107	185.8	511,826	99.4	0.6	NA	71.1	16,877	75.2
Polk	140	18.0	177	0.1	37.6	523,224	2,959	79,598	159.0	200,503	1.1	98.9	NA	71.2	331	2.4
Pope	159	3.1	173	6.7	56.8	553,957	3,210	74,378	169.8	184,764	5.8	94.2	2	77.9	909	7.1
Prairie	273	-0.9	779	171.3	213.1	2,274,086	2,920	291,350	127.1	363,197	93.0	7.0	2	76.3	13,847	76.9
Pulaski	79	-5.8	193	20.7	44.6	757,344	3,929	71,002	20.3	49,333	81.1	18.9	7	78.1	1,580	12.7
Randolph	223	5.8	339	59.5	104.3	995,660	2,936	144,033	157.0	238,977	25.7	74.3	5	62.6	7,048	20.2
St. Francis	259	-13.5	933	184.9	231.5	2,899,979	3,108	308,713	125.9	452,763	99.7	0.3	NA	69.1	9,903	61.5
Saline	42	-6.5	113	0.1	12.8	386,927	3,424	54,372	8.2	21,989	13.1	86.9	7	78.4	46	3.0
Scott	93	-6.8	177	D	25.9	434,292	2,454	71,379	136.7	258,813	1.2	98.8	NA	72.0	15	0.8
Searcy	195	15.8	310	0.1	30.1	583,263	1,883	64,568	18.0	28,564	7.4	92.6	2	68.9	579	11.9
Sebastian	101	-15.2	143	0.2	29.1	477,234	3,343	58,679	118.4	167,670	1.4	98.6	NA	80.6	74	2.7
Sevier	142	10.1	263	0.2	30.0	702,812	2,668	96,124	230.8	427,398	0.5	99.5	NA	84.8	184	4.4
Sharp	162	2.2	260	0.3	30.1	554,504	2,132	65,348	146.9	236,125	1.1	98.9	NA	69.9	663	15.6
Stone	160	18.0	303	0.2	31.2	655,942	2,163	74,294	60.2	114,435	1.6	98.4	NA	71.9	370	8.4
Union	36	-14.5	136	0.0	8.2	375,084	2,765	67,177	16.2	60,321	3.7	96.3	NA	74.6	13	2.6
Van Buren	128	3.9	209	0.1	21.6	575,172	2,754	63,590	16.3	26,755	6.6	93.4	NA	77.1	172	7.2
Washington	317	1.6	139	0.3	85.1	713,220	5,132	70,892	509.3	223,456	1.5	98.5	9	78.6	696	2.4
White	344	-3.2	213	41.7	153.2	593,386	2,779	74,101	124.7	77,319	27.4	72.6	2	71.5	7,172	19.5
Woodruff	255	-6.9	1,365	177.8	228.0	4,440,411	3,254	503,337	D	D	D	D	2	64.7	11,420	85.6
Yell	194	21.3	271	1.5	57.4	729,033	2,695	91,819	268.1	373,436	2.2	97.8	NA	73.7	989	13.2

Table B. States and Counties — **Water Use, Wholesale Trade, Retail Trade, and Real Estate**

STATE County	Water use, 2015		Wholesale Trade[1], 2012				Retail Trade[2], 2012				Real estate and rental and leasing,[2] 2012			
	Public supply water withdrawn (mil gal/day)	Public supply gallons withdrawn per person per day	Number of establishments	Number of employees	Sales (mil dol)	Average payroll (mil dol)	Number of establishments	Number of employees	Sales (mil dol)	Average payroll (mil dol)	Number of establishments	Number of employees	Sales (mil dol)	Average payroll (mil dol)
	133	134	135	136	137	138	139	140	141	142	143	144	145	146
ARKANSAS—Cont'd														
Cleveland	0.50	60.2	2	D	D	D	12	63	13.4	0.8	1	D	D	D
Columbia	2.15	89.2	22	D	D	D	103	1,010	197.0	20.1	28	139	20.1	5.4
Conway	4.16	197.9	15	212	150.8	6.7	78	903	287.6	19.8	8	43	5.0	1.7
Craighead	14.12	135.3	131	1,509	1,430.1	68.3	455	6,391	1,680.9	142.6	113	473	79.2	12.8
Crawford	28.86	467.7	62	775	380.8	29.6	153	1,922	525.4	42.0	40	198	32.4	7.6
Crittenden	7.13	145.6	57	987	1,938.0	42.7	144	2,158	813.3	44.7	38	180	22.0	5.3
Cross	1.81	104.7	17	268	265.7	11.4	70	789	180.8	16.5	19	101	9.5	2.3
Dallas	0.18	23.7	4	14	6.8	0.5	46	375	71.8	7.7	5	15	3.6	0.3
Desha	0.43	35.9	19	223	389.0	10.3	67	595	153.6	11.0	8	67	3.5	1.1
Drew	2.22	118.2	10	87	147.1	4.5	91	1,000	260.7	20.0	26	102	14.6	2.9
Faulkner	0.15	1.2	88	818	551.7	35.0	377	5,538	1,435.8	116.8	120	447	111.9	19.5
Franklin	3.00	169.5	6	14	3.8	0.4	51	450	163.0	11.3	6	12	0.9	0.2
Fulton	1.40	114.7	7	39	9.3	1.0	37	208	59.3	4.1	4	13	0.8	0.1
Garland	16.07	165.4	79	D	D	D	513	5,877	1,564.0	133.8	133	439	65.0	13.0
Grant	1.01	55.8	14	D	D	D	46	450	128.9	9.5	8	D	D	D
Greene	4.42	100.0	39	573	1,067.7	23.5	154	1,799	503.5	40.2	31	52	8.1	1.1
Hempstead	2.80	126.8	14	96	52.0	3.3	79	893	197.6	18.2	16	52	6.4	1.2
Hot Spring	2.27	67.9	11	D	D	D	89	903	254.2	19.9	16	44	4.1	1.0
Howard	6.09	457.9	11	63	34.2	3.1	66	619	162.5	13.4	11	23	2.2	0.3
Independence	5.82	157.1	26	D	D	D	164	1,703	441.1	37.3	23	88	10.8	2.3
Izard	0.79	58.8	5	D	D	D	50	401	108.7	8.2	6	50	5.6	0.7
Jackson	0.39	22.5	16	148	106.9	7.2	66	681	177.7	15.8	14	29	3.2	0.5
Jefferson	11.88	166.0	57	463	443.9	20.2	291	3,447	843.9	77.9	63	221	38.6	6.3
Johnson	4.79	183.2	5	D	D	D	72	903	237.3	19.6	18	32	5.1	0.8
Lafayette	0.37	52.9	NA	NA	NA	NA	21	142	30.5	2.3	2	D	D	D
Lawrence	1.09	65.0	18	162	159.1	5.8	58	615	196.3	14.4	10	28	3.0	0.6
Lee	1.28	132.6	9	109	123.5	4.6	19	166	43.8	3.7	10	28	4.6	0.8
Lincoln	0.51	36.9	6	D	D	D	26	209	57.5	3.7	6	D	D	D
Little River	2.80	224.5	4	D	D	D	39	383	104.2	8.7	2	D	D	D
Logan	3.39	156.1	8	43	7.4	0.7	66	658	152.8	13.9	11	18	1.7	0.4
Lonoke	6.01	83.9	36	291	217.9	12.2	171	2,265	613.4	49.6	49	127	16.7	3.9
Madison	0.00	0.0	3	D	D	D	32	402	130.2	9.5	6	11	1.2	0.2
Marion	0.81	50.0	8	18	16.5	0.8	36	444	94.8	8.7	11	13	1.6	0.3
Miller	0.09	2.0	38	579	308.2	31.3	125	1,393	435.7	30.7	27	D	D	D
Mississippi	1.44	32.9	48	D	D	D	166	1,748	437.8	40.1	36	137	30.5	3.3
Monroe	1.52	205.4	14	201	126.2	9.0	39	311	90.6	6.9	4	10	0.8	0.2
Montgomery	0.52	58.0	4	D	D	D	18	119	28.8	3.0	8	30	1.5	0.4
Nevada	0.22	25.7	5	15	8.6	0.4	25	277	159.1	5.3	5	11	0.6	0.2
Newton	0.02	2.5	3	D	D	D	17	86	17.0	1.5	1	D	D	D
Ouachita	3.26	133.8	22	D	D	D	108	1,104	222.0	21.2	21	D	D	D
Perry	0.06	5.9	2	D	D	D	18	153	30.5	2.5	2	D	D	D
Phillips	6.10	312.6	33	328	594.1	14.3	85	956	223.2	21.6	17	50	5.6	0.9
Pike	1.13	104.4	12	146	89.8	3.3	43	331	70.0	6.3	4	85	6.8	3.1
Poinsett	2.18	90.7	22	390	424.6	25.8	69	751	178.0	13.6	11	36	4.0	1.1
Polk	1.69	83.6	15	D	D	D	83	966	193.5	17.5	13	130	10.5	3.1
Pope	11.00	173.5	67	469	322.4	19.3	272	3,180	869.4	67.4	69	191	29.7	5.7
Prairie	0.39	47.0	8	65	67.2	2.9	33	206	54.3	3.3	3	D	D	D
Pulaski	39.60	100.8	659	11,024	8,414.5	576.5	1,715	25,070	7,234.4	622.7	592	3,397	606.5	119.4
Randolph	1.30	74.4	11	83	33.8	2.1	59	600	170.7	13.5	16	32	2.6	0.6
St. Francis	3.84	144.4	22	D	D	D	113	1,104	316.2	22.0	26	63	7.1	1.1
Saline	29.64	252.3	69	723	351.3	30.3	278	3,995	1,404.8	100.1	65	119	24.2	3.3
Scott	1.55	147.4	6	D	D	D	22	293	50.4	6.1	4	12	1.1	0.3
Searcy	0.31	39.4	2	D	D	D	34	265	49.8	4.7	5	D	D	D
Sebastian	0.13	1.0	194	2,362	1,713.4	105.7	574	7,899	1,944.5	174.1	170	888	133.9	28.2
Sevier	0.74	42.8	5	49	19.4	2.5	67	673	190.5	14.0	7	22	3.1	0.6
Sharp	0.98	57.9	6	D	D	D	58	650	152.6	12.1	10	20	1.7	0.5
Stone	1.77	142.1	7	59	34.1	1.2	46	526	107.5	12.1	6	6	0.6	0.1
Union	4.29	106.9	50	D	D	D	208	2,152	511.1	46.8	39	210	37.4	8.6
Van Buren	2.19	130.6	10	38	35.6	1.3	57	546	168.4	12.3	6	7	0.9	0.1
Washington	0.19	0.8	234	2,487	1,740.0	118.1	765	11,098	2,925.8	254.6	239	2,359	191.1	64.1
White	7.72	97.5	61	575	432.9	27.9	294	3,358	911.7	72.6	65	183	29.6	5.7
Woodruff	0.53	78.6	15	157	118.1	7.7	27	240	74.2	5.3	6	7	0.8	0.1
Yell	4.82	222.0	10	86	15.2	2.5	55	488	121.4	9.6	10	19	1.7	0.4

1   Merchant wholesalers, except manufacturers' sales branches and offices.   2. Employer establishments.

Professional Services, Manufacturing, and Accommodation and Food Services

STATE County	Professional, scientific, and technical services, 2012				Manufacturing, 2012				Accommodation and food services, 2012			
	Number of establish-ments	Number of employees	Sales (mil dol)	Average payroll (mil dol)	Number of establish-ments	Number of employees	Receipts (mil dol)	Annual payroll (mil dol)	Number of establis-hments	Number of employees	Receipts (mil dol)	Annual payroll (mil dol)
	147	148	149	150	151	152	153	154	155	156	157	158
ARKANSAS—Cont'd												
Cleveland	1	D	D	D	3	72	D	2.0	3	11	0.6	0.1
Columbia	33	218	22.7	8.0	32	2,118	602.8	97.6	41	674	30.8	6.9
Conway	31	86	8.6	2.8	24	904	384.4	45.9	25	333	13.9	3.6
Craighead	173	876	125.8	46.0	99	5,254	2,101.7	221.2	212	D	D	D
Crawford	87	283	27.6	8.3	63	4,126	1,207.8	127.1	82	1,502	64.8	18.1
Crittenden	55	264	23.5	8.4	40	1,484	849.0	60.9	89	1,565	82.8	19.8
Cross	24	70	5.4	1.8	10	588	238.8	17.3	24	322	14.3	3.5
Dallas	6	16	1.2	0.3	7	504	194.2	18.4	8	121	4.7	1.2
Desha	21	51	11.6	1.6	10	724	407.0	34.9	34	305	12.9	3.4
Drew	26	108	11.7	4.3	20	550	D	23.1	36	D	D	D
Faulkner	223	D	D	D	89	3,707	1,203.0	175.9	212	4,745	198.7	53.7
Franklin	19	94	7.0	2.0	19	1,049	D	36.1	23	255	11.3	3.0
Fulton	10	36	2.8	1.1	12	137	10.7	3.3	17	149	5.7	1.7
Garland	217	1,160	91.1	40.4	90	2,180	476.9	95.1	274	5,162	218.0	63.4
Grant	18	81	21.6	3.6	13	1,180	603.2	D	19	D	D	D
Greene	52	430	39.4	18.8	53	4,743	1,840.7	189.6	64	1,114	49.1	13.3
Hempstead	14	70	4.9	2.1	26	2,086	786.9	71.0	32	483	22.7	5.8
Hot Spring	29	93	6.6	2.1	34	1,409	728.0	61.1	34	476	21.5	5.3
Howard	14	36	2.8	1.0	19	3,455	1,022.9	93.8	19	D	D	D
Independence	59	223	20.7	6.2	34	3,891	1,211.4	137.6	66	1,173	48.8	12.2
Izard	7	22	2.7	1.0	6	215	D	8.2	13	D	D	D
Jackson	23	85	7.0	2.9	20	989	425.0	42.9	28	308	14.9	3.5
Jefferson	79	577	65.1	27.8	61	5,118	2,113.6	225.4	120	D	D	D
Johnson	29	87	9.3	2.9	32	2,791	657.3	77.5	35	439	20.4	5.3
Lafayette	5	12	1.3	0.3	5	42	D	1.4	5	55	3.1	0.7
Lawrence	14	40	4.9	1.0	20	328	73.2	10.8	19	242	9.2	2.3
Lee	10	33	3.0	0.9	3	14	5.2	0.8	6	56	3.1	0.7
Lincoln	7	D	D	D	6	343	D	16.1	11	D	D	D
Little River	9	54	6.5	1.7	14	1,239	D	87.5	11	D	D	D
Logan	31	71	9.7	2.7	16	1,138	D	52.3	26	242	9.3	2.5
Lonoke	88	313	31.8	9.7	32	D	628.5	59.1	91	1,369	60.0	15.9
Madison	15	39	2.7	1.0	22	1,066	D	32.2	13	182	7.4	1.9
Marion	17	45	3.7	1.4	16	1,539	244.8	42.5	30	166	8.5	1.9
Miller	43	226	25.7	7.8	29	2,331	D	142.1	75	D	D	D
Mississippi	40	135	10.7	3.7	46	5,306	5,231.1	340.9	77	1,178	51.5	12.4
Monroe	9	22	1.2	0.5	6	132	48.5	4.7	18	246	9.9	2.6
Montgomery	6	10	0.8	0.3	8	143	D	3.4	17	204	23.2	5.7
Nevada	7	41	1.8	0.9	7	D	D	D	7	D	D	D
Newton	4	D	D	D	9	32	5.3	1.3	11	D	D	D
Ouachita	24	D	D	D	32	2,566	D	128.1	31	500	19.1	5.1
Perry	8	D	D	D	NA	NA	NA	NA	8	D	D	D
Phillips	26	68	9.4	2.1	12	D	D	D	22	345	13.6	3.2
Pike	4	37	1.4	0.5	14	192	39.5	6.1	14	189	7.0	1.8
Poinsett	15	40	3.3	1.0	21	656	224.0	24.2	36	D	D	D
Polk	27	83	5.4	2.1	32	1,195	D	40.0	39	499	18.1	5.2
Pope	145	468	50.0	15.3	60	4,626	1,506.7	164.4	115	D	D	D
Prairie	8	30	2.9	0.8	NA	NA	NA	NA	12	84	4.0	0.7
Pulaski	1,529	10,113	1,616.1	552.9	327	13,328	6,515.9	655.6	985	19,810	961.9	281.2
Randolph	23	71	7.2	2.5	27	594	115.0	16.4	23	329	14.7	3.5
St. Francis	31	120	18.9	4.0	6	754	D	21.1	39	590	27.8	6.9
Saline	146	558	77.6	22.2	77	1,403	D	58.4	146	2,825	128.3	33.0
Scott	9	12	1.2	0.3	14	1,193	297.8	32.5	12	130	4.7	1.6
Searcy	8	28	1.4	0.3	11	96	D	2.8	9	D	D	D
Sebastian	320	1,452	244.6	61.5	183	13,713	5,156.5	560.3	270	5,467	242.1	70.0
Sevier	14	46	3.4	1.0	6	D	D	D	24	251	10.3	2.6
Sharp	17	41	2.7	0.8	13	77	D	2.3	32	288	13.1	3.4
Stone	13	43	2.7	0.9	14	88	10.5	2.8	34	395	14.8	4.1
Union	68	250	28.6	9.5	45	2,961	4,719.2	161.3	74	970	45.4	11.6
Van Buren	16	45	4.6	1.6	10	44	D	1.8	23	371	15.8	4.1
Washington	579	3,044	345.7	137.8	204	12,207	3,487.0	440.2	503	9,220	399.4	113.7
White	109	515	45.5	16.9	60	2,300	1,031.0	98.1	133	2,543	113.6	27.8
Woodruff	10	12	1.5	0.4	7	342	D	9.2	8	D	D	D
Yell	19	54	3.5	1.2	18	1,962	571.0	55.5	20	D	D	D

Table B. States and Counties — Health Care and Social Assistance, Other Services, Nonemployer Businesses, and Residential Construction

STATE County	Health care and social assistance, 2012				Other services, 2012				Nonemployer businesses, 2016		Value of residential construction authorized by building permits, 2018	
	Number of establishments	Number of employees	Receipts (mil dol)	Annual payroll (mil dol)	Number of establishments	Number of employees	Receipts (mil dol)	Annual payroll (mil dol)	Number	Receipts (mil dol)	New construction ($1,000)	Number of housing units
	159	160	161	162	163	164	165	166	167	168	169	170
ARKANSAS—Cont'd												
Cleveland	6	120	3.6	2.7	6	D	D	D	365	13.1	0	0
Columbia	77	1,212	77.7	32.7	44	178	11.9	3.4	1,292	49.7	3,436	19
Conway	46	649	31.4	16.2	22	78	11.1	2.4	1,343	51.3	1,917	22
Craighead	359	8,701	921.0	362.1	125	805	83.9	23.2	7,780	390.1	92,365	814
Crawford	97	1,665	140.4	59.4	65	327	32.3	8.7	3,841	167.6	11,372	124
Crittenden	117	2,181	170.6	69.4	59	379	33.3	8.9	3,624	131.9	10,834	50
Cross	46	810	42.0	21.0	19	D	D	D	1,413	56.1	0	0
Dallas	24	785	34.3	15.0	14	43	3.4	1.0	341	10.9	75	1
Desha	28	589	43.5	18.4	14	34	2.9	0.7	703	29.0	265	1
Drew	46	1,054	72.6	30.5	20	53	5.6	1.2	1,080	46.3	290	3
Faulkner	291	5,108	450.6	173.8	157	783	69.2	16.7	8,375	334.0	67,077	411
Franklin	32	623	47.9	19.3	14	40	3.8	1.0	1,001	39.0	100	2
Fulton	29	561	38.8	14.7	9	D	D	D	799	30.3	0	0
Garland	319	7,374	717.5	275.4	161	766	53.3	16.2	7,890	337.6	14,897	91
Grant	22	D	D	D	20	D	D	D	1,169	42.7	4,517	29
Greene	96	1,558	140.5	50.2	42	175	14.5	3.9	2,854	132.1	19,654	162
Hempstead	51	1,119	62.9	27.6	34	133	17.9	4.5	984	39.6	0	0
Hot Spring	46	1,334	85.6	38.7	23	D	D	D	1,917	71.1	1,250	10
Howard	33	D	D	D	25	86	9.4	2.3	760	36.2	0	0
Independence	98	3,010	282.1	111.5	53	276	17.8	6.0	2,378	103.0	2,975	32
Izard	28	593	32.7	15.4	11	34	3.1	0.7	859	31.8	863	5
Jackson	52	825	76.1	29.6	18	63	4.8	1.3	834	30.0	1,169	8
Jefferson	215	4,384	399.6	161.6	84	291	D	D	3,619	125.8	2,083	26
Johnson	40	996	65.7	28.5	28	112	5.6	2.5	1,319	51.5	5,376	39
Lafayette	9	177	8.1	4.3	4	30	2.0	0.7	329	11.3	0	0
Lawrence	32	623	40.4	19.8	15	D	D	D	1,131	50.3	1,604	16
Lee	17	323	31.4	11.0	6	18	1.0	0.3	662	26.3	0	0
Lincoln	16	323	26.6	9.4	15	D	D	D	482	20.4	684	4
Little River	14	D	D	D	13	36	3.6	0.9	562	21.1	473	8
Logan	43	613	44.4	17.4	23	81	6.6	1.9	1,198	40.5	400	4
Lonoke	98	1,274	78.5	32.0	62	235	18.1	5.6	4,565	197.1	34,694	371
Madison	18	279	13.5	6.0	15	D	D	D	1,221	49.0	1,110	7
Marion	18	D	D	D	15	39	3.9	0.6	1,141	37.0	8,282	63
Miller	67	D	D	D	45	238	20.1	5.6	2,588	107.9	6,242	29
Mississippi	125	1,895	131.4	53.5	43	190	15.8	4.4	2,181	68.5	4,497	33
Monroe	20	313	18.0	7.5	12	D	D	D	516	24.5	120	8
Montgomery	11	D	D	D	8	25	1.5	0.4	741	26.6	NA	NA
Nevada	15	443	19.8	9.7	9	41	2.9	0.7	442	17.4	0	0
Newton	13	216	7.8	3.8	3	D	D	D	668	25.8	0	0
Ouachita	62	D	D	D	30	D	D	D	1,239	40.4	172	2
Perry	13	D	D	D	5	D	D	D	669	27.6	73	2
Phillips	64	1,045	73.4	30.4	29	100	10.8	3.0	1,381	44.0	1,002	42
Pike	13	296	14.5	6.6	9	18	2.0	0.5	840	38.8	NA	NA
Poinsett	46	648	37.7	16.3	26	D	D	D	1,434	50.2	3,455	29
Polk	46	983	67.9	28.5	31	104	6.1	1.6	1,538	58.0	70	1
Pope	165	3,073	218.2	80.0	91	513	35.0	11.5	3,798	141.4	8,232	89
Prairie	11	D	D	D	10	27	2.0	0.5	456	19.2	731	5
Pulaski	1,446	41,716	5,078.9	2,013.0	807	6,109	823.4	190.7	28,663	1,304.2	208,653	941
Randolph	46	867	57.9	25.9	19	D	D	D	1,252	55.9	1,415	20
St. Francis	58	1,106	82.6	35.6	20	130	9.5	4.5	1,879	61.8	281	2
Saline	197	4,120	277.2	129.7	127	D	D	D	8,028	346.4	76,829	420
Scott	16	239	15.2	8.0	11	46	2.3	1.7	634	19.0	45	1
Searcy	14	D	D	D	2	D	D	D	780	30.5	0	0
Sebastian	410	11,295	1,192.7	466.3	203	963	80.5	22.8	8,681	448.8	58,391	340
Sevier	31	506	42.7	14.6	24	D	D	D	832	36.4	317	7
Sharp	46	540	29.7	13.4	22	108	7.5	1.8	1,247	43.3	2,161	10
Stone	23	509	31.9	15.1	15	D	D	D	1,127	42.1	470	9
Union	127	2,169	213.7	80.2	81	387	51.6	12.0	2,794	108.6	1,095	6
Van Buren	36	731	44.0	18.0	19	D	D	D	1,247	39.6	1,065	6
Washington	568	14,228	1,525.8	614.1	308	1,955	320.9	52.9	16,345	775.4	372,678	1,560
White	164	4,429	360.8	146.6	98	514	45.4	14.1	5,380	219.0	14,444	94
Woodruff	15	D	D	D	6	D	D	D	385	15.7	0	0
Yell	42	934	52.6	24.9	13	55	4.6	1.1	1,252	51.4	478	7

Table B. States and Counties — Government Employment and Payroll, and Local Government Finances

STATE County	Government employment and payroll, 2012									Local government finances, 2012				
			March payroll (percent of total)							General revenue				
													Taxes	
	Full-time equivalent employees	March payroll (dollars)	Adminis-tration, judicial, and legal	Police and corrections	Fire protection	Highways and transpor-tation	Health and welfare	Natural resources and utilities	Education and libraries	Total (mil dol)	Inter-govern-mental (mil dol)	Total (mil dol)	Per capita[1] (dollars)	
													Total	Property
	171	172	173	174	175	176	177	178	179	180	181	182	183	184

ARKANSAS—Cont'd

STATE County	171	172	173	174	175	176	177	178	179	180	181	182	183	184
Cleveland	330	806,962	9.0	5.0	0.0	5.3	0.7	2.9	76.0	20.0	15.3	2.4	280	186
Columbia	810	2,122,431	5.9	8.7	1.9	4.1	0.6	7.5	70.9	84.2	34.7	16.8	686	216
Conway	751	2,035,580	5.2	11.1	0.6	3.9	0.8	8.1	70.0	72.1	44.8	15.9	748	377
Craighead	3,565	10,924,637	4.8	9.2	2.9	3.7	1.2	10.0	67.7	285.0	164.7	77.8	780	344
Crawford	2,079	8,936,720	9.1	2.8	0.0	1.4	5.5	24.0	57.1	156.8	108.4	28.6	461	213
Crittenden	2,243	7,239,687	5.6	10.1	4.1	1.8	1.6	6.1	67.6	182.3	109.3	39.6	792	258
Cross	603	1,548,890	10.4	9.4	1.4	3.4	1.1	2.8	71.5	51.1	33.6	9.9	562	280
Dallas	261	612,066	9.1	13.5	0.3	5.1	2.7	7.1	61.9	19.8	11.6	4.3	544	186
Desha	795	2,143,489	5.0	5.6	0.5	2.7	22.4	3.6	59.5	57.2	28.7	12.9	1,031	405
Drew	969	2,684,507	3.1	4.7	1.1	2.3	30.7	2.1	55.8	79.4	41.6	12.6	671	211
Faulkner	3,393	11,696,206	5.6	8.1	3.7	2.3	1.7	2.7	75.5	324.2	171.2	77.9	656	297
Franklin	616	1,780,777	6.6	4.8	0.5	3.5	2.3	1.9	77.8	48.5	35.0	9.5	525	268
Fulton	446	1,158,320	4.4	3.4	0.7	4.9	23.0	2.8	60.2	31.9	18.9	3.9	319	163
Garland	2,929	9,379,603	4.7	8.8	4.0	3.5	3.4	5.5	68.3	270.5	155.0	62.1	640	262
Grant	736	2,167,090	4.0	5.7	0.2	2.7	0.5	2.6	83.3	54.6	40.7	8.6	480	234
Greene	1,593	4,613,388	4.1	5.9	2.2	3.0	2.1	8.3	68.5	112.0	67.4	19.6	455	189
Hempstead	991	2,866,901	6.3	9.8	1.5	3.8	2.3	7.5	64.3	63.0	40.8	14.1	629	190
Hot Spring	1,020	3,135,235	4.3	4.3	1.6	3.0	1.9	5.9	78.5	75.0	50.6	15.7	471	242
Howard	721	2,467,138	7.2	17.5	1.7	5.0	3.5	21.0	42.7	46.1	28.6	9.7	704	226
Independence	1,442	3,864,054	4.6	7.4	0.9	3.5	2.2	8.2	72.6	113.1	69.9	22.7	614	314
Izard	479	1,132,741	7.6	7.8	0.2	5.9	1.2	5.3	71.6	32.9	23.1	5.4	399	259
Jackson	623	1,641,667	7.2	8.7	4.1	4.3	2.8	5.1	65.5	43.2	27.4	9.3	528	229
Jefferson	2,803	8,103,678	6.2	13.3	4.7	3.4	1.8	1.9	66.2	217.6	136.9	51.2	686	285
Johnson	832	2,711,188	3.4	5.5	0.7	2.3	0.4	12.2	75.6	63.8	42.9	12.1	466	209
Lafayette	324	1,024,900	6.7	6.5	0.5	5.3	1.6	2.4	77.1	19.1	12.6	3.8	516	258
Lawrence	1,057	2,598,077	3.2	3.6	0.8	2.1	33.0	2.4	54.7	79.8	45.0	7.8	459	210
Lee	422	1,112,758	5.2	7.2	1.9	5.4	2.5	8.4	68.7	24.4	17.7	4.1	401	201
Lincoln	362	919,481	6.2	5.9	0.1	3.6	0.2	2.7	80.4	24.4	16.8	4.2	297	152
Little River	689	1,796,446	3.9	4.0	0.1	2.7	34.8	3.7	50.8	44.7	19.0	7.9	615	273
Logan	771	2,027,835	5.6	7.0	0.2	4.0	2.6	4.4	76.0	49.8	33.4	9.6	437	237
Lonoke	2,693	7,148,935	4.2	6.7	2.0	2.1	0.5	4.6	79.3	189.2	129.4	38.9	558	260
Madison	571	1,449,917	5.1	4.6	0.0	6.7	5.3	2.7	75.2	31.5	20.9	6.6	420	180
Marion	420	1,177,227	8.0	10.7	0.3	8.0	1.6	5.5	65.4	26.6	17.6	6.1	370	207
Miller	1,370	3,792,335	7.1	17.4	7.1	4.8	0.8	2.2	58.3	120.6	70.4	29.4	674	250
Mississippi	2,048	5,872,177	5.4	9.7	2.9	3.6	2.1	9.0	65.1	191.6	104.8	32.2	707	241
Monroe	360	1,055,919	8.0	11.9	0.8	5.2	0.9	10.4	61.7	25.7	17.8	4.5	571	283
Montgomery	294	752,749	7.1	6.2	0.0	6.4	2.9	4.0	72.7	19.1	14.5	3.0	317	201
Nevada	405	978,364	8.6	11.3	0.0	8.2	3.9	6.8	59.4	20.3	14.7	3.3	374	180
Newton	434	1,232,173	2.8	2.8	0.0	2.9	1.0	1.0	89.0	59.7	55.7	2.4	298	215
Ouachita	1,097	3,081,016	5.9	8.9	2.9	5.3	2.7	5.6	68.4	75.4	51.1	15.8	623	202
Perry	344	973,732	8.1	7.6	0.0	4.4	0.3	3.1	72.6	20.7	15.2	3.5	334	164
Phillips	872	2,319,840	6.4	8.7	2.9	4.6	0.0	7.6	68.3	70.5	48.6	14.3	689	239
Pike	507	1,198,447	2.9	2.6	0.0	2.3	0.6	3.0	88.0	32.5	23.2	6.0	533	207
Poinsett	959	2,599,342	5.4	11.1	1.0	3.7	0.5	5.4	72.6	69.5	51.1	10.0	411	173
Polk	1,139	3,233,326	3.5	4.4	0.5	3.3	0.1	3.1	84.0	84.7	45.1	10.6	516	173
Pope	2,245	7,108,185	4.8	9.2	3.2	2.4	3.2	4.5	71.3	165.6	100.1	42.3	674	270
Prairie	351	1,159,649	15.7	11.7	0.5	12.8	1.1	5.2	52.5	20.8	12.8	4.0	470	235
Pulaski	15,078	52,069,152	6.0	12.7	6.6	4.5	3.5	11.7	52.8	1,476.7	724.3	418.1	1,075	551
Randolph	552	1,387,909	7.5	7.1	2.0	4.5	1.7	6.7	68.7	37.2	24.0	9.9	551	358
St. Francis	1,036	3,954,323	5.7	6.9	1.6	2.0	2.7	7.1	73.4	75.8	52.5	14.7	527	164
Saline	2,671	8,478,497	6.2	7.9	4.2	2.4	0.6	6.1	71.0	238.1	147.9	54.6	489	267
Scott	364	909,428	4.1	3.6	0.0	5.1	1.8	4.7	79.2	25.0	18.3	4.3	391	127
Searcy	296	714,402	4.4	5.2	0.0	5.9	1.5	2.7	80.0	16.3	12.2	2.5	308	178
Sebastian	4,285	15,121,933	5.9	9.8	4.3	4.0	2.6	7.8	65.5	399.0	208.5	123.0	966	364
Sevier	764	2,036,880	4.0	5.6	0.4	2.6	1.5	12.6	72.8	59.3	43.9	8.4	490	157
Sharp	745	1,804,388	5.9	6.5	3.5	5.1	0.2	6.1	71.2	44.2	31.2	7.0	408	175
Stone	424	1,109,650	6.3	5.7	0.0	5.5	1.2	9.6	70.0	26.1	18.0	5.4	423	148
Union	1,719	4,970,357	4.4	7.3	3.6	3.5	2.6	4.4	72.2	125.7	71.2	35.1	859	292
Van Buren	757	1,902,959	7.4	21.6	1.0	6.7	1.1	2.5	58.5	49.1	26.5	14.0	822	502
Washington	7,560	23,284,035	5.1	10.7	3.9	4.1	1.3	4.1	69.5	691.8	396.1	183.9	870	333
White	2,609	7,296,125	4.8	6.2	2.5	2.4	2.0	5.5	75.7	192.0	122.5	42.8	545	227
Woodruff	367	874,741	9.7	5.0	0.3	4.3	1.5	8.7	68.2	25.9	19.0	3.7	521	309
Yell	877	2,241,720	3.8	7.4	0.3	4.0	0.5	4.0	79.4	58.7	42.0	10.7	489	268

1. Based on the resident population estimated as of July 1 of the year shown.

Table B. States and Counties — Local Government Finances, Government Employment, and Income Taxes

	Local government finances, 2012 (cont.)										Government employment, 2017			Individual income tax returns, 2016		
	Direct general expenditure							Debt outstanding								
			Percent of total for:													
STATE County	Total (mil dol)	Per capita[1] (dollars)	Education	Health and hospitals	Police protection	Public welfare	Highways	Total (mil dol)	Per capita[1] (dollars)	Federal civilian	Federal military	State and local	Number of returns	Mean adjusted gross income	Mean income tax
	185	186	187	188	189	190	191	192	193	194	195	196	197	198	199
ARKANSAS—Cont'd															
Cleveland	19.8	2,299	72.2	0.7	3.3	0.2	9.2	7.9	916	11	32	332	3,050	49,082	4,298
Columbia	85.3	3,484	43.3	28.4	3.6	0.1	3.9	107.4	4,388	36	85	2,002	8,800	48,234	5,089
Conway	70.4	3,308	65.7	1.5	5.0	0.2	8.3	39.8	1,868	57	81	1,501	8,250	46,916	4,480
Craighead	279.3	2,800	56.9	0.3	5.7	0.1	5.4	482.8	4,841	328	414	8,243	42,170	54,852	6,755
Crawford	160.3	2,588	67.2	0.0	5.0	0.0	7.4	203.0	3,277	96	246	2,206	23,970	45,810	4,097
Crittenden	177.1	3,540	57.7	0.2	7.9	0.0	4.9	305.8	6,114	98	189	2,636	20,540	43,652	4,586
Cross	50.3	2,847	65.6	4.4	4.9	0.2	5.5	15.3	867	57	87	1,063	7,120	41,226	3,675
Dallas	18.2	2,276	53.5	0.2	7.1	0.0	9.3	15.1	1,887	20	28	359	2,790	39,657	3,389
Desha	54.8	4,365	49.1	21.1	6.0	0.1	3.4	43.6	3,478	67	46	910	4,810	37,504	3,357
Drew	81.1	4,329	53.9	22.7	3.7	0.2	6.4	39.5	2,108	52	69	2,009	7,020	48,037	5,039
Faulkner	340.2	2,866	58.3	0.1	4.3	0.0	5.9	686.1	5,780	208	477	7,534	49,220	55,727	6,125
Franklin	46.2	2,558	73.0	3.3	3.8	0.3	6.5	43.4	2,406	156	69	877	6,740	44,205	3,943
Fulton	30.6	2,485	53.3	24.1	3.1	0.1	8.4	14.3	1,159	27	47	611	4,330	36,155	2,838
Garland	268.9	2,775	57.5	0.3	5.6	0.0	3.6	344.1	3,551	453	382	3,994	42,920	50,162	5,742
Grant	54.3	3,022	74.8	0.6	4.5	0.1	4.4	31.4	1,747	29	71	756	7,330	56,023	5,818
Greene	119.5	2,769	59.8	0.2	3.6	0.1	4.4	136.1	3,152	95	175	2,023	17,430	46,031	4,293
Hempstead	64.4	2,877	60.7	0.2	4.3	0.1	5.2	53.7	2,402	79	85	1,684	8,410	36,381	2,767
Hot Spring	76.2	2,283	72.0	1.7	3.4	0.1	4.0	94.3	2,823	63	123	1,934	12,350	43,231	3,689
Howard	46.0	3,350	63.9	0.8	4.9	0.1	4.2	74.9	5,451	62	52	772	5,450	40,216	3,696
Independence	118.5	3,202	52.8	0.2	3.5	0.1	6.2	274.1	7,403	105	144	2,113	14,520	48,684	5,330
Izard	33.6	2,497	65.3	1.3	4.8	0.2	6.9	26.2	1,942	26	50	964	4,760	39,515	3,251
Jackson	41.6	2,363	54.0	1.4	7.4	0.1	6.9	23.9	1,357	43	59	1,450	5,640	40,418	3,722
Jefferson	217.7	2,914	59.7	0.1	7.5	0.1	4.0	226.1	3,025	1,428	279	6,814	28,360	41,710	3,787
Johnson	65.1	2,514	63.3	0.2	4.4	0.0	7.2	48.8	1,883	85	102	1,063	9,770	40,683	3,351
Lafayette	20.9	2,805	68.4	0.2	6.4	0.1	6.3	10.0	1,344	27	27	407	2,520	39,025	3,588
Lawrence	75.1	4,412	56.5	22.2	3.3	4.3	3.1	40.2	2,361	50	63	1,139	6,190	39,063	3,508
Lee	21.6	2,110	53.3	0.4	9.2	0.2	10.8	5.6	551	33	29	690	2,820	39,958	4,394
Lincoln	25.2	1,788	68.0	0.1	4.2	0.0	7.9	12.9	913	23	39	1,166	3,790	42,440	3,566
Little River	45.4	3,511	41.4	20.9	4.1	6.7	4.1	77.9	6,027	44	48	771	4,920	45,921	4,147
Logan	50.5	2,295	64.1	5.2	5.3	0.1	5.4	41.6	1,893	97	83	1,308	8,460	39,379	3,191
Lonoke	184.1	2,636	69.9	0.2	4.3	0.0	2.8	172.0	2,463	135	285	2,772	29,740	53,141	5,226
Madison	31.6	2,021	66.4	3.3	5.6	0.0	11.6	24.7	1,576	43	64	560	6,450	40,905	3,665
Marion	28.0	1,688	60.5	0.2	8.4	0.2	11.9	19.4	1,172	34	64	522	6,300	38,098	3,056
Miller	112.1	2,568	56.8	0.3	9.6	0.0	4.3	109.3	2,504	53	168	1,930	17,310	46,486	4,887
Mississippi	189.3	4,154	49.4	0.5	5.1	0.1	2.9	796.0	17,471	101	163	2,595	16,200	41,065	3,723
Monroe	25.5	3,252	52.9	1.3	5.1	0.2	10.3	10.9	1,390	31	28	406	2,970	32,799	2,887
Montgomery	18.0	1,926	60.2	0.1	3.4	0.0	10.6	13.6	1,457	45	35	461	3,150	38,310	3,155
Nevada	20.5	2,300	61.8	0.3	6.5	0.2	8.5	12.4	1,394	25	32	419	3,320	37,967	2,914
Newton	30.3	3,746	81.8	0.1	1.5	0.1	7.3	72.1	8,919	44	31	386	2,900	35,758	2,570
Ouachita	71.1	2,801	66.5	0.1	4.9	0.0	5.4	60.6	2,386	93	93	1,808	9,570	42,805	3,864
Perry	19.2	1,861	72.5	0.1	5.9	0.3	7.5	14.0	1,359	22	40	375	3,850	45,479	3,979
Phillips	71.5	3,442	65.5	0.1	5.3	0.1	3.5	34.7	1,670	58	72	1,234	6,980	34,649	2,952
Pike	30.8	2,738	73.7	0.4	3.3	0.2	7.6	17.3	1,541	47	42	543	4,130	38,862	3,395
Poinsett	65.0	2,676	70.6	0.2	6.9	0.1	4.4	35.9	1,479	62	94	1,203	8,890	38,669	3,353
Polk	82.4	4,025	54.6	28.8	2.5	0.0	3.6	60.1	2,937	87	79	1,054	7,520	37,993	3,050
Pope	163.1	2,599	67.0	1.6	6.5	0.1	6.0	190.1	3,029	264	238	4,364	25,160	50,383	5,275
Prairie	19.8	2,343	62.2	2.0	6.4	0.0	9.5	17.3	2,050	43	32	421	3,310	42,751	3,903
Pulaski	1,448.1	3,723	46.0	4.2	6.9	0.0	3.8	1,780.8	4,578	9,059	5,009	44,611	177,780	63,478	8,974
Randolph	35.5	1,979	57.5	0.0	7.8	0.0	9.3	8.9	498	44	68	1,197	6,890	38,235	3,504
St. Francis	73.2	2,628	65.4	0.5	5.9	0.1	4.9	21.2	759	669	86	1,368	8,680	35,547	3,027
Saline	246.7	2,206	68.6	0.3	4.4	0.0	5.3	376.7	3,368	91	465	3,678	50,820	58,441	6,111
Scott	25.5	2,315	68.6	0.5	4.5	0.0	7.8	31.9	2,901	84	41	526	3,890	35,027	2,547
Searcy	16.1	2,010	62.9	0.2	4.8	0.2	10.4	2.8	353	38	31	345	2,930	30,899	2,157
Sebastian	398.6	3,131	51.6	0.2	5.7	0.1	6.2	717.8	5,639	920	530	6,822	53,050	52,759	6,303
Sevier	59.7	3,477	77.9	0.0	3.5	0.1	3.6	19.8	1,151	68	67	1,134	6,080	39,251	3,101
Sharp	43.7	2,563	62.6	0.1	5.0	0.0	10.0	23.8	1,398	49	68	768	6,350	36,443	2,975
Stone	24.5	1,931	63.3	0.1	5.7	0.2	9.7	8.6	681	67	49	506	4,610	35,753	2,776
Union	124.9	3,056	60.5	0.1	5.9	0.0	7.4	143.9	3,521	145	155	2,446	16,980	55,842	6,667
Van Buren	45.8	2,692	53.0	4.9	8.6	0.2	14.4	61.6	3,616	33	64	680	6,270	40,570	3,392
Washington	690.9	3,268	59.8	0.3	5.5	0.0	3.8	886.2	4,192	1,957	895	18,289	96,340	58,662	7,826
White	187.6	2,389	67.8	0.2	5.9	0.1	5.3	228.1	2,907	166	298	3,307	29,760	49,507	5,139
Woodruff	27.6	3,888	46.7	0.3	3.9	20.3	8.1	12.6	1,776	37	25	462	2,610	33,546	3,425
Yell	56.6	2,581	70.7	0.1	6.1	0.0	5.0	53.5	2,439	116	84	1,203	8,240	38,745	3,176

1. Based on the resident population estimated as of July 1 of the year shown.

Table B. States and Counties — Land Area and Population

State / county code	CBSA code[1]	County code[2]	STATE County	Land area[3] (sq. mi)	Population, 2018			Population and population characteristics, 2018										
					Total persons 2018	Rank	Per square mile	Race alone or in combination, not Hispanic or Latino (percent)				Percent Hispanic or Latino[4]	Age (percent)					
								White	Black	American Indian, Alaska Native	Asian and Pacific Islancer		Under 5 years	5 to 17 years	18 to 24 years	25 to 34 years	35 to 44 years	45 to 54 years
				1	2	3	4	5	6	7	8	9	10	11	12	13	14	15
06000		0	CALIFORNIA..................	155,793.7	39,557,045	X	253.9	39.3	6.5	1.0	17.0	39.3	6.2	16.6	9.5	15.3	13.3	12.8
06001	41,860	1	Alameda.........................	737.3	1,666,753	20	2,260.6	34.5	11.6	0.8	35.2	22.4	5.8	14.7	8.3	16.8	15.1	13.3
06003		8	Alpine...........................	738.3	1,101	3,104	1.5	66.6	1.3	21.2	2.5	11.4	4.0	13.5	7.8	9.9	7.5	12.1
06005		6	Amador.........................	594.6	39,383	1,194	66.2	79.6	3.1	2.8	2.7	14.4	4.1	10.9	5.7	10.9	11.8	13.2
06007	17,020	3	Butte.............................	1,636.5	231,256	290	141.3	75.1	2.6	3.0	6.7	16.7	5.5	14.4	14.3	13.1	10.9	10.5
06009		6	Calaveras......................	1,020.0	45,602	1,060	44.7	83.6	1.4	2.9	2.9	12.4	4.3	12.6	6.2	9.6	9.4	12.0
06011		6	Colusa...........................	1,150.7	21,627	1,745	18.8	35.6	1.5	1.8	2.2	60.3	7.1	20.2	9.2	13.3	12.1	11.7
06013	41,860	1	Contra Costa..................	717.1	1,150,215	39	1,604.0	46.8	10.0	1.0	20.9	25.8	5.6	16.9	8.1	12.8	13.5	14.0
06015	18,860	7	Del Norte......................	1,006.2	27,828	1,502	27.7	66.2	4.1	9.4	4.6	20.0	5.6	15.4	7.6	14.1	13.3	11.7
06017	40,900	1	El Dorado......................	1,707.8	190,678	350	111.7	80.5	1.4	1.8	6.6	12.9	4.6	15.3	7.1	10.2	11.2	13.4
06019	23,420	2	Fresno...........................	5,958.1	994,400	47	166.9	30.7	5.3	1.1	11.5	53.5	7.8	20.6	9.9	15.3	12.6	11.1
06021		6	Glenn............................	1,314.0	28,047	1,497	21.3	52.4	1.4	2.4	3.4	42.3	7.1	19.5	9.0	12.9	11.6	11.2
06023	21,700	5	Humboldt......................	3,568.2	136,373	469	38.2	78.5	2.4	7.5	4.9	11.8	5.3	13.9	12.6	13.3	13.1	10.6
06025	20,940	3	Imperial.........................	4,176.6	181,827	359	43.5	10.8	2.6	0.9	1.6	84.6	8.2	20.3	10.1	14.8	12.2	11.1
06027		7	Inyo...............................	10,180.9	17,987	1,922	1.8	64.0	1.4	11.9	2.5	22.7	5.6	14.8	6.6	10.9	11.3	10.9
06029	12,540	2	Kern..............................	8,132.3	896,764	61	110.3	35.2	5.9	1.2	5.8	54.0	7.8	21.1	10.1	15.6	12.8	11.2
06031	25,260	3	Kings.............................	1,390.3	151,366	435	108.9	33.7	6.9	1.4	5.3	55.0	7.5	19.6	11.0	17.0	13.8	11.5
06033	17,340	4	Lake..............................	1,256.5	64,382	827	51.2	72.6	2.7	4.2	2.7	21.3	5.9	15.1	6.6	11.4	10.5	11.9
06035	45,000	7	Lassen...........................	4,541.2	30,802	1,411	6.8	67.7	8.7	4.3	3.0	19.2	5.0	12.1	9.9	18.5	14.6	12.8
06037	31,080	1	Los Angeles	4,058.2	10,105,518	1	2,490.1	27.9	8.7	0.6	16.5	48.6	6.0	15.7	9.5	16.2	13.7	13.3
06039	31,460	3	Madera..........................	2,136.9	157,672	420	73.8	35.0	3.7	1.8	2.7	58.3	7.6	19.9	9.4	14.0	12.6	11.5
06041	41,860	1	Marin............................	520.5	259,666	263	498.9	74.5	3.3	0.8	8.7	16.1	4.6	15.4	6.5	8.7	11.7	15.5
06043		8	Mariposa........................	1,448.8	17,471	1,950	12.1	82.6	1.8	4.4	2.6	11.6	4.3	11.9	6.2	10.7	9.5	11.3
06045	46,380	4	Mendocino	3,506.4	87,606	661	25.0	67.2	1.5	5.4	3.1	25.6	5.9	15.5	7.3	11.3	12.0	11.6
06047	32,900	2	Merced	1,935.6	274,765	249	142.0	28.7	3.6	0.9	8.5	60.2	7.7	21.6	11.2	14.7	12.3	11.2
06049		6	Modoc...........................	3,915.4	8,777	2,518	2.2	80.2	1.8	4.5	2.1	14.2	5.0	14.5	6.0	10.1	10.2	11.1
06051		7	Mono............................	3,049.0	14,250	2,147	4.7	67.2	1.3	2.6	3.4	27.6	4.8	13.5	9.1	14.6	13.0	13.2
06053	41,500	2	Monterey.......................	3,281.7	435,594	162	132.7	31.5	3.2	0.8	7.9	59.1	7.1	19.0	9.9	14.3	13.0	11.8
06055	34,900	3	Napa.............................	748.3	139,417	464	186.3	54.1	2.7	1.1	10.1	34.5	5.1	15.6	8.5	12.3	12.6	13.2
06057	46,020	4	Nevada..........................	957.8	99,696	600	104.1	87.3	1.0	2.0	2.7	9.7	4.3	12.8	6.0	9.6	11.1	11.5
06059	31,080	1	Orange..........................	792.8	3,185,968	6	4,018.6	42.6	2.1	0.6	23.4	34.2	5.9	16.0	9.2	14.5	12.9	14.0
06061	40,900	1	Placer...........................	1,407.1	393,149	179	279.4	75.4	2.4	1.3	10.4	14.3	5.3	16.9	7.3	11.0	13.0	13.4
06063		7	Plumas..........................	2,553.1	18,804	1,883	7.4	86.4	1.7	3.8	2.1	9.2	4.6	12.3	5.9	10.0	9.6	10.6
06065	40,140	1	Riverside........................	7,206.6	2,450,758	10	340.1	36.8	7.1	1.0	8.2	49.6	6.5	18.7	9.7	14.0	12.9	12.5
06067	40,900	1	Sacramento....................	965.4	1,540,975	24	1,596.2	48.1	11.8	1.5	20.4	23.4	6.4	17.2	8.5	15.7	13.3	12.5
06069	41,940	1	San Benito	1,388.7	61,537	855	44.3	35.0	1.3	0.9	3.9	60.6	6.6	19.1	9.4	13.7	13.2	12.9
06071	40,140	1	San Bernardino...............	20,059.9	2,171,603	14	108.3	29.8	9.0	0.9	8.6	54.0	7.1	19.2	10.3	15.3	12.9	12.2
06073	41,740	1	San Diego	4,208.8	3,343,364	5	794.4	48.1	5.7	0.9	14.9	34.0	6.2	15.4	10.3	16.5	13.4	12.4
06075	41,860	1	San Francisco	46.9	883,305	64	18,833.8	43.3	6.0	0.8	38.4	15.2	4.5	8.9	7.0	23.6	15.8	13.0
06077	44,700	2	San Joaquin	1,392.4	752,660	88	540.5	33.9	8.2	1.2	18.6	41.9	7.1	20.1	9.6	14.1	13.0	12.2
06079	42,020	2	San Luis Obispo..............	3,300.6	284,010	245	86.0	71.0	2.3	1.3	5.3	22.8	4.6	13.0	15.2	11.5	11.1	10.9
06081	41,860	1	San Mateo.....................	448.6	769,545	84	1,715.4	42.1	3.0	0.6	34.0	24.3	5.7	14.9	7.3	15.0	14.3	13.8
06083	42,200	2	Santa Barbara.................	2,735.1	446,527	159	163.3	46.2	2.4	1.0	7.1	45.8	6.2	15.9	15.8	13.3	11.3	10.7
06085	41,940	1	Santa Clara....................	1,291.1	1,937,570	18	1,500.7	33.8	3.0	0.6	40.6	25.3	5.9	16.0	8.5	16.3	14.4	13.7
06087	42,100	2	Santa Cruz.....................	445.1	274,255	250	616.2	59.6	1.7	1.2	6.7	34.1	5.1	14.2	14.9	12.1	11.7	12.2
06089	39,820	3	Shasta...........................	3,775.4	180,040	365	47.7	83.0	2.0	4.1	4.6	10.3	5.9	15.5	7.6	12.9	11.1	11.5
06091		8	Sierra............................	953.2	2,987	2,968	3.1	84.9	1.5	2.2	1.4	12.1	4.7	11.4	4.9	8.3	9.6	10.7
06093		6	Siskiyou.........................	6,278.8	43,724	1,098	7.0	79.7	2.4	6.5	3.2	12.9	5.2	14.9	6.7	10.4	10.1	10.8
06095	46,700	2	Solano...........................	821.8	446,610	158	543.5	41.9	15.9	1.3	19.9	26.9	6.0	16.1	8.7	14.7	12.6	12.6
06097	42,220	2	Sonoma..........................	1,575.9	499,942	141	317.2	65.8	2.4	1.6	6.3	27.2	5.0	14.7	8.1	12.9	12.5	12.7
06099	33,700	2	Stanislaus	1,496.0	549,815	124	367.5	43.4	3.4	1.2	7.9	47.0	7.2	19.8	9.4	14.5	12.7	11.9
06101	49,700	3	Sutter	602.5	96,807	617	160.7	48.3	3.1	2.0	18.7	31.5	7.0	18.9	8.6	14.2	12.1	11.8
06103	39,780	4	Tehama..........................	2,949.1	63,916	836	21.7	70.0	1.4	3.4	2.3	25.7	6.4	17.6	7.6	12.1	11.0	11.7
06105		8	Trinity...........................	3,179.3	12,535	2,249	3.9	85.9	1.4	7.1	2.6	7.5	4.3	12.7	5.5	9.0	10.5	11.8
06107	47,300	2	Tulare............................	4,824.4	465,861	151	96.6	29.4	1.6	1.2	4.2	65.2	7.9	22.7	10.1	14.2	12.7	11.0
06109	43,760	4	Tuolumne.......................	2,220.9	54,539	934	24.6	82.2	2.4	3.0	2.5	12.7	4.4	12.4	6.6	12.0	11.1	11.2
06111	37,100	2	Ventura..........................	1,842.5	850,967	69	461.9	47.2	2.3	0.8	9.2	43.0	5.9	17.0	9.3	13.4	12.4	13.2
06113	40,900	1	Yolo..............................	1,014.7	220,408	308	217.2	49.8	3.4	1.3	17.9	31.9	5.6	15.3	20.1	13.6	11.8	10.6
06115	49,700	3	Yuba..............................	632.0	78,041	715	123.5	58.5	5.1	3.4	9.4	28.7	7.9	19.7	9.4	15.7	12.5	10.6
08000		0	COLORADO	103,638.7	5,695,564	X	55.0	70.0	4.9	1.3	4.5	21.7	5.9	16.3	9.2	15.7	13.7	12.5
08001	19,740	1	Adams...........................	1,166.3	511,868	138	438.9	51.4	4.0	1.1	5.1	40.4	7.1	19.5	8.7	16.4	14.8	12.4
08003		7	Alamosa.........................	722.6	16,683	1,999	23.1	50.1	2.1	2.3	1.8	45.8	6.5	17.5	17.4	13.9	10.8	9.4
08005	19,740	1	Arapahoe.......................	797.9	651,215	103	816.2	62.7	12.2	1.1	7.9	19.5	6.2	17.3	8.1	15.8	14.3	13.0
08007		7	Archuleta.......................	1,350.1	13,765	2,179	10.2	78.3	1.1	2.5	1.6	18.2	4.7	13.4	5.7	9.3	10.8	11.8
08009		9	Baca.............................	2,555.0	3,585	2,932	1.4	86.4	1.6	2.3	0.8	11.0	5.5	16.9	7.0	10.3	10.1	10.2
08011		7	Bent..............................	1,512.8	5,882	2,759	3.9	57.4	8.0	2.1	1.5	32.0	3.2	11.7	8.8	17.1	14.7	13.7

1. CBSA = Core Based Statistical Area. See Appendix A for explanation. See Appendix B for list of metropolitan areas with component counties.   2. County type code from the Economic Research Service of USDA Rural-Urban Continuum Codes. See Appendix A for definition.   3. Dry land or land partially or temporarily covered by water.   4. May be of any race.

Table B. States and Counties — **Population and Households**

STATE County	Population, 2018 (cont.) Age (percent) (cont.) 55 to 64 years	65 to 74 years	75 years and over	Percent female	Population change, 2000-2018 Total persons 2000	2010	Percent change 2000-2010	2010-2018	Components of change, 2010-2018 Births	Deaths	Net Migration	Households, 2013-2017 Number	Persons per household	Percent Family households	Female family householder[1]	One person
	16	17	18	19	20	21	22	23	24	25	26	27	28	29	30	31
CALIFORNIA	12.1	8.3	6.0	50.3	33,871,648	37,254,523	10.0	6.2	4,078,895	2,094,459	333,168	12,888,128	2.96	68.8	13.3	23.9
Alameda	12.2	8.2	5.6	50.8	1,443,741	1,510,258	4.6	10.4	159,649	80,638	77,770	569,070	2.81	66.7	11.9	24.5
Alpine	19.7	17.5	7.9	46.6	1,208	1,175	-2.7	-6.3	48	57	-70	304	3.84	67.8	9.5	28.9
Amador	16.5	16.5	10.5	45.6	35,100	38,091	8.5	3.4	2,372	3,511	2,383	14,185	2.37	66.8	7.6	29.2
Butte	12.7	11.0	7.6	50.6	203,171	220,002	8.3	5.1	20,190	18,934	10,103	86,167	2.54	59.8	11.3	28.8
Calaveras	18.4	16.7	10.8	50.2	40,554	45,578	12.4	0.1	2,941	4,082	1,183	17,812	2.50	66.8	9.5	27.5
Colusa	11.7	8.4	6.3	48.9	18,804	21,407	13.8	1.0	2,546	1,164	-1,173	7,047	3.02	75.3	10.1	20.9
Contra Costa	13.2	9.3	6.5	51.1	948,816	1,049,204	10.6	9.6	101,176	62,742	63,035	389,597	2.86	71.8	12.3	22.1
Del Norte	14.3	10.9	7.1	45.4	27,507	28,610	4.0	-2.7	2,596	2,279	-1,135	9,683	2.50	59.2	14.3	34.8
El Dorado	17.1	13.1	8.1	50.1	156,299	181,058	15.8	5.3	13,098	12,043	8,664	68,084	2.69	70.8	7.8	23.6
Fresno	10.4	7.2	5.1	50.1	799,407	930,496	16.4	6.9	128,424	54,033	-10,112	301,824	3.16	72.9	17.7	21.4
Glenn	12.8	9.0	6.8	49.2	26,453	28,122	6.3	-0.3	3,209	1,957	-1,336	9,936	2.78	72.4	11.6	23.4
Humboldt	13.3	11.3	6.6	50.2	126,518	134,611	6.4	1.3	12,236	10,797	368	53,966	2.43	56.3	11.5	32.2
Imperial	10.4	7.2	5.8	48.7	142,361	174,524	22.6	4.2	25,092	8,202	-9,701	45,198	3.77	77.6	19.3	19.1
Inyo	16.5	12.9	10.5	49.7	17,945	18,542	3.3	-3.0	1,665	1,547	-669	8,026	2.19	54.2	9.6	39.7
Kern	10.5	6.6	4.3	48.7	661,645	839,619	26.9	6.8	115,471	47,309	-10,776	264,993	3.20	74.7	16.5	20.1
Kings	9.5	5.9	4.3	45.0	129,461	152,982	18.2	-1.1	19,367	6,764	-14,567	42,349	3.18	76.0	17.9	18.0
Lake	15.9	13.9	8.8	50.1	58,309	64,664	10.9	-0.4	6,076	6,879	558	26,327	2.40	60.9	13.3	31.1
Lassen	12.0	9.4	5.8	37.8	33,828	34,895	3.2	-11.7	2,483	1,764	-4,926	9,441	2.28	64.5	9.3	28.9
Los Angeles	12.0	7.8	5.9	50.7	9,519,338	9,818,672	3.1	2.9	1,045,817	506,593	-250,269	3,295,198	3.01	66.9	15.2	25.6
Madera	11.0	8.4	5.6	51.8	123,109	150,841	22.5	4.5	19,209	8,729	-3,700	44,458	3.29	77.7	14.4	19.1
Marin	15.2	12.9	9.4	51.1	247,289	252,423	2.1	2.9	18,940	15,701	4,153	104,846	2.42	61.8	8.1	31.3
Mariposa	18.2	16.2	11.7	49.0	17,130	18,247	6.5	-4.3	1,205	1,454	-525	7,434	2.23	64.6	7.7	28.5
Mendocino	14.4	14.1	8.0	50.5	86,265	87,850	1.8	-0.3	8,641	7,018	-1,818	34,182	2.50	60.9	11.3	31.2
Merced	10.1	6.6	4.6	49.5	210,554	255,796	21.5	7.4	34,422	13,707	-1,666	79,261	3.30	76.3	18.1	18.9
Modoc	16.2	15.9	11.0	50.0	9,449	9,686	2.5	-9.4	673	908	-678	3,638	2.34	58.1	8.2	35.9
Mono	16.0	10.3	5.5	46.9	12,853	14,206	10.5	0.3	1,155	384	-745	4,899	2.80	50.1	4.5	37.0
Monterey	11.2	8.0	5.6	49.1	401,762	415,061	3.3	4.9	53,287	20,307	-12,323	125,939	3.30	72.4	13.5	21.7
Napa	13.6	10.8	8.3	50.2	124,279	136,578	9.9	2.1	11,958	10,052	1,043	49,044	2.79	68.8	10.4	25.1
Nevada	17.3	17.0	10.5	50.9	92,033	98,745	7.3	1.0	6,595	7,968	2,416	40,386	2.42	64.0	8.6	29.2
Orange	12.7	8.4	6.4	50.6	2,846,289	3,010,274	5.8	5.8	311,831	157,140	23,512	1,024,976	3.04	72.1	11.9	20.9
Placer	13.4	11.1	8.4	51.1	248,399	348,503	40.3	12.8	30,689	24,789	38,736	138,564	2.68	70.2	9.1	24.2
Plumas	18.6	17.8	10.6	50.2	20,824	20,007	-3.9	-6.0	1,285	1,792	-702	8,287	2.21	58.8	7.3	33.3
Riverside	11.5	8.2	6.2	50.2	1,545,387	2,189,765	41.7	11.9	250,404	129,124	140,099	711,724	3.26	73.4	13.2	21.3
Sacramento	12.2	8.4	5.8	51.1	1,223,499	1,418,735	16.0	8.6	161,827	90,712	52,256	532,050	2.76	66.1	14.6	26.4
San Benito	12.2	7.8	5.1	49.9	53,234	55,265	3.8	11.3	6,160	2,521	2,659	17,440	3.35	80.3	13.0	14.2
San Bernardino	11.3	7.1	4.5	50.2	1,709,434	2,035,201	19.1	6.7	253,293	109,472	-6,268	623,642	3.31	76.0	17.1	19.1
San Diego	11.8	8.1	5.9	49.7	2,813,833	3,095,349	10.0	8.0	358,797	172,073	64,089	1,111,739	2.87	67.2	12.0	24.0
San Francisco	11.5	8.7	7.0	49.0	776,733	805,184	3.7	9.7	73,844	48,143	52,066	358,772	2.35	47.0	8.1	36.7
San Joaquin	11.2	7.5	5.2	50.2	563,598	685,306	21.6	9.8	83,754	43,565	27,554	223,808	3.17	74.4	15.3	20.3
San Luis Obispo	13.7	11.9	8.2	49.3	246,681	269,597	9.3	5.3	21,563	19,077	12,023	105,044	2.51	63.3	8.3	26.1
San Mateo	13.0	9.1	7.0	50.6	707,161	718,518	1.6	7.1	74,206	39,596	16,727	261,796	2.88	69.5	10.4	23.2
Santa Barbara	11.3	8.4	6.9	50.0	399,347	423,947	6.2	5.3	46,545	24,980	1,215	144,015	2.94	65.1	11.1	24.2
Santa Clara	11.8	7.5	6.0	49.4	1,682,585	1,781,672	5.9	8.8	192,853	81,960	46,048	630,451	2.98	71.9	10.2	20.8
Santa Cruz	13.4	10.5	5.9	50.5	255,602	262,356	2.6	4.5	24,369	14,594	2,228	95,536	2.73	63.0	10.3	26.4
Shasta	14.7	12.2	8.6	50.9	163,256	177,221	8.6	1.6	17,094	17,421	3,343	70,486	2.49	64.3	11.6	28.7
Sierra	18.7	19.6	12.0	49.4	3,555	3,240	-8.9	-7.8	188	295	-146	1,208	2.36	58.2	5.3	36.7
Siskiyou	16.4	15.7	9.8	50.3	44,301	44,900	1.4	-2.6	3,700	4,432	-431	19,018	2.26	61.9	9.7	31.6
Solano	13.5	9.7	6.1	50.3	394,542	413,298	4.8	8.1	42,613	26,078	17,074	147,352	2.88	72.0	15.4	21.8
Sonoma	14.4	12.1	7.6	51.2	458,614	483,868	5.5	3.3	41,610	33,485	8,231	190,058	2.59	63.3	10.3	28.1
Stanislaus	11.3	7.7	5.4	50.5	446,997	514,451	15.1	6.9	63,394	33,011	5,279	171,324	3.10	74.2	15.3	20.4
	12.0	8.4	7.0	50.2												
Sutter	12.0	8.4	7.0	50.2	78,930	94,756	20.1	2.2	10,863	6,452	-2,404	32,188	2.94	73.0	12.8	22.0
Tehama	14.1	11.1	8.3	50.3	56,039	63,440	13.2	0.8	6,348	5,397	-435	23,712	2.63	68.4	11.8	24.8
Trinity	18.9	17.2	10.1	48.6	13,022	13,784	5.9	-9.1	910	1,332	-825	5,462	2.33	62.8	9.7	31.1
Tulare	9.9	6.7	4.7	50.0	368,021	442,181	20.2	5.4	62,255	23,912	-14,597	135,144	3.35	77.8	17.3	17.7
Tuolumne	16.2	15.5	10.7	48.1	54,501	55,368	1.6	-1.5	3,786	5,237	643	22,267	2.27	64.1	8.8	28.9
Ventura	13.2	9.0	6.6	50.5	753,197	823,393	9.3	3.3	84,239	45,315	-10,891	270,046	3.09	73.4	12.2	20.9
Yolo	10.3	7.3	5.2	51.6	168,660	200,855	19.1	9.7	19,898	10,329	10,009	72,845	2.81	62.3	10.1	23.8
Yuba	11.3	8.0	4.8	49.4	60,219	72,146	19.8	8.2	10,036	4,702	589	25,880	2.83	71.0	13.3	22.0
COLORADO	12.5	8.8	5.4	49.6	4,301,261	5,029,316	16.9	13.2	543,471	289,139	406,752	2,082,531	2.55	64.3	9.8	27.2
Adams	10.8	6.5	3.9	49.5	348,618	441,698	26.7	15.9	58,925	23,435	34,269	162,508	2.98	70.9	13.7	21.9
Alamosa	10.8	8.2	5.4	49.9	14,966	15,440	3.2	8.1	1,808	1,062	443	6,049	2.52	61.4	10.1	28.7
Arapahoe	12.2	8.2	4.9	50.4	487,967	572,130	17.2	13.8	65,291	30,645	44,253	235,263	2.64	66.1	11.3	26.6
Archuleta	18.2	17.9	8.1	49.9	9,898	12,084	22.1	13.9	984	744	1,428	5,553	2.24	66.3	6.8	28.0
Baca	15.3	12.3	12.4	49.8	4,517	3,787	-16.2	-5.3	335	453	-85	1,603	2.17	64.9	6.9	31.4
Bent	12.9	10.0	8.0	34.6	5,998	6,499	8.4	-9.5	327	474	-506	1,760	2.18	68.7	14.7	28.0

1. No spouse present.

Table B. States and Counties — Population, Vital Statistics, Health, and Crime

STATE County	Persons in group quarters, 2018	Daytime Population, 2013-2017		Births, 2018		Deaths, 2018		Persons under 65 with no health insurance, 2016		Medicare, 2018			Serious crimes known to police[2], 2016 Total	
		Number	Employment/ residence ratio	Total	Rate[1]	Number	Rate[1]	Number	Percent	Total beneficiaries	Enrolled in Original Medicare	Enrolled in Medicare Advantage	Number	Rate[3]
	32	33	34	35	36	37	38	39	40	41	42	43	44	45
CALIFORNIA..................	825,850	38,982,816	1.00	477,145	12.1	280,674	7.1	2,787,305	8.4	6,118,721	3,506,273	2,612,448	1,176,866	2,998
Alameda............................	36,417	1,602,833	0.96	19,132	11.5	11,150	6.7	74,359	5.3	238,274	136,143	102,131	69,871	4,227
Alpine...............................	24	1,496	1.80	8	7.3	6	5.4	59	7.1	255	233	22	40	3,656
Amador	4,398	37,537	1.02	296	7.5	427	10.8	1,479	6.0	11,060	8,649	2,411	761	2,080
Butte................................	5,457	225,507	1.00	2,480	10.7	2,395	10.4	12,937	7.1	49,786	47,629	2,157	8,097	3,599
Calaveras........................	493	39,367	0.65	382	8.4	539	11.8	2,068	6.3	12,956	11,131	1,825	834	1,878
Colusa.............................	268	21,538	1.01	314	14.5	120	5.5	1,969	10.7	3,611	3,264	347	403	1,888
Contra Costa....................	10,611	992,069	0.75	12,081	10.5	8,547	7.4	57,151	5.9	193,361	101,069	92,292	32,834	2,895
Del Norte.........................	3,064	27,842	1.05	308	11.1	279	10.0	1,546	7.7	6,100	5,586	514	776	2,894
El Dorado.........................	1,645	163,782	0.73	1,607	8.4	1,712	9.0	8,005	5.4	43,108	28,319	14,789	3,431	1,866
Fresno.............................	16,963	971,481	1.00	14,814	14.9	7,242	7.3	79,068	9.4	138,674	94,236	44,438	37,765	3,866
Glenn	317	26,851	0.90	365	13.0	219	7.8	2,301	9.9	5,617	5,370	247	662	2,381
Humboldt..........................	5,545	135,970	1.01	1,444	10.6	1,362	10.0	9,218	8.3	28,409	26,685	1,724	4,683	3,470
Imperial...........................	9,052	179,048	0.98	2,851	15.7	1,033	5.5	12,317	8.3	30,471	25,338	5,133	5,871	3,400
Inyo.................................	432	18,145	0.99	175	9.7	193	10.7	1,180	8.6	4,585	4,405	180	448	2,477
Kern................................	32,382	882,630	1.01	13,415	15.0	6,242	7.0	61,640	8.1	115,416	72,084	43,332	37,698	4,262
Kings...............................	16,066	151,589	1.03	2,225	14.7	900	5.9	9,837	8.3	16,975	13,923	3,052	3,806	2,543
Lake................................	1,124	60,136	0.82	736	11.4	822	12.8	4,263	8.7	17,064	16,130	934	2,125	3,314
Lassen	7,640	32,481	1.12	298	9.7	237	7.7	936	4.9	5,071	4,955	116	738	2,421
Los Angeles	178,334	10,238,711	1.03	119,254	11.8	68,907	6.8	926,957	10.7	1,463,089	746,936	716,153	308,575	3,034
Madera............................	7,905	151,131	0.93	2,336	14.8	1,039	6.6	12,189	9.7	23,921	15,829	8,092	4,729	3,056
Marin...............................	8,222	261,165	1.00	2,129	8.2	2,004	7.7	10,687	5.3	57,647	34,623	23,024	5,450	2,087
Mariposa..........................	728	17,187	0.93	147	8.4	157	9.0	990	7.8	4,763	4,418	345	321	1,859
Mendocino	1,977	87,872	1.01	1,007	11.5	875	10.0	6,772	9.9	22,690	20,677	2,013	2,050	2,356
Merced.............................	6,696	254,093	0.86	4,042	14.7	1,748	6.4	19,424	8.4	35,326	31,287	4,039	9,146	3,400
Modoc..............................	321	8,842	0.94	98	11.2	115	13.1	637	9.9	2,492	2,294	198	204	2,327
Mono...............................	337	14,997	1.12	128	9.0	46	3.2	1,221	10.3	1,653	1,581	72	199	1,447
Monterey	18,086	430,224	0.98	6,006	13.8	2,688	6.2	39,855	11.0	63,309	58,788	4,521	12,218	2,812
Napa................................	5,018	148,214	1.10	1,356	9.7	1,336	9.6	8,215	7.2	28,962	18,149	10,813	3,122	2,189
Nevada.............................	1,176	96,035	0.93	758	7.6	949	9.5	5,060	6.9	28,822	24,359	4,463	2,018	2,054
Orange.............................	44,926	3,252,325	1.06	37,050	11.6	21,220	6.7	221,792	8.2	491,674	243,918	247,756	73,329	2,306
Placer..............................	3,956	374,844	1.00	3,682	9.4	3,300	8.4	14,032	4.5	81,989	42,756	39,233	7,702	2,037
Plumas.............................	278	19,473	1.11	160	8.5	234	12.4	947	7.0	6,096	5,616	480	479	2,661
Riverside..........................	33,324	2,182,057	0.82	30,318	12.4	17,703	7.2	197,822	9.8	364,445	157,397	207,048	72,780	3,061
Sacramento......................	22,158	1,495,242	1.00	19,277	12.5	11,986	7.8	75,034	5.8	251,878	130,004	121,874	46,839	3,107
San Benito	289	49,111	0.64	787	12.8	333	5.4	3,836	7.4	8,484	7,544	940	698	1,182
San Bernardino.................	37,611	2,051,881	0.92	30,402	14.0	14,901	6.9	169,236	9.1	288,964	118,605	170,359	65,406	3,069
San Diego	108,137	3,315,480	1.02	41,635	12.5	23,022	6.9	226,877	8.1	516,596	271,576	245,020	72,315	2,180
San Francisco	24,235	1,084,683	1.45	8,953	10.1	6,620	7.5	34,411	4.7	145,658	86,845	58,813	54,706	6,280
San Joaquin	15,023	690,885	0.88	10,202	13.6	5,566	7.4	45,873	7.3	109,324	67,264	42,060	28,634	3,927
San Luis Obispo...............	16,232	278,827	0.99	2,518	8.9	2,375	8.4	15,158	7.0	61,960	52,650	9,310	7,802	2,768
San Mateo........................	8,815	767,262	1.01	8,774	11.4	5,331	6.9	33,832	5.2	124,263	69,163	55,100	16,527	2,149
Santa Barbara..................	19,626	456,199	1.06	5,353	12.0	3,234	7.2	37,611	10.3	74,641	62,440	12,201	11,306	2,536
Santa Clara......................	30,975	2,042,017	1.14	22,347	11.5	11,467	5.9	84,393	5.1	263,382	149,891	113,491	48,220	2,496
Santa Cruz.......................	14,048	262,092	0.91	2,709	9.9	1,961	7.2	15,954	7.1	48,719	45,187	3,532	10,586	3,857
Shasta.............................	2,834	179,748	1.01	1,995	11.1	2,144	11.9	9,511	6.7	47,010	45,919	1,091	6,894	3,857
Sierra..............................	33	2,700	0.83	32	10.7	46	15.4	147	7.1	905	873	32	40	1,380
Siskiyou...........................	576	44,131	1.04	456	10.4	559	12.8	2,637	8.1	13,251	12,152	1,099	1,037	2,412
Solano.............................	11,396	387,692	0.76	5,155	11.5	3,624	8.1	22,453	6.1	77,395	44,216	33,179	13,741	3,140
Sonoma............................	10,921	484,209	0.93	4,789	9.6	4,403	8.8	30,544	7.5	102,970	56,160	46,810	9,662	1,924
Stanislaus	6,458	513,551	0.90	7,717	14.0	4,050	7.4	31,825	6.8	85,341	46,900	38,441	21,284	3,946
Sutter	754	89,368	0.83	1,342	13.9	812	8.4	7,650	9.4	17,053	16,414	639	3,051	3,173
Tehama............................	842	60,593	0.89	774	12.1	644	10.1	3,921	7.7	14,593	14,243	350	2,297	3,656
Trinity	385	13,214	1.04	103	8.2	163	13.0	854	9.1	3,522	3,295	227	365	2,841
Tulare..............................	5,053	450,240	0.95	6,970	15.0	3,052	6.6	39,771	9.9	61,291	50,428	10,863	13,171	2,862
Tuolumne.........................	3,584	53,614	0.99	447	8.2	559	10.2	2,249	6.0	15,523	14,588	935	1,459	2,750
Ventura............................	11,371	805,510	0.89	9,370	11.0	6,204	7.3	69,811	9.7	145,310	97,052	48,258	18,608	2,190
Yolo................................	10,174	226,814	1.15	2,394	10.9	1,350	6.1	12,177	6.7	30,672	17,733	12,939	6,007	2,807
Yuba................................	1,138	70,281	0.85	1,242	15.9	522	6.7	4,607	7.1	12,337	11,348	989	2,262	3,040
COLORADO	121,148	5,425,806	1.00	66,249	11.6	38,367	6.7	401,879	8.6	880,478	547,567	332,911	170,833	3,083
Adams.............................	4,461	432,569	0.77	6,894	13.5	3,065	6.0	52,929	12.0	60,219	28,407	31,812	18,428	3,677
Alamosa...........................	1,272	17,911	1.24	206	12.3	111	6.7	1,658	12.7	2,880	2,339	541	149	897
Arapahoe.........................	4,303	619,714	0.98	7,870	12.1	4,128	6.3	47,210	8.5	90,145	49,991	40,154	19,796	3,080
Archuleta.........................	129	12,431	0.97	137	10.0	96	7.0	1,314	13.7	3,649	3,063	586	191	1,540
Baca................................	82	3,522	0.96	39	10.9	48	13.4	373	14.4	971	D	D	17	475
Bent................................	1,950	5,921	1.09	36	6.1	50	8.5	379	12.5	1,090	1,041	49	146	2,560

1. Per 1,000 estimated resident population.   2. Data for serious crimes have not been adjusted for underreporting; this may affect comparability between geographic areas and over time.   3. Per 100,000 population estimated by the FBI.

Table B. States and Counties — Crime, Education, Money Income, and Poverty

STATE County	Serious crimes known to police[2], 2016 (cont.)[1] Rate Violent	Property	Education — School enrollment and attainment, 2013-2017 Enrollment[3] Total	Percent private	Attainment[4] (percent) High school graduate or less	Bachelor's degree or more	Local government expenditures,[5] 2014-2015 Total current spending (mil dol)	Current spending per student (dollars)	Money income, 2013-2017 Per capita income[6]	Households Median income (dollars)	Percent with income of less than $50,000	with income of $200,000 or more	Income and poverty, 2017 Median household income (dollars)	Percent below poverty level All persons	Children under 18 years	Children 5 to 17 years in families
	46	47	48	49	50	51	52	53	54	55	56	57	58	59	60	61
CALIFORNIA......	445	2,553	10,518,223	13.9	38.1	32.6	65,177.1	10,475	33,128	67,169	38.3	9.7	71,785	13.3	18.1	17.4
Alameda............	613	3,614	416,674	14.9	30.4	44.7	2,209.0	9,819	41,363	85,743	30.4	14.6	95,550	9.3	10.5	10.1
Alpine...............	548	3,108	347	13.3	44.4	25.6	3.6	43,024	27,448	63,438	37.2	8.6	55,755	18.1	35.3	28.7
Amador.............	252	1,829	6,857	9.4	37.3	22.1	40.5	10,051	29,628	60,636	42.7	5.0	60,588	10.9	15.7	15.2
Butte................	351	3,248	64,792	7.3	33.9	26.6	335.4	10,820	26,304	46,516	53.1	3.8	48,634	18.1	22.6	21.2
Calaveras..........	401	1,478	7,595	8.4	37.6	19.3	65.4	11,362	31,652	54,800	45.3	4.6	58,536	13.1	21.1	20.9
Colusa..............	216	1,673	5,845	7.3	53.8	15.7	55.8	11,703	25,676	56,481	44.8	3.5	53,595	12.2	15.4	14.9
Contra Costa......	343	2,551	295,449	16.3	28.8	40.7	1,723.8	9,861	42,898	88,456	28.4	15.3	95,062	9.1	11.2	10.3
Del Norte..........	626	2,267	5,920	7.8	50.5	14.4	46.6	11,297	20,809	41,287	55.6	2.1	39,996	24.6	33.9	32.5
El Dorado..........	212	1,655	41,661	11.3	28.6	33.3	286.5	10,628	38,156	74,885	34.3	10.9	78,464	8.3	9.6	8.8
Fresno..............	612	3,254	290,845	7.8	48.2	20.1	2,127.9	10,858	22,234	48,730	51.0	4.0	51,452	21.1	28.3	26.7
Glenn...............	370	2,010	7,148	7.4	54.8	13.0	62.5	11,382	21,029	46,260	54.0	1.5	49,979	14.8	20.8	19.8
Humboldt...........	505	2,965	35,109	8.3	33.5	29.4	212.9	11,955	25,208	43,718	55.6	3.0	46,123	19.7	24.7	22.9
Imperial............	391	3,008	53,731	5.9	55.1	14.3	419.4	11,277	17,303	44,779	53.6	2.7	43,413	20.7	28.1	26.7
Inyo.................	630	1,847	3,714	10.1	41.7	25.3	65.7	12,640	30,323	51,500	49.1	3.2	53,528	11.8	17.6	17.1
Kern................	580	3,683	256,756	8.9	53.9	15.8	1,891.9	10,493	21,716	50,826	49.3	3.7	49,904	21.2	29.0	27.2
Kings...............	427	2,116	43,426	9.2	52.6	13.0	288.9	11,145	19,835	49,742	50.3	3.0	55,076	18.4	24.5	24.4
Lake................	591	2,723	13,724	10.4	45.6	15.3	101.3	11,781	23,345	40,446	57.6	2.2	45,797	20.2	30.1	29.9
Lassen.............	738	1,683	6,191	23.1	50.1	12.4	42.6	9,630	20,974	54,083	45.3	2.4	58,776	16.3	18.0	17.6
Los Angeles	554	2,480	2,704,769	15.3	42.6	31.2	17,145.4	11,138	30,798	61,015	42.2	8.4	64,912	14.9	20.9	20.4
Madera.............	662	2,395	43,026	7.1	53.2	13.8	313.5	10,157	19,975	48,210	51.3	2.9	50,783	21.2	28.6	27.4
Marin...............	182	1,905	61,579	24.2	18.0	57.5	426.5	12,843	66,748	104,703	25.5	24.5	112,735	7.9	8.2	7.3
Mariposa...........	463	1,395	2,909	9.4	38.1	24.4	22.2	12,299	28,241	51,385	49.0	2.4	52,387	15.2	21.2	21.0
Mendocino.........	696	1,659	19,779	9.5	39.3	24.8	155.8	12,064	27,093	46,528	52.9	3.2	50,453	16.3	22.8	21.6
Merced.............	553	2,847	86,441	5.0	56.2	13.8	611.8	10,806	20,120	46,338	53.4	3.2	48,036	23	33.7	31.7
Modoc..............	468	1,859	1,502	19.4	45.0	16.6	15.5	16,517	22,052	39,296	61.6	0.7	40,970	19.2	29.7	27.3
Mono...............	269	1,178	3,081	3.5	34.2	31.5	32.1	15,227	30,888	60,595	36.2	3.4	60,318	9.3	12.6	11.9
Monterey...........	419	2,393	122,521	9.0	49.5	23.9	822.9	10,838	27,168	63,249	38.6	7.1	70,294	11.9	16.2	16.1
Napa................	419	1,770	34,392	16.4	33.4	34.6	249.0	11,857	40,632	79,637	31.4	12.0	83,881	6.8	8.6	8.1
Nevada.............	216	1,839	19,490	10.8	25.0	35.8	182.5	11,210	35,581	60,610	42.0	6.3	64,901	11	14.4	13.4
Orange.............	229	2,078	862,152	15.0	32.6	39.1	4,817.7	9,691	37,603	81,851	30.6	13.0	86,031	11.5	15.7	15.9
Placer..............	165	1,873	95,847	13.0	24.6	37.5	610.6	9,257	39,734	80,488	30.4	10.2	81,366	7.8	7.2	6.7
Plumas.............	667	1,995	3,423	12.9	31.9	22.6	26.8	12,600	32,056	50,266	49.7	3.4	51,756	14.3	22.0	20.1
Riverside...........	313	2,748	668,113	11.7	45.3	21.5	4,264.1	10,012	25,700	60,807	41.8	5.3	63,776	12.9	16.2	15.8
Sacramento........	513	2,594	402,676	11.6	35.5	29.9	2,396.5	10,043	29,693	60,239	41.9	5.5	62,959	14.1	18.2	16.4
San Benito.........	262	919	17,130	10.6	45.6	19.2	114.0	10,237	30,012	80,760	29.2	8.4	77,200	8.4	11.9	11.3
San Bernardino....	491	2,578	621,531	11.1	47.0	19.8	4,023.5	9,801	22,867	57,156	43.8	4.1	60,270	16	23.0	22.0
San Diego..........	330	1,850	874,844	14.7	31.9	37.4	4,990.5	9,905	34,350	70,588	35.8	9.3	76,048	11.9	15.7	14.5
San Francisco.....	720	5,560	166,017	31.0	24.4	55.8	777.5	13,154	59,508	96,265	30.4	21.2	109,601	10.1	12.3	12.4
San Joaquin.......	824	3,104	206,340	12.4	48.9	18.1	1,377.5	9,803	24,694	57,813	43.5	4.9	60,950	15.5	21.6	20.3
San Luis Obispo...	396	2,373	77,327	8.7	29.3	34.0	359.7	10,343	33,972	67,175	37.2	7.3	70,634	11.9	12.3	11.6
San Mateo.........	212	1,936	187,289	22.3	26.6	48.5	1,106.3	11,622	53,516	105,667	23.0	22.5	115,908	6.4	7.0	6.9
Santa Barbara.....	342	2,193	134,744	9.5	37.0	33.3	726.3	10,591	32,872	68,023	37.7	9.6	70,651	14.2	17.4	16.3
Santa Clara........	281	2,215	510,417	21.0	27.2	50.0	2,943.9	10,659	48,689	106,761	23.8	22.4	118,468	7.5	8.1	8.0
Santa Cruz.........	401	3,455	79,763	11.9	29.1	39.8	444.5	10,820	36,388	73,663	35.6	11.7	76,533	12.6	13.7	13.0
Shasta..............	746	3,111	42,194	16.3	35.0	21.4	300.5	11,286	26,455	47,258	52.5	3.2	51,207	17	22.9	20.8
Sierra...............	483	897	462	12.3	32.5	21.4	6.4	17,218	31,750	44,190	53.9	4.6	49,495	13.7	20.2	19.9
Siskiyou............	375	2,038	8,988	10.2	35.8	22.7	84.5	13,663	24,605	40,884	58.0	1.8	44,013	17.7	25.7	23.9
Solano..............	462	2,678	110,210	13.2	35.7	25.6	620.4	9,372	31,934	72,950	34.2	7.0	75,931	10	14.0	12.6
Sonoma............	372	1,552	121,263	11.9	31.5	33.8	771.7	10,855	37,767	71,769	34.0	8.6	79,511	9.3	10.9	9.7
Stanislaus	624	3,322	151,991	7.9	50.5	16.7	1,127.1	10,685	24,007	54,260	46.1	3.8	58,925	14	18.6	17.8
Sutter	374	2,799	26,052	9.4	46.3	17.5	193.9	9,034	24,849	54,347	46.5	3.5	54,102	13.2	18.2	17.8
Tehama.............	573	3,083	15,460	7.6	48.4	14.4	122.3	11,561	22,631	42,512	56.1	2.9	41,819	20.1	29.0	26.5
Trinity..............	514	2,327	2,249	4.6	42.1	19.5	25.1	16,736	23,575	36,563	61.5	1.6	40,676	20.3	32.1	29.2
Tulare..............	349	2,513	139,076	6.4	57.2	13.8	1,073.9	10,507	18,962	44,871	54.9	3.1	46,377	24	31.9	30.9
Tuolumne..........	352	2,398	10,158	11.8	38.5	20.6	70.7	12,228	31,570	54,325	45.8	4.7	58,776	12.2	17.5	16.4
Ventura............	258	1,932	227,204	14.7	34.9	32.6	1,402.1	9,881	35,771	81,972	29.7	11.6	82,436	9.5	13.2	12.1
Yolo................	299	2,508	78,625	8.1	32.7	40.6	294.9	10,050	30,615	61,621	41.4	8.3	64,900	17.5	14.1	13.4
Yuba................	427	2,612	21,405	9.5	42.4	16.4	146.9	10,512	22,814	51,776	48.4	2.1	53,822	15.3	21.9	21.3
COLORADO	343	2,741	1,390,638	12.4	30.4	39.4	8,175.9	D	34,845	65,458	38.1	7.1	69,113	10.3	12.2	11.4
Adams..............	401	3,276	129,656	9.5	45.7	23.1	731.8	8,675	27,487	64,087	38.2	4.2	65,977	10.6	13.7	12.4
Alamosa............	66	831	5,371	7.6	42.0	26.2	26.5	10,709	19,217	36,315	64.1	1.9	43,121	21.3	26.6	25.4
Arapahoe..........	366	2,714	161,469	13.2	28.4	41.6	1,148.3	9,675	36,951	69,553	34.4	8.0	75,196	7.8	9.0	8.2
Archuleta..........	193	1,346	2,072	20.6	32.8	37.0	11.7	8,854	29,344	48,016	52.4	3.3	52,481	11.7	21.0	20.3
Baca................	56	419	716	5.9	41.2	21.4	8.7	13,534	22,853	35,898	63.8	1.4	35,725	19.7	32.1	28.9
Bent................	123	2,437	808	5.2	61.2	10.3	7.3	9,404	14,028	32,500	69.6	1.1	37,307	32	34.8	31.0

1. Data for serious crimes have not been adjusted for underreporting; this may affect comparability between geographic areas and over time.   2. Per 100,000 population estimated by the FBI.   3. All persons 3 years old and over enrolled in nursery school through college.   4. Persons 25 years old and over.   5. Elementary and secondary education expenditures.   6. Based on population estimated by the American Community Survey, 2013–2017.

Table B. States and Counties — **Personal Income and Earnings**

| | Personal income, 2017 | | | | | | | | | | Earnings, 2017 | | |
STATE County	Total (mil dol)	Percent change 2016-2017	Per capita¹ Dollars	Per capita¹ Rank	Wages and salaries (mil dol)	Supplements to wages and salaries, employer contributions (mil dol) — Pension and insurance	Government social insurance	Proprietors' income (mil dol)	Dividends, interest, and rent (mil dol)	Personal transfer reecipts (mil dol)	Total (mil dol)	Contributions for government social insurance (mil dol) — From employee and self-employed	From employer
	62	63	64	65	66	67	68	69	70	71	72	73	74
CALIFORNIA	2,364,129	4.6	60,004	X	1,187,476	191,481	77,389	240,975	508,393	331,432	1,697,321	93,774	77,389
Alameda	118,555	6.5	71,282	62	61,843	9,630	4,114	11,600	21,270	13,445	87,187	4,740	4,114
Alpine	74	-6.6	65,673	98	43	9	3	5	25	15	60	3	3
Amador	1,687	5.4	43,679	1,055	575	169	36	157	396	414	938	56	36
Butte	9,926	4.5	43,287	1,105	3,716	835	267	968	2,125	2,508	5,787	347	267
Calaveras	2,164	4.8	47,384	676	399	113	27	200	549	532	739	52	27
Colusa	1,048	7.0	48,056	622	394	90	32	241	224	179	756	30	32
Contra Costa	87,810	6.8	76,527	48	26,953	4,393	1,836	6,529	20,094	9,184	39,710	2,284	1,836
Del Norte	994	0.6	36,179	2,179	336	115	21	89	189	335	562	31	21
El Dorado	12,222	4.7	64,673	104	3,041	581	213	1,001	2,414	1,691	4,835	298	213
Fresno	41,024	4.1	41,470	1,338	17,888	3,928	1,327	4,207	7,368	9,380	27,350	1,462	1,327
Glenn	1,310	6.4	46,626	740	382	91	30	268	267	281	771	34	30
Humboldt	6,389	3.8	46,722	735	2,155	553	149	1,047	1,406	1,446	3,904	214	149
Imperial	6,619	4.1	36,206	2,172	2,631	759	197	1,036	912	1,679	4,623	217	197
Inyo	1,077	3.0	59,744	161	355	109	22	271	204	216	757	39	22
Kern	34,438	2.8	38,560	1,795	15,858	3,601	1,160	4,159	5,590	6,842	24,779	1,259	1,160
Kings	5,303	5.8	35,326	2,295	2,416	678	184	403	985	1,127	3,681	170	184
Lake	2,663	3.8	41,443	1,341	672	173	49	272	508	838	1,165	76	49
Lassen	1,143	1.7	36,686	2,094	500	192	33	79	230	282	804	38	33
Los Angeles	593,741	2.9	58,419	195	300,403	48,728	20,053	67,920	129,906	94,362	437,104	24,256	20,053
Madera	6,087	5.8	38,799	1,755	2,233	536	168	1,117	1,071	1,252	4,054	188	168
Marin	32,503	5.7	124,552	5	8,540	1,324	552	4,482	10,835	2,181	14,898	815	552
Mariposa	892	4.5	50,772	420	236	72	16	94	185	215	419	26	16
Mendocino	4,194	3.3	47,646	650	1,363	321	98	577	1,017	1,069	2,359	143	98
Merced	10,557	6.5	38,716	1,773	3,563	898	266	1,526	1,735	2,494	6,253	286	266
Modoc	402	4.0	45,338	865	102	34	8	61	91	123	204	11	8
Mono	732	10.4	51,631	391	358	74	26	101	215	74	559	29	26
Monterey	23,820	4.3	54,395	301	9,972	2,060	779	3,763	5,637	3,271	16,574	796	779
Napa	10,034	5.0	71,174	65	4,473	836	327	1,734	2,366	1,206	7,370	391	327
Nevada	5,960	3.8	59,715	162	1,511	323	107	803	1,572	1,071	2,744	173	107
Orange	208,653	4.6	65,400	99	107,138	16,021	7,496	22,182	49,466	22,381	152,837	8,616	7,496
Placer	24,527	4.9	63,515	123	9,710	1,530	697	1,957	4,814	3,180	13,894	833	697
Plumas	962	5.1	51,302	401	286	88	20	100	267	258	494	31	20
Riverside	95,141	5.4	39,261	1,679	34,558	7,283	2,455	7,469	15,914	17,774	51,765	3,033	2,455
Sacramento	76,832	3.9	50,197	450	41,643	9,554	2,677	6,216	13,695	14,611	60,090	3,110	2,677
San Benito	3,096	7.9	51,343	399	850	184	65	303	522	407	1,401	73	65
San Bernardino	83,742	4.5	38,816	1,753	37,693	7,843	2,775	6,107	13,107	16,979	54,418	3,109	2,775
San Diego	193,296	3.8	57,913	206	99,206	17,984	7,132	15,797	43,916	26,513	140,119	7,693	7,132
San Francisco	106,007	6.2	119,868	7	84,253	9,807	4,606	15,642	27,001	7,421	114,308	6,145	4,606
San Joaquin	31,920	6.0	42,822	1,165	12,327	2,598	912	2,594	5,109	6,970	18,431	1,029	912
San Luis Obispo	15,680	5.2	55,328	266	5,855	1,301	404	2,068	4,082	2,276	9,627	535	404
San Mateo	87,486	6.6	113,410	9	49,566	4,945	2,551	8,664	23,550	5,011	65,725	3,690	2,551
Santa Barbara	26,647	4.7	59,460	169	11,404	2,189	817	3,468	8,081	3,290	17,877	942	817
Santa Clara	190,002	6.7	98,032	13	143,997	13,238	7,235	13,088	39,574	13,059	177,557	10,044	7,235
Santa Cruz	17,665	5.4	64,028	113	5,595	1,109	403	2,284	4,115	2,150	9,391	497	403
Shasta	8,041	3.8	44,691	940	3,048	669	222	670	1,560	2,348	4,609	295	222
Sierra	134	4.6	44,584	952	23	10	1	11	37	32	45	3	1
Siskiyou	1,918	3.0	43,735	1,049	606	162	46	179	461	611	993	63	46
Solano	21,879	6.4	49,116	524	8,901	1,811	627	1,113	3,776	3,738	12,453	713	627
Sonoma	30,397	5.4	60,286	151	11,673	2,083	841	3,970	7,288	4,307	18,568	1,054	841
Stanislaus	23,446	4.9	42,793	1,170	9,314	1,866	691	2,361	4,001	4,840	14,232	781	691
Sutter	4,193	4.4	43,385	1,091	1,339	279	101	467	785	875	2,186	123	101
Tehama	2,558	4.7	40,016	1,548	826	189	62	255	549	689	1,333	79	62
Trinity	495	3.2	38,963	1,726	114	36	8	51	134	177	210	15	8
Tulare	18,467	5.1	39,756	1,599	6,822	1,627	510	2,700	2,974	4,230	11,659	561	510
Tuolumne	2,526	3.7	46,571	744	811	205	55	203	660	663	1,274	82	55
Ventura	50,551	4.5	59,178	179	19,343	3,535	1,384	4,916	10,627	6,479	29,178	1,613	1,384
Yolo	11,457	4.1	52,289	367	6,490	1,772	408	1,200	2,487	1,572	9,870	456	408
Yuba	3,045	3.9	39,525	1,633	1,175	338	89	231	453	878	1,833	95	89
COLORADO	306,411	5.8	54,561	X	160,372	20,805	11,485	28,501	68,190	39,530	221,162	12,295	11,485
Adams	20,738	5.2	41,215	1,378	11,809	1,640	833	1,954	2,620	3,221	16,235	843	833
Alamosa	591	4.0	35,721	2,243	332	58	25	44	113	154	460	24	25
Arapahoe	36,424	3.8	56,642	233	22,753	2,535	1,614	2,370	8,442	4,282	29,272	1,723	1,614
Archuleta	532	3.2	39,944	1,561	156	24	12	83	159	123	275	17	12
Baca	150	8.8	42,019	1,263	43	10	3	14	38	46	70	4	3
Bent	157	1.0	26,417	3,074	44	8	3	17	42	51	73	4	3

1. Based on the resident population estimated as of July 1 of the year shown.

Table B. States and Counties — Earnings, Social Security, and Housing

STATE County	Earnings, 2017 (cont.)									Social Security beneficiaries, December 2017			Housing units, 2018	
	Percent by selected industries											Supplemental Security Income recipients, 2017		
	Farm	Mining, quarrying, and extractions	Construction	Manu-facturing	Information; professional, scientific, technical services	Retail trade	Finance, insurance, real estate, and leasing	Health care and social assistance	Govern-ment	Number	Rate[1]		Total	Percent change, 2010-2018
	75	76	77	78	79	80	81	82	83	84	85	86	87	88
CALIFORNIA	1.3	0.2	5.4	9.1	18.8	5.3	9.1	9.4	16.2	5,858,780	148	1,261,217	14,277,157	4.4
Alameda	0.1	0	6.6	11.6	20.7	5	6	10.1	15.4	214,485	129	50,166	615,077	5.6
Alpine	0	0	D	D	D	0.9	2.4	1.4	30.1	240	214	36	1,778	1
Amador	2.7	0.8	7.4	4.9	6.3	6.9	3.5	D	41.5	11,455	297	722	18,450	2.3
Butte	4.3	0	6.8	5	5.8	8.9	6	20.3	21.9	52,370	228	11,063	100,033	4.4
Calaveras	1.8	D	14.2	2.3	D	7.9	4.3	D	31.3	13,270	291	1,026	28,065	0.5
Colusa	30.5	D	2.4	10.3	1.1	6	4.4	D	21.6	3,715	170	592	8,068	2.4
Contra Costa	0.2	-0.1	8.6	5.9	14	5.4	12.2	14.2	12.6	183,440	160	25,747	415,919	3.9
Del Norte	4.5	0	3.2	1.3	3.3	7	2.1	D	47.6	6,395	233	1,924	11,423	2.1
El Dorado	0.5	0	12.3	4.2	9.9	6.4	12.7	11.3	19.1	43,050	228	3,058	91,105	3.3
Fresno	6.7	0.2	5.8	6.2	5.6	6.5	5.5	14.3	22.3	138,195	140	43,836	333,769	5.8
Glenn	31.2	0.3	4.3	6.5	1.4	4.9	2.2	D	20.3	5,905	210	1,107	11,041	2.4
Humboldt	5.4	D	8.7	3.2	6.5	10	4.6	12.8	26.4	28,735	210	6,073	63,315	2.9
Imperial	16.9	0.9	2.5	1.7	2.3	7.3	2.4	5.9	36.7	32,605	178	10,455	57,895	3.3
Inyo	1.4	D	3.9	24.7	2.8	7	1.6	D	33.5	4,550	252	418	9,592	1.2
Kern	10.1	5.4	5.4	4.3	4.7	6.3	3.5	8.7	25.3	121,740	136	33,705	300,377	5.6
Kings	10.4	D	2.3	8.4	1.9	4.8	2.1	9.4	45.4	18,145	121	4,658	46,645	6.3
Lake	7.1	0.5	7.8	2	4	8.8	3.1	19	25.2	18,330	285	3,770	34,745	-2.1
Lassen	7.4	0	2.1	0.2	D	4.5	1.6	D	66.8	5,355	172	1,004	12,788	0.6
Los Angeles	0.1	0.1	3.7	7.7	19.5	5.2	10.9	9.8	14.6	1,346,075	132	405,771	3,561,069	3.4
Madera	20.4	D	4.4	6.6	2.1	4.6	2.2	14.1	22.2	25,300	161	4,775	50,966	3.7
Marin	0.3	D	7.1	5.6	20	6.2	11.7	10.6	12	51,835	199	3,371	113,182	1.8
Mariposa	2.5	D	5.7	1.8	5.2	8.6	2.1	3.6	42.8	4,985	284	457	10,404	2.1
Mendocino	3	0.1	8.6	7.4	5.1	10.4	3.9	12.8	21.8	21,645	246	3,395	40,926	1.5
Merced	20.2	D	3.6	9.6	2.1	5.7	2.9	8.9	26	37,790	139	11,070	85,756	2.5
Modoc	22	0	5.6	0.7	D	4.3	3.1	D	39.9	2,585	292	427	5,288	1.9
Mono	2.8	D	7	1	D	5.9	4.8	2.5	28.9	1,580	112	94	14,138	1.6
Monterey	12.6	0.4	4.4	2.5	5.1	5.2	4.8	7.7	23.6	62,705	143	8,493	142,399	2.4
Napa	3.3	D	7.2	23.7	5.5	4.8	5.9	9.1	14.5	27,050	192	2,198	55,460	1.3
Nevada	0.4	0.1	15.8	4.5	9.8	8.1	6.8	12.5	19.8	28,130	282	1,975	54,258	3.2
Orange	0.1	0.1	7.6	10.4	14.2	5.6	14.5	8.9	10.5	450,355	141	73,829	1,111,227	5.9
Placer	0.1	0.1	11.9	4.6	9.7	8.1	11.8	16.7	12.9	78,980	205	5,680	167,134	9.5
Plumas	1.4	D	8.3	7.8	4.4	6.5	3.3	6	37.7	5,995	320	651	15,864	1.9
Riverside	1.1	0.2	11.1	6.2	5.2	8.3	4.7	11	23.6	374,605	155	61,978	848,597	6
Sacramento	0.3	0	6.1	3.2	11.3	5.2	7.1	11.8	34.5	244,260	160	66,793	574,438	3.3
San Benito	8.9	0.1	11.2	19.1	D	4.6	4.5	4.1	20.6	8,775	145	921	19,438	8.8
San Bernardino	0.4	0.1	6.5	7.7	5	7.5	4.1	12.3	23.4	296,505	137	71,962	725,896	3.8
San Diego	0.5	0	5.4	8.6	17.3	5	7.9	8.7	23.6	496,190	149	83,185	1,224,375	5.1
San Francisco	0	0	2.9	1.7	35.2	3.5	16.3	4.6	12.4	123,830	140	42,499	401,452	6.5
San Joaquin	4.1	0.1	6	7.5	3.8	6.8	4.8	11.9	21.6	111,295	149	28,681	245,541	5
San Luis Obispo	4.1	0.1	9.8	5.6	9.5	8.1	5.8	10.4	20.9	59,855	211	4,532	122,979	4.8
San Mateo	0.1	0	4.6	7.7	38.2	3.7	11.8	5.9	5.8	113,485	147	10,168	279,457	3.1
Santa Barbara	5.4	1	4.9	7.4	13.7	5.6	7.4	11	19.9	72,830	163	8,807	158,333	3.6
Santa Clara	0.2	0	3.6	22.2	36.1	3.2	5	6.2	6.1	233,695	121	45,171	678,496	7.4
Santa Cruz	6	0	7.7	6.7	9	7.7	6.3	13.1	18.7	46,545	169	5,719	106,728	2.2
Shasta	1.3	0.2	6.9	3.8	6.7	9.5	5.6	19.2	23	49,275	274	9,858	79,194	2.4
Sierra	9.9	D	D	D	D	1	D	D	56.5	905	302	83	2,361	1.4
Siskiyou	6.9	D	5	6.3	4.7	6.7	2.7	13.7	32	13,540	309	2,580	24,214	1.3
Solano	1.2	0.2	9.8	13.1	4.3	6.6	3.6	15.9	25.1	77,730	174	12,068	158,808	4
Sonoma	2.9	0.1	9.6	12	9.6	7.2	7	13.3	13.9	99,625	198	9,121	205,225	0.3
Stanislaus	7.7	0	6.3	12.1	4.4	7.3	4.3	16.2	18.1	88,290	161	21,375	182,290	1.6
Sutter	9	0.6	5.6	5	3.8	9.4	6.4	12.5	18.5	17,610	182	4,077	34,477	1.8
Tehama	12	D	6.9	8.9	2.4	7.4	2.7	11.2	23	15,510	243	3,105	27,676	2.6
Trinity	2.8	D	7.8	8.3	4.4	9.5	D	D	39.5	3,770	297	649	8,945	3.1
Tulare	15.7	0	4.3	7.9	4.7	6.2	3.5	6.8	23.4	65,140	140	18,963	150,210	6
Tuolumne	1.2	0.6	7	4.6	D	7.5	4	16.6	32.7	16,160	298	1,646	31,628	1.2
Ventura	4.6	0.7	5.8	13.8	10.4	7	8.5	9.5	17	139,710	164	16,410	291,019	3.3
Yolo	3.4	0.1	4.8	5.4	6	4.1	3.7	6.4	43.5	29,335	134	5,345	78,531	4.6
Yuba	4.1	0.5	7.8	3.1	D	3.7	1.2	12.9	50.7	13,320	173	3,975	28,693	3.8
COLORADO	0.6	3.7	7.9	5.7	15.3	5.3	9	9.3	15.8	852,635	152	73,285	2,424,051	9.5
Adams	0.3	0.5	15.2	6.3	6.7	5.4	4	8.2	21.9	61,215	122	7,046	175,616	7.6
Alamosa	5.4	D	6	1.4	3.4	9.5	6.9	20	26.3	2,980	180	638	7,096	8.3
Arapahoe	0	1.2	8.1	1.6	18.3	5.9	15.2	10.7	9.6	85,900	134	7,498	254,242	6.7
Archuleta	2.5	1	17.5	1.8	6.7	11.2	7.6	6.2	19.7	3,675	276	129	9,521	8.7
Baca	17	D	4.3	0.1	D	5.7	D	D	42.3	980	275	73	2,257	0.4
Bent	24.9	0.4	D	D	0.5	3.8	D	4.4	30.3	1,075	181	251	2,269	1.2

1. Per 1,000 resident population estimated as of July 1 of the year shown.

Table B. States and Counties — **Housing, Labor Force, and Employment**

	Housing units, 2013-2017								Civilian labor force, 2018				Civilian employment[6], 2013-2017		
	Occupied units										Unemployment		Percent		
			Owner-occupied			Renter-occupied										
STATE County				Median owner cost as a percent of income			Median rent as a percent of income[2]	Sub-standard units[4] (percent)		Percent change, 2017-2018				Management, business, science, and arts	Construction, production, and maintenance occupations
	Total	Percent	Median value[1]	With a mort-gage	Without a mort-gage[2]	Median rent[3]			Total		Total	Rate[5]	Total		
	89	90	91	92	93	94	95	96	97	98	99	100	101	102	103
CALIFORNIA..............	12,888,128	54.5	443,400	25.9	11.0	1,358	33.1	8.6	19,398,212	1	815,410	4.2	17,993,915	38.1	20.1
Alameda.......................	569,070	53.0	649,100	24.4	10.0	1,547	30.5	7.7	848,215	0.9	25,446	3	826,310	48.0	15.5
Alpine...........................	304	83.2	343,800	34.6	11.9	1,083	23.1	3.3	547	-0.5	25	4.6	374	38.2	21.1
Amador.........................	14,185	77.0	278,600	24.4	13.3	1,056	35.4	2	14,706	-0.1	589	4	13,444	32.7	20.0
Butte............................	86,167	59.0	238,200	24.0	12.2	970	36.7	3.7	102,712	0.5	5,093	5	93,439	35.9	19.2
Calaveras.....................	17,812	78.2	273,400	28.5	13.6	1,195	33.8	1.7	21,351	1.4	845	4	16,721	35.6	23.1
Colusa.........................	7,047	64.2	223,600	24.7	10.0	896	28.3	8.8	10,969	1.3	1,418	12.9	9,470	24.2	40.0
Contra Costa................	389,597	65.5	522,300	25.0	11.0	1,600	31.7	5	564,570	1	17,792	3.2	535,401	43.0	15.9
Del Norte.....................	9,683	61.9	185,900	26.4	12.8	826	29.3	3.7	9,961	2.5	549	5.5	8,742	32.5	15.9
El Dorado.....................	68,084	76.3	405,900	25.5	13.3	1,122	31	2.5	91,589	1.8	3,270	3.6	80,373	41.4	15.3
Fresno..........................	301,824	53.0	220,600	23.9	10.7	931	34.4	9.7	448,353	0.7	33,427	7.5	392,003	29.1	28.3
Glenn...........................	9,936	57.6	214,600	25.4	12.4	775	29.6	6	12,779	-0.4	835	6.5	10,775	22.6	39.9
Humboldt......................	53,966	56.5	285,800	28.2	10.9	914	36	4.5	63,027	0.6	2,245	3.6	59,592	33.9	19.4
Imperial........................	45,198	56.4	167,700	23.6	11.5	805	32.3	10.8	71,055	-1.5	12,855	18.1	59,757	24.4	26.5
Inyo.............................	8,026	63.7	243,100	24.9	11.5	875	29.3	3.4	8,725	1.2	337	3.9	8,275	31.5	23.1
Kern	264,993	57.2	190,600	23.5	11.1	933	32.4	9.4	386,997	0.6	30,865	8	335,688	26.4	34.6
Kings............................	42,349	51.8	185,600	22.5	10.0	918	30.1	8.6	57,865	0.9	4,481	7.7	53,158	24.4	33.3
Lake.............................	26,327	65.9	182,000	28.8	14.7	914	37.4	3.2	29,116	-0.9	1,522	5.2	22,691	25.8	26.2
Lassen.........................	9,441	66.0	177,500	21.8	10.6	942	28.8	1.2	9,899	-1.5	474	4.8	9,052	28.4	21.9
Los Angeles	3,295,198	45.9	495,800	27.8	11.1	1,322	34.7	12	5,136,341	0.8	239,829	4.7	4,805,817	36.4	20.5
Madera.........................	44,458	62.3	220,400	24.2	11.2	980	34.4	9.8	61,528	0.8	4,316	7	56,076	23.9	36.8
Marin...........................	104,846	64.2	908,800	25.6	12.4	1,863	31.4	4.2	141,111	0.8	3,363	2.4	130,570	53.8	10.3
Mariposa......................	7,434	70.7	259,500	28.3	11.6	869	31.3	2.5	7,663	-0.1	406	5.3	7,009	30.5	16.2
Mendocino....................	34,182	59.2	338,000	29.2	12.1	1,048	35.3	5.7	39,715	0.2	1,564	3.9	37,084	32.5	22.9
Merced.........................	79,261	52.0	196,200	24.0	11.2	934	31.9	9.6	115,408	0	9,574	8.3	99,026	23.4	36.0
Modoc..........................	3,638	73.0	143,100	29.0	10.8	739	29.1	3	3,179	-0.6	240	7.5	3,231	36.5	26.6
Mono............................	4,899	56.1	311,700	30.7	12.6	1,103	24.1	1.8	8,524	0.2	328	3.8	7,864	37.0	14.6
Monterey......................	125,939	50.7	441,000	27.0	10.6	1,338	32.9	13.2	224,057	1.9	14,047	6.3	182,439	28.5	31.3
Napa............................	49,044	63.1	560,500	25.0	11.2	1,541	31.7	6.1	74,547	1.5	2,181	2.9	71,110	36.3	21.1
Nevada.........................	40,386	74.2	379,800	28.4	14.2	1,217	34.1	2.3	48,870	1	1,694	3.5	42,302	41.3	15.8
Orange.........................	1,024,976	57.4	620,500	26.1	10.0	1,693	33.8	9.1	1,625,426	1	47,541	2.9	1,560,997	40.9	16.9
Placer..........................	138,564	70.8	413,300	24.4	12.1	1,398	31	2.4	185,213	1.9	5,837	3.2	170,791	44.0	13.8
Plumas.........................	8,287	72.6	228,900	24.8	12.5	840	34	2.3	7,848	0.9	588	7.5	7,260	32.4	23.9
Riverside......................	711,724	65.0	304,500	26.6	12.8	1,251	35	7.3	1,092,371	1.8	47,808	4.4	978,726	29.4	24.6
Sacramento..................	532,050	55.5	299,900	24.2	10.2	1,122	32.6	5.2	710,442	1.8	26,948	3.8	666,790	38.4	17.2
San Benito...................	17,440	63.7	459,700	26.8	11.2	1,369	29.9	8.2	30,869	0.7	1,561	5.1	27,688	29.1	30.4
San Bernardino............	623,642	59.2	280,200	25.8	11.4	1,182	34.7	9.1	961,030	1.8	38,779	4	869,658	29.0	26.8
San Diego....................	1,111,739	53.0	484,900	26.4	10.9	1,467	33.4	6.8	1,592,193	1.1	52,663	3.3	1,536,073	41.3	16.1
San Francisco..............	358,772	37.3	927,400	25.5	10.0	1,709	25.9	8	575,567	2	13,545	2.4	504,914	55.0	9.0
San Joaquin.................	223,808	55.7	281,100	24.7	11.2	1,100	33.3	7.4	326,387	0.8	19,571	6	296,264	27.5	30.1
San Luis Obispo...........	105,044	60.0	499,800	26.4	10.7	1,326	32.6	3.7	140,920	0.2	4,151	2.9	129,277	39.2	18.2
San Mateo....................	261,796	59.7	917,700	25.1	10.3	1,973	29.8	8.1	454,875	2	10,007	2.2	404,882	47.4	13.4
Santa Barbara..............	144,015	52.3	509,400	25.2	11.6	1,496	33.6	10.5	216,698	0.6	8,437	3.9	211,793	35.2	22.2
Santa Clara..................	630,451	56.9	829,600	24.6	10.0	1,955	29	8.2	1,048,804	0.9	27,282	2.6	967,294	52.1	14.2
Santa Cruz...................	95,536	59.7	659,900	27.0	11.8	1,552	36.8	7.2	142,618	-0.2	6,984	4.9	133,847	40.7	19.1
Shasta..........................	70,486	62.6	233,500	25.0	13.2	966	34.5	4.2	74,215	0.2	3,669	4.9	72,195	31.7	20.0
Sierra...........................	1,208	79.7	157,100	25.2	16.4	919	31.7	0.2	1,278	-1.1	77	6	1,149	30.2	34.0
Siskiyou........................	19,018	65.5	176,600	26.5	12.1	829	34.2	4	17,410	-2.3	1,166	6.7	16,544	32.9	23.9
Solano..........................	147,352	60.0	342,000	24.3	10.4	1,407	32.8	5.2	209,721	0.6	8,168	3.9	196,309	32.7	22.6
Sonoma........................	190,058	60.3	513,300	25.9	11.6	1,456	32.9	5.5	262,348	0.7	7,187	2.7	249,134	37.2	20.4
Stanislaus	171,324	57.1	244,100	24.1	10.9	1,049	33.2	6.9	243,538	0.4	15,598	6.4	219,505	27.2	31.1
Sutter...........................	32,188	57.0	234,500	23.7	11.0	980	31.1	7.5	45,477	0.9	3,392	7.5	38,207	29.6	29.0
Tehama.........................	23,712	67.2	191,400	25.6	11.7	812	34.5	5.3	25,626	0.2	1,450	5.7	23,849	23.7	30.6
Trinity..........................	5,462	68.8	286,500	29.5	10.1	803	37.7	4.5	4,707	-2.2	268	5.7	4,800	30.3	20.9
Tulare...........................	135,144	56.2	180,200	24.7	10.0	877	33.4	10.3	204,589	-0.1	19,649	9.6	173,820	25.0	36.8
Tuolumne.....................	22,267	69.4	273,500	26.2	13.2	961	32.1	4	21,339	-0.4	982	4.6	20,401	32.8	20.4
Ventura........................	270,046	63.2	520,300	26.2	10.0	1,643	33.8	7	425,728	0.2	16,066	3.8	410,179	37.8	21.7
Yolo.............................	72,845	51.9	370,800	23.1	10.0	1,204	33.4	5.7	108,518	1.6	4,562	4.2	95,944	44.2	18.4
Yuba............................	25,880	58.2	207,100	24.4	11.7	923	33	7.3	29,078	1	1,863	6.4	27,832	29.3	26.8
COLORADO	2,082,531	64.7	286,100	21.7	10.0	1,125	30.6	3	3,096,358	3.5	101,606	3.3	2,760,076	41.2	18.4
Adams..........................	162,508	64.8	241,900	22.4	10.3	1,172	31.4	5.4	269,911	3.4	9,369	3.5	246,450	29.8	27.2
Alamosa.......................	6,049	56.9	152,900	24.6	10.0	675	29.9	5.1	8,447	3.7	352	4.2	6,593	30.6	24.5
Arapahoe......................	235,263	62.6	292,900	21.6	10.0	1,218	31.3	3.2	362,692	3.4	11,689	3.2	330,548	41.4	16.9
Archuleta......................	5,553	73.4	274,000	24.8	12.4	904	30.7	4.8	6,928	4.6	236	3.4	5,696	37.3	25.7
Baca............................	1,603	71.6	79,800	24.8	12.4	540	24.7	1.2	2,229	4.9	41	1.8	1,655	39.7	25.9
Bent.............................	1,760	62.6	77,700	19.7	12.0	669	41.8	3.4	2,017	4.7	64	3.2	1,370	31.0	23.2

1. Specified owner-occupied units.   2. A value of 10.0 represents 10 percent or less; a value of 50.0 represents 50 percent or more.   3. Specified renter-occupied units.   4. Overcrowded or lacking complete plumbing facilities.   5. Percent of civilian labor force.   6. Civilian employed persons 16 years old and over.

Table B. States and Counties — Nonfarm Employment and Agriculture

STATE County	Private nonfarm establishments, employment and payroll, 2016									Agriculture, 2017			
	Number of establishments	Employment						Annual payroll		Farms			Farm producers whose primary occupation is farming (percent)
		Total	Health care and social assistance	Manufacturing	Retail trade	Finance and insurance	Professional, scientific, and technical services	Total (mil dol)	Average per employee (dollars)		Percent with:		
										Number	Fewer than 50 acres	1000 acres or more	
	104	105	106	107	108	109	110	111	112	113	114	115	116
CALIFORNIA	922,477	14,600,349	1,928,468	1,154,342	1,711,363	611,298	1,190,717	886,644	60,728	70,521	64.0	6.3	46.6
Alameda	39,242	662,511	92,267	70,685	70,728	19,792	66,491	45,908	69,294	446	62.6	8.1	35.8
Alpine	35	549	D	D	D	D	D	8	14,299	6	33.3	16.7	40.0
Amador	824	8,224	1,308	805	1,557	190	302	295	35,918	482	54.6	6.2	44.5
Butte	4,627	60,432	15,032	4,271	10,238	2,564	2,471	2,302	38,087	1,912	65.2	2.9	51.3
Calaveras	908	6,251	1,075	363	1,263	138	214	212	33,986	699	59.7	6.3	35.9
Colusa	371	4,041	453	607	472	88	39	161	39,938	751	29.0	14.9	54.7
Contra Costa	23,591	325,864	55,403	15,101	45,925	23,924	24,629	21,469	65,883	459	75.6	6.1	46.7
Del Norte	401	4,093	1,152	100	974	100	120	133	32,401	90	58.9	4.4	41.6
El Dorado	4,439	45,023	6,892	2,682	6,137	3,010	2,330	2,043	45,377	1,390	83.4	1.3	39.6
Fresno	16,619	255,652	44,569	23,821	38,532	9,143	10,242	10,692	41,823	4,774	54.1	6.6	57.1
Glenn	468	5,198	480	794	865	120	329	254	48,814	1,173	48.3	8.5	53.9
Humboldt	3,170	34,455	7,019	2,172	7,003	1,167	1,798	1,219	35,382	849	46.6	14.6	52.4
Imperial	2,519	33,092	5,105	3,504	8,631	768	854	1,093	33,018	396	24.7	35.1	73.7
Inyo	509	5,119	1,119	168	935	75	126	189	36,924	85	41.2	25.9	37.9
Kern	12,724	190,503	30,127	11,832	32,769	5,802	10,631	8,342	43,788	1,731	40.3	17.6	51.1
Kings	1,596	23,824	4,613	4,169	4,205	520	868	952	39,939	963	48.9	9.2	54.1
Lake	1,085	9,583	2,462	307	2,289	258	236	366	38,172	636	69.3	2.8	41.4
Lassen	398	3,622	794	D	884	120	273	121	33,444	377	37.9	17.0	47.7
Los Angeles	269,489	3,871,716	534,449	338,448	425,475	159,566	283,794	212,489	54,882	1,035	89.9	1.0	46.1
Madera	1,950	26,668	5,884	3,824	3,750	475	467	1,102	41,325	1,386	41.6	8.7	52.7
Marin	9,963	100,530	15,417	3,855	14,804	4,747	8,118	6,555	65,206	343	44.9	14.0	42.6
Mariposa	296	3,220	469	90	386	32	47	84	26,166	299	34.8	23.1	46.1
Mendocino	2,439	23,414	4,422	2,751	4,671	561	634	864	36,888	1,128	44.6	11.1	43.2
Merced	3,041	43,152	7,035	9,361	8,589	1,066	830	1,702	39,453	2,337	53.5	7.4	56.3
Modoc	150	1,206	434	D	203	28	36	45	37,542	423	25.1	27.9	55.4
Mono	581	6,461	479	67	686	23	103	186	28,827	65	55.4	23.1	41.7
Monterey	8,632	107,865	15,749	7,660	17,472	2,793	7,115	4,836	44,837	1,104	45.6	20.2	44.3
Napa	4,216	62,535	10,068	11,266	7,000	1,414	1,901	3,189	50,994	1,866	74.9	2.8	32.2
Nevada	3,013	27,440	4,758	1,531	4,178	1,019	1,364	1,123	40,936	673	81.4	0.9	44.8
Orange	94,703	1,482,602	165,733	149,555	157,250	92,297	134,585	84,003	56,659	193	83.4	1.6	42.6
Placer	10,394	142,490	21,669	4,618	23,720	9,953	9,036	7,126	50,010	1,237	85.0	1.1	36.8
Plumas	587	3,679	929	490	557	128	134	159	43,136	162	45.1	16.0	44.1
Riverside	37,345	553,704	77,300	43,472	96,726	11,199	20,173	21,617	39,041	2,667	87.1	2.1	40.9
Sacramento	29,135	466,341	80,987	20,694	63,566	29,189	36,331	24,736	53,043	1,161	66.8	5.9	48.5
San Benito	965	11,803	1,461	2,745	1,386	229	246	512	43,353	610	60.0	10.8	45.5
San Bernardino	34,462	582,280	91,797	52,120	90,403	15,705	17,912	24,436	41,967	1,062	84.4	1.5	41.8
San Diego	83,146	1,248,369	167,831	100,498	155,358	55,355	124,846	69,458	55,639	5,082	90.8	0.8	36.2
San Francisco	34,314	627,915	64,301	7,894	47,392	54,001	107,780	60,460	96,312	10	100.0	NA	27.3
San Joaquin	11,237	177,161	28,448	17,986	26,507	6,256	5,011	7,604	42,921	3,430	62.1	5.4	55.0
San Luis Obispo	8,227	90,392	15,256	6,447	14,452	2,334	4,843	3,796	41,994	2,349	56.4	7.8	40.8
San Mateo	21,199	374,251	34,748	23,964	35,208	18,220	40,661	41,060	109,713	241	66.4	6.2	48.2
Santa Barbara	11,640	146,896	22,301	14,459	19,614	4,108	9,719	7,310	49,766	1,467	60.7	9.5	44.0
Santa Clara	48,278	1,021,748	110,903	83,313	85,613	22,728	139,191	114,930	112,484	890	78.1	5.2	44.9
Santa Cruz	7,028	77,903	13,290	5,158	12,527	2,364	4,360	3,561	45,715	625	80.5	2.1	43.2
Shasta	4,148	50,069	10,486	2,291	9,769	2,012	2,778	1,997	39,875	1,337	71.4	4.6	31.5
Sierra	68	197	33	D	19	D	2	7	37,305	38	23.7	26.3	56.9
Siskiyou	1,071	8,685	1,647	731	1,527	211	319	301	34,645	745	36.4	15.3	49.3
Solano	6,984	111,150	23,200	9,272	20,042	4,378	3,334	5,541	49,855	849	65.3	8.1	44.6
Sonoma	13,887	168,218	25,469	19,805	25,566	6,285	8,973	8,559	50,879	3,594	73.7	3.5	40.6
Stanislaus	8,866	139,192	24,819	19,633	22,899	3,390	6,209	6,240	44,827	3,621	65.3	3.5	51.3
Sutter	1,722	21,006	3,723	1,498	4,523	830	723	872	41,499	1,157	49.3	6.1	54.3
Tehama	975	12,628	2,127	1,941	1,999	231	219	511	40,501	1,479	61.9	7.6	44.7
Trinity	244	1,575	319	240	410	43	84	55	34,750	185	64.3	2.2	48.0
Tulare	6,301	94,534	15,764	13,440	16,450	3,060	2,711	3,706	39,198	4,187	57.6	5.4	52.3
Tuolumne	1,285	12,631	2,795	758	2,454	267	462	499	39,543	417	57.3	8.9	37.7
Ventura	20,909	256,376	38,214	24,647	40,861	11,666	22,432	13,358	52,103	2,135	78.4	2.2	43.0
Yolo	4,076	63,111	6,930	5,885	7,945	984	3,657	2,971	47,071	949	49.5	9.2	53.5
Yuba	802	9,781	2,470	468	1,503	177	659	404	41,337	764	59.8	3.8	51.0
COLORADO	165,264	2,318,190	307,955	121,428	281,435	106,462	194,466	120,399	51,937	38,893	46.2	14.9	38.2
Adams	9,442	162,819	24,196	12,269	20,338	3,042	5,660	7,768	47,709	905	62.0	10.9	32.2
Alamosa	482	5,749	1,621	94	1,137	334	163	188	32,689	280	23.2	20.7	46.9
Arapahoe	18,457	293,575	38,032	6,740	35,275	24,257	25,070	17,254	58,772	851	73.9	4.8	26.0
Archuleta	501	3,484	339	127	782	84	109	94	26,958	399	41.4	14.3	33.7
Baca	84	533	D	D	113	22	4	17	32,364	667	3.3	48.4	49.6
Bent	52	569	80	D	82	49	D	19	33,135	274	12.8	33.9	47.4

Table B. States and Counties — **Agriculture**

STATE County	Acreage (1,000)	Percent change, 2012-2017	Average size of farm	Total irrigated (1,000)	Total cropland (1,000)	Average per farm	Average per acre	Value of machinery and equipment, average per farm (dollars)	Total (mil dol)	Average per farm (acres)	Crops	Livestock and poultry products	Organic farms (number)	Farms with internet access (percent)	Total ($1,000)	Percent of farms
	117	118	119	120	121	122	123	124	125	126	127	128	129	130	131	132
CALIFORNIA................	24,523	-4.1	348	7,833.6	9,597.4	3,252,414	9,353	165,070	45,154.4	640,297	73.9	26.1	3,794	82.0	127,938	7.5
Alameda........................	183	3.1	411	7.5	17.3	2,920,388	7,106	58,016	46.2	103,509	77.4	22.6	13	84.5	201	6.3
Alpine..........................	3	D	529	D	D	2,418,390	4,573	104,011	D	D	D	D	NA	83.3	D	16.7
Amador	181	17.0	377	10.4	14.6	1,677,097	4,454	56,975	31.0	64,376	74.8	25.2	13	86.3	146	6.0
Butte............................	348	-8.6	182	192.5	214.2	2,193,553	12,042	163,066	524.2	274,140	96.8	3.2	100	80.4	6,677	6.1
Calaveras.....................	240	12.9	343	5.8	14.8	1,218,142	3,554	52,629	27.4	39,249	35.0	65.0	11	79.3	1,050	9.3
Colusa.........................	457	0.8	608	233.7	277.5	4,846,803	7,967	320,815	553.9	737,571	98.4	1.6	28	83.1	9,646	31.0
Contra Costa.................	156	21.9	339	22.6	41.5	2,346,158	6,922	93,600	83.2	181,327	77.4	22.6	9	84.5	503	6.1
Del Norte.....................	20	D	220	9.1	7.9	1,826,521	8,315	157,104	43.4	482,111	25.6	74.4	11	97.8	D	1.1
El Dorado......................	91	-29.1	65	5.6	8.4	649,878	9,926	41,388	24.5	17,650	87.0	13.0	27	87.6	82	1.3
Fresno........................	1,647	-4.3	345	972.6	1,142.7	3,917,829	11,359	234,782	5,742.8	1,202,926	71.1	28.9	183	75.6	8,894	7.7
Glenn..........................	467	-30.2	398	243.2	265.1	3,547,184	8,915	248,370	628.7	536,012	82.9	17.1	30	83.3	3,676	15.8
Humboldt......................	621	4.6	731	20.7	20.6	2,260,162	3,090	89,370	D	D	D	D	123	79.5	626	3.9
Imperial	522	1.2	1,317	456.1	504.0	14,670,312	11,135	884,987	1,859.7	4,696,157	65.7	34.3	45	90.7	3,640	27.5
Inyo............................	287	-13.3	3,375	17.1	13.6	2,093,360	620	70,430	10.6	124,800	14.3	85.7	1	83.5	1,101	16.5
Kern	2,295	-1.5	1,326	730.7	954.1	9,787,244	7,380	406,230	4,076.8	2,355,161	84.3	15.7	30	82.7	5,101	13.8
Kings	616	-8.6	640	371.7	488.5	6,917,469	10,815	349,654	1,649.3	1,712,640	50.1	49.9	25	80.4	5,849	29.8
Lake	138	-8.2	218	13.9	20.1	1,426,769	6,555	67,768	71.9	113,002	96.5	3.5	101	78.9	106	5.5
Lassen	473	-1.9	1,256	53.6	56.3	2,685,457	2,139	126,819	46.0	121,923	45.0	55.0	16	77.7	1,473	12.5
Los Angeles	58	-37.0	56	13.8	29.6	1,037,785	18,580	56,113	154.6	149,380	86.5	13.5	41	78.7	523	2.1
Madera.........................	645	-1.3	466	300.2	346.1	5,102,429	10,958	229,882	1,492.6	1,076,903	77.4	22.6	74	77.1	2,192	8.4
Marin	140	-18.0	408	5.0	13.7	2,393,811	5,862	102,186	95.3	277,962	11.6	88.4	67	86.9	712	13.1
Mariposa	301	6.3	1,008	2.8	5.8	2,080,275	2,064	55,341	24.7	82,706	7.7	92.3	4	87.3	1,670	23.4
Mendocino	782	1.5	693	27.9	64.3	2,653,485	3,829	87,962	173.0	153,362	86.6	13.4	131	81.6	226	3.3
Merced	946	-3.3	405	493.7	546.5	5,299,308	13,086	334,860	2,938.4	1,257,337	43.9	56.1	68	78.5	8,726	12.5
Modoc	571	9.1	1,350	142.1	159.9	2,640,981	1,956	195,540	114.8	271,357	70.2	29.8	24	82.5	2,537	31.2
Mono	73	29.5	1,124	41.7	7.9	2,158,060	1,921	140,666	9.6	147,277	65.6	34.4	NA	78.5	D	4.6
Monterey	1,340	5.7	1,214	294.6	366.7	8,944,364	7,368	805,557	4,116.1	3,728,396	99.1	0.9	191	75.5	1,269	7.4
Napa	256	1.0	137	60.9	67.7	6,052,361	44,154	94,303	573.2	307,198	97.7	2.3	117	84.7	924	2.1
Nevada	52	23.6	77	5.0	4.8	574,346	7,425	34,251	12.5	18,517	54.5	45.5	58	88.4	173	4.2
Orange	32	-46.4	168	4.2	9.6	3,205,502	19,094	162,436	82.5	427,497	99.5	0.5	7	79.8	6	3.1
Placer..........................	119	29.7	96	20.2	28.5	643,458	6,715	44,969	54.9	44,378	68.4	31.6	26	88.0	327	2.7
Plumas	191	9.6	1,179	18.3	29.2	2,707,681	2,298	86,429	9.6	59,235	35.1	64.9	4	82.1	120	6.8
Riverside	264	-23.3	99	126.2	179.7	1,794,629	18,144	102,551	932.0	349,450	75.9	24.1	228	80.4	1,621	2.4
Sacramento...................	260	5.4	224	100.4	118.8	2,252,041	10,048	129,041	430.5	370,759	70.1	29.9	27	83.2	1,966	9.7
San Benito	520	-13.9	853	18.1	35.6	3,043,028	3,569	98,840	368.4	267,057	79.9	20.1	75	81.3	575	9.8
San Bernardino..............	68	-11.6	64	22.2	29.3	1,278,283	19,897	78,028	373.9	352,096	25.2	74.8	25	75.9	647	2.6
San Diego	222	0.3	44	42.7	64.1	1,014,281	23,209	43,529	831.4	163,601	93.5	6.5	419	84.2	558	1.1
San Francisco................	0	650.0	9	D	D	699,840	77,760	28,864	D	D	D	D	NA	80.0	NA	NA
San Joaquin	773	-1.8	225	487.1	524.4	3,384,002	15,020	189,084	2,176.0	634,404	74.8	25.2	35	81.7	5,788	6.9
San Luis Obispo..............	931	-30.4	396	75.8	246.4	2,991,939	7,547	87,783	701.6	298,676	95.2	4.8	132	84.4	4,285	9.4
San Mateo.....................	46	-4.5	191	3.0	6.9	1,863,577	9,769	75,026	79.4	329,560	98.2	1.8	20	88.4	D	0.8
Santa Barbara................	715	2.0	487	119.9	146.3	5,060,150	10,381	183,019	1,519.9	1,036,090	98.0	2.0	163	87.7	854	5.2
Santa Clara...................	288	25.3	324	19.2	34.3	2,633,548	8,136	89,041	310.2	348,525	94.7	5.3	34	86.2	518	3.6
Santa Cruz....................	64	-36.1	102	20.1	23.5	2,183,024	21,352	116,842	606.5	970,464	98.7	1.3	130	85.1	37	1.9
Shasta..........................	410	8.9	307	48.8	38.9	895,229	2,919	51,324	62.2	46,546	35.0	65.0	16	81.5	547	2.0
Sierra	57	45.7	1,501	10.2	3.7	2,555,225	1,702	115,102	4.0	106,000	17.2	82.8	4	84.2	84	21.1
Siskiyou........................	687	-4.9	923	115.6	142.8	2,828,476	3,066	142,709	192.4	258,301	81.3	18.7	55	82.8	2,638	14.6
Solano..........................	343	-15.8	404	110.4	152.1	3,691,320	9,148	178,302	296.6	349,337	83.8	16.2	63	85.2	2,554	13.9
Sonoma........................	567	-3.8	158	86.4	129.9	3,501,852	22,186	77,715	919.1	255,719	66.9	33.1	332	87.7	2,410	3.8
Stanislaus	723	-5.9	200	380.6	404.7	3,116,617	15,619	182,695	2,526.3	697,690	53.0	47.0	35	82.2	5,006	7.5
Sutter	381	1.5	329	198.8	257.3	3,136,319	9,525	240,974	412.2	356,252	99.0	1.0	42	79.0	7,687	14.0
Tehama	614	-0.5	415	72.8	77.2	1,789,414	4,313	80,756	218.4	147,640	74.5	25.5	18	81.6	1,168	4.7
Trinity..........................	66	-62.6	356	D	1.7	683,288	1,921	35,076	D	D	D	100.0	9	82.2	D	2.2
Tulare	1,250	0.9	299	568.2	721.4	3,501,053	11,726	218,462	4,474.8	1,068,739	49.7	50.3	104	78.2	13,824	10.4
Tuolumne	123	39.5	294	2.6	1.5	1,091,612	3,715	52,254	32.3	77,384	3.5	96.5	3	81.5	397	8.4
Ventura	260	-7.5	122	98.1	123.4	3,106,351	25,498	127,982	1,633.3	765,008	99.2	0.8	128	80.6	830	2.5
Yolo	460	-0.3	484	234.7	312.8	4,699,589	9,703	240,642	571.6	602,266	97.1	2.9	98	86.4	2,850	19.2
Yuba............................	180	-4.3	235	72.5	79.3	1,931,854	8,221	157,292	179.1	234,438	88.9	11.1	21	82.5	2,828	4.6
COLORADO	31,821	-0.2	818	2,761.2	11,056.3	1,315,440	1,608	117,337	7,491.7	192,623	29.9	70.1	323	81.4	198,697	23.0
Adams..........................	705	2.1	779	21.6	586.8	1,256,762	1,613	129,421	126.5	139,779	81.9	18.1	17	80.3	5,037	26.1
Alamosa........................	192	5.3	686	79.5	81.1	1,453,990	2,120	272,790	89.3	319,050	90.9	9.1	13	83.2	836	22.9
Arapahoe	283	-0.1	332	1.2	136.8	751,389	2,260	63,650	26.7	31,370	78.0	22.0	3	87.7	1,705	15.0
Archuleta	210	0.0	527	18.3	12.5	1,634,748	3,104	67,028	11.2	27,965	12.6	87.4	2	79.4	143	2.5
Baca............................	1,472	-2.1	2,207	45.5	742.4	1,729,456	784	149,867	114.1	171,039	45.9	54.1	1	77.1	19,467	84.0
Bent............................	735	1.2	2,681	38.8	93.3	1,850,149	690	166,448	60.8	221,964	27.0	73.0	NA	69.0	1,854	51.5

Water Use, Wholesale Trade, Retail Trade, and Real Estate

STATE County	Public supply water withdrawn (mil gal/day)	Public supply gallons withdrawn per person per day	Number of establishments	Number of employees	Sales (mil dol)	Average payroll (mil dol)	Number of establishments	Number of employees	Sales (mil dol)	Average payroll (mil dol)	Number of establishments	Number of employees	Sales (mil dol)	Average payroll (mil dol)
	Water use, 2015		Wholesale Trade[1], 2012				Retail Trade[2], 2012				Real estate and rental and leasing,[2] 2012			
	133	134	135	136	137	138	139	140	141	142	143	144	145	146
CALIFORNIA..................	5,147.74	131.5	52,664	723,526	666,652.2	48,408.7	106,419	1,540,055	481,800.5	43,361.0	49,276	273,511	78,740.2	13,467.5
Alameda.........................	168.74	103.0	2,366	44,934	37,580.6	3,133.2	4,213	61,372	20,901.0	1,826.9	1,920	9,602	2,575.5	460.9
Alpine..............................	0.10	90.1	NA	NA	NA	NA	4	8	0.6	0.1	2	D	D	D
Amador...........................	8.64	233.5	20	D	D	D	121	1,489	321.5	35.7	38	100	17.3	3.5
Butte..............................	28.81	127.8	148	D	D	D	725	9,231	2,576.9	240.4	234	1,160	147.6	28.3
Calaveras.......................	6.59	147.0	18	D	D	D	133	1,044	252.3	27.2	44	170	23.2	3.5
Colusa...........................	2.46	114.5	27	338	428.7	18.7	59	434	127.9	10.6	19	40	7.8	1.2
Contra Costa..................	139.97	124.2	753	6,570	6,887.2	417.8	2,490	41,494	11,847.9	1,181.4	1,306	6,491	1,779.2	334.1
Del Norte........................	2.40	88.1	6	D	D	D	60	1,012	192.8	22.5	33	96	14.7	2.8
El Dorado.......................	27.80	150.7	107	553	316.7	28.7	530	5,841	1,597.8	155.8	242	856	176.1	27.6
Fresno............................	157.08	161.1	819	12,981	9,266.3	663.0	2,421	32,954	9,117.8	836.0	769	4,299	715.1	139.6
Glenn	2.55	91.0	17	224	160.1	11.8	73	688	191.2	16.3	20	41	5.4	1.4
Humboldt........................	11.49	84.7	105	1,028	361.9	41.5	578	6,600	1,759.2	170.3	174	536	89.9	15.2
Imperial..........................	24.47	135.8	197	1,801	1,599.1	72.5	446	7,322	1,676.9	160.3	119	574	92.6	15.9
Inyo................................	2.42	132.5	20	D	D	D	87	836	229.0	22.4	23	82	6.7	1.7
Kern................................	168.87	191.4	582	7,990	6,987.9	447.4	1,867	27,918	8,640.6	700.7	634	3,492	733.6	141.3
Kings..............................	29.07	192.6	69	684	746.6	36.3	285	3,961	1,032.0	92.2	97	371	71.0	9.9
Lake................................	2.93	45.4	24	D	D	D	167	2,041	522.3	49.8	59	160	24.5	4.1
Lassen	3.80	121.2	9	D	D	D	79	784	215.8	19.7	23	44	19.3	3.2
Los Angeles	1,256.44	123.5	21,270	237,644	199,804.8	12,881.4	28,427	385,441	121,389.4	10,699.7	13,874	82,043	29,586.3	4,476.1
Madera............................	15.63	100.8	76	815	508.9	37.8	326	3,455	1,012.9	84.3	75	336	38.4	8.5
Marin..............................	28.19	107.9	359	2,780	1,864.6	180.8	1,053	14,698	5,087.5	544.8	589	2,455	1,458.6	168.7
Mariposa........................	0.68	38.8	6	22	18.9	0.7	64	419	102.5	9.7	26	82	8.3	2.7
Mendocino	8.83	100.7	67	679	407.6	28.3	462	4,551	1,095.2	117.1	130	494	61.6	12.8
Merced...........................	50.17	186.9	112	1,635	2,260.2	71.2	528	7,497	1,959.5	173.3	152	532	79.1	14.6
Modoc.............................	0.60	66.9	7	D	D	D	30	203	45.7	4.9	7	15	1.3	0.2
Mono..............................	1.98	142.4	7	D	D	D	72	653	139.8	15.2	62	312	31.1	8.0
Monterey	38.23	88.1	346	4,574	5,775.2	278.9	1,316	16,335	4,457.4	437.2	444	1,873	436.3	69.6
Napa...............................	15.28	107.3	167	D	D	D	524	6,318	1,699.0	184.2	207	1,026	160.4	38.2
Nevada...........................	11.44	115.7	75	D	D	D	400	3,965	1,012.3	110.2	157	747	204.6	36.7
Orange...........................	457.54	144.3	6,434	79,685	97,796.0	5,200.7	9,390	143,012	45,193.6	4,135.3	5,320	38,952	9,259.7	1,921.2
Placer.............................	54.07	144.0	311	4,317	4,474.4	239.9	1,231	20,999	6,437.9	592.9	661	3,544	620.1	146.9
Plumas...........................	2.15	116.8	7	D	D	D	86	577	139.3	13.6	34	83	14.4	2.6
Riverside.........................	440.73	186.7	1,568	21,800	18,716.8	1,071.9	4,996	81,017	25,058.9	2,128.9	2,038	8,466	1,684.9	303.8
Sacramento.....................	231.29	154.1	1,096	14,448	18,746.3	816.5	3,512	55,910	15,227.3	1,484.7	1,650	8,879	1,621.2	364.9
San Benito......................	5.24	89.1	39	638	275.4	41.6	105	1,276	345.2	34.9	53	116	25.7	4.1
San Bernardino................	337.70	158.7	2,493	33,768	30,996.2	1,574.6	4,748	79,792	24,380.5	2,013.4	1,570	7,788	1,622.3	316.3
San Diego	408.82	123.9	3,883	59,227	35,937.4	4,055.0	9,219	138,929	39,786.1	3,787.5	5,401	28,321	7,895.7	1,308.8
San Francisco.................	67.54	78.1	1,066	12,056	11,121.7	850.7	3,573	43,378	14,632.7	1,455.0	1,828	15,000	6,000.9	1,071.1
San Joaquin....................	93.39	128.6	515	9,279	11,713.5	495.7	1,602	24,097	7,059.5	616.4	572	2,655	464.7	97.2
San Luis Obispo..............	29.10	103.4	289	D	D	D	1,177	13,992	3,624.0	361.5	430	1,552	278.4	52.2
San Mateo......................	68.39	89.4	1,050	15,030	15,969.7	1,249.1	2,041	34,069	11,330.6	1,062.8	1,142	7,018	2,227.1	348.4
Santa Barbara.................	49.94	112.3	406	5,325	3,475.6	397.1	1,509	18,781	4,853.8	501.5	691	3,047	570.7	113.7
Santa Clara.....................	194.59	101.5	2,310	84,304	91,859.0	10,822.2	4,927	84,158	40,336.7	3,212.4	2,426	12,827	4,458.9	763.7
Santa Cruz......................	18.45	67.3	266	5,614	5,898.2	297.2	887	11,120	4,368.0	294.7	363	1,271	264.1	41.8
Shasta............................	33.47	186.4	158	1,437	1,023.9	59.8	647	8,980	2,507.1	241.4	207	765	121.4	22.1
Sierra.............................	0.37	124.7	1	D	D	D	9	31	5.1	0.6	1	D	D	D
Siskiyou..........................	4.61	105.8	28	266	165.2	9.0	179	1,563	426.7	36.0	53	114	10.8	2.4
Solano............................	52.18	119.7	249	4,165	2,803.7	215.6	1,060	17,610	5,106.6	469.9	381	1,629	389.2	59.2
Sonoma..........................	40.49	80.6	593	8,047	4,443.2	557.8	1,768	23,032	6,016.3	655.8	679	2,824	631.1	103.4
Stanislaus.......................	80.48	149.5	405	6,087	5,295.1	313.6	1,374	20,970	5,933.6	527.1	433	2,141	387.9	73.2
Sutter.............................	13.61	141.1	70	1,658	1,197.3	99.6	287	4,188	1,069.5	101.8	89	436	50.5	11.1
Tehama...........................	5.26	83.1	25	190	88.8	6.4	151	1,696	654.6	45.5	48	152	25.7	4.6
Trinity	0.99	75.8	2	D	D	D	53	333	72.7	7.3	7	D	D	D
Tulare.............................	70.33	152.9	325	4,564	3,890.5	191.8	1,044	14,210	3,903.5	340.6	306	1,421	249.0	40.9
Tuolumne........................	5.47	101.8	31	D	D	D	173	2,219	573.3	54.5	82	174	32.6	4.4
Ventura...........................	130.02	152.9	985	D	D	D	2,562	37,012	11,194.2	1,011.0	1,008	4,568	983.6	196.5
Yolo................................	26.91	126.3	254	4,938	6,762.1	269.9	442	7,171	1,968.8	190.3	279	1,604	265.1	59.4
Yuba...............................	8.95	120.1	26	D	D	D	127	1,369	390.2	34.7	45	123	18.0	3.3
COLORADO	843.95	154.7	5,733	75,717	77,035.0	4,762.1	18,474	245,704	67,815.2	6,508.6	9,295	38,706	8,482.5	1,569.6
Adams............................	78.89	160.6	608	13,547	12,918.6	760.9	1,044	16,769	5,548.7	487.2	434	2,611	522.7	91.5
Alamosa..........................	2.09	126.7	18	166	78.8	6.0	85	1,091	280.7	27.7	18	83	11.1	2.6
Arapahoe........................	141.39	224.0	668	8,515	17,863.9	604.2	1,866	30,885	9,404.7	875.8	1,073	4,537	1,313.9	204.3
Archuleta........................	1.51	122.2	6	32	9.3	0.8	88	506	130.8	12.6	34	97	11.7	2.2
Baca...............................	0.45	124.5	23	57	86.1	2.0	16	128	38.4	3.1	3	D	D	D
Bent................................	0.81	138.9	NA	NA	NA	NA	12	73	17.4	1.3	NA	NA	NA	NA

1 Merchant wholesalers, except manufacturers' sales branches and offices.   2. Employer establishments.

Professional Services, Manufacturing, and Accommodation and Food Services

STATE County	Professional, scientific, and technical services, 2012				Manufacturing, 2012				Accommodation and food services, 2012			
	Number of establish-ments	Number of employees	Sales (mil dol)	Average payroll (mil dol)	Number of establish-ments	Number of employees	Receipts (mil dol)	Annual payroll (mil dol)	Number of establis-hments	Number of employees	Receipts (mil dol)	Annual payroll (mil dol)
	147	148	149	150	151	152	153	154	155	156	157	158
CALIFORNIA..................	114,321	1,303,232	234,371.2	90,437.3	38,741	1,163,341	512,303.2	69,316.8	78,560	1,394,984	90,830.4	25,147.8
Alameda......................	5,387	60,272	13,550.3	5,414.1	1,846	63,679	D	4,502.1	3,631	51,283	3,192.4	884.9
Alpine........................	3	D	D	D	NA	NA	NA	NA	9	D	D	D
Amador......................	80	277	29.1	9.8	38	599	139.6	31.6	100	2,088	242.0	53.1
Butte.........................	424	2,394	388.0	97.2	177	4,126	1,341.1	168.3	397	7,091	350.5	96.4
Calaveras...................	63	187	18.1	7.1	33	358	D	11.7	99	1,105	69.6	16.6
Colusa.......................	18	51	4.0	1.4	25	716	474.5	33.3	41	931	97.8	21.5
Contra Costa................	3,347	27,079	5,926.1	2,112.6	540	15,118	33,681.2	1,090.7	1,805	27,719	1,660.0	455.8
Del Norte...................	30	D	D	D	9	D	41.2	D	68	611	32.3	7.8
El Dorado...................	515	D	D	D	162	2,415	517.4	130.9	424	5,565	319.8	86.7
Fresno.......................	1,522	10,531	1,367.8	474.3	585	25,269	8,658.3	1,052.9	1,450	24,100	1,226.2	333.9
Glenn........................	33	278	45.0	21.2	26	636	D	24.4	55	598	33.2	8.4
Humboldt....................	244	1,996	164.6	62.4	134	2,149	D	80.9	374	4,746	257.5	70.0
Imperial.....................	179	787	79.1	30.4	50	2,218	1,466.0	95.4	258	3,516	182.6	47.9
Inyo..........................	35	D	D	D	13	161	D	7.4	91	1,525	99.6	26.7
Kern.........................	1,204	11,757	1,641.3	637.3	391	12,257	6,890.7	558.2	1,278	19,829	1,092.2	284.0
Kings........................	85	461	51.0	18.4	60	4,380	2,904.0	180.5	172	2,824	378.6	42.6
Lake.........................	66	243	22.2	7.6	32	265	80.5	11.1	130	1,460	88.8	24.9
Lassen......................	26	121	13.5	6.4	NA	NA	NA	NA	46	619	36.0	10.6
Los Angeles...............	31,324	521,067	66,261.5	26,244.3	12,760	359,532	163,829.6	19,852.8	20,298	355,736	22,965.1	6,390.6
Madera......................	116	493	66.9	21.6	92	3,298	1,441.1	168.0	193	2,461	150.1	37.1
Marin........................	1,744	9,095	2,037.3	698.0	219	1,935	D	92.7	751	11,578	729.7	225.6
Mariposa....................	19	D	D	D	14	78	D	3.5	56	1,473	157.9	32.3
Mendocino..................	206	729	68.1	22.9	123	2,066	453.4	82.1	339	3,369	182.6	50.8
Merced......................	142	791	67.1	26.2	116	9,973	4,435.6	405.4	298	4,585	232.9	60.2
Modoc.......................	12	60	5.3	1.5	3	D	D	D	21	149	8.3	1.9
Mono........................	23	80	10.5	3.4	7	39	D	1.2	141	3,450	246.9	67.4
Monterey....................	806	7,448	847.3	338.0	263	6,078	2,258.9	252.3	979	17,786	1,328.8	378.0
Napa.........................	395	1,801	280.5	101.5	431	10,837	4,623.5	622.5	375	10,466	774.1	247.7
Nevada......................	346	1,415	227.0	89.1	140	1,381	319.7	72.4	245	5,007	231.2	69.9
Orange.......................	14,120	112,581	24,110.2	8,899.6	4,701	150,020	47,299.4	8,879.0	7,141	143,519	9,050.6	2,599.9
Placer.......................	1,180	D	D	D	261	4,246	932.9	216.9	823	18,063	1,452.0	327.3
Plumas......................	51	D	D	D	17	444	D	19.8	100	D	D	D
Riverside....................	3,182	16,261	2,149.0	811.3	1,447	41,519	15,137.0	1,930.4	3,350	75,061	5,230.9	1,376.8
Sacramento.................	3,754	32,572	5,743.4	2,153.4	758	19,902	6,960.7	1,161.8	2,560	44,722	2,422.7	671.9
San Benito..................	70	213	26.4	8.9	62	2,222	591.1	95.6	80	925	49.9	13.5
San Bernardino.............	2,489	16,890	2,201.9	776.5	1,814	46,822	17,591.6	2,112.8	3,126	53,047	2,858.0	773.6
San Diego...................	12,528	134,334	24,111.3	9,099.2	2,891	97,346	33,320.5	6,196.1	6,880	147,457	10,403.8	2,857.4
San Francisco..............	6,295	84,841	29,389.5	9,033.5	693	7,506	D	327.6	4,059	73,417	6,142.7	1,841.6
San Joaquin................	780	4,463	491.1	190.0	517	18,703	9,212.4	879.0	997	15,422	808.6	211.0
San Luis Obispo............	868	4,914	673.1	269.5	382	6,107	2,854.0	285.7	865	14,254	824.8	229.5
San Mateo..................	2,999	32,982	8,831.3	3,659.8	633	22,708	D	2,299.6	1,910	33,203	2,552.9	710.9
Santa Barbara..............	1,347	9,785	1,751.7	654.0	458	13,896	4,157.6	851.5	1,087	20,623	1,428.9	400.1
Santa Clara.................	8,395	125,395	30,138.9	13,549.8	2,385	100,981	41,450.6	9,169.2	4,407	72,491	4,809.2	1,336.2
Santa Cruz..................	880	4,268	603.0	249.2	293	4,479	1,213.4	219.2	678	10,032	586.0	168.6
Shasta.......................	358	D	D	D	147	1,990	511.9	93.7	376	5,421	285.5	76.7
Sierra........................	1	D	D	D	3	D	D	D	14	D	D	D
Siskiyou.....................	96	362	38.8	12.0	31	667	203.4	28.2	135	1,317	71.5	19.7
Solano.......................	547	3,258	415.3	150.6	259	9,266	11,412.2	558.9	711	11,129	625.6	163.2
Sonoma......................	1,514	9,140	1,244.4	524.0	821	19,324	6,131.7	1,085.2	1,192	17,606	1,058.7	301.8
Stanislaus...................	649	5,111	507.5	196.0	395	19,963	11,703.6	1,007.8	813	13,611	705.7	192.6
Sutter........................	120	568	57.8	22.1	61	1,551	543.5	78.0	142	2,263	116.6	30.1
Tehama......................	61	211	27.9	8.6	38	1,648	449.5	70.1	121	1,367	65.1	16.6
Trinity.......................	19	74	7.0	2.5	14	194	D	7.9	46	205	13.4	3.3
Tulare.......................	407	D	D	D	237	11,412	8,362.4	538.0	568	8,540	451.9	118.1
Tuolumne....................	88	456	57.6	23.1	59	818	173.1	38.4	161	1,611	92.8	25.9
Ventura......................	2,634	22,377	3,185.4	2,063.2	867	23,166	8,334.0	1,295.4	1,598	27,725	1,597.4	442.6
Yolo..........................	411	3,207	484.6	184.3	167	6,236	2,538.4	311.3	414	8,216	656.6	177.5
Yuba.........................	84	410	60.6	24.1	39	540	107.2	20.9	82	1,111	54.8	14.8
COLORADO	23,872	180,064	33,740.7	12,932.1	4,898	114,632	50,447.1	6,230.1	12,744	240,484	13,617.7	3,994.6
Adams.......................	740	4,696	984.2	266.5	375	9,555	7,311.4	481.8	695	12,606	705.8	189.3
Alamosa.....................	43	169	16.8	6.4	14	108	13.8	3.5	44	790	35.4	9.7
Arapahoe....................	2,748	21,416	3,778.7	1,553.6	392	7,527	1,672.6	412.7	1,226	22,577	1,235.6	366.0
Archuleta....................	45	120	13.1	4.2	11	63	5.0	1.6	58	744	64.9	15.8
Baca.........................	5	D	D	D	NA	NA	NA	NA	7	D	D	D
Bent.........................	3	5	0.7	0.1	NA	NA	NA	NA	6	50	1.9	0.5

Health Care and Social Assistance, Other Services, Nonemployer Businesses, and Residential Construction

STATE County	Health care and social assistance, 2012				Other services, 2012				Nonemployer businesses, 2016		Value of residential construction authorized by building permits, 2018	
	Number of establish-ments	Number of employees	Receipts (mil dol)	Annual payroll (mil dol)	Number of establish-ments	Number of employees	Receipts (mil dol)	Annual payroll (mil dol)	Number	Receipts (mil dol)	New construction ($1,000)	Number of housing units
	159	160	161	162	163	164	165	166	167	168	169	170
CALIFORNIA..........	103,207	1,776,440	248,953.6	91,139.9	57,009	395,836	50,439.2	12,251.2	3,277,415	173,766.2	27,844,627	113,502
Alameda..............	4,273	82,510	12,949.1	4,762.2	2,761	19,955	2,642.5	739.4	143,612	7,204.4	2,034,826	8,056
Alpine...............	4	D	D	D	2	D	D	D	90	4.1	1,257	4
Amador..............	99	1,353	147.7	55.2	51	169	19.4	5.1	2,730	127.9	40,250	172
Butte................	716	12,868	1,434.5	560.2	321	2,158	190.0	56.0	13,739	663.1	141,164	703
Calaveras...........	97	985	108.9	41.7	60	265	20.4	5.6	3,604	170.6	29,518	112
Colusa..............	28	448	41.2	16.6	20	D	D	D	1,052	53.8	13,303	68
Contra Costa.......	2,877	50,689	8,262.6	3,051.1	1,515	10,368	1,238.8	338.4	94,711	5,353.0	773,679	2,907
Del Norte...........	68	1,214	121.3	44.7	21	D	D	D	1,292	51.8	7,601	25
El Dorado...........	461	6,504	680.9	276.7	289	1,393	129.6	38.2	16,779	863.1	184,804	543
Fresno..............	2,204	42,281	5,325.6	1,997.0	1,000	7,367	747.6	200.1	51,942	2,629.2	704,152	2,929
Glenn...............	42	546	52.0	22.2	24	70	12.7	1.8	1,390	65.6	11,752	59
Humboldt............	442	7,111	695.5	263.6	225	1,257	136.4	34.1	11,598	490.1	39,897	379
Imperial............	268	4,536	511.1	182.9	142	608	53.4	16.5	9,442	348.3	60,416	400
Inyo................	55	1,106	121.6	44.8	40	172	17.1	4.6	1,256	49.8	0	0
Kern................	1,550	27,833	3,675.0	1,265.4	835	5,099	567.8	153.6	45,491	2,273.4	488,476	2,452
Kings...............	231	4,770	587.8	203.5	94	382	37.4	9.9	4,520	200.5	84,402	352
Lake................	154	2,345	256.6	98.1	67	213	22.2	5.6	3,784	150.2	21,816	113
Lassen..............	59	838	84.1	31.0	29	D	D	D	1,106	38.6	1,555	7
Los Angeles........	29,822	498,944	67,261.3	24,116.1	15,843	110,674	13,562.1	3,278.3	1,046,426	55,988.4	5,526,501	22,009
Madera..............	204	5,871	761.0	321.0	112	489	45.2	11.8	7,272	354.2	122,117	503
Marin...............	1,117	15,860	2,102.3	848.3	643	4,539	583.8	160.1	37,856	2,817.1	99,630	164
Mariposa............	33	D	D	D	18	D	D	D	1,359	52.8	9,657	36
Mendocino...........	265	4,296	427.2	174.9	158	642	78.5	17.9	8,481	350.0	16,897	140
Merced..............	427	6,718	788.1	302.8	183	895	72.4	26.3	11,008	558.1	143,449	630
Modoc...............	17	477	33.9	13.4	12	D	D	D	549	23.7	1,008	6
Mono................	27	386	69.4	23.7	54	230	19.5	5.2	1,392	74.6	18,728	71
Monterey............	994	14,898	2,151.0	838.2	560	3,765	457.6	111.7	25,072	1,420.2	225,273	732
Napa................	404	10,222	1,360.7	553.3	241	1,359	127.7	40.0	11,857	725.8	78,080	269
Nevada..............	339	4,649	525.9	214.7	177	888	101.8	27.9	12,446	601.5	147,710	541
Orange..............	10,873	152,659	20,682.2	7,379.9	4,980	35,537	3,782.2	1,039.3	307,052	17,934.0	1,821,533	7,515
Placer..............	1,089	18,349	3,125.4	1,093.3	575	4,671	529.7	133.6	32,517	1,847.9	642,111	1,887
Plumas..............	49	900	85.2	32.9	39	124	12.9	3.3	1,584	73.1	8,701	41
Riverside...........	4,199	66,036	8,412.1	3,037.7	2,444	14,761	1,331.7	372.9	165,022	7,434.4	2,347,551	9,232
Sacramento..........	3,303	77,506	12,358.7	4,694.3	2,163	16,184	1,973.8	553.2	104,811	4,943.9	1,078,576	4,667
San Benito.........	96	1,309	143.2	61.4	68	249	22.4	5.3	3,617	188.9	174,389	553
San Bernardino......	3,784	81,285	11,199.3	4,102.6	2,244	15,260	1,344.6	415.7	143,379	6,200.6	1,191,305	5,577
San Diego...........	8,522	151,783	21,337.8	7,872.6	5,193	41,437	4,080.6	1,179.4	277,207	13,981.5	2,210,177	9,834
San Francisco.......	3,119	62,075	10,175.8	3,926.9	2,411	20,361	4,964.1	840.0	99,307	6,071.4	1,001,632	5,178
San Joaquin.........	1,361	27,052	3,447.7	1,264.8	841	5,038	445.0	135.0	38,315	2,028.6	1,003,804	3,280
San Luis Obispo.....	1,010	14,086	1,580.5	650.0	430	2,668	216.9	60.5	25,329	1,347.8	270,307	1,050
San Mateo...........	2,279	33,776	5,167.0	1,928.7	1,390	11,134	3,296.9	458.0	71,514	4,626.8	454,076	1,116
Santa Barbara.......	1,360	20,279	2,637.3	949.2	725	4,544	933.5	142.1	34,480	1,960.7	204,862	928
Santa Clara.........	5,410	99,127	17,021.0	6,095.5	3,008	20,859	3,493.8	728.5	143,480	8,416.4	1,849,046	8,191
Santa Cruz..........	893	12,989	1,689.9	622.3	451	2,973	328.1	98.5	25,079	1,268.8	59,874	426
Shasta..............	634	10,525	1,324.6	469.3	296	1,658	162.7	48.2	11,825	539.3	78,562	306
Sierra..............	8	D	D	D	NA	NA	NA	NA	233	6.6	1,991	6
Siskiyou............	115	1,630	174.1	72.8	72	242	17.3	5.0	3,321	135.7	13,356	54
Solano..............	861	21,490	3,241.8	1,204.0	552	3,228	326.8	102.6	24,790	1,026.7	241,759	990
Sonoma..............	1,462	23,222	3,156.2	1,198.4	853	4,845	494.1	146.9	45,132	2,320.8	1,065,855	3,279
Stanislaus..........	1,075	24,257	3,635.0	1,274.8	604	3,817	371.6	118.9	27,775	1,462.1	155,768	759
Sutter..............	249	3,369	392.4	147.2	108	571	53.1	16.5	5,773	385.2	30,073	97
Tehama..............	141	1,951	179.5	73.0	68	436	43.9	13.8	3,205	155.0	31,973	144
Trinity.............	24	315	27.9	11.8	12	34	3.4	0.9	971	38.8	7,599	55
Tulare..............	836	15,488	1,610.2	632.1	383	2,114	219.4	60.0	19,951	967.9	292,423	1,528
Tuolumne............	170	2,692	345.6	131.5	79	355	35.5	11.3	4,174	179.6	15,499	68
Ventura.............	2,557	32,438	3,987.6	1,434.5	1,176	7,150	763.3	188.6	69,019	3,743.8	285,879	1,204
Yolo................	371	6,923	847.0	333.6	300	2,124	256.0	72.3	13,162	646.8	188,488	776
Yuba................	80	2,197	396.9	106.0	47	153	14.0	4.3	3,535	129.3	89,540	379
COLORADO	14,869	257,898	29,488.2	11,877.0	10,246	64,398	8,519.0	2,100.1	497,109	23,693.4	10,230,540	42,627
Adams...............	659	14,707	1,732.1	715.9	651	4,571	456.1	138.6	32,870	1,488.8	763,507	2,797
Alamosa.............	64	D	D	D	39	178	11.8	3.2	1,102	47.0	4,558	44
Arapahoe............	1,885	27,029	2,888.9	1,245.0	1,114	7,534	1,008.0	267.0	57,046	2,955.0	788,724	3,592
Archuleta...........	35	248	15.8	6.6	18	102	8.6	2.8	1,965	88.2	36,520	162
Baca................	6	D	D	D	8	D	D	D	354	14.7	0	0
Bent................	7	43	2.8	1.4	3	D	D	D	234	9.9	1,312	3

— **Government Employment and Payroll, and Local Government Finances**

STATE County	Full-time equivalent employees	March payroll (dollars)	Administration, judicial, and legal	Police and corrections	Fire protection	Highways and transportation	Health and welfare	Natural resources and utilities	Education and libraries	Total (mil dol)	Intergovernmental (mil dol)	Total (mil dol)	Per capita[1] (dollars) Total	Per capita[1] (dollars) Property
			March payroll (percent of total)							General revenue		Taxes		
	171	172	173	174	175	176	177	178	179	180	181	182	183	184
CALIFORNIA	X	X	X	X	X	X	X	X	X	X	X	X	X	X
Alameda	56,184	365,163,607	5.7	11.5	5.1	11.1	17.4	11.1	35.4	11,581.0	4,300.9	3,665.4	2,358	1,599
Alpine	214	872,045	11.7	13.5	1.0	7.4	8.2	7.0	43.1	24.5	12.2	8.3	7,356	6,651
Amador	1,266	6,168,436	11.2	19.0	1.9	5.8	6.8	6.0	39.5	128.1	55.8	50.2	1,356	1,204
Butte	8,734	37,694,370	6.4	9.6	2.6	2.0	12.6	5.9	58.9	1,079.1	643.7	243.0	1,097	878
Calaveras	1,448	6,209,937	7.6	9.6	4.4	4.6	11.0	10.4	49.5	186.0	75.8	74.1	1,657	1,522
Colusa	1,069	4,506,211	9.2	12.0	1.8	3.7	9.6	7.3	55.3	146.1	73.1	36.5	1,707	1,430
Contra Costa	31,030	175,288,765	5.0	11.0	4.7	3.1	16.5	6.7	49.7	5,884.2	1,770.2	2,008.9	1,861	1,450
Del Norte	840	3,504,433	11.7	12.1	0.5	4.3	15.7	4.5	48.9	153.3	93.2	23.2	819	669
El Dorado	6,061	31,562,790	7.6	11.3	7.2	4.8	7.4	6.9	49.3	878.4	352.8	300.6	1,665	1,450
Fresno	34,954	165,436,346	4.1	10.3	2.1	3.3	9.7	4.5	65.0	5,127.4	3,047.2	1,071.6	1,131	789
Glenn	1,427	5,989,936	3.6	9.7	0.6	3.0	13.1	9.7	56.4	178.6	102.2	29.6	1,057	878
Humboldt	5,913	25,492,898	6.6	10.3	1.9	3.5	17.6	6.2	50.4	699.2	403.7	159.8	1,185	901
Imperial	10,122	49,143,599	4.2	6.0	1.7	1.1	19.5	16.2	45.5	1,293.3	740.8	180.2	1,019	733
Inyo	1,429	7,084,588	6.7	10.0	0.3	4.1	40.9	3.3	30.9	203.7	66.4	52.2	2,825	2,089
Kern	32,191	158,787,344	5.1	10.1	4.5	2.2	16.0	4.2	56.8	6,098.2	2,797.6	1,169.0	1,365	1,151
Kings	4,882	22,137,016	6.6	11.1	2.5	1.2	11.7	3.6	60.7	623.0	383.4	130.2	860	727
Lake	2,729	12,022,755	11.2	10.5	3.8	2.4	16.8	9.3	43.1	271.7	144.5	78.7	1,231	1,043
Lassen	1,280	5,212,652	7.9	9.0	1.2	3.2	10.4	8.7	58.1	128.4	89.5	24.8	738	648
Los Angeles	386,456	2,230,095,495	9.6	12.3	4.7	5.7	13.7	9.3	42.7	62,878.6	29,034.6	18,834.7	1,891	1,234
Madera	4,578	20,019,402	8.1	8.1	0.2	2.2	10.1	5.2	64.4	627.3	366.3	154.2	1,013	706
Marin	8,544	51,753,682	10.8	11.2	8.5	4.2	8.9	10.4	44.3	1,521.9	327.6	825.0	3,222	2,533
Mariposa	919	3,214,468	8.2	10.8	0.6	5.1	32.1	3.0	35.0	106.5	45.5	33.4	1,867	1,123
Mendocino	3,596	16,441,501	8.4	10.8	1.7	3.8	21.2	5.0	47.9	1,037.3	251.8	144.5	1,653	1,355
Merced	10,959	49,202,192	6.5	7.6	1.6	1.1	10.0	6.7	63.4	1,305.5	840.8	219.3	836	680
Modoc	586	2,160,529	8.3	8.7	1.4	11.9	22.7	4.7	40.8	67.3	46.4	10.6	1,140	1,021
Mono	1,012	5,526,104	7.8	11.4	5.1	6.0	35.5	9.2	22.9	195.2	38.3	79.1	5,511	4,023
Monterey	16,674	95,953,296	5.6	9.2	2.7	3.8	28.8	5.1	41.4	3,062.0	1,376.2	682.3	1,599	1,199
Napa	5,012	27,819,123	11.8	13.2	3.0	2.1	9.4	6.0	49.6	811.6	274.6	367.8	2,645	2,138
Nevada	3,125	16,593,333	8.7	9.9	4.8	4.6	26.3	10.1	30.7	498.3	165.7	159.3	1,620	1,417
Orange	85,251	527,595,855	5.4	11.0	4.8	3.1	7.4	5.7	58.4	14,543.9	5,867.6	5,580.4	1,806	1,406
Placer	12,015	67,291,627	7.1	9.6	4.2	2.3	5.5	9.5	58.5	1,867.4	613.0	730.0	2,018	1,673
Plumas	1,484	5,779,631	5.2	6.8	2.3	4.1	39.9	3.6	35.0	189.6	75.9	44.6	2,300	2,099
Riverside	68,997	380,597,495	8.6	11.0	1.9	2.3	12.6	7.6	54.4	10,975.4	5,598.2	3,090.1	1,362	1,054
Sacramento	50,509	274,337,834	5.2	13.3	5.5	4.2	8.8	13.3	46.1	7,904.0	3,980.4	1,968.0	1,357	948
San Benito	2,079	11,695,733	4.3	7.2	1.9	1.9	29.7	5.0	47.9	317.3	147.3	81.2	1,428	1,245
San Bernardino	68,989	370,218,367	5.5	10.6	4.1	2.1	13.3	5.1	56.9	11,897.3	6,945.9	2,679.6	1,287	987
San Diego	97,178	529,647,292	9.3	10.8	3.9	3.4	11.1	7.0	52.0	16,495.7	6,780.5	5,691.2	1,791	1,381
San Francisco	38,712	274,384,267	11.0	13.8	5.8	19.9	21.2	9.0	18.6	8,696.0	2,927.1	3,303.9	4,001	2,234
San Joaquin	23,911	123,453,125	6.5	12.7	3.3	2.6	14.7	5.0	53.3	3,894.7	2,276.8	855.2	1,217	851
San Luis Obispo	8,194	48,094,004	7.2	11.4	2.8	2.5	6.9	6.4	57.6	1,189.7	435.4	547.8	1,994	1,615
San Mateo	20,873	132,351,507	8.3	12.6	5.3	5.4	14.1	7.1	44.7	4,326.2	1,099.6	2,039.6	2,759	2,118
Santa Barbara	15,712	89,085,924	7.3	11.4	5.3	3.7	14.4	7.2	48.4	2,761.9	960.5	877.6	2,035	1,531
Santa Clara	59,919	402,121,133	7.6	10.2	5.0	5.0	20.4	6.5	42.7	12,701.2	3,946.9	4,816.5	2,621	1,963
Santa Cruz	9,292	50,504,116	8.1	10.1	3.9	7.3	13.5	7.9	47.1	1,432.9	632.4	483.8	1,813	1,441
Shasta	6,528	30,533,939	6.7	8.7	2.8	3.4	15.6	9.0	52.2	922.9	498.8	217.9	1,220	1,000
Sierra	204	851,638	16.3	12.9	0.1	11.6	17.0	3.1	35.4	28.6	16.9	7.5	2,443	2,207
Siskiyou	2,067	8,289,776	11.3	10.4	0.5	6.1	10.7	5.7	53.1	242.6	147.2	54.2	1,228	1,028
Solano	14,386	72,410,858	7.6	13.9	3.4	2.8	9.9	7.1	53.4	1,896.3	937.5	594.6	1,413	1,051
Sonoma	16,072	90,178,192	9.5	12.6	3.9	2.6	12.9	7.2	47.9	2,545.8	918.8	972.6	1,978	1,555
Stanislaus	19,446	94,702,481	5.9	8.3	2.5	1.6	11.8	9.4	58.2	2,696.4	1,547.9	554.1	1,062	825
Sutter	3,010	14,970,086	9.1	8.0	3.7	3.1	14.1	4.9	55.0	556.7	302.3	112.6	1,185	908
Tehama	2,320	9,999,317	7.1	9.2	1.1	3.3	13.4	2.6	61.2	246.2	160.2	57.2	902	755
Trinity	1,131	4,471,095	2.7	3.4	0.7	7.0	27.1	7.4	48.8	140.6	56.9	13.9	1,024	919
Tulare	21,502	97,324,423	4.7	7.2	1.7	1.1	30.4	3.5	50.1	3,132.9	1,499.7	450.9	998	665
Tuolumne	1,609	7,837,540	9.3	11.4	1.9	4.0	9.2	5.7	53.0	206.6	92.6	69.5	1,287	1,105
Ventura	27,714	159,457,912	10.1	10.8	4.6	3.0	13.0	7.6	49.2	4,630.9	2,005.3	1,379.1	1,650	1,378
Yolo	6,203	32,178,923	11.0	12.7	5.3	1.8	9.0	7.7	48.4	954.1	449.2	304.9	1,494	1,014
Yuba	3,659	17,894,536	5.9	8.6	0.7	1.5	7.2	2.0	71.6	385.0	230.2	77.0	1,056	932
COLORADO	X	X	X	X	X	X	X	X	X	X	X	X	X	X
Adams	14,341	67,598,280	8.2	13.6	4.3	2.6	4.0	12.3	52.8	1,856.9	785.2	806.6	1,755	1,137
Alamosa	647	1,959,302	10.3	10.3	0.7	4.6	18.5	7.3	47.7	73.8	42.5	23.1	1,428	843
Arapahoe	21,249	96,139,327	5.9	11.9	9.5	2.0	4.3	8.1	56.7	2,508.7	756.4	1,211.5	2,034	1,426
Archuleta	516	2,016,002	9.3	6.9	2.2	5.2	24.8	8.6	30.1	79.3	24.7	31.1	2,580	1,862
Baca	511	1,703,710	8.5	7.0	0.0	11.1	42.4	7.3	21.4	31.5	11.2	5.7	1,519	1,381
Bent	294	918,613	7.0	10.4	0.0	4.8	21.4	18.4	36.0	56.2	15.6	20.3	3,509	2,068

1. Based on the resident population estimated as of July 1 of the year shown.

Table B. States and Counties — Local Government Finances, Government Employment, and Income Taxes

STATE County	Local government finances, 2012 (cont.) Direct general expenditure							Debt outstanding		Government employment, 2017			Individual income tax returns, 2016		
	Total (mil dol)	Per capita[1] (dollars)	Education	Health and hospitals	Police protection	Public welfare	Highways	Total (mil dol)	Per capita[1] (dollars)	Federal civilian	Federal military	State and local	Number of returns	Mean adjusted gross income	Mean income tax
	185	186	187	188	189	190	191	192	193	194	195	196	197	198	199
CALIFORNIA	X	X	X	X	X	X	X	X	X	248,950	206,431	2,325,520	17,816,120	79,359	11,997
Alameda	12,422	7,990	22.9	13.4	5.2	5.4	2.3	24,528.0	15,776	9,162	3,879	108,109	784,180	93,718	14,725
Alpine	26	23,015	19.6	7.3	10.1	5.8	8.6	23.6	20,861	1	2	267	480	49,419	5,196
Amador	133.4	3,602	30.1	6.7	9.8	7.2	5.6	61.9	1,670	100	52	4,697	16,750	60,538	7,047
Butte	1,098.2	4,957	46.2	6.8	4.4	11.8	3.6	480.5	2,169	564	335	16,150	93,910	54,112	6,013
Calaveras	179.1	4,002	37.4	6.3	5.0	8.1	5.2	135.0	3,017	128	67	2,613	20,300	60,040	6,815
Colusa	142.2	6,642	35.7	6.2	5.7	4.9	6.5	51.5	2,404	69	32	2,177	9,800	57,679	6,488
Contra Costa	6,294.4	5,830	33.6	19.1	6.3	5.7	4.7	7,234.2	6,701	4,846	1,747	43,589	543,630	109,090	18,016
Del Norte	142.9	5,052	31.7	5.8	3.7	12.4	2.6	70.4	2,488	148	49	3,489	9,730	46,642	4,555
El Dorado	940.2	5,207	36.4	3.7	4.8	5.2	6.4	905.2	5,013	702	280	10,064	89,470	85,405	12,425
Fresno	5,031.5	5,308	44.7	7.0	5.6	10.3	3.4	3,847.5	4,059	9,924	1,632	62,586	393,330	52,038	5,767
Glenn	186.6	6,665	40.1	6.9	4.5	11.9	5.2	33.9	1,212	207	76	1,841	12,060	47,184	4,670
Humboldt	731.8	5,428	44.2	7.8	4.7	10.6	4.7	396.3	2,939	810	388	13,082	56,790	50,371	5,437
Imperial	1,172.3	6,625	40.7	23.6	4.1	7.5	2.9	1,408.8	7,962	2,111	367	16,532	78,510	40,026	3,307
Inyo	199.3	10,776	23.8	41.6	4.6	3.3	3.2	72.4	3,915	288	26	2,766	8,380	57,855	6,677
Kern	5,683.5	6,638	55.4	8.5	3.6	6.7	3.0	3,571.0	4,171	10,558	3,953	54,711	335,910	51,053	5,147
Kings	602.9	3,983	45.9	6.6	4.9	9.6	2.9	261.9	1,730	1,160	4,890	13,623	54,070	46,648	4,207
Lake	267.3	4,177	39.4	7.1	5.3	13.9	3.9	107.2	1,675	156	94	4,037	25,470	44,492	4,268
Lassen	133.2	3,956	45.5	7.1	5.0	10.9	6.5	58.3	1,734	1,858	36	4,584	9,860	54,050	5,242
Los Angeles	60,312.8	6,054	35.0	11.1	7.8	8.7	3.1	84,320.3	8,464	48,551	17,248	548,712	4,638,710	72,471	11,203
Madera	649.2	4,265	45.6	3.7	3.9	8.8	6.2	475.5	3,124	299	222	10,595	58,630	48,338	4,660
Marin	1,569.1	6,127	34.5	6.9	6.2	4.1	3.1	2,304.2	8,998	755	498	15,029	131,460	164,766	33,433
Mariposa	101.6	5,675	21.1	24.5	6.6	10.1	6.4	22.6	1,262	696	25	1,488	7,640	52,162	5,394
Mendocino	1,025.1	11,725	70.9	7.3	2.3	5.1	2.4	577.0	6,600	277	159	6,583	39,100	50,260	5,503
Merced	1,403.1	5,349	48.6	3.6	4.1	10.0	2.7	901.0	3,435	773	396	18,522	102,870	44,605	4,014
Modoc	67.1	7,198	38.4	16.9	4.0	6.8	8.8	4.6	497	225	13	900	3,490	42,504	4,019
Mono	192	13,383	15.1	34.5	6.6	4.9	8.7	76.3	5,321	217	211	1,411	6,410	56,222	6,731
Monterey	2,904.3	6,806	36.5	22.7	4.6	5.4	2.6	1,444.4	3,385	5,201	4,748	28,817	196,270	62,999	7,729
Napa	821.7	5,909	37.5	5.9	7.5	4.2	4.0	746.0	5,365	228	202	10,768	67,610	87,761	13,621
Nevada	537	5,464	23.8	31.3	4.9	5.6	4.7	392.6	3,994	371	147	5,713	49,430	67,326	8,610
Orange	13,915.7	4,503	41.4	2.9	7.7	7.3	4.5	22,316.3	7,222	11,375	5,099	147,611	1,500,510	86,686	13,775
Placer	1,896.3	5,243	41.7	2.8	5.8	5.9	6.0	2,500.4	6,913	718	595	18,256	181,310	86,864	12,201
Plumas	177.2	9,133	26.8	34.8	4.1	4.9	5.8	57.6	2,967	370	27	2,015	8,790	52,397	5,330
Riverside	11,682.2	5,149	39.3	8.1	6.7	7.1	4.3	13,164.6	5,802	7,200	3,931	125,804	988,750	55,672	5,875
Sacramento	7,966.3	5,494	34.4	6.0	4.9	8.6	5.8	16,350.5	11,275	9,265	2,969	167,551	681,990	61,018	7,287
San Benito	327.5	5,757	32.1	32.0	3.9	5.6	3.2	125.8	2,211	136	89	2,865	28,020	67,870	8,216
San Bernardino	11,798.5	5,669	38.7	15.6	6.0	7.5	5.5	11,574.3	5,561	13,635	19,837	111,176	898,910	51,761	5,158
San Diego	16,846	5,302	37.0	9.8	5.3	6.9	2.9	27,732.0	8,729	47,386	100,959	197,739	1,561,790	74,248	10,382
San Francisco	7,412.4	8,975	16.3	24.7	5.1	6.5	3.4	17,985.0	21,777	14,028	1,621	91,705	477,020	138,810	27,482
San Joaquin	3,717.2	5,291	40.5	9.2	5.9	8.8	3.5	3,309.2	4,710	3,085	1,145	39,884	309,720	56,746	6,155
San Luis Obispo	1,206.8	4,391	38.5	5.9	6.2	8.2	3.9	850.7	3,096	562	507	22,345	131,340	69,481	9,013
San Mateo	4,256.2	5,757	34.0	11.6	7.7	4.4	3.8	4,651.4	6,292	3,786	1,328	29,068	386,550	154,152	30,356
Santa Barbara	2,786.6	6,462	32.4	18.7	5.7	6.7	3.0	1,346.9	3,123	3,636	3,093	32,176	201,430	72,985	10,610
Santa Clara	11,865.9	6,458	32.5	21.8	5.2	5.2	2.2	17,898.2	9,740	10,174	3,322	83,837	916,070	153,436	28,468
Santa Cruz	1,415.2	5,305	36.6	6.6	6.3	8.5	2.3	1,074.8	4,029	543	390	19,407	130,730	79,736	11,812
Shasta	906.1	5,074	43.3	8.1	5.8	10.6	4.0	544.3	3,048	1,315	302	11,550	76,910	53,589	5,742
Sierra	29	9,401	28.7	10.0	10.3	10.1	12.9	6.1	1,986	41	4	325	1,230	47,743	4,690
Siskiyou	251	5,684	48.4	6.3	5.8	7.4	5.5	80.4	1,822	806	64	3,350	19,140	43,783	4,212
Solano	1,873.8	4,454	35.1	6.1	9.3	7.8	4.2	1,624.0	3,860	3,716	6,915	22,144	207,680	65,466	7,487
Sonoma	2,601.9	5,290	35.4	10.3	6.3	6.4	5.0	2,547.1	5,179	1,403	1,474	27,667	242,950	74,009	10,122
Stanislaus	2,792.3	5,352	50.1	6.9	4.9	10.2	3.4	4,496.8	8,619	870	811	28,940	225,840	53,305	5,666
Sutter	526.6	5,542	44.9	7.7	4.4	6.1	1.8	241.8	2,545	87	144	4,750	40,070	52,772	5,500
Tehama	244.9	3,862	49.8	6.6	5.9	14.9	4.0	28.9	456	213	94	3,891	25,150	48,477	4,763
Trinity	128.3	9,486	22.7	15.7	2.1	6.0	7.0	47.2	3,487	234	18	801	4,590	46,959	5,023
Tulare	3,186.6	7,050	39.0	24.4	3.2	8.0	4.7	1,380.8	3,055	1,062	685	31,225	178,610	44,391	4,279
Tuolumne	214.2	3,966	35.6	9.8	6.8	8.2	4.3	66.5	1,230	459	75	4,901	24,220	57,615	6,377
Ventura	4,471.8	5,349	38.6	13.1	7.5	4.6	3.5	3,011.8	3,603	7,273	4,902	38,837	404,630	78,185	11,168
Yolo	951.1	4,659	30.3	3.8	6.2	8.0	5.9	944.3	4,626	3,638	328	37,218	89,080	72,390	9,577
Yuba	436.2	5,982	54.3	2.1	4.1	10.8	4.0	399.0	5,472	1,549	3,929	5,017	29,100	46,127	3,784
COLORADO	X	X	X	X	X	X	X	X	X	53,607	52,203	386,937	2,648,690	73,452	10,488
Adams	1,860.3	4,048	42.2	0.3	5.7	9.9	5.6	2,579.2	5,612	1,121	1,634	41,383	231,160	55,186	5,865
Alamosa	68	4,210	38.8	5.3	7.5	20.9	5.9	38.4	2,379	141	38	2,274	6,640	45,249	4,616
Arapahoe	2,593	4,354	41.7	1.1	7.2	3.0	5.0	6,000.2	10,075	3,208	3,338	34,491	311,570	78,395	11,906
Archuleta	68.6	5,681	20.6	27.4	2.8	7.3	11.0	57.7	4,780	43	33	806	6,230	55,060	6,298
Baca	31.8	8,484	29.7	35.6	3.0	11.3	8.9	2.1	559	36	10	639	1,540	28,382	3,049
Bent	42.9	7,437	18.7	2.0	8.7	5.5	17.8	8.1	1,402	36	10	455	1,570	36,555	3,258

1. Based on the resident population estimated as of July 1 of the year shown.

Table B. States and Counties — Land Area and Population

State / county code	CBSA code[1]	County code[2]	STATE County	Land area[3] (sq. mi)	Total persons 2018	Rank	Per square mile	White	Black	American Indian, Alaska Native	Asian and Pacific Islancer	Percent Hispanic or Latino[4]	Under 5 years	5 to 17 years	18 to 24 years	25 to 34 years	35 to 44 years	45 to 54 years
				1	2	3	4	5	6	7	8	9	10	11	12	13	14	15
			COLORADO—Cont'd															
08013	14,500	2	Boulder	726.4	326,078	213	448.9	79.8	1.5	0.9	6.3	13.9	4.4	14.6	14.9	14.0	12.5	12.7
08014	19,740	1	Broomfield	33.0	69,267	777	2,099.0	78.9	1.9	1.0	8.2	12.6	5.4	17.7	7.5	15.2	14.9	13.8
08015		7	Chaffee	1,013.4	20,027	1,826	19.8	86.4	1.9	1.6	1.2	10.1	3.7	11.3	6.2	12.6	12.1	12.1
08017		9	Cheyenne	1,778.3	1,876	3,062	1.1	85.6	1.3	1.5	1.1	11.7	7.0	18.4	6.8	10.4	11.1	10.9
08019	19,740	1	Clear Creek	395.2	9,605	2,456	24.3	89.9	1.5	1.5	1.5	7.4	3.9	11.2	5.2	11.9	13.0	15.0
08021		9	Conejos	1,287.4	8,200	2,577	6.4	46.4	0.8	1.4	0.8	51.7	6.5	19.4	8.7	10.8	10.8	10.7
08023		9	Costilla	1,227.6	3,828	2,915	3.1	36.2	1.3	2.1	1.5	60.3	4.5	14.4	6.6	9.6	8.9	11.2
08025		8	Crowley	787.4	5,858	2,761	7.4	55.4	11.0	2.4	1.5	31.2	2.5	9.2	9.6	20.8	17.6	15.3
08027		8	Custer	738.6	4,954	2,835	6.7	91.8	1.8	2.0	0.8	5.5	3.3	10.5	4.7	7.4	8.3	10.4
08029		6	Delta	1,142.1	30,953	1,409	27.1	82.5	1.0	1.5	1.1	15.4	4.9	15.2	6.5	9.8	10.5	11.0
08031	19,740	1	Denver	153.3	716,492	90	4,673.8	56.5	10.1	1.2	5.1	29.7	6.0	13.5	8.0	23.3	16.0	11.6
08033		9	Dolores	1,067.2	2,074	3,041	1.9	90.3	0.9	4.3	0.7	6.2	3.5	16.5	5.6	8.1	11.3	12.5
08035	19,740	1	Douglas	840.3	342,776	207	407.9	84.1	2.0	0.7	6.6	9.0	5.9	20.1	7.7	11.1	14.8	16.0
08037	20,780	5	Eagle	1,684.5	54,993	927	32.6	67.6	1.2	0.6	1.6	29.8	5.6	16.2	7.4	15.9	15.6	14.9
08039	19,740	1	Elbert	1,850.8	26,282	1,556	14.2	89.8	1.8	1.2	1.7	7.2	4.7	17.1	7.1	8.8	11.3	15.9
08041	17,820	2	El Paso	2,126.8	713,856	91	335.6	72.3	7.8	1.5	5.2	17.5	6.7	17.4	10.9	16.1	12.7	11.7
08043	15,860	4	Fremont	1,533.1	48,021	1,022	31.3	80.3	4.1	2.3	1.3	13.5	4.3	12.1	6.6	14.5	13.2	13.0
08045	24,060	5	Garfield	2,947.5	59,770	873	20.3	69.2	1.0	1.2	1.3	28.8	6.9	18.4	8.0	13.8	13.9	12.8
08047	19,740	1	Gilpin	149.9	6,121	2,740	40.8	89.1	1.5	1.8	2.2	7.3	3.7	11.8	4.9	10.6	14.4	16.8
08049		7	Grand	1,846.4	15,525	2,067	8.4	88.5	1.2	1.3	1.4	9.0	4.1	12.7	6.9	14.1	12.7	13.2
08051		7	Gunnison	3,239.1	17,246	1,964	5.3	88.4	1.0	1.4	1.3	9.4	4.3	12.7	18.1	14.7	13.0	11.9
08053		9	Hinsdale	1,117.2	811	3,117	0.7	91.5	1.7	2.0	1.4	6.0	3.9	11.6	7.6	9.1	9.1	10.6
08055		6	Huerfano	1,591.0	6,889	2,686	4.3	63.2	1.2	2.2	1.2	34.0	3.7	12.6	5.1	8.8	8.7	10.9
08057		9	Jackson	1,613.7	1,399	3,082	0.9	85.7	0.1	1.6	1.0	12.6	4.9	12.2	5.4	11.7	12.4	12.9
08059	19,740	1	Jefferson	764.3	580,233	115	759.2	79.8	1.7	1.1	3.9	15.5	5.2	14.5	7.7	14.9	13.7	13.1
08061		9	Kiowa	1,767.8	1,383	3,086	0.8	89.9	0.7	1.2	0.4	8.9	7.9	14.5	8.0	9.8	10.0	9.4
08063		7	Kit Carson	2,160.8	7,163	2,650	3.3	79.1	1.1	1.1	1.0	19.0	6.4	19.0	7.2	11.6	11.3	10.3
08065		6	Lake	376.9	7,824	2,607	20.8	61.8	1.1	1.7	1.0	35.9	5.3	14.6	9.4	16.9	14.1	12.5
08067	20,420	4	La Plata	1,689.8	56,310	907	33.3	80.1	0.9	6.7	1.3	13.0	5.1	13.9	9.2	13.5	13.4	12.3
08069	22,660	2	Larimer	2,595.8	350,518	203	135.0	84.5	1.6	1.1	3.4	11.7	5.1	14.5	14.1	14.7	12.4	11.0
08071		7	Las Animas	4,772.9	14,503	2,129	3.0	54.6	2.1	1.9	1.4	41.2	4.7	14.1	8.3	11.2	10.5	11.2
08073		8	Lincoln	2,577.7	5,610	2,784	2.2	78.7	5.9	1.6	1.4	14.1	5.4	14.8	8.1	15.9	12.7	12.7
08075	44,540	7	Logan	1,838.6	21,528	1,753	11.7	78.3	4.0	1.5	1.2	16.3	5.3	13.2	10.6	15.3	12.7	11.8
08077	24,300	3	Mesa	3,328.9	153,207	433	46.0	82.7	1.3	1.4	1.6	14.8	5.7	15.9	9.2	13.1	12.1	11.0
08079		9	Mineral	875.8	776	3,120	0.9	91.9	0.6	1.8	0.9	6.4	4.3	10.6	3.5	11.1	9.0	10.8
08081	18,780	7	Moffat	4,743.2	13,188	2,218	2.8	82.0	1.2	1.5	1.4	15.7	7.1	18.8	7.4	12.8	12.4	11.7
08083		6	Montezuma	2,029.3	26,158	1,561	12.9	74.0	0.8	13.5	1.1	12.7	5.6	16.4	6.6	11.5	10.7	11.4
08085	33,940	4	Montrose	2,240.9	42,214	1,133	18.8	77.3	0.8	1.5	1.3	20.7	5.6	16.0	6.9	10.4	11.1	11.7
08087	22,820	6	Morgan	1,280.5	28,558	1,477	22.3	59.1	3.7	0.9	1.1	36.3	7.4	18.6	8.9	13.9	11.7	11.5
08089		6	Otero	1,261.9	18,432	1,904	14.6	55.1	1.5	1.6	1.4	42.1	6.0	17.9	9.2	11.2	11.4	10.7
08091		9	Ouray	541.6	4,833	2,844	8.9	91.9	0.6	1.3	1.4	6.5	2.9	12.4	4.7	8.1	11.2	12.6
08093	19,740	1	Park	2,193.9	18,556	1,897	8.5	90.9	1.3	1.8	2.0	6.2	3.6	11.5	4.9	9.4	12.0	15.0
08095		9	Phillips	687.9	4,286	2,878	6.2	77.8	0.8	0.7	0.9	20.6	6.7	17.9	7.0	10.1	11.1	10.6
08097	24,060	7	Pitkin	970.7	17,950	1,923	18.5	86.8	1.2	0.6	2.5	10.1	3.9	11.2	6.4	15.0	13.1	15.4
08099		7	Prowers	1,638.4	12,164	2,281	7.4	59.4	1.0	1.4	0.8	38.6	7.1	18.7	10.2	11.1	11.5	10.4
08101	39,380	3	Pueblo	2,386.1	167,529	390	70.2	53.4	2.3	1.4	1.4	43.1	5.8	16.6	8.9	13.1	11.8	11.8
08103		9	Rio Blanco	3,221.0	6,336	2,723	2.0	86.5	1.9	2.1	1.5	10.3	5.9	17.9	9.5	12.6	12.0	11.3
08105		7	Rio Grande	912.0	11,250	2,334	12.3	53.5	1.0	1.8	0.9	44.0	5.9	16.8	7.9	12.3	11.7	10.9
08107	44,460	7	Routt	2,362.0	25,733	1,574	10.9	90.7	1.2	0.8	1.6	7.0	4.5	13.6	7.8	14.9	14.4	13.8
08109		9	Saguache	3,168.6	6,843	2,687	2.2	60.7	1.4	2.6	1.6	35.9	5.8	15.6	6.2	8.5	11.2	11.5
08111		9	San Juan	387.5	762	3,122	2.0	86.0	0.8	1.7	1.4	12.3	3.7	8.9	4.7	12.9	14.4	13.1
08113		9	San Miguel	1,286.7	8,191	2,578	6.4	87.0	1.0	1.2	1.4	10.7	4.0	13.6	6.1	15.8	14.7	16.1
08115		9	Sedgwick	548.0	2,303	3,019	4.2	81.1	1.5	1.1	1.2	16.7	5.2	15.2	5.9	10.5	10.6	9.5
08117	14,720	5	Summit	608.3	31,007	1,407	51.0	82.8	1.3	0.7	1.8	14.6	4.5	11.7	6.9	20.3	15.0	14.1
08119	17,820	2	Teller	557.0	25,083	1,602	45.0	90.4	1.3	1.8	1.8	6.8	4.0	13.0	6.1	9.5	10.2	14.1
08121		9	Washington	2,518.1	4,909	2,839	1.9	87.7	1.6	0.8	0.8	10.5	5.9	16.7	7.5	11.9	11.2	11.4
08123	24,540	2	Weld	3,986.0	314,305	223	78.9	66.9	1.6	1.1	2.4	29.6	7.3	19.0	9.1	15.3	13.7	12.1
08125		7	Yuma	2,364.4	10,020	2,425	4.2	74.9	0.8	0.8	0.5	23.9	7.4	19.6	7.3	12.1	11.2	11.5
09000		0	CONNECTICUT	4,842.7	3,572,665	X	737.7	68.1	11.2	0.6	5.5	16.5	5.1	15.5	9.7	12.5	11.8	13.9
09001	14,860	2	Fairfield	625.0	943,823	54	1,510.1	62.8	11.7	0.4	6.5	20.2	5.5	17.0	9.1	11.4	12.4	14.7
09003	25,540	1	Hartford	735.0	892,697	62	1,214.6	62.2	14.3	0.6	6.3	18.5	5.4	15.6	9.0	13.3	12.3	13.4
09005	45,860	4	Litchfield	920.5	181,111	361	196.8	89.3	2.2	0.6	2.5	6.7	4.1	14.0	7.5	10.4	10.4	14.8
09007	25,540	1	Middlesex	369.3	162,682	406	440.5	85.3	5.7	0.6	3.9	6.4	4.1	13.6	8.8	11.5	10.8	14.6
09009	35,300	2	New Haven	604.5	857,620	68	1,418.7	63.9	14.0	0.6	4.8	18.6	5.1	15.0	10.0	13.4	11.7	13.4
09011	35,980	2	New London	665.1	266,784	257	401.1	77.9	7.4	1.8	5.4	10.9	5.0	14.4	10.0	13.1	11.1	13.3

1. CBSA = Core Based Statistical Area. See Appendix A for explanation. See Appendix B for list of metropolitan areas with component counties.   2. County type code from the Economic Research Service of USDA Rural-Urban Continuum Codes. See Appendix A for definition.   3. Dry land or land partially or temporarily covered by water.   4. May be of any race.

Table B. States and Counties — Population and Households

STATE County	55 to 64 years	65 to 74 years	75 years and over	Percent female	Total persons 2000	2010	Percent change 2000-2010	2010-2018	Births	Deaths	Net Migration	Number	Persons per household	Family households	Female family householder[1]	One person
	16	17	18	19	20	21	22	23	24	25	26	27	28	29	30	31
COLORADO—Cont'd																
Boulder	12.6	8.8	5.4	49.7	269,814	294,561	9.2	10.7	23,685	14,085	21,827	125,026	2.44	58.7	7.6	28.0
Broomfield	11.7	8.4	5.4	50.3	38,272	55,856	45.9	24.0	5,692	2,871	10,446	25,938	2.47	66.3	6.8	25.9
Chaffee	16.7	15.9	9.5	47.2	16,242	17,809	9.6	12.5	1,123	1,406	2,476	7,900	2.23	68.5	6.7	24.7
Cheyenne	14.9	11.5	9.1	49.1	2,231	1,833	-17.8	2.3	213	155	-15	776	2.69	65.3	3.1	32.5
Clear Creek	19.4	14.1	6.2	47.2	9,322	9,064	-2.8	6.0	582	475	429	4,374	2.09	60.8	8.1	32.9
Conejos	13.9	11.5	7.8	49.8	8,400	8,256	-1.7	-0.7	895	661	-292	2,992	2.70	68.3	10.3	30.4
Costilla	17.5	16.2	11.1	48.2	3,663	3,524	-3.8	8.6	253	301	349	1,568	2.31	58.9	11.5	38.3
Crowley	11.2	8.0	5.7	26.8	5,518	5,823	5.5	0.6	279	335	47	1,215	3.52	67.0	16.0	21.2
Custer	23.1	23.1	9.1	48.4	3,503	4,255	21.5	16.4	204	300	787	2,093	2.15	70.4	4.1	26.0
Delta	16.4	15.2	10.7	49.9	27,834	30,952	11.2	0.0	2,524	2,993	468	12,119	2.40	66.6	7.8	29.3
Denver	9.8	7.1	4.6	49.8	554,636	599,815	8.1	19.5	77,415	35,733	72,836	287,262	2.31	48.6	10.0	38.7
Dolores	17.4	15.1	10.0	47.4	1,844	2,064	11.9	0.5	138	136	7	707	2.46	60.8	13.4	27.7
Douglas	12.6	7.8	4.2	50.1	175,766	285,465	62.4	20.1	28,885	9,638	37,809	113,799	2.81	78.5	7.0	17.1
Eagle	12.8	8.3	3.2	47.0	41,659	52,196	25.3	5.4	5,348	907	-1,674	17,765	3.02	67.4	6.7	21.5
Elbert	18.7	11.5	4.9	49.5	19,872	23,088	16.2	13.8	1,555	1,039	2,673	8,866	2.76	77.2	5.6	17.7
El Paso	11.7	7.9	4.8	49.5	516,929	622,250	20.4	14.7	77,169	34,267	48,556	249,745	2.63	68.8	10.7	24.8
Fremont	14.8	12.8	8.9	42.3	46,145	46,824	1.5	2.6	3,097	4,438	2,510	16,762	2.14	69.4	9.5	27.4
Garfield	13.1	8.6	4.5	48.9	43,791	56,389	28.8	6.0	6,723	2,558	-816	21,055	2.71	72.6	9.6	20.3
Gilpin	20.9	12.8	4.1	47.5	4,757	5,453	14.6	12.3	353	218	518	2,603	2.19	55.8	2.8	35.5
Grand	18.7	12.6	5.0	46.4	12,442	14,843	19.3	4.6	976	514	183	5,724	2.53	61.1	7.4	27.4
Gunnison	12.4	8.9	4.1	46.1	13,956	15,324	9.8	12.5	1,222	582	1,249	6,495	2.36	56.4	8.8	28.8
Hinsdale	17.6	19.7	10.6	48.5	790	843	6.7	-3.8	41	36	-39	368	2.22	68.5	4.3	29.1
Huerfano	19.1	18.2	12.9	49.0	7,862	6,711	-14.6	2.7	395	827	604	3,173	1.99	54.1	9.6	38.0
Jackson	18.4	13.0	9.2	48.2	1,577	1,393	-11.7	0.4	99	91	-5	597	2.28	65.0	2.8	29.8
Jefferson	14.4	10.1	6.4	50.1	525,507	534,829	1.8	8.5	47,945	34,467	31,791	227,805	2.44	64.5	9.1	27.5
Kiowa	17.1	11.9	11.5	51.3	1,622	1,398	-13.8	-1.1	131	164	16	576	2.32	63.2	10.2	36.8
Kit Carson	14.8	10.0	9.3	50.0	8,011	8,270	3.2	-13.4	775	611	-1,313	2,995	2.37	70.3	6.6	27.6
Lake	12.9	9.6	4.6	46.2	7,812	7,310	-6.4	7.0	675	310	147	3,324	2.21	59.8	6.1	31.9
La Plata	15.4	11.5	5.7	49.5	43,941	51,335	16.8	9.7	4,472	2,700	3,168	21,818	2.41	61.4	7.7	30.3
Larimer	12.5	9.6	6.0	50.1	251,494	299,615	19.1	17.0	28,123	17,275	39,542	130,502	2.46	62.5	7.4	24.3
Las Animas	15.7	14.6	9.7	47.8	15,207	15,507	2.0	-6.5	1,120	1,416	-734	6,327	2.11	60.7	9.0	32.6
Lincoln	12.9	9.1	8.5	41.6	6,087	5,469	-10.2	2.6	481	423	80	1,477	2.38	66.6	10.0	29.5
Logan	13.3	9.6	8.2	44.1	20,504	22,709	10.8	-5.2	1,902	1,698	-1,486	8,151	2.55	58.9	9.0	33.6
Mesa	14.0	11.1	8.0	50.6	116,255	146,717	26.2	4.4	14,756	11,666	3,456	60,562	2.40	64.5	11.1	27.8
Mineral	19.6	20.7	10.4	50.4	831	712	-14.3	9.0	46	47	62	404	2.01	65.3	4.2	30.2
Moffat	14.4	9.5	5.8	48.7	13,184	13,791	4.6	-4.4	1,494	793	-1,331	5,103	2.53	65.9	7.8	28.6
Montezuma	15.7	13.6	8.5	50.7	23,830	25,541	7.2	2.4	2,446	2,193	383	10,520	2.43	64.3	9.0	29.0
Montrose	15.1	13.3	10.0	50.7	33,432	41,277	23.5	2.3	3,733	3,495	700	16,951	2.38	66.8	9.8	28.7
Morgan	12.5	8.3	7.2	49.5	27,171	28,159	3.6	1.4	3,593	2,129	-1,078	10,599	2.62	68.3	12.6	22.0
Otero	13.2	11.4	9.0	51.0	20,311	18,833	-7.3	-2.1	1,812	1,929	-282	7,490	2.38	67.1	14.4	30.2
Ouray	20.8	18.5	8.7	49.4	3,742	4,442	18.7	8.8	248	231	362	2,204	2.11	62.0	5.0	27.4
Park	23.1	15.4	5.1	47.4	14,523	16,204	11.6	14.5	902	716	2,130	7,389	2.27	64.2	5.0	28.0
Phillips	14.1	10.2	12.3	50.7	4,480	4,442	-0.8	-3.5	450	412	-200	1,696	2.51	65.3	7.8	30.8
Pitkin	15.6	12.9	6.5	48.3	14,872	17,149	15.3	4.7	1,167	415	40	7,340	2.40	49.6	8.5	38.4
Prowers	13.5	10.1	7.5	49.7	14,483	12,551	-13.3	-3.1	1,374	1,014	-760	4,913	2.38	68.1	11.9	27.9
Pueblo	13.5	10.8	7.7	50.7	141,472	159,063	12.4	5.3	15,428	13,937	7,051	63,489	2.50	64.2	14.2	29.9
Rio Blanco	15.3	8.7	6.8	48.9	5,986	6,673	11.5	-5.1	640	408	-577	2,417	2.57	67.2	5.8	28.8
Rio Grande	14.4	11.8	8.4	50.0	12,413	11,982	-3.5	-6.1	1,122	1,019	-839	4,750	2.36	63.8	10.4	33.1
Routt	15.5	10.8	4.7	47.9	19,690	23,506	19.4	9.5	1,836	859	1,223	9,478	2.53	59.4	4.7	29.5
Saguache	18.3	16.3	6.7	49.9	5,917	6,108	3.2	12.0	589	342	483	2,626	2.41	62.8	10.2	33.5
San Juan	18.9	15.5	7.9	44.0	558	699	25.3	9.0	40	32	55	255	2.23	45.9	9.8	40.4
San Miguel	15.1	11.2	3.5	46.8	6,594	7,359	11.6	11.3	560	177	447	3,301	2.36	54.1	7.8	35.0
Sedgwick	16.8	13.2	13.0	50.6	2,747	2,382	-13.3	-3.3	205	292	8	998	2.32	58.4	7.0	35.5
Summit	13.8	9.9	3.7	45.8	23,548	27,994	18.9	10.8	2,333	489	1,126	9,455	3.10	56.4	6.8	31.0
Teller	21.3	15.8	6.2	49.2	20,555	23,359	13.6	7.4	1,523	1,279	1,471	10,076	2.34	70.6	7.5	23.0
Washington	14.8	10.8	9.9	48.0	4,926	4,812	-2.3	2.0	384	403	116	2,012	2.25	70.2	9.3	25.4
Weld	11.5	7.7	4.5	49.6	180,926	252,847	39.8	24.3	33,427	13,595	41,180	99,817	2.80	73.2	10.3	20.5
Yuma	12.3	10.1	8.4	50.2	9,841	10,043	2.1	-0.2	1,203	816	-420	4,053	2.47	61.7	7.5	33.1
CONNECTICUT	14.3	9.6	7.6	51.2	3,405,565	3,574,147	5.0	0.0	298,938	247,536	-52,931	1,361,755	2.55	65.8	12.6	28.1
Fairfield	14.0	8.7	7.2	51.3	882,567	916,864	3.9	2.9	83,244	54,956	-1,185	337,678	2.75	70.0	12.1	24.4
Hartford	13.8	9.4	7.7	51.4	857,183	894,033	4.3	-0.1	77,815	65,517	-13,744	348,871	2.50	65.0	14.1	29.2
Litchfield	17.4	12.4	8.9	50.6	182,193	189,925	4.2	-4.6	11,956	14,586	-6,183	74,605	2.43	67.4	8.6	26.7
Middlesex	16.3	11.5	8.8	51.3	155,071	165,676	6.8	-1.8	11,335	12,313	-1,934	66,599	2.38	63.9	9.2	29.2
New Haven	14.0	9.7	7.7	51.8	824,008	862,456	4.7	-0.6	73,479	63,497	-14,814	327,402	2.55	62.7	13.8	31.4
New London	14.8	10.4	7.8	49.9	259,088	274,068	5.8	-2.7	22,191	19,816	-9,732	107,193	2.41	65.0	12.3	28.8

1. No spouse present.

Table B. States and Counties — Population, Vital Statistics, Health, and Crime

STATE County	Persons in group quarters, 2018	Daytime Population, 2013-2017 Number	Employment/ residence ratio	Births, 2018 Total	Rate[1]	Deaths, 2018 Number	Rate[1]	Persons under 65 with no health insurance, 2016 Number	Percent	Medicare, 2018 Total beneficiaries	Enrolled in Original Medicare	Enrolled in Medicare Advantage	Serious crimes known to police[2], 2016 Total Number	Rate[3]
	32	33	34	35	36	37	38	39	40	41	42	43	44	45
COLORADO—Cont'd														
Boulder	11,627	348,612	1.19	2,663	8.2	1,888	5.8	19,445	7.2	50,110	31,031	19,079	8,185	2,525
Broomfield	282	70,487	1.18	698	10.1	383	5.5	2,946	5.1	9,814	4,890	4,924	1,647	2,460
Chaffee	1,475	18,923	1.01	142	7.1	165	8.2	1,174	8.9	5,213	4,289	924	329	1,748
Cheyenne	43	2,316	1.20	23	12.3	18	9.6	196	13.4	382	365	17	4	219
Clear Creek	84	7,726	0.70	71	7.4	60	6.2	471	6.2	1,803	1,156	647	195	2,087
Conejos	36	7,264	0.69	90	11.0	70	8.5	601	9.2	1,890	1,407	483	68	938
Costilla	0	3,482	0.88	34	8.9	29	7.6	391	14.7	1,164	887	277	NA	NA
Crowley	2,811	5,250	0.85	23	3.9	39	6.7	198	8.3	855	727	128	63	1,144
Custer	150	4,387	0.91	31	6.3	37	7.5	364	12.1	1,672	1,330	342	106	2,367
Delta	713	28,811	0.87	294	9.5	386	12.5	2,291	10.3	8,940	6,799	2,141	524	1,998
Denver	16,311	828,550	1.41	9,619	13.4	4,916	6.9	61,876	10.3	89,912	45,432	44,480	29,856	4,270
Dolores	0	1,673	0.92	12	5.8	11	5.3	170	10.9	546	489	57	22	1,122
Douglas	630	282,554	0.77	3,541	10.3	1,397	4.1	10,784	3.7	43,155	25,387	17,768	4,885	1,481
Eagle	78	52,182	0.95	622	11.3	137	2.5	6,276	12.9	5,620	5,257	363	887	1,646
Elbert	73	17,157	0.43	220	8.4	142	5.4	1,572	7.4	4,440	3,011	1,429	11	47
El Paso	20,304	671,939	0.99	9,651	13.5	4,753	6.7	41,408	7.1	104,555	70,606	33,949	22,688	3,320
Fremont	8,412	46,127	0.97	376	7.8	539	11.2	2,535	8.6	12,158	7,915	4,243	328	703
Garfield	884	54,237	0.88	816	13.7	357	6.0	7,830	15.3	8,249	7,447	802	1,198	2,049
Gilpin	49	8,198	1.71	45	7.4	27	4.4	233	4.6	963	609	354	258	4,994
Grand	222	14,413	0.96	130	8.4	71	4.6	1,217	9.6	2,464	2,080	384	119	907
Gunnison	1,100	16,605	1.04	145	8.4	75	4.3	1,406	10.4	2,321	2,165	156	260	1,605
Hinsdale	56	826	1.02	2	2.5	4	4.9	69	11.8	226	215	11	10	1,314
Huerfano	165	6,391	0.95	46	6.7	97	14.1	391	8.7	2,351	1,918	433	237	4,156
Jackson	2	1,300	0.90	13	9.3	11	7.9	158	15.0	331	306	25	5	370
Jefferson	8,757	513,103	0.83	6,018	10.4	4,571	7.9	31,818	6.6	103,493	47,858	55,635	20,050	3,509
Kiowa	14	1,379	1.02	18	13.0	18	13.0	109	10.6	334	D	D	NA	NA
Kit Carson	58	8,073	1.06	86	12.0	72	10.1	759	13.1	1,477	1,420	57	132	1,723
Lake	152	6,001	0.64	77	9.8	28	3.6	791	12.1	978	898	80	97	1,289
La Plata	1,800	55,477	1.04	524	9.3	363	6.4	4,671	10.3	10,286	9,134	1,152	1,172	2,117
Larimer	9,369	324,438	0.96	3,395	9.7	2,261	6.5	20,618	7.3	59,706	41,244	18,462	8,273	2,430
Las Animas	862	14,366	1.04	131	9.0	157	10.8	1,029	10.3	4,115	3,380	735	524	3,797
Lincoln	1,011	6,115	1.41	57	10.2	45	8.0	380	10.3	1,037	986	51	44	790
Logan	3,057	21,191	0.93	231	10.7	202	9.4	1,609	10.7	4,167	3,649	518	693	3,149
Mesa	4,660	146,769	0.97	1,695	11.1	1,474	9.6	11,151	9.3	33,200	22,605	10,595	5,054	3,423
Mineral	0	808	0.93	6	7.7	6	7.7	45	8.6	270	236	34	0	0
Moffat	102	11,798	0.80	169	12.8	90	6.8	1,098	9.8	2,219	2,058	161	305	2,390
Montezuma	243	24,866	0.92	262	10.0	281	10.7	2,872	13.5	6,452	5,589	863	437	1,663
Montrose	542	40,698	0.99	441	10.4	451	10.7	3,954	12.5	10,799	8,410	2,389	1,106	2,830
Morgan	563	28,116	1.00	420	14.7	252	8.8	2,773	12.0	4,933	4,420	513	514	1,870
Otero	558	18,379	1.01	211	11.4	212	11.5	1,491	10.5	4,609	3,825	784	487	2,734
Ouray	0	4,520	0.94	27	5.6	24	5.0	334	9.3	1,305	1,114	191	21	560
Park	92	12,679	0.53	115	6.2	104	5.6	1,439	10.3	3,523	2,593	930	83	523
Phillips	60	4,496	1.02	52	12.1	53	12.4	415	12.6	937	919	18	55	1,272
Pitkin	72	25,325	1.68	148	8.2	45	2.5	1,773	12.1	2,919	2,797	122	447	2,496
Prowers	342	12,026	0.99	178	14.6	113	9.3	1,237	12.9	2,428	2,369	59	65	549
Pueblo	4,514	161,889	0.98	1,831	10.9	1,825	10.9	10,306	7.8	37,517	23,421	14,096	9,925	6,039
Rio Blanco	283	6,802	1.08	67	10.6	37	5.8	501	9.4	1,105	962	143	57	870
Rio Grande	198	11,008	0.91	119	10.6	127	11.3	1,095	12.2	3,118	2,561	557	280	2,526
Routt	338	25,705	1.09	234	9.1	130	5.1	1,775	8.4	3,777	3,447	330	406	1,674
Saguache	18	6,055	0.89	74	10.8	54	7.9	864	17.5	1,270	1,077	193	105	1,674
San Juan	0	525	0.86	6	7.9	1	1.3	53	10.0	159	D	D	10	1,429
San Miguel	9	8,592	1.17	61	7.4	13	1.6	803	11.5	1,055	959	96	84	1,052
Sedgwick	35	2,213	0.85	23	10.0	25	10.9	200	11.2	698	658	40	2	83
Summit	273	32,262	1.14	281	9.1	69	2.2	2,971	11.1	3,394	3,000	394	773	2,518
Teller	132	20,562	0.72	180	7.2	175	7.0	1,474	7.7	6,053	3,887	2,166	353	1,513
Washington	184	4,304	0.77	51	10.4	45	9.2	363	9.9	1,027	991	36	95	1,949
Weld	4,949	263,383	0.84	4,427	14.1	1,840	5.9	22,269	8.7	42,137	27,254	14,883	6,560	2,249
Yuma	197	10,405	1.06	145	14.5	94	9.4	974	12.1	1,900	1,849	51	27	266
CONNECTICUT	113,244	3,568,479	0.99	35,048	9.8	31,312	8.8	168,258	5.8	667,292	420,794	246,498	72,787	2,035
Fairfield	19,596	954,717	1.02	9,711	10.3	7,036	7.5	62,457	7.9	154,014	110,533	43,481	15,617	1,669
Hartford	26,012	968,919	1.16	9,213	10.3	8,316	9.3	36,306	5.0	169,878	94,455	75,423	22,420	2,570
Litchfield	2,474	158,018	0.72	1,396	7.7	1,822	10.1	6,805	4.7	41,341	27,578	13,763	NA	NA
Middlesex	4,656	150,861	0.85	1,269	7.8	1,536	9.4	5,099	3.9	35,570	20,837	14,733	NA	NA
New Haven	29,659	838,188	0.94	8,651	10.1	7,918	9.2	38,926	5.6	162,867	101,609	61,258	23,003	2,859
New London	11,134	270,730	1.00	2,581	9.7	2,572	9.6	9,730	4.5	54,518	37,556	16,962	NA	NA

1. Per 1,000 estimated resident population.   2. Data for serious crimes have not been adjusted for underreporting; this may affect comparability between geographic areas and over time.   3. Per 100,000 population estimated by the FBI.

Table B. States and Counties — Crime, Education, Money Income, and Poverty

STATE County	Serious crimes known to police[2], 2016 (cont.)[1] Rate Violent	Property	Education School enrollment and attainment, 2013-2017 Enrollment[3] Total	Percent private	Attainment[4] (percent) High school graduate or less	Bachelor's degree or more	Local government expenditures,[5] 2014-2015 Total current spending (mil dol)	Current spending per student (dollars)	Money income, 2013-2017 Per capita income[6]	Households Median income (dollars)	Percent with income of less than $50,000	with income of $200,000 or more	Income and poverty, 2017 Median household income (dollars)	Percent below poverty level All persons	Children under 18 years	Children 5 to 17 years in families
	46	47	48	49	50	51	52	53	54	55	56	57	58	59	60	61
COLORADO—Cont'd																
Boulder	239	2,286	96,142	11.9	17.8	60.4	[7] 606.0	[7]9,777	42,119	75,669	34.1	11.6	80,701	12.6	9.8	8.4
Broomfield	51	2,409	16,790	14.2	18.7	53.4	[7]	[7]	43,736	85,639	26.1	11.6	91,968	4.6	4.8	4.3
Chaffee	42	1,705	3,064	9.9	35.4	32.4	23.1	10,757	28,907	53,762	45.5	3.3	53,545	11.4	14.6	13.2
Cheyenne	55	164	564	10.5	42.4	21.9	4.7	16,079	23,698	54,907	44.7	2.2	50,571	13.6	21.4	22.2
Clear Creek	557	1,531	1,588	9.0	22.6	46.4	10.2	11,483	41,257	68,534	36.8	4.5	71,850	7.8	11.4	10.1
Conejos	83	855	2,116	6.9	45.4	19.2	15.1	9,629	19,047	35,657	61.7	0.7	36,852	21.2	28.2	26.7
Costilla	NA	NA	650	8.6	47.4	20.9	6.1	12,886	20,737	29,000	76.0	2.6	30,486	27.3	42.8	39.3
Crowley	91	1,053	854	13.6	58.8	8.1	5.1	11,556	14,393	35,292	62.8	0.5	38,112	47.4	37.6	34.2
Custer	156	2,211	701	27.5	26.3	33.3	4.0	10,010	26,032	41,330	55.8	1.4	54,080	13.2	24.9	22.9
Delta	103	1,895	5,656	13.4	48.7	19.4	40.6	8,001	25,546	42,487	56.4	3.6	43,528	16.7	21.2	19.9
Denver	659	3,611	154,790	17.8	30.9	46.5	1,052.2	10,227	38,991	60,098	42.0	8.2	64,974	12.5	17.4	16.9
Dolores	255	867	319	6.3	46.9	19.8	3.4	12,721	23,190	40,352	60.0	2.7	44,882	12.8	16.0	14.4
Douglas	140	1,341	93,714	15.1	14.3	58.0	554.2	8,309	48,725	111,154	16.5	17.1	112,386	3.2	2.7	2.3
Eagle	124	1,522	12,210	12.6	27.3	45.1	68.7	10,231	40,450	83,803	25.6	10.5	88,913	7.5	8.8	7.9
Elbert	8	38	5,976	16.5	28.9	35.0	25.2	8,256	42,522	92,849	24.6	12.7	102,731	4.9	7.2	6.1
El Paso	413	2,906	188,652	12.7	26.4	37.3	1,012.8	8,494	31,217	62,535	39.0	5.2	65,260	10.8	13.4	13.4
Fremont	75	628	8,105	11.9	49.2	17.1	46.6	8,967	20,919	44,712	55.8	2.2	48,820	16.6	22.8	21.4
Garfield	207	1,842	14,438	10.5	41.0	30.2	107.5	9,365	31,483	66,503	35.2	5.3	71,897	7.6	11.3	10.6
Gilpin	232	4,762	1,090	8.2	24.6	36.6	5.2	12,226	45,110	72,544	29.9	4.5	79,636	6.9	9.7	6.4
Grand	61	846	2,402	11.5	32.1	38.4	18.2	10,548	32,919	66,489	38.4	4.8	61,241	8.7	11.9	10.8
Gunnison	173	1,432	4,672	10.9	21.6	53.7	19.2	9,945	27,669	52,651	46.6	2.5	53,480	14.8	12.4	10.1
Hinsdale	526	788	141	21.3	27.9	40.8	1.4	14,729	29,574	53,056	49.2	3.0	59,157	8.6	16.8	15.8
Huerfano	456	3,700	1,209	13.6	36.1	23.6	7.8	10,334	25,547	35,801	65.5	2.8	37,424	20.8	37.8	32.2
Jackson	0	370	284	1.8	49.4	16.5	2.8	14,605	24,299	45,994	54.4	0.5	48,785	13.7	25.6	25.9
Jefferson	274	3,235	131,604	13.8	26.4	43.1	755.6	8,727	40,187	75,170	31.8	8.5	80,562	7.6	8.3	7.6
Kiowa	NA	NA	288	2.8	45.6	21.0	3.4	13,967	23,621	39,250	61.6	2.1	43,845	14	19.1	19.1
Kit Carson	209	1,514	1,579	4.2	52.5	15.8	14.2	10,042	26,125	45,881	54.4	3.0	44,028	11.6	19.3	18.7
Lake	159	1,129	1,427	9.6	46.6	31.2	15.4	14,112	28,492	46,176	54.2	1.5	49,799	12.2	18.5	16.8
La Plata	172	1,946	13,033	12.2	24.4	43.1	71.9	10,757	34,501	62,533	38.7	5.4	61,974	9.2	11.2	10.7
Larimer	211	2,219	95,048	9.4	23.7	45.9	429.9	9,283	34,087	64,980	39.2	6.0	69,443	11	8.9	8.5
Las Animas	232	3,565	2,887	15.4	41.5	20.2	22.3	10,080	24,268	40,586	58.1	1.7	39,552	23.7	31.5	29.9
Lincoln	126	664	894	4.4	65.4	13.2	12.9	18,572	14,765	44,725	55.0	2.2	45,308	17.6	23.5	22.9
Logan	295	2,854	4,638	4.8	43.8	19.0	28.8	9,709	24,595	44,876	53.2	3.4	50,246	15.8	18.3	17.3
Mesa	349	3,074	36,211	9.6	38.1	27.2	185.2	8,286	27,612	51,971	48.1	3.0	52,623	14.9	17.9	15.9
Mineral	0	0	89	12.4	22.0	39.3	1.4	18,377	33,018	50,385	49.5	2.5	55,906	8.5	12.5	12.9
Moffat	172	2,217	3,019	12.6	49.9	17.2	20.4	9,371	27,331	53,010	47.2	2.5	57,680	11	15.2	13.3
Montezuma	133	1,530	5,303	8.5	39.4	28.0	34.5	8,546	24,440	45,645	54.1	1.5	48,692	15.2	24.5	22.5
Montrose	105	2,725	8,732	11.9	44.2	23.4	55.1	8,667	24,308	44,865	54.1	1.3	51,031	12.9	18.3	17.2
Morgan	189	1,681	6,684	5.3	50.7	17.2	46.0	8,316	24,077	51,456	47.6	2.1	50,453	11.4	15.0	14.9
Otero	185	2,549	4,646	8.6	42.8	17.7	33.2	10,239	20,358	35,051	63.4	1.0	37,907	23.5	28.0	25.2
Ouray	0	560	687	24.2	19.4	49.4	8.4	15,393	35,544	61,333	40.6	3.9	63,627	7.7	11.1	9.8
Park	101	422	3,006	12.7	32.8	28.5	16.9	10,144	34,377	61,644	41.9	2.5	69,884	8.6	12.7	10.8
Phillips	162	1,110	1,018	5.7	42.2	21.6	13.4	14,467	27,790	50,076	49.9	3.8	52,096	10.9	15.6	15.4
Pitkin	61	2,435	3,252	24.1	19.0	61.2	26.5	15,118	65,800	67,755	32.8	11.5	78,596	5.9	6.8	6.2
Prowers	25	524	2,992	6.4	44.5	16.0	22.2	9,400	22,033	41,740	58.9	1.0	41,238	18.2	25.0	23.3
Pueblo	682	5,357	41,119	6.8	40.2	21.7	219.6	8,048	23,110	42,386	56.2	1.9	44,060	18.2	23.6	22.2
Rio Blanco	92	779	1,772	10.5	40.4	20.9	12.9	10,397	28,185	57,991	42.2	2.5	58,336	9.5	11.5	10.3
Rio Grande	244	2,282	2,668	6.8	45.0	23.7	18.3	9,304	22,412	38,534	61.6	1.5	41,693	18.4	26.3	26.0
Routt	177	1,496	5,054	6.9	24.6	51.6	40.7	12,421	38,111	67,472	37.9	8.4	76,505	6.9	7.4	7.0
Saguache	223	1,451	1,370	6.6	47.7	26.0	13.0	13,230	22,267	34,765	65.3	2.8	36,558	24.4	40.7	33.7
San Juan	0	1,429	88	0.0	40.9	29.8	1.4	22,226	28,889	46,397	55.3	2.7	46,985	13.6	21.3	21.1
San Miguel	113	939	1,401	19.3	20.4	54.1	14.9	12,614	42,015	62,243	41.2	6.7	70,418	7.7	9.6	8.8
Sedgwick	83	0	482	3.3	39.3	20.8	7.0	7,786	24,666	49,583	50.5	2.6	39,880	15.5	23.5	23.6
Summit	215	2,303	5,141	10.4	26.6	47.8	36.9	11,019	37,192	73,538	32.7	7.4	75,420	7.3	7.9	6.8
Teller	180	1,333	4,765	11.9	30.3	34.1	26.4	9,185	34,974	66,809	36.3	4.8	68,078	8.8	13.6	12.5
Washington	144	1,805	1,098	7.9	41.2	16.6	11.1	12,315	26,279	51,458	49.0	2.3	48,325	12.9	19.8	18.3
Weld	256	1,993	79,916	10.2	39.6	27.0	363.2	8,853	29,226	66,489	36.9	4.6	68,679	9.4	10.6	10.3
Yuma	0	266	2,508	13.6	47.0	21.0	18.4	10,251	24,789	44,668	58.0	2.2	48,893	13	17.1	16.0
CONNECTICUT	227	1,808	919,823	20.5	36.9	38.4	9,439.6	17,855	41,365	73,781	34.8	11.0	74,428	9.7	13.0	12.3
Fairfield	230	1,438	254,240	24.2	32.6	46.5	2,693.7	18,477	53,433	89,773	30.0	19.7	91,170	8.8	11.3	10.5
Hartford	264	2,306	225,913	17.0	37.8	37.4	2,439.8	18,418	37,817	69,936	36.9	8.9	70,433	11	15.3	14.8
Litchfield	NA	NA	39,809	18.7	37.1	35.0	432.5	18,663	40,619	76,438	31.6	8.0	77,968	6.9	7.9	7.5
Middlesex	NA	NA	38,410	24.5	33.3	40.8	395.5	12,432	43,695	81,673	30.3	10.5	81,533	6.8	7.4	6.7
New Haven	324	2,535	220,914	23.7	40.7	34.6	2,193.8	17,777	35,085	64,872	39.3	7.6	66,764	11	15.3	14.7
New London	NA	NA	62,904	19.4	38.2	32.9	650.4	17,695	36,881	69,411	34.6	6.8	71,721	8.6	12.3	10.8

1. Data for serious crimes have not been adjusted for underreporting; this may affect comparability between geographic areas and over time. 2. Per 100,000 population estimated by the FBI. 3. All persons 3 years old and over enrolled in nursery school through college. 4. Persons 25 years old and over. 5. Elementary and secondary education expenditures. 6. Based on population estimated by the American Community Survey, 2013–2017. 7. Broomfield county is included with Boulder county.

Table B. States and Counties — **Personal Income and Earnings**

STATE County	Personal income, 2017										Earnings, 2017		
	Total (mil dol)	Percent change 2016-2017	Per capita[1]		Wages and salaries (mil dol)	Supplements to wages and salaries, employer contributions (mil dol)		Proprietors' income (mil dol)	Dividends, interest, and rent (mil dol)	Personal transfer reeceipts (mil dol)	Total (mil dol)	Contributions for government social insurance (mil dol)	
			Dollars	Rank		Pension and insurance	Government social insurance					From employee and self-employed	From employer
	62	63	64	65	66	67	68	69	70	71	72	73	74

COLORADO—Cont'd													
Boulder	21,940	4.9	68,027	79	12,451	1,506	858	1,650	6,398	1,918	16,465	900	858
Broomfield	4,346	8.3	63,596	119	3,807	334	212	348	748	370	4,701	279	212
Chaffee	860	5.6	43,773	1,044	307	49	22	86	267	178	464	28	22
Cheyenne	106	16.1	57,212	220	34	7	2	33	23	15	76	3	2
Clear Creek	543	3.2	56,672	232	144	20	10	44	130	63	218	13	10
Conejos	284	4.1	34,726	2,384	51	11	4	49	44	87	115	7	4
Costilla	124	5.8	32,753	2,653	30	6	2	13	24	46	51	3	2
Crowley	113	-4.7	19,443	3,111	48	9	3	14	23	41	74	3	3
Custer	185	0.4	38,008	1,885	30	5	2	20	69	51	58	5	2
Delta	1,146	12.4	37,475	1,951	318	58	23	169	263	301	568	36	23
Denver	49,226	10.7	69,862	72	36,537	4,465	2,554	8,455	11,427	4,849	52,010	2,772	2,554
Dolores	71	7.2	34,214	2,457	21	4	1	3	17	19	29	2	1
Douglas	23,876	6.3	71,208	64	8,203	857	566	1,125	4,551	1,614	10,751	650	566
Eagle	3,855	4.1	70,384	70	1,608	166	123	498	1,398	208	2,395	127	123
Elbert	1,415	6.6	55,187	273	166	24	12	78	215	153	280	19	12
El Paso	32,522	5.2	46,511	750	16,509	2,678	1,292	1,936	6,702	5,489	22,415	1,211	1,292
Fremont	1,590	3.4	33,422	2,567	589	121	41	122	317	490	873	55	41
Garfield	3,270	4.4	55,305	267	1,322	187	97	260	1,243	354	1,867	101	97
Gilpin	274	3.7	45,531	845	247	19	18	23	55	36	307	18	18
Grand	705	5.0	46,013	793	291	40	22	68	217	88	421	23	22
Gunnison	752	5.3	44,365	974	339	55	24	85	250	85	503	26	24
Hinsdale	39	5.9	49,480	497	10	2	1	3	18	7	16	1	1
Huerfano	274	4.5	41,138	1,391	64	12	5	19	72	99	101	8	5
Jackson	64	5.7	46,248	772	22	4	2	9	16	11	36	2	2
Jefferson	34,705	4.7	60,398	149	14,064	1,859	1,037	2,779	7,124	4,300	19,739	1,143	1,037
Kiowa	74	11.6	53,959	312	25	5	2	12	19	15	44	2	2
Kit Carson	279	3.7	39,016	1,719	111	19	9	32	71	64	171	9	9
Lake	270	5.6	34,668	2,393	94	17	7	26	59	47	143	8	7
La Plata	2,933	1.0	52,759	351	1,281	179	91	348	893	366	1,898	103	91
Larimer	17,384	6.3	50,539	429	8,538	1,210	588	1,202	4,084	2,280	11,538	636	588
Las Animas	543	1.5	38,119	1,861	207	37	16	19	111	197	279	19	16
Lincoln	157	12.2	28,330	3,019	94	18	6	7	39	46	125	6	6
Logan	1,062	-1.8	48,521	588	349	61	26	228	201	184	665	33	26
Mesa	6,293	5.2	41,503	1,330	2,835	415	218	471	1,271	1,308	3,939	240	218
Mineral	51	4.2	66,047	94	19	2	1	6	19	8	28	2	1
Moffat	512	-0.7	39,007	1,720	245	44	18	45	88	104	352	19	18
Montezuma	1,054	2.5	40,336	1,495	356	64	26	66	269	255	512	32	26
Montrose	1,573	5.2	37,658	1,926	623	103	46	137	361	389	909	56	46
Morgan	1,230	4.5	43,632	1,060	552	85	43	178	184	232	858	44	43
Otero	682	4.2	37,214	1,997	251	45	21	48	126	233	366	23	21
Ouray	270	1.5	56,335	240	68	10	5	38	100	38	121	7	5
Park	765	6.7	42,703	1,186	106	17	7	57	167	122	188	13	7
Phillips	204	8.4	47,637	651	68	13	5	50	45	42	136	6	5
Pitkin	2,573	5.7	143,812	3	908	90	66	267	1,565	98	1,331	70	66
Prowers	498	1.9	41,247	1,374	165	31	12	88	97	125	296	14	12
Pueblo	6,198	3.7	37,231	1,995	2,770	427	213	307	1,096	1,836	3,717	233	213
Rio Blanco	284	2.4	44,189	998	145	29	10	14	59	49	197	10	10
Rio Grande	515	3.8	45,544	844	163	28	14	64	107	143	269	15	14
Routt	1,846	7.5	73,200	58	699	88	53	198	800	134	1,038	57	53
Saguache	200	2.9	30,134	2,919	63	12	5	19	49	49	100	5	5
San Juan	34	6.3	47,138	702	10	2	1	6	10	5	19	1	1
San Miguel	614	1.8	77,106	46	237	27	18	112	250	33	394	20	18
Sedgwick	123	9.8	52,363	363	29	6	2	26	23	28	63	3	2
Summit	1,971	5.2	64,446	107	929	101	70	265	671	122	1,365	72	70
Teller	1,159	4.3	47,030	710	314	44	23	57	252	223	438	30	23
Washington	203	3.8	41,019	1,404	58	12	5	30	41	40	104	5	5
Weld	13,428	4.3	44,080	1,011	5,539	765	415	1,519	1,933	1,876	8,238	442	415
Yuma	556	5.1	55,197	272	172	28	15	188	105	88	403	14	15
CONNECTICUT	257,714	3.3	72,110	X	114,743	17,649	7,951	27,965	57,328	33,288	168,309	9,151	7,951
Fairfield	104,590	3.3	110,104	10	38,308	4,826	2,362	13,413	30,677	7,948	58,909	3,144	2,362
Hartford	55,213	2.3	61,664	140	36,239	5,541	2,556	5,546	9,014	8,814	49,883	2,709	2,556
Litchfield	11,379	4.1	62,461	128	2,945	548	231	1,552	2,370	1,616	5,277	300	231
Middlesex	10,737	2.9	65,704	97	3,983	698	300	989	1,948	1,406	5,971	332	300
New Haven	46,931	4.0	54,543	295	21,927	3,607	1,670	4,146	8,216	8,748	31,349	1,754	1,670
New London	15,261	3.6	56,725	231	7,416	1,490	545	1,357	2,938	2,545	10,808	574	545

1. Based on the resident population estimated as of July 1 of the year shown.

Table B. States and Counties — Earnings, Social Security, and Housing

STATE County	Earnings, 2017 (cont.)									Social Security beneficiaries, December 2017		Supplemental Security Income recipients, 2017	Housing units, 2018	
	Percent by selected industries													
	Farm	Mining, quarrying, and extractions	Construction	Manu-facturing	Information; professional, scientific, technical services	Retail trade	Finance, insurance, real estate, and leasing	Health care and social assistance	Govern-ment	Number	Rate[1]		Total	Percent change, 2010-2018
	75	76	77	78	79	80	81	82	83	84	85	86	87	88
COLORADO—Cont'd														
Boulder	0.1	0.1	3.9	11.2	30.9	4.4	6.5	9.9	15.1	44,915	139	2,472	137,435	8.2
Broomfield	0	D	4.3	13.8	32.1	3.7	5.3	3	2.3	9,200	135	446	28,937	27.8
Chaffee	0.7	D	13.9	2.3	7.3	10.4	6.6	5.9	26	5,160	263	207	11,353	13.3
Cheyenne	36	9.1	D	D	D	4	D	D	18.1	355	192	11	1,005	3.2
Clear Creek	0	D	6	D	D	5.4	D	D	17.4	1,800	188	87	5,810	2.4
Conejos	19.6	1.9	10.4	2	D	5.1	D	9.9	21.3	1,950	238	354	4,449	3.8
Costilla	15.9	0.9	D	D	D	5.2	D	D	28	1,265	335	231	2,870	9.8
Crowley	20.3	0.2	D	0.1	0.3	4.6	D	4.5	41.4	865	149	161	1,593	2.2
Custer	3.6	0.7	18.7	5.2	8	10.8	3.7	D	21.1	1,665	342	60	4,426	11.9
Delta	2.7	19.3	7.9	4	4.4	8.3	4	9.2	25.3	9,100	298	546	14,839	1.8
Denver	0	10.4	4.5	3	17.3	2.7	10.9	7.2	12.3	85,520	121	14,402	330,862	15.8
Dolores	5	D	D	D	D	6.7	D	D	35.6	590	285	27	1,737	18.4
Douglas	0	1.3	8.3	1.6	19.6	6.6	17.5	8.7	7.8	39,835	119	1,073	128,727	20.5
Eagle	0.1	0.1	14.7	0.8	6.9	7.7	7.5	12.4	9.4	5,000	91	118	32,823	4.8
Elbert	-0.8	D	27.2	2.9	11.4	6.4	4.4	1.9	16	4,360	170	91	9,784	9.4
El Paso	0	0.1	7	4.6	14	5.9	7.3	10.5	31	105,415	151	9,156	275,396	8.9
Fremont	0.5	0.9	7	5	2.9	7	3.5	12.6	43.6	12,765	268	1,169	19,937	3.6
Garfield	0.2	6.8	16.9	1.7	6.6	7.4	6.7	11.6	17.5	8,020	136	414	24,217	3.9
Gilpin	0	0	2.6	D	D	D	D	D	10.4	970	161	28	3,724	4.4
Grand	1.6	0.8	15	1.7	D	7.4	7.3	3	19.8	2,340	153	60	16,944	5.5
Gunnison	0.5	7.2	11.9	1.2	6.9	6.9	5	3.9	24.8	2,190	129	57	12,073	5.8
Hinsdale	2.5	D	15.1	1.6	D	D	D	D	27.7	230	290	0	1,425	2.7
Huerfano	0.5	D	20.8	3.7	3.3	8.3	3.2	D	21.6	2,425	364	304	5,294	4.3
Jackson	16.7	D	D	D	D	6.8	D	D	22.3	320	231	12	1,327	3.3
Jefferson	0	0.6	8.2	11.5	15.8	6.9	6.3	11.1	14.5	96,980	169	5,422	243,009	5.6
Kiowa	40.1	D	1.2	0.8	D	6.3	2.2	D	25.4	315	229	16	827	2.7
Kit Carson	13.2	D	4.1	4.2	2.9	6.5	7.2	4.5	21.1	1,455	203	101	3,566	1.1
Lake	0	D	14.6	D	2.5	5.9	1.6	5.9	25.7	985	127	63	4,431	3.7
La Plata	0.1	3.7	10.4	2.3	9	6.5	8.7	13.7	19.5	9,895	178	388	28,267	9.3
Larimer	0.5	0.7	9.3	13	12.7	6.4	5.9	8.2	21.4	56,480	164	2,580	151,848	14.4
Las Animas	1.2	10.6	4.9	1.3	2.8	8.4	4.1	16.7	27.4	4,110	289	583	8,577	4.4
Lincoln	-1.2	0.2	3.6	1.2	D	9	5.9	6.4	48.1	1,035	187	62	2,491	2.9
Logan	11.2	4.7	4.9	6.6	-0.4	8.7	5.2	9.9	20.6	3,995	182	365	9,126	1.6
Mesa	0.4	6.5	11	4.1	5.5	7.6	7.6	16.8	16.6	32,865	217	2,590	67,215	7.3
Mineral	3.4	0.7	10.5	D	D	D	D	D	15.1	270	352	0	1,284	6.9
Moffat	2.1	14.9	5.9	0.9	D	7.2	3.4	D	18.1	2,340	178	184	6,318	2
Montezuma	0.7	4.9	7.6	3.7	3.6	9.9	4.3	16.5	26.8	6,650	254	453	12,407	2.6
Montrose	2.1	0.9	10.4	7.5	5.1	9	5.3	D	22.7	10,810	259	617	19,208	5.2
Morgan	13.3	4.6	5.3	21.7	3.5	4.3	3.1	D	12.9	4,905	174	439	11,850	3.1
Otero	7.4	D	4	7.8	4.6	6	3.7	D	23.4	4,450	243	859	8,994	0.3
Ouray	0.9	D	17.4	3.5	9.6	9.8	7.9	4.5	17.5	1,270	265	18	3,332	8
Park	-0.9	D	19.4	2.2	10.4	8.1	4	2.7	22.5	3,595	201	134	14,711	5.5
Phillips	19.1	D	7.4	1.1	D	5.1	D	D	23.3	900	210	53	2,152	3.1
Pitkin	0.1	D	6.2	0.6	7.8	5.2	15.4	2.4	13.9	2,625	147	29	14,141	9.2
Prowers	16.2	3.3	4.7	5.3	D	8	5.2	6.4	23.9	2,430	201	356	5,983	0.7
Pueblo	0.2	D	8	8.5	6.8	8.3	3.7	21.6	21.2	37,140	223	6,319	71,451	2.8
Rio Blanco	3.6	26	7.1	1.4	1.2	3	2.5	1.1	34.6	1,115	174	45	3,405	2.8
Rio Grande	15.3	D	7.5	2.3	2.1	4.5	4.9	D	19.1	3,240	287	482	6,824	2.9
Routt	0.9	10.3	11.8	0.6	6.2	7.4	8.5	9.2	12	3,410	135	78	16,951	4
Saguache	20.1	D	6.2	3	D	4.8	D	3.1	24.2	1,285	194	103	4,215	9.7
San Juan	0	1.3	D	D	D	18.6	D	D	20.1	155	217	0	787	4.1
San Miguel	0.5	D	15.4	2.2	6.6	6	7.6	3.9	12.5	970	122	34	6,943	4.6
Sedgwick	38.1	0.6	3	2.2	D	2.9	D	1	24	675	288	55	1,429	0.9
Summit	0	D	14.1	0.8	7.6	8.5	10.9	7.6	11.4	3,065	100	32	31,484	5.5
Teller	-0.3	D	6.9	D	8.1	8.2	4.8	D	15.5	6,200	252	232	13,349	5.5
Washington	20.6	D	3.4	1.5	D	6.5	3.6	1.5	20.7	1,025	208	63	2,473	1.6
Weld	5.2	9.1	14.3	11.2	4.3	5.8	5.7	7.3	11.6	42,050	138	3,306	112,465	16.8
Yuma	40.2	4.4	3.3	4	-0.1	5	5.5	D	13.5	1,865	185	90	4,550	1.9
CONNECTICUT	0.1	0.1	5.6	11.3	11.9	5.4	16.5	11.4	13.1	673,359	188	65,812	1,521,117	2.2
Fairfield	0	0.1	5	10.3	15	5.1	23.6	8.7	7.6	151,240	159	12,492	374,481	3.7
Hartford	0.1	0	4.3	11.5	12.1	4.4	21.3	11.7	13.5	172,830	193	21,474	380,471	1.7
Litchfield	0.2	0.2	14.7	D	7.2	9.7	D	11.5	12.7	41,940	230	1,820	88,383	1
Middlesex	0.3	D	D	17.4	8.2	6.5	5.4	14.4	15.9	35,310	216	1,687	76,537	2.3
New Haven	0.1	0.1	6.3	8.7	9.8	6.2	6.7	15.3	14.7	165,185	192	20,625	367,745	1.6
New London	0.4	0.1	5.4	18.7	8	5.5	3.2	11	25.8	56,025	208	4,467	123,635	2.2

1. Per 1,000 resident population estimated as of July 1 of the year shown.

Table B. States and Counties — Housing, Labor Force, and Employment

STATE County	Housing units, 2013-2017								Civilian labor force, 2018				Civilian employment[6], 2013-2017		
	Occupied units										Unemployment		Percent		
			Owner-occupied			Renter-occupied									
				Median owner cost as a percent of income			Median rent as a percent of income[2]	Sub-standard units[4] (percent)		Percent change, 2017-2018				Management, business, science, and arts	Construction, production, and maintenance occupations
				With a mort-gage	Without a mort-gage[2]	Median rent[3]									
	Total	Percent	Median value[1]						Total		Total	Rate[5]	Total		
	89	90	91	92	93	94	95	96	97	98	99	100	101	102	103
COLORADO—Cont'd															
Boulder	125,026	62.2	423,500	20.7	10.0	1,334	33.9	2	193,822	3.8	5,519	2.8	170,940	53.2	11.7
Broomfield	25,938	66.7	356,500	20.5	10.0	1,490	29.2	2.1	39,816	3.2	1,165	2.9	34,972	53.3	12.7
Chaffee	7,900	77.1	313,200	25.1	10.4	805	30.9	1.1	9,708	4.2	261	2.7	8,379	35.7	22.4
Cheyenne	776	73.5	90,000	20.1	10.0	613	17.2	1	1,166	2.8	21	1.8	931	37.1	31.6
Clear Creek	4,374	77.2	317,000	23.9	10.0	810	25.2	2.4	6,075	3.4	184	3	5,248	37.5	20.5
Conejos	2,992	78.1	113,100	25.0	10.4	533	26.7	4.5	4,080	3.9	179	4.4	2,899	30.3	31.6
Costilla	1,568	71.4	114,200	29.2	11.4	614	35.6	4.6	1,910	4.7	82	4.3	1,242	25.2	33.1
Crowley	1,215	73.9	79,700	25.5	13.2	827	29.5	2.7	1,533	4.1	67	4.4	1,747	22.2	32.7
Custer	2,093	81.9	248,300	32.9	10.2	660	30.7	4.1	2,106	3.5	77	3.7	1,389	30.1	34.4
Delta	12,119	71.0	206,200	24.5	11.0	847	34.4	3.3	14,851	3.9	585	3.9	11,209	34.5	28.2
Denver	287,262	50.1	322,900	21.4	10.0	1,131	29.4	3.7	412,817	3.4	13,146	3.2	374,043	46.1	15.6
Dolores	707	79.8	122,000	20.6	10.0	826	25.7	3.7	1,197	5.8	34	2.8	797	26.3	25.8
Douglas	113,799	79.5	407,100	20.3	10.0	1,574	26.3	1.3	191,240	3.4	5,472	2.9	169,625	53.7	9.6
Eagle	17,765	70.4	471,100	23.5	10.0	1,370	30.3	4.1	36,207	3.9	989	2.7	33,466	33.0	19.9
Elbert	8,866	89.8	380,000	23.1	10.0	1,029	25.3	1.5	14,963	3.8	425	2.8	13,086	42.3	23.2
El Paso	249,745	63.3	238,200	21.8	10.0	1,070	30.8	2.9	337,084	3.4	13,268	3.9	304,289	40.8	16.8
Fremont	16,762	74.9	160,000	22.4	10.0	786	29.6	2.1	15,342	2.5	798	5.2	14,406	30.8	19.9
Garfield	21,055	66.1	323,800	24.2	10.1	1,169	27.2	6.5	32,479	2.9	1,043	3.2	30,411	32.1	27.3
Gilpin	2,603	79.6	301,700	26.4	10.0	1,044	23.8	5.9	3,731	3.5	95	2.5	3,399	44.4	15.6
Grand	5,724	69.0	285,000	23.2	10.3	1,013	26.2	4.4	9,917	3.8	266	2.7	8,829	30.2	28.2
Gunnison	6,495	58.7	313,900	22.6	10.0	908	31.2	4.7	11,012	2.9	285	2.6	9,429	33.2	24.6
Hinsdale	368	69.8	325,400	25.1	12.2	700	25.6	3.8	459	-3	12	2.6	399	44.6	19.5
Huerfano	3,173	71.9	137,400	29.0	11.0	634	33.1	1.9	2,619	2.6	171	6.5	2,408	31.8	22.2
Jackson	597	70.4	171,300	23.9	10.0	706	29.7	0	1,029	7	27	2.6	707	30.6	37.3
Jefferson	227,805	70.8	334,100	21.1	10.0	1,205	30.3	1.6	334,242	3.3	10,118	3	305,799	45.6	15.1
Kiowa	576	76.0	83,200	22.8	11.1	619	18.2	0.3	963	4.1	17	1.8	632	33.1	25.3
Kit Carson	2,995	69.9	130,200	22.2	11.2	743	28.3	1.6	4,487	2.3	91	2	3,632	30.4	28.6
Lake	3,324	57.6	197,600	25.2	10.8	889	25.4	2.1	4,894	3.8	129	2.6	4,184	30.5	26.3
La Plata	21,818	68.2	356,700	23.4	10.0	1,090	31.3	2.5	32,091	2	971	3	29,184	40.1	18.8
Larimer	130,502	64.8	306,600	21.2	10.0	1,140	34.1	1.7	202,449	3.6	5,695	2.8	172,754	43.4	16.7
Las Animas	6,327	65.9	145,900	26.2	10.0	702	28.9	3.8	6,572	4.9	311	4.7	6,050	31.7	23.1
Lincoln	1,477	69.1	132,100	22.9	11.1	781	31.3	1.6	2,494	4.8	61	2.4	1,453	37.0	17.0
Logan	8,151	62.0	148,700	18.9	11.2	712	29.7	2.6	11,287	1.6	329	2.9	10,390	29.1	28.7
Mesa	60,562	67.0	207,900	22.8	10.0	907	32	2.4	76,060	3.2	3,111	4.1	68,918	33.8	24.1
Mineral	404	85.4	279,000	26.9	10.0	638	30.4	0.5	507	8.8	13	2.6	377	32.9	21.2
Moffat	5,103	69.8	169,200	20.3	10.0	732	26.4	2.7	7,579	3.4	277	3.7	6,373	27.7	31.2
Montezuma	10,520	70.2	197,900	23.2	10.0	774	27.1	3.4	13,338	3.7	632	4.7	11,258	31.8	23.0
Montrose	16,951	69.2	202,500	24.2	11.8	838	29.6	3.4	21,941	5.3	805	3.7	17,047	31.9	27.2
Morgan	10,599	64.2	162,900	21.7	10.6	780	25.9	5	16,473	5.7	483	2.9	13,280	24.5	37.5
Otero	7,490	64.3	91,800	22.0	12.0	703	32.1	2.6	8,635	4.3	430	5	7,177	35.1	24.3
Ouray	2,204	69.4	420,600	30.9	10.0	1,101	31.7	1.5	2,400	6	84	3.5	2,315	49.2	15.6
Park	7,389	81.3	262,300	23.9	10.0	1,098	34.6	2.4	10,859	3.7	314	2.9	9,044	33.8	23.7
Phillips	1,696	67.9	132,600	18.9	11.5	634	19	4.8	2,693	4.5	51	1.9	2,104	32.2	27.2
Pitkin	7,340	64.8	593,600	24.5	14.2	1,241	29.8	2	11,363	3.3	437	3.8	11,435	41.6	13.8
Prowers	4,913	65.1	94,400	19.0	10.3	677	30.5	2.2	6,387	3	212	3.3	5,372	32.9	25.4
Pueblo	63,489	63.2	148,000	22.8	12.0	788	32.5	3.1	75,912	1.5	3,726	4.9	66,165	31.3	21.7
Rio Blanco	2,417	69.0	201,000	17.5	10.0	731	23.8	3.4	2,854	2.4	127	4.4	3,061	27.8	37.4
Rio Grande	4,750	66.2	143,000	19.5	10.9	586	27	4.7	5,643	5	273	4.8	4,705	27.8	31.6
Routt	9,478	68.3	460,600	27.0	10.0	1,166	30.4	2.8	16,301	4.7	440	2.7	14,555	34.2	18.5
Saguache	2,626	70.6	150,100	22.9	12.2	633	30.8	7.5	3,638	5.8	169	4.6	2,465	30.5	39.4
San Juan	255	67.1	269,400	31.9	13.4	1,069	28.6	3.1	519	-1.7	16	3.1	305	28.9	21.0
San Miguel	3,301	59.8	485,000	28.8	10.0	1,160	33.2	3.9	5,520	3.2	194	3.5	4,746	37.8	19.9
Sedgwick	998	71.1	91,500	18.5	10.0	534	26.8	2.7	1,253	5.1	32	2.6	992	38.8	26.6
Summit	9,455	66.5	547,700	26.6	10.0	1,343	29.5	5.4	22,315	2.1	496	2.2	19,358	27.8	20.6
Teller	10,076	80.7	261,100	21.7	10.0	1,057	32.1	2.4	12,651	3.2	469	3.7	11,685	38.4	20.1
Washington	2,012	71.2	120,300	18.6	10.0	678	22.3	2.6	3,225	6.4	78	2.4	2,213	39.0	29.8
Weld	99,817	71.6	245,000	21.7	10.0	955	29.8	3.3	165,290	4.7	4,970	3	139,546	33.2	27.3
Yuma	4,053	62.0	148,800	23.0	10.0	705	25.4	3.1	6,142	8.1	125	2	4,940	29.4	34.0
CONNECTICUT	1,361,755	66.6	270,100	23.4	15.3	1,123	31.2	2.1	1,905,312	0.4	78,242	4.1	1,805,086	42.5	16.8
Fairfield	337,678	67.7	417,800	24.5	16.9	1,439	32.6	3.1	480,767	0.3	19,017	4	474,458	44.5	14.6
Hartford	348,871	64.6	235,300	22.5	14.9	1,044	30.1	2.1	480,319	0.6	20,380	4.2	445,468	43.4	16.5
Litchfield	74,605	76.8	250,100	23.3	14.6	995	29	1.2	105,014	0.9	4,014	3.8	98,166	40.8	20.6
Middlesex	66,599	73.7	283,700	22.4	14.7	1,132	30.4	1.2	93,078	0.6	3,267	3.5	88,344	45.4	15.9
New Haven	327,402	62.3	244,400	23.9	16.1	1,100	32.5	2	458,747	0.4	20,171	4.4	425,229	41.3	17.5
New London	107,193	66.7	238,900	23.2	14.0	1,071	29.5	1.8	137,463	0	5,431	4	133,786	40.1	17.5

1. Specified owner-occupied units.   2. A value of 10.0 represents 10 percent or less; a value of 50.0 represents 50 percent or more.   3. Specified renter-occupied units.   4. Overcrowded or lacking complete plumbing facilities.   5. Percent of civilian labor force.   6. Civilian employed persons 16 years old and over.

Table B. States and Counties — Nonfarm Employment and Agriculture

	Private nonfarm establishments, employment and payroll, 2016									Agriculture, 2017			
STATE County	Number of establishments	Employment						Annual payroll		Farms			Farm producers whose primary occupation is farming (percent)
		Total	Health care and social assistance	Manufacturing	Retail trade	Finance and insurance	Professional, scientific, and technical services	Total (mil dol)	Average per employee (dollars)	Number	Percent with:		
											Fewer than 50 acres	1000 acres or more	
	104	105	106	107	108	109	110	111	112	113	114	115	116
COLORADO—Cont'd													
Boulder	12,399	150,243	21,226	13,833	18,574	3,781	26,032	8,716	58,010	1,012	79.0	2.2	33.1
Broomfield	2,030	42,920	2,579	2,758	4,730	2,672	4,759	2,846	66,312	38	76.3	7.9	38.3
Chaffee	906	6,011	832	153	1,153	244	240	196	32,552	289	52.2	4.2	42.4
Cheyenne	62	503	D	D	57	D	6	23	45,690	377	4.8	53.1	47.2
Clear Creek	338	2,894	103	39	305	16	60	98	33,837	33	42.4	9.1	27.8
Conejos	113	736	212	61	204	D	10	24	32,072	524	33.4	14.3	49.2
Costilla	45	283	41	D	61	D	NA	7	23,127	229	51.5	9.6	38.2
Crowley	32	518	86	NA	86	13	D	17	33,699	246	21.1	30.9	51.7
Custer	135	569	28	38	154	14	27	18	32,004	315	35.6	8.6	39.0
Delta	820	6,514	1,550	386	1,241	212	163	200	30,746	1,615	69.7	2.8	41.8
Denver	24,986	439,602	56,626	17,189	32,963	25,187	43,405	26,348	59,935	12	100.0	NA	60.0
Dolores	48	250	49	D	42	D	2	9	36,120	313	21.7	10.5	38.1
Douglas	8,997	110,124	12,496	7,701	18,413	8,186	8,243	6,661	60,489	1,223	67.4	3.0	25.0
Eagle	3,415	32,362	2,035	355	4,339	832	1,398	1,237	38,221	257	44.7	7.8	34.2
Elbert	595	2,515	136	121	474	68	197	96	38,006	1,632	43.2	10.5	29.8
El Paso	17,097	235,480	37,138	10,999	32,284	10,643	22,496	10,500	44,589	1,345	45.5	10.6	34.9
Fremont	849	7,768	2,064	343	1,658	232	184	241	30,990	1,034	72.4	6.8	30.9
Garfield	2,406	20,023	2,724	216	3,258	670	1,017	940	46,941	661	49.5	13.2	45.1
Gilpin	120	4,665	56	D	23	D	30	181	38,722	37	51.4	NA	31.3
Grand	832	8,242	375	143	673	95	833	246	29,899	290	47.9	13.1	31.6
Gunnison	1,103	6,668	588	128	991	157	322	214	32,159	309	40.5	18.1	40.0
Hinsdale	66	125	D	NA	22	D	D	4	35,408	26	7.7	15.4	25.7
Huerfano	156	1,092	416	D	213	19	48	35	31,889	437	21.3	21.7	30.5
Jackson	68	254	D	D	60	D	18	11	41,846	131	15.3	37.4	46.2
Jefferson	17,046	187,897	28,351	9,073	31,068	8,569	21,228	8,823	46,957	597	77.7	2.7	28.6
Kiowa	38	222	D	NA	33	D	D	8	37,320	388	3.1	48.2	47.5
Kit Carson	270	2,090	263	123	353	118	37	67	32,280	574	11.0	40.4	47.0
Lake	210	1,291	129	D	208	20	30	34	26,500	33	42.4	6.1	25.0
La Plata	2,374	21,119	3,583	654	3,427	557	1,208	876	41,475	1,093	53.4	3.9	35.1
Larimer	10,577	125,796	20,875	10,965	19,329	3,740	9,143	5,853	46,527	2,043	71.0	4.4	31.6
Las Animas	361	3,122	747	29	737	146	80	92	29,365	549	19.1	37.7	44.8
Lincoln	136	1,358	293	D	322	69	35	48	35,166	489	8.4	51.5	48.9
Logan	573	5,280	1,085	323	1,211	189	118	178	33,806	861	16.6	33.1	45.7
Mesa	4,362	51,511	10,232	2,546	8,767	1,984	2,218	2,014	39,103	2,465	80.1	2.6	32.1
Mineral	65	231	D	D	60	D	6	8	35,450	19	NA	21.1	21.9
Moffat	402	3,214	513	52	753	83	73	145	45,103	462	24.5	28.1	29.9
Montezuma	753	6,900	1,385	265	1,294	160	331	246	35,610	1,123	49.2	5.9	37.0
Montrose	1,249	12,339	2,886	1,292	2,211	312	581	450	36,497	1,135	55.9	6.1	40.4
Morgan	664	9,198	1,304	2,826	1,084	250	126	373	40,546	740	28.4	19.5	51.8
Otero	411	4,216	1,212	477	722	160	112	132	31,327	444	30.4	16.9	42.7
Ouray	273	1,098	55	63	143	54	91	38	34,558	122	55.7	9.8	44.0
Park	451	1,430	126	47	323	24	90	51	35,398	278	30.2	14.4	30.1
Phillips	138	1,129	290	93	200	53	14	42	37,419	326	11.3	39.9	56.3
Pitkin	1,605	17,926	770	171	1,710	274	702	692	38,590	112	51.8	8.9	38.8
Prowers	349	3,113	670	182	742	212	85	93	29,897	472	10.2	36.9	47.6
Pueblo	3,086	49,911	13,215	4,353	8,263	1,143	2,132	1,901	38,081	839	41.7	14.2	37.6
Rio Blanco	210	1,713	214	D	202	42	34	106	62,078	320	35.3	22.2	41.4
Rio Grande	334	2,483	452	72	385	93	69	80	32,388	321	27.7	16.2	59.8
Routt	1,683	16,781	1,457	118	1,774	241	633	646	38,511	887	50.3	11.8	30.4
Saguache	125	932	89	91	128	10	9	27	28,692	288	23.6	25.3	52.4
San Juan	69	249	35	D	30	NA	5	6	22,578	NA	NA	NA	NA
San Miguel	627	5,067	165	110	553	67	180	163	32,081	133	30.1	17.3	35.0
Sedgwick	72	477	D	31	79	25	8	14	29,987	212	8.0	41.0	57.9
Summit	2,251	21,294	1,119	263	3,576	239	644	635	29,819	55	45.5	14.5	30.9
Teller	718	5,914	455	61	921	157	277	216	36,465	159	51.6	10.1	39.8
Washington	111	542	40	91	79	36	19	20	36,044	757	10.2	39.1	52.1
Weld	5,922	83,654	8,969	13,027	10,437	3,361	2,858	3,964	47,386	4,062	46.3	10.2	38.1
Yuma	380	2,823	603	92	477	146	83	97	34,391	774	16.0	42.5	57.9
CONNECTICUT	89,416	1,533,879	285,014	155,579	186,979	126,081	106,207	94,659	61,712	5,521	70.9	0.7	39.0
Fairfield	27,134	427,361	67,963	32,794	50,319	46,775	39,240	35,735	83,617	402	81.8	2.2	49.3
Hartford	22,795	456,617	86,011	50,757	50,684	53,792	29,936	27,195	59,558	786	70.9	0.5	39.3
Litchfield	4,762	52,751	9,431	8,889	8,828	1,352	1,688	2,205	41,800	1,217	67.7	0.7	33.8
Middlesex	4,208	63,220	14,797	9,504	9,296	1,833	2,733	3,038	48,055	441	79.4	0.2	42.1
New Haven	19,597	341,265	75,605	31,228	42,569	11,735	15,306	17,169	50,311	686	81.9	0.3	38.3
New London	5,865	105,998	17,290	13,522	15,036	2,075	8,216	5,249	49,522	823	63.1	0.6	43.3

Table B. States and Counties — **Agriculture**

STATE County	Land in farms					Value of land and buildings (dollars)		Value of machinery and equiopmnet, average per farm (dollars)	Value of products sold:				Organic farms (number)	Farms with internet access (percent)	Government payments	
			Acres								Percent from:					
	Acreage (1,000)	Percent change, 2012-2017	Average size of farm	Total irrigated (1,000)	Total cropland (1,000)	Average per farm	Average per acre		Total (mil dol)	Average per farm (acres)	Crops	Livestock and poultry products			Total ($1,000)	Percent of farms
	117	118	119	120	121	122	123	124	125	126	127	128	129	130	131	132
COLORADO—Cont'd																
Boulder	107	-19.5	106	27.2	38.1	1,329,691	12,571	67,305	43.9	43,378	87.4	12.6	29	90.7	501	5.6
Broomfield	9	-23.8	224	1.2	7.7	1,223,811	5,467	48,312	0.6	16,132	77.5	22.5	NA	63.2	D	2.6
Chaffee	66	-14.6	229	16.5	17.2	1,164,108	5,075	71,744	12.2	42,343	32.7	67.3	NA	83.7	56	3.5
Cheyenne	1,076	10.1	2,853	23.6	599.1	2,389,477	838	260,682	89.2	236,676	76.0	24.0	NA	73.7	10,125	82.0
Clear Creek	10	24.8	314	0.3	0.9	990,682	3,157	54,704	0.2	5,273	30.5	69.5	NA	81.8	NA	NA
Conejos	266	3.3	508	119.5	131.5	857,351	1,687	133,635	53.9	102,939	63.2	36.8	17	64.9	718	18.1
Costilla	358	-4.9	1,562	39.3	50.6	1,898,119	1,215	154,192	22.1	96,328	87.7	12.3	2	59.4	308	9.2
Crowley	484	-3.1	1,969	4.7	31.0	1,002,121	509	88,555	96.3	391,370	1.4	98.6	5	71.5	1,701	48.8
Custer	161	-14.5	512	22.6	29.0	994,967	1,943	81,523	9.7	30,733	47.3	52.7	NA	79.7	173	3.2
Delta	237	-5.5	147	66.8	69.4	705,824	4,813	67,981	67.1	41,559	45.2	54.8	33	83.7	897	6.3
Denver	0	-9.8	11	D	0.0	685,079	63,728	26,067	D	D	D	D	1	75.0	NA	NA
Dolores	158	-1.4	504	7.2	69.9	898,017	1,783	69,774	8.5	27,208	70.9	29.1	5	67.7	1,123	44.4
Douglas	202	0.8	165	2.3	26.5	1,112,035	6,747	50,523	18.9	15,428	62.0	38.0	3	87.3	428	3.4
Eagle	155	19.9	604	14.8	15.4	1,998,474	3,309	83,582	8.2	32,074	23.9	76.1	7	86.0	60	5.1
Elbert	1,018	-2.4	624	6.7	189.9	952,293	1,526	61,221	35.4	21,675	21.2	78.8	1	87.1	3,286	11.9
El Paso	630	-2.9	468	8.9	51.5	659,073	1,407	46,294	31.9	23,716	43.3	56.7	5	80.8	1,300	7.5
Fremont	278	-4.3	269	11.3	15.1	628,195	2,336	48,150	21.8	21,089	23.6	76.4	3	81.1	244	2.0
Garfield	475	52.9	719	52.0	77.4	1,724,785	2,399	89,572	35.9	54,256	24.5	75.5	4	80.0	360	7.3
Gilpin	4	-32.2	106	D	0.5	446,403	4,226	33,954	0.2	5,838	17.1	82.9	NA	81.1	28	16.2
Grand	241	6.2	831	36.3	36.5	1,827,034	2,199	92,591	14.4	49,793	23.5	76.5	NA	76.9	30	1.7
Gunnison	267	40.3	864	57.7	49.3	2,217,820	2,567	107,695	24.1	78,045	22.7	77.3	NA	83.2	51	3.9
Hinsdale	10	2.4	403	2.5	1.1	741,831	1,841	70,145	D	D	D	D	NA	76.9	D	3.8
Huerfano	582	0.1	1,331	8.6	19.4	1,280,062	962	58,781	13.2	30,174	10.8	89.2	1	70.7	311	7.8
Jackson	301	-12.0	2,301	70.4	67.4	3,045,594	1,323	196,274	24.5	186,924	18.5	81.5	3	71.8	35	6.9
Jefferson	69	0.4	115	1.2	5.4	885,635	7,715	36,831	9.0	15,144	77.8	22.2	2	86.1	151	3.0
Kiowa	1,092	-1.9	2,814	2.7	676.3	2,122,946	754	162,846	65.5	168,729	61.8	38.2	NA	72.2	10,450	82.0
Kit Carson	1,358	-1.4	2,366	117.8	890.7	2,883,863	1,219	375,287	474.3	826,268	32.4	67.6	NA	81.2	13,382	71.4
Lake	12	-1.9	362	1.9	0.5	743,849	2,055	46,972	D	D	D	D	NA	84.8	NA	NA
La Plata	549	-7.0	503	58.5	89.7	1,135,305	2,259	74,568	24.4	22,281	38.3	61.7	3	87.5	1,066	8.4
Larimer	482	7.1	236	60.2	98.6	1,095,047	4,637	76,905	150.7	73,772	45.7	54.3	20	85.1	633	5.5
Las Animas	1,796	-16.1	3,272	17.3	75.6	1,968,541	602	80,465	25.8	47,080	14.7	85.3	7	71.8	4,168	27.5
Lincoln	1,500	1.8	3,067	5.8	588.3	2,158,581	704	200,920	67.9	138,855	58.9	41.1	2	74.4	10,318	61.8
Logan	1,138	3.5	1,322	107.1	562.7	1,570,536	1,188	208,745	617.9	717,686	16.0	84.0	2	82.9	11,511	68.8
Mesa	343	-11.5	139	76.2	79.8	767,492	5,523	57,249	94.2	38,209	48.7	51.3	12	86.2	730	3.9
Mineral	8	27.2	444	2.9	0.7	1,526,408	3,441	31,306	D	D	D	100.0	NA	84.2	D	10.5
Moffat	953	2.5	2,063	30.1	123.4	1,648,562	799	107,741	33.1	71,727	11.7	88.3	2	71.9	2,109	26.4
Montezuma	691	0.0	615	79.0	117.2	744,860	1,211	85,128	46.4	41,339	64.3	35.7	6	79.0	1,237	13.3
Montrose	331	0.3	291	79.8	65.6	900,826	3,093	79,919	81.2	71,565	22.7	77.3	10	83.6	792	10.2
Morgan	659	1.9	891	132.3	340.4	1,546,382	1,735	241,369	559.5	756,130	16.1	83.9	5	82.0	6,040	53.9
Otero	688	-2.7	1,548	49.3	78.1	1,162,135	750	148,382	121.5	273,759	25.1	74.9	3	77.9	2,724	48.9
Ouray	85	4.7	698	8.6	8.6	2,130,534	3,054	88,951	4.2	34,459	17.2	82.8	1	89.3	64	4.1
Park	189	5.1	680	12.0	11.2	1,142,769	1,680	55,212	5.1	18,374	7.5	92.5	NA	78.1	26	2.5
Phillips	439	0.6	1,347	79.3	384.4	2,279,496	1,692	324,052	174.2	534,479	50.5	49.5	NA	86.2	8,706	79.4
Pitkin	33	1.9	292	10.1	5.9	2,225,232	7,617	88,246	2.9	26,000	34.9	65.1	NA	70.5	NA	NA
Prowers	1,011	-1.0	2,143	88.3	525.2	1,726,199	806	220,792	310.0	656,875	20.3	79.7	NA	65.7	9,185	75.6
Pueblo	896	0.0	1,067	18.1	72.0	1,097,156	1,028	76,147	52.0	62,033	41.0	59.0	7	77.5	2,117	13.9
Rio Blanco	411	-19.0	1,284	27.1	43.7	1,763,734	1,373	101,073	18.8	58,597	14.8	85.2	2	83.1	390	13.4
Rio Grande	177	-4.3	553	93.6	109.1	1,726,626	3,123	311,844	99.0	308,274	88.7	11.3	9	82.9	998	26.5
Routt	465	-24.1	524	42.7	81.0	1,647,039	3,141	69,340	31.6	35,679	16.2	83.8	4	81.1	962	10.8
Saguache	314	0.8	1,090	118.4	132.7	2,068,512	1,898	218,769	105.4	365,983	85.8	14.2	15	76.4	843	18.8
San Juan	NA	NA	NA	NA	NA	NA	NA	NA	NA	NA	NA	NA	NA	NA	NA	NA
San Miguel	136	7.5	1,023	15.9	14.3	1,524,124	1,490	79,047	6.4	47,925	14.0	86.0	NA	77.4	322	15.0
Sedgwick	349	3.8	1,645	40.4	228.1	2,226,323	1,353	321,028	93.9	442,693	49.3	50.7	2	82.1	4,776	81.6
Summit	27	4.8	483	5.5	6.8	2,041,182	4,225	90,529	1.5	27,127	35.1	64.9	NA	94.5	D	1.8
Teller	71	0.6	449	0.9	5.6	908,034	2,023	40,497	1.2	7,811	12.2	87.8	3	83.0	NA	NA
Washington	1,358	11.6	1,794	40.4	836.2	1,969,481	1,098	221,219	184.6	243,802	50.9	49.1	5	74.4	15,207	72.7
Weld	2,099	7.3	517	323.4	923.0	1,335,953	2,586	159,664	2,047.2	503,982	17.0	83.0	42	82.9	19,375	26.0
Yuma	1,400	3.5	1,809	209.0	628.2	2,953,997	1,633	313,588	918.7	1,186,972	21.8	78.2	4	82.4	19,612	69.8
CONNECTICUT	382	-12.6	69	7.4	148.6	862,636	12,483	62,250	580.1	105,074	72.4	27.6	113	82.4	1,850	4.4
Fairfield	52	-3.2	130	0.2	4.6	1,402,826	10,794	57,696	42.1	104,649	52.7	47.3	9	87.1	33	3.5
Hartford	48	-11.5	61	3.4	26.2	981,893	16,126	64,077	93.9	119,481	95.1	4.9	9	80.9	212	3.8
Litchfield	90	-0.7	74	0.5	37.4	840,256	11,322	56,949	41.1	33,800	51.0	49.0	28	83.3	363	3.8
Middlesex	16	-31.8	37	0.7	6.5	555,077	14,911	66,715	57.1	129,426	96.8	3.2	10	83.9	304	4.8
New Haven	27	-36.3	39	1.3	11.4	922,400	23,490	67,524	111.6	162,720	95.9	4.1	26	78.4	323	5.2
New London	60	-7.7	73	0.6	23.9	837,723	11,467	67,605	135.8	164,989	55.5	44.5	22	88.0	267	6.1

Table B. States and Counties — Water Use, Wholesale Trade, Retail Trade, and Real Estate

STATE County	Water use, 2015		Wholesale Trade[1], 2012				Retail Trade[2], 2012				Real estate and rental and leasing,[2] 2012			
	Public supply water withdrawn (mil gal/day)	Public supply gallons withdrawn per person per day	Number of establish-ments	Number of employees	Sales (mil dol)	Average payroll (mil dol)	Number of establish-ments	Number of employees	Sales (mil dol)	Average payroll (mil dol)	Number of establish-ments	Number of employees	Sales (mil dol)	Average payroll (mil dol)
	133	134	135	136	137	138	139	140	141	142	143	144	145	146
COLORADO—Cont'd														
Boulder	48.30	151.2	392	D	D	D	1,174	16,623	4,498.3	478.9	648	1,954	434.3	74.5
Broomfield	5.67	87.1	52	D	D	D	261	4,606	1,000.2	101.7	96	313	77.1	11.4
Chaffee	3.96	212.2	19	95	41.4	2.9	134	1,049	249.3	25.4	78	132	17.4	3.2
Cheyenne	0.36	196.8	3	D	D	D	13	73	18.5	1.3	2	D	D	D
Clear Creek	1.17	125.8	12	D	D	D	46	265	75.3	5.1	17	24	3.1	0.6
Conejos	3.38	415.7	4	19	4.6	0.9	18	203	35.9	4.3	4	11	0.4	0.1
Costilla	0.45	125.6	1	D	D	D	10	33	11.7	0.6	NA	NA	NA	NA
Crowley	1.00	179.8	1	D	D	D	8	89	17.0	2.3	1	D	D	D
Custer	0.38	85.5	3	2	0.4	0.0	25	164	48.6	3.4	10	9	1.9	0.3
Delta	5.00	166.8	28	174	47.2	6.7	116	1,158	309.8	27.6	36	254	16.5	4.6
Denver	163.27	239.2	1,175	17,997	14,625.8	1,090.1	2,282	26,469	7,111.4	725.7	1,451	9,373	2,723.8	488.3
Dolores	0.25	126.4	5	D	D	D	5	39	10.0	0.7	NA	NA	NA	NA
Douglas	38.48	119.4	241	2,398	2,701.7	205.2	851	15,688	4,308.8	398.1	476	1,154	283.5	48.3
Eagle	10.31	192.3	68	D	D	D	455	3,621	806.0	102.1	362	1,880	280.9	63.5
Elbert	0.85	34.4	14	D	D	D	38	406	105.7	8.7	16	19	3.7	0.7
El Paso	88.35	131.0	430	4,395	2,563.3	247.4	1,955	28,743	7,929.3	757.3	1,031	3,344	657.4	119.9
Fremont	6.42	137.5	27	D	D	D	130	1,594	334.9	34.9	39	159	15.9	3.2
Garfield	11.64	200.4	62	D	D	D	285	2,982	950.0	92.1	158	794	213.2	38.1
Gilpin	0.68	116.7	2	D	D	D	8	20	6.4	0.6	4	7	0.5	0.2
Grand	2.31	158.1	7	17	4.7	0.5	107	628	156.1	15.7	68	583	45.0	13.3
Gunnison	1.88	117.0	9	15	3.5	0.4	133	907	190.0	20.4	89	189	23.8	5.2
Hinsdale	0.24	310.1	NA	NA	NA	NA	17	27	9.0	0.9	4	3	1.2	0.1
Huerfano	2.97	457.5	4	D	D	D	31	215	62.9	4.7	7	15	2.3	0.3
Jackson	0.32	236.0	2	D	D	D	10	63	16.5	1.6	NA	NA	NA	NA
Jefferson	22.99	40.7	529	4,575	3,082.1	289.5	1,866	28,060	7,465.0	724.2	866	2,800	527.7	113.3
Kiowa	0.23	161.6	8	30	20.1	0.8	6	35	10.2	0.6	NA	NA	NA	NA
Kit Carson	1.27	163.7	20	184	271.9	8.5	41	312	115.0	7.6	7	24	2.9	0.7
Lake	4.47	597.2	4	D	D	D	30	199	37.4	4.5	13	51	2.9	0.9
La Plata	5.74	105.0	55	508	222.3	22.8	314	3,128	756.9	83.4	139	454	69.9	14.9
Larimer	30.58	91.7	295	4,294	5,143.6	368.5	1,244	17,307	4,341.3	414.2	526	2,112	307.0	71.4
Las Animas	3.46	246.1	9	D	D	D	60	679	178.9	16.7	22	66	8.6	2.5
Lincoln	0.78	140.4	1	D	D	D	31	330	183.9	7.1	3	5	0.3	0.0
Logan	3.26	147.9	24	D	D	D	100	1,124	320.0	26.3	15	40	7.1	1.3
Mesa	17.51	117.9	219	2,076	876.5	96.2	604	7,966	2,173.3	202.6	263	889	170.7	33.7
Mineral	0.22	303.0	NA	NA	NA	NA	13	60	13.5	1.4	3	3	0.4	0.1
Moffat	1.74	134.5	23	D	D	D	72	714	201.9	21.3	9	13	3.3	0.3
Montezuma	4.37	167.0	19	164	72.6	7.2	99	1,159	349.9	32.3	29	91	20.4	3.2
Montrose	9.13	223.0	47	313	156.2	11.7	180	2,152	583.8	55.9	53	125	18.0	3.6
Morgan	5.96	210.2	32	D	D	D	92	953	256.9	21.8	26	49	5.5	1.2
Otero	3.99	217.5	24	158	94.8	5.5	75	775	213.8	17.1	14	82	8.2	1.8
Ouray	1.80	383.7	1	D	D	D	38	145	22.6	2.5	9	16	1.8	0.5
Park	0.40	24.2	10	D	D	D	40	170	49.7	4.1	22	26	5.2	1.1
Phillips	0.80	184.0	10	D	D	D	21	158	46.1	4.0	3	3	0.1	0.2
Pitkin	8.13	457.1	11	D	D	D	235	1,504	344.4	46.4	203	959	167.3	38.7
Prowers	1.91	159.8	16	115	97.5	4.0	56	656	162.3	13.1	15	D	D	D
Pueblo	41.29	252.4	85	D	D	D	508	7,551	1,952.8	183.4	143	585	105.1	17.7
Rio Blanco	1.89	287.6	4	D	D	D	35	246	54.8	4.6	9	24	7.0	1.6
Rio Grande	1.20	104.0	25	313	238.4	13.2	48	369	99.8	9.5	18	52	4.8	1.2
Routt	2.88	119.4	35	250	131.2	12.7	215	1,616	360.9	41.4	131	530	57.0	14.3
Saguache	0.69	110.4	10	265	108.1	9.8	16	118	23.3	2.1	1	D	D	D
San Juan	0.24	342.4	NA	NA	NA	NA	14	29	6.8	0.6	2	D	D	D
San Miguel	0.68	86.3	5	15	4.0	0.9	72	478	79.7	10.5	78	196	32.5	7.1
Sedgwick	0.69	287.6	4	27	20.6	1.1	13	92	28.1	2.1	1	D	D	D
Summit	6.63	219.1	30	D	D	D	346	3,041	627.2	68.0	245	932	117.6	26.3
Teller	6.17	263.8	12	36	13.3	1.2	70	762	207.8	17.6	43	83	11.7	2.3
Washington	0.35	72.0	7	62	209.8	4.7	14	89	31.6	1.9	1	D	D	D
Weld	28.30	99.2	246	3,166	5,349.2	157.4	620	8,154	2,707.6	228.7	212	870	149.0	31.5
Yuma	1.42	140.0	29	215	855.5	10.0	63	456	125.6	9.6	12	17	1.9	0.4
CONNECTICUT	239.93	66.8	3,675	58,814	161,962.2	3,934.4	12,597	182,528	51,632.5	4,974.5	3,219	19,778	5,349.5	958.4
Fairfield	87.98	92.8	1,190	18,611	130,674.8	1,622.4	3,459	49,401	15,166.5	1,553.9	1,077	6,971	1,808.6	418.1
Hartford	59.22	66.1	970	19,033	15,797.2	1,086.7	3,134	49,862	13,762.4	1,257.3	868	5,027	1,087.0	230.9
Litchfield	10.18	55.4	162	D	D	D	692	8,669	2,655.0	241.2	137	388	60.3	13.6
Middlesex	7.31	44.6	167	2,288	1,537.6	146.7	659	8,548	2,202.6	215.5	124	809	126.4	30.3
New Haven	54.49	63.4	922	14,185	11,237.2	821.2	2,901	41,925	11,567.5	1,100.7	673	5,378	2,008.0	220.2
New London	8.11	29.8	150	D	D	D	1,023	14,372	3,679.3	364.3	204	765	182.6	32.0

1 Merchant wholesalers, except manufacturers' sales branches and offices.   2. Employer establishments.

Table B. States and Counties — **Professional Services, Manufacturing, and Accommodation and Food Services**

STATE County	Professional, scientific, and technical services, 2012				Manufacturing, 2012				Accommodation and food services, 2012			
	Number of establish-ments	Number of employees	Sales (mil dol)	Average payroll (mil dol)	Number of establish-ments	Number of employees	Receipts (mil dol)	Annual payroll (mil dol)	Number of establis-hments	Number of employees	Receipts (mil dol)	Annual payroll (mil dol)
	147	148	149	150	151	152	153	154	155	156	157	158
COLORADO—Cont'd												
Boulder	2,679	27,395	4,767.9	2,011.5	536	14,305	5,061.5	998.4	866	15,855	842.2	252.2
Broomfield	325	6,060	1,252.4	496.8	82	3,087	3,918.4	188.5	143	2,944	169.6	54.7
Chaffee	96	223	24.1	7.6	29	199	25.3	6.0	108	1,172	58.9	19.7
Cheyenne	4	5	0.3	0.1	NA	NA	NA	NA	4	28	1.1	0.2
Clear Creek	48	78	11.7	3.9	8	D	D	D	42	540	30.3	8.8
Conejos	5	9	0.8	0.2	5	53	D	2.6	11	38	3.9	1.0
Costilla	NA	NA	NA	NA	NA	NA	NA	NA	6	D	D	D
Crowley	3	D	D	D	NA	NA	NA	NA	3	12	0.8	0.0
Custer	16	21	3.8	0.8	7	32	D	1.3	12	56	3.2	0.7
Delta	76	D	D	D	50	619	168.1	27.4	76	623	27.2	8.0
Denver	4,291	42,123	9,140.6	3,409.8	759	17,032	5,343.9	761.4	1,982	42,906	2,884.9	823.2
Dolores	4	2	0.3	0.1	NA	NA	NA	NA	8	39	2.5	1.0
Douglas	1,623	10,273	2,561.7	798.6	133	2,169	460.4	119.3	522	10,295	541.8	167.0
Eagle	401	1,289	183.9	65.7	50	238	73.8	11.2	259	7,998	477.8	175.3
Elbert	87	176	22.0	8.5	21	143	D	6.5	26	190	9.3	2.5
El Paso	2,417	19,740	2,983.8	1,258.0	465	10,425	3,375.9	560.5	1,300	26,734	1,443.2	389.2
Fremont	64	178	14.1	4.3	34	409	116.8	20.5	85	878	39.2	11.2
Garfield	300	1,004	137.6	55.1	46	246	41.1	9.4	201	2,727	161.3	49.1
Gilpin	23	34	5.7	1.8	4	D	D	D	10	2,408	404.7	81.0
Grand	81	247	75.4	42.1	14	136	18.6	3.7	136	1,826	84.3	29.4
Gunnison	125	312	28.7	10.0	25	80	9.5	2.2	121	1,339	87.0	16.1
Hinsdale	1	D	D	D	NA	NA	NA	NA	17	75	4.1	1.3
Huerfano	14	35	2.7	1.2	3	26	D	1.4	26	172	9.0	2.4
Jackson	5	10	0.6	0.1	NA	NA	NA	NA	11	51	2.9	0.7
Jefferson	2,985	23,587	4,908.0	1,823.0	448	12,913	6,119.0	907.3	1,160	20,616	1,069.2	318.1
Kiowa	2	D	D	D	NA	NA	NA	NA	2	D	D	D
Kit Carson	18	41	3.8	1.2	8	165	D	4.6	23	261	12.8	3.4
Lake	11	40	3.6	1.6	4	36	D	D	37	268	13.1	3.7
La Plata	326	1,100	139.8	55.3	57	518	84.9	21.1	206	4,226	209.2	68.4
Larimer	1,493	8,727	1,031.1	450.9	403	10,163	4,275.7	642.6	847	14,821	756.5	218.0
Las Animas	24	93	7.2	2.8	6	56	9.0	2.6	50	656	30.9	8.4
Lincoln	10	25	2.2	0.6	NA	NA	NA	NA	19	222	9.6	2.3
Logan	30	101	10.9	3.4	20	308	213.0	11.9	46	595	26.2	7.5
Mesa	561	2,529	289.0	119.8	159	2,388	520.6	95.1	300	6,052	282.6	88.8
Mineral	3	4	0.3	0.1	NA	NA	NA	NA	19	66	7.9	2.5
Moffat	31	129	10.1	4.0	11	50	D	1.6	33	454	20.7	5.9
Montezuma	80	281	30.1	11.8	32	264	49.9	9.2	85	1,263	83.2	22.8
Montrose	110	438	46.3	20.6	66	1,167	210.7	39.2	78	1,007	49.6	15.4
Morgan	36	120	10.4	3.1	42	3,147	2,444.1	105.4	57	693	29.5	8.4
Otero	32	105	7.3	2.4	15	465	75.9	18.2	52	603	22.9	6.4
Ouray	47	78	10.4	3.7	11	36	4.9	1.2	47	280	21.5	6.3
Park	57	86	10.2	3.3	15	55	D	1.7	40	230	18.4	3.8
Phillips	10	18	2.2	0.5	3	16	4.1	0.7	15	76	2.6	0.8
Pitkin	224	636	154.3	43.7	17	104	16.7	4.5	160	5,089	305.3	118.2
Prowers	28	95	11.2	3.5	14	150	31.5	5.4	35	414	17.6	4.2
Pueblo	238	1,744	435.3	157.3	90	4,221	2,333.3	216.8	356	5,698	236.0	67.8
Rio Blanco	15	51	4.8	1.6	3	10	D	D	30	200	11.5	3.1
Rio Grande	28	72	6.1	2.1	10	59	10.5	2.4	32	278	12.8	3.9
Routt	193	531	81.9	25.5	24	118	17.4	4.8	146	5,159	241.4	80.0
Saguache	9	13	1.1	0.5	5	45	D	2.0	5	30	1.1	0.3
San Juan	6	D	D	D	3	8	D	0.4	24	86	6.2	1.5
San Miguel	75	129	19.7	5.6	14	84	10.9	4.9	72	1,439	77.2	29.2
Sedgwick	5	17	1.0	0.3	3	29	D	0.7	4	53	1.4	0.5
Summit	258	575	89.3	30.4	26	166	40.6	7.9	250	6,201	311.3	101.3
Teller	88	411	57.8	22.6	14	46	6.5	1.7	71	1,649	110.8	38.1
Washington	7	18	1.7	0.4	6	100	D	D	6	27	1.0	0.3
Weld	533	2,362	311.5	113.7	284	11,102	5,991.4	485.8	400	5,794	273.9	76.2
Yuma	27	62	6.6	2.0	11	78	164.8	2.8	26	231	8.5	2.5
CONNECTICUT	9,220	97,578	17,993.7	8,364.1	4,350	163,847	55,160.1	10,546.2	8,263	134,546	9,542.1	2,590.8
Fairfield	3,481	40,694	8,738.6	3,975.9	837	35,507	13,412.5	2,338.2	2,266	30,574	2,153.3	604.6
Hartford	2,238	26,427	5,239.4	1,968.7	1,261	57,332	16,965.5	3,899.3	2,043	32,877	1,905.3	549.8
Litchfield	372	D	D	D	382	9,062	2,615.3	463.3	411	4,426	265.2	75.3
Middlesex	374	2,735	425.1	166.9	243	8,920	3,605.4	543.1	421	5,434	329.5	99.3
New Haven	1,907	16,222	2,461.1	1,216.8	1,151	31,792	10,818.1	1,879.2	1,969	26,342	1,487.2	411.3
New London	529	8,100	666.1	862.0	172	12,435	4,693.7	950.2	698	28,347	3,023.8	748.7

Health Care and Social Assistance, Other Services, Nonemployer Businesses, and Residential Construction

STATE County	Health care and social assistance, 2012				Other services, 2012				Nonemployer businesses, 2016		Value of residential construction authorized by building permits, 2018	
	Number of establishments	Number of employees	Receipts (mil dol)	Annual payroll (mil dol)	Number of establishments	Number of employees	Receipts (mil dol)	Annual payroll (mil dol)	Number	Receipts (mil dol)	New construction ($1,000)	Number of housing units
	159	160	161	162	163	164	165	166	167	168	169	170
COLORADO—Cont'd												
Boulder	1,332	18,386	2,129.6	841.9	717	4,415	670.1	176.7	39,089	1,984.5	623,380	2,954
Broomfield	145	1,611	172.9	64.4	109	704	141.8	23.7	5,839	259.7	199,222	785
Chaffee	66	791	76.3	31.3	40	175	11.7	3.7	2,427	95.4	41,321	162
Cheyenne	1	D	D	D	4	6	1.0	0.2	201	7.3	978	6
Clear Creek	19	67	5.8	2.2	10	27	1.8	0.5	1,000	51.7	7,022	34
Conejos	11	254	17.1	6.9	4	D	D	D	625	28.2	8,427	22
Costilla	7	37	1.7	0.9	3	D	D	D	272	12.1	0	0
Crowley	3	D	D	D	1	D	D	D	171	5.7	219	1
Custer	2	D	D	D	10	120	5.3	2.6	683	29.3	21,399	77
Delta	89	1,716	115.7	48.9	50	185	15.2	4.1	2,964	131.8	8,348	48
Denver	2,093	54,161	7,316.9	3,008.8	1,607	13,247	1,868.2	472.2	68,929	3,715.0	1,452,879	7,878
Dolores	5	D	D	D	NA	NA	NA	NA	151	6.3	360	1
Douglas	743	8,339	1,137.4	412.4	508	3,075	270.0	80.6	31,744	1,613.7	1,016,081	4,065
Eagle	168	2,052	384.1	115.8	189	1,278	119.3	37.3	7,236	421.3	114,761	382
Elbert	25	132	8.2	3.9	42	118	11.9	3.2	2,796	134.8	66,406	217
El Paso	1,897	D	D	D	1,086	8,419	1,805.3	323.0	50,220	2,023.8	1,786,923	5,586
Fremont	93	1,982	128.3	60.6	46	214	13.1	4.4	2,796	102.9	27,703	137
Garfield	161	D	D	D	152	692	91.3	20.8	6,223	332.3	45,928	189
Gilpin	6	43	4.0	1.5	3	7	0.4	0.1	597	24.5	11,104	41
Grand	36	324	35.9	13.3	46	103	12.0	2.6	1,973	97.5	71,602	213
Gunnison	64	494	50.3	18.0	64	221	27.3	5.7	2,420	96.4	55,461	169
Hinsdale	1	D	D	D	6	D	D	D	133	5.2	3,793	9
Huerfano	18	424	31.2	15.3	7	D	D	D	575	21.2	6,941	38
Jackson	3	7	0.5	0.2	1	D	D	D	176	7.6	1,772	5
Jefferson	1,565	24,678	2,717.4	1,084.2	1,121	6,073	628.1	172.8	55,672	2,458.8	435,827	2,138
Kiowa	2	D	D	D	4	4	0.5	0.1	133	5.7	0	0
Kit Carson	26	284	22.2	9.0	13	D	D	D	703	33.0	539	3
Lake	14	195	18.3	6.8	12	32	2.1	0.5	631	26.0	8,962	51
La Plata	237	2,737	335.0	125.2	143	612	53.9	16.6	6,416	292.4	111,599	282
Larimer	1,021	18,142	1,988.2	783.2	658	3,536	374.1	96.2	31,698	1,420.8	645,800	2,944
Las Animas	36	D	D	D	36	129	11.0	3.0	966	36.9	5,430	40
Lincoln	7	245	21.3	8.4	11	41	3.4	0.9	371	13.0	1,809	18
Logan	65	1,027	88.3	33.5	53	203	21.5	5.2	1,315	62.1	4,837	20
Mesa	426	10,176	1,029.0	427.2	293	1,883	182.6	47.8	11,817	501.0	129,423	830
Mineral	2	D	D	D	3	D	D	D	158	8.4	3,660	19
Moffat	40	440	50.3	19.1	37	219	18.5	6.7	1,003	37.4	1,846	7
Montezuma	90	1,422	109.3	45.2	47	173	15.7	3.6	2,322	87.0	3,727	19
Montrose	172	2,338	221.5	83.5	86	368	36.5	9.4	3,744	159.1	48,400	386
Morgan	57	1,186	118.5	46.1	40	139	14.1	3.2	1,890	96.5	25,743	146
Otero	57	921	50.8	24.8	27	81	7.1	1.8	1,087	36.4	1,400	6
Ouray	18	52	3.9	1.6	8	35	2.6	0.8	954	53.4	21,469	61
Park	23	96	4.6	2.1	24	76	9.1	2.4	1,883	79.8	46,704	182
Phillips	9	298	21.2	8.8	12	24	3.2	0.7	398	21.1	1,534	11
Pitkin	74	D	D	D	115	913	122.3	36.8	3,687	259.5	140,486	83
Prowers	30	625	48.8	20.7	23	87	10.5	2.1	855	37.4	90	1
Pueblo	419	11,404	1,063.1	458.0	238	1,222	93.1	28.2	8,357	348.9	74,234	479
Rio Blanco	10	176	19.0	8.8	12	25	3.0	0.8	540	23.5	3,183	19
Rio Grande	34	420	28.7	11.9	24	94	12.6	2.9	1,053	35.9	3,987	20
Routt	118	1,170	141.6	51.0	86	438	37.7	10.9	3,693	181.4	93,972	170
Saguache	6	D	D	D	8	D	D	D	591	22.7	7,672	106
San Juan	3	D	D	D	3	17	0.7	0.4	129	7.3	1,307	7
San Miguel	28	132	10.0	4.2	44	270	29.1	7.8	1,739	101.0	74,267	53
Sedgwick	5	D	D	D	5	10	1.6	0.2	174	7.5	789	2
Summit	104	852	134.8	39.9	121	420	60.5	12.3	4,365	249.8	234,367	643
Teller	58	D	D	D	42	129	11.5	3.1	2,586	102.5	43,773	148
Washington	8	32	1.7	0.5	8	D	D	D	376	17.2	1,607	9
Weld	435	7,951	893.1	325.4	329	1,537	175.9	44.5	21,999	1,012.3	885,450	4,107
Yuma	26	584	53.7	22.6	22	D	D	D	993	45.8	0	0
CONNECTICUT	10,296	271,272	29,573.1	12,533.5	7,282	43,384	4,904.0	1,382.4	277,699	16,375.4	1,112,212	4,815
Fairfield	2,827	63,963	8,087.6	3,291.8	2,103	13,041	1,654.3	420.8	94,038	6,734.7	531,590	1,097
Hartford	2,771	79,917	8,536.4	3,723.3	1,935	12,855	1,454.4	450.4	58,805	3,202.1	145,131	1,134
Litchfield	515	9,500	929.2	374.9	359	1,621	163.1	46.6	17,224	955.6	48,637	126
Middlesex	470	13,869	1,411.2	645.8	339	1,650	163.1	49.9	13,390	726.6	40,086	164
New Haven	2,408	73,162	7,788.2	3,238.4	1,717	9,881	977.8	297.8	61,104	3,171.4	165,282	1,166
New London	734	17,357	1,728.0	751.2	459	2,498	274.7	61.9	16,925	826.8	104,339	666

Table B. States and Counties — Government Employment and Payroll, and Local Government Finances

			Government employment and payroll, 2012							Local government finances, 2012				
			March payroll (percent of total)							General revenue				
												Taxes		
													Per capita[1] (dollars)	
STATE County	Full-time equivalent employees	March payroll (dollars)	Adminis- tration, judicial, and legal	Police and corrections	Fire protection	Highways and transpor- tation	Health and welfare	Natural resources and utilities	Education and libraries	Total (mil dol)	Inter- govern- mental (mil dol)	Total (mil dol)	Total	Property
	171	172	173	174	175	176	177	178	179	180	181	182	183	184
COLORADO—Cont'd														
Boulder	11,666	48,102,144	8.2	10.8	5.0	2.7	5.3	10.3	53.3	1,374.3	334.5	816.3	2,674	1,840
Broomfield	687	3,465,698	16.4	35.0	0.0	2.4	10.3	27.3	3.9	167.6	16.5	123.6	2,120	775
Chaffee	981	3,205,729	12.3	6.1	0.6	3.3	43.6	2.3	30.5	122.6	43.2	31.0	1,707	1,041
Cheyenne	186	506,783	7.0	5.9	0.0	7.9	25.6	3.5	46.1	11.6	3.9	4.8	2,562	2,163
Clear Creek	426	1,607,157	17.1	24.4	1.0	10.4	10.2	4.5	29.9	55.5	7.7	41.0	4,539	4,152
Conejos	417	1,165,848	8.0	8.9	0.0	4.9	9.9	3.0	62.1	35.4	24.9	8.0	965	500
Costilla	216	594,990	12.8	7.1	0.6	14.3	13.6	6.0	39.9	21.5	11.8	7.4	2,049	1,959
Crowley	149	372,979	13.1	7.4	0.2	7.6	12.0	7.9	49.2	13.0	9.3	3.0	554	412
Custer	188	561,207	16.3	10.1	0.7	9.8	17.6	3.0	41.1	14.0	3.5	7.4	1,741	1,402
Delta	1,667	6,363,576	6.3	7.6	0.1	3.4	39.9	9.2	32.0	159.6	41.2	32.5	1,067	738
Denver	31,444	153,513,001	5.5	11.6	4.4	12.7	23.1	10.5	30.8	5,569.5	1,334.4	2,071.4	3,266	1,406
Dolores	125	332,266	21.5	7.7	0.0	17.4	6.7	1.6	42.7	5.7	2.5	2.8	1,418	1,324
Douglas	8,978	36,551,403	6.0	11.8	1.8	3.0	0.7	5.6	68.6	1,187.6	326.8	623.8	2,092	1,621
Eagle	1,753	9,241,964	10.1	13.6	8.4	9.4	9.0	14.1	30.0	388.1	36.2	240.3	4,632	3,109
Elbert	793	2,420,569	5.3	13.3	4.8	6.6	3.6	3.3	61.8	68.8	28.9	26.5	1,132	853
El Paso	24,223	94,407,600	4.8	9.4	3.9	2.0	15.6	15.5	46.2	2,544.0	807.4	804.8	1,248	728
Fremont	1,361	4,257,494	6.5	12.3	3.9	5.6	7.8	6.9	53.3	113.3	43.1	39.2	837	567
Garfield	2,715	10,773,217	7.9	10.4	4.9	3.5	18.8	8.7	43.3	377.7	79.3	217.3	3,815	3,060
Gilpin	323	1,493,439	17.4	31.0	11.0	10.9	2.8	6.6	15.7	64.3	18.7	33.2	6,047	1,928
Grand	899	3,399,937	11.0	8.9	1.9	8.6	29.9	12.4	25.0	112.4	11.3	66.9	4,715	3,643
Gunnison	938	4,262,174	12.1	9.1	1.5	9.8	23.1	10.8	16.9	118.1	21.2	51.6	3,335	2,295
Hinsdale	78	213,518	22.4	6.9	0.0	16.9	17.4	4.9	28.8	6.8	1.9	3.5	4,346	3,385
Huerfano	683	2,657,574	9.1	15.2	0.3	8.0	42.0	6.2	18.4	59.2	16.3	13.5	2,049	1,649
Jackson	109	283,034	16.2	7.4	0.3	12.1	6.1	7.8	43.4	7.5	4.3	2.3	1,700	1,447
Jefferson	16,292	67,925,819	8.0	14.5	6.3	2.7	4.7	8.0	53.4	1,796.8	529.1	959.0	1,758	1,296
Kiowa	195	518,331	6.2	3.4	0.1	6.2	53.7	0.0	26.7	13.7	4.6	3.5	2,400	2,321
Kit Carson	599	1,765,320	8.1	7.1	2.1	6.4	30.3	7.6	36.2	45.5	15.1	12.7	1,565	1,397
Lake	1,036	3,786,124	2.2	2.4	4.0	1.7	9.4	2.1	76.3	123.9	28.5	61.1	8,331	7,915
La Plata	2,067	7,718,347	12.2	16.8	4.4	5.9	9.2	7.1	41.1	215.9	60.0	121.8	2,324	1,552
Larimer	10,782	47,317,101	8.8	11.5	1.1	2.8	7.5	18.4	46.2	1,178.8	292.6	577.8	1,861	1,211
Las Animas	790	3,154,143	13.1	10.3	5.0	7.2	4.0	23.0	36.5	67.9	34.0	24.1	1,610	1,155
Lincoln	433	1,393,504	11.8	4.7	0.0	8.0	44.9	2.8	25.9	42.3	17.3	9.6	1,763	1,199
Logan	1,057	3,288,524	7.3	7.7	3.0	24.9	6.5	4.7	43.0	98.6	25.5	33.4	1,475	969
Mesa	5,197	18,735,519	8.2	13.3	5.0	4.1	7.0	9.6	48.8	498.4	180.8	228.0	1,542	966
Mineral	54	178,882	27.1	10.8	0.0	16.4	3.6	2.1	40.0	2.9	0.6	1.5	2,123	1,523
Moffat	596	2,538,838	9.9	13.4	0.2	10.3	6.2	10.3	44.2	92.8	17.6	36.4	2,760	2,173
Montezuma	1,215	5,805,045	11.6	22.2	1.0	7.2	7.7	14.6	27.4	95.8	39.0	40.1	1,577	1,113
Montrose	2,104	7,665,788	7.4	9.0	2.9	5.0	34.2	6.0	34.1	212.1	63.1	64.1	1,574	943
Morgan	1,340	3,811,946	7.6	9.5	0.4	4.0	9.8	9.7	57.0	108.9	39.6	44.8	1,573	1,252
Otero	1,005	2,762,692	7.5	7.2	2.0	3.8	7.9	18.7	51.8	77.3	47.6	18.6	995	589
Ouray	217	778,899	20.7	8.6	4.2	8.7	4.3	7.5	43.5	24.2	6.0	13.1	2,889	2,250
Park	565	1,709,266	7.9	11.7	9.4	8.8	7.9	2.6	45.3	79.9	43.2	27.9	1,739	1,620
Phillips	387	1,231,524	5.8	2.8	0.0	4.9	50.9	5.0	28.5	41.2	11.7	7.9	1,819	1,329
Pitkin	1,617	8,457,732	10.5	7.7	1.5	20.9	24.6	13.9	14.7	334.3	32.9	154.4	8,946	4,437
Prowers	976	3,070,921	6.7	5.7	0.9	3.5	37.0	8.6	32.8	89.1	35.2	16.6	1,340	781
Pueblo	5,698	21,434,409	5.8	12.3	11.0	3.0	6.6	9.0	49.7	552.8	247.0	223.3	1,388	895
Rio Blanco	743	2,764,159	6.3	7.4	0.2	5.5	52.7	8.3	15.4	118.7	16.4	59.8	8,716	7,064
Rio Grande	594	2,555,313	11.1	23.0	0.0	5.2	6.7	1.8	52.0	64.6	42.5	16.8	1,408	981
Routt	1,184	5,565,786	14.7	11.9	5.9	17.1	2.2	12.5	30.0	144.8	31.4	79.2	3,394	2,136
Saguache	347	1,034,643	14.8	8.6	0.3	8.8	6.1	10.3	48.3	55.6	45.0	6.6	1,042	909
San Juan	40	161,715	24.7	12.1	0.0	15.7	7.6	8.1	30.7	9.6	6.5	2.6	3,820	2,945
San Miguel	502	2,269,390	18.4	15.3	2.9	13.4	5.4	10.0	33.5	93.6	14.2	55.2	7,283	5,078
Sedgwick	255	812,165	5.4	2.7	1.9	4.4	48.8	7.8	27.6	22.9	7.9	4.8	2,001	1,581
Summit	1,631	6,095,822	12.4	10.1	11.6	10.3	3.7	14.3	28.7	206.4	13.5	141.5	5,044	2,991
Teller	955	3,818,256	16.1	19.9	2.6	7.0	8.6	7.5	33.5	87.9	28.6	45.4	1,942	1,236
Washington	385	1,126,606	13.3	11.8	0.0	8.2	7.0	2.5	56.0	43.4	28.9	10.2	2,145	1,945
Weld	8,663	35,763,495	8.2	17.4	4.0	5.2	6.6	11.0	45.5	919.9	308.8	411.9	1,562	1,194
Yuma	749	2,253,233	4.4	5.3	0.0	6.1	43.0	5.1	34.4	88.3	21.8	23.8	2,349	2,036
CONNECTICUT	X	X	X	X	X	X	X	X	X	X	X	X	X	X
Fairfield	32,029	179,963,079	3.5	9.1	5.1	3.1	3.2	3.7	70.6	4,597.7	963.2	3,193.1	3,419	3,370
Hartford	31,675	164,755,032	3.0	8.6	3.8	2.4	3.4	4.9	72.4	4,279.2	1,571.4	2,306.6	2,571	2,541
Litchfield	5,578	26,405,841	4.3	6.4	1.8	5.2	1.9	2.5	76.6	698.9	167.1	476.8	2,542	2,521
Middlesex	5,503	26,698,181	4.2	7.4	4.5	3.5	3.5	3.2	71.4	656.2	154.4	441.0	2,663	2,643
New Haven	28,448	140,929,161	3.5	10.1	6.3	2.6	2.7	5.4	68.7	3,790.8	1,443.5	2,034.2	2,358	2,333
New London	8,967	42,369,410	4.4	7.7	3.8	3.8	2.3	8.0	68.3	1,101.6	386.5	598.5	2,183	2,159

1. Based on the resident population estimated as of July 1 of the year shown.

— **Local Government Finances, Government Employment, and Income Taxes**

STATE County	Local government finances, 2012 (cont.)							Debt outstanding		Government employment, 2017			Individual income tax returns, 2016		
	Direct general expenditure														
	Total (mil dol)	Per capita[1] (dollars)	Percent of total for:					Total (mil dol)	Per capita[1] (dollars)	Federal civilian	Federal military	State and local	Number of returns	Mean adjusted gross income	Mean income tax
			Education	Health and hospitals	Police protection	Public welfare	Highways								
	185	186	187	188	189	190	191	192	193	194	195	196	197	198	199
COLORADO—Cont'd															
Boulder	1,414.6	4,633	43.6	2.5	8.2	2.3	4.6	1,940.0	6,354	2,077	848	32,749	157,470	95,151	15,835
Broomfield	144.5	2,479	0.0	1.3	11.0	7.9	6.3	650.9	11,165	171	171	1,507	33,340	90,274	13,618
Chaffee	126.2	6,953	33.9	30.5	2.8	4.5	3.0	96.2	5,298	71	46	1,929	9,310	58,479	6,971
Cheyenne	10.0	5,359	50.3	1.1	4.3	21.9	4.7	4.3	2,284	13	5	286	830	38,735	5,486
Clear Creek	50.3	5,569	22.6	4.4	10.8	5.5	14.8	19.7	2,186	32	24	611	4,750	78,041	11,250
Conejos	32.7	3,950	48.7	4.8	3.1	18.2	5.7	7.1	857	45	21	536	3,020	37,438	2,915
Costilla	19.3	5,383	36.1	8.6	3.1	5.2	18.0	10.6	2,962	10	10	370	1,400	34,689	3,064
Crowley	12.3	2,296	34.8	0.9	4.5	16.8	7.5	5.3	989	9	8	509	1,150	32,673	2,341
Custer	14.0	3,302	29.4	21.6	5.5	3.1	12.9	5.3	1,249	13	12	252	2,110	57,159	6,619
Delta	164.5	5,405	28.7	38.1	3.5	2.1	6.4	79.3	2,607	179	83	2,263	13,100	43,064	4,230
Denver	4,720.3	7,442	20.3	15.1	4.8	3.6	3.3	12,146.9	19,151	15,019	2,469	58,105	349,530	82,138	13,339
Dolores	8.4	4,230	38.7	1.5	9.3	1.7	28.9	3.1	1,535	9	5	226	830	43,388	4,116
Douglas	1,073.0	3,598	46.7	0.7	5.5	1.9	8.1	1,832.6	6,145	417	843	13,102	155,970	114,628	18,720
Eagle	360.2	6,944	19.9	3.1	5.6	0.9	7.0	691.4	13,329	127	138	3,170	28,640	87,726	14,516
Elbert	66.6	2,849	52.4	1.1	2.8	6.7	8.4	163.8	7,006	32	64	909	11,950	86,364	12,499
El Paso	2,502.2	3,880	37.1	21.9	6.0	2.0	8.1	4,398.1	6,819	12,130	37,056	38,918	319,200	61,763	7,367
Fremont	111.0	2,373	42.2	0.5	8.6	5.0	5.7	106.8	2,282	1,093	98	4,204	18,020	46,845	4,738
Garfield	343.8	6,036	29.4	12.6	5.3	5.4	6.2	453.7	7,965	268	147	4,951	27,210	68,390	9,629
Gilpin	50.9	9,270	11.0	2.3	12.0	3.9	11.8	57.5	10,467	11	15	451	2,800	61,779	7,370
Grand	101.5	7,151	19.1	14.0	6.2	1.0	9.3	159.5	11,235	111	38	1,241	7,640	63,255	8,489
Gunnison	122.5	7,917	13.3	24.8	4.1	3.0	11.9	140.6	9,086	174	40	2,068	8,020	59,278	7,437
Hinsdale	7.9	9,716	19.4	25.6	3.8	0.3	8.5	0.7	895	3	2	94	400	55,528	5,690
Huerfano	56.4	8,549	15.8	41.7	1.6	2.4	10.2	12.0	1,821	14	16	450	2,700	41,382	4,063
Jackson	7.0	5,173	38.5	4.4	6.1	2.3	23.7	0.7	487	32	3	136	640	43,605	4,238
Jefferson	1,793.4	3,289	42.8	1.2	9.3	2.3	4.8	1,397.5	2,563	8,662	1,490	28,247	293,820	79,802	11,546
Kiowa	14.6	10,098	23.1	43.2	3.7	4.8	11.6	4.6	3,195	22	3	230	610	37,902	3,697
Kit Carson	45.0	5,561	31.8	27.5	3.7	5.2	8.8	19.9	2,455	39	18	757	3,250	32,326	4,419
Lake	135.4	18,454	79.4	5.5	1.1	1.4	2.2	36.4	4,957	54	19	608	3,460	46,565	4,497
La Plata	202.8	3,869	35.0	1.1	7.0	2.7	5.9	291.6	5,566	317	135	5,525	26,890	71,130	9,990
Larimer	1,080.2	3,479	37.9	4.5	6.4	3.0	9.0	1,388.6	4,472	2,555	869	35,172	165,500	71,345	9,953
Las Animas	67.0	4,482	36.8	3.7	4.8	14.4	8.4	26.1	1,744	66	34	1,480	5,960	42,660	4,385
Lincoln	47.4	8,698	36.7	27.0	2.8	5.8	9.1	9.7	1,786	20	12	1,032	2,090	41,281	3,814
Logan	73.2	3,236	40.5	1.4	5.0	4.8	10.0	99.6	4,400	59	47	2,381	8,500	55,372	7,355
Mesa	517.8	3,502	35.4	1.7	13.1	5.6	9.4	476.5	3,223	1,573	385	8,487	68,820	54,254	6,163
Mineral	2.9	4,056	57.4	0.8	5.3	0.0	15.9	1.2	1,746	6	2	100	430	58,267	6,435
Moffat	93.2	7,060	24.3	30.6	5.6	6.2	10.7	40.3	3,050	135	33	946	5,740	53,684	5,502
Montezuma	95.7	3,762	36.0	3.0	10.1	11.6	6.2	60.5	2,379	354	65	2,377	11,580	51,759	6,025
Montrose	215.1	5,283	25.1	29.4	6.1	3.0	9.2	127.2	3,123	310	104	2,873	18,740	49,018	4,960
Morgan	102.1	3,585	44.8	1.5	4.7	4.6	7.3	72.8	2,556	118	70	2,097	12,830	47,837	4,913
Otero	73.8	3,949	48.8	9.4	2.9	2.4	5.4	37.0	1,981	103	45	1,779	7,520	38,592	3,338
Ouray	18.2	4,027	38.4	1.5	6.2	7.7	14.2	11.3	2,485	14	12	380	2,490	69,841	9,680
Park	79.6	4,968	50.7	2.8	3.8	4.7	6.8	28.9	1,800	49	45	771	7,700	62,161	7,178
Phillips	43.4	9,946	35.1	40.0	2.6	1.2	5.0	19.5	4,468	23	11	584	2,050	50,138	5,586
Pitkin	271.6	15,734	9.3	32.7	4.0	1.8	4.6	380.2	22,024	86	45	2,271	10,280	121,474	25,264
Prowers	85.2	6,880	36.9	27.3	5.4	4.4	4.5	184.4	14,887	37	30	1,344	4,860	42,089	4,155
Pueblo	566.4	3,521	40.3	1.5	6.6	5.3	3.7	456.3	2,837	1,106	423	11,706	70,430	48,976	5,199
Rio Blanco	94.0	13,703	15.7	31.1	5.7	2.8	9.7	113.7	16,584	70	15	1,189	2,710	56,178	5,686
Rio Grande	62.5	5,236	64.5	2.5	4.3	3.9	5.0	22.1	1,851	119	28	822	5,690	44,056	4,550
Routt	151.7	6,501	26.1	0.5	3.9	3.9	7.2	168.4	7,217	116	63	1,869	13,170	88,854	15,410
Saguache	54.4	8,636	66.9	1.8	1.8	8.1	6.5	14.0	2,225	44	17	494	2,020	34,810	3,949
San Juan	9.9	14,307	73.7	1.8	5.2	0.9	5.5	1.8	2,645	2	2	72	370	48,914	5,595
San Miguel	78.7	10,376	17.1	8.1	5.4	1.7	11.2	104.6	13,797	33	20	784	4,300	73,623	14,531
Sedgwick	21.9	9,187	35.7	36.4	2.6	2.8	4.4	1.7	700	17	6	324	1,020	40,619	3,960
Summit	193.3	6,894	18.6	1.3	5.5	1.0	7.9	128.1	4,569	53	76	2,483	16,960	75,805	11,237
Teller	84.7	3,621	35.6	6.2	7.8	2.8	8.5	55.5	2,371	52	62	1,239	12,050	61,189	6,882
Washington	40.7	8,539	68.2	2.8	2.6	6.4	6.5	14.9	3,135	42	12	456	2,020	43,814	4,273
Weld	839.9	3,185	42.6	1.2	7.3	4.0	6.6	868.6	3,294	662	755	15,983	132,160	61,915	7,268
Yuma	77.9	7,698	25.5	39.3	3.2	4.7	6.7	65.7	6,497	44	25	990	4,310	44,180	4,873
CONNECTICUT	X	X	X	X	X	X	X	X	X	18,089	13,526	222,540	1,754,130	92,838	15,701
Fairfield	4,616.9	4,944	50.9	1.2	6.6	1.0	3.1	4,013.1	4,297	2,862	1,907	44,076	459,130	148,397	31,256
Hartford	4,219.6	4,703	56.1	0.9	6.3	0.8	4.1	2,673.7	2,980	5,580	1,819	64,983	445,100	74,788	10,698
Litchfield	765.4	4,081	66.1	1.3	3.5	0.2	6.7	390.3	2,081	446	364	7,624	94,220	75,220	10,447
Middlesex	673.0	4,064	63.2	0.8	4.2	0.4	4.0	355.1	2,144	385	323	9,688	84,000	83,402	12,217
New Haven	4,427.8	5,132	58.4	0.6	4.3	0.3	2.5	3,649.0	4,229	5,478	1,918	44,839	413,190	71,243	9,930
New London	1142.0	4,165	60.1	0.7	5.5	0.6	6.1	911.5	3,324	2,787	6,651	28,095	134,930	69,035	9,124

1. Based on the resident population estimated as of July 1 of the year shown.

Table B. States and Counties — Land Area and Population

State / county code	CBSA code[1]	County code[2]	STATE County	Population, 2018				Population and population characteristics, 2018										
								Race alone or in combination, not Hispanic or Latino (percent)					Age (percent)					
				Land area[3] (sq. mi)	Total persons 2018	Rank	Per square mile	White	Black	American Indian, Alaska Native	Asian and Pacific Islander	Percent Hispanic or Latino[4]	Under 5 years	5 to 17 years	18 to 24 years	25 to 34 years	35 to 44 years	45 to 54 years
				1	2	3	4	5	6	7	8	9	10	11	12	13	14	15
			CONNECTICUT—Cont'd															
09013	25,540	1	Tolland..............	410.4	150,921	441	367.7	85.8	4.0	0.6	5.7	5.7	4.1	13.2	19.0	10.9	10.2	12.9
09015	49,340	2	Windham..............	512.9	117,027	532	228.2	83.9	2.7	1.1	2.0	12.3	4.9	14.9	9.8	12.8	12.0	13.8
10000		0	DELAWARE...............	1,948.2	967,171	X	496.4	63.9	23.4	0.9	4.7	9.5	5.7	15.4	8.7	13.3	11.5	12.7
10001	20,100	3	Kent....................	585.8	178,550	373	304.8	63.7	27.7	1.3	3.5	7.4	6.3	16.6	9.9	13.6	11.6	12.1
10003	37,980	1	New Castle.............	426.3	559,335	121	1,312.1	58.7	26.3	0.7	6.4	10.3	5.7	15.7	9.3	14.5	12.4	13.3
10005	41,540	2	Sussex	936.1	229,286	297	244.9	76.9	13.1	1.0	1.7	9.3	5.0	13.6	6.2	10.2	9.4	11.6
11000		0	DISTRICT OF COLUMBIA	61.1	702,455	X	11,496.8	38.8	46.3	0.8	5.4	11.3	6.5	11.7	10.6	23.4	15.0	10.7
11001	47,900	1	District of Columbia........	61.1	702,455	94	11,496.8	38.8	46.3	0.8	5.4	11.3	6.5	11.7	10.6	23.4	15.0	10.7
12000		0	FLORIDA....................	53,648.6	21,299,325	X	397.0	54.9	16.5	0.6	3.7	26.1	5.4	14.5	8.2	13.1	12.1	12.9
12001	23,540	2	Alachua................	875.0	269,956	255	308.5	63.1	21.3	0.6	7.4	10.3	5.2	12.8	20.8	15.6	10.9	9.8
12003	27,260	1	Baker..................	585.2	28,355	1,487	48.5	82.3	14.6	1.1	1.0	2.7	6.3	17.4	8.2	15.0	12.9	13.6
12005	37,460	3	Bay....................	758.5	185,287	355	244.3	78.8	12.5	1.5	3.7	6.7	6.1	15.3	7.9	14.4	12.1	12.8
12007		6	Bradford	294.0	27,732	1,504	94.3	74.9	20.7	1.0	1.1	4.3	5.4	14.2	7.9	15.3	13.2	12.9
12009	37,340	2	Brevard	1,015.2	596,849	113	587.9	76.2	11.1	0.8	3.7	10.7	4.7	13.6	7.2	11.4	10.4	12.7
12011	33,100	1	Broward	1,203.1	1,951,260	17	1,621.9	36.8	29.4	0.4	4.7	30.4	5.8	15.4	7.9	13.5	13.4	14.1
12013		6	Calhoun................	567.3	14,587	2,121	25.7	79.2	13.9	2.1	1.2	5.7	4.9	15.1	7.4	14.5	13.2	13.8
12015	39,460	3	Charlotte..............	681.1	184,998	356	271.6	85.3	6.2	0.7	1.9	7.4	3.0	8.9	5.1	7.8	7.3	10.5
12017	26,140	3	Citrus.................	581.9	147,929	446	254.2	89.1	3.5	0.9	2.1	5.9	3.8	11.1	5.2	8.6	7.7	11.0
12019	27,260	1	Clay...................	604.8	216,072	312	357.3	74.6	12.5	1.0	4.5	10.3	5.5	17.7	7.9	12.6	12.0	13.8
12021	34,940	2	Collier	1,996.3	378,488	186	189.6	63.2	7.2	0.4	2.0	28.2	4.4	12.7	6.6	9.5	9.7	11.5
12023	29,380	4	Columbia...............	797.6	70,503	769	88.4	73.9	19.0	1.1	1.5	6.4	5.9	15.8	8.7	13.1	11.7	12.1
12027	11,580	6	DeSoto.................	636.7	37,489	1,238	58.9	55.3	12.5	0.5	0.7	31.9	5.0	13.9	8.9	14.3	12.1	11.6
12029		6	Dixie..................	705.1	16,700	1,998	23.7	85.4	10.2	1.3	0.6	4.0	4.6	13.6	6.6	11.9	11.9	12.5
12031	27,260	1	Duval..................	762.9	950,181	52	1,245.5	54.7	30.8	0.8	6.2	10.1	6.8	15.8	8.8	16.6	12.7	12.5
12033	37,860	2	Escambia	657.0	315,534	222	480.3	66.9	24.1	1.6	5.0	5.8	6.0	14.8	11.4	14.7	11.0	11.6
12035	19,660	2	Flagler	485.1	112,067	543	231.0	76.5	10.9	0.8	3.3	10.5	3.9	13.0	6.1	9.0	9.6	12.0
12037		6	Franklin	545.1	11,736	2,310	21.5	81.2	13.4	1.1	0.7	5.6	4.5	11.6	6.4	14.6	11.3	12.7
12039	45,220	2	Gadsden	516.3	45,894	1,052	88.9	33.3	55.6	0.5	1.0	10.5	6.0	16.0	8.1	11.9	12.5	13.0
12041	23,540	2	Gilchrist	349.7	18,256	1,912	52.2	87.4	6.1	1.1	0.9	6.1	5.7	14.6	11.7	10.4	10.2	12.5
12043		6	Glades.................	806.6	13,724	2,184	17.0	61.1	13.5	4.5	0.9	21.1	3.1	12.0	6.6	13.0	12.3	12.5
12045	37,460	3	Gulf	553.4	16,164	2,031	29.2	77.5	17.7	1.3	0.8	4.6	4.0	11.5	7.3	14.4	12.5	14.2
12047		6	Hamilton	513.8	14,310	2,140	27.9	56.6	33.0	1.1	1.2	9.8	5.5	13.5	11.4	13.9	11.5	12.9
12049	48,100	6	Hardee.................	637.6	27,245	1,518	42.7	47.8	7.3	0.7	1.4	44.0	6.9	19.3	10.0	13.4	11.3	12.0
12051	17,500	4	Hendry	1,156.2	41,556	1,142	35.9	32.7	11.1	1.5	1.1	54.3	7.4	19.0	9.3	14.5	12.4	12.7
12053	45,300	1	Hernando	472.8	190,865	348	403.7	78.8	6.0	0.8	1.9	14.2	4.6	13.8	6.7	10.5	10.1	12.3
12055	42,700	3	Highlands	1,017.3	105,424	574	103.6	67.6	10.3	0.9	1.8	20.8	4.6	12.5	6.1	9.7	8.7	9.8
12057	45,300	1	Hillsborough	1,021.8	1,436,888	27	1,406.2	50.0	17.1	0.6	5.2	29.2	6.2	16.4	9.0	15.3	13.6	13.3
12059		6	Holmes	478.9	19,477	1,852	40.7	88.6	7.4	2.1	1.1	3.0	5.5	14.7	8.3	12.7	11.8	13.4
12061	42,680	3	Indian River...........	502.8	157,413	422	313.1	76.4	9.7	0.6	2.0	12.7	4.1	12.0	6.2	9.2	8.8	11.1
12063		6	Jackson................	918.2	48,305	1,017	52.6	66.8	27.6	1.3	1.3	5.0	5.0	13.5	8.3	13.5	13.8	13.0
12065	45,220	2	Jefferson	598.1	14,288	2,145	23.9	61.4	34.4	0.8	0.9	3.9	4.5	12.5	6.3	11.7	11.5	14.2
12067		9	Lafayette	543.4	8,732	2,525	16.1	72.0	13.8	0.7	0.6	14.2	4.2	16.0	10.2	14.3	14.5	13.4
12069	36,740	1	Lake	950.7	356,495	198	375.0	70.8	11.2	0.8	2.8	16.0	4.9	14.2	6.6	11.0	10.8	12.1
12071	15,980	2	Lee	782.0	754,610	87	965.0	67.9	8.8	0.5	2.2	21.9	4.6	13.0	6.9	11.0	10.3	11.7
12073	45,220	2	Leon	666.8	292,502	236	438.7	58.1	32.2	0.7	4.6	6.6	5.2	13.4	21.5	14.5	11.0	10.2
12075		6	Levy	1,118.2	40,770	1,157	36.5	81.1	9.7	1.2	1.0	8.6	5.1	14.4	6.4	11.2	9.9	12.3
12077		8	Liberty	835.6	8,457	2,547	10.1	72.6	19.9	1.3	0.5	7.2	4.7	13.2	8.2	17.0	15.6	14.5
12079		6	Madison	696.5	18,529	1,898	26.6	56.0	38.0	1.0	0.7	5.6	5.1	13.8	7.3	14.0	12.0	13.2
12081	35,840	2	Manatee	743.1	394,855	178	531.4	72.3	9.3	0.6	2.7	16.7	4.7	13.6	6.5	10.6	10.3	12.2
12083	36,100	2	Marion	1,588.4	359,977	197	226.6	71.5	13.4	0.8	2.3	13.6	4.9	13.6	6.6	10.9	9.8	11.4
12085	38,940	2	Martin	543.8	160,912	411	295.9	79.1	5.8	0.5	1.9	13.9	4.1	12.3	6.1	9.4	9.3	12.3
12086	33,100	1	Miami-Dade.............	1,898.8	2,761,581	7	1,454.4	13.5	16.0	0.2	2.0	69.1	5.8	14.4	8.4	14.3	13.7	14.7
12087	28,580	4	Monroe.................	983.0	75,027	738	76.3	67.0	6.7	0.9	1.9	24.9	4.6	10.5	6.2	12.4	12.2	14.5
12089	27,260	1	Nassau	648.7	85,832	672	132.3	88.3	6.4	0.8	1.6	4.5	5.1	14.7	6.6	11.5	11.3	13.2
12091	18,880	3	Okaloosa...............	930.2	207,269	323	222.8	76.5	11.2	1.3	5.4	9.7	6.6	15.7	8.9	16.1	12.1	11.3
12093	36,380	4	Okeechobee.............	768.9	41,537	1,144	54.0	63.9	9.1	1.2	1.3	25.5	6.0	15.3	7.8	13.3	12.3	12.2
12095	36,740	1	Orange	902.5	1,380,645	29	1,529.8	41.2	21.3	0.6	6.5	32.3	6.1	16.1	10.4	16.9	14.3	13.1
12097	36,740	1	Osceola	1,327.7	367,990	193	277.2	31.9	10.4	0.5	3.3	55.3	6.2	18.2	9.2	14.6	14.6	13.2
12099	33,100	1	Palm Beach.............	1,965.6	1,485,941	25	756.0	55.2	19.4	0.4	3.6	22.9	5.1	14.0	7.5	12.0	11.5	12.8
12101	45,300	1	Pasco	746.7	539,630	129	722.7	75.6	6.5	0.7	3.4	15.8	5.2	15.1	7.0	11.1	12.1	13.4
12103	45,300	1	Pinellas	273.7	975,280	49	3,563.3	75.5	11.4	0.7	4.4	10.0	4.3	11.8	6.6	12.1	10.9	13.3
12105	29,460	2	Polk	1,797.2	708,009	92	394.0	59.4	15.6	0.7	2.4	23.6	5.8	16.3	8.4	13.1	11.9	12.6

1. CBSA = Core Based Statistical Area. See Appendix A for explanation. See Appendix B for list of metropolitan areas with component counties.
Service of USDA Rural-Urban Continuum Codes. See Appendix A for definition.   3. Dry land or land partially or temporarily covered by water.

2. County type code from the Economic Research
4. May be of any race.

Table B. States and Counties — **Population and Households**

STATE County	Population, 2018 (cont.) Age (percent) (cont.) 55 to 64 years	65 to 74 years	75 years and over	Percent female	Population change, 2000-2018 Total persons 2000	2010	Percent change 2000-2010	2010-2018	Components of change, 2010-2018 Births	Deaths	Net Migration	Households, 2013-2017 Number	Persons per household	Family house-holds	Female family house-holder[1]	One person
	16	17	18	19	20	21	22	23	24	25	26	27	28	29	30	31
CONNECTICUT—Cont'd																
Tolland	13.9	9.1	6.7	49.9	136,364	152,744	12.0	-1.2	9,559	8,435	-3,019	54,878	2.47	65.1	8.9	25.2
Windham	15.2	9.8	6.8	50.5	109,091	118,381	8.5	-1.1	9,359	8,416	-2,320	44,529	2.50	66.5	12.3	27.1
DELAWARE	14.0	11.2	7.5	51.6	783,600	897,934	14.6	7.7	90,864	69,108	47,568	352,357	2.61	66.8	13.5	26.9
Kent	12.8	10.0	7.1	51.8	126,697	162,349	28.1	10.0	18,200	12,606	10,595	63,381	2.65	69.8	16.2	24.2
New Castle	13.5	9.1	6.5	51.5	500,265	538,479	7.6	3.9	54,040	36,988	4,279	202,654	2.65	65.0	13.6	28.2
Sussex	16.3	17.2	10.5	51.7	156,638	197,106	25.8	16.3	18,624	19,514	32,694	86,322	2.46	68.9	11.3	25.6
DISTRICT OF COLUMBIA	10.0	7.0	5.2	52.6	572,059	601,766	5.2	16.7	78,391	40,740	61,805	277,985	2.28	43.7	14.7	43.6
District of Columbia	10.0	7.0	5.2	52.6	572,059	601,766	5.2	16.7	78,391	40,740	61,805	277,985	2.28	43.7	14.7	43.6
FLORIDA	13.4	11.3	9.2	51.1	15,982,378	18,804,580	17.7	13.3	1,801,326	1,549,217	2,232,735	7,510,882	2.64	64.5	13.1	28.7
Alachua	10.8	8.4	5.6	51.7	217,955	247,337	13.5	9.1	23,654	15,148	14,179	97,485	2.50	52.3	10.8	34.9
Baker	12.4	8.5	5.6	47.4	22,259	27,115	21.8	4.6	2,807	1,966	401	8,299	3.02	75.9	12.3	19.2
Bay	14.2	9.9	7.2	50.4	148,217	168,852	13.9	9.7	18,769	15,002	12,584	68,667	2.59	64.9	12.1	28.7
Bradford	13.3	9.9	7.9	44.8	26,088	28,520	9.3	-2.8	2,507	2,479	-885	8,980	2.61	64.3	15.5	30.0
Brevard	16.4	12.8	10.9	51.1	476,230	543,372	14.1	9.8	42,504	55,817	66,747	227,223	2.47	63.9	11.5	30.0
Broward	13.4	9.3	7.3	51.3	1,623,018	1,748,146	7.7	11.6	179,562	122,233	146,904	675,828	2.77	64.2	15.6	28.9
Calhoun	13.0	10.1	7.9	45.4	13,017	14,625	12.4	-0.3	1,157	1,311	125	4,581	2.72	66.1	11.6	30.8
Charlotte	17.2	21.4	18.8	51.2	141,627	159,964	12.9	15.6	8,429	20,351	36,551	74,884	2.26	63.8	7.2	29.9
Citrus	16.3	19.5	16.8	51.5	118,085	141,229	19.6	4.7	8,626	20,255	18,293	62,488	2.22	63.3	9.8	31.8
Clay	13.8	9.9	5.9	50.7	140,814	190,865	35.5	13.2	17,655	13,439	21,021	71,939	2.81	75.9	13.0	19.7
Collier	13.4	15.8	16.4	50.7	251,377	321,521	27.9	17.7	26,632	26,056	56,188	138,131	2.55	67.6	9.0	26.9
Columbia	13.9	10.9	7.9	48.4	56,513	67,526	19.5	4.4	6,598	6,450	2,840	24,722	2.57	63.0	12.9	32.0
DeSoto	11.9	11.4	10.8	43.4	32,209	34,862	8.2	7.5	3,142	2,578	2,067	11,744	2.73	68.5	12.0	26.5
Dixie	15.3	13.7	10.0	44.6	13,827	16,422	18.8	1.7	1,267	1,769	777	6,431	2.30	65.7	12.1	26.6
Duval	12.8	8.6	5.5	51.5	778,879	864,267	11.0	9.9	105,198	64,255	45,365	347,783	2.57	62.2	15.6	30.6
Escambia	13.6	9.9	6.9	50.5	294,410	297,620	1.1	6.0	32,099	26,658	12,577	117,836	2.47	59.2	12.8	32.6
Flagler	15.7	17.8	12.9	51.9	49,832	95,703	92.1	17.1	6,671	9,884	19,384	39,433	2.65	69.7	9.9	23.9
Franklin	14.9	14.8	9.2	44.2	11,057	11,549	4.4	1.6	849	1,058	389	4,327	2.30	64.1	9.9	30.4
Gadsden	14.5	10.8	7.0	52.5	45,087	47,744	5.9	-3.9	4,624	3,790	-2,713	17,310	2.44	67.9	22.4	28.1
Gilchrist	14.4	11.3	9.2	48.4	14,437	16,941	17.3	7.8	1,565	1,511	1,260	6,399	2.48	68.4	11.8	27.8
Glades	13.1	14.2	13.1	43.8	10,576	12,881	21.8	6.5	563	904	1,171	4,297	2.74	65.3	9.9	29.8
Gulf	14.6	13.1	8.5	41.5	13,332	15,861	19.0	1.9	1,007	1,429	718	5,295	2.58	69.5	13.6	26.6
Hamilton	13.4	10.9	7.1	42.1	13,327	14,799	11.0	-3.3	1,293	1,120	-700	4,551	2.39	70.4	18.7	24.4
Hardee	10.5	9.2	7.4	47.2	26,938	27,731	2.9	-1.8	3,200	1,707	-2,004	7,718	3.26	74.2	14.9	22.1
Hendry	11.0	7.7	6.0	46.7	36,210	39,143	8.1	6.2	4,858	2,335	-207	12,098	3.07	69.2	19.5	24.6
Hernando	14.6	14.7	12.7	51.8	130,802	172,777	32.1	10.5	12,543	21,317	26,739	72,234	2.45	67.5	11.7	26.6
Highlands	13.4	16.6	18.7	51.1	87,366	98,786	13.1	6.7	7,488	12,394	11,590	41,350	2.38	64.1	9.3	31.0
Hillsborough	12.0	8.5	5.8	51.1	998,948	1,229,178	23.0	16.9	139,185	83,137	150,615	505,845	2.63	63.5	14.0	28.6
Holmes	13.8	11.0	8.9	46.9	18,564	19,924	7.3	-2.2	1,635	2,086	14	7,019	2.51	66.0	12.6	30.0
Indian River	15.6	17.3	15.8	52.1	112,947	138,028	22.2	14.0	10,375	15,786	24,647	57,911	2.53	63.2	7.8	31.4
Jackson	13.3	10.9	8.6	44.9	46,755	49,761	6.4	-2.9	4,125	4,789	-785	17,041	2.39	65.7	15.4	30.7
Jefferson	15.8	14.2	9.3	47.6	12,902	14,759	14.4	-3.2	1,058	1,295	-247	5,702	2.03	66.1	14.6	30.7
Lafayette	11.2	9.1	6.9	42.9	7,022	8,870	26.3	-1.6	607	613	-147	2,193	3.24	72.0	14.0	24.2
Lake	13.7	14.4	12.3	51.6	210,528	297,052	41.1	20.0	25,923	31,343	64,265	127,441	2.53	68.0	10.3	26.8
Lee	14.1	15.5	13.1	51.1	440,888	618,754	40.3	22.0	53,688	54,928	135,696	264,325	2.61	65.9	10.2	28.0
Leon	10.8	8.3	5.0	52.6	239,452	275,484	15.0	6.2	25,040	14,707	6,602	112,373	2.42	55.1	12.8	30.2
Levy	15.9	14.6	10.1	51.2	34,450	40,801	18.4	-0.1	3,263	4,408	1,115	15,806	2.49	65.3	13.5	29.2
Liberty	12.3	8.6	5.9	38.3	7,021	8,365	19.1	1.1	659	517	-61	2,325	2.96	69.6	8.0	27.3
Madison	14.1	12.1	8.4	47.1	18,733	19,230	2.7	-3.6	1,663	1,803	-560	6,743	2.44	65.3	14.0	32.3
Manatee	14.8	14.8	12.6	51.7	264,002	322,879	22.3	22.3	28,260	30,793	73,688	140,255	2.56	65.8	10.4	28.2
Marion	13.7	15.6	13.4	52.0	258,916	331,299	28.0	8.7	28,107	39,023	39,511	134,747	2.48	64.8	12.4	29.7
Martin	15.7	15.1	15.7	50.6	126,731	146,852	15.9	9.6	10,086	15,317	19,194	63,497	2.39	61.0	8.0	33.3
Miami-Dade	12.5	8.7	7.5	51.5	2,253,362	2,498,013	10.9	10.6	260,128	160,080	162,409	858,289	3.09	68.2	18.2	26.3
Monroe	16.6	14.1	8.9	48.0	79,589	73,090	-8.2	2.7	5,981	5,783	1,712	30,198	2.47	57.5	6.9	32.4
Nassau	15.5	13.9	8.3	50.8	57,663	73,310	27.1	17.1	6,444	6,379	12,382	30,454	2.55	72.8	10.0	22.7
Okaloosa	13.4	9.4	6.6	49.3	170,498	180,825	6.1	14.6	22,375	13,829	17,728	76,574	2.51	65.4	10.8	28.3
Okeechobee	12.9	10.6	9.2	46.3	35,910	39,996	11.4	3.9	4,315	3,524	755	13,333	2.79	68.0	12.6	26.9
Orange	11.2	7.2	4.7	50.9	896,344	1,145,954	27.8	20.5	132,723	61,847	163,402	451,960	2.78	65.2	15.3	25.7
Osceola	10.8	8.0	5.2	50.7	172,493	268,683	55.8	37.0	33,601	16,539	81,903	96,250	3.36	75.3	17.0	19.1
Palm Beach	13.3	11.6	12.3	51.5	1,131,184	1,320,135	16.7	12.6	118,679	115,982	163,082	543,591	2.59	62.4	11.8	31.0
Pasco	13.5	12.4	10.2	51.4	344,765	464,703	34.8	16.1	40,555	47,828	81,676	195,818	2.51	66.0	12.1	27.5
Pinellas	16.1	13.3	11.5	52.0	921,482	916,804	-0.5	6.4	69,574	96,406	85,133	406,871	2.29	55.5	10.7	36.9
Polk	12.3	11.3	8.9	51.0	483,924	602,098	24.4	17.6	61,773	52,726	96,548	226,604	2.82	68.8	13.5	25.5

1. No spouse present.

Table B. States and Counties — Population, Vital Statistics, Health, and Crime

STATE County	Persons in group quarters, 2018	Daytime Population, 2013-2017		Births, 2018		Deaths, 2018		Persons under 65 with no health insurance, 2016		Medicare, 2018			Serious crimes known to police[2], 2016 Total	
		Number	Employment/ residence ratio	Total	Rate[1]	Number	Rate[1]	Number	Percent	Total beneficiaries	Enrolled in Original Medicare	Enrolled in Medicare Advantage	Number	Rate[3]
	32	33	34	35	36	37	38	39	40	41	42	43	44	45
CONNECTICUT—Cont'd														
Tolland	15,020	125,187	0.66	1,156	7.7	1,060	7.0	4,116	3.6	26,172	13,936	12,236	NA	NA
Windham	4,693	101,859	0.74	1,071	9.2	1,052	9.0	4,819	5.1	22,931	14,289	8,642	NA	NA
DELAWARE	24,960	946,818	1.01	10,709	11.1	9,307	9.6	51,494	6.7	200,970	173,060	27,910	31,178	3,275
Kent	4,643	164,703	0.89	2,135	12.0	1,733	9.7	10,761	7.6	35,284	30,754	4,530	5,232	2,988
New Castle	17,474	575,855	1.08	6,308	11.3	4,813	8.6	26,342	5.7	98,195	81,807	16,388	19,714	3,530
Sussex	2,843	206,260	0.90	2,266	9.9	2,761	12.0	14,391	8.9	67,490	60,498	6,992	6,279	2,873
DISTRICT OF COLUMBIA	39,629	1,146,330	2.34	9,788	13.9	5,684	8.1	23,274	4.1	92,429	75,921	16,508	40,930	6,009
District of Columbia	39,629	1,146,330	2.34	9,788	13.9	5,684	8.1	23,274	4.1	92,428	75,920	16,508	40,613	5,962
FLORIDA	430,361	20,227,289	0.99	221,488	10.4	208,165	9.8	2,478,194	15.4	4,410,311	2,457,116	1,953,195	642,512	3,117
Alachua	14,487	275,994	1.14	2,813	10.4	2,001	7.4	26,422	12.2	42,931	32,618	10,313	9,210	3,502
Baker	2,724	24,096	0.66	320	11.3	262	9.2	2,438	11.2	4,738	3,332	1,406	434	1,576
Bay	3,841	182,406	1.03	2,253	12.2	1,996	10.8	21,705	14.5	37,349	27,979	9,370	7,464	4,044
Bradford	3,930	24,422	0.74	292	10.5	351	12.7	2,247	11.9	5,564	3,911	1,653	479	1,796
Brevard	6,717	558,564	0.96	5,230	8.8	7,377	12.4	57,971	13.2	150,933	91,414	59,519	17,727	3,087
Broward	16,295	1,810,066	0.91	21,943	11.2	16,035	8.2	242,930	15.3	315,011	139,897	175,114	65,701	3,404
Calhoun	1,887	13,124	0.71	127	8.7	156	10.7	1,453	14.3	2,814	1,831	983	114	818
Charlotte	3,171	165,377	0.86	1,031	5.6	2,802	15.1	16,698	15.6	66,335	42,548	23,787	3,062	1,737
Citrus	2,250	135,146	0.86	1,072	7.2	2,599	17.6	13,377	14.8	57,065	35,221	21,844	2,317	1,640
Clay	1,250	164,774	0.58	2,199	10.2	1,820	8.4	19,204	10.9	40,753	29,158	11,595	4,160	2,010
Collier	4,550	368,141	1.08	3,201	8.5	3,772	10.0	53,731	21.6	96,246	72,625	23,621	5,458	1,494
Columbia	4,988	68,916	1.02	784	11.1	845	12.0	6,595	12.6	15,435	10,973	4,462	2,245	3,271
DeSoto	3,575	36,789	1.09	380	10.1	344	9.2	5,782	23.0	7,049	4,798	2,251	974	2,733
Dixie	1,761	15,329	0.79	147	8.8	228	13.7	1,657	15.2	4,016	2,745	1,271	409	2,822
Duval	20,814	993,203	1.19	13,068	13.8	8,701	9.2	100,346	12.8	158,847	98,804	60,043	39,605	4,284
Escambia	17,839	328,783	1.13	3,888	12.3	3,453	10.9	28,046	11.4	68,414	46,059	22,355	12,380	3,939
Flagler	684	93,748	0.71	796	7.1	1,319	11.8	11,600	15.3	35,869	20,357	15,512	2,101	1,953
Franklin	1,464	11,883	1.05	96	8.2	100	8.5	1,145	15.2	2,934	1,958	976	164	1,386
Gadsden	3,157	41,362	0.71	541	11.8	479	10.4	5,469	15.5	10,048	4,543	5,505	601	1,581
Gilchrist	1,191	14,332	0.55	194	10.6	203	11.1	2,033	15.6	3,914	2,838	1,076	NA	NA
Glades	1,462	11,949	0.69	67	4.9	120	8.7	2,199	25.7	2,479	1,587	892	157	1,134
Gulf	2,983	15,199	0.86	119	7.4	184	11.4	1,295	13.4	3,765	2,852	913	269	1,690
Hamilton	2,645	13,990	0.93	156	10.9	140	9.8	1,337	14.4	2,845	2,089	756	311	2,182
Hardee	1,627	26,322	0.90	359	13.2	202	7.4	4,470	21.1	4,383	2,877	1,506	602	2,188
Hendry	696	38,557	0.97	569	13.7	314	7.6	8,284	24.9	5,730	3,895	1,835	1,069	2,726
Hernando	1,831	164,992	0.77	1,588	8.3	2,797	14.7	18,946	14.5	58,054	26,392	31,662	3,889	2,162
Highlands	1,734	98,378	0.94	906	8.6	1,637	15.5	11,995	18.5	32,497	20,743	11,754	2,994	2,998
Hillsborough	22,977	1,409,148	1.09	17,223	12.0	11,369	7.9	163,713	14.0	228,495	115,383	113,112	28,156	2,046
Holmes	1,776	17,099	0.62	202	10.4	229	11.8	2,204	15.8	4,737	3,562	1,175	305	1,843
Indian River	1,327	147,671	0.99	1,243	7.9	2,088	13.3	15,952	15.6	50,669	36,735	13,934	3,121	2,077
Jackson	7,784	47,898	0.96	507	10.5	612	12.7	4,434	14.0	11,213	8,326	2,887	1,043	2,275
Jefferson	1,284	11,971	0.56	123	8.6	159	11.1	1,295	13.3	3,512	1,823	1,689	294	2,103
Lafayette	1,481	7,656	0.58	65	7.4	79	9.0	1,145	20.3	1,064	812	252	73	844
Lake	3,869	291,717	0.73	3,301	9.3	4,367	12.4	34,599	14.2	99,911	61,132	38,779	7,500	2,356
Lee	8,484	684,185	0.94	6,692	8.9	7,875	10.4	88,839	17.2	186,099	121,317	64,782	14,199	1,969
Leon	15,162	305,249	1.14	3,027	10.3	1,946	6.7	24,285	10.2	43,430	22,431	20,999	16,269	5,631
Levy	332	34,942	0.66	400	9.8	551	13.5	5,183	17.2	11,501	7,698	3,803	1,175	3,010
Liberty	2,081	7,970	0.84	84	9.9	70	8.3	754	14.5	1,330	750	580	9	108
Madison	2,043	17,640	0.85	180	9.7	209	11.3	1,863	14.5	4,293	2,965	1,328	596	3,260
Manatee	4,810	338,770	0.83	3,453	8.7	4,178	10.6	40,663	14.8	97,080	61,465	35,615	9,527	2,556
Marion	9,018	334,765	0.92	3,449	9.6	5,014	13.9	38,184	15.9	111,618	61,555	50,063	9,097	2,626
Martin	4,205	157,683	1.03	1,256	7.8	2,035	12.6	17,598	16.3	44,706	31,812	12,894	2,865	1,807
Miami-Dade	42,228	2,776,859	1.06	31,268	11.3	21,861	7.9	433,868	19.4	457,618	148,960	308,658	111,149	4,061
Monroe	1,976	80,517	1.09	707	9.4	754	10.0	11,798	19.7	16,530	14,377	2,153	2,360	3,006
Nassau	543	65,712	0.63	831	9.7	945	11.0	7,436	11.8	20,797	14,559	6,238	1,371	1,722
Okaloosa	4,719	208,171	1.11	2,693	13.0	1,882	9.1	20,013	12.1	39,407	32,060	7,347	5,714	2,828
Okeechobee	2,989	39,761	0.97	496	11.9	471	11.3	6,527	21.8	8,208	4,986	3,222	1,428	3,621
Orange	35,267	1,449,427	1.25	16,625	12.0	8,545	6.2	169,689	14.9	181,214	92,866	88,348	55,329	4,190
Osceola	3,250	284,265	0.71	4,439	12.1	2,371	6.4	43,003	15.0	57,688	22,936	34,752	9,573	2,843
Palm Beach	21,625	1,449,692	1.04	14,776	9.9	15,455	10.4	177,174	16.3	315,761	194,507	121,254	48,613	3,361
Pasco	5,812	432,685	0.67	5,182	9.6	6,264	11.6	57,994	14.8	128,524	57,421	71,103	12,204	2,413
Pinellas	19,849	961,637	1.03	8,227	8.4	12,679	13.0	100,659	13.9	239,290	123,426	115,864	36,536	3,812
Polk	13,542	627,915	0.91	7,886	11.1	7,042	9.9	81,205	15.6	150,956	72,421	78,535	17,766	2,687

1. Per 1,000 estimated resident population.   2. Data for serious crimes have not been adjusted for underreporting; this may affect comparability between geographic areas and over time.   3. Per 100,000 population estimated by the FBI.

STATE County	Serious crimes known to police[2], 2016 (cont.)[1] Rate Violent	Property	Enrollment[3] Total	Percent private	High school graduate or less	Bachelor's degree or more	Total current spending (mil dol)	Current spending per student (dollars)	Per capita income[6]	Median income (dollars)	Percent with income of less than $50,000	Percent with income of $200,000 or more	Median household income (dollars)	All persons	Children under 18 years	Children 5 to 17 years in families
	46	47	48	49	50	51	52	53	54	55	56	57	58	59	60	61
CONNECTICUT—Cont'd																
Tolland................	NA	NA	48,305	9.3	33.0	39.7	357.7	17,696	37,830	81,312	30.1	9.5	75,571	7.4	6.5	5.9
Windham.............	NA	NA	29,328	10.1	44.4	24.4	276.2	17,544	29,993	62,553	39.8	3.5	62,606	11.5	15.6	15.4
DELAWARE........................	509	2,766	232,461	17.2	41.9	31.0	1,864.0	13,906	32,625	63,036	39.9	6.0	64,085	13	17.7	16.0
Kent.......................	473	2,515	47,229	15.1	45.7	23.5	333.0	12,738	27,420	57,647	43.6	3.3	57,112	13.2	20.2	19.0
New Castle............	570	2,961	144,240	19.6	38.7	35.7	1,124.1	14,487	34,541	68,336	37.4	7.5	66,839	13.4	15.6	14.4
Sussex..................	388	2,485	40,992	11.1	46.6	25.1	406.9	13,427	31,874	57,901	43.0	4.6	61,124	11.9	21.2	17.7
DISTRICT OF COLUMBIA...	1,206	4,803	166,054	42.0	27.3	56.6	1,621.3	20,037	50,832	77,649	35.7	15.4	80,153	16.6	26.2	26.0
District of Columbia.............	1,209	4,753	166,054	42.0	27.3	56.6	1,601.1	20,004	50,832	77,649	35.7	15.4	80,153	16.6	26.2	26.0
FLORIDA........................	430	2,687	4,707,573	17.5	41.4	28.5	24,366.7	8,838	28,774	50,883	49.1	4.8	52,582	14.1	20.6	19.6
Alachua..................	554	2,948	91,351	9.6	30.0	41.4	254.1	8,514	26,431	45,478	53.4	4.5	45,230	21.2	20.0	19.0
Baker......................	428	1,147	6,803	10.8	57.4	13.1	41.4	8,378	22,440	59,506	45.9	2.8	51,856	15.3	22.6	22.1
Bay........................	486	3,558	40,230	15.0	41.8	22.4	230.7	8,347	26,742	50,283	49.7	3.3	51,633	14.9	21.6	20.8
Bradford................	487	1,308	5,349	14.7	59.9	10.4	29.8	9,325	19,656	46,106	52.5	1.4	44,997	19.1	26.5	25.6
Brevard..................	500	2,587	121,680	17.0	36.8	28.4	601.8	8,326	29,405	51,536	48.3	3.9	52,596	12.4	18.8	18.3
Broward.................	387	3,017	478,405	21.0	38.6	31.5	2,331.4	8,704	30,109	54,895	45.8	5.9	56,702	13.1	18.0	17.4
Calhoun.................	215	603	3,248	5.5	63.0	9.6	20.8	9,159	15,927	36,237	66.8	0.7	37,612	21.1	30.2	28.2
Charlotte................	222	1,516	24,729	14.5	44.3	22.4	151.0	9,357	29,243	46,511	53.7	2.8	51,583	10.8	18.3	17.0
Citrus....................	239	1,401	21,815	13.6	50.4	17.8	132.2	8,740	25,034	40,574	60.2	1.9	43,147	14.4	27.1	25.4
Clay......................	268	1,742	54,571	13.3	40.1	23.7	291.6	8,138	28,599	61,971	38.8	3.5	65,375	9.9	13.2	13.1
Collier...................	263	1,230	65,008	16.4	39.9	34.9	466.0	10,304	41,239	62,407	39.2	10.2	66,709	11.7	21.8	20.1
Columbia...............	543	2,727	14,311	14.9	49.1	16.4	83.8	8,231	22,855	43,504	55.8	2.2	42,097	16.5	24.6	23.4
DeSoto..................	457	2,276	6,639	6.7	69.9	11.5	48.0	10,108	17,892	35,435	65.4	1.5	37,342	26.1	37.2	36.7
Dixie.....................	552	2,270	2,898	17.6	64.8	9.1	19.2	9,119	19,342	35,910	69.5	1.4	38,355	24.4	34.0	32.9
Duval....................	622	3,661	225,958	20.4	38.5	28.7	1,114.1	8,657	28,593	51,296	48.6	4.2	52,105	15.1	23.0	21.7
Escambia...............	630	3,309	77,214	21.0	36.7	26.0	356.6	8,754	25,666	47,361	52.8	2.5	48,289	16.4	26.6	26.0
Flagler..................	240	1,713	20,290	11.5	41.6	23.6	107.8	8,430	25,741	51,049	48.8	2.3	52,713	12	22.2	20.6
Franklin.................	237	1,150	1,886	14.9	55.4	18.4	13.9	10,825	23,524	41,267	56.1	3.7	40,158	21.3	34.0	32.9
Gadsden................	268	1,312	11,588	17.2	56.6	16.3	58.9	9,911	19,252	39,830	61.6	1.1	38,084	23.1	37.6	39.3
Gilchrist.................	NA	NA	3,595	9.0	55.4	12.4	27.8	10,631	21,145	42,934	56.1	1.6	42,880	16.1	24.4	24.8
Glades...................	209	924	2,491	10.0	65.9	10.9	15.5	9,674	20,476	37,385	64.2	2.1	42,865	18.9	29.4	25.4
Gulf.......................	377	1,313	3,108	13.2	52.3	18.5	18.4	9,842	21,085	44,647	55.2	1.6	44,135	21.6	27.2	25.7
Hamilton................	253	1,930	2,691	15.5	65.7	10.2	18.4	10,507	16,109	36,209	63.5	2.5	35,262	24	39.2	37.5
Hardee..................	294	1,894	6,517	8.1	72.0	10.5	48.5	9,282	18,643	39,063	61.1	1.7	40,056	23.3	32.7	30.8
Hendry..................	393	2,333	10,231	7.1	67.9	8.4	63.0	8,882	18,426	37,966	60.7	1.8	38,361	23.9	34.7	34.8
Hernando...............	260	1,902	35,519	15.0	49.0	17.1	190.2	8,609	23,495	44,324	56.7	1.6	44,710	14	20.8	17.8
Highlands..............	327	2,671	16,894	9.5	52.7	17.1	111.1	9,058	23,020	36,374	64.4	1.4	37,445	19.8	34.0	33.1
Hillsborough..........	298	1,748	350,891	17.3	39.0	32.0	1,908.9	9,201	29,806	53,742	46.4	5.6	54,741	15.5	21.4	19.9
Holmes..................	387	1,457	4,061	6.5	62.9	11.5	29.5	8,839	18,402	37,474	62.7	1.4	40,657	21.2	30.5	28.3
Indian River...........	230	1,848	26,889	15.2	42.4	27.8	156.1	8,636	33,122	49,009	51.0	6.2	51,797	10.6	18.2	17.4
Jackson.................	334	1,942	10,208	17.4	56.0	14.0	60.2	8,837	18,126	36,944	63.7	1.1	41,524	18	24.0	24.5
Jefferson...............	765	1,338	2,432	23.6	52.0	21.2	11.4	12,787	22,452	47,599	51.7	1.4	48,163	17.7	28.6	27.6
Lafayette...............	150	694	1,963	9.1	64.6	14.0	10.9	8,777	21,955	41,512	56.1	3.7	41,549	22.7	29.3	25.6
Lake......................	304	2,052	64,290	16.0	44.6	22.4	342.4	8,124	25,991	49,734	50.2	2.5	51,429	12.6	20.2	19.2
Lee........................	355	1,614	138,913	12.9	43.5	27.2	796.1	8,909	30,233	52,052	47.5	4.7	54,198	11.8	20.4	18.2
Leon.....................	731	4,900	104,264	12.0	25.4	45.5	290.8	7,952	28,548	49,941	50.0	4.6	51,716	18	18.0	17.6
Levy......................	1,076	1,934	8,277	12.6	57.8	11.9	51.0	9,276	21,043	36,554	64.8	1.1	37,272	20.8	28.9	28.9
Liberty...................	24	84	1,766	3.9	69.1	11.1	14.9	10,426	16,937	36,741	62.6	1.7	41,308	23	28.2	27.1
Madison.................	946	2,313	3,625	13.0	56.3	12.5	26.5	10,168	17,192	31,816	67.7	1.2	37,226	28.3	47.3	45.3
Manatee................	477	2,080	71,537	16.1	41.7	29.1	407.4	8,507	30,477	53,408	46.7	4.6	55,189	10.8	17.0	16.6
Marion...................	339	2,288	66,303	16.2	50.2	19.4	362.3	8,522	23,598	41,964	58.1	2.2	43,772	16.2	26.3	25.8
Martin....................	234	1,573	29,581	15.3	35.7	32.3	166.9	8,739	38,021	55,588	45.3	7.4	58,344	10.9	16.7	15.6
Miami-Dade............	571	3,490	661,957	20.9	47.2	27.8	3,166.6	8,871	25,481	46,338	53.0	5.4	49,758	16.7	22.0	21.5
Monroe..................	358	2,648	13,085	17.9	36.6	31.8	96.8	11,415	39,176	63,030	39.8	8.1	63,009	11.8	18.0	18.0
Nassau..................	215	1,507	16,306	16.9	41.7	27.2	93.9	8,408	33,337	64,294	38.5	5.3	70,590	9.1	12.9	12.4
Okaloosa...............	395	2,433	46,781	11.8	33.6	29.8	275.1	9,046	30,775	59,955	41.1	4.4	60,798	10.9	16.4	15.8
Okeechobee...........	396	3,225	8,588	12.1	64.4	11.0	57.0	8,946	18,611	39,059	63.2	1.5	42,524	21.8	31.3	30.2
Orange..................	616	3,574	356,288	17.8	36.9	32.7	1,774.3	8,972	27,394	51,586	48.4	5.1	54,021	15.3	21.9	20.8
Osceola.................	439	2,404	84,707	14.7	46.2	19.0	482.2	8,129	20,165	47,343	52.5	2.0	49,284	14	21.4	19.8
Palm Beach............	452	2,909	320,157	19.3	36.9	34.8	1,754.7	9,283	36,303	57,256	44.0	8.0	60,059	11.8	16.8	15.4
Pasco....................	327	2,087	106,364	15.0	44.4	22.7	577.3	8,331	26,624	48,289	51.5	3.1	51,247	13	18.1	17.9
Pinellas.................	425	3,387	182,940	19.2	37.8	30.1	940.7	9,065	32,120	48,968	50.8	4.4	51,488	12.2	17.2	16.4
Polk......................	333	2,354	151,515	16.4	51.2	19.5	879.5	8,820	22,579	45,988	53.7	2.4	48,328	16.1	25.5	25.9

1. Data for serious crimes have not been adjusted for underreporting; this may affect comparability between geographic areas and over time.   2. Per 100,000 population estimated by the FBI.   3. All persons 3 years old and over enrolled in nursery school through college.   4. Persons 25 years old and over.   5. Elementary and secondary education expenditures.   6. Based on population estimated by the American Community Survey, 2013–2017.

Table B. States and Counties — **Personal Income and Earnings**

STATE County	Personal income, 2017										Earnings, 2017		
			Per capita[1]			Supplements to wages and salaries, employer contributions (mil dol)						Contributions for government social insurance (mil dol)	
	Total (mil dol)	Percent change 2016-2017	Dollars	Rank	Wages and salaries (mil dol)	Pension and insurance	Government social insurance	Proprietors' income (mil dol)	Dividends, interest, and rent (mil dol)	Personal transfer receipts (mil dol)	Total (mil dol)	From employee and self-employed	From employer
	62	63	64	65	66	67	68	69	70	71	72	73	74
CONNECTICUT—Cont'd													
Tolland	8,303	3.1	54,818	289	2,149	561	148	580	1,345	1,100	3,438	182	148
Windham	5,300	4.3	45,553	842	1,777	377	139	382	822	1,111	2,675	155	139
DELAWARE	47,782	4.1	49,925	X	25,740	4,391	1,860	3,521	8,816	9,941	35,513	2,123	1,860
Kent	7,127	4.7	40,304	1,501	3,197	720	247	405	1,176	1,810	4,569	272	247
New Castle	29,992	4.4	53,577	322	19,192	3,067	1,355	1,962	5,531	5,271	25,575	1,500	1,355
Sussex	10,663	2.7	47,324	684	3,351	605	258	1,154	2,108	2,860	5,369	351	258
DISTRICT OF COLUMBIA	55,510	4.7	79,792	X	72,782	13,934	5,314	8,617	10,004	6,659	100,647	5,095	5,314
District of Columbia	55,510	4.7	79,792	35	72,782	13,934	5,314	8,617	10,004	6,659	100,647	5,095	5,314
FLORIDA	1,000,624	5.0	47,701	X	445,019	61,742	30,234	59,165	272,474	197,602	596,160	38,888	30,234
Alachua	11,286	4.5	42,280	1,234	6,548	1,217	450	359	2,535	2,096	8,574	506	450
Baker	871	5.1	30,804	2,868	282	59	19	29	112	235	389	27	19
Bay	7,797	3.1	42,476	1,206	3,660	629	269	410	1,724	1,795	4,968	316	269
Bradford	884	4.5	32,685	2,658	274	53	19	21	134	260	367	27	19
Brevard	25,683	5.7	43,592	1,064	11,294	1,668	785	1,167	5,688	6,337	14,914	1,028	785
Broward	94,239	5.2	48,680	571	46,364	5,900	3,105	5,279	22,363	15,212	60,648	3,790	3,105
Calhoun	378	4.4	26,108	3,079	100	21	7	13	58	136	141	12	7
Charlotte	7,383	4.8	40,557	1,463	1,987	287	138	404	2,227	2,415	2,817	250	138
Citrus	5,444	4.4	37,379	1,974	1,341	213	93	300	1,349	2,120	1,947	192	93
Clay	8,996	5.9	42,386	1,217	2,192	331	152	370	1,589	1,886	3,044	223	152
Collier	32,750	4.4	87,829	22	7,465	900	500	1,812	18,513	3,516	10,677	732	500
Columbia	2,365	5.0	33,973	2,487	1,005	196	72	129	380	717	1,401	95	72
DeSoto	886	4.5	24,040	3,099	388	67	28	68	179	310	550	37	28
Dixie	441	5.5	26,467	3,069	106	22	8	19	81	179	155	14	8
Duval	41,595	5.4	44,347	979	30,462	4,270	2,133	2,252	8,133	8,182	39,116	2,347	2,133
Escambia	12,808	3.4	40,855	1,424	7,077	1,217	519	569	2,830	3,147	9,383	585	519
Flagler	4,801	5.4	43,444	1,085	913	148	64	236	1,265	1,310	1,360	127	64
Franklin	404	3.9	34,447	2,420	121	23	8	31	132	115	183	14	8
Gadsden	1,538	3.3	33,383	2,573	501	103	35	78	284	455	717	50	35
Gilchrist	590	6.7	33,266	2,586	129	26	9	56	82	171	221	15	9
Glades	311	1.8	22,617	3,104	92	18	7	16	58	100	133	10	7
Gulf	544	4.7	33,665	2,533	151	29	10	23	130	154	213	17	10
Hamilton	357	3.9	25,192	3,087	146	33	11	5	51	137	195	14	11
Hardee	755	1.7	27,559	3,045	294	56	22	69	121	212	441	26	22
Hendry	1,218	1.1	30,190	2,913	533	86	44	93	171	326	756	40	44
Hernando	6,746	4.8	36,161	2,180	1,719	273	121	230	1,262	2,401	2,344	215	121
Highlands	3,441	3.5	33,446	2,562	1,070	179	77	140	767	1,325	1,466	124	77
Hillsborough	62,976	3.9	44,709	938	40,772	5,502	2,750	3,261	11,234	11,506	52,285	3,188	2,750
Holmes	572	4.9	29,242	2,974	121	28	8	25	96	212	183	17	8
Indian River	11,312	5.0	73,274	57	2,414	325	165	578	5,343	1,844	3,481	264	165
Jackson	1,482	3.2	30,660	2,877	555	118	39	63	271	528	775	57	39
Jefferson	577	4.9	40,762	1,438	95	19	7	40	130	150	160	12	7
Lafayette	209	4.9	24,767	3,096	49	12	4	20	39	55	85	5	4
Lake	14,028	5.8	40,541	1,465	3,939	606	276	562	2,771	3,880	5,383	434	276
Lee	36,787	5.6	49,764	475	12,480	1,742	848	3,769	13,467	7,347	18,840	1,319	848
Leon	12,442	4.7	42,862	1,158	7,318	1,317	495	710	2,642	2,031	9,840	576	495
Levy	1,397	5.4	34,614	2,400	325	62	23	86	234	466	497	41	23
Liberty	192	3.5	23,311	3,102	76	17	5	8	35	60	106	7	5
Madison	562	4.4	30,470	2,887	155	35	11	29	116	191	230	18	11
Manatee	17,690	5.1	45,880	807	5,691	783	393	1,062	5,354	3,781	7,930	569	393
Marion	12,709	4.5	35,864	2,216	4,252	673	295	642	2,904	4,379	5,862	480	295
Martin	12,651	4.7	79,104	38	3,108	433	213	569	6,093	1,726	4,322	301	213
Miami-Dade	126,716	4.3	46,048	789	66,925	8,953	4,465	11,197	28,941	25,387	91,540	5,727	4,465
Monroe	6,417	4.2	83,328	31	1,953	276	137	370	3,381	685	2,737	173	137
Nassau	4,599	6.4	55,594	260	1,000	150	69	215	1,271	806	1,433	108	69
Okaloosa	9,628	4.9	47,433	670	5,249	1,023	418	542	2,708	1,877	7,232	415	418
Okeechobee	1,257	4.8	30,203	2,912	524	81	38	91	186	414	733	49	38
Orange	57,386	5.8	42,541	1,199	44,811	5,548	2,984	4,581	9,268	9,536	57,924	3,435	2,984
Osceola	11,303	6.9	32,096	2,741	3,843	540	267	542	1,334	2,729	5,192	363	267
Palm Beach	109,974	5.6	74,754	55	35,975	4,418	2,352	5,970	50,104	14,024	48,715	3,155	2,352
Pasco	20,453	5.4	38,911	1,735	4,997	765	348	855	3,169	5,421	6,965	568	348
Pinellas	49,143	4.1	50,630	425	22,955	3,197	1,548	2,218	12,121	10,667	29,917	1,987	1,548
Polk	23,487	4.9	34,213	2,458	10,173	1,537	693	1,082	4,554	6,603	13,486	945	693

1. Based on the resident population estimated as of July 1 of the year shown.

Table B. States and Counties — Earnings, Social Security, and Housing

STATE County	Earnings, 2017 (cont.) Percent by selected industries									Social Security beneficiaries, December 2017		Supplemental Security Income recipients, 2017	Housing units, 2018	
	Farm	Mining, quarrying, and extractions	Construction	Manufacturing	Information; professional, scientific, technical services	Retail trade	Finance, insurance, real estate, and leasing	Health care and social assistance	Government	Number	Rate[1]		Total	Percent change, 2010-2018
	75	76	77	78	79	80	81	82	83	84	85	86	87	88
CONNECTICUT—Cont'd														
Tolland	0.4	D	9	D	6.2	6.5	4.1	10.4	38.8	26,495	175	1,149	60,032	3.5
Windham	0.4	D	D	18.3	4.6	8	D	14.7	19.9	24,335	209	2,098	49,833	1.6
DELAWARE	1.2	D	6.5	5.8	11.7	5.8	16.8	13.8	15.4	206,939	215	16,927	438,693	8.1
Kent	2.4	D	6	D	D	7.4	3.1	12.4	36.9	37,540	212	3,479	73,093	11.8
New Castle	0.1	D	5.4	4.5	14.3	4.8	21.5	13.6	12.4	101,365	181	10,139	224,499	3.2
Sussex	5.2	D	11.7	D	D	9.4	6	16.1	11.6	68,035	302	3,309	141,101	14.7
DISTRICT OF COLUMBIA	0	0	D	D	27.7	1	5.4	5.6	37.9	82,253	119	26,573	319,531	7.7
District of Columbia	0	0	D	D	27.7	1	5.4	5.6	37.9	NA	NA	NA	319,531	7.7
FLORIDA	0.4	0.1	6.8	4.8	12.6	7.5	9.6	12.6	14.5	4,531,636	216	578,891	9,547,305	6.2
Alachua	0.3	D	3.7	3.6	8.1	5.7	6.3	17.9	37.1	44,365	166	6,542	118,968	5.5
Baker	1.7	0	6.1	1.5	2.1	8.2	D	9.5	38.3	5,265	186	630	10,090	4.2
Bay	0	0.1	6.8	5	8.5	8.8	6.1	13.9	25.9	41,270	225	4,819	104,314	4.7
Bradford	0.8	6.2	5.6	4.2	3.4	9.7	3.4	9.7	32.3	6,140	227	824	11,029	0.2
Brevard	0.2	0	5.9	17.8	11.3	7.1	4.7	13.3	15.7	160,285	272	11,898	280,398	3.9
Broward	0.1	0	6.9	3.5	14.7	8.1	9.8	10.2	13.7	319,595	165	45,759	826,899	2
Calhoun	0.5	D	9.1	0.4	3	6.9	2.1	22.8	35.3	3,170	219	577	6,028	0.5
Charlotte	1.9	0.3	8.4	1.7	8.7	12.1	6.8	21.6	14.1	68,380	376	2,779	105,172	4.5
Citrus	0.1	0.2	12.1	1.6	6.4	11.4	4.8	21.8	12.8	60,020	412	3,441	79,988	2.5
Clay	0.1	D	11.7	3.3	11.4	9.5	6.2	18.5	15.2	42,900	202	3,073	81,785	8.4
Collier	1	0.1	10.1	2.9	12.1	8.5	11.6	13.1	9.7	93,940	252	4,169	218,281	10.6
Columbia	1.2	D	3.5	11	4.2	9.3	4.7	13.4	26.6	16,770	241	2,664	29,081	1.6
DeSoto	8.8	0	6.3	4.1	1.9	6.5	2.4	11.7	18.6	7,525	204	1,042	15,254	4.6
Dixie	3	0.3	4.4	16.3	D	8.5	0.3	3.6	36.7	4,590	275	756	9,463	1.6
Duval	0	0.1	6.4	5.3	11.7	5.8	15.5	13	13.8	166,300	177	25,977	412,590	6.2
Escambia	0	0.1	5.4	4.8	8.7	6.8	9.7	16.3	25.5	72,830	232	10,143	142,471	4.2
Flagler	0.2	D	7.5	4.6	9.4	10.5	7.2	12.6	16.7	37,205	337	1,759	52,530	8.1
Franklin	0	0.1	7.9	D	5.7	8.9	8.2	D	30	3,075	262	361	8,755	1.1
Gadsden	5.1	2.1	10.5	7.8	D	5.3	1.4	3.8	33.9	11,060	240	2,546	20,658	5.9
Gilchrist	19.2	0.2	9.1	1.9	2.3	3.1	1.5	15.6	26.7	4,275	241	505	7,578	3.7
Glades	11.4	D	5.7	10.2	1.2	2.5	1.2	D	22.1	2,610	190	186	7,061	1.2
Gulf	0	0.1	7	1.9	8.4	8.6	6.5	D	32	4,040	250	372	9,695	6.5
Hamilton	0.3	0	D	D	D	5.7	D	4	31.3	3,160	223	609	5,822	0.8
Hardee	15.2	D	3.1	4.7	1.8	5.7	4.2	D	21.4	4,840	177	774	9,750	0.3
Hendry	20.8	0.1	5.1	3.6	D	6.4	2.4	4.6	18.8	6,255	155	1,462	14,851	2
Hernando	0.1	0.1	5.9	5.8	D	11.3	4.1	23.3	16	62,375	334	4,450	87,526	3.6
Highlands	5.4	0	4.4	2.7	3.8	10.7	3.9	23.4	16.9	34,400	334	2,870	55,759	0.7
Hillsborough	0.3	0	5.8	4	16.6	7.1	14.6	11.4	13	238,470	169	40,939	590,779	10.2
Holmes	1.6	D	9	2.5	D	6.6	3.5	D	42.3	5,510	282	892	8,692	0.6
Indian River	0.7	D	7.3	4.1	12.6	9.3	9.4	17.4	10.3	51,485	333	2,548	81,043	6.2
Jackson	-0.7	1.1	6.9	6.6	D	8.2	3.4	8.7	39	12,575	260	1,999	21,113	0.5
Jefferson	14	0.1	8.2	0.3	D	5.5	4.3	D	22.8	3,725	263	589	6,769	2.1
Lafayette	18.5	D	D	4	D	5.9	D	D	40.4	1,185	140	151	3,377	1.5
Lake	1.2	0.2	10.5	3.9	6.1	11.6	5.6	19.2	15.7	103,990	301	7,512	160,467	10.7
Lee	0.3	0.1	10	2.1	10.5	8.9	7.3	10	16.7	189,485	256	12,863	399,729	7.7
Leon	0.1	D	3.8	1.2	15	5.7	6.7	13.4	35.7	44,900	155	6,368	131,211	5.7
Levy	7.7	0.6	13.2	8.4	3.7	9.5	4.2	6.7	20.5	12,450	309	1,444	20,661	2.7
Liberty	0.2	0.1	2.7	21	D	D	D	12.8	40	1,500	182	288	3,428	2.1
Madison	2.6	D	2.2	11.7	D	7.4	5.2	11.9	30.4	4,645	252	891	8,632	1.8
Manatee	1.4	D	9.7	7.5	8.6	9	7.4	14.3	11	98,855	256	5,970	194,539	12.6
Marion	1	0.2	7.3	8.5	6.6	10.9	5.3	18.8	15.2	116,970	330	9,999	170,504	3.9
Martin	0.9	D	8.3	5.6	10.8	8.2	8.4	18.4	9.3	45,540	285	1,607	80,410	2.6
Miami-Dade	0.4	0.1	6.9	2.9	14.7	6.8	9.9	11.4	13.3	425,610	155	164,076	1,031,955	4.3
Monroe	0	0	7	0.8	7.6	8.6	7.1	6.3	22.5	17,295	225	1,297	53,455	1.3
Nassau	0.3	0	5	8	7.8	7.5	5.7	8.5	18.8	21,195	256	1,182	39,982	14.2
Okaloosa	0	0	4.6	3.4	12.7	6.8	5	7.5	41.7	42,095	207	3,387	97,945	6
Okeechobee	7.7	D	16	4.1	4.9	7.6	3.2	D	18.5	8,960	215	1,107	18,730	1.2
Orange	0.2	0	5.7	4.8	14	5.9	8.8	10.1	10.2	193,435	143	35,290	544,417	11.6
Osceola	0.6	0	8.1	1.7	4.6	10.4	4.3	15.3	16.5	63,610	181	10,865	153,495	19.8
Palm Beach	0.4	0.2	6.4	3.7	14.8	6.9	10.9	12.7	10.6	316,825	215	24,176	689,908	3.8
Pasco	0.3	0.1	8.7	3.2	7.1	13.3	4.9	20.1	16	136,805	260	12,301	246,921	7.9
Pinellas	0	0	5.3	9.4	12.7	7.4	9.7	15.1	11.2	246,840	254	21,601	510,090	1.3
Polk	0.6	0.6	6.1	9	5.2	8.2	7.7	14.2	13.2	161,690	236	22,069	299,421	6.5

1. Per 1,000 resident population estimated as of July 1 of the year shown.

STATE County	Housing units, 2013-2017								Civilian labor force, 2018				Civilian employment[6], 2013-2017		
	Occupied units										Unemployment			Percent	
			Owner-occupied			Renter-occupied									
				Median owner cost as a percent of income			Median rent as a percent of income[2]	Sub-standard units[4] (percent)		Percent change, 2017-2018				Management, business, science, and arts	Construction, production, and maintenance occupations
				With a mort-gage	Without a mort-gage[2]	Median rent[3]									
	Total	Percent	Median value[1]						Total		Total	Rate[5]	Total		
	89	90	91	92	93	94	95	96	97	98	99	100	101	102	103
CONNECTICUT—Cont'd															
Tolland	54,878	72.4	247,500	21.7	13.0	1,093	30.5	0.9	86,499	0.8	3,097	3.6	80,613	42.7	17.8
Windham	44,529	69.9	196,800	23.3	13.5	869	31	2	63,426	0.5	2,866	4.5	59,022	33.1	23.4
DELAWARE	352,357	71.3	238,600	21.7	10.4	1,076	29.7	1.9	482,465	1.2	18,128	3.8	441,513	39.8	18.9
Kent	63,381	69.6	205,800	22.7	10.4	1,030	31.4	2.2	78,124	0.8	3,239	4.1	78,078	33.5	23.7
New Castle	202,654	68.4	248,100	21.0	10.2	1,104	29.5	1.7	298,915	1	10,938	3.7	269,164	43.9	15.8
Sussex	86,322	79.2	242,900	22.7	10.6	992	28.9	2.3	105,426	1.9	3,951	3.7	94,271	33.3	23.9
DISTRICT OF COLUMBIA.	277,985	41.7	537,400	21.3	10.0	1,424	29.2	3.8	404,610	0.8	22,470	5.6	357,701	61.7	6.3
District of Columbia	277,985	41.7	537,400	21.3	10.0	1,424	29.2	3.8	404,610	0.8	22,470	5.6	357,701	61.7	6.3
FLORIDA	7,510,882	64.8	178,700	23.8	12.4	1,077	33.6	3.2	10,234,770	1.4	365,097	3.6	9,018,570	34.6	18.4
Alachua	97,485	53.6	167,000	21.2	10.6	916	36	2.3	137,339	1.1	4,493	3.3	120,466	46.1	11.4
Baker	8,299	77.6	121,100	19.5	10.0	755	25.9	3.8	11,869	1.6	402	3.4	10,567	29.9	24.4
Bay	68,667	62.4	166,400	22.9	10.7	966	31.2	2.1	89,251	0.8	3,548	4	80,334	32.0	20.7
Bradford	8,980	71.1	90,500	19.2	10.0	755	29	2.4	11,304	0.2	371	3.3	9,118	31.7	21.8
Brevard	227,223	72.0	162,400	22.6	11.4	971	31.8	1.6	276,558	2.6	9,746	3.5	239,195	38.4	17.9
Broward	675,828	62.3	223,400	26.7	15.2	1,271	35.9	4.1	1,036,212	1.1	34,919	3.4	930,561	35.6	17.0
Calhoun	4,581	83.5	80,000	26.8	10.0	607	24.5	2.6	5,082	1.9	209	4.1	4,698	23.9	27.6
Charlotte	74,884	78.2	165,200	25.5	12.5	936	34.4	1.8	70,953	1	2,845	4	59,033	29.0	19.8
Citrus	62,488	80.9	117,400	22.9	11.0	778	33.1	1.9	47,799	-0.4	2,485	5.2	45,294	28.2	23.1
Clay	71,939	74.4	165,300	21.2	10.2	1,088	28.6	2.1	106,276	1.7	3,487	3.3	91,705	33.5	21.6
Collier	138,131	72.1	316,200	25.0	12.7	1,178	32.5	4.6	177,351	2	6,096	3.4	150,802	30.6	21.1
Columbia	24,722	73.0	112,500	21.7	10.6	797	27.9	3.4	29,540	0.4	1,106	3.7	25,911	30.3	24.0
DeSoto	11,744	68.9	83,700	24.4	10.9	672	31.7	6	13,955	-0.9	536	3.8	12,667	15.2	45.1
Dixie	6,431	78.2	71,600	22.1	10.3	661	29.2	4.7	5,773	0.1	244	4.2	4,798	25.9	32.1
Duval	347,783	57.7	156,200	22.4	11.2	991	30.9	2.4	487,844	1.7	17,433	3.6	430,830	36.6	18.1
Escambia	117,836	60.9	126,700	21.7	10.9	928	30.5	1.2	145,298	1.9	5,147	3.5	134,161	32.6	18.0
Flagler	39,433	77.0	188,400	24.9	11.9	1,118	32.1	1.7	47,077	1.7	1,904	4	39,278	31.6	17.2
Franklin	4,327	73.5	135,300	25.7	10.9	719	25.8	3.1	4,840	2.7	167	3.5	4,305	29.8	28.7
Gadsden	17,310	70.2	101,300	23.3	10.0	684	31.2	3.7	18,500	1.6	846	4.6	16,338	31.2	22.8
Gilchrist	6,399	81.7	96,700	21.5	10.8	632	25.1	2.2	6,869	0.4	258	3.8	6,444	24.5	28.5
Glades	4,297	75.0	80,100	24.8	10.7	729	32.9	4.3	5,206	4.8	208	4	4,052	27.8	30.7
Gulf	5,295	74.7	151,400	23.0	12.3	908	29.2	1.8	6,122	1.5	270	4.4	5,896	29.4	21.1
Hamilton	4,551	73.7	73,500	23.5	10.8	576	30.4	3.9	4,296	-0.7	182	4.2	3,849	28.3	25.7
Hardee	7,718	68.5	81,200	20.6	10.8	675	27.4	9.2	8,789	-2.2	467	5.3	9,857	22.9	36.1
Hendry	12,098	65.4	79,700	23.1	10.0	746	25.6	8.9	15,599	-2.8	947	6.1	16,313	20.7	46.6
Hernando	72,234	77.8	120,600	23.1	11.1	933	33.1	1.7	70,465	1.3	3,185	4.5	63,962	29.6	20.8
Highlands	41,350	74.7	87,900	22.8	11.0	745	31.2	3.2	36,472	-0.1	1,756	4.8	31,980	29.3	22.6
Hillsborough	505,845	58.0	179,500	22.1	10.7	1,040	31.3	3.6	735,690	1.2	24,886	3.4	647,075	38.4	17.2
Holmes	7,019	78.3	92,400	23.9	10.2	656	36.8	2.3	6,983	1	277	4	6,391	27.9	27.9
Indian River	57,911	75.8	172,600	23.3	11.8	928	34	1.6	65,104	1.5	2,786	4.3	56,016	32.6	19.3
Jackson	17,041	70.1	94,900	21.9	11.6	650	29.7	3.7	17,542	1.1	696	4	16,193	29.1	20.7
Jefferson	5,702	77.4	131,700	24.9	11.6	809	32.9	2.7	5,582	1.2	209	3.7	4,922	40.8	16.1
Lafayette	2,193	81.2	101,400	16.3	11.4	645	28.1	5.5	2,847	-3.5	91	3.2	2,532	32.4	30.2
Lake	127,441	73.5	155,100	22.7	11.4	979	31.8	2.3	155,273	2.5	5,455	3.5	131,532	32.0	18.9
Lee	264,325	69.8	190,200	24.1	12.8	1,035	31.1	2.7	342,684	1.9	11,634	3.4	287,128	30.4	20.1
Leon	112,373	52.6	187,400	21.3	10.0	968	34.8	2.2	154,655	1.3	5,177	3.3	143,570	45.1	10.3
Levy	15,806	75.0	88,700	24.4	11.4	691	29.3	2.7	16,926	0.6	649	3.8	14,623	23.3	28.6
Liberty	2,325	75.3	62,400	20.9	10.0	578	20.5	3.2	2,643	0.5	100	3.8	2,466	24.8	26.6
Madison	6,743	75.7	87,200	23.9	13.7	654	33.9	4.7	7,348	-0.6	286	3.9	5,985	27.6	28.0
Manatee	140,255	71.4	197,200	22.9	12.0	1,057	33.3	2.6	177,777	1.4	6,025	3.4	150,640	33.1	19.3
Marion	134,747	75.3	119,200	23.1	11.4	839	30.2	2	135,746	1.2	5,825	4.3	120,343	28.5	20.2
Martin	63,497	76.6	233,000	24.1	13.5	1,043	30.9	2.1	74,159	2.6	2,596	3.5	64,614	36.9	16.3
Miami-Dade	858,289	52.2	242,800	28.1	14.6	1,195	39	6.5	1,383,302	0.6	53,279	3.9	1,272,735	31.7	19.7
Monroe	30,198	58.7	429,000	29.8	13.3	1,507	34.4	3.9	45,307	-1.1	1,187	2.6	39,876	30.8	19.1
Nassau	30,454	77.8	203,500	20.6	10.0	1,084	32	1.6	39,910	1.7	1,281	3.2	34,780	34.5	23.7
Okaloosa	76,574	63.3	198,700	21.9	10.5	1,060	30.1	2	96,270	1.7	2,835	2.9	85,823	35.5	17.8
Okeechobee	13,333	72.2	89,900	21.3	10.0	726	30.7	4.6	17,697	-3.8	660	3.7	14,085	21.3	34.5
Orange	451,960	54.5	192,400	23.4	11.4	1,109	33.5	3.2	750,160	2.6	23,857	3.2	642,687	36.3	16.5
Osceola	96,250	60.4	164,500	25.3	12.6	1,129	35.5	3.7	177,919	2.5	6,456	3.6	146,390	24.8	21.2
Palm Beach	543,591	68.6	242,500	25.2	14.5	1,264	35.5	3.5	731,004	0.9	26,049	3.6	655,496	36.0	16.3
Pasco	195,818	71.9	134,300	22.7	11.4	971	31.6	2	231,983	1.3	8,906	3.8	202,690	36.1	17.6
Pinellas	406,871	65.3	167,100	23.7	13.8	1,007	32.2	2	492,704	1.5	16,163	3.3	438,915	37.7	15.8
Polk	226,604	68.3	121,100	22.7	11.7	913	30.6	3.9	298,759	1.5	12,156	4.1	263,208	29.9	23.9

1. Specified owner-occupied units.   2. A value of 10.0 represents 10 percent or less; a value of 50.0 represents 50 percent or more.   3. Specified renter-occupied units.   4. Overcrowded or lacking complete plumbing facilities.   5. Percent of civilian labor force.   6. Civilian employed persons 16 years old and over.

Table B. States and Counties — **Nonfarm Employment and Agriculture**

STATE County	Private nonfarm establishments, employment and payroll, 2016									Agriculture, 2017			
		Employment						Annual payroll		Farms			Farm producers whose primary occupation is farming (percent)
											Percent with:		
	Number of establish-ments	Total	Health care and social assistance	Manufac-turing	Retail trade	Finance and insurance	Professional, scientific, and technical services	Total (mil dol)	Average per employee (dollars)	Number	Fewer than 50 acres	1000 acres or more	
	104	105	106	107	108	109	110	111	112	113	114	115	116
CONNECTICUT—Cont'd													
Tolland	2,458	28,239	6,338	3,313	4,967	670	1,238	1,118	39,588	520	70.6	0.8	34.4
Windham	2,057	30,696	7,083	5,572	5,223	681	562	1,211	39,436	646	63.3	0.6	38.4
DELAWARE	25,366	400,069	67,806	27,189	56,173	42,232	29,556	21,196	52,982	2,302	55.7	6.9	52.8
Kent	3,422	53,196	10,879	4,810	9,317	1,581	2,452	2,040	38,349	822	53.4	6.3	48.5
New Castle	16,056	272,403	45,065	12,441	33,234	37,768	23,916	16,312	59,882	361	66.5	5.8	43.5
Sussex	5,601	66,704	11,674	9,938	13,615	1,897	1,853	2,470	37,035	1,119	54.0	7.6	58.9
DISTRICT OF COLUMBIA.	23,177	526,879	68,675	1,258	22,143	17,729	102,780	39,834	75,603	NA	NA	NA	NA
District of Columbia	23,177	526,879	68,675	1,258	22,143	17,729	102,780	39,834	75,603	NA	NA	NA	NA
FLORIDA	546,218	8,169,642	1,086,559	306,700	1,088,564	355,395	499,518	363,336	44,474	47,590	71.0	3.2	41.3
Alachua	6,114	93,371	25,190	3,708	14,191	4,130	5,637	3,662	39,225	1,611	72.1	2.5	34.5
Baker	383	5,728	1,865	153	888	137	72	187	32,635	328	69.2	1.2	35.0
Bay	4,627	61,535	9,768	4,101	11,712	1,464	6,833	2,125	34,529	190	69.5	4.2	23.2
Bradford	430	4,240	891	171	988	144	100	124	29,345	490	73.9	3.1	37.2
Brevard	13,927	176,190	29,695	18,301	29,198	4,653	14,471	7,665	43,506	522	81.0	3.1	43.5
Broward	60,204	693,194	93,960	24,305	110,165	34,234	53,439	32,246	46,518	640	97.2	0.2	41.5
Calhoun	184	1,782	653	43	307	56	12	47	26,520	289	56.4	3.8	29.7
Charlotte	3,883	37,640	8,823	499	9,256	1,091	1,401	1,263	33,560	306	66.3	6.2	37.2
Citrus	2,732	29,803	10,283	303	5,686	673	853	1,004	33,683	609	75.2	2.1	43.4
Clay	3,806	40,089	8,730	1,027	8,626	1,006	3,136	1,359	33,906	361	83.4	0.6	41.1
Collier	11,698	124,868	18,374	3,290	21,838	4,000	5,248	5,238	41,949	322	77.3	7.1	36.2
Columbia	1,320	19,130	4,538	716	3,279	486	586	709	37,055	979	66.4	1.7	40.6
DeSoto	466	5,491	1,104	485	1,048	159	150	188	34,198	761	57.4	7.4	44.5
Dixie	179	1,533	272	447	275	47	24	46	30,234	235	60.9	5.5	51.6
Duval	25,219	434,531	60,408	21,876	53,961	44,776	27,861	21,041	48,422	366	81.7	2.7	42.4
Escambia	6,813	104,620	21,384	3,986	16,067	7,901	7,478	4,217	40,303	649	72.7	2.2	36.1
Flagler	2,071	17,869	3,282	1,108	3,625	637	629	563	31,512	116	56.9	15.5	43.0
Franklin	313	2,265	296	D	447	63	73	63	27,955	15	66.7	6.7	20.0
Gadsden	664	8,956	2,494	1,010	1,260	148	128	328	36,583	522	54.0	1.3	33.6
Gilchrist	229	1,682	618	117	200	42	48	56	33,373	565	67.3	2.1	45.7
Glades	112	788	86	122	56	13	11	28	35,317	354	53.7	7.1	48.1
Gulf	286	2,749	551	41	418	86	181	87	31,476	46	30.4	4.3	26.4
Hamilton	169	1,846	255	D	444	20	20	79	42,746	338	43.5	3.0	43.2
Hardee	384	4,129	1,260	302	661	238	78	140	33,850	1,038	56.9	5.5	41.4
Hendry	579	6,115	1,060	792	1,305	211	352	215	35,175	436	50.9	10.8	47.3
Hernando	3,177	33,835	8,704	1,952	7,837	741	1,296	1,080	31,924	747	80.6	0.9	42.9
Highlands	1,913	20,419	5,793	764	4,643	596	690	635	31,108	989	66.4	6.1	45.7
Hillsborough	36,533	587,224	83,095	21,301	70,169	47,963	61,718	29,071	49,506	2,265	83.6	1.0	40.7
Holmes	251	1,865	570	94	392	51	57	50	26,559	721	41.5	1.7	34.5
Indian River	4,249	43,224	9,241	1,655	9,199	1,417	1,932	1,623	37,545	450	76.2	5.1	42.6
Jackson	768	9,305	1,840	556	1,998	331	258	288	30,898	1,154	45.6	4.3	41.5
Jefferson	236	1,596	239	42	363	111	61	47	29,430	592	62.8	4.1	36.3
Lafayette	97	686	137	50	78	52	21	18	26,246	257	43.2	4.7	50.0
Lake	7,132	81,265	18,500	3,086	16,098	2,034	2,881	2,718	33,451	1,703	75.1	2.7	37.6
Lee	18,143	209,788	35,633	5,278	40,208	6,018	12,271	8,205	39,111	800	81.6	2.4	38.5
Leon	7,603	98,267	18,175	1,563	16,690	4,414	10,354	3,882	39,506	325	67.4	3.7	32.5
Levy	722	5,867	792	512	1,482	232	184	177	30,174	1,058	66.4	3.9	49.4
Liberty	85	1,156	431	308	145	10	D	39	33,533	111	54.1	0.9	28.1
Madison	308	2,863	627	472	584	67	85	86	29,993	669	38.6	4.6	43.5
Manatee	8,729	99,027	16,031	8,002	19,583	2,498	4,309	3,614	36,498	753	66.3	7.0	45.7
Marion	7,004	79,752	15,888	6,725	16,289	2,094	2,894	2,751	34,496	3,985	81.2	1.2	43.8
Martin	5,462	57,067	11,133	2,542	10,111	1,904	3,696	2,201	38,566	594	79.0	5.9	40.5
Miami-Dade	83,903	972,716	138,060	35,960	142,824	49,973	69,970	46,078	47,370	2,752	93.2	0.3	47.1
Monroe	3,816	31,794	2,352	346	6,217	693	925	1,068	33,601	40	100.0	NA	26.8
Nassau	1,845	17,090	2,589	1,250	3,158	387	591	604	35,337	373	70.2	2.7	37.8
Okaloosa	5,280	59,443	8,502	1,817	12,372	2,425	6,423	2,255	37,937	481	64.4	1.0	33.4
Okeechobee	791	7,042	1,352	430	1,827	190	214	241	34,198	599	48.1	13.9	43.8
Orange	36,801	704,627	71,638	25,170	86,283	22,237	50,550	31,203	44,283	622	83.8	1.9	51.8
Osceola	6,000	76,881	11,810	1,637	16,364	1,246	1,804	2,456	31,941	392	65.1	10.2	37.7
Palm Beach	47,613	512,940	83,736	12,886	79,890	21,465	42,150	24,473	47,711	1,298	89.1	3.0	48.3
Pasco	9,377	96,501	20,997	3,206	23,363	2,547	4,221	3,332	34,531	1,165	71.7	4.0	36.5
Pinellas	28,117	374,390	72,554	29,033	52,728	24,657	29,654	16,585	44,298	148	97.3	0.7	31.2
Polk	11,530	181,761	28,214	16,638	27,610	11,624	6,072	7,236	39,810	2,080	63.2	4.8	37.6

Table B. States and Counties — Agriculture

	Land in farms		Acres			Value of land and buildings (dollars)		Value of machinery and equipment, average per farm (dollars)	Value of products sold:		Percent from:		Organic farms (number)	Farms with internet access (percent)	Government payments	
STATE County	Acreage (1,000)	Percent change, 2012-2017	Average size of farm	Total irrigated (1,000)	Total cropland (1,000)	Average per farm	Average per acre		Total (mil dol)	Average per farm (acres)	Crops	Livestock and poultry products			Total ($1,000)	Percent of farms
	117	118	119	120	121	122	123	124	125	126	127	128	129	130	131	132
CONNECTICUT—Cont'd																
Tolland	36	-25.4	69	0.2	16.2	665,187	9,703	62,379	53.4	102,725	62.3	37.7	3	79.2	215	3.5
Windham	52	-10.8	80	0.4	22.4	760,709	9,452	57,273	45.1	69,800	36.9	63.1	6	78.2	132	4.6
DELAWARE	525	3.3	228	163.3	452.2	1,920,109	8,414	198,096	1,466.0	636,826	22.2	77.8	13	78.7	15,162	35.4
Kent	182	5.9	222	57.8	155.7	1,758,029	7,923	179,332	391.3	476,038	27.9	72.1	4	76.6	4,531	34.3
New Castle	67	5.1	187	5.1	53.7	1,775,015	9,499	140,504	62.1	171,986	55.1	44.9	2	80.9	1,342	26.6
Sussex	275	1.2	246	100.3	242.8	2,085,980	8,473	230,459	1,012.6	904,900	18.0	82.0	7	79.4	9,289	39.1
DISTRICT OF COLUMBIA	NA	NA	NA	NA	NA	NA	NA	NA	NA	NA	NA	NA	NA	NA	NA	NA
District of Columbia	NA	NA	NA	NA	NA	NA	NA	NA	NA	NA	NA	NA	NA	NA	NA	NA
FLORIDA	9,732	1.9	204	1,519.4	2,825.8	1,206,788	5,901	72,754	7,357.3	154,599	77.5	22.5	251	76.3	59,120	8.4
Alachua	178	-5.2	111	10.4	55.9	866,214	7,832	55,524	99.9	62,019	75.3	24.7	23	79.1	661	5.6
Baker	33	1.1	102	0.2	3.6	465,756	4,588	38,815	13.2	40,256	16.1	83.9	NA	78.4	72	2.4
Bay	74	601.5	387	1.7	4.6	794,316	2,051	41,297	2.9	15,274	69.6	30.4	NA	73.2	23	3.2
Bradford	59	67.8	120	0.6	12.9	573,623	4,777	61,641	13.1	26,708	27.3	72.7	NA	75.3	85	1.6
Brevard	157	6.9	300	10.5	21.0	1,507,863	5,027	62,406	59.0	112,977	76.9	23.1	1	78.7	186	3.6
Broward	7	-53.5	11	0.7	1.6	348,907	33,140	31,890	24.9	38,883	94.2	5.8	NA	85.5	18	0.6
Calhoun	118	175.5	409	3.3	25.4	880,123	2,154	63,913	22.0	76,163	85.5	14.5	NA	75.4	876	10.7
Charlotte	113	-48.1	368	11.6	18.5	2,644,176	7,176	66,707	43.9	143,402	91.8	8.2	2	73.9	329	5.2
Citrus	56	37.5	92	0.9	9.6	726,032	7,929	49,552	13.5	22,118	67.3	32.7	NA	81.0	197	2.6
Clay	D	D	D	0.3	4.7	366,072	5,726	42,781	5.5	15,111	55.7	44.3	NA	72.9	23	2.2
Collier	148	20.1	461	37.3	82.7	2,189,706	4,749	121,437	189.7	588,994	96.8	3.2	2	83.5	141	5.3
Columbia	107	5.5	109	4.2	33.6	476,995	4,361	52,758	40.2	41,040	41.2	58.8	1	75.5	1,189	10.7
DeSoto	335	10.5	440	57.7	73.5	2,203,290	5,008	100,533	168.3	221,145	72.1	27.9	3	73.2	1,066	13.4
Dixie	56	24.8	240	3.3	16.3	892,927	3,722	65,150	10.8	46,034	84.6	15.4	NA	67.2	273	3.8
Duval	30	6.1	82	2.3	5.9	616,395	7,523	47,364	9.0	24,656	71.5	28.5	4	70.5	135	4.4
Escambia	59	-21.1	91	2.0	33.1	562,575	6,206	75,174	26.9	41,507	91.2	8.8	4	76.9	1,957	11.7
Flagler	79	81.8	683	3.4	5.8	3,801,926	5,565	81,473	14.3	123,388	90.2	9.8	3	73.3	55	8.6
Franklin	D	D	D	NA	0.1	D	D	126,657	D	D	D	D	NA	80.0	56	26.7
Gadsden	66	30.4	127	4.1	19.4	540,049	4,256	62,186	90.5	173,354	81.4	18.6	1	73.6	238	8.6
Gilchrist	82	-2.0	146	10.9	42.0	774,215	5,321	88,720	89.7	158,837	33.9	66.1	NA	73.5	462	8.7
Glades	429	-3.2	1,211	65.8	43.9	5,217,205	4,308	142,023	78.2	220,924	62.7	37.3	NA	66.1	869	12.7
Gulf	D	D	D	0.0	1.6	6,070,106	1,435	47,216	D	D	D	D	NA	56.5	17	8.7
Hamilton	88	22.9	261	8.9	33.6	1,009,713	3,865	157,590	42.4	125,364	69.9	30.1	3	76.6	1,825	18.6
Hardee	377	37.6	363	46.8	68.3	1,937,932	5,337	95,859	204.7	197,171	60.0	40.0	1	70.8	1,611	16.6
Hendry	433	-12.6	993	183.3	203.5	4,867,433	4,900	262,368	329.5	755,716	91.6	8.4	4	78.4	1,163	11.7
Hernando	50	-18.8	67	2.0	8.2	706,024	10,488	41,410	20.4	27,309	73.8	26.2	2	77.9	313	5.1
Highlands	376	-23.3	380	73.3	87.6	1,484,269	3,906	92,897	196.7	198,865	72.5	27.5	2	71.1	2,471	11.0
Hillsborough	180	-16.1	80	25.8	76.3	929,585	11,678	64,339	447.6	197,627	91.6	8.4	25	75.8	584	3.0
Holmes	101	-4.1	140	1.1	36.3	468,245	3,334	53,453	28.2	39,122	34.7	65.3	2	73.0	1,500	32.6
Indian River	183	12.4	406	52.9	55.5	2,330,717	5,745	90,645	106.5	236,611	89.3	10.7	9	68.2	426	7.1
Jackson	275	4.8	238	18.4	152.3	880,430	3,694	101,848	93.3	80,821	87.0	13.0	8	76.4	9,120	28.8
Jefferson	168	29.7	284	2.8	35.6	983,884	3,468	56,238	36.1	60,990	24.2	75.8	4	77.7	1,147	10.8
Lafayette	94	2.6	364	17.0	32.4	1,102,316	3,024	186,306	85.9	334,218	24.6	75.4	NA	68.9	1,200	14.0
Lake	184	20.8	108	19.6	43.5	856,367	7,932	60,783	215.7	126,665	91.1	8.9	21	81.0	890	5.9
Lee	87	0.1	109	10.5	22.2	1,330,329	12,206	53,238	104.4	130,449	93.8	6.2	7	76.0	163	1.8
Leon	92	12.8	282	2.3	7.6	1,204,029	4,266	50,879	5.5	17,034	73.4	26.6	7	84.6	54	4.6
Levy	187	12.0	177	20.8	79.1	816,534	4,608	90,455	131.0	123,818	38.5	61.5	2	83.8	2,571	7.0
Liberty	35	145.3	313	0.0	1.4	1,227,282	3,916	64,185	2.5	22,126	6.8	93.2	NA	79.3	106	19.8
Madison	168	17.3	251	16.4	47.5	884,049	3,527	87,915	88.3	131,945	40.1	59.9	6	65.6	1,002	16.9
Manatee	193	3.4	256	56.5	71.2	1,991,183	7,784	116,597	360.1	478,246	89.3	10.7	3	76.2	151	3.6
Marion	331	2.9	83	13.2	79.3	922,892	11,114	47,624	145.5	36,501	41.1	58.9	5	82.3	813	1.4
Martin	154	10.4	259	28.8	49.6	1,137,728	4,396	88,080	112.6	189,505	91.4	8.6	3	81.5	487	4.2
Miami-Dade	79	-3.4	29	36.8	55.2	1,068,826	37,450	51,638	837.7	304,409	98.8	1.2	35	70.6	1,733	1.8
Monroe	0	-64.9	4	0.0	0.1	D	D	67,514	3.9	98,375	22.1	77.9	NA	90.0	NA	NA
Nassau	55	38.8	146	0.2	4.6	547,982	3,744	52,065	12.9	34,525	5.5	94.5	NA	73.2	236	12.6
Okaloosa	47	-24.2	97	0.4	13.7	461,280	4,763	38,830	8.3	17,318	70.3	29.7	NA	71.9	992	14.3
Okeechobee	297	-32.7	497	23.2	42.2	2,096,854	4,223	135,425	235.9	393,791	13.6	86.4	NA	70.1	2,671	24.4
Orange	109	-17.5	176	8.1	15.7	1,482,493	8,432	70,712	232.0	372,932	96.6	3.4	2	77.0	205	4.5
Osceola	525	-4.0	1,339	36.5	40.2	5,196,486	3,880	121,645	85.4	217,982	52.4	47.6	3	78.6	1,048	9.4
Palm Beach	488	-5.1	376	370.7	438.9	3,149,296	8,379	179,904	901.7	694,699	98.3	1.7	10	84.2	114	1.1
Pasco	192	11.9	164	3.6	25.9	1,177,181	7,161	56,608	65.0	55,766	23.1	76.9	NA	77.8	876	11.8
Pinellas	2	64.3	16	0.1	0.7	943,499	57,464	29,146	1.9	13,068	73.5	26.5	3	81.8	D	1.4
Polk	487	-6.5	234	88.6	131.0	1,420,064	6,064	69,094	297.7	143,136	81.0	19.0	5	71.5	2,242	11.5

Table B. States and Counties — Water Use, Wholesale Trade, Retail Trade, and Real Estate

STATE County	Water use, 2015		Wholesale Trade[1], 2012				Retail Trade[2], 2012				Real estate and rental and leasing,[2] 2012			
	Public supply water withdrawn (mil gal/day)	Public supply gallons withdrawn per person per day	Number of establishments	Number of employees	Sales (mil dol)	Average payroll (mil dol)	Number of establishments	Number of employees	Sales (mil dol)	Average payroll (mil dol)	Number of establishments	Number of employees	Sales (mil dol)	Average payroll (mil dol)
	133	134	135	136	137	138	139	140	141	142	143	144	145	146
CONNECTICUT—Cont'd														
Tolland	4.93	32.6	55	516	230.0	27.9	373	4,932	1,303.1	120.4	90	312	55.7	9.5
Windham	7.71	66.1	59	1,048	289.3	48.4	356	4,819	1,296.2	121.2	46	128	20.9	3.7
DELAWARE	86.35	91.3	835	7,653	5,628.9	385.9	3,616	51,711	14,456.0	1,270.1	1,111	5,402	5,471.2	264.9
Kent	11.81	68.1	94	D	D	D	561	8,856	2,690.8	214.1	127	459	92.2	17.0
New Castle	60.61	108.9	589	D	D	D	1,948	30,756	8,623.2	768.5	717	3,548	5,144.4	199.0
Sussex	13.93	64.6	152	1,203	783.4	52.6	1,107	12,099	3,142.1	287.6	267	1,395	234.6	48.9
DISTRICT OF COLUMBIA.	0.00	0.0	335	3,415	2,591.9	260.6	1,710	19,780	4,439.9	525.2	1,112	10,103	3,213.9	673.7
District of Columbia	0.00	0.0	335	3,415	2,591.9	260.6	1,710	19,780	4,439.9	525.2	1,112	10,103	3,213.9	673.7
FLORIDA	2,384.85	117.6	27,109	252,418	252,626.6	12,867.6	71,189	947,877	273,867.1	24,033.5	29,845	139,955	30,560.1	5,337.4
Alachua	23.37	89.9	197	1,852	1,297.5	90.7	929	13,067	3,208.7	283.3	319	1,714	231.1	51.9
Baker	0.90	32.8	12	D	D	D	69	764	217.3	16.7	12	D	D	D
Bay	47.62	262.2	157	1,460	514.8	63.4	818	10,295	2,728.2	249.7	276	1,402	207.0	39.1
Bradford	0.95	35.3	15	D	D	D	82	830	241.2	20.2	22	155	9.8	2.1
Brevard	31.45	55.4	451	3,962	1,846.5	195.7	1,955	24,885	6,527.5	606.1	642	2,056	340.7	66.7
Broward	233.65	123.2	3,902	33,141	33,606.6	1,781.8	7,070	97,344	32,042.9	2,675.4	3,237	17,682	3,934.9	701.7
Calhoun	0.58	40.1	6	19	4.7	0.6	39	318	70.1	6.7	4	7	0.8	0.1
Charlotte	7.51	43.4	94	D	D	D	558	8,000	2,091.3	185.9	232	680	113.1	19.1
Citrus	14.15	100.3	80	D	D	D	455	5,122	1,421.0	121.8	172	415	54.4	10.4
Clay	13.51	66.2	105	897	329.7	35.0	580	8,009	1,909.5	182.3	181	584	117.2	18.1
Collier	51.82	145.0	306	2,417	2,306.5	163.1	1,418	18,924	5,304.1	511.0	907	2,610	546.6	109.8
Columbia	3.27	47.8	60	760	508.6	33.0	250	2,791	815.9	69.0	51	262	32.0	6.9
DeSoto	33.20	936.3	17	D	D	D	72	1,003	255.4	23.8	22	95	11.8	2.2
Dixie	0.62	38.3	3	7	0.6	0.1	39	251	56.9	6.0	4	3	0.4	0.0
Duval	109.03	119.4	1,126	19,090	19,018.9	1,081.3	3,231	45,707	12,985.3	1,164.5	1,204	7,127	1,839.1	321.6
Escambia	37.52	120.6	273	2,534	1,396.3	108.7	1,120	14,671	4,096.3	360.1	339	1,445	287.0	47.8
Flagler	9.17	87.0	54	239	70.5	10.0	235	3,094	773.3	73.3	137	355	75.7	13.2
Franklin	1.97	167.5	11	D	D	D	67	403	97.9	8.6	17	117	12.0	4.2
Gadsden	4.07	88.4	34	787	404.7	27.4	132	1,114	347.3	25.6	19	46	6.6	1.2
Gilchrist	0.23	13.4	8	44	58.4	2.0	29	178	52.5	3.5	6	13	1.4	0.4
Glades	0.51	37.3	3	D	D	D	13	38	11.7	0.7	2	D	D	D
Gulf	1.88	118.5	6	12	7.3	0.5	39	341	76.9	7.2	15	58	6.3	1.7
Hamilton	0.88	61.6	4	D	D	D	38	280	78.3	5.0	3	22	0.9	0.3
Hardee	1.64	59.6	19	282	176.8	9.6	76	667	172.1	14.3	21	58	6.1	1.4
Hendry	3.31	84.6	25	D	D	D	101	991	258.1	23.2	24	70	13.0	2.7
Hernando	18.25	102.3	92	367	149.2	14.4	431	6,620	1,749.4	155.2	138	394	50.4	9.1
Highlands	7.49	75.3	57	D	D	D	316	4,292	1,112.5	100.2	87	264	51.2	7.5
Hillsborough	196.38	145.6	1,727	25,316	21,082.8	1,237.1	4,389	63,643	18,274.2	1,670.9	1,848	9,476	2,483.5	414.7
Holmes	1.01	52.3	11	D	D	D	54	384	104.1	7.7	5	12	0.9	0.2
Indian River	16.94	114.5	125	D	D	D	659	7,958	1,881.3	189.1	231	1,213	162.3	36.9
Jackson	2.46	50.6	22	D	D	D	170	1,799	574.0	40.6	32	82	10.7	1.9
Jefferson	0.65	46.2	11	D	D	D	42	284	67.3	5.9	8	17	1.3	0.4
Lafayette	0.17	19.6	7	D	D	D	17	125	46.6	3.3	2	D	D	D
Lake	49.28	151.2	217	1,208	498.0	42.8	978	13,430	3,761.0	329.6	391	1,476	262.5	45.2
Lee	64.55	92.0	585	5,144	2,481.0	232.6	2,517	34,453	9,445.3	850.6	1,218	3,992	856.4	135.9
Leon	28.51	99.6	230	2,339	1,763.1	169.7	991	15,309	3,482.4	334.4	395	2,024	283.9	60.1
Levy	1.48	37.2	30	D	D	D	141	1,342	360.8	31.4	29	67	7.5	1.3
Liberty	0.46	55.2	2	D	D	D	15	111	30.2	2.3	1	D	D	D
Madison	1.23	66.8	8	D	D	D	62	447	171.2	9.5	11	19	2.3	0.5
Manatee	42.83	117.9	304	2,479	1,628.8	122.9	1,136	15,943	4,191.1	378.1	487	1,935	402.6	63.6
Marion	27.71	80.7	277	3,157	1,719.3	143.3	1,152	14,430	4,263.6	353.9	338	1,382	211.8	41.3
Martin	15.61	99.7	167	D	D	D	748	9,540	2,553.3	239.1	259	1,581	252.2	57.7
Miami-Dade	351.92	130.7	8,242	61,377	78,985.4	3,003.6	10,389	123,883	38,361.2	3,252.7	4,776	19,563	4,936.4	811.9
Monroe	0.00	0.0	88	276	259.4	12.3	639	5,576	1,467.1	149.1	317	948	193.1	30.5
Nassau	7.00	89.2	41	D	D	D	249	2,663	703.8	63.2	88	D	D	D
Okaloosa	21.81	109.8	137	1,029	429.7	52.2	850	11,135	2,886.5	266.9	342	1,385	252.9	54.9
Okeechobee	2.72	68.9	29	D	D	D	157	1,518	508.1	38.7	36	94	15.3	2.9
Orange	221.92	172.3	1,614	19,479	18,498.9	1,016.9	4,677	74,266	23,076.7	1,791.8	2,147	18,232	5,603.4	750.0
Osceola	42.19	130.2	134	1,288	2,461.0	57.6	845	12,399	3,236.2	272.3	448	4,095	433.7	119.5
Palm Beach	238.73	167.8	1,933	15,255	12,157.3	888.7	5,236	69,625	19,700.1	1,904.6	2,462	11,445	2,133.8	482.9
Pasco	61.15	122.8	303	1,725	709.2	72.5	1,385	18,940	5,278.2	450.4	438	1,432	234.6	41.9
Pinellas	23.86	25.1	1,122	13,166	12,411.5	703.1	3,562	47,381	14,578.2	1,253.7	1,517	5,979	1,035.5	206.6
Polk	67.54	103.9	544	8,056	10,601.3	394.0	1,756	22,988	6,495.3	558.8	651	2,928	510.6	93.1

1   Merchant wholesalers, except manufacturers' sales branches and offices.   2. Employer establishments.

Table B. States and Counties — Professional Services, Manufacturing, and Accommodation and Food Services

STATE County	Professional, scientific, and technical services, 2012				Manufacturing, 2012				Accommodation and food services, 2012			
	Number of establish-ments	Number of employees	Sales (mil dol)	Average payroll (mil dol)	Number of establish-ments	Number of employees	Receipts (mil dol)	Annual payroll (mil dol)	Number of establis-hments	Number of employees	Receipts (mil dol)	Annual payroll (mil dol)
	147	148	149	150	151	152	153	154	155	156	157	158
CONNECTICUT—Cont'd												
Tolland	189	1,152	166.2	65.5	134	3,251	903.6	179.2	221	3,719	219.1	57.1
Windham	130	D	D	D	170	5,549	2,146.1	293.6	234	2,827	158.6	44.6
DELAWARE	2,543	D	D	D	573	26,355	22,597.4	1,393.2	1,987	35,609	2,148.4	566.7
Kent	278	D	D	D	74	4,797	1,930.8	218.9	272	6,183	475.8	101.1
New Castle	1,912	D	D	D	364	12,721	17,046.7	856.3	1,102	20,628	1,128.3	312.6
Sussex	353	D	D	D	135	8,837	3,619.9	318.0	613	8,798	544.3	152.9
DISTRICT OF COLUMBIA	5,061	97,555	31,866.3	11,196.4	113	1,361	309.8	61.5	2,371	60,370	5,101.6	1,504.8
District of Columbia	5,061	97,555	31,866.3	11,196.4	113	1,361	309.8	61.5	2,371	60,370	5,101.6	1,504.8
FLORIDA	70,785	440,858	70,175.6	27,100.4	12,890	277,089	96,924.1	14,270.0	37,118	786,082	49,817.9	13,598.2
Alachua	819	4,648	547.7	219.4	149	3,166	D	167.8	569	D	D	D
Baker	20	100	8.6	3.1	4	126	D	D	35	581	23.7	6.4
Bay	407	3,335	466.0	177.0	100	3,840	1,473.8	195.3	465	9,994	565.2	161.3
Bradford	32	94	7.1	2.6	11	137	D	5.5	38	531	28.1	6.7
Brevard	1,669	13,893	2,433.6	981.2	407	19,152	5,441.9	1,311.3	1,042	18,994	902.6	257.7
Broward	9,583	46,815	8,286.6	2,833.0	1,454	21,057	6,010.6	1,054.7	3,685	72,428	5,129.2	1,322.2
Calhoun	8	32	2.1	1.3	7	51	D	1.6	14	D	D	D
Charlotte	381	1,295	138.5	50.5	69	402	90.4	14.6	261	4,804	219.2	61.7
Citrus	254	891	106.3	35.8	44	203	35.8	7.2	191	2,362	114.6	32.2
Clay	394	D	D	D	73	927	D	D	271	5,095	238.5	67.4
Collier	1,342	4,810	784.7	270.4	197	2,722	607.5	130.0	763	19,624	1,406.5	404.2
Columbia	113	433	43.7	14.4	42	608	249.0	26.7	116	2,331	106.6	29.5
DeSoto	32	114	15.1	3.7	8	235	D	11.4	31	402	19.6	5.2
Dixie	9	D	D	D	7	418	D	14.9	18	145	7.3	1.7
Duval	3,166	29,737	5,572.2	2,176.5	598	21,699	10,158.2	1,256.0	1,930	37,804	2,016.5	558.9
Escambia	774	7,159	939.6	359.4	174	4,026	2,427.8	242.5	558	11,548	598.4	162.5
Flagler	206	462	74.0	20.1	45	591	D	26.7	155	4,248	238.7	80.8
Franklin	27	52	7.8	2.3	NA	NA	NA	NA	45	555	28.8	9.0
Gadsden	36	D	D	D	31	840	178.6	31.9	53	559	28.8	7.7
Gilchrist	22	65	5.5	1.7	9	104	D	2.0	9	D	D	D
Glades	7	D	D	D	5	103	D	5.6	10	103	4.7	1.1
Gulf	27	130	27.8	7.2	10	64	8.6	2.2	32	324	16.5	4.4
Hamilton	9	22	1.9	0.5	5	D	D	D	16	165	6.1	1.7
Hardee	24	71	4.4	1.5	8	253	D	7.6	28	364	17.2	4.2
Hendry	40	D	D	D	20	887	D	44.0	65	760	37.4	9.3
Hernando	280	1,144	102.8	34.6	85	1,490	326.4	59.4	248	3,936	193.1	54.7
Highlands	132	602	57.5	18.4	44	570	214.0	22.7	147	2,331	110.6	30.7
Hillsborough	5,216	52,511	8,442.1	3,624.5	786	19,144	9,341.8	914.9	2,329	49,344	3,410.9	839.4
Holmes	17	87	14.8	3.3	14	103	14.6	3.9	16	203	9.4	2.4
Indian River	454	1,601	229.1	84.3	84	1,487	D	68.7	250	4,351	225.1	66.2
Jackson	43	233	22.7	9.5	16	459	D	18.0	70	1,044	52.2	11.9
Jefferson	17	49	5.4	1.6	4	D	D	D	17	D	D	D
Lafayette	8	D	D	D	4	62	D	2.1	7	D	D	D
Lake	622	2,090	238.2	87.7	145	2,439	D	99.3	451	8,045	394.9	109.9
Lee	1,893	12,312	2,202.7	844.3	366	4,010	812.8	165.1	1,189	25,851	1,346.6	402.6
Leon	1,363	11,176	1,519.5	766.3	97	1,462	400.0	72.0	644	13,783	629.0	170.3
Levy	42	149	15.8	4.8	20	385	D	13.9	66	661	28.8	7.9
Liberty	5	D	D	D	4	271	138.7	11.8	4	47	2.0	0.5
Madison	19	65	5.8	2.4	12	367	181.0	16.6	22	276	13.9	4.3
Manatee	928	12,131	728.3	402.2	283	8,121	2,338.0	403.9	593	9,987	532.9	155.6
Marion	669	3,676	415.5	157.2	178	4,806	1,471.2	212.9	437	7,369	375.2	102.5
Martin	697	3,071	403.4	149.0	162	2,869	1,103.3	151.9	334	6,215	312.7	91.6
Miami-Dade	12,008	58,711	11,734.8	4,018.8	2,070	30,387	7,192.9	1,318.2	5,052	104,467	7,696.6	2,078.4
Monroe	360	1,064	165.2	53.0	49	177	26.5	6.2	511	11,414	1,002.8	275.8
Nassau	184	559	80.2	28.5	37	1,239	929.1	80.9	158	3,378	203.3	71.5
Okaloosa	613	6,033	918.6	391.1	86	2,719	D	135.1	462	10,900	566.3	167.5
Okeechobee	45	164	15.4	4.9	17	197	D	6.8	56	912	40.1	10.3
Orange	4,882	44,689	6,856.9	3,044.6	747	23,702	8,280.9	1,531.7	2,715	102,733	8,326.4	2,131.0
Osceola	428	1,862	237.0	82.6	87	1,078	D	41.5	542	13,348	866.9	237.9
Palm Beach	7,364	36,924	6,189.1	2,368.7	928	11,731	3,550.4	614.2	2,665	57,739	3,467.3	1,044.3
Pasco	978	4,249	511.1	176.0	223	2,839	743.9	130.7	608	10,473	503.4	145.1
Pinellas	3,973	27,841	3,846.9	1,490.2	1,027	28,305	8,411.6	1,478.1	2,090	36,887	2,193.1	607.3
Polk	1,036	6,724	768.7	300.4	401	14,200	9,822.2	681.0	788	15,188	797.9	220.1

— **Health Care and Social Assistance, Other Services, Nonemployer Businesses, and Residential Construction**

STATE County	Health care and social assistance, 2012				Other services, 2012				Nonemployer businesses, 2016		Value of residential construction authorized by building permits, 2018	
	Number of establish-ments	Number of employees	Receipts (mil dol)	Annual payroll (mil dol)	Number of establish-ments	Number of employees	Receipts (mil dol)	Annual payroll (mil dol)	Number	Receipts (mil dol)	New construction ($1,000)	Number of housing units
	159	160	161	162	163	164	165	166	167	168	169	170
CONNECTICUT—Cont'd												
Tolland	302	5,920	501.9	227.1	188	1,110	141.8	37.2	9,435	449.4	47,662	289
Windham	269	7,584	590.7	280.9	182	728	74.7	17.8	6,778	308.9	29,485	173
DELAWARE	2,524	61,897	7,003.3	2,995.9	1,513	9,841	974.7	290.1	63,121	3,951.9	788,602	6,003
Kent	398	9,405	990.6	379.5	233	1,325	105.5	32.0	10,088	638.0	212,126	1,459
New Castle	1,603	41,861	4,843.5	2,154.2	931	6,651	703.0	207.5	36,809	2,423.8	125,307	1,364
Sussex	523	10,631	1,169.2	462.2	349	1,865	166.2	50.6	16,224	890.1	451,170	3,180
DISTRICT OF COLUMBIA	2,065	67,742	8,964.0	3,596.5	3,357	58,982	19,773.5	4,238.6	59,398	2,925.0	518,239	4,615
District of Columbia	2,065	67,742	8,964.0	3,596.5	3,357	58,982	19,773.5	4,238.6	59,398	2,925.0	518,239	4,615
FLORIDA	56,659	991,254	124,061.4	44,435.6	34,843	195,176	20,798.9	5,414.5	2,053,914	85,075.0	31,543,714	144,427
Alachua	736	21,940	2,707.5	1,027.7	384	2,650	463.7	92.8	17,973	656.9	225,324	1,504
Baker	38	1,783	117.8	66.7	32	D	D	D	1,259	38.9	20,517	118
Bay	490	9,575	1,034.4	396.1	305	1,892	157.5	42.5	13,923	667.3	334,206	1,520
Bradford	39	831	80.0	25.6	24	86	7.2	2.0	1,204	41.3	598	5
Brevard	1,522	31,218	3,727.6	1,387.7	958	4,563	372.7	117.7	41,969	1,596.3	860,729	2,958
Broward	6,273	89,756	12,193.7	4,272.6	4,124	21,448	2,245.9	602.5	252,396	10,014.7	719,415	3,332
Calhoun	29	475	40.6	14.1	7	37	3.6	0.8	765	26.3	1,309	12
Charlotte	485	8,927	1,119.6	401.0	297	1,326	113.0	33.0	12,658	553.1	529,176	2,068
Citrus	390	7,932	819.7	307.1	212	744	53.2	15.5	8,987	359.3	178,006	884
Clay	448	7,152	825.0	300.2	280	D	D	D	13,002	472.1	179,859	900
Collier	995	16,310	2,089.4	772.0	850	5,209	474.4	138.1	38,119	2,217.0	1,339,352	4,386
Columbia	175	4,387	567.3	215.6	70	299	27.1	6.3	3,917	165.7	21,197	147
DeSoto	44	1,009	96.8	38.3	25	78	4.4	1.5	1,563	62.6	15,791	88
Dixie	14	136	9.1	3.3	14	46	4.9	0.8	780	26.3	4,169	33
Duval	2,513	55,950	7,324.9	2,580.2	1,612	D	D	D	67,845	2,484.7	1,309,456	7,200
Escambia	758	20,561	2,476.2	948.2	439	2,685	260.9	73.5	21,040	877.2	238,688	1,055
Flagler	196	2,629	336.2	106.8	136	533	40.6	10.7	8,941	402.7	389,757	1,408
Franklin	21	303	22.2	8.1	15	59	4.1	1.4	1,300	48.3	17,305	79
Gadsden	54	2,437	155.6	99.5	32	111	9.1	2.6	2,980	84.5	24,864	1,111
Gilchrist	21	497	45.1	15.8	8	14	1.5	0.4	945	36.2	9,615	65
Glades	7	D	D	D	6	D	D	D	535	18.4	4,958	36
Gulf	25	476	43.8	16.4	16	44	3.0	0.9	1,147	53.1	36,731	148
Hamilton	17	D	D	D	13	41	3.8	1.1	574	21.2	0	0
Hardee	57	1,123	82.0	35.7	29	60	4.3	1.1	1,278	47.8	7,540	45
Hendry	69	1,081	85.1	35.8	46	172	13.0	3.7	2,880	99.0	19,167	79
Hernando	507	7,744	984.0	302.9	212	1,008	71.4	21.5	11,252	404.4	214,962	1,216
Highlands	325	5,021	576.5	194.8	134	504	37.4	9.1	5,715	221.0	55,084	271
Hillsborough	3,703	72,572	10,416.3	3,584.0	2,080	14,640	1,646.3	432.3	118,525	5,036.1	3,164,959	9,897
Holmes	33	511	36.0	12.2	14	49	3.1	1.1	1,086	39.6	1,198	9
Indian River	466	7,828	886.2	333.8	280	1,395	124.5	34.6	13,415	678.3	520,259	1,372
Jackson	83	1,796	157.4	64.3	53	225	22.9	6.0	2,765	89.5	9,386	57
Jefferson	26	238	12.0	5.1	12	31	2.0	0.5	1,012	36.4	3,772	62
Lafayette	11	135	7.7	3.4	3	D	D	D	347	11.5	1,761	14
Lake	825	15,150	1,648.7	639.5	449	2,246	194.7	57.9	24,468	939.6	826,343	3,330
Lee	1,488	26,009	3,362.1	1,226.1	1,209	6,696	580.1	164.2	63,568	2,979.7	1,869,044	9,721
Leon	745	16,817	1,893.7	744.3	615	4,445	666.4	170.7	20,580	788.3	274,633	1,806
Levy	62	566	35.3	14.5	48	111	13.2	2.3	2,686	115.2	17,716	176
Liberty	10	D	D	D	3	13	2.2	0.5	393	13.0	1,983	20
Madison	39	648	42.5	17.2	17	D	D	D	958	35.1	7,466	37
Manatee	877	14,956	1,512.5	582.0	534	2,743	196.5	59.5	29,976	1,392.0	813,267	4,490
Marion	878	15,494	1,874.0	674.9	455	2,315	196.6	54.0	24,317	977.6	433,239	2,817
Martin	536	8,591	946.3	388.8	399	2,032	181.9	54.8	15,319	834.6	221,222	441
Miami-Dade	9,030	132,886	17,547.4	6,100.1	4,903	28,561	3,116.7	758.0	469,992	18,147.3	2,260,848	11,703
Monroe	225	2,464	323.1	109.9	252	1,060	106.9	32.0	11,587	648.9	158,647	553
Nassau	168	2,337	230.5	89.6	123	D	D	D	5,874	260.6	337,208	1,322
Okaloosa	545	8,715	1,111.1	373.8	348	1,683	146.0	44.2	16,255	820.7	278,974	860
Okeechobee	99	1,305	162.4	52.9	54	225	17.6	5.0	2,197	84.5	18,377	52
Orange	3,056	66,554	8,920.9	3,080.9	2,033	15,498	1,676.9	435.9	129,056	4,991.5	2,714,752	13,757
Osceola	540	10,184	1,301.7	460.0	330	1,364	155.8	30.6	31,991	1,070.4	1,285,635	9,759
Palm Beach	5,319	75,097	9,756.7	3,371.0	3,204	18,011	1,831.0	493.9	170,587	8,106.8	1,312,556	4,518
Pasco	1,160	17,932	2,142.5	771.5	640	2,765	231.7	66.4	35,254	1,354.5	768,820	3,830
Pinellas	3,215	64,140	7,744.4	2,913.0	1,924	10,377	1,033.2	292.6	81,112	3,641.9	471,141	2,509
Polk	1,048	27,066	3,015.2	1,109.8	673	3,366	328.5	94.6	42,327	1,562.3	1,092,544	5,331

— **Government Employment and Payroll, and Local Government Finances**

STATE County	Government employment and payroll, 2012									Local government finances, 2012				
	Full-time equivalent employees	March payroll (dollars)	March payroll (percent of total)							General revenue				
			Adminis-tration, judicial, and legal	Police and corrections	Fire protection	Highways and transpor-tation	Health and welfare	Natural resources and utilities	Education and libraries	Total (mil dol)	Inter-govern-mental (mil dol)	Taxes		
												Total (mil dol)	Per capita[1] (dollars)	
													Total	Property
	171	172	173	174	175	176	177	178	179	180	181	182	183	184
CONNECTICUT—Cont'd														
Tolland	4,711	21,137,708	4.8	2.7	1.1	3.4	2.1	2.9	81.0	531.4	189.3	302.4	1,996	1,971
Windham	3,899	15,623,446	4.2	2.5	1.2	4.0	0.5	3.9	82.0	430.6	207.6	189.4	1,611	1,586
DELAWARE	X	X	X	X	X	X	X	X	X	X	X	X	X	X
Kent	4,210	17,226,252	4.7	6.0	0.1	0.6	1.6	5.6	79.4	494.8	323.1	88.0	525	459
New Castle	13,350	61,131,759	5.7	9.5	1.4	3.2	2.2	5.4	70.9	1,685.7	768.1	591.4	1,083	883
Sussex	5,143	20,898,662	5.1	4.6	0.0	1.2	3.3	4.3	80.0	633.4	356.0	169.5	833	671
DISTRICT OF COLUMBIA	X	X	X	X	X	X	X	X	X	X	X	X	X	X
District of Columbia	44,423	263,772,974	11.1	14.2	4.3	27.8	12.5	5.9	19.0	11,142.1	3,474.2	5,933.8	9,384	2,970
FLORIDA	X	X	X	X	X	X	X	X	X	X	X	X	X	X
Alachua	9,411	34,346,743	10.1	15.9	4.6	4.8	3.1	12.0	45.8	854.0	266.5	363.0	1,444	1,113
Baker	867	2,564,944	5.5	3.7	1.2	2.9	5.4	3.6	77.0	73.2	44.3	18.9	699	507
Bay	8,014	30,150,146	3.2	6.0	2.6	3.8	35.9	4.9	42.5	823.2	190.5	261.0	1,518	1,060
Bradford	881	2,067,161	5.4	1.3	0.4	2.7	7.1	1.3	75.8	71.8	37.9	23.1	853	598
Brevard	19,755	66,076,682	7.5	12.3	7.0	4.4	7.8	7.9	52.0	1,764.4	557.0	634.8	1,160	923
Broward	73,864	331,154,408	5.1	13.2	6.2	3.7	29.6	6.0	33.6	9,918.0	2,186.8	3,161.3	1,742	1,392
Calhoun	510	1,309,655	4.9	3.6	0.2	5.5	0.9	3.7	80.8	46.1	34.0	8.6	581	443
Charlotte	4,654	16,650,878	13.2	15.5	8.9	5.6	2.0	7.8	45.5	559.2	101.1	264.1	1,626	1,290
Citrus	3,890	11,674,757	8.6	11.3	0.1	3.6	5.4	3.4	65.1	322.4	98.7	162.1	1,163	1,064
Clay	6,995	21,858,185	5.6	10.0	3.5	1.9	1.2	5.5	71.3	556.6	210.2	185.3	953	696
Collier	9,918	41,162,175	6.9	15.7	6.7	3.5	4.2	9.1	52.0	1,300.6	231.7	737.4	2,218	2,006
Columbia	2,446	7,323,140	6.4	8.1	2.5	3.8	3.8	3.8	69.3	195.9	99.6	58.8	865	641
DeSoto	1,506	4,657,631	3.9	13.7	4.7	2.2	25.3	4.7	44.3	123.0	39.7	31.6	911	665
Dixie	584	1,731,414	9.6	25.5	0.3	3.8	8.6	2.7	49.0	42.4	22.0	12.7	789	669
Duval	26,681	104,173,723	5.7	15.6	6.2	2.1	1.2	7.3	52.4	3,353.2	1,044.0	1,351.0	1,536	1,039
Escambia	10,348	32,971,310	5.4	14.5	2.6	2.7	4.7	8.0	59.2	937.6	348.0	338.3	1,118	772
Flagler	2,869	10,004,315	13.0	9.5	8.0	1.8	3.2	8.7	53.9	286.1	72.0	141.3	1,437	1,235
Franklin	399	1,124,749	9.6	10.0	1.7	7.1	5.5	9.5	54.3	60.6	21.8	24.9	2,130	1,812
Gadsden	1,850	4,901,351	12.9	12.9	1.7	6.4	3.2	4.9	56.6	109.5	61.3	33.5	721	528
Gilchrist	624	1,705,173	8.0	8.7	0.9	3.7	4.8	1.4	69.5	43.8	24.4	13.1	781	660
Glades	401	1,250,845	13.0	0.2	0.5	3.3	5.2	7.6	67.4	65.1	17.5	12.8	974	884
Gulf	661	1,888,717	10.9	17.7	0.2	5.5	8.9	6.1	46.3	58.3	19.3	27.3	1,735	1,504
Hamilton	602	1,883,338	4.3	14.6	0.6	4.0	4.1	19.8	50.0	60.4	31.4	21.4	1,452	1,298
Hardee	1,238	3,660,532	9.3	12.4	2.4	3.4	4.4	4.8	59.9	83.9	40.3	30.3	1,103	950
Hendry	1,671	5,341,045	10.9	8.7	1.0	3.6	17.8	12.2	43.4	156.7	60.3	45.0	1,201	842
Hernando	5,261	17,523,253	4.9	11.1	6.5	1.8	0.9	20.4	52.8	557.9	169.7	301.2	1,737	1,597
Highlands	3,358	10,445,615	8.2	12.8	2.4	5.5	3.7	6.4	56.9	264.2	111.3	100.2	1,021	799
Hillsborough	45,811	168,419,971	6.8	14.7	5.5	5.2	2.8	7.1	56.0	4,882.0	2,046.8	1,736.7	1,359	996
Holmes	889	2,422,344	5.2	5.1	0.0	3.5	20.9	5.0	58.1	71.8	52.9	10.8	548	332
Indian River	4,188	14,858,891	4.7	16.3	4.8	5.0	5.1	12.6	48.7	445.1	88.8	266.5	1,896	1,553
Jackson	2,760	8,398,373	4.9	6.0	2.2	2.8	34.8	2.6	46.1	203.4	76.8	40.3	823	456
Jefferson	365	927,774	7.8	2.9	2.0	7.8	9.8	3.9	63.2	30.2	13.1	12.4	871	675
Lafayette	373	1,167,432	11.8	22.1	0.0	1.9	8.3	6.2	48.5	18.5	10.9	4.9	555	451
Lake	10,347	30,892,756	6.4	14.3	6.8	2.9	1.5	7.4	57.3	851.0	286.9	352.0	1,161	905
Lee	29,739	118,190,826	4.0	7.9	5.4	3.4	39.4	4.7	33.6	3,672.5	586.2	1,065.4	1,651	1,448
Leon	11,335	40,616,545	8.8	12.0	3.5	5.4	3.6	15.1	47.5	1,138.8	359.2	388.1	1,368	952
Levy	1,489	4,220,044	6.6	13.3	0.6	4.8	6.8	4.6	61.2	107.5	52.0	38.2	954	772
Liberty	390	1,120,616	1.3	0.1	28.3	3.3	4.3	2.5	59.6	26.9	19.5	5.1	613	482
Madison	949	2,696,175	4.6	8.3	1.1	3.0	18.6	2.7	58.5	73.1	37.0	16.5	874	617
Manatee	11,893	40,190,709	10.2	12.9	5.6	2.7	2.6	5.6	58.7	1,162.4	346.0	503.0	1,507	1,276
Marion	10,760	33,096,942	6.2	11.8	9.0	0.5	2.5	5.9	63.0	875.9	312.2	296.0	883	746
Martin	4,603	17,106,522	8.9	17.9	12.8	2.6	1.6	5.7	48.8	500.0	104.9	304.6	2,047	1,811
Miami-Dade	102,308	498,941,928	4.9	14.9	6.0	5.9	20.8	6.6	32.3	14,058.6	3,695.7	5,524.1	2,132	1,564
Monroe	3,585	14,624,150	5.7	22.6	8.9	2.9	3.9	19.5	34.7	567.8	118.5	263.2	3,519	2,437
Nassau	1,980	6,570,847	4.2	2.9	11.2	4.6	1.0	4.9	66.5	222.9	55.5	123.9	1,660	1,424
Okaloosa	6,391	22,546,268	5.1	9.5	4.5	3.0	2.3	7.4	65.4	596.0	213.5	239.6	1,260	1,023
Okeechobee	1,527	4,441,541	4.9	15.8	5.3	1.7	1.2	7.3	62.2	123.6	58.3	42.0	1,065	682
Orange	45,111	168,174,502	6.0	14.3	7.4	5.4	6.3	9.8	48.0	5,410.1	1,451.5	2,181.6	1,815	1,273
Osceola	10,876	36,955,599	7.4	13.0	6.2	2.3	1.1	9.5	58.0	1,052.2	358.1	406.0	1,412	1,006
Palm Beach	46,198	195,497,482	7.6	16.4	10.2	2.6	5.1	13.1	41.6	6,353.4	1,180.9	3,449.0	2,542	2,211
Pasco	14,918	46,238,730	6.6	11.6	5.0	1.2	1.2	4.8	67.1	1,276.0	533.4	417.6	888	715
Pinellas	32,162	118,407,394	7.7	19.5	5.8	3.8	3.8	10.1	45.5	3,227.6	836.8	1,470.9	1,597	1,224
Polk	22,910	75,047,946	7.9	12.5	4.2	2.1	2.6	10.6	56.6	1,844.2	710.5	644.8	1,047	726

1. Based on the resident population estimated as of July 1 of the year shown.

Table B. States and Counties — Local Government Finances, Government Employment, and Income Taxes

STATE County	Local government finances, 2012 (cont.)									Government employment, 2017			Individual income tax returns, 2016		
	Direct general expenditure							Debt outstanding							
	Total (mil dol)	Per capita¹ (dollars)	Percent of total for:					Total (mil dol)	Per capita¹ (dollars)	Federal civilian	Federal military	State and local	Number of returns	Mean adjusted gross income	Mean income tax
			Education	Health and hospitals	Police protection	Public welfare	Highways								
	185	186	187	188	189	190	191	192	193	194	195	196	197	198	199
CONNECTICUT—Cont'd															
Tolland	554.3	3,658	66.0	0.7	2.3	0.3	5.5	321.3	2,121	265	318	16,151	68,780	79,462	10,804
Windham	416.8	3,544	69.2	0.6	2.8	0.4	4.7	176.2	1,498	286	226	7,084	54,780	56,907	6,238
DELAWARE	X	X	X	X	X	X	X	X	X	5,754	8,566	59,882	455,660	64,393	8,244
Kent	527.3	3,145	73.4	1.1	4.4	0.0	1.5	478.7	2,856	1,680	4,266	17,168	80,670	50,842	5,184
New Castle	1,812.2	3,319	59.7	0.8	7.5	0.0	2.5	1,735.3	3,178	3,474	3,032	34,380	266,240	70,383	9,528
Sussex	613.0	3,014	69.2	2.1	4.3	0.1	1.7	515.0	2,532	600	1,268	8,334	108,770	59,769	7,370
DISTRICT OF COLUMBIA	X	X	X	X	X	X	X	X	X	195,159	13,834	41,159	343,030	93,024	16,325
District of Columbia	10,765.0	17,025	22.0	6.3	5.2	26.6	4.9	13,246.6	20,949	195,159	13,834	41,159	343,030	93,024	16,325
FLORIDA	X	X	X	X	X	X	X	X	X	139,250	91,582	955,564	9,667,760	61,980	9,071
Alachua	900.5	3,582	38.5	3.8	8.3	1.7	4.6	1,948.7	7,751	4,681	541	36,368	111,550	58,064	7,845
Baker	88.4	3,262	47.4	4.9	5.7	1.3	10.3	18.5	682	62	46	2,628	10,470	47,800	4,385
Bay	927.6	5,396	32.4	24.5	6.6	0.0	4.4	885.7	5,152	3,860	4,154	9,284	86,950	51,335	6,301
Bradford	72.8	2,691	44.9	6.1	6.5	0.0	6.2	13.5	501	32	46	2,202	9,970	43,995	4,255
Brevard	1,830.9	3,345	36.4	11.6	7.9	0.4	4.3	1,872.2	3,421	6,425	2,863	22,153	279,800	58,338	7,764
Broward	10,214.0	5,627	24.6	26.3	10.2	1.2	1.4	8,639.5	4,760	7,001	3,977	98,576	924,320	61,526	9,142
Calhoun	49.3	3,348	43.9	2.4	5.2	0.1	28.4	3.8	256	25	23	913	4,900	41,188	3,885
Charlotte	563.6	3,470	33.1	3.8	11.0	1.5	11.1	628.4	3,868	309	324	5,596	82,800	55,617	6,706
Citrus	362.7	2,602	47.4	5.5	9.1	2.5	6.6	493.5	3,541	235	258	4,075	65,200	47,080	5,251
Clay	560.4	2,884	52.3	0.7	8.2	0.5	6.0	488.9	2,515	377	381	6,675	97,370	57,805	6,445
Collier	1,313.8	3,952	37.5	3.0	12.1	0.6	6.0	2,257.5	6,791	707	673	12,696	177,550	125,451	25,354
Columbia	210.8	3,101	53.8	3.7	6.1	0.1	6.0	94.4	1,389	1,257	118	4,282	27,420	44,422	4,444
DeSoto	129.0	3,717	35.1	28.2	5.2	0.4	2.7	71.9	2,070	64	59	1,693	12,270	37,389	3,129
Dixie	42.5	2,637	45.4	10.3	7.8	0.0	6.5	11.2	694	10	42	1,006	5,060	37,879	3,157
Duval	3,336.4	3,793	39.0	1.9	9.4	1.4	4.4	11,704.3	13,306	16,430	12,242	38,630	446,100	55,384	7,005
Escambia	1,097.8	3,627	40.4	3.3	6.7	0.2	4.3	1,910.8	6,312	5,873	10,062	15,501	143,080	52,036	6,472
Flagler	307.1	3,122	38.2	1.4	7.1	0.2	6.7	437.4	4,447	149	197	3,558	51,500	56,921	7,344
Franklin	62.9	5,386	27.2	14.8	10.5	0.2	5.5	56.4	4,826	17	18	1,033	4,490	57,551	8,705
Gadsden	120.4	2,588	50.5	4.7	7.8	0.8	7.5	55.7	1,197	90	77	4,435	19,780	38,599	3,284
Gilchrist	44.2	2,629	55.7	5.0	6.8	0.4	8.4	4.7	282	35	30	1,090	6,610	43,982	4,159
Glades	69.5	5,305	21.6	4.0	6.8	0.1	6.4	202.1	15,417	10	22	491	4,060	48,691	5,748
Gulf	59.6	3,791	32.4	9.7	5.8	0.4	7.6	52.0	3,310	15	24	1,168	5,760	53,554	6,950
Hamilton	59.7	4,061	31.9	3.6	5.9	0.1	5.3	3.7	253	31	21	1,062	4,740	36,590	2,867
Hardee	86.6	3,149	54.2	4.1	11.3	0.2	5.3	9.9	360	47	46	1,570	9,740	38,028	3,026
Hendry	180.1	4,810	32.7	25.6	7.7	0.4	3.5	74.6	1,991	71	153	2,076	16,100	40,682	4,001
Hernando	566.7	3,268	33.0	2.6	5.9	0.1	3.9	365.6	2,108	358	334	5,480	80,870	43,705	4,352
Highlands	276.6	2,818	46.6	3.7	7.8	0.6	6.0	143.0	1,457	271	183	3,793	42,110	40,133	3,792
Hillsborough	5,230.4	4,093	38.8	3.2	7.5	2.6	3.9	6,006.8	4,701	15,196	8,053	65,280	642,880	61,805	8,820
Holmes	71.5	3,610	38.8	22.5	3.3	0.1	8.7	33.4	1,686	62	35	1,339	6,650	38,781	3,201
Indian River	470.0	3,343	38.2	4.8	9.4	0.8	8.2	436.2	3,103	365	275	4,729	74,040	87,256	14,924
Jackson	226.5	4,626	38.1	33.8	3.4	0.0	8.3	82.2	1,680	482	73	4,730	18,250	42,104	4,058
Jefferson	31.4	2,204	37.8	7.2	14.4	0.5	9.5	3.9	274	36	23	640	5,830	49,620	5,277
Lafayette	19.1	2,172	55.0	7.9	4.8	0.6	8.7	1.7	189	13	13	587	2,440	40,588	3,593
Lake	925.8	3,054	40.3	3.7	8.1	0.5	5.1	1,090.4	3,596	622	616	13,248	160,270	53,697	6,332
Lee	3,730.8	5,782	25.4	32.3	4.8	0.5	3.9	5,119.6	7,934	2,410	1,385	39,980	334,840	70,174	10,635
Leon	1,138.4	4,012	38.2	0.6	7.6	0.0	7.4	4,257.0	15,002	1,875	549	50,338	124,970	59,188	7,943
Levy	112.3	2,806	46.8	5.0	8.6	0.8	9.0	30.9	772	69	102	1,831	16,890	39,021	3,552
Liberty	27.8	3,361	51.9	8.1	3.7	0.3	10.1	4.7	568	40	11	763	2,620	42,718	3,619
Madison	78.8	4,166	46.8	15.6	5.2	0.4	9.1	16.3	861	44	29	1,335	6,930	39,542	3,415
Manatee	1,227.1	3,675	40.6	2.5	8.5	0.7	4.4	1,359.0	4,070	1,012	717	11,616	175,350	68,499	10,196
Marion	879.1	2,623	48.9	2.0	7.6	0.7	6.3	732.6	2,186	694	624	14,401	157,560	46,622	5,387
Martin	526.0	3,534	36.8	8.1	9.7	2.3	3.4	296.9	1,995	280	282	5,737	75,870	106,244	19,218
Miami-Dade	14,468.1	5,584	25.8	12.2	7.5	3.5	2.2	23,549.3	9,089	20,354	7,413	121,855	1,283,530	53,685	8,131
Monroe	536.4	7,170	22.9	4.6	11.0	0.5	2.3	1,453.0	19,423	1,204	1,381	4,698	42,820	111,727	21,035
Nassau	230.5	3,089	41.0	5.2	7.0	0.2	6.7	231.3	3,100	526	148	2,865	39,440	75,872	7,614
Okaloosa	687.4	3,616	51.5	2.4	6.6	0.3	2.9	368.2	1,937	8,678	16,093	8,298	100,230	58,286	7,614
Okeechobee	121.9	3,087	49.3	2.5	8.0	0.7	4.0	78.4	1,987	72	69	2,171	14,930	43,107	4,419
Orange	5,320.5	4,426	36.8	4.6	7.1	0.7	4.0	9,996.1	8,315	12,603	2,633	66,273	629,840	55,489	7,650
Osceola	1,153.9	4,015	42.2	1.2	7.2	1.7	8.7	2,678.5	9,319	435	628	12,709	161,730	39,674	3,483
Palm Beach	6,575.2	4,847	27.6	4.7	9.3	2.5	2.5	7,440.3	5,485	6,856	2,747	56,370	699,710	88,237	16,338
Pasco	1,277.5	2,716	49.4	2.0	7.9	0.8	5.8	1,324.5	2,816	848	935	16,762	229,430	52,616	6,035
Pinellas	3,402.6	3,693	34.6	4.2	11.2	3.0	4.2	3,555.7	3,859	7,192	2,755	37,403	469,170	63,435	9,343
Polk	1992.7	3,234	48.6	3.2	8.2	1.6	5.5	2,776.3	4,506	1,094	1,268	27,113	291,930	46,779	4,849

1. Based on the resident population estimated as of July 1 of the year shown.

Table B. States and Counties — **Land Area and Population**

State / county code	CBSA code[1]	County code[2]	STATE County	Land area[3] (sq. mi)	Population, 2018 Total persons 2018	Rank	Per square mile	White	Black	American Indian, Alaska Native	Asian and Pacific Islander	Percent Hispanic or Latino[4]	Under 5 years	5 to 17 years	18 to 24 years	25 to 34 years	35 to 44 years	45 to 54 years
				1	2	3	4	5	6	7	8	9	10	11	12	13	14	15
			FLORIDA—Cont'd															
12107	37,260	4	Putnam..........	727.9	74,163	742	101.9	72.7	16.6	1.0	1.0	10.2	5.8	15.6	7.0	11.2	9.9	11.8
12109	27,260	1	St. Johns..........	600.7	254,261	271	423.3	84.0	5.9	0.6	4.1	7.2	4.9	16.8	7.0	9.7	12.9	14.1
12111	38,940	2	St. Lucie..........	571.7	321,128	218	561.7	58.1	21.0	0.6	2.6	19.5	5.0	14.7	7.2	11.4	11.0	12.4
12113	37,860	2	Santa Rosa..........	1,012.4	179,349	369	177.2	85.0	7.2	1.6	3.7	5.7	5.6	16.3	7.7	14.0	12.9	13.6
12115	35,840	2	Sarasota..........	556.9	426,718	165	766.2	84.2	5.0	0.6	2.3	9.3	3.5	10.7	5.6	8.4	8.4	11.1
12117	36,740	1	Seminole..........	309.4	467,832	150	1,512.1	61.4	12.5	0.6	5.7	22.0	5.3	15.7	8.3	14.5	13.9	13.8
12119	45,540	3	Sumter..........	557.1	128,754	494	231.1	85.8	7.4	0.7	1.2	5.7	2.0	5.1	3.1	5.8	5.9	6.7
12121		6	Suwannee..........	688.6	44,191	1,090	64.2	76.8	13.1	1.0	1.0	9.6	5.4	15.9	7.5	12.4	10.9	12.4
12123		6	Taylor..........	1,043.3	21,623	1,746	20.7	74.3	20.3	1.7	1.3	4.5	5.7	14.5	7.2	14.6	11.7	12.5
12125		6	Union..........	243.6	14,940	2,100	61.3	71.1	23.0	0.8	1.0	5.7	5.3	14.2	8.8	15.2	13.3	13.7
12127	19,660	2	Volusia..........	1,101.2	547,538	125	497.2	72.7	11.3	0.8	2.5	14.5	4.7	13.0	8.1	11.8	10.4	12.3
12129	45,220	2	Wakulla..........	606.4	32,461	1,369	53.5	81.8	13.8	1.3	1.3	3.8	5.6	15.8	7.0	13.7	13.7	14.7
12131	18,880	3	Walton..........	1,037.7	71,375	758	68.8	86.4	5.8	1.7	2.1	6.4	5.7	14.5	5.9	12.1	12.2	13.3
12133		6	Washington..........	584.7	24,880	1,612	42.6	79.3	15.7	2.1	1.4	3.7	5.1	14.8	8.5	14.0	12.5	13.9
13000		0	GEORGIA..........	57,715.3	10,519,475	X	182.3	54.0	32.6	0.7	4.9	9.8	6.2	17.6	9.6	14.0	13.0	13.4
13001		7	Appling..........	508.3	18,507	1,900	36.4	69.8	19.8	0.5	0.9	10.2	6.8	17.9	8.2	11.9	11.9	12.5
13003		9	Atkinson..........	342.7	8,297	2,562	24.2	57.9	17.0	0.8	0.7	25.0	7.2	19.1	9.0	13.2	12.4	12.9
13005		7	Bacon..........	284.1	11,185	2,338	39.4	74.4	17.2	0.3	0.8	8.7	6.5	18.9	8.4	12.4	13.0	12.5
13007	10,500	3	Baker..........	342.0	3,092	2,959	9.0	48.6	44.7	0.6	1.2	6.0	5.3	14.0	7.6	11.0	9.9	13.0
13009	33,300	4	Baldwin..........	258.7	44,823	1,080	173.3	53.5	42.9	0.5	2.1	2.2	4.7	14.0	18.4	11.8	10.6	11.6
13011		8	Banks..........	232.1	18,988	1,874	81.8	88.8	3.3	0.9	1.4	7.1	5.9	16.4	8.0	11.8	12.5	14.3
13013	12,060	1	Barrow..........	161.0	80,809	700	501.9	72.4	13.1	0.7	4.4	11.5	6.7	19.2	8.0	14.6	14.1	13.4
13015	12,060	1	Bartow..........	459.5	106,408	570	231.6	78.9	11.8	0.8	1.4	8.8	6.5	17.7	8.3	13.6	12.5	14.3
13017	22,340	7	Ben Hill..........	250.1	16,787	1,991	67.1	56.8	36.4	0.7	1.0	6.2	6.4	18.3	8.1	12.2	11.5	12.6
13019		6	Berrien..........	453.4	19,252	1,864	42.5	82.7	11.3	0.7	1.4	4.9	6.4	17.9	7.6	12.6	11.4	13.5
13021	31,420	3	Bibb..........	249.4	153,095	434	613.9	39.0	55.9	0.6	2.6	3.4	6.8	17.8	10.1	13.7	11.6	11.9
13023		6	Bleckley..........	215.9	12,838	2,235	59.5	69.3	27.1	0.5	1.3	3.1	5.3	15.1	14.4	11.8	10.7	12.8
13025	15,260	3	Brantley..........	443.0	18,897	1,878	42.7	93.7	4.3	1.3	0.5	2.0	6.1	17.4	8.2	12.2	11.6	14.3
13027	46,660	3	Brooks..........	493.1	15,513	2,068	31.5	58.1	35.2	1.0	1.4	5.9	5.9	15.9	7.2	11.8	10.6	13.4
13029	42,340	2	Bryan..........	437.6	38,109	1,222	87.1	75.7	15.7	1.0	3.1	7.3	7.5	21.8	7.5	14.2	15.6	12.5
13031	44,340	4	Bulloch..........	675.9	77,296	718	114.4	64.9	30.2	0.6	1.9	4.1	5.8	14.2	23.5	14.1	10.6	10.2
13033	12,260	2	Burke..........	827.0	22,423	1,705	27.1	48.7	47.8	0.8	0.8	3.3	7.0	19.1	8.1	12.1	11.5	12.4
13035	12,060	1	Butts..........	183.7	24,193	1,636	131.7	67.2	29.1	0.7	0.8	3.5	5.8	15.0	9.4	14.4	13.1	13.7
13037		8	Calhoun..........	280.4	6,352	2,722	22.7	33.8	61.0	0.5	0.8	5.0	3.9	13.6	8.9	15.2	16.0	13.9
13039	41,220	4	Camden..........	630.3	53,677	943	85.2	72.1	20.1	1.2	2.6	7.0	7.2	17.2	11.7	16.3	11.3	11.0
13043		7	Candler..........	243.1	10,836	2,363	44.6	62.5	25.0	0.5	0.9	12.3	6.2	18.8	7.9	12.1	11.4	12.6
13045	12,060	1	Carroll..........	499.0	118,121	527	236.7	72.5	20.4	0.7	1.3	7.2	6.4	17.3	12.6	13.6	12.2	12.6
13047	16,860	2	Catoosa..........	162.2	67,420	793	415.7	92.3	3.6	0.9	1.9	3.1	5.5	17.4	7.7	12.1	12.6	13.9
13049		6	Charlton..........	780.1	12,968	2,231	16.6	63.1	29.7	3.0	1.2	4.7	5.1	14.1	9.5	16.2	13.0	13.4
13051	42,340	2	Chatham..........	433.1	289,195	242	667.7	49.9	41.3	0.7	3.7	6.6	6.3	14.9	11.0	16.4	12.4	11.5
13053	17,980	2	Chattahoochee..........	248.7	10,684	2,381	43.0	60.3	21.0	1.6	5.0	16.1	8.4	13.5	27.4	25.1	10.5	6.1
13055	44,900	6	Chattooga..........	313.3	24,790	1,617	79.1	84.0	10.8	0.7	0.8	5.4	6.0	16.4	8.3	12.7	12.2	13.3
13057	12,060	1	Cherokee..........	421.1	254,149	272	603.5	80.1	7.7	0.7	2.7	10.8	5.9	18.5	8.0	12.0	13.8	15.1
13059	12,020	3	Clarke..........	119.2	127,330	502	1,068.2	56.7	28.8	0.5	5.1	10.9	5.2	12.0	25.9	16.5	11.3	9.1
13061		9	Clay..........	195.4	2,887	2,976	14.8	37.0	60.8	0.6	0.8	1.7	5.2	15.2	5.9	10.6	10.8	10.2
13063	12,060	1	Clayton..........	141.7	289,615	241	2,043.9	11.0	71.4	0.7	5.6	13.3	7.5	20.3	9.9	15.7	13.1	13.1
13065		6	Clinch..........	815.0	6,648	2,700	8.2	66.4	27.7	0.9	0.6	5.9	6.6	18.9	8.4	12.8	11.8	13.0
13067	12,060	1	Cobb..........	339.8	756,865	85	2,227.4	53.4	28.8	0.7	6.3	13.2	6.2	17.4	8.9	14.7	14.1	14.2
13069	20,060	7	Coffee..........	592.3	43,093	1,114	72.8	58.8	28.8	0.6	1.1	12.0	6.9	17.5	9.8	14.5	12.9	13.1
13071	34,220	6	Colquitt..........	547.0	45,592	1,061	83.3	56.2	23.5	0.6	1.0	19.7	6.7	19.4	8.6	13.0	12.6	12.7
13073	12,260	2	Columbia..........	290.1	154,291	430	531.9	70.7	19.0	0.8	5.7	6.9	6.3	19.0	7.9	14.0	14.0	13.2
13075		6	Cook..........	228.3	17,162	1,967	75.2	65.7	28.2	0.6	1.0	5.7	6.4	18.7	8.6	12.2	12.1	13.1
13077	12,060	1	Coweta..........	440.9	145,864	450	330.8	72.4	18.8	0.7	2.8	7.1	6.0	18.5	8.2	12.4	13.2	15.1
13079	31,420	3	Crawford..........	324.9	12,318	2,266	37.9	74.3	21.2	1.0	1.3	3.5	4.9	15.7	7.0	11.9	10.8	14.1
13081	18,380	6	Crisp..........	272.7	22,601	1,701	82.9	50.6	44.9	0.5	1.6	3.5	6.3	17.9	7.8	11.7	11.7	12.2
13083	16,860	2	Dade..........	174.0	16,226	2,027	93.3	95.0	1.6	1.2	1.4	2.3	4.9	14.3	12.0	11.3	11.2	12.6
13085	12,060	1	Dawson..........	210.8	25,083	1,602	119.0	93.1	1.3	0.9	1.1	4.8	5.4	15.3	7.5	12.0	11.2	14.3
13087	12,460	6	Decatur..........	597.2	26,575	1,543	44.5	50.9	42.6	0.6	0.8	6.3	6.9	17.6	9.0	12.5	11.8	12.9
13089	12,060	1	DeKalb..........	267.7	756,558	86	2,826.1	30.6	54.9	0.7	7.3	8.6	6.9	16.2	8.4	16.9	14.3	13.1
13091		6	Dodge..........	496.0	20,705	1,788	41.7	66.0	30.4	0.6	0.8	3.6	4.9	14.5	8.3	13.2	12.6	14.8
13093		6	Dooly..........	392.6	13,706	2,186	34.9	43.3	49.5	0.5	0.8	6.9	3.8	13.4	7.7	12.6	13.3	14.0
13095	10,500	3	Dougherty..........	328.6	91,243	645	277.7	25.3	71.1	0.5	1.4	2.9	6.4	16.8	14.0	13.2	11.2	11.0
13097	12,060	1	Douglas..........	200.1	145,331	451	726.3	40.7	48.5	0.8	2.3	10.0	6.2	19.6	9.3	12.8	13.6	14.9
13099		6	Early..........	512.6	10,247	2,403	20.0	45.4	51.5	0.8	0.9	2.3	6.4	18.7	7.8	11.2	11.2	12.6
13101	46,660	3	Echols..........	420.4	4,000	2,899	9.5	63.3	5.4	2.3	0.8	30.1	6.3	20.4	8.0	14.7	13.4	12.8

1. CBSA = Core Based Statistical Area. See Appendix A for explanation. See Appendix B for list of metropolitan areas with component counties. Service of USDA Rural-Urban Continuum Codes. See Appendix A for definition. 3. Dry land or land partially or temporarily covered by water. 2. County type code from the Economic Research 4. May be of any race.

Table B. States and Counties — **Population and Households**

STATE County	Population, 2018 (cont.) Age (percent) (cont.) 55 to 64 years	65 to 74 years	75 years and over	Percent female	Population change, 2000-2018 Total persons 2000	2010	Percent change 2000-2010	2010-2018	Components of change, 2010-2018 Births	Deaths	Net Migration	Households, 2013-2017 Number	Persons per household	Family house-holds	Percent Female family house-holder[1]	One person
	16	17	18	19	20	21	22	23	24	25	26	27	28	29	30	31
FLORIDA—Cont'd																
Putnam	15.4	13.4	9.8	50.5	70,423	74,368	5.6	-0.3	6,934	7,945	842	27,951	2.54	61.4	13.4	33.1
St. Johns	14.3	12.3	7.9	51.2	123,135	190,034	54.3	33.8	16,654	14,424	61,213	83,744	2.68	71.7	8.6	22.6
St. Lucie	14.0	13.1	11.0	51.1	192,695	277,255	43.9	15.8	24,822	24,861	43,702	110,043	2.69	67.6	12.6	26.4
Santa Rosa	13.9	9.8	6.2	49.0	117,743	151,371	28.6	18.5	15,375	11,072	23,386	60,607	2.65	73.8	11.6	20.7
Sarasota	15.6	18.5	18.2	52.3	325,957	379,435	16.4	12.5	23,751	44,158	67,201	177,998	2.24	60.8	8.4	32.8
Seminole	13.0	9.1	6.4	51.7	365,196	422,713	15.7	10.7	37,492	26,573	34,452	161,371	2.76	66.0	11.3	27.4
Sumter	13.9	33.1	24.5	50.1	53,345	93,420	75.1	37.8	3,818	12,808	43,639	52,360	2.05	68.6	4.2	26.9
Suwannee	14.2	11.9	9.4	48.5	34,844	41,555	19.3	6.3	3,818	4,513	3,229	15,291	2.76	71.5	13.5	22.6
Taylor	13.4	12.0	8.4	45.4	19,256	22,571	17.2	-4.2	1,949	1,967	-938	7,406	2.48	70.5	13.0	25.7
Union	14.6	9.2	5.8	35.6	13,442	15,535	15.6	-3.8	1,327	1,764	-169	3,946	2.53	70.0	16.8	26.4
Volusia	15.3	13.7	10.7	51.2	443,343	494,596	11.6	10.7	39,680	55,104	68,077	209,885	2.42	61.2	11.1	31.5
Wakulla	13.9	10.1	5.5	46.6	22,863	30,783	34.6	5.5	2,692	2,126	1,110	11,075	2.53	71.8	11.6	22.7
Walton	15.7	12.9	7.7	49.5	40,601	55,043	35.6	29.7	5,961	4,847	14,990	25,449	2.41	65.9	10.8	28.2
Washington	13.7	10.5	7.1	46.3	20,973	24,896	18.7	-0.1	1,964	2,371	363	8,558	2.57	69.2	11.8	27.3
GEORGIA	12.2	8.5	5.4	51.4	8,186,453	9,688,709	18.4	8.6	1,074,297	634,603	387,595	3,663,104	2.71	67.6	15.0	26.8
Appling	13.5	10.2	7.0	50.1	17,419	18,236	4.7	1.5	2,079	1,618	-194	6,702	2.68	71.7	16.5	25.1
Atkinson	12.2	8.5	5.5	49.5	7,609	8,382	10.2	-1.0	1,027	583	-540	2,835	2.92	67.1	14.0	29.8
Bacon	12.2	9.8	6.2	51.1	10,103	11,089	9.8	0.9	1,244	1,062	-80	3,989	2.67	72.9	14.7	24.0
Baker	16.6	13.3	9.2	50.5	4,074	3,451	-15.3	-10.4	261	222	-405	1,321	2.46	63.5	13.6	33.8
Baldwin	12.8	9.7	6.3	49.3	44,700	45,840	2.6	-2.2	3,724	3,508	-1,306	16,330	2.54	58.5	15.8	32.4
Banks	13.7	11.0	6.5	49.2	14,422	18,375	27.4	3.3	1,597	1,261	278	6,489	2.83	74.9	9.8	23.4
Barrow	11.6	7.9	4.6	51.0	46,144	69,355	50.3	16.5	8,620	4,603	7,349	24,588	3.04	74.6	13.4	20.6
Bartow	13.1	8.8	5.2	50.7	76,019	100,128	31.7	6.3	10,795	7,064	2,584	37,120	2.74	71.8	13.1	22.5
Ben Hill	13.5	10.5	7.0	52.6	17,484	17,637	0.9	-4.8	1,903	1,771	-975	6,361	2.66	70.3	20.5	26.4
Berrien	13.6	10.0	7.1	50.9	16,235	19,291	18.8	-0.2	1,917	1,663	-298	7,240	2.60	70.7	14.9	24.8
Bibb	12.5	9.1	6.4	53.1	153,887	155,795	1.2	-1.7	18,008	13,477	-7,218	57,319	2.57	60.3	20.4	35.1
Bleckley	13.0	8.9	7.9	52.3	11,666	13,063	12.0	-1.7	1,096	1,178	-146	4,155	2.72	66.3	12.6	29.1
Brantley	13.6	10.3	6.3	50.7	14,629	18,414	25.9	2.6	1,759	1,541	263	6,658	2.75	74.1	11.3	22.1
Brooks	15.4	12.1	7.7	51.2	16,450	16,315	-0.8	-4.9	1,625	1,587	-860	6,337	2.45	65.0	12.0	30.8
Bryan	10.3	6.8	3.9	50.7	23,417	30,215	29.0	26.1	4,152	1,971	5,681	12,366	2.81	78.7	12.5	17.9
Bulloch	10.2	7.0	4.4	50.9	55,983	70,246	25.5	10.0	7,133	4,241	4,027	26,632	2.49	61.8	15.4	23.8
Burke	14.2	9.8	5.8	52.4	22,243	23,311	4.8	-3.8	2,615	2,007	-1,515	8,068	2.78	74.5	22.2	22.6
Butts	13.0	9.4	6.1	47.2	19,522	23,667	21.2	2.2	2,202	2,062	373	8,053	2.60	71.5	15.1	23.7
Calhoun	12.9	8.6	7.0	39.7	6,320	6,697	6.0	-5.2	454	498	-307	1,865	2.49	66.2	20.2	25.8
Camden	11.7	8.7	5.0	48.8	43,664	50,512	15.7	6.3	6,571	2,709	-723	18,913	2.68	75.9	13.4	19.3
Candler	13.1	11.2	6.8	51.0	9,577	10,995	14.8	-1.4	1,162	1,071	-252	4,061	2.62	71.9	19.6	24.4
Carroll	11.7	8.3	5.3	51.2	87,268	110,580	26.7	6.8	12,303	8,301	3,562	41,123	2.71	68.7	12.9	25.0
Catoosa	13.0	10.3	7.4	51.6	53,282	63,937	20.0	5.4	6,012	4,911	2,422	24,719	2.64	72.8	9.9	23.6
Charlton	12.7	9.1	6.9	42.7	10,282	12,171	18.4	6.5	1,012	820	479	3,537	3.34	77.9	11.5	18.2
Chatham	12.1	9.2	6.2	51.9	232,048	265,126	14.3	9.1	32,115	19,323	11,123	107,427	2.54	62.3	16.6	29.7
Chattahoochee	4.2	2.6	2.2	36.0	14,882	11,267	-24.3	-5.2	1,917	269	-2,301	2,505	3.05	73.1	10.1	17.0
Chattooga	13.6	10.1	7.4	48.9	25,470	26,017	2.1	-4.7	2,350	2,580	-1,009	9,253	2.50	66.4	13.2	28.7
Cherokee	12.7	9.1	4.9	50.8	141,903	214,372	51.1	18.6	23,109	11,344	27,850	83,150	2.82	74.2	9.4	20.8
Clarke	9.0	6.7	4.3	52.6	101,489	116,697	15.0	9.1	11,436	5,906	4,971	46,291	2.44	47.8	12.2	34.9
Clay	15.3	16.0	10.8	52.8	3,357	3,185	-5.1	-9.4	269	317	-254	1,154	2.57	60.8	19.9	35.4
Clayton	11.0	6.4	3.0	53.2	236,517	259,580	9.8	11.6	34,957	13,236	8,214	91,604	2.94	66.9	25.3	28.1
Clinch	12.3	10.2	6.0	51.4	6,878	6,798	-1.2	-2.2	794	620	-328	2,576	2.45	59.6	17.9	32.5
Cobb	12.2	7.8	4.5	51.6	607,751	688,071	13.2	10.0	77,577	33,533	25,137	274,361	2.66	68.3	13.2	25.0
Coffee	11.5	8.6	5.1	48.6	37,413	42,354	13.2	1.7	4,862	3,237	-929	14,329	2.73	67.2	15.9	29.5
Colquitt	11.5	9.2	6.2	50.5	42,053	45,499	8.2	0.2	5,516	3,844	-1,568	15,599	2.89	71.4	18.8	24.5
Columbia	12.0	8.4	5.1	51.2	89,288	124,041	38.9	24.4	14,207	7,116	22,917	45,823	3.13	77.4	10.4	19.6
Cook	12.3	9.7	6.8	51.8	15,771	17,209	9.1	-0.3	1,794	1,552	-297	6,065	2.81	72.5	16.8	22.9
Coweta	12.8	8.6	5.2	51.3	89,215	127,353	42.7	14.5	13,586	7,883	12,743	50,531	2.72	75.5	12.9	20.2
Crawford	16.7	12.1	6.7	49.6	12,495	12,630	1.1	-2.5	1,051	1,025	-342	4,715	2.59	70.2	13.1	26.6
Crisp	13.7	11.0	7.6	52.7	21,996	23,430	6.5	-3.5	2,447	2,019	-1,284	8,312	2.72	68.8	20.1	28.0
Dade	14.4	11.3	8.0	50.9	15,154	16,635	9.8	-2.5	1,336	1,445	-296	6,089	2.46	73.0	10.6	22.5
Dawson	14.3	12.8	7.3	50.6	15,999	22,337	39.6	12.3	1,977	1,578	2,334	8,557	2.71	75.0	8.8	21.6
Decatur	13.0	9.2	7.0	51.6	28,240	27,842	-1.4	-4.6	3,044	2,581	-1,740	10,311	2.50	65.6	20.8	32.0
DeKalb	11.8	7.8	4.6	52.7	665,865	691,971	3.9	9.3	90,659	36,594	10,741	273,614	2.64	58.7	17.3	33.0
Dodge	13.7	10.5	7.6	47.9	19,171	21,797	13.7	-5.0	1,901	1,863	-1,133	7,858	2.42	66.9	14.0	31.0
Dooly	15.2	11.6	8.5	45.6	11,525	14,923	29.5	-8.2	892	1,010	-1,119	5,171	2.37	66.6	21.1	31.0
Dougherty	12.0	9.1	6.2	54.1	96,065	94,562	-1.6	-3.5	10,923	7,447	-6,881	34,842	2.51	61.7	25.4	32.8
Douglas	12.0	7.4	4.1	52.5	92,174	132,305	43.5	9.9	14,321	7,527	6,233	48,426	2.87	71.9	18.2	23.0
Early	13.1	10.4	8.6	53.3	12,354	11,008	-10.9	-6.9	1,138	1,115	-793	4,032	2.54	66.3	22.2	30.1
Echols	11.5	7.6	5.5	48.3	3,754	4,027	7.3	-0.7	496	225	-300	1,502	2.67	72.2	14.6	24.9

1. No spouse present.

Table B. States and Counties — Population, Vital Statistics, Health, and Crime

STATE County	Persons in group quarters, 2018	Daytime Population, 2013-2017		Births, 2018		Deaths, 2018		Persons under 65 with no health insurance, 2016		Medicare, 2018			Serious crimes known to police[2], 2016 Total	
		Number	Employment/ residence ratio	Total	Rate[1]	Number	Rate[1]	Number	Percent	Total beneficiaries	Enrolled in Original Medicare	Enrolled in Medicare Advantage	Number	Rate[3]
	32	33	34	35	36	37	38	39	40	41	42	43	44	45
FLORIDA—Cont'd														
Putnam	1,422	67,621	0.80	846	11.4	989	13.3	9,034	16.5	19,124	12,297	6,827	2,272	3,167
St. Johns	3,042	204,571	0.78	2,115	8.3	2,010	7.9	18,115	9.6	53,053	38,387	14,666	4,141	1,763
St. Lucie	3,039	271,227	0.77	3,001	9.3	3,403	10.6	41,398	17.9	76,404	45,109	31,295	6,450	2,126
Santa Rosa	6,035	135,058	0.56	1,913	10.7	1,569	8.7	15,413	11.1	33,939	23,240	10,699	2,177	1,278
Sarasota	5,942	427,502	1.14	2,832	6.6	5,939	13.9	41,532	15.7	139,076	97,885	41,191	9,021	2,191
Seminole	3,512	422,483	0.88	4,710	10.1	3,626	7.8	46,722	12.1	78,182	44,909	33,273	11,911	2,615
Sumter	8,197	124,102	1.32	456	3.5	1,920	14.9	5,436	11.7	71,177	41,740	29,437	1,385	1,110
Suwannee	2,575	41,124	0.83	455	10.3	578	13.1	5,542	17.5	11,027	8,027	3,000	895	2,027
Taylor	2,424	22,594	1.04	219	10.1	234	10.8	2,105	14.1	4,876	3,573	1,303	716	3,179
Union	4,630	16,299	1.27	142	9.5	231	15.5	978	11.5	2,139	1,576	563	97	638
Volusia	14,427	496,568	0.89	4,984	9.1	7,166	13.1	57,998	14.8	143,449	72,364	71,085	18,428	3,519
Wakulla	2,592	24,564	0.48	330	10.2	263	8.1	2,813	11.7	5,929	2,856	3,073	556	1,752
Walton	2,074	63,881	1.02	770	10.8	655	9.2	9,012	17.6	14,766	10,720	4,046	1,612	2,464
Washington	2,464	22,848	0.81	241	9.7	295	11.9	2,644	15.0	5,506	4,106	1,400	381	1,541
GEORGIA	264,562	10,202,294	1.00	127,649	12.1	84,888	8.1	1,295,994	14.9	1,674,828	1,045,523	629,305	350,760	3,402
Appling	418	18,776	1.04	225	12.2	212	11.5	2,635	17.6	3,727	2,453	1,274	666	3,608
Atkinson	20	7,432	0.73	115	13.9	66	8.0	1,717	24.2	1,355	882	473	NA	NA
Bacon	324	11,354	1.02	150	13.4	115	10.3	1,742	18.6	2,147	1,396	751	NA	NA
Baker	0	2,609	0.48	30	9.7	27	8.7	405	16.1	671	404	267	NA	NA
Baldwin	5,686	45,111	0.98	390	8.7	489	10.9	4,975	15.0	8,678	4,753	3,925	1,830	4,034
Banks	0	15,370	0.61	196	10.3	155	8.2	2,633	17.2	3,683	2,286	1,397	535	2,893
Barrow	314	61,395	0.59	1,035	12.8	648	8.0	11,640	17.1	12,230	7,338	4,892	2,413	3,155
Bartow	979	96,684	0.87	1,333	12.5	910	8.6	14,515	16.3	18,096	11,679	6,417	3,819	3,728
Ben Hill	344	17,431	1.03	207	12.3	210	12.5	2,168	15.4	3,702	2,283	1,419	755	4,354
Berrien	178	16,492	0.64	235	12.2	225	11.7	2,663	17.1	3,763	2,564	1,199	521	2,761
Bibb	6,128	174,568	1.35	2,100	13.7	1,724	11.3	17,332	14.0	30,484	18,308	12,176	8,882	5,798
Bleckley	1,308	11,216	0.62	135	10.5	130	10.1	1,297	13.8	2,536	1,853	683	462	3,825
Brantley	78	14,789	0.43	229	12.1	219	11.6	2,724	17.7	3,366	2,383	983	524	2,842
Brooks	82	12,894	0.52	171	11.0	192	12.4	2,470	19.9	3,515	2,360	1,155	495	3,331
Bryan	99	26,421	0.47	538	14.1	262	6.9	4,021	12.4	5,361	3,373	1,988	670	1,854
Bulloch	5,501	70,989	0.91	882	11.4	570	7.4	10,427	17.0	10,131	7,004	3,127	2,012	2,780
Burke	286	24,499	1.22	297	13.2	229	10.2	2,541	13.4	4,542	2,546	1,996	1,063	4,702
Butts	2,676	22,186	0.84	272	11.2	264	10.9	2,516	14.3	4,714	2,616	2,098	562	2,388
Calhoun	1,712	6,493	0.99	53	8.3	54	8.5	721	18.8	1,191	755	436	56	871
Camden	1,961	49,339	0.88	779	14.5	361	6.7	6,004	13.6	8,387	6,265	2,122	NA	NA
Candler	283	9,991	0.78	128	11.8	129	11.9	1,802	20.5	2,276	1,425	851	NA	NA
Carroll	3,680	110,168	0.90	1,552	13.1	1,100	9.3	15,113	15.5	20,429	12,802	7,627	3,481	3,021
Catoosa	541	50,946	0.52	687	10.2	676	10.0	7,068	12.8	13,280	9,144	4,136	1,848	2,784
Charlton	2,231	11,369	0.63	114	8.8	90	6.9	1,203	14.5	2,097	1,503	594	223	1,718
Chatham	14,891	316,889	1.24	3,701	12.8	2,547	8.8	34,422	14.7	48,803	29,413	19,390	11,972	4,113
Chattahoochee	2,505	19,575	2.30	220	20.6	28	2.6	834	11.7	573	355	218	1	9
Chattooga	1,306	23,063	0.79	282	11.4	290	11.7	3,337	17.2	5,619	3,494	2,125	438	1,774
Cherokee	1,732	188,995	0.59	2,750	10.8	1,579	6.2	29,188	13.9	38,989	24,601	14,388	3,311	1,383
Clarke	10,109	140,505	1.30	1,368	10.7	777	6.1	15,722	15.5	16,644	10,768	5,876	5,002	3,998
Clay	58	2,714	0.64	23	8.0	39	13.5	368	16.8	770	462	308	NA	NA
Clayton	4,702	260,545	0.89	4,043	14.0	1,831	6.3	42,566	17.2	34,695	17,649	17,046	13,732	4,965
Clinch	126	6,952	1.08	83	12.5	67	10.1	907	16.0	1,445	982	463	239	3,459
Cobb	9,330	717,398	0.94	9,279	12.3	4,639	6.1	90,699	13.9	100,169	63,942	36,227	19,908	2,650
Coffee	3,167	43,973	1.06	590	13.7	404	9.4	6,281	18.4	7,066	4,671	2,395	NA	NA
Colquitt	1,052	44,251	0.91	604	13.2	467	10.2	8,649	22.8	8,810	5,835	2,975	NA	NA
Columbia	795	112,704	0.53	1,802	11.7	1,006	6.5	12,237	9.4	22,376	15,563	6,813	2,236	1,510
Cook	147	15,978	0.82	199	11.6	198	11.5	2,599	18.1	3,439	2,324	1,115	578	3,559
Coweta	585	114,725	0.65	1,677	11.5	1,066	7.3	14,075	11.5	22,473	13,918	8,555	2,835	2,018
Crawford	132	9,613	0.38	97	7.9	153	12.4	1,626	16.3	2,603	1,545	1,058	275	2,426
Crisp	438	23,762	1.09	270	11.9	285	12.6	2,809	15.4	4,414	2,663	1,751	932	4,096
Dade	1,019	14,170	0.72	151	9.3	189	11.6	1,773	14.3	3,551	2,426	1,125	38	235
Dawson	102	21,071	0.78	260	10.4	228	9.1	3,039	16.1	4,832	3,265	1,567	466	1,983
Decatur	1,034	26,256	0.92	376	14.1	341	12.8	3,647	17.0	5,636	3,854	1,782	829	3,099
DeKalb	11,521	700,520	0.90	10,866	14.4	4,972	6.6	98,243	15.3	100,806	54,464	46,342	38,108	5,130
Dodge	1,853	19,479	0.79	188	9.1	241	11.6	2,588	16.6	4,108	2,832	1,276	851	4,183
Dooly	1,935	13,402	0.86	88	6.4	117	8.5	1,696	17.9	2,302	1,425	877	196	1,414
Dougherty	6,917	104,491	1.38	1,203	13.2	950	10.4	11,430	15.7	17,238	10,663	6,575	5,110	5,640
Douglas	1,215	121,639	0.72	1,694	11.7	1,044	7.2	18,103	14.5	19,851	11,616	8,235	5,102	3,586
Early	134	10,020	0.90	127	12.4	149	14.5	1,229	15.0	2,361	1,499	862	244	2,326
Echols	0	2,765	0.25	35	8.8	17	4.3	922	26.8	520	378	142	30	743

1. Per 1,000 estimated resident population.   2. Data for serious crimes have not been adjusted for underreporting; this may affect comparability between geographic areas and over time.   3. Per 100,000 population estimated by the FBI.

Table B. States and Counties — Crime, Education, Money Income, and Poverty

STATE County	Serious crimes known to police[2], 2016 (cont.)[1] Rate — Violent	Property	Education — School enrollment and attainment, 2013-2017 — Enrollment[3] Total	Percent private	Attainment[4] (percent) High school graduate or less	Bachelor's degree or more	Local government expenditures,[5] 2014-2015 — Total current spending (mil dol)	Current spending per student (dollars)	Money income, 2013-2017 — Per capita income[6]	Households Median income (dollars)	Percent with income of less than $50,000	Percent with income of $200,000 or more	Income and poverty, 2017 — Median household income (dollars)	Percent below poverty level — All persons	Children under 18 years	Children 5 to 17 years in families
	46	47	48	49	50	51	52	53	54	55	56	57	58	59	60	61
FLORIDA—Cont'd																
Putnam	513	2,654	14,518	10.0	60.6	12.5	103.4	9,358	18,950	33,619	67.5	1.3	34,390	26.3	43.0	41.3
St. Johns	196	1,567	55,902	21.3	26.9	43.0	299.0	8,337	39,563	73,640	33.9	10.3	77,022	8.3	9.1	7.8
St. Lucie	272	1,854	66,687	15.0	47.8	19.6	344.5	8,596	24,940	47,132	52.6	2.9	49,995	12.8	19.1	18.0
Santa Rosa	140	1,138	40,461	11.1	36.5	27.1	212.1	8,057	28,908	62,731	38.3	4.0	65,434	10.2	14.3	13.1
Sarasota	219	1,972	64,707	15.7	37.0	33.9	445.1	10,620	37,054	55,236	45.1	6.3	58,423	9.2	14.8	13.4
Seminole	372	2,243	118,134	16.1	27.8	37.6	537.0	8,121	31,363	60,739	41.4	6.0	63,865	11.2	13.9	13.7
Sumter	234	876	9,062	17.2	38.5	30.9	77.3	9,303	33,168	54,771	45.8	3.5	57,931	9.1	26.0	25.3
Suwannee	546	1,482	9,308	16.8	59.5	13.7	52.4	8,660	21,565	40,600	58.0	2.3	44,144	20.3	30.0	28.2
Taylor	1,159	2,020	4,410	17.4	63.1	8.6	29.7	9,810	16,979	37,188	63.9	1.3	41,557	23.8	34.5	33.9
Union	243	395	2,528	6.1	61.7	8.3	20.9	8,764	13,485	37,460	61.2	0.9	47,373	22.2	23.0	22.0
Volusia	423	3,096	108,810	19.2	43.4	22.7	529.7	8,574	25,871	43,838	55.6	2.5	46,911	15.2	24.9	22.8
Wakulla	164	1,588	6,949	10.7	48.6	17.8	43.2	8,396	22,846	57,866	44.1	1.7	55,717	12.9	18.1	17.1
Walton	342	2,121	12,258	9.1	40.6	26.7	78.2	9,271	30,853	50,619	49.3	6.0	52,922	15.9	27.0	26.3
Washington	178	1,363	5,132	7.7	60.6	11.3	34.0	9,849	18,718	36,989	62.4	1.3	36,052	21.1	28.7	27.2
GEORGIA	398	3,004	2,756,619	14.4	41.8	29.9	16,346.0	9,371	28,015	52,977	47.3	5.1	56,117	15.1	21.5	20.3
Appling	336	3,272	4,021	6.4	65.0	11.5	36.7	9,945	19,936	37,089	62.3	1.4	40,862	22.2	33.5	32.2
Atkinson	NA	NA	2,179	2.2	70.3	8.2	17.0	10,037	19,904	33,063	67.6	1.8	34,821	24.2	36.5	35.7
Bacon	NA	NA	2,659	6.5	58.9	11.8	20.6	9,672	18,856	38,824	60.0	0.6	38,417	28.2	42.7	39.0
Baker	NA	NA	725	16.4	59.7	11.0	2.8	8,467	22,270	43,867	56.6	1.9	37,286	24.6	40.0	37.6
Baldwin	820	3,214	13,832	15.7	54.3	19.4	50.5	9,088	20,114	37,008	60.8	1.3	40,358	25.2	32.5	31.3
Banks	314	2,579	4,219	6.8	64.9	11.9	26.5	9,339	19,451	42,182	58.4	0.8	49,481	13.5	19.4	18.2
Barrow	527	2,628	20,380	14.7	50.9	17.3	115.9	8,640	22,978	56,119	44.0	2.0	60,028	12	15.7	15.7
Bartow	428	3,301	24,417	10.0	51.6	19.4	171.5	9,395	24,931	52,393	47.6	2.5	55,067	13.2	19.3	19.1
Ben Hill	404	3,951	3,965	5.6	62.1	10.2	30.5	9,218	16,635	32,344	70.8	0.6	32,370	24.5	38.8	36.6
Berrien	233	2,528	4,321	5.8	61.2	11.7	28.4	8,898	18,064	38,297	63.0	0.5	38,239	18.6	29.6	27.6
Bibb	501	5,297	41,454	22.5	47.1	25.4	239.4	9,789	23,426	38,183	59.5	3.5	39,047	25	36.7	36.5
Bleckley	339	3,486	3,862	6.3	57.4	17.2	22.3	9,036	20,667	40,688	58.8	1.4	44,262	20.3	29.4	28.3
Brantley	217	2,625	4,003	7.7	66.6	7.8	32.6	9,262	18,220	36,812	64.7	0.6	40,906	19	27.8	26.7
Brooks	599	2,732	3,665	9.5	57.2	13.6	22.2	10,160	20,964	34,890	63.2	1.4	36,030	23.7	37.6	37.3
Bryan	338	1,517	10,530	15.1	35.1	32.4	62.1	7,283	29,880	68,589	38.5	3.9	73,877	10.4	12.9	11.7
Bulloch	188	2,592	29,393	5.9	40.5	27.9	98.2	9,502	20,526	39,305	59.4	2.4	42,068	24.6	26.3	24.8
Burke	628	4,074	5,967	12.2	57.0	11.7	53.9	12,237	19,720	38,707	60.7	1.3	41,863	23.1	34.7	32.2
Butts	412	1,975	4,972	12.5	65.6	10.5	30.8	8,751	21,236	39,655	60.1	1.8	46,062	18.3	25.2	25.3
Calhoun	296	576	1,449	12.0	65.8	9.4	12.4	10,626	13,865	29,617	71.2	1.6	33,889	35.1	40.2	37.9
Camden	NA	NA	12,658	9.1	39.7	23.6	82.6	9,154	26,854	53,687	45.9	2.6	53,582	12.5	18.9	18.6
Candler	NA	NA	2,750	4.5	59.5	14.4	18.9	8,692	18,233	33,125	65.0	2.4	33,846	24.7	35.8	33.4
Carroll	325	2,696	33,908	8.9	52.0	19.6	172.8	8,797	23,139	46,844	53.0	2.5	51,388	17.2	24.4	23.1
Catoosa	236	2,547	16,102	16.0	45.5	20.3	104.2	9,591	25,643	54,537	44.9	2.3	53,833	12	17.3	15.2
Charlton	185	1,533	2,952	10.4	65.2	8.6	16.3	9,798	19,102	43,257	55.6	0.0	40,636	25.6	32.3	30.3
Chatham	483	3,630	79,547	24.6	34.8	33.2	366.9	9,624	28,765	52,215	47.9	4.8	54,667	16.3	24.2	23.8
Chattahoochee	0	9	2,757	8.3	33.6	33.0	9.8	10,836	22,774	46,096	52.1	2.7	44,439	19.6	22.6	25.0
Chattooga	113	1,660	5,232	8.1	65.8	10.1	38.6	9,040	17,716	35,718	66.3	1.0	39,325	20.2	26.3	23.2
Cherokee	96	1,287	64,629	15.1	33.1	35.7	357.6	8,600	33,466	75,477	31.6	6.7	78,247	7.5	9.2	8.0
Clarke	441	3,557	49,251	7.3	34.5	41.3	159.7	12,188	21,203	34,557	63.8	2.8	39,901	26.6	28.5	28.0
Clay	NA	NA	579	5.7	62.0	8.9	4.0	13,091	14,559	23,315	75.2	0.5	29,122	33.1	51.3	49.3
Clayton	675	4,290	81,164	10.9	49.0	19.1	540.0	8,035	19,498	44,106	56.6	1.2	44,757	16.3	25.5	24.4
Clinch	405	3,054	1,593	2.1	60.6	12.3	13.4	9,506	17,145	21,838	68.6	1.2	37,174	27.6	34.4	32.1
Cobb	276	2,374	205,673	16.7	27.7	45.5	1,128.6	9,361	36,587	72,004	35.0	8.8	75,485	9.5	11.8	10.9
Coffee	NA	NA	10,879	8.1	59.8	14.1	75.7	9,731	18,945	36,572	63.8	2.2	39,408	24.9	34.9	33.4
Colquitt	NA	NA	12,078	4.0	65.2	12.5	88.5	9,112	18,121	34,503	65.5	1.5	36,651	25.6	33.3	32.3
Columbia	52	1,458	39,132	13.2	32.4	34.4	210.3	8,237	31,720	74,162	29.9	6.4	75,832	6.6	7.9	7.4
Cook	443	3,115	4,350	9.2	58.5	14.8	31.4	9,422	17,587	35,539	62.6	1.0	36,463	21.3	31.7	29.9
Coweta	240	1,778	34,963	14.1	41.0	29.0	210.5	8,957	31,548	67,570	36.6	5.1	73,296	10.4	14.2	12.2
Crawford	203	2,223	2,825	14.6	52.5	13.2	16.3	9,201	22,212	41,032	57.3	1.6	47,422	17.6	27.7	26.2
Crisp	224	3,872	6,043	8.6	59.6	13.6	42.7	10,018	21,225	33,194	68.9	2.6	34,754	29.7	43.7	41.6
Dade	0	235	4,083	34.7	55.0	13.9	20.6	9,325	23,184	43,163	54.8	2.0	45,053	15.2	18.1	18.0
Dawson	102	1,881	5,059	11.9	41.8	31.1	39.6	11,424	31,954	62,284	38.8	7.2	64,930	9.4	14.4	13.1
Decatur	396	2,703	6,429	6.6	55.2	14.9	50.3	9,420	19,650	36,934	62.9	2.1	37,835	21.9	35.1	34.9
DeKalb	611	4,519	194,393	23.6	32.4	42.1	982.4	9,210	32,110	55,876	44.9	7.3	61,496	15.3	24.6	24.5
Dodge	339	3,844	4,408	5.6	59.0	14.6	36.2	11,013	18,563	35,290	63.5	0.7	36,067	21.8	29.3	29.1
Dooly	151	1,262	3,094	12.5	65.5	9.9	14.9	10,424	16,867	33,389	65.5	0.2	35,781	27.6	36.4	33.3
Dougherty	1,016	4,623	29,363	8.1	46.4	20.7	173.3	11,319	20,292	34,541	64.9	2.2	36,994	28.2	41.5	40.2
Douglas	323	3,263	41,275	15.0	43.2	26.7	226.5	8,739	25,449	59,333	42.2	2.7	60,177	11.8	17.1	16.3
Early	524	1,802	2,638	8.3	55.9	17.0	21.8	9,922	17,972	29,493	66.9	0.7	32,490	26.7	40.6	37.7
Echols	74	669	1,141	6.5	65.6	6.9	8.5	10,436	20,589	34,315	62.5	0.7	36,559	26.5	35.5	33.0

1. Data for serious crimes have not been adjusted for underreporting; this may affect comparability between geographic areas and over time.   2. Per 100,000 population estimated by the FBI.   3. All persons 3 years old and over enrolled in nursery school through college.   4. Persons 25 years old and over.   5. Elementary and secondary education expenditures.   6. Based on population estimated by the American Community Survey, 2013–2017.

Table B. States and Counties — **Personal Income and Earnings**

STATE County	Personal income, 2017										Earnings, 2017		
			Per capita[1]			Supplements to wages and salaries, employer contributions (mil dol)						Contributions for government social insurance (mil dol)	
	Total (mil dol)	Percent change 2016-2017	Dollars	Rank	Wages and salaries (mil dol)	Pension and insurance	Government social insurance	Proprietors' income (mil dol)	Dividends, interest, and rent (mil dol)	Personal transfer reecipts (mil dol)	Total (mil dol)	From employee and self-employed	From employer
	62	63	64	65	66	67	68	69	70	71	72	73	74

FLORIDA—Cont'd

STATE County	62	63	64	65	66	67	68	69	70	71	72	73	74
Putnam	2,282	5.0	31,057	2,849	680	125	48	89	370	872	943	77	48
St. Johns	15,647	6.5	64,177	110	3,611	486	245	634	4,231	1,980	4,976	346	245
St. Lucie	12,175	5.5	38,835	1,748	3,386	542	235	463	2,683	3,265	4,626	359	235
Santa Rosa	7,478	5.0	42,909	1,149	1,661	280	121	398	1,394	1,484	2,460	179	121
Sarasota	25,786	4.8	61,523	141	8,480	1,098	567	1,689	11,394	4,988	11,835	860	567
Seminole	21,389	5.5	46,231	773	10,073	1,298	680	878	3,774	3,461	12,929	819	680
Sumter	5,440	5.1	43,464	1,079	1,272	217	91	192	1,716	2,249	1,772	200	91
Suwannee	1,443	7.0	32,644	2,666	435	81	31	148	228	481	695	50	31
Taylor	640	3.7	29,298	2,966	292	53	20	28	115	216	394	28	20
Union	316	4.8	20,396	3,110	148	37	10	11	47	103	207	13	10
Volusia	21,902	5.1	40,658	1,447	7,473	1,105	522	930	5,014	5,904	10,030	752	522
Wakulla	1,128	5.2	35,129	2,329	223	47	16	47	178	239	333	26	16
Walton	3,834	5.3	56,076	247	1,083	145	75	368	1,238	563	1,671	113	75
Washington	704	4.0	28,676	3,006	230	45	16	27	108	244	319	25	16
GEORGIA	460,403	4.7	44,214	X	246,139	39,281	16,748	37,539	80,570	78,432	339,707	19,731	16,748
Appling	588	3.5	31,731	2,787	332	80	23	42	78	170	477	27	23
Atkinson	234	5.9	28,070	3,028	82	18	6	19	29	68	125	8	6
Bacon	366	2.9	32,310	2,713	154	33	11	40	44	109	237	13	11
Baker	109	-3.9	34,137	2,469	21	4	2	9	22	33	37	2	2
Baldwin	1,445	2.8	32,176	2,729	573	156	38	62	251	470	828	50	38
Banks	648	7.7	34,749	2,380	137	28	9	81	91	151	255	15	9
Barrow	2,780	5.4	35,164	2,323	805	143	54	179	332	537	1,182	76	54
Bartow	3,925	5.0	37,362	1,975	1,733	308	122	234	548	830	2,397	146	122
Ben Hill	514	3.1	30,247	2,907	208	45	16	21	90	183	289	20	16
Berrien	564	5.3	29,406	2,960	138	36	11	13	98	177	198	15	11
Bibb	6,119	2.8	40,031	1,546	3,963	661	273	445	1,175	1,612	5,342	320	273
Bleckley	420	3.5	32,704	2,656	92	29	6	5	86	117	133	10	6
Brantley	503	4.4	26,861	3,062	81	22	5	37	53	159	146	12	5
Brooks	523	0.9	33,571	2,543	120	25	8	19	98	161	173	13	8
Bryan	1,886	5.7	50,887	419	345	70	23	76	268	274	514	33	23
Bulloch	2,324	3.9	30,522	2,885	999	238	68	103	410	500	1,408	81	68
Burke	773	1.7	34,330	2,441	992	147	70	34	103	224	1,242	71	70
Butts	775	4.8	32,199	2,726	253	56	17	26	112	212	353	24	17
Calhoun	158	7.0	24,527	3,097	38	11	3	21	27	57	73	4	3
Camden	1,849	4.7	34,854	2,368	917	236	76	38	366	400	1,267	68	76
Candler	315	4.2	29,172	2,978	96	23	7	16	46	112	141	10	7
Carroll	4,334	4.7	36,790	2,078	1,871	348	129	260	742	954	2,608	158	129
Catoosa	2,273	3.5	34,158	2,466	567	106	40	145	262	543	857	62	40
Charlton	311	3.9	24,442	3,098	87	17	6	15	39	95	126	9	6
Chatham	12,873	3.0	44,313	985	7,968	1,354	573	822	2,787	2,408	10,717	612	573
Chattahoochee	319	1.2	30,857	2,864	917	256	94	4	139	37	1,271	46	94
Chattooga	734	3.7	29,621	2,952	234	55	17	41	96	251	347	25	17
Cherokee	12,148	5.2	49,067	531	2,736	441	186	871	1,530	1,525	4,233	268	186
Clarke	4,128	4.2	32,491	2,688	3,538	815	228	179	1,008	812	4,760	248	228
Clay	88	1.2	29,731	2,945	18	5	1	-2	20	38	23	2	1
Clayton	7,782	4.3	27,289	3,054	7,251	1,325	474	286	946	1,975	9,336	523	474
Clinch	242	-0.8	35,903	2,211	88	19	6	29	27	78	142	8	6
Cobb	40,281	4.6	53,300	334	23,229	2,974	1,562	2,482	6,798	4,513	30,248	1,742	1,562
Coffee	1,322	4.8	30,732	2,871	647	134	46	56	194	378	883	53	46
Colquitt	1,438	5.4	31,371	2,821	558	127	38	97	227	431	820	50	38
Columbia	7,277	5.7	48,009	625	1,422	258	98	373	1,212	1,066	2,151	138	98
Cook	529	3.9	30,632	2,879	134	34	9	13	84	162	190	14	9
Coweta	6,357	5.0	44,419	967	1,686	301	119	236	867	948	2,342	149	119
Crawford	401	2.6	32,597	2,677	50	12	4	26	53	110	91	7	4
Crisp	703	4.4	30,918	2,856	328	64	23	11	126	222	426	28	23
Dade	550	4.6	33,792	2,508	132	26	9	40	77	145	207	15	9
Dawson	1,058	6.1	43,380	1,092	299	53	21	80	181	185	453	29	21
Decatur	953	5.3	35,677	2,248	316	74	21	86	177	268	497	30	21
DeKalb	35,713	5.0	47,412	674	18,450	2,732	1,270	2,263	6,597	4,997	24,714	1,430	1,270
Dodge	618	3.2	29,806	2,941	179	50	12	25	101	188	265	18	12
Dooly	386	2.4	28,079	3,026	145	34	10	25	64	110	213	13	10
Dougherty	3,132	2.1	34,989	2,350	2,150	416	152	162	592	957	2,880	169	152
Douglas	4,913	4.5	34,147	2,467	1,817	309	125	108	589	994	2,359	148	125
Early	400	4.6	38,832	1,749	209	46	14	29	64	118	298	17	14
Echols	105	4.1	26,673	3,067	18	5	1	2	15	25	26	2	1

1. Based on the resident population estimated as of July 1 of the year shown.

Table B. States and Counties — Earnings, Social Security, and Housing

STATE County	Earnings, 2017 (cont.) — Percent by selected industries									Social Security beneficiaries, December 2017		Supplemental Security Income recipients, 2017	Housing units, 2018	
	Farm	Mining, quarrying, and extractions	Construction	Manufacturing	Information; professional, scientific, technical services	Retail trade	Finance, insurance, real estate, and leasing	Health care and social assistance	Government	Number	Rate¹		Total	Percent change, 2010-2018
	75	76	77	78	79	80	81	82	83	84	85	86	87	88
FLORIDA—Cont'd														
Putnam	1.9	0.4	5	12.6	D	10.2	3.4	14.4	25.6	21,000	286	3,044	37,359	0.1
St. Johns	0.2	D	6.5	6.8	10.1	9.1	10.5	11.6	12.8	52,765	216	2,489	110,825	23.4
St. Lucie	0.5	0	6.9	4.6	6.9	9	4.6	16.7	20	80,765	258	7,037	142,759	4.4
Santa Rosa	-0.2	0.5	8.3	2.5	10.7	8	4.6	14	23.3	36,110	207	2,593	73,067	12.8
Sarasota	0.1	0	9.2	5.1	13.4	8.9	9.7	17.1	9.1	138,365	330	4,694	243,994	6.8
Seminole	0.1	0	10.5	4.1	16.1	8.6	12.2	10.1	8.6	81,590	176	7,477	192,246	6
Sumter	1.2	0.5	10.8	4.4	5.8	8.4	6.9	15.3	20.8	69,110	552	1,664	72,385	36.5
Suwannee	8.3	D	8.6	14.7	D	10.4	2	8.2	21.6	12,160	275	1,458	19,344	0.9
Taylor	0.7	D	6.1	32.3	D	8.4	1.6	8.3	20.2	5,440	249	778	11,133	1.2
Union	1.1	D	5.4	4.9	D	D	0.9	D	54.3	2,420	156	394	4,628	2.7
Volusia	0.7	D	7.4	7.4	7	9.8	6	18.1	13.6	151,730	282	12,466	262,088	3.1
Wakulla	0.3	0	10	15.6	D	7	3.3	5.4	30.2	6,490	202	616	13,702	7
Walton	0.4	D	11.8	1.4	8.7	11.1	8.9	9.1	12.5	15,320	224	925	53,385	18.3
Washington	0.7	D	7.5	3.2	8.2	7.6	2.5	D	35.4	6,085	248	858	10,921	1.1
GEORGIA	0.6	0.2	5.6	9	15.9	5.9	8.4	9.7	16.1	1,790,398	172	259,792	4,326,105	5.8
Appling	6.2	0.1	4.3	9.2	1.6	10.4	2.1	D	15.4	4,145	224	659	8,563	0.6
Atkinson	8.3	D	D	41.2	D	3.6	3.3	D	17.9	1,560	187	358	3,499	-0.7
Bacon	13.2	D	1.4	19.9	D	6.6	D	D	14.1	2,340	207	407	4,796	0
Baker	29.7	0.1	D	0.4	D	2.5	D	5.2	18.1	770	241	149	1,657	0.3
Baldwin	0	0.1	D	11.3	D	9.6	3.9	14.1	39.7	9,390	209	1,471	20,624	2.2
Banks	21.2	0.3	7.3	8.5	D	7.5	D	3.5	18.5	4,030	216	354	7,762	2.3
Barrow	1.3	D	11.8	11.4	3.8	11.9	5	8.2	16.2	13,690	173	1,878	28,951	9.7
Bartow	1.5	0.4	7.8	27.4	4.7	6.6	4.1	7.6	13.4	20,065	191	2,323	41,532	4.3
Ben Hill	1.6	0	2	25.5	D	8.3	3.6	D	19.2	3,960	233	890	7,995	0.7
Berrien	0.5	0	4.9	30.9	2.6	7.2	5.4	D	27.2	4,205	219	801	8,814	1.2
Bibb	0	D	3.1	7.6	8.2	7.1	14.8	21.7	12	32,690	214	8,083	70,044	0.3
Bleckley	-4.4	0	9.3	2.6	2.2	10	D	5.7	49.2	2,695	210	443	5,314	0.2
Brantley	0	D	11.4	11.9	D	4.8	1.7	3.7	28.7	3,670	196	522	8,155	0.8
Brooks	8.1	0	2.1	7.6	2	5.4	4.6	8.1	20.1	3,830	246	751	7,808	1.4
Bryan	0.8	0.1	10	7.2	5.2	8.5	7.7	6.8	25.8	5,920	160	663	14,795	25
Bulloch	-0.4	D	5.6	8.1	D	8	5.5	13.5	33.5	10,995	144	1,693	31,407	9
Burke	1	0	18.2	3.2	35.1	1.9	1.3	D	7.4	5,115	227	1,063	10,072	2.1
Butts	0.5	0	D	14.8	D	8.8	3.5	D	27	5,295	222	750	9,452	1
Calhoun	25.4	D	D	D	D	5.5	D	D	35.2	1,300	201	306	2,399	-0.5
Camden	0.2	0.1	2.7	6.5	3.6	5.5	3.6	4.9	58.9	9,145	172	829	22,346	5.8
Candler	-0.5	0.1	9.4	3.5	9.3	10.9	D	D	27.4	2,490	231	458	4,767	0.2
Carroll	2.1	D	8.3	19.3	D	6.6	4.1	16.3	17.1	22,805	194	3,414	45,530	2
Catoosa	1.8	D	8.2	11.2	3.5	13.2	6.4	10.6	18.4	14,455	217	838	27,531	3.5
Charlton	4.1	D	5.8	12	D	4.8	D	1	21.8	2,345	184	381	4,527	1.2
Chatham	0	D	4.4	16	5.6	6.5	5.9	13.6	17.8	51,445	177	6,914	125,680	5.3
Chattahoochee	0.1	0	0.4	D	D	0.1	D	D	90.1	745	72	146	3,338	-1.1
Chattooga	2.3	0.3	4.3	40.4	2	6.8	4	D	21.8	6,380	258	1,014	10,952	-0.2
Cherokee	0.4	0.1	16.3	7.5	10.5	9.2	7.1	10.2	13.9	40,060	162	2,322	94,218	14.4
Clarke	0.2	D	2.7	10.6	4.9	6.6	6.4	15.6	35.3	17,560	138	3,193	53,143	4.1
Clay	-11.5	0.1	D	0.6	0.2	5.5	D	14.4	52.9	805	272	151	2,128	1.2
Clayton	0	D	3.4	3.6	1.9	4.6	2.4	5.9	11.3	39,325	138	9,153	105,859	1
Clinch	9.2	0	1.3	33	2.6	3.1	D	2.4	18	1,625	242	419	3,001	-0.2
Cobb	0	0.2	10	6.2	18.3	7.1	8.5	9	8.7	102,595	136	9,376	302,646	5.6
Coffee	2.2	0	6.3	19.5	2.4	8	3.8	D	17.2	7,920	184	1,633	17,337	1.6
Colquitt	5.7	0	4	14.5	D	10.1	5.1	8.7	27.7	9,690	211	1,953	18,620	1.7
Columbia	0.2	D	9.7	10.4	7.8	12	6.9	12.3	18.5	23,785	157	1,661	58,736	20.8
Cook	2.2	D	8.6	15.3	D	9.9	3	D	33	3,835	222	721	7,423	1,9
Coweta	0.1	D	7.7	14.5	5.6	9.3	5.8	17.2	15.6	24,100	168	2,140	55,398	10.4
Crawford	25.5	D	8.8	1.2	D	2.9	D	7.8	24.3	2,790	227	251	5,391	1.9
Crisp	-1.7	D	2.4	14.2	D	9.1	6.1	D	19.3	4,855	214	1,069	10,782	0.5
Dade	4.4	0.2	D	19.1	4.6	6.3	D	7.6	15.2	4,000	246	380	7,302	-0.1
Dawson	3.8	0.1	5.5	12	D	23.2	6.1	8.9	15.7	5,055	207	430	11,771	12.8
Decatur	10.8	D	4.5	9.3	3.1	8.7	6.8	D	26.4	6,260	234	1,375	12,224	0.8
DeKalb	0	D	4.8	4.2	14.8	6.1	7.7	12.1	14.6	103,500	137	18,535	314,302	3
Dodge	3.4	0.1	2.2	12.6	D	8.9	3.3	D	38.9	4,515	218	818	9,799	-0.6
Dooly	5.6	0.1	D	D	0.3	5.2	D	D	21.2	2,655	193	726	6,231	-1.6
Dougherty	0.4	0	4.9	9.5	6.5	6.6	4.8	18.8	23.5	19,040	213	5,152	40,593	-0.5
Douglas	0	D	5.3	11.4	3.7	10.9	5.9	10.9	16.5	22,250	155	2,903	53,033	2.7
Early	8.4	0	2.4	24.7	D	5.9	D	D	26.7	2,625	255	616	4,981	0.1
Echols	5.7	0	D	D	-0.1	1.5	D	D	39	565	144	38	1,586	1.9

1. Per 1,000 resident population estimated as of July 1 of the year shown.

Table B. States and Counties — Housing, Labor Force, and Employment

STATE County	Housing units, 2013-2017								Civilian labor force, 2018				Civilian employment[6], 2013-2017		
	Occupied units										Unemployment			Percent	
	Owner-occupied				Renter-occupied										
				Median owner cost as a percent of income		Median rent as a percent of income[2]	Sub-standard units[4] (percent)		Percent change, 2017-2018				Management, business, science, and arts	Construction, production, and maintenance occupations
	Total	Percent	Median value[1]	With a mort-gage	Without a mort-gage[2]	Median rent[3]			Total		Total	Rate[5]	Total		
	89	90	91	92	93	94	95	96	97	98	99	100	101	102	103
FLORIDA—Cont'd															
Putnam	27,951	72.7	82,800	23.1	10.0	679	35.9	2.8	27,097	-0.1	1,303	4.8	25,030	23.3	30.0
St. Johns	83,744	77.0	274,600	21.4	10.0	1,207	31.8	1	127,595	1.9	3,667	2.9	102,778	46.2	13.2
St. Lucie	110,043	72.2	150,700	24.8	13.4	1,088	36.1	2.6	142,635	2.2	6,245	4.4	122,153	27.5	21.8
Santa Rosa	60,607	74.3	170,500	21.2	10.3	1,059	28.3	2.4	80,654	1.7	2,678	3.3	70,810	37.7	20.4
Sarasota	177,998	73.4	215,300	24.0	12.3	1,116	32	1.6	188,038	1.5	6,331	3.4	160,224	34.2	17.3
Seminole	161,371	65.8	201,900	22.4	11.2	1,143	30.8	1.8	254,438	2.6	8,075	3.2	220,949	44.8	12.7
Sumter	52,360	90.1	239,800	23.5	10.0	831	32.9	1.4	31,241	2.9	1,592	5.1	23,889	30.4	20.0
Suwannee	15,291	70.8	92,400	20.8	10.0	702	25.4	3.5	18,286	-0.6	678	3.7	16,629	24.5	29.3
Taylor	7,406	79.2	84,900	23.3	11.7	621	25	3.8	8,735	-0.7	336	3.8	6,861	26.6	27.6
Union	3,946	67.7	89,000	24.0	10.0	616	22.9	2.7	4,670	-3.3	159	3.4	3,800	24.7	27.3
Volusia	209,885	69.4	149,900	24.4	12.6	972	35.3	1.8	253,439	1.2	9,472	3.7	212,016	31.3	21.1
Wakulla	11,075	80.4	133,700	20.1	10.0	840	27.5	2.9	14,767	1.6	460	3.1	13,589	33.3	21.7
Walton	25,449	71.2	203,100	24.3	10.0	936	30.5	4.6	30,644	1.7	946	3.1	27,853	35.5	18.5
Washington	8,558	78.9	102,700	22.2	11.5	699	29.9	2.7	9,920	1.1	379	3.8	8,860	28.9	26.4
GEORGIA	3,663,104	63.0	158,400	21.0	10.6	927	30.2	2.6	5,107,656	1	201,245	3.9	4,606,329	36.6	22.4
Appling	6,702	71.9	72,100	18.5	11.5	534	21.8	4	9,044	-2.4	393	4.3	6,951	26.0	41.4
Atkinson	2,835	74.1	62,500	21.3	10.9	485	24.8	1.7	4,358	4.6	154	3.5	3,289	21.6	46.5
Bacon	3,989	70.7	73,200	19.5	10.0	528	29.1	2.8	5,057	0.1	193	3.8	4,345	30.7	34.8
Baker	1,321	69.3	79,500	22.9	11.4	485	24	5.2	1,217	-1.6	62	5.1	1,286	28.5	32.3
Baldwin	16,330	55.1	108,800	21.1	11.9	687	38.5	1.9	17,286	-1.8	871	5	17,647	30.3	22.6
Banks	6,489	74.2	128,900	26.1	12.4	710	29	3.4	9,538	2.8	297	3.1	7,796	24.8	35.9
Barrow	24,588	72.9	134,300	21.0	10.0	941	27	2.7	39,665	1.2	1,303	3.3	34,265	28.0	29.1
Bartow	37,120	65.4	140,500	20.8	10.0	863	27.6	3	50,113	1.1	1,894	3.8	46,890	29.9	30.7
Ben Hill	6,361	60.7	81,200	24.8	12.6	630	27.6	1.4	5,508	0.7	324	5.9	6,132	24.3	38.9
Berrien	7,240	69.3	86,700	20.9	10.7	602	25.8	2.8	7,477	1.2	311	4.2	7,062	22.8	36.9
Bibb	57,319	52.7	117,300	21.1	11.3	774	33.7	2.4	69,212	-0.5	3,129	4.5	60,590	34.8	17.4
Bleckley	4,155	71.7	98,800	19.5	14.3	580	29.1	2.1	4,660	1.7	266	5.7	4,227	30.1	26.8
Brantley	6,658	78.3	68,200	23.8	12.7	579	26.8	3.1	7,351	0.7	329	4.5	6,430	24.4	36.8
Brooks	6,337	73.6	92,400	22.3	13.8	647	31.1	4.7	7,044	0	277	3.9	5,865	27.1	32.9
Bryan	12,366	68.9	201,700	21.1	10.0	1,229	32.9	1.9	17,868	1.5	608	3.4	15,250	37.6	21.7
Bulloch	26,632	53.2	131,200	18.8	10.3	787	35.7	2.6	37,503	2.3	1,568	4.2	32,662	32.9	23.6
Burke	8,068	69.2	86,500	19.8	12.2	581	31.1	3	9,367	0.3	562	6	8,671	28.0	34.2
Butts	8,053	69.9	121,500	23.7	11.8	796	32.3	1.2	10,744	1.2	434	4	8,655	27.3	31.1
Calhoun	1,865	67.4	49,000	23.0	15.8	543	25.4	2.1	2,256	0.4	96	4.3	1,612	30.3	30.8
Camden	18,913	60.1	154,500	21.7	10.0	957	28.6	2.3	20,982	0.6	872	4.2	21,015	33.0	23.6
Candler	4,061	58.4	88,600	23.1	10.5	577	36.5	5.5	5,358	2.5	184	3.4	4,279	25.8	30.7
Carroll	41,123	64.1	119,600	20.6	10.0	820	28.1	2.5	55,383	0.9	2,220	4	49,458	27.0	31.7
Catoosa	24,719	73.4	138,800	19.4	10.0	777	26	1.7	33,156	0.9	1,134	3.4	31,464	32.2	25.8
Charlton	3,537	72.5	82,200	19.0	10.0	551	22.2	0.6	4,805	-1.2	206	4.3	4,412	25.0	37.8
Chatham	107,427	53.9	177,900	22.5	11.9	993	30.4	2.4	140,971	1.5	5,252	3.7	132,386	36.2	20.1
Chattahoochee	2,505	26.9	81,700	16.3	15.4	1,267	29.7	2	1,988	0	111	5.6	2,210	31.9	28.4
Chattooga	9,253	65.7	68,500	20.6	12.2	594	25.5	7.7	10,487	-0.7	429	4.1	8,839	23.1	42.8
Cherokee	83,150	76.4	220,200	20.3	10.0	1,138	27.8	2	132,799	1.3	4,135	3.1	117,102	40.7	17.2
Clarke	46,291	38.5	154,600	20.8	11.1	816	36.4	2.9	61,475	0.9	2,430	4	57,801	40.7	18.2
Clay	1,154	64.7	59,900	26.7	13.3	403	38.6	3.6	858	-0.9	66	7.7	865	18.4	42.7
Clayton	91,604	50.5	89,400	23.0	10.5	921	32.5	3.8	136,502	1	6,688	4.9	122,985	23.2	28.6
Clinch	2,576	71.4	63,100	20.6	15.2	483	30.9	4.4	2,766	-0.3	126	4.6	2,163	27.0	37.6
Cobb	274,361	64.3	219,700	19.5	10.0	1,102	28.6	2	426,279	1.3	14,465	3.4	382,187	45.7	15.6
Coffee	14,329	66.1	87,600	22.6	11.4	575	27	2.6	18,709	1.4	845	4.5	16,232	33.1	30.2
Colquitt	15,599	59.5	84,500	21.7	11.0	624	32.3	4.2	21,551	-2.4	811	3.8	18,771	22.4	39.4
Columbia	45,823	78.5	183,800	19.7	10.0	1,117	27.6	1.4	74,950	0.9	2,609	3.5	63,139	42.9	17.3
Cook	6,065	69.0	87,800	24.3	13.7	703	28	1.8	7,886	2.2	298	3.8	6,902	24.8	34.3
Coweta	50,531	72.6	190,700	19.8	10.2	986	29.8	2.3	73,505	1.2	2,518	3.4	66,983	34.7	24.8
Crawford	4,715	76.8	93,300	22.7	11.2	706	31	3.1	5,703	-0.5	237	4.2	4,604	25.9	31.3
Crisp	8,312	59.1	83,900	22.7	13.0	624	34.5	3.9	9,399	0	456	4.9	8,481	28.7	26.2
Dade	6,089	75.3	122,500	19.4	10.8	665	30.7	2.9	8,274	0.8	300	3.6	7,719	26.1	30.8
Dawson	8,557	79.8	202,300	21.1	10.0	874	30.7	2	12,040	1.4	401	3.3	10,665	37.1	25.2
Decatur	10,311	59.7	109,800	23.1	10.0	622	28.3	8	11,551	-0.9	539	4.7	9,855	27.6	30.8
DeKalb	273,614	54.1	176,000	21.8	10.9	1,062	31.2	2.9	399,846	1.2	16,073	4	365,630	43.6	16.3
Dodge	7,858	66.2	73,400	20.9	10.3	538	24.9	2.7	7,176	0.6	372	5.2	7,684	33.6	28.3
Dooly	5,171	64.3	83,200	24.8	11.6	509	32	2.2	5,157	1.4	238	4.6	4,929	22.2	39.0
Dougherty	34,842	45.1	102,100	20.8	13.1	701	32	3.1	38,361	-1.4	1,966	5.1	34,494	30.3	24.5
Douglas	48,426	65.8	140,100	21.0	10.5	1,014	28.6	2.1	72,900	1.2	3,002	4.1	66,421	34.3	23.9
Early	4,032	68.1	82,700	26.6	14.8	627	27.2	6	4,560	0.6	209	4.6	3,682	29.9	38.3
Echols	1,502	62.1	57,000	18.9	12.0	670	32.5	3.3	1,900	-0.3	61	3.2	1,656	19.7	43.9

1. Specified owner-occupied units.   2. A value of 10.0 represents 10 percent or less; a value of 50.0 represents 50 percent or more.   3. Specified renter-occupied units.   4. Overcrowded or lacking complete plumbing facilities.   5. Percent of civilian labor force.   6. Civilian employed persons 16 years old and over.

Table B. States and Counties — Nonfarm Employment and Agriculture

	Private nonfarm establishments, employment and payroll, 2016									Agriculture, 2017			
													Farm producers whose primary occupation is farming (percent)
		Employment						Annual payroll		Farms			
											Percent with:		
STATE County	Number of establishments	Total	Health care and social assistance	Manufacturing	Retail trade	Finance and insurance	Professional, scientific, and technical services	Total (mil dol)	Average per employee (dollars)	Number	Fewer than 50 acres	1000 acres or more	
	104	105	106	107	108	109	110	111	112	113	114	115	116
FLORIDA—Cont'd													
Putnam	1,248	12,505	2,369	1,948	2,779	322	311	425	33,991	564	68.1	2.8	38.2
St. Johns	6,057	59,165	8,330	1,975	10,589	1,749	3,457	2,144	36,241	253	68.8	3.2	47.9
St. Lucie	5,540	58,914	11,420	2,813	13,403	1,270	2,354	2,059	34,956	415	55.7	13.3	49.2
Santa Rosa	2,622	24,931	3,861	509	5,229	731	1,590	859	34,472	699	63.2	2.9	38.6
Sarasota	13,671	142,030	28,289	7,510	23,669	5,080	10,380	6,044	42,555	292	71.2	5.8	41.7
Seminole	13,311	167,426	19,054	6,566	27,809	13,784	11,865	7,268	43,407	403	86.4	0.7	40.1
Sumter	1,453	20,883	4,277	1,219	3,710	685	679	757	36,272	1,307	75.7	1.9	37.0
Suwannee	680	8,172	1,492	1,946	1,587	141	187	250	30,620	1,079	56.3	2.8	48.2
Taylor	403	4,750	637	1,591	1,051	74	80	179	37,706	240	41.3	9.2	39.5
Union	135	1,848	698	D	172	20	33	63	34,361	308	62.7	3.6	40.5
Volusia	12,603	143,888	27,317	8,710	27,099	4,708	6,418	5,000	34,748	1,575	83.1	1.5	39.7
Wakulla	440	3,566	210	D	914	61	208	108	30,414	209	71.8	1.0	32.9
Walton	2,157	19,652	2,232	229	4,299	290	644	694	35,304	598	50.0	3.3	42.8
Washington	378	3,775	880	299	733	123	211	115	30,490	437	59.7	0.9	34.4
GEORGIA	228,330	3,804,433	497,019	367,902	485,488	177,532	263,554	182,911	48,078	42,439	42.3	5.3	39.4
Appling	365	5,940	970	551	1,107	152	37	280	47,199	548	43.8	6.6	39.2
Atkinson	87	1,385	D	685	126	66	2	47	33,814	215	34.4	11.6	45.3
Bacon	227	2,913	518	943	304	126	65	97	33,255	273	38.1	4.8	39.5
Baker	25	219	D	NA	26	7	D	9	39,694	147	29.3	21.8	56.1
Baldwin	801	13,107	3,912	1,546	2,462	384	222	445	33,956	139	36.0	6.5	23.4
Banks	284	3,212	140	287	905	30	37	85	26,387	463	40.0	0.9	48.9
Barrow	1,172	15,939	1,484	2,606	2,769	285	794	553	34,712	288	58.0	0.3	37.4
Bartow	1,964	31,827	2,770	8,505	4,145	652	696	1,295	40,696	469	56.5	1.9	39.9
Ben Hill	313	4,837	574	1,899	721	193	48	158	32,693	217	41.0	5.5	40.9
Berrien	248	3,271	290	1,603	446	134	34	100	30,452	349	33.5	8.6	48.4
Bibb	4,121	73,625	16,065	5,228	10,278	8,889	2,530	2,916	39,602	98	55.1	1.0	44.6
Bleckley	168	1,476	214	41	441	78	24	41	27,953	231	43.7	5.2	21.6
Brantley	189	1,254	130	174	254	33	22	40	31,609	235	49.4	NA	33.9
Brooks	207	2,133	564	174	359	73	37	67	31,218	360	31.1	11.9	43.8
Bryan	638	5,992	705	300	1,175	163	284	183	30,465	95	58.9	8.4	35.8
Bulloch	1,432	17,722	3,144	1,657	3,627	486	594	525	29,637	478	30.5	11.9	38.3
Burke	319	8,445	436	560	768	136	D	581	68,807	467	25.3	14.6	43.7
Butts	356	4,340	536	815	885	98	77	141	32,410	173	37.0	1.7	44.6
Calhoun	73	684	77	NA	76	31	D	23	33,712	169	20.1	16.0	40.1
Camden	803	8,044	864	157	2,327	277	501	240	29,835	47	70.2	2.1	28.4
Candler	215	2,264	569	172	419	84	82	62	27,438	197	32.0	6.1	30.5
Carroll	2,030	35,391	5,207	8,502	5,632	665	546	1,400	39,564	867	53.1	0.9	38.8
Catoosa	909	11,424	1,295	1,455	3,143	301	350	357	31,233	250	48.8	0.4	39.5
Charlton	149	1,919	260	340	226	33	53	61	31,962	120	50.8	5.0	28.1
Chatham	7,728	137,176	19,863	15,835	18,814	2,819	5,458	5,694	41,511	67	73.1	NA	44.0
Chattahoochee	111	1,883	71	D	143	18	855	83	43,989	12	58.3	NA	22.7
Chattooga	305	4,826	340	2,290	708	133	83	135	27,958	323	36.8	1.2	43.1
Cherokee	5,150	50,407	6,163	4,708	10,429	1,516	3,152	1,820	36,112	430	73.3	NA	39.3
Clarke	3,015	48,003	9,745	5,769	7,775	1,057	1,502	1,804	37,590	91	62.6	1.1	28.4
Clay	38	275	45	NA	53	D	D	8	29,582	67	14.9	20.9	42.5
Clayton	3,750	72,809	8,554	4,091	11,201	1,593	1,034	2,768	38,023	19	89.5	NA	47.2
Clinch	127	1,611	201	D	163	41	19	57	35,291	113	39.8	8.8	47.1
Cobb	20,180	338,473	34,067	17,868	39,315	17,074	28,925	18,306	54,083	116	92.2	NA	37.5
Coffee	833	13,281	2,152	2,969	1,990	309	221	431	32,423	608	34.7	9.2	40.2
Colquitt	899	11,135	2,362	2,748	1,977	294	170	355	31,864	498	31.9	8.8	47.7
Columbia	2,228	28,523	3,672	2,728	5,859	834	1,721	1,008	35,341	183	56.3	2.7	29.7
Cook	315	3,174	448	749	756	132	60	94	29,463	239	45.6	14.6	41.7
Coweta	2,386	32,336	5,274	4,926	5,993	713	932	1,198	37,035	368	56.3	1.6	35.0
Crawford	98	539	43	59	79	11	13	19	35,176	192	35.4	3.6	37.1
Crisp	510	6,737	1,150	1,085	1,394	210	135	222	32,975	236	32.6	14.0	33.1
Dade	217	2,795	262	542	522	102	44	97	34,682	198	41.9	1.5	40.6
Dawson	604	6,500	412	864	2,832	130	144	165	25,448	192	60.4	NA	38.4
Decatur	589	6,438	926	1,139	1,444	244	162	216	33,559	337	24.3	21.7	45.1
DeKalb	16,822	274,580	46,281	11,567	34,810	8,862	22,558	14,455	52,642	34	97.1	NA	42.3
Dodge	314	3,176	1,007	329	694	138	80	88	27,679	391	24.8	6.1	33.3
Dooly	165	2,871	57	D	319	65	10	91	31,820	297	30.3	18.9	45.8
Dougherty	2,276	37,007	8,338	2,869	6,486	1,113	2,145	1,398	37,780	110	40.0	10.0	38.9
Douglas	2,519	37,907	4,443	3,200	8,409	721	973	1,338	35,310	93	67.7	NA	34.7
Early	212	2,835	342	796	386	118	74	127	44,843	321	14.6	17.4	44.7
Echols	26	102	D	D	10	D	NA	4	38,108	66	37.9	13.6	43.4

Table B. States and Counties — **Agriculture**

			Land in farms			Value of land and buildings (dollars)		Value of machinery and equiopmnet, average per farm (dollars)	Value of products sold:				Organic farms (number)	Farms with internet access (percent)	Government payments	
				Acres							Percent from:					
STATE County	Acreage (1,000)	Percent change, 2012-2017	Average size of farm	Total irrigated (1,000)	Total cropland (1,000)	Average per farm	Average per acre		Total (mil dol)	Average per farm (acres)	Crops	Livestock and poultry products			Total ($1,000)	Percent of farms
	117	118	119	120	121	122	123	124	125	126	127	128	129	130	131	132
FLORIDA—Cont'd																
Putnam	85	20.3	150	6.7	13.5	596,965	3,977	65,825	46.1	81,681	76.0	24.0	NA	74.8	466	6.4
St. Johns	34	2.3	136	14.4	17.5	1,156,661	8,507	130,543	61.4	242,605	95.3	4.7	2	85.4	D	2.8
St. Lucie	226	15.8	545	48.2	68.7	3,254,221	5,976	109,557	139.6	336,446	89.3	10.7	2	68.9	947	14.5
Santa Rosa	85	-12.9	122	1.2	52.8	652,601	5,362	61,267	38.5	55,117	89.1	10.9	NA	79.3	4,549	23.2
Sarasota	71	-11.2	244	5.2	11.0	2,240,920	9,195	63,666	23.1	79,092	77.4	22.6	1	76.7	348	5.1
Seminole	35	61.0	87	1.2	7.1	716,815	8,271	38,395	21.3	52,965	91.2	8.8	5	78.7	136	3.2
Sumter	177	-3.4	135	2.0	21.3	816,314	6,025	50,217	54.5	41,666	36.7	63.3	8	74.7	1,099	16.7
Suwannee	170	-12.2	157	27.4	78.5	695,473	4,418	83,821	258.9	239,981	21.5	78.5	9	76.6	1,988	6.8
Taylor	59	56.8	245	0.2	4.5	892,861	3,650	55,626	11.8	49,113	21.1	78.9	NA	75.0	10	3.8
Union	54	16.3	175	1.5	10.3	649,755	3,722	54,492	7.7	25,010	47.7	52.3	NA	74.0	93	3.6
Volusia	114	7.8	73	9.2	25.1	748,025	10,309	51,317	196.4	124,693	93.4	6.6	6	76.3	1,139	5.8
Wakulla	24	-23.4	113	0.1	2.0	387,249	3,420	38,983	2.4	11,431	22.9	77.1	NA	65.6	161	7.7
Walton	89	-39.7	149	1.2	23.1	562,514	3,771	45,630	30.6	51,186	19.6	80.4	NA	80.1	1,007	16.7
Washington	45	-22.4	104	0.9	16.0	395,545	3,820	53,771	8.9	20,471	66.5	33.5	2	71.9	458	18.1
GEORGIA	9,954	3.5	235	1,287.5	4,372.1	822,958	3,509	115,773	9,573.3	225,577	34.2	65.8	139	76.0	247,428	31.8
Appling	128	4.4	234	13.7	85.1	760,709	3,249	136,171	166.6	303,936	36.6	63.4	7	71.5	2,462	31.9
Atkinson	72	-17.2	334	9.1	40.8	971,298	2,904	192,878	71.1	330,563	38.6	61.4	NA	72.1	2,132	34.0
Bacon	62	7.6	228	6.1	38.6	937,359	4,116	144,034	63.2	231,440	50.5	49.5	1	80.2	1,141	20.9
Baker	131	-10.6	891	26.2	53.2	1,980,216	2,222	343,799	57.0	387,469	63.5	36.5	2	62.6	5,182	59.9
Baldwin	34	81.5	244	0.1	8.0	527,772	2,165	66,743	1.4	10,216	33.7	66.3	NA	79.9	93	12.9
Banks	56	-5.5	122	0.5	12.1	655,689	5,381	95,826	169.5	366,194	2.3	97.7	NA	76.9	943	27.2
Barrow	22	-25.0	78	0.4	6.1	508,793	6,557	50,503	36.0	124,844	2.4	97.6	5	78.8	161	12.5
Bartow	77	21.2	165	1.0	16.9	994,446	6,025	65,838	71.4	152,292	12.5	87.5	NA	77.8	919	22.2
Ben Hill	53	-8.3	242	5.3	22.4	597,934	2,469	111,377	20.9	96,244	69.0	31.0	NA	71.0	891	44.2
Berrien	117	-18.6	335	21.4	61.2	1,046,386	3,128	170,691	85.5	244,931	70.7	29.3	NA	77.7	5,470	44.1
Bibb	9	-38.2	93	0.1	4.1	371,840	4,006	77,778	4.8	49,429	6.4	93.6	NA	83.7	27	9.2
Bleckley	48	-26.8	209	8.1	23.2	539,162	2,580	59,016	12.4	53,654	93.6	6.4	NA	58.9	638	53.7
Brantley	24	4.5	104	0.9	5.7	304,091	2,919	47,411	D	D	D	D	NA	78.7	127	17.4
Brooks	178	20.4	496	22.1	91.6	1,733,285	3,496	215,239	118.9	330,253	63.2	36.8	NA	72.5	3,288	55.0
Bryan	26	69.8	272	0.0	3.5	837,457	3,077	67,866	3.0	31,400	33.1	66.9	NA	74.7	33	7.4
Bulloch	197	9.4	413	17.7	126.1	1,181,592	2,864	202,153	89.9	187,992	82.2	17.8	1	76.8	9,661	46.9
Burke	223	38.3	478	43.2	123.3	1,357,912	2,843	266,151	118.1	252,972	57.2	42.8	3	76.4	7,072	45.6
Butts	31	48.0	181	0.0	6.4	704,674	3,897	61,476	4.3	24,694	37.7	62.3	NA	68.8	112	16.8
Calhoun	116	7.8	686	38.0	66.3	2,067,724	3,014	298,570	63.5	375,917	79.9	20.1	NA	66.3	6,347	72.2
Camden	6	-64.8	118	0.1	2.1	337,997	2,865	59,431	0.7	15,809	32.6	67.4	1	80.9	22	10.6
Candler	55	2.4	278	3.9	24.5	879,763	3,160	95,491	21.8	110,853	72.9	27.1	1	69.5	796	37.1
Carroll	85	-0.8	98	D	18.2	470,633	4,786	69,536	186.0	214,525	4.0	96.0	1	81.2	519	11.6
Catoosa	24	17.0	97	0.1	7.5	531,318	5,503	69,075	26.7	106,880	16.5	83.5	NA	78.0	360	25.2
Charlton	21	54.9	173	D	2.3	418,803	2,427	55,039	3.8	31,842	13.9	86.1	NA	66.7	41	18.3
Chatham	5	22.0	70	0.7	1.7	354,509	5,078	129,996	12.2	182,448	95.7	4.3	1	85.1	NA	NA
Chattahoochee	2	-57.4	145	D	0.1	428,469	2,958	70,000	D	D	100.0	D	NA	75.0	D	16.7
Chattooga	55	10.3	171	0.0	15.9	605,993	3,542	72,635	74.2	229,836	2.8	97.2	NA	78.0	403	25.4
Cherokee	24	-4.5	56	0.1	6.6	484,880	8,675	56,805	21.7	50,484	22.8	77.2	NA	89.8	182	10.0
Clarke	8	-9.5	88	0.1	1.6	683,725	7,735	52,373	44.7	491,385	9.5	90.5	NA	90.1	59	9.9
Clay	45	12.9	674	6.6	23.0	1,596,179	2,367	277,136	15.8	236,239	88.1	11.9	1	83.6	1,883	58.2
Clayton	1	-29.3	31	0.0	0.2	259,453	8,355	26,985	0.2	12,842	48.4	51.6	NA	89.5	D	5.3
Clinch	27	3.0	243	3.7	8.9	967,887	3,983	179,959	33.9	299,876	89.8	10.2	NA	72.6	290	31.0
Cobb	3	-50.9	22	0.0	0.4	248,584	11,425	38,141	D	D	D	D	NA	92.2	D	1.7
Coffee	189	12.6	311	35.3	103.5	938,419	3,016	187,887	185.5	305,051	39.0	61.0	4	75.8	8,386	37.2
Colquitt	186	-1.4	373	45.4	120.8	1,235,184	3,308	224,282	295.9	594,273	66.5	33.5	NA	72.7	8,659	55.6
Columbia	23	74.5	125	0.1	3.4	555,982	4,452	39,103	2.8	15,208	51.0	49.0	2	84.7	50	8.7
Cook	79	15.4	330	15.9	48.9	1,004,035	3,038	167,271	88.1	368,544	63.1	36.9	NA	70.7	4,636	50.2
Coweta	53	-3.8	145	0.3	12.5	699,043	4,825	67,682	11.7	31,793	36.4	63.6	NA	81.0	136	9.5
Crawford	35	3.9	184	2.7	10.7	739,529	4,029	103,828	61.0	317,745	20.6	79.4	3	82.8	243	18.8
Crisp	108	-7.8	458	20.2	66.9	1,403,992	3,065	198,462	60.0	254,085	82.0	18.0	NA	77.5	3,815	55.9
Dade	29	-10.6	147	0.0	4.8	584,184	3,981	58,107	25.1	126,631	3.2	96.8	3	68.7	198	24.7
Dawson	19	49.1	99	0.0	3.9	689,160	6,983	66,115	46.8	243,880	2.0	98.0	2	77.6	134	12.0
Decatur	192	-3.6	569	82.9	133.4	1,855,602	3,260	315,713	179.5	532,591	83.7	16.3	3	68.2	15,914	70.0
DeKalb	0	-84.1	14	0.0	0.0	646,015	46,933	17,575	0.5	16,059	71.1	28.9	NA	97.1	NA	NA
Dodge	103	14.4	264	11.6	36.3	685,800	2,600	81,427	30.5	78,115	73.9	26.1	NA	73.7	1,767	52.7
Dooly	186	46.6	626	29.7	121.2	1,830,024	2,922	240,010	99.2	334,020	86.0	14.0	1	76.1	4,446	67.3
Dougherty	64	-1.4	586	18.4	24.0	2,267,228	3,869	167,695	40.3	366,355	89.6	10.4	NA	85.5	1,747	38.2
Douglas	7	-15.1	76	0.2	1.9	509,840	6,695	49,702	0.7	7,398	46.4	53.6	NA	67.7	9	5.4
Early	168	-1.0	522	32.2	80.0	1,341,069	2,569	186,003	59.3	184,629	91.7	8.3	NA	73.5	4,866	74.5
Echols	23	71.6	346	3.4	9.2	965,776	2,791	147,334	17.9	271,697	82.0	18.0	NA	74.2	215	37.9

Table B. States and Counties — Water Use, Wholesale Trade, Retail Trade, and Real Estate

STATE County	Water use, 2015		Wholesale Trade[1], 2012				Retail Trade[2], 2012				Real estate and rental and leasing,[2] 2012			
	Public supply water withdrawn (mil gal/day)	Public supply gallons withdrawn per person per day	Number of establishments	Number of employees	Sales (mil dol)	Average payroll (mil dol)	Number of establishments	Number of employees	Sales (mil dol)	Average payroll (mil dol)	Number of establishments	Number of employees	Sales (mil dol)	Average payroll (mil dol)
	133	134	135	136	137	138	139	140	141	142	143	144	145	146
FLORIDA—Cont'd														
Putnam	2.10	29.2	24	D	D	D	239	2,429	633.5	56.8	52	136	16.2	3.3
St. Johns	16.83	74.3	163	1,429	1,426.3	81.2	760	9,003	2,502.6	205.6	302	1,076	199.0	34.0
St. Lucie	29.37	98.4	185	1,473	686.0	61.8	690	12,368	3,709.5	361.3	260	752	134.5	22.9
Santa Rosa	14.96	89.6	57	419	323.2	16.0	357	4,644	1,259.9	108.4	150	336	53.3	9.0
Sarasota	20.17	49.7	447	3,613	1,868.1	160.1	1,696	21,356	5,751.7	548.8	814	2,753	666.0	116.9
Seminole	57.59	128.2	617	6,435	2,813.7	295.8	1,666	24,591	6,972.0	608.4	705	3,850	609.2	131.7
Sumter	24.13	203.0	45	D	D	D	217	2,840	908.8	62.1	79	176	25.6	5.7
Suwannee	1.19	27.2	31	D	D	D	128	1,347	343.1	32.5	28	106	10.8	2.4
Taylor	1.75	77.8	20	D	D	D	87	816	205.2	17.5	12	27	2.8	0.7
Union	0.22	14.4	5	D	D	D	29	158	44.8	3.8	4	8	1.0	0.2
Volusia	55.45	107.1	420	2,983	1,655.1	144.8	1,869	23,642	6,168.3	569.3	655	2,511	402.4	75.0
Wakulla	2.31	73.3	10	D	D	D	62	738	176.1	16.1	16	25	3.3	0.5
Walton	11.17	175.9	47	595	454.1	27.0	344	3,638	817.4	79.6	186	915	151.9	31.4
Washington	0.95	38.5	11	D	D	D	67	736	174.7	15.7	12	22	2.7	0.6
GEORGIA	1,069.91	104.7	10,637	150,168	143,645.3	8,476.3	33,426	433,840	119,801.5	10,290.1	10,484	55,551	14,232.4	2,703.7
Appling	0.76	41.2	23	137	86.1	4.7	76	699	211.3	15.4	10	31	2.9	0.6
Atkinson	0.43	51.2	5	94	46.5	2.6	29	141	43.8	3.1	1	D	D	D
Bacon	0.98	86.7	16	230	160.9	6.9	40	280	72.7	5.4	2	D	D	D
Baker	0.15	47.2	2	D	D	D	5	25	4.7	0.4	2	D	D	D
Baldwin	3.82	84.0	23	D	D	D	182	2,187	554.5	46.6	34	D	D	D
Banks	2.61	141.1	13	158	110.3	7.1	58	795	213.7	16.9	5	D	D	D
Barrow	4.46	59.2	61	732	1,189.7	34.5	181	2,350	671.6	56.5	36	90	10.1	1.8
Bartow	52.41	510.1	103	995	861.5	44.9	302	3,590	1,264.9	87.7	92	301	40.0	8.2
Ben Hill	2.46	141.4	10	D	D	D	78	724	200.3	14.6	10	31	3.2	0.6
Berrien	0.78	41.1	18	68	58.5	2.8	67	465	127.1	10.8	6	8	2.0	0.2
Bibb	24.13	157.0	192	2,433	1,522.4	117.0	815	10,199	2,597.5	232.7	194	906	170.4	30.8
Bleckley	0.20	16.3	5	33	22.8	1.9	45	340	88.4	7.1	5	D	D	D
Brantley	0.24	13.0	4	D	D	D	40	299	74.0	5.2	3	6	0.3	0.1
Brooks	0.90	57.5	8	D	D	D	46	309	83.9	6.9	3	D	D	D
Bryan	2.59	73.7	20	D	D	D	96	1,051	352.3	23.8	28	D	D	D
Bulloch	4.77	65.7	44	273	311.2	11.2	266	3,203	796.8	67.6	72	304	48.8	7.7
Burke	0.85	37.4	18	248	210.7	9.2	54	712	196.7	17.2	8	D	D	D
Butts	2.74	116.1	10	187	534.9	8.1	79	681	333.8	13.9	16	28	3.7	0.6
Calhoun	0.44	67.9	8	70	26.4	2.2	15	100	19.6	2.0	1	D	D	D
Camden	3.94	75.6	10	D	D	D	158	2,314	600.1	50.2	43	173	23.1	3.7
Candler	0.41	37.7	7	D	D	D	51	401	120.0	9.2	6	13	0.7	0.2
Carroll	11.32	98.8	79	601	436.0	24.4	364	4,474	1,310.4	104.7	80	304	46.7	7.9
Catoosa	4.68	70.9	41	470	244.2	19.8	174	2,500	687.4	56.9	39	139	23.6	4.3
Charlton	0.76	58.6	9	97	51.5	2.7	32	224	58.8	3.8	3	D	D	D
Chatham	28.08	97.9	317	3,925	5,812.9	197.6	1,204	15,767	4,256.4	375.3	388	1,837	383.3	60.4
Chattahoochee	0.31	27.3	1	D	D	D	18	126	22.7	1.9	NA	NA	NA	NA
Chattooga	2.80	112.4	10	D	D	D	74	657	158.0	13.5	6	19	2.8	0.5
Cherokee	19.29	81.8	220	1,639	711.9	83.8	544	8,254	2,271.6	196.1	207	527	95.8	18.0
Clarke	11.48	92.6	99	1,801	1,947.0	85.0	516	6,963	1,684.2	145.6	190	926	140.6	27.0
Clay	0.25	79.6	2	D	D	D	13	76	12.5	1.1	1	D	D	D
Clayton	10.76	39.3	240	6,102	4,341.7	257.4	733	10,921	3,229.6	270.5	199	900	210.0	34.9
Clinch	0.45	65.3	5	67	13.1	1.8	22	176	44.7	3.3	3	D	D	D
Cobb	42.22	57.0	1,090	16,264	18,591.4	968.9	2,222	35,733	10,368.7	905.9	1,045	5,639	1,390.1	303.0
Coffee	4.05	94.0	45	447	487.9	19.7	191	1,784	487.5	38.7	29	99	11.4	2.4
Colquitt	3.11	67.8	48	501	513.5	19.9	184	1,784	460.0	40.0	37	89	14.1	2.4
Columbia	15.92	110.5	64	882	382.2	44.6	298	5,383	1,580.6	140.9	95	409	71.7	12.3
Cook	1.40	81.8	16	139	40.3	5.2	60	486	136.6	9.7	8	27	4.6	0.6
Coweta	7.45	53.8	73	830	1,518.7	38.1	329	5,166	1,479.5	120.0	120	300	61.3	11.3
Crawford	0.40	32.3	1	D	D	D	24	115	23.1	2.3	NA	NA	NA	NA
Crisp	2.01	87.8	32	D	D	D	119	1,365	303.5	24.7	27	188	13.4	3.8
Dade	2.02	124.2	3	D	D	D	61	455	184.6	8.5	3	7	0.5	0.1
Dawson	1.51	64.8	18	87	23.5	3.3	191	2,520	523.9	47.5	18	60	28.4	1.9
Decatur	2.43	89.4	29	D	D	D	136	1,333	324.7	28.8	22	D	D	D
DeKalb	0.00	0.0	756	9,390	5,554.7	488.9	2,217	30,430	7,956.5	738.7	890	6,039	1,710.5	263.3
Dodge	1.39	66.6	12	41	24.9	1.0	72	713	152.3	12.6	15	57	6.7	1.4
Dooly	2.28	162.5	11	79	67.5	3.1	39	250	147.1	6.1	1	D	D	D
Dougherty	11.57	126.7	120	1,451	841.3	65.1	494	6,397	1,529.9	135.0	141	537	98.4	17.1
Douglas	17.52	124.5	97	1,387	1,224.2	64.3	427	7,174	1,955.8	171.8	114	560	107.1	17.3
Early	1.21	114.4	12	58	85.6	2.5	51	388	86.1	6.8	5	21	2.9	0.8
Echols	0.05	12.4	1	D	D	D	3	D	D	D	1	D	D	D

1 Merchant wholesalers, except manufacturers' sales branches and offices.   2. Employer establishments.

STATE County	Professional, scientific, and technical services, 2012				Manufacturing, 2012				Accommodation and food services, 2012			
	Number of establishments	Number of employees	Sales (mil dol)	Average payroll (mil dol)	Number of establishments	Number of employees	Receipts (mil dol)	Annual payroll (mil dol)	Number of establishments	Number of employees	Receipts (mil dol)	Annual payroll (mil dol)
	147	148	149	150	151	152	153	154	155	156	157	158
FLORIDA—Cont'd												
Putnam	101	286	25.2	8.2	35	1,678	865.8	89.8	94	1,218	56.9	15.1
St. Johns	759	D	D	D	91	1,449	409.8	59.3	455	8,680	517.9	149.3
St. Lucie	514	2,173	281.6	97.3	134	2,015	605.7	85.4	390	6,652	329.3	91.3
Santa Rosa	289	1,851	295.2	126.7	55	407	124.1	19.7	189	3,219	145.7	41.4
Sarasota	1,775	8,573	1,216.7	439.1	308	5,559	1,200.1	267.0	853	16,450	896.2	263.7
Seminole	1,884	10,221	1,479.7	542.0	358	5,741	1,567.5	244.9	776	14,747	761.1	216.2
Sumter	128	500	53.9	21.0	36	942	461.9	40.7	106	2,464	117.2	35.9
Suwannee	49	204	18.8	5.3	19	D	D	46.9	53	679	34.1	8.2
Taylor	29	109	8.1	3.1	18	1,458	691.7	84.2	38	427	19.9	5.3
Union	8	D	D	D	4	D	D	D	9	82	3.6	0.9
Volusia	1,304	6,854	812.3	281.4	335	7,633	D	340.7	1,001	18,628	895.8	260.7
Wakulla	38	D	D	D	9	D	D	D	41	429	19.7	5.2
Walton	198	452	57.3	16.6	27	113	D	4.5	204	5,140	373.8	110.8
Washington	32	214	27.1	10.2	6	D	D	12.5	38	434	21.9	5.1
GEORGIA	28,112	D	D	D	7,456	333,837	155,836.8	15,316.6	18,815	353,638	18,976.6	5,173.4
Appling	20	55	5.7	1.7	25	529	407.3	23.1	29	410	18.8	5.0
Atkinson	2	D	D	D	10	468	144.8	15.3	7	52	2.4	0.5
Bacon	12	46	3.8	1.4	12	496	D	16.2	16	181	9.0	2.2
Baker	2	D	D	D	NA	NA	NA	NA	NA	NA	NA	NA
Baldwin	51	D	D	D	20	D	D	D	92	D	D	D
Banks	12	D	D	D	9	208	D	8.3	43	912	47.5	13.0
Barrow	101	3,525	137.7	87.7	69	1,940	889.2	76.1	81	D	D	D
Bartow	141	486	78.1	20.2	106	7,133	4,341.9	348.0	163	2,977	140.6	40.7
Ben Hill	12	66	5.1	1.4	28	1,408	512.4	51.6	35	361	17.7	3.9
Berrien	13	15	1.3	0.5	14	1,583	453.4	63.1	21	270	10.2	3.0
Bibb	382	2,581	340.7	118.9	119	4,441	1,573.5	213.4	403	7,905	352.5	98.9
Bleckley	11	52	2.7	1.7	8	303	D	12.3	14	202	10.2	2.5
Brantley	7	19	2.5	0.8	10	110	D	4.0	10	138	4.2	1.2
Brooks	12	53	5.8	2.1	10	187	D	7.4	16	D	D	D
Bryan	66	230	30.2	12.1	13	291	D	14.8	74	968	36.7	9.4
Bulloch	116	497	57.1	19.0	39	1,442	416.8	52.4	136	2,757	114.0	30.9
Burke	16	D	D	D	14	677	197.0	25.9	26	D	D	D
Butts	22	78	6.1	2.1	11	589	259.6	19.7	34	536	24.2	7.0
Calhoun	2	D	D	D	NA	NA	NA	NA	5	18	0.8	0.3
Camden	66	D	D	D	7	111	D	6.3	107	1,950	80.5	23.4
Candler	20	63	7.4	2.2	10	156	D	6.5	24	D	D	D
Carroll	147	716	74.8	23.5	112	7,174	6,237.8	299.1	198	3,261	157.7	42.4
Catoosa	64	300	26.4	10.4	43	1,537	D	71.1	89	1,733	87.5	23.4
Charlton	9	44	1.8	0.8	5	237	D	6.9	15	178	7.3	1.9
Chatham	708	5,871	640.2	253.4	175	13,829	D	1,015.1	897	18,046	1,024.7	277.3
Chattahoochee	28	232	26.4	11.4	NA	NA	NA	NA	9	42	2.0	0.5
Chattooga	13	58	7.1	2.2	14	2,156	403.9	56.9	31	318	17.4	3.8
Cherokee	740	2,735	421.6	133.0	144	3,813	1,027.8	145.6	323	6,256	281.7	81.2
Clarke	303	1,697	190.6	68.5	78	5,115	2,004.8	229.5	342	6,927	307.6	83.9
Clay	1	D	D	D	NA	NA	NA	NA	2	D	D	D
Clayton	221	982	119.9	39.9	100	3,676	1,873.4	165.7	388	8,178	450.9	129.9
Clinch	11	D	D	D	9	D	D	D	11	D	D	D
Cobb	3,387	33,011	5,509.8	2,097.4	460	19,738	8,587.2	1,180.3	1,451	27,543	1,516.1	418.6
Coffee	60	219	22.1	8.2	35	2,338	670.4	79.8	61	1,178	54.7	14.4
Colquitt	57	173	17.8	4.9	42	2,811	760.1	78.7	59	D	D	D
Columbia	208	1,348	626.9	70.9	55	2,978	2,023.7	168.7	182	3,389	153.2	41.0
Cook	15	44	3.7	1.9	25	517	201.8	17.9	29	D	D	D
Coweta	195	894	89.1	35.1	86	4,315	1,908.9	192.7	166	3,647	168.5	48.2
Crawford	3	D	D	D	7	D	D	D	4	33	1.4	0.3
Crisp	24	76	4.8	2.1	22	1,024	426.9	45.7	44	D	D	D
Dade	7	D	D	D	13	538	D	22.0	22	D	D	D
Dawson	54	135	19.6	5.4	21	1,161	263.5	37.0	40	697	39.9	10.9
Decatur	38	147	15.4	5.5	32	1,260	D	54.0	41	D	D	D
DeKalb	2,872	17,884	3,291.8	1,107.2	412	10,958	3,630.8	511.5	1,413	23,641	1,358.1	362.0
Dodge	21	90	6.7	2.3	18	639	193.9	27.3	25	360	15.3	4.4
Dooly	10	17	2.6	0.8	9	877	176.9	25.4	17	123	5.7	1.5
Dougherty	220	D	D	D	65	3,262	3,184.1	185.6	217	4,149	185.3	48.8
Douglas	226	1,000	102.4	37.2	88	2,512	690.3	101.7	202	4,276	210.1	56.6
Early	15	77	6.0	1.9	9	776	D	57.4	21	156	7.6	2.0
Echols	NA	NA	NA	NA	NA	NA	NA	NA	1	D	D	D

Health Care and Social Assistance, Other Services, Nonemployer Businesses, and Residential Construction

STATE County	Health care and social assistance, 2012				Other services, 2012				Nonemployer businesses, 2016		Value of residential construction authorized by building permits, 2018	
	Number of establish-ments	Number of employees	Receipts (mil dol)	Annual payroll (mil dol)	Number of establish-ments	Number of employees	Receipts (mil dol)	Annual payroll (mil dol)	Number	Receipts (mil dol)	New construction ($1,000)	Number of housing units
	159	160	161	162	163	164	165	166	167	168	169	170
FLORIDA—Cont'd												
Putnam	170	2,503	234.6	77.7	86	401	28.2	8.4	3,867	126.4	15,103	86
St. Johns	518	7,502	740.5	278.5	322	2,269	1,094.9	119.1	20,217	949.2	1,366,214	5,910
St. Lucie	655	10,230	1,342.1	441.1	362	1,779	148.2	42.0	24,859	901.8	644,868	3,529
Santa Rosa	261	3,479	429.1	143.2	155	732	46.8	15.0	11,745	501.4	262,445	1,513
Sarasota	1,516	25,814	2,976.0	1,087.1	914	4,738	451.7	117.4	40,328	2,044.8	1,220,982	5,799
Seminole	1,305	16,947	1,937.9	704.4	780	4,186	378.4	110.8	40,959	1,634.9	493,296	2,036
Sumter	146	2,956	381.2	123.8	64	304	22.2	6.7	6,367	254.4	552,266	2,076
Suwannee	65	1,342	104.8	38.7	37	186	20.1	5.5	2,417	85.8	11,589	63
Taylor	41	838	70.7	29.0	25	131	8.9	2.3	901	30.9	4,947	30
Union	15	D	D	D	5	D	D	D	576	23.3	348	32
Volusia	1,346	25,561	2,776.3	1,051.0	1,014	4,984	543.9	175.7	39,837	1,554.3	678,360	2,451
Wakulla	26	164	13.1	4.1	33	114	9.9	2.1	2,025	74.9	39,318	222
Walton	113	2,560	266.9	100.3	87	462	52.0	12.3	7,713	485.1	624,816	1,525
Washington	47	796	65.8	25.3	24	172	7.4	2.7	1,509	55.7	5,639	44
GEORGIA	22,734	448,460	51,800.6	19,515.2	13,828	89,302	10,617.1	2,703.1	877,908	35,007.7	11,146,199	59,315
Appling	36	D	D	D	28	99	8.6	2.2	1,160	42.3	444	4
Atkinson	3	D	D	D	2	D	D	D	541	22.0	0	0
Bacon	18	D	D	D	16	D	D	D	619	22.0	0	0
Baker	3	D	D	D	2	D	D	D	206	6.3	0	0
Baldwin	111	D	D	D	50	283	19.2	6.0	3,013	96.6	20,757	118
Banks	13	113	12.5	3.7	13	D	D	D	1,278	49.1	8,266	53
Barrow	91	1,292	117.4	44.6	79	322	34.7	9.0	6,011	244.3	101,618	867
Bartow	177	2,803	324.2	123.9	120	805	108.5	25.0	7,973	357.8	140,266	887
Ben Hill	31	698	49.9	18.9	22	D	D	D	1,053	34.8	5,304	58
Berrien	32	316	19.3	8.2	10	22	2.8	0.5	1,063	44.7	3,125	18
Bibb	540	14,875	1,757.6	642.6	256	1,605	183.0	51.2	12,338	398.7	24,851	145
Bleckley	20	291	19.7	8.0	10	33	3.8	0.9	810	24.1	1,860	7
Brantley	15	121	7.8	3.3	15	24	2.8	0.5	1,029	31.8	1,839	16
Brooks	17	D	D	D	18	D	D	D	916	31.0	5,392	43
Bryan	52	D	D	D	43	D	D	D	2,673	111.1	104,947	518
Bulloch	183	2,747	318.0	109.8	96	446	39.7	9.9	4,584	179.1	70,003	474
Burke	30	D	D	D	18	D	D	D	1,470	50.7	8,726	49
Butts	29	529	39.8	14.2	27	D	D	D	1,558	62.0	14,550	63
Calhoun	8	252	17.0	6.8	2	D	D	D	311	10.7	810	3
Camden	103	672	63.9	24.5	59	219	19.7	5.1	2,535	76.4	84,324	310
Candler	15	545	35.7	14.5	7	34	2.2	0.6	786	29.7	361	3
Carroll	214	4,784	634.3	238.3	122	D	D	D	8,334	307.7	153,544	706
Catoosa	100	D	D	D	40	272	18.5	5.2	4,124	182.8	53,899	254
Charlton	11	260	17.6	7.2	5	13	1.5	0.4	476	13.6	3,593	21
Chatham	721	18,354	2,327.4	860.8	414	D	D	D	20,730	897.9	394,316	2,067
Chattahoochee	5	20	2.6	1.0	5	D	D	D	248	5.3	0	0
Chattooga	28	382	27.7	10.9	17	65	11.5	2.0	1,353	70.8	5,916	73
Cherokee	447	5,141	471.4	208.8	324	1,402	118.2	35.1	23,616	1,046.0	784,560	3,500
Clarke	439	8,443	1,124.3	446.3	192	1,261	184.9	38.6	8,515	311.0	79,858	606
Clay	5	D	D	D	2	D	D	D	156	3.5	980	3
Clayton	400	7,024	810.1	306.3	270	1,349	144.9	36.5	28,491	671.0	143,421	720
Clinch	12	159	13.9	4.7	6	11	1.0	0.2	403	13.8	222	2
Cobb	1,803	28,679	3,519.7	1,393.8	1,237	9,389	847.7	295.9	76,862	3,345.1	622,866	2,790
Coffee	103	1,877	210.2	72.2	49	218	17.0	5.3	2,830	108.5	8,023	54
Colquitt	92	2,148	192.2	73.9	48	193	17.9	4.3	2,888	107.4	12,189	78
Columbia	215	3,078	254.4	102.3	134	794	69.6	22.5	10,016	413.5	233,893	1,273
Cook	31	D	D	D	12	50	3.7	1.1	1,025	43.5	5,898	51
Coweta	228	3,415	373.4	152.0	144	653	57.4	16.3	11,338	399.3	322,649	1,247
Crawford	7	D	D	D	7	51	5.0	1.9	791	27.4	3,073	13
Crisp	73	1,235	130.4	39.5	30	148	20.9	4.5	1,554	51.3	1,710	15
Dade	18	D	D	D	18	87	6.9	2.1	1,080	42.7	1,576	10
Dawson	41	D	D	D	35	161	11.0	2.9	2,180	117.7	77,267	446
Decatur	56	D	D	D	42	157	12.4	3.2	1,810	63.2	3,258	27
DeKalb	1,782	39,802	4,808.8	1,748.3	1,075	6,406	806.5	217.5	76,780	2,549.5	682,102	3,673
Dodge	51	893	65.8	27.5	17	124	6.0	1.7	1,433	41.7	2,504	13
Dooly	11	123	6.3	3.1	11	D	D	D	682	27.5	0	0
Dougherty	306	8,924	875.1	336.1	152	994	90.1	24.5	6,840	204.9	5,785	48
Douglas	266	4,639	498.1	185.7	183	796	87.3	22.3	12,531	393.5	73,294	399
Early	16	346	32.1	11.7	14	35	2.7	0.8	642	25.4	2,130	13
Echols	4	D	D	D	1	D	D	D	188	6.5	732	5

Table B. States and Counties — Government Employment and Payroll, and Local Government Finances

	Government employment and payroll, 2012									Local government finances, 2012				
			March payroll (percent of total)							General revenue				
												Taxes		
STATE County	Full-time equivalent employees	March payroll (dollars)	Administration, judicial, and legal	Police and corrections	Fire protection	Highways and transportation	Health and welfare	Natural resources and utilities	Education and libraries	Total (mil dol)	Inter-governmental (mil dol)	Total (mil dol)	Per capita[1] (dollars) Total	Per capita[1] (dollars) Property
	171	172	173	174	175	176	177	178	179	180	181	182	183	184
FLORIDA—Cont'd														
Putnam	3,846	14,358,652	7.4	13.9	0.8	1.5	2.5	26.1	46.6	395.8	157.9	190.3	2,597	2,417
St. Johns	6,382	21,674,061	7.3	12.2	6.8	2.0	1.9	5.0	59.5	671.6	162.3	311.6	1,541	1,380
St. Lucie	10,618	40,360,120	6.2	13.8	7.0	2.1	1.9	6.5	59.0	1,062.2	343.2	409.9	1,444	1,184
Santa Rosa	4,424	14,124,230	11.2	10.2	1.2	2.6	1.4	3.0	69.2	350.7	153.5	129.3	816	709
Sarasota	15,008	61,458,391	6.0	10.2	6.3	3.8	31.5	5.2	34.0	2,009.8	280.1	709.8	1,838	1,447
Seminole	13,257	48,666,111	6.8	14.5	7.5	2.5	1.1	6.0	60.1	1,274.8	440.7	579.9	1,346	977
Sumter	1,509	4,669,736	4.3	3.1	1.1	6.4	1.4	4.3	72.3	251.5	43.7	105.9	1,042	834
Suwannee	1,250	3,665,519	1.8	2.1	4.9	6.0	1.5	1.5	76.2	111.4	59.1	33.8	773	579
Taylor	786	2,148,026	10.9	14.9	3.3	3.6	2.4	3.5	59.2	67.3	33.3	26.1	1,148	904
Union	487	1,232,008	5.4	0.2	0.0	3.3	7.6	4.3	78.2	32.6	21.2	6.6	433	280
Volusia	20,784	73,359,257	5.4	11.5	4.2	2.1	24.3	6.2	44.1	2,117.9	503.9	753.8	1,517	1,158
Wakulla	827	2,245,238	3.1	0.4	1.1	0.0	4.2	3.1	87.4	79.8	43.2	24.2	784	664
Walton	2,328	7,662,784	10.7	15.8	12.5	4.9	2.3	2.2	47.4	217.6	48.3	141.1	2,450	1,824
Washington	925	2,765,292	6.8	13.6	0.1	3.5	2.8	2.9	69.5	77.2	44.1	22.4	901	681
GEORGIA	X	X	X	X	X	X	X	X	X	X	X	X	X	X
Appling	1,166	3,357,745	5.4	4.9	0.2	3.4	40.2	2.3	42.9	101.3	23.2	31.5	1,717	1,055
Atkinson	477	2,010,541	3.8	3.1	0.0	1.5	3.3	1.4	85.2	27.4	15.3	7.7	927	571
Bacon	457	1,275,084	6.8	7.3	3.9	3.1	3.3	3.9	70.6	31.3	15.9	11.6	1,032	637
Baker	109	265,135	10.3	11.8	0.0	4.2	6.9	0.3	66.0	7.6	2.8	4.1	1,214	935
Baldwin	2,074	6,857,034	4.5	7.7	2.8	1.2	39.8	4.6	38.7	195.7	44.2	53.0	1,143	638
Banks	669	1,937,141	7.1	10.1	4.9	1.5	0.8	3.5	69.3	49.3	16.9	23.2	1,267	661
Barrow	2,271	8,023,913	5.3	11.2	6.0	1.9	0.4	3.2	70.8	183.6	75.3	79.2	1,129	694
Bartow	3,986	13,981,683	6.0	7.9	4.2	1.8	11.2	5.6	61.8	329.5	108.9	176.5	1,753	972
Ben Hill	1,147	3,286,219	4.4	6.3	2.0	2.8	28.8	5.8	44.8	73.5	21.8	20.5	1,168	664
Berrien	719	2,060,957	6.9	9.8	0.2	4.4	3.1	4.2	71.1	50.3	26.7	17.3	911	561
Bibb	6,298	22,932,839	6.6	10.3	5.2	2.3	5.6	6.2	62.4	582.3	249.1	239.3	1,530	1,004
Bleckley	611	1,809,213	5.2	7.5	1.5	2.9	15.6	2.6	64.0	43.0	19.1	12.4	960	647
Brantley	674	1,858,203	5.0	7.6	1.1	3.5	4.4	0.6	76.4	47.4	24.7	17.9	963	714
Brooks	547	1,728,938	6.4	10.4	2.7	2.7	0.2	3.5	70.4	39.5	17.4	16.6	1,079	809
Bryan	1,408	4,117,520	6.2	9.0	3.9	3.1	0.9	1.8	72.5	105.5	39.0	54.1	1,679	990
Bulloch	2,932	8,670,844	4.4	9.3	1.3	2.3	13.2	5.4	62.9	203.4	80.5	82.0	1,128	580
Burke	1,329	4,107,904	4.5	7.8	10.8	4.1	1.0	2.7	66.7	98.4	35.0	53.8	2,324	1,816
Butts	841	2,814,107	8.3	12.6	6.9	3.6	1.8	7.2	58.7	67.2	18.6	39.3	1,671	1,021
Calhoun	366	979,335	10.2	7.4	0.7	2.9	40.9	1.9	35.5	30.9	10.8	7.0	1,076	732
Camden	2,030	7,548,391	6.8	8.0	6.1	2.8	1.4	3.1	70.2	151.8	54.9	73.4	1,428	963
Candler	567	1,831,024	5.7	4.7	0.3	2.6	32.8	2.7	50.3	45.3	16.5	11.4	1,029	561
Carroll	4,120	14,298,798	4.5	9.2	3.6	1.3	0.9	5.5	74.6	321.7	126.8	135.2	1,212	693
Catoosa	521	1,425,530	21.0	30.9	13.0	7.3	4.0	13.5	1.6	366.0	65.6	70.0	1,077	575
Charlton	616	1,655,066	4.2	6.4	0.0	3.2	24.8	3.3	57.2	42.4	11.9	18.8	1,412	1,079
Chatham	10,068	34,099,398	11.9	16.1	3.9	3.9	4.3	8.5	48.0	1,650.2	303.7	617.1	2,233	1,331
Chattahoochee	245	688,357	6.1	3.3	0.0	3.3	1.1	3.7	81.0	12.5	8.2	2.8	217	112
Chattooga	892	2,643,680	6.6	8.6	0.4	3.0	1.5	9.6	68.8	64.8	29.2	23.2	901	517
Cherokee	7,029	24,643,064	5.0	7.9	5.8	1.4	0.4	4.0	73.8	584.3	192.5	290.4	1,312	942
Clarke	4,598	14,811,444	7.4	13.2	5.1	3.9	6.5	8.9	52.4	786.3	118.3	156.8	1,304	951
Clay	153	338,738	12.0	11.6	0.0	5.9	10.5	4.9	53.7	11.6	5.8	4.5	1,443	1,081
Clayton	10,173	35,407,764	8.8	11.0	2.0	2.2	3.2	6.1	63.2	920.8	359.2	426.5	1,604	962
Clinch	408	1,264,709	7.4	6.1	2.4	2.4	26.1	1.7	53.7	37.6	11.7	10.4	1,552	1,170
Cobb	21,811	86,644,451	7.5	8.4	4.5	1.1	2.0	6.1	69.0	2,213.0	659.3	1,157.2	1,636	1,103
Coffee	1,488	4,411,069	6.7	9.4	3.0	2.6	0.9	5.5	70.9	107.8	47.8	44.0	1,020	537
Colquitt	2,449	7,687,804	4.2	6.3	1.7	2.0	30.8	3.3	49.7	222.7	74.9	47.4	1,028	553
Columbia	3,933	13,876,194	6.0	9.6	0.3	1.7	1.1	3.8	75.8	345.5	122.6	173.7	1,319	749
Cook	873	2,387,884	12.7	9.3	2.3	3.3	2.5	4.1	61.5	46.6	20.7	17.3	1,025	578
Coweta	4,492	16,492,046	4.9	10.2	4.8	1.9	0.7	3.7	71.5	348.5	120.9	183.0	1,397	887
Crawford	409	1,190,596	12.1	7.9	0.3	4.3	0.0	2.2	71.6	30.1	16.0	10.8	855	645
Crisp	1,725	5,432,319	3.5	6.3	2.7	2.0	36.6	9.1	38.4	77.9	34.1	32.8	1,391	767
Dade	530	1,479,400	6.8	9.6	0.2	3.2	0.6	3.0	72.4	34.2	13.9	16.9	1,027	529
Dawson	883	2,870,993	9.9	10.6	5.7	1.7	1.3	5.5	64.0	77.9	18.2	53.2	2,374	1,408
Decatur	1,769	5,577,746	4.6	10.6	0.9	2.4	30.0	3.0	47.3	136.5	40.7	37.7	1,372	723
DeKalb	26,888	103,868,526	7.1	8.8	3.1	0.8	23.2	3.6	52.3	2,945.3	639.0	1,074.5	1,520	1,096
Dodge	906	3,199,644	3.3	4.7	0.8	1.5	30.4	2.0	56.5	119.4	31.6	18.8	881	486
Dooly	464	1,464,602	8.7	18.6	0.6	3.5	5.3	4.9	57.6	43.0	17.6	16.5	1,150	731
Dougherty	4,532	14,341,822	8.6	11.0	5.2	3.2	6.8	9.3	52.1	390.9	181.4	135.1	1,429	878
Douglas	4,786	16,883,097	6.3	9.7	3.9	1.7	1.1	5.1	70.7	416.9	160.6	203.6	1,520	907
Early	569	1,743,416	4.9	3.4	2.7	3.8	5.9	5.5	72.8	41.8	16.7	18.3	1,726	1,066
Echols	193	553,759	4.6	9.7	0.0	4.1	4.2	1.7	75.0	10.7	5.7	4.4	1,110	953

1. Based on the resident population estimated as of July 1 of the year shown.

Table B. States and Counties — Local Government Finances, Government Employment, and Income Taxes

STATE County	Local government finances, 2012 (cont.)									Government employment, 2017			Individual income tax returns, 2016		
	Direct general expenditure							Debt outstanding							
			Percent of total for:												
	Total (mil dol)	Per capita¹ (dollars)	Education	Health and hospitals	Police protection	Public welfare	Highways	Total (mil dol)	Per capita¹ (dollars)	Federal civilian	Federal military	State and local	Number of returns	Mean adjusted gross income	Mean income tax
	185	186	187	188	189	190	191	192	193	194	195	196	197	198	199

FLORIDA—Cont'd															
Putnam	399.5	5,452	34.5	1.8	5.6	0.6	3.0	210.9	2,879	116	130	3,744	28,430	38,683	3,390
St. Johns	735.8	3,639	40.2	2.2	9.5	1.0	5.3	1,504.0	7,439	634	438	9,050	111,130	97,489	16,649
St. Lucie	1,134.8	3,998	41.4	1.0	7.9	0.9	6.3	2,450.5	8,632	738	632	12,799	142,070	48,878	5,419
Santa Rosa	415	2,618	54.4	1.5	8.3	0.0	4.4	1,574.0	9,930	828	1,334	5,622	76,020	60,685	7,416
Sarasota	2,019.2	5,229	26.3	30.5	5.5	0.1	4.4	1,927.4	4,991	1,032	801	13,413	204,610	80,827	13,583
Seminole	1,294.2	3,004	46.2	1.0	8.8	0.8	9.2	890.7	2,067	933	826	16,001	218,570	62,896	8,669
Sumter	263.4	2,592	27.3	1.6	6.0	0.5	7.8	594.1	5,846	1,734	211	3,047	57,090	76,131	10,808
Suwannee	116.7	2,674	46.6	3.1	7.6	0.8	7.6	34.0	778	102	74	2,371	16,380	40,606	3,956
Taylor	68.5	3,013	44.4	2.4	9.4	0.2	11.3	16.9	741	33	35	1,423	7,920	45,038	4,469
Union	34.6	2,273	56.6	4.9	7.0	1.2	3.9	2.9	192	18	19	1,983	4,540	43,793	3,748
Volusia	2,177.8	4,382	29.7	25.3	7.3	0.4	3.5	2,589.6	5,211	1,304	1,056	18,242	249,680	50,518	6,082
Wakulla	81.9	2,657	52.0	3.7	9.6	0.2	3.4	16.7	542	91	52	1,714	13,040	50,623	4,935
Walton	219.9	3,819	35.9	5.8	9.3	0.1	9.2	133.4	2,316	149	163	3,172	30,580	92,322	17,678
Washington	78.4	3,150	61.0	1.7	5.4	0.1	8.3	30.5	1,226	34	40	1,878	9,220	41,716	3,736
GEORGIA	X	X	X	X	X	X	X	X	X	101,246	90,626	584,317	4,434,440	60,753	7,804
Appling	103.6	5,642	37.2	40.4	3.0	1.1	5.8	23.1	1,257	43	50	1,324	7,180	41,125	3,733
Atkinson	26.9	3,242	60.6	0.2	3.6	0.4	3.5	11.0	1,324	17	25	441	3,020	29,657	1,968
Bacon	33.2	2,969	55.2	3.2	4.9	1.2	7.9	46.1	4,115	24	30	554	4,080	40,284	3,465
Baker	7.5	2,220	56.9	5.0	7.4	0.6	8.6	0.8	252	1	17	113	1,160	37,446	3,778
Baldwin	184.3	3,974	29.8	43.5	4.6	0.1	2.8	85.5	1,843	72	133	5,695	16,630	44,353	4,279
Banks	40.1	2,192	68.6	0.3	5.3	0.4	2.2	21.8	1,192	17	51	874	7,150	44,172	3,798
Barrow	186.4	2,657	60.5	0.7	6.9	0.3	2.8	222.6	3,172	154	216	2,699	33,560	48,899	4,708
Bartow	347.5	3,452	58.9	1.4	8.8	0.2	4.1	306.7	3,047	211	286	4,737	44,170	51,758	5,457
Ben Hill	81.8	4,663	37.3	32.7	4.5	0.4	3.3	18.0	1,027	27	46	1,024	6,440	37,952	3,090
Berrien	45.9	2,409	60.4	2.4	5.6	0.4	7.6	17.9	939	36	52	927	6,630	41,497	4,095
Bibb	601.4	3,844	44.1	7.1	6.5	0.3	1.9	510.5	3,262	1,061	405	8,661	64,820	48,702	5,609
Bleckley	45.7	3,536	52.6	19.3	4.9	1.0	4.6	14.9	1,152	27	32	1,328	4,670	46,384	4,213
Brantley	50.2	2,701	61.4	2.5	3.2	0.6	11.1	13.3	715	27	51	814	6,470	39,099	2,859
Brooks	42.2	2,737	55.7	1.6	6.5	0.4	4.6	12.1	786	26	43	660	6,200	39,024	3,605
Bryan	99.9	3,100	63.6	2.1	7.7	0.9	3.7	45.2	1,404	212	102	1,763	16,700	64,361	7,108
Bulloch	216.1	2,973	48.2	11.2	5.7	0.0	4.0	302.9	4,167	136	208	7,919	26,880	46,294	4,950
Burke	98.6	4,264	55.4	3.2	4.7	0.4	6.1	14.9	643	40	61	1,458	9,330	42,839	3,961
Butts	62.8	2,668	49.4	2.9	7.3	0.3	5.2	43.9	1,866	56	59	1,556	9,260	49,457	4,771
Calhoun	30.5	4,684	35.5	34.1	3.8	0.3	3.0	4.2	644	20	13	484	1,980	34,276	2,732
Camden	144.7	2,816	55.4	4.1	7.1	0.2	4.1	84.7	1,648	2,476	4,131	2,263	21,790	48,727	4,291
Candler	48.2	4,334	45.1	28.6	3.5	0.0	4.0	21.3	1,913	21	29	706	4,060	37,799	2,902
Carroll	329.8	2,956	58.0	0.6	6.4	0.2	2.6	335.3	3,005	211	312	7,083	46,960	52,256	5,421
Catoosa	277.3	4,263	51.2	31.2	2.8	0.4	2.1	143.9	2,212	73	181	2,578	26,940	49,685	4,765
Charlton	40.5	3,046	38.8	25.3	5.1	0.3	7.6	12.6	947	41	29	438	3,470	40,720	3,179
Chatham	1,559	5,640	26.6	30.7	10.1	0.3	2.2	741.4	2,682	2,642	5,138	16,972	125,870	58,125	7,170
Chattahoochee	16.1	1,234	73.5	1.4	3.7	4.7	3.0	4.9	376	99	14,252	254	2,890	39,335	2,453
Chattooga	68.3	2,655	56.6	0.3	5.8	0.3	4.1	31.8	1,237	37	64	1,278	9,130	39,217	3,001
Cherokee	581.9	2,629	63.6	3.8	4.8	0.4	2.5	701.9	3,172	339	676	8,225	111,070	72,172	9,375
Clarke	854.7	7,107	20.1	50.3	3.2	0.1	1.3	564.4	4,693	958	394	24,542	46,610	49,624	5,877
Clay	11.5	3,685	36.6	23.2	6.0	0.7	6.5	1.6	517	40	8	156	1,150	31,799	2,497
Clayton	908.8	3,418	54.3	3.7	8.1	0.7	2.7	457.9	1,722	1,405	812	13,729	126,510	32,874	2,236
Clinch	33.2	4,943	44.6	27.7	3.7	0.3	5.5	16.1	2,403	15	18	482	2,370	39,240	3,332
Cobb	2,261.5	3,197	56.3	1.0	7.2	0.7	7.3	3,722.8	5,262	2,543	2,400	33,551	345,900	77,037	11,229
Coffee	114.8	2,659	57.4	0.3	6.5	0.2	5.8	18.7	434	112	110	2,676	15,440	37,785	3,626
Colquitt	216.3	4,688	39.4	34.4	3.5	0.1	4.0	54.2	1,175	111	123	3,679	16,890	39,193	3,516
Columbia	330.5	2,511	64.3	0.9	6.4	0.3	6.0	242.1	1,840	391	414	5,397	63,670	71,536	8,828
Cook	49.1	2,900	54.5	1.3	8.1	0.5	6.5	18.8	1,112	30	47	1,177	6,390	36,624	3,494
Coweta	343	2,620	61.2	1.1	6.1	0.1	4.2	213.3	1,629	249	391	5,036	62,650	65,625	7,836
Crawford	30.2	2,394	59.2	1.1	4.7	0.3	5.5	12.0	952	7	33	419	4,930	41,334	3,315
Crisp	83.6	3,542	57.8	1.1	7.1	0.3	5.0	31.7	1,343	53	61	1,371	8,240	38,560	3,244
Dade	36.5	2,215	63.4	1.1	8.9	0.2	6.0	9.7	586	23	42	577	6,160	46,040	4,312
Dawson	84.8	3,783	48.5	2.7	4.7	0.9	3.3	124.1	5,535	44	67	1,191	10,510	63,253	8,010
Decatur	143.5	5,218	34.0	27.4	5.0	0.1	3.7	45.5	1,655	53	71	2,406	10,820	39,485	3,457
DeKalb	2,937.7	4,155	37.1	33.5	4.6	0.5	1.6	2,476.3	3,502	11,321	2,104	32,939	343,770	64,118	8,850
Dodge	77.8	3,646	46.0	31.2	3.4	1.0	3.8	21.4	1,005	38	52	1,836	7,180	36,332	2,874
Dooly	37.4	2,615	43.0	10.8	9.8	0.5	6.6	10.1	704	57	33	736	3,840	38,715	3,377
Dougherty	400.6	4,239	40.5	13.1	5.7	0.1	2.1	219.4	2,322	2,489	530	6,715	36,120	41,403	4,159
Douglas	492.1	3,674	53.7	0.9	4.5	0.4	2.1	632.2	4,719	191	392	5,495	62,680	48,170	4,678
Early	43.1	4,068	53.5	7.9	10.2	0.0	3.3	13.2	1,250	33	28	1,403	4,080	36,776	3,140
Echols	10.8	2,706	74.2	0.3	4.4	0.4	3.7	19.9	4,981	1	11	208	1,270	37,266	2,820

1. Based on the resident population estimated as of July 1 of the year shown.

Table B. States and Counties — **Land Area and Population**

State / county code	CBSA code[1]	County code[2]	STATE County	Land area[3] (sq. mi)	Population, 2018 Total persons 2018	Rank	Per square mile	Race alone or in combination, not Hispanic or Latino (percent) White	Black	American Indian, Alaska Native	Asian and Pacific Islander	Percent Hispanic or Latino[4]	Age (percent) Under 5 years	5 to 17 years	18 to 24 years	25 to 34 years	35 to 44 years	45 to 54 years
				1	2	3	4	5	6	7	8	9	10	11	12	13	14	15
			GEORGIA—Cont'd															
13103	42,340	2	Effingham	478.8	62,190	846	129.9	79.8	14.8	0.9	1.7	4.8	6.8	19.7	8.0	14.2	14.1	13.5
13105		6	Elbert	351.1	19,120	1,867	54.5	64.6	28.9	0.6	1.2	5.9	5.9	15.6	7.4	12.3	10.8	12.9
13107		7	Emanuel	680.6	22,612	1,699	33.2	60.1	35.0	0.6	0.9	4.5	6.6	18.1	9.2	13.5	12.2	11.7
13109		6	Evans	182.9	10,721	2,373	58.6	56.9	30.5	0.6	1.1	11.9	6.8	20.0	7.6	12.6	12.1	12.2
13111		8	Fannin	387.0	25,964	1,568	67.1	95.6	1.0	1.1	0.8	2.5	4.2	12.4	6.0	8.9	9.5	11.8
13113	12,060	1	Fayette	194.4	113,459	541	583.6	63.1	24.7	0.7	6.2	7.4	4.5	18.5	8.6	9.0	11.4	14.8
13115	40,660	3	Floyd	509.8	97,927	610	192.1	72.4	15.4	0.7	1.9	11.3	6.1	17.1	10.0	12.9	12.0	12.6
13117	12,060	1	Forsyth	224.6	236,612	284	1,053.5	71.7	4.4	0.6	15.3	9.7	6.0	21.4	7.4	9.7	16.0	16.5
13119		8	Franklin	261.6	23,023	1,679	88.0	84.6	10.2	0.8	1.4	4.6	5.9	15.8	9.7	12.4	10.7	12.6
13121	12,060	1	Fulton	526.7	1,050,114	43	1,993.8	41.1	44.8	0.6	8.3	7.3	5.9	16.0	10.1	17.0	14.2	13.8
13123		6	Gilmer	426.2	30,816	1,410	72.3	86.4	1.0	0.9	0.8	11.9	5.4	13.8	6.7	9.8	10.7	12.7
13125		9	Glascock	143.7	2,995	2,967	20.8	88.4	9.4	1.1	0.5	1.9	4.7	17.0	8.2	11.0	12.1	14.8
13127	15,260	3	Glynn	419.6	85,219	674	203.1	64.9	27.2	0.7	2.1	6.8	5.6	16.2	8.1	12.0	11.4	12.6
13129	15,660	4	Gordon	355.8	57,685	896	162.1	78.3	4.7	0.7	1.5	16.3	6.0	18.3	8.5	12.6	12.8	14.4
13131		6	Grady	454.5	24,748	1,619	54.5	58.7	28.9	1.0	0.8	11.7	6.5	18.3	7.5	11.5	11.7	12.9
13133		6	Greene	387.7	17,698	1,939	45.6	58.9	33.9	0.7	1.4	6.2	5.0	13.7	5.9	9.4	10.6	10.7
13135	12,060	1	Gwinnett	430.6	927,781	58	2,154.6	38.2	28.9	0.7	13.2	21.5	6.6	20.3	9.1	13.2	14.4	14.7
13137	18,460	6	Habersham	276.8	45,388	1,065	164.0	78.4	4.5	0.8	2.7	15.1	5.8	16.6	9.5	12.6	12.0	12.6
13139	23,580	3	Hall	393.0	202,148	332	514.4	61.4	8.0	0.6	2.4	29.0	6.6	18.8	9.1	13.0	12.5	13.5
13141	33,300	7	Hancock	471.1	8,348	2,556	17.7	25.3	71.3	0.7	1.1	2.4	3.8	11.7	7.9	13.9	10.9	13.3
13143	12,060	1	Haralson	282.2	29,533	1,442	104.7	92.3	5.4	0.9	1.1	1.8	6.0	18.0	7.7	13.0	12.0	14.4
13145	17,980	2	Harris	463.8	34,475	1,313	74.3	78.1	17.2	0.8	1.8	3.8	4.7	16.5	7.8	10.4	11.7	14.9
13147		6	Hart	232.4	26,099	1,564	112.3	75.9	20.0	0.5	1.2	3.9	5.3	15.6	7.4	11.4	10.8	13.4
13149	12,060	1	Heard	296.0	11,879	2,303	40.1	86.6	10.8	0.9	0.9	2.8	5.6	17.1	8.5	11.8	11.5	14.1
13151	12,060	1	Henry	318.6	230,220	293	722.6	43.6	46.8	0.8	4.2	7.2	5.9	19.8	9.4	12.3	13.6	15.3
13153	47,580	3	Houston	376.1	155,469	426	413.4	57.8	33.1	0.9	4.3	6.7	6.6	19.0	8.7	14.7	13.2	12.7
13155		7	Irwin	354.4	9,398	2,472	26.5	67.4	28.2	0.4	1.0	4.1	4.9	16.2	9.1	13.7	13.1	13.0
13157	27,600	4	Jackson	339.7	70,422	770	207.3	82.6	7.8	0.7	2.4	8.1	6.5	18.9	7.4	13.1	13.8	13.9
13159	12,060	1	Jasper	368.4	14,040	2,159	38.1	75.6	20.5	0.8	0.5	4.0	5.9	17.9	7.3	11.5	11.4	13.8
13161		7	Jeff Davis	330.9	15,029	2,094	45.4	72.2	15.3	0.6	0.8	12.2	6.9	19.6	8.4	12.3	12.1	12.7
13163		6	Jefferson	526.6	15,430	2,074	29.3	43.0	53.0	0.5	0.6	3.8	6.4	17.1	8.1	12.4	11.1	12.9
13165		6	Jenkins	347.3	8,683	2,530	25.0	51.7	42.4	0.6	0.7	5.6	5.3	15.0	9.8	14.6	12.5	12.7
13167	20,140	7	Johnson	303.0	9,708	2,451	32.0	62.9	34.2	0.5	0.6	2.6	5.1	13.7	7.9	13.4	13.3	14.1
13169	31,420	3	Jones	393.9	28,616	1,472	72.6	72.3	25.6	0.7	0.9	1.8	5.1	18.1	8.0	11.2	12.4	14.0
13171	12,060	1	Lamar	183.5	19,000	1,872	103.5	66.0	31.3	0.8	1.1	2.5	5.8	14.8	13.6	12.6	10.9	12.4
13173	46,660	3	Lanier	196.5	10,340	2,398	52.6	70.4	23.0	1.4	2.0	5.8	6.6	17.3	7.8	15.5	13.1	12.7
13175	20,140	5	Laurens	807.3	47,325	1,030	58.6	58.8	37.8	0.5	1.3	2.7	6.7	18.1	7.9	12.3	11.9	12.6
13177	10,500	3	Lee	355.9	29,764	1,437	83.6	72.0	22.4	0.6	3.3	3.0	6.1	19.9	7.8	12.9	14.6	13.8
13179	25,980	3	Liberty	516.5	61,497	856	119.1	41.6	44.9	1.2	3.9	12.8	10.4	17.7	14.0	19.4	10.8	9.1
13181	12,260	2	Lincoln	210.4	7,915	2,600	37.6	68.0	29.9	1.0	0.9	2.0	5.6	13.5	7.1	11.4	9.7	12.0
13183	25,980	3	Long	400.4	18,998	1,873	47.4	60.6	27.7	1.3	2.7	11.2	7.4	19.7	8.6	16.5	14.5	12.5
13185	46,660	3	Lowndes	497.2	116,321	535	234.0	55.1	37.5	0.7	2.9	5.9	6.8	17.2	16.8	15.2	11.2	10.4
13187		6	Lumpkin	282.9	32,955	1,360	116.5	91.9	2.1	1.4	1.2	5.0	4.5	13.1	18.9	11.0	10.3	11.2
13189	12,260	2	McDuffie	257.5	21,531	1,752	83.6	54.6	42.4	0.7	0.8	3.2	6.5	18.5	8.2	12.2	10.6	12.7
13191	15,260	3	McIntosh	431.4	14,340	2,137	33.2	63.3	34.4	0.8	0.7	2.2	4.1	12.0	6.6	10.5	9.4	13.3
13193		6	Macon	400.7	13,143	2,221	32.8	33.9	60.3	0.4	1.8	4.4	5.1	13.7	9.2	15.4	12.1	12.8
13195	12,020	3	Madison	282.3	29,650	1,440	105.0	82.9	9.9	0.8	2.2	5.8	6.0	17.1	7.6	12.5	12.1	13.6
13197	17,980	2	Marion	366.0	8,351	2,555	22.8	60.5	31.4	1.1	1.4	7.2	5.0	16.3	7.3	10.8	10.3	13.6
13199	12,060	1	Meriwether	501.2	21,068	1,771	42.0	58.0	39.8	0.8	0.8	2.2	6.0	15.3	8.2	11.8	10.8	12.4
13201		8	Miller	282.4	5,686	2,780	20.1	68.8	28.5	0.6	0.8	2.6	5.6	17.2	6.9	11.3	10.6	13.0
13205		6	Mitchell	512.2	22,192	1,714	43.3	46.4	48.3	0.6	1.1	4.6	5.9	16.8	8.7	13.4	12.8	13.1
13207	31,420	3	Monroe	396.1	27,520	1,511	69.5	73.6	23.3	0.7	1.3	2.4	5.1	15.4	8.5	11.7	11.6	14.0
13209	47,080	9	Montgomery	241.1	9,193	2,486	38.1	67.6	25.6	0.5	0.9	6.8	5.2	14.9	12.5	12.7	11.6	12.7
13211	12,060	1	Morgan	347.4	18,853	1,880	54.3	73.6	22.9	0.7	0.9	3.3	6.1	16.7	7.5	10.6	11.0	13.8
13213	19,140	3	Murray	344.5	39,921	1,184	115.9	82.8	1.3	0.7	0.6	15.6	6.5	18.3	8.4	12.7	12.2	14.4
13215	17,980	2	Muscogee	216.4	194,160	342	897.2	42.3	48.2	0.9	3.9	7.7	7.1	17.6	9.8	16.2	12.6	11.5
13217	12,060	1	Newton	273.7	109,541	556	400.2	46.8	46.8	0.7	1.7	5.9	6.4	19.5	9.7	12.6	12.9	14.3
13219	12,020	3	Oconee	184.3	39,272	1,198	213.1	85.5	5.7	0.4	4.8	5.1	5.6	21.2	7.9	9.1	13.6	14.7
13221	12,020	3	Oglethorpe	439.1	15,054	2,091	34.3	76.8	18.0	0.7	1.3	5.0	5.3	15.6	7.6	12.4	11.4	14.2
13223	12,060	1	Paulding	312.3	164,044	399	525.3	71.6	21.2	0.8	1.9	6.7	6.3	19.8	8.5	13.6	14.2	15.5
13225	47,580	3	Peach	150.3	27,297	1,515	181.6	46.6	45.1	0.8	1.6	7.8	5.6	15.3	14.2	12.4	10.7	12.0
13227	12,060	1	Pickens	232.1	31,980	1,382	137.8	94.8	1.6	1.0	0.9	3.1	5.1	15.3	6.9	11.2	11.0	13.4
13229	48,180	6	Pierce	340.4	19,389	1,857	57.0	85.2	9.3	0.9	1.0	5.1	6.4	18.4	7.9	11.7	12.6	13.3
13231	12,060	1	Pike	216.1	18,634	1,894	86.2	88.4	10.0	0.7	0.9	1.6	5.3	18.1	8.3	11.6	12.6	15.1
13233	16,340	4	Polk	310.3	42,470	1,129	136.9	73.1	13.4	0.6	0.9	13.7	6.8	18.6	8.4	13.7	12.1	12.5
13235	47,580	3	Pulaski	249.3	11,069	2,348	44.4	63.8	32.2	0.6	1.4	3.5	4.0	14.3	7.5	12.0	11.9	13.8

1. CBSA = Core Based Statistical Area. See Appendix A for explanation. See Appendix B for list of metropolitan areas with component counties.
Service of USDA Rural-Urban Continuum Codes. See Appendix A for definition. 3. Dry land or land partially or temporarily covered by water. 2. County type code from the Economic Research 4. May be of any race.

Table B. States and Counties — Population and Households

STATE County	Age (percent) (cont.)			Percent female	Total persons		Percent change		Components of change, 2010-2018			Households, 2013-2017		Percent		
	55 to 64 years	65 to 74 years	75 years and over		2000	2010	2000-2010	2010-2018	Births	Deaths	Net Migration	Number	Persons per household	Family households	Female family householder[1]	One person
	16	17	18	19	20	21	22	23	24	25	26	27	28	29	30	31
GEORGIA—Cont'd																
Effingham	12.1	7.3	4.3	50.2	37,535	52,257	39.2	19.0	6,086	3,342	7,154	19,584	2.90	75.2	11.2	19.8
Elbert	14.2	11.9	9.0	52.2	20,511	20,166	-1.7	-5.2	1,876	2,102	-817	7,730	2.46	65.9	15.8	30.5
Emanuel	12.7	9.6	6.5	50.8	21,837	22,600	3.5	0.1	2,574	2,346	-220	8,387	2.59	65.4	19.5	30.0
Evans	12.7	9.0	7.0	51.3	10,495	11,002	4.8	-2.6	1,284	914	-667	4,023	2.55	71.7	19.1	23.0
Fannin	17.7	18.2	11.3	51.4	19,798	23,700	19.7	9.6	1,641	2,612	3,220	10,175	2.39	66.4	7.9	28.8
Fayette	15.0	11.1	7.1	51.5	91,263	106,564	16.8	6.5	6,972	6,689	6,619	39,604	2.77	77.1	9.2	20.9
Floyd	12.6	9.5	7.2	51.7	90,565	96,314	6.3	1.7	9,880	8,606	398	35,506	2.60	69.6	14.8	25.9
Forsyth	10.9	7.4	4.6	50.4	98,407	175,511	78.4	34.8	19,003	8,573	50,075	70,468	2.99	82.0	8.1	14.4
Franklin	13.8	11.1	7.9	51.0	20,285	22,086	8.9	4.2	2,235	2,317	1,022	8,322	2.61	69.9	11.7	25.5
Fulton	11.3	7.2	4.5	51.6	816,006	920,441	12.8	14.1	103,963	51,056	75,919	391,850	2.49	54.0	14.0	38.4
Gilmer	16.0	15.7	9.1	49.9	23,456	28,281	20.6	9.0	2,626	2,377	2,269	11,468	2.56	71.6	8.7	24.0
Glascock	14.3	10.0	8.0	50.5	2,556	3,082	20.6	-2.8	232	316	-5	1,083	2.71	64.5	10.3	30.7
Glynn	14.0	12.2	8.0	52.9	67,568	79,625	17.8	7.0	8,036	6,932	4,515	33,200	2.47	65.4	15.3	30.4
Gordon	12.5	8.9	5.9	50.7	44,104	55,186	25.1	4.5	5,755	4,093	865	19,959	2.80	75.1	13.6	20.5
Grady	13.4	10.7	7.5	51.8	23,659	25,012	5.7	-1.1	2,840	2,088	-1,014	9,092	2.74	74.2	14.7	23.0
Greene	15.7	17.9	11.1	51.9	14,406	15,999	11.1	10.6	1,356	1,633	1,969	6,793	2.43	67.7	13.6	28.6
Gwinnett	11.6	6.5	3.5	51.2	588,448	805,326	36.9	15.2	95,751	32,671	59,737	283,256	3.12	75.9	14.0	19.6
Habersham	12.7	10.5	7.6	52.7	35,902	43,036	19.9	5.5	4,187	3,563	1,722	15,106	2.74	68.9	7.5	26.8
Hall	11.8	8.8	6.1	50.3	139,277	179,726	29.0	12.5	21,184	11,473	12,744	63,095	3.03	73.9	12.7	21.1
Hancock	15.2	14.0	9.3	45.0	10,076	9,401	-6.7	-11.2	598	801	-877	2,970	2.03	61.9	23.9	33.7
Haralson	12.7	9.6	6.6	51.5	25,690	28,777	12.0	2.6	2,841	2,921	836	11,033	2.57	72.9	12.2	23.0
Harris	15.1	12.2	6.6	50.0	23,695	31,998	35.0	7.7	2,402	2,139	2,228	12,088	2.70	80.0	10.4	18.0
Hart	14.4	12.3	9.3	50.5	22,997	25,214	9.6	3.5	2,244	2,365	1,016	9,848	2.51	71.1	14.3	24.9
Heard	13.9	10.7	6.7	50.2	11,012	11,825	7.4	0.5	1,061	1,021	15	4,379	2.62	69.1	12.7	25.7
Henry	12.1	7.5	4.1	52.3	119,341	203,830	70.8	12.9	19,833	11,323	17,912	72,697	2.98	77.5	17.3	19.5
Houston	12.4	7.7	5.0	51.5	110,765	139,914	26.3	11.1	16,682	9,111	7,989	55,200	2.69	70.9	15.1	24.2
Irwin	12.1	9.7	8.2	48.0	9,931	9,529	-4.0	-1.4	828	847	-135	3,323	2.70	64.2	13.4	32.0
Jackson	11.9	8.8	5.6	50.7	41,589	60,457	45.4	16.5	6,629	4,577	7,879	21,785	2.90	75.6	12.6	19.9
Jasper	14.7	10.8	6.7	51.1	11,426	13,898	21.6	1.0	1,392	1,111	-146	5,100	2.67	72.3	11.8	25.8
Jeff Davis	12.3	9.5	6.2	50.7	12,684	15,080	18.9	-0.3	1,729	1,304	-471	5,210	2.85	75.2	14.2	20.6
Jefferson	13.7	10.8	7.5	51.7	17,266	16,930	-1.9	-8.9	1,715	1,827	-1,400	5,797	2.66	63.2	19.8	34.3
Jenkins	13.2	10.1	6.7	46.4	8,575	8,336	-2.8	4.2	819	838	303	3,375	2.62	62.4	17.3	29.8
Johnson	13.7	10.8	8.0	44.0	8,560	9,972	16.5	-2.6	778	779	-259	3,277	2.92	65.6	15.6	32.4
Jones	13.7	10.7	7.0	51.6	23,639	28,667	21.3	-0.2	2,431	2,125	-354	10,472	2.70	75.1	15.0	21.1
Lamar	12.9	10.1	6.8	51.8	15,912	18,310	15.1	3.8	1,639	1,660	691	6,263	2.72	60.9	13.6	36.2
Lanier	12.9	8.5	5.5	49.5	7,241	10,070	39.1	2.7	1,122	707	-159	3,744	2.69	70.3	16.5	27.6
Laurens	12.8	10.0	7.6	52.7	44,874	48,445	8.0	-2.3	5,306	4,558	-1,867	17,437	2.66	65.8	17.3	30.0
Lee	12.1	8.4	4.2	49.9	24,757	28,298	14.3	5.2	2,885	1,668	233	10,292	2.74	77.6	13.4	19.2
Liberty	9.4	6.0	3.3	49.3	61,610	63,588	3.2	-3.3	11,797	2,763	-11,526	23,108	2.60	71.2	17.6	22.7
Lincoln	16.9	14.3	9.6	51.5	8,348	7,996	-4.2	-1.0	608	719	26	3,438	2.23	62.7	14.8	33.6
Long	11.3	6.3	3.3	49.6	10,304	14,331	39.1	32.6	2,052	734	3,278	5,399	3.28	73.4	17.5	22.2
Lowndes	10.1	7.3	5.0	51.6	92,115	109,248	18.6	6.5	13,406	6,986	502	40,318	2.73	63.1	15.1	28.1
Lumpkin	13.5	10.9	6.7	50.4	21,016	29,955	42.5	10.0	2,507	2,139	2,579	11,412	2.64	65.3	10.7	23.1
McDuffie	13.7	10.6	6.9	53.2	21,231	21,867	3.0	-1.5	2,407	1,978	-762	8,156	2.60	70.7	18.2	25.4
McIntosh	17.3	15.9	10.8	51.2	10,847	14,332	32.1	0.1	978	1,001	19	5,730	2.44	67.3	14.3	27.5
Macon	14.5	10.9	6.4	45.2	14,074	14,743	4.8	-10.9	1,128	1,277	-1,476	4,618	2.55	64.0	21.9	33.6
Madison	14.2	10.4	6.6	50.6	25,730	28,160	9.4	5.3	2,760	2,309	1,053	10,571	2.68	75.0	11.6	21.1
Marion	16.8	11.9	8.1	50.8	7,144	8,738	22.3	-4.4	732	648	-477	3,263	2.60	66.6	12.2	28.8
Meriwether	15.1	12.1	8.3	52.1	22,534	21,983	-2.4	-4.2	2,054	2,165	-805	8,108	2.57	69.6	18.8	27.1
Miller	13.2	11.1	11.2	52.1	6,383	6,125	-4.0	-7.2	556	651	-346	2,326	2.45	69.7	18.5	26.5
Mitchell	13.2	9.4	6.9	48.1	23,932	23,498	-1.8	-5.6	2,273	2,001	-1,592	7,991	2.55	67.1	23.0	30.0
Monroe	15.2	10.8	7.8	50.1	21,757	26,173	20.3	5.1	2,245	2,218	1,339	9,590	2.67	69.1	10.5	28.0
Montgomery	13.3	10.4	6.7	48.6	8,270	9,181	11.0	0.1	808	672	-132	3,077	2.66	69.1	10.7	27.1
Morgan	14.3	11.6	8.4	51.9	15,457	17,863	15.6	5.5	1,599	1,456	849	6,698	2.66	77.8	14.9	19.8
Murray	12.7	9.1	5.7	50.8	36,506	39,628	8.6	0.7	4,094	3,031	-768	14,176	2.77	75.1	11.9	20.1
Muscogee	11.7	7.8	5.6	51.4	186,291	190,573	2.3	1.9	25,017	15,255	-6,533	73,179	2.60	64.6	18.8	32.5
Newton	11.7	8.2	4.8	52.8	62,001	99,984	61.3	9.6	11,042	6,788	5,341	35,823	2.89	72.4	18.2	22.6
Oconee	12.8	9.3	5.8	50.9	26,225	32,831	25.2	19.6	2,807	1,867	5,495	12,693	2.82	79.9	9.6	18.6
Oglethorpe	14.6	11.0	7.9	50.6	12,635	14,876	17.7	1.2	1,277	1,143	38	5,642	2.57	68.5	12.5	27.0
Paulding	11.4	6.8	3.8	51.3	81,678	142,379	74.3	15.2	15,398	7,054	13,295	51,397	2.95	78.7	13.3	17.7
Peach	13.8	9.6	6.4	51.8	23,668	27,688	17.0	-1.4	2,513	2,044	-882	10,113	2.46	63.8	18.0	31.8
Pickens	15.3	13.8	8.1	50.9	22,983	29,425	28.0	8.7	2,505	2,621	2,656	11,379	2.64	75.0	8.5	19.8
Pierce	12.6	10.2	6.8	50.6	15,636	18,762	20.0	3.3	1,961	1,614	288	6,975	2.72	77.8	20.7	20.6
Pike	13.1	9.4	6.5	50.8	13,688	17,874	30.6	4.3	1,363	1,354	759	5,963	2.96	74.6	9.8	23.3
Polk	12.5	9.2	6.3	50.6	38,127	41,479	8.8	2.4	4,660	3,934	267	14,949	2.75	69.2	14.7	25.6
Pulaski	13.8	12.7	10.0	56.9	9,588	12,002	25.2	-7.8	728	882	-785	3,893	2.53	64.7	13.8	30.7

1. No spouse present.

Table B. States and Counties — Population, Vital Statistics, Health, and Crime

STATE County	Persons in group quarters, 2018	Daytime Population, 2013-2017		Births, 2018		Deaths, 2018		Persons under 65 with no health insurance, 2016		Medicare, 2018			Serious crimes known to police[2], 2016 Total	
		Number	Employment/residence ratio	Total	Rate[1]	Number	Rate[1]	Number	Percent	Total beneficiaries	Enrolled in Original Medicare	Enrolled in Medicare Advantage	Number	Rate[3]
	32	33	34	35	36	37	38	39	40	41	42	43	44	45
GEORGIA—Cont'd														
Effingham	606	41,653	0.42	767	12.3	478	7.7	6,031	11.7	8,737	5,694	3,043	932	1,606
Elbert	284	18,894	0.95	220	11.5	264	13.8	2,538	16.9	5,058	3,073	1,985	648	3,375
Emanuel	1,311	21,940	0.93	286	12.6	286	12.6	3,066	17.2	4,862	2,979	1,883	772	3,481
Evans	401	11,073	1.08	144	13.4	119	11.1	1,531	18.1	2,085	1,271	814	130	1,211
Fannin	164	23,579	0.90	193	7.4	347	13.4	3,283	18.2	7,938	5,663	2,275	327	1,340
Fayette	457	110,775	1.01	895	7.9	856	7.5	9,056	9.8	22,466	14,960	7,506	1,624	1,458
Floyd	3,759	100,714	1.10	1,177	12.0	1,100	11.2	12,532	16.2	20,256	14,003	6,253	3,133	3,249
Forsyth	665	191,833	0.81	2,397	10.1	1,247	5.3	19,170	9.8	27,654	17,414	10,240	1,836	834
Franklin	818	22,646	1.04	287	12.5	278	12.1	3,260	18.8	5,382	3,408	1,974	385	1,886
Fulton	34,253	1,403,278	1.80	12,662	12.1	7,382	7.0	114,269	13.0	133,058	77,702	55,356	54,405	5,296
Gilmer	176	26,571	0.74	316	10.3	372	12.1	5,204	23.1	8,174	5,740	2,434	580	1,960
Glascock	86	2,370	0.49	30	10.0	31	10.4	315	12.9	588	409	179	22	719
Glynn	1,606	89,051	1.15	915	10.7	950	11.1	11,809	17.4	18,421	12,969	5,452	3,071	3,644
Gordon	653	55,397	0.96	683	11.8	538	9.3	9,670	20.1	10,376	7,417	2,959	1,520	2,676
Grady	245	21,082	0.60	311	12.6	269	10.9	3,951	19.6	5,128	3,368	1,760	500	1,983
Greene	200	17,598	1.14	153	8.6	234	13.2	2,253	18.7	5,622	3,827	1,795	347	2,061
Gwinnett	5,571	835,365	0.87	11,455	12.3	4,568	4.9	136,064	16.7	101,678	58,922	42,756	21,647	2,370
Habersham	2,771	42,395	0.91	533	11.7	466	10.3	6,342	18.7	9,456	5,806	3,650	741	1,679
Hall	2,756	195,802	1.03	2,566	12.7	1,592	7.9	33,060	20.0	34,879	22,525	12,354	10,248	5,224
Hancock	1,211	7,857	0.62	53	6.3	127	15.2	761	13.7	2,279	1,162	1,117	175	2,088
Haralson	336	25,858	0.75	338	11.4	358	12.1	3,575	14.8	6,099	3,945	2,154	1,097	3,804
Harris	445	24,245	0.40	284	8.2	341	9.9	2,925	10.7	6,581	4,525	2,056	388	1,155
Hart	680	23,093	0.75	251	9.6	293	11.2	3,153	16.2	6,303	4,259	2,044	791	3,174
Heard	81	9,272	0.49	126	10.6	115	9.7	1,500	15.7	2,231	1,365	866	191	1,666
Henry	969	187,908	0.69	2,467	10.7	1,619	7.0	24,528	12.5	32,294	18,353	13,941	5,903	2,682
Houston	1,488	151,696	1.02	1,933	12.4	1,265	8.1	17,758	13.5	24,488	18,621	5,867	6,309	4,156
Irwin	996	8,488	0.76	97	10.3	115	12.2	946	13.9	2,030	1,299	731	238	2,596
Jackson	605	60,504	0.88	879	12.5	612	8.7	7,955	14.3	12,141	7,588	4,553	1,382	2,231
Jasper	98	11,038	0.50	148	10.5	137	9.8	1,988	17.6	2,921	1,777	1,144	222	2,024
Jeff Davis	121	14,330	0.88	209	13.9	154	10.2	2,371	19.0	2,781	1,931	850	428	2,878
Jefferson	522	14,837	0.81	196	12.7	229	14.8	2,283	18.3	3,808	2,366	1,442	440	2,761
Jenkins	1,175	7,854	0.66	90	10.4	102	11.7	1,113	18.1	1,741	1,012	729	NA	NA
Johnson	1,645	8,049	0.57	108	11.1	114	11.7	912	14.4	1,802	1,120	682	76	793
Jones	288	21,536	0.42	225	7.9	287	10.0	3,097	13.1	5,691	3,350	2,341	498	1,751
Lamar	1,251	16,305	0.71	201	10.6	211	11.1	2,061	14.5	3,868	2,240	1,628	433	2,383
Lanier	228	8,248	0.42	124	12.0	97	9.4	1,463	16.5	1,586	1,150	436	248	2,397
Laurens	1,037	49,317	1.11	623	13.2	573	12.1	5,443	14.2	10,592	6,852	3,740	1,641	3,633
Lee	929	21,460	0.42	314	10.5	249	8.4	2,984	11.9	4,620	3,156	1,464	616	2,340
Liberty	1,879	68,139	1.22	1,404	22.8	354	5.8	6,684	12.3	6,994	4,839	2,155	2,102	3,370
Lincoln	57	6,063	0.46	73	9.2	99	12.5	1,005	16.7	2,082	1,284	798	232	3,050
Long	329	13,111	0.28	235	12.4	99	5.2	2,978	17.9	1,655	1,175	480	203	1,104
Lowndes	5,993	121,274	1.15	1,578	13.6	937	8.1	14,561	15.4	17,799	13,130	4,669	4,380	3,862
Lumpkin	2,772	27,394	0.71	291	8.8	314	9.5	4,274	17.9	6,235	4,331	1,904	473	1,497
McDuffie	286	20,585	0.89	274	12.7	267	12.4	2,562	14.6	4,699	2,414	2,285	266	1,240
McIntosh	72	11,650	0.56	109	7.6	128	8.9	1,672	15.8	3,025	1,789	1,236	359	2,584
Macon	1,939	12,917	0.83	125	9.5	175	13.3	1,779	18.9	2,357	1,333	1,024	222	1,712
Madison	248	21,552	0.41	326	11.0	266	9.0	4,156	17.4	6,275	3,939	2,336	511	1,795
Marion	79	7,238	0.60	76	9.1	90	10.8	1,173	17.2	1,586	966	620	81	925
Meriwether	247	18,875	0.71	225	10.7	269	12.8	2,747	16.4	5,169	2,748	2,421	483	2,436
Miller	125	5,333	0.77	62	10.9	77	13.5	729	15.7	1,306	903	403	78	1,347
Mitchell	2,178	22,846	1.04	254	11.4	254	11.4	2,862	17.2	4,477	2,739	1,738	632	2,830
Monroe	1,201	24,124	0.75	254	9.2	321	11.7	3,001	13.9	5,820	3,870	1,950	528	1,941
Montgomery	810	7,068	0.45	89	9.7	76	8.3	1,200	17.6	1,751	1,121	630	NA	NA
Morgan	163	19,935	1.25	207	11.0	160	8.5	2,074	14.2	4,396	2,583	1,813	NA	NA
Murray	273	33,776	0.66	481	12.0	403	10.1	6,470	19.3	7,351	5,800	1,551	1,255	3,175
Muscogee	6,328	223,443	1.29	2,701	13.9	1,897	9.8	20,378	12.3	34,469	22,176	12,293	10,884	5,379
Newton	1,633	87,470	0.61	1,355	12.4	920	8.4	13,465	14.7	17,839	9,793	8,046	2,771	2,603
Oconee	142	33,539	0.85	368	9.4	249	6.3	3,046	9.6	6,609	4,584	2,025	605	1,654
Oglethorpe	177	10,451	0.34	139	9.2	152	10.1	2,034	16.8	3,166	2,025	1,141	339	2,283
Paulding	474	110,092	0.42	1,773	10.8	1,064	6.5	16,778	12.0	20,400	12,512	7,888	3,000	1,947
Peach	1,441	24,559	0.78	315	11.5	268	9.8	3,509	16.1	5,332	3,499	1,833	891	3,363
Pickens	398	28,282	0.84	306	9.6	355	11.1	3,601	14.9	8,832	5,919	2,913	610	2,052
Pierce	74	16,394	0.63	231	11.9	200	10.3	2,725	17.1	4,112	2,873	1,239	473	2,471
Pike	210	13,640	0.42	188	10.1	182	9.8	2,136	14.2	3,503	2,227	1,276	247	1,378
Polk	638	39,066	0.86	581	13.7	512	12.1	5,972	17.2	8,651	5,700	2,951	1,564	3,771
Pulaski	1,174	11,465	1.02	84	7.6	112	10.1	1,311	16.8	2,068	1,447	621	287	2,544

1. Per 1,000 estimated resident population.   2. Data for serious crimes have not been adjusted for underreporting; this may affect comparability between geographic areas and over time.   3. Per 100,000 population estimated by the FBI.

Table B. States and Counties — **Crime, Education, Money Income, and Poverty**

STATE County	Serious crimes known to police,[2] 2016 (cont.)[1] — Rate		Education — School enrollment and attainment, 2013-2017				Local government expenditures,[5] 2014-2015		Money income, 2013-2017				Income and poverty, 2017			
			Enrollment[3]		Attainment[4] (percent)					Households				Percent below poverty level		
	Violent	Property	Total	Percent private	High school graduate or less	Bachelor's degree or more	Total current spending (mil dol)	Current spending per student (dollars)	Per capita income[6]	Median income (dollars)	Percent with income of less than $50,000	Percent with income of $200,000 or more	Median household income (dollars)	All persons	Children under 18 years	Children 5 to 17 years in families
	46	47	48	49	50	51	52	53	54	55	56	57	58	59	60	61
GEORGIA—Cont'd																
Effingham	138	1,468	15,543	10.4	50.5	19.2	101.5	8,733	26,765	64,279	37.7	3.2	68,109	9.8	13.8	13.0
Elbert	406	2,969	4,471	8.8	66.6	11.1	30.8	10,100	21,138	35,207	64.1	1.9	35,452	22.9	34.9	31.2
Emanuel	469	3,012	5,568	7.7	63.2	12.5	39.1	9,052	17,944	33,089	67.2	1.2	33,551	27.6	39.4	38.6
Evans	196	1,016	2,632	21.8	63.0	15.5	17.6	9,243	20,736	38,736	60.3	3.2	34,464	28	41.3	38.4
Fannin	107	1,233	4,326	14.4	51.8	19.0	34.1	11,565	24,845	43,344	54.9	1.8	42,986	13.6	24.9	23.4
Fayette	71	1,387	30,161	16.0	25.5	46.7	182.1	9,072	39,936	84,861	27.1	10.9	87,831	5.7	7.8	7.1
Floyd	328	2,922	24,400	19.9	51.3	20.5	167.0	10,157	23,929	46,096	53.5	2.7	45,979	19.2	27.3	26.1
Forsyth	55	779	63,028	16.1	24.3	50.2	337.6	7,955	39,896	96,445	23.5	14.5	103,083	5.3	5.6	4.9
Franklin	162	1,724	4,807	13.9	61.8	12.8	34.1	9,534	19,663	39,246	61.4	1.4	42,703	18.7	25.4	24.7
Fulton	736	4,560	277,410	21.2	26.6	50.2	1,634.1	10,922	41,041	61,336	41.9	11.8	64,901	14.8	21.1	20.4
Gilmer	250	1,710	5,353	6.1	53.9	18.6	45.5	10,574	23,688	46,211	53.9	2.5	46,200	14.4	25.9	25.2
Glascock	131	588	719	5.3	64.8	9.4	6.2	10,171	19,815	45,273	54.3	0.6	43,529	17.3	22.3	20.2
Glynn	438	3,206	19,495	11.3	39.7	29.0	129.6	9,845	29,209	47,546	52.4	4.7	50,740	17	29.4	26.8
Gordon	264	2,412	13,690	6.0	57.8	13.7	94.2	8,715	21,208	43,452	57.6	1.8	46,868	14	19.7	18.2
Grady	179	1,805	6,043	3.4	58.5	13.7	40.4	8,648	20,864	39,462	59.9	2.1	41,095	20.3	31.5	27.4
Greene	303	1,758	3,023	7.3	50.3	25.6	33.8	14,409	32,890	45,069	54.1	6.9	50,736	17	30.2	28.9
Gwinnett	247	2,123	262,456	12.9	35.6	35.3	1,661.2	9,148	27,945	64,496	37.5	5.7	68,957	10.7	15.2	15.0
Habersham	174	1,504	10,025	17.0	55.8	18.4	67.6	9,741	20,656	44,474	55.6	1.8	49,292	13.3	18.1	17.2
Hall	452	4,772	50,501	9.2	49.3	23.5	312.5	8,904	26,283	55,622	44.7	4.6	61,320	13.3	20.8	17.9
Hancock	334	1,754	1,310	6.5	72.0	8.7	14.2	14,759	15,454	29,268	74.5	1.2	31,247	30.3	45.4	41.2
Haralson	583	3,221	7,033	6.0	57.8	14.1	55.0	9,636	23,141	43,663	55.1	1.7	45,167	15.3	22.5	20.2
Harris	173	982	7,779	10.1	35.4	27.4	49.1	9,240	32,373	69,539	37.3	5.4	72,811	8.3	11.5	10.5
Hart	365	2,809	5,412	10.5	58.0	13.8	33.0	9,355	21,668	41,216	58.2	2.1	44,603	18.9	26.6	25.2
Heard	201	1,465	2,724	8.9	64.6	10.8	20.2	10,066	20,946	44,897	55.8	1.0	44,575	18.9	28.1	25.5
Henry	177	2,505	64,308	14.7	40.1	28.0	355.2	8,605	26,924	64,752	38.2	3.6	67,493	9.8	14.6	13.0
Houston	433	3,723	43,351	11.3	38.2	25.4	268.5	9,539	26,305	55,965	44.6	3.2	59,291	13	20.2	19.2
Irwin	240	2,356	2,036	3.4	58.6	13.1	17.2	9,517	19,429	34,677	63.0	4.0	38,511	22	31.2	29.4
Jackson	289	1,942	16,077	10.9	50.2	19.7	105.3	8,655	25,598	57,999	41.8	3.2	63,422	11.5	14.8	13.4
Jasper	511	1,514	2,996	15.3	61.9	10.5	20.8	8,808	19,784	42,067	60.0	0.4	50,234	17.6	24.8	23.8
Jeff Davis	282	2,596	4,159	3.9	59.4	10.3	26.9	8,640	18,550	37,267	61.9	0.3	36,786	21.2	32.0	30.2
Jefferson	358	2,404	3,538	8.8	67.0	10.6	27.0	9,507	17,485	29,640	68.1	1.1	35,201	24	36.0	33.8
Jenkins	NA	NA	1,949	4.7	63.7	8.3	14.2	11,240	15,149	27,197	70.6	0.3	32,472	32.8	44.3	39.8
Johnson	167	626	2,027	7.1	67.6	9.6	11.5	9,806	19,706	36,423	62.5	0.0	35,243	29	35.5	31.7
Jones	98	1,653	6,951	9.9	50.1	20.7	51.1	9,404	26,098	55,110	47.3	2.6	56,039	12.9	19.0	17.1
Lamar	303	2,080	5,283	9.2	52.1	18.4	25.5	9,556	20,458	41,157	58.9	1.7	41,060	16.5	25.2	25.0
Lanier	435	1,962	2,646	8.5	53.4	15.8	17.8	10,024	17,739	31,109	67.1	0.4	39,165	20.5	30.3	28.1
Laurens	456	3,177	11,009	7.5	60.4	15.4	87.9	9,525	20,687	35,202	64.7	2.5	38,078	22.6	30.8	27.7
Lee	152	2,188	9,176	12.0	40.1	25.7	53.6	8,162	28,061	65,018	37.2	2.9	68,891	10.9	15.4	13.2
Liberty	561	2,809	17,409	10.3	40.4	19.4	98.1	9,734	20,966	43,493	57.2	1.2	45,655	16.8	24.8	26.0
Lincoln	421	2,629	1,447	7.0	60.9	12.1	12.3	10,353	24,529	37,711	61.2	2.1	44,819	18.1	27.8	27.1
Long	38	1,066	5,212	6.0	44.3	15.6	25.9	7,951	20,321	53,083	45.8	0.9	48,328	19.1	27.5	25.1
Lowndes	282	3,580	35,890	9.5	45.0	25.2	165.4	8,879	21,199	39,911	59.5	2.1	42,019	25.3	29.7	28.0
Lumpkin	38	1,459	9,460	5.4	45.6	26.7	35.8	9,612	23,364	43,039	56.5	3.0	55,453	13.9	19.2	18.3
McDuffie	144	1,095	5,168	5.1	58.5	15.3	42.4	9,912	20,436	40,469	59.3	1.7	40,814	21.2	31.2	30.2
McIntosh	180	2,404	2,755	9.5	53.2	14.0	16.2	9,987	25,226	43,285	57.3	2.0	40,832	19.5	34.3	31.7
Macon	247	1,465	3,089	11.1	61.0	8.6	17.8	11,055	15,919	30,851	73.6	1.8	32,974	29.6	38.7	36.8
Madison	207	1,588	6,313	15.2	55.5	16.7	51.2	10,552	22,885	47,653	52.3	2.2	47,956	15.9	22.5	21.7
Marion	57	868	1,874	7.7	59.9	12.5	13.5	9,323	20,154	39,015	60.2	1.3	39,408	23.9	38.7	34.6
Meriwether	368	2,068	4,586	10.6	62.0	10.7	31.4	10,493	19,679	36,368	60.1	1.9	38,442	19.9	33.3	31.8
Miller	104	1,243	1,229	15.5	56.9	11.4	10.9	10,749	21,002	37,255	63.7	2.7	37,878	23.8	36.2	33.2
Mitchell	246	2,584	5,680	8.9	61.9	12.3	37.7	9,660	16,088	34,122	68.7	1.0	36,234	27.5	37.9	35.3
Monroe	140	1,801	5,852	23.6	51.6	22.7	44.8	10,400	30,359	50,666	49.0	6.2	57,038	13.3	18.2	16.8
Montgomery	NA	NA	2,217	21.5	57.0	15.5	14.1	4,867	20,114	40,308	62.7	2.4	41,858	20.5	29.2	28.2
Morgan	NA	NA	4,053	7.2	48.1	22.1	31.1	9,652	28,830	59,572	43.6	4.5	55,251	12	19.8	19.0
Murray	673	2,502	9,051	7.1	69.5	9.6	62.9	8,155	19,084	41,617	58.1	0.9	45,975	17.2	25.5	24.5
Muscogee	601	4,778	56,715	10.6	40.3	26.0	300.5	9,301	24,604	43,239	55.6	3.4	42,610	22.6	33.4	30.7
Newton	422	2,181	29,890	14.6	47.4	19.9	177.7	9,045	23,611	52,784	47.6	2.6	55,632	13.4	20.1	19.1
Oconee	118	1,537	10,696	17.1	26.6	48.2	61.0	8,689	38,639	77,388	32.7	9.7	92,216	6.5	7.4	6.4
Oglethorpe	310	1,973	3,312	8.4	58.1	15.5	22.9	10,432	21,858	43,938	57.5	1.3	44,718	13.4	20.1	19.6
Paulding	134	1,813	43,277	12.9	42.9	24.4	240.7	8,449	26,636	63,669	36.6	2.5	67,906	8.3	11.2	10.5
Peach	506	2,858	8,451	8.5	45.0	20.3	35.6	9,693	22,388	43,645	55.1	1.2	46,608	19.6	30.0	27.0
Pickens	235	1,817	6,254	10.6	45.1	24.9	46.3	10,655	29,460	61,542	40.9	4.3	61,145	10.8	19.1	17.7
Pierce	475	1,996	4,306	5.9	58.3	12.7	33.9	9,064	23,754	39,863	56.2	1.1	42,140	19.4	28.1	25.2
Pike	67	1,311	4,437	14.9	52.1	16.5	27.4	7,980	25,176	52,377	47.6	2.7	62,250	10.7	14.0	12.1
Polk	304	3,467	10,310	9.9	61.5	12.7	67.0	8,674	22,314	40,652	58.4	1.5	43,488	19	27.3	26.1
Pulaski	479	2,065	2,226	10.4	60.0	12.6	13.1	9,264	18,623	38,750	62.0	0.4	39,743	22.5	31.1	27.4

1. Data for serious crimes have not been adjusted for underreporting; this may affect comparability between geographic areas and over time.   2. Per 100,000 population estimated by the FBI.   3. All persons 3 years old and over enrolled in nursery school through college.   4. Persons 25 years old and over.   5. Elementary and secondary education expenditures.   6. Based on population estimated by the American Community Survey, 2013–2017.

Table B. States and Counties — Personal Income and Earnings

STATE County	Personal income, 2017										Earnings, 2017		
	Total (mil dol)	Percent change 2016-2017	Per capita[1] Dollars	Per capita[1] Rank	Wages and salaries (mil dol)	Supplements to wages and salaries, employer contributions (mil dol) Pension and insurance	Supplements to wages and salaries, employer contributions (mil dol) Government social insurance	Proprietors' income (mil dol)	Dividends, interest, and rent (mil dol)	Personal transfer reecipts (mil dol)	Total (mil dol)	Contributions for government social insurance (mil dol) From employee and self-employed	Contributions for government social insurance (mil dol) From employer
	62	63	64	65	66	67	68	69	70	71	72	73	74
GEORGIA—Cont'd													
Effingham	2,372	5.0	39,545	1,627	467	95	31	65	233	400	658	45	31
Elbert	660	4.7	34,541	2,410	222	50	15	58	115	213	346	24	15
Emanuel	717	7.3	31,813	2,780	264	62	18	19	108	249	363	25	18
Evans	366	3.2	33,930	2,491	158	33	10	30	60	98	232	14	10
Fannin	864	5.7	34,110	2,472	229	44	16	92	180	290	381	31	16
Fayette	6,785	4.7	60,286	151	2,087	329	144	297	1,177	865	2,857	178	144
Floyd	3,632	4.0	37,204	2,000	1,803	320	126	296	614	966	2,544	158	126
Forsyth	13,703	4.9	60,110	155	4,064	565	274	944	1,812	1,054	5,848	342	274
Franklin	811	6.4	35,522	2,270	308	59	22	142	118	228	531	30	22
Fulton	82,058	6.1	78,794	39	70,557	8,639	4,560	14,773	18,266	6,584	98,528	5,426	4,560
Gilmer	1,032	5.6	33,648	2,538	245	53	17	139	190	313	454	31	17
Glascock	100	2.0	32,611	2,674	13	4	1	4	13	28	22	2	1
Glynn	3,639	3.3	42,673	1,189	1,761	317	124	214	972	780	2,416	150	124
Gordon	1,926	4.3	33,731	2,524	999	159	73	155	233	456	1,386	83	73
Grady	808	4.1	32,547	2,682	234	51	16	68	132	217	370	24	16
Greene	899	5.2	52,044	373	247	42	17	80	340	213	386	27	17
Gwinnett	36,677	4.9	39,856	1,580	21,046	2,875	1,408	3,016	4,790	4,700	28,345	1,626	1,408
Habersham	1,465	4.2	32,867	2,635	570	130	39	94	262	384	833	52	39
Hall	8,216	4.9	41,219	1,376	4,378	709	282	682	1,399	1,468	6,051	360	282
Hancock	240	2.0	27,998	3,030	60	18	4	4	38	96	86	7	4
Haralson	1,024	5.5	35,016	2,346	304	62	22	56	137	282	444	30	22
Harris	1,553	4.0	45,802	818	165	38	11	51	296	274	266	22	11
Hart	931	6.1	36,087	2,189	266	56	19	109	161	258	451	29	19
Heard	357	5.1	30,422	2,894	111	27	8	21	38	100	167	11	8
Henry	8,541	5.1	37,821	1,909	2,465	456	172	331	1,021	1,486	3,424	217	172
Houston	6,349	4.5	41,365	1,351	3,122	819	240	240	1,179	1,251	4,421	247	240
Irwin	284	5.7	30,230	2,910	75	19	6	6	53	95	105	8	6
Jackson	2,778	8.4	41,151	1,387	1,126	199	79	239	330	510	1,643	99	79
Jasper	506	4.1	36,270	2,154	80	20	6	36	75	126	141	11	6
Jeff Davis	430	1.0	28,634	3,010	166	36	12	7	65	136	221	15	12
Jefferson	510	2.6	32,593	2,678	205	44	14	26	84	181	288	20	14
Jenkins	246	0.9	28,073	3,027	52	14	4	5	42	87	74	6	4
Johnson	243	2.6	24,786	3,095	53	16	4	6	34	91	78	6	4
Jones	1,036	3.3	36,373	2,137	191	41	13	30	148	246	274	22	13
Lamar	604	4.3	32,483	2,689	141	35	10	39	77	179	225	16	10
Lanier	272	3.1	26,116	3,078	55	16	4	5	40	86	80	6	4
Laurens	1,691	3.2	35,729	2,241	769	168	56	81	275	489	1,074	69	56
Lee	1,329	4.0	45,096	887	262	52	19	40	182	212	372	24	19
Liberty	2,116	2.9	34,465	2,416	1,778	502	163	28	441	489	2,471	109	163
Lincoln	282	4.2	35,808	2,227	47	12	3	16	51	80	78	7	3
Long	491	2.6	25,838	3,081	39	14	3	10	73	116	65	5	3
Lowndes	4,152	4.3	35,950	2,207	2,229	494	164	195	817	928	3,082	170	164
Lumpkin	1,154	5.6	35,110	2,334	298	79	20	69	193	280	465	30	20
McDuffie	758	3.6	35,274	2,302	266	55	20	38	113	223	378	24	20
McIntosh	403	2.5	28,534	3,015	68	18	5	13	82	125	103	9	5
Macon	401	4.0	30,119	2,921	116	26	8	61	69	121	211	11	8
Madison	1,032	6.4	35,225	2,308	120	32	8	99	140	263	259	19	8
Marion	238	4.3	28,219	3,022	41	10	3	14	48	75	68	5	3
Meriwether	717	3.4	34,049	2,478	211	50	16	27	106	229	304	22	16
Miller	227	5.0	38,798	1,757	66	19	4	10	43	63	100	6	4
Mitchell	751	1.7	33,707	2,527	248	58	17	89	129	216	412	24	17
Monroe	1,169	3.7	43,125	1,126	318	81	21	64	189	241	483	30	21
Montgomery	262	1.0	28,994	2,986	57	13	4	7	37	77	81	7	4
Morgan	868	5.3	47,123	705	286	51	20	60	185	173	417	26	20
Murray	1,163	4.6	29,243	2,972	361	68	27	81	124	331	536	37	27
Muscogee	8,244	3.0	42,483	1,204	4,940	964	348	256	2,165	1,932	6,508	372	348
Newton	3,518	4.5	32,548	2,681	1,146	230	79	99	428	831	1,554	103	79
Oconee	2,334	5.1	61,379	142	493	85	34	180	486	237	792	47	34
Oglethorpe	547	4.7	36,773	2,082	65	17	5	80	81	126	166	10	5
Paulding	5,779	5.7	36,243	2,160	974	186	66	182	586	894	1,409	98	66
Peach	991	2.9	36,582	2,108	386	85	30	57	179	267	559	33	30
Pickens	1,444	6.2	45,717	829	378	63	25	92	273	336	558	41	25
Pierce	661	3.6	34,240	2,456	164	34	11	20	99	193	229	17	11
Pike	706	5.0	38,728	1,769	113	26	8	34	95	145	181	14	8
Polk	1,332	4.2	31,639	2,792	464	90	33	49	173	411	635	44	33
Pulaski	322	2.3	28,776	2,995	117	25	8	8	75	96	158	11	8

1. Based on the resident population estimated as of July 1 of the year shown.

Table B. States and Counties — Earnings, Social Security, and Housing

| STATE County | Earnings, 2017 (cont.) Percent by selected industries | | | | | | | | | Social Security beneficiaries, December 2017 | | Supplemental Security Income recipients, 2017 | Housing units, 2018 | |
| | Farm | Mining, quarrying, and extractions | Construction | Manufacturing | Information; professional, scientific, technical services | Retail trade | Finance, insurance, real estate, and leasing | Health care and social assistance | Government | Number | Rate[1] | | Total | Percent change, 2010-2018 |
	75	76	77	78	79	80	81	82	83	84	85	86	87	88
GEORGIA—Cont'd														
Effingham	0	D	7.5	18.3	6.2	5.9	3.7	D	24.2	9,630	161	877	23,469	18
Elbert	5	3.4	5.4	27	2.3	6.2	D	5.2	22.1	5,580	292	885	9,619	0.4
Emanuel	-2.6	0	3.2	23.7	D	6.8	7.3	D	30.6	5,365	238	1,070	9,920	-0.5
Evans	5.7	0	5.7	37.1	D	6.1	4.2	D	15.6	2,320	215	440	4,742	1.6
Fannin	1	0	D	4	4.9	13.5	8.5	D	15.1	8,580	339	686	17,486	7.8
Fayette	0.2	D	9.8	12	9	7.2	6.3	15.6	14.3	22,495	200	1,082	43,033	5.5
Floyd	0.7	D	2.7	18	5.5	6.9	4.4	25.3	14	22,280	228	3,335	40,636	0.2
Forsyth	0.2	0.1	10.9	9.7	18.9	5.7	6	9.9	9.5	27,505	121	980	84,142	31.4
Franklin	18.1	0	3.1	15.4	3.9	6.1	3.5	D	11.9	6,015	264	885	10,689	1.3
Fulton	0	0.2	2.8	3.8	31.8	3.7	12.6	7.5	9.9	132,655	127	27,327	480,341	9.9
Gilmer	15.3	D	8.4	13.8	D	8.9	4.8	4.7	15.9	8,810	287	623	17,247	4.1
Glascock	0.5	0	D	D	D	3.8	D	D	37.8	685	224	96	1,527	0.5
Glynn	0	D	4.4	6.3	5.5	7.7	4.4	15.5	24	19,710	231	1,910	43,512	6.9
Gordon	4	0	5.6	37.6	2	5.3	3.6	8.7	12.5	11,520	202	1,506	22,683	1.8
Grady	7.3	0.8	5.4	18.5	D	6.9	3.3	7	19.4	5,560	224	1,053	10,891	1.2
Greene	5.1	D	12.7	8.5	5.9	6.9	10.1	10.1	12.7	5,765	334	605	9,911	14.1
Gwinnett	0	D	9.1	8.5	15.1	7.6	9.3	6.9	9.3	104,260	113	11,902	312,896	7.3
Habersham	4.5	D	4	27.5	D	7	3.9	5.3	20.9	10,310	231	967	18,556	2.3
Hall	0.4	D	6.1	19.9	4.5	5.7	6.6	16.4	11.2	36,550	183	3,096	74,423	8.1
Hancock	0.9	D	D	D	D	3.4	D	D	48.7	2,455	287	445	5,390	1
Haralson	2.9	0	10.1	28.1	3.5	6.2	3.6	D	20.7	6,935	237	1,033	12,530	2
Harris	0	0	11.7	14.3	D	2.6	7	D	26.2	7,150	211	459	14,344	7.1
Hart	11.9	0.1	6	27.7	D	6.7	3.7	4.9	15.1	6,825	265	591	13,177	1.3
Heard	5	0	8.5	22.5	D	2	1.7	D	21.8	2,540	217	337	5,229	1.6
Henry	0	0.7	6.5	6.7	4.6	10.2	4.3	13.4	20.9	35,685	158	4,290	82,826	8.3
Houston	-0.1	D	3	8.1	7.3	5.5	2.5	6.2	56.7	25,750	168	3,677	63,958	9.7
Irwin	-0.6	0	7.4	10.6	D	6.6	D	6.4	33.1	2,240	238	391	4,091	1.5
Jackson	3.1	D	7.9	25	D	6.2	5.8	3.5	11	13,440	199	1,803	26,072	9.8
Jasper	3.9	0	8.7	19.3	D	4	3.2	D	24.6	3,235	232	339	6,505	5.7
Jeff Davis	-0.7	0	2.2	27.7	D	7.7	2.8	D	21.5	3,160	210	502	6,519	0.4
Jefferson	2.9	11.2	5.7	20.7	D	6.4	3.3	D	18.8	4,250	272	923	7,257	-0.6
Jenkins	-0.7	0	3.7	4	1.1	5.5	D	7.9	34.6	1,910	218	468	4,237	0.4
Johnson	0.1	0	6	7.1	D	5.8	D	18.8	40.5	2,090	214	571	4,114	-0.1
Jones	0.8	D	14.5	0.7	D	6.3	8.3	D	24.3	6,180	217	373	11,886	1.7
Lamar	8.5	0	4.2	16.8	2.4	6.9	4.8	5.5	29.7	4,365	235	548	7,615	1.9
Lanier	-0.1	0.3	2	10.2	D	D	D	2.2	48.3	1,775	170	352	4,442	4.6
Laurens	D	D	5.9	13.4	D	7.5	4.6	D	30.3	11,590	245	2,116	21,550	0.8
Lee	5.1	D	11.9	5.4	D	7.2	3.8	D	22.1	5,140	174	473	11,451	11.4
Liberty	0.1	0	1.2	7.6	D	2.9	1.6	1.8	75.1	8,140	133	1,292	28,570	6.7
Lincoln	0.7	0	21.4	5	2.7	6.2	6.6	3.2	26.6	2,275	289	227	4,914	2.7
Long	3.5	D	D	D	D	D	D	D	60	1,945	102	233	7,000	17
Lowndes	0.2	D	7.4	8.4	6.8	7.1	4	8.8	35.4	19,600	170	4,011	48,521	10.5
Lumpkin	1.6	D	8.1	10.9	3.5	6.7	4.8	D	37.6	6,710	204	484	13,824	7
McDuffie	4.8	D	6.3	25.1	D	8.9	4.9	D	22	5,165	240	947	9,361	0.5
McIntosh	2.9	D	5.3	D	D	7.1	1.2	2.1	35.3	3,295	234	382	9,612	4.3
Macon	24	D	3.6	22.8	D	3.6	2.6	D	22.4	2,500	188	432	6,089	-0.8
Madison	21.6	1.2	11.7	5	D	4.9	4.3	D	26.1	6,930	237	953	12,022	1.9
Marion	12.9	D	3.1	15.6	D	5.3	D	D	27.8	1,755	208	263	4,218	1.5
Meriwether	1.5	0	11.6	22	D	4.3	2.5	D	23.8	5,450	259	865	10,015	0.6
Miller	2.4	0	2.9	1.6	D	7.1	7.6	D	48.9	1,450	248	330	2,762	
Mitchell	14.6	D	2	27.3	D	5.5	4	D	19.9	4,945	222	1,065	9,076	0.9
Monroe	3.4	D	7.2	1.7	D	5.6	3.3	6.3	33.4	6,260	231	545	11,234	6.3
Montgomery	-0.3	D	4.5	4.4	D	5.7	D	D	24.2	1,930	214	328	3,972	0.8
Morgan	6.8	0.1	4.8	18.6	D	7.2	7.4	3.3	15.4	4,790	260	413	7,845	5
Murray	4.3	D	3.1	36.1	D	7.3	3.3	D	15.6	8,415	212	1,161	16,168	1.2
Muscogee	0	D	3.4	7.2	7	5.5	17.6	12.3	27	38,145	197	7,586	85,008	2.8
Newton	0	0	8.1	27.3	4.7	6.6	3.5	8	19.3	19,835	184	3,095	39,693	3.5
Oconee	4.9	D	5.4	4.8	10.4	6.6	10.8	14.3	12.3	6,750	178	327	14,593	17.7
Oglethorpe	37.4	2.8	12.6	6.1	D	2.3	4.3	D	17.6	3,390	228	304	6,681	3.1
Paulding	0.3	D	13.9	4.8	5.1	10.6	5.3	11.6	25	22,450	141	1,657	58,036	11.3
Peach	4.2	0	6.5	33.4	1.7	6.8	3.5	5.2	22	5,660	209	1,181	11,611	5.1
Pickens	2.5	D	8.4	9.7	5.1	7.7	6	24.1	14.3	9,240	293	576	14,107	3.1
Pierce	1.3	0	8.6	9.2	D	7.2	3.7	D	21.6	4,250	220	719	8,194	2.6
Pike	0.9	D	22	10.2	D	5.3	4.3	D	23.2	3,930	216	403	7,055	3.4
Polk	1.1	D	5.5	32.6	D	9.8	2	8.3	16.5	9,665	230	1,646	17,058	0.9
Pulaski	4	0	D	D	D	6.6	D	29.6	22	2,205	197	379	5,166	0.3

1. Per 1,000 resident population estimated as of July 1 of the year shown.

Table B. States and Counties — Housing, Labor Force, and Employment

STATE County	Total	Percent	Median value[1]	With a mortgage	Without a mortgage[2]	Median rent[3]	Median rent as a percent of income[2]	Sub-standard units[4] (percent)	Total	Percent change, 2017-2018	Total	Rate[5]	Total	Management, business, science, and arts	Construction, production, and maintenance occupations
	89	90	91	92	93	94	95	96	97	98	99	100	101	102	103
GEORGIA—Cont'd															
Effingham	19,584	76.7	155,500	19.7	10.0	957	29.6	2.4	29,925	1.6	989	3.3	26,904	32.1	33.2
Elbert	7,730	72.2	81,800	22.0	12.6	583	33.1	2.1	7,843	-0.2	378	4.8	7,327	25.8	38.5
Emanuel	8,387	68.2	78,500	21.8	12.1	569	30.3	4	8,324	-3.1	490	5.9	8,291	25.7	33.3
Evans	4,023	64.6	83,600	19.8	11.6	630	25.8	3.3	4,915	0.5	180	3.7	4,308	29.3	32.4
Fannin	10,175	76.8	171,500	23.3	11.9	738	28.7	1.1	11,207	2	442	3.9	9,299	29.6	26.3
Fayette	39,604	81.0	255,300	19.8	10.0	1,202	27.4	1.2	57,768	1.4	2,010	3.5	51,750	44.8	19.2
Floyd	35,506	60.2	126,600	19.8	10.9	711	28.7	2.7	44,274	0.1	1,906	4.3	41,473	29.0	28.7
Forsyth	70,468	84.3	301,100	19.3	10.0	1,249	27	1.3	118,048	1.4	3,717	3.1	103,649	51.1	12.8
Franklin	8,322	67.6	101,600	24.6	11.8	638	28.7	2.2	9,993	-0.9	383	3.8	8,353	29.8	36.3
Fulton	391,850	51.3	268,900	20.8	10.6	1,089	29.9	1.9	555,127	1.1	22,310	4	500,783	50.1	11.3
Gilmer	11,468	74.4	162,400	23.4	10.0	709	28.9	3.5	11,992	-0.1	507	4.2	12,120	26.1	30.2
Glascock	1,083	78.9	66,600	22.0	10.0	521	24.2	4.6	1,295	-0.3	54	4.2	1,307	32.4	39.0
Glynn	33,200	61.3	161,200	21.2	10.0	846	29.3	2.9	40,225	1	1,476	3.7	37,393	33.3	20.6
Gordon	19,959	64.2	119,500	19.7	10.9	676	27.3	3.4	27,993	5	1,053	3.8	25,142	23.2	39.8
Grady	9,092	61.0	110,500	21.3	13.3	748	33.2	3.3	10,684	-0.6	413	3.9	10,207	28.0	34.4
Greene	6,793	72.1	175,800	24.7	14.1	679	32.9	2.1	6,994	2.4	297	4.2	6,122	27.7	22.4
Gwinnett	283,256	66.6	185,200	21.8	10.0	1,142	31.2	3.3	487,986	1.2	17,073	3.5	439,634	37.3	20.4
Habersham	15,106	75.2	137,200	21.6	12.4	733	30.4	4	19,385	0.4	715	3.7	17,338	27.3	33.4
Hall	63,095	67.5	171,900	21.5	10.0	893	28.9	5.6	102,169	1.8	3,235	3.2	90,062	28.5	33.0
Hancock	2,970	78.5	66,100	28.1	18.4	795	38.7	1.4	2,479	-2	149	6	2,126	25.8	21.6
Haralson	11,033	68.3	117,000	18.3	12.9	666	30.2	2.1	12,508	1	482	3.9	11,808	27.2	34.8
Harris	12,088	84.7	194,800	21.5	12.1	909	29.2	1.8	16,736	0.5	571	3.4	15,123	36.8	24.2
Hart	9,848	74.7	131,200	23.8	12.2	666	29.9	2.1	11,681	3.8	423	3.6	9,989	26.8	34.2
Heard	4,379	69.6	100,500	22.9	13.0	642	27.5	4.6	5,208	0.8	202	3.9	4,797	23.6	40.9
Henry	72,697	72.0	154,900	21.8	10.0	1,111	29	1.4	113,843	1.3	4,716	4.1	100,413	33.5	23.8
Houston	55,200	64.1	135,800	19.2	10.0	882	29.7	3.1	70,197	1.5	2,803	4	65,928	35.2	22.9
Irwin	3,323	75.4	81,200	19.9	13.2	516	31.8	1.7	3,340	1.8	187	5.6	3,301	32.4	32.9
Jackson	21,785	77.0	163,200	20.7	10.9	798	29.6	2	36,248	2.7	1,083	3	28,016	32.3	26.8
Jasper	5,100	73.5	119,700	26.3	13.0	811	29.4	3.7	6,926	1	240	3.5	5,505	24.3	42.9
Jeff Davis	5,210	73.3	77,900	18.6	11.4	535	27.2	4.6	6,077	-0.8	296	4.9	5,472	26.4	35.0
Jefferson	5,797	64.3	69,200	22.0	13.1	536	31.6	3.3	6,747	0	359	5.3	5,783	22.4	41.2
Jenkins	3,375	68.7	59,100	22.8	14.7	528	29.9	4.4	3,206	1.3	173	5.4	3,296	25.5	32.1
Johnson	3,277	70.5	64,200	22.0	10.6	525	35.2	3.8	4,147	1.1	164	4	4,111	23.1	40.6
Jones	10,472	80.6	124,800	21.7	12.9	803	32	1.4	13,886	-0.4	508	3.7	12,241	33.8	26.3
Lamar	6,263	69.3	132,400	24.0	11.9	646	32.1	1.6	8,118	0.9	370	4.6	6,951	31.2	27.2
Lanier	3,744	61.6	102,000	25.5	10.0	681	29.9	1.7	3,845	0	169	4.4	3,551	29.2	22.9
Laurens	17,437	62.8	85,000	22.6	10.0	608	31.1	2.6	19,524	1.3	939	4.8	17,192	31.2	26.9
Lee	10,292	73.3	156,800	18.8	10.0	855	27.1	1.3	14,885	-1.1	530	3.6	13,503	39.9	23.5
Liberty	23,108	44.8	120,500	23.4	11.3	1,014	30.4	2	25,706	0.8	1,109	4.3	22,406	27.9	24.6
Lincoln	3,438	72.6	115,600	25.2	14.3	707	30.1	2.6	3,611	1.1	179	5	3,215	20.5	37.9
Long	5,399	68.7	117,500	19.8	10.0	759	31.4	2	8,028	0.7	318	4	5,999	29.0	31.2
Lowndes	40,318	52.2	129,700	21.9	10.0	760	31.3	3.4	51,746	0.1	2,106	4.1	46,445	30.9	20.7
Lumpkin	11,412	64.2	176,300	22.8	10.3	848	36.9	1.3	16,714	-0.1	600	3.6	14,549	28.8	26.2
McDuffie	8,156	61.4	102,500	20.8	10.7	625	33.2	2.7	8,973	0.9	499	5.6	8,204	29.0	32.0
McIntosh	5,730	78.8	112,700	25.1	13.5	754	33.7	2	6,190	0.9	247	4	5,716	23.0	32.1
Macon	4,618	63.6	61,300	21.9	13.3	562	36.5	2.6	4,731	0.3	295	6.2	4,524	19.6	40.7
Madison	10,571	74.1	121,600	19.5	10.0	716	26.7	3.3	13,689	0.9	483	3.5	12,065	29.7	33.1
Marion	3,263	72.5	86,300	25.1	12.7	554	22.5	2.4	3,435	0.3	174	5.1	3,413	28.5	37.1
Meriwether	8,108	68.2	91,300	21.6	15.1	749	37.6	2.6	8,947	0.9	447	5	8,165	23.7	40.5
Miller	2,326	66.0	88,500	19.8	14.5	665	40.8	5.6	2,813	-0.3	104	3.7	2,368	28.8	27.3
Mitchell	7,991	65.9	82,500	28.4	14.6	614	28.8	3.6	8,408		452	5.4	7,927	27.2	32.0
Monroe	9,590	77.1	159,900	20.8	10.1	692	28.1	2.7	13,043	-0.5	479	3.7	11,047	36.8	23.3
Montgomery	3,077	73.5	76,500	21.2	11.2	573	29.7	2.2	3,799	0.9	217	5.7	3,511	29.1	31.4
Morgan	6,698	74.7	208,200	22.0	13.3	839	24.6	2.1	9,067	0.9	323	3.6	8,011	31.1	31.3
Murray	14,176	67.9	91,700	20.6	10.0	670	29.6	4	15,943	0.5	847	5.3	16,748	17.0	44.8
Muscogee	73,179	48.4	140,200	22.6	11.1	856	31.3	2.4	79,354	0.4	4,029	5.1	79,022	33.3	20.0
Newton	35,823	69.0	123,300	21.8	10.0	936	31.6	2.1	51,780	1.1	2,306	4.5	46,324	28.9	28.4
Oconee	12,693	82.2	252,000	19.5	10.6	911	26.3	2.2	19,687	1.1	582	3	16,944	53.5	13.9
Oglethorpe	5,642	77.8	111,800	21.7	11.1	693	30.6	1.5	7,124	1	261	3.7	6,390	30.4	36.7
Paulding	51,397	77.7	150,400	20.3	10.7	1,074	28.7	2	83,868	1.3	2,887	3.4	74,446	34.6	22.7
Peach	10,113	65.6	126,000	21.5	10.0	715	31.7	1.9	11,911	1.3	607	5.1	11,282	29.0	30.2
Pickens	11,379	77.6	185,700	20.2	11.8	882	26.1	1.8	15,158	1.2	532	3.5	12,994	31.0	27.8
Pierce	6,975	73.4	99,000	20.6	12.4	625	29.7	1.5	8,686	-1.2	334	3.8	7,555	30.9	34.5
Pike	5,963	83.3	162,000	22.7	12.4	753	27.1	2.2	8,756	1.1	319	3.6	7,456	33.2	30.0
Polk	14,949	64.5	105,600	22.0	11.7	690	29.1	4.7	18,522	0.2	776	4.2	17,553	20.9	40.9
Pulaski	3,893	61.2	111,100	20.9	10.1	661	31.5	4.3	4,134	1	176	4.3	3,737	28.0	27.3

1. Specified owner-occupied units.   2. A value of 10.0 represents 10 percent or less; a value of 50.0 represents 50 percent or more.   3. Specified renter-occupied units.   4. Overcrowded or lacking complete plumbing facilities.   5. Percent of civilian labor force.   6. Civilian employed persons 16 years old and over.

Table B. States and Counties — Nonfarm Employment and Agriculture

STATE County	Private nonfarm establishments, employment and payroll, 2016									Agriculture, 2017			
	Number of establish-ments	Employment						Annual payroll		Farms			Farm producers whose primary occupation is farming (percent)
		Total	Health care and social assistance	Manufac-turing	Retail trade	Finance and insurance	Professional, scientific, and technical services	Total (mil dol)	Average per employee (dollars)	Number	Percent with:		
											Fewer than 50 acres	1000 acres or more	
	104	105	106	107	108	109	110	111	112	113	114	115	116
GEORGIA—Cont'd													
Effingham	704	7,738	930	1,705	1,398	167	272	305	39,404	254	55.5	6.7	35.4
Elbert	436	4,589	527	1,963	647	192	50	149	32,382	453	34.0	4.2	39.4
Emanuel	381	5,310	893	1,863	815	166	123	162	30,484	465	28.4	8.4	34.9
Evans	218	3,924	451	1,885	479	88	67	123	31,246	143	31.5	6.3	39.8
Fannin	608	5,434	916	466	1,376	150	239	148	27,311	211	64.0	0.9	44.2
Fayette	3,449	41,135	6,380	3,001	7,153	1,100	2,436	1,633	39,709	148	58.1	NA	53.4
Floyd	1,960	35,518	7,943	6,617	4,435	757	690	1,338	37,679	547	51.7	2.0	35.2
Forsyth	6,173	73,548	8,185	7,916	10,417	1,875	5,583	3,504	47,647	291	63.2	NA	49.9
Franklin	438	6,829	923	1,612	887	147	165	226	33,119	753	47.7	0.4	52.4
Fulton	35,950	784,738	85,698	18,535	54,928	62,012	99,298	55,206	70,350	195	75.9	NA	38.8
Gilmer	548	6,003	723	1,380	1,175	112	172	168	28,062	330	56.4	0.3	49.7
Glascock	24	216	D	D	19	D	D	5	25,190	76	35.5	3.9	38.2
Glynn	2,533	31,051	4,943	2,099	5,164	692	979	1,083	34,863	53	71.7	NA	25.0
Gordon	1,025	20,038	1,860	7,022	2,552	273	206	775	38,674	740	52.6	1.2	39.5
Grady	409	4,593	535	995	784	141	118	146	31,887	415	29.9	9.2	33.7
Greene	423	4,782	725	438	766	194	103	172	35,918	248	27.8	7.3	40.2
Gwinnett	23,151	330,163	28,427	23,501	46,993	14,912	27,695	16,332	49,467	177	67.2	0.6	39.7
Habersham	834	12,114	1,276	4,154	1,987	409	253	399	32,928	379	63.6	NA	42.2
Hall	4,205	74,898	12,645	20,491	9,097	2,021	1,951	3,324	44,381	551	63.5	0.4	38.1
Hancock	67	596	132	D	85	D	D	23	38,658	145	20.0	3.4	36.2
Haralson	435	5,462	844	1,556	1,032	114	108	209	38,319	321	49.2	NA	38.2
Harris	412	4,266	250	972	301	410	67	111	26,136	289	47.4	2.4	40.0
Hart	394	5,631	351	2,325	939	116	133	201	35,702	516	40.3	0.6	50.7
Heard	127	1,165	D	548	93	19	40	50	43,104	227	30.0	1.8	37.2
Henry	3,594	50,310	7,515	3,015	10,319	1,209	1,467	1,708	33,955	240	72.9	NA	39.7
Houston	2,506	37,793	6,195	4,415	7,567	1,073	3,855	1,281	33,892	277	55.2	2.9	21.5
Irwin	120	1,642	557	D	150	33	34	58	35,292	348	29.9	10.1	46.2
Jackson	1,256	20,249	1,212	6,241	3,054	231	524	772	38,122	734	52.7	0.8	38.2
Jasper	159	1,508	224	448	218	55	28	44	29,483	251	51.4	3.6	37.0
Jeff Davis	243	3,719	359	1,526	695	76	33	117	31,433	197	41.1	11.7	37.5
Jefferson	304	3,966	481	971	593	159	42	143	36,137	318	25.2	12.6	43.5
Jenkins	106	1,026	272	22	129	35	13	30	29,407	210	35.2	11.4	33.9
Johnson	117	949	211	111	175	35	14	28	29,563	284	28.9	7.4	28.5
Jones	319	2,665	440	55	533	53	70	84	31,703	165	33.3	5.5	29.3
Lamar	237	2,933	301	547	471	95	56	91	31,049	220	52.3	0.9	38.7
Lanier	89	819	188	139	124	72	21	24	29,284	103	45.6	19.4	38.1
Laurens	1,049	15,414	2,976	2,793	2,602	482	334	558	36,201	626	30.4	4.2	29.0
Lee	396	3,880	276	230	714	198	363	138	35,552	206	40.8	13.6	33.7
Liberty	824	12,194	2,207	1,724	2,158	347	607	480	39,339	69	63.8	1.4	23.3
Lincoln	133	804	26	81	153	43	29	24	30,205	104	40.4	1.9	25.6
Long	65	284	24	D	63	22	D	7	23,676	85	44.7	NA	28.9
Lowndes	2,750	41,159	7,561	3,298	6,751	1,038	1,246	1,314	31,915	380	52.6	3.2	30.9
Lumpkin	508	4,921	691	518	1,047	156	210	151	30,584	240	60.8	1.3	45.3
McDuffie	433	6,919	949	1,888	1,054	135	95	214	30,969	269	46.8	3.0	31.1
McIntosh	179	1,257	37	14	333	80	34	31	24,746	32	68.8	6.3	33.3
Macon	171	1,573	417	379	229	45	15	58	36,951	339	34.2	5.9	43.1
Madison	353	2,373	253	205	480	63	79	66	27,848	673	51.0	1.0	44.4
Marion	89	1,117	120	D	113	17	10	33	29,378	222	29.3	6.8	46.1
Meriwether	301	3,417	1,000	654	558	88	53	124	36,166	344	34.9	4.1	39.0
Miller	114	1,040	340	D	204	51	27	32	31,247	144	27.1	15.3	45.7
Mitchell	354	5,667	527	2,808	750	141	138	152	26,844	425	31.5	11.8	48.9
Monroe	495	6,071	931	640	861	144	161	219	36,054	219	38.8	4.1	35.9
Montgomery	101	864	108	81	161	30	29	22	25,498	179	27.4	10.1	32.3
Morgan	482	6,061	519	1,497	1,028	192	282	197	32,472	513	37.8	1.8	46.6
Murray	400	7,949	480	4,366	853	110	64	276	34,675	278	45.0	1.4	37.9
Muscogee	4,292	77,864	14,961	6,159	11,605	12,243	2,607	3,278	42,104	37	35.1	2.7	40.8
Newton	1,389	18,754	2,322	4,161	3,279	491	435	774	41,294	292	50.3	1.4	36.5
Oconee	1,118	11,237	1,561	674	2,212	474	837	413	36,785	329	49.2	1.2	29.7
Oglethorpe	174	1,019	110	81	124	30	50	33	32,805	427	38.6	2.8	39.9
Paulding	1,887	17,946	2,810	721	4,769	402	706	570	31,783	212	60.4	NA	26.3
Peach	464	6,237	638	2,434	885	131	110	252	40,399	228	51.3	3.5	43.9
Pickens	696	6,371	1,304	770	1,275	244	176	226	35,482	258	62.4	0.4	45.1
Pierce	340	3,321	240	392	471	97	73	107	32,362	352	46.6	6.5	36.6
Pike	254	1,741	184	185	188	164	65	56	32,298	286	45.1	1.0	30.2
Polk	592	9,903	1,106	3,600	1,530	167	115	354	35,707	401	51.4	3.0	38.8
Pulaski	174	1,976	722	D	371	75	43	80	40,564	189	41.8	7.9	40.5

STATE County	Acreage (1,000)	Percent change, 2012-2017	Average size of farm	Total irrigated (1,000)	Total cropland (1,000)	Average per farm	Average per acre	Value of machinery and equiopmnet, average per farm (dollars)	Total (mil dol)	Average per farm (acres)	Crops	Livestock and poultry products	Organic farms (number)	Farms with internet access (percent)	Total ($1,000)	Percent of farms
	117	118	119	120	121	122	123	124	125	126	127	128	129	130	131	132
GEORGIA—Cont'd																
Effingham	50	24.9	199	2.8	28.4	646,043	3,250	104,350	16.3	64,063	92.0	8.0	4	82.7	369	22.0
Elbert	79	39.3	175	1.0	19.2	687,827	3,925	83,075	107.1	236,494	4.9	95.1	4	64.7	919	28.3
Emanuel	139	-8.7	298	4.8	45.7	622,886	2,091	95,023	33.0	71,013	85.0	15.0	1	74.4	2,565	40.9
Evans	36	-1.2	249	5.6	14.4	671,882	2,699	104,565	32.2	224,979	60.7	39.3	NA	79.0	567	29.4
Fannin	16	17.9	78	0.2	4.0	457,536	5,902	48,477	23.0	109,175	21.7	78.3	NA	84.4	239	16.6
Fayette	11	-1.8	76	0.1	3.5	415,120	5,441	42,880	4.1	27,432	79.0	21.0	1	86.5	13	5.4
Floyd	75	6.7	137	0.7	21.7	665,897	4,866	88,749	53.4	97,700	10.2	89.8	NA	77.3	442	13.5
Forsyth	18	12.1	62	0.3	5.3	488,028	7,879	64,873	45.9	157,732	11.1	88.9	1	74.2	93	9.6
Franklin	79	1.9	105	0.2	21.0	601,312	5,748	100,018	371.8	493,734	0.6	99.4	1	78.6	928	27.5
Fulton	12	-13.3	63	0.2	2.2	1,195,368	19,063	42,330	2.3	11,641	39.9	60.1	7	91.8	110	10.8
Gilmer	28	11.0	86	0.1	6.9	658,366	7,657	86,301	205.4	622,530	1.5	98.5	NA	87.3	402	30.6
Glascock	21	-10.6	283	D	6.1	449,699	1,592	52,828	2.0	26,947	82.0	18.0	NA	86.8	187	23.7
Glynn	2	-46.5	36	0.1	0.2	559,751	15,411	68,477	0.3	5,887	26.0	74.0	1	54.7	8	9.4
Gordon	75	-12.1	101	1.0	29.8	660,422	6,545	73,663	294.2	397,519	2.9	97.1	1	73.1	1,580	29.5
Grady	124	-5.0	298	13.2	69.6	1,120,918	3,760	138,658	100.7	242,636	66.8	33.2	NA	69.2	5,132	52.0
Greene	76	55.8	305	0.2	9.0	1,094,410	3,586	98,364	79.1	319,073	3.0	97.0	NA	74.2	1,429	12.9
Gwinnett	11	1.9	60	0.1	3.0	563,058	9,339	53,633	16.8	95,068	96.5	3.5	NA	78.5	D	4.5
Habersham	26	-32.2	68	0.1	9.7	485,967	7,160	99,560	123.0	324,485	1.5	98.5	1	81.3	269	16.1
Hall	41	-21.7	74	0.1	13.8	689,173	9,332	79,541	128.5	233,156	2.3	97.7	1	80.9	789	20.3
Hancock	39	21.3	267	0.5	5.7	559,388	2,092	60,754	4.4	30,297	29.7	70.3	1	74.5	134	19.3
Haralson	27	0.5	84	0.2	7.7	398,850	4,750	59,412	75.4	234,754	1.8	98.2	NA	69.8	194	15.3
Harris	42	29.2	145	0.3	12.2	626,701	4,322	54,841	5.1	17,550	72.5	27.5	1	72.0	68	9.3
Hart	66	-2.9	129	2.2	26.1	722,492	5,622	116,647	215.1	416,953	6.2	93.8	NA	75.8	1,103	38.2
Heard	38	42.0	169	0.3	7.6	611,638	3,611	77,480	43.3	190,767	8.4	91.6	NA	84.1	346	18.9
Henry	12	-42.4	52	0.1	3.4	389,536	7,482	33,481	2.8	11,654	59.0	41.0	8	80.0	126	4.2
Houston	39	-17.5	141	7.6	18.3	567,998	4,021	86,680	18.2	65,588	55.0	45.0	NA	82.7	445	19.9
Irwin	123	-17.3	353	31.4	73.1	1,146,611	3,249	180,086	63.1	181,417	81.2	18.8	2	75.0	5,680	59.2
Jackson	75	-3.5	102	1.4	19.8	647,798	6,370	76,784	197.6	269,181	5.2	94.8	1	76.6	711	19.2
Jasper	43	-2.2	171	0.3	8.0	594,493	3,481	58,915	27.0	107,641	7.2	92.8	1	77.3	40	8.8
Jeff Davis	72	-9.2	363	10.3	46.3	910,689	2,505	215,420	40.6	205,914	70.9	29.1	NA	80.2	1,831	36.5
Jefferson	125	-14.2	393	33.6	69.7	1,017,736	2,590	140,667	58.5	183,912	73.0	27.0	NA	65.7	2,413	45.9
Jenkins	79	-13.2	378	7.3	33.4	989,382	2,620	96,519	21.6	103,071	87.2	12.8	NA	79.5	2,721	46.2
Johnson	75	31.2	263	9.1	25.0	551,537	2,093	59,306	12.3	43,447	82.2	17.8	NA	71.5	1,340	35.2
Jones	36	58.3	221	D	7.1	619,706	2,806	67,284	5.5	33,448	14.3	85.7	3	81.8	115	15.8
Lamar	32	-8.9	147	0.2	10.2	514,385	3,501	87,640	46.5	211,136	8.5	91.5	2	79.5	84	10.0
Lanier	47	12.4	454	7.3	25.4	1,376,047	3,030	220,587	22.9	222,184	98.9	1.1	NA	74.8	1,027	33.0
Laurens	155	-16.0	247	9.3	42.7	518,267	2,096	73,721	25.7	41,003	71.6	28.4	NA	74.3	2,465	57.2
Lee	120	14.1	584	19.1	60.1	1,976,595	3,384	150,525	60.4	293,097	77.3	22.7	NA	69.9	3,101	46.1
Liberty	6	2.5	92	0.1	1.0	488,481	5,289	36,656	0.5	6,986	61.0	39.0	NA	75.4	19	11.6
Lincoln	18	-22.5	176	D	3.3	549,595	3,125	64,987	4.2	40,346	17.0	83.0	NA	67.3	177	20.2
Long	10	-0.8	120	0.1	3.0	402,578	3,361	71,266	7.3	85,518	8.8	91.2	NA	85.9	63	9.4
Lowndes	62	-4.8	163	7.0	24.4	886,787	5,451	79,945	35.5	93,363	85.7	14.3	3	73.4	1,121	31.8
Lumpkin	27	55.1	112	0.2	6.9	665,565	5,925	82,836	51.3	213,658	7.6	92.4	NA	80.4	227	19.2
McDuffie	44	15.0	162	0.6	11.0	486,078	2,994	72,590	D	D	D	D	NA	74.0	255	20.4
McIntosh	10	-42.9	305	D	1.0	722,542	2,372	84,945	D	D	D	D	1	87.5	NA	NA
Macon	111	10.1	328	25.2	59.5	1,056,552	3,217	182,358	271.6	801,212	20.0	80.0	1	71.1	2,615	48.7
Madison	69	-3.7	102	0.3	23.0	577,100	5,664	83,713	239.6	355,947	1.7	98.3	1	77.4	569	21.2
Marion	64	35.0	288	1.8	14.4	684,034	2,375	99,628	20.6	92,599	24.6	75.4	NA	72.1	777	42.3
Meriwether	71	14.5	206	1.0	13.9	673,529	3,262	85,309	12.5	36,445	75.5	24.5	NA	75.9	261	15.7
Miller	80	-16.3	557	26.6	54.6	1,805,529	3,242	327,966	47.9	332,486	87.9	12.1	NA	75.0	6,028	70.1
Mitchell	190	-0.8	446	66.6	121.8	1,651,849	3,702	281,683	262.7	618,111	44.7	55.3	NA	72.7	6,948	51.1
Monroe	49	40.9	222	0.0	5.6	727,734	3,279	79,453	51.2	233,685	1.9	98.1	NA	84.0	94	10.5
Montgomery	60	3.2	333	7.2	22.5	859,810	2,584	96,589	15.5	86,732	87.2	12.8	NA	58.1	1,018	39.1
Morgan	88	-6.6	172	1.1	26.0	803,842	4,673	74,639	121.0	235,889	4.8	95.2	NA	76.8	922	19.1
Murray	47	0.5	170	0.9	11.9	860,300	5,068	105,708	122.7	441,428	3.5	96.5	NA	76.3	470	31.7
Muscogee	9	117.3	251	D	2.9	1,255,529	5,003	50,172	0.2	5,324	79.2	20.8	NA	94.6	D	2.7
Newton	43	5.0	146	0.1	8.5	655,436	4,475	74,446	12.4	42,308	15.1	84.9	2	79.8	245	12.0
Oconee	36	-21.2	108	0.6	7.9	784,386	7,235	69,487	42.2	128,210	33.7	66.3	1	79.6	383	26.1
Oglethorpe	73	-9.7	171	1.6	17.9	743,571	4,353	76,951	198.4	464,553	7.1	92.9	4	84.8	934	31.4
Paulding	15	77.2	70	0.1	4.1	404,436	5,781	52,413	9.5	44,967	5.7	94.3	NA	77.8	34	10.4
Peach	58	64.5	255	16.4	33.8	1,469,850	5,766	191,004	65.4	286,654	88.1	11.9	NA	81.6	254	14.5
Pickens	17	-1.5	64	0.1	4.0	548,090	8,529	101,132	77.1	298,841	1.2	98.8	NA	71.7	215	20.5
Pierce	81	3.4	230	8.3	47.6	661,340	2,877	151,848	42.1	119,608	82.5	17.5	NA	70.7	1,653	34.1
Pike	41	7.4	143	0.7	8.6	699,823	4,897	65,136	18.8	65,881	14.2	85.8	NA	78.7	225	18.2
Polk	62	38.4	155	0.1	28.7	561,506	3,616	116,950	46.0	114,691	29.2	70.8	1	73.3	232	15.7
Pulaski	53	-15.8	278	14.0	28.8	743,749	2,671	115,184	49.7	262,937	38.9	61.1	NA	87.3	703	57.1

Table B. States and Counties — Water Use, Wholesale Trade, Retail Trade, and Real Estate

STATE County	Water use, 2015		Wholesale Trade[1], 2012				Retail Trade[2], 2012				Real estate and rental and leasing,[2] 2012			
	Public supply water withdrawn (mil gal/ day)	Public supply gallons withdrawn per person per day	Number of establish-ments	Number of employees	Sales (mil dol)	Average payroll (mil dol)	Number of establish-ments	Number of employees	Sales (mil dol)	Average payroll (mil dol)	Number of establish-ments	Number of employees	Sales (mil dol)	Average payroll (mil dol)
	133	134	135	136	137	138	139	140	141	142	143	144	145	146
GEORGIA—Cont'd														
Effingham............	35.80	626.9	11	D	D	D	107	1,290	358.5	28.6	29	D	D	D
Elbert.................	1.59	82.1	41	309	61.8	8.3	79	611	142.0	13.1	3	D	D	D
Emanuel.............	1.59	70.0	18	143	89.1	4.2	82	778	203.3	16.4	15	D	D	D
Evans.................	0.54	50.1	5	33	4.4	0.6	56	453	178.8	12.5	3	11	1.6	0.2
Fannin................	1.75	72.0	18	73	21.1	2.5	104	943	256.6	20.3	29	55	11.2	1.4
Fayette...............	9.46	85.4	168	1,664	1,205.2	90.0	407	6,588	1,453.7	139.4	176	565	79.3	17.3
Floyd.................	11.80	122.3	74	812	691.5	33.8	386	3,986	1,022.4	89.3	76	252	41.7	8.2
Forsyth..............	20.61	97.0	384	5,014	3,722.6	349.7	581	8,463	2,366.8	230.9	232	507	105.3	21.6
Franklin.............	1.95	87.4	23	257	105.8	7.1	91	881	270.7	17.3	9	12	2.0	0.3
Fulton...............	196.32	194.3	1,496	27,530	29,149.1	1,970.4	3,368	49,050	13,382.7	1,292.8	2,068	17,597	5,968.3	1,241.3
Gilmer...............	2.50	85.0	23	134	63.5	4.3	91	1,103	291.8	23.6	32	53	8.6	1.4
Glascock............	0.07	22.8	NA	NA	NA	NA	5	14	5.7	0.3	NA	NA	NA	NA
Glynn................	9.31	111.4	66	446	270.0	19.9	452	4,567	1,407.1	111.2	143	512	70.6	16.4
Gordon..............	10.43	184.4	65	D	D	D	240	2,311	627.5	48.5	42	125	26.5	3.5
Grady...............	1.73	68.6	27	408	364.4	16.8	79	754	184.7	16.0	20	46	4.4	1.2
Greene..............	1.23	73.6	15	65	38.6	3.8	72	695	206.0	16.1	21	42	5.5	1.7
Gwinnett............	0.64	0.7	1,718	30,603	30,301.0	2,002.5	2,759	41,508	12,673.4	1,068.5	976	4,554	1,286.3	214.0
Habersham.........	5.66	128.6	35	179	99.2	6.3	158	1,795	462.1	41.2	22	50	6.8	0.9
Hall.................	88.18	455.6	235	3,265	9,022.6	173.1	579	7,640	2,231.9	193.5	164	450	116.5	17.1
Hancock............	1.20	140.3	1	D	D	D	21	99	24.8	2.1	2	D	D	D
Haralson............	2.53	87.7	20	142	52.6	7.4	84	851	321.2	23.5	8	D	D	D
Harris...............	6.26	187.5	9	D	D	D	43	260	70.2	4.9	13	D	D	D
Hart.................	1.46	57.2	15	154	33.9	6.0	75	849	173.6	15.9	10	D	D	D
Heard................	1.22	105.7	NA	NA	NA	NA	18	84	22.8	2.3	4	D	D	D
Henry...............	34.13	156.7	98	1,182	833.8	74.2	550	9,005	2,402.5	200.7	164	590	112.3	19.0
Houston............	23.75	158.3	48	377	220.6	13.3	442	6,625	1,762.8	150.4	124	447	68.8	12.0
Irwin................	0.44	47.6	9	136	79.6	4.1	30	149	32.3	2.9	2	D	D	D
Jackson.............	9.52	150.3	53	953	574.8	36.2	232	2,594	1,482.5	54.3	44	75	15.9	2.1
Jasper...............	0.75	55.0	2	D	D	D	26	213	47.6	4.0	4	2	0.3	0.0
Jeff Davis	0.90	60.3	10	131	64.4	4.3	67	726	251.9	17.8	5	D	D	D
Jefferson............	1.32	82.0	16	259	217.8	6.3	70	640	142.8	12.3	8	42	1.9	1.0
Jenkins.............	0.45	50.2	3	D	D	D	23	154	40.5	2.9	1	D	D	D
Johnson............	0.53	54.9	6	29	19.2	0.9	24	148	37.1	3.0	NA	NA	NA	NA
Jones...............	2.73	95.8	7	D	D	D	51	423	97.0	8.4	13	D	D	D
Lamar..............	1.87	102.7	5	84	20.6	2.6	43	421	107.2	9.1	4	D	D	D
Lanier..............	0.36	34.9	4	D	D	D	21	D	D	D	1	D	D	D
Laurens............	3.54	74.2	36	396	306.0	16.5	248	2,647	700.5	53.5	38	129	15.0	3.2
Lee.................	1.87	64.0	15	259	566.2	30.7	61	589	155.0	13.8	17	45	8.8	1.7
Liberty.............	6.42	102.8	11	D	D	D	171	1,938	564.1	40.9	48	183	24.6	5.5
Lincoln.............	0.01	1.3	7	33	11.1	0.8	22	160	38.8	3.2	4	D	D	D
Long................	0.51	28.8	1	D	D	D	12	52	16.2	1.1	3	4	0.4	0.1
Lowndes............	13.16	116.6	115	1,069	1,227.0	41.2	493	5,974	1,748.5	132.2	137	1,447	104.7	26.2
Lumpkin............	1.27	40.4	6	38	12.7	1.1	81	767	192.3	18.3	24	D	D	D
McDuffie............	2.59	120.2	9	29	21.9	1.3	103	1,027	295.0	23.9	15	54	5.4	1.3
McIntosh............	1.04	74.5	4	D	D	D	58	433	98.1	7.4	5	8	1.0	0.1
Macon..............	1.03	75.6	12	76	265.1	4.4	43	227	43.5	4.6	3	4	0.6	0.1
Madison............	0.53	18.6	13	D	D	D	57	403	135.7	8.7	13	D	D	D
Marion..............	1.41	160.9	2	D	D	D	22	104	35.3	2.2	NA	NA	NA	NA
Meriwether.........	0.31	14.6	6	19	16.8	0.8	90	622	116.1	11.8	5	D	D	D
Miller...............	0.26	44.4	5	63	54.6	2.4	33	237	77.4	5.0	5	7	0.3	0.1
Mitchell.............	3.77	167.0	22	394	172.9	10.2	96	735	156.8	14.6	9	21	1.6	0.5
Monroe..............	1.58	58.3	21	198	112.6	8.8	74	783	186.9	16.4	17	43	6.8	1.3
Montgomery.........	0.18	20.1	6	49	17.9	1.8	28	190	46.7	3.6	3	4	0.5	0.1
Morgan..............	1.34	74.3	15	190	117.0	6.6	69	893	309.2	19.5	18	31	4.2	1.0
Murray..............	1.89	47.8	26	399	123.5	17.1	90	711	198.1	16.0	12	D	D	D
Muscogee..........	36.77	183.3	157	1,843	1,550.1	80.6	796	11,371	2,847.8	250.2	237	1,461	258.1	55.7
Newton.............	13.73	130.2	53	518	278.2	20.9	210	2,778	747.3	60.7	52	182	36.8	6.6
Oconee.............	0.35	9.7	28	257	90.7	11.6	103	1,630	397.2	38.2	58	246	79.0	14.1
Oglethorpe.........	0.26	17.5	8	D	D	D	22	145	40.6	3.1	1	D	D	D
Paulding............	0.10	0.7	62	254	161.7	12.2	253	4,075	1,174.4	96.7	51	284	55.7	15.5
Peach...............	2.31	86.5	23	D	D	D	102	806	296.1	19.0	21	60	11.6	2.3
Pickens.............	2.77	91.4	18	87	56.6	2.7	97	1,177	327.4	26.9	34	D	D	D
Pierce..............	0.57	29.8	16	D	D	D	65	414	114.4	8.9	9	17	7.9	0.6
Pike................	2.97	165.5	11	D	D	D	31	165	36.2	3.1	5	D	D	D
Polk................	5.60	134.9	15	D	D	D	131	1,399	326.5	30.8	18	85	8.2	1.9
Pulaski.............	1.09	95.6	2	D	D	D	37	358	87.6	9.6	6	12	0.7	0.2

1 Merchant wholesalers, except manufacturers' sales branches and offices.   2. Employer establishments.

Table B. States and Counties — Professional Services, Manufacturing, and Accommodation and Food Services

STATE County	Professional, scientific, and technical services, 2012				Manufacturing, 2012				Accommodation and food services, 2012			
	Number of establishments	Number of employees	Sales (mil dol)	Average payroll (mil dol)	Number of establishments	Number of employees	Receipts (mil dol)	Annual payroll (mil dol)	Number of establishments	Number of employees	Receipts (mil dol)	Annual payroll (mil dol)
	147	148	149	150	151	152	153	154	155	156	157	158
GEORGIA—Cont'd												
Effingham	59	259	22.0	9.3	20	1,743	D	108.9	62	727	36.5	9.6
Elbert	21	50	4.1	1.2	89	2,028	379.6	70.7	24	325	13.7	4.0
Emanuel	26	D	D	D	29	1,694	706.3	50.5	32	416	17.4	4.2
Evans	11	54	3.9	1.6	14	1,769	D	45.0	14	D	D	D
Fannin	47	201	17.0	5.8	23	311	39.8	9.4	57	683	40.8	9.4
Fayette	422	2,127	275.0	130.8	92	2,230	853.7	112.5	217	4,857	211.5	64.6
Floyd	186	809	104.1	35.0	100	5,567	3,615.6	265.3	183	3,593	163.4	46.9
Forsyth	1,066	4,442	841.2	307.1	223	6,998	2,364.3	311.6	297	5,679	257.6	74.5
Franklin	25	109	8.1	2.7	30	1,204	434.5	49.5	43	643	29.4	7.9
Fulton	6,943	93,363	19,604.0	7,831.0	590	17,925	8,987.2	929.6	2,941	70,043	4,627.8	1,273.8
Gilmer	46	168	14.0	5.0	28	1,507	369.4	40.2	52	712	33.5	8.7
Glascock	2	D	D	D	NA	NA	NA	NA	1	D	D	D
Glynn	267	870	116.3	39.6	52	2,059	975.6	126.1	259	6,502	387.5	119.8
Gordon	62	337	66.0	23.5	104	6,492	2,499.1	260.5	92	1,371	70.9	18.0
Grady	19	61	7.3	1.9	19	511	141.2	21.4	28	310	14.2	3.2
Greene	39	92	12.0	4.0	11	414	557.6	19.3	29	887	56.7	19.0
Gwinnett	3,177	D	D	D	700	19,358	6,847.7	984.4	1,597	25,387	1,355.5	366.5
Habersham	63	257	36.1	8.6	52	4,122	1,219.0	137.8	75	1,145	53.5	13.7
Hall	402	D	D	D	225	17,020	7,629.2	647.1	283	4,742	298.3	67.4
Hancock	1	D	D	D	4	D	D	D	9	D	D	D
Haralson	33	86	8.3	2.2	33	1,364	834.1	55.2	38	D	D	D
Harris	30	D	D	D	18	D	D	D	28	523	25.0	6.7
Hart	38	104	11.9	3.6	28	2,115	602.1	91.1	29	D	D	D
Heard	4	D	D	D	10	419	D	17.4	8	D	D	D
Henry	294	1,380	198.3	57.5	69	2,872	2,035.1	137.2	340	5,783	281.5	73.1
Houston	271	3,288	437.6	169.5	54	3,105	2,051.0	129.1	270	5,726	259.0	69.1
Irwin	9	106	5.4	2.2	5	106	D	4.6	6	28	2.1	0.5
Jackson	99	468	75.5	21.3	70	4,420	1,924.1	183.9	68	1,015	46.9	13.3
Jasper	11	D	D	D	15	308	84.0	13.1	12	103	5.8	1.4
Jeff Davis	15	43	3.5	1.6	23	994	304.0	35.4	16	269	10.8	2.8
Jefferson	10	38	2.4	0.8	27	981	251.4	39.3	22	258	11.4	2.7
Jenkins	2	D	D	D	5	12	D	0.4	10	D	D	D
Johnson	6	16	0.8	0.2	5	167	14.9	3.5	9	54	2.7	0.6
Jones	20	68	5.1	1.8	12	68	D	3.2	20	D	D	D
Lamar	16	54	3.8	1.2	12	436	230.4	19.4	24	324	13.2	3.3
Lanier	4	17	0.8	0.2	4	124	D	3.4	12	103	4.6	1.4
Laurens	65	293	30.2	12.4	41	2,533	640.0	99.0	99	1,727	77.8	20.3
Lee	28	102	10.4	3.3	12	203	D	5.7	21	279	11.9	3.3
Liberty	74	D	D	D	18	D	D	D	99	D	D	D
Lincoln	10	D	D	D	4	93	10.7	2.8	15	D	D	D
Long	2	D	D	D	NA	NA	NA	NA	6	D	D	D
Lowndes	223	1,165	137.6	49.0	89	2,953	2,600.3	131.5	293	5,705	245.8	66.0
Lumpkin	59	159	15.4	5.5	25	569	100.0	22.3	59	974	46.7	12.3
McDuffie	24	D	D	D	32	1,627	554.4	63.2	38	515	24.7	5.9
McIntosh	18	23	2.6	0.7	7	28	D	0.9	29	402	17.9	4.3
Macon	6	13	1.1	0.3	16	547	478.5	31.9	14	D	D	D
Madison	25	75	5.9	1.9	24	210	21.4	7.3	20	D	D	D
Marion	4	D	D	D	3	D	D	D	6	16	1.3	0.2
Meriwether	13	43	3.6	1.3	14	688	320.5	27.6	29	D	D	D
Miller	8	22	1.7	0.6	NA	NA	NA	NA	10	78	3.1	0.7
Mitchell	20	253	17.4	7.8	16	2,928	D	80.3	29	354	18.6	5.1
Monroe	57	176	17.0	7.2	15	489	116.2	15.8	40	590	25.2	6.5
Montgomery	4	12	1.1	0.3	6	61	D	2.8	8	52	2.5	0.6
Morgan	44	479	56.9	19.3	26	1,097	314.1	50.0	52	830	35.4	10.3
Murray	19	D	D	D	65	3,656	1,306.6	122.5	41	D	D	D
Muscogee	350	2,520	301.3	113.9	122	6,977	1,937.2	297.0	442	10,453	519.3	149.2
Newton	103	392	43.9	12.8	77	3,759	1,854.8	186.1	108	1,718	112.9	23.6
Oconee	147	738	93.8	31.6	25	566	D	20.3	57	D	D	D
Oglethorpe	15	D	D	D	11	58	D	2.2	4	D	D	D
Paulding	165	565	65.6	22.3	48	775	191.0	31.9	129	2,645	121.1	33.8
Peach	27	101	7.6	2.7	28	D	D	D	55	764	40.8	9.4
Pickens	81	328	20.7	7.3	40	757	144.6	28.4	45	672	33.5	9.4
Pierce	15	73	4.7	1.6	14	380	D	13.6	21	239	11.2	2.9
Pike	18	D	D	D	8	160	D	6.0	9	D	D	D
Polk	36	113	9.5	2.8	31	3,234	D	132.0	65	903	40.6	10.9
Pulaski	14	56	4.9	2.1	3	D	D	D	18	229	10.5	2.3

Health Care and Social Assistance, Other Services, Nonemployer Businesses, and Residential Construction

STATE County	Health care and social assistance, 2012				Other services, 2012				Nonemployer businesses, 2016		Value of residential construction authorized by building permits, 2018	
	Number of establishments	Number of employees	Receipts (mil dol)	Annual payroll (mil dol)	Number of establishments	Number of employees	Receipts (mil dol)	Annual payroll (mil dol)	Number	Receipts (mil dol)	New construction ($1,000)	Number of housing units
	159	160	161	162	163	164	165	166	167	168	169	170
GEORGIA—Cont'd												
Effingham	57	D	D	D	41	D	D	D	3,629	140.3	129,280	573
Elbert	33	D	D	D	19	55	6.1	1.2	1,456	54.3	4,431	42
Emanuel	50	875	69.5	26.3	26	87	9.5	2.1	1,610	61.7	743	12
Evans	19	482	38.8	14.8	14	69	5.6	2.0	676	24.0	3,435	26
Fannin	66	1,039	115.7	39.3	29	106	9.7	2.4	2,707	128.5	54,272	293
Fayette	369	5,006	692.1	256.5	226	1,441	123.1	37.0	10,651	453.9	158,648	543
Floyd	281	8,058	1,049.2	412.6	104	831	64.9	19.5	6,742	254.1	33,901	210
Forsyth	463	6,830	704.5	283.8	307	1,541	188.7	50.8	20,464	1,002.7	405,556	3,650
Franklin	42	711	67.5	27.8	27	172	41.0	5.3	1,667	65.2	12,486	64
Fulton	3,542	71,584	9,875.8	3,610.7	2,108	21,451	3,833.9	763.1	107,036	5,393.4	2,002,488	10,051
Gilmer	46	577	46.2	20.2	37	169	16.4	4.8	2,662	114.2	32,289	188
Glascock	5	D	D	D	3	4	0.3	0.0	185	4.9	NA	NA
Glynn	262	5,031	645.8	235.5	141	746	84.3	17.9	6,504	277.6	167,307	568
Gordon	66	1,518	207.6	64.2	44	D	D	D	3,456	163.1	30,366	198
Grady	33	447	43.4	12.9	25	81	10.3	2.1	1,450	47.8	7,088	45
Greene	49	568	48.2	19.2	23	105	8.9	3.3	1,533	79.5	157,679	569
Gwinnett	1,834	25,079	2,700.3	1,067.6	1,382	8,424	840.6	245.4	102,719	4,268.5	828,646	3,716
Habersham	85	1,360	108.1	48.2	47	187	13.7	4.2	2,996	109.2	40,518	223
Hall	443	9,275	1,297.8	493.4	246	1,193	123.8	32.4	15,291	699.4	294,876	1,778
Hancock	6	D	D	D	7	D	D	D	577	11.9	3,513	18
Haralson	39	699	64.2	24.3	36	D	D	D	2,113	86.9	12,206	56
Harris	24	231	16.5	6.2	14	D	D	D	2,417	105.8	55,659	225
Hart	33	567	45.5	17.4	27	115	10.4	2.2	1,878	68.4	21,119	139
Heard	5	D	D	D	8	D	D	D	760	29.4	4,103	18
Henry	396	6,223	782.2	239.1	226	996	79.7	23.1	19,883	670.8	382,464	1,905
Houston	289	5,917	553.9	220.3	143	799	63.9	18.2	9,705	292.9	195,595	1,302
Irwin	20	758	42.8	20.1	7	25	3.5	0.8	600	22.5	2,004	23
Jackson	84	1,182	80.2	34.7	74	521	48.8	19.4	5,243	222.4	199,212	1,205
Jasper	14	D	D	D	7	29	1.5	0.5	1,108	40.0	9,646	72
Jeff Davis	18	316	24.0	9.5	10	19	1.6	0.3	828	30.4	0	0
Jefferson	22	430	32.2	16.4	14	D	D	D	1,168	37.6	3,101	17
Jenkins	8	393	14.6	9.7	6	14	1.8	0.4	513	18.8	1,607	16
Johnson	11	314	21.2	8.9	8	D	D	D	540	19.9	0	0
Jones	33	D	D	D	20	71	16.5	2.2	1,900	75.9	13,429	85
Lamar	22	D	D	D	13	216	14.4	7.2	1,194	37.2	7,968	64
Lanier	10	D	D	D	4	D	D	D	571	22.5	2,195	20
Laurens	142	4,233	600.0	214.6	64	D	D	D	3,835	156.3	2,310	21
Lee	32	360	21.7	10.8	27	D	D	D	2,167	75.5	12,037	99
Liberty	76	2,026	249.2	101.0	66	D	D	D	2,841	79.3	56,067	246
Lincoln	6	D	D	D	10	D	D	D	573	21.3	320	1
Long	5	29	1.9	0.6	2	D	D	D	671	20.4	30,400	152
Lowndes	369	D	D	D	151	881	60.2	17.1	6,993	343.7	185,401	1,058
Lumpkin	52	612	54.6	23.0	28	75	7.0	1.7	2,478	94.1	4,749	32
McDuffie	51	970	76.8	24.9	28	114	16.0	3.6	1,454	49.9	6,253	33
McIntosh	14	54	3.6	1.6	13	36	2.5	0.7	883	34.1	12,523	68
Macon	18	425	33.8	11.5	8	D	D	D	770	22.6	766	4
Madison	25	D	D	D	15	D	D	D	2,166	80.5	2,051	9
Marion	7	D	D	D	2	D	D	D	390	12.9	1,524	17
Meriwether	28	948	63.0	29.4	16	39	3.6	0.7	1,548	47.1	12,771	55
Miller	12	318	24.5	10.7	6	23	2.4	0.5	326	11.4	308	2
Mitchell	25	472	36.4	14.8	29	117	8.3	2.5	1,398	47.0	2,891	17
Monroe	55	D	D	D	29	D	D	D	2,062	85.8	2,176	135
Montgomery	4	24	1.2	0.5	3	4	0.2	0.1	555	20.0	1,807	13
Morgan	34	456	33.1	13.9	32	128	13.4	3.2	1,994	91.5	32,943	144
Murray	33	469	42.8	17.3	24	103	8.5	2.9	1,860	76.1	12,342	59
Muscogee	590	14,823	1,454.8	578.6	322	2,293	223.3	62.4	12,684	414.5	91,855	501
Newton	122	2,039	189.0	77.1	79	336	25.9	7.4	9,400	274.1	111,008	653
Oconee	126	1,525	127.0	56.1	53	380	44.3	11.8	3,964	204.0	119,311	402
Oglethorpe	12	D	D	D	11	D	D	D	986	34.6	780	52
Paulding	143	2,000	184.6	69.1	124	455	38.3	11.0	12,263	424.7	175,296	1,765
Peach	42	618	39.3	16.8	30	171	14.6	4.4	1,810	61.9	10,646	64
Pickens	64	1,186	118.7	48.4	39	D	D	D	3,109	146.8	33,267	125
Pierce	22	263	13.8	6.6	24	66	4.7	1.2	1,148	42.0	6,596	52
Pike	17	D	D	D	17	D	D	D	1,490	60.6	26,000	130
Polk	52	781	57.6	25.9	40	395	40.3	10.9	2,604	84.7	15,939	105
Pulaski	20	715	60.9	27.3	8	13	1.0	0.3	715	21.6	1,675	12

Table B. States and Counties — Government Employment and Payroll, and Local Government Finances

STATE County	Government employment and payroll, 2012									Local government finances, 2012				
			March payroll (percent of total)							General revenue				
												Taxes		
											Inter-govern-mental (mil dol)		Per capita[1] (dollars)	
	Full-time equivalent employees	March payroll (dollars)	Adminis-tration, judicial, and legal	Police and corrections	Fire protection	Highways and transpor-tation	Health and welfare	Natural resources and utilities	Education and libraries	Total (mil dol)		Total (mil dol)	Total	Property
	171	172	173	174	175	176	177	178	179	180	181	182	183	184
GEORGIA—Cont'd														
Effingham	2,486	7,934,109	4.0	6.9	1.7	0.8	16.1	2.9	65.1	191.3	66.5	72.8	1,366	843
Elbert	1,023	2,910,130	6.0	7.4	1.7	2.3	20.0	5.2	54.4	74.4	24.4	21.3	1,084	728
Emanuel	1,380	4,099,290	4.7	6.6	1.2	3.3	32.4	1.6	49.5	134.4	38.4	25.2	1,102	650
Evans	411	1,161,088	7.5	7.5	1.2	2.3	0.9	7.4	72.6	32.8	16.8	10.9	1,022	548
Fannin	760	2,415,781	6.9	7.2	1.6	5.7	4.3	5.2	68.0	63.1	21.3	34.9	1,484	927
Fayette	4,677	16,227,469	6.0	9.6	6.9	2.0	0.0	3.4	70.7	331.0	78.7	204.0	1,897	1,391
Floyd	3,631	12,476,709	5.7	9.3	4.2	4.2	1.7	5.5	67.7	620.3	284.0	151.4	1,574	957
Forsyth	5,440	15,768,647	8.4	9.3	5.1	2.1	0.8	5.4	66.7	548.8	158.2	323.5	1,721	1,160
Franklin	907	2,573,274	6.9	12.5	0.0	2.6	4.2	5.9	64.4	64.2	24.6	29.2	1,334	759
Fulton	43,801	165,333,873	9.4	12.0	4.7	15.4	3.4	6.1	47.6	5,335.6	1,131.9	2,739.7	2,802	1,941
Gilmer	920	2,851,278	9.0	12.0	2.0	3.3	4.8	1.4	67.0	76.9	24.5	43.0	1,524	1,036
Glascock	129	342,830	4.9	4.2	0.0	3.5	1.7	4.2	80.7	8.3	4.5	3.0	970	705
Glynn	4,919	18,972,711	4.6	6.1	2.8	0.9	46.3	3.8	35.3	515.4	78.5	158.8	1,960	1,234
Gordon	2,032	7,129,189	6.2	7.7	4.0	2.9	0.3	5.2	71.1	172.1	62.6	78.3	1,404	810
Grady	1,132	2,874,976	6.5	7.8	2.0	1.9	2.7	6.1	69.6	66.6	29.6	25.7	1,009	623
Greene	269	680,713	19.0	33.4	1.8	17.6	6.5	14.2	0.0	58.7	12.0	38.3	2,379	1,693
Gwinnett	27,778	103,170,776	5.7	8.0	3.3	0.8	1.5	3.8	75.9	2,774.6	950.1	1,287.6	1,529	1,100
Habersham	3,305	10,231,305	4.4	3.6	1.2	1.1	19.8	2.2	67.1	181.0	64.5	53.3	1,225	714
Hall	6,523	22,620,107	6.4	9.1	7.3	1.6	4.4	4.9	65.4	563.5	217.3	266.2	1,436	890
Hancock	382	962,206	6.0	11.2	0.0	2.9	5.0	4.4	68.0	28.6	10.2	16.3	1,811	1,568
Haralson	1,277	3,955,709	6.4	9.3	4.8	2.9	2.1	6.3	67.7	88.2	38.2	39.1	1,375	852
Harris	1,034	3,285,198	4.4	8.8	0.1	2.2	4.9	3.4	74.7	80.5	24.1	43.3	1,331	974
Hart	900	2,651,269	5.4	6.4	1.0	2.6	1.4	3.1	73.5	59.3	20.8	30.8	1,208	771
Heard	504	1,507,476	3.9	8.3	9.3	3.8	1.5	6.9	62.5	42.2	12.2	27.6	2,376	938
Henry	7,960	25,579,364	7.4	7.5	4.5	1.4	1.0	5.6	71.5	718.9	328.0	305.3	1,460	969
Houston	5,500	18,181,428	5.3	9.1	2.9	2.2	2.3	3.3	73.1	461.3	189.3	203.0	1,389	803
Irwin	623	2,698,793	4.3	21.9	4.3	7.8	23.1	6.2	32.3	40.3	14.0	9.7	1,013	702
Jackson	2,530	7,918,962	6.3	11.0	0.4	1.4	3.5	4.7	71.2	198.5	64.2	107.0	1,767	1,201
Jasper	596	1,714,273	5.5	6.8	0.6	0.7	23.1	3.8	56.7	44.3	14.2	16.0	1,176	880
Jeff Davis	671	2,209,748	5.1	5.1	1.9	1.6	22.2	2.5	60.6	64.7	22.7	14.5	959	451
Jefferson	926	2,709,948	7.4	10.5	1.1	0.9	22.0	2.9	53.3	61.2	24.1	20.9	1,273	787
Jenkins	429	1,431,503	7.7	9.7	1.7	6.7	21.4	3.0	48.9	28.0	15.0	8.5	923	581
Johnson	327	789,670	7.1	8.8	1.3	2.1	5.8	3.8	70.5	20.2	10.3	7.8	788	516
Jones	1,142	2,976,385	4.8	7.6	0.3	3.1	1.4	2.8	79.5	77.2	38.1	33.3	1,165	839
Lamar	637	1,432,522	7.9	19.7	2.3	3.0	3.1	7.3	55.8	44.4	15.3	19.3	1,069	698
Lanier	309	907,306	5.1	6.3	0.4	4.9	0.6	0.8	81.4	22.8	12.3	8.7	840	599
Laurens	2,333	6,680,665	4.4	7.5	2.2	2.2	14.7	4.0	62.8	168.6	86.7	55.3	1,151	626
Lee	1,281	3,572,458	6.0	9.8	3.1	2.1	3.3	1.7	73.1	83.1	33.8	38.4	1,337	897
Liberty	2,620	8,517,567	5.5	9.7	1.7	0.8	17.6	1.9	58.9	231.2	86.6	70.0	1,070	640
Lincoln	343	943,673	7.0	8.3	0.1	4.6	4.7	4.1	70.2	24.9	9.7	11.6	1,495	1,126
Long	484	1,237,309	6.2	6.7	0.0	3.9	0.5	1.1	81.0	41.0	26.8	10.9	678	497
Lowndes	6,045	19,639,563	3.1	7.2	1.9	1.4	42.6	2.7	39.9	581.5	129.5	139.2	1,215	637
Lumpkin	914	2,710,822	6.9	9.8	4.9	4.4	1.3	4.6	66.2	65.6	21.0	35.6	1,164	771
McDuffie	1,115	3,376,988	4.5	5.8	1.9	1.8	17.5	5.3	60.7	89.6	43.8	29.4	1,357	750
McIntosh	543	1,451,916	10.8	16.2	0.3	3.5	4.5	2.5	58.6	37.8	12.8	19.7	1,422	1,061
Macon	468	1,330,912	6.2	9.8	1.1	3.9	3.2	8.0	66.6	35.4	15.4	15.7	1,103	778
Madison	1,012	3,107,942	5.4	7.1	0.0	1.8	4.3	1.4	78.7	69.1	34.5	27.9	998	714
Marion	276	887,260	6.5	7.1	0.0	4.2	3.2	3.5	74.6	27.1	16.3	8.1	933	664
Meriwether	1,203	3,245,971	5.5	9.3	0.8	1.8	22.0	3.1	55.0	84.2	30.1	25.7	1,210	867
Miller	558	1,697,352	5.4	6.0	0.2	1.6	45.2	3.2	35.5	39.7	21.9	7.8	1,308	873
Mitchell	1,021	2,901,088	6.0	10.9	2.5	2.8	3.0	6.3	61.9	77.9	28.7	31.6	1,366	899
Monroe	1,172	3,579,175	4.2	11.4	1.2	4.4	12.1	3.3	61.1	93.8	21.4	53.1	1,992	1,362
Montgomery	230	587,331	8.4	7.4	0.5	6.6	3.1	1.4	72.5	17.7	8.0	7.4	835	546
Morgan	953	3,020,860	6.6	5.9	0.9	3.0	17.7	3.8	59.5	58.7	20.9	31.5	1,763	1,132
Murray	1,247	3,919,836	4.1	6.6	2.6	2.5	1.1	1.8	77.8	92.6	46.9	36.7	932	519
Muscogee	9,038	29,241,738	4.1	12.0	4.8	2.6	7.5	7.2	60.0	741.6	293.1	273.0	1,376	1,010
Newton	4,446	13,949,576	4.8	7.6	3.4	1.7	14.6	4.6	61.7	372.2	178.8	121.8	1,200	823
Oconee	1,252	3,915,501	7.1	6.7	0.4	2.2	1.3	3.9	74.9	100.2	32.7	57.1	1,698	1,106
Oglethorpe	532	1,614,557	5.6	5.6	0.8	1.8	3.5	1.4	81.2	31.8	13.7	15.1	1,034	808
Paulding	5,393	14,332,833	3.2	7.3	2.8	1.5	0.5	2.6	80.1	356.7	171.7	150.3	1,038	665
Peach	1,087	3,443,843	6.7	12.0	3.0	1.1	15.5	2.4	56.5	102.9	28.0	38.7	1,399	851
Pickens	1,155	3,419,594	7.3	9.4	3.0	2.8	3.9	5.3	64.6	83.1	24.1	47.4	1,618	1,120
Pierce	624	2,237,998	1.9	4.1	0.0	2.0	2.7	2.2	84.6	46.0	24.2	18.2	963	622
Pike	638	1,686,429	6.9	9.0	0.0	3.2	0.0	2.0	78.9	39.8	18.6	17.9	1,005	826
Polk	1,548	4,904,910	5.6	10.2	2.6	2.4	1.4	4.0	66.8	116.2	53.1	48.3	1,172	717
Pulaski	358	909,842	9.2	11.0	3.6	4.3	1.3	4.5	64.6	27.3	12.1	11.6	990	649

1. Based on the resident population estimated as of July 1 of the year shown.

Table B. States and Counties — Local Government Finances, Government Employment, and Income Taxes

STATE County	Local government finances, 2012 (cont.) Direct general expenditure — Total (mil dol)	Per capita[1] (dollars)	Percent of total for: Education	Health and hospitals	Police protection	Public welfare	Highways	Debt outstanding Total (mil dol)	Per capita[1] (dollars)	Government employment, 2017 Federal civilian	Federal military	State and local	Individual income tax returns, 2016 Number of returns	Mean adjusted gross income	Mean income tax
	185	186	187	188	189	190	191	192	193	194	195	196	197	198	199
GEORGIA—Cont'd															
Effingham	215.1	4,037	47.5	28.2	3.7	0.3	2.7	102.6	1,925	69	163	2,466	25,220	55,234	5,185
Elbert	78.1	3,967	39.3	26.1	4.2	0.7	4.5	17.7	901	120	52	1,158	7,970	40,072	3,428
Emanuel	128.4	5,609	29.9	50.2	2.4	0.2	2.9	34.5	1,507	64	59	2,001	8,770	36,683	2,862
Evans	39.2	3,664	67.4	1.1	4.4	0.0	3.4	8.1	760	42	28	609	4,180	41,489	3,873
Fannin	65.9	2,803	54.6	3.5	4.0	0.5	11.3	12.3	524	51	69	926	10,490	47,493	5,268
Fayette	360.7	3,354	57.2	1.1	6.8	0.2	4.4	279.1	2,596	482	349	4,632	53,290	87,831	12,786
Floyd	658.4	6,846	27.4	47.2	2.2	0.1	2.6	238.0	2,474	202	260	5,479	39,590	50,508	5,213
Forsyth	529.3	2,816	59.8	0.4	6.1	0.5	4.9	349.8	1,861	221	624	7,561	96,780	97,503	14,429
Franklin	58.5	2,670	56.1	3.0	9.3	0.4	6.3	16.0	730	48	61	1,082	9,080	42,626	3,757
Fulton	4,905.9	5,017	36.2	1.9	6.5	2.3	2.4	20,181.5	20,640	25,200	2,975	79,695	461,920	100,953	18,593
Gilmer	71.0	2,520	60.5	0.4	6.0	0.2	2.7	75.3	2,672	83	84	1,173	12,400	47,161	4,970
Glascock	8.8	2,789	73.4	1.9	3.4	1.5	6.9	0.4	113	2	8	190	1,040	44,621	3,718
Glynn	522.7	6,452	28.7	45.8	4.4	0.1	1.6	353.6	4,364	1,853	303	5,246	36,690	57,868	7,230
Gordon	172.7	3,096	59.5	1.2	6.0	0.4	3.7	114.7	2,057	89	155	2,621	22,570	46,170	4,330
Grady	73.3	2,881	53.7	1.8	4.8	0.0	6.5	41.6	1,635	78	68	1,159	9,760	39,221	3,311
Greene	66.3	4,122	48.1	0.3	8.8	1.2	6.7	33.3	2,068	44	47	778	7,660	87,043	13,781
Gwinnett	2,810.6	3,338	58.1	1.5	5.7	0.1	4.5	3,709.8	4,406	2,586	2,612	34,880	409,010	57,275	6,625
Habersham	168.2	3,865	41.0	30.6	3.5	0.3	3.1	147.2	3,382	99	115	2,863	17,730	47,921	4,340
Hall	566.0	3,053	55.8	6.1	4.5	0.8	2.5	1,522.9	8,213	474	540	10,413	86,160	57,746	6,874
Hancock	25.7	2,852	59.1	3.1	5.4	1.7	5.0	11.1	1,235	16	20	776	3,110	37,125	3,017
Haralson	90.4	3,182	64.8	1.4	5.5	0.3	2.9	42.6	1,502	47	79	1,505	11,420	47,838	4,339
Harris	77.2	2,371	65.4	3.4	5.0	0.0	4.2	45.3	1,392	58	92	1,218	14,380	70,365	8,364
Hart	58.4	2,289	53.1	3.2	5.6	0.4	4.4	16.0	628	86	69	1,086	10,290	45,938	4,956
Heard	36.5	3,133	56.5	4.4	5.1	2.9	4.3	21.9	1,878	16	32	604	4,210	44,644	4,080
Henry	565.4	2,705	60.8	0.4	5.5	0.9	6.1	704.9	3,372	944	619	8,518	100,770	52,883	5,427
Houston	446.8	3,057	57.5	4.7	6.4	0.0	5.5	209.8	1,435	14,869	3,682	9,655	68,000	53,079	5,261
Irwin	42.7	4,450	40.9	35.7	4.1	0.2	7.1	10.1	1,048	23	23	624	3,530	41,235	4,159
Jackson	211.8	3,497	53.3	2.4	5.8	0.3	7.5	505.9	8,352	159	183	2,907	28,960	55,029	5,685
Jasper	43.8	3,215	45.0	24.5	4.1	0.6	6.1	15.0	1,099	19	38	668	5,600	47,528	4,451
Jeff Davis	60.0	3,960	38.1	36.0	3.5	0.2	7.6	20.3	1,337	30	41	810	5,400	36,705	2,949
Jefferson	64.9	3,950	43.6	21.7	4.9	1.0	3.6	24.3	1,480	58	42	965	6,880	36,709	2,911
Jenkins	26.9	2,917	51.4	4.2	4.4	0.8	9.3	4.9	533	20	21	478	2,980	34,873	2,609
Johnson	19.4	1,960	61.3	3.0	5.3	0.3	6.1	0.9	88	18	22	610	2,900	36,659	2,694
Jones	72.0	2,520	65.4	0.6	5.4	0.6	6.1	11.5	403	36	77	1,122	11,830	51,095	4,683
Lamar	47.0	2,605	52.2	0.8	7.4	0.7	3.3	56.0	3,100	39	48	1,091	7,210	42,736	3,635
Lanier	22.1	2,125	69.1	0.5	7.1	0.4	6.2	11.4	1,096	17	28	649	3,310	36,404	2,475
Laurens	182.6	3,801	47.1	15.1	4.8	0.3	4.0	54.7	1,138	1,546	128	2,745	19,730	44,654	4,274
Lee	84.5	2,939	66.3	3.3	5.2	0.0	3.2	70.7	2,459	45	79	1,479	13,330	59,049	6,171
Liberty	250.0	3,818	53.4	19.3	4.8	0.0	2.3	82.6	1,262	3,730	15,465	3,180	26,360	37,765	2,667
Lincoln	23.8	3,082	54.0	3.7	3.6	2.7	6.6	35.4	4,577	14	21	415	3,240	47,310	4,517
Long	36.7	2,284	68.5	0.5	5.4	1.5	8.2	6.7	417	14	51	715	5,450	38,070	2,330
Lowndes	649.1	5,667	24.9	53.1	3.9	0.7	2.3	369.8	3,228	1,134	4,609	10,165	45,230	46,198	5,011
Lumpkin	67.2	2,197	60.3	1.9	7.6	0.1	3.6	75.2	2,455	74	131	2,870	12,270	50,760	5,176
McDuffie	90.0	4,153	49.0	21.0	4.1	1.3	2.2	31.7	1,464	29	229	1,218	9,090	42,906	3,680
McIntosh	35.7	2,581	47.5	2.9	9.5	0.0	4.1	3.4	246	41	42	593	4,870	43,734	4,238
Macon	36.4	2,549	51.7	1.7	6.1	0.5	5.1	4.5	314	27	31	838	4,400	34,815	2,834
Madison	72.1	2,583	67.3	2.6	3.1	0.5	4.4	51.6	1,850	43	80	1,166	12,020	44,261	3,754
Marion	31.7	3,643	77.5	1.8	2.4	2.2	1.7	21.1	2,425	16	23	349	2,700	40,155	3,716
Meriwether	85.0	3,997	44.3	21.9	5.5	0.2	2.8	60.8	2,859	49	57	1,276	8,720	41,964	3,701
Miller	38.7	6,487	24.8	50.2	3.2	0.1	3.5	25.7	4,303	18	16	833	2,200	38,552	3,800
Mitchell	87.6	3,783	42.9	4.0	5.8	0.0	7.0	58.1	2,509	79	55	1,390	8,200	37,589	2,966
Monroe	92.6	3,477	43.8	14.7	6.5	0.1	5.1	33.5	1,257	36	72	2,480	11,450	62,412	7,675
Montgomery	17.6	1,979	59.5	3.0	4.8	1.0	4.3	1.9	217	14	23	365	3,120	43,027	3,991
Morgan	72.8	4,070	44.7	20.5	4.7	0.9	5.4	29.9	1,674	38	50	1,113	8,440	59,403	7,080
Murray	90.2	2,289	67.5	2.4	4.0	0.9	5.5	39.4	1,001	97	109	1,252	15,140	40,116	3,219
Muscogee	832.5	4,196	45.9	7.7	5.9	2.3	4.4	677.3	3,413	6,365	4,744	13,116	84,120	49,818	5,609
Newton	383.8	3,782	52.5	20.5	4.2	0.0	2.1	387.3	3,816	237	292	4,309	46,130	44,500	3,994
Oconee	98.9	2,943	63.3	1.2	4.1	0.6	5.9	108.6	3,230	60	104	1,462	16,790	95,551	14,503
Oglethorpe	32.9	2,254	68.3	2.8	3.0	1.0	3.7	24.2	1,653	15	40	564	5,950	45,204	3,948
Paulding	341.1	2,355	68.6	0.9	5.0	0.1	7.3	260.6	1,800	133	468	4,997	67,220	55,088	5,301
Peach	89.7	3,247	45.2	13.6	6.8	0.2	2.5	47.6	1,722	112	77	2,023	11,270	47,940	4,571
Pickens	82.3	2,812	55.3	3.3	6.4	0.2	4.6	22.2	758	57	86	1,232	14,480	59,979	6,769
Pierce	44.8	2,375	64.8	2.3	3.1	0.8	6.5	18.5	982	53	53	713	7,590	47,050	4,451
Pike	37.6	2,114	69.3	2.4	7.0	0.2	3.7	11.8	662	31	49	720	7,640	56,477	5,587
Polk	111.7	2,712	59.9	1.2	7.3	0.3	4.7	44.4	1,079	71	114	1,561	16,320	41,632	3,373
Pulaski	35.2	3,007	42.6	2.6	5.9	0.2	5.4	5.9	508	15	27	638	3,550	43,435	4,228

1. Based on the resident population estimated as of July 1 of the year shown.

Table B. States and Counties — Land Area and Population

State / county code	CBSA code[1]	County code[2]	STATE County	Land area[3] (sq. mi)	Population, 2018			Population and population characteristics, 2018										
								Race alone or in combination, not Hispanic or Latino (percent)					Age (percent)					
					Total persons 2018	Rank	Per square mile	White	Black	American Indian, Alaska Native	Asian and Pacific Islancer	Percent Hispanic or Latino[4]	Under 5 years	5 to 17 years	18 to 24 years	25 to 34 years	35 to 44 years	45 to 54 years
				1	2	3	4	5	6	7	8	9	10	11	12	13	14	15
			GEORGIA—Cont'd															
13237		6	Putnam	344.7	21,809	1,732	63.3	66.5	26.8	0.5	1.0	6.4	5.0	14.9	6.8	10.7	10.0	12.6
13239	21,640	9	Quitman	151.2	2,279	3,022	15.1	50.5	47.7	0.7	0.7	1.7	5.2	12.6	5.5	8.9	7.8	11.8
13241		7	Rabun	370.1	16,867	1,983	45.6	88.9	1.9	1.1	1.4	8.2	4.3	12.7	6.8	10.2	10.0	12.6
13243		6	Randolph	428.2	6,833	2,690	16.0	36.0	61.5	0.3	0.6	2.3	5.6	14.6	9.0	10.6	9.8	10.8
13245	12,260	2	Richmond	324.3	201,554	334	621.5	36.3	57.6	0.9	2.9	5.0	6.7	16.1	11.3	16.6	11.6	11.1
13247	12,060	1	Rockdale	129.8	90,594	649	698.0	31.7	56.8	0.7	2.5	10.4	5.8	18.8	9.0	11.9	12.0	14.2
13249	11,140	8	Schley	166.9	5,236	2,815	31.4	73.0	20.3	0.5	1.1	6.2	5.1	19.9	7.6	10.3	11.7	16.0
13251		6	Screven	645.8	13,938	2,166	21.6	55.7	41.5	0.6	1.0	2.3	6.0	15.1	7.7	13.0	11.1	13.0
13253		6	Seminole	237.5	8,315	2,559	35.0	63.1	33.1	0.7	1.1	3.5	5.3	15.5	7.8	10.3	10.3	12.5
13255	12,060	1	Spalding	196.0	66,100	808	337.2	59.6	35.2	0.8	1.5	4.7	6.3	17.2	8.0	13.7	11.7	12.5
13257	45,740	7	Stephens	179.2	26,035	1,566	145.3	84.3	12.4	0.7	1.3	3.6	6.1	16.1	10.4	11.4	10.7	12.3
13259		8	Stewart	458.7	6,199	2,734	13.5	24.6	40.8	1.1	2.9	31.5	3.3	8.8	13.8	23.0	14.0	11.0
13261	11,140	6	Sumter	482.9	29,733	1,439	61.6	40.0	53.0	0.6	1.7	5.7	6.1	16.6	14.2	11.9	10.7	11.9
13263		8	Talbot	391.4	6,272	2,727	16.0	42.1	54.9	0.9	0.6	2.8	4.1	12.1	6.5	10.6	9.8	13.7
13265		8	Taliaferro	194.6	1,608	3,074	8.3	40.5	54.9	0.6	1.7	4.4	4.1	12.8	6.5	10.8	10.9	12.9
13267		6	Tattnall	480.8	25,391	1,589	52.8	58.6	29.5	0.5	0.8	11.6	5.0	15.2	9.4	16.2	14.0	13.8
13269		8	Taylor	376.7	8,039	2,587	21.3	58.0	38.9	0.5	1.1	2.7	5.0	15.3	7.3	11.7	11.1	14.0
13271		7	Telfair	437.3	15,876	2,047	36.3	50.0	35.0	0.4	0.9	14.7	3.9	12.0	7.7	15.5	15.5	13.9
13273	10,500	3	Terrell	335.7	8,611	2,539	25.7	36.5	60.7	0.6	0.7	2.7	5.9	17.2	7.9	12.7	10.4	11.8
13275	45,620	4	Thomas	544.6	44,448	1,088	81.6	58.7	36.5	0.8	1.3	3.9	6.3	17.4	8.0	11.9	11.6	13.0
13277	45,700	5	Tift	260.9	40,571	1,165	155.5	56.4	30.5	0.5	1.8	12.0	6.9	17.8	10.9	13.5	12.1	12.0
13279	47,080	7	Toombs	364.0	26,887	1,530	73.9	61.1	26.8	0.5	1.1	11.9	7.1	19.3	8.5	12.6	11.7	12.2
13281		9	Towns	166.5	11,852	2,305	71.2	94.8	1.6	0.7	0.9	2.9	3.6	9.1	13.6	7.4	7.1	10.0
13283		7	Treutlen	199.4	6,809	2,691	34.1	64.9	32.1	0.6	0.5	3.0	5.9	16.8	9.2	12.9	12.0	11.7
13285	29,300	4	Troup	414.0	70,034	772	169.2	57.4	37.4	0.6	2.5	3.7	6.4	17.8	9.6	13.9	12.1	12.8
13287		6	Turner	285.4	7,912	2,601	27.7	54.0	40.6	0.6	1.2	4.7	7.1	17.0	9.2	12.7	10.8	11.5
13289	31,420	3	Twiggs	359.3	8,188	2,580	22.8	56.8	40.6	0.8	0.6	2.5	5.2	14.1	6.2	11.6	10.2	13.2
13291		9	Union	322.1	24,001	1,642	74.5	94.7	1.1	1.0	0.9	3.4	3.7	12.1	6.0	8.2	8.6	11.1
13293	45,580	6	Upson	323.5	26,215	1,558	81.0	68.5	28.9	0.7	1.0	2.3	6.2	16.0	8.2	12.1	11.4	13.2
13295	16,860	2	Walker	446.4	69,410	776	155.5	92.2	5.3	0.8	0.9	2.3	5.6	16.1	7.7	12.1	12.5	13.4
13297	12,060	1	Walton	326.8	93,503	633	286.1	75.3	18.9	0.6	2.1	4.7	6.1	18.6	8.4	12.3	12.4	14.3
13299	48,180	5	Ware	899.2	35,680	1,284	39.7	64.4	30.7	0.8	1.2	4.5	6.8	17.2	8.4	13.6	11.6	12.3
13301		8	Warren	284.4	5,251	2,811	18.5	38.7	59.2	0.7	0.8	1.6	5.1	15.2	7.0	11.1	9.9	13.1
13303		7	Washington	678.5	20,386	1,801	30.0	43.4	53.9	0.3	0.8	2.6	5.7	15.9	8.4	13.4	11.9	13.1
13305	27,700	6	Wayne	641.9	29,808	1,436	46.4	72.8	20.7	0.8	1.0	6.5	6.5	17.9	7.7	13.4	12.8	13.2
13307		8	Webster	209.4	2,611	2,995	12.5	53.1	42.2	0.6	0.7	4.7	4.6	14.8	8.0	9.3	9.3	15.4
13309		9	Wheeler	295.5	7,879	2,604	26.7	57.1	37.5	0.4	0.6	5.6	4.5	12.5	9.9	17.8	14.8	14.5
13311		6	White	240.7	29,970	1,433	124.5	93.5	2.6	1.2	0.9	3.3	4.7	15.1	8.9	10.4	10.4	12.9
13313	19,140	3	Whitfield	290.4	104,062	580	358.3	58.8	4.2	0.6	1.7	35.9	6.5	19.3	9.3	13.4	12.6	13.4
13315		8	Wilcox	377.8	8,812	2,513	23.3	59.6	35.2	0.9	1.0	4.8	5.5	13.5	8.8	15.0	13.8	13.5
13317		6	Wilkes	469.5	9,876	2,437	21.0	52.9	42.3	0.5	1.0	5.3	5.2	16.0	7.4	10.6	9.9	12.7
13319		8	Wilkinson	449.2	9,036	2,496	20.1	58.1	39.2	0.7	0.8	2.7	5.6	17.1	7.7	11.0	10.8	12.7
13321	10,500	3	Worth	570.7	20,299	1,806	35.6	68.7	28.6	0.6	0.9	2.3	5.8	16.5	7.7	12.3	10.7	13.2
15000		0	HAWAII	6,422.4	1,420,491	X	221.2	36.2	3.0	1.7	75.3	10.7	6.2	15.2	8.5	14.3	12.7	12.0
15001	25,900	5	Hawaii	4,028.5	200,983	335	49.9	48.1	1.7	2.4	68.0	13.0	5.9	15.8	7.0	11.9	11.9	11.6
15003	46,520	2	Honolulu	600.6	980,080	48	1,631.8	31.8	3.7	1.5	78.6	10.0	6.3	14.9	9.3	15.2	12.8	11.9
15005	27,980	3	Kalawao	12.0	88	3,142	7.3	39.8	5.7	4.5	64.8	1.1	0.0	0.0	0.0	8.0	8.0	18.2
15007	28,180	5	Kauai	619.9	72,133	752	116.4	44.6	1.4	1.8	68.3	11.2	6.1	15.8	6.7	12.1	12.6	12.3
15009	27,980	3	Maui	1,161.5	167,207	391	144.0	43.9	1.4	1.7	67.7	11.5	5.9	15.9	6.8	12.7	13.4	13.0
16000		0	IDAHO	82,645.1	1,754,208	X	21.2	83.7	1.2	1.9	2.6	12.7	6.6	18.8	9.3	13.2	12.5	11.4
16001	14,260	2	Ada	1,052.0	469,966	148	446.7	86.9	1.9	1.1	4.5	8.3	5.8	18.0	8.6	14.3	14.1	12.7
16003		9	Adams	1,362.8	4,250	2,882	3.1	93.2	0.8	2.3	1.6	4.2	4.0	13.8	4.6	8.4	9.0	10.2
16005	38,540	3	Bannock	1,112.5	87,138	663	78.3	85.5	1.4	3.6	2.8	8.8	7.1	19.1	10.3	14.8	12.7	10.1
16007		9	Bear Lake	975.7	6,050	2,749	6.2	94.3	0.6	1.0	0.9	4.2	6.7	20.0	7.1	10.6	11.1	10.1
16009		6	Benewah	776.9	9,226	2,485	11.9	88.1	0.9	9.9	1.1	3.7	5.7	16.9	6.3	9.7	10.2	12.1
16011	13,940	4	Bingham	2,093.8	46,236	1,046	22.1	74.8	0.6	6.2	1.7	18.1	7.5	23.3	8.4	12.1	12.4	10.2
16013	25,200	7	Blaine	2,637.7	22,601	1,701	8.6	75.5	0.8	0.6	1.7	22.5	4.8	17.3	6.9	10.3	12.4	13.5
16015	14,260	2	Boise	1,899.6	7,634	2,622	4.0	92.6	0.9	2.4	1.5	4.9	3.6	13.3	5.1	8.0	10.0	13.3
16017	41,760	6	Bonner	1,733.2	44,727	1,084	25.8	94.9	0.5	2.1	1.5	3.2	5.1	14.6	6.0	9.6	11.0	11.8
16019	26,820	3	Bonneville	1,866.0	116,854	533	62.6	84.4	1.0	1.3	1.9	13.3	8.4	22.4	8.4	13.7	13.0	10.2
16021		7	Boundary	1,268.7	11,948	2,295	9.4	91.8	0.8	2.7	1.5	5.2	5.9	17.2	7.2	8.9	11.0	12.1
16023	26,820	3	Butte	2,236.5	2,611	2,995	1.2	93.5	0.8	2.7	0.6	4.5	5.5	18.5	7.1	8.7	10.4	10.0
16025	25,200	9	Camas	1,074.2	1,127	3,103	1.0	91.3	1.4	3.4	0.7	6.5	4.9	18.5	5.0	7.5	13.7	11.4
16027	14,260	2	Canyon	587.0	223,499	304	380.7	72.0	0.9	1.5	2.1	25.6	7.5	21.0	9.4	13.5	12.7	11.4

1. CBSA = Core Based Statistical Area. See Appendix A for explanation. See Appendix B for list of metropolitan areas with component counties. 2. County type code from the Economic Research Service of USDA Rural-Urban Continuum Codes. See Appendix A for definition. 3. Dry land or land partially or temporarily covered by water. 4. May be of any race.

Table B. States and Counties — Population and Households

STATE County	Population, 2018 (cont.) — Age (percent) (cont.) 55 to 64 years	65 to 74 years	75 years and over	Percent female	Population change, 2000-2018 — Total persons 2000	Total persons 2010	Percent change 2000-2010	2010-2018	Components of change, 2010-2018 Births	Deaths	Net Migration	Households, 2013-2017 Number	Persons per household	Family households	Female family householder[1]	One person
	16	17	18	19	20	21	22	23	24	25	26	27	28	29	30	31
GEORGIA—Cont'd																
Putnam	15.9	14.9	9.2	51.2	18,812	21,218	12.8	2.8	1,919	1,940	615	8,662	2.45	72.8	12.8	20.6
Quitman	17.1	18.0	13.2	52.2	2,598	2,511	-3.3	-9.2	204	232	-208	978	2.19	58.4	19.2	38.3
Rabun	15.8	16.4	11.2	50.8	15,050	16,276	8.1	3.6	1,233	1,657	1,025	6,506	2.45	64.1	9.6	31.0
Randolph	15.7	12.9	11.0	53.8	7,791	7,719	-0.9	-11.5	683	736	-854	2,864	2.45	62.7	27.3	30.3
Richmond	12.5	8.6	5.5	51.6	199,775	200,569	0.4	0.5	24,260	16,022	-7,181	72,361	2.66	60.0	20.9	34.2
Rockdale	13.8	9.2	5.3	53.0	70,111	85,176	21.5	6.4	8,193	5,337	2,575	29,937	2.93	73.2	18.6	22.4
Schley	12.2	9.9	7.2	52.6	3,766	5,010	33.0	4.5	419	292	98	1,925	2.68	76.2	18.4	23.2
Screven	15.4	11.5	7.3	50.5	15,374	14,592	-5.1	-4.5	1,505	1,421	-747	5,268	2.59	65.6	16.4	31.1
Seminole	15.2	13.0	10.0	52.1	9,369	8,729	-6.8	-4.7	817	954	-279	3,353	2.52	69.4	19.1	27.5
Spalding	12.8	10.7	7.1	52.0	58,417	64,098	9.7	3.1	6,882	6,048	1,179	23,475	2.68	68.7	19.8	26.4
Stephens	13.6	11.7	7.7	52.0	25,435	26,173	2.9	-0.5	2,514	2,833	190	9,427	2.64	68.9	9.6	29.6
Stewart	10.5	8.6	7.0	34.0	5,252	6,058	15.3	2.3	376	544	264	1,780	2.23	59.8	26.6	37.1
Sumter	12.0	10.2	6.6	53.0	33,200	32,817	-1.2	-9.4	3,271	2,901	-3,504	11,871	2.41	65.3	19.7	30.5
Talbot	19.0	15.0	9.4	52.1	6,498	6,874	5.8	-8.8	453	627	-431	2,801	2.29	66.8	16.7	30.3
Taliaferro	15.8	14.9	11.4	50.5	2,077	1,717	-17.3	-6.3	121	184	-48	710	2.59	62.1	21.4	30.0
Tattnall	12.0	8.6	5.7	42.3	22,305	25,517	14.4	-0.5	2,377	1,949	-566	8,044	2.38	71.7	16.2	25.4
Taylor	15.4	11.8	8.5	52.2	8,815	8,910	1.1	-9.8	710	814	-793	3,554	2.27	68.3	20.7	29.2
Telfair	13.4	10.0	8.1	41.5	11,794	16,490	39.8	-3.7	1,097	1,209	-522	5,167	2.52	65.7	15.7	31.4
Terrell	14.3	11.4	8.5	52.1	10,970	9,507	-13.3	-9.4	962	828	-1,041	3,290	2.63	67.8	26.4	28.5
Thomas	13.6	10.6	7.7	52.6	42,737	44,724	4.6	-0.6	4,756	4,165	-844	17,254	2.55	69.2	18.7	25.9
Tift	11.9	8.5	6.3	51.6	38,407	40,132	4.5	1.1	4,660	3,257	-1,025	14,999	2.57	71.2	20.5	24.2
Toombs	12.2	9.5	6.9	52.5	26,067	27,170	4.2	-1.0	3,246	2,542	-976	10,521	2.54	65.9	15.7	29.6
Towns	14.6	18.8	15.8	52.3	9,319	10,477	12.4	13.1	690	1,388	2,036	4,588	2.25	66.2	6.3	29.9
Treutlen	13.1	10.6	7.9	50.3	6,854	6,881	0.4	-1.0	632	574	-133	2,633	2.39	67.8	16.7	30.3
Troup	12.5	8.8	6.0	51.8	58,779	67,039	14.1	4.5	7,445	5,605	1,200	24,679	2.75	67.8	19.5	29.0
Turner	11.9	11.3	8.6	51.4	9,504	8,930	-6.0	-11.4	913	913	-1,051	3,103	2.47	73.3	16.1	22.7
Twiggs	16.8	14.0	8.8	50.9	10,590	9,022	-14.8	-9.2	750	880	-716	2,943	2.80	68.1	17.9	30.2
Union	17.2	19.4	13.6	51.6	17,289	21,356	23.5	12.4	1,356	2,491	3,760	8,788	2.47	70.6	10.4	27.4
Upson	14.5	10.7	7.8	52.5	27,597	27,151	-1.6	-3.4	2,674	2,964	-645	10,263	2.50	60.6	12.2	34.4
Walker	14.0	10.6	8.0	50.8	61,053	68,749	12.6	1.0	6,099	6,172	779	25,564	2.63	71.0	13.1	24.4
Walton	12.5	9.2	6.3	51.3	60,687	83,767	38.0	11.6	8,818	6,398	7,331	30,488	2.88	78.1	13.8	18.3
Ware	12.7	9.8	7.5	50.0	35,483	36,305	2.3	-1.7	4,021	3,693	-953	13,903	2.39	68.3	16.3	28.6
Warren	15.9	12.6	10.0	52.6	6,336	5,834	-7.9	-10.0	486	634	-437	2,274	2.34	61.0	19.3	37.6
Washington	14.3	10.0	7.4	49.0	21,176	21,183	0.0	-3.8	1,908	1,834	-894	7,384	2.54	70.7	22.7	26.4
Wayne	12.7	9.6	6.2	48.7	26,565	30,099	13.3	-1.0	3,275	2,711	-873	10,362	2.67	68.9	11.9	26.0
Webster	14.8	13.0	10.6	50.1	2,390	2,801	17.2	-6.8	180	159	-215	1,091	2.40	67.4	11.9	27.5
Wheeler	11.3	8.5	6.1	35.3	6,179	7,421	20.1	6.2	515	487	367	1,972	3.10	67.7	12.5	30.9
White	14.7	13.5	9.5	51.2	19,944	27,137	36.1	10.4	2,175	2,204	2,857	11,250	2.50	71.0	8.9	26.0
Whitfield	11.5	8.1	6.0	50.2	83,525	102,593	22.8	1.4	11,528	6,586	-3,429	35,384	2.90	72.0	12.1	22.8
Wilcox	11.9	9.9	8.1	40.3	8,577	9,256	7.9	-4.8	756	884	-323	2,676	2.55	64.5	13.9	33.0
Wilkes	15.2	12.4	10.8	52.0	10,687	10,593	-0.9	-6.8	873	1,128	-484	3,971	2.47	61.8	15.1	35.4
Wilkinson	15.7	10.5	8.9	52.2	10,220	9,568	-6.4	-5.6	893	972	-456	3,288	2.75	67.4	16.6	30.6
Worth	14.7	11.4	7.7	52.0	21,967	21,675	-1.3	-6.3	2,017	1,827	-1,580	7,899	2.61	73.4	19.5	23.0
HAWAII	12.7	10.5	7.9	49.9	1,211,537	1,360,307	12.3	4.4	152,292	90,763	-549	455,502	3.02	69.8	12.1	23.9
Hawaii	14.9	13.3	7.6	50.4	148,677	185,076	24.5	8.6	19,714	13,721	9,992	67,054	2.88	67.0	12.5	26.0
Honolulu	11.9	9.6	8.1	49.7	876,156	953,206	8.8	2.8	109,256	62,703	-19,098	311,451	3.06	70.6	12.3	23.5
Kalawao	23.9	14.8	27.3	53.4	147	90	-38.8	-2.2	0	2	0	53	1.40	28.3	0.0	66.0
Kauai	14.2	12.3	7.9	50.6	58,463	67,095	14.8	7.5	7,156	4,777	2,717	22,563	3.12	69.7	9.6	23.3
Maui	14.2	11.3	7.0	50.3	128,094	154,840	20.9	8.0	16,166	9,560	5,840	54,381	2.97	68.5	11.9	23.8
IDAHO	12.2	9.6	6.3	49.9	1,293,953	1,567,657	21.2	11.9	186,921	103,264	102,127	609,124	2.67	68.0	9.1	26.1
Ada	12.0	8.9	5.5	49.9	300,904	392,371	30.4	19.8	41,731	22,603	58,094	164,389	2.60	63.8	8.2	29.5
Adams	21.2	18.1	10.6	48.0	3,476	3,978	14.4	6.8	241	279	305	1,736	2.23	65.1	10.3	32.5
Bannock	11.5	8.7	5.5	50.3	75,565	82,842	9.6	5.2	10,543	5,588	-647	30,790	2.66	66.5	10.6	26.2
Bear Lake	13.7	12.1	8.6	50.1	6,411	5,986	-6.6	1.1	675	519	-94	2,313	2.55	75.0	8.3	22.4
Benewah	16.6	13.8	8.6	48.9	9,171	9,283	1.2	-0.6	888	981	38	3,508	2.56	66.4	8.9	28.0
Bingham	11.8	8.4	5.9	50.2	41,735	45,605	9.3	1.4	5,879	2,863	-2,419	14,903	3.03	74.8	10.0	22.2
Blaine	15.2	12.5	7.2	49.3	18,991	21,377	12.6	5.7	1,796	859	278	8,273	2.56	62.4	9.2	32.7
Boise	21.5	17.2	7.9	47.9	6,670	7,028	5.4	8.6	357	424	660	3,004	2.30	69.2	6.0	26.0
Bonner	17.4	15.5	9.0	50.1	36,835	40,877	11.0	9.4	3,353	3,442	3,917	17,563	2.36	65.8	7.5	29.0
Bonneville	10.7	7.9	5.4	50.0	82,522	104,294	26.4	12.0	15,879	6,625	3,354	38,400	2.83	72.2	10.0	23.5
Boundary	15.2	14.0	8.5	49.7	9,871	10,972	11.2	8.9	1,095	908	781	4,490	2.50	60.7	5.6	33.6
Butte	16.4	13.3	10.1	49.5	2,899	2,893	-0.2	-9.7	248	205	-333	1,049	2.45	67.9	9.3	29.2
Camas	16.8	14.8	7.6	49.4	991	1,117	12.7	0.9	87	50	-31	370	2.39	59.5	4.6	37.3
Canyon	10.7	8.4	5.3	50.5	131,441	188,922	43.7	18.3	25,805	11,417	20,108	69,303	2.94	69.9	11.1	24.9

1. No spouse present.

Table B. States and Counties — **Population, Vital Statistics, Health, and Crime**

STATE County	Persons in group quarters, 2018	Daytime Population, 2013-2017		Births, 2018		Deaths, 2018		Persons under 65 with no health insurance, 2016		Medicare, 2018			Serious crimes known to police[2], 2016 Total	
		Number	Employment/ residence ratio	Total	Rate[1]	Number	Rate[1]	Number	Percent	Total beneficiaries	Enrolled in Original Medicare	Enrolled in Medicare Advantage	Number	Rate[3]
	32	33	34	35	36	37	38	39	40	41	42	43	44	45

STATE County	32	33	34	35	36	37	38	39	40	41	42	43	44	45
GEORGIA—Cont'd														
Putnam	159	19,791	0.82	210	9.6	247	11.3	2,895	17.7	5,601	3,699	1,902	591	2,767
Quitman	0	1,897	0.66	24	10.5	27	11.8	274	16.8	732	460	272	41	1,813
Rabun	490	16,806	1.07	147	8.7	217	12.9	2,628	22.0	5,012	3,730	1,282	364	2,238
Randolph	310	6,991	0.92	72	10.5	77	11.3	758	14.6	1,640	965	675	120	1,691
Richmond	11,893	243,493	1.51	2,863	14.2	2,024	10.0	23,417	14.3	35,978	21,399	14,579	9,891	4,902
Rockdale	757	91,218	1.07	976	10.8	713	7.9	11,717	15.4	15,269	8,256	7,013	2,614	2,922
Schley	0	4,548	0.68	51	9.7	41	7.8	689	16.1	812	491	321	53	1,020
Screven	441	12,328	0.69	169	12.1	170	12.2	1,871	16.8	3,247	2,001	1,246	280	2,111
Seminole	96	8,357	0.93	92	11.1	101	12.1	942	14.5	2,285	1,583	702	162	1,879
Spalding	1,357	61,268	0.88	808	12.2	803	12.1	8,322	15.9	14,536	8,442	6,094	2,992	4,677
Stephens	775	25,830	1.02	287	11.0	355	13.6	3,106	15.4	6,572	4,311	2,261	837	3,289
Stewart	1,552	5,575	0.81	42	6.8	64	10.3	604	18.2	1,035	510	525	NA	NA
Sumter	1,627	31,889	1.11	378	12.7	365	12.3	3,799	16.0	6,152	3,542	2,610	1,601	5,271
Talbot	0	4,584	0.28	51	8.1	82	13.1	744	15.3	1,598	870	728	84	1,347
Taliaferro	7	1,479	0.42	12	7.5	21	13.1	231	19.2	472	251	221	NA	NA
Tattnall	4,677	24,256	0.84	270	10.6	256	10.1	3,225	18.6	4,014	2,444	1,570	417	1,658
Taylor	152	7,700	0.81	83	10.3	86	10.7	1,080	16.6	1,807	1,089	718	106	1,287
Telfair	3,202	16,353	1.00	131	8.3	165	10.4	1,568	15.5	2,383	1,566	817	NA	NA
Terrell	271	8,380	0.81	92	10.7	103	12.0	1,136	16.4	2,259	1,267	992	260	2,881
Thomas	630	47,016	1.12	559	12.6	528	11.9	5,829	16.0	10,396	6,739	3,657	1,568	3,687
Tift	1,554	45,432	1.29	550	13.6	411	10.1	5,796	17.4	7,600	5,006	2,594	1,966	4,815
Toombs	326	28,957	1.17	366	13.6	330	12.3	3,814	16.9	5,620	3,720	1,900	NA	NA
Towns	1,192	11,405	1.06	91	7.7	180	15.2	1,031	15.8	4,685	3,240	1,445	215	1,902
Treutlen	471	5,689	0.60	73	10.7	81	11.9	771	14.6	1,378	801	577	NA	NA
Troup	2,521	78,777	1.32	879	12.6	727	10.4	8,481	14.7	12,721	8,639	4,082	2,851	4,059
Turner	386	7,481	0.82	104	13.1	103	13.0	1,105	18.1	2,012	1,112	900	274	3,396
Twiggs	89	7,724	0.76	71	8.7	122	14.9	1,021	16.0	2,361	1,344	1,017	161	1,946
Union	306	23,077	1.10	168	7.0	309	12.9	2,633	17.3	8,384	5,875	2,509	290	1,292
Upson	373	25,360	0.91	310	11.8	369	14.1	3,131	14.8	6,507	3,678	2,829	928	3,542
Walker	1,318	55,924	0.56	725	10.4	812	11.7	7,921	14.3	14,665	9,798	4,867	1,841	2,714
Walton	761	74,794	0.64	1,131	12.1	847	9.1	10,825	14.2	16,545	9,970	6,575	2,203	2,469
Ware	2,379	40,181	1.34	471	13.2	449	12.6	4,075	14.7	8,134	5,601	2,533	1,748	4,975
Warren	85	4,448	0.53	58	11.0	69	13.1	649	15.4	1,409	768	641	NA	NA
Washington	1,866	20,587	1.01	209	10.3	223	10.9	2,155	14.0	4,474	2,523	1,951	464	2,266
Wayne	1,991	29,533	0.97	368	12.3	344	11.5	3,549	15.1	5,898	3,913	1,985	1,621	5,515
Webster	0	2,237	0.65	21	8.0	15	5.7	335	16.5	539	313	226	8	305
Wheeler	2,514	7,973	1.01	61	7.7	61	7.7	631	14.6	1,144	726	418	81	1,022
White	691	26,117	0.79	268	8.9	296	9.9	3,479	15.7	7,093	4,427	2,666	641	2,248
Whitfield	1,062	114,838	1.24	1,335	12.8	833	8.0	19,233	21.5	17,074	13,637	3,437	2,892	2,787
Wilcox	1,972	8,432	0.80	86	9.8	106	12.0	921	16.8	1,639	1,058	581	159	1,923
Wilkes	184	9,406	0.87	91	9.2	140	14.2	1,249	16.7	2,661	1,718	943	52	534
Wilkinson	175	9,161	1.00	102	11.3	128	14.2	1,016	13.9	2,292	1,436	856	78	1,012
Worth	89	16,833	0.51	205	10.1	232	11.4	2,915	17.4	4,119	2,691	1,428	640	3,125
HAWAII	43,754	1,423,109	1.00	17,326	12.2	12,660	8.9	48,641	4.2	266,717	145,251	121,466	47,170	3,302
Hawaii	3,819	196,030	1.00	2,270	11.3	2,020	10.1	8,067	5.0	42,954	28,111	14,843	5,395	2,747
Honolulu	35,936	991,955	1.00	12,368	12.6	8,600	8.8	30,330	3.8	179,460	93,156	86,304	32,558	3,270
Kalawao	3	85	0.98	0	0.0	0	0.0	NA	NA	0	0	0	NA	NA
Kauai	1,188	71,111	1.00	838	11.6	682	9.5	2,770	4.7	14,831	8,921	5,910	1,661	2,313
Maui	2,808	163,928	1.00	1,850	11.1	1,358	8.1	7,474	5.4	29,470	15,062	14,408	6,191	3,757
IDAHO	30,161	1,634,500	0.97	22,412	12.8	12,989	7.4	165,164	11.8	320,099	216,730	103,369	33,233	1,974
Ada	11,074	457,732	1.11	4,987	10.6	3,019	6.4	33,709	8.9	76,507	40,424	36,083	8,759	1,966
Adams	21	3,509	0.71	33	7.8	28	6.6	412	14.7	1,265	1,044	221	37	962
Bannock	1,995	82,096	0.94	1,173	13.5	677	7.8	6,949	9.8	14,707	10,364	4,343	2,459	2,913
Bear Lake	31	5,379	0.77	83	13.7	65	10.7	463	9.8	1,413	1,372	41	85	1,429
Benewah	70	9,471	1.13	100	10.8	109	11.8	910	13.1	2,623	2,559	64	NA	NA
Bingham	324	42,667	0.86	644	13.9	361	7.8	5,574	14.5	7,786	6,177	1,609	748	1,658
Blaine	258	22,372	1.07	194	8.6	107	4.7	2,922	16.2	4,565	3,774	791	187	858
Boise	34	5,938	0.62	55	7.2	55	7.2	621	11.5	2,044	1,205	839	86	1,209
Bonner	353	40,450	0.92	438	9.8	442	9.9	3,889	12.0	12,056	8,519	3,537	866	2,047
Bonneville	1,242	115,568	1.11	1,902	16.3	849	7.3	9,066	9.3	18,223	14,361	3,862	2,453	2,192
Boundary	73	11,001	0.92	148	12.4	123	10.3	1,460	16.1	3,204	2,359	845	141	1,231
Butte	18	4,840	3.29	31	11.9	20	7.7	273	14.0	621	D	D	3	123
Camas	0	845	0.90	10	8.9	8	7.1	134	15.9	231	188	43	8	752
Canyon	3,348	186,124	0.76	3,131	14.0	1,501	6.7	27,270	15.3	36,304	18,049	18,255	4,809	2,262

1. Per 1,000 estimated resident population.   2. Data for serious crimes have not been adjusted for underreporting; this may affect comparability between geographic areas and over time.   3. Per 100,000 population estimated by the FBI.

Table B. States and Counties — Crime, Education, Money Income, and Poverty

STATE County	Serious crimes known to police[2], 2016 (cont.)[1] Rate Violent	Property	School enrollment and attainment, 2013-2017 Enrollment[3] Total	Percent private	Attainment[4] (percent) High school graduate or less	Bachelor's degree or more	Local government expenditures,[5] 2014-2015 Total current spending (mil dol)	Current spending per student (dollars)	Money income, 2013-2017 Per capita income[6]	Households Median income (dollars)	Percent with income of less than $50,000	Percent with income of $200,000 or more	Income and poverty, 2017 Median household income (dollars)	Percent below poverty level All persons	Children under 18 years	Children 5 to 17 years in families
	46	47	48	49	50	51	52	53	54	55	56	57	58	59	60	61
GEORGIA—Cont'd																
Putnam	262	2,504	4,468	20.4	51.0	21.4	33.3	11,839	27,498	48,340	51.8	3.5	47,710	17.2	30.8	27.3
Quitman	221	1,592	380	15.3	68.3	8.3	4.8	14,944	18,921	26,750	73.5	0.5	31,151	26.1	43.0	41.7
Rabun	123	2,115	2,818	19.1	49.6	25.3	28.8	12,768	26,942	39,297	60.8	3.0	43,042	17.8	28.9	24.9
Randolph	268	1,424	1,580	11.8	61.4	12.1	11.8	11,441	19,781	30,640	75.9	1.2	30,847	33.6	49.1	44.7
Richmond	429	4,474	52,119	14.5	47.8	21.0	294.7	9,261	21,464	39,430	60.3	1.9	38,297	23.7	35.4	34.3
Rockdale	319	2,603	24,169	11.1	45.3	25.8	167.3	10,176	24,254	54,175	45.8	2.7	59,341	14.1	22.5	20.0
Schley	115	905	1,481	3.2	53.2	13.7	14.3	10,306	19,761	41,267	59.4	1.4	43,568	18	26.4	23.0
Screven	256	1,855	3,236	7.7	58.9	14.7	22.3	9,473	20,255	36,556	58.7	2.1	38,870	20.5	33.8	34.8
Seminole	383	1,496	1,792	9.0	56.9	15.1	15.8	9,589	21,257	33,999	65.9	1.5	35,527	29.2	44.8	43.4
Spalding	586	4,090	14,289	10.2	57.6	16.2	103.7	9,900	21,675	42,398	56.1	2.4	45,121	19.9	32.5	32.5
Stephens	271	3,018	6,660	16.2	54.4	19.6	35.5	8,691	21,657	39,756	59.4	2.6	40,483	18.7	28.4	26.8
Stewart	NA	NA	838	9.2	72.6	12.4	6.6	12,833	14,954	22,413	72.8	2.0	31,800	36.2	38.6	36.6
Sumter	691	4,580	9,204	6.2	55.0	16.8	45.9	9,649	18,785	34,219	65.4	1.7	36,611	25.5	38.3	35.7
Talbot	112	1,235	1,165	13.9	63.8	12.5	6.9	13,236	21,351	37,226	66.0	1.1	36,269	22.2	37.2	34.9
Taliaferro	NA	NA	316	12.7	78.3	6.8	3.6	D	17,939	30,500	72.0	0.4	30,586	26.5	44.1	44.2
Tattnall	155	1,503	5,112	11.0	64.6	12.3	32.9	8,745	16,279	36,355	63.7	1.8	38,672	27.3	35.7	34.0
Taylor	121	1,166	1,918	18.6	59.2	11.4	14.5	9,891	18,482	29,875	71.0	1.6	35,608	23.7	34.7	32.6
Telfair	NA	NA	2,750	4.5	77.0	8.1	16.2	9,491	13,594	28,044	77.0	0.3	31,354	34.6	42.8	36.0
Terrell	377	2,504	2,284	12.6	55.6	10.8	15.5	10,494	17,562	32,219	64.4	1.4	33,939	33	49.4	44.3
Thomas	238	3,450	11,536	14.7	48.7	22.2	82.9	9,601	24,047	41,336	57.6	3.0	43,257	17.9	25.4	24.5
Tift	578	4,237	10,846	6.8	52.6	16.8	75.2	9,474	20,800	38,728	60.1	2.1	41,544	21.7	31.5	32.5
Toombs	NA	NA	7,029	7.6	58.2	15.9	51.1	9,106	21,309	35,750	63.3	2.4	35,226	22.3	33.5	32.3
Towns	354	1,548	2,575	28.2	41.3	25.6	12.9	11,883	22,301	41,182	59.2	1.3	44,055	13.8	22.6	23.2
Treutlen	NA	NA	1,368	6.7	59.4	15.5	10.2	8,517	20,775	39,375	59.1	1.8	34,473	27.4	37.9	33.7
Troup	356	3,703	17,402	13.1	51.9	18.5	111.3	8,777	22,091	43,597	55.3	2.4	43,112	21.6	27.9	25.6
Turner	582	2,813	1,668	10.1	61.2	13.5	16.8	11,705	20,302	42,622	58.6	1.7	33,310	27.6	42.0	42.2
Twiggs	205	1,741	1,473	12.7	69.6	9.2	12.1	13,126	17,485	30,629	70.0	0.6	39,639	22.2	33.9	33.1
Union	103	1,190	3,743	22.7	45.9	22.0	30.7	11,236	26,755	42,767	55.1	2.7	46,097	15.4	24.8	20.5
Upson	359	3,183	5,874	6.6	57.8	12.9	41.4	9,731	19,624	35,375	66.3	1.3	39,780	20.5	31.1	29.7
Walker	293	2,421	14,875	15.5	55.7	15.5	97.8	9,309	22,564	43,581	56.9	2.4	44,176	15.6	24.2	21.2
Walton	241	2,228	23,140	13.4	51.3	19.0	132.5	8,546	25,184	55,876	43.3	3.8	58,028	12.3	16.8	15.4
Ware	524	4,451	7,903	9.5	59.0	13.5	62.1	10,159	19,246	36,962	62.3	0.9	38,412	22	35.1	33.7
Warren	NA	NA	877	15.4	68.8	13.7	7.5	11,355	20,712	32,860	66.6	1.1	34,680	27.9	43.1	40.1
Washington	220	2,046	4,774	11.6	63.1	13.1	34.7	11,118	19,238	38,097	62.7	1.4	37,464	26.7	33.9	33.0
Wayne	694	4,821	6,889	6.7	58.5	12.7	49.3	8,991	19,188	41,534	58.0	0.9	45,814	20.2	30.1	31.2
Webster	38	267	707	10.3	68.1	11.3	4.5	10,602	22,206	36,658	62.4	1.5	39,266	20	30.1	26.9
Wheeler	50	971	1,442	5.6	72.9	8.1	10.5	10,235	11,192	28,490	71.2	0.0	31,001	37.4	39.9	37.4
White	193	2,055	6,032	10.9	46.5	20.2	58.9	10,977	23,630	43,944	56.2	1.4	50,194	13.3	20.6	18.5
Whitfield	309	2,478	27,557	4.4	60.0	14.6	194.7	9,156	22,262	43,871	55.7	3.3	42,568	16.5	24.1	24.7
Wilcox	230	1,693	1,674	9.2	69.1	10.5	12.4	9,922	15,119	35,457	65.4	0.5	35,015	30.7	35.5	35.2
Wilkes	308	226	1,998	7.9	63.0	14.3	18.7	11,496	21,957	34,234	63.8	1.9	34,897	22.8	35.0	34.2
Wilkinson	195	817	2,106	11.2	69.5	9.0	18.0	11,717	19,823	38,711	58.8	0.6	40,906	23.5	31.7	30.1
Worth	498	2,627	5,017	7.8	61.0	11.0	30.7	9,050	20,783	40,369	59.4	1.7	42,913	21.6	32.5	32.1
HAWAII	309	2,993	330,239	22.9	36.1	32.0	2,344.5	12,855	32,511	74,923	32.7	8.4	77,936	9.5	11.9	10.7
Hawaii	238	2,509	42,731	18.0	38.9	28.6	(7)	(7)	26,959	56,395	45.1	4.1	56,540	15	20.9	18.8
Honolulu	238	3,033	238,821	24.6	34.8	34.0	(7)2,344.5	(7)12,855	33,776	80,078	29.6	9.6	80,947	8.3	9.9	9.0
Kalawao	NA	NA	5	40.0	38.0	22.8	(7)	(7)	46,024	61,750	32.1	0.0	0	0	0.0	0.0
Kauai	235	2,077	13,878	16.1	39.4	28.2	(7)	(7)	30,515	72,330	36.1	6.3	74,881	10.1	13.0	10.7
Maui	273	3,484	34,804	19.7	39.3	26.3	(7)	(7)	32,379	72,762	34.0	7.7	76,376	10	11.8	10.5
IDAHO	230	1,744	445,420	13.7	37.2	26.8	1,990.3	6,846	25,471	50,985	48.9	3.2	52,280	12.6	14.8	13.3
Ada	233	1,732	117,733	13.1	27.7	37.6	507.6	6,730	31,642	60,151	41.0	5.6	61,469	10.8	10.6	9.4
Adams	104	858	670	10.0	48.1	20.3	4.0	10,225	24,315	42,727	58.7	2.0	43,442	14.5	25.3	23.1
Bannock	285	2,628	25,898	8.4	34.0	28.1	91.0	6,293	23,872	47,390	52.1	2.1	51,093	14.2	15.5	14.1
Bear Lake	84	1,345	1,315	5.1	44.7	20.3	7.6	6,871	24,411	50,603	49.4	1.8	51,343	11.7	15.6	13.9
Benewah	NA	NA	1,800	15.0	52.8	14.1	12.5	9,565	23,120	43,472	56.4	1.4	43,570	14.3	22.8	20.6
Bingham	226	1,432	13,066	7.3	44.1	19.3	65.9	6,528	20,720	51,307	48.8	1.6	52,697	12.5	16.1	15.1
Blaine	202	656	4,284	7.5	32.8	40.4	54.0	15,620	32,736	58,835	43.8	5.5	68,101	8.5	9.8	7.7
Boise	211	998	1,267	11.9	34.8	29.2	7.9	9,492	29,648	49,964	50.0	2.8	56,067	12.1	19.3	17.5
Bonner	208	1,839	7,982	18.1	39.1	22.4	45.1	8,867	25,909	45,607	54.9	2.3	47,537	13.7	19.1	17.6
Bonneville	361	1,831	32,005	10.5	34.7	29.3	135.4	5,706	25,706	54,150	45.8	3.5	55,744	10.5	13.3	11.8
Boundary	114	1,118	2,195	28.5	47.5	18.2	10.7	7,734	24,606	39,512	57.8	3.4	43,835	15.5	23.3	22.8
Butte	0	123	608	10.9	44.3	15.5	3.2	7,549	26,227	43,207	56.7	3.9	45,226	16.9	22.1	18.1
Camas	0	752	190	10.2	42.1	20.6	2.0	12,818	29,193	36,667	61.1	9.2	51,045	9.2	12.6	10.0
Canyon	267	1,995	58,206	14.1	47.5	18.1	242.6	6,195	19,765	46,426	54.4	1.5	47,915	15.5	17.2	15.3

1. Data for serious crimes have not been adjusted for underreporting; this may affect comparability between geographic areas and over time. 2. Per 100,000 population estimated by the FBI. 3. All persons 3 years old and over enrolled in nursery school through college. 4. Persons 25 years old and over. 5. Elementary and secondary education expenditures. 6. Based on population estimated by the American Community Survey, 2013–2017. 7. Hawaii, Kalawao, Kauai, and Maui counties are included with Honolulu county.

Table B. States and Counties — Personal Income and Earnings

STATE County	Personal income, 2017 Total (mil dol)	Percent change 2016-2017	Per capita¹ Dollars	Per capita¹ Rank	Wages and salaries (mil dol)	Supplements to wages and salaries, employer contributions (mil dol) Pension and insurance	Government social insurance	Proprietors' income (mil dol)	Dividends, interest, and rent (mil dol)	Personal transfer receipts (mil dol)	Earnings, 2017 Total (mil dol)	Contributions for government social insurance (mil dol) From employee and self-employed	From employer
	62	63	64	65	66	67	68	69	70	71	72	73	74
GEORGIA—Cont'd													
Putnam	869	4.9	39,996	1,551	205	48	14	36	198	224	302	22	14
Quitman	68	5.3	29,036	2,983	14	4	1	4	10	28	23	2	1
Rabun	669	5.0	40,292	1,504	172	34	12	63	221	187	281	21	12
Randolph	219	5.7	30,910	2,857	68	17	5	17	36	78	107	7	5
Richmond	7,327	3.6	36,309	2,150	5,991	1,393	446	473	1,446	1,998	8,303	438	446
Rockdale	3,099	4.1	34,317	2,443	1,634	260	109	113	447	724	2,117	131	109
Schley	158	5.8	30,241	2,908	38	12	3	9	23	37	62	4	3
Screven	456	4.3	32,673	2,661	128	30	9	12	70	146	180	13	9
Seminole	328	1.8	39,506	1,640	87	19	6	56	50	103	169	12	6
Spalding	2,209	3.7	33,787	2,510	901	194	63	86	350	669	1,244	82	63
Stephens	976	2.9	37,709	1,921	384	76	27	54	159	284	541	36	27
Stewart	135	6.8	22,508	3,105	59	13	4	3	24	51	79	5	4
Sumter	1,020	2.9	34,174	2,462	450	111	32	30	199	309	623	39	32
Talbot	218	3.9	34,810	2,371	30	8	2	6	38	73	45	5	2
Taliaferro	54	1.9	33,003	2,615	6	3	0	5	9	19	15	1	0
Tattnall	697	4.9	27,503	3,047	226	60	16	91	103	197	392	20	16
Taylor	238	-7.0	29,213	2,976	65	15	4	8	41	85	93	7	4
Telfair	332	3.2	20,748	3,109	114	30	9	27	51	127	180	12	9
Terrell	342	3.9	39,175	1,693	88	20	6	21	76	102	135	9	6
Thomas	1,857	2.6	41,480	1,335	927	165	63	98	381	486	1,253	80	63
Tift	1,454	2.1	35,819	2,224	802	182	53	130	248	378	1,167	66	53
Toombs	927	0.6	34,337	2,438	440	87	32	50	137	280	609	38	32
Towns	403	1.9	35,014	2,347	112	27	8	22	112	158	169	15	8
Treutlen	194	1.5	28,750	2,998	39	11	3	9	26	69	62	5	3
Troup	2,536	3.7	36,335	2,145	1,837	311	134	105	432	620	2,386	141	134
Turner	264	2.7	33,218	2,591	75	17	5	13	39	98	110	8	5
Twiggs	308	4.9	37,713	1,920	72	14	5	40	35	101	131	10	5
Union	810	5.0	34,545	2,408	265	60	18	57	189	284	399	31	18
Upson	912	3.7	34,885	2,363	262	52	18	47	154	286	378	28	18
Walker	2,201	4.2	31,929	2,762	512	125	38	137	323	647	812	59	38
Walton	3,561	6.2	38,871	1,743	1,065	187	74	217	504	721	1,543	101	74
Ware	1,174	3.1	32,734	2,654	667	133	56	48	191	411	904	59	56
Warren	174	1.3	32,824	2,642	68	13	5	5	27	63	91	7	5
Washington	694	3.4	34,161	2,464	276	68	19	23	146	207	387	25	19
Wayne	907	3.8	30,427	2,892	351	77	24	46	123	292	499	33	24
Webster	81	2.9	31,190	2,840	22	5	2	5	16	21	33	2	2
Wheeler	153	2.1	19,220	3,112	44	10	3	14	20	55	71	5	3
White	980	4.8	33,262	2,587	296	57	21	75	164	269	449	32	21
Whitfield	3,909	3.5	37,351	1,978	2,675	417	193	486	781	786	3,771	219	193
Wilcox	228	6.0	25,934	3,080	43	13	3	23	38	82	81	5	3
Wilkes	383	4.3	38,698	1,775	111	26	8	31	71	115	175	11	8
Wilkinson	318	3.0	35,452	2,280	161	31	11	18	42	104	221	15	11
Worth	662	2.6	32,231	2,724	128	29	9	2	109	183	168	14	9
HAWAII	75,355	3.7	52,910	X	37,085	7,523	2,921	5,759	16,379	11,749	53,287	3,140	2,921
Hawaii	8,053	4.9	40,188	1,523	3,201	639	246	683	1,887	1,921	4,768	308	246
Honolulu	56,084	3.2	56,728	230	28,660	6,001	2,283	3,985	11,920	7,926	40,928	2,357	2,283
Kalawao	(2)7,856	(2) 5.4	(2) 47,226	(2) 693	(2)3,712	(2) 618	(2) 278	(2) 821	(2)1,764	(2)1,249	(2)5,428	(2) 337	(2) 278
Kauai	3,362	5.5	46,596	742	1,513	265	115	270	808	653	2,162	138	115
Maui	(2)	(2)	(2)	(2)	(2)	(2)	(2)	(2)	(2)	(2)	(2)	(2)	(2)
IDAHO	71,813	5.5	41,778	X	31,444	5,196	2,739	7,936	15,887	12,932	47,315	2,906	2,739
Ada	22,797	6.0	49,900	468	12,350	1,838	1,010	2,495	5,063	3,060	17,693	1,080	1,010
Adams	153	4.2	36,851	2,066	49	10	5	14	51	40	78	6	5
Bannock	3,154	4.8	36,987	2,037	1,371	270	124	166	529	709	1,931	126	124
Bear Lake	227	3.4	37,634	1,929	58	14	6	16	42	57	93	7	6
Benewah	326	3.4	35,520	2,271	147	28	13	20	66	95	210	15	13
Bingham	1,632	7.9	35,535	2,269	575	108	52	204	304	336	939	54	52
Blaine	2,258	6.0	102,546	11	588	76	53	232	1,283	151	949	57	53
Boise	317	6.5	43,549	1,071	48	11	5	17	71	69	81	7	5
Bonner	1,712	5.8	39,310	1,670	536	100	49	130	550	395	815	60	49
Bonneville	5,204	5.6	45,413	854	2,049	327	182	738	1,257	819	3,297	200	182
Boundary	412	5.0	34,576	2,405	142	28	14	45	92	107	227	16	14
Butte	99	0.6	37,885	1,902	739	65	54	7	18	25	864	53	54
Camas	41	4.6	37,216	1,996	22	3	2	3	12	8	30	2	2
Canyon	6,798	6.8	31,370	2,822	2,504	428	230	599	1,013	1,571	3,760	246	230

1. Based on the resident population estimated as of July 1 of the year shown.   2. Kalawao county is included with Maui county.

Table B. States and Counties — **Earnings, Social Security, and Housing**

STATE County	Earnings, 2017 (cont.) Percent by selected industries									Social Security beneficiaries, December 2017		Supplemental Security Income recipients, 2017	Housing units, 2018	
	Farm	Mining, quarrying, and extractions	Construction	Manu-facturing	Information; professional, scientific, technical services	Retail trade	Finance, insurance, real estate, and leasing	Health care and social assistance	Govern-ment	Number	Rate[1]		Total	Percent change, 2010-2018
	75	76	77	78	79	80	81	82	83	84	85	86	87	88

GEORGIA—Cont'd														
Putnam	1.6	0	10.1	11.3	D	8.9	7.4	D	29.4	6,020	277	531	13,270	3.6
Quitman	9.7	0	1.5	D	0.2	D	D	D	34.8	800	339	151	2,058	0.5
Rabun	2.1	D	12.4	7.7	3.8	12.9	7.2	D	18	5,320	320	429	12,680	3
Randolph	5.5	0	D	D	D	6.6	D	D	28	1,760	249	410	4,101	-1.2
Richmond	0	D	3.3	7.9	6.6	4.4	4.7	12.6	43.4	40,120	199	8,225	89,092	3.2
Rockdale	0	0	D	17.6	8.7	7.7	6.9	12	14.1	16,755	186	2,120	33,848	1.8
Schley	8.3	0	D	29	D	3	D	D	32.3	905	174	145	2,215	0.3
Screven	2	0.1	4	27.7	D	7	3.8	D	29.3	3,600	258	693	6,780	0.6
Seminole	4.7	0	1.7	21.6	D	4.2	7.5	12.8	14.5	2,535	306	435	4,833	0.8
Spalding	-0.2	D	4	16	3.3	7.2	4.1	15.4	24.7	15,790	242	2,790	27,580	2.9
Stephens	2.4	D	D	23.7	2.9	7.6	3.1	D	18.4	7,240	280	1,218	12,617	-0.4
Stewart	1.7	0	D	D	D	2.2	D	28.6	32.8	1,100	184	257	2,338	-1.9
Sumter	0.8	D	2.1	21.3	D	6.6	3.9	D	23.9	6,685	224	1,362	13,880	-0.2
Talbot	-1.1	16.3	28.5	0.2	D	1.5	D	D	27	1,715	274	317	3,426	0.7
Taliaferro	29.9	0	0.8	D	0.2	D	D	D	45.3	490	301	106	1,016	0.1
Tattnall	21.2	0	4.1	2.5	2.9	4.1	2.8	D	29.2	4,485	177	928	10,024	0.6
Taylor	3.5	D	5.1	3.3	D	7.8	2.9	15	24.5	1,985	244	400	4,611	1
Telfair	3.4	0.3	4.2	D	1.7	5.1	4.2	5	23.9	2,750	172	579	7,286	-0.1
Terrell	8.8	0.1	3.1	14.8	D	9.5	5.5	D	23.3	2,450	281	541	4,166	0.1
Thomas	-1.3	D	3.1	16.8	3.3	6.2	8.3	20.4	16.1	11,230	251	2,254	20,824	3.2
Tift	0.7	0.1	3.2	7	3.7	9.1	5.3	7.2	34.1	8,475	209	1,668	16,780	2.1
Toombs	1.8	0	5.6	10.7	D	9.3	4.6	D	14.6	6,150	228	1,295	12,232	0.9
Towns	-0.1	D	6.7	D	5.1	5.9	6.3	D	16.5	4,940	429	243	8,317	7.5
Treutlen	5.8	0	D	D	0.7	9.2	D	D	30.3	1,575	234	323	3,008	0.6
Troup	0	D	5.3	35.6	3.5	6.9	5.5	8.8	10.2	14,410	206	2,398	28,628	2.1
Turner	8.2	0	0.5	13.6	D	8.2	5.6	4.4	27.4	2,185	274	458	3,938	2.5
Twiggs	-0.7	D	D	D	D	D	D	D	3.9	2,535	310	419	4,252	0.4
Union	1.5	D	7.1	4.7	D	8.7	5.7	10.4	27	8,765	374	479	14,792	5.3
Upson	4.8	0.1	4.7	19.7	4.2	7.7	4.2	19.8	20.1	7,235	277	1,170	12,124	-0.3
Walker	3.3	0	5.9	31.4	D	5.3	5.5	4.7	22.1	16,420	238	2,199	30,458	1.2
Walton	0.7	0.2	14.9	15.7	3.8	6.4	4.8	7.9	16.1	18,045	197	2,529	34,265	5.6
Ware	0	0	3.1	12.1	D	9.8	4.4	16.2	20.8	8,185	228	1,797	16,778	2.8
Warren	0.5	D	1.6	28	D	3.8	0.7	D	14.7	1,560	294	257	2,975	-0.3
Washington	0.1	3.9	4.8	9.7	D	5.9	5	D	29.4	4,935	243	882	9,373	3.6
Wayne	1.1	0	8.6	20.6	D	8.6	2.8	10.6	31.2	6,625	222	1,097	12,284	0.7
Webster	12.9	D	0.9	D	0.1	8.5	1.3	D	19.9	595	228	92	1,533	0.6
Wheeler	11	0	4.2	0	D	2	D	D	22.3	1,255	158	228	2,621	-0.2
White	5.4	0	12.9	11.4	3.9	8.8	4.4	D	15.8	7,670	260	597	16,324	1.7
Whitfield	0.4	D	2.3	38.3	7.8	5.4	5.4	9.7	9.3	18,945	181	2,545	40,143	0.6
Wilcox	20.4	0	D	D	D	D	D	D	2.4	1,785	203	348	3,522	0.3
Wilkes	12.2	D	8.2	18.2	D	6.2	4.3	5.2	23.1	2,995	303	455	5,158	0
Wilkinson	0.4	41.7	9.7	5.9	D	1.9	D	3.1	11.4	2,585	289	369	4,483	-0.1
Worth	-2.1	0	6.4	11	D	9.7	4.8	D	30.8	4,525	220	660	9,337	0.9
HAWAII	0.5	0.1	8.1	1.8	7.1	6	6.2	10.1	28.9	266,523	187	23,930	546,213	5.1
Hawaii	2.4	D	D	1.6	5.5	8.5	4.4	9.6	23.5	44,870	224	5,237	88,558	7.6
Honolulu	0.2	0.1	7.8	1.9	7.8	5.3	6.6	10.5	31.8	175,700	178	15,735	352,527	4.6
Kalawao	(2) 1.4	(2) D	(2) 9.4	(2) 1.2	(2) 4.4	(2) 7.9	(2) 5.6	(2) 8.4	(2)16.0	15	170	0	113	0
Kauai	0.4	D	D	1.1	4.5	8.3	5.2	9	19.5	15,385	213	897	31,240	4.8
Maui	(2)	(2)	(2)	(2)	(2)	(2)	(2)	(2)	(2)	30,550	184	2,061	73,775	4.8
IDAHO	4.4	0.5	7.7	12.2	8.4	8.2	6.3	11.7	16.3	335,551	195	30,908	735,672	10.2
Ada	0.3	0.3	7.7	14.2	9.7	7.5	8.1	13.4	13.7	78,240	171	6,780	186,481	16.9
Adams	6	0.1	7.9	13.3	D	6	3.3	D	25.2	1,350	326	55	2,695	2.2
Bannock	0.7	D	6.8	8.7	5.3	7.8	7.4	15.3	24	15,010	176	1,998	34,450	3.8
Bear Lake	7.6	D	3.3	3.6	D	7.6	4.3	4.4	37.4	1,485	246	97	4,155	6.2
Benewah	-0.5	D	4.4	18.6	D	4.3	2.4	D	33.8	2,780	303	229	4,753	2.7
Bingham	13	D	6.6	14	D	5	5.8	10.1	21.7	8,505	185	917	16,857	4.4
Blaine	0.9	D	15.9	2.9	15	7.1	10.5	7.8	10	4,365	198	106	15,491	2.9
Boise	1.2	0.2	10.8	2.5	D	2.7	D	D	34	2,205	302	109	5,604	5.9
Bonner	0.7	1.2	8.8	18	7.1	9.7	5.6	7.5	18.3	12,570	289	815	25,262	2.4
Bonneville	1	D	6.5	8.4	7.2	17.8	5.6	15.7	11.9	19,450	170	2,293	43,775	10.2
Boundary	5.2	0.1	10	12.6	4	6.4	5.9	7.7	27.1	3,325	279	249	5,530	6.9
Butte	0.9	D	D	D	D	0.2	D	D	1.8	690	265	82	1,381	1.9
Camas	8.7	0.1	8.5	D	D	2.1	D	D	20.1	255	231	11	862	3.7
Canyon	3.9	0	12.4	16.3	4.8	9.4	4.1	9.9	13.9	38,520	178	4,637	77,867	12.2

1. Per 1,000 resident population estimated as of July 1 of the year shown.   2. Kalawao county is included with Maui county.

Table B. States and Counties — Housing, Labor Force, and Employment

STATE County	Housing units, 2013-2017								Civilian labor force, 2018				Civilian employment[6], 2013-2017		
	Occupied units							Sub-standard units[4] (percent)			Unemployment			Percent	
			Owner-occupied			Renter-occupied									Management, business, science, and arts	Construction, production, and maintenance occupations
				Median owner cost as a percent of income		Median rent[3]	Median rent as a percent of income[2]								
	Total	Percent	Median value[1]	With a mortgage	Without a mortgage[2]				Total	Percent change, 2017-2018	Total	Rate[5]	Total		
	89	90	91	92	93	94	95	96	97	98	99	100	101	102	103

STATE County	89	90	91	92	93	94	95	96	97	98	99	100	101	102	103
GEORGIA—Cont'd															
Putnam	8,662	74.9	168,700	22.1	11.3	693	32.5	0.9	8,223	0.6	408	5	9,127	25.6	29.5
Quitman	978	74.1	67,400	30.2	14.8	697	47.6	1.7	830	-0.4	46	5.5	729	13.7	38.7
Rabun	6,506	74.1	157,800	28.7	11.1	667	31	2.8	7,092	2.7	284	4	6,259	33.4	26.4
Randolph	2,864	60.5	67,300	25.0	13.4	564	24.9	2.8	2,489		146	5.9	2,639	27.7	32.5
Richmond	72,361	53.1	100,200	22.1	11.2	813	33	2.4	86,626	0.8	4,460	5.1	78,704	29.9	21.6
Rockdale	29,937	68.5	148,600	22.2	10.0	955	31.2	2.7	44,875	1.1	1,972	4.4	38,732	34.1	24.2
Schley	1,925	65.9	94,800	21.5	14.0	704	29.7	2.3	2,193	-0.8	102	4.7	2,027	31.2	31.0
Screven	5,268	69.2	78,900	22.3	11.1	594	28.8	3.5	5,330	1.2	288	5.4	5,631	27.8	33.6
Seminole	3,353	71.0	77,200	24.5	12.7	712	34.6	6	3,062	-0.8	162	5.3	2,853	34.1	25.3
Spalding	23,475	61.4	112,400	22.5	11.9	818	32.3	2.4	28,551	0.8	1,342	4.7	24,789	27.9	29.3
Stephens	9,427	70.2	98,500	20.7	11.9	638	33	3.3	10,964	-0.6	496	4.5	10,114	28.4	30.3
Stewart	1,780	68.0	51,800	24.7	17.9	515	38.1	1.8	2,352	3.1	110	4.7	1,369	31.6	27.8
Sumter	11,871	55.8	82,600	22.8	12.1	674	35.6	3.3	12,782	-0.9	757	5.9	11,558	31.2	30.3
Talbot	2,801	80.8	81,200	25.4	13.7	659	28.7	3.1	2,835	1.5	143	5	2,620	17.3	39.7
Taliaferro	710	69.7	59,100	26.4	17.6	520	27.8	3.9	585	1.7	30	5.1	627	19.5	41.9
Tattnall	8,044	68.2	88,100	21.7	12.4	543	22.9	5.3	9,692	1	407	4.2	7,655	29.6	30.0
Taylor	3,554	69.5	65,800	24.6	13.4	576	25.8	4.4	2,784	-1.2	182	6.5	2,974	28.2	30.4
Telfair	5,167	61.8	55,600	27.3	12.4	540	28	3.7	4,375	-8.5	297	6.8	4,823	24.5	38.3
Terrell	3,290	58.5	88,600	23.7	13.4	636	37	3.1	3,673	0.2	241	6.6	3,368	21.5	34.6
Thomas	17,254	64.4	131,400	22.6	13.6	808	31.2	2.9	16,925	-1.7	798	4.7	18,686	35.2	21.9
Tift	14,999	57.0	112,200	23.6	10.0	607	26.5	2.6	19,337	1.1	776	4	16,935	31.6	28.3
Toombs	10,521	60.6	97,500	21.4	12.1	567	28.5	6	11,945	1.1	694	5.8	10,574	26.3	32.7
Towns	4,588	80.8	197,900	28.0	12.7	689	32.4	1.3	3,886	3.2	213	5.5	3,955	30.3	18.4
Treutlen	2,633	71.0	71,000	27.3	10.6	573	16.6	3.2	2,704	-1.1	157	5.8	2,663	23.2	36.3
Troup	24,679	57.0	125,000	21.9	11.5	792	30.1	1.8	36,651	-1.9	1,356	3.7	29,630	28.6	34.1
Turner	3,103	69.9	72,700	19.7	14.7	548	36.7	6	3,185	-2.7	162	5.1	3,191	28.4	32.7
Twiggs	2,943	78.5	57,000	22.3	16.3	537	34.9	3.1	2,925	-1.4	172	5.9	2,591	20.5	38.6
Union	8,788	80.1	191,800	22.1	11.5	685	28.4	0.9	10,317	1.6	376	3.6	7,998	31.5	26.9
Upson	10,263	64.3	84,900	22.0	12.1	615	29.8	2.6	11,376	0.9	501	4.4	9,958	29.1	30.2
Walker	25,564	72.3	111,100	20.5	10.8	702	28.7	4.1	31,167	1	1,206	3.9	28,821	27.9	33.6
Walton	30,488	73.0	164,700	21.8	10.0	926	32.2	1.7	45,262	1.2	1,608	3.6	39,299	28.5	28.5
Ware	13,903	63.1	78,500	18.8	11.1	648	30.1	2	15,646	-1.1	616	3.9	13,208	25.6	33.1
Warren	2,274	67.1	62,300	22.7	15.2	548	32.2	2.1	2,748	0.9	137	5	2,104	21.3	36.5
Washington	7,384	68.8	82,400	21.4	13.0	656	31.1	4.2	7,157	-2.9	358	5	7,631	28.2	28.5
Wayne	10,362	63.1	107,300	20.1	10.8	609	25.2	3	11,398	0.4	530	4.6	10,402	30.8	32.5
Webster	1,091	78.0	57,200	20.1	10.0	571	20.4	0.5	1,001	0.8	63	6.3	1,116	29.7	33.1
Wheeler	1,972	63.8	46,800	24.5	10.0	477	32.5	2.8	1,670	-3.9	123	7.4	1,845	14.3	47.6
White	11,250	73.1	157,900	23.3	11.2	751	29.9	1.6	16,103	2.5	491	3	11,802	30.5	24.5
Whitfield	35,384	61.7	124,300	19.7	10.0	695	26.2	6.4	45,256	0.7	2,149	4.7	46,465	22.2	43.6
Wilcox	2,676	73.1	69,800	18.8	10.6	525	35.5	3.1	2,679	-3.1	140	5.2	2,392	28.7	31.0
Wilkes	3,971	67.7	83,400	23.9	14.8	639	32.5	0.3	3,891	2	178	4.6	3,866	24.1	36.8
Wilkinson	3,288	76.6	69,100	18.4	10.6	616	33.3	2.7	3,833	0.6	170	4.4	3,224	23.1	34.2
Worth	7,899	67.6	85,600	21.8	11.6	668	35.3	0.9	9,182	-0.9	404	4.4	8,153	27.1	33.2
HAWAII	455,502	58.1	563,900	26.2	10.0	1,507	33.2	9.5	678,734	-0.7	16,606	2.4	671,758	34.2	18.0
Hawaii	67,054	67.0	316,000	25.2	10.0	1,131	32.4	7.6	91,305	-0.3	2,728	3	84,962	32.0	19.5
Honolulu	311,451	55.6	626,400	26.0	10.0	1,653	34.3	9.7	465,193	-0.9	10,863	2.3	467,165	35.9	17.5
Kalawao	53	3.8	0	0.0	0.0	867	12.7	0	NA	NA	NA	NA	63	22.2	19.0
Kauai	22,563	63.0	520,100	28.6	10.0	1,308	29.3	8.3	36,100	0.1	907	2.5	35,783	28.7	19.0
Maui	54,381	59.3	569,100	27.3	10.0	1,336	29.6	11.2	86,137	-0.5	2,109	2.4	83,785	29.0	19.0
IDAHO	609,124	69.2	176,800	21.5	10.0	792	28.6	3.2	857,049	2.7	24,317	2.8	748,658	34.3	24.4
Ada	164,389	68.3	219,900	20.3	10.0	910	28.7	1.7	244,525	4.2	6,015	2.5	214,984	43.0	15.3
Adams	1,736	79.8	166,500	20.9	11.2	604	28.7	3.8	1,722	-1.7	94	5.5	1,539	33.1	26.4
Bannock	30,790	68.9	148,300	19.6	10.0	659	28.8	3	41,686	0.4	1,139	2.7	36,989	35.5	21.2
Bear Lake	2,313	78.6	142,100	18.6	10.0	583	23.8	2.6	2,835	0.1	82	2.9	2,523	23.1	32.5
Benewah	3,508	74.0	150,800	23.8	11.3	693	25.8	6.2	4,021	0.2	186	4.6	3,450	22.1	37.9
Bingham	14,903	74.8	147,400	19.7	10.0	652	26.5	4.3	23,357	1.3	633	2.7	19,417	31.2	30.6
Blaine	8,273	66.8	390,300	25.7	11.0	984	28.1	1.6	12,323	0.7	291	2.4	11,954	31.3	20.1
Boise	3,004	82.9	185,100	22.2	10.0	750	26	2.5	3,329	3.8	141	4.2	2,749	40.3	21.4
Bonner	17,563	72.8	222,700	26.5	10.0	752	29	3.6	19,610	1.7	803	4.1	17,199	26.6	32.3
Bonneville	38,400	70.6	161,000	20.0	10.0	759	28.3	3.7	55,403	3.4	1,326	2.4	48,734	35.8	23.4
Boundary	4,490	73.9	181,300	22.6	10.9	642	26.8	4	5,296	2.7	235	4.4	4,044	26.0	31.6
Butte	1,049	82.9	110,700	18.4	11.5	596	25.9	0.8	1,382	3.7	44	3.2	975	32.5	33.1
Camas	370	73.5	173,300	27.0	10.8	573	32.5	3.2	690	1	16	2.3	394	31.2	33.8
Canyon	69,303	67.6	144,000	22.3	10.0	812	28.8	4.5	100,275	3.8	3,087	3.1	88,055	26.5	30.7

1. Specified owner-occupied units.   2. A value of 10.0 represents 10 percent or less; a value of 50.0 represents 50 percent or more.   3. Specified renter-occupied units.   4. Overcrowded or lacking complete plumbing facilities.   5. Percent of civilian labor force.   6. Civilian employed persons 16 years old and over.

Table B. States and Counties — Nonfarm Employment and Agriculture

	Private nonfarm establishments, employment and payroll, 2016									Agriculture, 2017			
		Employment						Annual payroll		Farms			Farm producers whose primary occupation is farming (percent)
STATE County	Number of establishments	Total	Health care and social assistance	Manufacturing	Retail trade	Finance and insurance	Professional, scientific, and technical services	Total (mil dol)	Average per employee (dollars)	Number	Percent with:		
											Fewer than 50 acres	1000 acres or more	
	104	105	106	107	108	109	110	111	112	113	114	115	116
GEORGIA—Cont'd													
Putnam	425	4,365	416	475	973	144	72	130	29,750	186	24.7	2.2	42.6
Quitman	36	224	D	D	50	12	NA	5	23,674	37	8.1	10.8	22.2
Rabun	476	4,113	507	277	1,071	120	123	126	30,661	135	68.9	0.7	34.2
Randolph	130	1,393	297	D	159	38	26	45	32,385	153	5.9	21.6	42.5
Richmond	4,321	87,599	24,760	7,475	11,791	2,189	4,390	3,670	41,898	118	63.6	0.8	34.2
Rockdale	1,973	31,053	4,082	5,034	4,615	933	887	1,322	42,581	74	75.7	1.4	42.6
Schley	67	627	26	286	73	D	D	26	42,252	89	12.4	7.9	30.9
Screven	204	2,344	306	883	355	96	40	72	30,561	352	22.2	12.8	41.4
Seminole	195	1,478	340	26	295	75	77	48	32,702	157	25.5	12.1	68.4
Spalding	1,137	17,206	4,313	3,119	3,057	420	414	585	34,004	225	66.2	0.4	36.9
Stephens	544	7,942	1,384	2,242	1,158	177	116	263	33,116	227	45.8	NA	44.5
Stewart	63	682	101	D	62	20	3	22	32,028	104	13.5	8.7	22.9
Sumter	625	8,586	2,610	957	1,482	212	257	265	30,818	371	18.9	12.4	35.2
Talbot	60	543	D	D	48	31	D	21	38,392	102	22.5	4.9	38.3
Taliaferro	18	48	D	D	10	D	NA	1	28,063	48	4.2	4.2	40.5
Tattnall	296	3,304	848	116	402	139	152	108	32,666	547	37.7	3.3	44.8
Taylor	121	1,176	197	65	117	52	D	51	43,113	224	13.4	5.4	32.4
Telfair	180	2,730	207	D	340	94	27	67	24,552	255	25.5	3.5	41.6
Terrell	171	1,701	160	351	318	82	39	57	33,396	256	22.3	16.4	42.5
Thomas	1,113	16,241	3,576	2,557	2,344	614	295	676	41,596	408	31.1	12.5	41.3
Tift	1,022	15,846	2,357	1,421	2,694	427	542	543	34,271	306	38.2	16.3	44.0
Toombs	669	9,226	2,220	1,092	1,762	299	187	315	34,162	320	36.6	6.9	35.3
Towns	263	3,167	605	41	413	68	48	80	25,284	105	61.0	NA	46.8
Treutlen	86	680	172	66	216	27	D	19	28,454	148	26.4	4.7	26.8
Troup	1,416	33,465	3,021	11,593	3,095	1,121	633	1,456	43,511	261	46.7	1.5	36.0
Turner	151	1,441	158	394	192	72	51	45	31,048	246	30.1	9.3	35.2
Twiggs	69	1,502	166	NA	62	D	D	52	34,849	116	43.1	12.1	30.8
Union	547	5,755	1,290	330	1,275	613	160	193	33,537	251	61.8	NA	36.0
Upson	453	5,659	1,385	1,118	1,109	201	159	194	34,229	235	46.0	1.7	34.2
Walker	666	10,329	792	4,215	1,337	304	161	359	34,718	624	44.9	1.6	35.7
Walton	1,602	16,593	2,086	2,297	2,725	407	550	608	36,617	437	55.8	0.7	41.5
Ware	852	11,299	2,759	1,054	2,546	324	265	389	34,448	248	50.4	7.7	40.3
Warren	68	894	132	448	82	9	7	34	38,056	135	19.3	4.4	42.4
Washington	343	5,174	885	530	750	150	173	199	38,381	383	26.4	6.8	35.7
Wayne	551	5,769	1,146	913	1,217	181	104	199	34,459	316	46.8	3.8	36.9
Webster	26	280	D	D	48	5	D	13	45,043	109	18.3	20.2	45.2
Wheeler	64	821	55	NA	52	D	D	27	32,464	143	21.7	10.5	33.5
White	603	6,522	1,006	776	1,187	145	128	204	31,322	301	67.4	0.3	40.4
Whitfield	2,187	49,178	4,763	17,621	5,015	750	1,349	1,997	40,602	386	52.3	0.5	36.9
Wilcox	84	504	163	8	74	55	D	13	26,720	287	30.0	9.1	41.0
Wilkes	190	2,047	506	427	318	73	29	66	32,305	277	25.3	5.1	39.3
Wilkinson	130	2,175	187	681	165	40	33	102	47,041	140	22.1	3.6	24.0
Worth	255	2,607	380	555	528	63	70	85	32,642	469	32.0	15.4	44.9
HAWAII	32,350	528,415	71,052	13,040	70,647	19,060	22,782	22,892	43,323	7,328	89.5	1.7	46.7
Hawaii	4,032	54,561	8,508	1,489	9,654	1,151	1,485	2,028	37,167	4,220	89.4	1.4	46.4
Honolulu	21,404	359,766	53,010	10,060	47,049	16,355	18,257	16,369	45,499	927	91.3	1.7	55.4
Kalawao	2	D	NA	NA	D	NA	NA	D	D	NA	NA	NA	NA
Kauai	2,087	27,328	3,239	345	4,216	365	928	1,063	38,915	773	87.8	2.2	44.0
Maui	4,618	64,146	6,280	1,146	9,699	806	1,597	2,510	39,124	1,408	89.6	2.3	43.8
IDAHO	45,826	562,282	91,190	60,078	84,071	22,432	32,852	22,243	39,559	24,996	56.0	9.7	40.8
Ada	13,187	194,215	32,282	14,137	25,025	9,494	13,724	9,097	46,840	1,304	86.8	2.1	28.8
Adams	100	476	47	124	109	35	13	16	33,065	232	42.2	13.8	49.2
Bannock	2,017	24,676	5,215	1,738	4,517	2,435	1,289	806	32,660	757	51.9	9.0	35.1
Bear Lake	122	942	306	49	238	37	9	27	28,604	395	25.8	14.4	39.3
Benewah	235	2,170	392	D	286	64	39	82	37,629	288	42.7	8.7	41.2
Bingham	843	9,916	1,661	2,327	1,275	271	204	359	36,184	1,177	59.8	13.7	42.9
Blaine	1,412	11,001	889	430	1,429	268	700	437	39,734	190	47.4	23.2	42.8
Boise	157	609	26	14	110	D	11	15	25,348	90	68.9	7.8	45.0
Bonner	1,509	11,969	1,648	2,081	2,188	269	482	421	35,146	1,213	72.2	0.6	29.7
Bonneville	3,451	47,476	8,752	3,305	8,041	1,299	7,362	2,020	42,552	1,109	67.1	8.4	31.0
Boundary	367	2,458	528	438	434	54	100	82	33,340	348	48.9	4.6	39.1
Butte	56	942	D	D	78	11	D	34	35,872	189	24.3	27.0	58.1
Camas	31	174	10	D	21	D	NA	6	33,638	151	18.5	27.2	47.0
Canyon	3,979	50,955	7,072	9,198	8,488	1,057	1,400	1,707	33,507	2,289	77.7	2.6	36.8

Table B. States and Counties — **Agriculture**

STATE County	Acreage (1,000) [117]	Percent change, 2012-2017 [118]	Average size of farm [119]	Total irrigated (1,000) [120]	Total cropland (1,000) [121]	Average per farm [122]	Average per acre [123]	Value of machinery and equipment, average per farm (dollars) [124]	Total (mil dol) [125]	Average per farm (acres) [126]	Crops [127]	Livestock and poultry products [128]	Organic farms (number) [129]	Farms with internet access (percent) [130]	Total ($1,000) [131]	Percent of farms [132]
GEORGIA—Cont'd																
Putnam	38	34.3	206	1.8	14.7	865,498	4,206	100,518	34.7	186,780	20.0	80.0	NA	71.5	333	16.1
Quitman	19	111.8	521	D	4.2	1,201,990	2,307	64,583	D	D	D	D	NA	56.8	265	56.8
Rabun	8	-5.7	56	D	3.1	464,254	8,240	94,314	D	D	D	D	3	84.4	149	11.9
Randolph	122	2.2	797	33.6	66.3	2,256,188	2,832	275,608	43.4	283,784	85.0	15.0	NA	57.5	4,997	77.8
Richmond	13	-4.4	113	0.1	4.1	414,735	3,680	64,945	D	D	100.0	D	3	76.3	D	1.7
Rockdale	4	-22.8	57	0.0	1.0	402,413	7,060	38,569	0.5	6,108	49.6	50.4	NA	78.4	D	1.4
Schley	35	-1.5	392	D	8.5	1,116,611	2,848	60,512	14.8	166,843	18.9	81.1	NA	51.7	474	70.8
Screven	187	3.7	532	32.4	80.9	1,169,455	2,200	206,003	50.6	143,838	95.7	4.3	2	80.4	4,807	58.8
Seminole	105	19.0	669	41.0	79.5	2,100,309	3,141	286,662	61.9	394,401	92.3	7.7	1	69.4	6,536	65.6
Spalding	17	-9.5	76	0.1	4.8	387,738	5,121	32,050	9.3	41,338	34.9	65.1	NA	78.7	107	5.3
Stephens	20	6.0	86	0.0	4.8	496,202	5,774	112,819	114.3	503,595	0.3	99.7	NA	76.7	359	37.4
Stewart	51	-13.8	491	0.3	7.6	1,016,280	2,069	71,304	5.1	48,692	23.4	76.6	NA	59.6	534	56.7
Sumter	175	9.0	471	41.3	96.7	1,346,756	2,859	258,509	133.2	359,005	54.5	45.5	1	76.3	4,274	58.8
Talbot	30	-10.9	296	0.0	4.8	809,499	2,735	70,159	1.1	10,520	35.3	64.7	NA	79.4	242	18.6
Taliaferro	18	30.2	374	0.1	2.2	1,231,989	3,292	81,632	24.3	505,479	0.9	99.1	NA	70.8	323	39.6
Tattnall	114	5.7	208	14.6	52.5	804,395	3,874	140,385	387.7	708,722	28.7	71.3	5	77.3	1,663	32.7
Taylor	64	4.3	286	4.1	20.2	595,317	2,079	82,999	27.7	123,790	37.0	63.0	NA	72.8	686	52.2
Telfair	52	-21.7	205	6.4	17.5	452,315	2,210	59,880	10.3	40,475	91.7	8.3	NA	71.8	725	48.2
Terrell	134	11.1	524	32.0	88.2	1,468,061	2,803	285,046	53.1	207,543	92.9	7.1	NA	78.9	7,191	74.2
Thomas	187	8.1	459	11.4	85.3	1,670,886	3,640	166,382	78.7	192,958	68.1	31.9	1	78.9	5,807	52.2
Tift	121	42.8	394	33.3	77.0	1,251,034	3,174	203,433	84.0	274,425	95.4	4.6	3	79.4	6,522	56.2
Toombs	81	10.1	252	16.5	39.4	700,382	2,780	153,211	83.2	260,081	88.9	11.1	4	70.6	572	37.2
Towns	7	-20.0	64	0.0	2.0	352,577	5,497	70,921	2.2	21,257	70.8	29.2	NA	80.0	85	27.6
Treutlen	37	5.2	250	1.4	11.5	470,130	1,883	73,055	6.1	40,939	95.1	4.9	NA	62.2	233	34.5
Troup	45	38.2	172	0.2	6.4	557,147	3,246	64,542	5.9	22,778	46.6	53.4	6	83.1	288	15.7
Turner	92	6.4	376	27.9	58.2	1,159,576	3,084	220,779	65.2	265,240	57.1	42.9	1	76.8	4,558	58.1
Twiggs	39	1.4	338	3.5	14.0	817,257	2,417	82,020	7.1	61,362	88.8	11.2	1	69.8	495	35.3
Union	19	-6.1	77	0.0	7.3	446,988	5,771	77,107	37.4	148,940	15.0	85.0	5	74.9	158	27.9
Upson	32	-29.3	135	0.6	9.5	532,497	3,954	76,595	42.9	182,468	6.2	93.8	NA	77.4	113	10.2
Walker	91	13.9	145	0.2	26.1	616,558	4,239	72,803	152.4	244,223	3.1	96.9	1	80.9	1,100	27.7
Walton	47	-9.6	109	0.8	13.4	614,553	5,664	57,774	26.6	60,899	23.0	77.0	1	75.7	276	19.7
Ware	63	12.0	256	4.3	22.6	656,805	2,565	103,573	31.7	127,879	74.3	25.7	NA	71.0	1,210	20.6
Warren	38	10.7	282	D	11.3	841,802	2,982	57,368	3.1	22,807	48.2	51.8	NA	63.7	444	25.2
Washington	96	-3.8	251	8.8	35.1	528,574	2,106	87,028	19.9	51,893	65.0	35.0	1	70.2	1,684	47.5
Wayne	63	0.4	198	5.8	20.3	411,476	2,080	89,301	27.5	86,889	48.4	51.6	NA	72.2	539	19.0
Webster	60	24.3	548	10.4	33.3	1,338,185	2,442	377,331	22.8	209,394	79.6	20.4	NA	67.0	1,529	79.8
Wheeler	57	11.8	396	0.7	7.3	724,035	1,829	51,312	3.4	23,853	90.7	9.3	NA	74.1	269	54.5
White	19	-20.3	62	0.1	6.2	505,000	8,126	77,920	92.8	308,399	1.8	98.2	NA	84.1	388	13.6
Whitfield	37	-6.5	95	D	9.1	585,687	6,185	64,119	136.8	354,433	1.3	98.7	NA	79.0	565	33.7
Wilcox	91	-21.4	316	19.0	54.1	824,117	2,608	132,330	98.6	343,700	37.7	62.3	NA	72.1	3,486	71.1
Wilkes	91	-2.8	329	0.6	18.9	1,133,797	3,447	67,477	154.8	558,939	3.5	96.5	1	72.6	536	26.4
Wilkinson	30	90.8	217	0.4	11.0	444,442	2,050	50,675	6.2	44,186	40.0	60.0	1	52.9	183	20.7
Worth	218	-5.1	464	49.2	129.9	1,394,353	3,003	249,754	104.3	222,354	83.9	16.1	NA	77.0	9,709	54.2
HAWAII	1,135	0.5	155	45.5	191.2	1,445,188	9,328	50,701	563.8	76,938	74.0	26.0	167	76.1	8,362	9.0
Hawaii	664	-3.3	157	6.7	82.3	1,091,739	6,934	41,883	269.2	63,789	59.5	40.5	89	75.9	5,339	7.9
Honolulu	72	3.8	77	11.7	23.1	1,920,259	24,794	92,036	151.4	163,305	90.4	9.6	25	71.1	350	10.8
Kalawao	NA	NA	NA	NA	NA	NA	NA	NA	NA	NA	NA	NA	NA	NA	NA	NA
Kauai	150	4.2	194	22.3	29.3	1,744,739	8,982	47,852	61.0	78,946	75.2	24.8	13	70.4	499	12.5
Maui	249	8.6	177	4.8	56.6	2,027,299	11,466	51,466	82.2	58,385	90.3	9.7	40	83.5	2,174	9.4
IDAHO	11,692	-0.6	468	3,398.3	5,894.7	1,340,738	2,866	175,951	7,567.4	302,746	42.4	57.6	295	83.9	129,605	24.3
Ada	112	-22.0	86	57.3	62.9	819,575	9,511	80,276	131.6	100,936	32.5	67.5	9	88.3	471	4.4
Adams	163	19.7	703	22.2	16.9	1,089,369	1,550	83,372	12.6	54,306	25.4	74.6	NA	78.9	93	7.8
Bannock	315	6.8	416	40.0	181.5	812,963	1,953	97,293	37.8	49,943	56.8	43.2	1	81.6	5,606	33.9
Bear Lake	297	15.2	752	54.7	108.3	1,081,929	1,439	141,605	36.5	92,443	47.9	52.1	15	76.5	1,549	37.5
Benewah	140	-4.6	486	0.2	82.1	940,817	1,936	128,882	19.1	66,358	96.6	3.4	2	76.7	1,931	34.4
Bingham	933	7.3	793	333.9	397.7	2,016,632	2,544	258,056	453.1	384,999	77.8	22.2	6	84.9	13,317	24.8
Blaine	211	17.9	1,112	37.3	52.1	2,813,206	2,530	179,893	27.2	142,905	61.4	38.6	15	90.0	800	20.5
Boise	53	D	591	1.3	1.7	847,323	1,433	52,205	2.6	28,733	59.8	40.2	NA	75.6	6	3.3
Bonner	89	10.8	74	1.2	32.8	370,858	5,036	42,446	10.2	8,406	60.2	39.8	10	79.7	224	2.9
Bonneville	419	2.3	378	131.6	260.6	1,100,960	2,915	130,606	167.9	151,363	66.0	34.0	2	82.8	7,179	22.4
Boundary	69	-8.4	198	2.3	44.5	946,934	4,784	100,250	30.8	88,509	87.4	12.6	4	79.3	1,129	16.7
Butte	130	4.1	690	69.4	78.6	1,415,857	2,053	212,368	42.2	223,169	84.6	15.4	6	92.6	1,877	52.9
Camas	193	14.9	1,276	27.4	98.6	1,710,551	1,341	171,377	24.7	163,490	82.9	17.1	39	74.2	826	42.4
Canyon	275	-9.5	120	213.4	219.4	989,782	8,240	161,943	574.8	251,095	54.7	45.3	11	86.4	2,463	8.0

Table B. States and Counties — Water Use, Wholesale Trade, Retail Trade, and Real Estate

STATE County	Water use, 2015 Public supply water withdrawn (mil gal/ day)	Public supply gallons withdrawn per person per day	Wholesale Trade[1], 2012 Number of establishments	Number of employees	Sales (mil dol)	Average payroll (mil dol)	Retail Trade[2], 2012 Number of establishments	Number of employees	Sales (mil dol)	Average payroll (mil dol)	Real estate and rental and leasing,[2] 2012 Number of establishments	Number of employees	Sales (mil dol)	Average payroll (mil dol)
	133	134	135	136	137	138	139	140	141	142	143	144	145	146
GEORGIA—Cont'd														
Putnam	3.76	176.1	16	68	57.9	2.7	75	668	157.4	14.1	12	225	9.7	3.9
Quitman	0.17	73.8	1	D	D	D	10	55	12.1	0.9	1	D	D	D
Rabun	1.60	98.3	4	6	0.5	0.1	76	902	247.7	22.3	19	D	D	D
Randolph	0.88	122.3	5	40	70.8	1.7	27	191	47.6	4.2	5	5	1.8	0.1
Richmond	39.17	194.1	182	1,856	864.7	81.5	812	10,830	2,627.3	229.5	201	1,069	248.9	37.9
Rockdale	11.76	132.3	80	636	525.7	34.1	293	4,625	1,239.6	116.2	77	327	83.0	14.9
Schley	0.45	87.1	4	56	44.4	2.1	14	76	19.3	1.6	NA	NA	NA	NA
Screven	0.74	52.3	8	D	D	D	49	360	74.5	6.9	4	7	0.7	0.2
Seminole	0.50	57.8	13	76	109.1	4.2	52	331	73.0	6.4	4	7	1.4	0.1
Spalding	6.83	106.6	39	428	467.1	17.9	224	2,669	638.8	59.4	48	185	29.9	5.7
Stephens	3.38	132.1	19	D	D	D	99	1,113	262.5	24.5	14	46	6.2	1.2
Stewart	0.78	133.3	2	D	D	D	15	42	17.1	1.0	1	D	D	D
Sumter	2.48	80.6	35	425	305.9	13.2	137	1,382	311.0	29.1	22	57	8.1	1.3
Talbot	1.33	209.9	3	11	8.8	0.2	12	65	11.7	0.8	NA	NA	NA	NA
Taliaferro	0.05	30.5	NA	NA	NA	NA	5	10	2.3	0.1	1	D	D	D
Tattnall	1.22	48.4	21	459	212.9	18.1	64	444	103.0	8.0	6	17	2.0	0.3
Taylor	0.62	74.4	4	D	D	D	29	152	36.9	2.6	3	8	0.7	0.1
Telfair	1.22	74.4	11	48	35.7	1.4	43	290	59.8	4.8	1	D	D	D
Terrell	1.44	158.0	7	162	250.1	4.0	45	316	68.0	6.0	4	D	D	D
Thomas	5.64	125.2	60	441	406.8	18.4	218	2,154	564.6	48.0	42	123	82.2	4.6
Tift	4.78	117.3	67	1,041	634.1	42.8	221	2,405	805.6	54.4	36	136	21.8	4.5
Toombs	2.84	104.3	28	566	996.3	20.8	149	1,640	406.4	35.5	24	59	7.6	1.3
Towns	1.54	137.7	8	19	2.9	0.4	57	344	87.1	6.9	15	22	7.0	0.8
Treutlen	0.30	44.2	2	D	D	D	22	140	29.9	2.6	1	D	D	D
Troup	8.54	122.4	58	D	D	D	258	3,072	911.1	73.7	61	272	41.3	7.5
Turner	0.79	96.2	13	148	81.6	5.3	32	179	66.7	4.0	2	D	D	D
Twiggs	0.45	53.6	3	D	D	D	16	68	27.9	1.1	1	D	D	D
Union	1.82	81.7	9	57	26.8	1.9	93	1,007	242.9	22.0	32	71	9.9	2.1
Upson	3.02	114.5	7	D	D	D	93	970	207.9	20.6	11	26	3.4	0.6
Walker	6.62	97.3	34	D	D	D	151	1,441	355.1	28.1	16	29	4.4	1.0
Walton	3.16	35.7	74	620	295.0	28.5	196	2,403	744.5	57.9	65	149	23.0	5.0
Ware	2.74	77.5	33	D	D	D	204	2,356	627.4	52.4	26	85	10.2	2.2
Warren	0.32	58.6	1	D	D	D	14	86	14.5	1.7	3	10	0.5	0.2
Washington	2.00	96.1	12	105	133.5	4.1	72	766	187.0	17.3	14	117	9.2	3.2
Wayne	1.50	50.8	12	99	71.0	2.9	120	1,201	293.1	25.4	16	57	5.3	1.3
Webster	0.10	37.8	3	D	D	D	5	38	9.0	1.1	NA	NA	NA	NA
Wheeler	0.18	22.8	3	5	6.5	0.3	14	70	21.2	1.2	2	D	D	D
White	1.47	51.9	15	79	30.7	2.1	119	1,097	279.7	23.0	18	59	6.1	1.0
Whitfield	23.96	229.9	191	2,604	1,196.6	103.0	435	4,690	1,302.4	107.7	63	D	D	D
Wilcox	0.44	49.7	7	38	34.3	1.5	19	90	23.4	1.6	NA	NA	NA	NA
Wilkes	1.01	102.4	9	81	24.1	3.2	48	406	70.4	7.4	4	11	0.9	0.3
Wilkinson	0.70	76.5	8	35	8.4	1.1	24	150	32.5	2.4	1	D	D	D
Worth	1.01	48.8	22	D	D	D	56	430	117.1	10.9	9	D	D	D
HAWAII	266.92	186.4	1,561	16,686	9,608.0	724.5	4,643	68,360	18,901.7	1,835.0	1,919	11,369	3,411.2	483.9
Hawaii	39.70	202.1	178	D	D	D	648	9,084	2,390.8	241.3	245	1,172	226.5	39.1
Honolulu	168.78	169.0	1,167	13,446	8,052.8	596.9	2,889	46,165	13,036.4	1,233.1	1,219	7,213	2,553.5	340.7
Kalawao	0.01	112.4	NA	NA	NA	NA	1	D	D	D	NA	NA	NA	NA
Kauai	16.34	227.8	76	D	D	D	347	3,937	1,013.5	102.4	149	962	176.9	33.3
Maui	42.09	255.7	140	1,141	714.6	50.4	758	D	D	D	306	2,022	454.4	70.8
IDAHO	275.79	166.6	1,739	21,470	17,906.0	960.8	5,815	72,980	20,444.3	1,794.0	2,033	6,268	1,039.9	184.2
Ada	72.71	167.5	550	8,141	7,352.5	419.6	1,410	20,428	5,766.7	538.7	712	2,578	456.9	85.2
Adams	0.53	137.9	1	D	D	D	12	D	D	D	7	4	0.4	0.1
Bannock	16.91	201.9	80	D	D	D	299	4,330	1,155.3	95.7	80	221	31.5	5.2
Bear Lake	0.37	62.5	5	54	13.8	1.4	26	232	58.8	4.0	5	14	1.1	0.2
Benewah	0.52	57.4	4	D	D	D	34	286	76.5	7.3	6	9	1.2	0.2
Bingham	1.99	44.2	50	1,047	635.9	33.6	111	1,132	256.2	23.6	19	37	5.7	1.1
Blaine	5.44	251.9	31	D	D	D	183	1,348	298.6	38.7	92	D	D	D
Boise	0.48	68.0	1	D	D	D	15	107	20.0	1.5	5	11	1.4	0.2
Bonner	1.71	40.9	28	157	45.5	5.5	199	1,960	438.0	45.4	68	220	30.9	6.9
Bonneville	36.62	332.6	169	2,021	3,049.6	90.5	477	6,757	1,956.5	157.1	134	460	80.6	13.8
Boundary	0.39	34.5	7	D	D	D	47	386	100.1	9.0	7	5	0.8	0.1
Butte	1.43	571.8	3	D	D	D	13	86	21.8	1.6	2	D	D	D
Camas	0.14	131.3	NA	NA	NA	NA	3	D	D	D	NA	NA	NA	NA
Canyon	15.92	76.7	148	1,600	1,089.0	71.7	485	7,102	2,149.4	182.5	149	434	49.0	10.6

1 Merchant wholesalers, except manufacturers' sales branches and offices.   2. Employer establishments.

Table B. States and Counties — Professional Services, Manufacturing, and Accommodation and Food Services

STATE County	Professional, scientific, and technical services, 2012				Manufacturing, 2012				Accommodation and food services, 2012			
	Number of establish-ments	Number of employees	Sales (mil dol)	Average payroll (mil dol)	Number of establish-ments	Number of employees	Receipts (mil dol)	Annual payroll (mil dol)	Number of establis-hments	Number of employees	Receipts (mil dol)	Annual payroll (mil dol)
	147	148	149	150	151	152	153	154	155	156	157	158
GEORGIA—Cont'd												
Putnam	32	66	8.6	1.7	21	612	127.2	18.6	23	399	16.4	4.7
Quitman	1	D	D	D	NA	NA	NA	NA	1	D	D	D
Rabun	36	122	10.2	3.7	21	336	D	11.8	62	736	47.2	12.7
Randolph	8	28	2.5	0.6	4	D	D	D	11	66	2.7	0.7
Richmond	478	4,251	569.6	213.8	111	7,884	5,452.2	451.0	424	9,448	447.0	125.6
Rockdale	181	952	100.6	43.4	84	4,746	2,292.2	252.3	175	3,708	179.0	51.3
Schley	2	D	D	D	7	416	123.7	18.7	4	15	0.9	0.2
Screven	13	37	2.3	0.8	13	829	173.4	36.5	17	D	D	D
Seminole	8	D	D	D	3	6	D	D	15	D	D	D
Spalding	85	374	47.2	14.5	56	3,005	2,404.7	152.9	111	1,718	86.9	23.9
Stephens	39	205	28.1	15.2	54	1,807	511.6	73.5	42	595	24.9	6.4
Stewart	2	D	D	D	NA	NA	NA	NA	6	25	1.3	0.2
Sumter	39	D	D	D	25	1,103	492.5	37.8	59	882	37.2	10.2
Talbot	3	7	0.3	0.1	3	9	D	D	2	D	D	D
Taliaferro	NA	NA	NA	NA	NA	NA	NA	NA	1	D	D	D
Tattnall	20	76	5.4	1.7	9	59	7.3	1.5	15	D	D	D
Taylor	3	D	D	D	6	74	D	2.1	6	20	1.2	0.3
Telfair	10	37	2.7	1.0	8	D	D	D	15	D	D	D
Terrell	9	D	D	D	6	493	D	13.4	13	D	D	D
Thomas	74	331	41.1	12.2	41	2,677	674.9	109.0	82	1,240	59.3	15.0
Tift	81	533	47.6	23.0	39	1,289	528.1	51.5	98	2,175	100.8	26.9
Toombs	48	402	26.4	10.4	34	1,558	D	44.8	63	1,032	49.5	12.1
Towns	19	61	6.4	2.3	9	41	D	1.3	30	621	32.4	9.2
Treutlen	2	D	D	D	4	79	D	1.4	3	37	1.4	0.6
Troup	96	965	66.2	29.0	88	10,356	12,011.1	522.6	122	2,187	96.7	26.8
Turner	8	29	2.9	0.9	10	300	92.8	11.5	19	208	8.8	1.9
Twiggs	5	D	D	D	NA	NA	NA	NA	3	D	D	D
Union	43	165	15.3	5.5	27	260	54.0	10.2	46	547	28.4	7.1
Upson	30	126	15.3	3.8	19	1,252	D	51.1	39	512	25.3	6.6
Walker	51	497	16.1	7.1	55	3,652	1,753.7	129.3	49	D	D	D
Walton	158	516	65.3	18.8	56	1,800	777.9	84.4	103	1,603	72.9	19.9
Ware	61	252	23.2	6.9	31	1,118	D	35.1	66	1,317	59.3	14.8
Warren	4	6	0.7	0.2	NA	NA	NA	NA	3	7	0.4	0.1
Washington	24	170	14.2	7.8	17	565	157.5	21.4	27	409	18.3	5.0
Wayne	32	141	9.7	8.2	20	1,161	D	69.7	51	690	34.5	8.2
Webster	NA	NA	NA	NA	NA	NA	NA	NA	NA	NA	NA	NA
Wheeler	1	D	D	D	NA	NA	NA	NA	5	17	1.0	0.1
White	41	95	11.9	3.4	29	715	122.9	31.9	88	956	63.9	14.4
Whitfield	169	D	D	D	265	14,310	5,805.3	546.3	172	D	D	D
Wilcox	1	D	D	D	NA	NA	NA	NA	4	11	0.6	0.2
Wilkes	11	30	2.3	0.7	16	549	175.7	21.1	16	184	6.7	1.8
Wilkinson	5	38	2.9	0.9	12	763	D	52.9	6	25	1.0	0.2
Worth	16	55	5.4	1.7	11	256	D	10.2	14	D	D	D
HAWAII	3,226	21,629	3,334.1	1,265.6	796	11,440	D	465.0	3,518	98,364	9,536.7	2,536.0
Hawaii	294	1,502	193.3	72.1	112	1,182	283.3	46.4	430	12,297	1,124.5	324.7
Honolulu	2,399	18,234	2,895.1	1,105.4	544	9,076	D	370.8	2,355	57,486	5,273.2	1,333.0
Kalawao	NA	NA	NA	NA	NA	NA	NA	NA	NA	NA	NA	NA
Kauai	143	512	59.3	21.1	41	185	D	6.8	234	8,638	831.5	252.5
Maui	390	1,381	186.4	67.0	99	997	D	41.1	499	19,943	2,307.5	625.7
IDAHO	4,198	32,076	4,273.6	1,728.0	1,759	52,084	20,201.4	2,445.5	3,564	54,257	2,680.2	726.1
Ada	1,634	12,378	1,827.8	721.2	373	14,538	D	931.7	947	16,660	763.1	220.7
Adams	8	D	D	D	7	98	D	3.4	14	D	D	D
Bannock	165	1,277	84.2	40.3	44	1,633	916.3	67.7	197	3,199	135.5	37.2
Bear Lake	5	5	0.7	0.2	3	25	6.7	1.2	14	117	4.9	1.4
Benewah	9	D	D	D	11	548	D	D	23	D	D	D
Bingham	51	197	16.3	5.7	41	2,384	768.9	91.5	46	D	D	D
Blaine	154	652	91.7	45.5	45	298	57.8	12.8	111	2,628	138.2	49.2
Boise	9	8	0.6	0.1	4	13	4.2	0.7	23	D	D	D
Bonner	139	D	D	D	79	1,647	369.4	77.9	113	1,816	65.0	20.2
Bonneville	377	8,397	1,371.6	583.9	134	2,447	631.0	90.6	235	4,462	198.3	57.1
Boundary	23	90	6.0	2.2	24	293	D	11.6	23	D	D	D
Butte	2	D	D	D	NA	NA	NA	NA	11	D	D	D
Camas	NA	NA	NA	NA	NA	NA	NA	NA	7	32	1.4	0.2
Canyon	255	1,212	113.0	48.5	189	7,267	D	273.4	254	4,257	180.1	49.5

Health Care and Social Assistance, Other Services, Nonemployer Businesses, and Residential Construction

STATE County	Health care and social assistance, 2012				Other services, 2012				Nonemployer businesses, 2016		Value of residential construction authorized by building permits, 2018	
	Number of establishments	Number of employees	Receipts (mil dol)	Annual payroll (mil dol)	Number of establishments	Number of employees	Receipts (mil dol)	Annual payroll (mil dol)	Number	Receipts (mil dol)	New construction ($1,000)	Number of housing units
	159	160	161	162	163	164	165	166	167	168	169	170
GEORGIA—Cont'd												
Putnam	30	476	36.2	14.9	21	165	5.9	5.1	1,819	78.0	33,152	105
Quitman	3	D	D	D	2	D	D	D	145	3.9	329	5
Rabun	34	532	41.8	18.5	36	113	13.3	3.2	1,790	73.0	25,523	66
Randolph	8	D	D	D	8	18	2.8	0.4	408	11.3	1,000	4
Richmond	645	24,184	3,260.4	1,241.3	275	1,816	196.3	53.1	12,347	401.0	68,002	518
Rockdale	242	3,648	392.9	138.9	135	804	89.1	22.6	8,642	277.9	65,661	304
Schley	4	D	D	D	5	D	D	D	322	10.6	2,285	11
Screven	14	222	11.5	5.2	23	91	7.3	1.5	916	31.7	6,365	32
Seminole	22	D	D	D	11	D	D	D	578	23.0	125	2
Spalding	132	4,459	351.5	122.9	76	415	32.4	9.5	4,917	164.4	34,090	274
Stephens	52	1,390	110.8	47.2	29	222	12.1	3.9	1,655	65.2	500	1
Stewart	9	171	13.0	4.4	7	54	3.3	0.9	247	5.4	195	1
Sumter	80	D	D	D	45	D	D	D	1,822	54.5	2,315	17
Talbot	3	D	D	D	6	13	1.1	0.3	457	13.5	1,400	8
Taliaferro	1	D	D	D	4	D	D	D	110	3.3	NA	NA
Tattnall	27	720	99.8	26.5	15	D	D	D	1,294	48.0	3,492	26
Taylor	16	198	10.2	4.2	7	D	D	D	562	20.6	650	5
Telfair	18	476	25.2	12.3	14	51	6.4	1.4	644	29.9	0	0
Terrell	15	D	D	D	14	D	D	D	718	25.3	633	5
Thomas	146	3,668	404.9	149.3	63	483	52.9	11.5	3,123	139.4	21,847	100
Tift	110	3,122	399.3	149.5	56	290	26.7	7.8	3,029	132.4	16,146	177
Toombs	106	1,982	197.9	78.5	40	215	22.9	6.1	1,882	76.4	1,850	20
Towns	25	548	34.2	14.7	10	17	1.5	0.4	1,121	47.5	13,266	65
Treutlen	9	131	7.3	3.1	7	25	1.5	0.5	464	14.7	0	0
Troup	131	3,139	300.6	128.6	81	636	66.4	18.2	5,114	168.5	37,246	185
Turner	8	170	7.2	3.3	7	D	D	D	652	20.5	3,258	13
Twiggs	7	D	D	D	6	D	D	D	563	16.8	1,878	19
Union	66	1,110	97.3	39.7	28	168	20.5	4.3	2,231	87.1	54,654	211
Upson	65	1,433	130.3	53.2	40	D	D	D	1,712	54.6	2,154	14
Walker	53	957	64.0	26.6	39	258	22.2	7.7	4,133	199.8	23,356	135
Walton	133	1,554	176.9	57.5	113	346	33.7	8.0	7,986	317.3	103,395	618
Ware	119	2,883	284.9	112.7	53	261	25.1	7.1	1,881	67.3	16,461	133
Warren	5	134	6.5	3.2	4	D	D	D	366	11.3	0	0
Washington	33	1,001	56.1	27.1	29	71	6.4	1.7	1,208	38.8	9,083	81
Wayne	65	1,036	102.4	35.3	31	160	16.3	3.7	1,656	54.9	10,395	60
Webster	1	D	D	D	1	D	D	D	151	6.2	835	4
Wheeler	5	D	D	D	3	3	0.4	0.1	358	12.5	0	0
White	34	418	26.6	11.1	41	168	13.5	3.4	2,501	105.5	19,403	101
Whitfield	192	4,275	482.4	180.7	117	855	76.7	25.8	5,938	303.0	31,580	262
Wilcox	12	D	D	D	7	D	D	D	554	17.2	NA	NA
Wilkes	24	547	32.2	13.1	10	37	3.5	0.7	606	21.6	514	6
Wilkinson	15	D	D	D	10	29	2.2	0.6	601	14.9	1,148	8
Worth	26	D	D	D	27	64	7.4	1.8	1,273	46.8	5,469	36
HAWAII	3,559	66,772	8,136.9	3,290.6	2,808	19,348	2,004.8	538.7	108,308	5,285.5	1,359,881	4,659
Hawaii	469	7,503	781.2	356.4	288	1,387	166.1	41.0	17,590	786.4	322,391	1,043
Honolulu	2,520	50,049	6,302.6	2,481.0	2,012	14,967	1,522.4	411.8	66,902	3,377.8	645,840	2,410
Kalawao	NA	NA	NA	NA	NA	NA	NA	NA	NA	NA	NA	NA
Kauai	177	3,082	311.6	145.0	125	809	78.2	23.9	7,024	307.6	151,263	368
Maui	393	6,138	741.5	308.2	383	2,185	238.1	62.0	16,792	813.7	240,388	838
IDAHO	4,865	83,505	7,895.6	3,171.2	2,553	12,188	1,118.2	311.4	125,836	5,541.7	3,099,095	15,824
Ada	1,387	29,953	3,174.3	1,355.9	768	4,121	377.4	112.2	37,476	1,769.2	1,439,490	6,406
Adams	5	D	D	D	3	D	D	D	375	13.5	6,207	12
Bannock	335	3,819	314.1	115.4	120	591	61.6	15.7	5,106	202.1	46,617	404
Bear Lake	13	314	24.7	10.4	5	D	D	D	438	15.7	14,079	49
Benewah	16	391	28.2	12.2	14	D	D	D	576	23.0	5,109	32
Bingham	96	1,817	155.9	67.8	51	279	33.8	8.4	2,817	127.0	19,968	141
Blaine	72	687	73.4	31.9	89	299	46.6	11.2	3,620	216.7	62,279	104
Boise	5	18	1.3	0.5	8	D	D	D	668	24.9	25,749	95
Bonner	141	1,640	130.6	53.4	79	322	22.6	6.5	4,044	160.1	19,401	99
Bonneville	537	7,680	846.0	289.1	174	852	87.1	22.0	8,622	386.6	119,952	829
Boundary	28	536	30.2	14.8	18	40	3.4	0.9	961	38.7	16,316	68
Butte	7	D	D	D	6	D	D	D	184	4.6	0	0
Camas	4	13	0.4	0.2	NA	NA	NA	NA	91	3.3	1,556	12
Canyon	374	6,754	530.8	216.1	206	1,039	93.0	26.7	12,659	513.8	344,132	2,279

Table B. States and Counties — Government Employment and Payroll, and Local Government Finances

	Government employment and payroll, 2012									Local government finances, 2012				
			March payroll (percent of total)							General revenue				
													Taxes	
STATE County	Full-time equivalent employees	March payroll (dollars)	Adminis-tration, judicial, and legal	Police and corrections	Fire protection	Highways and transpor-tation	Health and welfare	Natural resources and utilities	Education and libraries	Total (mil dol)	Inter-govern-mental (mil dol)	Total (mil dol)	Per capita[1] (dollars)	
													Total	Property
	171	172	173	174	175	176	177	178	179	180	181	182	183	184

GEORGIA—Cont'd														
Putnam	984	3,113,107	7.0	8.5	2.1	1.9	21.4	3.9	53.4	77.1	16.7	40.8	1,927	1,196
Quitman	121	315,487	9.9	7.4	0.2	4.3	8.7	2.9	65.7	8.3	4.1	3.2	1,332	1,155
Rabun	712	2,242,761	6.8	10.9	2.2	4.4	7.2	5.6	61.5	63.4	12.6	43.0	2,638	1,882
Randolph	534	1,324,386	4.1	6.0	1.2	2.8	42.1	4.5	38.3	42.9	11.1	14.3	1,951	1,486
Richmond	7,950	24,545,151	7.9	10.6	4.4	2.7	3.5	7.3	62.0	723.6	324.4	222.4	1,098	673
Rockdale	3,955	12,355,812	6.2	9.9	4.2	1.3	0.7	4.5	71.2	266.8	93.9	129.0	1,503	1,071
Schley	221	708,164	2.4	6.6	0.0	3.3	4.8	4.1	78.8	16.0	8.4	5.0	1,011	733
Screven	656	1,803,310	6.3	10.5	2.8	3.9	4.8	5.5	64.2	45.6	23.1	16.0	1,128	780
Seminole	372	1,424,704	4.2	9.3	2.0	3.8	4.4	1.3	74.5	27.2	10.7	13.1	1,463	928
Spalding	2,703	8,758,007	4.7	13.1	5.5	2.0	7.8	7.1	56.8	223.0	90.1	90.6	1,418	906
Stephens	894	2,549,588	7.6	10.7	2.8	2.5	1.9	9.9	61.7	120.9	28.0	31.7	1,223	823
Stewart	231	632,898	9.4	19.7	2.8	4.9	5.1	4.7	52.5	14.0	5.9	5.5	915	668
Sumter	1,492	4,667,090	4.8	12.0	4.4	1.8	14.0	4.3	55.3	123.8	56.0	47.3	1,498	959
Talbot	263	648,950	15.0	7.1	0.0	6.9	4.5	5.3	60.1	16.0	5.2	8.8	1,350	1,039
Taliaferro	95	252,316	11.8	15.2	0.0	6.8	1.6	0.9	60.8	6.4	2.1	3.2	1,880	1,613
Tattnall	764	2,267,688	6.8	7.3	0.0	4.7	3.0	3.2	73.4	51.7	24.6	20.6	810	496
Taylor	402	1,087,805	6.6	7.8	0.7	2.6	1.3	2.5	76.3	24.2	12.5	8.6	1,017	618
Telfair	434	1,158,142	7.7	9.9	4.9	3.3	2.8	4.0	66.4	30.4	12.8	13.3	813	533
Terrell	443	1,230,523	6.4	14.1	3.6	2.3	4.9	4.0	64.2	29.7	13.0	12.4	1,376	912
Thomas	2,420	7,648,981	5.7	7.9	3.2	3.4	8.3	6.5	59.1	194.9	58.8	64.1	1,432	870
Tift	3,242	12,909,421	2.9	4.3	0.8	1.6	59.8	2.1	26.8	404.4	50.3	64.4	1,568	788
Toombs	1,085	3,290,743	4.9	9.0	1.7	1.4	3.9	3.2	74.9	191.8	42.5	32.2	1,177	561
Towns	518	1,438,233	4.8	7.4	0.8	3.1	0.3	24.8	49.8	26.3	6.4	15.9	1,518	962
Treutlen	241	645,937	7.5	7.8	0.4	3.2	1.3	4.5	74.0	28.8	21.1	5.0	740	446
Troup	3,339	10,586,640	4.7	11.9	4.4	1.8	9.1	6.2	59.3	240.0	99.8	101.3	1,480	879
Turner	509	1,317,091	10.3	7.4	1.7	4.5	3.8	5.8	62.7	31.0	13.3	10.2	1,209	826
Twiggs	296	826,420	11.0	20.1	0.5	4.9	0.4	1.5	60.0	20.2	6.9	10.5	1,247	910
Union	1,493	4,119,774	3.0	5.1	1.6	1.3	48.9	4.1	35.5	56.7	15.8	34.2	1,593	1,016
Upson	965	2,830,552	6.4	11.2	2.1	2.0	0.7	3.7	72.7	154.8	37.1	28.6	1,073	730
Walker	2,622	7,660,154	5.8	5.5	2.5	2.1	10.7	4.8	66.0	172.5	90.6	54.3	798	474
Walton	3,007	10,183,150	6.0	8.9	3.5	2.6	2.5	5.6	68.5	253.5	88.7	125.8	1,487	1,043
Ware	1,747	5,214,214	5.1	10.2	4.2	3.4	17.2	1.0	56.2	150.2	74.1	48.2	1,345	705
Warren	197	551,517	8.8	6.8	0.0	4.0	6.1	5.3	64.2	16.7	6.7	7.4	1,320	928
Washington	1,131	3,414,908	4.5	6.7	0.9	3.9	35.1	4.5	42.2	125.1	24.7	31.9	1,530	951
Wayne	1,486	4,440,469	3.8	6.1	0.9	3.2	35.1	2.4	45.9	139.5	38.9	37.7	1,243	759
Webster	104	294,610	7.7	5.3	0.0	3.0	2.2	1.0	80.8	9.5	3.7	4.2	1,493	1,310
Wheeler	259	643,558	10.3	8.6	0.0	6.2	1.6	4.0	68.1	17.9	10.2	6.1	772	542
White	868	2,678,650	6.8	11.0	0.9	2.2	1.2	3.4	72.6	77.2	27.9	40.3	1,464	942
Whitfield	4,096	14,180,499	3.9	6.7	4.0	3.4	7.2	11.9	61.8	347.4	152.6	112.5	1,088	733
Wilcox	281	825,846	7.4	8.9	0.0	5.0	0.3	1.5	76.4	20.6	10.9	7.4	819	578
Wilkes	700	2,101,724	4.1	4.7	2.3	3.1	36.0	3.8	45.3	48.7	11.7	15.5	1,540	1,102
Wilkinson	479	1,156,738	10.2	14.5	0.0	4.8	0.4	1.9	66.2	39.7	18.0	19.1	1,997	1,336
Worth	797	2,247,660	7.4	8.5	3.1	4.5	0.1	4.6	69.5	50.7	23.4	19.6	900	588
HAWAII	X	X	X	X	X	X	X	X	X	X	X	X	X	X
Hawaii	2,415	11,250,002	15.2	26.6	22.6	11.1	5.5	17.0	0.0	375.6	91.7	253.3	1,339	1,101
Honolulu	9,304	47,881,176	14.1	35.4	14.0	2.6	6.8	20.8	0.0	2,232.4	331.8	1,316.4	1,348	833
Kalawao	NA	NA	NA	NA	NA	NA	NA	NA	NA	NA	NA	NA	NA	NA
Kauai	1,232	5,830,608	20.2	19.2	15.5	10.5	6.2	20.4	0.0	188.8	66.9	100.2	1,465	1,179
Maui	2,328	11,762,934	19.0	23.7	16.4	6.9	6.2	25.4	0.0	252.6	23.1	224.7	1,420	1,317
IDAHO	X	X	X	X	X	X	X	X	X	X	X	X	X	X
Ada	12,112	39,983,613	9.7	14.3	6.3	4.1	3.0	5.8	55.5	1,138.5	454.6	413.3	1,010	956
Adams	147	443,031	15.8	17.4	0.0	11.4	1.6	4.6	45.7	11.9	6.2	4.4	1,132	952
Bannock	2,618	8,746,568	9.9	14.1	5.7	4.5	6.0	6.6	51.4	238.0	114.9	73.0	871	828
Bear Lake	229	654,192	13.1	9.9	0.2	7.8	3.3	5.5	57.6	22.6	13.4	2.6	441	419
Benewah	501	1,444,872	5.0	6.6	1.0	3.3	36.5	3.9	43.4	44.1	19.2	5.9	652	616
Bingham	1,565	4,338,272	6.4	11.2	2.5	4.1	0.9	3.8	70.0	101.5	63.5	23.4	514	501
Blaine	959	4,228,217	10.2	10.1	5.2	3.3	0.5	6.4	61.6	114.6	26.2	66.7	3,152	3,047
Boise	251	737,278	24.2	12.1	0.6	8.0	2.0	2.2	50.8	23.1	11.0	7.0	1,022	1,015
Bonner	1,368	4,223,862	11.1	13.5	5.6	4.8	4.5	6.4	51.1	107.8	42.8	46.9	1,158	1,112
Bonneville	3,464	10,839,917	6.9	10.9	5.5	3.6	4.1	8.8	57.9	271.5	135.2	82.8	776	747
Boundary	529	1,491,650	6.9	7.2	0.6	4.2	37.3	5.6	37.2	38.9	14.5	7.6	707	698
Butte	218	969,719	3.5	4.5	0.0	4.1	61.6	0.6	25.3	15.1	4.0	3.5	1,273	1,204
Camas	63	187,878	16.7	9.7	0.0	19.8	0.0	1.9	52.0	4.7	2.8	1.5	1,353	1,312
Canyon	5,895	18,424,410	6.4	13.6	4.1	2.0	2.4	5.1	63.5	487.9	253.1	149.0	768	705

1. Based on the resident population estimated as of July 1 of the year shown.

Table B. States and Counties — Local Government Finances, Government Employment, and Income Taxes

STATE County	Local government finances, 2012 (cont.) Direct general expenditure Total (mil dol)	Per capita[1] (dollars)	Percent of total for: Education	Health and hospitals	Police protection	Public welfare	Highways	Debt outstanding Total (mil dol)	Per capita[1] (dollars)	Government employment, 2017 Federal civilian	Federal military	State and local	Individual income tax returns, 2016 Number of returns	Mean adjusted gross income	Mean income tax
	185	186	187	188	189	190	191	192	193	194	195	196	197	198	199
GEORGIA—Cont'd															
Putnam	72.9	3,441	44.6	23.5	6.0	0.8	3.3	32.9	1,552	64	59	1,463	9,240	56,366	6,322
Quitman	8.2	3,406	52.3	7.2	6.2	1.8	4.5	6.3	2,614	8	6	144	860	32,594	2,291
Rabun	76.9	4,718	60.5	4.4	4.4	0.2	5.2	64.1	3,932	59	44	798	7,420	49,730	5,632
Randolph	40.0	5,457	32.6	34.8	3.1	0.0	2.6	8.5	1,166	21	18	585	2,500	33,335	2,825
Richmond	773.0	3,816	44.0	5.8	5.2	0.1	2.9	1,078.9	5,326	7,633	11,947	26,222	85,030	42,139	4,129
Rockdale	265.4	3,093	63.2	1.2	6.2	0.4	1.5	131.0	1,526	119	248	4,486	39,400	46,314	4,279
Schley	15.2	3,050	68.7	0.6	3.4	0.2	3.0	10.5	2,102	7	14	340	1,750	40,237	2,942
Screven	51.6	3,634	47.5	4.3	4.4	0.5	7.2	16.6	1,168	38	37	952	5,590	39,857	3,381
Seminole	28.0	3,127	58.5	3.1	7.8	0.0	6.4	2.0	222	22	23	436	3,270	41,439	3,893
Spalding	220.8	3,457	49.2	9.1	6.7	0.1	2.5	97.8	1,531	132	176	5,163	26,880	43,609	3,984
Stephens	131.2	5,068	39.4	38.7	2.9	0.3	1.2	65.0	2,510	65	70	1,670	10,440	43,085	4,072
Stewart	14.4	2,389	48.8	0.7	7.9	0.1	8.9	2.2	358	106	12	253	1,530	34,839	2,494
Sumter	189.6	6,009	27.5	40.2	3.7	0.1	1.5	43.4	1,374	120	77	2,600	11,600	38,868	3,409
Talbot	16.6	2,545	46.5	5.7	6.5	0.7	8.6	6.3	967	11	17	246	2,540	38,357	3,219
Taliaferro	6.4	3,816	48.9	2.7	14.8	2.5	5.5	0.7	438	4	4	136	640	32,041	1,977
Tattnall	52.9	2,082	60.1	2.7	5.1	0.1	7.0	17.8	701	50	57	2,021	7,940	40,242	3,793
Taylor	23.7	2,820	66.0	2.8	6.0	0.4	4.5	3.3	389	19	22	397	3,190	41,897	3,639
Telfair	30.5	1,866	55.4	3.3	8.2	0.4	6.3	11.0	675	30	35	775	3,800	35,380	2,806
Terrell	29.3	3,236	51.1	4.8	7.0	0.1	4.1	9.0	992	63	23	530	3,820	37,877	3,356
Thomas	190.8	4,266	41.2	9.8	5.5	0.1	5.3	245.9	5,499	180	121	3,127	18,460	52,442	6,188
Tift	381.3	9,285	20.1	64.4	1.5	0.1	1.9	195.8	4,767	204	107	5,471	16,580	45,350	4,509
Toombs	186.3	6,822	31.2	50.6	2.8	0.0	1.5	76.6	2,805	68	73	1,604	10,770	44,204	4,366
Towns	27.3	2,598	47.1	4.4	6.0	2.9	4.7	28.4	2,702	26	29	511	5,190	48,566	5,350
Treutlen	32.8	4,842	80.8	1.3	2.9	0.7	1.9	13.3	1,965	13	17	345	2,340	37,688	2,795
Troup	264.2	3,858	45.4	7.1	6.4	0.4	8.6	84.1	1,228	146	185	3,818	28,800	47,222	4,809
Turner	30.7	3,654	53.3	4.1	8.0	0.8	7.1	13.4	1,596	29	21	533	3,420	33,532	2,367
Twiggs	20.6	2,444	54.2	2.1	10.0	1.2	8.4	10.3	1,223	11	22	341	3,430	38,759	3,073
Union	54.6	2,546	54.2	3.2	5.7	0.9	3.8	28.4	1,326	55	64	1,865	10,120	49,006	5,045
Upson	143.4	5,384	30.0	51.3	2.2	0.0	1.4	37.4	1,403	43	71	1,268	10,630	41,889	3,684
Walker	177.3	2,604	57.4	15.8	4.9	0.8	3.6	84.0	1,233	105	186	2,944	25,860	43,660	3,921
Walton	248.4	2,937	56.6	1.1	6.4	1.4	4.9	295.1	3,490	151	250	3,513	38,690	55,719	5,728
Ware	150.8	4,210	40.9	26.4	5.2	0.2	4.1	43.3	1,209	98	92	3,251	13,560	41,393	3,820
Warren	15.9	2,855	53.9	0.2	11.9	1.1	8.2	9.0	1,620	19	14	261	2,260	35,611	2,713
Washington	93.4	4,474	37.1	33.1	4.7	0.1	6.2	65.8	3,153	49	51	2,249	7,920	43,609	4,224
Wayne	133.6	4,408	40.5	35.6	3.7	0.5	4.6	47.0	1,550	386	77	1,912	10,540	44,223	3,812
Webster	9.9	3,552	48.2	4.4	3.0	0.6	5.2	2.9	1,037	4	7	127	900	34,804	2,682
Wheeler	20.1	2,548	57.2	2.6	5.1	0.0	4.0	7.1	901	11	15	303	1,830	32,917	2,309
White	82.8	3,003	62.2	1.4	5.2	0.4	3.1	24.2	879	51	79	1,092	11,440	46,750	4,336
Whitfield	397.4	3,845	52.0	10.1	3.9	0.2	4.6	103.9	1,005	152	284	5,358	42,150	51,368	5,862
Wilcox	20.2	2,223	65.8	2.8	6.4	1.0	7.1	1.1	120	27	19	570	2,650	35,002	2,616
Wilkes	56.9	5,644	29.5	36.5	4.0	0.5	3.2	51.2	5,077	28	27	743	4,020	40,857	3,675
Wilkinson	52.8	5,509	73.3	2.0	4.8	0.6	3.6	25.9	2,707	19	24	466	3,880	41,344	3,546
Worth	55.0	2,532	54.0	1.3	8.3	0.1	10.1	14.9	684	35	56	884	8,210	40,737	3,583
HAWAII	X	X	X	X	X	X	X	X	X	33,426	55,415	93,533	685,220	62,493	7,602
Hawaii	354.9	1,876	0.0	0.0	13.4	1.9	13.5	415.5	2,196	1,318	1,418	11,915	87,740	53,523	6,175
Honolulu	1,596.7	1,635	0.0	1.5	15.2	0.0	7.8	5,300.0	5,428	30,692	52,182	69,038	481,540	65,538	8,105
Kalawao	NA	NA	NA	NA	NA	NA	NA	NA	NA	(2) 867	(2)1,191	(2)8,384	NA	NA	NA
Kauai	196.1	2,865	0.0	0.0	13.7	5.8	8.0	246.2	3,598	549	624	4,196	35,390	57,629	6,840
Maui	264.1	1,669	0.0	0.0	15.8	6.0	2.7	281.6	1,780	(2)	(2)	(2)	80,560	56,193	6,478
IDAHO	X	X	X	X	X	X	X	X	X	13,026	8,905	111,207	739,670	56,375	6,486
Ada	1,060.4	2,592	40.6	0.3	10.7	0.9	7.6	516.6	1,263	5,803	1,554	29,525	207,610	71,112	9,625
Adams	10.4	2,645	37.6	0.0	12.3	0.0	13.2	4.7	1,205	110	14	210	1,760	45,780	4,617
Bannock	221.0	2,637	41.2	2.7	8.1	1.0	5.5	54.8	654	555	277	7,900	34,650	49,044	4,583
Bear Lake	24.3	4,106	33.5	22.5	2.2	0.4	1.3	2.5	424	53	20	629	2,590	44,399	3,814
Benewah	38.9	4,264	35.2	40.0	2.3	0.7	4.2	11.6	1,277	47	30	1,290	3,940	42,183	3,427
Bingham	100.2	2,204	61.5	0.3	7.5	0.7	6.2	46.6	1,024	211	150	3,898	18,510	45,782	4,354
Blaine	113.0	5,346	53.5	2.2	8.7	3.0	3.7	69.4	3,281	101	72	1,324	12,010	93,240	15,778
Boise	17.6	2,582	45.9	0.8	0.9	0.9	9.6	15.5	2,261	145	24	329	3,440	58,690	6,915
Bonner	109.1	2,696	37.9	3.6	6.5	0.6	9.0	31.1	769	190	142	2,266	20,050	52,867	5,797
Bonneville	269.6	2,527	46.0	1.3	7.4	0.3	4.9	252.9	2,370	762	376	5,704	47,830	65,749	7,737
Boundary	40.5	3,751	26.8	27.6	9.8	1.0	7.6	14.5	1,345	153	39	946	5,160	44,620	4,135
Butte	12.7	4,635	28.6	45.0	2.1	0.8	3.4	2.7	1,003	59	28	161	1,020	42,290	3,619
Camas	4.6	4,281	41.0	0.3	12.3	0.2	19.9	3.6	3,301	24	4	93	450	56,127	5,282
Canyon	467.4	2,411	45.9	1.7	8.3	1.0	4.9	465.5	2,401	373	703	9,184	86,320	45,858	3,992

1. Based on the resident population estimated as of July 1 of the year shown.   2. Kalawao county is included with Maui county.

Table B. States and Counties — Land Area and Population

State / county code	CBSA code[1]	County code[2]	STATE County	Land area[3] (sq. mi)	Total persons 2018	Rank	Per square mile	White	Black	American Indian, Alaska Native	Asian and Pacific Islancer	Percent Hispanic or Latino[4]	Under 5 years	5 to 17 years	18 to 24 years	25 to 34 years	35 to 44 years	45 to 54 years
				1	2	3	4	5	6	7	8	9	10	11	12	13	14	15
			IDAHO—Cont'd															
16029		6	Caribou	1,764.2	7,060	2,660	4.0	93.1	0.4	1.1	1.0	5.7	6.9	21.7	7.3	11.2	12.8	10.3
16031	15,420	7	Cassia	2,565.6	23,864	1,652	9.3	70.6	0.7	1.2	1.4	27.4	7.9	23.8	9.0	12.2	12.1	9.8
16033		9	Clark	1,763.1	852	3,113	0.5	52.6	0.8	2.0	1.5	44.5	5.5	17.7	11.0	11.4	12.6	11.3
16035		6	Clearwater	2,457.3	8,758	2,521	3.6	91.9	1.0	3.5	1.3	4.4	3.8	12.8	5.9	10.5	10.3	12.8
16037		8	Custer	4,922.2	4,280	2,879	0.9	93.7	0.8	1.9	0.9	4.7	4.8	12.6	5.1	8.9	10.1	10.8
16039	34,300	6	Elmore	3,075.1	27,259	1,517	8.9	75.3	3.7	2.0	4.8	17.4	8.4	17.1	12.0	17.1	11.0	9.6
16041	30,860	3	Franklin	663.0	13,726	2,183	20.7	92.2	0.5	1.2	0.6	6.7	7.4	24.5	8.8	10.5	13.0	10.2
16043	39,940	6	Fremont	1,864.0	13,168	2,219	7.1	85.8	0.5	1.2	0.9	12.5	6.6	19.2	9.1	11.4	12.6	11.2
16045	14,260	2	Gem	559.8	17,634	1,942	31.5	89.5	0.5	1.9	1.7	8.4	6.0	16.9	6.9	10.4	10.8	12.2
16047		7	Gooding	729.3	15,196	2,081	20.8	68.6	0.6	1.6	1.1	29.5	7.1	20.4	8.4	11.5	11.5	11.2
16049		6	Idaho	8,477.5	16,513	2,008	1.9	92.6	0.8	4.1	1.1	3.5	4.7	15.0	6.6	8.6	9.8	10.6
16051	26,820	3	Jefferson	1,093.7	29,439	1,447	26.9	87.7	0.5	1.1	1.3	10.6	8.6	25.5	8.3	12.0	13.7	9.9
16053	46,300	7	Jerome	597.5	24,015	1,641	40.2	62.2	0.6	1.2	0.8	36.4	8.3	22.5	8.3	13.3	12.3	10.8
16055	17,660	3	Kootenai	1,237.8	161,505	408	130.5	92.6	0.8	2.2	1.9	4.8	6.0	16.8	7.5	12.9	12.0	12.1
16057	34,140	4	Latah	1,075.9	40,134	1,175	37.3	90.9	1.6	1.7	4.1	4.5	5.5	13.5	23.6	14.3	10.2	9.1
16059		7	Lemhi	4,563.7	7,961	2,597	1.7	94.9	0.6	1.8	0.9	3.5	4.9	13.7	5.4	8.7	9.9	9.7
16061		8	Lewis	478.8	3,861	2,912	8.1	86.8	1.3	8.0	3.0	4.7	5.1	17.6	5.8	8.9	9.2	10.5
16063	25,200	9	Lincoln	1,201.4	5,360	2,804	4.5	68.0	0.7	1.6	1.2	30.4	6.8	22.1	8.7	11.3	13.9	11.6
16065	39,940	4	Madison	469.3	39,304	1,197	83.8	89.6	0.9	0.8	2.6	7.8	9.6	17.3	31.1	15.1	7.7	6.0
16067	15,420	7	Minidoka	757.0	20,825	1,783	27.5	62.6	0.6	1.4	0.8	35.8	8.0	20.4	9.0	12.6	11.2	10.7
16069	30,300	3	Nez Perce	848.3	40,408	1,173	47.6	89.1	0.9	6.7	1.7	4.0	5.9	15.3	8.7	13.4	11.4	11.8
16071		8	Oneida	1,199.0	4,488	2,860	3.7	93.8	0.6	0.7	0.8	4.7	6.1	22.2	6.7	8.8	11.7	10.3
16073	14,260	2	Owyhee	7,668.2	11,693	2,315	1.5	69.8	0.7	3.6	1.0	26.3	6.4	19.6	8.3	11.0	11.5	11.7
16075	36,620	6	Payette	406.9	23,551	1,660	57.9	80.3	0.7	2.1	1.7	17.4	6.5	19.7	7.6	11.5	11.5	12.1
16077		6	Power	1,403.8	7,768	2,611	5.5	61.9	0.7	3.1	1.1	34.8	8.4	22.8	8.7	12.1	10.3	9.8
16079		6	Shoshone	2,637.4	12,796	2,237	4.9	93.5	0.8	3.4	1.2	3.6	6.0	14.5	6.9	10.8	10.3	12.2
16081	27,220	9	Teton	449.1	11,640	2,316	25.9	82.0	0.3	0.8	0.9	16.8	6.3	18.3	6.8	12.8	16.4	14.7
16083	46,300	5	Twin Falls	1,921.7	86,081	671	44.8	80.0	0.9	1.3	2.4	16.9	7.3	20.2	8.4	14.2	12.7	10.5
16085		8	Valley	3,665.1	11,041	2,351	3.0	93.5	0.6	1.6	1.2	4.7	4.6	13.5	5.1	9.9	12.3	12.0
16087		6	Washington	1,452.9	10,161	2,415	7.0	80.8	0.6	2.2	1.2	16.9	5.7	17.0	7.3	8.6	10.4	11.1
17000		0	**ILLINOIS**	55,514.0	12,741,080	X	229.5	62.5	14.9	0.5	6.5	17.4	6.0	16.5	9.2	13.9	12.9	12.9
17001	39,500	5	Adams	855.1	65,691	814	76.8	93.3	5.1	0.5	1.3	1.7	6.3	16.2	7.8	12.1	11.3	11.9
17003	16,020	3	Alexander	235.5	6,060	2,745	25.7	65.2	33.4	0.9	0.8	1.8	6.5	16.6	5.7	10.3	10.2	12.6
17005	41,180	1	Bond	380.3	16,630	2,003	43.7	88.9	6.8	0.9	1.2	3.6	4.8	14.7	7.5	14.0	13.2	12.5
17007	40,420	2	Boone	280.8	53,577	947	190.8	73.5	3.1	0.7	1.9	22.4	5.6	19.2	9.2	10.7	12.1	14.5
17009		7	Brown	305.7	6,556	2,706	21.4	74.3	18.8	0.4	0.5	6.7	4.4	11.5	10.3	19.5	15.4	13.5
17011	36,860	7	Bureau	869.1	32,993	1,358	38.0	88.5	1.5	0.5	1.2	9.5	5.3	16.1	7.3	10.8	11.3	12.6
17013	41,180	1	Calhoun	253.8	4,802	2,845	18.9	97.8	0.6	0.5	0.4	1.3	5.1	15.5	6.7	9.5	10.4	13.7
17015		7	Carroll	445.0	14,312	2,139	32.2	94.2	1.7	0.7	0.9	3.9	5.1	14.2	6.8	10.1	10.5	11.9
17017		6	Cass	375.8	12,260	2,275	32.6	76.3	4.2	0.4	0.8	19.2	6.6	17.2	7.9	11.9	12.4	12.7
17019	16,580	3	Champaign	996.1	209,983	319	210.8	69.3	14.5	0.5	12.4	6.1	5.5	13.3	23.1	14.3	10.9	9.6
17021	45,380	6	Christian	709.5	32,661	1,364	46.0	95.9	2.2	0.5	0.8	1.7	5.1	15.2	7.7	12.2	11.9	13.3
17023		6	Clark	501.4	15,596	2,064	31.1	97.3	0.8	0.6	0.7	1.6	5.9	16.8	7.3	11.0	11.6	12.9
17025		7	Clay	468.3	13,253	2,217	28.3	96.8	0.9	0.6	1.1	1.6	6.0	16.9	7.0	11.6	11.3	12.3
17027	41,180	1	Clinton	474.0	37,639	1,234	79.4	92.5	4.2	0.5	0.9	3.2	5.8	15.4	7.7	13.4	12.7	13.4
17029	16,660	5	Coles	508.3	50,885	978	100.1	92.1	4.7	0.5	1.5	2.7	4.9	13.1	16.9	13.3	10.8	10.8
17031	16,980	1	Cook	944.9	5,180,493	2	5,482.6	43.4	23.7	0.5	8.5	25.5	6.1	15.7	8.8	16.3	13.5	12.5
17033		7	Crawford	443.6	18,807	1,882	42.4	91.8	5.7	0.6	0.9	2.2	5.4	14.5	7.5	13.9	12.6	13.0
17035	16,660	9	Cumberland	345.9	10,808	2,364	31.2	97.6	0.9	0.6	0.9	1.1	6.0	16.1	6.9	11.5	11.7	12.5
17037	16,980	1	DeKalb	631.3	104,143	579	165.0	77.9	8.6	0.5	3.4	11.4	5.6	15.8	19.5	13.2	11.2	10.8
17039	14,010	3	De Witt	397.6	15,769	2,051	39.7	95.6	1.3	0.6	0.8	2.9	5.4	16.0	7.0	11.5	11.9	13.5
17041		6	Douglas	416.7	19,479	1,851	46.7	91.4	1.0	0.7	0.9	7.2	6.4	18.5	7.5	12.4	11.8	11.6
17043	16,980	1	DuPage	327.7	928,589	57	2,833.7	67.9	5.5	0.4	13.5	14.5	5.9	16.7	8.6	12.7	12.9	13.5
17045		6	Edgar	623.4	17,360	1,954	27.8	97.5	1.0	0.6	0.5	1.3	5.1	15.3	7.2	10.8	11.6	12.6
17047		9	Edwards	222.4	6,392	2,721	28.7	97.3	1.0	0.5	0.6	1.6	5.5	17.0	6.7	10.1	11.8	13.1
17049	20,820	7	Effingham	478.8	34,208	1,322	71.4	96.3	0.9	0.4	1.0	2.2	6.7	17.0	7.8	13.1	11.4	12.0
17051		6	Fayette	716.5	21,416	1,758	29.9	93.2	4.8	0.6	0.6	1.8	5.9	15.2	8.4	12.7	12.4	12.7
17053	16,580	3	Ford	485.6	13,264	2,215	27.3	94.7	1.5	0.7	0.9	3.6	6.1	16.8	7.7	11.6	11.6	12.2
17055		4	Franklin	408.9	38,701	1,209	94.6	97.0	1.1	0.8	0.7	1.8	6.1	16.2	7.2	11.4	11.7	13.0
17057	15,900	6	Fulton	865.7	34,844	1,307	40.2	92.5	4.2	0.6	0.5	3.1	5.0	14.8	7.7	12.2	12.7	12.9
17059		8	Gallatin	323.0	5,058	2,828	15.7	97.0	1.3	1.2	0.5	1.7	5.2	15.7	6.3	10.7	11.8	13.0
17061		6	Greene	543.0	13,044	2,227	24.0	96.9	1.7	0.6	0.4	1.3	5.2	16.0	7.5	11.4	11.9	13.3
17063	16,980	1	Grundy	418.1	50,972	974	121.9	87.1	2.0	0.4	1.3	10.2	6.3	19.1	8.1	12.5	13.9	13.4
17065		7	Hamilton	434.6	8,163	2,581	18.8	97.0	1.1	0.6	0.5	1.7	5.5	16.4	6.9	10.4	11.9	12.1
17067	22,800	7	Hancock	793.7	17,844	1,928	22.5	97.0	1.1	0.6	0.7	1.6	5.5	15.5	6.7	10.7	10.9	12.0

1. CBSA = Core Based Statistical Area. See Appendix A for explanation. See Appendix B for list of metropolitan areas with component counties.   2. County type code from the Economic Research Service of USDA Rural-Urban Continuum Codes. See Appendix A for definition.   3. Dry land or land partially or temporarily covered by water.   4. May be of any race.

Table B. States and Counties — Population and Households

STATE County	55 to 64 years	65 to 74 years	75 years and over	Percent female	2000	2010	2000-2010	2010-2018	Births	Deaths	Net Migration	Number	Persons per household	Family house-holds	Female family house-holder[1]	One person
	Age (percent) (cont.)				Total persons		Percent change		Components of change, 2010-2018			Households, 2013-2017		Percent		
	16	17	18	19	20	21	22	23	24	25	26	27	28	29	30	31
IDAHO—Cont'd																
Caribou	12.4	10.0	7.5	48.9	7,304	6,963	-4.7	1.4	748	538	-117	2,533	2.67	73.4	3.8	21.7
Cassia	11.1	7.9	6.3	49.1	21,416	22,964	7.2	3.9	3,164	1,597	-671	7,827	2.95	77.8	9.3	19.7
Clark	12.8	9.7	8.0	49.3	1,022	982	-3.9	-13.2	73	57	-148	313	3.31	78.0	11.8	22.0
Clearwater	16.6	15.8	11.5	45.0	8,930	8,761	-1.9	0.0	539	902	360	3,706	2.02	63.1	6.7	27.9
Custer	18.7	18.3	10.7	48.7	4,342	4,366	0.6	-2.0	325	331	-81	1,850	2.18	67.2	5.9	29.0
Elmore	11.4	8.1	5.4	47.6	29,130	27,040	-7.2	0.8	3,871	1,474	-2,251	10,062	2.54	69.4	8.2	24.4
Franklin	11.4	8.0	6.2	48.8	11,329	12,786	12.9	7.4	1,642	812	106	4,286	3.05	80.6	9.6	16.2
Fremont	13.1	9.7	7.1	47.7	11,819	13,236	12.0	-0.5	1,558	872	-770	4,383	2.81	78.2	8.7	19.5
Gem	15.2	12.7	9.2	50.0	15,181	16,719	10.1	5.5	1,638	1,621	899	6,404	2.61	68.3	12.1	26.6
Gooding	12.6	9.6	7.7	49.1	14,155	15,472	9.3	-1.8	1,722	1,186	-819	5,550	2.71	68.8	9.5	23.7
Idaho	16.8	16.5	11.4	47.5	15,511	16,267	4.9	1.5	1,289	1,468	439	6,480	2.40	66.6	5.5	28.7
Jefferson	10.5	7.0	4.5	49.2	19,155	26,142	36.5	12.6	3,966	1,255	580	8,470	3.23	80.5	5.1	16.4
Jerome	11.4	7.7	5.3	49.0	18,342	22,366	21.9	7.4	3,305	1,314	-348	7,741	2.95	74.7	10.4	19.6
Kootenai	13.7	11.5	7.5	50.6	108,685	138,466	27.4	16.6	14,532	10,710	19,111	58,873	2.52	69.7	10.2	24.1
Latah	10.3	8.2	5.2	49.2	34,935	37,243	6.6	7.8	3,687	1,856	1,069	15,448	2.29	55.0	6.4	29.7
Lemhi	17.4	17.3	12.9	49.4	7,806	7,936	1.7	0.3	612	788	198	3,703	2.04	62.2	5.7	35.2
Lewis	16.6	14.7	11.7	49.2	3,747	3,821	2.0	1.0	321	315	37	1,626	2.32	59.0	5.7	34.9
Lincoln	11.5	8.8	5.3	48.1	4,044	5,206	28.7	3.0	604	297	-157	1,609	3.26	71.9	7.8	23.9
Madison	6.2	4.0	3.0	49.4	27,467	37,551	36.7	4.7	8,974	1,052	-6,235	10,633	3.54	80.9	4.3	13.3
Minidoka	12.0	9.1	7.2	49.9	20,174	20,055	-0.6	3.8	2,655	1,407	-483	7,357	2.77	76.0	11.0	19.9
Nez Perce	13.5	10.9	9.1	50.6	37,410	39,270	5.0	2.9	3,952	4,093	1,306	16,308	2.39	66.3	12.4	27.6
Oneida	14.0	11.2	9.1	49.8	4,125	4,286	3.9	4.7	418	304	84	1,581	2.69	72.3	5.7	25.9
Owyhee	13.7	10.6	7.2	49.0	10,644	11,526	8.3	1.4	1,142	756	-222	4,190	2.68	68.7	8.9	27.3
Payette	12.8	10.3	8.1	50.1	20,578	22,622	9.9	4.1	2,523	1,670	83	8,571	2.65	69.3	8.4	24.9
Power	12.4	9.1	6.3	49.1	7,538	7,819	3.7	-0.7	1,070	488	-647	2,544	2.99	73.2	8.7	25.7
Shoshone	16.3	13.7	9.1	49.8	13,771	12,800	-7.1	0.0	1,126	1,499	364	5,614	2.17	63.4	9.7	32.2
Teton	12.1	8.8	3.7	47.5	5,999	10,165	69.4	14.5	1,253	317	521	3,764	2.86	64.7	6.3	26.7
Twin Falls	11.4	8.8	6.6	50.6	64,284	77,230	20.1	11.5	10,015	5,984	4,858	30,096	2.69	71.0	10.6	23.9
Valley	17.4	17.3	7.8	48.2	7,651	9,854	28.8	12.0	736	574	1,003	3,532	2.81	67.0	10.4	29.9
Washington	14.9	14.3	10.8	50.2	9,977	10,198	2.2	-0.4	884	964	47	3,979	2.48	65.0	9.7	29.7
ILLINOIS	13.1	9.0	6.7	50.9	12,419,293	12,831,572	3.3	-0.7	1,294,578	866,111	-519,943	4,818,452	2.61	64.8	12.4	29.2
Adams	14.1	10.4	9.8	50.8	68,277	67,097	-1.7	-2.1	6,760	6,536	-1,591	27,461	2.38	64.5	9.7	30.4
Alexander	16.2	12.3	9.6	51.6	9,590	8,238	-14.1	-26.4	775	805	-2,187	2,432	2.70	63.5	20.0	33.6
Bond	14.7	10.4	8.1	48.0	17,633	17,768	0.8	-6.4	1,301	1,416	-1,041	6,132	2.49	66.4	8.2	27.9
Boone	12.9	9.2	6.7	50.0	41,786	54,167	29.6	-1.1	4,784	3,198	-2,195	18,709	2.85	73.7	11.4	21.4
Brown	11.5	7.6	6.3	35.3	6,950	6,937	-0.2	-5.5	463	439	-406	2,066	2.33	62.7	7.1	30.3
Bureau	14.7	11.6	10.3	50.9	35,503	34,980	-1.5	-5.7	2,837	3,173	-1,658	13,816	2.40	69.5	10.2	26.8
Calhoun	15.7	12.4	11.0	50.2	5,084	5,089	0.1	-5.6	403	441	-251	1,881	2.54	67.3	5.0	29.1
Carroll	15.8	14.0	11.5	50.1	16,674	15,391	-7.7	-7.0	1,175	1,541	-710	6,573	2.20	62.2	7.3	32.4
Cass	13.5	9.6	8.2	49.5	13,695	13,641	-0.4	-10.1	1,432	1,206	-1,630	5,160	2.46	65.1	11.7	28.5
Champaign	10.5	7.5	5.3	50.2	179,669	201,081	11.9	4.4	19,622	10,485	-360	81,418	2.36	52.4	9.4	34.9
Christian	14.7	10.5	9.4	49.1	35,372	34,793	-1.6	-6.1	2,848	3,385	-1,594	13,892	2.27	64.3	11.5	30.1
Clark	14.6	10.9	8.9	50.3	17,008	16,335	-4.0	-4.5	1,555	1,685	-604	6,809	2.31	69.3	11.5	25.0
Clay	14.5	11.5	8.8	50.5	14,560	13,815	-5.1	-4.1	1,316	1,422	-447	5,624	2.32	67.3	8.1	29.7
Clinton	14.6	9.5	7.7	48.2	35,535	37,762	6.3	-0.3	3,424	2,850	-682	14,183	2.49	67.7	8.1	27.0
Coles	13.1	9.3	7.6	51.5	53,196	53,876	1.3	-5.6	4,191	4,204	-3,009	21,006	2.31	58.6	11.0	33.2
Cook	12.3	8.4	6.3	51.4	5,376,741	5,195,026	-3.4	-0.3	566,076	332,803	-247,645	1,956,561	2.63	60.5	14.5	32.6
Crawford	14.3	10.4	8.5	47.7	20,452	19,818	-3.1	-5.1	1,744	1,958	-794	7,665	2.25	65.0	8.2	30.2
Cumberland	15.6	10.8	8.8	50.3	11,253	11,045	-1.8	-2.1	1,013	927	-319	4,287	2.51	68.2	8.6	28.1
DeKalb	11.1	7.4	5.3	50.5	88,969	105,160	18.2	-1.0	9,676	5,786	-5,001	37,420	2.66	61.7	11.7	26.7
De Witt	15.4	10.9	8.3	50.5	16,798	16,558	-1.4	-4.8	1,448	1,525	-706	6,704	2.37	66.3	9.2	30.0
Douglas	13.7	9.7	8.4	50.6	19,922	19,977	0.3	-2.5	2,110	1,581	-1,024	7,580	2.59	66.1	8.4	28.4
DuPage	14.0	9.2	6.3	50.9	904,161	916,771	1.4	1.3	88,224	50,386	-26,236	340,669	2.70	70.1	9.1	25.0
Edgar	15.6	12.0	9.8	51.0	19,704	18,576	-5.7	-6.5	1,506	1,967	-751	7,669	2.25	68.7	12.1	27.9
Edwards	14.5	11.8	9.7	50.7	6,971	6,721	-3.6	-4.9	626	588	-369	2,810	2.32	66.0	10.4	30.1
Effingham	14.4	9.6	8.1	50.2	34,264	34,246	-0.1	-0.1	3,683	2,901	-812	13,450	2.50	67.8	8.5	27.8
Fayette	13.7	10.4	8.6	47.2	21,802	22,142	1.6	-3.3	2,045	1,818	-958	7,659	2.63	68.7	9.1	26.8
Ford	15.2	9.3	9.5	50.6	14,241	14,081	-1.1	-5.8	1,221	1,611	-428	5,684	2.30	64.2	12.5	31.4
Franklin	14.0	11.5	9.0	50.7	39,018	39,996	2.5	-3.2	3,887	4,412	-738	16,346	2.38	62.1	12.5	34.4
Fulton	14.1	11.3	9.3	48.0	38,250	37,069	-3.1	-6.0	2,882	3,724	-1,366	14,069	2.35	64.1	10.4	30.5
Gallatin	14.1	13.1	10.1	51.2	6,445	5,589	-13.3	-9.5	456	662	-325	2,272	2.30	65.2	12.7	31.8
Greene	15.1	10.8	8.8	49.7	14,761	13,886	-5.9	-6.1	1,138	1,284	-702	5,087	2.56	68.4	10.1	27.3
Grundy	12.8	8.3	5.7	50.1	37,535	50,077	33.4	1.8	5,072	3,208	-959	19,006	2.63	72.7	10.9	21.6
Hamilton	14.9	11.6	10.3	51.1	8,621	8,457	-1.9	-3.5	721	884	-122	3,413	2.39	68.9	8.3	26.8
Hancock	15.6	12.5	10.6	50.4	20,121	19,104	-5.1	-6.6	1,567	1,675	-1,156	7,523	2.39	69.7	8.7	26.2

1. No spouse present.

Table B. States and Counties — Population, Vital Statistics, Health, and Crime

STATE County	Persons in group quarters, 2018	Daytime Population, 2013-2017 Number	Employment/ residence ratio	Births, 2018 Total	Rate[1]	Deaths, 2018 Number	Rate[1]	Persons under 65 with no health insurance, 2016 Number	Percent	Medicare, 2018 Total beneficiaries	Enrolled in Original Medicare	Enrolled in Medicare Advantage	Serious crimes known to police[2], 2016 Total Number	Rate[3]
	32	33	34	35	36	37	38	39	40	41	42	43	44	45
IDAHO—Cont'd														
Caribou	79	7,546	1.24	90	12.7	72	10.2	523	9.2	1,326	1,284	42	45	665
Cassia	286	24,390	1.09	387	16.2	186	7.8	2,960	15.0	3,962	3,119	843	412	1,736
Clark	2	936	0.72	6	7.0	3	3.5	197	27.4	127	99	28	11	1,269
Clearwater	734	8,565	1.01	74	8.4	102	11.6	728	12.9	2,703	2,648	55	176	2,065
Custer	21	4,033	0.93	43	10.0	34	7.9	394	13.3	1,267	1,235	32	47	1,158
Elmore	620	25,751	0.96	468	17.2	180	6.6	2,934	13.4	4,373	3,487	886	352	1,364
Franklin	102	11,029	0.62	199	14.5	101	7.4	1,487	13.0	2,239	1,941	298	132	999
Fremont	456	11,467	0.72	180	13.7	96	7.3	1,518	14.9	2,477	2,102	375	116	905
Gem	151	14,340	0.60	200	11.3	189	10.7	1,768	13.4	4,606	2,539	2,067	177	1,042
Gooding	52	14,034	0.84	206	13.6	124	8.2	2,460	19.9	2,882	2,218	664	174	1,134
Idaho	518	15,904	0.94	151	9.1	164	9.9	1,610	14.0	4,217	4,124	93	172	1,051
Jefferson	111	22,724	0.60	473	16.1	156	5.3	3,134	12.8	3,918	3,177	741	195	709
Jerome	106	23,376	1.03	385	16.0	153	6.4	3,574	18.1	3,487	2,386	1,101	408	1,772
Kootenai	1,487	141,916	0.88	1,793	11.1	1,428	8.8	14,012	11.2	36,671	25,565	11,106	3,924	2,553
Latah	2,964	35,655	0.83	440	11.0	210	5.2	3,185	10.2	6,192	5,473	719	698	1,775
Lemhi	80	7,542	0.93	76	9.5	93	11.7	650	12.1	2,577	2,520	57	50	646
Lewis	74	3,793	0.98	34	8.8	36	9.3	445	15.8	1,911	1,872	39	53	1,392
Lincoln	37	4,509	0.66	68	12.7	27	5.0	770	17.2	1,000	803	197	23	430
Madison	629	39,409	1.07	1,084	27.6	125	3.2	3,124	8.8	3,000	2,456	544	298	771
Minidoka	82	19,316	0.88	312	15.0	168	8.1	3,096	18.2	3,511	2,611	900	289	1,398
Nez Perce	1,063	43,733	1.20	475	11.8	459	11.4	3,516	11.0	9,736	7,557	2,179	1,492	3,689
Oneida	50	3,939	0.79	51	11.4	34	7.6	377	10.9	966	944	22	39	906
Owyhee	160	10,426	0.79	142	12.1	86	7.4	2,084	22.8	2,272	1,403	869	144	1,269
Payette	94	19,864	0.69	305	13.0	211	9.0	2,439	13.1	5,382	3,353	2,029	292	1,264
Power	47	8,241	1.20	114	14.7	55	7.1	1,060	16.5	1,353	1,076	277	109	1,424
Shoshone	160	12,807	1.07	142	11.1	178	13.9	1,106	11.7	3,681	3,618	63	323	2,594
Teton	7	8,973	0.67	143	12.3	38	3.3	1,635	16.5	1,421	1,358	63	80	747
Twin Falls	963	82,462	1.01	1,231	14.3	746	8.7	8,546	12.3	15,613	10,585	5,028	1,650	1,967
Valley	66	10,604	1.12	100	9.1	76	6.9	1,055	13.2	2,769	1,989	780	235	2,296
Washington	119	9,224	0.79	111	10.9	95	9.3	1,125	14.9	2,915	2,185	730	130	1,299
ILLINOIS	296,779	12,839,459	1.00	148,117	11.6	110,092	8.6	801,267	7.5	2,192,385	1,634,082	558,303	318,160	2,485
Adams	2,022	69,104	1.07	788	12.0	844	12.8	2,665	5.1	14,839	12,629	2,210	1,731	2,627
Alexander	132	6,046	0.66	72	11.9	88	14.5	300	5.9	1,599	1,432	167	210	3,234
Bond	1,601	15,096	0.74	145	8.7	170	10.2	726	6.0	3,519	2,878	641	187	1,152
Boone	310	46,585	0.72	562	10.5	373	7.0	3,250	7.2	9,578	6,677	2,901	603	1,133
Brown	1,983	8,601	1.75	62	9.5	60	9.2	138	3.6	1,057	868	189	NA	NA
Bureau	457	30,673	0.82	335	10.2	383	11.6	1,701	6.5	7,781	6,499	1,282	382	1,224
Calhoun	90	3,731	0.45	45	9.4	63	13.1	205	5.5	1,209	989	220	NA	NA
Carroll	223	13,329	0.79	137	9.6	194	13.6	720	6.6	4,133	3,055	1,078	214	1,607
Cass	184	12,427	0.93	168	13.7	135	11.0	899	8.6	2,535	2,025	510	259	2,050
Champaign	16,398	217,371	1.09	2,302	11.0	1,389	6.6	10,119	6.0	28,723	15,983	12,740	6,952	3,327
Christian	1,596	30,205	0.77	319	9.8	387	11.8	1,489	5.8	7,683	6,057	1,626	NA	NA
Clark	221	13,745	0.71	172	11.0	202	13.0	646	5.0	3,719	2,959	760	98	745
Clay	305	13,191	0.97	156	11.8	176	13.3	616	5.8	3,169	2,920	249	148	1,114
Clinton	2,069	31,701	0.68	393	10.4	383	10.2	1,350	4.5	7,271	6,035	1,236	399	1,144
Coles	3,296	53,676	1.05	489	9.6	491	9.6	2,749	6.7	9,613	7,455	2,158	822	1,581
Cook	90,985	5,405,132	1.07	63,850	12.3	43,455	8.4	416,042	9.4	809,387	587,428	221,959	166,655	3,243
Crawford	1,493	19,892	1.09	207	11.0	237	12.6	832	5.8	4,301	3,874	427	236	1,262
Cumberland	117	8,750	0.57	123	11.4	111	10.3	527	6.0	2,277	1,785	492	74	685
DeKalb	5,645	96,494	0.84	1,061	10.2	723	6.9	5,791	6.7	15,218	11,828	3,390	2,501	2,447
De Witt	249	15,108	0.87	157	10.0	214	13.6	663	5.1	3,502	2,632	870	NA	NA
Douglas	168	19,238	0.93	238	12.2	179	9.2	1,471	9.1	3,861	2,539	1,322	175	1,110
DuPage	12,828	1,037,825	1.22	10,449	11.3	6,608	7.1	45,840	5.8	153,902	119,246	34,656	12,521	1,343
Edgar	283	18,176	1.07	174	10.0	226	13.0	834	6.0	4,252	3,489	763	213	1,318
Edwards	52	6,520	0.98	71	11.1	63	9.9	297	5.7	1,554	1,402	152	NA	NA
Effingham	440	38,563	1.26	435	12.7	342	10.0	1,443	5.1	7,281	6,405	876	628	1,924
Fayette	1,651	20,410	0.82	251	11.7	213	9.9	1,136	7.0	4,462	3,872	590	235	1,153
Ford	410	12,699	0.87	161	12.1	181	13.6	618	5.7	2,935	2,283	652	217	1,595
Franklin	517	34,151	0.66	457	11.8	521	13.5	2,075	6.7	9,617	7,611	2,006	629	1,739
Fulton	2,681	30,753	0.66	347	10.0	452	13.0	1,620	6.2	8,155	6,066	2,089	390	1,251
Gallatin	25	4,614	0.70	45	8.9	77	15.2	244	6.1	1,404	1,193	211	47	1,075
Greene	284	10,981	0.59	130	10.0	166	12.7	654	6.3	2,868	2,461	407	154	1,180
Grundy	254	45,696	0.81	587	11.5	409	8.0	1,887	4.3	8,448	7,321	1,127	578	1,170
Hamilton	117	7,182	0.70	87	10.7	109	13.4	378	5.9	1,874	1,648	226	NA	NA
Hancock	223	14,702	0.57	175	9.8	203	11.4	741	5.3	4,549	3,946	603	NA	NA

1. Per 1,000 estimated resident population. 2. Data for serious crimes have not been adjusted for underreporting; this may affect comparability between geographic areas and over time. 3. Per 100,000 population estimated by the FBI.

Table B. States and Counties — Crime, Education, Money Income, and Poverty

STATE County	Serious crimes known to police[2], 2016 (cont.)[1] Rate Violent	Property	School enrollment and attainment, 2013-2017 Enrollment[3] Total	Percent private	Attainment[4] (percent) High school graduate or less	Bachelor's degree or more	Local government expenditures,[5] 2014-2015 Total current spending (mil dol)	Current spending per student (dollars)	Money income, 2013-2017 Per capita income[6]	Median income (dollars)	Households Percent with income of less than $50,000	with income of $200,000 or more	Income and poverty, 2017 Median household income (dollars)	Percent below poverty level All persons	Children under 18 years	Children 5 to 17 years in families
	46	47	48	49	50	51	52	53	54	55	56	57	58	59	60	61
IDAHO—Cont'd																
Caribou	103	561	1,845	7.1	43.2	20.1	11.5	7,724	25,669	58,750	42.4	2.1	58,739	9.1	11.9	10.7
Cassia	206	1,529	6,546	6.1	48.2	18.1	33.2	6,199	20,007	48,162	52.4	1.9	51,323	12.7	15.7	14.3
Clark	346	923	268	1.5	57.6	17.0	2.0	13,755	15,283	31,927	62.9	0.0	42,226	14.5	21.4	19.2
Clearwater	235	1,831	1,298	12.8	45.7	17.4	12.6	11,520	22,169	41,122	59.9	2.2	46,214	15.7	22.6	20.2
Custer	74	1,084	653	1.5	41.8	22.6	5.3	9,271	23,290	37,976	62.8	0.5	44,100	14.7	22.9	22.2
Elmore	140	1,225	6,315	13.1	40.1	17.6	30.6	6,589	23,029	45,154	55.3	1.6	45,708	12.9	19.5	19.1
Franklin	45	954	3,767	7.9	42.3	20.2	18.5	5,830	20,454	51,583	49.1	1.4	55,056	8.2	10.8	9.4
Fremont	86	819	3,468	11.5	44.4	21.1	15.1	6,770	21,611	51,806	47.2	2.0	48,581	13.2	19.1	17.9
Gem	259	783	3,938	11.6	51.4	16.9	19.5	7,708	20,041	42,888	58.4	0.6	47,481	13.5	19.7	18.0
Gooding	143	991	3,800	9.0	56.8	14.7	21.9	6,745	20,821	42,626	56.4	1.3	46,218	14.9	19.6	18.3
Idaho	165	886	3,133	17.3	45.2	19.1	17.7	10,411	20,741	40,299	61.4	0.4	42,503	15.1	22.0	20.2
Jefferson	76	632	8,351	11.9	40.5	21.2	36.1	5,529	21,519	58,055	42.3	2.4	59,869	9.2	11.3	10.2
Jerome	317	1,455	6,256	9.1	56.6	13.0	27.7	6,096	19,329	46,421	53.4	1.7	50,728	13.7	18.9	16.9
Kootenai	232	2,321	34,686	14.9	34.3	24.5	144.1	6,599	28,275	53,189	45.8	3.6	56,921	10.6	14.7	13.3
Latah	127	1,648	14,922	9.2	22.8	46.4	41.3	8,713	24,166	43,310	55.8	2.9	49,445	16.5	12.4	10.3
Lemhi	90	556	1,271	13.6	42.2	22.3	8.2	8,387	22,489	36,031	64.2	0.9	41,153	16.1	25.9	22.8
Lewis	158	1,234	803	10.1	43.2	16.3	8.9	11,918	23,285	40,313	60.5	1.4	44,674	14.4	23.6	21.9
Lincoln	112	318	1,415	6.2	57.7	9.1	8.0	8,369	19,095	46,383	53.7	1.7	49,207	12.8	19.4	17.4
Madison	62	709	18,820	48.9	19.6	37.5	38.2	5,668	15,257	33,620	64.8	1.6	40,666	19.1	14.8	14.9
Minidoka	179	1,219	5,181	7.9	52.0	14.2	27.1	6,433	21,887	48,021	52.5	1.5	48,485	14.1	17.1	15.6
Nez Perce	134	3,556	8,907	13.6	39.4	22.7	50.1	8,984	26,799	51,804	48.0	1.6	54,729	12	15.7	13.9
Oneida	116	790	1,084	6.1	45.4	15.1	5.5	6,104	21,360	43,491	53.4	0.7	60,264	11.1	14.8	13.0
Owyhee	229	1,040	2,824	11.8	59.8	9.7	17.3	7,373	19,909	36,092	63.3	2.2	44,251	15.9	22.1	20.4
Payette	212	1,052	5,599	13.2	47.8	14.2	26.4	6,272	23,361	48,447	52.4	1.5	50,817	13	17.9	16.2
Power	131	1,293	2,121	9.6	56.4	15.8	14.5	8,706	21,513	47,602	54.6	1.6	45,922	14.6	20.0	19.3
Shoshone	450	2,144	2,212	8.1	52.2	12.4	18.6	10,522	23,834	39,835	61.1	1.2	46,793	17.4	25.9	24.7
Teton	56	691	2,513	17.0	24.6	42.5	12.7	7,399	28,004	55,986	44.2	2.3	63,168	8.3	12.0	11.1
Twin Falls	243	1,723	22,073	11.0	40.9	19.1	100.2	6,665	22,723	49,118	50.6	2.0	50,909	13.5	16.3	14.5
Valley	283	2,013	2,031	11.9	29.0	30.8	15.0	11,703	28,515	54,015	45.5	4.3	56,532	8.5	13.6	13.0
Washington	140	1,160	2,101	9.5	49.2	16.4	12.9	7,406	20,435	37,521	64.4	1.2	41,757	15.7	23.7	20.7
ILLINOIS	436	2,049	3,333,318	18.5	37.8	33.4	28,280.9	13,794	32,924	61,229	41.5	6.9	63,044	12.5	17.0	16.0
Adams	357	2,270	15,078	20.5	43.2	23.4	93.4	9,749	27,256	48,454	51.6	2.8	49,088	13.5	17.9	16.1
Alexander	1,201	2,033	1,503	2.7	56.3	10.7	13.3	13,587	18,564	31,014	70.1	0.5	33,985	30.3	50.5	49.1
Bond	37	1,115	4,369	20.3	50.2	19.3	23.7	10,061	24,473	54,393	43.7	1.8	54,831	13.3	16.9	15.5
Boone	186	947	15,006	17.0	48.8	21.7	105.9	10,732	29,029	62,701	38.9	5.1	69,413	8.8	12.7	11.0
Brown	NA	NA	1,373	10.6	54.1	13.2	7.4	9,435	21,906	56,289	43.5	3.0	53,875	14.9	15.2	14.8
Bureau	135	1,090	7,314	12.4	47.5	18.9	70.3	13,601	28,332	54,271	46.2	2.7	55,632	10.7	18.2	16.3
Calhoun	NA	NA	1,165	21.3	53.7	13.7	6.9	12,998	25,660	53,641	45.9	2.0	55,138	10.5	13.8	12.5
Carroll	75	1,532	2,903	8.5	50.9	17.4	26.1	11,111	27,605	50,555	49.4	2.0	49,744	11.5	19.2	18.1
Cass	522	1,528	2,866	9.4	61.3	13.4	22.9	9,735	25,451	50,156	49.8	1.9	50,568	13.3	18.1	17.0
Champaign	493	2,834	80,344	7.6	26.9	43.9	317.4	12,888	28,463	49,586	50.3	4.9	51,466	19.2	17.3	16.7
Christian	NA	NA	7,092	11.8	53.6	16.4	67.2	11,669	25,614	50,668	49.2	2.4	52,817	13.6	19.8	18.2
Clark	106	639	3,479	10.2	46.9	17.1	25.5	9,493	28,495	52,068	48.0	2.9	55,205	11	16.8	16.1
Clay	75	1,039	2,672	4.3	47.6	14.9	22.5	9,544	25,700	47,427	52.3	1.7	45,028	13.2	19.1	18.4
Clinton	163	980	8,519	14.4	42.7	22.1	52.0	9,838	30,382	64,543	37.2	3.4	65,586	8.2	10.5	10.0
Coles	335	1,246	16,853	5.4	39.8	26.0	84.9	13,006	26,060	41,907	56.5	2.8	46,011	19.5	22.5	23.6
Cook	677	2,566	1,331,311	23.2	37.3	37.2	11,792.0	15,259	33,722	59,426	43.2	7.7	61,401	14.6	20.5	19.8
Crawford	273	989	4,113	19.4	44.2	16.9	29.4	9,990	25,955	47,468	52.7	3.2	49,712	13.8	17.5	16.6
Cumberland	83	602	2,345	2.6	49.5	15.0	17.1	9,978	24,956	50,680	49.0	2.0	55,622	10.3	15.9	14.3
DeKalb	299	2,148	36,050	9.2	33.4	30.6	237.6	14,101	26,511	58,343	43.2	3.1	60,856	14.1	13.2	12.4
De Witt	NA	NA	3,508	9.1	45.6	20.3	30.1	10,771	27,866	55,411	45.2	1.7	56,091	11.7	18.5	16.5
Douglas	247	863	4,333	15.7	51.0	18.9	40.0	10,884	26,284	52,261	46.9	2.5	54,538	9.8	14.2	12.1
DuPage	92	1,251	246,274	22.1	26.1	48.0	2,492.7	15,987	42,050	84,442	28.6	12.4	89,536	6.2	7.6	7.3
Edgar	260	1,058	3,439	4.9	49.8	17.6	31.0	10,161	26,344	47,873	51.6	1.1	46,916	13.8	20.5	17.6
Edwards	NA	NA	1,408	5.7	46.2	12.5	8.4	8,948	26,549	49,632	50.4	2.0	48,649	10.9	17.3	16.4
Effingham	159	1,765	7,949	15.4	44.7	22.6	51.0	9,561	29,300	54,655	45.9	3.8	60,061	9.7	13.2	12.3
Fayette	132	1,020	4,812	18.8	58.7	11.9	30.7	10,775	21,844	45,193	55.6	1.5	45,193	18.2	23.7	22.1
Ford	287	1,309	2,990	10.3	48.4	19.2	37.1	12,929	26,611	50,851	49.2	2.4	55,356	11.6	17.3	16.1
Franklin	113	1,625	8,341	6.4	44.7	15.2	76.7	11,720	22,346	39,454	59.8	1.2	40,682	19.5	26.6	24.6
Fulton	99	1,151	8,002	4.9	46.0	17.7	50.6	10,342	24,269	48,599	51.4	1.9	49,315	15.2	20.5	18.8
Gallatin	183	892	1,128	4.6	52.7	12.8	8.1	10,914	24,538	42,450	58.1	1.1	42,533	18.9	30.5	29.2
Greene	237	942	2,779	13.6	55.5	12.0	20.2	9,964	22,836	44,502	56.1	1.5	47,188	14.8	21.0	19.4
Grundy	75	1,095	13,256	11.5	41.1	22.6	161.4	12,442	31,914	71,598	34.0	4.6	76,214	7.1	8.9	8.3
Hamilton	NA	NA	1,757	22.3	46.9	16.9	13.1	10,576	25,945	47,293	50.7	3.1	49,092	12.9	19.9	18.0
Hancock	NA	NA	3,798	7.5	46.1	19.7	32.5	10,654	26,118	51,460	47.9	2.4	52,625	11.7	18.8	18.6

1. Data for serious crimes have not been adjusted for underreporting; this may affect comparability between geographic areas and over time. 2. Per 100,000 population estimated by the FBI. 3. All persons 3 years old and over enrolled in nursery school through college. 4. Persons 25 years old and over. 5. Elementary and secondary education expenditures. 6. Based on population estimated by the American Community Survey, 2013–2017.

	Personal income, 2017										Earnings, 2017		
			Per capita[1]			Supplements to wages and salaries, employer contributions (mil dol)						Contributions for government social insurance (mil dol)	
STATE County	Total (mil dol)	Percent change 2016-2017	Dollars	Rank	Wages and salaries (mil dol)	Pension and insurance	Government social insurance	Proprietors' income (mil dol)	Dividends, interest, and rent (mil dol)	Personal transfer reecipts (mil dol)	Total (mil dol)	From employee and self-employed	From employer
	62	63	64	65	66	67	68	69	70	71	72	73	74

IDAHO—Cont'd

Caribou	267	4.6	38,020	1,880	194	39	17	13	51	55	263	16	17
Cassia	1,044	1.6	44,132	1,009	421	71	40	299	159	166	831	37	40
Clark	34	5.6	38,562	1,794	19	3	2	2	6	4	26	1	2
Clearwater	294	3.1	34,454	2,417	107	24	10	20	65	100	161	12	10
Custer	179	3.7	42,868	1,156	53	12	5	18	58	40	87	6	5
Elmore	972	4.2	36,239	2,162	455	114	46	82	243	205	697	34	46
Franklin	472	5.0	34,781	2,377	117	26	11	62	72	87	216	12	11
Fremont	467	4.9	35,638	2,251	119	24	11	75	103	98	230	13	11
Gem	630	5.8	36,225	2,167	137	27	14	37	143	172	215	18	14
Gooding	851	5.3	56,256	243	234	39	23	323	106	124	620	18	23
Idaho	530	2.5	32,369	2,707	168	37	15	38	150	142	259	20	15
Jefferson	961	6.1	33,779	2,512	235	44	22	129	154	164	429	25	22
Jerome	904	5.2	38,279	1,830	350	57	33	241	134	154	681	30	33
Kootenai	6,656	5.7	42,224	1,239	2,543	430	229	491	1,502	1,342	3,692	252	229
Latah	1,557	3.7	39,575	1,625	552	136	48	114	379	252	850	52	48
Lemhi	315	5.2	40,056	1,540	92	20	8	23	100	87	144	11	8
Lewis	173	0.3	44,577	954	57	12	5	13	33	70	87	7	5
Lincoln	183	5.5	34,342	2,436	60	12	6	48	27	35	127	5	6
Madison	984	5.4	25,132	3,088	527	97	47	114	166	232	786	45	47
Minidoka	782	3.1	37,706	1,922	319	55	30	100	153	146	503	28	30
Nez Perce	1,716	4.5	42,487	1,202	954	166	83	134	338	386	1,336	87	83
Oneida	154	6.0	34,831	2,369	36	9	3	11	27	38	60	4	3
Owyhee	412	5.3	35,410	2,283	95	18	9	74	81	89	197	9	9
Payette	894	4.1	38,509	1,801	255	46	24	134	162	200	459	28	24
Power	281	7.5	36,969	2,042	148	27	14	41	49	55	231	12	14
Shoshone	443		35,285	2,299	182	31	16	9	96	143	238	19	16
Teton	425	6.0	37,314	1,986	123	19	11	41	116	54	194	12	11
Twin Falls	3,259	5.5	38,291	1,828	1,443	243	132	484	600	655	2,302	137	132
Valley	497	4.4	46,550	747	171	31	16	48	187	91	265	18	16
Washington	347	2.8	34,313	2,445	100	20	9	31	76	101	161	12	9
ILLINOIS	693,914	3.0	54,271	X	367,621	60,977	24,752	50,558	141,541	103,970	503,909	27,595	24,752
Adams	2,939	2.8	44,373	973	1,466	288	103	207	631	619	2,063	120	103
Alexander	209	-0.1	33,018	2,613	54	15	4	10	31	94	82	6	4
Bond	587	3.5	34,664	2,394	216	54	15	20	109	150	305	19	15
Boone	2,403	1.9	44,908	909	886	176	67	82	346	382	1,211	71	67
Brown	218	3.8	32,435	2,698	193	39	12	12	41	41	256	14	12
Bureau	1,389	2.5	41,781	1,291	516	112	38	66	278	298	732	44	38
Calhoun	190	3.4	39,253	1,681	26	8	2	7	34	47	42	4	2
Carroll	622	-1.4	42,827	1,163	165	38	12	58	132	159	273	18	12
Cass	497	0.5	39,779	1,594	230	49	18	41	80	111	337	19	18
Champaign	9,126	0.9	43,584	1,065	4,970	1,297	301	657	1,967	1,213	7,224	334	301
Christian	1,313	2.9	39,651	1,609	403	90	29	117	226	331	639	38	29
Clark	629	3.5	39,888	1,572	195	50	14	36	115	150	295	18	14
Clay	491	3.0	37,030	2,030	214	55	15	-4	90	153	281	18	15
Clinton	1,675	1.8	44,533	959	441	101	31	117	298	304	690	39	31
Coles	2,022	3.4	38,902	1,736	1,077	255	72	130	387	437	1,534	81	72
Cook	308,704	3.0	59,238	175	184,199	27,575	12,214	26,942	68,842	45,348	250,931	13,615	12,214
Crawford	850	-0.2	44,838	921	364	114	24	95	142	174	597	31	24
Cumberland	451	3.4	41,388	1,348	106	25	8	31	71	92	170	10	8
DeKalb	4,066	2.2	38,827	1,750	1,778	445	116	168	775	661	2,507	128	116
De Witt	716	-2.7	44,888	914	292	66	19	64	118	151	440	24	19
Douglas	937	3.5	47,450	668	372	79	28	139	157	159	618	34	28
DuPage	64,479	3.7	69,323	74	42,987	6,010	2,941	4,852	13,045	6,104	56,790	3,076	2,941
Edgar	701	3.7	40,477	1,478	302	68	22	37	123	185	429	26	22
Edwards	254	5.7	39,128	1,699	100	24	7	22	47	57	152	9	7
Effingham	1,629	6.1	47,738	644	910	162	66	166	346	280	1,304	73	66
Fayette	724	2.5	33,229	2,590	190	48	13	44	135	196	295	19	13
Ford	660	-4.9	49,695	480	205	46	14	109	103	126	375	19	14
Franklin	1,409	2.9	36,093	2,188	341	83	25	78	223	439	527	37	25
Fulton	1,248	0.0	35,542	2,267	322	86	21	43	223	350	473	32	21
Gallatin	224	2.6	44,166	1,002	66	13	5	36	39	62	120	6	5
Greene	459	1.7	34,809	2,372	88	24	6	38	75	132	156	10	6
Grundy	2,482	3.5	49,070	530	1,170	235	79	196	343	343	1,680	91	79
Hamilton	350	5.5	42,710	1,183	97	23	7	52	64	88	179	9	7
Hancock	777	0.2	43,118	1,127	152	39	10	99	136	178	302	17	10

1. Based on the resident population estimated as of July 1 of the year shown.

Table B. States and Counties — **Earnings, Social Security, and Housing**

STATE County	Earnings, 2017 (cont.)									Social Security beneficiaries, December 2017		Supplemental Security Income recipients, 2017	Housing units, 2018	
	Percent by selected industries													
	Farm	Mining, quarrying, and extractions	Construction	Manufacturing	Information; professional, scientific, technical services	Retail trade	Finance, insurance, real estate, and leasing	Health care and social assistance	Government	Number	Rate[1]		Total	Percent change, 2010-2018
	75	76	77	78	79	80	81	82	83	84	85	86	87	88
IDAHO—Cont'd														
Caribou	4.3	16.8	8	34.9	3.4	3.1	1.7	D	15.1	1,460	208	81	3,308	2.5
Cassia	30	1	5.4	9.8	D	6.6	4.7	8.1	8.9	4,285	181	393	8,833	5.5
Clark	13.4	0	D	D	D	D	D	D	26.3	120	137	0	558	5.1
Clearwater	-0.7	D	6.3	5.6	2.6	6.8	1.8	D	34	2,825	331	250	4,638	4.2
Custer	10.1	D	8.5	D	6.6	4.8	2.6	D	29	1,360	326	58	3,137	1.1
Elmore	9.7	0	3.1	4.4	D	4.9	2.2	5.5	56.1	4,830	180	611	12,546	3.1
Franklin	16.2	D	8.5	6.6	D	9	4.4	D	21.4	2,425	179	159	4,901	8.2
Fremont	23.2	D	11.7	2.1	2.6	4.8	3.2	D	24.2	2,605	199	157	9,080	6.5
Gem	3.4	D	12.7	2.8	4.3	6.7	4.3	D	25.6	4,910	283	458	7,407	4.3
Gooding	58.6	0	2	8.6	D	2.2	D	D	9.3	3,110	206	302	6,232	2.2
Idaho	-1.3	1.8	11.5	8.6	3.1	6.8	4	10	30.4	4,400	269	324	8,769	0.3
Jefferson	10.4	0	12.8	12.4	D	9.7	6.1	D	13.1	4,295	151	316	9,561	9.6
Jerome	32.8	0	4	13.4	D	6.1	D	3.8	7.7	3,720	157	397	8,579	5.9
Kootenai	0.1	0.8	9.6	8	7	10.5	7	12.7	19.9	38,230	243	2,632	72,499	14.8
Latah	-0.5	D	5.3	2.7	7.7	7.4	4	10.3	44.5	6,395	163	518	17,168	7.4
Lemhi	5.1	0.4	11.4	3.1	5.2	7.6	3.2	8.1	36.9	2,735	347	188	4,910	3.8
Lewis	1.8	D	7	12.7	5.3	6.4	6.2	5.6	25	2,130	548	251	1,956	4
Lincoln	42.1	0	D	D	0.7	2.3	D	4.9	20.3	955	180	72	2,004	1.5
Madison	3.1	D	6	6.5	D	7.9	4.7	7.5	14.6	3,155	81	295	14,570	29.1
Minidoka	17.3	0	5.3	18.6	3.9	5.4	3.1	D	14.4	4,010	193	366	8,446	10.2
Nez Perce	-0.1	D	5.8	22	4.5	7.7	8.6	15.7	17.8	10,360	257	965	17,910	2.7
Oneida	12.6	D	D	2.2	3	6.1	D	6.5	29.8	1,030	233	56	2,008	5.4
Owyhee	42	D	5.3	4.8	D	4	D	D	15.8	2,485	214	270	4,941	3.3
Payette	15	D	5.4	13.8	D	4.2	7.2	D	10.9	5,695	245	589	9,533	6.6
Power	21.3	0.1	2	30.3	D	D	D	D	13.2	1,460	192	114	3,017	2.4
Shoshone	-0.1	19.5	4.8	3	5.3	22.1	2.8	8.4	19.3	3,970	317	458	7,153	1.1
Teton	3.1	D	19	3.2	11.2	7.1	4.1	8.3	14.5	1,405	123	50	5,959	8.8
Twin Falls	7.3	D	4.8	15.9	5.5	8	4.9	17.5	11.7	16,535	194	1,786	33,698	8.5
Valley	0.8	D	12.8	1.8	D	8.8	7.1	12	24.3	2,815	263	124	12,520	6.2
Washington	13.9	0	4.4	16	9.7	5.7	D	D	22.7	3,090	305	284	4,668	3.1
ILLINOIS	0.3	0.2	4.9	10.8	14.1	4.9	10.9	10.4	13.9	2,220,171	173	270,883	5,376,064	1.5
Adams	-0.1	0.9	6.8	15.7	5.2	7.9	7.5	19.3	12.2	15,510	234	1,344	30,278	1.5
Alexander	5.2	D	1.3	10.8	D	2.6	D	D	30.9	1,710	271	377	3,977	-0.7
Bond	0.6	0	5.9	25.5	3.2	3.4	2.9	D	26.2	3,720	219	320	7,286	2.8
Boone	0	D	8.3	50.8	2.8	3.5	2.4	4.1	13	10,275	192	571	20,097	0.6
Brown	1.2	0.1	6.9	0.5	D	1.3	D	4.2	13.1	1,080	161	78	2,451	-0.4
Bureau	2	D	5.5	15.5	3	4.8	3.3	D	19.5	8,090	243	427	15,680	-0.3
Calhoun	-1.5	D	12.6	2.9	2.5	9.1	9	D	34.3	1,330	275	76	2,895	2.1
Carroll	8.4	D	9.5	17	D	5.1	6.6	4.3	17.1	4,230	291	234	8,469	0.4
Cass	8.1	0	3.5	D	D	4.1	4.8	4.7	13.8	2,620	210	239	5,828	-0.1
Champaign	-0.1	0	5	6.3	8.2	6.2	5.3	14	39	27,710	132	3,198	93,396	6.7
Christian	7.8	D	6.6	14.3	D	7.1	4.1	14.7	17.1	8,230	249	630	15,601	0.3
Clark	4.3	1.5	7.7	30.4	7.7	5.5	4	4.1	16.5	3,900	247	290	7,827	0.7
Clay	-8.7	2.1	3	42.5	D	5.9	4	D	22.5	3,405	257	307	6,437	0.5
Clinton	6.2	D	13.8	7.6	D	9.2	5.3	11.6	23	7,410	197	321	15,934	4.1
Coles	0.9	0.2	4.9	12.3	D	5.9	5.9	17.2	25.3	9,980	192	1,203	23,489	0.3
Cook	0	D	3.2	6.7	19.2	4	14.5	9.8	11.9	798,435	153	150,817	2,200,221	0.9
Crawford	2.4	1.2	7.6	41.6	7.3	4.1	3.8	D	16.7	4,560	240	332	8,696	0.4
Cumberland	12.7	D	4.3	22.7	D	8.1	D	D	18	2,485	228	153	4,875	0
DeKalb	-0.8	D	10.3	11.5	D	7.3	4.1	D	31.7	15,215	145	1,008	41,248	0.4
De Witt	6.7	D	9.8	7.9	D	5.6	2.6	2.1	15.3	3,685	231	250	7,580	0.8
Douglas	3	D	11.4	42.4	D	4.9	3.3	3.6	10.1	3,965	201	229	8,467	0.9
DuPage	0	0	6.2	9.5	15.9	4.5	9.7	9.9	7.9	146,650	158	8,036	361,429	1.5
Edgar	3.3	0	4.4	36.4	2.7	4.5	10.2	D	14.2	4,490	259	436	8,833	0.3
Edwards	5.9	D	D	D	D	3.4	4.4	1.6	10.3	1,615	249	82	3,192	0.2
Effingham	2	0.1	7.8	15.6	D	7.6	5	19.5	8.6	7,620	223	474	14,906	2.3
Fayette	5.7	1.8	5.4	5.9	3.3	7.7	6.2	D	25.6	4,840	222	436	9,315	0.1
Ford	12.6	D	6.2	11.1	1.9	3.9	2.7	D	12.4	3,070	231	191	6,356	1.2
Franklin	3.8	0.5	9.4	6.5	D	8.3	3.6	12.9	27.7	10,430	267	1,311	18,630	-0.4
Fulton	0	0	6.1	3	4.2	8.3	5.9	19.2	30.6	8,710	248	683	16,372	1.1
Gallatin	27.6	25	2.2	1.1	D	2.5	0.9	D	11.5	1,545	304	209	2,752	0.2
Greene	14.3	D	6.2	3	3.5	7.4	D	D	26.2	3,215	244	391	6,426	0.6
Grundy	1.1	D	11.8	12.1	2.8	8	3.1	9.2	12.5	9,255	183	400	21,138	5.7
Hamilton	19.3	D	8.2	2.8	D	2.8	4.1	3.6	18.2	2,010	245	194	4,096	-0.2
Hancock	20.3	D	7.4	5.9	7.2	4	5.5	D	19.5	4,890	271	304	9,242	-0.3

1. Per 1,000 resident population estimated as of July 1 of the year shown.

Table B. States and Counties — **Housing, Labor Force, and Employment**

STATE County	Housing units, 2013-2017								Civilian labor force, 2018				Civilian employment[6], 2013-2017		
	Occupied units							Sub-standard units[4] (percent)			Unemployment			Percent	
	Owner-occupied					Renter-occupied									
				Median owner cost as a percent of income											
	Total	Percent	Median value[1]	With a mortgage	Without a mortgage[2]	Median rent[3]	Median rent as a percent of income[2]		Total	Percent change, 2017-2018	Total	Rate[5]	Total	Management, business, science, and arts	Construction, production, and maintenance occupations
	89	90	91	92	93	94	95	96	97	98	99	100	101	102	103
IDAHO—Cont'd															
Caribou	2,533	83.9	130,600	17.3	10.0	563	20.2	2.9	3,831	-0.9	108	2.8	2,967	31.5	34.5
Cassia	7,827	69.7	136,900	20.0	10.0	628	23.7	4.8	11,750	0.2	262	2.2	9,889	27.1	37.8
Clark	313	55.3	98,700	35.5	11.4	575	17.5	10.9	405	1.8	12	3	440	20.0	50.2
Clearwater	3,706	76.8	134,400	23.0	10.9	695	26.8	2.5	2,925	-2.9	197	6.7	2,796	31.8	31.7
Custer	1,850	76.2	173,300	23.8	10.0	624	29.8	3.1	2,190	1.3	88	4	1,722	32.3	30.7
Elmore	10,062	57.9	145,200	20.3	10.0	777	28	3.3	11,416	2	372	3.3	9,732	28.3	34.1
Franklin	4,286	80.5	168,200	23.1	10.2	683	23.2	3.8	6,920	2.4	148	2.1	5,679	27.1	37.0
Fremont	4,383	80.1	157,700	22.5	10.0	738	25.9	4.1	7,781	2.1	189	2.4	5,182	28.2	34.2
Gem	6,404	74.8	148,800	23.4	11.9	740	28.4	3.1	8,141	3.4	279	3.4	6,452	26.9	30.3
Gooding	5,550	67.8	134,400	21.0	10.6	689	27.4	6.6	8,105	1	195	2.4	6,886	28.4	37.0
Idaho	6,480	79.1	164,600	25.9	10.9	678	22.9	5.1	6,426	1.7	301	4.7	6,321	27.1	33.3
Jefferson	8,470	81.0	166,200	21.6	10.0	778	21.8	3.7	13,488	3.1	305	2.3	11,898	34.6	31.8
Jerome	7,741	64.1	144,400	23.4	10.3	735	27.5	5.8	11,963	2.7	304	2.5	10,195	23.0	42.3
Kootenai	58,873	70.9	212,900	22.9	10.2	902	28.6	2.7	77,765	2.6	2,700	3.5	67,680	32.0	22.3
Latah	15,448	53.3	207,200	19.9	10.0	675	34.6	2.4	20,267	1	498	2.5	19,118	43.8	18.3
Lemhi	3,703	70.5	173,400	23.8	10.4	616	29.9	3.1	3,511	0.8	157	4.5	3,109	30.7	26.1
Lewis	1,626	73.9	120,000	22.0	11.4	596	26.8	3.4	1,637	1.3	90	5.5	1,524	31.6	29.0
Lincoln	1,609	69.3	127,200	24.1	10.0	789	24.8	7	2,738	1.3	92	3.4	2,379	21.3	43.1
Madison	10,633	46.4	190,500	22.6	10.0	673	43.8	9.4	21,678	2.3	374	1.7	17,073	39.0	18.4
Minidoka	7,357	71.0	121,800	19.1	10.0	622	21.4	4.2	11,031	0.3	278	2.5	9,198	21.8	42.5
Nez Perce	16,308	70.9	172,500	21.1	10.2	693	28.3	3.1	21,053	-0.6	579	2.8	18,977	31.3	25.8
Oneida	1,581	78.6	151,600	25.1	12.0	730	21.3	4	2,339	3.7	51	2.2	1,693	30.3	38.1
Owyhee	4,190	68.4	125,700	23.5	10.0	624	29.4	5.6	5,448	2.6	196	3.6	4,687	24.1	42.6
Payette	8,571	74.0	138,900	22.6	10.6	714	24.8	5.3	11,535	0.3	413	3.6	9,679	23.8	34.1
Power	2,544	70.1	132,600	21.5	11.1	702	19.9	2.3	4,090	3.3	118	2.9	2,993	25.5	41.9
Shoshone	5,614	70.1	117,500	19.3	11.9	661	27.3	2.9	5,068	0.5	291	5.7	4,970	26.1	30.3
Teton	3,764	72.8	291,600	23.4	14.1	906	25.1	2.3	6,407	4.4	144	2.2	5,607	35.1	24.4
Twin Falls	30,096	68.0	154,200	22.1	10.0	754	28.3	3	40,747	1.5	1,096	2.7	38,869	29.6	29.3
Valley	3,532	75.7	258,000	28.9	10.0	803	29.4	2.8	5,313	3.2	200	3.8	4,244	35.0	24.0
Washington	3,979	73.1	149,100	23.3	11.2	658	34.1	3.3	4,632	0.5	192	4.1	3,693	26.5	32.6
ILLINOIS	4,818,452	66.1	179,700	22.1	13.0	952	29.6	2.9	6,469,668	-0.3	278,349	4.3	6,181,653	37.6	21.2
Adams	27,461	70.5	120,200	18.8	10.5	612	28.5	1.5	32,893	1.6	1,277	3.9	32,243	31.8	24.7
Alexander	2,432	70.5	53,200	27.8	12.6	465	22.7	3.2	2,153	1	171	7.9	2,164	26.8	19.5
Bond	6,132	78.3	115,200	19.7	12.6	668	24.4	4.1	7,929	0.1	347	4.4	7,483	24.5	30.9
Boone	18,709	79.2	145,700	22.5	12.6	852	27.4	3.2	26,473	1	1,523	5.8	25,060	29.0	32.4
Brown	2,066	78.8	88,600	17.1	10.5	577	23	1.9	2,896	1.3	78	2.7	2,418	27.4	27.5
Bureau	13,816	76.1	106,800	18.9	11.7	666	24.2	1	17,390	0	871	5	16,262	28.0	30.2
Calhoun	1,881	82.2	110,900	22.8	11.0	600	31.1	3.1	2,340	0.1	125	5.3	2,166	31.2	30.4
Carroll	6,573	76.8	99,400	19.1	12.0	616	25.9	1.4	7,525	-1.2	335	4.5	6,765	31.0	33.2
Cass	5,160	73.4	76,800	17.5	10.6	597	25.2	2.5	6,162	-0.3	277	4.5	6,152	23.8	38.7
Champaign	81,418	54.5	154,800	19.6	11.1	850	33.3	5	105,669	0.3	4,653	4.4	103,099	45.3	16.1
Christian	13,892	75.2	87,500	17.6	11.2	632	26.9	1.5	14,837	-0.2	785	5.3	14,987	30.8	28.1
Clark	6,809	74.3	87,400	17.9	11.6	669	26	1.9	7,775	-1.3	402	5.2	7,675	25.5	36.1
Clay	5,624	79.1	77,200	18.7	10.0	529	21.2	3.6	6,611	-0.5	351	5.3	6,348	24.5	40.6
Clinton	14,183	80.7	142,900	19.4	11.6	783	23.6	1.2	20,378	0.4	728	3.6	18,718	34.6	28.0
Coles	21,006	61.9	93,800	18.9	11.5	643	32.5	1.4	24,195	-1.5	1,171	4.8	24,725	31.2	24.6
Cook	1,956,561	56.9	227,600	24.3	14.9	1,044	30.5	3.8	2,611,512	1	105,409	4	2,521,437	39.3	19.1
Crawford	7,665	78.0	82,900	17.2	11.0	605	25.5	1.9	8,777	-0.6	470	5.4	8,102	28.6	33.7
Cumberland	4,287	79.1	94,000	18.3	12.0	560	22	2.4	6,080	-0.7	246	4	5,135	26.2	37.4
DeKalb	37,420	56.5	166,800	21.6	13.0	887	31.4	2.7	55,487	1.3	2,440	4.4	52,511	32.8	22.2
De Witt	6,704	77.9	98,000	18.2	10.1	562	26.2	1.9	7,582		385	5.1	8,112	29.5	27.8
Douglas	7,580	72.5	102,700	19.1	10.0	674	24.9	2.5	10,212	0.1	419	4.1	9,138	27.1	33.8
DuPage	340,669	73.3	289,900	22.8	13.5	1,224	28.6	2.6	508,650	-0.8	15,924	3.1	486,850	45.5	15.9
Edgar	7,669	74.0	80,000	18.5	10.4	608	28.8	1.2	9,200	-2.7	430	4.7	8,052	28.2	34.8
Edwards	2,810	83.5	73,500	17.3	10.0	487	24.8	1.6	2,779	-2.5	126	4.5	3,136	25.1	38.8
Effingham	13,450	77.6	137,300	18.9	10.6	610	23.6	1.5	19,119	1.2	716	3.7	17,229	30.6	30.0
Fayette	7,659	80.7	84,000	19.0	11.4	612	28.1	2.8	9,810	1.3	519	5.3	8,807	24.2	32.4
Ford	5,684	71.0	100,600	19.5	11.4	629	27.1	1.2	6,334	-0.5	305	4.8	6,177	31.1	32.0
Franklin	16,346	72.0	69,900	19.5	11.3	625	29.2	1.8	17,065	3.1	1,049	6.1	15,466	25.8	31.2
Fulton	14,069	77.5	84,800	18.3	11.7	631	27.1	1.6	15,224	-1.7	951	6.2	15,027	30.6	28.4
Gallatin	2,272	76.8	71,500	17.0	10.7	411	28.2	2	2,434	-1.3	140	5.8	2,133	33.8	29.5
Greene	5,087	78.2	76,900	19.5	12.1	588	26	1.5	6,015	-0.1	295	4.9	5,854	26.8	30.4
Grundy	19,006	72.1	188,300	21.1	12.7	971	24.3	1.7	25,255	-1.2	1,183	4.7	24,608	30.5	30.4
Hamilton	3,413	78.8	91,500	18.9	10.0	581	25.6	0.9	4,493	0.6	196	4.4	3,751	30.2	29.6
Hancock	7,523	80.7	85,100	18.1	10.0	621	20.9	1.5	8,469	-0.6	400	4.7	8,292	29.5	33.1

1. Specified owner-occupied units.   2. A value of 10.0 represents 10 percent or less; a value of 50.0 represents 50 percent or more.   3. Specified renter-occupied units.   4. Overcrowded or lacking complete plumbing facilities.   5. Percent of civilian labor force.   6. Civilian employed persons 16 years old and over.

Table B. States and Counties — Nonfarm Employment and Agriculture

STATE County	Private nonfarm establishments, employment and payroll, 2016									Agriculture, 2017			
	Number of establish- ments	Employment						Annual payroll		Farms			Farm producers whose primary occupation is farming (percent)
		Total	Health care and social assistance	Manufac- turing	Retail trade	Finance and insurance	Professional, scientific, and technical services	Total (mil dol)	Average per employee (dollars)	Number	Percent with:		
											Fewer than 50 acres	1000 acres or more	
	104	105	106	107	108	109	110	111	112	113	114	115	116

STATE County	104	105	106	107	108	109	110	111	112	113	114	115	116
IDAHO—Cont'd													
Caribou	186	2,744	278	751	244	48	26	178	64,868	411	28.2	23.6	48.2
Cassia	655	7,845	1,218	1,231	1,544	217	173	263	33,468	585	44.3	25.3	51.7
Clark	16	85	NA	D	40	D	D	3	29,965	68	19.1	38.2	52.1
Clearwater	231	1,812	486	297	240	39	37	69	38,312	312	50.6	3.8	36.9
Custer	165	704	63	27	169	20	30	26	36,700	267	34.8	12.0	50.6
Elmore	434	4,303	799	461	1,069	344	96	136	31,620	340	59.4	14.1	41.5
Franklin	299	2,120	308	303	545	60	83	67	31,766	787	44.7	7.6	33.9
Fremont	293	1,626	232	57	236	39	36	55	33,954	513	37.4	9.7	36.9
Gem	359	2,519	776	109	461	65	71	71	28,382	860	77.4	3.4	39.7
Gooding	356	2,683	559	539	397	71	73	99	36,820	538	58.6	7.6	50.9
Idaho	467	3,529	719	564	514	151	224	143	40,640	708	32.1	17.1	45.5
Jefferson	488	3,820	235	865	594	81	115	127	33,220	750	60.0	10.0	41.7
Jerome	538	6,351	463	1,544	899	104	90	234	36,767	486	49.8	7.8	55.3
Kootenai	4,659	50,135	9,532	5,278	8,929	2,194	2,233	1,915	38,196	1,073	68.7	2.1	32.1
Latah	888	8,870	1,347	383	1,935	225	485	258	29,131	1,041	48.7	9.1	34.3
Lemhi	277	1,728	492	61	400	31	79	50	28,752	351	48.1	8.8	42.8
Lewis	119	814	64	151	182	25	D	23	28,526	197	26.9	27.9	50.0
Lincoln	89	553	96	D	84	10	11	20	35,656	276	32.6	13.0	59.4
Madison	875	18,151	1,598	1,067	1,987	282	815	397	21,892	454	50.7	10.8	47.3
Minidoka	408	4,686	518	949	503	84	122	177	37,839	620	51.8	9.0	49.5
Nez Perce	1,108	17,627	3,120	4,260	2,579	1,043	498	679	38,534	446	47.3	24.2	42.4
Oneida	86	757	205	68	171	D	5	21	27,485	422	28.7	23.0	36.1
Owyhee	188	1,787	214	142	191	25	42	52	29,342	565	46.2	15.2	55.6
Payette	500	5,099	581	1,313	431	230	145	179	35,082	640	70.3	3.1	40.6
Power	170	2,150	160	D	156	51	46	81	37,694	295	29.2	39.3	52.6
Shoshone	354	4,176	519	128	1,114	61	161	184	44,134	48	75.0	NA	30.0
Teton	462	2,348	326	114	336	42	134	93	39,773	277	38.6	12.3	44.0
Twin Falls	2,584	30,292	6,409	3,479	5,105	937	1,112	999	32,979	1,211	51.6	5.9	49.6
Valley	593	3,296	487	91	488	80	95	105	31,962	188	57.4	6.4	33.4
Washington	208	1,892	356	478	268	43	53	58	30,777	535	49.7	15.0	50.2
ILLINOIS	319,605	5,513,071	805,338	535,830	631,937	346,002	389,970	295,308	53,565	72,651	35.6	10.8	43.4
Adams	1,802	30,925	5,757	5,177	4,997	1,495	693	1,203	38,916	1,308	26.8	9.9	42.8
Alexander	91	1,047	150	164	107	18	35	44	41,564	126	30.2	11.9	36.5
Bond	318	3,743	489	739	391	117	68	126	33,594	637	46.3	7.4	36.7
Boone	848	15,589	951	8,485	1,431	231	532	667	42,795	457	54.5	5.5	47.4
Brown	106	3,487	201	D	129	45	32	165	47,178	419	25.3	7.2	30.2
Bureau	744	9,992	2,097	1,697	1,100	346	293	403	40,342	1,038	28.9	13.8	46.5
Calhoun	87	541	93	13	83	57	7	13	24,140	474	25.7	5.3	34.2
Carroll	396	3,648	452	949	549	188	47	132	36,175	627	31.6	9.4	47.3
Cass	235	4,788	352	2,334	461	182	73	172	35,887	429	29.1	14.5	36.9
Champaign	4,176	69,416	12,845	6,788	10,071	3,112	2,751	2,840	40,919	1,214	33.1	16.0	50.0
Christian	701	8,282	1,679	861	1,385	332	445	297	35,803	794	33.8	16.5	48.2
Clark	333	3,979	361	1,274	477	148	138	141	35,550	733	37.8	10.8	38.2
Clay	374	4,763	582	2,235	521	153	94	179	37,512	732	37.8	8.6	37.4
Clinton	867	9,055	1,892	826	1,754	302	175	283	31,208	831	32.4	6.0	39.1
Coles	1,188	18,865	4,793	2,680	2,539	548	413	675	35,756	701	39.8	10.4	39.1
Cook	133,150	2,401,662	370,018	179,530	242,401	196,257	226,870	145,680	60,658	182	78.6	0.5	34.7
Crawford	417	6,949	760	1,772	768	227	310	284	40,800	566	38.0	11.3	41.4
Cumberland	187	2,086	583	544	202	118	12	56	26,905	724	40.2	4.8	34.3
DeKalb	1,957	27,297	5,332	3,875	4,448	901	1,053	1,044	38,241	779	35.3	14.2	53.7
De Witt	374	4,683	578	585	672	111	233	238	50,883	504	44.6	12.5	43.4
Douglas	589	6,620	319	2,624	1,207	194	90	252	38,015	600	45.5	12.5	40.5
DuPage	33,932	598,889	68,872	54,919	62,140	35,224	44,827	35,357	59,038	77	87.0	NA	41.8
Edgar	357	6,651	884	2,669	653	202	94	271	40,766	637	30.3	16.6	48.2
Edwards	143	2,042	90	D	180	79	23	75	36,785	291	31.3	11.3	40.8
Effingham	1,219	24,806	2,823	2,993	2,723	490	421	940	37,912	1,193	37.6	6.1	35.5
Fayette	464	4,394	802	344	817	225	119	129	29,363	1,239	38.7	8.2	37.1
Ford	356	4,184	1,172	657	480	142	113	158	37,859	564	29.8	13.8	49.5
Franklin	720	6,377	888	345	1,485	270	207	218	34,147	596	41.4	7.6	38.1
Fulton	626	6,325	1,909	176	1,402	329	168	182	28,852	973	27.9	12.7	45.4
Gallatin	98	715	95	15	67	26	25	25	34,425	165	20.0	21.8	60.6
Greene	218	1,760	343	105	394	142	93	66	37,385	733	25.9	14.2	43.0
Grundy	1,125	17,171	2,418	1,298	1,967	356	851	963	56,098	412	29.6	19.2	49.7
Hamilton	205	1,539	456	71	158	40	46	58	37,532	552	30.4	10.5	32.8
Hancock	382	2,767	501	306	425	184	157	102	36,995	1,109	26.1	12.4	47.5

Table B. States and Counties — **Agriculture**

STATE County	Land in farms — Acreage (1,000)	Percent change, 2012-2017	Acres — Average size of farm	Acres — Total irrigated (1,000)	Acres — Total cropland (1,000)	Value of land and buildings (dollars) — Average per farm	Average per acre	Value of machinery and equipment, average per farm (dollars)	Value of products sold: Total (mil dol)	Average per farm (acres)	Percent from: Crops	Percent from: Livestock and poultry products	Organic farms (number)	Farms with internet access (percent)	Government payments Total ($1,000)	Percent of farms
	117	118	119	120	121	122	123	124	125	126	127	128	129	130	131	132
IDAHO—Cont'd																
Caribou	366	-7.1	892	61.1	217.1	1,654,989	1,856	219,066	90.3	219,757	62.2	37.8	1	81.8	3,905	52.8
Cassia	643	5.3	1,100	259.3	385.0	3,508,509	3,190	512,076	926.7	1,584,137	27.6	72.4	4	87.9	11,088	38.6
Clark	149	-1.2	2,197	31.6	40.7	3,856,994	1,755	320,235	25.9	380,309	74.4	25.6	2	75.0	1,490	55.9
Clearwater	57	-22.1	181	D	24.8	447,579	2,469	54,776	7.3	23,487	46.8	53.2	NA	79.5	639	18.3
Custer	148	3.5	554	60.1	49.7	1,509,320	2,726	169,068	36.4	136,468	23.7	76.3	3	90.3	343	13.1
Elmore	358	4.0	1,054	113.2	148.9	2,626,980	2,492	400,675	429.9	1,264,462	27.8	72.2	7	82.6	684	11.5
Franklin	228	-13.0	290	65.3	132.1	674,740	2,325	128,763	82.8	105,187	31.1	68.9	26	83.5	2,730	39.6
Fremont	280	-11.6	545	101.9	171.0	1,507,845	2,767	225,633	138.2	269,419	84.7	15.3	NA	80.7	4,130	38.8
Gem	183	2.3	213	29.9	28.3	599,509	2,815	69,848	39.2	45,560	39.6	60.4	8	85.2	834	10.9
Gooding	188	-21.4	350	121.8	125.3	2,106,203	6,016	286,549	783.4	1,456,113	9.3	90.7	9	83.3	2,416	16.5
Idaho	537	-15.9	759	2.7	180.6	1,248,054	1,644	112,824	43.7	61,689	54.8	45.2	NA	79.2	3,060	36.4
Jefferson	334	3.3	445	198.3	228.3	1,566,390	3,522	264,821	294.6	392,743	58.7	41.3	6	86.9	4,603	24.4
Jerome	172	-8.7	353	134.9	134.6	2,132,761	6,039	418,233	639.6	1,316,016	18.9	81.1	16	84.2	2,050	33.5
Kootenai	140	12.4	130	13.7	62.2	719,383	5,525	49,847	21.5	20,057	81.0	19.0	3	81.7	1,211	9.9
Latah	350	-16.1	336	0.2	254.7	853,388	2,542	126,243	78.0	74,900	94.3	5.7	7	82.9	7,066	35.4
Lemhi	174	-7.2	496	72.2	46.4	1,251,971	2,526	116,297	33.3	94,818	16.6	83.4	3	89.7	295	10.0
Lewis	200	-9.4	1,017	D	151.1	1,997,866	1,964	238,202	37.8	191,787	90.2	9.8	NA	86.3	2,929	70.1
Lincoln	135	4.0	489	77.3	84.9	1,784,513	3,651	226,469	203.1	735,830	21.0	79.0	8	83.7	1,163	35.9
Madison	196	-2.6	432	125.9	160.0	1,797,444	4,162	289,620	157.0	345,855	93.2	6.8	1	90.3	3,919	39.0
Minidoka	268	9.6	432	232.7	242.6	1,958,696	4,539	300,481	354.4	571,692	73.4	26.6	6	81.9	4,319	40.2
Nez Perce	382	18.4	856	1.1	233.8	1,779,079	2,079	230,280	74.3	166,632	81.4	18.6	1	84.1	7,319	43.0
Oneida	320	-2.7	758	25.7	151.3	1,256,611	1,658	138,236	36.2	85,863	44.9	55.1	2	80.6	5,063	55.2
Owyhee	727	-2.9	1,287	119.0	137.8	2,096,160	1,628	232,705	273.4	483,851	22.6	77.4	7	82.8	2,365	21.4
Payette	163	3.5	254	59.2	57.4	890,516	3,505	141,684	167.4	261,563	30.0	70.0	3	88.1	900	12.0
Power	486	4.1	1,649	147.7	381.4	4,068,136	2,467	438,509	235.4	798,108	89.6	10.4	3	86.1	10,617	59.3
Shoshone	2	D	51	0.1	0.6	340,665	6,715	42,286	0.2	4,479	30.2	69.8	NA	77.1	NA	NA
Teton	117	-11.9	424	48.9	84.4	1,675,941	3,954	180,866	45.3	163,679	90.4	9.6	16	89.9	865	28.9
Twin Falls	469	-3.1	387	241.5	257.3	1,718,569	4,439	225,875	680.2	561,716	24.8	75.2	26	88.2	4,456	29.7
Valley	51	-16.8	271	22.1	4.3	703,011	2,594	62,528	10.5	56,069	8.7	91.3	1	67.6	84	4.3
Washington	468	9.8	876	38.8	80.4	1,185,859	1,354	132,560	50.2	93,918	41.8	58.2	6	80.7	1,591	28.4
ILLINOIS	27,006	0.3	372	612.5	24,003.1	2,705,291	7,278	220,485	17,010.0	234,133	81.4	18.6	328	76.9	521,229	66.9
Adams	478	22.9	365	11.0	382.8	2,376,117	6,506	227,632	269.4	205,979	73.2	26.8	9	75.7	4,870	60.0
Alexander	50	-19.1	401	2.6	43.1	1,371,640	3,423	144,673	16.6	131,889	98.5	1.5	NA	81.0	1,130	61.9
Bond	173	-12.9	271	0.0	149.8	1,865,147	6,874	180,014	84.8	133,047	89.7	10.3	2	76.9	3,877	60.3
Boone	114	-15.8	248	0.9	106.0	1,939,825	7,811	171,009	78.4	171,589	75.5	24.5	6	84.2	3,291	38.5
Brown	142	3.0	338	0.2	88.2	1,892,515	5,598	125,319	49.8	118,947	78.6	21.4	4	70.4	3,224	83.1
Bureau	437	-2.9	421	13.5	408.2	3,460,532	8,219	290,184	360.0	346,795	89.4	10.6	12	79.3	17,896	79.8
Calhoun	115	30.6	242	D	68.7	1,013,115	4,189	98,750	38.7	81,584	72.8	27.2	NA	63.5	2,393	68.6
Carroll	246	-4.1	392	10.6	210.0	3,150,456	8,039	269,522	216.8	345,845	69.0	31.0	NA	80.1	4,490	75.6
Cass	198	8.1	461	30.5	169.8	2,946,206	6,398	268,331	121.9	284,096	79.2	20.8	2	73.7	5,151	84.4
Champaign	583	-5.5	480	14.2	566.4	4,471,916	9,317	322,994	375.6	309,349	96.2	3.8	5	80.3	5,861	82.3
Christian	403	7.8	507	0.0	382.6	4,381,139	8,638	311,771	278.7	351,029	90.7	9.3	2	76.8	10,174	79.5
Clark	261	-2.1	356	11.8	227.7	2,032,961	5,708	205,302	163.3	222,795	73.9	26.1	1	71.8	4,408	77.8
Clay	294	8.9	402	D	258.7	2,058,866	5,121	214,709	116.1	158,626	86.9	13.1	NA	73.1	5,966	76.2
Clinton	236	-17.4	284	1.2	214.9	1,965,321	6,928	263,352	247.0	297,197	45.1	54.9	NA	78.1	6,067	74.8
Coles	237	-11.2	338	0.1	219.9	2,660,833	7,875	196,323	133.9	191,073	95.7	4.3	1	77.5	4,071	75.5
Cook	12	40.1	65	0.1	10.8	1,349,568	20,635	77,634	19.7	108,187	89.5	10.5	3	89.0	81	17.0
Crawford	220	2.2	388	9.1	193.5	2,039,041	5,254	213,282	108.4	191,594	90.4	9.6	NA	77.0	5,598	77.0
Cumberland	172	0.9	237	1.0	145.7	1,504,990	6,344	141,060	120.6	166,609	65.3	34.7	1	71.7	6,191	82.6
DeKalb	372	-6.5	477	0.5	362.6	4,495,730	9,420	299,674	384.2	493,178	60.9	39.1	11	87.2	8,773	71.6
De Witt	186	-4.9	369	0.2	177.1	3,094,024	8,387	202,905	120.4	238,875	91.6	8.4	5	79.6	4,331	69.0
Douglas	245	-6.9	408	0.0	236.6	3,701,396	9,071	203,298	159.5	265,888	93.9	6.1	7	64.3	3,836	57.2
DuPage	2	-70.2	28	0.0	1.6	471,456	16,807	38,061	3.9	50,377	97.6	2.4	NA	92.2	89	10.4
Edgar	318	-9.5	499	D	299.5	3,708,748	7,425	289,955	D	D	D	D	NA	80.4	7,464	82.4
Edwards	112	4.7	384	D	98.6	2,062,863	5,372	228,647	61.1	209,842	76.2	23.8	NA	78.0	3,203	80.4
Effingham	299	4.3	251	0.4	260.7	1,657,000	6,603	179,393	195.1	163,505	64.8	35.2	NA	79.2	9,626	73.8
Fayette	349	15.1	282	0.2	297.8	1,520,838	5,398	170,568	164.9	133,117	88.9	11.1	NA	70.2	6,528	63.9
Ford	270	-12.3	479	1.0	262.7	3,722,553	7,769	260,649	190.7	338,188	83.1	16.9	4	80.1	3,095	70.0
Franklin	174	-4.2	292	0.1	148.8	1,300,260	4,460	160,135	83.7	140,460	77.6	22.4	NA	67.6	3,569	54.4
Fulton	402	13.4	414	1.0	305.5	2,561,328	6,193	194,999	220.4	226,489	77.0	23.0	2	76.1	4,859	59.8
Gallatin	178	-4.5	1,078	28.0	161.3	5,719,128	5,307	451,878	92.4	559,933	97.9	2.1	NA	79.4	4,534	80.6
Greene	328	13.1	448	0.8	257.8	2,768,122	6,184	222,206	183.4	250,139	78.7	21.3	5	77.5	4,745	72.7
Grundy	233	7.4	566	D	224.9	5,018,301	8,868	344,786	135.5	328,791	97.6	2.4	NA	84.7	1,375	49.3
Hamilton	201	-10.2	363	NA	174.4	1,747,933	4,810	179,660	86.2	156,243	95.1	4.9	1	61.4	6,053	83.5
Hancock	455	17.9	411	6.8	378.2	2,911,061	7,091	222,490	320.2	288,772	69.7	30.3	NA	71.6	4,399	59.0

Table B. States and Counties — Water Use, Wholesale Trade, Retail Trade, and Real Estate

STATE County	Water use, 2015 Public supply water withdrawn (mil gal/day)	Public supply gallons withdrawn per person per day	Wholesale Trade[1], 2012 Number of establishments	Number of employees	Sales (mil dol)	Average payroll (mil dol)	Retail Trade[2], 2012 Number of establishments	Number of employees	Sales (mil dol)	Average payroll (mil dol)	Real estate and rental and leasing,[2] 2012 Number of establishments	Number of employees	Sales (mil dol)	Average payroll (mil dol)
	133	134	135	136	137	138	139	140	141	142	143	144	145	146
IDAHO—Cont'd														
Caribou	1.56	230.4	12	88	134.6	3.5	33	279	79.2	7.4	4	5	0.7	0.1
Cassia	3.66	155.7	30	360	702.9	15.6	116	1,301	323.9	29.8	23	38	6.0	0.8
Clark	0.17	193.2	1	D	D	D	4	D	D	D	1	D	D	D
Clearwater	1.04	122.4	4	94	54.1	5.5	36	279	55.5	6.4	6	10	0.5	0.1
Custer	0.95	232.4	NA	NA	NA	NA	29	212	39.4	3.5	6	D	D	D
Elmore	5.62	217.2	13	83	36.5	3.0	76	974	256.3	22.2	13	28	3.7	0.5
Franklin	11.62	888.8	10	D	D	D	45	511	116.4	9.7	9	D	D	D
Fremont	1.34	104.5	8	195	114.5	5.8	33	241	73.4	6.8	6	7	1.2	0.2
Gem	0.86	51.0	12	D	D	D	43	412	93.6	8.8	9	23	2.6	0.4
Gooding	3.59	234.9	21	178	217.6	6.4	44	355	91.5	7.1	7	D	D	D
Idaho	0.93	57.2	11	101	54.1	4.0	57	455	94.8	11.1	10	17	2.1	0.4
Jefferson	1.07	39.4	25	D	D	D	44	464	116.4	10.0	11	D	D	D
Jerome	3.67	160.9	36	308	217.3	14.1	71	845	277.0	20.3	22	73	8.0	1.9
Kootenai	34.69	230.7	132	D	D	D	574	7,996	2,501.7	207.0	201	623	122.6	19.1
Latah	4.20	108.3	21	D	D	D	139	1,874	356.1	37.2	44	159	19.3	3.5
Lemhi	1.63	210.7	5	D	D	D	42	335	98.4	8.0	16	33	2.5	0.7
Lewis	0.53	139.9	5	D	D	D	23	133	26.5	2.5	5	13	1.2	0.2
Lincoln	0.40	75.5	NA	NA	NA	NA	12	D	D	D	3	D	D	D
Madison	3.39	88.6	37	533	221.2	15.5	118	1,607	370.7	34.2	56	174	25.1	3.2
Minidoka	2.81	137.3	46	661	430.9	27.8	62	418	157.9	9.3	12	37	6.1	1.2
Nez Perce	10.07	251.4	42	D	D	D	200	2,249	682.9	56.9	39	137	25.5	4.5
Oneida	0.72	168.2	1	D	D	D	18	142	30.4	2.3	4	15	1.0	0.1
Owyhee	0.73	64.5	6	D	D	D	24	169	42.6	3.9	4	9	0.2	0.0
Payette	1.94	84.7	21	203	113.5	6.0	61	483	136.4	10.7	21	26	3.8	0.6
Power	2.15	281.1	13	212	221.7	7.3	16	164	29.6	3.1	7	D	D	D
Shoshone	2.48	199.5	11	D	D	D	61	846	518.2	31.2	13	35	4.4	0.4
Teton	0.78	73.8	9	D	D	D	38	299	66.1	6.3	34	51	7.6	1.5
Twin Falls	15.74	191.1	111	1,096	492.8	42.6	380	4,789	1,233.5	112.8	112	313	49.7	8.5
Valley	1.55	153.4	10	65	20.0	2.2	69	462	105.9	10.3	38	58	10.0	1.4
Washington	0.74	74.1	9	194	26.4	3.6	33	276	83.7	6.5	11	27	2.3	0.4
ILLINOIS	1,475.66	114.7	16,036	255,531	295,457.0	15,973.3	39,947	592,942	166,634.5	14,576.1	12,035	76,794	23,649.1	3,816.1
Adams	10.35	154.4	120	D	D	D	299	4,790	1,066.5	101.4	61	D	D	D
Alexander	1.61	237.5	5	16	8.0	0.5	23	135	24.2	2.3	3	8	0.8	0.2
Bond	1.30	76.7	21	247	182.4	11.2	46	363	124.2	6.5	8	D	D	D
Boone	3.56	66.4	31	239	202.6	12.4	108	1,369	395.4	31.6	24	61	9.9	1.6
Brown	0.04	5.9	10	D	D	D	20	149	32.8	3.0	NA	NA	NA	NA
Bureau	2.96	88.1	53	896	1,472.5	39.3	97	1,166	299.8	23.2	16	D	D	D
Calhoun	0.41	83.7	5	D	D	D	15	116	27.3	2.5	1	D	D	D
Carroll	1.03	70.5	28	243	285.8	9.1	50	427	95.5	8.8	7	21	1.5	0.2
Cass	1.10	85.6	18	179	501.0	8.7	48	491	119.8	10.3	5	16	2.0	0.4
Champaign	24.42	116.9	176	2,872	2,589.6	126.5	626	10,256	2,472.7	220.2	201	2,986	557.4	117.9
Christian	2.55	75.8	45	605	845.6	30.5	111	1,377	410.3	31.4	20	94	12.9	2.7
Clark	1.60	100.1	19	191	257.9	6.0	51	445	141.7	10.9	5	22	4.4	0.7
Clay	0.01	0.7	26	196	172.8	6.8	46	464	113.3	8.9	7	49	3.9	0.9
Clinton	6.98	184.7	48	541	451.0	20.9	141	1,561	425.9	40.3	21	181	14.7	8.9
Coles	4.10	78.1	50	553	627.4	25.3	198	2,645	701.3	59.5	50	166	29.4	4.8
Cook	834.08	159.2	6,130	94,754	100,829.6	6,169.4	15,225	222,918	62,767.4	5,733.8	5,629	40,439	12,377.8	2,244.4
Crawford	2.18	112.3	19	181	179.3	6.2	61	796	187.1	16.2	14	D	D	D
Cumberland	0.27	24.8	16	153	188.2	5.0	24	188	38.6	2.9	1	D	D	D
DeKalb	7.64	73.2	60	586	353.2	27.1	280	4,404	1,052.7	91.7	69	447	100.2	14.2
De Witt	1.31	80.6	30	352	603.6	23.8	52	677	220.6	17.3	9	30	2.5	0.4
Douglas	0.67	33.8	30	329	478.1	16.6	120	1,173	218.7	19.1	12	38	8.3	1.0
DuPage	6.80	7.3	2,322	45,595	65,510.4	3,110.6	3,336	59,068	17,758.8	1,543.7	1,310	11,880	6,433.2	673.0
Edgar	1.58	89.4	13	148	227.4	9.4	51	623	157.0	13.6	9	30	4.6	0.9
Edwards	0.04	6.1	15	D	D	D	28	202	55.0	3.9	2	D	D	D
Effingham	2.06	59.9	62	D	D	D	203	2,977	934.7	66.1	43	214	32.0	7.0
Fayette	1.27	57.6	25	321	398.4	13.1	85	929	256.4	19.5	12	25	3.1	0.7
Ford	1.44	104.8	34	354	566.7	19.9	51	537	119.1	10.1	8	D	D	D
Franklin	15.39	389.8	34	265	126.3	13.3	143	1,549	408.1	35.0	15	69	6.4	1.6
Fulton	2.55	71.4	22	247	184.1	11.7	115	1,378	316.6	27.8	15	49	6.7	1.1
Gallatin	3.25	617.3	4	43	25.0	1.5	13	76	16.1	1.7	1	D	D	D
Greene	0.70	52.9	18	152	321.5	5.9	49	408	125.6	9.1	3	2	0.1	0.0
Grundy	3.41	67.5	47	490	738.0	27.1	144	1,744	524.7	38.1	28	71	15.7	2.4
Hamilton	0.00	0.0	8	81	64.5	3.2	34	161	45.4	3.4	7	15	1.3	0.3
Hancock	1.32	71.2	31	233	361.4	9.8	67	474	97.0	9.0	4	10	1.2	0.2

1 Merchant wholesalers, except manufacturers' sales branches and offices. 2. Employer establishments.

Professional Services, Manufacturing, and Accommodation and Food Services

STATE County	Professional, scientific, and technical services, 2012				Manufacturing, 2012				Accommodation and food services, 2012			
	Number of establish-ments	Number of employees	Sales (mil dol)	Average payroll (mil dol)	Number of establish-ments	Number of employees	Receipts (mil dol)	Annual payroll (mil dol)	Number of establis-hments	Number of employees	Receipts (mil dol)	Annual payroll (mil dol)
	147	148	149	150	151	152	153	154	155	156	157	158
IDAHO—Cont'd												
Caribou	10	D	D	D	9	761	D	52.8	18	119	3.9	1.1
Cassia	49	146	12.1	4.1	31	1,345	917.1	53.3	51	D	D	D
Clark	2	D	D	D	3	D	D	0.3	1	D	D	D
Clearwater	11	46	2.4	1.1	21	251	D	8.5	27	175	6.5	2.1
Custer	8	D	D	D	5	D	D	D	31	D	D	D
Elmore	19	82	8.1	2.6	11	343	D	9.7	54	613	28.9	7.6
Franklin	17	51	6.2	1.5	19	247	39.9	8.7	16	204	5.6	1.6
Fremont	14	41	3.9	0.9	13	33	5.7	0.8	30	140	10.7	2.3
Gem	23	50	4.4	1.4	16	68	D	1.7	28	D	D	D
Gooding	21	D	D	D	23	405	D	20.5	30	183	7.3	1.9
Idaho	24	D	D	D	37	519	161.3	21.5	51	273	12.0	3.3
Jefferson	27	D	D	D	22	D	214.8	26.5	34	D	D	D
Jerome	25	113	13.4	3.8	24	1,301	D	52.9	30	329	16.7	4.0
Kootenai	442	D	D	D	241	4,011	D	170.2	362	D	D	D
Latah	80	D	D	D	26	277	D	12.3	121	D	D	D
Lemhi	19	62	3.1	1.2	9	60	12.2	1.5	35	223	10.3	2.5
Lewis	2	D	D	D	5	142	45.8	4.8	15	114	4.9	1.4
Lincoln	5	12	1.1	0.6	3	D	D	D	4	28	1.2	0.3
Madison	67	734	44.6	20.0	29	878	184.6	26.1	52	901	32.3	9.1
Minidoka	26	D	D	D	23	935	649.7	42.3	29	D	D	D
Nez Perce	80	D	D	D	35	2,791	1,124.5	133.9	99	2,096	108.5	30.1
Oneida	3	D	D	D	5	32	D	1.9	10	90	2.8	0.7
Owyhee	7	25	1.7	0.7	7	146	D	4.7	25	D	D	D
Payette	34	124	12.7	3.6	28	1,101	D	30.8	34	237	8.0	2.1
Power	8	D	D	D	7	D	D	D	12	52	2.2	0.5
Shoshone	27	D	D	D	16	182	D	7.4	42	D	D	D
Teton	39	103	11.1	3.8	9	76	D	2.6	37	257	15.0	5.0
Twin Falls	223	1,079	99.4	37.2	96	2,876	D	113.3	173	2,721	132.5	34.7
Valley	36	89	9.5	3.3	16	36	4.0	1.0	76	774	40.1	13.7
Washington	19	56	4.1	1.5	12	453	D	12.6	19	138	5.4	1.5
ILLINOIS	38,673	364,336	70,263.2	28,314.9	13,868	542,004	281,037.8	28,413.7	27,117	469,870	27,937.4	7,707.1
Adams	132	D	D	D	88	4,749	D	242.0	147	2,278	103.2	29.2
Alexander	7	37	1.7	0.8	4	145	D	6.2	14	61	2.2	0.7
Bond	25	D	D	D	16	838	419.8	37.4	33	332	14.9	3.8
Boone	59	639	57.0	29.4	78	7,619	5,906.2	404.0	69	796	41.8	10.6
Brown	6	26	2.0	0.7	5	138	36.3	5.9	11	D	D	D
Bureau	48	330	20.4	6.9	37	1,358	D	62.2	81	818	33.4	9.0
Calhoun	4	D	D	D	4	13	2.0	0.5	19	D	D	D
Carroll	24	62	6.6	1.6	26	784	293.1	31.4	39	317	15.0	3.7
Cass	11	54	6.0	1.7	13	2,297	D	83.4	28	D	D	D
Champaign	439	2,767	362.4	137.4	132	7,063	3,024.6	313.9	517	9,809	437.5	120.4
Christian	47	471	20.8	8.3	21	1,059	D	49.1	68	887	34.0	9.9
Clark	16	90	11.9	5.6	16	1,004	539.2	46.5	43	446	19.9	5.3
Clay	16	127	7.0	2.7	17	1,772	763.1	74.3	29	292	12.5	3.2
Clinton	46	208	18.6	7.1	33	732	D	26.3	98	1,090	41.4	10.8
Coles	67	405	40.7	13.1	40	2,615	D	109.0	130	2,232	84.7	24.1
Cook	19,017	217,861	48,255.4	18,955.5	5,120	181,315	79,527.0	9,622.8	11,329	207,364	14,553.1	4,023.7
Crawford	29	165	18.2	7.5	16	1,878	D	131.4	34	367	17.2	4.7
Cumberland	7	32	2.2	0.8	12	443	D	11.8	7	D	D	D
DeKalb	151	683	64.4	24.5	110	3,499	1,339.4	154.6	214	3,161	135.9	35.7
De Witt	23	90	9.1	2.7	14	513	181.4	20.7	38	489	19.8	5.7
Douglas	28	89	6.4	2.0	82	2,146	841.3	106.5	50	656	28.1	7.2
DuPage	5,117	46,480	8,120.0	3,347.2	1,680	53,913	18,896.7	2,921.6	2,132	40,549	2,424.3	690.5
Edgar	25	99	8.3	2.5	20	1,751	714.8	76.0	30	D	D	D
Edwards	7	22	1.7	0.5	9	D	D	D	11	103	2.8	0.8
Effingham	56	310	39.4	11.9	60	2,913	697.9	123.5	106	2,111	97.5	26.7
Fayette	21	134	9.9	4.2	13	439	113.9	15.6	45	506	21.0	6.0
Ford	18	104	10.2	3.1	17	562	D	24.7	31	D	D	D
Franklin	43	253	25.3	8.1	39	783	199.1	31.3	77	972	38.2	10.5
Fulton	38	187	17.6	7.7	19	218	47.5	6.8	72	856	28.7	8.1
Gallatin	7	22	1.5	0.7	4	7	1.0	0.2	8	29	1.4	0.3
Greene	16	65	6.6	2.6	12	167	D	6.0	28	D	D	D
Grundy	94	781	86.9	37.0	47	1,306	2,113.8	97.8	100	1,380	59.7	15.8
Hamilton	12	40	2.9	1.1	7	72	D	2.4	12	123	4.6	1.3
Hancock	21	173	32.3	7.4	24	1,217	D	D	32	227	10.5	2.8

Table B. States and Counties — Health Care and Social Assistance, Other Services, Nonemployer Businesses, and Residential Construction

STATE County	Health care and social assistance, 2012				Other services, 2012				Nonemployer businesses, 2016		Value of residential construction authorized by building permits, 2018	
	Number of establish-ments	Number of employees	Receipts (mil dol)	Annual payroll (mil dol)	Number of establish-ments	Number of employees	Receipts (mil dol)	Annual payroll (mil dol)	Number	Receipts (mil dol)	New construction ($1,000)	Number of housing units
	159	160	161	162	163	164	165	166	167	168	169	170
IDAHO—Cont'd												
Caribou	21	226	18.2	6.9	15	D	D	D	443	15.4	4,581	30
Cassia	83	1,246	95.1	34.2	37	D	D	D	1,530	80.6	17,248	93
Clark	1	D	D	D	NA	NA	NA	NA	66	1.4	307	2
Clearwater	24	515	40.4	19.1	14	D	D	D	504	20.7	2,822	23
Custer	8	D	D	D	5	6	0.5	0.1	451	15.0	200	1
Elmore	51	723	56.4	22.1	34	125	7.0	2.2	1,281	47.9	6,513	38
Franklin	25	325	25.1	9.1	19	D	D	D	1,027	42.0	8,735	48
Fremont	17	222	12.8	5.2	16	D	D	D	1,177	56.8	18,376	106
Gem	46	733	46.0	18.8	23	D	D	D	1,228	43.1	13,675	95
Gooding	35	496	39.5	15.0	23	D	D	D	857	35.9	6,469	36
Idaho	32	700	48.8	23.3	21	D	D	D	1,232	47.1	436	2
Jefferson	33	D	D	D	14	D	D	D	2,231	103.4	33,047	208
Jerome	36	502	35.3	17.7	48	162	17.0	4.1	1,155	59.6	12,674	85
Kootenai	509	8,630	806.2	308.4	236	D	D	D	12,316	545.7	451,559	2,210
Latah	85	1,360	115.0	49.3	52	D	D	D	2,574	94.1	36,929	193
Lemhi	27	366	28.2	10.7	22	75	7.7	1.5	725	24.9	4,572	32
Lewis	13	D	D	D	3	D	D	D	321	9.5	1,103	26
Lincoln	8	99	4.7	2.1	3	6	0.7	0.1	263	10.6	796	6
Madison	92	1,390	131.8	42.0	33	D	D	D	2,870	113.4	109,639	841
Minidoka	40	519	34.4	15.2	26	D	D	D	1,179	52.1	15,482	56
Nez Perce	138	3,029	341.2	123.0	85	D	D	D	2,123	84.3	21,004	86
Oneida	8	D	D	D	3	D	D	D	334	12.9	1,623	12
Owyhee	17	142	6.9	3.0	5	D	D	D	666	26.8	7,703	42
Payette	42	535	34.8	15.2	27	80	6.8	2.1	1,481	64.2	11,602	79
Power	12	190	11.5	5.4	11	58	6.6	1.4	360	15.4	4,371	18
Shoshone	33	488	35.7	13.6	17	58	5.0	1.6	736	20.7	1,727	10
Teton	29	250	21.1	9.0	20	61	6.0	1.8	1,510	57.4	40,748	208
Twin Falls	325	5,626	497.8	192.1	155	850	75.4	21.4	5,653	263.1	91,842	500
Valley	29	393	32.7	16.6	31	186	12.1	3.8	1,266	58.2	48,607	182
Washington	26	401	28.2	11.1	14	72	5.0	1.3	640	20.3	3,847	26
ILLINOIS	33,055	770,484	83,431.8	32,574.0	23,334	165,366	21,355.5	5,826.6	981,735	42,282.6	4,036,281	21,510
Adams	142	5,586	691.3	238.4	158	D	D	D	3,911	146.9	10,353	49
Alexander	8	237	12.2	6.6	6	10	0.8	0.2	292	7.6	0	0
Bond	30	593	47.3	21.9	21	99	8.8	2.6	976	27.5	1,671	10
Boone	73	1,077	80.1	30.0	67	372	30.0	9.4	3,085	123.2	7,609	45
Brown	9	D	D	D	12	D	D	D	333	9.1	175	1
Bureau	80	2,114	171.6	75.8	78	D	D	D	1,907	72.8	5,112	20
Calhoun	5	D	D	D	5	14	1.1	0.3	341	11.9	1,665	11
Carroll	26	616	23.8	9.5	32	191	13.4	4.0	987	34.5	5,060	17
Cass	17	379	15.7	7.3	25	D	D	D	749	20.6	1,194	9
Champaign	364	D	D	D	271	2,173	403.7	66.3	12,343	483.1	231,241	1,460
Christian	64	1,721	119.7	48.2	62	292	19.8	5.1	1,897	67.5	4,982	25
Clark	22	375	20.4	8.9	20	63	5.4	1.2	1,081	35.0	640	4
Clay	41	650	42.4	18.8	31	95	8.6	1.7	943	33.2	165	3
Clinton	84	1,624	128.7	52.6	66	284	25.0	6.1	2,353	84.3	18,341	73
Coles	155	3,981	367.2	149.0	96	465	35.2	11.2	2,637	95.8	2,161	13
Cook	14,637	358,374	39,639.9	15,523.6	9,887	78,562	12,262.7	3,166.7	483,757	20,961.3	1,280,759	8,199
Crawford	42	975	73.2	28.7	41	170	15.7	3.5	1,231	47.1	800	3
Cumberland	14	260	14.4	6.1	16	100	7.4	3.3	740	24.5	0	0
DeKalb	229	4,786	503.1	179.1	147	994	67.3	17.8	6,134	231.6	24,348	118
De Witt	28	581	38.5	17.1	27	98	9.5	2.5	897	27.9	4,412	19
Douglas	30	356	20.6	8.8	31	111	8.8	2.5	1,601	67.2	3,775	24
DuPage	3,215	62,644	7,846.5	3,116.4	2,047	17,768	2,184.8	676.0	83,927	4,501.6	477,043	1,439
Edgar	30	752	65.5	25.4	24	96	9.9	2.4	995	33.0	0	0
Edwards	14	120	5.9	3.2	14	D	D	D	445	14.2	NA	NA
Effingham	124	2,778	320.0	109.8	94	989	65.7	28.0	2,746	116.8	14,962	60
Fayette	42	987	48.3	20.2	33	157	14.7	3.6	1,295	49.0	836	5
Ford	35	1,053	88.1	37.9	28	D	D	D	958	33.1	1,669	13
Franklin	73	1,229	75.4	28.5	55	186	24.0	3.9	2,166	70.2	777	6
Fulton	70	2,037	171.7	66.2	50	260	14.2	4.2	1,668	50.4	9,987	45
Gallatin	7	109	5.3	2.0	11	D	D	D	297	11.8	NA	NA
Greene	22	378	22.9	11.7	15	D	D	D	798	28.7	511	3
Grundy	124	D	D	D	85	487	55.3	13.1	2,944	128.6	23,104	206
Hamilton	19	447	25.3	10.1	17	55	5.8	1.4	515	14.7	NA	NA
Hancock	28	493	34.1	15.0	29	70	5.7	1.5	1,339	50.6	644	3

Government Employment and Payroll, and Local Government Finances

STATE County	Government employment and payroll, 2012									Local government finances, 2012				
			March payroll (percent of total)							General revenue				
												Taxes		
			Adminis-tration, judicial, and legal	Police and corrections	Fire protection	Highways and transpor-tation	Health and welfare	Natural resources and utilities	Education and libraries	Total (mil dol)	Inter-govern-mental (mil dol)	Total (mil dol)	Per capita[1] (dollars)	
	Full-time equivalent employees	March payroll (dollars)											Total	Property
	171	172	173	174	175	176	177	178	179	180	181	182	183	184
IDAHO—Cont'd														
Caribou	536	1,743,847	5.7	7.1	0.0	5.1	23.6	2.6	54.8	30.0	15.1	9.8	1,451	1,424
Cassia	841	2,609,053	6.9	10.2	1.3	4.4	1.0	7.7	66.0	72.2	36.8	15.3	658	460
Clark	64	182,907	15.4	10.5	0.0	12.5	0.0	3.3	58.1	5.0	3.3	1.2	1,353	1,265
Clearwater	338	951,830	12.2	14.7	0.3	8.5	5.3	6.8	50.6	26.1	13.8	8.4	974	934
Custer	193	546,688	12.5	6.7	0.1	16.9	1.2	5.5	56.7	15.9	9.6	3.8	876	845
Elmore	1,019	3,030,975	6.9	10.0	0.6	5.4	25.3	5.0	45.8	85.0	33.0	18.8	717	631
Franklin	560	1,720,585	5.4	4.8	0.0	3.4	34.4	1.8	50.0	29.4	21.3	5.3	417	394
Fremont	515	1,419,098	11.6	16.1	2.7	6.1	2.9	5.3	54.6	35.8	16.2	14.1	1,086	1,034
Gem	557	1,566,566	7.1	9.6	1.2	2.9	21.3	5.1	50.7	48.1	18.9	14.1	844	831
Gooding	579	1,442,650	8.1	9.0	1.3	5.5	3.6	3.7	66.2	56.3	24.7	15.8	1,036	1,004
Idaho	626	1,781,949	5.1	6.7	0.0	7.5	28.5	2.9	44.8	45.1	21.7	8.0	491	490
Jefferson	872	2,231,238	5.7	8.4	1.8	4.0	1.4	0.9	76.4	54.6	35.5	14.4	541	538
Jerome	672	1,876,675	11.2	10.1	3.4	5.6	0.5	5.4	62.3	54.6	29.4	15.7	697	673
Kootenai	6,580	25,436,541	6.0	8.3	3.6	2.4	37.6	3.3	38.1	678.7	158.8	148.1	1,040	972
Latah	1,001	3,595,367	11.4	10.5	0.8	5.9	0.5	6.2	63.7	82.9	35.0	31.3	819	745
Lemhi	403	1,235,515	7.2	7.5	0.2	3.9	46.4	3.5	30.0	38.3	15.0	4.0	511	478
Lewis	228	620,176	8.8	8.6	0.0	7.6	0.3	4.4	69.1	19.4	10.6	6.1	1,560	1,538
Lincoln	225	639,708	10.8	7.0	0.8	6.1	0.7	4.7	69.2	12.7	7.9	3.6	675	614
Madison	1,018	2,964,631	10.1	13.1	1.9	4.4	1.9	2.7	63.6	142.6	48.3	21.2	565	517
Minidoka	971	2,994,496	5.6	6.8	1.4	1.2	25.7	9.8	49.0	70.9	29.8	11.3	562	530
Nez Perce	1,348	5,048,001	7.1	13.3	6.7	5.6	4.0	8.5	50.0	119.0	49.4	44.7	1,132	1,075
Oneida	180	488,815	12.4	9.4	0.2	6.7	2.2	3.2	65.1	13.7	7.2	3.0	709	690
Owyhee	420	1,130,203	5.4	8.3	0.9	4.7	0.4	2.7	73.7	36.6	20.4	12.9	1,130	780
Payette	742	2,179,486	8.8	11.0	1.4	4.1	2.9	4.4	66.6	54.2	28.9	16.9	747	643
Power	430	1,383,820	5.4	5.9	0.3	7.0	26.0	3.4	51.1	39.7	13.4	10.9	1,398	1,360
Shoshone	609	1,865,396	6.7	7.4	2.8	7.1	21.4	5.7	48.1	52.0	20.0	14.5	1,140	1,102
Teton	450	1,567,917	7.7	3.7	5.3	2.4	33.2	1.8	43.6	55.4	16.6	14.5	1,445	1,299
Twin Falls	3,114	9,543,688	6.8	11.2	2.7	2.8	5.5	3.6	66.3	357.5	212.6	68.8	876	846
Valley	517	1,760,075	11.5	14.1	6.6	9.0	7.9	8.9	39.9	49.2	15.8	24.3	2,542	2,475
Washington	545	1,653,304	6.7	8.4	0.8	4.2	28.1	6.1	43.6	48.8	16.8	12.1	1,202	1,131
ILLINOIS	X	X	X	X	X	X	X	X	X	X	X	X	X	X
Adams	2,703	8,715,868	5.5	10.4	4.2	4.1	5.0	6.1	62.7	223.4	108.4	76.6	1,140	966
Alexander	313	970,447	7.7	9.2	0.0	10.6	2.3	10.0	57.2	30.3	20.7	4.6	595	522
Bond	553	1,740,375	8.4	8.6	0.2	5.4	9.2	6.9	61.0	47.8	21.7	14.3	811	782
Boone	1,665	6,568,081	5.5	11.2	2.8	2.0	1.2	4.1	72.4	168.6	64.4	88.0	1,632	1,512
Brown	202	635,285	9.5	7.4	0.4	13.0	4.1	3.1	62.1	17.3	8.3	5.3	772	738
Bureau	1,639	5,498,491	7.7	6.6	1.2	2.6	22.0	6.1	53.1	152.9	48.9	47.1	1,371	1,315
Calhoun	170	503,707	8.6	7.8	0.2	10.3	6.6	2.8	63.7	12.8	6.7	4.6	917	910
Carroll	571	1,922,747	6.7	10.1	1.2	4.6	1.4	4.6	70.2	50.2	17.9	26.2	1,744	1,700
Cass	549	1,630,366	5.5	5.1	0.7	5.7	1.6	4.6	73.9	47.1	27.4	13.9	1,039	967
Champaign	7,295	27,910,700	5.6	8.8	3.9	7.8	5.7	5.8	60.6	779.8	297.9	355.6	1,749	1,502
Christian	1,070	3,699,842	8.2	9.1	2.1	5.7	2.0	6.3	66.0	97.0	49.7	35.0	1,009	963
Clark	656	1,941,162	6.3	7.0	1.4	5.2	2.5	7.5	65.2	49.9	25.6	16.5	1,017	965
Clay	731	2,318,318	7.1	5.7	0.1	3.7	25.1	6.3	51.0	65.8	22.2	11.1	807	758
Clinton	1,065	3,651,290	8.0	9.9	0.0	4.7	3.6	5.9	67.0	83.0	32.3	37.3	980	957
Coles	2,055	7,515,260	6.6	9.1	4.4	3.1	2.6	3.4	70.1	193.9	95.6	62.8	1,170	1,079
Cook	198,590	1,055,085,174	5.5	19.7	3.8	8.4	5.0	6.1	49.9	30,214.0	10,506.2	14,465.1	2,765	2,126
Crawford	1,004	3,546,258	3.9	4.8	1.2	4.9	40.2	1.7	42.6	92.3	22.6	23.8	1,214	1,192
Cumberland	489	1,701,831	5.1	5.3	0.6	4.4	1.3	6.8	75.7	24.9	13.2	8.4	765	749
DeKalb	3,677	13,579,842	6.4	11.5	5.3	3.7	5.7	4.9	61.7	427.7	136.1	235.3	2,247	1,839
De Witt	856	2,898,838	6.6	7.9	0.9	3.4	26.5	4.6	49.0	74.5	16.6	32.1	1,956	1,907
Douglas	604	1,931,336	13.2	8.9	0.8	4.9	0.1	2.9	68.4	57.7	23.4	26.8	1,352	1,325
DuPage	34,627	161,978,004	4.8	10.0	5.2	2.3	1.4	8.6	66.4	4,380.5	931.7	2,785.7	3,002	2,700
Edgar	762	2,449,135	5.9	7.4	2.5	12.8	1.9	5.1	63.4	53.8	26.7	21.4	1,175	1,081
Edwards	230	593,869	6.7	6.9	0.5	3.2	1.4	6.8	74.3	13.3	7.7	3.8	573	568
Effingham	1,139	4,092,064	7.6	10.0	2.5	4.1	2.3	4.6	67.2	103.7	48.7	39.5	1,151	1,088
Fayette	798	2,298,002	8.1	12.9	0.0	4.6	5.0	3.9	65.2	56.1	29.6	16.6	754	737
Ford	495	1,697,539	6.4	9.3	0.0	5.1	0.0	3.3	75.1	45.2	18.3	21.4	1,530	1,465
Franklin	1,582	5,056,096	5.7	8.6	1.7	3.6	12.7	9.1	58.0	140.8	72.3	25.5	646	571
Fulton	1,688	5,342,718	6.0	7.3	2.2	3.1	5.4	5.4	70.1	131.1	60.0	46.1	1,259	1,214
Gallatin	190	667,273	12.7	6.1	0.2	4.8	0.2	7.6	67.8	16.8	10.0	3.8	699	636
Greene	546	1,577,821	8.0	6.8	0.3	8.5	4.3	8.2	63.4	36.4	17.9	12.3	908	861
Grundy	1,993	7,671,944	5.9	9.9	3.1	2.7	1.3	1.8	74.1	223.4	53.5	147.8	2,939	2,877
Hamilton	413	1,340,057	6.2	3.3	0.0	3.7	34.5	5.5	46.3	33.7	13.2	5.1	604	603
Hancock	809	2,296,267	7.2	7.5	0.4	6.0	1.8	4.7	71.8	55.0	25.2	21.7	1,147	1,101

1. Based on the resident population estimated as of July 1 of the year shown.

Table B. States and Counties — Local Government Finances, Government Employment, and Income Taxes

STATE County	Local government finances, 2012 (cont.)							Debt outstanding		Government employment, 2017			Individual income tax returns, 2016		
	Direct general expenditure														
			Percent of total for:											Mean	
	Total (mil dol)	Per capita[1] (dollars)	Education	Health and hospitals	Police protection	Public welfare	Highways	Total (mil dol)	Per capita[1] (dollars)	Federal civilian	Federal military	State and local	Number of returns	adjusted gross income	Mean income tax
	185	186	187	188	189	190	191	192	193	194	195	196	197	198	199
IDAHO—Cont'd															
Caribou	29.0	4,268	41.5	0.2	10.7	0.5	13.5	1.0	151	39	23	696	2,830	53,008	5,118
Cassia	58.1	2,497	57.1	0.4	5.3	0.8	5.6	30.3	1,303	131	77	1,418	9,560	45,755	4,497
Clark	5.2	6,037	40.8	0.2	6.5	0.5	26.7	4.2	4,807	29	3	108	320	30,319	1,625
Clearwater	26.0	3,028	39.9	2.2	7.1	1.3	13.0	2.0	229	146	26	785	3,410	46,835	4,309
Custer	16.4	3,790	37.4	7.3	4.7	0.5	14.1	0.2	42	160	14	293	1,940	44,662	4,825
Elmore	76.8	2,930	37.5	27.0	6.8	0.0	7.2	27.5	1,049	855	3,299	1,048	11,470	41,542	3,512
Franklin	28.7	2,243	61.1	1.8	7.2	0.4	7.4	5.0	394	33	44	1,037	5,410	46,280	3,611
Fremont	39.0	3,014	39.0	1.3	7.0	0.8	11.9	29.5	2,277	73	42	950	5,530	40,251	3,179
Gem	41.4	2,481	43.1	21.4	5.8	0.6	5.5	23.5	1,409	77	57	895	7,450	43,822	3,804
Gooding	85.0	5,557	26.2	51.3	2.6	0.7	3.7	49.5	3,236	64	50	1,088	6,260	34,536	3,659
Idaho	41.4	2,537	44.3	2.9	4.7	1.4	20.3	6.4	391	324	52	907	6,380	42,684	4,113
Jefferson	64.3	2,411	54.0	0.0	6.7	0.2	4.6	89.0	3,335	51	93	1,229	10,880	49,806	4,437
Jerome	53.8	2,393	44.7	0.3	5.9	1.1	9.0	39.2	1,743	47	77	1,012	9,380	39,714	3,617
Kootenai	637.0	4,475	29.8	40.2	5.8	0.4	3.9	121.1	851	634	513	10,604	74,530	55,358	6,355
Latah	87.4	2,290	48.2	0.3	11.6	1.1	4.1	40.7	1,065	164	142	6,674	16,080	53,149	5,443
Lemhi	34.8	4,485	25.3	39.2	3.9	0.7	4.9	15.4	1,987	221	26	613	3,550	42,746	4,134
Lewis	21.4	5,498	42.3	0.7	5.0	0.7	11.4	4.3	1,109	60	13	385	1,810	41,969	3,679
Lincoln	12.3	2,332	69.2	0.0	4.6	0.1	9.2	6.3	1,194	84	17	387	1,980	41,218	3,288
Madison	144.7	3,862	27.9	37.4	3.3	0.2	4.1	137.2	3,662	57	127	2,098	13,110	40,921	3,183
Minidoka	75.3	3,760	38.1	24.8	4.2	0.5	5.7	46.9	2,341	86	68	1,354	8,660	44,200	3,977
Nez Perce	119.5	3,023	41.4	0.7	8.3	0.2	7.5	25.2	637	198	132	4,018	18,470	52,072	5,350
Oneida	14.2	3,368	42.9	22.5	6.2	0.3	7.9	2.7	633	19	14	419	1,820	42,266	3,119
Owyhee	32.2	2,814	58.3	0.0	6.5	0.9	6.7	21.0	1,836	47	38	643	4,670	36,541	3,643
Payette	52.4	2,315	48.3	3.5	7.4	1.5	7.7	25.3	1,117	32	76	1,034	9,790	52,104	5,580
Power	34.2	4,401	40.1	20.7	3.4	0.6	11.8	11.5	1,480	21	25	614	3,120	42,775	4,142
Shoshone	52.1	4,102	38.6	21.3	5.0	0.8	10.7	38.7	3,043	64	41	796	5,430	43,530	3,976
Teton	51.0	5,069	26.2	24.7	2.1	0.1	4.7	22.8	2,269	43	37	441	4,900	54,454	6,030
Twin Falls	356.9	4,541	65.8	1.8	3.6	0.9	4.2	190.1	2,418	378	278	4,779	36,330	46,239	5,003
Valley	50.0	5,243	33.1	0.0	8.0	0.2	14.2	52.4	5,495	252	35	728	5,230	58,977	6,975
Washington	43.6	4,322	34.4	33.0	5.6	1.2	5.7	9.6	952	51	33	695	4,180	40,069	3,354
ILLINOIS	X	X	X	X	X	X	X	X	X	80,111	42,947	748,859	6,099,590	71,613	10,509
Adams	201.0	2,991	56.5	3.5	5.7	0.2	5.8	99.6	1,482	234	130	3,953	31,570	55,758	6,600
Alexander	30.3	3,916	49.2	1.4	5.2	0.5	5.8	3.3	426	25	12	342	2,440	37,659	3,055
Bond	45.6	2,583	46.2	7.7	7.5	0.1	9.0	52.0	2,948	309	30	740	6,990	50,095	4,829
Boone	156.0	2,893	62.0	1.2	6.0	0.1	5.4	126.3	2,341	65	107	2,215	25,470	62,079	7,622
Brown	16.0	2,312	46.9	4.0	5.1	0.0	14.3	5.3	774	44	9	432	2,310	51,720	5,284
Bureau	156.2	4,551	37.8	25.0	3.8	0.0	9.0	77.1	2,245	111	66	2,187	16,590	51,879	5,696
Calhoun	11.5	2,294	52.1	0.5	3.8	0.1	22.6	8.5	1,693	21	10	233	2,160	53,726	5,600
Carroll	49.2	3,280	55.2	1.4	4.9	0.0	10.6	31.3	2,088	63	29	755	7,400	50,919	5,396
Cass	48.5	3,633	48.0	10.6	5.0	0.1	5.9	32.3	2,418	55	25	798	6,210	47,725	4,216
Champaign	826.4	4,066	48.3	2.5	5.1	1.9	5.6	670.9	3,301	1,254	413	35,838	84,500	63,041	8,206
Christian	110.2	3,182	62.3	1.4	5.2	0.2	6.9	48.6	1,404	73	70	1,735	15,320	50,792	5,274
Clark	50.6	3,123	49.6	1.9	5.8	0.2	12.5	27.6	1,705	54	31	828	7,500	50,848	5,949
Clay	65.1	4,732	32.8	32.8	3.4	0.1	5.2	24.2	1,756	42	26	958	6,140	44,403	3,937
Clinton	81.6	2,145	54.7	2.6	8.5	0.0	9.4	57.5	1,510	100	72	2,175	17,570	59,158	6,616
Coles	224.0	4,175	60.6	1.0	4.9	0.1	7.5	97.1	1,809	144	102	5,347	20,880	51,441	5,855
Cook	29,791.5	5,695	39.4	4.1	7.7	1.3	4.1	59,701.4	11,412	38,463	10,794	280,963	2,520,680	74,019	11,628
Crawford	103.4	5,277	28.7	46.8	2.5	0.1	5.6	46.4	2,366	55	35	1,784	8,570	53,188	5,885
Cumberland	25.4	2,316	59.2	2.1	4.8	0.2	11.9	9.6	878	28	32	442	4,900	47,724	4,412
DeKalb	465.9	4,450	45.9	1.7	5.4	3.0	4.9	394.6	3,769	199	203	12,098	45,760	56,171	6,182
De Witt	72.0	4,384	38.0	25.7	5.5	0.1	7.2	34.3	2,088	44	32	1,072	7,540	56,223	6,294
Douglas	56.1	2,825	47.8	1.8	6.3	0.3	11.0	34.9	1,760	56	40	1,028	9,900	51,480	5,300
DuPage	4,276.8	4,609	55.0	0.8	6.9	1.6	4.5	4,424.5	4,768	4,870	1,899	48,519	469,380	92,982	15,302
Edgar	59.4	3,263	54.0	3.0	5.0	0.0	11.2	50.5	2,777	48	34	919	8,060	48,648	5,222
Edwards	13.2	1,968	61.7	1.1	4.8	0.1	7.8	6.7	1,005	23	13	292	2,880	48,268	4,286
Effingham	107.8	3,137	47.2	2.6	6.9	0.7	10.6	58.0	1,688	149	70	1,555	17,430	58,673	7,156
Fayette	56.3	2,557	53.8	6.6	7.2	0.0	7.1	24.9	1,130	53	40	1,081	8,930	45,340	4,200
Ford	49.5	3,535	64.3	0.7	5.7	0.0	8.3	21.0	1,501	46	26	764	6,480	51,876	5,430
Franklin	143.4	3,639	47.5	12.4	7.3	0.3	5.1	32.0	811	189	78	1,941	16,380	44,724	4,074
Fulton	132.3	3,611	54.8	3.6	4.8	2.2	7.8	85.5	2,332	95	65	2,213	15,360	47,201	4,599
Gallatin	16.0	2,938	50.0	0.8	2.9	0.3	11.8	8.2	1,509	18	10	246	2,210	50,151	5,342
Greene	37.1	2,735	54.1	5.0	5.5	0.4	12.8	12.2	901	45	26	689	5,770	44,877	4,054
Grundy	239.2	4,757	60.5	1.0	4.2	0.0	7.5	311.7	6,199	107	102	2,962	25,000	66,484	8,377
Hamilton	35.0	4,183	33.6	40.5	2.7	0.1	8.6	25.1	3,002	36	16	507	3,560	49,311	4,898
Hancock	59.2	3,132	56.6	5.9	3.8	1.1	11.6	21.0	1,109	69	36	1,027	8,580	49,222	4,862

1. Based on the resident population estimated as of July 1 of the year shown.

Table B. States and Counties — **Land Area and Population**

State / county code	CBSA code[1]	County code[2]	STATE County	Population, 2018				Race alone or in combination, not Hispanic or Latino (percent)				Percent Hispanic or Latino[4]	Age (percent)					
				Land area[3] (sq. mi)	Total persons 2018	Rank	Per square mile	White	Black	American Indian, Alaska Native	Asian and Pacific Islander		Under 5 years	5 to 17 years	18 to 24 years	25 to 34 years	35 to 44 years	45 to 54 years
				1	2	3	4	5	6	7	8	9	10	11	12	13	14	15
			ILLINOIS— Cont'd															
17069		9	Hardin	177.5	3,910	2,909	22.0	95.9	1.2	1.2	0.8	2.3	4.2	13.9	6.6	8.8	10.5	14.0
17071	15,460	9	Henderson	378.8	6,709	2,695	17.7	96.9	1.0	0.7	0.6	2.0	5.0	13.1	6.7	9.4	10.3	12.6
17073	19,340	2	Henry	823.0	49,090	1,003	59.6	91.5	2.6	0.5	0.8	6.0	5.6	16.7	7.1	11.0	12.0	12.4
17075		6	Iroquois	1,117.4	27,604	1,509	24.7	91.0	1.7	0.6	0.8	7.2	5.5	16.1	7.5	10.3	11.4	12.3
17077	16,060	3	Jackson	584.1	57,419	899	98.3	76.3	16.3	1.0	4.7	4.5	5.4	12.8	21.5	13.4	10.1	9.7
17079		7	Jasper	494.6	9,611	2,454	19.4	97.6	0.7	0.4	0.5	1.5	6.0	17.0	7.1	10.8	11.5	12.6
17081	34,500	7	Jefferson	571.2	37,820	1,230	66.2	87.1	9.7	0.6	1.6	2.8	6.3	15.8	7.5	12.8	12.3	12.7
17083	41,180	1	Jersey	369.3	21,847	1,731	59.2	96.7	1.2	0.8	1.0	1.5	5.0	15.4	9.2	10.9	11.1	13.2
17085		6	Jo Daviess	600.9	21,366	1,759	35.6	95.4	1.1	0.5	0.8	3.1	4.2	14.6	6.3	8.7	10.1	11.7
17087		8	Johnson	343.9	12,456	2,252	36.2	89.5	7.2	0.7	0.6	3.1	4.8	13.7	8.2	12.7	11.8	13.1
17089	16,980	1	Kane	519.4	534,216	130	1,028.5	58.0	6.0	0.4	4.8	32.2	6.3	19.1	9.0	12.0	13.4	14.0
17091	28,100	3	Kankakee	676.5	110,024	552	162.6	73.5	15.7	0.5	1.4	10.6	5.9	16.8	11.0	12.2	11.7	12.4
17093	16,980	1	Kendall	320.3	127,915	499	399.4	70.0	8.0	0.3	3.9	19.5	6.7	21.7	8.2	12.5	16.3	14.2
17095	23,660	4	Knox	716.4	50,112	988	69.9	85.0	9.5	0.6	1.4	5.9	5.6	14.0	9.7	11.9	11.3	11.8
17097	16,980	1	Lake	443.9	700,832	95	1,578.8	62.6	7.6	0.5	9.1	22.2	5.7	18.4	10.2	11.2	12.5	14.0
17099	36,860	4	LaSalle	1,135.2	109,430	557	96.4	86.2	3.2	0.5	1.3	10.0	5.7	15.7	7.9	12.1	11.8	12.8
17101		7	Lawrence	372.2	15,765	2,052	42.4	85.7	10.2	0.6	0.6	3.9	5.1	13.6	8.9	15.2	13.9	12.6
17103	19,940	6	Lee	724.8	34,223	1,318	47.2	87.3	6.0	0.5	1.1	6.4	5.0	14.7	7.4	12.6	12.2	13.3
17105	38,700	4	Livingston	1,043.6	35,761	1,282	34.3	90.1	4.8	0.5	1.3	4.6	5.4	16.0	8.1	12.6	11.7	12.4
17107	30,660	6	Logan	618.1	28,925	1,461	46.8	87.4	8.8	0.5	1.1	3.5	5.3	14.1	10.2	13.8	13.1	11.9
17109	31,380	5	McDonough	589.4	29,955	1,434	50.8	89.2	6.1	0.7	2.9	2.8	4.4	12.6	22.0	11.8	9.7	9.8
17111	16,980	1	McHenry	603.4	308,570	227	511.4	81.9	2.0	0.5	3.6	13.4	5.5	18.0	8.4	11.4	12.6	15.1
17113	14,010	3	McLean	1,183.2	172,828	379	146.1	81.4	9.3	0.5	6.1	5.1	5.8	15.6	17.5	13.0	12.0	11.3
17115	19,500	3	Macon	580.6	104,712	577	180.4	78.8	19.5	0.6	1.7	2.3	6.1	16.0	8.8	11.9	11.5	11.6
17117	41,180	1	Macoupin	862.9	45,313	1,069	52.5	97.0	1.5	0.7	0.7	1.3	5.3	16.0	7.6	11.0	12.0	12.8
17119	41,180	1	Madison	716.0	264,461	260	369.4	86.6	9.9	0.6	1.6	3.4	5.7	16.1	8.1	13.4	12.2	12.9
17121	16,460	4	Marion	572.5	37,620	1,235	65.7	92.7	5.6	0.6	1.0	2.1	6.4	16.8	7.2	12.0	11.3	12.1
17123	37,900	2	Marshall	386.8	11,534	2,324	29.8	95.5	1.2	0.6	0.8	3.0	5.2	14.8	6.9	10.5	10.8	12.6
17125		6	Mason	539.3	13,565	2,193	25.2	97.4	1.2	0.7	0.7	1.1	5.1	15.7	7.1	10.3	11.5	12.9
17127	37,140	7	Massac	237.2	14,080	2,157	59.4	90.2	7.3	1.0	0.9	3.0	5.5	16.6	6.8	9.8	12.1	13.3
17129	44,100	3	Menard	314.4	12,288	2,270	39.1	96.8	1.5	0.8	0.7	1.6	5.5	16.5	7.1	10.9	12.4	12.9
17131	19,340	2	Mercer	561.2	15,601	2,062	27.8	96.0	1.3	0.5	0.7	2.5	5.1	16.3	7.0	10.3	11.6	13.0
17133	41,180	1	Monroe	385.3	34,335	1,316	89.1	97.2	0.7	0.5	1.0	1.5	5.6	16.5	7.1	10.8	12.8	13.7
17135		6	Montgomery	703.7	28,601	1,474	40.6	94.0	4.0	0.4	0.8	1.8	5.1	15.0	7.6	12.4	12.3	12.9
17137	27,300	4	Morgan	568.8	33,976	1,330	59.7	89.5	8.1	0.5	1.1	2.5	4.8	14.1	10.1	12.5	12.0	12.3
17139		6	Moultrie	336.0	14,717	2,114	43.8	97.3	1.0	0.5	0.5	1.5	6.7	18.7	7.4	11.5	11.9	11.6
17141	40,300	4	Ogle	758.6	50,923	976	67.1	87.8	1.8	0.5	0.9	10.3	5.5	16.9	7.7	11.4	11.5	13.4
17143	37,900	2	Peoria	618.7	180,621	363	291.9	72.3	20.3	0.6	4.8	4.9	6.8	16.8	9.0	13.6	12.1	11.9
17145		6	Perry	441.8	21,174	1,767	47.9	87.2	9.9	0.5	0.9	3.2	5.0	14.4	9.2	13.7	12.9	12.7
17147	16,580	3	Piatt	439.2	16,396	2,015	37.3	97.2	1.2	0.5	0.8	1.4	5.9	16.7	7.2	10.9	12.0	12.3
17149		7	Pike	831.4	15,611	2,060	18.8	96.8	1.8	0.5	0.5	1.2	6.1	16.3	7.4	11.4	11.1	12.3
17151		8	Pope	368.8	4,212	2,885	11.4	91.8	6.1	1.1	0.8	1.6	2.6	9.5	9.2	7.8	10.3	12.9
17153		8	Pulaski	199.2	5,463	2,797	27.4	66.2	32.1	1.3	0.9	2.3	6.2	15.3	6.7	11.4	10.6	11.4
17155	36,860	8	Putnam	160.1	5,740	2,777	35.9	92.5	1.3	0.6	1.0	5.9	4.9	15.2	7.0	10.0	11.3	12.4
17157		6	Randolph	575.3	32,106	1,379	55.8	85.8	10.9	0.5	0.8	3.1	5.2	14.1	7.7	13.9	13.1	13.0
17159		7	Richland	360.1	15,763	2,053	43.8	96.1	1.4	0.7	1.2	1.8	6.7	16.5	6.5	11.9	11.4	11.9
17161	19,340	2	Rock Island	427.4	143,477	454	335.7	73.4	12.1	0.6	3.3	13.1	6.2	16.0	8.6	12.4	12.0	11.7
17163	41,180	1	St. Clair	657.7	261,059	262	396.9	63.5	31.6	0.7	2.5	4.2	6.3	17.1	8.3	13.1	12.7	12.8
17165		6	Saline	379.9	23,906	1,648	62.9	93.1	4.9	0.9	1.1	1.9	6.4	15.3	7.2	12.3	11.2	13.1
17167	44,100	3	Sangamon	868.3	195,348	341	225.0	82.4	14.4	0.6	2.7	2.4	5.6	16.5	8.1	12.6	12.3	12.8
17169		7	Schuyler	437.3	6,907	2,682	15.8	94.0	3.8	0.3	0.6	1.9	4.0	14.2	6.6	10.5	12.3	14.7
17171	27,300	9	Scott	250.9	4,926	2,836	19.6	97.7	1.0	0.5	0.4	1.3	5.0	16.6	6.8	9.9	12.0	13.6
17173		6	Shelby	758.5	21,741	1,738	28.7	98.0	0.8	0.5	0.6	1.1	5.8	15.5	6.9	11.0	10.8	12.4
17175	37,900	2	Stark	288.0	5,427	2,801	18.8	96.3	1.5	0.6	1.1	2.0	5.4	16.1	7.4	10.1	11.2	12.3
17177	23,300	4	Stephenson	564.6	44,753	1,082	79.3	84.9	12.2	0.5	1.2	4.2	5.4	15.9	7.4	10.4	10.3	12.5
17179	37,900	2	Tazewell	646.4	132,328	482	204.7	95.2	1.9	0.6	1.4	2.3	5.8	16.9	7.0	12.1	12.9	12.6
17181		6	Union	413.5	16,841	1,987	40.7	92.4	2.0	0.9	0.9	5.3	5.3	15.7	6.7	11.8	11.6	12.9
17183	19,180	3	Vermilion	898.3	76,806	723	85.5	80.1	15.2	0.6	1.3	5.2	6.4	17.1	7.8	12.0	11.5	11.9
17185		7	Wabash	223.3	11,549	2,323	51.7	94.8	1.5	0.6	1.6	2.9	6.3	16.2	7.0	12.3	11.2	11.1
17187		6	Warren	542.4	17,032	1,976	31.4	85.0	3.5	0.6	2.9	9.7	6.1	15.8	12.2	10.4	11.0	11.2
17189		6	Washington	562.6	13,995	2,162	24.9	97.0	1.4	0.4	0.7	1.4	5.7	15.7	6.7	11.6	11.7	12.8
17191		7	Wayne	713.9	16,332	2,021	22.9	96.9	0.9	0.5	1.1	1.5	6.4	16.3	6.8	11.1	11.4	12.1
17193		6	White	494.8	13,665	2,187	27.6	97.1	0.9	0.6	0.8	1.5	5.7	16.1	6.4	11.3	11.3	12.0
17195	44,580	4	Whiteside	684.2	55,626	920	81.3	85.6	2.3	0.5	0.8	12.1	5.6	16.4	7.7	11.0	10.9	12.7
17197	16,980	1	Will	835.9	692,310	98	828.2	64.4	12.4	0.4	6.5	17.8	5.9	19.0	9.1	11.9	13.5	14.9
17199	16,060	1	Williamson	420.2	67,056	795	159.6	91.0	5.5	0.8	1.8	2.8	5.9	15.9	6.9	13.1	12.9	12.6

1. CBSA = Core Based Statistical Area. See Appendix A for explanation. See Appendix B for list of metropolitan areas with component counties. Service of USDA Rural-Urban Continuum Codes. See Appendix A for definition. 3. Dry land or land partially or temporarily covered by water. 2. County type code from the Economic Research Service of USDA Rural-Urban Continuum Codes. See Appendix A for definition. 4. May be of any race.

Table B. States and Counties — Population and Households

STATE County	Population, 2018 (cont.) Age (percent) (cont.)				Population change, 2000-2018				Population change, 2000-2018 Components of change, 2010-2018			Households, 2013-2017				
	55 to 64 years	65 to 74 years	75 years and over	Percent female	Total persons 2000	2010	Percent change 2000-2010	2010-2018	Births	Deaths	Net Migration	Number	Persons per household	Family house-holds	Female family house-holder[1]	One person
	16	17	18	19	20	21	22	23	24	25	26	27	28	29	30	31
ILLINOIS— Cont'd																
Hardin	16.2	15.2	10.5	49.3	4,800	4,323	-9.9	-9.6	282	511	-182	1,452	2.80	61.8	7.4	35.2
Henderson	17.7	13.3	11.8	51.2	8,213	7,328	-10.8	-8.4	536	689	-469	3,019	2.28	66.2	9.8	28.9
Henry	14.8	11.4	8.9	50.2	51,020	50,485	-1.0	-2.8	4,465	4,416	-1,438	19,991	2.45	68.6	8.6	27.7
Iroquois	15.4	11.4	10.1	50.9	31,334	29,719	-5.2	-7.1	2,544	3,054	-1,606	11,845	2.36	66.7	9.6	28.6
Jackson	11.4	9.0	6.7	50.3	59,612	60,209	1.0	-4.6	5,558	3,840	-4,619	23,942	2.28	52.7	10.9	36.3
Jasper	15.7	10.9	8.5	50.0	10,117	9,701	-4.1	-0.9	945	844	-188	3,723	2.56	68.9	7.9	26.9
Jefferson	13.4	10.9	8.3	48.6	40,045	38,825	-3.0	-2.6	3,963	3,650	-1,296	15,244	2.35	64.1	11.6	31.7
Jersey	15.7	10.6	8.9	51.1	21,668	22,986	6.1	-5.0	1,740	1,994	-894	8,831	2.40	70.3	10.8	25.8
Jo Daviess	16.3	16.4	11.7	50.0	22,289	22,681	1.8	-5.8	1,470	2,032	-739	9,795	2.23	65.3	6.9	28.7
Johnson	14.2	12.2	9.3	45.4	12,878	12,581	-2.3	-1.0	923	1,001	-55	4,486	2.37	68.6	9.7	27.7
Kane	12.6	8.3	5.4	50.2	404,119	515,378	27.5	3.7	56,030	25,441	-11,628	175,930	2.98	74.1	10.8	21.3
Kankakee	13.2	9.5	7.3	50.8	103,833	113,450	9.3	-3.0	11,073	9,119	-5,386	40,239	2.62	67.1	13.6	26.9
Kendall	10.1	6.5	3.8	50.4	54,544	114,803	110.5	11.4	13,660	4,467	4,016	39,882	3.07	79.8	11.1	16.0
Knox	14.0	11.9	9.7	49.6	55,836	52,925	-5.2	-5.3	4,544	5,518	-1,806	20,981	2.25	57.4	10.8	35.3
Lake	13.6	8.5	5.8	50.0	644,356	703,396	9.2	-0.4	64,747	36,318	-31,557	244,523	2.81	73.5	10.5	22.2
LaSalle	15.0	10.4	8.6	49.5	111,509	113,915	2.2	-3.9	10,004	10,618	-3,841	44,448	2.43	66.6	11.5	28.1
Lawrence	13.3	9.4	8.1	44.0	15,452	16,903	9.4	-6.7	1,363	1,690	-812	6,271	2.23	67.1	12.1	29.9
Lee	15.1	11.0	8.6	46.9	36,062	36,031	-0.1	-5.0	2,849	3,008	-1,655	13,416	2.34	63.7	9.1	29.4
Livingston	14.6	10.2	9.0	49.8	39,678	38,948	-1.8	-8.2	3,356	3,453	-3,144	14,379	2.38	66.2	10.7	28.8
Logan	13.3	9.7	8.6	49.2	31,183	30,305	-2.8	-4.6	2,474	2,715	-1,148	11,011	2.28	65.1	7.3	29.9
McDonough	12.1	9.8	7.9	51.0	32,913	32,610	-0.9	-8.1	2,349	2,509	-2,529	11,481	2.43	54.6	7.9	36.9
McHenry	14.6	8.9	5.7	50.2	260,077	308,827	18.7	-0.1	26,518	16,601	-10,276	110,860	2.76	74.9	9.8	20.3
McLean	11.5	7.7	5.5	51.4	150,433	169,577	12.7	1.9	17,108	9,468	-4,463	66,070	2.51	61.4	8.8	28.4
Macon	14.2	11.0	9.0	52.1	114,706	110,775	-3.4	-5.5	11,087	9,953	-7,220	44,310	2.34	60.9	13.5	34.5
Macoupin	15.5	11.2	8.7	50.5	49,019	47,765	-2.6	-5.1	3,796	4,633	-1,613	18,663	2.41	67.5	10.3	27.4
Madison	14.4	9.7	7.5	51.3	258,941	269,334	4.0	-1.8	25,534	22,836	-7,489	107,241	2.43	64.9	11.8	28.5
Marion	14.5	10.7	9.0	51.1	41,691	39,437	-5.4	-4.6	4,076	4,170	-1,715	16,001	2.35	65.4	12.7	30.7
Marshall	15.7	12.6	10.9	50.4	13,180	12,638	-4.1	-8.7	991	1,287	-808	4,900	2.38	64.6	6.4	31.8
Mason	15.1	12.2	10.0	50.7	16,038	14,666	-8.6	-7.5	1,137	1,527	-712	6,034	2.27	63.9	9.6	30.7
Massac	14.9	10.8	10.2	52.1	15,161	15,431	1.8	-8.8	1,326	1,717	-963	6,084	2.34	63.3	10.1	33.0
Menard	15.4	11.2	8.1	51.3	12,486	12,705	1.8	-3.3	1,012	1,062	-366	5,230	2.35	70.4	9.3	25.5
Mercer	15.0	11.8	9.8	50.1	16,957	16,434	-3.1	-5.1	1,223	1,491	-565	6,620	2.35	68.1	8.4	26.8
Monroe	15.8	9.8	7.9	50.3	27,619	32,951	19.3	4.2	2,764	2,350	999	13,227	2.53	75.7	7.2	21.6
Montgomery	14.6	10.6	9.6	47.6	30,652	30,105	-1.8	-5.0	2,409	2,946	-976	11,234	2.24	64.9	10.1	29.6
Morgan	14.2	10.9	9.1	49.2	36,616	35,545	-2.9	-4.4	2,932	3,203	-1,284	13,894	2.21	62.7	11.8	31.9
Moultrie	13.3	10.3	8.6	51.0	14,287	14,852	4.0	-0.9	1,550	1,528	-149	5,856	2.45	67.6	8.8	26.8
Ogle	14.8	10.5	8.2	50.3	51,032	53,497	4.8	-4.8	4,431	4,065	-2,975	20,830	2.45	68.3	9.4	26.7
Peoria	12.8	9.7	7.3	51.5	183,433	186,496	1.7	-3.2	21,434	14,858	-12,498	74,515	2.43	61.0	13.8	33.5
Perry	13.4	10.5	8.2	44.9	23,094	22,346	-3.2	-5.2	1,735	1,975	-937	8,223	2.29	62.8	12.2	33.6
Piatt	15.7	10.9	8.5	50.4	16,365	16,725	2.2	-2.0	1,459	1,406	-380	6,676	2.45	72.8	8.7	23.7
Pike	14.4	11.0	9.9	49.8	17,384	16,430	-5.5	-5.0	1,491	1,658	-648	6,629	2.32	63.8	9.8	32.6
Pope	19.7	15.8	12.2	48.3	4,413	4,470	1.3	-5.8	234	391	-104	1,639	2.50	63.9	5.4	35.9
Pulaski	15.9	12.8	9.6	51.4	7,348	6,157	-16.2	-11.3	545	656	-588	2,246	2.52	60.3	12.8	35.9
Putnam	16.7	13.6	9.0	49.1	6,086	6,006	-1.3	-4.4	416	461	-220	2,438	2.36	67.5	7.3	26.5
Randolph	14.4	10.0	8.6	45.0	33,893	33,480	-1.2	-4.1	2,807	3,087	-1,090	12,060	2.38	63.2	9.9	32.3
Richland	14.5	10.0	10.5	50.5	16,149	16,233	0.5	-2.9	1,649	1,683	-429	6,460	2.42	60.7	9.7	32.2
Rock Island	13.8	10.7	8.5	50.7	149,374	147,546	-1.2	-2.8	15,108	12,645	-6,523	60,064	2.35	62.7	13.0	32.7
St. Clair	14.0	9.1	6.7	51.8	256,082	270,062	5.5	-3.3	27,602	20,772	-15,930	103,125	2.53	64.9	16.3	30.6
Saline	14.1	11.2	9.0	50.6	26,733	24,913	-6.8	-4.0	2,636	2,926	-706	9,938	2.41	66.9	12.7	30.1
Sangamon	14.2	10.5	7.4	52.0	188,951	197,465	4.5	-1.1	18,860	15,922	-4,961	83,673	2.32	61.4	12.9	31.9
Schuyler	14.9	12.9	9.9	47.5	7,189	7,544	4.9	-8.4	513	704	-447	2,856	2.22	63.8	10.7	31.8
Scott	16.2	10.2	9.7	50.6	5,537	5,355	-3.3	-8.0	394	486	-338	2,111	2.40	65.8	9.1	29.4
Shelby	15.0	12.5	10.0	50.3	22,893	22,359	-2.3	-2.8	2,037	1,962	-679	9,183	2.36	68.6	7.7	27.0
Stark	15.1	12.0	10.3	50.5	6,332	5,992	-5.4	-9.4	515	638	-450	2,330	2.34	67.2	9.3	29.4
Stephenson	15.3	12.1	10.7	51.4	48,979	47,711	-2.6	-6.2	4,005	4,449	-2,528	19,604	2.30	64.4	11.9	30.6
Tazewell	13.8	10.4	8.3	50.8	128,485	135,392	5.4	-2.3	12,892	11,542	-4,363	54,751	2.41	67.7	9.7	27.5
Union	14.7	11.8	9.6	49.9	18,293	17,810	-2.6	-5.4	1,501	1,859	-604	6,686	2.51	71.2	11.5	26.1
Vermilion	14.0	10.8	8.6	50.2	83,919	81,625	-2.7	-5.9	8,537	7,908	-5,455	31,355	2.44	63.4	14.1	31.1
Wabash	15.2	11.3	9.3	49.6	12,937	11,947	-7.7	-3.3	1,188	1,154	-434	4,915	2.34	65.4	7.5	31.8
Warren	13.7	10.7	8.8	50.7	18,735	17,710	-5.5	-3.8	1,762	1,500	-945	6,802	2.38	66.3	11.7	29.6
Washington	15.7	10.7	9.4	50.1	15,148	14,716	-2.9	-4.9	1,262	1,250	-736	5,897	2.37	65.8	7.7	29.8
Wayne	14.4	11.4	10.1	50.8	17,151	16,760	-2.3	-2.6	1,691	1,743	-364	7,117	2.32	65.7	7.7	30.4
White	15.5	11.0	10.6	50.7	15,371	14,665	-4.6	-6.8	1,316	1,811	-498	6,144	2.25	64.8	10.1	31.4
Whiteside	14.8	11.5	9.4	50.4	60,653	58,494	-3.6	-4.9	5,186	5,267	-2,784	23,468	2.38	65.3	9.9	29.7
Will	12.6	7.9	5.2	50.4	502,266	677,560	34.9	2.2	65,151	34,746	-15,682	226,668	2.99	75.5	11.3	20.7
Williamson	13.6	10.9	8.1	50.3	61,296	66,365	8.3	1.0	6,460	6,232	503	26,862	2.43	66.0	12.3	29.1

1. No spouse present.

Table B. States and Counties — **Population, Vital Statistics, Health, and Crime**

STATE County	Persons in group quarters, 2018	Daytime Population, 2013-2017		Births, 2018		Deaths, 2018		Persons under 65 with no health insurance, 2016		Medicare, 2018			Serious crimes known to police[2], 2016 Total	
		Number	Employment/ residence ratio	Total	Rate[1]	Number	Rate[1]	Number	Percent	Total beneficiaries	Enrolled in Original Medicare	Enrolled in Medicare Advantage	Number	Rate[3]
	32	33	34	35	36	37	38	39	40	41	42	43	44	45
ILLINOIS— Cont'd														
Hardin	17	3,888	0.79	37	9.5	69	17.6	201	6.8	1,098	935	163	42	1,029
Henderson	51	5,211	0.47	68	10.1	90	13.4	350	6.7	1,670	1,401	269	NA	NA
Henry	721	42,404	0.68	514	10.5	563	11.5	2,137	5.4	11,273	8,110	3,163	710	1,584
Iroquois	468	25,443	0.77	312	11.3	334	12.1	1,551	7.0	6,804	5,757	1,047	462	1,874
Jackson	3,586	61,931	1.11	613	10.7	475	8.3	3,570	7.5	9,839	7,452	2,387	1,929	3,309
Jasper	54	8,047	0.65	111	11.5	98	10.2	472	6.1	2,215	1,924	291	NA	NA
Jefferson	2,141	43,618	1.34	469	12.4	433	11.4	1,691	5.8	8,396	7,204	1,192	1,233	3,237
Jersey	795	18,163	0.60	208	9.5	207	9.5	844	4.8	5,039	4,033	1,006	414	1,870
Jo Daviess	167	19,821	0.79	151	7.1	255	11.9	1,015	6.3	6,308	3,233	3,075	220	1,023
Johnson	1,273	12,055	0.80	111	8.9	138	11.1	498	5.8	3,061	2,335	726	109	934
Kane	6,811	496,444	0.87	6,516	12.2	3,446	6.5	43,137	9.4	75,995	57,565	18,430	7,537	1,445
Kankakee	6,272	107,433	0.93	1,302	11.8	1,181	10.7	5,918	6.6	21,515	17,096	4,419	2,624	2,718
Kendall	208	95,586	0.56	1,550	12.1	555	4.3	5,466	4.9	15,415	11,973	3,442	1,452	1,167
Knox	3,932	51,400	1.00	553	11.0	586	11.7	2,171	5.8	12,232	8,485	3,747	1,314	3,016
Lake	18,671	719,227	1.04	7,436	10.6	4,718	6.7	43,171	7.2	108,050	91,539	16,511	10,255	1,527
LaSalle	3,387	107,437	0.93	1,216	11.1	1,220	11.1	5,115	5.8	23,712	20,320	3,392	1,868	1,754
Lawrence	2,420	16,050	0.93	146	9.3	213	13.5	695	6.2	3,161	2,845	316	NA	NA
Lee	3,035	34,062	0.96	326	9.5	404	11.8	1,337	5.3	7,772	6,321	1,451	500	1,464
Livingston	2,315	36,877	1.00	381	10.7	374	10.5	1,495	5.4	7,643	5,914	1,729	567	1,572
Logan	4,143	27,567	0.84	283	9.8	308	10.6	951	4.7	5,863	4,356	1,507	434	1,575
McDonough	3,329	32,490	1.07	254	8.5	294	9.8	1,458	6.5	5,945	4,392	1,553	498	1,610
McHenry	1,648	258,536	0.69	3,043	9.9	2,143	6.9	14,516	5.5	50,519	43,170	7,349	3,218	1,070
McLean	10,507	178,480	1.06	1,936	11.2	1,209	7.0	6,133	4.3	25,683	18,176	7,507	3,141	1,826
Macon	4,009	114,407	1.14	1,268	12.1	1,174	11.2	4,653	5.6	23,982	20,644	3,338	3,388	3,227
Macoupin	863	37,456	0.59	462	10.2	570	12.6	2,060	5.7	10,917	9,098	1,819	673	1,515
Madison	3,951	247,781	0.85	2,930	11.1	2,842	10.7	11,491	5.2	53,573	34,913	18,660	5,661	2,377
Marion	759	37,279	0.94	484	12.9	416	11.1	1,706	5.6	9,234	8,157	1,077	1,135	3,125
Marshall	255	10,170	0.68	109	9.5	140	12.1	478	5.2	2,969	2,360	609	127	1,083
Mason	206	12,175	0.72	129	9.5	173	12.8	649	6.1	3,554	2,923	631	NA	NA
Massac	292	12,974	0.70	145	10.3	172	12.2	639	5.6	3,686	3,314	372	352	2,416
Menard	154	8,527	0.35	124	10.1	137	11.1	488	4.8	2,649	1,797	852	124	1,006
Mercer	185	11,858	0.46	150	9.6	179	11.5	639	5.2	3,969	2,684	1,285	121	772
Monroe	343	26,040	0.56	336	9.8	317	9.2	1,065	3.8	6,719	4,154	2,565	171	505
Montgomery	2,453	28,625	0.95	263	9.2	376	13.1	1,251	5.9	6,694	5,672	1,022	439	1,633
Morgan	3,327	35,051	1.04	310	9.1	362	10.7	1,252	4.9	7,811	6,100	1,711	793	2,407
Moultrie	395	13,534	0.83	201	13.7	144	9.8	824	6.9	3,102	2,621	481	NA	NA
Ogle	526	45,718	0.76	542	10.6	478	9.4	2,376	5.7	10,722	7,896	2,826	447	1,069
Peoria	4,811	207,166	1.25	2,361	13.1	1,800	10.0	8,871	5.8	35,276	24,120	11,156	6,780	3,668
Perry	2,473	19,758	0.79	202	9.5	226	10.7	851	5.6	4,514	3,429	1,085	171	827
Piatt	72	12,360	0.53	187	11.4	167	10.2	603	4.5	3,501	2,136	1,365	178	1,244
Pike	489	14,333	0.77	189	12.1	179	11.5	938	7.7	3,664	3,152	512	193	1,219
Pope	272	3,847	0.60	28	6.6	35	8.3	222	7.3	1,017	825	192	NA	NA
Pulaski	21	6,013	1.17	76	13.9	63	11.5	312	7.1	1,441	1,264	177	NA	NA
Putnam	2	4,746	0.65	51	8.9	64	11.1	253	5.7	1,367	1,065	302	NA	NA
Randolph	4,308	33,222	1.03	329	10.2	397	12.4	1,127	5.0	6,706	5,071	1,635	128	424
Richland	364	15,743	0.97	198	12.6	180	11.4	726	5.8	3,701	3,231	470	412	2,589
Rock Island	4,585	156,462	1.15	1,692	11.8	1,461	10.2	7,706	6.7	30,390	19,111	11,279	4,409	3,038
St. Clair	4,556	248,885	0.87	3,092	11.8	2,722	10.4	13,536	6.1	47,664	30,788	16,876	7,830	3,021
Saline	883	23,940	0.95	309	12.9	328	13.7	1,156	6.1	6,018	4,940	1,078	561	2,468
Sangamon	4,016	212,801	1.16	2,137	10.9	2,130	10.9	7,407	4.6	40,019	25,676	14,343	7,726	3,989
Schuyler	463	6,213	0.66	57	8.3	76	11.0	386	7.0	1,586	1,283	303	42	609
Scott	43	4,286	0.64	43	8.7	47	9.5	229	5.7	1,030	823	207	NA	NA
Shelby	205	18,228	0.64	254	11.7	253	11.6	864	5.1	5,076	4,519	557	32	189
Stark	92	4,720	0.67	60	11.1	64	11.8	238	5.5	1,259	946	313	NA	NA
Stephenson	836	44,358	0.93	440	9.8	551	12.3	2,064	5.8	11,420	6,825	4,595	872	2,116
Tazewell	2,566	127,351	0.88	1,435	10.8	1,440	10.9	4,415	4.1	28,002	20,232	7,770	2,458	1,930
Union	566	15,529	0.76	167	9.9	224	13.3	933	6.9	4,534	3,483	1,051	243	1,568
Vermilion	2,900	78,197	0.97	960	12.5	929	12.1	3,564	5.8	17,474	10,943	6,531	3,347	4,337
Wabash	88	10,075	0.71	155	13.4	127	11.0	554	6.0	2,708	2,380	328	214	1,875
Warren	978	16,882	0.93	203	11.9	179	10.5	980	7.5	3,492	2,786	706	312	1,792
Washington	246	14,222	0.99	140	10.0	137	9.8	587	5.2	3,133	2,635	498	163	1,219
Wayne	76	14,737	0.75	195	11.9	215	13.2	869	6.7	3,832	3,500	332	NA	NA
White	391	13,869	0.95	142	10.4	198	14.5	682	6.2	3,690	3,226	464	NA	NA
Whiteside	1,011	53,017	0.85	578	10.4	617	11.1	2,587	5.8	13,637	11,133	2,504	975	1,768
Will	8,739	611,051	0.77	7,619	11.0	4,690	6.8	34,207	5.7	101,186	76,624	24,562	9,409	1,386
Williamson	2,001	68,192	1.03	736	11.0	790	11.8	3,006	5.6	14,721	11,752	2,969	1,055	1,652

1. Per 1,000 estimated resident population. 2. Data for serious crimes have not been adjusted for underreporting; this may affect comparability between geographic areas and over time. 3. Per 100,000 population estimated by the FBI.

Table B. States and Counties — Crime, Education, Money Income, and Poverty

STATE County	Serious crimes known to police[2], 2016 (cont.)[1] Rate		Education: School enrollment and attainment, 2013-2017				Local government expenditures,[5] 2014-2015		Money income, 2013-2017				Income and poverty, 2017			
			Enrollment[3]		Attainment[4] (percent)					Households				Percent below poverty level		
	Violent	Property	Total	Percent private	High school graduate or less	Bachelor's degree or more	Total current spending (mil dol)	Current spending per student (dollars)	Per capita income[6]	Median income (dollars)	Percent with income of less than $50,000	Percent with income of $200,000 or more	Median household income (dollars)	All persons	Children under 18 years	Children 5 to 17 years in families
	46	47	48	49	50	51	52	53	54	55	56	57	58	59	60	61
ILLINOIS— Cont'd																
Hardin	147	882	755	4.6	53.0	11.1	5.6	9,113	20,025	39,524	60.3	0.8	40,160	21.6	36.2	32.2
Henderson	NA	NA	1,287	9.9	56.2	14.2	8.8	9,914	27,949	47,428	52.7	1.2	51,014	11.2	17.1	16.6
Henry	132	1,452	11,348	9.6	44.8	22.1	89.9	10,500	28,443	55,755	44.8	2.8	58,675	11	16.1	14.7
Iroquois	154	1,720	6,318	9.9	52.4	14.3	59.2	12,794	26,480	48,857	51.0	2.7	50,131	12.9	18.4	16.5
Jackson	410	2,899	21,757	5.4	32.4	36.2	96.6	13,071	23,455	36,008	61.9	2.9	38,157	29.2	31.8	29.0
Jasper	NA	NA	2,026	13.6	50.5	17.4	20.4	14,314	25,806	56,523	43.2	1.7	55,240	11.9	16.6	15.8
Jefferson	635	2,602	8,462	14.6	46.2	16.1	62.5	10,564	24,617	46,109	53.1	2.5	50,622	17.4	25.6	23.1
Jersey	163	1,707	5,812	29.6	44.4	19.7	27.2	10,156	27,528	56,320	44.8	1.8	58,928	10.3	14.8	13.1
Jo Daviess	153	869	4,538	12.1	45.2	23.5	46.0	13,871	32,401	55,532	45.3	3.3	51,866	9.3	13.7	12.7
Johnson	291	643	2,366	5.7	48.7	16.2	19.8	9,989	20,726	45,743	53.2	1.4	49,763	15	19.7	17.9
Kane	170	1,274	149,683	15.6	39.5	32.4	1,270.2	12,447	33,486	74,862	32.5	8.6	75,739	9.2	13.6	13.5
Kankakee	305	2,414	29,410	21.4	46.0	19.8	226.6	12,114	26,150	56,542	43.9	3.0	57,706	15	20.3	18.0
Kendall	109	1,058	36,631	13.6	30.3	34.8	313.9	11,754	33,369	89,860	23.0	6.9	97,039	4.8	5.8	5.5
Knox	372	2,644	11,806	19.2	47.7	17.9	90.6	11,841	23,676	41,972	57.5	1.6	44,686	16.1	23.4	23.1
Lake	153	1,374	194,575	16.1	30.8	44.2	2,212.6	16,216	42,388	82,613	30.2	14.6	86,242	7.7	10.0	9.2
LaSalle	130	1,625	25,544	11.4	47.4	17.8	218.7	13,156	27,959	54,693	45.9	2.7	56,854	14.3	22.0	18.7
Lawrence	NA	NA	3,225	11.2	54.2	11.6	20.0	8,788	21,072	44,504	55.5	1.6	45,235	17.3	23.4	22.7
Lee	190	1,274	7,494	18.0	46.3	17.8	50.6	11,817	28,179	58,319	43.0	3.1	59,450	11.4	15.9	14.5
Livingston	175	1,397	8,073	10.8	54.2	15.1	83.1	13,233	27,318	54,339	45.9	2.4	55,003	12.8	17.4	15.8
Logan	163	1,412	6,875	19.1	46.8	19.8	39.9	11,594	26,479	58,271	41.8	2.6	56,838	12.2	17.4	16.4
McDonough	285	1,326	11,561	6.0	37.8	32.6	46.7	13,501	22,527	42,911	55.1	1.5	44,524	18.6	22.0	20.5
McHenry	98	972	82,250	12.8	33.7	33.2	927.5	12,975	36,208	82,230	28.1	8.2	86,450	6.1	7.2	6.4
McLean	285	1,541	56,285	13.8	29.5	44.7	290.7	11,195	32,943	64,573	39.0	5.9	68,895	15.6	13.5	12.3
Macon	413	2,813	25,087	18.4	44.3	22.7	206.7	12,453	28,280	49,052	50.7	3.3	51,828	14.3	22.0	20.3
Macoupin	178	1,337	11,065	13.6	48.0	18.5	83.8	9,669	27,255	53,890	47.3	2.7	51,756	13.8	20.5	18.5
Madison	298	2,079	66,616	15.4	38.5	26.2	440.3	10,636	30,278	56,536	44.1	3.8	58,077	14.4	18.6	17.2
Marion	388	2,737	8,463	10.6	46.4	15.2	83.6	12,059	24,112	44,679	55.0	1.3	45,126	16.1	25.7	23.6
Marshall	128	955	2,265	8.4	48.5	17.4	15.8	11,931	29,025	55,173	45.3	2.6	55,337	9.7	14.9	14.6
Mason	NA	NA	2,842	7.6	54.8	15.4	31.2	11,297	25,952	44,695	53.7	1.7	51,731	13.7	21.4	19.9
Massac	329	2,086	3,221	4.8	48.8	12.1	26.7	10,950	23,434	42,160	56.3	1.6	47,646	15.3	24.7	23.4
Menard	89	916	2,771	9.7	42.2	24.6	24.1	9,631	32,839	62,368	39.2	4.1	65,367	8.7	14.0	12.5
Mercer	96	676	3,366	8.1	48.9	18.7	27.8	9,562	27,844	55,649	43.6	2.3	52,846	10.6	15.8	14.6
Monroe	24	481	7,984	21.1	35.9	30.6	53.1	10,249	37,043	74,410	32.9	7.3	83,767	4.9	4.8	4.0
Montgomery	104	1,529	6,113	9.9	53.3	14.4	43.6	9,693	23,172	47,807	52.9	2.4	51,206	15.5	22.9	20.8
Morgan	246	2,161	8,933	29.8	50.0	21.2	56.9	11,682	26,253	49,353	50.5	2.0	52,357	13.5	20.4	17.2
Moultrie	NA	NA	3,377	11.7	49.3	18.1	16.8	9,951	26,166	53,979	46.5	1.6	60,496	9	13.8	12.9
Ogle	60	1,010	12,546	10.1	44.6	19.7	116.5	12,595	29,239	57,655	43.2	3.1	60,656	9.7	14.0	12.8
Peoria	575	3,093	47,711	25.4	37.0	30.2	336.5	11,499	29,683	53,063	47.2	4.3	54,195	15.4	20.1	18.2
Perry	155	672	4,083	6.9	54.3	12.5	28.5	10,336	23,929	45,864	53.7	1.7	50,553	15.6	20.5	18.8
Piatt	189	1,055	3,884	13.5	39.9	28.5	30.4	11,239	33,672	67,360	39.6	4.3	67,173	6.3	8.2	7.6
Pike	95	1,124	3,551	7.2	52.7	16.1	25.8	9,734	23,218	41,387	58.7	1.6	43,301	15.9	22.9	22.1
Pope	NA	NA	724	9.3	45.7	13.1	5.6	10,133	22,191	41,139	57.3	1.5	43,119	18.4	27.8	26.3
Pulaski	NA	NA	1,191	12.9	50.2	11.2	15.0	16,566	20,195	34,655	63.9	0.9	38,846	22.9	36.1	33.7
Putnam	NA	NA	1,253	11.9	47.6	14.9	11.0	12,180	33,697	64,741	40.8	5.6	64,000	8	14.0	13.1
Randolph	70	354	6,290	15.2	56.7	13.1	50.2	12,129	24,716	49,717	50.3	2.6	52,749	15	22.3	18.4
Richland	390	2,199	3,570	11.6	43.5	21.5	22.7	9,269	25,262	46,454	53.5	3.0	48,489	15.4	20.7	19.2
Rock Island	365	2,673	34,905	16.8	42.0	22.7	263.5	11,851	27,822	51,426	48.2	2.7	51,805	12.9	19.7	18.1
St. Clair	590	2,430	68,647	14.7	38.2	26.6	501.9	12,180	28,643	51,103	49.1	4.1	51,937	16	24.1	22.7
Saline	405	2,063	5,042	6.0	43.4	16.4	42.3	9,907	22,725	40,722	58.0	1.5	41,394	18.6	29.0	29.4
Sangamon	793	3,197	49,601	16.5	35.3	34.2	368.5	12,389	33,277	58,687	43.1	5.0	61,519	15.4	22.9	21.0
Schuyler	145	464	1,348	5.4	47.7	17.9	11.5	9,690	23,670	47,321	52.1	1.1	52,946	11.8	16.3	15.0
Scott	NA	NA	1,167	11.6	56.0	13.9	9.1	10,283	26,914	48,542	50.5	2.6	49,745	12.2	17.3	16.4
Shelby	12	177	4,556	16.0	53.6	16.0	24.4	10,386	24,808	49,807	50.2	1.1	51,873	10.3	13.8	12.8
Stark	NA	NA	1,174	13.0	47.9	18.8	10.5	11,155	30,009	52,284	46.8	5.1	51,446	11.1	16.9	16.0
Stephenson	138	1,977	10,275	11.2	44.2	18.7	79.2	11,900	25,792	46,427	53.8	1.8	48,237	16.7	25.8	22.5
Tazewell	285	1,645	31,895	17.1	39.4	26.0	220.7	10,982	32,082	60,874	40.3	4.4	61,086	9.1	11.4	10.4
Union	219	1,349	3,588	7.2	45.1	22.3	29.6	10,264	24,646	46,716	54.3	3.0	45,847	19	25.1	23.9
Vermilion	813	3,525	17,708	6.5	53.5	14.6	151.8	11,542	23,416	44,930	54.2	1.8	43,649	19.4	31.0	28.6
Wabash	131	1,743	2,658	16.2	40.9	18.7	15.0	8,620	25,105	49,716	50.3	1.6	52,535	13.8	18.7	17.3
Warren	253	1,540	5,054	29.3	45.7	24.3	24.0	8,836	24,840	47,228	52.9	2.7	54,023	11.7	17.0	16.3
Washington	247	972	3,158	20.3	41.8	20.2	20.5	11,092	29,687	54,520	46.2	2.7	56,118	8.1	12.0	11.6
Wayne	NA	NA	3,426	7.3	49.9	13.2	25.8	9,822	25,046	46,405	53.1	2.1	46,339	14	21.0	20.5
White	NA	NA	2,907	7.8	48.0	15.6	34.8	14,117	26,522	46,279	53.5	2.1	48,202	15.3	23.5	21.2
Whiteside	205	1,563	12,631	11.4	46.9	18.1	105.9	11,148	28,188	51,969	48.2	3.0	54,284	12.9	19.2	16.8
Will	161	1,225	194,166	15.6	36.0	33.6	1,455.1	12,582	33,731	80,782	29.4	8.2	82,477	7	9.1	8.1
Williamson	135	1,517	14,566	8.2	39.2	22.5	110.2	10,593	26,023	48,600	51.4	2.2	49,993	15.3	21.0	19.2

1. Data for serious crimes have not been adjusted for underreporting; this may affect comparability between geographic areas and over time. 2. Per 100,000 population estimated by the FBI. 3. All persons 3 years old and over enrolled in nursery school through college. 4. Persons 25 years old and over. 5. Elementary and secondary education expenditures. 6. Based on population estimated by the American Community Survey, 2011–2015.

Table B. States and Counties — Personal Income and Earnings

STATE County	Personal income, 2017					Supplements to wages and salaries, employer contributions (mil dol)		Proprietors' income (mil dol)	Dividends, interest, and rent (mil dol)	Personal transfer receipts (mil dol)	Earnings, 2017	Contributions for government social insurance (mil dol)	
	Total (mil dol)	Percent change 2016-2017	Per capita[1] Dollars	Rank	Wages and salaries (mil dol)	Pension and insurance	Government social insurance				Total (mil dol)	From employee and self-employed	From employer
	62	63	64	65	66	67	68	69	70	71	72	73	74
ILLINOIS— Cont'd													
Hardin	143	0.7	35,344	2,294	26	7	2	12	21	55	47	4	2
Henderson	282	0.5	41,507	1,329	41	12	3	28	52	65	84	5	3
Henry	2,197	2.4	44,544	958	570	135	39	121	443	415	865	54	39
Iroquois	1,153	-1.8	41,365	1,351	306	70	22	113	225	290	512	31	22
Jackson	2,077	2.3	35,634	2,252	1,180	342	71	140	450	469	1,733	82	71
Jasper	403	3.5	42,052	1,258	89	26	6	64	80	85	184	9	6
Jefferson	1,429	2.8	37,438	1,961	914	173	66	72	244	377	1,226	71	66
Jersey	866	3.0	39,459	1,648	193	46	13	30	141	200	282	20	13
Jo Daviess	1,013	0.7	46,903	719	295	67	21	61	270	210	444	29	21
Johnson	424	1.3	32,881	2,633	84	27	5	14	64	113	130	9	5
Kane	26,186	4.2	48,975	541	11,368	2,103	787	1,606	4,067	3,237	15,864	852	787
Kankakee	4,369	2.3	39,862	1,579	2,025	423	145	176	641	1,026	2,768	159	145
Kendall	5,987	4.7	47,433	670	1,271	273	86	266	667	584	1,896	104	86
Knox	1,923	-0.4	37,983	1,889	798	167	70	100	361	570	1,135	73	70
Lake	53,627	4.1	76,227	49	27,311	4,279	1,745	3,324	13,778	4,519	36,658	1,953	1,745
LaSalle	4,687	2.8	42,582	1,196	2,054	416	145	209	814	979	2,823	167	145
Lawrence	462	0.1	28,574	3,012	184	48	13	21	100	160	265	16	13
Lee	1,388	3.1	40,333	1,497	592	118	41	63	252	313	814	50	41
Livingston	1,524	-3	41,727	1,296	632	133	44	154	267	310	964	53	44
Logan	1,044	-0.6	35,702	2,246	383	86	26	81	184	254	575	33	26
McDonough	1,127	-0.8	36,563	2,110	502	157	30	69	251	241	758	35	30
McHenry	16,557	4.4	53,562	324	4,886	932	342	804	2,648	1,927	6,963	396	342
McLean	8,197	0.9	47,578	659	5,024	890	311	560	1,404	1,031	6,784	359	311
Macon	4,835	0.2	45,701	830	2,734	494	198	298	885	1,084	3,725	217	198
Macoupin	1,756	1.6	38,639	1,784	430	100	29	56	320	443	615	44	29
Madison	11,883	3.8	44,768	934	4,645	978	334	684	2,022	2,380	6,642	384	334
Marion	1,514	3.2	39,935	1,563	567	128	43	88	251	464	826	52	43
Marshall	507	-3.8	43,248	1,111	124	28	9	31	97	120	192	13	9
Mason	546	0.5	39,789	1,591	126	36	8	50	97	147	221	13	8
Massac	528	-0.8	36,835	2,072	164	39	10	25	91	168	237	15	10
Menard	534	2.2	43,597	1,063	68	20	4	26	99	103	119	8	4
Mercer	687	4.0	43,994	1,023	116	30	9	33	124	146	187	14	9
Monroe	1,896	2.7	55,612	259	356	74	25	97	351	251	551	35	25
Montgomery	1,011	2.1	35,107	2,336	354	82	25	91	213	284	552	33	25
Morgan	1,333	1.7	39,429	1,654	600	119	42	80	280	333	841	51	42
Moultrie	773	2.5	52,624	356	174	37	13	193	110	130	417	23	13
Ogle	2,258	1.2	44,226	993	810	178	55	53	394	427	1,096	68	55
Peoria	8,833	0.2	48,263	603	6,040	1,012	414	400	1,766	1,593	7,867	443	414
Perry	747	0.6	35,117	2,333	194	54	13	100	127	193	361	21	13
Piatt	822	0.2	50,003	464	142	37	9	27	141	138	215	15	9
Pike	631	-0.3	39,896	1,570	169	39	12	80	114	154	300	17	12
Pope	122	3.7	28,262	3,021	24	8	2	9	22	40	42	3	2
Pulaski	200	3.0	36,215	2,171	115	28	8	10	29	75	161	9	8
Putnam	315	0.6	55,001	280	86	17	6	68	53	48	178	10	6
Randolph	1,134	2.2	34,989	2,350	479	117	32	39	223	294	667	39	32
Richland	643	2.8	40,424	1,485	249	57	18	41	127	164	363	22	18
Rock Island	6,394	5.1	44,155	1,004	4,578	832	310	517	1,293	1,270	6,236	349	310
St. Clair	11,266	2.9	42,923	1,148	4,881	1,077	373	461	2,099	2,493	6,792	381	373
Saline	933	4.3	38,690	1,777	333	78	24	81	156	296	517	31	24
Sangamon	9,101	1.9	46,325	765	5,101	1,051	341	445	1,924	1,672	6,938	372	341
Schuyler	289	0.1	41,117	1,394	74	20	5	34	48	61	131	7	5
Scott	192	0.8	38,362	1,816	40	11	3	19	32	41	72	4	3
Shelby	820	4.7	37,745	1,917	185	43	13	85	147	197	327	21	13
Stark	218	-1.8	40,153	1,529	57	14	4	14	47	53	89	6	4
Stephenson	1,854		41,144	1,388	833	163	60	87	372	448	1,143	71	60
Tazewell	6,021	0.3	45,096	887	2,760	495	201	267	1,112	1,120	3,723	220	201
Union	710	3.2	41,756	1,293	196	52	13	41	115	207	301	19	13
Vermilion	2,913	1.4	37,387	1,973	1,269	295	91	162	468	807	1,817	108	91
Wabash	492	3.8	42,812	1,168	132	38	8	33	102	111	212	12	8
Warren	670	1.7	39,006	1,721	255	53	18	70	126	146	397	22	18
Washington	657	4.1	46,795	728	325	73	23	89	127	124	511	27	23
Wayne	628	-1.9	38,059	1,876	151	40	11	87	116	161	289	16	11
White	638	5.2	45,742	827	174	39	13	86	126	159	311	18	13
Whiteside	2,373	3.5	42,290	1,231	888	228	61	111	470	578	1,287	75	61
Will	35,075	4.1	50,638	424	12,598	2,340	893	1,665	4,754	4,318	17,496	968	893
Williamson	2,881	2.6	42,787	1,172	1,260	297	91	157	491	628	1,804	104	91

1. Based on the resident population estimated as of July 1 of the year shown.

Table B. States and Counties — Earnings, Social Security, and Housing

STATE County	Earnings, 2017 (cont.)									Social Security beneficiaries, December 2017			Housing units, 2018	
	Percent by selected industries											Supplemental Security Income recipients, 2017		
	Farm	Mining, quarrying, and extractions	Construction	Manufacturing	Information; professional, scientific, technical services	Retail trade	Finance, insurance, real estate, and leasing	Health care and social assistance	Government	Number	Rate[1]		Total	Percent change, 2010-2018
	75	76	77	78	79	80	81	82	83	84	85	86	87	88
ILLINOIS— Cont'd														
Hardin	1	D	D	D	D	3	D	23.6	23.7	1,300	321	170	2,480	-0.4
Henderson	25.2	D	8.3	1.4	D	2.9	D	6	24.6	1,745	257	117	3,872	1.2
Henry	2.3	D	12	9.8	D	7.2	6.4	11.1	24.1	11,660	236	604	22,168	0
Iroquois	12.1	0.2	9.3	6.1	D	7.3	6.4	D	17	7,245	260	576	13,511	0.4
Jackson	0.7	D	4.7	3.3	4.1	5.9	3.2	17.8	42.4	9,980	171	1,622	29,026	1.6
Jasper	23.4	1.3	5.9	5.1	0.9	4.2	4.7	D	20.4	2,335	244	151	4,344	0
Jefferson	-0.5	0.6	3.1	25.4	3.9	6.1	5.5	19.5	13.3	8,820	231	953	17,009	0.3
Jersey	0.6	0	9.4	2	D	9.6	4.8	D	29.1	5,350	244	355	10,167	3.2
Jo Daviess	1.8	D	10.2	15.2	D	7.2	4.7	D	19.3	6,375	295	182	13,742	1.2
Johnson		D	7.3	2.3	3.1	4.4	D	D	50.4	3,210	249	263	5,642	0.8
Kane	0	0.1	8	17	9.1	5	5.7	10.5	17.2	75,970	142	5,220	189,472	4.1
Kankakee	1	D	4.6	21.2	4.2	6.3	4.9	17.3	16	22,720	207	2,693	45,652	0.9
Kendall	1.3	0.1	9.6	15.3	6.2	8.2	3.8	5.6	23.1	16,155	128	788	42,199	4.6
Knox	1.8	D	4.1	6.4	D	7.2	4.1	D	18.6	12,250	242	1,304	23,890	-0.8
Lake	0	D	4.9	21.8	9.8	7.1	6.9	6.4	13.1	105,900	151	8,306	265,150	1.9
LaSalle	0.4	3.5	7.1	19.4	4	7.2	5	8.8	15.4	25,425	231	1,704	50,147	0.3
Lawrence	1.6	4.6	D	D	2.3	4.2	11.1	10.7	21.8	3,495	216	301	7,172	3.4
Lee	-1.1	1	4.2	29.4	2.5	5.8	5.1	D	16.2	8,130	236	510	15,108	0.4
Livingston	7	D	6.5	18.8	10.8	7	4.2	9.3	16.2	8,140	223	523	15,919	0.2
Logan	6.6	0	3.8	19.1	3.6	6.4	4.8	11.5	17.6	6,330	216	404	12,045	-0.5
McDonough	3.2	0	4.8	12.5	2.9	5.7	3.4	D	49.7	5,750	187	573	14,411	0
McHenry	-0.4	0.1	12.2	17.7	6.4	7.6	3.7	10.9	16.2	51,175	166	2,055	118,814	2.4
McLean	0.8	0	3.7	2.8	5.1	5.1	38.8	9.5	15.4	26,495	154	1,815	72,680	4.3
Macon	0.3	D	7.2	30.1	4.5	5.3	4.5	13.1	11.1	25,215	238	3,297	50,393	-0.2
Macoupin	-2.9	D	8.3	7.8	D	8.4	6.2	D	23.8	11,645	256	981	21,787	0.9
Madison	0.2	0.2	9.3	15	7	6.9	4.4	11.4	17.1	56,555	213	5,747	119,630	2.2
Marion	2	1.3	6.7	18	D	4.9	4.3	16.7	17.9	9,410	248	1,220	18,225	-0.4
Marshall	5.5	0.7	9.5	31.2	D	3.8	3.4	7.7	16.1	3,125	266	127	5,905	-0.1
Mason	14.2	D	4.5	2.2	D	5.2	4.8	6	33.7	3,625	264	292	7,044	-0.5
Massac	5.5	0	3.2	12.8	1.5	4.3	3.4	5.9	27	4,065	283	450	7,150	0.5
Menard	5.1	0	12.3	1.7	D	6.4	6.4	D	32.2	2,795	228	160	5,749	1.7
Mercer	1.8	0	9.9	15	2.9	6.7	5.6	D	23.6	4,185	268	154	7,424	0.9
Monroe	-0.9	0.3	12.8	5	D	8.5	13.6	6.8	18.2	6,755	198	154	14,359	7.2
Montgomery	6.4	1.3	6.5	7.6	3.3	9	5.7	16.7	18.7	7,070	246	637	13,145	0.5
Morgan	0.6	0	5.4	19.8	4.2	7.8	7.2	15	16.2	8,220	243	882	15,457	-0.4
Moultrie	2.3	4.2	11.8	40.7	8.2	2.6	2.9	5.8	8	3,205	218	160	6,533	4.3
Ogle	-2.8	D	7.5	20.2	D	5	5.9	D	17.3	11,220	220	572	22,691	0.6
Peoria	-0.1	0	4.1	19.4	11.1	4.4	5.8	20.2	10.4	37,570	205	5,096	83,638	0.7
Perry	4.3	D	5.2	17	3.5	5.7	8	D	28.4	4,865	229	442	9,647	2.4
Piatt	-5.8	0.2	9	6.8	D	6.2	8	12	30.2	3,570	217	107	7,433	2.3
Pike	15.2	D	6.6	1.6	D	7.4	9.2	10.7	19.4	3,765	238	342	8,005	0.7
Pope	11	D	D	8	D	1.9	D	D	41.8	1,060	245	93	2,494	0.1
Pulaski	3.7	0	D	8	D	2.5	D	D	37.4	1,625	295	283	3,170	0.5
Putnam	7.4	D	D	24.3	D	4.3	6.7	1.9	10.3	1,430	250	41	3,163	2.9
Randolph	-0.7	D	5.8	21.7	D	8.1	3.5	D	25.7	7,165	221	495	13,958	1.8
Richland	3.6	2.1	4.4	8.3	2.6	6.2	5.6	15.9	17.1	3,965	249	415	7,513	0
Rock Island	0.2	0.3	4.2	12.1	7.1	4.7	4.2	9.3	19.1	31,685	219	2,687	66,171	0.6
St. Clair	0.3	0.1	5.8	6.4	9.7	6.5	3.8	13.6	31.1	49,880	190	7,984	120,596	3.7
Saline	3.5	7.2	12.5	3.5	4.8	7.5	6.1	15.2	20.5	6,520	271	1,083	11,691	-0.1
Sangamon	0.2	D	4.4	2.9	10.3	5.9	8.6	20.3	25	42,495	216	4,534	91,932	2.3
Schuyler	16.6	D	6.9	2.7	1.6	5.1	D	5.3	30.4	1,620	230	86	3,451	-0.2
Scott	15	0	5.5	D	1.2	3.8	D	D	22.2	1,025	205	70	2,457	-0.1
Shelby	12.2	D	6.2	14.8	D	5.8	8.7	8	15.4	5,485	253	351	10,626	2.2
Stark	5.5	0	13.2	21.7	D	7.9	D	3.9	18.8	1,420	261	91	2,660	-0.5
Stephenson	0.1	0.2	14	21.7	4	5.3	7.9	13.7	15.4	12,025	267	1,092	21,926	-0.7
Tazewell	0.4	0	8.7	29	4.2	6.6	5.3	6.1	14	29,985	225	1,811	59,036	2.6
Union	5.6	D	4.8	11.7	3	7.2	3.6	D	30.1	4,675	275	626	8,011	1.1
Vermilion	1.5	D	4.1	21.4	1.9	6.4	4.4	10	23.8	18,695	240	2,771	36,129	-0.5
Wabash	5.4	5.7	10.1	7	D	6.2	4.9	D	33.4	2,810	245	194	5,565	-0.4
Warren	7.9	D	4.9	32.6	D	5.2	3.7	D	13.2	3,670	214	294	7,689	0.1
Washington	7.1	D	5.4	D	3.2	8.2	3.8	D	9.4	3,160	225	154	6,665	2
Wayne	17.9	3.6	6.3	3.2	3.3	6.8	3.9	D	20.2	4,115	249	301	7,981	0.1
White	11	12.2	D	D	D	8.3	4.9	D	15.9	3,990	286	408	7,171	-0.1
Whiteside	0.7	D	4.4	21.8	4.3	6.4	4.5	6.2	28.5	14,480	258	1,081	25,820	0.2
Will	-0.1	0.1	8.8	12.8	6.8	6.6	4.2	10.4	15.1	103,665	150	6,978	245,200	3.2
Williamson	0.3	D	4.8	12	D	7.7	5.9	17.4	25.6	15,490	230	1,566	31,380	3.3

1. Per 1,000 resident population estimated as of July 1 of the year shown.

Table B. States and Counties — Housing, Labor Force, and Employment

STATE County	Housing units, 2013-2017								Civilian labor force, 2018				Civilian employment[6], 2013-2017		
	Occupied units										Unemployment			Percent	
	Owner-occupied					Renter-occupied									
				Median owner cost as a percent of income			Median rent as a percent of income[2]	Sub-standard units[4] (percent)		Percent change, 2017-2018				Management, business, science, and arts	Construction, production, and maintenance occupations
	Total	Percent	Median value[1]	With a mortgage	Without a mortgage[2]	Median rent[3]			Total		Total	Rate[5]	Total		
	89	90	91	92	93	94	95	96	97	98	99	100	101	102	103
ILLINOIS— Cont'd															
Hardin	1,452	80.2	63,200	19.4	11.1	352	24.9	2.4	1,343	-0.7	105	7.8	1,303	20.6	37.4
Henderson	3,019	79.4	88,100	18.1	10.0	584	22.3	1.9	3,664	0.4	183	5	3,331	25.0	35.3
Henry	19,991	78.2	115,800	18.4	12.0	624	24.1	0.7	25,083	0.4	1,259	5	22,901	30.8	29.4
Iroquois	11,845	76.0	96,800	20.7	11.9	632	26.6	2.6	14,394	-1.7	645	4.5	13,219	28.9	31.3
Jackson	23,942	53.1	108,600	19.1	11.5	665	36.4	1.7	28,137	0.2	1,290	4.6	25,594	37.9	18.8
Jasper	3,723	81.5	99,000	19.8	10.3	568	30.3	0.7	4,617	2.9	228	4.9	4,522	27.9	31.0
Jefferson	15,244	73.3	92,700	19.6	11.5	623	29.5	2.4	17,661	1	938	5.3	15,916	28.1	29.6
Jersey	8,831	81.3	135,400	19.3	12.0	613	32.1	1.4	11,007	0.5	534	4.9	10,387	33.0	25.7
Jo Daviess	9,795	78.4	143,300	21.1	13.0	653	22.4	1.6	10,983	-0.7	482	4.4	10,968	28.0	29.2
Johnson	4,486	81.5	96,600	19.5	12.8	602	27.8	1.6	4,100	-0.4	320	7.8	4,165	36.4	22.1
Kane	175,930	73.3	223,400	23.3	13.3	1,080	30	4.1	273,901	1.7	13,452	4.9	262,971	34.6	23.9
Kankakee	40,239	68.4	140,100	21.4	13.2	851	28.2	1.9	55,920	0.9	3,032	5.4	49,811	30.5	28.4
Kendall	39,882	81.9	214,700	23.0	13.7	1,249	28.3	2.2	67,661	-0.8	2,380	3.5	63,352	38.2	21.3
Knox	20,981	66.1	81,700	19.0	11.4	600	27.7	1.6	22,203	-1.3	1,183	5.3	21,330	30.2	28.0
Lake	244,523	73.4	251,400	22.7	13.9	1,127	29.8	2.7	378,401	1.4	17,099	4.5	347,792	42.3	17.5
LaSalle	44,448	72.7	126,100	19.9	11.5	736	29.1	1.3	56,230	0.1	3,262	5.8	50,811	28.0	30.3
Lawrence	6,271	71.1	72,400	17.3	10.0	608	25.1	2.9	5,981	-1.4	352	5.9	6,361	30.8	29.6
Lee	13,416	73.8	116,500	18.9	11.3	695	24.2	1.9	17,831	0.1	788	4.4	15,386	31.5	27.8
Livingston	14,379	72.6	109,500	19.4	12.2	655	27	1.8	16,610	-0.3	734	4.4	16,084	26.6	32.0
Logan	11,011	72.8	101,300	17.4	10.9	683	21.2	0.9	12,852	-0.3	606	4.7	12,625	30.3	26.8
McDonough	11,481	66.7	94,600	18.2	10.5	630	30.9	2.2	13,359	-1.2	684	5.1	13,837	32.2	21.1
McHenry	110,860	79.4	212,600	22.9	13.6	1,146	28.8	1.7	165,849	-0.9	5,799	3.5	162,177	36.6	21.2
McLean	66,070	64.9	163,800	18.8	10.6	811	27.2	1.8	87,889	-1.1	3,680	4.2	91,152	43.4	14.6
Macon	44,310	70.0	95,900	18.3	11.1	666	28.8	1.5	49,961	1.1	2,795	5.6	48,109	32.0	24.5
Macoupin	18,663	76.7	98,400	18.3	10.0	658	31.8	1.6	23,066	0.4	1,132	4.9	20,963	31.0	27.9
Madison	107,241	70.6	130,200	19.2	11.6	796	29.6	1.4	134,575	0.4	6,080	4.5	125,596	34.9	22.7
Marion	16,001	74.3	71,900	18.9	11.6	610	28.9	2.7	17,778	0.5	879	4.9	16,958	26.2	31.8
Marshall	4,900	83.1	103,300	18.7	10.8	636	25.6	1	5,510	0.8	286	5.2	5,514	29.4	30.9
Mason	6,034	77.3	81,000	18.9	12.3	615	24.6	0.9	6,318	-1.7	379	6	6,173	28.4	31.3
Massac	6,084	73.5	82,500	22.1	11.8	714	31.3	2	5,748	-1.7	403	7	5,563	26.8	27.8
Menard	5,230	76.0	132,500	18.3	10.3	702	23.8	2	6,689	-0.1	268	4	6,091	38.7	20.7
Mercer	6,620	77.4	105,100	18.4	11.3	622	23.8	0.7	8,103	0.4	428	5.3	7,327	29.9	33.3
Monroe	13,227	82.0	195,500	20.1	12.1	827	28.2	0.6	18,595	0.7	644	3.5	17,657	41.1	19.5
Montgomery	11,234	78.0	81,000	17.9	11.6	627	27.6	1.7	11,891	-0.6	706	5.9	10,750	34.2	23.6
Morgan	13,894	68.9	103,400	18.9	10.6	680	27.5	1.5	16,309	-1.2	719	4.4	15,777	31.9	23.4
Moultrie	5,856	75.8	107,500	19.1	10.9	617	25.6	1.8	7,524	2.7	289	3.8	6,993	29.0	35.9
Ogle	20,830	74.9	139,900	20.0	12.4	712	26.4	2.4	25,289	-0.5	1,275	5	24,713	30.5	31.8
Peoria	74,515	65.0	128,000	19.4	11.7	756	28.5	1.7	87,398	1.3	4,846	5.5	84,233	38.4	18.4
Perry	8,223	74.6	80,500	18.6	11.1	552	29.2	1.2	8,456	0.6	505	6	8,236	24.1	37.1
Piatt	6,676	81.7	128,100	17.9	10.0	779	23.1	0.9	8,430	0.1	363	4.3	8,673	36.3	25.5
Pike	6,629	77.5	74,700	18.6	11.8	542	26.8	2.1	7,256	-0.5	349	4.8	6,950	28.3	33.3
Pope	1,639	85.4	84,100	19.5	11.3	407	35.7	1.8	1,751	-1.6	107	6.1	1,330	22.1	35.6
Pulaski	2,246	73.7	63,500	21.0	10.0	525	30.8	1.6	2,055	-3.3	169	8.2	1,971	30.2	25.0
Putnam	2,438	79.8	120,800	19.1	10.0	645	22.6	0.9	3,040	1.2	159	5.2	2,983	31.8	34.1
Randolph	12,060	75.7	99,900	18.6	10.3	643	23.9	1.2	14,202	0.1	630	4.4	13,296	24.7	36.0
Richland	6,460	71.1	83,200	17.7	10.0	544	26.4	2.3	7,455	-1.2	350	4.7	7,229	28.6	33.5
Rock Island	60,064	69.0	115,600	19.5	11.8	692	27.7	2.4	71,847	0.9	3,757	5.2	68,461	29.5	28.0
St. Clair	103,125	65.1	122,600	20.3	12.1	824	31.7	1.7	127,192	0.6	6,423	5	117,401	34.4	21.7
Saline	9,938	72.5	70,500	17.7	10.8	584	27.9	2.5	9,879	1.1	643	6.5	9,723	26.8	27.8
Sangamon	83,673	69.4	136,100	19.0	10.6	779	29	1.7	104,949	0.2	4,506	4.3	95,417	41.2	15.5
Schuyler	2,856	79.7	83,400	18.2	12.2	608	21.8	0.7	3,334	0	149	4.5	2,919	27.9	26.6
Scott	2,111	75.7	87,500	17.1	11.9	543	24.3	2.1	2,481	0.7	133	5.4	2,349	30.2	32.1
Shelby	9,183	80.7	86,800	18.7	11.3	553	25.6	2.3	10,725	3	463	4.3	10,352	26.4	35.2
Stark	2,330	80.3	85,600	17.1	10.2	596	22.8	1.2	2,587	0.6	163	6.3	2,583	35.5	28.8
Stephenson	19,604	69.1	97,700	19.4	12.4	634	29.1	1.1	21,904	1.1	1,041	4.8	21,253	28.8	30.9
Tazewell	54,751	76.2	137,300	18.8	11.4	719	25.5	1.3	65,386	1	3,190	4.9	63,912	35.1	23.1
Union	6,686	80.2	98,600	19.9	11.8	517	23.7	3.2	7,423	0.9	480	6.5	7,245	31.1	30.6
Vermilion	31,355	69.9	75,900	18.3	10.8	657	27.7	2	33,578	-1.8	2,074	6.2	31,973	26.9	30.4
Wabash	4,915	75.5	79,000	18.8	10.0	586	27.3	1.6	5,728	1.7	255	4.5	5,291	27.9	37.6
Warren	6,802	74.7	83,900	19.1	11.4	589	26	3.6	8,691	0.4	367	4.2	8,248	31.4	29.6
Washington	5,897	78.5	108,100	20.2	11.3	640	22.4	1.3	9,625	-0.1	290	3	7,153	29.5	31.9
Wayne	7,117	76.6	78,600	18.4	10.0	582	24.8	3.2	6,949	-0.1	386	5.6	7,347	25.6	36.9
White	6,144	77.3	69,700	17.5	11.2	545	23.4	2.1	6,685	0.1	288	4.3	6,006	28.8	34.5
Whiteside	23,468	75.3	102,200	18.7	11.3	673	26.2	1.3	28,466	1	1,302	4.6	26,553	26.3	31.3
Will	226,668	81.2	216,400	23.1	13.6	1,112	31.1	2	357,226		14,441	4	342,710	36.6	22.5
Williamson	26,862	72.2	106,400	18.9	11.7	697	27.2	1.1	31,873	0.2	1,637	5.1	28,720	32.3	21.9

1. Specified owner-occupied units.   2. A value of 10.0 represents 10 percent or less; a value of 50.0 represents 50 percent or more.   3. Specified renter-occupied units.   4. Overcrowded or lacking complete plumbing facilities.   5. Percent of civilian labor force.   6. Civilian employed persons 16 years old and over.

Table B. States and Counties — **Nonfarm Employment and Agriculture**

STATE County	Private nonfarm establishments, employment and payroll, 2016									Agriculture, 2017			
	Number of establish-ments	Employment						Annual payroll		Farms			Farm producers whose primary occupation is farming (percent)
		Total	Health care and social assistance	Manufac-turing	Retail trade	Finance and insurance	Professional, scientific, and technical services	Total (mil dol)	Average per employee (dollars)	Number	Percent with:		
											Fewer than 50 acres	1000 acres or more	
	104	105	106	107	108	109	110	111	112	113	114	115	116

ILLINOIS— Cont'd

STATE County	104	105	106	107	108	109	110	111	112	113	114	115	116
Hardin	64	783	383	NA	72	16	D	23	28,849	161	21.7	3.1	30.6
Henderson	113	663	138	D	107	85	33	19	28,385	438	23.3	11.4	58.8
Henry	1,061	13,631	1,574	4,480	1,909	555	313	467	34,291	1,353	37.0	10.7	45.5
Iroquois	686	6,167	1,662	645	1,026	336	106	204	33,013	1,516	26.2	14.7	48.3
Jackson	1,305	16,827	3,766	929	3,757	608	656	564	33,519	772	34.7	6.9	40.4
Jasper	219	1,687	124	168	224	115	13	75	44,357	913	36.0	6.9	39.2
Jefferson	981	18,779	3,755	3,964	2,423	435	629	717	38,201	1,099	41.4	5.2	34.5
Jersey	424	4,538	917	179	926	209	99	131	28,778	519	35.5	9.2	43.2
Jo Daviess	709	6,654	680	978	958	214	185	242	36,346	947	31.0	6.0	42.3
Johnson	169	1,272	279	27	221	71	148	26	20,435	653	34.2	2.6	36.3
Kane	12,685	182,018	21,379	31,918	24,758	8,169	9,972	8,154	44,798	605	53.1	7.9	47.9
Kankakee	2,325	36,552	6,840	5,800	6,122	824	775	1,395	38,156	756	36.6	12.3	46.9
Kendall	2,158	23,941	1,889	2,324	5,849	660	730	835	34,887	313	39.9	13.7	52.5
Knox	1,033	15,988	3,476	1,252	3,510	422	268	472	29,505	853	22.5	14.3	50.7
Lake	19,817	323,110	35,081	35,794	38,639	14,487	34,246	23,742	73,479	302	77.8	2.6	40.6
LaSalle	2,639	38,539	5,369	5,100	6,424	1,340	1,391	1,587	41,181	1,496	33.4	11.4	45.9
Lawrence	258	3,399	569	1,013	403	106	42	118	34,771	426	34.7	15.3	44.0
Lee	702	10,693	2,162	3,276	1,335	338	244	431	40,298	832	33.5	14.5	50.8
Livingston	869	11,139	1,621	3,042	1,648	387	192	430	38,561	1,313	29.9	14.3	49.2
Logan	573	7,449	1,539	994	1,071	290	220	241	32,417	683	30.7	19.0	51.6
McDonough	676	9,024	1,877	1,447	1,633	335	239	266	29,487	760	29.3	13.2	47.2
McHenry	7,991	87,782	11,432	14,422	16,082	2,125	3,363	3,872	44,106	881	58.2	6.5	50.7
McLean	3,583	76,992	8,713	3,552	10,428	21,449	2,197	3,955	51,371	1,416	33.9	13.8	46.4
Macon	2,441	45,380	8,176	6,330	5,872	1,569	1,086	1,988	43,810	589	41.8	16.0	49.9
Macoupin	861	8,329	1,665	572	1,342	474	100	274	32,945	1,169	31.7	9.9	43.2
Madison	5,777	86,608	14,505	10,922	12,837	2,916	3,609	3,682	42,508	1,079	47.1	8.4	36.7
Marion	901	11,333	2,785	2,735	1,312	415	333	409	36,130	1,004	39.1	4.7	32.5
Marshall	264	2,732	478	918	275	101	28	94	34,494	472	21.2	11.0	45.6
Mason	275	2,276	482	91	425	137	25	81	35,707	548	25.2	18.4	47.8
Massac	229	3,566	910	449	328	110	169	146	40,928	417	34.3	7.9	50.3
Menard	212	1,351	87	34	263	109	86	41	30,618	386	32.4	12.7	46.5
Mercer	275	2,185	327	451	378	132	34	73	33,288	748	33.2	10.8	46.0
Monroe	783	8,429	1,007	335	1,359	332	592	287	34,056	568	46.0	10.9	41.2
Montgomery	696	7,015	1,329	682	1,457	389	176	221	31,491	1,067	33.3	13.8	47.9
Morgan	833	13,066	2,567	2,017	1,874	1,022	642	470	36,000	693	29.0	13.3	44.2
Moultrie	318	4,809	708	2,082	349	127	140	187	38,909	526	50.2	10.3	35.6
Ogle	1,048	13,243	1,459	3,225	1,521	505	343	576	43,514	1,011	43.0	10.8	46.7
Peoria	4,428	103,943	24,325	5,478	11,283	3,731	4,789	6,236	59,998	884	37.8	7.7	38.4
Perry	403	4,093	862	376	646	173	82	140	34,084	572	34.4	7.9	40.6
Piatt	326	2,356	394	184	418	145	117	79	33,701	422	36.0	21.1	53.6
Pike	361	3,089	693	149	605	210	66	98	31,870	956	24.7	15.2	40.4
Pope	47	236	89	D	41	11	4	4	17,678	322	25.2	2.5	32.9
Pulaski	84	599	134	D	116	56	D	16	27,109	222	26.1	15.3	38.6
Putnam	128	1,195	D	426	104	46	15	68	56,759	147	19.7	10.2	43.1
Randolph	677	10,912	2,174	2,869	1,405	294	294	398	36,470	808	34.7	7.9	36.7
Richland	455	5,391	1,181	441	668	178	80	191	35,355	596	41.9	8.4	35.9
Rock Island	3,135	62,287	9,631	7,198	8,223	2,949	3,224	3,077	49,407	649	38.1	6.0	42.5
St. Clair	5,261	78,081	14,833	4,847	13,511	2,347	5,095	2,905	37,202	793	46.0	9.5	42.3
Saline	574	6,853	2,013	360	1,291	348	157	253	36,875	452	39.6	9.5	36.6
Sangamon	4,969	86,003	23,987	2,702	12,528	5,670	4,820	3,482	40,487	1,083	46.4	13.0	44.5
Schuyler	148	1,032	272	D	214	66	20	35	33,570	544	21.5	11.2	33.5
Scott	77	595	21	D	79	61	8	24	40,274	300	25.0	15.0	45.3
Shelby	410	4,137	661	1,152	590	195	259	143	34,507	1,197	36.9	7.7	43.4
Stark	125	1,009	125	217	167	75	60	39	38,254	362	30.9	18.2	51.3
Stephenson	1,062	14,405	2,471	2,905	1,990	659	463	603	41,890	965	43.7	7.5	48.7
Tazewell	2,807	41,897	5,332	6,061	7,512	1,884	1,356	1,639	39,129	857	35.9	10.2	44.7
Union	359	3,652	1,341	258	706	142	73	100	27,353	590	30.7	5.4	37.2
Vermilion	1,411	24,530	5,336	4,861	3,872	1,101	428	973	39,647	1,049	38.9	14.1	47.8
Wabash	263	2,742	793	159	318	101	113	99	36,040	208	38.0	17.3	37.7
Warren	364	5,868	636	1,998	628	204	102	189	32,124	711	28.4	14.9	55.9
Washington	378	5,644	387	1,500	564	171	108	218	38,668	715	23.9	15.2	48.6
Wayne	376	3,191	944	264	593	130	73	92	28,966	1,025	31.6	11.0	42.8
White	386	3,487	639	279	519	158	81	125	35,965	496	34.9	17.3	46.3
Whiteside	1,218	17,410	3,239	3,599	2,666	581	317	631	36,260	959	33.5	10.4	45.6
Will	14,918	214,642	27,479	17,772	32,986	4,852	9,144	9,358	43,599	801	56.4	7.2	42.3
Williamson	1,627	24,099	6,389	3,029	3,924	1,218	616	894	37,115	610	45.7	4.6	28.7

Table B. States and Counties — **Agriculture**

STATE County	Land in farms — Acreage (1,000)	Percent change, 2012-2017	Average size of farm	Total irrigated (1,000)	Total cropland (1,000)	Value of land and buildings (dollars) Average per farm	Average per acre	Value of machinery and equipment, average per farm (dollars)	Total (mil dol)	Average per farm (acres)	Percent from: Crops	Livestock and poultry products	Organic farms (number)	Farms with internet access (percent)	Government payments Total ($1,000)	Percent of farms
	117	118	119	120	121	122	123	124	125	126	127	128	129	130	131	132
ILLINOIS— Cont'd																
Hardin	37	10.2	227	NA	21.2	745,489	3,281	84,639	D	D	D	D	1	90.1	679	38.5
Henderson	193	12.4	440	12.7	165.1	3,065,949	6,961	208,592	122.3	279,297	83.4	16.6	5	84.5	3,938	76.9
Henry	484	1.0	358	7.4	440.8	2,828,369	7,902	225,411	353.0	260,897	77.2	22.8	7	81.1	15,746	72.4
Iroquois	681	1.8	449	5.7	655.9	3,302,325	7,348	249,933	420.5	277,400	84.4	15.6	11	77.8	8,969	61.8
Jackson	222	3.5	287	1.7	176.8	1,546,191	5,386	149,783	87.2	112,920	85.9	14.1	3	69.3	4,446	47.8
Jasper	250	-0.5	273	D	218.7	1,540,385	5,634	162,342	165.9	181,690	61.6	38.4	2	75.0	7,045	84.2
Jefferson	269	25.9	245	0.1	222.6	1,019,111	4,158	108,307	94.6	86,101	82.8	17.2	6	69.9	5,256	64.8
Jersey	190	22.0	366	0.0	152.1	2,314,178	6,330	220,839	82.1	158,143	95.3	4.7	NA	75.0	4,326	64.5
Jo Daviess	289	6.5	306	0.8	202.1	1,867,551	6,110	196,260	151.9	160,415	65.0	35.0	3	75.1	6,275	67.9
Johnson	105	17.6	162	0.5	55.8	597,733	3,701	66,612	18.2	27,824	80.0	20.0	NA	65.4	2,524	45.2
Kane	170	1.0	281	1.3	161.9	2,971,109	10,558	229,206	183.1	299,633	84.8	15.2	10	83.6	3,782	45.6
Kankakee	313	-8.7	414	18.4	300.4	3,237,465	7,822	285,392	221.1	292,508	91.3	8.7	3	75.5	2,346	45.4
Kendall	138	6.3	441	D	133.6	3,991,102	9,059	260,029	101.6	324,655	92.4	7.6	3	85.6	2,128	60.7
Knox	414	19.1	485	0.0	355.5	3,553,390	7,319	247,401	284.4	333,419	78.5	21.5	2	82.6	7,150	73.0
Lake	31	1.8	101	0.4	23.9	1,230,772	12,149	102,194	39.1	129,364	85.2	14.8	8	77.8	423	10.9
LaSalle	573	-4.9	383	6.1	545.4	3,495,212	9,125	265,453	370.9	247,958	94.1	5.9	3	81.6	12,749	72.1
Lawrence	225	22.2	528	29.1	205.5	2,983,608	5,650	327,369	156.4	367,045	71.4	28.6	1	71.1	7,260	71.8
Lee	392	6.2	471	23.9	374.4	4,085,091	8,668	320,174	278.9	335,184	89.8	10.2	6	81.3	9,291	70.9
Livingston	601	-8.5	457	0.1	581.3	3,764,261	8,230	280,950	408.4	311,023	85.2	14.8	9	84.3	6,848	57.9
Logan	354	-2.5	518	2.6	338.1	4,343,867	8,380	297,104	245.7	359,712	90.5	9.5	2	79.9	4,262	79.8
McDonough	315	7.8	414	0.1	272.5	3,037,172	7,334	233,227	214.1	281,663	82.9	17.1	1	79.7	3,359	66.8
McHenry	208	-11.0	236	9.6	189.7	2,256,366	9,541	174,498	163.8	185,871	75.3	24.7	5	80.6	4,201	30.6
McLean	620	-10.4	438	3.2	599.9	4,310,555	9,844	280,498	457.1	322,784	85.0	15.0	3	81.1	9,368	73.0
Macon	277	-17.6	471	0.1	268.0	4,356,859	9,250	281,637	180.0	305,610	97.7	2.3	5	84.6	4,815	69.4
Macoupin	421	-4.1	360	0.0	355.3	2,589,379	7,195	203,190	236.5	202,305	82.6	17.4	1	74.7	4,907	63.5
Madison	319	3.8	295	0.5	287.8	2,571,906	8,706	176,232	174.7	161,912	89.9	10.1	6	79.0	6,378	56.1
Marion	249	-6.8	248	0.2	203.7	1,210,249	4,885	147,171	111.9	111,406	70.8	29.2	5	73.4	6,728	76.1
Marshall	199	-5.0	421	2.9	180.7	3,396,974	8,075	245,161	119.5	253,275	96.7	3.3	3	82.4	4,124	79.4
Mason	312	7.6	569	136.9	289.3	3,974,753	6,983	352,375	192.9	352,035	88.9	11.1	1	73.9	6,447	86.7
Massac	119	16.0	284	10.4	95.5	1,100,621	3,871	176,306	45.8	109,928	86.5	13.5	NA	77.7	3,252	63.1
Menard	168	6.5	435	3.8	139.0	3,399,115	7,807	261,654	89.7	232,267	93.2	6.8	NA	80.6	3,801	71.0
Mercer	282	12.0	377	7.8	247.3	2,471,925	6,551	197,201	217.5	290,807	71.9	28.1	3	78.2	6,604	76.7
Monroe	176	-8.8	310	3.2	151.0	2,065,789	6,659	215,520	88.2	155,195	74.5	25.5	NA	75.7	4,205	59.5
Montgomery	439	14.8	411	D	398.1	2,992,259	7,276	254,828	263.0	246,517	85.6	14.4	NA	79.9	6,978	76.9
Morgan	300	-2.9	433	7.7	265.2	3,573,396	8,247	266,790	172.0	248,221	88.5	11.5	11	81.8	4,846	75.8
Moultrie	202	-1.6	384	0.0	194.9	3,351,079	8,737	205,183	141.2	268,365	93.6	6.4	9	67.5	2,939	56.7
Ogle	355	-5.8	351	0.8	326.8	3,015,903	8,599	246,650	276.4	273,371	75.4	24.6	1	85.3	3,708	61.4
Peoria	250	-0.1	283	3.5	216.3	2,232,609	7,892	180,266	145.2	164,249	90.6	9.4	5	77.4	2,517	64.1
Perry	184	2.0	322	0.2	153.5	1,539,778	4,782	174,881	66.3	115,955	92.3	7.7	NA	62.9	3,806	73.8
Piatt	256	-1.2	607	1.1	251.2	5,617,953	9,260	341,248	165.3	391,673	99.5	0.5	2	85.5	3,844	68.0
Pike	447	8.6	468	3.1	342.9	2,766,090	5,916	203,650	278.9	291,705	64.8	35.2	NA	72.4	5,868	74.4
Pope	66	-15.3	205	D	30.9	715,861	3,491	75,796	8.9	27,503	76.5	23.5	NA	65.8	1,815	59.0
Pulaski	101	23.3	456	5.2	83.1	1,871,568	4,103	181,600	40.1	180,450	96.8	3.2	NA	68.9	2,466	64.9
Putnam	50	-17.3	339	0.2	43.7	2,833,889	8,372	272,212	D	D	D	D	NA	76.2	837	80.3
Randolph	262	-6.0	324	D	216.5	1,757,514	5,423	158,325	98.5	121,881	85.7	14.3	NA	73.0	5,839	66.2
Richland	178	-5.5	299	1.0	158.2	1,581,240	5,280	158,267	119.8	201,000	57.6	42.4	NA	82.0	5,629	76.2
Rock Island	160	7.0	246	4.8	132.4	1,712,532	6,965	179,885	99.9	153,954	80.3	19.7	2	76.6	3,685	60.9
St. Clair	237	-5.8	299	0.5	218.8	2,218,716	7,417	183,236	135.6	171,019	83.1	16.9	4	77.3	4,907	62.3
Saline	145	3.6	321	D	122.3	1,546,065	4,824	155,847	73.6	162,761	75.9	24.1	NA	72.1	3,646	51.5
Sangamon	531	3.4	491	0.8	496.8	4,381,113	8,931	259,349	352.6	325,599	92.4	7.6	3	78.8	6,498	63.3
Schuyler	212	16.3	389	2.4	153.8	2,135,913	5,484	176,634	116.3	213,836	64.6	35.4	NA	69.1	2,423	78.1
Scott	155	5.4	518	6.3	131.8	3,367,008	6,498	237,953	84.7	282,197	82.0	18.0	NA	70.7	1,621	65.3
Shelby	362	-10.7	303	D	325.7	2,133,632	7,047	191,064	219.1	183,081	79.9	20.1	1	75.1	8,283	75.1
Stark	179	6.3	494	D	169.2	4,103,207	8,314	302,743	117.0	323,246	96.1	3.9	1	79.3	3,618	82.9
Stephenson	305	-13.5	316	0.3	277.9	2,662,038	8,424	231,782	288.5	298,940	53.2	46.8	13	81.7	9,220	66.5
Tazewell	304	-9.8	355	39.7	282.2	2,938,881	8,272	216,559	220.4	257,216	82.6	17.4	19	78.5	3,523	58.0
Union	151	24.3	255	4.5	110.7	1,084,536	4,248	113,939	47.9	81,264	90.3	9.7	1	72.5	3,589	55.4
Vermilion	471	8.5	449	0.8	443.7	3,686,595	8,203	261,347	283.0	269,783	95.2	4.8	6	77.8	5,125	56.7
Wabash	115	8.5	555	2.7	105.6	3,070,471	5,533	310,687	52.6	252,793	96.1	3.9	NA	76.0	2,768	75.0
Warren	341	0.8	480	0.2	301.4	3,880,818	8,092	284,489	253.6	356,689	79.1	20.9	3	81.6	2,469	74.5
Washington	349	-1.7	488	1.8	325.7	3,134,730	6,422	325,140	203.8	284,987	69.0	31.0	NA	69.2	8,727	81.3
Wayne	368	-0.1	359	1.2	319.6	1,710,457	4,764	188,596	188.3	183,664	72.6	27.4	NA	72.4	10,861	76.5
White	289	-6.9	584	21.1	256.8	2,908,130	4,983	282,694	141.1	284,377	93.2	6.8	NA	73.6	7,825	71.8
Whiteside	371	-8.1	387	60.4	340.4	3,051,253	7,892	283,093	301.0	313,911	69.9	30.1	8	78.6	12,909	74.1
Will	217	-7.5	270	0.5	208.2	2,403,429	8,888	163,473	133.5	166,674	92.3	7.7	6	81.5	1,014	30.6
Williamson	104	0.4	170	0.0	73.3	673,017	3,953	94,199	34.7	56,907	74.4	25.6	NA	70.7	2,137	39.7

Items 117—132

STATE County	Water use, 2015		Wholesale Trade[1], 2012				Retail Trade[2], 2012				Real estate and rental and leasing,[2] 2012			
	Public supply water withdrawn (mil gal/day)	Public supply gallons withdrawn per person per day	Number of establishments	Number of employees	Sales (mil dol)	Average payroll (mil dol)	Number of establishments	Number of employees	Sales (mil dol)	Average payroll (mil dol)	Number of establishments	Number of employees	Sales (mil dol)	Average payroll (mil dol)
	133	134	135	136	137	138	139	140	141	142	143	144	145	146
ILLINOIS— Cont'd														
Hardin	0.13	31.4	NA	NA	NA	NA	8	57	14.5	1.0	2	D	D	D
Henderson	8.82	1,260.9	12	61	303.0	3.4	15	105	39.4	2.2	1	D	D	D
Henry	3.97	80.2	64	656	1,229.5	29.1	156	1,792	500.1	41.6	20	31	5.5	0.7
Iroquois	1.99	69.4	56	590	822.4	26.8	87	1,074	287.4	21.3	18	50	7.9	1.3
Jackson	5.96	100.4	26	239	187.6	9.7	225	3,684	1,008.3	76.4	77	350	49.9	7.4
Jasper	1.77	184.2	18	108	211.5	4.6	31	288	73.3	6.0	2	D	D	D
Jefferson	0.00	0.0	56	D	D	D	180	2,295	709.5	55.0	21	68	12.1	2.0
Jersey	1.08	48.3	24	D	D	D	69	909	230.6	21.3	10	16	3.0	0.5
Jo Daviess	2.03	91.9	21	135	94.8	5.3	118	880	293.7	21.2	18	27	6.7	1.3
Johnson	0.86	67.4	4	7	3.1	0.3	27	240	88.6	5.6	4	1	0.1	0.0
Kane	61.75	116.3	741	9,371	9,628.8	571.7	1,487	22,836	5,681.1	508.2	439	2,045	583.8	83.7
Kankakee	13.26	119.6	119	2,196	1,443.3	95.0	370	5,548	1,463.3	120.0	95	371	70.9	10.6
Kendall	7.66	62.1	75	1,327	2,125.6	64.4	237	4,777	1,151.5	106.6	60	139	21.8	4.0
Knox	0.49	9.5	48	680	502.4	29.0	193	3,463	791.3	75.6	35	123	18.6	2.7
Lake	59.65	84.7	1,106	27,371	26,255.5	2,227.7	2,309	37,702	14,900.5	1,112.0	745	3,386	994.6	193.0
LaSalle	9.07	81.5	124	1,719	2,344.1	78.3	420	6,168	1,689.5	142.3	86	533	63.6	16.9
Lawrence	0.62	37.6	14	233	113.8	7.5	38	406	117.3	9.0	7	14	1.4	0.3
Lee	3.94	113.9	28	D	D	D	100	1,264	379.9	30.1	21	112	13.8	2.6
Livingston	5.66	154.3	60	692	1,011.2	36.9	135	1,610	479.4	36.9	16	69	6.9	1.9
Logan	2.88	97.6	45	552	858.7	32.1	88	1,082	292.3	24.7	25	86	9.9	2.1
McDonough	2.63	83.9	29	D	D	D	121	1,554	340.8	32.9	26	110	16.3	2.1
McHenry	18.70	60.8	411	5,284	2,932.5	264.5	941	15,021	3,664.4	337.2	219	745	113.4	24.1
McLean	10.50	60.6	166	2,515	9,130.9	161.3	580	9,434	2,441.6	201.1	143	718	149.0	22.7
Macon	20.02	186.6	112	D	D	D	395	5,724	1,494.2	133.7	88	471	105.2	13.8
Macoupin	2.96	64.3	47	680	885.2	29.6	133	1,375	392.0	30.0	21	54	5.9	1.5
Madison	52.40	196.8	226	2,822	2,764.2	147.4	832	12,506	3,230.2	292.4	230	974	171.4	31.4
Marion	0.99	25.8	39	336	334.8	11.8	150	1,349	353.7	30.6	23	101	10.3	2.6
Marshall	1.67	139.4	16	D	D	D	42	384	85.7	6.7	6	D	D	D
Mason	0.57	41.6	27	306	664.8	14.7	45	445	130.5	8.9	5	11	1.2	0.2
Massac	4.73	320.3	8	D	D	D	37	319	84.9	7.5	5	36	3.0	0.6
Menard	0.81	65.1	10	87	153.4	4.7	31	319	76.8	5.9	4	7	0.9	0.2
Mercer	0.88	55.5	14	148	435.0	6.5	41	351	72.6	6.7	6	10	1.1	0.2
Monroe	0.37	10.9	21	284	182.7	13.4	96	1,393	481.7	41.7	28	151	18.8	5.4
Montgomery	2.69	93.1	47	314	372.9	13.3	128	1,518	432.5	34.1	15	53	6.5	1.2
Morgan	0.31	8.9	42	D	D	D	151	1,845	454.5	37.9	27	D	D	D
Moultrie	0.17	11.4	11	95	245.4	4.4	42	363	109.4	7.3	5	15	0.7	0.1
Ogle	5.09	98.5	53	D	D	D	138	1,466	408.1	29.2	36	104	11.3	1.9
Peoria	23.98	128.8	202	3,235	1,782.0	153.6	726	10,839	2,576.7	249.2	198	987	181.7	33.1
Perry	0.70	32.5	13	D	D	D	59	718	189.5	16.1	5	11	1.3	0.4
Piatt	1.12	68.3	25	275	429.7	15.4	47	446	143.4	10.6	4	D	D	D
Pike	1.90	118.8	24	193	340.6	9.4	53	566	174.3	12.2	7	16	7.6	0.3
Pope	0.00	0.0	NA	NA	NA	NA	11	52	11.5	0.8	2	D	D	D
Pulaski	0.17	29.9	6	D	D	D	18	85	35.0	2.2	NA	NA	NA	NA
Putnam	0.46	81.5	9	59	224.7	2.2	16	135	29.2	2.5	1	D	D	D
Randolph	2.43	74.0	33	429	406.4	20.0	100	1,440	373.4	32.9	9	21	3.8	0.6
Richland	1.42	88.6	25	329	566.0	12.1	62	720	176.4	15.2	6	20	1.6	0.4
Rock Island	17.39	119.0	152	2,826	3,164.9	182.9	479	7,931	1,859.1	186.9	119	526	108.1	14.3
St. Clair	17.32	65.6	177	1,846	2,643.8	85.8	910	13,296	3,234.2	305.3	230	1,005	171.6	31.4
Saline	0.00	0.0	14	104	51.3	3.5	111	1,245	353.6	31.5	9	39	10.1	1.3
Sangamon	23.21	116.8	196	3,346	3,372.0	151.3	754	11,950	3,128.6	277.1	211	842	153.5	25.5
Schuyler	0.92	130.8	7	67	68.6	3.1	28	207	39.0	4.6	3	D	D	D
Scott	4.82	946.6	3	D	D	D	9	98	39.1	2.4	1	D	D	D
Shelby	1.65	75.8	26	226	239.8	7.8	71	603	155.0	11.4	9	D	D	D
Stark	0.59	101.9	8	D	D	D	21	168	68.1	5.4	3	D	D	D
Stephenson	3.85	84.2	49	D	D	D	157	2,026	521.6	45.8	29	92	10.8	2.5
Tazewell	14.72	109.2	131	2,089	1,929.2	98.6	406	6,864	1,942.3	169.6	88	306	78.9	9.8
Union	1.28	73.5	12	130	40.2	3.8	64	649	167.1	15.3	11	34	3.8	0.8
Vermilion	8.95	112.9	77	1,788	3,136.5	84.3	255	3,401	850.3	74.3	45	158	28.7	4.5
Wabash	1.75	151.6	13	D	D	D	42	345	81.1	8.3	11	18	2.7	0.5
Warren	2.75	156.9	29	240	516.2	10.2	54	552	143.2	11.1	9	18	2.0	0.3
Washington	0.63	44.1	30	586	415.7	25.9	64	584	200.8	15.3	14	24	1.7	0.2
Wayne	1.12	68.2	22	196	214.0	8.6	68	602	157.6	13.7	7	13	1.5	0.4
White	1.08	75.4	25	218	161.9	7.4	58	510	142.9	11.2	10	52	14.2	2.1
Whiteside	3.62	63.4	61	597	689.1	24.7	190	2,676	578.0	57.9	38	111	15.1	2.5
Will	35.06	51.0	735	11,420	14,925.1	680.5	1,606	27,615	7,862.1	657.3	467	2,311	458.3	97.1
Williamson	1.22	18.1	60	723	255.2	28.5	271	3,783	1,116.3	93.8	51	187	29.2	5.3

1 Merchant wholesalers, except manufacturers' sales branches and offices.   2. Employer establishments.

Table B. States and Counties — Professional Services, Manufacturing, and Accommodation and Food Services

STATE County	Professional, scientific, and technical services, 2012				Manufacturing, 2012				Accommodation and food services, 2012			
	Number of establishments	Number of employees	Sales (mil dol)	Average payroll (mil dol)	Number of establishments	Number of employees	Receipts (mil dol)	Annual payroll (mil dol)	Number of establishments	Number of employees	Receipts (mil dol)	Annual payroll (mil dol)
	147	148	149	150	151	152	153	154	155	156	157	158
ILLINOIS— Cont'd												
Hardin	4	D	D	D	NA	NA	NA	NA	9	D	D	D
Henderson	6	29	2.3	0.7	NA	NA	NA	NA	11	D	D	D
Henry	69	289	21.2	7.2	55	4,230	D	155.3	85	D	D	D
Iroquois	33	206	12.6	4.4	30	642	515.2	21.9	60	537	22.5	6.6
Jackson	108	689	68.5	27.1	39	673	178.3	25.8	140	2,927	111.5	31.4
Jasper	10	22	1.9	0.5	12	288	101.6	10.7	15	122	4.4	1.2
Jefferson	76	523	48.4	20.2	32	2,998	D	144.3	81	1,647	71.1	20.9
Jersey	20	146	13.5	6.7	14	62	D	2.2	44	644	26.3	7.4
Jo Daviess	56	250	36.1	12.2	37	1,018	480.2	45.1	108	1,656	73.6	22.5
Johnson	13	259	5.4	2.5	9	36	D	1.7	17	D	D	D
Kane	1,539	9,323	1,603.3	573.6	799	30,327	10,338.7	1,548.3	850	15,058	720.3	207.4
Kankakee	152	735	64.1	24.5	100	4,889	4,842.8	269.7	219	3,675	160.3	47.4
Kendall	199	D	D	D	79	2,298	719.2	108.9	163	2,865	139.4	38.1
Knox	64	307	27.7	11.0	38	D	321.4	36.3	124	1,715	76.3	21.3
Lake	3,052	26,120	3,483.8	2,220.4	846	35,174	12,046.0	1,950.0	1,498	24,702	1,399.2	405.5
LaSalle	166	1,098	120.8	43.7	143	4,665	2,345.6	246.9	318	4,213	188.6	52.3
Lawrence	13	45	4.8	1.2	11	541	D	20.7	22	D	D	D
Lee	38	256	32.0	13.0	36	2,775	1,193.6	117.0	82	722	38.9	8.8
Livingston	55	229	27.4	9.1	60	3,376	1,210.5	166.3	76	855	36.2	9.2
Logan	34	180	16.6	6.4	18	1,034	555.3	46.3	63	853	31.0	9.5
McDonough	44	258	20.2	8.5	20	1,538	420.9	68.9	96	1,599	71.6	17.9
McHenry	898	D	D	D	491	15,508	5,163.2	820.7	558	9,074	435.7	125.5
McLean	363	2,852	280.7	125.2	92	3,881	1,590.2	199.5	379	8,136	393.0	108.7
Macon	157	1,216	142.7	54.0	109	8,240	13,379.3	435.3	225	4,331	189.8	55.6
Macoupin	40	149	15.3	4.3	33	567	D	24.6	89	D	D	D
Madison	549	3,711	748.1	216.0	193	12,308	19,140.5	841.4	582	9,920	431.2	124.6
Marion	60	250	18.1	8.2	42	2,567	710.6	101.5	77	848	38.2	11.1
Marshall	12	24	2.2	0.7	12	888	D	37.1	30	281	7.4	2.4
Mason	9	23	2.5	0.7	12	80	24.6	3.5	41	D	D	D
Massac	9	D	D	D	10	522	D	29.5	28	D	D	D
Menard	15	79	7.2	2.5	5	24	D	1.1	21	231	5.5	1.5
Mercer	11	28	2.5	0.7	12	669	D	25.8	22	D	D	D
Monroe	81	596	89.9	40.9	23	264	D	11.3	63	1,134	43.0	12.7
Montgomery	35	198	17.2	6.6	23	679	313.6	29.4	63	875	37.3	10.8
Morgan	39	642	60.3	29.9	30	1,867	D	82.1	90	1,353	63.7	15.9
Moultrie	16	67	5.9	3.1	36	1,621	533.4	65.0	26	D	D	D
Ogle	68	210	16.0	7.5	62	3,356	1,530.9	146.0	110	1,063	52.9	12.0
Peoria	429	5,236	719.2	311.0	157	7,747	6,197.5	466.3	470	8,372	383.5	109.8
Perry	19	52	4.9	1.4	19	412	D	19.0	37	492	15.5	4.8
Piatt	28	96	8.5	3.7	13	183	D	7.0	31	D	D	D
Pike	17	73	8.0	2.2	19	143	62.4	6.2	37	350	14.0	3.6
Pope	5	D	D	D	NA	NA	NA	NA	5	9	0.6	0.1
Pulaski	1	D	D	D	NA	NA	NA	NA	6	D	D	D
Putnam	5	20	1.7	0.6	8	440	D	16.8	14	69	2.5	0.5
Randolph	36	227	24.2	8.3	28	2,902	609.3	77.6	64	806	29.6	8.5
Richland	25	135	50.1	9.9	28	438	143.5	17.2	36	D	D	D
Rock Island	291	2,847	667.4	163.6	153	8,245	6,845.4	451.8	342	5,592	344.4	75.6
St. Clair	511	5,662	870.2	364.7	158	4,922	2,779.9	241.6	561	10,416	589.3	155.9
Saline	39	160	16.3	5.5	24	348	D	11.5	47	776	37.2	8.3
Sangamon	527	4,381	549.2	224.9	109	2,834	D	139.1	523	9,447	439.2	129.0
Schuyler	7	23	2.4	0.7	6	95	D	2.4	12	D	D	D
Scott	3	9	1.1	0.3	4	163	D	6.8	11	56	2.7	0.6
Shelby	21	184	21.6	8.5	21	1,042	D	45.2	41	375	14.2	4.0
Stark	8	66	5.0	1.9	7	248	D	11.5	3	6	0.3	0.1
Stephenson	81	454	55.4	19.6	62	3,037	1,145.2	155.4	89	1,033	47.6	12.0
Tazewell	180	1,187	118.5	52.8	110	8,215	5,850.3	443.8	306	6,143	358.5	92.3
Union	19	80	6.7	2.9	12	164	D	5.4	30	D	D	D
Vermilion	84	428	46.7	16.6	96	5,168	2,353.2	256.1	143	2,161	86.0	25.4
Wabash	22	140	14.2	5.7	9	188	43.3	8.9	21	296	11.8	3.5
Warren	20	85	8.1	2.2	17	1,803	632.7	71.2	36	481	20.6	5.4
Washington	22	105	12.2	3.9	14	D	445.6	D	30	D	D	D
Wayne	21	58	4.2	1.4	16	607	D	24.6	22	D	D	D
White	19	71	6.0	1.8	12	304	D	10.6	26	D	D	D
Whiteside	81	341	36.1	12.6	88	3,955	1,453.2	198.3	124	1,589	66.5	18.6
Will	1,586	D	D	D	588	20,377	20,627.2	1,191.0	1,108	20,582	1,313.5	320.8
Williamson	121	636	65.4	21.4	42	1,748	793.0	78.5	148	2,724	123.7	35.4

STATE County	Health care and social assistance, 2012				Other services, 2012				Nonemployer businesses, 2016		Value of residential construction authorized by building permits, 2018	
	Number of establish-ments	Number of employees	Receipts (mil dol)	Annual payroll (mil dol)	Number of establish-ments	Number of employees	Receipts (mil dol)	Annual payroll (mil dol)	Number	Receipts (mil dol)	New construction ($1,000)	Number of housing units
	159	160	161	162	163	164	165	166	167	168	169	170
ILLINOIS— Cont'd												
Hardin	12	252	18.3	7.9	3	3	0.3	0.1	218	5.3	0	0
Henderson	8	153	7.3	3.4	7	D	D	D	373	15.8	904	5
Henry	88	1,640	123.4	49.0	97	380	31.0	8.7	2,775	96.9	6,802	32
Iroquois	66	1,588	105.2	44.6	48	148	19.7	3.2	1,965	69.4	4,667	26
Jackson	167	3,463	517.9	159.6	93	396	41.7	8.4	3,151	118.9	1,196	9
Jasper	14	143	6.6	2.2	19	61	5.6	1.0	840	25.0	150	1
Jefferson	146	3,518	391.1	145.4	82	416	43.0	11.2	2,296	85.9	980	6
Jersey	48	D	D	D	35	109	8.5	2.3	1,284	38.1	4,338	27
Jo Daviess	41	656	43.1	17.8	57	247	22.8	6.0	1,962	75.4	7,363	26
Johnson	19	209	12.6	4.7	10	D	D	D	718	22.5	0	0
Kane	1,153	21,559	2,406.9	968.7	821	5,885	596.9	169.7	33,766	1,468.8	346,802	1,891
Kankakee	311	7,349	753.9	294.5	180	956	100.3	25.1	6,066	203.8	29,707	157
Kendall	177	D	D	D	164	795	73.6	21.5	8,277	307.2	99,239	732
Knox	122	3,696	338.7	125.8	77	562	125.9	15.1	2,299	68.3	2,954	22
Lake	1,949	33,669	4,026.3	1,549.4	1,276	7,626	728.2	224.2	54,571	3,028.9	236,265	696
LaSalle	284	5,993	448.1	188.7	237	1,205	109.6	31.7	5,848	213.6	27,208	130
Lawrence	23	617	30.3	13.5	22	111	11.0	3.5	779	27.1	8,625	50
Lee	80	2,137	166.8	72.1	60	345	33.1	9.5	1,897	71.1	5,369	22
Livingston	74	2,090	144.5	62.4	66	334	29.3	8.3	1,985	64.0	3,272	23
Logan	58	1,330	111.3	41.5	54	206	15.9	4.2	1,425	52.6	3,217	13
McDonough	71	1,768	138.8	58.5	65	D	D	D	1,481	47.6	99	1
McHenry	718	D	D	D	634	3,300	260.3	77.6	22,445	993.8	73,361	482
McLean	371	8,547	969.7	368.4	259	2,311	212.2	74.8	9,649	395.1	19,975	201
Macon	291	8,193	886.2	332.1	176	1,170	239.1	37.3	5,463	181.8	9,198	37
Macoupin	91	1,920	115.8	48.0	85	318	25.5	6.3	2,592	92.0	13,762	68
Madison	677	13,914	1,194.9	486.2	456	2,888	272.1	79.6	14,484	563.0	132,577	634
Marion	113	3,009	249.3	94.0	73	268	21.7	5.6	2,169	67.2	1,000	12
Marshall	19	468	22.1	9.5	15	D	D	D	618	20.7	1,117	6
Mason	26	506	36.7	16.5	27	90	6.8	1.6	674	29.3	844	4
Massac	26	755	53.8	24.4	21	65	7.9	1.8	795	24.8	0	0
Menard	12	75	6.3	2.1	16	64	5.6	1.3	817	25.3	4,046	18
Mercer	24	344	23.5	9.3	16	64	5.9	1.6	887	26.9	1,155	7
Monroe	79	846	57.1	24.2	71	407	25.0	9.6	2,166	87.9	30,058	122
Montgomery	73	D	D	D	57	233	20.8	5.6	1,579	51.4	2,574	12
Morgan	121	D	D	D	64	260	18.4	4.8	1,904	65.5	3,530	28
Moultrie	32	735	36.2	16.8	17	D	D	D	1,013	36.8	4,709	53
Ogle	82	1,505	103.9	41.0	75	343	36.6	10.3	3,301	117.4	13,029	73
Peoria	516	22,518	2,665.0	1,057.0	304	4,714	449.2	206.3	9,766	361.4	35,632	166
Perry	45	890	63.7	25.9	46	161	11.9	3.1	1,051	30.5	8,580	40
Piatt	21	D	D	D	18	D	D	D	1,168	41.7	10,087	33
Pike	25	586	49.0	18.0	26	109	12.8	3.2	1,093	40.8	3,069	21
Pope	11	D	D	D	3	D	D	D	220	5.1	0	0
Pulaski	14	151	6.8	2.6	14	43	3.6	0.9	289	7.3	900	9
Putnam	4	18	1.5	0.6	4	D	D	D	389	15.6	2,236	16
Randolph	73	2,170	260.4	123.7	61	266	28.4	8.6	1,418	49.8	5,821	23
Richland	50	1,014	71.7	31.3	40	162	17.2	4.0	1,131	39.7	454	2
Rock Island	416	8,883	802.3	345.0	265	1,600	138.9	43.0	6,898	261.9	19,688	117
St. Clair	595	15,933	1,363.8	594.9	387	2,528	213.0	73.6	14,360	479.6	137,931	664
Saline	78	1,808	143.9	60.3	47	172	22.0	4.0	1,551	54.0	0	0
Sangamon	445	20,510	2,559.6	892.3	474	3,319	416.7	124.8	12,284	477.5	80,363	488
Schuyler	14	323	28.2	10.7	12	D	D	D	468	15.6	0	0
Scott	4	D	D	D	4	10	1.4	0.3	310	9.3	NA	NA
Shelby	33	674	42.3	18.7	32	93	11.9	2.5	1,324	44.6	6,629	28
Stark	8	167	8.9	3.7	4	D	D	D	348	12.6	95	1
Stephenson	104	2,545	329.3	92.9	95	642	46.2	16.0	2,822	95.9	3,103	12
Tazewell	246	5,435	388.8	155.2	242	1,270	113.7	37.2	6,592	241.7	18,221	100
Union	52	1,215	72.6	30.4	22	80	7.1	2.1	1,027	34.0	2,049	11
Vermilion	143	4,736	514.4	235.4	121	540	47.4	13.3	4,158	129.9	6,270	65
Wabash	26	832	62.0	22.6	22	94	6.5	1.5	804	27.8	1,375	15
Warren	37	694	48.6	19.5	31	115	11.8	2.2	870	33.9	639	4
Washington	26	616	39.9	15.4	27	61	7.0	1.3	965	35.9	4,505	21
Wayne	32	799	53.9	22.2	27	113	14.4	3.2	1,245	42.9	0	0
White	43	638	36.5	14.9	33	160	16.2	4.7	1,078	41.6	0	0
Whiteside	99	3,068	261.2	99.1	109	608	54.1	13.5	2,817	99.3	4,760	28
Will	1,406	24,364	2,467.6	967.5	1,053	6,884	681.5	195.1	47,885	2,072.4	379,855	1,627
Williamson	204	5,977	677.0	251.1	93	519	52.4	14.1	4,231	148.9	28,193	229

Table B. States and Counties — Government Employment and Payroll, and Local Government Finances

STATE County	Full-time equivalent employees (171)	March payroll (dollars) (172)	Administration, judicial, and legal (173)	Police and corrections (174)	Fire protection (175)	Highways and transportation (176)	Health and welfare (177)	Natural resources and utilities (178)	Education and libraries (179)	Total (mil dol) (180)	Intergovernmental (mil dol) (181)	Taxes Total (mil dol) (182)	Taxes Per capita Total (183)	Taxes Per capita Property (184)
ILLINOIS— Cont'd														
Hardin	285	791,768	2.8	3.0	0.0	56.6	0.9	4.7	31.7	16.6	13.4	1.6	384	331
Henderson	266	806,748	8.3	7.3	0.3	7.4	10.9	2.4	62.8	21.4	9.7	7.4	1,047	1,030
Henry	1,997	6,801,070	4.9	8.8	1.9	3.9	16.2	5.8	57.8	199.6	66.8	68.8	1,372	1,289
Iroquois	1,017	3,877,441	5.9	6.3	0.5	4.2	0.4	1.9	79.8	90.3	38.3	39.1	1,337	1,242
Jackson	2,101	6,263,626	8.2	10.9	3.5	4.0	8.7	8.4	55.9	187.5	83.7	70.9	1,181	879
Jasper	379	1,198,050	10.1	7.5	0.4	7.8	10.7	3.7	59.8	34.3	16.7	13.8	1,437	1,424
Jefferson	1,638	5,345,187	5.0	7.6	2.9	4.0	1.2	3.6	74.9	147.2	83.4	43.3	1,119	882
Jersey	837	3,076,248	4.5	7.9	0.3	2.8	30.8	3.6	48.9	78.3	24.9	21.1	926	828
Jo Daviess	997	3,300,597	8.1	8.4	0.4	5.4	17.9	2.0	56.6	94.9	21.9	52.5	2,329	2,191
Johnson	372	1,081,737	6.4	5.0	0.0	5.0	0.2	4.9	77.4	26.5	15.8	7.0	547	545
Kane	21,805	101,252,430	5.2	10.1	5.2	2.0	0.9	6.8	68.3	2,745.0	798.1	1,591.7	3,046	2,837
Kankakee	4,413	16,356,166	7.8	13.5	3.6	3.7	1.5	3.4	65.4	441.9	208.0	169.2	1,496	1,433
Kendall	3,451	14,665,867	5.1	10.4	5.3	1.3	0.8	4.9	71.6	446.4	125.8	268.8	2,276	2,192
Knox	2,362	8,240,583	5.2	9.0	3.0	3.3	7.4	6.1	64.9	191.6	87.1	68.2	1,306	1,155
Lake	27,930	134,406,176	5.8	8.4	4.0	2.3	3.7	6.6	68.5	3,687.1	912.8	2,300.4	3,276	3,089
LaSalle	4,146	16,025,437	6.1	10.7	2.6	3.3	2.5	3.9	69.6	433.1	147.6	217.8	1,928	1,756
Lawrence	525	1,443,702	5.9	7.2	0.3	7.5	2.8	3.7	71.9	44.1	29.2	8.7	523	515
Lee	1,249	4,093,940	7.1	9.2	4.8	4.5	2.0	3.9	68.0	116.7	37.8	58.8	1,677	1,531
Livingston	1,564	5,591,107	6.4	8.8	1.4	4.2	3.1	3.6	72.0	146.1	52.6	67.2	1,738	1,641
Logan	897	2,996,965	7.7	10.0	3.8	5.0	4.3	2.9	65.3	74.1	29.9	31.4	1,045	1,003
McDonough	1,625	5,796,187	4.2	7.7	1.7	2.8	51.0	3.4	28.6	163.5	47.6	32.0	983	944
McHenry	11,260	47,454,823	5.9	10.6	5.0	2.9	2.6	5.6	65.8	1,313.1	295.8	821.5	2,666	2,473
McLean	6,296	24,583,518	6.5	10.3	4.7	4.3	5.2	5.3	61.6	657.7	182.2	354.7	2,059	1,702
Macon	4,204	17,133,160	5.9	11.8	4.5	3.0	2.0	8.2	63.3	407.1	180.7	163.9	1,488	1,260
Macoupin	1,579	5,464,855	7.7	8.5	0.5	3.9	2.1	5.6	71.2	159.2	103.8	40.1	850	818
Madison	8,550	34,777,691	7.6	11.4	3.9	3.8	1.5	6.9	63.4	966.9	418.8	400.7	1,496	1,338
Marion	1,941	6,738,024	6.0	6.5	2.0	6.9	1.1	4.0	73.0	188.6	94.3	42.9	1,104	1,038
Marshall	389	1,147,988	11.1	7.9	0.1	5.9	0.0	3.3	70.7	32.3	9.0	19.1	1,547	1,484
Mason	923	2,905,218	5.6	6.6	1.1	4.1	31.2	2.1	49.0	70.8	24.6	21.1	1,473	1,402
Massac	642	2,312,058	4.9	5.8	3.7	5.1	27.2	5.6	47.5	66.0	26.3	12.5	822	786
Menard	629	1,816,714	5.1	6.6	0.0	3.4	18.6	6.4	58.9	48.9	20.5	18.4	1,447	1,400
Mercer	808	2,500,408	4.4	7.5	0.1	4.2	27.9	2.7	52.0	60.4	20.7	22.0	1,356	1,324
Monroe	1,183	4,219,452	6.0	6.8	0.1	3.0	9.8	5.0	68.2	102.0	27.3	50.1	1,503	1,423
Montgomery	1,039	3,506,922	6.9	10.8	2.5	5.7	5.0	6.3	61.4	82.3	39.4	28.5	963	919
Morgan	1,212	4,876,454	5.8	9.2	2.8	3.7	1.9	5.1	70.1	101.9	48.0	40.0	1,135	1,038
Moultrie	521	1,796,777	7.8	7.6	2.7	4.3	1.3	9.1	66.3	36.7	14.6	17.0	1,135	1,079
Ogle	2,397	8,623,161	5.6	8.6	3.0	3.7	0.9	6.5	71.3	242.2	66.1	126.2	2,388	2,325
Peoria	6,795	26,829,973	7.0	12.3	5.0	5.9	4.2	8.9	54.4	819.7	356.0	319.4	1,706	1,383
Perry	777	2,700,659	4.7	8.5	1.5	3.8	27.6	5.4	47.3	84.4	42.3	13.8	627	594
Piatt	763	2,418,221	6.8	10.0	0.5	5.3	14.9	3.4	57.7	66.5	26.6	26.9	1,631	1,599
Pike	558	1,854,503	4.9	7.2	0.0	8.0	4.7	8.8	66.1	46.6	23.4	15.2	932	910
Pope	138	448,003	20.0	12.1	0.0	2.4	0.2	11.1	54.2	9.3	5.8	2.3	545	536
Pulaski	327	899,884	7.1	8.9	0.0	20.1	0.0	3.3	59.6	25.7	17.3	2.4	395	366
Putnam	225	602,290	16.8	7.7	4.2	6.1	0.0	5.9	58.5	21.9	11.9	8.0	1,357	1,315
Randolph	1,307	4,546,917	4.9	6.9	0.2	2.7	38.8	4.6	41.3	133.8	44.5	27.5	833	774
Richland	975	3,144,076	4.3	4.3	0.6	2.4	0.2	3.1	84.3	57.1	27.3	13.0	807	742
Rock Island	5,596	23,551,782	5.9	9.4	3.6	6.1	4.6	7.6	61.4	620.9	245.3	250.9	1,701	1,489
St. Clair	9,810	39,541,919	4.8	9.2	1.9	2.6	2.2	3.8	73.7	1,194.0	627.0	382.0	1,421	1,216
Saline	1,108	4,428,993	4.7	6.7	0.9	2.6	0.3	6.0	77.8	90.8	50.3	23.2	930	837
Sangamon	8,380	36,468,884	5.0	9.4	3.8	4.6	1.2	19.7	56.0	774.9	316.2	329.5	1,654	1,429
Schuyler	476	1,475,450	5.3	4.7	0.2	4.4	42.6	3.1	38.9	44.3	11.9	8.0	1,069	1,046
Scott	279	678,856	8.7	3.5	0.5	4.1	18.9	5.6	57.3	16.8	8.0	4.6	873	829
Shelby	598	1,947,657	9.5	8.9	1.8	7.6	2.8	6.4	62.1	47.8	23.5	17.9	808	790
Stark	247	745,997	7.9	3.6	5.2	4.9	5.8	1.4	71.0	24.8	11.5	10.9	1,837	1,825
Stephenson	2,084	7,077,197	4.5	9.2	3.6	2.9	5.4	4.5	68.9	190.9	85.0	73.4	1,563	1,449
Tazewell	4,864	18,067,473	5.1	9.0	3.1	2.4	2.6	4.8	70.8	521.3	190.4	225.1	1,655	1,450
Union	758	2,771,148	9.5	6.1	0.8	5.1	0.0	5.2	72.8	60.0	30.9	17.9	1,015	992
Vermilion	3,642	12,242,579	7.0	7.8	2.7	3.5	3.6	4.2	67.9	289.5	151.8	91.4	1,132	940
Wabash	629	2,227,140	2.9	4.6	1.3	1.8	48.4	3.1	37.5	63.3	16.1	9.7	830	795
Warren	522	1,914,920	7.4	10.5	4.1	3.6	0.2	4.0	69.9	49.1	22.4	18.5	1,044	1,001
Washington	568	1,952,729	6.8	5.6	0.6	5.3	31.1	4.1	46.3	61.8	13.6	15.4	1,056	1,044
Wayne	680	1,956,742	7.1	7.6	1.1	3.6	2.2	8.9	66.5	46.0	28.5	12.0	724	652
White	705	2,274,585	7.3	7.6	0.6	4.7	1.6	8.1	69.3	49.9	30.9	10.9	747	707
Whiteside	3,387	13,850,341	3.2	4.6	1.2	1.9	52.6	3.0	32.7	404.5	88.0	74.4	1,287	1,222
Will	22,376	101,738,743	4.7	11.4	5.8	2.2	2.7	5.6	66.5	2,654.5	767.6	1,489.2	2,182	2,004
Williamson	2,123	8,108,041	5.1	8.0	3.0	3.7	0.5	5.2	72.9	224.1	117.2	75.8	1,137	974

1. Based on the resident population estimated as of July 1 of the year shown.

— **Local Government Finances, Government Employment, and Income Taxes**

STATE County	Local government finances, 2012 (cont.)										Government employment, 2017			Individual income tax returns, 2016		
	Direct general expenditure							Debt outstanding								
	Total (mil dol)	Per capita¹ (dollars)	Percent of total for:					Total (mil dol)	Per capita¹ (dollars)	Federal civilian	Federal military	State and local	Number of returns	Mean adjusted gross income	Mean income tax
			Education	Health and hospitals	Police protection	Public welfare	Highways								
	185	186	187	188	189	190	191	192	193	194	195	196	197	198	199

ILLINOIS— Cont'd

STATE County	185	186	187	188	189	190	191	192	193	194	195	196	197	198	199
Hardin	9.4	2,219	53.6	4.3	2.9	0.3	6.9	3.9	917	9	8	195	1,530	44,941	4,712
Henderson	23.7	3,370	36.9	8.9	3.5	0.0	12.3	3.3	465	32	14	373	3,210	46,420	4,570
Henry	218.5	4,357	39.3	20.6	5.2	2.4	5.6	98.2	1,957	117	98	3,509	23,710	58,876	7,089
Iroquois	91.6	3,132	53.4	3.1	3.5	0.1	7.9	32.1	1,098	91	55	1,579	13,510	50,830	5,455
Jackson	186.2	3,100	49.6	4.1	7.0	4.9	4.5	96.1	1,600	144	121	10,791	22,350	50,000	5,818
Jasper	35.9	3,739	55.0	4.2	2.9	0.1	13.9	9.9	1,031	36	19	581	4,610	49,501	4,715
Jefferson	141.2	3,647	60.3	0.7	5.4	0.0	6.2	65.0	1,679	133	73	2,190	16,360	49,455	5,267
Jersey	88.3	3,885	32.7	37.7	3.8	0.1	7.5	73.1	3,212	42	43	1,120	10,080	53,997	5,753
Jo Daviess	84.9	3,767	44.0	15.8	6.1	0.0	11.0	34.5	1,528	64	43	1,322	12,530	50,899	5,724
Johnson	27.3	2,141	60.1	1.3	4.1	0.1	8.6	19.6	1,535	70	22	761	4,900	49,448	4,503
Kane	2,646.1	5,064	55.1	0.4	6.5	0.1	5.6	4,427.4	8,474	1,655	1,068	30,855	245,990	72,075	9,723
Kankakee	442.3	3,912	52.1	0.7	6.1	0.1	5.9	327.2	2,894	234	213	5,901	50,220	53,026	5,575
Kendall	434.1	3,676	60.8	0.5	5.2	0.9	3.7	902.1	7,638	114	254	6,383	58,070	71,188	8,316
Knox	198.6	3,801	51.6	1.5	5.0	4.2	8.6	156.9	3,002	168	94	3,063	22,940	49,444	5,275
Lake	3,519.2	5,012	56.6	2.1	5.9	0.6	4.2	3,079.5	4,386	5,370	13,501	37,768	342,650	110,274	20,696
LaSalle	473.9	4,195	57.8	1.3	5.1	1.1	6.6	284.6	2,520	347	216	5,948	53,970	54,179	6,158
Lawrence	51.2	3,083	63.6	1.4	3.9	0.1	9.0	34.7	2,091	43	27	831	6,250	46,549	4,474
Lee	113.4	3,238	58.0	1.7	5.2	0.1	7.1	71.5	2,040	85	64	1,798	16,140	54,104	6,118
Livingston	169.3	4,381	47.9	3.0	3.8	0.2	5.0	65.3	1,689	101	68	2,107	16,940	55,858	6,379
Logan	71.3	2,376	51.1	5.0	5.4	0.1	7.6	26.9	895	95	50	1,395	12,440	51,685	5,338
McDonough	169.8	5,218	27.4	39.5	3.7	3.4	9.6	21.4	657	96	58	5,212	11,810	48,671	5,118
McHenry	1,256.5	4,078	49.3	2.2	6.5	1.2	7.2	1,209.9	3,926	495	622	14,964	154,730	73,366	9,691
McLean	663.9	3,853	46.3	1.2	4.8	1.3	5.4	781.5	4,536	456	330	14,847	76,660	70,415	9,464
Macon	452.8	4,112	52.8	2.0	7.8	0.1	8.1	462.5	4,200	319	215	5,450	47,990	56,069	6,776
Macoupin	129.5	2,741	63.8	2.0	7.1	0.2	7.8	66.0	1,397	115	90	2,277	21,030	50,725	5,080
Madison	939.6	3,507	50.9	0.8	6.8	1.6	6.8	839.9	3,135	569	534	15,930	125,220	60,101	7,308
Marion	186.5	4,794	59.6	11.4	3.2	0.2	3.5	110.6	2,844	109	75	2,117	17,490	45,501	4,325
Marshall	33.3	2,698	45.3	2.0	5.5	0.1	16.2	9.4	759	38	23	485	5,830	54,532	5,968
Mason	72.0	5,027	41.2	33.1	3.0	0.0	4.5	27.4	1,914	58	27	1,110	6,360	48,877	4,893
Massac	63.9	4,197	33.1	34.0	4.6	0.0	6.8	35.3	2,315	45	28	882	6,280	45,353	4,186
Menard	46.5	3,652	52.7	4.5	4.3	13.7	7.4	27.0	2,121	29	24	655	6,070	62,929	7,131
Mercer	59.7	3,679	42.8	21.8	3.5	0.1	6.2	15.9	978	56	31	742	7,710	54,959	5,802
Monroe	99.7	2,990	44.6	3.1	5.8	10.1	10.9	136.3	4,085	70	68	1,510	17,220	78,692	10,340
Montgomery	84.4	2,851	51.5	3.4	7.1	0.1	10.4	52.7	1,779	105	53	1,438	12,490	51,709	5,311
Morgan	103.7	2,940	52.8	1.6	5.8	3.3	9.0	36.7	1,040	77	62	1,940	15,620	52,374	5,782
Moultrie	39.7	2,658	46.1	1.8	4.8	0.0	9.9	11.4	763	30	29	512	6,720	57,601	7,197
Ogle	280.5	5,307	64.6	0.8	3.1	0.0	5.5	269.6	5,101	117	102	2,904	25,160	58,379	6,613
Peoria	776.9	4,149	41.7	1.1	6.6	3.2	6.5	850.1	4,540	1,606	410	9,235	86,190	67,447	9,339
Perry	91.6	4,151	51.3	22.3	3.7	0.2	4.4	32.0	1,453	45	38	1,292	8,760	46,671	4,161
Piatt	65.0	3,940	47.2	2.6	3.6	12.4	9.9	36.4	2,205	39	33	1,060	8,030	65,820	8,352
Pike	48.7	2,986	53.6	6.0	6.0	0.3	9.7	27.7	1,701	56	31	916	6,930	47,100	5,054
Pope	9.6	2,241	48.1	0.0	2.7	0.0	16.4	0.3	64	67	8	193	1,600	43,446	3,891
Pulaski	23.9	3,981	59.8	1.8	6.4	0.3	6.2	12.7	2,118	56	11	907	2,310	41,468	3,465
Putnam	21.7	3,688	43.8	2.5	4.8	0.3	13.3	3.0	508	13	12	328	2,960	60,436	7,007
Randolph	140.7	4,269	35.0	36.0	4.5	2.8	6.9	54.6	1,657	89	56	2,339	13,530	51,444	5,365
Richland	75.7	4,677	78.3	0.4	3.6	0.1	5.2	28.2	1,746	49	31	950	7,390	46,590	4,337
Rock Island	636.7	4,318	45.3	1.1	6.6	3.0	5.2	418.1	2,835	4,954	662	7,824	69,290	53,351	5,977
St. Clair	1,159.8	4,314	54.3	1.3	5.1	0.1	4.2	908.3	3,378	6,004	4,979	12,742	120,780	56,667	6,565
Saline	95.1	3,814	54.7	1.0	5.6	0.6	5.5	54.8	2,197	97	47	1,755	10,160	47,723	5,113
Sangamon	823.4	4,132	52.9	1.4	7.6	0.2	4.4	2,513.3	12,612	1,801	439	18,184	98,460	64,451	8,461
Schuyler	47.2	6,325	29.5	48.7	2.2	0.1	10.2	10.5	1,403	21	13	611	3,120	50,531	5,254
Scott	17.4	3,281	46.2	2.2	3.3	13.9	8.8	6.2	1,174	15	10	327	2,400	51,373	5,178
Shelby	50.5	2,273	53.6	3.0	5.5	0.1	12.8	14.9	670	93	43	822	10,160	50,212	4,842
Stark	18.9	3,183	55.8	0.5	5.0	0.5	11.8	11.4	1,922	24	11	295	2,650	52,766	5,875
Stephenson	184.9	3,937	57.2	2.4	4.7	3.3	6.3	98.3	2,092	124	89	2,717	21,990	48,456	5,031
Tazewell	547.5	4,028	52.3	1.6	5.5	0.1	6.4	349.0	2,567	501	286	7,359	63,480	62,984	7,619
Union	60.8	3,445	72.9	2.7	4.1	0.0	5.3	53.7	3,042	66	33	1,195	7,650	48,974	4,905
Vermilion	308.3	3,819	56.4	0.7	6.4	3.5	6.3	102.1	1,265	1,461	151	4,459	33,190	45,952	4,560
Wabash	60.5	5,156	29.5	47.7	4.0	0.5	5.0	14.7	1,254	23	23	1,076	5,190	55,792	6,633
Warren	53.0	2,987	53.6	0.4	5.3	0.0	6.7	45.8	2,584	71	33	932	7,850	47,988	4,778
Washington	72.8	4,985	42.5	34.2	2.5	0.1	6.1	55.0	3,766	46	28	784	6,990	57,554	6,472
Wayne	47.3	2,854	59.1	1.9	4.8	0.1	9.4	21.3	1,285	53	33	955	7,210	46,678	4,228
White	56.9	3,908	63.4	1.7	4.0	0.1	9.2	23.5	1,610	51	27	809	6,190	50,720	5,470
Whiteside	392.0	6,777	27.5	52.5	2.6	0.2	2.3	129.8	2,244	156	111	4,884	27,550	50,109	5,256
Will	2,568.4	3,763	52.2	1.6	6.9	0.8	5.1	3,781.8	5,541	1,033	1,394	33,831	332,230	72,231	9,441
Williamson	279.8	4,196	65.4	0.0	3.9	0.1	4.9	229.8	3,447	1,667	132	4,221	29,760	52,269	5,721

1. Based on the resident population estimated as of July 1 of the year shown.

Table B. States and Counties — **Land Area and Population**

State / county code	CBSA code[1]	County code[2]	STATE County	Population, 2018			Population and population characteristics, 2018										
							Race alone or in combination, not Hispanic or Latino (percent)					Age (percent)					
				Land area[3] (sq. mi)	Total persons 2018	Rank	Per square mile	White	Black	American Indian, Alaska Native	Asian and Pacific Islander	Percent Hispanic or Latino[4]	Under 5 years	5 to 17 years	18 to 24 years	25 to 34 years	35 to 44 years	45 to 54 years
				1	2	3	4	5	6	7	8	9	10	11	12	13	14	15
			ILLINOIS— Cont'd															
17201	40,420	2	Winnebago	513.2	284,081	244	553.5	70.7	14.5	0.7	3.5	13.1	6.4	17.0	8.3	12.6	11.7	12.8
17203	37,900	2	Woodford	527.8	38,463	1,214	72.9	96.4	1.2	0.5	1.1	1.9	5.7	18.3	8.3	10.6	12.3	12.4
18000		0	INDIANA	35,826.2	6,691,878	X	186.8	80.6	10.6	0.7	3.0	7.1	6.3	17.2	9.8	13.1	12.3	12.5
18001	19,540	6	Adams	339.0	35,636	1,285	105.1	94.2	1.0	0.4	0.5	4.6	9.3	22.0	8.4	11.6	10.7	10.8
18003	23,060	2	Allen	657.3	375,351	187	571.0	76.1	13.5	0.8	4.9	7.6	7.0	18.7	9.0	13.9	12.3	12.2
18005	18,020	3	Bartholomew	406.9	82,753	687	203.4	82.8	3.0	0.6	8.2	6.9	6.6	17.2	8.1	14.5	12.4	12.6
18007	29,200	3	Benton	406.4	8,653	2,535	21.3	93.4	1.4	0.6	0.5	5.2	6.4	18.4	7.5	11.0	12.1	12.7
18009		6	Blackford	165.1	11,930	2,298	72.3	96.8	1.4	0.9	0.7	1.8	5.5	16.2	7.6	11.1	10.3	13.0
18011	26,900	1	Boone	422.9	66,999	796	158.4	91.6	2.6	0.6	3.7	3.2	6.8	19.7	7.8	11.9	13.8	13.8
18013	26,900	1	Brown	312.0	15,234	2,080	48.8	96.7	1.1	1.1	0.7	1.7	3.8	14.1	6.4	9.4	10.3	14.2
18015	29,200	3	Carroll	372.2	20,127	1,817	54.1	94.9	1.1	0.5	0.3	4.1	5.4	16.7	7.5	11.0	11.6	13.1
18017	30,900	4	Cass	412.2	37,955	1,227	92.1	80.1	2.2	0.7	2.2	15.9	6.3	16.8	8.2	11.4	12.3	13.2
18019	31,140	1	Clark	372.8	117,360	529	314.8	85.1	9.5	0.7	1.6	5.5	6.2	16.3	7.7	13.8	13.3	13.4
18021	45,460	3	Clay	357.6	26,170	1,559	73.2	97.2	1.3	0.7	0.6	1.4	6.2	16.8	7.4	12.2	12.0	12.8
18023	23,140	6	Clinton	405.1	32,250	1,374	79.6	82.3	1.0	0.5	0.5	16.4	7.0	19.2	7.9	12.3	11.6	12.1
18025		8	Crawford	305.6	10,558	2,388	34.5	97.2	1.1	1.1	0.5	1.4	5.3	16.2	7.0	10.8	11.3	13.5
18027	47,780	7	Daviess	429.5	33,147	1,355	77.2	92.3	2.7	0.5	0.6	4.9	8.1	21.2	8.3	12.6	11.3	10.9
18029	17,140	1	Dearborn	305.1	49,568	996	162.5	97.3	1.2	0.6	0.7	1.3	5.3	17.0	7.7	11.1	11.9	14.2
18031	24,700	6	Decatur	372.6	26,794	1,533	71.9	95.8	1.0	0.5	1.5	2.1	6.7	17.8	8.0	12.3	11.9	12.8
18033	12,140	4	DeKalb	362.8	43,226	1,109	119.1	96.0	0.9	0.5	0.8	2.8	6.5	17.7	8.3	12.6	11.9	13.0
18035	34,620	3	Delaware	392.1	114,772	538	292.7	88.7	8.3	0.7	2.0	2.6	4.9	13.4	19.6	11.5	10.0	11.4
18037	27,540	5	Dubois	427.3	42,565	1,126	99.6	90.7	0.9	0.3	0.8	7.8	6.7	17.5	8.1	11.2	11.6	12.9
18039	21,140	3	Elkhart	463.2	205,560	327	443.8	76.6	7.0	0.7	1.6	16.3	7.5	20.0	8.9	12.8	12.1	12.2
18041	18,220	6	Fayette	215.0	23,047	1,678	107.2	96.7	2.0	0.7	0.5	1.3	5.1	16.5	7.5	11.1	12.3	13.3
18043	31,140	1	Floyd	148.0	77,781	716	525.5	89.8	6.8	0.7	1.6	3.4	6.0	16.7	8.3	12.8	12.5	13.4
18045		6	Fountain	395.7	16,351	2,019	41.3	96.2	0.9	0.9	0.6	2.6	5.5	16.3	7.9	11.2	11.2	13.4
18047		6	Franklin	384.4	22,736	1,692	59.1	97.2	0.7	0.6	1.3	1.2	5.9	17.1	7.8	10.5	11.7	13.8
18049		7	Fulton	368.4	20,092	1,820	54.5	92.9	1.4	0.9	0.8	5.3	6.2	17.2	7.8	11.2	11.7	12.1
18051		6	Gibson	487.4	33,452	1,341	68.6	95.5	3.2	0.7	0.8	1.7	6.3	17.2	7.9	11.9	11.9	13.0
18053	31,980	4	Grant	414.1	65,936	809	159.2	87.2	8.6	0.8	1.4	4.4	5.4	15.3	12.8	10.9	10.4	12.0
18055		6	Greene	542.5	32,006	1,380	59.0	97.5	0.6	0.8	0.6	1.5	5.2	16.7	7.2	11.1	11.5	14.0
18057	26,900	1	Hamilton	394.3	330,086	211	837.1	85.2	5.1	0.4	7.2	4.1	6.6	20.4	7.7	11.9	14.8	14.6
18059	26,900	1	Hancock	306.0	76,351	730	249.5	93.6	3.4	0.7	1.3	2.4	5.8	17.6	7.7	11.9	13.0	14.0
18061	31,140	1	Harrison	484.5	40,350	1,174	83.3	96.6	1.2	0.7	0.8	2.0	5.9	16.6	7.1	11.6	12.5	13.6
18063	26,900	1	Hendricks	406.9	167,009	392	410.4	85.6	8.2	0.5	3.6	4.0	5.9	19.2	8.0	12.5	14.4	13.8
18065	35,220	4	Henry	391.9	48,271	1,018	123.2	94.7	3.3	0.6	0.7	1.9	5.0	15.5	8.1	12.3	12.1	13.8
18067	29,020	3	Howard	293.0	82,366	689	281.1	87.4	9.1	0.9	1.7	3.5	6.0	16.6	8.0	12.0	11.3	12.6
18069	26,540	6	Huntington	382.6	36,240	1,271	94.7	95.6	1.2	0.9	0.9	2.6	5.7	15.9	9.8	12.1	11.7	12.6
18071	42,980	4	Jackson	510.0	44,111	1,094	86.5	89.1	1.6	0.7	2.7	7.2	6.9	17.7	7.6	12.2	12.9	13.2
18073	16,980	1	Jasper	559.6	33,370	1,346	59.6	92.4	1.2	0.6	0.7	6.1	5.7	17.5	9.6	10.9	12.2	12.5
18075		6	Jay	383.9	20,764	1,786	54.1	95.7	0.8	0.6	0.7	3.2	7.2	18.3	8.1	10.9	11.0	13.2
18077	31,500	6	Jefferson	360.6	32,208	1,375	89.3	94.1	2.7	0.7	1.1	2.9	5.7	14.7	10.2	11.8	11.9	13.2
18079	35,860	6	Jennings	376.6	27,611	1,507	73.3	96.0	1.3	0.8	0.5	2.6	6.0	17.1	8.2	12.0	11.6	14.6
18081	26,900	1	Johnson	320.4	156,225	424	487.6	90.3	3.1	0.6	4.1	3.6	6.5	18.2	8.4	13.5	13.5	13.1
18083	47,180	5	Knox	516.0	36,895	1,253	71.5	93.7	3.6	0.7	1.2	2.2	6.0	15.5	12.7	11.6	10.9	11.6
18085	47,700	4	Kosciusko	531.4	79,344	706	149.3	89.1	1.6	0.6	1.9	8.1	6.5	17.3	9.0	12.9	11.5	12.2
18087		6	LaGrange	379.6	39,330	1,195	103.6	94.7	0.7	0.5	0.7	4.1	8.9	23.6	9.2	11.9	10.9	10.9
18089	16,980	1	Lake	498.8	484,411	144	971.2	55.3	24.3	0.6	2.0	19.4	5.9	17.4	8.7	12.3	12.7	12.7
18091	33,140	3	LaPorte	598.3	110,007	553	183.9	80.9	12.6	0.7	1.0	6.8	6.0	15.5	8.2	13.3	12.1	13.1
18093	13,260	6	Lawrence	449.2	45,668	1,058	101.7	96.6	0.9	1.0	1.0	1.7	5.6	16.2	7.5	11.1	11.7	13.5
18095	26,900	1	Madison	451.9	129,641	493	286.9	86.6	9.6	0.7	1.0	4.1	5.6	16.0	8.4	12.7	12.2	13.4
18097	26,900	1	Marion	396.4	954,670	51	2,408.4	57.2	30.0	0.7	4.2	10.6	7.2	17.4	9.2	16.9	12.9	11.7
18099	38,500	6	Marshall	443.6	46,248	1,045	104.3	88.1	1.2	0.7	0.9	10.4	6.3	18.7	8.3	10.9	11.6	12.6
18101		7	Martin	335.8	10,217	2,410	30.4	97.9	0.7	0.7	0.6	1.1	6.0	16.3	7.4	11.0	11.3	12.9
18103	37,940	6	Miami	373.8	35,567	1,288	95.1	90.5	5.9	1.6	0.8	3.3	5.2	15.9	8.3	13.2	13.1	13.4
18105	14,020	3	Monroe	394.5	146,917	448	372.4	85.7	4.5	0.7	8.1	3.5	4.4	11.2	26.3	14.3	10.7	9.6
18107	18,820	6	Montgomery	504.6	38,346	1,217	76.0	92.9	1.6	0.7	1.1	5.0	5.9	17.0	9.2	11.8	11.1	12.9
18109	26,900	1	Morgan	403.8	70,116	771	173.6	97.0	0.9	0.7	0.9	1.6	5.7	16.9	7.8	11.3	11.7	14.5
18111	16,980	1	Newton	401.8	14,011	2,161	34.9	91.9	1.1	0.8	0.7	6.4	5.3	15.7	7.2	11.5	11.9	12.9
18113	28,340	6	Noble	410.8	47,532	1,026	115.7	87.8	1.3	0.6	0.8	10.5	6.5	18.0	8.6	12.2	12.0	12.9
18115	17,140	1	Ohio	86.2	5,844	2,762	67.8	97.4	1.0	0.6	0.6	1.5	4.6	14.4	6.2	10.9	10.6	13.6
18117		6	Orange	398.4	19,489	1,850	48.9	96.0	1.9	0.9	0.6	1.8	5.9	16.8	7.8	10.9	11.3	12.7
18119	14,020	3	Owen	385.3	20,845	1,781	54.1	97.1	0.9	0.9	0.9	1.5	5.2	15.9	7.5	10.8	11.0	14.0
18121		6	Parke	444.7	16,927	1,979	38.1	95.1	3.0	0.7	0.3	1.6	6.0	15.5	7.7	12.9	11.3	12.7
18123		6	Perry	381.7	19,102	1,868	50.0	94.9	3.3	0.6	0.7	1.4	5.4	16.5	7.8	13.1	12.3	12.5

1. CBSA = Core Based Statistical Area. See Appendix A for explanation. See Appendix B for list of metropolitan areas with component counties.   2. County type code from the Economic Research Service of USDA Rural-Urban Continuum Codes. See Appendix A for definition.   3. Dry land or land partially or temporarily covered by water.   4. May be of any race.

Table B. States and Counties — **Population and Households**

STATE County	Population, 2018 (cont.) Age (percent) (cont.) 55 to 64 years	65 to 74 years	75 years and over	Percent female	Population change, 2000-2018 Total persons 2000	2010	Percent change 2000-2010	2010-2018	Components of change, 2010-2018 Births	Deaths	Net Migration	Households, 2013-2017 Number	Persons per household	Percent Family house-holds	Female family house-holder[1]	One person
	16	17	18	19	20	21	22	23	24	25	26	27	28	29	30	31
ILLINOIS— Cont'd																
Winnebago	13.7	10.1	7.5	51.2	278,418	295,264	6.1	-3.8	29,914	23,109	-18,180	114,491	2.47	65.1	14.0	29.7
Woodford	14.2	9.9	8.2	50.1	35,469	38,664	9.0	-0.5	3,528	3,101	-618	14,547	2.60	73.3	8.1	24.0
INDIANA	13.0	9.2	6.6	50.7	6,080,485	6,484,061	6.6	3.2	685,293	500,513	25,243	2,537,189	2.53	65.6	12.1	28.3
Adams	11.6	8.4	7.1	50.0	33,625	34,387	2.3	3.6	5,534	2,500	-1,793	12,453	2.77	69.0	11.1	25.9
Allen	12.4	8.6	5.9	51.1	331,849	355,335	7.1	5.6	42,781	25,234	2,769	142,696	2.54	64.9	13.1	29.4
Bartholomew	12.4	9.4	6.9	49.7	71,435	76,786	7.5	7.8	8,710	6,016	3,303	31,472	2.54	66.8	10.5	27.5
Benton	14.1	9.8	8.0	50.4	9,421	8,836	-6.2	-2.1	875	694	-367	3,397	2.52	65.6	8.8	29.2
Blackford	14.6	12.0	9.7	50.6	14,048	12,766	-9.1	-6.5	1,116	1,273	-685	5,199	2.32	66.8	12.1	28.9
Boone	12.8	8.0	5.4	50.3	46,107	56,638	22.8	18.3	6,292	4,070	8,079	24,228	2.57	72.7	8.6	23.1
Brown	17.7	15.3	8.8	50.7	14,957	15,245	1.9	-0.1	931	1,270	334	6,011	2.47	71.8	7.9	22.5
Carroll	15.1	11.5	8.2	49.7	20,165	20,155	0.0	-0.1	1,762	1,493	-294	7,819	2.54	70.3	7.4	24.1
Cass	14.0	9.9	7.9	50.1	40,930	38,966	-4.8	-2.6	4,038	3,254	-1,816	14,840	2.50	65.1	10.3	31.1
Clark	13.5	9.7	6.1	51.2	96,472	110,228	14.3	6.5	12,005	9,427	4,568	43,657	2.59	64.3	11.8	30.2
Clay	14.6	10.3	7.6	50.6	26,556	26,884	1.2	-2.7	2,591	2,474	-825	10,680	2.43	70.4	10.5	24.9
Clinton	13.2	9.1	7.6	50.3	33,866	33,219	-1.9	-2.9	3,672	2,929	-1,729	11,961	2.66	70.0	10.1	25.0
Crawford	16.3	12.2	7.4	49.1	10,743	10,713	-0.3	-1.4	917	954	-117	4,007	2.62	67.6	9.4	27.7
Daviess	12.2	8.7	6.6	49.6	29,820	31,654	6.2	4.7	4,369	2,758	-99	11,482	2.80	71.6	8.2	25.5
Dearborn	15.0	10.8	7.0	50.3	46,109	50,033	8.5	-0.9	4,250	3,763	-934	18,667	2.62	71.6	8.5	24.3
Decatur	13.9	9.6	7.1	50.3	24,555	25,739	4.8	4.1	2,844	2,165	398	10,354	2.52	68.1	8.4	26.5
DeKalb	13.7	9.6	6.6	50.4	40,285	42,229	4.8	2.4	4,380	3,325	-33	16,317	2.58	68.0	11.3	27.8
Delaware	12.0	9.5	7.6	51.7	118,769	117,664	-0.9	-2.5	10,028	9,998	-2,889	46,304	2.35	59.4	12.6	30.1
Dubois	14.7	9.7	7.8	50.0	39,674	41,888	5.6	1.6	4,485	3,302	-490	16,524	2.51	68.2	6.8	26.8
Elkhart	11.8	8.4	6.3	50.6	182,791	197,559	8.1	4.0	25,296	13,544	-3,676	71,733	2.78	71.9	12.7	22.5
Fayette	13.9	11.8	8.6	50.6	25,588	24,301	-5.0	-5.2	1,938	2,552	-629	9,410	2.44	69.0	14.0	24.5
Floyd	14.3	9.8	6.4	51.4	70,823	74,579	5.3	4.3	7,369	6,103	1,980	29,046	2.59	67.8	12.2	27.8
Fountain	14.5	11.0	9.1	50.1	17,954	17,240	-4.0	-5.2	1,516	1,642	-764	6,987	2.35	65.9	10.4	27.2
Franklin	14.8	10.8	7.6	50.0	22,151	23,096	4.3	-1.6	2,037	1,747	-651	8,843	2.56	76.9	9.1	20.4
Fulton	14.3	11.1	8.4	50.0	20,511	20,853	1.7	-3.6	2,051	1,948	-860	7,934	2.53	63.2	6.5	31.5
Gibson	14.2	9.8	7.7	50.0	32,500	33,503	3.1	-0.2	3,413	2,968	-473	13,336	2.46	69.6	10.7	25.4
Grant	14.0	10.6	8.6	52.1	73,403	70,063	-4.6	-5.9	6,095	6,715	-3,507	26,122	2.39	65.6	14.2	29.6
Greene	14.8	11.1	8.4	49.9	33,157	33,172	0.0	-3.5	2,761	3,172	-741	12,653	2.54	66.9	7.7	28.3
Hamilton	11.7	7.6	4.8	51.1	182,740	274,569	50.3	20.2	31,716	12,634	36,188	114,282	2.70	73.3	8.3	21.9
Hancock	13.7	9.8	6.5	50.8	55,391	70,043	26.5	9.0	6,420	5,113	5,036	27,576	2.62	72.7	9.1	22.3
Harrison	15.0	10.7	7.0	50.0	34,325	39,363	14.7	2.5	3,556	3,163	613	14,693	2.66	71.0	9.3	24.1
Hendricks	12.4	8.4	5.5	50.0	104,093	145,414	39.7	14.9	14,424	8,706	15,868	57,153	2.72	73.9	9.7	21.7
Henry	14.2	10.7	8.2	48.0	48,508	49,466	2.0	-2.4	3,893	4,695	-364	18,096	2.50	66.4	11.6	26.9
Howard	14.0	11.0	8.5	51.5	84,964	82,752	-2.6	-0.5	8,151	7,894	-584	34,538	2.36	64.2	12.7	31.3
Huntington	15.1	9.6	7.6	50.7	38,075	37,123	-2.5	-2.4	3,467	3,373	-966	14,616	2.40	69.1	8.3	25.7
Jackson	13.2	9.4	7.0	50.2	41,335	42,376	2.5	4.1	4,869	3,750	634	16,549	2.60	70.7	10.2	25.2
Jasper	14.1	10.3	7.3	50.3	30,043	33,481	11.4	-0.3	3,182	2,664	-619	12,220	2.66	71.5	9.4	24.5
Jay	13.4	10.4	7.5	50.2	21,806	21,253	-2.5	-2.3	2,465	1,912	-1,043	8,195	2.54	65.7	10.4	29.0
Jefferson	14.6	10.8	7.2	51.9	31,705	32,404	2.2	-0.6	3,022	3,039	-159	12,677	2.34	69.1	12.8	26.5
Jennings	14.1	10.0	6.5	49.9	27,554	28,529	3.5	-3.2	2,737	2,400	-1,256	10,753	2.56	67.2	11.5	27.5
Johnson	12.2	8.5	6.1	50.6	115,209	139,857	21.4	11.7	15,281	10,272	11,406	54,867	2.68	72.8	11.2	22.2
Knox	13.8	10.0	7.8	49.4	39,256	38,440	-2.1	-4.0	3,804	3,638	-1,706	14,986	2.36	65.0	12.7	29.5
Kosciusko	13.7	9.8	6.9	50.0	74,057	77,354	4.5	2.6	8,430	5,703	-680	30,265	2.55	71.5	10.3	22.3
LaGrange	11.0	8.0	5.6	49.2	34,909	37,130	6.4	5.9	6,101	2,150	-1,751	12,064	3.18	79.6	7.7	16.5
Lake	13.8	9.5	7.0	51.6	484,564	496,095	2.4	-2.4	48,764	39,279	-21,166	185,524	2.60	66.6	16.7	28.7
LaPorte	14.0	10.7	7.2	48.5	110,106	111,463	1.2	-1.3	10,803	9,750	-2,441	42,975	2.38	65.5	12.7	27.7
Lawrence	14.4	11.5	8.5	50.5	45,922	46,129	0.5	-1.0	3,994	4,529	119	18,432	2.44	71.3	10.9	24.7
Madison	13.4	10.6	7.7	50.0	133,358	131,639	-1.3	-1.5	12,388	12,215	-2,098	51,647	2.39	65.6	13.0	29.0
Marion	12.0	7.5	5.1	51.8	860,454	903,389	5.0	5.7	118,528	64,726	-1,902	367,215	2.51	56.3	15.7	36.0
Marshall	13.7	9.9	7.9	50.2	45,128	47,050	4.3	-1.7	4,785	3,778	-1,810	17,249	2.67	69.7	10.1	25.7
Martin	15.3	11.6	8.3	49.3	10,369	10,380	0.1	-1.6	1,042	870	-332	4,251	2.35	65.5	8.8	30.1
Miami	13.4	10.4	7.3	46.2	36,082	36,905	2.3	-3.6	2,975	2,998	-1,325	13,465	2.51	68.9	11.5	27.3
Monroe	10.4	7.7	5.4	50.3	120,563	137,959	14.4	6.5	10,734	7,479	5,743	55,014	2.35	51.9	9.8	32.6
Montgomery	14.2	9.7	8.2	49.3	37,629	38,121	1.3	0.6	3,777	3,197	-334	14,993	2.47	68.4	8.4	26.2
Morgan	15.1	10.3	6.6	50.3	66,689	68,943	3.4	1.7	6,366	5,365	231	25,805	2.66	71.5	10.2	22.8
Newton	16.0	10.9	8.6	49.5	14,566	14,239	-2.2	-1.6	1,181	1,273	-129	5,530	2.50	70.4	11.1	25.0
Noble	13.9	9.9	6.1	49.9	46,275	47,540	2.7	0.0	4,920	3,658	-1,256	18,205	2.56	71.2	10.3	25.5
Ohio	17.6	12.7	9.3	50.5	5,623	6,107	8.6	-4.3	432	513	-182	2,479	2.36	69.9	6.1	26.5
Orange	15.0	11.5	8.0	50.1	19,306	19,838	2.8	-1.8	1,886	1,843	-391	7,830	2.47	66.2	10.7	28.6
Owen	16.4	11.9	7.3	50.0	21,786	21,577	-1.0	-3.4	1,813	1,934	-611	8,551	2.43	69.6	9.2	25.7
Parke	14.5	11.7	7.7	52.7	17,241	17,354	0.7	-2.5	1,636	1,356	-720	6,112	2.55	70.5	9.1	23.5
Perry	14.4	11.0	7.8	46.4	18,899	19,338	2.3	-1.2	1,673	1,672	-231	7,460	2.35	67.4	10.9	28.2

1. No spouse present.

Table B. States and Counties — Population, Vital Statistics, Health, and Crime

STATE County	Persons in group quarters, 2018	Daytime Population, 2013-2017		Births, 2018		Deaths, 2018		Persons under 65 with no health insurance, 2016		Medicare, 2018			Serious crimes known to police[2], 2016 Total	
		Number	Employment/ residence ratio	Total	Rate[1]	Number	Rate[1]	Number	Percent	Total beneficiaries	Enrolled in Original Medicare	Enrolled in Medicare Advantage	Number	Rate[3]
	32	33	34	35	36	37	38	39	40	41	42	43	44	45
ILLINOIS— Cont'd														
Winnebago	4,743	291,208	1.03	3,559	12.5	2,781	9.8	15,892	6.7	57,697	37,887	19,810	11,052	3,939
Woodford	1,005	31,916	0.62	384	10.0	402	10.5	1,373	4.3	7,567	5,939	1,628	261	808
INDIANA	187,652	6,560,475	0.98	81,075	12.1	61,864	9.2	518,435	9.5	1,232,868	869,783	363,085	198,604	2,994
Adams	421	34,061	0.93	668	18.7	259	7.3	3,671	12.4	5,919	3,905	2,014	NA	NA
Allen	6,110	379,981	1.07	5,054	13.5	3,135	8.4	29,398	9.3	64,769	33,778	30,991	11,396	3,078
Bartholomew	1,148	90,574	1.24	1,044	12.6	723	8.7	6,720	9.8	15,344	12,269	3,075	2,578	3,148
Benton	92	7,427	0.68	112	12.9	79	9.1	834	11.7	1,850	1,527	323	NA	NA
Blackford	163	10,906	0.75	128	10.7	162	13.6	947	10.0	3,117	2,313	804	118	980
Boone	574	55,948	0.78	841	12.6	467	7.0	3,587	6.4	10,428	7,470	2,958	NA	NA
Brown	163	11,291	0.44	107	7.0	151	9.9	1,220	10.6	3,990	2,779	1,211	284	1,906
Carroll	106	16,359	0.61	210	10.4	192	9.5	1,618	10.0	4,339	3,280	1,059	NA	NA
Cass	1,047	36,405	0.89	466	12.3	409	10.8	3,678	11.9	7,926	5,916	2,010	682	1,809
Clark	1,326	109,684	0.91	1,432	12.2	1,184	10.1	8,332	8.5	22,847	17,109	5,738	3,805	3,277
Clay	341	21,974	0.63	299	11.4	286	10.9	2,019	9.4	5,789	4,655	1,134	NA	NA
Clinton	831	29,502	0.80	440	13.6	321	10.0	2,862	10.7	6,326	4,723	1,603	769	2,372
Crawford	62	8,455	0.49	98	9.3	120	11.4	908	10.6	2,525	2,047	478	144	1,383
Daviess	581	30,856	0.86	522	15.7	333	10.0	4,865	17.5	5,504	4,904	600	598	1,808
Dearborn	530	40,875	0.64	497	10.0	457	9.2	3,214	7.8	10,538	7,840	2,698	NA	NA
Decatur	377	29,491	1.23	366	13.7	276	10.3	1,913	8.6	5,413	4,112	1,301	NA	NA
DeKalb	615	43,960	1.07	533	12.3	412	9.5	3,185	8.9	8,527	4,555	3,972	530	1,245
Delaware	8,885	116,823	1.02	1,139	9.9	1,187	10.3	8,520	9.6	23,528	17,543	5,985	3,732	3,205
Dubois	894	48,083	1.26	559	13.1	406	9.5	3,038	8.6	8,621	7,698	923	NA	NA
Elkhart	3,669	230,470	1.30	3,054	14.9	1,665	8.1	25,222	14.7	33,882	23,499	10,383	NA	NA
Fayette	392	20,820	0.73	210	9.1	285	12.4	1,857	10.0	6,225	5,207	1,018	NA	NA
Floyd	1,330	69,489	0.81	889	11.4	754	9.7	4,683	7.3	15,509	11,925	3,584	1,642	2,226
Fountain	172	15,086	0.79	162	9.9	183	11.2	1,231	9.4	3,980	3,160	820	NA	NA
Franklin	187	17,028	0.46	250	11.0	210	9.2	1,707	9.0	5,483	4,075	1,408	190	834
Fulton	224	18,147	0.77	231	11.5	207	10.3	1,963	12.1	4,604	2,981	1,623	NA	NA
Gibson	738	38,942	1.33	405	12.1	383	11.4	1,945	7.1	6,763	4,842	1,921	NA	NA
Grant	4,826	69,521	1.07	657	10.0	807	12.2	4,879	9.8	15,638	11,493	4,145	1,756	2,603
Greene	281	26,313	0.57	309	9.7	417	13.0	2,540	9.8	7,157	5,897	1,260	451	1,625
Hamilton	1,868	288,271	0.87	3,791	11.5	1,801	5.5	14,924	5.3	44,165	31,161	13,004	NA	NA
Hancock	649	59,117	0.63	788	10.3	620	8.1	4,261	6.9	14,743	9,597	5,146	958	1,315
Harrison	461	33,120	0.64	443	11.0	361	8.9	2,976	9.1	8,392	6,673	1,719	NA	NA
Hendricks	4,053	140,929	0.79	1,740	10.4	1,104	6.6	9,146	6.7	25,609	17,129	8,480	2,360	1,471
Henry	3,556	42,675	0.70	456	9.4	550	11.4	3,111	8.6	11,217	7,523	3,694	NA	NA
Howard	1,281	86,883	1.12	969	11.8	940	11.4	5,775	8.7	19,405	13,952	5,453	2,565	3,157
Huntington	1,339	33,920	0.86	408	11.3	386	10.7	2,612	8.9	7,998	4,180	3,818	NA	NA
Jackson	595	46,133	1.12	610	13.8	448	10.2	3,687	10.1	8,737	6,142	2,595	1,288	2,909
Jasper	932	31,803	0.89	373	11.2	332	9.9	2,435	9.0	6,924	5,549	1,375	NA	NA
Jay	243	20,414	0.92	272	13.1	232	11.2	1,691	9.8	4,490	3,319	1,171	161	853
Jefferson	2,067	31,547	0.95	373	11.6	347	10.8	2,371	9.5	7,293	5,882	1,411	NA	NA
Jennings	298	24,159	0.71	305	11.0	305	11.0	2,186	9.4	5,913	4,404	1,509	593	2,139
Johnson	2,446	128,508	0.72	1,881	12.0	1,273	8.1	10,013	7.8	26,927	18,700	8,227	4,678	3,120
Knox	2,119	39,258	1.08	444	12.0	397	10.8	2,635	9.1	7,954	6,943	1,011	1,062	3,046
Kosciusko	1,575	79,235	1.01	1,005	12.7	709	8.9	7,497	11.5	15,117	8,684	6,433	1,171	1,588
LaGrange	325	37,443	0.92	712	18.1	262	6.7	7,422	22.0	5,603	3,647	1,956	196	502
Lake	6,417	472,239	0.92	5,422	11.2	5,015	10.4	34,921	8.6	91,736	65,653	26,083	15,238	3,352
LaPorte	6,347	106,918	0.92	1,252	11.4	1,225	11.1	8,090	9.5	22,671	18,170	4,501	3,106	2,893
Lawrence	653	40,262	0.73	485	10.6	555	12.2	3,227	8.9	10,533	8,100	2,433	724	1,764
Madison	6,175	118,230	0.79	1,452	11.2	1,445	11.1	9,612	9.5	28,862	17,763	11,099	3,378	2,668
Marion	16,470	1,066,462	1.28	14,009	14.7	8,190	8.6	86,091	10.6	143,225	94,271	48,954	55,553	5,884
Marshall	671	46,011	0.96	560	12.1	477	10.3	5,224	13.6	9,215	5,751	3,464	NA	NA
Martin	133	13,714	1.72	115	11.3	101	9.9	768	9.3	2,310	2,054	256	NA	NA
Miami	3,315	31,833	0.72	325	9.1	368	10.3	2,502	9.4	6,925	5,246	1,679	715	2,008
Monroe	15,007	153,261	1.13	1,268	8.6	937	6.4	10,522	9.2	20,917	16,470	4,447	4,366	2,997
Montgomery	1,176	36,869	0.92	451	11.8	385	10.0	3,257	10.7	7,879	5,497	2,382	NA	NA
Morgan	590	55,063	0.56	776	11.1	659	9.4	5,097	8.8	14,720	10,073	4,647	NA	NA
Newton	169	11,193	0.54	141	10.1	136	9.7	1,320	11.7	2,872	2,303	569	94	675
Noble	813	45,421	0.91	576	12.1	444	9.3	4,264	10.7	8,980	4,957	4,023	646	1,355
Ohio	52	4,548	0.54	49	8.4	73	12.5	371	7.9	1,304	968	336	NA	NA
Orange	258	19,103	0.94	223	11.4	230	11.8	1,596	10.3	4,599	3,637	962	NA	NA
Owen	197	17,675	0.65	203	9.7	258	12.4	1,851	11.0	4,822	3,608	1,214	NA	NA
Parke	1,556	14,683	0.64	195	11.5	176	10.4	1,532	12.5	3,524	2,756	768	NA	NA
Perry	1,514	18,207	0.87	199	10.4	180	9.4	1,210	8.4	4,081	3,516	565	NA	NA

1. Per 1,000 estimated resident population.   2. Data for serious crimes have not been adjusted for underreporting; this may affect comparability between geographic areas and over time.   3. Per 100,000 population estimated by the FBI.

Table B. States and Counties — **Crime, Education, Money Income, and Poverty**

STATE County	Serious crimes known to police[2], 2016 (cont.)[1] Rate — Violent	Property	Enrollment[3] Total	Percent private	High school graduate or less	Bachelor's degree or more	Total current spending (mil dol)	Current spending per student (dollars)	Per capita income[6]	Median income (dollars)	Percent with income of less than $50,000	Percent with income of $200,000 or more	Median household income (dollars)	All persons	Children under 18 years	Children 5 to 17 years in families
	46	47	48	49	50	51	52	53	54	55	56	57	58	59	60	61
ILLINOIS— Cont'd																
Winnebago	1,012	2,926	71,329	19.0	44.7	22.4	613.7	13,395	27,297	51,110	48.7	3.0	53,490	14.2	21.4	19.6
Woodford	68	740	10,401	15.6	38.7	31.1	87.5	11,075	34,198	69,507	33.7	5.7	75,733	5.8	7.7	6.9
INDIANA	405	2,589	1,697,392	16.4	45.4	25.3	10,061.7	9,619	27,305	52,182	47.8	3.4	54,134	13.3	17.8	16.3
Adams	NA	NA	8,574	26.2	57.0	14.9	44.7	10,400	21,534	48,290	51.7	2.1	51,488	15.4	24.8	23.8
Allen	334	2,744	98,348	23.1	39.8	27.5	520.8	9,588	26,932	51,091	48.7	3.2	52,661	13.1	19.0	17.2
Bartholomew	82	3,067	19,232	14.2	43.3	31.2	119.0	9,613	29,955	57,331	42.9	3.8	61,943	10.6	14.7	13.9
Benton	NA	NA	2,024	14.3	54.9	16.8	18.7	9,919	23,652	49,183	50.7	1.0	52,841	11.2	17.0	15.8
Blackford	58	922	2,568	7.7	62.2	11.1	16.8	8,815	22,328	40,622	60.0	0.8	42,636	14.3	22.3	20.5
Boone	NA	NA	16,513	13.7	29.7	47.2	110.3	9,409	42,844	75,591	32.6	11.9	82,670	5.7	5.9	5.3
Brown	309	1,597	3,105	9.8	44.7	25.5	23.9	11,078	31,365	59,292	40.8	2.8	56,979	10.9	16.5	15.2
Carroll	NA	NA	4,472	12.6	53.0	16.2	23.4	8,822	26,589	56,188	45.4	2.1	55,471	9.6	12.6	11.5
Cass	45	1,764	9,175	9.2	56.3	13.4	64.8	9,945	23,592	45,558	54.5	1.4	47,727	13.8	19.4	18.4
Clark	320	2,957	26,921	15.6	46.3	20.0	159.9	9,228	26,875	52,834	47.2	2.4	52,746	10.6	15.7	14.0
Clay	NA	NA	6,009	10.8	53.9	16.6	41.0	9,674	24,339	50,924	48.7	1.3	50,746	11.2	18.1	16.3
Clinton	102	2,270	7,758	11.1	58.4	15.7	57.1	9,105	23,722	51,659	48.4	1.7	51,540	13.4	19.2	16.5
Crawford	240	1,143	2,321	4.4	65.5	10.4	16.1	9,404	19,424	40,067	59.3	0.2	42,555	16.2	25.9	23.4
Daviess	136	1,672	7,265	23.6	60.2	14.2	42.8	9,670	21,794	48,355	51.3	2.0	46,292	13.4	18.9	17.7
Dearborn	NA	NA	11,968	13.0	49.2	21.7	74.9	8,719	30,228	62,905	38.4	4.2	65,005	9.7	12.6	11.2
Decatur	NA	NA	6,121	15.1	54.2	19.7	40.4	9,100	25,548	52,270	46.5	2.2	55,808	11.1	15.6	14.3
DeKalb	66	1,180	10,776	13.9	50.9	17.8	86.7	11,873	26,057	51,374	48.5	2.4	54,289	10.4	14.1	12.2
Delaware	261	2,944	35,609	6.6	45.5	23.9	155.8	10,048	23,271	41,208	58.1	2.3	41,874	20.6	22.2	20.7
Dubois	NA	NA	9,875	11.2	50.1	21.4	69.1	9,650	28,302	57,307	42.3	2.5	63,033	8.3	8.9	8.5
Elkhart	NA	NA	50,826	14.0	55.1	18.7	351.3	9,633	23,817	52,449	47.3	2.6	58,781	10.8	14.9	12.8
Fayette	NA	NA	5,072	8.2	61.5	11.1	39.9	10,491	22,428	41,476	58.3	1.6	44,970	15.5	21.6	19.0
Floyd	107	2,119	18,907	17.7	41.5	28.4	113.3	9,639	30,663	59,451	42.4	4.5	61,009	10.5	14.3	12.8
Fountain	NA	NA	3,620	8.8	54.6	14.4	26.1	8,979	25,383	46,669	53.0	1.5	50,817	12.9	18.2	16.7
Franklin	39	794	5,272	18.4	55.2	19.7	44.0	9,197	26,267	55,588	44.3	1.8	62,467	9.4	12.2	11.2
Fulton	NA	NA	4,438	11.3	55.3	12.8	23.7	9,183	23,557	47,108	54.0	0.7	51,088	12.2	17.8	17.3
Gibson	NA	NA	7,858	17.1	49.8	16.8	46.6	9,376	27,342	51,149	48.7	2.8	53,714	10.4	13.0	11.6
Grant	251	2,353	17,957	33.5	53.8	17.1	109.4	10,038	21,024	42,046	58.0	1.0	44,790	18.4	27.3	26.9
Greene	43	1,582	6,919	11.3	53.7	14.5	49.0	9,414	24,744	49,648	50.4	2.0	59,347	11.6	18.8	17.1
Hamilton	NA	NA	87,557	17.4	19.0	57.5	505.3	8,735	44,443	90,582	24.3	13.4	95,080	3.8	4.1	3.6
Hancock	150	1,166	17,868	14.9	38.6	30.1	106.6	8,863	31,428	70,973	34.3	4.3	73,294	5.5	6.8	6.1
Harrison	NA	NA	8,379	10.2	53.1	16.6	56.5	9,391	25,993	53,897	47.2	2.5	57,136	9.4	13.0	12.0
Hendricks	144	1,327	41,862	15.7	34.1	35.3	241.0	8,459	33,031	74,245	30.5	4.9	75,647	5.1	5.8	5.2
Henry	NA	NA	10,364	7.9	55.0	16.5	69.5	9,211	23,293	46,131	54.2	1.4	48,915	12.8	18.4	17.0
Howard	639	2,518	19,388	9.7	47.9	20.4	132.1	9,463	26,294	47,958	51.7	2.3	51,035	14.5	21.8	20.3
Huntington	NA	NA	8,901	19.0	52.9	18.1	49.0	8,801	24,222	50,063	49.9	1.4	53,635	10.2	14.0	13.7
Jackson	237	2,672	10,474	17.8	56.9	15.9	63.6	9,115	23,260	49,080	50.6	0.9	48,789	12.7	14.5	12.8
Jasper	NA	NA	8,338	17.5	54.4	14.9	43.1	8,396	24,953	56,574	43.6	1.8	58,891	10	13.3	13.0
Jay	101	752	4,746	9.2	65.0	10.5	36.8	10,467	20,193	42,878	56.4	0.7	46,740	14.3	23.2	21.4
Jefferson	NA	NA	7,161	25.9	51.2	17.4	43.6	9,873	25,429	50,722	49.3	1.4	51,163	13.7	20.4	18.3
Jennings	202	1,937	6,648	12.6	60.6	10.7	50.8	11,243	22,901	48,362	51.1	1.0	48,961	12.8	18.6	17.0
Johnson	308	2,812	38,399	15.3	39.8	30.9	230.7	9,044	31,101	65,272	36.7	4.9	70,690	8.8	11.5	10.4
Knox	109	2,937	9,749	5.8	47.2	16.1	48.8	9,207	23,441	44,837	55.0	1.8	44,044	18.9	23.6	21.0
Kosciusko	187	1,401	18,278	18.7	50.5	22.3	132.5	9,519	27,884	57,190	43.0	3.5	62,666	10.4	14.1	12.1
LaGrange	110	392	8,480	32.5	70.1	9.9	57.5	9,936	22,780	58,336	40.5	3.1	63,291	7.8	11.9	11.8
Lake	339	3,013	123,978	14.8	46.8	21.4	835.4	9,938	26,590	52,559	47.5	2.9	54,929	15.9	23.7	22.0
LaPorte	293	2,600	24,325	15.6	51.0	17.8	177.8	9,971	25,004	49,921	50.1	2.5	51,532	14.5	21.7	20.4
Lawrence	356	1,408	10,007	12.9	53.1	16.1	65.4	9,600	25,036	49,985	50.0	1.9	49,112	13.3	17.6	16.1
Madison	243	2,426	28,938	17.7	51.3	17.5	172.4	8,834	23,680	45,432	54.3	1.7	44,987	17.4	24.4	23.6
Marion	1,274	4,610	243,377	18.3	42.3	29.7	1,591.5	10,297	26,284	44,869	54.6	3.3	47,642	17.6	25.0	23.6
Marshall	NA	NA	10,755	16.3	54.6	19.8	69.7	9,321	24,289	51,869	48.1	1.9	53,387	11.6	14.8	13.4
Martin	NA	NA	2,270	7.1	59.2	11.0	13.8	8,798	25,138	49,372	51.1	1.2	50,203	12.5	16.7	16.0
Miami	129	1,879	8,294	5.7	55.8	12.6	47.8	8,542	22,890	46,666	53.3	1.6	47,225	14	22.2	19.9
Monroe	329	2,668	58,994	6.8	29.9	45.8	136.2	9,727	26,738	45,689	53.4	4.2	49,180	21.6	17.2	14.0
Montgomery	NA	NA	8,843	18.6	52.6	18.1	62.4	10,178	25,519	53,075	46.5	2.1	53,720	12.1	16.9	15.6
Morgan	NA	NA	16,376	13.2	53.5	16.1	97.3	8,627	27,402	60,317	40.4	2.3	61,068	9.9	13.8	12.8
Newton	22	653	3,068	7.8	59.5	11.0	22.7	9,775	24,315	52,193	47.3	1.9	58,384	10.9	16.5	15.2
Noble	210	1,145	11,415	13.1	56.7	14.0	66.9	8,958	25,260	52,393	47.2	2.3	52,764	9.8	13.9	12.8
Ohio	NA	NA	1,077	8.5	55.9	14.2	7.7	9,727	27,715	58,359	41.8	0.0	56,915	9.3	13.7	12.2
Orange	NA	NA	4,195	7.8	62.3	11.8	37.8	11,729	22,715	42,803	56.3	1.4	43,061	14.4	23.3	22.3
Owen	NA	NA	4,403	15.4	57.6	12.7	25.1	9,036	24,220	48,315	51.7	1.9	49,044	14.7	22.1	21.0
Parke	NA	NA	3,383	8.5	57.2	12.6	22.4	10,270	21,636	44,643	55.1	1.0	48,537	14.3	19.5	20.0
Perry	NA	NA	3,842	7.7	60.7	14.3	28.2	9,713	23,003	49,689	50.3	1.8	50,670	12.1	17.5	14.7

1. Data for serious crimes have not been adjusted for underreporting; this may affect comparability between geographic areas and over time. 2. Per 100,000 population estimated by the FBI. 3. All persons 3 years old and over enrolled in nursery school through college. 4. Persons 25 years old and over. 5. Elementary and secondary education expenditures. 6. Based on population estimated by the American Community Survey, 2011–2015.

Table B. States and Counties — Personal Income and Earnings

| | Personal income, 2017 | | | | | | | | | | Earnings, 2017 | | |
STATE County	Total (mil dol)	Percent change 2016-2017	Per capita[1] Dollars	Rank	Wages and salaries (mil dol)	Supplements to wages and salaries, employer contributions (mil dol) Pension and insurance	Government social insurance	Proprietors' income (mil dol)	Dividends, interest, and rent (mil dol)	Personal transfer receipts (mil dol)	Total (mil dol)	Contributions for government social insurance (mil dol) From employee and self-employed	From employer
	62	63	64	65	66	67	68	69	70	71	72	73	74
ILLINOIS— Cont'd													
Winnebago	11,870	3.4	41,682	1,305	6,490	1,212	460	506	1,888	2,573	8,668	501	460
Woodford	1,916	-2.0	49,474	498	455	95	32	107	396	287	689	42	32
INDIANA	301,008	4.1	45,196	X	149,369	25,273	10,909	28,191	47,283	57,689	213,743	12,804	10,909
Adams	1,311	3.9	36,934	2,052	572	112	44	236	192	257	964	55	44
Allen	16,602	4.4	44,525	960	9,185	1,512	679	1,375	2,837	3,114	12,751	762	679
Bartholomew	3,922	3.7	47,804	640	2,839	470	198	257	638	665	3,764	222	198
Benton	331	-3.2	38,447	1,807	100	19	7	28	60	74	155	10	7
Blackford	437	1.5	36,482	2,118	131	26	10	23	63	144	191	14	10
Boone	4,684	5.2	71,102	66	1,340	205	97	283	946	414	1,925	114	97
Brown	675	3.0	44,905	910	90	19	7	46	120	154	162	14	7
Carroll	814	0.5	40,642	1,450	212	38	15	65	130	165	329	22	15
Cass	1,409	2.2	37,077	2,020	594	114	43	58	206	406	809	53	43
Clark	4,927	3.4	42,121	1,251	2,377	430	177	295	626	1,055	3,279	203	177
Clay	964	3.0	36,801	2,076	295	62	22	47	138	263	425	30	22
Clinton	1,183	2.6	36,608	2,103	472	89	34	30	182	289	625	42	34
Crawford	340	2.0	32,141	2,735	69	16	5	15	41	115	105	9	5
Daviess	1,315	4.8	39,707	1,606	464	82	34	193	212	282	774	46	34
Dearborn	2,253	3.9	45,298	869	580	104	44	100	346	443	827	58	44
Decatur	1,091	3.5	40,820	1,430	676	120	49	64	167	234	909	55	49
DeKalb	1,783	2.6	41,622	1,317	1,092	187	82	109	280	372	1,469	90	82
Delaware	4,119	3.4	35,762	2,236	1,987	380	147	210	674	1,203	2,725	177	147
Dubois	2,291	4.8	53,825	317	1,308	214	95	170	557	349	1,787	105	95
Elkhart	9,051	6.0	44,143	1,007	7,330	1,235	542	875	1,303	1,565	9,982	573	542
Fayette	907	3.9	39,072	1,707	250	50	19	38	126	306	357	28	19
Floyd	4,172	3.5	54,129	308	1,368	236	101	272	907	721	1,977	124	101
Fountain	621	1.3	37,635	1,928	173	39	14	27	100	165	252	19	14
Franklin	1,007	2.6	44,500	961	165	35	12	72	179	207	284	22	12
Fulton	804	4.3	40,098	1,534	256	49	19	90	140	192	413	27	19
Gibson	1,466	4.4	43,653	1,057	1,130	201	83	112	207	302	1,525	88	83
Grant	2,521	1.0	37,921	1,894	1,143	216	87	132	359	818	1,578	105	87
Greene	1,209	3.7	37,575	1,934	250	50	19	55	196	330	374	29	19
Hamilton	23,108	6.1	71,377	60	8,393	1,136	591	2,028	4,205	1,659	12,147	694	591
Hancock	3,628	5.1	48,381	598	1,152	180	82	192	534	584	1,605	105	82
Harrison	1,604	2.7	40,212	1,518	424	75	31	63	229	347	594	43	31
Hendricks	7,808	5.4	47,699	645	2,910	476	216	430	1,006	1,006	4,031	247	216
Henry	1,771	3.7	36,530	2,114	503	99	37	73	250	531	712	54	37
Howard	3,306	3.1	40,135	1,532	2,040	347	147	138	498	908	2,673	171	147
Huntington	1,441	3.4	39,650	1,610	576	113	43	49	241	338	781	52	43
Jackson	1,811	2.9	41,263	1,372	984	196	74	78	255	378	1,332	81	74
Jasper	1,393	0.3	41,653	1,309	510	93	39	121	200	288	763	47	39
Jay	761	0.5	36,333	2,146	291	58	21	106	99	198	477	28	21
Jefferson	1,300	3.3	40,508	1,471	528	110	38	74	195	350	750	49	38
Jennings	1,034	3.5	37,421	1,965	306	58	23	30	119	329	417	30	23
Johnson	7,159	4.9	46,517	749	2,269	375	169	396	1,065	1,118	3,209	205	169
Knox	1,593	2.1	42,473	1,207	740	151	54	117	263	440	1,061	64	54
Kosciusko	3,578	4.2	45,177	881	1,974	407	143	192	580	618	2,717	160	143
LaGrange	1,521	5.5	38,697	1,776	675	122	52	244	187	225	1,093	60	52
Lake	20,931	4.0	43,099	1,130	9,629	1,630	708	1,276	2,966	4,766	13,244	829	708
LaPorte	4,429	3.4	40,253	1,511	1,772	317	135	282	686	1,021	2,506	163	135
Lawrence	1,775	4.1	38,879	1,741	565	101	42	64	246	481	773	56	42
Madison	4,751	2.6	36,691	2,092	1,681	289	125	232	639	1,392	2,327	165	125
Marion	48,413	3.7	50,957	414	36,645	5,609	2,613	10,864	6,761	8,021	55,731	3,052	2,613
Marshall	1,876	5.3	40,335	1,496	760	140	57	88	284	391	1,045	67	57
Martin	383	4.4	37,462	1,958	528	149	44	30	69	97	751	41	44
Miami	1,184	1.8	33,041	2,611	400	88	33	56	192	323	577	40	33
Monroe	5,862	5.9	39,880	1,576	3,061	656	219	435	1,274	954	4,370	250	219
Montgomery	1,500	1.5	38,940	1,732	713	126	53	100	218	348	992	63	53
Morgan	2,951	3.5	42,324	1,227	703	123	53	148	373	625	1,026	74	53
Newton	521	1.0	36,856	2,064	138	25	11	15	71	124	189	13	11
Noble	1,765	2.2	37,186	2,004	771	149	59	112	236	377	1,090	69	59
Ohio	226	1.7	38,856	1,745	50	9	4	13	29	53	76	6	4
Orange	703	6.0	36,195	2,175	290	46	22	57	98	212	416	28	22
Owen	794	3.2	38,093	1,869	212	54	16	47	108	217	329	23	16
Parke	593	2.5	35,097	2,339	119	26	9	61	94	166	215	15	9
Perry	689	2.1	36,121	2,185	285	56	20	52	105	178	413	27	20

1. Based on the resident population estimated as of July 1 of the year shown.

Table B. States and Counties — Earnings, Social Security, and Housing

STATE County	Farm	Mining, quarrying, and extractions	Construction	Manu-facturing	Information; professional, scientific, technical services	Retail trade	Finance, insurance, real estate, and leasing	Health care and social assistance	Govern-ment	Number	Rate[1]	Supplemental Security Income recipients, 2017	Total	Percent change, 2010-2018
	75	76	77	78	79	80	81	82	83	84	85	86	87	88
ILLINOIS— Cont'd														
Winnebago	-0.1	0	4.7	23.4	5	6	6.1	17.4	13	61,445	216	7,593	125,715	-0.2
Woodford	2.6	D	11.5	18	D	7.5	4.5	8.4	18	7,890	204	241	15,640	3.3
INDIANA	0.4	0.3	6.2	20.4	7.1	6.2	9.1	12.9	12	1,335,288	200	128,575	2,903,554	3.9
Adams	2.3	D	17.5	36	D	6	3.6	4.3	11.3	6,435	181	382	13,338	2.5
Allen	0	0.1	7.2	17	6.6	6.6	8.6	19.8	9.2	70,225	188	8,156	159,275	4.7
Bartholomew	0.3	D	3.8	46.6	4.9	4.4	4	7.4	9.1	16,575	202	1,257	34,531	4.3
Benton	7.3	0	6.6	14.5	D	4.5	9.2	D	18.1	2,020	235	163	3,928	0
Blackford	3.5	D	6.9	34.6	D	5.4	3.8	9.4	13.5	3,495	292	253	6,020	-0.5
Boone	1	D	10.1	8.1	9.1	19.1	5.8	6.5	11.9	10,915	166	446	27,553	21.1
Brown	0.9	0	12.2	5.5	6.7	8.5	4.4	10.7	22.3	4,365	290	196	8,743	5.5
Carroll	8.7	D	8.3	D	2.6	4.7	4.7	D	12.3	4,720	236	205	9,674	2.1
Cass	1	D	6	30.8	2.2	6.4	4	D	21.3	8,545	225	814	16,361	-0.7
Clark	0.1	0.3	6.6	18.5	3.1	10.9	7	12	11	24,770	212	2,221	51,086	6.9
Clay	0.6	D	4.3	42	2.5	6.8	3.3	6.8	14.2	6,450	246	627	11,784	0.7
Clinton	-0.4	0	5.9	40.8	D	4.8	4.7	8.6	13.7	6,870	213	542	13,412	0.7
Crawford	-1.4	D	5.5	D	1.6	5.3	D	4.8	20.9	2,920	276	365	5,562	0.8
Daviess	2.1	D	21.2	17.1	4.4	9.8	4.3	5.5	12.8	5,860	177	518	12,571	0.8
Dearborn	-0.2	D	8.3	14.7	D	8.7	5.6	8.5	22	11,235	226	618	20,615	2.2
Decatur	1	D	3.4	46.5	D	4.4	3.3	D	10.5	5,970	223	436	11,437	2
DeKalb	0.2	0.2	3.5	52.3	2.6	3.5	2.9	6.1	7.5	9,455	221	674	18,154	3.4
Delaware	-0.2	D	4.5	10.7	6.3	8.5	6.4	20.2	21.8	25,940	225	3,043	52,727	0.7
Dubois	1.5	D	3.8	39.6	3	6.7	3.9	D	6.2	8,945	210	374	17,938	3.2
Elkhart	0.3	0	3.5	53.1	2.9	3.8	2.7	6.9	5	35,975	175	3,057	79,492	2.2
Fayette	0.3	D	3.7	29.1	4.1	7.2	4.4	17.4	15.5	6,980	301	887	10,805	-0.8
Floyd	-0.1	D	7	20.5	7.7	5.5	5.2	22.1	11.7	16,460	214	1,480	33,014	3.3
Fountain	-0.4	0	4.5	41.4	D	6	5.1	D	15.1	4,415	267	319	7,943	1
Franklin	1.2	D	12.1	17.7	D	8.8	5.6	D	16.8	6,145	272	409	9,814	2.9
Fulton	2.1	D	15.6	26.7	D	7.2	5.1	D	18.5	4,965	248	372	9,726	0.1
Gibson	3.1	6.7	1.9	49.9	D	3.8	1.6	D	4.7	7,265	216	500	15,323	4.6
Grant	0	D	3.1	22.8	2.9	6.9	4.3	D	15.2	17,300	260	2,119	30,495	0.2
Greene	2.2	1.1	8.9	8.2	4.9	8.3	4	D	25.6	8,005	249	754	15,265	0.3
Hamilton	0.1	0.2	6.6	4.4	13.5	6.4	20	10.8	7	43,980	136	1,571	129,523	21.3
Hancock	0	0	9.9	16.1	19.2	5.6	4.4	6.5	14.8	15,420	206	693	30,589	8.7
Harrison	-0.2	1.1	6.7	17.7	2.7	7.6	4.9	D	19.1	9,175	230	612	17,187	4
Hendricks	0.1	D	7.3	6.9	3.5	13.3	3.6	7.5	13.7	26,740	163	930	63,176	14
Henry	-0.8	D	6.7	22.9	2.8	8.2	5.2	7.2	23.8	12,520	258	1,098	21,233	-0.3
Howard	0	D	3.1	46.2	2.7	6	3.8	13.5	9.3	21,590	262	2,187	39,567	2.3
Huntington	0.7	D	6.7	30.2	D	5.5	5.4	9.1	10.1	8,715	240	600	16,112	1.9
Jackson	1.7	D	3.7	39.9	1.7	5.9	3.1	D	14.6	9,715	221	807	19,327	6.2
Jasper	4.3	D	10.6	16.2	D	6.1	4.2	D	10	7,645	229	450	13,641	3.6
Jay	10.1	D	8.6	36.6	2.3	4.2	2.7	5	14.1	5,005	239	374	9,246	0.3
Jefferson	-0.6	0	4.5	28.2	D	10	3	14.1	15.3	7,950	248	742	14,495	1.3
Jennings	0.3	D	13.5	27	1.9	5.8	3.1	7.7	16	6,680	242	669	12,358	2.4
Johnson	-0.3	D	8	12.6	5.1	9.8	5.9	13.4	14.2	28,595	186	1,644	61,783	9.1
Knox	3.4	7.7	5	11.1	2.9	6.2	3.4	12.8	24.7	8,765	234	960	17,113	0.4
Kosciusko	1.5	D	4.2	48.5	2.6	5.2	3.5	6.5	6	16,380	207	929	38,738	4.6
LaGrange	5	D	6.1	51.5	1.8	6.6	2.5	D	6.1	6,050	154	319	14,922	5.9
Lake	-0.1	0.1	8.7	19.5	4.5	6.8	4.2	16.6	10.6	99,840	206	12,850	213,779	2.4
LaPorte	0	0	8.5	21	3.3	6.8	4.4	13.8	14.7	24,810	225	2,179	49,225	1.6
Lawrence	-0.4	2.1	7	25.3	6.5	8.5	5	14.6	13.4	11,590	254	1,063	21,175	0.5
Madison	0.1	D	6.8	15	3.7	6.5	5.6	17.5	14.9	32,120	248	3,351	59,132	0.1
Marion	0	0	5	11.4	11.2	5	18.2	14	10.7	156,275	164	26,432	424,371	1.6
Marshall	0.9	D	4	40.3	3.1	6.5	4.9	8.6	10.2	9,980	215	633	20,353	2.6
Martin	1.2	0	1.2	3.8	8.4	1.3	0.7	0.9	76.5	2,460	241	211	4,826	0.8
Miami	1.3	0.7	6.3	19.8	D	5.4	4.6	D	27.4	7,485	209	783	15,419	-0.4
Monroe	0	0.3	4.5	12.6	8.7	5.5	4.8	13.4	31.9	21,805	148	1,836	62,058	5
Montgomery	0.9	D	3.5	40.1	D	5.1	2.9	D	10.2	8,650	225	614	16,682	0.9
Morgan	1.2	0.5	17.4	16	D	7.5	5.5	8.8	13.2	16,145	232	966	28,470	2.5
Newton	3.5	D	9.9	17.8	D	3.5	D	6.1	17.6	3,145	223	218	6,095	1.1
Noble	0.7	D	4.4	53.6	D	5.8	2.6	5.7	9	9,925	209	648	20,634	2.6
Ohio	-1.5	0	D	2.8	D	2	D	3.7	21.3	1,415	243	77	2,860	3
Orange	0.3	D	20.1	14.3	D	4.7	2.4	D	11.1	5,050	260	498	9,229	0.6
Owen	2	0	6.7	47.5	D	4.5	3.2	D	11.2	5,415	260	369	10,221	1.3
Parke	4.1	D	11.6	17.4	D	6.8	6.3	D	23.1	3,850	228	259	8,260	2.1
Perry	0.6	0.3	3.7	40	2.8	5.1	7.5	5.3	18.8	4,550	238	330	8,739	2.9

1. Per 1,000 resident population estimated as of July 1 of the year shown.

Table B. States and Counties — **Housing, Labor Force, and Employment**

STATE County	Housing units, 2013-2017								Civilian labor force, 2018				Civilian employment[6], 2013-2017		
	Occupied units										Unemployment			Percent	
	Owner-occupied					Renter-occupied									
				Median owner cost as a percent of income			Median rent as a percent of income[2]	Sub-standard units[4] (percent)		Percent change, 2017-2018				Management, business, science, and arts	Construction, production, and maintenance occupations
	Total	Percent	Median value[1]	With a mort-gage	Without a mort-gage[2]	Median rent[3]			Total		Total	Rate[5]	Total		
	89	90	91	92	93	94	95	96	97	98	99	100	101	102	103
ILLINOIS— Cont'd															
Winnebago	114,491	66.1	115,900	20.7	12.4	753	29.2	2.3	141,196	1.3	8,095	5.7	132,190	30.8	27.5
Woodford	14,547	82.6	160,300	20.5	10.0	759	25.4	0.9	19,161	1.1	782	4.1	18,685	38.0	23.3
INDIANA	2,537,189	68.9	130,200	18.9	10.1	782	29	2	3,381,713	1.4	116,133	3.4	3,124,295	33.2	27.4
Adams	12,453	76.2	118,900	20.1	10.0	588	29.3	9.9	17,494	1.3	456	2.6	14,954	24.2	40.3
Allen	142,696	68.3	119,400	18.3	10.0	719	27.8	2.1	184,863	1.9	5,831	3.2	176,365	33.7	25.5
Bartholomew	31,472	71.0	139,400	19.0	11.1	854	24.1	3.4	45,295	1.7	1,185	2.6	39,722	40.7	26.0
Benton	3,397	73.9	84,900	18.3	10.0	707	27.7	2.1	4,574	1.7	147	3.2	4,126	25.2	37.4
Blackford	5,199	76.4	68,500	19.0	12.0	614	29.4	1.3	5,341	-0.1	206	3.9	5,251	22.7	41.7
Boone	24,228	75.8	207,500	18.7	10.0	888	26.9	1.4	35,904	1.4	971	2.7	32,690	48.2	18.7
Brown	6,011	83.5	174,800	20.5	13.0	886	30.6	3	7,659	1.3	243	3.2	6,754	33.3	27.0
Carroll	7,819	81.7	124,100	18.4	10.4	680	22.1	2.5	10,264	1.8	336	3.3	9,492	26.3	39.4
Cass	14,840	73.8	84,100	19.4	10.0	640	27.1	3.2	18,296	2.2	676	3.7	17,137	23.4	40.8
Clark	43,657	71.4	131,500	19.6	10.7	797	27.3	1	61,620	1.1	2,111	3.4	56,087	31.1	26.5
Clay	10,680	76.7	96,000	18.7	10.4	650	28.1	2	12,332	0.3	482	3.9	12,252	29.3	31.2
Clinton	11,961	71.5	103,700	18.0	10.2	704	25.7	2.3	17,200	1.2	485	2.8	15,228	24.2	42.9
Crawford	4,007	83.2	86,700	19.8	12.7	562	30.1	3	4,958	0.1	222	4.5	4,241	21.5	41.0
Daviess	11,482	73.8	115,400	18.5	10.0	641	27.6	3	16,531	3.6	447	2.7	14,200	25.0	40.3
Dearborn	18,667	79.1	160,800	19.7	10.8	735	27.3	1.6	26,132	1.4	950	3.6	24,597	31.5	29.0
Decatur	10,354	69.4	121,800	18.3	10.2	767	24.6	1.4	14,967	1.7	448	3	12,996	30.0	39.2
DeKalb	16,317	76.5	113,600	18.6	10.0	695	25	1.4	22,501	1	636	2.8	21,054	28.3	38.9
Delaware	46,304	64.2	88,600	18.1	11.0	708	33.9	1.1	54,159	-0.5	2,173	4	53,152	32.4	21.9
Dubois	16,524	77.0	146,000	18.1	10.0	586	25.9	2.7	23,357	0.6	580	2.5	21,928	31.6	32.4
Elkhart	71,733	68.6	130,800	18.1	10.0	747	26.7	2.8	116,267	3.4	3,012	2.6	94,516	25.5	38.8
Fayette	9,410	68.8	81,400	19.2	12.5	680	32	2.2	9,203	1.3	427	4.6	9,696	24.4	34.5
Floyd	29,046	72.3	159,700	18.6	10.0	767	28.2	0.9	41,401	1.2	1,375	3.3	38,137	36.7	23.7
Fountain	6,987	74.0	93,500	18.4	10.9	633	25.7	2	8,131	2.6	294	3.6	7,335	26.4	42.6
Franklin	8,843	80.3	152,200	19.8	10.0	668	26.3	1.7	11,395	1.5	423	3.7	11,012	31.6	34.0
Fulton	7,934	77.4	93,600	18.7	12.1	639	28.5	0.9	9,958	1.9	338	3.4	9,575	23.1	42.0
Gibson	13,336	77.3	105,700	17.4	11.0	671	25.2	2.5	19,475	1.8	521	2.7	16,210	26.7	38.8
Grant	26,122	68.4	87,600	19.3	10.0	676	29.4	1.4	32,239	1.1	1,243	3.9	29,436	28.1	28.2
Greene	12,653	79.7	95,900	18.1	11.4	604	26.2	3.9	13,754	1	609	4.4	14,248	29.3	29.6
Hamilton	114,282	78.0	240,000	18.2	10.0	1,103	25.7	1	181,103	1.5	4,879	2.7	163,999	53.3	11.0
Hancock	27,576	77.5	161,800	18.6	10.3	868	26.9	0.9	39,772	1.5	1,206	3	37,374	38.3	22.4
Harrison	14,693	82.6	136,400	19.5	10.0	696	26.3	2	20,172	1.2	698	3.5	17,769	29.0	31.0
Hendricks	57,153	78.7	171,600	18.3	10.0	1,026	25.9	1.4	88,595	1.5	2,554	2.9	81,408	40.4	20.8
Henry	18,096	73.1	94,800	19.2	10.0	687	28.8	0.8	22,475	1.3	792	3.5	20,044	28.9	29.7
Howard	34,538	68.3	101,300	17.5	10.0	678	27.1	0.7	37,645		1,529	4.1	36,774	28.7	31.7
Huntington	14,616	76.3	102,700	18.7	10.6	690	28.9	1.1	18,376	-0.2	654	3.6	18,256	27.4	34.5
Jackson	16,549	72.7	114,600	18.8	10.6	729	27.9	2.1	22,870	1.8	651	2.8	20,125	27.8	33.8
Jasper	12,220	76.4	153,200	18.3	10.0	764	28.4	2.2	16,509	0.6	649	3.9	15,315	25.3	38.2
Jay	8,195	74.1	85,000	19.7	10.2	608	26.3	4.2	9,843	0.5	327	3.3	9,315	22.4	45.6
Jefferson	12,677	71.7	120,000	19.1	10.2	723	25.3	3.8	15,100	0.1	518	3.4	14,465	30.0	36.3
Jennings	10,753	74.3	99,900	20.5	11.7	735	23.4	2.3	13,642	2.9	497	3.6	13,028	21.1	39.3
Johnson	54,867	71.0	149,700	18.3	10.0	896	27.3	2.1	82,164	1.4	2,362	2.9	74,247	39.1	22.0
Knox	14,986	64.0	87,200	17.9	10.0	663	27.5	1.8	18,898	1.4	615	3.3	18,338	27.1	32.5
Kosciusko	30,265	74.8	142,700	18.6	10.0	733	24.3	2.6	42,697	2.6	1,130	2.6	38,265	28.6	37.0
LaGrange	12,064	82.0	172,500	19.4	10.0	717	22.5	4.2	20,613	3	515	2.5	16,479	20.8	52.2
Lake	185,524	69.3	140,100	20.2	11.4	852	30.1	2.4	232,368	0.9	11,482	4.9	216,337	30.0	27.3
LaPorte	42,975	71.5	126,700	19.2	10.7	729	29.2	2.3	48,027	0.4	2,102	4.4	47,222	26.6	31.2
Lawrence	18,432	78.8	109,200	19.6	11.0	674	26.1	2.3	21,152	1.5	813	3.8	20,577	29.9	27.8
Madison	51,647	69.1	91,900	18.7	10.9	742	30.8	1.9	59,431	1.4	2,305	3.9	55,819	29.2	25.9
Marion	367,215	54.0	123,500	19.7	11.0	836	31.7	2.3	490,706	1.4	17,132	3.5	450,798	34.9	22.4
Marshall	17,249	75.5	130,100	19.3	10.0	681	29.1	4	23,481	-0.9	746	3.2	21,353	26.6	39.3
Martin	4,251	80.5	97,900	17.7	10.0	506	27.4	2.4	5,214	1.4	143	2.7	4,804	29.5	38.4
Miami	13,465	70.2	85,500	18.3	10.1	706	26.3	2.3	15,892	0.1	638	4	15,337	24.6	37.2
Monroe	55,014	54.2	163,900	18.7	10.0	869	36.8	1.6	69,690	1.7	2,510	3.6	71,839	43.3	15.2
Montgomery	14,993	71.6	118,400	18.4	10.0	661	24.9	1.5	19,157	0.8	582	3	18,802	25.6	37.5
Morgan	25,805	76.6	147,200	19.8	10.0	784	25.8	1.9	36,392	1.4	1,232	3.4	33,330	27.1	33.0
Newton	5,530	75.0	112,500	20.2	10.5	715	21.1	1.4	7,117	0.5	309	4.3	6,311	17.0	43.9
Noble	18,205	74.4	114,500	18.2	10.3	673	25.7	2.7	23,666	2.2	694	2.9	22,593	23.9	44.9
Ohio	2,479	79.0	142,400	21.1	12.6	716	22.4	0.8	3,201	1.5	112	3.5	3,041	24.9	33.7
Orange	7,830	75.4	90,400	19.4	11.2	589	26.3	3.8	8,597	-1.5	333	3.9	8,438	25.9	37.4
Owen	8,551	79.1	110,200	21.3	11.9	673	25.6	3.7	9,350	1.6	407	4.4	9,455	24.8	38.6
Parke	6,112	77.2	86,700	19.0	10.0	563	26.8	4.6	7,169	-0.4	286	4	6,734	22.0	38.2
Perry	7,460	77.3	103,000	17.8	10.0	585	26.2	1.3	9,323	0.6	344	3.7	8,199	23.7	39.6

1. Specified owner-occupied units.   2. A value of 10.0 represents 10 percent or less; a value of 50.0 represents 50 percent or more.   3. Specified renter-occupied units.   4. Overcrowded or lacking complete plumbing facilities.   5. Percent of civilian labor force.   6. Civilian employed persons 16 years old and over.

Table B. States and Counties — Nonfarm Employment and Agriculture

STATE County	Private nonfarm establishments, employment and payroll, 2016									Agriculture, 2017			
		Employment						Annual payroll		Farms			Farm producers whose primary occupation is farming (percent)
							Professional, scientific, and technical services				Percent with:		
	Number of establishments	Total	Health care and social assistance	Manufacturing	Retail trade	Finance and insurance		Total (mil dol)	Average per employee (dollars)	Number	Fewer than 50 acres	1000 acres or more	
	104	105	106	107	108	109	110	111	112	113	114	115	116

ILLINOIS— Cont'd

STATE County	104	105	106	107	108	109	110	111	112	113	114	115	116
Winnebago	6,442	118,132	20,785	24,052	14,926	3,677	4,568	4,998	42,309	736	50.5	6.5	39.6
Woodford	779	8,726	1,318	1,803	1,049	254	209	321	36,736	920	35.8	8.2	41.4
INDIANA	146,078	2,720,277	423,622	500,104	325,581	101,691	128,583	117,009	43,014	56,649	46.4	7.1	38.1
Adams	723	11,641	1,525	4,984	1,413	219	229	417	35,822	1,450	62.8	2.8	34.2
Allen	9,130	174,046	33,911	26,681	21,939	8,878	5,813	7,319	42,052	1,548	58.1	4.5	33.0
Bartholomew	1,835	47,791	4,940	13,008	5,023	994	2,923	2,241	46,884	564	47.0	8.7	36.6
Benton	174	1,436	58	360	181	94	49	49	34,026	358	30.2	23.2	52.2
Blackford	237	2,740	417	977	292	75	108	97	35,529	234	30.8	9.0	44.2
Boone	1,456	21,101	2,621	2,186	3,121	435	735	817	38,698	626	57.5	11.3	40.3
Brown	350	2,170	384	202	320	39	74	54	25,009	182	46.7	NA	31.2
Carroll	385	4,491	277	D	386	90	129	160	35,548	573	43.8	14.0	43.1
Cass	704	13,790	2,622	4,257	1,606	297	202	457	33,119	642	40.5	8.1	38.0
Clark	2,436	48,514	6,052	8,334	7,167	2,145	1,265	1,841	37,957	483	44.9	4.6	32.1
Clay	479	6,101	618	2,235	1,017	196	65	198	32,467	585	49.6	8.9	37.6
Clinton	600	9,860	1,221	3,845	1,030	205	125	346	35,056	560	41.6	15.4	48.7
Crawford	131	1,425	163	D	188	31	12	43	30,314	391	33.8	0.8	26.8
Daviess	897	10,480	1,454	2,185	1,558	261	364	361	34,408	1,230	62.4	4.7	28.3
Dearborn	917	13,047	2,744	1,767	2,080	330	250	459	35,175	598	38.5	0.8	30.6
Decatur	625	11,270	1,284	3,920	1,246	306	110	483	42,845	581	31.3	8.6	48.0
DeKalb	977	20,056	1,790	9,393	1,526	297	489	909	45,319	771	48.6	6.9	33.3
Delaware	2,435	42,283	10,360	4,293	6,276	2,902	1,605	1,465	34,658	546	52.9	8.1	45.0
Dubois	1,282	27,593	3,741	10,806	3,141	524	390	1,175	42,568	757	37.1	4.8	37.5
Elkhart	4,856	126,911	10,915	68,531	9,552	2,105	2,055	5,716	45,040	1,667	64.1	1.9	34.8
Fayette	450	5,981	1,605	1,327	978	159	228	204	34,188	343	39.9	7.3	39.3
Floyd	1,782	26,798	6,007	5,792	3,267	812	1,195	1,064	39,722	229	61.6	1.7	32.6
Fountain	303	3,635	418	1,560	581	142	77	122	33,536	497	35.4	12.5	42.5
Franklin	437	4,041	705	811	671	168	47	140	34,556	704	34.5	2.6	36.2
Fulton	452	4,982	769	1,595	927	169	120	172	34,505	635	42.8	11.5	44.4
Gibson	713	18,384	1,575	7,976	1,669	138	330	865	47,061	513	38.2	12.7	40.3
Grant	1,276	28,800	5,845	4,642	2,912	674	449	1,013	35,165	494	40.5	13.0	47.5
Greene	564	4,709	937	567	979	180	290	143	30,393	828	43.4	4.5	37.4
Hamilton	8,656	134,127	18,564	5,682	16,721	16,814	12,205	6,929	51,663	585	62.6	4.8	33.8
Hancock	1,406	19,402	2,570	3,136	2,135	352	2,370	814	41,970	551	56.4	10.2	34.7
Harrison	672	8,849	1,472	1,649	1,407	248	122	282	31,909	1,054	51.0	2.7	30.5
Hendricks	3,201	56,335	7,964	3,052	10,160	877	1,454	2,085	37,014	658	62.9	6.4	41.6
Henry	828	11,228	3,201	2,008	1,580	361	125	366	32,587	636	50.2	6.3	40.3
Howard	1,776	32,760	5,505	9,968	5,118	733	690	1,385	42,292	422	36.3	10.0	49.1
Huntington	866	13,280	1,797	3,951	1,374	337	205	432	32,563	611	41.6	10.8	33.7
Jackson	986	20,635	2,520	7,719	2,200	397	292	892	43,209	665	38.3	8.4	40.1
Jasper	751	9,675	1,424	1,511	1,546	296	177	345	35,639	611	39.1	13.7	47.5
Jay	396	6,073	940	2,666	620	150	95	216	35,558	770	45.3	8.3	37.4
Jefferson	661	11,853	2,125	3,249	1,680	146	223	428	36,090	684	39.8	2.2	30.5
Jennings	412	6,382	913	1,811	789	85	85	228	35,735	510	46.3	5.3	34.4
Johnson	3,095	47,132	7,182	6,225	9,195	1,046	1,574	1,681	35,660	642	62.9	5.9	37.8
Knox	883	14,079	3,622	1,624	2,004	308	237	530	37,656	496	30.0	19.8	53.4
Kosciusko	1,950	36,780	4,361	13,071	4,039	818	541	1,769	48,100	1,042	55.6	6.9	32.2
LaGrange	823	12,933	954	7,190	1,183	224	171	549	42,440	2,144	62.0	1.7	34.0
Lake	9,945	162,949	33,820	22,224	24,996	4,162	5,885	7,123	43,715	384	52.3	6.3	42.0
LaPorte	2,295	35,365	6,205	7,407	5,897	896	790	1,337	37,810	740	42.4	9.5	45.4
Lawrence	891	11,460	2,608	2,172	2,100	377	730	427	37,261	840	42.4	3.0	31.1
Madison	2,263	35,987	7,233	3,808	4,823	847	1,457	1,272	35,342	667	51.3	9.7	41.7
Marion	23,250	523,410	83,974	42,437	50,279	24,472	41,954	26,443	50,521	192	79.7	3.1	26.2
Marshall	1,046	17,556	1,969	6,319	2,236	561	265	645	36,742	829	47.8	6.4	39.3
Martin	190	2,182	114	347	276	44	755	91	41,501	260	39.2	7.3	29.2
Miami	577	6,768	1,093	1,970	888	311	118	229	33,909	629	37.8	7.9	43.5
Monroe	3,034	50,774	9,899	9,106	7,267	1,599	2,011	1,928	37,969	490	50.0	0.6	30.0
Montgomery	843	13,128	1,248	5,094	1,815	269	178	539	41,047	634	38.0	14.5	44.3
Morgan	1,188	12,268	1,767	2,353	2,247	403	320	452	36,840	501	49.1	7.0	38.1
Newton	244	2,419	252	662	253	105	64	80	33,105	358	28.2	17.3	50.7
Noble	856	16,454	1,370	9,347	1,647	252	172	612	37,171	1,015	52.4	5.6	33.6
Ohio	83	1,027	83	16	72	14	14	27	26,627	158	31.6	1.3	27.7
Orange	383	6,244	798	1,273	622	108	63	226	36,206	448	37.1	5.1	37.2
Owen	299	3,047	529	1,007	449	101	81	94	30,974	649	45.6	3.7	31.9
Parke	253	2,371	251	642	358	64	77	72	30,284	597	37.0	8.7	42.5
Perry	360	5,882	909	2,418	720	120	175	212	36,026	445	29.4	2.5	28.4

Table B. States and Counties — Agriculture

	Agriculture, 2017 (cont.)														
	Land in farms				Value of land and buildings (dollars)		Value of machinery and equiopmnet, average per farm (dollars)	Value of products sold:				Organic farms (number)	Farms with internet access (percent)	Government payments	
		Acres								Percent from:					
STATE County	Acreage (1,000)	Percent change, 2012-2017	Average size of farm	Total irrigated (1,000)	Total cropland (1,000)	Average per farm	Average per acre		Total (mil dol)	Average per farm (acres)	Crops	Livestock and poultry products			Total ($1,000)	Percent of farms
	117	118	119	120	121	122	123	124	125	126	127	128	129	130	131	132
ILLINOIS— Cont'd																
Winnebago	179	-2.3	243	1.6	161.0	1,732,196	7,137	145,947	107.2	145,644	78.1	21.9	9	81.7	6,961	54.9
Woodford	283	-12.3	308	D	259.0	2,761,299	8,972	205,867	216.1	234,897	75.2	24.8	23	77.6	3,479	73.6
INDIANA	14,970	1.7	264	555.4	12,909.7	1,737,741	6,576	163,136	11,107.3	196,073	64.1	35.9	657	71.9	342,914	47.9
Adams	213	1.3	147	0.5	194.4	1,215,197	8,274	101,610	283.1	195,266	34.9	65.1	15	50.8	3,926	35.4
Allen	282	4.0	182	0.4	249.5	1,446,442	7,950	113,983	175.8	113,581	71.1	28.9	19	65.6	5,389	47.2
Bartholomew	160	-6.5	284	15.5	142.2	1,902,512	6,688	159,738	93.0	164,929	88.3	11.7	NA	79.3	3,919	55.7
Benton	251	-1.3	701	6.6	246.4	5,422,824	7,734	405,595	178.9	499,765	86.9	13.1	NA	80.7	4,100	81.6
Blackford	92	4.7	394	NA	86.3	2,601,618	6,605	219,419	63.5	271,265	74.8	25.2	NA	76.5	1,567	67.9
Boone	230	3.8	367	0.1	219.9	2,800,238	7,621	206,909	134.6	215,045	92.9	7.1	3	89.8	6,471	42.0
Brown	15	1.4	81	0.1	5.7	356,748	4,390	44,535	1.9	10,527	85.4	14.6	1	81.9	162	18.7
Carroll	224	9.9	391	1.6	213.4	2,949,885	7,539	249,168	250.0	436,283	55.0	45.0	8	71.6	4,972	59.9
Cass	199	-0.4	311	0.8	182.7	1,939,195	6,243	212,168	149.5	232,807	66.4	33.6	2	77.4	3,933	66.5
Clark	94	19.6	195	0.7	68.6	1,072,932	5,515	113,762	41.7	86,244	84.3	15.7	NA	71.4	1,746	37.7
Clay	162	-0.5	277	0.6	139.1	1,412,114	5,100	142,144	76.2	130,309	96.4	3.6	1	72.6	3,616	63.8
Clinton	247	10.6	441	D	238.8	3,162,178	7,169	282,883	184.7	329,836	78.4	21.6	4	86.3	7,274	65.5
Crawford	53	13.4	135	D	18.7	416,192	3,094	51,196	9.3	23,754	41.1	58.9	NA	73.4	475	23.0
Daviess	225	0.0	183	4.8	193.2	1,395,457	7,620	144,028	270.9	220,211	41.6	58.4	1	52.3	6,725	23.3
Dearborn	65	14.2	108	0.1	29.8	525,303	4,861	56,517	12.2	20,390	69.6	30.4	NA	80.4	278	20.2
Decatur	202	8.3	348	0.0	179.2	2,461,834	7,083	231,518	178.9	307,904	57.8	42.2	NA	76.4	5,753	67.6
DeKalb	159	-1.2	206	3.6	140.1	1,143,430	5,547	121,735	93.8	121,624	65.3	34.7	NA	74.8	5,313	60.3
Delaware	168	-4.3	307	0.6	157.6	2,038,398	6,633	188,657	92.2	168,773	92.9	7.1	NA	83.5	4,044	56.4
Dubois	179	2.4	236	0.7	133.4	1,289,755	5,455	169,974	248.8	328,690	28.1	71.9	NA	71.9	6,327	60.1
Elkhart	175	1.2	105	25.0	146.5	1,173,021	11,178	98,422	298.3	178,936	23.4	76.6	86	45.5	3,082	16.3
Fayette	86	9.8	251	0.2	72.2	1,416,832	5,656	164,773	45.8	133,458	85.0	15.0	NA	73.8	2,463	51.9
Floyd	25	16.5	109	0.1	13.8	595,936	5,456	71,967	7.1	31,162	90.8	9.2	NA	72.5	335	18.3
Fountain	212	-1.1	427	D	187.4	2,871,619	6,732	224,601	112.7	226,809	94.0	6.0	3	77.7	4,181	66.6
Franklin	133	6.5	189	D	92.2	1,071,362	5,670	102,977	67.1	95,261	76.8	23.2	NA	69.2	3,190	50.4
Fulton	214	13.8	338	25.1	197.5	2,131,615	6,312	233,337	140.2	220,855	78.1	21.9	2	75.0	5,859	58.9
Gibson	220	-17.8	430	7.8	203.1	2,785,651	6,368	297,121	149.0	290,458	85.6	14.4	NA	76.4	6,226	64.9
Grant	190	3.7	385	D	181.4	2,716,186	7,059	216,027	118.6	240,095	83.3	16.7	3	82.4	1,747	60.1
Greene	169	-6.7	204	2.2	124.2	1,010,049	4,952	110,938	108.4	130,965	56.6	43.4	10	78.9	4,026	30.9
Hamilton	127	-2.7	218	D	117.4	1,903,729	8,750	168,283	104.6	178,853	97.5	2.5	2	83.9	1,209	39.5
Hancock	170	2.3	308	0.0	161.2	2,322,612	7,543	185,610	115.7	210,031	72.1	27.9	3	89.3	4,498	45.2
Harrison	149	10.1	141	0.3	100.7	644,972	4,575	84,004	88.7	84,114	51.9	48.1	NA	71.5	2,627	26.7
Hendricks	153	-30.0	232	0.1	141.5	1,774,141	7,638	128,330	84.4	128,293	96.2	3.8	6	82.1	3,541	36.9
Henry	168	-4.5	265	0.1	151.9	1,586,242	5,987	174,623	122.9	193,259	65.0	35.0	NA	80.3	5,297	51.3
Howard	146	1.1	345	D	138.0	2,681,236	7,765	219,981	97.1	230,078	83.1	16.9	3	79.9	4,286	68.2
Huntington	197	4.4	323	D	181.4	2,212,369	6,854	221,979	160.2	262,116	56.5	43.5	NA	81.7	2,019	62.7
Jackson	201	9.5	303	11.1	155.9	1,602,696	5,295	202,939	186.5	280,451	40.6	59.4	NA	73.1	4,533	56.2
Jasper	270	-4.5	442	25.9	251.6	2,854,205	6,456	251,325	298.7	488,939	47.7	52.3	1	78.4	4,951	67.6
Jay	208	18.1	270	D	190.3	2,044,970	7,585	180,334	372.6	483,891	23.7	76.3	2	75.2	3,566	60.8
Jefferson	107	11.7	156	0.0	66.9	645,429	4,141	87,775	31.4	45,975	84.6	15.4	1	74.4	1,417	33.0
Jennings	128	3.8	251	0.5	91.1	1,146,513	4,564	142,906	63.3	124,141	70.2	29.8	NA	73.1	2,427	39.8
Johnson	141	-2.4	220	2.4	122.0	1,482,614	6,745	148,278	75.3	117,271	88.6	11.4	2	82.7	4,292	37.9
Knox	311	-5.5	627	32.1	289.9	3,905,102	6,224	365,221	245.3	494,635	79.7	20.3	3	85.7	10,316	70.8
Kosciusko	262	2.7	251	30.1	229.7	1,788,066	7,120	177,429	298.0	286,019	42.0	58.0	7	68.2	8,572	43.7
LaGrange	195	-4.3	91	38.9	144.1	842,807	9,249	75,820	275.6	128,536	29.9	70.1	271	19.8	2,970	9.9
Lake	112	-15.5	293	4.7	106.0	2,040,013	6,966	155,636	65.4	170,253	93.0	7.0	NA	78.4	2,032	44.3
LaPorte	249	9.2	336	68.5	230.0	2,473,619	7,355	210,852	166.4	224,842	82.2	17.8	7	79.6	8,644	58.4
Lawrence	147	9.4	175	0.1	82.3	651,657	3,716	72,451	43.5	51,751	69.4	30.6	2	71.0	3,141	35.6
Madison	208	1.3	312	1.5	198.0	2,526,028	8,108	205,713	129.5	194,096	92.6	7.4	2	81.3	5,002	53.4
Marion	17	-13.5	90	0.1	15.5	955,725	10,564	62,277	12.1	62,844	92.2	7.8	3	81.8	423	19.3
Marshall	199	-3.5	240	16.5	177.3	1,503,166	6,259	151,905	145.2	175,111	65.2	34.8	21	63.3	5,212	45.7
Martin	62	-0.5	239	D	35.3	930,286	3,886	144,218	60.8	233,777	29.6	70.4	NA	62.3	879	35.4
Miami	194	10.4	308	3.4	175.1	2,076,888	6,750	165,044	179.5	285,297	51.5	48.5	1	80.1	5,973	71.1
Monroe	48	-9.5	97	0.1	22.2	640,303	6,569	62,244	9.4	19,196	73.7	26.3	16	83.3	493	19.8
Montgomery	282	-1.7	445	2.1	260.0	3,108,274	6,984	270,937	162.7	256,550	94.4	5.6	3	81.7	6,451	66.6
Morgan	137	-0.5	273	D	111.4	1,713,947	6,289	140,341	65.5	130,812	87.4	12.6	NA	79.0	2,760	41.9
Newton	181	-5.8	506	4.7	161.3	3,403,798	6,733	335,472	196.2	547,925	48.6	51.4	NA	84.4	1,666	57.0
Noble	200	10.2	197	21.1	172.3	1,259,845	6,394	141,041	158.5	156,156	53.2	46.8	35	69.1	5,315	46.5
Ohio	24	11.9	152	0.0	11.1	663,843	4,368	71,293	4.6	29,051	76.2	23.8	NA	75.3	445	17.7
Orange	102	4.3	229	0.1	72.2	1,026,470	4,489	136,262	122.5	273,498	31.1	68.9	NA	77.2	4,352	41.3
Owen	112	17.2	172	0.2	73.6	783,546	4,543	73,005	34.1	52,582	84.7	15.3	3	71.0	1,857	33.4
Parke	181	2.4	303	3.9	139.9	1,768,164	5,840	173,611	92.7	155,295	84.4	15.6	23	62.1	3,317	47.6
Perry	77	16.0	173	0.5	42.2	693,181	4,013	91,796	40.1	90,036	39.3	60.7	1	71.2	1,039	34.2

Table B. States and Counties — Water Use, Wholesale Trade, Retail Trade, and Real Estate

STATE County	Water use, 2015 Public supply water withdrawn (mil gal/day)	Public supply gallons withdrawn per person per day	Wholesale Trade[1], 2012 Number of establishments	Number of employees	Sales (mil dol)	Average payroll (mil dol)	Retail Trade[2], 2012 Number of establishments	Number of employees	Sales (mil dol)	Average payroll (mil dol)	Real estate and rental and leasing,[2] 2012 Number of establishments	Number of employees	Sales (mil dol)	Average payroll (mil dol)
	133	134	135	136	137	138	139	140	141	142	143	144	145	146
ILLINOIS— Cont'd														
Winnebago	29.23	101.8	333	4,123	2,700.4	207.0	986	14,298	3,752.1	326.5	212	1,512	169.0	43.7
Woodford	7.26	185.1	44	578	608.0	31.7	95	956	337.8	25.6	17	30	2.6	0.5
INDIANA	627.84	94.8	6,460	91,474	81,173.4	4,650.5	21,601	309,552	85,858.0	7,078.7	5,729	31,715	6,547.9	1,171.7
Adams	2.31	66.0	35	267	240.0	9.9	133	1,500	377.2	33.3	19	D	D	D
Allen	35.70	96.9	506	7,683	9,187.6	368.3	1,273	19,912	5,197.7	467.2	382	1,863	361.6	66.5
Bartholomew	9.49	116.9	77	998	774.4	52.7	306	4,701	1,113.1	99.4	72	303	57.0	9.4
Benton	0.40	46.1	15	201	203.4	8.0	31	199	53.3	3.8	3	2	0.3	0.1
Blackford	1.04	84.6	10	D	D	D	38	406	96.7	9.0	12	33	3.5	0.5
Boone	2.01	31.7	58	901	1,684.0	45.1	160	2,238	1,137.9	72.0	52	170	35.1	5.4
Brown	0.00	0.0	5	46	2.6	0.6	77	343	58.4	6.4	11	76	5.4	1.5
Carroll	1.31	66.0	18	161	302.4	7.1	51	395	99.8	8.0	11	38	5.1	1.3
Cass	5.94	156.4	39	434	570.0	19.0	118	1,502	341.6	33.5	17	59	8.2	1.3
Clark	22.11	191.6	95	1,011	1,024.5	52.3	426	6,966	1,814.3	158.5	79	502	87.5	17.1
Clay	0.33	12.5	13	D	D	D	84	878	312.7	19.0	15	24	5.2	0.6
Clinton	3.68	112.9	24	D	D	D	102	992	239.1	21.3	11	38	4.8	0.8
Crawford	1.64	156.4	5	80	42.5	2.5	24	201	89.9	3.8	3	D	D	D
Daviess	3.55	107.9	31	336	227.3	14.3	122	1,502	485.9	37.9	18	58	6.9	1.1
Dearborn	4.41	89.2	31	207	311.2	9.3	140	1,962	576.5	48.7	36	103	14.2	2.7
Decatur	2.59	97.7	32	391	455.7	17.2	110	1,259	357.2	27.8	17	45	8.1	1.2
DeKalb	3.17	74.4	41	D	D	D	125	1,469	383.3	32.2	25	118	14.5	4.9
Delaware	9.58	82.0	92	894	805.8	32.1	428	6,189	1,519.9	131.9	95	447	90.7	16.5
Dubois	5.84	137.5	74	1,053	637.0	50.3	217	3,332	919.2	79.8	31	D	D	D
Elkhart	12.95	63.6	340	5,803	3,329.9	249.5	678	8,754	2,440.4	206.9	157	768	134.5	25.4
Fayette	2.42	103.3	14	114	110.9	5.5	75	1,070	234.4	23.6	20	68	7.1	1.3
Floyd	1.21	15.8	69	579	323.3	23.3	206	3,146	772.3	69.6	69	205	34.4	5.9
Fountain	0.88	53.0	12	77	127.3	3.6	64	572	148.3	10.8	5	12	1.1	0.3
Franklin	2.62	114.6	7	33	14.8	1.3	68	662	170.2	13.4	8	14	1.6	0.3
Fulton	1.07	52.7	18	141	98.2	5.6	79	913	214.0	19.3	15	39	4.3	0.9
Gibson	1.71	50.6	20	267	188.5	11.3	120	1,643	557.6	37.8	17	47	11.8	1.4
Grant	3.95	58.1	37	367	251.0	15.6	244	3,113	793.3	65.7	43	154	17.7	3.8
Greene	2.87	88.5	17	130	107.2	4.5	103	1,054	252.4	20.2	19	59	5.2	1.3
Hamilton	35.69	115.2	357	4,138	3,403.7	291.1	865	15,746	4,338.4	397.7	395	2,349	1,394.5	144.2
Hancock	3.18	43.8	42	624	737.6	27.2	162	2,102	600.8	48.3	45	167	32.4	4.6
Harrison	2.64	66.7	20	D	D	D	114	1,423	470.2	30.7	18	36	5.8	0.8
Hendricks	5.10	32.2	101	2,980	2,723.4	141.5	441	8,760	2,561.4	201.3	108	506	82.6	16.7
Henry	4.68	95.5	31	D	D	D	152	1,551	466.2	33.1	25	73	7.5	1.7
Howard	8.47	102.6	62	559	512.7	31.6	328	4,927	1,193.3	104.0	71	311	50.4	8.9
Huntington	3.73	101.8	36	D	D	D	135	1,347	318.1	26.9	30	73	12.2	1.6
Jackson	5.39	122.3	35	D	D	D	183	2,225	592.7	49.9	45	115	17.7	2.5
Jasper	0.91	27.2	33	251	529.3	14.7	123	1,449	572.1	31.3	20	89	23.1	2.2
Jay	1.52	72.0	15	185	230.3	7.3	66	650	136.9	14.1	6	9	2.2	0.3
Jefferson	5.63	173.7	19	D	D	D	128	1,550	390.9	35.3	30	70	11.6	2.1
Jennings	1.03	36.9	15	D	D	D	66	751	196.9	16.9	10	32	3.2	0.8
Johnson	10.04	67.1	103	1,981	1,174.7	114.6	494	8,639	2,324.6	192.1	117	356	84.5	10.3
Knox	4.20	110.7	54	588	463.0	23.6	161	2,062	459.1	40.1	38	197	21.5	4.2
Kosciusko	3.33	42.4	89	D	D	D	298	3,566	921.5	82.7	72	162	24.7	3.8
LaGrange	0.97	25.0	33	313	182.4	10.4	151	1,127	284.4	24.7	26	47	7.4	1.2
Lake	76.05	155.9	413	4,472	4,599.1	219.2	1,513	23,986	7,495.3	551.0	373	2,090	371.9	74.3
LaPorte	9.35	84.3	100	1,161	694.9	46.8	457	5,845	1,367.8	116.2	84	367	95.2	10.6
Lawrence	5.05	111.0	22	D	D	D	160	1,897	519.2	42.6	21	68	8.1	1.8
Madison	14.98	115.5	73	974	1,301.2	50.0	346	4,944	1,378.7	107.9	81	348	58.2	10.3
Marion	111.30	118.5	1,295	23,766	18,700.3	1,359.0	2,952	46,739	14,421.7	1,155.9	1,244	11,355	2,105.2	465.9
Marshall	2.85	60.8	53	523	430.5	21.5	172	1,993	568.6	45.0	30	86	10.9	2.1
Martin	0.63	61.6	4	D	D	D	34	350	150.1	7.8	3	10	0.2	0.1
Miami	2.66	74.2	29	D	D	D	94	900	226.2	18.1	17	44	4.9	0.8
Monroe	15.78	109.0	82	D	D	D	458	7,390	1,661.3	145.2	163	865	152.5	27.7
Montgomery	3.61	94.4	41	343	365.7	16.0	129	1,651	446.6	34.4	29	63	12.0	1.9
Morgan	10.52	151.0	33	275	139.3	13.8	196	2,374	638.0	49.7	44	97	15.6	2.8
Newton	0.56	40.0	19	178	214.9	7.2	40	336	88.0	6.4	5	13	0.6	0.2
Noble	2.30	48.2	39	507	450.7	22.7	139	1,543	392.9	33.4	34	87	12.2	2.2
Ohio	0.74	124.6	4	D	D	D	13	88	15.3	1.3	3	D	D	D
Orange	0.00	0.0	12	74	63.7	2.9	61	668	156.0	13.6	11	35	2.3	0.6
Owen	1.40	67.1	10	D	D	D	38	424	111.9	9.3	7	7	1.5	0.2
Parke	0.93	55.0	7	97	47.6	2.8	43	304	70.1	5.7	11	66	6.2	2.2
Perry	0.33	17.1	9	66	13.3	1.9	65	718	157.2	13.2	11	33	4.3	0.7

1 Merchant wholesalers, except manufacturers' sales branches and offices. 2. Employer establishments.

Table B. States and Counties — Professional Services, Manufacturing, and Accommodation and Food Services

STATE County	Professional, scientific, and technical services, 2012				Manufacturing, 2012				Accommodation and food services, 2012			
	Number of establish-ments	Number of employees	Sales (mil dol)	Average payroll (mil dol)	Number of establish-ments	Number of employees	Receipts (mil dol)	Annual payroll (mil dol)	Number of establis-hments	Number of employees	Receipts (mil dol)	Annual payroll (mil dol)
	147	148	149	150	151	152	153	154	155	156	157	158
ILLINOIS— Cont'd												
Winnebago	608	3,779	660.0	191.5	600	25,024	8,145.6	1,491.8	566	10,168	490.0	137.0
Woodford	47	205	20.5	8.5	45	2,464	1,363.6	122.9	61	830	28.5	8.2
INDIANA	12,829	99,962	14,702.0	5,490.6	8,141	452,513	242,763.8	23,041.3	13,057	255,223	13,076.6	3,432.7
Adams	45	215	19.0	8.0	63	4,246	2,200.6	172.8	55	800	27.7	7.3
Allen	874	5,326	720.8	254.0	501	24,975	16,200.1	1,336.5	712	15,250	643.1	190.1
Bartholomew	159	3,550	299.0	234.7	142	11,663	5,636.4	553.6	201	4,243	198.6	54.2
Benton	8	31	3.5	0.8	15	341	D	13.3	9	51	1.8	0.4
Blackford	11	97	13.3	3.5	24	1,056	255.6	43.8	20	221	7.7	2.2
Boone	166	645	120.2	33.5	69	1,759	D	70.7	117	1,686	71.4	20.3
Brown	32	80	9.5	4.0	15	111	D	2.7	33	D	D	D
Carroll	23	90	7.0	2.2	25	1,963	D	76.1	32	407	19.4	5.6
Cass	44	224	17.7	5.9	50	4,197	1,768.1	144.2	79	1,062	40.8	11.0
Clark	177	1,021	126.2	37.9	143	7,708	2,376.6	340.7	219	D	D	D
Clay	23	D	D	D	33	2,198	520.4	82.3	45	531	21.4	5.7
Clinton	44	144	12.6	4.1	37	3,035	3,192.7	143.0	52	680	27.5	7.9
Crawford	4	12	0.4	0.1	5	D	D	D	21	D	D	D
Daviess	42	554	125.3	42.0	73	1,726	848.1	56.0	56	981	35.3	9.4
Dearborn	69	320	24.6	9.3	46	1,460	385.1	64.9	69	D	D	D
Decatur	31	131	12.6	4.2	56	4,722	4,663.4	208.9	51	953	38.1	10.8
DeKalb	71	449	40.5	14.5	111	8,128	4,742.1	414.3	81	1,387	53.1	14.7
Delaware	163	1,522	240.5	63.4	130	4,205	1,591.3	191.2	211	4,417	172.7	49.6
Dubois	83	355	34.8	12.1	103	9,834	D	363.1	100	1,727	65.8	18.1
Elkhart	313	2,004	220.2	81.0	795	53,705	14,833.3	2,288.0	348	6,500	280.7	75.8
Fayette	28	214	10.5	4.1	30	1,195	489.7	60.2	43	D	D	D
Floyd	195	1,068	151.9	45.7	108	5,421	1,726.9	264.2	130	D	D	D
Fountain	17	75	4.8	1.5	21	2,368	615.1	96.6	38	370	13.0	3.7
Franklin	17	52	9.1	1.3	18	551	258.0	26.2	40	589	27.1	7.3
Fulton	32	142	43.4	4.5	43	1,751	513.9	75.7	45	488	18.9	4.8
Gibson	48	281	29.9	16.3	41	6,144	6,041.4	368.0	68	1,192	45.9	13.2
Grant	75	359	31.6	10.8	68	4,770	2,013.0	278.8	129	2,061	89.8	24.7
Greene	47	253	25.7	9.6	23	449	118.7	23.9	54	702	22.1	6.5
Hamilton	1,260	6,790	1,168.3	472.1	196	5,171	1,641.7	242.7	579	11,974	588.2	166.1
Hancock	124	4,210	274.6	186.2	56	2,998	1,183.9	124.7	98	1,872	80.7	23.3
Harrison	40	159	11.1	4.6	41	1,613	473.0	64.4	61	2,442	349.8	49.6
Hendricks	285	1,105	127.4	44.7	96	3,336	2,660.1	148.1	298	6,387	292.8	82.5
Henry	50	209	17.5	5.4	42	1,845	579.9	78.3	64	921	42.8	11.5
Howard	114	631	61.2	22.6	70	7,671	D	593.4	186	3,866	159.9	46.1
Huntington	43	180	15.6	5.4	64	3,417	1,740.6	170.7	87	1,207	47.3	13.3
Jackson	54	294	25.9	8.4	64	5,395	2,307.5	268.1	86	1,536	65.4	18.3
Jasper	49	203	16.0	4.9	35	1,426	650.4	65.8	64	868	34.5	9.5
Jay	22	83	4.7	1.7	34	3,042	1,059.2	119.1	33	545	19.9	5.4
Jefferson	42	242	15.3	7.4	43	2,754	1,548.4	132.8	83	1,408	50.6	14.6
Jennings	19	88	11.1	3.3	37	1,712	425.6	68.3	31	453	17.8	4.9
Johnson	270	1,332	166.6	51.7	123	4,932	2,024.1	237.4	282	6,135	263.6	75.4
Knox	46	216	18.9	6.1	40	1,789	464.0	66.8	84	1,508	63.5	16.8
Kosciusko	138	475	44.8	14.4	173	13,247	7,235.4	750.6	167	2,452	113.3	31.3
LaGrange	39	178	10.8	4.3	134	5,141	1,416.3	234.2	68	907	39.6	11.2
Lake	886	6,003	709.3	261.6	349	23,122	30,831.9	1,746.0	983	18,097	1,167.0	265.5
LaPorte	158	1,069	85.0	40.4	172	7,589	2,644.0	350.5	235	4,992	357.0	78.7
Lawrence	66	784	87.5	34.2	60	2,008	437.3	100.3	69	1,177	52.2	13.6
Madison	182	769	70.8	23.0	94	2,701	1,391.1	129.3	229	3,885	165.5	47.6
Marion	2,747	32,947	5,954.4	2,344.4	881	42,808	28,049.4	2,579.2	2,130	47,455	2,645.5	734.8
Marshall	62	334	24.4	8.9	130	5,712	1,816.5	240.3	90	1,343	56.6	16.7
Martin	20	1,107	163.2	64.4	10	324	64.2	15.9	25	243	8.8	2.7
Miami	31	111	8.6	3.1	38	1,542	D	68.7	55	796	31.2	8.7
Monroe	289	2,014	240.8	98.8	94	6,578	1,548.5	283.0	368	7,805	335.9	92.3
Montgomery	53	187	15.3	5.1	64	4,658	2,719.5	230.0	91	1,150	49.5	12.6
Morgan	94	323	31.4	10.1	64	1,847	649.4	86.0	71	D	D	D
Newton	17	61	5.8	1.9	24	663	156.2	24.9	28	209	8.7	2.2
Noble	46	165	16.6	5.0	123	8,351	2,937.7	337.5	74	1,046	38.5	10.5
Ohio	4	D	D	D	4	16	D	D	12	D	D	D
Orange	18	75	4.5	1.8	24	1,216	208.9	43.5	39	1,921	148.8	37.4
Owen	22	68	5.3	1.9	27	1,117	169.4	48.8	18	363	12.3	3.4
Parke	10	62	4.0	1.4	13	402	D	20.2	24	211	9.1	2.3
Perry	24	78	10.4	2.9	29	1,883	945.5	102.1	40	500	23.7	6.1

Table B. States and Counties — Health Care and Social Assistance, Other Services, Nonemployer Businesses, and Residential Construction

STATE County	Health care and social assistance, 2012				Other services, 2012				Nonemployer businesses, 2016		Value of residential construction authorized by building permits, 2018	
	Number of establishments	Number of employees	Receipts (mil dol)	Annual payroll (mil dol)	Number of establishments	Number of employees	Receipts (mil dol)	Annual payroll (mil dol)	Number	Receipts (mil dol)	New construction ($1,000)	Number of housing units
	159	160	161	162	163	164	165	166	167	168	169	170
ILLINOIS— Cont'd												
Winnebago	665	19,871	2,398.9	923.1	534	3,186	306.6	82.3	17,830	640.5	25,741	220
Woodford	51	2,063	112.3	60.6	48	213	24.0	6.6	2,523	90.7	15,999	61
INDIANA	15,156	396,923	42,493.1	16,208.7	10,777	72,937	8,909.7	2,106.7	406,919	16,800.0	4,879,857	21,480
Adams	53	1,475	100.3	47.7	76	392	31.2	7.6	3,195	175.9	12,762	91
Allen	947	28,368	2,803.4	1,195.5	661	4,571	441.6	133.1	23,495	990.4	354,461	1,641
Bartholomew	221	4,824	512.8	203.1	111	692	82.5	19.7	4,212	172.2	37,313	170
Benton	13	67	4.0	2.2	10	29	3.5	0.8	627	25.5	2,497	16
Blackford	22	385	27.6	10.6	21	65	7.0	1.5	616	21.1	470	3
Boone	120	2,318	207.4	87.6	98	606	44.7	11.8	5,379	271.2	160,414	477
Brown	22	311	18.8	8.2	18	97	7.2	2.5	1,511	58.6	21,718	84
Carroll	26	255	18.4	7.9	26	85	6.8	1.8	1,316	51.4	9,645	51
Cass	65	2,332	180.8	88.4	59	328	22.5	5.1	1,787	63.5	941	5
Clark	239	5,916	591.2	239.0	173	1,192	138.5	33.2	6,859	307.2	139,862	753
Clay	44	574	59.5	17.3	40	360	23.0	6.4	1,405	46.9	305	2
Clinton	50	1,162	79.5	34.0	48	303	26.9	7.6	1,700	64.9	5,215	32
Crawford	14	D	D	D	8	D	D	D	646	26.5	0	0
Daviess	75	1,452	99.5	42.3	69	325	81.7	12.4	2,195	94.4	3,653	24
Dearborn	117	D	D	D	71	328	29.3	8.1	3,024	125.1	24,474	115
Decatur	59	1,064	99.7	42.2	40	242	22.8	4.7	1,577	62.6	7,250	58
DeKalb	87	1,613	126.8	53.2	70	353	26.5	6.2	2,640	105.7	30,950	119
Delaware	313	9,158	873.1	318.7	174	1,043	105.9	26.2	5,706	210.0	7,440	52
Dubois	124	3,358	314.6	124.1	82	462	58.1	13.4	2,774	113.2	25,701	72
Elkhart	362	10,105	1,160.8	413.6	336	2,069	261.0	61.1	12,573	568.5	96,206	351
Fayette	61	1,773	127.7	57.0	39	171	13.6	3.8	1,056	38.8	1,667	17
Floyd	238	5,715	577.4	218.7	127	864	81.9	18.4	5,257	222.8	61,324	206
Fountain	24	511	36.2	11.8	33	82	7.4	1.7	958	34.6	4,835	51
Franklin	52	833	55.8	19.3	38	107	10.4	2.6	1,566	68.2	14,073	69
Fulton	45	847	78.6	26.9	38	126	14.1	3.0	1,309	51.8	3,839	19
Gibson	77	1,923	150.9	61.2	53	246	21.9	6.2	1,604	55.7	19,738	133
Grant	192	5,281	508.2	211.7	106	475	50.7	13.4	3,208	111.4	11,278	74
Greene	66	1,049	75.4	27.6	50	176	14.2	3.2	1,819	53.0	NA	NA
Hamilton	897	16,978	2,311.3	740.4	498	3,201	249.8	74.1	28,302	1,470.3	966,651	3,005
Hancock	136	2,511	256.0	93.5	94	391	36.8	9.4	5,065	201.2	142,407	638
Harrison	68	1,346	103.6	39.4	39	127	13.8	3.4	2,534	93.5	22,172	96
Hendricks	296	7,036	763.3	293.4	206	1,574	114.9	37.1	11,101	451.2	222,429	935
Henry	90	2,718	194.9	82.2	66	323	31.9	6.7	2,365	91.0	7,593	51
Howard	221	5,417	456.4	182.6	129	922	68.2	18.9	4,238	150.1	46,802	349
Huntington	66	1,812	141.2	53.9	75	369	23.1	6.4	1,872	67.2	16,484	85
Jackson	106	2,528	237.0	87.4	75	435	38.5	9.3	2,164	82.9	18,913	168
Jasper	47	1,400	85.1	40.8	55	D	D	D	1,849	75.3	21,585	97
Jay	28	819	62.4	25.5	35	99	10.6	1.8	1,319	61.0	4,522	19
Jefferson	74	1,963	187.1	80.7	53	257	19.9	4.8	1,832	72.2	7,586	47
Jennings	74	933	70.5	30.0	24	84	6.5	1.7	1,477	50.6	8,146	50
Johnson	331	7,291	632.2	272.9	222	1,587	160.0	49.9	10,232	457.8	221,881	843
Knox	110	3,345	327.7	129.2	69	347	36.4	9.9	1,922	75.0	6,957	37
Kosciusko	149	3,711	321.4	118.8	145	934	108.8	24.1	5,017	192.5	59,777	324
LaGrange	46	807	69.7	25.4	44	197	20.3	5.8	3,708	168.3	45,567	150
Lake	1,254	31,946	3,812.7	1,353.0	876	6,336	638.4	185.0	28,205	1,075.1	316,476	1,287
LaPorte	228	5,626	611.2	208.3	194	1,090	79.0	22.5	5,937	213.4	32,150	140
Lawrence	94	2,646	202.8	80.1	73	361	30.7	8.6	2,515	87.3	2,997	19
Madison	251	6,498	697.3	262.5	199	1,088	77.1	21.6	6,651	236.3	24,401	106
Marion	2,414	83,226	10,235.0	4,151.7	1,625	17,182	3,477.5	665.9	61,939	2,555.8	430,363	2,398
Marshall	72	1,809	156.9	50.9	84	501	50.6	14.3	2,896	114.0	18,885	67
Martin	9	D	D	D	12	63	6.2	2.2	615	18.2	730	8
Miami	40	1,148	98.7	36.7	44	349	34.5	9.2	1,655	63.3	4,889	26
Monroe	329	8,906	927.6	356.4	204	1,905	265.5	55.8	9,318	356.4	73,232	369
Montgomery	84	1,332	106.2	43.3	83	304	24.1	5.8	2,134	78.2	13,346	67
Morgan	109	2,069	235.0	74.2	97	452	42.8	11.5	4,551	183.2	39,643	183
Newton	13	253	13.1	6.2	18	D	D	D	730	27.8	3,772	18
Noble	73	1,347	132.7	43.6	81	280	42.4	7.7	2,578	101.7	31,104	151
Ohio	8	D	D	D	6	D	D	D	314	10.7	6,490	32
Orange	42	862	69.7	25.6	31	138	11.1	2.3	1,152	45.9	404	3
Owen	23	422	22.9	10.0	27	68	4.8	1.1	1,402	54.8	12,411	48
Parke	19	D	D	D	29	71	8.0	1.6	1,124	63.6	6,216	40
Perry	36	846	80.3	26.4	26	83	6.8	1.8	848	33.0	4,023	24

— **Government Employment and Payroll, and Local Government Finances**

STATE County	Government employment and payroll, 2012									Local government finances, 2012				
			March payroll (percent of total)							General revenue				
												Taxes		
											Inter-govern-mental (mil dol)		Per capita[1] (dollars)	
	Full-time equivalent employees	March payroll (dollars)	Adminis-tration, judicial, and legal	Police and corrections	Fire protection	Highways and transpor-tation	Health and welfare	Natural resources and utilities	Education and libraries	Total (mil dol)		Total (mil dol)	Total	Property
	171	172	173	174	175	176	177	178	179	180	181	182	183	184
ILLINOIS— Cont'd														
Winnebago	10,237	41,731,581	5.0	11.9	6.0	3.7	3.9	7.5	61.2	1,183.6	493.6	527.0	1,804	1,627
Woodford	1,508	5,339,422	4.9	6.4	1.3	4.5	0.9	2.8	78.6	119.7	45.6	61.2	1,570	1,555
INDIANA	X	X	X	X	X	X	X	X	X	X	X	X	X	X
Adams	1,561	4,888,145	4.7	5.9	0.8	2.1	44.7	3.1	37.8	145.4	46.1	31.4	914	779
Allen	10,511	40,339,187	6.4	12.9	4.3	4.7	1.4	5.9	62.8	1,115.0	515.1	426.4	1,183	960
Bartholomew	4,371	15,688,309	3.2	6.6	2.9	1.3	44.5	3.1	37.7	469.7	111.3	106.7	1,348	1,076
Benton	555	1,313,464	8.3	7.4	0.0	6.3	5.5	2.3	69.0	40.6	19.2	16.2	1,838	1,489
Blackford	419	1,328,279	7.1	13.0	1.8	3.7	2.2	4.2	65.8	39.7	21.9	11.2	898	707
Boone	2,618	9,699,681	4.3	6.4	4.6	1.8	30.1	1.6	50.8	311.1	88.4	80.6	1,367	1,089
Brown	487	1,429,248	8.6	9.6	0.0	3.1	3.6	3.8	70.3	49.6	24.3	20.7	1,373	893
Carroll	613	1,723,537	7.5	7.8	0.0	5.1	6.1	5.3	66.8	54.7	26.6	20.7	1,030	776
Cass	2,403	7,224,020	3.1	5.7	1.4	1.6	31.7	7.4	48.9	182.8	62.7	46.0	1,192	797
Clark	4,732	18,084,071	3.7	7.9	2.7	2.4	38.3	3.7	41.0	466.1	142.4	134.5	1,201	884
Clay	1,049	2,619,145	6.8	6.9	1.9	3.0	1.0	5.5	72.4	75.7	42.8	22.3	831	529
Clinton	1,323	4,321,114	6.4	5.1	2.9	2.8	0.7	8.5	67.5	112.5	54.4	40.9	1,238	878
Crawford	416	1,229,568	6.6	5.4	0.0	4.7	3.2	1.7	77.0	32.3	18.4	8.3	783	640
Daviess	1,354	4,234,993	5.9	7.5	1.3	3.1	36.1	7.1	38.5	148.6	57.8	30.0	937	730
Dearborn	2,410	9,132,488	4.4	7.5	0.7	1.6	40.1	3.6	41.5	318.7	143.7	50.2	1,007	864
Decatur	1,237	4,252,343	4.4	5.2	2.3	2.0	40.2	2.9	42.7	119.2	37.5	26.3	1,009	794
DeKalb	1,614	5,058,353	9.1	8.5	2.6	3.0	1.3	8.0	66.9	153.8	68.7	51.5	1,216	955
Delaware	3,335	10,832,587	6.2	9.0	3.6	4.7	3.7	4.2	64.9	345.4	171.1	109.1	930	778
Dubois	1,643	4,804,962	7.3	8.1	0.8	5.6	2.5	16.6	59.1	155.2	64.9	49.7	1,180	905
Elkhart	6,985	24,411,992	5.4	8.4	4.1	2.5	1.6	3.6	73.6	630.5	315.1	218.4	1,094	907
Fayette	815	2,807,530	4.2	10.7	4.2	2.9	3.8	5.1	67.2	77.2	42.2	24.8	1,032	701
Floyd	4,128	15,144,305	3.0	3.9	2.2	0.8	54.1	2.1	33.3	467.4	119.9	81.4	1,081	846
Fountain	702	1,835,852	6.6	8.5	1.6	5.5	6.2	3.5	67.3	53.7	31.0	15.9	930	767
Franklin	568	1,607,664	8.0	8.8	0.0	4.5	1.5	2.6	73.5	47.8	26.1	16.2	704	477
Fulton	976	3,541,251	3.8	5.5	1.3	2.2	47.4	1.8	37.3	96.4	27.9	20.7	1,000	751
Gibson	1,093	3,390,759	8.4	7.1	3.0	3.7	4.8	4.6	68.3	107.6	54.3	38.1	1,140	1,012
Grant	2,226	7,247,230	7.6	13.8	3.6	3.3	0.8	2.9	67.7	198.6	103.6	70.9	1,023	759
Greene	1,299	4,191,866	4.9	6.2	1.0	2.4	23.5	4.2	56.9	123.7	53.8	24.9	756	573
Hamilton	9,749	38,707,131	4.7	8.4	7.3	2.0	14.0	2.7	59.9	1,219.3	387.4	488.6	1,688	1,330
Hancock	2,896	9,851,360	4.6	8.2	3.9	1.7	31.8	2.5	45.9	327.9	103.5	93.6	1,319	977
Harrison	1,349	4,713,395	5.2	4.9	0.0	2.6	36.7	2.0	47.0	155.4	72.7	26.9	689	469
Hendricks	6,025	22,075,204	3.7	5.6	5.8	1.4	30.4	2.6	50.1	681.2	209.2	213.8	1,421	1,074
Henry	2,369	7,555,604	4.3	5.2	1.2	2.3	32.1	3.4	50.6	241.5	75.8	42.1	853	643
Howard	4,091	15,459,399	5.0	6.2	3.5	2.0	35.8	3.0	42.2	435.8	136.7	118.7	1,433	1,170
Huntington	1,237	3,734,687	5.5	8.0	4.3	3.5	1.1	5.4	69.0	101.2	49.3	39.0	1,055	770
Jackson	2,118	8,012,413	3.8	6.5	2.3	1.6	47.5	1.4	36.3	212.1	54.8	30.5	707	506
Jasper	1,433	4,507,418	5.5	8.1	0.3	2.6	29.7	5.3	47.8	131.9	42.0	40.9	1,224	719
Jay	1,099	3,415,778	5.2	6.1	1.4	1.7	36.1	3.1	45.2	123.7	55.6	25.5	1,196	860
Jefferson	902	3,038,763	7.5	7.5	0.7	2.5	2.6	4.5	74.2	89.4	47.0	26.9	826	757
Jennings	908	2,922,410	4.4	7.4	0.6	3.0	2.6	5.4	75.0	78.7	47.6	22.3	793	611
Johnson	4,964	16,948,881	4.8	8.7	2.9	1.9	18.6	2.7	59.4	506.1	198.1	162.0	1,131	885
Knox	2,489	8,335,443	2.7	4.6	1.9	1.6	60.2	2.8	25.4	286.7	52.9	33.9	890	737
Kosciusko	2,569	8,158,465	6.1	8.0	0.4	2.3	0.9	3.7	77.8	243.0	119.1	85.5	1,101	909
LaGrange	1,149	3,367,799	4.8	6.5	0.3	3.1	0.6	2.5	80.6	95.5	51.4	32.4	865	663
Lake	18,892	64,877,066	9.2	9.9	4.1	4.4	2.1	8.2	60.1	2,367.0	1,042.1	989.0	2,003	1,956
LaPorte	4,264	12,639,630	5.9	11.9	4.3	3.5	3.5	6.6	63.1	369.8	180.5	137.0	1,231	1,055
Lawrence	1,833	6,258,969	4.2	7.1	2.2	2.7	24.3	3.4	55.6	143.8	73.1	50.7	1,100	799
Madison	3,695	12,894,572	8.1	13.7	4.5	3.9	1.5	11.3	55.4	411.1	191.4	142.7	1,095	811
Marion	34,223	145,267,021	3.8	7.6	6.1	1.6	14.0	18.4	48.0	4,321.3	1,815.1	1,329.5	1,447	1,014
Marshall	1,390	4,686,571	6.2	10.5	1.5	4.0	1.4	5.1	69.8	140.9	76.1	48.0	1,020	856
Martin	313	962,585	8.0	8.2	0.0	3.8	2.8	1.5	67.8	29.8	16.1	7.1	689	541
Miami	1,311	4,091,188	4.5	6.1	2.6	3.8	0.7	6.7	70.0	119.6	65.2	34.0	931	637
Monroe	3,589	12,483,781	10.4	10.4	5.5	5.0	2.7	8.7	56.9	339.2	139.6	147.6	1,046	827
Montgomery	1,366	4,441,185	3.7	7.5	4.2	3.9	1.0	10.2	68.9	131.4	58.1	56.2	1,468	1,078
Morgan	2,356	7,692,514	4.7	7.9	3.4	3.0	18.5	1.3	60.5	238.5	98.7	72.4	1,044	538
Newton	607	1,789,217	10.0	9.0	0.0	3.9	4.7	2.6	67.9	61.2	25.8	18.1	1,291	1,109
Noble	1,526	4,688,687	7.9	9.1	1.0	3.1	0.3	4.9	73.3	132.6	63.7	46.2	972	770
Ohio	248	804,741	9.9	6.7	0.0	5.5	3.4	20.4	52.3	29.4	20.3	4.8	786	579
Orange	656	2,087,602	7.2	6.3	0.2	4.7	1.4	5.5	73.3	74.2	49.7	16.5	838	620
Owen	478	1,467,231	7.6	11.8	0.0	5.3	4.5	1.2	68.4	51.9	27.2	15.9	742	538
Parke	550	1,469,526	6.3	9.1	0.8	4.5	3.5	4.2	69.9	47.3	28.5	14.7	862	531
Perry	892	2,938,269	4.0	4.8	0.4	4.2	35.8	7.7	42.5	92.9	30.5	18.1	929	744

1. Based on the resident population estimated as of July 1 of the year shown.

Table B. States and Counties — Local Government Finances, Government Employment, and Income Taxes

STATE County	Local government finances, 2012 (cont.)									Government employment, 2017			Individual income tax returns, 2016		
	Direct general expenditure							Debt outstanding							
			Percent of total for:											Mean	
	Total (mil dol)	Per capita[1] (dollars)	Education	Health and hospitals	Police protection	Public welfare	Highways	Total (mil dol)	Per capita[1] (dollars)	Federal civilian	Federal military	State and local	Number of returns	adjusted gross income	Mean income tax
	185	186	187	188	189	190	191	192	193	194	195	196	197	198	199
ILLINOIS— Cont'd															
Winnebago	1,135.0	3,886	50.2	1.7	8.1	3.0	5.4	750.7	2,570	835	592	13,876	134,770	52,375	5,904
Woodford	116.2	2,982	68.7	1.1	3.9	0.0	7.1	40.0	1,026	74	76	1,898	18,010	74,825	9,805
INDIANA	X	X	X	X	X	X	X	X	X	38,067	20,609	385,992	3,101,880	57,231	7,013
Adams	133.8	3,893	35.3	41.5	1.9	0.6	3.0	120.4	3,505	64	106	2,058	15,080	49,090	5,079
Allen	969.6	2,690	50.6	0.7	6.5	0.4	3.3	1,061.3	2,945	2,060	1,143	17,381	176,920	57,109	7,342
Bartholomew	465.6	5,883	32.7	40.9	1.8	0.5	0.9	364.3	4,603	173	245	6,360	39,530	62,360	7,576
Benton	35.9	4,079	50.7	2.9	2.6	0.5	7.6	27.8	3,163	25	26	583	4,150	43,417	4,203
Blackford	31.6	2,526	55.3	0.6	5.0	0.9	4.4	22.9	1,830	22	36	534	5,780	40,579	3,396
Boone	254.2	4,312	38.4	34.0	3.4	0.2	3.0	422.2	7,162	107	198	3,737	31,510	104,209	18,094
Brown	46.1	3,056	59.2	0.2	2.0	0.2	4.2	23.3	1,545	15	45	766	7,660	52,337	5,751
Carroll	44.9	2,233	56.6	1.7	3.2	1.1	6.3	15.9	791	66	60	793	9,660	50,736	5,096
Cass	169.3	4,387	43.5	32.2	4.5	0.2	2.9	80.8	2,094	91	112	2,986	17,800	44,373	4,140
Clark	456.8	4,081	34.1	34.1	3.8	0.2	1.1	411.3	3,674	1,603	353	4,575	57,090	51,460	5,271
Clay	70.5	2,627	57.4	1.1	2.7	0.5	3.4	38.3	1,426	65	78	1,237	12,000	45,713	4,133
Clinton	106.0	3,210	57.5	0.5	2.8	0.7	3.5	96.4	2,919	59	96	1,671	15,300	45,506	4,093
Crawford	28.5	2,676	60.9	2.8	2.1	0.1	4.3	20.9	1,955	21	32	467	4,600	39,952	3,250
Daviess	136.7	4,263	34.6	34.7	1.9	0.2	4.2	136.4	4,253	74	99	1,731	14,540	48,647	5,059
Dearborn	292.4	5,869	28.3	29.1	2.1	0.0	1.6	199.3	3,999	109	149	2,900	24,900	57,027	6,285
Decatur	123.9	4,759	32.1	32.1	1.8	0.1	1.8	144.4	5,545	63	80	1,568	12,880	48,571	4,816
DeKalb	141.5	3,344	61.2	0.3	3.3	0.3	3.6	92.5	2,185	81	128	2,000	20,890	50,435	5,293
Delaware	323.3	2,755	48.4	0.8	3.9	0.5	2.7	191.9	1,635	299	331	10,799	48,220	46,412	5,013
Dubois	122.5	2,913	62.4	0.6	3.1	0.1	4.8	195.3	4,641	106	127	2,082	22,250	67,632	9,757
Elkhart	609.8	3,055	58.2	1.0	3.9	0.2	3.5	758.8	3,801	278	611	8,288	93,820	61,910	8,238
Fayette	72.1	3,001	59.5	1.8	4.9	0.2	5.4	37.9	1,577	45	69	1,039	10,200	42,099	3,800
Floyd	441.6	5,865	25.8	49.3	1.8	0.0	1.1	309.6	4,113	215	230	4,070	38,080	67,768	9,578
Fountain	45.0	2,632	61.9	2.3	2.9	0.3	7.1	40.9	2,387	60	50	742	7,780	45,295	4,131
Franklin	38.8	1,688	69.0	0.1	2.0	0.3	4.9	26.8	1,166	42	68	922	10,770	55,141	5,939
Fulton	83.1	4,008	31.5	45.7	2.8	0.1	2.5	22.8	1,097	43	60	1,335	9,450	46,632	4,612
Gibson	99.3	2,969	54.6	1.5	3.1	0.1	6.2	186.7	5,581	92	100	1,368	15,940	51,739	5,299
Grant	175.3	2,529	54.4	0.3	7.8	0.2	3.4	108.6	1,566	1,086	187	2,941	29,080	43,470	4,086
Greene	110.5	3,356	48.9	22.9	1.7	0.1	3.4	52.3	1,587	76	97	1,760	14,330	46,377	4,271
Hamilton	1,098.2	3,794	43.5	16.9	3.8	0.1	2.9	2,131.8	7,364	421	977	13,681	151,960	107,707	18,652
Hancock	259.1	3,652	38.3	36.3	2.5	0.1	3.7	430.2	6,065	117	226	3,851	37,030	64,166	7,532
Harrison	142.1	3,631	38.8	32.2	0.5	0.1	1.6	105.0	2,682	103	120	2,037	18,280	52,172	5,219
Hendricks	586.7	3,900	37.8	29.3	2.6	0.1	1.7	985.7	6,552	271	486	8,329	77,950	67,504	7,994
Henry	226.4	4,588	34.1	40.7	1.5	0.1	1.6	118.3	2,397	94	136	2,962	21,570	44,933	4,277
Howard	406.5	4,907	32.7	36.7	3.9	0.3	1.8	200.3	2,417	185	247	4,896	40,280	49,484	5,092
Huntington	90.3	2,442	58.2	0.3	3.7	0.1	4.3	59.5	1,608	90	106	1,386	17,730	47,591	4,702
Jackson	185.0	4,294	31.0	55.4	1.0	0.1	1.1	103.4	2,400	91	131	3,083	21,390	49,553	5,004
Jasper	124.9	3,732	37.4	35.2	2.1	0.1	2.1	207.7	6,207	97	99	1,430	15,510	52,310	5,334
Jay	94.3	4,414	38.3	35.4	2.3	0.6	3.7	67.3	3,148	48	63	1,292	9,400	39,832	3,526
Jefferson	77.9	2,394	64.1	1.2	3.5	0.2	4.5	52.1	1,600	79	91	2,296	14,680	50,469	5,536
Jennings	82.7	2,935	66.8	0.7	2.7	0.2	2.8	49.5	1,758	81	83	1,183	12,930	42,022	3,668
Johnson	466.1	3,255	49.3	17.5	3.5	0.1	2.7	489.4	3,417	402	752	6,959	73,750	63,675	7,802
Knox	274.0	7,186	18.6	63.3	1.2	0.1	2.8	128.9	3,381	163	106	4,886	16,460	48,009	5,041
Kosciusko	216.4	2,788	61.0	1.0	3.8	0.1	4.8	226.2	2,915	160	235	2,903	38,350	56,027	6,545
LaGrange	85.5	2,278	67.1	0.1	1.4	0.1	3.8	71.2	1,896	57	118	1,236	17,280	51,199	5,138
Lake	1,850.2	3,748	45.8	0.6	5.4	1.1	1.8	1,929.7	3,909	1,395	1,457	24,029	228,140	54,103	6,231
LaPorte	330.9	2,974	53.0	1.0	4.1	0.3	2.3	311.4	2,799	182	334	6,588	51,030	50,455	5,550
Lawrence	114.9	2,494	59.2	0.4	4.2	0.2	6.0	97.1	2,107	117	137	2,066	20,860	46,349	4,475
Madison	322.0	2,470	48.2	0.7	5.0	0.2	3.7	497.2	3,814	258	376	6,042	59,120	45,785	4,573
Marion	4,896.8	5,329	31.1	23.0	4.5	0.2	0.9	11,765.5	12,803	15,170	3,117	65,998	454,100	52,783	6,536
Marshall	129.3	2,749	63.4	1.7	4.8	0.2	5.4	98.6	2,098	106	139	2,028	21,920	50,107	5,430
Martin	26.7	2,598	58.5	0.8	2.4	0.3	8.0	14.6	1,421	4,414	68	462	4,690	47,692	4,365
Miami	111.4	3,054	57.5	0.2	2.1	0.2	4.7	101.3	2,777	616	115	1,932	15,380	43,741	3,877
Monroe	289.9	2,055	45.2	1.2	4.9	0.4	4.3	383.5	2,719	324	419	22,426	56,880	60,142	7,798
Montgomery	110.0	2,875	52.3	0.3	3.9	0.5	5.8	103.4	2,703	77	113	1,944	18,040	47,572	4,558
Morgan	210.4	3,033	48.5	21.5	2.5	0.1	2.6	96.0	1,385	98	210	2,664	33,720	54,879	5,750
Newton	55.2	3,932	46.4	2.3	2.3	0.2	6.4	34.2	2,435	25	42	714	6,610	49,270	4,726
Noble	113.5	2,385	60.5	0.3	5.9	0.1	4.5	94.3	1,982	81	141	1,815	21,980	46,724	4,258
Ohio	23.6	3,888	36.5	0.1	3.4	0.1	3.1	15.6	2,573	15	18	357	2,750	48,928	4,932
Orange	63.7	3,235	54.0	0.2	0.9	0.1	3.8	72.0	3,654	44	64	912	8,750	40,616	3,569
Owen	40.1	1,878	63.7	0.0	2.5	0.2	4.4	41.4	1,939	37	63	755	9,550	44,139	3,953
Parke	44.2	2,588	55.1	0.9	2.6	0.1	6.9	39.4	2,308	49	47	1,043	6,920	45,724	4,416
Perry	80.3	4,126	33.1	41.5	1.7	0.0	3.6	65.0	3,340	73	54	1,395	8,490	46,950	4,599

1. Based on the resident population estimated as of July 1 of the year shown.

Table B. States and Counties — **Land Area and Population**

State / county code	CBSA code[1]	County code[2]	STATE County	Land area[3] (sq. mi)	Total persons 2018	Rank	Per square mile	White	Black	American Indian, Alaska Native	Asian and Pacific Islander	Percent Hispanic or Latino[4]	Under 5 years	5 to 17 years	18 to 24 years	25 to 34 years	35 to 44 years	45 to 54 years
				1	2	3	4	5	6	7	8	9	10	11	12	13	14	15
			INDIANA— Cont'd															
18125	27,540	8	Pike	334.3	12,410	2,258	37.1	97.0	0.8	0.7	0.9	1.4	5.8	16.2	6.7	11.0	11.5	13.2
18127	16,980	1	Porter	418.1	169,594	384	405.6	84.1	4.5	0.6	1.9	10.3	5.4	16.6	9.0	12.2	13.1	13.0
18129	21,780	2	Posey	409.4	25,540	1,583	62.4	96.8	1.7	0.6	0.8	1.3	5.4	16.6	7.5	11.1	11.7	13.0
18131		6	Pulaski	433.7	12,469	2,250	28.8	95.1	1.3	1.0	0.5	3.2	5.3	17.0	7.5	11.1	11.7	13.1
18133	26,900	1	Putnam	480.5	37,779	1,231	78.6	92.8	4.4	0.6	1.4	2.1	5.1	14.4	14.0	12.6	11.2	12.8
18135		6	Randolph	452.4	24,851	1,614	54.9	94.9	1.4	0.7	0.7	3.5	5.9	16.9	8.0	10.5	11.2	13.0
18137		6	Ripley	446.4	28,523	1,481	63.9	96.4	0.8	0.7	1.2	1.9	5.9	17.8	8.4	11.0	11.7	13.4
18139		6	Rush	408.1	16,663	2,002	40.8	96.5	1.6	0.6	0.6	1.7	5.8	16.9	8.1	11.1	11.2	13.7
18141	43,780	2	St. Joseph	457.9	270,771	254	591.3	74.8	15.0	0.9	3.3	8.9	6.4	17.2	10.9	13.3	11.8	11.8
18143	31,140	1	Scott	190.4	23,878	1,650	125.4	95.8	0.9	0.5	1.2	2.5	5.9	16.7	7.8	12.2	12.3	14.1
18145	26,900	1	Shelby	411.1	44,593	1,085	108.5	93.2	1.8	0.6	1.2	4.4	5.8	17.0	7.7	12.0	12.0	13.6
18147		8	Spencer	396.8	20,327	1,805	51.2	95.7	1.3	0.5	0.5	3.0	5.2	16.6	7.5	10.6	11.4	13.5
18149		6	Starke	309.1	22,935	1,684	74.2	95.0	0.8	0.8	0.5	3.9	5.9	16.9	7.5	11.5	11.5	12.9
18151	11,420	7	Steuben	308.8	34,586	1,312	112.0	94.7	1.1	0.6	1.0	3.7	5.7	14.9	10.1	10.6	10.1	13.3
18153	45,460	3	Sullivan	447.2	20,690	1,789	46.3	92.9	5.2	0.9	0.6	1.8	5.0	14.2	8.3	14.2	13.3	13.8
18155		8	Switzerland	220.7	10,717	2,376	48.6	96.2	1.7	0.6	0.6	2.0	6.3	18.4	7.3	10.9	12.1	13.6
18157	29,200	3	Tippecanoe	498.9	193,048	343	386.9	77.3	6.4	0.6	9.3	8.5	5.9	14.8	23.6	14.2	10.5	9.7
18159		6	Tipton	260.5	15,128	2,086	58.1	95.6	1.1	0.6	0.8	2.9	5.4	15.3	7.8	10.9	10.5	13.9
18161	17,140	1	Union	161.2	7,037	2,663	43.7	96.5	1.4	0.8	1.1	1.8	5.3	14.9	8.1	11.3	11.4	14.3
18163	21,780	2	Vanderburgh	233.7	180,974	362	774.4	86.0	11.3	0.6	2.0	2.7	6.0	15.5	9.7	14.3	11.8	11.7
18165	45,460	3	Vermillion	256.9	15,479	2,069	60.3	97.6	1.0	0.7	0.6	1.3	5.5	16.4	7.7	11.2	11.6	13.3
18167	45,460	3	Vigo	403.6	107,386	564	266.1	87.6	8.6	0.8	2.5	2.7	5.8	14.7	14.8	13.1	11.4	11.7
18169	47,340	6	Wabash	412.5	31,280	1,398	75.8	95.4	1.2	1.1	0.8	2.6	5.3	15.5	10.1	10.6	10.9	12.3
18171		8	Warren	364.7	8,263	2,569	22.7	96.7	0.8	0.7	0.8	2.0	5.3	17.1	6.6	10.9	11.1	13.8
18173	21,780	2	Warrick	384.8	62,567	842	162.6	93.5	2.3	0.5	3.1	1.9	5.5	18.4	7.4	10.9	13.0	13.5
18175	31,140	1	Washington	513.7	27,943	1,500	54.4	97.6	0.9	0.6	0.5	1.4	6.0	16.9	7.9	11.7	12.0	13.9
18177	39,980	5	Wayne	401.7	65,936	809	164.1	90.4	6.7	0.8	1.8	3.1	5.6	16.3	9.0	11.6	11.5	12.8
18179	23,060	2	Wells	368.1	28,206	1,493	76.6	95.2	1.3	0.6	0.9	3.2	6.5	18.2	7.6	11.4	11.5	12.1
18181		6	White	505.1	24,133	1,638	47.8	90.0	0.8	0.8	0.8	8.7	6.0	17.3	7.8	10.5	10.8	12.6
18183	23,060	2	Whitley	335.6	34,074	1,327	101.5	96.4	0.9	0.8	0.9	2.2	6.1	17.1	7.5	11.8	11.9	12.7
19000		0	IOWA	55,854.0	3,156,145	X	56.5	86.9	4.7	0.7	3.3	6.2	6.3	16.9	10.1	12.6	12.0	11.8
19001		8	Adair	569.3	7,063	2,659	12.4	96.6	0.8	0.5	0.6	2.2	5.4	16.2	6.5	11.1	10.6	11.4
19003		9	Adams	423.4	3,645	2,928	8.6	97.0	0.7	0.7	1.0	1.5	5.8	15.3	6.3	10.9	10.1	11.3
19005		6	Allamakee	639.0	13,832	2,173	21.6	90.6	1.9	0.5	0.7	7.0	6.9	16.6	6.9	10.1	10.0	11.4
19007		7	Appanoose	497.3	12,437	2,257	25.0	96.1	1.3	0.8	0.9	2.2	5.7	16.6	6.9	10.1	10.7	12.0
19009		8	Audubon	443.0	5,506	2,793	12.4	97.3	0.9	0.4	0.7	1.6	6.0	14.4	7.0	9.6	9.7	11.4
19011	16,300	2	Benton	716.1	25,642	1,577	35.8	97.2	1.2	0.5	0.6	1.5	6.1	17.3	7.1	10.3	11.8	13.5
19013	47,940	3	Black Hawk	565.9	132,408	481	234.0	83.0	11.0	0.6	3.4	4.5	6.3	15.4	14.8	13.1	11.4	10.4
19015	14,340	7	Boone	571.6	26,346	1,553	46.1	95.2	1.7	0.7	0.9	2.7	5.3	16.0	7.5	12.2	12.5	12.6
19017	47,940	3	Bremer	435.5	24,947	1,608	57.3	95.9	1.7	0.4	1.4	1.7	5.7	16.6	11.8	10.3	12.0	11.4
19019		6	Buchanan	571.1	21,199	1,765	37.1	97.0	1.1	0.5	0.8	1.7	6.5	19.6	7.0	11.4	12.1	11.8
19021	44,740	7	Buena Vista	574.9	19,874	1,832	34.6	59.7	3.5	0.5	11.6	26.0	7.5	18.0	10.6	13.0	11.4	10.6
19023		8	Butler	580.1	14,539	2,122	25.1	97.2	0.7	0.4	1.2	1.4	5.1	17.4	7.3	9.7	11.8	11.9
19025		9	Calhoun	569.8	9,699	2,452	17.0	95.0	2.9	0.6	0.4	1.9	5.7	15.7	7.3	11.5	11.1	10.6
19027	16,140	7	Carroll	569.4	20,154	1,815	35.4	95.6	1.7	0.5	0.8	2.5	6.6	17.9	7.5	10.6	10.9	11.6
19029		6	Cass	564.3	12,930	2,232	22.9	95.5	0.9	0.4	1.0	2.6	5.3	17.0	6.8	10.2	10.9	11.3
19031		6	Cedar	579.5	18,627	1,895	32.1	96.4	1.2	0.6	1.0	2.1	5.3	16.8	6.8	10.6	12.5	12.8
19033	32,380	5	Cerro Gordo	568.3	42,647	1,124	75.0	91.8	2.7	0.6	1.6	4.9	5.5	15.2	7.9	11.2	11.0	11.7
19035		6	Cherokee	576.9	11,321	2,331	19.6	93.9	1.6	0.6	0.6	4.0	5.8	16.0	6.2	10.6	10.0	11.0
19037		6	Chickasaw	504.3	11,964	2,293	23.7	96.1	1.0	0.4	0.5	2.8	6.0	17.5	7.4	9.6	11.0	12.0
19039		6	Clarke	431.2	9,423	2,467	21.9	83.3	1.6	0.8	1.3	14.3	7.1	18.7	7.3	11.4	11.5	11.5
19041	43,980	7	Clay	567.2	16,134	2,033	28.4	94.3	1.5	0.6	1.1	3.8	6.1	16.5	7.1	11.5	11.9	11.2
19043		8	Clayton	778.5	17,556	1,948	22.6	96.6	1.2	0.4	0.6	2.0	5.5	15.6	6.7	9.9	10.0	11.6
19045	17,540	4	Clinton	694.9	46,518	1,040	66.9	93.0	4.0	0.7	1.0	3.1	6.0	16.8	7.6	11.1	11.3	12.5
19047		7	Crawford	714.2	17,158	1,968	24.0	65.6	3.8	0.5	2.3	28.5	7.0	18.2	9.1	12.0	11.5	11.5
19049	19,780	2	Dallas	588.3	90,180	651	153.3	86.3	2.9	0.5	5.6	6.1	7.7	20.1	7.2	14.4	16.0	12.7
19051	36,900	9	Davis	502.2	9,017	2,497	18.0	97.6	0.6	0.7	0.6	1.7	9.0	20.4	7.6	10.8	10.8	10.7
19053		9	Decatur	531.9	7,890	2,602	14.8	93.6	2.4	1.0	1.2	3.2	6.4	15.4	17.2	9.4	9.4	9.4
19055		6	Delaware	577.7	17,069	1,975	29.5	97.1	1.3	0.4	0.5	1.6	6.3	17.3	7.6	9.7	11.0	12.5
19057	15,460	5	Des Moines	416.1	39,138	1,199	94.1	89.6	7.7	0.7	1.5	3.1	5.9	16.6	7.4	11.2	11.7	12.1
19059	44,020	7	Dickinson	380.5	17,153	1,969	45.1	96.5	0.8	0.4	1.2	2.0	4.8	14.4	6.3	10.1	10.6	11.4
19061	20,220	3	Dubuque	608.3	96,854	616	159.2	92.1	4.3	0.5	2.2	2.5	6.3	16.5	10.1	12.7	11.1	11.8
19063		7	Emmet	395.9	9,253	2,482	23.4	87.8	1.5	0.8	1.0	9.8	5.5	15.2	8.5	11.3	11.7	10.9
19065		6	Fayette	730.8	19,660	1,846	26.9	94.8	2.1	0.5	1.4	2.5	5.5	15.3	9.4	11.1	9.9	11.7
19067		7	Floyd	500.6	15,761	2,054	31.5	92.0	3.4	0.5	1.8	3.7	6.2	16.9	7.5	10.8	10.4	12.3

1. CBSA = Core Based Statistical Area. See Appendix A for explanation. See Appendix B for list of metropolitan areas with component counties. 2. County type code from the Economic Research Service of USDA Rural-Urban Continuum Codes. See Appendix A for definition. 3. Dry land or land partially or temporarily covered by water. 4. May be of any race.

Table B. States and Counties — Population and Households

STATE County	55 to 64 years	65 to 74 years	75 years and over	Percent female	Total persons 2000	2010	Percent change 2000-2010	2010-2018	Births	Deaths	Net Migration	Number	Persons per household	Family house-holds	Female family house-holder[1]	One person
	16	17	18	19	20	21	22	23	24	25	26	27	28	29	30	31
INDIANA— Cont'd																
Pike	15.5	11.5	8.5	50.1	12,837	12,710	-1.0	-2.4	1,164	1,195	-264	5,096	2.40	67.2	8.6	29.6
Porter	14.2	10.0	6.4	50.5	146,798	164,302	11.9	3.2	14,453	11,752	2,733	63,251	2.58	70.2	11.4	24.1
Posey	15.8	11.1	7.7	50.1	27,061	25,910	-4.3	-1.4	2,246	1,998	-622	10,140	2.50	72.2	9.7	23.5
Pulaski	14.8	10.9	8.7	49.0	13,755	13,386	-2.7	-6.9	1,117	1,232	-810	5,296	2.38	67.8	10.2	28.1
Putnam	13.2	9.3	7.2	47.5	36,019	37,952	5.4	-0.5	3,017	2,874	-312	13,162	2.44	70.3	12.2	23.7
Randolph	14.2	11.0	9.3	50.9	27,401	26,176	-4.5	-5.1	2,472	2,362	-1,444	10,495	2.36	65.6	10.2	29.2
Ripley	13.9	10.2	7.6	50.5	26,523	28,814	8.6	-1.0	2,765	2,494	-556	11,150	2.50	71.8	10.5	24.6
Rush	14.8	10.1	8.2	50.7	18,261	17,392	-4.8	-4.2	1,544	1,583	-693	6,672	2.48	73.1	9.6	23.3
St. Joseph	12.7	9.1	6.7	51.3	265,559	266,925	0.5	1.4	29,041	21,195	-3,930	100,694	2.55	63.8	13.1	30.5
Scott	14.3	10.0	6.6	50.9	22,960	24,187	5.3	-1.3	2,340	2,501	-144	8,892	2.63	71.7	9.2	23.2
Shelby	14.9	9.9	7.3	50.3	43,445	44,396	2.2	0.4	4,150	3,680	-245	17,603	2.48	67.0	10.2	26.8
Spencer	15.7	11.3	8.0	49.7	20,391	20,952	2.8	-3.0	1,766	1,648	-744	8,101	2.51	71.3	6.7	24.6
Starke	15.1	11.1	7.5	50.1	23,556	23,362	-0.8	-1.8	2,173	2,260	-324	8,792	2.61	69.4	11.3	25.2
Steuben	15.1	12.3	7.9	49.2	33,214	34,173	2.9	1.2	3,193	2,609	-144	13,810	2.40	67.8	8.3	25.8
Sullivan	13.2	10.6	7.4	45.7	21,751	21,475	-1.3	-3.7	1,821	1,950	-657	7,601	2.47	69.5	10.7	26.4
Switzerland	14.0	10.1	7.2	48.5	9,065	10,666	17.7	0.5	1,031	852	-130	4,259	2.47	69.2	10.2	24.6
Tippecanoe	9.5	6.8	4.9	48.9	148,955	172,803	16.0	11.7	18,922	9,465	10,858	68,771	2.47	56.8	10.1	29.2
Tipton	15.2	11.8	9.1	50.2	16,577	15,936	-3.9	-5.1	1,249	1,435	-626	6,365	2.37	67.1	9.2	27.9
Union	15.3	11.6	7.8	50.4	7,349	7,516	2.3	-6.4	593	580	-496	2,860	2.50	60.5	7.2	34.1
Vanderburgh	14.0	9.5	7.4	51.5	171,922	179,703	4.5	0.7	18,607	15,805	-1,365	74,923	2.34	59.6	12.4	33.2
Vermillion	14.4	11.7	8.4	50.3	16,788	16,210	-3.4	-4.5	1,315	1,739	-307	6,533	2.36	61.9	10.7	31.6
Vigo	12.2	9.3	7.0	49.3	105,848	107,848	1.9	-0.4	10,615	9,486	-1,532	41,164	2.40	60.5	13.2	31.7
Wabash	14.4	10.9	9.9	51.5	34,960	32,888	-5.9	-4.9	2,851	3,447	-1,009	12,920	2.32	65.3	9.8	29.8
Warren	15.0	11.1	9.1	50.6	8,419	8,511	1.1	-2.9	722	647	-326	3,395	2.41	73.5	8.3	23.4
Warrick	13.9	10.4	7.1	51.0	52,383	59,689	13.9	4.8	5,338	4,449	2,028	23,742	2.56	73.5	8.3	22.5
Washington	14.6	10.4	6.6	50.2	27,223	28,262	3.8	-1.1	2,591	2,498	-402	10,570	2.60	72.6	12.3	24.3
Wayne	14.0	10.6	8.6	51.6	71,097	68,996	-3.0	-4.4	6,383	6,944	-2,484	26,397	2.44	65.6	14.4	29.2
Wells	14.3	10.1	8.2	50.7	27,600	27,637	0.1	2.1	2,885	2,230	-70	10,944	2.49	70.7	9.7	26.1
White	14.8	11.8	8.3	50.2	25,267	24,643	-2.5	-2.1	2,413	2,262	-651	9,723	2.47	69.4	9.0	25.8
Whitley	15.0	10.7	7.3	50.2	30,707	33,290	8.4	2.4	3,245	2,510	70	13,469	2.45	71.2	8.7	24.8
IOWA	13.2	9.5	7.6	50.2	2,926,324	3,046,872	4.1	3.6	320,992	237,810	26,463	1,251,587	2.41	64.0	9.0	29.0
Adair	16.0	11.4	11.3	50.3	8,243	7,682	-6.8	-8.1	591	873	-340	3,210	2.19	65.4	7.1	30.1
Adams	17.3	12.3	10.8	49.9	4,482	4,029	-10.1	-9.5	352	403	-337	1,654	2.20	65.5	4.8	27.9
Allamakee	15.4	12.6	10.1	49.3	14,675	14,328	-2.4	-3.5	1,507	1,358	-646	6,037	2.25	64.1	5.6	30.5
Appanoose	15.3	12.4	10.3	50.6	13,721	12,887	-6.1	-3.5	1,211	1,379	-272	5,407	2.29	59.1	6.4	36.2
Audubon	17.1	12.0	12.8	51.5	6,830	6,119	-10.4	-10.0	508	651	-472	2,679	2.08	60.8	7.5	33.6
Benton	15.2	10.0	8.6	50.1	25,308	26,069	3.0	-1.6	2,407	1,907	-930	10,187	2.48	69.7	6.4	25.3
Black Hawk	12.2	9.3	7.1	50.8	128,012	131,090	2.4	1.0	14,091	9,847	-2,835	52,811	2.41	59.6	9.9	31.2
Boone	15.5	10.6	7.8	49.5	26,224	26,308	0.3	0.1	2,414	2,435	74	10,998	2.32	64.1	6.1	29.9
Bremer	12.6	10.3	9.3	50.5	23,325	24,276	4.1	2.8	2,115	1,758	335	9,445	2.45	69.6	5.5	25.7
Buchanan	13.8	10.0	7.9	50.3	21,093	20,958	-0.6	1.1	2,328	1,691	-383	8,212	2.53	67.1	8.0	27.5
Buena Vista	12.9	8.6	7.4	49.2	20,411	20,265	-0.7	-1.9	2,606	1,522	-1,490	7,561	2.56	67.8	9.2	27.2
Butler	14.5	12.0	10.4	50.1	15,305	14,869	-2.8	-2.2	1,240	1,506	-52	6,278	2.32	67.6	5.4	27.6
Calhoun	15.1	11.6	11.3	48.4	11,115	10,177	-8.4	-4.7	897	1,160	-211	4,229	2.13	64.2	10.3	30.2
Carroll	14.5	10.2	10.2	50.8	21,421	20,816	-2.8	-3.2	2,147	2,014	-795	8,675	2.31	63.0	7.2	34.0
Cass	15.4	11.9	11.3	50.8	14,684	13,952	-5.0	-7.3	1,184	1,591	-609	6,053	2.15	60.6	7.2	34.4
Cedar	15.5	10.7	9.0	50.2	18,187	18,495	1.7	0.7	1,506	1,462	97	7,546	2.39	66.9	5.3	27.8
Cerro Gordo	15.8	11.8	10.0	51.1	46,447	44,151	-4.9	-3.4	3,831	4,143	-1,177	19,201	2.18	59.6	9.5	35.0
Cherokee	16.3	11.9	12.2	49.7	13,035	12,067	-7.4	-6.2	1,056	1,307	-501	5,227	2.13	61.6	9.3	31.3
Chickasaw	15.7	11.2	9.6	49.4	13,095	12,442	-5.0	-3.8	1,153	1,100	-528	5,298	2.25	63.6	4.6	30.6
Clarke	14.1	10.2	8.3	49.4	9,133	9,286	1.7	1.5	1,026	880	-4	3,870	2.35	67.2	6.9	28.1
Clay	14.9	10.6	10.2	50.8	17,372	16,667	-4.1	-3.2	1,618	1,563	-579	7,264	2.21	63.5	9.4	30.6
Clayton	17.0	12.8	11.0	49.4	18,678	18,128	-2.9	-3.2	1,564	1,614	-516	7,625	2.28	63.7	7.5	30.5
Clinton	15.1	10.7	9.0	50.9	50,149	49,117	-2.1	-5.3	4,705	4,537	-2,777	19,877	2.35	62.7	10.6	30.7
Crawford	13.3	9.4	8.1	48.9	16,942	17,096	0.9	0.4	1,979	1,350	-567	6,389	2.60	71.1	9.2	22.4
Dallas	10.0	7.0	5.0	50.7	40,750	66,138	62.3	36.4	9,917	3,412	17,290	31,363	2.56	69.4	6.4	25.0
Davis	12.8	9.4	8.4	50.5	8,541	8,753	2.5	3.0	1,194	687	-242	3,255	2.68	73.2	8.3	24.0
Decatur	12.7	10.6	9.5	50.1	8,689	8,457	-2.7	-6.7	767	769	-569	3,172	2.31	62.3	9.0	30.9
Delaware	16.3	10.2	9.1	49.6	18,404	17,770	-3.4	-3.9	1,669	1,413	-963	6,926	2.47	70.6	7.1	25.7
Des Moines	14.3	11.4	9.4	51.3	42,351	40,325	-4.8	-2.9	3,775	3,773	-1,177	16,772	2.34	63.1	10.7	32.2
Dickinson	16.3	14.9	11.3	50.3	16,424	16,667	1.5	2.9	1,329	1,642	806	8,039	2.08	63.1	6.9	32.9
Dubuque	13.6	9.7	8.3	50.6	89,143	93,643	5.0	3.4	9,861	7,351	770	38,076	2.42	66.3	8.7	27.4
Emmet	15.6	11.3	10.1	49.8	11,027	10,302	-6.6	-10.2	910	1,030	-939	4,133	2.13	63.4	9.5	31.0
Fayette	15.6	11.1	10.4	49.6	22,008	20,882	-5.1	-5.9	1,749	2,048	-927	8,315	2.33	64.9	9.1	30.6
Floyd	14.2	11.6	10.2	50.6	16,900	16,295	-3.6	-3.3	1,583	1,581	-531	6,924	2.25	63.8	9.7	32.8

1. No spouse present.

Table B. States and Counties — Population, Vital Statistics, Health, and Crime

STATE County	Persons in group quarters, 2018	Daytime Population, 2013-2017		Births, 2018		Deaths, 2018		Persons under 65 with no health insurance, 2016		Medicare, 2018			Serious crimes known to police[2], 2016 Total	
		Number	Employment/ residence ratio	Total	Rate[1]	Number	Rate[1]	Number	Percent	Total beneficiaries	Enrolled in Original Medicare	Enrolled in Medicare Advantage	Number	Rate[3]
	32	33	34	35	36	37	38	39	40	41	42	43	44	45
INDIANA— Cont'd														
Pike	213	10,189	0.61	142	11.4	151	12.2	886	9.0	2,996	2,245	751	46	452
Porter	3,421	154,230	0.83	1,696	10.0	1,611	9.5	10,151	7.3	32,120	23,764	8,356	1,240	772
Posey	242	23,262	0.81	257	10.1	257	10.1	1,479	7.0	5,368	4,041	1,327	NA	NA
Pulaski	193	12,363	0.93	128	10.3	136	10.9	1,018	10.1	2,977	2,406	571	NA	NA
Putnam	5,022	36,009	0.90	402	10.6	345	9.1	2,197	8.2	7,208	5,105	2,103	NA	NA
Randolph	329	22,400	0.75	286	11.5	277	11.1	1,914	9.6	5,865	4,798	1,067	NA	NA
Ripley	449	26,148	0.84	336	11.8	294	10.3	2,086	8.9	5,688	4,433	1,255	NA	NA
Rush	178	14,640	0.71	198	11.9	185	11.1	1,568	11.6	3,583	2,803	780	NA	NA
St. Joseph	11,339	270,089	1.01	3,504	12.9	2,493	9.2	22,735	10.4	48,917	32,281	16,636	10,248	3,830
Scott	312	20,898	0.72	285	11.9	309	12.9	1,794	9.2	5,403	4,297	1,106	437	2,244
Shelby	683	41,391	0.86	484	10.9	442	9.9	3,427	9.4	8,934	6,211	2,723	1,176	2,648
Spencer	368	18,704	0.80	194	9.5	238	11.7	1,378	8.3	4,397	3,567	830	NA	NA
Starke	16	18,479	0.53	256	11.2	279	12.2	1,951	10.4	5,639	4,307	1,332	NA	NA
Steuben	1,309	33,268	0.93	406	11.7	344	9.9	2,403	9.0	7,658	4,425	3,233	NA	NA
Sullivan	2,228	19,236	0.79	191	9.2	204	9.9	1,398	9.2	4,361	3,486	875	200	1,201
Switzerland	107	8,553	0.52	118	11.0	110	10.3	961	11.2	1,761	1,402	359	NA	NA
Tippecanoe	15,858	197,743	1.13	2,318	12.0	1,190	6.2	16,330	10.6	24,401	18,942	5,459	4,800	2,583
Tipton	205	14,070	0.83	156	10.3	159	10.5	972	8.1	3,519	2,523	996	179	1,184
Union	67	5,525	0.50	67	9.5	70	9.9	548	9.4	1,498	1,223	275	NA	NA
Vanderburgh	7,077	202,816	1.25	2,158	11.9	1,890	10.4	12,807	8.7	36,650	26,280	10,370	7,337	4,033
Vermillion	209	14,156	0.77	148	9.6	199	12.9	1,104	8.8	3,767	3,169	598	NA	NA
Vigo	9,587	115,545	1.17	1,254	11.7	1,181	11.0	7,731	9.4	21,656	17,676	3,980	4,369	4,143
Wabash	1,843	30,970	0.94	343	11.0	404	12.9	2,367	9.9	8,062	4,753	3,309	NA	NA
Warren	84	6,488	0.54	80	9.7	85	10.3	523	8.0	1,827	1,532	295	NA	NA
Warrick	727	48,516	0.57	629	10.1	603	9.6	3,572	6.9	12,483	9,095	3,388	831	1,336
Washington	261	22,927	0.58	308	11.0	299	10.7	2,336	10.2	5,892	4,324	1,568	NA	NA
Wayne	2,705	69,102	1.07	712	10.8	877	13.3	5,813	11.1	15,733	13,780	1,953	NA	NA
Wells	472	26,245	0.88	363	12.9	244	8.7	1,780	7.8	5,824	3,360	2,464	536	1,917
White	307	23,067	0.89	301	12.5	286	11.9	2,204	11.6	5,537	4,418	1,119	103	426
Whitley	436	29,868	0.78	402	11.8	311	9.1	2,249	8.1	6,944	3,356	3,588	NA	NA
IOWA	98,932	3,121,048	1.00	38,417	12.2	28,803	9.1	126,746	5.0	612,111	490,593	121,518	74,501	2,377
Adair	151	6,584	0.83	80	11.3	87	12.3	246	4.5	1,701	1,523	178	56	785
Adams	69	3,459	0.82	33	9.1	43	11.8	172	6.0	945	923	22	33	881
Allamakee	230	12,527	0.79	196	14.2	183	13.2	758	7.2	3,408	2,966	442	119	864
Appanoose	134	12,192	0.93	135	10.9	157	12.6	552	5.8	3,281	2,650	631	387	3,110
Audubon	120	4,954	0.73	65	11.8	65	11.8	245	5.8	1,543	1,491	52	59	1,035
Benton	313	19,470	0.53	301	11.7	246	9.6	855	4.0	5,202	4,031	1,171	85	333
Black Hawk	4,976	141,740	1.13	1,659	12.5	1,210	9.1	5,661	5.3	25,564	17,024	8,540	3,786	2,832
Boone	737	23,250	0.77	266	10.1	294	11.2	881	4.1	5,827	4,847	980	280	1,050
Bremer	1,583	23,973	0.94	260	10.4	224	9.0	642	3.4	5,252	4,077	1,175	285	1,151
Buchanan	305	18,645	0.76	263	12.4	204	9.6	823	4.8	4,164	2,948	1,216	232	1,102
Buena Vista	817	21,249	1.08	300	15.1	149	7.5	1,514	9.3	3,513	3,303	210	409	1,996
Butler	198	11,969	0.61	131	9.0	177	12.2	517	4.5	3,640	2,965	675	6	40
Calhoun	720	8,570	0.71	100	10.3	128	13.2	371	5.2	2,545	2,396	149	83	853
Carroll	405	21,472	1.10	252	12.5	254	12.6	627	3.8	4,727	4,323	404	253	1,240
Cass	299	13,492	1.03	141	10.9	181	14.0	587	5.8	3,568	3,225	343	158	1,187
Cedar	312	14,129	0.56	179	9.6	172	9.2	569	3.8	3,894	3,118	776	108	591
Cerro Gordo	1,184	45,701	1.12	435	10.2	502	11.8	1,402	4.2	10,962	10,458	504	1,476	3,454
Cherokee	350	11,096	0.92	127	11.2	150	13.2	487	5.7	2,892	2,587	305	115	1,004
Chickasaw	95	11,438	0.89	139	11.6	113	9.4	523	5.5	2,756	2,521	235	75	624
Clarke	156	9,479	1.05	123	13.1	98	10.4	418	5.6	2,055	1,831	224	172	1,862
Clay	234	17,068	1.08	189	11.7	166	10.3	581	4.5	3,870	3,805	65	292	1,774
Clayton	270	16,437	0.86	183	10.4	195	11.1	853	6.3	4,514	3,460	1,054	47	268
Clinton	628	47,327	0.99	539	11.6	518	11.1	1,559	4.1	10,512	8,475	2,037	1,707	3,599
Crawford	565	16,841	0.96	249	14.5	166	9.7	1,287	9.3	3,311	2,991	320	58	340
Dallas	677	70,787	0.77	1,273	14.1	469	5.2	2,817	3.7	11,507	9,149	2,358	1,325	1,596
Davis	107	7,945	0.77	167	18.5	79	8.8	618	8.6	1,695	1,412	283	14	160
Decatur	695	7,371	0.80	90	11.4	81	10.3	386	6.6	1,730	1,505	225	24	294
Delaware	217	15,667	0.82	192	11.2	174	10.2	694	5.0	3,548	2,717	831	209	1,208
Des Moines	633	42,976	1.16	420	10.7	412	10.5	1,512	4.8	9,429	8,434	995	1,805	4,518
Dickinson	185	17,209	1.02	145	8.5	189	11.0	535	4.1	4,988	4,722	266	207	1,205
Dubuque	4,286	105,005	1.17	1,150	11.9	907	9.4	3,175	4.1	19,903	9,064	10,839	2,325	2,382
Emmet	399	9,052	0.87	109	11.8	118	12.8	511	7.0	2,242	2,163	79	172	1,781
Fayette	818	19,003	0.88	205	10.4	224	11.4	811	5.3	4,875	4,042	833	178	885
Floyd	249	15,092	0.90	192	12.2	188	11.9	689	5.6	3,836	3,545	291	198	1,248

1. Per 1,000 estimated resident population. 2. Data for serious crimes have not been adjusted for underreporting; this may affect comparability between geographic areas and over time. 3. Per 100,000 population estimated by the FBI.

Table B. States and Counties — Crime, Education, Money Income, and Poverty

STATE County	Serious crimes known to police[2], 2016 (cont.)[1] Rate — Violent	Property	Education — Enrollment[3] Total	Percent private	Attainment[4] (percent) High school graduate or less	Bachelor's degree or more	Local government expenditures,[5] 2014-2015 Total current spending (mil dol)	Current spending per student (dollars)	Money income, 2013-2017 Per capita income[6]	Households Median income (dollars)	Percent with income of less than $50,000	Percent with income of $200,000 or more	Income and poverty, 2017 Median household income (dollars)	Percent below poverty level All persons	Children under 18 years	Children 5 to 17 years in families
	46	47	48	49	50	51	52	53	54	55	56	57	58	59	60	61
INDIANA— Cont'd																
Pike	138	314	2,737	5.9	56.6	13.1	19.6	10,021	25,648	50,196	49.7	0.6	49,844	10.4	14.4	13.0
Porter	54	718	42,538	19.3	42.1	27.5	237.2	8,771	31,879	65,979	38.0	4.7	67,525	10.4	12.4	11.4
Posey	NA	NA	5,837	20.9	44.0	20.7	37.6	10,515	30,763	60,992	40.2	2.7	65,617	9.1	11.9	11.0
Pulaski	NA	NA	2,870	9.2	57.7	11.8	23.8	11,670	24,445	47,633	51.7	1.0	50,022	12.5	19.1	18.0
Putnam	NA	NA	9,169	30.3	54.8	15.4	59.4	10,036	23,842	55,295	44.0	2.2	57,402	12	16.0	15.0
Randolph	NA	NA	5,548	6.9	57.3	13.7	41.7	9,619	23,427	44,985	56.5	1.2	46,016	15.3	23.1	21.3
Ripley	NA	NA	6,566	11.7	55.2	18.2	37.2	11,689	25,385	53,698	46.7	1.9	52,562	10.9	14.4	13.2
Rush	NA	NA	3,705	8.4	61.2	14.8	24.0	9,998	23,749	47,955	51.6	1.9	51,113	12	17.4	16.1
St. Joseph	506	3,323	74,393	32.8	42.8	28.4	384.3	9,846	25,893	48,121	51.3	3.6	52,188	16	21.3	19.9
Scott	144	2,100	5,357	17.6	57.1	12.9	35.4	8,951	24,186	49,243	50.6	0.9	48,615	16.3	22.3	19.9
Shelby	572	2,076	10,650	8.8	55.0	18.0	64.5	8,750	27,317	57,216	42.6	2.6	61,327	8.4	13.5	12.5
Spencer	NA	NA	4,599	6.7	54.6	15.9	28.8	8,545	29,114	55,280	44.3	2.1	56,646	10.4	12.2	10.3
Starke	NA	NA	5,148	15.5	57.0	11.4	37.9	10,037	22,153	45,526	54.2	0.8	46,940	17.1	24.1	22.5
Steuben	NA	NA	8,234	21.8	48.2	20.3	36.2	9,526	26,902	52,749	46.5	2.1	55,184	11	16.5	15.1
Sullivan	108	1,093	4,049	13.1	57.1	12.5	28.3	9,595	22,239	45,031	54.5	1.4	46,810	14.6	19.0	17.5
Switzerland	NA	NA	2,488	7.1	66.1	8.7	14.8	9,340	21,511	43,468	56.1	1.2	47,478	16.3	26.5	25.0
Tippecanoe	258	2,326	70,782	9.4	34.3	36.9	220.8	9,672	25,481	50,486	49.4	3.3	52,858	18	16.1	14.8
Tipton	106	1,078	3,245	13.3	53.0	21.3	21.9	8,501	28,507	53,931	45.6	1.9	55,503	8.9	11.2	9.7
Union	NA	NA	1,625	3.7	59.0	17.6	15.5	11,304	22,527	45,531	55.2	0.5	48,206	10.7	17.7	16.7
Vanderburgh	450	3,584	44,192	20.5	43.2	26.2	246.4	10,671	26,917	44,815	54.1	2.7	47,456	17.5	22.9	19.4
Vermillion	NA	NA	3,502	8.3	55.7	13.0	24.9	9,809	23,891	45,440	55.1	1.3	46,330	13.3	17.9	15.7
Vigo	202	3,941	30,049	13.6	44.4	23.5	146.6	9,455	22,932	42,030	57.3	2.2	42,497	19.4	25.0	22.3
Wabash	NA	NA	7,493	20.3	53.3	18.7	55.3	10,796	24,700	49,052	51.2	1.8	50,177	13.3	17.7	15.7
Warren	NA	NA	1,773	8.9	53.2	19.4	10.7	9,059	29,312	58,950	38.5	2.9	58,045	10	13.6	11.9
Warrick	215	1,121	15,513	15.6	39.0	29.2	89.3	8,826	33,528	66,080	36.6	6.2	75,727	6.8	8.5	7.4
Washington	NA	NA	6,104	10.2	60.3	12.1	39.3	9,187	23,223	46,861	53.2	1.9	47,686	13.5	20.3	19.4
Wayne	NA	NA	15,756	18.6	52.3	18.2	97.4	9,121	23,895	41,813	57.0	2.9	44,179	16.6	24.7	22.6
Wells	21	1,895	6,717	12.1	47.6	18.6	41.6	9,379	25,850	53,038	46.1	2.4	55,221	8.6	11.7	10.6
White	91	335	5,390	7.6	52.1	16.6	45.2	9,690	26,275	51,404	49.0	1.7	52,377	10.5	16.3	15.8
Whitley	NA	NA	7,728	17.8	49.7	19.5	39.6	8,576	28,073	57,041	41.8	2.3	60,126	8.5	10.4	9.2
IOWA	291	2,086	807,407	15.7	39.7	27.7	5,530.1	10,944	30,063	56,570	44.2	3.8	58,706	10.8	12.6	10.9
Adair	140	645	1,530	5.6	50.9	15.7	8.9	10,063	28,861	49,477	50.6	2.6	52,155	10.2	13.3	11.1
Adams	0	881	749	6.0	45.5	17.3	6.4	12,341	27,022	49,745	50.3	2.1	48,191	12.3	18.7	18.1
Allamakee	80	784	3,024	19.6	52.8	17.5	23.0	10,312	27,377	47,895	51.9	3.0	49,445	11	15.8	15.3
Appanoose	217	2,893	2,499	12.2	46.7	18.2	19.8	9,734	25,543	40,377	60.8	2.4	42,274	16.9	23.4	20.8
Audubon	70	965	1,126	10.6	50.7	13.7	5.7	10,075	31,523	48,750	51.3	2.7	51,484	10.7	15.4	14.1
Benton	74	258	5,877	12.9	42.6	22.0	37.9	9,831	32,356	64,061	40.0	4.2	67,946	7.8	9.0	8.2
Black Hawk	465	2,366	37,997	10.7	40.4	27.5	243.1	12,790	27,669	50,916	49.0	2.9	50,426	15.3	16.5	13.7
Boone	244	806	6,202	10.6	40.0	24.2	38.1	9,818	30,190	57,906	42.6	2.5	60,558	7.3	10.3	8.9
Bremer	505	646	7,129	33.4	37.0	29.0	53.4	10,001	32,105	65,440	36.2	4.4	64,213	7.1	6.2	5.5
Buchanan	86	1,017	5,149	17.3	47.8	19.0	30.5	9,925	30,974	59,348	42.8	3.8	62,294	9	12.6	11.5
Buena Vista	327	1,669	5,518	13.9	50.3	20.1	44.8	10,706	26,345	52,784	45.5	2.7	53,230	12.8	16.3	15.0
Butler	13	27	3,271	7.4	47.2	16.9	19.1	9,800	28,584	53,937	45.1	2.5	58,386	9	10.6	9.0
Calhoun	51	801	1,934	7.0	43.7	19.0	18.9	11,047	27,370	46,302	53.1	3.2	51,754	12.4	15.5	14.2
Carroll	39	1,201	4,808	26.0	45.0	22.5	32.2	9,736	29,191	54,563	46.9	2.7	55,084	9.1	10.5	8.7
Cass	233	954	2,754	6.4	51.3	19.6	30.4	11,736	26,427	45,637	54.4	2.0	49,281	12.1	16.5	13.5
Cedar	126	465	4,122	6.9	41.8	22.4	33.9	9,719	30,362	62,555	35.9	3.5	63,430	6.9	7.5	6.8
Cerro Gordo	152	3,302	9,016	15.3	38.1	22.2	64.1	10,305	31,292	50,569	49.4	3.5	54,454	10.8	13.1	11.4
Cherokee	210	795	2,241	9.1	45.1	19.5	17.3	9,914	30,973	53,998	45.9	4.6	56,343	9.6	11.5	10.4
Chickasaw	150	474	2,674	12.9	51.9	15.5	16.9	9,675	27,973	50,688	49.2	1.7	56,819	9.5	13.3	12.1
Clarke	152	1,711	1,918	6.6	52.9	17.2	16.6	9,430	25,879	49,718	50.4	1.5	49,889	11	15.4	14.5
Clay	134	1,641	3,673	12.2	41.7	21.7	25.5	10,403	28,514	48,978	50.8	1.9	53,615	9.3	11.6	9.7
Clayton	40	228	3,689	12.5	53.0	15.7	49.3	20,868	27,719	51,114	49.1	1.9	54,740	9.6	13.4	11.9
Clinton	555	3,044	11,328	12.3	45.5	19.2	82.5	10,495	28,091	50,295	49.8	2.5	50,729	13.4	16.4	13.8
Crawford	47	293	4,210	11.7	58.1	13.0	31.9	10,477	27,270	51,091	48.6	2.7	53,806	11.8	14.3	12.3
Dallas	194	1,402	21,899	18.6	23.2	49.1	155.5	9,460	42,417	82,719	27.3	10.7	90,133	4.4	4.8	4.0
Davis	46	114	1,766	20.4	50.8	17.8	12.5	10,110	25,747	52,390	46.3	3.7	51,477	12.1	16.7	16.7
Decatur	98	196	2,397	36.1	50.9	21.5	12.2	11,287	21,110	41,042	59.9	1.0	41,843	17.1	22.3	21.2
Delaware	139	1,069	4,004	19.2	51.3	16.9	21.4	9,294	30,768	60,534	39.5	2.6	60,458	9.3	12.2	11.4
Des Moines	576	3,942	8,795	12.8	40.6	19.8	67.4	10,306	27,168	47,524	53.0	2.1	50,773	13.5	20.0	16.7
Dickinson	186	1,019	3,434	5.1	33.0	29.5	26.1	10,240	36,588	59,889	41.9	5.1	56,496	7.5	9.6	8.1
Dubuque	243	2,139	25,702	33.4	41.0	30.0	163.7	11,156	30,117	59,150	42.3	3.8	60,936	9.8	10.7	9.3
Emmet	394	1,388	2,553	5.1	43.5	20.6	19.1	9,999	29,396	47,419	51.0	2.9	49,353	10.3	13.9	13.0
Fayette	174	711	4,681	20.9	47.7	19.8	39.5	10,763	27,020	48,412	51.3	2.3	46,389	13.4	17.5	15.4
Floyd	170	1,078	3,519	11.5	43.4	20.9	22.1	10,812	28,323	48,607	51.1	3.0	51,901	11.8	16.5	15.0

1. Data for serious crimes have not been adjusted for underreporting; this may affect comparability between geographic areas and over time.   2. Per 100,000 population estimated by the FBI.   3. All persons 3 years old and over enrolled in nursery school through college.   4. Persons 25 years old and over.   5. Elementary and secondary education expenditures.   6. Based on population estimated by the American Community Survey, 2011–2015.

Table B. States and Counties — Personal Income and Earnings

STATE County	Personal income, 2017										Earnings, 2017		
			Per capita[1]			Supplements to wages and salaries, employer contributions (mil dol)						Contributions for government social insurance (mil dol)	
	Total (mil dol)	Percent change 2016-2017	Dollars	Rank	Wages and salaries (mil dol)	Pension and insurance	Government social insurance	Proprietors' income (mil dol)	Dividends, interest, and rent (mil dol)	Personal transfer receipts (mil dol)	Total (mil dol)	From employee and self-employed	From employer
	62	63	64	65	66	67	68	69	70	71	72	73	74
INDIANA— Cont'd													
Pike	484	4.3	39,153	1,695	186	36	13	26	64	130	261	17	13
Porter	8,351	4.4	49,586	493	2,906	475	215	482	1,262	1,395	4,078	259	215
Posey	1,193	4.4	46,613	741	497	112	34	68	194	228	712	43	34
Pulaski	525	3.4	41,906	1,272	200	40	15	39	96	127	293	18	15
Putnam	1,364	4.2	36,189	2,176	545	101	41	74	191	306	762	49	41
Randolph	902	-1.7	36,186	2,177	257	53	19	69	138	261	398	28	19
Ripley	1,133	4.0	39,826	1,585	591	112	42	56	192	236	802	49	42
Rush	728	3.1	43,763	1,046	206	42	15	76	109	162	339	21	15
St. Joseph	12,472	5.9	46,118	783	5,982	980	445	1,286	2,064	2,323	8,693	518	445
Scott	869	3.2	36,397	2,135	318	63	24	34	105	257	439	31	24
Shelby	1,874	4.1	42,222	1,240	845	145	63	121	261	413	1,174	73	63
Spencer	862	4.5	42,290	1,231	292	58	21	81	114	178	452	28	21
Starke	779	2.9	34,014	2,481	157	33	12	55	94	255	258	20	12
Steuben	1,386	4.1	40,203	1,520	610	117	47	65	263	307	839	55	47
Sullivan	699	3.3	33,697	2,529	243	54	17	21	104	207	335	24	17
Switzerland	309	3.4	28,933	2,989	85	13	6	13	42	81	117	9	6
Tippecanoe	7,034	4.3	36,907	2,056	4,309	827	311	462	1,317	1,135	5,908	339	311
Tipton	659	1.8	43,567	1,069	189	34	14	25	128	150	263	19	14
Union	261	2.9	36,298	2,151	48	10	4	20	43	67	81	6	4
Vanderburgh	7,996	3.7	44,028	1,019	5,304	854	392	527	1,458	1,772	7,076	430	392
Vermillion	575	2.4	37,089	2,017	222	41	16	22	85	172	301	21	16
Vigo	4,011	4.2	37,308	1,987	2,139	401	161	239	709	1,105	2,940	184	161
Wabash	1,274	0.0	40,503	1,472	471	89	35	96	241	367	690	46	35
Warren	342	-0.5	41,686	1,303	79	15	6	30	51	75	129	8	6
Warrick	3,348	4.6	53,549	325	793	133	57	258	538	516	1,242	80	57
Washington	998	2.3	35,873	2,215	233	46	18	61	126	268	358	26	18
Wayne	2,640	3.1	39,888	1,572	1,267	233	94	158	394	776	1,752	114	94
Wells	1,133	3.4	40,476	1,479	433	85	32	65	201	241	615	39	32
White	994	1.8	41,120	1,392	364	69	28	55	173	239	515	34	28
Whitley	1,442	4.0	42,715	1,182	554	110	40	73	220	276	777	50	40
IOWA	148,043	2.0	47,093	X	73,691	13,356	5,728	11,809	29,108	25,221	104,584	6,470	5,728
Adair	328	-2.4	46,459	759	106	21	9	9	67	62	146	10	9
Adams	219	-7.9	59,530	167	50	11	4	66	37	38	131	8	4
Allamakee	595	-0.1	42,852	1,160	186	42	15	66	121	122	309	20	15
Appanoose	447	0.2	36,161	2,180	173	38	15	20	80	131	245	18	15
Audubon	245	0.2	43,884	1,032	64	14	5	27	63	58	110	7	5
Benton	1,274	2.4	49,693	481	239	50	19	149	224	203	456	32	19
Black Hawk	5,596	2.7	42,187	1,244	3,502	630	275	313	1,043	1,130	4,720	294	275
Boone	1,214	1.9	45,854	812	402	85	34	67	224	252	588	40	34
Bremer	1,165	2.8	46,759	731	424	84	32	67	240	196	607	40	32
Buchanan	927	3.3	43,729	1,050	254	54	20	70	203	175	398	27	20
Buena Vista	879	0.3	43,713	1,052	439	85	34	135	165	152	693	38	34
Butler	678	0.6	46,419	762	139	31	12	92	130	141	273	17	12
Calhoun	435	-4.8	44,667	943	109	24	9	44	98	93	186	12	9
Carroll	1,018	1.3	50,112	457	462	86	35	150	218	179	732	44	35
Cass	587	1.5	44,648	945	233	50	18	44	132	142	344	23	18
Cedar	928	2.3	50,064	461	213	42	17	58	195	135	330	23	17
Cerro Gordo	2,165	-1.5	50,337	441	1,063	185	85	290	433	427	1,623	105	85
Cherokee	649	-4.6	57,318	216	192	39	15	193	120	107	440	26	15
Chickasaw	654	-4.1	54,448	299	204	39	17	152	129	106	412	26	17
Clarke	373	5.3	39,797	1,589	173	34	13	25	58	93	245	16	13
Clay	763	2.3	47,210	695	359	68	28	97	172	141	553	34	28
Clayton	821	3.1	46,549	748	281	56	24	94	193	167	454	29	24
Clinton	1,987	1.9	42,274	1,235	874	165	72	100	347	467	1,211	82	72
Crawford	654	0.7	38,373	1,813	302	58	22	51	138	131	434	27	22
Dallas	5,435	5.3	62,299	132	2,373	343	178	296	1,027	422	3,189	195	178
Davis	300	1.8	33,493	2,556	78	18	6	41	50	67	143	11	6
Decatur	258	3.3	32,453	2,694	82	18	7	20	44	70	128	9	7
Delaware	810	3.7	47,199	697	290	62	23	103	174	133	479	29	23
Des Moines	1,877	-4.2	47,623	656	963	175	81	211	348	398	1,431	92	81
Dickinson	962	3.1	55,945	251	366	74	31	96	270	166	567	37	31
Dubuque	4,463	2.7	45,990	797	2,649	448	208	257	976	791	3,562	224	208
Emmet	400	3.3	42,459	1,209	154	32	12	33	76	92	231	15	12
Fayette	818	2.6	41,312	1,363	268	53	22	79	172	212	422	28	22
Floyd	692	-0.3	43,932	1,029	261	58	20	43	143	157	382	25	20

1. Based on the resident population estimated as of July 1 of the year shown.

Table B. States and Counties — Earnings, Social Security, and Housing

STATE County	Earnings, 2017 (cont.) Percent by selected industries									Social Security beneficiaries, December 2017		Supplemental Security Income recipients, 2017	Housing units, 2018	
	Farm	Mining, quarrying, and extractions	Construction	Manufacturing	Information; professional, scientific, technical services	Retail trade	Finance, insurance, real estate, and leasing	Health care and social assistance	Government	Number	Rate[1]		Total	Percent change, 2010-2018
	75	76	77	78	79	80	81	82	83	84	85	86	87	88
INDIANA— Cont'd														
Pike	4.7	4.9	D	D	D	2.9	D	5.7	11.2	3,285	266	230	5,823	2.6
Porter	-0.1	0.1	9.5	21.9	6.2	6.7	4.6	13.5	9.5	34,745	206	2,003	69,388	4.9
Posey	4.4	0.3	5.7	46.7	D	5.3	2.5	D	8.3	5,880	230	334	11,544	3
Pulaski	9.1	D	3.5	33.1	1.7	6.1	4.7	D	19.9	3,305	264	277	6,118	1.1
Putnam	1.6	0.7	6.9	22.4	3	5.1	3.8	D	16.2	7,825	208	455	15,142	3
Randolph	2.2	D	9.4	30.1	5	4.2	3.3	D	14.5	6,540	262	519	11,701	-0.4
Ripley	1.6	0.3	5.2	18.4	3.9	4.1	3.1	D	8.3	6,015	211	337	12,453	4.2
Rush	8.2	D	8.9	22.8	3	6.8	4.2	D	16.5	4,005	241	292	7,503	-0.1
St. Joseph	0	0	5.6	15.2	10.3	6.1	5.3	15.6	8.9	52,300	193	5,879	117,088	2
Scott	0	D	3.9	39	2.2	7.3	3	D	14.2	6,235	261	832	10,645	1.9
Shelby	1.9	0.4	8.1	32.7	3.2	4.8	3.1	6.8	13.2	9,670	218	675	19,454	2
Spencer	6.2	D	6.6	21.1	D	2.7	3	6.8	10.6	4,815	236	269	9,139	3
Starke	8	0	5.6	17.4	2.8	8.1	2.8	D	18	6,350	277	560	11,190	2.1
Steuben	0.4	0.1	5.1	37.9	3	7.2	2.6	D	8.6	8,300	241	448	20,151	4
Sullivan	-1.2	D	3.3	11.9	3.7	5.8	2.8	4.1	28	4,785	231	383	8,958	0.2
Switzerland	-2	D	7.6	D	1.6	3.6	D	D	20.7	1,965	184	198	5,383	8
Tippecanoe	-0.1	D	4.8	22.7	5.1	5.3	5.1	14	26.7	25,930	136	2,282	76,722	7.9
Tipton	0.3	0	10.6	32.6	4.9	6.5	4.7	9.4	14.2	3,845	254	153	6,996	0
Union	1	0	8	17.4	2.4	7.4	D	D	24.4	1,670	232	136	3,259	0.6
Vanderburgh	0.1	0.1	7.5	16.4	6.7	6.4	5	19.3	8.8	39,605	218	4,544	84,507	1.8
Vermillion	0.6	D	20.2	22.8	2.2	7.3	D	11.3	10.8	4,140	267	326	7,489	0
Vigo	0.6	1.9	6.8	15.5	4	7.3	4.9	18.1	18.1	23,380	217	3,156	47,532	3.3
Wabash	3.7	D	6.4	29.7	3.8	7.4	4.4	D	10.7	8,730	278	574	14,196	0.2
Warren	17.3	D	6.5	22.5	D	3.1	1.2	12.4	13.9	2,005	244	80	3,769	2.4
Warrick	0.5	2.2	8.4	16	6.4	4.8	6.8	27.4	9.6	13,415	215	701	26,432	9.2
Washington	3.6	D	10.4	26.3	3.3	10.1	3.6	D	16.5	6,575	236	650	12,453	1.9
Wayne	0.6	D	4.1	21.6	3.1	7.3	4.9	21.7	13	17,440	264	2,157	31,450	0.7
Wells	2.6	D	5.6	28.3	D	5.5	5.4	10.8	10.7	6,295	225	313	11,924	2.3
White	4.6	0.3	9.3	27.9	D	7.6	4.6	7	12.3	6,010	249	325	13,134	1.3
Whitley	0.9	0	6.9	46.4	2	5.6	4.1	6.1	9.7	7,575	224	398	14,887	4.3
IOWA	2	0.2	7.2	16.4	6.6	6	10.3	10.7	16.5	638,322	203	51,138	1,409,650	5.5
Adair	-1.6	D	D	D	2.9	6.3	5.3	D	17.3	1,765	250	83	3,716	0.5
Adams	10.6	D	3.3	29.4	4.6	6	D	11.6	9.3	975	265	65	2,013	0.1
Allamakee	5.8	0.3	8.4	18.6	2.2	8.2	4	8.3	19.7	3,565	257	146	7,823	2.7
Appanoose	-3.2	D	2.9	26	D	8.3	3.6	D	16.1	3,535	286	430	6,647	0.2
Audubon	16.8	0	7.5	10.5	2.9	4.2	5.4	D	20.3	1,575	282	62	3,013	1.4
Benton	0.5	D	13.4	23.7	3.2	7.8	6	D	19.8	5,630	220	319	11,180	0.8
Black Hawk	0.3	D	4.9	25.3	5.9	6.7	6	13.6	15.5	27,145	205	3,233	58,320	4.4
Boone	1.2	D	8.7	6.6	6	6.9	4.2	7.9	26.3	5,925	224	312	12,034	2.4
Bremer	2.1	D	6.1	18	3.5	7	17.1	D	19.5	5,450	219	188	10,519	6.1
Buchanan	2.8	D	11.3	20.6	3	7.5	5.7	D	22.3	4,450	210	300	9,104	1.5
Buena Vista	12	0	4.6	29.6	D	5.3	3.8	D	15.4	3,645	181	256	8,290	0.6
Butler	21	D	4.9	16.4	2.6	4.7	5.2	D	15.7	3,915	268	171	6,810	1.9
Calhoun	13.7	0	5.9	3	D	6.2	5.2	D	20.2	2,660	273	150	5,134	0.5
Carroll	7.2	D	7	12.1	3.6	7.3	9.6	D	9.6	4,780	235	252	9,540	1.7
Cass	3.1	D	11.4	12.4	4.2	7.6	6.2	9.3	26.2	3,690	281	302	6,581	-0.1
Cedar	1.4	0.1	8.7	16	6.4	5.3	4.4	D	17.8	4,070	219	153	8,254	2.4
Cerro Gordo	0.2	D	5.4	17.4	6.2	7	6.1	23.8	11.5	11,390	265	829	22,361	0.9
Cherokee	8.6	D	5.9	29.4	5.4	4.1	2.9	D	13.7	3,025	267	116	5,783	0.1
Chickasaw	1.2	D	5.7	40.4	4.1	5.2	4	D	9.3	2,890	241	129	5,702	0.4
Clarke	3.8	D	D	33.5	D	7	2.6	6.5	19.2	2,155	230	146	4,326	5.9
Clay	6.6	D	6.6	8.6	D	12.6	3.9	12	18.4	4,030	249	218	8,300	3
Clayton	9.4	D	17.1	13.6	2.9	5.6	4	D	16.7	4,730	268	224	9,139	1.6
Clinton	-0.8	D	6.5	28.6	3.9	6.8	5.2	15.3	12.1	11,140	237	1,096	22,184	2.1
Crawford	4.2	0	5.5	31.4	2.7	5.8	4.8	5.9	19.1	3,520	206	203	7,053	1.6
Dallas	-0.2	0	5.7	4.8	6.7	7.1	41.3	8.3	7.9	11,550	132	424	38,278	40.4
Davis	-6.1	D	17.3	12.9	D	7	4.7	D	25.8	1,815	202	127	3,602	0.1
Decatur	6.9	D	8.1	4	3.1	5.9	D	D	23.5	1,830	230	195	3,856	0.6
Delaware	7.9	0.1	8.8	29	2.7	4.7	4.5	D	17.2	3,665	214	211	8,118	1.1
Des Moines	0	D	6.2	31.4	4.6	6.8	3.6	15.7	11.2	9,765	248	1,019	18,597	0.3
Dickinson	3.1	D	9.4	22.2	4.3	9.9	5.9	6.8	13	5,095	296	172	14,108	9.8
Dubuque	0.7	D	5.6	20.2	7.6	6.5	11.2	14.6	8.3	21,110	218	1,611	41,504	6.6
Emmet	7.1	D	6.8	17.5	D	6	D	D	18.2	2,360	250	118	4,820	1.3
Fayette	9	D	9.6	7	2.8	6.1	3.8	D	15.6	5,140	260	522	9,581	0.2
Floyd	2.9	D	4.9	35.1	2.9	6.4	5.6	D	15.9	4,050	257	322	7,591	0.9

1. Per 1,000 resident population estimated as of July 1 of the year shown.

STATE County	Total	Percent	Median value[1]	With a mortgage	Without a mortgage[2]	Median rent[3]	Median rent as a percent of income[2]	Sub-standard units[4] (percent)	Total	Percent change, 2017-2018	Total	Rate[5]	Total	Management, business, science, and arts	Construction, production, and maintenance occupations
	89	90	91	92	93	94	95	96	97	98	99	100	101	102	103
INDIANA— Cont'd															
Pike	5,096	82.8	89,300	16.2	10.9	634	24.2	1.3	6,140	-4.9	214	3.5	5,922	24.4	42.7
Porter	63,251	75.4	173,100	19.2	10.4	899	28.9	1.7	86,770	0.8	3,336	3.8	79,536	35.7	26.3
Posey	10,140	83.1	138,800	17.7	10.0	698	27.7	.2	13,731	1.4	388	2.8	12,454	31.7	31.2
Pulaski	5,296	76.4	92,600	19.5	10.0	665	25.6	1.8	6,528	2.2	204	3.1	5,654	26.8	42.4
Putnam	13,162	73.6	120,300	19.4	10.8	734	23	3.2	16,882	1.6	637	3.8	16,283	28.5	31.2
Randolph	10,495	75.9	79,500	18.8	11.3	623	24.4	1.2	11,614	-1.1	454	3.9	11,436	26.0	39.2
Ripley	11,150	76.7	139,500	19.2	10.0	682	26.5	3.5	14,080	0	507	3.6	13,646	27.7	35.7
Rush	6,672	72.6	100,000	17.9	11.4	650	27.1	1.8	9,038	1.1	260	2.9	7,403	24.4	38.6
St. Joseph	100,694	67.9	118,600	18.4	10.0	743	28.7	1.7	136,728	1.5	4,871	3.6	125,645	34.6	23.7
Scott	8,892	75.0	98,800	20.3	10.3	769	26.7	1	10,612	1.3	415	3.9	10,269	22.9	41.6
Shelby	17,603	73.4	125,300	18.4	10.7	754	27	2.3	23,195	1.3	719	3.1	22,045	28.7	34.3
Spencer	8,101	82.0	117,900	18.8	10.0	650	23.4	1	10,983	0.5	360	3.3	9,859	28.6	36.2
Starke	8,792	80.2	101,600	20.4	11.4	665	24.5	1.7	10,484	0.2	454	4.3	9,729	24.3	38.8
Steuben	13,810	77.8	136,300	19.5	10.1	729	23.4	1.3	20,351	1.9	542	2.7	17,154	25.6	35.3
Sullivan	7,601	72.7	80,900	18.2	11.0	668	32.2	2.9	8,616	0.3	402	4.7	8,087	26.2	37.1
Switzerland	4,259	70.6	114,300	24.1	14.1	763	24.4	3.6	5,096	1.9	198	3.9	4,378	16.6	40.3
Tippecanoe	68,771	54.2	144,300	18.2	10.0	823	32.6	1.8	97,693	2.1	3,081	3.2	91,869	39.2	22.5
Tipton	6,365	79.7	110,300	18.7	10.0	725	27.6	1	9,238	.8	259	2.8	7,430	32.3	35.4
Union	2,860	72.6	109,900	21.0	13.4	741	29.4	1.4	3,671	1.6	115	3.1	3,429	21.8	31.1
Vanderburgh	74,923	64.1	121,200	19.6	11.5	751	31.5	1.8	95,249	1.6	3,038	3.2	86,719	33.2	25.1
Vermillion	6,533	75.0	74,600	18.2	10.1	581	24.6	1.9	7,169	0.2	395	5.5	6,440	25.3	37.6
Vigo	41,164	60.5	90,700	18.2	11.4	717	32.6	1.8	49,142	0.3	2,153	4.4	47,559	32.5	24.4
Wabash	12,920	74.0	96,700	18.2	10.0	663	26	1.2	14,901	-1.6	520	3.5	15,079	30.3	31.5
Warren	3,395	83.9	112,500	17.9	10.0	763	25.3	3	4,219	3	136	3.2	4,012	30.9	39.3
Warrick	23,742	80.5	158,100	18.6	10.0	826	28.4	.2	33,148	1.4	972	2.9	31,003	39.3	24.7
Washington	10,570	76.0	106,200	19.1	10.5	639	27.1	2.2	13,767	0.9	485	3.5	11,952	28.0	40.2
Wayne	26,397	67.4	96,500	19.1	11.2	665	29.3	.2	31,319	1.4	1,126	3.6	29,078	30.2	29.0
Wells	10,944	79.4	121,000	18.0	10.0	662	27.4	1.1	14,396	1.9	405	2.8	13,703	27.3	34.1
White	9,723	78.4	105,800	18.4	10.6	703	24.6	1.9	13,639	2.1	419	3.1	11,428	26.7	38.5
Whitley	13,469	79.5	131,600	19.0	10.0	645	24.4	1.4	17,645	.2	504	2.9	16,513	27.0	36.6
IOWA	1,251,587	71.1	137,200	19.0	11.2	740	27.1	1.9	1,686,840	0.5	42,560	2.5	1,599,718	35.3	25.5
Adair	3,210	76.6	93,200	19.8	11.2	549	22.8	0.7	4,116	-0.3	98	2.4	3,680	28.2	34.8
Adams	1,654	77.8	84,900	19.7	11.1	476	19.8	1.7	2,119	-0.5	41	1.9	1,796	37.4	31.4
Allamakee	6,037	76.5	122,800	19.3	13.1	562	23.8	3.6	7,366	-1.8	226	3.1	6,881	29.8	37.4
Appanoose	5,407	76.0	78,000	20.5	14.2	569	26.5	3.1	5,856	-2.8	194	3.3	5,502	28.7	31.6
Audubon	2,679	78.5	68,800	16.5	10.0	560	23.2	0.6	3,116	-1.1	76	2.4	2,882	29.6	31.0
Benton	10,187	81.7	147,800	19.8	11.0	608	25.6	1.1	13,356	0.2	361	2.7	13,230	31.8	31.1
Black Hawk	52,811	66.0	139,300	19.2	11.3	747	29.6	1.7	68,953	1	1,909	2.8	68,771	31.8	25.5
Boone	10,998	75.5	130,500	19.2	11.4	670	25.2	2.5	14,816	0.1	317	2.1	13,803	31.5	26.9
Bremer	9,445	81.4	155,100	19.7	10.0	625	24.4	0.5	13,845	0.6	281	2	12,931	37.1	24.6
Buchanan	8,212	79.5	132,500	18.5	11.4	668	23.3	2.2	11,185	1	286	2.6	10,412	30.5	33.1
Buena Vista	7,561	66.2	111,100	17.7	10.0	640	23	7	11,349	-1.5	241	2.1	10,658	26.3	38.5
Butler	6,278	78.8	112,100	18.1	11.7	614	20.8	1.2	7,833	-0.2	215	2.7	7,431	29.9	32.1
Calhoun	4,229	77.1	77,800	16.9	10.7	541	26	1.9	4,290	-1.4	108	2.5	4,370	33.3	28.4
Carroll	8,675	75.1	127,400	17.2	10.0	575	28.1	1	10,811	-1.8	202	1.9	10,592	31.3	28.7
Cass	6,053	69.4	93,600	18.9	11.5	633	25	0.9	7,098	-0.3	190	2.7	6,544	29.4	31.5
Cedar	7,546	79.2	143,800	18.6	11.8	705	19.4	0.6	10,759	-0.1	260	2.4	9,872	34.9	27.9
Cerro Gordo	19,201	68.9	121,500	18.5	11.1	673	25.7	0.8	23,298	0.5	607	2.6	22,051	32.1	28.7
Cherokee	5,227	76.2	89,200	15.3	10.0	549	19.4	0.8	5,943	-1.5	128	2.2	5,990	27.7	33.3
Chickasaw	5,298	78.1	105,100	18.2	11.2	557	24.2	1.1	6,407	0.8	173	2.7	6,269	30.4	35.8
Clarke	3,870	68.3	105,000	20.1	12.1	730	24.5	3.8	4,801	0.5	136	2.8	4,610	31.1	36.6
Clay	7,264	69.2	115,700	19.0	11.2	629	26	2.4	8,583	0.4	273	3.2	8,247	33.2	28.6
Clayton	7,625	75.6	116,500	20.9	11.0	631	23.9	2.1	10,133	-0.3	321	3.2	9,050	27.6	36.6
Clinton	19,877	74.3	112,400	19.3	12.6	645	29.9	0.7	22,606	-2.3	728	3.2	22,825	28.6	32.2
Crawford	6,389	72.2	93,400	18.0	10.0	618	22	4.5	8,122	-1.4	276	3.4	8,112	25.9	45.5
Dallas	31,363	75.1	218,000	18.1	11.0	939	25.6	2.2	47,653	1.7	818	1.7	44,329	51.1	14.5
Davis	3,255	81.2	109,100	20.1	11.5	658	26.9	7.1	4,251	-0.1	113	2.7	3,949	35.0	32.3
Decatur	3,172	66.4	76,300	20.4	12.1	512	29	5.9	4,322	1.2	97	2.2	3,780	31.0	26.6
Delaware	6,926	82.2	126,000	17.9	12.1	593	25.4	1.1	10,411	-0.7	215	2.1	9,345	30.9	35.0
Des Moines	16,772	72.1	101,400	19.2	13.1	743	29.5	1.6	19,450	-0.8	634	3.3	19,302	27.8	30.3
Dickinson	8,039	75.9	175,900	20.1	11.1	743	26.2	0.7	9,865	-2.2	311	3.2	9,177	36.1	28.1
Dubuque	38,076	72.2	157,200	19.2	10.6	742	27.8	1.3	55,213	1.4	1,333	2.4	50,779	34.9	23.5
Emmet	4,133	77.4	85,700	18.9	12.1	662	25.3	3.1	5,292	-1.9	145	2.7	4,894	31.4	32.8
Fayette	8,315	75.8	90,800	18.7	12.0	602	26.9	1	10,572	1	313	3	10,036	30.2	31.6
Floyd	6,924	72.4	102,400	17.6	11.3	556	29.5	1.8	8,806	0.5	237	2.7	8,223	34.1	27.8

1. Specified owner-occupied units.   2. A value of 10.0 represents 10 percent or less; a value of 50.0 represents 50 percent or more.   3. Specified renter-occupied units.   4. Overcrowded or lacking complete plumbing facilities.   5. Percent of civilian labor force.   6. Civilian employed persons 16 years old and over.

Table B. States and Counties — Nonfarm Employment and Agriculture

	Private nonfarm establishments, employment and payroll, 2016									Agriculture, 2017			
	Employment							Annual payroll		Farms			Farm producers whose primary occupation is farming (percent)
							Professional, scientific, and technical services				Percent with:		
STATE County	Number of establishments	Total	Health care and social assistance	Manufacturing	Retail trade	Finance and insurance		Total (mil dol)	Average per employee (dollars)	Number	Fewer than 50 acres	1000 acres or more	
	104	105	106	107	108	109	110	111	112	113	114	115	116
INDIANA— Cont'd													
Pike	197	2,178	398	159	261	34	31	94	43,384	327	36.4	5.8	24.1
Porter	3,530	54,602	9,265	10,271	7,706	1,146	1,764	2,341	42,880	445	48.1	7.0	42.6
Posey	518	8,994	497	2,936	658	118	290	500	55,639	491	38.1	13.6	49.3
Pulaski	305	3,492	600	1,274	408	123	59	136	38,920	547	41.0	13.9	44.4
Putnam	698	11,763	1,834	2,747	1,275	250	184	396	33,662	828	44.8	4.5	30.8
Randolph	469	5,898	744	2,013	626	158	131	220	37,351	754	43.1	9.4	46.6
Ripley	635	10,619	1,377	2,115	829	242	173	487	45,833	879	36.9	4.7	34.3
Rush	360	3,423	536	657	387	94	126	118	34,569	557	30.9	9.2	51.3
St. Joseph	5,802	119,879	19,633	15,411	15,703	3,835	4,928	4,994	41,660	629	56.0	5.7	41.1
Scott	384	6,431	1,204	1,989	857	93	137	218	33,931	315	46.7	4.1	34.1
Shelby	927	16,479	1,893	5,495	1,480	197	215	701	42,536	567	44.4	11.8	44.8
Spencer	395	4,987	229	1,461	672	168	215	219	43,869	665	37.4	5.4	40.5
Starke	298	2,933	474	827	551	67	52	95	32,347	507	47.1	8.9	37.3
Steuben	960	14,380	1,371	5,116	2,139	215	200	472	32,850	472	40.3	6.1	35.4
Sullivan	333	4,125	567	468	569	106	99	164	39,729	450	30.7	9.3	43.5
Switzerland	125	1,570	150	87	135	25	15	51	32,208	410	38.3	1.0	30.5
Tippecanoe	3,570	66,250	10,961	15,671	9,450	1,666	2,663	2,812	42,444	693	53.7	9.1	35.4
Tipton	307	3,423	529	956	429	107	75	122	35,679	404	43.8	11.1	43.4
Union	111	930	76	344	196	19	23	27	29,033	238	26.5	9.2	51.2
Vanderburgh	4,995	102,062	19,775	11,076	12,805	4,882	3,918	4,325	42,377	251	47.8	6.4	43.4
Vermillion	270	3,192	567	677	620	54	39	176	55,032	283	36.7	14.5	49.8
Vigo	2,472	43,791	10,044	6,891	6,756	1,302	1,107	1,564	35,717	477	55.6	6.9	37.7
Wabash	727	11,072	2,149	2,713	1,371	297	214	380	34,300	724	41.0	7.6	40.6
Warren	125	1,394	270	582	106	35	14	49	34,933	417	37.9	11.5	36.4
Warrick	1,133	14,296	3,778	2,252	1,594	516	447	620	43,369	364	53.0	9.1	41.7
Washington	459	4,809	747	1,608	734	119	122	150	31,204	865	36.8	5.4	40.1
Wayne	1,471	25,068	5,374	5,598	3,727	793	430	933	37,202	768	38.5	4.2	40.4
Wells	622	10,584	1,717	2,844	985	164	249	364	34,369	581	39.1	14.3	44.9
White	590	7,321	772	2,881	1,129	186	90	255	34,793	539	37.3	14.8	48.8
Whitley	672	10,891	1,106	4,725	1,429	224	209	423	38,818	696	48.3	7.8	31.6
IOWA	81,563	1,354,487	224,133	208,831	187,275	98,251	55,168	56,930	42,031	86,104	31.7	9.8	45.0
Adair	191	1,795	330	D	264	78	76	59	32,752	738	22.2	14.5	44.4
Adams	106	1,073	412	222	95	34	22	44	41,215	509	21.2	10.4	51.2
Allamakee	403	4,034	857	948	595	204	66	138	34,103	997	26.7	6.0	38.2
Appanoose	297	3,832	662	1,093	713	111	82	126	32,770	675	35.9	6.4	36.4
Audubon	191	1,205	299	182	169	58	32	40	32,892	628	29.1	13.9	47.8
Benton	559	4,496	818	647	805	197	79	158	35,033	1,148	33.3	11.8	49.3
Black Hawk	3,189	68,598	15,570	12,168	9,351	2,255	3,508	2,540	37,031	968	42.3	8.9	42.5
Boone	566	7,070	1,733	501	1,059	162	162	249	35,228	967	44.0	10.2	36.5
Bremer	608	9,419	1,731	1,757	1,345	946	225	388	41,192	963	35.7	6.3	40.5
Buchanan	488	5,395	1,187	1,013	822	233	90	194	36,000	1,057	35.3	8.0	49.5
Buena Vista	554	8,898	1,298	3,261	1,084	292	237	313	35,230	802	24.9	12.7	52.4
Butler	328	2,402	533	631	389	138	58	81	33,657	1,074	40.3	8.8	46.9
Calhoun	282	2,234	639	101	398	110	39	73	32,497	813	33.1	16.1	52.0
Carroll	865	10,527	2,339	1,463	1,659	767	207	370	35,180	1,074	35.2	7.3	45.6
Cass	474	4,779	1,108	526	909	216	118	161	33,595	643	28.1	14.3	48.0
Cedar	464	4,449	621	663	683	148	83	150	33,748	933	37.6	9.4	45.9
Cerro Gordo	1,419	20,403	4,240	2,879	3,717	1,041	654	786	38,530	760	33.6	12.6	46.2
Cherokee	339	3,836	877	358	704	161	78	159	41,446	863	21.7	8.9	55.4
Chickasaw	410	3,887	577	1,394	448	170	57	152	39,202	973	33.4	7.5	44.4
Clarke	182	3,385	562	1,064	605	95	45	116	34,364	624	23.2	6.3	31.6
Clay	603	7,252	1,430	666	1,506	257	168	258	35,591	716	26.0	15.4	50.4
Clayton	528	5,341	1,143	973	682	178	95	188	35,196	1,525	26.8	5.0	42.2
Clinton	1,135	19,102	3,939	4,334	2,779	710	303	705	36,906	1,169	30.8	9.8	44.7
Crawford	431	6,375	1,175	2,243	781	215	111	229	35,947	915	26.6	12.0	49.3
Dallas	1,952	38,713	3,921	1,816	6,159	12,868	1,409	1,930	49,864	924	41.0	8.2	35.9
Davis	177	1,482	391	146	278	55	52	51	34,669	826	30.4	4.6	35.8
Decatur	133	1,742	317	50	223	41	29	41	23,512	659	25.2	9.0	39.1
Delaware	484	6,355	1,169	2,319	664	290	118	242	38,140	1,331	30.2	5.2	49.7
Des Moines	1,119	20,428	3,798	4,851	3,162	488	341	784	38,358	593	32.5	7.6	40.7
Dickinson	777	7,656	998	1,600	1,148	232	169	276	36,094	411	29.7	15.8	51.7
Dubuque	2,759	55,171	8,317	8,847	7,662	3,948	2,346	2,285	41,419	1,402	30.5	3.4	42.8
Emmet	314	3,275	768	822	488	125	61	103	31,310	488	26.2	13.9	56.7
Fayette	557	6,323	1,223	595	887	183	121	193	30,489	1,265	31.2	6.7	46.9
Floyd	418	4,574	1,214	639	802	204	109	169	36,965	917	33.9	10.9	45.2

Table B. States and Counties — Agriculture

STATE County	Acreage (1,000)	Percent change, 2012-2017	Average size of farm	Total irrigated (1,000)	Total cropland (1,000)	Value of land and buildings (dollars) Average per farm	Average per acre	Value of machinery and equiopmnet, average per farm (dollars)	Total (mil dol)	Average per farm (acres)	Crops	Livestock and poultry products	Organic farms (number)	Farms with internet access (percent)	Total ($1,000)	Percent of farms
	117	118	119	120	121	122	123	124	125	126	127	128	129	130	131	132
INDIANA— Cont'd																
Pike	81	0.7	246	D	63.3	1,214,424	4,931	138,768	42.6	130,343	68.1	31.9	NA	75.8	2,207	65.1
Porter	123	1.6	275	10.4	114.7	1,862,858	6,766	198,333	77.3	173,742	88.4	11.6	NA	79.6	3,698	53.9
Posey	194	-15.3	395	13.0	175.2	2,396,308	6,073	274,785	118.2	240,717	92.7	7.3	2	74.7	7,423	68.2
Pulaski	232	7.1	424	29.9	217.7	2,607,043	6,150	185,625	188.2	344,108	68.0	32.0	NA	73.9	5,770	72.2
Putnam	185	-6.4	223	0.5	140.4	1,437,116	6,435	103,171	85.1	102,793	84.7	15.3	NA	78.1	5,065	47.3
Randolph	242	0.3	321	0.2	224.5	2,057,555	6,417	207,262	213.1	282,635	55.4	44.6	10	75.9	5,720	59.3
Ripley	176	5.6	200	0.1	132.1	1,034,225	5,163	123,313	86.5	98,396	78.3	21.7	8	72.8	3,808	58.7
Rush	211	1.8	379	0.1	195.5	2,752,265	7,255	243,945	165.1	296,497	67.1	32.9	NA	79.4	4,579	63.4
St. Joseph	150	-1.3	238	28.1	133.8	1,928,345	8,087	164,410	103.9	165,261	80.0	20.0	3	74.4	4,335	44.7
Scott	59	15.2	188	3.7	45.7	1,010,422	5,368	116,543	23.8	75,695	88.9	11.1	NA	74.0	1,843	38.7
Shelby	220	-5.4	389	5.2	207.4	2,700,637	6,945	229,128	135.6	239,138	88.3	11.7	1	76.4	6,523	56.1
Spencer	169	-0.6	255	0.7	133.5	1,174,320	4,609	174,957	92.9	139,705	75.0	25.0	1	73.1	4,531	62.0
Starke	146	9.2	287	38.7	130.6	1,438,032	5,004	146,138	69.2	136,578	94.9	5.1	1	68.6	6,179	73.8
Steuben	120	15.1	255	13.0	101.7	1,411,595	5,537	144,619	64.0	135,672	71.0	29.0	NA	74.4	2,336	63.1
Sullivan	160	-6.0	356	7.1	139.6	1,770,624	4,977	190,307	88.9	197,533	90.3	9.7	2	82.2	4,194	69.3
Switzerland	55	8.9	134	D	27.8	549,933	4,098	67,288	14.8	36,127	74.6	25.4	9	68.0	711	24.4
Tippecanoe	222	0.9	321	4.6	197.0	2,893,652	9,027	188,551	143.0	206,338	83.1	16.9	1	85.6	3,070	51.9
Tipton	161	11.1	399	D	155.9	3,261,470	8,167	274,856	114.9	284,366	82.1	17.9	NA	85.6	2,684	67.6
Union	83	11.5	349	NA	71.0	2,211,666	6,340	200,911	41.9	175,992	91.5	8.5	NA	79.0	2,457	69.3
Vanderburgh	64	-16.5	255	1.3	61.0	2,013,091	7,906	184,217	39.0	155,339	98.0	2.0	NA	74.9	1,620	61.4
Vermillion	123	4.0	435	0.3	104.4	2,467,818	5,674	233,387	76.8	271,247	76.8	23.2	NA	71.0	1,888	53.7
Vigo	120	2.1	252	1.6	100.9	1,364,518	5,425	135,673	55.4	116,216	98.9	1.1	2	75.7	1,454	55.1
Wabash	211	6.9	292	1.8	190.3	1,835,188	6,290	192,429	161.2	222,664	59.1	40.9	2	76.8	3,814	62.3
Warren	188	6.8	450	7.1	167.9	3,057,183	6,786	239,741	130.6	313,293	79.7	20.3	2	78.9	4,075	62.8
Warrick	105	5.6	289	0.1	86.4	1,569,892	5,429	175,673	49.4	135,821	92.6	7.4	NA	77.2	2,445	46.4
Washington	212	6.2	245	0.2	147.0	1,102,858	4,501	129,743	160.6	185,609	42.5	57.5	2	70.4	3,910	36.0
Wayne	163	4.9	213	0.9	131.5	1,169,226	5,492	110,988	100.1	130,385	68.6	31.4	31	71.1	3,878	48.6
Wells	225	12.3	387	0.0	215.4	2,922,012	7,544	255,414	192.1	330,707	62.5	37.5	4	79.9	3,224	70.7
White	283	-1.8	525	5.0	266.5	4,101,696	7,815	319,127	256.8	476,384	61.8	38.2	NA	86.3	3,750	67.7
Whitley	176	25.8	253	1.6	154.1	1,606,248	6,343	187,714	120.9	173,774	65.3	34.7	NA	78.4	3,103	51.1
IOWA	30,564	-0.2	355	222.0	26,546.0	2,506,812	7,062	230,716	28,956.5	336,296	47.8	52.2	785	79.6	682,995	71.2
Adair	335	3.5	454	0.1	261.5	2,372,891	5,230	223,107	188.0	254,749	54.9	45.1	9	77.8	7,583	75.7
Adams	223	-2.5	439	D	174.1	2,189,535	4,987	197,021	108.3	212,764	59.2	40.8	NA	76.8	6,239	79.8
Allamakee	292	0.9	293	0.0	188.8	1,564,078	5,345	172,462	200.5	201,062	33.3	66.7	18	75.4	6,176	81.4
Appanoose	179	-4.5	266	NA	108.3	1,079,752	4,065	87,526	44.5	65,901	59.4	40.6	1	76.3	3,894	55.9
Audubon	276	-1.7	439	D	253.4	3,012,527	6,866	285,066	276.6	440,482	47.0	53.0	2	76.9	9,364	83.9
Benton	421	-0.4	366	0.2	384.2	2,706,668	7,387	245,776	347.7	302,895	62.8	37.2	11	80.7	7,127	77.0
Black Hawk	292	-1.6	302	0.4	275.6	2,632,645	8,723	250,907	261.2	269,871	61.9	38.1	5	84.2	6,532	73.1
Boone	315	0.5	326	0.2	288.7	2,595,336	7,966	205,330	218.4	225,806	73.9	26.1	4	83.1	5,716	70.4
Bremer	262	-3.5	272	0.5	240.8	2,174,810	7,991	227,554	229.9	238,769	59.4	40.6	10	81.0	5,871	77.8
Buchanan	330	-3.5	312	0.1	309.5	2,459,772	7,884	252,896	366.4	346,651	50.9	49.1	33	79.6	8,083	70.3
Buena Vista	357	-1.2	445	D	334.9	3,577,469	8,045	302,722	537.2	669,864	32.9	67.1	4	81.9	6,426	84.4
Butler	359	-1.0	334	1.6	333.5	2,397,864	7,169	202,064	291.5	271,395	62.8	37.2	3	81.3	11,840	80.4
Calhoun	351	-2.0	432	0.7	334.0	3,429,727	7,942	290,880	321.6	395,549	54.8	45.2	7	79.1	5,250	65.6
Carroll	349	-2.8	325	0.5	319.5	2,608,918	8,030	239,347	573.0	533,488	31.1	68.9	10	80.4	5,341	55.5
Cass	285	-1.8	443	D	241.9	2,610,781	5,895	236,918	203.4	316,264	56.9	43.1	7	77.1	5,293	73.4
Cedar	340	8.9	365	0.3	307.8	2,866,790	7,858	275,263	321.5	344,610	58.5	41.5	4	80.6	4,563	73.1
Cerro Gordo	320	-2.2	421	0.5	305.2	3,088,779	7,341	250,319	226.6	298,208	74.6	25.4	1	89.1	7,612	80.0
Cherokee	339	0.4	392	0.0	299.4	3,105,879	7,914	300,575	387.1	448,583	41.9	58.1	1	83.2	5,329	47.6
Chickasaw	293	-2.0	301	0.3	269.2	2,248,034	7,463	227,181	303.0	311,375	48.9	51.1	1	71.2	6,716	63.7
Clarke	193	14.1	309	D	112.2	1,319,833	4,271	98,535	123.2	197,500	17.4	82.6	1	71.8	7,147	68.6
Clay	329	3.2	460	0.7	306.8	3,670,430	7,985	310,588	348.7	487,042	46.9	53.1	1	85.9	9,744	84.8
Clayton	413	3.7	271	0.4	305.5	1,500,568	5,545	166,778	364.2	238,852	39.1	60.9	30	72.0	12,580	81.6
Clinton	403	-3.5	345	0.4	358.9	2,599,062	7,544	252,926	339.8	290,686	61.9	38.1	2	80.8	9,749	76.6
Crawford	440	-2.5	481	0.5	391.0	3,255,634	6,774	269,409	400.3	437,461	55.3	44.7	4	76.6	8,356	59.8
Dallas	293	-4.2	318	0.8	257.6	2,594,337	8,169	186,706	237.6	257,187	60.5	39.5	20	82.1	4,422	48.6
Davis	199	-7.2	240	0.1	121.8	941,546	3,916	125,282	91.9	111,274	31.0	69.0	39	59.9	2,701	50.6
Decatur	236	2.0	358	D	142.6	1,377,822	3,845	129,758	103.4	156,869	34.6	65.4	3	72.1	7,942	67.1
Delaware	365	-0.3	274	0.3	321.6	2,129,527	7,773	261,745	534.6	401,616	35.2	64.8	8	81.1	13,135	83.1
Des Moines	175	1.1	295	4.5	143.9	2,035,386	6,910	183,368	108.3	182,639	80.8	19.2	2	79.4	3,495	65.6
Dickinson	187	0.0	456	1.0	176.5	3,389,715	7,439	285,670	179.3	436,195	49.2	50.8	2	83.7	4,070	76.6
Dubuque	313	7.6	224	0.4	258.5	1,930,243	8,633	188,850	440.1	313,898	29.2	70.8	15	82.0	5,667	73.5
Emmet	230	4.9	471	0.8	211.9	3,382,133	7,182	356,936	234.9	481,395	49.9	50.1	1	86.3	4,554	83.4
Fayette	385	-0.9	304	1.3	337.6	2,183,246	7,176	222,654	372.9	294,761	46.1	53.9	9	79.5	14,587	84.3
Floyd	311	-2.2	339	2.1	286.3	2,493,726	7,359	238,169	281.0	306,482	55.1	44.9	6	79.6	10,269	77.1

Table B. States and Counties — Water Use, Wholesale Trade, Retail Trade, and Real Estate

STATE County	Water use, 2015		Wholesale Trade[1], 2012				Retail Trade[2], 2012				Real estate and rental and leasing,[2] 2012			
	Public supply water withdrawn (mil gal/day)	Public supply gallons withdrawn per person per day	Number of establishments	Number of employees	Sales (mil dol)	Average payroll (mil dol)	Number of establishments	Number of employees	Sales (mil dol)	Average payroll (mil dol)	Number of establishments	Number of employees	Sales (mil dol)	Average payroll (mil dol)
	133	134	135	136	137	138	139	140	141	142	143	144	145	146
INDIANA— Cont'd														
Pike	1.01	80.2	7	D	D	D	31	266	72.5	4.8	6	D	D	D
Porter	15.84	94.5	147	1,860	1,574.9	94.2	449	6,931	2,035.4	159.7	150	648	101.3	19.6
Posey	1.00	39.2	22	329	506.8	15.8	67	692	307.6	18.3	10	27	3.2	0.6
Pulaski	0.38	29.5	25	272	480.8	10.8	60	438	134.3	9.4	5	7	0.8	0.1
Putnam	4.03	107.2	16	141	48.5	6.3	106	1,211	349.0	25.4	24	69	7.4	1.5
Randolph	2.18	86.6	15	161	127.5	6.4	71	600	443.4	12.9	10	26	2.1	0.4
Ripley	1.19	41.5	17	D	D	D	102	844	222.9	19.9	19	D	D	D
Rush	0.99	59.4	23	516	527.1	32.5	49	420	108.1	9.0	12	15	2.6	0.3
St. Joseph	21.76	81.1	307	4,366	3,131.0	213.3	911	14,702	3,775.3	343.9	218	1,233	205.3	41.5
Scott	3.33	140.2	10	D	D	D	79	828	240.2	18.1	19	41	6.3	1.0
Shelby	5.66	127.3	37	676	370.9	25.8	118	1,392	502.4	37.0	41	126	18.5	3.6
Spencer	1.97	95.1	17	D	D	D	66	708	130.1	19.2	12	22	1.5	0.2
Starke	0.61	26.6	14	83	95.9	3.6	59	625	170.7	14.8	13	24	2.5	0.4
Steuben	1.36	39.6	37	279	185.1	10.7	185	2,028	613.8	41.1	44	102	16.9	3.0
Sullivan	1.36	65.0	18	162	164.4	6.9	54	553	138.2	11.7	8	16	1.2	0.4
Switzerland	1.04	98.8	3	7	2.3	0.4	15	108	20.2	1.6	2	D	D	D
Tippecanoe	12.84	69.1	109	1,275	751.1	54.5	529	8,815	2,225.7	189.2	167	852	142.9	28.6
Tipton	0.91	59.6	13	126	108.6	5.7	57	499	180.6	12.8	9	17	1.1	0.3
Union	0.35	48.7	4	D	D	D	21	191	32.9	3.4	1	D	D	D
Vanderburgh	17.40	95.7	259	4,815	2,679.5	295.9	791	12,637	3,141.7	290.9	208	1,500	247.1	45.5
Vermillion	1.25	79.7	13	D	D	D	52	591	194.1	12.8	4	6	0.7	0.2
Vigo	12.20	113.1	91	1,163	506.6	48.6	445	6,676	1,588.3	137.4	89	524	86.4	17.7
Wabash	3.48	108.3	31	275	348.5	12.0	130	1,332	324.5	29.8	15	95	8.9	2.7
Warren	0.43	52.0	9	146	206.2	6.7	14	86	22.1	1.5	2	D	D	D
Warrick	2.70	43.6	40	D	D	D	126	1,630	391.1	33.7	27	152	23.5	3.4
Washington	2.44	87.7	12	36	9.2	1.2	79	691	215.4	14.6	9	29	3.3	0.6
Wayne	5.01	74.8	55	678	868.2	27.3	267	3,664	950.8	80.7	53	190	37.5	5.9
Wells	2.44	87.3	26	D	D	D	84	982	231.5	21.6	23	66	6.8	1.5
White	0.97	39.9	34	324	339.4	16.7	97	1,099	302.9	25.5	17	53	5.9	0.9
Whitley	1.38	41.3	24	D	D	D	108	1,415	343.4	31.4	23	76	16.8	2.5
IOWA	390.38	125.0	4,302	58,872	62,318.3	2,841.8	12,046	174,556	44,905.6	3,865.3	2,742	12,031	2,268.3	425.9
Adair	0.67	92.7	10	132	183.2	5.2	30	252	63.0	4.3	5	D	D	D
Adams	1.00	263.4	5	46	36.3	1.5	19	101	21.3	2.1	2	D	D	D
Allamakee	0.91	65.5	33	443	275.9	16.0	59	563	144.6	11.2	13	36	2.5	0.5
Appanoose	6.65	530.8	9	64	40.4	1.9	58	636	138.8	13.0	8	D	D	D
Audubon	0.24	41.6	16	125	203.5	5.1	18	186	40.3	2.9	1	D	D	D
Benton	1.26	49.1	30	319	295.3	11.4	87	744	197.2	15.7	11	D	D	D
Black Hawk	16.56	124.1	151	2,687	1,980.4	126.8	509	8,793	2,110.5	191.0	138	617	118.1	17.5
Boone	2.39	89.7	23	D	D	D	69	978	217.2	22.9	15	26	2.3	0.6
Bremer	1.51	61.1	27	283	299.5	14.3	86	1,246	361.8	27.1	18	D	D	D
Buchanan	1.20	57.0	29	329	337.0	15.6	79	901	247.4	19.5	11	D	D	D
Buena Vista	3.57	174.2	25	256	514.6	12.7	94	1,149	281.0	24.8	18	71	8.9	2.6
Butler	0.83	55.6	29	225	407.7	8.6	58	372	104.9	7.0	7	4	1.0	0.1
Calhoun	1.02	103.9	20	235	353.0	11.6	48	340	127.0	8.3	4	23	3.1	0.9
Carroll	2.04	99.5	55	1,543	1,888.5	69.9	144	1,596	360.0	36.7	20	121	25.2	4.6
Cass	1.23	91.6	24	207	260.4	9.1	75	875	195.9	18.0	14	55	10.9	2.3
Cedar	1.04	56.7	28	384	387.3	15.0	59	611	208.1	12.2	13	18	2.7	0.4
Cerro Gordo	6.50	151.1	83	932	1,320.8	45.1	226	3,784	956.5	81.2	60	146	27.0	4.1
Cherokee	1.93	166.8	19	137	201.0	5.8	59	658	145.6	13.3	4	D	D	D
Chickasaw	1.06	87.6	33	292	469.7	14.8	51	437	116.9	9.3	5	9	1.2	0.2
Clarke	1.19	128.5	4	29	30.9	1.2	36	560	151.1	10.8	6	7	0.6	0.1
Clay	2.27	137.5	49	D	D	D	111	1,460	313.0	34.6	25	98	16.8	2.9
Clayton	0.73	41.4	26	310	917.2	15.2	82	654	211.6	13.4	9	16	2.8	0.5
Clinton	3.87	81.0	47	391	396.2	18.0	193	2,708	652.1	56.4	35	119	22.5	3.6
Crawford	2.96	173.2	19	208	318.8	10.4	72	853	184.4	15.8	7	8	1.1	0.2
Dallas	1.47	18.3	52	501	412.8	28.7	256	5,292	1,270.5	105.0	68	519	111.8	35.0
Davis	0.00	0.0	6	51	31.3	1.5	31	274	62.2	5.3	3	D	D	D
Decatur	0.55	66.9	7	82	34.8	1.6	24	210	35.6	3.1	4	6	0.7	0.1
Delaware	0.88	50.6	29	327	360.6	14.0	62	674	188.1	15.0	9	21	3.9	0.6
Des Moines	5.76	143.8	48	621	1,096.2	27.7	203	3,064	684.2	66.2	37	654	117.8	25.6
Dickinson	2.07	121.0	20	D	D	D	111	1,083	292.9	26.0	44	87	15.0	2.2
Dubuque	7.71	79.4	158	2,353	2,083.1	107.4	442	7,157	1,659.1	149.1	110	381	72.4	12.2
Emmet	1.17	119.8	17	107	222.5	4.1	50	467	90.0	8.6	6	13	0.7	0.1
Fayette	1.12	55.3	40	415	696.5	19.9	88	760	178.0	16.2	12	36	8.3	0.9
Floyd	2.22	139.1	20	380	295.8	20.4	62	723	188.8	14.0	10	35	3.3	0.7

1 Merchant wholesalers, except manufacturers' sales branches and offices. 2. Employer establishments.

Professional Services, Manufacturing, and Accommodation and Food Services

STATE County	Professional, scientific, and technical services, 2012				Manufacturing, 2012				Accommodation and food services, 2012			
	Number of establish-ments	Number of employees	Sales (mil dol)	Average payroll (mil dol)	Number of establish-ments	Number of employees	Receipts (mil dol)	Annual payroll (mil dol)	Number of establis-hments	Number of employees	Receipts (mil dol)	Annual payroll (mil dol)
	147	148	149	150	151	152	153	154	155	156	157	158
INDIANA— Cont'd												
Pike	9	28	2.1	0.7	7	247	D	11.7	17	138	5.2	1.4
Porter	350	2,035	273.7	101.0	137	9,239	9,469.9	695.2	319	5,925	270.6	72.2
Posey	37	518	44.5	21.6	26	2,689	6,454.3	235.2	35	463	18.8	5.8
Pulaski	24	58	4.9	1.1	21	1,274	498.6	65.4	21	166	8.0	2.0
Putnam	50	187	13.9	5.4	30	2,001	745.6	82.7	69	1,216	51.4	13.3
Randolph	34	100	10.5	2.8	49	2,045	847.6	93.2	40	512	18.8	5.2
Ripley	37	145	8.6	4.7	43	2,444	864.9	98.9	41	D	D	D
Rush	34	136	17.0	4.0	28	616	D	21.5	23	328	14.7	3.8
St. Joseph	516	4,882	1,359.4	273.9	365	13,831	6,508.6	733.1	559	10,899	485.6	139.1
Scott	28	178	14.5	5.3	21	1,594	866.1	72.8	39	D	D	D
Shelby	66	225	23.3	8.3	80	4,770	2,700.7	235.3	77	1,495	62.6	17.6
Spencer	20	84	7.2	2.0	24	1,399	1,634.2	64.3	27	335	19.4	4.4
Starke	19	51	4.4	1.3	20	853	253.1	30.2	30	326	14.2	3.7
Steuben	55	171	13.0	4.1	95	4,044	1,279.2	161.0	93	1,397	60.1	16.8
Sullivan	21	103	6.6	2.5	14	712	D	29.5	31	409	15.4	4.3
Switzerland	10	15	0.8	0.3	8	D	D	D	16	D	D	D
Tippecanoe	300	2,297	334.4	105.9	121	14,295	11,875.0	846.1	405	8,035	362.1	98.9
Tipton	19	56	4.4	1.4	17	777	236.3	33.9	26	295	12.9	3.3
Union	8	D	D	D	5	36	D	D	8	86	3.8	1.0
Vanderburgh	434	3,727	471.4	178.0	248	10,623	3,972.5	494.1	465	11,293	566.5	150.0
Vermillion	13	D	D	D	15	676	D	54.3	33	443	24.5	5.8
Vigo	200	1,162	120.3	44.0	112	8,872	3,512.9	438.4	276	5,439	230.1	66.6
Wabash	52	375	30.8	8.2	62	2,623	1,312.0	121.0	68	1,049	40.2	11.5
Warren	6	15	2.0	0.3	13	635	165.3	20.9	8	D	D	D
Warrick	98	389	44.3	14.7	48	2,631	1,853.2	174.2	71	1,087	44.1	13.0
Washington	27	111	11.9	3.2	36	1,395	339.0	55.5	30	D	D	D
Wayne	90	433	30.5	12.2	105	4,875	2,155.1	214.3	154	2,812	120.3	34.6
Wells	39	216	22.3	7.4	51	2,536	1,126.5	101.9	41	587	20.5	5.8
White	31	102	7.5	2.5	35	2,144	926.4	91.2	61	540	23.2	6.3
Whitley	37	179	14.4	4.7	69	4,541	2,199.7	220.0	64	851	39.5	8.7
IOWA	6,204	48,521	6,420.6	2,466.8	3,598	203,722	116,668.8	10,021.2	7,047	115,134	5,468.7	1,466.6
Adair	13	36	2.9	0.9	3	D	D	D	14	D	D	D
Adams	9	25	2.9	0.7	8	155	D	6.7	6	D	D	D
Allamakee	19	102	11.5	3.0	27	1,208	262.1	36.0	33	235	9.7	2.3
Appanoose	22	64	5.6	1.9	17	599	303.3	24.6	29	422	16.5	5.4
Audubon	9	16	1.9	0.3	7	172	D	8.0	6	D	D	D
Benton	30	76	7.2	2.4	29	717	166.5	24.6	33	D	D	D
Black Hawk	232	3,781	288.1	203.8	164	13,067	9,665.5	655.2	304	6,630	318.4	84.6
Boone	38	145	15.4	5.5	28	416	97.7	19.6	46	499	16.9	4.2
Bremer	36	180	17.7	5.5	36	1,714	883.7	86.3	46	562	20.0	5.5
Buchanan	22	83	10.3	2.9	41	1,124	677.4	45.2	33	399	12.2	3.1
Buena Vista	36	182	20.3	8.5	30	3,507	2,233.5	121.1	45	738	23.2	6.9
Butler	19	68	5.5	1.4	28	836	463.6	35.4	16	D	D	D
Calhoun	16	43	3.6	0.9	14	82	D	2.9	15	D	D	D
Carroll	46	197	27.4	6.9	38	1,286	904.3	60.2	59	687	22.5	6.4
Cass	27	115	12.3	4.8	21	513	157.5	20.5	36	371	14.4	3.8
Cedar	23	93	10.1	2.9	34	643	255.0	27.8	38	D	D	D
Cerro Gordo	95	613	73.7	29.9	52	2,687	1,361.7	122.5	129	D	D	D
Cherokee	18	77	10.4	2.0	23	1,109	653.3	38.9	28	344	11.6	3.3
Chickasaw	18	59	6.2	1.5	48	1,242	712.4	52.0	24	284	8.5	2.1
Clarke	13	45	3.3	1.0	13	887	D	34.8	22	571	67.5	8.7
Clay	39	179	18.9	6.4	27	999	320.1	44.5	55	645	24.9	6.4
Clayton	26	149	21.0	5.7	31	899	217.8	33.5	58	D	D	D
Clinton	60	295	35.6	10.2	53	4,405	4,731.1	228.3	108	1,664	103.5	22.7
Crawford	21	92	8.7	2.9	21	2,471	1,657.9	98.6	44	419	14.9	4.3
Dallas	184	1,361	229.7	70.2	39	2,067	740.2	77.8	149	2,911	148.0	44.0
Davis	14	52	5.3	1.5	8	145	D	5.5	15	100	3.2	0.9
Decatur	6	20	1.6	0.3	5	76	D	2.9	12	D	D	D
Delaware	27	105	11.2	4.6	37	1,831	872.7	78.1	29	246	8.4	2.3
Des Moines	60	317	31.9	11.6	52	4,367	1,626.7	194.1	97	D	D	D
Dickinson	46	148	15.2	5.2	37	1,491	719.8	55.8	94	978	56.8	16.6
Dubuque	166	2,956	450.9	147.7	144	8,498	6,036.4	434.6	242	4,456	169.5	49.8
Emmet	19	80	8.5	3.1	21	931	357.0	38.9	22	291	9.6	2.9
Fayette	34	112	8.6	3.4	25	530	D	21.5	45	570	18.4	4.8
Floyd	26	90	5.2	2.0	20	947	593.4	51.9	36	344	13.3	3.1

Table B. States and Counties — **Health Care and Social Assistance, Other Services, Nonemployer Businesses, and Residential Construction**

STATE County	Health care and social assistance, 2012				Other services, 2012				Nonemployer businesses, 2016		Value of residential construction authorized by building permits, 2018	
	Number of establish-ments	Number of employees	Receipts (mil dol)	Annual payroll (mil dol)	Number of establish-ments	Number of employees	Receipts (mil dol)	Annual payroll (mil dol)	Number	Receipts (mil dol)	New construction ($1,000)	Number of housing units
	159	160	161	162	163	164	165	166	167	168	169	170
INDIANA— Cont'd												
Pike	17	376	19.0	7.3	21	70	8.5	2.9	572	18.9	0	0
Porter	377	7,837	775.3	316.8	282	2,002	150.3	49.5	9,913	423.2	154,927	578
Posey	36	550	29.4	11.7	40	134	14.7	3.4	1,443	47.3	11,234	53
Pulaski	25	573	40.6	18.2	21	80	7.5	1.7	803	30.1	1,394	11
Putnam	71	1,649	110.7	46.2	66	278	18.9	5.5	2,054	76.3	32,375	142
Randolph	38	645	51.8	19.6	43	169	13.7	2.9	1,416	51.2	3,766	16
Ripley	67	1,404	130.5	53.0	49	178	17.3	4.0	1,740	69.9	14,820	97
Rush	31	555	50.8	17.7	28	88	8.9	1.7	1,115	47.2	2,542	18
St. Joseph	644	17,762	2,160.5	722.0	459	D	D	D	15,863	625.5	134,809	648
Scott	53	865	65.9	25.4	23	105	8.1	2.2	1,132	38.9	3,866	27
Shelby	77	2,008	194.2	70.0	69	452	41.0	10.7	2,770	125.8	17,392	83
Spencer	24	D	D	D	32	86	7.5	1.9	1,187	45.2	8,845	40
Starke	23	460	35.9	12.3	31	131	10.8	2.5	1,204	47.6	8,223	40
Steuben	84	1,384	97.2	36.3	76	424	53.0	12.3	2,153	98.8	46,262	155
Sullivan	31	647	50.7	20.5	21	113	6.9	1.7	967	26.5	2,224	22
Switzerland	15	D	D	D	13	39	4.1	0.9	573	22.1	3,554	61
Tippecanoe	385	10,859	1,194.7	423.0	240	1,793	208.1	46.8	9,217	410.0	304,119	1,751
Tipton	26	614	63.4	26.0	20	102	10.4	2.4	999	39.9	5,206	25
Union	11	D	D	D	12	D	D	D	500	21.3	1,260	7
Vanderburgh	554	18,044	2,025.2	775.4	360	2,889	300.6	86.0	9,458	390.2	45,787	267
Vermillion	23	534	61.6	19.5	23	54	5.4	0.9	710	23.0	1,658	13
Vigo	360	8,910	1,138.1	352.1	178	1,150	109.0	30.3	4,782	180.8	9,839	93
Wabash	76	2,143	141.7	52.9	60	303	25.0	5.5	1,737	57.6	4,688	25
Warren	10	D	D	D	6	D	D	D	518	20.4	3,861	18
Warrick	125	3,119	369.6	124.9	86	431	49.5	12.6	3,862	174.4	64,899	241
Washington	45	765	52.8	21.0	25	148	10.2	3.5	1,666	60.5	16,579	69
Wayne	205	5,350	523.3	204.3	117	509	47.0	10.5	3,676	149.9	16,660	122
Wells	57	1,641	128.3	51.5	61	280	21.2	5.7	1,732	65.1	14,775	59
White	36	852	63.3	25.2	33	121	12.6	2.7	1,446	63.3	11,262	50
Whitley	65	1,120	103.5	35.8	69	344	28.9	8.4	2,136	79.0	33,992	184
IOWA	8,131	206,906	18,583.8	7,894.4	5,866	30,672	3,343.2	847.7	209,794	9,279.3	2,249,100	11,518
Adair	16	336	21.7	8.4	15	D	D	D	638	27.2	2,529	10
Adams	17	327	27.3	9.5	9	32	1.9	0.5	331	15.8	993	3
Allamakee	48	1,022	51.1	24.2	33	90	12.2	2.5	1,164	54.6	5,670	37
Appanoose	37	714	52.5	21.7	25	71	7.5	1.5	827	36.1	951	10
Audubon	15	321	21.6	8.8	18	52	5.2	1.4	484	20.4	1,300	6
Benton	45	775	50.7	21.4	51	148	15.6	3.9	1,887	65.6	7,540	35
Black Hawk	362	10,530	990.2	416.7	225	1,484	137.5	36.7	7,361	351.5	53,124	227
Boone	53	1,623	110.8	48.8	48	171	19.1	5.0	1,805	70.1	10,657	61
Bremer	58	1,672	119.4	51.6	64	D	D	D	1,664	67.6	15,214	92
Buchanan	41	1,025	71.1	32.3	20	D	D	D	1,500	70.7	4,567	48
Buena Vista	46	1,341	90.4	41.8	32	129	13.0	2.9	1,262	55.2	2,859	19
Butler	28	513	24.4	11.6	22	D	D	D	1,121	39.7	3,743	21
Calhoun	33	685	51.2	20.8	14	D	D	D	769	30.2	4,560	16
Carroll	110	2,188	172.5	68.7	58	200	19.7	4.2	1,836	86.2	11,559	47
Cass	46	1,154	80.9	34.9	39	154	20.8	3.7	1,166	46.3	1,885	9
Cedar	51	617	29.3	13.6	33	D	D	D	1,320	55.3	11,932	52
Cerro Gordo	141	4,853	541.7	217.7	110	D	D	D	2,948	118.8	14,447	47
Cherokee	36	915	64.1	31.7	27	78	9.6	2.2	876	35.8	1,715	7
Chickasaw	36	561	50.0	16.7	31	98	14.3	1.9	932	34.4	1,930	7
Clarke	28	617	39.3	15.4	18	D	D	D	561	22.7	12,486	98
Clay	60	1,480	139.3	60.9	37	202	18.3	4.7	1,305	65.6	3,839	15
Clayton	57	999	54.8	24.3	35	D	D	D	1,409	56.2	7,572	35
Clinton	131	3,554	248.0	107.2	92	331	28.8	7.8	2,653	101.3	11,801	87
Crawford	37	1,008	67.8	28.2	38	D	D	D	943	42.9	4,215	17
Dallas	169	3,175	271.9	123.9	88	731	72.0	35.2	6,412	342.6	165,222	592
Davis	21	418	33.6	14.2	11	31	2.9	0.6	755	57.0	395	3
Decatur	20	335	21.0	10.2	5	D	D	D	601	22.7	10	1
Delaware	38	969	65.8	30.0	42	149	14.3	2.8	1,341	63.6	2,027	11
Des Moines	143	3,273	323.7	123.0	93	447	37.9	10.8	2,367	91.1	4,632	35
Dickinson	56	647	34.5	15.1	39	169	14.2	3.8	1,767	83.4	37,451	181
Dubuque	271	7,806	702.0	318.7	201	1,157	109.4	28.1	6,446	284.0	84,021	322
Emmet	35	941	72.2	28.6	26	76	6.4	1.7	659	25.0	2,427	10
Fayette	56	1,290	80.7	36.4	49	197	22.5	5.3	1,401	55.3	5,432	25
Floyd	49	969	62.3	28.7	36	119	8.8	2.2	1,140	39.3	3,764	15

Table B. States and Counties — Government Employment and Payroll, and Local Government Finances

STATE County	Government employment and payroll, 2012									Local government finances, 2012				
			March payroll (percent of total)							General revenue				
												Taxes		
	Full-time equivalent employees	March payroll (dollars)	Adminis- tration, judicial, and legal	Police and corrections	Fire protection	Highways and transpor- tation	Health and welfare	Natural resources and utilities	Education and libraries	Total (mil dol)	Inter- govern- mental (mil dol)	Total (mil dol)	Per capita[1] (dollars)	
													Total	Property
	171	172	173	174	175	176	177	178	179	180	181	182	183	184
INDIANA— Cont'd														
Pike	517	1,538,013	6.0	5.7	0.0	2.8	2.9	3.1	78.9	37.9	19.2	13.1	1,029	1,017
Porter	4,682	15,472,739	6.2	11.3	4.3	3.7	2.1	4.6	66.6	488.1	210.9	195.5	1,180	1,059
Posey	911	2,762,902	6.5	6.5	1.9	5.2	4.2	4.8	69.9	91.5	46.7	35.1	1,370	1,173
Pulaski	708	2,273,852	6.2	7.1	0.1	2.4	37.6	1.9	44.1	67.8	28.8	13.4	1,019	724
Putnam	1,642	4,711,936	4.0	5.6	1.1	2.5	24.9	2.7	57.3	152.8	52.1	46.2	1,223	1,010
Randolph	1,040	2,903,572	6.2	8.7	2.2	3.1	2.3	2.6	74.3	87.0	51.7	23.2	898	698
Ripley	1,010	3,272,378	6.6	6.7	0.8	3.3	2.0	5.4	74.4	92.3	48.8	27.6	967	752
Rush	863	2,783,719	5.3	5.5	1.8	3.6	34.1	2.2	47.2	62.7	23.4	13.5	788	596
St. Joseph	9,537	31,853,965	4.7	12.0	7.2	4.2	1.2	7.1	62.0	1,039.1	434.1	391.0	1,468	1,064
Scott	984	3,352,561	6.3	6.5	0.1	1.7	23.7	3.5	56.0	87.7	37.4	20.6	865	696
Shelby	1,997	6,919,558	3.0	7.4	2.7	1.5	36.5	2.1	46.2	272.2	100.9	54.8	1,233	968
Spencer	769	2,237,381	7.1	8.1	0.1	3.7	2.1	4.2	74.1	70.8	38.9	21.7	1,042	882
Starke	708	2,237,301	6.6	4.8	2.5	3.1	0.7	1.7	75.9	73.3	44.3	20.2	868	715
Steuben	1,096	3,394,672	9.6	9.3	2.3	3.8	4.4	6.2	63.6	108.5	47.5	40.3	1,182	873
Sullivan	911	2,516,743	6.1	5.1	1.0	4.1	30.7	3.5	49.0	93.6	35.3	20.1	951	859
Switzerland	398	1,091,343	11.4	6.6	0.0	5.1	2.6	5.1	68.7	40.0	28.0	6.9	658	486
Tippecanoe	4,468	15,188,885	7.3	12.7	5.8	5.8	2.2	5.7	59.5	457.5	213.5	170.7	962	767
Tipton	903	3,143,238	4.0	4.5	1.9	2.0	42.8	4.2	38.9	44.9	22.7	15.5	989	726
Union	448	1,183,280	9.6	3.8	1.0	2.9	1.2	2.3	78.6	26.8	13.9	8.2	1,116	890
Vanderburgh	5,583	20,513,638	6.9	13.0	6.2	3.9	1.5	8.7	57.8	578.5	275.8	204.6	1,131	901
Vermillion	614	1,596,357	7.0	7.2	0.5	4.5	1.0	2.1	76.9	49.4	28.3	15.4	963	931
Vigo	3,145	11,398,778	8.5	10.1	5.8	4.8	0.9	6.3	62.4	343.5	178.1	110.8	1,022	808
Wabash	1,443	4,610,578	4.1	7.2	4.2	2.4	29.9	2.5	49.7	143.9	51.1	32.9	1,017	612
Warren	295	823,372	8.8	8.6	0.0	7.3	2.3	2.0	70.9	26.8	11.8	11.6	1,393	1,027
Warrick	1,757	5,629,245	7.9	6.7	0.8	2.6	1.7	3.6	76.2	168.5	76.5	59.4	982	827
Washington	845	2,699,186	6.9	6.0	1.0	3.5	1.8	2.8	76.4	72.6	43.4	21.5	769	601
Wayne	2,355	8,196,624	6.3	10.4	3.9	3.3	3.6	11.9	58.9	225.2	109.7	75.5	1,104	906
Wells	917	2,758,659	6.4	11.3	1.0	3.1	1.4	4.9	70.3	82.1	43.3	25.6	927	656
White	1,059	3,072,979	5.9	7.0	4.5	4.1	1.4	4.8	71.6	119.7	51.9	36.9	1,509	1,286
Whitley	1,054	3,089,365	6.7	13.1	0.0	4.8	0.9	1.6	71.8	89.8	43.2	27.3	820	609
IOWA	X	X	X	X	X	X	X	X	X	X	X	X	X	X
Adair	361	1,122,671	8.0	6.1	0.0	8.8	28.8	3.4	44.3	37.5	13.2	12.9	1,725	1,407
Adams	179	522,990	8.9	6.5	0.0	10.7	6.7	3.3	62.4	16.9	7.2	7.4	1,901	1,634
Allamakee	647	2,079,591	5.0	5.7	0.1	6.8	25.3	3.2	53.2	65.4	22.8	22.7	1,596	1,243
Appanoose	443	1,437,537	5.8	7.1	0.8	6.8	1.1	3.0	74.6	41.7	21.0	16.6	1,308	1,005
Audubon	328	1,089,236	5.8	5.2	0.0	7.5	33.7	1.3	45.9	32.8	8.6	11.6	1,971	1,623
Benton	846	2,776,401	7.0	6.1	0.1	7.7	1.3	7.5	70.0	87.3	37.6	37.9	1,468	1,188
Black Hawk	4,471	16,944,268	4.8	10.2	4.6	4.7	6.0	11.4	55.6	566.6	249.4	219.9	1,668	1,325
Boone	1,271	4,353,230	3.6	5.2	1.3	4.7	29.4	4.3	50.3	126.6	35.0	39.6	1,510	1,205
Bremer	952	3,191,387	7.1	7.5	0.0	5.7	7.0	3.2	66.5	149.1	41.3	41.6	1,698	1,343
Buchanan	834	2,711,732	5.2	6.6	0.5	5.4	22.7	8.0	51.3	79.4	27.4	29.1	1,389	1,115
Buena Vista	1,236	4,037,429	5.3	5.7	0.3	4.3	36.7	2.1	45.6	128.8	34.8	37.1	1,802	1,417
Butler	352	1,075,176	10.9	10.2	0.1	14.2	6.9	7.8	48.7	80.8	53.4	20.5	1,365	1,136
Calhoun	506	1,374,475	7.1	6.8	0.0	9.4	7.0	3.4	64.2	42.3	15.6	21.9	2,208	1,889
Carroll	828	2,504,489	5.6	6.3	0.2	7.0	5.5	7.6	66.7	87.4	32.6	36.2	1,753	1,373
Cass	903	2,917,219	3.3	2.3	0.2	3.9	43.1	0.9	45.0	91.1	26.3	27.8	2,024	1,557
Cedar	668	1,997,014	6.7	9.8	0.1	8.4	4.5	4.8	63.2	67.2	27.0	32.7	1,774	1,427
Cerro Gordo	1,766	6,541,728	4.4	8.2	2.8	8.5	5.2	5.1	64.4	203.2	74.2	86.1	1,967	1,505
Cherokee	418	1,242,156	8.2	6.7	0.6	9.2	1.4	5.2	66.5	40.1	14.5	20.3	1,703	1,336
Chickasaw	502	1,552,970	6.1	5.4	0.0	7.3	4.9	6.3	69.5	40.9	17.3	18.5	1,511	1,176
Clarke	529	1,675,579	5.4	5.8	0.0	5.3	31.8	3.4	47.7	54.9	15.5	16.8	1,795	1,452
Clay	1,187	4,281,441	3.5	4.2	0.5	6.0	45.8	8.0	29.0	143.1	24.9	30.2	1,822	1,405
Clayton	718	2,326,866	6.3	6.5	0.1	7.1	14.8	3.5	61.2	88.3	36.5	28.8	1,614	1,312
Clinton	1,731	6,177,764	5.4	9.5	3.6	5.4	2.6	5.5	66.4	199.4	80.5	85.7	1,760	1,345
Crawford	917	3,208,303	4.3	4.0	0.1	5.6	29.6	4.8	49.8	89.7	30.6	26.4	1,524	1,243
Dallas	2,341	8,457,626	5.2	4.5	0.6	2.8	6.9	2.8	76.8	257.1	92.3	126.9	1,764	1,534
Davis	419	1,521,730	4.6	4.0	0.1	5.6	40.7	2.5	42.4	45.3	13.6	10.3	1,184	967
Decatur	476	1,395,435	5.0	5.3	0.0	7.8	24.8	1.6	54.5	38.0	14.7	12.4	1,498	1,205
Delaware	974	3,412,646	4.0	3.6	0.0	4.3	41.3	2.0	44.6	99.6	31.6	29.8	1,695	1,409
Des Moines	1,756	6,340,038	4.4	7.5	3.3	4.2	1.8	4.4	73.0	171.7	72.6	68.2	1,691	1,253
Dickinson	844	3,005,898	7.0	6.0	0.0	4.6	29.5	6.9	45.5	102.7	15.7	50.1	2,950	2,520
Dubuque	3,261	12,486,456	6.7	9.6	3.9	7.2	5.0	6.0	60.6	400.9	169.8	165.8	1,743	1,320
Emmet	840	2,701,635	4.3	4.2	0.0	4.0	1.6	3.9	81.5	71.8	26.5	22.1	2,185	1,847
Fayette	775	2,536,072	6.6	8.5	0.5	8.6	2.3	3.9	69.1	78.2	37.2	31.6	1,519	1,194
Floyd	655	2,381,344	4.8	5.4	1.3	6.9	31.5	3.8	44.8	76.5	22.6	24.9	1,552	1,207

1. Based on the resident population estimated as of July 1 of the year shown.

STATE County	Local government finances, 2012 (cont.)							Debt outstanding		Government employment, 2017			Individual income tax returns, 2016		
	Direct general expenditure														
	Total (mil dol)	Per capita[1] (dollars)	Percent of total for:					Total (mil dol)	Per capita[1] (dollars)	Federal civilian	Federal military	State and local	Number of returns	Mean adjusted gross income	Mean income tax
			Education	Health and hospitals	Police protection	Public welfare	Highways								
	185	186	187	188	189	190	191	192	193	194	195	196	197	198	199
INDIANA— Cont'd															
Pike	34.3	2,684	63.8	1.9	2.6	0.2	4.1	28.8	2,253	34	37	595	5,660	47,808	4,404
Porter	434.6	2,623	59.0	1.1	3.4	0.2	3.6	510.5	3,081	457	501	6,533	81,640	68,038	8,939
Posey	70.6	2,759	61.6	1.8	2.5	0.3	4.9	54.0	2,108	69	77	1,100	12,230	61,246	7,129
Pulaski	61.0	4,646	39.3	31.3	2.5	0.3	4.3	30.0	2,286	41	37	1,058	5,900	46,611	4,497
Putnam	123.0	3,258	52.6	25.9	2.2	0.1	3.9	99.5	2,636	73	99	2,338	16,070	49,808	4,873
Randolph	72.4	2,803	61.3	1.1	3.3	0.3	5.5	45.1	1,749	63	75	1,214	11,610	41,054	3,631
Ripley	77.1	2,698	69.6	0.9	2.4	0.1	3.5	73.8	2,582	71	85	1,295	13,500	52,226	5,543
Rush	60.9	3,561	39.7	33.6	2.8	0.2	6.5	41.7	2,438	42	50	1,022	8,010	46,077	4,279
St. Joseph	848.7	3,186	49.9	0.6	4.9	0.4	3.0	856.7	3,216	895	890	12,765	125,590	57,411	7,273
Scott	82.2	3,453	49.0	26.1	3.2	0.1	2.3	53.4	2,245	76	71	1,141	10,570	43,531	4,181
Shelby	217.7	4,896	31.6	43.4	3.2	0.1	2.2	156.3	3,515	126	133	2,460	21,390	52,008	5,444
Spencer	60.9	2,923	50.0	0.5	2.5	0.2	3.3	52.3	2,510	67	61	950	9,760	50,850	5,045
Starke	57.6	2,481	62.7	1.4	2.4	0.1	5.1	49.3	2,124	42	69	997	10,300	43,802	4,055
Steuben	88.6	2,597	53.3	1.0	3.4	0.2	3.8	103.6	3,037	62	101	1,442	16,440	51,899	6,078
Sullivan	83.4	3,936	37.2	35.1	0.9	0.2	3.7	81.5	3,848	53	56	1,764	8,700	47,172	4,256
Switzerland	38.7	3,712	40.1	0.3	1.1	0.2	3.1	17.5	1,683	19	32	461	4,170	42,084	3,641
Tippecanoe	406.1	2,288	50.8	0.2	6.3	0.6	5.9	369.7	2,083	432	600	23,663	74,340	57,639	7,028
Tipton	40.8	2,597	56.2	0.2	3.5	0.2	6.7	38.3	2,442	36	45	762	7,570	54,780	5,237
Union	23.2	3,150	73.7	0.1	2.6	0.0	4.3	25.2	3,429	13	22	396	3,380	43,699	3,930
Vanderburgh	605.3	3,347	39.0	0.7	7.5	0.3	2.7	673.3	3,723	1,040	562	9,788	85,360	54,165	6,652
Vermillion	47.0	2,933	53.2	0.4	2.5	0.4	5.1	23.9	1,493	32	46	660	7,310	44,928	4,039
Vigo	303.7	2,801	52.3	0.6	4.1	0.6	2.7	415.8	3,835	1,144	318	7,652	45,800	47,704	5,153
Wabash	128.9	3,983	46.9	29.1	2.8	0.1	3.3	49.4	1,525	72	90	1,480	15,080	48,751	5,357
Warren	25.3	3,032	48.5	1.2	1.6	1.1	6.3	5.8	698	13	25	350	3,960	53,532	5,599
Warrick	150.3	2,485	55.3	0.5	3.2	0.1	2.8	121.4	2,008	105	188	2,027	29,700	73,059	10,330
Washington	72.9	2,611	64.1	0.6	1.7	0.2	4.2	47.7	1,710	58	84	1,157	12,380	42,627	3,780
Wayne	192.9	2,822	52.8	1.7	4.5	0.3	3.0	101.7	1,489	166	193	4,578	30,130	43,550	4,345
Wells	73.2	2,646	66.0	0.6	4.1	0.1	4.5	54.7	1,977	53	83	1,294	13,210	51,916	5,320
White	92.9	3,804	53.9	0.2	2.1	0.1	3.9	122.7	5,024	56	72	1,361	12,090	47,933	4,908
Whitley	83.9	2,515	50.7	0.4	3.1	0.1	5.2	89.8	2,693	77	101	1,416	16,690	54,269	5,970
IOWA	X	X	X	X	X	X	X	X	X	17,782	11,476	240,696	1,447,460	60,995	7,295
Adair	35.9	4,797	29.3	28.1	3.8	0.1	14.9	30.8	4,112	32	25	440	3,400	48,156	4,771
Adams	18.9	4,842	43.4	5.1	6.6	0.8	17.5	25.1	6,408	26	13	196	1,810	44,695	4,778
Allamakee	60.7	4,262	38.8	26.8	3.5	0.2	12.3	42.3	2,969	70	50	1,100	6,640	45,589	4,360
Appanoose	38.5	3,030	55.1	4.8	8.0	0.2	13.4	8.5	670	48	45	629	5,390	40,369	3,592
Audubon	32.4	5,481	33.4	34.9	4.0	0.2	13.4	10.0	1,694	27	20	353	2,730	51,526	5,989
Benton	81.0	3,135	52.4	3.2	3.8	0.1	11.3	122.8	4,756	68	93	1,462	11,950	61,314	6,351
Black Hawk	637.5	4,836	53.7	3.2	4.6	0.3	7.4	430.8	3,268	531	491	11,248	58,630	57,293	6,638
Boone	124.1	4,739	36.1	35.5	3.3	0.4	7.7	248.4	9,484	122	95	2,263	12,660	59,069	6,289
Bremer	157.5	6,436	38.3	35.9	2.7	0.2	6.4	95.8	3,915	65	86	1,844	10,950	64,549	7,228
Buchanan	82.2	3,927	41.5	24.9	4.2	0.1	11.1	83.7	3,995	49	77	1,407	9,420	55,130	5,701
Buena Vista	124.9	6,065	34.7	32.6	3.3	0.1	7.7	93.1	4,522	92	71	1,682	9,580	53,922	5,823
Butler	80.9	5,400	24.9	40.1	2.8	0.3	13.2	30.8	2,054	43	53	754	6,740	52,309	4,804
Calhoun	44.1	4,453	58.6	8.7	3.3	0.5	11.4	14.8	1,490	33	33	640	4,480	51,982	5,230
Carroll	82.7	4,011	45.1	5.7	3.3	4.3	11.5	57.3	2,780	76	73	1,207	10,100	59,156	7,107
Cass	117.4	8,552	29.2	40.3	2.1	0.2	6.2	80.0	5,832	62	47	1,369	6,260	49,456	5,027
Cedar	69.5	3,774	57.4	5.4	4.1	0.0	10.6	54.8	2,977	84	67	984	8,840	58,622	6,051
Cerro Gordo	204.6	4,672	54.1	4.7	5.2	0.6	6.3	164.2	3,750	153	154	2,756	20,650	58,716	6,986
Cherokee	39.0	3,267	46.5	3.5	4.6	0.1	19.0	23.5	1,969	44	40	942	5,630	53,682	5,723
Chickasaw	44.7	3,641	56.0	3.0	4.0	0.2	13.2	29.3	2,390	56	44	604	5,690	53,738	6,215
Clarke	51.9	5,544	32.9	36.7	3.5	0.4	8.8	35.1	3,750	35	34	768	4,350	45,688	3,901
Clay	129.8	7,817	21.1	46.9	2.7	0.2	5.4	102.7	6,185	57	59	1,529	7,950	59,168	7,118
Clayton	98.8	5,538	51.9	15.0	3.1	0.4	9.5	56.2	3,150	78	64	1,233	8,290	47,689	4,960
Clinton	230.7	4,735	45.9	4.9	4.2	0.3	8.2	231.1	4,743	116	171	2,424	22,220	51,306	5,227
Crawford	93.1	5,378	36.5	33.2	2.6	0.1	10.1	85.1	4,916	63	61	1,225	7,880	48,780	4,750
Dallas	257.2	3,574	65.5	8.1	2.9	0.2	6.0	404.2	5,617	110	323	3,869	40,040	96,202	15,054
Davis	44.2	5,085	27.2	43.8	2.8	0.2	9.8	35.8	4,115	39	33	544	3,530	45,242	4,578
Decatur	44.9	5,439	33.8	43.0	3.1	1.0	8.7	35.6	4,310	32	27	528	3,060	42,823	3,984
Delaware	94.8	5,392	30.9	40.4	2.9	0.2	10.4	55.0	3,130	35	62	1,266	8,220	51,810	5,382
Des Moines	184.0	4,560	60.7	3.6	4.8	0.2	4.9	138.1	3,424	142	144	2,372	18,860	52,833	5,697
Dickinson	103.1	6,073	27.9	30.2	3.5	0.3	13.2	137.6	8,106	74	63	1,139	8,870	70,255	9,651
Dubuque	405.9	4,268	37.6	4.5	4.7	2.0	7.0	372.4	3,916	266	360	4,468	46,910	61,097	7,592
Emmet	70.6	6,975	75.4	3.2	3.2	0.1	6.0	24.8	2,448	34	33	701	4,420	49,875	5,184
Fayette	72.6	3,494	51.6	4.0	5.1	0.2	16.4	32.0	1,541	73	70	1,120	8,830	46,916	4,521
Floyd	71.8	4,475	33.5	31.9	2.8	0.9	9.2	26.4	1,647	41	57	1,010	7,310	51,480	5,169

1. Based on the resident population estimated as of July 1 of the year shown.

Table B. States and Counties — Land Area and Population

State / county code	CBSA code[1]	County code[2]	STATE County	Land area[3] (sq. mi)	Total persons 2018	Rank	Per square mile	White	Black	American Indian, Alaska Native	Asian and Pacific Islancer	Percent Hispanic or Latino[4]	Under 5 years	5 to 17 years	18 to 24 years	25 to 34 years	35 to 44 years	45 to 54 years
				1	2	3	4	5	6	7	8	9	10	11	12	13	14	15
			IOWA— Cont'd															
19069		7	Franklin	582.0	10,124	2,421	17.4	85.6	1.2	0.7	0.8	12.9	6.3	16.9	7.1	10.3	11.0	11.6
19071		8	Fremont	511.2	6,993	2,670	13.7	95.4	1.1	0.9	0.6	3.1	6.0	16.4	6.6	9.9	10.6	11.7
19073		6	Greene	569.6	8,981	2,504	15.8	95.3	0.9	0.9	0.9	3.2	6.3	16.8	7.1	10.4	10.4	11.7
19075	47,940	3	Grundy	501.9	12,304	2,269	24.5	97.7	0.9	0.4	0.5	1.3	5.5	17.4	7.2	10.8	11.8	11.9
19077	19,780	2	Guthrie	590.6	10,720	2,374	18.2	95.6	1.0	0.8	0.8	3.0	5.5	16.9	6.8	9.6	11.0	12.3
19079		6	Hamilton	576.8	14,952	2,099	25.9	89.9	1.8	0.8	2.8	6.3	6.4	16.3	7.4	10.7	11.6	12.1
19081		7	Hancock	571.0	10,712	2,379	18.8	93.7	1.1	0.6	0.9	4.6	5.7	16.0	7.3	10.2	11.3	11.0
19083		6	Hardin	569.3	16,868	1,982	29.6	92.8	2.0	0.7	1.3	4.5	5.0	15.0	8.5	10.6	11.3	11.6
19085	36,540	2	Harrison	696.8	14,134	2,154	20.3	97.1	0.8	0.9	0.6	1.8	6.2	17.0	7.0	10.7	11.0	12.5
19087		6	Henry	434.3	20,067	1,822	46.2	89.4	3.3	0.7	3.1	5.0	5.7	15.9	10.1	11.9	11.5	12.5
19089		6	Howard	473.2	9,187	2,487	19.4	97.3	1.0	0.4	0.6	1.6	6.5	18.3	6.9	10.3	11.1	11.4
19091		7	Humboldt	434.4	9,547	2,458	22.0	93.9	1.1	0.6	0.7	4.9	6.1	17.3	6.7	10.8	10.9	11.0
19093		8	Ida	431.5	6,841	2,689	15.9	96.2	0.8	0.7	0.9	2.5	6.0	18.2	7.3	10.2	10.7	10.3
19095		6	Iowa	586.5	16,141	2,032	27.5	95.6	1.1	0.5	0.7	3.1	5.9	17.4	7.4	10.7	11.6	12.5
19097		6	Jackson	636.0	19,432	1,855	30.6	96.5	1.2	0.7	1.2	1.6	5.8	16.5	7.3	10.1	10.7	12.8
19099	35,500	6	Jasper	730.4	37,147	1,246	50.9	94.3	2.7	0.6	1.1	2.5	5.6	16.8	7.2	11.9	12.3	12.7
19101	21,840	7	Jefferson	435.5	18,381	1,906	42.2	82.1	3.0	1.0	12.5	3.1	4.3	11.2	12.3	14.8	10.3	10.0
19103	26,980	3	Johnson	613.0	151,260	436	246.8	80.1	8.1	0.6	7.8	5.8	5.8	14.1	21.2	15.4	12.0	10.0
19105	16,300	2	Jones	575.6	20,744	1,787	36.0	93.9	3.1	0.5	1.1	2.1	5.2	16.2	7.0	11.4	12.0	12.7
19107		8	Keokuk	579.2	10,225	2,406	17.7	97.0	1.0	0.5	0.5	1.9	5.9	17.1	6.9	10.7	11.0	11.4
19109		7	Kossuth	972.7	14,908	2,103	15.3	95.3	1.5	0.5	0.9	2.9	5.7	16.2	7.1	10.1	10.0	10.9
19111	22,800	5	Lee	517.6	34,055	1,329	65.8	92.3	4.1	0.7	1.0	3.6	6.0	15.4	7.3	11.8	11.3	12.5
19113	16,300	2	Linn	717.1	225,909	300	315.0	88.0	7.3	0.6	3.4	3.4	6.3	16.9	9.1	13.6	13.0	12.5
19115		8	Louisa	401.8	11,169	2,340	27.8	78.7	1.3	0.7	4.1	16.2	6.1	16.5	8.0	10.9	12.9	12.5
19117		6	Lucas	430.6	8,645	2,537	20.1	96.8	0.6	0.6	0.6	2.2	6.5	16.7	7.4	10.1	10.2	12.0
19119		8	Lyon	587.7	11,811	2,307	20.1	96.4	0.7	0.6	0.7	2.6	7.6	20.7	7.2	10.3	12.7	10.6
19121	19,780	2	Madison	561.0	16,249	2,025	29.0	96.0	1.0	0.7	1.2	2.3	5.7	19.2	6.9	10.1	12.8	14.3
19123	36,820	7	Mahaska	570.9	22,000	1,722	38.5	94.0	2.3	0.6	2.0	2.4	6.6	17.4	9.3	11.6	12.0	11.2
19125	37,800	6	Marion	554.5	33,407	1,344	60.2	95.6	1.4	0.5	1.8	2.0	5.8	17.8	10.6	10.8	11.7	12.1
19127	32,260	4	Marshall	572.5	39,981	1,181	69.8	71.2	2.7	0.7	4.3	22.4	6.6	18.7	8.3	11.9	11.1	11.8
19129	36,540	2	Mills	437.4	15,063	2,090	34.4	94.9	1.1	1.0	0.8	3.3	5.7	17.9	7.1	9.8	12.2	13.5
19131		7	Mitchell	469.1	10,569	2,387	22.5	97.3	0.9	0.4	0.8	1.4	5.7	17.9	7.5	10.2	10.7	11.7
19133		6	Monona	694.1	8,679	2,532	12.5	95.6	1.3	1.6	0.6	2.2	5.7	16.3	6.9	9.7	10.4	10.8
19135		7	Monroe	433.7	7,790	2,609	18.0	95.9	1.1	0.5	0.7	2.8	5.6	18.1	7.3	10.1	11.7	12.7
19137		6	Montgomery	424.1	10,003	2,428	23.6	94.4	1.0	0.8	0.7	4.2	6.2	16.5	7.5	9.9	10.6	12.1
19139	34,700	4	Muscatine	437.4	42,929	1,118	98.1	77.6	3.1	0.7	1.6	18.3	6.5	18.4	8.2	12.7	11.9	12.2
19141		7	O'Brien	573.0	13,840	2,171	24.2	92.8	1.3	0.5	1.2	5.1	6.4	17.4	7.8	10.8	11.2	10.7
19143		7	Osceola	398.7	6,040	2,751	15.1	89.4	1.1	0.8	1.4	8.5	5.8	18.1	6.8	9.7	10.4	11.5
19145		6	Page	534.9	15,249	2,078	28.5	92.1	3.3	1.1	1.4	3.6	5.2	14.1	7.2	11.8	12.6	11.8
19147		7	Palo Alto	563.9	8,929	2,506	15.8	93.8	2.1	0.7	1.3	3.1	6.2	16.6	8.6	10.9	10.7	10.7
19149	43,580	3	Plymouth	862.8	25,095	1,601	29.1	92.3	1.4	0.7	1.2	5.7	6.5	18.5	7.9	10.3	12.0	12.1
19151		9	Pocahontas	577.2	6,740	2,694	11.7	94.2	1.5	0.6	1.2	3.9	5.8	17.1	6.6	9.9	10.1	10.7
19153	19,780	2	Polk	572.2	487,204	143	851.5	79.2	8.2	0.6	5.8	8.5	7.1	17.8	8.7	15.5	13.6	12.4
19155	36,540	2	Pottawattamie	950.5	93,533	632	98.4	89.0	2.5	1.0	1.4	7.8	6.3	17.3	8.4	12.1	12.0	12.1
19157		7	Poweshiek	584.9	18,699	1,891	32.0	92.5	2.1	0.6	2.9	3.4	5.0	14.5	15.4	9.8	9.8	11.0
19159		9	Ringgold	535.5	4,968	2,833	9.3	95.6	1.1	0.5	0.9	2.8	6.1	17.4	6.6	9.7	10.1	10.8
19161		9	Sac	575.0	9,719	2,450	16.9	95.8	0.9	0.5	0.7	3.3	6.1	16.3	6.7	9.8	9.9	11.9
19163	19,340	2	Scott	458.1	173,283	378	378.3	82.3	9.4	0.8	3.6	6.9	6.4	17.3	8.3	13.1	12.9	12.4
19165		6	Shelby	590.8	11,578	2,320	19.6	95.2	1.2	0.8	0.9	3.0	5.1	17.3	7.1	9.3	9.9	12.6
19167		7	Sioux	767.9	34,909	1,306	45.5	87.1	1.0	0.4	1.2	11.1	7.1	20.0	13.4	10.8	11.3	9.9
19169	11,180	3	Story	572.7	98,105	609	171.3	84.9	3.4	0.5	9.3	3.6	4.6	12.0	30.9	13.2	9.9	8.3
19171		6	Tama	721.0	16,904	1,980	23.4	81.9	1.3	7.5	0.9	10.3	6.5	17.6	7.8	10.4	10.5	12.5
19173		9	Taylor	531.9	6,191	2,736	11.6	90.8	0.9	0.6	0.6	8.2	6.6	16.9	7.3	10.5	11.3	11.3
19175		6	Union	423.6	12,359	2,262	29.2	94.6	1.5	0.6	1.1	3.2	5.4	16.8	9.4	11.1	11.3	11.6
19177		9	Van Buren	484.8	7,020	2,668	14.5	97.2	0.9	0.6	1.0	1.7	5.8	17.0	7.0	9.4	10.9	11.9
19179	36,900	5	Wapello	431.8	35,205	1,300	81.5	82.8	4.5	0.7	2.6	10.9	6.5	16.0	8.8	13.0	11.8	11.8
19181	19,780	2	Warren	569.8	51,056	973	89.6	95.1	1.4	0.6	1.2	3.0	6.1	18.6	9.4	11.4	12.9	12.9
19183	26,980	3	Washington	568.8	22,141	1,715	38.9	91.6	1.6	0.5	1.0	6.5	6.9	17.9	7.3	11.6	11.2	12.0
19185		9	Wayne	525.5	6,401	2,720	12.2	97.2	1.1	0.5	0.8	1.6	7.0	18.4	6.6	10.7	9.7	10.2
19187	22,700	5	Webster	715.7	36,277	1,268	50.7	88.8	5.8	0.7	1.6	5.1	6.0	15.8	11.5	12.0	10.9	11.1
19189		7	Winnebago	400.5	10,518	2,392	26.3	92.6	2.2	0.5	1.5	4.6	5.5	16.5	9.7	10.4	10.3	11.1
19191		7	Winneshiek	689.8	20,029	1,825	29.0	95.7	1.2	0.3	1.4	2.2	4.5	14.0	15.5	8.8	9.9	11.3
19193	43,580	3	Woodbury	872.9	102,539	594	117.5	74.6	5.0	2.3	3.8	17.0	7.2	18.9	9.8	12.9	12.2	11.7
19195	32,380	9	Worth	400.1	7,453	2,629	18.6	95.2	1.3	0.6	1.0	3.1	5.4	15.3	7.7	10.9	11.5	12.8
19197		7	Wright	580.4	12,690	2,244	21.9	85.9	1.1	0.6	0.8	12.7	6.4	17.6	7.0	10.0	10.8	10.5

1. CBSA = Core Based Statistical Area. See Appendix A for explanation. See Appendix B for list of metropolitan areas with component counties. 2. County type code from the Economic Research Service of USDA Rural-Urban Continuum Codes. See Appendix A for definition. 3. Dry land or land partially or temporarily covered by water. 4. May be of any race.

Table B. States and Counties — **Population and Households**

STATE County	55 to 64 years	65 to 74 years	75 years and over	Percent female	Total persons 2000	Total persons 2010	Percent change 2000-2010	Percent change 2010-2018	Births	Deaths	Net Migration	Number	Persons per household	Family house-holds	Female family house-holder[1]	One person
	16	17	18	19	20	21	22	23	24	25	26	27	28	29	30	31
IOWA— Cont'd																
Franklin	15.8	10.9	10.1	49.6	10,704	10,680	-0.2	-5.2	1,023	985	-598	4,232	2.40	67.6	10.3	25.9
Fremont	16.2	12.5	10.2	50.1	8,010	7,438	-7.1	-6.0	650	743	-360	2,997	2.28	67.2	8.8	27.1
Greene	15.2	11.6	10.5	50.7	10,366	9,337	-9.9	-3.8	873	986	-241	3,912	2.28	66.5	9.2	28.1
Grundy	14.5	10.7	10.2	50.7	12,369	12,453	0.7	-1.2	1,079	1,068	-153	5,155	2.37	68.7	6.0	26.5
Guthrie	15.4	12.3	10.1	50.1	11,353	10,955	-3.5	-2.1	893	1,027	-98	4,393	2.39	67.1	7.1	28.8
Hamilton	15.0	10.9	9.6	50.2	16,438	15,673	-4.7	-4.6	1,493	1,413	-807	6,367	2.35	66.3	7.6	30.1
Hancock	16.0	11.9	10.5	49.9	12,100	11,338	-6.3	-5.5	919	1,015	-530	4,809	2.24	65.9	6.6	28.5
Hardin	16.0	11.1	11.0	49.8	18,812	17,534	-6.8	-3.8	1,504	1,808	-349	7,183	2.28	62.5	5.6	33.9
Harrison	15.9	10.6	9.1	50.0	15,666	14,937	-4.7	-5.4	1,303	1,469	-641	6,068	2.29	65.8	9.2	26.8
Henry	13.4	10.6	8.4	48.4	20,336	20,145	-0.9	-0.4	1,900	1,779	-208	7,772	2.37	67.5	10.2	27.2
Howard	14.6	10.9	10.0	50.1	9,932	9,564	-3.7	-3.9	964	895	-446	3,883	2.34	63.6	7.3	32.3
Humboldt	15.6	10.7	10.8	50.7	10,381	9,814	-5.5	-2.7	881	964	-179	4,221	2.24	63.4	8.6	31.2
Ida	15.1	11.5	10.7	50.1	7,837	7,089	-9.5	-3.5	648	792	-103	3,043	2.25	65.9	5.3	28.2
Iowa	15.6	9.6	9.4	50.2	15,671	16,355	4.4	-1.3	1,541	1,466	-284	6,766	2.35	70.4	7.0	23.8
Jackson	15.9	11.5	9.4	50.1	20,296	19,853	-2.2	-2.1	1,744	1,857	-297	8,395	2.28	66.2	9.0	29.0
Jasper	14.2	10.3	8.8	48.9	37,213	36,842	-1.0	0.8	3,417	3,099	8	14,533	2.41	67.6	8.5	26.7
Jefferson	14.5	14.8	7.6	44.9	16,181	16,840	4.1	9.2	1,238	1,336	1,641	6,872	2.40	59.5	6.1	34.6
Johnson	9.8	7.2	4.5	50.4	111,006	130,882	17.9	15.6	14,866	5,615	11,134	57,423	2.37	54.7	7.1	28.6
Jones	14.8	11.0	9.6	48.3	20,221	20,636	2.1	0.5	1,721	1,646	41	8,264	2.32	67.9	6.8	26.7
Keokuk	15.7	11.0	10.4	49.1	11,400	10,511	-7.8	-2.7	1,013	938	-363	4,471	2.25	62.5	6.2	31.0
Kossuth	16.3	11.5	12.2	49.6	17,163	15,545	-9.4	-4.1	1,369	1,509	-491	6,674	2.23	65.8	5.9	31.6
Lee	15.3	11.8	8.5	49.6	38,052	35,862	-5.8	-5.0	3,401	3,544	-1,659	14,204	2.38	66.2	9.9	28.9
Linn	12.7	9.0	6.8	50.7	191,701	211,238	10.2	6.9	22,890	13,984	5,961	89,061	2.42	63.1	9.2	29.3
Louisa	14.6	10.4	8.1	49.0	12,183	11,387	-6.5	-1.9	1,124	871	-474	4,364	2.54	67.9	7.0	26.2
Lucas	15.3	11.8	10.0	49.0	9,422	8,900	-5.5	-2.9	852	883	-219	3,703	2.29	61.6	7.3	32.2
Lyon	12.7	9.2	8.9	49.3	11,763	11,581	-1.5	2.0	1,397	917	-251	4,489	2.58	74.8	5.8	22.9
Madison	13.9	9.7	7.3	50.1	14,019	15,679	11.8	3.6	1,372	1,221	417	6,357	2.44	72.3	5.8	24.1
Mahaska	13.7	10.0	8.3	49.4	22,335	22,382	0.2	-1.7	2,299	1,881	-791	8,955	2.41	66.4	9.9	29.2
Marion	13.4	9.8	8.1	50.0	32,052	33,307	3.9	0.3	3,062	2,783	-174	13,098	2.40	65.9	6.4	29.6
Marshall	13.4	9.9	8.3	49.4	39,311	40,648	3.4	-1.6	4,441	3,895	-1,218	15,541	2.54	66.3	9.6	28.0
Mills	15.3	11.5	6.9	49.7	14,547	15,059	3.5	0.0	1,260	1,102	-153	5,601	2.56	70.6	7.2	25.5
Mitchell	15.1	10.2	11.0	50.2	10,874	10,776	-0.9	-1.9	996	1,098	-96	4,302	2.42	65.7	5.4	31.3
Monona	15.6	11.9	12.7	51.2	10,020	9,242	-7.8	-6.1	726	1,191	-93	4,047	2.13	57.9	6.0	33.7
Monroe	14.5	11.2	8.7	50.5	8,016	7,972	-0.5	-2.3	722	852	-45	3,347	2.32	66.2	8.2	29.5
Montgomery	15.7	11.4	10.1	51.3	11,771	10,740	-8.8	-6.9	966	1,216	-488	4,614	2.17	66.8	14.4	29.6
Muscatine	13.5	9.8	6.9	50.0	41,722	42,749	2.5	0.4	4,478	3,223	-1,073	16,414	2.58	69.1	12.1	25.5
O'Brien	15.0	9.9	10.7	49.9	15,102	14,398	-4.7	-3.9	1,375	1,534	-396	6,101	2.22	64.2	6.0	29.9
Osceola	16.2	10.5	11.0	49.0	7,003	6,462	-7.7	-6.5	594	577	-445	2,617	2.31	64.3	6.4	29.0
Page	15.0	11.9	10.4	47.2	16,976	15,946	-6.1	-4.4	1,391	1,685	-399	6,405	2.24	63.1	5.9	32.5
Palo Alto	14.4	10.9	11.0	50.2	10,147	9,421	-7.2	-5.2	861	1,038	-318	3,823	2.29	63.1	6.3	31.0
Plymouth	14.2	10.0	8.3	50.1	24,849	24,984	0.5	0.4	2,354	2,010	-230	10,083	2.45	71.2	9.7	25.2
Pocahontas	16.7	11.8	11.3	50.2	8,662	7,310	-15.6	-7.8	637	763	-452	3,191	2.14	60.2	4.3	33.6
Polk	11.8	7.8	5.3	50.7	374,601	430,632	15.0	13.1	56,214	27,541	27,841	181,316	2.53	63.3	11.4	28.5
Pottawattamie	14.3	10.1	7.4	50.8	87,704	93,149	6.2	0.4	9,843	7,419	-1,999	36,926	2.46	65.6	11.9	28.2
Poweshiek	13.7	10.9	9.4	51.5	18,815	18,915	0.5	-1.1	1,454	1,821	156	7,571	2.20	63.4	9.7	30.3
Ringgold	14.7	12.1	12.4	50.6	5,469	5,130	-6.2	-3.2	458	627	9	2,063	2.31	67.3	6.1	28.3
Sac	16.0	11.8	11.6	50.7	11,529	10,350	-10.2	-6.1	914	1,140	-401	4,372	2.23	66.4	7.2	30.4
Scott	13.3	9.5	6.8	51.0	158,668	165,223	4.1	4.9	18,223	12,015	1,930	67,100	2.51	63.1	10.4	30.6
Shelby	16.0	11.1	11.5	50.6	13,173	12,169	-7.6	-4.9	972	1,197	-365	5,055	2.28	63.7	7.5	32.7
Sioux	11.7	8.0	7.8	49.7	31,589	33,704	6.7	3.6	4,150	2,080	-872	12,113	2.67	74.5	4.6	22.1
Story	9.2	6.8	5.3	47.8	79,981	89,542	12.0	9.6	7,670	4,128	4,993	37,106	2.32	51.5	5.4	27.2
Tama	14.9	10.4	9.3	49.9	18,103	17,767	-1.9	-4.9	1,812	1,688	-987	6,675	2.52	69.0	9.2	26.4
Taylor	14.0	12.1	10.0	49.3	6,958	6,317	-9.2	-2.0	621	634	-112	2,694	2.27	67.8	7.9	25.8
Union	13.9	10.8	9.8	51.5	12,309	12,534	1.8	-1.4	1,143	1,202	-114	5,309	2.30	60.7	8.5	31.6
Van Buren	15.5	12.6	9.8	48.5	7,809	7,571	-3.0	-7.3	741	732	-559	2,877	2.51	67.7	5.8	28.8
Wapello	14.1	10.0	8.0	50.2	36,051	35,624	-1.2	-1.2	3,615	3,311	-705	14,531	2.37	64.9	10.4	30.3
Warren	12.8	9.2	6.5	50.7	40,671	46,228	13.7	10.4	4,524	3,268	3,601	18,621	2.51	72.3	8.2	23.6
Washington	13.6	10.5	8.8	50.9	20,670	21,704	5.0	2.0	2,428	1,995	22	8,669	2.51	68.3	8.6	25.4
Wayne	15.2	10.8	11.3	50.9	6,730	6,403	-4.9	0.0	734	695	-38	2,631	2.39	62.5	7.3	34.1
Webster	14.4	10.1	8.3	48.2	40,235	38,013	-5.5	-4.6	3,633	3,670	-1,707	15,067	2.26	58.9	10.8	35.2
Winnebago	14.8	11.0	10.5	50.7	11,723	10,874	-7.2	-3.3	946	1,034	-275	4,590	2.17	63.1	7.4	31.1
Winneshiek	15.3	10.9	9.8	50.1	21,310	21,058	-1.2	-4.9	1,419	1,470	-975	8,123	2.24	65.8	5.9	28.9
Woodbury	12.2	8.8	6.3	50.4	103,877	102,175	-1.6	0.4	12,556	7,686	-4,513	38,962	2.55	65.9	13.1	28.4
Worth	15.9	11.3	9.2	49.5	7,909	7,591	-4.0	-1.8	641	683	-96	3,179	2.33	65.5	8.2	30.1
Wright	15.0	11.4	11.3	49.7	14,334	13,229	-7.7	-4.1	1,254	1,339	-454	5,579	2.26	61.9	9.1	32.0

1. No spouse present.

Table B. States and Counties — Population, Vital Statistics, Health, and Crime

STATE County	Persons in group quarters, 2018	Daytime Population, 2013-2017		Births, 2018		Deaths, 2018		Persons under 65 with no health insurance, 2016		Medicare, 2018			Serious crimes known to police[2], 2016 Total	
		Number	Employment/ residence ratio	Total	Rate[1]	Number	Rate[1]	Number	Percent	Total beneficiaries	Enrolled in Original Medicare	Enrolled in Medicare Advantage	Number	Rate[3]
	32	33	34	35	36	37	38	39	40	41	42	43	44	45
IOWA— Cont'd														
Franklin	193	10,197	0.97	131	12.9	115	11.4	549	6.9	2,301	2,204	97	20	196
Fremont	131	6,187	0.76	85	12.2	84	12.0	242	4.5	1,775	1,585	190	91	1,339
Greene	89	8,606	0.90	113	12.6	114	12.7	361	5.2	2,302	1,951	351	148	1,654
Grundy	152	10,323	0.67	128	10.4	125	10.2	345	3.5	2,804	2,228	576	82	661
Guthrie	168	9,236	0.73	113	10.5	132	12.3	458	5.5	2,779	2,280	499	35	330
Hamilton	199	14,267	0.88	186	12.4	178	11.9	626	5.2	3,368	3,011	357	172	1,141
Hancock	177	10,848	0.98	109	10.2	120	11.2	416	4.9	2,496	2,424	72	82	753
Hardin	761	17,099	0.98	162	9.6	225	13.3	677	5.2	4,111	3,714	397	220	1,271
Harrison	277	11,583	0.64	164	11.6	160	11.3	562	5.0	3,259	2,868	391	116	822
Henry	1,670	19,972	1.01	226	11.3	198	9.9	695	4.7	4,330	3,940	390	323	1,624
Howard	206	9,124	0.96	113	12.3	118	12.8	420	5.7	2,204	2,167	37	100	1,068
Humboldt	125	9,017	0.88	107	11.2	116	12.2	350	4.7	2,179	2,070	109	82	864
Ida	118	7,539	1.17	74	10.8	108	15.8	253	4.7	1,684	1,522	162	46	656
Iowa	284	16,512	1.03	180	11.2	183	11.3	532	4.0	3,486	2,888	598	108	659
Jackson	201	16,843	0.73	220	11.3	223	11.5	806	5.2	4,741	3,320	1,421	200	1,034
Jasper	1,743	31,066	0.67	401	10.8	389	10.5	1,120	3.9	8,075	6,602	1,473	786	2,138
Jefferson	1,715	19,034	1.13	152	8.3	186	10.1	938	7.3	4,276	3,684	592	394	2,229
Johnson	8,511	152,056	1.10	1,795	11.9	716	4.7	6,676	5.4	19,576	16,258	3,318	3,192	2,175
Jones	1,168	17,871	0.73	197	9.5	194	9.4	725	4.7	4,494	3,496	998	194	951
Keokuk	141	8,484	0.64	118	11.5	111	10.9	487	6.1	2,381	1,978	403	69	684
Kossuth	238	15,659	1.07	165	11.1	158	10.6	511	4.4	3,951	3,851	100	94	624
Lee	1,361	37,270	1.16	406	11.9	401	11.8	1,142	4.3	8,299	7,724	575	1,215	3,483
Linn	5,272	231,496	1.10	2,787	12.3	1,766	7.8	6,611	3.6	40,247	28,499	11,748	7,036	3,180
Louisa	122	9,507	0.68	133	11.9	117	10.5	722	7.9	2,276	1,905	371	100	898
Lucas	73	8,559	0.99	118	13.6	93	10.8	355	5.3	2,079	1,735	344	205	2,376
Lyon	169	10,875	0.85	169	14.3	116	9.8	530	5.5	2,168	2,001	167	80	680
Madison	170	12,186	0.55	163	10.0	144	8.9	600	4.6	3,134	2,461	673	160	1,017
Mahaska	690	19,971	0.78	258	11.7	227	10.3	788	4.4	4,578	3,875	703	456	2,047
Marion	1,402	34,876	1.10	375	11.2	344	10.3	990	3.8	6,970	6,028	942	273	1,049
Marshall	1,323	40,883	1.02	515	12.9	450	11.3	2,422	7.6	8,495	6,928	1,567	1,154	2,836
Mills	565	12,218	0.63	153	10.2	135	9.0	495	4.1	3,179	2,729	450	245	1,658
Mitchell	203	10,373	0.94	110	10.4	134	12.7	532	6.4	2,405	2,352	53	75	693
Monona	204	7,970	0.79	94	10.8	136	15.7	364	5.5	2,364	1,907	457	83	931
Monroe	115	7,751	0.96	80	10.3	87	11.2	341	5.4	1,758	1,400	358	108	1,357
Montgomery	192	10,375	1.03	121	12.1	134	13.4	477	6.0	2,660	2,384	276	NA	NA
Muscatine	539	45,647	1.13	527	12.3	365	8.5	2,014	5.7	8,338	6,366	1,972	857	1,993
O'Brien	398	13,215	0.90	168	12.1	177	12.8	554	5.0	3,261	3,084	177	131	944
Osceola	82	5,515	0.80	76	12.6	65	10.8	312	6.5	1,396	1,318	78	65	1,068
Page	1,488	16,185	1.11	154	10.1	192	12.6	592	5.5	3,881	3,540	341	307	1,991
Palo Alto	269	8,714	0.92	109	12.2	115	12.9	345	5.0	2,080	2,034	46	92	1,015
Plymouth	288	23,536	0.88	283	11.3	247	9.8	981	4.8	5,050	4,279	771	270	1,092
Pocahontas	99	6,822	0.95	78	11.6	83	12.3	315	6.0	1,794	1,725	69	65	936
Polk	9,468	507,899	1.17	6,896	14.2	3,630	7.5	20,758	5.1	73,392	54,821	18,571	15,540	3,276
Pottawattamie	2,116	86,013	0.84	1,160	12.4	949	10.1	3,869	5.1	19,184	14,286	4,898	4,492	4,800
Poweshiek	1,831	19,886	1.15	164	8.8	199	10.6	699	5.2	4,127	3,579	548	352	1,908
Ringgold	175	4,623	0.83	63	12.7	58	11.7	270	7.2	1,303	1,226	77	33	654
Sac	177	9,076	0.82	109	11.2	121	12.4	399	5.3	2,486	2,397	89	35	448
Scott	3,408	176,125	1.06	2,116	12.2	1,496	8.6	6,038	4.2	32,023	23,363	8,660	6,722	3,889
Shelby	213	12,004	1.04	110	9.5	132	11.4	424	4.7	3,043	2,783	260	10	84
Sioux	2,244	37,297	1.14	480	13.8	256	7.3	1,583	5.7	5,849	5,484	365	168	478
Story	11,339	98,950	1.06	900	9.2	525	5.4	3,529	4.7	13,065	11,116	1,949	1,659	1,836
Tama	291	14,772	0.70	213	12.6	182	10.8	887	6.4	3,830	3,045	785	240	1,393
Taylor	51	5,531	0.77	67	10.8	78	12.6	312	6.5	1,570	1,550	20	28	454
Union	455	13,106	1.10	146	11.8	129	10.4	472	4.9	2,910	2,644	266	239	1,921
Van Buren	57	6,541	0.76	89	12.7	88	12.5	361	6.4	1,816	1,559	257	37	507
Wapello	854	36,509	1.08	440	12.5	371	10.5	2,000	7.1	7,720	5,936	1,784	1,347	3,846
Warren	1,532	36,004	0.50	581	11.4	436	8.5	1,338	3.3	8,958	6,906	2,052	874	1,783
Washington	304	19,945	0.80	291	13.1	228	10.3	944	5.3	4,919	4,269	650	240	1,075
Wayne	93	5,932	0.83	92	14.4	87	13.6	368	7.4	1,530	1,291	239	64	1,004
Webster	2,720	38,769	1.11	428	11.8	421	11.6	1,383	5.0	8,043	7,010	1,033	1,268	3,441
Winnebago	439	10,901	1.07	107	10.2	109	10.4	334	4.1	2,499	2,380	119	31	294
Winneshiek	2,001	21,030	1.04	178	8.9	187	9.3	620	4.3	4,499	3,851	648	126	611
Woodbury	2,472	102,281	1.00	1,453	14.2	903	8.8	6,143	7.2	18,246	13,667	4,579	3,918	3,815
Worth	78	6,113	0.63	77	10.3	57	7.6	271	4.5	1,703	1,569	134	25	331
Wright	206	13,105	1.04	153	12.1	157	12.4	635	6.4	3,024	2,861	163	108	852

1. Per 1,000 estimated resident population.   2. Data for serious crimes have not been adjusted for underreporting; this may affect comparability between geographic areas and over time.   3. Per 100,000 population estimated by the FBI.

Table B. States and Counties — Crime, Education, Money Income, and Poverty

STATE County	Serious crimes known to police[2], 2016 (cont.)[1] Rate Violent	Property	School enrollment and attainment, 2013-2017 Enrollment[3] Total	Percent private	Attainment[4] (percent) High school graduate or less	Bachelor's degree or more	Local government expenditures,[5] 2014-2015 Total current spending (mil dol)	Current spending per student (dollars)	Money income, 2013-2017 Per capita income[6]	Median income (dollars)	Households Percent with income of less than $50,000	with income of $200,000 or more	Income and poverty, 2017 Median household income (dollars)	Percent below poverty level All persons	Children under 18 years	Children 5 to 17 years in families
	46	47	48	49	50	51	52	53	54	55	56	57	58	59	60	61
IOWA— Cont'd																
Franklin	59	137	2,342	3.0	47.5	16.1	17.0	10,739	25,248	48,172	52.1	1.4	53,157	11.1	15.5	13.8
Fremont	397	942	1,568	7.7	43.0	20.8	14.1	10,581	29,813	54,430	45.6	3.4	52,616	12.2	15.9	13.6
Greene	67	1,587	2,014	9.4	44.6	20.6	17.0	10,678	27,968	52,529	47.7	2.2	52,459	10.4	14.9	13.2
Grundy	81	580	2,832	10.6	36.9	26.3	27.5	10,053	35,662	65,170	38.4	4.8	72,184	5.9	6.8	6.0
Guthrie	0	330	2,483	6.6	46.5	21.1	25.5	9,849	30,646	56,306	42.8	4.3	57,635	9.5	11.2	10.0
Hamilton	172	968	3,425	6.8	38.2	23.5	29.1	10,782	27,963	55,836	44.9	2.4	57,106	8.7	11.6	10.7
Hancock	184	569	2,379	7.8	44.8	20.7	17.7	11,307	29,147	57,840	43.1	2.8	56,542	8.4	10.9	9.6
Hardin	69	1,202	3,982	9.0	41.6	20.7	33.7	10,517	28,445	52,207	45.7	2.7	52,662	11.4	16.1	14.0
Harrison	43	779	3,155	7.9	46.0	17.8	28.7	10,134	29,332	57,558	43.3	2.6	55,835	10	11.9	10.8
Henry	156	1,468	4,632	16.7	44.8	19.9	35.9	10,361	26,340	52,275	47.3	2.4	53,670	11.6	14.8	12.9
Howard	32	1,036	2,020	18.3	52.7	14.6	17.6	10,770	27,906	51,422	47.9	1.6	53,046	10.1	13.5	12.1
Humboldt	32	832	2,215	14.9	45.4	20.2	16.4	10,288	29,587	48,847	51.0	2.9	57,197	9.4	11.8	10.5
Ida	157	499	1,568	6.6	45.4	19.7	12.2	10,661	30,192	51,978	47.3	3.1	55,732	9.1	10.6	9.2
Iowa	110	549	3,731	8.4	46.6	20.2	27.4	10,154	29,881	58,077	44.2	2.6	64,091	7.2	7.7	6.9
Jackson	103	931	4,176	10.4	50.9	18.6	29.6	9,853	27,672	51,806	47.9	2.3	53,539	11.7	16.2	13.5
Jasper	237	1,901	8,095	11.5	48.9	18.1	57.5	9,867	27,214	56,363	43.9	2.2	56,134	9	10.8	9.4
Jefferson	107	2,121	5,064	42.6	33.6	33.4	25.2	10,688	26,630	44,516	54.1	2.7	47,907	14	18.0	15.2
Johnson	288	1,887	53,038	9.3	21.3	52.7	180.2	10,379	33,039	59,965	42.8	6.7	61,395	15.3	9.8	8.8
Jones	196	755	4,355	13.9	48.8	17.2	30.7	9,604	29,653	58,391	43.8	4.1	58,689	9.5	11.5	9.8
Keokuk	129	556	2,241	8.7	49.6	18.1	11.8	9,496	26,638	48,399	51.2	2.0	50,980	11.5	15.8	14.5
Kossuth	159	464	3,343	10.8	43.0	19.7	21.3	11,900	29,949	54,868	45.8	3.1	55,491	9.2	11.5	10.3
Lee	462	3,021	7,211	12.9	48.0	15.7	52.0	10,028	24,408	48,266	51.5	1.3	50,481	14.1	19.8	17.3
Linn	229	2,951	56,455	17.0	32.6	32.3	435.6	11,738	32,786	62,702	39.7	4.3	63,754	9	11.1	8.8
Louisa	207	692	2,572	4.3	54.3	14.9	27.0	10,265	27,234	54,393	46.6	3.2	56,067	9.9	12.8	11.6
Lucas	197	2,179	1,942	7.7	49.9	16.9	13.7	9,744	27,234	47,325	52.4	3.0	46,169	13.6	23.7	21.9
Lyon	119	561	2,888	20.4	46.1	21.7	20.4	9,353	28,356	62,012	37.1	3.1	61,749	7.6	9.0	8.0
Madison	108	909	3,912	6.3	41.5	23.5	31.9	9,138	31,449	60,077	38.8	3.6	66,012	7.4	8.4	7.2
Mahaska	274	1,773	5,995	28.4	46.9	23.8	30.2	9,831	26,575	50,568	49.3	2.1	55,947	13	15.2	12.9
Marion	273	776	8,474	29.9	42.7	26.1	55.8	9,989	27,815	57,917	41.2	2.3	61,175	7.9	8.6	7.5
Marshall	484	2,352	9,165	8.7	48.2	19.6	72.6	10,211	25,693	52,752	45.5	2.1	50,495	12.7	15.5	14.3
Mills	325	1,333	3,721	10.9	42.6	22.8	25.8	9,844	31,309	67,949	35.8	3.1	67,016	9.2	10.6	9.1
Mitchell	111	582	2,289	12.0	51.2	17.1	16.1	9,793	27,407	53,675	45.6	3.0	54,451	9.1	13.9	12.2
Monona	157	774	1,748	9.4	47.9	16.2	16.8	10,585	26,829	41,598	58.1	2.3	49,236	11.6	15.4	13.8
Monroe	113	1,244	1,693	6.6	55.7	15.8	11.9	9,611	25,929	50,179	49.9	0.6	52,047	10.9	16.1	13.8
Montgomery	NA	NA	2,094	6.0	47.9	16.1	18.3	10,549	25,005	43,674	55.6	1.9	51,317	12.5	17.7	15.9
Muscatine	453	1,540	10,699	8.0	47.3	21.1	74.1	9,561	28,028	56,398	43.5	2.5	59,042	10.7	13.9	12.1
O'Brien	187	756	3,045	19.9	44.0	19.8	25.5	10,516	32,051	56,314	45.3	4.9	60,375	7.7	10.0	9.0
Osceola	115	953	1,459	10.0	50.8	17.7	7.6	9,269	26,776	53,604	47.6	1.9	56,459	10.1	14.8	13.2
Page	266	1,725	3,219	12.4	45.0	20.6	25.7	10,749	25,739	46,708	52.5	1.5	47,994	14.5	20.8	17.6
Palo Alto	232	783	2,181	12.8	34.6	25.6	17.8	10,236	27,902	50,470	49.5	2.1	52,311	10.4	13.5	11.8
Plymouth	73	1,019	6,119	18.0	41.7	20.7	42.2	10,314	30,686	61,316	38.8	3.2	67,056	7.2	8.6	7.5
Pocahontas	130	806	1,359	12.4	47.4	15.7	35.6	33,269	27,553	45,969	53.1	2.1	47,919	12.9	18.1	16.5
Polk	422	2,854	121,120	18.3	33.7	35.3	876.5	11,460	33,524	63,530	38.9	5.7	66,112	9.5	11.9	10.5
Pottawattamie	256	4,543	23,214	11.2	44.3	21.2	196.9	12,451	29,085	56,291	44.9	3.2	57,867	10.6	13.9	12.2
Poweshiek	439	1,469	5,010	42.5	46.0	22.7	28.9	10,088	27,679	51,456	48.5	2.7	55,766	11.5	11.9	10.4
Ringgold	40	614	1,120	9.7	45.3	20.1	8.5	10,656	27,621	50,642	49.1	4.7	45,259	14.7	22.2	19.7
Sac	38	410	2,057	9.8	45.5	19.8	18.4	10,755	29,502	53,254	46.4	2.1	54,328	10.1	14.0	12.0
Scott	516	3,373	43,502	19.1	37.1	31.9	328.3	11,460	30,798	57,681	43.1	4.2	59,461	11.3	14.2	12.3
Shelby	8	76	2,689	8.3	46.2	21.2	20.8	11,135	30,799	55,638	45.2	4.0	56,373	8.4	10.6	8.9
Sioux	43	436	10,437	44.2	41.5	27.5	48.5	9,704	27,339	66,022	36.5	3.5	70,601	7.1	7.2	6.2
Story	157	1,679	43,483	3.6	22.0	50.6	114.3	10,199	27,392	52,671	47.9	4.3	61,381	16.9	7.6	6.1
Tama	296	1,097	3,963	8.9	49.2	16.5	25.6	10,573	27,074	56,110	43.5	1.6	52,685	9.5	13.4	11.9
Taylor	49	405	1,384	5.5	49.1	14.3	9.9	9,925	27,344	46,825	52.6	2.3	47,383	11.6	15.5	14.1
Union	265	1,656	2,916	14.6	44.7	16.1	21.0	10,052	25,098	47,597	53.0	1.8	47,814	14.6	17.9	15.2
Van Buren	96	411	1,508	29.2	51.2	13.8	10.8	10,110	24,952	47,197	52.4	3.0	47,667	14	20.7	18.9
Wapello	360	3,486	7,705	10.5	48.1	18.4	83.9	13,182	23,413	43,329	56.9	1.4	46,981	14.5	17.7	15.5
Warren	367	1,416	13,411	21.7	35.3	30.4	88.5	9,428	33,013	71,514	33.1	4.5	76,146	6.1	6.2	5.0
Washington	345	730	5,115	12.0	47.3	21.1	40.0	10,641	28,397	59,157	42.2	2.0	59,903	9.5	11.8	10.7
Wayne	94	910	1,286	18.9	56.1	13.8	11.0	10,077	23,367	42,434	56.3	2.4	45,384	16.6	24.7	23.7
Webster	442	2,998	9,266	12.3	41.9	20.4	52.5	10,110	24,629	42,148	56.4	2.0	48,712	15	16.5	14.2
Winnebago	57	237	2,553	22.2	42.8	20.8	25.5	11,079	26,558	50,072	49.9	0.8	54,045	9.4	13.0	11.6
Winneshiek	78	534	6,208	47.7	38.3	28.8	32.3	11,576	29,052	60,788	39.8	2.9	59,365	9	8.7	7.6
Woodbury	393	3,421	26,992	15.9	47.0	22.4	223.1	11,931	25,699	51,350	48.7	2.5	54,528	13.4	16.1	14.4
Worth	40	291	1,616	6.9	44.1	15.2	14.3	9,947	26,781	50,880	48.9	2.2	55,404	8.5	13.4	12.4
Wright	79	773	2,766	2.2	44.8	17.5	28.4	10,193	28,200	48,935	51.0	3.1	52,803	10	14.5	12.6

1. Data for serious crimes have not been adjusted for underreporting; this may affect comparability between geographic areas and over time.   2. Per 100,000 population estimated by the FBI.   3. All persons 3 years old and over enrolled in nursery school through college.   4. Persons 25 years old and over.   5. Elementary and secondary education expenditures.   6. Based on population estimated by the American Community Survey, 2011–2015.

Table B. States and Counties — Personal Income and Earnings

STATE County	Personal income, 2017										Earnings, 2017		
	Total (mil dol)	Percent change 2016-2017	Per capita Dollars	Per capita Rank	Wages and salaries (mil dol)	Supplements to wages and salaries, employer contributions (mil dol): Pension and insurance	Government social insurance	Proprietors' income (mil dol)	Dividends, interest, and rent (mil dol)	Personal transfer reecipts (mil dol)	Total (mil dol)	Contributions for government social insurance (mil dol): From employee and self-employed	From employer
	62	63	64	65	66	67	68	69	70	71	72	73	74
IOWA— Cont'd													
Franklin	488	2.4	47,980	626	168	36	13	81	113	91	298	16	13
Fremont	300	3.8	43,111	1,128	105	20	8	22	58	76	156	10	8
Greene	403	-1.9	44,895	912	143	31	12	30	96	90	216	14	12
Grundy	621	6.1	50,388	438	184	33	15	52	144	103	284	18	15
Guthrie	524	-0.4	49,143	523	127	28	10	59	112	103	224	15	10
Hamilton	702	-0.9	46,476	754	235	47	18	90	157	134	390	25	18
Hancock	529	3.3	49,114	525	290	59	23	42	109	97	414	24	23
Hardin	815	3.1	47,797	642	287	60	23	113	195	160	484	29	23
Harrison	612	-2.3	43,283	1,106	168	34	13	33	104	135	248	18	13
Henry	806	3.4	40,583	1,459	398	77	31	31	163	170	538	36	31
Howard	402	-1.1	43,608	1,062	150	33	13	35	102	79	231	15	13
Humboldt	449	-2.1	46,930	717	164	36	12	43	95	85	256	16	12
Ida	335	0.0	48,870	549	171	32	13	23	91	66	239	15	13
Iowa	811	2.2	50,333	442	400	101	37	55	195	131	593	35	37
Jackson	813	0.6	41,956	1,268	221	46	18	59	166	176	345	25	18
Jasper	1,503	2.2	40,662	1,446	458	94	37	72	278	306	661	47	37
Jefferson	698	0.8	37,910	1,899	306	70	24	43	229	144	442	30	24
Johnson	7,481	4.0	50,136	455	4,366	1,123	325	460	1,723	791	6,274	345	325
Jones	859	2.2	41,808	1,286	250	52	20	45	177	171	367	26	20
Keokuk	410	-3.2	40,419	1,486	86	19	7	40	82	92	153	11	7
Kossuth	739	2.6	49,266	513	307	57	23	102	173	139	489	31	23
Lee	1,339	-1.3	39,040	1,715	726	135	64	57	261	341	982	67	64
Linn	11,313	3.0	50,479	434	7,076	1,140	541	550	2,105	1,699	9,307	574	541
Louisa	425	1.7	38,010	1,883	159	33	12	26	69	85	230	15	12
Lucas	343	0.9	40,185	1,524	143	28	11	27	67	82	209	14	11
Lyon	657	2.1	55,732	255	180	35	14	184	123	79	413	18	14
Madison	751	3.1	46,911	718	153	32	13	47	126	116	244	17	13
Mahaska	888	2.6	39,931	1,565	323	69	26	58	184	181	476	31	26
Marion	1,501	3.2	45,340	863	829	146	61	77	295	261	1,112	71	61
Marshall	1,648	-0.8	40,906	1,414	772	148	62	71	321	406	1,051	70	62
Mills	772	3.0	51,217	404	167	39	12	93	118	176	311	21	12
Mitchell	580	-6.7	54,542	296	162	33	13	148	111	87	356	22	13
Monona	406	0.4	46,483	753	99	20	8	61	81	92	188	11	8
Monroe	316	2.6	40,278	1,506	173	32	14	13	65	69	232	15	14
Montgomery	401	2.1	39,526	1,632	168	35	13	29	84	109	246	16	13
Muscatine	1,930	2.3	45,010	899	1,181	198	90	82	382	351	1,551	97	90
O'Brien	761	0.2	55,168	274	240	49	18	150	168	128	457	23	18
Osceola	305	-2.0	50,513	432	94	18	8	73	59	48	192	10	8
Page	596	0.6	39,131	1,698	230	51	19	33	135	159	332	23	19
Palo Alto	433	-0.2	47,624	655	147	32	11	80	88	84	271	16	11
Plymouth	1,355	-2.6	53,746	319	537	94	44	172	287	184	846	48	44
Pocahontas	306	-12.9	44,728	936	131	25	12	41	66	65	209	12	12
Polk	24,640	3.7	51,138	408	17,241	2,571	1,291	1,779	4,444	3,241	22,881	1,379	1,291
Pottawattamie	3,996	0.5	42,787	1,172	1,668	288	136	280	662	859	2,372	156	136
Poweshiek	817	3.2	44,591	950	445	79	35	64	178	147	623	38	35
Ringgold	210	6.4	41,707	1,298	53	12	4	27	53	51	96	6	4
Sac	464	-2.8	47,227	692	124	26	10	68	112	94	228	15	10
Scott	8,904	3.0	51,612	393	4,142	685	332	590	1,680	1,510	5,750	362	332
Shelby	567	-0.2	48,804	558	233	49	18	54	129	119	354	23	18
Sioux	1,721	2.2	49,363	504	833	159	65	311	364	223	1,368	71	65
Story	3,885	2.6	39,848	1,581	2,317	564	169	229	938	516	3,280	188	169
Tama	738	1.6	43,239	1,114	218	46	16	46	152	152	326	23	16
Taylor	241	9.0	38,996	1,722	78	17	6	29	45	60	130	8	6
Union	464	-0.2	37,292	1,990	247	55	20	23	88	115	346	23	20
Van Buren	266	-1.6	37,170	2,006	70	18	6	19	59	72	113	9	6
Wapello	1,286	1.5	36,700	2,091	662	129	55	60	214	345	907	61	55
Warren	2,431	3.7	48,468	593	457	89	36	136	378	337	719	52	36
Washington	1,122	3.4	50,351	440	315	63	26	186	220	186	590	36	26
Wayne	260	2.0	40,085	1,537	73	20	6	41	52	60	140	9	6
Webster	1,564	-2.8	42,719	1,181	837	160	67	112	294	347	1,177	75	67
Winnebago	440	1.5	41,520	1,326	165	34	14	37	94	95	250	16	14
Winneshiek	935	-1.5	46,269	769	424	85	34	90	219	161	633	40	34
Woodbury	4,220	-1.3	41,202	1,379	2,167	388	174	326	687	838	3,055	193	174
Worth	295	-6.4	39,471	1,644	89	18	7	22	59	60	137	10	7
Wright	635	-0.1	49,661	484	233	50	18	116	120	134	417	23	18

1. Based on the resident population estimated as of July 1 of the year shown.

Table B. States and Counties — Earnings, Social Security, and Housing

STATE County	Earnings, 2017 (cont.) Percent by selected industries									Social Security beneficiaries, December 2017		Supplemental Security Income recipients, 2017	Housing units, 2018	
	Farm	Mining, quarrying, and extractions	Construction	Manufacturing	Information; professional, scientific, technical services	Retail trade	Finance, insurance, real estate, and leasing	Health care and social assistance	Government	Number	Rate[1]		Total	Percent change, 2010-2018
	75	76	77	78	79	80	81	82	83	84	85	86	87	88
IOWA— Cont'd														
Franklin	19.4	D	7.1	20.8	2.4	3.7	4.7	D	14.2	2,375	234	111	4,844	
Fremont	8.4	0	5.3	25.7	D	11.6	3.7	D	14.8	1,865	268	134	3,462	1
Greene	5.4	D	4.4	23.9	4.4	5.4	7	6.4	20.5	2,415	269	155	4,547	0
Grundy	9.3	0	18.8	7.4	D	4.1	D	D	13.3	2,975	241	98	5,584	1
Guthrie	6.8	0.2	11.3	12.6	6.3	3.2	12	6.8	22.8	2,890	271	120	5,815	1
Hamilton	3.6	D	5.7	19.9	4.6	5.9	7.7	D	18.7	3,570	236	197	7,194	-0.3
Hancock	8.4	D	2.2	49.2	D	2.4	2.2	D	8.6	2,570	239	77	5,344	0.3
Hardin	13.2	D	8.6	9	3.8	6.3	4.5	D	20.2	4,310	253	251	8,170	-0.7
Harrison	1.7	0	6.2	10.1	4.6	7.3	6.1	D	19.5	3,390	240	235	6,859	1.9
Henry	0.1	D	5.3	25.1	D	5.7	3.1	D	19.4	4,560	230	312	8,438	1.9
Howard	5.1	-0.1	7.9	29.3	2.3	7.5	4.5	D	17.2	2,285	248	102	4,372	0.1
Humboldt	5.8	D	7.6	25.7	3.4	5.7	3.8	D	16.6	2,295	240	147	4,739	1.2
Ida	3.5	0.1	6.4	42.8	D	4.5	7.2	9.6	8.5	1,720	251	67	3,446	0.6
Iowa	1.9	D	5.9	50.2	3	5.8	2.2	6	10.2	3,685	229	156	7,352	1.3
Jackson	2.5	0	9.1	15.4	4.6	9	7.3	D	17.8	5,020	259	388	9,581	1.7
Jasper	1.8	D	8.7	22.3	D	7.4	4.5	9.9	19.1	8,710	236	578	16,333	0.9
Jefferson	-0.7	D	4.4	12.5	8.7	7.7	20.2	D	16.8	4,185	227	342	7,633	0.5
Johnson	0.3	D	4.6	5.9	4.5	5.2	5	7.6	47.1	19,285	129	1,701	65,046	16.2
Jones	1.3	D	12.3	14.4	4.3	7.6	5.3	D	21.9	4,815	234	264	8,972	0.7
Keokuk	6.5	D	6.7	5.5	3	4.3	4.9	6.3	20.8	2,565	253	199	4,879	-1.1
Kossuth	7.9	0	9.4	19.6	5.4	4.9	10.7	D	13.5	4,135	276	192	7,522	0.5
Lee	-0.4	0.1	10.1	32.4	3.2	6.1	3.4	D	14	8,685	253	918	16,240	0.2
Linn	0.1	0.1	7	21.8	9.6	5.3	9.5	11.2	10.3	42,260	189	3,866	98,063	6.3
Louisa	5.9	D	2.2	38.8	D	2.4	3.1	D	17.4	2,410	215	189	5,047	0.9
Lucas	0.3	0	6.4	4.6	2.1	6.3	D	D	18.8	2,165	254	213	4,211	-0.7
Lyon	35.5	D	7	10.4	6.4	2.6	4	3.7	8.8	2,190	186	54	5,076	4.7
Madison	1.7	2.7	17.6	5.9	5.2	7.2	6.6	6.3	24.1	3,300	206	149	7,061	7.7
Mahaska	3.4	0	5.8	25.5	4.5	6.6	3.9	6	19.9	4,810	216	421	9,886	1.2
Marion	0.8	D	5	47.5	3.2	4.3	4.1	10.8	9.2	7,295	220	402	14,296	2.8
Marshall	0.1	D	5.9	31	D	6.2	3.3	11.1	20	9,035	224	662	16,816	-0.1
Mills	1.5	D	4.6	18.6	D	7.8	3.7	D	33	3,390	225	233	6,142	0.5
Mitchell	4.6	D	7.8	41.2	D	2.8	3.3	4.5	11.4	2,540	239	106	4,976	2.6
Monona	23.7	0	4.5	2.5	1.8	6.4	4.5	18.3	15.6	2,550	292	152	4,732	0.8
Monroe	1.3	D	8	43.5	D	3.2	3	D	15.4	1,865	238	99	4,002	3
Montgomery	4.5	D	7.7	16.9	D	6.2	5.3	D	24.1	2,800	276	251	5,236	-0.1
Muscatine	0	0.2	4.6	40.7	5.3	4.4	2.7	6.6	10.8	8,970	209	842	18,203	1.6
O'Brien	24.1	D	3.9	8.7	4.2	4.9	5.8	13.2	12.2	3,380	245	207	6,707	0.9
Osceola	26.7	D	5.7	17.3	2.5	3.1	3.4	7.3	8.7	1,460	242	52	2,960	
Page	1.4	D	5	18.8	D	7.3	4.2	D	25	4,180	275	367	7,193	0.1
Palo Alto	9.3	0.4	4.2	25.5	3.6	4.7	4.2	D	19.5	2,165	238	129	4,610	-0.4
Plymouth	12.5	D	5.3	24.2	D	4.2	4.6	D	11.2	5,290	210	194	10,901	3.3
Pocahontas	12.6	D	17.8	12.6	D	5.6	D	D	15.3	1,870	273	108	3,754	-1.1
Polk	0	0	7.4	5.7	10.9	5.3	20.8	10.8	12.7	75,510	157	7,936	204,633	12.3
Pottawattamie	1.7	0.2	7.6	14.4	5.2	8.2	4	13.6	15.9	19,615	210	2,165	40,020	1.8
Poweshiek	4.9	D	8.8	15.7	D	4.5	13.1	D	8.2	4,295	235	207	9,165	2.4
Ringgold	18.6	D	D	D	4.3	4.9	D	7.7	28.1	1,365	271	94	2,618	0.2
Sac	10.7	D	5.3	18.7	4.1	3.9	D	9.7	14.2	2,525	257	88	5,395	-0.6
Scott	0.1	0	9.3	17.3	5.8	7.5	6.5	14.4	10.8	33,535	194	4,042	74,659	3.9
Shelby	5.3	0	4.8	10.8	7.6	5.4	6.5	D	17.6	3,195	275	187	5,594	0.9
Sioux	15.5	0.3	8.2	25	4	4	5.7	6.3	9.6	5,890	169	183	13,027	6.1
Story	-0.3	D	6	11.4	8.3	4.9	4.5	8.2	39.9	12,910	132	653	40,766	10.8
Tama	3.4	-0.1	7.2	21.4	D	4.7	4.2	D	31.6	4,125	242	221	7,782	0.2
Taylor	11.4	0	6.5	27.1	D	2.6	3.5	D	15.7	1,600	259	112	3,106	0
Union	-0.3	D	5.4	23.3	D	7.1	4.4	6.3	26.4	3,050	245	264	5,948	0.2
Van Buren	-2.5	D	10.9	26.1	2.1	4.7	4.7	4.5	25.4	1,950	272	120	3,653	-0.5
Wapello	-1.2	D	7	27.1	2.3	7.9	4.1	14.3	17.5	8,295	237	1,077	16,106	0.1
Warren	-0.8	0.1	16.4	7	7.1	9.2	6	10.4	20.9	9,225	184	390	20,364	10.8
Washington	7.6	D	15.3	12	3.9	5.9	3.6	6.5	15.7	5,040	226	348	9,770	2.7
Wayne	5	0	D	21.3	3.1	4.2	D	4.8	25.9	1,640	253	128	3,192	-0.6
Webster	0.9	D	9.8	20.4	3.8	6.7	3.4	14.3	15.9	8,590	235	835	17,015	-0.1
Winnebago	8.4	D	9.3	16.2	4.6	8.8	6.3	D	16.3	2,665	252	142	5,209	0.2
Winneshiek	2.3	D	8.4	17	D	6	4.5	D	18.6	4,605	228	167	9,024	3.5
Woodbury	0.2	D	9.7	12.6	5.2	8.5	4.8	16.3	15.5	19,445	190	1,986	42,441	2.3
Worth	-5.2	1.3	10.2	24.6	D	3.5	D	4.4	15.3	1,765	236	70	3,521	-0.7
Wright	16.4	D	4	23.3	5.4	3.2	3.6	5.1	22.6	3,220	252	179	6,517	-0.2

1. Per 1,000 resident population estimated as of July 1 of the year shown.

Table B. States and Counties — Housing, Labor Force, and Employment

STATE County	Housing units, 2013-2017								Civilian labor force, 2018				Civilian employment[6], 2013-2017		
	Occupied units							Sub-standard units[4] (percent)			Unemployment			Percent	
			Owner-occupied			Renter-occupied									Management, business, science, and arts	Construction, production, and maintenance occupations
				Median owner cost as a percent of income			Median rent as a percent of income[2]			Percent change, 2017-2018					
	Total	Percent	Median value[1]	With a mortgage	Without a mortgage[2]	Median rent[3]			Total		Total	Rate[5]	Total		
	89	90	91	92	93	94	95	96	97	98	99	100	101	102	103

IOWA— Cont'd

STATE County	89	90	91	92	93	94	95	96	97	98	99	100	101	102	103
Franklin	4,232	72.6	87,100	22.0	10.0	649	22.1	1.7	5,783	0.2	123	2.1	4,801	31.1	35.5
Fremont	2,997	75.1	100,200	17.4	10.2	629	23.5	1.8	3,704	-2.6	69	1.9	3,363	34.8	30.0
Greene	3,912	74.2	88,900	18.4	10.0	605	24.5	1.1	5,400	-0.3	122	2.3	4,506	35.7	28.5
Grundy	5,155	80.4	129,900	17.5	10.0	634	23.2	1.3	6,544	0.3	162	2.5	6,295	36.7	26.4
Guthrie	4,393	80.2	112,600	19.6	11.6	627	23.8	1.3	5,570	0.4	144	2.6	5,350	33.8	28.0
Hamilton	6,367	71.6	98,900	17.9	10.2	653	23.1	1.4	6,936	-1.6	187	2.7	7,735	31.8	31.2
Hancock	4,809	78.1	97,600	18.2	10.0	579	25.9	0.6	5,974	-2.4	138	2.3	5,653	32.6	32.7
Hardin	7,183	76.3	91,300	16.7	11.6	607	21.7	1.4	8,248	-2.1	235	2.8	8,542	32.7	31.0
Harrison	6,068	76.9	107,600	18.3	10.1	678	24.6	1	7,291	0	161	2.2	7,308	31.4	32.1
Henry	7,772	71.2	107,900	18.3	11.5	673	25.9	1.5	9,580	-0.8	237	2.5	9,304	29.9	31.4
Howard	3,883	80.0	107,700	20.3	11.3	580	24.4	1	5,180	1.8	131	2.5	4,695	33.1	35.5
Humboldt	4,221	73.9	93,900	16.8	11.4	603	25.6	0.3	5,180	-1.4	130	2.5	4,698	31.0	31.7
Ida	3,043	74.9	91,900	15.9	10.0	453	19.9	0.3	4,091	1.8	80	2	3,533	34.3	31.2
Iowa	6,766	77.4	143,900	19.6	10.5	524	21.5	1.7	10,407	-0.1	215	2.1	8,623	30.3	29.7
Jackson	8,395	77.5	117,000	18.3	11.9	623	26.9	0.7	10,932	0.6	301	2.8	9,708	30.3	33.2
Jasper	14,533	73.7	122,800	18.6	12.3	696	24.6	1.9	19,266	0	506	2.6	17,428	28.2	31.6
Jefferson	6,872	67.3	114,300	19.4	12.3	661	26.7	1.8	9,203	0.8	219	2.4	8,372	36.5	24.7
Johnson	57,423	59.3	210,400	19.0	10.0	929	35.2	2.5	85,186	-0.1	1,635	1.9	81,701	47.0	14.4
Jones	8,264	75.8	130,700	20.1	10.3	660	24.7	1.4	10,484	-0.2	312	3	9,671	32.2	30.9
Keokuk	4,471	77.0	83,700	18.6	12.1	650	27.5	2.8	5,088	-1.9	147	2.9	4,922	33.4	33.6
Kossuth	6,674	79.1	104,300	18.4	10.0	636	27.7	1.1	8,514	-2.5	172	2	7,646	35.1	29.7
Lee	14,204	75.0	90,200	18.8	11.9	623	28.1	1.1	15,996	-1.1	638	4	16,022	24.9	35.0
Linn	89,061	74.2	150,600	19.3	12.2	727	26.7	1.5	119,524	0.8	3,313	2.8	117,384	38.6	21.7
Louisa	4,364	77.5	104,200	18.3	11.7	623	19.6	2.9	6,075	0.2	159	2.6	5,561	23.5	42.7
Lucas	3,703	77.0	84,900	19.0	12.5	675	25	1.1	4,467	2.5	89	2	4,076	26.9	28.1
Lyon	4,489	84.8	125,200	18.5	10.0	633	18.4	1.1	6,949	-0.5	107	1.5	6,004	37.7	27.4
Madison	6,357	76.7	160,400	21.2	13.3	831	25.4	0.8	8,397	1.4	265	3.2	7,971	37.8	26.3
Mahaska	8,955	70.5	110,100	19.3	10.1	613	26.4	1.4	11,695	0.8	289	2.5	10,897	32.9	29.9
Marion	13,098	71.1	146,900	19.0	11.7	654	24.1	1.2	17,849	3	363	2	17,090	35.8	27.9
Marshall	15,541	70.1	104,600	19.1	11.7	679	23.8	3.3	18,008		798	4.4	19,195	26.5	35.8
Mills	5,601	78.7	157,000	19.6	10.0	724	28.4	1.3	7,307	0.1	151	2.1	7,416	32.1	26.5
Mitchell	4,302	83.7	112,300	20.8	10.0	576	21.5	2	5,732	-0.5	107	1.9	5,180	29.6	33.2
Monona	4,047	70.0	84,300	17.7	10.8	572	28.1	1	4,456	-1.1	123	2.8	4,307	29.1	27.6
Monroe	3,347	76.2	99,100	19.0	12.4	613	21.7	1.4	3,898	0.3	114	2.9	3,780	29.7	32.1
Montgomery	4,614	67.9	81,800	19.5	10.8	664	26.3	3.1	4,923	-0.4	120	2.4	4,838	30.4	30.2
Muscatine	16,414	72.5	128,100	19.2	12.5	748	23.7	2.1	21,734	-0.4	575	2.6	21,645	29.2	34.8
O'Brien	6,101	71.0	108,000	16.9	10.0	617	24.4	1.2	8,111	1.2	161	2	7,418	29.2	34.6
Osceola	2,617	75.7	89,500	18.1	10.0	584	22.7	2.6	3,512	-2	68	1.9	3,197	32.0	35.0
Page	6,405	73.7	87,600	17.5	12.6	585	26.8	2.5	6,377	0.6	160	2.5	7,220	35.2	26.5
Palo Alto	3,823	75.0	98,100	17.6	11.1	562	22.5	1.4	4,895	0.2	107	2.2	4,819	33.3	27.0
Plymouth	10,083	79.1	150,200	17.4	10.0	628	23.2	0.6	14,786	0.9	279	1.9	13,100	31.8	27.8
Pocahontas	3,191	75.3	73,400	14.5	10.4	553	23	1.2	4,311	3.5	79	1.8	3,358	30.2	34.9
Polk	181,316	67.1	165,500	19.3	11.5	858	27.5	2.9	264,356	1.8	6,706	2.5	250,105	39.1	18.7
Pottawattamie	36,926	68.2	133,500	19.6	11.7	790	27.1	1.9	47,848	0.8	1,115	2.3	46,780	30.5	27.1
Poweshiek	7,571	69.8	131,100	20.8	12.4	697	24.6	0.9	10,435	0.4	242	2.3	9,622	32.4	27.0
Ringgold	2,063	74.9	79,600	20.1	13.1	561	23.5	0.9	2,524	-0.9	70	2.8	2,134	32.6	29.4
Sac	4,372	77.8	88,100	17.3	10.0	570	20.8	1.2	5,273	-1.1	125	2.4	5,011	29.7	30.0
Scott	67,100	69.2	153,200	19.2	11.8	748	29	1.5	86,878	0.8	2,567	3	83,710	36.4	22.8
Shelby	5,055	79.1	111,700	19.5	10.2	612	26	1	6,651	-0.3	132	2	6,043	35.2	26.8
Sioux	12,113	80.0	153,800	18.4	10.0	668	23.2	2.6	20,433	0.6	364	1.8	18,678	35.8	28.8
Story	37,106	51.6	172,900	18.3	10.0	857	35.4	1.8	57,756	0.9	916	1.6	51,305	46.7	16.0
Tama	6,675	77.4	105,300	18.7	10.9	672	24.6	3	9,509	-0.6	281	3	8,479	28.6	32.8
Taylor	2,694	76.1	76,100	17.8	11.4	603	22.6	1.7	3,227	-0.1	64	2	3,004	30.4	39.1
Union	5,309	70.7	94,300	18.1	13.6	594	26.8	2.1	6,375	-0.7	226	3.5	6,205	27.4	34.8
Van Buren	2,877	83.9	82,700	21.1	11.7	502	23.4	4.4	3,666	-1.3	99	2.7	3,240	29.4	37.3
Wapello	14,531	71.7	81,000	19.1	13.0	636	31.6	3.5	17,604	0	602	3.4	16,269	26.6	36.6
Warren	18,621	77.0	171,400	18.8	11.4	766	28	1.3	27,637	1.8	630	2.3	25,633	39.8	19.7
Washington	8,669	72.6	140,400	19.7	10.9	749	24.9	1.3	12,123	-0.7	283	2.3	11,244	29.7	30.1
Wayne	2,631	80.7	74,700	22.5	11.2	489	24.5	4.8	2,769	-0.1	76	2.7	2,796	30.9	38.7
Webster	15,067	67.7	95,300	18.9	11.4	614	28.8	0.9	19,109	-1.2	622	3.3	16,583	32.0	27.1
Winnebago	4,590	74.2	94,400	20.0	10.5	549	20.4	1.2	4,979	-3.4	129	2.6	5,119	29.8	36.6
Winneshiek	8,123	78.1	161,500	20.3	11.4	630	23.9	0.7	11,775	-0.4	315	2.7	11,957	36.4	25.3
Woodbury	38,962	66.5	110,700	18.5	11.0	723	26.8	3.1	55,149	1.5	1,372	2.5	51,486	30.0	30.5
Worth	3,179	80.7	98,000	17.6	11.1	536	24.5	1.9	4,162	-0.8	113	2.7	3,778	23.7	35.5
Wright	5,579	72.7	79,200	18.1	10.0	624	27	1.4	6,451		167	2.6	5,882	28.2	36.6

1. Specified owner-occupied units.   2. A value of 10.0 represents 10 percent or less; a value of 50.0 represents 50 percent or more.   3. Specified renter-occupied units.   4. Overcrowded or lacking complete plumbing facilities.   5. Percent of civilian labor force.   6. Civilian employed persons 16 years old and over.

Table B. States and Counties — Nonfarm Employment and Agriculture

	Private nonfarm establishments, employment and payroll, 2016									Agriculture, 2017			
	Employment							Annual payroll		Farms			Farm producers whose primary occupation is farming (percent)
STATE County	Number of establishments	Total	Health care and social assistance	Manufacturing	Retail trade	Finance and insurance	Professional, scientific, and technical services	Total (mil dol)	Average per employee (dollars)	Number	Percent with: Fewer than 50 acres	1000 acres or more	
	104	105	106	107	108	109	110	111	112	113	114	115	116

STATE County	104	105	106	107	108	109	110	111	112	113	114	115	116
IOWA— Cont'd													
Franklin	324	3,253	586	875	338	100	60	124	38,202	835	35.2	12.5	44.1
Fremont	185	1,923	281	518	574	70	45	64	33,467	527	25.4	17.6	45.4
Greene	274	3,123	627	489	509	118	82	105	33,586	700	25.7	18.3	50.8
Grundy	298	3,265	728	463	427	203	39	141	43,100	760	36.2	9.6	45.5
Guthrie	314	2,520	428	487	361	141	72	86	34,083	802	25.8	10.8	37.0
Hamilton	381	4,519	740	683	702	187	90	188	41,503	732	39.8	13.3	44.3
Hancock	304	3,605	496	1,142	397	82	346	142	39,278	801	30.5	13.5	48.0
Hardin	569	5,616	1,027	589	899	286	142	227	40,508	837	35.4	14.7	50.1
Harrison	352	3,295	948	282	426	141	86	115	34,796	794	29.5	16.4	48.8
Henry	511	8,712	1,190	2,835	950	172	127	310	35,542	908	30.1	5.9	34.6
Howard	262	3,057	626	1,009	417	128	44	97	31,801	879	32.5	7.7	46.2
Humboldt	312	3,528	455	1,011	492	126	59	143	40,464	572	31.1	14.3	51.4
Ida	246	3,004	482	1,149	250	169	56	134	44,575	525	31.2	17.1	49.8
Iowa	474	8,337	617	4,511	1,392	113	187	319	38,322	970	32.0	7.8	41.4
Jackson	533	4,763	611	841	863	278	91	148	31,095	1,107	30.3	5.7	45.4
Jasper	743	7,866	1,522	1,303	1,425	232	423	262	33,320	986	34.3	10.0	47.0
Jefferson	690	7,063	753	929	910	957	511	261	36,911	636	31.4	6.3	38.1
Johnson	3,279	62,217	17,163	4,887	9,608	2,452	2,982	2,622	42,146	1,257	38.0	5.3	46.5
Jones	497	4,728	866	777	1,069	210	157	153	32,331	1,110	34.5	8.6	45.1
Keokuk	235	1,774	370	150	253	91	41	59	32,986	927	25.2	9.6	47.3
Kossuth	554	6,000	888	1,402	871	494	221	235	39,167	1,347	25.2	13.4	53.4
Lee	888	14,704	2,165	4,019	1,998	342	1,900	571	38,808	837	32.6	5.1	38.5
Linn	5,467	121,595	16,541	16,445	15,526	11,092	6,185	5,793	47,641	1,374	44.0	5.9	38.2
Louisa	212	2,914	431	1,307	231	65	25	110	37,904	576	32.5	11.5	40.7
Lucas	178	3,159	571	138	496	102	39	126	39,801	567	25.7	7.9	38.0
Lyon	390	3,497	528	586	419	170	124	130	37,261	1,122	26.1	7.4	55.0
Madison	374	2,778	535	182	594	121	92	92	33,008	977	40.4	7.6	34.0
Mahaska	548	6,560	1,066	1,228	1,155	195	146	255	38,947	943	31.0	9.2	43.9
Marion	813	16,080	2,466	6,787	1,642	304	339	673	41,870	1,030	39.1	6.5	35.2
Marshall	803	14,097	1,980	4,920	2,221	311	341	562	39,871	886	38.6	10.7	43.6
Mills	298	2,194	606	28	334	110	119	71	32,287	520	38.8	13.1	41.6
Mitchell	313	3,165	648	930	406	120	66	111	35,033	789	29.0	10.6	52.6
Monona	232	2,182	685	65	432	113	42	67	30,776	619	20.8	17.6	53.3
Monroe	183	2,408	436	960	311	84	47	88	36,608	618	24.6	6.1	30.3
Montgomery	297	3,388	769	616	540	111	45	117	34,500	516	20.0	14.0	50.7
Muscatine	939	20,936	2,014	7,641	2,247	418	809	970	46,329	714	33.3	8.0	47.5
O'Brien	509	5,311	1,433	605	854	217	187	166	31,229	876	23.2	7.3	58.5
Osceola	193	1,759	255	330	188	84	28	65	37,004	591	26.7	11.0	55.7
Page	404	5,625	1,576	1,757	620	172	87	200	35,517	715	22.7	15.8	51.3
Palo Alto	283	2,877	692	589	326	103	51	94	32,838	785	28.9	13.6	45.1
Plymouth	713	10,095	1,330	2,676	1,024	301	195	439	43,453	1,219	24.6	10.7	54.3
Pocahontas	218	1,900	281	468	221	98	54	67	35,001	730	25.2	14.2	55.6
Polk	12,647	262,039	35,552	16,126	31,978	36,565	16,172	13,324	50,847	755	56.6	9.1	38.5
Pottawattamie	1,967	31,656	5,811	5,099	6,193	725	653	1,103	34,837	1,114	30.8	15.3	51.4
Poweshiek	532	9,279	1,203	1,485	1,260	879	119	353	38,043	852	29.5	10.3	47.8
Ringgold	140	1,073	352	28	212	47	45	32	29,565	675	12.9	11.0	41.9
Sac	322	2,296	530	441	332	126	52	83	36,116	889	31.3	12.9	47.5
Scott	4,402	81,853	13,146	11,453	12,171	2,569	2,878	3,340	40,803	684	35.4	8.8	46.6
Shelby	386	5,362	907	901	545	254	167	203	37,821	890	27.2	12.0	48.3
Sioux	1,282	18,760	2,719	5,170	1,579	580	1,100	711	37,909	1,724	35.6	4.9	48.6
Story	2,030	32,670	5,626	4,951	5,173	720	1,413	1,301	39,836	955	48.2	10.8	37.8
Tama	323	4,355	467	1,232	477	125	50	145	33,234	1,072	27.1	10.0	47.6
Taylor	138	1,672	295	648	133	35	26	64	37,983	667	21.9	12.0	41.2
Union	335	5,286	844	1,719	754	179	66	174	32,843	627	31.4	10.8	40.6
Van Buren	152	1,518	268	616	230	67	26	56	36,803	690	25.7	9.4	39.1
Wapello	746	14,577	2,859	3,974	2,556	387	222	514	35,257	715	33.7	6.9	38.1
Warren	835	8,573	1,243	475	1,767	349	254	304	35,441	1,214	45.3	5.7	31.0
Washington	694	6,845	1,336	957	975	242	178	232	33,954	1,129	31.0	4.3	46.2
Wayne	152	1,380	367	410	229	39	43	48	34,690	743	24.1	8.7	39.0
Webster	1,011	16,402	3,035	1,761	2,706	395	1,176	662	40,341	960	35.7	14.8	47.4
Winnebago	335	6,680	463	3,542	527	190	115	258	38,576	571	31.5	12.3	41.6
Winneshiek	618	9,579	1,481	1,437	1,235	259	251	318	33,179	1,458	30.1	5.5	46.7
Woodbury	2,668	46,184	9,172	4,829	7,550	1,172	1,067	1,688	36,558	1,037	30.9	13.1	42.5
Worth	176	1,853	224	496	160	61	13	61	33,055	582	33.5	15.6	48.3
Wright	385	4,192	822	1,379	509	133	146	189	45,186	735	35.9	16.9	50.6

Table B. States and Counties — **Agriculture**

STATE County	Land in farms: Acreage (1,000)	Percent change, 2012-2017	Acres: Average size of farm	Acres: Total irrigated (1,000)	Acres: Total cropland (1,000)	Value of land and buildings (dollars): Average per farm	Value of land and buildings (dollars): Average per acre	Value of machinery and equipment, average per farm (dollars)	Value of products sold: Total (mil dol)	Value of products sold: Average per farm (acres)	Percent from: Crops	Percent from: Livestock and poultry products	Organic farms (number)	Farms with internet access (percent)	Government payments: Total ($1,000)	Government payments: Percent of farms
	117	118	119	120	121	122	123	124	125	126	127	128	129	130	131	132
IOWA— Cont'd																
Franklin	349	-1.7	418	0.2	330.0	3,267,910	7,814	267,635	382.7	458,354	49.9	50.1	2	79.9	9,716	85.4
Fremont	274	-4.6	520	17.1	247.2	3,123,290	6,002	290,739	150.7	286,046	86.8	13.2	1	75.1	5,143	78.9
Greene	351	-1.6	502	0.1	323.0	4,163,712	8,297	298,887	299.4	427,783	58.3	41.7	13	84.0	4,531	63.9
Grundy	308	-3.1	405	0.0	296.3	3,682,729	9,086	287,687	266.7	350,933	70.8	29.2	NA	81.1	10,419	78.9
Guthrie	332	1.4	414	D	268.4	2,610,011	6,301	239,048	227.1	283,158	54.6	45.4	1	80.8	8,954	71.3
Hamilton	315	-3.6	431	D	296.2	3,495,669	8,115	303,864	586.8	801,623	28.7	71.3	5	86.1	5,877	59.2
Hancock	345	-2.2	431	3.6	334.9	3,286,656	7,621	331,122	422.6	527,586	44.7	55.3	NA	79.9	9,659	86.1
Hardin	337	1.3	402	D	310.6	3,142,054	7,813	299,034	484.6	578,983	39.0	61.0	5	82.2	4,740	79.3
Harrison	380	-3.6	478	43.4	336.2	2,945,210	6,161	275,156	216.2	272,293	81.1	18.9	NA	81.6	5,349	78.6
Henry	262	-2.9	288	0.0	213.8	1,807,194	6,267	167,085	177.8	195,843	58.8	41.2	7	74.2	6,564	73.2
Howard	299	-0.3	340	0.5	273.7	2,537,364	7,455	246,741	285.0	324,225	52.1	47.9	27	73.7	6,702	75.4
Humboldt	240	2.0	419	0.3	230.8	3,387,096	8,088	295,137	180.9	316,248	69.4	30.6	NA	79.0	4,733	83.0
Ida	263	0.8	501	D	239.3	3,681,819	7,347	326,692	222.8	424,358	63.3	36.7	11	78.5	3,738	77.9
Iowa	347	3.1	357	D	283.4	2,291,958	6,415	209,704	227.9	234,951	61.6	38.4	11	81.2	7,532	73.5
Jackson	316	2.2	285	0.2	228.4	1,703,564	5,973	189,407	264.1	238,539	37.5	62.5	7	78.1	7,264	73.4
Jasper	378	1.2	384	0.6	320.0	2,497,555	6,512	256,238	252.8	256,395	70.7	29.3	3	84.0	3,560	51.8
Jefferson	206	3.9	324	0.1	170.4	1,792,949	5,538	161,501	108.6	170,704	62.6	37.4	25	71.9	5,626	70.0
Johnson	304	-7.4	242	0.9	264.9	1,945,168	8,037	174,726	219.6	174,717	65.3	34.7	94	75.6	10,976	63.2
Jones	344	9.5	310	0.1	285.9	2,155,654	6,962	232,937	288.0	259,458	54.3	45.7	2	80.5	8,615	74.4
Keokuk	318	7.7	343	0.1	262.9	2,003,712	5,837	195,144	216.3	233,309	52.0	48.0	13	79.0	10,997	79.6
Kossuth	594	-0.9	441	2.1	573.4	3,480,288	7,892	300,789	588.1	436,566	54.3	45.7	15	80.3	14,891	87.8
Lee	220	-6.6	263	1.1	166.4	1,360,388	5,166	124,972	122.7	146,585	61.3	38.7	3	75.9	3,860	62.5
Linn	325	-4.4	236	0.7	284.6	1,966,919	8,328	167,553	218.8	159,214	74.0	26.0	1	84.2	7,745	63.5
Louisa	190	12.7	330	16.9	165.3	2,187,445	6,631	230,894	205.9	357,387	45.4	54.6	2	79.7	4,825	80.7
Lucas	175	-1.1	309	0.0	106.9	1,055,881	3,413	108,610	50.1	88,383	45.3	54.7	NA	74.3	4,943	65.8
Lyon	346	-6.4	309	1.4	318.2	3,082,560	9,988	287,450	923.6	823,148	20.6	79.4	4	83.1	3,718	75.7
Madison	271	-1.8	277	0.5	179.3	1,572,389	5,668	140,797	119.3	122,129	60.0	40.0	4	76.3	5,316	59.3
Mahaska	311	-3.7	330	0.1	262.9	2,043,469	6,193	198,211	280.7	297,707	43.4	56.6	1	80.2	7,046	76.6
Marion	255	-3.7	248	0.1	195.7	1,428,870	5,771	129,159	110.6	107,378	76.1	23.9	9	79.6	6,125	58.5
Marshall	316	1.3	357	0.0	289.6	2,714,523	7,600	259,796	266.0	300,265	65.9	34.1	4	84.2	4,640	49.8
Mills	208	0.6	399	1.9	188.9	2,391,040	5,992	221,104	98.8	189,944	97.9	2.1	2	82.5	5,150	73.1
Mitchell	289	-2.4	367	1.8	272.0	2,883,359	7,865	275,666	315.9	400,393	47.7	52.3	9	80.1	5,099	77.1
Monona	334	-1.3	539	60.4	293.2	3,107,691	5,762	317,189	192.6	311,189	80.1	19.9	NA	77.9	8,869	82.1
Monroe	193	-1.0	312	D	113.9	1,314,106	4,206	119,256	61.6	99,710	48.0	52.0	1	75.2	6,442	65.7
Montgomery	245	0.0	475	D	213.2	2,695,892	5,680	266,552	155.7	301,806	71.6	28.4	3	83.3	4,661	82.8
Muscatine	219	2.0	307	10.4	187.4	2,063,703	6,720	204,328	185.4	259,639	55.8	44.2	4	77.0	3,374	70.0
O'Brien	314	3.2	359	0.8	294.0	3,489,359	9,727	273,559	501.2	572,092	35.5	64.5	7	83.7	6,056	81.4
Osceola	235	-1.4	397	1.5	225.0	3,481,261	8,762	297,874	459.0	776,591	27.4	72.6	NA	85.3	5,537	83.9
Page	325	2.6	455	0.5	272.6	2,444,334	5,370	212,178	168.1	235,057	80.1	19.9	4	84.5	3,359	66.4
Palo Alto	342	-4.7	436	6.8	329.4	3,491,702	8,014	322,625	468.3	596,596	38.9	61.1	15	81.4	11,659	87.4
Plymouth	503	-7.1	413	2.8	452.6	3,535,476	8,561	285,527	738.2	605,578	33.9	66.1	5	80.3	7,240	79.2
Pocahontas	329	-0.8	451	0.4	319.5	3,638,642	8,064	311,860	356.0	487,684	48.3	51.7	5	78.6	5,254	89.5
Polk	194	-1.9	257	0.8	173.9	2,269,262	8,841	163,985	110.9	146,873	88.1	11.9	2	83.7	2,098	33.0
Pottawattamie	512	-4.0	459	2.6	465.2	3,116,311	6,784	285,570	409.3	367,376	69.8	30.2	9	80.6	4,495	48.1
Poweshiek	340	1.5	399	0.1	293.7	2,673,805	6,708	240,513	314.5	369,148	47.9	52.1	2	77.8	4,962	74.4
Ringgold	303	12.4	449	D	208.9	1,731,086	3,854	142,521	121.4	179,914	41.3	58.7	9	74.7	10,630	75.9
Sac	353	-1.1	397	0.7	330.7	3,155,661	7,943	295,984	459.5	516,830	39.9	60.1	11	81.2	5,280	64.0
Scott	220	-0.3	322	1.9	201.7	3,083,078	9,588	263,956	223.8	327,151	58.0	42.0	6	82.7	3,084	73.4
Shelby	371	-0.5	416	D	343.5	2,853,345	6,853	242,943	305.4	343,181	64.2	35.8	9	79.9	7,416	83.9
Sioux	484	-0.2	280	9.6	453.5	2,918,016	10,405	297,115	1,696.1	983,814	16.4	83.6	5	86.9	4,371	46.1
Story	304	-0.6	318	0.4	284.2	3,013,807	9,467	199,884	224.9	235,519	73.0	27.0	12	86.4	4,910	51.8
Tama	407	1.1	380	0.1	362.2	2,754,577	7,256	245,618	288.0	268,670	68.4	31.6	8	77.5	7,483	61.1
Taylor	289	3.6	433	D	225.3	2,081,546	4,812	169,533	128.0	191,942	65.8	34.2	2	72.4	10,007	77.4
Union	246	14.8	392	D	176.6	1,749,559	4,458	169,761	129.2	206,137	41.9	58.1	15	80.7	6,028	66.8
Van Buren	210	-1.4	305	0.0	139.8	1,424,733	4,674	130,212	97.8	141,791	40.4	59.6	5	70.1	5,276	57.2
Wapello	199	5.6	279	0.0	153.0	1,359,960	4,876	148,496	78.1	109,175	72.7	27.3	1	78.3	4,434	61.8
Warren	247	-6.2	204	0.0	181.7	1,147,348	5,636	105,972	79.0	65,045	85.0	15.0	3	78.3	6,028	48.2
Washington	310	-1.3	275	0.3	263.7	1,894,242	6,889	209,805	671.9	595,126	20.5	79.5	38	75.6	9,990	74.7
Wayne	285	4.2	384	0.0	201.8	1,632,207	4,252	159,124	91.8	123,524	57.9	42.1	7	64.6	7,493	71.3
Webster	409	0.1	426	0.0	387.1	3,388,576	7,948	258,965	320.7	334,043	67.0	33.0	1	79.8	11,444	83.4
Winnebago	246	4.5	431	0.0	234.5	3,012,461	6,989	297,495	239.9	420,168	54.5	45.5	1	83.0	8,604	84.9
Winneshiek	391	4.0	268	0.1	322.6	1,718,306	6,401	199,801	337.4	231,388	41.9	58.1	33	82.7	8,883	74.7
Woodbury	451	1.1	435	4.6	395.6	3,205,600	7,375	255,301	368.8	355,602	54.1	45.9	1	81.6	12,463	74.3
Worth	239	1.6	410	1.5	223.1	2,854,365	6,956	308,236	144.4	248,129	86.1	13.9	6	79.7	7,896	84.2
Wright	356	-0.9	485	NA	340.6	3,671,012	7,573	344,709	481.9	655,631	38.9	61.1	NA	81.0	9,844	84.5

STATE County	Water use, 2015		Wholesale Trade[1], 2012				Retail Trade[2], 2012				Real estate and rental and leasing,[2] 2012			
	Public supply water withdrawn (mil gal/day)	Public supply gallons withdrawn per person per day	Number of establishments	Number of employees	Sales (mil dol)	Average payroll (mil dol)	Number of establishments	Number of employees	Sales (mil dol)	Average payroll (mil dol)	Number of establishments	Number of employees	Sales (mil dol)	Average payroll (mil dol)
	133	134	135	136	137	138	139	140	141	142	143	144	145	146
IOWA— Cont'd														
Franklin	0.67	65.1	23	346	697.8	14.5	40	327	79.7	6.9	11	20	3.0	0.4
Fremont	0.50	72.4	14	202	212.1	9.7	30	534	145.6	10.6	6	10	0.2	0.1
Greene	0.66	73.1	12	449	1,016.7	24.4	39	367	94.1	7.0	4	10	0.6	0.1
Grundy	0.26	20.9	19	240	494.8	12.9	44	406	83.4	7.0	8	D	D	D
Guthrie	0.85	79.6	15	119	175.2	5.1	44	378	105.7	7.1	9	D	D	D
Hamilton	1.14	75.0	33	828	731.6	37.2	60	660	158.6	12.3	6	D	D	D
Hancock	0.58	52.9	26	176	333.3	8.1	47	424	216.1	8.2	8	28	1.9	0.5
Hardin	1.47	84.6	38	889	2,961.5	51.1	80	819	175.9	17.3	14	30	5.1	0.8
Harrison	0.92	64.5	28	452	263.2	17.9	52	467	197.2	10.8	9	15	1.3	0.5
Henry	2.04	102.3	31	279	224.8	9.9	63	880	229.1	19.3	16	32	2.8	0.3
Howard	0.54	57.4	18	165	262.0	6.3	45	363	100.7	7.4	4	D	D	D
Humboldt	0.94	98.4	31	238	274.0	11.6	50	480	108.9	9.4	9	19	1.8	0.4
Ida	0.42	59.8	17	184	272.8	7.5	36	305	64.1	5.5	8	12	1.4	0.4
Iowa	1.05	64.0	18	139	162.0	6.4	130	1,365	234.1	20.2	4	D	D	D
Jackson	1.10	56.6	26	230	201.6	8.5	76	946	258.0	18.9	13	20	2.8	0.4
Jasper	4.96	134.7	36	342	445.1	13.7	108	1,302	355.4	27.7	24	60	6.5	1.4
Jefferson	1.60	91.1	38	D	D	D	86	916	171.7	18.8	26	48	6.9	1.0
Johnson	10.04	69.6	85	1,389	1,011.8	61.0	509	8,743	1,861.7	195.8	134	538	131.1	20.8
Jones	0.89	43.5	24	301	903.0	12.0	79	1,062	269.3	26.3	14	D	D	D
Keokuk	1.24	122.0	25	229	214.3	9.9	36	240	55.0	3.5	4	12	1.4	0.1
Kossuth	1.25	82.4	38	388	500.1	19.6	93	879	246.8	19.2	11	48	2.4	0.7
Lee	12.38	352.8	39	390	482.8	18.1	151	2,014	474.3	43.4	22	72	9.9	1.7
Linn	41.89	190.5	310	4,863	3,030.7	261.4	716	14,387	4,483.3	351.2	214	944	203.0	34.1
Louisa	0.49	43.8	12	175	242.2	10.7	25	210	60.7	3.9	7	8	0.7	0.1
Lucas	0.47	54.1	5	D	D	D	29	381	86.1	8.0	4	6	1.0	0.1
Lyon	2.41	205.2	26	252	461.6	10.7	52	364	106.6	7.0	8	19	1.5	0.8
Madison	0.36	22.9	13	227	221.0	9.5	45	493	92.5	8.4	5	D	D	D
Mahaska	2.58	115.6	34	D	D	D	103	1,210	242.5	24.4	10	26	4.8	0.8
Marion	2.91	87.4	42	459	315.8	19.2	131	1,517	363.8	33.4	26	63	10.9	1.4
Marshall	5.01	123.0	39	D	D	D	150	2,059	438.0	43.6	32	394	74.0	14.1
Mills	0.87	58.6	16	222	173.7	10.5	36	315	96.4	6.1	15	50	7.1	1.4
Mitchell	0.75	69.2	23	294	514.0	14.8	55	365	73.8	6.1	7	50	0.9	0.2
Monona	0.82	91.3	12	105	140.9	4.7	43	392	119.6	9.0	2	D	D	D
Monroe	0.00	0.0	11	173	52.0	5.8	32	302	85.9	5.7	5	4	0.7	0.1
Montgomery	1.45	141.7	15	119	222.4	6.2	49	529	108.4	10.1	9	46	4.4	1.2
Muscatine	28.94	672.9	50	D	D	D	141	2,070	489.0	44.1	47	199	28.1	5.7
O'Brien	2.31	165.2	32	358	776.7	14.7	99	930	204.5	17.5	4	18	4.4	0.5
Osceola	4.30	698.7	8	D	D	D	29	164	81.0	3.5	1	D	D	D
Page	1.78	114.6	18	157	146.9	6.3	72	692	153.8	12.6	8	10	1.9	0.1
Palo Alto	0.78	85.4	17	138	262.9	6.2	41	340	81.1	6.9	7	17	4.0	0.3
Plymouth	3.34	134.7	35	351	469.0	13.8	97	1,013	270.0	20.9	18	57	5.9	1.3
Pocahontas	0.48	68.5	12	137	303.5	5.6	33	245	50.3	4.7	1	D	D	D
Polk	56.09	119.9	678	11,409	9,500.5	631.6	1,518	27,663	7,616.3	689.8	549	3,095	632.1	123.1
Pottawattamie	15.02	160.3	96	1,331	1,737.8	64.7	308	5,957	1,757.6	128.5	80	351	53.4	8.8
Poweshiek	1.33	71.7	21	182	226.5	7.6	84	1,107	432.9	33.4	13	28	2.9	0.5
Ringgold	0.00	0.0	7	55	90.7	2.2	28	194	79.6	4.3	2	D	D	D
Sac	1.14	113.8	29	229	275.3	13.3	57	381	101.6	7.5	4	4	1.4	0.1
Scott	17.82	103.5	266	4,020	2,642.1	195.5	638	11,210	3,098.7	266.1	181	744	194.3	27.8
Shelby	1.96	164.3	28	400	255.2	13.5	56	571	175.3	10.7	5	17	1.7	0.2
Sioux	9.13	261.3	87	1,554	1,401.0	60.6	149	1,622	433.3	35.3	24	106	18.4	5.8
Story	8.42	87.7	74	D	D	D	288	4,708	1,084.2	98.5	97	465	75.5	16.1
Tama	2.66	153.4	22	136	204.5	5.7	64	530	122.3	11.1	5	D	D	D
Taylor	0.00	0.0	5	D	D	D	18	147	32.6	2.2	3	D	D	D
Union	4.15	332.8	18	236	552.4	10.1	49	756	174.9	16.8	11	D	D	D
Van Buren	0.00	0.0	8	46	39.3	1.5	29	192	40.5	3.4	3	D	D	D
Wapello	7.94	225.7	29	211	314.3	7.9	135	2,290	538.4	48.5	23	91	12.5	2.9
Warren	1.00	20.6	37	549	287.1	24.6	103	1,513	367.8	32.3	23	69	10.4	1.6
Washington	1.81	81.4	42	306	273.0	13.4	103	1,091	256.1	22.1	12	22	1.6	0.3
Wayne	0.00	0.0	5	79	55.3	2.6	31	197	70.1	4.2	1	D	D	D
Webster	11.01	297.0	59	D	D	D	171	2,616	595.8	54.5	39	103	20.2	2.6
Winnebago	0.89	83.9	22	169	280.8	7.4	56	485	131.4	9.5	5	D	D	D
Winneshiek	1.33	64.2	33	271	281.9	14.5	121	1,185	293.0	26.8	11	23	1.9	0.4
Woodbury	13.97	135.9	149	2,253	2,107.1	101.7	432	7,336	1,776.1	155.7	90	516	65.2	13.3
Worth	0.45	59.5	14	103	189.5	4.8	20	183	36.7	3.6	1	D	D	D
Wright	1.24	97.1	18	286	628.1	15.4	61	606	117.9	10.4	14	21	2.7	0.3

1 Merchant wholesalers, except manufacturers' sales branches and offices.   2. Employer establishments.

Table B. States and Counties — Professional Services, Manufacturing, and Accommodation and Food Services

STATE County	Professional, scientific, and technical services, 2012				Manufacturing, 2012				Accommodation and food services, 2012			
	Number of establishments	Number of employees	Sales (mil dol)	Average payroll (mil dol)	Number of establishments	Number of employees	Receipts (mil dol)	Annual payroll (mil dol)	Number of establishments	Number of employees	Receipts (mil dol)	Annual payroll (mil dol)
	147	148	149	150	151	152	153	154	155	156	157	158
IOWA— Cont'd												
Franklin	20	76	5.6	2.2	24	719	229.3	36.4	18	154	5.6	1.6
Fremont	8	34	3.2	1.2	10	632	654.4	30.5	21	180	7.5	1.9
Greene	17	79	7.5	3.5	10	287	86.0	13.5	18	D	D	D
Grundy	12	37	4.4	1.3	13	504	153.9	20.5	20	138	4.4	1.2
Guthrie	17	68	10.2	2.5	9	354	D	15.4	18	D	D	D
Hamilton	24	99	12.1	4.1	22	639	275.3	22.3	29	286	10.1	2.7
Hancock	16	163	13.3	5.0	23	1,037	348.5	44.8	20	D	D	D
Hardin	34	164	14.1	4.7	25	535	1,272.7	24.5	34	441	14.6	3.8
Harrison	18	D	D	D	13	303	107.6	13.1	30	302	10.3	2.9
Henry	40	148	18.3	6.0	36	2,139	815.9	86.0	43	565	24.1	6.1
Howard	14	52	3.2	1.3	23	944	260.5	38.8	22	D	D	D
Humboldt	18	62	9.3	2.2	23	934	228.7	41.0	22	215	8.8	2.3
Ida	10	55	3.6	1.1	13	1,026	679.5	49.9	11	D	D	D
Iowa	26	147	26.7	15.9	27	3,254	1,475.9	168.2	41	567	21.6	6.8
Jackson	32	114	7.7	2.6	31	839	255.2	28.8	47	496	16.6	4.7
Jasper	55	469	116.8	18.6	37	1,576	306.3	53.5	59	846	33.6	9.3
Jefferson	133	697	69.8	25.1	36	1,134	266.2	50.4	46	467	19.0	5.9
Johnson	272	1,969	299.6	92.2	80	4,983	3,400.4	232.9	375	D	D	D
Jones	28	120	11.3	4.5	28	811	246.0	35.4	38	D	D	D
Keokuk	10	37	7.0	1.7	12	185	53.1	7.8	11	D	D	D
Kossuth	35	187	22.0	7.1	28	1,223	875.8	53.6	34	380	13.8	3.6
Lee	49	189	18.1	5.1	62	4,138	2,511.7	227.0	95	1,047	38.7	10.1
Linn	506	5,486	728.9	321.5	208	17,686	10,073.9	1,288.4	499	8,790	388.8	113.4
Louisa	11	33	2.6	0.8	12	1,401	D	49.0	19	99	4.1	1.0
Lucas	12	34	2.7	0.9	11	146	D	6.9	16	D	D	D
Lyon	21	120	17.2	9.7	27	589	111.8	26.8	18	D	D	D
Madison	31	102	9.7	3.3	15	162	D	6.6	23	D	D	D
Mahaska	35	136	12.5	6.2	33	1,211	969.9	60.6	38	D	D	D
Marion	58	360	32.5	11.9	43	6,128	2,031.6	378.0	68	935	30.8	8.7
Marshall	43	338	51.3	13.6	38	5,011	2,232.2	246.8	87	1,070	44.7	12.1
Mills	26	D	D	D	7	35	8.2	1.0	16	145	6.4	1.6
Mitchell	12	87	4.8	1.5	25	984	644.4	41.6	21	D	D	D
Monona	15	46	4.2	1.8	4	74	D	D	25	D	D	D
Monroe	10	40	5.0	1.2	12	426	D	14.0	21	D	D	D
Montgomery	15	68	9.5	2.5	9	417	242.8	21.1	25	254	10.0	2.9
Muscatine	59	678	71.9	36.2	63	6,623	3,982.7	339.5	88	1,129	47.1	12.6
O'Brien	27	158	21.2	5.6	25	522	D	24.1	27	D	D	D
Osceola	8	26	4.9	0.7	14	271	D	10.3	12	D	D	D
Page	19	110	6.4	2.8	17	1,355	303.3	60.0	31	369	14.4	3.9
Palo Alto	11	30	4.5	1.5	20	514	676.5	23.7	26	548	43.5	7.7
Plymouth	35	234	12.7	12.6	31	2,471	1,084.3	111.7	57	857	26.9	7.4
Pocahontas	17	52	3.2	1.2	13	342	75.3	15.3	15	D	D	D
Polk	1,398	14,140	2,345.9	878.5	337	16,660	10,472.9	834.2	1,100	20,540	1,012.6	290.6
Pottawattamie	130	686	77.2	27.1	62	4,787	3,929.2	205.4	207	5,282	412.8	90.8
Poweshiek	41	126	10.9	3.5	33	1,576	453.7	61.1	53	583	20.9	5.4
Ringgold	8	50	16.3	1.8	6	D	3.1	0.6	10	D	D	D
Sac	15	43	5.5	1.1	24	398	198.0	14.3	22	D	D	D
Scott	405	2,548	316.6	108.5	182	11,389	6,704.5	657.0	423	8,987	440.2	120.6
Shelby	20	136	13.3	4.2	19	666	176.3	27.1	25	D	D	D
Sioux	83	980	124.2	32.9	90	5,331	1,596.6	208.6	74	1,248	40.6	11.3
Story	203	1,114	118.0	53.3	77	4,821	2,787.2	256.8	229	4,269	172.6	48.0
Tama	22	61	5.2	1.5	19	280	116.9	12.7	27	D	D	D
Taylor	9	37	2.5	0.7	6	539	237.5	16.2	8	D	D	D
Union	17	63	5.0	2.1	13	1,654	284.0	61.1	28	366	14.3	3.7
Van Buren	7	25	2.1	0.7	11	901	203.7	39.9	12	D	D	D
Wapello	48	280	24.7	10.0	24	4,264	D	196.6	77	1,198	47.0	13.2
Warren	56	294	37.6	12.4	27	425	78.6	19.5	64	890	32.9	9.1
Washington	56	158	14.5	4.6	45	1,078	398.8	43.5	44	D	D	D
Wayne	8	39	4.1	1.0	9	408	102.1	14.3	11	80	2.1	0.6
Webster	71	1,053	35.7	52.8	44	1,246	1,549.8	68.0	83	1,365	61.9	16.6
Winnebago	23	168	10.4	4.7	18	2,588	734.7	109.0	23	D	D	D
Winneshiek	28	161	19.7	8.4	34	1,402	300.9	60.6	61	757	32.4	8.0
Woodbury	196	977	121.1	40.3	91	5,068	4,061.2	210.7	268	4,980	240.7	66.7
Worth	9	23	1.6	0.6	12	431	257.4	15.9	10	D	D	D
Wright	23	125	12.0	3.0	22	1,280	1,437.3	63.4	36	D	D	D

Health Care and Social Assistance, Other Services, Nonemployer Businesses, and Residential Construction

STATE County	Health care and social assistance, 2012				Other services, 2012				Nonemployer businesses, 2016		Value of residential construction authorized by building permits, 2018	
	Number of establishments	Number of employees	Receipts (mil dol)	Annual payroll (mil dol)	Number of establishments	Number of employees	Receipts (mil dol)	Annual payroll (mil dol)	Number	Receipts (mil dol)	New construction ($1,000)	Number of housing units
	159	160	161	162	163	164	165	166	167	168	169	170
IOWA— Cont'd												
Franklin	31	560	35.3	14.7	28	91	8.7	1.9	808	36.9	910	4
Fremont	17	415	25.6	11.0	12	D	D	D	468	18.5	1,980	8
Greene	30	588	39.3	16.5	26	88	8.6	1.7	700	30.5	1,000	7
Grundy	26	493	33.0	14.0	20	D	D	D	917	34.4	4,349	16
Guthrie	27	535	34.8	16.1	28	83	9.7	2.2	1,036	43.2	5,171	17
Hamilton	34	D	D	D	31	94	16.0	2.6	1,046	41.3	4,810	43
Hancock	18	463	30.9	12.8	26	253	26.4	10.1	882	33.0	2,405	15
Hardin	49	1,054	69.8	30.2	47	137	13.8	3.8	1,258	49.3	2,688	9
Harrison	33	858	59.3	23.9	25	63	5.4	1.2	1,046	43.1	7,797	33
Henry	54	1,141	85.2	39.3	43	137	9.5	3.3	1,309	44.7	7,291	37
Howard	22	547	28.3	11.9	16	46	4.0	1.0	802	43.0	1,400	4
Humboldt	24	472	27.1	11.1	16	49	6.1	1.2	717	32.4	2,710	16
Ida	22	503	31.8	12.6	14	D	D	D	565	23.0	1,770	9
Iowa	37	827	46.2	22.7	26	D	D	D	1,228	48.3	2,733	13
Jackson	41	855	51.8	23.7	49	120	17.7	2.7	1,523	64.0	6,898	40
Jasper	83	1,563	102.4	46.8	60	283	17.4	5.1	2,341	88.8	18,934	75
Jefferson	46	726	58.7	22.9	47	154	74.3	4.8	1,836	64.7	6,704	84
Johnson	383	15,739	1,967.8	768.9	217	1,519	187.4	42.4	9,841	477.5	221,615	1,295
Jones	36	842	55.1	21.8	41	108	12.6	2.4	1,345	56.0	5,491	32
Keokuk	21	374	21.0	10.5	19	D	D	D	720	36.0	445	4
Kossuth	44	829	66.4	25.6	49	126	15.2	3.0	1,433	61.3	2,256	11
Lee	108	2,268	166.4	74.7	74	232	24.8	5.6	1,915	78.4	4,533	18
Linn	582	14,939	1,451.7	615.2	377	2,610	253.6	77.3	13,452	604.7	101,239	892
Louisa	28	343	15.5	7.2	17	D	D	D	634	27.6	2,445	12
Lucas	25	595	33.6	15.2	13	26	3.7	0.7	643	28.4	100	1
Lyon	24	443	21.6	8.0	32	94	9.4	2.1	994	51.3	11,281	45
Madison	28	572	37.8	15.9	22	62	6.8	1.6	1,381	58.9	31,556	148
Mahaska	51	1,056	80.1	39.2	39	142	14.7	3.4	1,451	53.4	3,223	24
Marion	92	1,991	165.7	70.9	60	215	17.8	4.8	2,204	82.7	25,270	98
Marshall	82	1,930	155.4	70.4	61	284	25.3	6.0	1,920	72.6	17,857	111
Mills	37	740	32.8	17.2	24	62	6.4	1.6	960	34.6	360	2
Mitchell	33	590	37.3	15.3	33	73	6.9	1.7	893	37.3	7,047	41
Monona	21	698	60.5	21.2	14	49	3.4	1.1	653	24.0	1,950	8
Monroe	21	454	28.9	10.3	7	16	2.4	0.3	515	21.3	2,470	11
Montgomery	32	765	52.9	24.7	32	131	13.4	3.8	778	25.7	1,900	8
Muscatine	97	1,944	139.9	60.2	68	368	48.6	10.2	2,105	92.0	2,240	13
O'Brien	52	1,446	82.4	32.1	41	171	21.6	4.6	984	49.2	1,315	5
Osceola	14	260	16.5	6.5	11	D	D	D	442	20.3	1,200	4
Page	57	1,452	106.6	48.4	23	69	6.9	1.4	900	31.3	1,997	8
Palo Alto	30	705	48.2	20.4	15	D	D	D	702	30.4	155	1
Plymouth	56	1,139	81.9	30.9	59	277	30.5	8.1	1,715	82.9	20,113	107
Pocahontas	19	315	18.7	8.3	9	D	D	D	519	26.7	300	1
Polk	1,113	33,649	3,659.7	1,655.7	942	6,904	887.0	228.0	32,594	1,569.5	758,385	3,831
Pottawattamie	225	5,323	509.6	184.3	159	772	98.3	22.0	5,044	217.9	44,064	180
Poweshiek	55	1,098	87.2	38.0	35	112	13.2	3.0	1,309	49.6	4,706	19
Ringgold	14	399	27.5	12.2	13	40	5.3	0.9	457	20.8	280	1
Sac	28	560	32.8	15.3	16	43	4.9	1.1	847	38.0	3,732	17
Scott	482	12,086	1,132.3	490.6	306	2,165	188.8	52.9	10,619	508.3	86,222	403
Shelby	39	1,134	78.1	26.2	28	114	9.5	2.1	949	41.2	3,295	15
Sioux	78	2,437	149.6	62.7	83	306	36.2	7.4	2,715	127.1	25,497	139
Story	192	4,855	513.2	206.0	146	1,000	136.1	27.5	5,531	240.7	105,685	626
Tama	29	460	22.3	10.3	20	67	5.2	1.2	1,081	42.6	2,112	13
Taylor	15	D	D	D	11	D	D	D	565	25.6	947	5
Union	40	917	64.6	29.4	28	128	22.3	4.5	739	27.1	490	4
Van Buren	14	315	19.5	8.0	12	13	1.8	0.3	679	31.4	500	2
Wapello	92	2,615	214.4	90.0	50	249	19.9	6.7	1,659	61.4	1,810	21
Warren	77	1,232	73.9	33.0	63	227	17.4	4.6	3,611	147.6	89,936	335
Washington	67	1,252	78.5	34.9	53	148	20.3	4.0	1,744	71.2	11,134	72
Wayne	16	366	26.5	13.9	11	D	D	D	591	37.2	480	2
Webster	116	2,974	238.4	109.4	62	372	52.0	11.6	2,038	78.2	12,102	70
Winnebago	40	620	27.1	11.2	14	D	D	D	830	33.6	995	4
Winneshiek	61	1,422	105.8	51.0	42	D	D	D	1,883	69.2	13,133	49
Woodbury	331	8,431	820.1	310.1	181	1,331	92.1	29.0	5,651	248.2	29,872	161
Worth	12	179	8.5	3.9	12	D	D	D	535	18.1	570	4
Wright	38	924	83.8	34.0	24	57	5.3	1.1	891	36.9	2,774	14

Table B. States and Counties — **Government Employment and Payroll, and Local Government Finances**

STATE County	Government employment and payroll, 2012									Local government finances, 2012				
			March payroll (percent of total)							General revenue				
												Taxes		
											Inter-govern-		Per capita[1] (dollars)	
	Full-time equivalent employees	March payroll (dollars)	Adminis-tration, judicial, and legal	Police and corrections	Fire protection	Highways and transpor-tation	Health and welfare	Natural resources and utilities	Education and libraries	Total (mil dol)	mental (mil dol)	Total (mil dol)	Total	Property
	171	172	173	174	175	176	177	178	179	180	181	182	183	184

IOWA— Cont'd

Franklin	668	2,088,400	4.9	4.3	0.0	6.1	28.3	1.6	54.1	66.9	22.7	23.0	2,183	1,785
Fremont	347	973,340	7.5	7.8	0.0	11.0	2.0	3.1	66.2	34.7	15.8	16.0	2,243	1,866
Greene	666	2,223,582	5.3	3.9	0.1	5.8	41.2	3.9	39.3	57.4	14.6	19.1	2,082	1,727
Grundy	563	1,970,199	5.6	4.4	0.0	5.6	33.3	4.7	45.8	64.2	18.4	21.5	1,731	1,370
Guthrie	748	2,384,845	4.1	2.8	0.0	5.3	24.8	3.4	59.0	68.4	20.6	29.3	2,716	2,276
Hamilton	889	2,941,083	5.3	6.3	0.7	5.4	28.8	4.7	47.5	85.2	24.2	29.7	1,934	1,608
Hancock	533	1,678,758	4.9	4.9	1.1	7.4	29.0	1.1	50.1	52.6	15.5	18.7	1,678	1,364
Hardin	771	2,439,397	10.0	8.8	0.3	7.6	3.2	3.8	65.7	93.9	30.1	33.2	1,921	1,546
Harrison	661	2,116,699	6.1	6.5	0.0	7.4	2.6	6.5	68.9	60.2	26.0	28.5	1,960	1,608
Henry	1,101	3,801,450	6.1	5.0	0.3	3.4	27.7	5.1	50.9	103.1	34.1	30.0	1,484	1,188
Howard	610	1,837,491	3.8	4.1	0.0	6.3	32.8	4.1	48.6	53.0	15.0	18.0	1,887	1,526
Humboldt	551	1,979,695	10.2	4.3	0.1	15.7	23.2	4.8	41.3	51.5	15.8	17.9	1,843	1,479
Ida	324	944,758	6.5	5.6	0.0	8.7	0.4	3.6	73.9	24.5	9.5	11.8	1,661	1,328
Iowa	946	2,546,590	3.6	5.9	0.1	6.6	25.6	2.5	55.1	74.3	23.2	29.8	1,838	1,381
Jackson	760	2,545,154	6.2	8.0	0.2	6.2	18.9	3.4	56.7	78.0	28.3	27.5	1,395	1,119
Jasper	1,510	5,999,123	4.8	6.2	2.0	4.5	25.8	3.5	51.2	155.2	47.6	58.5	1,597	1,284
Jefferson	662	2,186,709	5.0	7.9	0.9	5.5	30.3	6.8	43.2	74.0	18.6	24.1	1,426	1,178
Johnson	2,791	12,750,946	7.7	8.1	1.5	4.7	5.9	5.3	62.3	508.5	160.5	263.7	1,934	1,579
Jones	764	2,287,665	6.5	6.6	0.0	6.9	3.4	2.6	72.1	73.5	35.1	28.3	1,369	1,067
Keokuk	574	1,571,936	7.3	3.7	0.0	8.5	14.2	3.5	62.2	51.8	19.5	19.7	1,897	1,573
Kossuth	791	2,418,144	8.4	5.5	0.2	7.0	33.0	4.1	41.0	91.7	21.6	29.7	1,937	1,582
Lee	1,300	4,660,014	5.4	7.2	3.1	4.7	4.4	9.0	64.9	121.2	55.2	48.2	1,353	989
Linn	9,095	37,187,147	3.6	5.9	2.8	6.2	2.3	4.9	72.4	1,182.6	511.6	437.3	2,031	1,562
Louisa	609	1,866,882	4.6	6.3	0.0	4.4	2.1	2.8	79.3	56.0	27.3	22.6	2,003	1,495
Lucas	520	1,767,462	3.7	2.9	0.0	5.3	32.1	16.9	38.6	45.7	14.5	12.3	1,406	1,112
Lyon	499	1,482,179	6.0	6.8	0.0	8.4	4.9	6.3	65.1	46.7	19.3	20.2	1,715	1,324
Madison	798	2,825,675	6.6	2.7	0.0	7.8	22.7	7.6	52.2	80.3	28.9	28.9	1,848	1,518
Mahaska	1,014	3,634,697	4.3	4.7	0.9	4.1	46.1	1.9	35.8	108.1	29.6	33.7	1,503	1,164
Marion	1,252	3,936,638	5.4	7.6	0.0	6.5	4.1	9.6	65.6	122.5	47.7	49.1	1,469	1,141
Marshall	1,954	7,209,585	3.6	6.6	1.9	3.7	0.6	4.3	78.3	184.2	83.4	70.1	1,715	1,332
Mills	661	1,998,540	5.5	6.9	1.4	7.4	5.2	1.1	71.4	51.3	23.3	23.3	1,569	1,336
Mitchell	526	1,692,873	5.0	4.8	0.0	5.4	33.0	2.6	47.2	57.0	14.0	18.3	1,705	1,409
Monona	396	1,218,905	10.0	7.1	0.0	11.2	2.6	8.7	59.5	37.4	15.9	15.8	1,736	1,419
Monroe	387	1,402,370	4.4	6.0	0.1	5.9	41.4	2.3	39.4	25.8	12.4	11.4	1,418	1,109
Montgomery	722	2,440,051	4.3	3.9	1.5	5.4	42.7	3.0	37.5	72.5	19.7	21.2	2,004	1,573
Muscatine	1,797	6,903,785	4.4	8.5	3.1	3.4	2.3	23.5	51.0	179.8	71.9	69.9	1,630	1,298
O'Brien	688	2,291,194	4.3	7.0	0.0	6.3	0.5	5.0	75.2	67.6	25.7	28.4	2,007	1,628
Osceola	225	737,061	10.1	8.0	0.0	13.2	1.6	6.2	60.4	21.0	8.0	9.8	1,588	1,342
Page	735	2,422,895	5.4	5.6	0.4	5.2	28.7	4.2	50.0	75.7	24.0	22.9	1,458	1,116
Palo Alto	595	1,986,443	5.8	3.7	0.8	6.9	35.4	3.3	43.7	67.2	16.0	23.3	2,512	2,103
Plymouth	1,172	4,151,413	4.7	5.6	0.3	5.4	25.2	3.7	54.8	126.6	33.5	46.1	1,850	1,539
Pocahontas	388	1,255,236	7.6	7.3	0.0	7.9	24.8	7.4	43.9	40.0	11.0	14.7	2,054	1,718
Polk	17,358	73,983,487	5.6	9.0	3.6	4.4	8.6	5.6	61.7	2,215.8	755.8	962.0	2,168	1,882
Pottawattamie	3,555	14,074,472	5.1	12.0	3.8	3.4	3.5	4.9	66.5	469.3	187.7	200.8	2,162	1,672
Poweshiek	616	2,161,055	7.6	7.8	1.1	6.4	2.2	6.6	67.8	70.4	26.8	32.7	1,745	1,368
Ringgold	380	1,133,677	4.5	3.2	0.0	9.7	40.0	2.0	40.3	38.0	10.1	11.1	2,172	1,874
Sac	370	1,168,894	8.0	8.4	0.0	9.1	4.9	9.7	53.3	38.8	16.2	16.8	1,655	1,346
Scott	6,132	26,019,745	5.1	9.3	3.9	3.8	2.4	4.0	69.8	729.6	283.5	333.3	1,974	1,565
Shelby	746	2,472,519	5.4	3.6	0.2	6.1	48.6	4.6	28.4	74.6	17.8	20.6	1,705	1,402
Sioux	1,410	5,040,852	7.0	4.6	0.0	3.5	32.1	5.9	45.0	155.5	40.9	50.2	1,466	1,159
Story	2,892	10,932,541	7.4	7.6	2.9	7.7	10.1	9.9	52.8	476.0	102.3	138.3	1,518	1,219
Tama	838	2,616,822	5.8	6.4	0.0	7.4	4.6	3.7	70.0	73.1	34.0	30.1	1,717	1,370
Taylor	283	832,177	7.3	5.5	0.0	10.1	5.8	4.1	65.8	26.1	12.6	9.8	1,572	1,285
Union	985	3,478,275	2.6	3.0	0.6	3.4	37.5	2.3	50.1	116.7	47.2	22.5	1,788	1,421
Van Buren	420	1,439,759	4.4	3.0	0.0	5.3	38.1	2.3	46.6	36.7	12.5	10.5	1,409	1,133
Wapello	1,563	6,980,218	2.5	3.5	1.9	4.5	2.0	4.5	80.0	186.1	86.6	52.4	1,482	1,084
Warren	1,608	6,242,328	5.6	5.6	1.1	3.5	2.5	5.3	75.5	156.4	71.0	65.1	1,387	1,216
Washington	1,128	3,614,174	5.4	6.2	0.4	4.7	26.2	4.4	52.3	111.8	34.7	38.8	1,771	1,403
Wayne	428	1,412,234	4.6	3.7	0.0	5.5	52.3	1.9	31.5	45.4	11.7	10.9	1,714	1,444
Webster	1,646	5,911,455	5.2	5.8	2.4	3.6	3.2	3.1	76.3	189.7	73.6	61.4	1,648	1,262
Winnebago	563	1,699,897	5.9	5.4	0.0	5.7	4.8	5.5	71.6	53.4	20.2	24.6	2,324	1,932
Winneshiek	1,453	4,847,620	2.3	3.4	0.2	3.7	28.1	2.1	59.9	162.1	45.6	40.6	1,928	1,635
Woodbury	3,937	16,380,806	4.5	9.7	4.1	5.4	2.2	5.6	67.1	475.0	216.3	177.2	1,732	1,265
Worth	353	1,078,114	9.5	7.7	0.0	8.8	3.7	3.5	65.9	35.3	14.3	16.5	2,191	1,830
Wright	944	3,639,368	3.1	3.8	0.0	4.6	48.9	2.0	37.6	120.8	27.5	28.8	2,216	1,856

1. Based on the resident population estimated as of July 1 of the year shown.

Table B. States and Counties — Local Government Finances, Government Employment, and Income Taxes

STATE County	Local government finances, 2012 (cont.)										Government employment, 2017			Individual income tax returns, 2016		
	Direct general expenditure							Debt outstanding								
			Percent of total for:												Mean	
	Total (mil dol)	Per capita[1] (dollars)	Education	Health and hospitals	Police protection	Public welfare	Highways	Total (mil dol)	Per capita[1] (dollars)	Federal civilian	Federal military	State and local	Number of returns	adjusted gross income	Mean income tax
	185	186	187	188	189	190	191	192	193	194	195	196	197	198	199
IOWA— Cont'd															
Franklin	74.7	7,078	38.7	27.4	2.8	0.1	7.5	53.7	5,092	41	37	726	4,530	52,790	5,611
Fremont	36.0	5,034	46.9	4.3	4.1	0.1	19.2	10.1	1,415	26	25	435	3,160	53,531	5,407
Greene	58.6	6,398	31.8	39.4	3.0	0.2	8.2	19.5	2,133	35	33	750	4,240	50,390	4,907
Grundy	60.9	4,889	35.4	29.1	3.1	0.1	12.1	34.5	2,773	31	45	709	5,770	64,170	7,124
Guthrie	64.7	6,005	45.4	24.0	2.4	0.1	9.0	71.3	6,614	58	39	866	5,090	62,895	7,301
Hamilton	89.3	5,820	41.9	27.7	3.4	0.2	7.1	95.4	6,215	39	55	1,214	7,150	54,492	6,016
Hancock	59.9	5,378	31.9	38.4	3.3	0.1	11.3	36.3	3,260	40	39	565	5,160	53,311	5,513
Hardin	98.1	5,668	39.4	22.8	3.6	0.1	10.4	60.0	3,470	73	60	1,761	7,730	54,317	6,456
Harrison	56.0	3,853	56.3	5.5	3.7	0.3	12.4	33.4	2,299	69	51	831	6,600	54,275	5,621
Henry	99.5	4,919	39.9	36.4	3.0	0.3	4.6	76.0	3,758	60	68	1,583	8,850	49,928	4,626
Howard	49.9	5,214	37.9	32.9	2.9	0.4	8.5	14.5	1,518	28	33	723	4,470	47,744	5,020
Humboldt	60.5	6,223	36.7	23.4	2.9	0.2	10.8	37.9	3,894	45	35	730	4,500	59,496	6,759
Ida	25.1	3,531	55.4	4.9	4.2	0.2	13.6	14.0	1,973	29	25	366	3,290	63,447	8,409
Iowa	74.5	4,600	48.3	23.2	3.7	0.4	9.2	69.2	4,275	55	58	987	7,960	56,336	5,812
Jackson	75.2	3,817	46.3	20.7	4.1	0.1	9.2	36.7	1,860	79	71	1,015	9,440	48,016	4,881
Jasper	146.8	4,011	39.1	28.3	4.3	0.3	6.0	102.6	2,802	94	130	1,893	16,690	55,243	5,577
Jefferson	72.9	4,323	28.0	30.9	3.6	0.2	10.0	71.8	4,254	61	62	1,113	7,270	53,109	6,108
Johnson	524.4	3,847	35.0	4.1	4.1	0.9	6.0	708.3	5,196	2,078	558	35,719	64,720	72,061	9,822
Jones	81.7	3,958	56.2	5.0	3.3	0.1	12.9	52.6	2,548	50	72	1,315	9,090	53,766	5,728
Keokuk	46.7	4,504	42.3	19.6	2.4	0.1	11.3	24.3	2,344	42	37	541	4,500	46,936	4,291
Kossuth	92.1	6,004	26.6	34.3	2.6	0.2	10.8	73.1	4,765	59	54	1,086	7,410	56,674	6,283
Lee	137.2	3,851	55.0	7.3	5.0	0.5	5.8	121.6	3,414	95	139	1,866	15,480	50,271	5,308
Linn	1,336.0	6,206	46.5	3.0	3.7	1.2	4.7	1,559.7	7,244	1,059	809	12,721	107,140	65,713	8,075
Louisa	54.0	4,790	58.9	3.9	3.7	0.1	10.4	92.9	8,237	61	41	657	5,030	50,845	4,687
Lucas	45.7	5,216	36.3	40.7	2.3	0.2	8.8	77.6	8,862	38	31	614	3,940	45,779	4,319
Lyon	43.5	3,701	45.1	4.4	4.6	0.1	20.2	26.6	2,260	39	43	654	5,190	57,856	6,335
Madison	80.3	5,130	45.0	29.6	2.4	0.1	8.2	120.8	7,718	39	58	963	7,290	67,027	7,687
Mahaska	103.0	4,588	32.3	43.1	3.7	0.2	7.0	35.6	1,584	56	79	1,393	9,560	54,742	5,670
Marion	110.4	3,302	53.4	5.1	4.5	0.3	11.9	105.0	3,142	129	117	1,710	14,880	63,020	7,137
Marshall	192.9	4,722	64.1	3.0	4.2	0.3	6.4	177.1	4,335	117	144	3,226	18,050	53,347	5,252
Mills	49.6	3,346	58.3	5.0	5.7	1.1	10.6	46.3	3,118	37	53	1,516	6,700	64,394	7,284
Mitchell	58.6	5,460	27.5	34.6	2.8	0.1	12.4	39.9	3,723	36	38	685	4,790	53,004	5,798
Monona	39.6	4,341	49.5	4.3	4.7	0.4	17.8	19.2	2,100	41	31	528	4,120	50,038	5,463
Monroe	25.6	3,175	52.7	6.3	5.3	0.3	19.1	18.5	2,294	40	28	545	3,390	46,227	4,183
Montgomery	75.5	7,150	27.3	38.4	8.7	0.2	5.5	34.3	3,246	40	37	914	4,820	48,769	4,955
Muscatine	169.3	3,949	47.2	3.6	5.1	0.4	6.8	78.4	1,828	86	156	2,563	20,380	56,071	5,979
O'Brien	67.2	4,738	61.1	4.1	3.9	0.2	8.1	45.7	3,226	46	49	1,063	6,630	58,543	6,998
Osceola	20.4	3,288	41.6	8.9	9.7	0.1	18.2	8.6	1,389	25	22	295	2,900	46,948	4,688
Page	86.1	5,483	33.4	39.4	2.8	0.1	7.4	65.9	4,192	72	51	1,250	6,470	50,339	5,033
Palo Alto	64.4	6,948	31.7	32.8	2.9	0.1	15.3	37.1	4,003	37	32	979	4,240	50,578	5,621
Plymouth	123.5	4,958	40.4	28.0	3.4	2.2	7.8	86.7	3,483	78	92	1,468	12,210	63,007	7,800
Pocahontas	41.8	5,851	31.5	27.7	4.1	0.5	11.0	23.7	3,313	33	25	545	3,290	51,259	5,408
Polk	2,428.8	5,474	46.0	7.6	4.5	1.5	5.2	2,789.0	6,286	6,015	1,851	30,169	226,530	69,483	9,195
Pottawattamie	475.8	5,121	56.9	3.4	5.2	0.3	4.5	433.2	4,662	209	338	5,254	42,630	54,895	5,821
Poweshiek	66.2	3,533	47.3	5.0	4.5	0.2	10.8	65.3	3,483	58	62	849	8,230	56,996	6,381
Ringgold	38.2	7,503	25.9	44.8	2.8	0.2	9.0	42.2	8,280	30	18	433	2,070	42,470	4,983
Sac	42.6	4,196	49.4	6.2	4.3	0.1	13.4	17.5	1,720	44	36	600	4,760	53,972	5,614
Scott	760.2	4,504	54.4	2.6	4.9	0.1	3.6	683.1	4,047	589	625	8,793	81,650	66,837	8,756
Shelby	87.3	7,233	22.6	50.5	1.7	0.1	7.8	52.5	4,348	43	42	1,055	5,790	57,070	6,695
Sioux	160.8	4,691	31.1	29.5	3.1	0.1	6.7	182.6	5,329	100	120	2,238	14,440	62,166	8,115
Story	440.2	4,830	30.3	42.8	3.2	0.5	3.7	391.5	4,295	949	345	19,275	36,690	67,234	8,304
Tama	71.1	4,056	60.3	5.1	3.5	0.1	12.6	36.6	2,088	67	62	1,961	8,330	49,674	4,777
Taylor	30.7	4,937	39.9	4.5	3.6	0.1	25.2	25.0	4,034	39	22	378	2,720	40,886	3,575
Union	122.3	9,707	35.7	41.6	1.4	0.1	4.0	91.1	7,230	51	44	1,360	5,580	46,304	4,352
Van Buren	35.9	4,821	31.7	41.5	2.3	0.1	11.2	9.2	1,230	34	26	510	3,130	45,527	4,487
Wapello	204.9	5,795	64.7	3.0	2.8	0.3	9.3	88.9	2,514	111	126	2,502	15,370	47,149	4,568
Warren	173.5	3,701	60.2	4.1	4.2	0.3	5.2	262.4	5,595	96	179	2,337	23,320	69,813	8,237
Washington	127.8	5,831	38.9	20.4	2.8	0.3	9.4	155.3	7,085	62	81	1,483	10,490	54,708	5,353
Wayne	43.2	6,809	20.6	52.3	2.4	0.2	7.7	24.6	3,877	32	24	594	2,720	41,470	3,320
Webster	231.6	6,213	65.0	3.5	2.6	0.2	5.7	235.4	6,314	191	125	2,848	16,320	52,229	5,600
Winnebago	54.8	5,168	50.8	4.8	4.2	0.1	18.2	51.9	4,900	46	41	722	5,120	50,962	4,837
Winneshiek	175.5	8,333	54.9	26.3	1.7	0.1	5.5	125.4	5,954	68	67	2,066	9,380	55,470	6,213
Woodbury	498.8	4,875	56.0	4.2	4.6	0.6	3.9	465.5	4,550	681	369	6,394	46,560	51,579	5,566
Worth	37.0	4,920	43.7	3.8	4.3	0.1	12.6	25.7	3,424	27	27	376	3,630	50,802	4,828
Wright	134.7	10,370	22.1	58.1	1.8	0.2	4.2	130.1	10,011	68	46	1,340	5,840	52,479	5,293

1. Based on the resident population estimated as of July 1 of the year shown.

State / county code	CBSA code[1]	County code[2]	STATE County	Land area[3] (sq. mi)	Total persons 2018	Rank	Per square mile	White	Black	American Indian, Alaska Native	Asian and Pacific Islancer	Percent Hispanic or Latino[4]	Under 5 years	5 to 17 years	18 to 24 years	25 to 34 years	35 to 44 years	45 to 54 years
				1	2	3	4	5	6	7	8	9	10	11	12	13	14	15
20000		0	KANSAS	81,759.2	2,911,505	X	35.6	78.1	7.0	1.8	3.8	12.1	6.5	17.7	10.1	13.2	12.2	11.5
20001		7	Allen....................	500.3	12,444	2,254	24.9	92.5	3.4	1.9	1.2	3.8	5.6	16.8	9.0	11.0	11.3	11.6
20003		6	Anderson................	579.6	7,878	2,606	13.6	96.1	1.2	1.6	0.9	1.9	6.6	18.8	7.1	9.8	11.1	11.1
20005	11,860	6	Atchison	431.2	16,193	2,029	37.6	90.7	6.3	1.4	1.1	3.1	6.0	17.4	13.7	10.5	10.7	11.5
20007		9	Barber	1,134.1	4,472	2,861	3.9	93.2	1.6	1.8	0.8	4.2	6.1	16.8	6.0	11.0	9.8	10.2
20009	24,460	7	Barton	895.3	26,111	1,563	29.2	82.6	2.1	1.2	0.5	15.2	6.3	17.5	8.5	11.8	10.9	10.6
20011		6	Bourbon	635.5	14,653	2,117	23.1	92.0	4.1	1.9	1.6	2.9	7.1	18.6	8.9	11.2	10.9	10.2
20013		6	Brown	570.9	9,598	2,457	16.8	85.4	2.3	9.5	0.8	4.7	6.3	18.9	6.8	10.7	10.8	11.2
20015	48,620	2	Butler	1,429.7	66,765	802	46.7	90.7	2.8	2.0	1.9	5.0	6.0	19.4	8.7	11.8	12.9	12.2
20017		9	Chase....................	773.1	2,629	2,993	3.4	92.7	1.8	1.5	0.8	5.1	5.1	14.8	8.3	10.7	10.0	11.3
20019		8	Chautauqua	638.9	3,309	2,949	5.2	89.8	2.2	8.0	0.5	4.0	5.0	14.9	6.6	10.2	9.9	10.6
20021		6	Cherokee	587.6	20,015	1,827	34.1	91.6	1.6	7.0	1.1	2.8	5.8	17.3	7.5	10.7	11.4	13.3
20023		9	Cheyenne	1,019.9	2,660	2,991	2.6	91.0	0.7	0.6	2.3	6.3	6.8	14.5	7.2	9.3	10.9	9.3
20025		9	Clark	974.6	2,005	3,047	2.1	86.4	1.3	2.0	2.0	10.8	5.3	18.8	8.2	10.6	11.7	10.4
20027		6	Clay	645.3	7,997	2,594	12.4	95.4	1.5	1.3	1.0	2.5	6.5	17.0	6.6	10.3	11.7	10.8
20029		7	Cloud	715.3	8,729	2,526	12.2	94.0	1.5	1.2	1.7	3.2	5.6	16.8	9.6	11.3	10.4	10.8
20031		6	Coffey	626.9	8,233	2,574	13.1	94.5	1.4	1.8	1.2	2.8	5.7	16.1	7.3	10.7	11.0	12.4
20033		9	Comanche................	788.3	1,748	3,069	2.2	90.6	1.1	1.4	0.6	8.2	4.9	18.9	6.4	9.2	10.0	10.9
20035	11,680	4	Cowley	1,125.7	35,218	1,299	31.3	82.1	4.0	3.3	2.8	11.0	6.1	17.5	10.0	12.1	11.5	11.5
20037	38,260	4	Crawford	589.8	39,019	1,204	66.2	88.9	3.3	2.0	2.6	5.8	6.2	15.5	18.1	11.6	11.1	10.5
20039		9	Decatur	893.5	2,871	2,977	3.2	95.3	1.5	1.1	0.5	3.1	5.7	13.8	6.0	10.7	8.5	10.4
20041		7	Dickinson	847.1	18,717	1,889	22.1	92.7	2.2	1.5	1.1	4.9	5.9	17.8	6.9	11.5	11.6	11.9
20043	41,140	3	Doniphan.................	393.5	7,682	2,617	19.5	92.3	4.1	2.2	0.8	2.8	5.3	15.9	11.1	11.0	11.4	11.7
20045	29,940	3	Douglas..................	455.8	121,436	517	266.4	81.8	6.0	3.6	6.2	6.4	5.0	13.2	23.3	14.6	11.8	9.6
20047		9	Edwards	621.9	2,849	2,979	4.6	77.7	1.1	2.1	0.5	20.4	6.0	17.3	7.2	9.2	10.8	11.9
20049		8	Elk	644.3	2,508	3,003	3.9	93.0	1.3	3.3	1.2	4.6	5.8	15.8	5.1	7.5	8.8	10.7
20051	25,700	5	Ellis	899.9	28,710	1,469	31.9	90.8	2.0	0.8	2.2	5.9	5.9	15.6	17.1	13.4	11.0	9.8
20053		7	Ellsworth	715.6	6,196	2,735	8.7	87.3	6.1	1.4	0.8	6.0	4.6	13.8	8.5	13.4	12.5	11.9
20055	23,780	5	Finney	1,302.0	36,611	1,262	28.1	41.4	3.9	0.8	4.4	50.5	8.7	21.4	10.9	14.2	11.9	11.2
20057	19,980	5	Ford	1,098.3	33,888	1,331	30.9	40.2	2.6	0.8	1.8	55.6	8.9	21.3	10.3	13.8	12.2	11.6
20059	36,840	6	Franklin	571.8	25,631	1,578	44.8	93.1	2.2	1.8	0.8	4.3	6.0	17.8	8.8	11.9	11.5	12.6
20061	27,920	4	Geary	384.7	32,594	1,367	84.7	60.8	20.2	2.0	6.4	16.6	11.9	18.9	15.4	21.4	11.6	6.5
20063		9	Gove	1,071.7	2,612	2,994	2.4	95.8	0.9	0.7	1.3	2.7	6.4	17.6	6.5	9.7	10.8	9.2
20065		9	Graham	898.5	2,492	3,006	2.8	90.4	4.5	1.7	2.5	3.5	4.1	15.4	5.6	9.6	10.6	9.5
20067		7	Grant	574.8	7,336	2,636	12.8	50.9	0.8	1.2	0.5	47.9	7.8	23.0	9.3	11.3	11.9	10.6
20069		9	Gray	868.9	6,033	2,752	6.9	82.2	0.9	0.9	0.6	16.4	7.6	21.4	9.0	11.0	12.6	10.7
20071		9	Greeley	778.4	1,227	3,099	1.6	79.0	0.3	0.7	0.7	19.9	5.9	20.1	5.9	11.7	11.7	8.7
20073		6	Greenwood	1,143.3	6,055	2,746	5.3	93.5	1.3	2.7	0.7	4.0	5.6	16.2	6.5	8.3	10.3	11.7
20075		9	Hamilton	996.5	2,607	2,998	2.6	62.3	1.0	1.8	0.5	36.0	7.6	21.1	8.2	13.7	11.7	11.4
20077		8	Harper	801.3	5,506	2,793	6.9	91.5	1.1	2.1	0.8	6.4	6.3	18.6	6.5	10.6	10.5	10.3
20079	48,620	2	Harvey..................	539.8	34,210	1,321	63.4	84.5	2.7	1.5	1.4	12.1	5.9	18.2	9.7	11.0	11.6	10.6
20081		9	Haskell	577.5	3,997	2,901	6.9	66.9	0.7	1.1	1.0	31.4	7.0	21.1	9.2	11.8	11.4	11.3
20083		9	Hodgeman	860.0	1,818	3,065	2.1	88.8	1.8	1.4	2.7	7.0	6.4	16.3	6.6	9.7	9.2	11.1
20085	45,820	3	Jackson	656.2	13,280	2,212	20.2	86.9	1.5	9.3	0.9	4.6	6.4	18.5	7.8	10.5	10.7	13.0
20087	45,820	3	Jefferson	532.6	18,975	1,875	35.6	95.1	1.2	2.0	0.7	2.9	5.5	17.3	7.2	10.3	11.7	13.1
20089		9	Jewell	910.0	2,841	2,981	3.1	96.1	0.6	1.1	0.7	2.5	5.5	13.5	6.3	9.3	8.3	9.9
20091	28,140	1	Johnson	473.6	597,555	112	1,261.7	81.9	5.8	0.9	6.1	7.8	6.4	18.0	8.0	13.7	14.0	13.0
20093	23,780	9	Kearny	870.5	3,943	2,907	4.5	65.2	1.7	2.2	0.8	32.3	8.0	21.0	8.6	13.8	11.2	10.6
20095	48,620	2	Kingman	863.4	7,310	2,638	8.5	94.2	0.9	1.7	0.9	3.9	5.7	16.3	7.2	10.1	10.8	11.8
20097		9	Kiowa	722.6	2,516	3,001	3.5	90.3	1.6	1.6	1.8	6.4	6.7	16.1	11.8	9.8	9.3	10.2
20099	37,660	7	Labette..................	645.4	19,964	1,828	30.9	88.8	5.4	3.9	1.0	4.7	6.7	17.3	7.6	11.8	10.4	12.7
20101		9	Lane.....................	717.4	1,560	3,076	2.2	89.6	2.1	2.1	0.6	7.8	5.7	16.4	6.7	10.4	8.7	12.6
20103	28,140	1	Leavenworth	463.4	81,352	697	175.6	81.7	10.2	1.6	2.7	7.0	6.5	17.2	8.1	13.8	14.4	12.6
20105		9	Lincoln..................	719.4	3,023	2,964	4.2	94.6	1.0	1.2	0.8	3.7	5.4	17.1	6.5	7.9	10.7	11.4
20107	28,140	1	Linn.....................	594.1	9,750	2,447	16.4	95.1	1.3	2.0	0.7	2.9	5.4	17.1	6.4	9.5	11.9	12.0
20109		9	Logan	1,073.0	2,844	2,980	2.7	91.8	1.5	1.2	0.9	6.2	7.4	16.7	7.2	11.6	11.6	9.0
20111	21,380	4	Lyon	847.5	33,406	1,345	39.4	73.0	3.3	1.5	3.2	21.5	6.0	16.3	17.6	12.4	10.3	10.1
20113	32,700	7	McPherson	898.3	28,537	1,479	31.8	93.2	1.9	1.1	1.2	4.3	5.6	17.3	8.7	11.7	11.6	10.8
20115		6	Marion	944.3	11,950	2,294	12.7	93.9	1.5	1.5	0.8	3.9	5.1	16.1	9.9	9.4	9.8	11.2
20117		6	Marshall	900.2	9,722	2,448	10.8	95.9	1.1	1.2	1.0	2.6	6.5	17.4	6.7	10.1	11.3	10.3
20119		9	Meade	978.1	4,146	2,891	4.2	79.4	1.4	1.5	1.1	17.8	6.6	19.0	9.4	10.5	9.7	12.3
20121	28,140	1	Miami...................	575.9	33,680	1,338	58.5	94.2	1.9	1.5	1.0	3.3	5.8	18.7	7.4	10.5	12.4	13.5
20123		7	Mitchell..................	701.8	6,150	2,738	8.8	95.6	0.6	1.0	1.4	2.6	6.9	16.4	9.2	9.6	10.3	10.1
20125	17,700	5	Montgomery..............	643.6	32,120	1,377	49.9	83.9	6.7	6.1	1.6	6.7	6.2	17.6	8.7	11.3	10.7	11.4
20127		8	Morris	695.3	5,521	2,790	7.9	93.0	1.2	1.4	1.0	5.3	5.4	15.1	6.6	10.3	10.3	11.2
20129		9	Morton..................	729.7	2,667	2,989	3.7	72.4	2.1	2.1	1.8	23.4	5.1	19.2	7.3	8.5	12.1	12.3
20131		6	Nemaha..................	717.4	10,155	2,416	14.2	96.1	1.1	1.0	0.7	2.4	7.3	18.7	8.1	10.7	10.2	11.2

1. CBSA = Core Based Statistical Area. See Appendix A for explanation. See Appendix B for list of metropolitan areas with component counties. 2. County type code from the Economic Research Service of USDA Rural-Urban Continuum Codes. See Appendix A for definition. 3. Dry land or land partially or temporarily covered by water. 4. May be of any race.

Table B. States and Counties — **Population and Households**

STATE County	Age (percent) (cont.) 55 to 64 years	65 to 74 years	75 years and over	Percent female	Total persons 2000	2010	Percent change 2000-2010	2010-2018	Components of change 2010-2018 Births	Deaths	Net Migration	Households 2013-2017 Number	Persons per household	Family households	Female family householder[1]	One person
	16	17	18	19	20	21	22	23	24	25	26	27	28	29	30	31
KANSAS	12.8	9.0	6.8	50.2	2,688,418	2,853,126	6.1	2.0	320,372	210,809	-50,988	1,121,943	2.52	65.5	10.1	28.7
Allen..............................	14.0	11.2	9.6	50.7	14,385	13,372	-7.0	-6.9	1,184	1,450	-663	5,325	2.32	60.3	8.3	33.7
Anderson.......................	14.3	10.7	10.6	50.4	8,110	8,102	-0.1	-2.8	816	788	-250	3,206	2.41	64.3	6.4	33.3
Atchison........................	13.0	9.1	8.0	51.5	16,774	16,921	0.9	-4.3	1,677	1,502	-909	5,967	2.52	61.8	10.1	33.1
Barber...........................	17.1	13.6	9.4	48.5	5,307	4,864	-8.3	-8.1	499	473	-420	1,967	2.47	61.0	7.0	34.0
Barton...........................	15.2	10.2	9.0	50.6	28,205	27,672	-1.9	-5.6	2,903	2,469	-1,993	11,288	2.36	66.1	10.9	28.4
Bourbon.........................	13.3	11.0	8.8	50.6	15,379	15,173	-1.3	-3.4	1,701	1,531	-691	5,622	2.55	67.4	10.4	28.1
Brown............................	14.8	11.5	9.0	50.6	10,724	9,984	-6.9	-3.9	1,060	1,007	-439	3,993	2.41	66.7	9.4	29.5
Butler............................	13.8	8.7	6.5	49.7	59,482	65,884	10.8	1.3	6,236	5,159	-191	24,358	2.61	72.0	9.2	24.0
Chase............................	14.6	13.4	11.7	49.1	3,030	2,790	-7.9	-5.8	224	275	-106	1,095	2.35	60.8	8.2	35.3
Chautauqua....................	16.2	13.5	13.2	48.5	4,359	3,669	-15.8	-9.8	274	447	-187	1,432	2.35	61.5	8.2	36.4
Cherokee.......................	14.7	10.9	8.4	50.8	22,605	21,607	-4.4	-7.4	1,903	2,176	-1,324	7,980	2.54	68.7	9.7	28.8
Cheyenne.......................	15.0	13.2	13.8	49.3	3,165	2,726	-13.9	-2.4	269	311	-23	1,248	2.12	60.3	5.7	37.3
Clark.............................	13.2	9.6	12.3	50.4	2,390	2,215	-7.3	-9.5	194	259	-148	912	2.23	61.3	10.5	34.6
Clay..............................	14.0	12.0	10.9	50.0	8,822	8,545	-3.1	-6.4	866	869	-544	3,406	2.36	71.2	7.9	26.2
Cloud............................	13.9	10.9	10.7	50.4	10,268	9,533	-7.2	-8.4	883	1,117	-570	3,896	2.26	62.0	9.0	32.5
Coffey...........................	15.4	12.3	9.1	50.6	8,865	8,598	-3.0	-4.2	724	805	-282	3,592	2.28	69.8	7.2	25.1
Comanche......................	14.2	14.2	11.3	51.4	1,967	1,891	-3.9	-7.6	166	248	-63	726	2.30	65.8	7.7	32.0
Cowley...........................	13.1	10.1	8.2	49.7	36,291	36,309	0.0	-3.0	3,605	3,548	-1,151	13,688	2.45	66.4	10.4	28.3
Crawford........................	11.5	8.5	7.0	49.8	38,242	39,135	2.3	-0.3	4,035	3,380	-761	14,974	2.49	59.4	10.6	30.9
Decatur..........................	16.8	13.1	15.1	49.7	3,472	2,965	-14.6	-3.2	264	372	14	1,439	1.95	53.6	7.4	41.1
Dickinson	14.6	10.1	9.6	49.6	19,344	19,749	2.1	-5.2	1,852	1,911	-974	7,781	2.42	66.8	7.0	29.4
Doniphan........................	14.0	11.0	8.6	49.7	8,249	7,948	-3.6	-3.3	658	619	-305	3,065	2.34	67.6	8.6	26.3
Douglas..........................	10.2	7.5	4.9	50.2	99,962	110,826	10.9	9.6	10,073	5,404	5,987	44,945	2.43	54.1	8.2	31.3
Edwards.........................	16.3	11.8	9.5	49.1	3,449	3,037	-11.9	-6.2	269	277	-185	1,273	2.23	64.7	6.8	32.1
Elk................................	17.1	14.6	14.4	49.5	3,261	2,882	-11.6	-13.0	235	331	-285	1,158	2.19	63.8	7.2	33.7
Ellis..............................	11.7	8.5	6.9	49.6	27,507	28,452	3.4	0.9	3,023	2,058	-713	11,647	2.38	56.1	8.6	33.2
Ellsworth........................	14.4	11.3	9.6	43.5	6,525	6,497	-0.4	-4.6	509	670	-139	2,500	2.17	63.4	8.6	33.3
Finney...........................	10.6	6.5	4.5	48.5	40,523	36,785	-9.2	-0.5	5,668	1,737	-4,156	12,648	2.89	73.8	14.4	21.7
Ford..............................	10.8	6.1	5.0	48.1	32,458	33,844	4.3	0.1	5,428	1,958	-3,474	11,339	3.00	73.0	11.3	21.3
Franklin	14.9	9.7	7.0	50.1	24,784	25,996	4.9	-1.4	2,574	2,140	-794	9,897	2.53	67.5	8.8	27.1
Geary............................	5.8	4.9	3.7	47.2	27,947	34,354	22.9	-5.1	8,328	1,701	-8,601	12,923	2.69	72.6	11.6	23.6
Gove	15.5	11.9	12.4	49.7	3,068	2,701	-12.0	-3.3	286	322	-56	1,193	2.17	69.4	4.5	27.5
Graham..........................	17.8	12.0	15.4	50.4	2,946	2,588	-12.2	-3.7	188	266	-22	1,239	2.03	59.3	6.7	37.0
Grant.............................	12.5	8.1	5.6	49.8	7,909	7,824	-1.1	-6.2	998	414	-1,086	2,628	2.91	74.0	6.1	19.7
Gray..............................	12.7	8.3	6.8	49.7	5,904	6,001	1.6	0.5	706	402	-277	2,141	2.76	75.1	6.6	22.4
Greeley..........................	15.2	9.7	11.0	52.1	1,534	1,248	-18.6	-1.7	144	148	-18	494	2.39	67.2	6.3	29.4
Greenwood......................	16.6	13.9	11.0	50.0	7,673	6,689	-12.8	-9.5	523	769	-387	2,772	2.22	64.5	7.1	32.6
Hamilton.........................	12.3	8.1	5.9	48.2	2,670	2,687	0.6	-3.0	331	209	-208	864	3.03	66.6	6.3	30.4
Harper............................	14.2	11.8	11.2	49.9	6,536	6,034	-7.7	-8.8	579	745	-361	2,357	2.37	64.5	6.6	32.3
Harvey...........................	13.4	9.8	9.7	50.6	32,869	34,684	5.5	-1.4	3,409	3,185	-691	13,355	2.49	69.4	7.5	27.1
Haskell	13.4	9.0	5.8	49.8	4,307	4,256	-1.2	-6.1	434	214	-489	1,330	3.04	75.4	7.8	21.7
Hodgeman.......................	16.7	10.7	13.3	50.2	2,085	1,918	-8.0	-5.2	184	159	-130	786	2.34	72.0	5.1	27.4
Jackson..........................	14.0	11.1	7.9	50.0	12,657	13,460	6.3	-1.3	1,372	1,101	-456	5,296	2.49	72.2	10.2	24.9
Jefferson........................	16.3	10.8	7.8	49.1	18,426	19,124	3.8	-0.8	1,580	1,470	-258	7,681	2.42	71.7	7.7	24.4
Jewell............................	17.2	15.4	14.7	48.9	3,791	3,073	-18.9	-7.5	242	332	-144	1,388	2.11	59.9	5.4	36.4
Johnson	12.5	8.7	5.8	50.9	451,086	544,181	20.6	9.8	60,834	30,451	23,420	224,248	2.56	68.4	8.8	26.0
Kearny...........................	11.3	8.3	7.2	50.1	4,531	3,982	-12.1	-1.0	502	303	-245	1,242	3.11	72.9	8.7	21.8
Kingman.........................	16.5	10.9	10.8	49.9	8,673	7,860	-9.4	-7.0	649	867	-333	3,148	2.36	65.1	8.3	32.2
Kiowa............................	14.2	12.0	10.0	51.0	3,278	2,553	-22.1	-1.4	283	200	-123	1,004	2.33	62.9	3.0	31.9
Labette..........................	14.5	10.6	8.5	50.3	22,835	21,606	-5.4	-7.6	2,249	2,180	-1,725	8,098	2.47	68.8	11.1	28.6
Lane..............................	16.0	12.3	11.2	49.5	2,155	1,749	-18.8	-10.8	150	207	-131	828	2.05	58.5	6.2	37.0
Leavenworth	12.9	8.8	5.7	46.8	68,691	76,211	10.9	6.7	8,036	4,842	1,999	27,233	2.69	72.0	9.8	25.0
Lincoln...........................	16.6	13.2	11.2	50.4	3,578	3,241	-9.4	-6.7	271	305	-186	1,275	2.40	61.6	9.1	34.2
Linn...............................	15.3	13.1	9.3	49.4	9,570	9,656	0.9	1.0	804	945	238	4,433	2.15	65.2	8.9	31.7
Logan............................	15.6	10.2	10.7	50.3	3,046	2,759	-9.4	3.1	324	271	34	1,168	2.36	64.6	5.0	32.3
Lyon..............................	12.2	8.4	6.7	51.4	35,935	33,692	-6.2	-0.8	3,435	2,297	-1,449	13,552	2.36	60.2	9.9	29.1
McPherson......................	14.5	10.3	9.5	51.0	29,554	29,181	-1.3	-2.2	2,693	3,044	-290	12,077	2.28	67.1	8.2	29.1
Marion...........................	15.3	11.8	11.5	50.3	13,361	12,660	-5.2	-5.6	956	1,337	-328	4,857	2.33	68.2	6.5	28.4
Marshall.........................	16.1	10.7	11.0	50.2	10,965	10,117	-7.7	-3.9	972	1,014	-348	4,209	2.30	65.9	5.8	30.0
Meade............................	13.3	9.4	9.9	49.3	4,631	4,575	-1.2	-9.4	473	371	-543	1,674	2.49	72.1	11.3	26.2
Miami............................	14.9	9.3	7.4	50.3	28,351	32,781	15.6	2.7	2,951	2,324	269	12,771	2.53	69.7	9.2	27.2
Mitchell..........................	13.9	12.1	11.5	49.4	6,932	6,373	-8.1	-3.5	656	723	-160	2,725	2.19	59.2	7.7	34.1
Montgomery....................	14.2	10.8	9.1	50.5	36,252	35,468	-2.2	-9.4	3,540	3,556	-3,368	13,619	2.39	65.1	9.3	31.1
Morris............................	16.5	12.6	12.1	50.0	6,104	5,923	-3.0	-6.8	498	623	-275	2,325	2.38	67.7	6.3	27.3
Morton...........................	15.1	9.6	10.7	50.4	3,496	3,233	-7.5	-17.5	275	286	-563	1,115	2.55	66.2	11.4	30.7
Nemaha..........................	13.7	9.2	11.0	49.4	10,717	10,178	-5.0	-0.2	1,145	1,009	-154	4,123	2.37	67.2	4.6	29.6

1. No spouse present.

Table B. States and Counties — Population, Vital Statistics, Health, and Crime

STATE County	Persons in group quarters, 2018	Daytime Population, 2013-2017		Births, 2018		Deaths, 2018		Persons under 65 with no health insurance, 2016		Medicare, 2018			Serious crimes known to police[2], 2016 Total	
		Number	Employment/ residence ratio	Total	Rate[1]	Number	Rate[1]	Number	Percent	Total beneficiaries	Enrolled in Original Medicare	Enrolled in Medicare Advantage	Number	Rate[3]
	32	33	34	35	36	37	38	39	40	41	42	43	44	45
KANSAS	79,632	2,922,764	1.01	36,637	12.6	25,272	8.7	239,482	9.9	522,921	434,052	88,869	89,427	3,076
Allen..............	382	13,172	1.07	129	10.4	163	13.1	866	8.8	3,042	2,806	236	375	3,693
Anderson..........	103	6,787	0.69	105	13.3	98	12.4	649	10.7	1,832	1,687	145	111	1,519
Atchison..........	1,385	16,182	0.96	194	12.0	168	10.4	920	7.3	3,105	2,775	330	470	2,898
Barber............	40	4,611	0.88	49	11.0	51	11.4	420	11.5	1,179	1,141	38	46	1,215
Barton............	672	26,637	0.97	315	12.1	310	11.9	2,642	12.3	5,497	5,394	103	716	2,667
Bourbon...........	409	15,080	1.05	190	13.0	154	10.5	1,172	10.2	3,266	2,796	470	484	3,326
Brown.............	116	10,113	1.08	111	11.6	121	12.6	813	10.6	2,290	2,211	79	217	2,241
Butler............	2,300	55,691	0.66	738	11.1	630	9.4	4,384	7.9	11,740	9,570	2,170	1,521	2,310
Chase.............	145	2,391	0.76	31	11.8	14	5.3	195	10.2	569	548	21	11	416
Chautauqua	79	3,114	0.78	27	8.2	46	13.9	399	16.0	950	910	40	NA	NA
Cherokee	202	18,289	0.74	213	10.6	260	13.0	1,750	10.7	4,550	3,938	612	463	2,364
Cheyenne..........	49	2,589	0.93	39	14.7	38	14.3	243	12.5	746	704	42	29	1,091
Clark.............	57	1,918	0.83	23	11.5	19	9.5	176	10.9	481	D	D	12	581
Clay..............	140	7,740	0.89	106	13.3	105	13.1	425	6.8	1,986	1,885	101	104	1,258
Cloud.............	498	8,857	0.93	81	9.3	131	15.0	664	9.7	2,225	2,148	77	225	2,470
Coffey............	130	8,970	1.16	90	10.9	80	9.7	498	7.4	2,103	2,018	85	103	1,331
Comanche..........	65	1,654	0.91	12	6.9	15	8.6	163	11.9	480	D	D	NA	NA
Cowley	2,009	35,082	0.96	374	10.6	407	11.6	2,936	10.5	7,323	6,853	470	1,194	3,461
Crawford	1,781	39,447	1.02	463	11.9	370	9.5	3,620	11.4	7,287	6,625	662	1,460	3,772
Decatur...........	81	2,612	0.79	31	10.8	38	13.2	234	11.5	814	770	44	NA	NA
Dickinson.........	307	17,630	0.83	208	11.1	197	10.5	1,402	9.2	4,270	4,154	116	350	1,832
Doniphan..........	427	6,855	0.75	70	9.1	72	9.4	568	9.7	1,594	1,533	61	93	1,204
Douglas...........	8,822	110,849	0.89	1,146	9.4	663	5.5	10,098	10.3	16,869	14,326	2,543	NA	NA
Edwards...........	35	2,617	0.77	29	10.2	26	9.1	362	15.6	705	688	17	22	878
Elk...............	40	2,396	0.81	29	11.6	31	12.4	241	13.5	806	767	39	11	433
Ellis.............	1,036	29,647	1.05	340	11.8	245	8.5	2,004	8.4	5,027	4,878	149	789	2,721
Ellsworth.........	978	6,340	1.00	64	10.3	70	11.3	321	7.7	1,417	1,374	43	64	1,257
Finney............	547	37,392	1.02	620	16.9	209	5.7	4,524	14.1	4,586	4,437	149	1,196	3,237
Ford..............	708	35,415	1.05	618	18.2	231	6.8	4,762	16.1	4,130	4,000	130	1,065	3,091
Franklin	479	23,506	0.84	287	11.2	250	9.8	1,604	7.6	5,233	4,633	600	613	2,414
Geary.............	845	44,206	1.50	869	26.7	194	6.0	2,827	8.9	3,862	3,569	293	813	2,185
Gove..............	56	2,758	1.10	35	13.4	38	14.5	248	12.7	682	664	18	11	420
Graham............	40	2,588	1.02	16	6.4	38	15.2	227	11.9	740	702	38	11	427
Grant.............	79	7,430	0.92	112	15.3	38	5.2	1,130	17.0	1,090	1,055	35	86	1,121
Gray..............	78	5,848	0.95	80	13.3	44	7.3	783	15.4	1,029	1,008	21	64	1,045
Greeley...........	26	1,328	1.21	14	11.4	12	9.8	151	14.9	295	D	D	10	747
Greenwood	90	5,457	0.72	65	10.7	75	12.4	504	11.0	1,711	1,621	90	97	1,583
Hamilton..........	0	2,557	0.95	36	13.8	19	7.3	466	21.3	405	D	D	8	331
Harper............	129	6,012	1.10	57	10.4	95	17.3	590	13.4	1,356	1,318	38	141	3,232
Harvey............	1,317	32,768	0.89	359	10.5	341	10.0	2,633	9.6	7,596	6,148	1,448	917	2,711
Haskell...........	33	4,246	1.09	54	13.5	27	6.8	670	19.3	601	586	15	29	725
Hodgeman	14	1,786	0.91	22	12.1	21	11.6	168	11.9	433	D	D	7	373
Jackson	133	11,359	0.68	167	12.6	134	10.1	998	9.3	2,956	2,449	507	189	1,542
Jefferson	235	13,905	0.46	200	10.5	150	7.9	1,332	8.7	3,925	3,245	680	286	1,588
Jewell............	27	2,707	0.80	31	10.9	35	12.3	239	11.7	882	841	41	NA	NA
Johnson...........	5,163	606,516	1.09	7,208	12.1	3,996	6.7	32,291	6.4	93,505	65,100	28,405	10,115	1,752
Kearny............	81	3,733	0.89	59	15.0	25	6.3	541	16.4	648	634	14	68	1,731
Kingman...........	190	6,795	0.78	70	9.6	100	13.7	490	8.6	1,797	1,737	60	167	2,337
Kiowa.............	149	2,728	1.16	36	14.3	22	8.7	228	12.5	569	554	15	20	784
Labette...........	480	21,285	1.08	278	13.9	227	11.4	1,695	10.4	4,844	4,331	513	734	3,572
Lane..............	3	1,680	0.97	15	9.6	16	10.3	153	12.2	400	388	12	13	789
Leavenworth	6,504	71,992	0.79	972	11.9	616	7.6	4,152	6.5	13,279	10,863	2,416	2,059	2,591
Lincoln...........	50	2,817	0.79	36	11.9	36	11.9	245	10.3	797	783	14	14	457
Linn..............	63	8,593	0.75	91	9.3	123	12.6	879	11.8	2,380	1,711	669	101	1,208
Logan.............	41	2,680	0.92	43	15.1	18	6.3	206	9.1	655	627	28	29	1,028
Lyon..............	1,450	32,813	0.97	406	12.2	272	8.1	3,513	12.8	5,947	5,500	447	772	2,332
McPherson.........	928	30,874	1.14	304	10.7	341	11.9	1,996	8.8	6,402	5,920	482	499	1,952
Marion............	727	10,566	0.73	118	9.9	141	11.8	1,033	11.6	3,008	2,933	75	129	1,174
Marshall..........	164	10,366	1.10	103	10.6	103	10.6	653	8.5	2,461	2,317	144	126	1,279
Meade.............	119	4,112	0.91	54	13.0	32	7.7	473	14.1	823	797	26	NA	NA
Miami.............	645	26,270	0.58	345	10.2	299	8.9	1,814	6.6	6,136	4,627	1,509	639	1,977
Mitchell..........	246	6,922	1.25	85	13.8	97	15.8	401	8.6	1,532	1,471	61	75	1,297
Montgomery........	1,113	34,630	1.08	362	11.3	363	11.3	3,006	11.8	7,475	6,752	723	1,397	4,267
Morris............	66	5,011	0.78	60	10.9	74	13.4	404	9.7	1,421	1,369	52	83	1,492
Morton............	83	3,007	1.06	22	8.2	27	10.1	303	13.3	577	562	15	62	2,104
Nemaha............	259	10,600	1.10	134	13.2	87	8.6	623	7.7	2,210	2,136	74	110	1,080

1. Per 1,000 estimated resident population.   2. Data for serious crimes have not been adjusted for underreporting; this may affect comparability between geographic areas and over time.   3. Per 100,000 population estimated by the FBI.

Table B. States and Counties — Crime, Education, Money Income, and Poverty

STATE County	Serious crimes known to police[2], 2016 (cont.)[1] Rate Violent	Property	Enrollment[3] Total	Percent private	Attainment[4] (percent) High school graduate or less	Bachelor's degree or more	Local government expenditures,[5] 2014-2015 Total current spending (mil dol)	Current spending per student (dollars)	Per capita income[6]	Median income (dollars)	Households Percent with income of less than $50,000	with income of $200,000 or more	Median household income (dollars)	Percent below poverty level All persons	Children under 18 years	Children 5 to 17 years in families
	46	47	48	49	50	51	52	53	54	55	56	57	58	59	60	61
KANSAS	380	2,696	783,160	13.5	35.7	32.3	4,989.0	10,033	29,600	55,477	45.1	4.4	56,382	11.9	14.7	13.4
Allen	483	3,211	3,040	5.2	40.9	19.2	26.5	10,804	23,011	43,031	56.9	1.6	42,957	16.7	23.0	19.8
Anderson	164	1,354	1,712	10.4	47.8	18.6	13.4	10,424	21,887	40,986	59.3	1.4	46,595	13.3	17.9	15.9
Atchison	290	2,608	5,186	40.0	47.1	20.7	24.6	10,710	25,494	46,640	52.9	2.3	45,941	14.3	18.9	17.0
Barber	238	978	997	13.4	42.8	19.9	8.5	11,547	28,840	52,075	47.9	3.9	47,948	12.2	19.1	17.3
Barton	264	2,403	6,581	10.2	45.1	16.9	42.9	9,519	26,264	46,070	52.4	1.9	46,934	15.6	18.9	17.3
Bourbon	467	2,859	3,685	8.9	40.7	19.1	23.4	9,920	20,707	39,379	59.5	1.7	41,847	18.3	25.6	23.3
Brown	186	2,055	2,220	11.4	46.0	21.2	17.0	11,569	24,319	46,964	53.2	2.5	45,637	15	21.0	19.3
Butler	176	2,134	18,671	13.0	33.9	29.3	138.7	7,376	28,478	62,324	40.5	3.8	65,561	10.1	11.6	10.3
Chase	114	303	577	13.2	35.6	25.1	4.4	12,343	24,469	42,772	54.9	2.0	47,436	11.2	15.3	14.1
Chautauqua	NA	NA	703	11.9	49.4	16.6	6.6	11,702	23,621	39,531	59.9	2.5	41,890	16.8	25.0	24.3
Cherokee	327	2,037	4,879	10.4	47.1	19.0	41.9	11,324	21,006	41,101	58.1	1.0	42,469	15.8	23.5	20.0
Cheyenne	151	941	550	2.9	38.2	25.8	5.3	12,505	27,934	47,167	53.0	1.6	42,247	12.8	19.8	18.6
Clark	97	484	460	7.8	33.5	33.1	6.1	13,144	27,087	46,094	53.8	2.1	51,621	12	18.6	16.3
Clay	145	1,113	1,914	9.4	37.6	23.9	13.7	9,744	28,115	55,434	43.5	3.8	50,634	10.6	14.6	13.7
Cloud	340	2,130	2,116	9.7	39.6	21.2	18.1	10,840	25,579	44,199	56.4	1.3	46,241	12.6	16.7	16.0
Coffey	142	1,189	1,779	8.0	44.0	20.9	17.7	11,239	31,679	58,662	41.8	3.6	57,021	10.2	13.3	12.5
Comanche	NA	NA	353	5.4	40.4	18.5	4.2	12,326	28,388	51,563	49.3	2.2	46,636	11.2	16.4	14.4
Cowley	368	3,093	9,445	10.7	41.5	20.3	61.1	9,802	23,130	46,624	53.2	1.7	46,703	17.6	23.2	19.7
Crawford	328	3,444	12,779	11.1	37.8	28.9	65.8	10,717	21,207	38,017	61.3	1.7	39,461	18.9	22.1	19.3
Decatur	NA	NA	491	9.0	40.8	21.9	4.3	12,120	30,890	41,230	61.2	3.6	42,077	14.5	22.2	22.2
Dickinson	162	1,670	4,430	10.4	44.2	20.8	36.8	10,229	24,434	49,663	50.3	1.4	52,562	9.9	14.3	13.6
Doniphan	65	1,139	2,057	4.7	48.0	17.0	15.9	11,025	24,520	50,300	49.6	2.0	48,553	14.8	20.6	19.2
Douglas	NA	NA	42,948	10.4	23.0	50.0	148.5	9,946	29,438	54,370	46.4	4.2	56,007	15.9	11.7	11.0
Edwards	80	798	647	2.8	44.5	18.8	6.1	12,701	27,966	50,229	49.6	2.3	47,725	11.2	17.0	16.1
Elk	79	354	472	6.1	48.9	15.8	7.2	14,491	21,156	39,405	57.9	0.8	39,556	15.8	29.2	27.8
Ellis	321	2,400	9,767	9.9	31.1	35.6	38.4	10,015	29,339	49,562	50.2	3.2	49,715	15.2	13.9	12.7
Ellsworth	98	1,159	1,159	6.6	42.6	20.3	13.6	11,578	24,102	48,550	51.2	2.0	51,355	11.5	14.0	13.6
Finney	484	2,752	10,772	4.3	51.6	17.3	90.3	10,262	23,074	51,703	47.4	2.4	54,534	13.2	17.8	16.6
Ford	334	2,757	9,106	6.4	54.0	18.3	75.7	9,823	22,053	49,890	50.1	3.1	50,080	12.7	16.6	15.9
Franklin	343	2,071	6,513	15.9	45.3	20.3	47.4	10,438	25,701	53,167	47.0	2.3	55,330	10.5	14.1	12.3
Geary	556	1,629	10,939	9.8	32.9	21.4	84.5	9,904	21,583	46,096	55.8	0.9	52,012	12	18.6	20.8
Gove	0	420	502	9.0	43.1	23.1	7.3	14,253	29,352	50,817	49.3	3.4	47,029	9.8	17.2	16.8
Graham	194	233	469	5.1	40.6	27.4	4.5	10,031	27,165	43,427	58.4	1.2	41,138	12.8	17.2	14.9
Grant	117	1,004	2,123	8.9	57.7	16.2	16.0	8,679	26,138	57,474	42.0	3.4	59,534	12.3	15.6	14.6
Gray	98	947	1,476	10.6	46.3	21.0	15.3	11,437	27,031	61,220	37.9	2.6	67,671	7.6	10.0	8.6
Greeley	149	598	286	4.9	46.2	30.3	3.1	11,425	25,775	47,045	53.4	2.6	48,647	10.8	16.7	16.4
Greenwood	310	1,273	1,304	3.7	46.0	18.9	12.0	11,786	24,837	41,648	58.3	1.0	40,741	15.3	23.7	20.7
Hamilton	124	207	667	6.0	55.7	17.8	5.8	10,542	21,694	48,160	54.5	1.3	47,454	13	18.1	16.6
Harper	344	2,888	1,235	6.8	50.6	17.5	12.5	11,474	25,698	48,059	51.3	3.1	44,594	14.5	21.5	20.5
Harvey	373	2,339	9,062	21.9	35.1	30.0	57.4	9,442	26,587	55,687	45.3	2.2	55,470	9.1	12.1	10.5
Haskell	75	650	997	13.0	49.1	17.6	9.9	11,828	24,141	53,780	45.6	3.0	54,145	10.1	14.5	13.0
Hodgeman	53	319	336	4.2	33.1	24.4	3.5	11,798	28,857	55,345	45.9	2.8	51,962	10.8	12.6	11.9
Jackson	163	1,379	3,293	8.2	45.7	19.9	25.9	10,333	25,920	53,592	46.4	2.5	49,779	11	14.4	12.2
Jefferson	211	1,377	4,359	7.6	46.8	21.2	41.1	11,307	27,783	58,935	39.3	1.1	66,044	8.5	11.3	9.6
Jewell	NA	NA	522	2.9	48.5	15.9	3.7	12,169	24,361	43,125	58.6	1.3	43,234	12.8	21.7	21.2
Johnson	172	1,580	155,377	19.8	18.8	54.6	899.0	9,421	43,061	81,121	29.2	10.7	83,516	5.3	5.8	5.4
Kearny	178	1,553	1,138	1.6	49.4	13.4	10.8	11,720	24,232	51,439	46.9	2.7	50,526	10.5	16.8	15.8
Kingman	182	2,155	1,672	16.4	38.7	23.3	13.2	11,275	30,927	57,593	44.0	3.9	50,081	12.1	18.7	17.3
Kiowa	39	745	604	23.5	36.7	27.6	6.9	12,781	24,961	48,226	52.2	1.8	44,374	11.6	18.2	17.7
Labette	457	3,115	4,555	7.7	44.9	17.6	40.4	10,016	22,841	45,706	53.4	1.6	46,819	15.3	24.1	22.3
Lane	243	546	332	0.0	37.6	23.9	4.4	13,447	29,768	51,765	48.6	3.0	55,083	10.2	15.0	14.0
Leavenworth	391	2,200	21,773	13.6	36.9	31.0	123.7	9,360	30,170	70,022	35.2	4.4	70,740	7.4	9.5	8.8
Lincoln	33	424	708	4.5	38.8	19.9	7.7	12,879	25,667	48,693	50.9	1.8	43,865	11.8	18.1	15.3
Linn	96	1,112	2,000	2.9	50.6	14.1	22.1	11,797	25,796	46,576	53.6	2.2	47,300	14.1	18.9	17.2
Logan	177	851	656	9.3	38.6	19.1	5.9	11,314	28,549	49,926	50.1	3.9	48,024	9.7	13.7	13.3
Lyon	202	2,130	10,499	4.7	43.1	27.1	56.4	10,199	24,307	42,992	56.4	2.3	47,279	15.9	16.9	15.1
McPherson	82	1,870	6,839	19.8	36.9	28.6	47.2	9,790	29,508	56,946	42.5	3.1	55,686	8.5	9.6	8.1
Marion	73	1,101	2,942	22.8	43.1	23.9	23.2	10,696	25,620	50,212	49.8	1.9	49,980	10.9	13.5	12.1
Marshall	152	1,127	2,180	16.0	49.4	18.6	19.8	10,566	27,908	50,420	49.6	2.7	49,466	10.8	14.1	14.0
Meade	NA	NA	993	9.9	47.6	20.7	7.2	12,114	25,173	54,167	43.4	2.2	56,397	9.9	13.6	12.9
Miami	238	1,739	8,425	10.5	37.6	25.9	47.8	9,389	31,611	63,501	36.9	5.1	69,327	7.3	9.1	8.1
Mitchell	69	1,228	1,548	20.5	37.1	24.1	13.2	11,340	26,108	44,591	55.9	2.6	43,743	12	16.8	17.2
Montgomery	476	3,790	7,904	11.4	39.4	18.7	56.9	10,175	22,823	43,977	57.0	1.3	45,808	16.8	25.2	22.8
Morris	72	1,420	1,187	8.2	48.3	18.1	12.1	11,326	26,569	50,338	49.4	3.3	49,561	11.2	16.8	16.2
Morton	441	1,663	580	0.0	51.1	13.1	10.7	8,553	23,038	43,813	53.3	2.1	50,698	10.9	16.3	14.4
Nemaha	118	962	2,421	12.8	49.1	23.7	18.5	10,098	27,438	53,368	46.6	2.7	58,729	8.2	10.3	10.6

1. Data for serious crimes have not been adjusted for underreporting; this may affect comparability between geographic areas and over time.   2. Per 100,000 population estimated by the FBI.   3. All persons 3 years old and over enrolled in nursery school through college.   4. Persons 25 years old and over.   5. Elementary and secondary education expenditures.   6. Based on population estimated by the American Community Survey, 2011–2015.

STATE County	Personal income, 2017										Earnings, 2017		
	Total (mil dol)	Percent change 2016-2017	Per capita[1] Dollars	Per capita[1] Rank	Wages and salaries (mil dol)	Supplements to wages and salaries, employer contributions (mil dol) Pension and insurance	Supplements to wages and salaries, employer contributions (mil dol) Government social insurance	Proprietors' income (mil dol)	Dividends, interest, and rent (mil dol)	Personal transfer receipts (mil dol)	Total (mil dol)	Contributions for government social insurance (mil dol) From employee and self-employed	Contributions for government social insurance (mil dol) From employer
	62	63	64	65	66	67	68	69	70	71	72	73	74
KANSAS	141,459	2.4	48,600	X	68,646	11,519	5,196	15,554	27,885	22,499	100,914	5,956	5,196
Allen	479	4.5	38,253	1,837	207	44	16	41	88	135	308	20	16
Anderson	296	-5.0	37,848	1,905	80	16	6	44	47	78	148	9	6
Atchison	582	2.7	35,619	2,254	254	44	20	32	102	140	350	23	20
Barber	182	1.5	39,718	1,604	65	14	5	15	44	46	99	7	5
Barton	1,197	1.5	45,222	878	478	89	36	150	268	247	753	46	36
Bourbon	584	2.0	39,604	1,620	250	48	19	75	82	140	392	25	19
Brown	418	4.3	43,352	1,096	217	41	16	39	84	99	314	19	16
Butler	2,940	2.1	43,964	1,026	766	171	58	276	466	491	1,271	78	58
Chase	123	5.4	46,007	795	36	8	3	20	35	23	67	4	3
Chautauqua	133	2.9	39,448	1,651	26	6	2	11	29	40	45	4	2
Cherokee	756	5.6	37,606	1,932	246	48	19	97	105	202	410	27	19
Cheyenne	119	2.5	44,248	990	32	7	2	25	24	29	66	4	2
Clark	118	2.1	59,001	184	31	7	2	31	24	21	71	3	2
Clay	339	3.6	42,548	1,198	102	22	8	45	77	80	178	11	8
Cloud	336	4.3	37,315	1,984	108	22	8	49	68	92	187	12	8
Coffey	415	-6.7	50,407	436	229	56	16	48	61	85	349	20	16
Comanche	78	4.4	43,437	1,086	21	5	2	12	16	20	40	2	2
Cowley	1,316	0.2	37,203	2,001	602	113	46	128	214	336	889	56	46
Crawford	1,389	3.3	35,591	2,257	667	137	51	69	289	348	925	60	51
Decatur	127	-4.2	44,177	1,000	28	6	2	26	29	31	63	3	2
Dickinson	747	2.6	39,510	1,638	247	54	20	63	144	174	385	25	20
Doniphan	282	1.9	36,542	2,112	85	19	7	17	49	67	128	9	7
Douglas	4,996	3.9	41,360	1,353	2,107	426	157	410	1,042	700	3,101	181	157
Edwards	139	-8.3	47,917	631	39	8	3	28	25	27	78	4	3
Elk	100	1.8	40,225	1,514	18	5	1	16	22	32	40	3	1
Ellis	1,246	-0.5	43,446	1,084	618	125	45	144	233	215	932	54	45
Ellsworth	250	12.2	39,492	1,641	88	20	7	17	55	57	132	9	7
Finney	1,493	0.1	40,272	1,507	805	137	58	221	202	225	1,221	66	58
Ford	1,287	3.4	37,429	1,962	747	130	52	141	181	199	1,071	61	52
Franklin	1,035	2.9	40,207	1,519	405	68	32	81	155	223	585	38	32
Geary	1,545		45,630	835	1,566	432	151	42	327	238	2,191	94	151
Gove	143	-11.6	54,224	304	44	9	3	44	26	26	101	6	3
Graham	110	4.3	43,995	1,022	34	7	3	12	21	31	56	4	3
Grant	356	-6.6	47,361	680	147	30	11	104	44	45	292	12	11
Gray	405	-6.2	67,986	80	127	23	10	159	51	37	319	11	10
Greeley	65	2.4	51,650	26	5	5	2	12	13	12	46	2	2
Greenwood	254	4.9	41,444	1,340	62	13	5	23	52	73	103	7	5
Hamilton	144	-3.6	54,707	292	39	7	4	58	20	18	108	3	4
Harper	244	-0.4	43,570	1,068	88	20	7	37	52	57	152	9	7
Harvey	1,400	2.0	40,521	1,469	590	105	49	124	224	306	868	56	49
Haskell	227	-9.4	56,037	248	76	14	7	77	37	25	173	6	7
Hodgeman	83	-0.1	45,227	877	21	5	2	13	18	16	41	2	2
Jackson	527	3.1	39,574	1,626	153	30	11	22	94	118	215	16	11
Jefferson	793	3.4	41,753	1,295	147	28	12	54	112	151	241	18	12
Jewell	131	-2.5	46,000	796	27	7	2	18	34	32	54	3	2
Johnson	41,369	2.9	69,977	71	20,877	2,639	1,502	4,475	8,779	3,601	29,492	1,726	1,502
Kearny	212	3.7	53,621	320	55	12	4	68	33	27	140	5	4
Kingman	317	-1.1	43,024	1,139	90	18	7	34	66	71	150	10	7
Kiowa	105	8.8	42,384	1,218	45	9	4	18	22	23	75	4	4
Labette	807	1.9	40,043	1,543	380	79	30	57	130	246	546	36	30
Lane	144	9.0	92,559	19	29	6	2	66	20	17	102	3	2
Leavenworth	3,333	3.8	41,101	1,396	1,417	343	124	137	635	585	2,021	114	124
Lincoln	123	7.2	40,481	1,477	33	8	3	14	29	32	58	4	3
Linn	337	4.2	34,694	2,390	109	25	8	5	58	93	146	12	8
Logan	130	2.0	45,961	800	47	11	4	18	27	27	80	5	4
Lyon	1,214	2.5	36,364	2,140	571	119	42	77	221	261	808	51	42
McPherson	1,355	1.6	47,213	694	674	142	50	174	241	253	1,040	61	50
Marion	518	6.9	43,207	1,117	156	29	11	73	80	116	270	17	11
Marshall	427	-1.5	43,790	1,043	198	37	17	56	95	96	308	19	17
Meade	256	5.6	59,533	166	72	14	5	86	47	33	177	7	5
Miami	1,547	4.8	46,231	773	357	62	28	121	242	255	568	38	28
Mitchell	324	1.2	52,899	345	122	24	9	100	53	63	255	13	9
Montgomery	1,145	2.6	35,172	2,321	559	119	45	93	184	339	816	53	45
Morris	237	0.2	43,460	1,081	52	11	4	44	46	55	112	6	4
Morton	121	13.7	43,997	1,021	45	9	4	34	21	24	91	4	4
Nemaha	518	0.6	51,162	405	204	38	15	69	145	84	326	18	15

1. Based on the resident population estimated as of July 1 of the year shown.

Table B. States and Counties — **Earnings, Social Security, and Housing**

STATE County	Earnings, 2017 (cont.) Percent by selected industries — Farm	Mining, quarrying, and extractions	Construction	Manu-facturing	Information; professional, scientific, technical services	Retail trade	Finance, insurance, real estate, and leasing	Health care and social assistance	Govern-ment	Social Security beneficiaries, December 2017 — Number	Rate[1]	Supplemental Security Income recipients, 2017	Housing units, 2018 — Total	Percent change, 2010-2018
	75	76	77	78	79	80	81	82	83	84	85	86	87	88
KANSAS	1.8	1.2	5.6	12.3	10.2	5.4	9.5	11.1	17.2	544,486	187	48,233	1,280,774	3.9
Allen	3.6	D	3.5	33.5	2.6	6	5.2	7.1	22.2	3,340	267	356	6,331	1.7
Anderson	8.6	3.2	15.3	7.4	2	10.6	6	11.9	17	1,995	255	136	3,741	0.6
Atchison	1.1	D	5.4	25.7	D	5.6	9	D	13	3,310	203	344	6,951	-0.5
Barber	-9	15.4	6.7	13.3	D	6.8	D	D	29	1,240	270	63	2,738	
Barton	3.7	13.3	7.1	7	3.6	7.2	10	D	14.9	5,910	223	509	12,757	0.5
Bourbon	-0.7	0.2	4.9	20.7	2.3	4.9	10.5	D	13.3	3,545	240	382	7,119	-0.7
Brown	4.9	D	3.1	27.6	4.4	4.7	4.6	14	21.7	2,415	250	216	4,740	-0.8
Butler	2.7	1.4	9.6	16.4	D	5.6	7.6	12.5	21.7	12,825	192	811	27,084	3.9
Chase	10.3	D	7.6	19	D	3	D	D	14.4	600	224	32	1,492	-0.7
Chautauqua	8.8	D	4.7	8.1	D	4.7	D	15.3	24.4	1,090	324	111	2,134	-0.7
Cherokee	2.4	D	10.1	23.7	2.7	4.4	12.2	12.5	15.4	5,070	252	621	9,861	-0.3
Cheyenne	21.5	2.2	3	3.8	D	2.7	D	15.1	15.1	765	285	18	1,500	-1.2
Clark	39.4	0.9	D	D	D	3.2	D	D	29.6	485	242	27	1,131	-0.4
Clay	13.4	D	6.4	8.7	4.2	7.4	5.3	D	26.3	2,090	263	111	4,083	0.9
Cloud	11.5	D	4.6	7.1	D	7.4	5.6	D	18.6	2,350	261	175	4,603	-1.2
Coffey	4.7	2.2	2.6	2.2	1.7	3.8	D	D	16.7	2,260	275	157	4,123	4
Comanche	12.5	3.5	2.8	6.6	D	6.7	D	D	27.9	480	268	33	1,030	-1.3
Cowley	3.4	1	3.8	34.4	2.7	5.3	4.3	D	19.3	7,985	226	713	16,195	1
Crawford	-1.8	0.3	3.9	15.4	4	6.5	6.2	12.9	25.9	7,780	199	1,013	18,165	2
Decatur	28.5	D	D	D	D	5	D	11.4	15.1	850	295	47	1,798	-1.2
Dickinson	6.3	D	5.2	23.3	3.3	6	6.2	D	21.3	4,395	233	289	9,185	2.4
Doniphan	1.7	D	7.9	18.5	D	4.4	6.5	6.1	30.8	1,710	221	94	3,576	0
Douglas	0.6	0.1	5.5	8.9	9.5	6.5	8.2	7.9	32.3	17,065	141	1,383	51,073	9.3
Edwards	25.9	D	2.1	7.7	D	3.4	2.7	10.4	13.8	715	247	55	1,620	
Elk	14.8	10.9	D	D	D	3.8	D	D	29.6	865	346	53	1,751	-0.5
Ellis	2.1	4.4	5.9	5.6	4.8	8	9.1	19	19.7	5,240	183	313	13,320	3.5
Ellsworth	0.4	D	3.3	13.4	D	4	D	7.4	34.9	1,495	236	69	3,225	-0.4
Finney	5.9	1.8	5.5	20	2.6	7.3	5.7	10.8	13.7	4,940	133	596	13,576	2.2
Ford	2.5	D	5	33.2	4.4	5.8	4.4	D	14.1	4,350	127	433	12,271	2.2
Franklin	1.4	1.2	7.6	9.6	3.2	7.7	3.9	D	19.4	5,650	220	502	11,254	1
Geary	-0.1	0	1.1	1.9	D	1.9	2	1.2	81.2	4,380	129	563	15,385	6
Gove	-0.2	1.8	2.6	12.2	1.6	17.1	10.5	11	17.3	690	262	21	1,473	7.1
Graham	-0.4	15.3	D	D	D	5.7	D	6.1	26.8	755	303	34	1,480	-0.2
Grant	28.2	11	5.8	3.4	D	3	3.6	4.7	10.8	1,180	157	83	2,955	0.4
Gray	39.6	0.1	8.6	1.7	2.2	2.6	6.8	3	11.6	1,030	173	29	2,444	4.5
Greeley	27.8	D	3.5	1	D	8.4	6.2	D	15.3	305	244	0	637	1.1
Greenwood	12.6	14.9	5.2	6.5	D	3.9	2.3	D	19.5	1,855	303	173	4,033	-0.9
Hamilton	60.6	D	D	D	D	3.1	7	D	9.6	425	161	31	1,229	-0.5
Harper	4.2	6.5	1.9	14.7	D	7.2	D	D	25.1	1,440	258	94	3,166	1.6
Harvey	1.7	1.3	7.3	27.8	3.8	5.6	5.6	D	11.5	7,530	218	481	14,878	2.4
Haskell	41.8	4.3	4.3	4.1	D	2	D	D	16	595	147	25	1,680	0.8
Hodgeman	19.7	D	1.9	D	D	D	5	D	32.6	455	247	11	970	-0.4
Jackson	-3.8	D	8.6	7.5	3.4	6.2	6.4	D	45	3,205	241	178	5,882	1.8
Jefferson	-0.1	D	26.7	7.7	D	3.7	4.9	D	21.4	4,170	219	253	8,424	3.2
Jewell	20.6	1.2	D	1.2	D	5.9	4.5	D	28.8	940	330	41	2,013	-0.9
Johnson	0	0.1	5.1	5.2	20.6	5.5	14.7	11	6.9	90,760	154	3,848	244,459	7.9
Kearny	40.9	D	D	D	D	2.6	D	0.3	25.1	670	169	51	1,571	0.9
Kingman	5.2	3.5	15	15.6	D	4.7	10.1	9.9	16.8	1,895	257	99	3,854	0.9
Kiowa	7.3	3.3	26	0.5	D	2.4	1.8	D	18.5	590	237	52	1,238	1.5
Labette	-0.1	D	2.6	22.2	2.5	5.4	3.7	13.6	25.9	5,115	254	712	10,038	-0.5
Lane	62.8	D	D	0	D	D	3.5	D	11.1	420	269	12	979	
Leavenworth	-0.1	D	5.3	4.2	6.2	3.5	5.5	4.7	59.5	13,710	169	915	29,991	4.5
Lincoln	16	0.2	D	D	D	2.7	4.3	D	32	810	266	39	1,844	-1.1
Linn	-10.1	3.4	17.7	4	D	6	5.2	D	25.1	2,625	270	184	5,660	3.9
Logan	5.4	D	D	D	D	5.7	D	D	41	670	238	31	1,447	0.3
Lyon	0	0.2	3.4	23.8	D	6.8	4.8	8	27.9	6,180	185	626	15,387	1
McPherson	1.5	0.7	7.8	36.2	D	4.1	4.3	9.3	9.3	6,660	232	313	13,384	5.2
Marion	7.2	0.5	4.2	28.5	3.6	3.8	2.9	D	15.4	3,105	259	157	6,008	1
Marshall	8.3	D	4.3	23.4	5.7	6	8	7.7	10.6	2,385	245	131	4,925	1.2
Meade	38.7	1.8	4.9	0.9	D	1.9	7.1	D	15.4	870	202	36	1,999	0.1
Miami	0.6	0.7	13.3	7	4.4	6.4	11.6	11	20.7	6,460	193	407	13,927	5.6
Mitchell	11.5	D	6.2	7.8	D	5.7	5.3	5	18.8	1,560	255	84	3,302	0.2
Montgomery	-0.2	0.7	6.7	28.9	D	6.6	4.6	D	15.1	8,265	254	1,122	16,455	-0.7
Morris	23.3	0.2	6.2	6.8	D	5.4	7.8	D	18.6	1,450	266	85	3,209	0.1
Morton	39.4	6.2	D	D	D	3.3	2.8	D	21.1	600	219	37	1,456	-0.7
Nemaha	11	D	5.4	20.5	3.1	4.6	D	D	10.4	2,230	220	83	4,609	1

1. Per 1,000 resident population estimated as of July 1 of the year shown.

Table B. States and Counties — Housing, Labor Force, and Employment

STATE County	Total [89]	Percent [90]	Median value[1] [91]	With a mortgage [92]	Without a mortgage[2] [93]	Median rent[3] [94]	Median rent as a percent of income[2] [95]	Sub-standard units[4] (percent) [96]	Total [97]	Percent change, 2017-2018 [98]	Total [99]	Rate[5] [100]	Total [101]	Management, business, science, and arts [102]	Construction, production, and maintenance occupations [103]
KANSAS	1,121,943	66.4	139,200	19.7	11.4	801	27.6	2.5	1,482,220	0.2	49,833	3.4	1,420,045	37.9	23.2
Allen	5,325	72.0	78,600	18.7	12.5	573	25.2	1.6	6,313	0.5	254	4	6,006	27.5	36.1
Anderson	3,206	71.2	88,200	20.9	14.6	652	25.3	2.6	4,133	-0.5	144	3.5	3,502	28.4	31.4
Atchison	5,967	70.1	92,900	20.6	12.5	626	24.5	1.8	6,985	-0.6	323	4.6	7,669	33.0	25.9
Barber	1,967	69.4	75,600	14.7	10.0	562	23.5	1.2	2,396	-2.1	62	2.6	2,391	29.3	35.2
Barton	11,288	68.7	87,600	18.9	10.3	626	23.9	3	13,413	-4.5	443	3.3	13,580	29.1	29.8
Bourbon	5,622	70.5	82,600	19.6	13.1	594	27.5	5	7,120	1.5	298	4.2	6,414	29.5	28.3
Brown	3,993	70.8	83,900	19.4	10.2	580	25.9	1.7	5,353	0.5	163	3	4,589	30.4	27.7
Butler	24,358	73.5	142,400	20.6	12.1	742	28	2.3	31,938	0.9	1,105	3.5	31,363	40.0	23.4
Chase	1,095	78.4	85,200	19.9	14.6	600	27.6	1.4	1,484	4.1	39	2.6	1,156	35.7	31.3
Chautauqua	1,432	77.8	63,300	21.1	13.6	575	28.1	2.5	1,417	-1.8	57	4	1,474	32.6	36.6
Cherokee	7,980	74.9	78,400	20.5	12.6	644	28	1.8	10,046	-0.6	377	3.8	8,713	32.4	30.4
Cheyenne	1,248	79.9	86,600	19.3	12.2	568	28.4	1	1,313	0.1	31	2.4	1,248	37.7	27.0
Clark	912	69.3	76,400	21.0	11.2	655	18	3.2	1,065	-1.8	26	2.4	1,029	44.3	22.1
Clay	3,406	79.5	100,200	18.4	11.6	619	24.1	2.4	3,791	-0.4	122	3.2	4,107	32.8	27.7
Cloud	3,896	73.4	73,200	18.9	10.4	616	24.7	1.5	3,784	-2.5	133	3.5	4,668	31.6	28.4
Coffey	3,592	76.1	111,000	18.2	10.7	620	23.8	1.8	4,030	-1.9	194	4.8	4,136	30.9	30.9
Comanche	726	81.7	73,200	15.8	11.8	517	15.7	0	882	-2.4	22	2.5	923	38.8	25.4
Cowley	13,688	65.9	85,700	19.4	12.0	677	26.8	2.2	16,735	-1.2	574	3.4	15,567	27.1	32.1
Crawford	14,974	59.5	87,300	19.7	11.9	702	34.6	4.4	18,746	-1.7	750	4	18,426	32.1	27.6
Decatur	1,439	71.7	63,400	19.6	11.7	596	23	0.4	1,251	-2.1	38	3	1,375	33.9	29.1
Dickinson	7,781	72.9	110,700	20.2	13.1	659	27.9	1.7	9,142	-1.2	321	3.5	8,736	29.2	30.5
Doniphan	3,065	72.0	95,300	21.0	12.7	614	21.7	2.6	4,181	-0.2	148	3.5	3,737	29.2	28.9
Douglas	44,945	51.6	188,100	19.6	11.3	869	31.9	1.8	65,199	0	1,995	3.1	64,647	45.2	13.3
Edwards	1,273	78.2	61,200	19.3	10.0	501	18.1	1.9	1,512	0.1	37	2.4	1,444	31.0	34.4
Elk	1,158	81.5	48,300	23.6	12.3	491	25.4	1.2	1,165	-1.7	39	3.3	1,022	34.7	30.3
Ellis	11,647	61.9	159,400	19.9	10.8	677	30.3	1.3	16,868	-0.5	402	2.4	15,862	33.1	21.1
Ellsworth	2,500	76.8	88,500	19.0	11.8	605	23.9	2.3	2,722	0.4	76	2.8	2,730	34.1	26.4
Finney	12,648	62.1	126,200	21.9	11.6	735	22.5	8.1	20,404	1.7	514	2.5	18,653	22.8	38.2
Ford	11,339	62.6	108,400	21.3	11.1	709	25.7	7.7	17,186	-3.4	443	2.6	16,655	24.3	45.2
Franklin	9,897	72.1	121,700	21.7	12.0	754	24.5	2.8	14,029	-0.8	503	3.6	12,784	29.9	31.3
Geary	12,923	39.0	141,900	23.8	13.2	1,052	29.8	4.2	11,492	0.1	551	4.8	11,575	31.8	24.6
Gove	1,193	77.3	78,900	18.1	10.0	593	23	1.6	1,436	1.1	31	2.2	1,295	39.5	25.9
Graham	1,239	80.8	69,600	19.7	12.1	446	27.8	0.2	1,121	0.8	36	3.2	1,207	32.9	23.3
Grant	2,628	78.6	102,800	20.2	10.0	637	28.5	3.2	3,340	-3.6	95	2.8	3,620	29.6	36.5
Gray	2,141	75.9	117,900	18.8	10.0	638	19.6	3.5	3,437	1.1	68	2	3,095	34.2	32.8
Greeley	494	64.8	86,100	20.3	12.6	692	19.2	3.2	855	-1.5	17	2	560	35.2	23.8
Greenwood	2,772	73.8	61,100	19.1	11.7	563	27.4	3.2	3,205	-0.2	116	3.6	2,773	28.4	31.4
Hamilton	864	68.6	86,800	21.7	12.8	593	15.5	3.4	1,637	0.6	32	2	1,284	33.5	35.5
Harper	2,357	73.1	66,700	17.9	12.1	664	24.2	0.7	2,748	4.1	79	2.9	2,608	29.3	32.3
Harvey	13,355	70.7	120,200	19.5	11.3	689	28.2	1.3	16,864	0.3	545	3.2	16,969	38.9	25.9
Haskell	1,330	75.9	102,600	19.1	10.0	700	18.4	5.8	2,211	-0.6	48	2.2	1,950	29.4	35.7
Hodgeman	786	72.3	86,700	18.9	10.0	610	22	0.9	991	0.6	25	2.5	991	42.6	26.0
Jackson	5,296	74.8	128,100	21.2	11.8	657	26.2	1.7	7,217	0.1	216	3	6,280	30.8	28.6
Jefferson	7,681	81.8	135,800	20.7	12.6	740	21.4	1.5	10,167	0	331	3.3	9,299	33.6	30.7
Jewell	1,388	80.2	53,700	18.7	11.2	490	24.9	0.3	1,287		36	2.8	1,324	41.4	28.5
Johnson	224,248	68.9	232,500	19.3	10.0	1,020	26.2	1.6	336,677	1	9,723	2.9	312,189	51.0	12.3
Kearny	1,242	78.1	98,200	20.6	14.9	662	17.9	0.7	2,083	1.2	49	2.4	1,803	39.0	35.3
Kingman	3,148	77.7	92,200	21.5	10.0	670	19.3	1.3	3,409	0.7	110	3.2	3,648	32.6	33.5
Kiowa	1,004	67.9	133,800	24.9	10.2	594	22.4	1.1	1,306	-2.7	31	2.4	1,273	40.2	25.8
Labette	8,098	70.7	74,900	18.7	12.2	612	28.9	4	10,272	-0.5	410	4	9,514	32.6	29.5
Lane	828	78.4	76,400	18.1	11.4	551	22.9	5.9	796	1.5	22	2.8	885	29.8	30.6
Leavenworth	27,233	68.0	171,000	20.7	11.6	950	24.8	1.6	36,546	0.9	1,330	3.6	34,678	37.8	21.5
Lincoln	1,275	80.9	68,900	18.5	12.0	524	25.4	3.1	1,684	0.2	42	2.5	1,494	38.6	29.3
Linn	4,433	76.4	89,400	19.8	14.4	653	21	5.3	4,448	1.1	261	5.9	4,141	24.7	36.2
Logan	1,168	75.1	83,100	18.9	11.1	777	25.9	2	1,670	0	36	2.2	1,398	34.0	30.0
Lyon	13,552	57.5	98,500	20.7	11.0	643	28.5	3.7	16,617	-0.8	587	3.5	17,399	30.9	30.8
McPherson	12,077	71.7	140,300	19.3	10.8	706	23.4	0.5	16,312	0.2	419	2.6	15,238	36.1	28.4
Marion	4,857	80.1	81,300	19.1	11.8	574	22	3.1	6,041	-3.3	188	3.1	5,697	30.6	32.6
Marshall	4,209	75.5	93,400	20.0	11.3	537	23.3	1.8	5,442	-0.5	143	2.6	4,875	30.7	33.8
Meade	1,674	71.9	88,700	17.8	10.3	620	26.1	1.7	2,291	0.8	48	2.1	2,055	37.5	32.7
Miami	12,771	78.0	181,100	21.0	13.0	797	29.1	2.1	17,469	1	629	3.6	16,285	35.6	26.9
Mitchell	2,725	72.3	85,700	18.7	12.5	561	26	2.3	3,426	-0.3	78	2.3	2,868	39.2	29.7
Montgomery	13,619	70.2	74,000	19.3	12.4	633	27.1	3	14,834	-0.8	640	4.3	14,522	29.5	32.3
Morris	2,325	77.8	95,100	20.8	10.2	619	24.5	1.2	2,985	-0.1	83	2.8	2,745	29.0	33.2
Morton	1,115	68.6	97,700	18.9	14.0	585	24	0	1,169	-2.2	38	3.3	1,275	29.5	37.8
Nemaha	4,123	74.4	116,500	17.4	10.6	581	21.8	1.6	5,499	-1.1	126	2.3	5,137	35.5	27.6

1. Specified owner-occupied units. 2. A value of 10.0 represents 10 percent or less; a value of 50.0 represents 50 percent or more. 3. Specified renter-occupied units. 4. Overcrowded or lacking complete plumbing facilities. 5. Percent of civilian labor force. 6. Civilian employed persons 16 years old and over.

Table B. States and Counties — Nonfarm Employment and Agriculture

STATE County	Private nonfarm establishments, employment and payroll, 2016									Agriculture, 2017			
	Number of establishments	Employment						Annual payroll		Farms			Farm producers whose primary occupation is farming (percent)
		Total	Health care and social assistance	Manufacturing	Retail trade	Finance and insurance	Professional, scientific, and technical services	Total (mil dol)	Average per employee (dollars)	Number	Percent with:		
											Fewer than 50 acres	1000 acres or more	
	104	105	106	107	108	109	110	111	112	113	114	115	116
KANSAS	74,884	1,184,710	191,669	160,006	153,917	60,819	65,414	51,016	43,062	58,569	21.8	20.2	41.9
Allen	382	4,410	561	1,885	598	120	118	147	33,293	505	24.0	13.5	41.3
Anderson	202	1,533	367	203	402	94	38	47	30,958	611	18.7	16.5	43.7
Atchison	351	5,451	880	890	607	114	86	172	31,633	595	17.5	9.1	44.4
Barber	201	1,352	261	170	195	54	54	49	36,096	362	11.6	36.7	54.7
Barton	954	10,236	2,133	1,293	1,641	649	331	357	34,829	628	19.9	24.8	46.0
Bourbon	346	4,851	974	1,423	733	230	117	153	31,626	813	18.0	10.6	41.9
Brown	266	3,436	778	572	408	210	91	113	33,022	510	22.4	19.2	47.5
Butler	1,335	13,557	2,840	1,479	2,259	528	447	481	35,444	1,471	38.0	12.8	33.4
Chase	66	529	D	174	42	15	D	19	35,488	238	13.4	33.6	51.4
Chautauqua	64	439	112	54	98	D	D	13	28,938	351	16.2	21.4	45.8
Cherokee	325	5,294	967	1,400	510	131	89	212	40,018	756	29.6	12.4	42.4
Cheyenne	105	573	D	27	92	29	15	18	30,981	384	11.2	31.8	40.6
Clark	61	477	D	D	85	36	20	19	38,895	230	2.2	33.5	41.7
Clay	267	2,251	515	338	366	94	64	71	31,487	547	19.6	22.5	42.7
Cloud	305	2,885	665	290	508	108	78	90	31,166	412	18.7	23.3	42.9
Coffey	239	3,007	435	135	381	105	36	206	68,468	699	16.5	15.2	38.3
Comanche	69	454	157	64	73	32	8	10	21,824	197	0.5	53.8	54.9
Cowley	746	11,113	2,079	3,636	1,494	367	223	385	34,616	921	24.1	15.0	44.2
Crawford	926	14,099	2,760	2,814	1,986	317	292	445	31,542	777	25.6	11.2	37.3
Decatur	104	593	175	D	55	32	27	15	25,688	270	12.6	40.0	52.4
Dickinson	447	4,997	884	1,147	747	187	127	154	30,914	919	22.0	18.2	43.4
Doniphan	156	1,570	173	467	151	56	15	57	36,387	430	23.3	13.3	45.2
Douglas	2,713	40,244	6,073	3,530	6,512	1,074	4,640	1,226	30,452	998	44.7	5.6	33.5
Edwards	84	609	160	128	83	19	11	21	34,875	249	6.8	32.9	49.0
Elk	67	334	D	D	50	24	16	8	22,799	318	12.6	22.3	48.3
Ellis	1,113	12,597	3,096	887	2,149	436	341	424	33,688	603	16.1	20.6	37.3
Ellsworth	174	1,964	464	337	245	105	70	73	36,968	384	10.7	28.6	45.5
Finney	991	14,921	1,813	3,348	2,880	449	264	528	35,353	450	11.3	41.8	55.7
Ford	773	14,013	1,301	5,379	1,788	282	506	515	36,751	505	11.9	32.9	44.1
Franklin	575	8,547	1,335	727	1,210	136	421	339	39,632	1,020	37.5	9.1	37.4
Geary	582	8,531	1,497	681	1,426	244	413	263	30,790	213	19.2	27.2	41.4
Gove	129	970	212	128	183	47	15	31	31,791	350	7.7	40.3	46.2
Graham	98	623	194	D	102	54	10	21	34,027	429	12.1	27.5	38.7
Grant	214	2,318	193	180	212	101	40	104	44,962	315	7.6	27.0	40.0
Gray	224	1,355	180	72	169	73	50	55	40,570	422	13.3	29.9	49.7
Greeley	40	320	D	NA	64	23	5	13	39,513	227	4.0	45.8	52.8
Greenwood	179	1,077	227	85	213	64	33	34	31,552	540	16.3	26.1	48.1
Hamilton	68	586	119	D	74	67	D	20	33,608	353	4.8	37.1	41.8
Harper	206	1,847	315	529	229	95	30	63	33,976	477	13.2	29.8	45.3
Harvey	760	13,173	3,112	3,833	1,491	322	287	450	34,150	752	38.2	14.2	40.5
Haskell	116	745	D	57	66	D	30	30	39,620	207	8.2	43.0	70.9
Hodgeman	46	259	D	NA	28	D	D	9	35,938	351	4.0	38.7	50.6
Jackson	256	3,224	538	232	378	121	68	89	27,451	972	23.7	8.1	34.9
Jefferson	306	2,340	384	271	303	52	64	93	39,777	1,012	33.1	6.1	33.7
Jewell	79	494	D	NA	65	34	13	14	27,530	455	12.1	30.3	53.3
Johnson	17,852	320,408	38,535	22,545	38,068	28,105	29,053	17,274	53,913	564	60.5	4.1	28.8
Kearny	85	668	D	D	54	73	12	25	37,680	299	6.4	34.1	45.4
Kingman	218	1,718	313	328	181	124	53	59	34,570	740	16.4	19.9	40.2
Kiowa	100	800	224	NA	68	32	D	25	31,565	359	6.4	25.9	39.9
Labette	454	7,317	2,095	2,121	1,008	255	86	258	35,317	997	26.5	11.4	38.0
Lane	65	336	D	D	30	30	11	12	36,473	242	8.3	39.3	48.4
Leavenworth	1,223	14,111	3,018	1,222	2,022	711	1,181	524	37,135	1,213	44.8	2.5	29.5
Lincoln	87	509	146	D	60	44	8	13	26,456	392	18.4	26.0	44.0
Linn	199	1,337	60	205	301	76	27	62	46,144	864	21.6	7.2	33.4
Logan	116	724	160	NA	127	59	21	23	32,140	270	7.8	45.9	54.9
Lyon	832	11,585	2,010	3,035	1,867	344	264	372	32,088	867	22.8	16.1	40.1
McPherson	894	13,669	2,292	4,595	1,305	616	244	582	42,609	988	25.0	17.8	40.2
Marion	288	2,608	623	287	279	95	81	67	25,850	892	26.3	17.3	40.5
Marshall	366	4,105	560	1,287	702	211	97	150	36,630	802	15.1	21.6	42.0
Meade	121	945	D	D	152	56	23	34	35,835	407	11.1	32.9	48.1
Miami	707	6,718	2,001	471	1,020	236	270	255	37,921	1,400	45.6	5.1	35.4
Mitchell	258	2,523	550	299	393	154	47	80	31,788	365	18.9	36.7	53.2
Montgomery	802	12,458	2,319	3,374	1,588	342	232	451	36,224	1,006	28.1	7.4	33.8
Morris	130	1,217	275	226	162	59	53	39	32,334	430	17.4	23.0	52.4
Morton	90	779	D	D	74	40	8	31	39,234	323	4.3	28.8	42.7
Nemaha	375	5,075	868	1,475	497	183	121	195	38,516	809	16.8	13.0	46.8

STATE County	Acreage (1,000)	Percent change, 2012-2017	Average size of farm	Total irrigated (1,000)	Total cropland (1,000)	Value of land and buildings: Average per farm	Value of land and buildings: Average per acre	Value of machinery and equipment, average per farm (dollars)	Value of products sold: Total (mil dol)	Value of products sold: Average per farm (acres)	Percent from: Crops	Percent from: Livestock and poultry products	Organic farms (number)	Farms with internet access (percent)	Government payments: Total ($1,000)	Government payments: Percent of farms
	117	118	119	120	121	122	123	124	125	126	127	128	129	130	131	132
KANSAS	45,759	-0.8	781	2,503.4	29,125.5	1,443,891	1,848	180,725	18,782.7	320,694	34.4	65.6	117	76.5	509,205	61.7
Allen	240	-2.2	475	0.5	133.0	964,120	2,029	104,166	47.9	94,921	65.1	34.9	NA	74.7	1,578	53.7
Anderson	365	-0.5	597	2.9	242.1	1,216,033	2,038	170,102	108.8	178,031	74.3	25.7	2	68.4	2,651	65.5
Atchison	236	7.0	396	1.0	174.3	1,205,388	3,040	161,609	85.2	143,200	78.5	21.5	NA	73.4	2,051	58.8
Barber	632	6.9	1,745	14.2	236.5	2,506,422	1,436	218,751	93.6	258,472	40.8	59.2	NA	79.8	4,125	60.8
Barton	558	-1.4	888	28.9	425.3	1,395,047	1,570	191,756	365.7	582,280	20.5	79.5	NA	72.1	7,953	75.8
Bourbon	336	0.5	413	0.6	132.0	830,177	2,008	97,866	78.9	97,090	31.6	68.4	NA	75.8	1,658	40.3
Brown	312	5.7	611	8.0	258.6	2,142,870	3,507	234,470	131.8	258,516	85.0	15.0	NA	81.0	5,985	75.3
Butler	798	3.9	543	2.7	323.5	1,231,054	2,268	125,659	266.2	180,942	29.7	70.3	4	78.9	3,696	31.2
Chase	360	-8.3	1,513	D	65.3	2,891,131	1,911	199,983	85.4	358,954	21.9	78.1	NA	89.9	650	51.7
Chautauqua	288	-7.1	822	0.0	41.6	1,340,024	1,631	97,412	31.3	89,268	32.9	67.1	NA	67.8	507	23.9
Cherokee	319	3.6	422	1.0	234.9	934,030	2,211	141,016	107.0	141,476	75.9	24.1	NA	77.2	2,126	48.0
Cheyenne	529	-3.2	1,378	43.6	340.7	2,035,736	1,477	237,954	132.8	345,714	51.1	48.9	3	67.4	2,764	77.6
Clark	434	-13.7	1,888	2.7	156.2	2,241,930	1,187	150,734	111.4	484,439	13.5	86.5	NA	59.6	6,014	87.8
Clay	386	6.5	706	30.9	259.7	1,914,257	2,712	226,844	121.2	221,528	67.5	32.5	NA	80.6	5,062	75.5
Cloud	322	0.0	782	16.9	203.2	1,799,344	2,302	219,484	77.5	188,070	73.8	26.2	NA	74.0	3,234	71.4
Coffey	386	17.3	553	1.1	219.0	1,008,529	1,825	128,316	71.7	102,564	65.4	34.6	1	76.5	3,260	68.5
Comanche	454	-6.5	2,302	5.0	152.3	2,669,162	1,159	228,061	51.8	262,959	31.6	68.4	NA	76.1	3,306	79.2
Cowley	563	-1.9	612	1.8	232.9	1,131,273	1,849	130,373	96.5	104,794	55.9	44.1	1	76.8	3,311	55.4
Crawford	335	3.7	431	1.4	208.4	868,757	2,014	127,884	85.9	110,605	72.6	27.4	NA	80.2	2,304	57.4
Decatur	420	-9.2	1,556	6.6	254.3	2,267,881	1,458	261,822	233.4	864,559	20.3	79.7	4	80.7	2,069	61.9
Dickinson	519	1.8	565	4.4	364.4	1,209,027	2,140	176,779	149.5	162,723	51.0	49.0	2	75.7	7,399	76.8
Doniphan	177	-1.1	413	1.8	144.9	1,416,197	3,431	214,601	81.2	188,902	94.3	5.7	NA	75.1	4,128	71.6
Douglas	230	9.3	231	3.5	159.3	939,826	4,072	94,196	65.9	65,999	76.7	23.3	11	78.3	1,316	38.8
Edwards	392	-0.6	1,574	71.3	275.1	2,902,328	1,843	359,573	228.8	918,795	30.5	69.5	NA	85.9	7,290	91.2
Elk	247	-22.0	777	0.0	56.9	1,199,924	1,545	92,972	37.7	118,428	21.6	78.4	NA	73.3	461	34.9
Ellis	502	1.0	832	1.6	270.4	1,122,301	1,349	133,106	65.0	107,813	48.9	51.1	NA	71.3	4,333	65.8
Ellsworth	390	2.3	1,016	0.5	200.0	1,632,908	1,608	200,669	48.3	125,828	55.6	44.4	NA	82.3	3,065	83.1
Finney	791	-3.1	1,757	186.4	679.5	2,749,764	1,565	507,327	823.1	1,829,091	22.0	78.0	NA	75.8	14,410	74.9
Ford	670	-4.3	1,326	67.1	529.2	2,051,886	1,547	293,262	515.3	1,020,301	21.1	78.9	NA	79.2	9,951	77.6
Franklin	355	-1.8	348	4.3	222.5	837,366	2,403	110,830	140.9	138,123	53.8	46.2	NA	76.4	1,602	37.1
Geary	155	6.5	728	2.8	65.1	1,676,183	2,301	148,272	31.8	149,451	46.7	53.3	NA	72.3	934	63.4
Gove	567	-1.9	1,621	13.4	362.3	2,108,777	1,301	243,452	201.5	575,757	29.7	70.3	NA	76.6	5,853	81.7
Graham	470	-2.6	1,097	12.3	278.7	1,409,160	1,285	160,299	58.2	135,676	76.5	23.5	NA	72.5	5,961	83.7
Grant	359	-1.3	1,139	83.2	304.6	1,794,738	1,576	356,803	814.1	2,584,575	9.9	90.1	1	78.4	5,423	86.3
Gray	556	1.6	1,318	116.9	439.4	2,103,461	1,596	317,212	990.7	2,347,519	12.0	88.0	NA	80.8	11,783	76.1
Greeley	475	-4.5	2,092	19.8	437.2	2,962,429	1,416	335,255	251.3	1,107,084	23.9	76.1	1	74.4	6,405	78.9
Greenwood	616	-12.1	1,141	D	112.4	1,901,459	1,667	128,315	105.5	195,311	16.4	83.6	NA	75.2	1,120	37.4
Hamilton	544	-14.3	1,541	20.5	435.4	1,642,940	1,066	242,221	335.7	950,878	12.3	87.7	NA	67.7	9,079	87.3
Harper	489	-3.3	1,026	3.3	337.1	1,684,429	1,642	198,557	93.1	195,279	50.3	49.7	NA	72.5	2,397	71.9
Harvey	344	1.3	457	40.4	297.9	1,448,397	3,167	188,621	140.0	186,137	57.4	42.6	11	82.0	7,020	59.8
Haskell	364	0.0	1,757	117.0	320.9	2,682,671	1,527	589,216	1,159.1	5,599,502	9.2	90.8	NA	84.1	8,597	90.8
Hodgeman	495	-8.8	1,410	27.3	319.9	1,658,340	1,176	271,148	191.9	546,698	20.8	79.2	NA	78.6	8,878	86.9
Jackson	335	1.6	344	0.9	168.6	921,574	2,677	103,920	71.0	73,086	56.6	43.4	NA	79.8	2,468	44.7
Jefferson	255	4.8	252	4.1	153.3	732,914	2,904	86,460	75.7	74,833	59.3	40.7	5	72.9	1,968	37.0
Jewell	463	-0.1	1,018	5.6	293.5	2,097,604	2,060	271,175	149.5	328,574	57.2	42.8	NA	79.8	5,204	80.7
Johnson	87	-12.3	154	0.5	56.4	582,891	3,773	81,219	D	D	D	D	NA	82.1	390	22.0
Kearny	516	-5.6	1,727	53.2	416.0	2,490,399	1,442	287,798	281.0	939,726	27.2	72.8	NA	83.6	8,766	86.3
Kingman	517	-4.7	698	16.6	316.5	1,130,791	1,619	137,458	78.8	106,458	62.8	37.2	NA	72.4	6,379	76.6
Kiowa	443	-2.7	1,234	56.8	256.3	1,938,782	1,571	193,895	72.3	201,340	74.2	25.8	NA	68.0	5,038	84.7
Labette	399	7.8	400	0.3	220.2	849,632	2,121	129,803	176.0	176,565	37.3	62.7	1	72.3	2,239	40.5
Lane	417	-7.8	1,723	10.2	311.4	2,195,555	1,274	220,218	D	D	D	D	NA	61.2	6,680	93.0
Leavenworth	195	5.5	160	0.1	112.0	548,881	3,421	69,466	44.0	36,235	70.3	29.7	1	77.8	1,027	22.5
Lincoln	385	-3.1	981	0.5	199.6	1,695,466	1,727	161,747	58.2	148,347	54.1	45.9	NA	76.3	3,203	72.7
Linn	302	-14.8	350	D	156.9	892,889	2,554	91,016	60.3	69,764	68.3	31.7	NA	73.5	2,040	51.4
Logan	605	6.7	2,239	11.3	340.1	3,014,159	1,346	268,005	70.9	262,481	67.3	32.7	NA	84.4	4,466	75.2
Lyon	523	-2.2	603	D	267.5	1,199,352	1,988	150,828	134.4	155,065	44.9	55.1	NA	76.2	3,709	58.7
McPherson	558	-2.4	565	39.3	415.5	1,547,157	2,739	198,986	155.0	156,919	60.8	39.2	3	81.4	9,838	71.2
Marion	568	-4.8	637	3.3	334.7	1,299,945	2,042	163,154	146.5	164,247	45.7	54.3	3	82.6	5,929	69.3
Marshall	500	14.0	623	5.0	361.5	1,928,648	3,094	224,692	125.4	156,353	74.1	25.9	1	80.5	6,159	74.1
Meade	588	-4.9	1,445	93.8	331.6	2,131,999	1,476	304,190	233.4	573,428	38.7	61.3	NA	77.9	10,913	76.9
Miami	296	0.0	211	1.6	181.6	653,977	3,095	85,262	71.8	51,285	73.9	26.1	2	81.1	1,356	28.3
Mitchell	414	-5.6	1,135	6.7	297.8	2,119,970	1,868	258,391	126.5	346,474	54.0	46.0	NA	79.5	5,379	79.5
Montgomery	366	8.9	364	2.8	202.9	730,827	2,010	112,280	95.3	94,683	58.6	41.4	NA	72.9	1,761	31.2
Morris	409	5.2	952	0.8	170.7	1,543,925	1,622	184,687	138.6	322,360	26.6	73.4	1	76.5	2,094	67.0
Morton	401	-12.2	1,242	32.0	331.0	1,272,145	1,024	161,831	134.8	417,381	29.7	70.3	NA	70.9	8,627	83.0
Nemaha	400	4.6	495	1.0	286.1	1,487,190	3,006	225,584	197.4	244,049	38.6	61.4	4	78.1	5,377	69.8

Table B. States and Counties — Water Use, Wholesale Trade, Retail Trade, and Real Estate

STATE County	Water use, 2015		Wholesale Trade[1], 2012				Retail Trade[2], 2012				Real estate and rental and leasing,[2] 2012			
	Public supply water withdrawn (mil gal/day)	Public supply gallons withdrawn per person per day	Number of establishments	Number of employees	Sales (mil dol)	Average payroll (mil dol)	Number of establishments	Number of employees	Sales (mil dol)	Average payroll (mil dol)	Number of establishments	Number of employees	Sales (mil dol)	Average payroll (mil dol)
	133	134	135	136	137	138	139	140	141	142	143	144	145	146
KANSAS	351.15	120.6	3,790	52,168	60,226.3	3,055.4	10,548	145,480	38,276.5	3,325.0	2,999	14,256	2,743.1	507.6
Allen............................	1.78	140.0	17	D	D	D	57	544	152.8	12.7	22	42	2.8	0.5
Anderson......................	0.60	76.8	12	54	69.0	2.3	38	268	92.1	5.8	2	D	D	D
Atchison......................	4.23	258.0	18	382	206.5	15.1	49	640	126.9	12.7	9	D	D	D
Barber..........................	0.63	130.6	11	94	89.0	5.5	32	222	76.4	4.5	5	8	1.0	0.1
Barton..........................	2.42	89.3	65	542	389.6	27.0	128	1,651	420.4	38.0	29	105	16.3	3.8
Bourbon........................	2.08	141.4	13	D	D	D	48	611	132.7	12.1	9	35	4.6	0.9
Brown............................	0.94	96.2	15	128	244.4	5.7	32	365	74.8	7.1	4	8	0.6	0.1
Butler............................	9.84	147.4	54	440	317.5	23.2	184	2,053	620.1	46.4	52	103	17.3	2.6
Chase............................	0.17	63.5	3	D	D	D	9	64	16.0	0.9	2	D	D	D
Chautauqua	0.42	123.5	2	D	D	D	15	96	20.0	1.4	NA	NA	NA	NA
Cherokee	1.83	89.1	17	154	209.1	6.5	56	497	125.4	10.3	4	16	2.0	0.4
Cheyenne......................	0.47	175.4	11	115	113.2	4.8	22	79	17.2	1.4	3	3	0.7	0.1
Clark..............................	0.30	143.1	1	D	D	D	9	53	9.1	1.0	NA	NA	NA	NA
Clay..............................	0.88	105.4	15	169	135.3	8.2	38	425	94.2	7.8	4	D	D	D
Cloud............................	0.89	96.5	20	264	199.1	10.6	56	558	136.5	12.5	5	9	1.2	0.2
Coffey............................	0.52	62.0	12	72	63.7	2.4	50	408	111.4	7.8	3	D	D	D
Comanche......................	0.36	195.3	2	D	D	D	17	69	18.7	1.6	1	D	D	D
Cowley	5.40	150.9	26	D	D	D	121	1,445	337.1	32.9	19	39	6.6	1.1
Crawford	4.90	124.9	39	577	297.7	20.8	165	1,915	406.1	37.0	38	108	15.2	2.3
Decatur	0.37	126.2	10	79	83.7	2.1	19	89	23.6	1.6	4	10	1.4	0.2
Dickinson	1.93	100.0	24	282	231.1	12.8	70	768	187.5	17.0	14	D	D	D
Doniphan......................	0.21	26.9	11	98	90.0	4.0	21	141	30.9	2.5	2	D	D	D
Douglas........................	12.67	107.3	71	610	282.9	24.6	373	6,066	1,354.2	122.6	157	761	97.7	20.9
Edwards........................	0.25	84.2	9	124	150.2	5.0	13	82	54.5	1.4	1	D	D	D
Elk................................	0.09	34.5	2	D	D	D	10	56	23.1	0.7	1	D	D	D
Ellis..............................	2.53	87.2	46	405	201.7	17.0	183	2,166	621.0	49.5	43	145	18.2	3.3
Ellsworth........................	1.40	220.7	9	73	80.9	2.8	29	238	53.6	4.0	1	D	D	D
Finney............................	7.62	205.3	79	D	D	D	174	2,393	577.0	53.7	36	132	33.5	5.1
Ford..............................	6.79	196.6	62	750	633.9	36.1	126	1,805	499.5	40.9	23	60	15.5	2.7
Franklin	1.93	75.4	15	148	138.8	6.9	90	1,054	271.1	21.9	13	D	D	D
Geary	4.49	121.3	8	D	D	D	96	1,309	345.9	27.4	37	292	77.1	11.6
Gove	0.30	113.6	11	D	D	D	20	184	91.5	4.8	NA	NA	NA	NA
Graham	0.54	208.4	9	24	29.2	1.3	21	132	35.5	2.8	2	D	D	D
Grant............................	1.22	157.8	13	123	87.6	6.9	33	269	52.8	5.0	6	D	D	D
Gray..............................	0.67	109.2	22	210	238.5	9.9	29	171	50.1	4.0	5	25	4.5	0.6
Greeley	0.25	188.0	3	D	D	D	6	44	11.8	1.1	NA	NA	NA	NA
Greenwood	0.63	100.9	9	D	D	D	32	193	49.5	4.0	2	D	D	D
Hamilton........................	0.70	282.9	6	58	89.5	2.6	11	95	19.1	1.9	NA	NA	NA	NA
Harper..........................	0.86	147.8	15	98	151.1	5.6	36	233	62.7	5.3	2	D	D	D
Harvey..........................	9.14	260.6	31	250	144.0	9.9	120	1,446	335.1	32.2	26	D	D	D
Haskell..........................	0.54	132.9	15	124	147.5	5.5	13	63	21.1	1.1	1	D	D	D
Hodgeman....................	0.15	79.2	5	D	D	D	8	D	D	D	NA	NA	NA	NA
Jackson........................	1.06	79.5	13	85	45.3	3.1	40	379	83.2	7.6	6	18	1.9	0.6
Jefferson......................	1.20	63.4	6	20	5.7	0.4	48	318	74.0	5.4	1	D	D	D
Jewell..........................	0.59	198.7	10	56	30.5	1.6	13	59	18.3	1.0	NA	NA	NA	NA
Johnson........................	11.53	19.9	915	18,267	27,613.7	1,397.4	1,868	35,648	10,481.4	897.6	914	4,765	1,271.2	217.1
Kearny..........................	0.55	139.0	5	D	D	D	9	51	12.2	0.7	3	D	D	D
Kingman........................	0.85	110.6	25	145	100.4	5.8	26	202	45.7	3.8	6	6	1.2	0.1
Kiowa............................	0.33	128.7	10	104	115.6	6.2	16	85	28.3	1.8	NA	NA	NA	NA
Labette..........................	2.62	125.9	15	D	D	D	89	931	198.6	19.8	12	34	4.0	0.8
Lane............................	0.27	161.7	9	54	52.5	1.8	12	50	9.6	0.8	NA	NA	NA	NA
Leavenworth	28.76	362.6	19	94	45.0	3.8	174	2,088	541.5	45.8	48	164	45.5	4.9
Lincoln..........................	0.15	48.3	7	74	31.1	1.8	11	57	9.2	1.0	1	D	D	D
Linn..............................	1.09	114.3	6	30	12.1	1.2	35	241	53.5	3.6	1	D	D	D
Logan............................	0.58	205.3	13	85	103.9	3.6	15	126	35.3	2.7	NA	NA	NA	NA
Lyon..............................	4.03	120.9	21	426	287.8	17.2	162	1,814	493.9	36.5	38	152	14.8	3.4
McPherson....................	4.33	149.6	37	264	560.9	14.9	130	1,197	295.5	27.0	24	75	5.4	1.1
Marion..........................	0.99	81.8	19	187	133.9	8.7	50	313	79.2	6.1	7	7	2.5	0.3
Marshall........................	1.11	111.7	25	159	229.5	7.3	70	687	234.9	13.9	6	12	0.5	0.1
Meade..........................	0.65	150.1	12	104	198.5	5.1	22	221	32.2	3.6	NA	NA	NA	NA
Miami	5.67	174.2	21	65	97.6	3.1	87	981	262.4	22.7	28	D	D	D
Mitchell........................	1.22	194.2	23	191	109.5	7.9	43	426	127.7	10.4	5	26	2.2	0.4
Montgomery..................	5.17	155.2	30	D	D	D	131	1,536	350.3	35.2	29	89	8.7	1.6
Morris..........................	1.62	287.0	4	13	11.1	0.6	28	185	44.0	3.8	NA	NA	NA	NA
Morton..........................	0.62	206.2	10	89	127.7	4.1	13	97	21.5	2.1	NA	NA	NA	NA
Nemaha	1.33	130.0	21	142	141.0	5.9	74	616	156.5	11.4	1	D	D	D

1 Merchant wholesalers, except manufacturers' sales branches and offices.   2. Employer establishments.

Table B. States and Counties — Professional Services, Manufacturing, and Accommodation and Food Services

STATE County	Professional, scientific, and technical services, 2012				Manufacturing, 2012				Accommodation and food services, 2012			
	Number of establishments	Number of employees	Sales (mil dol)	Average payroll (mil dol)	Number of establishments	Number of employees	Receipts (mil dol)	Annual payroll (mil dol)	Number of establishments	Number of employees	Receipts (mil dol)	Annual payroll (mil dol)
	147	148	149	150	151	152	153	154	155	156	157	158
KANSAS	7,110	60,989	8,716.1	3,596.2	2,875	152,423	86,076.3	7,578.3	5,943	106,850	4,873.4	1,342.9
Allen	27	97	7.1	2.6	25	1,875	470.9	65.1	25	315	13.2	3.2
Anderson	13	29	1.9	0.6	11	150	D	7.3	16	D	D	D
Atchison	21	D	D	D	19	1,333	635.0	79.6	34	D	D	D
Barber	13	54	4.1	1.5	7	119	39.6	5.9	14	110	5.3	1.0
Barton	58	332	38.4	13.9	47	D	337.4	D	62	934	41.1	11.1
Bourbon	28	116	9.4	3.6	27	980	174.9	35.9	32	386	15.2	4.1
Brown	12	68	8.5	3.4	17	530	248.8	20.4	22	289	7.9	2.4
Butler	104	838	49.7	17.5	46	1,306	D	84.7	102	1,590	74.7	18.0
Chase	6	D	D	D	4	88	D	3.6	5	D	D	D
Chautauqua	3	D	D	D	5	79	24.7	2.0	8	D	D	D
Cherokee	28	91	5.6	1.7	33	1,475	452.8	64.0	28	340	13.2	3.6
Cheyenne	7	20	1.7	0.6	3	11	D	D	6	D	D	D
Clark	6	30	3.7	0.9	NA	NA	NA	NA	5	34	0.5	0.1
Clay	15	63	5.6	1.6	10	339	D	13.3	18	162	6.9	1.9
Cloud	14	76	6.5	3.1	9	424	D	16.5	21	285	14.1	3.6
Coffey	14	D	D	D	6	131	D	4.4	22	176	7.2	2.0
Comanche	5	7	0.6	0.1	7	44	D	1.3	6	50	1.5	0.4
Cowley	64	218	21.6	5.6	39	3,333	2,043.9	161.6	62	1,008	48.0	11.7
Crawford	68	D	D	D	49	2,347	823.4	90.7	82	1,488	59.2	14.4
Decatur	6	26	2.6	0.7	NA	NA	NA	NA	7	D	D	D
Dickinson	31	160	14.4	4.1	15	1,146	280.6	42.1	41	442	17.8	4.9
Doniphan	10	D	D	D	13	375	110.8	16.6	8	D	D	D
Douglas	292	D	D	D	69	3,079	1,217.3	136.1	301	6,511	261.1	72.2
Edwards	6	13	0.7	0.2	6	133	D	4.6	5	22	0.9	0.2
Elk	7	15	0.9	0.3	NA	NA	NA	NA	7	D	D	D
Ellis	79	329	34.2	12.4	37	D	219.0	40.5	99	1,925	74.9	21.8
Ellsworth	6	69	6.9	2.7	10	296	52.4	13.7	12	132	4.4	1.3
Finney	58	263	28.5	9.9	26	3,711	D	124.1	76	1,412	74.5	18.5
Ford	45	488	50.8	23.1	23	6,272	5,948.2	220.2	73	1,032	56.1	14.4
Franklin	36	D	D	D	27	654	318.7	30.2	50	D	D	D
Geary	40	D	D	D	7	655	189.3	19.1	82	1,475	64.7	16.5
Gove	9	11	1.2	0.3	7	77	22.8	4.2	8	D	D	D
Graham	8	13	1.2	0.5	NA	NA	NA	NA	6	D	D	D
Grant	10	30	3.0	0.9	12	188	131.6	9.7	17	249	9.7	2.6
Gray	17	55	6.1	2.6	9	84	D	4.3	8	D	D	D
Greeley	4	5	0.7	0.3	NA	NA	NA	NA	2	D	D	D
Greenwood	9	24	2.2	0.7	6	68	D	4.2	12	107	3.4	0.9
Hamilton	3	10	0.5	0.1	NA	NA	NA	NA	5	D	D	D
Harper	12	20	2.1	0.5	21	424	154.1	16.3	17	191	10.7	2.5
Harvey	48	235	22.0	8.3	62	3,004	1,286.7	134.5	61	956	32.7	9.8
Haskell	8	29	2.9	1.0	3	D	D	2.3	8	D	D	D
Hodgeman	3	D	D	D	NA	NA	NA	NA	3	9	0.4	0.1
Jackson	21	78	5.0	1.4	6	214	D	7.6	21	D	D	D
Jefferson	23	54	9.8	1.7	10	282	D	10.5	23	D	D	D
Jewell	4	10	0.7	0.2	NA	NA	NA	NA	7	D	D	D
Johnson	2,669	29,498	4,846.6	2,133.2	478	20,164	7,140.8	1,058.6	1,158	25,214	1,225.3	365.9
Kearny	6	22	1.0	0.2	NA	NA	NA	NA	6	51	1.6	0.4
Kingman	11	47	4.1	1.3	9	403	D	18.2	13	168	7.2	1.5
Kiowa	3	D	D	D	NA	NA	NA	NA	6	D	D	D
Labette	22	105	9.9	3.4	40	1,908	415.1	80.8	36	481	18.7	4.9
Lane	6	14	1.3	0.6	NA	NA	NA	NA	2	D	D	D
Leavenworth	125	D	D	D	33	1,202	455.8	41.9	98	1,439	66.7	17.1
Lincoln	7	8	1.1	0.5	NA	NA	NA	NA	5	D	D	D
Linn	13	D	D	D	10	67	D	2.3	11	D	D	D
Logan	8	25	4.1	0.7	3	11	D	D	8	D	D	D
Lyon	45	D	D	D	37	2,723	2,034.0	119.9	88	1,358	50.0	15.1
McPherson	48	225	18.4	6.8	59	4,633	5,481.6	264.6	62	853	33.1	9.7
Marion	15	D	D	D	25	325	D	12.6	21	D	D	D
Marshall	22	93	13.3	3.3	16	1,391	341.7	67.1	25	221	10.6	2.6
Meade	6	26	1.3	0.4	NA	NA	NA	NA	9	D	D	D
Miami	67	D	D	D	25	447	D	26.7	44	D	D	D
Mitchell	16	53	4.6	1.3	13	574	144.2	22.9	14	D	D	D
Montgomery	49	182	15.5	5.2	52	3,468	6,105.5	196.5	85	1,265	46.3	13.0
Morris	10	53	5.1	1.6	7	171	D	7.4	13	D	D	D
Morton	5	16	1.3	0.3	3	D	D	D	7	D	D	D
Nemaha	22	80	11.4	3.1	26	1,307	413.2	59.7	25	282	8.2	2.0

Table B. States and Counties — Health Care and Social Assistance, Other Services, Nonemployer Businesses, and Residential Construction

STATE County	Health care and social assistance, 2012				Other services, 2012				Nonemployer businesses, 2016		Value of residential construction authorized by building permits, 2018	
	Number of establish-ments	Number of employees	Receipts (mil dol)	Annual payroll (mil dol)	Number of establish-ments	Number of employees	Receipts (mil dol)	Annual payroll (mil dol)	Number	Receipts (mil dol)	New construction ($1,000)	Number of housing units
	159	160	161	162	163	164	165	166	167	168	169	170
KANSAS	7,934	192,272	18,248.4	7,504.6	5,147	29,521	3,433.0	849.2	198,254	8,823.5	1,888,570	9,478
Allen	41	626	47.8	20.1	29	76	9.6	2.1	847	27.9	2,859	18
Anderson	21	359	24.2	9.8	11	17	1.7	0.3	634	22.4	2,928	18
Atchison	46	799	64.6	26.7	20	D	D	D	857	30.8	1,005	7
Barber	14	288	14.7	8.4	21	52	5.8	1.1	521	20.4	0	0
Barton	111	1,917	152.5	64.0	75	309	38.4	8.6	2,243	94.7	1,856	11
Bourbon	42	1,031	70.0	32.2	29	82	15.6	2.0	978	30.7	429	2
Brown	37	882	58.3	27.0	21	D	D	D	725	25.2	375	1
Butler	156	3,409	278.4	103.7	76	400	32.7	8.4	4,254	158.6	35,606	176
Chase	3	D	D	D	9	15	1.3	0.2	219	7.8	0	0
Chautauqua	7	138	8.1	4.0	2	D	D	D	301	10.8	0	0
Cherokee	40	984	70.6	25.8	22	118	5.8	1.5	1,063	47.6	2,974	27
Cheyenne	10	D	D	D	5	D	D	D	248	9.4	257	2
Clark	7	D	D	D	4	D	D	D	217	6.5	0	0
Clay	25	565	36.1	16.9	26	65	6.1	1.4	666	22.8	6,060	53
Cloud	35	744	38.1	19.1	25	78	5.9	1.6	645	24.4	0	0
Coffey	27	493	39.9	15.4	15	D	D	D	667	30.7	3,647	27
Comanche	7	166	7.1	3.2	6	9	0.7	0.2	155	5.9	0	0
Cowley	118	2,199	132.1	59.1	53	208	24.0	5.0	1,957	71.9	4,693	34
Crawford	129	3,042	233.8	97.9	63	261	20.0	5.5	2,074	71.1	15,864	97
Decatur	7	251	11.8	5.9	8	19	1.7	0.4	290	12.6	0	0
Dickinson	42	883	49.6	24.6	42	148	12.5	2.4	1,209	44.7	3,007	22
Doniphan	9	179	8.7	3.5	7	D	D	D	483	18.0	1,817	8
Douglas	289	6,580	545.8	211.1	181	1,423	230.7	37.2	8,281	341.6	126,151	823
Edwards	10	158	14.6	5.8	11	D	D	D	201	7.3	147	1
Elk	5	D	D	D	5	D	D	D	257	11.3	NA	NA
Ellis	117	3,239	319.4	128.5	85	362	40.8	8.9	2,936	119.0	6,622	31
Ellsworth	23	466	30.5	13.8	16	32	3.4	0.7	440	15.0	160	1
Finney	98	D	D	D	69	D	D	D	2,337	136.7	8,087	48
Ford	92	1,583	164.3	63.8	59	282	28.6	7.1	1,864	100.3	6,899	40
Franklin	68	1,733	93.7	42.1	43	179	14.3	4.6	1,594	67.7	15,506	85
Geary	51	1,577	153.3	58.7	55	241	18.9	5.5	1,405	42.6	3,052	12
Gove	11	237	18.0	6.9	11	D	D	D	295	17.7	1,816	21
Graham	12	237	14.1	6.1	5	D	D	D	298	11.4	0	0
Grant	17	104	7.3	2.7	15	43	5.5	1.3	512	28.2	435	2
Gray	11	149	6.5	3.1	11	D	D	D	657	34.7	2,160	8
Greeley	1	D	D	D	4	D	D	D	144	4.1	0	0
Greenwood	14	270	20.1	9.6	11	16	1.9	0.4	553	17.7	385	2
Hamilton	6	144	9.5	4.1	6	D	D	D	190	7.5	250	1
Harper	16	300	19.5	9.1	14	38	4.3	1.0	525	23.8	250	1
Harvey	117	2,967	251.3	102.3	56	262	26.2	7.2	2,407	76.8	7,029	34
Haskell	7	D	D	D	8	D	D	D	397	22.9	0	0
Hodgeman	7	D	D	D	5	D	D	D	179	8.4	0	0
Jackson	22	530	32.5	13.4	27	100	8.6	2.1	812	32.1	4,436	24
Jefferson	29	D	D	D	27	D	D	D	1,231	46.5	12,538	70
Jewell	4	D	D	D	6	16	1.9	0.3	263	10.2	0	0
Johnson	1,739	37,514	4,657.7	1,766.9	969	7,032	789.4	227.0	50,050	2,704.6	1,023,984	4,504
Kearny	5	D	D	D	4	D	D	D	308	17.0	0	0
Kingman	21	425	22.1	11.0	16	22	2.2	0.5	640	25.6	1,955	11
Kiowa	10	192	12.9	5.5	6	8	1.4	0.2	225	8.3	306	2
Labette	88	4,122	178.2	88.9	33	D	D	D	1,219	49.4	928	7
Lane	4	D	D	D	6	D	D	D	173	6.6	0	0
Leavenworth	137	2,981	288.2	114.7	99	447	36.5	11.6	3,943	135.1	60,475	309
Lincoln	7	D	D	D	7	22	0.9	0.2	239	7.4	100	1
Linn	10	D	D	D	14	71	6.7	1.4	678	22.5	4,249	45
Logan	7	D	D	D	13	23	1.9	0.4	276	11.4	0	0
Lyon	101	2,138	148.3	64.3	60	228	24.9	5.2	1,754	63.4	6,285	33
McPherson	100	2,333	128.2	58.7	84	364	36.0	9.6	2,450	94.3	6,556	56
Marion	31	608	38.3	14.8	26	88	14.9	2.3	957	28.2	1,970	10
Marshall	34	588	38.3	16.6	31	96	6.9	1.7	785	28.3	630	6
Meade	9	D	D	D	11	D	D	D	411	20.7	85	1
Miami	67	D	D	D	50	166	13.6	3.6	2,540	117.8	24,391	85
Mitchell	24	607	43.1	20.3	21	63	5.7	1.5	622	20.4	2,694	8
Montgomery	100	2,270	119.4	57.7	58	200	17.1	4.7	1,830	59.3	133	2
Morris	14	268	18.7	6.8	8	14	1.1	0.2	492	19.5	1,450	5
Morton	7	D	D	D	5	D	D	D	198	5.4	0	0
Nemaha	43	848	51.3	24.0	28	57	7.7	1.4	794	29.3	2,656	9

Government Employment and Payroll, and Local Government Finances

	Government employment and payroll, 2012									Local government finances, 2012				
			March payroll (percent of total)							General revenue				
												Taxes		
STATE County	Full-time equivalent employees	March payroll (dollars)	Administration, judicial, and legal	Police and corrections	Fire protection	Highways and transportation	Health and welfare	Natural resources and utilities	Education and libraries	Total (mil dol)	Inter-governmental (mil dol)	Total (mil dol)	Per capita[1] (dollars) Total	Per capita[1] (dollars) Property
	171	172	173	174	175	176	177	178	179	180	181	182	183	184
KANSAS	X	X	X	X	X	X	X	X	X	X	X	X	X	X
Allen	895	2,577,982	5.0	6.1	3.4	3.7	4.1	8.9	67.1	63.9	30.0	21.1	1,583	1,268
Anderson	497	1,619,637	6.2	5.4	1.6	4.7	1.1	6.1	73.7	23.0	11.7	7.8	980	756
Atchison	692	1,978,776	6.6	8.4	3.3	4.3	7.8	7.0	60.5	55.0	21.3	23.4	1,390	1,002
Barber	411	1,245,913	6.3	3.3	0.1	7.0	45.0	3.3	32.0	35.8	4.2	16.4	3,382	2,951
Barton	1,660	5,166,241	4.8	6.8	2.0	3.6	6.0	4.3	70.0	122.6	44.4	49.3	1,788	1,396
Bourbon	839	2,300,103	4.1	6.3	2.0	3.3	0.0	5.1	77.6	59.7	27.2	20.2	1,354	1,059
Brown	402	1,209,798	8.3	11.3	0.2	5.2	0.6	6.9	64.8	36.4	13.4	17.7	1,790	1,406
Butler	4,199	12,617,495	2.9	6.0	1.7	2.3	2.5	2.9	79.0	296.1	116.0	108.1	1,642	1,429
Chase	138	378,267	8.3	25.9	0.5	9.7	5.3	1.8	44.0	11.2	3.5	6.0	2,181	1,999
Chautauqua	172	502,746	9.7	7.9	0.0	8.5	6.3	5.4	60.4	13.8	5.5	6.9	1,943	1,619
Cherokee	874	3,187,294	11.0	10.0	0.6	9.2	3.4	2.6	61.3	64.1	33.3	21.8	1,027	758
Cheyenne	165	389,236	10.5	5.0	0.1	7.4	2.7	8.2	64.4	12.1	4.1	6.6	2,450	2,088
Clark	347	1,038,878	4.4	3.1	0.0	2.2	61.9	2.5	24.8	28.0	3.9	8.5	3,919	3,852
Clay	803	2,480,508	2.7	3.1	1.1	3.9	30.1	7.3	50.0	45.5	12.6	13.2	1,545	1,227
Cloud	581	1,796,777	3.3	5.8	1.8	7.0	2.6	3.3	72.8	44.9	18.4	15.2	1,616	1,216
Coffey	673	2,404,634	6.2	5.9	0.0	6.6	43.0	4.7	31.1	69.1	9.0	35.4	4,162	4,031
Comanche	187	510,886	10.4	5.9	0.0	8.5	34.5	11.2	28.4	18.5	6.5	6.4	3,350	3,116
Cowley	2,458	8,016,863	4.3	5.7	2.3	2.2	22.2	5.9	56.0	203.4	66.1	46.6	1,284	1,024
Crawford	1,777	5,700,396	5.1	9.6	2.5	3.3	21.7	6.6	49.1	136.9	53.7	45.9	1,166	827
Decatur	132	423,037	12.8	5.9	0.4	9.6	3.7	7.1	54.7	9.9	2.9	5.6	1,953	1,752
Dickinson	1,141	3,857,618	5.1	5.3	1.0	3.4	29.1	5.5	49.6	105.0	33.0	29.3	1,484	1,175
Doniphan	654	1,750,518	4.8	4.1	0.0	3.2	3.0	4.0	80.3	45.4	18.2	12.9	1,635	1,413
Douglas	4,535	18,551,008	5.6	11.2	5.0	2.9	33.2	7.9	33.4	537.2	114.0	188.6	1,671	1,239
Edwards	153	450,266	16.0	7.2	0.2	14.9	6.8	4.1	50.1	13.9	5.5	7.3	2,459	2,226
Elk	292	687,044	6.7	3.5	0.3	5.8	15.5	4.5	62.3	14.4	5.9	5.3	1,934	1,803
Ellis	1,003	3,461,008	7.9	9.4	2.7	5.0	5.7	5.6	61.1	88.4	23.1	51.1	1,759	1,232
Ellsworth	296	866,464	7.5	7.6	0.0	7.7	5.7	8.2	60.7	28.4	9.8	14.2	2,194	1,862
Finney	2,267	7,504,277	5.0	10.7	1.8	2.9	2.9	4.3	70.6	186.5	73.2	74.7	2,008	1,584
Ford	1,844	5,930,863	5.1	8.2	3.9	2.6	3.3	4.3	71.6	177.3	76.6	65.8	1,894	1,286
Franklin	1,501	5,023,604	6.2	8.2	1.6	2.3	29.7	5.6	44.5	115.7	36.0	39.3	1,518	1,176
Geary	2,097	7,346,708	3.8	7.7	1.7	1.2	23.2	1.3	60.2	186.7	68.2	47.0	1,236	779
Gove	329	918,512	4.3	1.7	0.0	4.8	54.5	0.9	32.9	24.5	5.7	7.8	2,849	2,457
Graham	232	804,031	8.2	3.8	0.6	8.9	44.4	4.5	28.5	22.4	4.0	9.8	3,805	3,282
Grant	403	1,281,935	6.8	7.4	0.2	7.9	5.9	5.1	65.0	41.0	11.0	26.3	3,319	3,166
Gray	309	995,915	8.2	7.4	0.0	6.0	2.2	5.2	67.3	26.3	10.8	12.0	1,998	1,829
Greeley	53	153,774	8.6	0.0	0.0	6.4	1.7	4.3	78.3	4.0	1.5	2.0	1,555	1,519
Greenwood	339	898,356	8.5	7.0	0.4	6.6	4.3	4.5	67.1	22.5	10.0	10.4	1,605	1,400
Hamilton	163	402,085	10.0	8.0	0.1	7.1	6.4	7.9	57.3	13.4	3.7	8.9	3,358	3,144
Harper	602	1,701,546	6.8	3.5	0.1	6.1	45.7	4.3	29.4	45.9	10.6	12.9	2,179	2,024
Harvey	1,517	4,865,931	8.6	8.1	5.6	3.6	3.0	5.5	65.1	120.5	49.4	44.5	1,277	900
Haskell	378	1,272,364	6.3	6.7	0.0	7.9	37.3	0.8	40.4	39.0	3.8	22.7	5,336	5,085
Hodgeman	127	312,316	11.2	6.4	0.0	12.3	7.7	10.6	49.0	11.5	3.2	6.7	3,390	3,354
Jackson	744	2,123,015	4.8	7.4	0.0	4.1	0.8	6.6	74.7	41.1	21.8	14.9	1,107	922
Jefferson	801	2,548,797	6.5	6.7	0.0	4.8	6.2	3.9	68.5	65.4	32.7	24.4	1,288	1,179
Jewell	228	595,682	6.9	3.1	0.0	12.6	38.5	5.3	30.9	15.8	4.4	6.1	2,003	1,819
Johnson	22,393	88,446,886	6.5	10.0	4.1	3.0	4.2	7.6	63.3	2,399.0	615.6	1,250.4	2,233	1,568
Kearny	501	1,624,976	4.9	5.2	1.0	3.4	47.9	3.2	32.3	40.1	5.1	19.2	4,834	4,739
Kingman	303	939,992	10.2	7.8	0.3	9.1	3.5	5.9	62.1	29.0	9.1	16.4	2,088	1,871
Kiowa	190	513,068	15.3	8.3	1.6	10.8	2.8	6.8	50.3	18.3	5.8	10.3	4,132	3,569
Labette	1,476	4,983,554	3.5	5.4	1.3	2.4	37.6	2.9	46.0	131.2	39.2	25.9	1,215	896
Lane	185	518,931	8.0	5.3	2.8	7.3	34.7	3.4	37.1	15.3	2.4	7.9	4,633	4,497
Leavenworth	2,924	9,219,623	4.7	9.0	2.4	3.1	3.7	5.2	70.5	234.3	105.0	92.8	1,194	954
Lincoln	278	791,585	5.0	2.8	0.1	6.6	36.5	5.0	42.1	16.1	5.5	7.6	2,408	2,131
Linn	469	1,414,132	7.1	7.1	0.7	5.0	2.4	6.1	70.4	38.3	14.7	20.4	2,163	2,067
Logan	328	920,118	5.1	3.8	0.2	3.2	54.6	2.9	29.9	24.5	3.1	9.2	3,298	2,915
Lyon	2,245	7,549,055	4.5	8.4	2.7	3.3	26.6	2.6	50.3	180.6	54.8	53.5	1,586	1,073
McPherson	1,486	4,467,777	5.3	7.9	1.7	5.1	4.7	13.1	58.6	102.2	34.2	49.8	1,697	1,261
Marion	702	1,972,669	7.2	6.2	0.1	6.0	17.8	6.6	54.8	54.7	18.7	20.1	1,630	1,376
Marshall	507	1,385,386	5.8	6.0	0.0	7.1	3.5	3.5	71.8	35.7	13.7	17.7	1,764	1,524
Meade	403	1,284,083	4.9	3.3	1.1	4.4	54.9	3.4	27.0	33.8	5.5	11.9	2,711	2,487
Miami	1,386	4,167,179	7.7	8.9	1.2	4.9	3.1	3.9	68.5	96.7	33.9	47.7	1,463	1,199
Mitchell	539	1,523,148	6.6	5.9	0.1	6.8	5.3	10.9	62.8	39.3	15.8	13.9	2,189	1,626
Montgomery	1,708	5,095,652	3.7	7.7	2.9	3.7	1.3	9.3	68.3	148.4	54.4	62.4	1,812	1,449
Morris	233	667,311	10.9	7.8	0.3	7.9	1.6	3.9	64.1	17.4	6.0	9.0	1,545	1,277
Morton	433	1,384,778	4.2	3.1	0.1	4.3	50.6	2.3	32.2	39.0	7.6	14.7	4,633	4,454
Nemaha	548	1,548,782	6.0	6.7	0.0	5.8	2.1	9.9	67.8	39.4	16.0	18.2	1,794	1,515

1. Based on the resident population estimated as of July 1 of the year shown.

Table B. States and Counties — Local Government Finances, Government Employment, and Income Taxes

STATE County	Direct general expenditure — Total (mil dol)	Per capita¹ (dollars)	Education	Health and hospitals	Police protection	Public welfare	Highways	Debt outstanding — Total (mil dol)	Per capita¹ (dollars)	Federal civilian	Federal military	State and local	Number of returns	Mean adjusted gross income	Mean income tax
	185	186	187	188	189	190	191	192	193	194	195	196	197	198	199
KANSAS	X	X	X	X	X	X	X	X	X	25,039	32,223	233,076	1,324,150	62,331	8,081
Allen	63.1	4,735	58.0	4.0	3.4	0.0	6.4	50.6	3,796	53	46	1,527	5,870	42,661	3,767
Anderson	40.1	5,062	61.6	2.1	2.8	0.0	8.0	28.9	3,654	35	29	551	3,490	43,541	4,015
Atchison	59.4	3,536	45.7	1.0	4.9	4.7	7.9	33.0	1,961	45	56	908	6,860	48,876	4,764
Barber	36.3	7,477	24.0	41.7	2.6	0.0	10.3	11.4	2,336	28	17	616	2,150	40,700	4,412
Barton	120.9	4,389	60.4	2.7	3.3	0.0	7.9	58.1	2,108	70	97	2,281	12,050	46,994	4,883
Bourbon	65.3	4,385	57.0	0.9	3.2	0.0	6.3	43.5	2,920	78	54	1,119	6,180	39,875	3,323
Brown	35.1	3,553	49.9	0.9	4.2	0.0	11.2	44.1	4,465	102	36	1,473	4,370	46,484	4,501
Butler	329.4	5,004	68.1	1.1	2.9	0.0	5.2	551.1	8,372	128	243	5,552	28,840	64,233	7,694
Chase	11.4	4,131	37.7	3.0	3.4	0.0	10.4	5.1	1,857	15	10	212	1,210	45,728	5,050
Chautauqua	13.5	3,787	47.9	5.7	3.6	0.0	9.6	9.2	2,578	18	12	240	1,360	42,301	3,721
Cherokee	63.8	3,007	60.9	2.7	4.3	0.0	8.9	20.0	944	55	75	1,313	8,490	44,647	4,120
Cheyenne	11.4	4,256	50.1	5.6	3.7	0.0	9.9	0.8	296	14	10	243	1,240	40,042	4,193
Clark	28.0	12,839	20.3	57.2	4.3	0.0	4.7	5.4	2,461	11	7	389	940	44,547	4,229
Clay	46.8	5,482	29.6	33.0	3.0	0.0	7.6	34.9	4,095	35	29	959	3,850	47,379	4,468
Cloud	46.3	4,930	66.5	3.2	3.3	0.0	6.9	13.5	1,434	39	33	766	4,050	42,757	3,817
Coffey	70.3	8,270	29.8	34.4	3.0	0.0	10.8	13.0	1,531	54	30	1,066	3,980	55,533	6,108
Comanche	19.2	10,056	20.4	23.8	2.0	0.0	6.2	6.1	3,165	5	6	254	830	39,024	3,451
Cowley	191.8	5,286	45.5	21.1	3.6	0.0	3.2	166.3	4,583	100	125	3,302	15,060	57,329	6,585
Crawford	135.7	3,448	45.0	17.8	5.0	0.0	3.9	114.8	2,916	85	143	5,015	16,040	47,771	5,549
Decatur	10.3	3,573	44.7	3.6	4.6	0.0	12.8	7.9	2,755	19	11	250	1,400	34,768	3,127
Dickinson	107.2	5,425	50.6	21.7	3.1	0.0	5.6	91.6	4,637	98	70	1,671	8,900	47,117	4,417
Doniphan	45.9	5,834	72.7	2.2	2.9	0.0	6.0	12.8	1,623	36	27	906	3,340	47,570	4,811
Douglas	474.7	4,206	28.6	35.1	4.9	0.0	3.3	544.9	4,828	439	451	16,043	50,540	62,339	8,063
Edwards	14.5	4,871	42.0	3.4	4.5	0.0	14.5	1.2	396	19	11	225	1,420	46,487	4,800
Elk	14.6	5,351	44.7	2.8	2.7	13.2	10.2	3.0	1,097	8	9	300	1,140	37,743	3,746
Ellis	86.9	2,990	45.4	3.2	5.5	0.0	7.4	38.7	1,332	138	104	3,639	13,080	52,628	5,963
Ellsworth	28.5	4,390	50.2	3.3	4.0	0.0	18.7	22.2	3,424	27	20	881	2,670	49,963	5,446
Finney	182.2	4,899	60.1	1.9	6.7	0.0	4.4	162.9	4,378	123	137	2,981	17,460	47,409	4,840
Ford	201.8	5,806	49.4	1.2	3.5	1.0	2.6	336.1	9,671	228	126	2,643	15,430	44,237	3,898
Franklin	118.9	4,591	39.4	30.1	1.6	0.0	5.7	81.1	3,129	68	95	1,952	11,900	49,263	4,756
Geary	176.2	4,635	47.3	25.0	6.0	0.0	2.9	273.5	7,194	3,160	15,333	2,541	17,220	39,766	2,820
Gove	24.9	9,123	26.3	51.1	1.8	0.0	8.5	1.5	532	13	10	407	1,350	40,783	4,722
Graham	21.4	8,308	22.0	38.9	2.6	0.0	9.1	0.4	152	22	9	314	1,250	35,325	3,394
Grant	35.6	4,496	41.9	5.9	4.7	0.0	7.6	27.3	3,445	19	28	650	3,170	50,554	4,947
Gray	25.6	4,246	56.7	2.7	4.4	0.0	11.9	24.2	4,013	21	22	908	2,760	53,605	6,200
Greeley	4.0	3,089	72.8	0.0	1.1	0.0	4.3	5.0	3,847	11	5	182	650	48,243	4,794
Greenwood	21.3	3,303	53.1	3.8	5.8	0.0	13.3	21.4	3,323	38	23	484	2,790	40,564	3,978
Hamilton	11.6	4,401	48.9	2.0	5.9	0.0	10.1	4.6	1,740	11	10	245	1,080	21,393	3,362
Harper	45.6	7,720	25.8	36.2	2.0	6.9	9.7	21.2	3,581	30	21	783	2,361	42,361	4,467
Harvey	109.6	3,145	50.9	2.7	5.6	0.1	5.4	180.9	5,190	71	125	1,967	15,650	53,786	5,416
Haskell	39.1	9,192	29.1	42.9	3.2	0.0	10.1	10.5	2,463	15	15	543	1,770	29,189	5,339
Hodgeman	10.7	5,451	37.8	5.5	4.6	0.0	12.0	11.5	5,870	17	7	264	860	42,921	3,870
Jackson	41.1	3,058	62.3	0.8	5.4	0.0	10.4	21.9	1,625	55	50	1,930	6,160	48,778	4,574
Jefferson	63.2	3,338	64.8	5.4	5.1	0.0	7.4	46.3	2,446	71	70	1,052	8,560	55,323	5,558
Jewell	13.7	4,485	29.6	21.3	2.8	0.0	17.3	0.8	250	27	11	342	1,440	40,156	3,610
Johnson	2,304.6	4,116	47.4	2.5	7.7	0.9	5.7	5,877.0	10,496	2,715	2,230	28,372	287,090	95,856	15,913
Kearny	42.8	10,778	27.2	45.6	2.8	0.0	6.2	5.6	1,409	15	15	681	1,830	44,239	4,747
Kingman	29.4	3,741	43.5	3.2	4.6	0.0	13.3	19.1	2,432	36	33	560	3,540	48,451	4,887
Kiowa	16.8	6,718	43.0	3.4	4.6	0.0	10.9	3.4	1,371	14	9	347	1,100	43,889	4,100
Labette	134.7	6,331	39.7	39.0	2.6	0.0	4.0	95.8	4,500	82	74	2,743	9,130	42,520	4,140
Lane	15.6	9,127	29.8	31.7	3.9	0.0	8.7	0.5	288	12	6	254	810	41,311	4,140
Leavenworth	188.5	2,425	61.8	0.0	5.1	0.0	3.5	316.9	4,076	4,287	3,577	4,013	33,860	61,141	6,576
Lincoln	16.5	5,197	44.3	7.0	2.8	0.0	13.6	1.8	569	28	11	376	1,430	37,538	3,304
Linn	38.3	4,053	55.6	3.0	4.7	0.0	10.2	11.7	1,244	47	36	748	4,280	46,783	4,598
Logan	27.7	9,951	22.7	51.3	2.8	0.0	4.7	6.2	2,220	22	10	716	1,400	50,776	5,899
Lyon	166.1	4,920	39.3	28.9	4.3	0.0	4.3	94.4	2,798	97	120	4,446	14,540	45,811	4,293
McPherson	101.4	3,454	45.5	2.3	4.3	0.0	12.0	90.9	3,097	87	104	1,955	13,820	57,715	6,464
Marion	54.2	4,388	42.4	18.1	3.1	0.0	9.1	43.6	3,528	62	42	949	5,390	49,554	5,202
Marshall	34.8	3,472	53.8	2.9	4.3	0.0	13.1	19.2	1,915	52	36	809	4,930	50,820	5,796
Meade	34.5	7,851	21.7	41.1	2.2	3.8	7.6	13.7	3,120	17	16	561	1,950	52,672	5,596
Miami	87.9	2,695	49.6	2.9	5.9	0.0	9.2	104.9	3,215	73	123	2,191	15,360	63,889	7,741
Mitchell	42.4	6,669	50.7	7.8	3.9	0.0	12.6	15.4	2,417	32	22	986	2,950	45,769	4,739
Montgomery	142.0	4,121	61.6	2.3	3.8	0.0	5.5	137.7	3,996	109	118	2,570	13,220	44,588	4,131
Morris	25.5	4,361	59.2	5.3	2.7	0.0	10.7	21.0	3,594	33	20	448	2,540	46,326	4,436
Morton	37.0	11,666	31.7	47.6	0.9	0.0	2.7	4.6	1,453	20	10	379	1,360	47,315	4,791
Nemaha	36.9	3,640	57.0	1.5	3.6	0.0	11.8	35.6	3,511	52	37	746	4,970	63,387	7,818

1. Based on the resident population estimated as of July 1 of the year shown.

Table B. States and Counties — Land Area and Population

State / county code	CBSA code[1]	County code[2]	STATE County	Population, 2018				Population and population characteristics, 2018										
								Race alone or in combination, not Hispanic or Latino (percent)					Age (percent)					
				Land area[3] (sq. mi)	Total persons 2018	Rank	Per square mile	White	Black	American Indian, Alaska Native	Asian and Pacific Islancer	Percent Hispanic or Latino[4]	Under 5 years	5 to 17 years	18 to 24 years	25 to 34 years	35 to 44 years	45 to 54 years
				1	2	3	4	5	6	7	8	9	10	11	12	13	14	15
			KANSAS— Cont'd															
20133		7	Neosho	571.5	15,951	2,040	27.9	91.8	2.1	2.0	1.1	5.1	6.6	18.1	8.5	10.7	10.8	11.3
20135		9	Ness	1,074.7	2,840	2,982	2.6	88.6	1.1	0.9	0.3	10.1	5.8	16.0	6.8	8.8	9.3	9.6
20137		7	Norton	878.0	5,430	2,800	6.2	90.2	4.0	0.9	1.3	5.4	5.3	13.8	8.2	13.2	11.6	13.7
20139	45,820	3	Osage	705.5	15,941	2,042	22.6	94.8	1.4	1.5	0.8	3.4	5.7	17.6	7.2	10.1	11.2	12.2
20141		9	Osborne	892.5	3,475	2,940	3.9	95.4	0.9	0.9	1.6	2.2	5.5	14.9	6.8	11.1	10.1	10.2
20143	41,460	9	Ottawa	720.7	5,802	2,768	8.1	95.1	1.7	1.2	0.6	2.9	4.9	17.7	7.6	9.6	11.8	12.2
20145		7	Pawnee	754.3	6,562	2,705	8.7	85.5	6.3	1.4	0.8	7.8	4.1	12.3	8.3	12.5	12.9	13.2
20147		7	Phillips	885.9	5,317	2,808	6.0	94.8	0.9	0.8	1.2	3.5	5.7	16.8	7.1	9.8	10.3	10.9
20149	31,740	3	Pottawatomie	840.8	24,277	1,632	28.9	92.0	2.0	1.5	1.7	5.1	7.8	21.4	8.2	12.5	13.2	10.7
20151		7	Pratt	735.0	9,378	2,475	12.8	89.6	2.2	1.4	1.3	7.3	7.0	17.7	9.7	11.0	10.9	9.5
20153		9	Rawlins	1,069.4	2,508	3,003	2.3	90.8	1.6	0.7	0.8	7.7	6.3	14.7	5.8	10.2	9.7	10.0
20155	26,740	4	Reno	1,255.5	62,342	844	49.7	86.0	4.2	1.4	0.9	9.7	5.5	16.9	8.5	12.4	11.6	11.4
20157		9	Republic	717.4	4,664	2,852	6.5	96.1	1.4	0.7	0.8	2.2	5.5	15.3	6.2	8.8	9.6	10.3
20159		7	Rice	726.2	9,531	2,461	13.1	85.2	2.0	1.8	1.6	11.5	5.9	16.8	11.9	11.2	10.0	10.6
20161	31,740	3	Riley	609.7	73,703	745	120.9	79.4	7.8	1.2	6.5	8.5	5.6	11.1	32.0	17.4	10.0	6.7
20163		9	Rooks	890.5	5,013	2,830	5.6	95.4	1.5	0.9	1.4	2.4	6.3	15.9	6.9	11.3	10.3	11.5
20165		9	Rush	717.8	3,093	2,958	4.3	94.1	1.0	1.3	0.7	4.2	5.4	15.5	6.9	9.2	10.3	11.6
20167		7	Russell	886.3	6,907	2,682	7.8	93.2	2.3	1.3	0.9	3.9	6.0	15.7	6.6	10.3	10.1	11.6
20169	41,460	5	Saline	720.2	54,401	937	75.5	82.5	4.7	1.1	3.0	11.4	6.1	17.1	9.0	12.4	11.5	12.1
20171		7	Scott	717.6	4,897	2,841	6.8	79.0	0.9	1.1	1.4	18.5	6.5	20.4	7.6	11.5	10.6	11.1
20173	48,620	2	Sedgwick	997.5	513,607	137	514.9	70.8	10.5	1.9	5.4	14.9	6.9	18.8	9.2	14.2	12.3	11.4
20175	30,580	5	Seward	639.7	21,780	1,734	34.0	30.6	4.7	0.9	3.2	62.0	9.2	22.5	10.5	15.1	11.9	11.2
20177	45,820	3	Shawnee	544.0	177,499	375	326.3	76.8	9.9	2.1	2.2	12.6	6.2	17.4	8.4	12.4	11.8	11.8
20179		9	Sheridan	896.0	2,533	3,000	2.8	93.2	0.8	0.7	0.6	5.6	6.8	18.4	6.8	9.3	10.5	9.8
20181		7	Sherman	1,056.1	5,899	2,758	5.6	85.6	1.7	1.0	0.8	12.6	6.8	17.0	8.4	12.2	11.3	10.1
20183		9	Smith	895.5	3,603	2,931	4.0	96.6	1.2	1.4	0.8	2.3	5.7	14.7	6.3	8.1	10.2	9.9
20185		9	Stafford	792.0	4,178	2,889	5.3	85.3	1.1	1.7	0.7	13.2	6.4	17.0	7.8	9.8	9.6	11.2
20187		9	Stanton	680.4	1,987	3,050	2.9	60.3	0.9	1.5	0.6	37.7	6.9	19.2	9.1	10.5	12.2	11.4
20189		7	Stevens	727.3	5,559	2,787	7.6	61.0	1.0	1.5	0.9	36.8	6.2	22.7	8.1	10.6	11.8	12.3
20191	48,620	2	Sumner	1,181.6	22,996	1,680	19.5	91.7	1.9	2.6	0.8	5.4	5.9	18.8	7.4	11.3	11.6	11.3
20193		7	Thomas	1,074.7	7,711	2,615	7.2	90.6	1.4	1.1	1.2	7.0	7.3	16.1	12.9	12.7	10.5	9.5
20195		9	Trego	889.5	2,793	2,986	3.1	95.9	1.4	1.0	0.6	2.4	4.8	13.1	6.2	10.1	9.7	11.6
20197	45,820	3	Wabaunsee	794.3	6,899	2,685	8.7	93.9	1.6	1.8	0.8	4.3	5.8	17.6	7.1	9.6	11.2	11.7
20199		9	Wallace	913.7	1,503	3,080	1.6	89.8	1.4	1.1	0.2	9.0	7.9	17.2	7.5	10.1	9.0	9.7
20201		9	Washington	894.8	5,420	2,802	6.1	94.9	1.1	0.6	1.0	3.6	6.6	15.7	7.7	9.2	10.4	11.3
20203		9	Wichita	718.6	2,105	3,039	2.9	68.6	1.7	0.5	0.3	29.9	5.6	20.5	8.2	9.6	10.9	11.0
20205		7	Wilson	570.4	8,665	2,533	15.2	94.1	1.2	2.9	0.9	3.4	6.3	17.8	6.8	10.6	10.8	11.3
20207		9	Woodson	497.8	3,183	2,957	6.4	94.9	1.4	2.4	0.6	3.0	5.3	15.8	6.3	10.3	11.0	10.7
20209	28,140	1	Wyandotte	151.6	165,324	396	1,090.5	42.6	23.5	1.4	5.8	29.3	8.0	19.9	8.5	15.1	13.0	11.4
21000		0	KENTUCKY	39,490.3	4,468,402	X	113.2	86.0	9.3	0.7	2.1	3.8	6.2	16.4	9.3	13.1	12.4	12.9
21001		7	Adair	405.3	19,215	1,865	47.4	94.4	3.7	0.7	0.5	2.0	5.5	14.8	11.7	11.7	10.7	13.1
21003	14,540	3	Allen	344.3	21,122	1,768	61.3	96.0	1.9	0.8	0.4	2.2	5.9	17.1	7.5	12.7	11.6	13.9
21005	23,180	6	Anderson	202.1	22,663	1,696	112.1	95.3	2.9	0.7	0.9	1.8	6.1	17.4	7.5	12.0	12.8	14.8
21007	37,140	9	Ballard	246.9	7,979	2,596	32.3	94.5	4.7	1.0	0.8	1.4	5.0	16.2	7.6	10.8	11.6	13.3
21009	23,980	6	Barren	487.6	44,176	1,091	90.6	91.5	5.0	0.6	1.1	3.3	6.6	16.9	7.7	12.1	12.2	13.1
21011	34,460	8	Bath	278.8	12,383	2,260	44.4	96.3	2.2	0.5	0.7	1.7	6.7	18.4	8.0	10.8	12.1	13.7
21013	33,180	7	Bell	359.1	26,569	1,545	74.0	95.7	3.2	1.0	0.6	1.2	5.9	15.4	8.0	12.4	11.4	13.5
21015	17,140	1	Boone	246.3	131,533	486	534.0	89.3	4.3	0.6	3.4	4.3	6.5	19.5	8.0	12.3	13.6	14.1
21017	30,460	2	Bourbon	289.7	20,184	1,813	69.7	86.5	7.1	0.6	0.6	7.1	6.1	16.9	7.7	11.4	11.5	13.5
21019	26,580	2	Boyd	159.9	47,240	1,032	295.4	94.4	3.6	0.7	0.8	1.9	5.6	15.7	6.9	12.1	12.4	13.3
21021	19,220	7	Boyle	180.4	30,100	1,430	166.9	87.4	9.2	0.7	1.4	3.5	5.3	14.7	12.0	12.0	11.3	12.8
21023	17,140	1	Bracken	202.7	8,239	2,573	40.6	97.1	1.5	0.6	0.4	1.9	6.0	17.4	7.3	11.8	11.8	14.1
21025		7	Breathitt	492.4	12,726	2,241	25.8	97.4	1.1	0.6	1.0	1.2	5.9	14.5	7.5	12.2	12.9	14.6
21027		8	Breckinridge	569.8	20,388	1,800	35.8	95.5	2.9	0.9	0.5	1.7	6.2	16.6	7.4	10.4	11.7	13.2
21029	31,140	1	Bullitt	297.0	81,069	699	273.0	95.7	1.8	0.9	1.0	2.1	5.3	16.6	7.8	13.0	13.2	14.5
21031	14,540	3	Butler	426.1	12,772	2,238	30.0	95.6	1.0	0.7	0.4	3.5	6.2	16.3	6.7	11.9	12.6	13.2
21033		7	Caldwell	344.8	12,715	2,242	36.9	92.2	6.4	0.7	0.6	1.6	5.8	16.6	7.3	11.5	11.3	12.7
21035	34,660	7	Calloway	385.0	39,135	1,200	101.6	91.1	4.9	0.7	2.3	2.7	5.2	12.9	19.7	12.0	10.2	11.1
21037	17,140	1	Campbell	151.3	93,152	635	615.7	93.7	3.8	0.5	1.4	2.2	5.8	15.0	9.9	14.9	12.1	12.4
21039		9	Carlisle	189.4	4,771	2,848	25.2	95.1	2.5	1.2	0.6	2.7	6.7	16.0	6.4	11.2	11.7	12.6
21041		6	Carroll	128.6	10,737	2,371	83.5	90.7	3.1	1.0	0.9	6.7	7.3	18.7	8.1	12.0	12.1	12.8
21043		6	Carter	409.5	27,004	1,526	65.9	97.5	1.0	0.7	0.5	1.3	6.4	16.1	8.5	11.4	11.7	13.4
21045		9	Casey	444.2	15,888	2,045	35.8	95.4	1.5	0.7	0.4	3.1	6.5	16.4	7.5	11.5	11.5	13.2
21047	17,300	2	Christian	717.5	71,671	755	99.9	68.0	23.2	1.1	2.7	8.1	9.6	17.3	16.7	16.6	10.0	8.6
21049	30,460	2	Clark	252.5	36,249	1,269	143.6	91.3	5.5	0.6	0.9	3.1	6.1	16.2	7.7	12.1	12.1	14.0

1. CBSA = Core Based Statistical Area. See Appendix A for explanation. See Appendix B for list of metropolitan areas with component counties. 2. County type code from the Economic Research Service of USDA Rural-Urban Continuum Codes. See Appendix A for definition. 3. Dry land or land partially or temporarily covered by water. 4. May be of any race.

STATE County	Age (percent) 55 to 64 years	65 to 74 years	75 years and over	Percent female	Total persons 2000	2010	Percent change 2000-2010	2010-2018	Components of change 2010-2018 Births	Deaths	Net Migration	Households Number	Persons per household	Family households	Female family householder[1]	One person
	16	17	18	19	20	21	22	23	24	25	26	27	28	29	30	31
KANSAS— Cont'd																
Neosho	14.2	10.5	9.3	50.5	16,997	16,511	-2.9	-3.4	1,761	1,630	-691	6,521	2.42	67.0	11.7	30.2
Ness	17.8	12.0	13.9	50.7	3,454	3,107	-10.0	-8.6	286	355	-196	1,327	2.22	68.0	3.8	29.6
Norton	13.7	9.9	10.6	44.1	5,953	5,669	-4.8	-4.2	460	519	-179	1,906	2.47	69.9	11.0	26.2
Osage	16.2	11.2	8.6	49.9	16,712	16,294	-2.5	-2.2	1,411	1,595	-163	6,604	2.38	68.8	7.6	28.1
Osborne	16.3	11.1	13.9	49.5	4,452	3,861	-13.3	-10.0	347	474	-256	1,713	2.09	57.2	5.5	37.8
Ottawa	15.8	11.0	9.4	48.1	6,163	6,091	-1.2	-4.7	488	559	-217	2,437	2.41	69.1	6.9	26.7
Pawnee	15.6	11.0	9.9	43.9	7,233	6,971	-3.6	-5.9	541	629	-319	2,590	2.19	62.1	11.7	33.0
Phillips	15.5	13.5	10.4	50.4	6,001	5,642	-6.0	-5.8	514	585	-255	2,326	2.30	64.3	5.8	31.7
Pottawatomie	12.1	8.3	6.0	50.3	18,209	21,608	18.7	12.4	3,053	1,420	1,048	8,510	2.69	72.7	7.2	24.1
Pratt	14.2	10.2	10.0	50.5	9,647	9,653	0.1	-2.8	1,110	952	-430	3,742	2.48	63.3	7.1	31.3
Rawlins	15.4	14.0	13.9	49.5	2,966	2,519	-15.1	-0.4	227	300	63	1,170	2.12	64.2	2.5	31.2
Reno	14.0	10.6	9.2	49.8	64,790	64,511	-0.4	-3.4	5,890	6,097	-1,929	25,015	2.42	65.0	10.5	28.9
Republic	16.6	13.3	14.5	50.6	5,835	4,980	-14.7	-6.3	373	704	17	2,307	2.00	56.7	4.1	40.3
Rice	14.2	10.2	9.1	50.1	10,761	10,082	-6.3	-5.5	973	981	-541	3,932	2.35	66.8	6.5	29.6
Riley	7.7	5.5	4.0	47.5	62,843	71,132	13.2	3.6	8,582	2,808	-3,453	26,686	2.46	54.6	7.2	28.7
Rooks	15.6	11.6	10.6	51.7	5,685	5,181	-8.9	-3.2	519	531	-152	2,144	2.31	64.9	9.1	32.2
Rush	16.3	12.6	12.2	48.7	3,551	3,307	-6.9	-6.5	256	405	-66	1,432	2.13	59.4	5.5	35.5
Russell	15.4	12.6	11.8	50.7	7,370	6,965	-5.5	-0.8	688	733	-9	3,161	2.17	64.1	7.9	28.2
Saline	13.9	9.9	8.1	50.4	53,597	55,609	3.8	-2.2	5,997	4,333	-2,857	22,294	2.41	62.6	11.1	31.2
Scott	12.8	10.3	9.1	49.6	5,120	4,936	-3.6	-0.8	513	450	-105	2,105	2.33	67.7	4.9	24.5
Sedgwick	12.6	8.6	5.9	50.5	452,869	498,358	10.0	3.1	61,799	35,441	-10,909	195,072	2.58	64.5	12.3	30.3
Seward	9.7	5.5	4.3	49.3	22,510	22,950	2.0	-5.1	3,602	1,079	-3,731	7,573	2.96	72.3	15.3	22.8
Shawnee	13.7	10.4	7.8	51.6	169,871	177,934	4.7	-0.2	19,160	14,727	-4,790	71,601	2.42	62.4	10.6	31.9
Sheridan	15.5	11.8	11.3	49.7	2,813	2,544	-9.6	-0.4	235	244	1	1,144	2.16	68.3	5.2	29.4
Sherman	14.9	10.0	9.3	49.8	6,760	6,010	-11.1	-1.8	639	587	-165	2,729	2.15	64.7	10.6	31.1
Smith	17.4	13.7	14.0	50.3	4,536	3,853	-15.1	-6.5	295	486	-60	1,662	2.18	64.0	4.2	32.9
Stafford	16.0	11.0	11.2	49.2	4,789	4,439	-7.3	-5.9	398	448	-211	1,804	2.29	68.2	6.8	27.5
Stanton	13.1	9.0	8.7	50.2	2,406	2,236	-7.1	-11.1	233	156	-331	798	2.61	67.3	2.6	32.2
Stevens	12.3	8.3	7.6	50.5	5,463	5,726	4.8	-2.9	652	360	-470	1,958	2.88	73.6	7.4	23.4
Sumner	15.0	10.4	8.3	49.9	25,946	24,137	-7.0	-4.7	2,214	2,143	-1,222	9,188	2.49	64.7	8.8	32.1
Thomas	13.4	9.2	8.5	51.0	8,180	7,902	-3.4	-2.4	936	601	-529	3,259	2.30	68.5	7.3	28.2
Trego	18.0	14.1	12.4	49.2	3,319	3,006	-9.4	-7.1	257	373	-96	1,389	2.03	62.7	8.1	33.8
Wabaunsee	17.1	11.6	8.4	48.9	6,885	7,055	2.5	-2.2	662	521	-297	2,732	2.50	70.7	6.8	25.5
Wallace	15.2	12.2	11.1	50.1	1,749	1,485	-15.1	1.2	166	144	-6	594	2.64	63.6	3.9	34.2
Washington	15.1	11.4	12.6	48.9	6,483	5,794	-10.6	-6.5	563	593	-348	2,339	2.32	66.2	6.8	30.8
Wichita	14.0	10.5	9.7	49.0	2,531	2,234	-11.7	-5.8	208	193	-143	890	2.39	70.7	7.3	26.4
Wilson	15.0	12.2	9.2	50.5	10,332	9,409	-8.9	-7.9	928	1,007	-665	3,873	2.25	63.1	10.7	30.2
Woodson	16.3	13.9	10.4	49.7	3,788	3,309	-12.6	-3.8	279	408	2	1,523	2.08	56.7	7.0	35.8
Wyandotte	11.8	7.4	4.9	50.4	157,882	157,525	-0.2	5.0	22,385	11,355	-3,148	59,355	2.73	63.9	17.1	30.4
KENTUCKY	13.4	9.7	6.6	50.7	4,041,769	4,339,333	7.4	3.0	456,319	369,344	42,993	1,724,514	2.49	65.9	12.5	28.4
Adair	14.0	10.9	7.7	50.5	17,244	18,661	8.2	3.0	1,723	1,621	435	7,101	2.54	68.5	10.4	29.1
Allen	13.7	10.7	7.0	50.5	17,800	19,968	12.2	5.8	2,045	1,837	957	7,705	2.65	73.9	11.6	23.5
Anderson	13.6	9.5	6.2	51.0	19,111	21,449	12.2	5.7	2,111	1,701	822	8,613	2.54	68.8	9.1	25.9
Ballard	14.6	11.9	9.0	50.2	8,286	8,246	-0.5	-3.2	667	864	-65	3,225	2.49	66.6	9.0	28.1
Barren	13.7	10.0	7.7	51.7	38,033	42,169	10.9	4.8	4,526	4,007	1,513	16,927	2.52	68.4	13.2	27.1
Bath	13.4	10.0	6.8	50.7	11,085	11,585	4.5	6.9	1,334	1,171	636	4,509	2.68	74.5	15.7	20.6
Bell	14.3	11.3	7.9	51.0	30,060	28,691	-4.6	-7.4	2,875	3,154	-1,851	11,063	2.39	63.1	16.2	31.9
Boone	12.5	8.5	5.1	50.5	85,991	118,815	38.2	10.7	13,603	6,728	5,901	46,095	2.75	75.4	11.7	19.8
Bourbon	14.0	10.5	8.4	51.3	19,360	20,010	3.4	0.9	1,892	1,780	79	8,116	2.44	66.7	11.2	26.7
Boyd	14.4	11.1	8.4	50.2	49,752	49,538	-0.4	-4.6	4,649	4,945	-1,988	19,119	2.43	67.5	11.8	28.1
Boyle	12.8	10.6	8.5	50.2	27,697	28,437	2.7	5.8	2,600	2,588	1,628	10,875	2.48	65.4	10.8	30.5
Bracken	15.0	10.2	6.4	49.9	8,279	8,488	2.5	-2.9	809	780	-277	3,427	2.42	64.8	9.6	28.6
Breathitt	15.2	11.0	6.2	50.0	16,100	13,876	-13.8	-8.3	1,341	1,604	-890	5,342	2.42	67.4	14.1	29.8
Breckinridge	15.2	11.8	7.5	49.7	18,648	20,051	7.5	1.7	1,914	1,884	311	7,467	2.64	67.5	8.6	26.0
Bullitt	14.0	9.7	5.9	50.3	61,236	74,308	21.3	9.1	6,551	4,694	4,898	29,014	2.70	73.4	11.3	22.2
Butler	14.3	10.8	8.0	49.8	13,010	12,697	-2.4	0.6	1,255	1,181	7	5,060	2.47	71.0	13.4	25.5
Caldwell	14.0	11.7	9.1	51.8	13,060	12,989	-0.5	-2.1	1,241	1,373	-132	5,309	2.37	71.8	14.7	25.1
Calloway	12.0	9.6	7.3	51.3	34,177	37,190	8.8	5.2	3,239	3,264	1,968	14,757	2.37	58.8	9.8	33.7
Campbell	14.2	9.2	6.4	50.9	88,616	90,338	1.9	3.1	8,887	6,921	890	35,870	2.46	64.2	12.4	29.1
Carlisle	13.9	11.4	10.0	50.7	5,351	5,098	-4.7	-6.4	538	543	-321	1,988	2.43	64.4	6.4	31.4
Carroll	13.7	9.1	6.1	49.6	10,155	10,807	6.4	-0.6	1,318	1,063	-334	3,962	2.61	66.5	12.6	27.5
Carter	13.8	11.1	7.7	50.8	26,889	27,721	3.1	-2.6	2,928	2,580	-1,049	10,460	2.55	70.9	13.9	26.3
Casey	13.2	12.0	8.2	51.5	15,447	15,960	3.3	-0.5	1,627	1,603	-85	6,398	2.41	67.7	7.5	29.1
Christian	9.0	6.8	5.5	46.5	72,265	73,938	2.3	-3.1	12,524	4,880	-9,999	25,275	2.61	67.4	13.8	27.4
Clark	14.0	10.5	7.4	51.2	33,144	35,603	7.4	1.8	3,508	3,317	471	14,216	2.49	68.4	12.9	24.3

1. No spouse present.

Table B. States and Counties — Population, Vital Statistics, Health, and Crime

STATE County	Persons in group quarters, 2018	Daytime Population, 2013-2017		Births, 2018		Deaths, 2018		Persons under 65 with no health insurance, 2016		Medicare, 2018			Serious crimes known to police[2], 2016 Total	
		Number	Employment/residence ratio	Total	Rate[1]	Number	Rate[1]	Number	Percent	Total beneficiaries	Enrolled in Original Medicare	Enrolled in Medicare Advantage	Number	Rate[3]
	32	33	34	35	36	37	38	39	40	41	42	43	44	45
KANSAS— Cont'd														
Neosho	450	15,878	0.95	207	13.0	175	11.0	1,075	8.5	3,547	3,355	192	346	2,132
Ness	70	3,149	1.10	34	12.0	37	13.0	289	13.0	773	756	17	35	1,179
Norton	820	5,557	1.01	62	11.4	68	12.5	343	9.4	1,162	1,116	46	44	800
Osage	194	11,739	0.42	183	11.5	208	13.0	1,213	9.5	3,676	3,254	422	188	1,332
Osborne	100	3,456	0.87	34	9.8	41	11.8	348	12.8	961	942	19	69	1,899
Ottawa	98	4,712	0.57	57	9.8	59	10.2	394	8.3	1,363	1,321	42	103	1,740
Pawnee	1,026	7,224	1.16	65	9.9	77	11.7	408	9.2	1,435	1,403	32	144	2,125
Phillips	68	5,410	0.99	63	11.8	65	12.2	427	10.2	1,457	1,413	44	31	578
Pottawatomie	299	22,465	0.93	396	16.3	193	7.9	1,474	7.2	3,876	3,482	394	343	1,459
Pratt	381	10,129	1.10	120	12.8	94	10.0	788	10.5	2,009	1,969	40	417	4,322
Rawlins	40	2,508	0.99	32	12.8	21	8.4	253	13.6	703	673	30	45	1,804
Reno	3,115	62,218	0.96	649	10.4	700	11.2	5,013	10.3	13,984	13,048	936	2,522	3,990
Republic	103	4,516	0.92	43	9.2	62	13.3	344	10.2	1,365	1,319	46	48	1,031
Rice	651	9,478	0.92	102	10.7	96	10.1	802	10.7	2,083	2,012	71	95	1,035
Riley	9,684	72,071	0.91	923	12.5	363	4.9	5,104	8.7	7,600	7,159	441	1,519	2,009
Rooks	72	5,053	0.96	63	12.6	72	14.4	403	10.2	1,263	1,221	42	14	272
Rush	66	2,996	0.92	35	11.3	27	8.7	228	9.9	856	834	22	78	2,534
Russell	89	6,605	0.89	77	11.1	93	13.5	616	11.5	1,799	1,770	29	140	1,997
Saline	1,470	57,162	1.07	625	11.5	495	9.1	4,811	10.7	11,282	10,311	971	2,204	3,980
Scott	105	4,777	0.92	59	12.0	65	13.3	459	11.3	1,025	997	28	60	1,214
Sedgwick	7,266	527,756	1.07	7,044	13.7	4,494	8.7	48,714	11.2	86,219	66,634	19,585	27,261	5,331
Seward	476	23,777	1.08	397	18.2	116	5.3	4,111	20.6	2,392	2,340	52	391	1,695
Shawnee	4,392	191,702	1.16	2,110	11.9	1,811	10.2	13,191	9.1	38,152	32,521	5,631	9,064	5,096
Sheridan	33	2,495	1.00	33	13.0	19	7.5	302	15.9	577	D	D	6	241
Sherman	102	5,933	0.98	71	12.0	76	12.9	484	10.3	1,299	1,273	26	94	1,581
Smith	56	3,672	0.99	41	11.4	45	12.5	299	11.4	1,129	1,086	43	15	410
Stafford	69	3,877	0.81	49	11.7	48	11.5	492	14.9	958	929	29	35	838
Stanton	47	2,187	1.08	20	10.1	18	9.1	270	16.1	343	D	D	0	0
Stevens	72	5,911	1.07	67	12.1	32	5.8	709	14.9	828	808	20	NA	NA
Sumner	409	20,779	0.76	250	10.9	253	11.0	1,753	9.3	4,983	4,261	722	618	2,652
Thomas	353	8,123	1.06	119	15.4	58	7.5	588	9.2	1,487	1,418	69	145	1,846
Trego	64	2,571	0.81	25	9.0	41	14.7	174	8.1	746	D	D	43	1,483
Wabaunsee	90	5,444	0.56	64	9.3	50	7.2	427	7.7	1,527	1,367	160	98	1,534
Wallace	19	1,548	0.94	25	16.6	10	6.7	116	10.0	351	D	D	0	0
Washington	114	5,074	0.82	66	12.2	84	15.5	511	12.2	1,469	1,420	49	28	506
Wichita	26	2,172	1.01	20	9.5	18	8.6	330	19.3	447	D	D	31	1,455
Wilson	121	8,704	0.96	107	12.3	113	13.0	735	10.8	2,286	2,177	109	161	1,850
Woodson	39	2,682	0.67	34	10.7	45	14.1	277	11.4	753	716	37	61	1,992
Wyandotte	1,335	178,726	1.21	2,616	15.8	1,442	8.7	24,087	17.0	24,232	14,377	9,855	NA	NA
KENTUCKY	131,697	4,446,264	1.01	53,803	12.0	45,778	10.2	218,900	6.0	911,928	631,240	280,688	107,466	2,422
Adair	1,185	17,184	0.73	207	10.8	235	12.2	1,037	7.2	4,305	3,356	949	41	215
Allen	197	18,334	0.72	230	10.9	253	12.0	1,127	6.7	4,440	3,272	1,168	262	1,263
Anderson	108	16,812	0.49	268	11.8	202	8.9	907	4.8	4,460	2,657	1,803	165	748
Ballard	127	7,042	0.67	70	8.8	108	13.5	360	5.7	1,910	1,494	416	62	757
Barren	703	43,014	0.98	550	12.5	517	11.7	2,470	6.9	9,857	7,337	2,520	687	1,568
Bath	103	10,051	0.51	159	12.8	163	13.2	762	7.5	2,819	1,794	1,025	45	365
Bell	945	28,631	1.16	333	12.5	365	13.7	1,560	7.4	6,865	5,360	1,505	755	2,792
Boone	834	148,187	1.32	1,660	12.6	1,001	7.6	4,303	3.8	20,524	12,174	8,350	2,557	1,977
Bourbon	236	18,634	0.85	235	11.6	236	11.7	1,239	7.7	4,482	2,808	1,674	353	1,754
Boyd	2,109	55,869	1.41	472	10.0	587	12.4	1,886	5.0	11,898	8,548	3,350	1,126	2,345
Boyle	3,267	32,924	1.26	321	10.7	323	10.7	1,145	5.3	6,925	4,854	2,071	383	1,276
Bracken	41	6,385	0.44	82	10.0	107	13.0	419	6.0	1,869	1,252	617	52	628
Breathitt	321	12,621	0.83	133	10.5	194	15.2	752	7.0	3,497	2,585	912	28	209
Breckinridge	300	16,887	0.59	254	12.5	210	10.3	1,232	7.7	4,709	3,767	942	84	420
Bullitt	340	64,566	0.63	842	10.4	660	8.1	3,182	4.7	15,225	9,856	5,369	1,477	1,858
Butler	203	11,262	0.71	149	11.7	128	10.0	766	7.4	2,908	1,995	913	105	810
Caldwell	148	12,130	0.88	154	12.1	165	13.0	573	5.8	3,281	2,506	775	318	2,522
Calloway	3,235	39,812	1.07	385	9.8	414	10.6	2,070	7.1	7,730	5,427	2,303	962	2,498
Campbell	3,253	76,877	0.67	1,096	11.8	903	9.7	3,751	4.9	16,555	9,723	6,832	1,789	1,939
Carlisle	60	3,942	0.51	60	12.6	55	11.5	280	7.4	1,271	938	333	24	497
Carroll	325	13,962	1.73	153	14.2	123	11.5	566	6.4	2,335	1,578	757	84	787
Carter	598	24,716	0.72	332	12.3	358	13.3	1,436	6.6	6,640	4,731	1,909	162	600
Casey	476	14,026	0.69	198	12.5	208	13.1	1,004	8.2	3,873	3,037	836	54	343
Christian	6,095	95,654	1.75	1,439	20.1	615	8.6	3,777	6.5	11,218	8,720	2,498	1,789	2,448
Clark	458	34,130	0.90	417	11.5	371	10.2	1,550	5.3	7,983	5,037	2,946	1,287	3,600

1. Per 1,000 estimated resident population.   2. Data for serious crimes have not been adjusted for underreporting; this may affect comparability between geographic areas and over time.   3. Per 100,000 population estimated by the FBI.

Table B. States and Counties — Crime, Education, Money Income, and Poverty

STATE County	Serious crimes known to police[2], 2016 (cont.)[1] Rate — Violent	Property	Education — School enrollment and attainment, 2013-2017 Enrollment[3] Total	Percent private	Attainment[4] (percent) High school graduate or less	Bachelor's degree or more	Local government expenditures,[5] 2014-2015 Total current spending (mil dol)	Current spending per student (dollars)	Money income, 2013-2017 Per capita income[6]	Households Median income (dollars)	Percent with income of less than $50,000	Percent with income of $200,000 or more	Income and poverty, 2017 Median household income (dollars)	Percent below poverty level All persons	Children under 18 years	Children 5 to 17 years in families
	46	47	48	49	50	51	52	53	54	55	56	57	58	59	60	61
KANSAS— Cont'd																
Neosho	277	1,855	4,089	10.5	39.3	19.4	26.2	10,542	23,589	44,402	54.3	2.2	44,073	15.5	22.4	20.8
Ness	67	1,111	627	17.4	43.5	19.0	5.6	12,611	30,761	48,412	51.8	3.1	49,258	11.1	15.1	14.1
Norton	73	727	1,223	6.5	46.6	16.1	10.4	11,276	22,935	50,673	49.6	1.2	47,697	12.3	16.2	16.0
Osage	170	1,162	3,521	7.1	46.7	20.7	30.0	11,046	27,209	54,186	47.2	1.7	53,537	11.7	15.3	13.9
Osborne	138	1,761	718	18.9	44.7	22.3	5.8	13,289	26,559	42,173	55.9	1.8	42,832	12.5	19.9	19.5
Ottawa	34	1,706	1,355	7.6	41.7	22.2	13.9	10,942	28,839	51,797	48.6	1.9	46,585	11.4	14.4	11.7
Pawnee	295	1,830	1,299	11.5	40.1	18.2	12.3	10,210	24,404	46,224	54.6	1.2	47,677	13	17.0	15.2
Phillips	205	373	1,276	6.4	43.1	21.5	9.1	11,480	24,795	46,806	54.6	0.6	47,196	11.6	16.3	15.2
Pottawatomie	238	1,221	6,484	17.5	34.5	33.5	41.3	10,083	27,978	64,410	38.3	2.9	65,956	9.8	10.9	10.5
Pratt	197	4,125	2,355	10.3	34.0	26.4	16.8	9,683	27,063	53,415	47.4	2.8	56,540	11.2	16.1	14.7
Rawlins	200	1,604	479	6.7	35.0	26.7	4.1	12,021	27,615	50,893	48.7	1.2	44,596	11.9	16.2	15.4
Reno	343	3,646	15,212	12.4	41.2	20.0	102.0	10,081	25,267	47,897	52.5	2.6	48,588	13.4	17.1	14.6
Republic	107	923	914	13.6	37.8	23.3	8.2	11,237	27,121	43,489	58.6	1.5	44,247	11.7	16.3	15.4
Rice	120	915	2,621	16.9	40.2	22.5	22.6	11,567	23,355	48,333	51.0	1.3	51,102	12.3	17.4	15.6
Riley	274	1,735	30,306	5.1	21.6	45.5	75.9	10,152	26,619	48,428	51.6	4.0	50,212	20.4	14.0	13.4
Rooks	19	253	1,173	11.8	39.8	25.7	10.2	12,145	25,415	48,352	51.4	2.3	44,086	10.9	13.4	13.0
Rush	130	2,404	640	5.0	39.4	23.1	6.7	11,829	25,983	43,594	54.3	1.9	44,203	12.1	17.2	16.1
Russell	371	1,626	1,278	4.9	40.2	24.2	10.1	12,672	25,686	48,427	52.4	1.3	43,139	14.2	21.3	19.5
Saline	417	3,563	13,814	13.3	42.8	25.0	91.3	10,624	27,951	49,728	50.3	3.1	50,072	11.8	16.5	15.3
Scott	263	951	1,095	20.1	44.9	26.7	9.1	9,389	31,825	62,198	39.1	3.2	59,798	7.6	11.0	10.3
Sedgwick	842	4,489	140,903	15.6	37.1	30.7	848.7	9,979	27,583	52,841	47.2	3.8	54,176	14.2	17.8	16.7
Seward	225	1,470	6,935	3.4	59.5	12.1	55.9	9,597	21,158	47,535	53.3	2.0	46,541	14.9	20.1	18.8
Shawnee	459	4,638	44,290	13.0	39.2	30.4	295.9	10,309	28,584	54,667	45.8	2.7	56,810	11.7	15.3	13.3
Sheridan	0	241	504	7.1	37.9	24.6	6.5	11,098	30,165	56,607	45.2	1.6	51,363	11.5	18.7	17.4
Sherman	185	1,396	1,456	1.1	40.6	18.2	10.3	9,402	25,653	52,030	46.3	1.9	45,991	13.2	20.3	19.0
Smith	27	383	721	4.7	42.6	20.1	8.3	12,936	28,122	45,357	55.9	4.0	41,047	12.8	19.9	18.7
Stafford	168	670	1,010	4.8	39.2	22.6	12.0	12,728	25,941	47,121	52.5	2.6	46,396	13.2	21.8	20.3
Stanton	0	0	613	6.0	48.2	22.6	5.4	11,646	21,062	42,222	59.8	0.4	57,769	10.2	11.9	11.2
Stevens	NA	NA	1,600	8.6	49.1	16.2	15.1	10,933	24,691	57,500	40.8	3.8	56,569	10.3	15.0	13.2
Sumner	163	2,489	6,056	10.5	42.5	20.9	40.5	10,555	25,393	52,695	48.4	1.6	53,212	11.8	16.1	14.2
Thomas	76	1,770	1,850	10.2	35.1	26.5	11.2	10,531	26,718	52,465	46.8	4.1	53,249	11.5	11.8	10.3
Trego	345	1,138	591	9.3	37.5	23.3	4.4	11,012	33,233	55,197	41.9	0.6	46,634	11.6	16.2	17.2
Wabaunsee	156	1,377	1,539	13.8	41.8	22.7	12.0	12,692	25,790	58,947	42.3	0.5	63,690	7.6	9.6	8.8
Wallace	0	0	389	2.8	38.7	26.4	4.4	14,973	29,931	60,000	45.8	3.5	52,621	11.2	15.3	14.6
Washington	72	434	1,150	16.3	45.8	19.1	9.2	11,528	26,927	47,992	53.4	2.0	47,889	10	13.6	13.6
Wichita	47	1,408	525	3.2	45.7	20.3	5.2	11,641	27,111	55,109	48.2	1.2	54,401	11.6	17.7	15.7
Wilson	207	1,643	1,755	6.6	48.3	15.5	18.4	11,111	25,107	44,468	55.8	2.2	41,866	15.3	21.3	19.1
Woodson	261	1,731	586	3.2	46.2	13.7	5.8	11,994	21,419	36,493	61.7	1.2	38,840	15.6	23.3	21.0
Wyandotte	NA	NA	42,296	10.1	54.3	16.7	333.8	10,736	20,192	42,783	58.4	1.0	46,032	18.4	24.6	21.5
KENTUCKY	232	2,190	1,074,127	15.2	47.9	23.2	6,630.3	9,628	25,888	46,535	52.9	3.2	48,332	17.1	22.1	20.6
Adair	16	199	4,997	28.6	60.6	15.8	24.4	8,979	18,408	36,575	65.0	1.0	35,026	22.5	33.5	31.3
Allen	121	1,143	4,337	13.6	59.2	14.4	26.3	8,504	21,652	40,598	58.2	1.8	40,955	21.8	30.2	24.9
Anderson	73	675	5,084	11.6	49.2	20.0	32.2	8,201	24,991	51,681	48.0	2.0	53,113	10.4	14.1	13.2
Ballard	61	696	1,825	11.3	51.3	14.1	13.2	9,274	25,063	42,988	56.6	1.7	44,010	16	23.7	21.4
Barren	119	1,449	10,034	7.9	58.3	16.2	76.8	9,426	20,493	39,658	61.8	1.0	41,477	22.1	32.8	29.5
Bath	16	348	2,818	6.6	64.2	11.7	18.8	8,746	20,059	38,763	62.0	1.8	40,507	23	34.0	32.2
Bell	163	2,629	5,752	6.7	68.7	9.3	46.5	9,412	14,754	23,558	78.2	0.5	28,150	36.7	45.5	43.2
Boone	111	1,866	33,840	16.8	34.2	31.5	190.9	8,689	33,553	72,731	32.6	6.7	78,163	7.1	8.7	8.0
Bourbon	99	1,654	4,355	12.8	52.1	19.0	34.1	9,332	25,994	47,886	51.4	2.2	46,281	16.7	23.0	21.0
Boyd	135	2,209	10,733	10.3	45.1	19.4	70.3	9,416	26,420	45,543	54.0	2.6	40,752	20.1	28.5	26.0
Boyle	97	1,179	7,458	26.7	48.8	23.0	43.8	9,342	23,822	43,076	56.4	3.2	48,290	15.5	19.5	18.2
Bracken	12	616	1,720	13.3	59.6	14.0	13.4	8,558	22,433	40,458	56.4	0.8	49,416	15.6	20.7	19.3
Breathitt	7	202	2,566	13.0	62.5	12.6	24.9	10,278	16,875	25,861	71.8	1.3	27,372	36.2	44.5	44.0
Breckinridge	55	365	4,518	14.6	64.2	9.9	31.0	9,377	20,735	44,057	55.3	0.6	43,148	17.9	25.5	23.9
Bullitt	112	1,746	17,567	14.1	54.0	13.9	111.2	8,288	26,643	59,917	41.2	1.8	62,550	9.2	12.2	11.2
Butler	39	771	2,611	17.9	64.1	11.7	19.3	8,501	21,787	39,362	58.6	1.1	47,146	17.1	23.0	21.8
Caldwell	182	2,340	2,542	6.5	57.4	16.5	17.3	8,099	25,272	46,182	53.1	2.3	42,857	16	24.6	23.9
Calloway	161	2,337	12,956	3.9	43.1	28.8	45.7	9,262	21,757	39,269	60.4	1.6	43,554	16.6	20.6	18.8
Campbell	112	1,827	23,028	21.7	40.8	31.9	116.9	9,798	31,065	57,208	43.5	4.4	61,384	10.9	11.7	11.0
Carlisle	21	477	1,048	7.5	51.3	15.5	7.8	9,675	24,015	38,860	58.8	2.2	42,019	15.1	22.4	21.5
Carroll	66	722	2,329	7.6	64.9	11.8	22.7	10,954	22,296	43,345	58.1	2.1	48,404	20.8	31.3	30.0
Carter	37	563	6,455	15.6	60.7	14.0	42.8	8,980	18,477	35,095	64.9	0.4	37,186	28.2	33.9	32.7
Casey	6	336	3,269	8.2	63.3	12.4	22.0	9,546	18,319	33,031	68.5	0.7	31,395	25.1	33.2	32.6
Christian	205	2,243	18,233	12.2	47.6	16.8	84.6	9,086	21,393	41,849	59.5	2.3	43,124	19.3	27.4	26.9
Clark	173	3,427	7,898	12.5	48.9	21.7	49.3	8,594	26,219	51,547	48.5	2.6	53,784	14.1	20.0	19.0

1. Data for serious crimes have not been adjusted for underreporting; this may affect comparability between geographic areas and over time. 2. Per 100,000 population estimated by the FBI. 3. All persons 3 years old and over enrolled in nursery school through college. 4. Persons 25 years old and over. 5. Elementary and secondary education expenditures. 6. Based on population estimated by the American Community Survey, 2011–2015.

Table B. States and Counties — Personal Income and Earnings

STATE County	Personal income, 2017					Supplements to wages and salaries, employer contributions (mil dol)		Proprietors' income (mil dol)	Dividends, interest, and rent (mil dol)	Personal transfer receipts (mil dol)	Earnings, 2017	Contributions for government social insurance (mil dol)	
	Total (mil dol)	Percent change 2016-2017	Per capita¹ Dollars	Per capita¹ Rank	Wages and salaries (mil dol)	Pension and insurance	Government social insurance				Total (mil dol)	From employee and self-employed	From employer
	62	63	64	65	66	67	68	69	70	71	72	73	74
KANSAS— Cont'd													
Neosho	605	3.8	37,792	1,914	236	49	18	41	93	166	343	23	18
Ness	151	11.8	52,680	353	46	10	3	35	38	30	94	5	3
Norton	219	-1.9	40,179	1,525	97	21	7	23	51	45	148	9	7
Osage	626	1.7	39,664	1,608	94	22	8	40	90	147	164	13	8
Osborne	164	4.1	45,402	856	49	10	4	28	35	38	90	5	4
Ottawa	235	-0.9	40,002	1,550	45	10	3	21	37	51	79	6	3
Pawnee	256	-13.5	38,307	1,826	110	26	8	38	50	65	181	10	8
Phillips	260	-1.4	48,355	599	93	25	7	24	62	57	150	9	7
Pottawatomie	1,272	3.0	53,216	337	411	72	31	94	180	154	609	37	31
Pratt	447	6.2	46,856	724	181	33	14	87	92	83	316	17	14
Rawlins	121	0.0	48,529	587	36	7	3	20	30	29	66	4	3
Reno	2,459	4.5	39,343	1,663	1,088	199	80	211	485	584	1,579	102	80
Republic	207	-5.1	44,049	1,014	65	14	5	37	40	50	122	7	5
Rice	402	0.3	41,642	1,311	162	35	12	54	68	84	263	15	12
Riley	3,039	1.6	40,974	1,409	1,242	283	91	214	729	369	1,829	102	91
Rooks	189	2.0	37,531	1,941	67	15	5	19	44	48	106	7	5
Rush	131	6.1	42,289	1,233	40	9	3	14	28	33	66	4	3
Russell	298	3.1	43,084	1,132	98	24	7	23	62	74	152	10	7
Saline	2,624	3.5	47,945	627	1,260	222	95	424	486	467	2,001	118	95
Scott	323	-2.2	65,178	101	87	14	7	134	52	43	243	8	7
Sedgwick	25,223	2.4	49,101	527	12,629	2,085	964	3,304	5,709	3,833	18,982	1,126	964
Seward	817	0.6	36,873	2,060	456	85	32	139	100	128	711	39	32
Shawnee	7,989	2.4	44,834	923	4,831	807	360	625	1,412	1,714	6,624	412	360
Sheridan	118	-2.7	46,736	734	41	8	3	25	29	23	77	4	3
Sherman	231	2.4	38,942	1,731	96	18	7	12	51	60	133	9	7
Smith	159	1.2	43,367	1,095	45	9	3	27	39	40	85	5	3
Stafford	175	-3.2	41,697	1,302	45	10	3	28	39	40	87	5	3
Stanton	102	-1.6	49,564	495	35	7	3	16	32	15	61	3	3
Stevens	202	0.4	36,020	2,198	73	15	6	38	41	34	131	6	6
Sumner	922	2.5	39,814	1,587	278	52	23	108	138	197	461	28	23
Thomas	318	0.6	40,874	1,422	160	27	12	29	63	59	228	15	12
Trego	132	5.7	45,878	808	48	11	4	20	25	33	83	5	4
Wabaunsee	337	2.9	48,957	543	51	10	4	25	90	57	90	6	4
Wallace	79	10.6	51,915	377	22	4	2	23	14	14	51	2	2
Washington	242		44,208	996	63	15	5	38	51	56	120	7	5
Wichita	131	-17.9	61,745	139	33	6	3	46	32	18	88	3	3
Wilson	374	4.2	43,056	1,136	154	35	12	51	62	99	252	16	12
Woodson	107	1.4	34,012	2,482	23	6	2	5	21	32	36	3	2
Wyandotte	5,303	3.1	32,085	2,743	5,215	823	417	421	625	1,341	6,876	414	417
KENTUCKY	180,827	3.3	40,600	X	90,230	15,488	6,945	11,888	29,449	43,740	124,550	7,860	6,945
Adair	576	3.6	29,562	2,954	155	32	12	24	73	216	223	18	12
Allen	654	3.8	31,222	2,836	166	32	13	54	76	201	265	19	13
Anderson	866	3.4	38,407	1,809	182	36	14	24	115	184	257	20	14
Ballard	296	3.5	36,849	2,067	83	13	7	26	45	85	130	9	7
Barren	1,541	2.8	35,184	2,316	638	113	51	150	215	442	952	64	51
Bath	367	2.9	29,669	2,949	74	15	6	11	40	132	106	10	6
Bell	764	3.4	28,395	3,017	296	63	23	11	94	397	393	32	23
Boone	5,930	4.5	45,358	860	4,310	629	329	252	706	844	5,520	331	329
Bourbon	865	3.3	43,186	1,120	286	47	24	124	156	191	481	28	24
Boyd	1,773	2.6	36,954	2,047	1,178	221	90	70	242	588	1,559	100	90
Boyle	1,087	2.0	36,312	2,149	596	105	48	53	206	294	802	53	48
Bracken	287	2.9	34,728	2,383	54	11	4	12	34	80	81	7	4
Breathitt	421	2.9	32,512	2,686	114	26	9	7	40	219	155	13	9
Breckinridge	668	3.8	33,214	2,592	133	28	10	51	117	207	222	18	10
Bullitt	3,165	4.3	39,440	1,652	974	160	77	149	303	627	1,360	94	77
Butler	431	5.8	33,562	2,545	111	25	9	32	47	142	177	13	9
Caldwell	427	1.7	33,824	2,504	149	27	12	32	64	143	220	16	12
Calloway	1,334	4.0	34,273	2,450	601	140	44	104	229	332	888	53	44
Campbell	4,266	4.1	46,127	782	1,418	231	104	180	676	760	1,933	125	104
Carlisle	207	3.5	42,704	1,184	35	7	3	36	37	55	82	5	3
Carroll	372	-9.2	34,715	2,385	369	58	28	13	47	115	469	29	28
Carter	808	3.0	29,783	2,943	194	39	15	31	91	319	279	24	15
Casey	480	2.4	30,446	2,891	130	30	10	20	58	194	190	15	10
Christian	2,649	2.5	37,622	1,931	3,115	803	301	220	552	623	4,439	200	301
Clark	1,392	2.6	38,608	1,790	649	107	51	67	206	359	875	59	51

1. Based on the resident population estimated as of July 1 of the year shown.

Table B. States and Counties — Earnings, Social Security, and Housing

STATE County	Farm	Mining, quarrying, and extractions	Construction	Manu-facturing	Information; professional, scientific, technical services	Retail trade	Finance, insurance, real estate, and leasing	Health care and social assistance	Govern-ment	Social Security beneficiaries, December 2017 Number	Rate[1]	Supplemental Security Income recipients, 2017	Housing units, 2018 Total	Percent change, 2010-2018
	75	76	77	78	79	80	81	82	83	84	85	86	87	88
KANSAS— Cont'd														
Neosho	0.5	3.3	4.9	19.9	D	8.1	5.8	D	28.8	3,805	238	350	7,731	2.9
Ness	20.1	19.1	3.2	1.5	D	2.4	D	D	21.8	770	268	21	1,726	-0.8
Norton	-0.1	D	3.6	10.7	3.6	6.1	D	6.9	28.3	1,245	229	52	2,547	0.2
Osage	5.1	D	10.7	4.5	D	6.4	D	D	31.2	3,905	248	344	7,599	1.3
Osborne	15.1	D	D	D	D	6.1	D	9	16.9	1,015	281	42	2,181	-1.2
Ottawa	7	0.2	3.9	10.7	D	3.2	12.2	10.6	24.4	1,400	239	95	2,788	0.3
Pawnee	11.9	D	6.5	1.4	2.1	3.8	7.2	8.9	45.2	1,490	223	79	3,152	0
Phillips	1.1	2.1	2.7	19.7	4.3	4.6	D	2.2	25.4	1,470	274	45	3,089	1.3
Pottawatomie	1.5	D	10.6	22.9	4.2	9.4	9.7	D	10	4,040	169	184	9,838	14
Pratt	12.4	5.5	4.5	2.7	3.8	10.2	7.8	D	17.3	2,100	220	121	4,474	-0.9
Rawlins	-6	0.6	6.6	3.7	8	16	D	5.8	20.7	730	292	26	1,460	0.1
Reno	2.2	0.6	5.6	12.3	5.7	6.7	8	14.6	16.9	14,905	238	1,277	28,516	0.9
Republic	20.2	D	6.8	9.5	4.3	5.5	5.1	D	15.9	1,430	305	71	2,881	0.1
Rice	8.5	4.1	3.3	16.5	4.5	3.3	D	D	18	2,210	229	132	4,596	1.1
Riley	0.5	D	5.4	2.1	7.7	5.9	9.8	11.8	39	7,700	104	574	31,337	11.1
Rooks	-3.4	9.2	D	D	3.7	3.9	1.7	5.5	28.5	1,345	267	68	2,750	-0.7
Rush	13.8	D	4	19	D	3	3.9	4.1	23.3	870	280	51	1,846	-1.2
Russell	-1.1	10.7	5.7	17.1	5.2	4.3	5.7	D	17.4	1,915	277	148	3,887	-0.5
Saline	0.9	D	5.6	16	6.6	6.4	7	18.3	11.9	11,850	217	1,075	24,421	1.3
Scott	47.3	0.3	2.2	2.6	D	3	D	D	7.3	1,030	208	51	2,226	1.5
Sedgwick	0.2	D	6	21.4	7.4	5.7	8.5	11.6	12.1	92,220	180	11,032	220,933	4.4
Seward	1.5	3.3	D	D	D	6.5	8.3	D	18.5	2,590	117	337	8,242	2.3
Shawnee	0.1	0.2	5.2	7	8.7	4.8	12.8	15.6	21.4	39,215	220	4,824	80,167	1.3
Sheridan	15.3	2.1	D	D	D	3.7	D	D	23.7	605	239	14	1,255	-0.5
Sherman	0.5	D	3.3	3.1	3.4	10	7.5	D	31.7	1,365	230	120	3,118	
Smith	21.9	D	4.1	1.6	D	5.8	3.7	12.7	18	1,145	312	50	2,239	0.3
Stafford	16	16.4	2.1	3.2	D	1.2	5	D	26.7	1,000	238	57	2,343	1
Stanton	16.3	0.2	D	D	D	3.2	D	D	26.7	350	170	14	991	0
Stevens	18.4	D	5.8	4.2	D	4	9.2	0.2	26.8	895	159	32	2,320	0.6
Sumner	14.1	0.8	3.8	14.5	3.6	4.8	5.7	D	19.2	5,230	226	360	10,989	1.1
Thomas	-5.9	D	6.9	3.2	6.2	10.4	14.9	D	14.8	1,485	191	80	3,602	1.8
Trego	10.9	D	3.1	2.7	D	3.9	D	D	29.5	810	281	29	1,664	-1.1
Wabaunsee	9	3	16.5	9.1	3.4	2.4	D	D	23.2	1,605	233	85	3,316	2.7
Wallace	29.6	0.8	D	D	D	4.1	D	D	16.1	360	236	21	775	-0.8
Washington	19	D	6.3	7.7	D	4	D	5.1	24.2	1,490	272	57	2,935	-0.6
Wichita	50.4	D	D	D	0.3	2.3	D	0.8	16.4	440	207	23	1,049	-0.5
Wilson	-0.8	1.3	7.8	39.6	D	3.4	5.5	D	19	2,460	284	242	4,653	-0.6
Woodson	-9.1	9	5.1	4.2	D	9.4	D	D	31.9	815	259	60	2,023	0
Wyandotte	0	D	6.5	13.1	6.8	4.3	2.6	15.2	20.6	26,385	160	5,282	68,297	2.3
KENTUCKY	0.8	0.4	6	14.8	7.1	6	7.2	12.6	18.4	980,991	220	177,858	1,995,182	3.5
Adair	0.3	0.3	7.9	7	D	11.2	6.4	D	22.5	4,710	242	973	8,620	0.6
Allen	5	0	7	24.5	D	6.1	4	D	16.4	4,900	234	849	9,507	2.1
Anderson	-1.7	D	D	30.2	4	8.9	4.4	4.6	18.5	4,880	216	429	9,462	3.5
Ballard	12.5	0	22.7	12	D	5.1	1.3	4.7	15.3	2,175	271	275	3,924	1.1
Barren	1	0	5.2	19	4.4	9.5	3.8	15	13.3	10,825	247	1,701	19,778	3.1
Bath	-2.9	0	17.7	D	D	4	2	6.7	27.3	3,155	255	856	5,497	1.7
Bell	-0.1	5.4	3.1	12.5	3.1	12.1	5.4	D	22.9	7,590	282	2,847	13,245	0.7
Boone	0	D	4.2	17.7	5.3	6.3	5.3	5.9	8.1	21,155	162	1,646	50,047	8.4
Bourbon	16.3	D	6.5	14.3	D	8.1	4.1	7.9	11.3	4,790	239	619	9,089	1.7
Boyd	-0.1	0.5	8.8	14.7	6.3	7.1	3.3	23.9	12.6	12,655	264	2,499	21,625	-0.8
Boyle	-0.6	D	4	15.8	D	7.2	5	D	12.9	7,245	242	1,147	12,501	1.5
Bracken	-3.6	0	7.5	D	D	2.9	2.7	8	25.4	2,095	253	321	3,880	1
Breathitt	0.2	D	1.6	D	2.1	8.9	4.4	33	33.5	3,835	296	1,950	6,356	2
Breckinridge	6.8	D	15.6	7.5	D	8.2	5.5	11.7	20.6	5,370	267	827	10,820	1.8
Bullitt	-0.2	D	12.7	15.2	3.1	4.9	2.9	4.7	12.3	16,670	208	1,318	31,940	9
Butler	5.8	D	8.4	32	D	3.3	3.9	D	17.9	3,235	252	450	5,965	1.5
Caldwell	2.7	D	5.5	24	D	10.4	5.2	D	14.9	3,495	277	482	6,280	-0.2
Calloway	4.8	D	5.5	16.1	5.1	6.9	4.2	4.8	30.3	8,315	214	842	18,982	5.1
Campbell	0	0	D	10.2	7.1	7.3	4.8	13	21.1	17,095	185	1,849	40,545	2.6
Carlisle	24.1	0	8.7	2.5	2.2	6.4	D	8.3	14.5	1,395	288	170	2,469	1.2
Carroll	0.2	0	3.6	53.8	D	4.6	1.3	D	8.7	2,655	248	521	4,715	0.4
Carter	-1.8	1.1	10.9	13	3.8	15.5	5	D	24	7,220	266	1,600	12,535	1.8
Casey	-0.9	D	8.1	27.7	D	5.7	D	11.4	18.2	4,185	266	898	7,527	0.5
Christian	0.6	0	1.5	9.1	2.2	2.4	1.6	5.2	66.9	12,475	177	2,331	30,007	1.9
Clark	0.3	D	5.8	22.3	6.1	6.4	3.7	11.6	10.5	8,590	238	1,356	15,952	1.6

1. Per 1,000 resident population estimated as of July 1 of the year shown.

Table B. States and Counties — Housing, Labor Force, and Employment

STATE County	Housing units, 2013-2017								Civilian labor force, 2018				Civilian employment[6], 2013-2017		
	Occupied units							Sub-standard units[4] (percent)		Percent change, 2017-2018	Unemployment			Percent	
	Owner-occupied					Renter-occupied									Management, business, science, and arts occupations	Construction, production, and maintenance occupations
	Total	Percent	Median value[1]	Median owner cost as a percent of income		Median rent[3]	Median rent as a percent of income[2]		Total		Total	Rate[5]	Total		
				With a mortgage	Without a mortgage[2]										
	89	90	91	92	93	94	95	96	97	98	99	100	101	102	103
KANSAS— Cont'd															
Neosho	6,521	69.8	77,300	18.7	11.4	601	24.5	3.8	6,010	-0.4	294	4.9	7,418	31.0	31.3
Ness	1,327	82.2	70,500	18.5	10.2	610	18.9	1.4	1,329	-1.8	37	2.8	1,447	32.9	34.1
Norton	1,906	77.0	73,700	18.1	10.9	719	22.9	1.2	2,746	-2.1	59	2.1	2,523	35.9	22.6
Osage	6,604	74.8	107,200	20.0	13.4	633	27.8	2.1	7,945	0.1	304	3.8	7,314	31.8	28.2
Osborne	1,713	71.9	61,300	17.6	10.0	497	20.9	1.2	2,004	-0.2	53	2.6	1,752	38.2	28.9
Ottawa	2,437	83.0	98,600	21.3	12.6	666	23.7	1.8	3,005	-1.4	87	2.9	3,002	34.8	26.5
Pawnee	2,590	70.5	75,600	19.7	11.4	549	21.1	0.5	2,940	-2.7	93	3.2	2,799	41.2	20.4
Phillips	2,326	78.2	76,900	17.8	10.5	545	25.6	2.7	2,800	-0.1	71	2.5	2,770	32.9	28.3
Pottawatomie	8,510	78.4	169,300	19.8	11.5	779	23.7	2.9	12,278	0.9	343	2.8	10,873	40.5	25.4
Pratt	3,742	71.2	87,600	17.4	10.0	709	22.9	2.8	4,952	0.3	137	2.8	4,617	32.9	29.9
Rawlins	1,170	74.3	81,700	19.8	11.5	611	21.7	0.3	1,467	1	31	2.1	1,240	41.9	24.4
Reno	25,015	68.7	96,600	19.2	11.8	698	27.2	3.3	29,916	-0.2	1,075	3.6	29,785	31.4	26.0
Republic	2,307	75.7	60,500	19.1	11.3	543	23.2	1.3	2,401	-2	66	2.7	2,390	38.9	26.9
Rice	3,932	72.6	74,800	18.3	10.1	548	25.5	2.7	5,287	-1.7	155	2.9	4,760	34.7	29.5
Riley	26,686	42.3	189,200	20.6	10.6	937	32.3	4.5	35,429	1	1,022	2.9	35,629	42.6	14.2
Rooks	2,144	79.9	75,400	21.1	11.5	526	21.5	1.8	2,522	1.3	81	3.2	2,495	33.7	26.5
Rush	1,432	77.8	69,900	15.9	10.8	574	30.4	1	1,660	0.8	45	2.7	1,505	35.1	27.0
Russell	3,161	76.4	90,100	17.5	12.5	560	27.4	1	3,352	-4.2	100	3	3,387	34.2	32.5
Saline	22,294	66.6	125,400	21.1	12.2	739	29.3	1.2	30,094	-1.5	924	3.1	27,700	33.1	28.4
Scott	2,105	74.5	135,900	22.3	10.0	830	26.6	3.4	2,858	0.5	57	2	2,564	44.2	30.3
Sedgwick	195,072	63.9	130,900	19.7	10.7	780	28.1	2.4	246,605	0.7	9,356	3.8	244,954	35.8	23.9
Seward	7,573	65.8	98,500	22.9	10.7	722	23.5	6.7	9,554	-2.6	315	3.3	10,866	20.6	44.1
Shawnee	71,601	64.8	127,600	19.0	11.6	762	28.8	2.6	91,125	0	3,184	3.5	84,423	38.2	21.5
Sheridan	1,144	77.7	101,000	17.0	10.4	545	19.3	0.6	1,398	2.2	32	2.3	1,219	40.9	29.9
Sherman	2,729	65.3	86,300	20.9	12.7	708	24	1.1	2,894	0.2	82	2.8	2,866	37.8	24.9
Smith	1,662	77.6	66,200	19.3	10.8	464	23.2	1.1	1,946		49	2.5	1,721	38.5	22.1
Stafford	1,804	83.8	61,800	17.4	10.7	659	23.3	3.1	1,952	-2.3	53	2.7	2,032	35.2	23.5
Stanton	798	78.1	71,900	23.8	10.4	554	23.2	2	1,010	1.3	26	2.6	999	40.1	29.6
Stevens	1,958	72.6	110,000	19.7	10.4	636	24	2.1	2,655	-0.4	75	2.8	2,569	33.0	39.4
Sumner	9,188	73.9	86,800	19.3	12.2	672	24.1	2.1	10,784	0.9	381	3.5	10,759	31.3	31.7
Thomas	3,259	74.4	114,000	18.8	13.1	495	24.7	0.9	4,230	-0.3	110	2.6	4,393	32.5	20.1
Trego	1,389	78.8	84,400	17.9	10.0	587	26	0	1,381	-3.6	44	3.2	1,747	29.1	31.5
Wabaunsee	2,732	84.5	111,900	20.0	13.1	649	23.8	2.2	3,648	0.4	115	3.2	3,376	35.5	25.1
Wallace	594	78.1	88,300	18.1	10.0	478	15.9	0.3	819	-3.4	21	2.6	776	46.0	19.6
Washington	2,339	80.3	75,300	17.5	10.7	448	18.8	1	2,927	-0.7	80	2.7	2,787	30.6	36.1
Wichita	890	70.4	84,000	17.7	13.2	683	18.2	4.2	1,265	8.3	28	2.2	1,095	34.9	36.7
Wilson	3,873	74.0	66,700	19.5	11.0	626	32	2.8	4,001	0.5	176	4.4	4,223	29.7	31.5
Woodson	1,523	81.5	53,200	19.2	14.2	563	23.6	2.4	1,594	0.5	69	4.3	1,500	33.4	35.5
Wyandotte	59,355	57.5	92,800	22.6	14.6	817	30.2	4.2	77,858	0.8	3,753	4.8	73,215	23.5	31.9
KENTUCKY	1,724,514	67.0	130,000	19.6	10.5	713	28.3	2.4	2,061,622	0.4	89,310	4.3	1,938,150	33.3	26.4
Adair	7,101	76.0	85,900	18.8	10.5	503	30.1	4	7,246	1	367	5.1	7,988	28.5	36.0
Allen	7,705	71.9	102,500	22.0	10.0	650	25.6	4.9	8,969	-0.1	336	3.7	8,443	24.5	37.2
Anderson	8,613	76.4	138,600	19.5	10.0	710	27.2	1.3	11,951	1	431	3.6	10,357	31.8	25.9
Ballard	3,225	78.5	102,600	18.8	10.0	611	25.6	2.2	3,583	-1.5	248	6.9	3,394	27.7	31.2
Barren	16,927	66.2	110,400	20.4	11.2	658	28.5	2.9	19,141	0.7	848	4.4	18,377	28.4	35.4
Bath	4,509	73.1	77,900	19.4	10.0	616	30.6	2.2	4,648	-1.6	313	6.7	4,462	26.3	38.3
Bell	11,063	65.0	59,400	22.2	11.8	496	36.1	2.6	8,513	-1.8	540	6.3	7,559	24.6	34.0
Boone	46,095	73.5	183,700	18.3	10.0	940	26.1	1.2	70,741	1.2	2,379	3.4	64,527	39.4	19.6
Bourbon	8,116	62.3	144,900	19.4	10.0	718	27.8	1.3	9,704	-1.9	387	4	9,357	29.4	28.0
Boyd	19,119	69.9	103,900	19.2	10.0	645	30.8	1.1	18,099	-1.2	1,071	5.9	18,235	36.3	22.2
Boyle	10,875	66.5	141,100	19.5	10.7	671	28.8	1.2	12,612	0	559	4.4	12,386	33.0	28.6
Bracken	3,427	72.4	102,300	19.8	11.7	616	30.3	2.7	3,851	0.4	187	4.9	3,498	27.0	36.4
Breathitt	5,342	73.1	50,000	21.8	11.7	478	29	4.3	3,643	-2.7	266	7.3	4,012	29.9	23.1
Breckinridge	7,467	78.1	95,200	19.1	10.0	550	24.4	3.4	7,990	-0.4	429	5.4	7,757	27.1	39.0
Bullitt	29,014	81.6	153,100	20.1	10.5	808	27.6	1.8	42,322	1.1	1,726	4.1	38,391	27.3	32.8
Butler	5,060	72.8	90,400	16.9	10.0	616	27.4	2.6	5,206	0.3	253	4.9	5,177	26.8	40.9
Caldwell	5,309	72.9	95,300	18.4	10.0	548	23.7	1.4	5,419	1.5	256	4.7	5,330	29.2	36.4
Calloway	14,757	63.6	130,100	19.2	11.5	651	35	0.9	18,864	0.4	737	3.9	17,382	31.1	24.2
Campbell	35,870	68.8	160,700	19.3	10.9	799	27.3	1.5	50,530	1.3	1,665	3.3	46,154	39.1	19.8
Carlisle	1,988	78.9	89,200	20.5	10.0	628	28.3	3.5	2,311	-3.1	113	4.9	1,978	27.9	28.2
Carroll	3,962	66.3	103,800	16.5	11.6	625	27.1	6.9	5,270	5.3	217	4.1	4,460	20.1	40.7
Carter	10,460	77.6	83,300	20.5	12.6	567	28.6	3.1	9,894	-0.3	912	9.2	9,584	24.6	29.0
Casey	6,398	80.0	77,600	21.5	11.7	480	23.8	2.4	6,734	0.7	314	4.7	5,769	28.0	37.2
Christian	25,275	47.6	112,200	19.2	10.2	771	29.3	2.9	24,853	1.5	1,304	5.2	24,118	27.8	29.7
Clark	14,216	65.7	139,200	19.8	10.1	699	28	2.2	17,202	-0.5	709	4.1	15,907	33.4	27.5

1. Specified owner-occupied units.   2. A value of 10.0 represents 10 percent or less; a value of 50.0 represents 50 percent or more.   3. Specified renter-occupied units.   4. Overcrowded or lacking complete plumbing facilities.   5. Percent of civilian labor force.   6. Civilian employed persons 16 years old and over.

Table B. States and Counties — Nonfarm Employment and Agriculture

	Private nonfarm establishments, employment and payroll, 2016									Agriculture, 2017			
		Employment						Annual payroll		Farms			Farm producers whose primary occupation is farming (percent)
							Professional, scientific, and technical services					Percent with:	
STATE County	Number of establishments	Total	Health care and social assistance	Manufacturing	Retail trade	Finance and insurance		Total (mil dol)	Average per employee (dollars)	Number	Fewer than 50 acres	1000 acres or more	
	104	105	106	107	108	109	110	111	112	113	114	115	116
KANSAS— Cont'd													
Neosho	446	5,064	1,174	891	815	202	144	171	33,736	687	25.5	9.3	36.3
Ness	137	915	257	38	68	54	24	33	35,730	523	8.2	33.8	39.8
Norton	184	1,784	458	242	198	93	37	65	36,708	328	14.0	39.6	52.1
Osage	247	1,678	484	D	357	116	53	42	25,078	1,042	24.8	12.7	36.1
Osborne	146	1,087	290	106	176	50	26	33	29,959	319	10.7	36.1	46.3
Ottawa	129	842	271	45	107	50	38	25	29,512	438	18.9	28.1	45.7
Pawnee	151	1,973	1,081	D	205	71	79	73	36,787	362	10.8	31.5	39.1
Phillips	235	1,648	266	204	225	116	117	60	36,108	415	11.8	33.3	50.1
Pottawatomie	607	8,699	1,338	1,420	1,690	202	181	341	39,216	774	27.4	14.6	34.4
Pratt	387	3,452	671	119	678	151	115	123	35,772	481	8.9	27.7	46.1
Rawlins	106	632	180	42	88	30	14	23	35,853	298	9.4	49.3	60.3
Reno	1,616	22,381	4,179	3,699	3,234	893	600	805	35,970	1,552	21.1	13.0	37.6
Republic	188	1,418	361	167	204	55	36	40	28,054	561	13.2	23.0	53.6
Rice	273	2,623	357	477	251	134	143	87	33,316	470	17.9	26.6	43.3
Riley	1,608	21,283	3,461	814	4,327	995	1,232	658	30,908	504	31.7	11.7	33.1
Rooks	189	1,477	286	107	210	73	48	47	31,819	412	10.9	32.3	45.5
Rush	99	1,052	152	338	68	40	17	35	33,538	488	10.5	25.4	38.9
Russell	257	1,803	323	98	262	72	46	55	30,546	500	15.0	23.0	38.1
Saline	1,512	27,684	5,107	4,975	4,154	892	1,140	998	36,055	609	25.1	17.1	41.5
Scott	205	1,497	415	50	282	92	55	47	31,594	236	17.8	39.4	58.9
Sedgwick	12,161	227,567	33,526	42,283	30,242	7,250	10,958	10,025	44,053	1,360	40.7	11.4	33.6
Seward	556	8,792	1,070	D	1,351	197	142	315	35,791	282	7.1	27.0	44.8
Shawnee	4,216	80,123	18,478	7,473	10,192	5,466	4,672	3,441	42,944	847	41.4	5.5	34.8
Sheridan	107	674	D	D	84	53	26	26	38,297	318	2.8	49.1	65.0
Sherman	256	1,977	382	68	379	99	64	66	33,275	386	10.6	33.7	54.5
Smith	139	873	263	12	166	59	27	23	26,216	425	11.1	33.9	55.9
Stafford	138	659	204	D	88	61	17	21	31,244	466	12.0	29.2	44.5
Stanton	66	496	D	D	61	50	20	19	38,133	220	2.7	42.3	51.2
Stevens	155	2,176	D	173	252	65	19	76	34,782	377	7.4	27.1	37.9
Sumner	481	4,328	932	849	634	211	68	145	33,580	953	21.9	24.3	43.3
Thomas	342	2,943	475	84	702	137	62	100	33,989	402	8.2	45.8	57.7
Trego	130	888	D	38	128	36	24	29	32,927	343	9.9	37.0	50.1
Wabaunsee	132	799	112	143	95	48	1	24	29,852	638	21.0	16.1	35.3
Wallace	56	356	53	D	40	15	D	13	36,806	281	5.0	39.9	47.0
Washington	211	1,591	397	189	189	70	57	42	26,593	694	13.0	23.2	50.0
Wichita	80	461	D	55	61	24	5	19	41,358	254	10.2	46.9	55.2
Wilson	215	3,699	743	1,005	246	87	49	153	41,327	420	14.3	21.7	49.6
Woodson	84	467	145	D	67	D	10	11	23,606	289	16.3	23.5	55.1
Wyandotte	3,171	70,230	14,555	10,468	7,981	1,109	2,509	3,420	48,692	158	74.7	2.5	32.1
KENTUCKY	92,000	1,603,173	255,345	235,487	214,356	74,742	74,749	65,243	40,696	75,966	40.1	2.5	36.4
Adair	301	4,138	521	564	718	185	50	104	25,175	1,154	30.4	1.1	37.1
Allen	249	3,194	443	514	378	126	111	102	32,033	1,127	36.6	1.8	43.0
Anderson	328	3,585	358	1,098	755	104	97	125	34,930	774	45.7	0.6	31.4
Ballard	124	1,419	107	601	152	17	101	58	40,955	295	33.6	8.1	42.9
Barren	878	14,811	2,426	3,966	2,483	332	269	481	32,496	1,899	42.5	1.5	38.3
Bath	140	1,612	204	D	152	62	22	48	29,694	728	30.1	1.4	33.3
Bell	474	6,854	1,457	1,159	1,485	259	124	207	30,152	110	49.1	1.8	24.0
Boone	3,086	79,697	4,725	13,819	10,100	3,779	1,630	3,410	42,781	721	54.5	1.0	25.7
Bourbon	399	5,236	704	1,434	927	229	237	224	42,692	915	38.6	2.1	45.1
Boyd	1,352	22,665	5,867	1,730	4,152	578	729	1,003	44,262	203	46.8	NA	33.6
Boyle	718	14,916	2,978	2,209	1,802	344	325	473	31,685	602	45.0	2.3	39.5
Bracken	94	911	76	D	134	31	12	29	31,786	531	29.0	0.6	35.8
Breathitt	243	3,055	925	33	458	116	92	90	29,573	160	36.9	1.3	29.2
Breckinridge	308	2,489	478	273	546	165	71	76	30,561	1,357	31.9	2.8	35.8
Bullitt	1,105	19,147	1,350	2,712	2,139	273	360	645	33,664	486	58.4	1.0	31.7
Butler	184	1,892	334	652	232	68	29	59	31,332	642	29.3	4.5	25.3
Caldwell	287	3,838	513	871	725	127	56	113	29,314	475	36.4	5.3	33.5
Calloway	823	14,516	2,308	2,531	1,960	405	291	433	29,851	710	48.9	3.8	36.9
Campbell	1,663	24,559	3,297	2,081	4,155	478	1,122	873	35,553	577	54.8	0.3	32.3
Carlisle	93	656	90	85	113	66	14	19	28,203	273	40.3	7.0	41.7
Carroll	233	5,893	385	2,767	625	64	93	337	57,154	308	25.6	1.0	32.5
Carter	441	4,891	539	700	923	194	117	132	27,031	718	27.7	0.4	38.3
Casey	217	3,259	538	1,523	382	85	156	88	27,133	1,106	33.3	2.1	40.7
Christian	1,356	24,095	3,127	6,616	3,279	655	715	862	35,764	1,137	33.3	6.9	42.4
Clark	745	12,839	1,582	2,825	1,626	293	1,145	483	37,584	871	41.8	2.3	37.7

Table B. States and Counties — **Agriculture**

STATE County	Acreage (1,000) [117]	Percent change, 2012-2017 [118]	Average size of farm [119]	Total irrigated (1,000) [120]	Total cropland (1,000) [121]	Average per farm [122]	Average per acre [123]	Value of machinery and equipment, average per farm (dollars) [124]	Total (mil dol) [125]	Average per farm (acres) [126]	Crops [127]	Livestock and poultry products [128]	Organic farms (number) [129]	Farms with internet access (percent) [130]	Total ($1,000) [131]	Percent of farms [132]
KANSAS— Cont'd																
Neosho	323	4.8	470	0.8	169.9	923,397	1,963	93,313	81.9	119,167	56.0	44.0	2	72.9	1,845	49.5
Ness	668	-1.4	1,278	3.7	404.6	1,385,852	1,084	159,980	60.8	116,216	61.4	38.6	NA	73.0	8,605	91.6
Norton	495	-1.4	1,509	20.3	284.0	2,053,567	1,361	299,003	143.3	436,744	43.0	57.0	NA	69.8	2,110	74.1
Osage	440	-0.6	422	1.3	252.6	840,108	1,992	126,651	92.4	88,677	72.4	27.6	NA	72.6	2,606	52.3
Osborne	437	-0.7	1,370	5.6	228.6	1,932,419	1,410	206,187	62.5	195,922	71.3	28.7	NA	75.5	2,266	81.8
Ottawa	439	4.6	1,003	6.5	242.2	2,017,300	2,011	217,607	108.4	247,436	46.7	53.3	2	74.7	3,278	74.9
Pawnee	474	-1.3	1,310	60.7	397.9	2,171,753	1,658	243,559	307.9	850,519	25.1	74.9	1	68.2	6,089	77.3
Phillips	497	0.5	1,198	6.4	254.1	1,728,534	1,442	208,663	107.6	259,294	54.5	45.5	NA	75.4	1,925	68.4
Pottawatomie	406	-0.9	525	19.6	158.7	1,290,997	2,461	124,388	101.4	130,961	41.3	58.7	NA	80.2	2,520	52.2
Pratt	465	0.1	967	63.8	366.5	1,987,147	2,055	245,812	271.3	564,046	33.6	66.4	NA	72.8	9,324	83.4
Rawlins	604	-0.9	2,025	14.3	356.0	3,123,663	1,542	323,136	100.4	336,748	66.6	33.4	1	84.2	3,971	79.5
Reno	789	-0.1	508	54.1	590.7	1,087,423	2,139	154,602	216.7	139,645	53.5	46.5	NA	69.3	14,557	69.5
Republic	373	3.4	665	40.2	269.1	1,720,315	2,586	200,912	187.5	334,275	51.9	48.1	2	73.4	5,249	77.4
Rice	463	1.2	986	29.9	366.1	2,006,778	2,036	254,152	235.5	501,162	36.0	64.0	1	81.5	6,079	73.8
Riley	214	-1.8	425	3.8	106.1	1,285,194	3,022	137,948	51.2	101,532	63.6	36.4	3	82.7	1,107	49.2
Rooks	559	1.3	1,356	5.7	320.2	1,696,528	1,251	189,770	76.6	185,934	64.1	35.9	NA	77.7	4,218	81.3
Rush	448	-1.1	919	8.6	323.2	1,193,377	1,299	146,600	59.5	121,994	69.4	30.6	NA	68.4	8,957	82.0
Russell	492	13.1	985	0.5	263.3	1,318,319	1,339	125,089	50.1	100,106	65.9	34.1	NA	70.4	5,057	79.6
Saline	358	-1.7	588	4.9	223.3	1,394,788	2,371	157,229	73.6	120,823	52.8	47.2	1	77.0	4,352	71.8
Scott	460	1.5	1,951	29.1	365.7	2,955,605	1,515	503,414	1,135.0	4,809,487	7.7	92.3	7	79.2	6,872	74.2
Sedgwick	497	2.0	365	40.4	408.9	1,264,948	3,464	135,560	118.9	87,440	79.9	20.1	1	79.9	7,283	52.6
Seward	361	-10.2	1,279	95.5	263.7	1,803,833	1,410	305,603	424.7	1,506,021	18.9	81.1	NA	69.9	7,997	76.2
Shawnee	202	3.8	238	14.7	126.5	712,656	2,993	88,748	49.2	58,035	79.8	20.2	2	81.3	1,312	33.4
Sheridan	512	-8.9	1,610	68.4	358.5	2,518,737	1,564	431,777	348.9	1,097,022	25.4	74.6	1	83.6	6,021	87.4
Sherman	618	4.0	1,602	97.1	491.6	2,821,024	1,761	358,514	139.2	360,567	72.8	27.2	4	74.6	8,255	78.2
Smith	541	8.2	1,274	7.4	363.2	2,431,582	1,909	275,597	129.3	304,144	75.9	24.1	5	84.0	4,089	86.4
Stafford	494	-1.0	1,059	76.4	393.0	1,909,862	1,803	300,164	198.6	426,120	41.5	58.5	NA	74.2	8,445	83.9
Stanton	435	1.4	1,978	54.3	396.1	2,105,893	1,064	364,126	133.5	606,786	54.5	45.5	NA	80.5	9,689	88.2
Stevens	455	0.0	1,208	138.4	370.0	1,675,641	1,387	330,668	340.6	903,358	32.3	67.7	NA	71.6	9,552	86.5
Sumner	758	5.3	795	25.7	630.3	1,461,530	1,838	204,872	155.7	163,348	87.8	12.2	NA	77.8	8,737	70.3
Thomas	670	-0.8	1,667	81.4	569.5	2,911,418	1,747	417,933	251.1	624,515	52.6	47.4	NA	84.8	6,720	79.6
Trego	515	15.4	1,503	5.5	276.3	1,714,222	1,141	222,541	57.2	166,706	59.5	40.5	NA	73.2	4,819	82.2
Wabaunsee	379	-4.4	594	8.7	114.2	1,144,196	1,927	113,289	63.1	98,975	40.0	60.0	NA	80.9	1,949	48.9
Wallace	446	-8.6	1,587	33.9	303.1	2,144,593	1,352	252,476	81.8	291,050	68.3	31.7	2	74.0	5,388	81.5
Washington	526	7.3	757	13.9	336.7	1,837,799	2,426	218,194	182.0	262,218	47.9	52.1	NA	76.9	4,929	80.3
Wichita	438	-5.6	1,724	40.9	367.9	2,416,112	1,401	385,925	559.3	2,202,157	12.8	87.2	16	76.0	6,749	84.3
Wilson	287	12.6	683	1.8	180.2	1,329,365	1,947	182,949	62.3	148,298	79.8	20.2	NA	71.2	1,941	51.0
Woodson	283	-4.0	979	D	135.4	1,627,566	1,662	184,288	52.6	181,834	52.8	47.2	2	78.2	1,573	55.4
Wyandotte	12	3.2	78	0.6	8.8	528,919	6,742	73,098	5.3	33,380	90.5	9.5	2	82.9	52	4.4
KENTUCKY	12,962	-0.7	171	83.9	6,630.4	643,019	3,769	82,740	5,737.9	75,533	44.3	55.7	227	72.4	126,697	22.2
Adair	172	1.1	149	0.0	76.8	448,542	3,008	72,779	69.4	60,101	26.2	73.8	1	68.5	2,151	33.6
Allen	169	15.8	150	0.2	74.2	518,199	3,462	70,602	88.6	78,613	26.4	73.6	8	68.1	2,489	24.2
Anderson	82	1.0	106	0.0	29.1	392,778	3,713	53,625	12.3	15,926	34.6	65.4	6	67.8	276	4.9
Ballard	94	-12.0	320	D	75.3	1,155,670	3,614	205,371	70.6	239,366	54.0	46.0	NA	87.5	1,653	49.8
Barren	254	2.1	134	0.1	141.4	481,503	3,602	90,193	127.2	66,982	38.3	61.7	NA	77.6	2,218	26.1
Bath	127	-10.6	175	0.0	46.7	412,199	2,360	61,331	18.3	25,161	30.8	69.2	4	76.2	217	6.2
Bell	15	87.3	137	0.0	3.4	273,172	1,990	43,893	0.5	4,591	48.5	51.5	NA	68.2	10	9.1
Boone	79	17.2	109	0.1	36.6	655,823	6,004	58,670	15.4	21,315	75.2	24.8	2	73.0	440	9.0
Bourbon	171	-7.0	187	0.6	74.9	1,061,516	5,684	104,627	209.6	229,030	21.9	78.1	3	76.2	695	17.9
Boyd	19	-10.7	96	0.0	3.5	230,681	2,405	57,311	1.2	5,842	38.0	62.0	NA	83.3	5	3.0
Boyle	89	-12.7	147	0.0	36.8	547,715	3,720	64,909	31.3	52,056	20.6	79.4	7	71.9	251	12.5
Bracken	87	0.0	164	0.1	32.4	408,483	2,498	60,419	10.7	20,190	60.2	39.8	1	64.6	84	10.0
Breathitt	23	4.4	145	0.0	3.6	227,411	1,569	54,188	0.5	3,175	59.4	40.6	NA	72.5	21	13.8
Breckinridge	275	5.9	203	0.1	126.8	625,871	3,087	92,986	99.4	73,279	47.0	53.0	6	68.8	3,162	37.1
Bullitt	44	-3.7	91	D	19.3	471,740	5,161	46,835	6.2	12,848	69.8	30.2	NA	78.8	41	2.5
Butler	147	-3.8	229	0.2	75.6	605,594	2,648	78,210	48.9	76,221	55.8	44.2	NA	65.1	2,423	34.6
Caldwell	130	-2.5	274	6.2	86.5	915,071	3,339	122,658	45.1	95,038	89.0	11.0	NA	71.8	2,555	40.8
Calloway	136	-23.0	191	2.9	102.5	786,844	4,122	115,703	97.7	137,631	60.0	40.0	NA	77.9	2,938	57.3
Campbell	46	9.3	80	0.0	15.9	404,186	5,060	51,900	7.1	12,334	48.3	51.7	NA	77.8	28	3.6
Carlisle	88	-10.8	322	1.7	73.1	1,224,443	3,798	170,980	67.6	247,681	56.3	43.7	NA	68.1	1,602	65.2
Carroll	51	-5.0	165	0.0	17.9	560,794	3,393	55,839	5.8	18,867	57.6	42.4	NA	68.8	140	10.4
Carter	92	-13.1	128	0.0	23.4	247,720	1,933	49,400	6.9	9,586	31.9	68.1	4	68.4	153	5.0
Casey	179	0.1	162	0.1	65.4	379,677	2,343	60,628	32.2	29,071	50.2	49.8	14	66.3	581	23.1
Christian	346	-4.1	304	5.1	245.8	1,464,184	4,817	152,416	205.3	180,542	81.1	18.9	13	56.6	6,215	42.9
Clark	147	7.2	169	0.1	66.4	749,313	4,431	74,443	34.0	39,068	45.5	54.5	2	78.5	289	10.1

Table B. States and Counties — Water Use, Wholesale Trade, Retail Trade, and Real Estate

STATE County	Water use, 2015		Wholesale Trade[1], 2012				Retail Trade[2], 2012				Real estate and rental and leasing,[2] 2012			
	Public supply water withdrawn (mil gal/day)	Public supply gallons withdrawn per person per day	Number of establishments	Number of employees	Sales (mil dol)	Average payroll (mil dol)	Number of establishments	Number of employees	Sales (mil dol)	Average payroll (mil dol)	Number of establishments	Number of employees	Sales (mil dol)	Average payroll (mil dol)
	133	134	135	136	137	138	139	140	141	142	143	144	145	146
KANSAS— Cont'd														
Neosho	1.08	66.1	28	223	96.2	8.2	86	800	197.7	18.8	11	18	2.0	0.4
Ness	0.32	106.5	16	D	D	D	19	98	15.4	1.6	1	D	D	D
Norton	0.75	135.1	8	68	38.3	2.5	27	183	51.2	3.9	1	D	D	D
Osage	1.52	95.9	15	73	48.6	2.9	42	360	74.0	5.8	5	D	D	D
Osborne	0.45	122.2	14	136	157.7	5.9	31	212	46.6	3.2	NA	NA	NA	NA
Ottawa	0.53	88.7	10	D	D	D	14	79	16.2	1.3	3	2	1.3	0.1
Pawnee	0.94	137.5	9	100	130.3	5.0	28	224	50.1	4.7	4	16	1.9	0.3
Phillips	0.98	180.5	13	63	69.7	2.8	35	227	51.5	4.1	1	D	D	D
Pottawatomie	6.22	267.0	30	549	224.8	23.5	81	1,819	338.9	48.4	18	D	D	D
Pratt	1.67	172.3	25	190	230.6	9.2	54	734	173.3	16.4	13	36	2.7	0.6
Rawlins	0.30	119.7	9	109	108.6	6.4	15	103	25.1	1.8	1	D	D	D
Reno	7.61	119.4	84	D	D	D	265	3,345	818.1	74.6	67	167	26.8	4.6
Republic	0.65	137.6	15	120	181.0	3.9	39	237	48.2	4.2	2	D	D	D
Rice	1.16	116.3	18	113	113.7	4.9	39	280	50.0	4.7	3	5	0.5	0.1
Riley	3.03	40.3	26	176	82.3	7.3	272	4,389	903.9	81.6	111	D	D	D
Rooks	0.68	131.4	17	159	178.2	6.9	28	200	69.2	3.8	2	D	D	D
Rush	0.51	162.9	14	74	58.6	2.9	10	65	29.1	1.8	NA	NA	NA	NA
Russell	0.44	62.5	14	114	101.2	4.3	39	267	76.5	4.7	8	25	3.1	0.6
Saline	5.90	105.9	95	1,195	996.5	54.7	250	3,989	1,120.4	87.4	64	208	52.5	6.4
Scott	0.84	169.2	19	126	192.1	6.1	33	223	56.8	3.9	4	3	0.5	0.1
Sedgwick	51.98	101.6	589	8,367	8,308.4	478.6	1,720	27,362	7,201.5	646.4	554	3,997	582.4	133.0
Seward	4.87	210.3	36	407	264.4	19.7	91	1,262	317.1	28.5	20	54	10.3	2.1
Shawnee	14.34	80.2	154	1,992	1,376.1	100.0	653	9,678	2,364.3	212.6	202	903	134.7	26.3
Sheridan	0.48	191.1	14	124	160.6	7.1	19	89	21.0	1.6	NA	NA	NA	NA
Sherman	1.34	224.0	23	225	341.0	9.3	34	409	132.3	8.9	4	D	D	D
Smith	0.49	132.3	10	134	128.2	4.8	24	169	67.4	3.4	2	D	D	D
Stafford	0.35	82.6	8	D	D	D	17	125	34.8	2.3	1	D	D	D
Stanton	0.40	193.1	9	D	D	D	5	D	D	D	1	D	D	D
Stevens	1.37	236.0	11	95	128.0	4.2	14	144	37.0	3.3	2	D	D	D
Sumner	2.10	89.2	28	167	157.4	7.0	65	592	159.8	11.1	12	D	D	D
Thomas	1.27	160.7	28	296	388.2	16.2	63	666	233.5	14.3	8	34	8.5	0.8
Trego	0.68	232.3	11	78	104.2	2.7	24	154	47.7	3.1	3	D	D	D
Wabaunsee	0.54	77.7	4	34	20.5	1.5	18	88	36.7	1.7	4	D	D	D
Wallace	0.22	144.9	5	D	D	D	7	42	7.6	1.0	2	D	D	D
Washington	0.78	139.3	21	183	264.8	6.3	36	215	45.6	4.1	6	9	0.4	0.0
Wichita	0.29	134.4	11	93	111.4	3.8	14	70	19.8	1.5	NA	NA	NA	NA
Wilson	1.36	153.6	5	20	31.7	0.7	43	234	57.7	4.5	3	3	0.2	0.0
Woodson	0.30	96.3	5	44	25.9	1.7	17	69	22.0	1.7	3	D	D	D
Wyandotte	62.15	380.4	225	5,758	5,611.1	302.2	452	6,929	1,769.4	172.6	136	593	112.2	20.2
KENTUCKY	552.83	124.9	3,690	57,630	71,745.9	3,090.3	15,224	202,615	54,870.0	4,619.2	3,534	18,250	4,845.5	637.3
Adair	0.00	0.0	15	72	42.1	1.6	64	691	204.3	16.2	5	D	D	D
Allen	0.95	46.0	9	D	D	D	59	410	111.3	8.4	9	23	2.4	0.6
Anderson	2.21	100.6	6	33	10.1	1.4	51	738	188.9	15.4	14	49	4.3	1.0
Ballard	0.58	70.6	4	D	D	D	26	162	57.6	3.6	3	D	D	D
Barren	7.76	178.1	39	D	D	D	188	2,193	562.8	49.5	23	71	9.9	1.6
Bath	0.00	0.0	3	D	D	D	31	182	47.8	3.8	8	D	D	D
Bell	3.83	140.1	18	189	212.9	5.9	128	1,515	365.1	31.2	19	71	9.2	1.6
Boone	0.04	0.3	170	6,614	21,688.2	542.7	470	9,132	2,564.6	208.6	102	719	175.3	25.2
Bourbon	2.10	104.4	4	D	D	D	65	876	248.2	21.8	10	16	4.0	0.5
Boyd	11.09	229.5	65	904	1,288.6	39.3	239	3,719	1,010.4	78.8	45	408	52.6	14.6
Boyle	5.58	187.2	20	140	114.1	5.7	134	1,717	431.4	39.6	23	66	8.7	1.5
Bracken	0.65	78.1	2	D	D	D	18	131	25.6	2.2	2	D	D	D
Breathitt	1.41	104.6	1	D	D	D	45	499	118.3	10.4	8	21	2.6	0.5
Breckinridge	1.80	89.9	8	72	36.0	2.3	55	543	148.2	12.2	9	23	2.2	0.8
Bullitt	0.00	0.0	28	564	519.7	22.0	144	1,550	586.4	36.0	31	118	19.6	4.0
Butler	1.21	93.5	6	D	D	D	33	232	49.9	4.3	4	5	0.3	0.1
Caldwell	0.00	0.0	9	D	D	D	57	687	159.9	15.0	6	9	1.7	0.3
Calloway	3.47	90.5	39	D	D	D	153	1,987	523.8	41.4	37	188	20.8	4.5
Campbell	26.34	286.1	60	1,036	835.3	60.6	265	4,285	1,105.2	94.3	62	544	93.9	26.4
Carlisle	0.14	28.7	4	20	4.2	0.5	12	81	19.9	1.6	7	8	2.3	0.2
Carroll	1.87	174.8	8	53	17.0	1.8	49	629	187.8	13.7	3	D	D	D
Carter	4.09	150.6	11	289	209.6	7.6	96	881	272.8	17.6	13	D	D	D
Casey	1.01	63.9	12	136	33.7	3.1	56	375	83.1	6.7	4	11	0.5	0.1
Christian	12.19	166.3	67	886	1,060.4	33.1	249	3,239	1,019.9	77.6	58	D	D	D
Clark	6.90	193.0	34	623	873.0	27.9	127	1,623	471.5	37.0	28	71	12.0	1.7

1 Merchant wholesalers, except manufacturers' sales branches and offices.   2. Employer establishments.

Table B. States and Counties — Professional Services, Manufacturing, and Accommodation and Food Services

STATE County	Professional, scientific, and technical services, 2012				Manufacturing, 2012				Accommodation and food services, 2012			
	Number of establishments	Number of employees	Sales (mil dol)	Average payroll (mil dol)	Number of establishments	Number of employees	Receipts (mil dol)	Annual payroll (mil dol)	Number of establishments	Number of employees	Receipts (mil dol)	Annual payroll (mil dol)
	147	148	149	150	151	152	153	154	155	156	157	158
KANSAS— Cont'd												
Neosho	33	123	42.9	5.5	31	922	223.1	39.6	27	D	D	D
Ness	5	20	1.7	0.5	4	23	7.5	1.0	7	D	D	D
Norton	14	46	3.8	0.8	5	D	D	D	13	140	6.1	1.8
Osage	17	54	6.0	1.6	3	D	D	D	20	D	D	D
Osborne	7	42	12.6	1.6	6	113	D	4.5	12	D	D	D
Ottawa	14	D	D	D	8	84	D	2.2	10	41	1.2	0.3
Pawnee	16	74	8.1	2.2	NA	NA	NA	NA	16	153	5.5	1.5
Phillips	16	97	11.6	4.0	10	178	D	11.1	14	140	4.3	1.0
Pottawatomie	52	198	15.5	5.8	30	1,368	377.5	74.6	35	422	17.7	4.5
Pratt	28	115	11.7	4.7	9	78	42.6	3.4	32	438	25.0	5.1
Rawlins	11	16	1.3	0.3	7	31	9.4	1.2	5	25	0.5	0.1
Reno	102	642	61.8	24.5	87	3,752	1,232.8	168.4	117	2,141	91.6	26.3
Republic	13	25	3.4	0.6	10	168	D	6.3	11	D	D	D
Rice	16	143	9.4	2.6	14	328	291.2	14.9	22	D	D	D
Riley	146	D	D	D	30	480	94.5	18.9	166	3,903	146.8	42.1
Rooks	13	43	4.9	1.9	6	130	D	4.1	17	88	3.1	0.8
Rush	6	14	1.4	0.7	6	320	D	11.3	7	36	1.5	0.3
Russell	12	44	4.7	1.2	7	114	D	5.1	18	283	11.6	3.3
Saline	112	D	D	D	75	5,497	D	237.2	137	3,047	119.6	31.8
Scott	19	52	7.7	1.6	6	20	D	1.0	14	D	D	D
Sedgwick	1,155	10,100	1,586.7	570.9	533	40,629	15,547.1	2,316.4	1,102	22,151	1,029.8	287.6
Seward	22	139	12.0	5.0	7	D	D	D	45	789	40.4	10.4
Shawnee	449	D	D	D	105	5,291	2,588.3	244.4	362	D	D	D
Sheridan	3	16	1.0	0.3	3	6	D	D	6	D	D	D
Sherman	22	79	6.6	1.9	5	46	D	2.1	25	D	D	D
Smith	8	21	2.6	0.4	6	107	D	3.3	8	D	D	D
Stafford	6	11	2.0	0.7	NA	NA	NA	NA	10	D	D	D
Stanton	5	16	1.2	0.4	NA	NA	NA	NA	4	D	D	D
Stevens	11	40	3.3	0.9	4	22	D	1.9	12	144	5.0	1.3
Sumner	32	114	13.9	5.6	37	827	D	35.6	42	458	19.3	5.0
Thomas	28	65	7.2	2.1	9	45	D	1.8	31	464	21.8	6.2
Trego	8	24	1.4	0.4	6	41	D	1.4	11	119	4.8	1.2
Wabaunsee	7	8	1.2	0.3	7	D	D	D	8	30	1.3	0.2
Wallace	3	D	D	D	NA	NA	NA	NA	3	D	D	D
Washington	10	24	3.4	0.8	8	174	35.1	5.4	12	110	3.2	0.8
Wichita	4	6	0.3	0.1	4	62	D	2.3	4	D	D	D
Wilson	13	34	4.1	1.1	19	888	181.5	35.0	20	D	D	D
Woodson	5	D	D	D	3	13	D	0.5	8	D	D	D
Wyandotte	191	2,703	305.9	93.5	174	10,537	11,105.9	666.4	265	5,206	284.6	75.1
KENTUCKY	8,101	62,851	7,782.5	2,816.7	3,782	213,545	129,284.4	10,140.1	7,678	156,965	7,500.1	2,083.5
Adair	17	D	D	D	25	323	153.1	10.9	19	D	D	D
Allen	7	84	3.4	1.7	10	D	D	D	16	D	D	D
Anderson	29	96	11.1	3.1	26	1,130	746.5	70.8	30	403	20.4	5.5
Ballard	10	D	D	D	11	678	D	49.0	10	D	D	D
Barren	47	265	22.5	7.9	45	3,480	929.5	139.8	86	1,554	71.9	18.6
Bath	10	D	D	D	8	D	D	4.8	12	D	D	D
Bell	29	104	9.2	3.3	19	1,075	304.4	34.6	44	855	36.7	9.5
Boone	224	2,184	228.4	72.6	188	12,910	5,069.7	653.0	286	D	D	D
Bourbon	32	321	35.0	14.7	24	1,731	1,066.6	78.2	27	D	D	D
Boyd	96	720	73.9	33.4	34	2,798	D	218.5	120	2,704	129.4	35.0
Boyle	55	275	34.6	10.2	22	1,881	673.6	77.7	61	1,325	59.6	17.2
Bracken	4	12	0.6	0.3	NA	NA	NA	NA	8	D	D	D
Breathitt	10	D	D	D	5	25	D	1.0	10	D	D	D
Breckinridge	19	77	6.0	2.0	13	248	29.7	9.4	15	195	8.7	2.4
Bullitt	77	336	31.4	11.4	42	2,117	811.5	85.7	90	1,930	82.9	22.4
Butler	10	31	1.6	0.7	13	573	185.8	24.0	13	D	D	D
Caldwell	18	45	3.5	0.8	12	864	391.2	31.8	25	393	13.2	3.5
Calloway	65	357	29.6	12.5	30	2,548	828.7	93.4	87	1,679	60.4	16.1
Campbell	146	950	125.1	41.8	78	2,651	994.7	123.9	208	D	D	D
Carlisle	2	D	D	D	4	80	10.4	1.8	6	31	1.3	0.3
Carroll	16	93	10.0	4.6	13	2,452	D	177.2	28	D	D	D
Carter	28	111	6.9	2.6	15	791	253.5	23.6	32	636	28.1	7.3
Casey	10	D	D	D	31	1,266	237.7	28.4	12	192	7.6	2.6
Christian	111	958	100.0	41.0	72	4,647	1,894.8	207.8	113	D	D	D
Clark	55	293	31.4	13.5	40	2,378	1,016.0	108.4	58	1,148	56.5	15.6

Health Care and Social Assistance, Other Services, Nonemployer Businesses, and Residential Construction

STATE County	Health care and social assistance, 2012				Other services, 2012				Nonemployer businesses, 2016		Value of residential construction authorized by building permits, 2018	
	Number of establishments	Number of employees	Receipts (mil dol)	Annual payroll (mil dol)	Number of establishments	Number of employees	Receipts (mil dol)	Annual payroll (mil dol)	Number	Receipts (mil dol)	New construction ($1,000)	Number of housing units
	159	160	161	162	163	164	165	166	167	168	169	170
KANSAS— Cont'd												
Neosho	52	1,148	94.8	36.3	31	102	8.7	1.7	1,073	38.3	415	3
Ness	9	257	15.5	7.4	14	D	D	D	300	10.9	300	1
Norton	22	497	26.3	13.1	11	D	D	D	426	14.0	185	1
Osage	27	1,648	40.6	25.0	18	D	D	D	1,025	39.9	4,896	49
Osborne	13	334	16.2	8.1	10	33	4.5	0.9	385	10.6	400	1
Ottawa	12	D	D	D	11	D	D	D	502	19.3	667	8
Pawnee	16	1,210	87.4	43.8	14	30	2.7	0.5	420	19.1	0	0
Phillips	19	346	21.3	10.5	25	84	11.0	1.6	517	16.2	95	1
Pottawatomie	50	1,048	78.1	29.6	53	152	14.6	3.8	1,795	86.5	38,078	143
Pratt	36	713	64.2	27.4	34	107	9.5	2.3	837	33.9	0	0
Rawlins	9	210	12.3	5.8	7	11	1.2	0.2	258	10.6	847	4
Reno	176	4,895	441.4	176.7	115	514	46.5	12.0	3,783	133.9	10,464	64
Republic	15	296	16.8	8.1	15	42	4.0	0.8	406	13.4	25	1
Rice	20	400	22.1	11.7	19	62	8.2	1.7	636	19.1	1,963	9
Riley	180	3,201	313.2	112.9	119	1,100	208.7	44.9	3,467	145.7	28,429	98
Rooks	12	245	17.8	7.2	10	39	3.5	0.7	567	20.2	390	2
Rush	7	163	9.1	3.7	5	D	D	D	267	8.5	0	0
Russell	13	132	8.1	3.6	18	71	7.4	1.7	848	37.6	1,581	10
Saline	181	D	D	D	113	D	D	D	3,402	142.9	7,671	38
Scott	11	341	19.6	10.4	17	42	6.5	1.0	440	16.0	1,075	3
Sedgwick	1,358	34,266	3,501.4	1,450.6	796	5,733	677.1	172.7	32,112	1,473.8	274,307	1,710
Seward	74	1,079	91.4	35.5	44	166	23.0	4.5	1,272	75.9	3,447	33
Shawnee	523	16,404	1,706.2	740.6	371	3,580	322.3	102.6	9,556	419.2	45,218	201
Sheridan	7	D	D	D	10	58	1.8	0.3	288	13.3	NA	NA
Sherman	38	353	23.9	11.7	20	71	7.4	1.7	512	17.5	0	0
Smith	7	D	D	D	13	D	D	D	328	9.7	0	0
Stafford	15	168	10.1	4.7	13	21	1.7	0.3	386	14.7	2,029	11
Stanton	3	D	D	D	5	D	D	D	195	9.1	0	0
Stevens	6	D	D	D	8	D	D	D	361	17.4	0	0
Sumner	58	947	58.2	25.4	39	116	9.9	2.6	1,452	50.6	2,553	27
Thomas	34	407	33.1	13.4	29	121	10.8	2.9	805	28.7	754	5
Trego	6	D	D	D	9	22	1.7	0.5	312	12.1	0	0
Wabaunsee	8	D	D	D	6	D	D	D	490	20.9	2,371	12
Wallace	4	D	D	D	6	D	D	D	166	5.0	0	0
Washington	25	317	16.3	7.6	19	D	D	D	473	19.3	0	0
Wichita	6	D	D	D	8	D	D	D	191	8.1	0	0
Wilson	33	695	46.6	18.8	17	35	3.8	0.8	595	19.2	935	4
Woodson	10	126	5.7	2.1	5	D	D	D	295	10.8	658	6
Wyandotte	320	13,552	1,568.6	707.1	222	1,320	270.7	42.0	7,496	308.7	40,673	232
KENTUCKY	11,425	251,878	26,264.7	10,184.1	5,849	38,364	4,071.4	1,090.0	285,053	12,267.2	2,267,765	13,826
Adair	36	739	48.8	20.2	14	D	D	D	1,571	64.0	0	0
Allen	23	D	D	D	17	D	D	D	1,477	61.0	1,425	16
Anderson	34	329	19.1	8.4	30	84	8.6	2.3	1,509	51.4	16,265	89
Ballard	6	D	D	D	5	D	D	D	453	12.2	NA	NA
Barren	105	D	D	D	59	223	14.9	4.7	3,295	128.7	32,011	198
Bath	9	296	10.1	4.3	8	D	D	D	805	25.4	0	0
Bell	78	D	D	D	35	154	11.2	2.9	1,339	39.2	3,547	34
Boone	243	4,772	446.2	181.8	180	D	D	D	7,608	332.7	104,419	702
Bourbon	47	714	59.3	22.2	21	D	D	D	1,335	57.7	9,627	42
Boyd	245	7,292	993.0	372.3	96	D	D	D	2,444	98.2	421	4
Boyle	132	2,917	297.4	130.9	53	208	16.8	4.2	2,010	69.1	6,234	34
Bracken	8	D	D	D	5	D	D	D	539	18.1	NA	NA
Breathitt	48	1,277	97.7	42.7	10	34	5.2	1.3	616	18.2	0	0
Breckinridge	31	589	39.9	13.5	19	38	3.7	0.8	1,291	57.3	380	3
Bullitt	108	1,386	95.1	39.7	90	1,584	46.3	42.7	4,381	178.0	94,147	403
Butler	20	352	19.9	9.7	18	D	D	D	827	33.3	0	0
Caldwell	34	570	44.7	16.4	17	D	D	D	750	27.4	255	2
Calloway	110	2,119	190.7	73.4	47	182	13.1	3.8	2,475	109.5	5,164	55
Campbell	158	3,490	334.3	130.9	126	D	D	D	5,586	228.6	78,557	469
Carlisle	6	D	D	D	5	10	1.1	0.2	404	18.5	NA	NA
Carroll	20	373	32.0	13.9	14	D	D	D	539	24.5	255	7
Carter	44	519	38.8	14.9	30	D	D	D	1,733	62.4	505	5
Casey	21	527	35.4	16.0	8	34	3.0	0.7	1,116	55.4	0	0
Christian	157	3,130	300.4	106.2	87	D	D	D	3,484	146.3	8,463	73
Clark	126	1,518	139.2	51.2	45	181	15.1	4.4	2,177	87.0	15,348	100

Table B. States and Counties — Government Employment and Payroll, and Local Government Finances

	Government employment and payroll, 2012									Local government finances, 2012				
			March payroll (percent of total)							General revenue				
												Taxes		
STATE County	Full-time equivalent employees	March payroll (dollars)	Administration, judicial, and legal	Police and corrections	Fire protection	Highways and transportation	Health and welfare	Natural resources and utilities	Education and libraries	Total (mil dol)	Intergovernmental (mil dol)	Total (mil dol)	Per capita[1] (dollars) Total	Per capita[1] (dollars) Property
	171	172	173	174	175	176	177	178	179	180	181	182	183	184
KANSAS— Cont'd														
Neosho	1,176	4,053,546	4.7	4.8	1.4	3.1	33.7	7.7	43.8	111.1	29.1	28.8	1,755	1,392
Ness	342	928,162	3.6	3.8	0.3	7.5	55.5	2.1	25.8	27.2	3.0	10.5	3,412	3,238
Norton	415	1,296,107	5.9	8.5	0.2	5.3	36.1	4.9	38.5	21.8	9.5	8.3	1,476	1,235
Osage	664	1,848,318	7.4	9.1	0.0	4.8	2.0	8.1	66.8	51.8	25.1	19.9	1,231	1,069
Osborne	160	407,550	12.5	11.0	0.0	10.3	6.0	16.5	39.9	12.2	3.9	6.3	1,668	1,374
Ottawa	333	902,710	6.3	6.6	0.0	8.3	3.0	8.5	63.2	26.0	12.4	11.0	1,813	1,494
Pawnee	440	1,250,370	6.8	9.0	0.2	6.2	4.7	6.2	62.4	27.5	10.2	13.2	1,900	1,520
Phillips	269	733,417	9.3	5.4	0.0	11.5	9.3	7.3	56.3	24.1	8.0	10.9	1,969	1,705
Pottawatomie	900	2,555,697	7.0	7.4	0.4	6.4	5.6	4.0	68.4	81.2	25.0	45.4	2,033	1,711
Pratt	620	2,089,279	5.5	7.1	0.6	5.9	5.9	8.3	64.6	48.5	14.6	24.6	2,526	2,145
Rawlins	120	323,307	14.0	8.7	0.1	13.4	2.7	5.2	54.9	9.2	3.2	4.8	1,855	1,554
Reno	3,036	10,310,558	4.2	9.4	4.3	3.9	2.4	5.3	68.8	260.0	97.6	109.2	1,695	1,318
Republic	280	743,094	10.6	6.2	0.0	10.1	3.1	14.2	51.3	22.0	7.1	12.0	2,465	2,116
Rice	740	2,211,947	5.2	5.5	0.1	4.7	28.7	3.7	50.7	54.4	18.2	18.8	1,885	1,542
Riley	2,188	7,227,365	9.0	12.5	5.2	5.3	2.9	8.2	55.4	194.7	54.3	101.1	1,339	930
Rooks	433	1,169,894	7.0	5.2	0.1	6.4	36.2	3.6	40.2	44.1	11.5	14.8	2,837	2,597
Rush	240	677,611	5.6	5.2	0.0	9.2	28.1	6.5	42.1	19.8	4.2	7.4	2,306	2,203
Russell	400	1,117,489	12.4	9.0	1.7	7.9	3.8	13.6	49.3	31.8	7.8	19.4	2,790	2,354
Saline	2,537	8,460,384	4.0	12.5	4.8	4.8	1.1	5.4	63.9	204.8	71.4	88.3	1,578	1,104
Scott	243	604,532	5.5	5.8	0.4	5.4	1.4	5.5	73.4	23.7	6.5	15.0	3,033	2,531
Sedgwick	17,666	64,762,573	6.4	12.0	4.9	3.5	5.0	4.5	61.8	1,873.6	724.4	682.0	1,354	1,041
Seward	1,811	5,549,695	5.2	6.6	1.4	2.3	29.2	3.6	49.3	146.4	48.8	38.4	1,629	1,116
Shawnee	8,380	28,121,726	3.6	11.0	4.3	2.8	2.6	4.9	70.3	768.6	263.0	299.3	1,672	1,189
Sheridan	256	590,482	3.7	3.2	0.0	5.6	53.2	2.1	27.9	10.1	2.5	6.2	2,430	2,074
Sherman	464	1,377,731	5.7	6.0	0.9	6.3	39.8	6.9	32.6	30.8	10.9	12.2	1,999	1,467
Smith	252	661,334	7.3	6.7	0.0	9.5	8.4	7.9	57.9	20.6	8.5	9.3	2,464	2,115
Stafford	276	853,136	9.9	5.7	0.8	9.4	3.5	6.5	62.0	24.1	7.5	12.6	2,881	2,680
Stanton	212	627,118	5.8	6.3	0.0	9.1	35.1	3.1	40.4	19.3	3.0	11.2	5,142	4,980
Stevens	518	1,610,255	4.2	4.8	0.3	4.7	38.6	4.1	41.0	50.0	6.3	27.4	4,762	4,526
Sumner	1,279	3,843,881	5.5	7.0	2.2	5.1	19.6	5.9	51.4	100.9	37.4	33.6	1,421	1,151
Thomas	600	1,667,889	4.5	6.5	1.4	4.8	3.5	6.7	70.3	44.9	12.3	19.0	2,396	1,891
Trego	344	1,000,545	5.7	4.2	0.2	6.3	56.4	2.5	22.3	13.1	3.4	7.5	2,518	2,196
Wabaunsee	308	821,494	10.9	7.3	0.0	6.3	2.4	6.6	65.2	27.8	12.1	10.7	1,521	1,395
Wallace	110	277,969	12.4	3.3	0.0	9.0	2.3	2.0	66.6	8.8	2.7	5.1	3,337	3,267
Washington	376	1,063,217	7.0	4.3	0.0	6.6	18.3	6.1	55.7	29.9	10.0	12.3	2,144	1,966
Wichita	216	654,420	4.5	3.3	0.1	4.9	41.8	2.5	39.5	16.5	3.9	5.9	2,609	2,207
Wilson	601	1,662,978	4.6	6.7	0.8	4.2	19.9	9.3	49.8	43.5	17.0	11.6	1,274	1,131
Woodson	181	419,389	10.5	9.6	3.3	11.4	2.2	8.1	52.8	13.3	5.4	6.7	2,052	1,782
Wyandotte	8,144	34,012,450	5.6	11.1	6.6	2.6	2.4	14.3	54.4	766.0	289.0	302.6	1,901	1,204
KENTUCKY	X	X	X	X	X	X	X	X	X	X	X	X	X	X
Adair	919	2,441,497	2.9	3.7	0.0	1.1	35.9	4.2	51.1	55.9	21.6	8.0	427	308
Allen	767	1,841,667	2.0	8.2	0.2	1.6	4.0	4.1	78.7	41.3	23.7	11.2	555	342
Anderson	809	2,162,986	6.1	5.8	0.3	3.2	5.0	4.0	75.1	51.0	24.5	18.4	846	649
Ballard	248	590,155	9.9	12.4	0.0	2.7	9.1	4.7	61.1	23.3	12.4	8.2	986	597
Barren	1,664	5,001,627	2.5	3.2	0.0	0.8	0.2	25.7	67.1	124.1	60.3	35.4	831	508
Bath	406	1,111,046	4.3	4.3	0.9	1.2	4.3	5.5	79.0	26.0	18.6	5.0	425	253
Bell	1,171	3,090,979	2.7	6.2	2.6	2.0	1.9	1.6	81.4	75.8	50.5	15.0	534	291
Boone	3,843	13,434,279	1.9	8.5	6.9	1.7	0.4	3.4	75.6	360.0	112.7	201.9	1,637	990
Bourbon	965	3,068,260	6.3	8.4	5.9	2.9	15.6	4.1	55.9	56.7	29.4	20.5	1,028	562
Boyd	2,063	6,328,157	3.3	7.1	4.8	2.9	12.1	6.5	61.5	147.1	62.5	56.2	1,143	583
Boyle	1,287	4,095,739	3.9	9.0	16.6	1.6	5.9	2.0	59.3	83.9	32.8	34.1	1,190	651
Bracken	356	894,119	6.9	4.0	0.0	2.5	7.4	5.6	73.1	19.7	12.1	5.3	621	450
Breathitt	629	1,632,815	3.0	3.4	0.6	2.7	1.6	1.3	86.6	44.7	30.3	8.4	615	272
Breckinridge	636	1,726,384	4.2	7.6	0.0	2.7	3.3	0.7	81.4	49.9	26.8	10.3	513	381
Bullitt	2,379	7,126,688	1.5	7.4	2.5	1.5	4.1	1.8	80.6	162.7	71.4	70.4	927	693
Butler	426	1,274,899	3.6	4.6	0.0	4.2	0.0	5.4	82.2	27.2	19.3	5.9	459	211
Caldwell	534	1,550,863	4.7	6.1	2.3	3.5	12.5	10.7	58.9	23.5	15.7	6.2	481	274
Calloway	2,147	6,749,443	2.1	4.3	1.7	1.6	54.4	1.7	34.0	317.2	34.5	23.7	628	447
Campbell	2,562	8,812,479	5.0	13.2	6.5	2.9	0.4	2.0	69.5	232.7	71.5	119.3	1,312	806
Carlisle	229	547,363	15.5	2.7	0.0	3.0	7.2	0.5	71.2	13.3	8.5	2.9	573	399
Carroll	523	1,513,204	6.2	11.6	1.6	2.3	2.6	4.1	71.1	176.6	16.1	13.1	1,202	549
Carter	1,152	2,867,307	1.7	3.7	0.0	1.6	9.7	2.9	78.0	60.6	42.8	11.2	410	234
Casey	760	1,971,527	2.7	6.8	0.5	1.5	27.9	2.2	58.2	51.9	25.0	6.6	412	269
Christian	1,972	5,973,027	3.9	11.1	5.4	1.2	2.6	9.3	61.0	153.9	80.7	50.3	666	318
Clark	1,289	3,897,749	3.3	8.0	8.0	1.8	7.1	3.9	65.0	104.2	43.5	36.8	1,029	594

1. Based on the resident population estimated as of July 1 of the year shown.

Table B. States and Counties — Local Government Finances, Government Employment, and Income Taxes

	Local government finances, 2012 (cont.)									Government employment, 2017			Individual income tax returns, 2016		
	Direct general expenditure							Debt outstanding							
			Percent of total for:											Mean	
STATE County	Total (mil dol)	Per capita[1] (dollars)	Education	Health and hospitals	Police protection	Public welfare	Highways	Total (mil dol)	Per capita[1] (dollars)	Federal civilian	Federal military	State and local	Number of returns	adjusted gross income	Mean income tax
	185	186	187	188	189	190	191	192	193	194	195	196	197	198	199

KANSAS— Cont'd

Neosho	113.5	6,916	38.0	33.2	2.1	0.0	7.7	154.6	9,423	59	58	1,832	6,960	43,641	4,138
Ness	25.4	8,281	22.4	50.3	3.1	0.0	8.6	2.1	688	24	11	427	1,420	44,018	4,263
Norton	22.4	3,997	48.1	6.0	4.3	0.0	6.6	10.5	1,866	25	17	805	2,330	46,472	5,129
Osage	52.1	3,229	56.9	1.1	5.3	0.0	9.4	54.0	3,346	73	59	1,150	7,400	47,484	4,281
Osborne	12.6	3,304	32.2	8.6	8.0	0.0	13.4	3.3	875	29	13	310	1,790	40,002	3,915
Ottawa	26.4	4,347	50.1	4.7	3.2	0.0	13.3	17.8	2,933	24	22	453	2,770	45,548	4,303
Pawnee	26.1	3,762	43.8	6.6	5.2	0.0	13.5	27.5	3,968	41	21	1,566	2,820	42,772	4,157
Phillips	25.4	4,596	38.5	5.1	3.7	0.0	12.6	4.9	881	36	20	882	2,650	41,935	4,054
Pottawatomie	89.9	4,029	54.4	5.8	3.3	0.0	7.9	77.1	3,455	57	92	1,236	10,910	60,301	6,546
Pratt	49.1	5,044	57.5	3.6	5.0	0.0	9.2	35.4	3,643	37	34	1,068	4,310	53,299	6,271
Rawlins	10.8	4,225	35.7	5.3	4.3	0.0	11.1	4.4	1,700	18	9	311	1,230	45,000	5,767
Reno	245.7	3,812	58.1	2.1	5.1	0.0	4.6	208.5	3,236	171	223	5,188	27,950	48,973	5,027
Republic	23.3	4,788	35.1	4.3	3.0	0.0	14.7	7.7	1,591	28	17	455	2,370	41,551	3,978
Rice	56.5	5,654	43.4	25.1	2.5	0.0	7.7	50.8	5,088	39	34	1,059	4,100	47,290	4,381
Riley	230.8	3,057	51.3	0.7	7.0	0.0	6.1	524.1	6,941	429	272	12,429	25,560	55,904	6,576
Rooks	50.5	9,668	22.1	22.3	3.3	5.5	5.9	39.4	7,551	32	19	641	2,410	38,490	3,880
Rush	21.5	6,668	27.9	26.9	0.9	0.0	10.6	8.4	2,621	24	11	348	1,550	39,677	3,400
Russell	31.0	4,458	38.8	4.9	4.7	0.0	12.1	17.1	2,459	32	26	661	3,220	39,172	3,559
Saline	211.2	3,772	45.1	1.4	5.3	0.0	7.8	251.6	4,493	239	201	4,157	26,480	54,984	6,278
Scott	22.4	4,533	43.6	4.5	6.5	2.3	7.7	37.8	7,650	23	18	365	2,400	57,180	6,932
Sedgwick	1,940.5	3,851	46.8	4.2	5.7	0.1	5.3	5,893.5	11,696	4,663	4,773	27,105	233,640	61,027	7,766
Seward	172.9	7,343	40.9	33.7	2.9	0.0	2.5	86.1	3,658	91	81	2,315	9,860	42,178	3,310
Shawnee	739.9	4,134	52.9	2.2	6.5	0.2	2.7	1,291.7	7,217	3,426	752	18,409	83,480	55,099	6,296
Sheridan	9.9	3,891	38.8	11.7	2.2	0.0	16.8	0.6	238	15	9	374	1,260	37,050	5,337
Sherman	28.9	4,724	57.7	3.1	3.6	0.0	7.8	18.3	2,989	48	22	722	2,650	44,968	4,220
Smith	21.3	5,645	40.2	5.3	2.0	0.0	17.3	2.0	535	34	14	341	1,830	37,600	3,701
Stafford	24.7	5,668	48.8	4.4	4.1	0.0	14.9	2.2	513	42	16	528	1,910	40,988	3,820
Stanton	28.2	12,976	20.1	52.9	1.2	0.0	8.9	15.2	6,985	9	8	328	920	47,292	4,574
Stevens	55.6	9,664	30.0	27.7	3.3	0.0	8.1	24.5	4,259	22	21	711	2,310	52,432	5,391
Sumner	97.3	4,110	41.6	20.7	4.1	0.0	7.7	85.1	3,595	74	85	1,815	10,280	50,881	5,037
Thomas	47.7	6,010	55.4	1.6	2.9	0.0	9.6	33.5	4,224	28	28	777	3,730	49,600	5,869
Trego	13.1	4,381	37.4	4.9	2.1	0.6	14.1	16.4	5,487	18	11	488	1,480	43,192	4,050
Wabaunsee	25.0	3,546	48.3	1.1	3.9	0.0	12.8	27.4	3,889	23	25	468	3,140	54,654	5,332
Wallace	9.8	6,453	40.5	2.8	3.1	2.3	13.0	5.2	3,412	11	6	211	700	47,037	4,521
Washington	29.5	5,125	44.0	14.4	0.8	0.0	17.0	3.2	559	43	20	682	2,750	45,605	4,704
Wichita	16.8	7,467	32.0	38.6	3.0	0.0	8.8	7.0	3,099	17	8	279	1,070	49,034	5,241
Wilson	43.9	4,825	41.2	25.8	5.1	0.0	6.6	43.5	4,772	35	32	955	3,840	43,966	4,245
Woodson	12.5	3,824	43.4	1.9	6.1	0.0	13.6	2.8	845	14	12	274	1,470	37,358	3,346
Wyandotte	733.0	4,606	51.2	1.5	7.1	0.0	1.3	2,162.3	13,588	1,340	616	14,212	70,660	40,600	3,351

KENTUCKY

KENTUCKY	X	X	X	X	X	X	X	X	X	36,245	44,911	272,287	1,906,090	54,529	6,348
Adair	60.0	3,213	34.8	41.3	2.1	0.0	3.2	137.2	7,348	47	55	895	7,060	35,520	2,985
Allen	49.2	2,435	63.1	7.8	3.4	0.1	4.2	71.1	3,516	43	63	783	7,860	43,729	4,857
Anderson	51.5	2,370	63.4	5.7	3.7	0.0	3.5	69.4	3,192	41	68	861	10,570	51,520	4,850
Ballard	29.1	3,486	40.4	3.5	3.4	0.0	6.5	122.6	14,712	25	24	385	3,380	49,948	5,026
Barren	120.1	2,816	69.4	1.0	3.9	0.7	2.6	241.8	5,673	105	131	2,199	18,330	43,240	4,122
Bath	23.4	1,987	68.5	4.7	2.1	0.0	5.2	23.4	1,980	24	37	498	4,660	37,726	2,904
Bell	70.9	2,517	61.7	2.1	3.4	0.0	2.6	42.0	1,492	121	79	1,604	8,650	34,783	2,658
Boone	317.2	2,573	54.9	0.6	4.8	1.9	8.0	852.8	6,915	1,163	397	5,362	60,800	67,994	8,449
Bourbon	58.2	2,912	60.5	5.7	3.8	0.1	3.2	52.5	2,629	35	60	1,006	9,010	46,669	5,128
Boyd	151.0	3,072	52.9	5.0	3.7	0.0	4.0	303.6	6,176	403	139	2,978	19,030	50,888	5,499
Boyle	80.8	2,820	48.5	3.9	4.6	0.3	3.0	210.1	7,332	61	81	1,765	12,040	51,231	5,541
Bracken	19.5	2,296	59.4	6.5	3.2	0.0	7.7	14.9	1,758	17	25	418	3,600	45,848	3,848
Breathitt	41.9	3,073	57.4	8.4	3.1	0.0	7.9	24.9	1,827	54	38	852	4,430	37,999	3,021
Breckinridge	54.2	2,698	52.5	2.3	2.2	0.1	4.0	265.6	13,235	61	60	849	7,970	44,791	3,989
Bullitt	164.4	2,166	55.3	3.4	4.5	0.0	2.2	188.8	2,488	74	244	2,721	37,770	53,222	5,168
Butler	27.0	2,105	61.6	0.3	3.5	0.1	7.5	53.2	4,145	28	38	632	4,980	42,118	3,250
Caldwell	28.0	2,163	70.3	2.5	2.0	0.1	6.9	20.0	1,544	36	38	633	5,420	43,501	3,873
Calloway	176.1	4,676	22.2	62.3	2.8	0.0	1.6	108.2	2,874	74	109	4,986	14,910	46,618	4,786
Campbell	217.1	2,389	52.4	0.5	8.0	0.4	4.4	506.2	5,568	294	272	5,937	43,390	64,438	8,096
Carlisle	16.7	3,315	59.4	5.5	1.6	0.0	10.4	23.2	4,601	14	15	241	2,060	52,805	5,304
Carroll	170.1	15,605	12.4	0.6	0.8	0.0	1.2	3,066.5	281,328	34	32	717	4,680	44,904	4,046
Carter	66.1	2,418	70.9	4.9	3.9	0.0	3.5	99.7	3,647	62	81	1,268	10,210	42,034	3,432
Casey	49.1	3,053	40.2	33.9	1.5	0.0	4.4	63.3	3,935	26	50	682	5,840	34,521	2,780
Christian	164.3	2,178	52.4	3.1	7.2	0.2	3.3	420.2	5,571	4,117	27,112	3,374	29,280	43,461	4,356
Clark	108.6	3,033	59.0	5.7	3.5	0.1	2.7	125.2	3,499	107	108	1,516	15,980	49,785	5,022

1. Based on the resident population estimated as of July 1 of the year shown.

Table B. States and Counties — Land Area and Population

State / county code	CBSA code[1]	County code[2]	STATE County	Land area[3] (sq. mi)	Total persons 2018	Rank	Per square mile	White	Black	American Indian, Alaska Native	Asian and Pacific Islancer	Percent Hispanic or Latino[4]	Under 5 years	5 to 17 years	18 to 24 years	25 to 34 years	35 to 44 years	45 to 54 years
				1	2	3	4	5	6	7	8	9	10	11	12	13	14	15
			KENTUCKY— Cont'd															
21051		7	Clay	469.3	20,105	1,819	42.8	93.6	4.3	0.7	0.4	2.1	5.9	15.2	7.1	15.3	13.6	14.2
21053		9	Clinton	197.3	10,206	2,412	51.7	96.0	1.0	0.8	0.5	3.0	6.0	16.5	7.1	11.6	11.4	13.4
21055		7	Crittenden	360.0	8,915	2,508	24.8	97.2	1.5	0.9	0.4	1.2	5.3	16.8	7.2	10.4	12.0	12.8
21057		9	Cumberland	305.2	6,659	2,698	21.8	95.4	4.2	0.6	0.3	1.5	6.1	15.6	6.5	10.9	10.3	12.7
21059	36,980	3	Daviess	458.4	101,104	597	220.6	89.8	6.5	0.4	2.2	3.2	6.8	17.7	8.1	12.9	11.8	12.3
21061	14,540	3	Edmonson	302.9	12,274	2,273	40.5	95.8	2.4	1.0	0.6	1.3	4.8	13.6	8.8	11.9	12.1	12.9
21063		9	Elliott	234.3	7,508	2,626	32.0	94.7	3.9	0.6	0.4	1.2	4.6	13.7	7.6	13.8	13.5	14.2
21065		6	Estill	253.1	14,198	2,149	56.1	98.0	0.9	0.7	0.2	1.2	5.4	16.1	7.1	11.5	12.0	14.6
21067	30,460	2	Fayette	283.6	323,780	216	1,141.7	73.3	16.3	0.7	5.0	7.4	6.0	14.9	14.1	15.4	13.1	11.7
21069		7	Fleming	348.5	14,432	2,133	41.4	96.8	2.0	0.5	0.4	1.4	6.3	17.8	7.6	11.3	12.0	13.8
21071		7	Floyd	393.3	35,845	1,279	91.1	97.6	1.4	0.5	0.4	0.8	5.8	16.0	7.4	11.8	12.5	13.5
21073	23,180	4	Franklin	207.8	50,815	980	244.5	83.6	12.0	0.7	2.4	3.5	5.6	15.2	9.2	12.8	12.1	13.4
21075	46,460	9	Fulton	205.9	6,120	2,741	29.7	72.6	25.4	1.1	1.0	2.2	6.6	15.4	7.2	13.4	10.8	11.8
21077	17,140	1	Gallatin	98.3	8,832	2,512	89.8	92.6	2.5	0.7	0.5	5.5	6.4	17.8	8.1	12.8	12.3	14.3
21079		6	Garrard	230.1	17,560	1,947	76.3	95.2	2.6	0.6	0.5	2.2	5.5	16.3	6.7	11.1	12.0	14.3
21081	17,140	1	Grant	258.0	25,121	1,599	97.4	95.5	1.5	0.6	0.8	2.7	7.5	19.0	8.6	12.5	12.2	13.7
21083	32,460	7	Graves	551.8	37,317	1,243	67.6	88.0	5.5	0.7	0.7	7.1	6.7	17.2	7.7	12.0	11.7	12.6
21085		6	Grayson	499.9	26,321	1,554	52.7	96.8	1.6	0.8	0.4	1.5	6.1	17.3	7.6	12.2	12.2	12.8
21087		8	Green	286.0	11,049	2,350	38.6	95.6	2.6	0.9	0.3	1.9	5.5	15.4	7.2	10.2	11.7	14.0
21089	26,580	2	Greenup	344.5	35,268	1,297	102.4	97.2	1.3	0.9	0.7	1.1	5.3	16.0	6.9	11.0	12.2	13.4
21091	36,980	3	Hancock	187.7	8,758	2,521	46.7	96.4	2.0	0.8	0.4	1.6	6.9	18.7	7.4	11.2	11.8	13.5
21093	21,060	3	Hardin	623.4	110,356	550	177.0	78.8	14.1	1.1	3.7	6.0	6.7	17.9	9.2	13.6	12.9	12.9
21095		7	Harlan	465.8	26,409	1,551	56.7	96.2	2.7	0.7	0.6	1.0	6.6	16.4	6.9	12.3	11.5	13.1
21097		6	Harrison	306.4	18,778	1,885	61.3	94.8	2.8	0.6	0.6	2.5	6.2	16.3	7.9	11.5	11.4	14.1
21099		8	Hart	412.6	18,906	1,877	45.8	92.8	5.5	0.7	0.6	1.9	7.0	17.5	7.8	11.8	11.4	13.3
21101	21,780	2	Henderson	436.5	45,591	1,062	104.4	88.3	9.6	0.5	0.9	2.7	6.0	17.1	7.5	12.3	12.1	12.8
21103	31,140	1	Henry	286.3	16,106	2,035	56.3	93.2	4.1	1.0	0.6	3.2	5.9	17.7	7.6	11.1	11.9	13.7
21105		9	Hickman	242.3	4,421	2,866	18.2	87.9	10.6	1.0	0.7	1.9	4.6	14.4	6.6	10.4	10.2	13.6
21107	31,580	5	Hopkins	542.1	45,068	1,076	83.1	90.1	8.0	0.7	1.0	2.2	5.9	16.7	7.4	12.2	12.2	12.8
21109		9	Jackson	345.2	13,442	2,196	38.9	98.5	0.5	0.5	0.2	0.9	6.4	16.3	7.2	11.6	13.0	13.9
21111	31,140	1	Jefferson	380.7	770,517	83	2,023.9	69.1	23.3	0.7	3.7	5.7	6.3	15.9	8.6	14.8	12.5	12.3
21113	30,460	2	Jessamine	172.2	53,920	940	313.1	90.5	5.4	0.8	1.8	3.5	6.5	17.7	9.7	12.7	12.4	13.0
21115		7	Johnson	262.0	22,386	1,709	85.4	97.9	0.8	0.7	0.7	0.9	5.4	16.4	7.6	11.5	12.5	14.1
21117	17,140	1	Kenton	160.3	166,051	395	1,035.9	90.3	6.0	0.5	1.9	3.4	6.8	17.1	8.0	14.8	13.1	12.6
21119		9	Knott	351.5	15,126	2,087	43.0	97.8	1.3	0.6	0.3	1.1	5.6	14.6	10.2	10.6	11.4	13.9
21121	30,940	7	Knox	386.3	31,304	1,397	81.0	96.9	1.7	0.8	0.5	1.3	6.3	17.1	9.1	12.6	11.7	13.2
21123	21,060	3	Larue	261.6	14,307	2,142	54.7	93.0	4.0	0.9	0.7	3.2	5.6	16.6	8.0	11.9	12.3	13.3
21125	30,940	5	Laurel	434.0	60,669	866	139.8	96.7	1.2	0.9	0.8	1.6	6.2	17.0	7.7	12.9	12.8	13.7
21127		6	Lawrence	415.6	15,571	2,066	37.5	97.8	1.1	0.8	0.6	1.3	6.3	17.5	7.0	11.5	12.4	13.4
21129		9	Lee	208.9	7,033	2,665	33.7	96.0	2.5	1.0	0.4	1.1	5.8	13.4	7.1	13.3	12.5	15.0
21131		9	Leslie	400.9	10,143	2,417	25.3	98.2	0.8	0.6	0.5	0.9	5.9	15.7	6.6	12.9	12.0	14.0
21133		9	Letcher	337.9	21,899	1,729	64.8	98.2	1.0	0.5	0.3	0.8	6.0	15.6	6.7	11.2	12.4	13.2
21135		8	Lewis	482.8	13,257	2,216	27.5	98.5	0.7	0.6	0.1	0.8	5.6	16.0	7.3	11.6	12.1	13.4
21137	19,220	7	Lincoln	332.8	24,644	1,623	74.1	95.6	2.9	0.8	0.4	1.7	6.7	17.1	7.3	11.8	11.3	14.0
21139	37,140	9	Livingston	313.1	9,242	2,484	29.5	96.5	1.1	1.1	0.7	2.0	5.5	14.9	6.7	10.7	10.5	13.8
21141		6	Logan	552.2	26,989	1,527	48.9	90.3	7.5	0.7	0.5	2.9	6.4	16.9	7.6	12.1	11.6	12.8
21143		9	Lyon	213.8	8,009	2,593	37.5	91.6	5.8	1.0	0.8	2.2	3.6	10.9	6.6	11.1	11.8	13.4
21145	37,140	5	McCracken	248.7	65,346	818	262.8	85.3	12.1	0.8	1.4	2.6	6.1	16.3	7.0	12.3	11.9	12.4
21147		9	McCreary	426.8	17,408	1,951	40.8	90.9	5.9	1.5	0.7	2.6	6.0	15.8	8.0	14.3	14.0	13.7
21149	36,980	3	McLean	252.5	9,252	2,483	36.6	97.0	1.3	0.8	0.5	1.6	5.7	18.1	6.8	10.7	11.7	13.3
21151	40,080	4	Madison	437.3	92,368	639	211.2	91.5	5.5	0.9	1.7	2.5	5.6	15.1	17.6	12.4	12.0	12.1
21153		9	Magoffin	308.4	12,362	2,261	40.1	98.3	0.5	0.6	0.3	1.1	5.9	16.4	7.1	11.9	12.0	14.3
21155		7	Marion	343.0	19,404	1,856	56.6	89.1	8.1	0.5	1.2	3.0	6.3	17.9	8.3	11.6	12.3	13.3
21157		7	Marshall	301.3	31,191	1,400	103.5	97.0	0.8	0.7	0.7	1.8	5.4	15.2	6.8	11.0	11.6	13.2
21159		9	Martin	229.6	11,323	2,330	49.3	89.5	6.9	0.7	0.4	3.3	4.7	14.9	7.1	16.3	13.8	13.4
21161	32,500	6	Mason	240.1	17,150	1,970	71.4	90.8	7.4	0.8	1.2	2.0	6.1	17.2	8.0	11.8	11.1	13.7
21163	21,060	3	Meade	305.4	28,715	1,468	94.0	91.0	4.6	1.2	1.6	3.7	5.3	17.1	8.3	13.4	13.7	14.2
21165	34,460	9	Menifee	203.6	6,451	2,715	31.7	95.5	3.3	0.9	0.3	1.2	5.2	13.3	8.8	10.6	11.5	13.9
21167		6	Mercer	249.1	21,774	1,735	87.4	92.4	4.6	0.7	1.0	3.2	5.9	16.1	7.5	11.4	11.0	14.0
21169	23,980	9	Metcalfe	289.6	10,030	2,422	34.6	96.0	2.1	0.7	0.4	1.9	6.2	17.3	7.3	11.3	11.2	13.5
21171		8	Monroe	329.4	10,718	2,375	32.5	94.2	2.7	0.6	0.4	3.2	6.3	16.3	7.7	11.1	11.7	13.4
21173	34,460	6	Montgomery	197.3	28,203	1,494	142.9	93.9	3.5	0.5	0.6	2.9	6.6	17.1	7.7	12.9	13.1	14.0
21175		9	Morgan	381.1	13,345	2,204	35.0	93.4	5.0	0.7	0.8	1.0	4.9	13.4	7.8	15.1	14.0	14.1
21177	16,420	6	Muhlenberg	467.4	30,774	1,414	65.8	93.1	5.4	0.6	0.5	1.5	5.6	15.0	9.0	12.1	12.3	13.0
21179	12,680	6	Nelson	417.5	45,851	1,053	109.8	92.0	6.1	0.6	0.8	2.2	6.2	17.4	7.8	12.7	12.5	13.5
21181		8	Nicholas	195.2	7,166	2,649	36.7	96.4	1.3	0.6	0.4	2.4	6.5	17.4	8.0	10.9	12.4	14.2

1. CBSA = Core Based Statistical Area. See Appendix A for explanation. See Appendix B for list of metropolitan areas with component counties.   2. County type code from the Economic Research Service of USDA Rural-Urban Continuum Codes. See Appendix A for definition.   3. Dry land or land partially or temporarily covered by water.   4. May be of any race.

Table B. States and Counties — **Population and Households**

STATE County	Population, 2018 (cont.)				Population change, 2000-2018							Households, 2013-2017				
	Age (percent) (cont.)				Total persons		Percent change		Components of change, 2010-2018						Percent	
	55 to 64 years	65 to 74 years	75 years and over	Percent female	2000	2010	2000-2010	2010-2018	Births	Deaths	Net Migration	Number	Persons per household	Family house-holds	Female family house-holder[1]	One person
	16	17	18	19	20	21	22	23	24	25	26	27	28	29	30	31
KENTUCKY— Cont'd																
Clay	13.5	9.5	5.7	47.9	24,556	21,729	-11.5	-7.5	2,242	2,167	-1,717	7,719	2.49	72.0	17.0	25.6
Clinton	14.4	11.3	8.2	50.9	9,634	10,267	6.6	-0.6	969	1,076	51	4,025	2.50	66.6	9.6	31.5
Crittenden	14.8	11.9	8.9	49.7	9,384	9,315	-0.7	-4.3	802	1,014	-178	3,711	2.41	68.4	9.1	28.8
Cumberland	16.0	12.6	9.3	51.3	7,147	6,849	-4.2	-2.8	640	851	26	2,709	2.46	66.7	9.6	30.9
Daviess	13.5	9.7	7.3	51.1	91,545	96,643	5.6	4.6	11,048	8,358	1,866	39,531	2.43	66.6	12.2	27.9
Edmonson	15.3	12.2	8.6	49.8	11,644	12,177	4.6	0.8	912	1,126	313	4,880	2.39	73.1	10.2	24.3
Elliott	12.8	11.5	8.2	43.5	6,748	7,850	16.3	-4.4	563	602	-305	2,635	2.39	73.1	14.8	23.6
Estill	14.3	11.7	7.3	50.5	15,307	14,679	-4.1	-3.3	1,273	1,545	-202	5,638	2.53	67.7	16.5	29.2
Fayette	11.5	8.0	5.3	50.9	260,512	295,867	13.6	9.4	33,374	18,483	13,113	127,336	2.37	57.4	12.4	31.4
Fleming	13.4	10.8	7.1	50.9	13,792	14,346	4.0	0.6	1,560	1,437	-27	5,849	2.48	73.8	12.4	22.9
Floyd	14.6	11.5	6.9	51.1	42,441	39,450	-7.0	-9.1	3,957	4,322	-3,345	15,108	2.42	69.1	14.9	27.5
Franklin	13.7	10.9	7.1	51.7	47,687	49,281	3.3	3.1	4,704	4,274	1,147	20,786	2.32	61.1	13.0	33.6
Fulton	14.7	12.2	8.0	50.3	7,752	6,813	-12.1	-10.2	665	833	-538	2,463	2.37	61.0	17.0	37.6
Gallatin	14.3	8.8	5.1	49.4	7,870	8,586	9.1	2.9	939	762	68	3,007	2.84	64.3	11.0	31.0
Garrard	15.9	10.7	7.4	50.7	14,792	16,905	14.3	3.9	1,536	1,355	477	6,925	2.47	72.6	13.2	23.2
Grant	12.7	8.4	5.3	49.9	22,384	24,658	10.2	1.9	3,017	1,876	-678	8,637	2.82	75.2	14.8	19.7
Graves	13.5	10.5	8.0	51.1	37,028	37,129	0.3	0.5	4,162	3,663	-296	14,299	2.56	66.2	11.3	30.3
Grayson	14.1	10.7	7.1	49.5	24,053	25,749	7.1	2.2	2,664	2,610	535	9,594	2.69	71.6	10.6	25.8
Green	15.3	11.9	8.8	50.7	11,518	11,273	-2.1	-2.0	962	1,136	-48	4,467	2.44	68.2	9.9	28.9
Greenup	14.2	12.1	8.9	51.4	36,891	36,902	0.0	-4.4	3,082	3,780	-914	14,089	2.53	72.9	11.5	23.1
Hancock	13.6	10.0	6.9	48.7	8,392	8,565	2.1	2.3	938	680	-59	3,375	2.54	75.1	9.6	21.7
Hardin	12.9	8.3	5.7	50.2	94,174	105,538	12.1	4.6	12,785	7,354	-760	41,051	2.56	67.1	11.8	28.1
Harlan	14.5	11.5	7.2	52.0	33,202	29,278	-11.8	-9.8	3,060	3,413	-2,533	11,249	2.39	69.1	15.9	27.9
Harrison	15.1	10.2	7.3	50.9	17,983	18,844	4.8	-0.4	1,765	1,829	7	7,107	2.57	69.3	11.7	26.4
Hart	14.7	9.7	6.8	50.8	17,445	18,190	4.3	3.9	2,073	1,721	376	7,346	2.49	68.3	10.6	27.6
Henderson	14.5	10.5	7.1	51.7	44,829	46,246	3.2	-1.4	4,635	4,179	-1,079	18,719	2.40	65.8	13.6	30.0
Henry	14.4	10.7	6.9	50.5	15,060	15,415	2.4	4.5	1,461	1,396	634	6,104	2.55	70.6	14.2	24.1
Hickman	14.6	13.8	11.8	52.9	5,262	4,902	-6.8	-9.8	336	529	-288	1,877	2.38	59.9	9.4	33.1
Hopkins	14.3	10.8	7.6	51.2	46,519	46,918	0.9	-3.9	4,389	4,872	-1,345	18,546	2.43	68.1	12.8	27.7
Jackson	14.4	10.8	6.4	50.3	13,495	13,490	0.0	-0.4	1,366	1,346	-64	5,435	2.44	71.4	12.0	25.6
Jefferson	13.4	9.5	6.7	51.7	693,604	741,075	6.8	4.0	82,348	62,345	10,143	309,888	2.42	59.6	14.1	33.6
Jessamine	13.0	8.9	6.1	51.3	39,041	48,582	24.4	11.0	5,521	3,498	3,317	18,537	2.69	76.2	15.4	18.5
Johnson	14.0	11.4	7.0	51.0	23,445	23,359	-0.4	-4.2	2,274	2,436	-803	8,771	2.57	68.4	10.3	28.6
Kenton	13.3	8.9	5.6	50.5	151,464	159,723	5.5	4.0	18,740	11,796	-486	62,929	2.57	64.8	12.9	28.7
Knott	15.2	11.5	7.0	50.6	17,649	16,371	-7.2	-7.6	1,432	1,680	-997	6,158	2.43	70.7	13.4	25.5
Knox	12.7	10.1	7.2	51.0	31,795	31,888	0.3	-1.8	3,304	3,303	-573	12,264	2.50	63.6	14.0	31.6
Larue	14.6	10.0	7.7	50.4	13,373	14,189	6.1	0.8	1,266	1,342	201	5,470	2.53	72.0	13.8	22.6
Laurel	13.4	10.0	6.4	51.0	52,715	58,849	11.6	3.1	6,108	4,932	692	22,976	2.57	69.0	14.2	27.3
Lawrence	14.6	10.8	6.6	50.2	15,569	15,859	1.9	-1.8	1,618	1,698	-200	6,254	2.52	68.5	9.4	28.1
Lee	15.3	11.6	5.9	45.8	7,916	7,887	-0.4	-10.8	620	835	-690	2,843	2.14	56.5	13.2	38.4
Leslie	15.0	10.8	7.2	50.1	12,401	11,310	-8.8	-10.3	1,103	1,341	-935	4,292	2.42	67.7	16.3	29.2
Letcher	15.3	12.3	7.3	51.1	25,277	24,511	-3.0	-10.7	2,302	2,639	-2,299	10,065	2.26	69.1	16.2	28.1
Lewis	15.4	10.9	7.7	50.0	14,092	13,883	-1.5	-4.5	1,201	1,291	-531	5,496	2.44	72.4	10.6	25.3
Lincoln	13.6	10.6	7.6	51.0	23,361	24,736	5.9	-0.4	2,733	2,360	-454	9,786	2.47	69.3	12.1	25.8
Livingston	16.3	12.6	9.1	50.9	9,804	9,519	-2.9	-2.9	821	1,059	-34	4,016	2.30	68.0	10.7	26.8
Logan	13.9	10.7	7.9	50.7	26,573	26,832	1.0	0.6	2,842	2,492	-182	10,780	2.46	64.3	10.2	30.1
Lyon	16.5	15.2	10.7	45.2	8,080	8,319	3.0	-3.7	454	943	175	3,376	2.04	58.9	7.3	35.6
McCracken	14.1	11.2	8.6	52.0	65,514	65,561	0.1	-0.3	6,521	6,697	19	27,557	2.32	58.9	12.4	36.1
McCreary	12.2	10.0	6.1	45.6	17,080	18,306	7.2	-4.9	1,864	1,639	-1,126	6,332	2.49	73.0	13.6	25.6
McLean	14.2	11.4	8.1	50.8	9,938	9,540	-4.0	-3.0	895	1,001	-179	3,826	2.42	71.2	8.9	25.8
Madison	11.4	8.4	5.4	51.4	70,872	82,913	17.0	11.4	8,252	5,906	7,018	33,036	2.48	62.8	11.5	27.9
Magoffin	15.1	10.5	6.7	50.0	13,332	13,333	0.0	-7.3	1,266	1,245	-993	5,057	2.50	68.8	9.4	29.7
Marion	13.8	9.7	6.8	50.5	18,212	19,823	8.8	-2.1	1,987	1,707	-728	7,365	2.51	62.1	13.1	33.0
Marshall	14.9	12.5	9.4	51.0	30,125	31,448	4.4	-0.8	2,609	3,501	656	13,117	2.33	70.2	8.8	26.3
Martin	13.0	10.2	6.4	45.1	12,578	12,929	2.8	-12.4	1,062	1,147	-1,535	4,316	2.49	68.1	10.2	28.6
Mason	13.7	11.0	7.4	50.7	16,800	17,490	4.1	-1.9	1,737	1,710	-365	6,737	2.51	68.8	13.4	28.7
Meade	14.0	8.6	5.4	49.6	26,349	28,613	8.6	0.4	2,202	1,910	-252	10,785	2.62	73.8	8.0	20.6
Menifee	15.7	12.5	8.4	49.1	6,556	6,304	-3.8	2.3	603	630	169	2,537	2.48	71.0	11.2	25.5
Mercer	15.3	11.0	7.8	50.9	20,817	21,317	2.4	2.1	2,078	2,151	548	8,645	2.46	69.2	10.7	26.1
Metcalfe	14.5	10.3	8.4	50.4	10,037	10,106	0.7	-0.8	1,066	1,063	-76	3,940	2.50	69.2	8.9	25.6
Monroe	14.7	11.1	7.8	50.1	11,756	10,963	-6.7	-2.2	1,042	1,261	-24	4,376	2.40	66.2	8.1	29.8
Montgomery	12.8	9.6	6.2	51.1	22,554	26,509	17.5	6.4	3,169	2,293	831	10,404	2.61	70.0	15.6	23.3
Morgan	14.0	10.2	6.5	42.8	13,948	13,924	-0.2	-4.2	1,087	1,224	-466	4,937	2.36	73.3	12.7	23.0
Muhlenberg	13.8	11.0	8.1	49.0	31,839	31,499	-1.1	-2.3	2,884	3,178	-423	11,416	2.63	70.3	12.4	26.2
Nelson	14.2	9.8	5.8	50.7	37,477	43,443	15.9	5.5	4,775	3,173	829	17,324	2.57	70.5	11.5	24.7
Nicholas	14.1	10.0	6.5	50.5	6,813	7,129	4.6	0.5	741	841	141	2,760	2.52	70.2	13.7	25.0

1. No spouse present.

Population, Vital Statistics, Health, and Crime

STATE County	Persons in group quarters, 2018	Daytime Population, 2013-2017		Births, 2018		Deaths, 2018		Persons under 65 with no health insurance, 2016		Medicare, 2018			Serious crimes known to police[2], 2016 Total	
		Number	Employment/ residence ratio	Total	Rate[1]	Number	Rate[1]	Number	Percent	Total beneficiaries	Enrolled in Original Medicare	Enrolled in Medicare Advantage	Number	Rate[3]
	32	33	34	35	36	37	38	39	40	41	42	43	44	45
KENTUCKY— Cont'd														
Clay	1,708	19,467	0.75	222	11.0	236	11.7	1,263	8.0	4,948	3,507	1,441	163	781
Clinton	136	10,676	1.12	110	10.8	113	11.1	639	7.9	2,504	1,994	510	34	335
Crittenden	210	8,213	0.74	82	9.2	100	11.2	442	6.1	2,204	1,695	509	91	995
Cumberland	86	6,318	0.82	70	10.5	119	17.9	355	6.8	1,770	1,349	421	16	238
Daviess	2,602	101,598	1.05	1,329	13.1	1,032	10.2	4,122	5.1	21,485	15,632	5,853	3,307	3,318
Edmonson	354	9,345	0.40	123	10.0	151	12.3	705	7.4	2,871	2,039	832	32	268
Elliott	1,034	6,997	0.69	74	9.9	72	9.6	322	6.3	1,602	970	632	0	0
Estill	118	11,992	0.51	135	9.5	183	12.9	785	6.8	3,608	2,673	935	29	203
Fayette	13,133	346,088	1.19	3,997	12.3	2,334	7.2	19,479	7.3	47,812	30,997	16,815	14,857	4,674
Fleming	22	12,539	0.65	177	12.3	173	12.0	872	7.3	3,490	2,510	980	70	477
Floyd	667	37,145	0.97	398	11.1	534	14.9	2,171	7.2	10,383	7,597	2,786	126	338
Franklin	1,873	58,502	1.37	542	10.7	506	10.0	2,582	6.4	13,793	8,211	5,582	1,535	3,037
Fulton	445	6,286	1.01	83	13.6	100	16.3	256	5.7	1,738	1,318	420	114	1,862
Gallatin	85	7,125	0.58	118	13.4	75	8.5	525	7.0	1,189	740	449	68	788
Garrard	109	12,585	0.35	192	10.9	181	10.3	1,019	7.2	3,871	2,809	1,062	117	677
Grant	456	20,359	0.55	394	15.7	247	9.8	1,165	5.5	5,095	2,945	2,150	211	853
Graves	463	33,949	0.78	504	13.5	414	11.1	2,176	7.2	8,628	5,963	2,665	624	1,667
Grayson	768	23,778	0.77	284	10.8	293	11.1	1,447	6.9	6,101	4,850	1,251	235	894
Green	113	8,850	0.52	126	11.4	133	12.0	664	7.6	2,818	2,104	714	44	402
Greenup	454	31,496	0.66	339	9.6	483	13.7	1,434	5.0	9,482	6,832	2,650	153	427
Hancock	90	9,361	1.19	115	13.1	81	9.2	317	4.4	1,931	1,578	353	24	275
Hardin	3,223	112,271	1.09	1,414	12.8	960	8.7	4,492	5.0	19,573	15,311	4,262	1,456	1,371
Harlan	627	27,686	1.02	330	12.5	392	14.8	1,466	6.7	7,572	5,656	1,916	98	358
Harrison	275	16,361	0.71	227	12.1	212	11.3	953	6.2	4,087	2,890	1,197	288	1,537
Hart	227	17,326	0.83	253	13.4	200	10.6	1,133	7.4	4,021	3,091	930	62	335
Henderson	1,165	45,595	0.97	537	11.8	536	11.8	2,106	5.6	9,973	6,599	3,374	990	2,134
Henry	80	12,297	0.52	183	11.4	162	10.1	893	6.8	3,499	2,135	1,364	45	288
Hickman	212	4,371	0.84	39	8.8	68	15.4	219	6.5	1,308	993	315	32	702
Hopkins	1,086	45,696	0.98	470	10.4	542	12.0	2,133	5.8	10,590	7,638	2,952	710	1,542
Jackson	110	11,704	0.60	168	12.5	163	12.1	789	7.2	3,097	2,319	778	73	548
Jefferson	16,630	848,516	1.23	9,649	12.5	7,598	9.9	35,430	5.6	145,058	94,189	50,869	38,172	4,975
Jessamine	1,719	48,375	0.86	656	12.2	425	7.9	2,813	6.5	9,228	6,019	3,209	1,434	2,727
Johnson	528	22,084	0.85	223	10.0	296	13.2	1,221	6.6	5,984	4,376	1,608	126	545
Kenton	2,445	147,663	0.80	2,267	13.7	1,487	9.0	7,280	5.1	27,851	16,703	11,148	3,010	1,815
Knott	815	13,849	0.60	149	9.9	196	13.0	841	6.9	3,901	2,706	1,195	10	64
Knox	691	31,436	1.00	384	12.3	444	14.2	1,701	6.7	7,820	6,105	1,715	245	774
Larue	313	11,544	0.57	158	11.0	149	10.4	736	6.5	3,269	2,474	795	55	386
Laurel	697	62,712	1.13	751	12.4	674	11.1	3,236	6.5	13,649	10,346	3,303	804	1,334
Lawrence	108	14,468	0.72	166	10.7	215	13.8	840	6.4	3,892	2,947	945	90	573
Lee	706	6,351	0.78	82	11.7	110	15.6	318	6.2	1,807	1,403	404	14	213
Leslie	227	9,740	0.66	105	10.4	161	15.9	577	6.8	2,885	2,017	868	15	142
Letcher	243	21,652	0.80	260	11.9	294	13.4	1,275	6.9	6,229	4,537	1,692	43	188
Lewis	139	11,677	0.58	138	10.4	151	11.4	832	7.6	2,942	2,234	708	19	139
Lincoln	219	20,216	0.55	358	14.5	283	11.5	1,477	7.5	5,858	4,195	1,663	101	414
Livingston	69	8,161	0.71	96	10.4	129	14.0	436	6.0	2,556	2,001	555	65	702
Logan	277	24,969	0.82	327	12.1	298	11.0	1,441	6.7	6,085	4,699	1,386	447	1,662
Lyon	1,005	7,612	0.76	54	6.7	123	15.4	285	5.6	2,311	1,678	633	61	735
McCracken	1,190	76,701	1.40	799	12.2	843	12.9	2,975	5.7	16,087	12,162	3,925	1,829	2,820
McCreary	1,936	16,264	0.66	207	11.9	171	9.8	1,024	7.8	3,907	3,026	881	68	382
McLean	82	7,795	0.58	96	10.4	111	12.0	504	6.6	2,341	1,599	742	52	547
Madison	6,673	85,555	0.93	991	10.7	743	8.0	4,003	5.6	16,052	10,033	6,019	2,617	2,951
Magoffin	127	11,644	0.68	137	11.1	156	12.6	847	8.1	3,214	2,244	970	20	158
Marion	505	20,217	1.12	238	12.3	199	10.3	918	5.8	3,966	3,046	920	191	992
Marshall	464	30,641	0.96	313	10.0	436	14.0	1,394	5.7	8,364	6,281	2,083	389	1,255
Martin	1,384	12,164	1.00	104	9.2	147	13.0	621	7.2	2,827	2,086	741	60	493
Mason	298	18,746	1.22	206	12.0	189	11.0	798	5.7	4,027	2,900	1,127	418	2,458
Meade	212	21,705	0.45	250	8.7	234	8.1	1,284	5.3	5,229	3,986	1,243	165	595
Menifee	272	5,174	0.51	75	11.6	91	14.1	457	8.9	1,723	1,104	619	22	346
Mercer	128	19,693	0.82	256	11.8	272	12.5	1,098	6.3	5,199	3,663	1,536	219	1,023
Metcalfe	121	9,013	0.75	117	11.7	139	13.9	579	7.2	2,530	1,740	790	114	1,157
Monroe	143	10,052	0.86	119	11.1	148	13.8	749	8.9	2,698	2,082	616	8	75
Montgomery	357	29,063	1.13	377	13.4	287	10.2	1,489	6.4	5,869	3,795	2,074	671	2,414
Morgan	1,944	12,729	0.84	125	9.4	156	11.7	762	8.1	2,967	1,878	1,089	16	121
Muhlenberg	2,094	28,728	0.78	353	11.5	424	13.8	1,524	6.4	7,588	5,398	2,190	190	612
Nelson	496	40,999	0.80	553	12.1	416	9.1	1,944	5.0	9,524	6,942	2,582	476	1,049
Nicholas	95	5,547	0.45	92	12.8	106	14.8	394	6.8	1,648	1,228	420	20	281

1. Per 1,000 estimated resident population.   2. Data for serious crimes have not been adjusted for underreporting; this may affect comparability between geographic areas and over time.   3. Per 100,000 population estimated by the FBI.

Crime, Education, Money Income, and Poverty

STATE County	Violent (Rate)	Property (Rate)	Enrollment Total	Percent private	High school graduate or less	Bachelor's degree or more	Total current spending (mil dol)	Current spending per student (dollars)	Per capita income	Median income (dollars)	Percent with income of less than $50,000	Percent with income of $200,000 or more	Median household income (dollars)	All persons	Children under 18 years	Children 5 to 17 years in families
	46	47	48	49	50	51	52	53	54	55	56	57	58	59	60	61
KENTUCKY— Cont'd																
Clay	77	705	4,156	7.0	70.2	9.5	34.6	10,197	15,388	24,596	74.3	0.9	26,386	41.7	55.7	56.2
Clinton	59	276	2,120	17.5	67.9	10.1	17.6	9,466	19,325	31,130	71.5	1.4	29,641	26.4	35.4	32.3
Crittenden	55	940	1,836	7.1	57.3	13.3	11.9	8,390	22,765	41,114	58.2	1.6	41,522	18.1	28.6	26.8
Cumberland	15	223	1,340	12.2	55.8	13.2	9.9	10,379	18,669	35,449	70.3	1.5	31,736	22.8	33.0	32.4
Daviess	165	3,153	24,474	15.5	46.3	21.6	155.4	9,298	26,501	48,371	51.5	3.3	50,359	16.1	21.7	19.0
Edmonson	50	217	2,175	5.4	62.5	11.1	17.5	9,013	21,851	41,114	59.1	2.2	39,490	16.9	24.5	23.2
Elliott	0	0	1,430	6.1	68.7	7.5	10.2	9,411	13,436	29,043	71.8	0.6	32,846	29.7	35.0	32.4
Estill	21	182	2,848	2.5	70.6	9.9	23.0	9,056	17,728	30,692	68.7	1.3	34,096	24.8	29.8	28.1
Fayette	350	4,324	91,564	14.9	30.0	41.8	437.1	10,767	31,653	53,013	47.6	5.5	56,192	16.5	17.1	16.4
Fleming	48	429	3,107	12.0	59.4	13.4	20.9	9,048	23,351	41,095	57.9	2.1	41,029	17.4	25.4	24.9
Floyd	29	308	7,906	11.3	60.2	12.6	61.0	9,771	18,366	31,196	69.2	1.0	32,841	32.2	39.0	37.6
Franklin	261	2,776	11,607	15.0	43.3	28.4	64.0	8,867	28,001	53,539	46.4	2.0	53,198	13.7	19.2	18.8
Fulton	49	1,813	1,265	9.9	54.9	14.9	11.1	11,173	18,111	28,274	71.5	0.4	30,761	29	42.8	40.1
Gallatin	35	753	2,008	12.5	64.7	11.9	15.8	9,183	22,508	50,250	49.6	0.4	47,907	14.7	21.8	19.8
						15.7	24.3	9,094	24,874	47,906	51.8	2.3	50,518	17	23.8	22.1
Garrard	69	608	3,585	11.1	58.0											
Grant	48	804	6,313	11.3	62.1	12.4	42.4	8,571	20,892	43,881	54.8	1.4	51,849	13.9	20.7	19.1
Graves	131	1,536	9,084	9.3	55.5	16.2	57.3	8,863	22,112	40,369	59.0	1.5	41,963	17.5	24.9	24.4
Grayson	65	830	5,789	8.9	63.2	9.9	37.7	8,520	19,520	35,944	62.8	1.2	38,133	22.5	29.6	27.7
Green	9	393	2,230	15.9	65.5	11.0	16.2	9,918	23,448	37,388	62.3	2.8	36,809	18.5	26.2	23.7
Greenup	28	399	7,925	5.5	49.4	17.2	54.2	8,717	25,378	47,517	52.7	2.6	46,699	16	22.2	20.1
Hancock	34	241	2,112	8.8	57.6	11.1	16.4	9,625	22,438	49,135	50.9	0.2	49,475	12.2	17.2	15.8
Hardin	162	1,209	29,044	14.6	40.1	23.5	155.5	8,992	26,436	51,923	48.0	2.3	52,673	12.8	16.8	15.5
Harlan	37	321	6,001	8.7	63.4	11.4	47.0	9,406	15,457	24,451	75.3	0.8	25,815	41.5	49.2	47.9
Harrison	117	1,420	3,739	8.4	58.9	15.4	26.9	8,859	22,497	44,620	54.6	1.2	49,694	15.3	21.1	19.4
						12.6	24.6	10,367	19,715	37,315	64.6	1.2	38,182	20	26.2	26.4
Hart	32	303	4,030	14.2	65.1											
Henderson	147	1,987	10,740	13.1	49.4	16.8	75.6	9,978	23,958	43,458	56.6	1.9	47,589	16.2	20.6	19.1
Henry	6	281	3,439	10.6	61.1	10.9	26.2	9,001	23,932	50,787	48.9	1.6	50,721	15.3	20.3	18.4
Hickman	88	614	899	8.7	65.0	9.3	8.1	9,855	19,764	38,036	66.9	0.2	40,902	19.1	27.6	24.9
Hopkins	104	1,438	9,962	10.5	55.0	15.7	70.4	9,071	23,288	44,048	54.9	1.8	44,419	19.3	25.2	23.1
Jackson	23	526	2,802	5.3	69.8	10.5	23.2	9,773	16,827	32,055	69.6	0.6	31,355	31.4	38.9	36.5
Jefferson	630	4,345	183,527	24.6	37.3	32.3	1,194.0	11,815	31,039	52,237	47.9	5.0	54,977	14.1	19.8	18.9
Jessamine	118	2,609	13,696	26.3	43.0	30.0	74.2	9,108	28,195	55,450	46.1	5.8	57,015	14.7	20.3	17.6
Johnson	48	498	5,078	10.8	54.9	15.1	46.2	10,059	19,925	35,629	63.3	1.2	37,724	23.3	29.7	25.4
Kenton	204	1,611	40,923	21.2	39.5	29.7	215.4	9,279	30,195	58,674	42.9	4.6	59,594	12	14.3	13.3
						12.9	25.7	10,479	17,670	30,503	67.7	0.6	31,788	34.6	42.0	38.4
Knott	0	64	3,471	20.0	61.6											
Knox	57	717	7,601	8.2	69.4	10.0	52.5	9,794	15,869	26,061	75.9	0.6	28,586	32.2	37.4	36.0
Larue	28	358	3,100	9.0	57.0	12.2	22.9	9,573	21,879	41,720	57.5	1.8	45,288	15.1	21.4	19.9
Laurel	81	1,253	13,575	8.9	60.5	13.0	83.6	8,364	20,446	37,235	62.6	1.8	39,830	24.3	30.4	26.8
Lawrence	32	541	3,273	4.9	64.9	11.6	22.7	8,658	18,885	32,703	66.3	1.3	28,672	32.8	38.9	32.8
Lee	0	213	1,484	4.2	69.5	8.9	10.0	9,699	16,489	23,297	74.2	1.0	28,084	33.7	48.0	43.4
Leslie	28	113	2,105	5.0	69.6	8.9	18.1	9,791	15,112	27,861	74.7	0.4	29,317	31	37.3	34.8
Letcher	53	136	4,820	7.2	63.3	11.7	38.1	10,038	18,085	30,293	71.5	0.6	32,635	30.8	38.3	36.3
Lewis	0	139	2,840	7.6	66.5	12.1	21.0	8,934	19,346	32,054	66.3	0.8	35,056	25.6	35.3	34.1
Lincoln	25	390	5,173	8.5	64.2	10.8	40.4	9,987	19,351	37,930	61.7	1.1	39,347	21	28.2	26.0
						8.9	13.4	10,802	24,464	43,472	55.1	1.8	44,435	15.4	23.4	22.1
Livingston	11	691	1,882	9.1	63.5											
Logan	164	1,498	5,794	8.1	58.3	14.8	42.2	8,980	21,465	40,982	58.0	1.1	47,174	17.9	24.4	23.3
Lyon	12	723	1,145	9.0	54.0	14.0	8.3	9,058	27,098	50,268	49.5	2.5	44,318	14.3	20.2	18.4
McCracken	234	2,586	14,782	10.4	42.0	24.2	94.0	9,313	29,881	42,894	55.1	3.6	48,994	15.2	21.2	20.5
McCreary	11	371	3,922	16.0	68.6	7.6	29.1	9,816	11,492	19,264	79.6	0.8	28,024	34.4	45.6	42.2
McLean	42	505	2,037	12.2	55.9	10.8	14.8	8,795	22,884	44,242	54.6	0.8	44,574	16.4	21.3	18.4
Madison	145	2,805	27,653	14.8	41.5	30.3	108.0	8,349	23,733	46,674	53.0	2.1	50,783	17	17.6	15.1
Magoffin	24	134	2,901	8.0	64.1	10.1	22.0	9,638	17,279	29,578	69.2	0.5	28,077	32.1	39.3	35.9
Marion	83	909	4,653	7.8	62.6	13.0	29.5	9,147	21,823	40,005	60.4	2.0	46,125	14.8	19.9	17.8
Marshall	68	1,187	6,346	7.3	51.2	17.5	43.8	8,898	27,391	49,126	50.9	2.3	50,786	12.1	16.9	15.8
						8.2	21.2	10,129	14,914	29,239	71.5	0.0	30,177	35.8	45.9	40.3
Martin	33	460	2,290	10.6	66.1											
Mason	165	2,294	3,675	8.4	52.2	18.5	25.0	8,800	25,285	43,082	56.5	2.4	45,608	18	26.3	25.3
Meade	43	551	7,114	10.0	47.9	17.4	41.1	8,097	25,119	53,732	45.3	1.5	58,873	11.2	15.1	13.4
Menifee	16	331	1,281	3.6	64.0	11.4	10.4	9,966	19,744	39,688	63.1	0.3	36,595	25.4	39.1	37.5
Mercer	70	953	4,924	12.6	53.4	17.0	32.0	9,349	24,981	47,574	52.5	1.7	47,611	13.4	19.3	17.5
Metcalfe	81	1,075	2,159	16.7	62.2	12.1	16.9	10,181	18,449	35,594	68.6	0.7	33,139	23.4	34.7	33.7
Monroe	19	57	2,286	6.6	64.1	14.8	19.5	10,335	21,985	35,665	63.3	3.2	32,518	24.3	33.1	31.3
Montgomery	122	2,292	6,434	9.7	54.8	17.0	43.8	8,901	21,371	42,172	56.9	1.3	43,890	17.7	22.3	22.0
Morgan	0	121	2,317	5.0	62.3	12.2	19.9	9,616	17,089	33,523	67.0	0.7	34,121	30.1	34.4	32.4
Muhlenberg	52	560	6,503	6.1	62.9	11.3	54.0	10,479	20,376	40,005	59.1	0.9	40,338	19.4	24.9	23.6
						17.5	68.3	9,092	28,156	55,182	44.3	3.6	58,960	9.8	15.1	13.5
Nelson	88	961	10,890	18.8	49.4											
Nicholas	70	210	1,510	10.7	64.4	10.4	9.8	8,268	21,519	38,900	59.1	1.7	40,264	18.8	27.6	27.3

1. Data for serious crimes have not been adjusted for underreporting; this may affect comparability between geographic areas and over time. 2. Per 100,000 population estimated by the FBI. 3. All persons 3 years old and over enrolled in nursery school through college. 4. Persons 25 years old and over. 5. Elementary and secondary education expenditures. 6. Based on population estimated by the American Community Survey, 2011–2015.

| STATE County | Personal income, 2017 | | | | | | | | | | Earnings, 2017 | | |
	Total (mil dol)	Percent change 2016-2017	Per capita[1] Dollars	Rank	Wages and salaries (mil dol)	Supplements to wages and salaries, employer contributions (mil dol) Pension and insurance	Government social insurance	Proprietors' income (mil dol)	Dividends, interest, and rent (mil dol)	Personal transfer receipts (mil dol)	Total (mil dol)	Contributions for government social insurance (mil dol) From employee and self-employed	From employer
	62	63	64	65	66	67	68	69	70	71	72	73	74
KENTUCKY— Cont'd													
Clay	609	2.9	29,924	2,937	158	38	12	32	59	309	240	19	12
Clinton	310	3.0	30,180	2,914	119	26	10	19	35	141	174	12	10
Crittenden	304	2.6	33,425	2,566	71	17	6	23	41	103	116	9	6
Cumberland	227	4.7	33,786	2,511	66	13	5	17	26	104	101	8	5
Daviess	4,008	2.6	39,933	1,564	2,009	335	153	161	698	1,019	2,658	174	153
Edmonson	385	4.7	31,494	2,807	58	15	5	20	45	129	97	9	5
Elliott	166	5.0	22,111	3,106	33	10	2	6	18	83	51	5	2
Estill	438	1.6	30,713	2,873	91	19	7	10	45	181	127	12	7
Fayette	15,052	2.0	46,753	732	9,908	1,724	736	1,039	3,389	2,244	13,406	764	736
Fleming	467	2.5	32,313	2,712	113	25	9	35	58	153	182	14	9
Floyd	1,274	3.7	35,137	2,327	447	84	35	113	141	588	679	51	35
Franklin	2,086	2.5	41,312	1,363	1,423	331	98	98	387	563	1,949	112	98
Fulton	200	3.4	32,258	2,717	76	16	7	11	33	86	110	8	7
Gallatin	266	3.8	30,286	2,904	125	21	9	6	25	71	161	10	9
Garrard	583	2.8	33,289	2,581	84	17	7	30	79	161	138	13	7
Grant	857	3.9	34,322	2,442	216	38	16	44	89	236	315	24	16
Graves	1,362	3.1	36,685	2,095	428	82	33	170	194	414	712	45	33
Grayson	848	3.1	32,168	2,730	281	58	23	50	109	278	412	30	23
Green	374	5.9	33,798	2,506	59	14	4	21	49	138	98	9	4
Greenup	1,360	2.7	38,285	1,829	361	66	32	59	154	441	518	43	32
Hancock	301	0.7	34,159	2,465	265	41	20	6	34	80	332	22	20
Hardin	4,561	4.4	42,204	1,242	2,469	554	205	369	776	1,031	3,597	202	205
Harlan	786	2.6	29,428	2,959	223	49	18	20	93	429	310	27	18
Harrison	634	3.1	33,751	2,516	213	41	17	32	87	172	302	22	17
Hart	587	4.3	31,319	2,830	193	38	15	88	77	191	334	23	15
Henderson	1,748	3.4	38,069	1,874	859	148	66	75	256	465	1,147	75	66
Henry	585	3.1	36,539	2,113	111	24	8	25	79	152	169	14	8
Hickman	185	5.9	40,895	1,418	32	7	3	49	27	61	90	5	3
Hopkins	1,735	2.6	38,097	1,864	767	134	61	99	260	495	1,062	71	61
Jackson	374	2.4	27,814	3,034	56	16	4	9	42	151	86	9	4
Jefferson	37,813	3.5	49,034	534	26,471	3,753	1,974	2,807	6,943	7,113	35,005	2,132	1,974
Jessamine	2,312	3.9	43,317	1,100	709	115	55	174	414	382	1,053	68	55
Johnson	729	2.4	32,255	2,718	188	39	15	31	94	309	273	23	15
Kenton	9,132	4.4	55,214	271	3,656	584	267	882	2,209	1,304	5,389	330	267
Knott	454	3.1	29,691	2,947	80	18	6	18	45	230	122	12	6
Knox	892	2.0	28,555	3,014	263	56	20	50	95	417	389	32	20
Larue	501	4.8	35,275	2,301	93	20	7	18	77	144	138	12	7
Laurel	1,992	3.8	33,096	2,604	1,024	172	83	118	213	647	1,397	95	83
Lawrence	481	2.2	30,585	2,883	122	23	10	20	52	210	175	15	10
Lee	206	2.0	31,422	2,816	54	11	4	11	24	105	80	7	4
Leslie	324	3.1	31,386	2,819	64	14	5	11	30	171	94	9	5
Letcher	660	1.9	29,549	2,956	157	32	12	28	66	351	229	21	12
Lewis	396	2.8	29,716	2,946	68	16	5	23	38	153	112	10	5
Lincoln	742	2.7	30,353	2,901	145	31	11	29	98	263	216	20	11
Livingston	338	1.5	36,412	2,133	117	21	9	19	46	109	167	12	9
Logan	933	5.1	34,478	2,414	395	70	30	87	133	275	581	39	30
Lyon	275	2.3	34,043	2,479	80	20	6	13	46	94	118	9	6
McCracken	3,191	2.1	48,797	561	1,752	282	137	467	592	723	2,639	165	137
McCreary	436	3.5	24,937	3,092	102	28	8	17	52	237	156	14	8
McLean	355	4.9	38,530	1,798	73	15	6	54	41	103	147	9	6
Madison	3,133	3.1	34,342	2,436	1,404	286	108	113	438	746	1,911	121	108
Magoffin	367	2.7	29,243	2,972	53	13	4	9	38	191	79	9	4
Marion	668	4.6	34,418	2,424	354	64	29	33	89	190	479	31	29
Marshall	1,225	1.9	39,039	1,716	562	97	45	75	199	344	779	53	45
Martin	329	6.7	28,740	2,999	118	28	9	18	49	170	174	13	9
Mason	671	4.3	39,056	1,712	365	70	29	35	121	183	500	32	29
Meade	1,076	2.4	38,225	1,840	172	37	13	50	160	233	273	21	13
Menifee	189	2.4	29,337	2,963	32	8	3	5	21	81	48	5	3
Mercer	776	1.6	36,079	2,191	312	56	24	50	115	216	442	31	24
Metcalfe	307	4.9	30,387	2,899	69	16	6	21	34	118	112	9	6
Monroe	372	4.1	34,888	2,362	112	23	9	42	41	139	186	13	9
Montgomery	942	2.4	33,733	2,522	432	75	34	49	118	261	591	40	34
Morgan	352	2.6	26,707	3,066	108	28	8	9	44	151	153	12	8
Muhlenberg	1,034	4.0	33,570	2,544	406	77	33	51	138	342	568	40	33
Nelson	1,914	3.2	41,941	1,270	671	115	52	79	256	390	916	62	52
Nicholas	236	4.1	33,170	2,597	31	7	2	11	29	82	52	5	2

1. Based on the resident population estimated as of July 1 of the year shown.

Table B. States and Counties — Earnings, Social Security, and Housing

STATE County	Earnings, 2017 (cont.)									Social Security beneficiaries, December 2017		Supplemental Security Income recipients, 2017	Housing units, 2018	
	Percent by selected industries													
	Farm	Mining, quarrying, and extractions	Construction	Manufacturing	Information; professional, scientific, technical services	Retail trade	Finance, insurance, real estate, and leasing	Health care and social assistance	Government	Number	Rate[1]		Total	Percent change, 2010-2018
	75	76	77	78	79	80	81	82	83	84	85	86	87	88
KENTUCKY— Cont'd														
Clay	-0.5	D	D	4.6	2.8	9.7	2.4	D	38.6	5,455	268	3,040	9,043	1.9
Clinton	2.3	D	5.3	34.1	1.3	7.2	2.3	14.7	17.6	2,735	266	820	5,303	-0.2
Crittenden	4	D	D	23.6	3.5	6	5	14.7	17.2	2,440	269	274	4,606	0.8
Cumberland	1.6	0	D	8.9	D	5.3	3.5	36.4	16.6	1,930	288	436	3,676	-0.3
Daviess	1.2	0.3	5.1	16.2	D	7.6	9.3	19.9	12.1	23,520	234	3,478	43,374	4.6
Edmonson	-3	0	18	D	D	5.1	D	D	40.8	3,155	258	400	6,607	2.1
Elliott	-0.6	0	4.9	0.4	D	3.7	D	10.9	60.4	1,755	233	462	3,443	2.1
Estill	-2.8	D	6.2	13	2.6	7.3	3.5	20.8	27.1	3,720	261	1,234	6,942	1.1
Fayette	2.2	-1.7	6.9	8.1	10.1	6	5.9	12.7	25.5	48,835	152	6,570	142,680	5.5
Fleming	-1.3	D	D	13.3	2.3	8.5	5.6	D	21.5	3,945	273	737	6,705	1.2
Floyd	0	6.4	7.2	4.1	9.4	6.9	2.3	19	18	11,865	327	3,967	18,518	1.9
Franklin	-0.1	D	3.6	9.8	6.2	4.2	4.3	D	46.7	14,035	278	1,505	23,287	0.5
Fulton	6.1	D	4.2	20.5	D	10.6	4.6	D	24.2	1,880	304	457	3,334	-1.1
Gallatin	-0.5	D	D	D	D	3.6	D	5	14.5	1,290	147	196	3,944	4.2
Garrard	-0.4	0	25.8	6.5	5.6	3.6	3.9	D	23.8	4,250	243	625	7,512	0.7
Grant	-1.3	0	7.5	15.3	7.6	10.4	3.2	D	20.7	5,725	229	868	10,258	3.2
Graves	14	D	5.2	13.8	4	7.7	4.4	11.3	16	9,445	254	1,538	16,840	0.4
Grayson	1.2	D	9.9	26.5	D	6.9	2.3	D	21.3	6,970	264	1,328	13,724	1.2
Green	5.4	0	6.3	2.7	4.8	7	5.6	21.4	25.1	3,100	280	559	5,319	-0.2
Greenup	-0.8	D	4.1	12	5.2	6.1	3.4	26.4	15.9	9,115	257	1,387	16,342	0.1
Hancock	1	D	5.2	71.7	D	1.9	0.7	D	7.3	2,190	249	268	3,753	0.5
Hardin	0.1	D	2.9	14.8	8.2	6	4.3	6.1	41.9	21,410	198	3,341	47,044	8.8
Harlan	-0.1	14.8	2.2	1.2	3.3	8.1	2.6	D	28.5	8,630	323	2,701	13,621	0.8
Harrison	-1.1	D	9.4	31.7	2.2	7.1	2.1	D	14.5	4,530	241	731	8,296	1.1
Hart	1.2	D	D	43.6	1.3	4.3	1.5	D	13.4	4,450	237	890	9,166	7.1
Henderson	1.4	0.1	5.8	31.1	3.1	6.6	3.6	D	12.8	10,975	239	1,629	20,619	1.5
Henry	-0.7	D	7.6	18.7	D	4.2	3.2	D	26.1	3,835	240	509	6,809	2.5
Hickman	45.4	0	D	D	D	3.1	D	D	13.5	1,390	308	171	2,363	0.9
Hopkins	2.1	5	7.1	14.6	D	11.1	3.6	17.1	16.2	11,665	256	1,888	21,494	1.5
Jackson	-7.8	D	D	5.5	D	5.2	3.7	D	39.3	3,430	255	1,258	6,632	1.7
Jefferson	0	-0.2	5	12.8	10.3	4.9	13.1	12.8	10.7	150,945	196	25,100	347,117	2.8
Jessamine	1.2	D	11.1	17.1	D	11.1	3.3	7	12.9	9,780	183	1,271	20,698	7.1
Johnson	-0.4	D	5.1	0.7	8.3	14.9	4.4	D	27.6	6,720	297	1,945	10,720	0.9
Kenton	-0.1	D	8.4	8.3	7.5	5	12.6	15.3	13.5	29,275	177	3,715	69,858	1.3
Knott	-0.6	D	8.2	D	8	7.5	D	D	29.8	4,190	274	1,487	7,628	2.1
Knox	-0.6	1.5	4.6	7.5	9	10.3	3.5	D	21.9	8,215	263	3,128	14,759	1.9
Larue	-1.4	0	12.6	16.9	D	4.6	5.3	11.3	24.4	3,605	254	524	6,402	3.7
Laurel	-0.2	1.3	4.5	16.7	4.4	9.2	4.1	12.8	11.8	14,860	247	3,125	25,988	2.1
Lawrence		D	8.6	D	D	9.9	2.4	25.6	20	4,325	275	1,368	7,431	2
Lee	-1.1	3.8	D	D	D	9.3	D	26.2	23.9	1,960	298	776	3,492	1.6
Leslie	-0.1	D	D	D	D	6.4	D	D	28.6	3,260	315	1,051	5,400	2.3
Letcher	0	3.2	2.9	2.5	D	9.4	2.6	D	24	7,185	322	2,041	11,793	1.7
Lewis	-0.3	0	D	14.9	1.7	4	D	11.4	26.5	3,160	237	965	6,581	1.5
Lincoln	-4.2	0	13.3	10.7	9.4	8.5	4.2	12.1	24.2	6,375	261	1,536	11,041	2.1
Livingston	3.4	D	15.8	3.1	D	3.7	D	9.5	17.6	2,840	306	322	4,901	1.6
Logan	3.4	D	6.6	42.3	2.8	5.4	2.7	5.8	11.2	6,640	245	916	12,412	0.6
Lyon	-1.4	0	7.5	D	D	5.7	2.4	10.4	46.6	2,475	306	166	4,919	2.7
McCracken	0	0	4.9	4.7	9.7	7.8	4.4	21.4	10.4	16,865	258	2,284	32,274	3.9
McCreary	-0.8	0	4.7	D	2.2	7.1	3.6	6.1	55	4,310	247	1,744	7,510	0
McLean	30.6	D	3.7	6.1	D	6.5	D	D	16.3	2,615	284	314	4,316	1.2
Madison	-0.4	D	5.5	20.1	9.6	7.2	3	10	26.1	17,285	189	2,985	37,059	5.8
Magoffin	-2.4	D	3.8	D	D	8	D	17.8	37.6	3,605	288	1,598	6,111	2.7
Marion	-0.6	0	4.4	51.2	D	4.3	2.5	D	10.4	4,405	227	947	8,319	1.7
Marshall	0.9	D	17	34.4	2.6	6.2	4.1	D	12.1	9,115	290	764	16,254	3.2
Martin	-0.6	21.1	D	D	D	6.5	D	9.3	39.8	3,280	286	1,229	5,301	2.7
Mason	0	0	8.1	20.8	D	7.9	3	15.7	13	4,380	255	717	8,159	0.7
Meade	2	2.6	14	14.3	5.4	9.1	5.2	5.9	20.4	5,985	213	571	12,562	6.8
Menifee	-2.2	D	D	13.9	D	4.3	D	D	37.8	1,900	294	533	3,810	1.8
Mercer	0.7	D	7.4	38.9	3.2	5.4	2.6	D	10.9	5,680	264	715	10,174	2.4
Metcalfe	5	0	D	31.8	D	4.5	2.5	4.4	22.3	2,815	279	614	4,757	1.6
Monroe	9.9	-0.1	9.5	15.7	D	7.6	4.7	D	16.1	2,960	278	676	5,257	1
Montgomery		D	5.8	36.7	D	8.6	4.3	D	12.1	6,430	230	1,221	12,012	2.7
Morgan	-3.5	D	D	12.1	D	6.4	D	9.1	35.8	3,270	248	940	6,064	4
Muhlenberg	3.2	14.2	11.7	7.2	D	6.4	2.4	D	24.9	8,340	271	1,299	13,810	0.8
Nelson	0.1	D	10.1	33.5	D	7.1	4.3	9.9	11.6	10,370	227	1,214	19,214	6.3
Nicholas	1.8	0	15.4	6.1	D	4	D	14.6	31.4	1,855	260	303	3,280	0.6

1. Per 1,000 resident population estimated as of July 1 of the year shown.

Table B. States and Counties — Housing, Labor Force, and Employment

STATE County	Housing units, 2013-2017								Civilian labor force, 2018				Civilian employment[6], 2013-2017		
	Occupied units										Unemployment		Percent		
			Owner-occupied			Renter-occupied									
				Median owner cost as a percent of income			Median rent as a percent of income[2]	Sub-standard units[4] (percent)		Percent change, 2017-2018				Management, business, science, and arts	Construction, production, and maintenance occupations
			Median value[1]	With a mort-gage	Without a mort-gage[2]	Median rent[3]			Total		Total	Rate[5]	Total		
	Total	Percent													
	89	90	91	92	93	94	95	96	97	98	99	100	101	102	103
KENTUCKY— Cont'd															
Clay	7,719	71.3	55,600	22.4	11.8	510	36.4	3.5	5,221	-2.6	369	7.1	5,762	24.8	29.3
Clinton	4,025	69.9	66,100	21.0	11.8	536	24.5	1.8	3,869	0.2	212	5.5	3,830	25.2	35.5
Crittenden	3,711	81.2	84,600	18.8	11.1	502	23.4	1.9	3,908	-1.9	202	5.2	3,690	28.3	35.9
Cumberland	2,709	70.2	90,300	26.4	10.7	437	22	0.6	3,134	6.6	140	4.5	2,401	34.7	27.8
Daviess	39,531	67.5	123,200	19.3	10.0	698	28.2	2.6	48,018	0.1	1,897	4	44,736	29.9	28.4
Edmonson	4,880	80.5	87,100	20.4	10.8	643	27.9	3.9	4,868	0.1	258	5.3	4,640	25.9	31.3
Elliott	2,635	76.9	72,700	21.3	12.4	532	41.5	1.1	2,070	-2.3	192	9.3	1,790	21.3	39.6
Estill	5,638	70.5	71,000	20.9	11.7	578	30.1	4.9	5,325	-0.5	292	5.5	5,015	24.5	41.2
Fayette	127,336	54.0	175,000	19.0	10.0	828	29.5	2.3	174,849	-0.3	5,801	3.3	162,280	42.9	16.1
Fleming	5,849	71.2	89,900	19.0	10.0	533	26.1	3.5	6,142	1.3	334	5.4	5,824	28.2	36.7
Floyd	15,108	70.4	72,900	22.7	11.4	579	33.4	3.3	10,907	-3.3	720	6.6	11,130	29.5	24.2
Franklin	20,786	63.2	139,300	19.3	10.0	727	25	2.1	25,051	1.1	936	3.7	23,685	37.4	22.4
Fulton	2,463	61.1	63,600	22.2	12.1	501	27.7	0.9	2,048	-0.9	118	5.8	2,287	29.9	26.6
Gallatin	3,007	71.3	109,900	20.1	10.3	678	20.4	2.4	4,073	0.8	166	4.1	3,728	20.2	34.4
Garrard	6,925	78.2	131,000	20.1	11.1	680	29.6	3.4	7,693	0.5	341	4.4	7,339	29.9	31.7
Grant	8,637	67.2	119,700	21.2	11.7	720	29.8	4.8	11,729	1	506	4.3	10,421	20.5	37.0
Graves	14,299	73.8	95,600	19.8	10.8	634	32	2.3	15,447	-1.5	777	5	15,661	27.7	30.5
Grayson	9,594	71.9	102,200	21.9	10.4	556	29.6	2.8	10,995	0.9	540	4.9	10,491	26.0	39.5
Green	4,467	76.8	75,800	19.1	10.0	542	29.5	1.1	5,076	-1.4	218	4.3	4,626	19.9	38.3
Greenup	14,089	76.2	103,300	19.3	11.5	681	28.3	1.7	13,459	-1.1	895	6.6	13,651	36.2	23.8
Hancock	3,375	75.9	109,100	17.0	10.0	593	21.6	1.4	4,089	-0.4	170	4.2	3,614	24.1	41.0
Hardin	41,051	61.6	148,000	19.1	10.0	783	25.9	2.1	49,149	0.8	1,991	4.1	47,636	32.6	24.4
Harlan	11,249	68.4	53,500	23.0	11.9	481	30.5	2.1	6,554	1.1	487	7.4	7,555	27.0	28.0
Harrison	7,107	69.6	132,900	20.1	12.1	622	28.7	2	8,699	0.1	360	4.1	7,850	25.5	36.2
Hart	7,346	74.3	90,200	19.8	10.2	508	27.2	2.8	8,085	-0.2	322	4	7,125	22.4	40.4
Henderson	18,719	61.9	118,000	19.2	10.5	643	28.8	1.7	22,154	0.8	851	3.8	20,942	28.6	31.5
Henry	6,104	67.8	126,100	20.4	10.6	745	29.1	3.1	8,183	0.6	318	3.9	7,143	22.5	36.3
Hickman	1,877	81.5	70,200	21.9	12.8	496	21	3.1	1,812	-0.4	104	5.7	1,631	24.3	39.2
Hopkins	18,546	70.5	96,600	18.0	10.0	657	26.4	1.5	19,281		852	4.4	18,920	28.4	30.9
Jackson	5,435	74.8	69,900	22.3	12.1	527	27	4.3	4,117	0.3	288	7	4,218	24.5	45.0
Jefferson	309,888	61.5	159,000	19.7	11.2	800	28.1	2.1	400,587	1	16,269	4.1	376,394	36.9	22.5
Jessamine	18,537	62.1	164,300	20.2	10.0	808	27.7	2.4	26,425	0	960	3.6	23,854	35.7	24.5
Johnson	8,771	72.3	90,300	19.3	13.0	609	31.8	3.9	6,763	-2.3	465	6.9	6,892	36.7	20.1
Kenton	62,929	65.7	149,700	18.8	10.0	763	26.3	2	87,686	1.2	3,025	3.4	82,552	37.1	22.0
Knott	6,158	76.8	52,000	20.0	10.0	470	35.1	4.8	4,425	-1.8	304	6.9	4,707	31.2	22.9
Knox	12,264	63.3	76,900	22.4	11.6	530	30.7	2.7	10,114	0.4	632	6.2	9,321	28.3	29.1
Larue	5,470	72.2	107,300	20.9	10.0	693	30.3	2.7	6,075	0.9	267	4.4	6,136	23.3	44.5
Laurel	22,976	69.1	102,000	20.1	11.8	615	30.1	2.9	24,947	1.1	1,268	5.1	22,550	25.4	30.4
Lawrence	6,254	76.5	80,400	22.4	11.2	571	30.4	3.7	5,085	1.5	368	7.2	5,065	26.2	30.0
Lee	2,843	73.5	64,200	25.9	13.5	550	48.6	3.8	2,033	7.1	129	6.3	1,713	29.9	36.0
Leslie	4,292	77.9	48,900	22.5	10.1	458	24.1	5.5	2,650	-3.2	188	7.1	2,774	29.3	30.2
Letcher	10,065	74.2	58,500	23.2	11.1	568	35.5	2.9	6,316	0.3	412	6.5	7,058	35.3	26.7
Lewis	5,496	74.8	68,300	19.0	12.4	445	28.3	3.4	4,727	0.4	396	8.4	4,561	28.0	39.4
Lincoln	9,786	73.5	96,100	19.6	11.3	620	27.9	3.1	9,366	-0.1	471	5	9,547	25.7	34.2
Livingston	4,016	74.3	90,800	19.4	10.0	633	27.9	2.7	3,702	-1.5	251	6.8	4,022	21.8	42.4
Logan	10,780	67.4	105,400	20.1	12.5	603	31	1.2	12,453	2.4	483	3.9	10,724	27.0	37.1
Lyon	3,376	82.5	122,900	20.7	10.0	481	30.6	1.9	3,063	2.3	156	5.1	2,829	25.6	29.7
McCracken	27,557	67.0	134,100	19.2	10.0	640	28.9	1.4	29,386		1,642	5.6	28,766	34.0	22.2
McCreary	6,332	70.8	61,300	27.2	14.2	574	44.8	2.1	4,654	-0.9	294	6.3	4,493	22.4	34.1
McLean	3,826	80.1	96,800	18.5	10.1	567	26.8	3.1	4,285	-0.4	211	4.9	3,838	25.1	40.1
Madison	33,036	59.0	151,000	19.2	10.5	679	28.9	1.3	46,892	1.5	1,809	3.9	41,594	36.3	21.7
Magoffin	5,057	68.7	63,300	21.3	11.0	556	42.6	3.7	2,855	-4.7	378	13.2	3,718	32.1	37.7
Marion	7,365	73.9	100,400	21.6	10.0	613	28.2	4.8	9,627	1.7	364	3.8	7,891	27.6	38.4
Marshall	13,117	78.9	118,100	19.0	10.0	643	26.9	2.4	15,078	0.2	798	5.3	13,089	28.6	33.8
Martin	4,316	72.2	65,500	27.9	11.2	483	31.8	5.1	2,788	-9.4	181	6.5	3,032	28.9	27.5
Mason	6,737	67.8	111,200	19.1	10.0	591	28.4	1.9	7,254	0.4	400	5.5	7,087	29.1	32.3
Meade	10,785	71.6	140,800	18.9	10.0	818	24	3.4	12,319	0.6	572	4.6	11,827	29.6	34.7
Menifee	2,537	82.2	77,800	23.4	10.0	573	22.2	2.5	2,340	-1.2	178	7.6	2,529	20.5	42.5
Mercer	8,645	71.8	139,900	20.2	10.1	619	28.6	1.7	9,871	-1.1	440	4.5	9,657	29.7	32.3
Metcalfe	3,940	76.3	75,200	22.7	11.7	534	23.6	2.2	4,201	0.5	173	4.1	3,875	24.9	39.7
Monroe	4,376	72.6	74,500	20.1	10.6	508	28.2	2.3	4,728	0	196	4.1	4,270	33.4	37.1
Montgomery	10,404	66.9	118,200	19.7	10.8	665	26.4	3.1	11,663	-0.6	696	6	11,384	26.0	34.1
Morgan	4,937	74.6	77,500	20.4	11.8	561	30.4	2.5	4,476	-0.8	283	6.3	3,662	30.8	33.9
Muhlenberg	11,416	77.8	82,000	18.8	10.0	540	27.3	2.1	10,604	-5.8	714	6.7	11,493	23.3	37.4
Nelson	17,324	78.4	144,800	19.6	10.3	693	26.6	2.7	22,711	1.9	985	4.3	21,251	28.3	35.9
Nicholas	2,760	69.6	82,100	18.1	10.5	578	26.3	5	3,287	-0.8	150	4.6	2,867	24.8	39.4

1. Specified owner-occupied units. 2. A value of 10.0 represents 10 percent or less; a value of 50.0 represents 50 percent or more. 3. Specified renter-occupied units. 4. Overcrowded or lacking complete plumbing facilities. 5. Percent of civilian labor force. 6. Civilian employed persons 16 years old and over.

STATE County	Private nonfarm establishments, employment and payroll, 2016									Agriculture, 2017			
		Employment						Annual payroll		Farms			Farm producers whose primary occupation is farming (percent)
	Number of establish-ments	Total	Health care and social assistance	Manufac-turing	Retail trade	Finance and insurance	Professional, scientific, and technical services	Total (mil dol)	Average per employee (dollars)	Number	Percent with:		
											Fewer than 50 acres	1000 acres or more	
	104	105	106	107	108	109	110	111	112	113	114	115	116
KENTUCKY— Cont'd													
Clay	227	2,583	838	275	636	74	46	73	28,084	233	28.3	3.0	33.6
Clinton	189	3,236	635	1,662	265	76	27	80	24,875	512	40.6	1.0	32.2
Crittenden	159	2,042	376	580	254	81	33	58	28,595	575	23.7	6.1	33.0
Cumberland	108	1,097	364	221	176	58	17	33	30,178	395	27.1	3.5	31.0
Daviess	2,334	41,409	8,357	5,063	6,150	3,230	935	1,595	38,507	919	52.6	7.7	39.9
Edmonson	122	848	223	D	162	66	13	23	27,636	578	37.0	0.5	33.1
Elliott	48	336	167	NA	62	16	NA	8	25,214	363	25.1	NA	41.8
Estill	185	1,577	404	186	285	67	40	45	28,822	367	31.1	1.4	37.9
Fayette	8,804	160,366	31,875	8,421	20,823	4,830	13,156	6,865	42,809	622	51.8	3.2	40.2
Fleming	232	2,099	552	418	442	100	35	66	31,562	1,013	32.0	1.8	39.8
Floyd	802	9,169	2,194	232	1,482	235	225	315	34,363	136	58.8	NA	31.7
Franklin	1,169	16,760	2,228	2,610	2,737	931	786	644	38,398	599	40.7	0.3	34.9
Fulton	116	1,479	291	446	206	73	24	47	31,564	146	41.1	19.9	53.6
Gallatin	94	889	D	D	180	26	21	23	25,505	235	43.8	3.0	25.5
Garrard	220	1,460	251	272	164	48	64	49	33,615	793	37.6	1.9	42.4
Grant	382	3,945	460	921	1,008	66	85	137	34,616	811	36.1	0.9	34.3
Graves	664	9,354	1,440	2,535	1,431	317	702	303	32,410	1,104	43.2	6.3	39.3
Grayson	493	6,319	1,010	1,776	1,037	227	68	192	30,366	1,339	33.8	2.1	35.9
Green	155	1,259	546	43	221	51	25	36	28,301	1,004	33.4	1.5	28.8
Greenup	506	4,897	1,188	541	695	183	147	180	36,716	584	37.0	0.9	34.4
Hancock	128	3,229	124	2,300	121	68	42	201	62,151	321	35.8	0.9	26.5
Hardin	2,292	36,218	7,602	6,302	6,284	1,260	1,162	1,300	35,901	1,305	49.0	2.9	34.3
Harlan	399	4,303	1,344	88	938	137	161	143	33,183	39	51.3	5.1	21.1
Harrison	284	4,024	974	1,298	616	83	112	160	39,826	1,138	36.7	1.1	39.0
Hart	288	4,503	587	2,686	459	74	49	139	30,811	1,287	40.9	1.2	36.7
Henderson	986	16,990	2,361	5,696	2,107	411	492	661	38,903	458	46.7	12.4	39.4
Henry	208	2,224	509	407	358	96	45	64	28,948	771	35.3	2.2	41.7
Hickman	73	998	156	156	286	67	D	33	33,214	246	34.6	10.2	54.8
Hopkins	1,010	14,935	3,252	1,962	2,674	428	380	611	40,891	656	43.9	5.0	34.6
Jackson	95	837	241	34	128	51	D	30	35,521	551	36.7	0.7	33.6
Jefferson	19,800	419,828	63,942	46,030	44,448	30,822	22,450	20,642	49,167	343	70.0	NA	35.8
Jessamine	1,095	15,817	1,288	2,744	2,621	237	686	564	35,631	671	56.9	1.2	35.7
Johnson	401	3,937	675	49	1,506	115	120	127	32,161	224	34.8	NA	24.8
Kenton	3,104	53,657	10,753	3,616	5,815	5,502	2,674	2,644	49,275	506	54.3	0.2	24.4
Knott	164	1,572	436	D	266	41	55	44	27,746	62	38.7	3.2	50.0
Knox	451	8,626	1,209	1,273	1,204	187	2,173	221	25,645	336	50.9	0.9	34.3
Larue	234	1,828	353	551	201	199	41	59	32,132	718	49.7	2.1	38.0
Laurel	1,155	23,945	2,499	3,793	3,464	941	2,811	745	31,132	955	48.6	0.3	33.0
Lawrence	205	2,437	800	D	655	71	52	82	33,521	284	25.4	2.1	32.8
Lee	90	1,333	829	D	151	20	18	29	21,392	144	36.8	2.8	38.4
Leslie	113	1,279	349	D	206	70	52	40	31,473	26	53.8	NA	12.5
Letcher	323	3,459	1,031	D	669	117	101	113	32,774	103	68.9	NA	27.3
Lewis	124	1,389	359	354	283	94	16	40	28,973	550	21.5	1.5	37.9
Lincoln	308	2,806	612	464	577	106	81	85	30,155	1,090	42.8	2.0	42.8
Livingston	139	1,900	351	88	184	36	34	86	45,311	365	20.3	5.5	36.3
Logan	510	6,712	744	2,863	975	179	182	272	40,488	1,078	37.9	4.0	41.6
Lyon	161	1,258	243	D	224	16	49	36	28,447	208	31.7	2.4	33.1
McCracken	2,074	34,307	7,067	2,025	6,217	1,230	1,072	1,331	38,786	318	52.5	6.3	36.8
McCreary	157	1,507	325	226	349	102	116	36	23,737	173	49.1	NA	35.5
McLean	168	1,279	170	133	214	88	18	45	35,558	439	42.8	8.4	39.5
Madison	1,666	23,139	3,310	4,908	4,265	573	718	815	35,230	1,187	37.3	1.9	38.6
Magoffin	159	1,123	197	D	214	56	103	30	26,989	335	36.7	0.9	30.4
Marion	362	7,852	1,472	4,131	670	135	107	268	34,189	954	35.6	1.5	38.0
Marshall	655	9,293	918	2,361	1,233	321	227	427	45,958	699	49.4	2.3	27.9
Martin	160	1,638	210	D	361	69	23	62	37,799	30	30.0	6.7	39.5
Mason	428	6,949	1,239	1,103	1,377	194	108	249	35,883	680	32.5	2.6	36.6
Meade	382	3,487	340	508	613	111	285	127	36,556	781	51.3	3.3	31.7
Menifee	58	488	190	88	75	D	D	16	32,893	283	36.7	0.4	27.8
Mercer	350	5,377	651	2,294	660	114	55	229	42,506	1,108	43.4	1.2	33.0
Metcalfe	119	1,150	92	610	158	43	15	35	30,331	945	38.7	1.6	40.4
Monroe	203	2,581	461	623	552	71	31	78	30,091	765	30.5	3.7	37.1
Montgomery	557	9,947	1,015	3,492	1,549	293	147	319	32,060	659	38.7	3.2	32.6
Morgan	154	1,832	356	244	354	115	78	62	34,039	657	26.2	2.1	37.5
Muhlenberg	575	6,356	1,402	718	1,207	187	263	213	33,538	549	32.8	4.0	37.6
Nelson	961	15,274	1,350	4,383	1,933	340	238	562	36,809	1,434	54.0	2.0	38.6
Nicholas	78	435	161	52	67	18	28	13	28,908	556	26.3	0.9	44.7

STATE County	Land in farms — Acreage (1,000) [117]	Percent change, 2012-2017 [118]	Acres — Average size of farm [119]	Total irrigated (1,000) [120]	Total cropland (1,000) [121]	Value of land and buildings (dollars) — Average per farm [122]	Average per acre [123]	Value of machinery and equipment, average per farm (dollars) [124]	Value of products sold — Total (mil dol) [125]	Average per farm (acres) [126]	Percent from: Crops [127]	Livestock and poultry products [128]	Organic farms (number) [129]	Farms with internet access (percent) [130]	Government payments — Total ($1,000) [131]	Percent of farms [132]
KENTUCKY— Cont'd																
Clay	44	26.3	190	0.0	8.3	345,381	1,814	53,754	5.2	22,399	75.2	24.8	2	74.7	9	3.9
Clinton	65	-12.0	127	0.0	23.8	354,745	2,788	72,223	40.6	79,334	7.5	92.5	NA	76.6	358	17.8
Crittenden	158	6.2	275	D	79.2	754,514	2,747	84,792	39.3	68,289	69.8	30.2	4	51.5	2,296	42.8
Cumberland	82	24.6	207	0.0	22.6	423,878	2,053	57,763	10.7	26,965	46.1	53.9	3	66.6	118	8.4
Daviess	238	0.3	259	10.9	190.8	1,291,082	4,986	163,634	185.9	202,262	64.4	35.6	NA	71.7	4,337	44.0
Edmonson	82	-4.0	141	0.0	38.1	448,629	3,178	75,656	27.5	47,500	40.9	59.1	NA	74.7	1,188	26.8
Elliott	55	-2.4	152	0.0	15.1	245,278	1,619	49,503	3.1	8,628	32.0	68.0	NA	79.3	72	9.9
Estill	53	1.6	145	0.0	14.2	347,874	2,404	48,838	4.1	11,183	35.4	64.6	1	75.5	126	16.1
Fayette	115	-0.2	184	0.3	33.7	2,694,042	14,619	122,300	215.5	346,492	5.9	94.1	6	90.0	576	10.1
Fleming	171	-6.4	169	D	77.3	447,405	2,643	71,101	48.8	48,124	38.3	61.7	2	68.4	783	46.5
Floyd	9	12.0	67	D	2.1	207,547	3,088	34,195	0.6	4,294	59.8	40.2	NA	88.2	D	1.5
Franklin	75	-5.1	124	0.2	29.4	493,851	3,967	53,515	18.9	31,482	42.3	57.7	10	77.6	666	7.3
Fulton	98	17.1	669	7.0	86.6	2,456,571	3,674	304,536	62.1	425,521	71.5	28.5	NA	76.7	2,263	73.3
Gallatin	33	17.0	138	0.0	14.2	393,568	2,845	61,824	7.7	32,936	85.7	14.3	NA	70.2	6	4.7
Garrard	141	10.8	178	0.0	56.8	518,773	2,917	76,025	35.4	44,608	32.0	68.0	5	70.6	345	12.4
Grant	97	-1.6	119	D	35.5	394,863	3,309	54,915	10.1	12,486	58.3	41.7	1	73.0	67	6.2
Graves	251	-13.9	228	5.1	194.8	870,326	3,825	144,824	346.2	313,547	29.7	70.3	NA	70.4	5,088	50.5
Grayson	212	5.7	159	0.2	95.3	468,818	2,956	64,374	59.6	44,494	37.4	62.6	11	65.1	2,219	30.1
Green	156	2.4	156	0.1	76.1	403,864	2,595	76,652	53.2	53,021	59.4	40.6	2	65.9	3,100	39.4
Greenup	74	-6.2	126	0.1	19.0	312,060	2,471	57,719	5.8	9,911	50.4	49.6	2	74.7	132	3.6
Hancock	48	-8.6	149	0.0	21.4	442,673	2,977	78,019	11.6	36,131	71.9	28.1	NA	80.1	472	38.9
Hardin	199	-1.9	153	D	109.6	701,236	4,594	81,201	59.2	45,396	70.1	29.9	1	73.9	1,777	22.1
Harlan	7	7.7	173	D	0.5	270,697	1,564	32,631	0.2	5,436	68.9	31.1	NA	79.5	D	5.1
Harrison	168	1.9	147	1.2	71.2	456,684	3,100	75,066	35.1	30,850	57.8	42.2	3	74.2	300	12.0
Hart	170	-6.9	132	0.2	73.8	406,053	3,078	59,043	36.8	28,584	51.6	48.4	3	65.3	3,457	29.1
Henderson	181	2.7	394	9.2	156.8	2,010,156	5,096	193,308	97.7	213,312	88.9	11.1	NA	83.2	4,739	53.1
Henry	131	1.9	170	0.2	65.2	656,023	3,861	79,554	30.6	39,696	53.9	46.1	2	73.9	195	10.1
Hickman	118	-16.1	482	9.5	103.9	1,933,385	4,014	317,655	159.6	648,817	35.7	64.3	NA	72.4	3,156	65.4
Hopkins	146	-10.2	223	0.1	91.0	752,392	3,372	98,293	119.6	182,309	32.6	67.4	2	73.6	1,661	31.9
Jackson	75	-3.3	136	0.0	26.1	321,560	2,356	50,666	5.7	10,430	35.2	64.8	4	73.7	55	6.4
Jefferson	20	-12.4	59	0.1	7.6	725,049	12,296	43,708	6.4	18,551	78.5	21.5	3	80.5	99	2.9
Jessamine	76	-8.8	114	0.0	32.4	754,661	6,640	57,978	79.9	119,028	7.4	92.6	1	85.5	387	7.7
Johnson	22	-9.4	98	0.0	3.8	294,847	3,001	37,113	0.7	3,152	29.7	70.3	NA	82.1	10	3.6
Kenton	37	-3.7	73	0.0	15.9	406,271	5,597	54,195	5.4	10,652	53.3	46.7	NA	77.7	38	5.3
Knott	13	89.1	206	D	0.6	263,055	1,279	38,779	0.4	6,581	8.6	91.4	NA	88.7	NA	NA
Knox	39	15.5	115	0.0	12.0	275,946	2,394	58,675	2.5	7,542	53.2	46.8	2	70.5	54	3.6
Larue	110	-1.4	154	0.0	67.7	545,514	3,549	93,130	41.1	57,259	78.9	21.1	NA	81.2	986	20.6
Laurel	90	-6.6	94	0.0	35.1	313,976	3,343	59,396	15.4	16,153	43.2	56.8	NA	69.0	147	7.0
Lawrence	51	22.9	180	D	7.9	288,449	1,599	47,327	1.3	4,423	40.8	59.2	NA	79.2	19	3.5
Lee	25	12.8	174	NA	8.5	356,475	2,047	49,063	1.4	9,667	25.2	74.8	NA	70.1	55	19.4
Leslie	2	D	63	D	0.2	242,308	3,820	23,981	0.0	1,269	69.7	30.3	NA	69.2	NA	NA
Letcher	6	95.5	55	NA	0.4	163,784	3,000	31,980	0.1	1,340	44.2	55.8	NA	82.5	NA	NA
Lewis	117	-0.5	213	D	41.7	447,476	2,096	58,968	12.7	23,065	68.7	31.3	NA	71.6	338	13.3
Lincoln	163	-9.7	150	0.0	69.0	486,123	3,246	73,186	59.0	54,136	31.5	68.5	20	70.1	939	21.8
Livingston	122	-1.2	333	0.0	61.6	937,557	2,812	108,341	24.2	66,178	63.8	36.2	NA	67.9	1,309	51.2
Logan	276	0.2	256	4.8	195.2	1,237,795	4,829	133,156	152.2	141,154	68.8	31.2	5	71.1	6,869	46.0
Lyon	33	-21.5	157	D	17.6	490,391	3,121	61,700	6.7	32,029	80.2	19.8	NA	64.4	391	28.8
McCracken	62	-7.6	195	0.2	50.6	869,914	4,456	123,106	28.9	90,953	77.4	22.6	NA	84.6	821	33.0
McCreary	18	1.3	106	D	3.8	259,977	2,455	59,199	2.6	14,740	23.6	76.4	1	63.0	44	21.4
McLean	129	4.0	295	D	108.1	1,315,544	4,466	184,326	190.8	434,711	29.7	70.3	NA	83.6	2,369	58.8
Madison	230	-1.3	194	0.1	74.8	671,408	3,468	71,336	50.6	42,592	15.3	84.7	6	72.4	361	14.7
Magoffin	44	-1.5	131	0.0	7.1	270,577	2,070	54,356	1.4	4,269	55.7	44.3	NA	76.7	7	3.3
Marion	163	-2.1	171	0.0	85.2	594,733	3,482	86,494	60.2	63,134	45.3	54.7	2	76.8	893	36.2
Marshall	85	-10.8	121	0.1	52.9	459,882	3,796	82,985	51.4	73,504	33.2	66.8	NA	73.8	1,139	40.1
Martin	11	D	368	NA	2.3	1,270,003	3,451	72,023	0.2	7,133	10.7	89.3	NA	70.0	NA	NA
Mason	132	4.3	194	0.0	68.7	574,464	2,957	76,841	31.3	46,081	63.5	36.5	4	75.3	557	25.3
Meade	141	18.0	181	0.0	80.4	781,623	4,328	98,021	45.8	58,634	61.2	38.8	NA	83.1	1,798	31.6
Menifee	35	-13.7	125	0.0	8.2	241,589	1,933	44,239	2.4	8,449	27.7	72.3	NA	73.5	6	1.8
Mercer	136	-5.4	123	0.0	59.7	483,392	3,925	61,328	45.9	41,428	26.2	73.8	3	73.6	2,019	12.4
Metcalfe	138	10.5	147	0.0	58.6	392,272	2,677	74,723	43.1	45,654	47.4	52.6	2	77.6	1,290	24.2
Monroe	160	-7.2	209	0.1	61.1	594,999	2,847	83,370	102.5	133,949	16.6	83.4	2	73.1	754	28.8
Montgomery	103	3.6	156	0.0	41.0	547,952	3,505	74,291	21.4	32,461	26.6	73.4	NA	71.9	114	13.1
Morgan	107	-10.3	162	0.1	23.2	315,781	1,948	55,320	5.8	8,804	38.4	61.6	NA	68.9	139	7.0
Muhlenberg	128	-1.0	232	0.0	69.3	695,899	2,996	102,576	94.5	172,069	30.3	69.7	NA	70.1	1,142	28.8
Nelson	214	13.7	149	0.2	114.0	604,664	4,061	76,095	67.1	46,791	62.7	37.3	NA	73.4	927	10.0
Nicholas	93	-9.1	167	0.0	39.4	387,800	2,322	66,211	25.9	46,653	49.3	50.7	1	60.1	139	8.6

Table B. States and Counties — Water Use, Wholesale Trade, Retail Trade, and Real Estate

STATE County	Water use, 2015 Public supply water withdrawn (mil gal/day)	Public supply gallons withdrawn per person per day	Wholesale Trade[1], 2012 Number of establishments	Number of employees	Sales (mil dol)	Average payroll (mil dol)	Retail Trade[2], 2012 Number of establishments	Number of employees	Sales (mil dol)	Average payroll (mil dol)	Real estate and rental and leasing,[2] 2012 Number of establishments	Number of employees	Sales (mil dol)	Average payroll (mil dol)
	133	134	135	136	137	138	139	140	141	142	143	144	145	146
KENTUCKY— Cont'd														
Clay	5.20	247.5	5	D	D	D	63	543	138.8	11.6	7	D	D	D
Clinton	3.75	368.6	11	64	87.1	2.3	39	296	59.4	4.4	7	19	3.0	0.4
Crittenden	0.47	51.2	5	118	11.8	2.5	31	273	58.8	5.1	6	13	1.7	0.3
Cumberland	0.63	93.2	NA	NA	NA	NA	30	181	46.0	3.4	3	7	0.3	0.1
Daviess	13.36	134.6	97	1,266	1,105.8	55.6	411	5,906	1,443.4	134.3	80	578	99.7	19.2
Edmonson	1.67	139.1	NA	NA	NA	NA	31	177	39.2	3.0	NA	NA	NA	NA
Elliott	0.19	24.8	NA	NA	NA	NA	12	D	D	D	NA	NA	NA	NA
Estill	1.31	91.1	3	D	D	D	42	299	75.3	5.9	5	D	D	D
Fayette	35.21	112.0	352	7,283	4,517.8	527.7	1,192	19,820	4,994.8	466.9	431	2,128	442.3	76.6
Fleming	0.21	14.3	10	D	D	D	61	455	134.8	11.2	10	15	1.9	0.2
Floyd	4.52	119.7	39	475	395.4	19.0	164	1,506	448.3	34.4	30	131	18.2	5.3
Franklin	16.10	319.6	28	282	372.8	15.5	178	2,477	654.2	54.0	38	191	22.2	4.6
Fulton	1.18	189.2	7	53	377.2	4.8	26	184	44.0	3.2	4	7	0.6	0.2
Gallatin	0.60	69.5	1	D	D	D	21	241	128.0	4.6	7	D	D	D
Garrard	1.43	83.0	6	23	7.4	0.8	35	167	59.1	3.3	7	10	2.0	0.2
Grant	1.70	68.7	8	D	D	D	74	943	284.4	21.2	17	38	4.0	1.0
Graves	2.62	70.0	38	613	767.9	25.6	123	1,374	403.7	32.0	34	70	10.9	1.5
Grayson	2.64	100.7	11	D	D	D	104	1,069	258.6	22.2	12	141	7.1	3.7
Green	0.84	76.3	6	29	15.1	0.9	32	246	62.1	5.2	3	D	D	D
Greenup	3.80	105.4	9	D	D	D	86	837	211.7	18.0	16	57	8.1	1.3
Hancock	0.53	61.0	3	D	D	D	17	138	43.5	2.6	5	13	2.5	0.3
Hardin	14.33	134.6	57	422	245.7	18.3	408	5,754	1,639.1	137.8	109	490	62.4	11.7
Harlan	3.40	122.7	25	204	177.3	9.5	101	1,043	205.4	21.2	14	46	4.8	0.9
Harrison	2.78	148.2	10	44	30.0	1.3	46	566	134.5	11.7	7	32	2.9	0.6
Hart	4.10	222.2	9	39	12.7	1.5	65	406	157.9	8.1	7	16	1.5	0.4
Henderson	8.68	187.0	45	D	D	D	170	2,174	729.9	53.7	44	275	23.4	5.2
Henry	0.00	0.0	13	D	D	D	36	342	171.4	6.3	4	D	D	D
Hickman	0.13	28.2	6	31	67.8	0.9	20	267	76.1	6.2	3	5	0.3	0.0
Hopkins	9.63	208.3	44	414	240.3	20.6	182	2,325	692.4	55.5	41	114	15.2	3.3
Jackson	1.47	110.1	NA	NA	NA	NA	25	187	45.7	2.7	5	14	1.4	0.4
Jefferson	133.75	175.2	1,006	15,867	13,048.4	836.7	2,659	41,294	10,964.4	1,004.0	926	7,168	2,895.1	289.1
Jessamine	5.34	102.8	40	D	D	D	158	2,638	920.3	71.1	31	124	14.0	3.3
Johnson	2.48	107.0	17	110	57.2	4.0	91	1,333	383.0	31.1	16	41	4.5	0.9
Kenton	0.00	0.0	119	1,888	886.0	92.5	394	5,422	1,331.7	120.4	129	656	161.3	27.0
Knott	1.84	117.2	NA	NA	NA	NA	39	297	72.5	5.4	3	D	D	D
Knox	0.30	9.5	11	70	39.9	2.0	106	1,194	343.1	26.2	11	51	4.8	1.0
Larue	0.67	47.0	7	D	D	D	30	255	63.9	4.6	3	3	0.1	0.1
Laurel	8.90	148.1	61	732	597.3	29.0	228	3,348	1,015.1	78.2	46	166	27.6	4.6
Lawrence	1.49	94.6	11	229	136.5	9.0	52	645	161.5	12.5	9	36	4.0	0.7
Lee	0.95	140.7	4	17	4.8	0.5	22	236	63.9	4.9	4	D	D	D
Leslie	1.06	99.0	NA	NA	NA	NA	26	220	55.6	3.7	NA	NA	NA	NA
Letcher	1.61	69.6	11	D	D	D	59	678	151.2	15.1	11	18	3.9	0.6
Lewis	2.42	176.9	3	D	D	D	32	252	70.5	4.1	2	D	D	D
Lincoln	2.11	86.3	14	D	D	D	61	623	145.9	10.9	6	10	1.1	0.2
Livingston	1.66	178.2	9	D	D	D	25	181	47.1	3.7	4	D	D	D
Logan	0.00	0.0	22	192	156.6	6.8	98	926	264.9	22.1	11	18	3.4	0.5
Lyon	2.67	321.5	3	D	D	D	20	190	65.1	4.0	3	4	0.9	0.1
McCracken	8.21	126.3	104	D	D	D	411	6,163	1,638.5	140.7	79	330	60.9	9.8
McCreary	1.96	109.6	2	D	D	D	42	378	81.9	7.5	8	13	0.8	0.2
McLean	0.69	72.5	8	D	D	D	28	185	61.0	4.1	NA	NA	NA	NA
Madison	11.42	130.0	38	308	262.0	9.6	299	4,171	1,080.7	85.1	68	D	D	D
Magoffin	0.78	60.9	2	D	D	D	34	241	61.1	4.8	2	D	D	D
Marion	4.13	213.3	11	68	34.4	2.1	65	649	171.0	14.0	9	19	3.1	0.8
Marshall	4.10	131.8	27	228	99.3	9.2	103	1,081	392.3	27.7	15	29	4.7	0.7
Martin	4.45	361.6	4	D	D	D	40	364	93.8	7.9	3	D	D	D
Mason	2.73	159.7	15	358	79.8	14.0	93	1,385	363.8	29.8	13	34	6.2	1.0
Meade	0.75	26.9	10	77	49.2	2.8	63	609	197.3	12.5	17	50	5.6	1.1
Menifee	1.08	169.9	NA	NA	NA	NA	15	123	23.2	1.4	3	D	D	D
Mercer	2.94	137.3	8	32	14.7	0.7	62	705	169.7	15.4	11	21	2.8	0.5
Metcalfe	0.00	0.0	2	D	D	D	27	233	49.6	4.7	3	4	0.9	0.1
Monroe	1.41	132.2	7	47	26.9	1.5	42	449	104.1	9.8	6	18	1.3	0.3
Montgomery	3.00	108.7	17	D	D	D	114	1,501	457.8	34.0	19	35	5.1	0.8
Morgan	1.00	75.3	NA	NA	NA	NA	45	390	93.9	7.9	2	D	D	D
Muhlenberg	3.47	111.3	13	151	33.9	6.2	115	1,291	304.1	27.5	15	58	6.8	1.4
Nelson	5.50	121.9	30	292	147.4	9.4	159	1,826	535.2	42.7	28	63	11.6	2.1
Nicholas	1.71	239.8	1	D	D	D	16	139	27.4	2.8	1	D	D	D

1   Merchant wholesalers, except manufacturers' sales branches and offices.   2. Employer establishments.

STATE County	Professional, scientific, and technical services, 2012				Manufacturing, 2012				Accommodation and food services, 2012			
	Number of establishments	Number of employees	Sales (mil dol)	Average payroll (mil dol)	Number of establishments	Number of employees	Receipts (mil dol)	Annual payroll (mil dol)	Number of establishments	Number of employees	Receipts (mil dol)	Annual payroll (mil dol)
	147	148	149	150	151	152	153	154	155	156	157	158
KENTUCKY— Cont'd												
Clay	19	62	5.1	1.4	8	236	D	4.0	20	D	D	D
Clinton	15	33	2.6	1.0	12	D	D	D	15	D	D	D
Crittenden	12	224	11.0	5.6	12	170	D	5.0	12	202	5.3	1.7
Cumberland	9	D	D	D	7	189	30.8	6.4	14	D	D	D
Daviess	155	1,499	100.4	42.9	104	5,092	3,773.5	238.6	173	D	D	D
Edmonson	5	13	1.1	0.3	3	D	D	D	13	D	D	D
Elliott	NA	NA	NA	NA	NA	NA	NA	NA	5	D	D	D
Estill	9	41	1.8	0.5	8	180	D	4.0	20	D	D	D
Fayette	1,072	10,073	1,441.2	561.1	224	8,005	2,922.0	351.1	772	17,490	939.4	270.7
Fleming	15	36	3.5	1.0	20	350	82.9	11.4	7	D	D	D
Floyd	69	D	D	D	13	145	30.7	5.0	49	851	36.3	9.1
Franklin	127	777	88.9	33.5	41	2,383	1,748.1	110.1	106	1,948	98.3	26.3
Fulton	7	19	1.3	0.5	9	366	240.7	14.0	13	170	7.2	1.9
Gallatin	10	37	10.3	1.2	4	D	D	D	10	D	D	D
Garrard	15	34	3.2	1.0	15	240	39.2	7.3	11	D	D	D
Grant	24	67	4.8	1.9	15	588	860.2	24.3	43	D	D	D
Graves	47	370	17.4	7.3	48	2,128	480.8	75.8	51	808	29.6	7.7
Grayson	27	77	5.5	1.8	28	1,507	441.0	52.9	30	D	D	D
Green	12	27	2.4	0.9	9	58	D	1.3	9	174	6.4	1.7
Greenup	31	208	13.3	5.0	17	557	D	27.2	36	676	30.4	9.1
Hancock	6	45	3.5	1.5	12	1,720	D	114.2	6	D	D	D
Hardin	217	1,492	168.9	63.4	68	4,931	2,078.1	230.9	182	4,504	192.0	54.4
Harlan	37	257	17.5	9.6	10	74	D	3.3	33	D	D	D
Harrison	16	90	6.8	3.5	19	1,182	559.7	66.4	22	334	13.1	3.3
Hart	16	62	4.2	1.5	18	2,113	D	75.1	24	D	D	D
Henderson	71	416	39.9	13.8	76	4,930	2,857.6	215.1	85	1,411	65.4	16.8
Henry	18	52	3.4	1.1	4	396	D	17.7	15	D	D	D
Hickman	4	D	D	D	3	D	D	D	4	D	D	D
Hopkins	60	380	38.7	14.3	46	2,270	964.5	127.5	73	1,415	54.3	15.0
Jackson	6	13	1.0	0.4	9	181	D	8.4	7	44	2.2	0.6
Jefferson	2,197	22,198	3,274.3	1,139.3	718	40,666	28,642.1	2,159.3	1,651	39,711	2,006.3	572.1
Jessamine	85	548	81.4	20.4	69	2,550	681.4	93.4	73	D	D	D
Johnson	30	141	23.9	6.1	6	53	D	1.4	40	D	D	D
Kenton	355	2,723	313.0	130.5	90	3,891	1,674.8	219.8	307	D	D	D
Knott	11	45	8.3	2.1	NA	NA	NA	NA	8	81	5.3	1.3
Knox	40	1,133	57.5	27.4	14	1,021	191.2	35.0	43	715	37.5	9.7
Larue	20	48	4.4	1.3	14	498	D	D	17	121	5.2	1.5
Laurel	93	467	40.0	15.7	54	3,237	924.1	129.5	94	2,181	101.9	28.3
Lawrence	12	66	5.1	2.3	3	7	D	0.3	20	D	D	D
Lee	5	17	0.9	0.4	NA	NA	NA	NA	5	D	D	D
Leslie	7	50	6.6	1.6	NA	NA	NA	NA	4	D	D	D
Letcher	19	177	10.0	5.6	8	21	D	0.7	23	D	D	D
Lewis	4	D	D	D	14	385	94.8	12.1	8	D	D	D
Lincoln	22	76	5.9	1.9	13	726	188.1	24.4	18	397	12.6	3.4
Livingston	7	D	D	D	6	73	D	3.5	10	D	D	D
Logan	29	148	11.8	5.0	39	2,271	2,571.5	118.6	34	D	D	D
Lyon	10	39	3.2	1.5	NA	NA	NA	NA	22	D	D	D
McCracken	203	1,194	219.4	56.2	58	3,077	2,308.6	164.2	213	4,111	181.7	52.4
McCreary	6	72	3.4	0.9	10	373	D	7.2	17	273	7.9	2.3
McLean	8	19	1.4	0.4	9	126	D	4.6	14	91	3.6	0.9
Madison	137	679	71.4	25.1	65	3,597	D	162.6	159	3,495	164.5	43.5
Magoffin	16	105	14.2	4.1	NA	NA	NA	NA	10	154	6.4	1.8
Marion	28	101	8.3	3.1	31	3,586	895.0	135.8	34	D	D	D
Marshall	36	197	20.6	9.3	36	2,172	3,212.2	171.1	79	1,224	45.9	12.6
Martin	11	23	2.7	0.8	3	27	D	0.6	12	152	6.3	1.6
Mason	25	110	9.3	3.5	11	1,249	D	57.1	40	774	35.6	10.1
Meade	33	269	11.2	4.4	6	250	D	D	30	409	23.1	5.9
Menifee	2	D	D	D	5	D	D	3.4	2	D	D	D
Mercer	23	58	4.7	1.4	12	2,096	2,130.5	131.8	38	D	D	D
Metcalfe	5	11	0.8	0.2	8	716	311.6	22.4	10	89	3.8	1.0
Monroe	8	16	0.8	0.3	18	547	85.9	17.4	16	D	D	D
Montgomery	35	149	14.0	4.5	35	3,919	1,040.4	140.0	35	D	D	D
Morgan	13	75	3.8	1.7	5	409	47.4	8.2	11	D	D	D
Muhlenberg	34	148	16.8	3.9	26	793	218.7	26.1	49	D	D	D
Nelson	68	243	18.9	5.2	53	3,434	1,820.0	164.9	59	1,198	48.3	13.3
Nicholas	6	11	1.1	0.4	4	39	4.5	1.2	6	30	1.2	0.2

Health Care and Social Assistance, Other Services, Nonemployer Businesses, and Residential Construction

STATE County	Health care and social assistance, 2012				Other services, 2012				Nonemployer businesses, 2016		Value of residential construction authorized by building permits, 2018	
	Number of establish-ments	Number of employees	Receipts (mil dol)	Annual payroll (mil dol)	Number of establish-ments	Number of employees	Receipts (mil dol)	Annual payroll (mil dol)	Number	Receipts (mil dol)	New construction ($1,000)	Number of housing units
	159	160	161	162	163	164	165	166	167	168	169	170
KENTUCKY— Cont'd												
Clay	36	943	106.1	37.7	10	34	3.9	0.9	1,119	31.8	0	0
Clinton	24	322	28.5	11.4	5	D	D	D	780	29.7	0	0
Crittenden	17	407	26.9	12.5	14	D	D	D	635	24.6	316	2
Cumberland	14	456	37.2	15.8	9	27	2.9	0.6	620	19.9	0	0
Daviess	324	7,657	744.6	296.5	150	D	D	D	5,810	253.8	24,115	247
Edmonson	18	D	D	D	8	D	D	D	882	34.9	NA	NA
Elliott	10	130	7.6	3.9	2	D	D	D	350	10.4	NA	NA
Estill	28	442	36.8	15.8	7	24	2.6	0.6	774	18.3	0	0
Fayette	1,048	29,625	3,726.0	1,437.5	553	4,405	738.6	141.8	23,083	1,138.3	183,119	1,789
Fleming	21	561	48.2	18.4	16	D	D	D	1,252	54.7	0	0
Floyd	131	1,939	198.7	75.6	43	298	34.9	9.8	2,341	99.4	950	5
Franklin	156	1,800	210.2	60.8	128	749	87.8	25.3	3,289	120.3	18,208	103
Fulton	15	D	D	D	6	D	D	D	330	11.2	42	1
Gallatin	9	D	D	D	5	D	D	D	403	14.0	4,709	21
Garrard	24	231	13.0	6.0	10	D	D	D	1,198	47.3	0	0
Grant	32	D	D	D	24	D	D	D	1,332	58.8	13,180	56
Graves	97	D	D	D	33	217	28.9	8.0	2,652	110.3	304	2
Grayson	58	1,131	86.6	34.8	29	D	D	D	1,871	99.0	1,250	8
Green	24	572	39.7	17.5	16	47	4.9	0.9	961	35.8	0	0
Greenup	104	D	D	D	25	D	D	D	1,840	61.7	6,144	17
Hancock	14	102	6.4	2.1	5	D	D	D	469	14.4	1,925	11
Hardin	341	7,473	697.5	304.9	145	D	D	D	5,515	216.5	58,279	336
Harlan	52	1,332	137.9	50.6	24	86	8.7	2.0	1,322	37.4	0	0
Harrison	46	909	84.0	30.6	21	D	D	D	1,043	42.2	10,322	54
Hart	27	470	32.1	14.9	16	46	4.4	1.1	1,670	94.9	13,475	127
Henderson	137	2,500	233.7	87.1	62	534	76.6	19.5	2,327	97.7	6,542	35
Henry	19	257	15.2	7.0	16	D	D	D	1,080	45.1	5,766	32
Hickman	10	179	12.6	5.7	2	D	D	D	331	11.4	NA	NA
Hopkins	122	3,143	289.1	117.6	68	498	56.4	15.7	2,388	94.1	9,035	73
Jackson	9	219	15.1	6.2	4	12	1.6	0.3	865	27.3	0	0
Jefferson	2,390	65,785	7,401.3	2,838.2	1,307	11,226	1,278.7	353.7	53,921	2,556.1	668,078	3,318
Jessamine	112	1,026	64.9	31.7	68	235	26.2	5.7	4,302	197.9	54,475	181
Johnson	56	828	84.6	29.5	30	D	D	D	1,380	48.7	501	2
Kenton	344	10,407	1,298.0	519.8	232	D	D	D	9,641	453.8	66,076	267
Knott	17	220	21.0	6.6	9	D	D	D	847	26.5	NA	NA
Knox	71	1,357	93.3	38.0	19	D	D	D	1,960	72.8	0	0
Larue	19	284	11.9	6.1	14	46	4.5	1.1	1,037	36.8	10,141	44
Laurel	136	2,528	320.2	128.2	67	D	D	D	3,935	184.1	797	4
Lawrence	30	702	69.8	25.8	18	D	D	D	807	25.3	NA	NA
Lee	19	612	21.3	10.6	1	D	D	D	426	12.9	NA	NA
Leslie	16	328	26.3	10.8	4	26	2.7	0.7	520	20.0	NA	NA
Letcher	45	937	96.7	36.6	13	D	D	D	1,201	35.9	0	0
Lewis	12	298	20.4	8.7	9	26	1.8	0.3	877	30.6	0	0
Lincoln	39	710	51.7	20.4	22	D	D	D	1,553	54.4	4,915	47
Livingston	20	D	D	D	9	D	D	D	569	18.7	NA	NA
Logan	48	677	68.6	19.4	34	105	9.5	2.9	1,790	83.5	1,095	15
Lyon	14	204	12.3	5.1	7	D	D	D	497	18.1	1,628	14
McCracken	276	6,441	782.5	281.4	129	D	D	D	4,391	182.3	26,784	113
McCreary	25	320	18.3	8.3	4	D	D	D	852	34.7	0	0
McLean	10	132	8.3	3.1	12	D	D	D	511	14.0	0	0
Madison	254	3,580	283.6	115.7	96	515	53.7	13.4	5,531	229.7	25,560	329
Magoffin	17	278	20.2	7.3	11	29	4.4	0.6	629	16.1	NA	NA
Marion	44	1,333	86.5	33.5	17	D	D	D	1,212	48.9	4,142	39
Marshall	64	986	59.3	25.8	38	174	15.1	4.3	2,272	89.1	24,928	78
Martin	23	237	18.3	6.8	7	24	2.9	0.9	470	13.3	NA	NA
Mason	65	1,200	109.4	40.9	42	160	10.7	2.9	1,198	48.5	2,687	18
Meade	38	363	19.3	8.6	23	D	D	D	1,519	60.6	14,243	78
Menifee	10	185	12.5	5.6	2	D	D	D	406	12.6	NA	NA
Mercer	42	696	60.8	24.2	29	D	D	D	1,493	61.5	7,661	45
Metcalfe	17	D	D	D	8	16	1.1	0.2	841	28.6	NA	NA
Monroe	29	494	34.3	14.7	9	44	5.3	0.9	919	37.6	NA	NA
Montgomery	73	913	83.4	30.2	29	D	D	D	1,782	62.7	11,683	109
Morgan	16	297	28.1	10.5	11	D	D	D	769	26.6	1,650	22
Muhlenberg	58	1,318	87.0	37.2	41	163	15.6	4.1	1,598	57.5	1,064	9
Nelson	97	1,577	126.8	49.4	46	182	15.5	4.0	3,043	122.1	32,807	203
Nicholas	13	269	15.2	7.2	4	23	1.7	0.5	464	15.4	586	3

STATE County	Full-time equivalent employees	March payroll (dollars)	Adminis-tration, judicial, and legal	Police and corrections	Fire protection	Highways and transpor-tation	Health and welfare	Natural resources and utilities	Education and libraries	Total (mil dol)	Inter-govern-mental (mil dol)	Total (mil dol)	Per capita[1] (dollars) Total	Per capita[1] (dollars) Property
					March payroll (percent of total)								Taxes	
	171	172	173	174	175	176	177	178	179	180	181	182	183	184
KENTUCKY— Cont'd														
Clay	994	2,631,167	3.1	5.8	0.0	2.7	3.9	4.3	79.7	47.7	34.9	7.4	345	209
Clinton	443	1,162,284	4.8	3.5	0.0	2.1	6.0	0.7	82.6	24.4	16.8	5.6	548	258
Crittenden	318	847,790	5.5	13.8	0.0	2.2	0.0	6.6	71.2	21.9	15.1	4.5	482	288
Cumberland	454	1,348,734	2.8	4.3	0.1	1.8	42.8	3.6	43.6	42.0	9.9	4.0	592	292
Daviess	4,233	13,420,532	3.9	7.2	3.3	2.8	7.4	14.6	60.1	320.6	123.3	99.0	1,012	595
Edmonson	508	1,172,078	2.9	4.0	0.4	1.8	3.8	6.2	80.7	24.3	16.3	5.3	442	332
Elliott	264	668,556	3.5	2.6	0.0	3.1	11.5	2.5	75.8	15.4	11.7	2.1	276	169
Estill	575	2,082,079	1.7	13.1	7.0	4.2	11.0	3.5	58.3	35.1	24.2	6.6	452	275
Fayette	9,962	37,856,745	4.3	13.5	7.8	2.1	6.3	4.9	58.5	920.0	203.8	539.7	1,767	835
Fleming	697	2,194,909	3.1	2.3	0.7	1.3	36.8	2.2	53.4	87.7	20.7	8.0	553	322
Floyd	1,386	3,755,718	2.5	3.5	2.7	1.3	3.7	4.8	81.3	96.9	62.9	22.7	584	472
Franklin	1,716	6,237,758	4.5	8.7	9.2	2.6	1.1	8.1	54.8	158.6	42.6	66.3	1,332	688
Fulton	418	1,044,790	3.3	7.0	5.9	10.5	0.4	9.6	58.4	26.4	17.0	5.5	847	491
Gallatin	332	954,873	7.1	3.3	0.0	2.1	2.1	3.8	81.6	30.0	13.7	8.5	1,007	632
Garrard	526	1,692,901	3.4	1.7	0.1	1.9	5.2	1.5	86.1	39.9	19.9	12.9	761	479
Grant	998	2,854,787	5.3	7.3	1.9	1.5	0.1	5.4	77.4	59.9	37.6	15.0	611	477
Graves	1,308	3,544,113	2.9	8.2	3.0	2.3	0.0	2.8	79.5	77.1	43.4	23.1	614	366
Grayson	956	2,669,148	4.8	14.5	0.3	2.2	2.1	3.6	70.5	66.8	40.3	15.8	608	317
Green	635	2,084,431	5.8	8.4	4.2	2.1	27.5	9.5	41.8	40.4	15.6	5.1	451	288
Greenup	1,220	4,273,541	2.1	6.9	1.4	1.9	0.4	3.3	82.5	86.3	43.9	29.1	793	654
Hancock	406	1,128,193	8.8	3.1	0.0	3.6	5.5	3.0	73.5	70.5	13.2	9.1	1,052	490
Hardin	5,176	17,598,804	1.2	3.7	1.8	1.2	45.7	3.6	41.7	459.3	132.4	90.3	844	479
Harlan	1,193	3,057,085	2.8	6.7	0.2	2.7	1.0	4.6	81.1	96.7	61.1	16.0	562	404
Harrison	635	1,973,639	6.3	9.3	3.0	3.0	0.0	2.3	76.0	38.3	20.2	14.4	771	361
Hart	599	1,691,514	2.9	6.7	0.1	2.1	4.8	5.2	76.9	36.5	22.7	9.6	522	293
Henderson	2,096	5,804,471	5.3	9.5	3.7	4.2	1.2	14.4	60.1	156.8	64.1	42.2	908	550
Henry	640	1,779,003	8.8	3.5	0.0	1.4	1.9	5.1	79.3	35.5	21.0	10.1	661	488
Hickman	198	524,720	7.5	5.4	0.0	2.2	2.3	1.0	80.8	11.7	7.7	3.0	622	421
Hopkins	1,879	5,461,945	4.2	9.4	3.9	3.0	5.6	7.9	65.5	126.7	65.8	37.0	791	444
Jackson	523	1,629,435	2.4	2.5	0.0	2.9	0.5	0.3	90.4	29.9	23.5	5.0	377	231
Jefferson	25,957	96,919,915	3.8	11.0	4.8	4.5	4.7	8.9	60.3	2,308.9	694.0	1,084.7	1,445	808
Jessamine	1,836	5,035,213	4.3	7.1	3.4	1.5	7.8	4.8	68.6	116.9	46.1	57.3	1,153	712
Johnson	862	2,638,353	2.4	1.8	1.1	1.5	0.7	2.6	86.7	69.4	42.9	14.0	598	338
Kenton	5,823	21,356,962	2.4	8.9	5.6	14.3	2.9	9.7	54.0	710.4	161.7	228.8	1,415	873
Knott	613	1,519,486	4.8	3.6	0.0	2.3	3.8	6.9	78.6	39.0	27.2	8.8	546	448
Knox	1,187	3,283,773	1.7	2.6	0.1	1.9	10.4	2.7	80.2	87.2	55.9	18.9	597	369
Larue	547	1,474,160	4.8	6.4	0.0	1.7	3.2	2.6	80.9	31.5	21.6	7.0	497	357
Laurel	2,042	5,388,170	2.8	6.5	0.3	2.5	3.9	3.5	79.3	125.4	73.3	38.1	641	329
Lawrence	604	1,562,126	4.8	3.3	1.1	2.8	4.5	4.0	78.6	54.7	23.2	8.2	517	381
Lee	279	772,061	4.6	4.7	0.0	3.4	11.0	4.8	71.3	19.3	12.6	4.2	539	364
Leslie	447	1,317,537	5.5	3.0	0.0	2.8	0.0	4.1	79.4	32.5	23.5	7.5	668	472
Letcher	1,021	2,457,149	1.7	4.3	0.4	2.2	3.8	4.0	81.9	57.9	40.2	11.8	493	377
Lewis	560	1,776,699	3.4	5.5	0.0	2.3	1.5	4.2	82.9	29.1	20.7	6.3	457	316
Lincoln	879	2,396,927	2.4	4.3	0.3	1.9	3.1	3.5	84.1	50.5	35.4	11.5	471	295
Livingston	346	854,563	7.6	3.0	8.2	3.7	4.9	4.1	68.4	22.0	13.3	6.5	688	436
Logan	972	2,732,295	5.2	7.8	1.4	1.6	0.3	3.8	78.6	68.7	39.7	21.0	787	379
Lyon	237	841,257	5.7	3.3	0.2	3.5	5.4	4.3	50.3	18.0	7.4	7.1	847	615
McCracken	2,541	8,688,735	3.1	9.6	3.2	4.7	11.0	11.5	55.4	229.1	82.8	78.2	1,193	632
McCreary	751	1,960,007	1.9	4.5	0.0	1.6	6.3	4.0	80.7	47.9	30.0	16.4	907	789
McLean	404	945,835	4.5	1.7	0.0	2.1	0.7	5.7	75.6	30.6	17.9	7.4	778	382
Madison	2,628	7,891,742	2.5	5.2	3.8	2.3	9.6	4.2	68.4	199.0	81.8	79.3	935	482
Magoffin	510	1,498,254	4.1	2.3	0.8	3.5	6.7	3.0	79.4	38.5	29.7	6.1	470	216
Marion	789	2,206,926	2.6	13.7	0.3	6.2	3.0	6.0	67.3	49.3	25.1	15.3	763	452
Marshall	1,233	3,676,388	2.4	4.3	0.0	2.0	23.4	5.4	61.5	138.8	34.7	36.4	1,160	589
Martin	565	1,560,146	7.3	3.2	0.0	2.3	6.6	3.2	77.0	32.7	22.1	7.2	566	272
Mason	917	2,257,527	7.8	11.9	3.1	2.4	6.1	5.7	59.4	62.2	21.7	18.3	1,043	494
Meade	931	2,688,037	3.4	5.7	0.1	1.5	3.2	3.3	81.9	56.8	35.1	14.8	508	380
Menifee	255	589,112	3.9	0.5	0.0	2.1	3.1	2.7	87.6	17.2	10.7	4.3	691	525
Mercer	736	2,237,637	6.9	9.4	2.9	5.4	2.8	4.1	67.1	50.4	24.0	20.1	944	596
Metcalfe	377	953,969	2.6	3.0	0.0	3.1	0.6	4.9	85.9	23.2	15.8	5.4	544	294
Monroe	585	1,493,674	4.7	6.7	0.0	1.6	5.1	5.9	75.8	28.4	19.3	6.0	550	323
Montgomery	853	2,642,340	1.3	2.9	6.2	0.8	6.6	1.1	80.9	69.6	34.6	22.4	832	434
Morgan	486	1,237,685	4.6	5.7	0.0	1.9	4.7	5.7	76.6	34.6	23.0	6.2	453	241
Muhlenberg	1,235	3,174,925	4.8	7.6	1.4	3.6	3.9	4.0	74.3	72.9	47.9	14.7	471	350
Nelson	1,501	4,602,823	4.7	5.8	0.7	1.6	4.5	4.2	76.6	108.2	44.4	36.8	829	669
Nicholas	219	557,957	7.9	3.1	0.4	3.0	1.0	7.7	75.2	15.4	10.3	3.1	437	281

1. Based on the resident population estimated as of July 1 of the year shown.

Table B. States and Counties — Local Government Finances, Government Employment, and Income Taxes

STATE County	Local government finances, 2012 (cont.)										Government employment, 2017			Individual income tax returns, 2016		
	Direct general expenditure							Debt outstanding								
		Per capita[1] (dollars)	Percent of total for:					Total (mil dol)	Per capita[1] (dollars)		Federal civilian	Federal military	State and local	Number of returns	Mean adjusted gross income	Mean income tax
	Total (mil dol)		Education	Health and hospitals	Police protection	Public welfare	Highways									
	185	186	187	188	189	190	191	192	193		194	195	196	197	198	199

STATE County	185	186	187	188	189	190	191	192	193	194	195	196	197	198	199
KENTUCKY— Cont'd															
Clay	48.2	2,236	66.0	2.1	3.1	0.0	7.1	33.2	1,542	353	57	1,103	6,270	34,670	2,488
Clinton	23.1	2,250	70.0	3.9	2.9	0.0	4.7	18.9	1,842	53	31	592	3,660	33,487	2,346
Crittenden	20.2	2,174	49.6	0.3	3.2	0.0	6.6	34.3	3,698	19	27	416	3,600	44,791	3,843
Cumberland	47.8	7,014	21.3	57.7	1.5	0.0	3.3	40.3	5,903	10	20	323	2,580	35,007	2,870
Daviess	344.4	3,519	39.4	6.6	4.3	0.1	2.9	1,124.1	11,488	258	318	5,354	45,260	53,004	5,702
Edmonson	23.8	1,975	69.3	5.0	2.8	0.0	5.3	36.6	3,036	221	36	503	4,820	40,483	3,140
Elliott	14.7	1,891	60.4	9.7	1.5	1.2	7.3	16.4	2,107	9	20	569	2,140	38,527	2,714
Estill	39.4	2,719	67.4	7.2	1.3	0.0	3.6	33.1	2,286	20	43	710	5,340	37,986	2,953
Fayette	871.4	2,852	47.8	1.8	5.5	1.0	1.3	1,402.6	4,591	4,238	1,000	39,823	141,550	65,335	9,050
Fleming	60.2	4,132	42.2	39.1	1.6	0.0	3.5	101.3	6,957	47	44	674	6,020	40,793	3,350
Floyd	95.8	2,460	58.7	3.2	3.0	0.0	4.7	77.1	1,979	121	108	2,181	12,460	40,422	3,750
Franklin	148.7	2,986	38.2	6.9	4.7	0.1	3.3	147.3	2,957	467	171	13,428	24,640	52,054	5,581
Fulton	26.8	4,114	37.8	0.2	5.2	0.0	5.6	13.8	2,107	27	35	488	2,310	36,472	3,116
Gallatin	31.5	3,721	44.7	3.1	3.1	0.0	2.2	306.7	36,176	34	26	410	3,550	43,220	3,523
Garrard	36.7	2,171	53.0	18.0	3.1	0.0	3.4	63.2	3,736	22	53	620	6,890	46,413	4,130
Grant	60.7	2,479	63.9	0.5	3.4	0.1	3.7	87.4	3,568	47	75	1,175	10,630	46,160	4,244
Graves	76.9	2,049	62.2	0.3	2.9	0.2	4.8	208.0	5,539	201	112	1,745	15,190	44,503	4,019
Grayson	62.1	2,391	54.7	1.0	2.5	0.6	4.1	106.8	4,113	93	78	1,625	10,390	40,240	3,475
Green	39.0	3,443	35.6	43.0	2.1	0.0	3.4	34.9	3,088	19	33	514	4,450	36,390	2,830
Greenup	85.0	2,315	62.5	3.4	4.2	0.0	4.8	61.8	1,684	55	107	1,467	14,680	52,396	5,529
Hancock	79.0	9,101	19.3	0.8	0.8	0.1	2.2	714.6	82,360	22	27	440	3,790	49,994	4,574
Hardin	430.7	4,025	34.9	44.6	2.8	0.0	2.0	304.8	2,848	5,281	4,731	7,721	48,190	51,216	5,087
Harlan	95.7	3,353	47.6	20.0	2.5	1.4	4.6	87.7	3,072	64	79	1,699	8,660	31,574	2,856
Harrison	37.7	2,026	62.3	1.1	5.4	0.2	9.1	17.8	956	35	56	773	7,890	45,894	4,193
Hart	35.3	1,923	58.3	4.8	2.9	0.1	5.4	51.6	2,807	43	56	805	7,410	36,321	2,763
Henderson	158.7	3,411	41.1	0.2	3.9	0.4	4.8	595.8	12,809	117	136	2,522	19,760	50,953	5,283
Henry	38.5	2,513	68.2	3.6	3.2	0.0	4.4	41.2	2,690	90	49	704	7,150	46,488	4,258
Hickman	12.5	2,633	61.6	0.0	3.3	0.0	8.4	15.6	3,280	20	13	225	1,840	44,101	4,049
Hopkins	127.9	2,738	50.6	2.9	4.8	0.7	5.6	336.3	7,198	170	135	3,117	18,870	50,123	5,062
Jackson	37.2	2,791	73.7	0.3	0.9	0.0	5.1	39.0	2,924	29	41	670	4,490	36,486	2,457
Jefferson	2,460.2	3,277	46.7	1.4	4.8	0.5	3.0	4,784.1	6,372	6,674	2,541	41,379	373,690	61,482	8,198
Jessamine	118.6	2,390	54.7	4.5	6.5	0.1	5.6	197.1	3,971	76	158	2,386	22,340	63,962	8,663
Johnson	63.4	2,713	62.6	7.2	2.4	0.0	4.6	48.3	2,065	41	67	1,394	7,740	44,155	4,007
Kenton	844.4	5,222	24.0	2.1	3.6	0.0	2.7	2,312.8	14,302	3,697	498	6,780	78,320	75,565	10,916
Knott	35.4	2,196	66.3	0.1	2.3	0.2	6.1	25.7	1,594	34	44	683	4,780	39,908	3,449
Knox	85.5	2,695	53.4	8.3	1.8	0.0	3.5	96.3	3,036	128	93	1,369	11,160	36,621	2,844
Larue	29.1	2,055	63.2	2.5	2.5	0.0	4.3	46.0	3,247	43	42	573	6,140	43,342	3,663
Laurel	122.8	2,066	64.1	2.4	3.8	0.9	3.4	206.4	3,470	244	181	2,604	23,450	43,653	4,165
Lawrence	56.4	3,560	42.6	2.7	1.4	0.0	5.0	323.0	20,378	33	48	638	5,430	42,127	3,396
Lee	18.2	2,364	53.5	6.3	4.4	0.1	10.1	9.1	1,180	9	19	392	2,150	37,262	2,988
Leslie	38.3	3,427	60.6	0.3	1.6	0.0	6.1	45.7	4,093	12	31	521	3,340	37,587	2,742
Letcher	57.7	2,407	65.1	0.2	2.3	0.0	4.0	48.6	2,030	48	67	1,022	7,210	39,225	3,315
Lewis	32.1	2,322	56.5	3.9	2.6	0.0	6.9	85.2	6,155	23	40	601	4,820	38,664	2,752
Lincoln	57.7	2,358	64.0	2.6	1.3	0.1	4.4	51.0	2,086	60	74	992	9,450	39,269	3,084
Livingston	21.9	2,329	53.2	2.8	2.6	0.0	6.2	29.9	3,170	89	28	455	3,950	45,415	4,204
Logan	70.1	2,633	53.7	15.9	4.9	0.0	4.2	64.5	2,421	64	82	1,186	11,430	46,990	4,904
Lyon	19.0	2,270	40.7	6.1	4.4	0.8	10.5	27.6	3,304	36	21	942	3,310	50,737	5,187
McCracken	222.0	3,387	53.7	0.1	3.1	0.1	3.3	760.9	11,608	562	223	3,649	30,040	58,255	7,250
McCreary	46.4	2,568	59.4	1.1	0.7	0.0	4.6	41.3	2,284	502	47	704	4,780	32,377	2,213
McLean	31.1	3,277	41.5	3.3	0.7	0.6	9.6	42.6	4,483	34	28	484	3,860	46,505	4,137
Madison	191.9	2,263	56.3	9.2	4.2	0.1	3.1	375.9	4,434	1,108	266	7,200	35,810	53,637	5,704
Magoffin	33.9	2,601	61.0	4.8	2.9	0.0	5.3	40.5	3,109	13	38	582	3,980	37,323	2,570
Marion	48.7	2,426	52.2	2.0	3.7	0.0	4.4	59.9	2,983	43	58	921	8,430	43,294	3,859
Marshall	146.0	4,657	26.1	18.0	3.9	0.3	2.3	483.2	15,417	88	94	1,604	14,010	52,615	5,437
Martin	33.5	2,633	63.8	9.1	1.1	0.0	5.6	13.4	1,048	420	31	520	3,070	35,144	3,209
Mason	67.9	3,879	34.1	4.5	4.5	0.0	7.5	293.2	16,743	50	51	1,362	7,390	49,272	5,063
Meade	55.3	1,892	66.3	2.2	2.1	0.0	3.0	96.2	3,291	35	85	1,028	12,680	50,154	4,592
Menifee	19.5	3,133	66.1	3.5	3.4	0.2	4.2	20.7	3,323	46	19	323	2,300	34,731	2,372
Mercer	48.2	2,267	58.2	3.7	3.9	0.0	4.4	86.2	4,054	46	65	854	9,710	46,454	4,335
Metcalfe	34.7	3,479	78.8	1.8	2.2	0.0	4.0	60.2	6,042	21	30	472	4,070	33,059	2,365
Monroe	27.3	2,526	64.8	9.0	3.4	0.0	4.9	27.3	2,518	22	32	605	4,270	36,811	3,242
Montgomery	73.1	2,716	63.0	9.0	4.6	0.0	2.4	73.0	2,713	71	84	1,212	11,640	44,424	4,177
Morgan	36.5	2,671	54.2	4.4	1.9	6.8	7.3	55.1	4,035	32	35	996	4,130	36,499	3,224
Muhlenberg	94.2	3,022	66.4	2.4	2.2	0.1	4.0	83.6	2,681	419	88	1,692	11,940	45,040	4,042
Nelson	117.2	2,645	59.2	2.1	3.0	0.2	2.8	245.4	5,537	82	138	1,815	21,860	54,819	6,495
Nicholas	15.9	2,269	62.2	1.2	3.9	0.5	10.0	17.4	2,481	14	21	314	2,950	36,919	2,843

1. Based on the resident population estimated as of July 1 of the year shown.

Table B. States and Counties — **Land Area and Population**

State / county code	CBSA code[1]	County code[2]	STATE County	Land area[3] (sq. mi)	Total persons 2018	Rank	Per square mile	White	Black	American Indian, Alaska Native	Asian and Pacific Islander	Percent Hispanic or Latino[4]	Under 5 years	5 to 17 years	18 to 24 years	25 to 34 years	35 to 44 years	45 to 54 years
				1	2	3	4	5	6	7	8	9	10	11	12	13	14	15
			KENTUCKY— Cont'd															
21183		6	Ohio	587.3	24,087	1,639	41.0	95.1	1.5	0.5	0.4	3.4	6.1	18.4	7.5	11.7	12.4	12.7
21185	31,140	1	Oldham	187.2	66,470	807	355.1	89.7	4.9	0.7	2.3	4.1	5.1	20.4	8.2	10.1	14.6	15.9
21187		8	Owen	351.1	10,880	2,361	31.0	95.6	1.5	0.6	0.4	3.0	5.1	17.0	7.5	10.9	12.3	13.5
21189		9	Owsley	197.4	4,472	2,861	22.7	97.4	0.8	0.7	0.3	1.6	6.7	15.9	6.8	12.1	11.1	13.5
21191	17,140	1	Pendleton	277.2	14,529	2,123	52.4	97.2	1.3	0.7	0.6	1.4	5.9	16.6	7.6	12.0	11.5	14.8
21193		7	Perry	339.7	26,092	1,565	76.8	96.5	2.3	0.6	0.7	1.0	6.7	16.2	6.7	12.4	12.7	13.8
21195		7	Pike	786.7	58,402	886	74.2	97.6	1.1	0.4	0.7	1.0	5.3	15.3	7.9	11.2	12.7	13.8
21197		6	Powell	179.0	12,442	2,255	69.5	96.8	1.5	0.6	0.6	1.8	6.7	17.4	7.8	12.2	13.0	13.3
21199	43,700	5	Pulaski	658.4	64,623	823	98.2	95.2	1.6	0.8	1.0	2.6	5.7	16.5	7.2	11.8	12.1	13.6
21201		8	Robertson	99.9	2,135	3,036	21.4	97.7	1.0	1.1	0.1	1.4	5.1	15.6	7.4	10.4	10.5	13.9
21203	40,080	7	Rockcastle	316.5	16,750	1,994	52.9	98.1	0.7	1.0	0.4	1.0	5.4	16.1	7.4	11.8	11.6	15.0
21205		7	Rowan	279.8	24,583	1,624	87.9	95.6	2.2	0.5	1.2	1.7	5.4	13.9	22.3	12.4	9.9	11.0
21207		9	Russell	253.7	17,821	1,932	70.2	94.7	1.4	0.6	0.7	3.8	6.1	16.6	6.9	10.9	11.2	14.0
21209	30,460	2	Scott	281.8	56,031	910	198.8	88.8	6.4	0.6	1.7	4.4	6.6	18.6	9.2	13.7	14.3	13.8
21211	31,140	1	Shelby	379.8	48,518	1,014	127.7	81.6	8.1	0.7	1.7	10.0	6.2	16.8	8.7	12.3	13.0	14.1
21213		6	Simpson	234.2	18,529	1,898	79.1	86.9	10.6	0.7	1.1	2.6	6.5	17.6	8.3	12.9	11.6	13.3
21215	31,140	1	Spencer	186.7	18,794	1,884	100.7	95.4	2.3	0.6	0.7	2.2	5.5	17.2	7.3	10.8	13.6	16.2
21217	15,820	7	Taylor	266.4	25,549	1,582	95.9	91.2	6.4	0.6	1.1	2.5	6.4	15.8	11.7	12.5	10.6	11.6
21219		8	Todd	374.5	12,311	2,267	32.9	87.9	8.6	0.7	0.5	3.9	7.0	19.7	8.1	11.8	11.6	12.7
21221	17,300	2	Trigg	441.6	14,643	2,118	33.2	90.0	8.2	0.9	0.8	2.3	5.4	16.5	6.5	10.0	10.4	13.4
21223	31,140	1	Trimble	151.6	8,515	2,542	56.2	95.0	1.1	0.9	1.0	3.4	5.7	16.5	7.7	11.2	11.9	14.7
21225		6	Union	342.9	14,505	2,128	42.3	83.8	14.4	0.7	0.9	2.0	5.1	13.5	16.0	11.3	11.7	12.1
21227	14,540	3	Warren	541.7	131,264	488	242.3	79.8	10.9	0.6	5.3	5.6	6.4	16.5	16.2	13.5	12.2	11.3
21229		9	Washington	297.0	12,084	2,289	40.7	88.9	6.6	0.5	1.1	4.6	6.6	17.2	7.9	11.0	11.3	14.0
21231		7	Wayne	458.2	20,468	1,797	44.7	94.2	2.3	0.7	0.6	3.5	5.5	14.9	7.4	11.6	11.4	13.5
21233		8	Webster	332.1	13,111	2,225	39.5	89.6	4.8	0.7	0.8	5.8	6.7	16.9	7.0	12.4	12.5	12.9
21235	30,940	7	Whitley	437.8	36,242	1,270	82.8	97.1	1.3	0.9	0.7	1.3	7.8	17.5	11.1	12.0	11.1	12.2
21237		9	Wolfe	222.2	7,177	2,647	32.3	98.2	0.9	0.8	0.2	1.0	6.2	16.8	6.7	10.7	12.4	12.9
21239	30,460	2	Woodford	190.1	26,533	1,546	139.6	87.3	5.7	0.5	1.0	7.0	5.8	16.3	8.1	10.3	12.1	13.3
22000		0	LOUISIANA	43,203.9	4,659,978	X	107.9	59.9	33.1	1.2	2.2	5.2	6.6	16.9	9.1	14.3	12.5	12.1
22001	29,180	2	Acadia	655.2	62,190	846	94.9	78.6	19.1	0.6	0.5	2.7	7.0	18.8	8.2	13.3	11.9	12.2
22003		6	Allen	761.8	25,605	1,580	33.6	72.5	23.3	2.8	1.0	2.3	5.9	16.1	8.2	15.8	13.9	13.1
22005	12,940	2	Ascension	290.1	124,672	512	429.8	69.2	23.9	0.7	1.7	5.7	7.1	19.7	8.0	13.9	14.1	13.6
22007		6	Assumption	338.6	22,300	1,712	65.9	66.4	30.0	0.9	0.6	3.1	5.6	15.9	8.1	12.7	11.7	13.4
22009		6	Avoyelles	832.0	40,462	1,170	48.6	66.3	30.9	1.8	0.9	2.0	6.7	16.9	8.2	13.7	12.4	12.3
22011	19,760	6	Beauregard	1,157.4	37,253	1,245	32.2	82.2	13.2	1.9	1.2	3.8	6.8	17.9	8.4	13.6	12.6	12.3
22013		6	Bienville	811.3	13,308	2,210	16.4	55.7	42.2	0.9	0.6	1.9	5.9	16.5	7.3	12.3	10.4	12.3
22015	43,340	2	Bossier	840.3	127,185	503	151.4	68.2	23.6	1.0	2.8	6.8	6.9	17.9	8.9	15.3	13.4	11.5
22017	43,340	2	Caddo	878.8	242,922	278	276.4	45.8	50.3	0.9	1.7	2.9	6.6	17.0	8.3	13.9	12.1	11.6
22019	29,340	3	Calcasieu	1,064.3	203,112	330	190.8	68.8	26.6	1.1	1.8	3.8	7.1	17.8	8.7	14.8	12.3	11.6
22021		8	Caldwell	529.4	9,960	2,430	18.8	80.2	16.4	0.8	0.6	3.2	6.2	16.9	7.5	13.1	12.3	12.8
22023	29,340	3	Cameron	1,284.9	6,968	2,672	5.4	90.7	4.6	1.2	0.5	4.3	5.2	17.0	8.0	12.7	11.9	13.3
22025		9	Catahoula	708.0	9,608	2,455	13.6	67.2	31.2	0.8	0.2	1.7	5.7	15.7	8.2	14.4	12.7	11.8
22027		6	Claiborne	754.9	15,944	2,041	21.1	45.8	52.2	0.9	0.7	1.5	5.3	12.7	8.1	15.5	12.4	12.9
22029	35,020	7	Concordia	697.0	19,572	1,848	28.1	58.0	40.1	0.7	0.6	1.5	6.3	17.6	8.9	13.7	11.5	11.0
22031	43,340	2	De Soto	876.4	27,436	1,512	31.3	60.0	36.4	1.4	0.6	3.0	6.1	17.8	7.6	12.2	12.1	12.5
22033	12,940	2	East Baton Rouge	455.3	440,956	161	968.5	45.5	47.3	0.6	3.8	4.2	6.5	16.1	13.7	14.6	12.0	10.9
22035		7	East Carroll	420.7	7,037	2,663	16.7	28.6	68.6	0.6	0.7	2.5	7.5	17.1	9.5	15.2	11.9	11.2
22037	12,940	2	East Feliciana	453.4	19,305	1,861	42.6	54.9	43.3	1.0	0.5	1.7	4.9	13.4	8.3	13.0	12.7	14.1
22039		6	Evangeline	662.4	33,443	1,342	50.5	67.8	28.2	0.7	0.7	3.8	7.0	18.0	9.4	13.8	11.7	12.0
22041		7	Franklin	624.6	20,156	1,814	32.3	66.0	32.1	0.6	0.6	1.7	7.2	18.4	7.8	12.3	11.6	11.3
22043	10,780	3	Grant	643.0	22,482	1,704	35.0	77.9	16.0	1.6	0.8	5.2	5.9	15.2	7.8	17.0	14.5	12.3
22045	29,180	2	Iberia	574.1	70,941	763	123.6	60.3	33.3	0.8	3.1	4.3	7.3	18.5	8.6	13.1	11.5	12.1
22047	12,940	2	Iberville	618.6	32,721	1,362	52.9	48.3	48.8	0.5	0.6	2.7	5.5	15.1	8.5	15.0	13.0	13.5
22049		6	Jackson	569.2	15,902	2,043	27.9	68.8	29.3	0.9	0.9	1.8	5.5	16.5	7.6	13.4	11.8	12.2
22051	35,380	1	Jefferson	295.7	434,051	163	1,467.9	53.6	27.5	0.8	4.7	14.9	6.5	15.5	7.5	14.5	12.5	12.5
22053	27,660	6	Jefferson Davis	651.4	31,582	1,389	48.5	79.8	17.9	1.1	0.7	2.5	6.9	18.8	8.1	12.6	11.7	12.0
22055	29,180	2	Lafayette	268.7	242,782	279	903.5	66.6	27.2	0.7	2.3	4.6	6.8	16.8	9.1	16.2	13.4	11.9
22057	26,380	3	Lafourche	1,068.4	98,115	608	91.8	78.4	14.3	3.6	1.1	4.4	6.4	16.8	8.4	14.2	12.3	13.0
22059		6	La Salle	624.7	14,917	2,101	23.9	83.5	12.4	1.6	0.5	2.9	6.1	16.8	8.4	14.2	13.4	11.8
22061	40,820	4	Lincoln	471.7	47,196	1,033	100.1	54.3	40.9	0.8	2.0	3.2	5.8	14.3	25.1	12.4	9.9	9.1
22063	12,940	2	Livingston	648.2	139,567	463	215.3	88.5	7.0	0.8	1.0	3.8	6.9	18.7	7.8	14.3	14.0	13.1
22065		7	Madison	624.4	11,161	2,341	17.9	34.7	63.0	0.7	0.5	2.2	6.9	16.9	8.9	17.0	11.3	12.7
22067	12,820	6	Morehouse	794.9	25,398	1,588	32.0	50.0	48.4	0.6	0.8	1.4	6.9	17.2	7.7	12.3	11.5	11.9
22069	35,060	6	Natchitoches	1,252.3	38,659	1,211	30.9	54.7	42.1	1.9	1.1	2.4	6.4	17.0	16.4	11.6	10.4	10.4

1. CBSA = Core Based Statistical Area. See Appendix A for explanation. See Appendix B for list of metropolitan areas with component counties.   2. County type code from the Economic Research Service of USDA Rural-Urban Continuum Codes. See Appendix A for definition.   3. Dry land or land partially or temporarily covered by water.   4. May be of any race.

Table B. States and Counties — **Population and Households**

STATE County	Age (percent) (cont.) 55 to 64 years	65 to 74 years	75 years and over	Percent female	Total persons 2000	2010	Percent change 2000-2010	2010-2018	Components of change, 2010-2018 Births	Deaths	Net Migration	Households, 2013-2017 Number	Persons per household	Family households	Female family householder[1]	One person
	16	17	18	19	20	21	22	23	24	25	26	27	28	29	30	31
KENTUCKY— Cont'd																
Ohio	13.4	10.4	7.4	50.2	22,916	23,854	4.1	1.0	2,438	2,289	105	9,055	2.62	70.8	9.6	23.8
Oldham	12.6	8.6	4.6	47.6	46,178	60,354	30.7	10.1	4,406	3,173	4,888	20,465	2.96	81.1	9.0	16.0
Owen	15.2	11.3	7.2	50.3	10,547	10,837	2.7	0.4	844	896	97	3,944	2.69	70.3	9.8	24.8
Owsley	14.3	11.3	8.3	50.6	4,858	4,755	-2.1	-6.0	426	617	-100	1,696	2.61	70.7	22.5	28.2
Pendleton	15.5	9.9	6.2	49.0	14,390	14,875	3.4	-2.3	1,370	1,248	-469	5,236	2.73	73.5	8.9	22.2
Perry	14.4	10.6	6.4	50.8	29,390	28,690	-2.4	-9.1	3,192	3,471	-2,334	11,037	2.42	68.9	15.1	27.4
Pike	15.1	11.6	7.2	51.2	68,736	65,029	-5.4	-10.2	5,649	6,754	-5,563	25,853	2.34	68.6	13.3	27.5
Powell	13.7	10.0	5.8	50.4	13,237	12,613	-4.7	-1.4	1,344	1,320	-194	4,878	2.48	68.0	15.2	26.3
Pulaski	14.2	11.2	7.6	51.2	56,217	63,061	12.2	2.5	6,082	6,558	2,088	25,810	2.44	65.1	13.4	29.4
Robertson	15.6	11.2	10.4	49.5	2,266	2,282	0.7	-6.4	189	264	-77	938	2.24	58.5	7.2	39.0
Rockcastle	14.6	10.8	7.3	51.1	16,582	17,056	2.9	-1.8	1,467	1,681	-86	6,552	2.52	72.1	12.5	25.4
Rowan	11.0	8.2	5.9	51.6	22,094	23,336	5.6	5.3	2,265	1,867	828	8,774	2.45	58.3	11.8	31.5
Russell	14.2	11.8	8.4	50.9	16,315	17,565	7.7	1.5	1,782	1,918	402	7,204	2.43	65.1	12.0	31.2
Scott	11.8	7.7	4.3	50.7	33,061	47,102	42.5	19.0	5,470	2,859	6,260	19,706	2.58	73.4	10.9	20.9
Shelby	13.4	9.6	5.8	51.4	33,337	42,048	26.1	15.4	4,991	2,863	4,327	16,369	2.70	72.4	11.2	23.1
Simpson	13.4	9.9	6.6	50.8	16,405	17,330	5.6	6.9	1,889	1,550	864	6,895	2.54	68.0	11.9	27.1
Spencer	15.4	9.2	4.8	49.4	11,766	17,063	45.0	10.1	1,534	1,144	1,336	6,678	2.68	82.4	9.0	13.0
Taylor	13.5	10.1	7.9	51.1	22,927	24,500	6.9	4.3	2,744	2,420	718	9,669	2.51	66.3	13.8	28.9
Todd	12.9	9.4	6.7	50.2	11,971	12,463	4.1	-1.2	1,462	1,086	-532	4,610	2.64	70.6	11.9	26.1
Trigg	15.6	13.3	9.0	50.4	12,597	14,329	13.7	2.2	1,230	1,430	515	5,982	2.37	68.5	10.9	25.5
Trimble	14.9	11.0	6.4	49.9	8,125	8,809	8.4	-3.3	824	743	-376	3,603	2.40	66.6	10.2	29.3
Union	13.7	10.4	6.2	47.9	15,637	15,007	-4.0	-3.3	1,400	1,416	-520	5,527	2.40	67.1	8.9	29.6
Warren	10.9	7.7	5.2	51.1	92,522	113,766	23.0	15.4	13,023	7,798	12,241	46,443	2.51	64.6	12.5	26.7
Washington	14.0	10.2	7.8	50.5	10,916	11,717	7.3	3.1	1,148	1,152	369	4,507	2.57	68.0	13.3	26.4
Wayne	14.7	12.4	8.7	50.3	19,923	20,813	4.5	-1.7	1,931	1,871	-393	8,011	2.55	63.4	9.2	33.4
Webster	14.2	10.3	7.1	50.5	14,120	13,621	-3.5	-3.7	1,354	1,399	-465	5,095	2.51	70.2	9.5	27.6
Whitley	12.3	9.3	6.7	50.8	35,865	35,633	-0.6	1.7	4,654	3,887	-143	12,583	2.72	73.9	12.8	22.5
Wolfe	14.9	11.7	7.6	51.0	7,065	7,357	4.1	-2.4	745	861	-66	2,853	2.50	66.5	14.2	29.4
Woodford	15.3	11.8	7.0	51.9	23,208	24,939	7.5	6.4	2,355	1,870	1,123	10,063	2.53	70.5	11.1	23.7
LOUISIANA	13.0	9.2	6.2	51.2	4,468,976	4,533,485	1.4	2.8	516,732	357,057	-34,167	1,737,645	2.61	64.6	16.1	29.9
Acadia	13.3	8.9	6.4	51.2	58,861	61,787	5.0	0.7	7,287	5,354	-1,490	22,675	2.71	68.4	13.8	27.4
Allen	12.0	8.6	6.4	43.3	25,440	25,763	1.3	-0.6	2,635	2,084	-700	7,834	2.71	65.6	11.7	32.5
Ascension	11.7	7.4	4.4	50.6	76,627	107,215	39.9	16.3	13,803	6,030	9,584	41,884	2.82	75.1	13.2	21.2
Assumption	14.7	10.6	7.4	51.5	23,388	23,416	0.1	-4.8	2,140	1,824	-1,439	8,710	2.60	67.9	14.5	27.8
Avoyelles	12.9	9.7	7.3	49.6	41,481	42,071	1.4	-3.8	4,561	4,025	-2,136	14,961	2.50	67.2	16.2	28.5
Beauregard	12.6	9.5	6.3	49.3	32,986	35,654	8.1	4.5	4,030	3,006	585	13,327	2.72	69.8	11.4	25.9
Bienville	14.5	11.1	9.9	52.1	15,752	14,353	-8.9	-7.3	1,424	1,703	-766	5,840	2.31	65.4	19.3	32.5
Bossier	11.8	8.2	6.1	50.5	98,310	117,027	19.0	8.7	14,770	8,287	3,614	48,142	2.54	66.6	14.0	27.9
Caddo	13.3	9.9	7.2	52.7	252,161	254,921	1.1	-4.7	29,751	22,514	-19,295	97,283	2.53	61.7	19.2	33.9
Calcasieu	12.8	8.7	6.1	51.1	183,577	192,773	5.0	5.4	23,167	16,191	3,517	77,130	2.53	65.3	15.1	29.5
Caldwell	13.4	10.4	7.4	48.6	10,560	10,129	-4.1	-1.7	1,017	1,010	-172	3,680	2.56	64.2	12.4	31.4
Cameron	15.7	9.7	6.8	50.2	9,991	6,868	-31.3	1.5	544	396	-59	2,686	2.53	76.4	9.9	18.2
Catahoula	14.1	10.3	7.2	47.1	10,920	10,407	-4.7	-7.7	1,022	1,118	-700	3,747	2.41	69.0	12.4	29.7
Claiborne	13.8	10.8	8.3	43.4	16,851	17,195	2.0	-7.3	1,406	1,557	-1,107	5,980	2.39	62.9	17.3	34.6
Concordia	13.6	9.9	7.3	49.3	20,247	20,822	2.8	-6.0	2,163	2,014	-1,405	7,440	2.44	67.0	20.1	29.3
De Soto	13.8	10.5	7.3	51.8	25,494	26,656	4.6	2.9	2,796	2,423	423	10,331	2.61	68.6	18.5	28.5
East Baton Rouge	11.9	8.7	5.5	52.2	412,852	440,169	6.6	0.2	49,948	30,763	-18,284	167,188	2.61	60.1	16.5	32.0
East Carroll	12.7	8.4	6.4	45.8	9,421	7,759	-17.6	-9.3	953	640	-1,045	2,417	2.06	60.4	29.7	36.3
East Feliciana	16.0	11.0	6.7	45.7	21,360	20,276	-5.1	-4.8	1,734	1,979	-722	6,817	2.34	71.4	19.0	24.9
Evangeline	12.7	8.8	6.5	49.2	35,434	33,988	-4.1	-1.6	3,993	3,074	-1,462	11,928	2.70	64.9	14.7	31.2
Franklin	13.5	9.8	8.1	51.6	21,263	20,767	-2.3	-2.9	2,397	2,257	-742	7,622	2.48	66.5	18.2	30.9
Grant	12.0	9.2	6.0	44.1	18,698	22,309	19.3	0.8	2,043	1,711	-143	7,271	2.60	64.3	11.0	32.6
Iberia	13.9	8.8	6.2	51.1	73,266	73,094	-0.2	-2.9	8,727	5,954	-4,929	26,420	2.74	69.7	18.4	25.0
Iberville	13.5	9.4	6.5	49.4	33,320	33,404	0.3	-2.0	3,277	2,642	-1,309	11,142	2.65	69.6	20.1	27.3
Jackson	13.2	10.9	9.0	48.7	15,397	16,272	5.7	-2.3	1,463	1,578	-243	6,032	2.44	68.1	15.8	28.0
Jefferson	13.9	10.1	7.0	51.6	455,466	432,573	-5.0	0.3	47,684	34,010	-12,046	168,786	2.57	63.3	15.8	31.2
Jefferson Davis	13.5	9.0	7.3	51.0	31,435	31,592	0.5	0.0	3,563	3,046	-511	11,435	2.70	67.9	15.9	27.8
Lafayette	12.6	8.0	5.2	51.3	190,503	221,724	16.4	9.5	27,307	14,232	7,970	89,677	2.60	62.8	14.6	29.0
Lafourche	13.4	8.8	6.6	51.0	89,974	96,662	7.4	1.5	10,242	7,175	-1,562	36,153	2.66	70.5	14.7	23.7
La Salle	12.4	9.7	7.2	48.2	14,282	14,890	4.3	0.2	1,434	1,362	-34	5,044	2.68	71.3	14.6	23.6
Lincoln	9.9	7.6	5.9	51.4	42,509	46,740	10.0	1.0	4,789	3,094	-1,243	17,370	2.54	60.3	16.9	26.4
Livingston	11.9	8.3	4.9	50.7	91,814	128,015	39.4	9.0	15,179	8,562	4,890	48,675	2.80	73.5	13.6	21.8
Madison	12.0	8.5	5.9	50.4	13,728	12,099	-11.9	-7.8	1,368	1,084	-1,243	4,073	2.43	58.9	23.9	37.4
Morehouse	13.7	11.1	7.7	51.9	31,021	27,979	-9.8	-9.2	2,981	3,053	-2,530	10,077	2.52	63.2	16.9	32.3
Natchitoches	11.2	9.6	7.0	51.9	39,080	39,569	1.3	-2.3	4,376	3,272	-2,006	14,549	2.63	55.7	13.9	35.0

1. No spouse present.

Table B. States and Counties — Population, Vital Statistics, Health, and Crime

STATE County	Persons in group quarters, 2018	Daytime Population, 2013-2017 Number	Employment/residence ratio	Births, 2018 Total	Rate[1]	Deaths, 2018 Number	Rate[1]	Persons under 65 with no health insurance, 2016 Number	Percent	Medicare, 2018 Total beneficiaries	Enrolled in Original Medicare	Enrolled in Medicare Advantage	Serious crimes known to police[2], 2016 Total Number	Rate[3]
	32	33	34	35	36	37	38	39	40	41	42	43	44	45
KENTUCKY— Cont'd														
Ohio	307	23,567	0.95	294	12.2	265	11.0	1,211	6.1	5,559	3,827	1,732	154	635
Oldham	4,587	52,790	0.61	571	8.6	411	6.2	1,885	3.5	9,637	6,651	2,986	664	1,010
Owen	0	8,889	0.54	104	9.6	105	9.7	523	6.0	2,367	1,531	836	52	486
Owsley	90	4,087	0.67	53	11.9	60	13.4	253	7.0	1,147	891	256	55	1,251
Pendleton	215	11,239	0.48	163	11.2	163	11.2	723	5.9	3,080	1,839	1,241	95	664
Perry	611	30,028	1.32	336	12.9	425	16.3	1,279	5.7	6,930	5,124	1,806	304	1,113
Pike	1,443	64,715	1.16	566	9.7	811	13.9	3,527	7.3	16,428	11,957	4,471	586	959
Powell	188	10,695	0.62	156	12.5	145	11.7	670	6.6	3,072	2,105	967	127	1,042
Pulaski	962	66,037	1.08	714	11.0	806	12.5	3,164	6.2	16,600	11,924	4,676	1,045	1,637
Robertson	57	1,718	0.49	20	9.4	28	13.1	101	6.1	479	344	135	3	142
Rockcastle	341	15,055	0.72	170	10.1	250	14.9	866	6.4	4,048	3,068	980	82	485
Rowan	3,005	26,016	1.16	264	10.7	211	8.6	1,089	6.1	4,560	2,849	1,711	276	1,151
Russell	177	17,918	1.03	209	11.7	229	12.9	1,125	8.0	4,343	3,267	1,076	113	640
Scott	1,091	56,400	1.15	695	12.4	417	7.4	2,187	4.7	8,022	4,912	3,110	1,200	2,246
Shelby	1,819	41,642	0.81	587	12.1	342	7.0	2,759	7.2	8,363	5,703	2,660	735	1,588
Simpson	327	19,378	1.19	228	12.3	165	8.9	796	5.4	3,878	2,940	938	343	1,893
Spencer	113	11,413	0.26	170	9.0	164	8.7	801	5.0	3,309	2,246	1,063	82	455
Taylor	1,338	26,859	1.14	339	13.3	320	12.5	1,217	6.2	6,049	4,663	1,386	580	2,268
Todd	195	10,376	0.57	158	12.8	129	10.5	825	8.2	2,384	1,930	454	108	861
Trigg	78	12,498	0.68	153	10.4	182	12.4	740	6.7	3,817	2,831	986	182	1,282
Trimble	41	6,600	0.44	98	11.5	96	11.3	405	5.7	1,923	1,344	579	12	137
Union	1,658	14,926	1.00	157	10.8	177	12.2	847	6.8	3,085	2,063	1,022	105	701
Warren	6,890	132,436	1.15	1,642	12.5	968	7.4	6,534	6.3	20,088	14,328	5,760	3,568	2,865
Washington	205	10,564	0.74	138	11.4	141	11.7	716	7.3	2,689	2,045	644	64	528
Wayne	331	19,659	0.85	233	11.4	217	10.6	1,173	7.3	5,095	3,768	1,327	148	726
Webster	393	11,779	0.72	171	13.0	147	11.2	839	7.8	3,037	2,052	985	51	390
Whitley	1,740	35,675	0.97	575	15.9	464	12.8	1,762	6.1	8,592	6,622	1,970	397	1,098
Wolfe	132	6,739	0.73	87	12.1	110	15.3	395	6.9	1,969	1,422	547	14	194
Woodford	413	23,483	0.82	287	10.8	233	8.8	1,307	6.1	5,674	3,421	2,253	443	1,709
LOUISIANA	129,499	4,678,164	1.01	60,341	12.9	46,256	9.9	460,244	11.8	848,502	547,080	301,422	180,888	3,864
Acadia	1,050	53,139	0.61	838	13.5	687	11.0	6,945	13.0	11,181	9,349	1,832	1,849	2,958
Allen	4,183	25,653	1.00	296	11.6	238	9.3	2,206	12.2	4,496	3,890	606	280	1,094
Ascension	790	106,532	0.78	1,717	13.8	911	7.3	8,909	8.3	16,779	7,381	9,398	4,234	3,484
Assumption	199	17,801	0.45	251	11.3	232	10.4	2,059	11.0	4,599	3,042	1,557	325	1,434
Avoyelles	3,346	37,542	0.75	531	13.1	455	11.2	3,818	12.1	8,774	7,412	1,362	1,186	3,068
Beauregard	1,296	32,304	0.70	460	12.3	414	11.1	3,954	13.1	6,997	6,053	944	347	952
Bienville	319	13,133	0.86	151	11.3	211	15.9	1,246	11.3	3,321	2,670	651	317	2,595
Bossier	2,545	117,401	0.86	1,708	13.4	1,108	8.7	9,957	9.3	20,317	15,803	4,514	4,785	3,788
Caddo	6,246	268,104	1.16	3,113	12.8	2,757	11.3	24,641	12.1	49,221	36,170	13,051	13,406	5,367
Calcasieu	3,794	206,578	1.09	2,958	14.6	2,034	10.0	18,790	11.1	36,521	29,606	6,915	10,003	5,020
Caldwell	584	9,310	0.80	114	11.4	124	12.4	1,047	13.3	2,155	1,608	547	269	2,709
Cameron	20	8,931	1.69	62	8.9	62	8.9	644	11.2	1,158	934	224	143	2,110
Catahoula	866	9,051	0.72	119	12.4	122	12.7	1,021	13.7	2,211	1,776	435	158	1,569
Claiborne	2,920	15,230	0.79	172	10.8	204	12.8	1,355	13.0	3,359	2,706	653	94	675
Concordia	1,480	19,337	0.87	249	12.7	249	12.7	1,860	12.2	4,125	3,405	720	618	3,099
De Soto	215	24,587	0.75	312	11.4	297	10.8	2,691	12.1	5,940	4,749	1,191	714	2,641
East Baton Rouge	11,106	500,009	1.25	5,846	13.3	3,909	8.9	40,062	10.6	72,916	38,037	34,879	21,214	4,752
East Carroll	1,067	7,384	1.04	102	14.5	66	9.4	575	11.1	1,373	996	377	86	1,194
East Feliciana	2,404	17,892	0.76	197	10.2	245	12.7	1,427	10.2	4,283	2,513	1,770	250	1,280
Evangeline	1,379	31,220	0.77	470	14.1	381	11.4	3,352	12.2	6,883	6,175	708	1,040	3,097
Franklin	732	18,904	0.79	290	14.4	279	13.8	2,445	15.0	4,491	3,503	988	164	809
Grant	2,958	18,506	0.46	230	10.2	184	8.2	1,922	11.8	4,255	3,374	881	154	715
Iberia	944	73,631	1.01	989	13.9	782	11.0	7,871	12.7	13,832	11,375	2,457	1,677	2,266
Iberville	3,989	37,983	1.38	360	11.0	312	9.5	2,574	10.6	6,166	2,805	3,361	1,281	3,890
Jackson	1,037	13,944	0.63	172	10.8	221	13.9	1,515	12.7	3,549	2,735	814	58	369
Jefferson	3,314	429,550	0.96	5,683	13.1	4,362	10.0	50,975	14.0	85,607	34,508	51,099	16,349	3,754
Jefferson Davis	567	28,090	0.72	423	13.4	404	12.8	3,329	12.7	5,865	5,202	663	NA	NA
Lafayette	5,155	266,981	1.24	3,194	13.2	1,977	8.1	24,568	11.8	37,041	29,917	7,124	9,993	4,342
Lafourche	1,626	93,288	0.89	1,203	12.3	893	9.1	13,018	15.7	17,784	12,300	5,484	2,879	2,928
La Salle	1,242	14,492	0.91	165	11.1	170	11.4	1,367	11.9	2,897	2,452	445	88	589
Lincoln	4,887	48,131	1.03	591	12.5	418	8.9	5,036	13.7	7,111	5,615	1,496	1,189	2,488
Livingston	1,191	104,935	0.47	1,788	12.8	1,139	8.2	12,430	10.2	21,102	9,664	11,438	4,237	3,055
Madison	1,596	11,315	0.92	142	12.7	149	13.4	918	10.9	1,958	1,663	295	94	827
Morehouse	768	23,914	0.74	339	13.3	341	13.4	2,390	11.5	6,242	4,421	1,821	1,420	5,458
Natchitoches	2,192	38,857	0.98	529	13.7	396	10.2	4,258	13.8	7,561	6,270	1,291	2,041	5,236

1. Per 1,000 estimated resident population.   2. Data for serious crimes have not been adjusted for underreporting; this may affect comparability between geographic areas and over time.   3. Per 100,000 population estimated by the FBI.

Table B. States and Counties — Crime, Education, Money Income, and Poverty

STATE County	Serious crimes known to police[2], 2016 (cont.)[1] Rate Violent	Property	Education — School enrollment and attainment, 2013-2017 Enrollment Total	Percent private	Attainment[4] (percent) High school graduate or less	Bachelor's degree or more	Local government expenditures,[5] 2014-2015 Total current spending (mil dol)	Current spending per student (dollars)	Money income, 2013-2017 Per capita income[6]	Households Median income (dollars)	Percent with income of less than $50,000	with income of $200,000 or more	Income and poverty, 2017 Median household income (dollars)	Percent below poverty level All persons	Children under 18 years	Children 5 to 17 years in families
	46	47	48	49	50	51	52	53	54	55	56	57	58	59	60	61
KENTUCKY— Cont'd																
Ohio	115	519	5,316	9.3	63.3	11.0	36.3	8,451	21,368	41,470	58.5	1.8	43,142	17.6	23.7	21.9
Oldham	68	942	18,389	17.7	29.1	40.4	106.4	8,677	38,063	92,237	24.7	12.7	97,960	5.1	4.8	4.0
Owen	0	486	2,391	7.7	65.5	9.6	16.6	8,439	22,802	44,031	58.2	1.9	48,362	15.7	20.9	18.6
Owsley	136	1,114	888	1.0	67.5	15.7	10.2	13,351	16,582	22,736	68.2	0.4	25,344	36.8	49.2	46.9
Pendleton	56	609	3,055	13.8	60.2	12.4	22.2	8,989	23,191	49,706	50.3	1.4	52,861	14.6	21.7	21.0
Perry	26	1,087	5,967	8.2	58.9	12.6	50.3	9,614	19,890	31,820	66.5	2.2	34,105	25.9	33.4	32.0
Pike	33	926	13,195	9.0	62.6	13.0	104.4	9,831	20,576	32,972	67.1	1.5	34,076	28.8	35.8	30.9
Powell	33	1,010	2,848	10.1	64.6	13.4	23.1	9,304	19,302	34,647	60.8	0.9	35,817	24.6	35.0	32.5
						15.2	94.4	8,988	21,036	35,022	64.6	1.3	36,295	23.7	29.4	27.7
Pulaski	88	1,549	13,816	9.2	57.3											
Robertson	0	142	419	8.4	58.7	17.2	3.6	9,435	21,764	30,694	60.8	2.5	43,227	21.1	29.2	26.1
Rockcastle	36	450	3,865	7.5	66.1	11.9	27.1	9,239	19,750	35,888	61.4	1.5	36,756	21.3	28.5	23.8
Rowan	88	1,063	8,230	3.7	46.2	26.7	28.7	8,478	19,032	36,411	63.5	2.2	41,050	23.7	26.7	24.6
Russell	45	594	3,420	7.8	60.8	13.4	28.5	9,296	18,857	34,660	67.2	1.1	33,575	23.3	32.1	31.0
Scott	127	2,119	13,981	22.1	41.2	28.1	74.7	8,286	30,702	65,598	38.2	4.2	67,234	10.4	12.7	10.9
Shelby	78	1,510	10,492	19.4	45.1	24.3	69.7	9,856	30,240	63,171	40.3	5.9	65,054	10.8	13.6	11.9
Simpson	182	1,711	4,042	14.2	57.0	15.1	27.6	9,087	22,663	44,989	55.3	2.4	47,542	14.4	21.3	18.9
Spencer	17	438	4,187	12.8	46.5	19.8	24.9	8,487	30,779	68,916	33.9	3.7	80,808	7.5	9.2	7.8
Taylor	153	2,116	6,217	22.6	54.8	18.8	35.6	9,321	19,885	36,455	62.8	1.1	41,087	18.2	25.6	24.8
						12.6	19.1	8,958	19,555	38,248	60.8	1.1	43,512	18	24.6	24.4
Todd	80	781	2,813	15.0	62.1											
Trigg	113	1,169	3,056	13.2	46.0	16.9	20.0	9,676	26,224	47,259	52.1	2.3	47,963	14	22.6	21.3
Trimble	23	114	1,972	13.1	64.0	11.8	13.6	9,270	26,542	50,998	48.2	2.0	53,024	13.5	19.1	18.6
Union	33	667	3,474	20.4	57.6	11.3	23.1	9,857	21,758	42,139	58.6	1.4	46,708	17.8	21.9	20.1
Warren	200	2,665	37,927	7.1	41.2	30.4	160.8	8,489	25,840	49,508	50.3	3.6	49,966	16.1	19.4	17.7
Washington	50	479	2,936	23.0	57.3	17.7	16.1	9,377	22,611	47,843	53.1	1.8	49,750	15.2	20.4	19.7
Wayne	59	668	4,477	8.1	65.5	11.4	32.4	9,416	17,627	33,715	69.0	1.0	34,382	24.9	35.4	33.4
Webster	23	367	2,862	11.1	64.4	9.0	19.5	8,464	21,150	39,273	60.6	1.6	42,968	14.7	20.0	19.3
Whitley	53	1,045	9,362	20.2	56.9	19.9	75.9	8,909	18,463	34,103	63.3	1.7	33,809	26.5	36.2	35.1
Wolfe	28	166	1,440	16.1	70.1	7.8	14.5	10,917	13,533	21,999	79.7	1.1	29,326	29.9	43.3	40.4
Woodford	58	1,651	6,423	17.9	38.8	32.8	37.5	9,106	31,208	60,604	41.4	4.6	64,177	9.3	13.2	12.2
LOUISIANA	566	3,298	1,167,557	19.5	49.5	23.4	7,899.1	11,021	26,205	46,710	52.6	4.0	46,283	19.6	27.7	26.0
Acadia	450	2,508	15,112	20.3	63.1	12.2	93.0	9,252	21,591	40,492	57.8	2.1	39,252	23.1	34.3	36.1
Allen	168	926	5,694	11.1	63.0	13.1	47.6	10,940	20,103	42,176	58.6	1.9	42,846	20.8	24.1	22.6
Ascension	341	3,144	32,157	21.1	45.6	27.6	238.5	11,043	31,520	74,748	33.7	5.3	72,154	12.6	14.6	13.4
Assumption	375	1,059	4,976	14.7	68.9	10.3	45.2	12,255	25,765	48,656	51.1	3.4	45,774	18.9	27.4	26.4
Avoyelles	525	2,543	9,252	15.3	65.4	11.3	61.9	9,371	20,199	36,763	60.8	1.6	36,177	24.6	33.0	30.1
Beauregard	101	850	8,227	12.0	55.6	16.3	64.3	10,795	24,551	47,350	52.1	2.8	51,422	14.6	17.9	16.9
Bienville	516	2,080	3,090	9.5	57.9	12.4	35.1	15,663	22,701	34,077	62.8	1.6	30,483	25.4	36.8	34.9
Bossier	550	3,238	30,614	12.6	39.8	25.7	221.3	10,064	27,235	52,145	47.9	3.4	52,158	16.8	23.9	21.7
Caddo	773	4,594	60,819	13.6	46.7	24.0	465.5	11,262	25,565	40,391	58.0	4.1	37,636	25.8	39.1	36.5
Calcasieu	672	4,347	50,480	12.7	47.8	21.7	355.4	10,499	26,569	48,219	51.5	3.7	52,407	14.2	20.8	18.8
Caldwell	211	2,497	2,233	8.8	65.9	12.4	19.5	11,567	20,961	31,933	67.1	1.4	39,863	23.4	32.1	29.5
Cameron	280	1,829	1,542	13.7	57.8	12.0	24.8	19,180	29,681	60,194	44.7	6.0	56,025	13.2	16.9	16.2
Catahoula	377	1,192	1,969	8.0	64.2	13.9	17.5	11,990	20,717	34,470	60.3	3.2	32,380	27.8	39.0	36.3
Claiborne	79	596	2,886	13.4	62.0	14.0	18.9	11,173	16,384	26,877	72.7	0.8	34,109	39.5	47.6	42.5
Concordia	622	2,477	4,529	3.8	64.2	11.4	41.9	10,655	17,551	30,028	66.3	1.5	33,873	27.7	38.6	36.4
De Soto	455	2,186	6,253	5.5	59.7	13.5	78.6	15,500	23,471	41,443	56.7	2.4	40,839	22.8	36.3	32.1
East Baton Rouge	602	4,150	129,161	21.5	36.9	34.5	758.8	11,819	30,162	51,436	48.7	5.6	54,494	18.9	26.3	24.5
East Carroll	750	444	1,008	15.9	68.8	9.8	13.3	12,133	14,694	20,795	81.4	0.4	26,431	46.7	62.3	60.1
East Feliciana	532	747	3,939	19.1	62.1	12.1	22.1	11,081	21,138	46,964	52.2	1.6	45,839	20.6	26.8	25.5
Evangeline	161	2,936	8,169	16.4	64.4	12.9	58.7	9,589	18,655	31,745	66.2	2.2	33,942	23.6	32.2	31.7
Franklin	188	622	4,783	19.0	67.1	11.4	31.9	10,858	18,786	34,722	62.6	1.5	32,485	27.9	40.7	38.1
Grant	42	673	4,631	12.4	60.5	8.5	28.7	9,005	18,509	40,577	58.9	0.9	44,298	21	26.0	24.3
Iberia	184	2,082	17,908	16.3	65.0	12.7	132.6	9,507	23,410	44,504	55.3	2.6	40,964	23.8	34.5	32.8
Iberville	1,102	2,788	7,311	21.6	61.3	15.0	72.2	15,339	22,252	47,128	51.8	2.2	44,410	22.9	31.0	29.3
Jackson	38	331	3,272	8.2	63.2	13.0	25.2	10,797	20,109	36,394	62.2	1.3	38,893	24.6	41.4	36.3
Jefferson	428	3,326	102,078	32.3	46.5	25.2	526.4	10,887	28,839	50,868	49.1	4.3	51,461	17.1	27.2	25.5
Jefferson Davis	NA	NA	7,673	12.4	61.7	15.8	61.3	10,560	23,068	40,744	56.9	3.0	43,317	19.3	24.4	23.3
Lafayette	446	3,896	60,797	21.5	42.0	31.8	320.8	10,297	30,656	53,950	46.6	6.4	52,827	17.4	22.6	22.4
Lafourche	418	2,510	23,616	17.6	63.6	16.3	158.5	10,634	26,331	52,705	47.8	3.5	53,081	15.8	21.9	21.4
La Salle	275	315	3,266	14.5	66.3	12.2	28.2	10,720	18,836	34,712	64.8	2.3	44,125	18.4	23.4	21.8
Lincoln	410	2,078	18,026	8.0	38.6	36.2	72.2	11,001	21,934	34,424	60.4	4.3	39,941	27.9	28.3	25.6
Livingston	267	2,788	34,821	11.9	55.1	17.4	230.3	8,944	27,280	60,456	41.5	3.0	61,297	11.4	14.7	14.3
Madison	255	572	2,330	13.3	64.0	13.4	21.1	11,879	15,134	29,424	72.8	0.5	29,507	38.9	52.0	50.4
Morehouse	588	4,870	5,308	15.4	64.0	13.9	48.9	11,138	18,776	31,672	68.2	1.7	32,988	28	40.3	39.4
Natchitoches	657	4,580	12,677	15.7	48.0	19.4	79.6	11,612	18,219	29,001	68.8	1.8	33,439	30.3	36.5	35.2

1. Data for serious crimes have not been adjusted for underreporting; this may affect comparability between geographic areas and over time. 2. Per 100,000 population estimated by the FBI. 3. All persons 3 years old and over enrolled in nursery school through college. 4. Persons 25 years old and over. 5. Elementary and secondary education expenditures. 6. Based on population estimated by the American Community Survey, 2011–2015.

Table B. States and Counties — **Personal Income and Earnings**

STATE County	Personal income, 2017										Earnings, 2017		
	Total (mil dol)	Percent change 2016-2017	Per capita[1] Dollars	Per capita[1] Rank	Wages and salaries (mil dol)	Supplements to wages and salaries, employer contributions (mil dol) Pension and insurance	Government social insurance	Proprietors' income (mil dol)	Dividends, interest, and rent (mil dol)	Personal transfer receipts (mil dol)	Total (mil dol)	Contributions for government social insurance (mil dol) From employee and self-employed	From employer
	62	63	64	65	66	67	68	69	70	71	72	73	74
KENTUCKY— Cont'd													
Ohio	760	3.4	31,431	2,815	266	57	21	54	92	257	398	28	21
Oldham	3,946	4.6	59,412	171	755	126	54	220	725	396	1,155	74	54
Owen	351	1.7	32,578	2,679	68	17	5	14	44	107	104	9	5
Owsley	135	2.2	30,453	2,890	21	6	2	5	13	80	33	3	2
Pendleton	647	-4.7	44,376	972	101	21	8	24	76	135	154	13	8
Perry	980	3.0	36,890	2,058	450	87	35	43	131	440	614	42	35
Pike	2,058	3.9	34,951	2,357	938	160	73	68	249	849	1,239	91	73
Powell	385	4.0	31,120	2,843	86	20	7	14	38	156	126	11	7
	2,280	3.6	35,382	2,288	935	174	76	139	280	891	1,324	94	76
Pulaski													
Robertson	68	2.6	31,885	2,767	10	3	1	1	9	25	14	1	1
Rockcastle	503	1.8	30,151	2,916	142	31	12	13	51	201	198	16	12
Rowan	732	1.7	29,866	2,938	368	84	28	26	101	244	505	32	28
Russell	581	4.6	32,691	2,657	185	42	15	84	86	214	326	24	15
Scott	2,313	4.6	42,144	1,247	1,492	223	116	128	257	343	1,960	117	116
Shelby	2,032	4.6	42,855	1,159	695	120	56	123	333	337	994	64	56
Simpson	679	3.5	37,491	1,948	372	61	30	67	90	177	531	33	30
Spencer	786	3.9	42,448	1,210	79	16	6	29	67	138	130	11	6
Taylor	868	4.3	34,074	2,477	442	81	36	32	133	286	591	39	36
	439	0.6	35,889	2,212	88	19	7	61	61	113	176	11	7
Todd													
Trigg	522	3.8	36,130	2,184	107	22	9	32	82	153	170	14	9
Trimble	300	2.5	35,041	2,345	54	13	4	1	32	85	71	7	4
Union	462	2.1	31,514	2,805	220	39	17	8	78	156	285	20	17
Warren	4,762	3.9	36,957	2,046	2,812	482	216	362	727	1,019	3,872	236	216
Washington	434	4.5	35,750	2,238	138	26	11	28	70	118	203	14	11
Wayne	570	3.1	27,494	3,049	185	38	16	25	79	245	265	21	16
Webster	510	4.2	39,143	1,697	156	31	12	67	67	139	265	16	12
Whitley	1,164	2.8	32,130	2,737	470	88	38	55	146	514	651	47	38
Wolfe	221	3.7	30,392	2,897	39	10	3	6	21	116	57	6	3
Woodford	1,290	3.4	48,906	546	420	70	34	143	237	211	667	38	34
LOUISIANA	204,517	2.5	43,786	X	97,391	17,774	6,289	16,468	35,866	45,659	137,922	7,674	6,289
Acadia	2,216	3.3	35,401	2,286	580	119	37	178	309	620	914	56	37
Allen	823	5.2	32,106	2,738	326	88	18	34	107	233	466	24	18
Ascension	5,862	3.4	47,679	648	2,693	462	173	275	663	838	3,604	202	173
Assumption	964	4.8	42,787	1,172	174	37	11	29	116	231	250	18	11
Avoyelles	1,501	4.1	36,626	2,100	376	91	23	101	191	510	591	37	23
Beauregard	1,522	3.9	41,218	1,377	367	76	22	51	198	374	516	34	22
Bienville	485	5.0	35,589	2,258	179	42	11	15	70	182	248	16	11
Bossier	5,317	1.1	41,655	1,308	2,219	467	163	303	873	1,156	3,151	168	163
Caddo	10,989		44,565	956	5,404	1,019	361	863	2,375	2,696	7,646	429	361
Calcasieu	9,412	5.2	46,491	751	5,153	973	333	783	1,329	1,890	7,242	396	333
Caldwell	327	2.4	32,861	2,637	88	22	6	11	42	126	126	9	6
Cameron	313	5.1	45,278	870	1,140	130	71	16	61	45	1,356	75	71
Catahoula	332	3.4	33,657	2,537	75	19	5	28	46	121	128	8	5
Claiborne	533	1.0	33,392	2,571	144	38	8	47	87	181	238	14	8
Concordia	633	3.9	31,881	2,768	194	47	12	56	94	231	309	18	12
De Soto	1,042	2.7	38,098	1,863	370	75	22	20	176	296	486	31	22
East Baton Rouge	21,765	2.8	48,771	563	14,735	2,549	921	1,826	4,366	3,940	20,031	1,046	921
East Carroll	258	3.1	36,206	2,172	62	16	4	32	46	104	113	5	4
East Feliciana	803	3.2	41,384	1,349	223	66	11	29	119	245	330	17	11
Evangeline	1,105	3.6	32,781	2,650	313	70	20	78	150	405	482	31	20
Franklin	635	3.8	31,348	2,826	167	44	10	45	85	268	267	16	10
Grant	692	0.3	30,971	2,853	155	44	11	31	79	212	241	17	11
Iberia	2,680	1.4	37,138	2,008	1,322	235	84	128	482	767	1,769	105	84
Iberville	1,290	3.9	39,045	1,714	1,233	220	77	49	172	336	1,579	86	77
Jackson	518	3.5	32,705	2,655	149	36	8	27	68	181	220	14	8
Jefferson	21,321	2.9	48,563	585	10,341	1,523	675	2,209	4,090	4,183	14,747	853	675
Jefferson Davis	1,265	5.2	40,176	1,526	340	75	21	64	177	324	499	30	21
Lafayette	11,128	2.0	45,892	806	6,502	1,026	425	1,090	2,184	1,926	9,043	497	425
Lafourche	4,350	3.3	44,192	997	1,782	350	111	367	943	874	2,609	146	111
La Salle	457	2.5	30,624	2,880	169	43	10	16	61	157	238	14	10
Lincoln	1,816	3.7	38,032	1,878	763	165	47	191	379	410	1,166	60	47
Livingston	5,321	1.3	38,493	1,803	1,142	219	72	242	549	1,065	1,675	107	72
Madison	360	0.1	31,834	2,776	117	31	8	37	45	131	193	10	8
Morehouse	963	-1.4	37,564	1,935	242	53	16	79	119	374	390	25	16
Natchitoches	1,456	4.2	37,325	1,982	508	129	30	173	214	418	839	44	30

1. Based on the resident population estimated as of July 1 of the year shown.

Table B. States and Counties — Earnings, Social Security, and Housing

STATE County	Farm	Mining, quarrying, and extractions	Construction	Manu-facturing	Information; professional, scientific, technical services	Retail trade	Finance, insurance, real estate, and leasing	Health care and social assistance	Govern-ment	Number	Rate[1]	Supplemental Security Income recipients, 2017	Total	Percent change, 2010-2018
	75	76	77	78	79	80	81	82	83	84	85	86	87	88
KENTUCKY— Cont'd														
Ohio	3.4	D	5.2	34.3	D	6.8	2.3	D	20.9	6,360	263	1,016	10,453	2.3
Oldham	0.4	D	10.1	7.4	11.1	5.7	15.4	12.7	17.9	9,795	147	489	22,293	7.7
Owen	-0.3	0	4	D	D	5.3	D	8.6	24.7	2,695	250	393	5,739	2
Owsley	-2	D	D	D	D	D	D	22.5	40.9	1,210	273	782	2,361	1.4
Pendleton	-2.1	D	D	14.3	D	3.3	3.4	7.9	21.3	3,415	234	530	6,396	0.9
Perry	0	D	2	0.2	D	9.7	3.6	D	20.3	7,790	293	2,791	12,999	1.7
Pike	-0.1	9.1	3	3.1	6.1	9.2	4.5	D	13.9	18,550	315	4,645	31,042	2.4
Powell	-1.2	D	D	13.1	D	8.8	2.3	9.2	28.9	3,495	282	1,049	5,713	2.1
Pulaski	-0.5	0.2	6.7	13.2	4.3	8.6	4.4	22.8	15	18,300	284	3,768	31,528	0.3
Robertson	-12	0	D	0.4	D	D	3.2	18.7	44.1	500	234	99	1,107	1.1
Rockcastle	-1.9	D	D	2.9	17.5	4.2	2.8	D	19.9	4,410	264	1,095	7,852	1.9
Rowan	-0.1	D	D	11.4	2.1	7.9	3.7	D	32.3	5,060	206	1,146	10,386	2.8
Russell	0	0.4	D	33.4	D	7.9	3.8	D	16.6	4,825	271	1,108	10,150	1.6
Scott	1.3	D	5	51.3	2.8	2.8	1.7	D	6.5	8,530	155	1,046	22,631	17.4
Shelby	1.1	0	5.5	27.2	D	8.7	5.1	7.6	12.8	8,800	186	717	18,257	10
Simpson	4.3	0	7.4	38.2	D	9.4	2.7	D	9	4,260	235	495	7,903	6.3
Spencer	-2	0	13.5	D	D	6.5	D	12.4	27.4	3,515	190	295	7,395	10.3
Taylor	0.4	D	D	10.2	2	7.8	4.7	D	19.2	6,620	260	1,284	10,988	1.2
Todd	13.9	0	9.2	13.9	D	9.5	D	D	16.5	2,640	216	373	5,358	1.3
Trigg	3.7	D	14.7	13.1	5.6	7.3	5.4	10.4	22.4	4,055	281	422	7,965	2
Trimble	-5.6	0	5.4	D	D	2.2	7.4	8.8	25.4	2,125	248	230	4,006	1.9
Union	-3.1	D	3.6	14.8	D	5.3	4.3	D	13.3	3,520	240	393	6,266	2
Warren	0.5	0	7.1	18	D	6.7	5.3	15	14.3	21,355	166	3,472	53,964	14.3
Washington	1.2	0	12.7	36.4	D	3.9	D	9.1	13.4	2,950	243	439	5,209	3.3
Wayne	2.4	D	4.5	24	D	8.4	4	D	19.8	5,505	266	1,698	10,906	-0.3
Webster	14.6	D	16.9	5.9	D	3.5	D	5.8	12.6	3,385	260	464	5,963	0.5
Whitley	-0.5	D	3.4	9	6	7	3.6	D	17.6	9,540	263	3,889	15,473	2
Wolfe	-3.3	D	D	2	D	8.8	D	D	37.1	2,245	309	1,206	3,746	2.3
Woodford	14.8	-0.2	5.7	19.2	6.8	4.4	2.9	D	12.7	5,885	223	397	11,228	4.8
LOUISIANA	0.4	3.2	9.7	9.5	8.5	6.5	6.3	12.4	17.3	895,826	191	177,338	2,076,028	5.7
Acadia	5	2.8	14.3	6.6	5.4	7.5	4.7	11.5	16.9	12,210	195	2,592	26,534	4.5
Allen	0.9	D	1.7	10.5	D	4.9	1.6	7.9	54.4	4,945	193	765	9,988	2.6
Ascension	0	0.1	21.6	26.4	D	6.5	4.7	5.4	9.5	18,190	148	2,106	48,680	19.4
Assumption	-0.5	1.5	13.4	13.7	D	6.6	7.9	D	22.9	5,070	225	923	10,867	5
Avoyelles	3.7	D	12.9	2.5	4.6	8.7	5.8	D	28.3	9,610	235	2,536	18,439	2.2
Beauregard	-0.7	0.4	5.3	20	4.1	7.4	8.2	13.1	18.8	7,610	206	1,090	15,890	5.7
Bienville	0.5	8.4	2.5	22	D	3.7	6.4	D	22.5	3,515	258	815	7,861	1.9
Bossier	0.1	3.5	4.9	5	4.2	9.8	4.7	9.2	34.7	21,370	167	3,437	57,828	17.1
Caddo	0	3.4	4.9	6.6	6.8	7	5.9	22.2	18.5	51,410	208	13,642	113,374	1.2
Calcasieu	0.1	0.3	17.6	18.5	7.2	7.5	4	11.5	12.7	39,455	195	6,212	92,047	12.2
Caldwell	0	0.8	D	2.3	D	5	D	26.5	25.9	2,310	232	507	5,192	4
Cameron	0.4	D	82.7	6.1	D	0.3	0.3	0.4	3.4	1,225	177	71	4,124	14.7
Catahoula	14.1	3.7	D	D	4.5	6.8	D	9.7	24.6	2,375	241	544	5,040	3.3
Claiborne	9.1	13.9	5.3	4.3	D	4.3	D	D	30.3	3,480	218	813	7,875	1.5
Concordia	9	2.3	2.5	3	D	10.8	4.2	D	27.6	4,565	230	1,216	9,621	2.5
De Soto	-1.4	21.5	D	D	1.8	6.1	2.4	D	21.6	6,365	233	1,308	13,174	7.2
East Baton Rouge	0	0.1	14.7	6.8	11.9	5.8	7.7	13.1	17.5	73,565	165	14,390	195,190	4.2
East Carroll	24.1	D	D	D	D	6.2	3.8	D	27.1	1,415	199	625	2,905	0
East Feliciana	0.1	1.3	4.5	7.4	D	3.5	3.8	10.6	52.3	4,180	215	847	8,552	6.7
Evangeline	5.8	0.7	3.9	11.7	2.4	7.6	4.8	D	18.1	7,420	220	2,146	15,068	2.8
Franklin	8.3	D	4.8	3.2	D	10.7	5.9	D	31.4	4,695	232	1,269	9,256	2.5
Grant	0.8	D	6.3	8.1	1	3.7	D	5.7	51.1	4,530	203	823	9,422	6
Iberia	-0.3	17.5	7.6	12.9	D	7.3	8	7.8	14.9	15,395	213	3,253	30,735	3.7
Iberville	0.1	1.1	24.9	36.1	D	2.2	3	2.3	12.5	6,625	201	1,357	13,583	6.9
Jackson	2.5	D	D	D	D	6.4	3.6	D	28.8	3,720	235	696	7,923	3.2
Jefferson	0	0.8	8	4.9	8.9	7.8	9.9	16.3	9.7	88,265	201	13,167	188,657	-0.3
Jefferson Davis	5.1	2.6	6.6	4.9	3.2	8.4	6.4	18.8	23.5	6,430	204	1,080	14,040	5.5
Lafayette	0	10.8	5.6	6.5	10.2	7.3	7.3	17.1	10.6	38,405	158	6,029	104,039	11
Lafourche	0.6	6.3	6.3	7.8	4.1	4.8	2.9	7	17.9	19,360	197	3,149	41,622	7.5
La Salle	-0.4	8.5	3.9	6.7	D	7.2	3.6	D	33.5	3,130	210	524	6,759	3
Lincoln	2.3	2.2	7.3	9.2	7.1	8	6.3	12.4	22.4	7,135	149	1,512	20,431	4.9
Livingston	0	0.4	16.6	11.2	D	9.9	8.6	7.2	19.9	22,825	165	2,618	58,274	16.2
Madison	11.5	0	1	9.1	D	7	3.3	D	25.8	2,135	189	714	5,171	7.6
Morehouse	11.4	D	7	7.6	3.1	7.9	4	20	16.5	6,845	267	1,781	12,642	1.8
Natchitoches	3	0.5	4.1	19.6	D	5.6	4.2	6.7	29.5	8,000	205	2,110	19,224	3.4

1. Per 1,000 resident population estimated as of July 1 of the year shown.

Table B. States and Counties — Housing, Labor Force, and Employment

STATE County	Housing units, 2013-2017								Civilian labor force, 2018				Civilian employment[6], 2013-2017		
	Occupied units							Sub-standard units[4] (percent)			Unemployment			Percent	
	Owner-occupied					Renter-occupied									
				Median owner cost as a percent of income			Median rent as a percent of income[2]							Management, business, science, and arts	Construction, production, and maintenance occupations
	Total	Percent	Median value[1]	With a mortgage	Without a mortgage[2]	Median rent[3]			Total	Percent change, 2017-2018	Total	Rate[5]	Total		
	89	90	91	92	93	94	95	96	97	98	99	100	101	102	103
KENTUCKY— Cont'd															
Ohio	9,055	76.6	88,300	20.4	10.0	536	23.7	2.8	9,914	1.2	566	5.7	9,324	26.7	36.7
Oldham	20,465	85.2	259,700	19.1	10.0	875	26.4	1.4	33,270	1	1,094	3.3	30,706	45.1	16.5
Owen	3,944	73.4	99,100	22.0	11.2	622	26.4	5.7	5,229	-4.1	255	4.9	3,975	27.7	35.5
Owsley	1,696	73.8	70,000	28.1	13.8	349	29.5	3.6	1,171	6.5	83	7.1	1,243	36.3	22.9
Pendleton	5,236	75.7	106,400	22.9	12.9	698	23.3	1.8	7,058	1	289	4.1	6,415	24.6	40.4
Perry	11,037	73.5	73,300	20.6	11.0	569	24.4	3.7	8,245	-2	522	6.3	8,819	31.8	25.1
Pike	25,853	72.9	75,400	22.0	10.8	651	30.8	2.4	19,933	-2.2	1,182	5.9	20,158	29.6	27.7
Powell	4,878	68.6	79,800	18.3	11.8	640	25.8	6	5,023	-0.1	299	6	4,615	21.1	42.1
Pulaski	25,810	69.2	109,100	21.2	11.6	627	33.1	1.9	25,726	1.3	1,305	5.1	24,928	29.3	28.0
Robertson	938	76.4	94,500	27.1	11.1	469	31.8	1.3	815	-0.4	40	4.9	881	30.6	38.4
Rockcastle	6,552	75.9	80,800	18.5	12.1	548	27.2	2.9	6,693	1	330	4.9	6,283	28.4	34.3
Rowan	8,774	59.5	121,100	21.2	10.8	625	29.4	1.8	10,706	0.4	553	5.2	10,073	34.3	21.7
Russell	7,204	74.1	87,300	22.2	11.3	541	28.3	3.4	6,270	0.1	364	5.8	6,282	28.3	37.7
Scott	19,706	69.5	170,800	18.2	10.0	813	24.7	3	28,607	-0.4	946	3.3	26,798	34.5	31.1
Shelby	16,369	69.3	184,900	19.6	10.0	824	27.6	3	24,920	0.9	868	3.5	22,446	33.3	26.5
Simpson	6,895	63.0	130,500	19.9	10.0	735	27.4	1.4	8,836	1.2	343	3.9	7,888	25.7	33.6
Spencer	6,678	83.1	190,900	18.9	10.8	630	22	1.8	10,061	1.1	367	3.6	9,070	33.3	33.7
Taylor	9,669	63.2	106,700	19.9	10.0	596	32.9	1.8	12,494	-3	535	4.3	10,454	26.1	30.9
Todd	4,610	71.2	94,800	23.5	11.7	612	25.8	2.2	5,312	-0.3	212	4	4,759	25.6	43.7
Trigg	5,982	82.6	119,500	21.1	10.0	598	30.1	2.8	6,001	0.9	284	4.7	5,709	30.8	31.1
Trimble	3,603	76.8	110,500	20.5	11.0	750	28.2	2.3	3,893	0.2	167	4.3	3,856	24.7	37.0
Union	5,527	67.9	83,100	16.5	12.0	585	26.3	1.6	6,039	-1.1	300	5	6,533	22.4	41.5
Warren	46,443	58.7	152,300	19.7	10.0	735	28	3.1	64,400	0.6	2,372	3.7	60,183	32.5	24.6
Washington	4,507	76.6	105,600	19.6	10.2	581	24.3	3	6,201	0.4	232	3.7	5,629	26.8	39.0
Wayne	8,011	72.8	81,400	19.6	10.0	519	29.9	3.8	7,598	2.5	534	7	6,992	25.8	32.6
Webster	5,095	72.8	80,800	20.6	10.9	545	24.6	2.8	5,862	0.9	246	4.2	5,098	26.7	39.4
Whitley	12,583	70.4	83,800	20.4	10.0	612	31	2.2	13,920	1.1	696	5	12,794	31.0	25.6
Wolfe	2,853	64.9	65,700	31.7	13.0	496	47.6	1.5	1,904	-1.2	146	7.7	1,895	18.7	29.8
Woodford	10,063	70.5	188,200	19.7	10.0	755	26.6	1.2	14,793	-1.2	457	3.1	13,099	40.0	24.2
LOUISIANA	1,737,645	65.5	152,900	20.0	10.0	825	32.1	2.8	2,103,495	0	102,704	4.9	2,031,238	33.1	24.0
Acadia	22,675	71.3	97,500	17.7	10.0	593	31.3	3.9	23,952	-0.3	1,287	5.4	24,982	27.6	29.8
Allen	7,834	75.9	84,800	18.1	10.0	570	29.7	5.1	8,784	-2	494	5.6	8,577	29.1	26.5
Ascension	41,884	80.2	179,800	17.8	10.0	972	25	2.4	62,979	0.4	2,609	4.1	57,496	37.3	24.1
Assumption	8,710	79.2	114,600	16.6	10.0	698	36.6	2.3	8,941	0.1	596	6.7	9,375	26.1	34.4
Avoyelles	14,961	69.7	90,600	19.1	10.0	638	31	4.1	15,313	-1.9	876	5.7	14,753	31.6	26.6
Beauregard	13,327	76.5	115,200	18.2	10.0	699	29.2	3.1	14,542	-0.8	773	5.3	14,174	29.2	33.4
Bienville	5,840	72.0	76,000	18.1	10.0	490	28.9	2.7	5,670	0.7	331	5.8	5,020	30.0	35.1
Bossier	48,142	62.9	164,600	20.2	10.0	952	30.2	2.8	57,620	0.1	2,464	4.3	54,751	37.0	21.3
Caddo	97,283	60.0	138,200	21.2	10.0	764	34.3	2.1	104,778	0	5,751	5.5	105,583	33.1	21.0
Calcasieu	77,130	67.6	138,100	18.4	10.0	792	30	2.7	109,878	1.4	4,195	3.8	90,318	30.6	25.8
Caldwell	3,680	73.7	67,800	18.6	11.8	577	26.9	3.4	3,826	-0.8	219	5.7	3,451	23.8	26.5
Cameron	2,686	89.9	110,900	15.0	10.0	803	30.3	3.8	4,057	1.4	143	3.5	3,118	24.9	36.3
Catahoula	3,747	75.3	78,700	19.5	10.0	486	32.5	4	3,381	-1.5	230	6.8	3,671	32.0	28.1
Claiborne	5,980	66.5	74,100	25.9	10.8	617	38.4	2	5,779	-1.3	303	5.2	5,311	24.8	36.1
Concordia	7,440	63.5	78,500	20.0	12.0	528	36	4.8	6,956	-2.5	489	7	6,768	24.1	25.5
De Soto	10,331	72.9	110,000	18.8	10.0	608	29.4	2.5	10,754	-0.2	618	5.7	10,301	28.0	31.3
East Baton Rouge	167,188	58.8	177,800	19.8	10.0	882	31.6	2.6	232,663	0.4	10,045	4.3	216,397	38.1	18.9
East Carroll	2,417	45.1	68,200	21.0	10.6	474	33.9	8.6	1,962	-4.4	203	10.3	1,697	32.7	20.9
East Feliciana	6,817	80.7	124,100	18.4	10.0	732	28.8	2.6	8,008	0.4	374	4.7	6,920	27.0	28.2
Evangeline	11,928	66.5	90,000	17.8	10.7	533	30.7	4.4	12,061	-3.8	697	5.8	11,578	27.7	30.4
Franklin	7,622	68.0	83,200	17.6	10.0	538	38.3	5	7,311	0.1	521	7.1	7,285	25.5	30.8
Grant	7,271	66.7	93,600	18.2	10.0	721	28.9	1.6	8,071	-1.3	476	5.9	7,248	25.7	32.4
Iberia	26,420	67.1	106,700	19.0	10.0	723	29.3	3.7	28,639		1,675	5.8	30,316	26.4	29.6
Iberville	11,142	75.8	127,500	20.5	10.0	712	31	4.7	14,190	0.3	878	6.2	12,825	26.9	25.8
Jackson	6,032	70.6	84,400	19.7	10.0	520	32.7	2.2	6,839	-2	315	4.6	5,664	27.0	29.4
Jefferson	168,786	61.9	176,000	22.6	10.0	936	32.1	2.4	215,064	0.1	9,404	4.4	210,435	32.6	23.7
Jefferson Davis	11,435	71.4	101,800	17.9	10.0	600	31	5.2	13,510	-0.7	637	4.7	12,173	27.0	31.3
Lafayette	89,677	65.5	172,500	18.8	10.0	834	29.4	2.6	113,337	0.3	5,072	4.5	119,324	35.7	21.4
Lafourche	36,153	75.1	144,300	18.9	10.0	764	28.4	2.4	41,816	-0.2	1,981	4.7	42,975	27.7	33.7
La Salle	5,044	73.9	76,700	17.9	10.0	544	23.7	3.6	6,289	2.4	276	4.4	4,829	29.0	31.8
Lincoln	17,370	54.5	145,900	17.2	10.0	679	39.3	3	21,791	1.1	1,138	5.2	21,219	36.3	18.2
Livingston	48,675	80.3	155,800	18.4	10.0	847	24.2	3.1	67,916	0.4	2,751	4.1	61,986	30.4	29.2
Madison	4,073	56.2	64,100	19.9	10.6	533	31.5	5	3,627	-3.7	301	8.3	3,767	25.6	23.4
Morehouse	10,077	66.0	84,900	22.7	10.0	574	34.8	2.9	10,193	-1.5	833	8.2	9,422	24.7	34.0
Natchitoches	14,549	50.0	114,100	19.8	10.0	681	39.4	2.3	16,527	1.2	961	5.8	12,941	27.7	31.6

1. Specified owner-occupied units. 2. A value of 10.0 represents 10 percent or less; a value of 50.0 represents 50 percent or more. 3. Specified renter-occupied units. 4. Overcrowded or lacking complete plumbing facilities. 5. Percent of civilian labor force. 6. Civilian employed persons 16 years old and over.

Table B. States and Counties — **Nonfarm Employment and Agriculture**

STATE County	Private nonfarm establishments, employment and payroll, 2016									Agriculture, 2017			
	Number of establishments	Employment						Annual payroll		Farms			Farm producers whose primary occupation is farming (percent)
		Total	Health care and social assistance	Manufacturing	Retail trade	Finance and insurance	Professional, scientific, and technical services	Total (mil dol)	Average per employee (dollars)	Number	Percent with:		
											Fewer than 50 acres	1000 acres or more	
	104	105	106	107	108	109	110	111	112	113	114	115	116
KENTUCKY— Cont'd													
Ohio	374	8,000	1,134	2,691	761	107	89	261	32,589	813	35.1	2.8	39.3
Oldham	1,222	12,953	2,611	1,043	1,536	1,507	709	494	38,104	466	54.3	1.5	28.0
Owen	122	1,507	257	D	135	47	7	50	33,268	821	28.4	2.9	33.7
Owsley	51	378	212	D	118	D	D	9	23,839	153	20.9	2.6	35.3
Pendleton	167	1,684	238	477	203	56	49	59	35,047	919	33.7	0.3	29.2
Perry	613	9,029	2,988	74	1,812	316	208	326	36,057	63	31.7	9.5	34.5
Pike	1,250	17,161	4,274	570	4,191	757	579	667	38,871	85	23.5	2.4	51.0
Powell	171	1,543	179	147	364	68	14	44	28,412	194	36.1	1.5	29.5
	1,358	20,771	4,990	3,792	3,403	649	546	714	34,356	1,704	41.4	0.8	37.8
Pulaski													
Robertson	22	133	87	NA	17	7	D	4	26,594	245	20.4	NA	35.8
Rockcastle	206	2,743	1,008	103	266	85	56	78	28,526	681	37.7	0.9	26.8
Rowan	508	7,806	2,060	1,215	1,477	232	76	242	31,011	329	45.3	0.3	34.7
Russell	339	4,430	939	873	727	144	50	133	30,024	672	45.5	1.9	37.7
Scott	939	22,540	1,683	10,942	1,904	322	409	1,191	52,855	851	47.5	2.1	38.1
Shelby	974	17,940	1,406	3,872	2,588	303	308	587	32,737	1,548	55.1	2.3	37.3
Simpson	394	7,219	384	2,716	1,105	148	60	278	38,557	471	53.1	6.6	40.9
Spencer	216	1,148	236	31	234	48	60	30	26,425	606	49.3	1.0	34.3
Taylor	613	9,324	1,359	1,413	1,543	238	108	289	30,946	803	47.3	1.9	34.1
	198	1,571	203	380	326	79	33	44	28,292	593	27.7	6.6	49.4
Todd													
Trigg	245	2,167	269	542	419	80	40	65	30,056	405	34.1	4.7	40.1
Trimble	72	675	122	D	74	60	7	34	50,689	469	43.3	2.1	37.5
Union	250	3,899	829	436	725	88	60	157	40,219	284	41.2	16.2	45.3
Warren	2,983	53,031	8,934	8,911	8,085	1,536	1,980	2,099	39,587	1,755	49.9	2.1	30.9
Washington	259	2,956	434	999	322	71	53	101	34,226	1,102	34.1	0.5	33.4
Wayne	273	4,213	600	1,368	738	161	48	141	33,473	710	39.2	1.1	39.1
Webster	214	2,079	286	238	311	83	24	91	43,702	499	33.9	8.2	34.5
Whitley	613	10,372	2,561	930	1,574	231	879	326	31,437	548	45.1	0.5	33.1
Wolfe	81	724	274	D	143	13	7	19	26,638	294	32.3	0.3	33.8
Woodford	544	6,998	649	2,073	856	197	439	288	41,195	689	44.8	2.8	46.3
LOUISIANA	105,732	1,709,226	294,641	118,352	240,119	64,521	97,108	75,125	43,953	27,386	46.5	7.6	37.7
Acadia	1,088	12,041	2,341	1,008	2,511	424	354	369	30,648	964	50.0	8.8	40.2
Allen	309	3,390	657	575	645	120	52	111	32,711	420	47.4	5.2	37.0
Ascension	2,238	38,203	3,404	5,627	6,161	1,032	2,173	2,063	54,005	221	69.7	6.8	31.5
Assumption	247	2,667	280	296	443	87	74	109	40,893	103	35.9	36.9	48.4
Avoyelles	700	8,830	2,298	268	1,512	347	226	273	30,882	770	40.1	8.6	38.0
Beauregard	602	7,057	1,305	918	1,368	724	183	265	37,554	730	40.8	3.4	31.2
Bienville	231	3,259	515	1,114	294	137	22	113	34,742	221	41.6	1.8	41.2
Bossier	2,477	37,328	4,410	1,408	7,792	1,043	1,315	1,189	31,864	519	54.5	5.6	44.2
Caddo	6,271	102,695	27,335	5,671	13,797	3,004	4,646	4,207	40,968	706	54.1	8.9	34.7
Calcasieu	4,537	74,546	13,952	8,584	11,404	2,030	4,415	3,261	43,742	931	50.2	7.0	28.2
Caldwell	174	1,829	733	29	304	134	81	54	29,673	329	42.9	4.0	30.4
Cameron	145	1,252	D	D	128	19	200	115	91,472	294	24.8	17.0	31.5
Catahoula	160	1,298	224	D	325	106	61	39	30,138	433	26.6	14.3	33.6
Claiborne	236	2,409	732	144	357	83	30	82	34,058	255	32.5	6.3	37.0
Concordia	363	3,923	880	224	841	209	155	131	33,426	371	24.0	22.6	36.3
De Soto	422	4,952	584	D	841	188	110	254	51,292	599	41.1	5.8	41.7
East Baton Rouge	12,259	246,150	38,310	10,051	30,196	12,137	19,971	11,983	48,682	449	58.4	1.3	40.5
East Carroll	117	1,266	314	107	128	36	11	41	32,320	209	18.2	35.9	62.4
East Feliciana	244	3,308	1,691	230	292	132	56	126	37,976	412	50.5	9.2	38.3
Evangeline	505	6,182	2,432	919	968	284	117	196	31,751	596	45.1	7.7	38.0
Franklin	370	3,547	937	204	917	221	118	94	26,385	797	31.0	8.7	36.7
Grant	166	1,885	232	D	264	76	7	60	31,977	207	35.7	8.2	28.4
Iberia	1,636	23,299	3,436	3,230	3,396	772	737	1,045	44,840	334	64.1	10.2	40.5
Iberville	549	11,681	819	4,270	1,111	291	769	883	75,553	151	31.8	27.2	55.6
Jackson	240	2,651	600	D	507	109	36	112	42,135	191	46.1	0.5	46.0
Jefferson	11,801	187,683	30,542	6,448	29,976	9,138	10,787	8,177	43,567	52	59.6	1.9	21.1
Jefferson Davis	663	7,007	1,535	522	1,409	271	264	241	34,379	703	37.8	12.4	37.7
Lafayette	8,402	127,110	24,652	6,183	17,866	3,591	8,312	5,503	43,292	549	73.4	2.9	33.3
Lafourche	1,772	26,469	4,014	1,949	4,242	840	814	1,201	45,357	379	53.0	6.9	27.1
La Salle	315	3,344	956	23	507	156	111	115	34,256	235	48.5	0.4	32.7
Lincoln	1,085	15,769	3,154	1,497	2,479	576	861	526	33,326	378	39.9	1.6	37.7
Livingston	1,756	22,147	2,337	1,729	5,267	638	1,134	821	37,085	436	74.5	0.2	38.0
Madison	196	2,680	1,113	149	391	60	17	75	28,000	250	16.4	32.4	50.2
Morehouse	439	5,481	1,908	562	957	198	94	152	27,734	409	27.1	18.6	49.0
Natchitoches	804	11,414	1,950	2,541	1,825	390	238	382	33,472	627	35.2	7.5	38.8

STATE County	Acreage (1,000)	Percent change, 2012-2017	Average size of farm	Total irrigated (1,000)	Total cropland (1,000)	Average per farm	Average per acre	Value of machinery and equiopmnet, average per farm (dollars)	Total (mil dol)	Average per farm (acres)	Crops	Livestock and poultry products	Organic farms (number)	Farms with internet access (percent)	Total ($1,000)	Percent of farms
	117	118	119	120	121	122	123	124	125	126	127	128	129	130	131	132
KENTUCKY— Cont'd																
Ohio	158	-0.4	194	D	86.4	662,879	3,418	96,947	135.8	166,998	27.8	72.2	3	67.2	1,810	29.5
Oldham	51	-14.7	110	0.1	21.3	879,589	7,964	66,919	18.5	39,730	46.2	53.8	1	80.3	252	4.7
Owen	157	19.3	192	0.5	61.7	542,771	2,831	72,383	23.9	29,107	54.9	45.1	NA	69.7	158	5.7
Owsley	29	5.7	190	D	10.3	255,706	1,342	37,727	1.3	8,458	64.0	36.0	NA	74.5	41	5.2
Pendleton	111	9.9	121	0.5	38.2	344,033	2,840	55,326	9.4	10,282	64.2	35.8	NA	71.3	112	8.7
Perry	16	49.3	260	0.0	5.6	297,441	1,146	49,250	0.3	5,175	27.6	72.4	Perry	77.8	D	1.6
Pike	19	45.5	229	0.0	3.4	324,062	1,414	56,010	0.7	8,753	49.6	50.4	NA	85.9	NA	NA
Powell	28	-6.8	144	0.0	9.6	336,855	2,334	46,794	2.7	13,938	73.4	26.6	NA	64.9	32	8.2
	226	-0.9	133	0.2	100.3	429,851	3,238	67,220	55.5	32,570	45.2	54.8	2	69.2	632	21.0
Pulaski																
Robertson	42	8.8	172	0.0	14.5	377,155	2,187	51,275	3.5	14,473	31.5	68.5	3	64.1	22	5.3
Rockcastle	81	-11.2	119	0.0	27.8	258,213	2,179	41,923	7.3	10,742	39.5	60.5	NA	71.5	215	13.1
Rowan	40	-6.4	120	0.0	13.1	333,138	2,770	56,262	4.1	12,605	40.1	59.9	NA	66.9	126	17.6
Russell	92	3.5	138	0.0	42.2	425,730	3,093	68,898	37.5	55,823	22.0	78.0	NA	69.8	456	20.7
Scott	131	2.4	153	0.3	56.1	858,492	5,595	78,301	51.7	60,734	30.2	69.8	1	78.7	224	6.8
Shelby	201	0.8	130	0.9	124.4	753,848	5,809	85,413	72.1	46,577	67.6	32.4	5	77.1	1,603	14.6
Simpson	111	9.2	235	0.3	88.3	1,335,785	5,675	146,265	79.0	167,658	64.5	35.5	NA	77.5	1,628	39.9
Spencer	74	7.3	122	0.1	34.8	556,079	4,542	62,736	18.3	30,163	75.1	24.9	NA	75.1	255	7.4
Taylor	112	-2.5	139	0.0	61.1	422,767	3,038	82,616	46.1	57,365	49.3	50.7	2	71.9	1,440	35.4
	168	-7.2	283	0.8	127.5	1,468,492	5,185	159,843	175.6	296,152	47.2	52.8	13	50.3	2,136	43.2
Todd																
Trigg	122	-5.3	302	2.2	75.9	1,239,797	4,110	130,967	58.8	145,183	74.6	25.4	5	60.2	2,747	35.8
Trimble	66	18.6	141	D	30.4	456,362	3,245	57,517	12.1	25,823	80.0	20.0	NA	65.9	356	8.3
Union	195	-0.1	685	3.8	172.8	3,453,444	5,039	337,598	108.9	383,285	92.5	7.5	NA	79.2	4,606	53.9
Warren	262	6.3	149	0.2	156.6	796,970	5,334	85,047	110.9	63,189	54.5	45.5	NA	75.6	5,481	21.8
Washington	161	14.5	147	0.1	67.5	470,574	3,212	62,124	34.4	31,208	34.9	65.1	2	68.1	459	18.2
Wayne	96	-25.3	135	0.1	34.5	360,738	2,666	63,632	58.0	81,655	17.2	82.8	NA	74.1	371	15.1
Webster	163	6.9	327	0.6	123.0	1,202,901	3,683	145,475	141.9	284,333	37.5	62.5	NA	73.9	4,513	64.5
Whitley	59	1.0	108	0.0	20.2	272,502	2,532	52,085	6.1	11,057	34.2	65.8	1	65.3	206	13.7
Wolfe	34	-20.6	115	0.0	10.2	231,135	2,016	53,278	1.5	5,044	56.4	43.6	NA	70.4	17	9.2
Woodford	112	0.2	163	0.0	42.0	1,320,705	8,111	92,879	132.6	192,441	9.7	90.3	2	88.2	403	9.3
LOUISIANA	7,998	1.2	292	1,235.8	4,345.8	889,146	3,045	121,758	3,173.0	115,861	65.0	35.0	29	69.9	177,399	28.4
Acadia	266	11.5	275	86.1	207.9	760,885	2,762	166,113	100.7	104,466	84.7	15.3	NA	62.1	13,935	59.1
Allen	95	7.9	226	18.9	46.4	580,390	2,566	68,258	19.8	47,055	71.2	28.8	NA	64.8	3,122	31.2
Ascension	38	-23.9	174	0.0	26.3	629,741	3,626	104,541	13.1	59,217	89.4	10.6	3	72.4	198	10.0
Assumption	92	47.8	892	D	86.5	2,626,865	2,944	469,713	45.6	442,806	98.8	1.2	NA	83.5	427	27.2
Avoyelles	282	-5.7	366	26.0	201.1	931,760	2,544	158,024	104.3	135,473	89.9	10.1	NA	69.5	7,776	39.0
Beauregard	148	0.9	202	3.3	39.1	614,319	3,039	69,645	15.8	21,705	45.4	54.6	1	76.7	2,855	12.9
Bienville	34	-39.0	154	D	10.0	392,811	2,547	59,842	32.3	146,068	2.6	97.4	NA	69.7	116	7.7
Bossier	107	31.4	206	2.0	34.0	642,592	3,122	73,951	14.4	27,825	65.7	34.3	NA	76.7	398	13.7
Caddo	199	42.5	282	22.6	84.7	841,843	2,983	110,644	61.1	86,482	62.7	37.3	NA	71.2	2,145	10.8
Calcasieu	354	4.8	380	13.1	77.5	1,323,640	3,480	77,967	25.8	27,676	51.6	48.4	NA	75.8	3,924	20.4
Caldwell	68	8.8	206	3.6	21.8	515,954	2,507	60,462	18.7	56,714	38.6	61.4	NA	60.2	1,822	36.2
Cameron	188	-20.1	639	5.9	50.9	1,584,171	2,478	87,142	12.0	40,667	46.1	53.9	NA	72.4	1,266	28.9
Catahoula	210	-6.3	485	58.5	145.7	1,309,375	2,702	184,305	70.6	163,046	97.6	2.4	NA	62.8	6,969	66.1
Claiborne	63	10.8	249	2.2	12.9	594,447	2,389	78,967	77.9	305,533	2.5	97.5	NA	60.4	324	7.8
Concordia	281	17.1	759	46.3	206.5	2,125,125	2,802	219,661	100.3	270,415	97.7	2.3	NA	66.0	8,888	78.7
De Soto	137	-16.9	228	0.2	28.3	676,324	2,966	97,326	20.6	34,347	12.6	87.4	NA	74.8	182	2.7
East Baton Rouge	58	1.3	130	0.5	13.4	1,071,013	8,251	89,008	12.6	28,058	22.3	77.7	1	83.1	132	5.8
East Carroll	221	-11.8	1,059	128.4	193.4	3,932,394	3,713	491,558	116.5	557,191	99.9	0.1	NA	76.6	9,631	86.6
East Feliciana	131	16.4	318	0.0	24.7	889,716	2,799	75,308	9.2	22,303	18.2	81.8	NA	80.3	511	11.2
Evangeline	159	-17.2	267	45.9	113.5	650,632	2,441	100,421	54.7	91,851	84.7	15.3	NA	74.2	6,872	41.4
Franklin	255	3.5	320	103.8	178.4	906,715	2,836	122,690	115.3	144,689	94.5	5.5	NA	64.0	8,085	64.9
Grant	51	6.0	246	D	17.0	672,574	2,738	75,464	7.7	37,411	74.8	25.2	NA	71.0	506	21.7
Iberia	115	7.0	344	2.6	88.2	985,830	2,868	215,874	57.9	173,263	96.5	3.5	NA	71.3	846	14.1
Iberville	182	11.2	1,203	D	76.8	2,159,687	1,796	484,293	48.3	320,126	95.3	4.7	NA	84.1	501	21.2
Jackson	21	10.5	108	0.2	3.2	431,104	4,003	76,776	42.8	223,874	1.1	98.9	NA	73.8	82	23.0
Jefferson	8	5.1	157	0.0	0.5	365,529	2,334	58,697	0.7	13,115	46.5	53.5	NA	75.0	11	9.6
Jefferson Davis	243	-8.1	346	68.2	167.7	771,190	2,227	119,746	73.3	104,239	78.3	21.7	NA	69.4	13,380	48.6
Lafayette	50	-10.8	90	5.1	29.9	504,748	5,581	86,348	21.4	38,998	79.0	21.0	2	71.8	1,039	8.2
Lafourche	157	-0.7	414	0.3	58.6	1,200,913	2,899	125,407	39.0	102,821	66.8	33.2	NA	72.8	124	3.2
La Salle	24	20.9	100	D	4.5	319,962	3,185	67,387	1.6	6,817	27.3	72.7	NA	74.9	166	24.3
Lincoln	72	28.6	190	0.6	14.8	609,592	3,210	84,608	134.2	354,944	1.0	99.0	NA	75.7	282	6.9
Livingston	30	7.5	68	0.1	5.8	363,820	5,351	57,006	10.6	24,232	8.2	91.8	NA	67.4	239	5.7
Madison	245	9.2	981	83.4	190.9	2,697,499	2,749	404,533	106.8	427,108	99.4	0.6	NA	63.2	8,445	84.0
Morehouse	257	-8.1	627	144.6	196.1	1,994,849	3,180	255,996	129.4	316,421	97.1	2.9	NA	71.4	10,044	63.6
Natchitoches	213	6.2	340	14.1	81.1	794,915	2,335	111,180	98.5	157,166	30.3	69.7	NA	67.5	2,910	37.8

Table B. States and Counties — Water Use, Wholesale Trade, Retail Trade, and Real Estate

STATE County	Water use, 2015 Public supply water withdrawn (mil gal/day)	Public supply gallons withdrawn per person per day	Wholesale Trade[1], 2012 Number of establishments	Number of employees	Sales (mil dol)	Average payroll (mil dol)	Retail Trade[2], 2012 Number of establishments	Number of employees	Sales (mil dol)	Average payroll (mil dol)	Real estate and rental and leasing,[2] 2012 Number of establishments	Number of employees	Sales (mil dol)	Average payroll (mil dol)
	133	134	135	136	137	138	139	140	141	142	143	144	145	146
KENTUCKY— Cont'd														
Ohio	2.62	108.2	7	77	22.6	2.4	67	724	190.0	14.6	11	26	2.5	0.5
Oldham	3.93	60.6	36	280	117.6	14.9	103	1,182	369.3	30.5	52	89	18.4	3.1
Owen	0.00	0.0	4	48	18.3	0.8	29	186	62.2	4.2	3	D	D	D
Owsley	0.53	118.8	1	D	D	D	8	100	16.1	1.6	2	D	D	D
Pendleton	0.97	67.3	8	D	D	D	26	202	51.5	4.1	4	D	D	D
Perry	4.18	151.6	29	448	254.1	24.0	146	1,950	525.1	42.1	20	96	60.5	4.0
Pike	6.09	98.6	50	512	483.2	26.0	281	3,734	936.2	86.0	40	164	25.7	5.2
Powell	1.45	118.2	5	39	10.0	1.6	41	451	100.4	7.4	5	9	1.9	0.2
Pulaski	7.56	118.5	66	D	D	D	282	3,304	864.1	76.4	51	211	22.4	5.0
Robertson	0.00	0.0	NA	NA	NA	NA	3	D	D	D	1	D	D	D
Rockcastle	1.95	115.1	9	44	13.1	1.3	50	323	95.2	6.2	3	D	D	D
Rowan	6.03	252.4	14	143	39.1	4.5	100	1,399	339.0	27.9	21	54	11.0	1.8
Russell	2.01	113.8	8	D	D	D	90	694	185.9	14.0	6	37	8.5	0.9
Scott	2.89	55.1	27	D	D	D	125	1,828	573.3	38.1	37	118	27.3	3.0
Shelby	2.93	64.2	33	D	D	D	126	1,654	569.1	39.3	39	155	27.2	4.3
Simpson	1.65	91.6	16	181	372.0	6.1	67	1,016	389.6	23.3	12	44	5.1	0.8
Spencer	0.00	0.0	NA	NA	NA	NA	26	233	81.1	4.8	3	D	D	D
Taylor	5.20	204.6	22	D	D	D	126	1,416	342.1	31.9	21	79	8.8	2.0
Todd	0.00	0.0	9	42	77.4	1.4	35	295	77.3	5.7	5	11	0.9	0.1
Trigg	2.09	146.8	3	15	5.2	0.4	46	405	95.2	7.8	8	D	D	D
Trimble	2.75	313.6	NA	NA	NA	NA	13	96	25.6	1.1	1	D	D	D
Union	1.87	124.3	15	214	278.4	9.9	67	703	195.9	16.7	7	D	D	D
Warren	17.47	142.2	131	1,800	2,822.5	83.0	489	7,103	1,692.1	154.7	125	427	84.0	12.7
Washington	1.17	97.0	9	D	D	D	37	285	76.0	5.4	4	D	D	D
Wayne	2.76	134.9	11	124	27.8	2.9	62	663	157.7	14.4	4	6	0.2	0.1
Webster	2.02	153.4	10	134	38.1	3.6	39	342	80.0	6.9	1	D	D	D
Whitley	4.84	134.0	22	351	172.0	17.7	132	1,432	442.6	32.5	23	62	9.3	1.7
Wolfe	0.47	64.7	2	D	D	D	29	185	58.2	3.8	2	D	D	D
Woodford	3.12	121.0	16	244	115.0	11.5	67	743	230.3	17.4	17	17	5.5	0.6
LOUISIANA	708.92	151.8	4,823	64,259	68,012.8	3,260.2	16,743	220,257	61,396.4	5,334.6	4,500	31,298	7,486.4	1,461.4
Acadia	5.62	89.8	44	709	528.8	24.4	192	2,383	602.7	55.5	34	163	20.4	5.3
Allen	4.24	165.1	8	24	18.8	0.6	65	623	157.6	12.2	5	14	1.3	0.3
Ascension	2.65	22.2	138	1,667	995.5	92.4	374	5,491	1,538.9	129.5	89	559	177.7	30.8
Assumption	4.19	183.4	11	64	79.4	1.8	42	475	121.0	10.4	5	8	3.1	0.4
Avoyelles	4.05	98.5	26	253	306.5	10.3	159	1,446	354.7	29.5	21	59	7.8	1.3
Beauregard	4.42	121.2	13	D	D	D	104	1,330	383.7	29.1	21	111	15.7	4.4
Bienville	2.72	197.3	8	68	27.6	3.1	47	344	66.5	6.0	4	D	D	D
Bossier	12.88	102.9	114	1,453	941.9	68.3	452	6,434	1,923.3	159.1	109	556	114.1	17.5
Caddo	43.28	172.1	328	5,258	5,800.1	258.1	958	13,053	4,034.9	331.3	307	2,379	445.9	94.5
Calcasieu	27.51	138.4	188	2,125	1,941.1	97.9	755	10,139	3,127.1	238.7	208	954	213.8	38.5
Caldwell	1.03	103.1	4	26	9.0	1.0	28	267	81.1	5.5	3	D	D	D
Cameron	1.50	220.0	11	71	29.9	4.8	17	101	28.3	2.3	8	64	21.9	2.9
Catahoula	1.17	115.3	15	89	315.8	3.5	35	268	66.6	5.4	2	D	D	D
Claiborne	3.01	184.7	11	152	134.7	6.4	48	362	83.7	7.9	5	D	D	D
Concordia	2.63	130.6	12	232	344.5	11.2	81	904	275.4	20.8	11	104	6.2	3.1
De Soto	3.08	113.9	11	36	13.2	1.4	68	873	251.6	20.2	13	116	25.6	5.3
East Baton Rouge	72.12	161.4	568	7,674	4,993.5	417.3	1,863	27,576	7,389.7	677.5	546	3,088	631.1	111.2
East Carroll	0.91	124.5	12	142	466.5	6.9	22	147	30.7	2.9	2	D	D	D
East Feliciana	2.21	112.2	10	D	D	D	42	276	80.3	5.9	5	12	2.8	0.4
Evangeline	6.50	192.6	15	112	72.2	3.2	108	986	213.7	18.8	24	75	9.2	1.7
Franklin	1.95	95.5	19	125	248.8	4.3	78	914	250.9	19.2	11	30	4.5	0.7
Grant	4.54	203.2	2	D	D	D	27	227	83.2	5.2	2	D	D	D
Iberia	8.65	116.7	94	1,192	560.5	57.3	285	3,524	970.7	89.3	104	2,038	915.5	192.9
Iberville	1.98	59.8	24	D	D	D	88	1,083	279.3	23.7	22	149	42.9	7.2
Jackson	1.73	109.1	4	D	D	D	40	547	128.1	11.2	7	12	0.7	0.2
Jefferson	61.79	141.6	719	9,641	8,453.9	518.4	1,807	27,991	8,112.3	737.5	498	3,605	896.5	141.6
Jefferson Davis	3.82	121.5	27	275	261.1	10.9	127	1,504	402.8	32.5	19	317	73.2	16.8
Lafayette	25.42	105.9	485	7,554	4,113.5	406.8	1,057	15,818	4,355.1	399.4	473	3,636	938.6	194.0
Lafourche	25.66	261.0	61	868	947.9	46.3	290	4,020	965.6	86.0	66	333	58.8	11.5
La Salle	1.72	114.9	10	153	257.8	5.5	51	563	142.3	11.8	10	26	3.5	0.7
Lincoln	7.18	150.3	34	500	197.0	15.2	166	2,243	592.6	52.9	48	235	25.7	6.2
Livingston	11.54	83.8	47	389	345.3	17.8	287	4,390	1,180.5	98.7	63	565	43.8	13.3
Madison	1.65	143.3	12	90	258.9	5.0	38	387	158.9	9.2	9	D	D	D
Morehouse	3.47	131.5	15	223	147.1	10.6	85	978	237.4	22.7	23	59	9.9	1.4
Natchitoches	7.72	197.0	24	157	77.8	5.8	145	1,676	404.8	33.6	46	223	28.7	3.6

1 Merchant wholesalers, except manufacturers' sales branches and offices.   2. Employer establishments.

Table B. States and Counties — Professional Services, Manufacturing, and Accommodation and Food Services

STATE County	Professional, scientific, and technical services, 2012				Manufacturing, 2012				Accommodation and food services, 2012			
	Number of establish-ments	Number of employees	Sales (mil dol)	Average payroll (mil dol)	Number of establish-ments	Number of employees	Receipts (mil dol)	Annual payroll (mil dol)	Number of establis-hments	Number of employees	Receipts (mil dol)	Annual payroll (mil dol)
	147	148	149	150	151	152	153	154	155	156	157	158
KENTUCKY— Cont'd												
Ohio	23	78	6.5	2.3	27	2,667	576.2	73.3	22	D	D	D
Oldham	170	516	69.3	25.6	45	785	304.0	36.9	70	1,322	72.8	16.8
Owen	5	D	D	D	NA	NA	NA	NA	10	D	D	D
Owsley	3	6	0.7	0.3	NA	NA	NA	NA	1	D	D	D
Pendleton	9	42	2.3	1.1	16	D	D	D	10	D	D	D
Perry	52	248	25.4	9.4	10	143	20.0	6.8	49	977	46.4	12.7
Pike	105	886	99.6	40.6	24	616	219.0	28.8	89	1,845	91.8	24.3
Powell	7	8	0.6	0.2	10	194	D	6.2	19	D	D	D
	97	390	41.2	12.6	74	3,470	1,411.6	132.3	100	1,837	88.2	23.8
Pulaski												
Robertson	1	D	D	D	NA	NA	NA	NA	NA	NA	NA	NA
Rockcastle	17	47	2.9	1.2	12	98	D	4.2	21	292	12.7	3.7
Rowan	22	82	5.7	2.0	20	981	291.9	30.5	51	1,057	46.4	11.9
Russell	21	66	4.3	1.1	25	1,610	404.0	42.8	32	376	16.2	4.1
Scott	77	311	36.7	14.1	37	8,525	10,844.2	552.2	88	1,795	89.7	24.1
Shelby	94	317	35.4	10.7	55	3,562	1,484.5	149.2	61	D	D	D
Simpson	16	112	9.2	2.9	34	2,958	1,387.3	137.3	41	868	40.0	10.9
Spencer	18	49	4.6	1.7	7	D	D	D	12	187	7.0	2.2
Taylor	51	97	9.5	2.6	26	1,191	D	37.7	45	818	35.2	8.7
	11	30	3.3	1.2	19	416	108.9	11.5	11	104	3.1	0.9
Todd												
Trigg	9	33	2.3	0.7	15	536	136.6	18.4	19	D	D	D
Trimble	4	7	0.4	0.1	3	D	D	D	4	D	D	D
Union	10	50	4.3	1.5	14	440	142.8	16.0	18	D	D	D
Warren	212	2,075	179.7	63.0	113	7,962	5,110.1	405.4	260	5,737	264.1	70.6
Washington	17	51	4.2	1.2	12	858	248.3	39.2	13	D	D	D
Wayne	18	52	3.8	1.4	24	1,498	267.2	44.9	26	D	D	D
Webster	10	23	1.4	0.3	12	259	189.4	10.8	14	D	D	D
Whitley	55	910	51.1	23.0	21	888	228.0	32.8	67	1,109	53.0	15.3
Wolfe	3	7	0.6	0.2	3	21	D	D	5	D	D	D
Woodford	63	496	76.6	29.7	29	1,828	644.1	103.0	33	D	D	D
LOUISIANA	11,728	88,093	13,546.2	5,022.9	3,308	136,327	271,191.1	8,489.3	9,019	193,928	11,697.9	3,110.7
Acadia	125	378	43.2	15.9	43	1,138	D	45.5	74	1,185	52.7	13.3
Allen	23	64	7.2	1.6	11	584	D	29.7	28	D	D	D
Ascension	162	922	137.4	53.2	100	4,518	14,208.5	427.9	173	3,211	167.2	43.5
Assumption	37	88	12.3	3.8	9	375	D	19.7	12	67	3.9	0.8
Avoyelles	60	224	28.0	7.4	20	279	D	8.4	51	1,842	153.8	39.6
Beauregard	50	189	15.6	5.9	18	757	D	57.2	40	720	35.0	8.7
Bienville	12	52	5.3	2.8	11	1,165	D	30.0	17	D	D	D
Bossier	197	1,032	116.1	42.2	70	1,534	911.8	74.6	235	7,792	667.0	135.9
Caddo	620	4,278	613.6	214.6	182	6,230	4,965.5	347.6	493	12,976	766.3	200.0
Calcasieu	423	5,141	451.3	218.1	126	D	D	D	353	10,769	983.3	210.5
Caldwell	26	74	13.4	1.9	6	24	D	0.8	10	D	D	D
Cameron	9	71	28.0	4.8	NA	NA	NA	NA	5	48	1.4	0.3
Catahoula	30	74	8.1	3.1	NA	NA	NA	NA	8	D	D	D
Claiborne	11	35	4.4	1.0	11	185	D	8.2	16	D	D	D
Concordia	28	162	19.6	6.6	11	234	79.7	9.9	25	382	17.9	4.5
De Soto	24	93	6.1	2.1	13	707	D	D	32	416	23.0	4.9
East Baton Rouge	1,693	17,189	2,800.2	1,013.8	334	11,176	53,388.8	774.5	1,000	23,462	1,230.7	345.7
East Carroll	5	18	1.6	0.5	5	D	D	1.3	13	64	3.5	0.7
East Feliciana	22	75	12.8	3.4	12	236	D	13.0	14	D	D	D
Evangeline	43	119	10.7	3.5	18	704	D	24.7	25	D	D	D
Franklin	34	163	13.8	4.2	9	178	D	4.1	22	D	D	D
Grant	6	D	D	D	11	307	D	10.8	5	76	2.6	0.8
Iberia	149	820	123.7	42.5	135	4,659	D	254.8	94	1,685	78.9	20.1
Iberville	33	208	23.6	13.8	30	3,165	8,877.1	287.6	36	497	22.5	6.6
Jackson	16	50	5.9	1.3	8	D	D	D	17	D	D	D
Jefferson	1,336	10,711	1,848.1	687.2	317	11,438	2,996.9	626.6	1,037	19,493	1,056.5	303.1
Jefferson Davis	65	344	33.4	17.7	17	534	D	21.4	43	669	29.4	7.3
Lafayette	1,269	8,970	1,597.9	547.4	295	10,996	D	717.5	665	14,444	782.6	230.2
Lafourche	160	1,635	138.6	73.0	59	2,575	864.1	119.7	159	2,654	115.3	29.1
La Salle	100	150	27.3	7.2	6	55	D	2.5	14	D	D	D
Lincoln	91	669	97.6	38.6	35	1,084	421.6	59.2	93	2,015	91.0	23.9
Livingston	140	627	65.0	24.5	67	1,772	504.0	81.0	156	2,737	115.9	31.5
Madison	11	29	1.5	0.8	5	D	D	D	20	D	D	D
Morehouse	23	96	12.4	3.4	14	111	D	4.2	26	D	D	D
Natchitoches	64	251	33.1	8.3	16	2,340	1,162.1	97.2	81	1,647	70.0	17.6

Health Care and Social Assistance, Other Services, Nonemployer Businesses, and Residential Construction

STATE County	Health care and social assistance, 2012				Other services, 2012				Nonemployer businesses, 2016		Value of residential construction authorized by building permits, 2018	
	Number of establishments	Number of employees	Receipts (mil dol)	Annual payroll (mil dol)	Number of establishments	Number of employees	Receipts (mil dol)	Annual payroll (mil dol)	Number	Receipts (mil dol)	New construction ($1,000)	Number of housing units
	159	160	161	162	163	164	165	166	167	168	169	170
KENTUCKY— Cont'd												
Ohio	39	1,020	65.6	28.4	30	89	9.8	2.5	1,131	40.4	1,314	9
Oldham	142	2,410	169.5	76.5	81	D	D	D	5,228	253.0	84,825	245
Owen	10	265	23.0	8.2	10	38	2.7	0.7	745	28.3	99	1
Owsley	9	192	10.5	5.2	3	16	1.3	0.3	261	10.9	NA	NA
Pendleton	18	249	14.7	6.5	11	D	D	D	725	28.7	0	0
Perry	128	2,853	304.5	107.6	27	D	D	D	1,417	47.9	0	0
Pike	213	4,427	579.9	210.9	78	389	41.9	11.3	2,806	112.6	1,513	5
Powell	19	213	17.6	6.6	8	42	3.5	0.9	789	27.1	0	0
	240	5,134	484.7	192.4	66	353	29.9	8.2	4,437	187.3	2,945	34
Pulaski												
Robertson	3	D	D	D	1	D	D	D	131	2.9	NA	NA
Rockcastle	36	808	66.5	31.2	11	76	6.0	1.6	888	29.1	NA	NA
Rowan	86	1,998	198.5	79.0	24	117	6.6	1.8	1,396	49.6	263	3
Russell	47	1,015	86.4	30.8	17	D	D	D	1,359	59.6	2,100	18
Scott	129	1,426	119.6	46.7	68	273	24.2	6.7	3,308	130.2	83,060	526
Shelby	85	1,415	110.8	44.5	67	501	50.2	13.4	3,304	150.5	51,526	232
Simpson	35	D	D	D	23	111	10.0	2.6	1,220	57.9	16,084	155
Spencer	17	219	13.4	6.1	14	D	D	D	1,240	46.8	27,491	132
Taylor	84	D	D	D	43	D	D	D	1,669	61.9	1,350	5
	17	215	14.6	5.3	9	D	D	D	812	41.4	706	8
Todd												
Trigg	22	378	23.4	9.7	14	D	D	D	937	40.5	1,444	7
Trimble	6	108	10.6	4.2	3	D	D	D	483	15.0	NA	NA
Union	33	896	83.6	28.0	12	56	9.5	1.7	718	28.0	628	3
Warren	383	7,745	852.6	320.8	199	1,035	86.7	25.8	9,213	526.3	275,188	2,183
Washington	27	410	18.6	8.7	16	110	7.5	2.1	768	29.9	797	14
Wayne	32	546	35.4	16.0	16	D	D	D	1,167	44.3	0	0
Webster	19	266	14.3	7.2	11	46	6.5	1.3	654	21.1	235	8
Whitley	97	2,467	272.1	98.8	31	D	D	D	2,199	87.7	1,481	11
Wolfe	12	230	14.7	6.1	3	D	D	D	423	16.8	NA	NA
Woodford	62	559	45.4	18.6	37	D	D	D	2,166	94.0	18,511	134
LOUISIANA	11,999	284,979	27,951.8	10,646.9	6,293	43,500	5,408.9	1,479.2	368,735	15,788.8	3,108,408	15,835
Acadia	128	2,215	157.2	62.7	70	346	26.4	7.1	4,388	184.1	3,860	34
Allen	43	907	61.8	22.1	20	D	D	D	1,163	32.7	4,384	35
Ascension	180	3,300	255.4	105.2	150	1,260	152.0	44.6	8,518	373.1	143,810	936
Assumption	22	675	25.3	13.4	17	D	D	D	1,546	56.3	5,369	19
Avoyelles	85	2,104	131.1	49.3	42	153	13.8	3.4	2,523	93.7	9,726	58
Beauregard	64	1,086	84.1	35.7	29	121	10.8	2.7	1,974	70.5	30,967	174
Bienville	15	486	30.7	10.9	11	D	D	D	795	24.6	0	0
Bossier	216	4,289	376.0	137.9	141	846	84.5	23.3	8,597	366.2	125,201	658
Caddo	818	28,245	2,809.9	1,111.3	381	D	D	D	20,511	825.7	76,504	300
Calcasieu	519	D	D	D	240	1,605	177.0	50.8	13,443	611.7	209,651	1,324
Caldwell	25	651	49.7	20.7	13	37	3.4	0.8	626	19.9	5,004	21
Cameron	2	D	D	D	4	12	1.0	0.3	664	30.8	9,810	67
Catahoula	15	526	19.1	9.8	14	D	D	D	671	22.0	838	3
Claiborne	21	791	46.2	19.7	13	63	4.2	0.8	782	25.9	0	0
Concordia	46	882	62.5	24.8	26	D	D	D	1,239	40.7	2,177	40
De Soto	30	722	54.5	19.8	20	D	D	D	1,925	67.4	26,121	106
East Baton Rouge	1,403	38,136	4,112.4	1,527.3	876	8,742	1,008.1	367.9	37,037	1,690.6	322,422	1,336
East Carroll	11	328	22.1	8.8	6	9	0.6	0.1	423	15.6	0	0
East Feliciana	32	1,821	117.2	64.9	16	54	9.1	1.7	1,334	49.7	8,574	44
Evangeline	95	2,618	184.3	72.9	26	55	4.7	1.0	1,658	59.1	8,881	54
Franklin	52	1,157	75.5	34.1	22	73	6.8	1.4	1,474	54.8	5,335	18
Grant	17	255	14.9	5.4	11	50	3.4	0.9	1,071	42.6	8,783	45
Iberia	207	3,985	309.5	122.6	124	868	111.9	29.7	6,027	215.4	17,676	80
Iberville	48	D	D	D	30	136	15.8	4.8	2,110	70.7	27,768	108
Jackson	22	555	41.0	15.6	17	71	5.2	1.6	835	25.8	17,108	34
Jefferson	1,318	26,711	3,077.9	1,178.8	730	5,002	551.7	161.5	43,078	2,012.6	140,413	599
Jefferson Davis	75	1,553	121.3	49.7	35	116	18.2	3.3	1,812	69.3	19,999	105
Lafayette	1,018	22,618	2,452.2	909.5	421	3,607	491.3	120.7	23,563	1,138.7	274,816	1,255
Lafourche	194	4,123	476.7	177.9	110	686	71.7	19.8	7,094	288.7	83,489	356
La Salle	22	747	69.1	23.3	12	D	D	D	960	40.1	1,519	7
Lincoln	115	3,306	304.1	106.2	52	214	15.2	4.7	2,954	144.5	11,037	79
Livingston	150	2,060	141.1	56.9	106	487	56.7	15.2	8,961	383.0	156,346	799
Madison	36	1,145	56.4	24.7	12	26	2.1	0.4	642	20.6	12,209	75
Morehouse	76	2,087	112.7	49.9	32	137	7.3	2.0	1,788	51.9	5,100	39
Natchitoches	102	1,758	138.0	50.9	41	150	12.0	2.7	2,389	91.0	17,903	78

Table B. States and Counties — Government Employment and Payroll, and Local Government Finances

STATE County	Government employment and payroll, 2012		March payroll (percent of total)							Local government finances, 2012				
												General revenue		
													Taxes	
	Full-time equivalent employees	March payroll (dollars)	Adminis-tration, judicial, and legal	Police and corrections	Fire protection	Highways and transpor-tation	Health and welfare	Natural resources and utilities	Education and libraries	Total (mil dol)	Inter-govern-mental (mil dol)	Total (mil dol)	Per capita[1] (dollars) Total	Property
	171	172	173	174	175	176	177	178	179	180	181	182	183	184
KENTUCKY— Cont'd														
Ohio	1,248	3,369,261	2.7	2.9	0.0	1.3	36.2	2.8	52.4	62.2	36.1	14.2	590	347
Oldham	2,024	6,660,606	0.3	5.8	2.0	0.6	3.6	1.6	84.6	158.6	58.3	71.9	1,171	957
Owen	363	1,105,970	4.6	2.3	3.8	2.1	0.7	0.2	83.4	23.3	14.0	7.1	661	495
Owsley	278	620,892	6.0	3.8	0.0	3.9	0.3	2.8	81.2	13.2	10.6	1.4	301	184
Pendleton	588	1,671,881	4.1	2.6	1.6	2.8	15.0	6.1	67.8	38.5	22.7	9.2	631	467
Perry	1,406	4,111,977	3.0	3.4	1.5	2.6	18.7	2.8	66.7	100.4	52.4	23.0	814	540
Pike	2,126	6,896,536	3.5	4.4	1.3	2.8	7.1	1.3	78.6	183.6	110.6	49.7	775	500
Powell	571	1,479,612	5.5	7.2	0.0	1.0	5.3	5.1	75.7	31.1	21.3	6.1	493	235
Pulaski	2,626	7,286,813	4.1	5.1	1.6	1.7	17.0	5.8	64.1	151.6	74.3	49.2	773	465
Robertson	124	297,631	8.0	3.4	0.0	4.9	0.2	0.6	83.0	5.9	4.4	1.2	557	414
Rockcastle	758	1,967,231	6.5	9.5	0.0	2.3	2.6	2.4	74.7	38.4	26.7	7.6	448	184
Rowan	813	2,389,386	2.9	7.6	0.4	3.5	14.9	2.7	67.0	61.6	29.3	19.7	841	374
Russell	920	2,454,498	2.9	5.5	0.4	0.9	28.6	4.1	57.3	61.4	21.4	14.1	807	422
Scott	1,616	5,156,528	2.9	7.7	7.0	2.1	6.1	0.1	73.2	151.0	48.9	60.2	1,227	530
Shelby	1,282	4,061,414	3.4	9.9	2.6	1.9	6.5	0.8	73.8	102.9	42.5	43.5	997	724
Simpson	616	2,092,237	8.9	11.0	1.5	2.3	5.8	3.3	66.5	48.7	23.2	18.0	1,026	501
Spencer	523	1,426,278	5.8	4.0	0.7	1.4	3.1	2.3	81.4	34.5	19.5	12.1	693	525
Taylor	1,374	4,732,730	2.1	2.7	0.9	1.1	51.8	2.5	38.2	123.7	56.5	19.0	769	374
Todd	505	1,331,511	3.1	7.5	0.2	1.9	3.5	7.4	76.3	31.2	20.1	6.9	544	268
Trigg	587	1,746,830	2.8	3.6	0.1	2.4	28.3	5.6	56.1	27.8	15.3	10.2	708	456
Trimble	305	972,373	7.5	3.6	0.0	1.9	2.3	5.1	78.5	32.6	10.9	5.6	634	445
Union	599	1,762,787	11.1	6.4	2.1	5.7	0.5	5.2	67.9	38.7	23.0	11.5	777	532
Warren	4,084	12,459,019	3.2	8.5	4.4	1.8	4.7	10.4	63.3	304.6	116.1	128.4	1,096	529
Washington	407	1,176,342	5.5	5.0	0.0	4.1	9.6	4.1	69.1	26.8	14.5	8.5	718	377
Wayne	760	2,029,072	4.1	6.1	0.2	1.7	4.0	0.3	83.0	44.7	31.3	10.0	478	288
Webster	605	1,592,385	5.5	8.5	4.2	2.0	2.8	7.4	66.8	37.5	24.0	7.8	574	425
Whitley	1,867	5,263,187	2.4	4.6	3.4	1.6	6.6	7.3	73.7	112.5	68.5	23.7	669	308
Wolfe	313	774,203	3.3	1.9	0.0	1.4	0.4	3.3	85.8	23.7	18.4	2.4	336	190
Woodford	911	3,023,818	4.5	9.8	2.1	1.8	8.6	2.9	68.0	69.9	26.8	32.2	1,286	739
LOUISIANA	X	X	X	X	X	X	X	X	X	X	X	X	X	X
Acadia	1,914	5,479,946	5.7	5.4	2.7	4.1	2.9	4.6	73.3	180.8	90.9	63.9	1,033	388
Allen	973	2,882,412	11.1	8.9	0.4	3.1	19.2	2.8	54.4	94.4	48.2	28.5	1,114	473
Ascension	4,531	13,738,983	6.7	8.8	2.0	2.3	2.8	3.8	71.9	408.3	139.8	213.9	1,905	870
Assumption	1,463	4,579,903	6.7	5.0	0.6	13.3	13.8	10.4	49.4	74.9	42.1	25.4	1,102	571
Avoyelles	1,542	3,784,025	3.9	22.1	1.3	2.7	13.2	4.5	52.2	121.6	72.1	26.8	644	144
Beauregard	1,561	4,516,320	4.2	3.0	1.7	3.0	29.5	1.5	56.6	146.5	59.0	50.2	1,382	629
Bienville	604	1,849,545	7.1	11.8	0.0	5.8	0.4	1.9	72.9	72.4	15.3	51.7	3,673	2,477
Bossier	4,814	15,229,557	8.2	15.0	5.4	2.1	0.4	3.1	64.8	444.2	156.3	238.0	1,948	757
Caddo	11,080	37,545,778	5.6	16.6	7.2	2.8	2.9	5.7	57.7	1,117.9	399.7	540.3	2,102	1,067
Calcasieu	9,145	28,598,210	5.0	14.5	3.5	5.7	7.9	5.4	56.0	961.3	315.0	432.3	2,223	866
Caldwell	302	782,732	5.3	3.7	0.3	0.5	0.0	1.0	89.3	33.5	19.0	10.2	1,019	536
Cameron	525	1,990,275	6.0	0.0	0.3	7.0	7.7	4.9	74.1	94.4	45.2	42.7	6,367	6,281
Catahoula	616	1,309,075	8.8	22.3	0.4	5.1	2.5	3.4	57.4	54.6	21.6	8.9	869	412
Claiborne	847	2,308,077	5.0	2.0	2.4	2.3	47.8	2.4	38.2	69.3	34.1	15.8	939	530
Concordia	1,328	3,662,764	3.6	24.2	2.0	3.1	16.5	5.2	44.7	109.8	52.5	25.5	1,253	622
De Soto	1,141	3,608,492	7.4	7.4	0.8	6.3	2.6	3.1	71.2	213.8	37.7	149.7	5,553	2,010
East Baton Rouge	16,122	60,516,124	9.3	10.2	6.8	4.4	7.2	8.9	49.7	1,776.4	573.7	866.4	1,949	820
East Carroll	291	819,177	9.3	8.7	1.7	2.4	46.3	8.0	23.1	47.3	28.8	7.1	947	459
East Feliciana	631	1,666,825	14.0	19.9	0.0	2.6	1.1	4.2	58.2	44.3	27.0	13.4	671	245
Evangeline	1,334	3,509,396	4.9	9.7	2.3	4.2	2.0	5.9	70.6	136.3	68.0	37.5	1,111	500
Franklin	1,046	2,791,309	5.1	15.1	1.2	2.0	28.2	2.9	45.4	84.3	40.9	21.5	1,046	283
Grant	604	1,502,745	8.0	3.6	0.0	2.3	3.2	5.7	76.5	50.6	32.7	12.2	551	301
Iberia	3,450	9,630,156	4.1	12.3	3.2	2.7	20.2	5.1	51.6	320.8	141.9	101.3	1,368	514
Iberville	1,742	4,067,035	7.6	14.8	2.5	5.7	1.5	5.6	57.3	154.3	45.0	93.6	2,817	1,287
Jackson	824	2,175,796	2.6	14.3	1.3	2.9	30.0	2.2	46.2	80.9	29.0	33.0	2,033	1,323
Jefferson	16,179	70,416,195	8.0	11.6	2.9	2.3	31.2	6.3	36.3	2,140.2	681.5	696.5	1,606	721
Jefferson Davis	1,386	3,583,234	4.3	9.8	2.0	2.1	0.3	3.8	76.9	101.8	54.3	35.4	1,127	532
Lafayette	8,193	26,367,258	8.2	13.8	4.3	3.8	0.8	11.2	56.6	791.5	255.4	391.9	1,726	692
Lafourche	4,602	16,739,494	5.8	10.8	0.0	3.9	32.6	3.4	42.1	526.8	177.3	149.9	1,545	846
La Salle	890	2,469,446	4.0	15.2	0.4	1.6	31.7	2.8	44.0	119.2	60.2	20.7	1,388	759
Lincoln	1,655	6,428,631	8.8	13.7	9.5	6.9	3.8	12.8	43.0	139.1	54.9	66.4	1,414	645
Livingston	4,067	13,075,838	6.4	8.4	0.8	1.6	0.8	3.2	78.1	359.5	202.1	123.4	935	334
Madison	681	1,378,550	9.2	30.1	0.1	5.0	0.3	1.6	53.3	76.9	38.0	17.4	1,428	929
Morehouse	1,347	4,002,380	5.9	10.2	2.9	1.8	23.0	0.9	54.6	125.8	64.1	30.3	1,099	513
Natchitoches	2,176	6,441,570	5.4	11.8	1.9	2.7	29.9	5.7	41.6	198.4	86.0	59.1	1,498	518

1. Based on the resident population estimated as of July 1 of the year shown.

Local Government Finances, Government Employment, and Income Taxes

STATE County	Local government finances, 2012 (cont.)									Government employment, 2017			Individual income tax returns, 2016		
	Direct general expenditure							Debt outstanding							
		Per capita[1] (dollars)	Percent of total for:					Total (mil dol)	Per capita[1] (dollars)	Federal civilian	Federal military	State and local	Number of returns	Mean adjusted gross income	Mean income tax
	Total (mil dol)		Education	Health and hospitals	Police protection	Public welfare	Highways								
	185	186	187	188	189	190	191	192	193	194	195	196	197	198	199
KENTUCKY— Cont'd															
Ohio	54.6	2,269	56.5	1.1	4.2	0.1	4.9	203.8	8,463	87	73	1,467	9,670	43,660	3,671
Oldham	156.7	2,552	60.0	4.3	4.0	0.4	2.1	428.5	6,978	74	188	3,269	28,130	96,794	14,749
Owen	24.6	2,286	63.4	3.3	2.4	0.5	6.5	37.0	3,440	20	33	453	4,340	44,245	3,772
Owsley	13.9	2,954	73.5	0.4	2.7	0.0	7.0	5.8	1,224	9	13	295	1,280	33,204	2,181
Pendleton	38.4	2,629	51.2	14.8	3.0	0.0	6.3	59.7	4,086	29	44	607	6,370	46,791	4,268
Perry	108.4	3,839	51.5	14.3	2.9	0.0	4.1	267.3	9,465	141	79	2,374	9,820	41,212	3,928
Pike	184.3	2,872	57.9	3.3	2.1	0.2	4.9	348.9	5,437	204	175	2,883	19,560	46,150	4,862
Powell	29.2	2,335	66.0	6.6	2.1	0.0	3.4	14.4	1,150	34	37	752	5,020	36,643	2,749
Pulaski	161.3	2,537	51.9	11.8	5.1	0.1	3.7	170.4	2,679	195	194	3,693	25,660	44,460	4,718
Robertson	15.0	6,849	83.7	0.5	0.9	0.0	3.9	36.7	16,787	1	6	148	830	40,237	3,129
Rockcastle	38.2	2,248	63.7	4.5	2.8	0.0	4.0	25.4	1,494	32	50	754	5,970	38,773	2,912
Rowan	57.8	2,467	44.0	13.0	4.0	0.6	5.0	89.2	3,802	87	69	3,062	8,650	43,857	4,029
Russell	56.8	3,247	41.5	34.9	2.6	0.4	3.2	42.4	2,424	63	54	989	6,980	37,575	2,989
Scott	139.0	2,834	46.7	7.0	4.0	0.2	2.7	633.9	12,922	58	164	2,295	24,050	60,826	6,618
Shelby	102.9	2,359	54.2	6.2	3.7	0.0	2.4	238.0	5,456	74	139	2,347	20,950	62,822	7,641
Simpson	44.9	2,560	53.3	3.9	5.1	1.0	3.9	71.7	4,088	35	54	842	8,210	45,385	4,075
Spencer	29.0	1,665	65.8	2.9	4.3	0.1	5.6	48.6	2,788	23	56	636	8,410	62,642	6,538
Taylor	135.0	5,469	23.2	57.5	1.9	0.0	2.1	111.7	4,523	86	73	1,818	10,370	42,669	4,053
Todd	33.7	2,664	60.0	5.0	3.2	0.0	4.5	102.5	8,103	35	37	626	4,810	44,899	4,120
Trigg	28.2	1,952	58.5	2.4	4.6	0.1	8.2	21.2	1,469	79	44	593	5,990	44,479	4,184
Trimble	33.1	3,770	40.0	1.5	0.6	0.0	3.9	423.4	48,190	18	26	326	3,720	46,837	4,225
Union	38.1	2,567	54.2	0.6	4.9	0.4	7.4	15.5	1,046	54	40	707	5,720	47,909	4,914
Warren	300.9	2,570	45.9	4.4	6.6	0.1	3.4	970.8	8,290	371	381	9,435	53,600	53,504	6,162
Washington	29.1	2,457	61.1	3.2	3.0	0.1	7.7	78.0	6,592	33	36	495	5,320	42,846	3,720
Wayne	46.9	2,252	65.2	3.1	3.1	0.0	3.8	44.3	2,129	36	62	955	7,450	36,643	2,850
Webster	36.1	2,657	46.4	1.2	2.4	0.0	5.6	63.7	4,692	39	38	617	5,300	47,809	4,335
Whitley	116.0	3,267	65.4	7.7	3.4	0.0	3.2	141.1	3,974	95	105	2,167	13,240	40,697	3,665
Wolfe	19.1	2,667	68.4	0.1	0.9	0.0	6.6	20.2	2,819	21	22	403	2,320	34,060	2,450
Woodford	67.4	2,689	51.3	5.2	8.7	0.0	4.7	133.5	5,323	42	79	1,467	12,580	58,005	7,376
LOUISIANA	X	X	X	X	X	X	X	X	X	31,067	33,652	292,812	1,968,190	57,214	7,380
Acadia	174.4	2,817	55.1	8.1	6.4	0.3	4.6	40.6	656	91	234	2,614	24,340	46,327	5,015
Allen	95.8	3,750	51.3	17.0	5.7	0.0	5.7	24.4	955	590	82	3,758	8,590	46,097	4,206
Ascension	402.3	3,583	57.6	3.1	6.1	0.0	4.1	796.9	7,097	143	465	4,861	52,500	72,115	9,011
Assumption	72.6	3,151	65.4	0.1	5.9	0.8	2.8	12.4	536	33	85	959	9,470	52,859	5,574
Avoyelles	119.8	2,877	51.1	10.8	10.3	0.0	2.9	26.7	640	80	143	3,312	15,780	42,919	4,102
Beauregard	151.0	4,161	49.3	23.5	4.9	0.0	5.2	90.4	2,493	70	137	1,689	13,810	55,276	5,583
Bienville	72.3	5,139	63.9	2.2	6.1	0.2	6.3	29.9	2,123	44	51	818	5,570	39,992	3,261
Bossier	464.2	3,799	47.3	1.0	9.1	0.1	5.0	486.1	3,978	1,983	5,562	6,422	53,440	54,775	5,941
Caddo	1,081.2	4,206	48.6	1.7	7.4	0.0	2.2	1,079.9	4,201	2,773	946	15,584	108,150	52,473	6,699
Calcasieu	908.6	4,671	38.0	7.0	6.7	0.4	7.0	2,311.6	11,885	548	834	13,324	87,550	59,589	7,419
Caldwell	34.6	3,461	63.2	7.2	3.0	0.2	3.0	14.9	1,485	27	36	607	3,640	49,765	4,816
Cameron	87.3	13,024	42.4	9.7	4.1	0.4	4.8	20.4	3,043	16	26	753	2,940	64,433	8,996
Catahoula	65.8	6,390	33.4	42.7	3.0	0.0	2.4	37.4	3,632	48	34	506	3,460	43,349	3,909
Claiborne	68.0	4,039	33.4	28.7	3.9	0.7	3.0	18.0	1,071	46	50	1,171	5,390	44,579	4,235
Concordia	116.6	5,726	35.0	12.7	6.4	0.0	2.6	38.7	1,899	60	70	1,435	7,300	41,939	3,895
De Soto	190.9	7,081	58.1	1.3	4.0	1.7	8.4	134.5	4,987	50	103	1,571	11,570	48,052	4,656
East Baton Rouge	2,083.6	4,687	38.7	5.0	6.4	0.1	5.2	2,247.5	5,056	2,385	1,855	46,015	196,010	70,432	10,922
East Carroll	50.8	6,748	38.0	18.4	3.5	0.0	2.7	36.4	4,836	20	23	514	2,500	37,687	3,688
East Feliciana	43.2	2,161	59.7	0.7	8.1	0.0	4.6	5.3	264	25	65	2,509	8,130	55,662	6,354
Evangeline	132.8	3,939	46.5	23.7	4.1	0.0	6.4	25.6	760	52	123	1,569	12,270	45,928	4,402
Franklin	83.8	4,076	38.5	25.0	7.6	0.3	4.2	14.2	691	53	74	1,409	7,720	37,728	3,439
Grant	55.3	2,505	70.8	0.2	6.0	0.0	2.2	23.9	1,085	727	83	820	7,920	48,760	4,342
Iberia	346.8	4,686	45.5	17.9	5.9	0.2	5.6	224.6	3,035	100	274	4,183	30,650	54,634	6,752
Iberville	172.3	5,186	44.7	0.6	7.8	1.5	10.8	142.1	4,275	85	111	2,864	13,390	54,186	6,412
Jackson	80.7	4,976	35.7	20.0	10.5	0.0	5.3	72.6	4,475	30	56	1,113	6,000	46,505	4,002
Jefferson	2,141.8	4,939	30.3	30.9	4.8	2.5	3.5	1,621.8	3,740	1,489	2,166	17,091	201,980	56,622	7,540
Jefferson Davis	102.5	3,259	62.2	1.3	8.7	0.1	3.0	56.9	1,811	90	118	1,921	13,340	50,365	5,512
Lafayette	816.4	3,596	40.1	0.7	7.8	0.1	5.7	1,609.2	7,087	1,010	947	12,511	106,440	65,130	9,615
Lafourche	483.7	4,985	32.9	32.8	5.3	0.5	2.6	200.2	2,064	137	390	6,677	39,880	53,379	7,459
La Salle	118.0	7,903	25.1	37.6	3.9	0.0	1.8	23.9	1,604	40	52	1,379	5,110	52,346	5,017
Lincoln	137.7	2,933	55.0	0.5	7.2	0.6	5.1	82.8	1,764	113	171	4,225	17,530	55,902	6,832
Livingston	373.0	2,827	65.1	0.6	5.1	0.0	2.6	445.0	3,373	156	521	5,487	55,410	58,191	5,728
Madison	79.7	6,557	26.6	19.8	12.1	0.1	3.5	74.6	6,141	38	37	788	3,970	32,039	2,707
Morehouse	124.7	4,525	44.2	20.5	4.1	0.1	2.7	101.1	3,668	56	95	1,122	10,730	39,212	3,469
Natchitoches	210.4	5,335	45.1	20.9	4.9	0.5	3.0	50.5	1,281	167	143	4,025	14,950	47,213	5,049

1. Based on the resident population estimated as of July 1 of the year shown.

State / county code	CBSA code[1]	County code[2]	STATE County	Land area[3] (sq. mi)	Total persons 2018	Rank	Per square mile	White	Black	American Indian, Alaska Native	Asian and Pacific Islancer	Percent Hispanic or Latino[4]	Under 5 years	5 to 17 years	18 to 24 years	25 to 34 years	35 to 44 years	45 to 54 years
				1	2	3	4	5	6	7	8	9	10	11	12	13	14	15
			LOUISIANA— Cont'd															
22071	35,380	1	Orleans	169.4	391,006	181	2,308.2	31.8	60.0	0.7	3.4	5.6	5.9	14.1	8.6	17.9	13.6	11.9
22073	33,740	3	Ouachita	610.4	154,475	429	253.1	59.0	38.0	0.6	1.4	2.2	6.9	18.0	9.6	14.3	12.3	11.8
22075	35,380	1	Plaquemines	780.3	23,410	1,666	30.0	65.2	22.1	2.4	5.2	7.8	6.8	19.1	8.6	13.1	13.1	13.3
22077	12,940	2	Pointe Coupee	557.2	21,940	1,725	39.4	61.2	35.9	0.5	0.5	2.9	6.1	15.7	8.0	11.2	10.9	12.1
22079	10,780	3	Rapides	1,320.3	130,562	490	98.9	62.7	32.7	1.5	1.9	3.2	6.8	17.9	8.7	13.0	12.1	12.1
22081		8	Red River	389.1	8,477	2,545	21.8	57.3	39.9	0.9	0.3	2.4	6.1	17.3	7.5	11.8	10.6	12.8
22083		6	Richland	555.7	20,192	1,811	36.3	61.7	35.9	0.6	0.5	2.3	6.1	17.2	8.3	13.2	12.4	11.6
22085		6	Sabine	866.7	24,032	1,640	27.7	70.5	17.8	10.5	0.8	4.0	6.1	17.5	7.1	11.8	11.2	12.0
22087	35,380	1	St. Bernard	377.5	46,721	1,038	123.8	63.8	23.9	1.2	2.9	10.2	7.1	19.5	7.6	16.5	13.5	11.7
22089	35,380	1	St. Charles	277.7	52,879	953	190.4	66.1	26.8	0.8	1.5	6.3	6.3	18.1	8.4	12.9	13.0	13.5
22091	12,940	2	St. Helena	408.4	10,262	2,402	25.1	45.3	52.5	0.9	0.7	1.9	5.5	15.6	7.7	14.0	10.5	12.5
22093	35,380	1	St. James	241.5	21,037	1,775	87.1	48.9	49.3	0.4	0.5	1.7	5.8	16.8	8.4	13.3	11.4	12.6
22095	35,380	1	St. John the Baptist	214.3	43,184	1,111	201.5	34.9	57.8	0.6	1.6	6.3	6.4	18.2	8.8	13.3	12.2	12.9
22097	36,660	4	St. Landry	923.9	82,764	686	89.6	55.5	42.1	0.6	0.7	2.3	7.6	19.2	8.2	12.7	11.2	11.6
22099	29,180	2	St. Martin	737.2	53,621	945	72.7	65.7	30.6	0.8	1.2	3.0	6.7	17.5	8.0	14.0	12.2	12.6
22101	34,020	4	St. Mary	555.6	49,774	992	89.6	57.9	32.6	2.4	2.0	7.1	6.8	17.0	8.0	12.9	11.1	12.9
22103	35,380	1	St. Tammany	846.2	258,111	266	305.0	79.9	13.1	1.0	2.0	5.7	6.1	17.8	7.6	11.5	12.7	13.2
22105	25,220	3	Tangipahoa	791.3	133,777	480	169.1	64.3	30.8	0.8	1.1	4.4	7.2	17.3	9.9	14.9	12.3	11.6
22107		9	Tensas	602.8	4,462	2,863	7.4	43.4	54.7	0.6	0.4	2.2	5.8	17.1	7.2	9.1	9.6	10.7
22109	26,380	3	Terrebonne	1,229.8	111,021	547	90.3	68.7	20.3	6.9	1.7	5.1	6.9	18.4	8.1	14.0	12.6	12.5
22111	33,740	3	Union	877.0	22,330	1,710	25.5	69.9	25.3	0.7	0.5	4.6	5.9	16.0	7.5	11.6	11.0	12.2
22113	29,180	2	Vermilion	1,173.2	59,830	872	51.0	79.7	15.1	0.7	2.3	3.7	6.6	18.9	7.8	12.9	12.6	12.3
22115	22,860	5	Vernon	1,327.9	48,860	1,008	36.8	72.8	15.4	2.2	3.6	9.4	8.1	16.7	14.3	17.3	12.3	9.9
22117	14,220	6	Washington	669.5	46,582	1,039	69.6	66.6	30.9	1.0	0.5	2.4	6.7	17.4	8.0	12.3	12.0	11.7
22119	43,340	2	Webster	593.2	38,798	1,206	65.4	62.9	34.8	1.1	0.7	2.0	6.2	16.4	7.9	12.2	11.1	12.4
22121	12,940	2	West Baton Rouge	192.4	26,427	1,550	137.4	56.4	40.2	0.6	0.9	3.2	7.1	17.4	7.9	15.5	12.9	12.4
22123		9	West Carroll	359.6	10,982	2,353	30.5	79.4	16.3	1.0	0.5	4.0	5.7	17.4	8.4	11.8	12.5	11.7
22125	12,940	2	West Feliciana	403.3	15,460	2,070	38.3	53.5	44.8	0.5	0.4	1.6	4.1	12.1	5.8	14.0	17.7	17.6
22127		6	Winn	950.1	14,134	2,154	14.9	65.9	31.5	1.4	0.6	2.2	6.0	14.9	7.7	13.9	12.3	13.4
23000		0	MAINE	30,844.7	1,338,404	X	43.4	94.8	2.1	1.4	1.8	1.7	4.8	13.9	8.0	12.0	11.4	13.5
23001	30,340	3	Androscoggin	467.9	107,679	562	230.1	92.5	5.3	1.1	1.5	2.0	5.8	15.8	8.4	12.4	11.8	13.6
23003		7	Aroostook	6,671.3	67,111	794	10.1	95.3	1.4	2.7	0.7	1.3	4.8	13.4	7.5	9.7	10.4	13.3
23005	38,860	2	Cumberland	835.7	293,557	234	351.3	92.2	3.7	0.9	3.1	2.1	4.9	13.8	8.6	13.7	12.3	13.6
23007		6	Franklin	1,697.0	29,897	1,435	17.6	97.1	0.9	1.3	0.9	1.3	4.2	13.3	9.6	10.8	10.1	12.8
23009		6	Hancock	1,587.1	54,811	930	34.5	95.9	1.2	1.1	1.6	1.5	4.4	12.7	6.6	11.1	10.4	13.0
23011	12,300	4	Kennebec	867.5	122,083	516	140.7	96.2	1.2	1.3	1.4	1.6	5.0	14.3	8.3	11.6	11.3	13.7
23013		7	Knox	365.1	39,771	1,185	108.9	96.6	1.1	1.4	1.0	1.5	4.4	13.4	6.4	10.5	10.9	12.6
23015		8	Lincoln	455.9	34,342	1,315	75.3	97.0	0.9	1.1	1.1	1.2	4.2	12.5	6.4	9.8	9.8	12.7
23017		6	Oxford	2,076.9	57,618	897	27.7	96.7	1.0	1.4	1.2	1.4	4.5	13.9	6.6	10.5	11.3	13.8
23019	12,620	3	Penobscot	3,397.2	151,096	438	44.5	95.3	1.4	2.1	1.6	1.4	4.7	13.4	10.2	13.2	11.4	13.2
23021		8	Piscataquis	3,961.0	16,800	1,990	4.2	96.4	0.8	1.5	1.2	1.5	4.4	12.4	6.0	8.6	10.0	13.2
23023	38,860	2	Sagadahoc	254.0	35,634	1,286	140.3	96.0	1.4	1.1	1.3	1.8	5.0	14.1	6.2	11.5	11.4	13.5
23025		6	Somerset	3,924.4	50,592	981	12.9	97.0	1.0	1.4	1.1	1.1	4.7	14.3	7.0	10.9	11.2	14.5
23027		6	Waldo	730.0	39,694	1,187	54.4	96.7	0.9	1.3	1.0	1.5	4.5	13.9	7.2	10.8	11.7	13.0
23029		7	Washington	2,562.7	31,490	1,393	12.3	91.2	1.0	6.5	0.8	2.4	4.8	14.1	7.3	9.6	10.3	12.5
23031	38,860	2	York	991.1	206,229	325	208.1	95.6	1.4	1.0	1.8	1.7	4.7	14.0	7.5	12.1	11.3	13.7
24000		0	MARYLAND	9,710.9	6,042,718	X	622.3	52.5	31.3	0.8	7.7	10.4	6.0	16.1	8.8	13.8	12.8	13.6
24001	19,060	3	Allegany	422.2	70,975	760	168.1	88.6	9.5	0.5	1.5	1.9	4.5	12.8	12.2	12.9	11.4	12.5
24003	12,580	1	Anne Arundel	414.8	576,031	116	1,388.7	70.0	18.7	0.8	5.5	8.1	6.1	16.1	8.7	14.2	13.3	13.6
24005	12,580	1	Baltimore	598.4	828,431	74	1,384.4	58.5	30.4	0.8	7.2	5.7	5.9	15.7	8.8	13.8	12.2	12.7
24009	47,900	1	Calvert	213.2	92,003	643	431.5	80.5	14.2	1.0	3.1	4.1	5.4	17.8	8.3	11.5	12.0	15.0
24011		6	Caroline	319.4	33,304	1,350	104.3	77.4	15.2	0.7	1.4	7.4	6.0	17.7	7.5	12.8	11.8	13.5
24013	12,580	1	Carroll	447.6	168,429	388	376.3	90.3	4.5	0.5	2.8	3.7	5.5	16.2	8.4	11.6	11.4	15.0
24015	37,980	1	Cecil	346.3	102,826	589	296.9	86.9	7.9	0.8	2.1	4.6	5.7	17.0	7.9	12.7	11.7	14.4
24017	47,900	1	Charles	457.8	161,503	409	352.8	41.3	50.4	1.6	4.6	6.0	6.0	18.0	8.7	13.0	12.8	15.8
24019	15,700	6	Dorchester	540.8	31,998	1,381	59.2	64.4	29.3	0.8	1.6	5.9	5.5	15.6	6.7	12.2	10.3	12.6
24021	47,900	1	Frederick	660.5	255,648	268	387.1	75.1	11.1	0.7	5.8	10.2	5.9	17.2	8.6	12.7	13.0	14.5
24023		6	Garrett	649.1	29,163	1,452	44.9	97.1	1.4	0.5	0.7	1.2	5.0	13.6	7.2	11.2	11.0	13.5
24025	12,580	1	Harford	437.1	253,956	273	581.0	77.7	15.4	0.7	4.0	4.7	5.6	16.5	8.2	12.5	12.4	14.2
24027	12,580	1	Howard	250.9	323,196	217	1,288.1	54.0	21.0	0.8	20.7	7.1	5.9	18.4	8.0	12.1	14.2	14.4
24029		6	Kent	277.0	19,383	1,859	70.0	79.6	15.6	0.5	1.4	4.3	4.1	11.7	11.4	10.7	8.8	11.0
24031	47,900	1	Montgomery	493.1	1,052,567	42	2,134.6	45.8	19.7	0.6	17.0	19.9	6.3	17.0	7.8	12.7	13.8	13.9
24033	47,900	1	Prince George's	482.7	909,308	60	1,883.8	13.9	63.4	0.9	5.1	19.1	6.5	15.7	9.6	14.6	13.4	13.8
24035	12,580	1	Queen Anne's	371.7	50,251	985	135.2	88.2	7.2	0.7	1.8	4.1	5.1	16.5	7.3	10.5	10.9	15.2

1. CBSA = Core Based Statistical Area. See Appendix A for explanation. See Appendix B for list of metropolitan areas with component counties. Service of USDA Rural-Urban Continuum Codes. See Appendix A for definition. 3. Dry land or land partially or temporarily covered by water. 2. County type code from the Economic Research 4. May be of any race.

Table B. States and Counties — **Population and Households**

STATE County	55 to 64 years	65 to 74 years	75 years and over	Percent female	2000	2010	2000-2010	2010-2018	Births	Deaths	Net Migration	Number	Persons per household	Family house-holds	Female family house-holder[1]	One person
	16	17	18	19	20	21	22	23	24	25	26	27	28	29	30	31
LOUISIANA— Cont'd																
Orleans	13.2	9.2	5.6	52.7	484,674	343,828	-29.1	13.7	39,449	26,286	32,967	154,895	2.42	49.0	17.9	43.4
Ouachita	12.4	8.6	6.2	52.1	147,250	153,731	4.4	0.5	18,459	12,653	-4,968	56,799	2.61	65.4	19.2	30.5
Plaquemines	12.6	7.9	5.6	49.6	26,757	23,039	-13.9	1.6	2,445	1,464	-622	8,759	2.63	73.4	16.4	22.8
Pointe Coupee	15.4	12.2	8.4	51.9	22,763	22,805	0.2	-3.8	2,297	2,066	-1,093	8,815	2.51	65.6	16.6	29.8
Rapides	13.0	9.4	7.0	51.6	126,337	131,609	4.2	-0.8	14,916	11,633	-4,269	48,032	2.66	66.9	17.8	29.3
Red River	14.8	10.7	8.4	51.9	9,622	9,091	-5.5	-6.8	944	875	-687	3,374	2.55	62.7	15.0	35.2
Richland	13.7	10.3	7.2	51.2	20,981	20,724	-1.2	-2.6	2,200	1,918	-806	7,500	2.62	68.2	18.3	28.0
Sabine	13.6	12.1	8.7	50.6	23,459	24,233	3.3	-0.8	2,435	2,218	-409	9,174	2.59	67.1	11.7	29.7
St. Bernard	12.6	7.2	4.2	51.0	67,229	35,897	-46.6	30.2	5,234	2,782	8,153	14,791	3.02	70.8	18.0	23.1
St. Charles	14.3	8.4	5.1	50.9	48,072	52,888	10.0	0.0	5,356	3,417	-1,976	18,925	2.75	75.2	16.3	20.9
St. Helena	14.2	11.7	8.3	51.8	10,525	11,207	6.5	-8.4	942	956	-943	3,990	2.60	69.8	22.5	28.5
St. James	14.6	10.0	7.1	51.7	21,216	22,101	4.2	-4.8	2,133	1,640	-1,568	7,887	2.70	70.2	21.5	26.5
St. John the Baptist	13.9	9.0	5.3	51.2	43,044	45,809	6.4	-5.7	4,743	3,325	-4,126	15,421	2.78	76.0	19.8	18.1
St. Landry	13.3	9.4	6.7	51.7	87,700	83,384	-4.9	-0.7	10,643	7,915	-3,305	30,467	2.70	67.0	18.0	29.1
St. Martin	13.9	9.1	6.0	50.8	48,583	52,160	7.4	2.8	5,994	3,886	-623	19,435	2.74	71.7	16.1	24.2
St. Mary	14.6	9.5	7.1	50.7	53,500	54,650	2.1	-8.9	6,097	4,572	-6,465	20,032	2.58	57.7	14.9	38.0
St. Tammany	14.1	10.4	6.5	51.5	191,268	233,754	22.2	10.4	23,847	17,445	18,007	91,353	2.70	72.0	12.6	23.2
Tangipahoa	12.5	9.0	5.4	51.6	100,588	121,107	20.4	10.5	15,846	9,880	6,704	47,598	2.63	67.1	17.6	27.1
Tensas	16.1	14.6	9.8	51.6	6,618	5,252	-20.6	-15.0	495	460	-834	1,930	2.46	57.3	19.8	38.6
Terrebonne	13.1	8.6	5.8	50.8	104,503	111,522	6.7	-0.4	13,425	8,439	-5,473	40,177	2.78	68.2	14.7	25.4
Union	15.3	11.9	8.7	50.5	22,803	22,774	-0.1	-1.9	2,302	2,116	-628	7,971	2.77	66.7	14.5	30.1
Vermilion	13.7	8.6	6.6	51.6	53,807	57,971	7.7	3.2	6,454	4,578	25	21,721	2.73	69.2	14.7	24.6
Vernon	9.1	7.2	5.0	46.7	52,531	52,334	-0.4	-6.6	8,551	3,183	-8,980	17,930	2.79	70.1	10.7	26.4
Washington	13.9	10.7	7.3	50.6	43,926	47,140	7.3	-1.2	4,889	4,789	-632	17,542	2.54	66.2	17.6	29.9
Webster	13.9	10.9	8.8	51.4	41,831	41,207	-1.5	-5.8	4,133	4,312	-2,226	15,854	2.46	61.9	14.6	35.2
West Baton Rouge	13.3	8.1	5.5	50.6	21,601	23,788	10.1	11.1	3,000	1,655	1,276	9,436	2.62	73.3	15.4	21.4
West Carroll	13.6	10.4	8.6	49.1	12,314	11,604	-5.8	-5.4	1,118	1,181	-555	4,182	2.55	70.1	15.1	27.7
West Feliciana	13.7	9.4	5.6	34.6	15,111	15,625	3.4	-1.1	984	971	-180	3,947	3.03	61.8	11.5	33.7
Winn	13.1	10.7	7.9	46.4	16,894	15,313	-9.4	-7.7	1,427	1,418	-1,191	5,382	2.37	68.5	15.8	29.6
MAINE	15.8	12.2	8.4	51.0	1,274,923	1,328,369	4.2	0.8	104,761	112,173	18,302	554,061	2.34	62.9	9.2	29.1
Androscoggin	14.4	10.4	7.4	51.1	103,793	107,710	3.8	0.0	10,531	8,762	-1,753	45,263	2.30	61.0	10.2	29.7
Aroostook	16.7	13.7	10.4	50.6	73,938	71,873	-2.8	-6.6	5,411	7,108	-3,060	29,844	2.23	62.7	8.4	32.5
Cumberland	14.7	10.9	7.6	51.5	265,612	281,676	6.0	4.2	23,054	21,136	10,151	118,807	2.36	61.1	8.7	29.3
Franklin	16.8	13.4	9.1	50.9	29,467	30,767	4.4	-2.8	2,083	2,640	-299	11,577	2.51	64.2	8.4	28.0
Hancock	17.2	14.9	9.7	51.6	51,791	54,408	5.1	0.7	3,877	4,834	1,408	23,674	2.23	63.0	8.1	30.1
Kennebec	15.9	11.8	8.1	51.2	117,114	122,154	4.3	-0.1	9,732	10,775	1,067	51,055	2.30	62.6	10.5	29.5
Knox	16.5	15.0	10.3	50.7	39,618	39,736	0.3	0.1	2,869	3,704	911	17,022	2.26	62.7	10.4	32.2
Lincoln	17.0	16.3	11.4	50.9	33,616	34,450	2.5	-0.3	2,256	3,418	1,083	15,241	2.19	63.1	7.5	29.0
Oxford	17.7	13.0	8.7	50.5	54,755	57,830	5.6	-0.4	4,249	5,260	840	20,756	2.72	65.6	8.7	28.3
Penobscot	15.2	10.9	7.8	50.5	144,919	153,932	6.2	-1.8	12,048	12,747	-2,043	61,848	2.35	62.1	9.4	28.6
Piscataquis	18.7	16.3	10.4	50.1	17,235	17,535	1.7	-4.2	1,192	1,867	-45	7,477	2.23	63.4	9.4	29.7
Sagadahoc	16.3	13.2	8.9	51.4	35,214	35,288	0.2	1.0	2,762	2,932	533	15,810	2.21	63.9	7.9	30.6
Somerset	16.6	12.6	8.2	50.3	50,888	52,226	2.6	-3.1	3,925	4,753	-781	21,392	2.35	64.2	10.7	28.6
Waldo	16.5	14.2	8.3	50.8	36,280	38,789	6.9	2.3	2,946	3,209	1,200	16,954	2.27	64.8	8.7	27.2
Washington	17.0	14.5	9.9	50.6	33,941	32,855	-3.2	-4.2	2,468	3,488	-322	14,017	2.20	63.0	10.2	30.6
York	16.2	12.1	8.4	51.2	186,742	197,140	5.6	4.6	15,358	15,540	9,412	83,324	2.38	65.3	9.1	26.7
MARYLAND	13.4	9.0	6.4	51.5	5,296,486	5,773,798	9.0	4.7	600,546	384,372	55,763	2,181,093	2.68	66.9	14.2	27.0
Allegany	13.2	11.0	9.3	47.9	74,930	75,047	0.2	-5.4	5,494	7,470	-2,076	27,759	2.34	61.7	11.2	32.1
Anne Arundel	13.3	8.7	5.9	50.5	489,656	537,631	9.8	7.1	57,088	33,947	15,604	205,395	2.67	69.5	11.4	24.5
Baltimore	13.7	9.6	7.6	52.6	754,292	805,229	6.8	2.9	80,734	65,943	9,086	312,859	2.58	63.5	14.5	28.4
Calvert	15.1	8.9	5.9	50.4	74,563	88,739	19.0	3.7	7,551	5,451	1,192	31,462	2.87	75.5	11.4	18.6
Caroline	14.5	9.6	6.7	51.0	29,772	33,078	11.1	0.7	3,219	2,736	-259	11,996	2.69	72.3	13.2	22.1
Carroll	15.0	9.7	7.1	50.5	150,897	167,142	10.8	0.8	13,382	12,270	249	60,432	2.71	75.1	9.0	20.8
Cecil	14.8	9.8	6.0	50.4	85,951	101,102	17.6	1.7	9,201	7,466	74	37,076	2.72	70.5	11.8	23.7
Charles	13.3	7.6	4.9	51.8	120,546	146,565	21.6	10.2	15,191	8,239	8,065	54,988	2.79	73.3	16.0	22.7
Dorchester	15.6	12.4	9.2	52.5	30,674	32,623	6.4	-1.9	3,071	3,098	-580	12,940	2.46	66.0	17.4	27.8
Frederick	13.5	8.5	5.9	50.7	195,277	233,391	19.5	9.5	23,008	14,066	13,480	90,022	2.68	72.3	10.0	21.7
Garrett	16.1	12.9	9.4	50.7	29,846	30,139	1.0	-3.2	2,377	2,589	-754	11,865	2.43	69.2	9.5	26.4
Harford	14.4	9.6	6.5	51.0	218,590	244,826	12.0	3.7	22,173	16,558	3,688	92,895	2.67	72.3	10.7	22.8
Howard	13.1	8.4	5.4	51.1	247,842	287,123	15.8	12.6	28,780	13,108	20,553	111,337	2.79	73.9	10.5	21.1
Kent	15.5	14.5	12.2	52.3	19,197	20,195	5.2	-4.0	1,339	2,088	-55	7,605	2.37	61.1	9.1	32.3
Montgomery	13.1	8.8	6.7	51.6	873,341	971,964	11.3	8.3	107,730	48,586	21,627	369,242	2.79	69.8	11.3	24.9
Prince George's	13.0	8.4	4.9	51.9	801,515	863,349	7.7	5.3	100,330	47,203	-6,730	306,694	2.89	66.0	19.7	28.3
Queen Anne's	15.7	11.2	7.6	50.4	40,563	47,789	17.8	5.2	3,889	3,334	1,946	17,995	2.70	72.2	9.0	22.6

1. No spouse present.

Table B. States and Counties — **Population, Vital Statistics, Health, and Crime**

STATE County	Persons in group quarters, 2018	Daytime Population, 2013-2017		Births, 2018		Deaths, 2018		Persons under 65 with no health insurance, 2016		Medicare, 2018			Serious crimes known to police[2], 2016 Total	
		Number	Employment/ residence ratio	Total	Rate[1]	Number	Rate[1]	Number	Percent	Total beneficiaries	Enrolled in Original Medicare	Enrolled in Medicare Advantage	Number	Rate[3]
	32	33	34	35	36	37	38	39	40	41	42	43	44	45

STATE County	32	33	34	35	36	37	38	39	40	41	42	43	44	45
LOUISIANA— Cont'd														
Orleans	13,453	437,781	1.28	4,583	11.7	3,655	9.3	38,100	11.6	62,235	29,514	32,721	20,200	5,085
Ouachita	5,538	162,517	1.10	2,083	13.5	1,659	10.7	14,557	11.2	28,031	20,394	7,637	10,394	6,901
Plaquemines	272	31,318	1.77	283	12.1	193	8.2	2,746	13.6	3,585	1,643	1,942	267	1,137
Pointe Coupee	116	19,716	0.72	261	11.9	251	11.4	2,053	11.5	4,787	2,480	2,307	356	1,722
Rapides	4,500	137,191	1.10	1,754	13.4	1,439	11.0	13,451	12.4	27,418	22,108	5,310	8,428	6,449
Red River	164	8,000	0.78	84	9.9	125	14.7	803	11.5	1,634	1,315	319	209	2,466
Richland	1,037	20,196	0.95	237	11.7	245	12.1	2,033	12.5	4,314	3,281	1,033	353	2,015
Sabine	438	22,940	0.85	291	12.1	237	9.9	2,879	15.1	5,411	4,464	947	333	1,382
St. Bernard	293	40,011	0.72	603	12.9	397	8.5	4,647	11.5	6,315	3,030	3,285	1,642	3,479
St. Charles	592	54,112	1.06	654	12.4	439	8.3	3,853	8.5	8,718	3,584	5,134	1,012	1,923
St. Helena	121	8,659	0.48	105	10.2	103	10.0	1,166	13.8	2,943	1,816	1,127	170	1,672
St. James	204	21,883	1.04	222	10.6	222	10.6	1,714	9.6	4,276	2,079	2,197	537	2,972
St. John the Baptist	471	41,753	0.90	542	12.6	423	9.8	4,031	10.8	8,056	3,534	4,522	1,059	2,457
St. Landry	1,105	77,432	0.79	1,225	14.8	1,022	12.3	8,414	12.0	18,526	14,894	3,632	3,400	4,215
St. Martin	701	45,114	0.64	699	13.0	527	9.8	5,576	12.2	10,128	7,867	2,261	1,182	2,190
St. Mary	868	56,641	1.20	653	13.1	563	11.3	5,940	13.7	10,468	8,079	2,389	2,129	4,071
St. Tammany	1,277	230,696	0.84	3,054	11.8	2,366	9.2	21,329	10.1	50,248	24,487	25,761	4,079	1,616
Tangipahoa	3,643	118,364	0.81	1,933	14.4	1,363	10.2	12,782	11.7	22,480	14,216	8,264	6,638	5,294
Tensas	16	4,563	0.86	52	11.7	62	13.9	504	14.2	1,171	956	215	15	324
Terrebonne	1,479	123,552	1.23	1,460	13.2	1,112	10.0	15,384	15.9	20,610	16,040	4,570	4,768	4,180
Union	476	19,828	0.67	253	11.3	252	11.3	2,282	12.9	5,115	3,748	1,367	306	1,370
Vermilion	537	51,500	0.66	716	12.0	608	10.2	6,624	12.9	10,896	9,226	1,670	1,481	2,467
Vernon	3,307	52,373	1.02	953	19.5	384	7.9	4,666	11.0	7,353	6,706	647	1,142	2,388
Washington	1,581	43,536	0.82	613	13.2	629	13.5	4,837	13.1	10,471	6,810	3,661	1,944	4,220
Webster	1,231	38,032	0.87	466	12.0	537	13.8	3,647	11.7	9,324	7,155	2,169	760	1,972
West Baton Rouge	556	27,224	1.14	386	14.6	221	8.4	1,896	8.7	4,260	1,928	2,332	625	2,430
West Carroll	434	10,056	0.67	125	11.4	158	14.4	1,188	13.8	2,618	1,931	687	357	3,188
West Feliciana	5,321	15,687	1.06	109	7.1	122	7.9	710	8.7	2,040	1,264	776	126	824
Winn	1,761	13,830	0.84	178	12.6	209	14.8	1,257	12.1	3,011	2,455	556	348	2,420
MAINE	35,836	1,314,339	0.98	12,438	9.3	14,079	10.5	105,736	10.1	331,086	226,314	104,772	23,560	1,769
Androscoggin	2,875	105,180	0.96	1,209	11.2	1,062	9.9	8,112	9.4	24,376	14,729	9,647	1,977	1,843
Aroostook	2,040	68,513	0.99	617	9.2	866	12.9	5,881	11.5	19,717	16,078	3,639	929	1,364
Cumberland	9,175	316,602	1.18	2,801	9.5	2,660	9.1	18,481	7.8	62,877	38,476	24,401	5,625	1,926
Franklin	1,107	29,544	0.96	229	7.7	337	11.3	2,614	11.6	7,695	4,759	2,936	364	1,218
Hancock	987	53,478	0.96	471	8.6	637	11.6	4,800	11.6	14,947	11,455	3,492	794	1,449
Kennebec	3,817	124,311	1.05	1,132	9.3	1,356	11.1	9,417	9.8	31,324	19,807	11,517	2,378	1,986
Knox	1,375	41,655	1.10	342	8.6	438	11.0	3,188	10.9	11,450	7,902	3,548	504	1,262
Lincoln	503	31,099	0.82	273	7.9	423	12.3	3,051	12.3	10,684	6,932	3,752	465	1,370
Oxford	839	50,785	0.74	512	8.9	686	11.9	4,839	10.9	15,387	10,565	4,822	1,204	2,106
Penobscot	6,982	155,347	1.04	1,437	9.5	1,573	10.4	14,179	12.0	36,184	26,043	10,141	3,110	2,037
Piscataquis	242	16,617	0.95	158	9.4	226	13.5	1,651	13.4	5,186	4,060	1,126	195	1,158
Sagadahoc	260	34,163	0.95	325	9.1	400	11.2	2,383	8.6	9,230	5,925	3,305	424	1,205
Somerset	705	48,524	0.89	444	8.8	544	10.8	4,767	12.0	12,801	9,904	2,897	1,036	2,033
Waldo	587	34,856	0.75	328	8.3	435	11.0	3,620	11.9	10,512	7,429	3,083	436	1,110
Washington	729	31,656	0.99	280	8.9	412	13.1	3,815	16.4	9,345	8,090	1,255	431	1,371
York	3,613	172,009	0.72	1,880	9.1	2,024	9.8	14,938	9.2	49,371	34,160	15,211	3,625	1,792
MARYLAND	140,447	5,730,452	0.91	71,029	11.8	51,184	8.5	353,248	7.0	1,010,800	887,237	123,563	165,845	2,757
Allegany	7,592	76,538	1.14	614	8.7	882	12.4	3,310	6.4	16,834	15,926	908	2,321	3,241
Anne Arundel	14,993	557,072	0.97	6,853	11.9	4,573	7.9	25,128	5.3	92,092	82,323	9,769	15,295	2,702
Baltimore	21,417	777,457	0.88	9,579	11.6	8,549	10.3	43,890	6.5	157,928	136,484	21,444	27,946	3,361
Calvert	642	69,493	0.53	897	9.7	744	8.1	3,260	4.2	15,289	14,407	882	1,324	1,465
Caroline	441	27,099	0.63	389	11.7	344	10.3	2,406	8.8	6,555	6,124	431	726	2,248
Carroll	3,365	138,297	0.67	1,655	9.8	1,553	9.2	5,977	4.3	32,106	29,455	2,651	2,257	1,354
Cecil	1,372	87,180	0.70	1,106	10.8	1,009	9.8	5,812	6.7	18,710	16,989	1,721	2,976	2,917
Charles	1,407	122,706	0.58	1,799	11.1	1,141	7.1	6,855	5.0	22,889	20,953	1,936	3,145	2,002
Dorchester	501	29,653	0.82	346	10.8	393	12.3	1,980	7.8	7,819	7,295	524	1,104	3,435
Frederick	4,348	226,609	0.85	2,792	10.9	1,804	7.1	11,655	5.5	40,558	37,180	3,378	3,777	1,534
Garrett	529	28,852	0.95	277	9.5	350	12.0	1,655	7.2	7,082	6,401	681	435	1,491
Harford	2,748	222,622	0.79	2,639	10.4	2,176	8.6	10,156	4.8	46,388	41,563	4,825	4,024	1,611
Howard	1,686	309,775	0.98	3,522	10.9	1,819	5.6	12,013	4.4	45,779	40,924	4,855	6,258	1,976
Kent	1,504	19,874	1.02	146	7.5	296	15.3	1,115	8.2	5,752	5,386	366	294	1,501
Montgomery	9,013	1,008,021	0.94	12,657	12.0	6,344	6.0	65,571	7.4	160,172	140,218	19,954	17,443	1,666
Prince George's	20,009	780,770	0.74	12,044	13.2	7,002	7.7	83,880	10.8	128,894	106,468	22,426	22,687	2,484
Queen Anne's	437	40,190	0.64	505	10.0	408	8.1	2,228	5.6	9,710	9,051	659	726	1,487

1. Per 1,000 estimated resident population.　　2. Data for serious crimes have not been adjusted for underreporting; this may affect comparability between geographic areas and over time.　　3. Per 100,000 population estimated by the FBI.

Table B. States and Counties — Crime, Education, Money Income, and Poverty

STATE County	Serious crimes known to police[2], 2016 (cont.)[1] Rate — Violent	Property	Education — School enrollment and attainment, 2013-2017 — Enrollment[3] Total	Percent private	Attainment[4] (percent) High school graduate or less	Bachelor's degree or more	Local government expenditures,[5] 2014-2015 Total current spending (mil dol)	Current spending per student (dollars)	Money income, 2013-2017 Per capita income[6]	Households Median income (dollars)	Percent with income of less than $50,000	Percent with income of $200,000 or more	Income and poverty, 2017 Median household income (dollars)	Percent below poverty level All persons	Children under 18 years	Children 5 to 17 years in families
	46	47	48	49	50	51	52	53	54	55	56	57	58	59	60	61
LOUISIANA— Cont'd																
Orleans	1,073	4,012	97,577	32.2	37.1	36.5	603.1	12,869	29,275	38,721	58.9	5.5	37,407	26.1	38.9	37.4
Ouachita	1,358	5,543	39,976	12.0	48.4	24.3	310.6	10,765	22,538	40,081	58.4	3.6	41,301	24.7	37.6	32.7
Plaquemines	162	975	6,247	19.8	54.1	19.3	82.6	16,541	26,177	49,635	50.3	3.7	56,199	16.2	19.0	17.4
Pointe Coupee	431	1,292	5,063	28.2	59.1	15.8	34.9	11,349	27,160	43,964	54.1	4.2	45,675	18.8	27.6	26.6
Rapides	1,075	5,374	33,723	17.1	52.4	20.1	229.7	9,688	23,486	42,655	57.2	2.8	42,238	19.9	26.0	24.4
Red River	507	1,959	2,039	15.7	61.2	15.6	21.4	14,371	25,154	41,510	59.4	4.9	35,662	23.3	34.8	33.0
Richland	457	1,558	4,444	9.0	59.6	15.4	41.2	10,266	19,975	34,745	62.2	2.1	36,432	27.8	44.4	39.9
Sabine	95	1,287	5,461	10.1	61.2	14.2	46.3	10,584	22,980	40,695	58.1	3.3	40,021	22.2	28.7	26.4
St. Bernard	286	3,193	12,312	12.1	57.4	12.1	78.4	10,561	20,431	45,265	54.1	1.6	44,553	20	28.7	25.7
St. Charles	333	1,590	13,713	14.0	47.2	22.3	154.9	16,339	30,378	64,707	39.0	4.8	65,335	11.4	16.7	15.7
St. Helena	344	1,328	2,228	11.5	67.4	11.2	12.3	10,933	21,148	35,254	65.7	1.0	36,723	23.2	36.6	36.6
St. James	609	2,364	5,006	17.4	60.3	14.0	61.4	16,179	25,724	52,055	48.4	3.5	53,045	16.7	23.9	22.6
St. John the Baptist	162	2,295	11,635	24.4	53.2	16.4	77.1	13,122	23,380	53,628	45.6	2.2	55,941	18.1	27.5	24.7
St. Landry	676	3,540	20,139	19.3	66.0	13.5	138.9	9,456	19,205	32,163	65.9	1.9	35,693	25.6	35.7	31.6
St. Martin	289	1,901	13,065	24.6	60.5	14.2	81.5	9,746	23,654	47,279	52.3	2.7	44,574	19.2	29.3	27.7
St. Mary	574	3,498	11,527	13.0	69.2	10.6	104.2	10,748	22,212	41,345	59.5	2.1	38,413	20.5	30.4	31.1
St. Tammany	173	1,443	63,517	27.4	36.4	32.5	433.6	11,459	33,149	66,539	38.3	7.2	67,926	11.1	15.0	13.7
Tangipahoa	933	4,361	34,476	13.0	54.2	19.9	187.3	9,396	23,520	45,901	53.3	2.3	44,256	20.9	31.0	30.1
Tensas	151	173	982	14.1	69.7	9.7	9.0	14,072	16,194	21,906	77.5	0.8	27,959	34.9	55.1	51.1
Terrebonne	476	3,704	26,855	17.1	61.3	14.4	175.6	9,536	24,017	47,650	52.0	3.2	47,971	19.7	24.7	23.6
Union	215	1,155	4,393	11.7	60.8	12.8	33.3	11,110	20,742	38,916	58.6	1.6	40,395	16.4	28.9	27.1
Vermilion	363	2,104	13,838	15.2	65.9	12.1	92.4	9,693	23,608	49,266	50.6	2.2	50,562	17	23.6	20.9
Vernon	301	2,087	13,166	10.8	49.1	17.7	95.0	10,172	22,583	46,620	55.2	2.0	45,711	18.3	23.8	23.4
Washington	784	3,436	10,916	12.1	64.5	12.2	82.8	11,133	18,345	32,962	67.1	2.0	37,792	23.1	33.1	30.9
Webster	337	1,635	8,617	11.7	58.1	15.5	63.0	9,723	19,256	30,891	69.4	1.3	32,522	20.3	29.1	27.4
West Baton Rouge	338	2,091	6,052	16.2	54.6	20.1	52.5	13,296	28,140	60,902	40.8	4.1	64,921	13.5	19.5	19.5
West Carroll	563	2,625	2,408	2.1	67.8	12.0	21.0	10,018	22,857	37,304	58.0	3.1	37,759	21.2	30.4	28.9
West Feliciana	255	569	4,552	7.1	52.4	23.0	28.1	13,242	23,041	55,647	46.5	4.1	56,584	21	20.2	18.3
Winn	438	1,982	3,023	12.1	63.8	13.1	25.5	10,328	18,417	29,472	65.6	1.6	39,474	23.7	31.5	30.8
MAINE	124	1,646	293,384	17.2	40.2	30.3	2,452.3	13,526	29,886	53,024	47.2	3.7	55,980	11.3	14.2	13.1
Androscoggin	137	1,706	25,297	19.6	47.3	22.1	204.0	12,096	26,276	49,538	50.4	1.8	48,446	12.4	15.8	13.9
Aroostook	137	1,227	14,090	9.9	50.4	18.5	133.7	13,665	23,631	39,021	60.4	1.5	42,600	14.4	17.5	16.3
Cumberland	136	1,790	67,816	20.2	28.3	45.0	532.5	14,169	36,780	65,702	38.3	6.8	70,661	8.1	9.2	8.9
Franklin	130	1,087	7,012	10.6	44.1	26.1	44.2	14,198	24,162	45,541	53.7	1.9	45,280	13.7	19.5	17.4
Hancock	55	1,394	10,553	16.7	38.8	32.4	103.9	16,163	31,178	51,438	48.8	4.0	51,009	11	15.0	14.1
Kennebec	152	1,834	26,804	19.0	42.0	26.7	199.4	12,518	27,336	50,116	49.9	2.3	52,265	12.4	14.2	13.0
Knox	73	1,189	7,391	13.0	41.5	30.5	90.8	15,313	29,806	53,117	47.0	3.4	51,723	10.7	14.7	13.7
Lincoln	141	1,229	5,798	20.2	39.5	33.1	55.6	13,976	31,522	54,041	46.1	3.9	52,019	11.4	15.3	14.2
Oxford	98	2,008	12,076	16.5	52.2	18.8	121.4	13,574	22,862	44,582	54.7	1.3	50,367	13.5	20.2	18.7
Penobscot	96	1,942	38,496	13.5	42.8	26.2	274.3	12,593	26,347	47,886	52.0	2.7	49,836	14.3	16.2	15.3
Piscataquis	113	1,046	3,260	17.2	50.9	17.8	18.8	10,642	23,464	38,797	61.6	1.8	40,841	15.5	23.4	21.7
Sagadahoc	45	1,160	7,064	11.1	36.1	34.5	68.5	14,855	32,947	60,457	41.2	2.7	61,047	9.7	14.0	12.3
Somerset	143	1,890	10,303	12.9	52.5	16.6	103.9	13,161	22,641	41,549	57.4	1.2	42,426	15.9	22.0	19.4
Waldo	64	1,046	8,031	23.8	39.9	30.3	56.0	14,932	27,763	50,162	49.8	2.3	54,547	13.1	18.8	16.6
Washington	121	1,250	6,277	10.4	50.3	20.9	65.4	15,401	24,311	40,328	60.2	1.5	37,943	21.1	26.8	25.3
York	148	1,644	43,116	19.5	38.2	30.9	372.8	12,989	33,635	62,618	39.7	5.1	66,025	7.8	9.7	8.8
MARYLAND	472	2,284	1,555,036	18.9	35.3	39.0	12,405.3	14,185	39,070	78,916	31.3	10.7	80,711	9.4	12.4	11.6
Allegany	345	2,896	17,416	8.6	52.2	18.2	126.4	14,256	22,355	42,771	56.2	1.8	42,564	17	22.8	22.3
Anne Arundel	471	2,231	145,793	19.6	32.2	40.1	1,051.2	13,220	43,258	94,502	23.7	12.9	96,133	6.1	8.0	7.6
Baltimore	531	2,830	209,286	21.7	35.5	37.8	1,474.3	13,424	37,270	71,810	33.7	7.8	73,309	8.3	10.4	9.7
Calvert	155	1,310	23,797	11.4	37.0	30.1	221.4	13,813	41,469	100,350	20.2	11.9	100,000	6	7.0	6.4
Caroline	192	2,056	7,454	6.6	57.5	16.6	70.3	12,576	25,355	52,469	47.3	2.8	56,338	13.8	20.5	18.3
Carroll	154	1,200	43,192	20.8	37.9	34.6	351.9	13,598	39,690	90,510	25.6	10.2	92,890	5	5.5	4.9
Cecil	366	2,551	24,332	18.4	48.1	23.0	201.6	12,858	32,542	70,516	35.0	5.9	72,259	9.7	13.2	12.4
Charles	359	1,643	40,650	11.7	39.3	28.5	363.2	13,831	38,890	93,973	24.1	10.8	94,478	7.5	9.8	9.2
Dorchester	479	2,956	6,591	10.8	53.0	20.1	66.6	13,880	28,911	50,532	49.6	2.9	47,011	15.7	26.9	26.5
Frederick	247	1,287	66,543	18.5	32.0	40.5	526.5	12,910	39,566	88,502	25.8	10.5	91,727	6.7	7.6	7.1
Garrett	206	1,286	5,916	17.7	54.5	19.6	55.8	14,454	26,303	48,174	52.5	2.7	46,899	11.8	18.7	18.3
Harford	221	1,390	62,498	17.6	34.2	35.2	476.5	12,695	37,972	83,445	28.5	8.8	80,922	7.1	8.5	8.0
Howard	228	1,748	89,888	17.3	18.7	61.2	843.6	15,714	51,045	115,576	17.0	20.6	111,576	5.9	6.4	6.1
Kent	209	1,291	4,421	38.9	42.4	33.2	30.0	14,252	32,217	56,638	43.5	5.6	57,760	12.8	20.4	20.1
Montgomery	175	1,490	274,602	21.6	22.7	58.3	2,340.0	15,152	51,162	103,178	22.4	19.8	102,944	7	9.3	8.9
Prince George's	360	2,124	243,667	16.8	39.7	31.9	1,866.6	14,531	34,391	78,607	29.0	8.2	80,858	8.6	11.8	11.2
Queen Anne's	242	1,245	11,548	13.1	37.6	35.3	97.2	12,579	40,553	89,241	25.9	10.2	90,696	7.7	9.5	8.0

1. Data for serious crimes have not been adjusted for underreporting; this may affect comparability between geographic areas and over time.   2. Per 100,000 population estimated by the FBI.   3. All persons 3 years old and over enrolled in nursery school through college.   4. Persons 25 years old and over.   5. Elementary and secondary education expenditures.   6. Based on population estimated by the American Community Survey, 2011–2015.

Table B. States and Counties — **Personal Income and Earnings**

STATE County	Personal income, 2017 Total (mil dol)	Percent change 2016-2017	Per capita Dollars	Per capita Rank	Wages and salaries (mil dol)	Pension and insurance	Government social insurance	Proprietors' income (mil dol)	Dividends, interest, and rent (mil dol)	Personal transfer receipts (mil dol)	Earnings, 2017 Total (mil dol)	From employee and self-employed	From employer
	62	63	64	65	66	67	68	69	70	71	72	73	74
LOUISIANA— Cont'd													
Orleans	19,359	3.0	49,222	516	11,144	1,858	751	2,061	4,687	3,517	15,814	844	751
Ouachita	6,179	2.1	39,643	1,613	3,091	570	198	482	1,004	1,625	4,342	243	198
Plaquemines	1,136	3.4	48,666	574	896	189	58	170	184	190	1,313	67	58
Pointe Coupee	946	3.5	42,469	1,208	215	43	15	45	138	240	319	22	15
Rapides	5,870	2.8	44,588	951	2,501	515	164	638	960	1,786	3,818	211	164
Red River	314	3.6	36,840	2,071	115	25	7	8	58	102	156	9	7
Richland	744	2.0	36,473	2,120	233	51	16	43	87	269	342	21	16
Sabine	784	3.5	32,635	2,667	202	47	13	70	124	268	331	21	13
St. Bernard	1,455	3.6	31,482	2,808	526	147	32	87	209	377	792	43	32
St. Charles	2,495	2.5	47,299	688	1,775	384	110	137	338	418	2,406	127	110
St. Helena	430	2.4	41,512	1,327	62	17	4	11	41	148	93	8	4
St. James	960	4.3	44,911	908	568	135	34	50	104	210	787	43	34
St. John the Baptist	1,692	1.6	38,945	1,730	892	197	56	89	183	427	1,235	70	56
St. Landry	3,300	1.3	39,519	1,635	954	205	60	174	490	1,076	1,393	89	60
St. Martin	1,973	1.7	36,420	2,129	529	100	34	96	269	521	759	50	34
St. Mary	1,903	0.6	37,341	1,980	1,096	205	68	71	359	563	1,441	83	68
St. Tammany	14,266	2.3	55,656	258	4,435	753	277	1,541	2,584	2,300	7,007	393	277
Tangipahoa	5,010	4.2	37,814	1,910	1,753	396	106	298	619	1,454	2,553	139	106
Tensas	165	3.3	35,824	2,222	40	9	2	16	39	61	67	4	2
Terrebonne	4,367	-1.1	38,958	1,728	2,641	417	172	259	746	1,053	3,489	204	172
Union	842	4.0	37,303	1,988	174	39	12	63	113	260	287	19	12
Vermilion	2,228	2.3	37,050	2,026	562	121	34	141	345	557	858	52	34
Vernon	1,994	2.5	39,306	1,671	1,060	285	93	48	370	459	1,486	70	93
Washington	1,530	3.2	32,799	2,648	415	96	25	58	185	601	594	41	25
Webster	1,464	0.7	37,179	2,005	467	96	30	65	220	489	657	44	30
West Baton Rouge	1,198	2.4	45,622	837	712	132	48	73	126	221	965	53	48
West Carroll	386	3.3	35,179	2,317	97	22	6	33	48	143	158	10	6
West Feliciana	569	3.2	37,005	2,033	307	84	16	50	111	107	456	20	16
Winn	504	2.2	35,191	2,314	183	38	12	69	59	166	303	18	12
MAINE	62,060	4.2	46,485	X	28,739	5,020	2,099	4,775	11,578	13,633	40,633	2,697	2,099
Androscoggin	4,292	4.3	39,873	1,578	2,210	364	164	226	589	1,132	2,964	200	164
Aroostook	2,664	3.5	39,377	1,660	1,090	234	81	145	409	876	1,550	109	81
Cumberland	17,156	4.9	58,654	190	10,236	1,494	736	1,360	3,623	2,578	13,825	872	736
Franklin	1,119	3.4	37,315	1,984	406	83	29	74	211	322	592	42	29
Hancock	2,684	3.4	49,256	515	927	163	71	416	643	559	1,577	110	71
Kennebec	5,274	3.6	43,292	1,103	2,737	566	189	341	855	1,267	3,833	238	189
Knox	1,950	4.3	49,005	538	748	136	55	269	507	417	1,208	84	55
Lincoln	1,663	3.8	48,619	577	437	76	32	160	452	377	705	55	32
Oxford	2,082	4.0	36,239	2,162	673	127	49	144	353	619	994	76	49
Penobscot	6,061	3.5	39,885	1,574	3,097	590	222	301	929	1,580	4,210	276	222
Piscataquis	608	3.0	36,224	2,169	206	49	15	36	111	212	307	23	15
Sagadahoc	1,758	4.8	49,679	483	827	157	64	109	388	344	1,157	76	64
Somerset	1,844	1.5	36,426	2,127	725	129	55	114	281	608	1,023	76	55
Waldo	1,541	4.2	38,681	1,781	493	82	37	130	290	414	742	56	37
Washington	1,226	1.3	38,799	1,755	409	92	31	137	200	438	668	47	31
York	10,139	4.9	49,653	485	3,517	678	269	815	1,738	1,888	5,279	358	269
MARYLAND	368,258	4.1	61,123	X	172,935	29,919	12,791	35,544	70,024	50,568	251,188	14,385	12,791
Allegany	2,816	2.6	39,320	1,669	1,293	274	107	136	519	934	1,810	120	107
Anne Arundel	37,059	4.0	64,648	105	21,552	4,191	1,654	2,486	7,208	4,247	29,884	1,662	1,654
Baltimore	49,224	4.2	59,130	180	22,790	3,772	1,675	3,578	10,270	7,722	31,815	1,895	1,675
Calvert	5,497	3.7	60,080	156	1,459	247	105	243	987	676	2,054	128	105
Caroline	1,488	5.8	44,832	924	416	85	32	158	221	364	691	41	32
Carroll	10,153	3.5	60,512	148	2,854	469	212	592	1,599	1,362	4,127	258	212
Cecil	4,732	3.8	46,059	788	1,663	332	129	239	728	950	2,363	147	129
Charles	8,820	4.5	55,231	269	2,145	434	164	324	1,434	1,140	3,067	187	164
Dorchester	1,452	4.0	45,141	885	484	104	37	122	275	416	747	47	37
Frederick	14,934	4.8	59,259	174	5,684	975	425	919	2,420	1,755	8,004	470	425
Garrett	1,281	3.1	43,824	1,040	452	93	35	108	267	323	689	45	35
Harford	14,263	3.8	56,564	234	5,398	1,090	422	629	2,261	2,096	7,539	453	422
Howard	24,064	4.3	74,938	53	12,575	1,569	893	1,923	4,173	1,910	16,959	976	893
Kent	1,153	4.6	59,466	168	345	65	27	116	370	256	552	36	27
Montgomery	91,202	4.8	86,136	26	38,155	5,949	2,739	16,570	19,566	6,680	63,412	3,443	2,739
Prince George's	43,233	3.5	47,365	679	20,406	4,056	1,549	1,797	7,242	6,343	27,808	1,602	1,549
Queen Anne's	3,085	4.7	61,995	137	663	121	50	264	609	425	1,097	68	50

1. Based on the resident population estimated as of July 1 of the year shown.

Table B. States and Counties — Earnings, Social Security, and Housing

STATE County	Earnings, 2017 (cont.) Percent by selected industries									Social Security beneficiaries, December 2017		Supple-mental Security Income recipients, 2017	Housing units, 2018	
	Farm	Mining, quarrying, and extractions	Construction	Manu-facturing	Information; professional, scientific, technical services	Retail trade	Finance, insurance, real estate, and leasing	Health care and social assistance	Govern-ment	Number	Rate[1]		Total	Percent change, 2010-2018
	75	76	77	78	79	80	81	82	83	84	85	86	87	88
LOUISIANA— Cont'd														
Orleans	0	2.4	2.5	2.4	17.1	3.6	7.2	9.9	19.8	63,325	161	20,496	191,627	0.9
Ouachita	0.4	0.5	5.9	8.9	9.8	7	7.7	19.2	15.8	29,755	191	6,988	69,018	7
Plaquemines	0.5	12.5	5.3	14.7	D	2.3	3.8	1.2	15	3,735	160	583	10,396	8.3
Pointe Coupee	1.4	2.1	5	8.1	D	10.6	9.2	D	19.9	4,970	223	1,008	11,613	4.4
Rapides	0.7	0.4	6.7	7.5	5.1	10.4	4.7	20.8	21.9	28,960	220	6,834	58,396	4.9
Red River	0.8	11.6	5.3	14.9	3.1	4.1	3.2	D	23.3	1,725	202	465	4,204	1.8
Richland	4.1	D	D	D	D	8.1	5.1	D	17.8	4,615	226	1,096	9,039	4.9
Sabine	9.6	1.5	5.1	16.8	5.7	7.7	4.8	D	21.1	5,780	241	1,009	15,198	7.6
St. Bernard	0.2	D	D	32.3	D	6.3	1.8	D	18.2	7,030	152	1,793	17,172	2.3
St. Charles	0	D	14.6	32.4	5	D	2.1	3	10.1	9,450	179	1,180	20,835	4.5
St. Helena	1.8	D	5.6	19	D	4.1	D	D	36	3,320	320	944	5,364	4.1
St. James	0.3	D	2.3	50.8	D	2.7	3.2	D	13.1	4,620	216	719	8,996	6.4
St. John the Baptist	0.1	2.5	14.4	31.9	3.4	5.1	3.3	D	11.9	8,920	205	1,776	17,851	2.3
St. Landry	0.1	1.8	7.4	6.9	5.8	11.2	4.2	15.1	21.6	20,100	241	5,411	36,928	3.5
St. Martin	0.1	5.1	6.5	22.3	D	8.9	7.2	8.9	14.7	11,120	205	1,762	23,619	7.7
St. Mary	-0.6	15.2	4.5	20.8	3	5	6.7	D	18.7	11,540	226	2,282	23,657	2.7
St. Tammany	0.1	8.6	8.8	4.2	8.7	7.6	7	12.4	14.8	51,410	201	4,905	104,826	9.9
Tangipahoa	0.2	0.4	5	5.1	6.4	11.5	5.6	10.4	28.9	23,970	181	5,150	56,361	12.6
Tensas	19	D	D	2.1	D	D	D	D	25.4	1,230	267	390	3,435	2.3
Terrebonne	0.2	12.9	7.7	10	7.4	6.6	6.1	13.1	9.8	22,750	203	4,769	45,711	4.4
Union	9.7	0.1	8.3	18.9	D	7.4	4.6	9.2	18.8	5,530	245	924	11,904	5
Vermilion	4.8	11.3	7.4	6.2	5.5	8.4	4.6	8.3	22.6	12,135	202	1,931	26,743	6
Vernon	-0.2	0	2.6	0.5	8.9	3.2	1.8	5.5	67.9	8,010	158	1,186	22,338	4.2
Washington	0.3	0.4	9.2	15.7	D	7.1	3.7	D	26.7	11,410	245	2,877	21,756	3.5
Webster	-0.2	4.2	8.4	13.5	D	10.2	5.3	D	18.3	10,055	255	1,983	19,745	2.1
West Baton Rouge	-0.4	D	24.4	26.3	D	5.3	D	D	11.3	4,545	173	802	11,223	20.4
West Carroll	12.2	D	D	D	D	7.4	2.5	7.1	29.9	2,750	250	503	5,190	2.9
West Feliciana	2.3	D	6.6	6.3	D	3.8	D	D	34.8	2,065	134	310	5,536	8.6
Winn	2.1	1.4	5.9	15.3	2	4.6	8.5	22.2	13.7	3,220	225	595	7,320	1.2
MAINE	0.4	0	7.2	9.1	8.3	7.7	7.2	16.1	17.7	338,770	254	37,309	746,596	3.4
Androscoggin	0.4	D	7.4	10.9	7.4	7.9	5.9	21	11.7	25,955	241	4,215	50,056	2
Aroostook	1.3	0	4.8	12.1	3.3	8.9	4.6	18.4	25.2	20,725	306	2,677	39,981	1.1
Cumberland	0.1	D	5.9	6.6	12.5	6.3	12.6	16.7	11.2	61,275	209	5,386	145,740	5.1
Franklin	0.6	0.1	7.2	14.3	D	9.7	3.8	D	20.5	8,100	270	940	22,277	2.6
Hancock	0.4	D	11.3	3.8	12	8.8	4.4	12.4	13.1	14,860	273	1,046	41,414	3.1
Kennebec	0.4	D	5	4.9	6.4	8.3	3.6	16.2	30.9	31,340	257	4,091	62,923	3.2
Knox	0.1	0	8.8	8.9	6.6	8.4	5	13.9	13.5	11,465	288	834	24,492	3.2
Lincoln	0.3	D	12.9	D	7.9	9.2	4.8	13.4	13.8	10,650	311	680	24,064	2.5
Oxford	0.3	0.1	9.6	16.2	4.1	9.3	3.3	13.6	17.9	16,480	287	1,997	37,114	2.9
Penobscot	0.2	D	5.9	3.9	5.3	9.2	4.7	23.8	20.7	37,695	248	5,545	76,136	3.1
Piscataquis	0.4	D	6.5	22.1	D	9.8	2.6	D	27.3	5,365	320	703	15,486	0.9
Sagadahoc	0.4	0	9.4	D	7.2	5.5	2.5	4.8	12.5	9,170	259	664	18,935	3.6
Somerset	3.4	D	14.5	15.8	3.4	8.2	3	14.5	15	14,780	292	2,160	30,968	1.3
Waldo	0.6	D	10.5	7.8	4.5	8.1	8.8	14.9	12.5	10,960	275	1,270	22,611	4.8
Washington	4.3	D	5	9.9	3.2	8.1	3.5	14	23.9	9,725	308	1,350	23,363	1.6
York	0.1	0.1	9.1	11.2	6.3	7.8	4.1	11	27.1	50,225	246	3,751	111,036	5
MARYLAND	0.2	0.1	6.7	4.2	16.3	5	10.9	10.8	23.3	983,736	163	122,312	2,458,801	3.4
Allegany	-0.1	0.3	3.8	9.7	4.5	7.4	5	22.4	25.3	17,485	244	2,350	32,826	-1.4
Anne Arundel	0	0	5.9	5.8	13.9	4.7	5.3	7.6	35	91,260	159	7,745	226,420	6.5
Baltimore	0.1	0	7.1	4.6	12.3	6.4	14.2	13.5	17.4	157,220	189	16,372	337,210	0.5
Calvert	-0.3	0	D	D	6.7	5.4	4.9	11.7	16.8	15,135	165	984	35,416	4.8
Caroline	9.4	D	10.7	9.9	D	8.2	D	D	17.9	7,140	215	840	13,655	1.3
Carroll	0.4	D	13.8	7.8	11.4	7.9	6.6	13.6	14.4	32,105	191	1,606	63,726	2.1
Cecil	1	0.4	7.1	19.9	D	5.6	2.7	9.9	23.4	19,925	194	1,873	42,676	3.8
Charles	-0.1	D	12.6	1.4	6.3	13.4	4.8	10.1	31.5	22,585	141	2,309	61,248	11.4
Dorchester	5.8	D	D	18.4	4.5	5	3.4	D	24.7	8,420	262	1,280	16,777	1.3
Frederick	0.2	D	D	D	D	D	D	D	19.6	39,785	158	2,297	99,041	9.9
Garrett	0.2	3.6	9.6	7.6	5.3	10.9	D	D	16.1	7,545	258	603	19,426	2.9
Harford	0.1	0.1	6.7	5.5	13.2	6.3	5.4	10.3	33	47,090	187	3,458	100,968	5.7
Howard	0	D	7.7	4.7	29.5	4.7	10	7.4	9.1	40,965	128	3,541	120,838	10.6
Kent	1.9	0	8.8	10.3	D	D	10.8	11	13.1	5,680	293	376	10,692	1.4
Montgomery	0	0	4.5	3.2	23.9	3.8	18.7	8.4	19.6	137,355	130	14,231	390,664	3.9
Prince George's	0	D	10.8	2.3	11.8	6.1	3.7	8	37.2	119,275	131	14,417	333,862	1.7
Queen Anne's	2.2	D	10.1	7.7	D	9	5.3	6.2	17.6	10,000	201	361	21,315	5.8

1. Per 1,000 resident population estimated as of July 1 of the year shown.

Table B. States and Counties — Housing, Labor Force, and Employment

STATE County	Housing units, 2013-2017 — Total	Occupied units — Percent	Owner-occupied — Median value[1]	Median owner cost as a percent of income — With a mortgage	Median owner cost as a percent of income — Without a mortgage[2]	Renter-occupied — Median rent[3]	Renter-occupied — Median rent as a percent of income[2]	Sub-standard units[4] (percent)	Civilian labor force, 2018 — Total	Percent change, 2017-2018	Unemployment — Total	Unemployment — Rate[5]	Civilian employment[6], 2013-2017 — Total	Percent — Management, business, science, and arts occupations	Percent — Construction, production, and maintenance occupations
	89	90	91	92	93	94	95	96	97	98	99	100	101	102	103
LOUISIANA— Cont'd															
Orleans	154,895	47.1	205,000	25.9	13.6	954	36.6	2.2	178,845	0.2	8,954	5	178,016	42.3	14.9
Ouachita	56,799	59.3	133,400	19.9	10.0	730	33	2.7	70,364	-0.3	3,661	5.2	64,288	33.8	20.7
Plaquemines	8,759	69.0	165,900	21.6	10.2	1,118	27.9	3.2	9,992	-0.1	462	4.6	9,849	32.4	30.3
Pointe Coupee	8,815	76.2	124,500	19.6	10.0	730	26.6	5.4	9,999	0.1	536	5.4	9,422	22.6	29.7
Rapides	48,032	61.3	133,800	19.6	10.0	780	32.6	2.6	55,281	-1.4	2,935	5.3	53,417	32.4	22.2
Red River	3,374	74.6	85,900	16.7	10.0	532	28.1	2.8	4,033	4.6	179	4.4	3,366	27.0	33.7
Richland	7,500	63.4	86,900	17.6	10.0	609	29.2	3.8	8,318	0.1	519	6.2	8,098	24.8	27.2
Sabine	9,174	74.2	84,200	16.5	10.0	530	30.8	2.5	9,009	2.1	467	5.2	8,598	29.0	35.1
St. Bernard	14,791	67.6	139,200	20.3	10.0	875	35.4	2.3	19,519	0.1	978	5	18,382	25.6	31.0
St. Charles	18,925	80.3	185,800	19.0	10.0	893	29.5	2	24,916	0.1	1,094	4.4	24,457	33.4	25.7
St. Helena	3,990	82.8	77,400	26.8	11.1	608	21.9	2.7	4,329	0.4	284	6.6	3,652	29.1	31.5
St. James	7,887	77.4	136,400	19.4	10.0	725	24.3	3.2	9,327	-0.5	576	6.2	9,193	22.3	35.5
St. John the Baptist	15,421	76.1	152,800	20.9	10.0	914	31.2	2.9	19,641	-0.3	1,117	5.7	19,280	28.9	29.6
St. Landry	30,467	69.8	99,200	20.2	10.6	616	36.5	3.4	31,933	-0.3	1,992	6.2	30,554	28.6	26.4
St. Martin	19,435	79.8	114,200	19.0	10.0	664	28.2	4.8	22,399	-0.5	1,173	5.2	23,899	26.2	32.1
St. Mary	20,032	62.5	97,000	19.5	10.8	752	26.7	3.5	20,103	-1.2	1,325	6.6	21,085	22.6	35.1
St. Tammany	91,353	78.2	206,600	21.5	10.0	1,012	31.1	1.8	117,656	0.3	4,928	4.2	115,543	39.4	18.2
Tangipahoa	47,598	68.2	149,300	19.4	10.0	783	34.4	2.8	54,353	-0.8	2,979	5.5	55,791	29.0	25.8
Tensas	1,930	62.0	62,200	24.5	13.3	441	43.8	6.1	1,460	-5.8	113	7.7	1,506	27.9	31.2
Terrebonne	40,177	71.1	143,700	19.8	10.0	876	28.6	3.4	46,432	-0.6	2,323	5	47,254	26.8	31.9
Union	7,971	81.6	88,700	21.1	10.0	466	33	3.5	9,153	-0.4	519	5.7	8,431	25.1	37.1
Vermilion	21,721	76.5	105,700	17.7	10.0	669	24.9	4.9	24,196	0	1,276	5.3	24,871	26.0	31.4
Vernon	17,930	52.4	116,600	17.2	10.0	952	28.6	1.8	16,040	-1.9	1,057	6.6	17,386	30.7	26.0
Washington	17,542	71.5	84,600	23.3	10.0	582	33.3	3.9	16,835	-0.5	968	5.7	16,259	24.7	29.7
Webster	15,854	70.0	81,600	22.8	11.3	633	34.9	3.5	14,668	-0.6	897	6.1	15,407	25.6	34.0
West Baton Rouge	9,436	73.4	177,000	17.5	10.0	815	26.7	2.7	13,528	0.4	601	4.4	12,225	31.9	28.7
West Carroll	4,182	74.2	79,400	16.7	10.0	523	26.6	3	3,890	-2.6	358	9.2	3,820	31.2	30.3
West Feliciana	3,947	73.5	209,600	22.3	10.7	853	21.6	1.9	5,334	0.2	212	4	5,504	34.3	19.1
Winn	5,382	65.2	72,700	16.7	10.1	580	35.3	1.3	4,925	-2.5	309	6.3	5,035	27.5	32.9
MAINE	554,061	72.0	179,900	22.1	13.2	808	29.7	2.1	698,745	0	23,524	3.4	658,693	36.6	21.9
Androscoggin	45,263	64.0	152,000	22.1	13.8	724	29.1	2.7	55,449	-0.2	1,828	3.3	53,532	33.2	23.9
Aroostook	29,844	71.7	97,000	19.8	12.3	565	28.9	1.8	31,085	-1.4	1,496	4.8	30,233	31.6	27.6
Cumberland	118,807	68.6	259,400	22.6	13.6	1,029	29.9	1.7	165,409	0.5	4,436	2.7	157,303	45.1	14.9
Franklin	11,577	79.8	136,300	20.8	11.7	596	27.7	2.2	14,471	0.2	581	4	14,426	32.0	25.2
Hancock	23,674	73.7	207,300	22.3	12.4	812	28.3	3.1	29,407	0.2	1,116	3.8	26,527	34.0	24.5
Kennebec	51,055	70.2	154,500	20.5	13.0	727	29	2.3	62,541	-0.3	2,024	3.2	58,332	37.1	19.7
Knox	17,022	76.3	199,600	23.7	13.5	790	28.3	2.4	20,584	-0.7	663	3.2	19,568	33.6	25.3
Lincoln	15,241	78.3	211,900	22.4	12.4	761	29.9	1.8	16,988	-0.4	568	3.3	16,588	34.5	26.7
Oxford	20,756	79.9	137,200	22.7	13.3	683	32	2.5	26,683	-0.6	1,065	4	25,524	27.7	30.6
Penobscot	61,848	69.7	137,900	20.7	12.9	777	31.5	2.2	77,127	0.2	2,920	3.8	72,746	35.5	19.9
Piscataquis	7,477	76.2	116,100	24.4	13.4	621	31.6	2.8	7,467	-0.5	311	4.2	6,545	29.3	34.1
Sagadahoc	15,810	75.8	199,400	22.1	12.7	843	29.8	1.3	19,440	0.2	527	2.7	18,266	36.8	23.6
Somerset	21,392	76.1	108,000	21.0	13.6	714	36.7	3.4	22,888	-0.8	1,101	4.8	22,217	27.4	31.4
Waldo	16,954	79.2	159,800	22.7	13.3	791	28.1	3.1	21,250	0.4	749	3.5	18,698	35.9	24.7
Washington	14,017	75.7	110,000	22.5	13.2	619	28.1	2.3	13,961	-0.7	687	4.9	12,881	28.9	33.2
York	83,324	74.5	233,000	23.2	13.8	926	29.5	1.5	113,999	0.5	3,455	3	105,307	35.6	22.5
MARYLAND	2,181,093	66.8	296,500	22.3	11.0	1,311	30.2	2.5	3,197,137	0.1	125,485	3.9	3,040,792	45.3	15.7
Allegany	27,759	68.8	119,900	19.5	13.0	672	29.4	1.2	31,984	-0.6	1,764	5.5	28,738	29.9	21.9
Anne Arundel	205,395	74.3	346,000	22.2	10.2	1,579	28.6	1.8	309,603	0.3	10,343	3.3	290,628	47.0	14.6
Baltimore	312,859	65.8	249,600	21.5	10.9	1,224	29.8	1.9	450,366	0.2	18,202	4	420,974	43.4	15.7
Calvert	31,462	83.4	347,200	22.4	10.0	1,612	29.8	1	49,121	-0.2	1,739	3.5	45,756	41.0	21.0
Caroline	11,996	71.2	201,200	25.6	13.7	924	33.2	2.1	18,028	0.5	688	3.8	15,674	27.6	29.0
Carroll	60,432	81.8	328,100	22.1	11.1	1,131	28.7	1.2	94,339	0.4	3,062	3.2	88,335	44.0	18.2
Cecil	37,076	73.1	238,000	22.2	12.4	1,071	29.3	2.1	52,632	-0.2	2,317	4.4	50,620	35.2	27.0
Charles	54,988	77.3	294,000	23.5	10.0	1,618	31.1	1.5	85,104	-0.4	3,299	3.9	78,635	42.2	16.0
Dorchester	12,940	65.8	179,300	23.3	13.2	869	33	2	15,347	-1.7	799	5.2	15,240	31.8	24.7
Frederick	90,022	74.8	315,400	22.1	10.0	1,338	30.1	1.3	130,831	0.2	4,598	3.5	130,387	46.1	16.1
Garrett	11,865	77.5	167,100	23.0	10.8	646	26	1.5	15,410	-0.4	737	4.8	13,937	33.8	29.9
Harford	92,895	78.6	281,400	21.7	11.3	1,197	29.9	1.3	138,162	0.1	5,005	3.6	129,108	43.3	17.0
Howard	111,337	73.7	439,900	21.7	10.0	1,661	27.8	2.1	183,889	0.4	5,529	3	167,493	60.9	9.2
Kent	7,605	70.1	237,400	24.0	12.9	938	34.4	0.7	10,254	0.5	444	4.3	9,131	36.5	20.4
Montgomery	369,242	65.6	467,500	21.7	10.0	1,693	30.6	3.3	554,989	0.5	17,560	3.2	554,085	56.1	10.5
Prince George's	306,694	61.8	272,900	24.0	11.0	1,385	30.7	4.3	504,423	-0.3	20,573	4.1	476,889	38.7	18.5
Queen Anne's	17,995	81.1	343,200	23.5	12.8	1,325	28	1.6	27,379	0.3	917	3.3	25,556	41.9	17.3

1. Specified owner-occupied units.   2. A value of 10.0 represents 10 percent or less; a value of 50.0 represents 50 percent or more.   3. Specified renter-occupied units.   4. Overcrowded or lacking complete plumbing facilities.   5. Percent of civilian labor force.   6. Civilian employed persons 16 years old and over.

Table B. States and Counties — Nonfarm Employment and Agriculture

STATE County	Number of establish-ments	Total	Health care and social assistance	Manufac-turing	Retail trade	Finance and insurance	Professional, scientific, and technical services	Total (mil dol)	Average per employee (dollars)	Number	Fewer than 50 acres	1000 acres or more	Farm producers whose primary occupation is farming (percent)
	104	105	106	107	108	109	110	111	112	113	114	115	116
LOUISIANA— Cont'd													
Orleans	9,311	175,310	23,414	2,985	14,825	7,073	13,604	7,978	45,506	39	94.9	NA	55.6
Ouachita	4,230	63,512	15,099	4,967	10,003	3,398	2,862	2,349	36,980	488	54.1	3.7	35.1
Plaquemines	681	10,169	432	1,724	561	107	409	658	64,718	113	52.2	11.5	38.3
Pointe Coupee	340	4,263	794	342	923	186	84	161	37,676	482	45.4	10.2	43.2
Rapides	3,130	47,406	13,962	3,667	8,175	1,441	1,931	1,798	37,937	856	51.1	6.2	45.1
Red River	128	1,999	460	370	133	83	29	84	41,973	197	25.9	13.2	46.8
Richland	410	5,727	1,692	D	871	220	86	184	32,144	626	33.1	10.5	30.2
Sabine	476	4,656	739	1,109	943	204	167	149	32,070	442	39.1	1.4	47.2
St. Bernard	681	8,197	653	1,394	1,882	175	161	340	41,519	33	30.3	21.2	28.6
St. Charles	985	21,331	1,516	4,640	1,394	274	2,070	1,422	66,653	67	32.8	NA	47.3
St. Helena	112	1,245	362	272	292	37	9	41	32,997	348	45.1	1.1	42.0
St. James	315	6,490	494	2,362	565	186	184	440	67,788	56	50.0	32.1	77.4
St. John the Baptist	721	17,758	1,061	2,440	1,729	307	369	893	50,315	22	45.5	31.8	62.5
St. Landry	1,618	22,342	5,467	1,320	4,026	709	564	836	37,418	1,200	53.7	6.5	37.1
St. Martin	914	11,836	1,595	1,570	1,662	331	301	475	40,137	360	70.0	6.7	34.1
St. Mary	1,273	19,625	1,928	3,625	2,266	550	782	946	48,212	98	48.0	36.7	50.0
St. Tammany	6,345	79,379	16,123	2,749	14,077	3,232	4,820	3,425	43,144	994	80.7	0.4	30.7
Tangipahoa	2,366	35,635	8,434	2,305	6,721	2,251	1,017	1,307	36,674	967	55.0	1.1	37.4
Tensas	79	472	70	21	85	43	D	15	31,703	231	16.9	24.7	42.5
Terrebonne	2,908	47,774	7,735	4,053	7,338	1,152	2,494	2,223	46,541	213	55.9	8.5	42.6
Union	339	4,145	796	D	582	115	57	119	28,791	426	36.6	3.1	36.4
Vermilion	1,002	10,111	1,615	558	2,204	373	293	356	35,218	1,304	41.9	8.5	34.6
Vernon	701	7,950	1,836	156	1,602	289	519	267	33,547	432	57.6	1.2	35.5
Washington	630	9,630	2,680	1,003	1,411	335	1,342	303	31,472	735	55.5	1.6	44.7
Webster	787	10,098	2,314	1,247	2,096	341	159	370	36,610	431	42.0	1.9	33.0
West Baton Rouge	549	11,806	452	2,432	1,139	150	253	562	47,573	111	61.3	11.7	44.3
West Carroll	172	1,774	526	D	346	73	11	54	30,334	548	27.7	8.2	34.9
West Feliciana	190	3,082	449	D	349	80	230	167	54,270	153	34.6	17.0	30.6
Winn	288	4,117	839	748	484	110	49	151	36,576	184	31.5	2.2	34.4
MAINE	41,178	511,936	111,720	49,793	83,847	28,305	23,182	21,349	41,703	7,600	47.2	2.4	43.2
Androscoggin	2,746	46,326	10,236	5,974	6,109	3,420	1,915	1,804	38,944	496	58.7	1.0	61.0
Aroostook	1,957	21,057	5,802	2,790	4,284	815	345	728	34,581	766	21.5	10.6	46.4
Cumberland	11,319	169,797	34,624	9,708	23,138	13,972	10,417	8,149	47,995	668	66.8	0.6	43.3
Franklin	827	8,833	1,744	1,098	1,681	675	121	276	31,214	354	49.4	2.0	38.1
Hancock	2,247	16,562	3,068	975	3,509	534	1,730	680	41,030	416	45.7	1.7	44.0
Kennebec	3,223	47,486	13,120	2,612	8,793	1,183	1,689	1,807	38,058	642	49.4	1.2	35.0
Knox	1,759	14,503	3,037	1,677	2,859	761	488	544	37,483	308	58.1	NA	44.4
Lincoln	1,402	8,782	1,866	782	1,628	288	302	323	36,780	309	53.4	0.3	45.5
Oxford	1,334	14,234	2,899	2,282	2,290	310	351	488	34,281	545	46.8	0.7	36.2
Penobscot	4,144	57,622	15,015	3,066	11,164	1,921	1,789	2,187	37,954	601	41.3	3.2	44.6
Piscataquis	430	4,604	1,282	1,101	936	67	56	148	32,079	188	29.8	3.7	45.7
Sagadahoc	919	13,874	1,177	D	1,997	310	716	646	46,545	209	49.3	1.0	52.1
Somerset	1,188	13,619	2,685	2,689	2,352	276	363	543	39,836	467	29.3	5.4	43.2
Waldo	994	9,639	1,833	1,123	1,480	854	199	422	43,786	517	49.1	0.6	42.5
Washington	843	7,070	1,708	935	1,695	311	132	246	34,815	379	44.6	1.6	33.8
York	5,556	54,168	11,271	7,084	9,901	1,644	2,010	2,135	39,414	735	59.0	0.8	43.0
MARYLAND	138,480	2,282,725	370,191	97,484	294,126	101,012	276,621	121,952	53,424	12,429	54.7	3.2	42.1
Allegany	1,542	24,654	5,997	2,369	3,922	863	1,082	860	34,889	290	43.8	0.3	35.5
Anne Arundel	14,191	236,879	27,939	12,005	34,173	6,310	34,208	13,507	57,023	390	67.7	0.3	38.2
Baltimore	19,895	323,939	58,280	14,328	48,286	20,695	28,268	15,967	49,290	708	67.1	1.7	40.0
Calvert	1,732	18,837	3,453	492	3,114	302	1,836	855	45,405	280	67.1	1.4	37.3
Caroline	613	7,349	752	1,218	1,215	159	299	284	38,676	588	48.3	4.9	50.7
Carroll	4,227	50,537	10,082	3,574	8,525	1,123	2,798	1,988	39,346	1,174	61.0	2.1	40.5
Cecil	1,761	24,780	4,776	4,064	3,835	358	424	1,115	44,978	533	55.7	1.7	42.3
Charles	2,628	34,040	4,561	474	8,722	761	2,359	1,275	37,468	385	58.7	1.3	44.3
Dorchester	689	9,659	1,763	2,455	1,351	225	190	353	36,560	371	39.1	11.1	53.1
Frederick	6,128	89,689	12,078	6,277	12,569	5,510	8,958	4,267	47,580	1,373	53.5	2.5	40.8
Garrett	892	9,734	1,804	1,010	1,650	355	382	316	32,476	707	37.3	0.8	32.7
Harford	5,480	70,975	11,034	4,574	14,034	1,866	7,884	3,049	42,964	628	64.0	1.6	38.4
Howard	9,374	176,059	16,515	5,647	16,261	7,383	42,102	10,814	61,423	321	72.9	1.6	35.9
Kent	605	7,341	1,169	1,228	983	178	258	246	33,553	346	32.9	11.6	48.2
Montgomery	27,421	424,372	69,747	7,656	46,783	18,898	71,088	27,230	64,165	558	69.7	2.3	39.2
Prince George's	15,042	256,974	32,015	6,990	39,434	5,898	31,348	11,938	46,455	367	71.9	2.2	31.5
Queen Anne's	1,387	11,808	1,019	1,161	2,554	293	599	434	36,734	483	40.2	8.9	47.3

Table B. States and Counties — Agriculture

	Agriculture, 2017 (cont.)															
	Land in farms					Value of land and buildings (dollars)		Value of machinery and equiopmnet, average per farm (dollars)	Value of products sold:				Organic farms (number)	Farms with internet access (percent)	Government payments	
			Acres								Percent from:					
STATE County	Acreage (1,000)	Percent change, 2012-2017	Average size of farm	Total irrigated (1,000)	Total cropland (1,000)	Average per farm	Average per acre		Total (mil dol)	Average per farm (acres)	Crops	Livestock and poultry products			Total ($1,000)	Percent of farms
	117	118	119	120	121	122	123	124	125	126	127	128	129	130	131	132
LOUISIANA— Cont'd																
Orleans	1	376.6	14	0.0	0.0	140,455	10,355	17,365	0.2	5,231	92.2	7.8	NA	87.2	8	10.3
Ouachita	93	0.1	191	16.1	49.0	813,699	4,261	89,169	45.3	92,887	52.5	47.5	3	81.6	2,315	22.7
Plaquemines	94	5.8	833	0.1	8.0	1,174,762	1,411	60,963	10.8	95,478	45.5	54.5	1	75.2	NA	NA
Pointe Coupee	188	3.0	389	5.9	132.7	1,203,401	3,091	191,613	80.2	166,309	89.8	10.2	NA	73.0	3,798	27.4
Rapides	203	-3.7	237	26.3	131.8	889,536	3,747	134,402	147.5	172,346	91.3	8.7	1	73.6	3,482	23.8
Red River	95	-29.5	485	2.4	26.8	1,084,557	2,238	150,566	17.6	89,589	38.6	61.4	NA	71.1	1,147	29.9
Richland	218	-21.7	349	73.0	135.5	987,603	2,831	141,410	74.7	119,335	94.3	5.7	NA	62.9	9,359	61.7
Sabine	62	20.0	141	0.1	14.9	531,768	3,779	81,312	145.9	330,118	1.2	98.8	NA	64.3	1,411	25.3
St. Bernard	32	1.7	983	NA	2.8	1,722,736	1,752	116,121	4.0	121,939	1.8	98.2	NA	78.8	D	3.0
St. Charles	14	-11.6	214	0.0	2.9	746,957	3,491	60,454	1.4	21,537	17.0	83.0	NA	61.2	D	3.0
St. Helena	37	-30.5	106	0.2	12.2	441,244	4,159	50,934	20.6	59,075	5.3	94.7	NA	62.4	102	12.1
St. James	51	26.6	903	D	45.0	2,765,668	3,062	645,194	27.0	481,393	99.7	0.3	NA	76.8	49	7.1
St. John the Baptist	20	84.8	904	0.0	18.0	3,163,313	3,500	651,269	7.2	328,364	99.5	0.5	NA	59.1	NA	NA
St. Landry	267	-11.1	223	24.3	195.2	650,514	2,919	110,986	93.1	77,605	85.4	14.6	2	65.9	6,348	28.0
St. Martin	83	10.0	232	3.9	63.7	743,147	3,205	182,286	39.6	109,994	88.3	11.7	NA	66.1	1,723	16.4
St. Mary	80	5.4	818	D	72.2	2,697,959	3,298	552,607	45.1	460,510	99.0	1.0	NA	73.5	368	15.3
St. Tammany	43	26.2	43	0.4	7.7	464,732	10,731	39,617	10.0	10,063	55.7	44.3	1	77.4	NA	NA
Tangipahoa	98	-8.1	101	1.2	29.6	513,368	5,061	63,007	42.4	43,845	47.3	52.7	5	67.6	208	5.0
Tensas	202	2.7	874	55.5	166.0	2,450,887	2,803	324,337	93.5	404,827	99.7	0.3	NA	64.5	7,907	82.3
Terrebonne	79	-15.2	370	0.1	35.8	1,523,117	4,118	175,237	30.1	141,479	56.8	43.2	NA	75.1	131	3.8
Union	75	20.2	177	0.0	19.5	538,032	3,044	85,109	121.1	284,319	1.5	98.5	NA	70.7	185	3.5
Vermilion	410	44.4	314	68.1	217.0	903,947	2,877	117,984	117.3	89,923	57.1	42.9	NA	61.8	13,719	53.5
Vernon	41	-16.5	95	0.3	8.1	350,847	3,703	53,429	25.5	59,113	2.7	97.3	NA	70.4	184	15.3
Washington	81	-0.9	110	0.5	30.8	396,447	3,612	80,648	32.4	44,020	36.4	63.6	8	69.5	255	4.6
Webster	58	11.0	135	0.2	11.7	395,957	2,939	68,771	9.4	21,717	13.6	86.4	NA	66.6	74	4.4
West Baton Rouge	34	12.5	307	0.1	29.8	865,851	2,820	203,536	25.6	230,991	63.0	37.0	NA	80.2	225	18.0
West Carroll	168	1.4	307	69.8	111.1	1,010,538	3,296	115,396	62.5	114,117	96.2	3.8	NA	54.9	5,591	79.4
West Feliciana	86	-14.8	564	0.1	24.7	1,655,865	2,935	110,413	9.2	60,261	42.3	57.7	1	72.5	329	20.3
Winn	30	21.1	164	0.0	5.1	460,561	2,804	97,682	20.2	110,049	2.5	97.5	NA	76.1	282	11.4
MAINE	1,308	-10.1	172	32.3	472.5	446,614	2,596	81,792	667.0	87,758	61.3	38.7	621	83.6	8,947	10.9
Androscoggin	56	-6.4	112	1.0	24.6	395,349	3,526	68,417	40.5	81,726	37.6	62.4	18	85.1	481	10.5
Aroostook	317	-9.6	414	12.7	174.0	720,511	1,741	194,251	202.0	263,674	92.9	7.1	49	79.6	2,817	28.6
Cumberland	50	-20.2	75	0.8	15.3	511,437	6,830	59,232	25.6	38,389	60.8	39.2	38	90.6	539	5.1
Franklin	47	-4.5	133	0.1	11.1	331,253	2,484	59,248	D	D	D	D	37	87.0	277	15.5
Hancock	65	22.2	157	0.2	15.2	438,042	2,794	65,383	18.4	44,163	57.0	43.0	65	80.8	247	7.2
Kennebec	82	5.2	128	0.2	36.5	386,694	3,023	77,600	49.0	76,333	23.4	76.6	48	83.5	422	10.6
Knox	26	-12.9	83	0.3	9.9	392,714	4,725	49,648	9.1	29,597	69.9	30.1	25	78.9	46	3.6
Lincoln	25	-19.3	82	0.1	6.5	382,809	4,644	50,811	12.9	41,689	35.2	64.8	32	86.7	177	5.5
Oxford	77	2.1	141	0.8	17.5	410,809	2,914	65,022	24.1	44,253	78.5	21.5	31	85.7	836	13.8
Penobscot	105	-6.6	175	1.6	41.1	432,698	2,466	93,820	50.9	84,717	35.6	64.4	33	79.0	603	9.2
Piscataquis	51	9.4	272	0.0	8.7	382,344	1,408	84,800	9.1	48,447	47.2	52.8	24	79.8	107	16.0
Sagadahoc	18	-12.0	85	0.1	5.2	349,864	4,134	52,958	D	D	D	D	31	85.2	379	8.1
Somerset	146	4.1	312	0.3	35.8	460,950	1,476	117,809	83.9	179,724	66.3	33.7	53	84.2	475	13.7
Waldo	57	-56.7	109	D	21.5	327,769	2,998	52,008	23.0	44,400	36.9	63.1	81	85.9	908	9.5
Washington	125	-16.2	329	D	31.2	505,172	1,534	65,445	D	D	D	D	19	78.6	55	3.2
York	61	-5.4	83	1.6	18.3	425,179	5,120	60,944	28.6	38,846	82.5	17.5	37	83.9	578	5.4
MARYLAND	1,990	-2.0	160	124.8	1,426.7	1,258,691	7,861	124,871	2,472.8	198,955	38.3	61.7	134	76.9	44,410	28.7
Allegany	35	-2.7	122	0.0	13.2	680,294	5,592	53,733	4.2	14,362	73.0	27.0	1	61.4	245	22.8
Anne Arundel	27	-3.9	69	0.2	14.6	713,958	10,312	65,583	18.2	46,549	70.7	29.3	1	85.9	322	7.2
Baltimore	76	8.1	108	0.7	50.5	1,594,001	14,825	103,714	67.5	95,367	86.9	13.1	10	80.5	1,327	14.8
Calvert	25	-23.6	90	0.3	12.7	921,361	10,257	67,836	6.3	22,579	90.2	9.8	NA	76.4	147	9.6
Caroline	128	-14.8	218	32.4	109.0	1,551,852	7,126	175,992	277.4	471,815	25.5	74.5	3	68.5	3,482	46.8
Carroll	147	10.7	125	1.6	109.4	1,022,466	8,178	117,957	110.4	94,078	65.6	34.4	5	81.9	3,501	33.4
Cecil	74	-3.7	138	1.5	54.6	1,109,934	8,017	139,348	136.8	256,700	57.0	43.0	8	79.5	1,475	22.1
Charles	41	-12.1	107	0.5	26.0	1,007,714	9,458	100,760	14.1	36,532	88.4	11.6	4	76.1	789	17.7
Dorchester	132	4.5	356	29.9	97.0	2,022,110	5,676	229,945	188.7	508,553	30.5	69.5	NA	70.4	4,484	70.6
Frederick	189	3.9	137	1.2	140.7	1,307,843	9,522	122,029	131.6	95,835	48.3	51.7	31	80.3	3,980	26.5
Garrett	90	-5.1	128	0.1	42.7	582,887	4,561	82,214	29.0	41,068	42.4	57.6	11	63.6	260	7.4
Harford	74	13.4	118	0.6	51.7	1,289,892	10,906	107,318	45.9	73,065	74.3	25.7	2	84.7	1,411	20.7
Howard	32	-13.4	101	0.4	17.8	925,165	9,156	86,214	27.3	84,919	86.3	13.7	NA	85.7	240	10.6
Kent	134	0.8	388	10.1	109.2	2,564,409	6,609	248,381	111.2	321,428	61.6	38.4	16	82.1	3,429	69.7
Montgomery	66	3.2	117	1.2	48.7	964,640	8,213	102,089	42.6	76,310	88.8	11.2	4	90.0	1,179	14.3
Prince George's	34	5.5	94	0.8	17.7	762,242	8,132	76,284	17.6	47,872	86.8	13.2	NA	80.4	135	8.4
Queen Anne's	163	3.9	337	16.7	135.8	2,476,771	7,339	191,888	180.6	373,822	50.7	49.3	15	84.7	4,235	59.2

Table B. States and Counties — Water Use, Wholesale Trade, Retail Trade, and Real Estate

STATE County	Water use, 2015		Wholesale Trade[1], 2012				Retail Trade[2], 2012				Real estate and rental and leasing,[2] 2012			
	Public supply water withdrawn (mil gal/day)	Public supply gallons withdrawn per person per day	Number of establishments	Number of employees	Sales (mil dol)	Average payroll (mil dol)	Number of establishments	Number of employees	Sales (mil dol)	Average payroll (mil dol)	Number of establishments	Number of employees	Sales (mil dol)	Average payroll (mil dol)
	133	134	135	136	137	138	139	140	141	142	143	144	145	146
LOUISIANA— Cont'd														
Orleans	140.90	361.6	256	3,794	2,687.0	191.5	1,275	12,371	3,245.1	337.8	379	2,156	411.6	79.1
Ouachita	24.18	154.2	182	D	D	D	710	9,203	2,387.1	205.9	185	1,145	228.0	37.9
Plaquemines	7.14	303.9	54	982	2,228.3	57.5	66	499	134.1	13.3	41	364	116.3	23.0
Pointe Coupee	3.54	159.1	10	140	436.2	6.3	77	775	201.2	17.0	12	37	10.7	1.7
Rapides	18.91	143.1	123	D	D	D	584	7,769	2,211.5	188.3	137	D	D	D
Red River	1.00	116.4	7	70	22.9	2.3	18	154	37.3	2.6	3	D	D	D
Richland	3.64	177.4	21	234	529.8	13.8	65	715	250.4	16.9	16	113	8.1	2.0
Sabine	2.34	96.8	14	123	55.8	4.6	79	860	217.2	19.3	13	23	3.1	0.4
St. Bernard	7.16	157.7	26	D	D	D	137	1,432	392.2	35.7	19	60	8.9	2.2
St. Charles	9.09	172.1	73	1,944	4,939.9	105.6	112	1,184	402.9	31.0	35	172	49.9	9.3
St. Helena	0.90	85.2	2	D	D	D	29	345	80.0	4.4	2	D	D	D
St. James	4.00	185.5	10	D	D	D	50	490	128.6	10.7	6	14	1.8	0.3
St. John the Baptist	7.45	170.8	29	D	D	D	118	1,586	479.2	36.4	29	199	58.2	8.7
St. Landry	10.31	123.0	59	578	782.4	24.5	305	3,806	976.8	86.8	53	674	124.3	31.0
St. Martin	4.67	86.7	52	795	458.3	43.5	142	1,615	559.0	33.9	38	814	352.9	59.5
St. Mary	9.32	176.5	75	D	D	D	198	2,295	605.2	54.2	80	1,141	259.8	65.0
St. Tammany	23.64	94.5	244	2,224	5,060.2	125.1	915	12,433	3,550.7	301.2	215	1,112	250.7	55.5
Tangipahoa	15.06	117.0	86	1,701	1,300.4	68.5	438	6,290	1,769.7	144.7	94	498	86.5	18.5
Tensas	1.16	244.7	9	72	195.4	3.7	15	78	27.7	1.8	NA	NA	NA	NA
Terrebonne	1.88	16.5	196	2,102	996.0	113.8	503	7,070	1,929.4	170.2	167	1,690	471.5	101.9
Union	4.40	195.8	5	D	D	D	66	609	141.3	14.4	5	9	1.3	0.2
Vermilion	7.07	118.1	33	307	235.8	15.1	180	2,057	577.3	47.8	39	224	41.9	9.0
Vernon	4.35	85.6	18	90	57.3	3.3	134	1,537	426.7	34.7	31	268	70.5	11.3
Washington	4.63	99.8	20	118	128.3	3.5	138	1,152	297.0	26.5	15	41	4.0	0.8
Webster	5.36	133.9	34	394	204.7	15.4	163	2,193	549.4	47.2	33	155	34.4	6.7
West Baton Rouge	7.21	282.9	43	755	967.9	41.2	85	1,173	455.5	25.3	11	121	29.2	5.9
West Carroll	1.39	123.1	5	D	D	D	34	397	87.4	7.8	5	12	1.8	0.3
West Feliciana	1.67	108.5	3	D	D	D	28	283	86.6	5.7	6	D	D	D
Winn	2.01	138.0	10	108	65.2	3.8	48	543	113.9	11.3	8	29	3.3	0.8
MAINE	84.97	63.9	1,344	14,753	12,961.3	691.5	6,351	80,155	21,521.7	1,884.6	1,580	6,242	1,100.4	220.6
Androscoggin	7.92	73.9	102	1,236	473.9	54.6	439	6,018	1,818.1	138.5	111	376	62.9	11.6
Aroostook	4.11	59.9	72	503	308.9	21.8	346	4,186	1,119.4	90.0	76	252	50.4	6.5
Cumberland	25.35	87.4	456	5,956	5,925.3	308.3	1,448	21,738	5,751.4	522.3	516	2,787	519.6	109.3
Franklin	1.36	45.3	14	D	D	D	161	1,623	395.5	34.4	27	68	8.2	1.6
Hancock	6.69	122.4	59	464	244.5	14.7	379	3,471	852.6	86.4	80	185	27.2	5.5
Kennebec	6.15	51.3	96	1,990	1,613.7	96.4	526	8,111	2,179.3	201.2	99	429	65.5	14.1
Knox	3.02	75.8	49	256	165.9	9.6	257	2,656	632.9	60.7	69	151	22.2	5.5
Lincoln	0.73	21.5	30	D	D	D	210	1,648	421.7	39.6	49	114	15.2	3.2
Oxford	2.85	49.8	34	D	D	D	224	2,212	611.4	53.6	37	129	14.6	3.5
Penobscot	4.79	31.4	162	1,794	955.4	82.3	735	10,931	3,203.1	249.6	172	692	123.3	22.9
Piscataquis	0.88	52.0	8	D	D	D	91	823	212.2	19.0	12	27	3.3	0.6
Sagadahoc	1.41	40.1	22	108	43.5	3.8	141	1,864	465.5	42.8	32	60	8.7	1.9
Somerset	1.82	35.6	28	176	61.1	6.6	213	2,353	611.0	51.9	31	219	48.7	10.0
Waldo	0.99	25.3	23	D	D	D	163	1,479	365.7	34.4	29	59	7.1	2.1
Washington	1.57	49.6	45	230	125.4	5.2	150	1,670	433.1	37.1	20	46	4.1	1.2
York	15.33	76.2	144	1,163	818.2	55.2	868	9,372	2,448.7	223.0	220	648	119.4	21.0
MARYLAND	749.52	124.8	4,768	73,369	60,734.2	4,378.5	18,179	281,678	76,379.7	7,168.5	6,001	42,838	13,410.1	2,253.2
Allegany	0.67	9.2	45	D	D	D	288	3,854	922.8	81.5	52	199	29.3	5.6
Anne Arundel	39.49	70.0	492	8,187	7,606.5	484.5	2,005	33,052	8,758.8	831.2	566	4,232	1,254.5	203.5
Baltimore	209.46	252.0	749	10,796	5,548.5	609.6	2,745	47,973	12,645.7	1,235.1	855	6,432	3,201.7	344.6
Calvert	2.49	27.5	42	268	91.8	13.6	205	2,955	848.4	72.4	80	285	79.2	15.3
Caroline	0.98	30.1	21	186	118.9	8.3	86	980	476.2	28.7	15	D	D	D
Carroll	7.05	42.1	150	1,286	723.9	61.7	495	7,901	2,245.2	184.3	137	474	83.1	15.7
Cecil	3.60	35.2	60	D	D	D	264	3,895	1,146.3	87.9	72	191	27.7	5.5
Charles	7.32	46.9	56	435	950.4	21.1	495	8,729	2,245.0	207.7	107	394	97.3	13.3
Dorchester	2.65	81.8	32	276	234.2	12.2	100	1,133	288.7	25.4	37	92	8.3	2.6
Frederick	13.79	56.2	199	2,212	1,185.8	119.4	736	11,814	3,267.7	299.3	246	864	207.0	39.8
Garrett	2.74	93.0	23	D	D	D	136	1,714	517.9	39.1	34	D	D	D
Harford	9.84	39.3	170	1,865	2,420.7	99.4	723	13,420	3,792.9	342.6	215	751	192.9	27.9
Howard	0.01	0.0	478	11,707	9,266.7	784.1	854	15,811	4,867.7	427.7	379	3,356	1,025.9	181.9
Kent	1.09	55.1	24	172	127.1	6.9	99	848	185.9	18.6	25	57	18.0	2.0
Montgomery	354.94	341.3	676	9,113	10,456.8	672.7	2,702	46,240	13,706.2	1,333.7	1,324	12,342	4,534.5	829.3
Prince George's	52.34	57.5	536	11,108	7,639.8	651.0	2,217	36,414	9,358.1	907.2	640	6,216	1,186.5	281.3
Queen Anne's	1.77	36.2	70	778	353.0	37.8	210	2,305	547.5	49.1	47	155	36.1	4.8

1 Merchant wholesalers, except manufacturers' sales branches and offices.   2. Employer establishments.

Table B. States and Counties — Professional Services, Manufacturing, and Accommodation and Food Services

STATE County	Professional, scientific, and technical services, 2012				Manufacturing, 2012				Accommodation and food services, 2012			
	Number of establish-ments	Number of employees	Sales (mil dol)	Average payroll (mil dol)	Number of establish-ments	Number of employees	Receipts (mil dol)	Annual payroll (mil dol)	Number of establis-hments	Number of employees	Receipts (mil dol)	Annual payroll (mil dol)
	147	148	149	150	151	152	153	154	155	156	157	158
LOUISIANA— Cont'd												
Orleans	1,450	13,212	2,613.2	971.7	144	6,049	4,352.7	335.6	1,300	35,510	2,765.4	764.7
Ouachita	435	2,696	373.8	123.8	126	D	D	D	294	D	D	D
Plaquemines	51	382	114.7	28.9	37	2,174	D	192.2	61	737	59.8	18.8
Pointe Coupee	30	99	15.8	5.4	8	385	D	16.0	37	344	18.5	3.8
Rapides	285	D	D	D	72	3,851	D	217.3	237	4,330	216.8	58.3
Red River	9	29	4.0	1.0	4	194	D	8.2	10	D	D	D
Richland	27	92	10.4	2.8	11	904	396.5	37.5	24	D	D	D
Sabine	50	185	19.8	7.6	16	753	D	36.1	25	D	D	D
St. Bernard	34	148	14.2	4.3	33	1,195	11,904.0	109.8	81	D	D	D
St. Charles	95	1,402	162.3	75.5	40	4,695	29,174.8	471.2	82	995	49.3	12.7
St. Helena	6	16	2.2	0.4	5	257	D	D	8	D	D	D
St. James	17	75	8.0	3.3	24	2,156	D	201.7	25	D	D	D
St. John the Baptist	57	335	46.3	15.3	24	2,788	D	234.5	75	1,235	58.5	14.4
St. Landry	142	553	78.8	25.3	57	1,353	3,421.2	60.8	99	1,594	76.6	21.0
St. Martin	100	325	50.6	13.5	69	1,911	D	86.0	75	1,321	63.2	15.5
St. Mary	104	614	97.7	34.5	81	4,170	1,901.2	249.1	107	2,823	201.1	55.7
St. Tammany	844	5,154	700.8	292.6	123	3,676	D	205.3	556	9,615	443.8	128.0
Tangipahoa	208	889	93.5	33.6	79	2,389	681.2	84.4	213	4,285	185.8	50.9
Tensas	2	D	D	D	3	13	D	D	6	D	D	D
Terrebonne	287	2,797	353.6	138.9	143	6,301	1,538.3	343.2	235	5,138	295.2	84.7
Union	14	41	5.3	1.4	10	D	D	24.9	16	D	D	D
Vermilion	118	291	33.0	11.6	40	636	D	24.9	61	928	49.4	11.3
Vernon	86	725	70.3	32.6	14	200	D	6.4	66	1,412	58.8	16.2
Washington	43	133	19.4	5.2	27	1,027	616.1	65.5	61	713	33.5	8.5
Webster	53	247	21.0	6.4	29	1,436	D	D	61	807	34.8	8.7
West Baton Rouge	26	238	22.2	8.1	36	2,300	7,272.3	151.5	56	878	49.1	10.9
West Carroll	11	D	D	D	3	D	D	D	11	186	6.3	1.8
West Feliciana	26	77	7.9	4.3	8	324	D	D	27	341	14.7	3.9
Winn	21	47	4.4	1.4	14	606	D	28.1	18	D	D	D
MAINE	3,492	22,943	3,352.6	1,238.0	1,650	49,238	16,044.5	2,424.3	3,958	49,672	2,901.3	850.8
Androscoggin	183	1,652	359.2	80.1	150	5,205	1,886.9	251.6	209	3,021	153.3	44.5
Aroostook	97	343	31.4	11.9	92	2,689	1,037.9	121.1	156	1,897	83.2	23.9
Cumberland	1,410	10,188	1,627.5	641.9	380	8,691	D	433.9	973	15,001	839.9	254.8
Franklin	43	D	D	D	25	1,454	D	72.7	92	1,114	41.4	12.8
Hancock	138	1,773	268.7	99.5	90	1,463	520.2	73.7	301	2,040	211.1	54.9
Kennebec	302	D	D	D	95	2,386	634.2	114.8	302	4,055	222.9	66.8
Knox	132	440	53.5	20.8	94	1,443	377.8	63.4	166	1,663	96.8	30.9
Lincoln	108	D	D	D	72	742	D	31.9	149	1,127	84.6	24.3
Oxford	75	307	32.8	10.9	61	2,434	860.6	138.6	133	2,562	103.8	32.5
Penobscot	328	1,831	179.4	84.5	134	3,749	977.7	164.0	315	5,639	313.9	86.7
Piscataquis	13	D	D	D	22	1,045	177.5	37.8	47	259	14.9	3.6
Sagadahoc	99	917	103.0	52.7	39	D	D	D	81	1,053	54.9	17.1
Somerset	59	332	37.1	13.4	72	3,330	1,607.3	177.8	92	846	43.8	12.8
Waldo	60	187	15.7	7.1	45	1,163	168.4	36.4	93	789	46.2	13.3
Washington	31	D	D	D	36	994	359.2	40.7	80	558	28.2	7.8
York	414	2,078	356.0	106.6	243	D	2,762.3	D	769	8,048	562.4	164.0
MARYLAND	19,714	244,710	50,024.9	20,161.2	3,096	100,079	39,533.0	5,908.9	11,344	204,222	12,516.8	3,410.5
Allegany	96	486	42.7	18.3	52	2,547	D	119.2	181	D	D	D
Anne Arundel	2,027	24,815	5,787.2	2,467.9	275	11,547	4,456.9	993.6	1,158	25,939	1,564.0	419.4
Baltimore	2,692	24,678	3,990.9	1,657.7	451	16,807	8,066.7	1,003.7	1,578	27,158	1,555.8	415.4
Calvert	215	1,286	162.5	54.7	38	455	84.1	18.8	146	D	D	D
Caroline	38	D	D	D	28	1,167	302.3	42.8	36	D	D	D
Carroll	494	2,471	324.9	125.6	124	3,402	1,019.4	178.4	262	5,810	246.8	73.1
Cecil	155	570	52.7	19.1	49	4,496	1,989.9	312.3	176	2,792	154.1	41.7
Charles	273	1,979	311.6	127.5	43	399	84.0	18.4	244	D	D	D
Dorchester	53	169	17.8	5.2	44	2,546	843.1	93.7	58	D	D	D
Frederick	845	6,686	1,098.7	427.9	163	6,026	3,236.1	354.3	441	8,452	449.6	130.0
Garrett	53	397	37.4	17.3	50	1,128	D	39.6	74	D	D	D
Harford	697	D	D	D	137	4,058	1,866.8	207.2	394	7,960	390.9	104.7
Howard	1,883	35,086	10,616.5	3,126.2	186	5,013	1,538.2	276.8	543	11,000	610.9	177.1
Kent	51	D	D	D	29	945	360.0	50.7	74	D	D	D
Montgomery	5,701	74,255	14,389.0	6,751.1	381	8,233	2,172.6	619.7	1,818	31,526	2,080.0	571.8
Prince George's	1,662	26,331	4,349.1	1,903.9	264	7,291	2,216.8	424.1	1,269	23,872	1,685.5	436.2
Queen Anne's	158	D	D	D	49	921	208.3	41.8	94	2,111	113.0	33.7

Table B. States and Counties — Health Care and Social Assistance, Other Services, Nonemployer Businesses, and Residential Construction

STATE County	Health care and social assistance, 2012				Other services, 2012				Nonemployer businesses, 2016		Value of residential construction authorized by building permits, 2018	
	Number of establishments	Number of employees	Receipts (mil dol)	Annual payroll (mil dol)	Number of establishments	Number of employees	Receipts (mil dol)	Annual payroll (mil dol)	Number	Receipts (mil dol)	New construction ($1,000)	Number of housing units
	159	160	161	162	163	164	165	166	167	168	169	170
LOUISIANA— Cont'd												
Orleans	861	21,761	2,667.4	964.2	578	4,297	791.8	139.5	37,858	1,592.9	264,117	1,303
Ouachita	629	14,085	1,354.2	483.6	229	1,533	141.0	41.4	12,583	528.0	93,631	486
Plaquemines	21	468	40.0	17.7	44	D	D	D	2,479	137.1	12,718	48
Pointe Coupee	35	709	49.3	19.3	28	D	D	D	1,582	68.2	12,805	54
Rapides	506	14,112	1,514.4	554.9	198	1,018	104.1	27.5	8,132	370.9	56,462	260
Red River	15	444	37.8	11.4	6	D	D	D	518	18.1	0	0
Richland	80	1,783	100.9	40.6	18	D	D	D	1,444	49.2	7,332	25
Sabine	44	846	53.5	20.5	22	79	19.5	2.2	1,357	52.3	8,810	49
St. Bernard	51	D	D	D	37	D	D	D	3,613	146.4	32,062	178
St. Charles	65	D	D	D	50	D	D	D	4,055	169.6	35,777	196
St. Helena	14	D	D	D	7	D	D	D	924	21.4	5,652	33
St. James	28	764	69.8	29.3	16	D	D	D	1,235	36.7	17,340	63
St. John the Baptist	70	D	D	D	39	367	57.3	16.1	3,111	94.5	7,786	47
St. Landry	289	6,071	433.5	172.0	77	361	31.7	8.9	5,732	208.6	26,027	121
St. Martin	79	1,675	79.2	37.7	44	126	20.5	4.3	4,608	154.3	32,080	171
St. Mary	115	2,094	164.1	64.7	89	523	65.0	19.2	3,815	128.2	4,060	15
St. Tammany	791	14,504	1,581.8	607.7	356	1,993	219.0	60.3	24,503	1,295.3	349,027	1,430
Tangipahoa	301	8,143	655.2	261.4	149	966	98.1	25.5	10,120	365.0	186,102	1,322
Tensas	9	66	5.1	2.1	2	D	D	D	349	10.6	1,355	16
Terrebonne	284	6,992	704.8	288.9	175	1,449	232.6	73.0	8,277	365.7	33,640	149
Union	32	851	53.6	20.7	14	35	3.3	0.7	1,513	57.6	1,000	4
Vermilion	101	1,764	122.8	46.2	56	252	24.6	6.2	4,591	153.0	28,295	147
Vernon	77	2,010	222.5	85.8	41	170	15.3	3.6	2,078	76.8	8,896	50
Washington	84	2,309	171.6	73.6	28	106	10.0	2.3	3,171	112.2	420	6
Webster	86	2,332	173.5	65.1	39	250	29.9	7.2	2,589	104.1	4,618	155
West Baton Rouge	32	443	26.4	11.3	38	263	40.4	10.7	1,785	68.8	69,892	571
West Carroll	16	549	35.9	14.9	15	60	4.2	1.1	690	24.4	1,757	9
West Feliciana	24	462	36.9	13.6	10	D	D	D	763	34.2	13,949	41
Winn	38	957	67.2	29.2	18	D	D	D	685	34.5	0	0
MAINE	4,730	109,231	10,297.0	4,393.0	2,786	13,755	1,462.8	376.3	114,473	5,215.7	10,093	76
Androscoggin	385	9,531	947.5	402.8	211	1,024	84.6	23.5	6,302	292.1	52,289	300
Aroostook	229	6,120	471.8	207.2	122	397	45.8	9.1	4,048	162.7	7,328	55
Cumberland	1,339	33,687	3,348.8	1,475.2	734	4,502	518.8	130.4	28,716	1,499.9	308,274	1,401
Franklin	106	1,882	156.4	74.4	44	214	19.8	4.8	2,370	78.8	21,805	136
Hancock	159	3,144	306.6	127.7	140	686	101.2	21.7	7,769	377.0	61,367	297
Kennebec	464	13,374	1,293.6	552.0	289	1,265	139.0	37.9	8,478	321.6	63,415	306
Knox	163	3,022	256.5	104.8	126	593	66.9	19.1	5,937	310.1	27,202	103
Lincoln	113	1,800	144.6	51.5	81	547	51.7	16.2	4,675	192.6	21,216	100
Oxford	125	2,777	198.2	85.1	90	335	31.1	8.4	4,386	182.6	39,484	182
Penobscot	547	14,740	1,570.2	624.9	273	1,395	142.7	36.9	9,258	359.0	46,344	261
Piscataquis	36	1,508	106.4	51.6	25	92	6.6	1.9	1,177	40.6	8,815	22
Sagadahoc	116	1,375	80.7	36.0	59	266	27.3	6.9	3,298	127.0	23,879	112
Somerset	144	2,809	208.6	96.4	88	286	26.2	6.3	3,163	114.2	12,269	83
Waldo	113	1,622	148.9	65.4	82	264	26.3	6.4	3,893	140.3	19,615	105
Washington	108	2,058	137.6	66.4	51	209	19.7	4.3	3,750	190.5	6,446	47
York	583	9,782	920.8	371.5	371	1,680	155.0	42.5	17,253	826.7	229,458	1,111
MARYLAND	16,000	359,734	40,821.9	16,319.9	9,978	79,391	10,879.7	2,928.5	487,540	21,477.8	3,701,849	18,647
Allegany	250	6,283	616.1	235.0	139	780	58.0	16.9	2,985	112.2	6,797	30
Anne Arundel	1,272	26,683	2,975.3	1,196.9	1,077	8,665	902.9	291.8	42,701	2,138.5	346,028	2,046
Baltimore	2,619	58,216	6,062.4	2,458.5	1,376	9,983	1,044.2	295.7	66,764	3,002.6	387,843	2,107
Calvert	181	3,475	342.2	149.7	122	773	59.6	20.1	6,549	287.1	43,135	184
Caroline	46	826	44.6	23.3	48	226	23.7	7.6	2,610	116.3	10,592	59
Carroll	459	9,821	950.3	358.3	355	2,195	180.2	57.5	12,517	540.9	98,303	399
Cecil	196	4,679	534.5	259.0	164	867	68.1	20.9	5,607	251.0	36,921	155
Charles	325	4,598	456.6	190.4	213	1,353	113.6	35.7	11,031	382.7	148,402	734
Dorchester	84	1,826	158.1	65.8	68	360	19.7	5.3	2,386	93.2	11,618	54
Frederick	613	11,380	1,206.1	516.3	426	2,837	348.7	93.7	18,994	868.1	487,668	2,000
Garrett	76	1,797	118.6	52.0	73	1,219	106.6	47.9	2,345	106.9	36,641	92
Harford	594	10,550	1,029.1	406.1	422	2,691	227.0	90.5	16,889	743.6	168,483	863
Howard	928	14,235	1,406.4	600.2	509	4,399	552.9	179.8	27,662	1,426.8	355,091	2,046
Kent	74	1,374	115.6	47.4	44	172	19.5	4.8	1,810	85.0	7,185	28
Montgomery	3,584	61,807	7,227.2	3,069.1	1,891	19,109	4,325.3	1,001.8	112,683	5,777.6	371,593	1,947
Prince George's	1,812	31,493	3,126.4	1,249.8	1,126	8,923	996.2	297.7	76,805	2,299.6	523,165	2,267
Queen Anne's	85	1,064	74.1	34.4	103	526	45.1	12.7	4,819	265.9	56,984	279

STATE County	Government employment and payroll, 2012									Local government finances, 2012				
			March payroll (percent of total)							General revenue				
													Taxes	
			Adminis-tration, judicial, and legal	Police and corrections	Fire protection	Highways and transpor-tation	Health and welfare	Natural resources and utilities	Education and libraries	Total (mil dol)	Inter-govern-mental (mil dol)	Total (mil dol)	Per capita[1] (dollars)	
	Full-time equivalent employees	March payroll (dollars)											Total	Property
	171	172	173	174	175	176	177	178	179	180	181	182	183	184
LOUISIANA— Cont'd														
Orleans	7,189	28,500,562	12.7	30.3	9.1	2.5	3.8	25.1	9.9	1,968.9	669.4	766.2	2,075	1,020
Ouachita	7,210	21,316,630	7.2	10.3	3.6	2.2	3.7	5.2	67.2	636.4	302.9	268.8	1,730	618
Plaquemines	1,620	5,259,702	13.4	13.1	0.6	7.9	7.0	6.2	48.6	320.9	176.8	96.4	4,031	2,274
Pointe Coupee	1,063	2,905,856	7.3	13.8	0.0	1.6	21.6	5.3	50.2	93.0	34.1	31.6	1,391	766
Rapides	5,615	17,417,361	10.4	15.6	7.9	3.6	1.4	5.7	52.6	487.4	230.0	195.3	1,475	567
Red River	533	1,454,876	5.8	37.4	0.0	1.9	0.9	1.0	50.4	43.6	18.0	22.1	2,455	992
Richland	1,229	3,799,353	5.9	17.8	0.1	3.2	35.8	2.3	34.3	105.4	49.7	25.9	1,238	508
Sabine	818	2,028,527	9.4	18.3	0.0	4.8	3.6	7.0	55.7	96.4	47.5	40.6	1,668	405
St. Bernard	1,804	5,761,067	8.7	16.2	6.9	6.4	1.4	5.2	54.8	484.3	396.4	68.9	1,655	655
St. Charles	3,451	12,023,950	5.4	15.1	0.0	1.8	10.8	8.5	57.6	387.0	80.9	211.6	4,016	2,217
St. Helena	456	1,219,647	8.6	9.7	0.0	3.8	45.3	1.3	30.5	32.8	13.8	7.5	676	349
St. James	1,306	4,803,097	7.4	11.1	0.0	2.6	16.4	8.2	49.6	231.2	42.5	70.5	3,247	1,994
St. John the Baptist	1,701	5,496,602	10.6	10.0	0.0	8.8	0.1	9.7	60.5	229.3	53.3	82.6	1,845	913
St. Landry	4,416	14,852,877	5.9	10.1	3.0	2.4	26.6	3.1	48.4	409.3	165.3	100.0	1,196	372
St. Martin	1,824	5,579,531	5.5	14.8	0.1	2.7	7.9	2.9	65.6	147.8	80.2	54.1	1,026	489
St. Mary	3,043	9,174,661	6.1	12.3	1.5	2.5	10.9	8.1	57.1	251.5	102.3	102.4	1,907	1,061
St. Tammany	10,707	35,822,862	5.7	10.3	0.3	2.6	33.9	2.1	44.3	1,250.6	404.2	450.6	1,882	995
Tangipahoa	6,393	23,444,209	4.2	6.0	1.2	1.7	46.4	1.8	37.5	621.2	213.8	128.9	1,044	366
Tensas	264	627,291	16.3	4.0	0.0	4.9	1.7	3.9	68.6	27.3	17.2	7.3	1,474	872
Terrebonne	5,509	18,140,503	3.6	8.6	1.2	1.4	31.1	4.6	49.2	603.6	234.4	173.9	1,554	551
Union	834	2,308,579	6.3	18.6	0.2	2.1	11.0	6.9	53.9	62.9	32.1	20.7	923	359
Vermilion	2,406	8,239,940	6.2	8.3	1.8	3.2	23.4	6.7	50.2	227.6	95.5	73.9	1,258	572
Vernon	2,133	5,249,110	6.4	9.9	1.2	3.6	0.1	1.9	76.0	155.1	98.2	46.0	855	294
Washington	1,946	5,729,429	5.2	6.2	1.5	2.7	14.9	1.9	66.9	160.0	81.0	45.0	964	454
Webster	1,523	4,175,873	6.3	15.2	1.4	3.3	0.1	7.0	65.3	133.5	64.2	57.4	1,402	613
West Baton Rouge	1,000	3,133,887	7.9	4.1	2.2	2.9	2.9	12.2	62.7	112.9	36.3	55.4	2,296	1,199
West Carroll	438	1,121,168	6.5	2.8	0.0	4.1	3.9	2.4	79.0	46.7	23.8	13.0	1,133	428
West Feliciana	748	2,572,616	10.2	10.9	0.2	3.9	16.8	3.4	53.6	68.8	21.1	29.6	1,922	1,366
Winn	679	1,633,669	7.5	13.5	1.8	3.1	0.7	8.9	63.3	42.7	25.9	13.6	909	416
MAINE	X	X	X	X	X	X	X	X	X	X	X	X	X	X
Androscoggin	3,959	13,779,680	4.1	8.3	4.8	4.2	2.0	5.1	70.2	355.6	153.6	163.3	1,517	1,507
Aroostook	3,302	10,418,372	5.5	4.9	2.0	3.8	16.3	5.3	61.4	264.2	111.0	83.6	1,180	1,174
Cumberland	10,861	40,790,587	5.2	9.0	5.8	4.8	5.4	6.8	61.0	1,129.5	280.4	610.0	2,149	2,117
Franklin	1,043	3,602,511	5.4	8.2	1.3	4.4	1.5	4.1	73.6	80.5	29.1	43.4	1,418	1,414
Hancock	1,982	6,326,482	6.8	6.5	2.5	3.7	1.0	4.2	73.3	197.6	39.3	137.4	2,518	2,502
Kennebec	4,312	13,281,549	5.2	7.6	3.0	3.6	1.2	5.8	72.6	343.2	144.3	155.9	1,280	1,266
Knox	1,307	4,815,634	8.9	8.8	3.1	4.4	3.3	2.5	67.5	129.9	19.5	90.5	2,283	2,267
Lincoln	1,389	4,505,799	5.7	4.0	0.5	2.0	2.2	3.4	80.2	135.6	34.2	88.2	2,582	2,572
Oxford	2,319	7,212,500	4.7	5.3	2.5	4.9	0.8	2.5	78.4	186.7	69.4	103.9	1,807	1,800
Penobscot	5,352	18,128,721	5.6	7.8	5.2	7.6	1.3	6.1	64.9	466.9	185.2	205.7	1,338	1,324
Piscataquis	1,109	4,071,817	4.7	4.0	0.2	1.9	47.9	1.9	38.2	99.6	35.5	26.2	1,514	1,504
Sagadahoc	1,209	4,568,672	5.0	6.6	2.7	2.7	1.0	3.8	74.9	131.3	38.0	73.7	2,093	2,078
Somerset	2,667	8,560,527	3.4	6.5	1.2	2.5	0.5	1.6	82.6	185.9	90.8	84.4	1,626	1,622
Waldo	1,256	3,892,726	8.1	6.4	0.8	2.8	1.9	2.4	74.8	102.4	36.3	56.7	1,460	1,455
Washington	1,219	3,492,782	6.9	7.3	1.2	2.6	3.5	5.0	70.9	100.0	42.2	47.1	1,450	1,445
York	7,047	25,948,699	5.4	9.0	4.1	3.0	1.2	5.9	70.5	637.1	181.5	390.3	1,961	1,938
MARYLAND	X	X	X	X	X	X	X	X	X	X	X	X	X	X
Allegany	2,826	11,858,505	3.5	6.0	2.0	3.5	0.4	6.3	75.4	272.3	133.1	86.3	1,167	773
Anne Arundel	17,468	83,267,035	4.0	8.6	6.2	4.4	2.8	3.8	67.7	2,076.5	568.1	1,135.3	2,062	1,152
Baltimore	26,532	122,265,325	4.1	12.0	5.2	1.3	3.0	2.6	69.5	2,786.6	910.6	1,567.3	1,917	1,039
Calvert	3,256	15,584,064	4.8	7.8	0.1	1.9	2.8	4.8	74.3	388.6	117.7	224.0	2,500	1,684
Caroline	1,269	4,767,293	5.8	8.2	0.0	2.2	3.3	4.6	71.4	117.5	59.9	45.1	1,379	973
Carroll	5,844	23,979,765	5.5	5.5	0.7	1.6	1.0	2.9	80.6	641.8	205.1	366.2	2,190	1,331
Cecil	3,436	14,149,378	4.6	8.1	1.2	1.6	2.8	2.0	76.9	375.0	153.4	172.0	1,691	1,137
Charles	5,864	27,330,417	4.8	12.4	0.0	0.6	3.1	3.7	73.5	663.0	226.7	318.3	2,114	1,346
Dorchester	1,251	4,831,214	5.1	13.0	0.0	3.8	4.8	2.5	66.5	134.8	62.3	54.8	1,683	1,219
Frederick	10,553	47,827,090	4.3	6.4	4.0	1.9	4.9	3.7	73.1	1,033.9	315.3	529.5	2,210	1,385
Garrett	1,283	4,466,807	6.7	4.8	0.8	10.6	1.8	3.9	70.1	214.5	59.8	111.5	3,734	2,998
Harford	8,483	39,111,192	6.1	9.6	0.3	2.6	1.8	4.3	73.8	952.9	307.2	524.4	2,109	1,291
Howard	12,202	62,646,998	4.3	7.7	1.9	1.0	4.2	4.1	75.2	1,532.5	372.1	962.2	3,214	1,692
Kent	708	2,731,612	8.4	10.5	0.0	4.3	1.1	5.9	64.0	74.9	18.1	46.4	2,298	1,677
Montgomery	38,590	236,750,984	3.3	7.6	4.0	3.0	6.2	10.6	64.3	5,240.0	1,125.4	3,182.9	3,168	1,422
Prince George's	27,062	140,810,958	4.4	15.2	3.4	1.2	4.0	1.6	67.6	3,399.7	1,344.2	1,551.8	1,761	1,007
Queen Anne's	1,906	8,133,110	4.6	6.4	0.2	2.6	7.3	5.6	72.6	207.2	65.4	111.4	2,293	1,412

1. Based on the resident population estimated as of July 1 of the year shown.

Table B. States and Counties — Local Government Finances, Government Employment, and Income Taxes

	Local government finances, 2012 (cont.)										Government employment, 2017			Individual income tax returns, 2016		
	Direct general expenditure							Debt outstanding								
			Percent of total for:												Mean	
STATE County	Total (mil dol)	Per capita[1] (dollars)	Education	Health and hospitals	Police protection	Public welfare	Highways	Total (mil dol)	Per capita[1] (dollars)	Federal civilian	Federal military	State and local	Number of returns	adjusted gross income	Mean income tax
	185	186	187	188	189	190	191	192	193	194	195	196	197	198	199
LOUISIANA— Cont'd															
Orleans	1,848.6	5,006	12.2	0.7	7.8	0.1	6.6	2,707.7	7,333	9,656	3,526	25,306	160,470	60,636	9,386
Ouachita	687.9	4,428	53.4	2.3	5.8	0.1	2.6	489.7	3,152	432	573	10,112	65,130	52,473	6,254
Plaquemines	321.2	13,429	37.8	2.1	4.1	0.5	1.0	163.7	6,844	659	415	1,495	10,070	69,698	9,938
Pointe Coupee	90.9	4,001	37.3	22.2	6.6	0.4	2.1	45.9	2,021	59	84	1,009	9,660	52,761	6,139
Rapides	504.4	3,810	49.3	0.1	8.4	0.1	5.3	504.4	3,811	2,143	495	9,882	55,670	52,842	6,136
Red River	47.2	5,251	59.8	0.0	3.7	0.0	1.4	5.0	560	24	32	537	3,300	47,435	5,608
Richland	109.4	5,231	36.1	29.1	3.4	0.1	5.6	51.6	2,464	77	74	958	8,140	44,179	4,457
Sabine	85.0	3,493	69.8	0.2	4.8	0.0	5.6	27.9	1,145	38	90	1,255	8,700	50,079	5,008
St. Bernard	516.0	12,393	31.7	3.5	2.5	0.2	1.3	186.9	4,490	48	175	2,224	16,920	41,622	3,805
St. Charles	382.3	7,256	43.1	9.6	4.8	0.3	5.3	894.4	16,978	152	198	3,218	23,800	63,297	7,628
St. Helena	32.3	2,917	31.4	38.0	4.6	0.0	8.8	5.1	457	9	39	604	5,470	40,127	3,412
St. James	156.3	7,194	43.5	11.8	3.9	0.6	2.5	1,439.8	66,281	34	81	1,489	9,710	56,415	6,231
St. John the Baptist	252.0	5,630	34.8	0.5	4.6	0.5	5.1	1,281.3	28,626	100	163	2,006	19,390	46,931	4,474
St. Landry	414.8	4,958	43.1	29.0	4.8	0.0	3.0	98.9	1,182	164	314	4,860	35,170	46,824	4,929
St. Martin	141.4	2,682	59.3	0.9	8.4	0.2	5.1	123.9	2,349	63	203	1,803	23,050	47,235	5,096
St. Mary	245.0	4,562	42.6	10.2	6.7	0.2	3.8	139.7	2,602	134	300	4,354	21,240	45,509	4,768
St. Tammany	1,244.6	5,198	37.0	28.1	5.6	0.3	4.8	977.9	4,084	515	971	14,052	115,360	70,907	10,659
Tangipahoa	692.4	5,610	29.5	47.0	3.7	0.0	2.7	361.5	2,929	372	491	10,682	51,830	50,148	5,647
Tensas	26.2	5,284	36.9	2.0	4.8	0.0	4.9	26.6	5,361	21	17	301	1,720	41,535	4,635
Terrebonne	620.6	5,546	29.9	28.6	4.4	0.3	2.9	301.9	2,698	282	476	5,073	45,580	53,802	6,396
Union	60.2	2,685	49.1	8.9	5.4	0.2	6.0	5.9	265	97	84	795	8,710	47,497	4,658
Vermilion	223.8	3,812	42.2	20.8	4.9	2.1	5.1	37.7	643	152	238	3,003	24,210	49,515	5,193
Vernon	159.1	2,953	69.0	0.3	5.5	0.1	5.4	78.1	1,451	2,060	7,911	2,302	19,890	45,643	3,803
Washington	160.8	3,445	54.9	14.8	4.7	0.0	5.1	63.6	1,363	100	171	2,506	16,480	40,007	3,243
Webster	135.1	3,299	55.0	0.5	6.2	0.1	4.2	123.2	3,010	107	145	1,994	15,930	45,345	4,962
West Baton Rouge	118.0	4,896	36.6	0.9	8.9	0.6	4.0	182.2	7,559	92	98	1,560	11,850	59,514	7,028
West Carroll	47.4	4,114	52.9	20.0	3.8	2.1	3.9	8.1	701	29	40	738	4,090	44,999	4,137
West Feliciana	67.9	4,410	41.6	23.6	6.1	0.1	2.4	71.0	4,612	16	38	2,355	4,580	78,619	12,042
Winn	46.7	3,110	63.7	0.5	5.9	0.0	4.7	11.5	766	57	48	733	4,910	46,228	4,305
MAINE	X	X	X	X	X	X	X	X	X	15,257	6,800	85,265	650,850	56,987	6,685
Androscoggin	348.5	3,239	53.0	0.2	4.0	0.4	5.6	353.5	3,285	277	327	5,142	49,530	48,757	4,909
Aroostook	269.7	3,805	46.4	17.9	2.8	0.3	7.2	101.0	1,426	1,200	204	4,867	43,986	43,986	4,110
Cumberland	1,113.8	3,923	43.9	0.9	4.4	2.5	5.5	1,208.5	4,257	1,969	2,273	18,299	153,010	73,969	10,399
Franklin	104.7	3,419	60.2	0.7	3.7	0.2	8.5	100.7	3,287	118	89	2,063	13,040	45,770	4,417
Hancock	188.4	3,453	54.5	0.6	3.0	0.2	9.3	154.0	2,823	341	265	3,105	27,590	55,539	6,257
Kennebec	348.6	2,861	58.7	0.5	3.4	0.3	6.1	214.9	1,764	2,159	406	14,222	58,350	52,100	5,573
Knox	129.2	3,257	48.4	1.5	4.4	0.2	9.5	77.3	1,950	114	203	2,405	20,420	53,903	6,107
Lincoln	134.0	3,920	66.7	0.7	2.9	0.4	7.8	90.9	2,659	79	127	1,551	17,950	55,596	6,332
Oxford	185.2	3,222	64.2	0.5	2.9	0.4	8.6	87.1	1,516	137	175	3,028	25,980	43,649	3,988
Penobscot	527.2	3,429	48.1	1.1	3.8	0.2	4.2	409.3	2,662	1,169	461	12,847	67,980	51,210	5,675
Piscataquis	98.3	5,686	30.4	44.3	1.9	0.2	4.5	37.9	2,194	53	51	1,318	7,260	41,440	3,711
Sagadahoc	124.2	3,528	56.8	0.2	3.5	0.3	5.7	98.8	2,807	370	124	1,499	18,550	59,994	6,712
Somerset	179.7	3,461	69.3	0.2	2.5	0.2	6.3	81.7	1,574	198	155	2,357	22,070	44,639	4,288
Waldo	97.2	2,504	58.5	1.5	3.5	0.6	10.7	48.3	1,244	89	130	1,491	18,540	47,010	4,643
Washington	103.7	3,194	54.3	2.0	2.7	0.1	8.6	31.8	979	350	160	2,337	13,880	40,608	3,600
York	629.4	3,163	57.4	0.5	5.3	0.3	6.4	355.5	1,787	6,634	1,650	8,734	106,840	59,174	6,817
MARYLAND	X	X	X	X	X	X	X	X	X	175,887	50,172	342,854	2,950,710	76,084	10,550
Allegany	267.9	3,619	60.6	0.8	3.3	0.6	4.9	173.8	2,348	490	253	5,540	28,770	47,300	4,609
Anne Arundel	2,207.3	4,010	54.8	2.4	5.2	1.0	4.4	1,723.1	3,130	42,387	18,274	34,154	284,430	86,558	12,676
Baltimore	3,004.9	3,676	56.3	1.7	6.9	0.4	2.5	3,573.5	4,372	14,704	2,708	40,942	410,740	74,678	10,510
Calvert	401.4	4,479	58.4	0.8	3.8	1.0	3.2	210.1	2,344	135	331	4,181	44,720	80,972	10,161
Caroline	111.8	3,416	59.2	0.3	4.3	0.1	4.2	60.3	1,842	72	107	1,718	15,410	47,845	4,608
Carroll	634.2	3,793	62.1	0.8	3.5	1.2	4.4	467.0	2,793	321	543	7,849	84,070	78,281	9,806
Cecil	362.9	3,569	58.9	0.9	5.1	1.4	5.0	330.6	3,251	1,871	332	4,477	46,660	61,576	6,871
Charles	647.7	4,301	63.4	0.9	8.5	0.6	1.8	442.9	2,941	2,301	1,058	7,470	79,860	70,015	7,711
Dorchester	119.9	3,683	50.4	0.7	6.1	0.1	5.4	66.4	2,040	172	104	2,104	15,130	46,678	4,737
Frederick	1,022.3	4,267	56.6	0.7	5.2	3.4	3.4	1,148.1	4,792	3,651	1,912	11,938	124,880	76,136	9,717
Garrett	204.6	6,852	39.8	0.8	9.6	0.1	12.7	131.5	4,404	65	94	1,637	13,590	48,907	4,968
Harford	983.7	3,957	58.8	0.5	6.5	0.7	5.0	907.9	3,652	10,967	1,891	9,466	126,160	73,315	9,025
Howard	1,583.8	5,289	57.3	0.6	5.3	0.9	2.7	1,520.4	5,078	646	1,199	16,240	154,280	104,521	16,307
Kent	68.7	3,405	43.8	1.6	9.3	1.4	5.8	56.0	2,776	61	59	990	9,230	68,782	8,688
Montgomery	5,475.9	5,450	50.5	1.8	5.2	3.2	3.5	5,936.8	5,909	48,937	7,711	42,754	525,630	105,866	18,028
Prince George's	3,659.3	4,153	49.8	1.7	6.7	0.8	3.4	2,724.6	3,092	27,318	7,647	65,102	480,840	55,812	5,553
Queen Anne's	220.6	4,540	56.7	1.1	3.1	1.6	2.2	152.9	3,146	97	161	2,532	24,500	81,824	11,224

1. Based on the resident population estimated as of July 1 of the year shown.

Table B. States and Counties — Land Area and Population

State / county code	CBSA code[1]	County code[2]	STATE County	Land area[3] (sq. mi)	Total persons 2018	Rank	Per square mile	White	Black	American Indian, Alaska Native	Asian and Pacific Islander	Percent Hispanic or Latino[4]	Under 5 years	5 to 17 years	18 to 24 years	25 to 34 years	35 to 44 years	45 to 54 years
				1	2	3	4	5	6	7	8	9	10	11	12	13	14	15
			MARYLAND— Cont'd															
24037	15,680	3	St. Mary's	358.7	112,664	542	314.1	76.8	16.2	0.9	4.2	5.3	6.4	17.8	9.2	14.1	12.4	14.0
24039	41,540	2	Somerset	319.7	25,675	1,575	80.3	53.4	43.0	0.9	1.5	3.6	4.9	12.2	16.8	13.3	11.3	11.5
24041	20,660	6	Talbot	268.6	36,968	1,249	137.6	79.1	13.3	0.5	1.8	6.8	4.6	13.5	6.0	9.9	9.3	12.0
24043	25,180	2	Washington	457.8	150,926	440	329.7	80.7	13.5	0.6	2.5	5.4	5.7	16.2	8.1	13.1	12.1	14.2
24045	41,540	2	Wicomico	374.4	103,195	585	275.6	64.6	28.2	0.6	3.8	5.4	6.1	16.0	14.9	12.0	10.9	11.6
24047	41,540	2	Worcester	468.3	51,823	965	110.7	81.6	13.9	0.7	2.0	3.6	4.2	13.0	6.7	10.4	9.3	12.5
24510	12,580	1	Baltimore city	80.9	602,495	109	7,447.4	29.2	63.2	0.9	3.4	5.5	6.3	14.1	9.5	19.2	12.6	11.6
25000		0	**MASSACHUSETTS**	7,801.2	6,902,149	X	884.8	73.1	8.2	0.6	7.9	12.3	5.2	14.6	10.2	14.4	12.2	13.4
25001	12,700	3	Barnstable	394.2	213,413	314	541.4	91.3	4.0	1.2	2.2	3.2	3.7	11.4	7.0	8.9	8.7	12.1
25003	38,340	3	Berkshire	926.9	126,348	506	136.3	89.8	4.3	0.6	2.4	5.1	4.2	12.7	9.5	10.7	10.4	13.0
25005	39,300	1	Bristol	553.1	564,022	120	1,019.7	84.1	5.7	0.7	3.1	8.4	5.2	15.4	9.1	13.0	12.1	14.2
25007	47,240	7	Dukes	103.2	17,352	1,955	168.1	89.5	5.4	2.2	1.9	3.8	4.7	12.8	6.5	10.7	11.2	13.3
25009	14,460	1	Essex	492.5	790,638	81	1,605.4	70.8	4.2	0.4	4.2	21.9	5.6	15.7	9.2	12.5	11.9	13.8
25011	24,640	4	Franklin	699.2	70,963	761	101.5	92.1	2.0	1.0	2.6	4.2	4.4	13.1	6.9	12.0	11.7	13.0
25013	44,140	2	Hampden	617.0	470,406	147	762.4	63.2	8.8	0.6	3.0	26.1	5.4	16.1	10.4	13.4	11.5	12.8
25015	44,140	2	Hampshire	527.2	161,355	410	306.1	85.2	3.7	0.6	6.8	5.8	3.4	11.3	23.2	10.6	9.7	11.4
25017	14,460	1	Middlesex	817.8	1,614,714	22	1,974.5	73.5	6.0	0.4	14.0	8.3	5.3	14.4	9.9	15.6	13.1	13.4
25019		7	Nantucket	46.1	11,327	2,329	245.7	73.3	10.5	0.5	2.1	15.3	6.4	14.7	6.8	14.2	15.0	14.8
25021	14,460	1	Norfolk	396.1	705,388	93	1,780.8	76.1	7.8	0.4	12.8	4.8	5.3	15.6	8.8	12.9	12.6	14.0
25023	14,460	1	Plymouth	658.9	518,132	134	786.4	83.2	11.7	0.7	2.2	4.1	5.3	16.1	8.6	11.0	11.4	14.6
25025	14,460	1	Suffolk	58.2	807,252	78	13,870.3	46.6	21.5	0.7	10.0	23.4	5.2	11.4	13.7	23.4	12.9	11.0
25027	49,340	2	Worcester	1,510.7	830,839	71	550.0	77.7	5.6	0.6	6.0	11.9	5.4	15.7	9.7	13.0	12.1	14.2
26000		0	**MICHIGAN**	56,602.9	9,995,915	X	176.6	76.9	14.9	1.3	4.0	5.2	5.7	15.9	9.6	13.0	11.6	12.9
26001		9	Alcona	674.7	10,362	2,396	15.4	96.8	0.9	1.3	0.6	1.6	3.0	9.7	4.8	6.9	7.6	11.8
26003		7	Alger	915.0	9,097	2,492	9.9	86.4	8.1	6.3	0.8	1.6	3.7	11.3	7.2	11.2	11.3	12.1
26005	26,090	4	Allegan	825.2	117,327	530	142.2	89.8	2.1	1.2	1.2	7.4	6.2	18.0	7.8	11.9	11.9	13.2
26007	10,980	7	Alpena	571.9	28,360	1,485	49.6	96.8	1.1	1.2	0.8	1.4	4.8	13.7	7.0	10.5	10.8	12.5
26009		9	Antrim	475.7	23,365	1,667	49.1	95.8	0.7	1.8	0.6	2.4	4.6	13.5	6.4	9.3	9.0	12.2
26011		8	Arenac	363.2	15,041	2,093	41.4	95.9	1.1	1.8	0.7	2.0	4.8	13.4	6.3	9.9	10.0	12.1
26013		9	Baraga	898.4	8,320	2,558	9.3	76.6	8.9	16.6	0.8	1.6	3.9	13.6	8.1	11.9	11.6	13.5
26015	24,340	2	Barry	553.1	61,157	859	110.6	95.3	1.1	1.1	0.8	3.1	5.5	16.6	7.9	11.3	11.4	13.2
26017	13,020	3	Bay	442.2	103,923	581	235.0	91.7	2.8	1.1	0.9	5.4	5.0	15.2	7.6	12.3	11.4	12.7
26019	45,900	9	Benzie	319.7	17,753	1,938	55.5	94.9	1.2	2.1	0.7	2.6	4.7	13.5	6.1	10.3	9.8	12.0
26021	35,660	3	Berrien	567.8	154,141	431	271.5	76.9	15.9	1.2	2.8	5.7	5.7	16.1	8.1	11.8	11.3	12.6
26023	17,740	6	Branch	506.4	43,622	1,100	86.1	91.7	2.7	1.0	1.4	5.0	6.0	17.2	7.7	11.9	11.8	12.8
26025	12,980	3	Calhoun	706.3	134,487	475	190.4	80.2	12.9	1.4	3.5	5.3	6.2	16.7	9.0	12.3	11.7	12.5
26027	43,780	2	Cass	490.1	51,653	967	105.4	89.0	6.7	2.1	1.3	4.0	4.9	15.8	7.8	10.3	10.3	13.7
26029		7	Charlevoix	416.3	26,244	1,557	63.0	95.4	0.9	2.4	0.9	2.1	4.2	14.6	7.1	10.0	10.1	12.3
26031		7	Cheboygan	715.3	25,413	1,587	35.5	94.6	1.1	4.8	0.7	1.5	4.0	12.4	6.7	9.4	9.7	12.9
26033	42,300	7	Chippewa	1,558.5	37,517	1,237	24.1	74.5	7.3	19.8	1.7	2.0	4.8	13.5	11.8	13.3	12.5	12.3
26035		6	Clare	564.4	30,757	1,416	54.5	96.2	1.2	1.6	0.5	2.0	5.4	14.4	6.8	10.5	10.2	12.2
26037	29,620	2	Clinton	566.4	79,332	707	140.1	91.4	2.7	1.0	2.3	4.5	5.6	16.8	8.4	12.1	12.3	13.7
26039		7	Crawford	556.4	13,901	2,169	25.0	95.6	1.3	1.4	1.1	2.0	4.6	13.3	6.2	9.4	9.2	13.2
26041	21,540	5	Delta	1,171.1	35,857	1,278	30.6	95.1	0.9	4.1	0.9	1.4	5.0	14.7	6.9	9.8	10.6	12.3
26043	27,020	7	Dickinson	760.9	25,383	1,590	33.4	96.3	0.9	1.5	1.0	1.6	5.5	14.8	7.0	10.6	10.6	12.6
26045	29,620	2	Eaton	575.2	109,826	555	190.9	84.9	7.8	1.1	3.0	5.5	5.4	15.3	8.7	13.0	11.7	12.7
26047		7	Emmet	467.5	33,308	1,349	71.2	93.2	1.2	5.0	1.0	1.7	4.8	14.4	7.7	11.4	10.8	12.3
26049	22,420	2	Genesee	637.0	406,892	173	638.8	74.8	21.6	1.3	1.5	3.5	5.9	16.6	8.6	12.3	11.6	13.2
26051		6	Gladwin	501.8	25,337	1,593	50.5	96.7	0.9	1.1	0.6	1.8	5.3	13.4	6.3	9.5	9.3	12.6
26053		7	Gogebic	1,102.1	15,096	2,089	13.7	91.4	4.3	3.6	0.6	1.5	3.9	11.7	7.5	11.0	10.7	12.5
26055	45,900	5	Grand Traverse	464.3	92,573	636	199.4	94.3	1.3	1.9	1.3	2.9	5.2	15.0	7.5	12.5	11.8	12.5
26057	10,940	6	Gratiot	568.4	40,599	1,162	71.4	86.8	6.2	1.0	0.8	6.3	4.8	14.8	11.1	13.1	12.6	13.0
26059	25,880	6	Hillsdale	598.2	45,749	1,057	76.5	96.0	1.2	1.2	0.8	2.3	6.0	15.9	9.4	10.5	10.8	12.5
26061	26,340	5	Houghton	1,009.1	36,219	1,272	35.9	93.4	1.4	1.4	3.8	1.7	5.1	14.9	21.8	10.1	9.4	9.6
26063		7	Huron	836.0	31,166	1,402	37.3	96.0	0.8	0.8	0.8	2.5	5.0	14.2	6.9	9.6	9.6	12.5
26065	29,620	2	Ingham	556.1	292,735	235	526.4	72.7	13.9	1.3	8.2	7.9	5.7	14.3	19.0	14.3	11.2	10.6
26067	26,960	4	Ionia	571.3	64,210	831	112.4	89.7	5.1	1.0	0.8	4.8	5.8	16.5	9.2	13.7	13.0	13.6
26069		7	Iosco	549.1	25,081	1,604	45.7	95.1	1.3	1.8	1.2	2.4	4.4	11.9	5.9	9.4	8.8	11.8
26071		7	Iron	1,166.0	11,117	2,345	9.5	95.4	0.9	2.0	0.8	2.3	4.3	12.3	5.6	7.9	9.3	11.0
26073	34,380	4	Isabella	572.7	70,562	768	123.2	87.8	3.9	4.7	2.6	4.0	4.6	12.6	27.2	12.5	9.8	9.8
26075	27,100	3	Jackson	701.9	158,823	418	226.3	87.1	9.7	1.0	1.3	3.6	5.6	15.8	8.7	12.7	11.6	13.2
26077	28,020	2	Kalamazoo	562.1	264,870	259	471.2	80.2	13.5	1.2	3.5	5.0	6.0	15.6	15.4	13.6	11.6	11.0
26079	45,900	7	Kalkaska	559.7	17,824	1,931	31.8	95.5	1.3	2.0	1.0	2.2	5.2	15.8	7.0	11.5	11.5	12.9
26081	24,340	2	Kent	848.0	653,786	102	771.0	75.8	11.3	1.0	3.9	10.7	6.7	17.4	9.5	15.8	12.6	12.0

1. CBSA = Core Based Statistical Area. See Appendix A for explanation. See Appendix B for list of metropolitan areas with component counties. Service of USDA Rural-Urban Continuum Codes. See Appendix A for definition. 2. County type code from the Economic Research 3. Dry land or land partially or temporarily covered by water. 4. May be of any race.

Table B. States and Counties — Population and Households

STATE County	Population, 2018 (cont.) Age (percent) (cont.) 55 to 64 years	65 to 74 years	75 years and over	Percent female	Population change, 2000-2018 Total persons 2000	2010	Percent change 2000-2010	2010-2018	Components of change, 2010-2018 Births	Deaths	Net Migration	Households, 2013-2017 Number	Persons per household	Family house-holds	Percent Female family house-holder[1]	One person
	16	17	18	19	20	21	22	23	24	25	26	27	28	29	30	31
MARYLAND— Cont'd																
St. Mary's	13.0	7.8	5.3	50.2	86,211	105,143	22.0	7.2	11,699	6,290	2,134	39,276	2.75	70.4	12.0	24.1
Somerset	13.1	9.8	7.1	45.9	24,747	26,470	7.0	-3.0	2,110	2,166	-757	8,362	2.36	62.9	18.2	32.1
Talbot	15.4	15.2	14.0	52.8	33,812	37,777	11.7	-2.1	2,769	3,620	81	16,498	2.25	66.4	12.2	27.4
Washington	13.4	9.6	7.6	49.1	131,923	147,430	11.8	2.4	14,155	12,311	1,723	55,999	2.51	66.8	12.7	27.3
Wicomico	12.7	9.3	6.6	52.6	84,644	98,733	16.6	4.5	10,213	7,756	2,067	37,415	2.62	65.3	13.7	26.2
Worcester	16.1	15.6	12.2	51.5	46,543	51,451	10.5	0.7	3,577	5,139	1,977	21,190	2.40	63.7	10.7	30.2
Baltimore city	12.7	8.3	5.7	53.1	651,154	620,862	-4.7	-3.0	71,466	52,938	-36,572	239,791	2.48	51.5	21.9	38.7
MASSACHUSETTS	13.6	9.5	7.0	51.5	6,349,097	6,547,790	3.1	5.4	592,466	458,279	224,482	2,585,715	2.53	63.7	12.3	28.5
Barnstable	17.6	17.4	13.2	52.2	222,230	215,875	-2.9	-1.1	12,928	23,732	8,544	95,011	2.22	61.5	8.8	32.7
Berkshire	16.2	13.1	10.1	51.6	134,953	131,275	-2.7	-3.8	8,866	12,121	-1,606	55,063	2.19	59.4	12.1	33.7
Bristol	14.1	9.7	7.2	51.6	534,678	548,254	2.5	2.9	46,913	43,047	12,392	215,903	2.51	65.9	14.1	27.9
Dukes	16.4	15.6	8.8	50.7	14,987	16,535	10.3	4.9	1,330	1,152	641	6,139	2.77	63.0	10.8	32.1
Essex	14.3	9.8	7.2	51.8	723,419	743,081	2.7	6.4	69,796	53,885	32,276	291,659	2.60	66.9	13.6	27.4
Franklin	16.9	14.0	8.0	51.5	71,535	71,377	-0.2	-0.6	5,024	5,697	302	30,512	2.27	58.7	9.7	31.8
Hampden	13.7	9.6	7.2	51.7	456,228	463,625	1.6	1.5	42,996	36,313	166	178,931	2.54	64.7	17.8	29.3
Hampshire	13.2	10.5	6.8	53.3	152,251	158,056	3.8	2.1	8,801	10,135	4,567	58,782	2.35	59.4	10.2	29.5
Middlesex	12.9	8.6	6.6	51.0	1,465,396	1,503,123	2.6	7.4	143,340	92,352	61,788	593,784	2.57	64.9	9.7	26.5
Nantucket	13.2	8.9	5.9	49.1	9,520	10,172	6.8	11.4	1,212	517	447	3,761	2.83	61.1	7.7	29.8
Norfolk	13.9	9.4	7.5	51.9	650,308	670,907	3.2	5.1	59,661	47,036	22,380	262,324	2.58	66.2	9.6	27.0
Plymouth	14.9	10.8	7.4	51.4	472,822	494,937	4.7	4.7	42,389	36,372	17,652	184,195	2.70	71.2	12.5	24.0
Suffolk	10.4	6.9	5.1	51.7	689,807	722,190	4.7	11.8	77,839	39,005	46,489	303,676	2.41	49.9	16.3	35.7
Worcester	14.2	9.1	6.6	50.7	750,963	798,383	6.3	4.1	71,371	56,915	18,444	305,975	2.58	66.0	12.1	27.1
MICHIGAN	14.0	10.1	7.1	50.8	9,938,444	9,884,117	-0.5	1.1	933,558	767,504	-53,152	3,888,646	2.49	64.5	12.4	29.2
Alcona	20.3	19.5	16.3	49.6	11,719	10,942	-6.6	-5.3	502	1,530	448	4,979	2.06	61.9	6.1	34.1
Alger	17.7	15.4	10.3	44.7	9,862	9,601	-2.6	-5.2	480	932	-47	3,244	2.53	64.4	5.8	31.4
Allegan	14.5	10.1	6.5	50.0	105,665	111,407	5.4	5.3	11,244	7,779	2,504	42,556	2.65	72.4	8.6	22.6
Alpena	17.2	12.9	10.5	50.7	31,314	29,601	-5.5	-4.2	2,147	2,998	-367	12,789	2.20	61.8	10.4	31.8
Antrim	17.9	15.8	11.4	50.3	23,110	23,574	2.0	-0.9	1,648	2,247	407	9,732	2.35	70.5	7.7	25.0
Arenac	18.6	14.8	10.1	49.6	17,269	15,899	-7.9	-5.4	1,034	1,724	-155	6,663	2.26	65.0	9.2	29.9
Baraga	15.3	12.8	9.3	44.9	8,746	8,866	1.4	-6.2	611	861	-293	3,009	2.23	63.1	10.5	32.4
Barry	15.6	11.0	7.4	49.7	56,755	59,175	4.3	3.3	5,224	4,396	1,183	23,539	2.50	70.9	7.3	23.5
Bay	15.3	11.6	8.8	50.9	110,157	107,773	-2.2	-3.6	8,770	9,820	-2,745	44,070	2.36	63.4	12.2	30.4
Benzie	17.4	15.1	11.1	50.4	15,998	17,524	9.5	1.3	1,260	1,711	688	6,911	2.48	64.5	6.3	30.5
Berrien	14.7	11.2	8.5	51.1	162,453	156,811	-3.5	-1.7	14,784	14,097	-3,322	63,035	2.38	64.4	13.3	30.1
Branch	14.5	10.6	7.6	48.5	45,787	45,248	-1.2	-3.6	4,325	3,630	-2,361	16,415	2.51	67.4	10.1	26.4
Calhoun	13.8	10.2	7.7	51.1	137,985	136,148	-1.3	-1.2	13,638	12,114	-3,178	53,528	2.43	63.4	13.8	31.3
Cass	15.7	12.9	8.1	49.8	51,104	52,288	2.3	-1.2	3,885	4,229	-259	20,686	2.46	69.4	10.1	25.7
Charlevoix	17.3	14.4	10.0	50.5	26,090	25,956	-0.5	1.1	1,927	2,284	668	11,234	2.30	65.2	7.3	29.2
Cheboygan	17.7	16.0	11.2	50.1	26,448	26,145	-1.1	-2.8	1,636	2,647	298	11,348	2.22	65.3	8.9	29.8
Chippewa	13.8	10.2	7.7	44.8	38,543	38,669	0.3	-3.0	2,869	2,977	-1,062	14,004	2.42	61.1	9.7	32.1
Clare	16.7	14.3	9.6	50.0	31,252	30,924	-1.0	-0.5	2,686	3,348	515	12,726	2.37	65.2	10.3	29.9
Clinton	14.2	10.0	6.9	50.5	64,753	75,367	16.4	5.3	6,626	4,880	2,262	29,163	2.63	70.1	8.4	24.2
Crawford	18.5	14.8	10.9	49.2	14,273	14,081	-1.3	-1.3	983	1,390	240	6,025	2.26	65.5	8.8	28.1
Delta	16.7	13.7	10.5	50.3	38,520	37,069	-3.8	-3.3	2,953	3,560	-579	15,920	2.25	63.0	9.8	31.4
Dickinson	16.9	12.0	10.0	49.9	27,472	26,168	-4.7	-3.0	2,114	2,549	-337	11,269	2.24	65.1	10.5	30.6
Eaton	14.6	11.2	7.4	50.9	103,655	107,763	4.0	1.9	9,599	8,013	553	44,323	2.41	65.5	11.0	29.0
Emmet	16.1	13.4	9.2	50.7	31,437	32,694	4.0	1.9	2,470	2,828	1,002	14,496	2.24	63.1	8.4	28.8
Genesee	14.3	10.1	7.4	51.8	436,141	425,789	-2.4	-4.4	40,445	36,323	-23,255	166,838	2.43	64.2	16.0	30.2
Gladwin	17.0	15.6	11.2	49.4	26,023	25,695	-1.3	-1.4	2,101	2,838	390	10,990	2.28	65.0	9.3	30.4
Gogebic	16.8	14.6	11.3	46.2	17,370	16,424	-5.4	-8.1	1,022	1,752	-597	6,660	2.11	57.8	9.5	36.9
Grand Traverse	15.5	11.9	8.0	51.1	77,654	86,981	12.0	6.4	7,624	6,796	4,756	36,519	2.42	65.3	8.4	27.9
Gratiot	13.1	9.6	7.9	46.3	42,285	42,476	0.5	-4.4	3,304	3,596	-1,594	14,736	2.41	66.3	12.3	27.5
Hillsdale	15.4	11.4	8.2	50.2	46,527	46,686	0.3	-2.0	4,503	3,886	-1,541	17,896	2.47	66.8	8.5	28.3
Houghton	11.6	10.0	7.5	45.9	36,016	36,625	1.7	-1.1	3,071	2,884	-614	13,157	2.58	57.3	6.8	32.5
Huron	17.0	13.9	11.2	50.5	36,079	33,118	-8.2	-5.9	2,504	3,682	-754	13,880	2.25	64.4	8.8	31.9
Ingham	11.4	8.2	5.3	51.3	279,320	280,891	0.6	4.2	27,257	17,061	1,545	111,894	2.39	54.5	11.5	33.3
Ionia	13.5	9.1	5.6	46.4	61,518	63,899	3.9	0.5	6,037	4,255	-1,452	22,625	2.66	69.9	9.4	23.8
Iosco	18.1	16.7	12.9	50.4	27,339	25,888	-5.3	-3.1	1,837	3,293	653	11,457	2.18	61.9	8.6	32.4
Iron	19.0	16.9	13.7	50.1	13,138	11,817	-10.1	-5.9	754	1,537	94	5,315	2.06	53.9	7.4	40.7
Isabella	10.9	7.5	5.1	51.3	63,351	70,313	11.0	0.4	5,363	3,870	-1,278	24,898	2.57	56.3	10.9	27.3
Jackson	14.5	10.4	7.4	48.9	158,422	160,245	1.2	-0.9	14,728	13,450	-2,622	61,418	2.43	65.8	12.6	29.1
Kalamazoo	11.7	8.7	6.2	51.0	238,603	250,327	4.9	5.8	25,886	17,163	6,024	102,362	2.45	59.7	11.2	29.9
Kalkaska	15.8	12.7	7.7	48.7	16,571	17,147	3.5	3.9	1,411	1,569	839	7,019	2.45	67.7	8.8	26.7
Kent	12.4	8.0	5.7	50.7	574,335	602,628	4.9	8.5	72,673	37,606	16,454	236,929	2.64	66.4	12.0	26.0

1. No spouse present.

Table B. States and Counties — Population, Vital Statistics, Health, and Crime

STATE County	Persons in group quarters, 2018	Daytime Population, 2013-2017 Number	Employment/ residence ratio	Births, 2018 Total	Rate[1]	Deaths, 2018 Number	Rate[1]	Persons under 65 with no health insurance, 2016 Number	Percent	Medicare, 2018 Total beneficiaries	Enrolled in Original Medicare	Enrolled in Medicare Advantage	Serious crimes known to police[2], 2016 Total Number	Rate[3]
	32	33	34	35	36	37	38	39	40	41	42	43	44	45
MARYLAND— Cont'd														
St. Mary's..........................	2,791	106,331	0.92	1,365	12.1	851	7.6	5,412	5.6	16,111	15,725	386	2,302	2,057
Somerset...........................	5,308	24,449	0.84	248	9.7	275	10.7	1,537	9.2	4,890	4,558	332	607	2,382
Talbot	373	41,980	1.26	335	9.1	482	13.0	2,147	8.0	11,066	10,354	712	790	2,122
Washington	8,314	151,190	1.02	1,644	10.9	1,521	10.1	8,448	7.1	30,628	27,118	3,510	3,632	2,436
Wicomico..........................	4,881	103,581	1.03	1,247	12.1	1,049	10.2	6,734	8.1	19,080	18,019	1,061	3,505	3,420
Worcester.........................	722	53,880	1.10	405	7.8	691	13.3	2,733	7.3	15,003	13,930	1,073	1,985	3,873
Baltimore city	26,054	726,833	1.39	7,965	13.2	6,928	11.5	39,346	7.6	99,460	80,381	19,079	40,689	6,580
MASSACHUSETTS..........	248,396	6,861,424	1.02	70,297	10.2	58,506	8.5	165,417	3.0	1,303,797	992,416	311,381	132,016	1,938
Barnstable........................	4,108	210,621	0.97	1,552	7.3	2,907	13.6	4,663	3.1	74,491	63,535	10,956	4,118	1,933
Berkshire..........................	5,889	128,924	1.02	985	7.8	1,480	11.7	3,117	3.3	34,045	31,344	2,701	2,756	2,387
Bristol..............................	15,523	505,290	0.81	5,632	10.0	5,480	9.7	14,881	3.3	118,754	95,846	22,908	12,520	2,252
Dukes..............................	142	17,427	1.02	164	9.5	130	7.5	566	4.2	4,753	4,594	159	278	1,600
Essex...............................	19,527	712,982	0.84	8,444	10.7	6,903	8.7	21,253	3.3	155,181	119,665	35,516	13,297	1,715
Franklin............................	1,511	63,909	0.81	577	8.1	708	10.0	1,587	2.8	17,869	14,054	3,815	1,080	1,770
Hampden...........................	15,129	465,508	0.98	4,877	10.4	4,536	9.6	13,665	3.6	100,573	68,266	32,307	14,913	3,236
Hampshire.........................	22,324	156,112	0.94	994	6.2	1,274	7.9	2,992	2.6	33,036	26,383	6,653	2,700	1,717
Middlesex..........................	56,809	1,650,555	1.08	16,769	10.4	11,849	7.3	35,016	2.7	266,426	198,397	68,029	21,430	1,347
Nantucket..........................	56	11,087	1.03	162	14.3	54	4.8	387	4.1	1,872	1,807	65	335	3,036
Norfolk..............................	17,045	674,342	0.94	7,171	10.2	5,936	8.4	11,891	2.1	129,457	101,594	27,863	8,779	1,354
Plymouth...........................	11,373	450,993	0.77	5,127	9.9	4,680	9.0	10,660	2.5	108,132	88,594	19,538	7,368	1,552
Suffolk..............................	50,684	1,043,337	1.63	9,302	11.5	5,277	6.5	25,518	3.9	105,897	76,885	29,012	23,645	3,009
Worcester..........................	28,276	770,337	0.88	8,541	10.3	7,292	8.8	19,221	2.8	153,310	101,450	51,860	16,130	2,085
MICHIGAN......................	226,269	9,889,666	0.99	110,676	11.1	95,614	9.6	519,190	6.4	2,023,274	1,213,122	810,152	235,192	2,369
Alcona..............................	127	9,272	0.65	57	5.5	174	16.8	563	8.5	4,315	2,851	1,464	112	1,094
Alger................................	1,051	8,975	0.91	59	6.5	111	12.2	474	7.9	2,618	1,804	814	76	813
Allegan.............................	955	105,154	0.83	1,363	11.6	921	7.8	6,171	6.4	22,354	10,580	11,774	1,710	1,484
Alpena..............................	513	29,408	1.05	240	8.5	343	12.1	1,341	6.1	8,712	6,684	2,028	494	1,725
Antrim...............................	226	20,075	0.68	206	8.8	274	11.7	1,333	7.9	7,191	4,635	2,556	406	1,759
Arenac.............................	207	14,200	0.82	123	8.2	204	13.6	872	7.7	4,654	3,010	1,644	160	1,057
Baraga	1,010	8,801	1.09	63	7.6	113	13.6	523	8.9	1,977	1,439	538	NA	NA
Barry................................	605	46,778	0.53	636	10.4	580	9.5	2,736	5.6	12,920	6,562	6,358	648	1,101
Bay..................................	1,439	95,639	0.79	1,026	9.9	1,163	11.2	5,048	6.0	26,067	16,674	9,393	2,378	2,260
Benzie..............................	252	14,956	0.67	156	8.8	210	11.8	970	7.5	5,261	3,365	1,896	179	1,026
Berrien..............................	3,488	153,879	0.98	1,659	10.8	1,709	11.1	9,340	7.6	35,236	23,134	12,102	4,304	2,792
Branch..............................	1,979	41,210	0.87	493	11.3	420	9.6	2,766	8.1	9,449	6,678	2,771	835	1,926
Calhoun.............................	4,326	140,627	1.11	1,615	12.0	1,389	10.3	7,020	6.5	30,456	21,500	8,956	5,109	3,815
Cass................................	611	42,249	0.59	429	8.3	521	10.1	3,129	7.7	12,305	8,204	4,101	848	1,856
Charlevoix.........................	279	25,189	0.92	226	8.6	290	11.1	1,495	7.4	7,199	4,823	2,376	375	1,426
Cheboygan........................	390	22,852	0.75	190	7.5	366	14.4	1,674	9.1	8,072	5,519	2,553	367	1,451
Chippewa..........................	4,641	38,006	1.00	316	8.4	371	9.9	2,387	8.9	8,028	5,601	2,427	563	1,485
Clare................................	391	28,264	0.78	318	10.3	404	13.1	2,038	8.8	9,168	5,999	3,169	597	1,961
Clinton..............................	630	61,283	0.56	824	10.4	574	7.2	2,939	4.5	14,348	8,827	5,521	707	909
Crawford	197	13,241	0.89	114	8.2	166	11.9	731	7.2	3,891	2,661	1,230	247	1,797
Delta................................	623	35,701	0.96	320	8.9	432	12.0	1,956	7.1	10,560	7,181	3,379	781	2,156
Dickinson	433	27,655	1.18	278	11.0	306	12.1	1,127	5.7	6,814	4,709	2,105	NA	NA
Eaton...............................	1,770	104,915	0.93	1,118	10.2	981	8.9	4,661	5.2	23,125	14,738	8,387	1,872	1,718
Emmet..............................	505	36,440	1.22	286	8.6	308	9.2	1,907	7.4	8,773	6,105	2,668	364	1,095
Genesee............................	5,860	394,197	0.90	4,653	11.4	4,558	11.2	21,574	6.4	88,552	45,647	42,905	11,919	2,922
Gladwin............................	289	22,345	0.66	264	10.4	379	15.0	1,549	8.4	8,101	5,067	3,034	278	1,110
Gogebic............................	1,313	15,713	1.02	120	7.9	216	14.3	751	7.3	4,385	3,019	1,366	175	1,149
Grand Traverse..................	1,455	100,308	1.20	910	9.8	847	9.1	5,027	6.8	21,412	13,189	8,223	1,199	1,295
Gratiot..............................	5,423	40,700	0.96	364	9.0	431	10.6	1,768	6.0	8,594	5,813	2,781	613	1,483
Hillsdale	1,579	42,577	0.82	555	12.1	484	10.6	2,449	6.8	10,177	7,060	3,117	516	1,127
Houghton	3,047	36,067	0.98	348	9.6	344	9.5	1,945	7.0	7,494	4,770	2,724	470	1,295
Huron...............................	524	32,311	1.04	313	10.0	457	14.7	1,656	7.0	9,134	6,694	2,440	321	1,053
Ingham..............................	17,194	320,672	1.26	3,359	11.5	2,213	7.6	16,185	6.9	47,351	33,211	14,140	8,377	2,919
Ionia................................	5,134	55,529	0.68	699	10.9	541	8.4	3,192	6.4	11,345	6,831	4,514	780	1,214
Iosco...............................	400	26,281	1.11	205	8.2	390	15.5	1,383	7.8	8,855	5,904	2,951	464	1,838
Iron.................................	355	10,909	0.91	95	8.5	185	16.6	538	6.9	3,823	2,728	1,095	167	1,484
Isabella.............................	5,846	73,876	1.10	604	8.6	459	6.5	5,075	8.9	10,615	7,348	3,267	1,167	1,650
Jackson.............................	8,665	153,459	0.92	1,737	10.9	1,628	10.3	7,513	6.1	33,884	24,070	9,814	4,338	2,761
Kalamazoo........................	8,460	265,684	1.05	3,125	11.8	2,194	8.3	14,403	6.6	47,607	26,166	21,441	9,213	3,515
Kalkaska...........................	138	15,136	0.67	161	9.0	180	10.1	1,042	7.6	4,540	3,106	1,434	337	1,950
Kent.................................	11,539	687,202	1.16	8,703	13.3	4,780	7.3	38,088	6.9	104,666	47,769	56,897	14,339	2,230

1. Per 1,000 estimated resident population.   2. Data for serious crimes have not been adjusted for underreporting; this may affect comparability between geographic areas and over time.   3. Per 100,000 population estimated by the FBI.

Table B. States and Counties — Crime, Education, Money Income, and Poverty

STATE County	Serious crimes known to police[2], 2016 (cont.)[1] Rate		Education School enrollment and attainment, 2013-2017 Enrollment[3]			Attainment[4] (percent)		Local government expenditures,[5] 2014-2015		Money income, 2013-2017		Households		Income and poverty, 2017		Percent below poverty level	
	Violent	Property	Total	Percent private	High school graduate or less	Bachelor's degree or more	Total current spending (mil dol)	Current spending per student (dollars)	Per capita income[6]	Median income (dollars)	Percent with income of less than $50,000	Percent with income of $200,000 or more	Median household income (dollars)	All persons	Children under 18 years	Children 5 to 17 years in families
	46	47	48	49	50	51	52	53	54	55	56	57	58	59	60	61
MARYLAND— Cont'd																
St. Mary's	203	1,854	30,421	15.7	40.1	30.4	218.2	12,201	37,528	86,508	27.7	9.1	82,433	8.5	11.4	11.5
Somerset	451	1,931	7,457	7.6	60.2	14.4	44.9	15,272	18,395	39,239	58.6	1.1	40,320	24.7	32.6	31.8
Talbot	220	1,902	7,464	19.3	36.2	37.4	55.4	11,962	44,785	65,595	39.6	8.8	70,620	9.1	14.8	14.1
Washington	302	2,134	34,512	13.2	49.8	21.5	293.8	13,159	28,742	58,260	43.3	3.9	59,828	13.3	18.7	16.4
Wicomico	489	2,931	30,759	10.4	44.7	27.8	190.7	13,108	27,755	54,493	46.7	4.0	52,341	15	20.5	20.1
Worcester	297	3,576	9,970	16.3	41.9	30.1	112.8	16,954	34,425	59,458	42.5	5.0	61,405	9.9	16.1	16.2
Baltimore city	1,802	4,778	156,859	23.7	45.6	30.4	1,344.2	15,743	28,488	46,641	52.7	4.6	46,762	22.1	31.8	29.8
MASSACHUSETTS	377	1,561	1,737,576	26.7	34.4	42.1	15,044.5	15,740	39,913	74,167	35.4	10.8	77,385	10.5	13.5	12.7
Barnstable	367	1,565	39,018	15.3	29.4	41.7	452.5	17,796	40,886	68,048	37.1	6.8	70,576	7.6	11.2	10.2
Berkshire	534	1,853	28,439	24.2	39.1	33.2	288.7	17,481	33,245	55,190	45.9	5.1	56,063	10.6	16.2	15.1
Bristol	464	1,788	135,245	17.4	45.5	27.3	1,120.7	14,185	32,406	62,514	41.6	5.8	67,085	11.1	17.1	15.0
Dukes	294	1,306	3,206	16.5	25.4	46.3	64.1	27,585	42,956	67,535	36.9	11.2	67,390	7.6	10.6	10.1
Essex	350	1,365	191,338	21.5	36.0	38.8	1,752.3	15,137	38,604	73,533	35.5	10.5	75,309	10.2	13.9	12.8
Franklin	380	1,390	15,018	14.0	35.1	36.8	162.3	16,528	33,010	57,307	44.0	3.8	57,930	10.4	14.4	11.8
Hampden	633	2,603	120,867	16.5	44.8	26.5	1,115.4	15,283	28,072	52,205	48.1	4.1	51,850	17.1	25.9	25.5
Hampshire	278	1,439	56,788	21.0	30.0	45.6	292.5	15,765	32,198	64,974	39.6	6.2	67,774	10.2	9.8	8.8
Middlesex	180	1,167	413,398	31.8	27.2	54.1	3,538.3	16,365	47,616	92,878	27.8	16.2	97,851	8	8.9	8.3
Nantucket	236	2,800	2,203	24.5	28.2	45.1	32.8	21,234	47,924	91,942	24.9	13.8	92,347	5.7	6.1	5.8
Norfolk	194	1,160	178,866	31.2	26.2	52.5	1,598.0	15,584	49,816	95,668	26.4	16.9	100,710	6.7	7.1	6.4
Plymouth	379	1,173	127,500	16.6	35.6	35.7	1,194.9	14,040	39,247	82,081	31.0	10.6	86,026	7.3	8.6	7.8
Suffolk	734	2,276	215,479	45.8	38.0	43.6	1,607.3	19,849	38,031	61,242	43.0	9.4	65,999	17.9	25.1	26.5
Worcester	438	1,646	210,211	20.8	38.4	35.3	1,824.7	14,137	34,691	69,313	37.1	7.9	70,222	10.4	12.6	11.6
MICHIGAN	459	1,910	2,522,019	12.9	39.0	28.1	16,801.9	11,248	28,938	52,668	47.4	4.3	54,840	14.1	19.6	17.7
Alcona	146	947	1,378	5.2	50.7	15.2	7.4	10,157	24,463	39,424	62.3	1.0	41,615	14.6	28.7	26.4
Alger	161	653	1,491	12.7	54.4	17.8	12.0	11,213	21,771	42,647	55.7	1.3	46,991	13	18.4	17.0
Allegan	277	1,207	27,099	11.5	47.3	22.3	179.0	10,165	27,172	58,487	42.2	2.9	62,421	9.5	12.5	10.7
Alpena	342	1,382	5,822	10.1	42.9	17.3	43.5	11,015	24,030	40,954	60.4	1.2	40,603	13.8	21.5	20.2
Antrim	91	1,668	4,255	8.2	42.1	26.9	33.7	9,964	29,307	50,988	48.7	4.0	50,583	11.1	17.8	16.3
Arenac	271	786	2,627	5.7	56.2	11.6	21.1	9,650	22,622	39,947	61.2	1.4	41,275	15.7	25.9	24.6
Baraga	NA	NA	1,471	9.0	56.9	15.5	11.8	10,739	18,975	42,757	58.6	2.1	42,180	16.7	23.6	21.2
Barry	204	897	13,437	12.4	45.5	19.5	83.7	9,294	27,166	57,312	42.4	1.8	59,460	8.8	11.7	10.8
Bay	373	1,888	24,336	11.8	45.2	19.0	164.4	11,440	25,462	45,983	53.2	2.0	45,771	14.5	19.4	16.1
Benzie	138	889	3,302	11.6	39.6	28.6	20.7	9,960	26,790	53,185	48.0	1.9	54,065	9.4	15.2	14.3
Berrien	453	2,339	37,655	21.1	40.0	26.7	288.0	11,423	27,505	47,132	52.2	3.5	48,924	17.3	26.6	23.9
Branch	272	1,654	9,553	13.6	52.2	14.0	76.5	11,886	22,977	48,192	51.6	1.5	49,387	12.6	19.1	16.8
Calhoun	742	3,074	32,139	12.5	45.1	21.0	251.4	12,503	24,859	46,213	53.2	2.3	46,113	19.1	28.4	24.9
Cass	232	1,624	11,277	9.4	46.4	18.1	68.9	10,233	28,019	50,699	49.2	3.2	52,063	12	17.9	16.8
Charlevoix	179	1,247	5,398	10.7	36.8	30.3	59.9	16,169	31,730	51,567	48.7	4.4	51,457	10.1	15.2	13.3
Cheboygan	146	1,305	4,626	8.5	48.8	19.5	37.6	13,144	24,956	42,876	57.0	1.7	43,724	14.3	25.8	24.2
Chippewa	303	1,182	8,405	10.7	47.1	20.7	63.0	12,974	21,958	44,030	55.8	1.4	44,586	17	21.7	19.2
Clare	378	1,583	5,799	11.8	54.2	12.1	53.5	12,380	21,198	35,913	64.0	1.2	36,661	22.3	37.8	35.0
Clinton	108	801	20,533	11.4	33.2	31.5	107.1	10,747	32,792	64,903	37.3	5.5	66,000	7.4	7.7	6.7
Crawford	269	1,528	2,577	7.7	47.1	17.6	15.8	9,949	22,891	42,666	56.9	0.3	47,068	16.6	30.5	27.5
Delta	215	1,941	7,334	9.5	40.1	20.7	53.7	11,422	25,582	44,639	54.2	1.7	50,802	12.6	18.2	16.9
Dickinson	NA	NA	5,028	10.5	41.8	25.5	43.8	11,741	25,998	45,681	54.1	2.2	48,291	12.1	15.7	14.2
Eaton	279	1,439	25,661	17.2	35.0	26.1	184.9	10,506	30,064	59,244	42.2	2.8	64,318	8.7	12.7	11.8
Emmet	144	950	7,172	11.4	30.9	32.9	50.9	10,381	31,356	51,475	48.3	4.2	52,796	8.5	12.1	11.2
Genesee	653	2,270	102,274	9.6	41.8	20.4	742.4	11,028	25,180	45,231	54.5	2.7	46,457	18.3	26.3	21.6
Gladwin	228	882	4,527	12.0	54.6	13.6	26.6	9,063	23,491	40,871	59.5	1.5	41,667	16.6	27.3	27.2
Gogebic	112	1,037	2,678	8.3	46.5	18.4	18.6	11,151	22,297	36,689	63.6	1.5	38,343	18.7	28.0	27.5
Grand Traverse	231	1,064	20,491	16.4	29.9	34.2	170.0	13,470	31,701	58,229	42.1	4.6	59,674	9.3	11.4	10.4
Gratiot	189	1,294	9,880	22.2	51.2	14.7	80.4	12,306	20,597	42,256	57.6	2.0	42,653	19.5	22.5	19.5
Hillsdale	186	941	10,910	27.1	51.1	16.8	68.7	11,290	23,831	46,160	53.9	1.9	47,610	14	20.2	19.0
Houghton	193	1,102	12,271	6.5	41.0	32.9	58.7	10,768	21,462	41,379	57.8	2.2	45,127	14.9	15.3	13.5
Huron	125	929	6,129	11.4	53.6	15.5	61.4	12,314	26,352	45,191	54.7	2.4	46,627	13.4	20.4	19.2
Ingham	632	2,287	98,822	7.5	28.8	38.4	496.5	11,902	27,399	49,109	50.8	3.7	51,186	19.8	23.7	22.8
Ionia	252	962	15,421	11.7	48.9	16.2	96.1	11,760	22,715	51,980	47.5	1.6	57,318	11.6	14.5	13.6
Iosco	321	1,517	4,242	8.6	50.5	16.6	41.0	10,686	24,099	41,414	60.8	1.3	41,755	17	28.1	25.9
Iron	231	1,253	1,820	6.1	53.2	18.5	12.7	9,884	23,658	36,773	63.3	1.2	42,082	13.5	24.0	21.7
Isabella	312	1,337	29,729	6.2	38.7	29.4	62.8	9,726	22,009	42,771	56.5	2.3	45,683	23.8	17.0	14.7
Jackson	537	2,224	38,295	15.0	42.6	21.1	277.3	11,984	25,952	49,715	50.2	2.7	50,895	13.3	21.2	18.9
Kalamazoo	569	2,947	80,035	10.1	28.6	37.2	390.4	11,440	29,258	51,945	48.2	4.5	56,199	14	16.1	14.9
Kalkaska	411	1,539	3,441	11.6	54.9	12.5	21.5	9,784	22,822	43,431	58.1	1.3	43,357	17.1	24.0	22.0
Kent	380	1,850	169,307	20.3	34.7	34.7	1,200.2	11,171	29,433	57,302	43.4	4.5	61,146	10.4	14.1	12.6

1. Data for serious crimes have not been adjusted for underreporting; this may affect comparability between geographic areas and over time.   2. Per 100,000 population estimated by the FBI.   3. All persons 3 years old and over enrolled in nursery school through college.   4. Persons 25 years old and over.   5. Elementary and secondary education expenditures.   6. Based on population estimated by the American Community Survey, 2011–2015.

STATE County	Personal income, 2017										Earnings, 2017		
	Total (mil dol)	Percent change 2016-2017	Per capita[1] Dollars	Rank	Wages and salaries (mil dol)	Supplements to wages and salaries, employer contributions (mil dol) Pension and insurance	Government social insurance	Proprietors' income (mil dol)	Dividends, interest, and rent (mil dol)	Personal transfer receipts (mil dol)	Total (mil dol)	Contributions for government social insurance (mil dol) From employee and self-employed	From employer
	62	63	64	65	66	67	68	69	70	71	72	73	74
MARYLAND— Cont'd													
St. Mary's	6,188	3.8	54,921	283	3,292	703	262	269	1,113	819	4,526	255	262
Somerset	812	5.3	31,327	2,829	332	89	24	80	147	278	525	30	24
Talbot	2,643	4.0	71,246	63	902	149	68	229	863	458	1,349	85	68
Washington	6,868	3.6	45,610	838	3,108	563	235	536	1,138	1,467	4,442	273	235
Wicomico	4,209	3.8	40,896	1,417	2,163	421	158	368	725	1,044	3,110	184	158
Worcester	3,008	4.5	58,191	200	947	170	78	374	825	625	1,569	99	78
Baltimore city	30,074	2.5	49,168	521	23,855	3,998	1,710	3,487	5,062	8,279	33,051	1,882	1,710
MASSACHUSETTS	463,931	4.3	67,596	X	254,642	37,251	16,753	41,300	92,100	67,100	349,945	18,838	16,753
Barnstable	15,033	4.3	70,430	69	4,828	879	352	1,499	4,336	2,822	7,559	449	352
Berkshire	6,833	2.6	54,095	310	2,995	541	215	527	1,414	1,673	4,277	248	215
Bristol	28,803	4.2	51,298	402	11,718	2,204	840	1,898	3,848	6,293	16,660	931	840
Dukes	1,530	5.2	88,295	21	482	82	36	299	567	168	899	47	36
Essex	50,309	4.3	64,071	112	19,842	3,250	1,377	4,221	9,307	7,762	28,690	1,573	1,377
Franklin	3,700	3.1	52,332	365	1,169	261	83	290	704	900	1,803	104	83
Hampden	23,171	2.6	49,319	507	10,680	2,077	751	1,260	3,088	6,615	14,768	814	751
Hampshire	8,186	3.4	50,582	427	3,248	794	205	776	1,623	1,230	5,023	244	205
Middlesex	126,975	4.7	79,214	37	77,960	9,584	5,085	10,431	28,364	12,209	103,060	5,578	5,085
Nantucket	1,341	5.0	119,379	8	439	60	34	302	513	73	834	41	34
Norfolk	60,750	4.1	86,746	23	23,842	3,399	1,637	4,571	14,255	5,550	33,450	1,811	1,637
Plymouth	32,980	4.4	64,020	115	10,534	1,920	731	2,451	5,702	5,127	15,636	858	731
Suffolk	58,974	4.3	73,909	56	67,077	8,612	4,035	9,403	12,075	8,962	89,128	4,633	4,035
Worcester	45,346	4.7	54,891	286	19,828	3,588	1,371	3,371	6,302	7,718	28,159	1,506	1,371
MICHIGAN	460,270	3.5	46,136	X	231,748	38,237	17,078	30,622	82,505	94,679	317,685	20,022	17,078
Alcona	378	4.0	36,474	2,119	69	16	5	12	89	158	103	12	5
Alger	294	2.4	32,253	2,719	100	23	8	11	59	100	141	11	8
Allegan	4,938	4.3	42,406	1,214	1,907	350	141	272	799	918	2,670	171	141
Alpena	1,118	2.3	39,288	1,675	475	103	37	67	187	387	681	49	37
Antrim	1,016	2.7	43,615	1,061	189	44	16	58	281	289	307	27	16
Arenac	546	3.3	36,296	2,152	174	34	14	25	84	199	248	20	14
Baraga	263	1.1	31,211	2,838	110	33	8	11	51	85	162	11	8
Barry	2,590	3.6	42,745	1,178	542	127	40	149	431	501	858	62	40
Bay	4,276	3.9	41,024	1,403	1,577	299	118	170	695	1,216	2,164	155	118
Benzie	718	3.3	40,874	1,422	154	30	12	45	190	196	241	20	12
Berrien	7,116	4.9	46,133	781	3,145	636	239	360	1,251	1,610	4,379	279	239
Branch	1,528	3.8	35,200	2,312	593	122	44	60	265	424	820	57	44
Calhoun	5,188	1.9	38,683	1,780	3,073	546	233	200	832	1,414	4,052	261	233
Cass	2,229	5.2	43,379	1,093	410	87	31	90	395	505	618	51	31
Charlevoix	1,272	2.5	48,678	572	486	91	38	90	354	272	705	48	38
Cheboygan	952	2.5	37,539	1,939	235	47	20	50	218	321	351	30	20
Chippewa	1,224	1.8	32,459	2,693	487	142	38	48	234	371	714	47	38
Clare	1,002	2.9	32,680	2,660	306	69	24	58	161	388	457	38	24
Clinton	3,473	3.5	44,270	989	784	132	60	161	577	559	1,137	81	60
Crawford	454	3.7	32,627	2,671	168	34	13	31	85	156	246	19	13
Delta	1,381	2.0	38,390	1,811	577	110	47	55	249	427	789	58	47
Dickinson	1,150	2.5	45,248	876	684	140	53	27	230	298	904	57	53
Eaton	4,447	2.6	40,784	1,435	2,081	374	152	182	725	942	2,790	183	152
Emmet	1,769	3.4	53,296	335	784	133	60	137	517	358	1,113	72	60
Genesee	16,147	2.7	39,636	1,615	6,539	1,151	497	795	2,451	4,753	8,982	614	497
Gladwin	903	5.3	35,770	2,234	163	35	13	45	153	328	255	26	13
Gogebic	583	1.7	38,016	1,881	212	51	16	20	138	199	299	22	16
Grand Traverse	4,330	3.5	47,165	699	2,334	399	177	419	987	830	3,330	208	177
Gratiot	1,440	1.6	35,104	2,338	562	122	43	63	227	401	790	54	43
Hillsdale	1,556	1.6	33,908	2,493	598	119	46	69	246	428	832	58	46
Houghton	1,291	1.6	35,570	2,263	513	125	39	54	284	365	730	48	39
Huron	1,352	1.6	43,223	1,115	465	95	37	74	365	397	671	48	37
Ingham	11,258	2.7	38,795	1,759	7,788	1,603	566	577	1,979	2,381	10,534	619	566
Ionia	2,111	2.9	32,840	2,641	679	156	52	72	270	482	960	65	52
Iosco	911	4.2	36,220	2,170	311	64	25	43	182	368	442	37	25
Iron	470	1.3	42,236	1,238	147	32	11	14	86	176	204	16	11
Isabella	2,349	0.7	33,053	2,607	1,189	303	88	94	444	631	1,674	100	88
Jackson	6,039	2.4	38,069	1,874	2,843	553	213	319	954	1,571	3,929	257	213
Kalamazoo	12,200	3.6	46,389	764	6,499	1,143	476	799	2,380	2,153	8,917	541	476
Kalkaska	578	2.8	32,780	2,651	218	40	16	33	97	184	309	23	16
Kent	33,598	3.7	51,801	383	20,253	3,176	1,497	2,675	8,126	4,735	27,601	1,636	1,497

1. Based on the resident population estimated as of July 1 of the year shown.

STATE County	Farm	Mining, quarrying, and extractions	Construction	Manu-facturing	Information; professional, scientific, technical services	Retail trade	Finance, insurance, real estate, and leasing	Health care and social assistance	Govern-ment	Social Security beneficiaries, December 2017 Number	Rate[1]	Supplemental Security Income recipients, 2017	Housing units, 2018 Total	Percent change, 2010-2018
	75	76	77	78	79	80	81	82	83	84	85	86	87	88
MARYLAND— Cont'd														
St. Mary's	-0.2	D	4	0.9	23.4	4	2.8	6.3	46.7	16,275	144	1,663	46,013	11.5
Somerset	10.8	0	4.4	3.7	1.5	D	D	D	45.8	5,410	209	900	11,490	3.2
Talbot	0.9	D	7.2	D	11	6.8	11.1	21.6	10.9	11,055	298	564	20,245	3.4
Washington	0.4	D	5.6	11.4	4.6	9.3	12.3	14.8	14.4	32,400	215	3,660	61,638	1.4
Wicomico	2.2	D	5.9	6.1	5.9	8.6	7.3	19.3	17.7	20,590	200	2,738	42,470	3.1
Worcester	2.9	D	6.2	2.8	6.6	9.5	9.6	9.1	17.6	15,475	299	855	56,532	1.4
Baltimore city	0	D	3.6	2.7	13.6	1.8	10.4	18	19.9	103,560	169	37,289	293,653	
MASSACHUSETTS	0	0.1	6.1	7.8	19.8	4.5	11.5	13.2	11.9	1,260,786	184	186,405	2,914,929	3.8
Barnstable	0	D	12.7	D	8.6	9.2	6.6	16.2	18	71,395	334	3,201	164,321	2.5
Berkshire	0	D	D	8.9	9.2	7.3	5.7	19.1	14.3	34,390	272	4,007	69,400	1.3
Bristol	0	0	7.8	D	7.1	7.9	3.8	15.2	15.1	121,775	217	18,939	236,274	2.5
Dukes	0.1	0	D	D	D	9.2	5.1	9.3	14.7	4,430	256	125	18,023	4.9
Essex	0	0	7.4	15.8	12.8	5.9	5.6	15.7	12.8	149,980	191	22,436	313,958	2.4
Franklin	-0.2	D	9.5	13.3	6.1	6.9	2.8	13	19.4	17,205	243	2,045	34,172	1.2
Hampden	0	0.1	6.3	9.8	5.6	6.2	9	21	18.8	102,465	218	30,875	193,870	0.9
Hampshire	0	D	5.7	4.4	6.6	D	3.6	12.9	31	30,905	191	2,945	64,057	2.3
Middlesex	0.1	0	5.5	10.1	30.6	3.4	5.7	8.7	8.6	248,170	155	25,080	641,398	4.8
Nantucket	0	0.5	25.1	D	D	D	6.4	5.2	10.2	1,705	152	35	12,514	7.7
Norfolk	0	0	8.6	6.9	16.5	6.5	12	11.5	9.9	121,500	173	10,483	280,291	3.7
Plymouth	0.1	0.1	11.3	5.6	8.9	7.8	7	13.5	18.1	106,225	206	9,237	208,114	4
Suffolk	0	D	2.6	D	23.3	2.1	25.5	15.4	10.3	97,560	122	34,094	342,052	8.4
Worcester	0	0.1	7.5	12.2	10.2	5.7	7	15.8	15.9	153,080	185	22,903	336,485	3
MICHIGAN	0.1	0.2	5.6	16.6	12.4	5.8	7.3	12.3	14	2,186,709	219	274,877	4,614,380	1.8
Alcona	-2.8	0	D	12.9	D	9.3	4	26	17.9	4,750	459	322	11,196	1.1
Alger	0.1	0	3.9	25.4	D	5.2	5	6.9	29.7	2,960	325	172	6,704	2.3
Allegan	1.8	0.1	9.2	37	3.2	5.2	3.3	4.3	12.9	24,505	210	1,655	51,523	4.2
Alpena	-0.5	1.2	5	16.7	4.2	9.8	4.8	9.8	29.3	9,750	343	1,139	16,067	0.1
Antrim	0.8	D	10.6	16.5	5.2	8	5.8	D	23.7	7,795	335	484	18,111	1.6
Arenac	-0.1	D	4.8	19.1	D	8.6	4.4	14.6	15	5,255	349	612	9,856	0.5
Baraga	0.1	D	3.6	18.1	2.9	D	D	D	51.9	2,245	266	160	5,309	0.7
Barry	2	0	7.1	30.7	D	4.6	7.6	7.9	18.3	14,055	232	705	27,791	2.9
Bay		0	4.4	15.6	11	8	4.5	17.1	18	29,035	279	3,218	48,336	0.2
Benzie	0.7	D	15.3	9	D	8.1	6.7	10.7	18.3	5,630	320	298	12,611	3.4
Berrien	0.8	0.2	4.5	30.5	3.9	5.3	4.8	11.7	13.8	37,685	244	4,668	77,648	0.9
Branch	-1.2	D	6.2	18.5	D	7.4	5.3	5.7	24.2	10,615	245	958	20,910	0.3
Calhoun	0.1	D	3.8	24.9	10.1	4.8	2.4	14	21	32,920	245	4,894	60,864	-0.3
Cass	-1.1	D	8	23.6	4.1	4.6	5.6	D	22.2	13,035	254	956	26,432	2.1
Charlevoix	0	D	10.1	26.3	D	4.7	4	12.8	16.8	7,685	294	484	17,758	2.9
Cheboygan	0.3	D	14.8	2.6	5.9	11.3	5.1	D	21.1	8,925	352	671	18,614	1.7
Chippewa	-0.4	D	4	4.9	2.7	7.6	2.8	4.5	57	8,910	236	902	21,489	1.1
Clare	-0.1	D	9.3	15.4	5.5	8.8	3.3	8.5	24.4	10,285	336	1,331	23,371	0.6
Clinton	0.5	0.5	13.9	14.7	D	8.3	8.5	7	14.7	15,530	198	673	31,952	4.1
Crawford	0	D	D	13.1	4	6.4	3.9	D	21.5	4,300	309	381	11,241	1.3
Delta	0.1	D	8.2	19.7	D	8.8	4.8	12.8	17.3	11,585	322	999	20,393	0.9
Dickinson	-0.1	0	19.2	21.9	3.1	6.5	2.5	D	25.2	7,470	294	506	14,106	0.8
Eaton	-0.6	0.1	5.7	18.4	5	7.1	17	5.5	14.9	25,280	232	1,731	47,668	1.3
Emmet	0	D	9.4	11.4	D	9.8	5.3	18.7	15.2	9,070	273	498	21,772	2.2
Genesee	0.1	0	5.9	11.2	7.4	8.5	6.2	18.8	16.4	99,615	245	16,841	192,637	0.2
Gladwin	-0.9	D	14.2	19.5	D	11.3	5.1	D	19.5	9,090	360	892	17,952	1.6
Gogebic	-0.1	0	5.2	14.6	3	6.9	2.6	D	33.6	4,890	319	457	10,795	0
Grand Traverse	0.1	0.4	8.1	10.9	8.1	9.5	10.2	21.3	12.7	22,585	246	1,429	44,494	7
Gratiot	-0.2	D	3.4	19.2	D	5.7	4.4	D	20.9	9,515	232	1,111	16,348	0.1
Hillsdale	1.1	D	4.6	34.3	D	6.3	3.3	D	18.3	11,235	245	1,141	22,090	1.5
Houghton	0.1	D	6.1	5.8	5.9	7.2	3.6	15.3	41.7	8,185	225	621	18,923	1.6
Huron	1	D	7.1	15.6	D	6.8	5.9	D	17.2	9,915	317	712	21,304	0.5
Ingham	-0.1	D	3.9	8.7	9.1	4.7	7.1	15.1	31.5	50,870	175	8,035	124,140	2.4
Ionia	1.4	D	7.9	25.4	2.4	7.3	5.1	6.3	24	12,725	198	1,276	25,028	1
Iosco	0	D	7.2	10.6	3.3	7.7	4.7	D	21.5	9,785	389	833	20,553	0.5
Iron	0.3	0	7.9	5	D	12.8	4.3	14	26.7	4,245	382	285	9,331	1.5
Isabella	-0.6	1.7	9.4	10.5	3.4	6.4	6	7.6	38.7	11,625	164	1,233	29,284	3.2
Jackson	-0.3	0.1	5	19.2	4.6	6.1	4.8	16	14.2	37,230	235	4,545	69,685	0.3
Kalamazoo	0.4	0	6.5	22.5	6.4	6.1	8.6	15.5	13	50,895	194	6,397	112,800	2.5
Kalkaska	0.2	12.7	17.4	6.2	D	5.3	2.6	2.3	21.3	5,035	286	376	12,408	2
Kent	0.2	0	6.1	20.3	8.1	5.5	8.1	15.3	7.5	111,485	172	13,896	257,370	4.2

1. Per 1,000 resident population estimated as of July 1 of the year shown.

Table B. States and Counties — Housing, Labor Force, and Employment

STATE County	Total	Percent	Median value[1]	With a mortgage	Without a mortgage[2]	Median rent[3]	Median rent as a percent of income[2]	Sub-standard units[4] (percent)	Total	Percent change, 2017-2018	Total	Rate[5]	Total	Management, business, science, and arts	Construction, production, and maintenance occupations
	89	90	91	92	93	94	95	96	97	98	99	100	101	102	103
MARYLAND— Cont'd															
St. Mary's	39,276	71.9	291,500	21.6	10.6	1,288	28.1	1.8	55,295	0.6	2,102	3.8	54,121	44.8	19.0
Somerset	8,362	64.6	131,000	23.3	14.3	673	40.1	3.3	9,353	0.9	644	6.9	8,593	28.9	22.8
Talbot	16,498	70.3	326,300	22.9	10.7	1,084	35.4	0.8	19,562	-0.5	733	3.7	17,863	43.2	17.1
Washington	55,999	64.5	205,300	21.2	11.4	889	27.7	2	74,742	-0.5	3,249	4.3	67,375	33.2	23.9
Wicomico	37,415	60.7	171,700	21.2	12.3	1,042	32.2	3.6	51,041	0.6	2,676	5.2	49,785	32.7	22.0
Worcester	21,190	74.4	252,100	25.7	13.1	994	30.3	1.9	25,525	0.5	2,050	8	23,915	35.5	16.6
Baltimore city	239,791	47.4	153,200	23.2	13.8	1,009	31.8	2.6	289,758	-0.1	16,454	5.7	277,954	42.1	15.3
MASSACHUSETTS	2,585,715	62.4	352,600	23.0	14.2	1,173	30.1	2.3	3,805,450	3	127,048	3.3	3,525,672	45.3	15.4
Barnstable	95,011	78.8	375,000	26.2	14.6	1,199	32.6	1.3	116,225	2.5	4,974	4.3	104,246	37.9	17.6
Berkshire	55,063	69.0	203,300	21.8	13.6	802	30.3	0.9	66,109	1.1	2,669	4	63,947	37.7	17.8
Bristol	215,903	62.6	280,400	23.0	14.0	855	29	1.6	302,918	2.4	12,963	4.3	278,538	36.2	21.9
Dukes	6,139	77.7	674,600	35.0	15.8	1,441	31.4	2.8	9,780	2.3	449	4.6	9,172	45.2	21.5
Essex	291,659	63.8	373,400	23.6	14.7	1,135	31.5	2.7	429,887	2.7	14,703	3.4	397,621	41.2	17.6
Franklin	30,512	68.9	226,600	23.9	13.9	899	31.5	1.3	41,365	2.5	1,250	3	36,953	41.5	19.6
Hampden	178,931	61.2	198,500	22.4	14.6	866	32.6	2.8	231,265	2.5	10,659	4.6	215,324	34.2	20.6
Hampshire	58,782	66.1	272,700	22.6	13.9	1,040	32.7	1.2	91,522	2.6	2,768	3	84,348	45.7	13.7
Middlesex	593,784	62.6	453,300	22.2	13.6	1,455	28.4	2.2	923,768	3.3	24,982	2.7	862,873	55.0	11.5
Nantucket	3,761	64.8	995,900	27.7	15.5	1,689	28.9	4.4	7,526	4.4	332	4.4	6,408	32.3	25.5
Norfolk	262,324	69.3	433,000	22.5	14.0	1,450	29.5	1.5	393,159	3.4	11,654	3	367,385	52.8	11.6
Plymouth	184,195	75.9	344,400	23.8	14.8	1,185	31.1	1.4	284,938	3.2	9,970	3.5	261,653	38.8	17.4
Suffolk	303,676	36.3	430,900	24.1	14.2	1,419	31.1	3.9	456,319	3.4	13,720	3	423,215	45.5	12.2
Worcester	305,975	64.7	260,800	22.3	14.1	987	29.5	2.4	450,670	2.6	15,956	3.5	413,989	41.7	18.5
MICHIGAN	3,888,646	71.0	136,400	20.1	12.5	824	30.3	2	4,902,069	0.3	203,224	4.1	4,524,874	35.6	23.6
Alcona	4,979	88.2	96,000	22.9	12.8	601	29.5	1.2	3,830	-0.9	252	6.6	3,357	23.5	32.8
Alger	3,244	86.6	119,000	23.1	12.3	611	32.8	1.9	3,243	-1.6	254	7.8	3,160	27.9	25.8
Allegan	42,556	81.9	150,600	20.3	10.8	775	24.7	2.4	62,239	1.2	2,033	3.3	54,028	30.3	35.0
Alpena	12,789	77.0	94,000	20.4	12.2	568	28.4	1.1	13,459	-1.4	684	5.1	12,665	29.5	24.5
Antrim	9,732	84.7	151,500	22.8	12.7	701	28.5	1.9	10,111	-0.1	568	5.6	9,771	27.5	28.4
Arenac	6,663	82.7	88,900	23.3	13.1	610	28.8	1.5	5,974	-1.6	425	7.1	5,842	25.6	31.3
Baraga	3,009	83.3	93,100	22.5	12.4	567	27.9	2.7	3,176	-0.5	194	6.1	2,485	25.8	27.6
Barry	23,539	80.3	146,300	20.9	11.2	815	26.7	1.9	31,664	1.1	1,079	3.4	27,877	29.0	32.1
Bay	44,070	78.1	96,800	20.4	13.0	637	29.8	1.1	50,352	-0.9	2,410	4.8	46,195	29.4	25.2
Benzie	6,911	88.0	162,200	22.5	11.8	722	28.6	1.8	8,790	-0.8	484	5.5	7,679	31.0	25.5
Berrien	63,035	69.3	140,900	19.8	12.0	709	29.9	2	73,328		3,152	4.3	70,439	34.2	25.0
Branch	16,415	75.4	97,700	20.1	12.1	708	26.9	2.7	19,641	1.3	720	3.7	18,861	22.8	36.7
Calhoun	53,528	69.8	102,600	19.8	13.1	714	31.1	1.7	62,865	-1.5	2,646	4.2	58,179	29.0	30.0
Cass	20,686	80.5	127,600	21.0	11.7	721	28.7	2.8	24,378	0.3	992	4.1	23,277	28.6	35.4
Charlevoix	11,234	81.1	158,800	22.3	12.1	702	27.8	1	13,128	0.5	622	4.7	11,902	30.7	26.3
Cheboygan	11,348	81.7	116,900	22.2	11.4	655	28.3	1.4	10,682	-1.2	983	9.2	10,443	26.8	27.7
Chippewa	14,004	70.0	111,100	19.9	11.8	628	27	1.3	16,312	-0.1	1,081	6.6	14,986	29.1	20.4
Clare	12,726	81.5	85,000	23.2	12.5	597	34.5	3.1	11,843		721	6.1	10,985	25.1	30.7
Clinton	29,163	79.3	164,700	19.5	11.4	796	27.6	0.9	41,047	-0.1	1,303	3.2	37,136	40.4	21.2
Crawford	6,025	80.6	91,900	21.0	12.7	733	31.1	1.6	5,512	1.9	331	6	5,107	26.1	28.5
Delta	15,920	79.9	105,900	19.9	12.1	558	30.6	1.6	17,030	-0.3	905	5.3	15,821	28.1	30.3
Dickinson	11,269	77.9	92,100	18.4	12.6	672	27.3	1.3	12,449	-0.6	479	3.8	11,154	35.4	26.7
Eaton	44,323	70.8	142,300	19.5	12.2	823	26.3	1.9	56,986	-0.2	1,977	3.5	52,647	34.2	24.4
Emmet	14,496	73.5	171,100	20.8	12.4	779	28.6	1.9	17,604	0.1	1,037	5.9	16,237	35.0	20.1
Genesee	166,838	70.1	96,500	21.1	13.2	738	32.9	1.6	181,781	0	8,894	4.9	166,919	31.5	24.8
Gladwin	10,990	83.6	100,500	22.8	12.3	601	30	3.2	9,952	0.2	560	5.6	8,896	24.7	34.9
Gogebic	6,660	77.1	70,100	19.9	13.3	512	30.1	0.9	6,207	-2.1	317	5.1	5,968	27.3	31.1
Grand Traverse	36,519	76.6	183,000	21.9	12.2	917	27.2	1.7	49,157	-0.2	1,811	3.7	45,390	36.7	19.0
Gratiot	14,736	72.7	92,100	21.3	12.3	658	32.4	1	17,766	-1.1	832	4.7	15,236	29.9	29.3
Hillsdale	17,896	76.5	105,600	20.0	12.1	702	28	2.7	20,738	-1.5	834	4	19,345	27.9	36.1
Houghton	13,157	68.5	102,400	19.5	11.9	664	35.8	2.7	16,179	-1.7	824	5.1	15,228	39.4	18.0
Huron	13,880	81.6	96,200	20.8	11.9	596	29.4	1.5	15,826	-0.5	729	4.6	14,090	28.9	33.9
Ingham	111,894	58.2	123,700	20.0	12.5	841	31.5	1.8	150,474	-0.2	5,483	3.6	137,687	40.8	17.2
Ionia	22,625	77.9	117,000	20.0	12.5	731	28.3	2.5	30,119	0.3	1,037	3.4	27,980	27.0	32.6
Iosco	11,457	80.1	89,000	20.8	11.6	621	27	2	10,076	-0.4	642	6.4	8,924	23.4	34.7
Iron	5,315	82.6	76,700	22.4	14.4	500	29.4	1.2	5,147	-0.7	287	5.6	4,376	23.3	29.7
Isabella	24,898	61.5	128,400	20.7	11.1	723	39	2	34,817	-1.1	1,363	3.9	33,890	31.0	19.8
Jackson	61,418	73.2	120,100	20.1	11.7	738	31	1.5	74,281	0.2	2,930	3.9	67,486	30.5	26.5
Kalamazoo	102,362	63.7	146,100	19.4	12.1	762	29.3	1.5	132,886	0.3	4,537	3.4	128,938	39.3	19.1
Kalkaska	7,019	80.5	105,300	21.6	12.4	674	27.3	2.6	7,816	-0.8	458	5.9	6,968	20.9	33.2
Kent	236,929	68.9	153,500	19.2	11.2	828	29.5	2.3	358,900	1.2	10,654	3	321,583	36.2	24.2

1. Specified owner-occupied units. lacking complete plumbing facilities.   2. A value of 10.0 represents 10 percent or less; a value of 50.0 represents 50 percent or more.   3. Specified renter-occupied units.   4. Overcrowded or   5. Percent of civilian labor force.   6. Civilian employed persons 16 years old and over.

Table B. States and Counties — Nonfarm Employment and Agriculture

	Private nonfarm establishments, employment and payroll, 2016									Agriculture, 2017			
		Employment						Annual payroll		Farms			Farm producers whose primary occupation is farming (percent)
							Professional, scientific, and technical services				Percent with:		
STATE County	Number of establishments	Total	Health care and social assistance	Manufacturing	Retail trade	Finance and insurance		Total (mil dol)	Average per employee (dollars)	Number	Fewer than 50 acres	1000 acres or more	
	104	105	106	107	108	109	110	111	112	113	114	115	116

STATE County	104	105	106	107	108	109	110	111	112	113	114	115	116
MARYLAND— Cont'd													
St. Mary's	1,937	29,819	4,765	335	4,741	454	8,199	1,484	49,765	615	57.2	1.5	43.7
Somerset	361	3,888	1,222	391	411	80	108	143	36,788	255	42.4	3.9	56.2
Talbot	1,441	17,217	3,262	1,231	2,791	492	1,063	654	37,963	317	44.5	10.4	43.7
Washington	3,403	60,322	9,844	5,942	10,150	6,734	1,788	2,296	38,070	877	50.3	1.1	45.1
Wicomico	2,469	36,295	9,044	2,459	6,683	1,183	1,387	1,421	39,141	494	53.0	4.9	48.6
Worcester	2,127	18,178	2,224	602	3,676	538	593	635	34,931	369	49.3	7.9	45.9
Baltimore city	12,555	295,343	75,924	11,002	18,236	16,775	21,930	18,040	61,082	NA	NA	NA	NA
MASSACHUSETTS	177,631	3,254,781	644,071	221,424	373,471	189,009	283,863	204,747	62,907	7,241	67.8	0.3	42.8
Barnstable	8,596	76,683	16,339	1,957	15,886	2,276	4,922	3,430	44,724	321	93.5	0.0	46.5
Berkshire	3,896	53,308	11,591	5,141	8,396	1,895	2,520	2,379	44,620	475	50.9	1.3	42.6
Bristol	12,799	201,964	42,329	26,135	34,323	4,632	6,133	9,060	44,860	688	75.9	NA	50.7
Dukes	1,087	5,679	814	103	1,137	228	235	330	58,057	108	90.7	0.9	45.5
Essex	18,715	288,887	68,167	36,622	40,456	11,171	14,211	14,773	51,137	419	78.0	0.5	46.9
Franklin	1,583	20,265	3,761	3,659	2,956	501	534	823	40,620	830	46.7	0.5	41.6
Hampden	9,675	170,884	41,474	19,271	23,448	9,649	6,455	7,650	44,770	523	64.1	0.4	37.0
Hampshire	3,628	62,356	21,306	2,797	7,841	1,783	2,017	2,108	33,809	692	59.2	NA	41.2
Middlesex	44,154	887,777	136,116	53,481	85,243	30,420	117,249	67,139	75,626	620	73.9	NA	41.3
Nantucket	1,014	4,697	512	49	847	116	183	331	70,425	21	90.5	NA	59.7
Norfolk	20,112	347,909	72,396	17,433	47,455	27,982	22,879	19,295	55,461	197	81.2	0.5	41.0
Plymouth	12,464	167,363	34,123	10,681	29,021	7,202	10,427	7,760	46,364	758	74.8	0.8	47.4
Suffolk	21,204	612,391	123,222	10,504	36,281	72,492	74,266	51,557	84,189	21	100.0	NA	43.8
Worcester	18,053	300,840	68,658	33,591	39,746	16,448	18,166	14,557	48,388	1,568	67.7	0.1	38.6
MICHIGAN	220,412	3,805,578	615,103	579,509	470,993	160,029	266,869	183,193	48,138	47,641	46.3	4.5	43.1
Alcona	170	1,197	200	200	282	34	52	39	32,221	223	37.7	1.3	51.4
Alger	230	1,672	224	512	273	78	21	68	40,960	126	48.4	4.8	39.4
Allegan	2,285	36,388	3,271	13,439	3,855	373	1,500	1,655	45,483	1,172	52.2	5.0	43.9
Alpena	780	10,431	2,802	1,272	1,941	323	227	354	33,951	415	38.6	2.4	38.1
Antrim	540	3,697	336	805	581	122	123	119	32,135	333	37.8	2.4	47.4
Arenac	332	3,295	574	820	503	63	90	116	35,220	350	34.0	5.7	36.7
Baraga	180	1,676	267	494	267	46	9	55	32,524	65	29.2	7.7	40.8
Barry	902	10,375	1,233	3,367	1,308	732	318	400	38,585	938	48.8	4.1	34.2
Bay	2,195	30,973	7,257	4,090	5,450	968	1,550	1,216	39,250	726	36.8	8.8	48.8
Benzie	445	3,587	429	675	501	152	62	116	32,466	197	59.9	0.5	38.7
Berrien	3,520	54,222	9,392	9,337	7,077	1,396	1,983	2,383	43,951	872	57.8	3.3	48.8
Branch	812	11,748	1,556	2,604	1,793	406	519	431	36,690	789	38.7	7.5	39.9
Calhoun	2,558	53,966	9,228	14,614	6,161	1,015	2,516	2,716	50,327	958	42.6	5.8	44.2
Cass	723	7,556	940	2,551	902	200	185	260	34,412	747	51.1	5.2	43.1
Charlevoix	782	8,288	1,336	2,523	891	190	205	343	41,337	271	45.8	1.1	39.0
Cheboygan	734	4,628	767	277	1,168	219	112	162	34,903	330	37.0	0.9	32.3
Chippewa	805	8,985	2,072	570	1,729	277	228	274	30,501	427	26.7	3.5	36.1
Clare	564	6,176	1,320	1,114	1,098	134	153	218	35,302	396	40.9	2.3	48.5
Clinton	1,310	16,486	1,937	2,413	2,484	1,056	513	611	37,082	1,017	46.7	5.9	41.5
Crawford	303	3,501	1,057	571	527	50	60	132	37,616	45	62.2	NA	19.2
Delta	1,019	12,134	1,903	2,140	2,310	734	367	423	34,865	253	29.2	5.5	41.6
Dickinson	837	12,473	2,733	1,996	1,938	317	334	546	43,795	158	32.9	1.3	34.9
Eaton	2,092	39,769	3,632	7,408	5,915	3,807	1,032	1,863	46,841	962	41.6	5.0	42.2
Emmet	1,502	14,731	2,960	1,255	2,823	322	435	584	39,638	324	43.8	0.9	33.5
Genesee	7,684	120,175	27,279	10,873	19,837	4,072	4,355	5,010	41,686	820	59.4	3.4	46.2
Gladwin	401	3,834	661	919	712	99	43	131	34,235	459	37.5	1.5	39.6
Gogebic	379	4,066	649	729	724	102	92	122	29,897	54	51.9	1.9	18.8
Grand Traverse	3,409	44,949	9,243	4,898	7,989	2,128	2,358	1,849	41,132	497	57.3	0.8	38.4
Gratiot	736	10,746	2,373	2,392	1,396	392	251	388	36,120	812	38.3	9.7	49.8
Hillsdale	751	10,914	1,369	4,191	1,454	266	203	399	36,598	1,205	44.3	5.8	40.8
Houghton	839	8,950	1,970	817	1,644	509	516	285	31,807	208	36.5	0.5	38.7
Huron	937	10,742	1,982	3,237	1,410	491	238	395	36,748	1,153	29.7	14.0	52.0
Ingham	6,104	109,635	23,565	8,984	13,725	8,616	6,364	4,958	45,224	912	60.2	4.4	39.6
Ionia	889	11,192	1,311	3,811	1,958	572	164	394	35,223	954	44.3	5.6	46.3
Iosco	616	6,495	1,001	1,139	1,352	224	164	215	33,090	244	42.2	0.8	37.0
Iron	352	2,566	407	315	427	120	113	83	32,279	133	32.3	2.3	49.0
Isabella	1,375	23,489	3,073	2,574	3,437	531	604	794	33,805	959	36.9	3.6	42.1
Jackson	2,897	50,505	10,043	9,290	7,378	1,312	2,931	2,310	45,746	923	52.1	3.9	41.5
Kalamazoo	5,561	107,303	19,560	16,991	13,557	5,762	4,088	5,049	47,052	707	61.8	5.1	43.2
Kalkaska	337	3,611	546	469	607	73	57	166	45,935	225	39.1	1.3	35.5
Kent	16,349	358,249	52,360	65,032	35,806	15,691	15,778	16,272	45,421	1,010	54.1	3.5	43.1

STATE County	Land in farms					Value of land and buildings (dollars)		Value of machinery and equiopmnet, average per farm (dollars)	Value of products sold:				Organic farms (number)	Farms with internet access (percent)	Government payments	
			Acres								Percent from:					
	Acreage (1,000)	Percent change, 2012-2017	Average size of farm	Total irrigated (1,000)	Total cropland (1,000)	Average per farm	Average per acre		Total (mil dol)	Average per farm (acres)	Crops	Livestock and poultry products			Total ($1,000)	Percent of farms
	117	118	119	120	121	122	123	124	125	126	127	128	129	130	131	132

MARYLAND— Cont'd																
St. Mary's..........................	62	-7.9	100	0.7	37.0	999,805	9,949	75,425	26.0	42,203	78.8	21.2	2	58.0	970	19.5
Somerset........................	59	-8.9	233	0.3	38.0	1,334,676	5,726	173,390	262.2	1,028,239	8.4	91.6	2	76.9	1,875	51.8
Talbot	94	-21.6	295	8.3	81.1	2,075,678	7,028	158,736	68.5	216,199	63.0	37.0	3	80.4	3,891	58.4
Washington	119	-8.0	136	0.6	82.2	1,095,597	8,057	121,316	153.7	175,285	24.8	75.2	12	69.1	995	17.8
Wicomico........................	89	5.8	179	11.0	65.6	1,261,012	7,034	158,378	304.0	615,350	22.5	77.5	3	75.3	2,410	44.1
Worcester........................	99	-0.1	269	5.9	71.6	1,425,500	5,300	184,865	249.1	675,154	15.1	84.9	1	72.1	3,630	51.8
Baltimore city	NA	NA	NA	NA	NA	NA	NA	NA	NA	NA	NA	NA	NA	NA	NA	NA
MASSACHUSETTS	492	-6.1	68	23.9	171.5	739,711	10,894	65,382	475.2	65,624	76.5	23.5	208	84.1	4,004	7.3
Barnstable......................	7	40.4	20	1.1	1.6	624,807	30,555	60,762	23.1	72,019	40.4	59.6	11	90.0	197	4.7
Berkshire........................	59	-4.9	123	0.3	19.1	943,835	7,644	72,649	23.5	49,453	42.8	57.2	16	85.5	447	7.8
Bristol............................	32	-8.2	47	2.0	13.0	846,518	18,186	68,617	35.0	50,901	79.0	21.0	18	75.3	429	12.6
Dukes............................	8	-39.3	71	0.3	0.8	816,456	11,429	88,694	5.4	49,917	61.5	38.5	5	91.7	NA	NA
Essex............................	21	-7.5	49	1.3	11.0	863,169	17,450	69,643	32.9	78,439	86.6	13.4	6	89.7	54	2.1
Franklin	88	-1.7	106	1.8	24.6	682,435	6,419	67,251	68.9	83,000	73.0	27.0	32	84.3	476	8.6
Hampden........................	36	-7.0	69	1.0	12.0	711,793	10,343	55,643	25.9	49,507	83.3	16.7	7	79.3	362	6.3
Hampshire.......................	51	-6.1	73	0.8	20.2	560,780	7,662	75,215	46.0	66,512	76.8	23.2	28	85.7	473	9.0
Middlesex.......................	27	-3.2	44	1.2	13.0	702,873	15,944	61,303	63.4	102,177	88.1	11.9	26	84.5	172	4.8
Nantucket.......................	1	-37.6	37	0.3	0.5	1,432,672	39,124	53,243	D	D	D	D	2	42.9	NA	NA
Norfolk...........................	8	-19.3	39	0.5	3.1	663,973	17,150	57,310	D	D	D	D	6	85.8	64	5.1
Plymouth........................	60	-6.2	79	11.9	18.2	758,347	9,575	73,670	71.9	94,900	86.4	13.6	20	89.3	316	5.7
Suffolk...........................	0	-12.5	1	0.0	0.0	229,899	229,899	12,756	0.5	24,810	96.7	3.3	5	95.2	NA	NA
Worcester........................	95	-6.4	61	1.5	34.5	747,474	12,297	57,372	65.2	41,579	70.9	29.1	26	82.7	1,015	8.4
MICHIGAN	9,764	-1.9	205	670.2	7,924.5	1,015,631	4,955	154,740	8,220.9	172,560	56.5	43.5	764	77.2	167,189	32.2
Alcona...........................	36	-4.9	163	0.1	24.1	423,042	2,590	106,156	11.5	51,543	43.6	56.4	8	65.9	268	21.5
Alger.............................	21	17.9	166	0.0	9.9	339,285	2,040	69,429	4.2	33,532	29.9	70.1	3	81.0	12	6.3
Allegan..........................	230	-15.0	196	24.8	196.9	1,172,374	5,981	223,117	584.4	498,612	30.2	69.8	12	80.5	4,521	24.2
Alpena...........................	65	-5.6	158	0.0	42.2	401,054	2,545	95,421	25.9	62,400	29.5	70.5	8	74.9	861	23.1
Antrim............................	56	-13.4	167	4.0	34.2	701,340	4,203	107,992	35.5	106,520	81.7	18.3	9	73.3	226	14.7
Arenac...........................	87	6.7	249	0.2	73.0	835,592	3,355	186,941	43.0	122,860	67.5	32.5	12	74.3	2,256	71.4
Baraga	18	-0.7	271	0.0	9.5	592,800	2,189	89,014	2.2	34,000	58.4	41.6	3	67.7	7	26.2
Barry	155	-6.4	165	4.9	119.2	791,437	4,801	119,827	139.7	148,915	30.9	69.1	6	82.2	2,959	28.1
Bay...............................	210	8.3	289	5.2	197.1	1,460,329	5,052	242,520	116.5	160,519	88.3	11.7	NA	69.3	4,501	67.8
Benzie...........................	19	-10.3	94	0.7	8.7	372,275	3,961	66,072	10.0	50,898	78.5	21.5	2	84.8	189	12.2
Berrien	145	-7.6	166	20.0	123.5	1,068,559	6,445	142,166	171.3	196,501	91.4	8.6	15	76.4	2,594	20.6
Branch...........................	239	-2.0	303	55.7	204.3	1,285,432	4,236	207,759	162.3	205,697	65.9	34.1	6	73.9	5,703	45.5
Calhoun..........................	214	-4.9	223	13.3	174.6	1,185,546	5,309	139,254	113.9	118,861	61.1	38.9	20	71.5	4,522	36.7
Cass..............................	199	5.2	266	71.2	163.7	1,228,314	4,622	191,044	153.4	205,339	65.1	34.9	10	79.8	4,103	42.6
Charlevoix.......................	30	-20.2	110	0.1	14.1	416,535	3,770	59,479	8.4	31,052	59.3	40.7	6	69.0	104	11.8
Cheboygan......................	44	-3.4	133	D	22.1	341,794	2,562	72,788	7.1	21,655	58.8	41.2	7	69.1	112	10.9
Chippewa........................	89	-4.3	209	0.0	53.2	451,403	2,164	75,495	10.7	25,000	37.7	62.3	1	79.9	447	23.7
Clare.............................	55	-12.6	138	D	30.4	415,261	3,011	76,135	22.1	55,705	21.9	78.1	13	56.6	384	21.7
Clinton...........................	230	-5.8	226	2.6	200.9	1,277,549	5,655	194,330	224.3	220,535	32.2	67.8	20	80.3	4,392	41.7
Crawford	3	6.8	65	NA	0.3	228,867	3,502	36,385	0.2	4,778	10.2	89.8	NA	71.1	NA	NA
Delta.............................	59	-17.0	232	0.8	29.0	414,631	1,785	89,494	10.8	42,688	59.9	40.1	4	75.5	133	24.1
Dickinson	22	-23.0	140	0.3	8.7	380,435	2,727	84,219	4.4	27,671	54.4	45.6	NA	77.8	33	11.4
Eaton............................	210	-5.9	218	0.7	177.1	912,095	4,176	132,342	83.3	86,595	89.3	10.7	20	74.1	4,192	37.6
Emmet............................	39	-1.4	121	0.3	20.5	456,379	3,767	63,450	8.7	26,895	70.3	29.7	15	78.1	97	12.7
Genesee.........................	124	0.5	151	1.5	104.3	795,230	5,262	103,908	70.4	85,871	86.5	13.5	11	84.8	2,561	25.0
Gladwin..........................	59	-12.8	128	0.1	36.5	498,882	3,909	74,943	15.8	34,333	56.1	43.9	3	63.6	680	34.6
Gogebic..........................	6	-8.9	103	D	1.8	266,642	2,601	41,304	0.7	13,833	29.0	71.0	NA	83.3	D	1.9
Grand Traverse	51	-6.7	102	2.8	36.1	651,401	6,362	85,866	34.1	68,610	83.2	16.8	3	81.7	501	17.3
Gratiot...........................	297	2.5	365	15.9	272.4	1,984,846	5,432	280,110	281.4	346,607	43.3	56.7	13	80.9	5,365	60.7
Hillsdale	254	-3.1	211	8.8	212.3	909,201	4,309	149,441	165.1	137,021	51.4	48.6	18	73.0	7,375	50.0
Houghton	26	-4.3	125	0.0	13.4	294,396	2,354	49,491	6.3	30,322	36.3	63.7	4	70.2	52	13.0
Huron............................	495	9.5	430	3.1	458.8	2,597,983	6,048	360,764	610.8	529,729	43.1	56.9	20	76.6	12,201	75.5
Ingham..........................	178	-11.2	195	1.8	152.2	1,040,491	5,325	143,901	113.8	124,780	64.1	35.9	12	85.1	3,921	19.7
Ionia.............................	234	-5.8	245	5.1	200.1	1,215,280	4,955	206,048	382.9	401,410	21.9	78.1	15	79.5	5,053	45.5
Iosco.............................	34	-11.0	139	0.2	22.9	437,110	3,153	103,020	14.9	61,037	27.3	72.7	6	69.7	503	33.2
Iron..............................	23	2.2	176	0.5	10.6	348,316	1,976	64,714	3.7	27,564	88.6	11.4	NA	74.4	38	7.5
Isabella..........................	212	12.4	221	2.9	174.2	905,013	4,099	156,666	116.8	121,844	52.8	47.2	27	75.2	3,450	41.8
Jackson..........................	160	-12.4	174	4.7	125.8	866,522	4,986	116,065	70.8	76,714	61.6	38.4	6	78.2	3,526	25.9
Kalamazoo	139	-3.5	196	43.0	111.8	1,382,696	7,055	206,186	236.9	335,109	74.5	25.5	2	83.7	2,664	21.6
Kalkaska........................	27	5.1	121	1.6	16.3	320,046	2,654	88,846	8.3	37,000	92.3	7.7	4	83.1	170	20.0
Kent..............................	157	0.0	156	15.3	124.8	1,150,595	7,380	134,311	262.8	260,213	77.0	23.0	12	85.0	2,199	18.7

Table B. States and Counties — Water Use, Wholesale Trade, Retail Trade, and Real Estate

STATE County	Water use, 2015		Wholesale Trade[1], 2012				Retail Trade[2], 2012				Real estate and rental and leasing,[2] 2012			
	Public supply water withdrawn (mil gal/day)	Public supply gallons withdrawn per person per day	Number of establishments	Number of employees	Sales (mil dol)	Average payroll (mil dol)	Number of establishments	Number of employees	Sales (mil dol)	Average payroll (mil dol)	Number of establishments	Number of employees	Sales (mil dol)	Average payroll (mil dol)
	133	134	135	136	137	138	139	140	141	142	143	144	145	146
MARYLAND— Cont'd														
St. Mary's	4.15	37.2	39	397	189.5	17.6	294	4,835	1,227.0	109.5	83	312	94.7	11.4
Somerset	1.09	42.3	14	D	D	D	61	434	112.2	9.5	17	42	4.8	0.7
Talbot	2.24	59.7	56	443	277.4	19.9	222	2,635	670.2	64.6	55	179	34.7	6.3
Washington	17.27	115.5	137	1,917	1,804.2	89.0	612	9,244	2,457.6	207.6	141	755	216.5	29.4
Wicomico	6.86	67.0	108	1,122	1,231.4	49.9	390	6,375	1,608.3	145.0	126	624	86.3	20.7
Worcester	7.68	149.0	47	D	D	D	401	3,370	835.6	81.9	152	467	75.3	15.1
Baltimore city	0.00	0.0	544	8,592	7,954.3	495.2	1,839	15,747	3,647.7	379.0	596	4,055	883.7	187.6
MASSACHUSETTS	648.06	95.4	6,619	114,195	123,904.4	8,035.1	24,311	351,598	92,915.4	9,161.7	6,485	42,788	13,628.4	2,357.9
Barnstable	31.84	148.6	178	1,152	563.1	57.0	1,503	14,395	3,856.9	401.4	331	1,361	260.5	53.1
Berkshire	14.33	112.1	105	1,242	455.0	58.0	711	8,482	1,916.5	201.7	108	715	99.5	23.1
Bristol	26.60	47.8	517	10,556	9,375.8	626.2	2,192	33,806	8,403.5	813.8	418	1,382	293.7	53.1
Dukes	3.07	177.5	16	D	D	D	205	1,276	373.6	43.7	63	142	41.6	6.6
Essex	77.15	99.4	726	11,128	15,101.2	768.2	2,585	37,792	10,037.9	995.4	602	2,734	629.9	113.9
Franklin	3.73	52.8	64	D	D	D	262	2,903	703.7	73.3	37	110	16.9	2.9
Hampden	45.38	96.4	385	6,581	6,028.9	355.0	1,573	22,637	5,753.0	540.3	364	1,839	289.2	66.0
Hampshire	18.09	112.2	85	1,676	1,807.0	81.2	546	7,914	1,750.0	187.6	114	435	279.8	15.5
Middlesex	70.26	44.3	1,760	36,339	46,631.4	3,169.0	5,156	80,738	21,344.6	2,155.0	1,567	11,979	5,087.1	616.2
Nantucket	2.00	183.1	7	D	D	D	155	998	317.5	35.8	53	157	59.7	7.9
Norfolk	35.88	51.6	890	15,930	13,702.9	1,083.4	2,548	43,010	11,801.1	1,163.3	774	6,263	1,778.1	382.1
Plymouth	68.09	133.4	488	5,947	9,622.7	353.9	1,892	26,703	6,889.6	698.5	364	1,550	341.1	69.6
Suffolk	0.00	0.0	630	11,314	12,840.7	809.3	2,411	31,965	8,851.0	892.5	1,093	11,366	3,821.2	826.9
Worcester	251.64	307.3	768	11,502	7,126.8	636.8	2,572	38,979	10,916.5	959.5	597	2,755	630.2	120.8
MICHIGAN	1,030.44	103.8	9,392	132,490	115,704.9	7,474.6	34,858	441,190	119,302.0	10,527.3	7,826	48,706	11,974.5	1,806.9
Alcona	0.06	5.8	4	14	3.2	0.4	35	236	52.5	4.9	3	5	0.8	0.1
Alger	0.41	43.7	3	D	D	D	45	272	64.6	5.6	3	4	0.7	0.1
Allegan	4.03	35.2	106	1,354	609.4	130.1	335	3,354	949.9	76.3	69	210	38.9	8.0
Alpena	2.02	70.1	32	409	223.9	17.6	146	1,731	448.8	41.5	18	111	7.3	2.1
Antrim	1.19	51.4	9	40	15.7	1.2	88	530	169.6	13.4	22	D	D	D
Arenac	42.16	2,762.6	10	D	D	D	71	459	150.8	9.6	5	D	D	D
Baraga	0.51	59.5	3	9	3.3	0.2	29	275	53.1	5.3	5	D	D	D
Barry	1.57	26.5	26	179	122.5	7.3	124	1,198	286.0	24.0	24	68	8.1	2.8
Bay	8.97	84.9	87	D	D	D	419	5,526	1,303.0	124.5	65	212	29.3	4.7
Benzie	0.68	39.0	5	D	D	D	73	535	128.0	11.2	15	33	3.3	0.7
Berrien	12.42	80.3	133	D	D	D	587	6,783	1,681.1	147.2	152	614	78.3	19.5
Branch	2.77	63.4	28	265	124.3	11.3	132	1,612	435.2	39.0	31	77	15.0	2.2
Calhoun	12.53	93.3	94	D	D	D	488	5,858	1,702.3	133.4	87	373	53.9	10.5
Cass	1.15	22.3	45	321	316.2	15.8	116	876	256.9	18.9	28	48	7.9	1.0
Charlevoix	2.66	101.4	15	51	9.6	1.4	116	823	196.8	18.0	29	115	18.0	3.9
Cheboygan	0.98	38.5	13	89	37.4	3.1	147	1,161	310.2	27.3	17	D	D	D
Chippewa	2.69	70.7	25	295	145.4	11.0	148	1,725	454.1	36.8	26	96	8.9	1.8
Clare	1.12	36.7	11	D	D	D	118	1,027	261.3	22.5	9	24	2.5	0.4
Clinton	1.16	15.0	52	869	659.2	39.7	170	2,090	749.2	53.0	53	204	34.7	6.8
Crawford	0.66	47.8	4	34	21.5	1.3	60	531	214.6	12.0	13	22	3.7	0.7
Delta	2.81	77.2	45	331	157.1	12.3	183	2,160	507.1	45.0	29	64	6.8	1.2
Dickinson	2.35	91.1	42	D	D	D	154	1,824	431.2	40.4	28	D	D	D
Eaton	2.63	24.2	71	1,474	1,076.7	65.4	330	5,619	1,453.0	129.9	79	380	78.8	12.4
Emmet	3.84	115.8	34	217	95.8	9.4	293	2,606	627.8	63.5	41	204	24.8	3.9
Genesee	4.22	10.3	272	3,969	3,673.6	218.5	1,459	19,368	5,307.9	444.9	318	1,843	255.8	57.1
Gladwin	0.45	17.9	7	38	11.2	1.4	82	598	141.0	11.6	13	102	6.1	2.6
Gogebic	1.48	95.9	9	66	74.3	2.1	79	764	159.6	15.1	14	104	7.2	1.6
Grand Traverse	7.33	80.0	134	1,146	454.0	52.5	560	7,184	1,767.8	174.8	151	488	96.5	17.0
Gratiot	1.60	38.5	27	D	D	D	135	1,339	344.2	28.2	19	60	7.5	1.3
Hillsdale	2.01	43.8	33	301	407.9	12.7	139	1,330	370.2	32.1	25	54	12.0	1.4
Houghton	3.87	106.4	21	D	D	D	149	1,638	329.4	32.7	25	D	D	D
Huron	2.58	80.9	38	518	523.6	26.4	161	1,481	361.9	29.1	9	11	2.6	0.4
Ingham	26.09	91.2	204	2,701	5,407.9	130.9	916	13,217	3,260.5	293.0	253	1,946	236.4	68.8
Ionia	4.99	77.7	26	D	D	D	143	1,589	430.4	34.8	17	45	6.9	1.1
Iosco	1.20	47.3	5	D	D	D	115	1,302	327.2	28.8	19	37	4.3	0.6
Iron	1.26	111.0	10	44	11.7	1.3	61	433	101.6	9.1	17	37	3.5	0.7
Isabella	3.01	42.6	51	504	362.3	19.7	215	3,322	769.9	71.5	55	1,077	70.7	27.6
Jackson	10.84	68.0	137	D	D	D	526	7,003	1,841.7	163.5	99	567	82.0	15.5
Kalamazoo	24.35	93.6	234	3,668	1,553.7	197.3	863	12,708	3,129.4	284.2	210	2,328	223.7	71.6
Kalkaska	0.41	23.8	18	167	75.7	7.1	54	525	155.9	12.7	9	D	D	D
Kent	9.01	14.2	976	22,090	17,703.0	1,235.3	2,116	31,615	8,698.6	803.1	640	3,990	698.0	143.7

1 Merchant wholesalers, except manufacturers' sales branches and offices. 2. Employer establishments.

— **Professional Services, Manufacturing, and Accommodation and Food Services**

STATE County	Professional, scientific, and technical services, 2012				Manufacturing, 2012				Accommodation and food services, 2012			
	Number of establish-ments	Number of employees	Sales (mil dol)	Average payroll (mil dol)	Number of establish-ments	Number of employees	Receipts (mil dol)	Annual payroll (mil dol)	Number of establis-hments	Number of employees	Receipts (mil dol)	Annual payroll (mil dol)
	147	148	149	150	151	152	153	154	155	156	157	158
MARYLAND— Cont'd												
St. Mary's.......................	309	8,327	1,654.0	640.7	28	225	D	9.6	184	3,670	166.6	48.1
Somerset......................	20	D	D	D	13	340	223.2	13.2	29	272	12.8	3.1
Talbot	134	1,678	260.2	97.6	41	1,465	D	57.9	133	2,476	131.4	42.1
Washington	234	1,726	190.6	72.1	127	5,612	2,735.0	307.2	290	5,083	258.7	73.8
Wicomico	227	1,661	238.8	91.0	79	3,108	1,216.8	127.2	208	3,871	187.1	48.7
Worcester......................	142	642	65.5	28.7	36	604	241.7	24.6	413	6,050	552.3	153.6
Baltimore city	1,555	21,994	4,747.0	1,890.5	409	11,748	5,043.3	574.0	1,541	21,832	1,607.8	435.6
MASSACHUSETTS..........	21,422	255,022	60,370.0	23,826.5	6,806	234,168	81,927.8	14,395.3	16,898	273,185	17,509.0	5,019.8
Barnstable......................	733	4,806	932.9	341.7	187	2,157	478.6	119.4	1,143	13,117	1,000.4	291.5
Berkshire......................	338	2,688	397.7	162.8	151	5,275	1,288.9	310.7	522	7,006	418.7	124.2
Bristol..........................	1,045	6,050	823.3	295.3	674	26,935	8,015.0	1,552.1	1,241	19,755	969.1	276.1
Dukes...........................	62	221	38.5	13.6	21	108	D	D	138	878	120.3	36.7
Essex..........................	2,137	15,135	2,330.9	1,075.8	869	38,451	12,747.9	2,517.9	1,797	25,502	1,536.1	431.0
Franklin	132	584	153.6	27.6	105	3,615	1,682.5	171.4	147	1,864	85.5	25.4
Hampden	854	6,893	883.2	358.6	583	20,588	6,259.4	1,100.7	928	14,276	714.2	198.4
Hampshire......................	360	1,834	228.2	87.6	134	2,939	1,096.3	140.0	384	5,977	264.4	78.5
Middlesex......................	6,817	111,444	28,751.6	11,746.3	1,652	59,454	22,760.7	4,255.8	3,662	59,109	3,940.3	1,125.1
Nantucket......................	56	176	35.7	11.0	18	75	D	2.0	111	849	119.4	36.6
Norfolk..........................	2,640	20,674	4,096.5	1,498.9	628	20,613	10,798.9	1,248.1	1,596	27,505	1,613.3	463.8
Plymouth	1,245	7,134	1,125.5	426.1	487	10,374	2,493.2	521.2	1,038	18,005	909.4	272.8
Suffolk..........................	3,188	61,414	17,726.5	6,606.9	335	8,908	3,805.2	472.0	2,469	54,643	4,551.0	1,304.5
Worcester......................	1,815	15,969	2,846.1	1,174.2	962	34,677	10,475.8	1,979.4	1,722	24,699	1,266.9	355.4
MICHIGAN......................	21,650	D	D	D	12,444	514,058	238,892.4	27,611.4	19,491	347,337	17,962.4	4,871.7
Alcona..........................	7	29	5.0	1.6	17	175	27.5	8.0	26	102	3.9	1.1
Alger............................	10	17	2.3	1.1	11	471	D	24.9	40	260	16.8	3.7
Allegan.........................	161	1,387	171.6	85.8	202	13,273	5,286.6	633.9	207	2,697	131.9	37.1
Alpena.........................	40	193	16.8	6.9	43	1,227	480.3	56.0	72	879	35.1	10.4
Antrim...........................	36	128	9.8	3.3	40	776	175.0	29.6	59	946	42.6	15.5
Arenac.........................	15	83	11.1	5.4	28	694	145.7	28.0	48	457	28.2	8.0
Baraga.........................	3	11	0.9	0.3	21	440	150.3	17.1	17	D	D	D
Barry	63	308	20.7	8.9	49	2,725	1,115.7	122.9	80	982	38.5	11.3
Bay..............................	152	1,360	111.0	57.1	123	3,650	1,149.4	190.6	233	4,039	172.0	47.6
Benzie..........................	31	61	5.6	1.8	21	363	D	10.8	56	1,068	50.4	16.9
Berrien	284	2,149	201.0	108.3	289	8,330	1,962.8	388.9	365	5,323	241.7	69.4
Branch..........................	45	391	114.4	18.1	72	2,604	812.7	115.1	78	1,071	47.2	12.8
Calhoun.........................	191	1,058	93.0	55.5	148	11,179	5,445.1	599.3	280	6,023	471.2	104.3
Cass............................	47	191	15.4	5.8	70	2,249	721.7	96.4	65	778	30.9	8.5
Charlevoix......................	61	224	23.7	8.3	47	2,266	728.4	109.2	75	1,288	61.9	18.6
Cheboygan.....................	41	112	11.2	4.2	31	248	57.1	10.2	119	689	67.4	18.0
Chippewa.......................	42	D	D	D	27	498	90.1	22.1	111	2,157	136.3	38.3
Clare	30	144	16.5	7.9	26	811	254.0	42.7	64	812	34.7	9.1
Clinton	132	576	82.5	26.7	60	1,868	625.5	98.0	98	1,504	55.9	16.5
Crawford	17	62	10.3	2.1	21	499	184.2	24.2	43	550	22.6	5.6
Delta............................	78	499	57.8	12.1	68	2,364	854.3	137.4	99	1,213	45.3	12.4
Dickinson	53	358	31.3	12.4	41	2,224	983.6	109.6	73	809	31.6	8.7
Eaton...........................	177	883	100.9	37.8	91	7,872	10,600.6	488.1	206	4,230	169.2	50.6
Emmet..........................	110	394	61.3	22.2	54	984	281.2	40.1	139	2,280	122.4	37.5
Genesee	639	3,544	370.3	143.2	273	10,675	9,418.1	684.4	704	13,207	563.9	157.4
Gladwin	26	51	4.5	1.2	27	771	185.0	33.5	43	476	17.8	5.1
Gogebic	18	90	7.3	3.3	19	641	90.8	22.7	59	968	42.1	11.7
Grand Traverse.................	369	2,118	295.2	109.2	176	4,464	1,153.9	216.1	249	5,649	343.1	93.6
Gratiot	29	142	14.2	7.0	51	2,401	809.7	116.7	72	1,009	42.5	12.4
Hillsdale........................	46	166	17.1	5.4	77	3,673	1,445.7	149.8	68	786	31.8	8.7
Houghton	72	455	47.8	20.3	41	552	D	D	110	1,372	51.0	14.0
Huron...........................	48	227	22.2	10.9	65	3,285	891.7	132.1	102	885	38.0	9.8
Ingham..........................	742	5,940	1,026.8	344.1	190	7,572	4,972.9	416.5	609	11,266	483.0	134.6
Ionia	46	159	15.0	6.6	70	3,251	1,363.0	135.5	77	976	35.5	10.2
Iosco	30	218	11.9	5.5	41	869	226.7	33.2	80	677	34.0	9.1
Iron..............................	29	105	9.9	4.2	17	395	D	16.7	33	293	12.5	3.0
Isabella.........................	104	677	62.2	26.0	59	2,197	616.7	95.8	125	5,523	447.4	98.9
Jackson.........................	217	2,504	367.1	180.4	268	8,414	2,621.3	409.3	275	4,788	201.5	57.3
Kalamazoo......................	544	3,689	576.8	203.2	311	15,557	7,385.6	911.1	546	11,663	477.9	146.3
Kalkaska	18	38	7.6	2.1	13	430	146.4	20.5	31	345	16.6	4.6
Kent.............................	1,635	13,433	2,016.6	777.1	1,068	57,371	17,535.6	2,899.2	1,192	25,307	1,154.4	335.4

Table B. States and Counties — Health Care and Social Assistance, Other Services, Nonemployer Businesses, and Residential Construction

STATE County	Health care and social assistance, 2012				Other services, 2012				Nonemployer businesses, 2016		Value of residential construction authorized by building permits, 2018	
	Number of establishments	Number of employees	Receipts (mil dol)	Annual payroll (mil dol)	Number of establishments	Number of employees	Receipts (mil dol)	Annual payroll (mil dol)	Number	Receipts (mil dol)	New construction ($1,000)	Number of housing units
	159	160	161	162	163	164	165	166	167	168	169	170
MARYLAND— Cont'd												
St. Mary's	179	4,110	379.9	172.2	142	865	80.7	30.1	6,914	271.6	178,932	931
Somerset	38	1,121	74.7	35.1	30	101	11.8	2.2	1,471	49.0	6,751	36
Talbot	173	3,517	387.0	147.2	118	610	74.4	17.4	4,433	233.1	32,715	107
Washington	440	10,210	1,056.4	428.4	261	1,594	136.6	38.4	8,625	384.8	74,471	310
Wicomico	361	8,798	935.1	385.7	189	1,286	99.0	31.1	6,274	272.9	29,721	187
Worcester	140	1,956	196.1	80.4	143	868	82.8	23.4	5,146	273.7	47,783	239
Baltimore city	1,471	79,915	11,349.2	4,158.7	939	8,989	1,303.0	305.5	39,520	1,494.8	235,027	1,547
MASSACHUSETTS	18,386	587,485	63,583.1	27,696.7	14,008	93,489	10,455.1	2,931.3	529,496	28,441.7	4,157,964	17,044
Barnstable	811	15,781	1,766.8	730.5	590	3,176	320.4	95.6	26,068	1,347.3	281,588	1,005
Berkshire	438	11,415	1,091.4	488.4	278	1,675	144.1	39.5	9,985	442.2	81,411	262
Bristol	1,414	39,217	3,485.9	1,573.5	1,085	5,614	479.1	138.6	32,628	1,596.4	137,701	669
Dukes	61	784	91.1	42.7	54	164	25.6	6.4	3,974	253.7	88,472	134
Essex	2,080	62,430	5,324.0	2,497.2	1,449	8,386	727.3	225.5	62,522	3,231.9	236,030	870
Franklin	194	3,671	291.8	121.8	132	578	52.4	15.2	6,112	227.7	13,523	59
Hampden	1,161	37,660	3,822.0	1,659.5	809	5,662	497.1	138.7	24,516	1,193.4	67,675	291
Hampshire	435	18,108	875.9	459.1	301	1,627	164.1	48.9	13,126	558.2	84,468	368
Middlesex	4,489	124,041	15,136.6	6,421.7	3,397	24,727	2,984.3	890.7	139,021	7,825.9	897,561	4,309
Nantucket	35	392	53.4	23.0	44	155	39.9	8.1	2,531	199.7	159,755	169
Norfolk	2,234	66,785	5,406.8	2,524.8	1,576	10,253	1,184.0	321.8	58,833	3,684.2	540,737	2,009
Plymouth	1,213	31,032	2,904.1	1,305.7	969	5,915	500.5	163.9	38,088	2,058.0	360,133	1,565
Suffolk	1,816	116,274	16,983.3	7,058.9	1,988	17,967	2,602.9	629.2	59,300	3,241.3	882,651	3,738
Worcester	2,005	59,895	6,350.0	2,790.0	1,336	7,590	733.5	209.4	52,792	2,581.8	326,260	1,596
MICHIGAN	26,231	585,530	63,018.8	25,556.5	15,919	96,150	10,407.7	2,719.9	703,595	30,685.0	12,202	65
Alcona	12	D	D	D	8	D	D	D	645	24.2	2,612	26
Alger	20	299	22.2	8.6	13	37	4.0	0.9	570	22.0	4,870	25
Allegan	172	3,225	265.9	111.8	172	795	92.5	22.7	8,031	349.5	118,844	436
Alpena	83	1,724	122.6	47.4	65	258	23.5	5.3	1,941	77.0	4,861	24
Antrim	54	302	15.9	7.7	39	160	13.5	3.8	2,051	90.2	19,186	102
Arenac	34	647	58.7	20.6	24	D	D	D	894	38.3	2,145	10
Baraga	18	324	27.2	10.4	16	36	3.5	0.7	381	12.9	1,264	8
Barry	82	1,336	123.4	50.3	83	402	42.0	11.3	3,651	161.8	45,712	216
Bay	329	7,152	682.5	261.2	190	928	70.8	21.3	5,465	210.3	29,838	85
Benzie	30	D	D	D	25	86	5.6	1.7	1,758	75.5	19,736	72
Berrien	399	9,410	816.5	329.2	251	1,199	116.0	32.2	9,862	392.2	92,060	302
Branch	100	1,497	143.0	57.1	67	276	18.4	6.8	2,454	116.3	16,364	82
Calhoun	323	9,313	966.4	421.9	208	1,173	448.4	41.7	6,261	233.3	11,040	54
Cass	60	904	66.3	30.0	58	D	D	D	3,043	127.8	28,849	90
Charlevoix	74	1,187	104.5	48.7	65	247	25.4	6.3	2,564	112.3	28,306	118
Cheboygan	54	1,025	87.3	35.4	74	208	17.6	5.1	1,927	72.5	14,218	55
Chippewa	79	1,939	170.1	68.1	53	D	D	D	1,934	53.0	5,957	31
Clare	59	1,106	86.2	28.5	38	159	14.1	3.3	1,767	76.9	1,255	15
Clinton	112	1,664	140.4	50.3	94	495	37.7	11.6	5,445	238.2	49,843	235
Crawford	32	971	111.5	41.9	21	155	16.7	5.7	867	33.7	4,588	24
Delta	104	2,016	167.7	67.1	84	392	37.7	9.2	2,018	69.7	9,941	44
Dickinson	118	D	D	D	66	249	21.5	5.6	1,461	53.2	7,088	36
Eaton	236	3,506	282.4	117.2	157	1,093	136.7	45.4	6,986	264.7	30,942	159
Emmet	185	2,962	345.5	151.9	109	651	67.7	17.6	3,598	167.8	27,378	125
Genesee	1,294	25,418	2,787.5	1,148.7	562	3,406	376.2	91.1	27,464	988.5	107,825	630
Gladwin	39	611	55.8	17.0	26	154	11.1	2.9	1,523	76.2	0	0
Gogebic	32	661	63.0	25.8	42	131	10.2	2.6	913	32.4	2,291	14
Grand Traverse	396	8,782	995.6	397.1	199	1,327	133.2	37.5	9,518	455.3	96,804	661
Gratiot	104	2,339	236.7	82.4	46	223	35.1	6.4	2,178	86.8	5,903	29
Hillsdale	104	D	D	D	51	D	D	D	2,855	114.7	11,653	66
Houghton	92	D	D	D	67	D	D	D	2,013	64.2	11,662	58
Huron	97	1,741	159.2	59.9	60	234	24.6	5.6	2,228	98.4	5,529	37
Ingham	807	22,354	2,566.1	999.5	566	5,094	633.8	183.6	18,957	899.9	79,381	431
Ionia	103	1,226	105.2	39.0	66	271	22.9	5.7	3,239	117.1	30,533	116
Iosco	52	814	81.5	29.8	50	176	12.6	3.1	1,511	55.7	9,788	36
Iron	18	431	52.4	19.1	24	D	D	D	777	24.0	7,456	30
Isabella	202	3,040	222.1	94.7	111	601	46.0	12.3	3,539	155.0	10,569	45
Jackson	351	9,060	936.8	409.4	210	1,361	129.7	37.1	8,958	349.1	32,711	172
Kalamazoo	653	18,751	2,261.9	865.0	427	3,007	384.4	91.0	16,080	696.1	107,523	460
Kalkaska	27	475	42.9	15.0	26	136	17.2	5.2	1,217	48.9	5,421	29
Kent	1,581	50,294	5,244.9	2,133.2	1,083	8,294	765.1	220.5	46,154	2,293.7	520,956	2,366

Table B. States and Counties — Government Employment and Payroll, and Local Government Finances

| | Government employment and payroll, 2012 | | | | | | | | | Local government finances, 2012 | | | | |
| | | | March payroll (percent of total) | | | | | | | General revenue | | | | |
STATE County	Full-time equivalent employees	March payroll (dollars)	Administration, judicial, and legal	Police and corrections	Fire protection	Highways and transportation	Health and welfare	Natural resources and utilities	Education and libraries	Total (mil dol)	Intergovernmental (mil dol)	Taxes Total (mil dol)	Per capita[1] (dollars) Total	Per capita[1] (dollars) Property
	171	172	173	174	175	176	177	178	179	180	181	182	183	184
MARYLAND— Cont'd														
St. Mary's........................	3,187	14,069,480	5.9	10.5	0.0	2.3	1.5	4.3	73.2	356.5	125.4	191.8	1,760	923
Somerset..........................	890	3,320,415	5.7	9.8	0.0	2.6	2.1	5.5	67.9	83.1	45.3	26.3	1,002	735
Talbot	1,356	5,353,079	6.3	12.0	0.0	3.6	4.8	9.8	53.9	135.2	24.3	75.9	1,992	1,178
Washington	5,270	21,889,886	4.2	7.2	2.7	2.6	0.7	8.0	73.2	547.6	234.3	228.4	1,531	989
Wicomico	4,063	15,857,286	4.2	10.7	1.8	1.7	1.9	5.3	73.7	376.1	166.7	134.3	1,334	842
Worcester........................	2,609	11,789,178	8.3	14.2	2.1	3.0	6.7	9.7	51.9	340.0	56.3	227.1	4,403	3,313
Baltimore city	27,461	126,508,297	5.8	15.9	7.5	3.3	8.2	10.7	47.4	3,714.0	1,967.9	1,238.8	1,994	1,229
MASSACHUSETTS.........	X	X	X	X	X	X	X	X	X	X	X	X	X	X
Barnstable......................	7,548	35,968,725	7.2	11.5	10.0	4.2	3.5	6.4	53.6	1,003.5	207.7	645.0	2,994	2,809
Berkshire........................	4,790	19,230,480	4.3	8.5	3.3	5.5	1.3	4.1	71.5	506.3	218.2	246.7	1,897	1,828
Bristol............................	17,070	76,423,100	3.0	10.6	7.2	2.1	2.0	5.3	68.1	2,032.5	942.1	830.7	1,507	1,453
Dukes............................	1,048	4,632,999	7.6	11.3	1.4	6.7	6.9	4.4	59.7	141.2	27.4	88.5	5,195	4,963
Essex............................	25,587	123,574,109	3.4	8.7	6.1	2.3	1.3	6.5	69.6	2,861.5	1,081.5	1,475.0	1,952	1,898
Franklin..........................	2,963	11,147,283	5.4	6.1	2.8	5.5	1.3	4.8	71.6	305.5	144.0	135.0	1,887	1,847
Hampden	18,660	82,237,236	2.8	9.5	5.8	2.3	1.5	8.2	68.6	2,010.8	1,105.6	711.6	1,527	1,484
Hampshire.......................	5,845	24,568,656	4.7	9.8	7.3	3.2	2.8	5.3	64.6	489.0	185.2	236.2	1,478	1,434
Middlesex.......................	51,015	257,135,128	5.3	9.1	7.3	2.5	5.9	5.3	61.9	7,258.0	1,991.8	3,798.4	2,471	2,386
Nantucket.......................	564	3,317,115	5.0	8.7	5.6	10.9	11.3	6.7	48.7	127.3	11.0	80.2	7,784	6,281
Norfolk...........................	21,584	108,297,457	3.8	9.0	7.0	2.5	1.4	5.7	68.8	2,684.4	649.6	1,685.1	2,471	2,399
Plymouth.........................	17,576	78,325,658	3.7	8.5	6.3	2.3	1.5	4.3	71.8	1,886.5	696.4	1,001.7	2,004	1,943
Suffolk...........................	22,999	131,415,091	3.4	16.9	11.5	2.0	7.1	7.2	49.6	3,908.1	1,488.3	1,972.4	2,650	2,442
Worcester.......................	28,380	132,203,123	3.5	8.3	5.1	3.2	1.5	4.3	73.0	3,064.8	1,424.8	1,314.3	1,630	1,589
MICHIGAN	X	X	X	X	X	X	X	X	X	X	X	X	X	X
Alcona............................	260	869,231	18.9	12.8	2.7	13.1	5.9	0.9	43.1	26.7	8.8	13.3	1,250	1,247
Alger..............................	293	1,015,817	13.5	7.1	0.5	18.5	0.2	4.4	52.0	30.8	13.5	10.2	1,071	1,037
Allegan...........................	3,023	10,951,667	9.1	7.0	1.3	3.2	8.0	2.2	67.1	353.3	194.8	109.8	980	962
Alpena...........................	2,199	8,769,942	4.0	2.3	1.9	3.0	58.9	0.8	28.5	257.0	79.4	32.4	1,109	1,087
Antrim............................	795	2,618,552	12.6	9.1	1.8	7.2	4.1	3.3	59.1	89.8	22.9	43.1	1,841	1,822
Arenac...........................	446	1,462,195	13.6	6.7	0.0	5.4	0.6	3.4	66.5	44.9	24.2	14.4	928	920
Baraga...........................	413	1,533,081	10.5	4.7	0.2	7.7	36.0	3.8	36.1	56.1	20.1	9.9	1,142	1,141
Barry	1,440	5,121,005	9.4	7.0	1.4	5.4	12.9	2.3	58.3	149.7	79.8	42.0	711	706
Bay................................	4,027	15,471,429	6.7	5.7	2.4	4.8	13.5	5.1	61.1	536.8	284.0	123.7	1,157	1,137
Benzie............................	473	1,629,367	11.3	8.6	1.6	6.8	9.1	2.1	57.3	57.9	16.6	24.9	1,423	1,407
Berrien...........................	4,813	18,604,576	9.6	10.9	2.0	2.9	2.9	4.5	64.6	601.1	301.4	200.9	1,288	1,264
Branch............................	1,691	6,939,089	6.6	5.2	1.3	3.6	38.9	3.2	38.5	226.8	88.1	39.0	889	873
Calhoun..........................	4,008	16,572,500	10.0	11.0	3.1	3.3	5.9	4.4	61.4	671.0	371.6	175.1	1,296	1,142
Cass..............................	1,418	4,769,730	10.8	7.3	0.6	2.9	0.9	2.2	72.4	172.3	89.2	43.1	825	808
Charlevoix.......................	1,150	4,194,441	10.6	5.9	1.3	5.8	28.6	3.6	42.0	158.1	43.7	73.2	2,813	2,799
Cheboygan......................	787	2,583,533	17.3	8.3	0.3	7.1	0.7	3.5	58.4	82.5	33.6	37.9	1,467	1,464
Chippewa........................	1,196	4,184,040	10.1	7.0	2.7	11.4	6.7	6.0	52.6	135.4	67.2	34.8	894	891
Clare.............................	1,104	4,192,533	8.2	5.7	0.9	5.4	0.8	1.5	74.1	127.0	64.5	31.2	1,013	1,002
Clinton...........................	1,742	6,413,165	10.6	9.9	0.7	3.5	0.4	3.2	69.3	200.2	105.1	60.4	794	775
Crawford	409	1,431,323	13.6	11.5	1.6	16.3	4.0	2.0	47.9	39.4	16.7	15.9	1,133	1,086
Delta..............................	1,241	4,680,702	6.7	9.5	0.0	5.2	3.8	6.7	65.7	127.4	66.1	38.2	1,037	1,028
Dickinson	1,535	6,348,874	4.3	5.6	1.0	3.4	58.2	2.3	23.9	184.8	56.0	31.4	1,196	1,182
Eaton.............................	2,554	9,735,640	10.8	10.4	3.7	4.1	3.2	4.4	60.8	310.5	152.5	99.7	923	899
Emmet............................	1,325	5,336,908	10.4	6.0	0.7	4.0	16.4	3.6	56.1	264.7	141.6	74.6	2,266	2,213
Genesee	15,234	64,330,939	5.5	5.9	1.4	3.5	24.1	3.5	55.1	2,005.4	1,056.8	353.2	844	786
Gladwin..........................	706	2,311,382	11.6	6.0	5.6	5.3	0.0	6.6	61.0	64.7	29.2	22.5	882	866
Gogebic..........................	622	2,249,336	12.5	6.4	0.2	9.6	0.9	8.4	60.0	90.5	45.8	17.4	1,082	1,078
Grand Traverse.................	3,921	13,601,114	7.7	6.2	1.5	4.9	19.6	4.5	54.3	484.0	209.1	154.5	1,733	1,707
Gratiot............................	1,175	3,955,893	11.4	7.1	0.6	5.7	0.5	4.7	67.3	148.7	93.4	35.9	853	831
Hillsdale	1,203	4,074,488	12.8	8.9	1.5	5.5	0.3	8.2	59.8	131.8	71.6	31.6	684	680
Houghton	1,000	3,212,799	11.7	7.0	0.3	9.7	5.5	5.2	58.7	146.4	70.0	29.8	815	804
Huron	1,172	3,974,661	13.7	7.4	3.0	6.1	17.1	4.5	45.7	144.4	58.3	49.0	1,508	1,483
Ingham	10,953	47,886,830	7.3	7.2	3.2	4.6	11.6	7.8	53.9	1,384.5	665.7	427.0	1,516	1,387
Ionia..............................	1,653	5,904,984	8.9	6.9	0.5	4.2	2.6	4.1	71.7	208.2	123.1	53.2	832	780
Iosco	1,129	3,442,430	9.4	4.0	0.3	4.8	27.8	2.2	46.8	108.8	50.8	33.6	1,326	1,313
Iron................................	408	1,333,527	19.7	8.3	1.1	6.9	9.9	12.6	38.2	67.8	34.2	17.2	1,482	1,471
Isabella...........................	1,686	5,798,126	10.7	6.7	1.2	7.0	29.5	4.2	39.4	236.5	148.6	46.1	653	641
Jackson..........................	4,304	17,626,740	7.6	8.1	2.4	4.2	3.5	3.4	69.5	585.1	325.3	139.2	868	809
Kalamazoo	6,988	32,644,262	7.1	11.8	16.7	2.9	2.7	3.6	54.2	970.9	521.9	297.6	1,169	1,137
Kalkaska.........................	695	2,106,824	12.6	6.6	0.4	8.0	43.8	2.8	23.7	84.6	15.9	18.4	1,075	1,058
Kent...............................	16,442	72,374,352	7.5	10.6	3.2	4.8	1.8	4.9	66.1	2,471.0	1,223.4	763.8	1,243	1,084

1. Based on the resident population estimated as of July 1 of the year shown.

Table B. States and Counties — Local Government Finances, Government Employment, and Income Taxes

STATE County	Local government finances, 2012 (cont.)										Government employment, 2017			Individual income tax returns, 2016		
	Direct general expenditure							Debt outstanding								
			Percent of total for:												Mean	
	Total (mil dol)	Per capita[1] (dollars)	Education	Health and hospitals	Police protection	Public welfare	Highways	Total (mil dol)	Per capita[1] (dollars)	Federal civilian	Federal military	State and local	Number of returns	adjusted gross income	Mean income tax
	185	186	187	188	189	190	191	192	193	194	195	196	197	198	199
MARYLAND— Cont'd															
St. Mary's	331.8	3,045	62.8	2.2	6.2	0.9	2.7	197.3	1,810	9,628	2,476	4,597	51,910	74,587	9,057
Somerset	126.9	4,833	34.0	0.9	3.5	0.2	3.0	52.4	1,996	49	97	2,794	8,730	41,187	3,526
Talbot	130.3	3,419	40.1	3.0	8.2	0.8	5.1	87.8	2,304	199	137	1,647	19,000	80,779	12,000
Washington	564.3	3,783	59.9	0.7	4.0	0.4	4.5	391.3	2,623	584	480	8,062	69,090	55,338	5,945
Wicomico	357.2	3,549	57.8	1.0	6.3	3.1	2.6	203.7	2,024	283	328	7,687	45,320	50,602	5,609
Worcester	300.6	5,827	35.7	2.9	10.6	0.7	4.0	284.8	5,522	179	198	3,595	27,560	62,636	8,150
Baltimore city	4,080.5	6,567	34.4	2.9	9.1	0.0	5.1	2,807.8	4,519	10,770	2,072	55,378	260,260	51,708	6,390
MASSACHUSETTS	X	X	X	X	X	X	X	X	X	46,592	19,257	396,903	3,409,490	88,430	14,411
Barnstable	1,041.6	4,835	45.9	1.1	5.3	0.2	3.5	892.5	4,143	1,645	1,163	13,336	126,520	73,120	10,150
Berkshire	629.4	4,841	60.3	0.5	3.2	0.3	5.9	274.5	2,111	390	296	7,997	64,680	59,768	7,542
Bristol	1,991.8	3,614	57.9	0.9	5.0	1.0	2.5	1,318.2	2,392	1,164	1,343	27,688	274,910	62,534	7,818
Dukes	159.8	9,379	47.0	2.7	4.8	0.1	3.1	92.7	5,440	48	64	1,539	11,390	73,851	10,528
Essex	2,925.1	3,871	57.7	0.4	4.6	0.2	2.8	1,876.8	2,484	3,529	1,920	38,077	397,980	82,029	12,790
Franklin	333.5	4,661	58.8	0.4	2.7	0.4	4.8	96.2	1,344	209	166	5,044	35,610	55,669	6,060
Hampden	2,073.1	4,449	58.0	0.5	4.5	0.6	2.9	1,537.4	3,300	3,848	1,302	30,174	219,210	55,924	6,641
Hampshire	545.4	3,413	56.1	0.8	5.8	0.5	3.8	283.7	1,775	1,463	343	17,772	72,380	68,784	8,989
Middlesex	7,035.9	4,577	49.7	11.6	4.1	0.2	2.6	4,420.3	2,876	11,670	4,819	78,450	797,830	111,281	19,878
Nantucket	106.8	10,369	26.6	0.4	4.0	6.2	0.6	224.6	21,811	53	51	732	7,750	88,905	15,119
Norfolk	2,651.4	3,889	55.1	0.5	5.1	0.2	3.0	2,012.1	2,951	1,580	1,647	33,979	354,220	124,491	23,589
Plymouth	1,986.2	3,974	61.8	0.6	4.6	0.3	2.6	1,305.2	2,612	3,398	1,249	27,497	262,710	84,108	13,008
Suffolk	3,805.2	5,112	33.9	7.5	8.8	1.3	1.5	2,110.9	2,836	14,528	2,969	64,939	381,910	89,405	15,728
Worcester	3,304.7	4,099	61.5	0.4	4.0	0.2	3.4	2,495.3	3,095	3,067	1,925	49,679	402,430	71,253	9,755
MICHIGAN	X	X	X	X	X	X	X	X	X	52,685	17,849	542,757	4,718,510	60,747	8,065
Alcona	27.1	2,545	30.2	4.5	5.3	0.9	24.2	3.8	359	19	16	315	4,880	42,122	3,981
Alger	32.4	3,395	36.3	4.6	2.9	0.0	17.5	26.3	2,754	85	13	614	4,070	47,644	4,905
Allegan	347.7	3,103	55.1	7.4	3.5	3.5	7.8	410.3	3,662	177	187	5,215	56,110	56,773	6,531
Alpena	248.9	8,516	25.0	59.1	1.5	0.3	2.8	47.7	1,630	140	46	2,769	14,080	45,575	5,067
Antrim	88.3	3,774	40.2	3.4	4.7	14.5	8.8	44.8	1,913	59	37	1,112	11,680	56,361	7,016
Arenac	43.2	2,790	50.7	2.2	3.0	0.5	12.9	32.8	2,122	43	24	554	7,200	42,470	4,283
Baraga	72.9	8,401	19.5	53.3	1.1	0.2	10.4	63.4	7,303	28	12	1,473	3,460	42,814	3,549
Barry	150.3	2,547	48.0	5.6	3.7	9.3	7.8	79.7	1,352	82	97	2,416	28,650	58,311	6,604
Bay	521.5	4,877	44.7	20.6	3.3	4.5	4.2	246.5	2,305	252	225	5,545	52,920	47,921	5,087
Benzie	56.3	3,226	36.8	7.9	2.1	12.2	8.7	30.3	1,734	37	42	666	9,170	50,003	5,199
Berrien	618.7	3,965	53.9	7.1	5.5	1.4	5.2	398.2	2,551	332	263	8,984	72,730	55,823	7,065
Branch	225.6	5,144	34.9	36.1	2.4	5.3	5.0	73.0	1,664	84	67	2,805	18,900	45,732	4,364
Calhoun	680.5	5,037	45.5	17.6	4.3	2.6	5.4	473.1	3,502	3,060	267	7,959	61,020	49,750	5,298
Cass	179.5	3,436	58.6	7.1	3.5	4.6	5.4	185.2	3,544	77	82	2,086	23,370	57,678	7,528
Charlevoix	145.4	5,587	41.5	16.3	2.3	9.8	7.0	79.2	3,043	54	64	1,761	13,720	60,869	9,114
Cheboygan	82.0	3,173	52.2	1.5	4.4	1.1	11.7	35.0	1,356	56	100	996	12,720	45,392	5,122
Chippewa	142.9	3,672	42.0	7.3	3.4	0.4	14.8	140.9	3,620	464	225	5,627	15,760	42,338	3,977
Clare	130.5	4,244	66.9	0.3	2.7	0.5	8.1	36.5	1,188	93	49	1,614	12,970	39,549	3,436
Clinton	197.5	2,598	55.6	0.4	4.2	0.6	7.3	261.6	3,442	244	131	2,027	37,330	64,993	8,040
Crawford	38.5	2,750	41.0	1.0	4.9	1.1	14.9	20.3	1,451	140	22	608	6,220	41,077	3,673
Delta	137.3	3,722	63.6	3.6	2.1	0.2	6.5	110.1	2,984	200	57	1,795	17,580	48,566	5,032
Dickinson	190.3	7,257	25.2	50.0	2.2	0.1	4.5	120.1	4,580	770	56	2,113	12,870	51,545	5,659
Eaton	316.4	2,929	51.9	3.6	5.8	6.6	6.0	453.6	4,200	189	203	5,511	54,040	55,017	5,971
Emmet	280.3	8,515	27.0	38.8	1.4	4.8	4.5	162.6	4,941	105	53	2,432	17,920	69,408	11,162
Genesee	2,064.7	4,935	41.9	28.1	3.5	1.1	3.3	995.9	2,380	1,094	649	19,375	190,860	50,338	5,826
Gladwin	61.5	2,415	46.1	2.0	3.8	0.6	13.3	37.6	1,474	52	40	802	11,200	44,643	4,211
Gogebic	91.1	5,666	31.9	7.4	3.1	10.2	9.5	75.9	4,719	162	23	1,531	6,690	44,217	4,050
Grand Traverse	471.3	5,288	46.6	17.8	2.7	5.6	3.8	445.4	4,998	493	271	5,674	48,800	61,339	8,241
Gratiot	152.9	3,635	57.9	7.3	3.1	1.2	8.1	103.0	2,449	73	57	2,301	16,910	46,510	5,012
Hillsdale	131.8	2,850	51.6	0.9	3.3	14.1	8.6	74.2	1,605	88	71	2,303	19,750	45,029	4,286
Houghton	140.9	3,858	41.4	5.6	2.0	13.7	7.0	113.0	3,095	163	88	3,497	14,740	47,322	4,735
Huron	148.9	4,587	35.1	11.1	2.9	10.7	18.5	113.5	3,496	99	65	1,741	16,360	47,439	5,131
Ingham	1,371.5	4,868	44.9	13.6	4.2	3.1	3.5	1,588.9	5,640	1,570	593	40,383	124,830	56,792	7,282
Ionia	225.2	3,523	60.0	7.0	2.6	0.5	5.8	294.7	4,610	118	95	3,105	27,470	48,463	4,751
Iosco	108.1	4,265	39.8	17.8	2.4	6.7	7.8	52.0	2,052	116	63	1,482	12,050	40,478	3,667
Iron	59.7	5,151	21.7	4.9	2.7	29.2	9.9	46.6	4,026	30	17	923	5,540	42,060	3,971
Isabella	230.9	3,270	25.5	39.2	3.2	5.6	6.2	128.0	1,812	163	110	10,567	26,460	51,157	5,754
Jackson	586.0	3,655	54.4	10.1	2.6	3.6	6.4	539.6	3,366	332	244	7,458	70,940	52,836	5,966
Kalamazoo	958.5	3,765	47.3	14.6	7.5	1.0	4.4	1,168.8	4,591	692	420	14,281	120,640	64,532	8,724
Kalkaska	63.6	3,721	23.4	42.5	3.6	0.2	7.4	40.1	2,342	27	28	1,038	8,250	41,883	4,111
Kent	2442.6	3,975	51.3	6.7	4.7	1.7	3.6	3,992.0	6,497	2,908	1,081	24,577	308,680	66,848	8,946

1. Based on the resident population estimated as of July 1 of the year shown.

Table B. States and Counties — **Land Area and Population**

State / county code	CBSA code[1]	County code[2]	STATE County	Land area[3] (sq. mi)	Total persons 2018	Rank	Per square mile	White	Black	American Indian, Alaska Native	Asian and Pacific Islander	Percent Hispanic or Latino[4]	Under 5 years	5 to 17 years	18 to 24 years	25 to 34 years	35 to 44 years	45 to 54 years
				1	2	3	4	5	6	7	8	9	10	11	12	13	14	15
			MICHIGAN— Cont'd															
26083	26,340	9	Keweenaw	540.1	2,113	3,038	3.9	97.8	0.8	0.9	0.2	1.3	4.2	10.6	4.7	6.9	8.2	9.8
26085		9	Lake	567.6	11,881	2,301	20.9	87.8	9.8	1.9	0.7	2.6	4.4	11.8	5.5	8.2	9.1	12.5
26087	19,820	1	Lapeer	644.6	88,028	659	136.6	93.1	1.6	1.0	1.0	4.7	4.8	15.8	8.0	10.8	11.2	14.8
26089	45,900	9	Leelanau	347.2	21,764	1,736	62.7	91.3	1.0	3.8	1.0	4.5	4.0	12.1	6.3	8.6	9.1	10.5
26091	10,300	4	Lenawee	749.6	98,266	607	131.1	88.3	3.5	1.1	0.9	8.2	5.5	15.6	9.0	11.6	11.7	13.2
26093	19,820	1	Livingston	565.2	191,224	347	338.3	95.5	0.9	0.9	1.5	2.5	5.1	16.2	8.2	10.8	11.4	15.1
26095		7	Luce	899.1	6,283	2,726	7.0	81.3	12.4	7.4	0.7	1.6	4.0	12.5	7.8	13.3	13.1	13.2
26097		7	Mackinac	1,021.9	10,787	2,365	10.6	77.9	3.8	20.3	1.2	1.9	4.0	11.7	6.6	9.4	9.2	12.9
26099	19,820	1	Macomb	479.2	874,759	65	1,825.5	80.7	13.1	0.9	5.0	2.7	5.5	15.6	8.2	13.4	12.0	14.0
26101		7	Manistee	542.3	24,528	1,629	45.2	90.7	4.1	3.2	0.7	3.3	4.4	13.0	7.3	10.5	9.7	12.3
26103	32,100	5	Marquette	1,809.0	66,516	806	36.8	94.1	2.1	3.0	1.3	1.6	4.8	13.3	15.4	11.4	11.0	10.9
26105	31,220	7	Mason	495.0	29,100	1,455	58.8	92.8	1.5	1.6	1.1	4.6	5.2	15.1	6.8	10.7	10.5	11.8
26107	13,660	6	Mecosta	555.1	43,545	1,104	78.4	93.2	3.9	1.6	1.3	2.4	4.8	13.6	18.7	10.9	9.3	10.7
26109	31,940	7	Menominee	1,044.0	22,983	1,681	22.0	94.1	1.2	3.6	0.8	1.9	4.5	13.6	6.7	9.7	10.5	13.0
26111	33,220	3	Midland	516.3	83,209	685	161.2	92.9	1.9	1.0	2.9	2.8	5.4	15.9	8.3	12.4	11.8	13.4
26113	15,620	9	Missaukee	564.8	15,113	2,088	26.8	94.9	1.0	1.4	1.0	3.2	6.3	16.7	7.2	11.4	10.2	12.3
26115	33,780	3	Monroe	549.3	150,439	442	273.9	92.8	3.4	0.9	1.1	3.7	5.3	16.1	7.9	11.7	11.6	13.8
26117	24,340	2	Montcalm	705.3	63,968	834	90.7	93.0	3.0	1.2	0.7	3.6	5.7	16.5	8.0	12.5	12.0	13.5
26119		9	Montmorency	546.7	9,265	2,481	16.9	97.3	1.0	1.6	0.5	1.3	3.6	11.4	5.2	7.6	8.2	11.8
26121	34,740	3	Muskegon	503.9	173,588	377	344.5	78.8	15.4	1.6	1.1	5.8	6.1	17.0	8.2	13.1	12.0	12.3
26123		6	Newaygo	838.9	48,892	1,007	58.3	91.9	1.7	1.3	0.8	5.8	5.8	16.7	7.3	11.6	10.8	12.7
26125	19,820	1	Oakland	867.4	1,259,201	33	1,451.7	73.6	14.8	0.8	8.9	4.2	5.4	15.5	8.1	13.3	12.5	14.0
26127		6	Oceana	538.1	26,625	1,541	49.5	82.6	1.6	1.7	0.5	15.1	5.6	17.2	7.8	10.6	10.6	12.0
26129		9	Ogemaw	563.5	20,952	1,777	37.2	95.7	0.7	1.6	1.0	2.4	4.5	14.0	6.3	9.7	9.6	11.7
26131		9	Ontonagon	1,311.0	5,795	2,769	4.4	95.9	0.8	2.0	1.1	1.6	2.7	10.0	4.8	5.4	7.4	12.6
26133		9	Osceola	566.3	23,341	1,669	41.2	96.1	1.6	1.5	0.7	2.0	5.4	17.0	7.0	11.1	10.7	12.4
26135		9	Oscoda	565.7	8,276	2,565	14.6	96.7	0.9	1.7	0.6	1.7	5.7	13.7	6.0	8.8	8.4	10.4
26137		7	Otsego	515.0	24,665	1,622	47.9	95.9	1.1	1.7	1.3	1.7	5.3	15.8	7.7	11.3	10.2	13.3
26139	24,340	2	Ottawa	563.5	290,494	240	515.5	85.2	2.3	0.7	3.6	10.0	6.2	17.8	13.3	12.2	11.8	11.6
26141		7	Presque Isle	658.7	12,738	2,240	19.3	96.5	0.9	1.4	0.8	1.5	4.1	11.9	5.8	7.6	8.9	11.2
26143		7	Roscommon	519.9	23,884	1,649	45.9	95.8	1.0	1.6	0.9	2.1	3.6	11.1	5.2	8.0	7.9	11.5
26145	40,980	3	Saginaw	800.5	190,800	349	238.4	71.0	19.8	0.9	1.8	8.5	5.7	15.6	9.4	12.5	10.9	12.5
26147	19,820	1	St. Clair	721.3	159,337	416	220.9	93.0	3.5	1.1	1.0	3.4	5.0	15.8	7.8	11.1	11.1	14.5
26149	44,780	4	St. Joseph	500.6	61,043	860	121.9	88.3	3.7	1.0	1.1	8.1	6.5	18.0	7.9	12.0	11.4	12.1
26151		6	Sanilac	962.6	41,182	1,147	42.8	94.9	0.9	0.9	0.5	3.7	5.4	16.0	7.4	10.2	10.6	12.7
26153		7	Schoolcraft	1,171.9	8,068	2,584	6.9	89.1	1.2	11.7	0.6	1.1	4.0	13.0	6.4	7.9	9.3	12.7
26155	37,020	4	Shiawassee	531.0	68,192	784	128.4	95.3	1.2	1.1	0.9	3.0	5.4	15.7	8.4	11.6	11.3	13.8
26157		6	Tuscola	804.5	52,516	956	65.3	94.4	1.6	1.2	0.6	3.5	5.1	15.3	7.4	11.1	11.1	13.5
26159	28,020	2	Van Buren	607.8	75,448	735	124.1	83.1	4.9	1.6	1.1	11.7	5.9	17.3	7.8	11.0	11.6	12.9
26161	11,460	2	Washtenaw	706.0	370,963	189	525.4	73.0	13.6	1.0	11.0	4.8	4.9	13.7	18.8	14.5	11.4	11.6
26163	19,820	1	Wayne	612.0	1,753,893	19	2,865.8	51.5	39.6	1.1	4.3	6.1	6.5	17.1	8.7	14.2	11.7	13.0
26165	15,620	7	Wexford	564.9	33,466	1,340	59.2	96.0	1.2	1.4	1.0	2.1	6.1	17.1	7.3	11.7	11.1	12.7
27000		0	MINNESOTA	79,625.4	5,611,179	X	70.5	81.6	7.7	1.8	5.9	5.5	6.3	16.9	8.9	13.6	12.7	12.3
27001		8	Aitkin	1,821.8	15,902	2,043	8.7	95.2	1.1	3.1	0.7	1.5	3.7	13.0	5.2	7.7	8.3	10.8
27003	33,460	1	Anoka	422.0	353,813	200	838.4	83.1	7.9	1.4	5.7	4.7	6.3	17.6	7.7	13.2	13.3	13.8
27005		6	Becker	1,315.1	34,371	1,314	26.1	89.2	1.1	9.9	0.9	2.1	6.2	18.2	7.3	10.4	11.3	11.0
27007	13,420	7	Beltrami	2,504.7	46,847	1,037	18.7	74.8	1.6	23.0	1.3	2.4	7.1	18.0	13.4	12.5	10.8	9.9
27009	41,060	3	Benton	408.3	40,545	1,166	99.3	91.2	5.5	1.0	1.7	2.5	7.2	18.0	8.1	14.8	13.7	12.2
27011		9	Big Stone	499.2	4,989	2,832	10.0	96.5	0.9	0.8	0.5	2.3	5.6	15.5	6.3	9.7	9.0	10.6
27013	31,860	3	Blue Earth	747.8	67,427	792	90.2	89.3	5.0	0.7	3.1	3.8	5.5	14.2	21.5	13.7	11.0	9.5
27015	35,580	6	Brown	611.1	25,111	1,600	41.1	93.9	0.9	0.4	1.0	4.6	5.6	16.3	9.7	10.6	10.8	11.0
27017	20,260	2	Carlton	861.3	35,837	1,280	41.6	90.3	2.2	7.2	1.0	1.8	5.2	17.2	7.4	12.2	12.7	13.4
27019	33,460	1	Carver	354.2	103,551	584	292.4	90.2	2.6	0.6	4.1	4.3	6.6	20.2	8.1	10.6	14.4	14.8
27021	14,660	9	Cass	2,021.5	29,519	1,443	14.6	85.0	1.0	13.2	0.9	2.4	5.5	15.7	6.0	9.3	9.6	11.1
27023		7	Chippewa	581.1	11,924	2,299	20.5	88.1	1.4	1.9	2.7	7.7	6.8	16.7	7.7	11.4	10.9	10.9
27025	33,460	1	Chisago	414.9	55,922	915	134.8	94.5	1.9	1.2	1.7	2.3	5.8	16.9	7.6	12.2	12.6	14.8
27027	22,020	3	Clay	1,045.2	63,955	835	61.2	88.7	4.7	2.2	2.1	4.6	7.4	17.3	14.6	13.8	12.7	10.2
27029		8	Clearwater	998.7	8,810	2,514	8.8	87.8	1.3	11.3	0.8	2.4	6.2	18.6	6.8	10.4	11.5	11.2
27031		9	Cook	1,452.4	5,393	2,803	3.7	87.7	1.6	9.8	1.2	2.5	4.7	11.0	5.6	10.1	10.1	11.5
27033		7	Cottonwood	640.0	11,277	2,333	17.6	86.5	1.5	0.9	4.3	8.2	6.9	17.6	7.6	9.5	10.5	11.2
27035	14,660	4	Crow Wing	998.4	64,889	821	65.0	96.2	1.4	1.5	0.9	1.5	5.6	16.0	6.7	11.1	11.2	11.6
27037	33,460	1	Dakota	562.4	425,423	166	756.4	80.2	8.2	0.9	6.1	7.4	6.5	17.9	7.9	13.1	13.4	13.4
27039	40,340	3	Dodge	439.3	20,822	1,784	47.4	93.2	1.1	0.8	1.4	5.1	6.2	19.5	8.0	11.7	13.3	13.3
27041	10,820	6	Douglas	636.8	37,964	1,226	59.6	96.8	0.9	0.7	0.8	1.8	5.9	15.7	7.0	11.3	11.2	11.3
27043		6	Faribault	712.5	13,758	2,180	19.3	91.4	1.0	0.8	0.7	7.3	6.4	16.4	6.9	9.9	11.3	11.1

1. CBSA = Core Based Statistical Area. See Appendix A for explanation. See Appendix B for list of metropolitan areas with component counties. Service of USDA Rural-Urban Continuum Codes. See Appendix A for definition. 3. Dry land or land partially or temporarily covered by water.   2. County type code from the Economic Research   4. May be of any race.

Table B. States and Counties — Population and Households

STATE County	55 to 64 years	65 to 74 years	75 years and over	Percent female	Total persons 2000	Total persons 2010	Percent change 2000-2010	Percent change 2010-2018	Births	Deaths	Net Migration	Number	Persons per household	Family households	Female family householder[1]	One person
	16	17	18	19	20	21	22	23	24	25	26	27	28	29	30	31
MICHIGAN— Cont'd																
Keweenaw	18.8	22.0	14.8	48.7	2,301	2,156	-6.3	-2.0	150	169	-23	1,013	2.09	62.2	9.0	32.7
Lake	19.9	17.6	11.0	49.2	11,333	11,539	1.8	3.0	807	1,292	815	4,555	2.48	60.8	6.9	34.3
Lapeer	16.4	11.1	7.0	49.3	87,904	88,318	0.5	-0.3	6,693	6,735	-231	33,152	2.60	73.7	9.4	22.0
Leelanau	18.5	17.9	13.0	50.6	21,119	21,713	2.8	0.2	1,400	1,898	555	9,022	2.35	69.3	6.4	26.5
Lenawee	14.4	11.3	7.7	49.5	98,890	99,892	1.0	-1.6	8,633	8,212	-2,044	38,115	2.45	65.9	11.1	28.8
Livingston	16.0	10.6	6.6	49.9	156,951	180,961	15.3	5.7	14,629	11,502	7,280	70,831	2.62	73.4	7.6	22.0
Luce	15.5	10.7	9.8	41.1	7,024	6,631	-5.6	-5.2	414	612	-153	2,253	2.37	61.8	7.0	33.4
Mackinac	18.1	16.1	11.9	48.9	11,943	11,117	-6.9	-3.0	692	1,114	97	5,132	2.06	60.1	8.9	33.6
Macomb	14.4	9.7	7.3	51.3	788,149	841,039	6.7	4.0	76,453	69,158	27,106	341,532	2.50	66.0	13.4	28.8
Manistee	17.1	15.0	10.7	48.3	24,527	24,747	0.9	-0.9	1,678	2,577	679	9,810	2.34	62.8	7.5	32.7
Marquette	14.0	11.3	7.8	49.9	64,634	67,071	3.8	-0.8	5,324	5,435	-412	26,199	2.39	59.5	8.1	31.1
Mason	16.5	13.6	9.9	50.4	28,274	28,691	1.5	1.4	2,386	2,728	773	12,186	2.32	64.0	9.8	30.7
Mecosta	13.6	10.8	7.5	49.8	40,553	42,798	5.5	1.7	3,435	3,111	428	15,641	2.57	61.2	8.7	29.7
Menominee	17.3	13.9	10.7	49.1	25,326	24,029	-5.1	-4.4	1,654	2,214	-467	10,593	2.17	60.7	7.7	34.6
Midland	14.5	10.0	8.3	50.7	82,874	83,626	0.9	-0.5	7,000	5,930	-1,474	33,986	2.42	67.8	8.7	26.3
Missaukee	15.5	12.0	8.5	49.2	14,478	14,851	2.6	1.8	1,472	1,340	137	5,941	2.49	68.5	8.1	26.8
Monroe	15.5	10.6	7.5	50.6	145,945	152,024	4.2	-1.0	12,611	11,597	-2,597	58,652	2.53	68.8	10.2	26.7
Montcalm	14.3	10.3	7.2	48.3	61,266	63,342	3.4	1.0	5,953	4,937	-383	23,556	2.56	68.3	10.8	26.6
Montmorency	19.8	19.0	13.3	49.0	10,315	9,760	-5.4	-5.1	537	1,297	269	4,074	2.24	63.4	9.5	31.4
Muskegon	14.3	10.2	6.8	50.3	170,200	172,194	1.2	0.8	17,385	13,948	-2,065	65,216	2.55	67.1	14.5	26.9
Newaygo	15.9	11.3	7.9	49.8	47,874	48,460	1.2	0.9	4,522	4,043	-33	18,772	2.51	68.5	8.9	25.2
Oakland	14.3	9.9	6.9	51.0	1,194,156	1,202,384	0.7	4.7	110,653	84,872	31,832	499,617	2.46	64.8	10.1	29.3
Oceana	15.6	12.1	8.5	49.3	26,873	26,570	-1.1	0.2	2,537	2,200	-276	10,176	2.52	72.2	9.7	23.6
Ogemaw	18.4	14.8	11.1	50.2	21,645	21,699	0.2	-3.4	1,561	2,518	230	9,325	2.22	65.6	10.6	30.2
Ontonagon	20.8	20.9	15.3	49.2	7,818	6,780	-13.3	-14.5	258	830	-415	2,945	2.03	57.4	4.8	37.7
Osceola	15.3	12.4	8.8	49.6	23,197	23,528	1.4	-0.8	2,136	2,009	-304	9,010	2.53	66.7	10.7	28.6
Oscoda	19.8	15.9	11.3	48.7	9,418	8,636	-8.3	-4.2	730	1,029	-60	3,728	2.21	60.7	7.0	35.3
Otsego	15.1	12.5	8.6	50.4	23,301	24,166	3.7	2.1	2,051	2,160	626	9,880	2.41	69.6	10.1	25.7
Ottawa	12.0	8.6	6.4	50.6	238,314	263,795	10.7	10.1	27,807	14,981	14,031	99,721	2.72	72.8	8.3	20.9
Presque Isle	19.1	17.8	13.6	50.3	14,411	13,376	-7.2	-4.8	797	1,598	171	5,929	2.13	65.9	6.9	30.0
Roscommon	20.1	19.4	13.2	49.9	25,469	24,448	-4.0	-2.3	1,398	3,280	1,307	11,131	2.13	62.1	10.4	33.1
Saginaw	14.1	10.9	8.3	51.4	210,039	200,169	-4.7	-4.7	18,492	17,084	-10,863	78,482	2.39	62.6	14.4	31.4
St. Clair	15.9	11.1	7.7	50.3	164,235	163,049	-0.7	-2.3	12,965	14,156	-2,496	64,387	2.45	66.4	10.3	27.6
St. Joseph	14.2	10.5	7.5	50.1	62,422	61,295	-1.8	-0.4	6,614	5,156	-1,695	23,831	2.52	69.8	10.9	25.2
Sanilac	16.2	12.3	9.1	50.1	44,547	43,101	-3.2	-4.5	3,639	3,907	-1,656	17,121	2.39	65.5	9.1	29.2
Schoolcraft	19.9	15.5	11.3	50.7	8,903	8,485	-4.7	-4.9	557	893	-78	3,282	2.43	62.9	7.6	32.7
Shiawassee	15.4	10.9	7.5	50.6	71,687	70,663	-1.4	-3.5	5,860	5,848	-2,498	27,623	2.46	69.0	10.3	24.4
Tuscola	16.2	11.6	8.6	49.8	58,266	55,730	-4.4	-5.8	4,479	4,769	-2,947	21,624	2.42	69.3	8.6	25.6
Van Buren	15.3	11.0	7.1	50.4	76,263	76,264	0.0	-1.1	7,361	6,097	-2,097	29,151	2.53	67.2	10.6	27.3
Washtenaw	11.3	8.4	5.4	50.4	322,895	345,104	6.9	7.5	30,655	18,048	13,480	138,947	2.46	57.3	8.9	30.2
Wayne	13.3	9.0	6.4	51.8	2,061,162	1,820,539	-11.7	-3.7	191,941	149,228	-111,147	673,143	2.59	61.9	19.0	33.0
Wexford	15.0	11.1	8.0	49.9	30,484	32,735	7.4	2.2	3,304	2,887	335	13,105	2.49	68.0	10.7	25.9
MINNESOTA	13.4	9.1	6.8	50.2	4,919,479	5,303,925	7.8	5.8	570,171	341,882	81,671	2,153,202	2.49	64.6	9.3	28.3
Aitkin	18.3	18.7	14.3	49.5	15,301	16,192	5.8	-1.8	949	1,752	519	7,709	2.02	65.3	6.4	29.9
Anoka	14.0	8.6	5.5	50.0	298,084	330,858	11.0	6.9	34,531	16,077	4,749	126,072	2.71	72.0	10.4	22.3
Becker	15.1	12.1	8.4	50.1	30,000	32,504	8.3	5.7	3,482	2,853	1,267	13,489	2.45	67.9	10.1	27.2
Beltrami	12.2	9.2	6.9	50.0	39,650	44,442	12.1	5.4	5,696	3,384	120	17,076	2.55	63.9	14.0	28.7
Benton	11.9	7.7	6.4	50.1	34,226	38,451	12.3	5.4	4,700	2,753	158	16,005	2.40	64.9	11.2	26.1
Big Stone	16.9	12.3	14.2	50.4	5,820	5,268	-9.5	-5.3	465	612	-128	2,264	2.16	64.2	6.1	31.2
Blue Earth	10.8	7.7	6.2	49.7	55,941	64,013	14.4	5.3	6,083	3,910	1,265	25,558	2.42	57.3	8.1	26.6
Brown	15.1	10.5	10.4	50.2	26,911	25,893	-3.8	-3.0	2,253	2,418	-612	10,668	2.26	65.4	7.2	29.5
Carlton	14.6	9.6	7.6	47.8	31,671	35,386	11.7	1.3	3,015	3,047	510	13,413	2.49	67.4	8.6	26.3
Carver	13.3	7.2	4.8	50.4	70,205	91,086	29.7	13.7	9,560	3,905	6,855	35,342	2.77	75.1	6.7	20.1
Cass	16.9	15.4	10.5	48.9	27,150	28,567	5.2	3.3	2,729	2,556	785	12,965	2.19	68.9	10.4	25.5
Chippewa	14.2	11.0	10.2	49.8	13,088	12,441	-4.9	-4.2	1,320	1,238	-605	5,019	2.35	65.5	9.4	30.6
Chisago	14.7	9.3	6.1	48.4	41,101	53,890	31.1	3.8	4,660	3,208	586	19,871	2.64	72.6	7.9	21.9
Clay	10.8	7.1	6.1	50.5	51,229	58,999	15.2	8.4	6,968	3,849	1,859	23,453	2.48	63.7	8.4	28.2
Clearwater	15.2	10.7	9.5	48.9	8,423	8,695	3.2	1.3	894	811	36	3,428	2.54	64.8	7.5	30.5
Cook	18.3	18.3	10.3	50.0	5,168	5,176	0.2	4.2	377	378	216	2,700	1.92	63.2	7.3	29.9
Cottonwood	14.0	11.4	11.4	50.0	12,167	11,687	-3.9	-3.5	1,238	1,122	-526	4,837	2.30	64.9	7.7	31.8
Crow Wing	15.4	12.7	9.8	50.2	55,099	62,510	13.5	3.8	5,893	5,386	1,930	26,314	2.38	66.7	9.2	27.6
Dakota	13.7	8.5	5.7	50.7	355,904	398,583	12.0	6.7	43,090	19,624	3,549	158,777	2.59	69.4	10.4	24.5
Dodge	13.2	8.4	6.4	50.1	17,731	20,087	13.3	3.7	2,063	1,157	-166	7,690	2.64	73.0	8.6	22.6
Douglas	14.9	12.4	10.3	50.0	32,821	36,009	9.7	5.4	3,414	3,329	1,896	16,175	2.25	64.5	5.1	30.0
Faribault	15.7	11.7	11.1	50.0	16,181	14,553	-10.1	-5.5	1,219	1,546	-471	6,245	2.19	63.1	7.8	32.5

1. No spouse present.

Table B. States and Counties — Population, Vital Statistics, Health, and Crime

STATE County	Persons in group quarters, 2018	Daytime Population, 2013-2017 Number	Employment/ residence ratio	Births, 2018 Total	Rate[1]	Deaths, 2018 Number	Rate[1]	Persons under 65 with no health insurance, 2016 Number	Percent	Medicare, 2018 Total beneficiaries	Enrolled in Original Medicare	Enrolled in Medicare Advantage	Serious crimes known to police[2], 2016 Total Number	Rate[3]
	32	33	34	35	36	37	38	39	40	41	42	43	44	45
MICHIGAN— Cont'd														
Keweenaw	10	1,897	0.71	19	9.0	19	9.0	96	6.7	756	523	233	30	1,381
Lake	370	10,288	0.60	99	8.3	161	13.6	697	8.7	3,809	2,559	1,250	215	1,886
Lapeer	1,618	75,083	0.65	779	8.8	876	10.0	4,866	6.8	18,907	10,917	7,990	1,154	1,306
Leelanau	284	19,726	0.81	173	7.9	223	10.2	1,208	7.9	6,949	4,108	2,841	99	449
Lenawee	5,120	87,672	0.75	1,026	10.4	997	10.1	4,794	6.3	22,426	14,074	8,352	766	833
Livingston	1,392	153,995	0.65	1,772	9.3	1,550	8.1	6,168	3.9	36,870	22,363	14,507	1,779	944
Luce	1,172	6,786	1.19	43	6.8	86	13.7	341	8.6	1,591	1,115	476	131	2,055
Mackinac	95	10,928	1.02	85	7.9	130	12.1	909	11.7	3,477	2,297	1,180	345	3,181
Macomb	7,517	802,434	0.85	9,267	10.6	8,510	9.7	44,965	6.2	172,818	103,712	69,106	16,986	1,956
Manistee	1,369	23,963	0.95	241	9.8	310	12.6	1,383	8.1	7,354	5,030	2,324	531	2,174
Marquette	4,101	67,716	1.02	648	9.7	678	10.2	2,775	5.4	14,900	10,086	4,814	1,091	1,623
Mason	442	28,668	0.99	269	9.2	306	10.5	1,599	7.2	8,117	5,363	2,754	514	1,786
Mecosta	3,342	42,637	0.97	383	8.8	364	8.4	2,441	7.5	9,215	5,566	3,649	912	2,116
Menominee	382	20,832	0.75	186	8.1	247	10.7	1,334	7.5	6,303	4,045	2,258	336	1,433
Midland	1,274	86,011	1.07	813	9.8	743	8.9	3,796	5.6	17,677	10,732	6,945	994	1,189
Missaukee	194	13,400	0.74	181	12.0	162	10.7	988	8.3	3,676	2,523	1,153	185	1,240
Monroe	1,463	127,712	0.68	1,501	10.0	1,454	9.7	6,260	5.1	31,822	19,478	12,344	2,506	1,728
Montcalm	3,055	56,924	0.76	704	11.0	609	9.5	3,603	7.2	13,905	8,404	5,501	1,147	1,865
Montmorency	156	8,839	0.85	64	6.9	167	18.0	529	8.4	3,788	2,503	1,285	37	404
Muskegon	5,490	164,699	0.89	2,072	11.9	1,761	10.1	8,475	6.1	38,207	20,086	18,121	5,973	3,455
Newaygo	557	43,724	0.78	548	11.2	522	10.7	2,912	7.6	11,620	5,720	5,900	764	1,608
Oakland	13,244	1,323,370	1.13	13,360	10.6	10,875	8.6	54,115	5.2	236,800	148,405	88,395	18,223	1,458
Oceana	303	23,926	0.77	299	11.2	265	10.0	2,138	10.4	6,527	3,966	2,561	859	3,670
Ogemaw	244	20,953	1.00	192	9.2	285	13.6	1,248	8.0	6,741	4,699	2,042	476	2,289
Ontonagon	83	5,564	0.75	31	5.3	111	19.2	327	8.5	2,361	1,693	668	56	955
Osceola	454	21,940	0.85	234	10.0	250	10.7	1,336	7.4	6,052	3,912	2,140	396	1,725
Oscoda	65	7,961	0.87	90	10.9	112	13.5	546	9.1	2,788	1,929	859	190	2,323
Otsego	347	25,802	1.15	243	9.9	278	11.3	1,360	7.1	6,364	4,375	1,989	580	2,390
Ottawa	9,069	268,734	0.92	3,413	11.7	1,935	6.7	12,039	5.1	49,769	19,230	30,539	4,321	1,526
Presque Isle	230	12,021	0.81	106	8.3	182	14.3	708	8.1	4,697	3,184	1,513	80	628
Roscommon	277	23,997	1.01	164	6.9	382	16.0	1,288	8.0	9,382	6,119	3,263	524	2,204
Saginaw	6,728	205,976	1.15	2,119	11.1	2,139	11.2	9,104	6.0	44,823	25,178	19,645	4,527	2,359
St. Clair	1,999	141,724	0.74	1,519	9.5	1,728	10.8	8,588	6.6	36,346	22,786	13,560	2,742	1,726
St. Joseph	765	58,311	0.90	749	12.3	576	9.4	4,127	8.3	12,870	8,633	4,237	1,140	1,915
Sanilac	565	38,392	0.82	423	10.3	493	12.0	2,673	8.2	10,407	7,265	3,142	508	1,269
Schoolcraft	140	8,019	0.96	67	8.3	108	13.4	532	9.1	2,383	1,632	751	NA	NA
Shiawassee	821	58,199	0.65	712	10.4	731	10.7	3,323	5.9	15,592	9,498	6,094	1,055	1,560
Tuscola	1,078	46,021	0.67	506	9.6	648	12.3	2,657	6.3	13,302	8,447	4,855	749	1,413
Van Buren	877	67,710	0.77	825	10.9	808	10.7	5,055	8.2	16,643	10,000	6,643	1,607	2,148
Washtenaw	22,604	398,942	1.21	3,637	9.8	2,395	6.5	14,526	4.9	57,596	38,670	18,926	7,113	1,968
Wayne	22,715	1,825,561	1.09	22,418	12.8	18,489	10.5	103,958	7.1	325,601	185,189	140,412	73,035	4,179
Wexford	389	34,874	1.14	366	10.9	333	10.0	2,064	7.7	8,026	5,438	2,588	982	3,103
MINNESOTA	131,278	5,504,140	1.00	68,617	12.2	42,847	7.6	220,535	4.8	995,561	417,614	577,947	131,150	2,376
Aitkin	274	14,486	0.78	120	7.5	213	13.4	722	6.9	4,608	1,770	2,838	359	2,304
Anoka	2,961	285,435	0.68	4,210	11.9	2,140	6.0	13,375	4.5	55,617	20,525	35,092	8,019	2,315
Becker	458	32,246	0.92	419	12.2	379	11.0	1,834	6.9	8,364	3,554	4,810	317	946
Beltrami	2,095	46,436	1.03	661	14.1	433	9.2	3,231	8.7	8,633	4,587	4,046	1,531	3,340
Benton	1,049	35,565	0.81	552	13.6	315	7.8	1,401	4.1	7,044	3,143	3,901	819	2,052
Big Stone	137	4,751	0.88	61	12.2	71	14.2	209	5.6	1,483	681	802	34	681
Blue Earth	3,938	70,787	1.14	715	10.6	461	6.8	2,599	4.8	10,901	5,044	5,857	1,643	2,487
Brown	1,120	27,037	1.13	273	10.9	285	11.3	721	3.7	6,101	2,680	3,421	177	703
Carlton	1,993	32,936	0.85	355	9.9	355	9.9	1,423	5.0	7,388	3,308	4,080	945	2,658
Carver	877	85,487	0.76	1,174	11.3	530	5.1	2,611	2.9	13,420	4,944	8,476	1,011	1,009
Cass	223	26,975	0.85	304	10.3	305	10.3	1,685	7.8	9,064	4,051	5,013	493	1,719
Chippewa	237	12,014	1.00	143	12.0	138	11.6	590	6.2	2,638	1,038	1,600	161	1,339
Chisago	1,675	43,449	0.61	593	10.6	399	7.1	1,759	3.9	9,865	3,688	6,177	648	1,193
Clay	2,921	51,417	0.68	903	14.1	473	7.4	2,190	4.2	9,748	4,822	4,926	1,279	2,033
Clearwater	115	8,166	0.82	112	12.7	89	10.1	560	8.1	2,001	863	1,138	109	1,237
Cook	51	5,404	1.05	47	8.7	47	8.7	286	7.4	1,673	736	937	120	2,310
Cottonwood	244	11,605	1.03	139	12.3	150	13.3	516	5.9	2,918	1,416	1,502	89	774
Crow Wing	736	65,554	1.07	675	10.4	683	10.5	2,577	5.2	17,203	6,822	10,381	1,707	2,688
Dakota	2,824	373,034	0.82	5,185	12.2	2,627	6.2	14,416	4.0	66,499	27,234	39,265	8,827	2,115
Dodge	149	16,497	0.64	238	11.4	147	7.1	694	3.9	3,372	1,678	1,694	163	800
Douglas	522	38,284	1.07	426	11.2	419	11.0	1,314	4.5	10,310	3,545	6,765	583	1,565
Faribault	336	13,152	0.88	148	10.8	161	11.7	602	5.7	3,641	1,455	2,186	133	954

1. Per 1,000 estimated resident population.   2. Data for serious crimes have not been adjusted for underreporting; this may affect comparability between geographic areas and over time.   3. Per 100,000 population estimated by the FBI.

Table B. States and Counties — Crime, Education, Money Income, and Poverty

STATE County	Serious crimes known to police[2], 2016 (cont.)[1] Rate Violent	Property	School enrollment and attainment, 2013-2017 Enrollment[3] Total	Percent private	Attainment[4] (percent) High school graduate or less	Bachelor's degree or more	Local government expenditures,[5] 2014-2015 Total current spending (mil dol)	Current spending per student (dollars)	Money income, 2013-2017 Per capita income[6]	Median income (dollars)	Households Percent with income of less than $50,000	with income of $200,000 or more	Income and poverty, 2017 Median household income (dollars)	Percent below poverty level All persons	Children under 18 years	Children 5 to 17 years in families
	46	47	48	49	50	51	52	53	54	55	56	57	58	59	60	61
MICHIGAN— Cont'd																
Keweenaw	138	1,243	324	6.2	41.7	25.1	0.2	29,143	28,700	41,118	58.8	2.4	43,812	12.2	15.5	14.2
Lake	289	1,596	1,920	11.6	59.2	11.4	8.7	14,408	18,199	32,309	68.9	0.7	35,005	22.1	38.8	38.1
Lapeer	220	1,086	19,799	9.2	45.9	18.4	125.2	10,134	26,650	56,186	43.2	2.6	57,621	8.7	11.9	10.9
Leelanau	73	377	4,046	17.4	28.0	40.8	29.0	13,437	37,061	62,646	39.9	6.8	66,372	7.1	10.9	10.3
Lenawee	137	696	23,750	16.2	46.1	20.5	179.2	11,758	25,649	51,339	48.7	2.0	56,416	10.4	14.3	13.9
Livingston	132	812	46,109	13.4	30.3	34.7	270.5	10,088	36,845	78,430	29.5	7.2	82,076	5.3	6.3	5.8
Luce	455	1,600	1,089	5.7	52.0	15.1	7.1	9,775	19,442	41,221	58.1	0.9	44,479	19	26.3	23.4
Mackinac	332	2,849	1,878	6.0	47.1	19.1	15.0	11,137	26,967	42,559	58.8	2.0	43,427	14.3	21.9	20.5
Macomb	297	1,659	208,278	11.6	40.6	24.2	1,390.3	10,922	29,740	58,175	43.1	3.5	60,475	11.2	15.7	14.1
Manistee	291	1,883	4,577	17.1	45.4	20.5	50.6	10,464	24,398	44,882	55.5	1.9	45,504	13.5	22.1	20.3
Marquette	232	1,391	18,265	8.3	36.4	30.8	95.0	11,517	25,550	48,491	51.4	2.1	49,472	16.7	17.7	15.0
Mason	257	1,529	5,954	11.9	41.4	22.2	54.5	13,625	26,251	45,524	54.6	2.4	46,579	13.3	21.2	19.4
Mecosta	668	1,448	14,238	5.5	46.0	21.7	73.0	12,473	21,978	43,470	56.9	2.0	45,785	20.3	26.7	22.8
Menominee	247	1,185	4,477	11.7	51.1	15.8	39.5	10,965	26,151	44,480	55.7	1.5	48,627	11.8	17.0	15.4
Midland	128	1,061	20,332	15.9	35.1	34.1	133.6	11,093	33,013	57,117	43.8	6.5	61,290	10.7	13.0	11.6
Missaukee	215	1,026	3,080	13.5	53.0	13.4	19.7	9,288	21,805	42,370	58.4	1.4	44,553	14.2	21.7	20.7
Monroe	255	1,473	35,478	13.1	45.6	18.6	252.8	10,890	29,245	59,479	42.3	2.9	61,121	11.7	14.4	12.2
Montcalm	400	1,465	14,356	11.7	51.0	12.8	100.0	11,204	21,509	44,651	56.8	1.1	46,664	14.9	21.2	19.7
Montmorency	98	306	1,428	9.6	56.9	12.0	7.7	10,348	23,155	39,152	63.5	1.1	40,170	14.1	28.5	27.1
Muskegon	437	3,018	41,371	10.2	44.9	18.6	304.8	10,737	22,829	46,077	53.6	2.0	48,885	15.2	21.5	20.4
Newaygo	286	1,322	10,654	11.7	54.2	15.0	86.5	11,036	22,735	45,645	54.2	1.5	47,521	14.4	21.4	20.3
Oakland	181	1,277	309,352	16.4	25.4	45.7	2,170.3	11,787	40,941	73,369	34.3	9.9	77,558	7.8	9.3	8.0
Oceana	718	2,953	5,728	10.7	49.0	18.1	33.4	10,210	22,185	44,382	55.7	1.3	46,243	14.6	21.5	20.8
Ogemaw	529	1,760	3,943	8.3	53.7	11.8	19.4	9,356	22,028	38,149	62.8	1.1	38,220	16.2	27.0	25.5
Ontonagon	324	631	868	6.6	48.8	17.4	12.7	23,299	22,958	36,073	64.8	0.6	37,208	15.6	27.2	24.6
Osceola	348	1,376	4,881	11.6	57.6	12.4	37.4	9,315	21,090	41,099	60.3	1.3	41,268	14.7	22.8	21.1
Oscoda	342	1,981	1,439	18.3	56.5	10.9	8.7	10,132	22,343	36,833	66.9	1.0	39,253	18	29.4	29.7
Otsego	354	2,036	5,092	17.0	44.2	22.0	36.2	9,388	26,012	50,823	49.2	1.9	51,814	12	18.6	17.0
Ottawa	252	1,275	82,262	19.2	36.3	32.5	489.8	10,929	29,121	63,962	37.9	4.2	68,816	8.2	8.2	7.3
Presque Isle	71	557	2,149	13.1	51.3	16.2	14.0	9,513	24,793	43,758	57.0	1.0	43,244	15.4	27.0	22.5
Roscommon	341	1,863	3,610	8.8	51.9	14.2	38.0	13,250	22,333	37,834	65.4	1.1	40,306	18.8	37.8	35.6
Saginaw	608	1,751	49,305	10.9	44.7	21.1	303.0	10,773	25,348	45,034	55.2	2.7	45,433	17.5	24.2	21.4
St. Clair	351	1,375	35,891	10.3	44.5	18.0	295.2	10,312	27,807	53,641	46.4	2.6	56,671	12.4	18.6	16.7
St. Joseph	296	1,620	13,969	8.8	51.5	15.4	111.7	10,414	23,702	47,856	52.2	1.8	50,854	13	19.4	17.6
Sanilac	262	1,007	8,795	10.4	54.6	13.9	66.2	10,103	23,924	44,417	55.6	1.6	47,287	14.5	22.1	20.4
Schoolcraft	NA	NA	1,426	8.3	55.0	15.2	8.3	9,755	21,534	37,428	61.9	1.2	41,973	14.6	23.2	21.1
Shiawassee	288	1,271	16,324	12.1	45.0	16.2	125.9	10,858	25,218	50,967	48.9	1.5	53,055	11.1	16.5	15.3
Tuscola	321	1,092	11,462	15.6	52.4	13.8	93.2	11,895	23,573	45,495	54.9	1.5	47,357	14.2	19.8	19.3
Van Buren	389	1,759	18,105	9.3	45.3	20.6	187.5	11,990	25,433	49,119	50.7	2.4	52,114	12.8	18.1	16.0
Washtenaw	318	1,650	125,917	9.8	20.2	54.3	518.7	11,840	37,455	65,618	38.8	8.9	70,509	12.9	11.4	10.1
Wayne	1,036	3,143	454,295	11.6	44.6	22.8	3,162.1	11,190	24,847	43,702	55.1	3.4	45,182	22.6	33.4	31.1
Wexford	499	2,604	7,156	13.3	48.5	17.6	69.7	13,786	22,028	42,793	57.7	1.2	46,072	13.5	20.9	18.3
MINNESOTA	243	2,133	1,396,256	16.0	32.6	34.8	10,174.4	11,899	34,712	65,699	37.9	6.4	68,364	9.5	11.7	10.8
Aitkin	96	2,208	2,596	5.3	47.4	16.7	22.0	11,306	26,883	45,860	54.8	1.7	44,344	12.1	18.8	16.2
Anoka	129	2,186	87,792	12.0	34.7	28.7	702.8	11,103	34,321	76,796	30.0	5.2	79,097	5.4	7.3	6.5
Becker	84	862	7,757	10.9	39.5	24.0	50.0	10,665	28,525	55,884	45.4	3.3	54,502	11.7	17.3	16.1
Beltrami	271	3,069	12,850	8.7	37.5	27.0	115.1	14,235	23,748	45,923	53.2	2.2	47,336	18.8	24.8	22.1
Benton	138	1,914	9,792	9.2	39.3	22.1	54.9	8,930	27,018	53,574	47.4	2.3	58,572	9.7	10.1	9.0
Big Stone	20	661	965	2.7	52.9	16.8	10.4	12,579	29,035	48,299	52.2	3.3	48,553	12.3	16.0	15.3
Blue Earth	201	2,286	22,400	9.5	33.3	32.2	108.0	10,211	28,283	53,752	46.6	3.8	56,137	16.3	12.4	12.1
Brown	79	624	6,075	34.7	46.0	19.8	39.9	11,937	29,696	55,764	42.6	3.1	57,742	8	9.9	9.1
Carlton	186	2,472	8,859	10.6	41.8	21.5	64.5	9,986	26,900	58,478	41.7	2.5	60,740	9.3	9.8	8.4
Carver	64	945	27,711	16.8	23.5	47.5	167.6	10,087	44,212	93,095	23.3	14.5	102,511	4	3.9	3.4
Cass	192	1,527	5,484	9.4	42.6	21.6	52.0	12,207	28,004	50,162	49.8	2.7	51,884	15.1	23.5	22.6
Chippewa	42	1,297	2,542	5.3	45.2	17.8	24.9	12,416	29,354	57,601	44.7	3.0	60,039	10.5	14.0	13.8
Chisago	61	1,133	13,219	9.2	39.4	21.2	80.3	10,740	32,105	76,747	28.9	3.5	82,118	6.1	6.9	5.5
Clay	134	1,900	18,833	20.9	31.1	33.2	96.4	9,821	28,122	61,409	44.1	3.3	60,213	12	12.8	12.7
Clearwater	182	1,055	2,068	9.2	51.2	15.3	15.9	10,766	24,515	45,638	53.8	2.2	48,115	14.8	18.4	16.6
Cook	96	2,214	799	7.9	25.6	40.4	7.8	13,108	31,831	51,903	48.1	1.9	51,146	8.8	15.3	14.7
Cottonwood	87	687	2,499	12.4	45.3	20.4	23.1	11,925	27,206	50,524	49.5	2.4	48,976	11.3	15.8	15.2
Crow Wing	208	2,480	13,389	10.0	37.0	24.6	104.3	10,900	30,013	53,121	47.2	3.4	54,065	9.8	12.7	11.2
Dakota	163	1,952	106,346	15.3	26.4	41.1	840.0	11,311	38,863	79,995	28.7	8.5	81,004	5.8	6.5	6.3
Dodge	44	756	5,438	10.5	39.0	24.6	38.6	9,440	31,417	71,078	32.1	3.3	70,431	5.8	6.5	5.9
Douglas	110	1,455	7,890	11.1	34.7	25.2	55.6	10,517	33,336	58,667	42.2	4.0	62,809	7.3	8.8	8.3
Faribault	57	896	2,777	9.4	48.6	17.3	21.9	11,386	29,116	50,847	49.1	3.3	45,963	12.1	18.0	16.5

1. Data for serious crimes have not been adjusted for underreporting; this may affect comparability between geographic areas and over time.   2. Per 100,000 population estimated by the FBI.   3. All persons 3 years old and over enrolled in nursery school through college.   4. Persons 25 years old and over.   5. Elementary and secondary education expenditures.   6. Based on population estimated by the American Community Survey, 2013–2017.

Table B. States and Counties — Personal Income and Earnings

STATE County	Personal income, 2017										Earnings, 2017		
			Per capita[1]			Supplements to wages and salaries, employer contributions (mil dol)						Contributions for government social insurance (mil dol)	
	Total (mil dol)	Percent change 2016-2017	Dollars	Rank	Wages and salaries (mil dol)	Pension and insurance	Government social insurance	Proprietors' income (mil dol)	Dividends, interest, and rent (mil dol)	Personal transfer receipts (mil dol)	Total (mil dol)	From employee and self-employed	From employer
	62	63	64	65	66	67	68	69	70	71	72	73	74

STATE County	62	63	64	65	66	67	68	69	70	71	72	73	74
MICHIGAN— Cont'd													
Keweenaw	93	1.6	43,993	1,024	13	3	1	4	26	29	21	2	1
Lake	358	2.7	29,790	2,942	63	15	5	14	74	160	97	11	5
Lapeer	3,612	3.4	40,960	1,410	898	181	69	185	479	810	1,334	98	69
Leelanau	1,319	0.7	60,914	145	258	55	21	113	468	231	446	33	21
Lenawee	3,757	3.3	38,094	1,867	1,212	240	92	137	562	933	1,681	122	92
Livingston	10,582	4.6	55,799	254	2,866	490	217	569	1,591	1,399	4,142	273	217
Luce	190	2.2	29,812	2,940	70	20	5	9	38	72	104	8	5
Mackinac	454	2.7	42,367	1,221	156	32	14	24	119	137	226	17	14
Macomb	39,081	3.9	44,850	919	19,296	2,980	1,446	2,484	5,521	7,671	26,206	1,669	1,446
Manistee	890	2.0	36,416	2,132	302	73	23	40	188	314	438	33	23
Marquette	2,533	1.5	38,096	1,866	1,175	244	90	103	461	679	1,612	106	90
Mason	1,118	2.6	38,460	1,806	435	90	34	60	218	340	619	44	34
Mecosta	1,383	2.5	31,868	2,770	582	142	44	36	238	399	803	55	44
Menominee	926	2.2	40,163	1,528	272	66	21	46	184	242	405	30	21
Midland	4,581	16.6	54,922	282	2,668	377	157	339	863	756	3,541	222	157
Missaukee	493	4.4	32,878	2,634	132	26	11	45	82	147	214	16	11
Monroe	6,789	4.0	45,363	859	2,097	381	153	376	913	1,371	3,007	207	153
Montcalm	2,098	3.3	33,018	2,613	690	148	53	102	283	581	992	71	53
Montmorency	331	2.9	35,747	2,239	76	17	6	14	77	143	114	12	6
Muskegon	6,453	3.0	37,149	2,007	2,814	526	214	332	943	1,781	3,885	261	214
Newaygo	1,765	3.9	36,589	2,105	520	107	40	97	271	480	763	57	40
Oakland	86,271	4.1	68,971	77	48,538	6,217	3,525	9,070	16,969	10,334	67,350	4,038	3,525
Oceana	955	2.4	36,109	2,186	272	58	22	47	172	280	399	30	22
Ogemaw	690	3.7	32,885	2,631	218	41	17	31	124	280	307	26	17
Ontonagon	220	1.5	37,473	1,952	42	12	3	9	45	93	66	7	3
Osceola	793	1.9	34,096	2,475	324	59	25	44	116	244	452	33	25
Oscoda	260	1.3	31,412	2,817	54	13	4	21	51	113	92	9	4
Otsego	940	2.4	38,327	1,819	430	76	33	56	172	246	596	41	33
Ottawa	13,252	4.2	46,275	768	6,162	1,111	458	933	2,526	1,900	8,664	525	458
Presque Isle	473	3.2	36,945	2,048	123	28	10	12	98	169	173	16	10
Roscommon	841	2.4	35,187	2,315	193	46	15	35	185	378	289	29	15
Saginaw	7,311	3.6	38,090	1,872	3,939	713	299	348	1,098	2,187	5,299	351	299
St. Clair	6,693	3.1	42,002	1,265	2,138	418	165	289	1,006	1,585	3,010	213	165
St. Joseph	2,194	2.3	36,005	2,201	945	185	72	79	338	565	1,281	87	72
Sanilac	1,456	1.0	35,272	2,303	437	91	35	67	266	469	630	48	35
Schoolcraft	303	3.7	37,696	1,923	114	29	8	8	58	110	160	12	8
Shiawassee	2,557	1.8	37,355	1,976	689	147	52	113	352	688	1,001	76	52
Tuscola	1,882	0.1	35,676	2,249	477	106	37	88	297	602	708	58	37
Van Buren	2,935	1.1	38,953	1,729	998	207	75	166	450	752	1,446	97	75
Washtenaw	20,715	4.5	56,348	239	11,788	2,497	835	1,293	4,493	2,497	16,414	934	835
Wayne	73,133	2.7	41,704	1,300	46,289	6,962	3,364	4,190	11,578	19,688	60,806	3,798	3,364
Wexford	1,152	3.2	34,633	2,399	564	120	44	58	184	350	785	53	44
MINNESOTA	303,141	4.0	54,442	X	165,543	25,072	12,112	21,511	58,508	47,380	224,237	13,516	12,112
Aitkin	598	4.6	37,793	1,913	151	32	12	27	135	204	222	18	12
Anoka	17,107	4.3	48,687	569	6,770	1,056	518	878	2,278	2,598	9,222	577	518
Becker	1,533	3.5	44,959	904	585	107	46	129	291	375	867	57	46
Beltrami	1,827	3.3	39,275	1,677	839	165	65	92	336	503	1,161	73	65
Benton	1,682	3.5	42,119	1,252	754	127	60	96	245	328	1,037	65	60
Big Stone	243	-5	48,320	600	73	15	6	4	63	69	98	8	6
Blue Earth	2,907	4.6	43,407	1,089	1,819	312	140	238	566	511	2,508	147	140
Brown	1,261	3.5	50,038	462	578	114	46	86	289	266	824	51	46
Carlton	1,446	3.1	40,723	1,440	620	121	49	45	214	366	834	55	49
Carver	6,911	5.1	67,680	81	2,259	371	166	553	1,098	541	3,349	195	166
Cass	1,320	4.6	44,951	905	353	76	29	85	329	413	542	42	29
Chippewa	536	-0.5	44,726	937	238	48	19	14	122	128	319	21	19
Chisago	2,567	4.8	46,421	761	713	120	57	136	349	431	1,025	68	57
Clay	2,607	2.1	41,018	1,405	862	158	72	160	394	521	1,251	81	72
Clearwater	360	2.7	40,527	1,468	120	24	10	28	62	98	182	12	10
Cook	275	2.9	50,943	416	95	20	8	36	76	59	159	11	8
Cottonwood	488	2.6	43,161	1,122	186	39	16	46	108	132	287	19	16
Crow Wing	2,755	3.6	42,770	1,177	1,249	215	100	212	532	722	1,776	120	100
Dakota	24,309	4.5	57,638	208	10,814	1,680	804	1,480	3,911	2,984	14,778	890	804
Dodge	886	3.5	42,682	1,188	283	52	22	37	137	142	395	26	22
Douglas	1,898	-1.8	50,521	430	820	151	63	201	385	410	1,234	80	63
Faribault	515	1.4	37,398	1,971	173	36	14	-12	133	160	211	19	14

1. Based on the resident population estimated as of July 1 of the year shown.

Table B. States and Counties — Earnings, Social Security, and Housing

STATE County	Earnings, 2017 (cont.)									Social Security beneficiaries, December 2017		Supplemental Security Income recipients, 2017	Housing units, 2018	
	Percent by selected industries													
	Farm	Mining, quarrying, and extractions	Construction	Manu-facturing	Information; professional, scientific, technical services	Retail trade	Finance, insurance, real estate, and leasing	Health care and social assistance	Govern-ment	Number	Rate[1]		Total	Percent change, 2010-2018
	75	76	77	78	79	80	81	82	83	84	85	86	87	88
MICHIGAN— Cont'd														
Keweenaw	0	D	7.3	D	D	4.6	D	0.6	31.8	830	394	30	2,500	1.3
Lake	-0.7	0	7	3.2	D	D	4.8	22.5	32.6	4,310	359	645	15,390	2.8
Lapeer	0	0.6	9.6	23.4	3.2	8.7	4.9	6.9	20.8	21,290	241	1,294	36,802	1.3
Leelanau	2.2	D	13.9	4.6	D	5	6.9	9.4	23.9	7,060	326	114	15,758	5.5
Lenawee	0	0	5.9	28.3	3.3	7.1	6.1	9.9	18.8	24,690	250	2,018	43,874	1
Livingston	0.1	0.1	10.7	19.3	9.6	8.3	6.9	9.6	11.1	39,010	206	1,215	76,997	5.8
Luce	0.9	0	3.8	5.6	D	7.9	D	D	50.9	1,805	284	223	4,381	0.9
Mackinac	0.6	D	6.8	2.1	D	9.3	4.1	D	24.6	3,770	352	198	11,290	2.5
Macomb	0	0	7.4	23.1	14.9	6.6	4.4	9.9	12.8	184,095	211	22,218	367,901	3.2
Manistee	0.1	D	6.1	17.2	2.9	8.1	2.8	D	39.5	7,905	324	655	15,877	1.1
Marquette	-0.1	8.6	5.8	4.3	6.4	6.7	5.3	20.7	22.8	16,470	248	1,095	34,941	1.8
Mason	1	D	7.3	20.9	D	8.2	4.2	11.3	19.2	8,670	298	749	17,647	2.1
Mecosta	-1.1	0.1	7	16	D	10.4	3.7	8.4	37.5	10,240	236	1,084	21,623	2.3
Menominee	1.8	0.1	4.2	32.7	D	4.5	3.4	D	26.1	6,905	300	469	14,352	0.9
Midland	-0.3	D	5.2	25	3.4	3.6	3.1	10.3	6.3	19,405	233	1,555	37,114	3.2
Missaukee	7.8	D	11.7	17	3.3	8.3	4.9	D	15.9	4,055	270	323	9,258	1.5
Monroe	0.1	D	7.5	18.8	8.5	6.3	3.2	8.5	12.5	35,240	235	2,523	64,785	2.9
Montcalm	2	D	7.3	21.7	2.9	8.4	3.6	D	21.3	15,650	246	1,805	28,681	1.6
Montmorency	0	D	10.1	13.6	2.1	5.5	24	5.4	19	4,190	453	355	9,596	0
Muskegon	0.5	0.1	6.6	26.2	4.6	9.8	3.9	17.2	13.9	42,360	244	6,212	74,305	1
Newaygo	1.1	D	8.3	21.9	5.4	9.8	9	8.2	18.9	12,995	269	1,349	25,567	2
Oakland	0	0	4.8	11.1	22.6	5.7	13	10.9	5.9	242,210	194	21,512	542,802	2.9
Oceana	4.4	0.6	7.5	25.2	1.7	5.3	3.7	3	23.5	7,230	273	784	16,159	1.4
Ogemaw	2	0.4	12.5	4.4	3	15	3.7	D	15.6	7,560	360	791	16,216	1.1
Ontonagon	-0.9	0	6.5	D	D	14	4.5	13.8	33.2	2,605	443	152	5,702	0.5
Osceola	0.4	1.3	19.5	25.6	D	3.8	2.3	9.9	14.1	6,815	293	860	13,815	1.4
Oscoda	0.3	0	11.5	22.8	3.2	8.8	3.5	2.4	22.5	3,120	376	286	9,207	1
Otsego	0	3.5	7.7	11.5	3.3	14.8	4.8	D	16	6,935	283	566	14,905	1.2
Ottawa	1	0	7.7	36.7	5.4	5.2	5.1	5.5	13.4	51,995	182	2,636	110,845	8.1
Presque Isle	-1.2	D	5.5	4.4	2.7	7.5	4.5	D	21.7	5,200	407	370	10,472	0.4
Roscommon	-0.2	D	8.7	9.2	D	16.4	4.9	D	29.6	10,455	438	959	24,574	0.5
Saginaw	-0.6	0.1	4.5	19.8	5.8	7.4	6.2	19.4	14.3	49,570	258	8,422	87,817	1.1
St. Clair	-0.4	D	7.6	20.4	4.4	7.8	3.8	15.4	17.6	40,010	251	3,603	72,374	0.8
St. Joseph	-1.3	0	5.4	43.5	2.5	6.9	2.3	8.7	14.7	14,285	234	1,282	28,015	0.9
Sanilac	0.6	0.8	7.4	24.4	2.7	8.1	5.4	D	19.2	11,450	277	972	23,090	1.6
Schoolcraft	-0.2	9.6	5.7	8.3	D	7.6	6.5	4.8	39.4	2,685	334	263	6,387	1.2
Shiawassee	-1.3	0.1	8.1	13.4	5.7	9.2	4.4	13.5	20.4	17,410	254	1,668	30,271	-0.2
Tuscola	-2	D	7.2	16.4	D	6.8	4.4	D	26.8	14,995	284	1,396	24,512	0.2
Van Buren	3.1	D	8.8	11.4	9.5	5.8	3	D	23	18,410	244	2,189	37,381	1.6
Washtenaw	0	0	2.8	7.5	17.8	4	4.7	11	34.9	58,325	159	5,575	151,550	2.7
Wayne	0	0.1	4	14.2	13.4	4.3	5.9	13.5	12.2	357,250	204	84,810	815,803	-0.7
Wexford	-0.4	0.2	3.9	25.7	D	7.6	4.4	13.2	18.4	9,050	272	1,155	16,980	1.5
MINNESOTA	0.2	0.3	6.1	12.2	11.4	5.3	10	13.3	13	1,012,620	182	93,892	2,456,064	4.6
Aitkin	-0.5	2.5	8.9	10.4	1.6	8.4	4.8	D	22.9	4,790	303	294	16,931	5.7
Anoka	0.2	0	10.1	23.8	5	6.4	4.8	11.8	12.5	57,175	163	4,358	133,192	5.1
Becker	0.9	D	10.2	14.6	D	7.6	6.6	14.9	22.9	8,840	259	665	19,884	5.9
Beltrami	-0.2	D	9.2	4.6	4.6	8.2	3.7	21.1	31.1	9,325	200	1,249	21,886	6.6
Benton	0.8	0	17	23.1	D	6.2	3.9	8.4	10.7	7,180	180	393	17,265	7
Big Stone	-13	D	20	0.9	D	4.6	6.3	D	34.8	1,510	300	96	3,166	1.6
Blue Earth	2	D	6.9	12.1	8	7.6	5.6	21.5	15.2	11,205	167	1,016	28,825	10
Brown	1.5	0	8.4	25.3	6.6	6.3	4.6	14.3	12.9	6,320	251	269	11,799	2.7
Carlton	-0.5	D	10.9	14.7	3	5.1	5.1	10.8	36.2	7,980	225	567	16,091	2.8
Carver	0.8	0.1	8.3	25.3	6.7	4.1	6	10.8	10.4	13,255	130	539	38,848	12.5
Cass	-0.7	0	10.2	6.5	D	7.7	4.5	D	37.4	9,835	335	680	26,101	4.8
Chippewa	-3	D	8.1	23.3	D	6.4	7.4	D	23.7	2,705	226	147	5,713	-0.1
Chisago	0.2	D	11.7	14.4	9.4	7.7	2.9	21.1	15.7	10,435	189	566	22,174	4.7
Clay	-0.4	D	7.2	7	5	7.3	5.4	10.8	23.2	10,095	159	1,146	26,804	11.9
Clearwater	3.2	0	17.3	20.1	D	3.9	D	D	16.4	2,215	249	205	4,781	0.2
Cook	0	0	10.6	D	2.7	7.8	3.6	4	32.8	1,685	312	41	6,174	5.7
Cottonwood	4.4	D	7.6	22.2	D	6	5	D	17.5	3,080	273	212	5,431	0.4
Crow Wing	-0.1	D	11.5	8.5	6.4	9.7	7.9	20.1	14.4	17,995	279	1,158	42,179	5
Dakota	0	0.1	7.3	12.7	11.2	7.4	12.8	8.3	12	66,670	158	4,489	168,117	5.3
Dodge	-3.9	D	13.8	28.5	3.4	3.6	4.3	D	18	3,530	170	169	8,339	4.9
Douglas	-0.7	D	10.2	19.4	4.5	8.2	5.9	9.3	18.8	10,530	280	478	21,385	7.4
Faribault	-21.1	0	7.4	27.7	5.7	8	10.1	14.9	21.7	3,770	274	240	7,051	-0.6

1. Per 1,000 resident population estimated as of July 1 of the year shown.

Table B. States and Counties — Housing, Labor Force, and Employment

STATE County	Housing units, 2013-2017							Sub-standard units⁴ (percent)	Civilian labor force, 2018		Unemployment		Civilian employment⁶, 2013-2017		
	Occupied units									Percent change, 2017-2018			Percent		
	Owner-occupied			Median owner cost as a percent of income		Renter-occupied								Management, business, science, and arts	Construction, production, and maintenance occupations
	Total	Percent	Median value¹	With a mortgage	Without a mortgage²	Median rent³	Median rent as a percent of income²		Total		Total	Rate⁵	Total		
	89	90	91	92	93	94	95	96	97	98	99	100	101	102	103
MICHIGAN— Cont'd															
Keweenaw	1,013	86.1	95,800	20.8	13.8	519	25.3	3.8	882	-2.8	61	6.9	856	33.6	18.1
Lake	4,555	84.4	80,800	25.9	14.1	571	37.9	2.3	3,666	-2	252	6.9	3,514	23.0	31.4
Lapeer	33,152	82.5	151,400	21.9	11.4	805	31	2.1	41,369	0.6	2,137	5.2	38,577	29.5	32.3
Leelanau	9,022	86.9	248,900	23.5	11.3	899	26.2	1.3	10,533	-0.4	445	4.2	9,734	35.9	21.9
Lenawee	38,115	77.7	124,900	21.6	12.9	756	28.8	1.3	46,956	-0.6	1,918	4.1	44,355	28.4	29.6
Livingston	70,831	85.4	218,700	19.7	10.8	966	29.1	1.2	102,785	1	3,383	3.3	94,735	40.0	20.5
Luce	2,253	77.3	83,200	19.5	12.2	632	26.3	1.8	2,417		150	6.2	2,064	29.5	21.3
Mackinac	5,132	74.0	125,100	23.1	13.0	570	24.5	2.6	5,129	-1.5	495	9.7	4,552	24.6	25.8
Macomb	341,532	72.9	146,700	19.9	12.8	916	30.1	1.9	445,483	0.7	18,038	4	414,453	34.4	23.5
Manistee	9,810	82.3	116,200	22.1	12.2	691	31.9	1.2	10,454	0.2	600	5.7	9,372	29.4	23.5
Marquette	26,199	70.0	142,900	19.2	11.2	669	30.9	1.7	32,422	-1.2	1,583	4.9	29,746	32.5	21.2
Mason	12,186	77.1	126,600	23.4	12.6	689	29	1.3	13,835	-1.7	676	4.9	12,418	30.1	26.0
Mecosta	15,641	74.0	114,700	21.6	11.8	647	32.3	2.6	18,562	-1.5	920	5	18,219	28.1	28.2
Menominee	10,593	78.9	95,900	19.8	11.8	550	28	1.5	11,019	-0.2	446	4	10,638	24.8	35.2
Midland	33,986	75.9	133,000	19.1	11.2	744	29.6	1.6	40,611	0.5	1,618	4	37,913	39.9	21.4
Missaukee	5,941	82.0	107,100	22.7	12.6	730	28.8	3.6	7,067	-0.4	355	5	6,209	24.7	38.4
Monroe	58,652	80.2	149,500	19.6	11.7	790	29.4	1.7	75,765	-0.1	3,169	4.2	69,205	30.3	31.1
Montcalm	23,556	77.9	101,000	21.1	13.2	700	29.8	2.2	28,474	0.8	1,204	4.2	25,787	24.5	36.1
Montmorency	4,074	88.3	93,800	24.2	12.1	607	31	1.5	3,037	-0.9	262	8.6	2,971	23.9	31.0
Muskegon	65,216	74.3	105,300	19.6	11.9	717	32.7	2.1	78,196	0.6	3,557	4.5	73,192	28.0	30.7
Newaygo	18,772	82.6	104,500	21.4	13.0	670	30.6	2.8	23,333	-0.5	1,012	4.3	19,256	25.8	36.1
Oakland	499,617	70.6	209,800	19.5	12.0	1,003	27.2	1.3	670,739	0.9	22,462	3.3	629,551	48.9	14.3
Oceana	10,176	80.6	106,300	21.9	12.2	674	27.2	5.1	12,456	-0.8	760	6.1	10,693	26.1	38.9
Ogemaw	9,325	82.5	89,600	23.2	13.3	664	32.9	2.8	8,137	-1.3	570	7	7,739	26.1	28.8
Ontonagon	2,945	88.2	69,500	23.7	13.4	447	28.7	1.7	2,110	-3.2	165	7.8	2,021	26.3	28.6
Osceola	9,010	81.2	91,400	21.8	12.9	587	30	2.7	10,884	1.8	483	4.4	8,960	23.7	39.3
Oscoda	3,728	85.0	83,400	23.4	13.2	648	30.2	3.9	2,976	1.1	191	6.4	2,815	21.5	36.9
Otsego	9,880	79.6	124,100	20.2	11.9	756	29.4	2.5	11,584	-0.5	606	5.2	10,894	29.4	25.1
Ottawa	99,721	77.4	168,000	18.9	10.8	854	28.5	2.3	160,101	1.1	4,508	2.8	143,295	34.3	27.9
Presque Isle	5,929	87.3	97,800	20.1	12.2	564	28.5	1.5	5,114	-2.3	407	8	4,530	27.5	32.2
Roscommon	11,131	81.5	94,000	24.6	11.9	644	35.1	1.3	7,814	0	608	7.8	7,657	25.1	27.0
Saginaw	78,482	71.7	94,900	19.9	12.4	731	31.7	1.7	86,849	-0.9	4,152	4.8	82,297	30.5	23.5
St. Clair	64,387	76.1	135,000	20.6	12.3	781	30.5	1.4	75,778	0.7	3,595	4.7	72,419	27.8	31.5
St. Joseph	23,831	74.0	111,200	20.5	11.1	695	27.9	3.1	28,268	-2.1	1,055	3.7	27,605	24.4	41.9
Sanilac	17,121	79.9	101,300	20.5	12.3	643	29.1	1.9	19,579	-0.5	1,004	5.1	17,631	27.0	36.1
Schoolcraft	3,282	79.0	105,000	21.2	13.6	617	36.6	1.6	3,387	0.5	242	7.1	2,724	25.5	28.3
Shiawassee	27,623	75.7	111,000	20.3	11.6	705	28.5	1.5	33,151	-0.8	1,432	4.3	30,786	28.0	32.6
Tuscola	21,624	82.0	98,800	21.2	12.8	670	30	1.7	23,860	-0.8	1,304	5.5	22,987	26.1	32.7
Van Buren	29,151	77.2	123,100	21.0	12.5	673	28.8	3	35,681	-0.2	1,726	4.8	33,499	28.9	30.9
Washtenaw	138,947	60.2	231,500	19.9	11.6	1,025	30.5	1.7	194,621	0.6	5,928	3	183,919	52.6	13.3
Wayne	673,143	62.2	92,400	20.8	14.0	826	33.8	2.8	794,466	0.4	41,540	5.2	722,115	31.9	24.3
Wexford	13,105	76.4	96,500	22.0	12.7	723	29.1	2.4	14,766	-0.1	688	4.7	13,834	27.3	34.2
MINNESOTA	2,153,202	71.6	199,700	20.4	10.8	906	28.8	2.5	3,070,224	0.4	89,339	2.9	2,904,103	40.1	20.8
Aitkin	7,709	82.6	169,300	26.2	12.4	638	30.7	3.2	7,162	-0.2	402	5.6	6,274	30.7	26.2
Anoka	126,072	80.1	205,000	20.4	10.0	1,034	29.3	2.1	196,586	0.7	5,432	2.8	187,986	36.6	23.2
Becker	13,489	78.1	182,100	21.9	11.4	700	26.4	2.3	18,591	0.2	661	3.6	16,143	32.8	30.7
Beltrami	17,076	68.2	153,100	21.2	11.7	689	31.2	2.7	24,088	1.8	988	4.1	20,931	33.7	20.9
Benton	16,005	68.7	162,600	22.5	11.4	687	31	2.8	21,666	-0.3	757	3.5	20,468	31.1	28.8
Big Stone	2,264	77.2	97,000	18.6	11.2	498	24.8	1.3	2,517	-2.1	96	3.8	2,388	31.7	31.8
Blue Earth	25,558	62.0	170,800	20.1	10.4	815	30.7	1.4	40,277	0.6	1,011	2.5	37,072	33.7	22.7
Brown	10,668	77.8	135,300	18.9	10.5	592	25.8	1.5	14,535	1.1	488	3.4	13,588	30.1	31.4
Carlton	13,413	79.7	162,800	21.1	12.0	710	26.8	2.6	17,655	-0.2	729	4.1	16,758	31.3	25.8
Carver	35,342	81.2	287,200	19.9	10.4	1,003	26.4	1.5	57,859	0.8	1,422	2.5	55,757	46.5	15.0
Cass	12,965	80.7	178,700	22.7	11.3	692	26.4	3.3	14,333	-0.1	731	5.1	12,264	29.2	26.4
Chippewa	5,019	70.3	104,500	18.9	10.0	594	23.6	1.2	6,887	-0.5	220	3.2	6,270	32.1	29.3
Chisago	19,871	85.4	206,400	21.8	11.9	844	28.6	1.2	29,662	0.6	997	3.4	28,244	34.0	25.9
Clay	23,453	68.7	173,100	19.9	10.9	771	32.9	1.9	35,791	0.4	1,025	2.9	33,502	36.1	21.0
Clearwater	3,428	79.6	122,800	21.7	12.5	612	29.4	4.2	4,475	-2.7	364	8.1	3,667	27.4	36.8
Cook	2,700	75.0	241,400	25.6	10.7	690	21.5	7	3,029	-2.5	105	3.5	2,636	39.4	18.6
Cottonwood	4,837	77.4	89,400	18.3	10.4	616	25.6	2.9	5,826	1.9	207	3.6	5,365	28.9	36.7
Crow Wing	26,314	75.7	188,100	21.9	11.5	781	29.5	1.2	32,232	0.1	1,264	3.9	30,124	32.9	22.8
Dakota	158,777	74.4	238,000	19.8	10.0	1,063	28.1	1.6	239,835	0.7	6,091	2.5	231,109	42.4	17.6
Dodge	7,690	82.5	167,900	20.6	10.8	639	22.8	1.7	11,834	1.1	352	3	11,109	34.6	28.6
Douglas	16,175	75.1	197,200	21.5	11.8	737	29.7	0.9	20,604	0.4	581	2.8	19,119	35.4	26.0
Faribault	6,245	75.9	86,500	18.4	10.4	585	23.6	1	7,006	-1.9	243	3.5	7,091	32.7	32.1

1. Specified owner-occupied units.   2. A value of 10.0 represents 10 percent or less; a value of 50.0 represents 50 percent or more.   3. Specified renter-occupied units.   4. Overcrowded or lacking complete plumbing facilities.   5. Percent of civilian labor force.   6. Civilian employed persons 16 years old and over.

Table B. States and Counties — Nonfarm Employment and Agriculture

	Private nonfarm establishments, employment and payroll, 2016									Agriculture, 2017			
		Employment						Annual payroll		Farms			Farm producers whose primary occupation is farming (percent)
							Professional, scientific, and technical services				Percent with:		
STATE County	Number of establishments	Total	Health care and social assistance	Manufacturing	Retail trade	Finance and insurance		Total (mil dol)	Average per employee (dollars)	Number	Fewer than 50 acres	1000 acres or more	
	104	105	106	107	108	109	110	111	112	113	114	115	116

MICHIGAN— Cont'd

Keweenaw	60	204	NA	D	16	D	D	6	29,093	9	100.0	NA	NA
Lake	160	1,115	249	91	257	63	D	32	28,576	168	37.5	1.2	32.5
Lapeer	1,639	18,318	2,788	5,282	3,300	428	546	642	35,059	1,013	52.0	3.4	46.5
Leelanau	751	4,572	629	393	669	210	217	188	41,113	470	50.6	0.9	46.9
Lenawee	1,805	23,382	2,997	5,219	3,825	824	454	854	36,507	1,361	42.7	7.6	41.9
Livingston	4,319	51,969	5,915	9,509	9,311	3,525	2,725	2,029	39,035	724	61.7	2.6	41.9
Luce	171	1,526	383	253	284	57	19	54	35,193	71	56.3	1.4	35.5
Mackinac	440	2,112	385	106	350	88	38	113	53,545	101	37.6	7.9	32.0
Macomb	18,905	298,365	40,754	69,651	42,581	6,029	29,648	14,497	48,589	404	55.7	4.7	53.3
Manistee	563	5,891	1,015	871	1,255	167	104	218	37,088	274	37.6	1.1	41.2
Marquette	1,625	21,405	5,712	928	3,800	979	635	818	38,218	179	49.7	3.4	41.6
Mason	732	9,263	1,326	2,233	1,510	222	165	343	37,056	472	41.5	2.8	38.7
Mecosta	716	9,471	1,446	2,359	2,041	209	274	325	34,273	694	31.7	2.2	45.6
Menominee	459	5,125	230	1,709	676	143	137	181	35,322	353	29.7	3.4	42.9
Midland	2,081	35,682	6,644	6,859	4,066	1,125	978	2,271	63,646	530	51.3	4.2	39.2
Missaukee	297	2,383	405	399	406	55	36	75	31,648	406	35.7	6.9	46.1
Monroe	2,285	37,503	4,751	7,359	4,933	810	1,285	1,623	43,270	1,085	57.7	4.1	40.5
Montcalm	995	12,232	3,044	2,382	2,467	355	235	425	34,746	962	45.2	4.6	40.1
Montmorency	203	1,647	247	438	229	73	19	57	34,508	178	34.8	1.7	38.1
Muskegon	3,114	52,661	10,271	13,060	7,940	1,075	1,474	2,129	40,422	476	61.1	2.3	44.0
Newaygo	803	9,374	1,664	1,525	1,615	583	348	337	35,961	850	46.2	3.4	42.8
Oakland	38,944	692,833	107,764	52,089	76,020	37,676	100,586	41,487	59,880	514	68.9	0.6	38.1
Oceana	492	4,878	705	1,522	644	126	93	161	32,914	545	36.7	5.0	47.3
Ogemaw	547	5,268	1,086	300	1,434	129	111	169	32,166	294	34.4	4.8	50.6
Ontonagon	161	894	208	D	225	58	10	25	27,885	114	11.4	1.8	33.7
Osceola	425	6,073	1,010	2,170	591	119	94	245	40,378	625	37.4	2.2	36.9
Oscoda	176	1,459	136	328	230	36	20	47	31,920	144	54.9	0.7	21.6
Otsego	754	8,863	1,794	1,054	2,128	176	167	308	34,739	193	43.5	2.6	36.9
Ottawa	6,013	109,415	10,969	37,004	10,396	2,557	4,027	4,586	41,916	1,130	56.8	3.0	50.4
Presque Isle	321	2,300	326	222	374	102	40	79	34,183	322	25.5	3.4	40.6
Roscommon	539	4,716	561	591	1,335	158	57	130	27,607	48	43.8	2.1	32.5
Saginaw	4,261	78,672	17,499	11,722	12,759	2,770	2,470	3,159	40,154	1,250	44.2	5.8	42.1
St. Clair	3,096	42,187	7,816	8,957	7,219	1,281	1,012	1,608	38,123	1,077	52.6	3.0	42.8
St. Joseph	1,161	19,614	1,678	9,511	2,525	371	474	761	38,813	896	45.5	8.3	39.7
Sanilac	816	8,346	1,290	2,791	1,582	362	185	286	34,294	1,315	33.7	8.1	58.9
Schoolcraft	236	1,877	447	69	358	188	35	69	36,643	62	37.1	6.5	24.5
Shiawassee	1,126	13,299	2,533	2,202	2,525	332	270	458	34,447	972	51.1	4.9	41.5
Tuscola	824	8,628	2,401	1,271	1,614	293	199	305	35,372	1,241	42.4	6.5	50.3
Van Buren	1,303	16,763	2,651	2,954	2,861	327	1,914	672	40,079	953	52.2	2.3	42.4
Washtenaw	8,119	150,135	37,479	15,005	17,704	3,911	15,217	8,233	54,838	1,245	59.7	2.7	39.8
Wayne	32,224	637,407	107,608	84,269	69,675	34,809	41,534	34,371	53,924	248	79.8	NA	47.5
Wexford	840	12,142	1,795	3,120	2,036	316	245	435	35,813	304	43.1	1.6	45.3
MINNESOTA	150,115	2,661,627	460,279	305,782	307,266	163,505	183,069	137,136	51,523	68,822	28.8	9.3	45.5
Aitkin	400	3,180	832	397	610	95	34	103	32,529	462	19.3	2.4	34.9
Anoka	7,750	114,048	17,467	20,998	16,803	2,257	3,987	5,292	46,400	360	60.0	1.7	37.4
Becker	932	10,740	2,441	2,285	1,984	267	178	383	35,689	943	20.5	7.7	39.9
Beltrami	1,170	14,490	3,793	950	3,090	406	417	501	34,565	583	25.6	4.3	32.8
Benton	900	15,199	2,473	3,260	2,098	202	225	610	40,107	816	32.2	4.0	41.3
Big Stone	190	1,646	762	14	196	89	32	60	36,615	438	17.8	19.4	47.9
Blue Earth	1,956	36,969	8,851	4,233	6,371	974	1,096	1,346	36,410	983	30.9	10.9	49.2
Brown	772	13,095	2,370	3,015	1,717	439	447	502	38,330	1,040	25.1	5.9	44.8
Carlton	710	8,015	2,033	1,283	1,397	429	168	318	39,719	529	25.7	0.9	35.4
Carver	2,517	39,358	5,610	10,723	3,734	753	2,053	1,968	50,009	689	38.3	5.2	45.0
Cass	820	7,007	1,254	305	1,016	190	557	212	30,212	432	20.8	4.4	45.8
Chippewa	387	5,030	1,188	1,025	653	194	80	174	34,673	623	26.6	15.4	52.3
Chisago	1,246	13,579	3,976	2,149	1,899	271	872	573	42,216	821	52.1	1.7	34.8
Clay	1,317	17,915	4,377	800	2,901	422	543	604	33,737	694	20.2	23.9	55.2
Clearwater	211	2,478	592	D	234	70	60	127	51,204	414	23.9	8.7	36.6
Cook	278	2,022	221	58	306	42	29	67	32,917	32	78.1	NA	20.4
Cottonwood	346	3,921	742	1,278	501	95	73	124	31,603	744	22.4	17.7	55.9
Crow Wing	2,178	26,295	6,154	2,353	4,694	1,307	983	980	37,251	494	29.8	2.6	34.0
Dakota	10,530	177,935	24,923	17,404	24,775	12,181	9,356	8,817	49,552	820	48.5	6.1	49.1
Dodge	414	4,759	355	1,682	453	106	94	207	43,400	611	40.9	13.3	47.9
Douglas	1,348	18,089	3,863	3,899	3,146	404	423	730	40,332	960	27.8	5.7	36.6
Faribault	415	4,094	739	1,226	608	235	78	150	36,659	822	28.6	14.4	55.0

Table B. States and Counties — **Agriculture**

STATE County	Land in farms — Acreage (1,000)	Land in farms — Percent change, 2012-2017	Acres — Average size of farm	Acres — Total irrigated (1,000)	Acres — Total cropland (1,000)	Value of land and buildings (dollars) — Average per farm	Value of land and buildings (dollars) — Average per acre	Value of machinery and equiopmnet, average per farm (dollars)	Value of products sold: Total (mil dol)	Value of products sold: Average per farm (acres)	Percent from: Crops	Percent from: Livestock and poultry products	Organic farms (number)	Farms with internet access (percent)	Government payments — Total ($1,000)	Government payments — Percent of farms
	117	118	119	120	121	122	123	124	125	126	127	128	129	130	131	132
MICHIGAN— Cont'd																
Keweenaw	0	-24.5	27	NA	0.1	90,000	3,375	26,667	0.0	222	100.0	NA	NA	66.7	NA	NA
Lake	22	-16.9	129	0.1	11.8	316,975	2,462	52,897	3.2	19,321	41.7	58.3	NA	69.6	49	6.5
Lapeer	165	-5.8	163	2.4	128.7	752,544	4,607	141,624	87.0	85,838	72.9	27.1	16	76.8	1,424	18.0
Leelanau	50	-15.9	106	2.3	29.9	779,662	7,321	111,622	42.4	90,302	93.7	6.3	12	87.7	376	14.0
Lenawee	386	12.0	283	9.8	345.2	1,481,398	5,226	196,185	259.9	190,951	64.7	35.3	6	81.3	11,691	53.3
Livingston	89	3.7	123	1.1	67.2	703,733	5,701	85,997	48.5	66,965	62.5	37.5	7	84.0	1,444	13.3
Luce	10	-14.7	139	D	4.0	351,299	2,521	64,881	3.8	53,113	88.4	11.6	NA	60.6	D	11.3
Mackinac	25	11.7	248	0.0	13.2	495,340	1,997	74,432	7.1	70,683	11.5	88.5	3	76.2	173	13.9
Macomb	74	8.4	182	4.3	66.6	928,906	5,095	149,403	78.8	195,111	87.2	12.8	1	81.9	800	25.0
Manistee	41	-6.6	151	1.0	19.3	435,471	2,884	81,371	10.3	37,686	75.6	24.4	7	72.6	246	15.0
Marquette	30	-1.4	169	0.1	11.3	372,759	2,206	85,310	3.7	20,536	30.8	69.2	8	83.2	46	9.5
Mason	85	8.1	181	4.2	63.0	563,138	3,111	132,221	56.7	120,097	58.1	41.9	21	75.8	943	25.8
Mecosta	115	-6.4	166	17.6	81.5	581,429	3,505	145,703	180.1	259,458	21.5	78.5	6	64.3	909	27.2
Menominee	80	-13.4	226	0.1	47.2	479,385	2,125	113,385	37.6	106,507	11.5	88.5	2	78.5	610	26.9
Midland	88	-2.1	165	0.6	69.9	916,909	5,542	121,112	46.9	88,483	57.1	42.9	5	80.2	2,366	40.0
Missaukee	114	14.2	280	8.5	88.7	1,023,840	3,658	205,707	148.7	366,276	14.8	85.2	4	77.1	759	25.6
Monroe	210	-2.2	193	4.3	194.1	1,190,516	6,156	150,143	174.5	160,833	96.2	3.8	NA	83.5	4,555	43.7
Montcalm	230	-2.9	239	59.5	191.9	955,776	3,991	170,672	180.5	187,598	71.2	28.8	9	73.5	2,732	27.4
Montmorency	26	7.2	147	0.0	16.3	314,723	2,146	110,173	9.2	51,511	39.4	60.6	NA	71.9	177	21.9
Muskegon	63	-14.9	133	3.6	45.8	852,881	6,425	112,539	74.7	156,884	58.9	41.1	5	82.8	173	11.1
Newaygo	136	8.4	160	12.0	96.7	623,318	3,889	126,490	128.3	150,958	37.6	62.4	16	78.4	296	13.3
Oakland	29	-9.0	56	0.6	17.4	652,488	11,623	67,181	22.3	43,442	88.0	12.0	9	85.0	161	4.1
Oceana	127	-0.5	233	13.1	93.6	969,750	4,159	183,666	124.7	228,791	66.2	33.8	9	81.3	699	14.9
Ogemaw	70	2.8	238	D	47.7	666,927	2,797	177,989	49.8	169,429	25.1	74.9	NA	63.9	677	41.8
Ontonagon	27	-6.7	238	D	12.5	379,699	1,597	68,540	3.1	27,167	80.5	19.5	NA	77.2	14	15.8
Osceola	104	-6.3	166	2.0	67.4	497,961	3,003	79,214	43.5	69,650	26.8	73.2	4	63.4	1,101	18.6
Oscoda	16	-3.4	112	D	6.5	307,892	2,741	39,097	5.6	38,653	23.9	76.1	7	41.7	20	4.9
Otsego	33	3.0	172	1.1	17.5	479,329	2,780	80,181	6.2	32,311	80.9	19.1	6	80.8	64	18.7
Ottawa	172	-7.7	152	23.0	145.2	1,258,057	8,271	167,813	506.7	448,373	55.7	44.3	6	85.2	2,675	19.6
Presque Isle	64	-20.9	200	1.8	41.0	469,658	2,345	93,591	18.9	58,661	68.9	31.1	1	62.1	374	26.4
Roscommon	6	-22.5	120	0.7	2.9	293,961	2,451	76,198	0.8	16,292	38.4	61.6	1	70.8	30	16.7
Saginaw	327	5.6	262	1.7	300.5	1,518,681	5,805	162,379	170.3	136,206	87.9	12.1	12	79.4	6,853	63.1
St. Clair	182	1.2	169	1.0	160.3	888,682	5,254	132,186	80.9	75,105	88.6	11.4	11	73.4	2,041	22.1
St. Joseph	245	10.5	273	123.1	212.3	1,562,992	5,717	235,762	230.7	257,450	68.8	31.2	16	64.6	5,839	39.7
Sanilac	437	-4.5	332	1.7	401.0	1,636,584	4,930	274,204	357.7	271,993	54.3	45.7	52	72.5	7,801	49.4
Schoolcraft	15	-22.6	242	0.0	5.9	441,401	1,820	65,397	2.1	34,016	48.7	51.3	NA	85.5	98	21.0
Shiawassee	210	-5.8	217	1.5	187.1	976,860	4,511	151,599	97.5	100,284	67.4	32.6	21	80.9	3,670	45.8
Tuscola	330	1.4	266	8.7	298.5	1,386,278	5,217	226,605	231.0	186,103	69.4	30.6	79	79.7	7,168	52.8
Van Buren	152	-13.3	159	35.6	118.1	921,952	5,789	150,630	205.5	215,686	81.5	18.5	7	74.5	1,602	14.4
Washtenaw	179	5.2	144	4.0	150.4	1,124,667	7,823	112,400	91.2	73,227	76.3	23.7	29	84.3	3,438	24.6
Wayne	10	-36.3	40	0.6	7.8	467,878	11,561	70,633	23.1	93,274	96.8	3.2	2	88.3	56	4.8
Wexford	40	-0.3	132	4.3	26.2	445,486	3,368	60,875	18.1	59,701	48.0	52.0	8	67.8	164	9.5
MINNESOTA	25,517	-2.0	371	611.6	21,786.8	1,799,201	4,853	223,666	18,395.4	267,289	55.4	44.6	735	79.0	394,491	59.9
Aitkin	106	-13.8	229	3.0	54.1	482,701	2,109	72,031	12.5	26,970	56.5	43.5	1	68.2	282	16.5
Anoka	39	-12.9	108	3.0	29.4	823,272	7,590	122,561	67.8	188,222	51.9	48.1	5	85.6	239	9.2
Becker	368	-15.4	390	13.4	256.0	1,133,301	2,906	151,842	174.5	185,081	59.4	40.6	4	73.6	5,253	58.4
Beltrami	169	-6.6	289	3.5	79.8	568,690	1,966	67,182	23.8	40,823	55.8	44.2	NA	81.0	775	21.1
Benton	195	3.2	239	16.7	155.8	1,048,133	4,390	181,337	207.2	253,893	30.8	69.2	5	75.4	1,702	43.5
Big Stone	269	8.0	614	4.1	246.4	2,667,748	4,348	308,736	138.8	316,790	77.1	22.9	2	78.1	3,315	75.1
Blue Earth	383	1.7	389	4.3	355.5	2,804,263	7,202	284,239	483.5	491,860	41.9	58.1	7	82.3	12,899	76.4
Brown	356	9.1	342	4.1	330.8	2,248,890	6,574	241,577	381.5	366,838	45.8	54.2	3	80.1	6,242	82.2
Carlton	93	0.9	177	D	41.3	380,506	2,155	70,143	11.0	20,766	43.5	56.5	7	80.5	196	4.3
Carver	159	2.2	230	0.6	136.1	1,552,374	6,742	218,040	111.4	161,652	61.9	38.1	7	82.0	963	47.2
Cass	134	-15.1	309	8.4	57.9	773,837	2,503	83,876	26.5	61,259	28.3	71.7	1	75.0	325	14.1
Chippewa	341	1.8	547	4.5	320.5	3,226,230	5,894	352,983	256.7	412,037	73.3	26.7	7	76.6	7,059	84.6
Chisago	116	1.5	141	4.0	82.7	643,553	4,575	94,546	52.8	64,358	74.6	25.4	6	83.3	1,379	31.5
Clay	577	-5.6	831	2.9	538.1	3,280,220	3,948	367,559	277.8	400,218	86.5	13.5	12	84.7	5,759	73.5
Clearwater	156	-6.7	376	4.9	76.1	761,920	2,026	113,597	30.1	72,609	65.7	34.3	3	77.1	417	27.1
Cook	1	-38.7	44	0.0	0.2	258,025	5,927	19,944	0.4	11,906	95.8	4.2	2	84.4	D	3.1
Cottonwood	370	-0.6	498	2.1	345.5	3,146,803	6,321	388,964	382.2	513,669	50.8	49.2	4	86.7	5,155	85.5
Crow Wing	89	-10.8	181	4.5	41.8	485,403	2,688	93,161	19.1	38,571	48.6	51.4	6	73.5	159	21.1
Dakota	227	3.3	277	62.8	205.4	1,911,437	6,902	227,421	235.4	287,091	76.3	23.7	13	78.2	2,990	43.4
Dodge	248	10.0	406	4.9	231.9	2,797,971	6,892	283,496	238.4	390,185	58.0	42.0	6	83.6	6,605	64.6
Douglas	263	-1.6	274	3.3	205.3	1,082,155	3,946	138,654	100.3	104,526	73.9	26.1	9	75.5	3,133	66.6
Faribault	408	4.5	496	D	388.9	3,372,928	6,799	352,244	337.7	410,869	68.4	31.6	5	82.8	5,464	81.8

Table B. States and Counties — Water Use, Wholesale Trade, Retail Trade, and Real Estate

STATE County	Water use, 2015		Wholesale Trade[1], 2012				Retail Trade[2], 2012				Real estate and rental and leasing,[2] 2012			
	Public supply water withdrawn (mil gal/day)	Public supply gallons withdrawn per person per day	Number of establishments	Number of employees	Sales (mil dol)	Average payroll (mil dol)	Number of establishments	Number of employees	Sales (mil dol)	Average payroll (mil dol)	Number of establishments	Number of employees	Sales (mil dol)	Average payroll (mil dol)
	133	134	135	136	137	138	139	140	141	142	143	144	145	146
MICHIGAN— Cont'd														
Keweenaw	0.05	23.1	2	D	D	D	11	39	3.9	0.5	1	D	D	D
Lake	0.26	22.8	4	D	D	D	30	243	60.2	4.8	4	D	D	D
Lapeer	0.40	4.5	50	438	282.1	20.7	239	2,859	867.1	66.0	56	219	24.5	5.2
Leelanau	0.50	22.7	11	D	D	D	124	568	139.3	12.4	30	D	D	D
Lenawee	6.10	61.9	56	D	D	D	304	3,804	961.6	86.9	57	169	30.5	8.2
Livingston	6.92	36.9	198	2,435	3,092.5	144.1	599	8,695	2,410.2	205.7	124	544	95.4	18.5
Luce	0.50	77.9	4	D	D	D	26	256	84.2	5.9	7	36	2.4	0.6
Mackinac	1.29	118.5	8	48	65.3	1.9	93	366	121.9	10.3	12	D	D	D
Macomb	3.97	4.6	787	10,277	5,776.1	580.9	2,786	40,305	11,304.2	1,006.0	617	3,018	572.1	99.2
Manistee	1.54	63.0	13	117	225.6	6.6	107	905	231.9	19.0	18	42	5.8	0.9
Marquette	5.16	76.8	47	370	203.2	15.9	275	3,741	789.3	77.2	64	266	37.8	6.3
Mason	2.45	85.1	19	135	190.9	5.8	113	1,428	370.3	32.4	30	560	117.8	31.7
Mecosta	1.27	29.5	19	D	D	D	142	1,881	488.2	40.3	38	94	15.8	2.4
Menominee	1.07	45.4	18	297	144.1	11.9	68	584	155.5	11.9	16	D	D	D
Midland	0.14	1.7	44	297	703.7	16.7	314	4,050	1,015.7	88.4	63	257	36.8	8.4
Missaukee	0.38	25.5	16	111	69.6	4.5	39	332	120.0	8.9	4	5	0.5	0.1
Monroe	9.27	62.0	89	D	D	D	377	4,977	1,471.2	110.5	78	306	43.8	7.9
Montcalm	3.06	48.6	39	314	144.6	12.0	214	2,231	601.8	50.2	22	64	9.5	1.4
Montmorency	0.12	13.0	2	D	D	D	33	224	66.7	4.9	3	D	D	D
Muskegon	16.08	93.1	121	D	D	D	552	7,597	1,919.4	171.2	91	457	71.7	14.8
Newaygo	1.87	39.0	29	201	105.1	8.7	149	1,423	377.1	31.9	26	65	9.0	1.7
Oakland	19.11	15.4	2,048	28,521	25,910.5	1,806.5	4,880	70,570	20,886.2	1,879.2	1,644	15,464	3,085.1	678.8
Oceana	1.16	44.4	10	65	31.2	2.7	88	606	160.5	12.8	17	43	6.2	1.2
Ogemaw	0.38	18.1	21	441	155.5	17.4	119	1,574	387.6	35.3	21	58	9.0	1.6
Ontonagon	0.44	73.2	4	9	1.9	0.3	30	242	48.4	5.2	3	5	0.3	0.2
Osceola	1.37	59.4	13	116	134.7	5.2	73	601	176.1	15.4	9	9	2.3	0.4
Oscoda	0.07	8.5	2	D	D	D	37	241	59.5	4.6	7	14	1.8	0.2
Otsego	1.11	45.8	42	379	167.4	15.1	148	2,025	528.6	46.1	21	66	9.7	1.8
Ottawa	88.23	315.2	295	3,659	2,645.2	190.1	764	9,714	2,666.6	230.5	196	825	143.8	27.3
Presque Isle	0.46	35.8	5	8	2.0	0.2	64	388	110.9	8.6	7	D	D	D
Roscommon	0.28	11.7	10	48	12.6	1.4	111	1,220	331.4	28.7	15	63	9.7	1.6
Saginaw	0.42	2.2	181	1,975	1,264.9	96.7	870	12,210	2,913.3	262.8	132	602	101.1	16.3
St. Clair	137.89	862.5	89	924	548.7	40.4	532	6,745	1,760.0	148.7	94	272	56.4	8.2
St. Joseph	3.25	53.3	42	D	D	D	196	2,254	631.8	51.7	40	133	18.7	2.7
Sanilac	1.56	37.6	33	315	248.9	16.9	156	1,502	374.2	30.7	18	41	5.3	1.0
Schoolcraft	0.35	42.8	6	5	2.8	0.1	46	376	124.6	7.9	1	D	D	D
Shiawassee	2.89	42.1	40	457	201.1	18.2	200	2,413	713.9	58.1	35	77	11.2	2.0
Tuscola	1.89	35.1	39	465	404.6	23.0	157	1,581	481.9	34.8	19	75	8.7	1.4
Van Buren	3.55	47.3	53	D	D	D	252	2,285	634.6	54.1	32	102	15.3	1.9
Washtenaw	18.36	51.2	276	3,580	4,695.9	221.8	1,106	16,577	4,461.1	411.4	306	2,409	727.2	115.9
Wayne	466.55	265.2	1,483	23,525	25,358.3	1,417.5	6,091	65,409	17,409.4	1,539.9	1,070	6,044	4,464.6	225.3
Wexford	2.65	80.3	25	409	162.6	19.5	163	1,922	497.4	42.8	34	105	15.6	2.9
MINNESOTA	515.24	93.9	6,569	108,467	104,485.1	7,170.1	19,109	288,888	78,898.2	6,857.5	6,300	34,499	7,827.9	1,396.0
Aitkin	0.27	17.2	12	114	125.1	4.8	69	647	173.3	13.3	9	9	1.4	0.2
Anoka	108.23	314.5	326	12,633	7,485.0	1,617.5	884	15,209	3,982.1	355.7	345	1,149	249.9	34.9
Becker	1.66	49.7	37	263	150.8	10.1	132	1,731	459.7	38.9	34	77	17.8	2.5
Beltrami	1.45	31.7	44	D	D	D	220	3,106	702.7	66.5	30	83	14.5	2.4
Benton	2.08	52.4	42	1,130	911.7	58.9	119	1,800	510.3	42.9	35	80	13.5	2.4
Big Stone	0.49	97.2	8	74	208.2	3.9	27	209	38.2	3.7	3	3	0.3	0.1
Blue Earth	6.23	94.7	89	1,383	953.2	65.6	321	6,061	1,413.1	128.0	83	557	66.5	13.3
Brown	1.07	42.3	28	376	701.3	19.2	109	1,606	347.1	32.6	18	59	7.5	1.5
Carlton	1.51	42.5	17	287	226.0	11.4	107	1,344	351.8	28.3	16	51	10.5	1.1
Carver	8.32	84.3	127	2,247	1,699.4	200.5	210	3,484	907.8	80.6	96	603	123.4	29.1
Cass	0.54	18.8	14	187	87.9	10.0	131	913	255.7	19.8	37	236	13.3	5.9
Chippewa	1.17	96.6	19	313	532.2	15.7	54	650	198.9	13.9	14	122	6.5	2.4
Chisago	2.00	36.8	45	435	176.2	18.3	154	1,722	469.2	37.1	44	D	D	D
Clay	4.92	78.9	68	900	1,175.4	47.0	160	2,682	665.1	57.7	41	160	19.2	3.7
Clearwater	0.22	25.0	2	D	D	D	34	245	48.8	4.1	NA	NA	NA	NA
Cook	0.29	55.8	3	D	D	D	52	337	66.7	7.8	15	43	4.3	0.9
Cottonwood	1.76	152.4	25	168	287.4	9.6	51	506	102.8	9.8	6	19	3.3	0.8
Crow Wing	3.40	53.6	67	450	265.1	18.4	365	4,518	1,125.0	101.2	89	203	46.4	6.3
Dakota	40.71	98.2	524	7,768	11,786.0	484.9	1,122	21,719	6,485.6	576.6	479	2,310	439.8	83.3
Dodge	0.92	45.2	21	521	406.7	28.5	48	452	87.9	7.1	7	D	D	D
Douglas	2.20	59.3	48	997	502.2	44.5	234	3,078	743.4	65.8	43	146	36.6	4.5
Faribault	0.92	65.5	25	227	227.0	6.6	66	618	122.3	11.8	5	10	1.0	0.2

1 Merchant wholesalers, except manufacturers' sales branches and offices.   2. Employer establishments.

Table B. States and Counties — Professional Services, Manufacturing, and Accommodation and Food Services

STATE County	Professional, scientific, and technical services, 2012				Manufacturing, 2012				Accommodation and food services, 2012			
	Number of establishments	Number of employees	Sales (mil dol)	Average payroll (mil dol)	Number of establishments	Number of employees	Receipts (mil dol)	Annual payroll (mil dol)	Number of establishments	Number of employees	Receipts (mil dol)	Annual payroll (mil dol)
	147	148	149	150	151	152	153	154	155	156	157	158
MICHIGAN— Cont'd												
Keweenaw	NA	NA	NA	NA	4	10	D	D	19	99	5.4	1.5
Lake	4	16	1.1	0.5	8	D	D	D	30	D	D	D
Lapeer	132	623	74.6	25.7	125	4,923	1,303.5	198.8	117	1,933	80.2	22.4
Leelanau	72	223	32.2	10.0	35	240	D	8.8	72	718	46.5	17.0
Lenawee	119	613	50.9	20.1	131	4,569	2,047.2	234.5	167	2,658	105.7	30.4
Livingston	502	2,276	402.4	129.3	248	8,508	3,252.3	420.4	264	5,085	226.3	62.0
Luce	8	12	0.9	0.4	6	171	69.2	7.7	22	180	7.0	1.9
Mackinac	16	32	3.5	1.4	19	143	D	4.6	115	749	122.1	35.2
Macomb	1,581	30,331	3,348.4	2,177.3	1,593	59,114	27,017.3	3,495.8	1,565	28,350	1,263.1	347.5
Manistee	40	108	11.6	4.1	24	816	419.5	46.5	54	1,406	155.4	25.1
Marquette	113	676	66.7	28.6	49	871	275.7	45.3	174	2,806	114.4	34.9
Mason	44	156	13.1	5.0	38	1,800	432.2	86.2	88	980	50.2	13.9
Mecosta	46	281	34.3	16.4	32	1,880	677.0	77.4	78	1,178	45.7	13.5
Menominee	28	88	6.4	2.5	47	1,665	461.7	76.7	47	575	21.8	6.0
Midland	154	785	87.9	34.9	62	6,241	3,591.1	466.1	138	2,861	136.2	40.7
Missaukee	11	18	2.0	0.7	21	363	99.4	12.7	20	168	10.0	2.6
Monroe	147	828	129.9	40.6	128	6,591	2,976.5	351.3	259	4,280	179.9	49.6
Montcalm	51	220	16.1	5.6	74	2,738	528.3	121.1	82	1,003	44.9	12.2
Montmorency	10	21	1.8	0.7	15	369	74.5	12.6	22	D	D	D
Muskegon	223	1,513	182.5	65.7	259	12,483	3,727.0	608.0	335	5,450	236.1	67.6
Newaygo	54	348	52.1	17.4	40	1,897	663.4	84.6	76	906	39.9	10.5
Oakland	6,134	82,960	13,269.4	6,209.6	1,669	47,243	18,446.3	2,707.5	2,755	51,669	2,567.3	739.9
Oceana	28	123	14.4	5.5	41	1,324	473.2	46.6	57	599	29.3	8.2
Ogemaw	31	118	9.5	3.4	30	265	79.0	8.1	65	789	38.1	11.0
Ontonagon	6	9	0.8	0.2	NA	NA	NA	NA	27	156	6.2	1.4
Osceola	25	88	8.5	2.7	41	1,898	968.5	92.5	39	543	25.4	8.0
Oscoda	9	58	2.8	1.4	17	246	70.0	8.9	23	196	8.0	2.4
Otsego	55	205	31.2	9.7	37	682	141.4	25.9	60	1,037	54.4	14.7
Ottawa	466	3,228	471.5	190.5	544	31,831	11,067.3	1,529.6	381	7,573	321.8	89.8
Presque Isle	14	32	1.9	0.6	13	166	D	7.0	43	286	10.6	3.0
Roscommon	30	160	5.4	2.1	16	602	131.7	29.2	71	987	39.8	12.2
Saginaw	318	2,226	299.2	109.3	206	11,249	4,523.3	653.2	368	7,829	373.8	97.6
St. Clair	222	982	112.8	39.8	235	8,080	4,027.0	384.7	283	4,635	191.5	53.3
St. Joseph	74	4,239	44.9	63.4	132	7,683	3,542.4	350.7	104	1,368	57.9	15.8
Sanilac	51	210	15.3	5.3	74	2,385	729.7	95.7	61	567	27.8	6.9
Schoolcraft	9	45	2.9	1.2	9	185	104.4	11.4	35	261	11.6	3.1
Shiawassee	66	308	33.5	10.8	60	1,811	466.5	71.7	109	1,491	61.7	16.8
Tuscola	50	193	19.6	7.9	44	1,216	513.6	54.5	61	753	29.3	8.0
Van Buren	77	1,348	195.0	65.4	87	2,781	1,224.1	140.8	149	1,967	97.2	26.8
Washtenaw	1,284	13,390	2,329.9	928.1	332	13,232	5,419.9	725.8	766	14,879	764.9	216.3
Wayne	2,848	46,825	7,135.0	3,444.6	1,483	71,526	56,638.5	4,413.5	3,184	61,446	4,238.8	1,050.2
Wexford	60	298	28.1	13.2	49	3,890	1,119.0	173.9	78	1,064	46.6	12.8
MINNESOTA	16,348	140,927	23,449.1	9,739.3	7,313	297,884	123,076.3	15,822.6	11,345	221,859	11,722.6	3,238.0
Aitkin	14	D	D	D	27	298	62.1	11.4	51	448	18.8	5.1
Anoka	720	3,290	511.7	176.0	611	20,086	6,716.2	1,164.4	470	9,467	434.0	123.0
Becker	53	181	24.5	7.1	43	2,240	455.7	97.3	88	1,097	57.7	14.6
Beltrami	64	359	34.3	13.6	37	732	D	25.3	94	1,711	76.2	22.1
Benton	48	217	31.1	12.6	70	2,975	681.7	124.1	59	1,072	45.0	12.6
Big Stone	11	D	D	D	5	20	1.1	0.3	18	D	D	D
Blue Earth	147	1,090	127.2	52.6	88	3,896	3,938.5	189.7	156	3,584	143.6	39.2
Brown	43	405	43.4	15.9	38	2,935	1,506.6	129.7	61	955	32.5	9.4
Carlton	45	178	15.3	5.1	27	1,397	D	85.8	67	887	34.6	9.5
Carver	319	2,820	373.5	97.0	144	9,666	3,992.3	572.5	145	D	D	D
Cass	35	131	10.9	4.6	36	300	56.4	10.2	136	2,297	144.7	38.5
Chippewa	19	77	6.9	2.9	27	1,085	358.5	47.3	29	406	14.1	3.5
Chisago	72	D	D	D	80	1,952	552.9	88.0	86	D	D	D
Clay	77	D	D	D	38	832	409.3	D	81	1,824	68.8	20.2
Clearwater	11	53	3.1	1.0	13	443	D	14.1	21	D	D	D
Cook	15	D	D	D	5	43	12.5	1.9	62	637	46.8	14.0
Cottonwood	19	72	7.4	2.2	26	1,780	1,059.6	60.6	21	272	9.7	2.6
Crow Wing	143	940	125.8	50.7	104	2,480	496.6	103.9	209	3,003	169.5	45.9
Dakota	1,385	8,495	1,552.6	595.7	432	16,946	17,442.9	921.0	688	15,357	762.1	211.9
Dodge	22	D	D	D	23	1,123	719.7	57.8	27	336	12.6	3.3
Douglas	83	508	84.5	21.4	89	3,174	920.1	157.1	117	2,023	89.8	25.7
Faribault	20	79	7.9	2.8	24	1,134	326.0	46.6	34	260	11.8	2.5

Table B. States and Counties — Health Care and Social Assistance, Other Services, Nonemployer Businesses, and Residential Construction

STATE County	Health care and social assistance, 2012				Other services, 2012				Nonemployer businesses, 2016		Value of residential construction authorized by building permits, 2018	
	Number of establishments	Number of employees	Receipts (mil dol)	Annual payroll (mil dol)	Number of establishments	Number of employees	Receipts (mil dol)	Annual payroll (mil dol)	Number	Receipts (mil dol)	New construction ($1,000)	Number of housing units
	159	160	161	162	163	164	165	166	167	168	169	170
MICHIGAN— Cont'd												
Keweenaw	1	D	D	D	2	D	D	D	158	4.7	1,896	13
Lake	12	248	13.8	7.4	10	23	1.9	0.3	615	20.5	0	0
Lapeer	201	2,532	239.7	91.1	103	420	37.5	9.3	6,540	286.2	31,578	149
Leelanau	55	D	D	D	34	84	9.3	2.3	2,840	133.4	43,857	189
Lenawee	231	3,168	274.6	112.9	146	758	50.6	14.1	5,877	227.5	23,745	105
Livingston	376	5,161	522.1	191.9	281	1,853	146.9	48.3	14,968	721.0	197,291	742
Luce	16	414	37.4	15.9	10	D	D	D	333	11.2	295	3
Mackinac	19	332	47.3	13.9	15	D	D	D	901	31.5	4,539	19
Macomb	2,308	37,149	4,079.6	1,683.2	1,391	7,991	736.6	223.6	63,638	2,767.7	501,550	1,971
Manistee	65	906	93.7	35.5	44	179	13.7	4.4	1,663	60.5	3,312	11
Marquette	237	5,537	592.1	252.1	131	564	52.6	13.2	3,476	102.6	20,176	75
Mason	93	1,446	124.1	56.5	57	203	16.5	4.7	1,957	71.6	14,793	74
Mecosta	84	1,528	112.8	51.6	62	336	29.4	7.1	2,214	80.8	34,539	245
Menominee	40	334	18.5	8.2	30	161	16.5	4.0	1,312	61.0	4,736	30
Midland	239	6,268	682.2	242.8	147	882	113.0	23.2	5,003	195.3	16,537	88
Missaukee	26	326	14.1	6.6	19	50	4.8	1.2	1,119	48.6	3,366	21
Monroe	282	5,347	457.9	193.6	156	727	67.6	17.0	8,280	362.2	73,573	492
Montcalm	106	3,054	276.4	110.5	88	317	32.7	7.5	3,679	151.5	21,677	123
Montmorency	12	219	15.7	6.1	13	D	D	D	556	21.8	3,446	19
Muskegon	369	11,494	982.3	483.8	250	1,315	120.8	29.6	9,279	361.7	47,920	233
Newaygo	76	1,706	168.0	69.7	66	211	40.0	5.2	2,813	119.1	17,829	100
Oakland	5,120	100,125	10,835.6	4,461.3	2,371	16,548	1,962.1	474.5	114,295	6,697.4	751,898	2,642
Oceana	45	628	44.7	18.8	37	93	8.7	2.0	1,704	63.4	17,570	100
Ogemaw	66	1,321	102.6	45.5	44	152	11.1	2.9	1,319	50.1	7,356	10
Ontonagon	18	243	17.0	6.9	12	44	7.2	0.8	359	13.0	675	4
Osceola	50	1,106	90.0	34.5	30	109	12.4	2.8	1,396	63.7	3,080	20
Oscoda	14	164	9.9	3.6	12	50	3.3	0.8	598	26.1	3,684	20
Otsego	83	1,420	211.2	58.3	61	238	21.0	5.8	2,012	84.2	1,377	17
Ottawa	516	9,453	895.3	314.2	436	2,569	261.1	73.9	19,132	1,023.3	303,471	1,149
Presque Isle	26	331	22.9	9.0	23	45	5.3	0.9	930	27.9	8,151	38
Roscommon	45	531	38.0	15.3	56	176	14.5	3.9	1,513	51.9	6,689	43
Saginaw	582	17,262	1,766.5	712.8	328	1,943	161.3	45.2	10,443	403.3	47,805	333
St. Clair	378	7,828	696.4	292.1	201	912	87.1	20.5	10,243	407.7	50,380	262
St. Joseph	108	2,062	187.0	74.5	97	330	31.6	9.0	3,462	147.5	17,786	67
Sanilac	90	1,317	114.8	37.9	55	153	18.0	3.9	3,138	133.6	4,992	42
Schoolcraft	22	D	D	D	14	71	5.0	1.4	472	14.5	3,124	13
Shiawassee	134	2,549	217.0	87.8	97	463	37.7	9.1	4,246	163.3	14,646	69
Tuscola	107	2,444	186.7	78.4	55	168	13.0	3.2	3,420	128.5	6,971	35
Van Buren	107	2,497	195.5	81.3	89	360	30.1	6.6	4,865	197.3	30,227	119
Washtenaw	964	36,873	4,710.2	2,219.2	537	3,891	489.6	143.2	29,801	1,313.9	193,830	805
Wayne	4,091	101,848	12,420.4	4,712.3	2,645	16,865	1,763.8	497.5	126,180	4,117.0	379,405	1,397
Wexford	96	2,022	169.8	70.1	68	254	25.5	6.6	2,148	87.9	14,491	74
MINNESOTA	15,107	440,195	40,403.6	17,514.4	10,832	72,715	7,877.3	2,017.1	403,926	18,727.4	5,720,813	25,673
Aitkin	29	720	67.2	25.3	35	127	14.7	2.1	1,042	46.5	23,911	112
Anoka	625	15,314	1,631.1	710.6	535	3,642	350.2	102.1	22,809	999.6	370,420	1,693
Becker	78	1,800	149.8	65.9	82	371	39.4	7.1	2,892	148.5	34,076	192
Beltrami	138	3,934	434.5	151.1	90	415	49.8	12.1	2,861	116.7	13,961	141
Benton	84	3,071	116.7	56.0	79	588	48.9	15.2	2,639	123.1	35,611	227
Big Stone	20	898	56.9	24.6	15	33	3.7	0.5	390	18.7	1,279	9
Blue Earth	223	9,080	671.0	323.3	130	D	D	D	4,137	187.1	71,160	406
Brown	64	2,350	172.1	74.3	70	269	35.9	7.3	1,795	71.4	9,868	47
Carlton	88	2,058	145.3	68.3	62	243	22.2	5.8	1,878	70.8	22,758	155
Carver	201	4,828	471.1	202.5	171	1,051	84.6	24.4	8,136	414.2	235,224	973
Cass	68	1,227	65.1	27.7	59	228	18.4	3.7	2,599	126.3	54,719	230
Chippewa	39	1,100	69.6	29.2	41	156	20.1	3.9	863	36.6	1,053	8
Chisago	131	4,202	313.6	152.4	95	400	29.8	8.6	3,815	162.4	48,032	263
Clay	167	3,955	186.6	87.0	105	491	38.3	10.8	4,096	159.5	66,698	396
Clearwater	16	551	22.9	12.0	13	34	3.8	0.6	621	26.9	1,433	10
Cook	15	233	20.9	8.1	9	D	D	D	769	30.7	16,907	86
Cottonwood	34	818	50.1	19.9	27	89	8.0	2.0	799	35.6	3,789	17
Crow Wing	231	5,938	482.6	215.6	141	694	54.5	13.7	5,146	241.4	99,872	509
Dakota	1,012	23,031	1,679.6	745.8	729	6,034	582.8	183.3	29,230	1,340.4	446,186	2,057
Dodge	31	245	15.0	6.9	41	264	29.3	7.6	1,381	72.3	16,604	86
Douglas	129	3,480	266.1	105.0	109	464	42.6	9.5	3,354	169.3	43,350	198
Faribault	38	807	56.7	23.5	32	141	14.8	3.5	1,158	58.2	2,048	9

Table B. States and Counties — Government Employment and Payroll, and Local Government Finances

STATE County	Full-time equivalent employees	March payroll (dollars)	Adminis-tration, judicial, and legal	Police and corrections	Fire protection	Highways and transpor-tation	Health and welfare	Natural resources and utilities	Education and libraries	Total (mil dol)	Inter-govern-mental (mil dol)	Total (mil dol)	Per capita[1] (dollars) Total	Per capita[1] (dollars) Property
	171	172	173	174	175	176	177	178	179	180	181	182	183	184
MICHIGAN— Cont'd														
Keweenaw	94	226,587	43.0	12.5	0.3	32.4	0.3	5.4	3.3	7.1	2.2	2.4	1,085	1,064
Lake	335	1,121,895	29.9	22.5	0.7	15.2	0.2	4.0	24.4	41.5	20.4	15.6	1,355	1,353
Lapeer	2,193	8,102,009	9.7	7.1	0.9	3.7	6.5	3.4	67.0	261.5	141.1	64.1	727	687
Leelanau	610	2,337,768	17.9	7.8	10.1	6.0	1.3	2.0	50.2	66.0	15.8	38.3	1,774	1,747
Lenawee	2,916	10,906,000	8.3	8.7	1.9	4.7	2.7	5.5	65.8	340.2	180.3	97.9	989	958
Livingston	3,683	15,206,225	8.3	7.3	2.3	3.3	1.3	2.2	69.7	518.2	264.0	170.8	934	916
Luce	511	1,851,870	3.9	1.5	0.5	3.4	68.0	1.9	19.9	52.1	10.7	6.0	924	922
Mackinac	650	2,008,291	8.8	6.7	0.6	5.6	41.9	4.0	30.0	45.0	12.9	23.1	2,077	1,972
Macomb	20,477	98,514,743	5.7	8.9	3.4	3.3	4.1	2.4	70.5	3,154.9	1,534.9	942.2	1,112	1,087
Manistee	1,223	4,900,512	8.6	4.0	2.1	5.6	46.5	1.1	31.4	89.4	31.4	32.7	1,326	1,315
Marquette	2,307	8,582,841	9.4	7.9	1.6	8.1	17.8	11.0	40.6	242.6	106.7	75.0	1,105	1,084
Mason	951	3,483,823	12.1	7.3	0.1	7.1	0.9	4.3	66.7	123.3	40.6	57.2	1,996	1,980
Mecosta	1,566	5,890,046	7.7	5.5	1.5	4.1	36.2	3.2	40.3	182.4	76.2	42.5	980	926
Menominee	588	2,056,771	19.0	9.3	2.8	9.0	0.0	3.2	55.6	62.8	33.4	19.2	806	799
Midland	2,175	9,622,686	11.4	7.8	3.3	4.0	3.3	5.7	62.5	271.7	113.5	103.5	1,235	1,220
Missaukee	422	1,353,016	12.8	7.9	0.0	5.9	3.8	2.5	64.8	51.3	27.9	11.7	775	714
Monroe	3,882	16,268,085	7.1	8.4	1.4	3.3	1.1	4.8	72.4	475.7	225.8	166.5	1,102	1,074
Montcalm	1,898	7,424,584	9.0	5.3	0.5	3.4	5.9	1.9	72.7	230.7	138.4	56.8	901	887
Montmorency	201	694,558	20.5	8.4	2.1	11.4	4.4	2.8	43.7	25.7	7.3	10.4	1,095	1,081
Muskegon	5,428	21,789,876	7.5	7.4	2.5	3.3	9.1	3.1	65.4	721.5	413.6	168.4	989	913
Newaygo	1,567	5,734,250	9.2	6.4	0.9	3.1	12.6	1.5	64.0	180.6	100.9	46.4	967	962
Oakland	32,137	148,761,141	8.1	11.5	4.0	2.5	1.6	3.0	67.0	4,845.3	2,149.8	1,849.8	1,515	1,468
Oceana	787	2,716,638	12.5	6.8	0.6	9.1	6.1	3.2	57.2	91.5	36.3	30.4	1,156	1,142
Ogemaw	842	2,976,350	8.9	6.3	0.2	5.1	44.2	1.3	31.8	88.5	51.5	18.2	849	836
Ontonagon	240	749,123	19.9	5.8	0.6	28.7	0.1	8.1	33.5	31.1	13.6	12.2	1,900	1,897
Osceola	733	2,622,547	9.4	6.1	0.6	5.1	5.4	1.4	70.9	69.7	41.4	19.9	853	849
Oscoda	244	725,038	18.2	5.2	0.5	9.3	2.2	2.3	61.4	22.2	10.6	9.0	1,046	1,036
Otsego	766	3,112,250	10.4	4.0	0.5	8.3	0.2	1.8	71.3	77.8	31.0	34.0	1,415	1,413
Ottawa	6,822	27,516,658	8.5	6.3	1.4	2.9	4.0	6.4	67.9	866.8	436.0	302.6	1,125	1,104
Presque Isle	353	1,093,950	16.9	10.3	0.0	9.1	0.4	3.7	54.2	39.4	19.9	14.6	1,112	1,107
Roscommon	871	3,202,024	11.2	10.4	2.9	8.2	2.8	1.9	61.8	97.6	32.0	44.6	1,849	1,841
Saginaw	5,686	21,466,345	8.3	8.5	2.2	2.7	9.8	4.8	61.7	786.5	475.8	154.2	777	684
St. Clair	4,714	19,193,428	9.3	10.1	2.3	4.7	2.9	4.1	64.9	638.8	345.1	182.6	1,136	1,082
St. Joseph	2,407	8,504,558	8.9	6.1	1.5	3.5	17.3	3.9	56.9	263.0	120.1	64.5	1,061	1,051
Sanilac	1,146	3,992,557	10.8	9.0	0.7	4.8	2.5	4.3	65.5	164.8	92.6	39.4	932	918
Schoolcraft	461	1,943,689	9.8	4.5	1.3	9.9	52.0	3.2	18.6	62.6	11.5	8.5	1,020	1,018
Shiawassee	2,564	9,090,340	7.2	7.6	1.3	2.6	17.5	2.4	59.3	229.5	141.1	48.8	706	694
Tuscola	1,649	6,143,983	21.0	6.5	0.2	4.3	0.6	1.4	64.0	203.6	117.9	44.3	810	798
Van Buren	2,988	10,792,044	6.7	6.5	1.0	3.0	15.9	2.4	63.8	369.9	183.5	110.9	1,470	1,455
Washtenaw	9,997	45,620,706	8.5	10.1	3.0	4.2	5.2	5.4	62.0	1,472.6	631.4	577.8	1,646	1,596
Wayne	52,078	243,918,311	7.3	16.2	6.7	6.5	2.2	6.4	52.0	9,260.6	4,384.4	2,686.6	1,499	1,195
Wexford	861	3,131,204	9.3	8.2	2.0	8.9	0.5	6.9	62.4	121.3	63.1	38.8	1,190	1,183
MINNESOTA	X	X	X	X	X	X	X	X	X	X	X	X	X	X
Aitkin	582	2,073,612	15.2	11.2	0.4	6.7	11.2	4.6	46.4	60.1	32.6	17.4	1,089	1,074
Anoka	10,501	53,828,905	6.5	8.8	1.4	2.5	5.0	3.0	71.0	1,331.2	702.4	418.5	1,244	1,193
Becker	932	4,604,178	7.8	4.6	0.0	8.2	10.4	5.5	61.2	127.6	63.7	39.1	1,185	1,161
Beltrami	1,932	6,706,796	6.4	7.1	0.7	3.3	9.3	2.1	68.3	213.6	142.5	38.4	846	783
Benton	983	5,694,288	6.7	6.0	0.2	10.1	6.5	2.2	67.4	129.9	70.8	39.7	1,023	988
Big Stone	457	1,386,890	7.6	3.9	0.1	6.3	36.5	4.2	39.3	61.1	19.6	7.4	1,429	1,407
Blue Earth	2,214	8,872,355	7.8	8.8	1.3	4.6	6.9	5.2	63.0	311.6	161.3	79.4	1,221	1,080
Brown	1,088	4,160,686	9.0	10.8	0.0	6.2	20.5	12.8	39.2	121.7	52.1	29.1	1,145	1,070
Carlton	1,862	6,624,488	5.4	5.5	3.7	4.3	24.0	2.7	53.1	175.9	81.0	37.5	1,060	1,044
Carver	2,896	13,125,660	8.3	9.1	0.5	3.7	9.7	7.6	58.3	405.9	156.2	153.3	1,636	1,556
Cass	1,234	4,242,722	11.4	8.7	0.0	4.7	8.0	7.4	56.2	139.1	77.1	36.0	1,270	1,262
Chippewa	807	3,441,530	7.9	4.1	0.2	6.5	37.5	2.9	37.6	70.5	36.6	15.5	1,281	1,255
Chisago	1,385	5,404,860	10.1	10.6	0.1	5.4	10.2	3.2	57.7	193.7	95.4	66.1	1,237	1,214
Clay	2,229	9,153,639	5.8	9.5	2.1	3.2	9.3	7.6	60.6	275.2	152.5	52.4	871	834
Clearwater	344	1,650,939	7.5	7.1	0.0	4.2	13.2	2.5	62.5	36.7	20.9	8.5	982	979
Cook	357	1,321,609	10.7	6.6	0.1	6.3	41.6	8.6	23.6	43.3	14.6	10.6	2,035	1,721
Cottonwood	572	1,944,398	8.0	7.4	0.1	6.3	7.4	9.1	58.7	74.4	30.9	14.0	1,205	1,195
Crow Wing	2,463	11,443,269	7.2	9.3	0.8	3.7	30.0	2.2	44.6	346.9	130.2	91.9	1,461	1,378
Dakota	12,238	59,978,327	5.3	8.3	1.1	2.3	5.3	4.9	70.7	1,651.5	821.5	536.9	1,325	1,284
Dodge	717	3,409,832	6.5	6.4	0.0	3.9	12.4	1.9	67.9	88.6	44.2	22.9	1,131	1,119
Douglas	1,101	6,909,728	5.8	7.2	0.1	2.6	9.8	5.5	66.7	237.1	64.8	46.8	1,286	1,248
Faribault	667	3,058,474	6.0	6.7	0.1	5.1	34.0	6.2	39.8	90.8	34.3	16.1	1,130	1,101

1. Based on the resident population estimated as of July 1 of the year shown.

Table B. States and Counties — Local Government Finances, Government Employment, and Income Taxes

STATE County	Local government finances, 2012 (cont.) Direct general expenditure Total (mil dol)	Per capita[1] (dollars)	Percent of total for: Education	Health and hospitals	Police protection	Public welfare	Highways	Debt outstanding Total (mil dol)	Per capita[1] (dollars)	Government employment, 2017 Federal civilian	Federal military	State and local	Individual income tax returns, 2016 Number of returns	Mean adjusted gross income	Mean income tax
	185	186	187	188	189	190	191	192	193	194	195	196	197	198	199
MICHIGAN— Cont'd															
Keweenaw	6.9	3,101	2.6	1.3	7.4	0.3	34.9	4.3	1,951	24	3	114	1,040	49,220	4,852
Lake	31.5	2,738	24.3	2.6	4.3	1.0	15.0	21.8	1,898	53	18	429	4,610	38,126	3,465
Lapeer	274.0	3,108	46.0	7.1	3.5	8.9	6.8	238.6	2,706	139	139	4,110	42,700	53,580	5,790
Leelanau	61.1	2,829	43.8	4.2	3.6	0.7	9.8	51.6	2,388	134	34	1,686	12,030	74,717	11,384
Lenawee	351.5	3,551	55.5	5.5	3.4	4.6	6.5	276.7	2,796	195	150	4,536	45,390	50,290	5,076
Livingston	530.7	2,902	57.0	7.6	3.3	0.5	5.0	1,200.5	6,566	261	304	6,396	96,590	77,880	10,999
Luce	51.6	7,912	15.9	60.1	0.9	0.2	7.0	15.2	2,335	15	8	752	2,560	41,822	3,791
Mackinac	45.6	4,094	32.8	5.3	3.6	0.1	14.6	33.1	2,975	63	62	887	5,990	44,433	5,006
Macomb	3,200.9	3,777	51.2	8.3	6.2	1.5	3.9	3,701.0	4,368	8,232	1,786	29,693	444,570	55,255	6,512
Manistee	95.8	3,885	34.2	1.9	3.0	12.4	11.2	104.6	4,240	111	55	2,550	11,620	45,104	4,697
Marquette	235.2	3,464	37.8	1.8	6.5	6.4	9.7	135.1	1,989	280	124	5,307	30,400	52,610	5,606
Mason	115.8	4,037	56.0	0.9	2.9	9.4	8.9	57.5	2,005	76	59	1,835	14,170	47,621	5,251
Mecosta	174.1	4,018	38.9	30.3	3.2	0.8	5.0	74.8	1,726	99	66	4,476	17,100	47,047	5,057
Menominee	61.6	2,585	51.9	0.5	6.7	0.2	12.8	22.8	958	56	37	2,033	11,150	48,750	4,605
Midland	272.5	3,250	51.0	2.8	4.1	2.1	7.6	318.6	3,800	158	132	3,059	40,010	72,793	10,587
Missaukee	54.0	3,591	36.3	33.2	2.2	0.6	9.3	4.1	276	27	24	513	6,590	40,965	3,591
Monroe	515.6	3,414	53.6	6.7	3.7	0.2	9.1	557.6	3,691	244	239	5,407	74,070	58,219	6,662
Montcalm	236.5	3,748	58.8	7.6	2.3	0.4	7.4	191.1	3,029	132	98	2,992	27,690	43,183	3,968
Montmorency	24.1	2,539	34.8	1.0	4.8	1.0	13.9	10.5	1,103	18	15	376	4,390	39,970	3,451
Muskegon	746.4	4,386	51.2	13.2	3.2	3.6	4.5	688.6	4,046	360	294	7,361	78,670	48,182	5,138
Newaygo	194.0	4,046	57.6	5.7	2.5	6.5	7.1	159.0	3,316	73	77	2,205	21,520	46,229	4,614
Oakland	4,863.5	3,984	50.4	6.9	6.5	0.2	4.9	4,726.4	3,872	4,895	2,076	46,325	635,870	90,621	15,452
Oceana	89.5	3,401	42.0	4.4	3.7	17.2	11.9	48.9	1,859	166	42	1,259	12,130	45,358	4,861
Ogemaw	91.5	4,268	23.9	47.2	2.2	0.7	7.5	60.2	2,807	58	33	720	9,340	38,464	3,469
Ontonagon	29.7	4,631	39.8	1.3	2.4	0.1	24.2	24.8	3,875	32	9	339	2,760	41,189	3,705
Osceola	69.8	2,999	56.1	2.5	3.0	0.3	11.7	41.1	1,765	58	37	938	10,050	41,398	3,579
Oscoda	22.1	2,573	44.7	4.2	4.0	8.4	11.5	3.6	419	54	13	285	3,540	38,366	3,439
Otsego	81.5	3,391	48.3	3.2	2.7	0.6	12.1	42.7	1,777	142	41	1,100	12,420	47,762	5,126
Ottawa	885.8	3,292	57.1	5.1	3.6	0.9	6.5	1,000.3	3,717	424	506	15,733	133,250	67,518	8,739
Presque Isle	40.5	3,081	35.5	1.1	3.7	0.7	13.8	21.2	1,618	60	20	590	6,430	43,233	4,200
Roscommon	94.2	3,908	58.3	2.5	4.2	1.6	7.4	44.3	1,836	31	38	1,394	11,270	41,570	4,139
Saginaw	801.9	4,043	42.8	14.5	5.8	0.7	5.8	494.0	2,490	1,457	314	9,317	89,760	48,021	5,364
St. Clair	651.8	4,058	44.3	15.8	3.9	0.1	6.4	526.8	3,280	732	330	6,297	78,780	53,154	5,957
St. Joseph	268.7	4,420	49.4	24.1	3.0	0.3	4.3	186.9	3,074	112	97	2,814	28,140	47,241	4,790
Sanilac	165.3	3,911	47.1	12.6	4.3	6.0	11.0	127.3	3,011	104	66	1,786	19,010	43,286	4,197
Schoolcraft	58.9	7,054	15.2	41.3	2.0	13.4	8.4	36.7	4,402	40	13	981	3,920	45,589	4,541
Shiawassee	236.8	3,421	55.9	8.0	3.1	6.2	8.8	102.4	1,479	133	109	3,202	32,990	47,569	4,774
Tuscola	211.4	3,867	51.0	9.0	3.1	9.1	9.0	137.5	2,515	135	83	2,808	24,980	44,401	4,069
Van Buren	365.1	4,839	52.4	18.4	2.7	0.9	6.5	300.6	3,984	154	120	4,720	34,970	48,395	5,050
Washtenaw	1,495.8	4,262	46.0	12.6	6.5	0.9	4.9	2,033.3	5,794	4,135	629	71,379	165,230	80,390	12,655
Wayne	9,500.3	5,300	36.3	3.3	7.0	5.2	2.9	21,084.6	11,764	13,918	3,243	74,000	796,330	52,903	6,806
Wexford	112.1	3,437	54.4	1.5	4.1	1.5	9.9	59.5	1,825	125	53	2,018	15,300	43,330	4,027
MINNESOTA	X	X	X	X	X	X	X	X	X	32,314	19,975	376,550	2,737,290	71,417	9,716
Aitkin	64.5	4,049	33.1	1.4	4.3	8.2	22.4	16.8	1,053	45	55	834	7,250	49,206	4,968
Anoka	1,279.3	3,803	53.7	0.9	5.4	5.1	9.5	1,587.7	4,720	456	1,238	15,250	175,740	66,289	7,912
Becker	136.5	4,137	44.4	1.1	4.2	11.3	12.3	95.6	2,898	232	119	3,017	16,010	55,234	5,997
Beltrami	237.7	5,239	45.5	1.1	3.5	7.4	8.2	329.6	7,264	396	158	5,079	19,600	49,582	5,023
Benton	105.9	2,726	49.8	1.2	5.5	8.3	10.1	177.0	4,555	56	139	1,732	19,590	53,081	5,446
Big Stone	57.1	11,056	19.8	43.6	2.3	4.0	9.5	316.3	61,258	32	17	606	2,520	48,031	4,873
Blue Earth	298.5	4,586	38.2	0.6	4.8	5.4	14.5	311.4	4,785	261	244	5,284	30,790	57,930	6,945
Brown	114.6	4,507	33.1	12.3	4.8	7.0	11.5	109.7	4,315	75	85	1,649	13,150	56,235	5,467
Carlton	170.7	4,830	39.9	19.7	3.8	7.4	8.0	194.2	5,495	65	119	5,238	16,250	54,295	5,230
Carver	420.3	4,485	43.0	0.6	4.3	4.9	9.0	930.8	9,933	212	360	4,865	49,010	99,710	15,610
Cass	150.7	5,316	45.3	1.8	4.4	6.4	12.0	129.6	4,571	254	103	3,625	14,190	51,076	5,613
Chippewa	70.8	5,832	38.1	1.0	3.7	12.0	12.1	81.7	6,730	67	42	1,188	6,040	52,929	5,375
Chisago	182.5	3,415	43.9	1.5	4.9	4.7	15.5	291.7	5,458	95	190	2,402	27,140	64,588	7,391
Clay	286.2	4,758	32.4	1.9	4.5	6.9	10.4	437.1	7,267	111	215	4,403	28,390	55,601	5,620
Clearwater	40.3	4,626	44.8	0.2	5.1	9.0	18.1	19.0	2,179	38	31	514	3,760	54,485	6,322
Cook	44.8	8,644	13.1	30.8	6.2	4.2	13.3	40.0	7,721	127	19	787	3,030	51,725	5,303
Cottonwood	74.7	6,441	31.9	19.0	3.8	5.3	14.2	80.5	6,940	62	39	806	5,580	48,491	4,682
Crow Wing	333.5	5,303	34.0	22.0	4.7	6.2	6.0	491.9	7,822	205	249	3,574	31,450	55,321	6,114
Dakota	1,670.9	4,125	51.3	0.8	5.2	4.3	6.8	2,383.8	5,885	3,407	1,490	18,689	216,620	76,250	10,260
Dodge	88.6	4,380	46.8	2.3	6.2	13.6	9.3	114.3	5,648	41	73	1,222	10,140	60,595	6,548
Douglas	244.5	6,713	25.3	35.9	2.8	3.2	7.4	374.7	10,290	140	132	3,434	19,070	61,967	7,640
Faribault	106.3	7,456	21.6	34.8	2.4	1.7	14.0	77.3	5,420	57	48	846	6,930	46,851	4,499

1. Based on the resident population estimated as of July 1 of the year shown.

Table B. States and Counties — **Land Area and Population**

State / county code	CBSA code[1]	County code[2]	STATE County	Land area[3] (sq. mi)	Total persons 2018	Rank	Per square mile	White	Black	American Indian, Alaska Native	Asian and Pacific Islander	Percent Hispanic or Latino[4]	Under 5 years	5 to 17 years	18 to 24 years	25 to 34 years	35 to 44 years	45 to 54 years
				1	2	3	4	5	6	7	8	9	10	11	12	13	14	15
			MINNESOTA— Cont'd															
27045	40,340	3	Fillmore	861.3	21,058	1,773	24.4	96.9	0.8	0.4	0.9	1.8	6.6	18.0	6.8	10.1	11.4	11.5
27047	10,660	7	Freeborn	707.3	30,444	1,423	43.0	85.8	1.7	0.7	3.2	9.9	5.7	16.3	6.8	11.0	11.2	11.5
27049	39,860	4	Goodhue	756.9	46,403	1,043	61.3	93.2	1.9	1.7	1.3	3.5	5.6	16.5	7.2	11.2	11.8	12.4
27051		9	Grant	547.8	6,021	2,753	11.0	96.1	1.2	0.9	0.7	2.4	6.2	16.4	6.1	10.4	11.9	10.2
27053	33,460	1	Hennepin	553.8	1,259,428	32	2,274.2	71.3	15.0	1.4	8.5	7.0	6.5	15.5	8.5	17.0	13.6	12.2
27055	29,100	3	Houston	552.0	18,578	1,896	33.7	97.2	1.3	0.6	0.9	1.2	5.6	16.1	6.5	10.1	11.3	12.1
27057		7	Hubbard	926.0	21,332	1,760	23.0	94.3	1.0	3.4	0.9	2.2	5.4	15.8	5.9	8.9	10.6	11.6
27059	33,460	1	Isanti	435.7	39,966	1,182	91.7	95.3	1.3	1.3	1.7	2.1	5.9	17.6	7.4	12.7	12.4	13.3
27061	24,330	6	Itasca	2,667.3	45,108	1,075	16.9	93.9	1.1	5.1	0.8	1.6	5.2	15.5	6.7	9.7	11.1	11.8
27063		7	Jackson	703.0	9,911	2,435	14.1	93.1	1.5	0.9	2.1	3.9	5.5	16.1	6.7	10.5	11.6	11.2
27065		6	Kanabec	521.6	16,207	2,028	31.1	96.3	1.1	1.6	1.0	1.7	5.4	16.1	7.1	9.9	11.3	12.8
27067	48,820	4	Kandiyohi	797.4	42,855	1,120	53.7	80.4	6.1	0.6	1.4	12.3	6.8	17.7	8.0	12.0	11.1	11.1
27069		9	Kittson	1,098.8	4,248	2,883	3.9	96.4	0.7	0.7	1.1	2.2	5.5	15.9	7.2	9.2	9.3	11.6
27071		6	Koochiching	3,104.2	12,440	2,256	4.0	94.8	1.2	3.7	0.9	1.3	4.4	13.8	6.6	9.6	10.0	12.5
27073		9	Lac qui Parle	765.0	6,658	2,699	8.7	95.6	1.3	0.7	1.2	2.6	4.8	15.3	6.6	8.1	10.0	10.7
27075		6	Lake	2,109.3	10,658	2,384	5.1	96.3	1.2	1.5	0.8	1.7	4.9	13.9	6.0	9.8	10.5	11.1
27077		9	Lake of the Woods	1,297.9	3,758	2,920	2.9	95.0	1.5	2.3	2.6	1.4	4.9	14.1	5.9	8.7	10.3	12.4
27079	33,460	1	Le Sueur	448.7	28,494	1,482	63.5	92.1	1.0	0.8	1.0	6.2	6.1	17.8	7.3	11.0	12.3	13.5
27081		9	Lincoln	536.8	5,673	2,782	10.6	96.6	0.6	0.6	0.7	2.3	6.0	17.4	5.9	9.6	9.6	11.0
27083	32,140	7	Lyon	714.4	25,629	1,579	35.9	84.6	4.1	0.8	4.9	7.1	7.4	18.4	9.5	13.0	12.2	10.8
27085	26,780	6	McLeod	491.5	35,873	1,276	73.0	91.6	1.1	0.6	1.1	6.5	5.9	17.1	7.7	12.0	11.6	13.1
27087		8	Mahnomen	557.9	5,519	2,792	9.9	53.7	1.6	49.0	0.7	4.0	8.7	23.0	7.4	9.8	10.3	10.5
27089		8	Marshall	1,775.1	9,390	2,474	5.3	94.0	0.8	1.1	0.5	4.8	6.5	16.4	7.2	10.8	10.5	11.9
27091	21,860	7	Martin	712.3	19,785	1,840	27.8	93.7	1.0	0.7	1.0	4.5	5.7	16.0	7.0	10.4	10.4	11.1
27093		6	Meeker	608.1	23,141	1,674	38.1	94.7	1.0	0.5	0.7	4.0	6.1	18.0	7.4	10.2	11.2	11.8
27095	33,460	1	Mille Lacs	572.4	26,139	1,562	45.7	90.5	1.2	6.7	1.0	2.5	6.5	17.6	7.2	11.5	11.8	12.6
27097		6	Morrison	1,125.1	33,169	1,354	29.5	96.7	1.1	0.8	0.7	1.8	6.0	17.4	7.1	10.8	11.6	12.2
27099	12,380	4	Mower	711.3	40,011	1,178	56.3	79.3	4.4	0.6	5.6	11.9	6.7	18.6	7.7	12.3	11.9	11.6
27101		9	Murray	704.7	8,276	2,565	11.7	93.5	0.7	0.6	1.8	4.3	5.8	16.1	6.7	9.1	10.5	11.0
27103	31,860	3	Nicollet	448.6	34,220	1,319	76.3	89.6	4.3	0.7	2.3	4.7	5.8	16.3	12.6	12.6	12.6	11.3
27105	49,380	7	Nobles	715.1	21,924	1,728	30.7	59.2	5.5	0.7	7.3	28.4	8.2	19.2	8.8	12.3	11.4	11.6
27107		8	Norman	872.8	6,475	2,712	7.4	91.9	1.3	3.3	1.1	4.9	5.9	18.2	6.9	9.8	11.5	11.5
27109	40,340	3	Olmsted	653.5	156,277	423	239.1	81.9	7.3	0.6	7.5	5.0	6.9	17.6	7.7	14.6	13.2	11.6
27111	22,260	6	Otter Tail	1,971.8	58,812	879	29.8	93.5	1.9	1.2	1.0	3.6	6.0	15.9	6.9	9.8	10.2	11.0
27113		6	Pennington	616.6	14,178	2,151	23.0	92.4	2.0	2.5	1.4	3.8	6.3	16.5	8.0	13.0	12.2	11.8
27115		6	Pine	1,411.3	29,483	1,445	20.9	90.9	2.8	4.1	1.2	3.0	4.8	14.8	6.7	11.2	12.2	13.0
27117		6	Pipestone	465.1	9,047	2,494	19.5	88.6	1.8	2.3	1.4	7.7	7.3	18.5	7.1	10.0	10.5	11.5
27119	24,220	3	Polk	1,971.1	31,529	1,391	16.0	88.3	3.2	2.4	1.5	6.6	7.0	17.2	8.8	12.1	11.2	11.4
27121		8	Pope	669.6	11,097	2,347	16.6	97.0	1.0	0.8	0.9	1.5	5.5	15.2	6.1	11.1	10.7	10.8
27123	33,460	1	Ramsey	152.2	550,210	123	3,615.0	64.2	14.0	1.4	16.2	7.6	6.9	16.4	9.8	16.7	12.4	11.1
27125		8	Red Lake	432.4	3,999	2,900	9.2	93.4	1.3	2.3	0.6	4.0	5.8	18.3	6.0	9.5	12.2	11.6
27127		7	Redwood	878.6	15,249	2,078	17.4	88.4	1.1	5.4	3.3	3.8	6.5	18.2	7.4	10.4	10.8	11.3
27129		8	Renville	982.9	14,612	2,119	14.9	88.5	1.1	1.5	1.2	9.0	6.3	16.9	7.5	10.2	10.8	11.8
27131	22,060	4	Rice	495.8	66,523	805	134.2	83.4	6.2	0.7	3.1	8.1	5.8	16.1	14.5	11.4	11.6	12.2
27133		6	Rock	482.5	9,414	2,468	19.5	94.3	1.4	1.0	1.2	3.5	6.1	19.5	7.3	10.3	11.7	11.2
27135		7	Roseau	1,671.6	15,150	2,084	9.1	93.3	1.1	2.6	3.4	1.4	6.0	18.1	7.7	10.1	11.0	13.7
27137	20,260	2	St. Louis	6,247.8	199,754	337	32.0	93.2	2.5	3.3	1.7	1.8	5.1	13.9	12.5	11.6	11.3	11.2
27139	33,460	1	Scott	356.3	147,381	447	413.6	82.8	5.5	1.4	7.2	5.3	6.8	20.6	7.9	12.0	14.7	14.9
27141	33,460	1	Sherburne	432.9	96,036	621	221.8	92.7	3.6	1.0	2.0	2.7	6.8	19.7	8.2	13.4	14.0	14.4
27143	33,460	1	Sibley	588.6	15,028	2,095	25.5	88.9	1.2	0.5	1.0	9.4	5.6	18.0	7.6	10.9	11.8	12.6
27145	41,060	3	Stearns	1,342.8	159,256	417	118.6	87.0	7.7	0.6	2.9	3.5	6.4	16.7	14.8	12.2	11.3	11.3
27147	36,940	5	Steele	429.6	36,803	1,256	85.7	87.2	3.9	0.6	1.4	8.1	6.2	18.7	7.6	11.8	11.9	12.5
27149		7	Stevens	563.6	9,753	2,446	17.3	88.8	1.6	2.5	2.7	6.7	5.5	15.5	20.4	11.1	10.3	8.7
27151		7	Swift	742.0	9,345	2,476	12.6	91.7	1.8	0.9	1.4	5.6	6.1	17.0	6.5	10.8	11.2	11.8
27153		6	Todd	945.0	24,582	1,625	26.0	92.1	1.0	1.0	1.1	6.2	6.8	17.0	7.3	9.7	10.4	11.6
27155		9	Traverse	573.9	3,308	2,950	5.8	90.1	1.2	6.5	0.9	3.3	5.7	15.3	7.6	8.6	10.6	11.2
27157	40,340	3	Wabasha	523.0	21,645	1,744	41.4	95.6	1.1	0.6	1.0	2.9	5.7	16.1	6.7	10.5	10.8	12.9
27159		7	Wadena	536.3	13,773	2,177	25.7	95.5	1.9	1.6	1.0	2.0	7.0	18.7	7.2	10.3	10.9	11.1
27161		6	Waseca	423.4	18,691	1,892	44.1	90.2	2.9	0.9	1.2	6.3	5.6	17.5	7.9	12.1	12.8	12.2
27163	33,460	1	Washington	384.4	259,201	264	674.3	84.3	5.8	0.9	7.1	4.3	6.0	18.6	7.9	11.4	13.3	13.9
27165		6	Watonwan	435.0	10,980	2,354	25.2	71.7	1.0	0.6	1.3	26.2	7.0	17.4	8.6	10.4	11.2	10.8
27167	47,420	6	Wilkin	751.0	6,254	2,728	8.3	94.3	1.2	2.2	0.7	3.1	6.1	16.3	7.7	10.0	11.6	12.5
27169	49,100	4	Winona	626.1	50,825	979	81.2	92.1	2.3	0.7	3.1	3.1	4.8	13.2	20.2	11.4	10.2	10.5
27171	33,460	1	Wright	661.1	136,349	470	206.2	93.7	2.3	0.7	1.9	3.1	6.9	21.0	7.5	11.7	14.2	13.8
27173		9	Yellow Medicine	759.1	9,795	2,443	12.9	90.1	1.1	4.2	0.9	5.1	6.2	17.3	7.8	11.0	10.6	11.4

1. CBSA = Core Based Statistical Area. See Appendix A for explanation. See Appendix B for list of metropolitan areas with component counties.   2. County type code from the Economic Research Service of USDA Rural-Urban Continuum Codes. See Appendix A for definition.   3. Dry land or land partially or temporarily covered by water.   4. May be of any race.

Table B. States and Counties — Population and Households

STATE County	55 to 64 years	65 to 74 years	75 years and over	Percent female	Total persons 2000	2010	Percent change 2000-2010	2010-2018	Births	Deaths	Net Migration	Number	Persons per household	Family house-holds	Female family house-holder[1]	One person
	16	17	18	19	20	21	22	23	24	25	26	27	28	29	30	31
MINNESOTA— Cont'd																
Fillmore	14.6	11.0	9.9	49.8	21,122	20,871	-1.2	0.9	2,123	1,901	-23	8,614	2.37	68.2	5.5	27.0
Freeborn	15.4	11.5	10.7	50.2	32,584	31,254	-4.1	-2.6	2,810	2,990	-618	12,958	2.32	65.0	10.2	28.5
Goodhue	15.6	11.0	8.7	50.4	44,127	46,185	4.7	0.5	4,236	3,916	-75	19,345	2.34	67.4	9.9	26.2
Grant	15.4	11.9	11.4	49.8	6,289	6,018	-4.3	0.0	575	575	6	2,536	2.30	68.8	7.3	26.9
Hennepin	12.6	8.2	5.8	50.5	1,116,200	1,152,385	3.2	9.3	135,393	68,118	40,498	499,104	2.40	57.3	9.4	33.1
Houston	16.8	12.0	9.5	49.8	19,718	19,022	-3.5	-2.3	1,592	1,426	-610	8,114	2.27	68.3	8.6	27.3
Hubbard	16.8	15.0	10.1	49.2	18,376	20,428	11.2	4.4	1,798	1,649	764	8,758	2.35	70.7	7.4	24.1
Isanti	14.5	9.2	6.8	49.4	31,287	37,810	20.8	5.7	3,712	2,498	948	14,571	2.61	69.1	9.9	24.0
Itasca	16.4	13.6	9.8	49.5	43,992	45,051	2.4	0.1	3,843	4,236	499	19,356	2.27	67.1	7.6	27.2
Jackson	16.0	11.2	11.2	48.8	11,268	10,266	-8.9	-3.5	912	862	-407	4,350	2.29	65.7	6.7	28.3
Kanabec	16.8	12.1	8.4	49.7	14,996	16,244	8.3	-0.2	1,294	1,243	-84	6,353	2.47	68.2	7.7	25.9
Kandiyohi	14.4	10.2	8.6	49.7	41,203	42,239	2.5	1.5	4,788	3,134	-1,037	16,765	2.47	69.4	8.9	25.6
Kittson	16.9	12.7	11.7	49.7	5,285	4,552	-13.9	-6.7	390	544	-147	1,891	2.21	60.8	7.6	35.9
Koochiching	17.6	14.5	11.0	50.0	14,355	13,317	-7.2	-6.6	872	1,227	-521	5,629	2.21	64.1	8.7	32.7
Lac qui Parle	16.8	13.3	14.3	49.7	8,067	7,259	-10.0	-8.3	537	723	-419	3,171	2.11	64.8	6.2	30.6
Lake	17.8	14.2	11.8	48.5	11,058	10,862	-1.8	-1.9	880	1,153	77	5,082	2.03	64.3	6.0	29.4
Lake of the Woods	19.5	14.2	10.0	47.7	4,522	4,045	-10.5	-7.1	285	380	-193	1,533	2.47	63.7	5.1	33.5
Le Sueur	14.4	10.1	7.4	49.6	25,426	27,701	8.9	2.9	2,642	1,787	-57	10,844	2.53	70.7	7.4	24.0
Lincoln	14.6	11.0	13.8	49.6	6,429	5,896	-8.3	-3.8	573	643	-148	2,484	2.23	62.7	4.5	32.9
Lyon	12.9	8.3	7.6	50.1	25,425	25,857	1.7	-0.9	3,016	1,823	-1,452	10,060	2.44	64.1	8.6	29.4
McLeod	13.9	9.9	8.8	50.0	34,898	36,645	5.0	-2.1	3,440	2,757	-1,472	14,760	2.40	66.8	8.5	27.6
Mahnomen	13.2	9.3	7.9	49.6	5,190	5,413	4.3	2.0	861	513	-239	1,947	2.80	66.1	16.2	28.9
Marshall	15.2	10.9	10.6	49.5	10,155	9,439	-7.1	-0.5	922	648	-321	3,953	2.35	64.6	7.1	28.8
Martin	15.9	12.0	11.5	50.4	21,802	20,843	-4.4	-5.1	1,835	2,070	-819	8,685	2.27	63.3	8.4	32.0
Meeker	15.2	11.0	9.0	49.1	22,644	23,298	2.9	-0.7	2,256	1,805	-606	9,164	2.48	67.9	5.9	27.4
Mille Lacs	14.6	10.0	8.3	49.7	22,330	26,097	16.9	0.2	2,700	2,388	-266	10,116	2.48	67.9	11.4	26.4
Morrison	15.3	10.6	8.9	49.5	31,712	33,198	4.7	-0.1	3,178	2,599	-595	13,327	2.43	68.0	7.8	27.8
Mower	12.9	9.3	9.1	49.7	38,603	39,163	1.5	2.2	4,159	3,179	-110	15,524	2.49	65.8	8.4	28.8
Murray	15.3	13.4	12.1	50.0	9,165	8,725	-4.8	-5.1	730	834	-344	3,713	2.22	63.4	3.9	31.4
Nicollet	12.5	9.4	6.9	49.5	29,771	32,729	9.9	4.6	3,157	1,814	157	12,662	2.41	66.8	8.2	26.6
Nobles	12.2	8.2	8.1	48.5	20,832	21,378	2.6	2.6	3,018	1,468	-1,034	7,917	2.71	69.4	10.5	26.8
Norman	15.1	10.9	10.2	49.6	7,442	6,852	-7.9	-5.5	595	798	-174	2,733	2.36	65.1	7.7	30.2
Olmsted	13.0	8.5	7.1	51.2	124,277	144,260	16.1	8.3	17,761	8,157	2,490	59,804	2.49	67.0	9.7	26.3
Otter Tail	16.3	13.1	10.6	49.7	57,159	57,303	0.3	2.6	5,402	5,553	1,721	24,300	2.33	67.6	6.6	28.3
Pennington	14.0	9.6	8.7	50.4	13,584	13,930	2.5	1.8	1,484	1,100	-125	5,883	2.37	61.1	10.5	34.1
Pine	16.6	11.8	8.9	46.3	26,530	29,747	12.1	-0.9	2,328	2,269	-319	10,752	2.54	63.8	8.0	30.3
Pipestone	14.1	9.7	11.2	51.3	9,895	9,597	-3.0	-5.7	998	915	-638	4,019	2.25	64.9	9.1	31.3
Polk	14.4	9.6	8.4	49.8	31,369	31,600	0.7	-0.2	3,417	2,807	-671	12,609	2.40	62.7	6.9	32.5
Pope	16.0	13.5	10.9	49.0	11,236	10,995	-2.1	0.9	1,021	1,020	107	4,898	2.19	65.3	5.4	30.2
Ramsey	12.2	8.4	6.0	51.2	511,035	508,639	-0.5	8.2	63,626	33,392	11,716	208,504	2.51	58.5	11.7	33.0
Red Lake	15.8	11.2	9.8	48.9	4,299	4,089	-4.9	-2.2	410	295	-207	1,718	2.32	64.4	8.1	31.4
Redwood	14.1	10.6	10.5	50.1	16,815	16,058	-4.5	-5.0	1,562	1,543	-829	6,310	2.38	64.9	7.6	31.3
Renville	15.7	10.5	10.3	49.2	17,154	15,728	-8.3	-7.1	1,498	1,559	-1,068	6,219	2.32	64.0	6.3	30.7
Rice	12.9	8.7	6.7	49.0	56,665	64,142	13.2	3.7	6,070	3,936	265	22,899	2.49	68.4	9.6	26.4
Rock	14.1	10.1	9.7	50.8	9,721	9,686	-0.4	-2.8	919	973	-215	3,985	2.30	64.9	7.7	28.0
Roseau	15.8	9.7	7.8	48.5	16,338	15,629	-4.3	-3.1	1,553	1,124	-923	6,123	2.50	67.8	6.4	27.2
St. Louis	15.0	11.2	8.2	49.8	200,528	200,231	-0.1	-0.2	16,702	17,084	103	85,662	2.23	57.2	8.7	34.5
Scott	12.2	6.6	4.2	50.2	89,498	129,912	45.2	13.4	15,609	5,081	7,004	47,864	2.92	77.0	8.3	18.3
Sherburne	12.2	7.1	4.3	48.8	64,417	88,492	37.4	8.5	9,794	4,072	1,856	31,181	2.88	77.1	8.2	16.7
Sibley	15.3	9.7	8.7	49.7	15,356	15,232	-0.8	-1.3	1,379	1,181	-404	5,993	2.45	68.9	6.5	27.0
Stearns	12.2	8.4	6.7	49.5	133,166	150,642	13.1	5.7	16,262	8,072	463	58,657	2.51	64.0	8.8	26.6
Steele	13.6	9.5	8.2	50.2	33,680	36,581	8.6	0.6	3,790	2,496	-1,081	14,450	2.50	67.3	8.1	27.9
Stevens	11.2	8.5	8.8	50.3	10,053	9,722	-3.3	0.3	947	687	-226	3,630	2.58	60.2	4.0	29.4
Swift	14.7	11.1	10.8	49.4	11,956	9,783	-18.2	-4.5	903	918	-423	4,217	2.20	61.5	8.7	35.3
Todd	15.7	12.0	9.6	48.5	24,426	24,895	1.9	-1.3	2,650	1,712	-1,258	9,777	2.46	66.9	5.5	28.8
Traverse	15.9	11.2	14.0	49.8	4,134	3,558	-13.9	-7.0	272	428	-96	1,576	2.07	65.2	6.5	30.8
Wabasha	15.6	12.3	9.5	49.9	21,610	21,664	0.2	-0.1	1,950	1,517	-445	8,867	2.39	69.3	7.5	25.3
Wadena	13.8	10.6	10.4	50.5	13,713	13,843	0.9	-0.5	1,496	1,619	60	5,704	2.31	62.6	8.9	33.0
Waseca	13.5	10.3	7.9	51.8	19,526	19,138	-2.0	-2.3	1,743	1,341	-851	7,375	2.40	67.1	9.4	28.3
Washington	13.9	9.0	6.0	50.6	201,130	238,114	18.4	8.9	23,376	12,257	10,167	92,005	2.69	72.7	9.7	22.1
Watonwan	14.5	9.5	10.5	50.6	11,876	11,211	-5.6	-2.1	1,251	983	-501	4,327	2.49	63.6	9.2	31.6
Wilkin	16.6	9.8	9.4	48.4	7,138	6,576	-7.9	-4.9	597	637	-284	2,852	2.18	64.4	8.1	33.5
Winona	13.0	9.7	7.3	50.5	49,985	51,461	3.0	-1.2	3,890	3,402	-1,125	19,228	2.44	59.6	7.2	30.5
Wright	12.2	7.5	5.1	49.5	89,986	124,697	38.6	9.3	14,845	6,160	3,055	46,568	2.79	75.4	8.1	19.7
Yellow Medicine	15.5	9.8	10.4	49.5	11,080	10,438	-5.8	-6.2	945	976	-617	4,157	2.32	67.8	9.1	28.2

1. No spouse present.

Table B. States and Counties — Population, Vital Statistics, Health, and Crime

STATE County	Persons in group quarters, 2018	Daytime Population, 2013-2017		Births, 2018		Deaths, 2018		Persons under 65 with no health insurance, 2016		Medicare, 2018			Serious crimes known to police[2], 2016 Total	
		Number	Employment/ residence ratio	Total	Rate[1]	Number	Rate[1]	Number	Percent	Total beneficiaries	Enrolled in Original Medicare	Enrolled in Medicare Advantage	Number	Rate[3]
	32	33	34	35	36	37	38	39	40	41	42	43	44	45
MINNESOTA— Cont'd														
Fillmore	359	17,591	0.69	268	12.7	223	10.6	1,254	7.6	4,850	2,210	2,640	83	399
Freeborn	637	28,801	0.88	321	10.5	359	11.8	1,314	5.6	7,670	2,988	4,682	432	1,418
Goodhue	891	45,077	0.95	500	10.8	455	9.8	1,796	4.8	10,270	4,086	6,184	909	1,958
Grant	110	5,278	0.77	68	11.3	54	9.0	258	5.7	1,640	693	947	16	272
Hennepin	25,918	1,450,923	1.34	16,322	13.0	8,771	7.0	52,533	5.0	193,047	79,396	113,651	40,613	3,286
Houston	257	15,179	0.64	202	10.9	176	9.5	704	4.7	4,522	2,220	2,302	116	620
Hubbard	154	18,633	0.78	207	9.7	194	9.1	907	5.9	5,715	2,442	3,273	545	2,636
Isanti	465	31,205	0.62	433	10.8	311	7.8	1,464	4.5	7,406	2,865	4,541	778	2,021
Itasca	1,017	43,589	0.92	450	10.0	478	10.6	2,239	6.5	12,104	5,478	6,626	460	1,012
Jackson	110	10,364	1.05	108	10.9	98	9.9	341	4.4	2,342	1,391	951	43	429
Kanabec	246	13,303	0.64	170	10.5	152	9.4	704	5.6	3,890	1,814	2,076	259	1,645
Kandiyohi	1,047	43,371	1.04	574	13.4	343	8.0	1,920	5.6	9,699	4,135	5,564	658	1,546
Kittson	111	4,119	0.88	46	10.8	65	15.3	171	5.2	1,181	505	676	23	523
Koochiching	241	12,562	0.96	99	8.0	131	10.5	635	6.7	3,708	1,732	1,976	58	455
Lac qui Parle	154	6,356	0.86	64	9.6	92	13.8	273	5.5	1,862	688	1,174	47	694
Lake	224	10,184	0.92	101	9.5	127	11.9	337	4.3	3,104	1,464	1,640	39	369
Lake of the Woods	53	3,412	0.79	37	9.8	40	10.6	187	6.4	1,047	498	549	7	180
Le Sueur	270	22,595	0.64	340	11.9	224	7.9	1,164	5.1	5,124	2,044	3,080	303	1,097
Lincoln	135	4,999	0.74	69	12.2	68	12.0	239	5.6	1,466	847	619	12	209
Lyon	900	27,525	1.13	359	14.0	224	8.7	1,113	5.3	4,800	2,730	2,070	321	1,254
McLeod	476	34,794	0.95	400	11.2	340	9.5	1,282	4.4	7,534	2,660	4,874	530	1,482
Mahnomen	79	5,875	1.18	105	19.0	68	12.3	371	8.4	917	525	392	1	18
Marshall	76	7,743	0.65	115	12.2	88	9.4	425	5.8	2,124	920	1,204	49	521
Martin	348	19,848	0.98	223	11.3	225	11.4	839	5.5	5,360	2,534	2,826	242	1,220
Meeker	354	19,925	0.72	262	11.3	218	9.4	957	5.2	5,093	1,667	3,426	247	1,072
Mille Lacs	522	24,306	0.89	338	12.9	265	10.1	1,338	6.5	6,085	2,468	3,617	711	2,767
Morrison	529	29,592	0.80	383	11.5	341	10.3	1,473	5.6	7,451	2,781	4,670	212	649
Mower	632	38,048	0.93	503	12.6	391	9.8	2,028	6.4	8,396	4,254	4,142	758	1,941
Murray	163	7,702	0.83	94	11.4	98	11.8	355	5.7	2,148	1,234	914	100	1,198
Nicollet	2,829	31,725	0.90	360	10.5	252	7.4	986	3.8	5,939	2,534	3,405	388	1,161
Nobles	385	22,304	1.04	374	17.1	178	8.1	1,802	10.0	3,881	2,480	1,401	245	1,123
Norman	149	5,952	0.79	78	12.0	99	15.3	315	6.2	1,608	795	813	2	30
Olmsted	2,372	168,061	1.21	2,108	13.5	1,031	6.6	6,011	4.6	26,474	15,429	11,045	3,024	1,981
Otter Tail	1,184	54,536	0.88	690	11.7	670	11.4	2,367	5.4	15,553	5,874	9,679	915	1,585
Pennington	327	16,992	1.37	163	11.5	132	9.3	524	4.5	2,858	1,173	1,685	126	884
Pine	1,654	26,526	0.80	263	8.9	272	9.2	1,405	6.5	6,780	2,819	3,961	942	3,259
Pipestone	205	9,390	1.04	128	14.1	115	12.7	518	7.2	2,011	1,215	796	63	685
Polk	1,260	29,249	0.85	430	13.6	326	10.3	1,294	5.1	6,546	3,094	3,452	531	1,687
Pope	184	10,277	0.88	119	10.7	100	9.0	386	4.6	2,799	1,136	1,663	64	580
Ramsey	17,442	599,357	1.23	7,648	13.9	4,226	7.7	24,725	5.5	88,772	36,568	52,204	18,798	3,459
Red Lake	34	3,244	0.61	39	9.8	27	6.8	193	6.0	883	224	659	8	198
Redwood	373	15,425	1.00	186	12.2	174	11.4	840	7.1	3,401	1,491	1,910	251	1,636
Renville	342	13,945	0.88	196	13.4	173	11.8	710	6.2	3,458	1,733	1,725	262	1,780
Rice	7,308	62,084	0.91	774	11.6	516	7.8	2,801	5.7	11,495	4,540	6,955	1,012	1,544
Rock	260	8,590	0.82	117	12.4	105	11.2	385	5.2	2,196	1,165	1,031	106	1,107
Roseau	191	16,275	1.09	171	11.3	131	8.6	640	5.0	3,095	1,091	2,004	169	1,070
St. Louis	9,127	208,683	1.09	1,962	9.8	2,065	10.3	6,849	4.3	45,271	19,997	25,274	6,622	3,307
Scott	1,313	120,194	0.72	1,845	12.5	659	4.5	4,744	3.7	17,787	6,876	10,911	2,161	1,503
Sherburne	2,187	69,450	0.54	1,205	12.5	539	5.6	3,113	3.8	13,218	5,139	8,079	1,378	1,495
Sibley	230	12,032	0.63	154	10.2	118	7.9	706	5.9	3,083	1,274	1,809	101	683
Stearns	7,293	166,839	1.14	2,021	12.7	999	6.3	5,828	4.6	26,970	10,984	15,986	4,154	2,674
Steele	594	39,051	1.13	421	11.4	324	8.8	1,285	4.2	7,411	2,935	4,476	761	2,070
Stevens	1,005	10,828	1.21	113	11.6	76	7.8	340	4.8	1,747	999	748	141	1,439
Swift	150	9,098	0.93	112	12.0	108	11.6	402	5.5	2,156	1,029	1,127	47	508
Todd	346	21,215	0.71	328	13.3	192	7.8	1,400	7.3	5,563	1,819	3,744	304	1,261
Traverse	100	3,119	0.85	35	10.6	34	10.3	156	6.3	917	480	437	64	1,899
Wabasha	246	18,125	0.70	240	11.1	183	8.5	778	4.6	4,804	2,050	2,754	164	776
Wadena	482	14,282	1.11	198	14.4	184	13.4	642	6.1	3,706	1,430	2,276	46	332
Waseca	959	16,732	0.77	193	10.3	143	7.7	718	4.9	4,055	1,620	2,435	267	1,410
Washington	3,553	214,094	0.72	2,790	10.8	1,673	6.5	6,455	3.0	43,018	15,782	27,236	5,311	2,092
Watonwan	150	10,269	0.88	155	14.1	108	9.8	732	8.5	2,273	1,167	1,106	130	1,194
Wilkin	152	5,668	0.78	80	12.8	80	12.8	224	4.4	1,433	668	765	87	1,370
Winona	4,084	50,359	0.98	458	9.0	447	8.8	1,871	4.8	9,473	4,907	4,566	1,046	2,062
Wright	1,105	106,976	0.65	1,734	12.7	840	6.2	3,989	3.4	19,519	6,987	12,532	2,233	1,686
Yellow Medicine	290	9,578	0.93	115	11.7	109	11.1	465	5.9	2,374	1,264	1,110	84	861

1. Per 1,000 estimated resident population.   2. Data for serious crimes have not been adjusted for underreporting; this may affect comparability between geographic areas and over time.   3. Per 100,000 population estimated by the FBI.

Table B. States and Counties — Crime, Education, Money Income, and Poverty

STATE County	Serious crimes known to police[2], 2016 (cont.)[1] Rate		School enrollment and attainment, 2013-2017				Local government expenditures,[5] 2014-2015		Money income, 2013-2017				Income and poverty, 2017			
			Enrollment[3]		Attainment[4] (percent)					Households			Percent below poverty level			
											Percent					
	Violent	Property	Total	Percent private	High school graduate or less	Bachelor's degree or more	Total current spending (mil dol)	Current spending per student (dollars)	Per capita income[6]	Median income (dollars)	with income of less than $50,000	with income of $200,000 or more	Median household income (dollars)	All persons	Children under 18 years	Children 5 to 17 years in families
	46	47	48	49	50	51	52	53	54	55	56	57	58	59	60	61
MINNESOTA— Cont'd																
Fillmore	38	360	4,620	11.5	42.8	20.7	26.1	10,501	28,441	57,093	44.0	2.6	56,165	10.3	14.4	13.4
Freeborn	72	1,346	6,556	8.1	47.1	16.8	49.7	12,100	27,603	51,174	48.5	1.9	52,117	11.8	15.8	15.9
Goodhue	151	1,807	10,410	14.4	38.9	24.7	77.6	11,438	33,477	62,431	40.6	4.0	65,953	8	9.0	8.4
Grant	17	255	1,223	9.0	41.3	18.6	11.9	10,907	30,359	53,727	47.5	3.9	50,943	9.2	13.1	13.2
Hennepin	470	2,816	308,128	17.3	24.2	48.2	2,155.8	13,096	41,794	71,154	35.9	9.9	74,568	10.5	13.7	13.0
Houston	37	583	4,128	16.7	39.2	23.2	46.0	10,928	30,150	56,837	43.5	2.8	55,558	7.6	8.9	8.3
Hubbard	140	2,496	4,188	9.3	38.9	26.6	25.3	10,427	28,073	52,941	47.4	2.6	56,129	11.5	16.8	15.7
Isanti	104	1,917	9,271	12.7	44.2	17.3	65.7	10,967	30,145	67,565	35.6	2.7	70,594	7.9	10.1	8.9
Itasca	119	893	9,807	10.3	38.0	22.7	80.6	11,783	27,497	52,050	48.4	1.6	49,934	11.2	14.9	12.6
Jackson	20	409	2,231	6.9	42.2	20.2	17.0	11,210	31,010	55,122	45.7	3.7	55,981	8.6	11.9	11.2
Kanabec	140	1,506	3,376	8.1	51.1	14.8	22.2	9,969	26,345	50,509	49.4	2.3	53,181	9.4	16.5	15.4
Kandiyohi	169	1,377	9,690	10.3	38.3	22.6	63.9	11,598	29,375	56,604	43.7	3.2	59,816	10.6	14.3	14.1
Kittson	23	500	854	10.2	43.1	23.2	9.3	13,871	30,525	52,304	46.6	2.2	52,327	9.4	11.9	10.9
Koochiching	71	385	2,490	9.1	46.0	18.7	22.8	12,523	26,804	47,131	52.5	1.7	48,942	12.7	20.4	18.8
Lac qui Parle	15	679	1,342	6.6	44.4	19.0	15.2	11,580	31,427	50,195	49.7	4.5	53,046	9.8	13.0	12.0
Lake	19	350	1,843	7.8	35.7	29.0	15.1	10,671	32,319	56,078	44.9	2.1	55,622	8.4	11.7	10.4
Lake of the Woods	26	154	656	3.2	51.7	17.0	6.2	13,403	24,964	46,943	52.8	0.0	49,828	9.7	13.8	13.4
Le Sueur	36	1,061	6,625	13.5	42.7	21.9	42.8	9,913	31,135	65,500	37.2	4.0	69,581	7.7	8.4	7.6
Lincoln	209	0	1,211	10.4	46.9	19.7	11.4	12,187	28,382	51,102	49.0	2.2	51,278	10.4	12.2	11.6
Lyon	82	1,172	7,059	11.5	41.0	26.5	75.4	16,776	30,203	54,181	46.0	3.9	55,255	12.2	13.5	12.9
McLeod	92	1,390	8,195	13.5	44.8	18.0	55.0	10,445	30,145	59,869	40.2	2.8	61,822	7.7	8.6	8.1
Mahnomen	0	18	1,420	5.6	49.9	12.1	18.5	13,852	20,720	42,439	56.7	1.5	43,591	21	33.0	30.0
Marshall	53	468	1,931	6.9	47.8	20.1	18.9	14,136	28,585	57,289	43.6	2.3	56,330	9.4	10.5	9.5
Martin	106	1,114	4,058	14.4	45.7	20.0	36.4	12,356	30,806	53,627	46.8	4.8	53,805	11.1	16.7	15.8
Meeker	104	968	5,294	10.4	44.0	19.1	35.5	10,267	29,216	59,611	39.9	3.0	56,068	9.1	10.2	8.9
Mille Lacs	117	2,650	5,801	12.3	48.6	15.5	65.4	10,272	25,732	53,737	46.2	1.9	53,273	11	15.3	13.3
Morrison	21	628	7,361	11.7	48.6	16.4	55.9	10,423	28,040	52,855	46.9	3.1	55,709	10.5	13.8	12.2
Mower	197	1,744	9,906	9.1	44.8	20.7	73.1	11,696	28,613	53,700	47.2	3.5	55,772	10.6	13.7	12.8
Murray	60	1,138	1,660	11.3	47.1	18.1	12.8	11,869	30,553	54,211	45.4	3.2	60,682	8.2	10.7	10.7
Nicollet	60	1,101	9,602	37.7	33.7	32.2	37.4	15,297	29,722	62,593	39.8	4.0	66,944	8.8	9.5	8.7
Nobles	115	1,008	5,302	8.1	55.9	14.5	43.6	11,015	24,935	53,267	46.8	2.7	49,935	12.8	17.8	16.4
Norman	0	30	1,414	9.3	49.1	17.5	13.2	12,280	27,099	53,034	47.2	2.4	50,481	12.7	17.9	16.3
Olmsted	174	1,807	38,988	17.6	26.0	43.1	260.3	11,115	37,956	72,337	33.8	7.6	77,110	8.3	9.9	8.8
Otter Tail	80	1,505	11,753	13.4	38.9	24.7	127.8	16,640	29,932	55,181	45.6	3.4	53,033	10.3	14.2	12.9
Pennington	56	828	3,127	6.4	44.9	18.7	81.6	37,435	28,562	53,893	47.1	2.4	56,015	10.3	12.7	11.0
Pine	270	2,989	6,064	10.7	51.5	13.9	41.3	10,810	24,044	47,285	52.5	2.1	52,226	12.2	16.7	15.0
Pipestone	33	652	1,954	15.5	47.5	20.5	17.7	11,563	28,706	48,909	51.1	3.5	50,784	9.7	13.3	12.4
Polk	178	1,509	7,710	9.4	40.2	24.5	55.7	11,211	28,260	55,393	45.2	3.2	54,717	11.6	13.4	13.0
Pope	45	534	2,196	8.2	38.5	22.2	15.9	12,920	32,454	58,198	43.3	3.2	59,903	8	10.6	10.1
Ramsey	425	3,034	145,498	24.5	31.2	41.5	1,229.2	14,078	32,544	60,301	42.0	5.9	61,924	14	19.6	18.7
Red Lake	0	198	880	5.1	47.2	16.6	10.3	13,941	26,988	52,500	47.5	1.8	51,785	10.3	12.4	11.4
Redwood	143	1,493	3,539	12.6	48.6	18.4	27.4	11,144	27,543	51,871	48.3	2.7	53,985	10	13.4	12.2
Renville	136	1,644	3,126	11.3	47.6	14.5	19.5	10,776	31,215	56,721	43.7	3.7	54,758	10.4	14.3	13.9
Rice	154	1,390	19,865	38.2	40.8	26.8	97.3	11,446	28,603	63,311	39.7	4.5	65,011	11.1	13.8	12.2
Rock	376	731	2,259	16.9	44.2	21.8	15.6	9,961	29,000	56,753	42.7	3.4	60,041	9.3	11.3	10.1
Roseau	6	1,064	3,450	6.9	42.7	19.2	31.0	10,689	27,935	56,273	43.7	2.7	58,742	8.3	11.0	10.2
St. Louis	236	3,071	49,814	12.4	34.8	28.4	289.5	11,647	29,197	50,936	49.2	3.2	53,013	14.5	14.5	13.1
Scott	105	1,398	39,769	16.6	28.0	38.9	245.7	10,340	38,322	93,151	23.8	11.0	99,685	4	4.7	4.4
Sherburne	115	1,380	25,099	11.3	33.2	27.4	191.9	9,679	33,048	83,895	26.6	5.4	87,094	4.3	5.4	5.1
Sibley	108	575	3,535	16.1	49.5	16.6	25.4	10,568	29,884	60,848	41.6	3.1	59,378	7.7	10.7	9.3
Stearns	211	2,463	45,957	19.4	36.7	27.2	269.2	11,080	29,148	59,564	41.9	3.8	63,017	11	12.3	11.5
Steele	144	1,926	9,002	11.2	42.6	24.6	66.1	10,109	29,930	58,882	41.4	3.5	60,143	9.3	12.4	11.6
Stevens	163	1,276	3,288	6.5	34.6	28.8	16.7	10,958	31,419	57,552	44.5	6.5	59,406	10.3	8.8	7.7
Swift	86	422	2,018	3.0	46.5	17.0	15.3	10,274	29,470	49,556	50.3	3.6	53,561	11.5	14.0	12.7
Todd	120	1,141	5,220	18.3	50.1	14.5	51.4	16,169	24,988	49,213	50.6	2.0	49,962	13.3	17.1	16.4
Traverse	178	1,721	651	4.9	45.7	17.6	6.3	12,253	30,234	48,889	50.5	4.4	50,692	13	19.8	18.2
Wabasha	66	710	4,619	12.4	43.5	21.6	43.6	9,774	32,307	61,973	39.1	4.2	63,374	7	8.8	8.2
Wadena	36	296	3,129	4.3	47.6	12.9	29.7	9,945	24,200	45,018	55.4	2.2	45,716	15.7	20.7	17.4
Waseca	100	1,310	4,422	11.4	42.6	20.2	38.1	10,159	27,383	55,189	43.6	2.4	59,246	10.3	12.8	11.3
Washington	103	1,989	66,283	15.7	25.6	42.3	425.6	10,617	41,591	89,598	23.9	11.0	92,582	4.2	4.9	4.3
Watonwan	202	992	2,404	6.4	57.8	15.2	21.8	12,370	26,884	50,044	50.0	2.0	50,678	11.2	15.7	13.9
Wilkin	79	1,291	1,450	8.3	36.3	20.8	11.6	10,784	28,575	52,917	45.5	2.0	58,118	9.3	12.8	12.0
Winona	120	1,942	15,993	18.1	34.4	29.6	69.5	13,001	27,200	53,975	46.7	2.9	55,577	13.8	12.7	10.9
Wright	91	1,596	35,244	12.3	34.3	27.4	272.5	10,162	32,506	77,953	29.8	4.7	80,855	5.4	5.2	4.8
Yellow Medicine	133	728	2,217	6.6	45.4	15.8	19.3	12,868	28,182	54,645	44.8	2.6	53,596	9.9	13.0	12.4

1. Data for serious crimes have not been adjusted for underreporting; this may affect comparability between geographic areas and over time.   2. Per 100,000 population estimated by the FBI.   3. All persons 3 years old and over enrolled in nursery school through college.   4. Persons 25 years old and over.   5. Elementary and secondary education expenditures.   6. Based on population estimated by the American Community Survey, 2013–2017.

Table B. States and Counties — **Personal Income and Earnings**

STATE County	Personal income, 2017										Earnings, 2017		
	Total (mil dol)	Percent change 2016-2017	Per capita[1]		Wages and salaries (mil dol)	Supplements to wages and salaries, employer contributions (mil dol)		Proprietors' income (mil dol)	Dividends, interest, and rent (mil dol)	Personal transfer reecipts (mil dol)	Total (mil dol)	Contributions for government social insurance (mil dol)	
			Dollars	Rank		Pension and insurance	Government social insurance					From employee and self-employed	From employer
	62	63	64	65	66	67	68	69	70	71	72	73	74

MINNESOTA— Cont'd

Fillmore	855	0.5	40,766	1,437	220	45	18	50	169	197	333	26	18
Freeborn	1,264	3.0	41,405	1,347	514	90	40	35	246	325	679	50	40
Goodhue	2,300	3.5	49,682	482	1,053	185	81	198	416	422	1,517	97	81
Grant	283	-3.5	47,693	646	80	15	7	31	60	75	133	9	7
Hennepin	88,978	5.2	71,067	67	68,139	8,968	4,772	7,814	20,382	10,207	89,693	5,186	4,772
Houston	920	3.0	49,289	511	190	41	15	66	175	177	313	22	15
Hubbard	860	4.6	40,899	1,415	232	44	18	66	180	235	361	28	18
Isanti	1,689	4.8	42,673	1,189	463	90	36	86	224	336	676	46	36
Itasca	1,816	1.5	40,225	1,514	671	134	54	97	350	540	955	68	54
Jackson	483	1.9	48,601	580	208	45	18	45	122	99	315	19	18
Kanabec	663	3.0	41,384	1,349	157	33	13	70	94	172	273	19	13
Kandiyohi	2,200	4.1	51,466	396	989	180	78	340	407	427	1,587	97	78
Kittson	210	-0.7	49,294	509	63	13	5	24	50	49	106	6	5
Koochiching	493	2.7	39,378	1,659	193	38	17	19	87	167	267	20	17
Lac qui Parle	310	-6.6	46,306	766	81	19	6	15	81	87	121	10	6
Lake	481	5.5	45,746	826	188	37	16	26	95	131	267	19	16
Lake of the Woods	189	0.8	50,391	437	59	13	5	23	34	49	99	7	5
Le Sueur	1,323	4.5	47,050	708	398	74	33	62	246	229	567	37	33
Lincoln	240	-5.4	42,324	1,227	67	14	5	7	60	64	93	7	5
Lyon	1,183	0.3	45,797	819	652	121	48	90	242	227	911	56	48
McLeod	1,717	3.5	47,841	638	776	136	59	177	292	322	1,148	70	59
Mahnomen	191	-7.0	34,207	2,460	72	17	5	10	37	67	104	7	5
Marshall	444	0.1	47,475	666	101	21	8	40	84	100	171	11	8
Martin	973	3.3	49,015	536	376	68	28	71	246	232	542	35	28
Meeker	963	2.8	41,638	1,312	298	58	24	52	172	222	431	30	24
Mille Lacs	1,053	3.5	40,685	1,445	358	71	28	66	157	288	523	36	28
Morrison	1,303	1.2	39,410	1,657	419	86	34	102	227	334	641	43	34
Mower	1,757	2.9	44,403	970	823	135	59	75	335	402	1,092	73	59
Murray	422	-4.1	50,520	431	117	24	9	65	94	91	216	12	9
Nicollet	1,612	4.3	47,449	669	672	129	51	105	323	265	957	57	51
Nobles	925	1.9	42,144	1,247	455	81	34	105	181	182	674	39	34
Norman	247	-4.5	37,412	1,967	71	14	6	3	68	77	93	8	6
Olmsted	8,396	4.1	54,194	307	6,032	830	435	415	1,424	1,159	7,712	461	435
Otter Tail	2,650	2.5	45,415	853	946	187	74	199	573	637	1,407	96	74
Pennington	726	1.1	51,016	411	490	84	37	40	175	138	651	38	37
Pine	1,043	3.6	35,722	2,242	284	64	23	67	177	312	438	31	23
Pipestone	484	3.1	53,314	333	176	34	14	111	90	93	336	18	14
Polk	1,424	2.5	45,040	895	506	97	41	90	248	337	734	47	41
Pope	510	1.8	46,488	752	200	38	16	12	125	123	266	19	16
Ramsey	28,654	3.9	52,291	366	22,044	3,228	1,555	1,747	5,941	5,045	28,574	1,683	1,555
Red Lake	192	2.8	47,637	651	40	9	3	33	28	38	85	5	3
Redwood	688	-7.3	45,061	894	240	50	19	81	162	164	390	25	19
Renville	712	-0.5	48,651	576	254	50	21	58	180	160	382	23	21
Rice	2,757	4.2	41,787	1,288	1,182	196	91	137	492	510	1,606	103	91
Rock	460	1.5	48,510	589	156	30	11	80	95	94	276	15	11
Roseau	737	4.9	48,110	614	374	75	29	54	162	133	533	30	29
St. Louis	8,911	3.4	44,556	957	4,644	825	364	410	1,636	2,210	6,243	400	364
Scott	8,276	5.1	56,753	229	2,731	423	212	649	1,120	775	4,017	239	212
Sherburne	4,270	4.8	45,157	882	1,194	218	95	216	507	611	1,722	109	95
Sibley	676	1.4	45,467	847	159	33	14	48	133	139	254	17	14
Stearns	6,998	3.8	44,344	980	4,241	722	327	526	1,217	1,296	5,817	344	327
Steele	1,606	4.1	43,549	1,071	1,008	168	75	43	286	324	1,293	82	75
Stevens	429	-4.3	44,580	953	226	45	18	32	117	82	322	18	18
Swift	405	-8.6	43,024	1,139	157	34	13	20	90	106	223	16	13
Todd	935	2.7	38,130	1,860	273	53	21	97	147	262	444	31	21
Traverse	154	-10.5	46,448	760	50	10	4	2	51	43	66	5	4
Wabasha	963	3.7	44,577	954	261	53	21	66	178	194	400	27	21
Wadena	518	2.8	37,892	1,901	217	45	17	40	90	178	318	22	17
Waseca	786	-2	41,814	1,285	278	55	24	68	141	175	425	28	24
Washington	16,324	4.4	63,681	116	4,273	688	317	915	3,142	1,721	6,193	389	317
Watonwan	457	5.6	42,173	1,246	164	33	13	18	93	107	228	15	13
Wilkin	323	-0.2	51,110	409	89	15	8	50	66	69	162	11	8
Winona	2,420	3.1	47,561	661	1,068	225	83	104	662	420	1,480	89	83
Wright	6,389	4.3	47,577	660	1,926	343	153	418	836	851	2,841	176	153
Yellow Medicine	486	-10.2	49,296	508	154	33	12	58	131	116	258	16	12

1. Based on the resident population estimated as of July 1 of the year shown.

Table B. States and Counties — Earnings, Social Security, and Housing

STATE County	Earnings, 2017 (cont.)									Social Security beneficiaries, December 2017		Supplemental Security Income recipients, 2017	Housing units, 2018	
	Percent by selected industries													
	Farm	Mining, quarrying, and extractions	Construction	Manufacturing	Information; professional, scientific, technical services	Retail trade	Finance, insurance, real estate, and leasing	Health care and social assistance	Government	Number	Rate[1]		Total	Percent change, 2010-2018
	75	76	77	78	79	80	81	82	83	84	85	86	87	88
MINNESOTA— Cont'd														
Fillmore	-11.6	D	10.9	23	3.7	8.2	7.1	D	19.7	5,005	239	192	10,028	3
Freeborn	-5.6	D	6.7	22.6	3	10.8	8.1	D	14.3	8,045	263	563	14,371	1
Goodhue	-1.2	D	6.8	24.5	2.9	5.8	3.6	12.3	16.9	10,490	227	486	20,692	1.7
Grant	4.8	0	12	6.4	D	5.1	D	D	17.6	1,705	287	61	3,303	-0.6
Hennepin	0	0.1	4	8.1	18.7	4.2	14.5	10.1	9	187,645	150	26,756	537,756	5.6
Houston	2.8	0	12.7	10.1	D	5.3	4.3	10.8	20.2	4,670	250	199	8,777	2.1
Hubbard	0.2	D	11.2	19.3	2.6	8.8	4.6	16.7	17.6	6,075	289	375	14,917	2
Isanti	-0.5	0	9	14.8	D	8.4	4.2	20.3	18.7	7,935	200	402	16,212	5.8
Itasca	-0.2	D	7.2	8.9	3.2	8.3	4.8	17.4	22.4	13,070	290	896	27,789	2.7
Jackson	6	0	4.9	31.3	3.4	2.4	3.4	D	13	2,405	242	103	5,082	1.8
Kanabec	3	0.5	21.9	8.4	2.3	6.5	4.8	9	28.6	4,250	265	236	7,983	1.7
Kandiyohi	0.7	D	7.9	19.7	4	6.7	4.9	D	16.3	9,755	228	759	19,982	2.6
Kittson	13.3	D	5.6	7.8	D	4.7	D	D	18.8	1,180	278	59	2,612	0.3
Koochiching	0.3	0	6.4	24.2	2.2	7.3	3.9	D	23.3	3,950	315	303	7,934	0.4
Lac qui Parle	-9.9	0	9	7.6	D	9.9	9.7	11.6	33	1,930	289	80	3,701	0.2
Lake	0	D	4.1	16.8	2.4	4.5	4	D	20.8	3,120	296	124	7,995	4.1
Lake of the Woods	-3.6	0	D	16	1.4	5.9	D	14.9	18.3	1,145	306	32	3,817	3.9
Le Sueur	1.2	D	11	38.4	2.5	4.4	4.1	5.7	12.9	5,380	191	238	12,809	3.2
Lincoln	-6.3	0	20.7	3.3	D	6.3	4	D	17.6	1,510	266	55	3,147	1.3
Lyon	-2	0.1	4.8	16.9	3.9	6.8	12.6	8.7	21.6	4,995	193	402	11,285	1.7
McLeod	3.5	D	5.8	33.7	2.3	5.6	4.5	13.9	10.2	7,815	218	360	15,939	1.1
Mahnomen	-1.2	0	3.1	D	D	3.7	D	D	59.4	980	175	136	2,781	-0.2
Marshall	6.4	D	9.1	14.8	1.9	4.5	D	7.6	22.2	2,225	238	90	4,816	0.1
Martin	5.2	0	5.4	14.2	3.8	7	7.3	16	13.6	5,615	283	391	9,971	-0.4
Meeker	-0.2	0.2	12.1	21.2	D	6.1	4.9	8.7	17.9	5,365	232	224	10,952	2.6
Mille Lacs	0.4	D	9.8	8.3	5.7	6.5	4.3	D	34.3	6,600	255	452	12,971	1.7
Morrison	3.7	0.2	10.3	9.3	6.1	8	4.3	D	23.6	7,965	241	634	16,255	3.3
Mower	-4.1	D	4.5	20.5	D	5	3.2	D	15.4	8,970	227	774	17,058	0.2
Murray	16.9	D	9	D	3	6.4	4.5	D	16.8	2,215	265	86	4,658	2.2
Nicollet	2.4	-0.1	4.3	24.7	D	4.1	4.4	D	21.6	5,980	176	331	13,621	5.8
Nobles	5.8	-0.1	5.1	30.1	3.6	7	5.4	D	13.2	4,005	183	318	8,698	1.9
Norman	-7.5	0	D	0.1	10.1	6.3	D	19.6	25	1,710	259	108	3,442	0.6
Olmsted	-0.3	0	4.7	8.7	4.2	4.9	3.2	54.2	8.6	26,805	173	2,224	66,672	10.2
Otter Tail	0.6	0.1	10.5	18.2	4.5	7	4.2	14.6	16.7	16,335	280	774	36,282	1.9
Pennington	2.2	0	2	9.1	D	4.5	2.2	D	12.7	2,930	206	191	6,552	4
Pine	3.1	D	11.1	2.7	D	6.9	3.6	9.3	38.9	7,260	249	541	17,635	2.1
Pipestone	14.6	D	10.3	9.5	8.1	5.2	2.5	D	15.6	2,020	222	137	4,511	0.6
Polk	2.7	0.2	8.7	15.7	3.6	6.4	4.2	D	21.3	6,855	217	579	15,039	2.9
Pope	-5.6	D	5.9	23.8	3	7.3	5.9	D	20.8	2,785	254	129	6,697	4.1
Ramsey	0	0	4.2	10.6	9.3	3.9	8.8	13.3	16.6	87,455	160	16,699	220,680	1.6
Red Lake	25.7	0	6.3	D	D	4.6	D	4.2	18.3	940	233	37	1,944	-0.2
Redwood	1.5	D	4.8	26.5	2.3	5.8	7.7	6.9	19.4	3,550	232	190	7,340	0.9
Renville	8.4	0.1	5.7	18.5	4	3.4	D	D	23.1	3,610	247	211	7,353	0
Rice	-0.5	0.2	7.5	21.9	D	5.6	4.3	10.4	15.1	11,920	181	766	25,125	2.7
Rock	19.4	D	5.8	7.5	3.9	4.7	14.7	11.6	14.5	2,310	243	103	4,327	1.5
Roseau	6.3	0	1.7	53.1	1.5	3.8	3.3	8.5	12.2	3,325	217	131	7,649	2.4
St. Louis	0	5.4	5.6	5	6.5	7.3	5.8	25.8	17.5	47,420	237	5,051	105,002	1.9
Scott	0.1	0.2	14.6	16.7	5.7	5.5	4.6	7.4	16.1	17,885	123	1,304	51,946	10.2
Sherburne	0	D	13.9	15.4	3.1	7.2	3.5	10.5	17.6	14,000	148	1,013	34,312	6
Sibley	6.1	0	9.4	18.6	2.1	2.8	3.4	D	16.5	3,205	216	147	6,611	0.4
Stearns	1.2	0.2	9.3	12.5	6.3	7.6	7.2	19.2	14.8	27,605	175	2,425	65,265	5.3
Steele	-2.4	D	4.1	30.3	D	7.2	17.7	10.6	11.4	7,710	209	514	15,689	2.2
Stevens	7.4	D	7.2	19.8	4.4	6.6	3.2	D	22	1,735	180	119	4,263	2.5
Swift	-9.5	D	7.5	23.2	3.8	6.1	4.5	D	24.1	2,235	238	155	4,837	0
Todd	3.2	D	5.7	30	1.6	4.5	3.8	17.4	17.4	5,985	244	385	13,293	2.9
Traverse	-13	0	4.1	3.5	D	7.9	D	13.6	26.7	960	289	76	2,105	1.5
Wabasha	2	D	7.4	22.9	2.6	5.7	5.7	D	16.5	4,970	230	210	10,257	2.6
Wadena	1.3	0	9.4	9.4	3.2	6.1	3.6	D	24.4	3,855	282	403	7,123	3.2
Waseca	1.9	D	6.7	30.2	3.8	4.8	5.6	9.7	21	4,260	227	233	7,943	0.5
Washington	0.3	0.1	6.7	13.8	8.1	7.5	8	13.5	12.9	42,395	165	2,082	99,459	7.7
Watonwan	0.6	D	8.6	27.2	2.2	3.6	5.5	10.3	18	2,325	214	118	5,054	0.1
Wilkin	-8.4	D	4.5	1.3	D	3.1	8.6	13.4	14.5	1,460	231	93	3,146	2.2
Winona	1.6	D	4	29.1	D	5.5	3.9	9.7	15.7	9,780	192	616	21,237	2.3
Wright	0.3	D	15.4	16	3.3	8.1	4.7	11	13.9	20,420	152	880	52,458	7.1
Yellow Medicine	6.1	D	9.4	5.3	5.1	4.5	7.3	D	28.7	2,485	252	154	4,768	0.2

1. Per 1,000 resident population estimated as of July 1 of the year shown.

STATE County	Housing units, 2013-2017								Civilian labor force, 2018				Civilian employment[6], 2013-2017		
	Occupied units										Unemployment			Percent	
			Owner-occupied			Renter-occupied									
				Median owner cost as a percent of income			Median rent as a percent	Sub-standard						Management, business, science, and arts	Construction, production, and maintenance occupations
	Total	Percent	Median value[1]	With a mort-gage	Without a mort-gage[2]	Median rent[3]	of income[2]	units[4] (percent)	Total	Percent change, 2017-2018	Total	Rate[5]	Total		
	89	90	91	92	93	94	95	96	97	98	99	100	101	102	103

MINNESOTA— Cont'd

STATE County	89	90	91	92	93	94	95	96	97	98	99	100	101	102	103
Fillmore	8,614	79.8	148,300	21.0	11.2	606	26.4	3.2	11,534	1.1	357	3.1	10,671	34.8	29.5
Freeborn	12,958	76.8	105,100	19.2	10.3	642	27.1	1.9	16,044	-0.6	512	3.2	15,278	27.5	33.0
Goodhue	19,345	74.6	191,400	20.0	11.9	779	28.4	2	26,823	-0.1	737	2.7	23,976	35.9	26.2
Grant	2,536	79.3	104,900	20.5	11.4	580	27.3	1.2	3,303	0.7	131	4	2,853	31.7	30.3
Hennepin	499,104	62.4	245,400	20.4	11.4	1,031	28.9	2.9	703,310	0.7	17,457	2.5	674,973	48.5	13.6
Houston	8,114	80.3	164,200	20.3	12.1	677	27.1	1.1	10,460	0	299	2.9	10,094	35.6	29.2
Hubbard	8,758	82.3	182,700	22.9	12.3	648	26.8	3	9,851	0.3	490	5	9,611	32.3	26.0
Isanti	14,571	81.6	172,900	21.6	12.1	914	28.8	2.3	21,134	0.7	788	3.7	19,857	29.2	31.1
Itasca	19,356	80.4	156,100	21.7	11.8	655	28.8	3.1	21,820	0.4	1,175	5.4	20,287	31.7	26.7
Jackson	4,350	78.8	114,100	17.6	10.2	629	22.7	1.3	5,733	-0.4	167	2.9	5,279	34.5	31.0
Kanabec	6,353	81.5	147,200	23.0	14.0	789	29.9	2.7	8,934	-1.1	489	5.5	7,655	27.6	31.9
Kandiyohi	16,765	73.9	167,000	21.2	12.1	709	28.2	2.2	24,821	-0.1	726	2.9	21,874	33.4	28.7
Kittson	1,891	80.4	71,800	18.1	10.0	554	24.4	1.3	2,346	-0.9	69	2.9	2,189	32.8	31.8
Koochiching	5,629	78.7	108,300	20.0	10.0	595	33.3	1.4	5,956	-0.2	362	6.1	5,832	27.1	29.5
Lac qui Parle	3,171	80.5	81,100	18.7	10.0	560	24.9	1.3	3,528	0.1	128	3.6	3,458	37.3	26.3
Lake	5,082	83.8	165,800	21.8	10.2	644	30	3.6	5,478	-0.5	172	3.1	4,803	42.0	24.2
Lake of the Woods	1,533	81.6	128,400	21.1	12.7	623	26.5	2.1	2,405	0.9	91	3.8	2,053	22.0	42.5
Le Sueur	10,844	81.9	190,700	21.2	11.4	779	27	1.9	15,962	0.7	662	4.1	14,665	31.9	33.2
Lincoln	2,484	78.9	95,300	19.8	11.7	596	23.7	0.8	3,269	-2.7	98	3	2,816	35.2	29.3
Lyon	10,060	68.2	135,900	18.5	10.0	621	26.7	2.5	14,818		426	2.9	13,863	35.4	28.4
McLeod	14,760	78.3	150,400	20.5	11.0	777	27.2	1.3	19,500	0	610	3.1	19,282	30.2	32.2
Mahnomen	1,947	69.6	97,300	20.2	13.0	567	27.5	3.7	2,329	-1.4	106	4.6	2,193	27.3	24.8
Marshall	3,953	81.1	104,500	17.8	10.5	565	23.4	1.6	5,440	-0.6	315	5.8	4,832	32.6	32.3
Martin	8,685	74.6	112,400	18.6	10.2	593	27.5	1.8	10,303		323	3.1	10,236	32.5	27.6
Meeker	9,164	78.7	161,600	21.3	11.9	714	26.3	2.4	13,143	-0.7	458	3.5	11,589	32.2	34.0
Mille Lacs	10,116	73.9	151,400	22.9	13.1	735	27.7	2.7	12,788	0.5	619	4.8	12,117	27.8	32.9
Morrison	13,327	79.3	159,100	21.8	12.1	689	28.2	1.8	17,576	-0.5	823	4.7	16,502	29.1	32.1
Mower	15,524	73.3	114,700	18.8	10.0	704	29.1	2	20,450	-0.5	547	2.7	19,157	29.2	32.7
Murray	3,713	81.3	107,700	18.1	10.5	601	24.1	0.6	4,906	0.5	182	3.7	4,222	34.8	29.6
Nicollet	12,662	72.8	178,000	20.9	10.3	829	27	0.9	20,756	0.7	456	2.2	18,581	38.3	21.1
Nobles	7,917	71.1	118,300	20.2	10.0	690	26.6	4.5	11,284	-0.5	296	2.6	10,580	23.9	41.6
Norman	2,733	80.9	88,500	17.5	11.5	555	26.5	3.3	3,379	-0.5	145	4.3	3,144	34.1	28.6
Olmsted	59,804	73.8	188,300	19.0	10.0	884	28.6	2.7	87,757	1.2	2,009	2.3	80,838	49.6	15.3
Otter Tail	24,300	78.8	170,900	20.0	11.2	656	28.1	2.1	31,441	-0.3	1,128	3.6	28,208	32.9	29.9
Pennington	5,883	73.6	133,300	19.5	10.5	627	25.9	1.4	8,797	0	369	4.2	7,502	30.0	28.7
Pine	10,752	78.4	151,600	24.3	13.4	713	29.6	3	14,850	-0.9	720	4.8	12,594	25.1	30.7
Pipestone	4,019	74.9	91,200	19.5	10.0	594	24	2.8	4,971	2.3	143	2.9	4,328	30.3	34.5
Polk	12,609	73.3	152,600	19.5	11.6	689	29.5	1.5	16,786	-1.2	615	3.7	15,866	35.0	25.6
Pope	4,898	79.2	163,600	21.1	11.5	659	27.2	1.6	6,431	1.1	166	2.6	5,510	36.2	26.9
Ramsey	208,504	59.3	208,700	20.9	11.1	934	30	4.4	288,814	0.7	7,742	2.7	278,185	43.6	16.5
Red Lake	1,718	82.0	107,300	18.5	10.4	495	27.7	1.6	2,231	-0.8	115	5.2	2,044	30.4	30.7
Redwood	6,310	77.2	97,400	18.7	10.0	617	24.8	1	7,614	-0.8	274	3.6	7,533	33.1	28.6
Renville	6,219	79.5	100,100	19.1	10.0	599	27.8	1.2	8,787		345	3.9	7,443	32.8	33.9
Rice	22,899	74.3	188,400	22.3	10.8	796	30	2	36,852	0.9	1,020	2.8	34,378	35.6	26.6
Rock	3,985	74.5	133,600	19.9	10.5	631	22	1.9	5,726	-2.5	132	2.3	4,779	35.3	28.4
Roseau	6,123	78.7	118,500	20.4	10.3	650	25.2	3.6	7,989	-1.9	265	3.3	8,329	27.8	43.2
St. Louis	85,662	70.9	146,700	20.2	11.2	730	30.6	2.4	101,957	-0.5	3,755	3.7	98,224	35.6	20.8
Scott	47,864	83.0	272,000	20.5	10.0	1,130	28.7	2	82,820	0.8	2,062	2.5	77,624	41.2	20.9
Sherburne	31,181	83.1	204,100	20.3	10.0	963	29.3	1.8	51,700	0.7	1,631	3.2	49,701	34.9	26.4
Sibley	5,993	78.2	142,800	19.9	10.8	679	24.8	1.6	8,473	0.7	268	3.2	7,794	29.1	37.9
Stearns	58,657	68.7	171,300	20.1	10.6	774	26.7	3	89,884	-0.2	2,643	2.9	85,604	32.7	25.3
Steele	14,450	76.5	154,300	19.9	11.2	758	29.4	2.5	20,563	0.1	605	2.9	18,539	32.8	29.0
Stevens	3,630	66.5	150,800	16.4	10.0	689	37.9	1.3	5,457	-0.9	129	2.4	5,248	33.9	25.1
Swift	4,217	69.2	102,100	18.3	10.1	615	23.9	1.5	5,037	-0.2	184	3.7	4,751	30.0	32.9
Todd	9,777	81.8	141,000	22.5	12.7	630	25.7	4.7	13,587	0.7	525	3.9	11,260	28.3	38.1
Traverse	1,576	80.4	79,800	20.7	10.0	607	23.3	1.4	1,760	-0.6	57	3.2	1,640	36.2	23.2
Wabasha	8,867	80.9	167,300	21.2	11.4	694	25.5	1.4	12,295	1.1	361	2.9	11,379	34.4	28.0
Wadena	5,704	77.6	118,900	21.6	12.6	635	28.8	2.7	5,917	1.5	306	5.2	6,060	23.9	34.6
Waseca	7,375	77.8	147,800	19.6	11.0	611	27.9	1.9	9,002	-3.2	366	4.1	9,516	31.3	31.3
Washington	92,005	81.3	264,300	20.1	10.0	1,246	28.5	1.4	141,974	0.7	3,558	2.5	133,811	46.0	16.2
Watonwan	4,327	73.5	94,500	18.9	11.0	616	21	1.6	6,509	0.2	225	3.5	5,641	28.1	38.2
Wilkin	2,852	76.0	114,400	19.0	10.0	496	29.4	1.2	3,558	0.2	107	3	3,286	37.6	26.7
Winona	19,228	70.0	158,400	20.5	10.7	647	29.5	1.9	28,804	-0.6	753	2.6	28,578	35.1	25.0
Wright	46,568	82.4	211,500	20.5	10.2	924	27.2	2	74,674	0.7	2,219	3	70,509	34.0	26.8
Yellow Medicine	4,157	77.9	99,100	19.6	10.3	603	27.6	1.2	5,379	0.5	161	3	5,014	33.4	29.9

1. Specified owner-occupied units.　　2. A value of 10.0 represents 10 percent or less; a value of 50.0 represents 50 percent or more.　　3. Specified renter-occupied units.　　4. Overcrowded or lacking complete plumbing facilities.　　5. Percent of civilian labor force.　　6. Civilian employed persons 16 years old and over.

Table B. States and Counties — **Nonfarm Employment and Agriculture**

STATE County	Private nonfarm establishments, employment and payroll, 2016									Agriculture, 2017			
	Number of establishments	Employment						Annual payroll		Farms			Farm producers whose primary occupation is farming (percent)
		Total	Health care and social assistance	Manufacturing	Retail trade	Finance and insurance	Professional, scientific, and technical services	Total (mil dol)	Average per employee (dollars)	Number	Percent with: Fewer than 50 acres	1000 acres or more	
	104	105	106	107	108	109	110	111	112	113	114	115	116
MINNESOTA— Cont'd													
Fillmore	600	4,686	850	857	757	239	133	158	33,653	1,401	31.7	5.1	42.6
Freeborn	781	11,569	2,498	2,739	1,999	522	192	428	36,999	1,076	35.4	11.8	51.8
Goodhue	1,312	20,628	3,478	4,808	2,562	442	453	875	42,428	1,461	36.6	4.4	45.2
Grant	199	1,431	360	104	247	72	37	51	35,324	524	20.6	16.6	42.4
Hennepin	40,301	888,172	135,045	74,644	77,584	84,038	85,258	55,619	62,622	467	68.7	1.7	45.1
Houston	426	4,023	1,010	476	575	103	98	126	31,374	891	21.4	2.2	41.5
Hubbard	575	4,545	822	853	1,036	146	106	161	35,533	384	21.9	2.1	34.6
Isanti	835	8,978	2,009	1,395	1,890	309	205	340	37,863	805	46.0	3.4	34.7
Itasca	1,164	14,132	3,641	1,009	2,424	421	558	520	36,815	337	27.0	2.4	36.1
Jackson	312	4,767	1,287	1,169	355	91	53	174	36,460	799	25.4	13.0	55.1
Kanabec	292	2,966	912	525	543	91	77	114	38,316	624	33.2	1.6	41.2
Kandiyohi	1,408	19,658	5,419	2,674	3,104	547	565	709	36,083	1,220	32.3	9.3	39.9
Kittson	143	1,261	325	203	298	57	22	44	35,256	528	8.3	28.6	47.2
Koochiching	392	3,788	680	D	779	129	63	136	35,916	181	9.9	6.1	36.7
Lac qui Parle	204	1,717	553	144	300	92	18	53	30,824	853	20.2	14.8	44.9
Lake	298	2,868	490	507	343	115	50	110	38,259	42	54.8	NA	32.9
Lake of the Woods	159	1,373	D	165	236	30	14	42	30,744	134	14.2	14.2	35.2
Le Sueur	702	7,406	779	2,945	717	219	186	327	44,112	937	39.7	6.7	35.4
Lincoln	211	1,515	520	19	244	53	35	42	27,496	672	20.5	13.2	48.9
Lyon	807	12,785	2,381	1,928	1,945	1,106	373	523	40,946	893	19.9	12.1	50.6
McLeod	978	16,258	3,118	5,590	2,264	412	412	687	42,280	880	38.4	7.8	46.1
Mahnomen	101	1,785	340	D	143	56	17	54	30,055	311	19.0	19.9	46.4
Marshall	260	1,573	305	223	249	119	28	67	42,429	1,086	7.2	22.4	42.9
Martin	635	8,078	1,706	1,478	1,317	331	189	316	39,135	911	23.6	16.4	56.7
Meeker	565	6,467	1,353	1,777	922	199	96	235	36,350	1,028	35.1	7.4	44.2
Mille Lacs	696	8,547	1,823	1,057	1,309	206	112	263	30,777	707	40.0	2.7	36.3
Morrison	871	7,919	1,530	1,124	1,592	260	182	274	34,566	1,760	25.0	2.4	46.7
Mower	846	14,602	2,624	3,817	1,733	312	226	700	47,936	1,068	34.9	12.5	47.7
Murray	307	2,650	433	D	326	153	75	87	32,797	864	24.1	14.0	53.2
Nicollet	658	12,832	2,359	3,641	1,040	215	434	511	39,808	689	22.5	7.7	51.9
Nobles	601	9,148	1,450	3,011	1,558	242	255	323	35,309	885	27.0	15.0	55.6
Norman	183	1,284	439	D	185	82	30	51	39,665	505	13.5	35.8	55.1
Olmsted	3,575	95,956	19,904	4,307	11,594	1,703	D	5,349	55,741	1,139	43.2	6.2	43.2
Otter Tail	1,673	18,780	3,997	4,099	2,862	546	398	666	35,456	2,544	19.4	7.2	41.7
Pennington	397	9,350	1,290	941	1,143	130	335	371	39,652	409	15.4	20.8	44.6
Pine	616	7,223	1,464	332	1,106	177	114	191	26,409	823	26.6	1.8	43.7
Pipestone	339	3,114	480	491	591	112	81	103	33,199	595	32.9	8.9	49.9
Polk	768	9,406	2,199	1,726	1,478	243	210	329	34,978	1,258	14.2	25.4	56.8
Pope	370	3,858	642	915	376	120	248	156	40,501	837	25.9	12.1	42.7
Ramsey	13,536	307,529	62,278	23,081	27,738	18,528	15,057	16,980	55,214	55	96.4	NA	59.8
Red Lake	103	607	91	D	118	61	20	21	34,578	263	11.0	19.8	48.1
Redwood	525	5,721	877	904	813	339	80	195	34,037	1,134	23.2	12.0	55.1
Renville	467	4,632	892	1,245	554	174	162	177	38,154	1,026	24.2	19.3	54.6
Rice	1,543	24,908	3,308	4,014	2,864	450	470	889	35,702	1,242	42.1	3.0	37.7
Rock	264	2,826	863	292	408	276	91	91	32,176	701	26.5	9.3	53.0
Roseau	415	6,854	772	3,812	850	174	79	248	36,249	842	14.4	16.2	39.0
St. Louis	5,339	88,503	24,822	4,126	12,618	4,411	3,721	3,668	41,449	779	27.3	1.8	36.1
Scott	3,338	44,084	4,949	6,688	5,215	709	2,411	2,141	48,568	740	50.0	2.7	32.4
Sherburne	2,039	22,123	4,271	3,559	3,199	417	610	942	42,590	501	47.7	5.8	40.7
Sibley	350	3,520	610	898	366	136	56	125	35,453	898	30.7	10.9	49.2
Stearns	4,428	83,525	16,872	11,748	11,363	4,135	2,864	3,615	43,282	2,951	24.4	2.3	49.8
Steele	1,005	19,226	2,665	4,997	2,729	2,168	247	864	44,962	746	39.9	9.9	47.4
Stevens	314	4,675	1,461	1,031	557	102	108	167	35,754	553	27.3	19.7	52.9
Swift	304	3,041	641	611	398	105	82	104	34,312	760	25.0	13.8	49.4
Todd	544	5,796	1,559	1,758	783	208	83	210	36,188	1,604	22.1	2.1	42.0
Traverse	123	839	282	47	191	39	2	25	29,757	411	22.4	30.9	59.1
Wabasha	552	5,448	1,013	1,237	789	157	111	197	36,170	809	22.9	4.8	50.5
Wadena	402	4,040	944	306	746	154	120	144	35,639	516	19.8	4.1	37.3
Waseca	460	5,133	889	1,657	710	170	167	200	38,956	729	33.2	9.1	48.8
Washington	5,870	81,510	12,925	8,466	14,185	6,193	3,818	3,409	41,822	612	64.4	3.4	44.4
Watonwan	294	3,721	498	1,343	458	130	40	117	31,561	497	27.8	15.1	52.0
Wilkin	156	1,763	463	D	183	55	D	61	34,832	391	16.9	37.9	64.5
Winona	1,156	23,755	3,467	5,109	2,844	549	489	899	37,855	1,034	25.0	4.5	49.5
Wright	3,285	36,834	5,711	5,744	7,255	731	1,013	1,515	41,141	1,338	45.1	3.3	37.2
Yellow Medicine	328	3,329	876	224	384	121	D	133	39,837	852	23.8	13.6	47.1

Table B. States and Counties — **Agriculture**

STATE County	Acreage (1,000)	Percent change, 2012-2017	Average size of farm	Total irrigated (1,000)	Total cropland (1,000)	Value of land and buildings — Average per farm	Average per acre	Value of machinery and equipment, average per farm (dollars)	Total (mil dol)	Average per farm (acres)	Crops	Livestock and poultry products	Organic farms (number)	Farms with internet access (percent)	Total ($1,000)	Percent of farms
	117	118	119	120	121	122	123	124	125	126	127	128	129	130	131	132
MINNESOTA— Cont'd																
Fillmore	376	-11.1	268	0.7	287.6	1,488,701	5,554	185,396	291.7	208,242	48.4	51.6	44	73.7	8,723	67.1
Freeborn	394	3.1	366	1.7	374.9	2,208,230	6,030	250,401	364.0	338,289	60.7	39.3	12	84.3	11,605	74.9
Goodhue	385	-3.4	263	6.0	325.8	1,633,399	6,204	219,974	348.6	238,596	49.9	50.1	41	83.4	11,779	59.3
Grant	324	7.0	619	5.9	303.0	2,724,030	4,403	298,988	190.3	363,141	75.6	24.4	NA	74.8	7,264	90.6
Hennepin	46	-33.4	98	0.3	36.6	1,322,909	13,464	133,330	58.6	125,418	88.7	11.3	4	77.5	193	27.0
Houston	217	-5.3	244	0.2	125.8	1,044,963	4,290	130,913	116.2	130,386	38.7	61.3	22	78.0	3,372	68.5
Hubbard	95	-19.1	246	24.5	53.4	651,843	2,646	107,044	44.2	115,221	88.6	11.4	2	82.8	495	18.5
Isanti	132	-7.0	164	4.0	96.3	639,469	3,887	100,672	48.7	60,463	74.2	25.8	10	81.7	635	12.5
Itasca	72	-14.7	213	D	36.6	604,662	2,842	67,203	8.0	23,751	64.7	35.3	NA	77.7	D	5.9
Jackson	356	-0.4	446	D	335.5	2,870,744	6,438	308,732	314.5	393,630	58.2	41.8	1	88.2	9,173	78.2
Kanabec	119	-7.8	190	2.2	66.2	504,920	2,652	89,170	29.8	47,808	60.2	39.8	7	69.2	109	19.7
Kandiyohi	456	9.8	374	26.6	402.8	1,949,625	5,218	260,271	424.1	347,605	47.0	53.0	7	76.4	10,884	81.2
Kittson	479	1.9	908	2.4	408.6	2,041,371	2,249	319,681	128.3	243,081	95.6	4.4	NA	76.3	12,450	91.5
Koochiching	56	4.5	308	D	28.2	444,918	1,443	85,478	6.9	38,050	64.6	35.4	NA	72.4	320	14.4
Lac qui Parle	420	-6.0	492	5.1	375.2	2,204,166	4,478	275,311	249.9	292,939	68.3	31.7	11	81.2	6,064	88.2
Lake	4	-4.6	85	0.0	1.4	308,042	3,629	49,065	0.4	8,524	83.0	17.0	2	92.9	41	7.1
Lake of the Woods	91	1.1	681	1.2	67.8	1,156,249	1,697	172,314	17.3	128,940	95.9	4.1	NA	67.2	772	46.3
Le Sueur	249	3.1	266	1.8	224.2	1,643,885	6,175	180,636	181.4	193,551	64.0	36.0	8	75.5	4,652	72.8
Lincoln	298	2.4	443	D	269.8	2,143,527	4,836	261,768	186.0	276,847	60.5	39.5	3	75.3	7,124	80.4
Lyon	395	-4.3	442	0.4	366.3	2,589,529	5,852	300,380	412.3	461,736	44.3	55.7	3	84.3	5,565	63.0
McLeod	269	1.8	305	0.1	248.9	1,747,482	5,724	226,601	185.6	210,928	69.3	30.7	9	78.5	4,093	66.4
Mahnomen	221	2.5	711	D	186.3	2,102,461	2,955	251,243	70.1	225,392	94.4	5.6	2	76.8	2,742	69.8
Marshall	902	10.0	831	D	824.1	2,056,182	2,474	274,618	261.5	240,750	94.2	5.8	2	71.3	18,205	85.7
Martin	449	4.8	493	0.5	434.3	3,308,478	6,712	386,978	635.5	697,610	41.8	58.2	4	86.2	8,613	79.7
Meeker	301	-0.8	293	8.8	262.1	1,521,946	5,190	204,806	265.2	257,930	44.7	55.3	7	76.7	5,200	72.9
Mille Lacs	126	-1.5	178	0.5	86.9	552,471	3,102	103,477	43.9	62,139	52.9	47.1	6	77.2	190	24.0
Morrison	382	-12.4	217	30.3	232.8	719,062	3,310	156,473	394.7	224,273	17.3	82.7	10	75.7	2,301	39.8
Mower	447	-0.6	419	5.0	420.9	2,852,833	6,813	279,549	413.2	386,915	58.7	41.3	15	84.5	10,064	74.3
Murray	395	-3.1	457	D	362.6	2,819,738	6,166	316,318	337.8	391,005	54.5	45.5	10	82.1	5,522	65.5
Nicollet	265	-3.4	384	0.0	249.5	2,691,522	7,002	299,514	339.3	492,462	40.6	59.4	1	83.5	2,277	47.8
Nobles	414	8.9	468	0.1	392.3	3,236,081	6,911	399,982	519.0	586,400	39.6	60.4	1	82.4	8,236	81.5
Norman	526	-1.2	1,041	1.4	498.9	3,437,726	3,301	410,892	218.3	432,202	94.3	5.7	4	76.0	5,243	78.4
Olmsted	286	8.1	251	0.1	239.1	1,671,227	6,657	184,486	214.4	188,248	56.7	43.3	15	83.5	9,079	61.1
Otter Tail	794	-10.0	312	75.5	576.2	927,172	2,969	150,686	349.9	137,547	57.4	42.6	33	72.9	8,675	64.2
Pennington	286	5.2	699	D	249.2	1,347,472	1,928	231,758	66.5	162,484	91.6	8.4	NA	77.0	5,293	75.3
Pine	160	-21.3	195	0.4	81.7	460,529	2,364	73,400	39.0	47,361	38.6	61.4	2	75.8	174	18.1
Pipestone	240	-0.8	403	2.2	210.6	2,352,844	5,833	343,986	326.1	547,988	30.0	70.0	5	88.1	1,582	49.2
Polk	1,023	-6.6	813	5.6	938.5	2,667,646	3,280	391,409	429.8	341,630	93.8	6.2	18	76.1	17,113	77.8
Pope	333	-0.3	398	32.0	280.3	1,648,542	4,144	254,858	199.3	238,106	63.8	36.2	8	75.7	4,173	74.8
Ramsey	1	-10.8	12	0.1	0.4	312,488	26,646	45,670	3.0	53,655	74.7	25.3	8	94.5	D	1.8
Red Lake	209	5.1	794	1.1	189.3	1,881,249	2,370	305,925	65.6	249,426	89.0	11.0	NA	80.6	2,688	81.0
Redwood	524	0.5	462	0.0	494.9	2,882,387	6,239	315,623	453.2	399,613	58.2	41.8	4	80.2	6,220	66.6
Renville	624	0.4	608	1.2	598.2	3,990,664	6,560	376,170	609.2	593,752	61.1	38.9	1	80.9	5,570	84.6
Rice	226	-4.3	182	2.8	192.6	1,249,054	6,857	145,442	205.0	165,042	49.6	50.4	13	76.9	6,228	62.0
Rock	288	2.6	411	D	266.4	3,133,759	7,631	322,110	419.1	597,825	34.2	65.8	1	89.7	2,105	73.9
Roseau	558	0.4	663	0.0	463.1	1,155,325	1,743	183,983	129.5	153,853	84.3	15.7	3	78.3	10,057	71.9
St. Louis	139	9.0	178	D	67.1	354,725	1,992	61,899	16.1	20,718	57.1	42.9	8	77.3	48	3.3
Scott	116	-18.2	156	0.0	98.0	1,184,671	7,590	120,351	75.6	102,122	58.9	41.1	15	80.4	900	38.9
Sherburne	103	-8.7	205	36.4	78.5	1,055,081	5,155	187,885	89.6	178,838	83.9	16.1	4	84.2	1,068	25.0
Sibley	350	1.1	390	0.5	326.6	2,629,735	6,746	283,199	318.7	354,924	57.2	42.8	8	82.4	4,299	62.0
Stearns	651	-14.1	221	51.8	515.9	1,135,611	5,149	185,876	748.0	253,466	23.9	76.1	57	78.0	5,926	56.4
Steele	251	5.6	337	2.0	233.5	2,088,084	6,201	251,529	251.8	337,586	60.7	39.3	11	79.5	5,216	71.0
Stevens	330	3.4	597	21.3	308.0	3,032,762	5,077	289,508	327.4	592,118	42.6	57.4	4	85.7	3,945	75.9
Swift	345	-4.4	454	26.8	316.4	2,289,023	5,043	305,866	284.2	373,895	53.0	47.0	NA	81.2	4,405	84.3
Todd	333	-15.4	208	12.9	210.5	570,580	2,745	111,342	179.5	111,884	31.6	68.4	23	70.4	1,987	45.0
Traverse	365	4.6	887	0.8	350.9	4,415,585	4,979	484,191	210.5	512,088	78.3	21.7	NA	76.6	4,735	83.5
Wabasha	231	-6.1	285	1.7	175.8	1,574,440	5,519	244,686	186.3	230,295	43.0	57.0	11	83.3	6,359	70.1
Wadena	128	-13.9	249	15.7	75.3	546,823	2,200	88,995	52.8	102,411	56.5	43.5	15	71.1	865	41.3
Waseca	247	6.6	339	D	231.0	2,243,731	6,621	279,994	275.0	377,284	48.2	51.8	9	77.9	5,793	80.9
Washington	76	-5.9	124	4.1	57.8	1,081,821	8,695	111,931	59.8	97,676	90.7	9.3	10	83.0	1,036	25.0
Watonwan	252	6.5	508	6.8	241.1	3,604,518	7,097	382,501	269.5	542,310	54.2	45.8	NA	82.3	9,171	87.3
Wilkin	428	-3.6	1,095	1.2	414.6	4,239,436	3,872	442,751	185.6	474,673	99.5	0.5	3	79.0	4,555	85.9
Winona	269	-3.1	260	0.0	180.8	1,494,722	5,753	181,789	228.2	220,662	30.6	69.4	58	78.9	3,952	60.3
Wright	241	-16.5	180	6.8	203.7	1,158,403	6,441	150,834	196.5	146,867	57.5	42.5	20	79.8	1,301	38.1
Yellow Medicine	384	-2.9	450	0.5	355.3	2,435,244	5,408	275,914	256.4	300,971	66.4	33.6	5	81.3	5,699	74.2

Water Use, Wholesale Trade, Retail Trade, and Real Estate

STATE County	Water use, 2015 Public supply water withdrawn (mil gal/day)	Public supply gallons withdrawn per person per day	Wholesale Trade[1], 2012 Number of establishments	Number of employees	Sales (mil dol)	Average payroll (mil dol)	Retail Trade[2], 2012 Number of establishments	Number of employees	Sales (mil dol)	Average payroll (mil dol)	Real estate and rental and leasing,[2] 2012 Number of establishments	Number of employees	Sales (mil dol)	Average payroll (mil dol)
	133	134	135	136	137	138	139	140	141	142	143	144	145	146
MINNESOTA— Cont'd														
Fillmore	1.28	61.4	24	256	362.7	12.1	90	653	189.5	14.2	6	D	D	D
Freeborn	3.49	114.0	43	516	479.1	24.3	137	1,806	559.8	43.7	22	73	10.2	1.6
Goodhue	3.09	66.5	42	566	582.2	25.8	222	2,356	737.9	55.5	39	109	21.1	3.5
Grant	0.31	52.5	10	131	957.4	7.9	32	202	60.9	4.4	2	D	D	D
Hennepin	73.39	60.0	2,046	36,257	32,265.1	2,340.4	4,184	74,958	23,926.9	2,033.8	2,218	17,614	4,192.5	829.4
Houston	0.86	45.8	16	132	108.0	4.4	70	624	136.2	12.1	4	10	2.4	0.3
Hubbard	0.67	32.4	3	D	D	D	103	947	216.1	19.3	14	D	D	D
Isanti	1.32	34.3	24	172	79.9	6.5	97	1,522	482.8	36.8	29	D	D	D
Itasca	2.02	44.5	31	234	133.0	11.1	198	2,347	568.6	50.9	30	82	12.9	2.1
Jackson	0.56	55.6	14	270	297.2	10.5	43	327	85.2	5.8	7	D	D	D
Kanabec	0.38	24.0	6	27	9.0	0.8	44	527	130.7	10.1	2	D	D	D
Kandiyohi	4.56	107.2	70	D	D	D	224	2,988	666.4	61.3	47	130	15.5	2.7
Kittson	0.56	126.6	15	77	191.2	4.3	31	268	128.4	4.9	2	D	D	D
Koochiching	0.71	55.3	11	50	15.2	1.8	78	749	189.5	16.0	13	33	4.5	0.9
Lac qui Parle	0.37	54.0	12	122	235.9	5.3	38	309	67.5	5.2	3	7	0.4	0.1
Lake	0.78	73.4	2	D	D	D	43	358	136.0	9.8	9	D	D	D
Lake of the Woods	0.17	43.3	4	20	18.2	0.7	27	204	53.2	3.7	4	7	0.6	0.1
Le Sueur	2.32	83.9	28	246	268.8	10.7	86	783	210.7	14.5	23	32	5.6	0.8
Lincoln	0.99	171.5	6	61	106.9	3.5	38	242	66.9	4.7	4	9	1.3	0.1
Lyon	2.70	105.2	36	D	D	D	134	2,020	458.9	41.4	29	119	10.3	4.6
McLeod	2.74	76.3	32	504	260.1	27.3	156	2,113	501.4	42.3	35	92	15.4	2.4
Mahnomen	0.27	49.5	6	D	D	D	20	161	26.8	2.8	3	D	D	D
Marshall	0.45	47.8	20	227	431.5	11.2	36	271	123.0	7.2	2	D	D	D
Martin	1.61	80.4	40	712	1,166.5	44.7	96	1,242	294.5	27.5	17	37	17.3	0.9
Meeker	1.25	54.1	20	206	224.9	8.8	83	809	250.0	19.3	12	26	5.9	0.9
Mille Lacs	0.43	16.7	26	238	180.0	7.9	99	1,141	252.6	21.2	26	71	7.8	1.3
Morrison	1.95	59.5	26	337	238.0	10.6	135	1,487	419.9	32.3	16	49	5.5	0.8
Mower	5.87	150.1	28	D	D	D	132	1,826	370.0	35.4	21	126	20.1	1.8
Murray	0.55	65.4	11	131	354.5	6.2	42	266	46.8	4.4	6	26	1.7	0.6
Nicollet	4.22	126.5	34	415	372.2	19.5	74	869	232.6	23.1	21	135	9.0	3.6
Nobles	2.15	98.8	35	D	D	D	111	1,471	328.0	30.1	13	46	3.2	0.5
Norman	0.29	43.4	16	148	171.2	5.6	28	214	47.0	4.3	4	6	0.7	0.1
Olmsted	12.86	84.9	102	1,210	715.3	58.1	598	10,457	2,447.2	232.4	173	749	143.4	23.0
Otter Tail	3.44	59.6	56	385	738.6	16.8	253	2,903	776.5	64.3	57	95	24.1	2.7
Pennington	1.07	75.3	20	D	D	D	76	1,028	233.5	20.3	12	D	D	D
Pine	0.85	29.2	15	60	12.9	1.3	96	1,030	262.9	20.7	15	50	6.0	0.9
Pipestone	1.81	195.2	20	237	573.1	8.5	52	478	135.5	9.7	3	D	D	D
Polk	8.57	271.8	44	469	960.5	20.0	109	1,377	331.6	28.5	9	50	3.1	1.2
Pope	0.55	49.8	56	D	D	D	41	311	138.5	7.7	6	7	1.6	0.2
Ramsey	52.58	97.7	617	10,538	8,499.7	647.1	1,639	26,639	6,557.0	643.7	684	3,885	1,421.2	176.0
Red Lake	0.64	157.8	5	D	D	D	19	151	61.8	3.5	1	D	D	D
Redwood	0.97	62.7	30	430	287.2	22.3	72	735	169.6	15.9	15	26	3.1	0.3
Renville	1.02	68.5	27	261	559.4	13.4	67	514	120.6	9.0	4	8	1.7	0.4
Rice	5.54	84.7	62	1,013	2,093.8	55.6	202	2,664	683.4	59.6	50	185	48.5	4.0
Rock	1.51	157.3	17	220	726.3	8.8	40	391	104.0	8.1	10	23	3.0	0.5
Roseau	0.71	45.0	7	D	D	D	88	876	271.2	16.7	11	32	2.3	0.5
St. Louis	35.28	176.0	206	2,363	1,301.6	114.0	911	11,842	3,008.1	263.3	207	937	154.8	26.9
Scott	7.84	55.3	152	2,134	2,117.5	132.7	318	4,704	1,337.1	104.4	143	332	72.6	10.9
Sherburne	4.95	54.0	65	497	353.4	23.2	186	2,778	795.5	65.2	74	162	27.9	4.5
Sibley	1.45	97.5	17	D	D	D	54	363	75.9	5.7	11	D	D	D
Stearns	14.58	94.2	183	3,672	2,063.4	161.2	671	10,874	2,917.9	244.9	161	820	132.8	22.7
Steele	4.04	109.9	44	598	531.4	31.4	178	2,699	568.1	55.5	27	292	18.3	5.4
Stevens	0.79	80.6	19	99	522.7	4.8	50	545	210.1	12.8	7	18	1.2	0.3
Swift	0.79	84.6	13	D	D	D	45	373	93.7	7.4	5	73	2.8	1.4
Todd	1.18	48.6	14	132	178.2	5.1	94	722	156.8	13.0	22	D	D	D
Traverse	0.20	58.8	11	103	130.5	5.2	23	182	46.7	3.1	2	D	D	D
Wabasha	1.85	87.1	24	250	191.1	9.7	87	867	223.9	17.7	8	24	2.3	0.3
Wadena	0.93	67.0	17	391	246.9	17.1	74	750	164.3	17.9	6	D	D	D
Waseca	1.67	87.9	24	185	180.0	10.0	61	682	180.6	19.1	12	23	2.5	0.4
Washington	19.23	76.4	176	1,817	4,760.1	103.6	699	12,623	2,976.4	267.4	284	1,069	184.9	38.9
Watonwan	1.29	117.8	14	104	190.1	3.9	40	392	64.3	6.5	5	23	1.1	0.5
Wilkin	0.29	45.3	13	188	315.2	10.6	26	188	68.4	4.8	6	5	2.7	0.5
Winona	3.76	73.9	56	D	D	D	164	2,742	681.9	58.1	41	129	21.2	3.0
Wright	8.09	61.6	100	1,135	636.9	61.6	428	6,934	1,713.5	142.5	93	179	48.6	5.5
Yellow Medicine	2.24	226.8	15	200	647.8	8.3	48	377	100.0	7.0	4	D	D	D

1 Merchant wholesalers, except manufacturers' sales branches and offices.   2. Employer establishments.

Professional Services, Manufacturing, and Accommodation and Food Services

STATE County	Professional, scientific, and technical services, 2012				Manufacturing, 2012				Accommodation and food services, 2012			
	Number of establish-ments	Number of employees	Sales (mil dol)	Average payroll (mil dol)	Number of establish-ments	Number of employees	Receipts (mil dol)	Annual payroll (mil dol)	Number of establis-hments	Number of employees	Receipts (mil dol)	Annual payroll (mil dol)
	147	148	149	150	151	152	153	154	155	156	157	158
MINNESOTA— Cont'd												
Fillmore	36	D	D	D	47	800	332.9	31.9	72	437	16.5	4.4
Freeborn	37	235	24.3	9.5	54	2,572	806.5	106.0	73	1,000	36.7	10.4
Goodhue	74	401	53.9	21.9	87	4,839	1,869.4	223.3	111	3,145	246.2	62.6
Grant	12	D	D	D	14	98	16.7	3.0	14	D	D	D
Hennepin	6,831	74,416	14,339.4	5,730.4	1,675	72,307	22,020.7	4,518.2	2,735	66,296	3,791.2	1,108.5
Houston	24	94	7.7	2.5	22	287	54.9	11.3	35	192	8.3	2.2
Hubbard	32	77	6.2	2.1	35	933	325.8	37.7	83	646	30.3	7.3
Isanti	60	D	D	D	70	1,518	394.8	80.0	53	D	D	D
Itasca	78	D	D	D	44	1,231	471.9	63.9	108	1,294	58.9	16.4
Jackson	16	67	7.5	2.0	14	1,359	D	75.3	21	258	8.7	2.2
Kanabec	18	90	6.6	2.1	17	622	116.0	22.5	27	269	11.1	2.6
Kandiyohi	95	538	60.4	21.5	73	2,916	1,140.0	115.0	91	1,427	55.4	15.4
Kittson	7	D	D	D	6	129	D	5.2	8	D	D	D
Koochiching	17	67	4.5	1.7	18	1,021	D	59.8	47	479	24.2	5.8
Lac qui Parle	9	D	D	D	12	283	D	12.1	13	D	D	D
Lake	13	34	3.9	1.5	18	553	167.8	27.4	66	681	36.6	11.0
Lake of the Woods	6	9	0.5	0.2	5	120	D	7.1	38	487	27.7	6.7
Le Sueur	36	D	D	D	52	2,130	883.4	101.4	48	466	18.2	4.9
Lincoln	7	D	D	D	5	15	D	0.5	12	D	D	D
Lyon	49	360	29.8	20.1	36	1,882	1,131.2	76.3	66	1,194	40.1	11.9
McLeod	64	392	32.3	15.5	80	5,465	1,882.5	277.2	64	1,043	39.6	11.2
Mahnomen	3	D	D	D	NA	NA	NA	NA	13	D	D	D
Marshall	11	30	6.9	1.5	17	251	59.7	11.0	23	D	D	D
Martin	39	193	21.3	7.9	39	1,313	1,576.5	59.8	38	749	26.9	7.3
Meeker	33	115	10.8	3.8	55	1,753	828.4	75.9	38	450	14.6	3.9
Mille Lacs	29	D	D	D	40	852	400.9	37.2	67	D	D	D
Morrison	35	195	18.2	8.2	51	1,319	397.7	50.4	89	911	35.5	9.5
Mower	44	D	D	D	36	3,752	D	151.6	71	1,052	44.0	11.3
Murray	15	D	D	D	8	387	D	9.5	24	D	D	D
Nicollet	42	450	46.7	25.0	50	3,678	965.1	131.9	52	759	26.5	7.6
Nobles	34	D	D	D	25	2,856	1,585.0	123.2	42	616	27.9	6.9
Norman	12	D	D	D	NA	NA	NA	NA	14	50	2.1	0.5
Olmsted	278	10,867	1,070.1	668.3	90	9,046	3,209.0	591.8	331	7,596	391.7	111.1
Otter Tail	95	482	48.6	19.3	83	3,875	1,464.5	156.1	149	1,471	69.7	19.7
Pennington	16	D	D	D	17	884	D	38.2	37	1,023	53.8	16.3
Pine	28	D	D	D	26	276	44.3	9.2	65	2,524	232.7	48.8
Pipestone	14	58	13.0	1.5	13	385	92.1	11.3	24	394	10.8	3.1
Polk	48	D	D	D	34	1,526	1,187.8	63.8	61	1,171	48.7	14.9
Pope	23	D	D	D	23	616	113.4	25.8	28	283	11.7	2.7
Ramsey	1,724	13,007	2,300.4	893.6	591	22,817	6,172.0	1,343.7	1,102	21,792	1,080.4	320.4
Red Lake	4	D	D	D	3	D	D	D	14	D	D	D
Redwood	19	58	8.3	2.7	31	1,021	371.8	34.9	39	1,122	98.0	20.8
Renville	24	123	17.8	6.4	23	1,028	559.3	49.6	31	265	8.5	1.9
Rice	137	642	54.3	22.5	77	3,907	1,741.9	189.7	124	2,082	82.6	24.4
Rock	16	85	10.5	4.3	13	267	86.4	9.8	16	205	7.5	1.8
Roseau	24	85	7.8	2.4	24	3,941	2,082.2	147.1	36	533	28.2	7.5
St. Louis	393	D	D	D	213	4,380	D	210.9	530	9,670	525.9	125.7
Scott	426	2,207	229.3	381.8	182	5,671	2,301.5	330.9	193	6,476	581.2	139.3
Sherburne	157	582	60.7	22.1	149	3,078	857.7	157.6	116	2,114	86.3	23.5
Sibley	26	D	D	D	23	1,028	1,018.4	44.3	21	D	D	D
Stearns	311	D	D	D	248	11,231	3,539.4	480.1	360	6,378	266.7	72.2
Steele	59	D	D	D	63	4,535	1,539.8	209.2	84	1,614	61.5	17.4
Stevens	16	99	11.4	4.5	16	776	D	36.1	25	413	16.5	3.9
Swift	16	69	7.7	2.4	16	814	D	46.5	28	252	8.8	2.2
Todd	27	96	6.3	2.6	43	1,509	885.9	63.1	45	384	18.3	4.8
Traverse	3	D	D	D	7	22	5.4	0.9	8	D	D	D
Wabasha	32	D	D	D	34	1,506	523.1	60.1	63	594	20.6	5.6
Wadena	19	54	7.8	2.8	18	342	43.1	10.6	30	322	11.2	2.9
Waseca	31	149	10.1	3.8	28	2,263	1,061.5	99.8	34	351	12.5	3.0
Washington	783	3,673	535.3	207.7	188	6,928	5,767.1	427.3	399	8,618	399.0	115.3
Watonwan	9	36	4.3	1.1	19	1,231	343.2	39.5	23	D	D	D
Wilkin	7	D	D	D	5	11	D	D	13	152	4.3	1.3
Winona	79	360	32.1	11.5	102	4,996	1,567.9	232.0	125	2,124	76.4	20.2
Wright	305	881	98.2	31.7	196	4,776	1,184.9	234.7	190	3,095	123.8	34.0
Yellow Medicine	16	D	D	D	21	261	177.9	11.5	25	605	41.5	10.3

Health Care and Social Assistance, Other Services, Nonemployer Businesses, and Residential Construction

STATE County	Health care and social assistance, 2012				Other services, 2012				Nonemployer businesses, 2016		Value of residential construction authorized by building permits, 2018	
	Number of establishments	Number of employees	Receipts (mil dol)	Annual payroll (mil dol)	Number of establishments	Number of employees	Receipts (mil dol)	Annual payroll (mil dol)	Number	Receipts (mil dol)	New construction ($1,000)	Number of housing units
	159	160	161	162	163	164	165	166	167	168	169	170
MINNESOTA— Cont'd												
Fillmore	49	D	D	D	44	147	12.5	2.5	1,713	73.2	16,046	87
Freeborn	71	2,569	208.3	94.6	66	369	20.1	5.2	1,842	86.1	6,296	25
Goodhue	141	3,780	254.3	123.6	103	483	41.6	10.5	3,067	135.5	27,351	136
Grant	20	511	32.7	16.4	15	39	3.8	0.5	536	22.3	570	2
Hennepin	3,899	128,451	14,036.0	6,012.9	2,651	22,081	2,761.6	721.7	106,061	5,473.0	1,768,792	7,057
Houston	45	1,047	35.7	18.7	41	106	9.8	2.0	1,396	68.3	7,395	46
Hubbard	52	917	85.4	37.0	38	187	14.0	3.0	1,745	66.7	3,977	21
Isanti	78	2,198	217.6	91.0	61	D	D	D	2,733	114.7	53,342	301
Itasca	151	3,495	248.9	112.8	85	387	56.8	9.9	2,938	107.7	18,288	90
Jackson	31	1,421	49.5	23.6	24	95	8.9	1.4	793	34.6	1,473	6
Kanabec	32	938	79.3	32.3	26	85	6.8	1.7	993	46.7	6,596	42
Kandiyohi	179	5,189	303.2	164.6	98	599	52.4	10.8	3,151	150.3	25,227	135
Kittson	11	359	19.0	8.7	10	50	4.0	0.7	342	12.8	212	1
Koochiching	41	668	49.7	19.1	27	109	9.4	1.7	853	25.5	5,757	32
Lac qui Parle	15	585	31.6	15.4	15	60	9.0	1.1	630	24.0	1,032	5
Lake	29	473	28.5	11.9	20	177	13.6	4.1	841	32.4	10,955	54
Lake of the Woods	8	D	D	D	10	54	5.3	0.9	350	12.0	9,218	55
Le Sueur	57	844	46.3	19.8	63	D	D	D	1,979	89.2	21,462	85
Lincoln	16	535	32.7	14.1	14	87	10.5	2.0	481	16.3	1,339	6
Lyon	82	2,006	164.5	63.0	51	D	D	D	1,739	77.6	11,265	77
McLeod	113	2,714	223.3	93.4	79	500	38.0	9.3	2,326	108.9	23,588	134
Mahnomen	8	176	12.8	5.0	7	48	4.9	0.9	326	13.2	0	0
Marshall	17	283	13.1	7.1	23	D	D	D	635	22.9	635	3
Martin	64	2,030	139.3	57.1	52	156	14.5	3.0	1,522	68.8	5,179	23
Meeker	57	1,240	81.2	32.4	42	181	14.7	2.6	1,686	72.8	17,881	104
Mille Lacs	71	1,845	104.2	45.5	54	D	D	D	1,749	66.1	19,454	81
Morrison	83	1,749	134.0	54.5	86	341	40.4	7.1	2,399	114.8	10,730	91
Mower	86	2,920	201.5	93.2	91	537	46.7	10.0	1,804	84.7	11,639	68
Murray	17	455	32.6	13.7	22	67	11.2	1.6	731	37.3	3,365	14
Nicollet	78	2,303	152.6	93.6	56	D	D	D	2,177	96.7	19,761	81
Nobles	63	1,298	66.4	31.0	51	294	24.5	5.7	1,229	62.7	2,336	12
Norman	15	401	22.6	11.1	12	38	3.0	0.5	466	20.9	2,447	9
Olmsted	412	20,014	2,408.0	854.4	240	1,846	155.2	46.2	9,888	440.7	330,266	1,581
Otter Tail	172	4,540	285.9	126.7	130	517	46.0	10.3	4,810	214.0	18,728	127
Pennington	40	1,255	108.3	42.5	45	260	15.4	3.9	883	31.4	11,518	108
Pine	76	1,035	73.6	26.3	42	186	22.5	3.8	1,732	70.8	16,060	85
Pipestone	28	738	49.6	19.0	22	71	6.8	1.5	694	35.0	3,840	17
Polk	90	2,512	154.4	71.4	56	301	23.2	5.4	2,230	90.8	22,181	95
Pope	25	666	43.0	20.7	25	75	7.1	1.5	949	39.3	10,671	38
Ramsey	1,850	57,676	5,557.3	2,429.7	1,090	9,996	1,273.8	320.8	37,772	1,587.8	177,832	1,001
Red Lake	6	D	D	D	5	D	D	D	242	10.4	1,106	7
Redwood	38	865	62.8	23.7	53	237	18.9	4.7	1,044	42.4	4,247	16
Renville	33	1,020	48.1	21.9	33	D	D	D	1,074	52.0	2,570	12
Rice	159	3,193	215.8	101.4	129	606	48.6	12.3	4,218	170.0	45,173	187
Rock	15	634	29.9	11.9	20	75	4.8	1.2	740	35.4	6,759	24
Roseau	30	841	60.8	21.9	36	129	13.1	1.8	1,149	38.8	2,611	16
St. Louis	729	24,700	2,210.0	1,048.0	386	2,505	239.0	58.7	11,652	458.8	89,172	481
Scott	238	4,719	395.9	170.5	221	1,260	108.5	31.7	10,716	545.8	237,088	853
Sherburne	146	4,147	216.9	112.8	147	727	71.0	21.0	6,460	284.9	110,467	487
Sibley	23	568	28.5	13.4	25	D	D	D	1,064	43.5	8,619	30
Stearns	413	14,979	1,619.6	743.1	359	2,344	237.3	58.0	10,626	527.6	128,783	543
Steele	125	2,486	218.1	92.0	89	525	55.0	12.6	2,409	103.6	30,102	161
Stevens	37	1,392	77.0	37.9	22	106	9.8	2.1	668	29.5	3,690	13
Swift	24	674	40.8	16.0	28	114	13.7	2.7	675	26.0	1,926	10
Todd	58	1,546	121.8	63.8	44	129	13.8	2.2	1,623	72.3	22,777	123
Traverse	11	294	14.5	5.8	8	D	D	D	250	9.7	740	3
Wabasha	57	D	D	D	43	149	11.3	2.8	1,607	71.0	12,697	62
Wadena	46	1,073	92.7	34.5	27	117	9.9	1.8	1,033	44.0	6,869	66
Waseca	50	975	56.4	22.0	33	114	10.1	2.2	1,144	55.7	6,330	27
Washington	580	10,469	1,052.7	428.2	397	2,671	194.9	63.4	18,294	861.8	405,835	1,699
Watonwan	20	484	41.4	15.7	27	115	13.5	2.0	630	23.6	1,126	7
Wilkin	20	743	61.1	23.4	12	D	D	D	466	40.2	3,959	19
Winona	122	3,195	220.1	90.3	84	429	44.4	10.5	2,969	120.6	24,002	135
Wright	266	6,437	397.7	187.1	225	1,238	90.3	24.3	9,790	425.4	239,063	926
Yellow Medicine	28	1,122	67.3	31.0	22	52	5.8	1.3	782	30.1	1,442	7

Government Employment and Payroll, and Local Government Finances

STATE County	Full-time equivalent employees	March payroll (dollars)	Adminis-tration, judicial, and legal	Police and corrections	Fire protection	Highways and transpor-tation	Health and welfare	Natural resources and utilities	Education and libraries	Total (mil dol)	Inter-govern-mental (mil dol)	Total (mil dol)	Per capita (dollars) Total	Per capita (dollars) Property
					March payroll (percent of total)							General revenue	Taxes	
	171	172	173	174	175	176	177	178	179	180	181	182	183	184
MINNESOTA— Cont'd														
Fillmore	743	2,541,608	12.4	9.9	0.0	8.7	11.1	6.0	50.3	79.4	42.2	20.8	999	988
Freeborn	1,073	4,355,329	8.3	11.4	1.9	7.2	10.0	5.7	54.1	127.7	69.2	36.7	1,183	1,110
Goodhue	1,720	6,840,668	9.9	13.6	2.1	4.3	9.2	6.0	53.4	204.8	92.0	69.5	1,500	1,468
Grant	273	953,527	13.2	7.0	0.0	7.4	8.2	5.8	57.5	34.1	18.5	9.7	1,624	1,620
Hennepin	35,312	195,123,070	8.9	12.4	2.0	3.7	9.4	8.3	54.2	6,392.6	2,496.9	2,262.3	1,910	1,724
Houston	731	2,758,225	7.6	7.3	0.3	4.4	7.9	2.9	66.7	81.1	51.4	19.2	1,022	1,012
Hubbard	660	2,206,385	9.8	10.0	0.0	6.0	8.6	2.6	59.7	84.9	48.1	26.6	1,305	1,278
Isanti	1,257	4,796,343	6.7	9.3	0.1	4.0	7.5	2.3	68.0	131.8	76.3	35.3	924	904
Itasca	1,538	7,554,704	6.6	8.1	0.4	8.7	15.2	3.8	55.3	301.4	126.6	54.1	1,196	1,185
Jackson	515	1,776,829	11.8	7.0	0.2	8.4	20.7	6.0	44.4	50.6	24.7	15.9	1,544	1,531
Kanabec	867	2,925,087	5.0	6.1	0.0	4.3	35.1	1.6	43.5	90.0	33.3	14.7	920	889
Kandiyohi	2,286	9,769,471	6.3	8.2	0.4	2.9	40.7	4.1	36.3	282.7	84.2	49.6	1,170	1,089
Kittson	282	1,417,262	8.1	3.9	0.0	6.1	5.8	4.7	69.0	29.6	16.1	6.4	1,432	1,411
Koochiching	528	2,114,323	5.7	6.7	1.6	5.8	7.4	7.8	61.4	61.1	35.8	8.3	632	626
Lac qui Parle	625	1,888,050	6.9	3.8	0.0	5.1	33.9	3.0	45.7	46.7	21.4	8.4	1,176	1,141
Lake	361	1,980,601	12.9	10.1	0.3	9.4	6.4	8.7	48.8	64.0	33.4	15.7	1,454	1,414
Lake of the Woods	143	726,420	14.0	7.3	0.0	9.2	10.2	5.3	51.7	20.3	13.0	5.1	1,272	1,255
Le Sueur	871	2,940,497	8.0	8.1	0.0	4.7	11.3	5.1	60.6	96.7	50.3	31.2	1,128	1,088
Lincoln	199	603,609	18.2	11.9	0.1	15.9	1.7	6.8	38.3	21.7	9.6	8.1	1,392	1,384
Lyon	1,012	3,496,744	7.5	9.5	0.1	6.3	1.3	11.7	60.6	145.6	71.4	30.6	1,199	1,151
McLeod	1,516	6,615,440	5.8	6.3	0.2	3.2	37.7	10.6	34.8	212.6	66.7	39.1	1,084	1,063
Mahnomen	413	1,411,273	11.1	5.4	0.0	2.8	22.1	3.6	50.5	40.8	24.5	6.0	1,085	1,083
Marshall	459	1,668,424	9.8	5.5	0.5	7.6	16.1	9.7	49.9	55.9	36.6	9.4	991	982
Martin	655	3,114,449	10.3	9.8	0.1	7.4	3.2	9.6	56.8	92.7	49.5	24.0	1,170	1,158
Meeker	1,226	4,903,007	5.1	5.4	0.1	2.7	21.6	3.2	60.7	139.5	63.7	28.6	1,239	1,222
Mille Lacs	1,239	4,213,762	8.0	10.1	0.2	3.3	6.5	3.4	67.4	113.5	71.6	30.4	1,182	1,162
Morrison	1,124	4,203,099	7.6	8.2	0.9	5.8	10.1	2.5	63.7	118.8	71.3	29.8	903	875
Mower	1,542	6,255,175	7.7	8.0	0.8	4.4	8.9	12.3	56.6	166.8	93.6	36.0	915	853
Murray	420	2,070,204	5.7	4.9	0.0	4.6	33.5	2.7	42.5	54.5	22.6	10.9	1,273	1,259
Nicollet	835	3,375,650	8.8	10.9	0.1	6.1	20.8	7.8	43.0	108.0	39.0	29.6	899	839
Nobles	747	5,019,216	4.9	6.5	0.1	3.1	5.4	4.5	73.5	104.9	59.6	21.9	1,019	964
Norman	410	1,309,952	11.1	4.4	0.2	8.7	6.0	6.0	61.5	40.3	26.4	8.4	1,266	1,263
Olmsted	4,101	28,521,111	5.6	8.4	2.3	3.1	9.3	7.4	60.7	672.3	289.4	201.9	1,373	1,242
Otter Tail	2,164	8,240,552	8.0	7.4	0.2	4.7	21.9	3.4	52.3	298.8	109.1	62.1	1,083	1,068
Pennington	640	2,304,729	5.4	8.5	1.6	4.2	7.5	11.0	56.5	114.3	37.7	13.8	984	963
Pine	879	3,660,809	9.4	7.3	0.3	7.0	4.0	1.4	67.8	103.3	61.8	27.4	938	920
Pipestone	661	2,186,364	6.7	4.4	0.1	5.7	33.1	2.8	46.0	72.9	31.8	11.0	1,175	1,146
Polk	1,733	5,824,889	5.7	5.8	1.5	3.5	29.5	8.1	43.7	191.1	112.8	36.5	1,161	1,082
Pope	553	2,333,307	3.9	5.8	0.0	8.4	42.6	1.9	32.2	48.8	23.1	14.2	1,302	1,287
Ramsey	16,492	141,646,187	5.1	8.3	2.7	4.8	6.3	4.1	67.7	2,881.4	1,248.1	805.8	1,549	1,417
Red Lake	258	709,610	7.9	6.0	0.0	6.6	6.3	5.2	67.6	24.0	15.3	4.3	1,044	1,038
Redwood	739	3,232,367	9.3	5.7	0.2	4.8	7.0	5.7	65.2	101.1	39.6	20.4	1,287	1,261
Renville	704	2,316,532	18.7	8.2	0.0	9.5	12.1	4.4	43.1	88.9	34.9	21.9	1,424	1,401
Rice	2,519	10,254,560	4.8	6.6	0.7	2.9	41.2	2.9	39.9	352.9	102.9	62.2	959	916
Rock	396	1,387,361	10.8	6.2	0.1	8.3	1.0	11.6	59.9	45.4	21.6	11.5	1,203	1,152
Roseau	687	2,591,371	8.0	6.4	0.0	5.4	6.6	3.1	69.0	74.6	50.8	14.1	909	899
St. Louis	7,560	37,760,893	7.0	10.6	2.8	7.2	13.4	8.3	44.2	1,073.0	545.0	233.2	1,164	1,026
Scott	3,486	17,619,282	8.6	9.3	0.5	3.5	6.2	5.2	64.4	500.4	232.5	180.8	1,338	1,287
Sherburne	3,233	14,013,536	5.6	10.8	0.4	2.4	4.7	3.2	71.3	366.7	185.3	126.0	1,408	1,391
Sibley	636	2,194,050	9.3	7.3	0.3	6.5	27.2	1.9	46.6	76.3	33.5	18.9	1,250	1,235
Stearns	4,907	24,879,439	7.5	10.1	1.5	2.8	14.9	4.1	56.2	676.6	322.4	196.7	1,297	1,129
Steele	1,297	5,726,547	5.5	10.8	0.9	4.1	6.2	10.3	60.3	147.4	81.6	42.4	1,167	1,112
Stevens	479	1,791,149	11.2	17.4	0.6	6.2	9.0	11.6	40.3	43.2	23.3	12.2	1,258	1,229
Swift	748	2,235,013	8.5	5.5	0.0	5.7	37.9	3.6	34.8	82.8	25.2	13.2	1,379	1,363
Todd	994	3,435,036	8.2	8.5	0.0	4.5	12.5	2.3	58.8	94.8	59.3	21.3	869	840
Traverse	251	735,078	9.6	10.4	0.4	13.3	21.2	2.5	41.3	26.6	9.8	7.7	2,242	2,236
Wabasha	717	2,663,637	12.2	9.5	0.1	4.8	7.6	8.0	55.6	95.1	50.4	27.4	1,278	1,244
Wadena	723	2,230,614	6.7	2.7	0.1	5.3	11.7	4.2	66.3	67.0	41.7	12.2	887	870
Waseca	839	2,685,918	9.1	9.2	1.4	6.3	7.1	5.6	60.1	83.8	42.3	21.8	1,133	1,094
Washington	6,573	28,742,198	7.5	9.9	1.5	2.6	4.9	4.1	68.0	850.9	369.3	318.3	1,304	1,251
Watonwan	544	1,961,440	9.4	7.3	0.3	6.3	9.4	7.3	57.7	52.1	29.2	12.3	1,097	1,083
Wilkin	308	1,120,394	10.9	8.0	0.0	10.2	10.2	7.3	51.6	36.4	21.4	9.3	1,417	1,407
Winona	1,299	5,244,944	8.6	10.3	2.2	4.6	9.2	8.7	54.4	161.3	88.3	44.7	866	816
Wright	4,086	18,042,110	5.5	7.7	0.2	3.1	16.3	2.4	60.5	548.1	243.1	150.9	1,185	1,154
Yellow Medicine	412	1,492,491	12.8	9.7	0.0	10.5	8.7	6.7	48.7	72.8	27.5	13.9	1,364	1,345

1. Based on the resident population estimated as of July 1 of the year shown.

Table B. States and Counties — Local Government Finances, Government Employment, and Income Taxes

STATE County	Local government finances, 2012 (cont.) Direct general expenditure Total (mil dol)	Per capita¹ (dollars)	Education	Health and hospitals	Police protection	Public welfare	Highways	Debt outstanding Total (mil dol)	Per capita¹ (dollars)	Government employment, 2017 Federal civilian	Federal military	State and local	Individual income tax returns, 2016 Number of returns	Mean adjusted gross income	Mean income tax
	185	186	187	188	189	190	191	192	193	194	195	196	197	198	199
MINNESOTA— Cont'd															
Fillmore	76.1	3,651	36.6	4.1	4.6	4.1	17.1	66.9	3,213	70	73	1,216	9,890	51,049	5,173
Freeborn	125.1	4,028	42.5	2.8	6.6	6.1	15.4	132.0	4,249	74	106	1,465	14,890	53,299	5,864
Goodhue	204.0	4,403	43.7	3.7	6.0	4.9	10.8	184.3	3,977	123	161	4,134	23,640	61,749	7,071
Grant	31.2	5,248	38.6	0.9	4.1	11.4	16.0	31.1	5,236	23	21	372	2,930	52,710	5,602
Hennepin	7,135.3	6,024	29.8	13.2	5.5	5.6	5.3	9,944.8	8,395	13,529	4,733	86,769	636,450	91,442	14,979
Houston	81.7	4,339	53.8	2.6	5.0	5.5	10.5	57.5	3,052	69	65	1,123	9,470	57,989	6,763
Hubbard	78.2	3,842	35.6	0.3	3.6	14.6	18.2	83.3	4,093	43	74	1,092	9,560	52,794	5,347
Isanti	136.1	3,558	50.4	3.4	6.9	7.7	11.0	169.3	4,426	77	139	2,036	19,440	55,805	5,712
Itasca	350.2	7,744	24.1	20.6	2.5	8.1	14.2	319.0	7,054	170	157	3,423	20,600	53,290	5,385
Jackson	50.2	4,887	33.0	4.1	3.8	7.8	19.0	50.8	4,943	25	35	768	5,030	52,708	5,274
Kanabec	84.8	5,300	27.0	37.5	2.3	6.2	8.2	63.2	3,950	35	56	1,305	7,350	49,053	4,707
Kandiyohi	300.9	7,100	20.9	38.3	5.5	4.8	6.1	333.7	7,875	141	148	3,898	21,190	56,479	6,351
Kittson	33.3	7,415	39.2	0.7	3.3	4.6	22.4	21.5	4,785	43	15	289	2,120	51,601	5,562
Koochiching	70.6	5,344	34.8	3.6	4.7	13.7	11.0	39.7	3,002	182	44	779	5,930	47,189	4,460
Lac qui Parle	48.9	6,880	33.1	26.2	3.0	4.0	16.2	28.8	4,046	36	23	751	3,380	55,855	6,196
Lake	63.2	5,838	24.4	5.5	5.8	10.5	17.5	119.8	11,076	23	37	919	5,210	53,227	5,330
Lake of the Woods	20.1	5,071	32.1	0.5	4.1	7.7	23.1	304.4	76,625	31	13	280	1,980	47,399	4,137
Le Sueur	119.9	4,333	53.4	2.4	3.8	5.4	10.2	161.8	5,845	76	99	1,315	14,150	60,589	6,792
Lincoln	25.1	4,309	25.1	0.5	6.1	11.4	20.4	39.0	6,710	31	20	291	2,680	50,514	4,977
Lyon	146.3	5,727	52.4	0.4	7.1	3.1	11.6	165.7	6,486	118	88	2,886	11,990	57,039	6,279
McLeod	206.8	5,737	26.6	34.0	4.4	4.9	10.2	191.4	5,309	78	126	1,846	18,450	55,268	5,834
Mahnomen	39.5	7,142	44.6	20.1	5.7	5.9	9.3	26.1	4,718	24	20	1,340	2,240	41,435	3,391
Marshall	64.2	6,790	36.8	0.4	2.9	5.0	21.2	37.9	4,006	51	33	596	4,510	54,323	5,921
Martin	94.4	4,613	46.0	0.5	6.6	4.8	14.2	96.9	4,732	59	69	1,329	10,270	53,433	6,126
Meeker	131.9	5,719	44.6	17.9	4.5	5.3	7.4	173.9	7,539	76	81	1,234	11,160	54,995	5,747
Mille Lacs	118.0	4,583	57.3	0.6	3.7	6.4	6.8	133.7	5,195	64	90	3,358	12,200	48,332	4,631
Morrison	121.6	3,680	48.7	1.8	3.7	7.1	14.7	122.4	3,704	410	116	1,966	15,730	47,164	4,389
Mower	168.0	4,268	46.1	1.1	4.6	8.4	11.8	1,198.8	30,447	139	138	2,525	18,730	56,650	6,938
Murray	54.4	6,337	23.7	28.8	4.7	2.0	15.6	37.9	4,418	45	29	574	4,140	52,850	5,421
Nicollet	111.3	3,380	30.7	17.7	4.8	6.8	10.6	144.3	4,383	33	110	2,925	15,890	62,574	7,504
Nobles	104.2	4,852	42.9	3.4	7.6	7.3	10.8	69.0	3,210	85	77	1,462	10,260	48,069	4,451
Norman	40.7	6,134	33.4	1.1	3.5	8.1	19.4	17.3	2,601	31	23	445	3,210	50,071	4,861
Olmsted	687.5	4,675	34.2	1.9	4.8	7.4	9.9	2,857.8	19,432	805	545	8,110	77,970	74,353	10,064
Otter Tail	312.8	5,461	45.3	8.8	3.2	5.1	10.5	310.4	5,419	218	203	3,652	28,440	54,809	5,833
Pennington	122.4	8,695	70.1	0.0	2.8	3.6	4.7	105.6	7,504	55	49	1,532	6,990	52,431	5,225
Pine	95.3	3,262	45.6	1.9	5.8	7.4	12.1	136.2	4,662	296	98	3,022	12,850	47,157	4,316
Pipestone	70.7	7,570	36.9	25.0	2.8	5.3	9.6	31.4	3,359	45	32	905	4,480	48,766	4,861
Polk	182.0	5,792	29.6	1.4	3.7	10.5	14.8	169.8	5,406	96	108	2,640	14,670	54,538	5,615
Pope	48.7	4,470	30.5	12.3	9.7	6.5	14.2	36.7	3,368	40	38	832	5,520	58,029	6,989
Ramsey	2,823.6	5,428	39.6	2.3	6.4	6.6	5.2	4,373.6	8,408	2,362	1,956	55,588	266,340	65,822	8,707
Red Lake	25.7	6,285	56.4	0.3	4.3	4.4	15.8	18.7	4,565	19	14	272	1,880	50,416	4,590
Redwood	94.9	5,987	30.0	25.7	4.1	7.3	11.4	93.1	5,876	52	53	1,345	7,720	51,287	5,322
Renville	96.1	6,251	25.3	21.0	3.3	5.9	14.5	80.0	5,207	60	51	1,683	7,440	54,078	5,993
Rice	342.7	5,285	25.9	37.7	3.6	2.9	5.8	303.1	4,673	134	208	3,440	29,460	61,470	7,046
Rock	42.6	4,461	42.5	0.6	4.4	8.4	12.8	74.6	7,811	27	33	725	4,510	52,350	5,235
Roseau	80.9	5,225	41.7	0.5	3.6	5.4	18.9	44.4	2,870	95	54	971	7,570	58,082	7,544
St. Louis	1,223.1	6,106	33.5	5.6	5.4	6.8	9.4	959.9	4,792	1,411	808	15,298	93,730	57,121	6,535
Scott	487.6	3,608	45.0	0.4	4.6	4.1	15.6	1,025.8	7,590	129	513	9,629	69,790	86,810	12,666
Sherburne	342.7	3,831	57.6	0.7	4.6	4.0	8.4	655.5	7,328	133	328	4,211	44,820	66,248	7,418
Sibley	82.9	5,484	34.0	16.4	4.2	4.8	14.5	70.1	4,636	40	52	745	7,460	51,273	4,847
Stearns	692.0	4,565	39.7	8.6	5.0	4.9	11.1	994.2	6,558	2,337	539	9,396	73,550	63,152	8,380
Steele	144.4	3,975	47.3	1.6	5.1	5.6	14.0	145.9	4,016	76	129	2,170	18,560	56,302	5,947
Stevens	43.9	4,548	36.6	0.3	5.8	5.7	19.8	77.2	7,986	73	31	1,374	4,460	57,563	6,744
Swift	86.6	9,024	19.1	41.7	2.8	4.8	8.8	45.2	4,715	50	33	947	4,610	48,935	5,064
Todd	111.4	4,544	53.4	2.6	3.5	6.4	11.8	81.6	3,330	82	86	1,300	10,950	44,469	3,986
Traverse	29.5	8,562	21.2	13.2	3.7	4.8	17.5	15.5	4,502	27	11	326	1,640	51,773	6,055
Wabasha	100.8	4,696	37.3	2.8	5.5	4.0	15.3	103.1	4,800	54	76	1,066	11,150	55,086	5,730
Wadena	92.1	6,693	61.5	1.4	3.3	12.6	6.8	28.2	2,051	54	47	1,442	6,270	44,067	3,850
Waseca	84.8	4,408	42.7	2.1	5.7	11.6	9.7	75.0	3,897	266	63	1,094	9,080	50,425	4,878
Washington	872.4	3,574	51.1	1.8	5.9	3.6	8.8	1,195.5	4,898	392	898	10,912	128,690	88,476	12,949
Watonwan	57.4	5,127	43.4	1.2	4.2	7.5	11.1	64.3	5,747	50	38	768	5,290	49,084	4,638
Wilkin	36.2	5,494	38.6	2.9	5.1	6.0	20.9	19.1	2,900	19	22	405	3,230	54,236	6,140
Winona	157.7	3,054	44.7	2.6	5.6	6.4	13.8	84.9	1,645	134	166	3,491	22,520	57,533	6,620
Wright	554.0	4,351	45.4	11.5	4.5	3.5	7.8	1,170.5	9,192	195	475	6,042	64,000	68,610	8,187
Yellow Medicine	83.2	8,190	26.8	22.5	2.0	9.0	12.3	76.0	7,477	40	34	1,462	4,950	54,357	5,184

1. Based on the resident population estimated as of July 1 of the year shown.

Table B. States and Counties — Land Area and Population

State / county code	CBSA code[1]	County code[2]	STATE County	Land area[3] (sq. mi)	Total persons 2018	Rank	Per square mile	White	Black	American Indian, Alaska Native	Asian and Pacific Islander	Percent Hispanic or Latino[4]	Under 5 years	5 to 17 years	18 to 24 years	25 to 34 years	35 to 44 years	45 to 54 years
				1	2	3	4	5	6	7	8	9	10	11	12	13	14	15
28000		0	MISSISSIPPI..................	46,924.4	2,986,530	X	63.6	57.5	38.1	0.9	1.4	3.4	6.2	17.4	9.8	13.2	12.2	12.3
28001	35,020	5	Adams..........................	462.3	31,192	1,399	67.5	35.4	53.0	0.6	0.7	11.3	5.8	14.2	7.5	13.3	13.3	11.7
28003	18,420	7	Alcorn..........................	400.0	36,925	1,252	92.3	83.7	12.9	0.7	0.6	3.4	5.7	17.0	8.1	12.4	12.1	13.1
28005	32,620	8	Amite..........................	730.1	12,326	2,264	16.9	57.9	40.6	0.6	0.3	1.4	5.4	15.0	7.0	10.2	9.9	11.7
28007		6	Attala..........................	735.0	18,365	1,908	25.0	54.0	43.5	0.5	0.5	2.1	6.3	18.8	8.1	11.3	11.1	12.3
28009	32,820	1	Benton..........................	406.6	8,271	2,567	20.3	61.5	35.7	0.9	0.3	2.8	5.9	15.8	7.7	12.1	11.4	13.7
28011	17,380	7	Bolivar..........................	876.7	31,333	1,396	35.7	33.1	63.9	0.3	1.1	2.2	6.6	17.7	10.9	14.0	11.2	11.5
28013		9	Calhoun..........................	586.6	14,436	2,132	24.6	65.4	28.7	0.5	0.3	6.2	5.6	17.8	7.8	11.0	11.4	13.7
28015	24,900	9	Carroll..........................	628.3	9,911	2,435	15.8	65.2	33.1	0.6	0.4	1.7	4.3	14.2	7.1	10.6	11.3	12.8
28017		7	Chickasaw..........................	501.8	17,171	1,966	34.2	50.1	44.6	0.5	0.7	5.3	6.6	18.2	8.7	13.0	11.5	12.1
28019		9	Choctaw..........................	418.2	8,278	2,564	19.8	67.9	30.5	0.5	0.7	1.6	5.7	16.0	7.4	11.6	10.9	12.7
28021	46,980	8	Claiborne..........................	487.4	9,002	2,500	18.5	11.9	85.9	0.5	1.2	1.4	6.0	15.0	20.7	10.8	10.2	9.3
28023	32,940	9	Clarke..........................	691.6	15,604	2,061	22.6	63.6	34.9	0.6	0.3	1.1	5.7	16.3	8.0	11.7	10.8	12.5
28025	48,500	7	Clay..........................	410.1	19,386	1,858	47.3	39.3	58.8	0.5	0.5	1.6	6.3	16.9	8.4	13.2	11.5	11.7
28027	17,260	7	Coahoma..........................	552.5	22,628	1,697	41.0	21.0	77.0	0.3	0.6	1.7	7.9	19.1	10.3	12.3	10.9	11.2
28029	27,140	2	Copiah..........................	777.3	28,543	1,478	36.7	44.5	51.8	0.5	0.7	3.6	6.0	17.0	10.4	12.0	11.4	11.7
28031		8	Covington..........................	413.8	18,853	1,880	45.6	61.2	36.2	0.5	0.7	2.4	6.5	18.1	8.2	12.9	11.8	12.4
28033	32,820	1	DeSoto..........................	476.3	182,001	358	382.1	64.4	29.5	0.5	1.9	5.1	6.1	19.5	8.7	13.0	14.0	14.0
28035	25,620	3	Forrest..........................	466.0	75,036	737	161.0	58.1	38.4	0.6	1.4	2.9	6.5	16.6	14.3	15.1	11.9	10.9
28037		9	Franklin..........................	564.0	7,788	2,610	13.8	63.9	35.2	0.7	0.3	1.1	5.4	17.8	7.5	10.6	11.2	12.2
28039		6	George..........................	478.7	24,250	1,635	50.7	87.7	8.3	1.0	0.9	3.2	7.7	18.7	8.4	14.0	11.9	12.7
28041		8	Greene..........................	712.7	13,586	2,192	19.1	72.8	25.8	0.7	0.3	1.3	4.7	14.8	8.9	16.5	14.2	14.0
28043	24,980	7	Grenada..........................	422.1	21,055	1,774	49.9	55.3	43.0	0.6	0.6	1.4	6.4	17.5	8.3	12.2	11.6	12.9
28045	25,060	2	Hancock..........................	474.0	47,334	1,029	99.9	86.4	8.9	1.4	1.4	4.0	5.1	15.4	7.2	11.9	11.3	13.5
28047	25,060	2	Harrison..........................	573.6	206,650	324	360.3	65.7	26.5	1.0	3.8	5.6	6.5	17.4	9.6	14.2	12.3	12.1
28049	27,140	2	Hinds..........................	869.8	237,085	282	272.6	24.9	73.1	0.4	1.0	1.6	6.4	17.7	11.3	14.6	11.9	11.5
28051		6	Holmes..........................	756.7	17,622	1,943	23.3	16.4	82.4	0.4	0.4	1.1	6.6	18.7	12.2	13.0	10.5	11.1
28053		6	Humphreys..........................	418.5	8,257	2,571	19.7	21.0	75.2	0.5	0.5	3.7	5.7	20.3	8.4	11.8	10.9	11.5
28055		8	Issaquena..........................	413.0	1,308	3,093	3.2	34.5	63.1	0.5	0.5	1.7	2.8	8.9	13.1	16.4	12.7	13.5
28057	46,180	7	Itawamba	532.8	23,517	1,664	44.1	90.8	7.4	0.6	0.6	1.6	5.6	16.1	10.7	12.6	11.5	13.4
28059	25,060	2	Jackson..........................	722.8	143,277	456	198.2	69.0	22.1	0.9	3.0	7.0	5.8	17.6	8.1	13.2	12.7	13.2
28061	29,860	9	Jasper..........................	676.2	16,428	2,014	24.3	45.2	53.5	0.5	0.3	1.4	6.0	16.5	8.0	11.6	11.2	12.2
28063		8	Jefferson..........................	519.9	7,106	2,655	13.7	13.8	85.2	0.4	0.3	1.0	6.4	16.2	8.6	13.4	11.7	11.8
28065		8	Jefferson Davis	408.4	11,234	2,336	27.5	38.1	60.1	0.6	0.5	1.6	5.4	14.4	8.3	11.2	11.1	12.4
28067	29,860	4	Jones..........................	694.8	68,461	781	98.5	65.3	29.7	0.8	0.7	4.5	6.7	18.4	9.3	12.2	11.6	11.8
28069	32,940	9	Kemper..........................	766.2	10,027	2,423	13.1	34.6	61.1	3.8	0.4	0.9	4.4	13.7	14.6	12.0	10.6	11.8
28071	37,060	4	Lafayette......................	631.7	54,793	931	86.7	71.4	23.8	0.5	2.7	2.8	5.0	13.1	23.1	14.1	11.6	10.2
28073	25,620	3	Lamar..........................	496.7	62,447	843	125.7	74.8	21.3	0.6	1.9	2.7	6.5	18.2	8.4	14.6	14.1	12.6
28075	32,940	5	Lauderdale....................	703.7	75,317	736	107.0	52.8	44.4	0.4	1.1	2.2	6.3	17.1	8.7	13.3	11.8	12.4
28077		8	Lawrence..........................	430.7	12,455	2,253	28.9	65.4	32.3	0.5	0.5	2.1	6.3	18.1	7.3	11.4	11.9	12.5
28079		6	Leake..........................	582.9	22,763	1,690	39.1	47.6	42.3	5.9	0.5	4.7	6.4	19.3	8.2	12.8	12.3	12.2
28081	46,180	5	Lee..........................	450.0	85,202	675	189.3	66.0	30.8	0.5	1.2	2.7	6.8	18.4	8.3	13.3	12.8	13.0
28083	24,900	5	Leflore..........................	594.1	28,919	1,462	48.7	22.4	74.4	0.4	0.7	2.8	7.7	18.7	11.3	12.8	11.3	10.6
28085	15,020	5	Lincoln..........................	586.1	34,205	1,323	58.4	68.0	30.7	0.6	0.6	1.1	6.1	17.4	7.9	12.1	12.8	12.9
28087	18,060	5	Lowndes..........................	505.4	58,930	877	116.6	51.9	45.2	0.5	1.3	2.1	6.4	17.1	9.9	13.9	11.7	11.8
28089	27,140	2	Madison..........................	714.5	105,630	573	147.8	55.9	38.5	0.4	3.0	3.1	6.3	18.7	8.7	12.9	13.6	13.3
28091		6	Marion..........................	542.4	24,715	1,620	45.6	66.0	32.2	0.5	0.6	1.8	5.8	17.3	7.9	12.2	12.4	12.2
28093	32,820	1	Marshall..........................	706.2	35,451	1,291	50.2	48.4	47.7	0.6	0.4	3.9	5.6	15.3	9.5	12.4	11.6	13.1
28095		7	Monroe..........................	765.1	35,564	1,289	46.5	67.8	30.8	0.5	0.4	1.3	5.4	17.0	7.8	12.1	11.5	13.0
28097		7	Montgomery....................	407.0	10,023	2,424	24.6	52.8	45.1	0.6	0.8	1.4	6.0	16.6	7.1	11.6	10.3	12.2
28099		7	Neshoba..........................	570.1	29,125	1,454	51.1	59.3	22.3	17.1	0.8	2.1	7.2	20.7	8.6	12.0	11.7	11.7
28101		7	Newton..........................	577.9	21,443	1,757	37.1	61.3	31.5	5.7	0.7	2.0	6.4	18.8	10.3	11.8	11.7	12.3
28103		7	Noxubee..........................	695.2	10,535	2,391	15.2	26.2	72.2	0.5	0.5	1.4	7.3	17.1	9.5	13.0	10.9	11.8
28105	44,260	5	Oktibbeha.......................	458.2	49,599	995	108.2	57.5	37.9	0.5	3.6	1.7	5.4	12.4	30.4	13.9	9.2	8.1
28107		7	Panola..........................	685.2	34,178	1,324	49.9	47.4	50.2	0.6	0.4	2.5	6.9	17.9	8.7	13.3	11.5	12.6
28109	38,100	6	Pearl River	811.3	55,387	924	68.3	83.2	13.2	1.3	0.9	3.2	5.8	16.8	8.9	11.8	11.4	12.9
28111	25,620	3	Perry..........................	647.2	11,931	2,297	18.4	78.5	19.9	0.8	0.5	1.6	5.8	16.0	8.0	11.9	12.2	12.5
28113	32,620	8	Pike..........................	409.0	39,563	1,190	96.7	43.8	53.6	0.7	0.9	2.0	6.7	19.1	9.1	11.9	11.7	11.6
28115	46,180	7	Pontotoc........................	497.8	31,833	1,383	63.9	77.6	15.5	0.7	0.6	7.0	7.1	19.5	8.1	12.7	12.4	12.8
28117		7	Prentiss........................	415.0	25,315	1,595	61.0	83.5	15.3	0.4	0.5	1.5	6.0	16.2	10.2	12.7	11.3	12.8
28119		6	Quitman	405.0	7,051	2,661	17.4	26.7	71.6	0.8	0.6	1.7	6.0	16.8	9.2	12.0	11.4	13.0
28121	27,140	2	Rankin...........................	775.5	153,902	432	198.5	74.4	21.7	0.5	1.7	2.8	5.9	17.3	7.8	14.0	14.3	13.1
28123		6	Scott...........................	609.2	28,287	1,489	46.4	50.2	38.1	0.5	0.7	11.5	7.8	18.9	8.2	12.9	11.9	12.4
28125		8	Sharkey...........................	431.7	4,377	2,868	10.1	26.6	70.7	0.3	1.0	2.2	6.0	18.2	7.6	10.8	10.9	11.4
28127	27,140	2	Simpson..........................	589.2	26,758	1,536	45.4	62.4	35.4	0.5	0.8	1.8	5.6	18.1	8.1	12.1	12.0	12.3
28129		8	Smith...........................	636.3	16,002	2,038	25.1	74.3	24.1	0.4	0.2	1.7	5.7	17.4	7.8	11.2	11.5	12.9
28131		6	Stone...........................	445.5	18,717	1,889	42.0	77.0	20.3	0.9	0.9	2.2	5.6	15.5	13.7	12.2	11.6	12.3

1. CBSA = Core Based Statistical Area. See Appendix A for explanation. See Appendix B for list of metropolitan areas with component counties. Service of USDA Rural-Urban Continuum Codes. See Appendix A for definition.   3. Dry land or land partially or temporarily covered by water.   2. County type code from the Economic Research   4. May be of any race.

Table B. States and Counties — **Population and Households**

STATE County	55 to 64 years	65 to 74 years	75 years and over	Percent female	2000	2010	2000-2010	2010-2018	Births	Deaths	Net Migration	Number	Persons per household	Family households	Female family householder[1]	One person
	16	17	18	19	20	21	22	23	24	25	26	27	28	29	30	31
MISSISSIPPI..................	12.9	9.4	6.5	51.5	2,844,658	2,968,118	4.3	0.6	316,072	251,454	-46,825	1,103,514	2.62	67.5	17.9	28.2
Adams.......................	15.3	10.9	7.9	47.9	34,340	32,299	-5.9	-3.4	3,090	3,365	-875	11,509	2.53	64.6	24.7	33.1
Alcorn.......................	13.0	10.7	7.7	51.2	34,558	37,060	7.2	-0.4	3,593	3,769	72	14,675	2.50	65.9	12.2	30.1
Amite........................	17.1	13.2	10.3	51.6	13,599	13,128	-3.5	-6.1	1,079	1,226	-657	4,994	2.50	61.2	13.7	36.5
Attala.......................	13.0	10.5	8.6	52.6	19,661	19,562	-0.5	-6.1	2,035	2,256	-973	7,174	2.56	70.1	22.1	28.5
Benton......................	14.7	10.4	8.3	50.4	8,026	8,728	8.7	-5.2	793	844	-415	2,960	2.78	71.8	14.2	26.4
Bolivar......................	12.4	9.9	5.9	53.5	40,633	34,153	-15.9	-8.3	4,110	3,371	-3,578	12,267	2.57	63.5	26.8	32.1
Calhoun.....................	13.9	10.4	8.5	51.9	15,069	14,962	-0.7	-3.5	1,414	1,471	-460	5,853	2.46	66.8	17.1	30.5
Carroll......................	16.0	13.7	9.9	49.4	10,769	10,597	-1.6	-6.5	725	865	-544	3,592	2.80	73.2	8.5	26.0
Chickasaw..................	12.7	9.7	7.5	50.9	19,440	17,392	-10.5	-1.3	2,025	1,503	-741	6,454	2.63	68.9	20.0	28.9
Choctaw.....................	14.2	11.9	9.7	51.1	9,758	8,551	-12.4	-3.2	747	758	-258	3,198	2.57	61.6	12.4	36.6
Claiborne....................	11.8	9.7	6.7	52.6	11,831	9,597	-18.9	-6.2	959	804	-778	3,187	2.66	61.5	28.5	36.5
Clarke.......................	14.6	11.7	8.7	53.2	17,955	16,732	-6.8	-6.7	1,546	1,705	-968	6,365	2.52	67.9	15.4	29.3
Clay.........................	14.2	10.8	7.7	53.2	21,979	20,634	-6.1	-6.0	1,869	1,941	-1,174	7,681	2.57	66.6	23.6	26.3
Coahoma....................	12.9	9.1	6.3	53.7	30,622	26,145	-14.6	-13.5	3,411	2,481	-4,490	8,969	2.63	66.6	30.7	30.6
Copiah......................	14.0	10.5	7.2	51.9	28,757	29,447	2.4	-3.1	2,994	2,685	-1,212	9,778	2.83	70.0	20.5	27.8
Covington...................	13.1	9.6	7.3	51.3	19,407	19,573	0.9	-3.7	2,174	2,155	-733	6,919	2.74	71.5	16.9	24.5
DeSoto......................	11.8	8.0	4.9	51.8	107,199	161,267	50.4	12.9	17,306	10,441	13,886	61,158	2.82	73.6	14.7	21.7
Forrest......................	11.2	7.8	5.8	52.5	72,604	74,928	3.2	0.1	8,691	6,041	-2,564	28,063	2.56	62.7	19.2	27.9
Franklin.....................	15.3	11.1	8.8	50.8	8,448	8,118	-3.9	-4.1	706	801	-240	3,097	2.48	74.6	15.9	24.7
George......................	12.2	9.0	5.5	49.4	19,144	22,579	17.9	7.4	2,995	2,130	812	7,220	3.19	70.6	7.7	27.9
Greene......................	12.0	8.8	6.1	42.2	13,299	14,395	8.2	-5.6	1,070	1,066	-828	4,174	2.51	67.4	8.6	27.4
Grenada.....................	13.4	10.5	7.3	52.4	23,263	21,905	-5.8	-3.9	2,242	2,395	-692	7,889	2.66	64.0	21.0	32.4
Hancock.....................	15.8	12.0	7.8	51.1	42,967	44,014	2.4	7.5	3,920	3,894	3,282	19,145	2.40	66.5	13.4	27.5
Harrison.....................	13.0	9.1	5.9	51.0	189,601	187,105	-1.3	10.4	22,748	15,622	12,443	77,630	2.52	66.7	17.7	28.3
Hinds........................	12.6	8.4	5.6	53.3	250,800	245,365	-2.2	-3.4	27,002	17,384	-18,049	89,153	2.63	64.4	24.7	31.0
Holmes......................	12.8	8.6	6.4	52.2	21,609	19,483	-9.8	-9.6	2,173	1,794	-2,268	6,280	2.80	66.0	36.1	31.8
Humphreys..................	14.4	9.8	7.1	52.9	11,206	9,375	-16.3	-11.9	970	782	-1,328	3,119	2.75	63.3	31.4	32.9
Issaquena	16.1	8.0	8.7	40.8	2,274	1,399	-38.5	-6.5	106	93	-106	437	2.38	65.7	20.1	27.0
Itawamba	12.4	9.7	7.9	50.7	22,770	23,401	2.8	0.5	2,174	2,252	210	8,813	2.54	70.4	13.3	26.4
Jackson......................	13.6	9.5	6.3	50.8	131,420	139,668	6.3	2.6	13,410	10,868	1,130	50,994	2.75	66.2	14.6	28.6
Jasper.......................	14.1	11.6	8.8	51.6	18,149	17,065	-6.0	-3.7	1,796	1,616	-824	6,817	2.42	76.1	19.6	23.1
Jefferson	14.9	9.4	7.5	50.9	9,740	7,732	-20.6	-8.1	866	681	-824	2,453	2.86	64.5	28.3	33.9
Jefferson Davis	14.6	13.1	9.6	52.7	13,962	12,481	-10.6	-10.0	1,125	1,266	-1,111	4,798	2.40	63.6	21.7	32.1
Jones........................	13.1	9.8	7.1	51.4	64,958	67,769	4.3	1.0	7,896	6,137	-1,030	24,663	2.70	69.8	16.1	26.7
Kemper......................	12.8	10.8	9.4	49.9	10,453	10,446	-0.1	-4.0	732	825	-330	3,695	2.46	61.1	20.6	34.9
Lafayette....................	10.2	7.8	4.8	51.5	38,744	47,359	22.2	15.7	4,540	3,123	5,897	19,767	2.41	57.3	13.8	28.8
Lamar.......................	11.8	8.2	5.6	52.0	39,070	55,668	42.5	12.2	6,446	3,427	3,708	22,022	2.73	71.6	14.5	23.1
Lauderdale..................	13.0	9.9	7.5	51.5	78,161	80,267	2.7	-6.2	8,355	7,084	-6,248	29,892	2.51	67.5	17.5	31.1
Lawrence	14.5	10.4	7.6	51.5	13,258	12,929	-2.5	-3.7	1,337	1,205	-611	4,822	2.63	70.2	15.2	28.0
Leake........................	12.5	9.6	6.8	48.4	20,940	23,803	13.7	-4.4	2,480	2,036	-1,488	8,228	2.70	69.7	21.1	27.9
Lee..........................	12.6	8.7	6.1	52.2	75,755	82,910	9.4	2.8	9,612	7,535	256	32,485	2.58	67.7	15.2	28.3
Leflore......................	12.0	8.3	6.2	53.4	37,947	32,382	-14.7	-10.7	3,989	3,006	-4,520	10,477	2.74	61.1	27.7	36.3
Lincoln......................	13.6	10.0	7.1	52.4	33,166	34,870	5.1	-1.9	3,639	3,382	-905	12,806	2.64	70.5	16.4	26.9
Lowndes.....................	13.2	9.3	6.6	52.4	61,586	59,779	-2.9	-1.4	6,481	4,928	-2,388	22,630	2.56	68.3	18.2	27.9
Madison.....................	13.2	8.5	4.7	52.1	74,674	95,203	27.5	11.0	10,594	8,164	7,969	38,405	2.61	72.7	15.6	24.3
Marion......................	13.6	10.6	7.9	51.7	25,595	27,085	5.8	-8.8	2,603	2,833	-2,153	9,667	2.56	68.4	15.2	28.5
Marshall.....................	14.9	10.8	6.8	50.4	34,993	37,145	6.1	-4.6	3,547	3,401	-1,837	13,084	2.60	68.1	16.4	26.9
Monroe......................	13.7	11.0	8.2	52.4	38,014	36,989	-2.7	-3.9	3,449	3,502	-1,367	14,042	2.53	67.5	16.3	29.7
Montgomery.................	14.6	12.2	9.4	52.3	12,189	10,926	-10.4	-8.3	1,063	1,176	-794	4,524	2.25	70.9	21.8	26.5
Neshoba.....................	12.3	9.3	6.5	52.4	28,684	29,685	3.5	-1.9	3,534	3,056	-1,028	10,773	2.69	69.2	20.0	28.8
Newton......................	11.9	9.7	7.1	52.2	21,838	21,720	-0.5	-1.3	2,384	2,233	-424	8,010	2.58	72.6	19.1	25.7
Noxubee.....................	13.9	9.3	7.1	52.8	12,548	11,545	-8.0	-8.7	1,294	1,003	-1,315	4,002	2.68	67.4	25.5	30.4
Oktibbeha...................	9.1	6.4	5.1	50.1	42,902	47,671	11.1	4.0	4,647	2,480	-268	17,393	2.54	50.9	11.3	34.0
Panola......................	13.4	9.4	6.3	51.9	34,274	34,698	1.2	-1.5	4,138	3,317	-1,333	12,449	2.73	65.3	18.1	32.4
Pearl River..................	13.7	11.4	7.4	50.8	48,621	55,752	14.7	-0.7	5,232	5,143	-437	20,710	2.58	72.0	13.5	24.5
Perry........................	14.7	10.7	7.6	51.1	12,138	12,249	0.9	-2.6	1,171	1,094	-393	4,476	2.66	68.8	13.9	29.0
Pike.........................	12.5	10.2	7.1	52.9	38,940	40,407	3.8	-2.1	4,554	4,131	-1,253	14,962	2.59	64.1	18.3	34.1
Pontotoc....................	12.4	8.6	6.4	51.1	26,726	29,957	12.1	6.3	3,600	2,377	647	10,845	2.84	71.0	13.5	25.4
Prentiss.....................	12.6	9.9	8.3	51.0	25,556	25,276	-1.1	0.2	2,621	2,382	-194	9,533	2.55	68.6	13.5	28.0
Quitman	14.3	10.0	7.4	53.5	10,117	8,222	-18.7	-14.2	800	815	-1,172	3,072	2.40	61.4	25.8	34.9
Rankin.......................	12.3	9.1	6.2	51.9	115,327	142,054	23.2	8.3	15,296	9,022	5,645	55,226	2.61	72.2	12.8	23.4
Scott........................	12.8	8.7	6.4	50.9	28,423	28,260	-0.6	0.1	3,812	2,402	-1,381	10,096	2.79	69.4	22.8	27.7
Sharkey.....................	16.1	11.1	8.0	52.2	6,580	4,916	-25.3	-11.0	522	501	-570	1,809	2.48	60.0	17.3	36.7
Simpson	14.2	10.1	7.4	51.5	27,639	27,498	-0.5	-2.7	2,649	2,494	-883	9,322	2.85	71.3	19.5	25.3
Smith........................	13.9	11.1	8.5	51.9	16,182	16,491	1.9	-3.0	1,563	1,365	-686	5,850	2.74	71.5	13.0	26.2
Stone........................	13.0	10.1	5.8	49.5	13,622	17,788	30.6	5.2	1,746	1,471	645	5,979	2.89	75.6	13.5	22.2

1. No spouse present.

Table B. States and Counties — Population, Vital Statistics, Health, and Crime

STATE County	Persons in group quarters, 2018	Daytime Population, 2013-2017 Number	Employment/residence ratio	Births, 2018 Total	Rate[1]	Deaths, 2018 Number	Rate[1]	Persons under 65 with no health insurance, 2016 Number	Percent	Medicare, 2018 Total beneficiaries	Enrolled in Original Medicare	Enrolled in Medicare Advantage	Serious crimes known to police[2], 2016 Total Number	Rate[3]
	32	33	34	35	36	37	38	39	40	41	42	43	44	45
MISSISSIPPI	98,060	2,934,967	0.96	36,319	12.2	31,356	10.5	342,668	14.0	590,782	479,860	110,922	91,115	3,049
Adams	2,322	32,788	1.12	347	11.1	407	13.0	3,274	14.1	7,233	6,022	1,211	NA	NA
Alcorn	733	37,515	1.02	411	11.1	459	12.4	4,278	14.2	8,992	8,618	374	NA	NA
Amite	116	10,522	0.54	124	10.1	149	12.1	1,648	17.2	3,204	2,734	470	NA	NA
Attala	358	17,189	0.77	232	12.6	227	12.4	2,069	13.8	4,218	3,290	928	NA	NA
Benton	78	6,535	0.38	102	12.3	97	11.7	981	14.8	1,934	1,622	312	NA	NA
Bolivar	1,671	32,933	0.98	423	13.5	408	13.0	3,652	14.1	7,045	6,178	867	NA	NA
Calhoun	217	13,023	0.69	148	10.3	167	11.6	2,232	18.9	3,553	3,240	313	NA	NA
Carroll	363	7,621	0.29	80	8.1	100	10.1	1,206	15.8	2,691	2,456	235	NA	NA
Chickasaw	496	16,285	0.85	222	12.9	200	11.6	2,406	17.3	4,070	3,560	510	NA	NA
Choctaw	122	7,475	0.70	87	10.5	111	13.4	888	13.7	1,754	1,583	171	99	1,204
Claiborne	1,207	9,437	1.14	110	12.2	95	10.6	923	14.0	1,862	1,421	441	95	1,245
Clarke	53	13,382	0.55	188	12.0	192	12.3	1,887	14.8	4,020	3,336	684	NA	NA
Clay	304	17,739	0.71	216	11.1	245	12.6	2,498	15.7	4,447	3,867	580	373	1,875
Coahoma	756	24,475	1.02	349	15.4	288	12.7	2,585	13.1	4,969	4,416	553	NA	NA
Copiah	1,034	26,089	0.74	324	11.4	324	11.4	3,324	14.4	6,066	4,270	1,796	NA	NA
Covington	237	17,755	0.80	247	13.1	229	12.1	2,643	16.6	4,136	3,249	887	NA	NA
DeSoto	607	147,496	0.70	2,152	11.8	1,397	7.7	15,900	10.3	27,781	22,282	5,499	4,120	2,351
Forrest	2,918	84,663	1.28	962	12.8	758	10.1	9,723	15.5	13,334	10,312	3,022	2,817	3,711
Franklin	67	6,966	0.71	83	10.7	75	9.6	869	13.8	1,875	1,688	187	NA	NA
George	635	20,344	0.58	356	14.7	264	10.9	2,713	13.8	4,375	3,369	1,006	NA	NA
Greene	2,589	12,222	0.59	132	9.7	136	10.0	1,392	15.1	2,311	2,018	293	26	202
Grenada	257	23,050	1.22	269	12.8	280	13.3	2,590	15.0	5,352	4,609	743	NA	NA
Hancock	550	44,992	0.93	444	9.4	481	10.2	5,749	15.1	9,607	6,391	3,216	NA	NA
Harrison	5,215	212,562	1.14	2,675	12.9	1,962	9.5	26,077	15.4	38,205	29,403	8,802	9,390	4,611
Hinds	9,612	258,354	1.15	2,978	12.6	2,145	9.0	27,658	13.8	41,634	28,499	13,135	10,255	4,835
Holmes	989	16,915	0.72	235	13.3	238	13.5	2,239	15.7	4,056	3,174	882	NA	NA
Humphreys	82	8,180	0.81	94	11.4	110	13.3	1,045	14.9	1,884	1,677	207	NA	NA
Issaquena	295	1,295	1.00	14	10.7	9	6.9	144	17.8	170	142	28	NA	NA
Itawamba	1,032	20,851	0.72	258	11.0	254	10.8	2,874	15.5	5,457	5,100	357	NA	NA
Jackson	1,419	136,935	0.93	1,619	11.3	1,386	9.7	16,058	13.4	27,508	20,378	7,130	4,365	3,417
Jasper	87	14,115	0.62	195	11.9	190	11.6	2,098	15.9	3,929	3,072	857	NA	NA
Jefferson	359	7,120	0.80	87	12.2	81	11.4	981	17.1	1,655	1,347	308	NA	NA
Jefferson Davis	114	9,612	0.47	118	10.5	159	14.2	1,581	17.9	2,637	2,246	391	NA	NA
Jones	2,233	71,077	1.10	877	12.8	802	11.7	8,816	15.9	13,936	11,134	2,802	1,835	2,923
Kemper	1,200	10,546	1.13	92	9.2	110	11.0	1,350	19.0	2,012	1,619	393	68	772
Lafayette	5,966	53,891	1.05	540	9.9	416	7.6	5,719	13.8	7,786	7,107	679	NA	NA
Lamar	327	54,536	0.78	772	12.4	426	6.8	6,692	12.5	9,023	7,203	1,820	1,119	1,896
Lauderdale	3,683	83,509	1.16	923	12.3	836	11.1	7,910	12.8	15,020	12,516	2,504	2,704	3,470
Lawrence	0	11,375	0.72	161	12.9	155	12.4	1,626	15.4	3,212	2,700	512	NA	NA
Leake	1,680	19,996	0.65	283	12.4	270	11.9	3,383	19.3	4,414	3,457	957	NA	NA
Lee	1,063	98,606	1.37	1,153	13.5	987	11.6	9,147	12.7	17,055	15,547	1,508	NA	NA
Leflore	1,490	33,376	1.36	446	15.4	355	12.3	3,379	13.9	5,978	5,637	341	NA	NA
Lincoln	710	33,057	0.88	412	12.0	418	12.2	4,077	14.3	7,422	6,174	1,248	NA	NA
Lowndes	1,468	63,764	1.17	749	12.7	610	10.4	6,984	14.2	11,660	10,345	1,315	NA	NA
Madison	1,754	109,628	1.15	1,257	11.9	1,082	10.2	8,648	9.5	17,568	13,775	3,793	1,361	1,527
Marion	729	25,548	1.01	286	11.6	336	13.6	3,197	15.9	5,759	4,579	1,180	337	1,770
Marshall	1,843	30,861	0.63	383	10.8	439	12.4	3,897	13.9	7,651	5,922	1,729	600	1,686
Monroe	405	31,824	0.71	403	11.3	425	12.0	3,912	13.5	8,559	7,691	868	NA	NA
Montgomery	100	9,328	0.76	127	12.7	121	12.1	1,278	15.8	2,688	2,540	148	NA	NA
Neshoba	390	29,737	1.03	417	14.3	379	13.0	4,278	17.3	5,747	5,029	718	NA	NA
Newton	734	19,420	0.75	288	13.4	281	13.1	2,832	16.3	4,808	4,012	796	NA	NA
Noxubee	157	10,168	0.80	159	15.1	128	12.1	1,748	19.5	2,456	2,351	105	NA	NA
Oktibbeha	4,570	50,443	1.05	571	11.5	353	7.1	5,663	14.2	6,750	6,103	647	1,117	2,230
Panola	315	32,930	0.90	482	14.1	426	12.5	4,200	14.7	7,342	5,807	1,535	1,207	3,765
Pearl River	1,355	46,430	0.59	603	10.9	651	11.8	6,289	14.3	13,432	9,694	3,738	NA	NA
Perry	102	10,619	0.66	130	10.9	117	9.8	1,700	17.1	2,812	2,332	480	NA	NA
Pike	898	41,187	1.10	530	13.4	525	13.3	4,679	14.5	8,697	6,610	2,087	NA	NA
Pontotoc	234	29,488	0.88	439	13.8	281	8.8	4,311	16.1	6,203	5,550	653	NA	NA
Prentiss	929	23,384	0.79	301	11.9	277	10.9	3,140	15.6	5,491	5,185	306	NA	NA
Quitman	115	6,894	0.72	85	12.1	104	14.7	984	16.5	1,652	1,461	191	NA	NA
Rankin	5,893	143,574	0.91	1,716	11.1	1,217	7.9	12,832	10.2	26,938	21,059	5,879	1,227	1,068
Scott	228	28,958	1.05	468	16.5	342	12.1	4,572	19.2	5,526	4,214	1,312	NA	NA
Sharkey	108	4,327	0.79	52	11.9	54	12.3	573	15.5	1,134	959	175	NA	NA
Simpson	607	23,684	0.65	292	10.9	320	12.0	3,211	14.6	5,836	4,599	1,237	14	57
Smith	112	14,137	0.68	182	11.4	169	10.6	1,935	14.9	3,417	2,792	625	NA	NA
Stone	1,914	16,095	0.75	207	11.1	179	9.6	1,886	13.5	3,707	2,795	912	424	2,349

1. Per 1,000 estimated resident population.   2. Data for serious crimes have not been adjusted for underreporting; this may affect comparability between geographic areas and over time.   3. Per 100,000 population estimated by the FBI.

Table B. States and Counties — Crime, Education, Money Income, and Poverty

STATE County	Serious crimes known to police[2], 2016 (cont.)[1] — Rate Violent	Property	Education — School enrollment and attainment, 2013-2017 — Enrollment[3] Total	Percent private	Attainment[4] (percent) High school graduate or less	Bachelor's degree or more	Local government expenditures,[5] 2014-2015 Total current spending (mil dol)	Current spending per student (dollars)	Per capita income[6]	Money income, 2013-2017 Households Median income (dollars)	Percent with income of less than $50,000	Percent with income of $200,000 or more	Income and poverty, 2017 Median household income (dollars)	Percent below poverty level All persons	Children under 18 years	Children 5 to 17 years in families
	46	47	48	49	50	51	52	53	54	55	56	57	58	59	60	61
MISSISSIPPI.................	280	2,768	789,622	13.0	47.0	21.3	4,163.5	8,482	22,500	42,009	56.9	2.4	43,595	19.9	27.6	27.0
Adams.......................	NA	NA	7,371	13.2	55.2	17.4	34.1	9,570	17,721	30,359	70.8	2.2	31,044	32.5	44.4	38.8
Alcorn.......................	NA	NA	8,684	13.0	52.7	15.9	46.2	7,629	20,527	38,919	62.9	1.4	39,528	19.1	25.2	24.7
Amite........................	NA	NA	2,748	28.5	60.1	13.2	12.5	11,854	19,665	30,129	68.2	1.9	35,422	23.3	31.6	29.1
Attala.......................	NA	NA	4,504	6.5	53.6	12.3	29.3	8,487	20,617	33,815	65.0	2.3	35,158	24.1	31.8	31.8
Benton......................	NA	NA	1,727	5.7	62.4	10.3	11.5	9,592	18,599	40,605	64.6	0.7	35,797	21.8	33.9	34.0
Bolivar.....................	NA	NA	9,811	7.0	48.3	22.9	58.6	9,184	16,984	28,468	69.9	1.5	34,216	32.4	41.5	40.6
Calhoun....................	NA	NA	3,401	6.9	60.5	11.2	19.9	7,812	17,837	33,370	66.3	0.6	35,886	21.8	30.4	29.8
Carroll.....................	NA	NA	2,385	24.9	52.4	16.4	7.9	7,894	22,995	43,068	54.6	4.5	40,798	17.6	24.4	23.3
Chickasaw.................	NA	NA	3,888	8.1	62.0	11.8	25.5	8,546	19,609	33,579	64.1	1.6	37,231	18.2	29.6	28.1
Choctaw....................	73	1,131	2,033	6.0	54.2	17.3	14.4	10,045	19,816	34,542	64.8	1.3	37,561	22.1	32.6	31.2
Claiborne..................	288	956	2,993	6.8	52.9	18.8	15.2	9,433	13,095	24,601	77.8	0.2	28,518	42.6	53.5	55.6
Clarke......................	NA	NA	3,666	4.7	55.9	13.3	25.4	8,453	20,564	37,626	61.1	2.1	38,840	20.8	32.1	31.4
Clay.........................	206	1,669	5,347	11.9	52.0	19.3	28.9	8,671	19,220	34,118	63.7	1.0	36,044	25.4	37.7	37.7
Coahoma...................	NA	NA	7,146	11.2	48.5	16.9	47.7	9,862	16,699	28,728	70.6	1.4	28,921	34.8	50.4	51.5
Copiah......................	NA	NA	7,594	10.4	52.2	13.3	30.9	7,197	18,756	38,046	62.1	1.2	39,107	22.5	34.6	34.6
Covington..................	NA	NA	4,385	14.0	55.1	16.1	25.0	8,378	18,749	36,471	62.3	0.4	39,644	23	34.7	34.5
DeSoto......................	118	2,234	48,206	13.2	40.1	23.5	235.1	7,065	28,316	62,595	39.0	3.5	66,125	8.7	12.8	12.7
Forrest.....................	196	3,514	23,702	13.2	41.0	26.7	110.7	9,493	20,783	39,555	60.0	1.8	39,394	22.7	27.5	27.5
Franklin....................	NA	NA	1,811	10.3	53.2	16.2	13.6	9,380	24,864	42,388	55.8	2.8	38,370	20.6	28.5	25.9
George......................	NA	NA	5,925	17.3	57.7	11.9	31.4	7,656	20,973	47,640	51.9	2.9	51,185	16	22.5	22.5
Greene......................	16	186	2,547	11.2	60.8	8.7	17.2	8,155	18,002	48,029	51.6	3.3	44,337	21.7	24.4	22.7
Grenada....................	NA	NA	5,343	10.6	50.2	18.1	32.8	7,859	20,150	34,876	63.8	1.4	38,827	20.4	29.6	29.5
Hancock....................	NA	NA	10,248	17.6	42.9	20.9	55.0	8,511	24,373	47,518	51.8	1.9	45,535	17	24.4	23.6
Harrison...................	248	4,363	49,445	11.1	42.3	22.2	268.4	8,431	23,127	44,684	54.9	2.0	46,709	19.7	30.5	29.9
Hinds.......................	739	4,096	73,338	17.4	38.9	28.6	354.9	8,769	22,397	41,011	57.9	2.5	44,076	20.2	28.6	27.0
Holmes.....................	NA	NA	5,321	7.3	65.7	10.7	29.3	8,376	12,394	20,330	80.1	0.7	24,783	40.8	52.5	52.7
Humphreys................	NA	NA	2,324	10.3	62.8	13.6	15.7	8,997	15,696	26,188	77.3	2.4	26,489	38.4	56.2	53.0
Issaquena	NA	NA	141	19.9	72.6	6.1	NA	NA	16,348	25,609	75.5	1.6	28,075	38.1	50.0	54.0
Itawamba..................	NA	NA	5,814	3.0	52.4	13.0	27.5	7,707	20,859	38,358	59.7	1.1	45,718	14.5	19.7	19.0
Jackson....................	197	3,219	36,509	12.5	43.7	20.7	222.1	9,077	24,665	50,274	49.7	2.4	49,699	14.5	21.6	22.0
Jasper......................	NA	NA	3,616	20.3	53.2	13.9	22.1	8,974	20,619	35,271	64.3	2.5	35,916	23.8	32.5	34.4
Jefferson	NA	NA	1,596	0.1	63.6	12.7	12.8	9,904	13,758	21,779	74.9	0.9	27,925	34.1	45.6	47.8
Jefferson Davis	NA	NA	2,565	16.7	60.1	15.0	15.4	10,086	17,035	26,736	75.3	1.3	28,043	28.7	40.1	41.1
Jones.......................	352	2,571	16,279	12.2	48.9	18.4	93.5	7,906	20,958	38,656	61.0	2.2	39,459	21.3	27.6	28.0
Kemper.....................	114	659	2,776	4.0	53.0	13.1	12.9	11,227	15,790	27,016	74.0	1.8	32,026	29.8	40.6	38.4
Lafayette..................	NA	NA	20,315	5.0	29.4	41.9	60.3	8,773	25,719	45,019	53.1	4.5	47,899	21.1	18.4	18.7
Lamar......................	191	1,704	18,138	14.8	33.0	35.9	82.7	7,936	28,342	56,129	44.1	4.4	57,125	15.5	18.6	18.7
Lauderdale................	368	3,102	19,989	10.0	44.5	20.1	107.9	8,615	23,339	41,340	58.9	2.4	43,538	20.5	30.0	28.5
Lawrence..................	NA	NA	3,012	7.4	56.0	13.8	17.7	8,013	21,826	40,432	58.4	1.1	38,446	19.7	28.9	28.1
Leake.......................	NA	NA	5,853	14.8	60.0	12.1	23.1	7,810	18,825	35,578	63.0	3.7	36,031	21.7	33.5	33.8
Lee..........................	NA	NA	21,790	11.5	42.7	23.5	141.2	8,551	23,968	45,985	53.5	2.8	51,559	14	20.4	19.5
Leflore.....................	NA	NA	9,129	11.2	57.2	17.9	47.0	8,749	15,403	25,210	71.8	0.8	25,569	42.2	60.2	57.7
Lincoln.....................	NA	NA	8,436	12.6	50.1	15.0	51.1	8,139	20,627	37,308	60.0	1.7	40,898	18.2	24.1	24.6
Lowndes....................	NA	NA	15,893	12.1	46.0	23.6	88.9	9,101	23,141	43,198	54.8	2.0	42,277	22.2	32.6	32.9
Madison....................	141	1,385	29,052	25.0	25.3	46.5	138.7	8,492	36,627	68,600	37.3	8.5	69,820	10.7	14.3	14.0
Marion......................	215	1,554	5,964	21.0	59.5	12.9	35.2	9,171	19,610	30,998	65.6	1.6	28,967	24.7	33.0	30.7
Marshall...................	374	1,312	8,207	14.9	61.9	13.1	39.1	8,211	19,775	41,134	58.4	1.0	38,498	22.8	34.2	32.5
Monroe.....................	NA	NA	8,027	7.3	55.7	16.5	44.1	8,169	21,643	39,444	59.0	2.0	40,371	18.2	25.6	23.6
Montgomery...............	NA	NA	2,289	25.3	53.4	21.0	14.0	9,712	22,666	34,983	62.2	1.2	36,182	23.2	33.7	31.5
Neshoba....................	NA	NA	7,923	6.5	54.5	14.1	34.3	7,542	19,243	36,755	61.4	1.9	38,728	22.4	31.0	29.7
Newton.....................	NA	NA	6,114	9.1	46.6	16.3	32.5	8,515	21,177	37,643	62.4	1.2	39,898	20.4	27.2	26.0
Noxubee...................	NA	NA	2,623	14.7	61.8	12.9	16.5	9,308	16,591	30,808	67.5	0.8	30,130	34.5	45.8	44.7
Oktibbeha.................	168	2,063	22,176	7.9	33.0	42.6	49.3	9,488	21,322	37,348	60.0	3.0	39,387	25.5	26.2	26.6
Panola......................	377	3,388	8,240	11.4	60.4	14.4	52.7	8,705	20,191	35,891	64.7	1.2	35,927	22.7	34.0	33.7
Pearl River................	NA	NA	13,417	12.1	45.8	15.0	73.0	8,390	22,136	44,734	53.7	1.4	47,757	17.2	24.9	22.7
Perry........................	NA	NA	2,914	7.8	57.8	10.6	17.1	8,945	19,308	35,374	64.8	0.7	38,997	20.5	31.3	30.6
Pike.........................	NA	NA	10,366	10.7	53.9	15.9	59.7	8,540	17,470	30,949	68.9	1.1	32,525	28	37.8	36.4
Pontotoc...................	NA	NA	7,779	6.2	54.9	14.9	44.8	7,707	20,421	41,865	57.9	1.5	45,396	14.6	21.0	20.7
Prentiss....................	NA	NA	6,557	2.4	55.0	12.3	31.1	8,337	19,016	32,854	66.0	1.4	36,654	17.7	24.3	23.6
Quitman....................	NA	NA	1,799	14.2	61.8	11.8	11.7	9,862	15,189	25,671	74.6	0.3	26,740	40.9	57.5	56.8
Rankin.....................	64	1,004	37,617	20.8	36.5	29.2	189.1	8,090	29,055	61,605	39.9	4.1	65,504	9.3	11.9	11.9
Scott........................	NA	NA	7,005	6.9	62.1	12.7	42.5	7,367	20,520	33,601	65.8	2.4	37,201	21.9	29.0	29.5
Sharkey....................	NA	NA	1,149	16.1	50.0	21.5	9.7	10,760	17,192	30,033	74.2	0.9	28,842	35.5	51.0	47.5
Simpson...................	4	53	7,169	17.7	56.0	13.3	32.5	8,377	19,336	37,591	66.2	1.8	38,385	23	33.6	29.6
Smith.......................	NA	NA	3,556	8.2	62.1	11.0	24.0	8,463	21,864	37,697	59.6	1.6	42,517	16.3	24.0	23.0
Stone.......................	227	2,122	4,393	10.4	52.3	15.0	22.4	8,501	21,615	46,283	52.2	2.6	44,159	16.3	24.3	23.5

1. Data for serious crimes have not been adjusted for underreporting; this may affect comparability between geographic areas and over time.   2. Per 100,000 population estimated by the FBI.   3. All persons 3 years old and over enrolled in nursery school through college.   4. Persons 25 years old and over.   5. Elementary and secondary education expenditures.   6. Based on population estimated by the American Community Survey, 2013–2017.

Table B. States and Counties — **Personal Income and Earnings**

STATE County	Personal income, 2017										Earnings, 2017		
			Per capita[1]			Supplements to wages and salaries, employer contributions (mil dol)						Contributions for government social insurance (mil dol)	
	Total (mil dol)	Percent change 2016-2017	Dollars	Rank	Wages and salaries (mil dol)	Pension and insurance	Government social insurance	Proprietors' income (mil dol)	Dividends, interest, and rent (mil dol)	Personal transfer receipts (mil dol)	Total (mil dol)	From employee and self-employed	From employer
	62	63	64	65	66	67	68	69	70	71	72	73	74
MISSISSIPPI	109,324	2.3	36,567	X	48,366	8,211	3,623	7,391	18,045	28,632	67,591	4,679	3,623
Adams	1,026	0.5	33,099	2,603	410	63	30	87	192	355	591	45	30
Alcorn	1,289	3.5	34,644	2,396	558	91	41	67	184	410	757	57	41
Amite	393	3.3	31,542	2,804	75	13	6	25	49	139	118	11	6
Attala	610	1.8	33,002	2,617	166	29	12	48	83	206	256	21	12
Benton	241	2.9	29,022	2,985	40	8	3	8	25	88	60	6	3
Bolivar	1,154	-0.6	36,131	2,183	450	82	34	42	208	406	609	45	34
Calhoun	458	2.3	31,576	2,798	113	20	9	37	59	162	179	14	9
Carroll	361	1.2	35,649	2,250	45	9	3	3	56	115	60	8	3
Chickasaw	563	4.0	32,817	2,644	197	33	15	50	96	185	296	22	15
Choctaw	260	0.8	31,461	2,812	100	21	7	14	34	86	142	10	7
Claiborne	265	-1.3	29,657	2,950	191	44	14	8	32	119	257	17	14
Clarke	567	1.6	35,815	2,225	106	20	8	24	63	192	158	15	8
Clay	707	1.6	35,998	2,202	218	34	16	73	112	205	341	24	16
Coahoma	790	-2.9	34,125	2,470	308	50	23	14	138	325	395	32	23
Copiah	917	1.9	32,140	2,736	290	59	23	54	102	301	425	32	23
Covington	638	6.3	33,449	2,561	206	37	15	66	86	198	324	23	15
DeSoto	7,054	4.7	39,461	1,647	2,371	340	176	439	739	1,146	3,327	233	176
Forrest	2,879	2.7	38,141	1,858	1,829	320	134	258	568	749	2,540	163	134
Franklin	258	0.7	33,209	2,593	67	14	5	14	35	92	100	8	5
George	767	2.5	31,850	2,773	184	34	14	24	91	204	256	21	14
Greene	381	0.4	28,556	3,013	73	16	5	10	40	120	105	9	5
Grenada	741	1.9	35,122	2,331	408	73	31	49	102	255	561	40	31
Hancock	1,627	4.0	34,580	2,403	760	143	61	52	369	418	1,016	71	61
Harrison	7,453	2.3	36,350	2,143	4,048	728	320	469	1,562	1,808	5,565	359	320
Hinds	9,282	0.7	38,758	1,765	6,207	1,068	455	755	1,962	2,268	8,485	541	455
Holmes	492	-2.1	27,715	3,038	130	26	10	-3	63	247	162	16	10
Humphreys	232	-4.4	27,775	3,035	72	14	6	-11	46	108	81	9	6
Issaquena	16	-32.1	11,937	3,113	7	1	1	-15	9	10	-6	1	1
Itawamba	778	3.9	33,116	2,601	246	43	18	27	89	246	334	28	18
Jackson	5,181	2.0	36,449	2,123	2,651	525	202	251	875	1,199	3,629	242	202
Jasper	584	4.8	35,220	2,309	169	30	13	45	71	183	257	19	13
Jefferson	230	1.8	31,628	2,794	44	11	4	2	24	96	60	6	4
Jefferson Davis	331	3.6	29,287	2,970	71	13	5	19	42	133	109	10	5
Jones	2,547	3.5	37,501	1,945	1,189	228	85	187	408	784	1,689	112	85
Kemper	289	3.1	29,224	2,975	152	29	11	15	36	112	208	14	11
Lafayette	2,177	2.9	40,037	1,544	1,023	181	74	219	532	373	1,497	96	74
Lamar	2,398	2.3	39,076	1,706	677	100	50	237	417	406	1,064	75	50
Lauderdale	2,878	0.7	37,796	1,912	1,427	245	111	192	590	772	1,975	134	111
Lawrence	410	3.2	32,468	2,690	116	20	8	37	45	155	181	14	8
Leake	665	5.5	29,289	2,969	174	31	14	82	71	219	301	20	14
Lee	3,387	2.8	39,882	1,575	2,328	337	174	267	517	744	3,106	206	174
Leflore	1,030	1.5	35,241	2,307	544	102	42	45	217	352	733	51	42
Lincoln	1,274	2.5	37,087	2,019	497	76	36	92	159	354	702	51	36
Lowndes	2,193	2.4	37,061	2,023	1,230	210	95	96	405	562	1,631	108	95
Madison	6,475	2.9	61,895	138	2,791	366	199	667	1,427	740	4,024	263	199
Marion	816	8.4	32,535	2,684	340	51	25	74	122	292	490	37	25
Marshall	1,113	1.8	31,238	2,835	290	44	22	43	117	355	398	35	22
Monroe	1,185	2.4	33,047	2,608	434	75	34	65	166	375	608	48	34
Montgomery	338	1.8	33,194	2,595	90	16	7	13	54	133	126	11	7
Neshoba	1,026	3.5	34,943	2,359	468	78	34	117	150	304	698	44	34
Newton	720	2.2	33,989	2,484	200	39	15	54	97	239	309	23	15
Noxubee	353	2.5	32,862	2,636	91	18	7	37	42	134	152	11	7
Oktibbeha	1,617	0.9	32,464	2,692	842	169	61	79	332	343	1,151	73	61
Panola	1,096	2.0	32,246	2,720	428	69	32	77	143	350	607	46	32
Pearl River	1,943	2.3	35,164	2,323	388	72	28	99	262	573	587	53	28
Perry	371	2.2	30,856	2,865	111	17	8	13	40	131	148	13	8
Pike	1,209	1.7	30,641	2,878	527	93	39	67	177	436	727	54	39
Pontotoc	1,002	3.2	31,672	2,791	470	71	37	58	118	258	637	47	37
Prentiss	760	2.2	30,084	2,924	268	47	20	31	101	256	366	30	20
Quitman	182	-7.4	24,999	3,090	39	8	3	-11	33	95	38	6	3
Rankin	6,609	1.7	43,459	1,082	2,874	418	207	498	991	1,223	3,997	270	207
Scott	862	5.5	30,336	2,902	483	85	39	79	91	281	687	44	39
Sharkey	124	-3.6	27,895	3,032	39	8	3	-12	26	63	37	5	3
Simpson	942	3.7	34,969	2,353	220	41	17	98	100	320	375	27	17
Smith	539	6.8	33,550	2,549	120	23	9	90	55	161	242	15	9
Stone	557	0.4	30,731	2,872	158	29	12	21	77	186	219	18	12

1. Based on the resident population estimated as of July 1 of the year shown.

Items 62—74

Table B. States and Counties — Earnings, Social Security, and Housing

STATE County	Earnings, 2017 (cont.)									Social Security beneficiaries, December 2017		Supplemental Security Income recipients, 2017	Housing units, 2018	
	Percent by selected industries													
	Farm	Mining, quarrying, and extractions	Construction	Manufacturing	Information; professional, scientific, technical services	Retail trade	Finance, insurance, real estate, and leasing	Health care and social assistance	Government	Number	Rate[1]		Total	Percent change, 2010-2018
	75	76	77	78	79	80	81	82	83	84	85	86	87	88
MISSISSIPPI	1.1	0.8	5.8	13.6	5.7	7.7	5.1	11.9	22.8	661,656	222	119,553	1,332,577	4.5
Adams	1.2	5.7	4.3	6	5.1	13.8	5.8	D	13.8	8,095	261	1,760	14,691	0.2
Alcorn	0.6	0	4.6	19.8	2.6	10.6	3.6	11.9	20.9	10,165	273	1,665	17,279	1.2
Amite	11.9	D	4.9	12.8	D	5.4	D	D	16.8	3,525	283	606	6,788	2.3
Attala	-0.4	0.5	16.8	12.8	D	11.4	4.7	D	20.3	4,970	269	900	9,244	1.3
Benton	1.7	0	6.1	13	5.6	9.5	1.4	11.9	38	2,175	262	410	4,252	1.6
Bolivar	0.2	0	3.5	16.3	D	10.7	4.4	15.3	20.3	8,095	253	2,893	14,410	2.4
Calhoun	12.7	0.1	3	20.5	1.9	6.9	3.8	D	15.8	4,050	279	648	6,998	1.2
Carroll	-23.6	D	20.1	12.7	D	4.2	D	D	28.9	3,050	301	445	5,196	2.9
Chickasaw	8.2	0.1	4.4	39.4	1.9	8.7	2.8	D	14.1	4,695	274	974	7,655	1.9
Choctaw	2.2	D	2.3	8.7	D	3.1	D	D	31	1,955	236	330	4,210	1.4
Claiborne	0.4	0	D	2.7	D	2.5	D	D	29.5	2,215	247	667	4,314	2.2
Clarke	5.7	8.4	11.1	10.3	2.7	5.7	D	D	22.9	4,630	293	716	8,032	2
Clay	14.3	D	4.9	14.9	3.2	10.1	3.1	D	13.1	5,055	257	1,015	9,304	1.4
Coahoma	-5.4	0.1	3.3	6.5	5.3	7.5	11	19.8	23.6	5,655	244	1,996	10,707	-0.8
Copiah	3.7	1.4	3.3	35.3	2.5	6.6	2.4	D	18.4	6,895	242	1,522	12,265	0.7
Covington	11.6	D	8.9	19	D	6	3.2	6	18.7	4,665	245	963	8,739	2.8
DeSoto	0	D	9.1	8.3	2.9	11.3	4.4	11.4	12	30,240	169	2,868	68,518	11.2
Forrest	0	0.3	5.4	9	3.6	6.7	4.7	17	28.7	15,025	199	2,704	33,215	2.9
Franklin	4.3	D	4.8	1	D	9.3	D	D	35.6	2,150	277	374	4,252	2.4
George	2	D	8.4	6.3	3.8	11.4	4.1	D	31.1	5,095	211	784	9,565	2.5
Greene	3.5	0.3	D	D	D	5.6	D	D	44.4	2,770	208	430	5,265	2.8
Grenada	0.5	0	2.4	28.9	D	10.3	4.2	D	19.8	6,040	286	1,326	10,269	1.1
Hancock	-0.1	D	4	7.5	11.2	4.6	1.8	4.6	40.4	10,235	218	1,235	25,918	18.5
Harrison	0	D	5.5	4.2	6	7.1	4.3	8.5	34.6	42,095	205	6,494	93,911	10.2
Hinds	0.1	1	3.1	3.5	8.3	5.1	7	16.7	32.3	46,445	194	10,977	104,318	0.9
Holmes	-13.1	D	4.3	17	D	8.8	5.9	D	41	4,640	262	1,871	8,598	2.2
Humphreys	-25.5	0.2	6.5	26.6	D	7.2	12.9	D	25.8	2,215	266	1,035	3,826	-0.8
Issaquena	231.7	0	D	0	D	D	D	D	-65.4	190	142	57	568	2
Itawamba	0.8	0	11.6	32.2	D	6.1	2.7	7.8	17.8	6,365	271	855	10,339	2.1
Jackson	-0.2	0.1	7.2	38.2	6.5	4.8	3	7.2	18.7	31,005	218	3,287	62,727	4.4
Jasper	11.7	2.6	8.6	30.8	3.8	4.6	D	D	18.6	4,485	270	793	8,409	2.4
Jefferson	-1.3	0	D	D	D	D	D	14.1	46.1	1,940	267	683	3,776	2.7
Jefferson Davis	9.9	D	27.6	3.5	2.2	7	D	D	26	2,955	261	545	5,990	2
Jones	3.3	7.1	6.2	22.3	3.4	5.8	3.6	5.4	20.8	15,715	231	2,493	29,142	2.5
Kemper	3.8	D	18.4	6.8	D	1.7	D	D	16.6	2,315	234	491	4,833	2.5
Lafayette	0	D	4.1	7.7	10.5	6.9	5.5	14.9	33.9	8,225	151	857	26,458	16.4
Lamar	0.9	0.7	9.1	1.4	D	13.7	7.5	22.7	11.5	10,210	166	1,470	24,770	2.9
Lauderdale	0.1	0.1	4.2	7.2	4.2	9.1	5.3	19.6	21.2	16,685	219	3,020	35,349	1.9
Lawrence	14	D	4.1	33.7	D	4.8	2.6	6.1	18.1	3,680	291	611	6,116	2.4
Leake	19.3	0.2	D	D	D	8.1	3.4	D	13	5,145	227	985	9,559	1.5
Lee	0	0.1	3.2	19.8	7.1	9.2	6.1	21.3	9.8	19,385	228	2,949	37,052	3.3
Leflore	-1.5	D	6.9	13.5	5.1	7.1	5.5	9.7	29.9	6,910	236	2,532	13,128	-0.5
Lincoln	3	1.2	8.6	8.7	3.3	9.9	4.5	15.1	12.8	8,405	245	1,291	15,562	2
Lowndes	-0.3	D	5.5	19.1	3.8	6.8	4.9	14.1	23.2	13,075	221	2,439	27,489	3.5
Madison	-0.2	0.9	5.5	16.8	14.7	9.4	9.7	9.1	6.9	18,315	175	2,089	44,047	14.2
Marion	5.1	4	11.7	6.4	4.6	8	4.1	D	13.2	6,585	263	1,149	12,018	1.5
Marshall	0.1	0.1	11.8	13.5	D	8.7	5.4	D	16.3	8,595	241	1,755	15,820	6.3
Monroe	0.8	0.5	12.3	32.3	D	5.5	2.5	D	13.1	9,555	266	1,159	16,649	1.2
Montgomery	-2.3	0.1	D	D	5.9	10.1	D	D	24.3	3,040	299	714	5,765	11
Neshoba	9.5	D	11.1	4.2	1.8	9.7	2.8	D	41.2	6,630	226	1,256	12,562	1.6
Newton	10.6	D	7	16.5	1.6	5.5	2.1	D	30.1	5,345	252	663	9,533	1.7
Noxubee	12.7	D	D	23.7	D	10.1	2.1	D	25.7	2,780	259	914	5,232	1.2
Oktibbeha	0	D	3.5	7.8	4.3	5.9	4.2	7.1	49.7	7,370	148	1,457	22,201	6
Panola	0.7	D	6.7	13.1	D	10.3	5.6	D	18.6	8,365	246	2,035	15,129	3
Pearl River	0.5	D	10.3	5.9	4.4	13.5	4.8	D	28.6	14,640	265	1,886	25,689	7.3
Perry	-0.3	0.7	5	32.8	D	5.1	D	9.2	16	3,160	263	505	5,671	2.8
Pike	1.1	1.2	3.4	15.7	3.7	10.8	5.4	9	26	9,685	245	2,260	18,689	4.6
Pontotoc	-0.2	0.1	3.2	47.4	D	6.2	2.4	D	10.3	7,025	222	862	12,922	3.9
Prentiss	0.1	0	8.5	21.9	D	7.4	4.2	D	21	6,295	249	707	11,220	1.5
Quitman	-47.4	D	D	D	D	8.8	13.7	D	54.9	1,840	253	618	3,594	0.2
Rankin	0.7	D	9.5	6.8	5.3	10.6	7.5	12.2	13.1	28,985	191	2,691	61,483	8.8
Scott	7.8	0	5.7	46.5	D	5.5	2	D	11.3	6,305	222	1,313	11,735	2.3
Sharkey	-43.4	0.4	1.5	-0.1	D	12.2	11.3	D	57.8	1,270	286	399	2,142	2
Simpson	14.3	0.3	7.6	1.8	D	8	5.7	D	20.9	6,380	237	1,281	12,198	2.2
Smith	26.8	D	3.2	24.6	D	2.5	D	4.7	12	3,970	247	514	7,425	2.6
Stone	2.1	D	5.1	12.8	3.9	9.4	3.8	D	28.4	4,140	229	642	7,532	5.2

1. Per 1,000 resident population estimated as of July 1 of the year shown.

Table B. States and Counties — **Housing, Labor Force, and Employment**

STATE County	Housing units, 2013-2017								Civilian labor force, 2018				Civilian employment[6], 2013-2017		
	Occupied units							Sub-standard units[4] (percent)		Percent change, 2017-2018	Unemployment			Percent	
	Owner-occupied					Renter-occupied								Management, business, science, and arts	Construction, production, and maintenance occupations
	Total	Percent	Median value[1]	Median owner cost as a percent of income		Median rent[3]	Median rent as a percent of income[2]		Total		Total	Rate[5]	Total		
				With a mort-gage	Without a mort-gage[2]										
	89	90	91	92	93	94	95	96	97	98	99	100	101	102	103
MISSISSIPPI	1,103,514	68.1	109,300	21.0	11.1	740	30.1	3.2	1,275,721	-0.4	60,729	4.8	1,221,828	31.5	27.4
Adams	11,509	62.5	90,800	24.1	11.5	583	34.8	3	11,202	-0.1	696	6.2	10,190	30.5	25.3
Alcorn	14,675	70.2	86,100	20.2	10.4	607	24	1.9	16,123	0.8	667	4.1	14,884	29.2	33.1
Amite	4,994	85.8	77,500	27.8	12.3	643	26.5	2.1	4,470	-1.3	270	6	4,550	24.4	39.8
Attala	7,174	70.5	72,700	19.0	10.1	534	31.4	4.3	6,927	-0.3	393	5.7	6,776	26.1	35.8
Benton	2,960	82.7	70,300	23.5	12.1	527	22	1.9	3,078	0.8	171	5.6	2,923	24.4	42.6
Bolivar	12,267	55.4	89,100	22.3	13.2	604	31.4	3.1	12,472	-3.9	764	6.1	11,228	31.1	23.9
Calhoun	5,853	71.2	66,600	20.2	12.6	550	30.4	3.3	5,976	-2	257	4.3	5,260	21.4	47.1
Carroll	3,592	81.5	90,900	19.1	11.9	421	34	4	3,593	-1.3	196	5.5	3,737	33.9	33.3
Chickasaw	6,454	70.8	63,800	21.0	10.0	545	30	2.9	7,036	-0.7	349	5	6,746	19.7	44.9
Choctaw	3,198	76.5	77,200	21.8	11.8	547	29.6	2.7	3,792	3.3	182	4.8	3,046	31.0	34.7
Claiborne	3,187	68.7	61,000	24.0	14.9	597	34.7	7.3	2,952	-1.9	271	9.2	2,394	25.0	29.2
Clarke	6,365	83.0	72,000	19.8	11.5	612	28.8	1.6	5,938	-2.7	334	5.6	6,137	26.2	36.2
Clay	7,681	71.8	81,200	23.7	12.3	714	41.9	2	7,826	-0.2	470	6	7,663	27.6	33.7
Coahoma	8,969	51.2	62,400	19.7	13.6	578	29.6	3.3	8,680	-2.5	592	6.8	8,402	29.9	25.0
Copiah	9,778	77.9	93,800	21.9	12.0	715	29.5	5.4	11,251	-0.7	614	5.5	10,312	28.1	28.7
Covington	6,919	81.7	77,600	23.0	10.0	666	28.8	2.8	8,288	0.1	362	4.4	7,377	24.4	35.1
DeSoto	61,158	73.2	158,600	19.5	10.0	1,000	27.7	2.7	89,980	0.8	3,384	3.8	85,681	32.7	26.2
Forrest	28,063	55.1	114,700	20.0	11.5	747	33.1	2.6	33,763	0.2	1,494	4.4	32,089	34.0	22.7
Franklin	3,097	76.5	74,700	18.7	10.0	488	31	1.5	2,766	-2.2	167	6	2,883	28.2	39.5
George	7,220	85.2	98,200	20.6	10.0	671	22.9	2	8,892	-0.4	565	6.4	8,011	30.4	35.1
Greene	4,174	87.6	80,700	18.0	11.5	635	20.5	5	4,289	-1.9	264	6.2	3,972	34.9	33.7
Grenada	7,889	68.3	93,200	22.7	10.7	626	26.9	2.8	9,591	-0.8	410	4.3	7,958	32.5	26.0
Hancock	19,145	73.5	132,800	22.7	10.9	787	28.1	2.5	18,839	-0.1	937	5	19,009	34.2	24.2
Harrison	77,630	55.8	144,300	23.0	10.5	861	31	3.4	86,579	-0.1	3,917	4.5	84,351	28.6	22.9
Hinds	89,153	59.3	109,400	21.8	10.8	812	33.2	3.6	109,294	-0.7	5,037	4.6	105,853	32.2	22.0
Holmes	6,280	61.0	50,600	30.2	15.3	490	32.5	5.3	5,700	-2.3	507	8.9	4,891	24.4	36.6
Humphreys	3,119	58.2	64,200	32.2	13.3	522	31.1	4.5	2,306	0	193	8.4	2,730	21.9	40.6
Issaquena	437	46.0	50,200	34.1	14.1	389	28	7.3	378	-4.8	34	9	333	11.4	47.4
Itawamba	8,813	75.3	87,000	21.6	10.9	647	25.8	3.1	10,302	-0.9	419	4.1	9,392	23.0	40.0
Jackson	50,994	70.2	125,100	21.4	10.1	847	28.7	1.5	58,725	-0.3	3,246	5.5	60,574	31.9	27.0
Jasper	6,817	84.1	67,300	22.3	12.2	680	29.7	4.8	6,106	-0.2	357	5.8	6,470	23.9	39.2
Jefferson	2,453	65.3	57,100	19.1	15.4	415	36.8	4.6	1,998	-4.4	265	13.3	1,833	21.8	27.8
Jefferson Davis	4,798	74.9	80,600	26.9	15.4	587	36.4	1.6	4,113	-2.5	275	6.7	3,914	17.9	39.7
Jones	24,663	72.6	85,600	20.9	10.9	639	31.6	4.1	25,613	0.2	1,222	4.8	26,883	28.7	31.5
Kemper	3,695	76.4	70,900	29.7	11.7	363	25.9	5.1	3,454	-3	256	7.4	3,538	22.3	42.2
Lafayette	19,767	58.4	177,300	19.4	10.0	862	40.6	2.9	28,216	3.1	1,095	3.9	24,493	40.6	16.7
Lamar	22,022	68.1	169,000	19.5	10.0	904	28.7	2.9	30,510	0.4	1,109	3.6	27,791	39.0	18.7
Lauderdale	29,892	65.6	88,500	21.6	11.0	709	27.7	3.2	30,550	-2.9	1,538	5	32,021	34.0	23.5
Lawrence	4,822	79.2	89,100	17.3	14.0	718	27.5	4.5	4,605	-0.8	274	6	4,722	28.3	39.1
Leake	8,228	72.0	80,800	20.5	11.4	636	26.8	4	7,927	2.8	389	4.9	8,855	24.2	35.0
Lee	32,485	67.3	125,600	20.2	10.0	686	29.4	3.8	40,297	-0.9	1,566	3.9	38,185	31.0	28.5
Leflore	10,477	49.1	76,100	22.5	13.4	542	37.5	4.1	10,251	-1.8	692	6.8	9,106	28.1	27.9
Lincoln	12,806	74.9	94,800	20.5	11.8	688	30.7	2.5	14,663	0.5	691	4.7	13,056	32.6	27.0
Lowndes	22,630	61.3	123,400	20.9	10.0	750	30	2	25,329	-0.3	1,219	4.8	24,054	29.6	29.1
Madison	38,405	70.7	213,400	19.1	10.0	919	28.3	2.4	53,303	-0.6	1,950	3.7	51,194	46.3	17.6
Marion	9,667	78.6	78,500	24.6	12.1	616	40.6	4.5	10,130	-1.3	521	5.1	9,171	28.2	31.7
Marshall	13,084	75.9	94,300	22.9	12.7	637	28.2	2.6	14,591	0.8	730	5	14,304	23.2	37.7
Monroe	14,042	74.9	87,100	21.5	11.2	601	30.5	2.1	15,351	-0.6	754	4.9	14,499	26.5	36.9
Montgomery	4,524	74.0	77,900	20.4	13.4	498	27.4	2.5	4,047	-3.1	213	5.3	4,071	30.6	32.0
Neshoba	10,773	73.5	80,400	20.4	12.0	645	28.3	6.6	10,307	-2.3	510	4.9	12,292	30.5	26.4
Newton	8,010	77.6	80,300	20.7	12.3	635	30.7	4.6	8,422	-1.3	410	4.9	8,108	31.4	32.9
Noxubee	4,002	74.0	57,400	22.7	12.0	535	33.8	4.8	3,845	-1.7	259	6.7	3,953	21.6	43.1
Oktibbeha	17,393	53.2	146,400	20.1	10.0	755	39.3	2	22,521	1.4	1,061	4.7	20,717	44.8	16.4
Panola	12,449	72.8	73,800	21.6	13.2	673	30.2	4.7	12,970	-1.1	770	5.9	12,653	29.7	34.8
Pearl River	20,710	76.6	122,900	22.3	10.3	744	27	3.6	23,312	0.2	1,098	4.7	21,083	29.4	29.0
Perry	4,476	82.0	81,100	22.0	12.8	614	30.3	4.8	4,355	0.1	255	5.9	4,282	24.5	36.7
Pike	14,962	68.4	87,500	23.7	12.5	651	31.3	2.8	14,572	-0.8	833	5.7	14,021	24.1	33.9
Pontotoc	10,845	72.4	102,100	19.3	10.9	674	24.6	4.1	14,423	-0.5	559	3.9	13,673	22.8	38.4
Prentiss	9,533	70.9	90,500	22.3	11.2	525	28.4	1.7	11,207	0.4	485	4.3	9,519	21.7	35.4
Quitman	3,072	65.5	51,400	28.9	15.4	580	31.7	4.9	2,432	-2.1	184	7.6	2,333	28.9	24.3
Rankin	55,226	75.2	158,400	18.9	10.0	948	25.6	2.5	76,149	-0.6	2,595	3.4	71,953	40.1	19.6
Scott	10,096	71.1	71,500	19.0	13.7	663	30.7	6.1	13,152	-1.7	515	3.9	10,960	24.1	38.4
Sharkey	1,809	62.1	51,100	31.0	10.1	414	33.7	4.8	1,686	-0.6	118	7	1,509	46.3	16.2
Simpson	9,322	79.0	86,800	24.1	14.2	661	34.5	6.5	10,931	-0.8	492	4.5	10,299	27.8	34.9
Smith	5,850	81.0	79,700	19.4	10.5	609	24.9	2.6	6,752	0.2	296	4.4	6,463	23.2	40.9
Stone	5,979	78.4	113,900	23.3	10.0	697	26.6	4.8	6,791	2.3	369	5.4	7,588	22.7	37.3

1. Specified owner-occupied units.　2. A value of 10.0 represents 10 percent or less; a value of 50.0 represents 50 percent or more.　3. Specified renter-occupied units.　4. Overcrowded or lacking complete plumbing facilities.　5. Percent of civilian labor force.　6. Civilian employed persons 16 years old and over.

Table B. States and Counties — Nonfarm Employment and Agriculture

	Private nonfarm establishments, employment and payroll, 2016									Agriculture, 2017			
		Employment						Annual payroll		Farms			Farm producers whose primary occupation is farming (percent)
							Professional, scientific, and technical services					Percent with:	
STATE County	Number of establishments	Total	Health care and social assistance	Manufacturing	Retail trade	Finance and insurance		Total (mil dol)	Average per employee (dollars)	Number	Fewer than 50 acres	1000 acres or more	
	104	105	106	107	108	109	110	111	112	113	114	115	116
MISSISSIPPI	58,850	939,322	165,677	143,226	146,030	35,414	30,209	34,357	36,576	34,988	31.6	6.4	37.8
Adams	795	10,047	1,843	529	2,208	355	225	332	33,094	171	40.4	7.6	41.7
Alcorn	771	11,858	2,630	2,178	2,220	324	522	402	33,934	457	39.4	3.1	29.5
Amite	171	1,370	189	334	166	35	26	46	33,857	484	26.9	2.7	43.1
Attala	341	4,332	531	668	715	148	55	154	35,435	468	28.0	4.7	33.5
Benton	53	971	175	200	114	11	D	29	29,713	285	24.2	3.9	29.9
Bolivar	717	9,166	1,703	1,752	1,535	258	184	302	32,910	412	21.4	27.9	63.1
Calhoun	251	2,506	470	823	417	59	28	71	28,475	518	26.4	6.8	31.4
Carroll	109	661	121	D	86	22	10	17	25,902	446	18.2	10.1	32.4
Chickasaw	323	5,157	386	2,968	697	113	61	149	28,817	506	22.7	7.5	33.7
Choctaw	111	1,124	88	246	144	18	11	53	47,230	227	17.6	4.8	33.7
Claiborne	101	2,206	570	105	164	42	D	126	57,091	224	17.0	8.0	35.9
Clarke	225	3,346	444	526	338	89	31	121	36,253	300	27.3	3.3	33.4
Clay	353	4,341	580	614	813	120	250	151	34,686	354	19.2	7.9	27.9
Coahoma	531	6,234	1,687	668	1,034	229	207	207	33,235	206	18.0	42.2	63.4
Copiah	434	5,846	811	1,934	866	169	83	168	28,679	478	28.0	3.6	40.4
Covington	325	4,018	452	1,383	613	115	45	130	32,266	523	33.7	2.1	43.6
DeSoto	2,814	51,301	6,153	3,858	9,747	1,016	962	1,674	32,627	398	51.0	9.0	39.1
Forrest	1,866	32,734	8,581	3,705	4,627	991	1,106	1,274	38,917	376	51.3	1.3	30.9
Franklin	122	1,175	364	28	156	54	38	42	35,348	198	32.3	2.5	38.2
George	313	3,668	780	299	1,043	72	101	124	33,802	492	57.3	1.2	36.6
Greene	114	807	23	11	215	D	13	31	38,343	436	44.3	2.8	35.5
Grenada	550	7,652	684	2,658	1,420	220	196	256	33,461	245	24.1	6.1	28.0
Hancock	717	9,489	994	834	1,539	248	1,451	378	39,825	287	51.9	1.4	40.7
Harrison	4,192	73,655	14,298	2,998	12,254	2,634	2,286	2,659	36,097	322	72.0	NA	26.1
Hinds	5,257	98,678	32,383	3,576	11,067	4,782	4,813	4,390	44,486	872	39.8	4.8	34.1
Holmes	237	1,981	396	465	445	77	37	52	26,145	496	12.1	11.3	34.1
Humphreys	136	1,600	172	D	294	50	4	45	28,414	179	17.3	29.6	52.3
Issaquena	9	57	D	NA	NA	D	NA	2	30,088	119	16.8	35.3	46.7
Itawamba	368	5,512	566	2,296	711	157	29	178	32,270	364	28.0	2.2	30.1
Jackson	2,266	46,761	5,548	15,700	5,163	977	1,749	2,186	46,746	473	72.1	0.4	33.4
Jasper	204	2,931	319	1,231	339	104	46	121	41,329	507	26.4	3.0	46.8
Jefferson	53	630	291	D	77	14	NA	22	35,519	236	20.3	5.9	42.8
Jefferson Davis	152	1,267	70	D	247	32	14	37	29,227	355	32.1	1.7	47.7
Jones	1,304	24,855	3,093	6,596	3,072	525	450	919	36,972	882	40.4	1.5	40.0
Kemper	122	1,540	317	256	138	48	6	86	55,888	313	23.3	6.4	46.9
Lafayette	1,214	17,020	2,682	1,887	2,915	581	1,121	577	33,907	443	21.0	4.1	31.7
Lamar	1,334	17,205	3,168	162	4,975	590	748	491	28,517	491	51.5	1.8	36.5
Lauderdale	1,919	29,940	7,356	1,966	5,367	1,599	822	1,027	34,287	305	32.1	4.6	23.6
Lawrence	161	1,792	218	748	268	66	14	83	46,408	354	34.5	1.4	43.6
Leake	280	4,122	559	D	734	129	38	115	27,941	573	31.2	2.1	48.4
Lee	2,435	47,530	7,827	9,107	7,128	2,333	1,249	1,751	36,846	436	31.2	4.8	34.6
Leflore	704	12,407	2,975	2,242	1,901	389	274	396	31,925	257	11.3	35.0	51.7
Lincoln	802	10,751	1,636	1,035	2,011	331	302	379	35,257	611	32.6	1.3	35.8
Lowndes	1,496	21,599	3,151	4,038	3,910	521	536	861	39,845	444	34.5	6.3	27.6
Madison	3,011	51,000	4,514	8,233	7,352	3,266	3,411	2,152	42,187	524	29.0	8.4	34.7
Marion	561	6,887	1,023	596	1,192	284	194	235	34,128	511	39.1	2.0	41.5
Marshall	414	6,970	1,463	794	880	284	83	220	31,612	634	32.5	7.4	33.6
Monroe	625	7,557	1,286	2,490	1,057	199	90	309	40,834	644	34.6	5.6	28.7
Montgomery	205	2,400	612	225	468	103	25	65	27,235	270	26.7	3.7	31.5
Neshoba	498	7,954	818	421	1,313	280	397	324	40,688	652	30.8	1.8	44.9
Newton	332	3,734	712	922	664	128	42	117	31,273	527	28.3	3.2	41.4
Noxubee	175	1,767	336	564	318	71	10	55	31,388	517	19.5	8.5	39.1
Oktibbeha	881	12,825	1,748	1,429	2,363	417	509	367	28,644	412	27.2	3.2	28.5
Panola	590	7,850	1,189	1,532	1,638	338	139	256	32,627	627	18.7	9.7	32.4
Pearl River	802	7,873	1,162	579	2,193	318	382	241	30,561	717	47.4	2.1	37.9
Perry	142	1,633	247	634	279	31	16	77	47,366	306	43.1	1.3	41.9
Pike	942	13,065	2,504	2,486	2,669	376	263	386	29,535	508	38.8	0.2	45.2
Pontotoc	493	11,635	815	7,423	1,084	219	110	373	32,085	745	31.9	3.0	26.0
Prentiss	486	5,805	721	1,924	910	186	170	171	29,404	486	28.8	6.4	29.7
Quitman	104	756	286	D	116	54	14	17	22,063	275	15.6	23.3	43.0
Rankin	3,644	55,571	8,146	4,144	9,836	2,654	1,449	2,114	38,050	577	38.1	3.8	37.2
Scott	475	10,502	649	5,740	1,240	194	74	363	34,542	660	34.5	2.1	39.6
Sharkey	124	771	221	NA	141	D	16	21	27,774	142	14.8	39.4	48.7
Simpson	414	5,670	2,156	378	1,016	461	88	157	27,704	498	25.7	2.6	47.2
Smith	171	2,300	238	935	257	61	93	83	35,917	540	25.6	1.1	48.4
Stone	270	3,088	561	501	726	123	100	93	30,183	323	46.7	1.2	44.6

STATE County	Acreage (1,000)	Percent change, 2012-2017	Average size of farm	Total irrigated (1,000)	Total cropland (1,000)	Average per farm	Average per acre	Value of machinery and equipment, average per farm (dollars)	Total (mil dol)	Average per farm (acres)	Crops	Livestock and poultry products	Organic farms (number)	Farms with internet access (percent)	Total ($1,000)	Percent of farms
	117	118	119	120	121	122	123	124	125	126	127	128	129	130	131	132
MISSISSIPPI..................	10,415	-4.7	298	1,814.5	4,960.6	817,041	2,745	109,875	6,196.0	177,088	37.0	63.0	37	66.0	213,785	40.8
Adams.........................	69	5.2	406	D	21.8	1,197,343	2,950	84,618	7.6	44,363	79.9	20.1	NA	74.9	464	34.5
Alcorn........................	83	-11.8	181	D	39.4	385,117	2,131	65,906	19.1	41,755	78.7	21.3	NA	65.2	1,186	52.1
Amite.........................	92	-23.9	190	0.2	19.3	607,952	3,192	69,786	85.2	176,112	2.4	97.6	NA	65.3	412	19.4
Attala........................	118	-5.9	252	0.3	22.1	465,417	1,846	47,727	14.3	30,585	30.4	69.6	NA	54.1	1,532	53.8
Benton........................	76	-7.9	267	D	25.6	513,315	1,926	75,492	11.7	41,098	65.9	34.1	NA	67.0	510	35.8
Bolivar.......................	409	4.8	993	275.0	374.6	3,004,756	3,025	475,613	208.0	504,847	99.9	0.1	NA	78.2	17,899	76.5
Calhoun.......................	148	-15.6	286	0.8	73.8	507,660	1,776	142,990	61.8	119,373	90.9	9.1	NA	61.0	3,916	74.3
Carroll	177	5.0	398	24.5	71.9	850,650	2,138	112,567	39.4	88,312	83.1	16.9	NA	64.3	4,063	51.3
Chickasaw.....................	172	3.8	340	5.6	92.4	681,863	2,003	127,343	103.8	205,227	41.0	59.0	2	64.6	2,850	55.5
Choctaw.......................	64	1.5	284	1.8	10.5	522,082	1,841	53,109	12.7	55,859	43.5	56.5	NA	65.6	858	58.1
Claiborne.....................	72	-13.0	323	2.2	18.8	874,076	2,708	100,254	8.6	38,438	73.9	26.1	NA	56.7	1,285	52.7
Clarke........................	103	82.8	344	0.4	9.5	768,676	2,237	65,877	29.5	98,260	4.8	95.2	NA	61.7	373	35.0
Clay..........................	124	-4.4	351	0.1	30.6	659,679	1,877	72,201	64.0	180,720	6.5	93.5	NA	59.0	1,977	58.2
Coahoma.......................	267	2.2	1,294	165.8	237.5	4,279,639	3,307	617,813	156.3	758,699	91.3	8.7	NA	76.2	9,650	87.9
Copiah........................	122	5.3	255	0.8	22.5	654,533	2,563	76,441	92.1	192,770	3.3	96.7	1	63.0	1,412	38.1
Covington.....................	89	-15.8	170	0.1	17.0	614,485	3,605	82,308	253.8	485,304	1.3	98.7	NA	67.5	691	22.8
DeSoto........................	121	1.9	304	10.7	74.2	914,718	3,009	116,103	39.4	98,912	85.9	14.1	NA	64.1	2,188	23.6
Forrest.......................	48	12.5	128	0.4	10.7	543,054	4,244	65,447	12.4	33,016	33.5	66.5	NA	70.2	544	23.4
Franklin......................	41	-19.1	205	0.1	6.9	650,912	3,174	55,584	3.9	19,904	32.3	67.7	NA	68.7	240	18.2
George........................	55	-10.0	111	1.1	24.5	415,726	3,731	68,803	18.2	36,988	80.1	19.9	NA	77.4	425	10.8
Greene........................	69	0.9	159	0.1	9.0	402,646	2,528	62,767	31.2	71,502	8.9	91.1	NA	66.7	376	31.7
Grenada.......................	73	-17.2	299	1.0	21.2	657,052	2,200	89,278	11.7	47,833	76.0	24.0	NA	64.1	1,271	50.2
Hancock.......................	32	28.4	113	0.1	7.3	436,624	3,861	66,054	4.5	15,603	24.3	75.7	NA	79.8	66	5.2
Harrison......................	16	-34.3	49	0.1	4.1	412,695	8,374	52,978	3.4	10,519	70.0	30.0	3	72.4	39	4.3
Hinds.........................	213	-15.1	244	0.5	54.1	804,312	3,292	61,962	57.4	65,637	29.1	70.9	NA	61.2	3,604	42.7
Holmes........................	241	1.6	487	58.4	118.6	1,180,015	2,425	120,527	66.3	133,647	96.1	3.9	NA	61.3	5,626	58.5
Humphreys.....................	164	-15.3	917	72.1	134.1	2,998,513	3,270	419,098	95.9	535,721	75.7	24.3	NA	82.1	6,512	81.6
Issaquena	131	5.5	1,103	26.3	87.2	3,018,677	2,737	610,300	D	D	D	D	NA	63.9	2,740	71.4
Itawamba	75	-20.5	207	0.1	25.7	354,780	1,712	59,971	7.9	21,791	82.0	18.0	1	69.0	950	51.9
Jackson.......................	36	-3.0	77	0.2	8.4	386,270	5,012	64,869	7.6	16,163	47.1	52.9	3	75.7	97	7.0
Jasper........................	111	14.3	219	0.1	15.1	614,597	2,805	98,483	191.2	377,083	0.9	99.1	NA	64.9	1,301	43.6
Jefferson	60	-30.4	253	0.1	11.4	636,903	2,520	51,954	30.5	129,186	9.8	90.2	NA	53.8	541	26.7
Jefferson Davis	55	-6.4	156	0.1	12.6	399,812	2,570	58,480	47.8	134,758	4.1	95.9	NA	71.3	158	14.1
Jones.........................	123	-2.5	139	0.5	22.7	527,503	3,786	71,665	221.1	250,719	1.8	98.2	NA	68.6	1,299	17.7
Kemper........................	112	-9.5	358	D	15.5	723,481	2,022	59,748	19.3	61,802	5.7	94.3	NA	60.1	1,199	46.3
Lafayette.....................	105	-3.9	236	0.6	29.0	646,938	2,740	57,637	9.4	21,176	72.0	28.0	2	69.1	1,031	42.7
Lamar.........................	73	14.3	149	0.2	11.0	529,531	3,548	59,665	53.2	108,360	5.4	94.6	NA	81.9	510	16.7
Lauderdale....................	82	19.0	269	0.7	18.1	553,284	2,055	56,867	3.9	12,767	18.7	81.3	NA	73.4	312	20.7
Lawrence......................	56	-22.4	159	0.2	17.5	511,947	3,211	81,082	91.2	257,644	3.6	96.4	NA	68.9	490	11.0
Leake	95	-10.7	165	0.0	27.2	500,892	3,027	76,068	328.0	572,438	1.4	98.6	NA	64.2	793	43.6
Lee...........................	123	-7.5	282	0.8	72.9	517,010	1,832	102,991	32.6	74,773	75.5	24.5	NA	70.6	2,112	37.2
Leflore.......................	299	1.9	1,163	167.0	243.8	3,373,801	2,902	470,366	210.0	817,062	67.8	32.2	NA	67.7	13,507	85.6
Lincoln.......................	101	-7.2	165	0.1	14.9	506,676	3,071	60,954	72.2	118,187	2.5	97.5	7	66.6	239	12.6
Lowndes.......................	139	16.6	314	7.6	64.6	793,469	2,530	119,488	60.8	136,890	38.5	61.5	NA	75.9	2,939	50.7
Madison	157	-22.5	300	D	50.1	789,468	2,628	65,717	20.1	38,353	78.5	21.5	NA	66.2	2,653	38.7
Marion........................	81	-0.5	159	0.1	18.8	458,585	2,881	75,413	91.2	178,462	2.5	97.5	3	67.1	1,174	27.6
Marshall......................	212	4.4	335	2.3	72.4	804,766	2,403	72,214	24.7	38,882	76.2	23.8	NA	60.3	2,168	35.0
Monroe........................	186	-18.6	288	0.3	90.4	633,479	2,198	97,367	39.7	61,691	71.7	28.3	NA	62.4	3,401	45.7
Montgomery....................	68	-30.4	251	0.5	20.9	501,369	1,999	67,717	14.7	54,567	55.2	44.8	NA	62.2	840	51.1
Neshoba.......................	112	10.8	172	0.1	25.9	459,112	2,664	77,883	248.7	381,434	1.5	98.5	2	71.0	741	29.0
Newton........................	105	-3.7	199	0.8	25.1	472,560	2,371	79,938	116.6	221,264	4.6	95.4	NA	71.2	1,325	37.6
Noxubee.......................	203	-4.7	393	24.4	98.1	995,194	2,533	173,217	124.7	241,246	39.2	60.8	NA	62.7	4,890	59.8
Oktibbeha.....................	95	-9.1	231	0.3	21.0	645,315	2,796	69,080	17.1	41,398	17.5	82.5	NA	69.4	1,124	38.6
Panola........................	226	-17.2	360	29.5	113.2	886,959	2,463	108,817	55.0	87,748	86.9	13.1	NA	61.7	7,916	55.2
Pearl River...................	105	-11.2	147	1.1	17.8	519,572	3,545	56,063	17.5	24,379	45.8	54.2	3	74.1	402	9.2
Perry	44	1.3	144	0.4	10.6	462,067	3,210	67,901	33.7	110,196	11.6	88.4	NA	60.8	209	27.5
Pike..........................	66	-8.6	130	0.1	15.7	482,938	3,726	83,431	70.4	138,594	3.9	96.1	2	65.2	285	12.6
Pontotoc......................	137	-10.1	184	D	65.1	362,339	1,968	64,218	20.8	27,858	80.2	19.8	NA	52.1	2,165	51.9
Prentiss......................	109	16.5	223	0.5	41.5	457,174	2,046	70,477	21.2	43,621	58.6	41.4	NA	52.7	1,606	62.1
Quitman.......................	199	-4.9	722	80.1	150.4	2,065,226	2,861	210,343	D	D	D	D	NA	61.5	9,821	93.5
Rankin........................	121	-3.6	210	0.1	37.3	693,646	3,300	90,066	114.0	197,615	7.7	92.3	NA	72.1	2,052	28.9
Scott.........................	120	4.2	182	0.2	30.7	462,657	2,546	95,592	272.7	413,121	2.1	97.9	NA	65.3	884	35.9
Sharkey.......................	172	10.9	1,214	70.6	140.8	4,016,682	3,310	476,427	86.5	608,972	93.3	6.7	NA	67.6	5,700	81.0
Simpson.......................	95	-13.2	191	0.3	21.8	526,657	2,758	81,714	227.4	456,665	2.4	97.6	NA	63.9	535	29.7
Smith.........................	83	-23.6	153	0.7	24.0	440,459	2,873	82,278	218.6	404,798	1.8	98.2	NA	61.5	1,135	31.5
Stone.........................	46	-0.1	141	0.3	10.4	467,314	3,308	57,118	12.4	38,387	67.5	32.5	NA	74.3	408	11.8

Table B. States and Counties — Water Use, Wholesale Trade, Retail Trade, and Real Estate

STATE County	Water use, 2015		Wholesale Trade[1], 2012				Retail Trade[2], 2012				Real estate and rental and leasing,[2] 2012			
	Public supply water withdrawn (mil gal/day)	Public supply gallons withdrawn per person per day	Number of establishments	Number of employees	Sales (mil dol)	Average payroll (mil dol)	Number of establishments	Number of employees	Sales (mil dol)	Average payroll (mil dol)	Number of establishments	Number of employees	Sales (mil dol)	Average payroll (mil dol)
	133	134	135	136	137	138	139	140	141	142	143	144	145	146
MISSISSIPPI.................	400.36	133.8	2,484	30,351	28,303.0	1,373.6	11,594	136,032	37,053.2	2,968.4	2,374	10,235	1,709.3	334.1
Adams.............................	4.92	157.4	35	265	169.6	10.0	176	2,119	488.7	47.6	36	135	17.6	3.9
Alcorn.............................	4.75	127.0	35	D	D	D	172	2,119	538.0	49.0	23	225	12.2	3.8
Amite..............................	1.34	106.6	7	62	14.0	1.5	30	162	39.2	3.5	3	4	0.5	0.1
Attala.............................	2.24	117.6	13	D	D	D	78	807	192.5	15.5	10	29	3.8	0.8
Benton...........................	0.49	59.9	NA	NA	NA	NA	16	112	24.4	2.5	NA	NA	NA	NA
Bolivar...........................	4.16	124.8	29	329	763.8	15.0	161	1,535	371.2	31.5	45	126	18.6	3.2
Calhoun..........................	2.28	154.9	14	175	81.1	5.2	58	401	95.2	8.1	4	10	0.7	0.3
Carroll............................	0.86	84.0	4	D	D	D	15	87	22.1	1.5	1	D	D	D
Chickasaw......................	1.81	104.5	15	90	69.8	3.1	83	687	153.4	11.7	8	17	2.6	0.5
Choctaw.........................	0.96	115.7	2	D	D	D	27	152	25.1	2.7	1	D	D	D
Claiborne........................	0.66	72.1	1	D	D	D	24	152	35.3	3.4	NA	NA	NA	NA
Clarke............................	2.00	125.0	4	D	D	D	51	322	63.6	5.5	2	D	D	D
Clay...............................	2.53	126.2	12	119	158.4	5.8	78	792	165.4	15.2	8	20	3.5	0.6
Coahoma	3.83	155.6	28	D	D	D	117	1,043	295.4	24.6	42	255	23.4	5.0
Copiah...........................	3.79	131.7	15	87	46.3	2.8	83	834	181.5	15.7	8	75	5.0	1.6
Covington.......................	1.86	95.2	12	68	116.9	2.4	68	522	188.3	12.1	8	27	3.2	0.5
DeSoto...........................	19.51	112.6	120	2,840	3,232.4	127.2	495	7,957	2,320.9	193.3	97	331	83.8	11.6
Forrest...........................	12.10	159.3	86	857	574.3	32.9	367	4,470	3,680.2	107.7	92	377	66.1	12.8
Franklin	0.98	126.6	4	D	D	D	17	113	29.0	2.4	4	30	1.1	0.8
George	1.23	52.6	11	75	54.2	2.5	77	900	229.5	17.2	6	D	D	D
Greene...........................	1.86	137.6	3	D	D	D	26	211	48.3	3.9	3	11	0.6	0.1
Grenada	3.96	183.5	28	D	D	D	120	1,305	415.1	32.2	17	61	13.0	2.4
Hancock	4.39	94.6	15	64	10.3	3.3	126	1,328	346.2	30.2	28	90	10.0	2.3
Harrison	20.84	103.5	161	1,537	664.4	65.1	805	10,872	2,859.1	243.0	249	1,100	210.9	35.5
Hinds	50.54	208.1	270	3,476	2,274.4	166.5	869	11,093	3,072.3	276.4	278	1,544	319.8	66.3
Holmes...........................	2.20	120.0	8	26	32.7	1.0	66	467	98.1	8.9	13	29	2.8	0.4
Humphreys	0.92	106.1	4	D	D	D	34	288	100.4	6.9	2	D	D	D
Issaquena	0.12	89.8	2	D	D	D	NA	NA	NA	NA	NA	NA	NA	NA
Itawamba	10.39	440.1	8	138	41.9	4.6	70	614	157.1	13.2	4	10	0.7	0.2
Jackson	14.50	102.5	60	564	236.3	22.5	426	4,828	1,220.5	109.0	98	424	49.4	12.7
Jasper	3.29	198.6	5	D	D	D	39	360	73.0	7.8	5	47	5.2	1.2
Jefferson	0.72	95.9	NA	NA	NA	NA	14	108	22.0	1.5	1	D	D	D
Jefferson Davis	1.45	124.3	2	D	D	D	39	207	61.6	4.4	2	D	D	D
Jones	11.75	172.2	75	D	D	D	241	3,000	796.4	61.7	54	228	64.8	13.0
Kemper	1.78	178.6	3	D	D	D	25	156	37.8	2.8	4	D	D	D
Lafayette	5.28	99.3	31	249	161.2	9.1	211	2,576	548.8	53.2	43	97	24.5	3.3
Lamar............................	5.92	97.7	36	D	D	D	282	4,802	1,041.4	86.7	61	D	D	D
Lauderdale	10.95	139.4	78	1,649	1,701.4	74.1	406	5,061	1,488.2	113.4	75	266	58.2	7.9
Lawrence	1.72	136.3	1	D	D	D	36	342	62.5	6.1	1	D	D	D
Leake	2.21	97.1	6	60	16.9	1.8	78	776	173.0	15.9	4	6	0.2	0.1
Lee	4.29	50.3	153	1,526	1,049.1	63.6	510	7,242	1,628.1	154.7	96	413	76.0	12.7
Leflore	4.15	133.9	31	D	D	D	154	1,637	465.6	36.2	42	D	D	D
Lincoln...........................	4.04	116.6	31	D	D	D	159	1,783	540.6	40.8	26	86	13.8	2.9
Lowndes.........................	8.37	140.2	80	D	D	D	311	3,578	736.5	73.2	63	186	26.3	4.8
Madison	16.52	159.7	135	2,220	4,549.4	118.2	497	6,698	1,616.9	148.1	139	909	133.7	32.4
Marion	3.62	141.6	16	163	121.6	5.1	134	1,182	280.1	25.6	25	110	18.3	3.6
Marshall	2.53	70.4	17	180	96.9	9.5	95	881	185.4	16.8	9	16	1.8	0.3
Monroe	3.63	101.3	18	182	150.2	8.0	136	1,213	259.2	22.9	14	51	6.0	1.6
Montgomery	1.30	128.1	3	D	D	D	51	478	144.4	9.0	4	18	1.7	0.4
Neshoba.........................	4.47	151.7	20	277	448.0	13.2	110	1,180	288.5	25.0	11	256	9.3	6.8
Newton...........................	2.47	113.6	8	39	8.0	1.1	70	707	137.4	14.2	5	12	1.9	0.2
Noxubee.........................	1.37	124.1	10	80	58.4	1.8	43	320	93.5	7.0	NA	NA	NA	NA
Oktibbeha.......................	7.58	152.2	15	436	187.3	17.5	163	1,924	472.0	38.3	59	178	30.5	4.8
Panola	3.35	98.0	31	536	576.6	24.2	170	1,555	471.8	33.0	15	66	10.0	2.1
Pearl River	4.58	83.0	25	D	D	D	172	1,793	477.3	43.4	19	52	7.7	1.1
Perry	1.23	100.2	4	D	D	D	34	250	62.4	4.4	3	D	D	D
Pike...............................	5.89	147.4	52	383	206.4	13.9	223	2,458	603.8	51.1	39	140	27.1	3.6
Pontotoc.........................	3.45	111.6	16	148	65.2	3.9	88	950	259.3	19.6	8	18	1.9	0.3
Prentiss..........................	3.28	128.8	15	72	11.5	1.2	103	948	189.1	17.1	32	61	7.6	1.2
Quitman..........................	0.74	98.9	4	D	D	D	23	128	28.6	2.3	6	D	D	D
Rankin............................	17.66	118.5	224	3,551	2,354.5	186.9	509	8,324	2,361.2	190.2	167	818	143.3	28.9
Scott..............................	8.02	283.7	17	72	56.4	2.3	126	1,188	243.8	23.6	9	35	4.0	1.0
Sharkey..........................	0.52	113.4	9	82	86.7	3.4	24	174	31.5	3.1	13	24	2.7	0.4
Simpson	3.60	132.2	13	79	27.0	2.6	90	1,020	234.7	20.5	12	41	5.8	1.0
Smith.............................	1.18	73.5	5	42	15.5	1.2	35	210	47.2	4.0	NA	NA	NA	NA
Stone.............................	1.46	80.8	10	29	10.9	1.0	54	582	166.6	13.4	8	22	1.5	0.3

1 Merchant wholesalers, except manufacturers' sales branches and offices.   2. Employer establishments.

Table B. States and Counties — Professional Services, Manufacturing, and Accommodation and Food Services

STATE County	Professional, scientific, and technical services, 2012				Manufacturing, 2012				Accommodation and food services, 2012			
	Number of establishments	Number of employees	Sales (mil dol)	Average payroll (mil dol)	Number of establishments	Number of employees	Receipts (mil dol)	Annual payroll (mil dol)	Number of establishments	Number of employees	Receipts (mil dol)	Annual payroll (mil dol)
	147	148	149	150	151	152	153	154	155	156	157	158
MISSISSIPPI	4,747	30,205	4,023.3	1,449.9	2,252	132,789	66,441.6	5,919.1	5,177	116,238	6,999.2	1,765.0
Adams	52	225	24.8	8.8	18	650	155.0	27.4	89	1,698	89.3	24.0
Alcorn	51	358	27.0	11.2	41	2,118	1,092.7	89.7	69	1,200	55.3	17.0
Amite	9	23	1.6	0.5	6	177	48.3	7.8	3	24	1.4	0.4
Attala	28	62	7.0	2.3	18	656	175.6	20.3	23	D	D	D
Benton	2	D	D	D	6	151	D	5.4	NA	NA	NA	NA
Bolivar	44	173	20.6	7.3	18	1,458	405.8	65.4	53	911	39.4	9.4
Calhoun	18	26	2.3	0.7	18	883	271.1	29.0	10	D	D	D
Carroll	8	16	2.4	0.7	NA	NA	NA	NA	3	16	0.3	0.1
Chickasaw	15	63	4.5	1.7	44	2,817	483.8	87.7	20	D	D	D
Choctaw	8	16	1.5	0.6	6	205	56.8	7.8	8	D	D	D
Claiborne	7	13	1.3	0.3	4	83	D	3.3	11	153	7.7	1.7
Clarke	11	D	D	D	16	494	D	16.1	13	D	D	D
Clay	22	247	20.3	9.7	20	704	656.6	37.9	37	499	22.6	5.9
Coahoma	41	202	31.5	9.9	19	757	288.4	28.5	46	1,244	82.3	20.3
Copiah	28	103	12.1	3.3	20	2,106	626.8	67.6	34	436	16.8	4.1
Covington	18	87	4.3	1.8	11	1,337	432.0	35.0	31	D	D	D
DeSoto	183	989	99.0	27.1	102	3,453	1,269.5	157.5	292	6,498	311.3	80.7
Forrest	187	998	116.5	42.2	64	3,248	942.4	123.6	186	4,332	181.0	50.5
Franklin	9	37	2.6	1.5	3	D	D	D	5	17	0.5	0.1
George	17	100	8.7	2.7	15	300	D	22.1	26	378	15.4	3.6
Greene	4	9	1.0	0.5	4	12	D	0.4	7	D	D	D
Grenada	30	182	21.0	9.4	28	2,239	717.9	90.9	59	940	42.0	10.1
Hancock	96	2,163	316.6	135.0	31	819	D	58.5	86	D	D	D
Harrison	388	2,313	296.4	103.5	109	3,179	1,989.8	163.3	447	18,209	1,537.7	378.0
Hinds	657	5,244	815.6	320.2	131	3,730	1,374.4	183.1	473	9,261	475.6	126.7
Holmes	14	40	7.6	1.8	4	436	D	11.7	16	122	5.5	1.5
Humphreys	5	8	1.2	0.2	4	D	D	D	9	116	4.3	1.0
Issaquena	NA	NA	NA	NA	NA	NA	NA	NA	NA	NA	NA	NA
Itawamba	12	30	3.8	0.9	42	1,542	930.6	50.7	27	404	17.2	4.7
Jackson	208	1,545	179.8	74.1	75	15,152	D	1,119.9	256	D	D	D
Jasper	17	85	9.2	3.4	16	1,599	327.7	52.4	9	D	D	D
Jefferson	NA	NA	NA	NA	NA	NA	NA	NA	5	25	0.9	0.3
Jefferson Davis	13	22	2.5	0.8	4	13	D	D	10	111	4.7	1.1
Jones	95	456	57.2	17.4	61	6,427	1,656.1	245.6	101	D	D	D
Kemper	5	D	D	D	8	415	D	11.2	12	D	D	D
Lafayette	115	924	167.9	52.6	20	1,248	167.6	59.8	128	2,797	135.6	36.9
Lamar	115	740	94.0	35.9	20	177	D	5.8	121	2,475	118.1	31.9
Lauderdale	141	1,063	98.7	40.7	58	2,141	779.4	82.0	175	3,628	174.0	45.7
Lawrence	10	13	1.8	0.4	8	646	D	49.1	11	102	4.0	1.0
Leake	15	40	4.2	1.2	7	D	D	D	22	D	D	D
Lee	187	1,105	109.8	46.2	134	9,087	3,414.0	372.8	205	4,596	199.3	55.5
Leflore	45	317	46.2	13.1	29	D	D	D	73	1,285	63.4	16.6
Lincoln	57	265	42.5	13.1	33	1,189	D	53.2	61	984	43.6	10.8
Lowndes	102	514	54.5	26.2	66	4,223	3,543.9	231.2	121	2,163	98.5	26.6
Madison	367	2,907	546.2	180.0	63	5,749	4,568.0	338.7	239	4,681	230.1	60.9
Marion	46	236	22.2	9.1	18	508	75.1	17.3	45	507	22.4	5.5
Marshall	13	D	D	D	27	543	182.5	23.5	31	383	16.3	4.0
Monroe	33	94	11.5	2.5	51	2,356	1,592.6	104.8	47	D	D	D
Montgomery	9	32	3.2	0.7	9	268	D	10.1	21	D	D	D
Neshoba	28	168	22.4	9.1	12	529	175.3	21.6	42	640	27.1	6.6
Newton	21	38	3.9	1.5	15	1,077	D	43.3	26	D	D	D
Noxubee	5	21	1.2	0.2	19	475	139.0	15.6	9	148	6.1	1.7
Oktibbeha	76	441	46.1	15.1	23	1,210	569.1	55.3	108	2,744	125.2	32.8
Panola	31	139	21.1	4.2	31	1,579	631.5	70.7	53	901	42.7	11.2
Pearl River	56	347	28.3	12.9	42	562	224.1	26.2	86	1,158	49.0	13.4
Perry	7	39	4.4	2.1	7	645	D	41.3	6	43	1.9	0.5
Pike	69	291	27.5	11.9	29	2,287	514.9	69.1	76	1,478	68.5	16.2
Pontotoc	24	100	9.8	3.4	71	6,199	1,469.9	185.6	33	492	20.3	5.1
Prentiss	38	165	22.6	5.8	34	1,818	814.2	61.7	28	435	21.8	4.9
Quitman	4	D	D	D	NA	NA	NA	NA	6	D	D	D
Rankin	311	1,356	176.7	54.7	118	3,655	1,553.2	165.9	286	5,399	278.5	71.4
Scott	30	104	6.4	2.4	22	4,883	D	164.6	37	551	26.4	6.2
Sharkey	7	17	1.1	0.3	NA	NA	NA	NA	6	D	D	D
Simpson	27	106	10.0	3.6	11	249	D	8.8	39	599	31.7	6.7
Smith	12	126	11.5	1.7	14	886	321.1	37.3	7	D	D	D
Stone	23	91	6.6	2.4	12	593	251.9	25.3	32	440	21.0	5.2

Table B. States and Counties — Health Care and Social Assistance, Other Services, Nonemployer Businesses, and Residential Construction

STATE County	Health care and social assistance, 2012				Other services, 2012				Nonemployer businesses, 2016		Value of residential construction authorized by building permits, 2018	
	Number of establish-ments	Number of employees	Receipts (mil dol)	Annual payroll (mil dol)	Number of establish-ments	Number of employees	Receipts (mil dol)	Annual payroll (mil dol)	Number	Receipts (mil dol)	New construction ($1,000)	Number of housing units
	159	160	161	162	163	164	165	166	167	168	169	170
MISSISSIPPI..................	6,211	157,620	16,630.6	6,544.7	3,540	19,232	1,951.9	548.9	214,804	8,608.7	1,193,505	6,883
Adams...........................	89	1,903	223.0	80.8	43	196	16.1	4.6	2,517	92.7	1,085	6
Alcorn..........................	103	2,447	271.4	79.4	41	167	13.1	3.5	2,518	130.7	2,456	14
Amite...........................	10	166	12.5	4.5	8	38	4.9	0.8	845	36.5	0	0
Attala..........................	24	D	D	D	22	D	D	D	1,198	49.0	130	1
Benton..........................	8	152	9.5	3.9	5	D	D	D	587	21.6	0	0
Bolivar.........................	90	1,919	149.1	62.5	52	194	15.5	3.8	1,965	67.2	3,921	34
Calhoun.........................	23	468	32.0	13.6	14	D	D	D	924	35.5	450	3
Carroll.........................	5	88	5.5	2.1	7	11	0.9	0.2	656	26.4	NA	NA
Chickasaw.......................	21	391	31.9	15.0	20	D	D	D	1,121	40.6	100	1
Choctaw.........................	8	203	16.5	6.2	8	D	D	D	623	21.2	517	4
Claiborne.......................	13	301	19.2	7.4	6	11	1.1	0.2	376	12.6	0	0
Clarke..........................	18	421	32.9	13.0	17	D	D	D	1,010	33.1	0	0
Clay............................	27	696	62.2	25.8	26	113	9.0	2.5	1,238	49.2	1,171	16
Coahoma	82	1,733	184.7	66.0	34	131	8.0	2.2	1,659	57.1	2,954	18
Copiah..........................	34	701	48.0	20.5	25	D	D	D	1,847	55.9	1,017	7
Covington.......................	30	582	48.1	20.7	24	108	9.3	2.4	1,449	57.6	0	0
DeSoto..........................	266	5,597	637.8	225.0	167	893	88.1	23.2	13,285	587.6	227,168	1,323
Forrest.........................	202	7,779	873.5	421.1	100	648	54.6	15.5	5,256	228.8	18,077	99
Franklin........................	8	D	D	D	3	D	D	D	515	14.3	0	0
George..........................	36	821	74.9	31.3	17	53	6.3	1.4	1,380	50.3	515	3
Greene..........................	7	D	D	D	7	D	D	D	660	22.0	150	1
Grenada.........................	74	1,323	115.4	45.4	27	103	10.8	2.5	1,381	53.1	0	0
Hancock.........................	52	D	D	D	40	291	26.0	9.0	3,416	133.7	91,181	600
Harrison........................	460	12,318	1,560.5	648.9	271	1,604	155.7	42.7	14,780	581.3	194,734	1,178
Hinds...........................	742	27,244	3,150.9	1,279.8	405	2,731	299.2	94.4	20,633	775.3	36,584	213
Holmes..........................	35	395	26.9	10.8	12	191	6.2	2.1	1,168	34.3	848	9
Humphreys.......................	20	242	19.7	7.7	11	36	2.0	0.6	589	18.6	0	0
Issaquena	1	D	D	D	NA	NA	NA	NA	76	2.3	NA	NA
Itawamba	29	D	D	D	19	D	D	D	1,342	48.1	897	6
Jackson.........................	277	D	D	D	151	768	65.8	21.6	9,113	342.9	68,648	381
Jasper..........................	12	299	20.5	8.9	11	D	D	D	966	29.5	0	0
Jefferson.......................	14	305	19.6	9.1	5	D	D	D	538	12.3	0	0
Jefferson Davis	12	D	D	D	8	D	D	D	911	22.1	0	0
Jones	108	3,252	283.3	128.7	81	D	D	D	4,482	175.3	2,374	11
Kemper..........................	10	249	14.5	6.9	3	D	D	D	547	16.1	NA	NA
Lafayette.......................	126	2,671	363.2	110.3	63	397	87.9	19.1	4,402	242.1	42,333	260
Lamar...........................	147	3,066	344.9	133.1	61	262	25.9	6.2	4,578	236.7	933	6
Lauderdale......................	222	7,919	883.6	347.0	131	663	63.0	16.1	5,084	171.5	14,018	77
Lawrence........................	20	192	14.0	4.8	7	27	3.8	1.0	750	23.7	0	0
Leake...........................	25	598	36.8	16.0	11	40	3.5	1.1	1,224	44.3	0	0
Lee.............................	284	7,976	1,089.4	387.2	128	1,144	105.3	41.5	6,255	272.1	23,873	135
Leflore.........................	81	2,882	245.8	104.8	44	163	12.4	2.8	1,520	68.4	2,424	7
Lincoln.........................	70	1,784	181.2	61.2	48	290	24.6	8.9	2,516	100.3	301	4
Lowndes.........................	158	2,949	323.8	111.7	87	462	42.4	11.5	3,931	139.7	12,856	123
Madison	262	4,940	339.3	129.9	156	1,298	151.4	48.5	11,167	648.4	160,566	598
Marion..........................	45	940	63.9	25.3	26	113	10.6	2.8	1,947	65.2	0	0
Marshall........................	28	1,405	90.8	30.3	29	193	19.3	5.5	2,789	106.9	16,443	122
Monroe..........................	78	1,773	153.8	58.3	42	102	11.3	2.6	1,965	74.0	980	6
Montgomery......................	20	D	D	D	18	70	5.7	1.4	598	19.9	2,460	87
Neshoba.........................	40	1,070	102.3	43.5	36	146	13.4	3.2	1,834	60.4	0	0
Newton..........................	25	702	57.3	19.6	19	57	4.3	1.0	1,297	45.3	0	0
Noxubee.........................	13	293	22.5	9.9	10	19	1.9	0.4	849	25.5	0	0
Oktibbeha.......................	90	1,733	158.0	63.7	64	325	65.7	6.4	3,106	110.1	18,690	119
Panola..........................	67	1,416	136.4	48.9	22	72	7.7	1.7	2,635	101.8	1,928	21
Pearl River.....................	101	1,041	73.9	32.7	49	328	20.7	8.3	4,059	155.5	31,083	256
Perry	19	263	19.3	7.8	7	33	2.6	0.8	744	27.6	245	1
Pike............................	125	2,758	280.6	119.4	56	299	22.0	6.2	3,258	102.7	16,654	188
Pontotoc........................	39	D	D	D	32	D	D	D	1,996	81.2	2,309	42
Prentiss........................	42	858	65.4	25.7	29	101	9.8	2.1	1,574	49.2	1,106	9
Quitman	14	283	15.7	7.5	9	D	D	D	537	13.3	195	1
Rankin..........................	316	8,559	1,023.6	371.7	214	1,114	125.0	35.2	12,612	582.0	115,147	489
Scott...........................	34	D	D	D	39	95	9.7	2.4	1,603	57.1	1,031	7
Sharkey.........................	12	219	18.9	8.0	11	59	7.0	1.1	377	12.6	1,200	7
Simpson.........................	51	2,448	150.8	64.9	26	D	D	D	1,835	78.5	6,509	34
Smith...........................	8	221	10.8	4.8	8	22	2.3	0.5	968	35.6	263	3
Stone...........................	22	498	42.5	16.7	9	D	D	D	1,231	49.6	6,466	43

Table B. States and Counties — Government Employment and Payroll, and Local Government Finances

	Government employment and payroll, 2012									Local government finances, 2012				
			March payroll (percent of total)							General revenue				
												Taxes		
STATE County	Full-time equivalent employees	March payroll (dollars)	Administration, judicial, and legal	Police and corrections	Fire protection	Highways and transportation	Health and welfare	Natural resources and utilities	Education and libraries	Total (mil dol)	Inter-governmental (mil dol)	Total (mil dol)	Per capita[1] (dollars) Total	Per capita[1] (dollars) Property
	171	172	173	174	175	176	177	178	179	180	181	182	183	184
MISSISSIPPI	X	X	X	X	X	X	X	X	X	X	X	X	X	X
Adams	1,489	4,260,491	9.2	8.0	2.4	5.1	26.3	5.5	41.4	139.6	46.8	32.7	1,016	894
Alcorn	2,243	7,489,226	3.0	3.6	1.7	1.3	54.6	4.0	31.8	263.0	70.9	24.2	650	610
Amite	299	736,289	14.3	7.8	0.1	5.8	2.2	1.8	66.9	23.6	11.3	6.5	502	498
Attala	932	2,477,820	6.6	4.7	2.3	3.4	21.1	4.4	56.3	69.8	32.7	16.3	850	818
Benton	295	719,394	10.6	6.4	0.0	3.6	0.4	1.7	76.1	18.5	13.0	3.5	406	392
Bolivar	1,582	4,628,258	5.5	13.0	0.3	4.9	0.3	3.0	72.0	119.8	63.2	35.1	1,036	985
Calhoun	797	2,771,233	3.3	2.8	0.0	1.3	49.8	1.3	39.9	46.2	18.3	8.5	575	564
Carroll	314	861,917	13.2	17.2	0.2	6.8	1.7	0.3	60.4	21.1	8.8	6.4	617	604
Chickasaw	881	2,154,461	7.6	9.3	1.7	3.6	8.8	5.2	62.6	53.0	32.3	11.7	673	613
Choctaw	408	952,647	11.6	4.1	0.2	1.9	1.6	2.0	76.1	22.8	12.4	4.5	537	521
Claiborne	496	1,465,091	5.5	6.2	1.5	4.2	22.1	1.6	57.8	34.3	20.9	6.0	640	605
Clarke	690	1,711,804	10.0	5.8	0.8	4.0	1.9	7.4	68.8	41.5	20.7	15.2	917	894
Clay	763	1,943,802	4.0	6.9	4.0	3.4	11.5	2.8	66.9	50.0	29.0	16.2	791	775
Coahoma	1,488	4,098,825	5.5	7.7	3.1	2.8	0.4	13.9	66.3	114.9	75.2	21.5	837	778
Copiah	1,481	4,154,517	5.1	5.7	0.7	2.2	11.5	2.3	72.0	103.1	56.6	17.6	609	584
Covington	1,021	2,828,948	4.9	4.0	0.1	11.3	32.9	1.7	44.1	78.2	25.0	13.0	663	643
DeSoto	5,452	16,140,720	6.4	11.9	7.2	2.5	2.2	3.5	65.3	471.9	208.5	194.3	1,169	1,065
Forrest	6,510	21,206,976	3.1	4.5	2.3	1.8	60.8	2.2	24.8	662.3	117.6	91.2	1,187	1,057
Franklin	363	888,524	9.6	4.0	0.0	5.2	1.8	1.0	78.1	35.6	14.5	5.9	746	704
George	1,085	2,865,559	4.2	7.1	0.4	2.7	30.9	0.7	53.5	89.3	31.9	12.7	553	528
Greene	532	1,305,598	6.9	3.9	0.0	3.1	15.5	1.6	67.6	37.4	20.6	9.4	654	637
Grenada	1,382	4,096,902	5.7	4.4	2.9	2.1	40.8	1.9	40.3	116.3	39.5	20.6	949	909
Hancock	1,924	6,676,661	5.8	6.9	3.4	2.2	23.0	4.5	52.3	287.9	169.1	47.6	1,052	1,011
Harrison	8,736	32,935,719	4.4	8.9	5.2	4.2	30.6	3.3	42.1	1,243.7	542.0	244.1	1,258	1,055
Hinds	10,525	28,655,948	5.9	10.5	4.8	2.2	1.5	4.8	70.4	878.7	450.7	268.0	1,078	1,017
Holmes	1,272	3,625,794	5.9	6.2	0.7	2.4	0.9	1.6	81.9	86.9	59.2	11.7	625	598
Humphreys	384	897,846	4.1	7.0	1.7	2.5	13.2	3.0	68.3	30.0	17.0	9.1	991	961
Issaquena	19	50,080	41.5	24.8	0.0	24.5	6.1	1.7	0.0	5.7	0.8	1.6	1,159	1,141
Itawamba	1,223	4,512,156	2.7	2.6	0.2	1.5	0.6	1.9	90.4	109.5	57.9	13.4	576	538
Jackson	7,975	28,632,767	3.0	5.8	2.5	2.0	45.3	2.4	38.2	857.2	237.3	174.7	1,245	1,188
Jasper	861	2,242,650	7.4	4.2	0.0	4.5	26.0	3.0	54.5	55.7	24.4	18.0	1,092	1,057
Jefferson	478	1,235,476	6.8	10.4	0.0	2.4	29.1	1.1	48.4	43.5	13.0	6.2	816	767
Jefferson Davis	567	1,467,224	8.3	4.6	0.9	4.0	30.4	1.6	49.8	39.7	17.1	8.1	672	658
Jones	4,753	12,100,544	2.7	3.7	2.3	2.1	35.5	1.9	50.3	341.0	127.5	54.3	791	752
Kemper	712	2,430,022	3.8	6.4	0.1	2.1	1.0	0.6	85.7	67.6	39.0	6.3	610	594
Lafayette	1,452	4,109,506	5.9	10.5	4.9	4.1	3.5	5.7	63.4	177.9	50.8	51.3	1,036	964
Lamar	2,053	4,821,922	4.0	6.2	0.6	4.8	0.9	0.5	81.5	123.2	59.9	53.4	924	906
Lauderdale	3,227	9,470,298	9.1	5.9	3.6	6.1	0.0	4.9	68.9	246.0	129.7	76.1	949	901
Lawrence	479	1,248,756	9.0	6.6	0.7	3.8	1.7	1.5	76.3	29.2	16.0	11.0	873	858
Leake	684	1,880,375	16.5	12.0	1.7	3.7	1.5	2.2	61.0	53.2	27.1	11.1	478	447
Lee	4,000	11,007,645	6.2	9.1	3.5	3.3	2.8	6.2	68.2	257.6	136.9	85.3	1,003	974
Leflore	2,494	8,995,576	3.1	4.0	1.8	1.7	57.3	2.3	29.6	240.0	68.2	28.3	913	861
Lincoln	1,177	3,186,542	7.5	6.9	3.7	3.9	0.6	2.4	74.6	84.1	45.5	26.5	760	721
Lowndes	2,233	7,025,354	8.5	12.2	3.9	4.4	1.2	8.3	59.4	183.3	105.0	53.8	901	845
Madison	2,936	9,496,425	7.8	11.0	5.2	3.3	1.3	2.9	67.0	279.8	105.3	131.7	1,337	1,266
Marion	1,327	2,909,454	6.2	11.0	1.8	3.7	1.7	1.0	73.2	79.0	36.5	17.5	662	635
Marshall	1,090	3,348,828	7.9	14.8	1.8	9.2	0.0	8.4	56.4	69.4	40.2	23.0	629	608
Monroe	1,425	3,622,413	13.2	8.0	3.4	7.1	1.1	4.6	60.5	97.7	48.7	27.8	764	733
Montgomery	546	1,639,820	6.9	4.5	1.6	3.8	37.3	2.7	42.6	35.2	16.1	7.1	672	642
Neshoba	938	2,330,410	5.2	9.8	3.5	4.9	0.8	6.3	69.2	84.7	35.9	14.6	489	471
Newton	1,105	3,232,369	4.5	4.7	0.6	1.9	0.9	5.5	81.6	80.7	53.7	13.3	616	581
Noxubee	657	1,978,193	6.6	1.5	0.5	2.2	28.3	0.4	59.1	39.8	18.4	8.4	752	729
Oktibbeha	1,842	5,582,328	2.8	4.7	3.1	1.1	47.2	4.4	36.2	155.8	47.9	35.8	744	726
Panola	1,433	4,200,779	4.8	10.0	2.0	2.8	2.1	3.6	74.4	97.6	58.1	28.7	832	760
Pearl River	2,574	7,161,607	5.5	5.4	1.8	2.1	8.1	3.0	73.4	183.3	100.0	38.8	702	666
Perry	466	1,122,268	9.5	5.9	0.4	5.6	1.3	2.1	74.8	33.9	18.6	9.5	788	759
Pike	2,872	9,325,024	3.8	4.6	1.6	1.6	46.9	2.2	38.5	249.1	83.4	32.7	816	780
Pontotoc	982	3,251,798	6.3	8.7	2.5	3.4	1.2	4.1	73.1	74.0	42.6	18.2	594	546
Prentiss	1,158	3,605,727	3.3	4.8	2.1	1.8	1.3	1.1	85.6	87.2	54.3	15.2	598	572
Quitman	519	1,364,995	6.8	5.4	0.1	5.5	31.8	1.2	49.1	23.7	13.9	7.2	919	878
Rankin	4,244	12,845,764	5.1	11.8	6.8	3.4	0.1	3.9	68.2	344.6	160.2	130.8	901	859
Scott	1,071	2,578,316	6.0	10.4	1.4	2.8	0.9	4.7	73.7	65.2	39.7	17.6	624	583
Sharkey	279	713,380	12.1	7.5	0.1	4.4	1.2	10.7	63.5	17.4	9.5	5.1	1,064	1,028
Simpson	898	2,221,618	6.8	8.7	0.2	5.6	1.2	1.8	73.3	56.8	33.6	17.5	639	614
Smith	568	1,449,509	9.4	8.8	0.0	4.1	1.0	2.8	73.8	37.3	21.8	10.9	667	654
Stone	1,427	5,071,678	2.8	2.3	0.5	0.8	0.4	0.4	92.7	126.2	75.9	12.5	691	645

1. Based on the resident population estimated as of July 1 of the year shown.

Local Government Finances, Government Employment, and Income Taxes

STATE County	Total (mil dol)	Per capita[1] (dollars)	Education	Health and hospitals	Police protection	Public welfare	Highways	Total (mil dol)	Per capita[1] (dollars)	Federal civilian	Federal military	State and local	Number of returns	Mean adjusted gross income	Mean income tax
	185	186	187	188	189	190	191	192	193	194	195	196	197	198	199
MISSISSIPPI..................	X	X	X	X	X	X	X	X	X	25,354	27,218	219,283	1,230,160	48,584	5,232
Adams.............................	139.6	4,345	30.8	31.5	5.2	0.2	5.9	55.9	1,739	105	186	1,486	12,120	45,633	5,402
Alcorn.............................	255.2	6,866	20.1	53.1	2.1	0.1	2.6	317.3	8,537	108	215	3,018	13,760	45,141	4,457
Amite..............................	19.7	1,524	56.2	1.8	6.7	0.0	13.8	0.3	25	30	72	387	4,840	44,352	3,937
Attala.............................	75.3	3,933	38.1	28.5	2.8	0.2	5.1	32.6	1,702	57	106	1,013	7,330	41,506	3,585
Benton...........................	19.4	2,227	67.1	0.9	4.4	0.2	12.1	3.9	444	47	48	349	3,240	34,849	2,429
Bolivar...........................	121.4	3,582	53.7	4.8	5.9	0.2	8.4	52.7	1,553	75	177	2,646	13,060	43,424	4,323
Calhoun..........................	49.9	3,364	39.2	32.8	3.2	0.1	5.9	14.4	971	31	84	550	5,750	36,438	2,753
Carroll............................	20.6	1,974	43.6	0.9	2.8	0.0	14.4	13.5	1,292	19	57	382	4,160	46,777	4,463
Chickasaw......................	52.1	2,994	52.7	1.8	5.1	8.9	7.0	31.3	1,795	48	98	881	7,450	37,374	3,259
Choctaw..........................	30.5	3,651	50.2	10.5	5.3	0.1	10.2	32.0	3,838	57	48	703	3,240	40,951	3,035
Claiborne........................	35.4	3,783	50.8	3.0	3.9	0.2	5.8	129.3	13,835	26	46	1,475	3,360	31,779	2,220
Clarke.............................	40.6	2,452	65.6	0.9	5.4	0.1	8.0	10.9	661	32	93	760	6,520	43,449	3,739
Clay...............................	52.7	2,577	56.9	0.6	7.8	0.6	8.0	34.3	1,677	58	113	861	8,320	39,470	3,730
Coahoma........................	119.1	4,634	63.3	0.9	4.4	0.0	4.0	151.1	5,877	60	132	1,765	9,270	37,647	3,847
Copiah...........................	112.0	3,869	65.2	13.0	4.2	0.0	7.0	26.9	930	70	161	1,635	11,560	39,192	3,179
Covington.......................	69.3	3,537	37.9	38.8	3.9	0.1	7.3	13.5	688	69	111	1,196	7,870	39,026	3,301
DeSoto...........................	452.7	2,723	48.5	1.1	8.4	0.0	5.1	539.6	3,246	230	1,046	6,634	80,600	53,947	5,466
Forrest...........................	657.8	8,555	16.6	64.3	2.3	0.0	3.0	378.3	4,920	745	771	11,164	31,040	50,262	6,375
Franklin..........................	33.3	4,206	42.1	31.8	4.6	0.0	7.5	3.6	454	49	45	609	3,100	46,190	4,375
George............................	87.3	3,806	33.7	44.6	2.8	0.1	6.5	28.7	1,250	45	138	1,447	8,850	50,647	4,438
Greene............................	39.0	2,727	52.3	0.8	6.9	16.0	9.3	7.5	522	13	64	1,030	4,210	48,254	3,975
Grenada..........................	114.7	5,290	29.2	42.6	4.9	0.0	4.5	98.3	4,534	235	122	1,611	9,410	43,687	4,363
Hancock.........................	284.4	6,285	23.0	16.2	2.7	0.1	4.9	96.7	2,137	1,963	747	2,032	18,230	50,646	5,505
Harrison.........................	1,263.3	6,511	21.1	29.5	4.6	0.2	4.8	919.9	4,741	5,648	8,025	13,552	87,160	47,101	5,150
Hinds.............................	892.8	3,591	57.8	0.8	5.7	0.3	4.2	1,035.1	4,163	4,518	1,412	34,277	104,430	46,459	5,212
Holmes...........................	104.3	5,551	78.5	1.3	3.6	0.2	4.5	35.2	1,870	53	99	1,315	7,140	29,798	1,851
Humphreys......................	30.1	3,277	50.7	1.4	6.0	0.1	15.6	10.5	1,144	22	48	484	3,340	32,871	3,215
Issaquena	5.9	4,234	0.9	5.4	10.5	0.0	13.4	1.8	1,275	2	6	98	430	36,942	2,974
Itawamba	111.8	4,790	82.2	0.5	2.0	0.0	3.7	48.6	2,082	48	132	1,086	9,330	44,661	3,799
Jackson..........................	885.7	6,313	30.2	41.1	3.1	0.1	3.7	521.2	3,715	1,140	1,047	8,775	60,540	52,689	5,645
Jasper............................	52.0	3,145	47.2	13.8	3.9	0.1	13.0	21.9	1,327	49	97	928	6,980	39,625	3,305
Jefferson	38.6	5,053	32.5	24.2	4.3	10.8	4.1	5.0	653	19	44	609	3,140	31,626	1,942
Jefferson Davis	43.5	3,615	47.4	27.4	3.9	0.0	7.0	9.1	759	24	66	600	4,760	35,737	2,742
Jones.............................	365.6	5,326	40.2	37.4	2.4	0.8	3.6	230.8	3,362	218	387	7,023	26,580	44,594	4,376
Kemper...........................	67.4	6,517	80.0	0.6	1.8	0.1	3.5	9.1	878	32	52	639	3,760	34,549	2,579
Lafayette........................	126.1	2,548	52.3	0.9	7.5	0.0	9.3	146.9	2,968	329	306	8,120	20,130	75,648	11,676
Lamar.............................	128.5	2,224	68.5	0.7	6.9	0.2	7.3	76.2	1,319	50	358	2,366	23,980	61,948	7,989
Lauderdale......................	232.7	2,900	60.0	3.5	5.9	0.0	5.1	138.1	1,722	804	1,319	5,154	30,990	51,674	6,376
Lawrence	30.1	2,396	64.4	1.7	4.0	0.4	8.9	8.0	634	40	74	672	4,850	44,056	3,634
Leake.............................	54.6	2,344	49.9	15.0	4.7	0.0	8.2	21.7	931	61	124	713	8,520	39,397	3,163
Lee................................	265.1	3,118	54.1	0.9	7.2	0.2	8.9	210.0	2,470	461	522	4,936	37,160	54,231	6,612
Leflore...........................	246.7	7,972	21.8	53.9	3.5	0.0	2.9	171.6	5,546	108	163	3,976	11,670	38,415	4,322
Lincoln...........................	82.3	2,359	58.3	1.7	7.0	0.0	9.8	29.6	848	105	197	1,771	13,580	48,547	4,819
Lowndes.........................	180.6	3,026	47.7	0.8	6.3	0.1	7.7	210.1	3,521	845	1,605	3,332	24,610	47,445	4,887
Madison	302.7	3,074	49.9	0.4	6.9	0.1	12.3	478.1	4,855	224	603	4,540	48,640	85,761	14,076
Marion	79.2	2,994	45.6	21.5	5.3	0.0	4.2	27.0	1,020	44	143	1,286	9,500	44,028	3,915
Marshall	73.1	1,995	56.1	1.7	6.9	0.1	12.7	20.0	545	76	198	1,165	15,320	37,229	3,006
Monroe...........................	96.6	2,653	58.9	1.2	7.3	0.4	7.6	47.3	1,299	125	208	1,414	14,740	42,505	3,658
Montgomery....................	37.1	3,497	42.0	24.7	4.2	0.3	9.9	11.3	1,062	27	59	591	4,280	39,320	3,095
Neshoba..........................	87.8	2,947	41.8	32.2	3.5	0.0	5.2	30.9	1,037	77	170	6,126	11,690	42,300	3,996
Newton...........................	81.2	3,757	66.9	1.0	5.1	0.0	5.2	11.7	539	83	121	1,923	8,810	41,812	3,357
Noxubee..........................	40.0	3,569	46.0	25.3	3.7	0.1	6.1	6.0	537	41	62	732	4,510	32,765	2,251
Oktibbeha........................	178.0	3,694	32.7	38.4	3.7	0.0	4.9	104.4	2,167	236	276	9,701	17,830	51,484	5,870
Panola...........................	102.7	2,980	56.0	1.3	6.9	0.2	7.0	38.1	1,104	110	197	2,112	14,360	39,565	3,832
Pearl River......................	195.3	3,533	60.8	8.4	3.0	0.1	6.4	65.6	1,186	121	316	3,092	21,130	46,467	4,290
Perry..............................	35.3	2,921	48.4	1.5	4.7	0.1	17.1	88.9	7,358	20	70	552	4,600	41,148	3,280
Pike...............................	242.6	6,051	34.8	43.8	2.9	0.0	2.6	84.1	2,098	107	226	3,337	16,000	40,294	3,617
Pontotoc.........................	80.2	2,621	56.4	1.0	4.0	0.1	6.4	30.1	983	49	184	1,187	12,960	42,822	3,667
Prentiss..........................	89.5	3,525	81.0	0.8	4.2	0.0	3.0	31.5	1,242	42	143	1,498	9,530	40,602	3,291
Quitman..........................	33.0	4,231	64.9	0.9	4.1	0.0	8.6	7.5	959	20	42	333	2,770	32,556	2,586
Rankin............................	365.9	2,521	50.1	0.9	7.2	0.1	9.8	417.1	2,873	627	865	8,756	65,280	59,624	6,523
Scott..............................	65.3	2,311	62.2	1.9	5.4	0.0	7.7	22.0	779	210	165	1,259	11,710	37,905	2,967
Sharkey..........................	21.1	4,406	71.8	0.6	4.2	0.0	8.3	5.6	1,159	22	25	449	1,810	32,843	2,792
Simpson..........................	63.8	2,330	55.8	1.6	3.8	2.0	6.9	28.1	1,027	43	154	1,822	10,480	40,847	3,474
Smith.............................	36.8	2,253	63.0	1.0	5.3	0.0	13.3	9.9	606	26	94	588	6,010	44,110	4,003
Stone.............................	142.2	7,887	79.3	0.5	3.6	0.0	2.5	30.7	1,701	65	98	1,144	6,640	43,391	3,819

1. Based on the resident population estimated as of July 1 of the year shown.

Table B. States and Counties — Land Area and Population

State / county code	CBSA code[1]	County code[2]	STATE County	Land area[3] (sq. mi)	Total persons 2018	Rank	Per square mile	White	Black	American Indian, Alaska Native	Asian and Pacific Islancer	Percent Hispanic or Latino[4]	Under 5 years	5 to 17 years	18 to 24 years	25 to 34 years	35 to 44 years	45 to 54 years
								Race alone or in combination, not Hispanic or Latino (percent)					Age (percent)					
				1	2	3	4	5	6	7	8	9	10	11	12	13	14	15
			MISSISSIPPI— Cont'd															
28133	26,940	7	Sunflower	697.8	25,735	1,573	36.9	24.1	73.6	0.5	0.6	1.9	5.6	16.5	9.9	16.6	13.1	12.7
28135		7	Tallahatchie	645.2	13,987	2,164	21.7	35.5	56.7	0.7	1.3	7.0	5.6	14.0	10.4	17.5	13.0	12.5
28137	32,820	1	Tate	404.8	28,759	1,465	71.0	65.5	31.5	0.6	0.7	3.0	5.8	16.9	11.8	12.4	11.0	12.5
28139		6	Tippah	457.8	21,995	1,723	48.0	78.0	17.7	0.5	0.5	4.8	6.4	18.1	9.1	11.9	12.0	13.1
28141		8	Tishomingo	424.3	19,454	1,853	45.8	93.5	3.0	0.5	0.3	3.6	5.5	16.0	7.7	11.6	11.4	13.6
28143	32,820	1	Tunica	454.7	9,944	2,432	21.9	19.3	77.7	0.5	1.1	2.5	8.6	20.7	8.9	13.9	12.6	11.4
28145		6	Union	415.6	28,606	1,473	68.8	79.3	16.1	0.6	1.4	4.3	6.7	18.3	8.0	12.6	12.8	12.8
28147		9	Walthall	403.9	14,465	2,130	35.8	53.6	43.8	0.8	1.0	2.1	5.8	17.0	8.4	11.4	12.0	11.9
28149	46,980	4	Warren	588.5	46,176	1,048	78.5	47.5	49.4	0.5	1.1	2.4	6.4	17.5	8.4	12.4	12.3	12.2
28151	24,740	5	Washington	724.7	45,063	1,077	62.2	25.4	72.3	0.4	0.9	1.7	7.2	18.6	8.9	12.4	11.2	11.8
28153		7	Wayne	810.7	20,298	1,808	25.0	58.1	40.3	0.6	0.5	1.6	6.8	17.7	8.5	12.6	11.5	11.9
28155		9	Webster	420.9	9,788	2,444	23.3	79.0	19.8	0.5	0.4	1.4	6.0	17.7	7.7	12.1	11.5	13.0
28157		8	Wilkinson	678.1	8,792	2,516	13.0	28.4	70.6	0.5	0.3	0.9	5.3	15.9	8.0	15.6	11.9	11.7
28159		7	Winston	607.3	18,165	1,918	29.9	50.4	47.2	1.4	0.4	1.3	5.3	17.3	7.6	11.9	11.7	12.1
28161		7	Yalobusha	467.2	12,392	2,259	26.5	59.1	39.4	0.7	0.4	1.8	6.1	16.3	7.2	11.8	11.1	12.8
28163	27,140	2	Yazoo	922.3	28,248	1,491	30.6	34.9	57.2	0.6	0.8	7.5	5.6	16.4	8.3	17.9	15.7	11.6
29000		0	MISSOURI	68,745.8	6,126,452	X	89.1	81.3	12.7	1.2	2.8	4.3	6.1	16.4	9.2	13.4	12.2	12.3
29001	28,860	7	Adair	567.3	25,339	1,592	44.7	91.9	3.8	0.7	3.0	2.6	5.0	13.3	27.7	10.3	8.5	9.7
29003	41,140	3	Andrew	432.6	17,607	1,944	40.7	95.4	1.7	0.8	0.8	2.6	5.7	17.2	7.3	11.4	12.3	12.8
29005		9	Atchison	547.3	5,171	2,821	9.4	97.6	0.9	0.8	0.6	1.3	4.9	15.2	5.9	10.2	10.8	12.9
29007	33,020	6	Audrain	692.2	25,473	1,584	36.8	89.0	8.0	0.8	0.9	3.1	6.3	16.6	8.0	13.0	12.6	12.2
29009		6	Barry	778.3	35,886	1,275	46.1	86.4	0.9	2.0	2.3	10.0	6.1	16.6	7.5	11.1	10.6	12.5
29011		6	Barton	592.0	11,798	2,308	19.9	94.7	1.3	2.7	1.0	2.7	5.7	17.6	8.0	10.5	11.3	11.7
29013	28,140	1	Bates	836.7	16,320	2,022	19.5	95.7	1.8	1.6	0.5	2.2	5.9	17.4	7.7	11.2	11.5	12.1
29015		7	Benton	704.0	19,278	1,862	27.4	96.2	0.9	1.7	0.8	2.1	4.4	12.9	5.3	8.2	8.4	12.1
29017	16,020	3	Bollinger	617.9	12,169	2,279	19.7	97.0	0.9	1.4	0.5	1.4	4.8	16.4	7.0	10.7	11.3	13.6
29019	17,860	3	Boone	685.5	180,005	366	262.6	81.1	11.2	1.0	6.3	3.5	5.8	14.5	19.2	15.3	11.8	10.3
29021	41,140	3	Buchanan	408.2	88,571	657	217.0	85.0	7.3	1.1	2.3	6.9	6.3	16.2	9.2	14.2	12.5	12.1
29023	38,740	5	Butler	694.7	42,639	1,125	61.4	90.9	6.7	1.5	1.2	2.2	6.4	17.1	7.7	12.4	11.6	12.3
29025	28,140	1	Caldwell	426.4	9,108	2,491	21.4	96.3	1.4	1.4	0.9	2.1	5.8	18.0	8.1	10.3	11.1	12.7
29027	27,620	3	Callaway	834.6	44,889	1,078	53.8	92.1	5.4	1.3	1.1	2.2	5.5	15.5	10.5	13.2	12.3	12.9
29029		7	Camden	656.0	45,815	1,054	69.8	95.2	1.1	1.2	1.0	2.9	4.5	13.2	5.7	9.3	9.2	11.9
29031	16,020	3	Cape Girardeau	578.5	78,753	711	136.1	87.8	8.9	0.8	2.3	2.4	5.8	15.5	14.0	12.8	11.3	11.3
29033		6	Carroll	694.6	8,743	2,524	12.6	96.1	2.6	0.8	0.5	1.6	5.8	17.2	7.8	10.1	11.3	12.3
29035		9	Carter	507.4	6,054	2,747	11.9	95.6	1.0	2.1	0.6	2.8	6.4	17.0	7.3	10.1	11.4	12.6
29037	28,140	1	Cass	696.6	104,954	575	150.7	89.8	5.1	1.4	1.6	4.6	6.1	18.0	7.7	11.9	12.5	12.9
29039		6	Cedar	474.5	14,165	2,152	29.9	96.0	0.8	1.7	0.7	2.4	6.9	17.2	6.9	9.8	9.9	11.7
29041		9	Chariton	751.2	7,451	2,630	9.9	96.0	3.1	0.8	0.4	1.0	6.0	16.8	6.3	9.9	10.5	11.0
29043	44,180	2	Christian	562.6	86,983	665	154.6	94.8	1.4	1.4	1.3	3.0	6.3	19.0	7.2	13.0	13.6	12.6
29045	22,800	9	Clark	504.6	6,842	2,688	13.6	98.0	1.0	0.8	0.7	1.0	6.1	16.7	6.8	10.6	11.1	12.4
29047	28,140	1	Clay	397.7	246,365	276	619.5	83.1	7.9	1.2	3.5	7.0	6.4	17.7	8.0	14.6	13.8	13.0
29049	28,140	1	Clinton	419.0	20,470	1,796	48.9	95.2	2.1	1.3	0.8	2.3	6.1	17.4	7.2	11.3	11.8	13.2
29051	27,620	3	Cole	391.5	76,796	724	196.2	83.1	13.3	0.8	1.9	2.9	6.0	16.3	8.7	13.6	12.8	12.9
29053		6	Cooper	564.8	17,603	1,945	31.2	89.7	8.2	1.1	0.9	2.1	5.4	16.0	9.9	13.5	11.9	11.8
29055		6	Crawford	742.5	23,957	1,645	32.3	96.5	1.0	1.4	0.6	2.0	5.7	17.0	7.5	11.1	11.3	12.5
29057		8	Dade	490.0	7,569	2,624	15.4	95.9	1.1	2.6	0.8	2.1	4.8	15.7	6.8	9.3	11.0	12.5
29059	44,180	2	Dallas	541.0	16,762	1,993	31.0	96.3	0.8	2.0	0.6	2.2	6.5	17.1	6.9	10.8	10.6	12.0
29061		8	Daviess	563.3	8,313	2,560	14.8	97.0	1.1	1.0	0.7	1.6	6.7	18.8	7.7	10.3	10.7	11.3
29063	41,140	3	DeKalb	421.4	12,630	2,247	30.0	84.6	12.0	0.8	0.8	2.8	4.9	12.4	8.0	16.0	15.1	14.5
29065		7	Dent	752.8	15,441	2,072	20.5	95.7	1.0	2.0	1.2	1.8	5.9	16.6	6.6	10.6	11.0	12.0
29067		6	Douglas	813.6	13,373	2,202	16.4	96.7	0.8	2.2	0.7	1.8	5.7	16.2	6.1	9.9	10.2	11.6
29069	28,380	7	Dunklin	541.1	29,423	1,448	54.4	81.9	11.3	0.9	0.8	7.0	6.8	18.8	7.7	11.1	11.3	12.1
29071	41,180	1	Franklin	922.7	103,670	583	112.4	96.3	1.5	0.9	0.9	1.8	6.1	16.9	7.5	12.4	11.3	13.3
29073		6	Gasconade	519.0	14,705	2,115	28.3	97.2	1.0	0.9	0.8	1.5	5.3	15.3	7.0	10.7	10.3	12.7
29075		8	Gentry	491.4	6,628	2,701	13.5	96.9	1.1	0.8	0.8	1.7	7.2	17.5	7.2	12.0	10.8	11.7
29077	44,180	2	Greene	675.3	291,923	237	432.3	89.8	4.6	1.6	3.0	3.9	6.0	14.8	13.6	14.1	11.7	11.3
29079		7	Grundy	435.3	9,914	2,434	22.8	95.1	1.3	1.2	1.2	2.6	7.3	16.7	8.1	12.4	9.6	10.9
29081		7	Harrison	722.5	8,414	2,551	11.6	96.2	1.1	0.9	0.8	2.4	6.4	17.8	6.7	10.5	10.4	11.2
29083		6	Henry	696.9	21,792	1,733	31.3	94.9	1.9	1.5	0.7	2.6	5.9	16.1	7.0	11.2	10.7	12.3
29085		8	Hickory	398.8	9,509	2,462	23.8	96.2	0.9	2.3	0.5	1.9	4.5	12.7	5.1	7.6	8.2	11.8
29087		8	Holt	462.7	4,404	2,867	9.5	96.8	0.8	1.5	0.7	1.3	5.2	15.6	5.4	9.8	10.2	13.1
29089		6	Howard	463.8	10,137	2,419	21.9	92.4	6.1	1.4	0.7	1.6	5.9	15.8	12.3	11.0	10.5	11.1
29091	48,460	7	Howell	927.2	40,076	1,177	43.2	95.8	0.9	1.8	1.1	2.2	6.3	17.5	7.8	12.0	11.3	11.9
29093		7	Iron	550.3	10,177	2,414	18.5	95.9	1.9	1.7	0.5	1.7	5.2	15.7	6.9	10.3	12.0	12.8
29095	28,140	1	Jackson	604.5	700,307	96	1,158.5	64.8	25.0	1.3	2.9	9.1	6.6	17.0	8.2	15.6	12.6	12.1

1. CBSA = Core Based Statistical Area. See Appendix A for explanation. See Appendix B for list of metropolitan areas with component counties. 2. County type code from the Economic Research Service of USDA Rural-Urban Continuum Codes. See Appendix A for definition. 3. Dry land or land partially or temporarily covered by water. 4. May be of any race.

Table B. States and Counties — Population and Households

STATE County	55 to 64 years	65 to 74 years	75 years and over	Percent female	Total persons 2000	Total persons 2010	Percent change 2000-2010	2010-2018	Births	Deaths	Net Migration	Number	Persons per household	Family house-holds	Female family house-holder[1]	One person
	16	17	18	19	20	21	22	23	24	25	26	27	28	29	30	31
MISSISSIPPI— Cont'd																
Sunflower	11.8	8.2	5.5	46.6	34,369	29,383	-14.5	-12.4	2,667	2,466	-3,942	8,505	2.70	66.3	29.5	30.1
Tallahatchie	12.0	8.4	6.5	44.4	14,903	15,385	3.2	-9.1	1,307	1,274	-1,445	4,296	2.48	64.7	22.7	32.7
Tate	12.9	10.1	6.6	51.8	25,370	28,878	13.8	-0.4	2,772	2,315	-591	10,016	2.65	71.5	20.1	24.5
Tippah	12.8	10.0	6.6	51.3	20,826	22,232	6.8	-1.1	2,239	2,213	-254	8,204	2.64	72.9	12.0	23.1
Tishomingo	13.8	11.9	8.5	51.4	19,163	19,601	2.3	-0.7	1,669	2,349	547	7,606	2.53	71.3	12.0	26.1
Tunica	11.7	7.9	4.3	53.2	9,227	10,778	16.8	-7.7	1,567	846	-1,576	3,983	2.55	67.7	28.0	29.8
Union	12.1	9.6	7.1	51.0	25,362	27,134	7.0	5.4	3,021	2,337	800	9,927	2.81	71.1	13.0	26.8
Walthall	13.9	10.7	9.0	51.8	15,156	15,447	1.9	-6.4	1,474	1,505	-956	5,903	2.46	61.5	15.0	36.0
Warren	14.3	10.1	6.5	52.4	49,644	48,771	-1.8	-5.3	5,093	4,329	-3,369	18,559	2.53	65.8	18.3	30.9
Washington	14.1	9.8	6.0	53.6	62,977	51,135	-18.8	-11.9	6,092	4,841	-7,402	18,249	2.60	63.0	26.5	33.3
Wayne	14.1	9.7	7.4	52.0	21,216	20,747	-2.2	-2.2	2,359	1,832	-975	7,762	2.61	73.8	18.2	23.2
Webster	14.3	10.3	7.5	51.2	10,294	10,249	-0.4	-4.5	1,001	1,141	-320	3,842	2.55	71.2	14.7	27.3
Wilkinson	14.3	9.9	7.3	46.4	10,312	9,878	-4.2	-11.0	881	962	-1,019	2,882	2.79	61.1	25.4	36.7
Winston	14.1	11.4	8.6	51.2	20,160	19,198	-4.8	-5.4	1,623	1,850	-800	7,411	2.43	70.1	20.8	28.0
Yalobusha	14.6	11.9	8.0	52.1	13,051	12,678	-2.9	-2.3	1,278	1,415	-147	5,196	2.35	67.6	17.0	29.2
Yazoo	11.1	7.5	5.8	42.4	28,149	28,065	-0.3	0.7	2,839	2,404	-280	8,642	2.71	66.0	27.0	30.3
MISSOURI	13.5	9.7	7.2	50.9	5,595,211	5,988,952	7.0	2.3	617,794	478,044	-331	2,386,203	2.47	64.5	11.8	29.2
Adair	10.5	8.2	6.7	51.9	24,977	25,604	2.5	-1.0	2,154	1,736	-684	9,595	2.36	53.5	7.1	34.2
Andrew	14.8	10.5	8.0	50.3	16,492	17,297	4.9	1.8	1,502	1,393	207	6,874	2.50	71.4	5.7	23.3
Atchison	14.7	13.7	11.7	50.3	6,430	5,685	-11.6	-9.0	437	628	-331	2,492	2.10	57.6	6.4	35.8
Audrain	13.5	10.1	7.7	54.1	25,853	25,529	-1.3	-0.2	2,838	2,414	-469	9,457	2.51	64.1	10.7	30.3
Barry	15.1	11.8	8.8	49.4	34,010	35,603	4.7	0.8	3,443	3,347	213	13,091	2.68	71.8	9.8	24.1
Barton	14.7	11.1	9.4	50.8	12,541	12,400	-1.1	-4.9	1,141	1,144	-606	4,939	2.39	66.9	9.5	27.8
Bates	14.8	10.3	9.1	50.6	16,653	17,049	2.4	-4.3	1,515	1,702	-546	6,704	2.40	68.1	8.2	28.1
Benton	18.0	18.0	12.8	49.9	17,180	19,056	10.9	1.2	1,291	2,384	1,319	7,982	2.34	66.1	6.2	29.2
Bollinger	15.7	12.0	8.6	49.7	12,029	12,363	2.8	-1.6	1,068	1,110	-148	4,805	2.53	71.3	10.6	25.0
Boone	10.8	7.4	4.8	51.5	135,454	162,645	20.1	10.7	17,323	8,572	8,607	68,898	2.40	57.4	9.9	29.9
Buchanan	13.3	9.1	7.0	49.5	85,998	89,190	3.7	-0.7	9,615	7,783	-2,439	33,304	2.56	62.2	13.1	31.3
Butler	13.6	10.4	8.4	51.4	40,867	42,794	4.7	-0.4	4,593	4,645	-63	16,550	2.53	67.2	14.9	26.8
Caldwell	14.4	11.1	8.7	49.3	8,969	9,424	5.1	-3.4	779	818	-286	3,741	2.36	65.8	8.7	29.4
Callaway	13.9	9.8	6.5	48.9	40,766	44,334	8.8	1.3	4,095	3,154	-362	16,105	2.54	66.0	11.0	29.1
Camden	18.0	17.5	10.6	50.3	37,051	44,017	18.8	4.1	3,310	3,959	2,436	16,340	2.71	72.9	7.2	22.9
Cape Girardeau	12.5	9.4	7.4	51.5	68,693	75,673	10.2	4.1	7,453	6,175	1,854	29,613	2.52	62.9	10.1	28.0
Carroll	13.8	12.3	9.5	51.4	10,285	9,295	-9.6	-5.9	884	994	-444	3,618	2.43	67.5	9.6	28.4
Carter	15.2	12.1	7.8	51.7	5,941	6,265	5.5	-3.4	645	660	-198	2,403	2.58	62.8	12.4	31.3
Cass	14.0	9.4	7.4	51.3	82,092	99,505	21.2	5.5	9,878	7,539	3,176	38,706	2.61	73.1	9.5	22.5
Cedar	14.2	12.8	10.5	50.1	13,733	13,982	1.8	1.3	1,463	1,662	392	5,879	2.33	63.3	10.6	32.1
Chariton	15.9	11.8	11.9	50.4	8,438	7,830	-7.2	-4.8	696	783	-292	2,842	2.59	65.1	5.2	30.8
Christian	12.6	9.4	6.3	50.9	54,285	77,417	42.6	12.4	8,318	4,903	6,137	30,774	2.68	74.0	10.1	21.1
Clark	15.4	11.3	9.5	48.9	7,416	7,129	-3.9	-4.0	641	684	-244	2,907	2.32	68.4	7.3	27.8
Clay	12.4	8.5	5.7	50.9	184,006	221,943	20.6	11.0	25,097	13,857	13,229	89,709	2.60	67.3	10.7	25.8
Clinton	14.9	10.2	7.8	49.7	18,979	20,743	9.3	-1.3	1,924	2,035	-167	8,185	2.45	72.2	9.3	23.0
Cole	13.2	9.8	6.8	49.5	71,397	75,975	6.4	1.1	7,613	5,280	-1,480	29,642	2.43	63.5	11.1	30.6
Cooper	13.6	10.0	8.0	47.8	16,670	17,604	5.6	0.0	1,576	1,570	1	6,410	2.50	64.2	10.3	30.4
Crawford	15.3	11.5	8.2	50.4	22,804	24,703	8.3	-3.0	2,303	2,418	-624	9,286	2.58	66.1	9.4	29.0
Dade	16.2	13.2	10.5	48.9	7,923	7,882	-0.5	-4.0	569	856	-31	3,107	2.39	68.6	9.6	25.7
Dallas	15.7	11.5	8.8	50.1	15,661	16,770	7.1	0.0	1,694	1,576	-129	6,156	2.64	73.3	9.4	20.9
Daviess	14.1	12.1	8.3	49.6	8,016	8,433	5.2	-1.4	939	737	-319	3,083	2.63	67.3	6.3	27.7
DeKalb	12.6	8.5	8.1	37.4	11,597	12,892	11.2	-2.0	923	940	-244	3,854	2.34	65.0	7.5	30.9
Dent	15.6	11.9	9.9	50.2	14,927	15,656	4.9	-1.4	1,444	1,631	-25	6,087	2.52	67.5	9.1	27.8
Douglas	16.2	13.8	10.6	50.3	13,084	13,684	4.6	-2.3	1,228	1,347	-191	5,173	2.56	70.2	7.4	28.2
Dunklin	13.5	10.3	8.4	52.2	33,155	31,953	-3.6	-7.9	3,619	3,599	-2,561	12,760	2.37	63.9	16.1	31.5
Franklin	15.2	10.1	7.3	50.3	93,807	101,495	8.2	2.1	10,200	8,229	278	40,612	2.50	70.6	10.5	24.4
Gasconade	16.0	12.3	10.4	50.1	15,342	15,213	-0.8	-3.3	1,287	1,666	-115	6,135	2.36	69.4	7.0	25.5
Gentry	13.8	9.5	10.4	51.8	6,861	6,740	-1.8	-1.7	758	710	-158	2,662	2.42	66.3	7.5	30.6
Greene	11.9	9.1	7.3	51.4	240,391	275,178	14.5	6.1	29,302	22,146	9,688	119,989	2.30	58.8	10.0	31.4
Grundy	13.5	10.7	10.9	51.3	10,432	10,261	-1.6	-3.4	1,210	1,138	-418	4,018	2.43	63.7	11.3	32.2
Harrison	14.6	11.3	11.2	50.6	8,850	8,957	1.2	-6.1	908	942	-507	3,528	2.36	68.3	10.9	27.7
Henry	15.1	12.3	9.4	50.9	21,997	22,270	1.2	-2.1	2,139	2,568	-33	9,294	2.32	62.2	9.8	31.1
Hickory	17.4	19.0	13.8	50.6	8,940	9,627	7.7	-1.2	658	1,211	435	3,983	2.33	64.9	7.1	30.1
Holt	15.6	13.1	12.1	51.1	5,351	4,912	-8.2	-10.3	422	525	-408	2,111	2.08	66.1	7.1	29.2
Howard	14.1	10.7	8.6	50.0	10,212	10,144	-0.7	-0.1	978	775	-213	3,713	2.53	66.8	9.7	28.7
Howell	13.4	11.2	8.6	51.3	37,238	40,398	8.5	-0.8	4,147	4,137	-299	16,204	2.44	67.0	10.2	28.1
Iron	15.7	12.1	9.3	50.2	10,697	10,630	-0.6	-4.3	863	1,201	-115	4,062	2.44	66.4	9.6	28.0
Jackson	13.0	8.7	6.3	51.6	654,880	674,134	2.9	3.9	78,178	51,470	5	280,174	2.42	58.5	14.6	34.3

1. No spouse present.

Table B. States and Counties — Population, Vital Statistics, Health, and Crime

STATE County	Persons in group quarters, 2018	Daytime Population, 2013-2017 Number	Daytime Population, 2013-2017 Employment/ residence ratio	Births, 2018 Total	Births, 2018 Rate[1]	Deaths, 2018 Number	Deaths, 2018 Rate[1]	Persons under 65 with no health insurance, 2016 Number	Persons under 65 with no health insurance, 2016 Percent	Medicare, 2018 Total beneficiaries	Medicare, 2018 Enrolled in Original Medicare	Medicare, 2018 Enrolled in Medicare Advantage	Serious crimes known to police[2], 2016 Total Number	Serious crimes known to police[2], 2016 Total Rate[3]
	32	33	34	35	36	37	38	39	40	41	42	43	44	45
MISSISSIPPI— Cont'd														
Sunflower....................	4,108	26,755	0.98	279	10.8	303	11.8	2,904	15.3	4,893	4,347	546	NA	NA
Tallahatchie....................	2,441	13,668	0.77	150	10.7	161	11.5	1,580	16.1	2,730	2,455	275	NA	NA
Tate....................	1,452	23,169	0.55	342	11.9	302	10.5	3,256	14.4	5,782	4,554	1,228	NA	NA
Tippah....................	337	20,595	0.84	264	12.0	255	11.6	2,838	15.6	5,257	4,859	398	NA	NA
Tishomingo....................	280	18,239	0.84	209	10.7	290	14.9	2,351	15.3	5,071	4,801	270	NA	NA
Tunica....................	104	14,957	2.12	171	17.2	100	10.1	1,018	11.5	1,812	1,402	410	451	4,406
Union....................	283	28,614	1.04	369	12.9	259	9.1	3,914	16.6	6,249	5,713	536	NA	NA
Walthall....................	129	12,510	0.60	171	11.8	175	12.1	2,069	17.6	3,311	2,683	628	NA	NA
Warren....................	524	49,560	1.11	589	12.8	529	11.5	4,802	12.2	9,521	7,702	1,819	1,845	3,918
Washington....................	732	48,149	1.01	603	13.4	606	13.4	5,556	14.2	10,285	8,109	2,176	2,400	5,886
Wayne....................	137	18,543	0.75	268	13.2	217	10.7	2,563	15.1	4,214	3,453	761	NA	NA
Webster....................	47	8,883	0.71	121	12.4	141	14.4	1,113	13.9	2,838	2,650	188	NA	NA
Wilkinson....................	1,112	8,510	0.75	87	9.9	120	13.6	986	15.2	1,926	1,619	307	NA	NA
Winston....................	452	17,135	0.81	183	10.1	235	12.9	2,356	16.5	4,603	4,073	530	NA	NA
Yalobusha....................	156	10,770	0.68	147	11.9	170	13.7	1,380	13.8	3,709	3,304	405	NA	NA
Yazoo....................	5,560	26,078	0.81	299	10.6	279	9.9	2,949	15.1	4,935	4,074	861	NA	NA
MISSOURI	174,441	6,110,186	1.01	72,508	11.8	59,825	9.8	526,350	10.6	1,204,203	795,514	408,689	202,193	3,318
Adair....................	2,915	26,148	1.06	267	10.5	189	7.5	2,320	12.3	4,530	4,110	420	790	3,123
Andrew....................	192	11,804	0.34	179	10.2	178	10.1	1,487	10.4	3,331	2,993	338	204	1,181
Atchison....................	98	4,861	0.82	51	9.9	78	15.1	432	10.9	1,432	1,340	92	31	592
Audrain....................	2,323	25,563	0.98	335	13.2	268	10.5	2,322	11.9	5,509	4,474	1,035	531	2,028
Barry....................	296	36,546	1.08	414	11.5	379	10.6	4,538	16.3	8,257	5,028	3,229	867	2,422
Barton....................	90	10,691	0.76	122	10.3	122	10.3	1,389	14.6	2,938	2,236	702	291	2,473
Bates....................	311	14,001	0.66	164	10.0	181	11.1	1,702	13.0	3,826	2,796	1,030	388	2,379
Benton....................	244	17,193	0.71	154	8.0	303	15.7	1,817	13.9	6,584	4,723	1,861	476	2,565
Bollinger....................	163	9,934	0.49	107	8.8	146	12.0	1,358	14.0	2,918	2,461	457	205	1,690
Boone....................	9,034	180,781	1.07	2,045	11.4	1,127	6.3	13,730	9.2	26,216	18,231	7,985	4,902	2,767
Buchanan....................	4,348	98,618	1.22	1,100	12.4	881	9.9	7,439	10.4	17,382	14,905	2,477	5,207	5,852
Butler....................	858	46,231	1.20	546	12.8	561	13.2	4,484	13.1	10,346	8,895	1,451	1,793	4,178
Caldwell....................	214	7,147	0.49	97	10.6	89	9.8	871	12.2	1,961	1,540	421	123	1,379
Callaway....................	3,684	39,541	0.73	450	10.0	417	9.3	3,590	10.4	8,822	6,884	1,938	1,175	2,619
Camden....................	774	45,835	1.06	363	7.9	543	11.9	4,883	15.0	12,303	9,904	2,399	1,028	2,325
Cape Girardeau....................	3,841	83,210	1.14	859	10.9	706	9.0	7,172	11.4	15,557	13,807	1,750	2,396	3,033
Carroll....................	88	8,047	0.76	105	12.0	119	13.6	824	11.9	2,292	1,886	406	121	1,356
Carter....................	40	5,649	0.75	80	13.2	98	16.2	757	15.4	1,569	1,354	215	123	1,969
Cass....................	1,045	80,670	0.57	1,195	11.4	992	9.5	7,385	8.6	19,666	11,715	7,951	2,654	2,606
Cedar....................	156	12,603	0.74	195	13.8	199	14.0	1,501	14.3	3,845	2,410	1,435	352	2,532
Chariton....................	213	6,641	0.70	78	10.5	107	14.4	683	12.1	1,918	1,666	252	99	1,315
Christian....................	582	63,318	0.49	991	11.4	655	7.5	6,965	9.8	16,187	8,637	7,550	1,337	1,586
Clark....................	90	5,583	0.61	71	10.4	64	9.4	681	12.8	1,525	1,380	145	65	966
Clay....................	2,653	213,479	0.81	2,983	12.1	1,801	7.3	16,424	8.0	40,578	28,173	12,405	10,121	4,253
Clinton....................	445	15,636	0.49	252	12.3	236	11.5	1,756	10.4	3,943	3,109	834	324	1,576
Cole....................	4,917	90,650	1.38	890	11.6	683	8.9	5,532	9.1	14,608	12,302	2,306	1,896	2,471
Cooper....................	1,543	15,459	0.72	181	10.3	183	10.4	1,430	10.8	3,651	2,783	868	327	1,855
Crawford....................	332	21,703	0.71	246	10.3	296	12.4	2,703	13.9	5,807	3,673	2,134	582	2,378
Dade....................	133	7,027	0.81	75	9.9	109	14.4	851	14.7	2,032	1,176	856	123	1,633
Dallas....................	199	13,139	0.43	216	12.9	206	12.3	1,973	15.2	4,245	2,176	2,069	339	2,079
Daviess....................	152	7,042	0.64	111	13.4	87	10.5	1,050	16.4	1,873	1,584	289	68	829
DeKalb....................	3,460	12,354	0.95	118	9.3	91	7.2	763	10.6	2,220	1,879	341	168	1,330
Dent....................	201	14,490	0.81	163	10.6	211	13.7	1,859	15.5	3,871	3,341	530	254	1,634
Douglas....................	123	11,722	0.66	149	11.1	163	12.2	1,542	15.3	3,517	1,837	1,680	158	1,188
Dunklin....................	671	29,916	0.91	389	13.2	450	15.3	3,386	13.9	7,316	6,065	1,251	1,132	3,694
Franklin....................	858	93,428	0.82	1,207	11.6	1,042	10.1	8,580	10.0	22,046	10,242	11,804	2,741	2,675
Gasconade....................	250	14,358	0.94	155	10.5	203	13.8	1,387	12.1	3,879	2,602	1,277	209	1,416
Gentry....................	177	6,418	0.91	86	13.0	89	13.4	658	12.5	1,548	1,421	127	43	644
Greene....................	11,279	323,915	1.27	3,498	12.0	2,713	9.3	26,418	11.4	57,398	31,542	25,856	18,725	6,451
Grundy....................	350	10,275	1.04	137	13.8	132	13.3	944	12.1	2,430	2,247	183	161	1,602
Harrison....................	145	8,234	0.90	104	12.4	120	14.3	960	14.5	2,118	1,941	177	158	1,851
Henry....................	233	21,344	0.94	255	11.7	305	14.0	1,968	11.7	6,151	4,420	1,731	665	3,138
Hickory....................	75	8,178	0.63	102	10.7	142	14.9	970	15.6	3,137	1,791	1,346	90	988
Holt....................	101	4,058	0.79	49	11.1	68	15.4	439	13.0	1,187	1,064	123	72	1,637
Howard....................	718	8,375	0.63	111	10.9	69	6.8	863	11.3	2,128	1,642	486	143	1,412
Howell....................	608	41,760	1.10	462	11.5	505	12.6	4,382	13.7	10,381	7,751	2,630	1,023	2,560
Iron....................	276	10,183	0.97	100	9.8	168	16.5	1,000	12.8	2,771	2,345	426	139	1,388
Jackson....................	11,067	742,524	1.16	9,244	13.2	6,694	9.6	67,366	11.5	122,407	72,228	50,179	32,878	4,771

1. Per 1,000 estimated resident population. 2. Data for serious crimes have not been adjusted for underreporting; this may affect comparability between geographic areas and over time. 3. Per 100,000 population estimated by the FBI.

Table B. States and Counties — Crime, Education, Money Income, and Poverty

STATE County	Serious crimes known to police[2], 2016 (cont.)[1] Rate Violent	Property	Education — School enrollment and attainment, 2013-2017 Enrollment[3] Total	Percent private	Attainment[4] (percent) High school graduate or less	Bachelor's degree or more	Local government expenditures,[5] 2014-2015 Total current spending (mil dol)	Current spending per student (dollars)	Money income, 2013-2017 Per capita income[6]	Households Median income (dollars)	Percent with income of less than $50,000	Percent with income of $200,000 or more	Income and poverty, 2017 Median household income (dollars)	Percent below poverty level All persons	Children under 18 years	Children 5 to 17 years in families
	46	47	48	49	50	51	52	53	54	55	56	57	58	59	60	61
MISSISSIPPI— Cont'd																
Sunflower	NA	NA	6,534	14.9	57.2	14.5	35.8	8,645	14,427	28,556	71.6	1.7	29,704	36.2	47.8	49.3
Tallahatchie	NA	NA	2,366	16.8	63.8	10.1	18.6	8,893	14,163	30,000	70.3	1.2	30,998	35.2	41.7	42.2
Tate	NA	NA	7,872	13.3	51.0	16.1	34.2	7,254	21,671	46,233	53.1	2.7	47,296	16.5	24.0	22.7
Tippah	NA	NA	5,590	7.1	56.1	14.5	34.1	8,061	19,780	39,351	58.6	1.5	39,695	17.9	23.1	22.7
Tishomingo	NA	NA	4,160	9.0	61.8	11.5	28.2	8,929	19,379	36,672	65.3	1.3	35,031	17.9	21.0	20.7
Tunica	332	4,074	3,111	8.2	50.9	17.1	25.8	11,552	18,486	32,052	70.1	0.6	31,492	29.1	44.6	47.9
Union	NA	NA	6,954	6.1	54.8	14.7	40.4	8,043	19,518	40,076	60.0	1.5	46,979	14.5	19.4	18.9
Walthall	NA	NA	3,455	21.2	64.9	10.3	20.0	9,338	20,155	31,077	69.5	1.7	32,078	26.1	37.2	36.1
Warren	323	3,596	12,004	14.5	45.0	22.9	73.0	8,797	22,542	41,635	57.4	1.4	44,227	21.4	31.7	28.9
Washington	265	5,621	12,683	12.2	51.8	19.0	85.8	9,483	19,247	29,387	68.5	2.4	30,865	32.7	45.3	48.1
Wayne	NA	NA	4,956	10.7	62.4	12.6	30.6	9,076	21,515	35,215	58.9	2.6	36,339	23	33.8	34.2
Webster	NA	NA	2,393	11.2	50.9	18.1	14.9	7,817	20,662	35,634	60.3	2.4	39,479	23	33.0	34.5
Wilkinson	NA	NA	1,824	17.4	66.7	14.9	11.4	9,311	12,722	23,340	78.0	0.7	27,962	33.1	40.5	40.4
Winston	NA	NA	4,292	14.7	54.4	15.9	24.3	8,397	23,527	33,313	64.3	3.0	36,305	22.5	33.3	31.1
Yalobusha	NA	NA	2,684	18.3	56.0	14.0	15.5	8,668	20,037	37,647	60.0	0.7	36,834	21.3	30.7	31.3
Yazoo	NA	NA	6,664	18.8	59.6	14.3	34.1	8,422	16,927	28,330	70.5	0.9	33,051	33.9	41.7	38.3
MISSOURI	519	2,799	1,514,505	18.8	41.7	28.2	9,305.0	10,125	28,282	51,542	48.5	3.9	53,506	13.4	18.5	17.2
Adair	202	2,922	10,007	9.9	45.1	31.0	28.7	9,537	21,778	38,750	59.6	1.9	38,784	25.6	22.2	20.2
Andrew	226	956	3,929	8.4	46.3	25.1	24.5	8,496	28,003	56,658	45.8	3.7	60,759	8	11.0	10.2
Atchison	76	516	969	8.2	49.7	23.3	10.1	13,863	28,209	45,259	54.4	2.6	49,469	11.9	17.0	16.6
Audrain	164	1,864	5,351	12.2	62.4	13.7	30.2	9,024	21,226	44,056	57.1	1.5	44,212	17.2	26.7	26.1
Barry	210	2,213	8,105	12.3	60.1	12.8	58.7	8,718	20,840	40,638	58.5	1.7	40,765	16.1	25.7	23.7
Barton	340	2,133	2,626	10.2	54.1	17.4	18.7	9,494	24,628	41,184	59.5	2.3	41,796	14.7	21.4	19.2
Bates	454	1,926	3,642	13.0	59.9	15.0	25.0	9,091	25,873	45,605	55.0	1.9	45,392	14.4	21.3	20.4
Benton	501	2,064	3,454	14.0	58.6	11.6	22.1	8,624	20,163	35,097	66.8	0.6	39,588	17.2	28.5	26.7
Bollinger	750	940	2,696	12.9	66.5	9.4	15.7	8,290	20,687	40,791	58.1	2.3	43,611	14.8	22.5	20.4
Boone	380	2,386	61,145	12.0	27.5	45.9	233.1	9,977	28,495	52,005	47.8	4.4	52,179	15.1	13.6	12.9
Buchanan	515	5,338	21,492	12.9	49.4	19.9	121.9	9,465	24,271	48,652	51.1	2.4	46,516	15.6	21.6	19.2
Butler	508	3,670	9,990	5.9	52.8	15.9	54.6	7,893	20,855	37,878	62.9	2.7	39,642	22.7	32.0	29.8
Caldwell	269	1,110	2,134	4.9	53.8	17.4	16.6	10,326	24,200	44,975	54.8	1.2	44,252	13.9	19.6	17.5
Callaway	397	2,222	10,702	21.9	52.0	21.6	43.2	8,813	24,208	53,180	46.7	1.9	53,317	12.3	18.1	16.4
Camden	278	2,047	8,461	14.3	47.7	22.0	53.9	10,070	25,492	50,496	49.4	3.7	51,489	13.6	23.8	23.3
Cape Girardeau	380	2,653	22,680	14.6	41.5	29.8	88.1	8,707	25,965	49,554	50.4	2.9	51,955	14.6	17.7	15.9
Carroll	112	1,244	1,846	4.3	60.1	17.1	15.8	10,862	24,642	43,583	54.1	3.6	45,404	13.9	19.7	18.2
Carter	592	1,377	1,679	6.0	56.5	12.3	11.6	8,957	21,569	37,875	61.3	3.2	33,793	20.9	35.0	33.8
Cass	203	2,403	25,610	15.1	41.4	25.8	162.9	8,893	30,618	65,352	36.0	4.0	65,839	9.2	12.2	10.7
Cedar	446	2,086	3,099	14.4	57.6	13.8	19.2	8,832	20,228	35,930	67.3	1.9	37,958	17.2	29.5	28.6
Chariton	199	1,116	1,517	13.2	60.7	16.4	12.0	11,097	23,463	43,186	58.2	1.5	44,587	12.7	17.6	17.4
Christian	180	1,406	22,105	12.5	39.8	27.9	123.9	8,346	26,628	55,761	44.0	3.3	58,931	9.9	12.4	10.6
Clark	193	773	1,430	14.5	58.6	13.2	9.5	8,686	26,253	45,216	55.6	1.5	43,130	16	23.6	22.9
Clay	974	3,278	59,969	15.5	36.2	31.9	399.8	9,788	31,953	65,675	36.6	4.6	67,666	7.4	9.6	8.8
Clinton	321	1,255	4,692	10.6	46.5	18.5	40.0	9,472	27,655	57,591	41.6	2.1	57,807	11.1	14.1	12.4
Cole	296	2,175	18,502	26.2	40.3	31.4	103.8	7,888	27,559	54,216	44.6	2.5	55,315	11.7	15.7	13.8
Cooper	85	1,770	4,066	12.9	50.7	20.7	23.3	9,331	22,371	46,547	52.9	1.0	48,851	11.5	17.7	15.4
Crawford	168	2,211	5,263	10.1	64.0	11.2	27.9	8,019	20,799	37,171	61.0	0.4	39,306	19.4	27.8	25.6
Dade	398	1,235	1,581	12.1	56.3	15.1	11.4	10,303	20,468	38,880	63.2	1.2	39,127	16.6	26.5	23.5
Dallas	245	1,834	3,250	18.1	60.2	12.1	20.7	8,421	19,647	41,441	58.1	1.9	38,685	18.5	27.8	26.6
Daviess	171	658	1,702	19.6	56.4	17.3	13.2	10,120	22,642	45,707	53.9	1.7	45,342	13.8	22.4	21.5
DeKalb	238	1,093	2,364	11.4	60.3	14.5	10.8	9,922	18,994	46,517	52.5	1.7	48,060	15.5	14.8	14.2
Dent	109	1,524	3,240	6.7	61.4	12.9	18.0	7,969	20,908	38,829	62.0	2.0	35,445	20.2	31.4	29.7
Douglas	180	1,008	2,945	14.3	64.7	9.4	13.4	8,574	18,095	33,003	69.5	0.9	34,265	20.4	30.8	28.3
Dunklin	532	3,162	7,335	3.0	62.2	12.9	50.1	8,643	18,878	32,348	68.7	1.2	33,721	24.6	35.6	32.6
Franklin	209	2,466	23,049	17.9	45.5	20.4	156.2	9,482	27,209	53,849	46.7	2.8	55,937	10.4	14.6	13.1
Gasconade	190	1,226	3,004	9.9	54.8	17.1	23.8	8,150	25,963	50,687	49.1	1.0	48,711	11.9	16.4	15.1
Gentry	90	554	1,390	14.0	53.9	20.0	11.9	10,605	20,903	43,777	56.3	0.6	43,182	14	19.4	19.2
Greene	824	5,628	78,851	16.3	36.8	30.5	334.4	8,693	25,529	43,175	56.0	2.7	45,608	16.2	20.7	18.9
Grundy	90	1,513	2,306	9.7	53.5	17.9	15.1	9,496	22,014	41,092	56.9	1.3	40,305	17.9	26.8	25.1
Harrison	47	1,804	1,833	8.1	61.6	14.5	14.4	9,116	20,947	42,889	56.9	1.0	40,139	16.7	25.8	23.4
Henry	378	2,760	4,716	11.1	54.8	15.9	26.8	9,126	24,371	44,089	58.1	1.7	43,615	16.1	24.1	23.1
Hickory	0	988	1,753	18.3	59.4	9.8	8.9	9,906	19,711	34,746	69.0	0.5	35,170	19.3	36.8	34.3
Holt	114	1,523	742	5.3	51.6	21.7	7.2	11,913	25,306	43,981	55.0	1.0	46,560	13.9	19.1	18.2
Howard	148	1,264	2,828	35.7	49.2	25.5	12.0	8,231	23,430	50,356	49.5	2.2	45,858	13.3	19.0	17.7
Howell	308	2,252	9,568	8.2	52.7	15.4	47.2	8,319	20,274	34,984	65.5	1.7	35,483	22.3	29.9	28.1
Iron	190	1,198	1,980	4.4	61.3	11.7	19.4	10,305	19,414	36,457	63.4	0.8	35,682	22.6	35.8	31.6
Jackson	929	3,842	167,394	16.9	38.9	30.2	1,169.0	10,871	28,965	50,652	49.4	3.6	52,585	13.8	20.7	20.5

1. Data for serious crimes have not been adjusted for underreporting; this may affect comparability between geographic areas and over time.   2. Per 100,000 population estimated by the FBI.   3. All persons 3 years old and over enrolled in nursery school through college.   4. Persons 25 years old and over.   5. Elementary and secondary education expenditures.   6. Based on population estimated by the American Community Survey, 2013–2017.

Table B. States and Counties — **Personal Income and Earnings**

STATE County	Personal income, 2017					Supplements to wages and salaries, employer contributions (mil dol)					Earnings, 2017	Contributions for government social insurance (mil dol)	
	Total (mil dol)	Percent change 2016-2017	Per capita¹ Dollars	Per capita¹ Rank	Wages and salaries (mil dol)	Pension and insurance	Government social insurance	Proprietors' income (mil dol)	Dividends, interest, and rent (mil dol)	Personal transfer receipts (mil dol)	Total (mil dol)	From employee and self-employed	From employer
	62	63	64	65	66	67	68	69	70	71	72	73	74
MISSISSIPPI— Cont'd													
Sunflower	755	-0.9	29,057	2,982	303	59	23	36	128	287	421	30	23
Tallahatchie	405	3.4	28,695	3,005	116	20	9	40	59	142	185	14	9
Tate	992	3.3	34,873	2,365	211	38	16	49	117	277	312	26	16
Tippah	714	3.1	32,520	2,685	245	44	19	29	88	237	337	27	19
Tishomingo	625	2.5	31,981	2,752	224	42	17	27	79	216	309	26	17
Tunica	319	-6.7	31,814	2,779	307	34	24	16	56	105	381	26	24
Union	900	3.1	31,512	2,806	491	76	36	60	121	252	662	48	36
Walthall	450	4.3	31,006	2,851	84	16	6	37	62	161	143	12	6
Warren	1,802	1.9	38,525	1,799	953	188	74	82	301	465	1,297	86	74
Washington	1,675	0.4	36,248	2,159	656	111	50	115	267	559	933	69	50
Wayne	665	4.0	32,511	2,687	204	36	15	90	100	205	345	23	15
Webster	356	0.2	36,500	2,116	71	13	5	13	46	129	102	10	5
Wilkinson	254	1.4	28,850	2,992	61	12	5	7	39	102	84	8	5
Winston	618	4.0	33,875	2,499	203	33	15	43	85	207	294	23	15
Yalobusha	436	1.3	34,863	2,366	111	22	8	19	55	163	161	15	8
Yazoo	743	-0.1	27,455	3,050	286	62	22	-5	118	269	365	29	22
MISSOURI	274,976	3.6	45,014	X	143,084	21,938	10,157	21,260	51,507	54,381	196,439	12,077	10,157
Adair	813	3.4	32,037	2,749	370	73	26	44	191	204	514	32	26
Andrew	751	3.6	42,782	1,175	95	20	7	40	124	129	162	12	7
Atchison	243	0.1	45,975	798	59	12	4	51	48	53	126	7	4
Audrain	980	-0.3	38,228	1,838	361	74	26	183	158	218	644	39	26
Barry	1,187	5.1	33,277	2,583	614	99	45	88	256	320	847	56	45
Barton	410	3.7	34,589	2,401	109	23	8	57	68	116	197	13	8
Bates	605	5.5	37,037	2,028	139	30	10	65	99	159	244	17	10
Benton	643	1.7	33,736	2,520	126	27	9	46	114	246	208	20	9
Bollinger	387	3.9	31,478	2,809	62	13	4	26	56	128	105	9	4
Boone	7,986	3.2	44,797	929	4,514	926	302	462	1,570	1,203	6,204	339	302
Buchanan	3,365	2.6	37,779	1,915	2,302	373	165	188	537	855	3,027	185	165
Butler	1,484	2.3	34,789	2,374	719	137	54	104	232	526	1,014	67	54
Caldwell	320	4.3	35,121	2,332	66	13	5	22	48	80	106	8	5
Callaway	1,640	3.5	36,418	2,131	647	142	46	58	257	381	893	57	46
Camden	1,624	4.4	35,598	2,256	595	92	45	141	385	480	872	64	45
Cape Girardeau	3,404	3.9	43,556	1,070	1,763	289	126	446	597	667	2,625	158	126
Carroll	383	-2.3	43,508	1,077	90	18	7	82	69	93	196	12	7
Carter	192	2.2	31,090	2,845	48	11	4	14	29	75	77	6	4
Cass	4,675	3.7	45,075	891	1,037	177	75	275	619	827	1,565	106	75
Cedar	426	4.3	30,262	2,906	92	21	7	46	72	167	166	14	7
Chariton	312	4.0	41,686	1,303	68	14	5	38	68	81	125	8	5
Christian	3,273	4.6	38,310	1,823	640	115	47	219	453	619	1,021	75	47
Clark	231	-1.4	34,332	2,440	43	10	3	13	42	63	69	6	3
Clay	11,178	3.6	46,026	792	5,702	816	412	625	1,452	1,705	7,554	460	412
Clinton	854	5.8	41,554	1,323	160	32	11	43	140	173	247	17	11
Cole	3,435	3.4	44,783	931	2,444	521	164	230	634	630	3,359	184	164
Cooper	651	3.9	36,872	2,061	190	36	14	50	108	159	289	19	14
Crawford	850	4.5	35,282	2,300	303	49	21	74	131	256	447	32	21
Dade	256	2.6	33,748	2,519	60	13	4	31	43	77	109	8	4
Dallas	539	5.3	32,308	2,714	79	17	6	64	81	169	166	15	6
Daviess	285	5.6	34,028	2,480	49	11	3	43	54	77	106	7	3
DeKalb	343	6.7	27,236	3,055	148	30	10	24	52	85	212	13	10
Dent	487	2.5	31,454	2,814	130	27	9	30	82	176	197	16	9
Douglas	352	3.3	26,463	3,070	81	17	6	21	55	130	125	12	6
Dunklin	988	1.6	32,790	2,649	292	56	22	36	135	407	406	32	22
Franklin	4,328	3.8	41,887	1,275	1,722	290	127	233	690	914	2,372	156	127
Gasconade	552	4.7	37,472	1,954	182	37	13	31	112	158	263	19	13
Gentry	275	6.9	41,287	1,367	87	15	6	35	46	77	144	8	6
Greene	11,982	3.7	41,344	1,356	7,741	1,192	552	1,154	2,210	2,527	10,639	650	552
Grundy	333	1.8	33,508	2,553	131	27	10	31	59	111	198	13	10
Harrison	315	8.0	36,931	2,053	85	18	6	55	60	92	164	10	6
Henry	875	4.6	40,307	1,500	297	63	21	80	152	266	461	31	21
Hickory	250	3.7	26,346	3,075	40	9	3	11	47	120	62	8	3
Holt	204	-0.6	46,194	777	50	10	4	46	35	45	111	7	4
Howard	380	1.8	37,470	1,955	95	18	7	15	67	104	135	10	7
Howell	1,281	2.9	31,931	2,761	547	103	41	90	209	443	781	56	41
Iron	336	4.4	32,894	2,629	145	27	10	11	44	144	194	14	10
Jackson	31,053	3.9	44,432	966	22,606	3,237	1,594	2,759	4,912	6,107	30,197	1,799	1,594

1. Based on the resident population estimated as of July 1 of the year shown.

STATE County	Earnings, 2017 (cont.)									Social Security beneficiaries, December 2017			Housing units, 2018	
	Percent by selected industries											Supplemental Security Income recipients, 2017		
	Farm	Mining, quarrying, and extractions	Construction	Manu-facturing	Information; professional, scientific, technical services	Retail trade	Finance, insurance, real estate, and leasing	Health care and social assistance	Govern-ment	Number	Rate[1]		Total	Percent change, 2010-2018
	75	76	77	78	79	80	81	82	83	84	85	86	87	88
MISSISSIPPI— Cont'd														
Sunflower	1.4	0	2.9	3.6	2	6	4.9	6.1	41.7	5,715	220	1,935	9,679	-0.1
Tallahatchie	11.4	0	2.4	1.2	D	6.9	3	D	28.5	3,180	225	1,002	5,624	1.6
Tate	-0.8	D	8.3	10.1	7.4	9.6	4.3	D	27.5	6,525	229	923	11,593	5.9
Tippah	-0.3	D	6.6	29.6	D	7.3	3.1	D	17.1	6,055	276	1,007	9,865	1.7
Tishomingo	0	0	8	40.5	1.5	6.7	2.9	D	14.4	5,790	296	718	10,452	1.5
Tunica	-0.3	0.1	2.2	6.4	D	3	3.5	2.4	10.4	2,145	214	757	4,948	3
Union	0.8	0	5.2	39.9	D	5.5	2.2	D	10.4	7,080	248	753	11,974	3.9
Walthall	10.3	0.7	10.6	11.5	D	9.4	2.6	D	21.3	3,705	256	667	7,284	2.1
Warren	-0.1	0.3	3.5	15	6	6.3	3.4	11.3	31.2	10,585	226	2,040	22,065	0.8
Washington	-0.2	D	3.9	8.7	5.3	8.4	5	11.5	25.2	11,870	257	4,307	21,609	-0.5
Wayne	14.9	3	3.3	10.2	2.1	8.3	5	D	19.6	4,790	234	864	9,481	2.9
Webster	-2.4	0	7.4	11	D	7.2	1.9	D	20.3	3,220	330	661	4,864	1.3
Wilkinson	1.1	D	1.7	8.5	D	8.9	4.5	D	33.6	2,205	250	651	5,182	2.9
Winston	7.3	0	4.4	25.2	2.7	8.5	2	D	13.3	5,110	280	852	8,913	1.9
Yalobusha	-2.9	D	9.7	34.3	D	5	3.8	D	27.1	4,245	340	898	6,548	3.2
Yazoo	-8	D	3.1	13.3	2	6.4	3.1	D	43.6	5,630	208	1,683	10,189	1.1
MISSOURI	0.5	0.1	6.2	10.8	11.6	6	9	12.4	15.3	1,281,534	210	137,796	2,806,371	3.5
Adair	0.4	0	4.3	10.9	3.2	9	4	D	25.4	4,910	193	649	11,602	3
Andrew	6.7	D	11.9	2.3	D	8.5	4.2	D	23.1	3,500	199	174	7,337	0.4
Atchison	27.7	0	3.7	0.7	D	5.1	7.1	11.1	14.8	1,500	284	85	2,956	
Audrain	4.1	0	4	35.3	2.2	6.5	4.1	D	19.3	5,900	230	579	10,936	0.8
Barry	2.1	0.2	6.1	33.2	16.7	6.3	5	D	9.9	9,040	253	949	17,638	0.7
Barton	13.8	D	10.2	5.6	D	8.7	5.4	8.9	23	3,230	273	324	5,591	-0.1
Bates	7.9	D	11.6	2.5	D	9.7	6.7	7.7	25.8	4,100	251	396	7,842	0
Benton	1.5	0	11	6.7	2.5	10.6	10.3	D	27	7,130	374	618	14,216	0.5
Bollinger	3.3	D	14.4	6.3	2.6	6.7	D	D	21.7	3,285	267	408	5,883	0.1
Boone	0.2	0	4.4	4.7	7.2	6.5	9.2	11.5	36.1	26,770	150	2,750	78,940	13.5
Buchanan	0.4	D	6.4	26.8	4.9	6.1	6.3	15.6	13.2	18,640	209	2,451	38,804	1
Butler	0.6	D	4.4	11.4	5.4	9.3	5.8	D	22.1	11,230	263	2,182	19,854	0.6
Caldwell	5.2	D	12.7	2.1	5.1	18.6	4.6	5	26.8	2,160	237	161	4,716	2.4
Callaway	0.9	0.4	6.7	13.9	4.1	4.9	2.7	D	22.8	9,830	218	884	18,997	2.6
Camden	-0.2	D	10.7	4.1	5	13.8	7.4	19	11.8	13,155	288	683	41,970	1.9
Cape Girardeau	0.5	D	5.4	16.3	6.6	8.2	5.8	23.8	13.1	16,385	210	1,594	34,213	4.9
Carroll	14.7	0	8.2	18.7	D	5.1	5.5	D	15.3	2,365	269	210	4,650	0.4
Carter	-1.3	D	13.7	12.1	1.1	4.3	D	9.5	29.8	1,835	297	336	3,264	0.5
Cass	2.5	0.4	12.7	7.5	5	9.5	5.4	9	18.8	20,550	198	982	42,427	6
Cedar	4.3	D	16.7	6.9	3	9	4.2	D	23.9	4,395	312	429	7,255	0.4
Chariton	16.5	0	9.9	3.8	D	7.6	8.6	6.7	17.3	1,935	259	149	4,151	-0.4
Christian	-0.1	D	15	7.3	7.1	9.4	6.8	6.6	17.7	17,120	200	1,075	34,786	10.2
Clark	1.1	D	D	9.5	2.5	11.6	D	5.5	30.5	1,635	243	108	3,499	0.8
Clay	0	D	6.1	16.1	17.3	6.7	4.8	7.6	15	42,005	173	2,604	98,926	5.3
Clinton	5.6	0	7.9	5.3	D	5.4	5.8	20.8	23.8	4,255	207	350	9,033	1.8
Cole	0.1	D	6.7	4.8	8.4	6.2	6.6	11	37	16,530	215	1,298	33,508	3.9
Cooper	6.6	D	11	5.4	3.1	8.6	6.8	8.4	23.1	3,960	224	342	7,505	0.5
Crawford	-0.8	0.8	5.6	30.3	2.1	13.8	3.3	D	11	6,530	271	698	12,078	1
Dade	12.8	0.4	10	11	D	5	2.9	2.5	21.6	2,195	289	169	3,951	-0.3
Dallas	-3.1	D	D	5.7	2.2	9.9	5.8	D	19.7	4,585	275	488	7,679	0.2
Daviess	10	0.1	18.1	8.6	2.4	9.1	4.2	D	22.4	2,045	245	148	4,195	-0.1
DeKalb	3.5	0	5.2	1.6	D	7.8	7.2	D	31	2,365	188	108	4,350	0.5
Dent	-0.9	D	4.8	13.9	2.3	10.5	6.3	D	25.8	4,290	277	580	7,308	0.3
Douglas	-1.2	D	9.1	21.4	D	10.3	3.1	D	19.3	3,855	290	365	6,527	0.1
Dunklin	-2.1	0	4.8	4.8	3.3	11.1	6.7	D	21.2	8,300	276	2,150	14,437	0.1
Franklin	0.3	0.2	8.9	27.4	5.6	7.5	5.3	11	11	24,160	234	1,905	45,533	4.9
Gasconade	-1.5	D	6.1	28.2	D	7.5	5.2	6	21	4,275	290	285	8,194	-0.1
Gentry	17.6	0	4.7	11	D	5.6	D	21.5	14.4	1,650	248	161	3,211	0
Greene	0	D	4.7	9.4	10.7	7	6.2	18.9	12.3	59,825	206	6,543	134,568	7.3
Grundy	3	D	6.2	20.7	2.6	6.3	4.1	13.7	24.1	2,520	253	263	5,006	-0.3
Harrison	14.2	D	4.1	1.8	D	22.2	4.9	5.9	25.5	2,270	266	213	4,383	-0.5
Henry	1.8	D	6.8	16	3.3	10.3	6.1	10.9	24.5	6,735	310	679	10,970	0.8
Hickory	-5.2	D	D	D	D	13.9	D	12.3	26	3,465	366	263	6,865	0.4
Holt	12.2	D	0.9	20.7	D	11.6	4.3	4.7	13.7	1,220	276	69	2,795	-0.4
Howard	-2.9	D	6.5	13.5	D	7.3	5.9	D	17.2	2,280	225	223	4,592	0.2
Howell	-0.1	0.2	3.7	14.5	5.8	8.1	5.6	20.7	15.7	11,550	288	1,653	18,299	1.5
Iron	-0.3	D	2.4	14.3	D	6.9	1.9	10.7	19.9	3,065	300	591	5,322	-0.1
Jackson	0	0	6.8	6	18.7	4.4	12.1	11.8	15.5	129,030	185	17,222	326,019	4.5

1. Per 1,000 resident population estimated as of July 1 of the year shown.

STATE County	Housing units, 2013-2017								Civilian labor force, 2018				Civilian employment[6], 2013-2017		
	Occupied units										Unemployment			Percent	
			Owner-occupied			Renter-occupied									
				Median owner cost as a percent of income			Median rent as a percent of income[2]	Sub-standard units[4] (percent)		Percent change, 2017-2018				Management, business, science, and arts	Construction, production, and maintenance occupations
	Total	Percent	Median value[1]	With a mortgage	Without a mortgage[2]	Median rent[3]			Total		Total	Rate[5]	Total		
	89	90	91	92	93	94	95	96	97	98	99	100	101	102	103

STATE County	89	90	91	92	93	94	95	96	97	98	99	100	101	102	103
MISSISSIPPI— Cont'd															
Sunflower	8,505	56.2	71,600	25.8	13.2	608	32.1	4	7,837	-2.5	611	7.8	8,371	28.0	28.2
Tallahatchie	4,296	77.4	63,400	22.7	13.1	462	28.4	3.6	5,399	-3.8	285	5.3	3,960	31.6	29.9
Tate	10,016	76.2	107,400	21.8	10.9	685	29.4	4.5	12,259	0.6	600	4.9	11,649	28.9	32.1
Tippah	8,204	74.1	86,000	20.0	10.1	551	23.3	2.9	9,443	-0.1	410	4.3	9,077	25.7	41.2
Tishomingo	7,606	75.9	82,700	19.5	11.2	554	26.3	3.8	8,461	1.9	393	4.6	7,890	22.3	38.6
Tunica	3,983	37.5	96,000	22.5	11.5	725	28.5	9.9	4,477	-0.1	237	5.3	4,213	22.9	21.1
Union	9,927	72.2	92,500	20.4	10.5	654	23.4	4.1	14,034	0.5	494	3.5	11,565	24.3	36.9
Walthall	5,903	89.4	101,900	28.1	15.1	537	26.9	4.8	5,024	0.1	325	6.5	5,553	29.8	33.6
Warren	18,559	63.7	114,600	21.4	10.7	666	30.6	3.1	20,405	-1.6	1,113	5.5	19,407	34.3	24.4
Washington	18,249	54.5	74,400	22.5	12.4	664	34.5	2.9	16,727	-2.8	1,180	7.1	17,213	31.5	22.6
Wayne	7,762	80.8	80,100	19.5	11.7	523	30.6	3.4	7,506	-0.1	403	5.4	7,800	26.7	39.1
Webster	3,842	74.5	77,400	22.2	11.1	525	34.6	3.3	3,907	1.3	194	5	3,502	37.4	30.3
Wilkinson	2,882	80.7	60,400	31.1	16.4	503	31.6	0.8	2,765	-2.1	235	8.5	2,355	33.9	28.5
Winston	7,411	72.1	77,600	22.7	12.4	643	31.8	4.2	7,407	2.3	413	5.6	7,303	27.2	32.8
Yalobusha	5,196	74.8	75,200	20.3	10.9	559	29	2	5,119	1.5	254	5	5,274	21.7	41.7
Yazoo	8,642	61.9	78,700	23.4	12.1	589	33.9	4.5	9,073	-0.9	503	5.5	7,778	30.8	29.6
MISSOURI	2,386,203	66.9	145,400	19.9	11.2	784	28.4	2	3,052,386	-0.3	97,578	3.2	2,867,393	35.9	22.2
Adair	9,595	59.3	117,700	18.8	10.8	610	36.7	1.8	10,672	1.8	375	3.5	11,274	36.8	20.9
Andrew	6,874	77.4	136,400	19.9	10.0	765	25.9	2.1	9,685	-1.2	258	2.7	8,504	35.4	27.1
Atchison	2,492	70.7	82,000	20.3	12.1	518	20	0.3	2,771	-2.9	69	2.5	2,666	31.9	28.1
Audrain	9,457	68.1	95,800	19.3	10.0	625	25.5	1.9	10,804	-2.6	334	3.1	10,622	26.8	31.8
Barry	13,091	74.5	112,600	20.4	11.3	630	29.6	3.8	15,592	0.6	463	3	14,330	24.7	39.6
Barton	4,939	69.2	97,500	21.5	11.1	527	27.1	3.3	5,181	-0.6	160	3.1	5,304	32.7	32.8
Bates	6,704	73.7	108,300	19.7	11.9	656	27.2	2.8	7,960	-0.3	303	3.8	7,261	27.1	31.9
Benton	7,982	81.4	114,600	22.4	12.9	608	31.5	2.8	7,143	-2.1	323	4.5	6,177	31.0	29.1
Bollinger	4,805	80.6	97,100	19.9	10.6	584	28.6	2.9	5,498	-0.1	198	3.6	4,995	24.4	39.1
Boone	68,898	54.8	177,800	19.2	10.0	826	31.8	1.7	97,114	-0.4	2,206	2.3	92,859	44.8	14.2
Buchanan	33,304	63.2	114,800	19.4	11.3	737	27.1	2.6	44,570	-1.3	1,319	3	42,011	28.0	29.1
Butler	16,550	63.3	104,600	20.3	12.3	672	29.3	1.6	18,127	-2.2	830	4.6	16,983	29.2	28.0
Caldwell	3,741	75.1	103,600	20.2	12.8	629	26.4	4.9	4,404	-0.7	138	3.1	3,840	28.2	32.0
Callaway	16,105	71.8	132,500	19.2	10.0	690	26.1	2.3	21,087	-1.7	618	2.9	20,199	31.9	25.8
Camden	16,340	79.8	176,300	22.5	10.0	703	28.7	1.7	18,578	-1.7	783	4.2	17,136	29.1	22.0
Cape Girardeau	29,613	65.4	151,900	19.6	10.8	743	27.9	1.8	40,008	0.3	1,102	2.8	37,488	34.4	21.8
Carroll	3,618	73.6	81,800	17.4	13.0	542	28.8	1.7	4,683	-2.3	147	3.1	3,700	28.7	33.5
Carter	2,403	72.7	90,400	22.4	10.8	564	27.5	5	2,513	-0.8	129	5.1	2,484	29.8	32.9
Cass	38,706	75.5	165,800	19.9	11.5	931	27.8	2.2	54,386	0.2	1,660	3.1	49,809	35.3	24.8
Cedar	5,879	70.4	92,700	21.7	13.8	614	34.6	1.4	5,691	-1.2	196	3.4	4,908	29.0	29.5
Chariton	2,842	76.9	81,300	18.6	12.6	536	26.4	1.8	3,760	-2.5	105	2.8	3,129	29.6	32.8
Christian	30,774	74.1	154,400	19.7	10.8	762	28	2.4	43,619	0.9	1,124	2.6	39,399	35.9	20.5
Clark	2,907	75.1	85,000	19.6	11.2	577	21.8	2.6	3,187	-0.7	123	3.9	3,135	27.7	40.7
Clay	89,709	69.1	160,900	19.4	10.0	887	26.1	1.2	134,903	0	3,904	2.9	123,139	37.0	21.0
Clinton	8,185	75.1	142,000	19.1	12.4	798	24.7	1.4	10,852	-0.3	342	3.2	9,661	29.2	30.8
Cole	29,642	67.2	154,200	19.6	10.0	627	23.3	1.3	38,229	-1.6	956	2.5	36,629	37.6	20.6
Cooper	6,410	71.2	128,900	19.8	10.9	659	27.2	1.5	7,424	-0.6	230	3.1	7,804	31.3	24.7
Crawford	9,286	71.5	116,100	20.6	12.4	616	30	3	10,832	0.1	425	3.9	9,420	24.2	35.0
Dade	3,107	78.7	75,700	22.6	12.0	612	29.2	2.8	3,576	-0.1	97	2.7	3,137	31.7	32.1
Dallas	6,156	73.2	107,400	19.7	10.0	593	23.9	2.7	6,966	0.2	273	3.9	5,978	26.5	33.2
Daviess	3,083	78.7	101,100	19.6	12.7	539	26.7	3.8	4,048	-0.8	122	3	3,571	27.9	30.7
DeKalb	3,854	66.5	111,600	18.5	12.5	622	23.5	1.5	4,829	-1.7	152	3.1	4,325	31.1	30.3
Dent	6,087	70.3	107,300	22.8	11.1	510	25	2.7	6,199	0.2	205	3.3	5,930	28.0	32.0
Douglas	5,173	76.6	101,700	22.5	11.7	549	28	3.8	5,009	-1.3	229	4.6	4,997	16.3	41.2
Dunklin	12,760	63.3	69,500	19.2	12.2	535	30	2.8	12,102	-2.8	666	5.5	11,669	27.9	30.3
Franklin	40,612	74.1	156,800	20.4	10.9	736	26.2	1.9	52,287	-0.4	1,604	3.1	49,855	30.2	31.6
Gasconade	6,135	76.4	123,000	19.4	10.5	624	27.7	1.7	7,752	-0.6	225	2.9	6,793	27.0	35.6
Gentry	2,662	72.5	85,600	19.8	12.3	575	23.8	3	3,584	-1.1	87	2.4	3,037	31.5	31.1
Greene	119,989	58.1	136,300	19.5	10.2	732	30.2	1.8	148,502	0.9	3,787	2.6	138,083	35.9	18.5
Grundy	4,018	67.3	85,100	18.2	12.1	583	23.4	5.4	4,536	-5.6	164	3.6	4,506	30.2	33.1
Harrison	3,528	73.0	72,800	22.0	11.2	548	25.9	4.8	3,828	-2.4	118	3.1	3,821	29.5	28.2
Henry	9,294	73.3	92,200	20.7	12.4	666	28.9	3.7	9,795	-1.1	349	3.6	8,906	29.8	31.4
Hickory	3,983	82.0	90,200	26.5	12.0	580	30.3	1.7	3,834	1.8	158	4.1	3,207	25.9	33.4
Holt	2,111	71.6	93,700	18.6	11.3	443	22	2.1	2,644	-2	63	2.4	2,119	35.0	29.1
Howard	3,713	75.9	116,300	19.7	10.0	610	25.5	2.8	4,973	-2.2	141	2.8	4,804	35.1	26.2
Howell	16,204	69.2	102,200	21.5	10.6	603	27.7	2.9	16,233	1.9	580	3.6	16,463	29.5	28.4
Iron	4,062	72.2	83,100	19.0	11.5	542	27	3.1	3,544	-1.2	191	5.4	3,829	18.9	33.3
Jackson	280,174	58.7	131,500	20.4	12.3	849	29	1.9	363,146	0.1	13,558	3.7	338,110	36.5	20.3

1. Specified owner-occupied units. 2. A value of 10.0 represents 10 percent or less; a value of 50.0 represents 50 percent or more. 3. Specified renter-occupied units. 4. Overcrowded or lacking complete plumbing facilities. 5. Percent of civilian labor force. 6. Civilian employed persons 16 years old and over.

Table B. States and Counties — Nonfarm Employment and Agriculture

STATE County	Private nonfarm establishments, employment and payroll, 2016									Agriculture, 2017			
	Number of establishments	Employment						Annual payroll		Farms			Farm producers whose primary occupation is farming (percent)
		Total	Health care and social assistance	Manufac-turing	Retail trade	Finance and insurance	Professional, scientific, and technical services	Total (mil dol)	Average per employee (dollars)	Number	Percent with:		
											Fewer than 50 acres	1000 acres or more	
	104	105	106	107	108	109	110	111	112	113	114	115	116

MISSISSIPPI— Cont'd													
Sunflower	439	5,439	1,022	354	1,005	242	57	179	32,841	311	17.7	42.1	51.3
Tallahatchie	173	1,814	446	D	270	34	44	59	32,626	436	14.7	17.7	40.3
Tate	378	3,923	600	491	830	175	89	118	30,156	593	33.6	5.9	40.1
Tippah	356	5,280	564	2,151	650	137	78	165	31,187	557	25.7	3.1	33.5
Tishomingo	358	5,003	588	2,287	631	119	101	156	31,112	274	25.2	2.9	28.2
Tunica	204	7,319	227	513	342	70	18	215	29,427	91	15.4	54.9	80.5
Union	507	9,608	1,090	3,901	1,179	218	95	351	36,579	618	33.8	3.2	27.2
Walthall	214	1,911	256	369	352	66	14	58	30,221	635	33.5	1.1	46.7
Warren	1,013	16,058	2,452	3,066	2,557	375	394	621	38,679	160	20.0	15.6	29.7
Washington	1,136	14,338	2,922	1,173	2,853	343	340	456	31,812	273	12.8	37.7	66.7
Wayne	373	4,226	654	808	975	217	98	143	33,810	562	40.9	2.5	41.4
Webster	155	1,363	289	209	210	50	73	52	38,081	292	21.6	5.5	30.8
Wilkinson	134	1,359	318	132	271	37	11	39	28,472	163	28.2	16.6	23.4
Winston	378	4,990	663	1,465	941	92	74	166	33,335	483	32.3	3.5	36.9
Yalobusha	182	2,429	354	984	328	96	12	75	30,891	348	21.0	3.7	33.7
Yazoo	386	4,116	977	546	769	140	148	136	33,017	574	17.2	14.6	32.7
MISSOURI	160,912	2,494,720	420,073	260,451	324,717	131,863	156,958	112,072	44,924	95,320	29.6	6.2	38.8
Adair	630	7,929	2,105	586	1,485	216	275	252	31,784	816	27.5	6.0	33.4
Andrew	314	1,758	334	32	352	59	52	51	29,176	706	32.6	7.8	40.8
Atchison	202	1,296	282	18	292	87	29	38	29,171	401	19.0	23.7	54.7
Audrain	545	6,998	1,063	1,819	1,135	248	129	256	36,579	911	24.6	12.4	47.1
Barry	738	14,648	2,180	4,963	1,605	291	D	573	39,146	1,392	34.2	2.9	41.0
Barton	264	2,667	473	358	506	145	107	80	30,126	865	25.7	10.3	44.5
Bates	365	2,773	785	70	581	219	77	86	30,887	1,160	30.0	9.6	43.1
Benton	383	2,254	365	172	738	115	63	54	23,963	749	21.5	5.5	47.2
Bollinger	215	1,443	364	167	307	49	31	40	27,541	756	23.3	4.0	39.6
Boone	4,671	77,527	17,549	4,133	12,833	7,279	3,869	2,946	38,005	1,184	47.1	3.0	30.5
Buchanan	2,284	44,180	8,638	10,317	5,713	1,680	1,315	1,837	41,574	797	40.4	6.0	35.8
Butler	1,242	15,479	4,266	2,345	3,006	575	332	508	32,834	441	30.8	20.6	47.1
Caldwell	143	1,118	109	38	410	57	18	35	30,979	924	32.5	6.0	34.0
Callaway	738	12,098	2,515	1,734	1,319	277	308	490	40,492	1,438	30.0	3.5	30.9
Camden	1,442	13,229	2,420	430	3,246	401	914	434	32,783	516	20.3	2.3	40.6
Cape Girardeau	2,446	38,503	10,591	3,735	6,207	1,253	1,231	1,430	37,149	1,111	32.3	5.1	41.8
Carroll	223	1,636	400	191	285	103	36	48	29,373	1,016	18.0	10.1	39.8
Carter	182	1,006	265	210	164	53	12	24	23,762	160	31.9	11.3	37.3
Cass	1,972	21,209	3,084	2,799	4,439	605	493	675	31,848	1,477	47.1	3.7	34.9
Cedar	281	2,420	586	364	414	94	59	65	26,788	854	26.3	2.9	44.0
Chariton	218	1,354	295	90	274	77	28	41	30,604	985	21.9	9.8	41.4
Christian	1,760	14,957	1,777	1,468	2,891	598	965	446	29,820	1,169	42.2	0.8	40.4
Clark	145	943	130	43	266	68	11	22	23,558	547	19.4	9.1	37.2
Clay	5,079	100,582	13,915	14,301	12,441	2,342	15,693	5,114	50,842	552	55.6	6.0	32.4
Clinton	378	2,968	992	157	467	125	77	96	32,389	684	41.1	8.8	36.4
Cole	2,262	35,026	6,746	2,289	5,586	1,963	1,533	1,373	39,190	1,169	30.2	0.8	32.1
Cooper	403	3,934	841	220	800	137	76	112	28,538	883	22.2	8.3	34.3
Crawford	505	5,741	896	2,014	650	155	129	197	34,371	628	21.8	3.7	34.6
Dade	141	1,251	41	304	165	35	18	37	29,644	699	22.2	9.7	50.9
Dallas	316	2,440	1,000	161	533	116	40	45	18,373	1,176	34.3	1.8	40.2
Daviess	150	924	83	214	230	57	29	26	27,708	1,015	20.8	6.1	31.5
DeKalb	215	1,956	400	38	515	218	20	64	32,755	708	28.2	5.8	33.2
Dent	397	3,632	839	665	509	175	48	125	34,544	694	27.4	5.8	37.7
Douglas	204	2,090	283	615	463	69	33	51	24,454	994	22.8	3.8	46.3
Dunklin	797	7,157	2,203	458	1,394	302	137	185	25,790	283	25.1	34.3	54.8
Franklin	2,663	35,408	4,735	8,946	4,983	1,054	926	1,315	37,125	1,818	42.2	2.3	30.5
Gasconade	415	4,246	878	964	673	174	84	110	25,928	823	17.4	2.3	36.0
Gentry	192	1,818	808	D	275	60	13	47	26,004	686	22.4	7.9	40.1
Greene	8,671	154,610	29,063	12,645	20,178	7,371	7,111	6,132	39,663	1,857	51.8	1.2	34.5
Grundy	246	2,631	632	725	469	75	51	84	32,089	662	24.5	8.5	36.3
Harrison	204	2,004	513	48	660	115	22	50	25,128	974	21.0	7.8	40.1
Henry	581	6,900	1,830	1,083	1,202	229	126	246	35,658	898	24.1	11.7	45.7
Hickory	152	842	213	D	311	41	21	20	23,633	529	17.4	4.2	46.4
Holt	135	928	179	182	161	40	D	32	35,001	380	24.2	14.2	50.5
Howard	204	2,226	615	270	266	72	66	63	28,464	690	16.8	6.1	36.4
Howell	1,123	12,416	3,268	2,265	2,207	406	319	386	31,075	1,451	33.7	2.4	39.8
Iron	239	1,839	618	73	299	63	16	61	33,331	270	24.8	4.1	35.1
Jackson	19,144	338,535	56,859	24,887	37,550	24,955	28,012	17,037	50,325	706	67.1	3.5	30.1

Table B. States and Counties — **Agriculture**

STATE County	Land in farms Acreage (1,000) [117]	Percent change, 2012-2017 [118]	Acres Average size of farm [119]	Total irrigated (1,000) [120]	Total cropland (1,000) [121]	Value of land and buildings (dollars) Average per farm [122]	Average per acre [123]	Value of machinery and equipment, average per farm (dollars) [124]	Value of products sold: Total (mil dol) [125]	Average per farm (acres) [126]	Percent from: Crops [127]	Livestock and poultry products [128]	Organic farms (number) [129]	Farms with internet access (percent) [130]	Government payments Total ($1,000) [131]	Percent of farms [132]
MISSISSIPPI— Cont'd																
Sunflower	389	4.3	1,249	217.7	325.9	3,977,773	3,184	518,720	223.8	719,566	86.2	13.8	NA	72.3	14,647	80.7
Tallahatchie	310	-9.1	710	130.4	234.5	2,002,926	2,820	212,704	134.9	309,404	99.0	1.0	NA	61.9	7,579	72.2
Tate	158	3.0	266	4.7	67.5	751,443	2,825	93,215	40.1	67,575	71.1	28.9	NA	72.2	2,548	37.1
Tippah	109	-12.1	195	0.2	39.0	404,978	2,072	80,929	23.2	41,655	58.9	41.1	NA	62.3	1,086	64.3
Tishomingo	47	-4.7	172	0.3	19.5	325,832	1,890	55,001	7.0	25,445	90.2	9.8	NA	61.3	484	51.5
Tunica	186	-12.2	2,041	99.0	177.1	6,030,602	2,955	663,152	D	D	D	D	NA	64.8	5,159	86.8
Union	112	-7.5	181	0.0	45.4	362,278	1,999	60,172	16.3	26,299	74.7	25.3	NA	65.4	1,906	57.8
Walthall	100	-15.2	158	0.1	30.1	489,851	3,104	76,957	85.3	134,307	4.9	95.1	6	55.7	1,002	32.0
Warren	99	-20.3	621	9.3	40.4	1,508,216	2,427	174,355	18.8	117,469	95.2	4.8	NA	68.8	2,283	59.4
Washington	371	8.2	1,357	238.6	349.2	5,033,096	3,708	634,141	D	D	D	D	NA	77.3	12,792	86.1
Wayne	97	4.2	173	0.6	27.8	536,506	3,096	84,892	242.6	431,692	3.1	96.9	2	69.2	759	35.8
Webster	74	-8.0	254	0.4	29.6	464,975	1,833	90,512	19.7	67,548	76.6	23.4	NA	58.2	1,211	55.8
Wilkinson	87	-15.8	532	D	11.7	1,278,484	2,401	86,434	4.6	28,258	48.4	51.6	NA	70.6	345	26.4
Winston	108	10.2	223	0.6	17.4	507,990	2,277	66,860	80.1	165,925	3.7	96.3	NA	64.0	804	41.4
Yalobusha	81	-14.2	233	2.8	26.5	434,275	1,864	84,136	13.9	40,009	88.3	11.7	NA	56.6	741	42.5
Yazoo	308	-12.3	536	62.8	167.5	1,495,962	2,789	170,781	105.2	183,207	84.9	15.1	NA	63.1	8,817	70.9
MISSOURI	27,782	-1.7	291	1,529.2	15,599.4	986,481	3,385	104,066	10,525.9	110,427	52.0	48.0	415	72.5	323,801	32.8
Adair	268	-1.9	328	0.1	141.9	916,811	2,792	94,641	52.8	64,721	65.3	34.7	1	68.3	2,179	36.8
Andrew	205	3.2	290	1.2	158.6	1,115,611	3,843	113,518	75.0	106,218	85.2	14.8	NA	82.3	3,325	55.4
Atchison	302	15.0	754	19.9	275.1	3,698,611	4,903	367,596	147.8	368,566	97.2	2.8	NA	81.3	5,332	78.1
Audrain	405	-7.1	445	17.0	334.6	1,894,323	4,256	167,943	247.1	271,233	61.4	38.6	31	68.4	5,722	58.6
Barry	290	8.0	208	4.3	96.9	713,417	3,429	85,578	403.1	289,563	4.2	95.8	1	74.8	391	4.9
Barton	331	-0.4	383	21.7	221.5	1,053,331	2,753	167,455	132.0	152,652	61.0	39.0	NA	74.1	6,312	48.6
Bates	460	2.5	396	3.6	281.7	1,224,243	3,090	137,790	159.8	137,752	63.3	36.7	3	71.6	4,732	49.1
Benton	224	-7.0	299	0.7	77.4	817,792	2,737	78,088	82.7	110,463	19.5	80.5	2	72.9	785	21.6
Bollinger	180	-10.0	238	13.1	77.9	597,725	2,507	75,632	32.1	42,450	56.9	43.1	NA	62.7	1,470	37.0
Boone	213	-11.6	180	3.8	128.5	1,015,839	5,654	74,663	105.0	88,688	44.2	55.8	4	82.4	1,827	20.6
Buchanan	184	-2.5	231	1.2	146.3	936,040	4,053	107,515	66.9	83,923	89.3	10.7	NA	70.3	2,939	45.5
Butler	242	3.3	548	154.3	207.0	2,573,693	4,695	233,342	112.8	255,841	98.6	1.4	NA	81.2	9,945	42.0
Caldwell	250	2.1	270	D	168.1	856,166	3,170	81,607	67.2	72,720	70.9	29.1	1	71.9	5,068	57.8
Callaway	297	-6.2	206	8.8	166.6	816,689	3,960	97,888	124.5	86,602	47.6	52.4	4	81.1	3,457	27.6
Camden	123	-11.0	239	0.0	25.9	527,680	2,208	59,654	15.1	29,250	11.3	88.7	NA	66.1	243	4.1
Cape Girardeau	290	14.6	261	36.8	208.5	1,132,758	4,343	120,048	99.3	89,351	75.8	24.2	NA	69.6	4,195	48.2
Carroll	426	-1.4	419	3.9	333.2	1,500,209	3,580	151,887	144.7	142,399	87.4	12.6	4	72.1	10,429	79.1
Carter	72	-2.7	448	D	9.1	854,925	1,909	68,650	3.8	23,844	11.2	88.8	NA	81.3	73	11.9
Cass	317	-0.7	215	3.5	201.7	807,084	3,759	76,607	120.5	81,576	82.0	18.0	2	74.3	3,599	27.6
Cedar	207	9.4	243	0.8	62.2	604,805	2,489	65,465	49.5	58,000	13.4	86.6	13	69.7	665	13.8
Chariton	388	-4.5	394	1.0	273.9	1,354,347	3,439	155,013	162.8	165,317	60.4	39.6	1	67.5	5,119	54.1
Christian	154	-14.2	132	0.1	43.9	530,251	4,027	54,661	28.9	24,687	18.0	82.0	NA	72.3	105	2.5
Clark	256	6.2	468	4.3	193.8	1,673,148	3,575	177,466	99.8	182,404	77.0	23.0	NA	68.7	2,967	66.0
Clay	111	0.5	201	4.5	64.4	839,612	4,169	90,403	34.7	62,951	55.6	44.4	NA	81.3	1,272	18.7
Clinton	222	16.1	325	0.0	150.2	1,209,500	3,721	128,331	81.8	119,642	78.8	21.2	NA	77.3	2,035	33.3
Cole	186	5.3	159	0.4	70.5	578,816	3,646	69,979	36.8	31,506	36.0	64.0	6	73.7	919	26.3
Cooper	282	-8.2	319	0.2	167.3	1,043,246	3,268	121,276	97.5	110,428	64.1	35.9	9	72.6	3,451	56.6
Crawford	160	-17.6	255	0.4	37.7	658,502	2,583	58,391	14.8	23,556	25.2	74.8	1	73.1	261	8.9
Dade	266	8.2	380	3.7	113.5	1,067,218	2,807	117,152	70.2	100,418	42.2	57.8	3	66.2	1,928	25.0
Dallas	207	-5.1	176	0.2	57.9	446,303	2,538	56,030	51.3	43,648	9.5	90.5	28	66.3	425	5.4
Daviess	307	-2.7	302	0.6	192.8	985,987	3,265	98,261	131.1	129,122	36.7	63.3	9	64.5	7,048	65.2
DeKalb	202	-17.0	285	D	133.5	932,047	3,273	89,075	64.8	91,479	65.4	34.6	1	76.4	3,612	54.5
Dent	190	0.8	273	0.3	27.3	571,102	2,091	62,969	21.8	31,438	11.8	88.2	7	79.0	204	9.7
Douglas	267	5.0	268	0.1	46.6	562,982	2,100	60,494	33.8	33,970	4.4	95.6	1	72.8	220	2.7
Dunklin	283	1.1	1,000	179.3	277.9	5,087,191	5,090	465,745	196.6	694,749	98.4	1.6	NA	75.3	7,431	68.9
Franklin	266	-8.8	146	1.6	120.1	565,029	3,864	61,725	60.0	32,980	43.6	56.4	2	74.0	1,172	18.6
Gasconade	207	-0.8	252	0.1	75.4	701,975	2,787	82,115	32.3	39,273	46.3	53.7	3	72.2	1,118	31.1
Gentry	239	-5.8	348	0.0	152.0	1,077,559	3,098	118,270	120.2	175,265	31.3	68.7	22	75.7	4,896	69.2
Greene	223	6.0	120	0.5	78.3	570,292	4,745	53,364	38.7	20,854	21.2	78.8	2	74.3	807	6.1
Grundy	225	10.5	341	2.1	160.2	997,041	2,928	110,989	92.8	140,210	53.0	47.0	8	71.6	4,553	58.2
Harrison	392	-2.2	403	D	259.3	1,114,054	2,768	101,414	92.7	95,181	74.1	25.9	NA	71.4	10,309	67.0
Henry	382	6.8	425	3.3	213.4	1,143,536	2,690	129,133	98.7	109,924	59.9	40.1	3	73.7	4,645	42.0
Hickory	164	-9.7	310	D	50.9	654,352	2,108	79,880	29.9	56,609	18.8	81.2	2	67.9	301	14.6
Holt	209	4.2	550	31.9	188.3	2,688,737	4,893	253,959	108.8	286,195	96.4	3.6	4	76.3	4,386	75.0
Howard	219	-10.2	317	4.6	133.3	957,809	3,023	115,515	55.9	81,077	76.1	23.9	2	71.4	2,818	59.1
Howell	333	-5.8	230	0.6	54.7	492,355	2,144	62,506	56.9	39,193	7.8	92.2	NA	78.2	285	4.6
Iron	65	-7.4	242	D	12.9	499,202	2,065	50,579	4.3	16,052	8.7	91.3	NA	75.2	32	4.1
Jackson	106	-4.5	150	1.0	73.3	872,579	5,814	73,951	37.6	53,244	80.9	19.1	21	79.7	702	18.8

Table B. States and Counties — Water Use, Wholesale Trade, Retail Trade, and Real Estate

STATE County	Water use, 2015		Wholesale Trade[1], 2012				Retail Trade[2], 2012				Real estate and rental and leasing,[2] 2012			
	Public supply water withdrawn (mil gal/ day)	Public supply gallons withdrawn per person per day	Number of establishments	Number of employees	Sales (mil dol)	Average payroll (mil dol)	Number of establishments	Number of employees	Sales (mil dol)	Average payroll (mil dol)	Number of establishments	Number of employees	Sales (mil dol)	Average payroll (mil dol)
	133	134	135	136	137	138	139	140	141	142	143	144	145	146
MISSISSIPPI— Cont'd														
Sunflower	3.01	111.5	15	330	443.3	13.5	100	922	244.1	18.8	10	20	3.5	0.5
Tallahatchie	1.31	89.8	7	76	67.2	2.7	40	262	54.1	7.0	5	8	0.8	0.1
Tate	1.81	64.0	13	44	16.9	1.9	73	799	191.9	17.9	8	17	3.7	0.5
Tippah	2.69	121.5	15	143	247.8	6.4	77	628	133.8	11.8	6	37	2.7	1.2
Tishomingo	2.55	130.4	18	166	59.7	4.3	81	597	114.3	12.3	12	20	2.0	0.5
Tunica	3.10	299.7	6	62	84.2	3.2	68	511	107.4	9.0	11	27	10.0	0.9
Union	2.57	90.4	17	166	200.6	6.7	101	1,039	297.2	22.1	16	37	4.1	0.8
Walthall	2.64	180.4	4	D	D	D	41	364	111.3	7.4	5	17	2.2	0.6
Warren	7.99	168.3	41	D	D	D	207	2,588	606.9	53.5	43	186	33.5	6.5
Washington	11.55	240.0	70	638	1,152.7	32.8	232	2,937	656.6	56.4	47	159	21.4	4.8
Wayne	2.62	127.4	21	153	205.9	9.9	83	863	183.9	17.4	9	D	D	D
Webster	1.40	141.4	4	9	1.8	0.2	43	225	52.6	4.4	NA	NA	NA	NA
Wilkinson	1.02	111.8	10	48	46.8	1.6	32	283	54.4	6.0	4	D	D	D
Winston	2.00	109.2	15	247	198.6	9.0	87	870	209.6	18.4	13	116	5.0	2.7
Yalobusha	2.22	178.4	4	D	D	D	45	354	72.0	6.3	3	26	2.1	0.2
Yazoo	5.49	200.5	19	245	282.1	13.2	94	707	177.4	14.7	18	47	4.7	1.2
MISSOURI	797.09	131.0	6,557	96,683	91,916.4	4,978.9	21,456	302,568	90,546.6	7,278.2	6,165	33,447	6,730.0	1,297.9
Adair	2.50	98.5	21	D	D	D	121	1,538	336.2	30.3	22	78	14.2	2.5
Andrew	18.06	1,044.2	14	D	D	D	41	332	103.8	6.9	10	D	D	D
Atchison	0.49	92.3	14	133	228.9	5.1	41	316	109.8	7.7	3	5	0.3	0.1
Audrain	2.16	82.8	20	D	D	D	102	1,108	253.7	21.9	13	37	5.4	0.9
Barry	4.57	127.6	25	419	321.4	22.5	133	1,439	379.2	29.2	27	80	11.3	1.9
Barton	1.83	154.0	12	191	192.1	6.8	44	501	146.1	9.6	4	8	1.0	0.2
Bates	1.21	73.6	10	124	90.3	5.2	60	650	171.7	14.2	5	9	0.6	0.2
Benton	0.71	38.0	10	71	25.8	1.9	67	662	183.0	13.8	9	16	2.9	0.3
Bollinger	0.16	13.1	14	99	66.5	6.5	30	316	73.3	6.6	4	9	0.4	0.1
Boone	17.85	102.0	135	1,461	631.4	73.2	627	11,563	3,741.0	287.7	227	920	160.6	28.8
Buchanan	0.00	0.0	102	1,711	1,506.6	76.6	339	5,467	1,369.3	120.6	100	329	59.6	9.9
Butler	1.38	32.1	49	371	193.1	11.7	203	2,610	758.1	56.4	41	181	21.8	6.5
Caldwell	0.34	37.7	6	62	46.3	2.2	24	208	47.8	3.8	4	D	D	D
Callaway	3.60	80.3	22	244	100.9	8.7	126	1,259	377.6	25.2	28	83	7.3	1.9
Camden	3.87	87.5	45	349	169.4	11.6	302	3,072	648.1	67.0	83	232	40.2	6.4
Cape Girardeau	7.86	100.0	128	1,450	861.4	58.4	415	5,855	1,611.4	131.1	110	340	55.2	9.4
Carroll	0.81	90.1	12	140	448.8	5.7	40	285	83.3	5.8	7	D	D	D
Carter	0.46	73.4	7	D	D	D	23	181	31.1	2.5	3	3	0.3	0.1
Cass	1.55	15.3	59	562	333.5	23.8	252	3,658	984.7	85.0	66	162	35.2	5.2
Cedar	0.86	61.7	7	58	29.3	1.3	48	483	104.9	9.2	5	22	1.6	0.6
Chariton	0.37	48.8	14	155	222.3	5.9	43	269	103.7	6.1	12	23	1.1	0.3
Christian	6.55	78.7	65	550	200.2	23.0	237	2,764	696.8	59.1	67	144	33.4	4.1
Clark	0.69	101.5	11	154	88.9	5.5	36	258	117.2	4.8	3	5	0.3	0.1
Clay	124.21	527.1	280	4,156	4,129.6	235.5	582	11,592	3,862.1	299.5	245	1,166	197.5	39.5
Clinton	0.30	14.6	10	84	132.0	3.0	57	449	158.0	10.8	13	42	4.3	1.0
Cole	8.18	106.6	77	2,154	974.4	62.8	301	5,114	1,257.9	115.0	62	247	45.8	7.2
Cooper	1.33	75.4	15	86	102.7	2.8	61	757	301.2	15.8	16	50	6.5	1.0
Crawford	1.28	52.2	14	110	47.6	5.6	76	636	205.0	14.1	22	71	10.7	2.1
Dade	0.37	48.7	8	506	254.4	15.6	28	181	37.7	2.6	3	4	0.3	0.1
Dallas	0.47	28.7	9	61	75.0	1.2	47	476	134.8	9.5	7	11	1.9	0.2
Daviess	0.59	71.5	9	58	31.1	1.8	36	186	70.9	3.8	4	3	0.3	0.1
DeKalb	0.14	11.0	6	D	D	D	39	529	123.6	10.7	12	D	D	D
Dent	0.90	57.7	6	D	D	D	55	538	127.7	11.2	14	51	2.9	0.7
Douglas	0.56	41.9	8	36	5.3	0.8	40	460	96.9	8.7	4	4	0.4	0.0
Dunklin	3.06	99.0	33	355	218.5	14.0	140	1,495	427.6	32.9	26	529	26.6	9.9
Franklin	6.94	67.8	99	981	574.7	36.9	378	4,653	1,396.4	107.9	89	288	28.4	7.8
Gasconade	0.82	55.2	21	204	86.7	6.7	66	657	171.4	14.4	9	13	1.1	0.3
Gentry	0.62	92.6	10	56	53.3	2.4	39	283	78.1	6.0	4	131	1.9	0.8
Greene	33.20	115.2	398	7,106	5,120.2	315.7	1,143	18,649	4,984.2	434.1	406	2,373	329.9	68.8
Grundy	1.34	132.7	8	88	107.3	3.1	43	413	89.6	8.0	8	24	2.5	0.4
Harrison	0.91	105.6	14	117	62.9	3.5	47	558	166.0	12.1	7	14	2.3	0.3
Henry	2.00	92.0	22	199	129.1	7.7	117	1,170	275.0	25.7	19	68	9.2	2.0
Hickory	0.31	33.7	4	15	3.8	0.3	29	236	59.9	4.7	2	D	D	D
Holt	0.40	89.2	9	103	117.3	3.7	22	146	46.4	3.0	2	D	D	D
Howard	1.04	102.6	9	D	D	D	34	245	53.4	3.5	3	D	D	D
Howell	3.01	75.0	41	398	229.2	13.2	232	2,085	561.3	45.6	41	131	14.8	3.3
Iron	0.42	41.5	3	D	D	D	38	262	70.8	4.9	7	19	2.4	0.7
Jackson	26.90	39.1	832	11,496	10,325.8	676.6	2,228	34,276	9,164.9	846.3	819	5,036	1,232.2	235.8

1 Merchant wholesalers, except manufacturers' sales branches and offices.   2. Employer establishments.

STATE County	Professional, scientific, and technical services, 2012				Manufacturing, 2012				Accommodation and food services, 2012			
	Number of establish-ments	Number of employees	Sales (mil dol)	Average payroll (mil dol)	Number of establish-ments	Number of employees	Receipts (mil dol)	Annual payroll (mil dol)	Number of establis-hments	Number of employees	Receipts (mil dol)	Annual payroll (mil dol)
	147	148	149	150	151	152	153	154	155	156	157	158
MISSISSIPPI— Cont'd												
Sunflower	23	71	6.6	2.1	14	293	137.8	9.3	33	358	18.3	4.8
Tallahatchie	10	42	3.7	1.0	4	50	D	1.5	10	90	3.4	0.8
Tate	22	D	D	D	14	784	303.8	30.9	28	403	17.5	4.7
Tippah	15	72	5.6	2.6	27	1,286	400.3	46.5	22	D	D	D
Tishomingo	21	103	5.1	1.5	29	1,345	298.8	49.6	33	D	D	D
Tunica	10	D	D	D	5	319	D	9.8	35	8,231	873.2	204.4
Union	27	84	7.9	3.1	37	3,660	2,379.3	136.5	38	536	26.2	7.1
Walthall	10	22	2.4	0.7	16	469	D	17.0	15	172	8.1	1.6
Warren	96	845	159.4	41.2	37	2,699	D	116.0	111	4,091	345.5	79.0
Washington	80	358	33.5	13.6	34	1,050	711.3	46.6	88	1,868	121.9	29.5
Wayne	40	110	13.7	3.6	11	1,057	279.9	35.6	28	D	D	D
Webster	10	66	4.9	1.5	11	352	D	10.2	10	140	5.7	1.4
Wilkinson	6	D	D	D	5	115	D	4.9	4	D	D	D
Winston	21	95	15.0	2.6	15	1,450	328.9	52.7	30	444	20.8	5.0
Yalobusha	8	45	2.6	0.9	7	857	D	30.9	11	64	4.3	1.0
Yazoo	22	160	11.5	4.3	12	497	D	29.7	25	331	18.2	4.0
MISSOURI	13,279	137,981	24,292.6	8,614.9	6,097	243,208	111,535.4	11,920.8	12,459	239,264	12,430.3	3,409.2
Adair	42	D	D	D	15	638	282.2	24.1	58	D	D	D
Andrew	13	58	3.1	2.0	4	13	2.3	0.5	15	112	4.5	1.1
Atchison	10	D	D	D	5	D	D	0.4	13	132	5.3	1.5
Audrain	22	147	9.1	4.6	36	1,702	1,124.1	68.5	40	441	17.2	4.6
Barry	43	D	D	D	39	4,713	1,391.4	158.8	57	776	33.0	9.0
Barton	13	119	10.6	5.7	17	411	101.9	15.6	17	D	D	D
Bates	21	D	D	D	14	99	D	3.2	28	D	D	D
Benton	23	D	D	D	20	167	D	4.5	47	D	D	D
Bollinger	7	D	D	D	14	154	23.6	5.0	10	110	4.4	1.1
Boone	414	3,570	424.0	156.7	99	3,994	2,042.1	173.3	419	9,006	373.2	104.7
Buchanan	153	D	D	D	89	12,338	D	474.4	183	4,062	180.1	48.6
Butler	48	386	38.3	14.4	46	2,178	545.4	66.9	80	1,678	67.4	18.7
Caldwell	8	D	D	D	6	37	D	0.8	9	D	D	D
Callaway	35	268	33.8	9.5	34	1,605	506.6	69.1	72	910	37.1	10.3
Camden	90	397	51.2	18.1	45	604	131.2	23.2	157	2,633	142.9	40.4
Cape Girardeau	158	1,137	109.6	38.5	95	3,700	2,884.5	181.9	168	4,167	171.0	48.7
Carroll	16	40	3.2	0.8	12	160	D	6.2	13	D	D	D
Carter	5	34	1.4	0.7	18	92	36.1	4.0	12	139	4.3	1.2
Cass	157	D	D	D	59	1,901	557.3	74.0	131	2,133	89.4	25.7
Cedar	14	38	3.1	0.8	20	301	149.1	12.8	32	302	11.0	3.0
Chariton	11	D	D	D	4	78	D	D	16	85	3.0	0.8
Christian	141	D	D	D	100	1,295	274.9	46.1	111	1,774	73.4	23.5
Clark	7	10	0.6	0.2	6	176	D	D	11	102	4.4	1.4
Clay	499	9,242	2,515.1	805.3	195	10,152	8,645.4	579.9	409	9,827	756.4	161.0
Clinton	24	D	D	D	13	105	D	3.1	20	303	13.2	3.7
Cole	231	1,587	238.9	81.4	56	2,293	1,877.5	101.3	166	3,172	132.4	39.4
Cooper	24	80	4.9	2.1	13	374	D	14.0	38	D	D	D
Crawford	26	148	7.4	3.2	47	1,922	345.0	57.9	58	484	23.9	6.7
Dade	3	D	D	D	12	205	64.6	7.2	13	80	2.6	0.8
Dallas	15	D	D	D	15	105	D	2.9	25	254	9.9	2.5
Daviess	5	D	D	D	8	231	D	D	13	82	2.8	0.8
DeKalb	8	20	1.8	0.7	4	23	D	1.3	17	159	7.9	2.0
Dent	16	51	3.5	1.3	21	615	D	30.4	26	D	D	D
Douglas	11	33	3.0	0.8	11	712	D	15.8	16	D	D	D
Dunklin	31	463	11.7	4.4	11	500	D	18.2	44	647	29.6	7.4
Franklin	185	1,174	144.2	42.6	221	9,002	2,617.3	382.3	184	3,157	126.4	38.1
Gasconade	29	117	7.0	2.5	40	1,161	193.2	41.2	46	449	19.4	5.5
Gentry	9	D	D	D	7	228	D	D	13	78	2.2	0.7
Greene	801	5,862	830.7	281.9	295	11,900	4,623.8	521.5	723	14,502	628.1	185.1
Grundy	14	47	2.9	0.9	8	707	D	32.3	13	217	6.9	2.0
Harrison	11	29	1.5	0.6	5	32	D	1.0	21	281	11.4	2.8
Henry	35	141	12.0	3.3	25	1,164	694.8	52.5	56	770	29.7	8.3
Hickory	8	D	D	D	5	D	D	D	17	75	3.1	0.8
Holt	2	D	D	D	7	210	D	6.7	14	112	4.1	1.0
Howard	16	45	4.2	1.4	10	245	57.5	10.2	14	171	5.2	1.7
Howell	64	306	24.9	10.3	69	2,483	672.0	78.5	89	1,241	54.1	14.3
Iron	8	D	D	D	15	88	D	2.2	22	107	4.7	1.3
Jackson	2,044	24,922	5,811.2	1,804.1	634	25,870	10,193.5	1,396.4	1,453	30,594	1,649.0	485.7

Table B. States and Counties — Health Care and Social Assistance, Other Services, Nonemployer Businesses, and Residential Construction

STATE County	Health care and social assistance, 2012				Other services, 2012				Nonemployer businesses, 2016		Value of residential construction authorized by building permits, 2018	
	Number of establish-ments	Number of employees	Receipts (mil dol)	Annual payroll (mil dol)	Number of establish-ments	Number of employees	Receipts (mil dol)	Annual payroll (mil dol)	Number	Receipts (mil dol)	New construction ($1,000)	Number of housing units
	159	160	161	162	163	164	165	166	167	168	169	170
MISSISSIPPI— Cont'd												
Sunflower	63	1,199	104.8	39.0	34	164	13.2	3.7	1,785	46.9	1,275	11
Tallahatchie	15	362	29.6	12.0	14	44	6.4	1.0	772	20.4	48	1
Tate	37	544	51.5	21.3	17	101	7.7	2.7	2,105	89.4	22,728	125
											836	4
Tippah	31	628	44.5	17.6	10	42	2.5	0.7	1,454	63.3		
Tishomingo	32	D	D	D	22	D	D	D	1,151	43.7	480	5
Tunica	16	190	12.3	4.8	8	D	D	D	705	23.9	25,278	110
Union	51	1,223	111.7	40.7	18	D	D	D	2,008	84.1	1,774	9
Walthall	21	285	14.0	5.4	14	D	D	D	1,121	38.5	0	0
Warren	114	2,997	293.1	108.1	58	307	29.8	7.9	2,998	111.5	900	3
Washington	164	3,083	249.4	99.9	80	556	57.1	16.3	3,366	125.3	3,047	11
Wayne	22	607	45.0	21.8	20	D	D	D	1,435	48.5	450	12
Webster	12	D	D	D	7	D	D	D	810	30.7	220	4
Wilkinson	14	350	29.1	11.5	7	D	D	D	579	17.9	0	0
											1,054	5
Winston	28	393	34.8	12.4	17	D	D	D	1,294	46.6		
Yalobusha	16	328	23.3	11.0	6	D	D	D	816	28.7	426	14
Yazoo	41	872	73.8	27.5	27	D	D	D	1,593	53.0	0	0
MISSOURI	17,766	399,940	40,089.3	15,746.9	10,357	62,825	6,979.9	1,834.9	409,303	18,268.7	3,167,067	16,875
Adair	101	1,929	159.3	63.3	61	D	D	D	1,524	55.9	12,249	61
Andrew	28	D	D	D	19	D	D	D	1,237	47.1	400	1
Atchison	14	270	16.9	6.7	15	D	D	D	421	16.1	309	1
Audrain	71	1,414	99.4	40.4	45	249	18.8	7.4	1,377	58.7	1,494	16
Barry	71	1,788	99.2	42.8	65	222	15.6	3.9	2,293	81.4	3,664	22
Barton	25	457	30.0	13.2	18	48	4.9	1.3	917	36.4	375	3
Bates	36	D	D	D	21	D	D	D	1,213	44.8	0	0
Benton	34	400	21.4	9.7	32	91	8.3	1.6	1,425	63.0	1,105	10
Bollinger	20	312	15.2	6.0	16	56	5.3	1.1	733	30.6	0	0
Boone	602	16,725	2,033.5	699.4	327	1,985	187.4	53.2	11,783	570.4	127,986	557
Buchanan	315	7,704	852.1	346.6	172	D	D	D	4,050	163.5	14,944	78
Butler	209	4,378	527.8	163.1	65	296	24.0	5.9	2,529	128.6	483	10
Caldwell	14	D	D	D	15	D	D	D	632	24.1	6,451	25
Callaway	64	2,368	128.3	64.9	66	229	19.6	5.5	2,474	92.1	10,303	69
Camden	121	2,143	262.5	84.9	102	358	30.7	8.1	3,845	193.6	38,371	163
Cape Girardeau	317	10,920	1,149.2	455.5	159	798	78.1	19.9	5,281	234.7	29,489	816
Carroll	22	375	24.9	7.9	18	D	D	D	635	22.1	900	4
Carter	39	237	8.5	3.9	4	9	1.7	0.3	524	27.7	0	0
Cass	159	3,056	250.2	98.6	140	522	41.2	12.2	6,996	277.1	112,237	521
Cedar	30	646	32.0	15.1	19	34	3.4	0.7	1,148	47.3	543	9
Chariton	14	261	10.8	4.5	14	36	5.9	1.2	590	20.0	530	2
Christian	115	1,434	89.7	37.4	119	429	31.5	9.0	6,735	298.4	137,643	608
Clark	13	60	4.0	1.6	11	37	4.5	0.7	440	19.8	249	5
Clay	553	12,953	1,393.1	591.2	329	1,826	171.1	54.5	15,177	641.6	91,988	466
Clinton	47	D	D	D	33	102	6.7	1.9	1,369	50.7	12,495	63
Cole	252	6,480	711.7	280.5	227	1,441	173.3	52.7	4,794	233.7	34,487	171
Cooper	52	773	45.3	18.7	28	106	8.5	2.2	1,094	44.5	0	0
Crawford	60	955	77.2	33.2	28	117	8.4	2.1	1,561	55.6	395	5
Dade	10	D	D	D	10	18	2.2	0.6	505	16.6	75	1
Dallas	30	1,021	26.9	13.1	20	D	D	D	1,377	55.6	259	1
Daviess	16	78	6.0	2.2	8	D	D	D	793	31.9	110	1
DeKalb	28	D	D	D	10	D	D	D	638	30.6	1,051	6
Dent	55	712	42.7	17.8	20	45	3.9	0.9	913	35.2	0	0
Douglas	20	313	16.1	7.0	14	41	4.5	0.8	1,067	42.2	130	2
Dunklin	87	3,270	167.8	57.4	39	136	13.0	2.6	1,797	114.4	3,483	19
Franklin	262	3,747	322.4	153.2	185	869	81.7	23.3	6,777	285.9	88,481	457
Gasconade	34	701	40.7	17.3	33	D	D	D	1,210	46.1	544	4
Gentry	34	777	38.0	17.2	11	26	2.5	0.7	535	20.0	390	4
Greene	820	28,578	3,027.6	1,240.2	599	4,433	401.4	117.0	20,677	1,006.3	244,404	1,271
Grundy	34	656	48.5	18.8	27	61	5.0	1.2	674	27.9	379	4
Harrison	24	488	29.4	12.1	21	D	D	D	652	31.2	0	0
Henry	55	1,569	122.3	55.1	42	163	10.4	3.2	1,460	56.4	1,136	11
Hickory	9	98	5.4	2.1	11	22	1.9	0.4	702	24.3	NA	NA
Holt	9	D	D	D	9	D	D	D	407	17.1	0	0
Howard	24	493	16.4	8.3	13	D	D	D	674	26.4	515	2
Howell	156	3,669	294.1	127.4	66	381	38.9	8.4	3,115	133.9	3,615	39
Iron	93	656	34.8	15.3	27	D	D	D	531	16.3	0	0
Jackson	2,040	54,553	6,169.9	2,405.2	1,236	9,447	1,762.1	312.8	44,923	1,993.6	552,281	3,564

Table B. States and Counties — Government Employment and Payroll, and Local Government Finances

STATE County	Government employment and payroll, 2012									Local government finances, 2012				
			March payroll (percent of total)							General revenue				
												Taxes		
	Full-time equivalent employees	March payroll (dollars)	Administration, judicial, and legal	Police and corrections	Fire protection	Highways and transportation	Health and welfare	Natural resources and utilities	Education and libraries	Total (mil dol)	Intergovernmental (mil dol)	Total (mil dol)	Per capita[1] (dollars) Total	Per capita[1] (dollars) Property
	171	172	173	174	175	176	177	178	179	180	181	182	183	184
MISSISSIPPI— Cont'd														
Sunflower	2,017	5,682,629	3.7	5.0	1.7	2.5	30.7	1.5	53.7	155.8	63.4	20.6	724	694
Tallahatchie	772	1,986,175	8.5	7.5	0.2	4.7	29.5	0.9	48.6	34.1	21.3	8.2	542	517
Tate	1,430	4,623,219	2.1	2.6	1.1	1.1	0.9	1.2	90.6	106.6	62.4	20.6	724	690
Tippah	915	2,435,046	6.8	3.3	0.2	2.1	22.7	2.8	61.0	68.1	38.2	11.3	512	467
Tishomingo	694	1,807,779	8.5	7.3	1.2	2.3	1.2	4.4	73.2	46.2	29.7	10.1	515	495
Tunica	738	1,778,465	10.4	23.6	0.0	4.7	6.1	9.7	45.3	86.8	57.0	21.4	2,043	1,507
Union	1,025	2,626,662	4.5	7.6	2.0	3.0	1.3	10.2	71.3	61.0	37.8	16.4	596	576
Walthall	518	1,141,649	3.1	5.7	0.2	3.0	2.1	0.6	83.4	45.4	21.5	8.4	559	539
Warren	1,819	5,138,472	4.6	6.1	7.5	3.0	0.3	7.0	69.2	170.1	68.3	68.7	1,429	1,171
Washington	3,566	9,118,481	5.7	7.2	2.5	3.0	32.4	4.6	43.1	298.0	98.6	52.7	1,060	977
Wayne	1,112	3,158,182	4.3	5.0	0.4	2.8	39.5	1.7	44.9	88.7	32.9	10.5	508	496
Webster	496	1,240,223	6.4	4.4	0.1	3.7	24.5	1.5	58.9	36.7	19.1	6.3	623	599
Wilkinson	427	1,032,081	12.7	10.5	0.3	7.1	2.1	3.0	61.9	56.6	14.2	5.9	630	607
Winston	620	1,506,689	8.7	16.0	2.1	4.3	1.9	2.4	64.2	46.2	24.1	11.5	602	576
Yalobusha	708	1,878,214	6.3	4.5	1.3	4.5	39.0	4.3	40.1	42.2	18.6	8.6	691	675
Yazoo	1,019	2,766,051	5.8	9.4	4.3	6.7	2.3	10.2	60.9	70.1	40.4	21.3	755	728
MISSOURI	X	X	X	X	X	X	X	X	X	X	X	X	X	X
Adair	916	2,496,611	7.3	5.8	2.8	3.2	13.2	5.6	59.0	68.7	23.1	26.9	1,051	570
Andrew	515	1,433,245	5.1	4.2	0.9	3.0	4.0	5.7	76.7	48.4	17.6	23.4	1,345	1,199
Atchison	319	829,091	7.7	5.0	0.1	22.0	10.0	5.1	49.6	22.0	10.2	9.7	1,755	1,294
Audrain	1,347	4,107,516	4.1	5.9	0.2	2.5	49.7	3.5	33.4	133.2	34.7	34.4	1,343	940
Barry	1,307	3,855,776	4.7	5.7	1.8	2.3	1.6	5.6	77.7	94.7	45.3	37.8	1,063	636
Barton	723	2,240,324	3.5	2.9	0.7	1.9	43.2	5.8	41.8	83.5	14.1	10.7	866	674
Bates	840	2,585,067	4.7	5.8	0.3	2.0	37.0	4.7	45.0	43.7	19.9	13.4	805	577
Benton	748	1,949,137	5.2	5.4	0.1	2.8	27.9	2.2	53.8	41.5	16.6	13.2	696	514
Bollinger	361	902,476	5.5	5.4	0.3	4.6	0.0	1.6	82.4	21.6	12.4	7.2	585	414
Boone	6,008	20,052,275	7.9	5.3	3.3	2.8	2.7	11.3	63.5	497.3	161.0	228.2	1,354	805
Buchanan	3,079	9,642,143	5.9	9.4	5.3	3.7	2.5	5.0	66.6	296.5	114.1	129.1	1,439	812
Butler	1,617	4,243,462	2.3	5.6	2.5	3.4	0.0	4.2	79.9	124.9	58.1	43.7	1,015	498
Caldwell	485	1,279,896	6.3	9.6	0.0	2.5	7.8	5.3	68.5	29.5	14.3	7.8	847	648
Callaway	1,265	3,154,685	6.9	9.5	2.6	4.3	5.4	8.0	63.0	88.2	36.4	34.7	782	576
Camden	1,451	4,272,326	7.8	13.4	5.1	5.6	4.2	2.2	60.3	116.5	32.4	68.3	1,557	990
Cape Girardeau	2,602	6,797,882	6.6	9.1	5.9	6.5	1.2	10.3	58.6	207.7	74.1	101.6	1,320	702
Carroll	390	1,096,814	9.3	3.7	1.4	4.2	4.3	6.6	70.1	26.7	11.7	10.0	1,101	852
Carter	278	723,988	1.6	5.8	0.0	2.9	3.2	2.5	72.4	15.4	9.6	3.9	625	446
Cass	4,195	14,748,324	5.3	6.9	4.3	2.7	12.2	4.5	63.7	380.9	126.2	139.6	1,391	927
Cedar	643	1,585,692	4.7	5.5	0.2	3.0	25.1	6.6	54.3	50.4	15.5	11.7	850	590
Chariton	295	762,719	8.8	6.7	0.2	3.7	5.8	6.0	68.4	20.7	8.4	9.5	1,240	969
Christian	2,200	6,653,224	5.3	7.1	2.0	1.8	0.2	4.7	77.8	188.4	89.3	71.0	890	611
Clark	372	840,780	6.1	5.8	0.0	4.4	21.9	7.3	53.6	21.0	7.2	6.3	911	738
Clay	12,186	43,650,964	3.1	4.3	2.0	0.8	42.4	2.3	44.6	1,333.0	239.3	340.1	1,495	1,078
Clinton	670	2,036,971	7.0	9.3	0.4	4.7	2.3	8.2	67.6	52.6	24.6	20.4	993	788
Cole	2,439	7,947,888	7.8	8.8	4.1	4.5	3.5	5.9	65.1	213.9	62.0	116.3	1,523	890
Cooper	744	2,121,619	5.8	7.9	1.4	3.1	23.2	4.8	52.9	62.0	16.7	23.7	1,353	687
Crawford	756	1,998,530	5.7	8.1	0.0	3.7	7.3	5.6	68.1	45.1	21.5	17.0	683	512
Dade	452	949,754	5.1	2.9	0.0	1.2	37.3	2.9	50.6	20.8	9.6	6.2	824	608
Dallas	463	1,037,873	7.3	5.8	0.3	5.2	0.8	2.2	78.1	31.3	18.2	10.5	627	394
Daviess	341	863,936	7.8	3.3	0.0	3.1	2.5	7.8	74.9	20.0	9.8	7.4	895	719
DeKalb	227	666,095	6.8	3.3	0.0	4.5	3.8	6.9	74.5	18.0	7.8	6.8	522	356
Dent	677	1,899,125	6.9	2.7	0.2	3.0	33.8	4.1	48.4	46.0	16.0	9.7	622	406
Douglas	383	1,073,499	10.7	2.4	0.0	4.9	5.0	5.3	70.1	32.6	12.6	16.6	1,225	824
Dunklin	1,473	3,567,888	5.4	6.8	1.4	3.0	1.6	10.3	68.2	82.8	44.0	27.3	859	614
Franklin	3,292	11,002,286	4.9	8.8	2.3	3.4	4.3	2.7	72.9	276.7	102.6	133.5	1,317	868
Gasconade	880	2,347,282	3.9	4.6	0.0	3.4	28.6	4.8	53.1	70.3	15.8	18.8	1,257	905
Gentry	345	893,935	12.0	4.7	0.4	7.4	4.6	5.3	65.1	20.8	9.7	7.8	1,144	911
Greene	10,039	36,380,689	4.7	8.2	3.7	4.6	1.4	13.2	55.1	880.5	308.6	410.2	1,462	763
Grundy	761	1,960,447	2.6	5.1	1.0	3.5	14.2	6.8	64.8	55.4	22.3	10.8	1,048	654
Harrison	594	1,570,497	5.2	2.6	0.2	3.0	37.3	7.0	42.9	43.2	13.0	10.7	1,229	806
Henry	1,267	4,585,264	3.2	3.7	1.3	1.0	61.3	2.7	26.7	117.2	50.1	23.1	1,045	588
Hickory	326	851,720	6.0	4.2	0.0	2.3	0.0	2.3	84.9	21.9	12.6	6.7	714	572
Holt	184	461,150	11.3	6.1	0.0	5.3	1.7	7.2	68.0	16.0	6.1	7.4	1,595	1,143
Howard	396	983,070	7.8	7.5	0.4	5.0	4.3	9.4	64.8	23.9	8.7	11.5	1,135	911
Howell	1,537	3,973,191	5.5	5.3	1.4	3.4	4.8	7.9	71.2	100.7	49.7	31.7	781	439
Iron	459	1,303,360	4.7	4.4	0.6	6.5	6.1	1.8	75.7	26.1	13.0	10.3	991	765
Jackson	27,447	101,433,064	7.4	14.7	9.5	6.2	0.7	5.5	54.6	3,343.9	905.1	1,696.2	2,504	1,116

1. Based on the resident population estimated as of July 1 of the year shown.

Table B. States and Counties — Local Government Finances, Government Employment, and Income Taxes

STATE County	Local government finances, 2012 (cont.)									Government employment, 2017			Individual income tax returns, 2016		
	Direct general expenditure							Debt outstanding							
			Percent of total for:											Mean	
	Total (mil dol)	Per capita¹ (dollars)	Education	Health and hospitals	Police protection	Public welfare	Highways	Total (mil dol)	Per capita¹ (dollars)	Federal civilian	Federal military	State and local	Number of returns	adjusted gross income	Mean income tax
	185	186	187	188	189	190	191	192	193	194	195	196	197	198	199

MISSISSIPPI— Cont'd															
Sunflower	160.1	5,631	46.7	34.5	2.9	0.1	5.4	30.8	1,085	48	129	3,381	9,440	35,558	3,228
Tallahatchie	39.2	2,596	54.2	1.1	5.0	0.0	7.9	12.7	843	43	68	1,004	4,870	34,221	2,682
Tate	144.1	5,057	68.2	0.5	2.9	0.0	3.0	96.6	3,389	84	159	1,552	11,740	44,577	4,069
Tippah	68.2	3,095	49.3	23.7	3.2	0.2	8.8	13.9	629	55	127	1,221	8,700	40,331	3,316
Tishomingo	53.8	2,746	50.8	1.1	4.8	0.0	7.0	25.8	1,315	61	113	858	7,420	42,978	3,550
Tunica	103.7	9,896	24.0	1.9	8.0	0.7	5.8	114.9	10,965	22	58	762	4,580	30,833	2,240
Union	59.7	2,178	65.6	1.4	6.1	0.0	5.6	32.4	1,180	43	166	1,217	11,460	44,467	3,978
Walthall	45.0	2,981	52.1	26.1	4.3	0.2	4.8	1.9	128	32	84	622	5,570	38,775	3,107
Warren	169.5	3,526	45.5	1.1	6.6	0.2	7.1	264.3	5,496	2,382	315	2,239	20,770	47,517	4,844
Washington	305.6	6,143	28.7	43.2	3.9	0.1	4.1	140.1	2,816	413	286	3,506	19,270	38,556	3,657
Wayne	70.5	3,414	47.5	34.9	3.4	0.1	5.6	14.5	700	39	119	1,275	8,260	43,769	3,666
Webster	31.4	3,130	63.8	1.3	4.6	0.0	7.8	7.1	706	35	57	435	3,900	42,645	3,590
Wilkinson	55.4	5,871	26.6	28.9	2.5	0.1	3.6	35.9	3,804	9	45	539	3,430	36,655	2,726
Winston	45.6	2,397	54.2	1.3	6.9	0.1	7.3	5.2	272	37	104	762	7,350	41,969	3,963
Yalobusha	40.4	3,257	39.3	27.4	4.0	0.0	10.5	17.9	1,447	66	72	819	5,340	38,151	3,214
Yazoo	75.1	2,663	51.5	1.3	5.5	0.3	5.8	42.6	1,510	842	134	1,424	9,360	39,105	3,587
MISSOURI	X	X	X	X	X	X	X	X	X	58,416	35,716	377,249	2,781,110	59,280	7,546
Adair	66.2	2,589	44.3	3.2	5.6	7.5	7.7	43.5	1,700	77	81	2,384	9,550	44,736	4,460
Andrew	36.8	2,114	65.6	3.0	5.9	1.0	6.2	25.6	1,468	34	59	725	8,290	56,836	6,176
Atchison	22.0	3,990	52.6	2.6	2.8	0.0	17.0	6.5	1,173	31	18	350	2,500	50,753	5,328
Audrain	139.4	5,440	36.1	40.4	2.1	3.8	3.0	68.4	2,669	80	79	2,218	10,520	43,338	3,989
Barry	100.1	2,815	59.9	3.2	4.9	0.0	15.0	67.2	1,892	101	121	1,434	14,300	43,459	4,246
Barton	83.6	6,780	22.2	65.7	1.4	0.0	2.7	35.3	2,861	41	40	845	5,120	40,107	3,383
Bates	44.5	2,660	58.6	0.1	9.7	6.8	7.3	46.0	2,754	56	61	1,115	7,060	43,429	4,023
Benton	41.9	2,209	51.5	5.5	3.4	22.2	5.5	22.9	1,210	98	64	930	7,990	38,373	3,259
Bollinger	21.1	1,700	73.8	1.0	4.3	0.0	7.9	3.1	248	23	41	445	4,790	39,338	2,888
Boone	580.4	3,444	44.8	3.1	4.3	0.2	6.2	2,592.5	15,382	2,532	605	29,235	77,800	64,254	8,777
Buchanan	261.5	2,915	51.6	2.2	9.4	0.7	5.3	599.9	6,688	540	306	6,237	38,890	50,390	5,626
Butler	122.1	2,837	60.0	0.0	6.4	0.0	5.4	48.6	1,129	757	142	2,745	17,380	41,351	4,135
Caldwell	28.6	3,124	59.8	1.8	3.5	5.7	7.6	9.9	1,087	42	30	593	3,940	45,522	3,833
Callaway	85.8	1,936	53.8	4.3	8.4	0.0	6.7	57.3	1,293	116	141	3,732	19,680	47,746	4,625
Camden	113.7	2,593	47.6	3.7	9.0	0.0	11.7	112.7	2,570	74	152	1,878	20,260	51,676	6,040
Cape Girardeau	211.7	2,751	54.0	0.3	5.4	0.0	9.9	197.3	2,564	372	279	5,959	34,840	57,887	7,105
Carroll	27.9	3,076	59.3	3.2	3.9	0.0	11.1	12.4	1,360	42	30	564	4,080	43,737	4,024
Carter	15.8	2,520	74.5	2.8	1.9	0.0	3.9	29.2	4,657	88	21	358	2,430	35,674	2,818
Cass	400.2	3,987	50.4	13.7	3.1	0.3	5.8	468.7	4,669	275	349	4,655	48,830	63,123	7,536
Cedar	37.7	2,733	50.1	29.0	5.1	0.0	2.8	32.6	2,361	67	47	711	5,580	35,271	2,769
Chariton	22.7	2,968	52.9	4.1	2.8	0.0	14.2	3.5	456	39	25	432	3,370	44,541	4,124
Christian	179.8	2,252	67.4	0.5	4.7	1.0	5.5	246.9	3,093	111	288	3,109	37,080	56,252	6,079
Clark	23.6	3,386	46.2	6.2	1.8	17.9	8.0	8.6	1,234	33	23	439	2,860	42,539	3,530
Clay	1,296.4	5,696	31.9	48.7	2.3	0.0	1.9	934.2	4,105	1,347	877	14,869	117,310	62,934	7,417
Clinton	50.6	2,467	62.4	1.9	7.3	0.0	8.9	42.6	2,078	82	68	987	9,670	53,795	5,484
Cole	222.3	2,911	50.1	2.6	10.7	0.0	10.0	194.9	2,552	617	270	18,892	36,360	59,443	7,272
Cooper	65.2	3,719	36.8	19.0	3.7	4.9	5.9	51.2	2,925	46	55	1,255	7,490	43,822	3,926
Crawford	44.2	1,780	63.0	8.1	3.6	0.0	5.8	29.0	1,169	33	81	930	10,230	41,159	3,928
Dade	20.9	2,758	51.9	1.1	3.6	23.8	6.9	4.0	526	29	25	521	3,130	39,340	2,989
Dallas	39.6	2,358	42.6	3.7	4.9	0.0	39.8	4.3	254	34	56	572	6,650	36,561	2,867
Daviess	19.9	2,419	62.2	3.1	3.1	0.1	12.4	10.1	1,231	30	28	480	3,530	40,852	3,629
DeKalb	17.0	1,315	62.4	3.4	4.1	0.0	6.0	6.2	478	27	31	1,198	4,140	43,541	3,878
Dent	47.9	3,058	43.1	38.7	4.1	0.0	4.2	2.6	166	56	52	899	5,950	38,528	3,253
Douglas	34.6	2,550	64.0	1.9	3.6	0.0	13.6	7.5	553	49	45	382	4,900	33,627	2,400
Dunklin	76.5	2,405	65.8	1.0	6.7	0.0	5.4	33.5	1,052	97	100	1,516	11,010	38,062	3,313
Franklin	286.0	2,820	58.5	2.0	6.4	0.0	9.3	497.8	4,909	223	348	4,269	49,940	54,611	6,230
Gasconade	55.7	3,719	45.7	31.4	2.9	0.5	4.5	60.7	4,054	51	49	1,018	7,110	41,672	3,657
Gentry	20.3	2,997	59.9	3.6	3.3	0.0	10.5	8.2	1,217	37	22	394	2,850	43,690	3,790
Greene	855.2	3,047	50.1	1.1	8.7	0.2	6.0	1,601.3	5,706	2,169	963	18,746	129,120	56,558	7,351
Grundy	48.8	4,722	61.4	3.0	2.3	10.7	6.0	28.4	2,746	59	33	951	4,210	41,786	3,810
Harrison	40.5	4,640	35.7	40.6	3.2	0.0	7.4	11.6	1,333	40	28	774	3,670	35,572	2,770
Henry	113.3	5,114	25.1	59.5	2.3	0.1	3.3	36.1	1,629	76	73	1,685	9,430	44,038	4,046
Hickory	21.4	2,275	79.2	1.5	2.4	0.0	5.9	11.7	1,244	39	32	284	3,530	33,840	2,412
Holt	15.2	3,273	49.5	0.6	2.4	0.0	13.7	0.8	182	34	15	298	2,110	46,747	5,150
Howard	22.1	2,174	53.2	3.8	5.5	0.3	6.2	33.3	3,276	37	32	461	4,400	44,632	4,384
Howell	94.2	2,317	67.7	2.1	5.1	0.0	5.1	39.4	970	131	135	2,142	15,800	41,119	4,089
Iron	27.4	2,641	71.9	1.5	3.9	0.0	5.6	10.9	1,046	15	63	630	3,840	37,646	2,831
Jackson	3093.9	4,567	37.7	2.6	9.6	0.3	7.4	6,245.9	9,221	16,621	2,496	42,459	329,590	55,949	6,762

1. Based on the resident population estimated as of July 1 of the year shown.

Table B. States and Counties — **Land Area and Population**

State / county code	CBSA code[1]	County code[2]	STATE County	Land area[3] (sq. mi)	Total persons 2018	Rank	Per square mile	White	Black	American Indian, Alaska Native	Asian and Pacific Islancer	Percent Hispanic or Latino[4]	Under 5 years	5 to 17 years	18 to 24 years	25 to 34 years	35 to 44 years	45 to 54 years
				1	2	3	4	5	6	7	8	9	10	11	12	13	14	15
			MISSOURI— Cont'd															
29097	27,900	3	Jasper	638.5	120,636	520	188.9	86.6	3.2	2.9	2.0	8.3	6.9	18.1	9.1	14.1	12.4	11.6
29099	41,180	1	Jefferson	656.5	224,347	303	341.7	95.7	1.7	0.8	1.2	2.0	5.9	17.3	7.4	12.9	13.2	13.6
29101	47,660	4	Johnson	829.3	53,652	944	64.7	88.1	5.9	1.4	2.9	4.5	6.2	15.1	20.1	14.5	10.6	9.7
29103		9	Knox	504.0	3,947	2,906	7.8	97.6	1.0	1.0	0.7	1.1	5.9	17.4	7.7	9.6	9.7	12.1
29105	30,060	6	Laclede	764.7	35,713	1,283	46.7	95.2	1.5	1.6	1.1	2.5	6.9	17.8	7.5	11.7	11.6	12.9
29107	28,140	1	Lafayette	628.4	32,598	1,366	51.9	93.8	3.0	1.3	1.0	2.9	5.8	17.1	7.6	11.8	11.1	13.1
29109		6	Lawrence	611.7	38,359	1,216	62.7	90.5	0.9	1.9	0.8	7.7	6.7	18.5	7.8	11.1	11.6	12.5
29111	39,500	9	Lewis	505.0	9,855	2,440	19.5	94.1	4.0	1.1	0.7	1.8	5.7	16.3	12.6	10.4	10.8	11.7
29113	41,180	1	Lincoln	626.6	57,686	895	92.1	94.6	2.7	0.9	0.9	2.6	6.9	18.5	7.8	13.8	12.5	13.1
29115		7	Linn	615.6	12,037	2,291	19.6	96.0	1.6	0.7	0.5	2.5	6.1	17.5	7.5	10.8	11.0	11.2
29117		6	Livingston	532.3	15,146	2,085	28.5	93.2	4.5	0.9	1.0	1.9	5.6	15.3	7.6	13.9	13.5	12.3
29119	22,220	2	McDonald	539.5	23,078	1,677	42.8	80.1	2.7	4.6	4.2	11.7	7.4	18.4	8.2	11.7	12.1	13.3
29121		7	Macon	801.2	15,153	2,083	18.9	95.1	3.3	0.9	0.8	1.6	5.7	17.2	7.1	10.2	11.0	11.9
29123		6	Madison	494.4	12,188	2,277	24.7	95.8	1.0	1.1	1.1	2.4	6.0	17.1	7.1	11.9	11.3	13.1
29125		8	Maries	527.0	8,769	2,519	16.6	96.9	1.2	1.6	0.7	1.2	4.4	15.9	7.5	10.2	11.2	13.4
29127	25,300	5	Marion	436.9	28,592	1,475	65.4	92.3	6.1	0.8	1.2	1.9	6.5	16.8	9.2	12.2	11.6	12.0
29129		9	Mercer	453.8	3,641	2,929	8.0	95.7	0.9	1.2	1.0	2.5	6.4	17.4	7.6	9.6	9.6	11.6
29131		6	Miller	592.6	25,336	1,594	42.8	96.2	1.1	1.5	0.8	2.0	6.3	17.1	7.5	11.8	11.5	12.5
29133		6	Mississippi	411.6	13,336	2,208	32.4	72.6	25.2	0.7	0.5	2.2	5.1	16.0	8.2	13.7	13.3	13.5
29135	27,620	3	Moniteau	415.0	16,121	2,034	38.8	90.4	4.4	1.0	0.7	4.8	6.3	18.1	7.9	13.6	13.6	12.8
29137		9	Monroe	647.7	8,664	2,534	13.4	94.7	3.9	1.1	0.7	1.7	5.9	16.0	6.3	9.9	10.5	11.8
29139		6	Montgomery	535.0	11,534	2,324	21.6	95.4	2.3	1.0	0.9	2.0	5.3	16.6	6.6	10.8	11.1	12.7
29141		8	Morgan	597.6	20,358	1,803	34.1	95.6	1.2	1.7	0.8	2.4	6.4	16.5	6.5	10.3	9.6	11.6
29143		7	New Madrid	674.9	17,296	1,960	25.6	81.7	16.8	0.8	0.7	2.0	6.2	17.0	6.9	11.8	11.4	12.8
29145	27,900	3	Newton	624.8	58,266	887	93.3	88.7	1.7	4.3	2.9	5.6	6.1	17.6	8.2	11.8	11.4	12.9
29147	32,340	6	Nodaway	877.0	22,304	1,711	25.4	93.4	3.4	0.7	1.9	1.8	4.8	11.1	28.6	10.9	9.4	9.3
29149		9	Oregon	789.8	10,541	2,390	13.3	96.0	0.9	2.8	0.7	1.8	6.0	16.6	6.6	9.7	9.8	12.2
29151	27,620	3	Osage	606.6	13,714	2,185	22.6	98.0	0.7	0.7	0.4	1.0	6.1	17.1	8.5	11.3	11.8	13.3
29153		9	Ozark	745.0	9,017	2,497	12.1	96.9	0.7	1.9	0.6	1.7	4.2	14.6	5.2	8.3	9.4	11.5
29155		7	Pemiscot	492.6	16,272	2,024	33.0	70.8	27.1	0.8	0.7	2.7	7.2	18.5	8.0	12.0	11.4	12.1
29157		6	Perry	474.4	19,150	1,866	40.4	96.1	0.9	0.8	0.8	2.4	5.9	17.4	7.8	11.8	11.8	12.9
29159	42,740	4	Pettis	682.2	42,542	1,128	62.4	86.5	4.2	0.9	1.5	9.0	6.7	17.9	8.4	13.3	11.9	11.5
29161	40,620	5	Phelps	671.8	44,732	1,083	66.6	90.7	2.9	1.5	4.5	2.6	5.6	15.2	16.6	11.7	10.8	10.9
29163		6	Pike	670.4	18,504	1,901	27.6	89.3	8.6	0.7	0.6	2.3	6.1	15.9	8.1	14.0	12.4	12.9
29165	28,140	1	Platte	419.8	102,985	587	245.3	82.8	8.1	1.1	4.2	6.2	6.2	17.6	8.0	13.4	14.0	13.3
29167	44,180	2	Polk	635.5	32,201	1,376	50.7	94.9	1.4	1.4	1.2	2.6	6.2	16.6	13.0	10.9	10.8	11.8
29169	22,780	5	Pulaski	547.1	52,014	960	95.1	72.8	13.1	2.0	5.2	11.3	6.6	15.3	22.1	17.8	12.0	9.1
29171		9	Putnam	517.3	4,757	2,849	9.2	96.8	0.6	0.7	0.9	2.2	6.2	16.0	6.2	10.3	9.9	11.7
29173	25,300	9	Ralls	469.8	10,212	2,411	21.7	96.7	1.9	0.8	0.7	1.3	4.8	16.3	6.7	10.1	11.4	13.2
29175	33,620	6	Randolph	482.7	24,763	1,618	51.3	91.1	6.9	1.1	1.2	2.2	5.8	15.9	9.1	13.8	12.6	13.2
29177	28,140	1	Ray	568.8	22,883	1,686	40.2	95.2	2.1	1.1	0.7	2.5	5.5	17.0	7.6	11.2	11.5	13.4
29179		9	Reynolds	808.5	6,254	2,728	7.7	96.1	1.6	2.7	0.6	1.7	4.3	15.2	6.7	9.7	11.2	13.3
29181		9	Ripley	629.5	13,401	2,198	21.3	96.6	1.0	1.9	0.7	1.5	6.1	16.9	6.4	11.5	11.6	12.3
29183	41,180	1	St. Charles	560.5	399,182	177	712.2	88.7	6.0	0.6	3.3	3.4	5.9	17.3	8.4	13.0	13.5	13.1
29185		8	St. Clair	675.0	9,395	2,473	13.9	96.1	1.1	1.8	0.6	2.2	6.1	13.9	5.9	9.8	9.2	12.0
29186		6	Ste. Genevieve	499.2	17,888	1,927	35.8	96.6	1.4	0.7	1.3	1.2	5.5	16.2	7.3	11.0	11.2	12.8
29187	22,100	4	St. Francois	451.9	66,692	804	147.6	93.0	5.1	0.9	0.7	1.6	5.5	15.7	8.2	14.5	13.6	13.1
29189	41,180	1	St. Louis	507.4	996,945	46	1,964.8	67.5	25.8	0.6	5.4	3.0	5.9	16.1	8.5	12.9	12.0	12.4
29195	32,180	6	Saline	755.5	22,895	1,685	30.3	82.1	6.4	1.1	2.3	10.4	5.7	16.7	11.0	11.8	11.5	11.4
29197	28,860	9	Schuyler	307.3	4,599	2,855	15.0	97.8	0.6	0.7	0.6	1.5	8.0	17.2	8.3	11.5	9.9	11.7
29199		9	Scotland	436.5	4,966	2,834	11.4	98.2	0.6	0.8	0.5	1.0	8.8	20.6	8.4	11.2	10.6	10.4
29201	43,460	4	Scott	420.0	38,458	1,215	91.6	84.8	12.9	1.0	0.7	2.5	6.4	17.7	7.5	12.8	11.5	12.7
29203		9	Shannon	1,003.8	8,189	2,579	8.2	95.9	1.0	2.8	0.7	2.1	5.2	16.3	6.7	10.9	9.4	12.6
29205		9	Shelby	500.9	6,050	2,749	12.1	96.3	1.8	0.8	0.5	2.2	6.5	17.6	7.1	10.2	12.1	10.6
29207		6	Stoddard	823.2	29,206	1,450	35.5	96.3	1.6	0.9	0.5	1.8	5.7	16.1	7.7	11.9	12.0	12.7
29209	14,700	6	Stone	464.0	31,749	1,385	68.4	96.0	0.8	1.7	0.6	2.4	3.8	12.6	5.9	8.0	8.9	11.9
29211		9	Sullivan	648.0	6,221	2,732	9.6	77.8	3.6	1.0	0.5	18.0	6.6	15.8	8.1	10.0	11.3	13.9
29213	14,700	4	Taney	632.4	55,852	916	88.3	90.4	2.1	1.8	1.6	6.2	5.7	15.4	9.6	11.4	10.9	11.9
29215		9	Texas	1,177.3	25,571	1,581	21.7	92.9	4.2	2.1	0.6	2.1	5.6	15.7	7.6	11.6	11.5	12.1
29217		7	Vernon	826.4	20,528	1,794	24.8	95.5	1.5	1.7	0.9	2.1	6.1	17.5	8.9	10.8	11.0	12.3
29219	41,180	1	Warren	428.6	34,711	1,310	81.0	93.5	3.3	0.9	0.8	3.4	6.4	17.4	7.3	12.1	11.2	12.7
29221		6	Washington	759.9	24,943	1,609	32.8	95.3	2.9	1.1	0.5	1.5	5.8	17.0	7.4	12.2	12.2	14.2
29223		9	Wayne	759.3	13,122	2,224	17.3	96.5	1.1	1.7	0.6	1.9	5.2	15.3	6.0	10.3	10.0	13.3
29225	44,180	2	Webster	592.6	39,109	1,202	66.0	95.8	1.5	1.6	0.7	2.1	7.6	19.7	7.6	12.3	12.1	12.7
29227		9	Worth	266.6	2,040	3,045	7.7	96.9	1.1	0.6	0.4	1.6	5.3	15.0	6.9	10.4	9.3	11.3
29229		6	Wright	681.8	18,378	1,907	27.0	96.3	0.9	1.5	0.7	2.0	7.3	18.3	7.2	10.7	10.7	12.0

1. CBSA = Core Based Statistical Area. See Appendix A for explanation. See Appendix B for list of metropolitan areas with component counties.   2. County type code from the Economic Research Service of USDA Rural-Urban Continuum Codes. See Appendix A for definition.   3. Dry land or land partially or temporarily covered by water.   4. May be of any race.

Table B. States and Counties — **Population and Households**

STATE County	Population, 2018 (cont.) Age (percent) (cont.)				Population change, 2000-2018 Total persons		Percent change		Components of change, 2010-2018			Households, 2013-2017		Percent		
	55 to 64 years	65 to 74 years	75 years and over	Percent female	2000	2010	2000-2010	2010-2018	Births	Deaths	Net Migration	Number	Persons per household	Family households	Female family householder[1]	One person
	16	17	18	19	20	21	22	23	24	25	26	27	28	29	30	31

STATE County	16	17	18	19	20	21	22	23	24	25	26	27	28	29	30	31
MISSOURI— Cont'd																
Jasper	12.1	8.9	6.8	51.2	104,686	117,391	12.1	2.8	13,899	9,610	-1,019	46,009	2.52	65.4	11.2	27.5
Jefferson	14.8	9.3	5.7	50.4	198,099	218,708	10.4	2.6	21,630	16,117	308	83,744	2.63	73.5	11.4	21.0
Johnson	11.1	7.4	5.3	48.6	48,258	52,595	9.0	2.0	5,894	3,296	-1,553	19,918	2.48	64.4	9.5	24.0
Knox	15.6	11.4	10.7	50.0	4,361	4,131	-5.3	-4.5	405	412	-178	1,602	2.43	67.0	9.4	30.0
Laclede	13.7	10.2	7.7	50.9	32,513	35,571	9.4	0.4	3,934	3,158	-628	13,825	2.54	71.1	10.1	23.9
Lafayette	14.5	9.9	9.0	50.4	32,960	33,370	1.2	-2.3	3,054	3,032	-788	13,224	2.42	70.2	9.8	25.7
Lawrence	13.5	9.9	8.4	50.4	35,204	38,641	9.8	-0.7	4,105	3,653	-726	14,636	2.56	69.9	10.2	25.8
Lewis	14.0	10.0	8.5	49.8	10,494	10,209	-2.7	-3.5	925	904	-375	3,754	2.47	64.8	6.9	30.0
Lincoln	13.9	8.1	5.3	50.0	38,944	52,565	35.0	9.7	6,010	3,662	2,806	18,698	2.89	73.4	11.6	22.0
Linn	14.9	11.8	9.3	51.3	13,754	12,761	-7.2	-5.7	1,129	1,396	-454	4,997	2.42	67.3	10.8	29.0
Livingston	12.6	9.9	9.4	56.5	14,558	15,195	4.4	-0.3	1,333	1,600	208	5,813	2.35	63.9	8.3	29.2
McDonald	13.6	9.1	6.2	49.5	21,681	23,083	6.5	0.0	2,679	1,804	-892	8,137	2.77	74.6	11.3	21.2
Macon	14.2	12.2	10.6	50.5	15,762	15,566	-1.2	-2.7	1,410	1,559	-257	6,023	2.50	62.5	9.8	33.0
Madison	14.4	10.5	8.6	51.1	11,800	12,224	3.6	-0.3	1,165	1,381	185	4,867	2.47	67.2	10.2	25.5
Maries	15.9	11.9	9.6	49.8	8,903	9,180	3.1	-4.5	664	833	-240	3,667	2.42	65.1	8.1	29.8
Marion	13.6	10.0	8.1	51.3	28,289	28,781	1.7	-0.7	3,005	2,636	-534	11,311	2.40	65.1	11.7	28.9
Mercer	15.7	11.1	11.0	49.2	3,757	3,785	0.7	-3.8	367	353	-157	1,390	2.59	65.8	7.9	31.5
Miller	14.2	11.3	8.0	50.1	23,564	24,752	5.0	2.4	2,469	2,281	415	9,514	2.59	67.0	9.7	30.5
Mississippi	12.6	10.0	7.8	45.9	13,427	14,358	6.9	-7.1	1,300	1,481	-843	5,128	2.37	70.9	20.9	23.8
Moniteau	11.9	8.9	6.8	46.9	14,827	15,605	5.2	3.3	1,679	1,209	57	5,373	2.71	73.2	8.9	23.2
Monroe	16.3	12.8	10.6	49.4	9,311	8,840	-5.1	-2.0	796	771	-206	3,615	2.36	64.7	8.8	30.7
Montgomery	15.6	11.2	10.0	49.8	12,136	12,234	0.8	-5.7	1,097	1,299	-502	4,844	2.32	66.3	9.8	29.0
Morgan	15.7	13.4	10.1	49.9	19,309	20,565	6.5	-1.0	2,105	2,470	164	7,774	2.54	63.9	9.1	30.0
New Madrid	14.7	11.0	8.2	52.0	19,760	18,960	-4.0	-8.8	1,884	1,971	-1,581	7,309	2.42	67.0	15.8	27.2
Newton	14.0	10.4	7.7	50.1	52,636	58,118	10.4	0.3	5,914	5,068	-665	22,151	2.58	71.0	9.1	24.6
Nodaway	10.7	7.9	7.3	49.6	21,912	23,370	6.7	-4.6	1,912	1,557	-1,436	8,493	2.30	58.4	7.2	27.6
Oregon	15.9	12.9	10.4	50.9	10,344	10,881	5.2	-3.1	1,039	1,160	-216	4,375	2.43	66.4	8.3	28.2
Osage	14.5	9.5	8.0	48.5	13,062	13,883	6.3	-1.2	1,303	1,040	-429	5,108	2.61	70.8	5.6	23.9
Ozark	17.9	16.2	12.7	49.8	9,542	9,717	1.8	-7.2	693	1,043	-346	4,075	2.26	66.2	6.6	28.5
Pemiscot	13.7	9.8	7.3	52.8	20,047	18,296	-8.7	-11.1	2,243	1,920	-2,360	6,875	2.49	63.2	19.7	31.5
Perry	14.2	10.2	7.9	50.0	18,132	18,971	4.6	0.9	1,815	1,686	67	7,529	2.50	70.9	8.5	23.5
Pettis	13.6	9.2	7.6	50.4	39,403	42,201	7.1	0.8	4,703	3,492	-849	16,031	2.58	66.8	11.5	28.2
Phelps	12.6	9.2	7.3	47.8	39,825	45,156	13.4	-0.9	4,291	3,626	-1,115	17,330	2.41	62.0	9.4	28.8
Pike	13.4	9.6	7.7	44.5	18,351	18,515	0.9	-0.1	1,804	1,636	-178	6,741	2.40	65.7	11.0	27.9
Platte	12.9	8.9	5.6	50.7	73,781	89,325	21.1	15.3	9,731	5,229	9,171	38,147	2.52	66.6	8.9	27.5
Polk	12.7	10.0	8.0	50.9	26,992	31,137	15.4	3.4	3,125	2,902	858	11,717	2.55	68.0	9.2	23.5
Pulaski	8.1	5.3	3.7	43.5	41,165	52,274	27.0	-0.5	6,710	2,447	-4,621	15,375	2.83	66.8	10.5	26.6
Putnam	15.2	13.2	11.3	49.6	5,223	4,979	-4.7	-4.5	472	512	-178	1,956	2.44	69.0	13.7	28.6
Ralls	15.7	13.3	8.4	49.8	9,626	10,167	5.6	0.4	799	779	28	3,994	2.53	73.2	8.9	22.4
Randolph	12.8	9.5	7.3	47.8	24,663	25,414	3.0	-2.6	2,346	2,230	-771	8,348	2.72	67.6	8.4	29.1
Ray	15.3	10.4	8.1	50.1	23,354	23,494	0.6	-2.6	2,048	2,086	-575	8,684	2.60	70.1	10.2	24.4
Reynolds	16.4	12.6	10.6	48.5	6,689	6,694	0.1	-6.6	465	707	-197	2,628	2.34	72.0	7.4	24.3
Ripley	14.9	11.5	8.9	50.3	13,509	14,106	4.4	-5.0	1,442	1,579	-560	5,397	2.55	67.5	12.9	27.4
St. Charles	13.6	8.9	6.3	50.8	283,883	360,494	27.0	10.7	37,229	21,307	22,908	142,554	2.65	72.7	9.6	22.6
St. Clair	16.0	14.3	12.7	49.7	9,652	9,805	1.6	-4.2	820	1,216	-13	4,135	2.21	64.0	7.9	30.3
Ste. Genevieve	16.6	11.2	8.3	49.3	17,842	18,157	1.8	-1.5	1,477	1,599	-143	7,185	2.45	71.4	10.2	25.7
St. Francois	13.0	9.3	7.1	46.6	55,641	65,367	17.5	2.0	5,983	6,300	1,656	24,661	2.40	64.9	10.1	29.2
St. Louis	14.2	10.1	8.0	52.6	1,016,315	998,986	-1.7	-0.2	95,754	79,612	-17,937	402,307	2.44	64.4	13.9	30.4
Saline	13.6	9.9	8.4	50.1	23,756	23,370	-1.6	-2.0	2,293	2,054	-711	8,754	2.47	64.7	11.7	30.9
Schuyler	13.6	10.2	9.6	50.3	4,170	4,431	6.3	3.8	535	415	47	1,669	2.64	66.9	8.6	28.5
Scotland	11.9	9.4	8.7	50.5	4,983	4,853	-2.6	2.3	683	476	-95	1,870	2.56	66.7	9.7	28.0
Scott	13.4	10.3	7.7	51.4	40,422	39,188	-3.1	-1.9	4,113	3,591	-1,230	15,241	2.51	68.7	14.3	27.0
Shannon	16.8	12.5	9.6	50.0	8,324	8,439	1.4	-3.0	743	741	-248	3,158	2.58	64.6	12.5	29.1
Shelby	14.8	11.4	9.9	50.2	6,799	6,373	-6.3	-5.1	614	655	-282	2,446	2.38	66.8	7.8	29.5
Stoddard	13.9	10.9	9.2	50.6	29,705	29,968	0.9	-2.5	2,841	3,173	-406	11,773	2.48	64.0	9.0	29.8
Stone	18.0	18.7	12.3	51.0	28,658	32,210	12.4	-1.4	2,058	3,127	633	12,880	2.41	70.7	6.1	24.3
Sullivan	13.9	11.4	8.8	48.6	7,219	6,714	-7.0	-7.3	700	605	-594	2,283	2.73	61.9	9.3	32.8
Taney	13.5	12.5	9.2	51.6	39,703	51,675	30.2	8.1	5,239	4,428	3,363	22,142	2.37	69.0	12.7	25.1
Texas	14.8	11.5	9.5	47.5	23,003	26,010	13.1	-1.7	2,421	2,415	-430	9,303	2.62	66.6	9.9	28.7
Vernon	14.1	10.7	8.6	51.1	20,454	21,161	3.5	-3.0	2,054	2,023	-659	8,170	2.44	68.0	9.9	26.9
Warren	15.4	10.0	7.6	50.1	24,525	32,512	32.6	6.8	3,405	2,351	1,160	12,032	2.76	74.3	10.5	21.5
Washington	14.5	10.0	6.7	48.5	23,344	25,199	7.9	-1.0	2,433	2,255	-420	9,048	2.64	71.5	12.3	22.1
Wayne	16.4	13.1	10.4	50.8	13,259	13,523	2.0	-3.0	1,175	1,622	52	5,482	2.41	67.3	13.8	26.7
Webster	12.7	8.9	6.5	49.0	31,045	36,207	16.6	8.0	4,472	2,705	1,156	13,311	2.75	73.5	9.9	22.4
Worth	17.0	11.8	12.9	51.8	2,382	2,169	-8.9	-5.9	191	248	-74	888	2.25	70.8	6.8	25.3
Wright	14.2	10.9	8.8	50.9	17,955	18,815	4.8	-2.3	2,031	1,853	-615	7,488	2.42	66.9	12.7	29.9

1. No spouse present.

Table B. States and Counties — Population, Vital Statistics, Health, and Crime

STATE County	Persons in group quarters, 2018	Daytime Population, 2013-2017		Births, 2018		Deaths, 2018		Persons under 65 with no health insurance, 2016		Medicare, 2018			Serious crimes known to police[2], 2016 Total	
		Number	Employment/ residence ratio	Total	Rate[1]	Number	Rate[1]	Number	Percent	Total beneficiaries	Enrolled in Original Medicare	Enrolled in Medicare Advantage	Number	Rate[3]
	32	33	34	35	36	37	38	39	40	41	42	43	44	45
MISSOURI— Cont'd														
Jasper	2,487	124,035	1.10	1,624	13.5	1,178	9.8	13,150	13.2	23,015	16,491	6,524	5,624	4,742
Jefferson	1,984	166,958	0.48	2,522	11.2	2,173	9.7	17,938	9.4	42,265	21,812	20,453	4,360	1,939
Johnson	3,684	50,771	0.88	687	12.8	382	7.1	4,304	9.8	7,929	5,898	2,031	1,231	2,274
Knox	87	3,757	0.86	46	11.7	45	11.4	470	15.6	967	889	78	20	518
Laclede	345	35,808	1.02	496	13.9	362	10.1	3,777	13.1	8,324	4,383	3,941	849	2,399
Lafayette	724	28,742	0.74	356	10.9	352	10.8	2,772	10.6	7,214	4,956	2,258	371	1,152
Lawrence	559	33,060	0.69	514	13.4	433	11.3	4,301	13.9	8,683	5,001	3,682	1,016	2,671
Lewis	788	8,369	0.64	108	11.0	105	10.7	933	12.1	2,205	1,961	244	102	1,001
Lincoln	632	43,131	0.53	737	12.8	454	7.9	4,622	9.7	9,827	6,101	3,726	767	1,394
Linn	152	11,886	0.93	123	10.2	155	12.9	1,141	11.9	3,154	2,798	356	199	1,630
Livingston	1,997	15,745	1.11	156	10.3	187	12.3	1,382	13.0	3,410	2,973	437	234	1,561
McDonald	157	20,880	0.79	355	15.4	221	9.6	4,139	21.9	3,939	2,562	1,377	613	2,721
Macon	286	14,310	0.84	157	10.4	167	11.0	1,518	13.0	4,006	3,593	413	246	1,612
Madison	167	11,191	0.79	145	11.9	186	15.3	1,294	13.1	3,169	2,581	588	163	1,311
Maries	67	6,774	0.41	65	7.4	98	11.2	1,045	15.0	2,009	1,658	351	88	988
Marion	1,371	30,963	1.17	341	11.9	295	10.3	2,351	10.3	6,599	5,728	871	1,026	3,556
Mercer	51	3,778	1.07	51	14.0	33	9.1	404	14.1	878	782	96	30	817
Miller	271	21,522	0.68	305	12.0	263	10.4	2,622	13.0	5,411	4,182	1,229	523	2,079
Mississippi	1,846	12,917	0.79	133	10.0	191	14.3	1,185	12.4	2,937	2,648	289	308	2,207
Moniteau	1,377	13,583	0.65	193	12.0	164	10.2	1,841	15.0	2,957	2,392	565	135	843
Monroe	128	7,363	0.66	103	11.9	94	10.8	830	12.5	2,172	1,899	273	92	1,079
Montgomery	394	10,109	0.70	116	10.1	147	12.7	1,187	13.2	2,874	2,240	634	201	1,735
Morgan	302	19,088	0.86	249	12.2	289	14.2	2,702	18.0	5,855	4,729	1,126	348	1,734
New Madrid	332	17,997	1.00	215	12.4	231	13.4	1,787	12.5	3,758	3,210	548	228	1,264
Newton	880	56,643	0.94	678	11.6	593	10.2	6,852	14.5	12,050	8,666	3,384	2,221	3,788
Nodaway	3,652	22,692	1.00	237	10.6	170	7.6	1,837	11.5	3,859	3,586	273	279	1,231
Oregon	121	9,944	0.80	109	10.3	143	13.6	1,150	14.0	2,822	2,273	549	100	914
Osage	405	11,414	0.68	183	13.3	122	8.9	1,077	9.8	2,580	2,146	434	65	479
Ozark	123	8,082	0.59	78	8.7	137	15.2	1,136	17.3	2,890	1,904	986	94	1,007
Pemiscot	202	16,989	0.94	246	15.1	234	14.4	1,645	11.7	3,813	2,967	846	772	4,460
Perry	286	19,571	1.05	215	11.2	231	12.1	1,460	9.2	4,033	3,511	522	296	1,542
Pettis	851	44,006	1.09	522	12.3	404	9.5	4,592	13.2	8,601	6,887	1,714	1,440	3,413
Phelps	3,014	47,009	1.11	477	10.7	430	9.6	4,734	13.5	8,686	6,889	1,797	1,220	2,734
Pike	2,372	18,308	0.97	215	11.6	192	10.4	1,711	12.9	3,737	3,010	727	200	1,093
Platte	869	92,149	0.91	1,261	12.2	670	6.5	5,981	7.1	15,834	11,391	4,443	3,672	3,774
Polk	1,514	28,912	0.82	378	11.7	413	12.8	3,161	12.9	6,614	3,580	3,034	1,129	3,619
Pulaski	9,953	55,310	1.08	744	14.3	285	5.5	4,282	11.2	6,245	5,389	856	930	1,747
Putnam	57	4,257	0.71	57	12.0	56	11.8	494	13.5	1,309	1,165	144	9	186
Ralls	54	8,721	0.70	93	9.1	78	7.6	852	10.5	2,455	2,101	354	139	1,365
Randolph	2,255	25,407	1.04	289	11.7	240	9.7	2,118	11.3	5,181	4,161	1,020	502	2,008
Ray	311	17,499	0.48	247	10.8	284	12.4	2,009	10.9	4,890	3,432	1,458	563	2,486
Reynolds	101	6,605	1.10	43	6.9	85	13.6	677	14.0	1,919	1,625	294	57	894
Ripley	63	12,163	0.68	157	11.7	219	16.3	1,599	14.7	3,479	2,960	519	408	2,973
St. Charles	5,448	330,607	0.73	4,404	11.0	2,863	7.2	19,275	5.8	66,982	37,475	29,507	6,109	1,567
St. Clair	207	8,615	0.76	115	12.2	152	16.2	1,034	15.6	2,636	1,826	810	188	2,153
Ste. Genevieve	277	15,618	0.73	182	10.2	194	10.8	1,591	10.9	3,990	3,075	915	227	1,271
St. Francois	7,019	65,662	0.98	683	10.2	788	11.8	5,352	10.8	14,941	11,062	3,879	1,774	2,663
St. Louis	19,326	1,100,168	1.21	11,309	11.3	10,025	10.1	66,336	8.1	200,539	118,475	82,064	28,282	2,820
Saline	1,488	22,852	0.98	223	9.7	240	10.5	2,234	12.6	4,840	3,782	1,058	521	2,246
Schuyler	47	3,672	0.57	72	15.7	41	8.9	581	16.4	907	804	103	36	813
Scotland	76	4,554	0.85	94	18.9	43	8.7	727	18.3	896	839	57	54	1,114
Scott	559	39,763	1.05	461	12.0	464	12.1	3,532	11.2	9,555	8,194	1,361	1,313	3,375
Shannon	80	7,525	0.73	88	10.7	87	10.6	955	15.0	2,098	1,667	431	106	1,291
Shelby	198	5,451	0.78	76	12.6	53	8.8	607	12.8	1,489	1,322	167	41	675
Stoddard	689	27,840	0.86	294	10.1	385	13.2	2,790	11.8	7,422	6,083	1,339	487	1,635
Stone	300	27,904	0.70	240	7.6	392	12.3	3,327	15.2	9,729	5,614	4,115	674	2,197
Sullivan	108	6,845	1.17	83	13.3	68	10.9	744	14.8	1,467	1,319	148	76	1,212
Taney	1,754	57,994	1.15	651	11.7	532	9.5	6,669	16.0	13,677	8,074	5,603	2,144	3,894
Texas	1,894	24,742	0.89	283	11.1	274	10.7	2,698	14.4	5,746	4,779	967	446	1,743
Vernon	868	20,584	0.99	223	10.9	218	10.6	2,176	13.4	4,527	3,523	1,004	981	4,731
Warren	317	26,824	0.54	418	12.0	315	9.1	3,108	11.2	6,939	3,714	3,225	758	2,252
Washington	1,092	21,537	0.61	282	11.3	279	11.2	2,658	13.6	5,205	3,470	1,735	601	2,436
Wayne	133	12,397	0.78	139	10.6	205	15.6	1,454	14.5	3,424	2,756	668	288	2,155
Webster	927	31,475	0.59	580	14.8	382	9.8	4,430	14.2	7,788	3,820	3,968	711	1,887
Worth	52	1,718	0.65	23	11.3	22	10.8	197	12.8	510	473	37	9	442
Wright	195	16,942	0.79	261	14.2	222	12.1	2,282	15.8	4,772	2,827	1,945	353	1,947

1. Per 1,000 estimated resident population.   2. Data for serious crimes have not been adjusted for underreporting; this may affect comparability between geographic areas and over time.   3. Per 100,000 population estimated by the FBI.

Table B. States and Counties — Crime, Education, Money Income, and Poverty

STATE County	Serious crimes known to police[2], 2016 (cont.)[1] Rate — Violent	Property	School enrollment and attainment, 2013-2017 Enrollment[3] Total	Percent private	Attainment[4] (percent) High school graduate or less	Bachelor's degree or more	Local government expenditures,[5] 2014-2015 Total current spending (mil dol)	Current spending per student (dollars)	Money income, 2013-2017 Per capita income[6]	Median income (dollars)	Households Percent with income of less than $50,000	with income of $200,000 or more	Income and poverty, 2017 Median household income (dollars)	Percent below poverty level All persons	Children under 18 years	Children 5 to 17 years in families
	46	47	48	49	50	51	52	53	54	55	56	57	58	59	60	61
MISSOURI— Cont'd																
Jasper	413	4,329	30,295	14.9	47.5	22.7	174.8	8,015	23,390	45,328	54.1	2.0	46,611	16.8	24.0	22.1
Jefferson	165	1,774	53,455	15.4	43.8	19.8	322.4	9,153	27,443	60,765	40.0	2.4	62,334	10.7	14.0	12.1
Johnson	214	2,060	17,562	8.5	38.5	28.4	69.5	9,393	23,304	50,689	49.4	1.2	54,417	12.8	14.0	13.6
Knox	0	518	888	22.5	58.9	15.9	5.2	10,135	22,171	39,674	64.3	1.1	36,866	18.6	31.4	30.3
Laclede	325	2,074	8,084	13.4	56.4	13.7	48.7	7,988	20,534	42,646	58.0	1.2	45,267	15.6	23.6	22.0
Lafayette	115	1,037	7,122	15.7	53.7	18.3	50.3	9,486	27,260	52,557	46.8	2.6	51,745	12.5	18.4	18.8
Lawrence	407	2,263	8,898	14.4	53.4	15.9	48.3	8,078	21,022	41,673	59.5	1.6	42,856	16	25.2	23.3
Lewis	167	834	2,612	30.6	57.5	14.4	13.6	8,850	22,083	47,148	53.1	1.1	46,517	16	22.3	19.6
Lincoln	349	1,045	13,398	12.3	54.7	15.7	78.4	8,592	24,023	58,603	42.3	2.2	67,986	9.8	13.7	12.3
Linn	246	1,385	2,735	9.8	59.1	14.8	22.7	9,819	22,361	41,652	58.9	1.3	42,331	13.5	21.9	20.6
Livingston	267	1,295	3,184	9.4	55.0	18.8	20.8	9,636	22,248	45,929	54.3	2.0	45,448	16.3	20.9	19.4
McDonald	550	2,171	5,381	12.9	59.6	12.7	32.0	8,229	19,577	41,207	59.0	1.7	38,468	19.1	30.5	26.7
Macon	203	1,409	3,418	13.0	57.2	15.3	22.3	9,623	20,890	38,903	60.4	1.5	40,037	12.6	20.7	18.6
Madison	257	1,054	2,680	10.0	55.0	12.5	17.4	8,076	20,081	37,484	60.4	1.1	38,206	18.6	26.7	25.1
Maries	146	842	1,894	14.9	57.8	13.6	11.2	8,483	22,087	41,715	57.7	1.5	44,366	13.9	20.8	19.1
Marion	291	3,264	6,671	21.0	50.7	20.9	43.9	8,564	22,662	44,098	54.8	1.7	45,064	17.2	22.1	21.3
Mercer	0	817	788	15.7	59.5	17.6	6.8	11,047	20,374	43,314	58.7	0.0	42,048	14.5	19.6	18.6
Miller	366	1,713	5,835	6.8	56.9	16.0	46.9	9,319	23,346	41,461	59.5	2.8	42,042	15	23.4	22.0
Mississippi	408	1,798	2,845	5.1	65.4	11.4	18.3	8,223	17,918	32,212	68.8	1.4	34,185	28.5	37.8	34.3
Moniteau	144	700	3,590	19.8	59.1	17.5	20.7	8,549	21,305	50,897	48.7	1.4	49,452	12	16.6	15.8
Monroe	141	938	1,837	20.4	56.8	14.4	14.4	9,683	22,255	42,011	61.4	0.5	42,299	13.5	23.1	22.1
Montgomery	294	1,442	2,318	9.9	60.7	12.9	14.9	9,169	21,757	43,094	57.7	0.9	47,044	15.2	21.5	19.7
Morgan	264	1,470	3,656	29.4	62.0	12.6	16.7	8,157	20,055	34,776	62.3	0.6	41,908	19.7	30.2	29.8
New Madrid	222	1,042	3,798	4.2	66.4	12.6	27.6	10,167	20,261	33,846	63.3	1.0	38,542	25.4	38.2	34.8
Newton	341	3,447	13,687	12.6	47.3	19.4	70.7	8,119	25,837	46,723	53.0	3.1	49,161	13.2	19.0	17.1
Nodaway	199	1,032	8,128	6.8	47.6	26.8	30.0	10,800	21,056	41,370	59.8	1.3	44,273	17	15.0	13.8
Oregon	137	777	2,268	8.2	58.2	12.8	16.5	9,730	18,309	32,070	69.5	0.2	31,714	24.3	37.1	34.6
Osage	37	443	3,210	26.5	54.4	18.8	14.8	8,808	24,995	54,503	46.1	1.0	57,694	9.2	10.6	9.8
Ozark	161	846	1,900	8.7	61.5	13.6	15.1	9,752	17,857	32,021	70.3	0.3	33,284	21.5	35.4	31.2
Pemiscot	919	3,542	4,301	2.6	63.7	12.0	36.9	10,487	18,883	32,468	68.7	1.1	32,224	26.4	43.4	40.6
Perry	401	1,141	4,528	25.9	57.2	16.3	21.3	8,812	24,846	54,935	44.7	1.1	52,132	9.7	14.7	13.9
Pettis	351	3,062	10,306	11.9	49.3	17.7	57.4	8,506	22,304	43,097	57.7	1.8	44,867	16	21.5	19.8
Phelps	258	2,476	14,524	10.1	44.8	28.7	59.1	8,953	23,691	41,681	57.3	3.0	41,330	18.4	21.4	19.9
Pike	98	995	3,419	10.8	62.2	15.5	24.3	9,519	20,947	45,112	55.7	1.0	44,040	16.4	23.4	23.3
Platte	875	2,900	25,077	17.5	26.7	41.5	175.0	10,878	37,443	74,199	32.7	6.6	75,651	6.2	7.1	6.2
Polk	417	3,202	8,328	28.5	50.4	20.3	47.0	8,992	21,357	44,805	56.0	2.1	44,214	15.1	22.0	20.7
Pulaski	241	1,507	15,641	11.3	38.6	25.8	88.6	9,702	21,716	51,137	48.4	1.0	53,168	13	15.1	15.2
Putnam	0	186	842	6.5	52.1	18.1	6.9	9,825	20,729	37,028	62.8	1.0	38,024	16.5	27.1	25.9
Ralls	236	1,129	1,976	12.4	59.6	13.2	5.6	7,373	24,687	50,161	49.8	1.5	53,965	9.6	14.1	12.2
Randolph	76	1,932	6,356	20.7	50.0	14.6	37.4	9,983	19,984	44,754	54.3	1.4	47,327	16.9	25.5	20.7
Ray	671	1,815	5,292	13.6	58.5	14.4	28.8	8,672	26,781	57,270	43.8	1.7	61,592	10.3	15.1	12.9
Reynolds	173	722	1,185	6.2	63.8	9.8	13.8	12,351	21,593	40,265	59.9	0.8	34,424	20.4	33.4	29.5
Ripley	423	2,550	2,872	7.3	61.1	11.9	18.9	8,266	18,434	33,849	65.9	0.3	32,331	23.9	35.2	32.4
St. Charles	128	1,439	103,865	27.6	30.8	37.1	604.3	10,350	35,628	78,380	29.2	6.6	81,827	5.3	6.7	5.8
St. Clair	309	1,844	1,582	16.4	59.9	13.6	12.4	9,641	20,827	35,066	66.2	0.8	35,230	20.4	31.1	30.0
Ste. Genevieve	230	1,042	4,178	19.7	54.5	15.6	21.4	11,415	26,418	50,959	49.1	1.7	58,797	10.8	15.7	14.2
St. Francois	303	2,360	14,556	10.1	54.2	13.3	93.0	8,649	20,944	42,873	57.7	1.0	41,708	17.7	24.3	22.2
St. Louis	380	2,441	254,671	28.3	28.2	42.8	1,890.0	13,495	38,081	62,931	39.4	8.6	64,926	10	13.1	12.1
Saline	224	2,022	5,884	24.7	55.8	18.7	32.6	8,900	21,729	41,567	58.9	1.2	43,235	15.6	22.3	20.4
Schuyler	158	655	1,130	8.5	55.2	14.0	5.6	8,729	19,882	38,848	62.4	1.4	32,860	15.9	28.8	28.1
Scotland	186	928	998	21.4	61.2	12.6	6.2	9,955	23,785	42,939	56.7	2.7	40,900	15.6	24.8	25.2
Scott	799	2,576	8,373	13.1	59.2	13.6	56.0	8,222	22,939	41,628	59.5	2.0	42,581	20.2	31.8	28.1
Shannon	414	877	1,713	8.9	62.4	14.2	17.7	8,818	17,903	31,202	69.8	0.9	29,152	35.9	53.1	49.7
Shelby	99	577	1,307	21.5	53.8	15.7	10.6	9,913	22,349	42,593	57.6	1.3	42,444	15.7	22.6	21.3
Stoddard	131	1,504	6,257	11.4	58.8	14.1	43.7	8,571	21,684	40,076	61.9	1.3	41,824	17.1	23.5	22.5
Stone	479	1,718	5,538	15.1	49.0	18.4	40.7	10,346	26,052	43,292	57.4	2.3	44,384	15.5	27.4	24.9
Sullivan	207	1,004	1,350	3.5	66.4	10.7	10.7	10,540	21,168	42,034	56.2	0.9	40,517	16.1	22.8	21.3
Taney	380	3,514	12,599	23.8	46.9	17.8	72.0	9,090	21,381	39,661	60.5	1.4	43,110	13.8	22.2	21.2
Texas	141	1,603	5,900	20.5	58.8	13.8	33.6	8,517	17,918	35,571	64.8	0.4	33,457	21.2	31.2	29.8
Vernon	612	4,118	4,784	17.8	53.0	17.3	27.9	8,931	22,369	41,479	57.9	2.4	41,284	15.6	24.7	23.2
Warren	431	1,822	7,455	18.2	48.6	18.7	43.8	9,044	26,845	56,193	45.2	3.8	59,723	10.1	14.4	13.3
Washington	450	1,986	5,347	4.6	63.1	8.9	33.4	8,823	18,314	37,810	62.5	0.8	37,318	22.8	30.9	27.8
Wayne	157	1,998	2,489	11.0	60.9	12.1	15.1	8,181	18,897	35,135	68.1	0.4	33,390	22.9	35.3	34.6
Webster	162	1,725	8,885	16.9	53.2	15.7	56.0	8,026	20,468	45,185	55.0	1.1	46,039	15.5	26.4	25.6
Worth	49	393	391	7.2	55.5	19.1	3.1	9,574	22,961	48,214	52.8	1.1	41,017	14.8	22.0	19.9
Wright	281	1,666	4,035	13.8	63.3	11.8	28.0	8,179	19,805	31,290	70.9	3.0	33,191	24.3	36.0	33.5

1. Data for serious crimes have not been adjusted for underreporting; this may affect comparability between geographic areas and over time.   2. Per 100,000 population estimated by the FBI.   3.   All persons 3 years old and over enrolled in nursery school through college.   4.   Persons 25 years old and over.   5.   Elementary and secondary education expenditures.   6. Based on population estimated by the American Community Survey, 2013–2017.

Table B. States and Counties — **Personal Income and Earnings**

STATE County	Personal income, 2017										Earnings, 2017		
	Total (mil dol)	Percent change 2016-2017	Per capita[1] Dollars	Per capita Rank	Wages and salaries (mil dol)	Supplements to wages and salaries, employer contributions (mil dol) Pension and insurance	Government social insurance	Proprietors' income (mil dol)	Dividends, interest, and rent (mil dol)	Personal transfer reecipts (mil dol)	Total (mil dol)	Contributions for government social insurance (mil dol) From employee and self-employed	From employer
	62	63	64	65	66	67	68	69	70	71	72	73	74
MISSOURI— Cont'd													
Jasper	4,586	2.7	38,150	1,854	2,502	411	178	459	699	1,061	3,550	217	178
Jefferson	8,995	3.4	40,192	1,522	2,007	336	150	399	1,037	1,855	2,892	211	150
Johnson	1,862	3.3	34,550	2,406	844	228	69	89	351	383	1,230	65	69
Knox	128	-1.4	32,165	2,731	34	8	3	13	28	39	58	4	3
Laclede	1,216	5.8	34,317	2,443	510	103	40	125	182	359	777	52	40
Lafayette	1,327	4.1	40,657	1,448	321	65	23	103	205	352	512	35	23
Lawrence	1,245	4.3	32,399	2,703	363	69	27	69	195	355	528	40	27
Lewis	327	1.6	32,809	2,645	89	18	7	21	52	90	135	10	7
Lincoln	2,168	4.5	38,584	1,793	513	90	37	119	231	462	760	52	37
Linn	452	2.5	37,090	2,016	159	28	13	45	89	136	245	17	13
Livingston	577	3.4	38,010	1,883	241	46	17	74	105	151	378	23	17
McDonald	618	3.8	27,094	3,059	269	47	19	31	78	175	366	25	19
Macon	620	1.8	40,631	1,454	185	41	13	97	98	163	336	22	13
Madison	434	3.2	35,432	2,282	123	26	10	24	61	164	182	14	10
Maries	283	3.0	31,955	2,755	45	10	3	10	53	85	68	7	3
Marion	1,114	2.9	38,916	1,734	556	91	43	71	176	321	761	50	43
Mercer	125	7.2	33,890	2,494	35	6	3	27	22	33	72	4	3
Miller	874	3.8	34,635	2,397	250	48	19	82	140	234	399	27	19
Mississippi	436	5.7	32,093	2,742	130	27	9	66	68	148	233	14	9
Moniteau	568	7.0	35,375	2,289	147	31	11	66	98	117	255	15	11
Monroe	338	-5.1	39,260	1,680	74	17	5	28	59	89	123	9	5
Montgomery	467	5.9	40,795	1,434	110	21	8	53	73	121	192	12	8
Morgan	804	4.4	39,893	1,571	141	28	10	94	269	237	273	21	10
New Madrid	550	3.9	31,290	2,833	251	45	19	6	85	198	322	23	19
Newton	2,170	3.2	37,232	1,994	871	147	63	155	340	505	1,236	81	63
Nodaway	653	1.6	29,079	2,981	297	68	21	47	134	160	433	27	21
Oregon	296	0.7	28,022	3,029	89	17	9	20	45	127	136	12	9
Osage	585	1.2	42,816	1,166	149	29	11	89	100	102	278	17	11
Ozark	268	2.6	29,142	2,979	46	11	3	16	49	110	76	8	3
Pemiscot	561	3.4	33,326	2,578	181	40	13	36	79	216	270	18	13
Perry	743	1.9	38,628	1,786	403	67	29	44	107	178	543	34	29
Pettis	1,540	3.2	36,186	2,177	751	135	55	139	237	425	1,080	67	55
Phelps	1,674	3.3	37,422	1,964	779	166	53	90	318	424	1,089	65	53
Pike	626	2.8	33,735	2,521	201	44	14	68	127	165	328	20	14
Platte	5,554	4.4	54,893	285	2,419	324	170	387	842	648	3,299	199	170
Polk	1,015	4.3	31,938	2,759	325	69	23	66	163	309	483	33	23
Pulaski	2,059	3.4	39,542	1,628	1,159	325	108	42	395	390	1,634	76	108
Putnam	167	2.3	34,693	2,391	38	9	3	21	35	55	70	5	3
Ralls	411	2.8	40,220	1,516	169	28	12	46	59	93	255	16	12
Randolph	966	5.0	38,726	1,770	386	77	29	129	130	265	621	39	29
Ray	917	3.3	40,116	1,533	173	40	13	52	122	217	278	21	13
Reynolds	202	3.5	32,238	2,722	75	15	6	5	41	80	101	8	6
Ripley	410	2.3	30,206	2,911	80	18	6	27	55	175	131	12	6
St. Charles	19,888	4.8	50,284	444	7,288	1,040	523	1,046	2,571	2,712	9,896	621	523
St. Clair	271	2.8	28,955	2,988	52	12	4	19	51	114	87	8	4
Ste. Genevieve	662	4.0	37,106	2,012	42	174	20	14	118	164	342	24	20
St. Francois	2,158	3.7	32,349	2,708	845	174	60	82	317	711	1,161	80	60
St. Louis	66,809	3.7	67,029	84	39,176	4,830	2,693	5,193	18,648	8,834	51,891	3,122	2,693
Saline	866	2.0	38,228	1,838	332	62	24	112	142	238	529	31	24
Schuyler	124	4.3	27,614	3,042	19	6	1	7	23	38	34	3	1
Scotland	161	3.6	32,434	2,699	41	11	3	25	33	42	81	5	3
Scott	1,474	2.7	38,255	1,836	641	107	49	122	236	455	919	62	49
Shannon	233	2.3	28,210	3,023	42	10	3	18	39	85	73	7	3
Shelby	225	-0.5	37,346	1,979	56	13	4	22	46	59	95	7	4
Stoddard	1,040	1.5	35,407	2,284	393	69	30	70	159	328	562	41	30
Stone	1,135	3.8	35,794	2,229	236	39	18	64	240	344	356	33	18
Sullivan	242	5.5	38,892	1,739	119	19	8	30	34	66	176	10	8
Taney	1,904	3.7	34,394	2,429	1,012	145	78	235	300	526	1,470	98	78
Texas	680	2.8	26,425	3,071	195	49	14	30	126	239	287	22	14
Vernon	726	4.7	35,519	2,273	279	64	20	87	116	219	450	26	20
Warren	1,344	4.5	39,093	1,703	310	54	23	66	187	295	453	33	23
Washington	704	3.3	28,139	3,025	164	39	12	21	75	266	236	19	12
Wayne	384	2.5	28,879	2,991	79	18	6	16	65	166	120	12	6
Webster	1,209	4.1	31,268	2,834	260	53	19	87	160	311	418	33	19
Worth	75	4.3	36,236	2,164	12	3	1	13	15	19	28	2	1
Wright	565	3.3	30,848	2,866	140	30	10	39	90	204	219	18	10

1. Based on the resident population estimated as of July 1 of the year shown.

Table B. States and Counties — Earnings, Social Security, and Housing

STATE County	Earnings, 2017 (cont.)									Social Security beneficiaries, December 2017			Housing units, 2018	
	Percent by selected industries											Supplemental Security Income recipients, 2017		
	Farm	Mining, quarrying, and extractions	Construction	Manu-facturing	Information; professional, scientific, technical services	Retail trade	Finance, insurance, real estate, and leasing	Health care and social assistance	Govern-ment	Number	Rate[1]		Total	Percent change, 2010-2018
	75	76	77	78	79	80	81	82	83	84	85	86	87	88
MISSOURI— Cont'd														
Jasper	1.2	0.2	4.7	23.8	4.4	8	4.2	9.9	10.4	25,190	210	3,562	51,797	2.2
Jefferson	0	0.5	13.3	10.6	4.4	8.9	5.5	11.8	18.3	46,320	207	2,909	91,627	4.6
Johnson	0.2	D	4.8	6.1	2.3	4.6	3.8	4.3	59.7	8,575	159	744	22,388	4
Knox	4.7	D	10.9	12.6	D	5.3	D	2.8	21.3	1,035	260	102	2,273	-0.7
Laclede	0	0.1	5	42.8	D	9	4	8.5	10.9	9,250	261	1,205	16,034	1.6
Lafayette	5	0	11.4	10	D	8.3	5.4	8.6	22.1	7,730	237	575	14,826	0.7
Lawrence	1	D	10	18.1	4.7	8.9	4.6	D	22.1	9,635	251	863	16,716	0.4
Lewis	4.2	D	8.1	6.9	D	5.8	4	D	20.7	2,390	240	191	4,544	0.2
Lincoln	2	1.3	14.1	17.1	D	6.3	5.7	7.8	17	11,015	196	862	21,847	4
Linn	2.3	0.1	D	19.7	5.5	6.6	5.5	9.9	16.6	3,250	267	368	6,386	-0.7
Livingston	6.8	D	7.5	8.6	2.6	10.1	4.8	D	19.9	3,590	237	330	6,836	1.6
McDonald	-0.3	D	9.7	41.8	D	7.7	2.2	2.7	14.8	4,535	199	595	9,966	0.4
Macon	0.2	0.1	5.6	25.9	7.4	5.6	4.5	D	25.5	4,255	279	313	7,672	0.1
Madison	2.9	D	10.1	12.6	D	9.8	2.6	9.8	24.4	3,660	299	545	5,988	0.3
Maries	-1.8	0.1	7	20.2	D	8.5	D	7.8	22.9	2,365	267	137	4,627	0.3
Marion	0.4	D	7	9.2	D	8.9	5.6	D	13.6	6,925	242	1,021	13,079	2
Mercer	30.7	D	D	D	D	4.4	3.4	6.2	17.4	955	260	66	2,128	-0.3
Miller	6.8	D	11.6	8.5	2.9	12	4.5	D	19.1	5,960	236	571	12,956	1.5
Mississippi	20	0	1.7	4.6	D	6	6.4	D	22.7	3,285	242	694	5,723	0.2
Moniteau	12.1	D	15.2	15.6	2.1	6.4	3.6	D	21.3	3,255	203	216	6,178	0
Monroe	11.5	D	6.1	10.3	2.1	2.9	7.5	D	27.4	2,350	273	180	4,853	1.1
Montgomery	15.8	0.7	9.9	18.8	2.9	6.2	D	5.4	17.3	3,110	272	271	6,263	2.2
Morgan	8.8	D	14.6	8.3	D	15.7	5.3	D	17.3	6,380	317	592	15,593	0.5
New Madrid	-3.6	0	2.7	16.1	D	14	2.6	D	15.7	4,255	242	849	8,608	0.9
Newton	2.4	D	7.4	13.8	2.5	7.4	3.1	29.6	11.3	13,120	225	937	24,790	2
Nodaway	-2	D	5.2	19.9	3.3	8.4	4.8	12.5	29.7	4,060	181	296	9,779	2.7
Oregon	2.9	D	3.5	5.5	D	8.4	3.1	12.8	18.7	3,075	291	579	5,479	-0.1
Osage	5.2	0.7	11.2	40.3	D	4.7	2.7	3.9	13.9	2,855	209	130	6,686	1.4
Ozark	-4.8	0.1	9.2	9.3	D	7	8.3	D	26.6	3,255	354	284	5,700	0.9
Pemiscot	7.2	D	D	D	D	7.1	4.2	12.1	27.5	4,360	259	1,281	8,175	0.2
Perry	0.9	0	10.3	30.1	3.9	6.6	5	D	13.7	4,505	234	364	8,808	2.8
Pettis	1.4	D	4.7	25.3	6.9	7.5	3.8	8.7	17.7	9,285	218	1,260	18,253	0
Phelps	-0.4	0.1	3.9	7.1	3	8.1	4	15.1	37.6	9,250	207	1,175	20,475	4.8
Pike	6.4	D	12	7.8	4.3	11.3	3.2	6.3	27.3	4,105	221	409	7,929	0.7
Platte	0.3	D	8.3	11.7	7.2	7.3	6.6	6.3	10.4	15,995	158	702	42,366	8
Polk	0.4	D	7.2	2.5	D	7.9	4.3	10.7	32.8	7,035	221	888	13,618	2.4
Pulaski	-0.1	D	1.8	D	D	3.3	1.8	2.5	79.3	6,935	133	883	19,165	7
Putnam	17.9	0	D	D	D	7.7	7.3	2.8	28.8	1,325	275	134	2,983	0
Ralls	9.7	0	D	48.9	D	3.2	D	D	8.3	2,575	252	115	5,197	0.3
Randolph	1.2	D	3.6	10	2.4	15.8	7.1	9.3	17.9	5,400	216	838	10,772	0.5
Ray	0.2	D	9.8	13.9	D	8.7	4.4	D	26.8	5,310	232	326	10,106	1.2
Reynolds	-1.5	D	D	15.4	D	3.6	D	10.1	18.6	1,920	306	248	4,029	0
Ripley	1.3	0	6.2	15.5	1.9	10.2	3.7	14.5	27	4,000	295	767	6,627	0.4
St. Charles	0.2	D	8.8	13.7	11.4	7.6	10.1	10	11.2	69,630	176	2,737	156,324	10.8
St. Clair	5	D	6.3	4.2	D	10.9	4.7	9.9	29.1	2,900	310	264	5,651	0.2
Ste. Genevieve	-0.7	4.9	8.9	11.8	D	5.6	3.9	D	18.7	4,335	243	300	8,730	1.1
St. Francois	-0.2	0.5	7.2	8.9	2.7	9.3	7	14.8	27.1	16,505	247	2,500	30,244	6.3
St. Louis	0	0.1	5.7	9.7	13.5	5.6	12.1	12.8	7.7	204,355	205	18,012	441,973	0.9
Saline	11.3	0.1	3.1	23.5	2.2	6.5	3.6	D	16.7	5,100	225	610	10,189	0.7
Schuyler	-8.1	0	22.4	D	D	8.9	3.2	3.3	37.8	960	213	113	2,095	-0.3
Scotland	8.7	D	6.8	6.1	D	8.3	D	D	38.1	970	195	56	2,369	0
Scott	1.4	0.2	6.1	15.3	5.4	5.2	5.1	D	14	10,395	270	1,729	17,300	1.8
Shannon	-3.4	D	D	26.9	D	5.4	3.9	7.6	22	2,255	273	355	4,162	0
Shelby	2.5	D	7.2	12.4	4.1	11.7	4.9	D	26	1,560	259	124	3,202	-0.1
Stoddard	-2.9	D	8	28.6	D	8.4	7	D	13.9	8,185	279	1,105	13,751	1
Stone	0.1	D	13.5	1.6	4.3	8.9	5.5	6.5	16.6	10,240	323	566	21,257	4.3
Sullivan	19	0	3.1	D	3.3	3.5	2.8	3.2	13.6	1,560	250	196	3,341	-0.5
Taney	0	D	4.7	2.2	4	10.3	4.4	D	9.8	14,775	267	1,152	31,005	6
Texas	0.8	D	6.6	16.4	D	8.1	4	5.9	34.9	6,325	246	760	11,727	0.4
Vernon	11.8	0.2	4.5	21.5	2.5	5.8	6.6	D	20.7	4,880	239	619	9,590	1
Warren	0.1	D	13.6	25.4	3.4	5.7	5.5	D	16.4	7,530	219	526	15,714	7
Washington	-1.1	D	6.6	10.7	D	6.5	5.4	D	37.4	6,045	242	1,146	11,051	0.3
Wayne	-1.1	D	4.8	11.5	D	6.7	3.2	13.7	24.7	4,125	310	752	8,096	0.1
Webster	-0.9	D	13.3	15.2	D	9.1	4.1	D	18.3	8,635	223	834	14,831	2.9
Worth	27.6	D	D	D	D	7.1	3.2	3.8	26.6	555	270	42	1,270	-0.8
Wright	-1.4	D	9.3	11.1	D	13.3	5.1	D	20.4	5,375	293	832	8,717	0.2

1. Per 1,000 resident population estimated as of July 1 of the year shown.

Table B. States and Counties — Housing, Labor Force, and Employment

STATE County	Housing units, 2013-2017 Owner-occupied Total	Percent	Median value[1]	Median owner cost as a percent of income With a mortgage	Without a mortgage[2]	Renter-occupied Median rent[3]	Median rent as a percent of income[2]	Sub-standard units[4] (percent)	Civilian labor force, 2018 Total	Percent change, 2017-2018	Unemployment Total	Rate[5]	Civilian employment[6], 2013-2017 Total	Percent Management, business, science, and arts	Construction, production, and maintenance occupations
	89	90	91	92	93	94	95	96	97	98	99	100	101	102	103
MISSOURI— Cont'd															
Jasper	46,009	64.6	112,700	19.3	11.1	748	28.5	2.5	56,624	-0.4	1,555	2.7	56,319	30.3	27.7
Jefferson	83,744	79.9	154,100	20.4	10.9	824	28	2	116,200	-0.2	3,620	3.1	109,196	31.3	25.7
Johnson	19,918	59.8	147,000	19.5	10.0	754	29.5	2.5	22,777	-2.3	844	3.7	24,278	32.3	24.0
Knox	1,602	79.0	72,400	22.4	12.8	503	23.6	3.4	1,922	-3.6	54	2.8	1,642	33.3	32.6
Laclede	13,825	67.6	112,700	19.6	10.7	633	30.5	3.2	16,785	0.9	620	3.7	14,894	26.6	36.5
Lafayette	13,224	72.9	122,600	19.8	10.9	648	25.4	2.1	16,991	-0.1	545	3.2	15,277	27.4	31.9
Lawrence	14,636	70.7	98,000	19.6	11.8	650	25.2	3.3	18,100	1.2	552	3	16,701	27.7	31.5
Lewis	3,754	72.9	85,500	18.1	10.7	522	22	2.8	5,099	-0.4	145	2.8	4,814	23.6	36.5
Lincoln	18,698	77.0	154,100	20.9	10.3	828	29	2.1	27,367	-0.2	904	3.3	25,119	25.6	35.0
Linn	4,997	73.0	80,400	18.4	11.2	528	26.8	1.8	5,133	-2.6	241	4.7	5,516	26.3	31.9
Livingston	5,813	66.8	106,000	18.3	10.5	630	24	2.3	7,500	0.4	187	2.5	6,637	29.5	24.4
McDonald	8,137	70.7	97,000	19.9	11.0	600	24.4	7.9	10,507	1	319	3	9,010	20.0	41.1
Macon	6,023	74.1	89,000	19.1	12.9	492	25.9	1.7	7,661	0.9	225	2.9	6,388	27.9	33.6
Madison	4,867	71.2	99,800	20.5	10.2	564	30.5	3.1	5,464	-0.7	194	3.6	4,976	20.9	36.2
Maries	3,667	73.0	122,800	23.2	10.0	585	27.7	3.2	3,874	-1.3	128	3.3	3,705	24.6	38.7
Marion	11,311	64.0	113,500	19.4	11.3	643	25.6	1.7	14,450	-0.8	447	3.1	13,150	30.3	30.5
Mercer	1,390	76.0	82,500	17.6	11.6	527	22.1	6.5	1,910	-2	60	3.1	1,594	32.4	34.6
Miller	9,514	74.8	126,500	22.0	10.1	638	28.2	2.2	12,112	0.6	443	3.7	11,068	25.6	27.2
Mississippi	5,128	60.6	73,400	20.4	12.8	586	30.1	4.5	5,937	-2	227	3.8	4,796	21.9	31.9
Moniteau	5,373	76.8	118,400	18.8	10.0	564	23.2	2.2	7,223	-2	216	3	6,715	29.0	31.2
Monroe	3,615	74.4	103,100	19.9	10.0	556	25.2	2	3,960	-2.8	141	3.6	3,893	24.6	33.2
Montgomery	4,844	72.2	105,300	21.1	11.6	653	25.3	2.3	5,693	0.5	164	2.9	5,012	28.3	35.6
Morgan	7,774	75.4	115,600	23.3	13.3	609	27.8	2	7,945	-0.1	339	4.3	7,121	23.8	30.4
New Madrid	7,309	62.6	74,500	17.1	13.6	598	29.3	2.8	8,046	0.4	384	4.8	6,939	24.0	33.1
Newton	22,151	71.6	118,200	19.3	11.3	666	26	2.6	27,232	-0.5	821	3	27,120	28.9	31.3
Nodaway	8,493	56.1	117,800	19.1	11.2	627	26.4	1.9	10,650	-0.1	312	2.9	11,535	29.9	24.0
Oregon	4,375	77.3	87,200	22.1	10.0	458	37	1.5	3,936	-2.2	136	3.5	4,158	26.1	35.5
Osage	5,108	82.6	140,500	19.4	10.0	564	23.2	1.5	6,996	-1.8	169	2.4	6,890	27.6	31.1
Ozark	4,075	78.4	91,800	20.1	11.6	608	35.5	3.6	3,461	-3.1	179	5.2	3,107	28.5	37.3
Pemiscot	6,875	52.8	73,300	19.3	12.2	568	28.8	3.7	6,349	-3.3	352	5.5	6,326	24.7	34.2
Perry	7,529	76.5	131,900	19.1	10.0	651	26.6	1.5	10,173	0.5	238	2.3	9,166	29.3	35.3
Pettis	16,031	67.2	111,400	20.3	11.1	695	27.4	2.9	20,716	-0.9	857	4.1	18,739	27.9	32.7
Phelps	17,330	60.9	126,100	18.8	10.0	701	29.4	1.8	19,662	-0.3	606	3.1	19,096	39.4	20.3
Pike	6,741	71.3	106,500	19.6	11.2	636	23.7	2.7	7,674	-3.4	277	3.6	7,527	26.5	32.4
Platte	38,147	65.2	204,900	19.4	10.9	953	25.3	1.5	57,812	0.1	1,482	2.6	51,998	43.5	16.4
Polk	11,717	66.6	122,600	20.0	10.0	667	28.8	2.8	14,329	0.8	523	3.6	13,901	34.4	26.7
Pulaski	15,375	48.2	141,700	21.8	10.0	991	24	2.1	14,629	-0.7	526	3.6	16,142	34.4	24.0
Putnam	1,956	72.8	84,500	23.9	13.2	540	27.6	1.7	2,440	-0.4	84	3.4	2,041	29.2	37.5
Ralls	3,994	82.3	126,000	20.8	10.7	715	23.7	2.2	5,618	-0.7	158	2.8	5,003	27.1	32.4
Randolph	8,348	75.4	93,800	18.8	11.5	624	30.4	1.6	10,257	-0.3	394	3.8	10,098	29.0	27.1
Ray	8,684	77.5	129,700	19.5	10.6	673	28	2.1	11,048	-0.6	397	3.6	10,601	26.0	36.9
Reynolds	2,628	78.5	90,300	19.5	10.0	562	27.3	2.1	3,039	-3	94	3.1	2,527	25.6	39.7
Ripley	5,397	76.8	87,800	22.6	11.8	514	30.1	2.1	5,129	-2.5	267	5.2	5,364	27.7	28.4
St. Charles	142,554	80.2	198,500	19.2	10.8	993	26.6	0.9	221,947	-0.1	5,637	2.5	206,974	42.8	16.9
St. Clair	4,135	75.2	78,500	22.1	13.0	483	26.1	6	3,781	-2.8	165	4.4	3,406	29.1	31.9
Ste. Genevieve	7,185	77.2	148,800	19.3	10.7	666	28.9	1.7	9,195	1	257	2.8	8,510	24.7	38.3
St. Francois	24,661	68.6	110,200	19.9	11.3	636	28.1	2.8	26,504		969	3.7	26,288	26.1	28.2
St. Louis	402,307	69.5	181,100	20.0	11.7	937	28.8	1.3	525,125	-0.2	15,801	3	496,931	44.4	14.2
Saline	8,754	68.6	96,700	20.6	12.9	628	27.9	3	10,732	0.4	326	3	10,546	29.8	31.5
Schuyler	1,669	72.4	72,500	19.6	13.9	476	25.3	3.3	1,977	0.8	82	4.1	1,911	27.1	33.9
Scotland	1,870	71.4	82,000	23.6	10.0	475	21.9	4	2,380	-3.2	68	2.9	2,156	34.5	30.4
Scott	15,241	68.9	103,300	18.4	10.2	624	27.1	4	20,017	-0.7	684	3.4	17,102	27.3	30.2
Shannon	3,158	71.7	101,400	21.9	10.7	559	27.3	5.6	3,241	-1.4	162	5	2,901	24.3	47.8
Shelby	2,446	73.8	70,300	19.9	11.5	554	18.8	2.4	3,018	-2.6	92	3	2,938	27.7	35.4
Stoddard	11,773	69.3	91,300	20.8	11.4	594	27.6	1.8	13,090	-1.3	581	4.4	12,837	26.5	33.8
Stone	12,880	80.0	160,600	22.1	11.1	723	30.4	1.8	13,763	-0.6	644	4.7	12,223	27.8	27.3
Sullivan	2,283	73.9	77,700	19.7	12.8	584	19.2	3.4	2,811	1.9	88	3.1	2,681	28.0	42.3
Taney	22,142	59.5	124,400	23.4	12.2	761	28.1	3	26,828	-0.6	1,395	5.2	24,422	27.3	17.4
Texas	9,303	74.1	105,800	20.4	10.7	566	33.2	3.2	9,043	-3.7	370	4.1	8,748	25.7	32.6
Vernon	8,170	68.3	97,100	20.0	11.3	642	27.7	2.7	9,557	-1.1	301	3.1	9,505	31.6	29.5
Warren	12,032	79.7	166,100	19.7	10.8	803	30.7	4.2	17,560	-0.3	493	2.8	14,824	26.2	33.3
Washington	9,048	81.9	90,400	21.2	11.4	498	27.3	3.3	10,205	-1.1	453	4.4	9,112	21.4	38.4
Wayne	5,482	76.7	72,700	20.2	10.1	557	28.7	2.8	5,322	-4.1	258	4.8	4,501	26.0	31.7
Webster	13,311	72.8	122,500	19.2	10.0	614	26.8	6.2	16,916	0.4	525	3.1	15,097	24.9	35.0
Worth	888	75.6	60,600	17.9	10.0	503	20.5	2.3	1,193	0	34	2.8	965	32.4	28.3
Wright	7,488	68.3	89,500	21.1	10.4	531	28.3	4.2	7,425	-2.7	307	4.1	6,631	22.9	38.4

1. Specified owner-occupied units.   2. A value of 10.0 represents 10 percent or less; a value of 50.0 represents 50 percent or more.   3. Specified renter-occupied units.   4. Overcrowded or lacking complete plumbing facilities.   5. Percent of civilian labor force.   6. Civilian employed persons 16 years old and over.

Table B. States and Counties — Nonfarm Employment and Agriculture

STATE County	Private nonfarm establishments, employment and payroll, 2016									Agriculture, 2017			
		Employment						Annual payroll		Farms			Farm producers whose primary occupation is farming (percent)
							Professional, scientific, and technical services				Percent with:		
	Number of establishments	Total	Health care and social assistance	Manufacturing	Retail trade	Finance and insurance		Total (mil dol)	Average per employee (dollars)	Number	Fewer than 50 acres	1000 acres or more	
	104	105	106	107	108	109	110	111	112	113	114	115	116
MISSOURI— Cont'd													
Jasper	2,823	48,567	6,337	9,526	8,342	1,164	1,017	1,842	37,920	1,315	42.1	3.3	38.1
Jefferson	4,058	41,468	5,976	4,359	7,598	1,279	1,432	1,472	35,488	721	43.7	1.1	37.2
Johnson	942	10,548	2,282	1,531	1,751	317	439	312	29,566	1,626	37.8	5.0	36.2
Knox	95	709	36	D	120	48	30	18	25,433	637	18.8	9.3	41.9
Laclede	782	11,681	1,601	4,344	2,022	320	171	371	31,754	1,304	27.7	2.3	36.5
Lafayette	712	6,389	1,143	944	944	250	204	196	30,602	1,175	38.5	7.7	39.2
Lawrence	735	7,174	1,446	1,194	1,447	186	136	235	32,819	1,697	41.8	3.2	40.0
Lewis	187	2,140	280	128	324	95	47	54	25,145	636	27.8	9.6	33.5
Lincoln	916	8,943	1,216	1,260	1,764	338	190	327	36,565	1,092	41.9	4.3	36.0
Linn	292	3,251	482	956	522	149	91	104	32,042	994	23.7	7.7	36.9
Livingston	424	4,982	937	513	1,250	189	131	158	31,705	784	22.1	9.3	35.9
McDonald	311	5,228	279	2,702	936	116	33	164	31,436	940	26.9	1.9	40.2
Macon	352	3,733	535	538	707	178	316	112	29,897	1,163	22.0	8.1	37.7
Madison	299	3,330	1,058	265	600	73	75	87	26,131	361	19.9	2.5	39.9
Maries	131	1,065	158	159	234	104	17	31	29,175	879	14.9	3.1	36.6
Marion	843	12,304	2,997	1,891	1,959	395	252	429	34,889	587	26.9	9.5	36.6
Mercer	69	452	66	D	135	34	14	11	25,423	493	16.0	8.3	40.2
Miller	673	6,331	512	706	1,869	246	160	187	29,610	1,023	19.7	3.4	36.7
Mississippi	268	2,342	394	86	428	142	75	68	29,069	159	13.8	53.5	70.4
Moniteau	324	2,762	334	625	451	121	64	88	31,845	1,135	28.7	3.2	40.5
Monroe	189	1,573	242	499	262	67	19	43	27,403	978	23.6	7.3	35.1
Montgomery	258	2,218	383	508	349	104	24	75	33,762	698	26.8	9.5	38.8
Morgan	488	3,330	328	582	866	116	87	89	26,779	962	29.4	3.5	46.8
New Madrid	488	6,342	971	1,573	1,508	166	57	203	31,949	290	15.2	50.3	62.3
Newton	1,218	21,028	6,086	2,952	2,135	535	414	793	37,712	1,588	37.1	1.7	38.0
Nodaway	477	6,062	1,083	1,443	1,109	166	145	186	30,762	1,133	24.4	10.5	42.7
Oregon	224	1,726	503	173	485	47	30	37	21,177	564	19.5	8.0	44.6
Osage	273	3,329	319	1,446	462	121	24	113	33,977	1,277	15.8	3.4	33.2
Ozark	170	979	117	99	197	72	41	21	21,355	705	15.0	4.7	46.4
Pemiscot	436	4,407	1,391	D	730	134	50	138	31,311	184	14.1	49.5	63.6
Perry	516	10,012	1,107	4,139	1,181	252	184	340	33,960	921	27.3	4.3	37.4
Pettis	1,043	17,480	3,042	4,015	2,661	379	1,470	598	34,196	1,259	34.3	8.2	40.8
Phelps	1,121	13,867	3,394	1,035	2,396	436	314	455	32,835	728	32.1	2.6	32.0
Pike	409	4,480	824	659	686	151	86	142	31,678	926	26.0	9.1	36.0
Platte	2,389	39,824	3,420	3,192	6,700	1,817	1,540	1,675	42,048	490	41.6	8.0	30.9
Polk	594	7,627	2,014	451	1,087	206	710	320	41,995	1,562	32.8	2.9	42.0
Pulaski	718	8,539	1,704	211	1,834	384	341	258	30,167	502	25.7	1.6	36.8
Putnam	91	630	127	83	211	59	D	18	28,762	585	14.5	10.1	46.1
Ralls	201	2,492	187	1,338	177	44	18	126	50,376	672	25.0	10.1	37.3
Randolph	592	7,679	1,309	955	1,247	585	90	271	35,252	783	32.4	5.5	31.8
Ray	360	2,990	592	380	623	105	101	97	32,342	1,070	30.7	5.0	33.1
Reynolds	157	1,410	244	331	127	35	4	57	40,662	341	22.0	1.8	31.6
Ripley	446	2,548	992	441	489	75	25	49	19,323	438	25.1	5.3	37.4
St. Charles	8,541	134,424	17,016	14,008	20,992	10,054	7,394	5,701	42,408	604	45.0	8.1	39.1
St. Clair	168	1,385	505	68	367	91	28	35	25,471	734	18.1	7.4	43.8
Ste. Genevieve	401	5,032	899	1,496	492	161	80	199	39,605	660	26.4	3.6	39.4
St. Francois	1,552	18,703	4,962	1,770	3,256	970	338	581	31,060	688	34.9	1.9	31.7
St. Louis	33,603	588,926	92,665	41,765	70,417	31,897	46,566	31,755	53,921	184	67.4	3.8	33.7
Saline	485	7,774	1,442	2,443	986	249	90	236	30,338	882	21.5	14.9	45.2
Schuyler	68	342	D	D	109	16	D	10	27,789	541	23.7	6.3	42.4
Scotland	139	842	D	92	175	48	21	25	29,570	713	24.1	7.0	41.1
Scott	1,126	13,952	3,500	2,510	1,525	398	338	484	34,670	450	35.1	15.6	39.9
Shannon	181	1,171	163	594	153	53	6	26	22,190	435	25.3	6.0	37.0
Shelby	164	939	92	161	228	46	45	27	28,920	628	20.2	13.5	31.4
Stoddard	716	8,663	1,754	2,641	1,287	408	183	306	35,273	792	31.1	22.6	46.4
Stone	688	4,147	432	97	854	150	76	127	30,724	628	35.7	1.8	34.9
Sullivan	104	2,023	208	D	154	49	15	77	38,124	671	11.6	10.6	46.3
Taney	1,833	25,056	2,105	458	5,069	506	688	722	28,830	395	26.6	4.8	38.1
Texas	527	4,238	965	871	779	157	66	123	28,919	1,371	25.2	4.2	43.1
Vernon	525	5,895	1,536	1,059	952	405	128	187	31,702	1,265	24.5	8.3	39.8
Warren	579	6,190	652	1,230	983	234	130	214	34,496	568	37.7	4.8	32.7
Washington	372	3,347	765	456	586	129	45	93	27,687	502	27.5	3.0	41.8
Wayne	298	1,692	386	442	344	68	32	38	22,193	340	15.9	4.7	41.6
Webster	662	5,411	547	889	1,183	230	220	165	30,569	1,837	37.5	1.3	39.0
Worth	47	225	22	46	80	14	D	5	22,516	336	17.6	9.8	35.2
Wright	401	3,484	507	482	963	187	51	96	27,462	1,115	20.4	3.9	45.0

Table B. States and Counties — **Agriculture**

STATE County	Land in farms					Value of land and buildings (dollars)		Value of machinery and equiopmnet, average per farm (dollars)	Value of products sold:				Organic farms (number)	Farms with internet access (percent)	Government payments	
	Acreage (1,000)	Percent change, 2012-2017	Acres			Average per farm	Average per acre		Total (mil dol)	Average per farm (acres)	Percent from:				Total ($1,000)	Percent of farms
			Average size of farm	Total irrigated (1,000)	Total cropland (1,000)						Crops	Livestock and poultry products				
	117	118	119	120	121	122	123	124	125	126	127	128	129	130	131	132
MISSOURI— Cont'd																
Jasper	265	7.2	201	5.3	141.2	647,953	3,221	94,672	97.2	73,947	48.1	51.9	NA	75.6	1,639	26.0
Jefferson	91	-6.5	126	0.2	34.6	531,201	4,200	50,306	12.9	17,870	58.2	41.8	NA	76.1	263	10.0
Johnson	384	-1.8	236	3.0	227.5	789,475	3,344	92,874	139.9	86,061	45.1	54.9	5	78.2	3,545	32.8
Knox	235	-16.2	370	0.4	161.7	1,124,020	3,042	140,644	97.9	153,615	52.8	47.2	8	60.8	4,645	66.4
Laclede	298	-6.8	229	0.3	75.0	575,705	2,517	64,847	45.5	34,913	11.6	88.4	NA	70.7	208	6.5
Lafayette	341	4.2	290	1.4	265.3	1,314,426	4,535	155,252	163.3	138,955	80.6	19.4	3	79.2	2,775	36.9
Lawrence	302	-2.8	178	2.9	124.1	569,764	3,198	87,304	241.0	142,032	8.9	91.1	2	69.7	1,526	12.9
Lewis	214	-24.8	336	D	153.0	1,112,669	3,312	120,524	83.6	131,465	72.2	27.8	13	68.6	3,114	58.2
Lincoln	227	-19.1	208	1.3	157.0	908,336	4,361	98,978	86.3	79,056	69.5	30.5	3	75.9	2,891	42.1
Linn	331	-1.5	333	1.3	206.7	958,778	2,883	107,802	76.4	76,814	59.7	40.3	12	68.8	7,019	56.0
Livingston	285	0.6	364	D	215.1	1,227,229	3,372	133,506	86.1	109,776	88.0	12.0	5	72.3	6,686	62.0
McDonald	191	2.6	204	0.1	44.8	546,226	2,682	77,040	197.5	210,061	2.3	97.7	7	75.7	409	7.3
Macon	393	1.7	338	0.6	236.9	1,078,661	3,194	101,249	116.9	100,521	59.9	40.1	6	69.1	4,513	50.6
Madison	94	-12.1	261	D	22.3	547,402	2,099	56,907	16.3	45,169	4.9	95.1	NA	65.9	120	8.9
Maries	248	2.9	283	0.5	64.3	557,083	1,971	69,007	32.4	36,879	14.6	85.4	NA	70.0	513	13.5
Marion	233	5.0	396	4.8	182.5	1,571,407	3,966	156,078	99.1	168,853	76.7	23.3	1	68.3	2,268	59.6
Mercer	194	-14.6	393	0.0	99.5	1,058,158	2,693	74,366	82.2	166,748	28.4	71.6	2	74.8	3,029	59.2
Miller	258	3.8	252	1.6	68.1	629,480	2,497	77,397	96.7	94,539	6.4	93.6	NA	72.5	256	10.0
Mississippi	251	2.3	1,576	116.8	243.1	9,200,783	5,837	631,538	D	D	D	D	NA	78.6	5,337	90.6
Moniteau	227	-3.6	200	0.4	104.6	713,079	3,570	84,169	144.7	127,456	21.3	78.7	7	69.2	2,023	31.4
Monroe	340	-4.4	348	1.2	226.8	1,237,626	3,559	106,640	133.8	136,833	59.6	40.4	4	69.1	5,907	61.8
Montgomery	221	-20.8	317	3.3	144.7	1,194,722	3,771	123,954	93.7	134,219	63.5	36.5	7	71.8	2,612	50.1
Morgan	210	6.2	219	0.2	85.4	839,556	3,837	87,885	199.4	207,225	9.9	90.1	9	61.9	1,243	13.7
New Madrid	418	21.4	1,443	257.3	410.5	8,066,767	5,591	659,481	231.5	798,286	100.0	0.0	NA	78.6	11,682	91.4
Newton	261	5.5	165	0.5	91.3	598,888	3,639	75,574	246.0	154,909	6.2	93.8	1	73.0	776	12.1
Nodaway	440	3.8	388	1.6	325.4	1,557,349	4,012	144,528	152.2	134,308	84.0	16.0	6	76.8	5,833	54.8
Oregon	201	-20.7	357	0.0	27.3	635,970	1,781	65,952	23.3	41,250	4.5	95.5	2	72.5	349	11.3
Osage	320	13.0	251	1.3	101.5	605,323	2,415	79,274	80.7	63,186	21.5	78.5	NA	68.8	1,009	21.1
Ozark	227	-0.8	322	1.0	30.4	686,823	2,133	68,929	25.1	35,644	6.3	93.7	1	73.3	332	6.1
Pemiscot	296	-2.9	1,610	148.1	286.7	8,426,555	5,235	614,890	159.2	865,217	100.0	0.0	1	77.2	6,158	89.1
Perry	219	-3.4	237	1.4	124.6	776,958	3,273	100,770	62.8	68,172	57.0	43.0	NA	64.7	3,033	56.8
Pettis	389	-7.2	309	0.7	240.0	1,082,193	3,500	118,802	239.1	189,934	35.5	64.5	17	69.7	5,057	42.2
Phelps	160	1.4	219	0.1	29.4	577,647	2,636	70,254	14.0	19,231	17.7	82.3	1	79.5	287	10.3
Pike	311	-14.1	336	5.0	207.8	1,179,923	3,516	141,497	133.2	143,811	59.4	40.6	2	62.7	2,795	50.2
Platte	161	5.6	330	4.5	126.9	1,459,303	4,429	144,958	60.0	122,516	88.5	11.5	1	77.8	1,255	34.1
Polk	359	6.9	230	2.4	103.4	581,099	2,525	66,217	99.4	63,609	11.1	88.9	23	71.1	613	10.7
Pulaski	111	-0.9	222	0.2	24.2	496,821	2,237	58,444	27.2	54,127	4.7	95.3	NA	73.7	60	4.8
Putnam	264	-9.7	452	D	132.6	1,138,477	2,520	103,874	93.9	160,557	23.9	76.1	NA	73.8	1,964	52.6
Ralls	243	-14.2	362	D	181.4	1,392,728	3,850	138,653	79.5	118,344	81.3	18.7	NA	73.4	3,524	68.2
Randolph	213	1.6	272	0.7	123.7	940,599	3,461	84,856	81.3	103,847	45.5	54.5	9	74.1	2,853	43.9
Ray	267	-2.49	249	4.6	179.5	876,483	3,516	98,521	79.0	73,842	80.9	19.1	3	73.2	3,613	46.2
Reynolds	87	-10.8	254	D	13.2	406,440	1,599	49,387	D	D	D	D	NA	70.7	105	8.5
Ripley	143	3.9	327	12.8	41.1	799,801	2,446	78,726	26.2	59,721	28.7	71.3	NA	73.3	1,303	20.8
St. Charles	156	-1.7	258	1.7	124.2	1,257,799	4,885	137,288	61.8	102,308	87.1	12.9	NA	77.8	1,080	37.9
St. Clair	249	4.2	339	0.0	116.0	830,734	2,453	99,643	48.4	65,917	59.5	40.5	2	67.8	1,906	20.4
Ste. Genevieve	169	3.6	255	0.2	77.1	753,601	2,951	76,204	31.8	48,171	57.3	42.7	NA	65.3	2,166	39.2
St. Francois	125	7.4	182	0.3	37.6	532,762	2,933	62,812	14.6	21,150	53.7	46.3	3	68.9	203	7.4
St. Louis	46	54.3	249	0.9	13.6	1,082,987	4,348	60,124	20.5	111,560	95.4	4.6	3	84.8	215	15.2
Saline	441	-4.3	500	7.2	355.8	2,007,141	4,010	214,564	257.4	291,841	70.4	29.6	3	74.9	4,231	68.8
Schuyler	167	4.7	309	0.0	80.8	796,550	2,581	77,623	38.4	71,002	38.8	61.2	NA	64.3	1,729	47.1
Scotland	250	2.5	351	0.0	181.5	1,182,524	3,370	135,426	156.7	219,724	36.7	63.3	19	63.5	4,814	56.1
Scott	223	-0.1	495	91.5	203.4	2,518,197	5,087	274,600	184.8	410,682	55.0	45.0	NA	70.0	8,463	65.1
Shannon	130	4.7	298	0.0	29.1	585,434	1,963	69,516	11.6	26,632	7.8	92.2	NA	71.7	233	8.3
Shelby	278	-7.2	442	1.4	204.8	1,648,469	3,729	163,179	105.5	168,002	72.4	27.6	NA	72.3	3,894	65.1
Stoddard	476	6.1	600	281.7	437.9	3,214,252	5,353	259,498	291.9	368,573	82.0	18.0	NA	69.6	17,568	63.9
Stone	106	-10.0	169	0.0	20.9	489,224	2,894	47,276	35.2	55,989	4.3	95.7	NA	78.2	145	4.1
Sullivan	310	-4.0	462	D	159.7	1,079,907	2,338	114,353	178.4	265,927	15.9	84.1	NA	70.5	5,031	57.8
Taney	108	-6.6	274	0.1	18.8	612,082	2,235	50,546	13.1	33,225	9.3	90.7	NA	73.9	235	5.3
Texas	391	-0.4	285	1.1	82.1	588,769	2,066	63,440	45.2	32,992	11.5	88.5	1	74.5	489	6.3
Vernon	436	4.1	344	12.2	272.2	978,555	2,841	126,119	215.6	170,442	38.2	61.8	10	69.3	4,835	37.4
Warren	128	-6.1	225	0.9	81.8	911,284	4,048	105,482	46.5	81,917	77.9	22.1	3	80.6	1,442	36.3
Washington	104	-16.3	207	0.1	20.4	490,458	2,372	50,335	10.0	19,859	16.3	83.7	NA	75.1	206	3.2
Wayne	98	-16.2	287	0.5	33.2	675,333	2,350	60,230	12.6	37,156	61.9	38.1	NA	70.6	637	14.1
Webster	265	-2.5	144	0.1	77.0	447,850	3,102	59,669	54.4	29,625	12.5	87.5	8	74.6	437	5.2
Worth	125	0.2	373	NA	72.8	1,061,053	2,844	106,629	41.9	124,705	37.9	62.1	NA	75.0	2,694	69.9
Wright	285	-3.1	256	0.5	67.5	551,501	2,158	59,321	44.8	40,158	7.0	93.0	1	70.9	294	5.7

Water Use, Wholesale Trade, Retail Trade, and Real Estate

STATE County	Water use, 2015		Wholesale Trade[1], 2012				Retail Trade[2], 2012				Real estate and rental and leasing,[2] 2012			
	Public supply water withdrawn (mil gal/day)	Public supply gallons withdrawn per person per day	Number of establish-ments	Number of employees	Sales (mil dol)	Average payroll (mil dol)	Number of establish-ments	Number of employees	Sales (mil dol)	Average payroll (mil dol)	Number of establish-ments	Number of employees	Sales (mil dol)	Average payroll (mil dol)
	133	134	135	136	137	138	139	140	141	142	143	144	145	146
MISSOURI— Cont'd														
Jasper	18.54	156.3	143	1,695	972.5	70.6	514	7,769	1,987.5	166.1	114	506	75.5	13.2
Jefferson	28.68	128.0	132	1,302	798.0	65.5	484	6,756	1,952.6	162.7	143	465	62.2	14.1
Johnson	5.14	95.3	20	108	45.6	4.0	148	1,827	508.2	40.2	36	129	25.1	3.4
Knox	0.00	0.0	8	42	61.2	0.8	16	113	38.1	2.1	NA	NA	NA	NA
Laclede	3.79	106.8	27	305	196.2	11.3	174	1,813	502.4	42.1	28	72	10.9	1.6
Lafayette	2.31	70.6	34	319	184.0	11.6	106	1,055	375.5	20.5	16	D	D	D
Lawrence	2.77	72.6	26	239	92.5	7.1	122	1,320	449.0	31.3	20	48	4.2	0.8
Lewis	0.69	67.6	8	D	D	D	32	288	85.7	6.1	3	D	D	D
Lincoln	2.51	45.9	34	245	91.1	9.8	144	1,473	447.8	34.5	28	71	9.0	1.3
Linn	2.10	170.6	8	50	51.1	1.9	56	535	150.0	11.8	9	D	D	D
Livingston	1.89	125.8	22	272	126.7	11.4	76	1,167	359.1	26.5	11	37	9.8	0.7
McDonald	1.86	82.1	10	D	D	D	65	933	221.2	18.6	8	9	2.0	0.3
Macon	1.86	121.3	14	111	65.7	5.2	67	631	146.5	11.5	12	38	3.5	0.7
Madison	0.62	50.0	11	185	28.7	6.1	38	505	138.0	11.8	6	23	1.1	0.4
Maries	0.30	33.5	8	D	D	D	25	222	50.1	3.4	2	D	D	D
Marion	3.66	126.7	26	321	479.7	14.1	143	1,797	508.5	38.3	27	D	D	D
Mercer	0.13	35.2	1	D	D	D	13	64	25.0	1.1	1	D	D	D
Miller	0.78	31.1	13	167	94.6	5.7	119	1,651	377.4	38.8	51	203	30.1	5.3
Mississippi	1.90	135.4	18	191	256.2	6.9	52	474	182.1	9.5	2	D	D	D
Moniteau	1.47	92.1	10	173	69.8	5.0	55	457	136.2	8.5	5	8	0.5	0.1
Monroe	4.71	548.8	9	67	78.7	2.2	35	277	80.0	4.8	3	10	1.3	0.2
Montgomery	0.44	37.6	19	135	110.7	4.8	36	315	98.1	6.1	8	10	1.7	0.2
Morgan	0.70	34.7	17	56	22.2	1.9	91	762	195.1	16.3	19	39	4.8	0.8
New Madrid	1.95	107.1	32	428	436.0	18.3	77	1,319	495.7	28.0	9	21	3.2	0.5
Newton	4.33	73.9	41	1,200	1,674.4	48.3	196	2,090	853.8	49.2	29	77	10.5	1.7
Nodaway	1.88	82.4	17	221	181.4	8.9	72	1,122	260.0	21.2	20	35	5.7	0.6
Oregon	0.88	80.3	6	D	D	D	44	419	98.8	8.3	7	14	1.5	0.2
Osage	0.55	40.4	6	24	9.3	0.8	49	423	152.5	10.3	5	6	0.5	0.1
Ozark	0.24	25.5	6	32	17.3	0.7	33	214	49.6	3.4	9	16	1.0	0.2
Pemiscot	2.13	121.8	21	233	550.6	10.3	70	688	274.3	13.2	10	D	D	D
Perry	1.48	77.2	12	348	174.5	15.2	75	978	270.2	23.0	12	19	5.0	0.4
Pettis	3.55	84.0	35	350	175.4	15.7	174	2,323	615.1	54.4	44	358	37.0	9.4
Phelps	2.83	63.2	36	365	108.9	13.7	190	2,401	689.2	53.0	40	146	20.0	4.0
Pike	1.13	61.6	25	314	312.7	11.7	66	686	191.0	15.0	3	8	0.6	0.1
Platte	2.42	25.2	103	1,288	4,053.0	85.4	313	6,054	1,986.7	144.3	126	1,164	178.1	41.4
Polk	1.31	41.9	23	531	63.0	9.3	110	1,099	299.5	26.3	14	69	6.2	1.3
Pulaski	5.85	109.9	6	D	D	D	138	1,655	455.2	36.4	46	167	40.6	4.1
Putnam	0.25	51.5	3	D	D	D	24	176	50.3	3.1	4	14	0.8	0.2
Ralls	0.00	0.0	16	168	153.4	7.2	34	185	52.4	3.8	2	D	D	D
Randolph	1.12	44.6	17	D	D	D	97	1,118	296.7	25.3	19	63	9.9	1.6
Ray	2.36	103.5	9	114	186.2	5.7	56	607	138.7	12.6	9	21	1.7	0.4
Reynolds	0.13	20.2	4	D	D	D	20	122	29.6	2.0	4	9	0.4	0.1
Ripley	0.63	45.6	5	D	D	D	43	435	120.2	8.1	11	136	4.6	1.8
St. Charles	17.94	46.5	336	4,305	9,006.9	246.4	1,085	18,318	4,971.7	437.2	350	1,398	438.4	53.2
St. Clair	0.32	33.9	4	9	0.6	0.1	33	317	87.9	5.8	3	4	0.2	0.0
Ste. Genevieve	1.43	79.8	12	133	137.0	6.1	49	462	103.4	10.1	9	27	3.5	0.6
St. Francois	5.07	76.2	32	657	285.0	24.2	229	3,421	882.8	84.5	61	229	24.4	5.4
St. Louis	226.20	225.4	1,587	30,594	32,424.2	1,822.0	3,826	67,577	25,262.7	1,882.4	1,309	10,461	2,048.1	504.3
Saline	2.88	123.8	31	358	382.5	16.0	97	981	253.0	19.1	12	D	D	D
Schuyler	0.00	0.0	2	D	D	D	24	165	48.4	2.7	NA	NA	NA	NA
Scotland	0.15	30.9	6	D	D	D	28	162	39.8	3.0	2	D	D	D
Scott	5.94	152.3	53	823	717.9	30.8	181	1,555	415.7	33.2	40	141	17.5	4.0
Shannon	0.44	53.3	7	D	D	D	19	125	28.4	2.0	7	D	D	D
Shelby	0.23	37.5	15	97	69.7	3.5	35	223	58.9	4.4	4	5	0.5	0.1
Stoddard	3.23	108.2	37	366	428.5	13.4	118	1,277	424.0	29.6	26	51	6.7	1.2
Stone	3.15	101.8	17	D	D	D	99	795	216.8	18.9	38	164	19.0	5.8
Sullivan	0.65	102.3	2	D	D	D	27	184	50.4	3.4	5	4	0.5	0.1
Taney	8.29	151.9	32	D	D	D	414	4,936	939.9	88.7	116	1,023	152.0	35.8
Texas	1.72	67.0	22	102	36.7	2.8	83	742	172.5	14.3	10	33	2.7	0.7
Vernon	2.02	97.0	18	180	80.3	5.7	85	897	238.6	19.1	12	37	6.3	0.8
Warren	1.63	48.6	25	279	153.3	14.6	88	879	298.0	18.8	25	74	13.8	1.7
Washington	0.66	26.6	15	46	15.2	1.3	49	510	122.3	9.9	7	16	1.9	0.5
Wayne	1.33	99.2	11	D	D	D	36	319	72.3	6.3	3	3	0.4	0.0
Webster	1.11	29.6	32	134	69.6	5.0	109	1,123	376.7	23.8	26	50	4.0	0.9
Worth	0.01	4.9	4	D	D	D	12	68	18.2	1.2	2	D	D	D
Wright	0.97	53.1	17	223	89.9	6.9	83	952	245.6	20.0	15	41	3.6	0.6

1 Merchant wholesalers, except manufacturers' sales branches and offices. 2. Employer establishments.

Table B. States and Counties — Professional Services, Manufacturing, and Accommodation and Food Services

STATE County	Professional, scientific, and technical services, 2012				Manufacturing, 2012				Accommodation and food services, 2012			
	Number of establishments	Number of employees	Sales (mil dol)	Average payroll (mil dol)	Number of establishments	Number of employees	Receipts (mil dol)	Annual payroll (mil dol)	Number of establishments	Number of employees	Receipts (mil dol)	Annual payroll (mil dol)
	147	148	149	150	151	152	153	154	155	156	157	158
MISSOURI— Cont'd												
Jasper	180	D	D	D	171	9,161	3,558.8	397.3	261	4,960	214.4	60.2
Jefferson	245	941	88.6	32.7	173	4,369	1,420.5	224.6	279	5,461	228.4	66.2
Johnson	66	D	D	D	30	1,252	D	43.0	100	1,672	66.3	16.4
Knox	4	D	D	D	NA	NA	NA	NA	6	D	D	D
Laclede	41	169	14.0	4.6	59	4,120	1,327.5	139.4	79	1,099	47.9	12.7
Lafayette	47	D	D	D	40	793	D	28.5	61	696	24.2	6.4
Lawrence	44	123	10.7	3.3	47	1,357	629.9	53.6	50	676	24.9	7.2
Lewis	13	D	D	D	6	104	D	3.9	14	113	4.1	1.2
Lincoln	51	184	15.4	5.5	49	981	387.2	51.3	58	D	D	D
Linn	22	98	9.7	3.1	15	1,003	207.5	27.4	20	226	7.8	2.2
Livingston	31	133	10.5	3.4	16	554	152.7	21.4	25	D	D	D
McDonald	13	44	2.6	0.9	23	2,974	611.6	81.9	33	264	13.3	3.3
Macon	23	D	D	D	9	472	D	15.9	32	366	18.4	5.2
Madison	13	74	5.2	1.5	14	281	D	10.2	22	D	D	D
Maries	6	D	D	D	9	165	D	8.4	11	41	1.5	0.4
Marion	45	258	24.9	8.6	39	1,475	1,488.5	72.2	74	1,115	47.0	12.7
Mercer	3	D	D	D	NA	NA	NA	NA	7	D	D	D
Miller	38	274	20.9	10.3	21	488	D	14.5	54	634	31.9	10.0
Mississippi	9	71	7.7	4.3	6	126	D	6.2	20	267	11.5	3.0
Moniteau	15	65	4.8	1.7	28	677	D	28.1	21	D	D	D
Monroe	10	D	D	D	9	218	D	D	18	141	4.7	1.3
Montgomery	8	D	D	D	19	499	154.8	17.1	21	194	6.7	1.9
Morgan	27	86	6.4	2.0	21	609	D	18.1	53	453	19.0	5.3
New Madrid	15	63	5.0	1.9	15	1,561	883.0	89.5	34	474	26.8	5.5
Newton	70	375	38.0	14.8	72	2,499	724.0	89.2	97	1,684	82.8	21.3
Nodaway	27	124	13.3	4.1	22	1,675	D	69.5	45	1,074	36.7	10.5
Oregon	10	D	D	D	11	137	24.0	3.6	14	171	5.8	1.5
Osage	9	17	1.7	0.4	29	988	D	40.1	20	D	D	D
Ozark	9	D	D	D	8	70	D	1.9	22	187	7.5	2.3
Pemiscot	11	44	3.5	0.9	12	825	D	37.0	29	311	15.1	3.3
Perry	27	118	8.8	4.2	37	3,627	1,142.3	115.6	39	618	20.9	5.8
Pettis	67	1,532	101.8	40.6	49	3,955	1,522.4	152.5	80	1,475	59.4	16.6
Phelps	77	327	35.9	11.5	50	912	484.4	43.1	114	1,810	78.1	21.6
Pike	18	522	43.8	11.5	21	555	324.3	22.8	25	D	D	D
Platte	260	D	D	D	49	2,644	1,870.0	127.4	202	5,779	394.3	101.0
Polk	43	D	D	D	22	343	D	12.1	44	780	27.0	7.3
Pulaski	58	639	99.0	45.5	15	123	24.5	D	99	2,280	91.8	39.3
Putnam	3	D	D	D	5	72	D	2.2	4	D	D	D
Ralls	5	19	1.9	0.5	15	1,272	1,405.4	66.2	11	87	3.0	1.0
Randolph	25	106	5.4	1.7	30	1,128	219.0	40.9	51	582	26.5	6.6
Ray	30	D	D	D	14	305	D	16.7	21	229	9.0	2.2
Reynolds	4	D	D	D	26	259	44.2	8.0	15	D	D	D
Ripley	10	D	D	D	30	446	D	11.6	15	195	7.7	1.9
St. Charles	765	6,210	720.9	239.7	256	10,982	6,851.7	614.3	712	16,108	918.4	227.3
St. Clair	9	25	3.3	1.0	8	28	4.9	1.2	16	78	5.4	0.8
Ste. Genevieve	23	81	6.1	2.5	30	1,467	400.4	74.7	29	D	D	D
St. Francois	79	300	33.6	8.7	49	1,474	272.2	55.7	115	1,802	76.3	21.6
St. Louis	3,618	46,440	8,274.0	3,139.6	950	35,884	15,922.9	2,621.7	2,219	47,895	2,628.8	713.8
Saline	29	D	D	D	21	1,948	747.5	68.9	43	522	17.5	5.3
Schuyler	1	D	D	D	3	9	2.9	0.4	3	D	D	D
Scotland	8	D	D	D	9	49	D	1.5	10	60	1.9	0.6
Scott	66	360	47.3	21.5	54	2,412	847.7	94.9	69	1,189	52.8	15.7
Shannon	4	D	D	D	24	372	51.1	8.9	15	64	3.4	0.8
Shelby	11	45	4.7	1.1	8	239	D	8.9	12	85	2.3	0.7
Stoddard	30	157	17.4	5.5	36	2,506	1,242.8	111.5	42	585	24.5	6.9
Stone	34	76	5.6	1.7	22	108	11.6	3.4	92	584	48.9	10.0
Sullivan	4	D	D	D	4	D	D	D	6	D	D	D
Taney	101	413	31.2	12.3	40	360	84.2	14.8	302	7,039	553.0	144.2
Texas	25	80	5.4	1.8	45	698	157.8	24.1	41	D	D	D
Vernon	34	120	11.1	2.9	20	894	D	46.8	36	456	22.3	4.8
Warren	38	145	14.4	4.9	34	1,383	453.2	58.7	49	D	D	D
Washington	13	35	2.0	0.7	19	533	290.1	17.6	22	D	D	D
Wayne	9	D	D	D	25	335	63.1	11.7	20	166	8.9	2.9
Webster	42	D	D	D	45	696	206.2	24.9	35	526	23.5	5.9
Worth	4	D	D	D	3	D	D	0.4	3	D	D	D
Wright	21	51	5.4	1.2	26	381	D	13.8	23	307	10.8	3.0

Health Care and Social Assistance, Other Services, Nonemployer Businesses, and Residential Construction

STATE County	Health care and social assistance, 2012				Other services, 2012				Nonemployer businesses, 2016		Value of residential construction authorized by building permits, 2018	
	Number of establishments	Number of employees	Receipts (mil dol)	Annual payroll (mil dol)	Number of establishments	Number of employees	Receipts (mil dol)	Annual payroll (mil dol)	Number	Receipts (mil dol)	New construction ($1,000)	Number of housing units
	159	160	161	162	163	164	165	166	167	168	169	170
MISSOURI— Cont'd												
Jasper	333	6,521	629.5	315.1	225	1,277	99.9	29.8	6,630	368.6	77,886	602
Jefferson	381	6,119	478.7	186.3	334	1,558	143.2	42.4	13,040	517.9	130,893	677
Johnson	100	2,309	200.4	78.6	62	D	D	D	3,006	109.1	6,376	45
Knox	8	38	2.3	0.8	9	D	D	D	351	16.9	200	2
Laclede	78	1,475	135.0	55.4	49	D	D	D	2,559	130.4	2,396	20
Lafayette	62	D	D	D	46	135	11.3	3.0	2,143	83.8	10,723	60
Lawrence	71	1,279	99.0	46.0	38	109	9.2	2.8	2,645	100.7	1,963	11
Lewis	24	311	12.4	5.9	12	D	D	D	611	24.5	150	1
Lincoln	73	D	D	D	61	D	D	D	3,354	131.2	25,846	140
Linn	24	523	37.9	15.2	27	90	9.6	1.9	878	33.2	180	1
Livingston	43	861	74.4	27.8	22	D	D	D	985	35.8	5,400	39
McDonald	26	296	16.7	7.3	17	D	D	D	1,355	54.5	965	7
Macon	31	550	40.5	15.4	26	D	D	D	1,089	43.9	1,931	9
Madison	29	886	38.9	20.7	16	43	3.4	0.8	712	24.6	1,010	15
Maries	12	138	8.6	3.0	4	15	2.0	0.2	577	25.0	215	1
Marion	136	2,858	286.2	109.4	57	332	18.2	5.2	1,634	66.9	7,186	50
Mercer	7	D	D	D	8	D	D	D	267	11.4	0	0
Miller	37	495	33.0	13.3	41	D	D	D	1,644	71.8	4,656	14
Mississippi	25	409	19.9	8.0	19	56	4.3	1.1	590	31.9	511	8
Moniteau	32	D	D	D	18	53	3.2	0.8	983	40.3	720	4
Monroe	29	D	D	D	13	D	D	D	611	28.0	0	0
Montgomery	17	382	19.7	8.2	17	D	D	D	845	37.6	17,552	21
Morgan	28	256	13.9	5.2	29	D	D	D	1,726	70.8	270	2
New Madrid	52	886	48.4	17.6	22	58	5.7	1.0	743	23.7	1,406	10
Newton	141	6,401	607.1	273.5	63	219	19.1	5.1	3,799	166.8	4,364	38
Nodaway	51	1,239	94.2	39.5	40	163	10.6	3.1	1,405	47.8	5,003	40
Oregon	38	458	18.1	8.9	15	D	D	D	765	26.0	0	0
Osage	22	D	D	D	14	37	4.2	0.6	979	42.9	460	5
Ozark	10	100	5.8	2.4	13	42	2.7	0.6	773	24.4	0	0
Pemiscot	75	1,276	74.9	32.8	14	45	3.9	1.1	811	24.5	362	9
Perry	51	1,164	86.5	31.9	38	570	17.9	22.3	1,228	47.9	11,073	85
Pettis	136	3,111	229.9	97.5	91	482	34.5	11.2	2,737	123.1	2,500	14
Phelps	148	3,820	343.0	120.7	71	323	24.2	8.3	2,631	101.9	16,242	131
Pike	52	802	49.6	21.5	21	39	5.2	1.2	1,146	46.8	710	13
Platte	201	3,319	354.3	139.8	163	877	94.7	27.0	7,513	374.3	94,227	346
Polk	74	1,924	159.2	63.7	42	218	9.8	2.5	2,346	92.8	8,272	32
Pulaski	62	1,773	158.5	62.7	58	248	19.2	5.9	2,008	71.4	7,428	49
Putnam	10	94	10.1	3.1	6	17	2.0	0.4	431	21.3	0	0
Ralls	13	162	10.0	4.5	12	52	4.9	1.2	735	33.3	200	2
Randolph	72	1,504	128.3	48.0	45	140	10.6	2.5	1,311	54.2	5,746	56
Ray	36	D	D	D	24	D	D	D	1,267	46.0	9,962	48
Reynolds	29	158	7.0	3.0	6	D	D	D	447	17.7	0	0
Ripley	69	796	36.3	16.8	16	46	4.2	0.8	827	32.3	65	3
St. Charles	939	15,694	1,482.9	576.5	592	3,967	336.9	102.9	25,591	1,123.6	511,422	2,326
St. Clair	28	486	22.3	10.4	13	44	4.7	1.0	687	26.0	0	0
Ste. Genevieve	46	815	59.5	23.8	34	138	9.8	2.4	1,112	34.9	797	4
St. Francois	244	5,279	379.4	164.4	99	441	32.0	8.9	3,151	121.7	18,124	181
St. Louis	4,190	86,410	9,445.2	3,803.8	1,961	15,935	1,682.2	529.5	76,527	3,952.9	400,156	1,136
Saline	73	1,618	110.8	47.6	35	152	16.8	4.1	1,223	44.8	355	3
Schuyler	3	20	1.2	0.7	7	D	D	D	334	18.0	852	4
Scotland	7	D	D	D	15	D	D	D	508	29.7	215	1
Scott	139	2,990	200.0	90.4	61	322	25.5	6.9	2,264	100.8	5,755	52
Shannon	19	215	13.0	4.7	6	15	1.7	0.4	747	28.4	0	0
Shelby	7	102	5.1	2.1	15	38	4.8	0.9	474	18.3	135	1
Stoddard	90	1,499	84.2	36.2	41	137	9.7	3.0	1,956	108.8	1,690	14
Stone	45	458	39.5	12.1	52	273	21.8	6.5	2,772	116.9	39,293	170
Sullivan	10	254	13.9	6.1	10	21	2.8	0.5	367	14.4	0	0
Taney	125	2,363	247.5	91.8	101	556	49.6	12.9	4,418	177.2	40,241	244
Texas	52	968	70.6	28.2	34	69	6.5	1.4	1,760	66.8	620	7
Vernon	71	1,468	91.0	38.0	34	122	7.5	1.8	1,319	52.8	630	7
Warren	56	D	D	D	36	D	D	D	2,051	78.3	75,873	332
Washington	76	776	66.3	22.9	16	56	4.2	1.1	1,017	35.3	65	1
Wayne	40	379	18.1	7.5	10	48	2.1	0.6	682	27.6	0	0
Webster	56	500	26.9	12.2	35	D	D	D	3,044	123.6	6,222	41
Worth	2	D	D	D	5	D	D	D	207	6.9	0	0
Wright	43	492	30.5	11.7	23	77	6.4	1.5	1,399	61.7	1,033	8

Table B. States and Counties — Government Employment and Payroll, and Local Government Finances

	Government employment and payroll, 2012									Local government finances, 2012				
STATE County			March payroll (percent of total)							General revenue				
												Taxes		
	Full-time equivalent employees	March payroll (dollars)	Adminis-tration, judicial, and legal	Police and corrections	Fire protection	Highways and transpor-tation	Health and welfare	Natural resources and utilities	Education and libraries	Total (mil dol)	Inter-govern-mental (mil dol)	Total (mil dol)	Per capita[1] (dollars)	
													Total	Property
	171	172	173	174	175	176	177	178	179	180	181	182	183	184

MISSOURI— Cont'd

STATE County	171	172	173	174	175	176	177	178	179	180	181	182	183	184
Jasper	4,406	12,579,406	4.8	9.9	4.0	3.6	1.3	3.8	71.5	389.2	139.5	146.6	1,272	589
Jefferson	6,669	24,871,942	2.8	6.2	4.1	2.5	3.8	3.1	76.7	560.9	238.8	255.4	1,160	796
Johnson	2,208	7,565,488	3.1	4.7	2.1	2.3	37.3	2.7	47.4	195.3	49.7	52.6	967	584
Knox	221	492,621	7.9	5.4	0.0	7.2	22.0	5.2	52.2	12.1	7.0	4.4	1,068	756
Laclede	1,413	3,701,221	5.5	5.9	1.6	12.4	1.2	6.8	65.2	72.4	35.3	26.3	742	477
Lafayette	1,188	3,488,934	7.8	8.3	0.6	3.5	2.3	9.3	67.9	88.1	38.4	34.2	1,034	710
Lawrence	1,155	3,231,901	5.5	6.1	0.7	2.7	6.5	2.7	75.5	76.5	38.1	27.2	706	425
Lewis	450	1,137,169	6.6	5.6	0.1	4.4	19.6	4.3	58.6	29.3	13.4	9.1	892	661
Lincoln	1,917	6,064,837	5.5	7.0	1.3	2.6	24.9	0.7	57.6	159.5	58.6	49.5	928	677
Linn	590	1,568,941	6.7	5.1	0.0	4.8	4.2	7.5	69.7	39.5	19.0	13.4	1,074	641
Livingston	654	1,837,354	4.6	6.8	5.3	2.6	13.9	14.2	51.7	49.5	19.1	16.1	1,073	702
McDonald	606	1,598,982	8.5	7.8	0.1	4.5	1.5	6.0	70.3	51.8	29.8	17.6	770	427
Macon	1,039	2,633,830	3.7	3.4	0.8	3.2	42.4	2.9	43.4	92.8	45.8	29.8	1,914	1,610
Madison	682	1,827,224	2.1	3.5	0.1	2.1	44.4	2.8	42.9	25.4	13.9	8.3	667	425
Maries	323	761,125	7.6	6.0	0.0	6.9	9.4	3.4	66.1	18.2	8.6	7.6	847	638
Marion	1,348	3,816,108	4.3	7.2	3.7	3.7	10.5	8.5	58.2	94.9	33.0	39.1	1,361	752
Mercer	176	501,591	15.9	5.2	0.1	7.0	6.8	4.3	59.8	9.5	4.4	3.9	1,038	887
Miller	1,205	3,202,179	4.4	4.5	1.6	2.3	11.6	1.8	73.2	80.0	30.4	36.5	1,472	1,081
Mississippi	496	1,277,944	12.1	11.0	0.1	3.6	4.4	7.4	61.1	39.2	20.9	12.9	904	600
Moniteau	498	1,342,360	7.0	4.0	0.2	3.3	8.9	4.9	70.4	34.2	15.0	12.7	813	528
Monroe	490	1,220,603	5.4	5.4	0.3	4.2	22.2	8.5	53.6	28.8	12.5	9.7	1,109	878
Montgomery	414	1,189,713	7.9	12.4	0.0	5.3	4.0	3.0	66.0	27.1	9.4	13.0	1,088	730
Morgan	588	1,595,566	8.3	9.3	0.7	4.5	8.1	2.2	61.6	37.0	13.2	17.9	892	558
New Madrid	720	1,973,525	9.1	7.8	0.4	5.1	5.0	6.0	65.2	48.9	21.7	21.3	1,153	837
Newton	1,886	5,757,934	4.6	4.8	2.8	1.7	3.3	2.2	80.6	121.7	59.7	39.0	661	405
Nodaway	726	2,001,480	9.5	5.9	0.8	3.6	4.2	6.4	68.6	62.2	22.3	27.8	1,186	755
Oregon	416	986,254	6.1	4.7	0.0	3.9	0.0	4.8	79.9	22.3	13.8	6.1	554	379
Osage	364	958,029	5.9	4.6	2.7	4.1	8.7	5.2	68.3	23.3	8.9	9.6	696	471
Ozark	375	902,737	3.5	3.0	0.0	3.7	2.8	1.2	83.1	20.2	12.4	5.9	612	453
Pemiscot	869	2,608,472	5.8	7.8	0.7	1.4	2.9	7.8	73.3	61.3	38.4	13.9	770	506
Perry	569	1,561,790	6.3	12.2	0.0	3.8	5.0	9.4	63.2	42.8	15.7	20.2	1,064	628
Pettis	2,440	8,051,066	2.4	3.6	1.7	1.5	41.8	2.5	45.8	222.9	54.6	51.1	1,207	624
Phelps	2,804	9,025,924	2.3	3.7	1.2	1.5	51.9	4.5	33.4	301.2	46.2	39.1	869	478
Pike	681	2,031,713	2.7	3.7	0.2	0.7	28.4	3.3	60.9	45.8	18.4	20.6	1,109	754
Platte	2,626	11,215,330	4.0	6.6	2.9	2.1	4.0	1.9	78.0	290.1	82.7	172.3	1,871	1,274
Polk	1,882	6,311,305	2.0	2.0	0.1	1.6	60.7	1.1	32.3	164.9	36.7	18.1	584	439
Pulaski	1,731	5,423,451	3.5	3.9	1.1	2.3	7.4	5.5	75.3	125.6	76.5	29.6	556	371
Putnam	314	940,189	4.5	2.1	0.0	2.4	55.0	5.9	29.6	17.4	5.2	7.7	1,554	1,199
Ralls	284	692,452	21.1	12.6	0.0	13.9	2.2	4.0	41.7	13.1	5.3	6.2	600	404
Randolph	1,211	3,641,751	3.9	5.9	1.9	2.1	2.9	4.9	77.8	104.1	32.8	33.6	1,328	821
Ray	1,243	21,423,521	0.8	0.5	0.3	0.3	89.8	0.8	7.3	87.1	25.3	21.5	933	704
Reynolds	325	775,935	7.0	5.6	0.0	5.7	4.1	1.6	75.1	20.4	10.7	7.5	1,131	997
Ripley	665	1,587,309	4.3	3.8	0.5	1.9	28.8	2.6	58.2	27.1	17.6	6.3	449	337
St. Charles	12,474	44,955,774	5.7	9.4	5.0	2.8	3.2	4.3	66.6	1,191.7	344.4	666.4	1,808	1,183
St. Clair	558	1,434,103	4.2	10.9	0.0	2.8	35.5	3.2	42.1	48.9	23.1	6.2	654	535
Ste. Genevieve	472	1,571,579	6.8	13.6	0.1	3.5	5.8	7.1	62.2	37.1	12.7	20.0	1,125	724
St. Francois	2,385	7,190,551	2.7	4.3	0.6	1.6	5.1	5.3	80.0	178.1	78.4	65.4	993	571
St. Louis	35,141	147,062,201	4.5	10.0	7.3	2.5	1.6	2.8	69.6	3,629.3	1,051.6	2,133.5	2,133	1,497
Saline	749	2,090,138	7.0	10.8	3.2	5.2	6.6	26.6	39.7	61.0	25.6	21.0	898	647
Schuyler	276	469,325	6.5	3.5	0.0	3.7	25.1	6.2	54.3	12.0	5.3	3.2	735	541
Scotland	479	1,508,783	7.5	3.0	0.0	5.6	60.2	4.1	19.3	31.5	5.9	4.5	918	718
Scott	1,609	5,229,887	4.1	7.7	1.4	1.8	4.2	23.8	53.9	108.4	50.7	38.1	973	559
Shannon	529	555,611	8.1	5.1	0.0	7.2	7.0	5.1	67.1	13.2	8.0	2.9	343	223
Shelby	432	1,223,611	12.6	7.4	0.3	6.2	25.9	5.7	38.5	23.5	9.7	6.6	1,064	756
Stoddard	1,139	2,920,419	5.2	6.2	0.8	8.7	6.5	5.3	66.9	72.2	30.2	21.0	704	560
Stone	846	2,351,044	6.0	5.6	1.1	2.7	0.1	2.1	82.4	74.2	35.5	30.6	969	612
Sullivan	370	985,283	6.2	4.1	0.2	3.8	27.9	5.8	50.1	23.6	9.0	6.6	1,012	748
Taney	1,787	5,327,466	7.7	9.1	3.9	4.1	8.3	6.6	58.2	198.6	59.2	103.3	1,952	978
Texas	1,227	3,278,813	3.7	3.2	0.1	3.2	31.5	5.3	50.4	84.8	28.4	20.4	791	654
Vernon	1,038	3,438,287	4.3	4.0	1.4	1.5	36.6	4.4	47.6	48.3	21.1	19.4	934	559
Warren	943	2,742,942	5.8	9.6	2.2	1.6	5.8	4.1	68.2	70.7	27.9	32.8	1,001	734
Washington	953	2,869,920	3.5	2.5	0.3	2.7	34.5	4.9	50.7	69.6	27.6	13.6	541	368
Wayne	459	1,011,584	9.4	3.6	0.0	7.6	5.0	3.2	71.2	25.2	14.3	7.7	573	378
Webster	946	2,669,213	5.5	5.0	0.3	2.8	11.0	3.5	71.2	63.4	29.0	20.2	556	309
Worth	134	294,433	8.2	2.8	0.0	3.4	21.0	5.8	57.6	6.8	2.2	2.2	1,037	834
Wright	792	2,007,501	4.3	3.8	0.3	2.7	11.1	4.2	73.0	47.2	25.3	12.2	656	392

1. Based on the resident population estimated as of July 1 of the year shown.

Local Government Finances, Government Employment, and Income Taxes

STATE County	Local government finances, 2012 (cont.)									Government employment, 2017			Individual income tax returns, 2016		
	Direct general expenditure							Debt outstanding							
			Percent of total for:											Mean	
	Total (mil dol)	Per capita¹ (dollars)	Education	Health and hospitals	Police protection	Public welfare	Highways	Total (mil dol)	Per capita¹ (dollars)	Federal civilian	Federal military	State and local	Number of returns	adjusted gross income	Mean income tax
	185	186	187	188	189	190	191	192	193	194	195	196	197	198	199
MISSOURI— Cont'd															
Jasper	396.9	3,443	54.1	10.7	5.4	0.1	5.6	243.6	2,113	301	427	6,557	50,760	49,168	5,481
Jefferson	583.0	2,648	64.1	2.8	6.2	0.0	7.7	577.7	2,623	297	753	8,315	106,120	54,424	5,673
Johnson	233.9	4,299	31.0	47.8	3.5	0.0	4.6	246.2	4,525	1,296	3,821	6,067	22,230	48,860	4,654
Knox	10.9	2,667	49.1	8.8	4.0	18.8	5.9	0.6	147	29	13	269	1,700	32,611	2,648
Laclede	68.0	1,919	74.1	0.0	4.7	0.0	6.3	34.1	962	77	119	1,439	15,130	39,426	3,397
Lafayette	87.7	2,650	57.3	1.7	5.6	0.1	7.0	105.1	3,177	105	111	2,144	14,910	48,199	4,488
Lawrence	78.1	2,031	67.8	0.8	3.9	5.7	6.5	98.6	2,562	243	129	1,746	16,020	42,170	3,747
Lewis	26.7	2,624	50.7	1.4	3.7	15.5	8.9	11.0	1,085	47	31	566	4,160	42,056	3,630
Lincoln	153.2	2,871	47.7	26.4	4.4	0.0	4.4	139.5	2,615	111	189	2,094	25,730	51,994	5,037
Linn	37.6	3,014	60.3	3.0	4.4	0.0	11.3	26.2	2,102	55	41	796	5,420	42,332	3,956
Livingston	59.6	3,966	50.2	2.8	4.8	8.2	7.4	28.8	1,918	74	45	1,338	6,260	44,853	4,543
McDonald	44.0	1,922	69.8	0.0	4.1	0.0	8.0	31.9	1,393	89	77	883	9,000	37,185	2,698
Macon	48.3	3,102	46.4	1.1	3.5	22.2	8.9	21.2	1,363	67	51	1,544	7,060	41,447	3,812
Madison	30.2	2,426	68.9	0.0	6.2	0.0	6.2	3.9	310	38	41	832	5,050	39,833	3,099
Maries	18.1	2,013	61.7	4.7	4.0	0.0	9.9	10.7	1,187	10	30	338	3,830	40,514	3,268
Marion	99.0	3,444	54.3	3.1	3.7	6.3	4.7	133.0	4,628	103	93	1,768	12,670	47,369	4,890
Mercer	9.9	2,650	69.6	5.6	1.5	0.0	12.0	8.6	2,310	30	12	224	1,530	37,107	3,237
Miller	78.5	3,161	59.5	4.2	3.5	6.0	5.7	46.2	1,860	45	85	1,435	10,510	39,575	3,437
Mississippi	35.3	2,466	49.4	5.6	5.4	0.6	6.5	20.3	1,418	18	40	1,030	4,910	41,840	4,477
Moniteau	32.1	2,054	63.0	5.8	3.2	0.0	6.8	31.2	1,994	46	50	1,007	6,650	43,982	3,664
Monroe	28.8	3,309	49.1	3.2	3.9	16.0	10.7	54.4	6,255	72	29	621	3,870	42,489	3,668
Montgomery	28.9	2,411	56.1	3.6	5.3	0.0	7.9	11.0	913	49	37	591	5,180	43,043	3,667
Morgan	40.7	2,025	46.7	0.1	7.7	7.9	8.7	22.0	1,093	40	67	982	8,490	38,483	3,149
New Madrid	46.5	2,517	59.4	2.4	6.4	0.0	7.6	18.4	995	44	59	912	6,950	41,766	4,206
Newton	127.6	2,161	69.8	3.0	3.0	0.5	3.4	106.0	1,794	134	195	2,443	24,350	52,051	5,824
Nodaway	59.7	2,551	52.7	3.7	4.8	0.0	11.8	64.8	2,766	83	64	2,553	8,500	46,663	4,484
Oregon	21.9	1,990	73.6	1.6	2.2	0.0	5.3	3.9	358	32	35	508	3,820	33,376	2,593
Osage	23.1	1,669	59.8	6.0	2.4	0.0	5.6	11.0	794	28	45	824	6,090	48,484	4,330
Ozark	20.7	2,155	78.4	2.7	3.2	0.1	6.5	0.7	69	12	31	429	3,620	34,930	3,151
Pemiscot	61.8	3,411	67.4	1.6	4.6	0.0	5.4	11.3	624	48	56	1,380	6,290	38,722	3,654
Perry	43.0	2,261	53.4	1.8	6.3	0.0	8.0	19.0	1,001	48	64	1,249	9,120	46,291	4,202
Pettis	213.3	5,041	37.6	44.8	2.5	0.0	4.2	106.8	2,524	138	144	3,260	18,600	43,339	3,970
Phelps	295.8	6,576	23.7	59.1	2.1	0.3	2.9	165.9	3,688	331	259	6,059	17,550	48,151	5,042
Pike	43.7	2,354	53.0	1.6	7.4	0.0	9.9	24.3	1,308	64	55	1,660	7,330	44,672	4,232
Platte	285.1	3,097	65.5	0.9	4.8	0.2	5.0	434.8	4,724	721	366	3,958	48,500	79,697	11,492
Polk	168.1	5,419	28.7	60.0	1.0	0.0	3.1	55.0	1,774	71	103	2,435	12,220	42,305	3,651
Pulaski	139.6	2,621	69.4	2.9	2.8	0.0	4.4	141.0	2,648	3,494	10,908	2,071	17,860	43,904	3,424
Putnam	17.9	3,623	40.9	1.9	1.7	18.6	8.7	7.6	1,551	18	16	419	2,070	37,871	3,127
Ralls	12.4	1,207	50.3	3.6	5.3	0.0	17.2	14.9	1,451	28	35	344	4,660	49,989	5,306
Randolph	103.6	4,090	59.4	15.6	4.7	0.0	3.9	94.5	3,731	68	76	2,083	10,380	45,482	4,606
Ray	82.9	3,594	35.4	24.2	3.6	15.3	8.2	32.9	1,426	49	77	1,375	10,640	50,678	4,907
Reynolds	20.8	3,118	70.7	4.1	2.1	0.5	3.4	4.8	719	16	21	394	2,430	35,849	2,693
Ripley	26.6	1,894	72.9	5.2	4.9	0.0	4.4	1.2	88	54	46	568	5,100	33,379	2,493
St. Charles	1,188.4	3,223	54.5	2.1	6.5	0.1	9.4	1,722.2	4,671	745	1,327	16,069	194,290	70,802	8,917
St. Clair	44.1	4,651	28.5	34.9	1.9	0.0	5.3	16.1	1,703	41	31	472	3,660	36,480	2,870
Ste. Genevieve	38.8	2,184	67.5	3.0	6.6	0.0	7.8	28.1	1,581	29	60	1,006	8,310	51,110	4,882
St. Francois	177.6	2,694	64.6	4.1	6.8	0.1	6.3	112.4	1,705	141	202	5,857	25,840	44,340	4,171
St. Louis	3,854.3	3,853	55.7	1.6	7.0	0.9	5.2	4,175.7	4,174	5,748	3,372	48,695	500,790	86,478	14,265
Saline	61.1	2,617	55.2	5.4	6.9	0.3	7.5	7.5	323	77	73	1,629	9,690	42,934	3,952
Schuyler	11.1	2,542	46.7	3.1	1.3	22.3	14.5	7.8	1,793	30	15	284	1,750	31,010	2,325
Scotland	35.5	7,289	17.7	58.8	1.2	11.4	5.9	18.8	3,848	21	17	552	2,070	40,231	3,250
Scott	109.3	2,794	52.1	2.0	13.1	0.0	3.9	182.4	4,661	101	129	2,126	16,990	48,752	5,377
Shannon	12.9	1,551	60.4	0.2	2.3	0.0	12.2	2.7	326	20	28	326	3,050	31,902	2,371
Shelby	24.1	3,872	42.9	4.0	2.6	27.1	7.7	6.0	969	31	20	595	2,880	40,593	3,493
Stoddard	67.4	2,263	63.7	5.5	2.6	0.0	6.1	41.2	1,384	159	97	1,312	12,210	45,342	4,894
Stone	68.6	2,173	57.5	0.0	4.0	0.0	7.1	49.4	1,566	40	107	1,082	14,000	46,436	4,866
Sullivan	22.7	3,475	48.2	30.8	2.2	0.1	5.6	9.1	1,389	44	21	420	2,650	35,324	2,606
Taney	188.6	3,561	41.8	3.4	3.9	0.0	6.1	593.9	11,215	179	182	2,303	24,890	38,394	3,815
Texas	72.4	2,804	46.8	37.3	2.0	0.1	3.4	30.6	1,185	65	81	1,871	9,200	35,957	2,830
Vernon	45.8	2,207	64.9	3.0	3.5	0.0	7.3	60.2	2,903	93	67	1,648	8,290	39,254	3,413
Warren	69.9	2,135	57.6	4.6	6.2	0.0	5.1	59.4	1,815	46	117	1,253	15,780	53,207	5,388
Washington	67.9	2,707	49.1	31.2	3.2	0.0	3.5	32.5	1,294	55	81	1,510	8,790	36,760	2,613
Wayne	23.2	1,734	66.5	1.8	4.6	0.0	10.8	24.4	1,824	76	45	513	4,630	33,086	2,247
Webster	62.8	1,727	65.3	0.3	4.1	9.7	6.4	23.5	648	87	128	1,330	15,140	44,895	4,223
Worth	7.6	3,657	53.1	2.9	3.3	20.3	3.2	1.0	466	23	7	147	930	34,852	2,819
Wright	48.4	2,598	61.6	0.2	2.3	10.5	5.3	14.9	799	43	62	872	6,960	33,996	2,522

1. Based on the resident population estimated as of July 1 of the year shown.

Table B. States and Counties — **Land Area and Population**

State / county code	CBSA code[1]	County code[2]	STATE County	Population, 2018			Population and population characteristics, 2018										
							Race alone or in combination, not Hispanic or Latino (percent)					Age (percent)					
				Land area[3] (sq. mi)	Total persons 2018	Rank	Per square mile	White	Black	American Indian, Alaska Native	Asian and Pacific Islander	Percent Hispanic or Latino[4]	Under 5 years	5 to 17 years	18 to 24 years	25 to 34 years	35 to 44 years	45 to 54 years
				1	2	3	4	5	6	7	8	9	10	11	12	13	14	15
			MISSOURI— Cont'd															
29510	41,180	1	St. Louis city..................	61.7	302,838	231	4,908.2	46.2	47.0	1.0	4.3	4.1	6.2	12.8	9.1	20.1	13.2	11.6
30000		0	MONTANA	145,546.1	1,062,305	X	7.3	88.3	1.0	7.7	1.6	4.0	5.9	15.7	9.3	12.9	11.9	11.3
30001		7	Beaverhead..................	5,542.7	9,404	2,470	1.7	92.1	0.8	2.7	1.5	5.0	4.6	12.8	14.6	10.7	10.2	10.0
30003		6	Big Horn......................	4,997.8	13,338	2,207	2.7	29.4	0.8	64.9	0.9	7.0	9.3	24.3	8.4	13.0	10.4	10.3
30005		9	Blaine.........................	4,227.1	6,807	2,692	1.6	46.9	0.8	50.5	0.7	3.8	8.3	21.3	8.5	12.6	11.1	10.5
30007		9	Broadwater...................	1,192.4	6,085	2,743	5.1	94.7	0.7	2.5	0.8	3.0	4.9	15.0	6.2	9.5	10.6	13.1
30009	13,740	3	Carbon........................	2,047.7	10,714	2,378	5.2	95.4	0.8	1.9	0.7	2.5	3.6	13.8	5.8	8.5	11.7	12.1
30011		9	Carter.........................	3,340.5	1,238	3,097	0.4	97.7	0.7	1.5	0.4	1.4	7.4	13.0	5.9	11.9	8.8	9.1
30013	24,500	3	Cascade.......................	2,698.2	81,643	695	30.3	88.3	2.4	6.4	2.1	4.6	6.7	15.7	9.3	14.4	11.1	10.8
30015		8	Chouteau.....................	3,972.5	5,745	2,776	1.4	78.5	0.6	19.2	0.7	2.6	5.1	18.2	7.2	11.7	11.4	10.1
30017		7	Custer	3,783.3	11,586	2,319	3.1	93.2	0.8	3.1	1.2	3.6	6.0	15.4	8.1	12.2	11.7	11.7
30019		9	Daniels........................	1,426.0	1,747	3,070	1.2	93.3	1.0	3.7	0.5	3.6	5.2	16.3	5.0	10.7	10.1	9.7
30021		7	Dawson.......................	2,371.9	8,680	2,531	3.7	93.8	0.8	3.2	0.9	3.1	6.1	15.6	8.4	12.6	11.2	11.1
30023		7	Deer Lodge	736.7	9,131	2,490	12.4	92.0	0.9	5.0	0.9	3.7	3.6	10.7	8.1	11.8	11.4	13.4
30025		9	Fallon	1,620.6	2,920	2,974	1.8	96.5	0.7	1.5	1.1	1.7	7.4	19.7	6.1	12.3	11.5	11.2
30027		7	Fergus........................	4,339.3	11,113	2,346	2.6	95.6	0.5	2.6	0.6	2.4	5.5	15.3	6.2	10.7	11.1	11.2
30029	28,060	5	Flathead	5,087.2	102,106	596	20.1	94.8	0.6	2.5	1.5	2.8	5.8	16.2	6.7	12.1	12.5	11.9
30031	14,580	5	Gallatin.......................	2,605.0	111,876	544	42.9	93.0	0.8	1.7	2.5	4.0	5.8	14.3	15.8	16.4	13.5	10.5
30033		9	Garfield	4,676.6	1,268	3,095	0.3	98.1	0.6	0.9	0.2	0.9	5.8	16.3	6.9	9.1	13.2	10.6
30035		7	Glacier........................	2,994.9	13,747	2,181	4.6	33.3	0.5	65.3	0.7	3.1	9.2	22.0	9.0	13.5	11.5	10.3
30037	13,740	3	Golden Valley...............	1,174.4	826	3,114	0.7	93.0	1.2	4.0	1.5	4.0	5.2	16.0	6.4	8.2	10.8	10.4
30039		8	Granite........................	1,727.2	3,378	2,944	2.0	95.9	0.9	2.0	0.7	2.3	3.4	11.9	5.3	8.0	10.5	10.5
30041		7	Hill.............................	2,899.2	16,347	2,020	5.6	72.1	0.9	25.4	1.2	3.6	9.0	18.6	9.4	13.6	11.4	9.9
30043	25,740	9	Jefferson	1,656.9	12,097	2,286	7.3	94.8	0.6	3.1	0.9	2.6	4.3	16.1	6.5	8.4	11.3	13.8
30045		8	Judith Basin	1,869.7	1,952	3,053	1.0	97.2	0.2	1.4	0.4	1.6	4.5	14.9	4.9	8.1	10.1	11.7
30047		6	Lake...........................	1,490.5	30,250	1,426	20.3	71.6	0.8	28.7	1.0	4.6	6.1	17.2	7.5	10.6	10.6	10.7
30049	25,740	5	Lewis and Clark	3,458.4	68,700	779	19.9	93.4	0.8	3.4	1.3	3.4	5.8	15.7	7.9	12.5	12.2	12.1
30051		9	Liberty........................	1,430.0	2,430	3,010	1.7	97.7	1.0	1.8	0.5	0.9	6.0	15.2	7.4	12.4	11.3	11.1
30053		7	Lincoln........................	3,612.5	19,794	1,838	5.5	94.6	0.7	2.8	0.9	3.3	4.5	13.8	5.0	8.3	9.7	11.5
30055		9	McCone.......................	2,642.2	1,675	3,073	0.6	96.1	1.3	2.4	0.7	1.7	5.6	14.6	7.3	9.9	9.5	9.5
30057		9	Madison	3,588.2	8,768	2,520	2.4	91.7	0.8	1.7	0.8	6.6	4.0	11.6	5.8	11.5	10.4	11.1
30059		9	Meagher......................	2,391.9	1,866	3,063	0.8	96.1	0.7	1.7	0.5	2.4	5.3	14.1	5.4	8.5	9.5	10.1
30061		8	Mineral	1,219.6	4,316	2,876	3.5	94.0	0.9	3.8	0.9	2.9	4.8	13.3	4.8	8.9	9.5	11.4
30063	33,540	3	Missoula......................	2,593.0	118,791	524	45.8	91.9	1.0	3.9	2.9	3.3	5.1	13.6	14.0	15.6	12.9	10.9
30065		8	Musselshell..................	1,869.0	4,651	2,854	2.5	92.3	1.1	3.0	2.1	3.3	4.3	14.3	5.7	9.1	9.0	12.3
30067		7	Park...........................	2,802.5	16,736	1,995	6.0	94.9	0.6	2.2	1.0	3.2	4.5	13.1	5.6	11.8	12.4	12.7
30069		9	Petroleum....................	1,655.6	513	3,135	0.3	96.7	1.8	2.3	0.8	2.1	3.7	14.2	8.2	8.0	8.4	13.5
30071		9	Phillips........................	5,140.5	4,074	2,895	0.8	87.5	0.9	11.9	0.9	3.2	7.1	16.7	6.8	9.0	10.5	10.6
30073		7	Pondera	1,624.6	5,972	2,755	3.7	83.3	0.9	15.4	0.9	2.0	7.3	16.7	7.9	12.1	9.8	11.0
30075		9	Powder River	3,298.2	1,716	3,071	0.5	96.2	0.9	3.1	0.9	1.8	4.4	12.3	7.2	9.3	9.6	11.1
30077		6	Powell.........................	2,326.0	6,968	2,672	3.0	90.4	1.4	6.1	0.9	2.8	3.9	10.7	8.1	12.8	13.5	15.0
30079		9	Prairie........................	1,736.6	1,087	3,105	0.6	93.9	1.1	2.9	1.7	4.0	4.5	12.8	5.3	8.3	9.7	10.4
30081		6	Ravalli	2,391.0	43,172	1,112	18.1	94.4	0.6	2.2	1.1	3.6	4.8	14.3	6.4	9.3	10.7	12.2
30083		7	Richland......................	2,084.3	10,913	2,358	5.2	91.7	1.0	3.6	0.9	5.3	6.8	18.5	7.7	13.5	12.4	11.9
30085		7	Roosevelt....................	2,354.3	11,059	2,349	4.7	36.8	0.7	60.8	1.1	4.2	10.2	23.3	8.5	13.8	11.0	9.7
30087		9	Rosebud......................	5,008.1	9,063	2,493	1.8	57.4	0.8	37.9	1.7	4.9	8.4	20.6	8.3	11.8	10.0	11.3
30089		8	Sanders.......................	2,760.4	11,844	2,306	4.3	92.4	0.6	5.5	0.8	3.2	4.8	12.8	5.4	7.8	8.8	10.5
30091		9	Sheridan......................	1,675.8	3,424	2,942	2.0	92.1	1.0	3.2	1.0	4.8	5.2	15.2	6.4	9.8	13.1	10.7
30093	15,580	5	Silver Bow...................	718.0	34,993	1,304	48.7	91.5	1.0	3.1	1.3	5.1	5.8	14.5	11.5	12.3	11.0	11.3
30095		8	Stillwater.....................	1,796.7	9,534	2,460	5.3	93.7	0.6	2.0	1.1	4.4	4.5	17.3	6.2	8.4	11.2	12.4
30097		9	Sweet Grass.................	1,855.5	3,710	2,924	2.0	95.5	0.9	2.3	1.2	2.5	4.6	15.2	7.9	8.7	9.9	11.9
30099		8	Teton	2,271.6	6,162	2,737	2.7	95.5	0.6	3.1	1.5	1.6	6.9	17.4	6.9	9.9	10.3	11.3
30101		7	Toole..........................	1,915.0	4,853	2,843	2.5	88.9	1.7	6.7	1.4	4.3	6.6	14.0	7.3	13.2	13.0	11.6
30103		8	Treasure......................	977.8	679	3,129	0.7	92.2	0.4	3.8	1.6	3.8	8.1	12.8	5.0	9.7	8.8	8.4
30105		7	Valley.........................	4,926.1	7,437	2,632	1.5	86.8	0.9	10.4	1.6	2.7	5.9	17.0	6.4	10.5	10.7	10.8
30107		9	Wheatland	1,422.5	2,236	3,026	1.6	91.2	0.9	2.4	1.3	6.9	6.3	18.5	9.5	8.5	9.2	10.0
30109		9	Wibaux.......................	888.6	1,034	3,106	1.2	93.9	0.1	1.7	1.3	4.1	6.2	15.2	7.3	8.5	11.4	11.2
30111	13,740	3	Yellowstone..................	2,633.5	160,137	414	60.8	88.6	1.4	5.5	1.5	5.8	6.3	17.2	7.9	13.9	12.6	11.7
31000		0	NEBRASKA..................	76,817.6	1,929,268	X	25.1	80.3	5.8	1.4	3.3	11.2	6.9	17.8	9.9	13.3	12.4	11.4
31001	25,580	4	Adams........................	563.3	31,511	1,392	55.9	86.2	1.6	0.9	1.6	10.9	6.6	17.1	11.0	11.8	10.9	11.0
31003		9	Antelope......................	857.2	6,336	2,723	7.4	95.8	0.7	0.6	0.5	3.2	6.9	16.9	7.1	9.6	10.1	10.0
31005		9	Arthur.........................	715.4	465	3,138	0.6	95.1	0.2	0.6	0.9	4.3	5.2	20.6	8.8	11.0	11.6	9.7
31007	42,420	9	Banner........................	746.2	730	3,125	1.0	92.1	2.2	0.3	0.3	5.8	6.7	16.8	6.6	9.6	10.1	9.0

1. CBSA = Core Based Statistical Area. See Appendix A for explanation. See Appendix B for list of metropolitan areas with component counties. 2. County type code from the Economic Research Service of USDA Rural-Urban Continuum Codes. See Appendix A for definition. 3. Dry land or land partially or temporarily covered by water. 4. May be of any race.

Table B. States and Counties — Population and Households

STATE County	Population, 2018 (cont.) Age (percent) (cont.)				Population change, 2000-2018							Households, 2013-2017				
	55 to 64 years	65 to 74 years	75 years and over	Percent female	Total persons 2000	Total persons 2010	Percent change 2000-2010	Percent change 2010-2018	Births	Deaths	Net Migration	Number	Persons per household	Family house-holds	Female family house-holder[1]	One person
	16	17	18	19	20	21	22	23	24	25	26	27	28	29	30	31
MISSOURI— Cont'd																
St. Louis city.....................	13.2	8.3	5.4	51.6	348,189	319,275	-8.3	-5.1	37,676	24,933	-29,115	139,741	2.18	46.2	17.5	44.8
MONTANA	14.3	11.3	7.5	49.7	902,195	989,409	9.7	7.4	100,933	78,277	49,992	419,975	2.38	62.1	8.2	30.4
Beaverhead...................	15.0	12.4	9.6	48.6	9,202	9,246	0.5	1.7	734	690	115	3,978	2.23	57.0	5.1	36.2
Big Horn.......................	11.5	8.1	4.7	50.2	12,671	12,865	1.5	3.7	2,200	1,076	-649	3,710	3.54	79.4	20.4	17.0
Blaine..........................	12.3	8.7	6.7	49.8	7,009	6,491	-7.4	4.9	895	555	-23	2,314	2.82	67.4	15.9	28.3
Broadwater...................	17.1	14.8	8.8	48.8	4,385	5,607	27.9	8.5	427	451	497	2,405	2.37	64.5	5.3	27.5
Carbon........................	18.7	15.9	9.9	49.4	9,552	10,078	5.5	6.3	626	797	803	4,565	2.27	62.8	5.7	32.2
Carter.........................	18.2	13.1	12.7	50.3	1,360	1,160	-14.7	6.7	117	108	68	565	2.29	65.1	4.2	32.7
Cascade.......................	13.5	10.4	8.2	49.4	80,357	81,323	1.2	0.4	9,484	6,875	-2,252	34,383	2.30	62.5	9.7	31.7
Chouteau	15.9	12.1	8.3	50.0	5,970	5,813	-2.6	-1.2	413	491	8	2,290	2.50	68.5	8.1	28.8
Custer.........................	15.0	11.0	9.0	49.9	11,696	11,699	0.0	-1.0	1,250	1,162	-196	4,875	2.35	65.6	9.6	29.5
Daniels........................	16.5	13.2	13.3	48.4	2,017	1,751	-13.2	-0.2	147	185	33	876	2.01	56.4	2.1	40.0
Dawson........................	15.2	10.9	9.0	48.5	9,059	8,963	-1.1	-3.2	935	803	-434	4,045	2.19	68.0	6.8	23.7
Deer Lodge...................	17.1	14.5	9.4	46.6	9,417	9,292	-1.3	-1.7	604	1,033	271	3,984	2.03	58.2	7.0	39.6
Fallon.........................	14.9	9.0	7.9	49.3	2,837	2,890	1.9	1.0	391	244	-120	1,241	2.30	64.1	10.1	32.1
Fergus........................	15.4	14.1	10.4	48.7	11,893	11,593	-2.5	-4.1	997	1,310	-162	4,953	2.19	62.6	7.9	34.2
Flathead......................	15.3	12.3	7.3	50.2	74,471	90,927	22.1	12.3	9,246	6,936	8,833	38,006	2.50	65.4	6.7	28.9
Gallatin.......................	11.1	8.1	4.5	48.1	67,831	89,513	32.0	25.0	9,687	4,406	16,853	40,723	2.38	58.5	5.9	27.5
Garfield.......................	14.7	13.3	9.9	49.6	1,279	1,209	-5.5	4.9	122	100	35	451	2.40	72.3	3.5	25.9
Glacier........................	12.5	7.2	4.8	51.6	13,247	13,399	1.1	2.6	2,013	1,221	-445	4,181	3.07	65.4	17.0	34.5
Golden Valley................	15.9	16.2	10.9	50.0	1,042	884	-15.2	-6.6	66	74	-52	325	2.30	68.9	8.0	24.6
Granite........................	19.9	18.1	12.5	49.0	2,830	3,079	8.8	9.7	160	268	405	1,309	2.40	61.7	2.8	32.2
Hill.............................	12.9	9.0	6.2	49.7	16,673	16,096	-3.5	1.6	2,466	1,224	-994	6,208	2.58	65.0	14.3	28.2
Jefferson.....................	18.2	14.7	6.7	49.5	10,049	11,403	13.5	6.1	730	830	802	4,512	2.52	71.3	6.4	23.8
Judith Basin	18.7	15.1	12.0	48.3	2,329	2,072	-11.0	-5.8	124	148	-96	925	2.12	65.2	6.2	29.6
Lake...........................	15.2	13.2	8.9	50.7	26,507	28,746	8.4	5.2	3,001	2,387	910	11,796	2.45	65.5	10.5	29.6
Lewis and Clark	15.1	11.7	7.1	50.6	55,716	63,395	13.8	8.4	6,342	4,798	3,762	27,534	2.34	62.5	9.6	30.6
Liberty........................	16.0	9.3	11.2	51.8	2,158	2,339	8.4	3.9	198	182	73	859	2.54	64.1	4.8	33.5
Lincoln........................	18.6	17.4	11.2	49.6	18,837	19,683	4.5	0.6	1,437	1,977	661	8,244	2.31	59.6	4.8	33.6
McCone........................	17.4	14.0	12.2	48.7	1,977	1,734	-12.3	-3.4	138	150	-45	720	2.37	67.6	2.6	31.1
Madison.......................	17.4	18.3	9.9	46.5	6,851	7,691	12.3	14.0	501	621	1,197	3,487	2.18	68.4	4.0	36.4
Meagher.......................	16.5	19.2	11.5	49.5	1,932	1,891	-2.1	-1.3	154	209	31	777	2.54	60.9	9.3	32.4
Mineral........................	18.4	16.9	12.0	49.0	3,884	4,226	8.8	2.1	358	421	152	1,694	2.43	55.9	7.9	38.6
Missoula.......................	12.2	9.8	5.8	49.9	95,802	109,296	14.1	8.7	10,052	6,985	6,448	47,963	2.31	55.9	8.5	31.8
Musselshell...................	18.7	16.4	10.1	49.6	4,497	4,538	0.9	2.5	341	453	224	2,073	2.28	64.2	6.0	30.5
Park...........................	17.1	14.3	8.4	49.6	15,694	15,636	-0.4	7.0	1,213	1,237	1,119	7,552	2.09	56.3	5.1	36.7
Petroleum.....................	19.1	10.5	14.4	45.6	493	488	-1.0	5.1	21	28	35	206	2.20	61.7	2.9	29.1
Phillips........................	17.0	11.9	10.4	49.8	4,601	4,252	-7.6	-4.2	427	413	-193	1,791	2.27	60.2	4.9	37.0
Pondera	14.9	11.0	9.4	50.2	6,424	6,155	-4.2	-3.0	631	555	-258	2,218	2.61	63.8	11.8	32.9
Powder River	18.9	15.7	11.5	50.5	1,858	1,743	-6.2	-1.5	114	168	24	764	2.05	64.1	6.5	31.9
Powell.........................	15.4	12.1	8.5	37.6	7,180	7,034	-2.0	-0.9	444	620	108	2,400	2.18	67.4	7.5	28.0
Prairie.........................	17.2	19.3	12.5	49.1	1,199	1,179	-1.7	-7.8	100	147	-49	549	2.37	66.1	1.5	29.1
Ravalli.........................	16.6	15.7	10.1	50.4	36,070	40,212	11.5	7.4	3,169	3,570	3,370	16,936	2.42	66.3	7.5	28.4
Richland.......................	14.4	9.0	6.0	47.8	9,667	9,746	0.8	12.0	1,274	751	589	4,523	2.51	66.1	7.5	30.1
Roosevelt.....................	12.1	6.9	4.5	50.0	10,620	10,425	-1.8	6.1	1,916	1,121	-170	3,203	3.42	65.2	19.8	30.0
Rosebud.......................	13.9	10.0	5.8	49.6	9,383	9,235	-1.6	-1.9	1,315	705	-789	3,205	2.87	69.8	7.9	25.5
Sanders.......................	18.7	19.3	12.0	48.8	10,227	11,413	11.6	3.8	882	1,137	693	4,994	2.24	66.8	6.0	26.5
Sheridan......................	17.0	11.9	10.7	49.3	4,105	3,384	-17.6	1.2	326	444	149	1,661	2.10	60.0	5.3	34.6
Silver Bow....................	14.5	10.8	8.3	49.8	34,606	34,209	-1.1	2.3	3,265	3,387	925	15,256	2.19	54.3	10.1	38.0
Stillwater.....................	17.4	14.4	8.3	48.8	8,195	9,105	11.1	4.7	686	715	456	3,797	2.42	72.1	3.7	24.8
Sweet Grass	15.3	14.6	11.9	48.9	3,609	3,652	1.2	1.6	265	332	129	1,531	2.37	66.2	5.4	32.7
Teton..........................	14.4	11.7	10.9	50.8	6,445	6,071	-5.8	1.5	644	532	-19	2,413	2.43	63.9	5.1	32.5
Toole..........................	15.8	10.3	8.2	44.1	5,267	5,324	1.1	-8.8	470	379	-573	1,871	2.28	64.0	8.1	31.8
Treasure......................	18.6	15.9	12.7	49.9	861	718	-16.6	-5.4	73	70	-42	365	2.16	72.9	4.7	26.0
Valley.........................	15.3	11.9	11.4	49.9	7,675	7,369	-4.0	0.9	701	659	26	3,432	2.16	63.7	7.0	29.5
Wheatland.....................	14.2	13.5	10.4	48.5	2,259	2,168	-4.0	3.1	199	193	61	820	2.52	58.5	6.8	36.7
Wibaux........................	16.0	13.2	11.1	48.3	1,068	1,017	-4.8	1.7	92	124	44	497	2.21	70.8	5.8	28.4
Yellowstone...................	13.4	9.8	7.1	50.8	129,352	147,982	14.4	8.2	16,350	11,820	7,644	64,020	2.39	62.9	8.8	29.3
NEBRASKA.................	12.6	8.9	6.8	50.1	1,711,263	1,826,305	6.7	5.6	216,048	130,333	17,767	748,405	2.46	64.5	9.8	29.0
Adams..........................	13.5	10.2	8.0	50.2	31,151	31,367	0.7	0.5	3,368	2,543	-674	12,659	2.35	61.8	7.4	32.5
Antelope.......................	15.7	12.1	11.5	49.7	7,452	6,685	-10.3	-5.2	694	619	-427	2,748	2.30	69.9	8.0	26.5
Arthur..........................	11.2	11.6	10.3	50.5	444	460	3.6	1.1	36	34	3	177	2.38	54.2	4.0	40.1
Banner..........................	17.3	15.6	8.2	52.1	819	690	-15.8	5.8	51	36	22	300	2.43	79.0	8.3	20.3

1. No spouse present.

Table B. States and Counties — Population, Vital Statistics, Health, and Crime

STATE County	Persons in group quarters, 2018	Daytime Population, 2013-2017 Number	Employment/ residence ratio	Births, 2018 Total	Rate[1]	Deaths, 2018 Number	Rate[1]	Persons under 65 with no health insurance, 2016 Number	Percent	Medicare, 2018 Total beneficiaries	Enrolled in Original Medicare	Enrolled in Medicare Advantage	Serious crimes known to police[2], 2016 Total Number	Rate[3]
	32	33	34	35	36	37	38	39	40	41	42	43	44	45
MISSOURI— Cont'd														
St. Louis city......................	11,551	424,197	1.73	4,047	13.4	3,222	10.6	32,997	12.6	49,417	28,720	20,697	25,236	8,024
MONTANA	28,965	1,027,347	0.99	12,050	11.3	9,726	9.2	84,231	10.0	222,949	181,667	41,282	31,816	3,052
Beaverhead......................	442	9,385	1.01	82	8.7	94	10.0	762	10.9	2,265	2,019	246	56	601
Big Horn...........................	137	13,861	1.12	240	18.0	153	11.5	2,105	18.5	1,878	1,672	206	482	3,619
Blaine...............................	220	6,515	0.95	99	14.5	61	9.0	924	16.8	1,113	D	D	21	318
Broadwater......................	52	4,984	0.69	56	9.2	54	8.9	478	10.8	1,426	1,234	192	65	1,139
Carbon.............................	53	9,063	0.72	75	7.0	86	8.0	846	10.7	2,716	2,120	596	129	1,230
Carter..............................	11	1,250	0.88	18	14.5	13	10.5	119	13.4	317	293	24	0	0
Cascade..........................	2,488	81,822	1.00	1,067	13.1	843	10.3	6,647	10.2	17,500	13,061	4,439	3,349	4,060
Chouteau.........................	135	5,439	0.85	54	9.4	62	10.8	732	15.9	1,197	1,006	191	19	330
Custer..............................	431	11,719	0.97	138	11.9	142	12.3	790	8.4	2,579	2,465	114	237	1,937
Daniels............................	41	1,788	1.00	15	8.6	16	9.2	134	10.3	440	426	14	2	113
Dawson...........................	498	9,285	0.99	88	10.1	88	10.1	553	7.6	1,837	1,750	87	202	2,066
Deer Lodge	854	9,013	0.97	74	8.1	112	12.3	598	9.2	2,571	2,239	332	374	4,104
Fallon..............................	34	3,035	1.07	39	13.4	25	8.6	170	6.5	530	512	18	20	614
Fergus.............................	465	11,385	1.01	121	10.9	142	12.8	785	9.3	3,020	2,449	571	205	1,798
Flathead...........................	992	95,922	1.00	1,144	11.2	884	8.7	7,557	9.5	22,997	17,620	5,377	3,292	3,382
Gallatin............................	3,273	100,114	0.99	1,282	11.5	569	5.1	6,846	7.6	15,311	12,295	3,016	2,394	2,320
Garfield...........................	0	1,074	0.98	17	13.4	11	8.7	107	10.8	279	266	13	9	670
Glacier............................	690	13,793	1.03	230	16.7	180	13.1	2,463	21.0	1,923	1,906	17	163	1,190
Golden Valley..................	89	675	0.79	10	12.1	2	2.4	66	11.0	296	237	59	8	979
Granite............................	40	3,134	0.94	18	5.3	30	8.9	298	12.6	961	857	104	64	1,953
Hill..................................	593	16,991	1.07	300	18.4	150	9.2	1,693	12.3	2,926	2,896	30	620	3,719
Jefferson	230	9,327	0.56	92	7.6	116	9.6	808	8.6	2,866	2,413	453	179	1,529
Judith Basin	0	1,873	0.90	13	6.7	10	5.1	152	10.4	558	447	111	14	736
Lake................................	586	28,116	0.88	359	11.9	331	10.9	3,570	15.5	7,180	5,921	1,259	890	3,005
Lewis and Clark	1,960	69,351	1.09	785	11.4	634	9.2	4,136	7.6	14,750	11,669	3,081	1,986	2,962
Liberty.............................	403	2,312	1.06	25	10.3	18	7.4	256	13.5	440	425	15	8	330
Lincoln.............................	209	19,101	0.98	166	8.4	252	12.7	1,724	12.4	7,133	5,125	2,008	328	1,732
McCone...........................	19	1,653	0.91	20	11.9	17	10.1	193	14.7	336	D	D	13	777
Madison	163	8,070	1.05	67	7.6	78	8.9	634	11.3	2,388	2,215	173	51	640
Meagher..........................	174	2,015	1.02	14	7.5	19	10.2	145	11.1	570	545	25	15	824
Mineral............................	22	3,934	0.83	39	9.0	41	9.5	332	11.3	1,413	1,201	212	4	94
Missoula...........................	3,645	117,024	1.05	1,174	9.9	878	7.4	9,106	9.5	21,531	17,288	4,243	4,577	3,972
Musselshell......................	52	4,768	1.00	38	8.2	63	13.5	408	11.7	1,369	1,183	186	121	2,634
Park.................................	108	14,886	0.86	151	9.0	157	9.4	1,277	10.1	3,976	3,871	105	374	2,329
Petroleum........................	0	439	0.94	2	3.9	1	1.9	53	14.1	104	88	16	NA	NA
Phillips............................	127	3,933	0.87	53	13.0	38	9.3	456	14.3	1,017	961	56	50	1,203
Pondera	645	5,968	0.96	86	14.4	60	10.0	610	12.8	1,343	1,159	184	49	791
Powder River	35	1,626	1.02	19	11.1	16	9.3	145	11.1	385	355	30	NA	NA
Powell.............................	1,708	6,867	1.01	53	7.6	72	10.3	413	10.2	1,561	1,395	166	165	2,423
Prairie.............................	21	1,249	0.88	8	7.4	11	10.1	87	10.5	357	331	26	15	1,298
Ravalli.............................	478	37,978	0.80	379	8.8	466	10.8	3,559	11.3	12,694	9,790	2,904	553	1,329
Richland..........................	34	12,142	1.13	138	12.6	84	7.7	869	8.7	1,839	1,824	15	274	2,198
Roosevelt........................	186	11,341	1.03	221	20.0	153	13.8	1,739	17.9	1,649	1,615	34	188	1,606
Rosebud..........................	65	10,080	1.20	149	16.4	102	11.3	995	12.7	1,691	1,534	157	50	530
Sanders...........................	188	11,168	0.94	109	9.2	139	11.7	1,226	15.3	4,073	3,505	568	152	1,341
Sheridan..........................	85	3,723	1.09	38	11.1	41	12.0	282	9.8	925	871	54	65	1,731
Silver Bow	998	34,568	1.00	389	11.1	412	11.8	2,517	9.2	7,882	6,706	1,176	1,857	5,348
Stillwater.........................	112	8,758	0.87	79	8.3	83	8.7	567	7.6	2,321	1,845	476	91	951
Sweet Grass	45	3,975	1.21	33	8.9	28	7.5	257	9.5	957	831	126	17	467
Teton...............................	461	5,701	0.88	80	13.0	54	8.8	514	11.0	1,514	1,075	439	69	1,129
Toole	673	5,051	1.01	58	12.0	38	7.8	399	11.6	923	899	24	94	1,865
Treasure..........................	0	725	0.83	10	14.7	5	7.4	66	13.3	197	168	29	NA	NA
Valley..............................	126	7,511	0.99	85	11.4	62	8.3	738	12.7	1,783	1,724	59	64	829
Wheatland........................	147	2,036	0.92	25	11.2	24	10.7	227	14.6	546	483	63	16	761
Wibaux............................	24	1,051	0.87	10	9.7	10	9.7	82	10.1	264	D	D	2	173
Yellowstone.....................	3,698	158,780	1.03	1,916	12.0	1,496	9.3	11,016	8.4	30,337	23,187	7,150	6,662	4,191
NEBRASKA..................	51,115	1,913,285	1.02	25,899	13.4	15,565	8.1	153,934	9.7	337,817	288,120	49,697	48,713	2,554
Adams.............................	1,296	31,415	0.99	406	12.9	309	9.8	2,246	9.0	6,692	6,353	339	1,104	3,495
Antelope..........................	60	6,084	0.90	91	14.4	66	10.4	548	11.3	1,511	D	D	35	551
Arthur..............................	0	404	0.90	4	8.6	2	4.3	44	11.9	109	D	D	0	0
Banner.............................	0	645	0.79	7	9.6	3	4.1	52	9.6	207	D	D	NA	NA

1. Per 1,000 estimated resident population.   2. Data for serious crimes have not been adjusted for underreporting; this may affect comparability between geographic areas and over time.   3. Per 100,000 population estimated by the FBI.

Table B. States and Counties — Crime, Education, Money Income, and Poverty

STATE County	Serious crimes known to police[2], 2016 (cont.)[1] — Rate		School enrollment and attainment, 2013-2017 — Enrollment[3]		Attainment[4] (percent)		Local government expenditures,[5] 2014-2015		Money income, 2013-2017		Households — Percent		Income and poverty, 2017	Percent below poverty level		
	Violent	Property	Total	Percent private	High school graduate or less	Bachelor's degree or more	Total current spending (mil dol)	Current spending per student (dollars)	Per capita income[6]	Median income (dollars)	with income of less than $50,000	with income of $200,000 or more	Median household income (dollars)	All persons	Children under 18 years	Children 5 to 17 years in families
	46	47	48	49	50	51	52	53	54	55	56	57	58	59	60	61
MISSOURI— Cont'd																
St. Louis city......................	1,943	6,081	75,442	32.6	37.5	34.1	452.8	11,223	26,739	38,664	60.5	3.0	40,876	21.4	32.6	32.2
MONTANA	368	2,683	236,695	12.6	36.3	30.7	1,593.0	11,025	28,706	50,801	49.2	3.7	53,262	12.7	15.9	14.0
Beaverhead.....................	64	537	2,291	3.4	37.0	33.0	13.4	11,680	28,420	43,880	53.5	3.6	55,842	13.8	17.9	16.6
Big Horn..........................	533	3,086	3,901	7.0	47.1	17.6	35.2	14,180	17,905	47,276	52.8	2.5	41,957	26.8	30.2	27.7
Blaine..............................	167	152	1,748	9.4	40.1	20.7	19.6	14,971	17,059	35,506	65.0	1.0	37,653	26.2	31.3	27.2
Broadwater.......................	491	648	1,017	6.9	42.6	28.6	6.1	9,344	32,268	55,295	43.7	4.2	54,523	9.8	13.6	11.9
Carbon.............................	238	992	1,770	4.5	34.1	31.1	17.0	12,737	31,697	56,988	44.1	3.3	52,726	9.4	13.2	10.9
Carter..............................	0	0	250	31.2	45.9	16.6	2.4	18,217	30,659	45,347	54.7	5.1	44,774	12.9	20.4	21.4
Cascade...........................	234	3,826	18,035	12.8	39.2	27.3	114.8	9,779	28,350	46,827	52.9	3.7	47,882	11.9	14.7	13.2
Chouteau..........................	52	278	1,427	6.4	39.1	25.6	10.4	16,025	22,014	39,577	61.4	1.6	42,598	14.5	20.8	17.2
Custer.............................	229	1,708	2,472	11.7	36.2	22.4	16.7	9,766	28,501	53,050	46.9	2.7	47,675	13	15.4	14.2
Daniels............................	0	113	312	4.5	44.5	23.0	3.2	11,658	36,108	53,591	43.2	5.0	47,032	10.2	10.7	9.7
Dawson............................	286	1,780	1,951	7.3	43.4	19.8	15.7	11,260	29,130	59,622	43.5	4.4	54,210	10.7	11.6	10.5
Deer Lodge	406	3,698	1,640	7.1	47.8	17.1	11.9	11,063	25,107	41,235	60.8	2.2	44,295	15.9	19.8	18.1
Fallon..............................	154	461	663	13.3	40.8	15.9	10.4	18,370	32,371	56,806	43.9	4.2	60,495	9.1	11.9	11.5
Fergus.............................	640	1,158	2,233	6.0	39.0	29.5	21.4	13,618	27,491	47,110	52.6	2.5	49,892	12.7	16.8	15.2
Flathead...........................	314	3,068	19,694	14.6	34.8	29.1	135.7	9,791	28,379	51,410	48.5	3.5	57,389	11	13.9	12.5
Gallatin............................	260	2,060	29,528	11.9	22.0	48.8	118.8	9,654	33,181	59,397	42.5	5.6	61,446	9.8	8.0	7.1
Garfield............................	74	596	167	2.4	47.2	17.5	2.5	13,714	29,896	47,188	52.1	4.7	43,753	16.4	25.6	23.6
Glacier.............................	285	905	3,781	6.0	51.7	18.4	36.7	13,185	16,737	29,201	68.7	2.2	38,345	26.2	32.7	30.0
Golden Valley....................	245	734	135	18.5	52.3	20.6	2.6	22,902	25,110	43,854	59.7	3.7	35,850	19	29.9	27.8
Granite.............................	153	1,800	666	5.4	43.1	25.0	4.8	12,412	29,144	49,063	50.6	4.1	44,834	12.2	19.1	16.0
Hill.................................	540	3,179	4,414	7.2	40.2	23.7	40.7	13,304	21,780	45,269	55.3	1.9	48,470	15.7	20.0	19.1
Jefferson	350	1,179	2,535	15.8	33.4	32.9	16.0	10,101	32,387	64,911	37.8	5.3	66,813	8.4	9.5	7.8
Judith Basin	105	631	317	9.5	40.2	28.3	5.2	20,699	28,709	43,281	54.1	2.4	43,748	12.7	19.0	16.4
Lake................................	452	2,553	6,465	12.4	38.4	26.0	50.4	11,610	24,348	42,582	56.8	3.7	42,265	18.8	25.2	22.5
Lewis and Clark	473	2,490	14,692	24.0	29.5	37.5	94.5	9,951	31,252	60,789	41.5	3.1	59,819	8.3	10.6	9.7
Liberty.............................	330	0	329	14.9	49.5	16.3	3.6	14,224	36,525	46,641	51.5	6.1	41,798	18.5	27.0	24.1
Lincoln.............................	211	1,521	3,582	13.9	47.2	20.4	26.8	11,288	22,483	36,934	63.7	1.7	38,257	15.6	28.3	25.4
McCone............................	120	658	328	12.5	48.2	17.4	3.2	13,351	28,230	46,193	53.2	4.9	44,001	14.7	19.0	17.2
Madison...........................	100	540	1,171	15.2	36.9	30.3	12.3	14,506	31,620	47,900	52.5	5.9	50,248	10	13.5	12.0
Meagher...........................	110	714	427	6.3	49.9	19.6	3.1	14,477	20,095	41,343	62.2	0.0	43,001	16	31.3	30.6
Mineral............................	94	0	633	8.4	52.2	15.2	9.2	15,886	22,894	40,117	59.9	1.8	42,452	14.5	23.2	20.6
Missoula..........................	415	3,557	31,273	9.5	26.3	42.6	142.8	10,496	29,681	49,412	50.4	4.0	53,141	14.3	14.7	12.0
Musselshell......................	675	1,960	886	7.7	52.0	15.0	7.9	10,957	23,908	38,156	58.8	1.1	42,255	17.2	26.8	24.8
Park................................	212	2,117	2,761	13.7	36.0	34.1	22.3	11,368	29,181	44,920	54.0	3.0	49,550	12.9	15.9	13.5
Petroleum.........................	NA	NA	65	0.0	49.7	25.3	1.4	15,849	31,549	46,429	52.9	4.4	43,669	14.1	24.0	20.5
Phillips............................	265	939	739	10.7	45.1	18.1	10.8	16,025	22,369	42,101	57.5	2.0	44,168	14.4	20.5	20.5
Pondera...........................	113	678	1,424	14.8	44.2	22.1	13.6	14,626	22,866	44,597	54.2	1.7	42,175	17.7	24.7	21.6
Powder River	NA	NA	256	15.6	35.4	25.6	4.0	15,684	31,211	51,136	49.3	0.9	49,446	12.2	16.8	15.6
Powell.............................	382	2,041	966	14.3	49.4	18.2	10.7	14,633	23,990	44,352	56.2	4.8	45,418	18.7	19.1	17.0
Prairie.............................	260	1,038	235	21.7	47.3	20.5	2.1	13,828	28,366	50,850	48.5	1.8	43,238	12	17.2	15.8
Ravalli.............................	214	1,115	8,758	12.2	40.6	26.5	54.3	9,819	25,151	44,733	53.4	1.8	49,997	12.5	18.1	16.4
Richland...........................	377	1,821	2,447	6.5	45.1	19.7	25.6	12,588	33,709	66,572	35.8	5.0	63,343	8.7	10.6	9.5
Roosevelt..........................	632	974	2,961	3.2	51.7	15.5	37.6	14,995	18,030	39,219	59.0	1.8	42,379	26.1	32.8	29.7
Rosebud...........................	85	445	2,212	11.0	45.3	18.8	27.6	16,913	23,832	54,709	45.6	3.3	54,998	17.3	22.7	21.1
Sanders...........................	238	1,103	1,843	12.6	53.1	17.3	19.5	14,165	23,020	36,445	64.5	2.5	40,582	20.5	29.8	28.0
Sheridan...........................	160	1,571	604	10.3	40.6	20.8	9.3	17,513	32,833	51,940	48.6	5.1	49,862	11	11.2	9.7
Silver Bow........................	282	5,066	7,696	12.7	41.9	25.9	43.6	9,942	26,248	40,480	58.0	2.6	44,762	16.3	18.9	16.7
Stillwater	272	679	1,952	11.2	42.1	25.0	17.4	12,308	31,583	61,998	39.2	3.0	63,140	8.5	10.4	8.6
Sweet Grass......................	137	330	766	7.8	42.7	25.4	5.9	11,313	28,065	49,761	50.3	2.4	52,303	10	13.4	11.9
Teton...............................	311	818	1,309	15.6	39.4	23.7	13.7	13,385	26,884	51,060	49.2	2.6	47,750	13.5	19.7	17.9
Toole...............................	436	1,428	955	18.3	51.8	14.8	9.1	13,933	26,354	46,735	52.5	2.6	46,896	15.7	18.0	16.1
Treasure...........................	NA	NA	144	2.8	42.0	23.1	1.6	27,439	22,880	42,454	61.1	0.5	50,432	11.7	18.8	20.3
Valley..............................	194	634	1,446	11.6	44.6	21.1	17.6	14,377	29,096	55,267	46.4	2.8	47,676	11.8	16.1	15.0
Wheatland.........................	476	285	445	3.6	57.6	17.8	4.7	16,599	20,165	37,222	63.9	0.4	36,771	18.5	25.6	22.4
Wibaux............................	0	173	220	18.6	46.4	22.7	3.1	17,699	24,662	47,132	54.7	0.0	48,092	10.8	12.6	11.5
Yellowstone.......................	388	3,803	35,758	15.5	37.5	30.2	223.2	9,639	32,296	57,955	43.0	5.0	58,031	10.3	12.6	10.8
NEBRASKA.....................	291	2,263	506,803	16.3	35.8	30.6	3,730.4	11,932	29,866	56,675	43.8	4.1	59,913	10.7	13.7	12.6
Adams..............................	212	3,283	8,620	24.1	39.7	23.5	65.7	12,977	28,085	51,721	48.7	3.1	53,321	12.1	16.0	15.3
Antelope...........................	142	409	1,381	11.6	41.8	18.6	22.9	21,605	28,091	46,949	52.1	3.5	46,560	11.2	17.9	17.8
Arthur..............................	0	0	149	9.4	34.8	29.9	2.2	20,841	21,799	41,250	61.0	1.7	44,109	13.8	19.5	16.5
Banner.............................	NA	NA	149	2.7	36.9	17.4	3.2	19,444	30,736	55,000	45.3	4.7	53,040	11.7	21.3	21.3

1. Data for serious crimes have not been adjusted for underreporting; this may affect comparability between geographic areas and over time.   2. Per 100,000 population estimated by the FBI.   3. All persons 3 years old and over enrolled in nursery school through college.   4. Persons 25 years old and over.   5. Elementary and secondary education expenditures.   6. Based on population estimated by the American Community Survey, 2013–2017.

Table B. States and Counties — **Personal Income and Earnings**

STATE County	Personal income, 2017										Earnings, 2017		
	Total (mil dol)	Percent change 2016-2017	Per capita[1] Dollars	Per capita[1] Rank	Wages and salaries (mil dol)	Supplements to wages and salaries, employer contributions (mil dol) Pension and insurance	Supplements to wages and salaries, employer contributions (mil dol) Government social insurance	Proprietors' income (mil dol)	Dividends, interest, and rent (mil dol)	Personal transfer receipts (mil dol)	Total (mil dol)	Contributions for government social insurance (mil dol) From employee and self-employed	Contributions for government social insurance (mil dol) From employer
	62	63	64	65	66	67	68	69	70	71	72	73	74
MISSOURI— Cont'd													
St. Louis city	13,449	1.1	43,577	1,066	14,706	2,204	1,049	1,663	2,186	3,131	19,622	1,129	1,049
MONTANA	47,677	4.2	45,274	X	20,615	3,273	1,726	4,444	11,678	9,336	30,057	1,985	1,726
Beaverhead	419	-0.2	44,381	971	151	29	13	39	118	96	232	14	13
Big Horn	383	3.3	28,698	3,004	189	40	15	15	71	140	258	16	15
Blaine	193	-0.5	28,810	2,994	57	14	5	7	53	64	82	6	5
Broadwater	230	4.2	38,717	1,772	54	9	5	13	52	55	81	6	5
Carbon	486	3.9	45,444	850	102	17	9	30	131	97	158	13	9
Carter	55	-8.9	44,869	917	13	3	1	13	15	9	30	1	1
Cascade	3,753	4.1	45,959	801	1,723	300	147	238	840	806	2,409	156	147
Chouteau	191	3.3	33,066	2,606	50	9	4	4	68	45	68	5	4
Custer	512	2.9	43,680	1,054	206	35	17	74	105	106	333	21	17
Daniels	54	-20.8	31,067	2,848	29	5	2	-18	23	17	18	3	2
Dawson	372	1.0	41,576	1,321	180	27	17	8	67	77	231	17	17
Deer Lodge	348	4.0	38,219	1,842	126	23	10	15	72	106	174	13	10
Fallon	142	0.1	47,322	685	74	11	6	17	31	23	109	7	6
Fergus	476	4.5	42,200	1,243	177	31	15	53	126	110	276	19	15
Flathead	4,576	6.1	45,760	824	1,900	262	165	510	1,172	895	2,837	194	165
Gallatin	5,579	5.1	51,751	387	2,589	365	214	725	1,518	578	3,893	238	214
Garfield	48	-7.4	37,318	1,983	12	3	1	7	18	10	23	1	1
Glacier	450	2.4	32,960	2,621	169	39	14	25	96	148	246	15	14
Golden Valley	43	2.7	52,800	348	7	2	1	7	15	9	16	1	1
Granite	136	3.5	40,572	1,461	33	6	3	10	41	31	52	4	3
Hill	714	3.4	43,393	1,090	327	57	32	39	181	163	456	30	32
Jefferson	550	3.3	46,256	771	113	19	9	33	121	103	174	13	9
Judith Basin	93	-2.5	47,411	675	19	4	2	21	27	17	45	2	2
Lake	1,120	4.6	36,982	2,039	332	60	27	80	302	331	499	37	27
Lewis and Clark	3,208	4.2	47,328	683	1,709	305	136	243	739	592	2,392	152	136
Liberty	86		35,320	2,296	23	4	2	11	31	18	40	2	2
Lincoln	667	5.4	34,299	2,448	198	38	18	48	151	254	301	27	18
McCone	55	-21.6	32,104	2,739	25	5	2	-9	22	12	22	2	2
Madison	393	5.6	48,035	623	171	21	16	46	130	77	253	17	16
Meagher	83	0.5	44,763	935	19	4	2	12	28	23	36	2	2
Mineral	163	7.9	38,312	1,822	36	7	3	16	29	52	63	5	3
Missoula	5,500	5.3	46,829	725	2,654	403	223	489	1,534	929	3,769	244	223
Musselshell	183	3.9	39,433	1,653	60	10	4	10	43	57	85	7	4
Park	769	5.5	47,033	709	225	31	20	73	259	149	350	25	20
Petroleum	18	-10.8	34,407	2,428	5	1	0	3	5	3	10	0	0
Phillips	147	-3.3	35,634	2,252	47	9	4	3	44	42	63	5	4
Pondera	243	-3.1	40,688	1,444	62	12	6	13	77	64	92	7	6
Powder River	59	-5.1	33,759	2,514	18	4	2	8	19	11	31	2	2
Powell	278	3.4	40,884	1,420	98	22	8	17	92	65	146	10	8
Prairie	48	1.9	43,463	1,080	12	3	1	5	13	12	21	2	1
Ravalli	1,793	5.4	42,123	1,250	452	75	39	121	496	446	687	56	39
Richland	609	-1.8	55,167	275	301	44	24	59	123	74	428	27	24
Roosevelt	350	1.3	31,565	2,800	149	30	12	-8	70	126	182	14	12
Rosebud	381	2.9	41,167	1,384	216	43	19	8	63	91	285	18	19
Sanders	391	4.0	33,426	2,565	103	21	10	32	97	151	166	15	10
Sheridan	159	-13.9	45,855	811	60	11	5	9	47	32	85	6	5
Silver Bow	1,659	5.9	47,943	628	688	114	56	255	338	356	1,112	73	56
Stillwater	462	4.2	49,040	532	195	29	14	37	110	83	276	18	14
Sweet Grass	155	2.5	42,048	1,259	80	12	6	6	56	32	104	7	6
Teton	268	-1.5	43,992	1,025	67	13	6	38	82	59	123	8	6
Toole	211	3.2	43,255	1,110	92	18	8	24	62	38	141	9	8
Treasure	32	-0.4	46,863	722	7	1	1	6	9	7	15	1	1
Valley	307	-4.1	41,337	1,358	136	24	13	-11	87	80	161	13	13
Wheatland	75	-2.3	35,177	2,318	23	4	2	8	22	22	37	2	2
Wibaux	48	10.2	46,683	739	11	3	1	12	8	10	27	2	1
Yellowstone	7,955	5.0	50,035	463	4,043	583	331	895	1,530	1,334	5,851	375	331
NEBRASKA	97,557	3.0	50,875	X	48,428	8,132	3,687	11,998	19,771	14,550	72,246	4,178	3,687
Adams	1,494	3.5	47,158	701	659	118	49	150	336	282	977	59	49
Antelope	335	5.0	52,682	352	94	17	7	72	73	61	191	9	7
Arthur	20	1.9	43,247	1,112	6	1	1	4	5	4	11	0	1
Banner	42	-17.2	56,007	249	8	1	1	17	6	6	28	1	1

1. Based on the resident population estimated as of July 1 of the year shown.

Table B. States and Counties — Earnings, Social Security, and Housing

STATE County	Earnings, 2017 (cont.)									Social Security beneficiaries, December 2017		Supplemental Security Income recipients, 2017	Housing units, 2018	
					Percent by selected industries									
	Farm	Mining, quarrying, and extractions	Construction	Manu-facturing	Information; professional, scientific, technical services	Retail trade	Finance, insurance, real estate, and leasing	Health care and social assistance	Govern-ment	Number	Rate[1]		Total	Percent change, 2010-2018
	75	76	77	78	79	80	81	82	83	84	85	86	87	88
MISSOURI— Cont'd														
St. Louis city	0	D	D	7.3	16.8	1.6	10.9	16.1	14.8	53,145	172	15,543	177,156	0.7
MONTANA	1	3.2	8.9	4.4	8.3	8.3	7.2	14.6	20	228,685	218	18,215	515,175	6.7
Beaverhead	12.5	D	6.7	1	4	8.6	6.3	12.5	27.2	2,300	244	125	5,347	1.4
Big Horn	3.3	21.5	D	D	2.5	4.8	2.1	D	43.4	2,215	166	352	4,735	0.8
Blaine	2.2	D	2.9	0.8	D	12.4	D	D	51.1	1,180	176	201	2,853	0.4
Broadwater	6.2	D	D	17.6	D	7.3	7.8	7.5	18.7	1,475	248	65	2,742	1.8
Carbon	0.3	2.8	15.4	2	D	5	6.6	9.5	21.5	2,795	261	110	6,572	2.1
Carter	48.4	0.1	D	0.4	D	5.1	D	D	17.6	305	250	7	834	3
Cascade	0.4	0	7.9	3.5	6	8.2	7.7	17.4	27.2	18,455	226	1,849	39,036	4.7
Chouteau	10.7	0.1	3.6	1.5	D	10	7	6.9	29.9	1,225	212	63	2,929	1.7
Custer	4.1	0.3	7.4	0.9	D	12.4	7.4	D	21.3	2,620	224	239	5,700	2.5
Daniels	-138.6	D	5.4	D	D	D	D	D	34.5	465	268	12	1,126	1.4
Dawson	-3.8	7	3.8	1.1	5.3	8.4	4.3	D	17.4	1,760	197	104	4,443	5
Deer Lodge	0.3	0	8.8	D	6.6	5.1	2.6	30.6	30.7	2,645	290	271	5,217	1.9
Fallon	6.3	25.6	12.5	0.9	2.2	4.1	3	7	15.1	555	184	11	1,685	14.6
Fergus	2.4	D	15.8	7.3	3.7	8.2	7.8	D	20.7	3,065	271	194	5,905	1.1
Flathead	0.3	0.6	11	6.5	7.6	8.8	9.2	19.4	12	23,565	236	1,303	49,096	4.5
Gallatin	1.2	0.5	13.7	5.1	13.4	11.5	7.6	9.5	15.1	15,135	140	581	51,011	20.6
Garfield	28.7	0.1	D	D	D	7.1	D	1.6	31.7	285	220	11	864	2.4
Glacier	4.6	2.9	2.2	0.4	D	7.6	1.2	D	56.1	2,130	156	588	5,391	0.8
Golden Valley	12.1	D	D	D	D	D	3.4	D	19.9	295	359	15	484	1.7
Granite	7.6	0.6	7.2	4.4	D	5.8	D	D	26	1,005	299	47	2,835	0.5
Hill	4.6	0.1	5.4	0.4	6.4	7.3	4.8	D	31.3	2,710	165	427	7,343	1.3
Jefferson	2.1	9.8	11.2	6.5	D	3.4	4.9	9	26.5	3,070	258	145	5,115	1.2
Judith Basin	44.2	0	6.8	0.4	D	3.6	D	D	18.2	550	280	23	1,357	1.6
Lake	1.5	0.7	9.3	5.2	6.5	8.5	3.7	13.7	35.4	7,425	245	724	16,939	2.1
Lewis and Clark	0.4	0.7	5.6	2.3	10.3	6.4	9	13.2	35	15,400	227	1,112	31,793	5.3
Liberty	28.3	D	3.7	0.6	D	5.2	D	D	16.5	405	167	53	1,045	0.2
Lincoln	0.3	0.8	10.9	2.6	3.8	9.8	3.3	15.6	28.7	7,005	360	590	11,676	2.3
McCone	-47.6	0.1	8	0.4	D	7.5	D	D	30.9	345	201	0	1,022	1.3
Madison	6.3	7	8.8	1.9	3.6	4.4	4	D	10.7	2,370	290	66	7,017	1.1
Meagher	17.7	D	D	D	D	D	5	D	19.7	580	313	50	1,449	1.2
Mineral	-0.4	2.3	9.4	14.2	D	11.9	1.4	D	28.2	1,485	349	132	2,502	2.2
Missoula	0.1	0.1	7	3.2	9.7	8.9	7.4	18.3	18.9	21,760	185	2,097	54,926	9.6
Musselshell	-0.7	41.7	8.3	0.6	2.5	4.4	D	9.1	15.3	1,445	311	111	2,704	1.9
Park	3.1	0.1	11	7.2	6.6	6.5	6.5	12.4	12.8	3,850	235	226	9,665	3.1
Petroleum	29.7	D	2.8	0	D	D	1.5	D	26.5	115	220	0	332	3.1
Phillips	-6.1	D	10	1.8	D	8.9	8.3	D	34.4	1,050	255	86	2,353	0.8
Pondera	2.1	1.4	12.4	1.9	4.6	9.4	D	15.1	21.8	1,330	223	191	2,674	0.5
Powder River	15.5	D	D	D	D	9.7	D	D	31.2	375	214	0	1,033	1.1
Powell	2.5	D	D	D	2.6	4.1	2.2	10.4	48.8	1,585	233	109	3,254	4.7
Prairie	8.8	0.1	D	D	D	4.6	D	D	50.1	360	325	16	679	0.9
Ravalli	-0.5	0.7	13.5	5.4	9.5	7.5	6	13.4	19.3	12,950	304	754	19,846	1.3
Richland	0.9	19.7	11.9	5.5	3.2	7.9	7.5	D	11	1,880	170	97	5,255	15.5
Roosevelt	-15.5	4.5	4.3	0.5	D	8.9	2.6	D	55.4	1,790	161	393	4,137	1.8
Rosebud	1.2	18.1	D	D	D	2.8	D	D	34.3	1,815	196	226	4,182	3.1
Sanders	0.7	2.4	10.8	5.9	3	7.3	4.3	13.3	24	4,315	368	306	6,765	1.3
Sheridan	2.1	6.2	D	D	4.4	8	D	D	24.6	935	270	35	2,166	3.7
Silver Bow	0.1	10.4	3.5	4.3	5	12.6	6.9	15.9	15.9	8,485	245	980	17,291	3.4
Stillwater	4.7	D	D	4.9	3	3.1	1.7	4	9.4	2,365	251	79	4,879	1.7
Sweet Grass	-2.2	D	9.5	3.3	2	5	3.6	4.6	11.4	955	259	25	2,169	0.9
Teton	9.5	D	12.3	0.9	D	6.9	7.2	6.8	18.4	1,535	252	121	2,920	1
Toole	4.8	6	D	D	D	3.8	3.9	5.2	28.8	930	190	98	2,381	1.9
Treasure	48.8	0	2.2	0	D	D	D	D	15.3	210	309	11	432	2.4
Valley	-14.1	D	6	1.3	D	7.8	7	D	29	1,815	244	128	4,896	0.3
Wheatland	18.3	D	10.6	6.9	D	6.4	4.2	D	21	520	243	54	1,210	1.1
Wibaux	21.4	D	D	D	D	5.6	3.4	D	25.2	255	250	5	571	6.1
Yellowstone	0.5	3.8	8.9	6.3	9.5	7.4	8.3	17.5	11.6	31,240	197	2,583	72,392	13.2
NEBRASKA	4.9	0.2	5.6	9.2	8.1	5.6	9	11	16.2	340,251	177	28,272	845,042	6.1
Adams	7.9	0.1	7.2	14.9	3.5	6	4.9	D	14.8	6,810	215	553	13,955	4.5
Antelope	32	D	9.9	3.7	D	4	6.5	8.4	12.8	1,535	241	85	3,340	1.7
Arthur	50.4	0	D	0.2	D	D	2	D	22.4	110	241	0	254	0
Banner	65.4	0.3	D	0.6	0.8	3.5	D	D	12.1	235	317	0	367	-0.5

1. Per 1,000 resident population estimated as of July 1 of the year shown.

Table B. States and Counties — Housing, Labor Force, and Employment

STATE County	Housing units, 2013-2017								Civilian labor force, 2018				Civilian employment[6], 2013-2017		
	Occupied units							Sub-standard units[4] (percent)			Unemployment			Percent	
	Owner-occupied					Renter-occupied									
				Median owner cost as a percent of income		Median rent[3]	Median rent as a percent of income[2]			Percent change, 2017-2018				Management, business, science, and arts	Construction, production, and maintenance occupations
	Total	Percent	Median value[1]	With a mortgage	Without a mortgage[2]				Total		Total	Rate[5]	Total		
	89	90	91	92	93	94	95	96	97	98	99	100	101	102	103
MISSOURI— Cont'd															
St. Louis city	139,741	43.5	123,800	20.9	13.4	780	30.9	2.4	153,678	-0.4	5,878	3.8	152,079	40.6	15.2
MONTANA	419,975	67.7	209,100	22.2	10.8	751	28.1	2.6	528,244	0.6	19,656	3.7	497,995	36.5	22.2
Beaverhead	3,978	65.9	192,600	19.6	10.0	591	32	2.2	5,043	-0.1	158	3.1	4,647	34.1	24.7
Big Horn	3,710	61.3	100,000	18.3	10.0	661	23.2	16.6	5,098	-7.5	489	9.6	4,789	33.9	20.8
Blaine	2,314	59.0	85,800	22.8	13.1	480	21.1	7.5	2,291	-2.6	98	4.3	2,494	37.2	27.5
Broadwater	2,405	84.0	195,000	23.0	10.0	640	23.6	1.7	2,628	1.7	104	4	2,621	36.4	30.6
Carbon	4,565	79.0	227,400	21.1	11.6	754	26.3	2	5,487	-0.2	193	3.5	5,127	38.5	23.3
Carter	565	83.0	97,900	27.1	10.0	700	25.6	1.2	672	-3.4	17	2.5	607	49.8	24.7
Cascade	34,383	65.6	168,100	20.9	11.1	694	28	2.1	37,848	0.3	1,362	3.6	36,927	35.6	20.9
Chouteau	2,290	62.5	123,000	23.6	11.2	398	18.1	2.8	2,481	-0.4	75	3	2,490	39.0	21.8
Custer	4,875	70.3	157,000	18.4	10.0	723	25	1.6	6,068	-1.5	188	3.1	6,417	33.8	21.8
Daniels	876	76.8	123,500	17.4	12.6	677	19.7	2.1	881	-2.9	19	2.2	925	47.7	17.7
Dawson	4,045	69.4	154,300	18.0	10.0	650	19.7	5.1	4,639	-0.8	126	2.7	4,805	33.9	28.8
Deer Lodge	3,984	70.1	116,700	18.7	10.0	522	26.9	2.3	5,143	0.2	183	3.6	3,881	29.6	25.6
Fallon	1,241	67.7	154,200	17.3	10.0	738	18.9	1.5	1,704	-1.8	32	1.9	1,601	25.3	39.1
Fergus	4,953	70.0	133,700	19.4	12.4	710	22.4	3.6	5,779	0.3	215	3.7	5,593	36.9	20.9
Flathead	38,006	72.0	246,500	24.3	10.8	798	28.4	2.9	47,793	2.2	2,289	4.8	46,250	34.0	21.6
Gallatin	40,723	61.6	303,700	22.8	10.6	948	31.2	1.9	66,429	2.9	1,674	2.5	56,751	40.3	20.0
Garfield	451	80.9	116,300	20.0	10.0	500	18.8	3.3	738	-2.9	20	2.7	576	53.3	21.0
Glacier	4,181	59.0	105,000	17.3	10.3	511	26	4.8	5,713	-0.1	445	7.8	4,539	36.5	22.0
Golden Valley	325	72.0	98,300	26.3	10.2	820	19.4	2.5	369	-1.3	17	4.6	351	37.6	32.5
Granite	1,309	72.4	218,900	22.5	10.1	516	19	0.7	1,675	3.6	90	5.4	1,206	34.3	25.0
Hill	6,208	62.4	128,000	20.9	10.8	594	27.3	2.3	7,613	-2.3	274	3.6	7,144	35.7	23.9
Jefferson	4,512	85.1	264,000	21.2	10.0	714	23	2.3	5,630	0.1	216	3.8	5,302	43.4	21.1
Judith Basin	925	71.6	138,500	19.1	10.0	527	20.3	1	920	-0.3	31	3.4	965	43.6	27.2
Lake	11,796	71.8	224,100	27.9	11.2	665	24.1	3.6	13,135	0	563	4.3	11,866	34.8	25.0
Lewis and Clark	27,534	68.7	220,600	21.0	10.0	819	27.3	1.6	35,455	0.6	1,178	3.3	34,118	45.2	15.8
Liberty	859	61.1	108,000	25.7	10.0	542	23.8	2	964	-1.5	24	2.5	1,129	33.3	27.6
Lincoln	8,244	79.5	175,500	26.1	12.8	664	30.1	2.1	8,060	2.2	595	7.4	6,529	28.9	27.6
McCone	720	80.7	111,900	23.5	12.3	600	16.9	3.9	980	-4.1	18	1.8	798	53.4	22.4
Madison	3,487	76.9	252,200	25.8	11.6	734	25.9	4.1	4,488	2.2	159	3.5	3,873	33.8	26.3
Meagher	777	70.4	136,300	27.8	14.9	600	27.2	0	955	2.7	37	3.9	902	35.5	29.7
Mineral	1,694	70.7	159,800	26.4	12.1	564	29.1	2.1	1,718	2	123	7.2	1,583	26.2	24.4
Missoula	47,963	58.9	259,600	23.1	12.0	792	31.3	2.2	63,099	1.2	2,100	3.3	61,644	39.3	17.2
Musselshell	2,073	70.1	161,400	24.6	10.8	680	34.1	4.2	2,267	-0.9	97	4.3	1,853	27.4	31.0
Park	7,552	70.9	235,600	25.8	12.7	723	27.9	1.2	8,822	2.3	338	3.8	8,162	34.8	24.8
Petroleum	206	65.0	112,000	26.3	10.0	481	30	0	287	-1.7	12	4.2	256	54.7	23.8
Phillips	1,791	71.2	117,800	19.9	11.1	514	19.3	2.5	1,918	1.5	87	4.5	1,716	33.4	29.8
Pondera	2,218	72.3	122,100	20.1	11.2	591	26	3.2	2,712		110	4.1	2,652	34.9	25.3
Powder River	764	63.9	110,900	20.6	10.0	551	22.7	0	971	-3.5	28	2.9	954	39.6	30.2
Powell	2,400	69.2	141,000	20.7	10.0	571	22.8	5	2,880	-0.2	119	4.1	2,552	40.7	25.2
Prairie	549	88.7	100,700	14.7	10.0	444	33.3	0	492	1.2	18	3.7	626	44.1	25.9
Ravalli	16,936	74.0	246,600	26.9	12.0	756	29.7	2.3	19,913	0.8	835	4.2	17,549	34.9	25.3
Richland	4,523	62.6	213,000	15.9	10.0	833	21.1	3.6	5,889	-1.4	180	3.1	6,013	28.2	35.1
Roosevelt	3,203	57.8	116,400	16.8	10.0	389	17.5	5.6	4,461	-2.3	204	4.6	3,835	29.3	25.8
Rosebud	3,205	72.1	118,600	18.1	10.0	558	22.3	5.1	3,893	-3.2	206	5.3	4,032	33.5	31.8
Sanders	4,994	75.8	205,000	30.6	11.8	633	29.5	3.6	4,765	-0.2	304	6.4	4,084	29.3	29.5
Sheridan	1,661	75.9	146,500	21.3	11.5	712	28.5	1.4	1,769	-5	42	2.4	1,879	36.2	22.9
Silver Bow	15,256	66.5	133,800	20.4	11.0	606	31.5	1.9	17,238	0.6	692	4	16,310	33.8	22.4
Stillwater	3,797	77.8	225,200	19.8	10.8	697	23.4	3.7	4,932	1.9	168	3.4	4,508	31.8	33.5
Sweet Grass	1,531	74.6	225,900	21.3	12.3	683	19.6	1.3	1,772	-1.3	54	3	1,621	32.9	35.5
Teton	2,413	69.7	156,600	22.2	10.3	676	28.2	3.5	2,702	-2.8	91	3.4	2,746	37.3	28.4
Toole	1,871	58.0	125,200	18.5	10.0	562	22.7	0.3	2,120	-1.3	56	2.6	2,202	31.7	24.4
Treasure	365	69.3	105,500	35.7	14.4	590	20.5	1.4	337	-0.9	10	3	388	35.6	29.4
Valley	3,432	73.8	135,600	16.6	11.1	609	18.4	0.7	4,129	-0.7	126	3.1	3,832	37.7	23.6
Wheatland	820	64.5	89,300	21.3	11.0	575	22.9	4.9	782	-0.3	39	5	974	32.3	34.8
Wibaux	497	79.3	110,100	20.5	11.9	825	19.9	1.6	464	-3.7	16	3.4	563	41.6	25.4
Yellowstone	64,020	68.0	210,500	21.7	10.4	825	27.9	2.8	81,269	0	2,715	3.3	80,238	34.0	23.6
NEBRASKA	748,405	66.0	142,400	19.7	11.5	773	26.6	2.4	1,020,197	0.8	28,509	2.8	987,216	36.8	23.4
Adams	12,659	68.3	115,300	19.1	11.2	655	27.9	1.2	16,547	-0.7	475	2.9	15,890	33.4	26.8
Antelope	2,748	77.1	78,500	17.7	10.7	529	25.1	1.7	3,574	0.5	85	2.4	3,203	36.2	29.9
Arthur	177	63.3	101,500	25.0	11.5	658	25.8	0	219	-0.5	11	5	177	46.9	32.2
Banner	300	68.3	137,200	25.4	12.0	513	26.3	4.3	381	-2.1	13	3.4	398	52.0	25.1

1. Specified owner-occupied units.   2. A value of 10.0 represents 10 percent or less; a value of 50.0 represents 50 percent or more.   3. Specified renter-occupied units.   4. Overcrowded or lacking complete plumbing facilities.   5. Percent of civilian labor force.   6. Civilian employed persons 16 years old and over.

Table B. States and Counties — Nonfarm Employment and Agriculture

STATE County	Private nonfarm establishments, employment and payroll, 2016									Agriculture, 2017			
	Number of establish-ments	Employment						Annual payroll		Farms			Farm producers whose primary occupation is farming (percent)
		Total	Health care and social assistance	Manufac-turing	Retail trade	Finance and insurance	Professional, scientific, and technical services	Total (mil dol)	Average per employee (dollars)	Number	Percent with:		
											Fewer than 50 acres	1000 acres or more	
	104	105	106	107	108	109	110	111	112	113	114	115	116
MISSOURI— Cont'd													
St. Louis city	12,812	223,259	39,973	16,638	10,146	13,284	16,366	12,744	57,084	NA	NA	NA	NA
MONTANA	37,626	378,463	70,286	18,355	59,582	16,982	20,616	14,543	38,426	27,048	30.9	31.7	48.5
Beaverhead	384	2,532	492	58	552	99	114	77	30,342	494	40.9	30.0	54.7
Big Horn	211	2,365	597	D	379	71	43	109	46,160	353	19.0	46.2	55.8
Blaine	140	987	286	31	190	40	18	40	41,024	491	7.5	50.7	62.0
Broadwater	148	885	114	D	152	36	33	27	30,447	296	25.3	29.7	50.9
Carbon	408	2,164	283	53	276	59	84	58	26,602	725	28.0	23.7	52.8
Carter	33	151	D	D	39	NA	6	5	30,298	323	4.3	71.8	66.0
Cascade	2,410	30,825	7,140	1,453	4,964	1,627	1,199	1,120	36,342	1,027	37.7	22.6	42.1
Chouteau	155	692	217	37	99	41	12	22	32,038	633	4.3	61.5	66.0
Custer	424	4,415	950	47	923	274	97	142	32,120	441	24.3	39.0	48.1
Daniels	68	611	122	D	88	40	10	26	42,398	277	4.0	54.5	50.7
Dawson	333	2,740	619	33	542	96	51	109	39,722	487	12.3	41.9	48.7
Deer Lodge	251	2,766	1,338	D	302	68	98	108	39,052	77	15.6	22.1	32.6
Fallon	150	1,036	133	D	138	48	14	53	50,730	289	13.5	55.4	60.7
Fergus	443	3,267	764	381	485	117	81	117	35,874	845	18.6	48.3	56.3
Flathead	4,087	38,091	6,485	2,632	6,126	1,985	1,579	1,468	38,536	1,146	64.7	4.3	34.3
Gallatin	5,448	45,778	5,778	3,067	7,971	1,495	2,990	1,793	39,170	1,123	57.3	10.1	36.5
Garfield	25	130	D	D	50	D	NA	4	28,223	260	3.1	72.7	72.7
Glacier	224	2,234	437	D	506	45	41	84	37,441	637	16.0	31.1	45.1
Golden Valley	15	85	D	D	D	D	D	2	22,365	157	10.8	52.2	58.2
Granite	104	635	D	38	99	D	10	21	32,517	151	17.2	41.7	50.8
Hill	520	5,191	1,299	39	1,050	239	136	176	33,934	698	9.3	51.0	50.3
Jefferson	279	1,945	225	261	181	36	50	73	37,441	370	37.0	16.8	32.1
Judith Basin	59	201	9	NA	31	D	8	7	33,771	357	13.7	53.5	59.6
Lake	795	5,534	1,258	186	1,180	204	358	177	31,928	1,170	55.7	6.6	43.6
Lewis and Clark	2,243	25,535	5,930	644	3,993	1,605	1,747	1,034	40,486	707	66.1	11.2	32.0
Liberty	73	356	D	NA	51	19	9	9	26,146	246	2.0	75.6	70.4
Lincoln	592	3,948	988	192	762	122	101	115	29,068	345	53.0	2.3	39.7
McCone	51	351	D	D	78	22	D	13	37,895	437	4.1	59.0	60.1
Madison	358	1,446	155	84	241	65	52	52	36,283	605	29.4	28.4	49.7
Meagher	71	298	D	D	59	D	D	8	28,047	145	21.4	60.7	63.5
Mineral	118	844	124	D	220	13	14	21	24,404	93	44.1	4.3	19.9
Missoula	4,386	49,585	9,849	1,896	8,499	1,955	3,019	1,793	36,152	576	66.1	3.6	32.9
Musselshell	115	876	178	12	110	23	17	40	45,686	346	14.5	34.4	54.1
Park	799	5,083	891	420	743	182	192	166	32,744	575	39.8	22.6	46.2
Petroleum	12	29	D	NA	5	NA	D	0	12,759	104	12.5	64.4	68.4
Phillips	135	821	176	D	235	47	38	23	27,615	445	11.5	54.2	58.8
Pondera	176	1,327	264	70	229	61	31	43	32,068	486	14.0	39.9	54.3
Powder River	71	309	D	D	82	D	21	9	28,440	325	8.9	64.3	70.5
Powell	157	1,019	240	D	165	45	29	33	32,604	254	24.4	28.7	43.7
Prairie	36	146	D	D	24	16	6	4	24,760	179	4.5	65.9	67.0
Ravalli	1,452	9,181	1,597	778	1,524	360	482	296	32,282	1,576	74.6	3.0	39.1
Richland	528	5,841	621	504	582	143	138	359	61,399	527	13.5	50.7	53.2
Roosevelt	214	1,994	D	D	469	83	30	63	31,374	501	7.4	51.9	51.7
Rosebud	178	2,429	206	D	300	57	21	130	53,507	414	15.0	44.4	53.6
Sanders	365	2,125	522	224	333	51	43	61	28,687	521	37.2	9.6	44.3
Sheridan	169	950	304	D	166	73	34	28	29,207	458	4.6	55.9	67.1
Silver Bow	1,140	12,935	3,011	618	2,212	280	548	470	36,330	142	45.8	11.3	24.9
Stillwater	268	2,640	260	426	246	50	48	170	64,433	562	22.8	28.8	42.0
Sweet Grass	171	1,130	18	67	154	41	42	59	52,235	301	19.3	36.9	45.6
Teton	212	1,095	146	10	191	84	39	33	30,268	686	23.6	26.2	46.5
Toole	172	1,562	309	D	217	48	26	56	36,055	362	4.4	62.7	62.4
Treasure	19	52	D	NA	D	D	D	1	28,635	121	16.5	52.1	62.3
Valley	274	2,314	557	33	424	98	61	76	32,983	557	9.3	48.5	56.1
Wheatland	55	397	D	9	74	20	D	12	29,637	174	11.5	51.1	60.1
Wibaux	36	127	D	D	25	10	6	4	33,315	137	10.2	56.9	54.5
Yellowstone	5,614	70,372	14,309	3,266	10,826	4,361	3,422	3,023	42,955	1,314	45.9	14.5	35.7
NEBRASKA	54,265	884,450	129,977	91,984	112,718	63,100	40,375	37,715	42,642	46,332	23.8	23.8	51.6
Adams	971	13,612	2,983	2,460	1,969	389	276	487	35,753	545	25.1	25.1	61.7
Antelope	230	1,498	285	115	276	92	27	51	33,750	704	20.7	22.2	58.5
Arthur	11	68	NA	NA	D	D	D	2	28,118	95	4.2	63.2	62.9
Banner	7	33	NA	NA	NA	D	NA	1	36,970	239	6.3	41.4	48.0

Table B. States and Counties — **Agriculture**

STATE County	Land in farms Acreage (1,000)	Percent change, 2012-2017	Acres Average size of farm	Total irrigated (1,000)	Total cropland (1,000)	Value of land and buildings (dollars) Average per farm	Average per acre	Value of machinery and equipment, average per farm (dollars)	Value of products sold: Total (mil dol)	Average per farm (acres)	Percent from: Crops	Livestock and poultry products	Organic farms (number)	Farms with internet access (percent)	Government payments Total ($1,000)	Percent of farms
	117	118	119	120	121	122	123	124	125	126	127	128	129	130	131	132
MISSOURI— Cont'd																
St. Louis city......................	NA	NA	NA	NA	NA	NA	NA	NA	NA	NA	NA	NA	NA	NA	NA	NA
MONTANA	58,123	-2.7	2,149	2,061.2	16,406.3	1,968,381	916	164,524	3,520.6	130,162	45.0	55.0	221	81.4	284,244	38.9
Beaverhead......................	1,234	-10.7	2,498	263.8	162.8	3,290,191	1,317	201,987	118.2	239,277	31.5	68.5	2	85.6	577	8.5
Big Horn	3,188	1.2	9,032	44.1	223.8	3,546,651	393	218,911	83.6	236,833	39.5	60.5	NA	76.2	2,444	36.5
Blaine	2,040	-7.4	4,155	44.2	599.0	2,460,670	592	215,403	90.0	183,253	44.0	56.0	29	79.0	10,435	63.5
Broadwater......................	467	-2.1	1,577	47.1	112.5	1,844,915	1,170	166,279	39.7	134,081	56.7	43.3	1	77.4	2,336	44.9
Carbon	816	3.1	1,125	98.8	135.0	1,669,647	1,484	154,004	99.0	136,585	33.4	66.6	NA	82.3	1,388	32.6
Carter	1,768	-0.6	5,473	2.3	247.5	2,943,872	538	270,868	70.6	218,663	8.5	91.5	1	79.6	7,229	68.7
Cascade......................	1,270	1.2	1,237	35.7	420.0	1,499,361	1,212	134,128	107.3	104,453	47.7	52.3	9	80.2	7,780	42.7
Chouteau	2,071	-0.1	3,271	14.2	1,309.7	3,053,370	933	353,122	170.7	269,733	84.1	15.9	14	84.4	21,813	83.3
Custer	2,089	-4.6	4,737	37.2	118.5	2,539,839	536	170,666	76.6	173,744	15.2	84.8	1	84.1	3,114	37.6
Daniels	770	0.2	2,779	0.6	533.7	1,762,211	634	297,586	42.2	152,300	77.3	22.7	1	78.7	7,683	85.6
Dawson......................	1,133	-9.9	2,326	21.2	368.1	1,554,263	668	191,646	58.2	119,485	44.0	56.0	NA	74.5	7,569	64.9
Deer Lodge	74	11.3	962	13.1	11.8	1,869,813	1,943	145,035	6.5	84,247	11.3	88.7	NA	68.8	169	14.3
Fallon	902	-7.9	3,121	1.4	191.8	1,883,893	604	196,591	45.3	156,706	15.0	85.0	NA	79.6	3,853	59.9
Fergus	2,188	11.6	2,589	16.3	623.9	2,833,620	1,094	184,680	133.6	158,135	26.9	73.1	2	84.3	12,281	51.8
Flathead	182	7.1	159	22.1	92.5	1,014,016	6,389	64,906	35.9	31,286	76.6	23.4	10	84.7	1,823	10.0
Gallatin	700	-0.3	624	81.3	208.5	1,889,690	3,030	117,382	112.1	99,825	61.6	38.4	11	88.4	3,106	15.9
Garfield	2,215	1.1	8,519	2.8	294.2	3,441,672	404	239,724	54.5	209,765	16.6	83.4	1	79.2	5,608	64.6
Glacier......................	1,186	-24.5	1,862	27.4	493.8	2,171,691	1,167	151,623	106.5	167,248	54.8	45.2	7	70.3	5,948	34.5
Golden Valley	683	-3.5	4,351	7.3	108.0	2,914,246	670	142,583	18.6	118,478	27.9	72.1	NA	69.4	3,049	65.0
Granite	286	0.1	1,892	31.9	28.9	3,060,313	1,618	143,069	17.9	118,530	16.5	83.5	NA	90.1	268	32.5
Hill	1,616	1.1	2,315	4.1	1,223.3	1,992,745	861	259,353	130.8	187,322	81.9	18.1	12	81.5	20,360	75.9
Jefferson	352	-5.1	952	33.5	57.9	1,619,472	1,702	88,418	20.2	54,497	20.1	79.9	NA	89.7	634	11.6
Judith Basin	860	-16.8	2,409	13.7	278.9	2,237,680	929	226,807	88.9	249,022	28.2	71.8	4	86.0	3,687	58.3
Lake	641	15.4	548	100.4	93.4	880,495	1,606	72,903	64.8	55,381	34.0	66.0	32	82.8	1,442	13.4
Lewis and Clark	801	-5.0	1,132	48.2	78.7	1,479,324	1,306	78,842	43.2	61,085	31.1	68.9	3	86.3	1,081	11.7
Liberty	914	1.7	3,714	7.0	698.3	3,329,506	897	424,336	88.3	358,911	78.2	21.8	6	83.3	10,873	90.7
Lincoln......................	48	1.1	139	4.9	12.5	727,103	5,250	54,620	3.1	9,017	32.5	67.5	NA	78.8	47	1.2
McCone	1,340	-2.4	3,065	7.3	592.0	1,619,356	528	237,370	61.3	140,222	49.0	51.0	NA	76.4	13,400	80.5
Madison	923	-14.9	1,526	130.3	151.2	2,610,305	1,710	149,921	83.6	138,238	27.6	72.4	NA	81.3	1,458	15.7
Meagher......................	882	8.6	6,084	52.1	85.2	5,524,417	908	270,602	36.8	253,586	12.1	87.9	NA	71.7	887	26.2
Mineral	18	8.0	198	0.6	5.4	989,976	5,002	42,783	0.6	6,495	37.7	62.3	2	73.1	82	12.9
Missoula......................	260	5.3	452	15.5	21.6	1,262,721	2,796	42,356	9.8	17,099	57.3	42.7	5	82.8	417	6.1
Musselshell	1,103	8.4	3,189	12.9	145.1	2,038,138	639	140,313	37.3	107,760	20.8	79.2	NA	78.6	2,231	30.1
Park......................	712	-8.0	1,238	62.0	110.7	3,230,902	2,609	98,425	33.5	58,287	28.1	71.9	1	83.5	935	15.3
Petroleum......................	593	-14.1	5,698	10.9	84.8	3,863,919	678	194,528	17.8	170,779	18.4	81.6	NA	86.5	861	51.9
Phillips......................	1,937	-6.3	4,352	31.4	508.8	2,306,077	530	224,289	74.6	167,719	34.0	66.0	17	83.1	9,471	66.1
Pondera	805	-15.9	1,656	69.8	551.1	1,998,397	1,207	272,432	111.5	229,477	68.2	31.8	1	80.7	10,629	69.5
Powder River	1,627	2.4	5,005	16.0	145.7	2,755,267	551	223,710	62.1	191,058	4.9	95.1	1	79.4	2,797	48.3
Powell	572	-2.9	2,253	51.7	58.0	2,917,797	1,295	135,021	31.8	125,370	20.5	79.5	NA	79.5	377	23.2
Prairie......................	747	-2.8	4,175	14.6	129.8	3,229,966	774	170,306	43.3	241,899	24.9	75.1	1	78.2	4,610	77.7
Ravalli	241	2.7	153	71.0	52.1	877,618	5,734	54,698	42.7	27,070	29.8	70.2	8	84.5	245	3.9
Richland	1,270	-1.8	2,410	53.5	479.5	2,112,650	877	242,969	100.1	189,949	55.3	44.7	8	79.5	10,227	66.6
Roosevelt	1,307	5.5	2,610	24.3	757.3	1,883,016	722	268,384	64.1	128,004	69.4	30.6	2	76.6	13,696	76.2
Rosebud......................	2,732	-13.0	6,600	38.7	169.8	2,835,966	430	161,371	86.6	209,271	19.6	80.4	NA	78.7	3,759	34.1
Sanders......................	643	89.7	1,233	21.5	43.3	1,219,226	988	65,694	16.9	32,457	30.6	69.4	8	76.4	570	8.6
Sheridan......................	1,064	2.1	2,323	4.6	786.1	1,611,743	694	443,294	70.6	154,083	82.8	17.2	3	86.2	11,702	80.6
Silver Bow	60	-13.5	425	2.4	3.7	956,028	2,251	52,803	2.7	19,218	20.7	79.3	NA	78.9	NA	NA
Stillwater	763	-5.8	1,357	23.2	175.7	1,823,923	1,344	103,840	51.5	91,557	30.4	69.6	NA	79.0	4,175	40.0
Sweet Grass	826	-3.5	2,745	38.8	57.2	3,117,975	1,136	121,775	25.7	85,375	12.2	87.8	NA	84.7	617	19.6
Teton	887	-9.0	1,294	93.8	460.1	1,533,701	1,186	159,196	107.2	156,277	64.1	35.9	8	82.4	8,367	57.0
Toole	1,095	-3.0	3,025	5.3	734.5	2,653,458	877	280,722	84.2	232,547	79.5	20.5	4	77.1	11,549	82.9
Treasure	614	-0.6	5,076	36.6	55.8	2,934,450	578	340,275	45.0	372,116	60.1	39.9	NA	77.7	1,197	47.1
Valley	1,630	-0.3	2,926	45.1	779.2	1,883,822	644	274,232	96.6	173,345	55.2	44.8	3	74.0	13,469	74.9
Wheatland	860	-1.6	4,944	23.0	138.8	3,425,165	693	199,401	43.1	247,718	20.3	79.7	NA	77.6	2,221	50.6
Wibaux	515	-5.5	3,762	2.9	98.3	2,321,989	617	224,104	18.0	131,467	31.0	69.0	NA	77.4	2,083	83.2
Yellowstone......................	1,603	-3.9	1,220	76.8	299.0	1,223,832	1,003	104,007	135.3	102,958	31.8	68.2	3	83.0	5,615	22.5
NEBRASKA......................	44,987	-0.8	971	8,588.4	22,242.6	2,674,492	2,754	268,968	21,983.4	474,476	42.4	57.6	292	81.3	639,975	66.6
Adams......................	340	-0.2	624	237.0	300.5	3,321,098	5,323	366,765	392.5	720,206	44.2	55.8	5	88.4	11,978	69.9
Antelope......................	492	3.6	699	255.3	364.4	3,205,709	4,588	385,363	529.5	752,134	36.3	63.7	4	86.5	10,289	72.4
Arthur	453	0.0	4,766	8.7	31.7	3,817,883	801	169,891	27.5	289,632	8.7	91.3	NA	89.5	506	25.3
Banner	423	0.2	1,770	26.1	191.2	1,543,874	872	205,818	100.5	420,540	20.7	79.3	12	83.7	4,845	80.3

Table B. States and Counties — Water Use, Wholesale Trade, Retail Trade, and Real Estate

STATE County	Water use, 2015		Wholesale Trade[1], 2012				Retail Trade[2], 2012				Real estate and rental and leasing,[2] 2012			
	Public supply water withdrawn (mil gal/day)	Public supply gallons withdrawn per person per day	Number of establishments	Number of employees	Sales (mil dol)	Average payroll (mil dol)	Number of establishments	Number of employees	Sales (mil dol)	Average payroll (mil dol)	Number of establishments	Number of employees	Sales (mil dol)	Average payroll (mil dol)
	133	134	135	136	137	138	139	140	141	142	143	144	145	146
MISSOURI— Cont'd														
St. Louis city......................	92.67	293.6	452	7,692	5,916.4	423.3	923	9,422	2,471.9	231.1	411	2,432	1,003.0	102.5
MONTANA	153.19	148.3	1,288	13,034	12,645.8	577.1	4,831	55,418	15,623.6	1,346.5	1,726	5,207	835.4	162.3
Beaverhead......................	1.82	195.7	6	D	D	D	49	423	124.5	9.6	15	72	8.7	2.4
Big Horn..........................	1.21	91.4	6	26	20.8	1.1	47	341	101.4	7.7	8	18	1.8	0.4
Blaine..............................	0.93	141.4	11	53	197.2	1.6	21	165	46.9	3.3	2	D	D	D
Broadwater......................	1.03	181.1	7	28	17.7	1.3	15	131	77.7	3.1	1	D	D	D
Carbon............................	1.76	169.1	15	D	D	D	50	D	D	D	24	30	2.5	0.5
Carter..............................	0.04	33.9	NA	NA	NA	NA	6	34	14.7	0.8	3	D	D	D
Cascade..........................	12.79	155.4	112	D	D	D	352	4,859	1,359.7	117.4	121	349	62.1	9.8
Chouteau........................	0.88	152.6	15	79	195.8	3.0	22	114	46.8	2.5	4	3	0.5	0.0
Custer..............................	1.39	114.5	19	161	64.3	5.3	54	806	256.7	21.1	16	23	3.3	0.5
Daniels............................	0.21	119.3	5	16	38.4	0.7	16	96	51.4	2.5	NA	NA	NA	NA
Dawson............................	1.75	181.8	17	181	323.9	6.9	47	493	151.8	11.9	12	41	11.3	3.2
Deer Lodge......................	2.30	251.7	1	D	D	D	28	290	75.2	6.2	8	14	1.0	0.3
Fallon..............................	0.28	87.8	6	D	D	D	15	137	34.7	3.0	5	2	0.3	0.1
Fergus..............................	1.06	92.8	15	D	D	D	65	464	150.3	11.0	21	53	6.0	1.1
Flathead..........................	11.43	118.9	103	958	1,283.5	38.6	473	5,317	1,515.9	138.3	223	791	86.9	21.0
Gallatin...........................	11.93	118.4	127	1,025	600.7	40.2	582	6,760	1,710.3	166.7	332	824	152.6	25.9
Garfield...........................	0.04	30.4	NA	NA	NA	NA	6	78	13.1	1.0	NA	NA	NA	NA
Glacier............................	1.76	129.0	8	52	108.7	2.2	44	448	128.7	11.2	7	5	1.0	0.1
Golden Valley..................	0.04	48.4	1	D	D	D	1	D	D	D	NA	NA	NA	NA
Granite............................	0.05	15.4	3	16	5.8	0.7	19	101	24.3	1.9	3	D	D	D
Hill..................................	2.15	129.7	26	221	367.1	9.3	88	1,029	286.4	23.9	24	64	7.1	1.4
Jefferson.........................	1.28	109.9	8	30	13.6	1.3	28	185	51.7	3.5	7	13	0.7	0.2
Judith Basin	0.09	46.7	5	25	13.0	0.9	6	20	5.6	0.3	2	D	D	D
Lake................................	2.39	81.1	20	59	21.8	1.5	122	1,069	268.3	26.4	37	39	6.0	0.9
Lewis and Clark	7.93	119.4	63	516	332.7	21.3	276	3,735	998.6	91.5	98	315	68.3	11.9
Liberty.............................	0.22	91.4	7	49	59.3	1.9	10	44	12.8	1.3	2	D	D	D
Lincoln............................	2.28	119.7	11	47	35.4	1.1	83	693	172.6	15.2	24	51	5.7	0.8
McCone...........................	0.08	47.5	3	D	D	D	10	73	24.8	1.6	1	D	D	D
Madison	1.10	139.0	3	D	D	D	44	225	59.5	4.1	25	D	D	D
Meagher..........................	0.24	131.1	1	D	D	D	13	64	14.3	1.0	2	D	D	D
Mineral............................	0.33	77.6	2	D	D	D	16	215	49.3	4.1	2	D	D	D
Missoula..........................	30.41	266.3	151	1,838	1,220.7	81.5	570	7,931	2,044.0	180.0	206	918	130.6	29.7
Musselshell......................	0.25	54.6	4	14	6.7	0.5	19	186	42.0	3.2	3	D	D	D
Park................................	2.42	151.5	8	18	6.0	0.6	100	669	205.4	17.6	33	41	5.8	1.1
Petroleum........................	0.01	21.1	NA	NA	NA	NA	2	D	D	D	1	D	D	D
Phillips............................	0.47	112.7	4	44	98.9	1.8	26	212	39.2	4.0	3	2	1.0	0.1
Pondera	0.84	135.8	13	133	244.5	7.3	25	227	55.9	4.7	2	D	D	D
Powder River	0.08	45.1	1	D	D	D	12	107	24.6	1.9	2	D	D	D
Powell.............................	1.37	200.3	2	D	D	D	18	181	46.0	5.1	4	7	1.1	0.2
Prairie.............................	0.01	8.6	NA	NA	NA	NA	5	24	6.5	0.3	1	D	D	D
Ravalli.............................	3.25	78.6	42	151	182.9	5.6	166	1,482	330.6	31.3	44	90	8.6	1.7
Richland...........................	1.18	98.7	24	238	470.5	9.8	57	652	215.8	17.1	23	184	54.7	11.7
Roosevelt.........................	1.72	149.9	10	D	D	D	41	530	159.2	11.0	10	23	1.0	0.2
Rosebud...........................	1.52	161.7	1	D	D	D	28	240	56.4	4.4	7	26	8.1	0.7
Sanders...........................	0.71	62.6	9	52	9.6	0.9	53	325	78.0	6.4	10	20	1.2	0.2
Sheridan..........................	0.04	10.8	5	D	D	D	27	193	61.1	4.0	1	D	D	D
Silver Bow	7.73	223.3	37	348	189.3	14.3	172	2,203	610.1	51.7	47	137	15.1	3.2
Stillwater	0.38	40.1	5	14	74.9	0.9	33	243	103.2	4.7	4	8	1.0	0.1
Sweet Grass	0.51	140.3	4	22	2.9	0.5	21	139	39.5	2.8	6	9	1.4	0.2
Teton...............................	1.13	185.1	11	48	114.0	1.8	27	190	69.7	4.9	5	D	D	D
Toole	1.21	237.9	9	50	222.3	3.0	24	221	83.5	5.2	8	15	1.6	0.2
Treasure..........................	0.07	100.4	1	D	D	D	3	D	D	D	NA	NA	NA	NA
Valley..............................	1.61	210.2	14	203	248.0	9.6	47	366	158.7	8.7	6	17	1.6	0.5
Wheatland........................	0.32	151.7	1	D	D	D	9	71	16.7	1.2	NA	NA	NA	NA
Wibaux............................	0.07	61.9	NA	NA	NA	NA	4	22	6.3	0.4	NA	NA	NA	NA
Yellowstone......................	25.09	159.8	306	4,690	3,193.3	231.3	734	10,298	3,272.2	277.7	271	914	164.3	30.2
NEBRASKA......................	275.18	145.1	2,720	34,409	42,619.0	1,675.4	7,279	105,953	30,470.7	2,440.4	2,001	10,068	1,732.0	388.5
Adams.............................	6.50	205.8	63	703	949.4	32.0	144	1,876	453.3	42.7	60	131	24.2	2.9
Antelope..........................	0.67	104.5	22	225	535.0	9.7	37	275	70.2	4.7	4	2	0.5	0.1
Arthur..............................	0.00	0.0	NA	NA	NA	NA	2	D	D	D	NA	NA	NA	NA
Banner............................	0.02	25.4	NA	NA	NA	NA	NA	NA	NA	NA	NA	NA	NA	NA

1 Merchant wholesalers, except manufacturers' sales branches and offices.   2. Employer establishments.

Table B. States and Counties — Professional Services, Manufacturing, and Accommodation and Food Services

STATE County	Professional, scientific, and technical services, 2012				Manufacturing, 2012				Accommodation and food services, 2012			
	Number of establish-ments	Number of employees	Sales (mil dol)	Average payroll (mil dol)	Number of establish-ments	Number of employees	Receipts (mil dol)	Annual payroll (mil dol)	Number of establis-hments	Number of employees	Receipts (mil dol)	Annual payroll (mil dol)
	147	148	149	150	151	152	153	154	155	156	157	158
MISSOURI— Cont'd												
St. Louis city.....................	1,009	17,461	3,015.1	1,200.0	484	17,422	10,737.0	975.2	1,036	22,069	1,255.7	371.4
MONTANA	3,545	16,660	2,191.9	798.8	1,237	15,729	11,535.2	714.5	3,458	46,251	2,420.5	649.5
Beaverhead......................	25	72	5.3	1.5	13	37	6.8	1.2	48	425	18.3	5.0
Big Horn.........................	15	39	3.0	1.2	3	15	D	D	27	234	17.2	3.5
Blaine............................	13	26	4.8	1.6	5	13	3.4	0.5	12	56	2.6	0.6
Broadwater......................	9	28	2.5	0.7	6	159	D	6.8	21	118	5.4	1.4
Carbon...........................	28	D	D	D	10	D	D	D	51	490	24.8	7.4
Carter............................	5	9	0.6	0.1	NA	NA	NA	NA	2	D	D	D
Cascade..........................	202	1,159	131.8	50.3	62	964	955.3	45.0	240	3,887	194.7	51.5
Chouteau	9	27	2.2	0.6	7	17	5.9	0.7	18	D	D	D
Custer............................	28	99	7.9	3.1	13	79	D	2.2	39	543	28.5	6.8
Daniels...........................	3	D	D	D	NA	NA	NA	NA	9	D	D	D
Dawson...........................	24	71	6.5	2.3	4	37	D	1.6	34	502	25.7	6.4
Deer Lodge......................	26	112	15.6	4.9	4	87	D	D	30	275	10.9	2.6
Fallon.............................	9	16	2.3	0.5	3	9	D	D	18	104	6.9	1.4
Fergus............................	34	82	7.8	2.0	26	273	60.6	11.9	47	413	18.5	4.9
Flathead..........................	375	1,347	184.6	56.1	182	2,367	620.8	105.3	363	4,362	247.9	67.7
Gallatin..........................	655	2,415	298.0	113.5	188	2,363	491.0	99.5	410	7,193	348.1	96.5
Garfield..........................	NA	NA	NA	NA	NA	NA	NA	NA	5	28	1.1	0.2
Glacier...........................	11	64	6.8	1.8	4	20	2.3	0.5	51	335	38.3	8.7
Golden Valley...................	1	D	D	D	NA	NA	NA	NA	4	13	0.5	0.1
Granite	5	3	0.7	0.2	5	15	2.2	0.5	16	101	8.3	2.9
Hill................................	30	206	20.6	10.4	7	18	2.9	0.7	56	758	35.0	9.2
Jefferson.........................	25	36	5.2	1.7	12	234	D	14.6	21	191	7.1	2.1
Judith Basin	4	11	2.1	0.3	NA	NA	NA	NA	10	27	1.4	0.3
Lake..............................	52	352	71.8	20.2	35	497	72.4	15.4	76	630	33.5	8.6
Lewis and Clark	250	1,661	209.8	84.0	58	525	D	22.1	198	3,083	142.0	39.6
Liberty	4	10	0.6	0.2	NA	NA	NA	NA	5	32	0.7	0.2
Lincoln...........................	35	84	8.2	2.5	24	137	16.8	4.0	64	488	26.4	7.3
McCone..........................	1	D	D	D	NA	NA	NA	NA	5	18	0.6	0.1
Madison..........................	28	60	5.5	1.9	11	69	D	1.8	55	220	15.8	4.0
Meagher..........................	3	3	0.2	0.1	NA	NA	NA	NA	15	52	2.2	0.5
Mineral	6	37	2.7	1.1	7	200	D	7.6	19	120	4.8	1.4
Missoula..........................	501	2,865	325.4	137.2	102	1,351	310.6	49.1	342	6,106	317.4	84.0
Musselshell......................	8	15	1.5	0.5	3	6	1.7	0.3	13	D	D	D
Park..............................	74	181	23.7	7.6	29	338	58.9	14.1	118	1,130	75.2	22.3
Petroleum........................	1	D	D	D	NA	NA	NA	NA	2	D	D	D
Phillips...........................	9	28	2.4	0.7	5	13	1.9	0.5	16	109	4.7	1.2
Pondera	10	36	3.0	1.2	8	89	D	3.1	16	141	4.8	1.2
Powder River	4	D	D	D	NA	NA	NA	NA	12	57	2.9	0.6
Powell	9	32	3.3	0.9	8	185	D	D	22	D	D	D
Prairie............................	4	5	0.8	0.3	NA	NA	NA	NA	6	19	0.6	0.1
Ravalli	122	514	27.3	25.5	84	703	132.4	25.7	96	841	38.4	11.6
Richland..........................	40	228	46.6	13.6	12	371	D	14.6	44	569	38.4	8.9
Roosevelt.........................	11	21	2.0	0.8	NA	NA	NA	NA	24	256	13.7	3.1
Rosebud..........................	5	15	1.4	0.3	3	7	D	D	33	247	10.8	2.6
Sanders..........................	24	35	3.5	0.9	20	185	37.6	6.4	39	320	12.5	3.6
Sheridan..........................	11	28	3.3	1.1	NA	NA	NA	NA	15	137	6.9	1.7
Silver Bow	107	654	73.9	30.8	35	492	D	31.5	147	2,244	102.4	28.7
Stillwater.........................	24	55	6.0	1.7	11	441	D	25.6	25	174	11.0	2.6
Sweet Grass	12	28	4.4	1.0	10	53	D	2.0	16	140	6.4	2.0
Teton	10	36	3.7	1.0	7	15	3.0	0.5	19	107	5.2	1.2
Toole	12	36	5.0	1.5	4	30	7.0	1.3	27	202	12.0	2.7
Treasure..........................	2	D	D	D	NA	NA	NA	NA	4	13	0.4	0.1
Valley	19	75	6.5	2.5	6	39	D	1.0	34	367	16.4	4.4
Wheatland........................	3	7	1.4	0.2	NA	NA	NA	NA	11	54	3.5	0.6
Wibaux...........................	4	8	0.8	0.4	NA	NA	NA	NA	4	37	1.5	0.5
Yellowstone......................	604	3,578	618.7	198.5	183	3,185	6,880.3	185.8	404	7,935	452.2	121.3
NEBRASKA..................	4,448	74,514	5,726.7	3,639.3	1,844	92,409	57,499.2	4,002.8	4,326	70,128	3,094.5	855.4
Adams............................	62	306	31.4	12.2	57	2,448	1,858.9	101.8	81	1,354	53.0	13.7
Antelope..........................	12	29	4.6	1.1	9	85	D	4.1	15	D	D	D
Arthur............................	1	D	D	D	NA	NA	NA	NA	1	D	D	D
Banner............................	NA	NA	NA	NA	NA	NA	NA	NA	NA	NA	NA	NA

Table B. States and Counties — Health Care and Social Assistance, Other Services, Nonemployer Businesses, and Residential Construction

STATE County	Health care and social assistance, 2012				Other services, 2012				Nonemployer businesses, 2016		Value of residential construction authorized by building permits, 2018	
	Number of establishments	Number of employees	Receipts (mil dol)	Annual payroll (mil dol)	Number of establishments	Number of employees	Receipts (mil dol)	Annual payroll (mil dol)	Number	Receipts (mil dol)	New construction ($1,000)	Number of housing units
	159	160	161	162	163	164	165	166	167	168	169	170
MISSOURI— Cont'd												
St. Louis city..................	1,219	35,572	4,162.1	1,389.0	629	4,529	647.7	151.1	21,332	829.7	62,601	661
MONTANA	3,512	65,657	6,469.5	2,555.4	2,278	10,917	1,222.0	302.8	88,689	3,977.0	0	0
Beaverhead....................	40	487	41.1	19.0	21	58	4.0	1.0	860	33.2	2,400	15
Big Horn.......................	21	D	D	D	9	22	2.3	0.6	540	17.7	0	0
Blaine...........................	15	366	31.1	12.7	10	D	D	D	340	9.0	380	4
Broadwater....................	7	106	7.0	3.0	9	D	D	D	494	22.0	0	0
Carbon.........................	32	D	D	D	20	D	D	D	1,182	50.5	2,950	10
Carter...........................	2	D	D	D	2	D	D	D	123	7.3	0	0
Cascade........................	262	6,363	711.9	269.1	155	871	76.6	21.7	4,775	200.1	34,820	144
Chouteau......................	11	130	9.5	4.9	6	9	0.3	0.1	359	13.2	5,526	33
Custer..........................	49	978	67.2	31.3	27	123	14.2	3.2	861	37.3	182	1
Daniels.........................	4	D	D	D	5	D	D	D	131	6.8	715	3
Dawson........................	29	631	45.0	20.7	30	97	9.4	2.3	635	22.4	127	1
Deer Lodge....................	52	1,278	110.6	51.7	12	45	5.0	1.3	473	15.8	1,766	8
Fallon..........................	5	D	D	D	9	21	3.6	0.7	305	11.9	6,238	56
Fergus..........................	47	855	52.9	25.3	32	122	11.1	2.1	1,000	40.1	722	3
Flathead........................	339	5,537	572.5	232.6	227	937	87.1	22.7	10,648	503.5	91,331	466
Gallatin........................	385	4,387	437.5	173.1	269	1,314	155.9	40.3	12,559	618.3	343,388	1,620
Garfield.........................	1	D	D	D	2	D	D	D	136	5.2	0	0
Glacier.........................	18	962	55.3	22.5	17	85	28.6	2.7	719	25.9	0	0
Golden Valley.................	2	D	D	D	1	D	D	D	84	4.4	NA	NA
Granite.........................	4	D	D	D	3	6	0.3	0.1	327	12.7	NA	NA
Hill..............................	58	1,374	102.1	44.4	37	173	18.3	3.9	963	31.7	245	1
Jefferson	22	225	13.9	5.3	10	34	4.1	1.3	1,007	42.7	2,284	9
Judith Basin	3	6	0.1	0.0	1	D	D	D	190	7.3	NA	NA
Lake............................	77	1,182	98.1	43.7	50	141	11.0	2.9	2,373	90.5	2,203	15
Lewis and Clark	271	5,376	610.0	219.5	200	1,156	126.8	41.6	5,492	253.5	32,586	186
Liberty..........................	3	D	D	D	3	D	D	D	146	4.8	NA	NA
Lincoln.........................	56	866	60.1	27.3	36	114	10.5	2.5	1,558	55.5	764	7
McCone.........................	3	D	D	D	2	D	D	D	164	5.3	20	1
Madison........................	19	141	12.3	5.2	15	D	D	D	1,060	43.1	1,276	5
Meagher........................	7	D	D	D	2	D	D	D	168	7.3	NA	NA
Mineral.........................	13	145	8.7	4.9	7	4	1.4	0.3	338	10.3	570	2
Missoula........................	489	9,292	965.9	351.1	287	1,889	258.2	56.0	10,111	471.2	120,594	689
Musselshell....................	9	178	11.1	3.8	8	17	1.7	0.3	335	13.7	125	2
Park.............................	55	850	60.0	27.7	49	181	16.3	4.8	2,205	87.6	10,793	69
Petroleum......................	1	D	D	D	1	D	D	D	35	1.6	NA	NA
Phillips.........................	9	184	9.5	4.8	13	37	3.9	0.9	372	11.3	300	1
Pondera........................	18	317	20.9	9.1	12	28	3.1	0.5	433	15.2	0	0
Powder River	1	D	D	D	7	D	D	D	175	6.1	NA	NA
Powell..........................	16	184	14.7	5.6	5	18	1.9	0.5	493	20.8	10,155	38
Prairie..........................	3	D	D	D	2	D	D	D	82	2.6	NA	NA
Ravalli..........................	133	1,459	103.3	46.0	81	246	22.3	5.2	4,364	192.1	3,427	27
Richland........................	32	676	59.1	21.2	30	117	12.6	3.4	953	41.5	1,841	13
Roosevelt......................	12	D	D	D	11	58	3.1	0.6	490	19.3	430	2
Rosebud........................	17	300	13.0	6.1	14	77	5.3	1.9	468	14.3	0	0
Sanders........................	39	407	28.1	12.0	14	60	5.4	1.2	1,033	43.7	0	0
Sheridan........................	12	366	18.0	7.9	9	20	3.2	0.6	327	14.0	0	0
Silver Bow.....................	159	3,303	287.5	127.1	72	289	34.1	7.2	2,215	96.8	19,667	185
Stillwater......................	24	259	14.5	5.4	10	18	3.0	0.5	821	36.5	570	2
Sweet Grass	6	24	1.1	0.3	10	28	2.1	0.5	434	17.0	0	0
Teton...........................	18	238	11.8	5.6	11	14	2.8	0.6	580	25.6	158	1
Toole	12	D	D	D	11	25	2.2	0.4	309	11.6	0	0
Treasure........................	1	D	D	D	1	D	D	D	48	1.4	NA	NA
Valley...........................	24	603	43.1	19.5	20	63	6.9	1.5	520	16.2	983	5
Wheatland......................	4	D	D	D	3	5	0.3	0.1	145	5.4	NA	NA
Wibaux.........................	3	D	D	D	NA	NA	NA	NA	70	1.9	1,237	9
Yellowstone....................	558	12,676	1,527.6	583.0	368	2,134	234.8	58.7	11,661	599.9	169,124	1,466
NEBRASKA....................	5,410	125,469	12,869.4	4,907.3	3,989	21,832	2,841.3	612.5	134,524	5,876.1	1,309,845	7,866
Adams..........................	116	2,495	247.7	103.7	55	307	33.0	6.8	2,274	91.9	10,721	38
Antelope........................	15	305	22.9	8.8	20	40	4.5	0.8	675	30.9	720	4
Arthur...........................	NA	NA	NA	NA	2	D	D	D	44	3.3	NA	NA
Banner..........................	NA	NA	NA	NA	1	D	D	D	44	2.2	NA	NA

Government Employment and Payroll, and Local Government Finances

STATE County	Government employment and payroll, 2012									Local government finances, 2012				
			March payroll (percent of total)							General revenue				
												Taxes		
											Inter-govern-mental (mil dol)	Total (mil dol)	Per capita[1] (dollars)	
	Full-time equivalent employees	March payroll (dollars)	Adminis-tration, judicial, and legal	Police and corrections	Fire protection	Highways and transpor-tation	Health and welfare	Natural resources and utilities	Education and libraries	Total (mil dol)			Total	Property
	171	172	173	174	175	176	177	178	179	180	181	182	183	184
MISSOURI— Cont'd														
St. Louis city	15,033	62,103,817	5.6	17.2	5.7	20.6	1.5	12.9	34.1	2,385.3	762.8	924.8	2,907	1,228
MONTANA	X	X	X	X	X	X	X	X	X	X	X	X	X	X
Beaverhead	518	1,862,160	5.1	4.6	0.4	2.9	54.8	1.7	29.5	66.4	12.9	10.3	1,104	1,099
Big Horn	748	2,839,698	3.5	4.0	0.0	3.4	4.1	1.1	82.8	62.2	38.7	13.7	1,049	1,040
Blaine	358	1,163,514	11.3	3.8	0.0	6.0	0.6	3.7	73.6	31.5	20.8	7.2	1,083	1,053
Broadwater	160	477,725	12.8	12.5	0.0	5.0	4.9	1.1	62.3	14.4	6.3	5.4	935	924
Carbon	377	1,229,196	11.7	8.3	1.5	6.6	1.7	4.4	62.9	33.2	13.2	15.7	1,547	1,457
Carter	67	178,052	5.5	6.2	0.0	11.1	1.6	2.3	58.2	7.1	3.5	2.6	2,229	2,201
Cascade	2,704	9,771,107	6.8	13.0	3.8	5.6	3.7	6.9	59.0	238.3	103.2	77.2	944	913
Chouteau	318	956,267	6.0	6.6	0.0	4.7	29.2	2.6	49.0	26.4	10.3	9.2	1,565	1,560
Custer	539	1,661,688	7.8	7.4	3.4	4.8	3.2	3.6	68.6	42.2	19.5	9.9	832	817
Daniels	99	271,126	13.7	7.5	0.1	5.3	5.9	3.5	61.2	10.7	3.8	5.1	2,865	1,845
Dawson	486	1,501,541	7.2	15.3	1.5	5.5	7.5	3.6	57.4	42.3	16.8	12.8	1,387	1,374
Deer Lodge	264	898,579	8.3	14.8	4.3	3.9	1.1	6.9	59.7	28.1	15.5	7.9	855	847
Fallon	190	709,670	11.6	5.6	3.4	9.5	5.9	6.1	55.5	33.9	25.4	5.0	1,645	1,614
Fergus	520	1,621,405	6.8	8.4	2.1	15.7	1.2	2.9	61.6	43.5	22.6	14.7	1,286	1,268
Flathead	2,820	10,913,778	6.6	7.4	3.2	3.5	3.5	3.7	70.8	292.8	116.8	111.5	1,216	1,179
Gallatin	2,434	9,405,208	8.1	11.0	3.8	2.9	5.0	5.6	60.7	253.4	77.2	121.2	1,309	1,215
Garfield	115	230,472	8.7	3.3	2.9	6.0	24.2	7.0	41.9	7.0	2.6	2.3	1,862	1,861
Glacier	700	2,311,773	4.2	4.6	0.0	3.2	3.2	2.5	81.1	52.7	34.1	13.8	1,008	1,004
Golden Valley	58	147,171	10.6	3.5	0.0	4.0	0.0	0.3	80.9	4.9	2.7	1.9	2,302	2,299
Granite	179	573,451	9.2	4.8	0.0	3.8	33.5	2.9	44.5	15.4	5.5	4.2	1,364	1,358
Hill	793	2,599,436	4.3	6.6	2.9	3.9	3.3	3.7	74.5	62.6	35.3	17.8	1,085	1,070
Jefferson	303	957,909	14.8	9.2	0.0	4.0	5.0	1.6	64.0	29.3	15.5	10.6	927	924
Judith Basin	121	355,407	6.9	3.6	0.0	13.7	0.1	1.1	72.7	9.7	4.7	3.9	1,915	1,915
Lake	962	3,993,744	4.2	5.9	0.2	1.6	3.5	2.9	80.7	85.3	44.4	27.2	940	933
Lewis and Clark	1,872	7,755,463	7.5	9.0	2.6	3.9	8.6	5.4	59.9	213.1	82.3	69.8	1,076	1,054
Liberty	111	316,696	12.4	8.7	0.0	7.1	6.6	4.8	58.9	8.2	3.8	3.3	1,372	1,372
Lincoln	599	1,992,630	12.4	7.4	0.5	3.8	2.7	4.3	65.2	57.6	31.7	14.9	766	754
McCone	168	326,681	15.1	4.8	0.1	1.2	1.9	4.1	42.3	8.6	3.2	4.3	2,540	2,486
Madison	459	1,488,288	7.5	4.1	0.2	3.8	40.5	2.0	39.5	41.8	10.9	17.1	2,205	2,194
Meagher	122	326,266	10.3	7.3	0.0	3.7	0.0	4.5	46.8	8.8	3.1	3.4	1,746	1,742
Mineral	297	957,709	7.9	6.9	0.3	1.9	33.5	1.3	47.5	23.2	8.6	6.0	1,442	1,403
Missoula	3,035	11,623,602	8.8	11.6	6.2	6.3	5.7	3.6	55.2	333.0	140.7	131.9	1,189	1,156
Musselshell	259	845,308	4.5	3.3	0.0	3.2	25.2	1.6	61.7	22.2	9.1	7.4	1,596	1,532
Park	528	1,727,963	10.9	8.8	4.3	3.9	4.6	4.7	62.0	50.7	22.2	18.0	1,154	1,123
Petroleum	36	121,984	11.4	0.0	0.0	5.5	0.0	6.6	74.9	4.7	3.4	0.9	1,705	1,703
Phillips	229	653,111	10.8	5.9	0.1	6.4	3.3	8.6	61.5	21.3	11.3	6.4	1,542	1,503
Pondera	212	607,909	10.4	10.1	0.2	5.9	1.8	7.3	62.5	34.1	12.3	7.0	1,132	1,127
Powder River	137	334,388	14.5	7.2	0.0	8.8	27.7	1.7	37.3	12.1	5.0	3.7	2,074	1,968
Powell	199	625,409	10.4	7.0	0.5	5.1	2.6	2.8	69.0	21.5	10.6	6.4	906	902
Prairie	95	225,508	8.2	3.7	0.0	5.1	32.5	1.7	42.7	7.5	2.4	1.9	1,617	1,608
Ravalli	1,130	3,297,468	9.0	9.9	0.2	2.5	1.0	3.9	72.3	96.2	49.5	36.0	885	874
Richland	560	1,708,186	7.9	8.6	0.2	7.8	4.4	8.1	58.4	72.7	47.2	9.4	866	853
Roosevelt	704	2,186,188	5.4	5.6	0.2	3.3	10.8	2.9	70.0	63.5	42.5	12.7	1,161	1,154
Rosebud	641	1,932,124	5.8	8.0	0.0	6.1	4.9	5.7	68.6	65.9	31.0	16.0	1,705	1,689
Sanders	390	1,112,745	8.1	9.8	0.3	5.2	3.6	1.9	69.3	33.6	16.5	12.8	1,123	1,122
Sheridan	333	1,098,598	7.7	3.6	1.6	5.2	44.9	1.5	34.4	19.8	10.2	5.6	1,551	1,542
Silver Bow	995	3,780,881	7.3	11.3	8.8	7.4	1.2	11.1	51.5	120.3	54.8	39.2	1,139	1,112
Stillwater	340	1,123,218	10.5	6.8	1.0	7.0	2.4	1.8	70.1	29.0	12.6	12.5	1,360	1,350
Sweet Grass	197	563,456	9.7	3.8	0.0	3.5	28.6	2.5	49.1	22.0	6.9	6.1	1,698	1,696
Teton	434	1,416,652	5.6	3.0	0.1	2.9	31.7	6.4	49.4	34.6	11.1	9.4	1,552	1,512
Toole	386	1,266,882	7.5	5.0	0.0	3.8	44.2	2.8	34.4	36.1	9.0	7.8	1,492	1,473
Treasure	44	114,460	17.8	4.4	0.0	4.5	6.2	7.2	53.1	3.7	1.5	1.7	2,261	2,258
Valley	402	1,205,227	6.6	9.6	0.0	6.9	3.9	4.9	66.3	36.1	17.0	11.6	1,551	1,486
Wheatland	160	440,257	19.4	6.3	0.0	12.1	3.4	4.6	49.3	9.4	4.2	4.2	1,974	1,965
Wibaux	61	199,748	22.1	5.7	0.0	16.7	2.2	0.8	52.4	6.8	4.9	1.2	1,174	1,124
Yellowstone	4,840	19,590,185	5.0	8.6	4.7	4.9	8.9	6.0	55.1	469.5	175.3	161.7	1,065	989
NEBRASKA	X	X	X	X	X	X	X	X	X	X	X	X	X	X
Adams	2,340	8,844,524	2.4	3.7	1.5	2.0	0.5	13.9	70.2	174.2	49.6	89.6	2,849	2,506
Antelope	558	1,836,977	2.9	2.2	0.0	3.6	29.5	1.6	60.0	30.0	8.2	17.8	2,718	2,366
Arthur	35	130,066	6.4	2.0	0.0	4.7	0.0	27.0	59.3	5.8	0.9	4.6	9,488	9,335
Banner	61	179,960	9.3	1.7	0.0	7.8	0.0	0.0	79.6	4.4	1.3	2.8	3,726	3,499

1. Based on the resident population estimated as of July 1 of the year shown.

— **Local Government Finances, Government Employment, and Income Taxes**

STATE County	Total (mil dol)	Per capita[1] (dollars)	Education	Health and hospitals	Police protection	Public welfare	Highways	Total (mil dol)	Per capita[1] (dollars)	Federal civilian	Federal military	State and local	Number of returns	Mean adjusted gross income	Mean income tax
	Local government finances, 2012 (cont.) — Direct general expenditure — Percent of total for:							Debt outstanding		Government employment, 2017			Individual income tax returns, 2016		
	185	186	187	188	189	190	191	192	193	194	195	196	197	198	199
MISSOURI— Cont'd															
St. Louis city	2,326.2	7,311	33.4	1.7	10.8	0.0	1.1	3,993.6	12,552	14,191	1,522	20,162	142,480	47,207	5,932
MONTANA	X	X	X	X	X	X	X	X	X	13,214	7,810	75,130	500,640	55,932	6,625
Beaverhead	83.3	8,915	24.9	55.9	2.2	0.0	3.8	91.0	9,739	200	40	827	4,390	45,732	4,563
Big Horn	70.6	5,404	65.3	1.6	3.9	0.0	4.8	34.0	2,603	408	59	1,661	4,650	38,603	3,049
Blaine	33.0	4,932	63.3	2.3	5.1	0.0	8.2	3.4	513	183	29	487	2,620	35,193	3,102
Broadwater	14.1	2,447	49.7	2.6	9.1	0.2	5.3	4.7	809	41	26	213	2,660	50,777	5,092
Carbon	34.2	3,380	55.4	0.7	7.0	0.2	11.0	23.7	2,339	80	48	499	5,170	51,760	5,770
Carter	7.6	6,469	34.7	9.5	5.5	0.1	25.5	0.4	371	14	5	104	560	49,279	4,170
Cascade	242.5	2,968	53.0	1.0	9.7	1.4	5.2	90.0	1,101	1,675	3,472	4,040	39,330	50,718	5,428
Chouteau	26.7	4,530	44.1	21.5	3.3	0.0	8.4	4.1	697	33	25	413	2,220	46,368	4,816
Custer	40.6	3,415	62.2	2.4	7.6	0.1	8.1	9.5	801	198	51	895	5,530	52,077	5,268
Daniels	9.9	5,552	39.1	7.1	5.2	0.0	8.9	3.2	1,792	14	8	115	880	53,009	6,251
Dawson	38.5	4,159	54.9	3.1	5.4	1.0	7.1	8.2	884	34	38	726	4,090	53,734	5,489
Deer Lodge	30.1	3,259	41.6	2.0	6.6	2.8	4.8	4.9	531	86	37	1,001	4,150	45,851	4,338
Fallon	38.0	12,574	45.8	4.0	2.8	0.0	17.5	0.2	57	12	13	277	1,370	63,732	7,749
Fergus	44.0	3,847	53.6	2.3	4.8	0.0	11.5	9.5	831	134	49	897	5,490	46,453	4,423
Flathead	299.8	3,272	56.2	3.9	5.8	1.2	5.0	178.9	1,952	771	446	4,229	49,260	58,412	7,381
Gallatin	262.4	2,834	48.1	1.3	10.1	4.2	4.1	247.8	2,676	578	479	9,380	55,300	67,866	9,472
Garfield	7.3	5,772	36.8	2.4	2.5	23.3	14.2	0.6	450	26	6	124	530	39,960	3,134
Glacier	51.7	3,768	77.0	2.8	4.0	0.1	4.7	22.4	1,630	447	58	2,036	5,150	35,770	2,905
Golden Valley	4.5	5,323	65.4	0.9	4.3	0.5	4.7	0.0	5	5	3	76	440	35,977	3,443
Granite	15.6	5,012	35.1	0.6	6.3	26.8	7.6	2.0	654	38	15	217	1,460	49,791	5,628
Hill	62.8	3,840	76.1	0.8	4.8	0.0	3.2	16.7	1,020	164	71	2,109	7,480	47,052	4,703
Jefferson	31.9	2,799	57.0	3.8	8.3	0.0	5.0	4.6	400	34	52	623	5,550	63,970	7,302
Judith Basin	9.6	4,741	53.8	0.9	3.4	0.0	18.1	3.4	1,658	29	9	144	930	41,646	3,884
Lake	86.4	2,980	61.8	0.9	5.2	0.3	4.0	23.2	799	102	133	3,089	12,900	43,810	4,328
Lewis and Clark	212.2	3,270	47.9	4.1	8.6	3.1	5.3	156.7	2,415	1,908	309	8,911	33,990	60,160	6,776
Liberty	7.9	3,293	47.0	5.3	10.3	0.0	12.1	1.8	772	17	9	129	950	37,619	3,065
Lincoln	58.1	2,979	51.4	6.8	7.7	0.1	7.8	18.2	932	413	86	755	8,200	42,895	4,031
McCone	8.6	5,082	52.1	3.7	4.1	0.8	13.0	2.4	1,422	17	8	131	880	38,478	4,174
Madison	42.1	5,447	35.2	13.7	4.0	18.5	7.6	7.0	907	55	36	456	3,980	55,306	6,476
Meagher	10.9	5,666	29.5	3.3	0.7	0.0	6.7	0.3	179	29	8	109	830	44,489	4,335
Mineral	24.9	5,975	42.3	33.5	3.9	0.0	3.9	5.6	1,346	55	19	269	1,910	44,625	4,299
Missoula	338.7	3,052	44.0	5.5	7.0	0.8	5.2	188.8	1,701	1,399	538	9,148	57,390	59,888	7,493
Musselshell	23.0	4,926	37.1	29.7	2.1	0.0	4.3	1.8	390	15	21	252	2,010	45,377	4,867
Park	60.3	3,873	58.7	2.2	5.8	0.5	3.5	26.2	1,681	75	73	647	8,810	51,148	5,943
Petroleum	4.6	8,926	53.5	1.5	1.5	0.0	8.0	0.4	812	3	2	58	190	40,126	2,984
Phillips	22.5	5,449	53.5	1.7	4.2	0.0	11.5	7.9	1,903	76	18	303	1,960	39,205	3,702
Pondera	34.1	5,531	42.2	35.4	3.5	1.5	3.2	14.5	2,348	33	24	385	2,920	37,650	3,172
Powder River	12.1	6,877	33.4	1.6	5.0	22.2	16.5	0.1	69	11	8	191	830	46,305	4,093
Powell	23.3	3,289	58.1	0.9	6.4	0.4	8.2	1.7	234	78	24	996	2,700	44,253	4,123
Prairie	7.4	6,390	28.9	2.4	3.9	29.4	8.6	2.0	1,732	36	5	142	580	43,459	3,922
Ravalli	99.9	2,460	64.0	1.1	7.3	0.5	5.0	31.4	773	530	189	1,415	20,040	52,646	6,015
Richland	76.0	7,032	41.5	1.4	4.3	0.9	22.5	6.1	568	78	49	709	5,600	64,654	8,479
Roosevelt	58.9	5,389	63.9	10.7	5.5	0.5	4.5	9.1	836	180	49	1,671	3,990	41,073	3,920
Rosebud	68.3	7,269	51.2	7.9	4.8	0.3	4.7	257.2	27,372	223	41	1,570	3,910	51,465	5,197
Sanders	36.1	3,162	60.5	4.1	6.1	0.0	8.2	4.9	428	142	52	521	5,010	40,365	3,873
Sheridan	21.8	6,087	50.6	2.2	6.1	1.6	16.8	1.9	517	67	15	254	1,900	52,125	5,796
Silver Bow	113.4	3,297	39.5	4.4	5.9	0.1	4.1	60.4	1,757	221	163	2,176	16,270	52,224	5,806
Stillwater	30.5	3,315	64.5	0.6	4.5	0.1	6.8	2.6	287	34	42	452	4,370	60,100	6,632
Sweet Grass	22.6	6,259	30.6	0.8	5.2	32.8	6.0	1.4	398	27	16	200	1,760	50,613	5,243
Teton	35.3	5,826	43.7	23.0	0.8	4.8	5.1	8.3	1,372	49	25	430	3,000	42,866	4,104
Toole	36.4	6,970	29.7	40.6	6.4	0.0	6.6	14.4	2,766	154	19	436	2,210	43,257	4,585
Treasure	3.8	5,182	44.6	5.5	3.4	0.1	10.4	0.5	679	6	3	54	360	50,233	4,022
Valley	35.4	4,717	51.9	2.2	5.0	0.1	10.3	8.7	1,160	154	33	618	3,660	46,422	4,913
Wheatland	8.9	4,252	54.8	5.6	6.4	0.1	6.6	3.2	1,505	19	9	139	890	41,790	3,431
Wibaux	6.5	6,114	36.4	10.7	5.5	0.0	16.1	1.2	1,157	8	4	137	450	46,680	3,860
Yellowstone	506.3	3,333	47.8	7.1	5.8	0.2	6.1	224.5	1,478	1,796	741	7,284	77,220	61,634	7,746
NEBRASKA	X	X	X	X	X	X	X	X	X	16,867	12,630	146,317	898,140	61,556	7,597
Adams	180.4	5,735	72.7	0.4	3.1	0.2	6.2	136.0	4,322	105	105	2,227	14,610	55,957	6,489
Antelope	34.5	5,275	71.6	0.0	2.2	0.0	12.9	7.4	1,136	27	22	460	2,940	46,659	5,148
Arthur	4.1	8,356	45.4	0.2	0.8	0.0	11.7	0.0	0	2	2	51	210	23,052	2,190
Banner	4.4	5,725	68.1	0.3	1.3	0.0	14.7	0.0	0	1	3	65	270	39,463	2,989

1. Based on the resident population estimated as of July 1 of the year shown.

Table B. States and Counties — Land Area and Population

State / county code	CBSA code[1]	County code[2]	STATE County	Land area[3] (sq. mi)	Total persons 2018	Rank	Per square mile	White	Black	American Indian, Alaska Native	Asian and Pacific Islander	Percent Hispanic or Latino[4]	Under 5 years	5 to 17 years	18 to 24 years	25 to 34 years	35 to 44 years	45 to 54 years
				1	2	3	4	5	6	7	8	9	10	11	12	13	14	15
			NEBRASKA— Cont'd															
31009		9	Blaine	710.7	476	3,137	0.7	97.7	1.1	0.6	0.0	1.7	5.5	13.7	8.0	10.9	7.6	12.0
31011		9	Boone	686.6	5,239	2,813	7.6	96.6	0.6	0.5	0.4	2.4	6.2	17.0	7.3	9.9	9.9	10.5
31013		7	Box Butte	1,075.3	10,772	2,367	10.0	82.9	1.6	3.6	1.2	12.7	6.7	18.4	7.3	11.4	11.7	10.1
31015		9	Boyd	539.9	1,955	3,052	3.6	95.5	0.4	1.4	0.9	2.3	4.5	14.5	7.3	7.7	8.6	10.0
31017		9	Brown	1,221.4	2,973	2,969	2.4	96.4	0.7	1.4	0.6	1.9	4.4	16.9	7.0	8.7	9.8	11.2
31019	28,260	4	Buffalo	968.2	49,615	994	51.2	87.6	1.7	0.7	2.1	9.2	7.0	16.4	15.1	13.5	11.9	10.2
31021		8	Burt	491.6	6,488	2,711	13.2	93.7	1.0	2.3	1.0	3.4	5.4	17.0	6.8	10.2	9.9	11.7
31023		6	Butler	584.9	8,058	2,586	13.8	94.9	0.8	0.6	0.7	3.7	5.8	17.4	7.5	10.4	10.8	12.0
31025	36,540	2	Cass	557.4	26,159	1,560	46.9	95.0	1.2	1.1	0.9	3.4	5.9	18.2	7.2	10.4	12.4	13.2
31027		9	Cedar	740.2	8,446	2,548	11.4	97.1	0.6	0.8	0.4	2.0	6.7	18.7	7.2	9.3	9.4	11.2
31029		9	Chase	894.4	3,977	2,902	4.4	84.2	0.9	0.4	0.3	15.1	6.5	19.1	6.6	9.9	11.5	10.9
31031		7	Cherry	5,960.2	5,761	2,773	1.0	90.9	1.2	7.0	1.1	3.0	6.8	16.7	7.0	10.1	11.9	11.2
31033		7	Cheyenne	1,196.3	9,310	2,478	7.8	90.6	0.9	1.4	1.4	7.0	6.1	17.3	6.7	12.1	12.0	11.9
31035		8	Clay	572.3	6,214	2,733	10.9	89.7	0.8	0.7	0.4	9.3	7.1	17.6	7.1	11.2	10.2	11.1
31037		7	Colfax	411.6	10,881	2,360	26.4	48.2	4.1	0.6	0.7	47.0	9.0	20.7	8.3	12.6	13.2	11.0
31039		7	Cuming	570.5	8,940	2,505	15.7	88.4	0.6	0.7	0.5	10.5	6.7	18.1	7.9	9.8	10.4	11.2
31041		7	Custer	2,575.6	10,840	2,362	4.2	95.3	1.0	1.0	0.4	3.5	6.5	17.5	6.9	10.6	10.7	10.8
31043	43,580	3	Dakota	264.3	20,083	1,821	76.0	49.2	6.0	3.1	4.5	39.0	8.7	19.8	9.5	13.6	11.4	11.7
31045		7	Dawes	1,396.5	8,716	2,529	6.2	87.0	2.4	4.3	3.2	5.4	5.0	12.6	22.7	10.2	9.4	9.0
31047	30,420	7	Dawson	1,013.1	23,709	1,656	23.4	58.8	5.9	0.7	1.3	34.1	8.0	19.2	8.3	12.7	11.8	11.2
31049		9	Deuel	439.9	1,825	3,064	4.1	91.8	0.6	1.5	0.6	6.7	5.3	16.4	5.2	9.2	10.7	12.2
31051	43,580	3	Dixon	476.1	5,709	2,779	12.0	83.9	0.8	0.9	0.4	14.9	7.2	18.4	8.0	9.7	10.6	11.5
31053	23,340	4	Dodge	529.1	36,791	1,257	69.5	84.4	1.5	1.0	1.2	13.4	6.8	17.6	9.0	11.1	11.6	11.6
31055	36,540	2	Douglas	326.4	566,880	117	1,736.8	71.2	12.5	1.1	4.9	12.8	7.5	18.1	9.1	15.5	13.4	11.7
31057		9	Dundy	919.7	1,770	3,067	1.9	90.1	1.3	1.2	0.7	8.2	4.9	14.3	8.5	8.5	10.5	11.4
31059		8	Fillmore	575.4	5,527	2,789	9.6	94.1	1.0	0.9	0.7	4.1	5.4	14.5	6.9	11.5	11.0	12.1
31061		9	Franklin	575.8	3,023	2,964	5.3	97.1	0.6	0.9	0.7	2.2	5.1	14.3	6.2	9.6	9.2	10.5
31063		9	Frontier	974.6	2,608	2,997	2.7	96.5	0.7	1.0	0.4	2.3	5.0	14.0	11.2	10.0	9.5	10.8
31065		9	Furnas	719.1	4,715	2,850	6.6	94.1	0.8	1.1	0.6	4.5	5.7	16.1	7.1	9.5	10.1	11.1
31067	13,100	6	Gage	851.5	21,493	1,755	25.2	95.5	1.2	1.1	0.8	2.7	5.9	16.6	7.0	10.4	11.5	12.1
31069		9	Garden	1,705.4	1,897	3,059	1.1	92.8	0.7	1.7	0.5	5.9	4.6	15.0	6.1	10.2	8.0	11.0
31071		9	Garfield	569.3	1,987	3,050	3.5	98.0	0.3	0.6	0.1	1.4	4.8	13.6	8.1	8.5	9.2	9.6
31073	30,420	9	Gosper	458.2	1,996	3,049	4.4	92.5	1.0	1.4	0.8	5.9	5.9	16.5	6.1	9.5	9.9	11.5
31075		9	Grant	776.9	660	3,130	0.8	98.2	0.5	0.5	0.8	1.2	8.5	16.1	5.0	10.9	11.7	8.2
31077		8	Greeley	569.8	2,356	3,016	4.1	96.6	0.8	0.3	0.3	2.5	6.4	16.4	7.2	9.9	10.4	11.6
31079	24,260	3	Hall	546.4	61,607	853	112.8	66.7	3.5	0.7	1.7	28.5	7.8	19.6	8.3	13.1	12.5	11.6
31081	24,260	3	Hamilton	541.9	9,280	2,479	17.1	95.7	0.6	0.6	0.5	3.4	6.3	17.8	7.9	10.7	11.1	12.2
31083		9	Harlan	553.5	3,401	2,943	6.1	96.8	0.6	0.8	0.4	2.3	5.4	15.8	6.3	8.3	9.6	11.4
31085		9	Hayes	713.1	916	3,110	1.3	94.0	0.7	0.9	0.7	4.7	7.4	15.1	7.0	9.3	8.7	6.9
31087		9	Hitchcock	709.9	2,806	2,984	4.0	94.9	0.4	1.0	0.4	4.2	5.4	17.4	6.0	8.6	11.8	10.1
31089		7	Holt	2,412.4	10,178	2,413	4.2	93.6	0.6	0.7	0.6	5.3	7.0	18.1	7.0	9.7	10.1	10.3
31091		9	Hooker	721.2	682	3,128	0.9	96.3	0.3	0.9	0.3	2.9	6.2	16.0	5.7	8.5	10.7	8.2
31093	24,260	9	Howard	569.3	6,468	2,714	11.4	96.0	0.8	0.6	0.6	2.7	6.2	18.1	6.2	10.6	11.2	12.3
31095		7	Jefferson	570.2	7,097	2,656	12.4	94.4	0.8	1.1	0.6	4.2	5.6	16.4	6.3	9.9	10.5	11.3
31097		8	Johnson	376.1	5,134	2,822	13.7	81.0	6.4	1.5	1.5	10.3	4.7	14.1	7.7	13.9	13.3	13.0
31099	28,260	7	Kearney	516.2	6,544	2,708	12.7	92.6	0.5	0.7	0.5	6.5	6.3	18.3	7.2	11.2	11.4	11.6
31101		7	Keith	1,061.6	8,021	2,590	7.6	90.7	1.1	1.2	0.9	7.6	5.6	14.2	6.3	9.7	9.7	11.3
31103		9	Keya Paha	773.1	810	3,118	1.0	98.1	0.2	0.7	0.5	0.7	4.1	15.4	5.3	6.8	10.0	8.8
31105		8	Kimball	951.8	3,618	2,930	3.8	86.9	1.2	2.7	1.6	10.1	6.0	15.6	6.9	9.9	10.0	11.3
31107		9	Knox	1,108.4	8,419	2,550	7.6	87.2	0.8	10.3	0.7	2.9	6.5	17.8	6.8	8.8	9.5	10.3
31109	30,700	2	Lancaster	837.6	317,272	220	378.8	83.3	5.4	1.2	5.6	7.2	6.3	16.5	14.9	13.9	12.5	10.7
31111	35,820	5	Lincoln	2,564.1	35,185	1,301	13.7	88.6	1.5	1.0	1.3	8.7	6.0	17.5	7.4	11.6	12.6	11.5
31113	35,820	9	Logan	570.7	749	3,123	1.3	96.0	0.4	1.6	0.4	2.4	6.4	19.5	5.3	7.6	13.5	9.5
31115		9	Loup	563.5	618	3,133	1.1	95.3	1.1	0.2	0.2	3.2	4.9	14.1	7.1	8.6	7.9	9.1
31117	35,820	9	McPherson	859.0	492	3,136	0.6	98.6	1.2	0.4	0.0	1.0	3.3	15.2	8.5	5.9	9.8	14.8
31119	35,740	5	Madison	572.6	35,392	1,293	61.8	80.0	1.9	1.5	2.2	15.8	7.3	18.0	9.5	12.8	11.7	10.8
31121	24,260	3	Merrick	485.9	7,733	2,612	15.9	93.3	0.8	1.0	1.4	4.7	5.9	16.7	7.4	11.0	11.0	12.6
31123		9	Morrill	1,423.8	4,686	2,851	3.3	82.8	0.6	1.3	1.0	15.4	5.5	17.5	7.2	10.7	11.4	11.7
31125		8	Nance	441.6	3,532	2,936	8.0	95.6	0.8	1.2	0.3	3.1	5.5	16.9	6.4	10.4	10.9	11.3
31127		7	Nemaha	407.4	6,958	2,676	17.1	94.9	1.9	0.9	0.9	2.8	5.9	15.8	12.1	11.6	10.8	10.1
31129		9	Nuckolls	575.2	4,195	2,887	7.3	95.9	0.5	0.8	1.0	2.9	5.1	14.9	6.8	9.2	10.1	10.3
31131		6	Otoe	615.7	15,985	2,039	26.0	89.6	1.4	0.9	1.2	8.3	6.6	17.4	7.5	10.8	11.4	12.0
31133		9	Pawnee	431.1	2,632	2,992	6.1	97.0	1.1	0.9	0.8	1.9	6.4	15.2	6.2	8.7	8.9	10.1
31135		9	Perkins	883.3	2,929	2,972	3.3	94.7	0.8	0.4	0.3	4.3	6.8	18.3	6.7	9.8	11.8	9.2
31137		7	Phelps	539.8	8,996	2,501	16.7	92.8	0.7	0.8	0.8	5.9	5.9	17.8	7.7	11.1	10.8	12.0
31139	35,740	9	Pierce	573.2	7,142	2,652	12.5	96.8	0.8	0.7	0.7	2.0	6.3	18.4	7.2	10.4	11.3	12.1

1. CBSA = Core Based Statistical Area. See Appendix A for explanation. See Appendix B for list of metropolitan areas with component counties. 2. County type code from the Economic Research Service of USDA Rural-Urban Continuum Codes. See Appendix A for definition. 3. Dry land or land partially or temporarily covered by water. 4. May be of any race.

Table B. States and Counties — Population and Households

STATE County	Age (percent) (cont.)				Population change, 2000-2018							Households, 2013-2017				
	55 to 64 years	65 to 74 years	75 years and over	Percent female	Total persons		Percent change		Components of change, 2010-2018						Percent	
					2000	2010	2000-2010	2010-2018	Births	Deaths	Net Migration	Number	Persons per household	Family house-holds	Female family house-holder[1]	One person
	16	17	18	19	20	21	22	23	24	25	26	27	28	29	30	31

NEBRASKA— Cont'd

STATE County	16	17	18	19	20	21	22	23	24	25	26	27	28	29	30	31
Blaine	17.0	13.4	12.0	49.6	583	478	-18.0	-0.4	44	33	-17	232	2.16	65.1	0.9	27.2
Boone	16.3	10.8	12.0	49.9	6,259	5,505	-12.0	-4.8	510	535	-241	2,277	2.31	66.2	6.2	30.0
Box Butte	15.4	11.3	7.7	50.3	12,158	11,308	-7.0	-4.7	1,241	951	-832	4,610	2.39	66.4	5.5	30.7
Boyd	16.8	15.8	14.8	49.8	2,438	2,099	-13.9	-6.9	148	249	-41	905	2.23	66.3	2.7	31.6
Brown	16.0	13.2	12.9	51.2	3,525	3,143	-10.8	-5.4	230	317	-85	1,475	2.04	62.0	9.2	33.8
Buffalo	11.4	8.3	6.2	50.0	42,259	46,099	9.1	7.6	5,765	2,859	621	18,923	2.46	61.8	8.6	27.8
Burt	15.0	12.3	11.8	50.4	7,791	6,858	-12.0	-5.4	575	786	-160	2,885	2.23	66.9	7.4	28.7
Butler	15.2	11.2	9.7	49.4	8,767	8,395	-4.2	-4.0	725	816	-245	3,400	2.33	66.7	6.5	30.1
Cass	15.3	10.7	6.8	49.6	24,334	25,241	3.7	3.6	2,328	1,961	563	9,894	2.55	69.8	7.6	25.2
Cedar	16.0	10.5	10.9	49.4	9,615	8,852	-7.9	-4.6	872	840	-444	3,508	2.40	67.9	4.0	27.9
Chase	14.9	9.8	10.7	50.5	4,068	3,966	-2.5	0.3	400	416	30	1,671	2.23	65.7	4.0	30.6
Cherry	14.5	11.2	10.6	49.3	6,148	5,713	-7.1	0.8	585	509	-28	2,652	2.14	65.0	5.0	29.9
Cheyenne	14.5	10.5	8.9	49.7	9,830	9,998	1.7	-6.9	1,033	777	-950	4,400	2.25	58.2	6.8	38.7
Clay	15.4	11.4	8.9	48.7	7,039	6,539	-7.1	-5.0	652	580	-400	2,616	2.36	67.7	7.0	27.3
Colfax	11.6	7.3	6.1	46.7	10,441	10,515	0.7	3.5	1,530	635	-541	3,681	2.86	69.4	7.3	24.7
Cuming	14.0	10.4	11.5	49.9	10,203	9,139	-10.4	-2.2	913	796	-318	3,790	2.35	65.6	6.1	32.5
Custer	14.6	12.0	10.4	50.2	11,793	10,943	-7.2	-0.9	1,049	1,088	-57	4,792	2.23	66.3	8.5	30.2
Dakota	11.7	7.8	5.8	49.3	20,253	21,006	3.7	-4.4	3,016	1,326	-2,647	7,427	2.73	75.5	16.0	18.5
Dawes	12.7	9.3	9.3	50.1	9,060	9,182	1.3	-5.1	789	692	-570	3,557	2.22	60.2	8.4	29.9
Dawson	12.2	9.5	7.2	48.0	24,365	24,326	-0.2	-2.5	3,237	1,717	-2,164	8,898	2.65	72.0	11.8	23.2
Deuel	17.6	12.6	10.9	50.4	2,098	1,932	-7.9	-5.5	130	185	-53	833	2.26	65.9	9.1	28.8
Dixon	14.6	11.5	8.6	49.1	6,339	6,000	-5.3	-4.9	623	518	-400	2,307	2.46	69.6	7.2	27.7
Dodge	13.2	9.9	9.3	50.4	36,160	36,685	1.5	0.3	4,011	3,589	-306	15,090	2.36	66.0	9.4	27.4
Douglas	11.7	7.8	5.2	50.6	463,585	517,114	11.5	9.6	70,109	32,338	12,435	213,689	2.51	61.8	11.8	31.1
Dundy	16.7	13.3	11.9	50.0	2,292	2,008	-12.4	-11.9	137	232	-146	875	2.25	62.4	9.8	33.9
Fillmore	16.0	11.5	11.2	50.0	6,634	5,890	-11.2	-6.2	477	705	-134	2,443	2.20	63.8	6.1	32.1
Franklin	16.9	14.7	13.6	50.8	3,574	3,225	-9.8	-6.3	240	310	-130	1,367	2.15	66.2	7.5	30.6
Frontier	15.8	12.6	11.3	48.9	3,099	2,756	-11.1	-5.4	200	147	-202	1,113	2.24	68.1	5.3	27.8
Furnas	15.2	13.8	11.3	50.2	5,324	4,959	-6.9	-4.9	415	558	-97	2,172	2.18	59.3	4.7	37.8
Gage	15.7	10.6	10.2	50.1	22,993	22,311	-3.0	-3.7	1,981	2,270	-531	9,255	2.27	64.0	6.5	31.6
Garden	17.2	13.3	14.6	47.7	2,292	2,057	-10.3	-7.8	161	231	-94	897	2.08	60.6	2.7	36.2
Garfield	17.6	13.9	14.8	50.1	1,902	2,049	7.7	-3.0	128	270	81	893	2.14	67.2	8.4	31.2
Gosper	16.7	12.5	11.4	48.7	2,143	2,044	-4.6	-2.3	183	197	-33	885	2.24	68.4	8.2	26.7
Grant	17.1	13.3	9.2	47.1	747	614	-17.8	7.5	78	44	10	274	2.34	70.1	3.3	29.2
Greeley	14.6	12.0	13.6	50.8	2,714	2,538	-6.5	-7.2	234	237	-183	1,015	2.37	66.1	5.0	32.7
Hall	12.2	8.4	6.4	49.6	53,534	58,607	9.5	5.1	7,823	4,415	-383	22,817	2.64	67.9	14.2	25.7
Hamilton	14.1	10.8	9.1	49.8	9,403	9,114	-3.1	1.8	857	658	-31	3,722	2.42	73.3	7.1	24.0
Harlan	16.9	14.2	12.0	48.2	3,786	3,417	-9.7	-0.5	315	337	6	1,590	2.15	59.5	4.5	35.7
Hayes	18.1	13.5	14.0	48.3	1,068	960	-10.1	-4.6	110	39	-118	423	2.26	70.0	0.7	26.5
Hitchcock	15.4	13.4	11.9	49.6	3,111	2,908	-6.5	-3.5	255	307	-51	1,273	2.22	59.2	6.1	37.4
Holt	16.2	11.4	10.2	50.0	11,551	10,435	-9.7	-2.5	1,151	1,015	-390	4,569	2.21	64.6	5.0	30.1
Hooker	14.2	14.2	16.3	51.8	783	736	-6.0	-7.3	57	102	-12	316	1.96	63.6	6.3	32.3
Howard	14.3	11.4	9.7	49.3	6,567	6,274	-4.5	3.1	630	527	97	2,656	2.40	66.0	6.9	28.4
Jefferson	16.1	12.6	11.3	50.5	8,333	7,547	-9.4	-6.0	645	873	-221	3,308	2.16	60.6	8.4	35.5
Johnson	14.6	9.7	9.1	41.2	4,488	5,217	16.2	-1.6	361	493	45	1,869	2.14	67.1	9.6	28.7
Kearney	14.3	10.4	9.2	50.1	6,882	6,489	-5.7	0.8	662	606		2,745	2.36	63.4	6.9	31.3
Keith	16.5	15.1	11.6	49.6	8,875	8,368	-5.7	-4.1	675	765	-254	3,989	2.02	62.7	7.3	34.6
Keya Paha	18.6	14.6	16.4	51.5	983	824	-16.2	-1.7	58	53	-19	334	2.16	68.3	3.9	25.4
Kimball	15.9	12.0	12.4	49.8	4,089	3,821	-6.6	-5.3	340	403	-140	1,546	2.35	65.6	11.4	27.5
Knox	15.6	12.2	12.5	50.5	9,374	8,701	-7.2	-3.2	835	950	-164	3,662	2.26	65.4	5.9	30.5
Lancaster	11.2	8.4	5.5	49.8	250,291	285,407	14.0	11.2	33,375	16,826	15,439	120,962	2.42	60.3	9.6	29.7
Lincoln	14.2	10.8	8.6	50.5	34,632	36,288	4.8	-3.0	3,538	2,963	-1,681	15,025	2.31	65.3	9.4	30.4
Logan	15.6	12.7	9.9	47.1	774	763	-1.4	-1.8	83	50	-49	366	2.51	70.5	4.9	24.3
Loup	21.7	15.7	11.0	49.0	712	628	-11.8	-1.6	48	47	-12	245	2.19	75.9	7.3	20.0
McPherson	18.3	13.2	11.0	49.0	533	539	1.1	-8.7	23	30	-41	192	2.23	71.4	2.1	28.6
Madison	13.9	8.5	7.5	50.5	35,226	34,876	-1.0	1.5	4,284	2,940	-822	14,236	2.39	64.7	11.1	28.7
Merrick	14.9	10.6	10.0	49.9	8,204	7,855	-4.3	-1.6	757	695	-185	3,251	2.34	66.5	6.6	27.1
Morrill	14.7	10.8	10.3	48.7	5,440	5,042	-7.3	-7.1	430	478	-311	2,017	2.35	61.9	9.8	32.8
Nance	17.2	11.4	10.0	50.3	4,038	3,735	-7.5	-5.4	339	395	-150	1,553	2.20	62.9	8.6	34.6
Nemaha	13.7	11.2	8.9	50.0	7,576	7,248	-4.3	-4.0	634	674	-251	2,814	2.31	66.9	8.4	27.9
Nuckolls	16.5	14.0	13.1	50.3	5,057	4,500	-11.0	-6.8	346	495	-151	1,985	2.13	63.1	4.1	32.9
Otoe	14.7	9.9	9.5	50.4	15,396	15,740	2.2	1.6	1,626	1,533	162	6,439	2.43	66.8	10.1	28.8
Pawnee	15.8	14.4	14.3	50.8	3,087	2,773	-10.2	-5.1	247	291	-97	1,238	2.15	63.7	8.5	32.9
Perkins	13.9	12.7	10.8	49.1	3,200	2,970	-7.2	-1.4	315	258	-100	1,247	2.30	67.8	4.4	31.5
Phelps	14.0	10.3	10.4	49.9	9,747	9,188	-5.7	-2.1	929	940	-177	3,870	2.30	63.2	4.3	32.0
Pierce	15.1	10.0	9.3	49.4	7,857	7,266	-7.5	-1.7	690	572	-242	2,985	2.36	67.6	5.7	28.5

1. No spouse present.

Table B. States and Counties — **Population, Vital Statistics, Health, and Crime**

STATE County	Persons in group quarters, 2018	Daytime Population, 2013-2017 Number	Employment/ residence ratio	Births, 2018 Total	Rate[1]	Deaths, 2018 Number	Rate[1]	Persons under 65 with no health insurance, 2016 Number	Percent	Medicare, 2018 Total beneficiaries	Enrolled in Original Medicare	Enrolled in Medicare Advantage	Serious crimes known to police[2], 2016 Total Number	Rate[3]
	32	33	34	35	36	37	38	39	40	41	42	43	44	45
NEBRASKA— Cont'd														
Blaine	0	439	0.77	4	8.4	2	4.2	56	15.6	120	D	D	NA	NA
Boone	102	5,345	1.00	61	11.6	66	12.6	401	9.6	1,228	1,168	60	NA	NA
Box Butte	136	11,591	1.07	131	12.2	110	10.2	887	9.7	2,265	2,153	112	140	1,236
Boyd	34	2,008	0.96	17	8.7	20	10.2	150	10.9	622	D	D	NA	NA
Brown	18	3,038	0.99	28	9.4	30	10.1	277	12.4	771	D	D	25	861
Buffalo	1,975	49,811	1.04	693	14.0	372	7.5	3,396	8.3	7,981	7,245	736	973	1,972
Burt	117	5,842	0.76	70	10.8	92	14.2	538	10.8	1,786	1,580	206	37	647
Butler	166	6,713	0.65	82	10.2	82	10.2	518	8.2	1,856	1,711	145	19	236
Cass	267	18,522	0.47	272	10.4	235	9.0	1,472	6.9	5,055	4,180	875	339	1,328
Cedar	128	7,715	0.81	107	12.7	103	12.2	610	9.0	1,858	1,535	323	27	318
Chase	64	4,025	1.11	55	13.8	47	11.8	429	13.8	854	D	D	17	430
Cherry	40	6,025	1.07	68	11.8	63	10.9	644	14.1	1,280	D	D	71	1,210
Cheyenne	98	10,918	1.17	112	12.0	81	8.7	591	7.1	2,059	1,928	131	170	1,668
Clay	74	5,553	0.77	80	12.9	65	10.5	592	12.2	1,460	D	D	23	477
Colfax	77	10,596	1.00	196	18.0	58	5.3	1,426	16.0	1,467	1,408	59	NA	NA
Cuming	126	8,715	0.93	104	11.6	90	10.1	810	11.5	2,128	2,007	121	17	187
Custer	132	10,930	1.02	130	12.0	128	11.8	937	11.2	2,506	2,473	33	143	1,328
Dakota	244	22,201	1.17	353	17.6	144	7.2	2,760	16.0	3,212	2,515	697	632	3,102
Dawes	1,005	8,991	1.00	88	10.1	80	9.2	798	12.2	1,757	1,551	206	151	1,675
Dawson	294	23,702	0.98	394	16.6	195	8.2	2,917	15.0	4,180	3,765	415	381	1,604
Deuel	0	1,699	0.80	14	7.7	21	11.5	164	11.7	489	D	D	5	261
Dixon	70	4,465	0.55	78	13.7	56	9.8	471	10.4	1,160	953	207	50	930
Dodge	1,178	35,797	0.96	482	13.1	406	11.0	3,070	10.7	8,076	6,859	1,217	778	2,122
Douglas	12,595	603,115	1.19	8,488	15.0	3,960	7.0	49,376	10.3	85,150	61,783	23,367	20,516	3,699
Dundy	32	2,020	1.00	18	10.2	29	16.4	193	14.3	477	D	D	5	285
Fillmore	186	5,541	0.98	62	11.2	81	14.7	361	8.5	1,520	1,502	18	16	288
Franklin	46	2,622	0.73	33	10.9	31	10.3	215	9.8	847	D	D	9	307
Frontier	113	2,491	0.89	21	8.1	13	5.0	203	10.6	569	D	D	NA	NA
Furnas	78	4,799	0.99	55	11.7	56	11.9	390	10.9	1,317	D	D	64	1,323
Gage	489	20,180	0.87	240	11.2	251	11.7	1,446	8.5	5,379	4,821	558	523	2,566
Garden	24	1,897	0.98	21	11.1	15	7.9	158	11.6	604	592	12	NA	NA
Garfield	54	1,976	1.02	18	9.1	26	13.1	137	9.7	483	470	13	2	99
Gosper	41	1,644	0.66	23	11.5	21	10.5	130	8.4	498	434	64	13	664
Grant	3	681	1.00	11	16.7	6	9.1	45	8.8	178	178	0	NA	NA
Greeley	56	2,227	0.82	24	10.2	32	13.6	276	15.5	575	575	0	NA	NA
Hall	1,039	65,680	1.14	926	15.0	532	8.6	7,153	13.9	10,307	9,556	751	1,978	3,181
Hamilton	116	8,463	0.86	120	12.9	78	8.4	539	7.2	2,066	1,983	83	105	1,143
Harlan	40	3,207	0.83	38	11.2	32	9.4	271	10.5	870	857	13	NA	NA
Hayes	0	743	0.57	18	19.7	3	3.3	151	22.9	196	D	D	7	756
Hitchcock	26	2,457	0.69	25	8.9	38	13.5	240	11.4	783	D	D	25	870
Holt	112	10,295	1.00	139	13.7	119	11.7	798	10.0	2,555	2,542	13	31	302
Hooker	22	699	1.05	6	8.8	8	11.7	42	8.4	239	D	D	2	274
Howard	66	5,212	0.64	72	11.1	62	9.6	480	9.4	1,389	1,362	27	NA	NA
Jefferson	88	7,519	1.07	80	11.3	88	12.4	503	9.3	1,945	1,770	175	NA	NA
Johnson	1,026	4,973	0.89	39	7.6	54	10.5	331	10.1	883	845	38	11	213
Kearney	72	6,250	0.91	75	11.5	67	10.2	427	8.1	1,204	1,153	51	105	1,592
Keith	34	8,109	1.00	92	11.5	79	9.8	605	10.0	2,176	1,998	178	224	2,803
Keya Paha	0	631	0.79	6	7.4	1	1.2	73	12.8	245	D	D	1	125
Kimball	45	3,668	0.99	37	10.2	46	12.7	340	12.2	963	947	16	19	519
Knox	221	7,922	0.86	105	12.5	101	12.0	912	14.2	2,186	1,985	201	28	329
Lancaster	14,984	315,192	1.05	3,964	12.5	2,106	6.6	23,240	9.1	48,444	41,287	7,157	10,161	3,276
Lincoln	606	36,279	1.04	427	12.1	348	9.9	2,530	8.8	7,686	6,429	1,257	1,084	3,055
Logan	0	790	0.71	9	12.0	6	8.0	85	13.3	154	142	12	NA	NA
Loup	0	474	0.76	6	9.7	8	12.9	54	12.2	149	D	D	NA	NA
McPherson	0	364	0.70	2	4.1	2	4.1	37	9.3	91	74	17	NA	NA
Madison	1,267	38,843	1.21	497	14.0	374	10.6	3,067	10.7	6,703	5,927	776	673	1,923
Merrick	195	6,755	0.73	90	11.6	92	11.9	575	9.2	1,816	1,719	97	47	606
Morrill	78	4,581	0.86	44	9.4	46	9.8	500	13.0	958	901	57	61	1,268
Nance	143	3,254	0.82	39	11.0	41	11.6	269	9.6	707	674	33	NA	NA
Nemaha	467	7,174	1.04	80	11.5	63	9.1	381	7.3	1,553	D	D	71	1,015
Nuckolls	50	4,058	0.88	43	10.3	63	15.0	270	8.7	1,193	1,157	36	NA	NA
Otoe	278	14,900	0.88	196	12.3	162	10.1	1,117	8.7	3,457	3,080	377	351	2,193
Pawnee	39	2,656	0.96	31	11.8	30	11.4	241	12.5	653	D	D	45	1,709
Perkins	35	3,003	1.07	37	12.6	21	7.2	277	12.4	695	672	23	21	716
Phelps	239	9,542	1.08	102	11.3	100	11.1	608	8.3	2,075	2,053	22	164	1,763
Pierce	90	6,018	0.68	79	11.1	66	9.2	422	7.3	1,395	D	D	20	367

1. Per 1,000 estimated resident population. 2. Data for serious crimes have not been adjusted for underreporting; this may affect comparability between geographic areas and over time. 3. Per 100,000 population estimated by the FBI.

Table B. States and Counties — **Crime, Education, Money Income, and Poverty**

STATE County	Serious crimes known to police[2], 2016 (cont.)[1] Rate Violent	Property	School enrollment and attainment, 2013-2017 Enrollment[3] Total	Percent private	Attainment[4] (percent) High school graduate or less	Bachelor's degree or more	Local government expenditures,[5] 2014-2015 Total current spending (mil dol)	Current spending per student (dollars)	Money income, 2013-2017 Per capita income[6]	Median income (dollars)	Households Percent with income of less than $50,000	with income of $200,000 or more	Income and poverty, 2017 Median household income (dollars)	Percent below poverty level All persons	Children under 18 years	Children 5 to 17 years in families
	46	47	48	49	50	51	52	53	54	55	56	57	58	59	60	61
NEBRASKA— Cont'd																
Blaine	NA	NA	102	15.7	38.5	24.2	2.4	20,974	28,503	52,000	41.4	2.2	44,016	14.5	21.4	21.4
Boone	NA	NA	1,217	20.3	42.0	19.8	15.4	15,386	28,861	53,854	45.9	3.2	55,493	9.2	13.0	13.0
Box Butte	203	1,033	2,576	13.5	42.9	17.4	21.8	11,059	28,483	56,328	43.7	3.0	58,728	11.6	16.2	14.9
Boyd	NA	NA	414	4.8	44.5	20.2	6.1	17,504	26,413	48,750	50.5	1.7	43,189	12.6	24.7	23.0
Brown	0	861	623	10.3	48.3	18.2	10.2	21,453	29,664	42,773	56.9	2.0	46,768	12.1	18.2	16.2
Buffalo	182	1,790	14,743	9.9	31.5	33.6	92.3	11,842	28,553	55,053	45.4	3.4	58,800	12.7	12.1	10.1
Burt	70	577	1,333	10.2	46.2	19.1	16.8	13,254	26,421	50,174	49.8	1.2	52,879	11.5	15.5	13.7
Butler	62	174	1,836	26.3	46.7	18.7	14.7	14,747	27,216	52,448	45.9	1.8	52,033	8.5	10.0	8.6
Cass	110	1,219	6,282	11.6	36.0	26.8	44.3	11,732	32,509	68,284	34.8	4.4	71,166	6	8.2	7.1
Cedar	35	282	2,036	17.5	44.1	18.4	19.2	16,376	29,694	57,208	44.5	3.4	61,159	8.3	10.7	10.1
Chase	51	380	804	4.7	36.4	19.4	10.5	12,505	33,708	54,568	42.5	2.8	57,965	9.3	11.4	10.0
Cherry	307	903	1,035	8.3	41.5	20.1	12.1	27,891	28,553	53,226	47.1	2.6	46,894	11.7	16.9	16.7
Cheyenne	206	1,462	2,336	7.5	32.4	26.3	21.8	12,480	32,995	58,770	40.7	5.3	59,971	10.2	12.9	12.0
Clay	124	352	1,356	5.2	44.2	17.8	20.8	14,466	27,275	54,167	45.0	2.3	51,775	10.8	14.9	14.3
Colfax	NA	NA	2,697	3.9	60.2	14.4	31.4	12,137	23,393	54,876	42.5	2.0	61,176	9.2	12.6	12.2
Cuming	22	165	2,104	19.3	48.4	21.2	20.7	13,071	28,762	50,734	49.3	3.4	55,465	8.3	11.4	10.2
Custer	139	1,189	2,273	9.4	39.8	21.7	27.2	15,414	32,605	48,836	51.1	4.0	50,627	12.1	18.2	17.7
Dakota	304	2,798	5,437	9.5	61.5	12.6	50.9	11,712	22,463	52,401	46.6	2.9	52,055	12.7	18.9	18.5
Dawes	144	1,530	2,915	7.6	31.2	37.0	14.4	11,981	24,811	46,146	51.9	2.2	43,627	17	21.0	18.3
Dawson	160	1,444	5,829	5.0	56.2	15.8	63.1	11,633	24,912	51,238	48.3	2.6	46,395	11.5	15.8	15.2
Deuel	0	261	368	5.4	42.9	18.1	7.5	18,863	28,225	53,438	46.2	2.9	47,584	12.2	21.5	19.9
Dixon	56	875	1,421	2.7	49.2	18.8	13.3	14,150	26,094	57,036	43.2	2.5	54,941	8.8	11.2	10.3
Dodge	207	1,915	8,743	21.3	46.6	19.0	70.3	11,518	27,162	51,748	47.5	2.4	53,152	13.7	18.5	15.9
Douglas	490	3,209	151,104	21.1	31.8	37.9	1,064.7	11,176	32,023	58,640	42.9	5.9	61,706	11.4	15.7	15.0
Dundy	0	285	471	12.1	39.8	21.1	5.7	16,690	26,949	44,653	53.8	3.4	45,680	14.9	23.8	22.6
Fillmore	18	270	1,094	11.1	45.7	19.2	14.1	15,285	30,874	56,750	44.2	3.2	57,539	8.2	12.3	12.0
Franklin	68	239	548	2.9	42.1	20.0	4.9	15,997	28,635	49,453	50.8	3.4	47,002	13.7	22.9	22.2
Frontier	NA	NA	685	4.2	37.1	19.5	9.9	16,570	27,900	52,090	45.2	2.2	49,455	13.1	20.0	19.4
Furnas	62	1,261	1,041	8.9	45.2	18.2	16.0	14,234	24,522	43,400	57.0	1.0	50,675	11.2	18.8	18.1
Gage	378	2,188	4,565	14.1	44.1	20.3	42.6	12,953	27,424	52,223	47.8	1.8	53,305	10.7	12.8	11.9
Garden	NA	NA	357	6.7	35.1	24.2	4.2	16,237	35,602	48,215	51.5	4.7	39,446	15.6	26.1	24.4
Garfield	49	49	339	6.8	38.3	19.5	4.8	13,202	25,856	46,509	56.7	1.0	43,478	11.6	16.4	15.5
Gosper	102	562	439	2.1	39.7	24.1	3.4	15,408	31,901	61,769	39.9	1.7	54,787	9.2	16.1	14.7
Grant	NA	NA	153	21.6	40.6	23.0	2.6	16,788	22,693	45,833	54.7	2.2	52,665	10	12.5	13.5
Greeley	NA	NA	507	24.5	43.2	17.3	5.7	18,900	25,544	47,218	50.8	1.5	45,037	12.5	19.9	19.9
Hall	333	2,849	15,124	10.3	47.3	19.8	141.1	11,696	26,419	53,807	45.6	2.8	54,546	12	17.3	15.6
Hamilton	261	881	2,187	12.1	38.0	25.7	20.7	13,134	31,989	61,944	37.5	4.1	68,296	6.5	8.8	8.1
Harlan	NA	NA	693	4.3	41.8	18.7	4.3	15,272	26,375	46,750	52.1	1.4	47,829	10.4	16.8	15.1
Hayes	324	432	193	3.1	36.1	17.2	2.6	24,305	27,183	44,946	51.8	5.7	45,136	16.7	27.2	29.0
Hitchcock	174	696	606	13.4	45.3	17.4	6.2	20,929	25,290	41,582	57.8	1.3	42,567	13.7	19.3	17.6
Holt	58	243	2,036	16.7	42.4	21.0	25.1	15,288	27,858	52,050	46.7	2.1	50,370	10.8	15.6	15.3
Hooker	0	274	120	5.8	37.6	25.6	3.0	17,017	27,714	41,607	54.1	2.8	47,327	8.6	12.5	13.3
Howard	NA	NA	1,493	11.5	47.3	20.1	16.3	12,452	26,734	53,648	45.4	2.1	54,671	10	13.0	12.5
Jefferson	NA	NA	1,440	3.4	50.8	14.7	21.2	13,681	26,859	46,576	54.7	3.1	48,930	11.5	15.2	13.6
Johnson	0	213	1,002	4.6	53.9	17.3	10.4	22,398	22,398	49,564	50.4	1.7	48,518	12.7	15.8	14.9
Kearney	61	1,531	1,508	7.6	40.5	22.3	18.1	14,297	31,234	53,207	46.2	3.1	62,499	8.4	11.5	10.6
Keith	163	2,640	1,503	12.0	42.3	22.0	21.5	19,724	27,890	45,078	55.9	1.8	47,598	12.3	19.9	18.0
Keya Paha	0	125	144	6.3	43.0	20.6	2.3	22,941	28,981	48,864	51.5	2.7	45,688	17.7	27.4	25.5
Kimball	109	410	748	5.6	46.2	17.5	6.6	12,336	24,011	43,017	55.9	1.6	46,571	13.8	21.0	19.3
Knox	24	306	1,905	12.3	42.9	20.8	24.9	16,467	27,283	48,072	51.7	2.4	46,163	12.6	18.3	17.0
Lancaster	336	2,939	92,556	16.1	28.9	37.9	476.6	10,749	29,901	55,747	44.6	4.1	59,681	11.4	11.5	10.2
Lincoln	290	2,765	8,903	13.0	35.8	22.2	60.7	10,535	29,687	55,875	44.7	2.9	55,934	11.6	16.3	13.1
Logan	NA	NA	225	11.1	35.2	22.7	2.9	13,537	24,624	50,278	49.7	0.8	48,579	8.9	13.0	12.9
Loup	NA	NA	86	2.3	41.6	22.9	2.0	25,766	29,248	58,625	41.2	2.4	46,875	15.8	26.1	25.0
McPherson	NA	NA	75	8.0	32.0	25.2	1.9	23,134	27,241	60,714	43.8	3.6	49,875	12.7	24.5	21.3
Madison	143	1,780	9,089	18.8	41.6	20.4	65.9	11,590	26,093	49,865	50.1	2.4	51,184	13.1	15.7	14.7
Merrick	64	541	1,678	14.5	41.4	17.6	12.7	13,014	27,223	53,536	44.9	3.3	59,984	10.2	14.3	13.1
Morrill	83	1,185	1,205	8.8	45.5	18.9	13.7	14,845	25,120	44,201	57.4	2.5	44,062	14.3	21.2	18.8
Nance	NA	NA	786	12.3	46.0	18.3	10.8	13,551	26,852	45,428	54.3	3.0	48,972	11.8	15.4	14.1
Nemaha	143	872	2,112	8.7	39.6	28.0	19.7	16,833	28,572	55,536	45.2	4.0	52,229	12.6	14.6	12.9
Nuckolls	NA	NA	850	3.9	48.4	19.1	6.3	13,380	24,426	42,055	58.3	1.4	43,712	11.5	18.1	17.0
Otoe	75	2,118	3,398	12.2	47.0	21.4	29.9	11,430	28,567	54,605	46.0	2.4	60,469	9.1	12.9	10.6
Pawnee	38	1,671	465	10.8	53.2	15.9	7.5	15,794	27,196	42,176	55.9	1.8	42,962	13.2	21.4	21.8
Perkins	0	716	565	18.4	39.0	22.9	6.5	15,309	30,923	58,135	42.5	3.2	55,033	9.3	12.4	11.9
Phelps	107	1,655	2,049	10.0	38.6	26.0	24.0	15,082	30,166	56,408	44.3	2.9	60,695	8.8	12.0	10.8
Pierce	73	294	1,734	17.7	41.8	22.5	16.0	13,213	28,766	55,417	44.4	2.6	58,375	9.5	12.7	11.8

1. Data for serious crimes have not been adjusted for underreporting; this may affect comparability between geographic areas and over time. 2. Per 100,000 population estimated by the FBI. 3. All persons 3 years old and over enrolled in nursery school through college. 4. Persons 25 years old and over. 5. Elementary and secondary education expenditures. 6. Based on population estimated by the American Community Survey, 2013–2017.

Table B. States and Counties — **Personal Income and Earnings**

STATE County	Personal income, 2017										Earnings, 2017		
			Per capita[1]		Wages and salaries (mil dol)	Supplements to wages and salaries, employer contributions (mil dol)		Proprietors' income (mil dol)	Dividends, interest, and rent (mil dol)	Personal transfer receipts (mil dol)		Contributions for government social insurance (mil dol)	
	Total (mil dol)	Percent change 2016-2017	Dollars	Rank		Pension and insurance	Government social insurance				Total (mil dol)	From employee and self-employed	From employer
	62	63	64	65	66	67	68	69	70	71	72	73	74
NEBRASKA— Cont'd													
Blaine	28	-10.7	58,373	196	6	1	1	8	8	5	16	0	1
Boone	312	1.6	58,370	197	89	18	7	95	71	45	209	8	7
Box Butte	486	2.5	44,603	948	260	41	33	49	83	112	383	25	33
Boyd	100	2.2	50,489	433	19	5	1	31	19	24	56	3	1
Brown	156	-9.5	51,850	380	47	10	4	43	31	31	103	5	4
Buffalo	2,567	5.3	51,614	392	1,166	207	86	261	754	330	1,720	100	86
Burt	325	2.1	49,697	479	76	15	6	75	51	70	172	8	6
Butler	371	4.3	46,107	784	109	22	8	41	78	69	180	11	8
Cass	1,320	4.1	51,000	412	246	46	18	113	237	207	423	26	18
Cedar	460	1.5	53,946	314	106	22	8	122	90	65	259	11	8
Chase	192	-0.5	48,397	596	74	14	6	33	49	35	126	7	6
Cherry	288	6.0	49,467	499	85	17	7	84	66	47	193	8	7
Cheyenne	463	-2.5	47,875	634	347	45	22	31	96	80	446	28	22
Clay	277	3.8	44,691	940	110	23	9	20	59	56	162	10	9
Colfax	441	-1.1	41,629	1,316	231	40	17	73	73	62	360	19	17
Cuming	571	-13.0	63,125	126	157	28	12	210	100	78	407	15	12
Custer	516	8.0	47,380	677	180	38	14	103	102	99	335	17	14
Dakota	806	-0.5	39,912	1,567	600	99	43	99	93	146	841	49	43
Dawes	330	0.7	37,093	2,015	120	29	9	34	68	73	193	12	9
Dawson	986	0.0	41,575	1,322	475	89	36	137	158	178	737	40	36
Deuel	74	-2.2	39,469	1,645	20	4	2	0	22	19	26	2	2
Dixon	258	-0.8	44,819	927	69	14	5	42	46	41	130	7	5
Dodge	1,669	3.7	45,463	849	725	129	54	189	335	338	1,097	67	54
Douglas	33,379	4.1	59,433	170	19,620	2,855	1,473	4,968	7,108	3,899	28,916	1,682	1,473
Dundy	98	-0.8	54,590	293	27	5	2	14	31	21	49	3	2
Fillmore	313	5.4	56,095	246	97	20	7	66	74	58	190	10	7
Franklin	134	3.0	44,931	906	27	6	2	4	45	34	40	3	2
Frontier	115	-1.7	43,548	1,073	34	7	3	26	22	21	70	3	3
Furnas	224	-0.7	46,863	722	79	16	6	30	46	55	131	8	6
Gage	1,039	4.6	48,079	619	361	75	27	102	191	256	565	35	27
Garden	83	4.9	43,663	1,056	25	5	2	11	18	23	43	3	2
Garfield	90	-14.3	44,411	969	28	6	2	20	24	20	56	3	2
Gosper	99	5.0	48,595	581	19	4	2	8	28	19	33	2	2
Grant	31	-13.4	48,481	592	7	1	1	7	11	6	15	1	1
Greeley	113	6.8	47,426	673	24	5	2	25	29	22	57	3	2
Hall	2,552	4.5	41,476	1,337	1,511	267	113	190	513	462	2,080	126	113
Hamilton	481	5.7	52,244	368	171	29	13	61	112	74	274	16	13
Harlan	144	-4.7	41,834	1,284	32	7	3	19	31	34	61	4	3
Hayes	43	-12.4	48,490	591	9	2	1	12	10	6	23	1	1
Hitchcock	105	-2.7	37,209	1,998	29	8	2	4	26	32	43	3	2
Holt	579	6.1	56,789	227	185	34	15	180	101	106	413	20	15
Hooker	35	-18.9	51,749	388	11	2	1	12	6	8	26	1	1
Howard	280	2.7	43,528	1,075	63	14	5	36	51	53	118	7	5
Jefferson	335	-0.1	46,719	736	132	24	10	42	81	74	208	12	10
Johnson	197	8.4	37,921	1,894	67	17	5	43	33	37	133	6	5
Kearney	364	-12.1	55,680	257	92	18	7	83	75	63	200	9	7
Keith	344	-0.4	42,669	1,191	127	24	10	47	76	78	208	13	10
Keya Paha	53	-7.1	66,206	93	6	1	1	23	11	8	31	1	1
Kimball	163	8.9	44,960	903	60	13	5	7	44	38	85	6	5
Knox	387	3.8	45,669	832	109	24	8	70	78	84	211	12	8
Lancaster	14,735	3.6	46,874	721	8,325	1,511	626	941	3,102	2,094	11,402	683	626
Lincoln	1,643	-0.6	46,578	743	793	129	81	202	266	363	1,204	77	81
Logan	36	-12.8	46,952	715	6	2	1	12	5	7	20	1	1
Loup	32	-21.8	53,044	342	4	1	0	12	6	6	18	1	0
McPherson	26	-10.4	52,627	355	4	1	0	11	6	3	16	0	0
Madison	1,690	3.6	48,087	617	944	168	68	218	311	294	1,399	81	68
Merrick	360	-3.2	45,683	831	99	18	8	76	60	71	201	11	8
Morrill	241	0.0	49,765	474	65	13	5	68	42	45	151	6	5
Nance	144	7.1	39,899	1,569	47	10	4	21	28	33	81	4	4
Nemaha	340	2.8	48,894	547	167	36	12	45	68	69	261	14	12
Nuckolls	202	2.2	47,321	686	54	11	4	33	42	50	103	6	4
Otoe	805	3.3	50,212	448	254	50	19	88	173	141	410	24	19
Pawnee	116	-1.6	44,048	1,015	34	7	3	24	25	24	68	4	3
Perkins	156	1.8	53,568	323	57	11	4	39	33	25	111	5	4
Phelps	501	-8.9	55,277	268	214	43	16	117	96	88	391	18	16
Pierce	384	5.2	53,771	318	81	16	6	104	62	54	207	10	6

1. Based on the resident population estimated as of July 1 of the year shown.

Table B. States and Counties — Earnings, Social Security, and Housing

STATE County	Earnings, 2017 (cont.)									Social Security beneficiaries, December 2017		Supplemental Security Income recipients, 2017	Housing units, 2018	
	Percent by selected industries													
	Farm	Mining, quarrying, and extractions	Construction	Manufacturing	Information; professional, scientific, technical services	Retail trade	Finance, insurance, real estate, and leasing	Health care and social assistance	Government	Number	Rate[1]		Total	Percent change, 2010-2018
	75	76	77	78	79	80	81	82	83	84	85	86	87	88

NEBRASKA— Cont'd														
Blaine	61.4	0	D	0	0.2	D	D	D	26.5	125	259	0	325	-0.3
Boone	41.9	0	4.3	6.4	D	3.7	D	4.1	17.5	1,235	231	38	2,633	-0.6
Box Butte	8.7	0	3.6	5.5	2.9	4.1	3.1	D	16.1	1,880	173	179	5,449	-0.5
Boyd	36.8	D	2.6	3.1	D	3	4.7	4.6	18.6	630	319	28	1,376	
Brown	34.7	0.2	5.9	3.2	D	7.3	D	3	24.6	790	262	53	1,843	-1.1
Buffalo	3.6	0.2	6.2	15	5.5	7.6	5	17.4	15.3	8,085	163	454	20,637	8.3
Burt	38.5	0	5.6	4.2	D	3	D	4.2	17.2	1,840	282	122	3,487	0.6
Butler	14.5	D	4.3	19.1	D	2.9	D	D	22	1,880	233	82	4,090	0.9
Cass	14.2	D	8.2	9.3	3	6.5	5.4	4.4	18.6	5,140	199	232	11,659	4.9
Cedar	35.4	D	6.4	5.2	2.8	3.2	8.6	D	15.6	1,890	222	62	4,169	0.5
Chase	16.5	0.1	4.6	2	4.2	9.1	D	3.9	19.2	865	218	40	1,959	0.7
Cherry	38.6	0.1	6.2	1.5	3.5	7.1	1.5	5	17.8	1,265	217	69	3,264	3.4
Cheyenne	2.1	D	2.4	3.2	2.4	8.3	1.9	8.4	10.3	2,030	210	138	5,008	2.5
Clay	5.5	D	9.5	12.5	D	4.6	D	4.4	28.7	1,485	239	70	3,021	0.7
Colfax	14.3	D	D	D	1.2	D	2.5	D	11.6	1,465	138	68	4,215	2.9
Cuming	45.4	D	3.9	6	3	2.9	6.2	D	9.7	2,150	238	70	4,257	1.3
Custer	23.5	0	6.6	16.2	3.1	4.9	5.4	D	14.9	2,520	231	127	5,658	1.4
Dakota	3.5	0.1	4.8	41.3	D	3.9	8.7	3.4	9.1	3,545	176	265	7,871	3.1
Dawes	8.4	D	4.3	0.3	3.2	11.5	3.8	12	36.6	1,695	191	89	4,256	0.1
Dawson	13.8	D	3	26.4	2.8	5.5	4.1	D	19.3	4,315	182	308	10,301	1.8
Deuel	-10.5	0.4	D	1.6	D	11.7	D	6.7	36.9	510	271	29	1,025	-1.6
Dixon	27.8	0	6.9	D	D	1.2	2.4	2.8	15.8	1,160	202	44	2,709	0.8
Dodge	6.4	0.1	5.3	20.7	3.4	8.2	4.5	D	18.3	8,425	230	563	16,796	1.3
Douglas	0	0.1	4.6	5.1	11.8	4.8	11.9	12.5	10.8	85,405	152	10,413	237,306	8.1
Dundy	27.4	0.3	3.7	1.8	D	6.2	4.1	4	28.4	510	283	23	1,121	-0.4
Fillmore	21.2	0.1	8.9	8.6	D	4.2	10.7	4.1	20.5	1,510	271	42	2,935	0.8
Franklin	4.5	0.2	D	D	D	9.4	8.4	D	39.2	895	299	50	1,714	-1.2
Frontier	30.6	D	8.2	2.2	D	2.6	10.8	0.8	24.1	580	220	32	1,583	0.6
Furnas	15.2	0	4.6	6.1	6.6	6.3	D	10.7	19.6	1,385	290	86	2,710	-0.4
Gage	10.8	D	4	19.9	2.5	6.8	3.9	D	20.4	5,425	251	403	10,492	0.4
Garden	22.8	0.3	D	D	D	11.4	D	12.5	19.4	610	320	38	1,303	-0.8
Garfield	26	D	4	5.2	D	5.9	D	D	15.8	510	253	20	1,208	2.5
Gosper	28.6	0	D	D	D	1.8	D	D	23.5	510	251	17	1,308	3.2
Grant	42.3	0.1	3.4	3.6	D	9.6	1.8	D	22.5	155	239	0	388	-0.8
Greeley	32.6	0.1	3.4	2.4	D	D	6.5	0.8	21.4	585	246	27	1,311	0.8
Hall	1.3	0.1	6.7	20.8	3.5	8.7	6.5	11.6	16.6	10,850	176	942	25,076	6.5
Hamilton	14	0.1	5.6	15.4	D	6.1	3.9	D	10.5	2,110	229	67	4,143	4.5
Harlan	29.8	D	2.5	2.4	D	5.2	D	D	27.5	910	264	45	2,397	1
Hayes	55.2	D	2.9	0	D	D	D	D	17	180	202	9	512	0.8
Hitchcock	-8.3	D	17.1	14.8	D	4.8	1.8	1	34.3	800	282	49	1,740	-1.3
Holt	17.7	0.3	5.4	2.6	D	17.7	7.2	D	11.1	2,600	255	136	5,270	1.1
Hooker	28.1	0.1	D	D	D	D	D	D	16	230	341	0	443	2.8
Howard	24.6	D	5.5	2.2	D	5.6	4.8	5.6	31.2	1,465	228	51	3,120	5.7
Jefferson	15.2	D	8.5	16.7	3.3	6.8	3.5	10.5	14.6	1,925	268	146	3,909	-0.2
Johnson	24.4	0	5.9	D	D	3.5	D	4.3	39.4	915	176	46	2,172	-0.9
Kearney	30.7	0.5	4.3	16.1	D	2.8	D	D	13.7	1,210	185	84	2,974	3
Keith	9.7	D	7.6	4.5	4.3	9.7	5.7	9.7	14.7	2,220	275	113	5,468	0.8
Keya Paha	70.9	0.3	D	D	D	D	D	D	9.8	255	322	8	547	-0.4
Kimball	1.4	8.4	4.5	11.7	D	6.2	D	1.2	26.8	1,000	276	53	1,950	-0.7
Knox	22	0	6.1	3.6	D	5.9	4.3	D	26.3	2,300	271	136	4,984	4.1
Lancaster	0.5	D	6.1	7.7	10.2	5.8	10.2	13.2	22.2	47,800	152	4,965	133,479	10.4
Lincoln	6.1	D	5.3	3	3.6	6.8	4.8	16	16.5	6,590	187	699	16,858	1.7
Logan	37.1	0	D	D	D	8.4	4.7	0.8	20.2	160	208	0	394	-0.3
Loup	66.2	0.2	0.6	3.9	0.4	D	D	D	15.2	155	255	9	461	8.5
McPherson	62.8	0	0.7	D	D	D	D	0	13.3	70	140	0	282	-0.4
Madison	5.6	D	5.7	15.7	3.8	7.6	8.2	15.3	16.3	7,125	203	531	15,333	2.1
Merrick	19.4	D	18.7	8.6	2	4	5.2	D	17.1	1,855	235	134	3,830	3.5
Morrill	32	D	2.3	5.8	D	4.2	4.2	D	22.3	975	202	84	2,438	-0.2
Nance	23.3	D	D	D	D	3.3	5.3	7.5	26.1	735	204	57	1,869	3.8
Nemaha	12.3	0	2.6	6.6	D	2.7	2.3	4.8	56.3	1,575	227	123	3,499	0
Nuckolls	19	0.1	3.5	D	D	6.2	5.6	17.3	17.9	1,200	281	53	2,451	-0.6
Otoe	11.8	D	6.3	20	2.6	6.7	4.4	8.2	22.9	3,530	220	179	7,217	2.7
Pawnee	28.2	D	D	14.6	0.6	3.3	D	4	21.9	650	246	34	1,643	3.5
Perkins	21.4	0	10.3	4.6	D	3.7	D	3.3	20.2	680	234	16	1,449	-0.1
Phelps	26.3	D	D	D	2.9	5.6	4.7	D	11.9	2,120	234	115	4,283	2.6
Pierce	15.2	1.3	7.5	23.1	3.7	3.9	5.3	6.6	10.3	1,425	200	55	3,284	1.9

1. Per 1,000 resident population estimated as of July 1 of the year shown.

STATE County	Housing units, 2013-2017								Civilian labor force, 2018				Civilian employment[6], 2013-2017		
	Occupied units							Sub-standard units[4] (percent)			Unemployment			Percent	
	Owner-occupied					Renter-occupied									
				Median owner cost as a percent of income		Median rent[3]	Median rent as a percent of income[2]		Total	Percent change, 2017-2018			Total	Management, business, science, and arts	Construction, production, and maintenance occupations
	Total	Percent	Median value[1]	With a mortgage	Without a mortgage[2]						Total	Rate[5]			
	89	90	91	92	93	94	95	96	97	98	99	100	101	102	103
NEBRASKA— Cont'd															
Blaine	232	60.8	85,900	23.1	10.0	705	13.9	4.7	262	0.4	12	4.6	282	44.7	34.0
Boone	2,277	77.9	105,600	18.5	10.7	596	20.3	1.8	2,922	0.1	65	2.2	2,769	34.3	30.4
Box Butte	4,610	71.7	105,400	19.0	10.3	575	25.2	1.1	5,399	-0.3	149	2.8	5,509	30.0	38.6
Boyd	905	81.8	63,800	17.7	10.9	475	26	0.7	1,083	0.6	32	3	1,020	43.4	29.4
Brown	1,475	72.9	80,200	15.5	14.0	492	18.8	2.2	1,392	-0.5	46	3.3	1,584	40.2	21.9
Buffalo	18,923	63.1	161,200	19.9	11.1	755	26.7	1.7	27,695	1.7	649	2.3	27,447	33.4	23.0
Burt	2,885	75.8	91,600	19.9	12.5	613	23.4	2.4	3,465	-0.8	116	3.3	3,011	33.2	27.4
Butler	3,400	79.9	111,500	20.3	11.9	674	23.6	2.6	4,533	-0.2	105	2.3	4,121	27.8	37.0
Cass	9,894	81.8	166,200	20.6	13.4	779	24.3	1.6	13,275	.1	393	3	13,311	34.2	24.5
Cedar	3,508	80.7	113,600	18.4	10.5	621	21.7	1	4,459	-0.1	104	2.3	4,599	34.9	28.2
Chase	1,671	80.5	109,900	20.3	10.6	613	23.6	0.5	2,268	-1.4	49	2.2	2,007	34.3	33.6
Cherry	2,652	61.8	119,800	21.1	10.0	699	22.7	0.8	3,375	-0.4	72	2.1	3,267	39.0	25.6
Cheyenne	4,400	70.7	114,100	18.1	11.4	685	22.5	1.5	4,731	-7.1	133	2.8	5,587	39.3	18.8
Clay	2,616	77.3	85,000	18.7	10.0	559	21.4	1.8	3,239	-1.1	100	3.1	3,112	28.7	37.0
Colfax	3,681	68.4	94,300	20.7	10.0	591	16.8	7.6	5,556	-0.1	129	2.3	5,305	24.5	48.6
Cuming	3,790	68.1	113,200	17.6	10.6	652	23	1.6	4,713	-0.2	116	2.5	4,819	32.2	34.9
Custer	4,792	71.9	92,800	19.7	12.2	608	25.2	2.8	6,425	0.8	136	2.1	5,636	32.8	28.7
Dakota	7,427	65.9	116,400	19.6	11.0	686	22.9	7.6	10,777	1.6	373	3.5	10,163	20.1	41.7
Dawes	3,557	62.5	107,500	20.8	13.5	632	22.8	3.1	5,040	-2.2	135	2.7	4,590	37.9	17.4
Dawson	8,898	66.8	101,000	18.7	11.9	699	25.1	5	12,934	0.1	356	2.8	12,196	25.4	40.0
Deuel	833	75.2	76,300	18.6	10.8	658	18.3	1.4	974	-5.8	29	3	1,002	32.9	24.5
Dixon	2,307	80.3	87,600	18.1	10.9	671	22.1	2.7	3,046	1.2	91	3	2,955	29.3	34.8
Dodge	15,090	63.9	119,600	19.3	12.2	719	24.3	2.3	19,361	1.2	529	2.7	18,495	27.2	28.6
Douglas	213,689	61.1	155,100	20.3	12.4	871	28.8	2.5	293,923	1.2	8,994	3.1	285,735	40.5	17.9
Dundy	875	68.0	73,900	18.5	10.0	507	18.3	0.9	1,161	-1.4	26	2.2	927	45.1	25.1
Fillmore	2,443	74.9	76,100	16.5	10.2	590	20.3	0.7	3,159	1.9	78	2.5	2,893	34.2	30.2
Franklin	1,367	83.5	62,000	18.9	10.6	560	18	1	1,468	-0.3	44	3	1,496	34.8	31.4
Frontier	1,113	76.7	98,200	18.1	11.4	613	22.3	0.2	1,506	-3.3	38	2.5	1,253	35.4	27.1
Furnas	2,172	71.8	65,300	21.8	10.2	556	23.7	2.6	2,627	-1.8	67	2.6	2,394	37.3	27.9
Gage	9,255	68.5	108,800	19.5	10.5	656	22.8	1	10,916	-1.4	345	3.2	11,118	33.3	30.3
Garden	897	80.4	81,800	21.6	10.8	581	22.9	1.8	1,192	0.3	28	2.3	921	42.6	23.3
Garfield	893	78.6	96,100	21.7	11.3	369	24.6	1.8	1,173	1.6	28	2.4	1,006	34.6	28.0
Gosper	885	69.6	116,300	19.8	10.4	621	15.9	0	1,064	2.1	27	2.5	1,129	30.7	28.9
Grant	274	81.4	55,300	28.8	10.7	425	19.4	0	416	-5.2	11	2.6	338	38.8	30.5
Greeley	1,015	80.5	69,400	20.9	12.1	549	19.2	3.4	1,214	-0.3	32	2.6	1,183	36.5	30.5
Hall	22,817	61.7	136,500	19.6	10.0	708	25.2	4.6	31,628	0.3	999	3.2	31,740	26.3	34.6
Hamilton	3,722	81.3	136,000	19.0	11.3	690	22.2	1.1	4,682	0.2	116	2.5	4,856	35.7	25.9
Harlan	1,590	77.1	83,200	18.9	12.4	572	22.6	0.7	1,772	0.1	41	2.3	1,613	32.9	29.3
Hayes	423	66.9	77,500	21.5	11.8	491	15.5	0.7	595	4.2	13	2.2	502	42.8	27.9
Hitchcock	1,273	73.5	58,400	17.6	13.1	627	28.1	1.3	1,252	-0.6	42	3.4	1,349	26.2	28.8
Holt	4,569	72.0	102,900	18.6	10.8	598	23.1	1.1	5,725	-0.3	146	2.6	5,662	36.9	25.9
Hooker	316	74.7	85,800	21.1	10.6	625	29.4	0.9	401	1.8	15	3.7	304	38.8	20.7
Howard	2,656	76.8	119,600	20.3	13.5	609	25	1.5	3,316	0.1	100	3	3,307	34.7	28.7
Jefferson	3,308	73.5	75,500	18.7	12.4	563	21.6	0.6	4,155	0	103	2.5	3,694	30.7	29.5
Johnson	1,869	73.9	82,200	19.6	11.0	611	25.8	1.8	2,074	0	74	3.6	1,998	36.1	25.3
Kearney	2,745	69.4	128,600	18.7	10.0	713	25.9	1.7	3,743	-0.2	77	2.1	3,470	31.3	31.3
Keith	3,989	67.5	108,400	20.1	12.5	600	27.2	1	4,548	-0.7	136	3	4,103	30.0	25.9
Keya Paha	334	72.5	72,000	14.8	11.6	575	13.6	1.8	586	-3.3	13	2.2	428	48.4	24.1
Kimball	1,546	66.7	83,200	22.2	13.2	684	23	1.7	2,016	2.3	53	2.6	1,738	28.0	29.9
Knox	3,662	73.5	85,100	18.0	11.8	510	22.8	3.3	4,635		141	3	4,271	36.5	26.5
Lancaster	120,962	60.1	162,900	19.6	11.0	787	29.4	2.5	173,384	1.8	4,408	2.5	166,689	40.0	19.0
Lincoln	15,025	64.3	130,800	19.4	11.6	683	24.5	2.3	18,306	-0.6	543	3	17,442	29.7	29.9
Logan	366	69.1	110,900	28.3	10.9	553	13.8	3	469	-0.2	13	2.8	450	28.0	40.9
Loup	245	81.6	159,100	23.6	10.3	546	13	0	395	-0.8	12	3	295	49.5	29.2
McPherson	192	66.7	137,500	15.0	11.3	644	16.3	3.6	440	-2.7	11	2.5	225	33.3	28.0
Madison	14,236	65.4	126,100	19.3	12.1	643	24.7	3.3	19,398	0.9	484	2.5	18,419	29.1	32.0
Merrick	3,251	74.8	90,900	18.6	10.0	601	20.9	1.3	4,053	0.1	113	2.8	4,194	29.3	32.7
Morrill	2,017	71.3	87,400	20.9	13.4	690	24.3	2.5	2,599	-0.1	69	2.7	2,417	28.9	32.5
Nance	1,553	78.5	80,400	18.7	12.4	500	22.3	0.2	2,026	0.8	49	2.4	1,792	35.3	26.5
Nemaha	2,814	71.9	114,600	18.6	13.0	616	22.5	1.3	3,608	0.3	124	3.4	3,444	32.2	24.7
Nuckolls	1,985	75.6	62,300	18.1	11.3	505	27.3	1.2	2,388	1.3	63	2.6	2,224	34.8	25.5
Otoe	6,439	72.4	130,700	20.3	11.6	659	23.7	1.2	8,134	-0.1	230	2.8	8,201	29.7	29.6
Pawnee	1,238	80.3	71,100	17.2	12.6	522	24.4	3.6	1,472	-2	37	2.5	1,205	35.5	28.5
Perkins	1,247	78.8	105,600	17.8	11.4	686	25	0.2	1,808	0.2	35	1.9	1,464	37.7	28.8
Phelps	3,870	70.4	120,000	18.7	10.5	574	23.7	0.3	4,903	0.1	110	2.2	4,780	33.9	30.4
Pierce	2,985	80.6	102,600	18.2	11.3	594	21.4	0.9	4,089	-0.5	106	2.6	3,706	33.3	32.8

1. Specified owner-occupied units.   2. A value of 10.0 represents 10 percent or less; a value of 50.0 represents 50 percent or more.   3. Specified renter-occupied units.   4. Overcrowded or lacking complete plumbing facilities.   5. Percent of civilian labor force.   6. Civilian employed persons 16 years old and over.

Table B. States and Counties — Nonfarm Employment and Agriculture

STATE County	Private nonfarm establishments, employment and payroll, 2016									Agriculture, 2017			
	Number of establishments	Employment						Annual payroll		Farms			Farm producers whose primary occupation is farming (percent)
		Total	Health care and social assistance	Manufacturing	Retail trade	Finance and insurance	Professional, scientific, and technical services	Total (mil dol)	Average per employee (dollars)	Number	Percent with:		
											Fewer than 50 acres	1000 acres or more	
	104	105	106	107	108	109	110	111	112	113	114	115	116

NEBRASKA— Cont'd

STATE County	104	105	106	107	108	109	110	111	112	113	114	115	116
Blaine	9	11	NA	NA	D	D	NA	0	30,545	101	5.9	72.3	70.0
Boone	203	1,471	316	133	277	85	31	49	33,560	524	15.6	23.5	57.3
Box Butte	315	2,791	592	295	432	124	103	94	33,810	431	13.7	33.4	54.1
Boyd	70	397	116	14	77	39	D	11	27,990	286	15.7	34.3	64.6
Brown	131	842	141	D	270	42	19	27	32,024	268	21.6	40.7	51.2
Buffalo	1,633	23,040	4,232	3,187	4,270	707	841	804	34,913	953	27.7	18.4	48.0
Burt	206	1,166	170	40	198	62	69	42	36,154	521	28.0	17.5	49.4
Butler	206	2,083	399	672	259	129	40	76	36,723	723	23.9	14.9	50.1
Cass	551	3,853	409	490	612	234	157	148	38,480	766	37.9	15.7	43.2
Cedar	303	1,888	160	222	350	131	88	64	34,113	784	19.5	16.3	54.0
Chase	164	1,107	129	15	324	71	20	39	35,336	325	13.8	41.5	59.8
Cherry	227	1,574	282	46	383	47	77	42	26,995	567	10.8	61.9	63.9
Cheyenne	295	4,687	510	279	819	147	61	231	49,209	572	8.6	37.6	49.2
Clay	185	1,118	93	46	211	76	32	40	35,584	441	25.4	24.0	58.5
Colfax	264	3,712	249	D	339	88	51	149	40,034	516	22.5	16.7	59.1
Cuming	358	2,603	350	356	367	201	129	95	36,414	804	23.9	13.2	53.0
Custer	387	2,954	625	D	589	178	98	100	33,906	1,108	18.1	36.2	55.9
Dakota	437	11,397	538	5,113	1,064	673	100	453	39,706	267	28.5	16.9	43.4
Dawes	262	2,155	528	19	638	77	63	64	29,871	491	16.7	35.0	50.4
Dawson	698	9,800	1,183	3,501	1,802	242	188	335	34,215	686	26.4	25.1	56.1
Deuel	56	312	52	NA	108	26	NA	8	26,708	225	12.0	35.1	50.8
Dixon	107	1,065	94	D	69	41	D	36	33,869	567	28.7	14.3	47.1
Dodge	1,027	15,878	2,892	3,374	2,747	428	210	559	35,230	676	28.4	14.3	52.5
Douglas	15,610	311,016	48,539	20,156	36,201	37,284	19,738	15,439	49,641	367	61.3	6.8	32.5
Dundy	59	315	96	19	31	14	23	13	40,410	268	6.0	51.1	68.3
Fillmore	223	1,758	302	284	223	132	27	61	34,772	439	14.4	27.1	65.7
Franklin	75	411	117	NA	104	41	21	13	31,616	317	16.1	30.0	61.5
Frontier	72	428	45	D	71	63	15	14	32,960	371	22.4	34.5	54.8
Furnas	164	1,347	317	138	211	73	14	47	34,924	377	12.7	34.2	54.1
Gage	665	7,514	1,812	1,714	1,088	224	149	242	32,176	1,188	33.2	14.8	42.3
Garden	53	249	D	D	57	20	D	5	21,353	221	15.4	46.2	54.6
Garfield	94	601	117	109	115	21	22	16	26,829	202	27.7	31.7	54.4
Gosper	61	195	12	D	24	27	D	7	34,687	287	8.7	28.9	56.4
Grant	30	108	NA	D	25	D	D	2	22,778	64	1.6	64.1	80.0
Greeley	67	316	9	17	104	34	NA	9	29,345	369	8.4	28.5	59.8
Hall	1,881	30,454	4,300	6,814	5,105	1,241	621	1,103	36,214	582	28.9	18.6	54.7
Hamilton	311	2,820	336	628	305	123	108	113	39,999	586	31.2	17.9	55.4
Harlan	105	609	155	D	101	37	37	19	31,067	281	23.5	38.4	54.9
Hayes	17	53	D	NA	12	D	D	2	29,264	220	9.5	43.2	53.9
Hitchcock	66	440	D	95	75	27	D	18	41,211	288	9.0	38.9	51.7
Holt	427	3,451	832	187	558	181	77	112	32,505	1,142	15.7	33.3	55.5
Hooker	32	95	D	D	28	9	D	4	40,979	97	7.2	67.0	62.3
Howard	170	1,068	340	26	208	111	33	32	30,264	617	25.9	13.0	49.6
Jefferson	238	2,656	442	685	419	81	65	88	33,280	590	20.2	20.0	50.8
Johnson	113	862	254	D	153	46	12	28	31,958	502	24.1	11.2	41.9
Kearney	170	1,710	550	289	166	73	19	58	34,169	342	14.3	34.8	68.6
Keith	344	2,640	256	225	690	190	118	81	30,666	318	19.8	32.7	45.4
Keya Paha	22	55	NA	NA	14	D	D	7	24,618	237	6.3	46.0	68.9
Kimball	124	949	D	213	157	45	9	41	43,157	443	8.1	32.1	42.5
Knox	257	1,621	263	42	333	157	65	46	28,387	956	18.0	19.2	50.2
Lancaster	8,427	136,325	25,404	12,557	18,835	10,127	8,471	5,595	41,043	1,786	54.9	7.3	34.1
Lincoln	1,054	11,970	2,938	291	2,127	478	389	417	34,826	1,040	26.3	29.5	45.6
Logan	22	58	D	NA	D	NA	D	2	26,862	117	24.8	33.3	61.6
Loup	11	24	NA	D	D	D	NA	0	19,167	130	19.2	37.7	62.9
McPherson	7	22	NA	NA	D	D	NA	1	24,136	109	8.3	63.3	62.1
Madison	1,322	18,045	2,800	2,825	3,012	716	587	669	37,076	659	24.6	16.4	52.3
Merrick	233	1,660	300	220	187	87	32	63	37,933	483	28.0	16.6	52.7
Morrill	106	632	75	D	198	46	8	23	35,877	426	20.0	31.5	55.7
Nance	101	496	149	NA	104	44	18	13	26,617	375	21.1	25.1	58.7
Nemaha	183	1,502	341	D	249	110	49	46	30,348	410	24.6	21.5	49.2
Nuckolls	180	1,130	353	9	237	80	30	32	28,692	431	9.3	27.1	59.3
Otoe	467	5,031	818	1,414	786	152	80	157	31,201	815	28.6	16.6	42.5
Pawnee	64	506	108	D	69	51	11	18	34,678	460	15.2	18.7	47.0
Perkins	126	887	232	50	146	37	22	34	38,545	418	10.0	36.1	55.7
Phelps	330	3,913	861	D	447	123	87	144	36,684	371	12.4	33.7	66.6
Pierce	234	1,538	296	105	223	111	49	52	33,939	625	23.0	18.2	51.4

Table B. States and Counties — Agriculture

STATE County	Land in farms		Acres			Value of land and buildings (dollars)		Value of machinery and equipment, average per farm (dollars)	Value of products sold:				Organic farms (number)	Farms with internet access (percent)	Government payments	
	Acreage (1,000)	Percent change, 2012-2017	Average size of farm	Total irrigated (1,000)	Total cropland (1,000)	Average per farm	Average per acre		Total (mil dol)	Average per farm (acres)	Percent from: Crops	Percent from: Livestock and poultry products			Total ($1,000)	Percent of farms
	117	118	119	120	121	122	123	124	125	126	127	128	129	130	131	132
NEBRASKA— Cont'd																
Blaine	367	-8.9	3,630	8.5	28.8	3,603,549	993	173,445	32.1	317,376	6.6	93.4	NA	89.1	979	43.6
Boone	432	-0.5	825	169.8	319.2	3,669,838	4,449	399,375	473.8	904,158	34.1	65.9	1	79.6	9,212	73.3
Box Butte	677	0.3	1,571	138.5	346.6	2,096,463	1,334	311,694	176.9	410,517	60.9	39.1	2	81.0	7,657	72.2
Boyd	323	11.0	1,129	13.9	135.6	2,290,609	2,028	258,985	104.3	364,577	38.7	61.3	2	76.6	2,160	72.4
Brown	615	-15.2	2,295	40.1	108.1	2,689,620	1,172	259,836	290.7	1,084,873	7.8	92.2	NA	85.8	809	39.6
Buffalo	528	-9.0	554	214.1	324.5	2,435,697	4,393	241,065	332.7	349,120	52.1	47.9	NA	80.9	8,917	62.4
Burt	298	-3.8	572	47.5	275.2	3,524,417	6,160	318,618	263.7	506,226	55.1	44.9	6	80.4	8,438	73.5
Butler	374	1.1	517	102.3	319.1	2,946,211	5,693	273,973	259.8	359,288	62.2	37.8	10	79.4	11,674	77.3
Cass	346	0.4	452	3.9	306.4	2,534,769	5,607	202,195	164.2	214,405	92.5	7.5	9	82.4	5,164	62.9
Cedar	474	1.5	604	163.2	393.2	3,129,654	5,182	295,573	423.1	539,617	44.0	56.0	2	80.1	14,856	75.8
Chase	569	5.1	1,750	168.9	323.0	3,647,226	2,085	480,540	440.1	1,354,191	34.6	65.4	NA	88.3	10,653	72.9
Cherry	3,563	-5.2	6,284	53.0	383.7	5,862,309	933	240,960	230.9	407,279	14.6	85.4	7	85.4	3,302	22.6
Cheyenne	759	8.0	1,328	52.6	528.8	1,354,420	1,020	193,548	163.9	286,594	37.2	62.8	15	73.6	13,034	83.6
Clay	319	-3.5	723	190.6	259.5	3,508,217	4,850	345,579	356.1	807,372	44.2	55.8	2	90.0	10,804	68.3
Colfax	262	1.8	508	81.0	240.4	3,149,351	6,194	354,733	364.5	706,298	34.6	65.4	6	85.5	7,546	76.2
Cuming	364	0.2	452	53.1	330.1	2,752,249	6,087	334,881	1,132.0	1,407,956	15.7	84.3	3	76.5	9,249	76.9
Custer	1,505	0.1	1,358	258.0	481.9	3,361,912	2,475	269,342	781.2	705,014	23.5	76.5	NA	81.9	14,411	48.5
Dakota	167	5.4	624	29.2	151.1	3,527,505	5,656	268,570	85.0	318,180	91.7	8.3	NA	73.0	4,211	69.7
Dawes	750	-9.0	1,528	17.8	174.5	1,358,907	889	115,299	60.9	124,100	22.9	77.1	1	84.1	2,924	63.5
Dawson	610	-3.2	889	235.0	303.7	3,034,516	3,412	336,300	748.4	1,091,000	22.9	77.1	16	84.4	15,112	60.5
Deuel	276	-0.2	1,227	17.4	226.8	1,601,034	1,305	277,172	71.3	316,960	49.5	50.5	NA	74.7	4,297	76.9
Dixon	279	-6.6	492	28.1	221.8	2,303,075	4,676	232,241	271.6	478,968	38.0	62.0	2	83.8	8,379	68.1
Dodge	337	2.2	499	132.6	312.5	3,199,731	6,412	286,042	270.5	400,151	65.3	34.7	9	76.3	9,943	74.1
Douglas	91	5.4	247	24.6	81.6	1,891,447	7,644	169,943	55.5	151,324	93.7	6.3	NA	88.8	2,205	35.7
Dundy	540	3.7	2,016	78.4	210.5	3,082,953	1,530	404,375	161.1	601,254	37.9	62.1	NA	88.1	5,558	76.1
Fillmore	329	0.3	750	219.9	305.3	4,088,900	5,448	460,510	240.9	548,850	74.9	25.1	NA	84.5	12,680	79.5
Franklin	316	10.0	998	97.5	187.0	3,456,445	3,462	273,977	106.9	337,088	84.8	15.2	NA	82.0	5,786	75.7
Frontier	484	7.1	1,305	50.2	203.8	2,452,811	1,879	262,770	121.4	327,332	50.0	50.0	NA	84.6	4,408	57.7
Furnas	450	3.3	1,194	64.1	291.5	2,946,660	2,467	338,139	240.4	637,637	42.2	57.8	NA	75.9	5,050	79.3
Gage	539	0.9	454	90.8	449.4	2,008,444	4,427	195,339	280.2	235,836	64.4	35.6	NA	83.0	14,883	70.6
Garden	1,018	-0.8	4,608	34.6	166.3	3,992,706	866	240,357	81.2	367,416	40.8	59.2	3	86.9	1,939	61.1
Garfield	342	-1.0	1,696	15.3	66.4	2,513,876	1,483	142,181	54.7	270,891	19.7	80.3	NA	83.7	671	36.6
Gosper	282	-2.7	983	79.2	150.2	2,763,817	2,812	361,583	105.7	368,397	69.4	30.6	1	83.3	5,134	61.3
Grant	495	0.4	7,736	1.7	50.6	6,476,796	837	236,936	D	D	D	D	NA	90.6	D	3.1
Greeley	339	0.3	919	91.9	156.5	2,726,640	2,965	274,794	193.3	523,957	34.2	65.8	NA	82.1	4,895	77.8
Hall	328	-0.4	564	230.8	272.0	2,866,675	5,083	354,102	302.4	519,589	57.7	42.3	1	85.2	13,806	69.8
Hamilton	312	2.6	533	248.1	286.7	3,379,235	6,341	333,006	275.7	470,561	69.3	30.7	9	85.0	13,043	69.1
Harlan	334	6.7	1,188	86.6	220.6	3,417,433	2,878	370,997	160.3	570,374	58.6	41.4	2	83.6	5,397	69.4
Hayes	437	13.4	1,985	55.8	195.7	2,809,923	1,415	293,526	167.2	760,155	35.8	64.2	NA	84.1	2,946	83.2
Hitchcock	393	-1.7	1,363	24.3	228.3	2,145,874	1,574	230,905	59.6	207,024	76.5	23.5	1	71.9	3,038	75.3
Holt	1,393	-1.5	1,220	303.7	608.0	2,904,705	2,380	268,044	453.5	397,144	49.4	50.6	5	75.7	11,202	49.0
Hooker	427	-2.2	4,402	2.5	6.8	3,237,188	735	109,284	D	D	D	D	NA	72.2	451	24.7
Howard	281	-10.1	455	115.6	178.0	1,587,631	3,491	215,883	235.2	381,172	35.2	64.8	NA	78.3	7,045	63.5
Jefferson	359	1.9	608	105.4	283.7	2,525,053	4,151	262,657	219.6	372,158	52.0	48.0	NA	77.6	8,991	76.1
Johnson	197	-0.1	393	19.4	137.7	1,427,986	3,631	151,986	83.1	165,602	59.2	40.8	1	72.1	4,348	80.1
Kearney	291	-0.8	852	189.5	244.9	4,456,076	5,232	482,408	369.7	1,081,094	42.4	57.6	1	93.3	10,195	72.8
Keith	491	-9.2	1,546	79.9	226.7	2,513,223	1,626	294,853	161.9	508,972	48.5	51.5	9	88.4	4,957	60.4
Keya Paha	423	-9.2	1,784	25.0	95.6	2,527,270	1,416	200,328	52.3	220,810	34.8	65.2	NA	84.0	1,305	38.0
Kimball	603	1.0	1,362	33.8	410.7	1,464,107	1,075	141,161	40.0	90,237	75.9	24.1	26	65.9	9,488	81.0
Knox	601	-4.3	628	70.8	323.6	2,102,065	3,345	223,437	288.5	301,768	37.5	62.5	11	76.8	12,233	72.6
Lancaster	423	-13.5	237	21.3	362.9	1,325,789	5,598	125,910	188.8	105,730	82.3	17.7	11	85.8	9,485	53.1
Lincoln	1,357	-4.7	1,305	242.8	421.6	2,184,451	1,674	221,829	755.2	726,188	24.5	75.5	7	83.4	13,167	44.2
Logan	298	-9.7	2,547	16.2	41.9	3,055,685	1,200	227,088	28.6	244,564	35.6	64.4	NA	68.4	1,227	41.9
Loup	280	-1.1	2,152	9.4	24.0	2,502,612	1,163	167,861	30.8	236,946	14.3	85.7	NA	85.4	765	46.2
McPherson	489	3.9	4,486	8.1	22.7	3,675,404	819	168,099	28.4	260,541	7.5	92.5	NA	84.7	471	28.4
Madison	353	0.5	536	130.7	312.1	3,120,513	5,819	324,775	276.1	418,948	57.0	43.0	2	79.5	7,543	69.7
Merrick	243	3.3	503	163.8	201.5	2,551,386	5,074	278,229	240.3	497,573	47.4	52.6	5	80.7	8,619	67.1
Morrill	829	3.7	1,945	121.8	242.5	2,226,414	1,145	237,293	319.7	750,451	25.1	74.9	1	73.0	5,034	67.4
Nance	220	5.7	587	75.6	158.8	2,480,621	4,227	240,847	155.3	414,141	48.6	51.4	6	77.3	6,113	73.9
Nemaha	261	2.9	636	15.4	230.0	2,893,077	4,548	234,596	114.4	279,090	93.3	6.7	6	74.6	6,373	79.5
Nuckolls	357	2.2	829	76.7	248.7	2,975,636	3,588	321,294	147.5	342,276	79.0	21.0	9	82.6	8,084	81.9
Otoe	390	0.6	479	12.8	331.0	2,372,053	4,957	203,937	170.5	209,232	85.3	14.7	9	83.1	5,740	73.3
Pawnee	273	1.4	593	11.4	183.7	1,921,924	3,244	194,408	78.9	171,454	72.0	28.0	NA	68.7	3,568	76.5
Perkins	556	-0.1	1,330	131.9	432.1	2,847,060	2,140	350,487	196.8	470,794	74.6	25.4	2	84.9	11,277	80.4
Phelps	342	3.1	921	225.4	277.1	4,707,223	5,114	603,438	578.2	1,558,601	29.8	70.2	NA	85.7	13,067	81.7
Pierce	344	4.4	550	127.1	275.2	2,679,363	4,872	300,420	255.5	408,749	48.8	51.2	2	72.6	10,199	71.8

— **Water Use, Wholesale Trade, Retail Trade, and Real Estate**

STATE County	Public supply water withdrawn (mil gal/day)	Public supply gallons withdrawn per person per day	Wholesale Trade[1], 2012 Number of establishments	Number of employees	Sales (mil dol)	Average payroll (mil dol)	Retail Trade[2], 2012 Number of establishments	Number of employees	Sales (mil dol)	Average payroll (mil dol)	Real estate and rental and leasing,[2] 2012 Number of establishments	Number of employees	Sales (mil dol)	Average payroll (mil dol)
	133	134	135	136	137	138	139	140	141	142	143	144	145	146
NEBRASKA— Cont'd														
Blaine	0.02	41.1	NA	NA	NA	NA	2	D	D	D	NA	NA	NA	NA
Boone	0.63	118.5	16	213	518.4	10.3	38	257	85.8	4.6	5	D	D	D
Box Butte	1.58	139.4	20	196	173.0	8.2	47	412	96.5	7.8	10	16	2.8	0.3
Boyd	0.15	74.8	3	16	8.4	0.5	11	74	14.4	1.0	1	D	D	D
Brown	0.49	166.3	4	D	D	D	31	259	68.1	5.3	2	D	D	D
Buffalo	6.45	132.0	77	902	1,254.5	43.0	236	3,677	967.0	78.9	55	156	39.0	4.4
Burt	0.85	129.1	16	180	128.0	6.2	29	179	33.8	2.5	4	5	0.3	0.0
Butler	0.68	83.8	14	129	216.5	6.9	27	298	64.2	4.8	4	3	0.3	0.1
Cass	13.53	530.3	17	D	D	D	70	627	177.8	13.2	20	21	3.3	0.5
Cedar	0.65	75.9	24	161	120.3	7.2	46	377	111.0	8.0	8	14	1.4	0.3
Chase	0.91	230.0	16	222	536.5	10.0	30	260	92.3	7.4	4	7	0.2	0.1
Cherry	0.61	104.3	7	102	222.5	2.3	38	422	87.3	7.6	9	7	1.4	0.2
Cheyenne	2.16	212.5	13	113	194.6	5.6	52	1,508	1,081.6	46.1	7	9	1.5	0.2
Clay	1.25	198.1	24	174	289.5	8.6	25	200	135.9	4.1	2	D	D	D
Colfax	1.11	105.5	17	131	214.2	7.6	43	342	106.0	7.6	6	14	1.4	0.2
Cuming	1.61	176.4	24	163	220.5	7.4	50	378	206.0	7.5	4	5	0.9	0.1
Custer	1.18	109.2	15	120	77.8	5.4	63	483	143.4	10.6	7	10	0.7	0.1
Dakota	2.02	97.2	15	249	219.1	12.3	68	897	198.7	18.5	13	D	D	D
Dawes	1.18	130.3	4	23	10.4	0.7	58	581	169.9	13.8	10	10	1.1	0.2
Dawson	5.97	249.9	34	433	680.1	19.5	107	1,398	423.4	34.4	19	D	D	D
Deuel	0.50	260.3	3	D	D	D	11	118	94.8	2.1	1	D	D	D
Dixon	0.75	129.4	8	35	93.3	1.7	9	61	11.7	0.8	1	D	D	D
Dodge	0.70	19.1	63	640	1,127.7	31.8	162	2,427	1,097.3	59.0	36	172	24.1	4.2
Douglas	56.63	103.0	750	10,775	12,685.1	594.8	1,749	34,754	8,586.0	839.3	713	5,700	977.6	258.1
Dundy	0.28	155.6	5	D	D	D	10	46	12.3	1.1	1	D	D	D
Fillmore	0.78	138.8	24	199	281.1	8.1	30	234	65.0	3.9	5	4	0.4	0.0
Franklin	0.67	224.5	9	68	90.2	2.2	12	102	20.4	2.0	1	D	D	D
Frontier	0.27	102.9	6	D	D	D	12	65	19.2	1.2	1	D	D	D
Furnas	0.58	119.3	10	D	D	D	33	204	52.9	3.8	1	D	D	D
Gage	3.60	164.4	36	349	369.5	15.5	112	1,036	262.4	23.0	14	23	3.7	0.6
Garden	0.22	114.7	3	D	D	D	12	65	11.9	0.9	NA	NA	NA	NA
Garfield	0.18	88.8	3	D	D	D	22	138	29.6	2.1	1	D	D	D
Gosper	0.28	141.9	6	41	101.4	1.6	5	24	3.7	0.3	4	D	D	D
Grant	0.05	78.0	3	D	D	D	4	20	3.3	0.2	NA	NA	NA	NA
Greeley	0.23	94.7	4	49	50.4	2.4	15	92	41.6	1.9	2	D	D	D
Hall	11.94	193.6	98	1,296	910.4	66.9	297	4,864	1,256.3	110.1	77	296	54.3	9.0
Hamilton	1.24	134.9	14	284	545.3	14.7	40	309	116.5	6.1	7	9	3.1	0.7
Harlan	0.45	130.4	10	46	63.2	2.0	18	97	34.4	2.0	1	D	D	D
Hayes	0.09	96.6	NA	NA	NA	NA	2	D	D	D	NA	NA	NA	NA
Hitchcock	0.37	128.3	5	D	D	D	13	71	15.8	1.4	NA	NA	NA	NA
Holt	1.15	111.5	30	374	424.0	16.2	80	615	159.9	11.2	13	17	4.2	0.4
Hooker	0.18	245.9	NA	NA	NA	NA	5	34	7.2	0.6	NA	NA	NA	NA
Howard	0.56	87.4	8	55	43.7	1.9	27	212	52.9	3.8	NA	NA	NA	NA
Jefferson	1.11	152.8	13	D	D	D	33	570	176.9	10.1	4	15	0.7	0.3
Johnson	1.00	193.3	4	D	D	D	26	144	44.8	2.9	4	23	3.6	0.3
Kearney	0.86	130.6	14	182	246.1	8.5	20	160	33.4	3.0	3	3	0.6	0.1
Keith	1.08	133.9	19	154	135.2	6.7	63	560	241.5	12.3	17	44	3.9	0.7
Keya Paha	0.05	62.2	2	D	D	D	3	9	5.0	0.2	NA	NA	NA	NA
Kimball	0.52	141.0	4	D	D	D	22	173	50.3	4.2	3	D	D	D
Knox	0.97	113.5	13	118	151.0	4.4	54	384	82.2	6.5	7	29	1.7	0.6
Lancaster	1.52	5.0	278	4,169	3,139.7	169.3	1,016	17,165	4,322.6	388.1	344	1,715	255.1	56.5
Lincoln	5.63	157.9	46	D	D	D	194	2,180	728.8	49.2	43	104	17.8	2.6
Logan	0.05	64.4	2	D	D	D	2	D	D	D	NA	NA	NA	NA
Loup	0.00	0.0	1	D	D	D	1	D	D	D	NA	NA	NA	NA
McPherson	0.00	0.0	NA	NA	NA	NA	2	D	D	D	NA	NA	NA	NA
Madison	4.94	141.0	64	1,730	2,252.8	78.7	212	3,061	815.2	67.6	59	172	24.8	4.2
Merrick	0.80	102.7	24	198	369.2	9.5	33	204	72.1	3.7	5	10	1.1	0.5
Morrill	0.43	88.6	12	120	71.0	5.9	20	163	37.2	2.9	3	3	0.4	0.0
Nance	0.37	102.9	5	23	52.0	0.9	16	100	25.4	2.0	1	D	D	D
Nemaha	0.89	126.3	9	57	69.5	2.5	37	235	57.7	4.6	5	10	0.8	0.1
Nuckolls	0.55	127.1	16	114	172.0	5.4	26	231	73.8	4.8	1	D	D	D
Otoe	2.54	158.9	21	171	239.4	8.0	80	833	202.5	16.9	15	63	11.9	1.9
Pawnee	0.37	139.2	1	D	D	D	10	76	15.7	1.4	NA	NA	NA	NA
Perkins	0.68	231.0	14	121	218.7	6.0	19	120	56.8	3.5	3	15	1.0	0.1
Phelps	1.62	174.3	28	378	851.6	17.3	48	404	116.5	9.3	9	13	2.7	0.2
Pierce	0.69	95.7	14	D	D	D	36	200	69.6	3.5	3	3	0.5	0.1

1   Merchant wholesalers, except manufacturers' sales branches and offices.   2. Employer establishments.

Table B. States and Counties — Professional Services, Manufacturing, and Accommodation and Food Services

STATE County	Professional, scientific, and technical services, 2012				Manufacturing, 2012				Accommodation and food services, 2012			
	Number of establishments	Number of employees	Sales (mil dol)	Average payroll (mil dol)	Number of establishments	Number of employees	Receipts (mil dol)	Annual payroll (mil dol)	Number of establishments	Number of employees	Receipts (mil dol)	Annual payroll (mil dol)
	147	148	149	150	151	152	153	154	155	156	157	158
NEBRASKA— Cont'd												
Blaine	NA	NA	NA	NA	NA	NA	NA	NA	1	D	D	D
Boone	8	25	5.5	0.9	11	112	D	5.4	11	94	3.2	0.8
Box Butte	22	93	8.8	2.6	8	328	D	16.2	32	339	14.7	3.9
Boyd	1	D	D	D	5	16	D	0.3	6	20	0.6	0.1
Brown	6	19	1.5	0.4	3	24	D	D	10	87	2.9	0.7
Buffalo	104	630	77.1	27.0	58	3,306	1,785.0	147.3	143	3,084	121.7	33.9
Burt	8	72	20.8	3.8	8	76	22.2	2.8	15	67	2.8	0.6
Butler	9	D	D	D	10	571	D	23.9	15	D	D	D
Cass	37	127	10.3	5.2	19	381	170.5	19.2	41	D	D	D
Cedar	13	D	D	D	12	198	D	9.3	12	87	2.2	0.5
Chase	8	D	D	D	4	22	D	D	9	D	D	D
Cherry	18	62	7.4	1.7	8	23	5.1	0.9	23	300	14.0	3.8
Cheyenne	15	D	D	D	8	273	120.8	15.0	35	520	28.1	6.9
Clay	7	D	D	D	7	67	D	2.5	8	31	1.0	0.3
Colfax	11	58	8.0	1.6	3	D	D	D	19	D	D	D
Cuming	22	104	15.7	3.3	14	323	245.8	14.3	25	290	15.4	2.6
Custer	27	96	9.9	2.6	9	D	D	D	31	313	10.7	3.1
Dakota	25	D	D	D	36	D	D	D	40	526	25.1	7.2
Dawes	18	D	D	D	4	10	1.5	0.3	37	457	17.4	4.9
Dawson	57	D	D	D	26	D	D	D	61	D	D	D
Deuel	3	4	0.3	0.1	NA	NA	NA	NA	5	D	D	D
Dixon	1	D	D	D	NA	NA	NA	NA	6	17	1.1	0.1
Dodge	49	183	20.6	7.0	60	3,402	1,955.3	140.1	97	1,476	56.3	15.8
Douglas	1,742	55,558	3,260.3	2,757.2	431	20,560	10,990.1	904.0	1,258	24,758	1,170.2	342.9
Dundy	5	D	D	D	5	15	2.7	0.4	4	27	1.2	0.3
Fillmore	10	24	2.5	0.7	13	221	415.1	8.7	13	81	2.7	0.6
Franklin	4	15	1.5	0.4	NA	NA	NA	NA	6	33	1.3	0.3
Frontier	3	15	0.9	0.3	NA	NA	NA	NA	3	D	D	D
Furnas	5	18	1.2	0.4	7	98	D	4.4	12	D	D	D
Gage	33	125	10.6	3.8	40	1,252	727.0	56.1	49	628	27.4	6.7
Garden	3	D	D	D	NA	NA	NA	NA	3	32	1.0	0.2
Garfield	7	D	D	D	8	117	D	3.7	9	63	1.8	0.3
Gosper	3	D	D	D	NA	NA	NA	NA	3	D	D	D
Grant	2	D	D	D	NA	NA	NA	NA	5	12	0.1	0.0
Greeley	NA	NA	NA	NA	3	9	D	D	4	9	0.6	0.1
Hall	109	638	69.7	25.2	74	7,241	6,021.9	280.1	156	2,515	114.9	33.0
Hamilton	16	69	13.0	2.7	19	443	D	21.7	19	169	6.8	2.0
Harlan	8	D	D	D	5	37	D	D	14	91	3.6	0.8
Hayes	2	D	D	D	NA	NA	NA	NA	2	D	D	D
Hitchcock	NA	NA	NA	NA	3	85	188.0	3.6	5	17	0.6	0.1
Holt	21	63	7.7	2.8	20	190	D	6.8	41	386	12.8	3.2
Hooker	1	D	D	D	NA	NA	NA	NA	4	7	0.3	0.0
Howard	10	26	3.5	0.9	5	10	2.1	0.3	10	69	2.5	0.5
Jefferson	11	D	D	D	16	572	178.4	20.6	19	160	6.7	1.5
Johnson	4	11	0.7	0.2	4	D	D	D	10	57	2.0	0.5
Kearney	10	27	2.0	0.6	9	260	209.2	12.2	12	118	3.1	1.0
Keith	28	119	9.9	3.6	15	254	D	8.0	46	514	22.9	6.1
Keya Paha	4	5	0.2	0.0	NA	NA	NA	NA	NA	NA	NA	NA
Kimball	9	20	1.5	0.3	8	263	38.7	8.9	16	110	4.0	0.9
Knox	17	D	D	D	6	23	6.4	D	22	98	3.5	0.7
Lancaster	842	9,135	1,292.4	460.9	235	12,011	5,963.3	596.5	672	13,483	598.3	156.9
Lincoln	78	D	D	D	17	D	200.8	D	94	D	D	D
Logan	1	D	D	D	NA	NA	NA	NA	1	D	D	D
Loup	NA	NA	NA	NA	NA	NA	NA	NA	1	D	D	D
McPherson	NA	NA	NA	NA	NA	NA	NA	NA	1	D	D	D
Madison	88	702	51.5	20.6	55	3,092	D	132.6	101	1,644	64.6	17.8
Merrick	8	34	4.2	1.4	16	254	D	11.8	13	99	4.4	1.0
Morrill	1	D	D	D	3	36	D	1.4	18	147	4.2	1.1
Nance	5	D	D	D	NA	NA	NA	NA	14	D	D	D
Nemaha	8	36	2.1	0.7	3	D	D	D	20	253	7.0	2.5
Nuckolls	14	31	2.6	0.7	3	6	D	D	9	D	D	D
Otoe	26	85	7.3	2.1	17	1,512	D	66.9	40	398	13.9	4.4
Pawnee	4	D	D	D	5	D	D	D	5	33	0.8	0.2
Perkins	7	25	1.6	0.5	3	10	D	D	3	7	0.6	0.1
Phelps	25	89	11.2	3.6	7	D	D	D	22	316	11.3	3.1
Pierce	11	D	D	D	11	D	D	D	10	99	2.2	0.6

Table B. States and Counties — Health Care and Social Assistance, Other Services, Nonemployer Businesses, and Residential Construction

STATE County	Health care and social assistance, 2012				Other services, 2012				Nonemployer businesses, 2016		Value of residential construction authorized by building permits, 2018	
	Number of establishments	Number of employees	Receipts (mil dol)	Annual payroll (mil dol)	Number of establishments	Number of employees	Receipts (mil dol)	Annual payroll (mil dol)	Number	Receipts (mil dol)	New construction ($1,000)	Number of housing units
	159	160	161	162	163	164	165	166	167	168	169	170
NEBRASKA— Cont'd												
Blaine	NA	NA	NA	NA	NA	NA	NA	NA	46	1.2	NA	NA
Boone	19	244	14.0	4.7	10	26	3.1	0.8	557	22.4	1,882	6
Box Butte	29	607	50.5	20.0	31	105	11.7	2.3	727	26.2	350	2
Boyd	9	108	5.2	2.1	4	11	1.6	0.2	224	8.4	423	2
Brown	11	181	11.5	4.8	11	28	3.1	0.8	322	10.1	0	0
Buffalo	177	4,012	453.6	165.4	112	D	D	D	3,872	185.3	49,519	189
Burt	17	227	12.5	5.6	13	72	8.5	2.4	519	22.2	800	3
Butler	15	373	28.3	13.0	15	D	D	D	685	26.1	679	4
Cass	29	423	26.6	9.8	35	120	9.0	2.4	1,861	78.2	18,862	113
Cedar	13	191	10.2	4.2	25	D	D	D	732	36.4	1,479	10
Chase	10	142	11.6	5.2	12	D	D	D	434	23.8	2,774	12
Cherry	19	345	23.9	9.5	18	36	4.8	0.8	593	28.4	2,957	17
Cheyenne	19	510	45.6	16.9	23	67	6.6	1.8	653	27.9	2,835	25
Clay	16	154	5.4	2.6	8	D	D	D	514	24.9	2,225	13
Colfax	15	344	36.0	8.6	27	76	8.1	1.9	556	27.5	4,713	38
Cuming	26	385	40.9	14.6	33	132	21.1	3.8	745	37.1	5,059	22
Custer	41	713	44.0	19.8	28	59	7.2	1.2	1,209	45.0	5,229	27
Dakota	32	520	33.7	12.2	36	240	54.8	14.1	1,036	50.9	6,807	31
Dawes	33	630	44.1	21.3	19	51	3.1	0.8	644	21.2	1,118	10
Dawson	73	1,143	92.1	34.5	62	D	D	D	1,492	63.3	8,198	43
Deuel	3	19	1.0	0.4	3	D	D	D	182	9.6	0	0
Dixon	11	99	4.6	1.8	11	D	D	D	503	18.5	1,567	7
Dodge	114	2,662	231.7	85.4	92	377	36.4	8.9	2,265	100.7	17,957	64
Douglas	1,742	47,573	5,673.5	2,121.5	1,067	8,179	1,287.2	251.7	37,087	1,819.9	312,837	2,994
Dundy	8	D	D	D	3	D	D	D	170	6.8	0	0
Fillmore	14	288	20.5	8.7	22	63	9.4	1.4	503	20.7	1,147	7
Franklin	7	166	9.1	3.6	7	19	1.4	0.2	269	9.3	772	5
Frontier	8	40	1.0	0.5	4	D	D	D	219	9.7	0	0
Furnas	20	359	24.6	10.9	14	D	D	D	452	20.0	1,330	5
Gage	58	1,780	114.4	48.2	66	242	21.6	5.6	1,587	59.8	11,991	58
Garden	4	D	D	D	4	9	0.5	0.1	191	7.7	710	4
Garfield	7	D	D	D	8	17	1.7	0.4	226	8.3	884	8
Gosper	7	9	0.4	0.2	1	D	D	D	199	9.1	350	2
Grant	NA	NA	NA	NA	2	D	D	D	78	3.5	0	0
Greeley	3	10	0.1	0.1	2	D	D	D	269	13.4	503	4
Hall	185	D	D	D	145	987	92.7	21.6	3,868	174.5	17,551	117
Hamilton	19	D	D	D	23	D	D	D	834	37.4	10,199	44
Harlan	8	172	11.2	5.0	6	D	D	D	329	10.2	1,865	14
Hayes	1	D	D	D	NA	NA	NA	NA	83	4.2	0	0
Hitchcock	2	D	D	D	2	D	D	D	241	10.2	0	0
Holt	33	870	75.4	29.2	37	D	D	D	1,306	74.3	1,460	5
Hooker	1	D	D	D	4	4	0.5	0.1	104	3.3	340	2
Howard	10	D	D	D	12	D	D	D	533	22.5	3,822	17
Jefferson	16	411	28.1	11.9	17	D	D	D	472	19.2	1,990	10
Johnson	14	274	22.3	9.4	8	21	1.8	0.3	322	12.0	0	0
Kearney	14	604	27.7	13.2	13	D	D	D	520	20.6	3,005	14
Keith	23	339	32.1	10.6	24	94	8.7	2.2	788	36.5	6,184	35
Keya Paha	NA	NA	NA	NA	3	D	D	D	114	4.0	0	0
Kimball	7	97	9.1	4.0	10	D	D	D	274	10.9	0	0
Knox	19	375	24.2	9.1	12	29	3.3	0.6	666	25.0	3,816	21
Lancaster	971	23,204	2,364.8	939.4	667	4,152	578.3	130.7	21,173	859.6	330,376	1,740
Lincoln	140	D	D	D	79	398	38.3	10.1	2,325	93.1	7,533	42
Logan	1	D	D	D	3	15	0.3	0.2	67	2.3	NA	NA
Loup	NA	NA	NA	NA	1	D	D	D	81	2.9	445	5
McPherson	NA	NA	NA	NA	NA	NA	NA	NA	42	1.7	0	0
Madison	164	D	D	D	106	542	44.3	14.0	2,709	118.3	26,460	140
Merrick	17	343	24.3	9.1	22	48	7.3	1.2	673	28.1	6,385	27
Morrill	8	135	12.6	4.3	6	D	D	D	391	14.2	0	0
Nance	10	165	7.4	3.5	13	D	D	D	264	10.4	1,009	5
Nemaha	21	369	30.8	13.6	17	73	4.5	1.1	512	20.4	1,611	7
Nuckolls	15	385	28.3	11.4	23	48	4.4	0.8	348	13.2	450	3
Otoe	42	853	66.9	26.5	36	129	11.4	2.9	1,229	46.4	11,863	33
Pawnee	7	116	8.8	3.9	5	14	0.9	0.2	271	10.0	1,050	6
Perkins	7	230	16.5	6.2	10	D	D	D	310	17.4	600	3
Phelps	21	813	59.7	24.7	30	104	21.1	2.9	853	36.3	2,231	13
Pierce	17	D	D	D	13	22	2.6	0.6	662	29.1	4,073	14

Table B. States and Counties — Government Employment and Payroll, and Local Government Finances

	Government employment and payroll, 2012									Local government finances, 2012				
			March payroll (percent of total)							General revenue				
													Taxes	
STATE County	Full-time equivalent employees	March payroll (dollars)	Adminis-tration, judicial, and legal	Police and corrections	Fire protection	Highways and transpor-tation	Health and welfare	Natural resources and utilities	Education and libraries	Total (mil dol)	Inter-govern-mental (mil dol)	Total (mil dol)	Per capita[1] (dollars)	
													Total	Property
	171	172	173	174	175	176	177	178	179	180	181	182	183	184

NEBRASKA— Cont'd														
Blaine	38	116,097	9.8	2.6	0.0	4.4	0.0	0.8	82.3	3.5	0.8	2.4	4,720	4,449
Boone	460	1,692,880	3.4	2.8	0.0	3.1	53.1	1.6	35.2	48.2	4.1	17.4	3,205	2,668
Box Butte	797	2,934,530	5.1	4.9	0.6	2.6	34.3	4.7	46.8	73.9	15.5	21.5	1,898	1,550
Boyd	117	356,840	12.6	1.7	0.0	16.0	0.2	10.9	57.9	9.3	3.1	5.0	2,429	2,227
Brown	260	870,487	5.2	3.3	0.0	3.3	24.0	16.3	47.5	23.9	5.2	7.5	2,470	2,176
Buffalo	1,737	6,480,217	6.2	9.5	0.9	3.9	2.1	3.9	71.0	175.2	52.8	86.9	1,830	1,377
Burt	405	1,151,444	8.6	6.4	0.0	7.3	1.0	16.5	58.3	32.4	6.0	19.8	2,978	2,657
Butler	460	1,583,569	5.4	4.9	0.0	7.3	25.9	17.6	38.5	51.3	15.3	24.0	2,892	2,645
Cass	930	3,065,349	8.2	11.0	0.0	5.1	1.0	3.6	70.6	95.9	27.6	43.8	1,744	1,516
Cedar	483	1,415,097	8.1	3.5	0.0	8.8	0.8	13.3	64.8	39.6	9.7	20.9	2,385	2,173
Chase	332	1,110,424	4.3	4.0	0.0	4.7	35.2	7.8	44.0	41.9	4.1	13.9	3,412	3,043
Cherry	255	767,776	8.8	7.8	0.0	8.5	0.8	7.7	65.2	38.3	6.2	15.0	2,611	2,227
Cheyenne	473	1,711,606	5.9	6.9	0.1	6.1	2.1	17.6	59.6	50.6	16.3	25.0	2,484	1,966
Clay	462	1,297,168	6.4	2.9	0.0	4.4	10.6	4.8	67.8	36.0	7.3	21.7	3,380	3,083
Colfax	471	1,687,680	7.1	4.2	0.1	3.4	0.0	8.5	76.2	45.8	15.6	25.2	2,364	2,089
Cuming	453	1,421,997	8.3	5.2	0.0	7.6	0.8	11.8	65.0	41.8	8.7	22.9	2,521	2,184
Custer	710	2,846,682	7.1	7.6	0.6	7.7	7.1	24.5	41.2	53.1	11.4	26.7	2,483	2,199
Dakota	972	3,563,243	6.5	7.2	0.4	2.2	0.4	6.2	75.7	80.5	44.9	26.9	1,286	955
Dawes	367	1,249,160	8.1	6.9	0.0	5.6	4.6	6.3	67.5	30.8	10.5	13.6	1,487	1,140
Dawson	1,718	5,640,576	3.0	5.6	0.0	2.6	22.8	12.1	52.5	153.2	47.5	40.1	1,657	1,368
Deuel	141	507,062	13.6	7.1	0.0	10.8	0.8	3.1	63.8	13.1	2.9	7.5	3,787	3,435
Dixon	423	1,293,730	7.0	5.2	0.0	4.4	0.1	2.3	78.0	31.8	9.3	14.9	2,525	2,324
Dodge	2,164	10,158,631	3.6	5.2	1.1	2.6	42.4	7.4	36.3	221.5	79.5	60.9	1,672	1,359
Douglas	24,079	100,381,103	3.6	9.6	4.0	3.5	4.4	25.2	48.9	2,457.4	796.5	1,177.7	2,217	1,587
Dundy	208	669,425	6.4	3.2	0.0	3.8	42.5	2.5	41.3	17.3	2.2	6.8	3,356	3,043
Fillmore	362	1,220,014	6.9	3.1	0.1	6.7	29.9	2.4	49.5	43.0	5.2	18.2	3,154	2,687
Franklin	266	1,622,165	12.8	12.9	0.0	7.6	20.4	27.8	17.9	14.4	3.0	5.2	1,628	1,517
Frontier	255	1,135,230	18.7	2.7	0.0	9.6	0.0	22.2	46.4	17.7	4.4	9.4	3,436	3,195
Furnas	443	1,409,219	6.3	2.7	0.2	3.0	18.5	17.2	51.3	28.8	8.9	13.3	2,701	2,216
Gage	894	3,582,464	6.7	7.0	2.9	7.2	0.7	19.7	53.9	82.2	27.8	39.6	1,814	1,546
Garden	214	658,334	5.9	3.2	0.9	5.3	49.9	2.8	31.7	16.1	1.9	6.4	3,289	2,928
Garfield	99	296,601	11.6	3.8	0.0	6.2	0.0	8.4	68.2	7.8	2.6	4.1	2,026	1,771
Gosper	141	396,475	7.9	4.8	0.0	10.0	27.7	9.6	37.4	12.4	1.6	6.8	3,334	3,090
Grant	58	138,009	9.1	2.9	0.0	8.9	0.0	0.0	78.7	4.2	0.6	3.2	5,083	4,808
Greeley	162	445,160	7.7	2.9	0.0	5.1	0.0	6.8	77.0	13.4	3.4	7.4	3,018	2,769
Hall	2,737	10,820,863	5.4	7.6	3.9	3.5	0.6	18.3	59.8	240.9	94.1	101.1	1,675	1,264
Hamilton	408	1,264,730	9.1	7.2	0.0	7.2	3.0	5.2	67.5	39.3	8.1	21.3	2,363	2,061
Harlan	208	554,731	9.8	4.8	0.0	6.6	36.0	7.8	31.8	21.6	4.7	5.2	1,526	1,274
Hayes	59	140,504	6.9	0.0	0.0	17.5	0.0	1.1	74.5	4.9	1.1	3.3	3,501	3,306
Hitchcock	135	502,076	5.5	9.7	0.0	8.5	0.6	32.9	42.8	12.2	2.7	6.3	2,166	1,952
Holt	457	1,501,263	9.1	4.7	0.0	9.6	2.1	8.2	65.9	52.2	11.5	29.0	2,791	2,328
Hooker	94	243,859	6.4	2.5	0.0	3.0	31.7	0.0	53.1	6.6	1.1	3.3	4,499	4,234
Howard	489	1,673,314	3.0	2.5	0.0	3.5	30.8	15.6	43.1	39.6	8.7	12.1	1,910	1,679
Jefferson	388	1,330,833	4.5	5.1	0.5	4.1	1.7	10.5	71.7	34.4	8.5	21.1	2,812	2,496
Johnson	311	1,042,290	4.4	2.9	0.0	4.2	35.4	11.8	40.5	31.4	6.4	12.0	2,329	2,119
Kearney	491	1,419,422	5.9	3.6	0.2	4.7	23.6	1.7	59.6	37.0	4.9	21.7	3,345	3,061
Keith	405	1,305,826	7.9	6.0	2.7	4.6	0.5	4.9	72.0	34.2	10.9	18.9	2,304	1,808
Keya Paha	48	112,765	9.7	2.6	0.0	8.1	0.1	0.9	76.3	3.9	0.8	2.8	3,476	3,285
Kimball	327	1,077,444	7.5	4.5	0.0	4.9	31.5	6.3	43.8	23.2	8.1	9.0	2,386	2,123
Knox	455	1,410,392	6.9	5.2	0.0	6.0	0.5	11.5	69.5	39.5	15.7	18.5	2,154	1,898
Lancaster	10,733	45,755,791	5.1	7.8	4.0	4.4	4.3	11.6	61.0	979.6	313.6	469.5	1,600	1,150
Lincoln	1,720	6,235,856	4.7	7.5	3.4	4.1	1.7	7.3	69.6	279.7	58.1	71.6	1,983	1,637
Logan	59	160,033	10.8	4.2	0.0	4.3	0.0	2.4	77.5	4.8	1.4	3.0	3,927	3,676
Loup	40	120,306	13.9	4.4	0.0	11.3	0.0	1.2	68.0	3.9	1.3	2.1	3,615	3,416
McPherson	37	88,185	16.1	0.0	0.0	8.0	0.0	0.1	75.8	3.0	0.5	2.2	4,361	4,232
Madison	1,848	7,112,436	4.2	6.2	2.5	3.0	2.2	7.2	74.5	181.2	50.7	86.6	2,472	2,061
Merrick	402	1,076,825	8.5	3.7	0.0	5.6	31.5	5.5	44.2	35.9	7.1	13.5	1,732	1,569
Morrill	306	1,053,262	7.6	5.7	0.1	4.9	0.1	9.8	68.4	37.2	13.6	10.5	2,152	1,947
Nance	276	922,483	9.8	3.4	0.0	6.6	22.8	3.9	52.2	23.2	3.7	11.8	3,167	2,896
Nemaha	407	1,469,356	4.6	3.0	0.0	3.2	23.9	9.1	55.9	43.7	12.6	14.0	1,959	1,690
Nuckolls	283	687,707	10.1	4.5	0.0	6.4	0.3	41.3	36.3	18.3	8.3	7.3	1,653	1,451
Otoe	850	2,831,957	5.7	5.8	1.1	4.0	15.2	13.1	52.1	63.3	14.6	30.7	1,948	1,590
Pawnee	199	600,056	5.0	2.2	0.0	4.6	35.8	3.6	47.4	19.2	4.6	6.3	2,267	2,041
Perkins	326	1,063,703	7.6	5.6	0.0	8.0	47.1	0.7	29.4	27.8	2.7	9.8	3,327	2,981
Phelps	471	1,581,446	8.2	8.0	0.0	6.4	0.6	7.7	68.6	46.7	11.6	24.5	2,663	2,090
Pierce	446	1,313,225	5.7	3.6	0.0	4.0	19.8	2.4	64.0	35.8	6.4	16.9	2,364	2,111

1. Based on the resident population estimated as of July 1 of the year shown.

Table B. States and Counties — Local Government Finances, Government Employment, and Income Taxes

STATE County	Total (mil dol) 185	Per capita¹ (dollars) 186	Education 187	Health and hospitals 188	Police protection 189	Public welfare 190	Highways 191	Total (mil dol) 192	Per capita¹ (dollars) 193	Federal civilian 194	Federal military 195	State and local 196	Number of returns 197	Mean adjusted gross income 198	Mean income tax 199
NEBRASKA— Cont'd															
Blaine	3.5	6,794	68.8	0.0	1.3	0.1	13.6	0.2	409	29	2	46	240	31,038	2,996
Boone	44.3	8,176	31.0	48.5	1.6	0.2	8.2	3.3	617	30	18	645	2,600	53,716	5,955
Box Butte	77.0	6,806	35.7	37.0	2.5	2.0	3.9	22.0	1,940	37	37	1,014	5,090	51,586	5,181
Boyd	9.7	4,699	58.5	0.6	1.5	0.2	13.1	3.5	1,709	16	7	220	920	32,117	3,262
Brown	24.8	8,204	40.4	26.1	2.3	0.3	10.6	32.9	10,893	19	10	401	1,410	36,026	3,600
Buffalo	185.9	3,916	56.3	0.0	5.0	0.1	9.3	209.9	4,423	133	168	3,975	22,020	60,729	7,324
Burt	33.4	5,018	48.1	0.0	2.4	7.6	14.7	21.0	3,159	33	22	537	3,100	49,876	4,753
Butler	46.9	5,656	32.0	32.2	1.7	0.4	12.1	67.8	8,175	43	27	625	3,930	49,917	4,894
Cass	93.1	3,704	51.2	0.3	3.0	4.3	10.9	110.7	4,404	61	89	1,339	12,590	64,407	7,310
Cedar	36.7	4,202	50.3	0.2	2.2	11.6	13.5	12.1	1,386	102	29	613	4,020	51,039	5,784
Chase	45.4	11,179	31.0	33.0	1.0	7.2	9.0	27.2	6,701	27	14	429	1,790	45,903	5,564
Cherry	38.0	6,630	32.1	37.2	1.7	0.3	10.5	8.0	1,401	50	20	564	2,840	42,510	4,336
Cheyenne	49.4	4,909	41.1	0.6	3.5	0.7	11.0	57.6	5,724	33	33	779	4,600	58,016	6,792
Clay	34.4	5,370	60.7	0.6	1.7	7.2	11.3	9.1	1,421	150	21	588	2,900	53,735	5,900
Colfax	46.8	4,390	67.4	0.0	2.2	0.1	9.4	40.1	3,760	63	37	696	4,960	46,365	4,047
Cuming	41.2	4,546	53.9	0.1	3.2	10.9	11.1	33.8	3,720	34	31	728	4,360	53,540	6,086
Custer	58.1	5,407	49.7	9.3	2.4	0.2	14.8	69.4	6,462	42	37	883	5,230	42,991	4,113
Dakota	78.7	3,764	62.6	0.2	7.4	0.1	7.6	134.6	6,433	78	69	1,092	9,830	44,321	4,001
Dawes	29.9	3,268	45.6	1.0	4.2	5.9	7.9	6.6	723	131	27	1,114	3,610	40,330	3,836
Dawson	147.3	6,083	43.0	30.0	3.4	0.3	4.0	105.3	4,347	104	82	2,183	11,400	45,379	4,163
Deuel	13.9	7,026	54.5	0.2	3.3	12.7	8.4	6.2	3,140	4	6	211	850	44,433	4,146
Dixon	37.0	6,247	66.9	0.5	2.1	6.9	10.0	11.9	2,016	39	20	408	2,780	45,409	4,418
Dodge	228.6	6,277	38.1	39.7	2.7	0.1	4.4	108.2	2,971	113	124	3,005	17,330	51,824	5,142
Douglas	2,356.0	4,435	50.4	2.4	4.8	0.7	3.5	5,801.4	10,920	5,882	2,198	35,236	266,440	71,928	10,140
Dundy	16.6	8,200	35.5	42.3	1.9	0.1	6.9	4.4	2,201	11	6	228	820	41,682	4,650
Fillmore	52.3	9,062	29.1	41.2	1.9	5.3	7.7	42.5	7,369	27	19	712	2,760	57,153	6,588
Franklin	15.0	4,719	33.2	32.0	1.8	0.8	12.7	4.5	1,407	20	10	310	1,390	46,970	5,123
Frontier	20.5	7,466	46.9	0.1	2.3	0.1	8.9	3.3	1,221	16	9	314	1,170	37,168	4,105
Furnas	28.2	5,750	56.4	1.0	2.4	0.6	7.4	29.1	5,927	32	16	493	2,230	43,431	5,096
Gage	86.9	3,984	52.5	1.0	5.5	0.3	9.7	60.4	2,770	84	73	1,881	10,260	51,311	5,223
Garden	15.6	7,995	28.9	43.5	2.2	0.1	10.1	6.3	3,250	17	7	139	900	34,621	2,938
Garfield	7.9	3,915	57.3	0.0	2.5	0.1	10.1	2.3	1,144	10	7	153	860	38,269	3,573
Gosper	10.9	5,386	31.3	0.1	3.2	25.6	12.4	14.3	7,034	7	7	164	940	54,597	6,110
Grant	3.8	6,037	69.2	0.0	2.1	0.4	9.7	0.6	886	4	2	76	330	47,773	4,058
Greeley	13.1	5,331	58.5	0.6	2.1	10.6	11.9	0.6	256	7	8	253	1,060	32,357	3,927
Hall	244.4	4,050	57.3	0.2	5.0	0.4	4.7	235.9	3,910	653	210	4,362	29,570	52,024	5,945
Hamilton	38.8	4,301	50.9	10.9	3.5	0.3	6.8	21.3	2,363	28	32	503	4,540	64,195	7,653
Harlan	18.5	5,430	23.7	38.1	1.7	0.1	10.0	8.8	2,568	35	12	266	1,520	46,336	4,968
Hayes	4.6	4,815	56.7	0.0	1.7	0.1	23.0	3.0	3,102	6	3	78	380	19,039	3,511
Hitchcock	14.2	4,921	60.3	0.0	1.9	12.2	13.1	25.6	8,853	10	10	289	1,240	39,178	3,492
Holt	51.3	4,932	45.5	0.4	1.7	4.7	17.2	22.9	2,199	49	35	815	5,050	43,818	5,048
Hooker	6.6	9,034	46.4	0.1	1.6	24.9	5.3	2.7	3,706	3	2	104	370	36,678	2,527
Howard	38.9	6,142	41.7	32.5	1.3	0.1	6.8	35.9	5,667	33	22	599	3,010	47,271	4,707
Jefferson	40.6	5,402	53.7	1.6	3.4	0.3	20.6	11.0	1,468	30	25	580	3,380	49,780	5,234
Johnson	34.2	6,653	29.7	38.9	1.2	0.3	9.9	24.3	4,729	37	14	756	2,080	44,365	3,773
Kearney	35.5	5,473	48.5	23.6	1.5	0.3	10.0	27.7	4,274	23	22	495	3,050	57,069	6,355
Keith	39.6	4,813	60.0	0.5	6.0	0.4	7.6	23.7	2,887	37	28	525	3,930	47,742	5,118
Keya Paha	3.8	4,669	59.2	0.1	1.4	0.2	21.0	0.1	63	1	3	70	390	30,036	2,095
Kimball	23.1	6,099	29.0	29.9	2.7	0.3	7.3	8.6	2,260	15	12	436	1,580	43,461	4,438
Knox	36.1	4,212	62.9	0.2	2.2	0.2	15.1	13.8	1,609	49	29	1,103	3,930	42,747	4,071
Lancaster	1,063.8	3,626	52.7	2.0	4.3	0.9	6.6	2,798.4	9,538	3,299	1,080	30,494	143,310	63,149	7,864
Lincoln	277.0	7,674	31.2	44.8	2.8	0.1	3.5	165.3	4,578	263	121	2,616	16,600	53,862	5,820
Logan	4.4	5,741	67.1	0.1	2.1	0.1	12.6	0.0	0	5	3	75	330	38,321	2,803
Loup	3.6	6,161	52.9	0.1	1.5	0.1	13.6	0.2	387	1	2	58	300	33,643	2,827
McPherson	2.7	5,281	63.8	0.0	1.7	0.0	16.4	0.2	424	1	2	39	210	38,271	2,329
Madison	170.2	4,860	59.2	2.5	5.3	4.1	7.9	156.1	4,457	177	119	3,565	16,740	61,743	7,693
Merrick	35.5	4,565	36.4	31.5	2.4	0.0	9.6	24.0	3,084	22	27	593	3,570	48,017	4,595
Morrill	33.2	6,781	39.2	26.6	3.3	9.2	5.8	13.5	2,752	21	17	582	2,130	41,972	4,312
Nance	23.3	6,270	46.3	24.6	3.0	0.1	9.3	5.5	1,467	17	12	383	1,630	37,353	3,675
Nemaha	44.9	6,283	42.5	30.4	2.7	0.2	5.5	29.2	4,079	29	23	1,592	2,990	55,821	6,224
Nuckolls	18.8	4,230	39.6	0.3	2.4	0.5	14.2	17.6	3,963	23	15	361	2,020	45,504	4,373
Otoe	67.1	4,260	45.5	16.1	3.2	0.4	12.3	89.9	5,710	58	55	1,305	7,550	59,330	6,551
Pawnee	19.3	6,965	36.0	32.5	1.5	0.2	10.3	5.3	1,916	23	9	249	1,210	41,745	4,258
Perkins	25.8	8,812	27.1	49.1	2.1	0.3	6.5	3.1	1,070	16	10	400	1,320	47,579	5,233
Phelps	43.9	4,769	54.3	0.1	2.5	4.2	9.8	37.5	4,071	58	31	725	4,380	59,131	7,063
Pierce	33.9	4,731	50.9	15.7	2.6	6.0	10.0	8.7	1,213	28	25	390	3,390	51,459	5,883

1. Based on the resident population estimated as of July 1 of the year shown.

Table B. States and Counties — **Land Area and Population**

State / county code	CBSA code[1]	County code[2]	STATE County	Land area[3] (sq. mi)	Population, 2018 Total persons 2018	Rank	Per square mile	White	Black	American Indian, Alaska Native	Asian and Pacific Islander	Percent Hispanic or Latino[4]	Under 5 years	5 to 17 years	18 to 24 years	25 to 34 years	35 to 44 years	45 to 54 years
				1	2	3	4	5	6	7	8	9	10	11	12	13	14	15
			NEBRASKA— Cont'd															
31141	18,100	5	Platte	674.1	33,363	1,347	49.5	78.1	0.9	0.6	1.3	19.8	7.3	18.7	8.3	12.1	11.7	11.1
31143		9	Polk	438.3	5,278	2,809	12.0	92.8	0.5	0.8	0.5	6.3	4.9	17.7	7.4	8.9	10.5	12.7
31145		7	Red Willow	717.0	10,726	2,372	15.0	92.6	1.8	0.8	0.7	5.1	5.9	16.0	9.4	11.1	11.0	10.8
31147		7	Richardson	551.8	7,937	2,599	14.4	94.3	1.0	4.1	1.0	2.0	5.7	15.4	6.9	9.7	9.7	11.7
31149		9	Rock	1,008.3	1,360	3,090	1.3	97.2	0.2	1.0	0.4	1.5	6.0	14.0	6.1	9.1	10.4	7.4
31151		6	Saline	574.1	14,350	2,136	25.0	69.4	1.4	0.8	3.7	25.9	6.7	18.5	12.7	11.2	11.7	12.1
31153	36,540	2	Sarpy	238.2	184,459	357	774.4	83.1	5.3	0.9	3.9	9.8	7.2	20.2	8.5	14.4	14.3	12.4
31155	36,540	2	Saunders	750.3	21,303	1,761	28.4	96.4	1.0	0.8	0.9	2.3	6.2	18.1	7.1	10.9	11.4	12.6
31157	42,420	5	Scotts Bluff	739.4	35,989	1,274	48.7	72.6	1.2	1.9	1.1	24.3	6.8	18.2	8.1	11.9	11.7	10.7
31159	30,700	2	Seward	571.4	17,318	1,958	30.3	95.5	1.2	0.8	0.9	2.8	5.8	17.8	13.2	10.6	11.3	11.4
31161		9	Sheridan	2,441.0	5,190	2,820	2.1	85.0	1.0	11.1	1.4	5.3	6.4	15.7	6.6	8.5	10.6	10.9
31163		8	Sherman	565.8	3,038	2,962	5.4	96.6	0.4	0.5	0.7	2.5	5.3	15.7	6.6	8.5	9.0	11.7
31165	42,420	9	Sioux	2,066.7	1,187	3,101	0.6	92.8	0.5	1.4	0.8	5.7	3.8	14.8	7.3	7.1	10.2	9.7
31167	35,740	9	Stanton	427.6	5,970	2,756	14.0	92.7	1.3	1.1	0.7	5.5	6.4	18.7	7.4	10.7	11.7	11.8
31169		9	Thayer	573.8	5,039	2,829	8.8	96.5	1.0	0.9	0.6	2.4	6.2	16.7	6.3	9.8	9.7	11.0
31171		9	Thomas	712.9	720	3,127	1.0	94.4	1.3	1.9	0.6	2.6	6.0	17.9	5.1	10.7	9.3	11.4
31173		8	Thurston	393.6	7,303	2,639	18.6	37.6	1.2	56.5	1.1	6.1	10.7	25.5	10.0	12.8	9.4	9.2
31175		9	Valley	568.1	4,190	2,888	7.4	95.9	0.7	0.6	0.7	3.0	6.1	16.8	6.7	9.7	10.3	11.5
31177	36,540	2	Washington	390.0	20,667	1,790	53.0	95.3	1.2	0.8	0.9	3.1	5.9	18.4	7.3	9.9	12.5	13.2
31179		6	Wayne	442.9	9,403	2,471	21.2	90.5	1.9	0.9	1.2	6.8	5.4	14.6	21.4	10.6	9.8	9.5
31181		9	Webster	574.9	3,533	2,935	6.1	92.6	1.0	1.0	1.6	5.5	4.8	17.2	7.2	9.9	10.2	11.7
31183		9	Wheeler	575.2	805	3,119	1.4	97.8	0.4	0.4	0.9	1.7	5.8	13.5	7.1	8.7	9.2	10.4
31185		6	York	572.5	13,772	2,178	24.1	91.6	2.1	1.0	1.3	5.3	6.5	17.0	9.0	12.0	10.8	10.5
32000		0	NEVADA	109,780.2	3,034,392	X	27.6	51.6	10.4	1.5	11.2	29.0	6.1	16.6	8.2	14.7	13.3	13.0
32001	21,980	6	Churchill	4,930.6	24,440	1,630	5.0	75.8	3.2	5.3	5.0	14.3	6.5	16.3	8.0	13.6	10.8	11.8
32003	29,820	1	Clark	7,891.7	2,231,647	13	282.8	45.3	13.1	1.1	13.2	31.4	6.3	16.9	8.2	14.9	13.8	13.3
32005	23,820	4	Douglas	709.7	48,467	1,015	68.3	82.5	1.4	2.7	3.1	13.0	3.4	12.9	5.7	9.5	10.0	11.6
32007	21,220	5	Elko	17,169.2	52,460	957	3.1	68.3	1.5	5.6	2.1	24.4	7.4	19.9	8.5	15.1	12.9	12.5
32009		9	Esmeralda	3,581.9	826	3,114	0.2	70.6	4.7	8.1	2.1	18.6	3.3	12.0	3.8	9.6	10.5	9.3
32011	21,220	9	Eureka	4,175.7	2,003	3,048	0.5	81.8	1.3	3.4	1.9	13.5	5.0	18.8	6.1	10.5	12.0	14.3
32013	49,080	7	Humboldt	9,640.8	16,786	1,992	1.7	66.9	1.5	4.7	1.7	27.5	7.1	19.9	7.7	13.8	12.4	12.1
32015		7	Lander	5,490.1	5,575	2,786	1.0	70.8	1.4	4.8	1.9	22.6	7.7	18.9	6.9	13.7	11.6	12.9
32017		8	Lincoln	10,633.4	5,201	2,818	0.5	86.3	3.8	2.3	1.8	8.2	4.1	15.7	8.5	11.1	11.5	11.4
32019	22,280	4	Lyon	2,001.2	55,808	917	27.9	77.0	1.9	3.5	2.8	17.7	5.5	15.9	6.6	12.7	11.4	12.0
32021		7	Mineral	3,752.8	4,514	2,857	1.2	64.8	4.8	16.7	4.3	13.0	5.6	14.1	6.4	12.2	10.0	10.3
32023	37,220	4	Nye	18,181.9	45,346	1,067	2.5	78.2	4.0	2.5	3.3	15.0	4.4	12.4	6.3	9.4	8.8	11.4
32027		9	Pershing	6,036.6	6,666	2,697	1.1	66.6	4.8	3.8	2.3	24.5	4.0	12.3	7.9	15.1	14.7	16.1
32029	39,900	2	Storey	264.0	4,029	2,898	15.3	86.3	2.3	2.7	3.6	7.6	2.4	9.6	4.8	8.1	8.9	12.9
32031	39,900	2	Washoe	6,301.4	465,735	152	73.9	65.3	3.1	2.0	7.9	24.8	5.9	15.7	8.8	15.2	12.3	12.5
32033		7	White Pine	8,874.6	9,475	2,465	1.1	73.4	5.5	5.0	1.9	16.3	5.3	14.6	7.5	15.2	13.5	12.0
32510	16,180	3	Carson City	144.7	55,414	923	383.0	68.8	2.4	2.9	3.6	24.5	5.7	14.6	7.9	13.2	11.1	12.6
33000		0	NEW HAMPSHIRE	8,953.5	1,356,458	X	151.5	91.5	2.0	0.8	3.6	3.9	4.7	14.3	9.3	12.5	11.4	14.0
33001	29,060	4	Belknap	401.8	61,022	861	151.9	96.3	1.0	0.8	1.6	1.7	4.4	14.1	6.8	10.7	10.9	13.4
33003		6	Carroll	931.9	48,779	1,009	52.3	96.8	0.9	0.9	1.0	1.6	3.7	12.0	6.1	9.1	9.2	13.1
33005	28,300	4	Cheshire	706.7	76,493	726	108.2	95.3	1.2	0.8	2.2	1.9	4.4	13.4	11.6	12.0	10.4	12.0
33007	13,620	7	Coos	1,794.6	31,589	1,388	17.6	96.3	1.2	1.2	0.9	1.8	4.0	12.3	6.9	11.0	10.8	14.0
33009	17,200	5	Grafton	1,708.6	89,786	653	52.5	92.2	1.5	1.0	4.5	2.5	4.1	12.1	13.1	12.2	10.2	12.1
33011	31,700	2	Hillsborough	876.5	415,247	170	473.8	85.8	3.2	0.7	5.2	7.0	5.2	15.2	8.6	13.7	12.2	14.4
33013	18,180	4	Merrimack	932.9	151,132	437	162.0	93.6	1.9	0.9	2.9	2.3	4.7	14.4	9.1	12.3	11.7	13.9
33015	14,460	1	Rockingham	695.4	309,176	226	444.6	93.6	1.2	0.6	2.8	3.2	4.6	14.8	7.5	11.9	11.5	15.3
33017	14,460	1	Strafford	367.6	130,090	492	353.9	92.3	1.9	0.8	4.5	2.6	4.8	13.8	15.7	13.3	11.1	12.8
33019	17,200	7	Sullivan	537.5	43,144	1,113	80.3	96.2	1.1	1.2	1.5	1.7	4.7	14.2	6.7	11.4	11.0	14.0
34000		0	NEW JERSEY	7,354.4	8,908,520	X	1,211.3	56.2	13.7	0.5	10.6	20.6	5.8	16.1	8.6	13.0	12.8	13.9
34001	12,100	2	Atlantic	555.5	265,429	258	477.8	57.5	15.6	0.6	9.1	19.2	5.4	15.8	9.0	12.0	11.1	13.7
34003	35,620	1	Bergen	232.8	936,692	55	4,023.6	56.9	6.1	0.3	17.7	20.6	5.3	15.9	8.1	11.6	13.2	14.5
34005	37,980	1	Burlington	799.3	445,384	160	557.2	69.0	18.2	0.7	6.3	8.3	5.1	15.7	8.3	12.5	12.4	14.3
34007	37,980	1	Camden	221.4	507,078	139	2,290.3	57.8	19.8	0.6	6.6	17.2	6.1	16.6	8.2	13.9	12.7	13.3
34009	36,140	3	Cape May	251.5	92,560	637	368.0	86.7	5.0	0.5	1.5	7.9	4.6	12.9	7.5	10.4	9.2	12.0
34011	47,220	3	Cumberland	483.4	150,972	439	312.3	47.5	20.1	1.4	1.9	31.4	6.3	17.6	8.1	14.3	13.0	13.1
34013	35,620	1	Essex	126.1	799,767	79	6,342.3	31.6	39.6	0.5	6.3	23.5	6.6	17.1	8.8	13.8	14.0	14.0
34015	37,980	1	Gloucester	322.0	291,408	239	905.0	79.8	11.5	0.5	3.8	6.4	5.2	16.6	8.8	12.4	12.5	14.4
34017	35,620	1	Hudson	46.2	676,061	100	14,633.4	29.9	11.5	0.4	16.8	42.9	6.9	13.5	8.0	21.1	15.8	12.2
34019	35,620	1	Hunterdon	427.8	124,714	511	291.5	86.2	2.9	0.3	5.0	6.8	4.1	15.2	8.8	9.1	10.7	16.1

1. CBSA = Core Based Statistical Area. See Appendix A for explanation. See Appendix B for list of metropolitan areas with component counties.   2. County type code from the Economic Research Service of USDA Rural-Urban Continuum Codes. See Appendix A for definition.   3. Dry land or land partially or temporarily covered by water.   4. May be of any race.

STATE County	55 to 64 years	65 to 74 years	75 years and over	Percent female	Total persons 2000	2010	Percent change 2000-2010	2010-2018	Births	Deaths	Net Migration	Number	Persons per household	Family house-holds	Female family house-holder[1]	One person
	16	17	18	19	20	21	22	23	24	25	26	27	28	29	30	31
NEBRASKA— Cont'd																
Platte	13.7	9.2	8.0	49.3	31,662	32,237	1.8	3.5	3,985	2,261	-595	12,937	2.51	65.5	8.1	30.3
Polk	15.0	12.6	10.3	50.6	5,639	5,406	-4.1	-2.4	443	507	-62	2,038	2.53	72.0	4.8	25.1
Red Willow	15.0	10.4	10.4	50.2	11,448	11,055	-3.4	-3.0	1,062	1,001	-388	4,598	2.28	60.7	6.1	31.9
Richardson	16.2	12.6	12.1	49.7	9,531	8,363	-12.3	-5.1	735	940	-220	3,798	2.08	62.3	6.9	33.8
Rock	20.4	15.0	11.7	49.6	1,756	1,528	-13.0	-11.0	124	185	-110	655	2.02	62.4	5.2	30.8
Saline	12.0	8.2	6.9	48.8	13,843	14,200	2.6	1.1	1,575	1,175	-254	5,073	2.62	67.8	7.0	27.9
Sarpy	11.2	7.1	4.7	50.0	122,595	158,835	29.6	16.1	21,117	7,358	11,900	63,851	2.73	73.3	10.0	21.8
Saunders	14.9	10.7	8.0	49.4	19,830	20,778	4.8	2.5	2,036	1,655	150	8,150	2.54	69.4	7.8	25.9
Scotts Bluff	13.5	10.3	8.7	51.3	36,951	36,970	0.1	-2.7	4,081	3,425	-1,634	14,425	2.48	65.1	12.5	28.8
Seward	13.1	9.3	7.5	48.9	16,496	16,750	1.5	3.4	1,579	1,384	377	6,496	2.40	68.3	5.8	25.6
Sheridan	14.5	14.3	12.5	50.9	6,198	5,469	-11.8	-5.1	482	594	-164	2,306	2.22	62.1	8.6	35.6
Sherman	16.2	13.9	13.2	50.9	3,318	3,152	-5.0	-3.6	257	312	-60	1,378	2.17	63.7	6.2	30.1
Sioux	18.5	14.5	14.1	48.7	1,475	1,311	-11.1	-9.5	78	60	-145	579	2.17	65.3	5.9	30.7
Stanton	15.4	9.9	8.0	49.3	6,455	6,128	-5.1	-2.6	599	349	-413	2,351	2.54	76.1	12.9	19.9
Thayer	14.9	12.8	12.5	50.2	6,055	5,228	-13.7	-3.6	450	633	-5	2,337	2.13	64.1	4.2	31.4
Thomas	13.6	15.6	10.4	48.6	729	647	-11.2	11.3	65	40	49	293	2.19	64.8	4.4	30.0
Thurston	10.5	6.4	5.5	50.6	7,171	6,939	-3.2	5.2	1,261	619	-282	2,142	3.27	73.0	22.1	23.9
Valley	13.5	13.1	12.2	50.4	4,647	4,260	-8.3	-1.6	407	446	-31	1,934	2.16	70.4	6.0	26.3
Washington	15.0	10.7	7.1	49.9	18,780	20,234	7.7	2.1	1,759	1,440	74	8,133	2.47	72.8	8.7	23.7
Wayne	12.3	8.2	8.1	49.7	9,851	9,595	-2.6	-2.0	836	497	-543	3,602	2.25	65.3	6.4	23.2
Webster	16.1	11.6	11.4	50.2	4,061	3,812	-6.1	-7.3	286	481	-84	1,499	2.35	61.0	4.9	36.1
Wheeler	19.4	12.8	13.0	48.9	886	818	-7.7	-1.6	68	39	-43	378	2.24	64.8	7.4	31.0
York	13.8	10.8	9.6	51.0	14,598	13,665	-6.4	0.8	1,427	1,256	-61	5,623	2.29	65.2	6.6	31.2
NEVADA	12.4	9.7	6.0	49.9	1,998,257	2,700,679	35.2	12.4	294,505	183,602	221,704	1,052,249	2.71	63.8	12.8	28.4
Churchill	14.0	11.4	7.6	49.2	23,982	24,877	3.7	-1.8	2,560	2,173	-844	9,734	2.41	64.0	8.1	28.9
Clark	11.8	9.1	5.7	50.1	1,375,765	1,951,271	41.8	14.4	221,151	124,882	183,271	749,858	2.79	64.1	13.8	28.2
Douglas	18.4	17.2	11.3	49.7	41,259	46,997	13.9	3.1	2,685	3,853	2,674	20,376	2.32	70.0	9.5	22.8
Elko	12.4	7.1	4.3	48.1	45,291	48,942	8.1	7.2	5,865	2,345	-78	17,882	2.88	71.4	8.8	23.1
Esmeralda	14.8	20.9	15.9	44.8	971	784	-19.3	5.4	43	88	81	494	2.22	47.4	7.3	49.4
Eureka	17.0	10.1	6.2	47.2	1,651	1,987	20.4	0.8	143	117	-19	765	2.25	62.5	4.4	33.6
Humboldt	13.4	8.7	5.0	47.9	16,106	16,521	2.6	1.6	2,093	1,027	-828	6,261	2.69	64.8	8.4	31.3
Lander	12.5	9.1	6.7	48.8	5,794	5,775	-0.3	-3.5	716	327	-597	2,183	2.67	70.4	12.1	23.3
Lincoln	12.9	14.5	10.3	46.3	4,165	5,339	28.2	-2.6	285	422	-9	1,930	2.43	66.2	6.8	33.1
Lyon	14.8	13.4	7.8	48.9	34,501	51,980	50.7	7.4	4,687	4,643	3,754	20,127	2.59	66.2	10.1	26.6
Mineral	16.8	13.5	11.2	50.5	5,071	4,770	-5.9	-5.4	405	631	-37	1,859	2.36	57.2	15.6	41.6
Nye	17.3	17.8	12.3	48.8	32,485	43,945	35.3	3.2	3,068	5,600	3,904	18,077	2.37	60.9	8.4	32.1
Pershing	14.0	9.3	6.7	35.6	6,693	6,752	0.9	-1.3	440	391	-150	2,018	2.33	65.1	7.0	26.6
Storey	21.8	21.1	10.4	48.8	3,399	4,014	18.1	0.4	152	224	81	1,665	2.31	61.3	5.4	30.8
Washoe	13.2	10.3	6.0	49.6	339,486	421,425	24.1	10.5	44,453	30,416	30,233	173,519	2.53	61.7	10.8	29.4
White Pine	14.1	10.2	7.8	41.9	9,181	10,026	9.2	-5.5	861	770	-648	3,343	2.50	61.8	6.5	32.5
Carson City	14.6	11.9	8.5	48.7	52,457	55,274	5.4	0.3	4,898	5,693	916	22,158	2.36	60.2	13.2	33.1
NEW HAMPSHIRE	15.7	10.8	7.3	50.4	1,235,786	1,316,464	6.5	3.0	102,554	93,479	31,684	526,710	2.45	66.6	9.4	25.5
Belknap	17.5	13.4	8.8	50.6	56,325	60,073	6.7	1.6	4,370	5,531	2,159	24,579	2.42	66.4	9.3	25.6
Carroll	18.9	17.1	10.8	50.4	43,666	47,825	9.5	2.0	2,893	4,277	2,377	21,203	2.21	66.3	6.5	26.2
Cheshire	15.6	12.0	7.9	51.1	73,825	77,122	4.5	-0.8	5,586	5,802	-379	30,529	2.34	62.9	9.8	28.4
Coos	17.2	13.8	9.9	47.2	33,111	33,052	-0.2	-4.4	2,045	3,543	-12	13,879	2.16	62.9	10.0	31.8
Grafton	15.5	12.1	8.6	50.6	81,743	89,137	9.0	0.7	6,146	6,636	1,196	34,856	2.37	61.4	8.0	31.3
Hillsborough	14.9	9.6	6.4	50.2	380,841	400,699	5.2	3.6	35,319	26,060	5,493	158,139	2.52	67.1	10.7	24.6
Merrimack	15.5	10.7	7.5	50.7	136,225	146,457	7.5	3.2	11,099	10,997	4,679	57,247	2.47	66.7	8.7	25.8
Rockingham	16.5	11.0	7.0	50.4	277,359	295,211	6.4	4.7	21,628	18,631	11,231	119,955	2.50	69.9	8.8	23.2
Strafford	13.6	9.0	6.0	51.0	112,233	123,149	9.7	5.6	10,160	8,420	5,233	48,543	2.43	64.4	8.5	24.9
Sullivan	16.6	12.9	8.6	50.6	40,458	43,739	8.1	-1.4	3,308	3,582	-293	17,780	2.38	65.2	11.2	28.2
NEW JERSEY	13.7	9.1	7.1	51.1	8,414,350	8,791,962	4.5	1.3	852,207	595,714	-140,088	3,199,111	2.74	69.3	13.3	25.7
Atlantic	15.0	10.3	7.6	51.6	252,552	274,521	8.7	-3.3	25,415	21,754	-12,869	100,660	2.65	66.7	15.9	27.6
Bergen	14.2	9.3	7.9	51.5	884,118	905,143	2.4	3.5	76,860	58,496	13,791	337,819	2.74	72.3	11.0	23.6
Burlington	14.7	9.5	7.4	50.7	423,394	448,730	6.0	-0.7	37,321	32,511	-8,010	164,404	2.66	70.1	11.8	25.0
Camden	13.5	9.0	6.7	51.8	508,932	513,719	0.9	-1.3	51,779	38,115	-20,458	187,012	2.70	67.3	16.9	27.8
Cape May	16.8	15.2	11.3	51.1	102,326	97,261	-4.9	-4.8	7,299	10,708	-1,206	39,861	2.30	65.1	9.8	29.7
Cumberland	12.3	8.7	6.5	49.0	146,438	156,633	7.0	-3.6	16,548	12,164	-10,118	50,596	2.81	68.7	20.0	25.7
Essex	12.3	7.7	5.8	51.9	793,633	783,885	-1.2	2.0	85,425	49,002	-20,918	280,327	2.78	64.9	19.3	30.2
Gloucester	14.3	9.4	6.4	51.3	254,673	288,570	13.3	1.0	24,523	20,825	-685	104,810	2.74	71.5	12.1	23.4
Hudson	10.7	6.7	5.1	50.2	608,975	634,245	4.1	6.6	84,798	32,062	-11,148	252,352	2.66	62.0	16.1	28.3
Hunterdon	17.5	10.9	7.6	50.5	121,989	127,357	4.4	-2.1	7,582	7,406	-2,855	46,822	2.59	73.2	7.3	22.7

1. No spouse present.

Table B. States and Counties — Population, Vital Statistics, Health, and Crime

STATE County	Persons in group quarters, 2018	Daytime Population, 2013-2017 Number	Employment/ residence ratio	Births, 2018 Total	Rate[1]	Deaths, 2018 Number	Rate[1]	Persons under 65 with no health insurance, 2016 Number	Percent	Medicare, 2018 Total beneficiaries	Enrolled in Original Medicare	Enrolled in Medicare Advantage	Serious crimes known to police[2], 2016 Total Number	Rate[3]
	32	33	34	35	36	37	38	39	40	41	42	43	44	45
NEBRASKA— Cont'd														
Platte....................	447	35,040	1.12	473	14.2	278	8.3	2,702	10.0	6,271	5,966	305	624	1,896
Polk.......................	111	4,348	0.67	59	11.2	55	10.4	383	9.4	1,269	D	D	34	659
Red Willow..........	428	11,297	1.08	134	12.5	118	11.0	741	9.0	2,473	2,452	21	240	2,229
Richardson..........	148	7,007	0.73	84	10.6	113	14.2	639	10.5	2,177	2,156	21	63	785
Rock.....................	27	1,361	0.97	18	13.2	15	11.0	124	11.9	247	D	D	0	0
Saline...................	959	14,328	1.00	194	13.5	139	9.7	1,586	14.1	2,448	2,388	60	246	1,724
Sarpy....................	1,241	149,815	0.73	2,504	13.6	1,012	5.5	10,004	6.3	24,507	19,632	4,875	2,622	1,467
Saunders..............	334	16,492	0.59	252	11.8	194	9.1	1,179	6.9	4,215	3,565	650	153	728
Scotts Bluff.........	884	37,029	1.03	476	13.2	416	11.6	3,572	12.3	8,072	7,329	743	1,012	2,871
Seward..................	1,321	15,421	0.81	181	10.5	152	8.8	858	6.5	3,377	3,167	210	93	619
Sheridan...............	136	4,814	0.84	59	11.4	71	13.7	568	14.5	1,373	1,240	133	NA	NA
Sherman...............	53	2,744	0.79	35	11.5	39	12.8	272	12.2	818	733	85	15	488
Sioux....................	0	1,047	0.68	10	8.4	3	2.5	109	11.5	259	D	D	NA	NA
Stanton................	0	4,519	0.52	67	11.2	33	5.5	396	10.0	986	877	109	47	798
Thayer..................	121	5,497	1.15	51	10.1	80	15.9	378	10.0	1,354	1,342	12	56	1,089
Thomas................	2	634	0.97	5	6.9	3	4.2	50	9.0	186	174	12	NA	NA
Thurston..............	50	7,601	1.22	165	22.6	79	10.8	1,058	17.3	997	966	31	23	372
Valley...................	45	4,286	1.02	43	10.3	50	11.9	334	10.7	1,057	1,045	12	33	800
Washington..........	143	19,314	0.90	214	10.4	189	9.1	945	5.6	4,071	3,319	752	176	871
Wayne...................	928	9,672	1.05	97	10.3	47	5.0	617	8.8	1,486	1,351	135	NA	NA
Webster................	155	3,305	0.83	31	8.8	54	15.3	296	11.0	924	902	22	13	363
Wheeler................	0	858	1.03	10	12.4	4	5.0	63	10.3	159	D	D	3	408
York......................	786	14,763	1.13	172	12.5	138	10.0	788	7.5	3,070	3,049	21	266	1,925
NEVADA..............	37,615	2,891,608	1.00	36,042	11.9	25,041	8.3	323,527	13.1	511,342	326,118	185,224	95,983	3,265
Churchill..............	304	24,103	1.01	290	11.9	253	10.4	2,647	13.6	5,593	4,963	630	460	1,904
Clark.....................	22,978	2,118,093	1.01	27,244	12.2	17,506	7.8	246,022	13.5	345,424	202,854	142,570	75,316	3,493
Douglas................	230	46,263	0.93	245	5.1	532	11.0	4,230	12.0	14,935	12,818	2,117	862	1,795
Elko.....................	792	50,435	0.93	713	13.6	362	6.9	5,953	12.8	6,281	6,125	156	1,090	2,068
Esmeralda............	1	1,168	1.15	6	7.3	4	4.8	96	16.8	263	252	11	6	713
Eureka..................	1	5,540	5.22	17	8.5	10	5.0	114	7.0	336	D	D	43	2,120
Humboldt..............	183	17,213	1.01	230	13.7	114	6.8	2,203	15.0	2,646	2,579	67	275	1,602
Lander..................	16	6,029	1.05	80	14.3	36	6.5	639	13.1	884	873	11	152	2,555
Lincoln.................	290	5,208	1.00	37	7.1	60	11.5	474	12.8	1,110	1,042	68	40	801
Lyon	361	44,498	0.62	572	10.2	607	10.9	5,767	13.9	13,828	10,676	3,152	724	1,369
Mineral................	52	4,586	1.07	47	10.4	97	21.5	410	12.4	1,310	1,170	140	27	609
Nye.......................	1,165	42,573	0.95	369	8.1	728	16.1	3,716	12.5	15,809	8,059	7,750	995	2,349
Pershing...............	1,800	6,903	1.11	39	5.9	45	6.8	565	14.3	1,001	976	25	151	2,276
Storey..................	5	3,385	0.71	19	4.7	19	4.7	272	9.6	1,298	1,016	282	116	2,901
Washoe................	5,308	444,508	1.00	5,392	11.6	3,943	8.5	44,439	11.7	85,358	59,140	26,218	13,720	3,025
White Pine............	1,301	10,276	1.12	101	10.7	93	9.8	742	10.8	1,824	1,771	53	95	970
Carson City	2,828	60,827	1.28	641	11.6	632	11.4	5,238	12.7	13,443	11,475	1,968	1,152	2,110
NEW HAMPSHIRE	42,542	1,293,939	0.95	12,149	9.0	11,935	8.8	78,021	7.2	290,038	251,816	38,222	22,831	1,710
Belknap................	1,008	56,720	0.88	500	8.2	766	12.6	3,872	8.1	17,334	15,182	2,152	1,628	2,677
Carroll..................	440	46,737	0.97	322	6.6	552	11.3	3,275	9.5	15,178	13,472	1,706	852	1,920
Cheshire...............	4,624	73,787	0.94	644	8.4	717	9.4	4,743	8.3	17,974	15,595	2,379	1,203	1,964
Coos.....................	2,439	31,368	0.95	224	7.1	415	13.1	2,081	9.2	9,846	9,311	535	482	1,679
Grafton.................	7,102	101,474	1.27	702	7.8	823	9.2	5,612	8.5	20,687	18,496	2,191	1,542	1,862
Hillsborough........	7,759	389,680	0.92	4,193	10.1	3,393	8.2	25,164	7.3	77,050	64,574	12,476	7,290	1,809
Merrimack............	6,799	150,986	1.04	1,304	8.6	1,336	8.8	8,390	7.1	33,165	29,197	3,968	1,984	1,500
Rockingham..........	2,504	289,797	0.92	2,667	8.6	2,420	7.8	14,206	5.6	63,490	54,505	8,985	3,768	1,246
Strafford..............	9,137	116,361	0.84	1,200	9.2	1,069	8.2	8,053	8.0	24,593	21,505	3,088	2,666	2,088
Sullivan	730	37,029	0.71	393	9.1	444	10.3	2,625	7.7	10,722	9,979	743	574	1,547
NEW JERSEY.................	182,113	8,641,087	0.93	100,226	11.3	76,370	8.6	681,347	9.2	1,583,575	1,212,979	370,596	160,066	1,790
Atlantic................	6,037	275,103	1.02	2,722	10.3	2,805	10.6	23,502	10.6	55,867	45,199	10,668	7,850	2,878
Bergen	10,436	908,155	0.94	9,296	9.9	7,336	7.8	65,960	8.5	167,417	134,542	32,875	9,925	1,056
Burlington............	11,736	432,653	0.93	4,326	9.7	4,101	9.2	20,360	5.6	87,240	66,388	20,852	7,265	1,621
Camden................	7,497	469,873	0.83	6,040	11.9	4,771	9.4	32,981	7.7	94,264	72,649	21,615	14,668	2,888
Cape May.............	2,601	94,642	1.00	804	8.7	1,298	14.0	5,824	8.4	27,128	23,103	4,025	3,047	3,250
Cumberland	9,974	155,480	1.01	1,774	11.8	1,447	9.6	14,695	12.1	28,059	21,601	6,458	6,450	4,166
Essex....................	23,476	809,505	1.03	10,198	12.8	6,526	8.2	82,345	12.2	117,429	79,917	37,512	19,493	2,449
Gloucester............	4,239	254,768	0.74	2,753	9.4	2,676	9.2	13,950	5.7	54,316	42,155	12,161	5,749	1,979
Hudson.................	9,477	620,219	0.83	10,199	15.1	4,474	6.6	83,679	14.1	81,053	54,121	26,932	12,593	1,854
Hunterdon............	3,682	116,139	0.85	921	7.4	992	8.0	4,790	4.7	24,625	19,936	4,689	748	601

1. Per 1,000 estimated resident population.   2. Data for serious crimes have not been adjusted for underreporting; this may affect comparability between geographic areas and over time.   3. Per 100,000 population estimated by the FBI.

Table B. States and Counties — Crime, Education, Money Income, and Poverty

STATE County	Serious crimes known to police[2], 2016 (cont.)[1] Rate Violent	Property	School enrollment and attainment, 2013-2017 Enrollment[3] Total	Percent private	Attainment[4] (percent) High school graduate or less	Bachelor's degree or more	Local government expenditures,[5] 2014-2015 Total current spending (mil dol)	Current spending per student (dollars)	Money income, 2013-2017 Per capita income[6]	Median income (dollars)	Households Percent with income of less than $50,000	Percent with income of $200,000 or more	Income and poverty, 2017 Median household income (dollars)	Percent below poverty level All persons	Children under 18 years	Children 5 to 17 years in families
	46	47	48	49	50	51	52	53	54	55	56	57	58	59	60	61
NEBRASKA— Cont'd																
Platte	122	1,775	8,241	21.7	42.9	21.5	61.0	12,761	28,187	58,679	43.1	3.2	57,693	8.6	11.3	10.6
Polk	19	640	1,227	7.7	39.1	20.9	19.6	15,290	32,424	63,667	37.3	5.4	61,422	6.9	10.7	9.6
Red Willow	121	2,108	2,553	8.6	39.8	18.7	20.6	11,926	25,006	42,882	55.7	2.6	49,447	10.9	14.6	13.3
Richardson	37	747	1,694	8.9	45.6	19.4	18.0	14,340	28,109	46,839	54.2	2.6	48,087	13	18.3	17.0
Rock	0	0	213	4.2	45.7	18.9	3.3	15,802	33,867	52,361	46.1	6.9	48,373	14.3	24.1	22.9
Saline	364	1,359	4,069	15.1	50.1	13.4	35.4	12,255	22,324	50,932	49.2	1.7	53,662	10.6	11.6	11.0
Sarpy	99	1,368	51,472	15.6	26.2	39.5	275.2	10,357	33,103	75,752	29.2	5.3	80,842	5.1	5.9	5.3
Saunders	71	657	5,297	16.2	37.4	26.5	33.6	11,671	31,163	65,015	37.7	3.2	63,849	7.6	9.2	8.1
Scotts Bluff	247	2,624	9,103	11.3	41.4	22.1	79.7	12,039	26,532	47,975	51.7	2.7	48,662	13.3	19.8	18.3
Seward	60	559	4,845	32.1	34.7	28.1	38.1	14,900	29,398	63,095	39.0	3.9	68,762	7.5	8.0	7.4
Sheridan	NA	NA	1,220	9.1	41.3	25.8	12.1	14,350	25,817	41,209	60.0	1.7	41,247	14.3	23.4	21.4
Sherman	33	455	658	10.2	45.5	18.3	7.2	16,151	27,983	48,704	51.0	1.4	55,432	11.7	21.7	19.9
Sioux	NA	NA	240	6.3	39.7	26.6	2.6	26,616	26,852	45,375	52.7	2.1	50,910	17.1	28.8	26.3
Stanton	102	696	1,595	12.5	41.7	17.6	5.8	12,413	29,517	57,534	42.8	2.1	58,295	7.8	10.0	9.1
Thayer	19	1,069	982	11.2	44.5	20.7	14.6	17,071	31,129	48,151	52.2	3.1	51,757	11.6	16.2	15.5
Thomas	NA	NA	155	12.3	32.2	29.0	2.3	19,772	29,243	53,173	47.1	1.4	46,927	13.5	21.8	19.7
Thurston	97	275	2,409	5.4	45.9	16.0	29.9	16,185	19,380	44,701	55.1	2.7	45,328	23.3	32.6	30.0
Valley	73	727	788	3.9	46.0	20.3	10.2	13,721	27,271	50,270	49.8	4.0	44,907	12.1	15.7	15.3
Washington	69	802	5,382	15.2	33.2	30.8	36.3	10,271	33,136	66,485	37.7	4.4	72,385	7.2	8.0	7.0
Wayne	NA	NA	3,626	5.5	30.8	32.4	28.7	18,536	27,292	58,093	45.3	3.7	54,548	12.2	10.5	9.5
Webster	56	307	817	9.8	44.1	22.8	8.3	14,125	26,136	43,831	56.0	3.6	45,768	13	17.4	15.4
Wheeler	408	0	145	20.0	46.2	19.1	2.3	25,239	28,257	49,706	50.5	2.4	55,906	9.2	15.8	16.4
York	22	1,904	3,512	20.0	35.5	28.1	24.4	12,264	28,298	59,966	41.8	3.0	55,950	10.1	13.5	12.5
NEVADA	678	2,587	693,218	11.1	42.5	23.7	3,928.1	8,555	28,450	55,434	45.1	4.1	57,932	13.3	19.2	17.9
Churchill	186	1,718	5,250	10.1	41.9	18.3	38.2	10,937	25,211	46,914	52.1	2.0	53,302	11.5	17.8	17.4
Clark	770	2,723	510,031	11.7	43.5	23.3	2,675.1	8,254	27,719	54,882	45.7	4.0	57,217	14	20.5	19.3
Douglas	140	1,656	9,053	10.8	31.2	27.2	61.9	10,220	35,727	61,176	39.0	5.6	66,092	8.2	12.7	11.4
Elko	353	1,715	13,436	5.2	44.7	17.7	95.4	9,679	32,498	76,178	31.5	4.6	76,439	10.6	12.1	10.4
Esmeralda	119	594	172	2.3	54.3	14.7	2.0	27,176	23,755	39,405	62.6	0.0	47,053	14.6	22.1	21.8
Eureka	296	1,824	422	18.5	51.7	13.5	7.1	28,628	35,606	67,159	34.5	4.2	67,976	9	7.9	7.1
Humboldt	332	1,270	4,050	5.6	51.3	15.2	35.4	10,196	29,215	69,324	36.6	2.7	68,753	10.5	14.4	13.2
Lander	672	1,883	1,345	1.6	55.9	13.3	13.3	12,639	30,256	79,865	34.1	0.8	75,943	11.1	14.7	14.4
Lincoln	60	741	1,187	5.6	44.8	21.7	13.9	13,734	27,218	52,971	46.3	1.6	54,844	13.8	19.1	17.3
Lyon	263	1,107	11,540	9.9	46.1	14.7	80.2	9,929	25,063	50,920	48.6	2.0	54,588	10.8	18.0	17.6
Mineral	135	473	758	3.8	48.4	14.0	7.1	14,896	22,791	39,375	57.1	1.7	45,589	17.5	28.3	26.6
Nye	189	2,161	7,229	12.7	51.4	11.5	56.6	10,960	23,740	44,225	54.8	0.6	48,513	15.8	26.8	25.5
Pershing	814	1,462	1,651	4.8	54.4	13.7	9.9	14,290	19,201	52,308	48.8	1.3	57,885	18.2	20.0	18.5
Storey	1,075	1,825	557	3.4	36.7	22.9	7.1	17,659	36,388	63,607	36.4	4.4	61,751	7	9.2	8.2
Washoe	504	2,521	111,687	10.0	36.2	29.8	583.7	8,869	31,879	58,595	43.0	5.4	61,506	11.1	14.1	12.3
White Pine	133	837	2,161	9.6	51.2	14.6	17.0	13,552	25,350	60,358	40.3	1.6	53,765	13.8	16.8	15.2
Carson City	288	1,822	12,683	7.7	41.8	21.6	224.1	8,023	28,044	49,341	50.7	3.0	55,228	11	17.3	15.8
NEW HAMPSHIRE	198	1,513	312,824	22.0	35.1	36.0	2,690.1	D	36,914	71,305	34.6	7.3	73,638	7.7	10.0	9.1
Belknap	248	2,429	12,818	20.1	37.1	31.5	135.0	15,759	33,849	65,834	38.1	5.0	63,902	8.3	12.7	11.2
Carroll	162	1,757	8,236	15.5	36.5	34.0	98.9	18,411	35,646	58,139	42.4	5.1	58,005	9.3	14.8	13.9
Cheshire	181	1,782	18,937	21.2	38.7	32.6	142.4	17,377	32,072	60,148	41.7	4.5	60,844	9.4	11.9	10.7
Coos	174	1,505	5,863	12.9	51.8	18.3	66.3	16,437	25,895	45,386	54.2	1.9	43,836	11.7	19.2	17.3
Grafton	176	1,686	22,341	32.6	35.5	39.3	212.3	19,550	35,255	61,036	41.5	7.3	63,322	9.4	12.4	11.6
Hillsborough	274	1,535	97,392	25.5	35.0	36.5	771.2	13,354	37,622	75,777	32.6	8.0	78,171	7.9	10.6	9.7
Merrimack	168	1,332	34,807	26.0	34.7	35.2	335.3	14,181	34,475	69,856	35.3	6.4	70,408	7.3	9.5	8.5
Rockingham	116	1,130	67,892	19.1	30.4	40.6	618.1	14,362	43,474	85,619	26.5	11.0	89,049	5.1	5.6	5.4
Strafford	223	1,865	36,099	12.6	35.2	35.7	219.3	14,072	32,540	67,805	37.5	4.3	68,864	9.4	10.2	9.2
Sullivan	189	1,359	8,439	17.4	46.8	25.9	101.0	16,811	31,301	59,419	42.2	3.4	59,493	10.3	15.7	13.8
NEW JERSEY	245	1,545	2,257,674	18.7	38.8	38.1	25,044.1	18,187	39,069	76,475	33.9	11.9	80,106	10	13.8	13.1
Atlantic	360	2,518	67,755	12.5	46.7	26.6	842.3	18,511	29,941	57,514	44.3	5.5	59,309	14.4	21.1	20.8
Bergen	86	970	230,965	21.8	31.9	47.9	2,565.8	18,915	46,601	91,572	27.8	16.6	93,805	6.6	6.8	6.4
Burlington	157	1,464	110,302	17.7	35.5	36.8	1,279.7	18,066	39,528	82,839	28.4	10.3	86,777	6.5	8.2	7.3
Camden	464	2,425	128,970	17.5	42.2	31.1	1,452.5	17,815	32,931	65,037	39.7	6.9	65,817	11.7	16.6	16.3
Cape May	231	3,019	18,440	14.7	42.2	31.3	256.4	20,181	36,256	62,332	40.1	6.2	64,450	10.4	16.3	16.1
Cumberland	520	3,646	36,337	8.0	61.3	14.4	480.7	17,340	23,012	50,000	50.0	3.0	51,786	18.4	28.1	27.8
Essex	563	1,886	215,841	17.5	43.1	34.0	2,581.3	19,383	35,133	57,365	45.0	10.8	60,284	15.7	21.2	19.0
Gloucester	116	1,863	75,662	14.0	41.3	31.0	822.6	16,968	36,205	81,489	30.4	8.3	84,639	6.7	9.2	8.8
Hudson	322	1,531	155,432	18.9	42.4	39.3	1,572.2	17,946	35,910	62,681	41.2	10.1	65,673	14.1	21.9	23.1
Hunterdon	39	561	30,490	17.6	26.8	50.7	412.9	20,362	54,200	110,969	20.6	21.3	113,083	3.9	3.5	3.2

1. Data for serious crimes have not been adjusted for underreporting; this may affect comparability between geographic areas and over time. 2. Per 100,000 population estimated by the FBI. 3. All persons 3 years old and over enrolled in nursery school through college. 4. Persons 25 years old and over. 5. Elementary and secondary education expenditures. 6. Based on population estimated by the American Community Survey, 2013–2017.

	Personal income, 2017										Earnings, 2017		
			Per capita[1]			Supplements to wages and salaries, employer contributions (mil dol)							Contributions for government social insurance (mil dol)	
STATE County	Total (mil dol)	Percent change 2016-2017	Dollars	Rank	Wages and salaries (mil dol)	Pension and insurance	Government social insurance	Proprietors' income (mil dol)	Dividends, interest, and rent (mil dol)	Personal transfer reecipts (mil dol)	Total (mil dol)	From employee and self-employed	From employer
	62	63	64	65	66	67	68	69	70	71	72	73	74
NEBRASKA— Cont'd													
Platte	1,600	3.7	48,233	606	857	171	65	202	325	238	1,295	72	65
Polk	267	8.1	50,165	453	58	12	4	61	51	45	135	6	4
Red Willow	476	1.6	44,356	977	213	41	17	44	113	107	315	19	17
Richardson	376	3.7	47,160	700	96	21	8	51	75	88	175	11	8
Rock	83	-1.2	57,659	207	22	5	2	31	18	9	59	2	2
Saline	592	2.4	40,998	1,407	326	58	24	66	98	109	474	27	24
Sarpy	8,732	4.2	48,129	613	3,950	712	310	305	1,373	1,108	5,277	312	310
Saunders	1,047	2.7	49,725	476	227	44	17	99	193	170	387	23	17
Scotts Bluff	1,522	0.2	41,864	1,281	739	130	59	129	262	341	1,057	68	59
Seward	821	5.1	47,842	637	279	50	21	92	160	132	443	26	21
Sheridan	238	3.5	45,072	892	61	14	5	45	51	49	125	6	5
Sherman	129	4.7	41,869	1,279	29	6	2	19	25	31	57	3	2
Sioux	61	-22.4	50,458	435	9	2	1	24	13	7	36	1	1
Stanton	283	3.4	47,261	691	85	14	6	60	49	36	165	8	6
Thayer	255		50,596	426	98	20	8	37	65	54	163	9	8
Thomas	40	-13.5	55,014	279	11	2	1	13	8	6	26	1	1
Thurston	318	2.8	44,034	1,017	134	30	10	107	42	62	281	11	10
Valley	194	2.4	46,100	786	71	15	6	32	44	42	124	7	6
Washington	1,116	3.0	53,838	316	432	71	31	91	214	158	625	38	31
Wayne	423	4.9	45,371	858	165	36	12	76	90	65	289	14	12
Webster	161	-5.3	45,805	817	36	8	3	33	30	39	79	4	3
Wheeler	68	-22.9	82,615	32	11	2	1	42	10	5	55	1	1
York	678	6.5	49,105	526	333	58	25	85	156	126	501	28	25
NEVADA	138,386	5.8	46,557	X	67,630	10,836	4,898	8,593	33,725	22,929	91,956	5,227	4,898
Churchill	1,001	5.9	41,332	1,360	422	93	34	62	180	256	611	35	34
Clark	97,457	5.1	44,217	994	49,313	7,433	3,580	5,671	22,989	16,191	65,996	3,761	3,580
Douglas	3,342	6.3	69,188	75	904	144	65	275	1,292	479	1,387	89	65
Elko	2,343	4.5	44,497	962	1,153	200	78	93	296	297	1,524	81	78
Esmeralda	35	-1.1	41,168	1,382	17	4	1	-4	7	8	19	1	1
Eureka	73	6.9	37,003	2,035	443	65	30	2	14	11	539	29	30
Humboldt	766	3.8	45,548	843	445	88	31	27	111	118	591	31	31
Lander	335	4.2	58,807	188	268	47	18	-2	32	41	331	18	18
Lincoln	187	5.5	35,711	2,244	66	22	4	2	36	54	93	5	4
Lyon	1,992	7.2	36,806	2,075	496	111	38	79	309	505	724	51	38
Mineral	165	3.6	36,925	2,054	81	18	6	2	33	61	107	6	6
Nye	1,614	5.2	36,521	2,115	595	105	43	101	274	572	843	62	43
Pershing	214	5.5	32,944	2,624	112	31	7	5	33	48	155	7	7
Storey	210	18.1	52,348	364	641	115	57	21	39	34	834	44	57
Washoe	25,556	8.5	55,487	263	10,925	1,879	799	1,911	7,426	3,574	15,514	880	799
White Pine	413	7.9	43,098	1,131	234	61	15	15	65	93	325	16	15
Carson City	2,682	9.3	48,997	539	1,516	419	93	335	589	585	2,362	111	93
NEW HAMPSHIRE	80,122	5.1	59,360	X	37,058	5,561	2,549	8,012	14,281	11,844	53,180	3,295	2,549
Belknap	3,588	4.6	59,032	183	1,198	201	84	368	780	654	1,852	123	84
Carroll	2,699	4.0	56,145	245	789	132	57	331	794	568	1,309	91	57
Cheshire	3,886	4.4	51,153	406	1,538	268	107	338	842	732	2,251	149	107
Coos	1,324	3.2	41,866	1,280	485	103	35	77	243	439	700	51	35
Grafton	5,306	3.2	59,356	172	3,219	474	229	556	1,335	855	4,478	273	229
Hillsborough	24,608	5.2	60,064	157	13,197	1,851	893	2,296	3,844	3,334	18,237	1,110	893
Merrimack	8,497	5.2	56,948	223	4,232	730	293	814	1,505	1,429	6,069	366	293
Rockingham	21,687	5.9	70,788	68	9,014	1,201	617	2,536	3,573	2,373	13,368	823	617
Strafford	6,346	5.4	49,339	505	2,753	481	186	515	969	1,023	3,935	242	186
Sullivan	2,182	3.5	50,644	423	634	120	46	181	397	436	982	66	46
NEW JERSEY	581,199	4.6	65,387	X	265,376	38,247	19,481	57,926	107,193	81,905	381,030	22,677	19,481
Atlantic	12,566	3.6	46,557	746	6,237	1,053	497	1,100	2,173	2,907	8,885	556	497
Bergen	77,013	4.9	81,203	34	31,084	4,121	2,320	9,082	17,248	7,775	46,606	2,721	2,320
Burlington	26,763	3.9	59,659	163	12,876	2,004	1,006	2,067	4,374	4,085	17,953	1,085	1,006
Camden	26,495	4.1	51,878	379	11,747	1,850	921	1,903	4,128	5,390	16,420	1,019	921
Cape May	5,456	4.0	58,324	198	1,756	345	152	589	1,389	1,259	2,842	187	152
Cumberland	5,933	3.0	38,893	1,738	2,911	563	241	490	874	1,685	4,206	260	241
Essex	51,370	4.3	63,554	121	24,997	3,939	1,787	3,991	11,161	8,235	34,714	2,028	1,787
Gloucester	15,342	4.0	52,506	359	5,327	968	429	1,010	2,028	2,581	7,734	484	429
Hudson	41,238	5.3	59,623	164	21,326	2,921	1,461	5,721	5,276	5,685	31,428	1,792	1,461
Hunterdon	10,829	4.1	86,589	24	3,564	472	238	959	2,049	990	5,233	314	238

1. Based on the resident population estimated as of July 1 of the year shown.

Table B. States and Counties — Earnings, Social Security, and Housing

STATE County	Earnings, 2017 (cont.)									Social Security beneficiaries, December 2017		Supplemental Security Income recipients, 2017	Housing units, 2018	
					Percent by selected industries									
	Farm	Mining, quarrying, and extractions	Construction	Manu-facturing	Information; professional, scientific, technical services	Retail trade	Finance, insurance, real estate, and leasing	Health care and social assistance	Govern-ment	Number	Rate[1]		Total	Percent change, 2010-2018
	75	76	77	78	79	80	81	82	83	84	85	86	87	88
NEBRASKA— Cont'd														
Platte	9.9	0.2	6	31.7	3.1	5.9	4.9	7.8	13.5	6,480	195	307	13,867	3.7
Polk	35	D	4.5	1.9	D	5.1	D	6	21.4	1,250	235	37	2,734	0.1
Red Willow	7.1	1.1	5	10.6	3.5	8.8	5.9	13.7	19.7	2,470	230	145	5,327	1.1
Richardson	15.7	D	4.9	10.9	3.7	5.7	4.1	D	18.3	2,250	282	169	4,413	0.5
Rock	49.2	0.2	D	D	D	3	D	0.9	19.3	210	146	10	915	0.1
Saline	7.1	0	2.4	40.5	D	4.5	3.1	D	16.9	2,545	176	172	5,862	1.7
Sarpy	0.1	D	9	4.3	8.2	5.8	9.2	5.3	25.5	24,870	137	1,356	69,959	13
Saunders	14.9	D	11.1	6.2	6.4	6.2	5.6	D	22.3	4,180	199	184	9,792	6.2
Scotts Bluff	2.9	D	7.2	5.4	4.5	7.3	5.2	17.5	19	8,340	229	830	16,384	-0.1
Seward	9.9	0	8.9	18.3	D	4.9	5.3	D	15.6	3,340	195	137	7,213	4.9
Sheridan	27.1	D	2.1	7.8	2.6	7.1	D	3.6	25.4	1,390	263	74	2,911	-0.9
Sherman	19.8	0	3.2	3.3	D	7.9	3.9	7	21.5	835	271	37	1,946	0.3
Sioux	73	0.1	0.5	2.5	D	2.3	D	D	12.4	235	195	5	829	1.7
Stanton	27	D	D	D	D	1	2.8	0.8	9.9	1,000	167	24	2,700	2.6
Thayer	18.4	0	4.3	19.4	1.1	3.4	6.5	4.2	22.1	1,350	268	74	2,755	0.9
Thomas	35.9	D	D	D	D	D	D	D	17	160	221	0	405	0.7
Thurston	30.1	0	2.3	5.4	D	4.5	2.4	5.8	36.2	1,140	158	241	2,445	1.6
Valley	16	D	6.1	4.2	D	8.3	D	D	27	1,060	252	61	2,302	1.3
Washington	7.4	D	10.5	18.1	4.9	9.8	5.2	D	19.5	4,095	198	168	8,693	4.7
Wayne	19.6	0	2.2	16.1	2.1	4.5	8.2	8.2	23.7	1,495	160	69	3,991	5.7
Webster	35.2	D	D	D	5.2	4.1	D	5.5	20.2	995	282	103	1,911	-0.1
Wheeler	79.5	0	D	D	D	D	D	0	6.2	155	189	0	583	1.2
York	11.2	D	5	12	4.5	5.3	6.7	D	14.8	3,095	224	175	6,327	1.5
NEVADA	0.1	1.7	7.4	3.8	9.1	6.9	5.7	9.3	16.4	521,297	174	56,143	1,268,633	8.1
Churchill	1.6	0.2	10.2	6.8	3.7	5.6	3	9.1	32.7	5,730	236	523	10,967	1.3
Clark	0	0	6.4	2.5	9.1	7.2	6.6	9.1	15.5	354,170	161	43,628	913,260	8.7
Douglas	0	D	14	9.5	10.8	5	6.8	8.1	13.4	14,535	301	371	24,543	3.7
Elko	1.4	15.7	8.9	0.8	3.1	6.6	2.4	6.5	19.5	6,510	124	498	21,755	11.2
Esmeralda	-18.2	D	D	D	D	D	0.2	0	28.2	265	312	19	852	0
Eureka	0.2	D	D	D	D	0.2	D	D	2.9	330	168	19	1,080	0.4
Humboldt	0.9	38.5	4.3	2.7	D	5.7	0.9	D	20.7	2,725	162	226	7,549	6.1
Lander	-0.6	75.2	D	D	0.2	2.1	D	0.3	12.8	910	160	74	2,717	5.5
Lincoln	-1.8	1	D	D	D	D	2	D	51.8	1,110	213	70	2,812	3.1
Lyon	1.5	2.7	10.8	19.7	5.6	6.6	3.1	D	21.7	14,455	267	926	23,702	5.1
Mineral	-1.6	5.7	D	0.3	D	3.9	D	D	35.2	1,320	296	139	2,840	0.4
Nye	4.3	13.5	5.6	1.4	17.6	6.5	2	6.7	15.9	16,390	371	1,160	22,390	0.2
Pershing	7.1	42.4	D	D	D	3.2	0.7	D	37.2	1,025	157	68	2,486	0.9
Storey	0	D	20.3	41	D	D	D	D	2.5	1,315	328	12	2,054	3.1
Washoe	0.1	0	11	6.3	10.7	6.4	4.1	11.7	16.4	85,410	185	7,192	201,081	8.8
White Pine	-0.9	39.8	4.4	0.4	D	3	1.4	D	35.1	1,830	191	157	4,519	0.5
Carson City	0.2	D	6.3	8	8.2	6.4	4.2	14.3	36.4	13,265	242	1,061	24,026	2.1
NEW HAMPSHIRE	0.1	0.1	7.6	11.7	12.8	7.8	8.6	12.4	12.1	300,267	224	19,032	638,091	3.8
Belknap	0.1	0.3	12.7	8.9	7.2	11.4	4.4	13	14.4	18,030	297	1,026	38,783	3.8
Carroll	-0.2	D	14.5	4.2	8.8	11.2	5.2	11.3	14	15,510	323	706	41,413	4
Cheshire	0.4	D	9.9	14.8	6.1	10.2	7.1	11.3	14.5	19,170	252	1,240	35,722	2.7
Coos	-0.2	0.1	D	D	2.6	8.9	4.4	18.4	26.9	10,715	339	928	21,612	1.4
Grafton	0.2	0.1	4.6	8.9	10.9	5.9	5	24.9	10.3	21,105	236	1,022	53,083	3.8
Hillsborough	0	D	D	14.7	14.9	7.4	11.5	11.3	9.5	80,435	196	7,108	172,031	3.6
Merrimack	0.2	0.3	7.6	7.6	8.6	7.4	9.7	14.2	20.6	34,460	231	2,044	65,253	2.7
Rockingham	0.1	0.1	8.3	10.5	15.5	7.9	7.4	8.9	7.9	63,950	209	2,193	133,178	5.1
Strafford	0.1	D	D	D	13.8	7.7	8	13.5	20.3	25,735	200	1,966	54,307	5
Sullivan	0.2	D	10.3	25	6.1	9.2	5.3	8.1	14.7	11,155	259	799	22,709	1.7
NEW JERSEY	0.1	0.3	5.5	7.6	14.9	6.1	10.7	11.3	14.4	1,613,096	179	181,512	3,628,302	2.1
Atlantic	0.6	0.5	7.1	1.6	6.9	7.4	4.5	16.3	23.6	59,315	220	7,270	128,409	1.4
Bergen	0	D	5.5	6.9	14.7	7.1	8.4	14.7	9.6	163,140	172	12,425	359,291	2
Burlington	0.2	D	5.4	8.1	11.7	7.9	12	13.6	17.2	90,420	202	6,018	179,893	2.4
Camden	0	0	5.9	7.3	10	7	5.2	18.8	17.7	99,270	194	16,839	206,146	0.6
Cape May	0.2	0.1	10.9	1.7	5.1	9.4	7.3	9.9	27	28,715	307	1,724	99,436	1.1
Cumberland	1.5	0.4	6.5	15	D	7.3	3	15.9	25.9	30,885	202	5,919	56,490	1.1
Essex	0	0.3	4	4.3	12.2	3.5	14	11	20.4	119,570	148	28,573	318,813	1.9
Gloucester	0.6	D	9.7	9.5	D	11.1	3.8	10.9	20.8	57,770	198	4,472	113,903	3.7
Hudson	0	D	2.3	2.4	12.9	4.9	29.9	5.7	12.4	82,000	119	21,047	284,142	5.1
Hunterdon	0.4	D	10.3	4.4	15.7	6.9	17.5	9.6	13.2	24,225	194	835	50,463	2

1. Per 1,000 resident population estimated as of July 1 of the year shown.

Table B. States and Counties — Housing, Labor Force, and Employment

STATE County	Housing units, 2013-2017								Civilian labor force, 2018				Civilian employment[6], 2013-2017		
	Occupied units							Sub-standard units[4] (percent)		Percent change, 2017-2018	Unemployment			Percent	
	Owner-occupied					Renter-occupied									
				Median owner cost as a percent of income		Median rent[3]	Median rent as a percent of income[2]		Total		Total	Rate[5]	Total	Management, business, science, and arts	Construction, production, and maintenance occupations
	Total	Percent	Median value[1]	With a mortgage	Without a mortgage[2]										
	89	90	91	92	93	94	95	96	97	98	99	100	101	102	103
NEBRASKA— Cont'd															
Platte	12,937	71.2	136,600	18.9	10.8	684	21.7	2.7	17,328	2.5	458	2.6	17,730	29.9	36.1
Polk	2,038	80.3	100,200	18.0	10.0	612	19.7	2.2	2,902	0.8	68	2.3	2,732	35.0	29.8
Red Willow	4,598	75.1	91,500	18.8	13.2	605	25.2	0.8	5,826	-0.1	137	2.4	5,598	28.6	26.3
Richardson	3,798	77.4	69,300	15.9	12.4	499	19.8	1.6	4,231	0.6	126	3	3,954	33.5	33.7
Rock	655	76.0	83,700	17.3	10.0	528	17	0.3	906	0.3	22	2.4	760	37.6	26.3
Saline	5,073	68.3	95,000	20.9	11.9	723	23.9	3.8	7,441	0.8	224	3	7,053	24.6	41.0
Sarpy	63,851	69.6	173,900	20.0	10.7	943	25.3	2.5	94,057	1.1	2,499	2.7	91,916	43.0	17.7
Saunders	8,150	79.1	159,400	20.3	12.5	747	21.2	2.1	10,948	1.2	298	2.7	11,034	35.6	26.4
Scotts Bluff	14,425	68.9	116,600	21.5	12.8	729	27.8	1.8	18,422	0.4	591	3.2	17,568	31.4	26.4
Seward	6,496	70.9	159,700	18.8	11.4	699	24.5	1.2	8,730	1.5	225	2.6	8,759	36.6	27.6
Sheridan	2,306	70.3	70,900	20.5	13.2	604	21.8	3.3	2,690	-0.7	69	2.6	2,619	38.6	24.2
Sherman	1,378	81.6	85,400	22.1	11.0	510	18.2	1	1,701	0.7	45	2.6	1,515	37.8	31.4
Sioux	579	75.6	103,200	27.0	12.3	592	20.3	0.5	743	-1.5	19	2.6	660	55.6	19.7
Stanton	2,351	83.4	111,900	17.8	10.4	777	25.4	2.2	3,468	-0.1	85	2.5	3,207	28.7	34.1
Thayer	2,337	77.6	67,500	18.0	10.0	555	18.8	1.6	2,866	0.3	64	2.2	2,560	35.1	27.7
Thomas	293	69.6	82,300	17.0	10.5	531	20.3	0.7	440	1.1	13	3	364	41.8	28.8
Thurston	2,142	59.9	79,100	17.8	10.0	578	26.7	12.2	2,968	-1.3	120	4	2,589	38.9	22.3
Valley	1,934	71.6	92,700	17.5	12.5	614	27.3	0.8	2,084	-1.1	60	2.9	2,349	36.9	24.4
Washington	8,133	76.5	182,400	21.4	12.0	706	27.7	0.9	11,209	0.8	315	2.8	10,805	37.1	23.6
Wayne	3,602	63.5	133,000	16.5	10.7	680	22.9	2.9	5,665	0.4	136	2.4	5,224	34.4	25.6
Webster	1,499	80.1	75,600	18.9	11.7	460	18.6	0.7	1,645		46	2.8	1,764	35.9	30.2
Wheeler	378	70.1	104,300	25.9	10.7	529	13.9	2.1	562	-3.6	14	2.5	494	32.2	38.9
York	5,623	70.7	128,400	19.8	10.0	647	25.7	0.8	7,309	-0.1	182	2.5	7,132	39.6	25.5
NEVADA	1,052,249	55.4	216,400	22.7	10.0	1,017	29.5	4.5	1,500,377	2.9	68,418	4.6	1,341,358	28.4	18.9
Churchill	9,734	64.3	169,100	21.3	10.0	792	28.5	4.3	11,214	3	436	3.9	9,228	30.3	29.4
Clark	749,858	52.7	212,300	22.9	10.0	1,048	30	4.6	1,098,114	2.7	52,643	4.8	982,033	27.2	17.5
Douglas	20,376	69.4	311,400	25.1	10.8	1,094	28.2	2.2	22,882	1.7	993	4.3	20,744	36.1	18.7
Elko	17,882	70.6	198,100	18.1	10.0	904	23.1	3.9	27,148	0.7	888	3.3	26,482	25.8	33.2
Esmeralda	494	54.5	73,500	14.7	12.1	497	22	4	433	-12.7	21	4.8	449	31.0	43.9
Eureka	765	69.0	83,100	15.3	10.0	695	25.4	2.9	1,064	1.3	29	2.7	904	30.6	38.1
Humboldt	6,261	76.9	163,500	18.2	10.0	832	23.5	3.8	8,170	-1.9	276	3.4	8,394	22.5	40.3
Lander	2,183	81.4	151,900	16.4	10.0	625	22	4.5	3,151	0	117	3.7	2,683	22.1	47.9
Lincoln	1,930	69.2	132,900	20.4	10.0	592	18	2	2,088	1.6	93	4.5	1,793	37.1	19.3
Lyon	20,127	70.8	158,000	23.5	10.6	919	26.6	2.8	22,467	1.3	1,212	5.4	20,991	25.1	30.7
Mineral	1,859	65.1	90,900	17.8	10.0	518	21.3	9.4	1,929	-1.1	106	5.5	1,685	23.8	32.2
Nye	18,077	69.3	125,100	22.5	11.3	792	27.9	4	16,801	2.8	960	5.7	14,551	24.3	28.5
Pershing	2,018	70.1	101,100	20.9	10.0	648	22.9	6.8	2,586	-1.3	106	4.1	2,211	35.1	33.5
Storey	1,665	82.9	187,100	21.3	10.1	747	21.5	0	2,005	4.7	89	4.4	1,768	30.3	17.9
Washoe	173,519	57.7	268,100	22.8	10.0	947	28.8	4.8	250,005	4.8	9,064	3.6	219,548	33.8	19.5
White Pine	3,343	76.3	130,600	17.9	10.0	696	22.4	3.7	4,604	1.3	170	3.7	3,567	34.1	25.1
Carson City	22,158	55.0	217,400	23.6	11.5	868	27.9	4.4	25,718	1.4	1,216	4.7	24,327	30.3	23.7
NEW HAMPSHIRE	526,710	70.7	244,900	23.1	15.3	1,052	28.8	1.9	761,752	1	19,240	2.5	713,424	40.3	19.9
Belknap	24,579	75.8	220,400	23.6	15.9	933	28.9	1.6	31,291	0.6	788	2.5	30,674	37.5	21.1
Carroll	21,203	79.6	227,600	23.7	14.4	920	30	2.4	23,607	0.2	598	2.5	23,324	32.5	22.6
Cheshire	30,529	70.3	188,700	23.6	16.9	934	29.8	2.1	41,020	0.1	1,030	2.5	40,037	37.4	22.9
Coos	13,879	71.2	123,200	22.1	15.5	711	28.2	1.5	14,606	1	467	3.2	14,728	31.6	23.9
Grafton	34,856	68.3	215,600	23.2	14.9	904	28.8	2.2	49,592	0.6	1,032	2.1	45,847	41.9	19.1
Hillsborough	158,139	65.9	256,300	22.8	14.8	1,132	28.8	2.3	236,915	1.2	6,223	2.6	219,781	41.4	19.0
Merrimack	57,247	70.9	226,700	23.1	15.5	1,007	28.9	1.7	82,759	0.8	1,832	2.2	77,527	39.3	20.2
Rockingham	119,955	76.7	295,900	23.1	15.4	1,164	28.3	1.3	185,379	1.2	5,100	2.8	170,757	43.6	18.3
Strafford	48,543	65.6	220,900	23.1	15.5	1,018	28.8	2.7	73,309	1.1	1,676	2.3	69,103	38.1	20.6
Sullivan	17,780	73.4	171,100	24.4	16.6	893	28.8	1.5	23,272	0.1	493	2.1	21,646	35.0	26.7
NEW JERSEY	3,199,111	64.1	321,100	25.2	17.2	1,249	31.5	3.4	4,422,942	-0.7	183,375	4.1	4,388,024	41.7	17.6
Atlantic	100,660	67.4	219,000	27.9	18.9	1,070	35	3.7	118,969	0.3	7,001	5.9	127,737	31.0	16.6
Bergen	337,819	64.6	451,200	26.1	18.0	1,419	29.7	2.4	472,001	-0.7	16,228	3.4	473,672	47.9	14.3
Burlington	164,404	76.4	245,300	23.9	15.9	1,263	30.3	1.6	227,445	-1.2	8,568	3.8	223,990	43.8	16.3
Camden	187,012	66.8	193,500	24.4	17.8	1,018	32.2	2.2	249,945	-1.3	11,588	4.6	248,241	39.3	17.6
Cape May	39,861	77.5	295,500	26.6	17.6	1,086	36.8	1.5	45,785	-0.7	3,840	8.4	42,170	34.6	17.9
Cumberland	50,596	63.7	160,500	24.5	16.3	1,003	37.3	3.9	64,289	-1.5	4,161	6.5	62,714	26.1	30.5
Essex	280,327	44.5	362,300	27.0	18.9	1,107	32.9	4.5	364,346	-0.8	18,851	5.2	371,793	37.9	18.4
Gloucester	104,810	79.6	213,800	23.8	16.9	1,134	33.2	1.4	147,175	-1.3	6,235	4.2	145,749	41.7	18.5
Hudson	252,352	31.4	349,500	21.9	19.8	1,286	29	7.6	357,639	-0.7	13,852	3.9	354,105	39.9	19.5
Hunterdon	46,822	83.7	393,800	23.2	15.3	1,388	31.3	0.8	63,020	-0.7	2,049	3.3	66,382	51.7	12.2

1. Specified owner-occupied units.   2. A value of 10.0 represents 10 percent or less; a value of 50.0 represents 50 percent or more.   3. Specified renter-occupied units.   4. Overcrowded or lacking complete plumbing facilities.   5. Percent of civilian labor force.   6. Civilian employed persons 16 years old and over.

Table B. States and Counties — Nonfarm Employment and Agriculture

	Private nonfarm establishments, employment and payroll, 2016									Agriculture, 2017			
STATE County		Employment						Annual payroll		Farms			Farm producers whose primary occupation is farming (percent)
	Number of establishments	Total	Health care and social assistance	Manufacturing	Retail trade	Finance and insurance	Professional, scientific, and technical services	Total (mil dol)	Average per employee (dollars)	Number	Percent with:		
											Fewer than 50 acres	1000 acres or more	
	104	105	106	107	108	109	110	111	112	113	114	115	116
NEBRASKA— Cont'd													
Platte	1,016	15,936	1,877	4,985	2,257	502	379	624	39,153	836	26.0	12.3	52.7
Polk	151	1,023	236	49	203	53	26	28	27,322	432	18.5	17.8	60.7
Red Willow	415	3,778	629	313	906	235	111	121	32,042	333	34.5	32.7	48.3
Richardson	268	1,877	419	298	296	57	69	54	28,885	708	22.2	15.7	44.0
Rock	53	333	D	D	38	D	D	12	36,787	220	7.7	52.3	70.5
Saline	303	6,005	505	2,958	537	157	47	247	41,126	717	19.1	19.7	52.3
Sarpy	3,598	52,676	5,539	2,613	9,426	1,738	4,096	2,133	40,493	417	60.7	8.4	34.5
Saunders	537	3,993	746	405	625	215	132	132	32,963	1,118	35.1	12.6	42.7
Scotts Bluff	1,082	13,095	2,549	835	2,547	849	339	462	35,261	760	29.7	13.2	48.0
Seward	463	5,669	886	1,097	518	217	126	191	33,604	944	39.4	12.7	40.8
Sheridan	169	951	190	13	226	80	32	26	27,162	525	11.2	45.3	60.0
Sherman	89	561	179	D	129	18	10	16	27,904	384	16.4	22.4	48.2
Sioux	17	32	D	NA	D	D	D	1	36,344	307	8.1	53.7	62.5
Stanton	115	1,967	D	D	89	32	8	115	58,682	571	22.1	12.3	48.9
Thayer	212	1,974	367	D	244	112	34	68	34,644	414	20.3	29.0	54.6
Thomas	23	220	NA	D	9	D	D	7	33,545	90	12.2	63.3	55.6
Thurston	118	1,425	173	241	162	64	D	67	46,744	309	21.7	26.5	59.7
Valley	182	1,306	360	81	298	67	67	41	31,598	362	18.0	29.0	53.1
Washington	591	6,807	885	1,273	1,057	253	217	307	45,041	747	44.4	11.5	41.2
Wayne	241	3,194	499	834	369	330	142	94	29,564	485	22.9	16.1	55.0
Webster	96	638	167	NA	148	40	3	19	30,301	406	16.7	26.1	49.8
Wheeler	24	134	NA	D	D	D	NA	2	16,485	215	10.7	32.6	57.0
York	518	6,381	1,133	847	932	373	126	224	35,152	521	16.3	22.1	61.4
NEVADA	64,815	1,165,298	121,037	43,023	146,445	36,955	59,623	49,208	42,228	3,423	51.7	13.7	50.4
Churchill	479	5,518	776	416	895	145	352	201	36,379	504	59.3	5.4	53.1
Clark	44,564	847,203	86,056	19,629	108,100	26,494	44,256	34,904	41,199	179	77.1	0.6	30.5
Douglas	1,612	16,841	1,492	1,638	2,051	352	751	627	37,256	239	69.5	7.9	41.0
Elko	1,110	20,350	1,560	233	2,564	283	450	1,097	53,906	526	42.0	21.3	49.1
Esmeralda	12	201	NA	D	D	NA	NA	11	53,990	24	37.5	29.2	55.3
Eureka	33	D	D	D	31	D	D	D	D	86	14.0	40.7	65.6
Humboldt	392	5,611	421	240	964	81	65	315	56,128	298	33.9	24.5	59.3
Lander	94	1,413	D	D	210	13	D	90	63,951	117	41.0	21.4	60.3
Lincoln	83	618	124	D	204	31	14	17	28,265	166	36.1	9.6	48.4
Lyon	806	10,218	552	2,213	1,325	143	380	391	38,227	312	56.1	8.7	54.1
Mineral	60	1,009	117	D	85	D	10	44	43,425	59	71.2	1.7	51.2
Nye	662	8,752	755	87	1,634	145	D	378	43,192	211	53.6	12.8	53.3
Pershing	72	1,071	D	D	140	14	14	55	51,226	154	32.5	24.0	55.3
Storey	88	653	D	95	76	NA	19	19	29,505	2	100.0	NA	100.0
Washoe	12,170	186,628	24,429	15,585	24,137	5,947	10,164	8,172	43,786	353	69.7	7.4	43.3
White Pine	185	2,728	291	16	353	39	22	148	54,148	176	42.0	19.9	46.4
Carson City	1,916	21,862	3,730	2,586	3,523	1,125	1,188	935	42,754	17	70.6	NA	53.3
NEW HAMPSHIRE	37,868	594,243	91,765	68,645	100,563	28,757	32,287	29,193	49,127	4,123	57.1	0.8	38.6
Belknap	1,805	21,310	3,969	2,704	5,085	627	627	899	42,168	256	50.8	0.4	41.5
Carroll	1,877	16,502	2,534	807	3,764	382	524	574	34,761	285	51.6	1.1	41.5
Cheshire	1,899	27,234	3,701	4,498	5,750	1,346	628	1,119	41,077	420	49.8	0.7	32.1
Coos	853	9,053	2,137	633	1,852	257	124	308	33,987	272	40.4	2.2	36.8
Grafton	2,845	49,080	11,637	5,203	7,506	887	1,626	2,489	50,710	462	39.8	1.7	42.5
Hillsborough	10,944	184,677	30,117	26,458	29,088	9,189	11,802	10,001	54,153	605	63.3	0.2	42.0
Merrimack	4,050	64,576	12,558	5,644	10,454	3,404	2,802	2,924	45,283	545	58.9	0.6	38.5
Rockingham	9,667	139,449	16,380	14,537	28,176	7,030	10,065	6,886	49,381	618	73.6	0.2	42.6
Strafford	2,620	38,715	7,316	5,240	6,442	3,647	1,312	1,776	45,864	310	65.5	0.3	32.1
Sullivan	915	11,804	1,249	2,921	2,431	430	202	493	41,742	350	61.1	1.1	32.7
NEW JERSEY	231,974	3,636,293	584,649	218,742	464,603	198,374	328,347	214,758	59,060	9,883	75.2	1.1	39.6
Atlantic	6,302	105,922	19,072	1,800	15,978	2,377	4,368	4,072	38,442	450	75.3	0.9	52.1
Bergen	31,645	437,598	74,952	29,407	59,519	15,805	35,178	25,995	59,404	74	98.6	NA	50.4
Burlington	10,440	182,219	27,533	14,104	25,043	19,076	12,808	9,495	52,110	915	72.3	2.0	47.3
Camden	11,417	178,732	41,541	12,134	24,605	4,828	14,919	8,756	48,987	197	81.2	NA	38.8
Cape May	3,841	27,491	4,326	577	7,032	1,104	976	1,073	39,031	164	73.8	NA	48.5
Cumberland	2,815	46,097	9,750	7,815	7,412	1,071	1,005	1,818	39,439	560	63.6	2.0	48.0
Essex	18,763	289,030	55,798	18,994	26,939	19,919	22,356	17,434	60,320	22	100.0	NA	28.9
Gloucester	5,958	93,340	15,080	8,037	17,466	1,799	3,718	3,885	41,622	580	72.6	1.2	46.5
Hudson	13,389	219,848	28,683	8,101	26,679	35,922	12,358	15,385	69,982	4	100.0	NA	50.0
Hunterdon	3,769	43,742	7,155	3,535	7,035	3,137	5,190	2,781	63,586	1,604	75.3	0.7	34.7

Table B. States and Counties — **Agriculture**

STATE County	Land in farms Acreage (1,000)	Percent change, 2012-2017	Acres Average size of farm	Acres Total irrigated (1,000)	Acres Total cropland (1,000)	Value of land and buildings (dollars) Average per farm	Value of land and buildings (dollars) Average per acre	Value of machinery and equipment, average per farm (dollars)	Value of products sold: Total (mil dol)	Value of products sold: Average per farm (acres)	Percent from: Crops	Percent from: Livestock and poultry products	Organic farms (number)	Farms with internet access (percent)	Government payments Total ($1,000)	Government payments Percent of farms
	117	118	119	120	121	122	123	124	125	126	127	128	129	130	131	132
NEBRASKA— Cont'd																
Platte	384	-10.0	459	191.8	336.4	2,903,960	6,328	345,260	688.6	823,639	27.8	72.2	6	79.7	12,585	75.1
Polk	251	2.3	581	164.2	225.0	3,434,576	5,911	369,062	330.7	765,505	39.4	60.6	1	85.6	7,235	83.1
Red Willow	439	4.7	1,319	52.7	248.2	2,568,525	1,947	307,287	188.2	565,150	38.2	61.8	NA	82.6	4,049	57.1
Richardson	342	7.1	483	11.2	272.4	2,061,048	4,267	202,966	149.3	210,944	78.5	21.5	3	79.4	8,915	75.3
Rock	584	-9.4	2,655	35.2	121.4	3,019,965	1,138	221,861	108.1	491,364	20.6	79.4	1	87.3	1,581	41.4
Saline	360	-0.4	503	135.7	305.0	2,370,146	4,716	285,163	206.9	288,576	69.9	30.1	1	77.3	9,762	80.6
Sarpy	99	8.5	239	11.5	93.0	1,774,545	7,439	127,332	54.9	131,707	91.8	8.2	9	83.2	1,930	47.0
Saunders	480	2.2	429	135.6	436.2	2,420,851	5,641	235,724	360.5	322,419	62.6	37.4	7	79.2	12,010	68.5
Scotts Bluff	442	-0.8	581	170.7	218.1	1,184,110	2,038	231,435	322.7	424,641	30.6	69.4	3	84.1	5,405	54.2
Seward	363	2.4	385	138.7	310.5	2,198,064	5,710	252,569	251.0	265,841	61.5	38.5	NA	79.3	10,627	71.6
Sheridan	1,562	1.8	2,974	74.1	301.5	2,884,505	970	210,422	150.6	286,863	38.2	61.8	2	80.8	5,522	62.9
Sherman	311	10.5	809	93.3	159.0	2,165,691	2,676	223,342	139.3	362,885	58.1	41.9	NA	82.0	3,109	62.5
Sioux	1,230	0.4	4,006	41.8	97.6	3,607,478	901	175,807	133.3	434,283	13.2	86.8	NA	86.3	2,690	49.8
Stanton	266	4.6	466	34.5	203.7	2,327,041	4,991	214,703	208.4	364,956	45.4	54.6	2	79.3	7,411	79.5
Thayer	326	-0.2	787	128.4	251.0	3,083,516	3,920	360,804	227.7	550,041	56.5	43.5	2	77.5	8,364	79.0
Thomas	388	5.6	4,313	2.6	7.4	3,364,667	780	159,890	24.4	271,067	8.3	91.7	NA	94.4	D	20.0
Thurston	232	-6.3	751	14.9	206.8	3,625,111	4,827	377,357	207.3	670,731	49.1	50.9	1	76.7	6,000	79.3
Valley	351	0.4	969	111.3	172.6	2,788,775	2,878	303,059	223.9	618,483	34.7	65.3	4	82.6	4,664	68.8
Washington	248	-0.1	332	22.4	215.9	2,163,878	6,519	197,031	150.4	201,325	71.8	28.2	1	86.7	2,839	58.0
Wayne	281	0.5	580	61.6	253.6	3,196,693	5,512	310,983	223.8	461,466	57.7	42.3	1	85.8	8,593	70.9
Webster	329	8.8	810	68.1	206.2	2,219,552	2,739	254,116	347.9	856,778	22.3	77.7	2	78.3	5,547	71.9
Wheeler	357	0.0	1,662	36.9	87.8	2,539,799	1,528	258,222	283.1	1,316,963	7.4	92.6	2	88.4	2,418	54.9
York	347	2.1	665	275.4	327.3	4,575,694	6,878	498,031	340.9	654,309	59.8	40.2	NA	84.6	14,518	77.2
NEVADA	6,128	3.6	1,790	790.4	794.7	1,627,858	909	155,033	665.8	194,495	41.5	58.5	51	82.9	5,049	9.1
Churchill	250	26.7	496	45.0	47.4	949,440	1,915	106,008	90.7	179,938	21.9	78.1	3	85.1	427	11.9
Clark	D	D	D	3.7	4.0	1,439,603	3,109	76,922	12.7	70,676	90.2	9.8	1	74.9	16	2.2
Douglas	118	17.2	495	34.7	22.0	1,017,364	2,055	108,770	23.5	98,464	25.6	74.4	NA	89.5	130	4.6
Elko	2,180	2.5	4,145	199.9	215.0	2,276,052	549	136,223	72.2	137,213	15.4	84.6	1	85.0	351	3.6
Esmeralda	D	D	D	15.0	14.4	2,138,151	2,083	517,623	12.0	498,083	96.2	3.8	NA	83.3	98	45.8
Eureka	579	-9.4	6,729	50.4	59.8	3,362,856	500	423,423	40.4	470,128	73.2	26.8	1	84.9	1,066	11.6
Humboldt	990	22.4	3,323	162.6	158.3	2,945,636	887	309,287	105.7	354,534	71.2	28.8	5	89.6	747	19.5
Lander	329	4.9	2,815	37.7	46.7	2,951,893	1,049	227,081	31.8	272,043	67.1	32.9	7	74.4	144	12.8
Lincoln	66	D	399	24.2	20.6	1,028,189	2,576	237,470	22.0	132,404	58.6	41.4	2	73.5	10	3.0
Lyon	181	-50.5	581	55.8	65.1	1,328,718	2,286	147,374	102.7	329,179	28.3	71.7	13	85.3	839	9.9
Mineral	D	D	D	2.0	2.2	1,168,722	293	66,181	D	D	D	D	NA	57.6	150	27.1
Nye	93	43.4	442	21.9	22.4	766,261	1,732	128,095	65.0	307,924	8.0	92.0	3	71.6	30	1.9
Pershing	330	10.4	2,145	42.0	56.8	1,717,125	801	189,476	33.8	219,610	58.3	41.7	NA	83.8	689	26.0
Storey	D	D	D	NA	NA	D	D	D	D	D	NA	D	NA	100.0	NA	NA
Washoe	501	13.2	1,420	43.6	22.2	1,457,532	1,026	62,049	19.9	56,484	45.8	54.2	14	86.4	174	5.1
White Pine	165	-14.5	939	51.5	37.2	1,245,500	1,326	168,506	30.0	170,682	38.8	61.2	NA	79.5	177	5.7
Carson City	1	D	57	0.4	0.6	D	D	D	D	D	D	D	1	100.0	NA	NA
NEW HAMPSHIRE	425	-10.3	103	2.2	108.0	539,732	5,231	68,629	187.8	45,548	57.4	42.6	156	87.2	3,494	7.5
Belknap	25	6.4	99	0.1	5.2	487,697	4,914	62,719	7.6	29,754	56.7	43.3	5	85.9	148	9.0
Carroll	32	10.6	114	0.3	4.4	447,525	3,929	47,048	5.5	19,446	67.5	32.5	15	82.8	295	8.4
Cheshire	54	-15.3	128	0.1	10.7	484,018	3,791	72,235	14.6	34,683	47.6	52.4	23	91.7	473	7.6
Coos	47	-17.4	172	0.1	15.4	442,111	2,564	70,608	16.4	60,301	32.5	67.5	9	81.6	420	7.0
Grafton	74	-10.7	159	0.1	16.3	622,137	3,907	74,022	23.4	50,587	30.3	69.7	10	84.6	426	9.5
Hillsborough	44	-7.3	73	0.6	11.7	568,208	7,775	67,925	18.8	31,030	77.2	22.8	18	93.1	281	7.8
Merrimack	54	-16.4	100	0.4	17.5	577,576	5,798	99,615	49.3	90,541	74.1	25.9	29	87.3	492	6.6
Rockingham	32	-10.5	52	0.3	10.3	588,366	11,281	53,046	22.4	36,243	72.6	27.4	21	86.2	621	6.0
Strafford	23	-24.4	75	0.1	5.6	485,607	6,493	53,461	10.5	33,803	61.6	38.4	13	91.3	171	5.8
Sullivan	39	1.2	113	0.1	10.9	540,738	4,792	71,638	19.3	55,146	34.4	65.6	13	81.4	168	8.0
NEW JERSEY	734	2.7	74	86.8	463.0	1,000,464	13,469	86,532	1,098.0	111,095	89.7	10.3	122	80.9	7,503	7.5
Atlantic	29	306.2	64	11.6	17.8	823,031	12,764	135,393	120.7	268,162	98.7	1.3	10	85.3	198	7.8
Bergen	1	-26.6	14	0.1	0.3	1,412,811	99,475	48,545	D	D	100.0	D	1	79.7	D	1.4
Burlington	96	0.4	105	12.4	49.7	1,057,462	10,052	92,669	98.6	107,738	92.4	7.6	6	82.2	828	7.4
Camden	9	26.5	47	2.3	5.0	774,929	16,419	81,602	22.9	116,208	99.6	0.4	5	83.2	D	1.5
Cape May	8	-87.4	50	1.4	3.8	722,281	14,561	59,087	9.8	59,988	89.2	10.8	NA	81.1	D	1.2
Cumberland	66	53.1	118	20.0	49.6	1,159,637	9,801	150,219	212.6	379,730	97.5	2.5	8	77.5	665	9.6
Essex	0	49.2	9	0.0	0.1	733,010	84,431	108,943	D	D	D	100.0	NA	59.1	NA	NA
Gloucester	49	-51.5	85	8.7	35.6	1,079,229	12,676	107,289	102.5	176,645	92.6	7.4	1	78.6	1,196	12.6
Hudson	0	-100.0	7	NA	D	327,000	50,308	35,385	D	D	D	D	NA	100.0	NA	NA
Hunterdon	101	600.6	63	1.8	65.6	986,211	15,617	66,403	92.2	57,510	85.5	14.5	31	82.6	524	5.9

Table B. States and Counties — Water Use, Wholesale Trade, Retail Trade, and Real Estate

STATE County	Water use, 2015		Wholesale Trade[1], 2012				Retail Trade[2], 2012				Real estate and rental and leasing,[2] 2012			
	Public supply water withdrawn (mil gal/day)	Public supply gallons withdrawn per person per day	Number of establishments	Number of employees	Sales (mil dol)	Average payroll (mil dol)	Number of establishments	Number of employees	Sales (mil dol)	Average payroll (mil dol)	Number of establishments	Number of employees	Sales (mil dol)	Average payroll (mil dol)
	133	134	135	136	137	138	139	140	141	142	143	144	145	146
NEBRASKA— Cont'd														
Platte	4.96	151.0	51	543	851.1	26.9	161	2,112	541.2	45.6	38	120	21.7	2.8
Polk	0.39	75.0	8	115	211.9	6.2	24	128	50.2	2.8	1	D	D	D
Red Willow	2.34	216.1	22	246	193.8	12.5	80	929	329.2	21.6	15	37	2.7	0.4
Richardson	0.74	91.4	26	137	473.1	5.0	44	331	94.1	7.2	6	16	1.7	0.5
Rock	0.16	115.9	4	D	D	D	7	44	6.8	0.7	NA	NA	NA	NA
Saline	1.36	95.2	21	175	316.6	9.1	43	536	129.2	11.1	8	18	2.6	0.3
Sarpy	30.65	174.5	183	2,932	4,040.2	161.1	367	7,301	2,926.4	174.8	146	580	163.2	22.0
Saunders	49.56	2,358.2	31	193	235.6	9.0	67	566	161.7	12.3	17	22	1.8	0.4
Scotts Bluff	5.66	156.1	56	D	D	D	178	D	D	D	46	116	19.8	3.0
Seward	1.39	81.2	27	258	528.2	14.1	47	521	105.6	10.7	9	11	2.6	0.3
Sheridan	0.59	113.0	12	206	104.3	4.8	42	236	55.7	3.8	2	D	D	D
Sherman	0.23	74.4	3	32	15.2	1.2	17	134	59.1	3.0	1	D	D	D
Sioux	0.08	63.5	1	D	D	D	3	D	D	D	NA	NA	NA	NA
Stanton	0.36	60.6	3	D	D	D	13	83	17.9	1.4	NA	NA	NA	NA
Thayer	0.81	156.9	25	215	524.6	12.3	31	173	56.1	3.4	3	D	D	D
Thomas	0.11	160.8	1	D	D	D	4	25	8.0	0.4	NA	NA	NA	NA
Thurston	0.60	84.9	8	99	103.3	3.5	24	219	73.0	4.7	4	D	D	D
Valley	1.25	300.9	8	76	225.5	3.3	33	267	116.5	6.0	2	D	D	D
Washington	12.18	601.5	18	D	D	D	56	1,106	747.4	42.4	15	20	2.6	0.5
Wayne	0.87	92.9	12	122	63.4	3.2	40	352	69.6	5.9	7	16	1.2	0.5
Webster	0.39	107.6	13	D	D	D	19	163	29.3	2.4	NA	NA	NA	NA
Wheeler	0.04	53.3	3	D	D	D	2	D	D	D	NA	NA	NA	NA
York	1.87	135.4	37	390	427.0	17.6	70	979	290.2	20.9	19	47	5.6	0.9
NEVADA	558.26	193.1	2,501	27,649	19,841.7	1,516.2	8,135	129,977	38,234.2	3,454.1	3,866	22,412	4,981.2	814.7
Churchill	3.38	139.7	15	78	39.1	2.9	69	966	235.1	23.4	32	113	12.5	2.6
Clark	432.47	204.5	1,630	16,747	11,597.1	958.8	5,712	95,369	27,971.7	2,531.6	2,794	17,855	3,700.3	647.4
Douglas	14.08	295.1	41	341	211.6	18.3	172	1,793	516.6	46.8	126	D	D	D
Elko	12.61	242.8	57	D	D	D	161	2,359	946.5	63.8	41	249	35.0	7.3
Esmeralda	0.11	132.7	1	D	D	D	1	D	D	D	NA	NA	NA	NA
Eureka	0.32	158.7	2	D	D	D	7	29	10.2	0.6	NA	NA	NA	NA
Humboldt	3.68	216.2	18	122	71.4	8.1	78	989	325.3	25.6	9	D	D	D
Lander	1.56	264.3	4	34	38.4	2.2	20	235	52.0	6.0	3	4	0.8	0.1
Lincoln	1.16	230.3	2	D	D	D	16	D	D	D	3	D	D	D
Lyon	9.39	178.6	38	749	206.4	24.6	97	1,188	465.5	29.1	33	D	D	D
Mineral	1.05	234.5	2	D	D	D	15	95	31.3	3.0	NA	NA	NA	NA
Nye	6.29	148.1	9	96	55.4	4.5	117	1,404	397.1	34.1	34	79	7.7	1.8
Pershing	1.27	191.4	2	D	D	D	16	131	48.4	3.3	1	D	D	D
Storey	0.53	132.9	NA	NA	NA	NA	20	41	6.0	0.9	1	D	D	D
Washoe	57.68	129.1	584	8,064	6,401.9	414.6	1,391	21,603	6,167.0	580.0	671	D	D	D
White Pine	1.18	120.3	7	64	33.7	2.2	31	408	111.0	9.6	7	D	D	D
Carson City	11.50	210.9	89	519	276.4	25.2	212	3,139	918.2	92.6	111	304	51.7	9.5
NEW HAMPSHIRE	95.52	71.8	1,543	21,140	18,029.2	1,307.9	6,127	95,660	26,018.2	2,403.6	1,338	7,044	1,593.1	309.7
Belknap	3.12	51.5	50	447	214.2	23.9	342	4,907	1,357.5	127.0	78	420	62.0	12.3
Carroll	3.45	73.0	39	310	99.2	14.5	363	3,558	877.7	88.9	69	237	36.1	8.6
Cheshire	4.12	54.3	59	1,151	637.4	47.0	368	5,839	1,692.5	150.1	60	229	45.1	8.0
Coos	4.20	134.6	21	295	89.3	7.5	182	1,800	566.6	45.2	25	68	11.9	2.5
Grafton	7.57	84.8	78	713	487.9	42.6	519	7,712	2,034.2	199.5	144	454	70.5	15.3
Hillsborough	38.74	95.3	537	6,822	4,749.3	470.5	1,584	26,984	7,724.7	700.9	387	2,697	565.9	123.8
Merrimack	8.26	55.8	148	3,176	2,823.3	162.5	624	10,124	2,819.7	243.0	143	848	319.9	41.4
Rockingham	15.35	50.9	487	6,804	8,203.7	455.3	1,587	26,066	6,764.5	625.5	303	1,286	316.8	55.9
Strafford	8.00	63.1	85	1,037	385.9	58.1	385	6,378	1,619.4	166.9	93	560	78.1	22.7
Sullivan	2.71	63.1	39	385	339.1	26.0	173	2,292	561.2	56.5	36	245	86.7	19.2
NEW JERSEY	1,175.42	131.2	12,760	208,830	288,467.8	14,976.8	31,722	436,299	133,665.7	12,676.0	8,749	53,751	17,327.6	2,813.1
Atlantic	30.20	110.1	188	D	D	D	1,227	16,099	4,292.7	394.9	227	1,383	351.1	52.0
Bergen	127.42	135.8	2,720	36,346	77,906.6	2,730.3	3,807	56,423	20,349.2	2,662.1	1,357	7,550	2,481.5	417.9
Burlington	54.20	120.4	492	10,202	14,927.4	618.5	1,428	23,654	6,868.6	645.4	364	3,340	886.7	201.7
Camden	42.83	83.8	572	8,133	4,906.7	442.3	1,730	23,577	6,445.8	593.9	398	2,660	601.1	116.3
Cape May	13.61	143.7	60	D	D	D	669	5,803	1,639.4	166.2	218	681	148.7	26.0
Cumberland	15.72	100.9	152	3,223	2,422.4	133.6	512	7,201	2,049.0	175.0	120	471	96.2	15.8
Essex	31.22	39.2	987	14,029	13,657.7	913.7	2,710	26,114	9,204.6	720.2	879	5,267	1,258.8	214.8
Gloucester	17.52	60.1	296	7,307	16,524.4	437.2	954	16,728	4,452.9	398.7	171	1,228	256.1	63.9
Hudson	0.00	0.0	757	15,906	26,043.1	1,009.8	2,118	23,126	6,647.6	611.5	636	3,698	1,238.8	199.0
Hunterdon	119.90	955.5	143	1,868	1,030.6	150.0	493	6,561	2,350.0	190.2	104	415	123.8	25.3

1 Merchant wholesalers, except manufacturers' sales branches and offices.   2. Employer establishments.

Table B. States and Counties — Professional Services, Manufacturing, and Accommodation and Food Services

STATE County	Professional, scientific, and technical services, 2012				Manufacturing, 2012				Accommodation and food services, 2012			
	Number of establishments	Number of employees	Sales (mil dol)	Average payroll (mil dol)	Number of establishments	Number of employees	Receipts (mil dol)	Annual payroll (mil dol)	Number of establishments	Number of employees	Receipts (mil dol)	Annual payroll (mil dol)
	147	148	149	150	151	152	153	154	155	156	157	158
NEBRASKA— Cont'd												
Platte	65	465	55.7	23.1	74	5,492	4,438.5	261.6	75	968	40.9	10.5
Polk	12	18	1.9	0.4	6	53	D	1.6	6	37	1.4	0.2
Red Willow	28	123	13.9	4.4	14	293	D	14.3	30	524	21.5	6.0
Richardson	13	63	4.2	1.5	14	193	40.4	7.1	21	193	6.1	1.7
Rock	2	D	D	D	NA	NA	NA	NA	4	15	0.4	0.1
Saline	16	43	4.6	1.2	19	2,654	2,175.0	125.9	27	309	10.6	2.6
Sarpy	297	2,588	354.6	156.8	76	2,699	791.9	139.3	255	4,718	224.7	62.7
Saunders	45	119	15.0	4.9	22	288	104.6	9.5	42	D	D	D
Scotts Bluff	68	D	D	D	39	847	270.7	33.7	100	D	D	D
Seward	29	106	21.4	3.3	20	1,197	576.8	57.3	30	453	18.6	4.4
Sheridan	8	29	3.8	0.7	NA	NA	NA	NA	21	133	4.8	1.3
Sherman	6	13	0.9	0.3	3	10	D	D	8	61	2.5	0.6
Sioux	1	D	D	D	NA	NA	NA	NA	2	D	D	D
Stanton	2	D	D	D	NA	NA	NA	NA	5	60	1.7	0.4
Thayer	9	18	2.3	0.6	11	524	D	15.3	12	115	7.6	1.1
Thomas	1	D	D	D	NA	NA	NA	NA	NA	NA	NA	NA
Thurston	9	D	D	D	6	246	D	10.1	8	65	2.5	0.5
Valley	14	D	D	D	9	74	D	3.2	9	D	D	D
Washington	47	163	20.1	6.5	26	1,134	1,549.7	69.9	52	441	16.1	4.4
Wayne	16	56	10.7	2.7	12	893	217.6	28.6	23	393	11.5	2.5
Webster	2	D	D	D	NA	NA	NA	NA	4	24	0.6	0.2
Wheeler	NA	NA	NA	NA	NA	NA	NA	NA	5	8	0.2	0.1
York	29	122	14.5	4.8	28	777	359.3	34.9	39	710	32.2	8.7
NEVADA	8,102	47,934	7,758.5	2,832.1	1,706	38,123	14,719.1	1,979.3	5,815	296,762	27,481.5	8,555.6
Churchill	43	354	23.4	10.4	18	248	D	12.8	50	586	35.9	9.4
Clark	5,645	35,253	5,825.0	2,128.2	894	17,390	5,673.8	782.0	4,050	250,601	24,283.8	7,612.3
Douglas	238	786	115.6	37.2	74	1,129	713.0	55.1	126	5,326	445.8	125.1
Elko	98	666	123.7	32.7	24	D	D	D	138	5,036	442.7	121.4
Esmeralda	1	D	D	D	NA	NA	NA	NA	1	D	D	D
Eureka	4	D	D	D	NA	NA	NA	NA	5	34	1.5	0.4
Humboldt	19	96	10.3	3.6	13	241	120.0	12.0	62	1,161	84.1	15.7
Lander	1	D	D	D	NA	NA	NA	NA	14	145	6.2	1.6
Lincoln	6	20	2.4	0.6	NA	NA	NA	NA	19	D	D	D
Lyon	62	324	34.8	13.1	81	1,708	729.9	85.9	67	613	31.2	7.9
Mineral	5	22	1.5	0.6	NA	NA	NA	NA	10	D	D	D
Nye	50	155	12.5	4.3	14	60	D	1.7	81	1,401	96.5	22.5
Pershing	2	D	D	D	6	128	D	D	13	113	5.8	1.8
Storey	6	7	0.5	0.2	6	91	17.3	3.1	14	71	9.4	2.4
Washoe	1,619	9,029	1,435.4	539.9	442	13,974	6,427.4	840.4	973	28,138	1,860.8	580.8
White Pine	8	25	2.1	0.9	6	23	D	0.8	33	553	31.2	9.4
Carson City	295	1,180	170.1	60.0	122	2,798	634.0	162.7	159	2,740	133.4	41.2
NEW HAMPSHIRE	3,825	30,159	3,947.8	1,697.5	1,851	66,636	18,895.6	3,923.8	3,606	54,047	2,942.3	890.9
Belknap	147	D	D	D	86	2,483	673.3	117.2	223	2,603	157.9	50.7
Carroll	133	D	D	D	74	1,069	225.8	41.2	313	4,034	247.0	70.6
Cheshire	147	628	69.2	30.0	127	4,719	1,101.6	230.1	172	2,543	128.7	40.0
Coos	37	114	11.3	4.3	37	731	189.3	31.0	111	1,747	81.0	31.2
Grafton	254	1,537	210.1	98.4	115	5,758	1,593.9	300.2	378	5,112	296.7	92.2
Hillsborough	1,335	10,986	1,721.0	737.1	554	25,287	7,450.8	1,732.0	897	14,781	762.2	229.8
Merrimack	433	2,850	402.7	171.8	206	5,548	1,577.3	291.1	307	4,965	238.7	75.2
Rockingham	1,049	8,202	1,109.2	462.4	425	14,055	4,580.4	824.8	853	13,804	810.2	237.3
Strafford	235	1,720	217.6	95.3	137	4,428	924.4	228.1	282	3,676	182.8	52.2
Sullivan	55	180	21.1	9.0	90	2,559	578.8	128.0	70	782	37.1	11.8
NEW JERSEY	29,390	307,549	58,738.2	24,013.0	7,758	230,697	108,855.0	14,094.8	20,127	291,933	19,673.6	5,386.8
Atlantic	579	D	D	D	96	1,730	285.4	72.3	860	46,661	4,008.5	1,282.5
Bergen	4,067	37,178	6,945.7	2,557.1	1,107	33,434	12,577.6	2,133.9	2,331	28,682	2,016.7	518.2
Burlington	1,323	D	D	D	343	15,380	5,496.6	1,046.9	914	14,391	771.4	206.5
Camden	1,444	D	D	D	389	11,340	D	613.9	998	14,598	789.4	210.9
Cape May	214	D	D	D	66	615	98.2	21.5	903	5,888	593.0	160.0
Cumberland	207	D	D	D	162	8,055	2,812.0	351.2	265	3,555	173.7	43.6
Essex	2,213	28,745	6,117.7	2,678.1	720	17,556	5,942.0	921.7	1,550	20,633	1,378.7	368.3
Gloucester	514	D	D	D	235	8,056	12,683.6	440.2	483	7,832	406.6	108.0
Hudson	1,335	11,261	1,961.4	898.8	378	7,865	2,682.9	363.9	1,381	15,540	1,214.5	287.1
Hunterdon	561	4,111	888.9	350.4	141	3,485	1,400.2	198.5	312	3,518	206.3	54.9

Health Care and Social Assistance, Other Services, Nonemployer Businesses, and Residential Construction

STATE County	Health care and social assistance, 2012				Other services, 2012				Nonemployer businesses, 2016		Value of residential construction authorized by building permits, 2018	
	Number of establishments	Number of employees	Receipts (mil dol)	Annual payroll (mil dol)	Number of establishments	Number of employees	Receipts (mil dol)	Annual payroll (mil dol)	Number	Receipts (mil dol)	New construction ($1,000)	Number of housing units
	159	160	161	162	163	164	165	166	167	168	169	170
NEBRASKA— Cont'd												
Platte	82	1,551	179.9	55.9	78	360	26.7	8.4	2,260	99.7	15,656	60
Polk	9	273	17.4	7.2	9	17	2.8	0.5	461	17.9	1,432	7
Red Willow	50	604	60.9	22.5	33	90	10.1	2.4	870	32.6	1,918	3
Richardson	26	D	D	D	22	66	4.8	0.8	581	17.7	0	0
Rock	4	D	D	D	5	7	0.9	0.2	220	10.3	750	6
Saline	26	525	37.9	16.4	26	96	6.2	1.8	870	37.2	6,202	38
Sarpy	302	4,733	387.5	146.4	225	1,219	110.5	30.3	10,528	403.6	266,048	1,242
Saunders	31	672	38.8	17.6	27	D	D	D	1,783	69.4	30,035	137
Scotts Bluff	128	D	D	D	76	D	D	D	2,433	104.8	2,448	14
Seward	36	761	53.7	24.0	38	134	15.4	3.5	1,344	45.9	14,712	64
Sheridan	17	208	12.2	6.4	18	42	3.1	0.6	441	16.2	212	3
Sherman	6	D	D	D	6	11	0.9	0.1	266	11.3	2,325	10
Sioux	1	D	D	D	1	D	D	D	97	2.8	0	0
Stanton	7	D	D	D	4	23	2.7	0.4	478	20.8	1,480	7
Thayer	11	416	25.8	11.1	21	60	16.3	1.4	404	19.9	2,562	11
Thomas	NA	NA	NA	NA	1	D	D	D	99	4.3	429	2
Thurston	9	277	32.6	14.7	8	24	3.2	0.8	288	12.5	810	3
Valley	18	111	5.9	2.5	14	67	6.0	1.3	391	19.1	1,585	6
Washington	40	926	67.4	31.7	41	D	D	D	1,649	71.0	24,880	87
Wayne	24	458	31.7	14.2	20	D	D	D	628	25.6	2,124	15
Webster	9	189	10.7	4.7	5	17	2.1	0.3	271	7.4	80	2
Wheeler	NA	NA	NA	NA	1	D	D	D	94	3.5	0	0
York	41	1,063	79.9	35.5	57	253	20.6	5.0	1,046	42.5	12,444	65
NEVADA	6,308	108,585	13,928.5	5,094.7	3,538	25,386	2,608.9	706.5	220,786	11,200.4	3,400,610	17,645
Churchill	41	714	81.1	30.6	42	171	12.2	3.5	1,236	50.6	15,269	73
Clark	4,426	75,019	9,714.9	3,493.8	2,344	17,926	1,602.8	476.8	167,624	8,150.3	2,246,485	12,044
Douglas	121	1,310	165.9	59.1	69	514	41.2	15.1	5,226	344.9	97,576	235
Elko	125	D	D	D	70	D	D	D	2,429	109.2	25,988	170
Esmeralda	NA	NA	NA	NA	1	D	D	D	64	1.5	NA	NA
Eureka	1	D	D	D	1	D	D	D	119	4.4	NA	NA
Humboldt	37	628	55.0	22.2	36	D	D	D	851	30.4	1,729	12
Lander	9	D	D	D	4	D	D	D	260	6.9	331	2
Lincoln	6	128	7.4	3.3	2	D	D	D	292	7.4	1,996	7
Lyon	38	D	D	D	42	202	20.7	5.3	2,702	123.9	81,807	331
Mineral	6	D	D	D	4	D	D	D	152	4.8	0	0
Nye	61	821	82.6	24.3	49	203	16.8	4.4	2,294	90.9	NA	NA
Pershing	6	107	9.0	3.6	4	D	D	D	194	4.7	131	2
Storey	1	D	D	D	3	D	D	D	307	12.2	1,798	13
Washoe	1,190	D	D	D	728	D	D	D	31,711	1,843.2	864,825	4,437
White Pine	16	301	44.6	16.7	13	D	D	D	475	16.7	2,774	9
Carson City	224	3,744	510.8	182.9	126	660	62.8	19.0	4,850	398.4	59,901	310
NEW HAMPSHIRE	3,578	87,099	9,616.5	4,086.4	2,879	16,603	1,554.9	473.3	105,503	6,044.0	875,243	4,445
Belknap	137	3,536	358.6	148.0	147	626	49.1	13.8	5,647	329.7	41,764	173
Carroll	142	2,693	267.9	100.4	111	432	39.6	11.1	5,612	300.8	92,011	234
Cheshire	157	3,954	334.7	156.5	144	938	77.2	22.6	5,867	304.8	26,059	162
Coos	102	2,469	214.2	91.1	68	377	40.5	12.6	2,231	91.8	11,940	70
Grafton	273	10,236	1,482.4	659.8	207	D	D	D	8,035	436.8	59,912	297
Hillsborough	1,094	28,561	3,089.1	1,339.9	824	5,516	490.3	160.3	28,882	1,698.6	207,436	1,406
Merrimack	410	12,310	1,239.7	550.0	411	1,995	257.0	68.2	11,080	608.7	85,996	348
Rockingham	866	15,640	1,697.7	671.8	676	3,639	335.9	104.1	26,905	1,720.0	254,449	1,160
Strafford	302	6,486	834.3	327.4	204	1,192	111.9	32.9	8,051	408.6	82,449	532
Sullivan	95	1,214	97.8	41.4	87	D	D	D	3,193	144.3	13,226	63
NEW JERSEY	26,935	540,875	60,375.2	24,325.0	18,327	108,216	11,607.8	3,150.1	693,239	40,396.8	4,220,431	27,942
Atlantic	846	17,487	1,969.3	780.4	563	3,588	293.9	85.2	17,231	838.9	131,881	833
Bergen	3,664	70,990	9,303.0	3,642.8	2,423	12,297	1,376.8	366.9	95,446	6,536.3	453,012	2,849
Burlington	1,215	25,242	2,710.6	1,006.5	778	4,560	363.7	118.9	28,443	1,621.8	139,735	1,268
Camden	1,535	38,296	4,238.4	1,821.5	920	5,873	478.1	149.4	30,385	1,600.0	70,833	765
Cape May	278	4,767	443.7	186.8	296	1,237	96.3	32.4	8,248	506.0	214,575	643
Cumberland	417	8,593	872.1	338.7	240	1,253	97.1	27.3	5,987	281.7	7,332	74
Essex	2,534	53,168	6,274.3	2,462.1	1,639	12,502	1,220.6	360.6	66,727	3,551.0	230,233	2,053
Gloucester	689	13,076	1,298.2	541.2	502	2,838	223.8	66.5	16,391	781.7	83,635	640
Hudson	1,412	26,740	2,397.6	1,000.5	1,092	5,024	439.1	125.3	55,682	2,576.8	892,520	4,617
Hunterdon	363	7,216	794.4	323.9	272	1,466	120.6	38.5	12,122	810.8	59,516	621

Table B. States and Counties — **Government Employment and Payroll, and Local Government Finances**

STATE County	Full-time equivalent employees	March payroll (dollars)	March payroll (percent of total) Administration, judicial, and legal	Police and corrections	Fire protection	Highways and transportation	Health and welfare	Natural resources and utilities	Education and libraries	Local government finances, 2012 — General revenue Total (mil dol)	Intergovernmental (mil dol)	Taxes Total (mil dol)	Per capita[1] (dollars) Total	Property
	171	172	173	174	175	176	177	178	179	180	181	182	183	184
NEBRASKA— Cont'd														
Platte	3,477	20,266,212	1.3	2.8	0.3	1.8	0.3	79.5	13.4	163.8	34.4	61.8	1,892	1,373
Polk	420	1,380,326	5.6	2.1	0.0	3.0	15.0	11.8	58.7	37.3	5.7	21.1	3,974	3,451
Red Willow	459	1,542,403	5.5	7.0	2.8	3.6	3.4	14.8	59.2	39.4	13.2	18.3	1,666	1,234
Richardson	419	1,193,885	9.7	4.8	0.6	7.6	0.0	12.0	63.6	30.7	8.7	18.1	2,182	1,949
Rock	140	411,891	13.3	2.7	0.0	6.6	35.8	2.2	35.4	13.0	2.1	4.8	3,482	3,134
Saline	632	2,291,344	7.0	11.3	0.3	4.0	0.9	7.0	67.4	70.4	19.1	28.7	1,969	1,723
Sarpy	5,078	18,211,968	6.6	10.7	1.5	2.7	1.0	2.9	72.0	450.7	142.5	250.1	1,508	1,248
Saunders	810	2,374,236	6.4	9.1	0.3	4.5	15.3	6.0	56.4	83.3	19.9	36.4	1,747	1,563
Scotts Bluff	2,061	7,164,008	4.8	7.4	1.1	2.8	2.5	7.6	73.3	182.1	72.1	64.7	1,751	1,338
Seward	680	2,373,107	7.0	6.7	0.0	6.0	0.7	9.6	68.9	55.3	12.4	35.6	2,103	1,821
Sheridan	512	1,548,088	13.3	3.5	0.0	6.0	29.3	9.8	37.6	40.3	9.6	11.2	2,111	1,872
Sherman	144	428,471	12.6	3.9	0.0	9.3	0.2	2.5	70.1	13.6	4.9	7.3	2,338	2,074
Sioux	56	132,554	19.8	4.1	0.0	17.1	0.0	2.1	56.8	4.9	1.0	3.0	2,305	2,122
Stanton	142	497,786	10.8	7.3	0.0	12.3	0.9	19.3	48.7	13.2	4.4	6.8	1,111	1,047
Thayer	412	1,461,621	5.5	2.0	0.0	5.1	41.8	4.4	38.2	41.8	5.4	16.6	3,236	3,029
Thomas	60	133,894	17.6	0.2	0.0	4.3	2.3	11.2	63.8	4.0	0.7	2.8	4,143	3,988
Thurston	545	1,799,779	5.2	2.2	0.0	2.7	22.5	1.8	65.3	52.7	28.4	8.7	1,244	1,115
Valley	518	1,666,812	3.3	2.5	0.0	3.6	47.1	17.8	25.3	53.3	10.2	13.7	3,233	2,920
Washington	750	2,779,921	6.4	9.0	0.0	4.2	8.1	3.5	68.0	69.7	16.2	43.5	2,146	1,843
Wayne	341	1,199,613	9.9	5.1	0.0	9.4	0.0	6.2	69.3	36.1	12.9	18.5	1,940	1,746
Webster	258	1,370,728	10.8	2.2	0.0	8.5	14.9	37.0	25.2	25.0	5.9	8.3	2,228	1,836
Wheeler	43	129,479	13.7	4.4	0.0	13.0	0.0	0.4	68.2	4.3	0.9	3.2	3,984	3,805
York	557	2,016,974	7.4	11.4	2.9	4.0	1.6	20.2	51.6	58.5	16.3	32.4	2,356	1,736
NEVADA	X	X	X	X	X	X	X	X	X	X	X	X	X	X
Churchill	944	3,773,220	10.4	12.8	0.4	2.3	1.9	7.4	51.3	114.7	52.6	27.8	1,142	921
Clark	51,796	300,546,553	8.1	16.4	5.9	3.4	8.6	10.1	45.3	8,606.7	3,678.4	2,735.1	1,367	869
Douglas	1,543	6,734,261	11.5	13.8	10.6	2.6	1.1	9.0	47.4	190.9	73.5	79.1	1,682	1,414
Elko	1,843	7,360,751	11.7	10.6	2.2	3.0	2.9	4.9	62.8	202.1	112.9	62.5	1,220	871
Esmeralda	82	243,932	21.0	20.4	0.0	9.4	1.5	2.3	37.8	7.7	4.9	1.6	2,030	2,012
Eureka	151	777,513	15.5	14.0	0.0	9.5	5.9	8.6	42.4	52.6	15.1	33.5	16,737	16,592
Humboldt	805	3,278,576	10.2	13.2	0.3	2.8	19.5	2.9	48.7	119.3	53.7	33.6	1,972	1,745
Lander	301	1,258,391	12.7	11.1	0.0	4.5	25.4	3.4	42.8	97.8	10.8	72.9	12,271	11,925
Lincoln	324	1,339,919	8.9	8.4	0.1	6.3	17.9	11.0	44.6	43.9	32.2	5.0	930	812
Lyon	1,568	6,140,208	8.1	8.1	3.5	1.3	1.3	10.4	64.0	160.6	98.5	45.8	892	708
Mineral	326	1,115,225	7.2	7.3	1.2	2.2	44.5	6.8	29.7	44.0	21.3	4.5	977	861
Nye	1,197	5,104,254	15.1	13.0	3.6	2.6	5.5	2.8	53.7	149.5	78.9	54.1	1,259	1,117
Pershing	319	1,109,998	11.6	9.0	0.3	4.2	22.5	5.0	44.3	34.1	14.3	8.8	1,300	1,263
Storey	188	901,189	19.1	15.5	16.1	3.8	0.0	4.0	34.8	29.3	7.0	16.6	4,219	4,028
Washoe	13,423	56,391,305	10.3	14.1	5.5	4.2	4.2	8.5	50.6	1,707.2	748.2	591.5	1,376	997
White Pine	513	2,356,531	8.8	7.1	1.5	3.7	40.7	2.2	32.8	71.2	22.1	18.0	1,791	1,611
Carson City	1,396	6,652,347	9.5	13.4	7.3	4.2	3.5	6.4	53.3	189.1	96.1	54.9	1,001	717
NEW HAMPSHIRE	X	X	X	X	X	X	X	X	X	X	X	X	X	X
Belknap	2,709	10,085,919	5.6	9.4	4.9	3.9	5.2	2.9	67.2	286.0	77.2	174.6	2,894	2,867
Carroll	2,191	7,449,385	6.3	9.2	2.5	4.0	7.7	3.0	65.3	220.7	71.1	131.4	2,763	2,740
Cheshire	3,313	11,134,351	6.0	8.9	2.9	3.9	7.7	4.1	65.0	326.6	110.7	178.9	2,328	2,314
Coos	1,565	5,117,863	3.6	6.6	2.3	4.9	20.1	3.2	58.8	159.6	71.8	67.1	2,091	2,079
Grafton	4,014	15,506,186	5.7	9.6	3.8	4.9	5.6	2.9	66.7	413.3	113.5	253.8	2,845	2,823
Hillsborough	13,991	56,054,764	4.1	10.8	6.0	4.5	3.9	3.8	65.8	1,458.9	470.6	808.2	2,006	1,981
Merrimack	5,875	21,465,982	6.0	10.6	5.3	4.2	7.6	3.1	61.7	555.7	176.5	328.2	2,236	2,219
Rockingham	10,620	43,247,180	4.5	10.2	6.0	2.4	3.9	2.7	68.4	1,174.1	314.0	771.3	2,590	2,568
Strafford	4,327	16,109,116	5.0	11.0	4.3	2.9	5.3	4.6	64.6	465.8	153.2	257.6	2,076	2,027
Sullivan	1,670	6,151,956	5.3	6.7	2.1	4.8	8.2	3.5	67.8	169.0	64.2	91.6	2,126	2,114
NEW JERSEY	X	X	X	X	X	X	X	X	X	X	X	X	X	X
Atlantic	14,001	71,971,044	5.3	13.7	4.7	1.7	5.3	3.8	63.4	1,749.6	507.4	1,016.6	3,691	3,639
Bergen	32,531	187,619,946	3.6	14.1	2.2	2.4	3.4	3.1	69.8	4,811.6	664.9	3,480.7	3,788	3,728
Burlington	17,657	91,624,216	4.0	9.2	2.6	2.9	2.3	3.0	75.0	2,079.2	596.9	1,183.3	2,622	2,584
Camden	20,756	110,518,829	3.6	10.7	3.0	3.5	5.8	2.8	67.4	3,281.1	1,305.1	1,230.4	2,396	2,359
Cape May	5,885	27,086,618	8.8	13.8	3.3	3.6	9.4	7.3	49.4	701.1	152.6	449.5	4,667	4,561
Cumberland	7,697	36,180,326	5.2	9.1	0.8	1.2	4.3	5.3	72.5	886.9	544.0	234.1	1,483	1,435
Essex	27,848	164,987,769	6.6	19.3	7.5	1.4	6.3	6.8	50.7	4,140.4	1,433.6	2,242.3	2,846	2,712
Gloucester	12,453	61,264,381	3.9	10.6	0.6	1.8	6.9	3.4	70.7	1,465.5	472.5	747.5	2,581	2,536
Hudson	18,627	101,485,405	7.4	23.1	8.9	1.9	5.7	4.8	45.5	2,886.1	1,144.0	1,243.6	1,906	1,849
Hunterdon	5,140	25,927,699	5.8	5.6	0.8	4.7	2.2	2.5	77.1	623.8	82.1	477.9	3,762	3,722

1. Based on the resident population estimated as of July 1 of the year shown.

Table B. States and Counties — Local Government Finances, Government Employment, and Income Taxes

STATE County	Local government finances, 2012 (cont.) Direct general expenditure Total (mil dol)	Per capita[1] (dollars)	Percent of total for: Education	Health and hospitals	Police protection	Public welfare	Highways	Debt outstanding Total (mil dol)	Per capita[1] (dollars)	Government employment, 2017 Federal civilian	Federal military	State and local	Individual income tax returns, 2016 Number of returns	Mean adjusted gross income	Mean income tax
	185	186	187	188	189	190	191	192	193	194	195	196	197	198	199
NEBRASKA— Cont'd															
Platte	113.1	3,461	56.1	0.4	3.7	0.6	15.1	2,372.1	72,585	89	114	2,544	16,650	52,674	5,770
Polk	34.4	6,457	55.6	18.0	1.4	0.1	7.2	36.4	6,843	24	18	520	2,560	52,466	5,426
Red Willow	41.1	3,746	48.6	0.9	4.2	0.6	6.1	41.9	3,815	78	36	1,053	4,890	49,803	5,518
Richardson	30.5	3,684	56.0	0.2	3.6	0.5	13.4	14.8	1,787	33	27	605	3,790	46,703	4,616
Rock	12.2	8,902	28.5	45.3	2.3	0.2	9.0	0.5	363	3	5	232	650	34,749	3,835
Saline	69.9	4,800	47.6	15.1	3.0	5.7	7.4	56.7	3,893	61	47	1,417	6,440	49,939	4,521
Sarpy	475.3	2,866	55.1	0.8	7.4	0.2	4.2	984.0	5,933	3,095	6,425	7,033	85,430	68,633	7,936
Saunders	75.5	3,628	42.1	21.4	3.2	0.2	8.3	105.7	5,074	101	72	1,503	10,090	67,668	8,307
Scotts Bluff	188.1	5,089	58.5	0.3	4.2	1.6	3.8	124.2	3,361	157	124	3,170	16,350	48,768	4,985
Seward	66.4	3,923	62.3	0.1	3.8	0.8	11.4	73.7	4,351	50	55	1,072	7,650	63,153	6,934
Sheridan	37.7	7,085	31.7	24.7	2.1	9.8	6.1	9.5	1,782	24	18	597	2,350	36,483	3,289
Sherman	13.4	4,324	49.2	0.3	3.1	0.3	17.7	6.5	2,098	13	11	243	1,450	37,130	3,381
Sioux	4.8	3,666	52.8	0.0	2.8	0.0	23.8	0.0	0	9	4	77	530	28,304	2,904
Stanton	13.6	2,232	42.0	0.7	4.3	0.5	31.8	14.5	2,388	19	21	285	2,730	51,944	5,399
Thayer	43.3	8,429	33.8	38.7	2.7	0.2	7.2	11.5	2,243	28	17	668	2,420	53,238	6,318
Thomas	4.0	5,904	53.0	0.5	3.1	0.0	7.9	0.8	1,214	10	3	92	340	35,153	2,991
Thurston	60.1	8,565	48.8	36.6	1.1	0.1	3.6	70.6	10,050	202	25	1,583	2,740	42,634	4,585
Valley	51.9	12,276	20.8	38.7	0.9	0.1	4.8	58.0	13,716	31	15	573	1,950	34,636	4,244
Washington	65.2	3,221	57.9	0.1	4.7	0.2	11.9	202.8	10,013	47	70	1,334	9,810	74,933	9,292
Wayne	43.1	4,516	51.6	0.3	2.5	0.4	9.5	23.9	2,503	36	29	961	3,770	52,844	5,915
Webster	23.9	6,404	33.4	19.3	2.3	5.0	13.2	9.5	2,548	24	12	305	1,590	41,945	3,512
Wheeler	4.1	5,045	61.1	0.0	2.5	0.0	23.7	0.6	806	3	3	66	400	37,183	3,103
York	55.4	4,034	45.6	2.4	5.0	0.3	13.4	105.0	7,641	57	45	1,119	6,580	55,572	6,249
NEVADA	X	X	X	X	X	X	X	X	X	19,208	18,220	137,834	1,377,430	64,596	9,414
Churchill	117.7	4,831	40.0	0.3	7.9	1.8	3.2	48.9	2,005	594	635	1,292	11,090	48,237	5,176
Clark	9,171.7	4,584	29.1	8.3	9.6	2.7	7.2	21,727.8	10,860	13,093	15,498	88,167	999,150	63,607	9,281
Douglas	187.5	3,990	36.5	0.3	5.7	2.5	2.5	82.9	1,764	84	130	2,219	26,020	78,589	13,036
Elko	209.5	4,091	47.0	0.9	7.2	0.7	5.0	51.6	1,008	350	140	3,537	23,250	66,934	8,169
Esmeralda	8.2	10,566	34.9	3.8	14.2	0.4	10.2	1.0	1,279	5	2	106	380	46,608	4,671
Eureka	40.5	20,245	25.6	2.0	4.9	0.3	18.1	0.0	0	9	5	182	740	60,886	8,080
Humboldt	102.4	6,005	35.6	26.8	6.8	1.0	6.9	5.9	344	156	45	1,373	7,690	59,857	6,968
Lander	42.2	7,095	31.4	24.0	6.2	2.0	4.2	0.0	0	69	15	464	2,450	66,324	8,573
Lincoln	42.9	7,928	28.0	0.6	5.4	1.6	11.1	9.9	1,834	53	13	598	1,660	49,914	4,341
Lyon	173.5	3,380	52.1	0.6	14.8	3.1	4.1	198.7	3,872	72	145	2,127	25,610	46,418	4,605
Mineral	39.6	8,513	17.4	39.2	5.2	0.6	3.6	14.3	3,064	55	13	474	1,940	45,297	4,464
Nye	174.9	4,071	43.6	4.0	14.2	1.5	4.9	134.2	3,123	120	117	1,685	18,510	47,961	4,916
Pershing	35.1	5,199	33.9	28.5	4.8	1.5	1.5	18.6	2,751	15	13	731	1,940	51,810	5,448
Storey	27.2	6,900	26.2	0.0	10.5	0.8	8.2	58.6	14,880	3	11	248	1,950	60,191	7,194
Washoe	1,673.2	3,892	35.9	1.1	6.6	4.3	3.3	4,470.2	10,398	3,730	1,273	24,404	223,790	73,546	11,484
White Pine	67.7	6,746	27.2	38.8	5.4	1.6	6.0	14.1	1,407	165	22	1,146	3,910	54,847	5,956
Carson City	205.0	3,738	48.3	2.1	8.1	1.2	5.3	391.1	7,131	635	143	9,081	27,420	53,397	6,659
NEW HAMPSHIRE	X	X	X	X	X	X	X	X	X	7,631	4,679	82,069	698,570	73,891	10,603
Belknap	273.9	4,541	53.3	0.3	6.3	6.1	4.4	96.2	1,595	138	201	4,077	33,260	65,478	8,867
Carroll	240.5	5,057	57.3	1.0	4.6	7.3	6.0	161.9	3,404	135	160	2,855	26,220	70,408	11,035
Cheshire	326.5	4,248	59.3	0.8	4.3	5.5	5.6	178.9	2,328	166	241	5,168	37,410	62,846	7,927
Coos	150.6	4,691	46.4	1.2	3.9	16.3	6.1	37.2	1,158	402	98	2,638	14,960	44,298	4,336
Grafton	440.6	4,940	56.2	0.8	4.4	4.8	5.7	258.1	2,895	532	280	6,704	44,250	79,639	12,423
Hillsborough	1,496.1	3,713	52.0	0.6	6.1	3.8	4.7	1,157.0	2,872	3,985	1,415	17,455	214,430	73,723	10,442
Merrimack	608.7	4,147	55.4	0.5	5.3	7.4	4.5	341.5	2,327	821	487	16,009	75,740	68,905	9,189
Rockingham	1,129.6	3,793	60.9	0.4	6.4	4.0	3.7	523.7	1,758	1,055	1,239	13,272	168,280	87,511	13,634
Strafford	444.5	3,582	51.7	0.1	5.7	7.3	4.8	294.8	2,375	305	416	11,513	62,640	62,915	7,857
Sullivan	166.1	3,857	51.2	0.5	4.3	11.4	5.9	81.8	1,900	92	142	2,378	21,430	63,544	8,869
NEW JERSEY	X	X	X	X	X	X	X	X	X	49,435	25,011	536,221	4,384,460	84,547	13,331
Atlantic	1,718.6	6,240	52.7	0.6	6.1	2.1	1.7	1,314.6	4,773	2,623	826	19,736	132,660	53,739	6,109
Bergen	4,857.2	5,286	54.3	5.8	7.0	1.3	2.6	3,581.0	3,897	2,582	1,873	46,315	465,350	111,181	20,424
Burlington	2,064.4	4,574	62.3	1.5	4.2	2.2	3.1	2,370.1	5,251	4,953	6,012	24,345	225,050	77,912	10,947
Camden	3,129.5	6,094	51.5	4.2	4.5	3.4	4.0	3,660.4	7,128	2,313	1,042	29,575	245,100	65,281	8,418
Cape May	808.9	8,400	33.8	1.5	5.3	4.4	4.9	673.4	6,992	450	1,224	8,600	49,930	61,696	7,904
Cumberland	880.4	5,580	60.1	2.7	3.8	3.4	2.5	354.4	2,246	621	284	11,921	66,150	47,683	4,692
Essex	4,300.2	5,459	38.9	3.3	8.3	2.9	1.3	3,851.1	4,889	8,921	1,632	61,340	372,130	85,621	14,647
Gloucester	1,410.5	4,871	58.9	0.8	4.6	2.2	1.9	1,385.8	4,785	520	576	19,329	140,720	70,463	8,759
Hudson	2,833.2	4,343	33.2	3.1	8.5	2.8	1.8	3,638.2	5,577	5,677	1,506	36,409	332,760	69,103	10,399
Hunterdon	605.4	4,765	66.0	1.2	3.5	0.8	6.1	565.1	4,448	265	248	7,621	64,920	121,101	21,561

1. Based on the resident population estimated as of July 1 of the year shown.

Table B. States and Counties — Land Area and Population

State / county code	CBSA code[1]	County code[2]	STATE County	Land area[3] (sq. mi)	Total persons 2018	Rank	Per square mile	White	Black	American Indian, Alaska Native	Asian and Pacific Islancer	Percent Hispanic or Latino[4]	Under 5 years	5 to 17 years	18 to 24 years	25 to 34 years	35 to 44 years	45 to 54 years
				1	2	3	4	5	6	7	8	9	10	11	12	13	14	15
			NEW JERSEY— Cont'd															
34021	45,940	2	Mercer..................	224.4	369,811	191	1,648.0	50.3	20.5	0.5	12.6	18.1	5.7	15.6	11.4	12.5	12.7	13.9
34023	35,620	1	Middlesex..................	309.2	829,685	72	2,683.3	43.4	10.3	0.5	25.7	21.6	5.8	16.0	9.3	13.5	13.8	13.7
34025	35,620	1	Monmouth..................	468.2	621,354	108	1,327.1	76.2	7.5	0.4	6.4	11.1	5.0	16.2	8.4	10.8	11.4	14.9
34027	35,620	1	Morris..................	460.6	494,228	142	1,073.0	72.2	3.8	0.3	11.7	13.7	5.0	16.1	8.6	11.0	12.2	15.3
34029	35,620	1	Ocean..................	628.4	601,651	110	957.4	85.4	3.6	0.3	2.4	9.5	7.1	16.9	7.4	11.0	10.0	11.6
34031	35,620	1	Passaic..................	186.0	503,310	140	2,706.0	41.8	10.8	0.4	6.0	42.3	6.7	17.1	9.7	13.5	12.6	13.1
34033	37,980	1	Salem..................	331.8	62,607	841	188.7	75.6	14.7	0.7	1.5	9.5	5.4	16.0	8.1	11.8	11.7	13.6
34035	35,620	1	Somerset..................	301.9	331,164	210	1,096.9	56.9	10.1	0.3	19.4	15.0	5.1	16.8	8.2	11.2	12.8	15.5
34037	35,620	1	Sussex..................	518.7	140,799	461	271.4	87.0	2.6	0.4	2.7	8.6	4.5	15.3	8.1	10.9	11.1	15.7
34039	35,620	1	Union..................	102.8	558,067	122	5,428.7	40.9	21.7	0.4	6.2	32.3	6.3	17.1	8.4	12.8	13.7	14.2
34041	10,900	2	Warren..................	356.5	105,779	572	296.7	82.4	5.4	0.4	3.5	9.7	4.6	15.1	8.5	11.2	11.1	15.2
35000		0	NEW MEXICO	121,311.9	2,095,428	X	17.3	38.5	2.4	9.5	2.2	49.1	5.9	17.1	9.4	13.5	12.0	11.5
35001	10,740	2	Bernalillo..................	1,161.3	678,701	99	584.4	40.1	3.2	4.8	3.5	50.3	5.6	16.2	9.1	14.9	12.9	12.0
35003		9	Catron..................	6,924.2	3,578	2,934	0.5	77.3	1.1	4.3	0.7	18.7	3.1	9.1	5.3	6.4	6.1	7.9
35005	40,740	5	Chaves..................	6,067.2	64,689	822	10.7	39.5	1.7	1.2	1.3	57.2	6.6	19.7	9.6	12.8	11.9	11.2
35006	24,380	6	Cibola..................	4,540.0	26,746	1,538	5.9	20.3	1.3	40.4	0.9	38.4	6.3	17.3	8.9	14.2	12.7	11.3
35007		7	Colfax..................	3,758.0	12,110	2,284	3.2	47.9	0.9	2.1	1.0	49.3	4.8	13.3	6.9	10.8	9.3	11.4
35009	17,580	5	Curry..................	1,405.5	49,437	999	35.2	49.0	6.6	1.4	2.7	42.7	8.1	18.2	12.2	17.2	11.7	9.7
35011		9	De Baca..................	2,323.1	1,781	3,066	0.8	53.8	1.0	2.3	0.4	44.3	4.8	17.6	6.5	8.6	9.8	9.7
35013	29,740	3	Dona Ana..................	3,808.2	217,522	311	57.1	27.8	1.9	1.2	1.5	68.6	6.4	18.1	14.4	13.0	11.0	10.2
35015	16,100	5	Eddy..................	4,176.4	57,900	891	13.9	47.1	1.7	1.5	1.1	49.8	7.4	19.1	8.8	14.3	12.3	11.1
35017	43,500	7	Grant..................	3,961.2	27,346	1,514	6.9	46.7	1.0	1.7	1.1	50.7	5.2	14.7	7.9	9.6	10.1	10.0
35019		7	Guadalupe..................	3,029.8	4,341	2,871	1.4	16.4	1.8	2.1	1.5	79.2	4.9	16.0	8.2	14.9	12.8	10.2
35021		9	Harding	2,125.5	655	3,131	0.3	54.0	0.3	0.6	0.0	45.5	3.8	8.4	5.2	8.2	8.5	8.9
35023		9	Hidalgo..................	3,438.5	4,240	2,884	1.2	40.2	1.4	0.9	0.8	57.7	6.3	16.4	8.3	11.2	8.7	12.2
35025	26,020	5	Lea..................	4,391.5	69,611	774	15.9	35.8	3.8	1.2	0.7	59.4	7.8	22.0	9.7	14.6	12.8	10.9
35027	40,760	7	Lincoln..................	4,831.1	19,556	1,849	4.0	62.0	0.9	3.6	0.8	33.8	4.7	13.7	6.0	9.4	9.5	11.0
35028	31,060	6	Los Alamos..................	109.2	19,101	1,869	174.9	73.0	1.8	1.4	7.3	18.2	5.3	17.0	7.0	12.4	12.3	13.3
35029	19,700	6	Luna..................	2,965.2	23,963	1,644	8.1	29.9	1.3	1.1	1.1	67.6	7.6	18.5	8.9	12.3	9.7	10.2
35031	23,700	5	McKinley..................	5,450.7	72,290	751	13.3	9.8	1.0	75.3	1.3	14.4	7.2	21.6	9.6	15.0	11.4	11.2
35033		9	Mora..................	1,926.2	4,506	2,858	2.3	17.7	0.5	0.8	0.5	81.0	4.6	13.3	6.6	9.2	9.6	11.9
35035	10,460	4	Otero..................	6,612.6	66,781	801	10.1	50.2	4.1	6.9	2.3	38.7	6.9	16.4	10.3	15.3	11.3	10.1
35037		7	Quay..................	2,873.9	8,253	2,572	2.9	50.3	2.0	1.7	1.5	45.9	5.1	16.2	6.3	10.0	10.3	11.5
35039	21,580	4	Rio Arriba..................	5,860.9	39,006	1,205	6.7	13.4	0.6	14.7	0.7	71.2	6.2	17.2	8.0	11.7	10.9	12.1
35041	38,780	7	Roosevelt..................	2,446.1	18,743	1,888	7.7	52.5	2.6	1.8	1.7	42.9	7.1	17.2	17.8	13.1	10.1	10.0
35043	10,740	2	Sandoval..................	3,710.1	145,179	452	39.1	44.7	2.6	13.0	2.2	39.4	5.5	17.7	7.8	12.4	12.6	12.4
35045	22,140	3	San Juan..................	5,517.2	125,043	508	22.7	39.8	1.1	39.8	1.0	20.5	6.7	19.8	8.3	13.8	12.5	11.0
35047	29,780	6	San Miguel..................	4,721.5	27,591	1,510	5.8	18.7	1.8	1.6	1.4	77.5	4.7	13.7	10.2	11.8	10.2	12.0
35049	42,140	3	Santa Fe..................	1,910.1	150,056	443	78.6	44.1	1.1	3.1	1.9	51.1	4.3	13.7	7.3	11.2	11.2	12.4
35051		6	Sierra..................	4,181.2	10,968	2,355	2.6	66.2	1.2	2.8	1.0	30.9	5.0	10.5	5.5	8.5	7.9	10.2
35053		6	Socorro..................	6,646.4	16,735	1,996	2.5	35.1	1.4	12.9	2.3	49.8	5.7	16.7	11.1	11.8	10.4	10.7
35055	45,340	7	Taos..................	2,202.4	32,835	1,361	14.9	36.6	0.7	6.0	1.0	56.9	4.4	13.2	6.6	10.1	11.1	12.3
35057	10,740	2	Torrance..................	3,345.2	15,591	2,065	4.7	51.9	1.9	3.1	1.1	43.8	5.0	15.7	8.2	11.7	11.4	11.9
35059		9	Union..................	3,825.1	4,118	2,893	1.1	53.4	2.3	2.0	1.0	42.6	4.7	14.2	7.1	14.9	13.3	11.3
35061	10,740	2	Valencia..................	1,066.7	76,456	728	71.7	33.3	1.3	4.5	1.0	61.0	5.7	17.8	8.8	12.5	11.5	12.2
36000		0	NEW YORK	47,123.4	19,542,209	X	414.7	56.9	15.5	0.7	9.7	19.2	5.8	15.0	9.2	14.7	12.4	13.1
36001	10,580	2	Albany..................	522.8	307,117	229	587.4	73.9	14.2	0.5	7.8	6.1	5.0	13.4	14.7	13.3	11.5	12.1
36003		7	Allegany..................	1,029.4	46,430	1,042	45.1	95.4	1.8	0.6	1.8	1.7	5.2	15.0	14.7	10.2	10.1	11.4
36005	35,620	1	Bronx..................	42.1	1,432,132	28	34,017.4	9.8	30.0	0.6	4.4	56.4	7.2	17.6	9.9	16.1	12.7	12.5
36007	13,780	2	Broome..................	705.8	191,659	346	271.5	85.4	7.0	0.7	5.4	4.3	5.2	14.1	14.2	11.3	10.3	11.5
36009	36,460	4	Cattaraugus..................	1,308.4	76,840	722	58.7	92.2	2.4	3.9	1.3	2.1	5.6	16.5	9.1	11.0	10.9	12.6
36011	12,180	4	Cayuga..................	691.6	77,145	719	111.5	91.9	5.3	0.8	1.0	3.0	5.0	14.7	8.3	12.6	11.5	13.4
36013	27,460	4	Chautauqua	1,060.2	127,939	498	120.7	88.8	3.3	0.9	1.0	7.8	5.4	14.9	9.8	11.6	10.6	12.4
36015	21,300	3	Chemung..................	407.4	84,254	680	206.8	88.9	8.0	0.7	2.1	3.2	5.6	15.8	8.2	12.4	11.7	12.7
36017		6	Chenango..................	893.6	47,536	1,025	53.2	95.8	1.4	0.9	1.0	2.2	5.4	15.3	7.5	11.3	10.7	13.4
36019	38,460	5	Clinton..................	1,037.8	80,695	701	77.8	91.0	4.6	0.8	1.9	3.0	4.9	13.1	13.0	12.6	11.8	13.2
36021	26,460	6	Columbia..................	634.7	59,916	870	94.4	88.2	5.9	0.6	2.5	4.9	4.2	13.1	6.9	10.8	10.5	14.0
36023	18,660	4	Cortland	498.8	47,823	1,023	95.9	94.1	2.5	0.8	1.7	2.7	5.3	14.0	18.1	11.1	10.3	11.8
36025		6	Delaware..................	1,442.4	44,527	1,087	30.9	92.9	2.2	0.6	1.4	4.0	3.8	12.7	10.0	10.2	9.6	12.6
36027	35,620	1	Dutchess..................	795.6	293,718	233	369.2	72.9	11.6	0.6	4.5	12.5	4.5	14.2	10.7	11.9	11.5	14.3
36029	15,380	1	Erie..................	1,042.7	919,719	59	882.1	76.8	14.1	0.9	4.3	5.7	5.4	14.8	9.2	14.3	11.2	12.7
36031		6	Essex..................	1,794.1	37,300	1,244	20.8	93.4	2.8	0.9	1.2	3.0	3.9	12.4	6.9	11.9	11.2	13.5
36033	31,660	7	Franklin..................	1,629.2	50,293	984	30.9	82.9	6.0	7.9	0.8	3.6	4.8	14.6	9.7	14.2	12.4	13.4
36035	24,100	4	Fulton..................	495.5	53,591	946	108.2	93.7	2.7	0.6	1.1	3.2	5.0	15.1	7.4	12.2	11.6	14.1

1. CBSA = Core Based Statistical Area. See Appendix A for explanation. See Appendix B for list of metropolitan areas with component counties.   2. County type code from the Economic Research Service of USDA Rural-Urban Continuum Codes. See Appendix A for definition.   3. Dry land or land partially or temporarily covered by water.   4. May be of any race.

Table B. States and Counties — Population and Households

STATE County	55 to 64 years	65 to 74 years	75 years and over	Percent female	2000	2010	2000-2010	2010-2018	Births	Deaths	Net Migration	Number	Persons per household	Family house-holds	Female family house-holder[1]	One person
	16	17	18	19	20	21	22	23	24	25	26	27	28	29	30	31
NEW JERSEY— Cont'd																
Mercer	13.1	8.5	6.6	51.1	350,761	367,511	4.8	0.6	34,662	23,990	-8,539	129,546	2.75	67.9	13.6	26.8
Middlesex	13.1	8.6	6.4	50.7	750,162	809,924	8.0	2.4	79,013	48,202	-11,410	283,794	2.84	73.0	11.8	22.7
Monmouth	15.7	10.1	7.5	51.4	615,301	630,374	2.4	-1.4	49,462	44,833	-13,645	232,482	2.67	69.4	10.4	25.7
Morris	14.7	9.4	7.7	50.9	470,212	492,314	4.7	0.4	38,576	30,842	-5,743	180,124	2.72	72.0	8.7	23.6
Ocean	13.5	11.9	10.6	51.7	510,916	576,546	12.8	4.4	68,365	58,750	16,078	223,135	2.61	67.0	9.7	28.7
Passaic	12.7	8.3	6.3	51.2	489,049	501,609	2.6	0.3	57,091	30,192	-25,562	162,440	3.09	73.1	18.3	22.9
Salem	14.9	10.6	8.0	50.9	64,285	66,066	2.8	-5.2	5,601	5,985	-3,096	24,038	2.59	66.6	13.5	27.7
Somerset	14.8	8.6	7.0	51.1	297,490	323,433	8.7	2.4	27,841	19,293	-757	115,970	2.84	72.5	9.2	23.7
Sussex	17.0	10.8	6.5	50.3	144,166	148,909	3.3	-5.4	10,195	9,699	-8,719	53,618	2.64	72.2	8.9	22.5
Union	13.0	8.1	6.3	51.2	522,541	536,567	2.7	4.0	55,999	32,889	-1,511	187,916	2.93	71.7	15.9	24.5
Warren	16.1	10.2	8.0	51.0	102,437	108,645	6.1	-2.6	7,852	7,996	-2,708	41,385	2.54	68.5	9.5	25.8
NEW MEXICO	13.1	10.4	7.1	50.5	1,819,046	2,059,180	13.2	1.8	213,795	142,845	-34,628	770,435	2.65	63.8	13.8	30.3
Bernalillo	13.0	9.8	6.6	50.9	556,678	662,487	19.0	2.4	65,780	44,300	-4,801	263,551	2.53	60.3	13.5	32.6
Catron	20.6	25.2	16.3	47.2	3,543	3,729	5.2	-4.0	159	296	-17	1,433	2.36	60.4	5.2	38.4
Chaves	12.2	9.0	7.0	50.4	61,382	65,648	6.9	-1.5	7,562	5,418	-3,083	23,343	2.72	69.1	16.6	27.7
Cibola	13.2	9.4	6.7	48.9	25,595	27,215	6.3	-1.7	3,042	2,130	-1,388	9,068	2.77	67.7	18.9	27.7
Colfax	16.5	15.6	11.2	49.3	14,189	13,750	-3.1	-11.9	1,033	1,185	-1,507	5,591	2.15	57.0	13.2	35.3
Curry	10.4	7.0	5.6	48.1	45,044	48,376	7.4	2.2	7,428	3,200	-3,238	18,470	2.67	65.6	14.6	28.4
De Baca	15.0	16.1	11.8	50.5	2,240	2,022	-9.7	-11.9	128	227	-146	666	2.99	56.5	8.4	36.8
Dona Ana	11.1	9.1	6.7	50.9	174,682	209,202	19.8	4.0	24,508	12,451	-3,755	76,740	2.72	68.3	15.5	24.5
Eddy	12.5	8.3	6.2	49.7	51,658	53,823	4.2	7.6	6,840	4,555	1,775	21,273	2.64	70.6	13.0	24.0
Grant	14.7	16.1	11.7	50.9	31,002	29,510	-4.8	-7.3	2,516	2,792	-1,876	11,879	2.33	61.1	14.1	32.7
Guadalupe	13.4	9.8	9.8	43.0	4,680	4,686	0.1	-7.4	352	353	-350	1,253	2.98	48.1	11.6	46.7
Harding	19.2	20.0	17.7	48.9	810	695	-14.2	-5.8	41	62	-21	203	2.69	56.7	5.4	41.9
Hidalgo	14.6	12.5	9.8	50.4	5,932	4,898	-17.4	-13.4	454	379	-744	1,761	2.47	66.0	13.7	30.7
Lea	10.8	6.7	4.8	48.6	55,511	64,727	16.6	7.5	9,131	4,356	43	22,029	3.04	74.5	12.0	22.1
Lincoln	17.0	17.1	11.6	51.2	19,411	20,495	5.6	-4.6	1,507	1,675	-775	7,902	2.45	63.3	6.0	32.1
Los Alamos	14.9	10.1	7.7	49.2	18,343	17,950	-2.1	6.4	1,413	994	709	7,525	2.38	66.0	6.0	30.5
Luna	11.7	11.5	9.6	49.7	25,016	25,095	0.3	-4.5	3,215	2,452	-1,893	9,088	2.63	58.9	13.3	36.1
McKinley	11.5	7.3	5.1	51.6	74,798	71,485	-4.4	1.1	9,114	4,829	-3,491	19,764	3.65	69.4	24.8	27.7
Mora	16.1	17.3	11.5	48.9	5,180	4,881	-5.8	-7.7	347	351	-375	1,513	3.04	54.7	4.8	31.0
Otero	12.5	9.6	7.6	48.3	62,298	63,832	2.5	4.6	7,536	4,791	122	23,657	2.61	63.4	12.3	32.2
Quay	15.2	14.7	10.8	51.2	10,155	9,040	-11.0	-8.7	787	972	-613	3,085	2.72	51.6	9.7	47.2
Rio Arriba	14.5	11.3	8.1	51.1	41,190	40,220	-2.4	-3.0	4,388	3,320	-2,286	12,852	3.02	59.3	13.6	35.5
Roosevelt	10.5	7.9	6.4	50.0	18,018	19,840	10.1	-5.5	2,338	1,257	-2,231	7,125	2.54	60.9	12.7	30.8
Sandoval	13.8	11.2	6.5	51.0	89,908	131,620	46.4	10.3	12,136	8,380	9,811	49,265	2.80	70.2	12.6	24.7
San Juan	13.0	8.7	6.2	50.5	113,801	130,045	14.3	-3.8	14,824	8,045	-11,873	41,999	3.01	70.6	16.7	24.8
San Miguel	15.7	12.9	8.8	50.5	30,126	29,379	-2.5	-6.1	2,481	2,295	-2,000	11,041	2.41	51.6	15.2	43.0
Santa Fe	15.6	15.6	8.8	51.5	129,292	144,227	11.6	4.0	10,938	9,193	4,218	61,651	2.34	59.6	11.5	34.0
Sierra	15.8	19.7	16.8	50.0	13,270	11,996	-9.6	-8.6	829	1,959	99	5,400	2.04	51.6	9.4	44.9
Socorro	14.3	11.5	7.8	49.8	18,078	17,861	-1.2	-6.3	1,756	1,426	-1,481	4,698	3.53	53.8	13.1	38.4
Taos	15.9	16.3	10.2	50.8	29,979	32,935	9.9	-0.3	2,502	2,412	-168	12,603	2.55	57.3	12.7	37.5
Torrance	15.4	12.9	7.8	47.0	16,911	16,375	-3.2	-4.8	1,307	1,236	-875	5,598	2.66	62.5	14.4	35.2
Union	13.6	11.2	9.7	44.1	4,174	4,554	9.1	-9.6	330	373	-398	1,424	2.53	57.4	11.7	37.9
Valencia	13.9	10.8	6.9	49.8	66,152	76,582	15.8	-0.2	7,073	5,181	-2,020	26,985	2.76	69.6	14.3	24.7
NEW YORK	13.3	9.3	7.2	51.4	18,976,457	19,378,124	2.1	0.8	1,954,011	1,264,995	-523,216	7,302,710	2.63	63.4	14.3	29.7
Albany	13.2	9.7	7.3	51.6	294,565	304,208	3.3	1.0	25,759	22,159	-527	125,376	2.32	54.4	10.7	35.8
Allegany	14.4	11.1	7.9	49.2	49,927	48,917	-2.0	-5.1	4,089	3,853	-2,747	18,124	2.34	65.2	10.5	29.1
Bronx	11.2	7.1	5.7	52.9	1,332,650	1,384,603	3.9	3.4	175,469	79,404	-49,646	495,356	2.85	65.9	30.4	30.1
Broome	14.3	10.1	8.9	50.8	200,536	200,675	0.1	-4.5	16,752	17,267	-8,551	78,821	2.36	59.3	11.5	32.1
Cattaraugus	15.2	11.2	8.0	50.4	83,955	80,343	-4.3	-4.4	7,343	6,841	-4,022	31,723	2.38	63.0	10.8	30.0
Cayuga	15.5	11.0	8.1	48.8	81,963	80,017	-2.4	-3.6	6,396	6,196	-3,068	31,428	2.36	63.1	12.0	29.7
Chautauqua	15.2	11.1	9.0	50.6	139,750	134,907	-3.5	-5.2	11,373	11,871	-6,506	52,983	2.35	62.3	11.4	31.0
Chemung	14.7	10.6	8.3	50.3	91,070	88,849	-2.4	-5.2	8,067	7,715	-4,950	34,664	2.37	62.5	12.0	30.3
Chenango	16.1	11.7	8.6	49.9	51,401	50,511	-1.7	-5.9	4,261	4,624	-2,615	20,373	2.36	62.4	9.8	28.8
Clinton	14.4	9.9	7.2	48.5	79,894	82,131	2.8	-1.7	6,358	5,788	-2,006	31,680	2.32	63.4	11.1	27.0
Columbia	16.7	13.7	10.1	49.9	63,094	63,057	-0.1	-5.0	4,338	5,488	-1,959	25,470	2.32	62.9	11.6	29.7
Cortland	13.0	9.5	7.0	51.1	48,599	49,294	1.4	-3.0	3,961	3,607	-1,826	17,925	2.50	61.4	9.6	28.8
Delaware	16.7	13.9	10.6	49.5	48,055	47,963	-0.2	-7.2	3,168	4,460	-2,127	19,098	2.28	61.6	10.0	32.4
Dutchess	15.2	9.9	7.7	50.2	280,150	297,462	6.2	-1.3	21,780	20,008	-5,503	107,384	2.58	67.1	10.8	26.8
Erie	14.4	10.0	7.9	51.6	950,265	919,129	-3.3	0.1	82,129	80,224	-693	386,371	2.32	59.4	13.3	33.6
Essex	16.8	13.5	10.0	48.4	38,851	39,363	1.3	-5.2	2,560	3,321	-1,299	15,257	2.32	64.9	10.3	29.9
Franklin	14.1	9.9	6.9	45.0	51,134	51,607	0.9	-2.5	4,099	3,782	-1,656	18,956	2.38	63.8	11.4	29.5
Fulton	15.1	11.3	8.3	50.2	55,073	55,520	0.8	-3.5	4,357	4,971	-1,304	22,535	2.34	64.1	11.5	28.7

1. No spouse present.

Table B. States and Counties — Population, Vital Statistics, Health, and Crime

STATE County	Persons in group quarters, 2018	Daytime Population, 2013-2017 Number	Employment/residence ratio	Births, 2018 Total	Rate[1]	Deaths, 2018 Number	Rate[1]	Persons under 65 with no health insurance, 2016 Number	Percent	Medicare, 2018 Total beneficiaries	Enrolled in Original Medicare	Enrolled in Medicare Advantage	Serious crimes known to police[2], 2016 Total Number	Rate[3]
	32	33	34	35	36	37	38	39	40	41	42	43	44	45
NEW JERSEY— Cont'd														
Mercer	20,371	427,464	1.30	4,198	11.4	3,018	8.2	26,707	8.9	64,746	45,186	19,560	8,075	2,181
Middlesex	23,360	824,392	0.97	9,038	10.9	6,328	7.6	60,638	8.7	133,123	102,146	30,977	11,774	1,397
Monmouth	6,782	587,882	0.87	5,834	9.4	5,860	9.4	38,177	7.4	122,154	99,924	22,230	9,572	1,531
Morris	8,565	537,060	1.15	4,557	9.2	3,865	7.8	23,232	5.6	88,261	73,225	15,036	4,366	876
Ocean	6,880	522,412	0.73	8,426	14.0	7,153	11.9	34,389	7.5	150,903	114,997	35,906	7,686	1,307
Passaic	10,232	463,101	0.80	6,626	13.2	3,866	7.7	57,808	13.5	82,265	58,311	23,954	10,277	2,015
Salem	1,258	58,406	0.81	630	10.1	748	11.9	4,069	7.9	14,062	11,774	2,288	1,224	1,927
Somerset	5,281	351,466	1.11	3,185	9.6	2,613	7.9	16,720	5.9	54,691	44,643	10,048	3,775	1,131
Sussex	1,694	114,414	0.61	1,168	8.3	1,259	8.9	6,875	5.8	28,479	24,266	4,213	1,243	876
Union	6,560	527,185	0.89	6,589	11.8	4,264	7.6	57,638	12.1	85,708	60,796	24,912	11,888	2,136
Warren	1,975	90,768	0.70	942	8.9	970	9.2	7,008	8.0	21,780	18,098	3,682	1,282	1,210
NEW MEXICO	42,923	2,080,787	1.00	23,803	11.4	18,198	8.7	189,965	11.2	409,451	267,560	141,891	96,550	4,640
Bernalillo	11,913	704,368	1.09	7,319	10.8	5,897	8.7	54,217	9.6	124,626	61,727	62,899	49,115	7,261
Catron	106	3,556	1.01	14	3.9	26	7.3	193	8.9	1,382	1,149	233	24	708
Chaves	1,782	63,170	0.91	850	13.1	656	10.1	6,608	12.3	11,903	10,023	1,880	2,749	4,197
Cibola	2,565	26,569	0.95	305	11.4	273	10.2	2,599	12.4	4,717	3,677	1,040	557	2,046
Colfax	408	12,662	1.03	107	8.8	127	10.5	836	9.4	3,546	2,865	681	297	2,646
Curry	1,492	51,684	1.06	824	16.7	381	7.7	4,426	10.3	7,282	6,469	813	2,790	5,527
De Baca	9	2,022	1.01	13	7.3	25	14.0	212	16.0	537	513	24	33	1,849
Dona Ana	4,394	206,971	0.92	2,750	12.6	1,614	7.4	22,842	12.9	39,562	24,687	14,875	6,551	3,058
Eddy	995	60,254	1.13	799	13.8	537	9.3	4,000	8.1	9,700	9,341	359	2,308	3,972
Grant	588	28,624	1.02	271	9.9	320	11.7	1,594	7.8	8,383	6,129	2,254	NA	NA
Guadalupe	573	4,471	1.03	45	10.4	48	11.1	261	8.9	999	898	101	88	2,051
Harding	0	605	1.30	4	6.1	5	7.6	42	9.2	202	186	16	NA	NA
Hidalgo	64	4,632	1.11	52	12.3	48	11.3	362	10.8	1,095	747	348	54	1,249
Lea	2,067	70,843	1.05	1,014	14.6	497	7.1	7,289	12.1	8,950	8,693	257	2,992	4,140
Lincoln	116	19,311	0.97	168	8.6	205	10.5	1,798	13.0	5,899	4,671	1,228	576	3,010
Los Alamos	94	25,302	1.80	183	9.6	101	5.3	474	3.2	3,358	3,073	285	NA	NA
Luna	550	24,489	1.02	372	15.5	277	11.6	2,587	13.8	6,400	3,774	2,626	996	4,099
McKinley	775	73,260	1.02	878	12.1	625	8.6	10,861	16.5	10,727	9,627	1,100	2,404	3,105
Mora	8	4,083	0.58	37	8.2	32	7.1	357	10.6	1,443	1,300	143	30	663
Otero	2,321	64,411	0.97	952	14.3	585	8.8	6,252	11.9	12,625	9,757	2,868	1,583	2,470
Quay	22	8,458	1.00	80	9.7	103	12.5	560	8.9	2,537	2,372	165	108	1,301
Rio Arriba	425	36,417	0.78	442	11.3	443	11.4	3,920	12.0	9,185	6,144	3,041	840	2,146
Roosevelt	1,078	17,966	0.83	254	13.6	157	8.4	1,830	11.9	2,989	2,714	275	NA	NA
Sandoval	761	116,648	0.62	1,440	9.9	1,118	7.7	11,780	10.0	28,970	15,498	13,472	3,278	2,337
San Juan	1,743	127,918	0.99	1,543	12.3	1,078	8.6	13,546	14.0	20,476	18,531	1,945	3,995	3,441
San Miguel	1,299	27,428	0.92	252	9.1	285	10.3	2,009	9.4	6,681	4,693	1,988	NA	NA
Santa Fe	2,632	149,201	1.02	1,243	8.3	1,158	7.7	14,723	13.0	37,993	25,642	12,351	4,717	3,167
Sierra	265	11,548	1.08	100	9.1	233	21.2	730	10.3	4,332	2,826	1,506	341	3,074
Socorro	581	16,549	0.91	189	11.3	155	9.3	1,635	12.2	3,657	2,598	1,059	743	4,351
Taos	470	32,802	1.00	287	8.7	324	9.9	3,307	13.4	9,316	6,895	2,421	693	2,115
Torrance	612	14,200	0.75	162	10.4	148	9.5	1,253	10.8	3,473	1,899	1,574	361	2,367
Union	666	4,171	0.97	37	9.0	34	8.3	270	9.9	951	910	41	36	874
Valencia	1,549	66,194	0.66	817	10.7	683	8.9	6,592	10.7	15,557	7,533	8,024	3,283	4,365
NEW YORK	572,948	20,179,743	1.04	227,099	11.6	165,728	8.5	1,151,995	7.1	3,555,595	2,116,595	1,439,000	379,466	1,922
Albany	17,576	376,514	1.44	2,990	9.7	2,787	9.1	10,741	4.4	59,582	32,686	26,896	8,765	2,842
Allegany	4,266	44,265	0.84	474	10.2	465	10.0	1,936	5.6	10,276	6,290	3,986	570	1,243
Bronx	44,498	1,260,654	0.66	20,331	14.2	11,267	7.9	116,497	9.4	204,150	85,425	118,725	(4)	(4)
Broome	10,915	201,716	1.07	1,923	10.0	2,119	11.1	8,158	5.4	44,140	25,666	18,474	5,403	2,789
Cattaraugus	2,598	74,865	0.90	782	10.2	858	11.2	4,441	7.2	17,877	9,415	8,462	1,275	1,678
Cayuga	3,850	70,476	0.78	751	9.7	704	9.1	3,361	5.5	16,061	10,394	5,667	1,423	1,837
Chautauqua	6,071	130,601	1.00	1,281	10.0	1,417	11.1	5,619	5.6	30,516	16,382	14,134	3,312	2,565
Chemung	3,945	87,811	1.03	905	10.7	942	11.2	3,076	4.6	19,738	11,763	7,975	2,064	2,397
Chenango	753	46,652	0.90	500	10.5	546	11.5	1,985	5.1	11,761	7,035	4,726	965	2,001
Clinton	6,636	80,940	0.99	774	9.6	729	9.0	3,798	6.1	18,254	13,922	4,332	1,389	1,724
Columbia	1,962	57,092	0.85	477	8.0	661	11.0	2,991	6.4	15,204	10,315	4,889	801	1,317
Cortland	3,820	47,435	0.96	499	10.4	421	8.8	1,702	4.6	9,222	6,431	2,791	820	1,708
Delaware	2,410	45,810	0.99	322	7.2	567	12.7	2,160	6.5	11,168	7,646	3,522	671	1,504
Dutchess	19,657	272,990	0.84	2,503	8.5	2,726	9.3	12,198	5.3	58,570	45,597	12,973	4,092	1,401
Erie	27,667	953,974	1.07	9,758	10.6	9,837	10.7	33,803	4.5	195,505	77,651	117,854	25,757	2,808
Essex	2,098	37,590	0.96	296	7.9	413	11.1	1,491	5.3	9,276	6,890	2,386	417	1,095
Franklin	6,186	51,489	1.02	480	9.5	523	10.4	2,434	6.6	10,954	8,083	2,871	683	1,362
Fulton	1,433	48,297	0.76	490	9.1	574	10.7	2,528	5.9	12,929	6,438	6,491	1,182	2,216

1. Per 1,000 estimated resident population.   2. Data for serious crimes have not been adjusted for underreporting; this may affect comparability between geographic areas and over time.   3. Per 100,000 population estimated by the FBI.   4. Bronx, Kings, Queens, and Richmond counties are included with New York county.

Table B. States and Counties — Crime, Education, Money Income, and Poverty

STATE County	Serious crimes known to police², 2016 (cont.)¹ Rate Violent	Property	Education School enrollment and attainment, 2013-2017 Enrollment³ Total	Percent private	Attainment⁴ (percent) High school graduate or less	Bachelor's degree or more	Local government expenditures,⁵ 2014-2015 Total current spending (mil dol)	Current spending per student (dollars)	Money income, 2013-2017 Per capita income⁶	Median income (dollars)	Households Percent with income of less than $50,000	with income of $200,000 or more	Income and poverty, 2017 Median household income (dollars)	Percent below poverty level All persons	Children under 18 years	Children 5 to 17 years in families
	46	47	48	49	50	51	52	53	54	55	56	57	58	59	60	61
NEW JERSEY— Cont'd																
Mercer	402	1,779	100,554	24.1	36.8	41.5	1,104.2	18,651	40,064	77,027	33.5	13.7	78,161	11.4	15.1	14.0
Middlesex	140	1,257	221,335	13.9	36.5	42.0	2,075.5	16,718	36,558	83,133	29.8	11.3	85,187	8.5	11.0	10.9
Monmouth	156	1,375	159,733	20.7	31.9	44.0	1,817.6	18,143	46,736	91,807	28.3	16.2	97,627	7.3	9.3	8.7
Morris	65	811	125,804	21.2	27.1	52.6	1,410.4	18,334	53,491	107,034	21.1	21.0	114,269	4.9	5.1	4.8
Ocean	97	1,210	143,982	34.3	43.2	28.4	1,195.8	16,804	33,312	65,771	38.6	6.2	70,493	10.2	15.7	15.1
Passaic	368	1,647	135,428	14.5	51.6	27.0	1,553.6	18,566	29,393	63,339	41.4	7.7	63,127	16.5	24.4	23.6
Salem	271	1,657	14,455	10.9	50.9	21.0	201.5	17,934	31,681	63,934	40.4	4.7	61,322	13.3	21.7	18.5
Somerset	68	1,063	84,370	19.2	26.8	53.1	953.7	17,635	51,923	106,046	21.9	21.6	111,838	5.3	5.5	5.1
Sussex	56	819	34,390	17.2	37.0	34.4	431.2	19,932	41,272	89,238	25.4	10.4	89,744	5.3	6.2	5.8
Union	336	1,800	142,235	15.0	43.3	34.1	1,681.0	17,922	38,163	73,376	35.3	12.3	76,830	9.3	13.4	12.8
Warren	69	1,141	25,194	17.2	40.7	31.7	304.5	17,742	37,001	75,500	32.3	8.5	79,633	7.4	9.7	8.9
NEW MEXICO	702	3,937	549,233	10.0	41.4	26.9	3,303.3	9,705	25,257	46,718	52.8	3.4	47,086	19	25.9	24.6
Bernalillo	1,039	6,222	179,187	13.5	34.7	33.4	918.9	9,044	28,340	50,386	49.6	4.1	51,091	14.6	18.7	17.4
Catron	207	502	415	7.5	43.6	25.8	6.3	24,525	22,487	42,047	64.1	2.6	34,458	21.2	45.4	44.2
Chaves	573	3,625	17,474	12.0	48.9	19.0	109.2	9,094	21,177	42,177	57.9	2.2	43,341	18.9	25.0	22.9
Cibola	511	1,536	6,773	10.1	52.3	12.4	39.4	10,513	17,768	36,089	62.6	0.5	37,753	30.1	37.3	37.0
Colfax	303	2,343	2,311	7.6	44.2	20.5	22.5	13,175	21,785	33,042	65.3	0.4	39,372	19.8	28.8	28.1
Curry	477	5,049	13,924	7.3	43.7	19.9	80.3	8,607	22,628	41,941	57.8	1.7	43,590	18.9	29.1	27.4
De Baca	112	1,737	552	7.4	48.9	10.4	4.7	14,750	24,571	31,439	64.1	1.5	33,095	22	33.9	31.1
Dona Ana	232	2,826	68,704	5.0	43.0	27.4	390.0	9,480	21,050	39,114	60.3	2.6	38,562	26.3	37.5	37.8
Eddy	484	3,489	13,536	4.8	51.9	16.2	105.8	9,546	28,419	60,703	43.2	4.3	52,932	16.9	21.5	20.4
Grant	NA	NA	6,327	7.9	38.6	27.0	48.5	11,053	23,898	40,470	59.9	1.5	40,684	20.3	30.6	29.5
Guadalupe	326	1,725	968	10.6	61.0	13.1	11.1	14,986	18,086	26,060	75.5	1.3	31,915	22.6	29.4	27.3
Harding	NA	NA	86	7.0	45.3	24.0	3.4	34,260	30,782	35,096	68.5	6.9	35,441	15.1	23.9	26.6
Hidalgo	486	763	878	5.6	54.5	14.4	10.2	15,580	18,338	31,829	63.4	0.1	33,557	24.8	36.3	34.8
Lea	378	3,762	18,777	6.2	58.3	13.1	128.3	8,356	24,507	59,285	41.5	4.4	52,358	16.1	21.1	19.2
Lincoln	444	2,566	3,790	8.9	37.7	29.6	31.3	10,793	26,820	42,145	56.9	3.4	47,141	15.8	30.6	28.7
Los Alamos	NA	NA	4,665	12.8	12.1	65.5	40.7	11,609	52,125	110,190	19.5	13.9	118,380	3.7	3.5	3.2
Luna	539	3,560	5,583	7.1	63.6	14.1	56.2	10,292	16,622	27,602	71.7	1.0	30,621	28.3	40.1	41.1
McKinley	634	2,471	20,926	6.2	59.7	10.8	146.7	10,903	14,077	30,336	66.3	1.3	31,746	37.8	45.9	46.2
Mora	111	553	1,202	2.2	48.7	12.7	9.7	18,951	16,019	26,644	74.2	0.7	33,671	22.6	34.1	31.7
Otero	387	2,083	15,909	9.3	44.3	18.3	66.0	9,089	21,876	43,533	58.0	1.0	43,338	18.5	29.4	30.1
Quay	157	1,144	1,850	1.4	55.9	15.4	19.1	13,031	18,220	26,663	73.2	0.6	29,600	23.9	37.5	34.7
Rio Arriba	613	1,533	9,297	7.8	47.5	18.5	65.4	11,967	19,602	33,422	65.9	1.7	36,977	28.9	32.6	30.9
Roosevelt	NA	NA	6,492	2.2	47.4	24.5	37.5	10,872	18,954	35,928	63.6	1.2	37,767	25.7	32.4	32.2
Sandoval	254	2,083	37,161	10.9	34.9	30.1	205.8	9,399	27,406	60,345	41.5	3.9	56,937	15.3	18.6	16.9
San Juan	843	2,598	35,472	8.7	48.0	14.6	244.5	9,975	22,665	49,686	50.3	2.3	46,977	23.1	29.2	26.8
San Miguel	NA	NA	6,986	12.5	47.7	19.6	47.7	12,356	18,012	29,168	71.8	0.9	33,205	29.2	37.3	37.5
Santa Fe	362	2,805	32,307	14.4	33.4	41.4	185.9	9,847	35,801	57,945	43.5	6.7	58,639	12.2	18.6	16.6
Sierra	514	2,560	1,757	7.7	47.1	19.2	16.2	11,652	22,749	29,690	72.3	1.4	30,356	26.6	42.8	41.9
Socorro	515	3,836	5,142	3.9	57.1	19.5	27.1	12,146	17,017	34,008	66.8	1.1	34,880	28.3	40.2	37.7
Taos	366	1,748	7,097	7.8	39.1	27.7	48.3	11,583	23,229	35,314	65.1	1.8	34,980	22.8	32.0	29.9
Torrance	459	1,908	3,373	9.9	48.9	17.7	43.5	10,958	19,129	35,543	64.2	1.2	36,886	26.7	36.4	34.0
Union	146	728	841	8.7	61.6	15.9	9.1	15,972	23,180	38,240	62.9	2.1	38,627	17.6	26.5	25.6
Valencia	905	3,459	19,471	9.3	51.0	16.3	124.1	9,553	20,572	43,428	56.7	1.3	46,155	17.5	24.8	21.7
NEW YORK	376	1,546	4,869,327	23.5	40.2	35.3	56,862.0	20,746	35,752	62,765	41.2	8.9	64,783	14.1	19.9	18.9
Albany	357	2,485	83,298	23.3	32.1	40.5	667.7	16,093	35,278	62,293	40.5	6.3	65,659	11.3	13.2	12.2
Allegany	177	1,066	13,739	23.6	48.4	19.8	135.2	19,474	22,377	45,359	54.8	1.4	46,491	16.3	25.0	22.7
Bronx	(7)	(7)	406,578	16.6	56.1	19.4	(7)	(7)	19,721	36,593	61.4	2.2	37,377	27.9	39.3	38.5
Broome	330	2,459	53,058	8.2	40.9	28.0	497.3	18,068	26,790	49,064	50.7	2.9	47,910	17.5	21.2	18.8
Cattaraugus	184	1,494	18,171	19.4	51.1	18.9	248.9	18,518	23,984	45,571	53.9	1.6	47,875	15.8	23.4	20.0
Cayuga	238	1,599	16,827	16.0	45.0	22.4	169.7	17,527	27,957	54,664	46.1	2.6	55,460	12.6	19.7	18.3
Chautauqua	276	2,289	30,183	8.1	47.1	21.2	345.9	17,162	23,962	44,304	55.5	1.4	45,840	17.7	27.5	26.0
Chemung	200	2,197	19,043	17.1	44.9	25.1	185.7	15,711	27,209	51,251	48.7	3.3	50,562	15.3	23.7	20.9
Chenango	205	1,796	10,270	12.1	51.1	18.6	155.5	19,888	25,233	48,567	51.3	1.8	48,161	12.6	18.2	16.4
Clinton	166	1,558	18,975	7.2	50.3	21.9	219.6	20,004	25,833	52,759	47.6	2.1	56,436	13.7	17.3	16.2
Columbia	160	1,158	11,465	16.4	41.4	30.1	164.3	22,205	34,737	61,093	40.8	5.3	60,629	10.5	16.2	15.4
Cortland	90	1,618	14,388	7.0	43.6	26.0	117.7	17,790	26,271	52,451	47.6	2.9	52,038	15.7	20.1	18.4
Delaware	220	1,285	9,571	5.1	49.9	21.6	141.5	22,321	26,016	47,921	51.8	2.0	45,385	17.9	30.0	28.0
Dutchess	193	1,208	76,198	27.8	35.7	34.6	846.9	20,240	36,704	75,585	33.2	8.4	76,955	10.1	12.9	11.6
Erie	413	2,395	223,313	17.3	36.9	32.9	2,070.2	15,999	31,083	54,006	46.6	4.0	55,581	14.5	21.4	19.9
Essex	158	938	6,703	12.6	42.4	26.7	92.4	23,576	29,008	55,294	45.2	2.2	52,741	10.6	16.8	15.8
Franklin	209	1,153	10,145	19.0	51.0	18.7	151.5	20,036	24,294	50,733	49.1	2.4	50,187	18.9	26.7	22.9
Fulton	279	1,936	10,845	7.7	48.7	17.7	150.4	16,870	26,298	48,033	51.7	2.1	46,984	15.9	25.3	22.7

1. Data for serious crimes have not been adjusted for underreporting; this may affect comparability between geographic areas and over time. 2. Per 100,000 population estimated by the FBI. 3. All persons 3 years old and over enrolled in nursery school through college. 4. Persons 25 years old and over. 5. Elementary and secondary education expenditures. 6. Based on population estimated by the American Community Survey, 2013–2017. 7. Bronx, Kings, Queens, and Richmond counties are included with New York county.

STATE County	Personal income, 2017										Earnings, 2017		
	Total (mil dol)	Percent change 2016-2017	Per capita[1] Dollars	Per capita[1] Rank	Wages and salaries (mil dol)	Supplements to wages and salaries, employer contributions (mil dol) Pension and insurance	Supplements to wages and salaries, employer contributions (mil dol) Government social insurance	Proprietors' income (mil dol)	Dividends, interest, and rent (mil dol)	Personal transfer receipts (mil dol)	Total (mil dol)	Contributions for government social insurance (mil dol) From employee and self-employed	Contributions for government social insurance (mil dol) From employer
	62	63	64	65	66	67	68	69	70	71	72	73	74
NEW JERSEY— Cont'd													
Mercer	24,861	4.8	66,343	91	16,414	2,352	1,189	1,912	5,227	3,463	21,867	1,282	1,189
Middlesex	48,543	4.1	57,598	210	29,217	4,103	2,183	3,728	7,863	6,538	39,232	2,323	2,183
Monmouth	47,224	4.3	75,395	51	15,314	2,279	1,186	4,275	9,365	5,737	23,054	1,396	1,186
Morris	47,101	5.3	94,259	17	26,094	3,037	1,767	5,984	9,587	3,805	36,881	2,136	1,767
Ocean	30,007	5.2	50,184	452	7,906	1,417	648	2,814	5,462	6,810	12,785	890	648
Passaic	24,683	2.4	48,152	611	9,557	1,594	749	2,115	3,907	4,986	14,015	859	749
Salem	2,963	3.0	47,191	698	1,258	251	98	149	446	732	1,756	112	98
Somerset	32,385	6.5	96,548	14	17,302	1,978	1,175	5,361	6,010	2,389	25,817	1,458	1,175
Sussex	8,387	3.9	59,193	177	1,924	347	153	678	1,281	1,184	3,103	200	153
Union	36,322	5.0	64,413	108	16,766	2,350	1,139	3,583	6,461	4,683	23,839	1,403	1,139
Warren	5,717	4.0	53,531	326	1,799	303	142	415	884	985	2,660	172	142
NEW MEXICO	83,127	2.4	39,709	X	38,565	7,023	3,035	5,035	16,422	19,547	53,658	3,523	3,035
Bernalillo	28,551	1.6	42,186	1,245	16,888	2,907	1,325	1,355	5,727	5,881	22,475	1,440	1,325
Catron	111	2.7	30,895	2,858	24	7	2	9	30	44	41	4	2
Chaves	2,630	9.7	40,537	1,466	796	152	63	550	411	669	1,560	96	63
Cibola	742	1.2	27,620	3,041	302	64	23	27	111	268	416	29	23
Colfax	478	0.9	39,272	1,678	164	34	12	37	105	153	247	18	12
Curry	2,231	3.2	44,791	930	1,031	221	97	326	367	462	1,675	80	97
De Baca	72	-3.1	39,220	1,688	18	4	2	8	17	27	32	2	2
Dona Ana	7,623	3.2	35,362	2,291	2,968	618	236	798	1,306	2,006	4,620	298	236
Eddy	2,752	2.6	48,280	602	1,622	285	123	163	543	524	2,193	137	123
Grant	1,073	1.2	38,737	1,768	393	88	30	38	215	386	549	42	30
Guadalupe	145	-4.2	32,848	2,639	51	10	4	7	23	56	72	5	4
Harding	27	-12.7	39,588	1,623	7	2	1	3	8	7	12	1	1
Hidalgo	160	1.0	37,255	1,992	65	17	5	5	30	55	91	7	5
Lea	2,573	6.8	37,419	1,966	1,553	261	117	54	320	551	1,984	133	117
Lincoln	797	2.6	41,111	1,395	222	41	17	57	239	238	338	27	17
Los Alamos	1,275	4.4	68,053	78	1,437	145	112	40	246	87	1,735	109	112
Luna	701	-2.0	29,131	2,980	280	64	24	12	116	293	381	31	24
McKinley	1,947	1.1	26,837	3,064	786	195	64	84	292	688	1,129	74	64
Mora	160	-15.8	35,258	2,305	25	7	2	4	32	66	37	4	2
Otero	2,224	2.3	33,792	2,508	957	226	83	80	465	593	1,346	84	83
Quay	308	2.3	37,060	2,024	102	21	8	15	57	129	146	12	8
Rio Arriba	1,315	1.0	33,590	2,541	374	78	29	36	196	468	517	41	29
Roosevelt	753	5.4	39,974	1,555	209	48	16	105	117	187	378	19	16
Sandoval	5,757	3.1	40,396	1,490	1,315	223	102	258	902	1,150	1,898	146	102
San Juan	4,284	1.4	33,751	2,516	2,318	436	181	110	651	1,042	3,044	199	181
San Miguel	929	-0.1	33,494	2,555	278	71	21	26	168	400	396	30	21
Santa Fe	8,264	2.8	55,553	261	2,904	499	214	572	2,764	1,361	4,189	288	214
Sierra	424	2.2	38,137	1,859	116	25	10	27	95	194	177	15	10
Socorro	566	-0.1	33,675	2,531	214	53	16	39	99	189	322	20	16
Taos	1,209	2.6	36,853	2,065	389	70	32	78	317	384	570	45	32
Torrance	453	0.1	29,192	2,977	130	26	10	17	68	175	183	15	10
Union	144	-0.4	34,498	2,412	54	10	4	16	28	46	84	6	4
Valencia	2,449	1.6	32,244	2,721	575	113	50	80	357	769	818	68	50
NEW YORK	1,281,082	6.0	65,392	X	673,153	106,776	47,722	130,995	268,993	226,704	958,647	52,092	47,722
Albany	17,972	3.6	58,048	204	13,997	3,304	1,123	1,303	3,523	3,322	19,727	1,025	1,123
Allegany	1,592	3.8	33,942	2,490	536	169	46	87	239	490	838	52	46
Bronx	52,321	6.9	35,564	2,264	16,435	3,524	1,364	2,980	6,066	18,312	24,303	1,456	1,364
Broome	8,293	4.7	42,825	1,164	3,861	975	320	493	1,403	2,155	5,650	329	320
Cattaraugus	2,989	4.2	38,644	1,783	1,208	345	101	185	450	875	1,839	110	101
Cayuga	3,166	4.4	40,797	1,433	1,123	286	98	159	505	775	1,666	100	98
Chautauqua	5,113	4.7	39,624	1,618	1,968	495	172	337	753	1,557	2,972	181	172
Chemung	3,643	4.5	42,577	1,197	1,682	379	139	173	530	1,001	2,374	142	139
Chenango	1,968	5.2	41,118	1,393	835	215	69	110	300	537	1,229	74	69
Clinton	3,459	4.8	42,720	1,180	1,557	411	135	232	497	868	2,334	133	135
Columbia	3,238	2.6	53,436	329	909	223	79	265	702	723	1,476	89	79
Cortland	1,886	4.6	39,465	1,646	739	203	63	107	290	466	1,112	64	63
Delaware	1,709	5.3	37,981	1,890	647	187	55	98	337	518	988	61	55
Dutchess	15,988	5.7	54,093	311	6,154	1,246	506	903	2,971	2,924	8,810	504	506
Erie	45,656	4.7	49,230	506	23,912	4,951	1,956	3,108	7,663	9,989	33,927	1,902	1,956
Essex	1,665	5.8	43,857	1,036	620	172	53	102	337	438	946	57	53
Franklin	1,872	5.4	36,617	2,101	801	264	67	95	302	539	1,227	71	67
Fulton	2,264	6.1	42,020	1,262	695	177	59	152	335	661	1,083	69	59

1. Based on the resident population estimated as of July 1 of the year shown.

Table B. States and Counties — Earnings, Social Security, and Housing

STATE County	Earnings, 2017 (cont.)									Social Security beneficiaries, December 2017		Supplemental Security Income recipients, 2017	Housing units, 2018	
	Percent by selected industries													
	Farm	Mining, quarrying, and extractions	Construction	Manufacturing	Information; professional, scientific, technical services	Retail trade	Finance, insurance, real estate, and leasing	Health care and social assistance	Government	Number	Rate[1]		Total	Percent change, 2010-2018
	75	76	77	78	79	80	81	82	83	84	85	86	87	88
NEW JERSEY— Cont'd														
Mercer	0	0.6	3.1	4.9	21.1	3.8	11.6	9	17.9	65,520	175	9,683	145,121	1.4
Middlesex	0	0	4.6	8.3	18.2	5.3	8	9	13.5	132,975	158	13,474	302,239	2.5
Monmouth	0.1	0.1	9.7	3.6	17.2	7.3	8.7	15.8	13.8	123,625	197	8,024	262,161	1.5
Morris	0	D	4.3	7.7	22.3	5.7	11	8.9	8.7	85,810	172	4,360	194,282	2.3
Ocean	0	1.1	10.1	3.2	8.2	10.3	5.8	17.7	19.9	156,920	262	7,442	284,906	2.5
Passaic	0	0.2	7.8	11	7.5	8.1	6.4	13.7	19.6	84,615	165	14,567	177,278	0.7
Salem	0.9	0.1	8.3	13.4	D	5	2.5	10.8	19.5	15,465	246	1,715	27,603	0.7
Somerset	0	0.2	3.8	21.3	20.5	4.5	7.8	6.3	6.7	52,765	157	2,916	127,012	3.2
Sussex	0	0.6	11.5	6.1	8.8	7.8	4.5	13.4	20.9	29,445	208	1,646	62,464	0.9
Union	0	D	D	11.3	16.4	4.9	7.6	9.8	13.2	87,770	156	11,010	202,688	1.6
Warren	0.6	D	D	11.5	7.8	9.1	3.2	12.3	17.3	22,875	214	1,553	45,562	1.5
NEW MEXICO	1.8	4.7	6.3	3.1	12.7	6.6	5.2	12.4	26.4	427,426	205	63,706	943,208	4.6
Bernalillo	0	0.1	6.4	3.8	17.2	6.3	6.8	13.4	25.3	127,455	188	18,002	295,216	3.9
Catron	11.6	D	4.9	2.6	D	D	D	D	45.2	1,470	410	75	3,383	2.8
Chaves	10.3	21.8	3.6	3.5	4.1	7.5	4	11.5	17.4	13,045	201	2,166	27,428	2.7
Cibola	0.9	D	3.4	1	1.2	6.9	2.1	D	41.2	5,210	194	959	11,401	2.6
Colfax	5.4	2.1	5.9	2.2	2.8	8.5	4.6	D	33.1	3,710	305	422	10,295	2.7
Curry	17.2	D	3.6	2.5	2.9	4.8	2.6	8.9	37.3	7,595	152	1,517	21,389	6.6
De Baca	5.2	1.5	D	D	D	11.4	D	D	27.9	565	309	82	1,377	2.5
Dona Ana	4	0.1	6.8	3.4	7.1	5.9	4.8	15.9	29.8	41,375	192	8,264	89,049	9.3
Eddy	1.4	31.1	7.6	5	4	4.7	3.8	7.4	14.1	10,740	188	1,214	24,782	9.8
Grant	0.9	D	4	0.7	3	6.5	2.8	8.5	34.3	8,875	321	871	15,078	2.6
Guadalupe	6.7	0.2	1.6	D	D	12.9	D	12.8	28.8	1,105	249	239	2,446	2.3
Harding	30.5	0.1	D	D	D	D	D	D	41.3	210	303	11	538	1.9
Hidalgo	-2.6	0.6	D	D	D	7.6	D	D	58.1	1,190	276	178	2,460	2.7
Lea	4.7	29.9	12.5	-7.2	3.1	6.6	5.2	6.6	12.5	9,840	143	1,545	26,764	7.4
Lincoln	1.4	D	7.5	0.9	D	12.8	6.6	13	21.6	6,085	314	377	18,271	4.3
Los Alamos	0	D	1	D	D	1.1	2	3.5	7.6	3,130	167	81	8,403	0.6
Luna	-2.9	0.2	6.1	9.9	D	7.7	2.7	D	38.6	7,025	292	1,502	11,310	2.8
McKinley	-0.5	D	2.9	3.3	2	10.3	3.4	13.3	45.4	11,405	157	4,603	26,344	2.1
Mora	8.2	D	D	D	D	5.6	1.8	D	40.4	1,555	342	283	3,315	2.6
Otero	0.5	0.4	5.4	0.2	4.6	5.5	2.4	11.3	55.1	13,215	201	1,461	31,834	2.7
Quay	-0.8	D	4.8	D	2.8	8.9	4.6	13.7	31	2,655	320	393	5,698	2.3
Rio Arriba	0.7	1.1	4	1	3.6	6.7	2.1	17.1	43.9	10,075	257	1,734	20,172	2.8
Roosevelt	26.3	0.2	3.5	5.8	D	5.8	2.9	5.1	30.7	3,195	170	574	8,519	4.4
Sandoval	0.1	D	7.4	14.5	6.2	6.4	3.6	10	23	30,115	211	2,752	57,328	9.6
San Juan	-0.6	18.6	8.4	2.4	D	8.4	3.3	14	22.7	22,745	179	4,020	51,276	3.9
San Miguel	1.1	0.1	4	0.8	3.1	6.5	4.1	D	49.2	7,255	261	1,803	15,967	2.4
Santa Fe	-0.1	0.8	5.1	1.2	12.5	8.5	6.8	14.2	27	37,345	251	2,669	73,456	3
Sierra	10.9	D	8.4	2.3	2.8	7.6	2.5	D	30.7	4,515	406	599	8,570	2.5
Socorro	10.7	D	0.8	2.3	8.9	4.2	1.6	D	46	3,845	229	1,026	8,243	2.3
Taos	-0.2	0.6	7.6	1.5	7.6	9.1	4	16.9	21.1	9,620	293	1,116	21,037	3.8
Torrance	3.8	D	5.8	3.2	D	9.3	D	D	28.6	3,760	242	582	8,098	3.9
Union	9.1	1.5	D	D	D	8.4	5.7	D	20.6	1,015	242	116	2,353	1.9
Valencia	1	0.3	12.9	5.5	4	10.1	3.2	8.9	28.1	16,485	217	2,470	31,408	4.4
NEW YORK	0.1	0.3	4.6	4.2	17.3	4.6	19	10.9	14.9	3,586,883	181	637,595	8,363,934	3.2
Albany	0.1	D	4.4	3.5	12.8	4.9	9.5	11.6	32.9	61,445	198	7,210	142,305	3.3
Allegany	1.5	0.3	7.3	15.7	2.9	5.1	1.8	8.4	36.6	11,295	241	1,362	26,388	1
Bronx	0	D	5.8	1.6	2.7	5.8	3.9	26.5	26	201,400	137	105,283	532,487	4.1
Broome	0.1	0.1	5.9	11.3	6.4	6.8	5.4	17.6	25.7	47,495	245	7,033	91,234	0.7
Cattaraugus	0.6	0.5	4.7	14.7	3.6	8	3.4	D	36.6	19,675	254	2,462	41,652	1.3
Cayuga	2.1	D	6.7	14.7	4.5	6.9	2.9	14	29.2	17,615	227	1,789	37,158	1.9
Chautauqua	1.8	0.2	5.1	22.7	3.5	7.6	2.6	13.6	24.1	33,485	259	4,453	67,677	1.1
Chemung	0	0.5	5.4	16.6	4	7.1	5.5	16.9	23.7	21,575	252	3,102	38,916	1.4
Chenango	1.3	0.1	5.1	30	4.1	5.4	9.8	6	25	13,000	272	1,652	25,790	4.3
Clinton	2	D	6.3	9.8	3.6	8.3	2.3	17.4	31.5	20,030	247	2,812	36,734	2.4
Columbia	1.3	D	8.7	6.4	7.8	7.3	2.9	17	24.6	15,835	261	1,367	33,614	2.6
Cortland	0.9	0.3	4.9	15.2	5.6	7.1	4.2	D	28.7	10,030	210	1,103	20,805	1.2
Delaware	0.9	2.3	4.5	28.1	4.4	5.5	3.3	8.8	28.9	12,140	270	1,087	31,646	1.4
Dutchess	0.2	0.3	6.4	11.4	7.3	6.9	4	16.1	22.5	60,295	204	5,271	121,158	2.1
Erie	0.1	0.2	4.4	10.8	9.3	6	9.5	13.1	20.4	205,795	222	27,454	429,714	2.3
Essex	0.2	1.2	6.9	7.9	3.7	7.2	2.9	11.2	35.9	9,955	262	818	26,393	3.1
Franklin	1.2	D	3.9	D	3.5	5.8	2	19.2	50.3	11,975	234	1,792	25,840	2.1
Fulton	0.1	0.5	5.3	9.6	3.8	13.4	3.2	16.9	25.6	14,190	263	1,898	29,130	2

1. Per 1,000 resident population estimated as of July 1 of the year shown.

Table B. States and Counties — Housing, Labor Force, and Employment

STATE County	Total [89]	Percent [90]	Median value[1] [91]	With a mortgage [92]	Without a mortgage[2] [93]	Median rent[3] [94]	Median rent as a percent of income[2] [95]	Sub-standard units[4] (percent) [96]	Total [97]	Percent change, 2017-2018 [98]	Total [99]	Rate[5] [100]	Total [101]	Management, business, science, and arts [102]	Construction, production, and maintenance occupations [103]
NEW JERSEY— Cont'd															
Mercer	129,546	64.2	281,900	24.1	15.2	1,191	31.7	2.4	196,494	0.5	7,217	3.7	181,602	44.7	15.6
Middlesex	283,794	63.6	329,000	24.8	16.4	1,384	29.5	4.4	435,053	-0.4	15,791	3.6	408,838	45.1	17.8
Monmouth	232,482	73.8	396,200	25.0	15.6	1,315	33.6	1.7	323,106	-0.4	11,870	3.7	314,470	44.6	15.1
Morris	180,124	75.1	438,100	23.9	15.7	1,420	27	1.7	252,984	-0.7	8,288	3.3	262,461	51.0	12.2
Ocean	223,135	80.0	267,900	26.5	17.9	1,368	36.7	2.7	266,971	-0.5	11,515	4.3	253,628	35.1	18.3
Passaic	162,440	53.5	333,200	28.4	19.8	1,238	36	7.7	239,206	-0.9	12,205	5.1	238,552	32.3	26.2
Salem	24,038	71.4	185,800	23.2	16.5	981	34.5	1.8	28,795	-1.3	1,569	5.4	29,365	32.5	28.6
Somerset	115,970	76.0	412,800	24.0	14.2	1,499	28.6	1.5	169,129	-0.7	5,811	3.4	174,463	52.2	12.5
Sussex	53,618	82.7	264,100	25.2	16.6	1,244	31.2	0.9	72,560	-0.9	2,871	4	75,370	39.5	18.7
Union	187,916	58.9	351,800	26.4	18.4	1,219	32.5	4.9	272,683	-0.8	11,748	4.3	278,003	37.1	21.8
Warren	41,385	71.3	256,700	24.0	17.1	1,056	30.4	1.8	55,348	-0.5	2,118	3.8	54,719	36.5	20.5
NEW MEXICO	770,435	67.9	163,900	22.1	10.0	809	30	4.3	940,359	0.4	46,536	4.9	879,201	35.7	20.2
Bernalillo	263,551	62.8	189,700	22.1	10.0	834	31.6	3.2	329,380	0.5	14,850	4.5	313,658	40.2	16.0
Catron	1,433	92.9	164,600	24.9	11.1	840	29.3	0.5	1,117	-3.7	72	6.4	919	39.2	18.7
Chaves	23,343	68.0	106,400	20.4	10.0	727	28.7	4.2	27,137		1,319	4.9	26,659	28.3	26.6
Cibola	9,068	71.1	89,800	22.4	10.0	611	28.6	12.1	8,927	-1.7	561	6.3	9,600	28.1	22.5
Colfax	5,591	67.4	105,900	23.1	13.6	589	32.9	2.7	5,480	-3.5	271	4.9	4,663	33.0	18.5
Curry	18,470	57.7	131,200	23.1	10.0	836	29.5	3.4	21,629	-2.7	878	4.1	20,509	28.5	32.2
De Baca	666	66.5	67,700	25.9	10.0	671	28	0.9	768	-9.2	35	4.6	675	32.9	36.3
Dona Ana	76,740	62.7	140,700	22.6	10.0	735	31.9	4.8	96,769	1.3	5,470	5.7	88,633	32.2	19.2
Eddy	21,273	70.6	143,100	16.9	10.0	841	22	5.1	31,376	7.8	1,045	3.3	26,191	26.4	33.0
Grant	11,879	72.3	125,300	22.0	10.1	679	29.4	4	12,248	0.2	601	4.9	10,647	32.3	22.0
Guadalupe	1,253	66.5	81,100	19.9	12.6	430	27	2.8	1,624		90	5.5	1,374	32.2	9.0
Harding	203	73.4	67,800	32.5	12.1	525	31	0	283	0.7	15	5.3	201	42.8	23.9
Hidalgo	1,761	72.8	81,200	32.5	11.4	526	20.6	3.2	2,190	3	84	3.8	1,614	21.6	27.7
Lea	22,029	68.1	118,500	17.8	10.0	831	21.3	6.1	29,873	7.6	1,231	4.1	28,672	25.0	37.8
Lincoln	7,902	78.3	171,900	25.5	12.1	727	24.7	3.7	8,702	0.1	396	4.6	7,057	28.1	21.2
Los Alamos	7,525	73.7	285,300	16.5	10.0	1,004	21.3	0.9	9,098	-0.1	308	3.4	9,122	67.7	6.6
Luna	9,088	61.8	83,800	25.0	10.4	549	28.9	3.2	10,107	-3.6	1,203	11.9	7,895	21.7	32.2
McKinley	19,764	71.5	62,800	20.1	10.0	651	23.9	19.6	23,810	-1.7	1,699	7.1	23,207	29.4	23.5
Mora	1,513	76.2	109,100	18.4	14.0	688	50	6.9	2,266	2.9	139	6.1	1,245	24.0	22.7
Otero	23,657	64.1	106,300	21.5	10.0	818	28.7	2.7	24,601	-1.2	1,203	4.9	23,707	27.5	21.7
Quay	3,085	68.6	72,200	21.9	11.4	524	28.2	0.7	3,202	-1.3	155	4.8	3,015	33.8	24.4
Rio Arriba	12,852	76.6	167,100	22.0	10.0	597	35.1	2.8	16,670	-0.5	868	5.2	13,786	37.4	15.5
Roosevelt	7,125	61.2	114,300	21.4	10.8	762	38.1	3.9	7,875	-1.3	342	4.3	7,650	33.5	23.1
Sandoval	49,265	80.8	183,300	22.9	10.0	1,057	31.7	4.4	64,633	0.3	3,217	5	59,556	39.7	16.9
San Juan	41,999	73.0	143,300	20.0	10.0	778	27.1	8	52,537	-2.4	3,029	5.8	51,379	28.3	28.4
San Miguel	11,041	70.4	132,900	26.7	14.6	647	35.4	3	10,939	0	650	5.9	9,230	33.6	17.0
Santa Fe	61,651	70.3	277,700	23.9	10.0	987	28.7	2.9	73,974	0.9	3,065	4.1	69,630	44.2	14.6
Sierra	5,400	74.4	99,600	22.9	11.3	568	28.9	2.1	4,097	-1.4	289	7.1	3,740	32.5	22.1
Socorro	4,698	76.1	103,000	20.9	10.7	591	30.2	4	6,455	-1.9	343	5.3	5,856	35.7	25.0
Taos	12,603	74.3	218,400	27.2	12.3	716	34.6	3.6	14,985	-0.4	975	6.5	13,739	34.7	16.1
Torrance	5,598	80.2	111,700	24.3	12.5	810	34.6	4	5,603	0.6	427	7.6	5,326	34.2	21.9
Union	1,424	65.8	89,500	18.9	12.1	530	18.4	0.3	1,773	-7.2	59	3.3	1,535	31.7	25.3
Valencia	26,985	80.5	133,100	24.8	10.6	781	32.9	2.9	30,234	0.5	1,650	5.5	28,511	27.6	27.8
NEW YORK	7,302,710	54.0	293,000	23.8	14.0	1,194	31.9	5.4	9,574,706	0.1	393,648	4.1	9,467,631	40.2	16.5
Albany	125,376	56.8	214,400	20.4	11.5	969	29.6	1.1	158,835	0.6	5,844	3.7	158,961	44.7	13.0
Allegany	18,124	74.3	73,300	19.2	12.6	633	30.9	3.2	19,461		1,096	5.6	20,132	31.4	27.2
Bronx	495,356	19.7	371,800	29.6	12.0	1,133	35.6	12.8	605,864	-0.4	34,319	5.7	593,858	25.0	18.1
Broome	78,821	65.7	113,100	20.6	12.4	734	32.6	1.6	84,592	0.2	4,115	4.9	87,365	37.7	18.3
Cattaraugus	31,723	71.3	86,500	19.6	13.0	626	29.1	3.1	34,020	-0.6	1,820	5.3	33,732	30.5	26.1
Cayuga	31,428	70.8	120,000	20.1	12.6	715	27	1.7	35,954	0.4	1,610	4.5	37,196	33.8	25.2
Chautauqua	52,983	70.0	85,800	19.4	12.6	631	31.8	2	54,993	-0.6	2,766	5	56,416	29.9	28.6
Chemung	34,664	68.1	105,500	18.9	11.6	764	32	1	35,373	-0.7	1,649	4.7	37,726	35.8	20.9
Chenango	20,373	74.9	95,900	19.6	13.2	645	28.8	2.7	22,416	0.5	1,047	4.7	21,665	32.7	28.9
Clinton	31,680	68.0	129,000	20.6	11.0	762	28.9	2	36,428	1	1,597	4.4	36,091	31.6	23.3
Columbia	25,470	72.4	224,600	23.2	14.5	886	28.3	1.5	31,426	1.2	1,043	3.3	30,164	38.4	20.7
Cortland	17,925	64.7	113,900	19.2	12.8	742	27.6	1.7	22,927	0	1,165	5.1	24,251	34.4	21.7
Delaware	19,098	73.3	138,000	22.0	13.9	696	32.5	3.5	19,244	1.6	928	4.8	19,919	31.9	26.4
Dutchess	107,384	69.2	275,200	25.6	15.1	1,174	32.9	3.8	143,934	0.6	5,305	3.7	144,934	39.7	17.4
Erie	386,371	65.0	139,900	19.2	12.5	778	29.9	1.6	443,446	0	19,574	4.4	448,392	38.7	17.5
Essex	15,257	76.0	146,900	19.7	13.3	798	27.3	1.9	17,078	-0.4	834	4.9	17,544	32.2	22.1
Franklin	18,956	72.9	102,200	20.0	11.9	670	28.3	2.4	19,647	-0.4	1,014	5.2	19,960	31.6	21.6
Fulton	22,535	71.4	107,600	19.5	13.4	734	31.6	1.5	22,877	-1.1	1,166	5.1	24,239	30.7	25.5

1. Specified owner-occupied units. 2. A value of 10.0 represents 10 percent or less; a value of 50.0 represents 50 percent or more. 3. Specified renter-occupied units. 4. Overcrowded or lacking complete plumbing facilities. 5. Percent of civilian labor force. 6. Civilian employed persons 16 years old and over.

Table B. States and Counties — Nonfarm Employment and Agriculture

STATE County	Private nonfarm establishments, employment and payroll, 2016									Agriculture, 2017			
	Number of establishments	Employment						Annual payroll		Farms			Farm producers whose primary occupation is farming (percent)
		Total	Health care and social assistance	Manufacturing	Retail trade	Finance and insurance	Professional, scientific, and technical services	Total (mil dol)	Average per employee (dollars)	Number	Percent with:		
											Fewer than 50 acres	1000 acres or more	
	104	105	106	107	108	109	110	111	112	113	114	115	116

STATE County	104	105	106	107	108	109	110	111	112	113	114	115	116
NEW JERSEY— Cont'd													
Mercer	9,675	190,694	29,108	6,182	23,562	14,882	21,617	12,290	64,448	323	72.1	0.6	35.1
Middlesex	21,826	387,607	53,531	26,362	40,096	13,586	58,331	25,199	65,011	217	82.0	0.9	38.4
Monmouth	19,133	241,367	45,161	9,350	40,272	10,763	20,458	11,908	49,337	838	85.3	0.7	46.4
Morris	16,704	296,580	36,391	13,570	29,753	19,899	42,676	22,932	77,321	418	81.6	NA	29.9
Ocean	12,931	142,730	35,445	4,986	28,768	3,663	7,491	5,371	37,630	260	87.3	NA	38.4
Passaic	12,111	146,408	27,607	16,484	25,273	4,918	7,438	6,949	47,466	89	88.8	NA	39.0
Salem	1,141	17,727	3,086	2,948	1,927	452	554	903	50,958	781	67.3	3.1	39.9
Somerset	9,970	190,814	23,201	14,958	18,731	10,337	28,761	16,228	85,045	452	76.8	2.0	31.5
Sussex	3,221	32,680	6,424	2,292	6,124	877	1,342	1,337	40,897	1,008	75.6	0.7	32.1
Union	13,741	201,299	33,296	13,827	26,073	6,012	14,161	12,379	61,494	9	100.0	NA	69.2
Warren	2,428	28,038	5,426	3,279	5,873	551	1,133	1,222	43,589	918	70.7	1.3	35.6
NEW MEXICO	43,771	628,723	121,840	25,757	97,171	24,135	57,997	25,029	39,810	25,044	52.2	18.2	42.1
Bernalillo	15,795	268,851	51,110	12,471	36,656	11,432	31,486	11,300	42,032	1,248	89.8	1.8	32.2
Catron	59	418	D	D	80	D	D	11	26,708	341	22.9	29.0	41.3
Chaves	1,398	16,623	3,626	829	3,271	584	740	563	33,848	560	41.3	25.7	44.5
Cibola	319	4,830	1,325	60	926	97	25	165	34,165	640	47.5	18.9	44.9
Colfax	402	3,492	463	113	624	162	79	97	27,916	304	17.8	34.9	38.9
Curry	1,068	12,940	2,710	627	2,583	459	784	396	30,590	641	21.2	32.4	41.6
De Baca	47	249	D	D	62	D	D	6	25,036	226	44.2	33.2	53.5
Dona Ana	3,615	51,225	14,177	2,241	8,289	1,563	3,885	1,580	30,852	1,946	86.7	1.8	33.1
Eddy	1,429	22,717	3,021	1,068	3,053	526	609	1,120	49,289	507	47.1	18.9	41.7
Grant	602	6,909	1,580	125	1,199	179	161	251	36,401	404	30.4	25.2	44.4
Guadalupe	92	1,013	87	D	254	21	D	28	27,163	297	20.2	46.5	54.7
Harding	13	38	D	NA	9	D	NA	1	20,500	184	4.9	54.9	49.0
Hidalgo	99	893	208	D	240	D	27	21	23,587	151	11.3	45.7	51.5
Lea	1,682	23,098	2,286	690	3,324	468	475	1,074	46,500	555	36.6	28.6	42.9
Lincoln	677	5,080	529	106	1,189	268	144	145	28,463	454	29.7	30.2	36.0
Los Alamos	366	13,079	986	61	509	304	9,762	1,119	85,560	2	100.0	NA	20.0
Luna	382	4,457	1,059	447	1,033	128	85	116	26,000	211	39.8	25.1	53.0
McKinley	992	16,491	4,726	526	3,508	427	233	501	30,406	2,441	42.4	22.6	53.1
Mora	44	319	152	D	72	10	NA	8	25,210	700	40.4	9.1	36.0
Otero	962	12,243	2,565	139	2,471	312	567	381	31,116	473	56.0	15.4	43.7
Quay	224	1,900	359	59	424	117	59	49	26,015	613	12.6	36.2	40.7
Rio Arriba	543	6,134	1,934	103	1,103	181	60	218	35,577	1,439	61.8	11.3	36.0
Roosevelt	329	3,498	603	299	645	120	60	106	30,190	742	18.3	31.3	40.7
Sandoval	1,717	25,825	3,910	2,400	3,552	934	1,208	985	38,143	1,007	69.0	10.9	33.8
San Juan	2,651	37,010	6,875	1,315	6,193	927	1,226	1,587	42,871	2,965	56.5	21.0	54.9
San Miguel	451	6,271	3,280	48	926	172	114	162	25,863	1,170	35.9	18.6	38.0
Santa Fe	4,726	46,628	8,833	820	9,424	1,600	2,423	1,847	39,613	639	67.9	9.7	35.7
Sierra	217	2,411	701	101	463	61	62	64	26,565	257	38.5	25.3	56.7
Socorro	229	3,087	915	124	436	79	225	88	28,419	658	69.6	12.0	45.7
Taos	1,072	8,603	1,441	180	1,566	184	278	239	27,827	824	78.4	4.1	34.5
Torrance	219	1,724	150	88	523	35	54	56	32,335	716	18.7	22.6	43.2
Union	98	946	179	D	142	67	14	28	29,752	369	1.1	59.9	47.8
Valencia	914	10,702	1,835	665	2,400	325	321	294	27,488	1,360	91.7	1.5	32.0
NEW YORK	544,073	8,178,455	1,544,405	418,987	945,066	553,058	647,503	521,873	63,811	33,438	36.7	3.3	48.1
Albany	9,531	181,194	36,785	8,334	23,209	12,535	17,601	8,676	47,882	440	37.7	0.9	42.6
Allegany	779	11,776	1,735	2,213	1,311	191	241	376	31,897	789	29.4	2.5	42.7
Bronx	18,025	260,629	100,523	6,049	32,529	4,320	4,282	11,697	44,880	NA	NA	NA	NA
Broome	4,247	71,043	15,768	7,357	11,006	2,030	3,758	2,770	38,996	494	37.2	1.0	41.5
Cattaraugus	1,627	22,925	3,436	3,943	3,949	655	708	827	36,074	956	31.1	1.5	42.9
Cayuga	1,619	19,993	4,384	3,160	3,463	304	497	715	35,773	842	38.7	6.7	53.5
Chautauqua	2,880	40,961	8,456	8,865	6,475	769	920	1,354	33,059	1,228	34.6	2.4	45.3
Chemung	1,791	30,971	6,589	5,345	5,300	934	804	1,228	39,640	398	29.1	1.3	37.8
Chenango	924	14,213	1,856	4,373	1,701	1,186	377	638	44,861	770	28.4	2.5	50.2
Clinton	1,826	24,672	5,071	3,835	4,997	439	555	924	37,448	588	27.7	5.8	46.6
Columbia	1,783	16,156	4,409	1,318	2,974	311	659	644	39,888	518	45.4	3.1	46.7
Cortland	1,005	15,477	3,275	2,650	2,377	353	1,001	511	32,985	536	33.2	2.8	43.6
Delaware	1,058	10,593	1,950	3,462	1,525	339	217	403	38,072	689	28.6	1.6	46.7
Dutchess	7,581	96,151	19,397	5,865	14,916	2,792	7,496	4,302	44,738	620	53.1	3.5	45.5
Erie	22,795	417,701	74,219	43,609	54,940	28,526	29,322	18,392	44,031	940	51.9	2.7	48.7
Essex	1,177	9,865	1,914	783	1,876	198	207	379	38,406	285	40.7	5.6	37.5
Franklin	959	10,733	3,739	519	1,944	212	315	368	34,253	636	25.8	3.3	52.0
Fulton	1,194	14,203	3,466	1,983	2,419	282	298	507	35,692	207	39.6	NA	39.1

Table B. States and Counties — **Agriculture**

STATE County	Agriculture, 2017 (cont.)															
	Land in farms					Value of land and buildings (dollars)		Value of machinery and equiopmnet, average per farm (dollars)	Value of products sold:				Organic farms (number)	Farms with internet access (percent)	Government payments	
		Acres									Percent from:					
	Acreage (1,000)	Percent change, 2012-2017	Average size of farm	Total irrigated (1,000)	Total cropland (1,000)	Average per farm	Average per acre		Total (mil dol)	Average per farm (acres)	Crops	Livestock and poultry products			Total ($1,000)	Percent of farms
	117	118	119	120	121	122	123	124	125	126	127	128	129	130	131	132
NEW JERSEY— Cont'd																
Mercer	25	27.8	78	1.0	15.8	1,414,874	18,114	83,438	25.0	77,344	80.1	19.9	12	73.4	149	8.0
Middlesex	16	-7.2	74	2.0	11.2	1,607,661	21,773	112,644	38.4	176,770	98.0	2.0	2	77.9	92	7.8
Monmouth	39	0.6	47	3.6	23.8	981,430	20,982	79,157	80.6	96,221	83.6	16.4	3	80.5	366	3.3
Morris	15	898.2	35	1.0	6.7	743,975	21,426	68,480	24.8	59,388	93.1	6.9	11	86.4	60	3.1
Ocean	9	6.8	33	0.8	4.4	622,892	19,031	60,677	24.6	94,769	81.1	18.9	3	81.2	59	3.1
Passaic	2	-94.6	21	0.1	0.3	679,638	31,953	47,779	2.9	32,169	95.0	5.0	NA	85.4	8	3.4
Salem	98	-95.0	126	17.1	80.9	1,059,096	8,420	139,528	102.3	131,040	88.3	11.7	4	79.1	1,869	19.3
Somerset	36	-41.2	79	0.9	19.9	1,569,021	19,776	65,277	20.1	44,509	71.5	28.5	13	81.0	148	7.3
Sussex	60	62,156.3	59	0.4	25.7	683,936	11,535	47,928	18.2	18,081	59.4	40.6	9	80.0	310	3.9
Union	0	-99.9	8	0.0	D	1,303,684	156,442	118,929	D	D	D	D	NA	100.0	NA	NA
Warren	74	150.6	80	1.4	46.8	980,498	12,184	76,777	93.2	101,542	72.0	28.0	3	80.7	952	10.6
NEW MEXICO	40,660	-5.9	1,624	626.0	1,825.8	845,740	521	63,619	2,582.3	103,112	25.2	74.8	183	60.5	63,660	13.8
Bernalillo	221	-85.8	177	4.3	6.5	489,688	2,759	34,855	9.3	7,466	51.8	48.2	23	70.5	2	0.4
Catron	1,261	18.4	3,697	1.8	5.1	1,551,601	420	52,857	9.5	27,774	1.4	98.6	5	68.0	970	9.1
Chaves	2,318	251.2	4,140	42.8	62.2	1,957,270	473	164,614	404.5	722,348	10.6	89.4	NA	83.0	2,236	17.0
Cibola	1,594	9,374,482.4	2,490	0.9	5.4	789,275	317	36,619	D	D	100.0	D	4	46.6	476	9.2
Colfax	2,073	135.4	6,819	16.7	19.2	3,442,286	505	77,901	D	82,543	3.0	97.0	5	73.4	237	7.9
Curry	902	-15.5	1,407	58.8	428.4	977,762	695	163,697	480.6	749,735	6.6	93.4	5	78.5	14,607	69.4
De Baca	1,182	-28.1	5,231	7.6	10.1	1,962,324	375	85,317	28.1	124,487	19.5	80.5	NA	87.6	1,989	36.7
Dona Ana	528	-53.7	271	73.7	93.1	674,302	2,484	91,093	370.3	190,284	61.8	38.2	23	73.7	578	4.0
Eddy	1,088	-45.1	2,146	31.5	49.3	1,268,345	591	145,419	97.3	191,870	49.5	50.5	NA	82.4	385	9.5
Grant	894	-3.9	2,213	2.0	6.5	1,077,324	487	62,151	14.7	36,507	4.2	95.8	NA	77.7	945	8.4
Guadalupe	1,444	39.7	4,862	4.2	13.3	1,512,859	311	59,332	13.3	44,643	2.3	97.7	NA	65.0	1,851	25.3
Harding	938	20.6	5,100	0.9	14.8	1,868,529	366	D	13.4	73,054	0.3	99.7	NA	70.7	951	33.2
Hidalgo	849	54.3	5,622	18.5	25.5	D	D	157,031	23.4	155,099	55.3	44.7	NA	79.5	1,565	40.4
Lea	1,938	24.8	3,492	42.9	111.9	1,439,038	412	115,880	192.2	346,382	17.3	82.7	4	71.2	2,204	27.7
Lincoln	1,466	19.8	3,230	2.1	6.7	1,607,027	498	56,708	15.9	34,930	2.5	97.5	1	74.9	1,665	17.4
Los Alamos	D	D	D	NA	NA	D	D	D	D	D	NA	D	NA	100.0	NA	NA
Luna	576	-53.9	2,729	20.1	30.0	1,404,258	515	168,893	79.3	375,725	61.1	38.9	1	83.4	2,313	43.1
McKinley	2,570	79.3	1,053	2.5	38.7	450,977	428	26,248	8.1	3,334	7.8	92.2	NA	19.4	600	12.2
Mora	931	-38.7	1,329	11.7	21.2	734,372	552	49,430	18.2	25,931	12.7	87.3	7	52.7	548	4.6
Otero	1,019	-5.4	2,155	4.7	8.6	946,804	439	52,864	18.2	38,395	51.8	48.2	5	79.3	783	8.5
Quay	1,548	14.8	2,526	13.1	199.6	889,432	352	83,453	39.5	64,388	16.2	83.8	1	71.3	7,352	61.3
Rio Arriba	1,362	-47.2	947	26.1	41.7	812,334	858	51,633	14.6	10,172	35.7	64.3	32	60.7	1,114	7.9
Roosevelt	1,500	-36.2	2,021	44.5	317.1	923,240	457	118,420	290.6	391,699	10.4	89.6	12	74.5	10,555	56.5
Sandoval	784	9.2	778	6.9	17.5	415,220	534	33,172	12.4	12,286	63.8	36.2	6	52.2	487	4.1
San Juan	2,551	168.5	861	73.6	107.9	345,734	402	39,425	74.1	24,998	91.5	8.5	1	44.9	1,383	8.3
San Miguel	2,270	21.7	1,940	13.3	22.4	870,177	449	37,470	19.1	16,323	3.7	96.3	7	50.0	1,385	9.2
Santa Fe	D	D	D	15.6	23.7	932,062	881	65,568	25.4	39,798	54.5	45.5	14	77.0	367	5.5
Sierra	1,012	-20.4	3,939	5.8	8.5	1,422,045	361	87,711	31.9	124,093	30.8	69.2	3	75.1	316	9.7
Socorro	912	282.7	1,387	16.2	17.7	870,620	628	65,960	65.1	99,009	14.1	85.9	1	63.1	265	2.3
Taos	285	-57.4	346	15.9	16.6	565,648	1,635	45,157	7.6	9,266	55.0	45.0	17	66.3	270	3.6
Torrance	1,561	-20.7	2,180	16.1	29.8	1,038,912	477	55,855	45.9	64,096	24.7	75.3	NA	63.5	2,311	18.6
Union	1,887	438.1	5,114	15.4	48.9	2,110,381	413	89,284	83.1	225,295	9.8	90.2	NA	66.9	2,896	27.4
Valencia	518	-79.1	381	16.0	18.0	442,410	1,162	47,173	46.1	33,886	10.3	89.7	6	70.1	52	1.1
NEW YORK	6,866	-4.4	205	53.3	4,291.4	663,082	3,229	135,626	5,369.2	160,572	39.3	60.7	1,497	77.1	59,106	19.3
Albany	60	86.9	135	1.1	34.5	601,883	4,446	78,697	47.3	107,564	76.6	23.4	10	79.1	250	16.1
Allegany	162	7.5	205	0.4	88.7	412,662	2,013	85,322	69.3	87,853	37.1	62.9	45	64.6	1,280	28.4
Bronx	NA	NA	NA	NA	NA	NA	NA	NA	NA	NA	NA	NA	NA	NA	NA	NA
Broome	62	-21.6	126	0.5	33.5	390,574	3,089	72,467	32.1	64,953	32.4	67.6	10	73.9	346	14.8
Cattaraugus	166	-15.7	174	0.2	88.7	398,333	2,291	102,151	93.4	97,711	21.3	78.7	11	65.1	650	24.0
Cayuga	225	34.7	267	0.3	177.9	1,057,750	3,955	211,196	287.9	341,868	24.3	75.7	27	76.5	3,092	28.7
Chautauqua	224	-5.5	182	1.0	126.9	481,615	2,645	128,191	161.0	131,081	45.5	54.5	42	78.1	1,621	11.8
Chemung	67	15.1	168	0.1	35.0	440,268	2,619	91,732	19.0	47,771	50.6	49.4	5	78.6	384	19.1
Chenango	149	29.5	193	0.3	77.1	397,806	2,056	104,336	67.9	88,212	26.3	73.7	42	76.2	539	20.6
Clinton	162	9.8	275	0.8	85.1	727,023	2,645	179,004	167.8	285,355	26.6	73.4	8	80.4	127	7.0
Columbia	99	4.0	191	2.1	64.5	801,814	4,188	123,888	88.4	170,718	55.9	44.1	33	83.0	913	12.9
Cortland	114	-19.1	212	0.2	58.5	491,363	2,320	128,057	69.5	129,675	19.7	80.3	46	80.6	592	31.0
Delaware	140	-3.7	204	0.2	67.9	586,225	2,880	89,482	45.7	66,335	29.1	70.9	38	83.3	871	26.1
Dutchess	102	-9.4	164	0.8	40.1	1,486,434	9,040	84,120	43.9	70,818	64.8	35.2	15	88.5	242	8.4
Erie	143	0.3	152	2.0	96.4	696,510	4,576	137,967	131.0	139,333	47.3	52.7	28	81.6	1,405	19.1
Essex	58	5.1	202	0.1	22.7	481,641	2,382	84,723	13.2	46,239	51.4	48.6	12	87.0	209	12.3
Franklin	141	-3.0	221	0.5	74.8	550,272	2,487	114,437	86.4	135,822	18.6	81.4	49	68.9	446	15.9
Fulton	22	-83.1	107	0.1	12.8	299,090	2,791	84,953	10.3	49,609	42.2	57.8	4	78.7	107	11.1

Table B. States and Counties — Water Use, Wholesale Trade, Retail Trade, and Real Estate

STATE County	Water use, 2015		Wholesale Trade[1], 2012				Retail Trade[2], 2012				Real estate and rental and leasing,[2] 2012			
	Public supply water withdrawn (mil gal/day)	Public supply gallons withdrawn per person per day	Number of establishments	Number of employees	Sales (mil dol)	Average payroll (mil dol)	Number of establishments	Number of employees	Sales (mil dol)	Average payroll (mil dol)	Number of establishments	Number of employees	Sales (mil dol)	Average payroll (mil dol)
	133	134	135	136	137	138	139	140	141	142	143	144	145	146
NEW JERSEY— Cont'd														
Mercer	37.62	101.3	354	D	D	D	1,305	18,794	5,127.4	477.9	347	1,934	729.3	91.8
Middlesex	39.08	46.5	1,580	33,984	40,540.7	2,614.2	2,611	38,315	11,869.8	982.7	680	5,893	2,421.8	349.8
Monmouth	71.17	113.2	803	6,856	4,888.8	409.3	2,627	38,150	11,026.1	1,008.7	672	3,948	824.6	164.5
Morris	90.03	180.2	912	14,194	21,280.6	1,103.1	1,823	29,044	9,346.9	854.7	606	5,457	2,863.2	427.4
Ocean	52.45	89.1	388	2,761	1,295.7	127.9	1,869	26,568	7,695.4	724.1	546	2,525	468.2	92.8
Passaic	270.78	530.0	755	11,293	9,132.5	774.4	1,834	22,841	7,294.0	580.7	412	2,274	942.0	120.4
Salem	4.24	66.1	36	713	1,825.4	36.6	176	1,932	627.0	43.4	42	174	28.5	6.1
Somerset	2.71	8.1	495	12,184	25,544.7	1,040.4	1,086	18,878	5,609.3	510.5	294	1,286	442.8	62.4
Sussex	5.94	41.3	122	1,083	459.6	58.0	413	5,658	1,819.8	146.0	86	316	62.9	11.1
Union	141.52	254.6	853	15,361	14,069.6	1,380.5	1,941	24,757	7,376.3	646.2	532	3,070	1,058.3	147.7
Warren	7.26	67.9	95	D	D	D	389	6,076	1,573.8	143.0	58	181	43.1	6.6
NEW MEXICO	254.10	121.9	1,646	17,448	10,720.4	814.6	6,590	90,792	25,179.3	2,214.5	2,369	9,754	1,960.4	368.7
Bernalillo	87.60	129.5	791	10,150	5,620.8	495.7	2,076	33,334	9,548.2	857.5	942	4,274	818.2	150.5
Catron	0.15	43.4	1	D	D	D	13	68	10.7	0.9	NA	NA	NA	NA
Chaves	11.57	175.9	46	446	190.4	17.8	233	3,138	895.1	72.7	78	267	45.8	10.1
Cibola	2.38	87.1	7	D	D	D	70	864	256.7	19.1	12	36	5.8	1.1
Colfax	1.80	145.0	9	D	D	D	77	640	151.6	13.5	26	104	6.7	1.4
Curry	5.20	103.2	46	425	199.8	15.4	190	2,492	624.4	56.0	61	207	30.8	5.6
De Baca	0.24	131.3	1	D	D	D	8	54	13.0	1.2	1	D	D	D
Dona Ana	33.99	158.6	102	D	D	D	496	7,916	1,965.4	167.7	209	690	116.6	18.9
Eddy	13.45	233.6	54	558	1,075.3	23.3	191	2,674	798.7	67.0	55	283	89.5	14.7
Grant	2.49	87.0	14	109	43.3	4.1	114	1,222	257.1	25.1	40	126	15.2	2.8
Guadalupe	0.58	132.7	1	D	D	D	16	258	126.6	4.2	2	D	D	D
Harding	0.08	114.6	NA	NA	NA	NA	3	D	D	D	NA	NA	NA	NA
Hidalgo	1.73	391.1	2	D	D	D	26	237	157.7	4.8	1	D	D	D
Lea	10.19	143.2	92	D	D	D	214	2,830	919.8	71.1	91	774	247.8	53.2
Lincoln	4.39	226.1	10	D	D	D	135	1,184	279.7	26.9	60	152	22.8	3.3
Los Alamos	3.06	172.1	3	D	D	D	28	472	103.2	10.9	22	66	17.1	2.6
Luna	2.99	122.0	14	D	D	D	74	972	210.0	19.2	23	47	7.7	1.3
McKinley	3.40	44.3	44	D	D	D	227	3,271	996.7	72.6	42	158	28.4	5.4
Mora	0.33	71.8	NA	NA	NA	NA	7	D	D	D	1	D	D	D
Otero	6.69	103.9	24	D	D	D	186	2,185	567.7	50.6	52	151	18.7	3.5
Quay	1.26	149.0	2	D	D	D	41	461	263.9	8.7	8	13	0.9	0.4
Rio Arriba	1.83	46.4	10	55	43.7	1.0	83	1,068	254.6	27.4	24	64	7.2	1.4
Roosevelt	2.72	142.3	11	87	70.7	2.8	52	650	156.8	14.8	11	26	3.9	0.6
Sandoval	11.24	80.6	40	235	88.8	8.7	189	3,397	942.3	79.4	75	198	39.7	7.8
San Juan	18.83	158.6	156	1,412	663.0	73.8	450	6,210	1,801.6	157.4	107	750	205.0	36.8
San Miguel	2.19	78.3	8	D	D	D	81	921	220.9	20.5	18	49	6.3	1.2
Santa Fe	10.57	71.1	111	867	773.2	37.4	813	8,981	2,324.5	250.1	280	933	181.8	36.9
Sierra	1.53	135.6	2	D	D	D	43	474	102.1	9.0	9	17	2.5	0.4
Socorro	1.99	115.3	1	D	D	D	39	483	119.8	10.6	11	32	3.1	0.6
Taos	2.41	73.2	17	D	D	D	211	1,438	304.1	32.0	62	213	19.3	4.4
Torrance	1.76	113.7	9	D	D	D	43	494	154.0	9.8	2	D	D	D
Union	0.52	123.8	NA	NA	NA	NA	21	131	33.2	2.5	1	D	D	D
Valencia	4.94	65.2	18	D	D	D	140	2,212	601.3	50.0	43	D	D	D
NEW YORK	2,424.65	122.5	28,853	325,663	341,735.0	19,833.3	77,463	905,325	251,167.7	23,641.2	32,033	166,315	56,409.8	8,654.4
Albany	45.78	148.0	394	4,810	4,329.6	252.9	1,305	21,436	5,762.8	538.6	412	2,637	565.5	101.6
Allegany	3.12	65.7	18	131	94.9	4.5	145	1,396	271.1	26.8	19	34	6.1	1.3
Bronx	0.00	0.0	676	10,510	10,994.5	587.4	3,932	27,777	6,872.8	616.4	2,235	8,856	1,899.7	302.1
Broome	18.73	95.3	196	3,870	2,968.8	163.5	719	11,290	2,741.2	246.2	160	834	180.3	27.5
Cattaraugus	9.45	121.3	49	709	637.7	26.4	339	4,084	1,091.5	90.4	45	257	29.1	7.7
Cayuga	5.43	69.4	63	912	623.4	43.6	260	3,535	874.7	78.5	59	178	29.1	4.4
Chautauqua	12.58	96.2	109	1,405	693.2	58.8	508	6,313	1,437.9	132.3	88	560	447.5	19.9
Chemung	8.37	96.1	85	1,193	765.0	51.5	350	5,044	1,174.8	115.8	84	382	106.6	17.0
Chenango	2.22	45.5	24	D	D	D	170	1,953	512.8	41.7	24	D	D	D
Clinton	4.93	60.7	90	1,293	709.1	56.4	368	5,354	1,385.3	115.3	76	280	45.0	8.4
Columbia	2.97	48.3	53	729	306.1	30.1	267	2,770	748.8	67.9	58	181	21.7	4.2
Cortland	3.80	78.4	33	D	D	D	177	2,415	694.4	54.0	40	146	24.4	4.2
Delaware	405.54	8,805.9	30	573	256.8	29.6	183	1,784	472.7	39.1	30	75	10.7	1.8
Dutchess	18.97	64.1	214	1,909	4,342.1	130.8	1,046	14,155	3,792.7	349.9	325	1,324	246.3	45.7
Erie	171.43	185.8	998	18,454	19,343.2	1,011.2	3,343	52,423	12,106.1	1,139.3	785	5,883	862.2	190.9
Essex	5.45	141.6	15	169	82.5	4.9	214	2,192	514.0	49.2	31	D	D	D
Franklin	3.83	75.6	23	203	149.2	6.8	185	1,855	501.8	45.2	33	94	12.6	2.3
Fulton	5.46	101.1	50	465	244.9	21.2	205	2,382	675.3	57.4	30	118	18.2	3.6

1 Merchant wholesalers, except manufacturers' sales branches and offices.   2. Employer establishments.

Table B. States and Counties — Professional Services, Manufacturing, and Accommodation and Food Services

STATE County	Professional, scientific, and technical services, 2012				Manufacturing, 2012				Accommodation and food services, 2012			
	Number of establish-ments	Number of employees	Sales (mil dol)	Average payroll (mil dol)	Number of establish-ments	Number of employees	Receipts (mil dol)	Annual payroll (mil dol)	Number of establis-hments	Number of employees	Receipts (mil dol)	Annual payroll (mil dol)
	147	148	149	150	151	152	153	154	155	156	157	158
NEW JERSEY— Cont'd												
Mercer	1,591	21,394	5,318.1	2,127.7	246	7,070	2,220.3	378.2	812	11,894	731.4	201.0
Middlesex	4,053	50,970	10,318.6	3,919.9	742	28,277	15,784.9	1,765.7	1,685	21,988	1,387.2	361.2
Monmouth	2,621	20,213	3,516.5	1,446.3	426	8,551	3,053.1	440.2	1,652	23,082	1,318.9	356.7
Morris	2,665	36,232	8,207.1	3,128.9	529	14,358	5,178.0	835.8	1,284	18,783	1,235.0	337.9
Ocean	1,091	5,988	839.5	301.7	278	5,069	1,400.0	231.1	1,145	12,911	801.5	203.7
Passaic	1,051	7,060	1,023.8	413.3	716	18,337	5,214.5	1,030.3	975	10,172	648.0	156.1
Salem	80	D	D	D	38	2,617	D	187.3	106	1,691	89.2	22.8
Somerset	1,827	25,815	5,063.6	2,307.5	300	12,329	4,974.7	1,007.3	798	11,509	739.9	210.9
Sussex	335	1,357	181.3	67.8	119	1,932	465.8	100.1	294	3,455	222.3	52.7
Union	1,389	16,181	1,875.4	1,171.6	619	20,790	20,139.4	1,727.9	1,134	12,856	819.1	211.9
Warren	230	D	D	D	108	3,854	2,050.3	227.0	245	2,294	122.2	32.1
NEW MEXICO	4,687	44,175	7,618.8	2,771.8	1,389	26,731	29,102.4	1,349.2	4,177	82,601	4,349.7	1,250.4
Bernalillo	2,261	18,714	3,488.9	1,101.8	575	11,976	D	569.9	1,394	31,736	1,702.6	495.5
Catron	4	D	D	D	4	13	D	0.6	12	38	1.7	0.4
Chaves	108	994	172.6	64.1	37	877	770.2	37.5	128	2,300	107.8	28.5
Cibola	17	D	D	D	6	38	D	1.1	36	584	27.5	7.7
Colfax	23	D	D	D	13	98	D	3.7	64	1,091	67.0	21.9
Curry	88	535	49.7	19.0	25	534	D	28.5	83	1,949	78.2	22.3
De Baca	1	D	D	D	NA	NA	NA	NA	5	D	D	D
Dona Ana	339	D	D	D	128	2,520	D	87.1	319	6,813	285.2	80.7
Eddy	77	593	54.1	33.5	35	1,459	D	112.1	111	2,083	118.0	31.0
Grant	47	D	D	D	14	121	D	3.6	78	862	33.1	9.6
Guadalupe	2	D	D	D	NA	NA	NA	NA	23	302	15.4	4.3
Harding	NA	NA	NA	NA	NA	NA	NA	NA	1	D	D	D
Hidalgo	4	D	D	D	NA	NA	NA	NA	16	207	9.6	2.7
Lea	82	569	82.1	30.8	37	854	D	68.0	138	2,261	132.1	30.2
Lincoln	53	D	D	D	17	67	D	2.6	99	1,185	60.5	18.0
Los Alamos	65	D	D	D	8	47	D	2.0	37	450	23.8	6.3
Luna	20	D	D	D	12	287	D	9.0	56	770	32.4	8.7
McKinley	43	D	D	D	24	383	D	26.7	143	2,508	119.4	31.5
Mora	NA	NA	NA	NA	NA	NA	NA	NA	3	D	D	D
Otero	71	D	D	D	28	190	D	5.1	108	2,422	164.7	45.1
Quay	12	D	D	D	4	24	D	1.3	33	536	22.9	6.0
Rio Arriba	35	D	D	D	22	95	D	2.9	66	1,089	70.7	20.3
Roosevelt	16	D	D	D	14	329	449.8	14.6	30	587	20.5	6.2
Sandoval	172	760	94.1	39.6	60	3,747	D	243.4	156	3,482	161.0	50.9
San Juan	256	D	D	D	85	1,318	268.6	62.8	197	4,253	201.8	56.3
San Miguel	35	D	D	D	9	48	9.1	1.5	58	719	34.4	8.9
Santa Fe	625	2,604	356.9	151.5	138	719	131.0	27.5	421	9,049	592.4	179.9
Sierra	15	D	D	D	5	121	D	3.0	39	390	15.8	4.7
Socorro	24	D	D	D	5	64	D	2.2	41	621	24.8	6.8
Taos	97	D	D	D	39	104	D	2.6	151	1,974	92.2	31.5
Torrance	13	D	D	D	11	132	D	4.5	26	D	D	D
Union	7	D	D	D	NA	NA	NA	NA	14	171	6.3	1.8
Valencia	75	D	D	D	27	523	D	23.6	91	D	D	D
NEW YORK	59,302	588,820	133,638.8	49,200.3	16,475	426,621	148,879.9	22,073.3	49,731	679,146	49,285.5	13,734.3
Albany	1,116	14,737	3,110.3	1,023.3	231	7,327	3,547.4	423.5	1,011	15,417	866.6	240.8
Allegany	49	199	20.4	7.2	46	2,433	841.8	108.8	92	1,175	50.0	12.4
Bronx	671	3,704	376.9	147.0	323	6,197	1,477.9	251.5	1,735	15,924	1,005.1	250.4
Broome	312	D	D	D	173	7,718	2,200.8	403.1	522	7,985	387.4	104.5
Cattaraugus	96	518	67.8	23.8	74	4,669	1,558.6	286.1	213	2,835	128.6	36.4
Cayuga	92	477	44.4	19.9	88	3,143	1,065.7	155.1	182	1,977	89.5	25.5
Chautauqua	194	1,108	87.5	33.3	197	9,474	5,107.5	428.6	347	4,735	208.7	57.7
Chemung	111	774	83.5	36.1	85	5,495	1,247.0	278.8	202	3,534	154.5	43.3
Chenango	64	316	26.3	8.8	74	3,443	1,661.4	165.3	94	769	34.7	10.0
Clinton	128	734	67.1	26.7	78	3,161	1,279.4	138.5	187	2,648	139.2	38.3
Columbia	175	562	73.5	27.5	73	1,290	462.6	53.7	161	1,419	72.7	20.8
Cortland	82	1,036	99.7	51.1	66	3,163	711.4	146.5	134	2,574	101.0	28.7
Delaware	75	219	21.2	5.8	36	3,593	1,557.2	195.7	124	1,060	44.6	12.4
Dutchess	775	4,010	624.7	224.1	198	8,544	2,481.9	668.2	784	9,107	499.5	136.0
Erie	2,138	28,912	3,598.2	1,656.1	1,008	42,606	15,835.4	2,250.2	2,279	41,143	1,871.9	551.5
Essex	71	D	D	D	28	782	213.1	56.6	201	2,360	150.3	47.2
Franklin	65	410	33.4	17.3	28	460	250.2	19.9	115	846	51.2	13.0
Fulton	77	300	26.2	8.9	71	1,724	712.2	66.3	131	1,209	56.1	15.8

Health Care and Social Assistance, Other Services, Nonemployer Businesses, and Residential Construction

STATE County	Health care and social assistance, 2012				Other services, 2012				Nonemployer businesses, 2016		Value of residential construction authorized by building permits, 2018	
	Number of establishments	Number of employees	Receipts (mil dol)	Annual payroll (mil dol)	Number of establishments	Number of employees	Receipts (mil dol)	Annual payroll (mil dol)	Number	Receipts (mil dol)	New construction ($1,000)	Number of housing units
	159	160	161	162	163	164	165	166	167	168	169	170
NEW JERSEY— Cont'd												
Mercer	1,165	28,970	2,981.0	1,326.6	815	6,403	1,245.5	239.1	25,163	1,388.3	54,987	501
Middlesex	2,195	46,302	5,084.5	2,039.8	1,569	10,342	1,635.7	398.2	57,590	3,297.7	429,196	2,737
Monmouth	2,382	40,905	4,809.5	1,842.3	1,477	8,532	738.0	223.9	55,531	3,726.4	345,298	1,897
Morris	1,727	34,457	4,235.4	1,784.5	1,200	7,548	802.0	232.2	43,758	3,056.4	230,239	1,589
Ocean	1,537	30,984	3,185.9	1,246.7	1,061	5,433	489.4	129.6	41,690	2,394.5	442,360	2,283
Passaic	1,431	25,884	2,516.8	1,059.9	956	4,962	443.6	118.5	40,074	2,058.6	57,403	624
Salem	165	3,312	319.9	122.3	100	386	29.1	7.5	2,830	127.7	9,460	63
Somerset	1,173	21,653	2,475.7	980.8	714	4,882	643.1	156.7	27,536	1,768.4	149,698	1,309
Sussex	361	6,319	551.2	232.3	300	1,285	112.4	33.1	11,135	617.5	19,665	156
Union	1,551	31,943	3,370.8	1,367.2	1,188	6,710	646.0	211.4	44,132	2,499.9	182,343	2,312
Warren	295	4,571	543.1	218.3	222	1,095	112.9	29.0	7,138	356.3	16,511	108
NEW MEXICO	4,967	116,557	11,236.6	4,588.0	2,962	17,464	1,798.6	501.4	122,042	4,803.1	114,651	423
Bernalillo	1,893	48,404	5,278.0	2,143.7	1,096	7,326	750.0	217.2	40,613	1,697.7	291,352	1,284
Catron	7	120	2.7	1.7	5	D	D	D	356	12.0	NA	NA
Chaves	176	3,778	331.1	133.6	79	396	33.7	9.6	3,025	126.4	9,489	57
Cibola	49	1,532	150.8	53.9	23	85	7.3	2.0	1,135	31.9	NA	NA
Colfax	39	593	52.5	25.4	28	87	8.6	2.1	797	27.9	5,894	13
Curry	118	2,829	225.6	87.1	76	468	40.0	9.4	1,999	78.6	19,182	110
De Baca	5	D	D	D	3	D	D	D	111	5.2	NA	NA
Dona Ana	496	12,122	1,010.7	418.4	234	1,124	86.4	26.3	12,557	476.8	199,003	965
Eddy	114	2,875	275.8	112.9	85	501	48.4	12.5	2,464	112.7	46,312	284
Grant	81	1,645	139.1	58.5	45	172	10.9	2.9	1,531	42.8	1,455	9
Guadalupe	9	D	D	D	9	D	D	D	182	4.9	NA	NA
Harding	1	D	D	D	NA	NA	NA	NA	61	3.8	NA	NA
Hidalgo	10	133	7.6	3.3	3	D	D	D	219	7.0	NA	NA
Lea	112	2,329	207.9	78.7	105	800	122.2	31.3	3,094	149.1	35,130	166
Lincoln	47	598	63.8	25.4	40	204	14.8	3.9	1,863	71.9	29,671	87
Los Alamos	67	1,095	102.6	41.2	24	203	11.2	2.8	1,064	39.6	3,382	11
Luna	50	855	76.3	30.1	28	83	6.6	1.6	982	33.4	3,383	19
McKinley	107	4,407	374.3	155.3	78	469	55.3	10.8	3,428	79.3	658	4
Mora	5	119	4.3	2.5	4	D	D	D	301	8.3	NA	NA
Otero	101	2,241	210.4	81.4	67	357	21.3	6.3	3,298	113.9	0	0
Quay	26	406	37.9	11.9	23	112	13.1	2.8	387	13.7	NA	NA
Rio Arriba	84	1,878	141.5	63.0	23	115	12.2	3.3	1,856	58.4	NA	NA
Roosevelt	32	752	57.3	23.2	17	69	8.1	1.7	860	30.8	3,232	21
Sandoval	201	3,058	284.8	107.2	109	583	45.2	16.1	8,046	294.7	158,499	781
San Juan	275	6,819	682.5	291.7	226	1,571	164.1	54.5	5,104	193.9	15,779	71
San Miguel	73	2,950	178.1	80.2	28	150	7.5	2.1	1,342	40.7	140	1
Santa Fe	513	8,697	961.0	384.4	335	1,892	268.6	66.4	16,294	757.5	65,954	273
Sierra	20	784	40.2	19.4	19	106	10.1	2.1	713	24.0	0	0
Socorro	29	736	48.7	24.6	12	D	D	D	746	20.3	359	2
Taos	103	1,476	120.9	53.7	57	229	18.3	5.3	3,293	105.0	13,591	111
Torrance	21	273	10.0	5.1	8	D	D	D	774	26.1	NA	NA
Union	13	D	D	D	10	34	2.9	0.6	291	8.8	NA	NA
Valencia	90	2,685	117.5	57.7	63	D	D	D	3,256	106.2	20,441	121
NEW YORK	56,734	1,468,987	155,666.1	65,180.0	45,646	271,689	39,709.2	9,395.1	1,708,374	89,515.1	6,692,382	37,778
Albany	1,017	33,297	3,522.5	1,396.7	810	5,994	691.9	220.5	17,933	960.7	229,740	679
Allegany	100	1,793	119.8	50.7	75	263	20.0	4.4	2,442	82.8	4,673	42
Bronx	2,145	98,945	10,001.3	4,584.1	1,757	8,242	782.4	224.0	115,123	3,521.5	484,404	3,698
Broome	435	14,852	1,527.8	612.6	341	1,937	151.1	43.6	9,824	404.2	29,851	283
Cattaraugus	175	3,585	324.5	123.1	123	666	53.8	13.7	3,748	144.5	11,693	85
Cayuga	198	4,036	302.4	136.8	131	518	41.1	9.8	4,192	167.8	18,161	116
Chautauqua	279	8,791	623.9	263.5	253	1,448	105.7	24.1	7,018	267.9	24,456	135
Chemung	211	6,421	621.6	294.0	128	670	57.3	15.6	3,870	141.5	30,006	186
Chenango	107	2,025	158.6	65.3	77	256	22.5	6.4	2,729	102.5	8,284	160
Clinton	239	5,147	499.7	231.6	116	560	50.1	13.0	3,949	157.4	21,804	137
Columbia	153	3,929	330.5	150.5	99	335	35.2	9.5	6,015	268.1	26,482	97
Cortland	127	3,591	231.6	106.1	93	401	35.2	9.0	2,264	90.4	12,043	93
Delaware	114	2,167	152.1	63.3	83	417	75.1	10.5	3,547	138.4	6,749	40
Dutchess	901	18,607	2,004.6	847.0	591	2,592	279.2	73.3	21,564	1,035.5	148,667	521
Erie	2,675	74,944	7,532.5	3,154.4	1,752	11,023	1,059.9	283.5	47,797	2,191.2	305,839	1,249
Essex	151	1,978	140.3	61.6	67	282	29.4	7.4	3,017	110.1	26,029	98
Franklin	170	3,276	285.0	126.0	72	225	19.5	5.0	2,688	105.6	19,099	117
Fulton	182	4,128	260.4	113.7	85	486	38.5	11.5	2,715	101.5	8,878	51

Table B. States and Counties — Government Employment and Payroll, and Local Government Finances

STATE County	Full-time equivalent employees	March payroll (dollars)	Adminis-tration, judicial, and legal	Police and corrections	Fire protection	Highways and transpor-tation	Health and welfare	Natural resources and utilities	Education and libraries	Total (mil dol)	Inter-govern-mental (mil dol)	Taxes Total (mil dol)	Taxes Per capita[1] Total	Taxes Per capita[1] Property
	171	172	173	174	175	176	177	178	179	180	181	182	183	184
NEW JERSEY— Cont'd														
Mercer	15,352	84,285,619	4.4	12.4	3.3	2.0	4.4	4.9	64.8	2,164.5	711.0	1,168.1	3,172	3,117
Middlesex	26,592	147,425,663	4.2	13.0	2.6	1.8	4.3	3.9	68.2	3,819.6	965.9	2,247.0	2,730	2,672
Monmouth	27,427	142,190,760	5.3	14.3	0.7	3.0	5.2	3.7	66.3	3,459.7	822.0	2,117.8	3,365	3,308
Morris	19,889	108,738,326	4.6	10.9	0.8	2.8	3.7	5.8	68.0	2,618.5	372.1	1,893.1	3,801	3,744
Ocean	20,430	99,202,051	5.5	14.5	0.4	3.0	4.9	5.2	63.9	2,394.3	580.3	1,531.1	2,638	2,603
Passaic	15,817	88,473,333	5.1	16.3	5.0	2.0	8.1	4.7	57.7	2,251.4	742.8	1,305.1	2,595	2,566
Salem	3,305	15,720,003	5.8	12.2	0.0	2.4	4.8	2.4	69.6	394.8	172.3	152.1	2,313	2,287
Somerset	13,026	68,430,732	3.9	11.5	0.6	3.4	3.0	2.1	73.5	1,611.4	277.0	1,174.0	3,583	3,530
Sussex	5,561	30,640,722	5.9	8.8	0.2	3.9	3.0	1.3	75.3	772.0	189.2	484.5	3,286	3,255
Union	23,222	130,750,946	5.8	13.4	5.4	2.2	5.9	2.3	63.3	3,230.4	1,130.6	1,723.2	3,168	3,100
Warren	4,346	20,547,388	6.3	9.9	0.9	3.6	6.8	2.0	68.4	536.8	183.8	292.4	2,716	2,688
NEW MEXICO	X	X	X	X	X	X	X	X	X	X	X	X	X	X
Bernalillo	22,833	89,838,327	6.2	16.3	6.5	6.3	5.2	6.3	51.7	2,451.4	1,173.3	882.0	1,310	743
Catron	146	386,239	12.7	8.6	0.0	7.4	4.7	1.5	64.1	15.7	10.9	2.6	698	511
Chaves	2,443	7,710,245	4.6	11.3	4.7	3.4	1.7	6.7	65.0	249.1	177.0	44.9	682	436
Cibola	909	2,491,571	7.4	11.5	1.3	2.3	1.9	3.3	70.0	97.5	46.9	12.3	451	248
Colfax	652	2,023,377	9.7	9.4	4.3	3.0	9.7	10.8	51.3	63.7	33.7	19.3	1,463	839
Curry	2,120	6,374,697	3.9	9.1	4.6	2.6	2.3	2.7	74.0	176.6	105.3	49.5	991	345
De Baca	134	371,334	8.8	11.3	0.0	8.7	3.7	10.9	56.5	13.8	7.8	2.5	1,319	841
Dona Ana	7,916	26,726,295	5.8	10.4	2.7	2.6	2.1	5.9	66.7	732.8	425.3	209.7	978	447
Eddy	2,143	8,178,370	5.4	14.2	5.2	4.3	2.1	6.4	59.3	275.0	129.3	115.7	2,126	1,225
Grant	1,747	5,905,715	4.3	7.8	1.4	2.5	44.2	2.7	35.9	187.1	80.4	29.7	1,009	473
Guadalupe	390	1,120,471	7.2	4.4	2.0	4.0	2.5	2.3	74.8	29.2	18.8	6.1	1,319	617
Harding	70	190,631	18.3	3.6	0.0	12.0	4.9	3.4	55.3	10.0	6.0	3.0	4,246	2,506
Hidalgo	293	795,504	9.1	17.5	0.0	4.5	3.0	5.4	58.2	28.3	19.6	4.7	976	778
Lea	3,191	11,349,323	4.4	10.8	3.6	2.9	15.4	4.7	55.7	413.1	170.9	153.5	2,314	1,380
Lincoln	853	2,783,245	8.5	11.0	3.3	4.9	5.2	9.6	53.8	99.8	41.5	37.7	1,857	1,135
Los Alamos	1,400	5,075,436	10.8	6.3	17.0	4.7	1.3	11.9	40.5	138.8	77.2	49.3	2,712	875
Luna	1,233	3,637,272	6.8	12.9	1.8	1.9	2.6	2.4	66.6	103.9	67.8	23.4	936	513
McKinley	3,373	9,383,425	3.6	7.5	2.2	1.6	1.9	3.4	78.5	249.0	155.9	62.8	861	271
Mora	208	516,517	10.0	3.6	0.0	4.3	0.8	0.5	79.2	16.8	10.9	2.4	506	430
Otero	1,662	5,122,202	6.3	14.5	0.3	2.5	2.3	4.7	67.9	147.4	86.7	40.4	612	307
Quay	563	1,605,317	7.9	9.3	0.4	3.2	4.0	8.7	65.3	54.3	38.6	8.0	912	461
Rio Arriba	1,378	4,062,743	9.2	7.6	1.7	2.7	5.6	3.5	67.3	133.9	69.5	50.2	1,244	819
Roosevelt	849	2,598,517	4.7	9.9	3.2	3.4	1.0	3.2	73.2	65.0	40.9	14.6	714	505
Sandoval	3,959	13,152,644	7.2	11.4	4.7	3.3	1.2	5.4	66.3	399.2	201.9	135.8	1,002	605
San Juan	5,857	21,149,302	4.2	11.0	2.6	2.0	1.9	8.4	68.4	491.8	290.9	126.9	987	702
San Miguel	1,294	3,946,008	6.9	7.5	1.7	1.8	1.8	6.1	72.8	102.3	63.7	27.0	933	408
Santa Fe	4,848	18,022,225	9.3	12.0	6.4	3.8	4.1	9.6	48.1	527.4	253.9	199.3	1,361	807
Sierra	644	2,455,286	6.7	6.0	0.0	1.9	22.5	6.1	54.0	49.9	22.0	12.6	1,060	582
Socorro	721	1,882,356	6.5	9.1	3.0	3.6	4.4	6.7	63.5	61.4	43.7	9.7	551	305
Taos	1,245	3,508,311	12.0	9.6	1.7	3.3	3.5	5.5	61.6	118.8	59.8	45.9	1,400	624
Torrance	904	2,576,995	5.9	5.6	0.5	2.0	1.4	1.7	82.4	69.5	50.0	14.8	923	704
Union	203	666,897	11.2	10.4	3.2	8.9	2.6	4.7	56.6	23.5	13.2	5.9	1,327	768
Valencia	2,378	6,663,270	5.6	7.4	1.3	1.2	2.2	2.4	79.8	195.8	120.3	56.4	736	383
NEW YORK	X	X	X	X	X	X	X	X	X	X	X	X	X	X
Albany	12,459	58,755,137	5.6	15.4	3.5	2.8	8.7	5.3	57.2	1,776.2	540.6	885.9	2,900	2,024
Allegany	2,326	8,539,230	7.1	8.0	0.7	8.2	7.3	2.7	64.1	300.9	162.2	113.9 (2)	2,356 (2)	1,929 (2)
Bronx	(2)	(2)	(2)	(2)	(2)	(2)	(2)	(2)	(2)	(2)	(2)	(2)	(2)	(2)
Broome	9,618	36,733,525	4.9	8.4	2.7	4.4	10.5	3.0	64.3	1,182.8	494.6	520.5	2,628	1,756
Cattaraugus	4,623	18,563,190	6.2	8.6	1.7	8.0	12.2	3.6	59.1	526.9	273.4	184.2	2,318	1,675
Cayuga	3,237	14,564,325	6.1	8.2	3.3	5.0	9.9	3.2	63.1	427.9	185.0	169.5	2,131	1,441
Chautauqua	6,787	27,243,053	4.8	7.7	2.9	6.8	9.0	2.9	65.0	772.7	364.8	268.8	2,013	1,539
Chemung	3,853	14,858,297	5.0	9.7	2.9	4.0	13.2	3.8	59.7	476.3	219.3	175.3	1,971	1,236
Chenango	2,731	10,005,930	6.4	7.7	1.8	9.2	7.9	1.6	64.4	295.2	157.3	105.1	2,106	1,541
Clinton	3,949	16,260,748	5.3	6.0	0.9	6.0	11.3	2.6	65.0	458.8	198.9	190.2	2,329	1,643
Columbia	3,025	13,243,189	8.0	8.1	0.4	9.6	12.9	2.0	57.7	374.6	114.6	212.1	3,394	2,596
Cortland	2,146	9,594,343	7.0	14.5	2.0	8.9	10.2	5.2	50.7	258.6	118.1	110.0	2,223	1,645
Delaware	2,262	8,403,397	8.5	6.5	0.1	11.8	10.9	1.5	59.1	286.6	118.1	136.3	2,883	2,410
Dutchess	12,054	60,953,575	5.6	9.6	3.0	3.7	5.7	1.9	69.4	1,683.1	521.2	964.5	3,244	2,611
Erie	35,259	161,616,876	3.7	12.8	3.3	2.9	5.3	5.1	65.4	5,298.2	2,255.2	2,176.7	2,368	1,547
Essex	1,990	7,313,826	9.9	6.1	1.3	9.8	14.0	4.4	53.3	255.8	76.1	132.5	3,401	2,621
Franklin	2,713	9,538,618	5.8	5.4	0.9	6.2	10.0	2.2	68.0	305.3	153.8	104.0	2,008	1,575
Fulton	2,664	9,331,227	4.7	7.9	2.7	4.8	13.2	1.3	64.4	301.1	138.6	121.2	2,207	1,595

1. Based on the resident population estimated as of July 1 of the year shown.   2. Bronx, Kings, Queens, and Richmond counties are included with New York county.

Table B. States and Counties — Local Government Finances, Government Employment, and Income Taxes

STATE County	Local government finances, 2012 (cont.) Direct general expenditure — Total (mil dol)	Per capita¹ (dollars)	Education	Health and hospitals	Police protection	Public welfare	Highways	Debt outstanding Total (mil dol)	Per capita¹ (dollars)	Government employment, 2017 Federal civilian	Federal military	State and local	Individual income tax returns, 2016 Number of returns	Mean adjusted gross income	Mean income tax
	185	186	187	188	189	190	191	192	193	194	195	196	197	198	199
NEW JERSEY— Cont'd															
Mercer	2,145.5	5,825	52.3	0.9	5.3	4.3	1.4	1,928.9	5,237	2,347	730	37,533	174,760	92,659	15,431
Middlesex	3,874.0	4,707	54.1	1.1	5.8	2.4	1.7	4,163.4	5,059	2,428	1,754	53,133	404,770	76,604	10,459
Monmouth	3,411.5	5,420	54.8	1.1	6.0	2.1	2.9	2,733.3	4,343	2,026	1,403	33,807	321,630	101,483	17,355
Morris	2,580.5	5,182	55.7	1.5	5.7	1.5	3.1	2,056.9	4,130	5,511	1,103	26,680	253,750	125,309	23,220
Ocean	2,437.7	4,200	51.2	0.6	6.8	3.2	3.4	2,209.0	3,805	3,210	1,401	25,331	286,100	64,762	7,814
Passaic	2,262.2	4,499	45.8	2.5	6.7	5.0	2.2	1,387.8	2,760	1,060	1,002	28,639	249,170	58,074	7,020
Salem	408.1	6,204	53.4	1.9	3.9	2.2	4.2	399.9	6,081	154	123	4,052	30,320	58,937	6,474
Somerset	1,638.3	4,999	58.6	2.0	5.3	1.0	4.6	1,441.4	4,399	1,779	661	16,762	168,810	122,100	22,852
Sussex	733.7	4,976	63.4	1.4	3.9	2.2	4.2	551.0	3,737	325	282	7,541	72,640	78,374	10,538
Union	3,281.6	6,033	53.5	2.9	6.2	1.6	1.8	2,546.6	4,681	1,454	1,120	32,164	274,290	84,019	13,535
Warren	573.8	5,330	58.0	1.8	4.0	3.5	3.9	237.2	2,203	216	209	5,388	53,550	68,159	8,221
NEW MEXICO	X	X	X	X	X	X	X	X	X	29,288	17,348	159,649	907,830	51,290	5,889
Bernalillo	2,337.5	3,471	48.0	2.0	9.0	1.6	5.0	3,333.0	4,949	14,004	5,108	55,444	306,870	55,578	6,667
Catron	17.1	4,674	36.7	2.0	4.1	0.6	7.9	9.9	2,693	96	9	199	1,340	35,643	3,349
Chaves	248.0	3,771	52.6	0.0	6.6	2.3	4.4	107.2	1,630	236	174	4,090	25,000	43,548	5,003
Cibola	102.5	3,749	38.6	30.4	2.4	3.0	2.9	41.6	1,521	290	63	2,867	9,320	37,324	3,067
Colfax	65.2	4,931	40.3	5.9	6.4	0.7	7.3	52.6	3,979	45	30	1,234	5,420	39,255	3,689
Curry	185.3	3,711	57.6	0.2	5.2	0.7	4.3	71.0	1,422	871	4,751	2,419	20,370	40,595	3,874
De Baca	13.6	7,072	35.8	17.8	4.5	0.1	4.9	5.2	2,717	12	5	172	820	52,894	3,954
Dona Ana	719.6	3,356	57.5	1.3	6.7	1.9	4.1	440.1	2,052	3,401	559	16,476	91,660	42,947	4,403
Eddy	252.5	4,640	47.2	2.8	8.5	1.6	5.2	120.4	2,213	692	145	3,256	23,640	71,318	10,125
Grant	196.6	6,690	26.5	40.7	4.6	2.8	2.6	102.5	3,489	197	70	3,051	12,060	43,446	4,152
Guadalupe	26.2	5,682	37.7	0.7	4.4	6.5	5.2	22.0	4,789	24	10	374	1,810	29,017	1,822
Harding	10.9	15,478	46.4	1.6	4.0	0.1	7.1	5.9	8,396	12	2	77	320	35,353	3,206
Hidalgo	27.3	5,693	43.1	2.0	15.9	0.6	2.6	9.5	1,987	255	11	369	1,770	35,427	2,679
Lea	416.5	6,278	45.5	12.6	5.6	1.1	7.8	219.2	3,304	89	173	3,675	26,920	50,846	5,451
Lincoln	102.5	5,048	37.3	4.2	6.6	0.5	5.9	89.0	4,382	95	50	1,075	9,000	46,144	5,260
Los Alamos	168.1	9,258	31.9	0.0	4.1	1.6	6.7	190.8	10,505	236	50	1,644	9,260	103,121	15,321
Luna	99.5	3,974	55.3	2.0	7.7	1.0	3.5	25.7	1,027	407	61	1,626	10,420	31,647	2,219
McKinley	255.3	3,497	63.0	1.1	4.0	1.8	3.8	145.8	1,997	2,509	186	4,730	30,850	33,119	2,588
Mora	17.2	3,658	55.5	0.3	2.6	0.0	3.0	10.3	2,189	36	12	246	2,030	31,896	2,523
Otero	149.2	2,258	50.7	0.5	8.4	3.1	9.6	138.3	2,094	1,720	4,167	4,545	26,310	40,611	3,561
Quay	53.7	6,124	48.7	5.9	4.7	3.6	4.1	28.0	3,197	30	21	814	3,610	29,786	2,561
Rio Arriba	130.8	3,245	54.4	0.5	4.5	1.1	2.9	101.6	2,519	276	100	4,456	16,450	41,129	3,716
Roosevelt	64.4	3,152	61.8	0.1	6.6	2.2	4.8	18.8	922	40	46	2,051	7,460	34,762	3,183
Sandoval	384.6	2,836	51.6	0.1	6.8	1.0	6.1	599.5	4,422	366	367	7,200	64,490	57,107	6,330
San Juan	551.0	4,287	55.6	3.3	6.3	1.2	4.3	2,140.3	16,652	1,510	327	9,635	48,640	48,945	5,153
San Miguel	108.9	3,769	60.5	0.3	4.2	0.7	4.8	73.4	2,539	128	69	3,373	11,740	34,250	2,879
Santa Fe	578.2	3,950	45.8	1.3	6.0	2.2	3.5	916.2	6,259	988	387	14,463	75,700	69,520	10,082
Sierra	50.5	4,245	27.8	29.9	10.1	1.0	8.1	29.4	2,475	86	28	803	4,860	34,806	2,983
Socorro	72.0	4,091	47.8	0.2	3.8	0.0	4.6	25.8	1,466	175	42	2,444	6,660	38,027	3,309
Taos	129.6	3,953	49.9	1.4	3.2	2.6	3.3	125.3	3,823	260	84	1,809	15,260	42,426	4,535
Torrance	69.7	4,348	66.8	0.8	2.8	0.8	2.9	231.1	14,425	63	39	914	5,710	34,889	3,043
Union	21.1	4,754	42.4	8.0	5.7	1.5	6.6	13.0	2,941	42	9	277	1,590	37,342	3,696
Valencia	184.9	2,413	64.8	0.5	5.8	0.6	3.4	196.9	2,570	97	193	3,841	30,590	43,903	3,962
NEW YORK	X	X	X	X	X	X	X	X	X	116,538	55,540	1,286,867	9,588,900	80,281	13,112
Albany	1,817.9	5,952	40.0	3.9	5.2	11.2	3.9	2,211.1	7,239	5,098	679	57,475	152,380	72,666	10,366
Allegany	309.4	6,398	47.0	2.5	1.8	9.8	11.7	294.0	6,080	115	66	3,960	18,650	46,444	4,547
Bronx	(2)	(2)	(2)	(2)	(2)	(2)	(2)	(2)	(2)	4,072	2,347	57,926	653,330	36,817	3,148
Broome	1,232.1	6,221	48.7	3.4	2.9	12.0	3.8	1,229.8	6,209	523	286	18,053	87,450	52,748	5,961
Cattaraugus	550.0	6,922	49.6	5.9	2.3	13.2	7.5	513.3	6,460	258	122	9,498	33,990	47,518	4,804
Cayuga	442.3	5,560	52.0	4.7	3.2	9.3	6.8	308.3	3,875	150	115	5,652	35,100	51,949	5,557
Chautauqua	806.8	6,042	50.1	3.0	2.9	12.8	6.0	665.7	4,985	311	193	8,706	56,620	45,631	4,413
Chemung	467.0	5,252	42.9	3.0	3.0	18.1	8.9	490.6	5,518	211	128	5,817	38,630	52,861	5,779
Chenango	297.2	5,953	57.1	3.1	1.6	8.2	7.3	216.1	4,329	88	73	4,147	22,490	46,264	4,490
Clinton	495.0	6,062	54.0	4.9	1.9	11.3	5.6	401.8	4,921	688	118	7,283	36,370	51,712	5,431
Columbia	381.3	6,100	48.0	4.5	2.2	13.2	9.0	225.4	3,607	153	91	4,443	29,980	66,289	8,910
Cortland	277.6	5,611	47.3	4.6	3.0	10.4	8.5	199.2	4,027	112	69	4,144	20,470	49,982	5,165
Delaware	281.8	5,961	44.9	3.5	1.5	9.4	12.5	208.3	4,406	121	66	4,174	19,720	47,985	4,970
Dutchess	1,642.8	5,525	55.5	3.6	3.3	7.6	4.0	1,417.6	4,768	1,304	432	18,494	141,840	74,168	9,925
Erie	5,644.5	6,141	44.0	10.5	3.7	9.5	3.2	5,158.7	5,613	8,425	1,608	65,892	448,110	60,499	7,721
Essex	273.6	7,022	36.7	6.8	1.3	10.7	9.0	306.9	7,877	324	55	3,992	17,770	51,923	5,839
Franklin	335.9	6,486	56.1	3.6	1.2	11.1	5.6	277.2	5,352	169	69	7,437	20,120	47,534	4,875
Fulton	288.3	5,250	49.7	2.7	2.5	16.8	5.0	192.0	3,496	82	83	3,482	24,910	48,009	4,662

1. Based on the resident population estimated as of July 1 of the year shown.   2. Bronx, Kings, Queens, and Richmond counties are included with New York county

Table B. States and Counties — Land Area and Population

State / county code	CBSA code[1]	County code[2]	STATE County	Land area[3] (sq. mi)	Total persons 2018	Rank	Per square mile	White	Black	American Indian, Alaska Native	Asian and Pacific Islancer	Percent Hispanic or Latino[4]	Under 5 years	5 to 17 years	18 to 24 years	25 to 34 years	35 to 44 years	45 to 54 years
				1	2	3	4	5	6	7	8	9	10	11	12	13	14	15
			NEW YORK— Cont'd															
36037	12,860	4	Genesee	492.9	57,511	898	116.7	92.0	3.9	1.4	1.1	3.4	5.2	15.1	8.3	12.4	11.1	13.8
36039		6	Greene	647.2	47,491	1,027	73.4	86.6	6.6	0.8	1.8	6.0	4.1	12.3	9.1	11.8	10.9	13.7
36041		8	Hamilton	1,717.4	4,434	2,864	2.6	96.1	1.6	0.9	1.1	1.7	2.6	10.3	5.8	7.6	8.7	12.9
36043	46,540	2	Herkimer	1,411.5	61,833	852	43.8	95.6	1.9	0.6	0.9	2.2	5.1	15.5	8.3	11.4	10.8	13.0
36045	48,060	3	Jefferson	1,268.7	111,755	545	88.1	83.5	7.5	1.0	2.8	7.8	7.8	16.2	12.3	17.1	11.6	10.4
36047	35,620	1	Kings	69.4	2,582,830	9	37,216.6	37.8	31.0	0.6	13.6	19.1	7.2	15.6	8.1	18.4	13.9	11.7
36049		6	Lewis	1,274.6	26,447	1,549	20.7	96.7	1.1	0.6	0.8	1.8	6.2	16.7	7.5	11.6	11.1	12.8
36051	40,380	1	Livingston	631.8	63,227	840	100.1	92.1	3.1	0.7	1.9	3.7	4.3	13.4	15.1	10.8	10.4	13.1
36053	45,060	2	Madison	654.9	70,795	764	108.1	94.4	2.4	1.0	1.4	2.3	4.6	14.4	12.8	10.6	10.5	13.2
36055	40,380	1	Monroe	656.9	742,474	89	1,130.3	72.2	16.0	0.6	4.5	9.0	5.5	15.3	9.9	14.2	11.3	12.7
36057	11,220	4	Montgomery	403.1	49,455	998	122.7	81.8	2.9	0.6	1.2	14.9	6.2	16.5	8.0	12.5	11.4	12.5
36059	35,620	1	Nassau	284.6	1,358,343	30	4,772.8	60.4	12.2	0.4	11.2	17.2	5.5	16.0	8.8	11.7	12.0	13.9
36061	35,620	1	New York	22.7	1,628,701	21	71,748.9	48.7	13.5	0.5	13.7	25.9	4.7	9.6	8.9	22.3	14.3	12.2
36063	15,380	1	Niagara	522.4	210,433	318	402.8	87.5	8.6	1.6	1.6	3.1	5.3	14.7	8.2	12.6	11.1	13.2
36065	46,540	2	Oneida	1,212.3	229,577	296	189.4	83.3	7.3	0.6	4.7	6.1	5.6	15.6	9.4	12.5	11.1	12.9
36067	45,060	2	Onondaga	778.4	461,809	154	593.3	79.1	12.7	1.4	4.7	5.1	5.7	15.6	10.3	13.3	11.2	12.7
36069	40,380	1	Ontario	644.0	109,864	554	170.6	91.1	3.1	0.5	1.8	5.0	5.0	15.2	9.0	11.2	11.0	13.5
36071	35,620	1	Orange	812.3	381,951	183	470.2	65.3	11.6	0.7	3.5	21.0	6.6	18.8	10.5	11.8	11.8	13.7
36073	40,380	1	Orleans	391.3	40,612	1,161	103.8	87.8	7.0	1.0	0.9	4.9	5.1	14.3	8.7	12.8	11.5	14.0
36075	45,060	2	Oswego	951.6	117,898	528	123.9	95.2	1.6	0.9	1.1	2.7	5.4	15.6	10.7	12.4	10.9	13.8
36077	36,580	7	Otsego	1,001.7	59,749	874	59.6	92.3	2.7	0.6	2.0	3.8	4.2	11.7	16.7	10.0	9.4	11.8
36079	35,620	1	Putnam	230.3	98,892	605	429.4	79.0	3.3	0.4	2.8	15.8	4.5	15.3	8.5	11.0	11.7	15.8
36081	35,620	1	Queens	108.8	2,278,906	11	20,945.8	26.2	19.1	0.8	28.0	28.1	6.2	13.9	7.6	16.1	13.7	13.5
36083	10,580	2	Rensselaer	652.5	159,442	415	244.4	84.7	8.2	0.6	3.4	5.2	5.3	14.3	10.0	14.2	11.8	13.1
36085	35,620	1	Richmond	57.5	476,179	146	8,281.4	61.5	10.2	0.5	10.8	18.7	5.8	16.1	8.3	13.6	12.5	13.8
36087	35,620	1	Rockland	173.4	325,695	214	1,878.3	64.0	12.2	0.4	6.8	18.1	8.1	20.1	9.2	11.6	11.0	12.2
36089	36,300	4	St. Lawrence	2,679.3	108,047	561	40.3	93.2	2.8	1.4	1.6	2.4	5.1	15.1	13.2	11.8	10.9	12.5
36091	10,580	2	Saratoga	810.0	230,163	294	284.2	91.7	2.4	0.5	3.8	3.4	5.1	14.9	8.2	12.2	12.3	14.7
36093	10,580	2	Schenectady	204.6	155,350	427	759.3	75.9	12.8	1.1	6.3	7.4	5.8	15.7	9.0	13.2	12.3	13.0
36095	10,580	2	Schoharie	621.8	31,097	1,404	50.0	94.2	1.9	0.7	1.2	3.3	4.1	13.3	10.5	10.6	10.4	13.2
36097		6	Schuyler	328.3	17,912	1,925	54.6	96.1	1.6	0.8	1.0	1.9	5.1	14.1	6.8	11.3	11.0	13.8
36099	42,900	6	Seneca	323.7	34,300	1,317	106.0	90.3	5.9	0.9	1.1	3.5	5.2	14.7	8.7	13.5	11.1	12.5
36101	18,500	4	Steuben	1,390.5	95,796	622	68.9	95.0	2.3	0.7	1.9	1.7	5.4	16.0	7.7	11.7	11.3	13.4
36103	35,620	1	Suffolk	911.8	1,481,093	26	1,624.4	68.3	8.1	0.5	4.7	19.8	5.4	15.8	9.0	11.9	11.7	14.8
36105		4	Sullivan	968.1	75,498	733	78.0	73.0	9.4	0.8	2.3	16.6	5.7	15.5	7.9	11.9	11.5	13.8
36107	13,780	2	Tioga	518.6	48,560	1,013	93.6	95.8	1.4	0.6	1.2	2.1	5.2	15.9	7.3	10.8	11.3	13.0
36109	27,060	3	Tompkins	474.6	102,793	591	216.6	79.6	5.2	0.8	12.1	5.3	3.8	10.8	26.5	12.8	10.4	10.1
36111	28,740	3	Ulster	1,124.2	178,599	372	158.9	80.9	7.4	0.8	2.8	10.5	4.4	13.3	9.1	12.6	11.6	13.8
36113	24,020	3	Warren	867.2	64,265	828	74.1	94.8	1.9	0.7	1.3	2.7	4.5	13.8	7.1	11.9	10.6	13.7
36115	24,020	3	Washington	831.2	61,197	858	73.6	93.3	3.4	0.7	0.9	2.8	4.7	14.1	7.9	12.3	11.8	14.3
36117	40,380	1	Wayne	603.8	90,064	652	149.2	91.7	4.0	0.7	1.1	4.5	5.4	15.9	7.6	11.5	10.9	14.1
36119	35,620	1	Westchester	430.6	967,612	50	2,247.1	54.4	14.6	0.4	7.1	25.1	5.6	16.3	8.8	11.5	12.8	14.3
36121		6	Wyoming	592.8	40,085	1,176	67.6	90.7	5.5	0.6	0.8	3.3	4.9	14.0	7.4	14.1	12.4	14.5
36123	40,380	1	Yates	338.1	24,841	1,616	73.5	95.6	1.5	0.6	1.0	2.3	6.0	15.9	10.9	10.8	9.4	11.0
37000		0	**NORTH CAROLINA**	48,619.4	10,383,620	X	213.6	64.5	22.5	1.7	3.7	9.6	5.9	16.3	9.5	13.4	12.5	13.3
37001	15,500	3	Alamance	423.4	166,436	394	393.1	64.9	21.1	0.9	2.1	12.9	5.8	16.5	10.4	12.5	11.5	13.5
37003	25,860	2	Alexander	260.0	37,353	1,240	143.7	88.0	6.8	0.7	1.2	4.8	4.9	15.3	7.4	11.7	12.0	14.5
37005		9	Alleghany	234.4	11,161	2,341	47.6	87.5	2.2	0.9	0.8	9.9	4.6	12.8	6.3	9.4	10.0	13.0
37007		6	Anson	531.5	24,877	1,613	46.8	45.3	49.0	1.1	1.6	4.3	5.1	14.5	8.4	14.3	12.1	13.2
37009		7	Ashe	425.1	27,109	1,519	63.8	93.2	1.2	0.8	0.7	5.2	4.1	13.6	6.3	9.9	11.1	13.2
37011		8	Avery	247.3	17,505	1,949	70.8	89.4	4.9	0.9	0.7	5.2	3.7	11.2	9.4	12.5	12.6	14.1
37013	47,820	6	Beaufort	832.0	47,079	1,035	56.6	66.8	25.2	0.7	0.6	8.0	4.8	15.3	7.1	10.1	10.8	12.6
37015		7	Bertie	699.2	19,026	1,871	27.2	35.5	61.4	1.0	0.9	2.2	4.3	13.3	7.7	12.7	10.5	12.3
37017		6	Bladen	874.9	33,190	1,353	37.9	55.9	34.3	2.9	0.6	7.8	5.1	15.4	7.5	10.8	11.4	12.8
37019	34,820	2	Brunswick	849.2	136,744	468	161.0	83.5	10.9	1.3	1.1	4.9	3.9	11.4	5.3	9.0	9.5	11.2
37021	11,700	2	Buncombe	656.5	259,103	265	394.7	85.3	7.1	1.0	1.9	6.7	5.0	13.5	7.6	14.0	13.3	12.8
37023	25,860	2	Burke	506.2	90,382	650	178.5	82.9	7.6	0.8	4.1	6.2	4.8	14.1	8.7	11.7	11.1	14.4
37025	16,740	1	Cabarrus	361.2	211,342	316	585.1	66.5	19.3	0.8	4.8	10.8	6.5	19.2	8.0	12.6	14.2	14.6
37027	25,860	2	Caldwell	471.9	82,029	693	173.8	88.6	5.8	0.7	0.9	5.7	5.1	15.0	7.6	11.4	11.3	14.9
37029	21,020	8	Camden	240.3	10,710	2,380	44.6	82.6	13.1	1.2	2.9	3.0	5.3	17.5	6.6	11.2	13.4	14.7
37031	33,980	4	Carteret	507.6	69,524	775	137.0	88.3	6.4	1.1	2.0	4.3	4.1	13.4	6.3	10.2	10.9	13.3
37033		8	Caswell	425.4	22,698	1,694	53.4	62.7	33.0	0.9	1.0	4.2	4.8	14.0	7.1	11.5	11.0	14.1
37035	25,860	2	Catawba	401.4	158,652	419	395.2	76.9	9.7	0.6	4.7	9.9	5.6	16.5	8.4	11.9	11.7	14.2
37037	20,500	2	Chatham	681.7	73,139	747	107.3	73.2	12.8	0.7	2.5	12.3	4.9	15.3	6.3	9.0	11.4	13.8
37039		9	Cherokee	455.5	28,383	1,484	62.3	93.1	2.1	2.8	0.9	3.3	4.2	12.6	6.0	8.9	9.8	12.4

1. CBSA = Core Based Statistical Area. See Appendix A for explanation. See Appendix B for list of metropolitan areas with component counties. Service of USDA Rural-Urban Continuum Codes. See Appendix A for definition. 2. County type code from the Economic Research Service of USDA Rural-Urban Continuum Codes. See Appendix A for definition. 3. Dry land or land partially or temporarily covered by water. 4. May be of any race.

Table B. States and Counties — **Population and Households**

STATE County	Population, 2018 (cont.) Age (percent) (cont.)				Population change, 2000-2018							Households, 2013-2017				
					Total persons		Percent change		Components of change, 2010-2018						Percent	
	55 to 64 years	65 to 74 years	75 years and over	Percent female	2000	2010	2000-2010	2010-2018	Births	Deaths	Net Migration	Number	Persons per household	Family house-holds	Female family house-holder[1]	One person
	16	17	18	19	20	21	22	23	24	25	26	27	28	29	30	31
NEW YORK— Cont'd																
Genesee	15.5	10.3	8.4	50.3	60,370	59,943	-0.7	-4.1	4,892	5,090	-2,231	23,951	2.41	64.9	9.1	29.1
Greene	16.0	13.0	9.1	47.7	48,195	49,215	2.1	-3.5	3,319	4,236	-785	17,106	2.60	61.9	8.3	32.4
Hamilton	20.8	19.4	11.9	49.9	5,379	4,841	-10.0	-8.4	234	477	-163	1,095	4.13	66.0	7.6	30.2
Herkimer	15.3	11.8	8.9	50.5	64,427	64,461	0.1	-4.1	5,311	5,599	-2,327	25,187	2.45	64.3	10.3	29.4
Jefferson	10.9	8.0	5.7	47.4	111,738	116,234	4.0	-3.9	17,056	7,329	-14,329	43,206	2.54	67.6	10.6	26.4
Kings	11.1	7.9	6.0	52.6	2,465,326	2,504,717	1.6	3.1	341,232	134,716	-127,883	944,650	2.75	62.0	18.6	29.2
Lewis	15.7	10.4	7.9	49.3	26,944	27,090	0.5	-2.4	2,705	2,064	-1,288	10,236	2.59	70.2	8.2	23.0
Livingston	15.1	10.4	7.5	49.8	64,328	65,207	1.4	-3.0	4,379	4,407	-1,944	24,432	2.38	63.2	10.9	28.4
Madison	15.6	10.6	7.7	50.7	69,441	73,451	5.8	-3.6	5,409	5,086	-2,986	26,307	2.53	64.1	10.0	28.3
Monroe	13.8	9.8	7.4	51.7	735,343	744,399	1.2	-0.3	68,160	54,083	-15,927	300,496	2.40	60.6	13.9	32.0
Montgomery	14.3	10.6	8.0	50.8	49,708	50,258	1.1	-1.6	4,842	4,754	-882	19,700	2.46	63.5	14.0	30.1
Nassau	14.3	9.8	8.0	51.3	1,334,544	1,339,885	0.4	1.4	117,313	90,708	-7,453	444,136	3.02	76.6	11.4	20.2
New York	11.3	9.0	7.5	52.7	1,537,195	1,586,360	3.2	2.7	151,330	85,624	-22,964	758,345	2.10	42.3	11.2	46.3
Niagara	15.9	10.9	8.2	51.3	219,846	216,485	-1.5	-2.8	17,759	19,508	-4,180	87,978	2.37	62.1	12.5	32.2
Oneida	14.1	10.3	8.5	50.2	235,469	234,869	-0.3	-2.3	21,164	20,672	-5,771	90,472	2.43	62.4	13.1	31.6
Onondaga	14.1	9.6	7.4	51.8	458,336	467,064	1.9	-1.1	43,563	34,902	-13,924	185,840	2.41	61.1	13.1	31.1
Ontario	15.2	11.8	8.2	51.0	100,224	108,090	7.8	1.6	8,483	8,741	2,139	44,269	2.39	64.5	10.2	29.2
Orange	12.7	8.3	5.8	49.9	341,367	372,829	9.2	2.4	40,187	21,869	-9,268	126,460	2.90	70.5	11.9	24.8
Orleans	15.8	10.5	7.4	50.1	44,171	42,883	-2.9	-5.3	3,430	3,470	-2,245	16,214	2.38	66.4	13.2	26.8
Oswego	15.0	9.8	6.5	49.9	122,377	122,105	-0.2	-3.4	10,772	8,760	-6,246	45,881	2.51	67.0	11.8	25.0
Otsego	14.9	12.1	9.1	51.5	61,676	62,277	1.0	-4.1	4,277	4,963	-1,826	23,627	2.33	63.5	9.0	27.8
Putnam	15.9	10.3	7.1	50.0	95,745	99,650	4.1	-0.8	6,919	5,743	-1,931	34,316	2.82	75.3	8.1	20.6
Queens	13.2	8.8	6.9	51.5	2,229,379	2,230,578	0.1	2.2	249,732	121,110	-80,804	777,904	2.97	67.5	15.9	26.2
Rensselaer	14.4	10.1	6.9	50.6	152,538	159,433	4.5	0.0	13,902	12,498	-1,303	64,456	2.39	60.9	11.9	31.0
Richmond	13.8	9.5	6.7	51.5	443,728	468,730	5.6	1.6	44,629	29,980	-7,049	166,150	2.82	74.2	14.6	22.5
Rockland	12.1	8.5	7.2	50.9	286,753	311,694	8.7	4.5	40,873	17,653	-9,278	99,935	3.18	74.8	10.5	21.2
St. Lawrence	13.9	10.1	7.3	48.9	111,931	111,940	0.0	-3.5	9,654	8,274	-5,296	41,638	2.38	63.2	11.4	28.9
Saratoga	14.5	10.8	7.3	50.5	200,635	219,593	9.4	4.8	18,321	14,628	7,028	93,129	2.39	65.6	8.9	27.3
Schenectady	13.8	9.5	7.6	51.3	146,555	154,751	5.6	0.4	14,715	12,568	-1,452	53,825	2.80	61.1	11.5	33.2
Schoharie	16.0	12.9	9.0	49.8	31,582	32,729	3.6	-5.0	2,110	2,356	-1,396	12,539	2.41	63.2	10.1	28.8
Schuyler	16.6	12.7	8.6	50.1	19,224	18,353	-4.5	-2.4	1,405	1,617	-226	7,444	2.39	64.1	10.0	28.9
Seneca	15.1	11.3	7.9	47.5	33,342	35,243	5.7	-2.7	3,039	2,781	-1,189	13,536	2.34	62.0	10.0	29.8
Steuben	14.9	11.3	8.4	50.2	98,726	98,990	0.3	-3.2	8,841	8,107	-3,909	40,351	2.37	64.6	10.7	29.3
Suffolk	14.6	9.5	7.4	50.8	1,419,369	1,493,147	5.2	-0.8	130,331	98,616	-43,698	489,328	3.00	73.5	11.3	22.0
Sullivan	14.8	11.4	7.5	48.5	73,966	77,504	4.8	-2.6	6,950	6,046	-2,942	27,679	2.59	63.1	11.0	30.7
Tioga	16.3	11.3	9.0	50.3	51,784	51,049	-1.4	-4.9	4,056	3,629	-2,933	19,996	2.44	67.6	11.0	27.4
Tompkins	11.2	8.9	5.6	50.8	96,501	101,580	5.3	1.2	7,004	5,514	-343	38,986	2.33	52.4	8.7	32.4
Ulster	15.5	11.6	8.2	50.4	177,749	182,512	2.7	-2.1	12,978	13,758	-3,069	69,662	2.42	62.3	11.0	30.3
Warren	16.1	12.9	9.3	50.9	63,303	65,698	3.8	-2.2	4,789	5,600	-573	27,249	2.34	60.9	10.8	31.9
Washington	15.4	11.3	8.2	48.2	61,042	63,243	3.6	-3.2	4,885	5,074	-1,832	23,988	2.46	67.5	11.7	25.6
Wayne	15.8	11.2	7.7	50.4	93,765	93,754	0.0	-3.9	7,933	7,060	-4,586	36,578	2.45	66.9	10.4	26.5
Westchester	13.6	9.1	8.0	51.6	923,459	949,220	2.8	1.9	87,127	58,614	-9,738	345,885	2.74	69.4	12.4	26.3
Wyoming	14.9	10.9	7.0	45.9	43,424	42,150	-2.9	-4.9	3,203	3,038	-2,244	15,686	2.39	66.3	9.8	27.9
Yates	15.2	12.3	8.5	51.4	24,621	25,364	3.0	-2.1	2,539	2,094	-965	9,338	2.55	67.0	8.9	25.9
NORTH CAROLINA	12.9	9.7	6.5	51.4	8,049,313	9,535,736	18.5	8.9	990,630	708,132	560,003	3,874,346	2.53	65.9	13.2	28.3
Alamance	13.1	9.5	7.4	52.6	130,800	151,160	15.6	10.1	14,876	13,010	13,430	63,035	2.43	65.8	15.0	28.9
Alexander	14.2	11.7	8.4	49.1	33,603	37,185	10.7	0.5	2,923	3,028	297	13,744	2.61	70.6	11.5	25.9
Alleghany	16.9	15.6	11.5	50.5	10,677	11,154	4.5	0.1	784	1,072	303	4,742	2.27	72.3	8.1	25.3
Anson	13.8	10.9	7.6	48.0	25,275	26,929	6.5	-7.6	2,104	2,476	-1,708	9,647	2.46	63.9	17.2	29.5
Ashe	16.2	15.0	10.7	50.9	24,384	27,240	11.7	-0.5	1,887	2,810	815	11,995	2.20	70.4	11.0	25.4
Avery	14.2	12.9	9.3	45.6	17,167	17,812	3.8	-1.7	1,159	1,601	141	6,725	2.17	66.2	8.1	27.6
Beaufort	15.4	14.4	9.6	52.2	44,958	47,768	6.3	-1.4	3,946	4,801	205	18,978	2.47	65.6	12.8	30.3
Bertie	16.1	12.9	10.1	49.5	19,773	21,275	7.6	-10.6	1,485	2,042	-1,706	7,988	2.32	61.5	20.7	35.8
Bladen	15.3	13.2	8.6	52.3	32,278	35,181	9.0	-5.7	2,872	3,405	-1,455	14,394	2.33	65.4	18.8	32.2
Brunswick	18.2	21.3	10.2	52.2	73,143	107,429	46.9	27.3	8,462	10,800	31,120	53,104	2.29	69.0	9.3	26.6
Buncombe	13.8	11.9	8.1	52.1	206,330	238,331	15.5	8.7	21,147	20,616	20,006	105,407	2.33	58.1	8.5	34.1
Burke	15.0	11.5	8.7	50.0	89,148	90,832	1.9	-0.5	7,235	8,414	782	34,568	2.49	66.7	12.8	29.1
Cabarrus	11.7	8.0	5.3	51.3	131,063	178,087	35.9	18.7	19,741	12,406	25,752	70,598	2.76	73.2	12.6	22.7
Caldwell	14.8	11.8	8.1	50.5	77,415	83,060	7.3	-1.2	6,602	7,673	105	32,150	2.51	69.3	12.6	27.2
Camden	14.9	9.5	6.8	50.2	6,885	9,980	45.0	7.3	736	602	598	3,796	2.71	81.8	15.0	15.7
Carteret	16.8	15.2	9.8	51.0	59,383	66,463	11.9	4.6	4,886	6,443	4,616	30,000	2.25	64.3	10.7	29.8
Caswell	16.0	12.8	8.8	49.2	23,501	23,734	1.0	-4.4	1,682	2,184	-540	9,160	2.38	69.5	13.0	27.0
Catawba	13.9	10.7	7.2	51.2	141,685	154,753	9.2	2.5	14,305	13,232	2,935	60,238	2.55	68.6	11.3	26.1
Chatham	15.0	14.0	10.4	52.2	49,329	63,481	28.7	15.2	5,247	5,368	9,698	28,148	2.40	69.0	9.6	27.2
Cherokee	16.4	17.6	12.0	51.3	24,298	27,444	12.9	3.4	1,848	2,989	2,083	11,206	2.41	67.4	10.4	28.7

1. No spouse present.

Table B. States and Counties — Population, Vital Statistics, Health, and Crime

STATE County	Persons in group quarters, 2018	Daytime Population, 2013-2017 Number	Employment/ residence ratio	Births, 2018 Total	Rate¹	Deaths, 2018 Number	Rate¹	Persons under 65 with no health insurance, 2016 Number	Percent	Medicare, 2018 Total beneficiaries	Enrolled in Original Medicare	Enrolled in Medicare Advantage	Serious crimes known to police², 2016 Total Number	Rate³
	32	33	34	35	36	37	38	39	40	41	42	43	44	45
NEW YORK— Cont'd														
Genesee	1,947	54,581	0.86	566	9.8	635	11.0	2,472	5.3	12,812	5,579	7,233	1,263	2,165
Greene	3,210	44,223	0.82	378	8.0	529	11.1	2,001	5.7	11,719	7,399	4,320	540	1,189
Hamilton	79	4,241	0.79	16	3.6	69	15.6	217	6.7	1,575	1,028	547	54	1,160
Herkimer	1,400	53,489	0.66	604	9.8	656	10.6	2,585	5.2	14,661	8,698	5,963	1,059	1,771
Jefferson	6,135	120,144	1.07	1,859	16.6	920	8.2	5,656	6.1	19,849	13,447	6,402	2,362	2,017
Kings	35,539	2,317,483	0.73	39,259	15.2	18,550	7.2	198,931	8.8	366,408	205,096	161,312	(4)	(4)
Lewis	313	23,611	0.72	310	11.7	265	10.0	1,307	5.9	5,377	3,586	1,791	236	882
Livingston	5,876	58,504	0.80	501	7.9	542	8.6	2,210	4.6	13,141	5,210	7,931	882	1,374
Madison	4,582	62,872	0.73	605	8.5	614	8.7	2,682	4.9	14,085	8,289	5,796	1,022	1,438
Monroe	25,919	779,054	1.08	7,798	10.5	6,697	9.0	29,587	4.9	154,339	51,958	102,381	18,755	2,515
Montgomery	916	47,769	0.92	559	11.3	544	11.0	2,372	6.0	12,103	6,361	5,742	1,024	2,082
Nassau	20,482	1,272,557	0.86	14,117	10.4	11,419	8.4	56,454	5.0	262,188	199,341	62,847	15,144	1,117
New York	68,019	3,325,276	2.88	16,906	10.4	12,280	7.5	85,635	6.3	281,505	174,138	107,367	(4)175,814	(4)2,052
Niagara	3,991	190,024	0.77	2,066	9.8	2,374	11.3	8,540	5.0	48,911	19,809	29,102	6,092	2,894
Oneida	13,150	239,502	1.07	2,422	10.5	2,484	10.8	8,892	5.0	52,086	31,201	20,885	5,222	2,266
Onondaga	17,032	497,076	1.13	5,068	11.0	4,266	9.2	19,703	5.2	93,146	49,723	43,423	11,133	2,391
Ontario	3,243	109,642	1.00	972	8.8	1,085	9.9	3,911	4.5	25,232	10,195	15,037	1,866	1,776
Orange	11,265	351,130	0.85	4,905	12.8	2,873	7.5	19,544	6.1	62,266	48,881	13,385	7,328	1,952
Orleans	2,670	37,721	0.78	388	9.6	414	10.2	2,053	6.4	8,599	3,681	4,918	748	1,822
Oswego	4,808	105,418	0.72	1,284	10.9	1,082	9.2	5,083	5.3	24,428	14,371	10,057	2,310	1,942
Otsego	5,266	61,695	1.03	482	8.1	642	10.7	2,670	6.1	14,074	10,428	3,646	777	1,297
Putnam	2,582	76,810	0.55	822	8.3	763	7.7	3,959	4.8	18,529	14,571	3,958	591	614
Queens	27,770	1,965,446	0.66	29,144	12.8	16,669	7.3	225,096	11.3	354,001	186,899	167,102	(4)	(4)
Rensselaer	5,869	137,828	0.72	1,690	10.6	1,608	10.1	6,332	4.9	31,843	17,765	14,078	3,655	2,293
Richmond	7,055	397,574	0.63	5,355	11.2	4,146	8.7	21,728	5.4	87,456	52,376	35,080	(4)	(4)
Rockland	6,947	298,732	0.82	5,345	16.4	2,476	7.6	17,759	6.5	56,301	44,003	12,298	3,542	1,084
St. Lawrence	10,616	108,522	0.95	1,029	9.5	1,082	10.0	5,360	6.6	23,288	16,883	6,405	1,729	1,626
Saratoga	3,400	203,035	0.80	2,190	9.5	2,011	8.7	8,005	4.3	47,069	25,326	21,743	2,816	1,246
Schenectady	4,581	151,065	0.94	1,738	11.2	1,518	9.8	6,130	4.8	31,521	16,093	15,428	4,681	3,049
Schoharie	1,268	28,624	0.78	228	7.3	305	9.8	1,353	5.7	6,685	4,528	2,157	385	1,248
Schuyler	201	15,931	0.73	157	8.8	189	10.6	804	5.6	4,623	2,745	1,878	114	632
Seneca	2,749	33,446	0.91	327	9.5	318	9.3	1,649	6.3	7,505	4,228	3,277	635	1,839
Steuben	1,838	96,440	0.97	980	10.2	1,026	10.7	4,594	5.9	21,993	14,089	7,904	1,519	1,571
Suffolk	29,238	1,411,106	0.88	15,210	10.3	13,061	8.8	74,327	6.0	286,316	229,841	56,475	22,237	1,491
Sullivan	3,791	70,992	0.85	835	11.1	777	10.3	4,087	6.9	16,708	13,904	2,804	1,225	1,658
Tioga	520	41,471	0.65	493	10.2	474	9.8	1,869	4.7	11,201	6,706	4,495	462	947
Tompkins	13,094	116,232	1.24	769	7.5	630	6.1	4,429	5.6	16,429	11,833	4,596	1,805	1,721
Ulster	11,815	164,592	0.82	1,451	8.1	1,738	9.7	9,049	6.5	39,967	29,687	10,280	2,633	1,475
Warren	641	70,855	1.19	555	8.6	674	10.5	2,623	5.2	17,376	9,747	7,629	1,195	1,865
Washington	3,068	52,026	0.64	549	9.0	668	10.9	2,636	5.5	13,612	7,667	5,945	574	932
Wayne	1,083	79,313	0.71	903	10.0	870	9.7	3,992	5.3	21,505	9,077	12,428	1,614	1,786
Westchester	27,966	953,117	0.95	10,041	10.4	7,616	7.9	61,342	7.7	173,563	125,689	47,874	12,431	1,275
Wyoming	3,422	38,025	0.84	386	9.6	344	8.6	1,632	5.4	8,605	3,836	4,769	324	799
Yates	1,251	23,378	0.85	301	12.1	269	10.8	1,816	9.5	5,818	2,657	3,161	320	1,289
NORTH CAROLINA	275,434	10,050,817	1.00	118,784	11.4	93,060	9.0	1,023,107	12.2	1,930,529	1,263,801	666,728	315,534	3,110
Alamance	6,014	149,729	0.89	1,895	11.4	1,623	9.8	17,976	13.9	32,379	14,521	17,858	4,369	2,736
Alexander	1,508	30,805	0.60	356	9.5	391	10.5	3,705	12.9	8,098	5,115	2,983	747	2,000
Alleghany	111	10,785	0.97	97	8.7	135	12.1	1,339	16.8	3,274	2,143	1,131	102	1,126
Anson	2,039	23,502	0.80	256	10.3	267	10.7	2,437	13.2	5,411	3,882	1,529	700	3,324
Ashe	323	24,323	0.79	207	7.6	355	13.1	3,251	16.1	7,666	5,580	2,086	327	1,212
Avery	2,456	18,439	1.14	130	7.4	215	12.3	2,126	18.5	4,319	3,054	1,265	229	1,330
Beaufort	515	46,722	0.97	439	9.3	620	13.2	4,734	13.0	13,110	10,373	2,737	1,194	2,535
Bertie	1,320	19,009	0.87	172	9.0	262	13.8	1,797	12.8	5,289	4,462	827	364	1,867
Bladen	322	35,412	1.10	322	9.7	466	14.0	4,408	16.6	7,860	5,553	2,307	NA	NA
Brunswick	844	114,175	0.82	983	7.2	1,649	12.1	13,022	14.6	45,079	35,296	9,783	1,607	1,393
Buncombe	7,682	271,358	1.16	2,455	9.5	2,668	10.3	22,904	11.3	58,651	41,166	17,485	7,235	2,832
Burke	3,324	84,392	0.88	892	9.9	1,018	11.3	9,950	14.2	20,421	12,544	7,877	2,104	2,438
Cabarrus	1,364	178,060	0.80	2,551	12.1	1,650	7.8	17,123	9.8	32,206	19,300	12,906	3,939	1,966
Caldwell	941	74,298	0.78	787	9.6	965	11.8	9,097	13.9	19,012	11,025	7,987	2,665	3,306
Camden	17	7,060	0.28	90	8.4	57	5.3	909	10.3	1,981	1,689	292	77	742
Carteret	999	65,789	0.90	529	7.6	882	12.7	6,452	12.3	18,432	15,312	3,120	1,039	1,499
Caswell	1,363	17,140	0.39	197	8.7	243	10.7	2,227	13.2	5,895	3,022	2,873	454	1,991
Catawba	2,565	168,882	1.18	1,638	10.3	1,682	10.6	16,641	13.0	35,078	22,007	13,071	4,716	3,046
Chatham	762	56,300	0.60	650	8.9	746	10.2	7,245	13.5	18,072	10,958	7,114	1,214	1,675
Cherokee	436	26,852	0.94	233	8.2	371	13.1	3,073	15.4	9,340	6,738	2,602	854	3,148

1. Per 1,000 estimated resident population.   2. Data for serious crimes have not been adjusted for underreporting; this may affect comparability between geographic areas and over time.   3. Per 100,000 population estimated by the FBI.   4. Bronx, Kings, Queens, and Richmond counties are included with New York county

Items 32—45

Table B. States and Counties — Crime, Education, Money Income, and Poverty

STATE County	Serious crimes known to police[2], 2016 (cont.)[1] Rate		Education School enrollment and attainment, 2013-2017				Local government expenditures,[5] 2014-2015		Money income, 2013-2017				Income and poverty, 2017			
			Enrollment[3]		Attainment[4] (percent)						Households Percent			Percent below poverty level		
	Violent	Property	Total	Percent private	High school graduate or less	Bachelor's degree or more	Total current spending (mil dol)	Current spending per student (dollars)	Per capita income[6]	Median income (dollars)	with income of less than $50,000	with income of $200,000 or more	Median household income (dollars)	All persons	Children under 18 years	Children 5 to 17 years in families
	46	47	48	49	50	51	52	53	54	55	56	57	58	59	60	61
NEW YORK— Cont'd																
Genesee	218	1,947	12,958	11.9	44.7	21.4	153.5	17,974	27,499	54,033	46.1	2.3	55,522	10.8	14.5	13.1
Greene	227	962	7,740	12.4	50.6	22.0	133.7	21,775	27,402	53,214	47.2	3.4	54,635	12.7	19.5	18.4
Hamilton	107	1,052	740	12.4	44.3	20.0	18.5	47,250	24,891	55,587	45.2	2.1	51,520	9.8	15.8	13.6
Herkimer	201	1,570	13,753	10.9	46.7	20.7	153.2	15,889	24,932	49,077	50.8	1.8	46,733	14.3	21.2	19.6
Jefferson	240	1,777	27,217	13.0	43.3	21.4	238.1	15,742	24,717	50,322	49.6	2.0	47,436	15.1	21.0	21.0
Kings	(7)	(7)	662,415	29.0	45.0	35.2	(7)	(7)	29,928	52,782	47.8	7.2	56,548	19.8	26.7	26.3
Lewis	112	770	5,758	14.1	56.1	16.3	130.0	17,055	25,779	51,475	48.5	2.8	51,857	12.5	20.2	19.4
Livingston	142	1,232	16,933	9.2	44.3	23.7	142.4	17,627	25,882	53,654	46.6	2.4	56,407	12	14.6	12.9
Madison	172	1,266	18,098	25.8	43.3	27.0	175.9	17,304	28,010	58,365	42.6	3.4	56,477	10.8	14.4	13.1
Monroe	333	2,183	191,316	25.5	34.0	37.1	2,020.0	18,307	31,291	55,272	45.6	4.7	57,660	14.6	22.2	21.9
Montgomery	169	1,913	11,306	15.2	50.1	17.0	121.0	17,335	25,307	47,449	52.4	2.1	46,601	17.8	28.7	26.7
Nassau	133	983	345,888	26.2	32.3	44.4	5,183.1	25,265	46,839	105,744	23.1	19.6	107,465	6.2	7.7	7.3
New York	(7) 575	(7) 1,477	334,583	44.6	25.6	60.7	(7) 21,874.7	(7) 21,491	69,529	79,781	36.1	20.1	84,133	16.3	23.4	24.9
Niagara	399	2,495	47,654	16.6	43.7	23.5	486.7	16,492	28,395	51,656	48.7	2.5	54,317	12.4	17.6	16.0
Oneida	286	1,980	53,195	14.6	45.3	23.9	565.0	16,292	27,283	51,316	48.8	2.9	53,234	16.1	24.9	23.0
Onondaga	304	2,087	122,742	25.7	34.7	35.0	1,251.8	17,400	31,436	57,271	44.1	4.7	57,641	13.7	19.9	18.5
Ontario	156	1,620	26,130	20.7	34.9	33.7	283.8	17,182	33,685	61,710	40.8	5.1	65,271	9.3	13.1	11.5
Orange	248	1,704	105,528	24.5	39.8	29.5	1,272.4	20,804	32,616	75,146	34.4	7.8	77,606	10.9	16.5	15.0
Orleans	190	1,632	8,021	11.2	52.5	15.9	105.9	17,077	23,929	49,223	50.6	1.8	48,799	15.2	23.7	22.0
Oswego	223	1,719	30,159	7.5	51.4	18.3	386.1	19,055	25,791	51,755	48.4	2.4	52,732	16.3	23.2	21.1
Otsego	150	1,146	16,391	15.5	41.7	29.6	145.2	19,819	26,688	51,254	48.6	3.0	51,561	13.1	19.6	18.8
Putnam	38	575	23,593	18.2	35.0	38.5	371.6	24,898	44,063	99,608	22.5	14.6	98,765	5.4	5.9	5.4
Queens	(7)	(7)	548,550	20.5	46.6	30.8	(7)	(7)	28,814	62,008	40.9	5.7	64,046	12.2	16.3	15.3
Rensselaer	296	1,998	38,904	30.3	37.1	29.8	368.8	17,618	33,067	63,166	40.4	4.7	63,457	11.5	15.4	14.1
Richmond	(7)	(7)	118,932	23.4	42.6	32.1	(7)	(7)	33,922	76,244	35.1	9.0	78,466	11.9	16.8	15.6
Rockland	117	968	96,359	44.2	34.9	40.4	990.6	24,123	36,898	88,571	30.3	15.1	87,873	13.3	21.8	21.4
St. Lawrence	163	1,463	30,277	22.8	48.1	23.1	294.7	19,051	23,554	48,300	51.3	2.2	49,607	18.9	28.8	25.1
Saratoga	112	1,135	51,625	20.7	30.9	40.4	501.3	16,176	39,653	77,548	30.9	7.3	82,732	6.6	7.9	7.4
Schenectady	454	2,595	37,641	19.1	39.3	30.8	427.0	16,910	29,981	61,315	41.5	4.1	61,841	12.8	18.8	18.6
Schoharie	117	1,131	7,439	9.8	48.3	21.6	93.6	21,102	26,953	51,842	48.1	2.7	51,007	13.9	19.1	16.7
Schuyler	72	560	3,544	12.7	48.8	22.1	40.8	18,791	25,285	47,810	51.6	1.1	48,782	13.9	23.0	20.9
Seneca	194	1,645	6,678	17.6	49.5	20.5	79.7	19,227	26,541	51,601	48.0	2.7	54,563	12	19.2	19.4
Steuben	193	1,377	20,915	12.7	47.3	22.6	289.0	19,297	27,731	50,157	49.9	2.7	50,807	12.8	19.1	17.1
Suffolk	121	1,369	375,657	15.1	38.2	35.0	5,718.0	23,116	40,277	92,838	26.4	13.9	94,108	7	8.9	8.1
Sullivan	268	1,390	16,334	14.1	46.8	23.4	252.2	25,744	28,224	53,877	47.2	3.9	52,504	14.9	24.8	23.7
Tioga	129	817	10,704	13.2	45.6	24.7	134.5	17,193	30,252	57,153	43.8	3.9	57,190	9.9	15.8	14.3
Tompkins	139	1,582	41,321	51.1	25.4	52.6	225.0	20,066	29,759	56,200	45.4	6.2	56,539	18.6	15.0	13.6
Ulster	164	1,311	39,349	14.7	39.8	31.4	529.3	22,491	32,453	61,652	41.5	5.6	62,531	13.7	17.4	16.6
Warren	173	1,692	13,283	9.2	41.1	29.3	172.7	18,816	33,127	60,222	42.0	3.9	58,859	9.7	15.4	14.4
Washington	154	777	12,476	13.1	50.8	19.8	161.5	18,137	26,064	52,527	47.2	2.1	53,609	11.7	17.6	16.3
Wayne	175	1,611	20,043	11.0	45.7	21.7	273.7	18,740	27,318	53,693	46.0	2.4	52,709	12.1	16.3	15.9
Westchester	215	1,060	251,266	25.9	31.9	47.7	3,686.8	24,510	52,049	89,968	30.1	19.5	90,483	8.5	10.6	10.2
Wyoming	113	686	7,920	13.2	53.0	15.4	75.7	18,014	25,635	55,459	45.2	1.4	53,986	11.2	15.0	14.1
Yates	68	1,221	5,222	36.6	48.3	23.9	44.6	19,606	26,608	51,758	48.6	3.5	49,198	13.9	24.4	23.7
NORTH CAROLINA	372	2,737	2,526,271	14.6	39.2	29.9	13,238.5	8,622	28,123	50,320	49.7	4.3	52,797	14.7	21.0	19.6
Alamance	391	2,345	40,622	22.1	43.0	22.9	197.9	8,061	25,157	44,281	55.4	2.2	47,914	14.4	20.6	19.4
Alexander	228	1,773	7,559	14.8	58.0	13.9	44.3	8,424	22,655	44,523	55.5	1.8	48,577	11.7	16.1	15.4
Alleghany	143	982	1,922	5.1	51.9	18.7	16.7	11,298	21,153	38,944	63.7	1.0	38,994	20.9	34.7	30.3
Anson	451	2,873	5,381	5.5	61.2	9.2	36.3	10,287	19,105	38,123	64.2	1.1	41,266	22.2	33.0	30.7
Ashe	107	1,105	4,895	8.4	46.4	19.5	31.4	9,697	23,650	40,293	60.5	1.1	40,611	15.9	25.1	22.1
Avery	215	1,115	3,869	25.4	49.5	20.2	25.7	11,191	21,704	37,109	63.4	3.0	40,682	18.6	27.5	25.8
Beaufort	295	2,240	10,164	6.2	47.6	19.6	66.6	8,867	24,657	41,101	57.8	2.3	43,497	22	31.1	28.6
Bertie	190	1,677	4,103	11.8	61.0	12.3	31.9	11,634	18,319	31,287	70.6	0.9	33,022	27.2	39.2	35.9
Bladen	NA	NA	7,394	10.4	53.7	14.5	45.9	9,121	20,839	32,396	65.3	1.0	38,059	20.7	28.4	26.0
Brunswick	91	1,302	20,479	12.2	38.3	28.0	126.0	9,303	29,707	51,164	48.8	3.1	56,227	11.9	21.5	19.3
Buncombe	281	2,551	55,021	16.9	33.1	38.5	284.4	9,178	29,590	48,464	51.3	3.8	50,271	11.5	17.6	17.0
Burke	202	2,236	18,364	11.3	49.8	16.7	110.0	8,303	21,885	40,854	59.5	1.5	42,179	16.6	22.1	20.3
Cabarrus	128	1,838	53,616	13.0	36.1	30.0	302.1	7,933	29,143	60,716	40.1	4.9	62,167	11.1	13.6	12.5
Caldwell	201	3,105	17,341	7.0	53.5	14.8	104.9	8,652	21,991	40,735	58.7	1.8	44,798	16.3	22.1	18.8
Camden	96	646	2,834	7.1	40.9	18.1	17.2	8,870	27,468	68,327	35.5	2.1	64,086	8	10.7	9.6
Carteret	120	1,379	13,785	11.4	34.9	26.7	79.9	9,155	30,903	51,584	48.6	3.6	53,192	13.3	20.9	19.3
Caswell	320	1,671	4,756	13.3	55.6	13.7	25.9	9,177	21,692	39,428	61.5	1.9	44,998	19.3	28.8	27.1
Catawba	280	2,766	36,670	14.7	46.3	21.5	206.0	8,379	25,960	48,649	51.2	3.1	53,348	12.5	18.7	17.1
Chatham	152	1,524	14,163	15.0	34.0	40.1	89.1	9,150	36,933	59,684	41.9	8.8	63,373	10.3	16.0	14.2
Cherokee	203	2,945	4,943	11.5	48.8	19.2	34.4	9,584	21,152	38,115	62.2	0.5	38,283	17.2	28.8	27.1

1. Data for serious crimes have not been adjusted for underreporting; this may affect comparability between geographic areas and over time.   2. Per 100,000 population estimated by the FBI.   3. All persons 3 years old and over enrolled in nursery school through college.   4. Persons 25 years old and over.   5. Elementary and secondary education expenditures.   6. Based on population estimated by the American Community Survey, 2013–2017.   7. Bronx, Kings, Queens, and Richmond counties are included with New York county.

Table B. States and Counties — Personal Income and Earnings

STATE County	Personal income, 2017										Earnings, 2017		
	Total (mil dol)	Percent change 2016-2017	Per capita[1] Dollars	Per capita[1] Rank	Wages and salaries (mil dol)	Supplements to wages and salaries, employer contributions (mil dol) Pension and insurance	Supplements to wages and salaries, employer contributions (mil dol) Government social insurance	Proprietors' income (mil dol)	Dividends, interest, and rent (mil dol)	Personal transfer receipts (mil dol)	Total (mil dol)	Contributions for government social insurance (mil dol) From employee and self-employed	Contributions for government social insurance (mil dol) From employer
	62	63	64	65	66	67	68	69	70	71	72	73	74
NEW YORK— Cont'd													
Genesee	2,455	4.1	42,365	1,223	962	252	86	132	369	586	1,432	83	86
Greene	2,194	4.6	46,210	776	643	188	55	157	379	548	1,041	64	55
Hamilton	235	4.6	52,436	360	65	26	6	12	64	60	109	7	6
Herkimer	2,510	5.4	40,320	1,498	671	183	58	126	365	723	1,037	69	58
Jefferson	5,146	4.2	45,069	893	2,669	749	251	216	924	1,077	3,885	191	251
Kings	129,149	6.8	48,758	564	34,018	6,852	2,840	9,351	18,504	32,573	53,061	3,038	2,840
Lewis	1,137	4.6	42,814	1,167	263	89	24	78	167	253	454	26	24
Livingston	2,748	9.6	43,071	1,135	822	246	72	355	386	600	1,496	85	72
Madison	3,007	3.9	42,380	1,219	904	225	78	188	490	645	1,395	84	78
Monroe	38,050	4.2	50,894	417	20,479	3,759	1,672	2,809	6,471	8,142	28,720	1,606	1,672
Montgomery	2,023	5.4	41,070	1,400	810	178	71	109	279	634	1,168	72	71
Nassau	116,084	5.5	84,763	27	40,437	6,800	3,217	10,776	27,469	14,155	61,231	3,319	3,217
New York	292,925	7.4	175,960	2	306,975	33,492	17,953	58,757	94,129	22,184	417,177	21,605	17,953
Niagara	9,270	5.0	43,866	1,033	3,098	716	268	447	1,317	2,382	4,530	284	268
Oneida	9,993	5.5	43,198	1,118	4,676	1,177	388	575	1,621	2,669	6,815	395	388
Onondaga	23,383	4.1	50,244	446	12,804	2,633	1,046	1,914	3,815	4,918	18,397	1,009	1,046
Ontario	5,640	4.5	51,321	400	2,666	531	216	291	971	1,096	3,704	213	216
Orange	19,155	5.7	50,113	456	7,206	1,622	606	1,039	2,800	3,751	10,473	580	606
Orleans	1,547	4.3	37,736	1,918	533	167	48	124	201	430	871	51	48
Oswego	4,582	4.1	38,671	1,782	1,600	441	129	146	562	1,269	2,316	142	129
Otsego	2,520	4.6	41,941	1,270	1,053	256	88	180	431	622	1,577	93	88
Putnam	6,304	5.1	63,469	124	1,441	297	119	339	1,074	877	2,195	130	119
Queens	110,449	6.5	46,829	725	36,762	7,112	3,042	9,136	14,993	28,940	56,052	3,181	3,042
Rensselaer	7,608	4.6	47,633	653	2,870	660	236	336	1,169	1,608	4,102	239	236
Richmond	26,326	6.4	54,908	284	5,961	1,223	499	1,446	3,647	6,596	9,130	557	499
Rockland	19,118	5.6	58,133	202	6,752	1,299	551	1,310	3,386	3,529	9,913	556	551
St. Lawrence	3,987	5.4	36,371	2,138	1,626	466	140	162	594	1,160	2,394	143	140
Saratoga	15,008	5.5	65,288	100	4,629	885	385	848	3,188	1,930	6,747	386	385
Schenectady	7,683	4.7	49,389	502	3,783	688	304	321	1,289	1,682	5,096	294	304
Schoharie	1,221	4.9	38,855	1,746	374	105	31	78	181	304	588	37	31
Schuyler	728	3.2	40,458	1,481	197	51	18	47	108	210	314	21	18
Seneca	1,278	4.8	37,037	2,028	566	146	48	73	206	347	834	49	48
Steuben	4,191	4.6	43,528	1,075	2,135	411	168	202	653	1,038	2,915	173	168
Suffolk	98,174	5.1	65,758	95	40,941	7,560	3,225	6,837	17,401	15,733	58,563	3,232	3,225
Sullivan	3,375	6.6	44,707	939	1,115	286	96	167	581	996	1,664	102	96
Tioga	2,134	3.8	43,928	1,030	692	152	56	158	308	493	1,057	66	56
Tompkins	4,441	4.9	42,373	1,220	2,823	482	230	340	903	725	3,875	210	230
Ulster	8,758	5.5	48,811	556	2,764	685	232	643	1,636	2,025	4,324	258	232
Warren	3,271	5.2	50,690	422	1,745	338	147	286	603	737	2,515	145	147
Washington	2,390	5.0	38,783	1,761	690	207	61	128	347	628	1,087	68	61
Wayne	4,020	4.6	44,332	983	1,186	334	103	347	492	989	1,969	119	103
Westchester	99,536	5.8	101,542	12	32,219	5,039	2,381	8,886	26,893	10,064	48,525	2,611	2,381
Wyoming	1,572	5.1	38,825	1,752	583	175	53	112	242	377	923	52	53
Yates	963	5.1	38,601	1,791	261	69	23	121	181	250	474	28	23
NORTH CAROLINA	454,307	4.7	44,233	X	232,255	35,087	16,987	34,424	84,973	88,932	318,754	19,990	16,987
Alamance	6,307	5.2	38,839	1,747	2,681	386	198	336	1,061	1,418	3,601	246	198
Alexander	1,336	5.5	35,839	2,218	342	61	26	127	196	352	556	39	26
Alleghany	417	5.0	37,836	1,907	108	21	8	50	99	134	188	14	8
Anson	834	4.4	33,379	2,574	267	56	20	82	107	276	424	27	20
Ashe	963	4.6	35,707	2,245	287	49	22	97	181	305	455	34	22
Avery	612	4.0	34,885	2,363	245	43	19	44	149	175	351	24	19
Beaufort	1,927	3.7	40,926	1,411	652	117	49	113	372	574	930	69	49
Bertie	658	4.3	34,212	2,459	216	44	16	22	90	260	298	23	16
Bladen	1,153	4.9	34,439	2,421	510	91	37	116	157	400	754	47	37
Brunswick	5,379	6.1	41,092	1,399	1,370	232	104	393	1,243	1,565	2,099	175	104
Buncombe	11,876	4.7	46,102	785	5,967	913	444	1,126	2,910	2,378	8,451	545	444
Burke	3,063	5.4	34,304	2,446	1,172	221	89	156	515	885	1,637	117	89
Cabarrus	9,086	6.0	43,920	1,031	3,516	536	253	535	1,235	1,477	4,840	311	253
Caldwell	2,772	5.2	33,815	2,505	1,043	175	77	132	445	815	1,428	106	77
Camden	469	4.5	44,290	986	54	11	4	18	81	90	87	7	4
Carteret	3,297	2.6	47,871	635	896	155	67	224	851	754	1,342	99	67
Caswell	786	3.8	34,704	2,387	116	25	9	62	110	247	212	18	9
Catawba	6,896	5.6	43,651	1,058	4,043	626	304	494	1,242	1,489	5,466	348	304
Chatham	4,297	5.3	60,127	154	614	97	46	209	1,147	675	966	78	46
Cherokee	877	3.6	31,207	2,839	296	53	22	62	154	357	433	36	22

1. Based on the resident population estimated as of July 1 of the year shown.

STATE County	Earnings, 2017 (cont.)									Social Security beneficiaries, December 2017		Supple-mental Security Income recipients, 2017	Housing units, 2018	
	Percent by selected industries													
	Farm	Mining, quarrying, and extractions	Construction	Manu-facturing	Information; professional, scientific, technical services	Retail trade	Finance, insurance, real estate, and leasing	Health care and social assistance	Govern-ment	Number	Rate[1]		Total	Percent change, 2010-2018
	75	76	77	78	79	80	81	82	83	84	85	86	87	88
NEW YORK— Cont'd														
Genesee	2.5	0.7	5.9	15.4	3.1	7.2	3.4	10.4	30.2	13,950	241	1,099	25,848	1.2
Greene	0.4	D	5.4	7.1	4.6	7.5	3.3	5.8	36	12,520	264	1,353	29,833	2.2
Hamilton	0	D	D	D	D	6.3	D	D	58.1	1,650	368	56	8,967	3.1
Herkimer	1.4	2	7.4	15.6	2.6	7.3	2.4	9.7	29.4	16,190	260	1,559	33,873	1.5
Jefferson	1	0.4	4.5	3.6	2.6	6	2.2	10.6	57.4	22,005	193	2,636	60,049	3.6
Kings	0	D	6.2	2.2	9.5	7	6	21.8	19.1	340,835	129	129,406	1,053,767	5.3
Lewis	7.6	D	5.9	15.8	2.2	5.3	2	D	38.3	5,960	224	567	15,749	4.2
Livingston	1.6	D	7.7	8.7	D	5.5	2	8	30.2	14,285	224	1,255	27,616	2.2
Madison	1.4	D	6.4	14	4.9	8.2	3.2	D	23	14,955	211	1,276	32,394	2
Monroe	0.1	0	5	11.7	13	5.1	6.7	14.9	14.2	160,940	215	25,713	329,190	2.7
Montgomery	1.1	0.4	5.7	15.9	3.4	9.2	2.2	22.7	18.4	13,510	274	1,990	23,540	2
Nassau	0	D	6	3.2	12.4	7.3	11.6	19.1	15.8	259,100	189	16,750	473,496	1.1
New York	0	0.5	1.6	0.7	27.8	2.5	33.5	4.8	7	258,120	155	68,565	886,249	4.6
Niagara	0.8	D	5.7	16.3	4.6	8.5	2.9	13.5	25.4	53,255	252	5,795	100,614	1.5
Oneida	0.3	0.4	3.5	8.7	6.9	5.9	7.9	17.3	30.3	55,465	240	8,035	105,454	1.2
Onondaga	0.1	0.1	4.8	9.4	11.4	5.6	8	13.8	19.4	98,135	211	14,300	209,347	3.4
Ontario	0.7	0.1	7.9	14.5	5.9	8.1	4.1	11.9	18.8	26,520	241	1,792	51,204	6.1
Orange	0.3	0.1	5.9	6.1	7.8	8.6	3.6	15	29.3	66,195	173	6,883	144,232	5.3
Orleans	2.8	5.2	4.8	18.6	D	5.2	3.5	D	38.1	9,625	235	925	18,598	0.9
Oswego	0.4	0.2	6.7	11.8	D	7.3	2.5	10.7	28.4	27,440	232	3,261	54,610	1.9
Otsego	0.9	D	4.5	4.9	3.4	8.2	7.2	27.6	22.4	14,740	245	1,324	31,341	1.8
Putnam	0.1	D	D	D	9.6	5.2	4	17.8	23.9	18,865	190	801	38,680	1.2
Queens	0	D	12	2.5	4.9	5.5	7.5	14.5	18.8	338,250	143	70,599	865,878	3.7
Rensselaer	0.2	0.3	7.8	13	8.9	5.4	3.6	11.6	24.6	34,000	213	4,128	73,264	2.5
Richmond	0	0	12.2	D	6.1	7.4	4.7	23.3	20.9	90,485	189	14,776	181,199	2.6
Rockland	0	D	7.8	7.6	11.5	7.3	4.1	15.7	20	55,815	170	5,005	106,747	2.6
St. Lawrence	1.7	0.2	4.2	8.5	3.1	6.8	2.5	D	37.6	25,925	236	3,665	53,386	2.4
Saratoga	0.3	0.3	8.5	13.5	10.8	6.2	10.4	10.3	16.6	48,885	213	2,709	107,374	8.8
Schenectady	0	D	4.8	13	19.7	5.3	4.7	14.1	17.9	33,470	215	5,281	69,954	2.6
Schoharie	0.8	D	12.5	3.7	3.5	6.6	5.9	9	32.7	7,220	230	665	17,593	2.1
Schuyler	3.9	D	10.2	14	D	7.2	D	11.8	25.2	4,945	275	388	9,839	4
Seneca	1.2	D	3.7	23.8	D	8.2	2.2	D	30.4	8,195	238	767	16,388	2.2
Steuben	1.3	0.2	2.4	15	17.8	5	3.7	9.5	20.8	23,815	247	2,822	49,695	1.7
Suffolk	0.3	0.2	8.9	8	10	6.4	9.8	12	20.1	294,950	198	20,025	576,873	1.2
Sullivan	0.3	0.6	5.7	4.5	3.9	6	4.3	20.3	32.2	18,010	239	2,730	50,942	3.6
Tioga	0.6	5.3	4.1	37.4	D	5.3	2.2	5.1	18.4	12,325	254	1,131	22,600	1.9
Tompkins	0.3	D	D	7.3	11.1	4.6	3.5	D	12.9	16,265	155	1,516	43,879	5.3
Ulster	0.6	0.2	7	6.4	5.9	8	4.7	13.7	28.8	41,500	231	4,068	85,421	2.1
Warren	0.1	0.6	7.8	11.2	8.5	8.8	6	16.1	14.4	18,585	288	1,548	40,199	3.8
Washington	3.3	0.9	8	18.3	2.1	7.1	1.9	D	37.1	15,045	244	1,616	29,592	2.6
Wayne	3	0.2	7.8	23	2.7	6.6	2.5	7.3	27.3	23,140	255	2,258	41,798	1.8
Westchester	0	D	7	6.4	14.8	4.6	13.1	13.6	15.9	168,990	172	17,499	375,852	1.3
Wyoming	5.9	D	4.5	12.5	D	6.7	2.5	D	39.9	9,320	230	638	18,282	1.8
Yates	7.8	D	10.5	14.5	D	7.4	3.6	D	19.2	6,255	251	472	13,887	2.9
NORTH CAROLINA	1	0.1	6.3	11.2	11.1	6	8.9	10.1	18.4	2,059,436	200	232,386	4,684,876	8.3
Alamance	0	0.1	6.2	15.6	4.5	8.6	6	19.8	11.1	34,775	214	3,545	71,660	7.6
Alexander	12.1	D	4.9	31.3	D	4.2	3.2	4.6	19.5	9,470	254	621	16,500	1.9
Alleghany	8.1	D	12	15.2	2.9	6.6	4.2	D	16.6	3,530	320	327	8,172	1.4
Anson	13.2	D	4.1	18.1	D	4.9	1.6	4.3	26.4	6,000	240	1,002	11,628	0.5
Ashe	8.7	D	15	9.9	D	7.8	5	11	13.6	8,215	305	798	17,787	2.9
Avery	3.6	D	8.4	1.1	D	7	4.3	D	23.4	4,600	262	408	14,275	2.7
Beaufort	1.4	D	5	21.2	3.7	7.6	5	9.4	16.1	14,345	305	1,810	26,265	6.4
Bertie	6.8	D	D	D	D	2.8	D	D	25.3	5,980	311	1,184	9,870	0.5
Bladen	12.7	0	2.8	40.7	1.4	3.4	2	D	17.3	8,630	258	1,487	17,926	1.2
Brunswick	1.5	0	12.2	4.8	6.8	8.3	5.8	10.9	15.7	45,360	347	2,230	92,264	19.1
Buncombe	0.4	0.1	6.3	10.2	9	7.7	6.5	21.1	13.3	59,940	233	5,571	126,567	11.6
Burke	1	D	3.6	25.9	3	5.5	3.9	17.5	24.1	22,395	251	1,997	41,314	1.2
Cabarrus	0.5	D	6.9	7.6	5.6	8.3	4.3	6.9	21.2	34,780	168	3,207	80,873	12.4
Caldwell	0.4	D	4.8	24.8	2.8	6.4	2.6	11.1	15.6	20,795	254	1,926	38,073	1.1
Camden	3.2	0.1	11	3.8	D	5.1	D	D	29.2	2,145	203	122	4,303	4.8
Carteret	0.2	D	8.6	4.2	5.8	12.3	7.3	10.4	23.3	19,430	282	1,232	50,725	5.3
Caswell	14.4	D	9.9	7.7	D	3.7	D	D	31.4	6,485	286	708	10,846	2.1
Catawba	0.6	D	3.9	27.9	5.1	8.1	3.6	9.7	11.3	37,930	240	3,069	69,263	1.8
Chatham	2.9	D	8.2	10.5	11.4	7.6	2	12.9	15.7	18,480	259	907	33,013	14.8
Cherokee	2.6	D	9.2	10.2	8	9.7	5.6	D	20.7	10,145	361	813	18,407	5.1

1. Per 1,000 resident population estimated as of July 1 of the year shown.

Table B. States and Counties — Housing, Labor Force, and Employment

STATE County	Housing units, 2013-2017								Civilian labor force, 2018				Civilian employment[6], 2013-2017		
	Occupied units							Sub-standard units[4] (percent)		Percent change, 2017-2018	Unemployment			Percent	
	Owner-occupied					Renter-occupied								Management, business, science, and arts	Construction, production, and maintenance occupations
				Median owner cost as a percent of income			Median rent as a percent of income[2]								
	Total	Percent	Median value[1]	With a mortgage	Without a mortgage[2]	Median rent[3]			Total		Total	Rate[5]	Total		
	89	90	91	92	93	94	95	96	97	98	99	100	101	102	103

STATE County	89	90	91	92	93	94	95	96	97	98	99	100	101	102	103
NEW YORK— Cont'd															
Genesee	23,951	72.5	111,900	19.6	12.3	748	28	1.6	29,796	1.1	1,245	4.2	29,386	31.0	28.7
Greene	17,106	75.8	176,100	24.4	13.4	876	37.5	1.8	20,735	1.3	935	4.5	20,009	35.5	23.8
Hamilton	1,095	84.7	164,000	22.8	12.7	713	21.8	2.1	2,296	-0.7	157	6.8	1,991	25.3	29.4
Herkimer	25,187	71.7	95,800	19.7	12.8	657	26.2	1.9	27,990	0	1,374	4.9	28,650	31.4	24.6
Jefferson	43,206	55.6	149,300	20.6	12.3	966	29.1	2.2	44,691	-0.5	2,510	5.6	44,883	32.2	22.1
Kings	944,650	30.0	623,900	30.4	14.3	1,314	32.8	10.8	1,211,721	-0.3	51,220	4.2	1,217,976	40.8	14.7
Lewis	10,236	78.0	121,700	19.6	12.1	742	31.4	1.8	11,677	0.8	647	5.5	11,838	31.0	34.2
Livingston	24,432	73.2	125,000	20.5	13.3	755	35.2	1.8	30,827	0.8	1,333	4.3	29,390	34.4	25.7
Madison	26,307	76.0	132,800	21.0	13.3	755	26	1.3	32,630	0.9	1,564	4.8	33,640	36.6	22.6
Monroe	300,496	63.8	142,300	20.5	13.1	872	32.6	1.4	362,858	0.4	15,459	4.3	367,859	42.7	15.9
Montgomery	19,700	68.9	99,900	21.3	14.9	732	31.8	2.6	22,436	-0.2	1,155	5.1	21,956	30.0	27.3
Nassau	444,136	80.6	460,700	27.0	18.0	1,663	33.6	2.7	707,875	0.4	25,027	3.5	682,063	44.7	13.7
New York	758,345	24.1	915,300	18.6	10.0	1,615	28.2	6.2	919,101	-0.2	33,750	3.7	906,389	60.0	6.0
Niagara	87,978	71.5	114,800	19.6	13.3	669	29.4	1.2	99,138	-0.2	5,197	5.2	100,990	32.8	22.8
Oneida	90,472	66.6	120,000	20.0	13.0	735	30	1.9	101,729	0.1	4,498	4.4	102,889	35.3	20.9
Onondaga	185,840	64.9	139,400	19.5	12.4	823	29.6	2	220,771	0.6	8,826	4	223,207	41.2	16.0
Ontario	44,269	73.2	156,500	19.6	13.1	837	29.8	1.5	55,149	0.7	2,172	3.9	54,398	40.4	19.9
Orange	126,460	68.4	260,300	25.6	16.5	1,187	34.7	4.1	182,241	1	7,155	3.9	174,770	35.6	19.6
Orleans	16,214	75.0	93,600	22.4	14.5	683	32.2	2.5	17,616	0.7	870	4.9	17,976	28.7	31.7
Oswego	45,881	72.6	97,800	19.7	12.8	748	31.7	3	52,824	0.4	2,892	5.5	53,211	29.2	27.4
Otsego	23,627	74.3	141,900	21.2	12.3	808	32.6	2.8	28,170	0.7	1,225	4.3	28,545	36.6	20.6
Putnam	34,316	81.9	357,700	26.2	16.2	1,334	32.1	1.6	51,085	0.6	1,886	3.7	51,775	41.5	16.6
Queens	777,904	44.5	481,300	29.8	14.3	1,456	33.2	9.7	1,162,225	-0.2	41,766	3.6	1,142,363	33.3	18.9
Rensselaer	64,456	63.4	183,400	21.4	13.1	908	29.1	1.7	81,358	0.6	3,166	3.9	80,468	39.9	18.9
Richmond	166,150	69.5	460,200	27.1	15.0	1,229	33.3	4.5	220,621	-0.3	9,112	4.1	212,253	40.7	16.8
Rockland	99,935	68.9	425,100	27.8	17.8	1,420	37.7	6.5	154,676	0.9	5,775	3.7	149,868	44.3	13.4
St. Lawrence	41,638	72.5	88,000	19.4	12.5	723	30.4	3.1	43,515	0.6	2,448	5.6	44,013	34.2	21.8
Saratoga	93,129	71.5	243,600	20.5	11.9	1,046	25.9	1	118,982	0.7	4,187	3.5	117,053	45.8	16.4
Schenectady	53,825	67.8	164,100	21.9	12.9	894	31.7	1.4	76,303	0.7	3,063	4	73,044	38.1	16.9
Schoharie	12,539	75.5	143,300	23.4	14.7	781	29.2	1.3	14,774	0.9	712	4.8	14,198	33.9	25.5
Schuyler	7,444	76.4	114,700	20.4	13.1	741	28.4	3.1	8,268	0.8	423	5.1	8,224	35.0	26.1
Seneca	13,536	73.2	98,400	19.6	13.0	750	28.2	1.8	16,087	0.2	622	3.9	15,488	33.0	25.4
Steuben	40,351	71.8	95,300	19.6	12.4	691	27.3	2.2	42,816	0.5	2,106	4.9	43,232	34.3	26.9
Suffolk	489,328	80.3	379,400	27.6	18.7	1,646	36.2	2.8	777,784	0.3	29,952	3.9	744,660	38.4	18.8
Sullivan	27,679	66.9	167,900	24.5	15.2	860	29.4	2.1	35,947	5	1,472	4.1	32,610	31.1	22.3
Tioga	19,996	77.1	113,000	19.2	12.6	695	30.2	1.8	22,772	0.3	999	4.4	23,012	34.9	22.8
Tompkins	38,986	55.5	190,100	21.3	12.3	1,055	34.8	2.1	50,112	0.6	1,829	3.6	50,390	51.4	11.4
Ulster	69,662	69.4	221,600	25.2	15.6	1,053	35.1	2.1	88,712	0.9	3,452	3.9	86,552	39.6	18.5
Warren	27,249	71.9	192,800	22.4	12.4	881	30.5	1.3	31,709	-0.3	1,473	4.6	32,518	35.7	19.4
Washington	23,988	72.7	144,900	22.3	14.0	823	31.8	1.9	28,164	0.3	1,165	4.1	28,741	28.1	28.9
Wayne	36,578	76.8	118,900	20.9	14.1	742	30.9	1.8	43,877	0.7	1,823	4.2	43,209	33.4	27.2
Westchester	345,885	61.5	513,300	24.8	16.9	1,444	32.9	4.5	484,256	0.9	18,828	3.9	479,696	47.3	12.8
Wyoming	15,686	75.8	108,500	19.4	12.1	634	26.4	1	18,093	1.2	838	4.6	18,372	28.0	31.1
Yates	9,338	77.1	128,900	21.8	12.8	732	32.3	2.4	11,783	1.5	447	3.8	11,331	30.6	29.0
NORTH CAROLINA	3,874,346	65.0	161,000	20.7	11.0	844	29.4	2.7	4,981,834	0.9	194,514	3.9	4,571,020	36.9	22.6
Alamance	63,035	65.4	145,500	20.7	11.2	774	30.3	2.7	80,583	0.7	2,958	3.7	73,906	33.0	26.6
Alexander	13,744	75.5	131,800	18.3	10.5	620	27.8	3.9	18,023	0.2	570	3.2	16,393	26.8	40.1
Alleghany	4,742	75.0	136,000	23.8	11.5	635	30.3	1.3	4,305	-1.4	194	4.5	4,447	29.7	29.7
Anson	9,647	65.0	83,700	19.9	13.7	687	30.3	4.4	10,407	-1.2	465	4.5	10,153	23.4	40.0
Ashe	11,995	74.1	150,300	22.2	10.3	641	28	1	12,750	0.6	458	3.6	12,174	26.2	28.8
Avery	6,725	77.0	138,800	24.8	10.9	723	35	2.6	7,639	-0.1	278	3.6	6,778	29.8	23.9
Beaufort	18,978	70.8	123,600	22.9	13.1	691	31.7	1.1	19,739	-1.3	900	4.6	19,051	31.5	30.2
Bertie	7,998	73.6	78,900	24.5	17.3	644	33.1	3.1	7,832	-3.1	387	4.9	7,307	23.7	41.7
Bladen	14,394	68.9	89,500	24.1	13.2	630	30	2.7	14,418	-0.1	759	5.3	13,263	25.2	35.4
Brunswick	53,104	77.2	194,700	23.8	11.8	883	33	1.8	52,867	2.9	2,723	5.2	48,982	29.0	24.2
Buncombe	105,407	63.7	209,800	22.3	11.0	897	30.2	3.6	139,319	1.9	4,134	3	123,090	39.6	18.8
Burke	34,568	71.5	115,400	21.8	10.4	635	29.1	3.3	40,579	0.2	1,446	3.6	37,149	28.3	31.1
Cabarrus	70,598	70.8	180,300	19.7	10.0	856	25.9	4.1	106,601	1.8	3,794	3.6	95,894	37.4	21.0
Caldwell	32,150	71.6	112,400	19.7	11.4	635	28.3	2.5	36,595	0.2	1,402	3.8	35,011	24.5	35.8
Camden	3,796	80.1	222,500	25.5	10.0	1,122	30.5	1.7	4,650	-1.7	173	3.7	4,528	37.4	21.6
Carteret	30,000	72.7	197,700	23.7	11.8	864	27.1	1.5	31,755	-0.6	1,369	4.3	30,098	35.1	21.9
Caswell	9,160	76.4	104,700	21.9	12.0	557	36.7	2	9,820	0.5	429	4.4	9,512	27.8	29.4
Catawba	60,238	69.3	139,900	19.3	10.0	700	27	3.5	78,802	0.1	2,761	3.5	72,258	30.5	30.8
Chatham	28,148	76.2	251,600	20.3	10.7	783	28.4	2.3	34,637	1.3	1,158	3.3	30,832	41.8	21.7
Cherokee	11,206	80.0	145,500	23.1	11.2	694	25.9	2.7	11,235	0.5	495	4.4	9,925	30.1	24.8

1. Specified owner-occupied units.   2. A value of 10.0 represents 10 percent or less; a value of 50.0 represents 50 percent or more.   3. Specified renter-occupied units.   4. Overcrowded or lacking complete plumbing facilities.   5. Percent of civilian labor force.   6. Civilian employed persons 16 years old and over.

Table B. States and Counties — Nonfarm Employment and Agriculture

STATE County	Private nonfarm establishments, employment and payroll, 2016									Agriculture, 2017			
	Number of establishments	Employment						Annual payroll		Farms			Farm producers whose primary occupation is farming (percent)
		Total	Health care and social assistance	Manufacturing	Retail trade	Finance and insurance	Professional, scientific, and technical services	Total (mil dol)	Average per employee (dollars)	Number	Percent with:		
											Fewer than 50 acres	1000 acres or more	
	104	105	106	107	108	109	110	111	112	113	114	115	116
NEW YORK— Cont'd													
Genesee	1,294	16,567	2,772	3,091	2,846	371	309	582	35,121	485	38.8	7.8	51.5
Greene	1,147	10,475	1,167	852	2,220	336	215	348	33,227	206	35.9	2.9	50.3
Hamilton	199	861	30	D	170	14	4	27	31,455	14	35.7	NA	33.3
Herkimer	1,112	12,489	2,330	3,130	2,041	315	156	434	34,750	596	24.3	1.2	47.4
Jefferson	2,443	30,183	6,395	2,339	6,710	686	931	1,085	35,961	792	26.5	5.6	51.5
Kings	57,621	606,738	198,133	20,927	75,955	18,402	21,266	24,612	40,564	19	100.0	NA	15.4
Lewis	532	4,812	1,119	1,138	848	85	85	191	39,794	625	23.8	5.0	56.6
Livingston	1,234	14,046	2,185	2,066	2,544	255	410	454	32,315	661	43.9	8.9	47.4
Madison	1,411	17,284	3,079	2,775	2,554	390	654	610	35,318	691	27.4	4.5	54.0
Monroe	17,744	358,650	67,599	35,726	41,706	13,273	25,274	16,016	44,657	527	56.4	6.1	51.8
Montgomery	1,081	15,201	4,055	3,391	2,611	280	270	550	36,197	564	28.4	2.8	62.4
Nassau	48,260	557,159	119,768	15,892	79,399	33,675	42,030	29,787	53,462	32	81.3	NA	23.1
New York	104,691	2,245,903	240,993	17,702	149,397	301,457	326,941	241,159	107,377	7	100.0	NA	50.0
Niagara	4,584	60,907	11,184	8,619	11,307	1,320	1,498	2,170	35,635	690	50.1	5.2	43.0
Oneida	4,902	87,875	19,318	9,595	12,205	6,630	3,695	3,456	39,332	967	34.1	2.5	45.5
Onondaga	11,709	218,730	41,919	17,112	29,584	10,782	14,180	9,614	43,956	623	44.6	5.1	48.9
Ontario	2,920	46,743	8,473	6,557	9,349	906	1,405	2,180	46,634	833	40.3	5.2	49.2
Orange	9,456	117,570	23,294	7,822	24,283	2,996	4,470	4,597	39,098	621	43.6	1.8	53.1
Orleans	650	8,144	1,454	2,339	1,113	581	107	274	33,701	498	43.4	5.8	56.8
Oswego	2,138	24,454	4,782	3,081	4,514	615	925	1,021	41,748	612	40.2	1.1	43.4
Otsego	1,409	19,436	5,949	935	3,127	1,136	589	770	39,640	880	27.0	1.8	45.1
Putnam	2,875	20,972	4,951	1,349	3,252	554	1,084	908	43,313	89	64.0	NA	32.8
Queens	49,597	563,339	127,918	20,396	65,305	22,839	16,748	26,655	47,316	4	100.0	NA	20.0
Rensselaer	2,997	43,574	8,843	3,501	5,738	1,430	3,576	2,005	46,003	470	37.0	1.9	44.6
Richmond	9,240	101,055	31,303	1,169	16,432	2,578	3,811	4,199	41,547	6	100.0	NA	6.1
Rockland	10,023	110,957	25,303	7,324	14,436	3,128	5,972	5,112	46,074	14	71.4	NA	59.5
St. Lawrence	1,921	26,637	6,345	2,048	5,161	662	602	988	37,098	1,253	16.7	3.9	49.0
Saratoga	5,278	69,665	9,801	6,259	11,400	3,795	4,542	3,281	47,094	591	54.0	2.0	47.3
Schenectady	3,060	52,478	11,930	4,256	7,249	2,128	3,953	2,366	45,090	185	43.8	NA	41.7
Schoharie	578	5,411	947	293	1,078	248	191	193	35,664	541	27.7	1.3	51.2
Schuyler	383	3,604	794	632	652	56	58	134	37,297	408	38.5	2.2	46.4
Seneca	717	8,697	1,216	1,501	2,303	173	102	288	33,081	516	39.7	3.5	55.6
Steuben	1,806	25,943	6,938	3,926	4,067	1,030	1,083	1,269	48,919	1,542	21.8	4.5	44.9
Suffolk	49,149	578,418	98,447	51,925	83,692	22,673	45,817	31,145	53,846	560	74.1	0.4	58.1
Sullivan	1,899	20,221	6,491	970	2,829	624	586	676	33,413	366	50.3	2.2	45.0
Tioga	787	7,691	1,130	1,170	1,217	224	229	265	34,400	535	29.0	2.2	46.4
Tompkins	2,370	49,767	5,710	2,954	4,991	1,119	1,947	1,833	36,841	523	47.6	2.9	39.6
Ulster	4,814	46,586	9,586	3,530	9,247	2,040	1,640	1,649	35,405	421	51.8	0.7	51.0
Warren	2,317	31,682	6,666	3,330	6,050	1,291	856	1,248	39,383	80	58.8	NA	40.8
Washington	1,052	10,292	1,778	2,932	1,785	207	232	411	39,928	915	37.2	2.8	43.6
Wayne	1,726	19,996	3,060	5,993	3,415	517	701	785	39,246	829	43.4	4.0	53.0
Westchester	31,941	389,632	81,294	12,031	51,054	21,030	25,573	25,047	64,284	115	81.7	1.7	49.5
Wyoming	779	8,752	1,222	1,819	1,432	362	327	302	34,488	729	41.0	6.4	51.9
Yates	518	5,016	907	914	746	90	111	157	31,275	867	30.8	1.4	60.4
NORTH CAROLINA	227,347	3,794,926	582,346	432,538	496,375	182,063	220,467	170,980	45,055	46,418	47.9	3.8	42.7
Alamance	3,215	59,118	12,604	9,922	9,079	1,430	1,320	2,308	39,047	720	45.8	0.7	40.6
Alexander	553	7,620	630	3,737	795	167	244	235	30,786	544	50.0	0.9	45.4
Alleghany	245	2,185	398	496	340	63	37	62	28,311	448	37.3	3.1	38.2
Anson	379	5,274	770	1,698	735	81	92	158	29,930	412	32.8	4.4	41.7
Ashe	540	5,663	1,212	841	1,122	214	68	182	32,121	864	42.0	1.9	43.5
Avery	474	4,565	847	107	852	101	76	132	28,994	351	50.4	1.7	44.7
Beaufort	1,099	13,552	2,137	2,397	2,321	406	254	462	34,075	310	38.7	15.5	46.1
Bertie	303	4,473	944	1,663	365	73	33	125	27,919	323	26.9	10.8	65.4
Bladen	509	10,307	1,161	5,872	880	141	136	344	33,398	512	35.9	7.4	48.6
Brunswick	2,448	25,315	3,819	1,409	5,051	635	756	898	35,483	231	42.0	5.2	43.9
Buncombe	8,252	116,660	24,852	11,950	18,956	2,745	4,579	4,564	39,120	1,073	67.3	0.5	38.0
Burke	1,403	22,598	4,476	7,381	3,089	379	401	770	34,060	508	56.1	0.6	38.9
Cabarrus	4,234	61,850	9,030	5,975	12,603	916	1,669	2,350	37,988	629	56.6	1.6	34.8
Caldwell	1,309	19,092	3,668	6,661	2,892	342	313	631	33,047	411	57.2	0.5	39.6
Camden	121	622	43	D	94	14	28	16	25,712	81	48.1	24.7	59.1
Carteret	1,931	18,618	3,301	1,011	4,311	530	532	585	31,408	158	78.5	2.5	29.8
Caswell	235	1,549	369	160	309	47	38	42	27,191	493	28.6	3.4	44.9
Catawba	4,090	82,642	11,950	22,806	10,098	1,281	1,904	3,336	40,368	638	53.8	1.1	36.7
Chatham	1,405	14,023	2,640	2,088	2,253	255	573	469	33,464	1,116	48.7	0.4	37.8
Cherokee	579	6,486	1,093	1,324	1,438	189	319	194	29,964	277	57.4	0.7	39.0

Table B. States and Counties — **Agriculture**

STATE County	Acreage (1,000)	Percent change, 2012-2017	Average size of farm	Total irrigated (1,000)	Total cropland (1,000)	Average per farm	Average per acre	Value of machinery and equipment, average per farm (dollars)	Total (mil dol)	Average per farm (acres)	Crops	Livestock and poultry products	Organic farms (number)	Farms with internet access (percent)	Total ($1,000)	Percent of farms
	117	118	119	120	121	122	123	124	125	126	127	128	129	130	131	132
NEW YORK— Cont'd																
Genesee	177	-5.5	365	3.3	148.6	1,220,292	3,345	312,434	234.9	484,402	34.4	65.6	13	77.5	2,668	44.7
Greene	35	-18.6	170	0.3	13.7	535,865	3,156	74,288	19.8	95,927	46.7	53.3	7	72.3	138	14.1
Hamilton	1	-55.1	67	D	0.1	222,415	3,341	32,734	D	D	D	NA	NA	92.9	D	14.3
Herkimer	118	-37.2	198	0.2	69.5	452,284	2,289	111,551	58.0	97,277	23.4	76.6	28	67.1	467	18.3
Jefferson	247	-14.9	312	0.4	168.8	836,501	2,677	170,553	165.1	208,404	21.6	78.4	31	74.7	1,986	22.3
Kings	0	D	1	0.0	0.0	536,994	443,604	12,004	D	D	D	D	NA	73.7	NA	NA
Lewis	182	0.4	292	0.1	105.0	586,534	2,009	171,441	153.1	244,917	13.8	86.2	12	72.8	416	22.9
Livingston	189	-2.8	287	0.2	145.9	1,064,151	3,712	196,665	183.7	277,905	30.1	69.9	5	82.8	4,427	30.7
Madison	172	-16.2	249	0.5	105.5	652,012	2,621	142,460	113.6	164,444	24.7	75.3	64	79.7	1,418	22.0
Monroe	107	8.2	203	0.6	85.7	872,523	4,306	155,561	76.6	145,433	86.9	13.1	20	88.4	2,627	17.6
Montgomery	115	29.5	204	0.1	84.5	506,591	2,485	129,396	75.0	132,906	23.8	76.2	55	70.7	404	14.9
Nassau	1	-66.1	28	0.1	0.2	493,741	17,362	39,261	D	D	D	D	2	56.3	NA	NA
New York	0	D	2	D	0.0	D	D	4,336	0.0	6,429	100.0	NA	NA	100.0	NA	NA
Niagara	140	-1.8	203	1.5	116.2	624,058	3,070	161,032	118.6	171,909	63.6	36.4	19	82.3	2,095	21.3
Oneida	193	28.3	199	0.7	119.2	530,131	2,659	118,065	100.5	103,883	29.8	70.2	15	77.4	1,066	19.6
Onondaga	161	70.6	258	1.3	113.1	1,063,488	4,122	196,839	178.4	286,371	22.2	77.8	20	86.2	1,815	25.8
Ontario	200	3.9	240	0.8	163.8	967,405	4,027	189,335	205.2	246,291	30.8	69.2	53	72.6	3,712	29.7
Orange	81	-7.8	131	2.5	49.1	906,875	6,936	113,299	87.9	141,572	75.7	24.3	17	81.3	463	11.0
Orleans	130	-4.1	260	3.2	107.7	825,545	3,173	225,733	155.3	311,811	85.8	14.2	23	71.7	3,323	39.0
Oswego	86	-52.3	141	0.8	40.3	311,560	2,213	87,168	41.2	67,369	50.7	49.3	11	80.1	126	14.4
Otsego	155	143.9	176	0.4	81.5	468,529	2,666	79,321	56.2	63,840	34.5	65.5	62	75.2	619	13.6
Putnam	7	26.5	84	0.1	2.6	503,785	6,001	55,525	3.1	35,337	91.1	8.9	3	97.8	NA	NA
Queens	D	D	D	D	D	679,231	48,517	6,091	0.1	23,500	61.7	38.3	NA	75.0	NA	NA
Rensselaer	83	5.0	176	1.0	46.8	618,709	3,513	107,314	41.0	87,255	59.2	40.8	26	81.9	1,040	22.8
Richmond	D	D	D	0.0	D	D	D	7,145	D	D	D	NA	2	66.7	NA	NA
Rockland	1	9.5	41	0.1	0.3	1,183,762	28,772	115,774	2.1	153,071	95.9	4.1	2	100.0	NA	NA
St. Lawrence	343	-4.0	273	0.4	176.7	500,868	1,832	111,812	191.1	152,496	17.6	82.4	100	77.5	1,130	12.1
Saratoga	72	260.4	121	0.7	41.6	713,614	5,890	125,743	76.8	129,968	24.8	75.2	5	88.0	369	5.1
Schenectady	17	-82.4	94	0.2	9.2	402,340	4,288	59,097	5.5	29,519	64.3	35.7	NA	78.4	21	8.1
Schoharie	100	-47.3	185	0.1	61.1	449,208	2,435	108,434	47.9	88,590	42.0	58.0	28	76.0	259	21.6
Schuyler	79	13.8	193	0.3	48.4	631,614	3,270	127,031	45.8	112,140	33.1	66.9	23	73.5	203	13.5
Seneca	119	-9.0	230	0.2	96.7	862,800	3,756	170,204	90.8	176,052	51.9	48.1	42	68.6	2,029	20.2
Steuben	397	-2.1	258	0.9	240.4	540,734	2,099	128,101	196.0	127,075	35.5	64.5	59	76.6	3,739	29.4
Suffolk	30	-16.5	54	12.1	23.1	655,303	12,219	153,042	225.6	402,818	90.4	9.6	30	86.1	76	2.1
Sullivan	60	11.3	164	0.2	26.2	689,944	4,213	78,765	28.4	77,549	19.7	80.3	15	82.0	152	7.7
Tioga	113	4.9	212	0.4	54.8	483,358	2,285	99,481	40.9	76,368	29.9	70.1	16	83.0	971	25.2
Tompkins	91	0.6	175	0.4	62.1	661,192	3,789	138,310	64.7	123,715	24.6	75.4	45	85.9	1,575	22.6
Ulster	59	-17.3	140	3.7	24.1	965,681	6,899	95,712	54.3	129,088	88.3	11.7	24	86.9	164	8.1
Warren	10	5.9	126	0.0	0.9	526,197	4,174	60,826	D	D	D	D	1	85.0	D	2.5
Washington	185	D	203	1.0	103.0	565,739	2,794	133,639	135.8	148,428	18.0	82.0	18	83.9	1,418	18.7
Wayne	159	-11.2	192	1.5	115.5	659,498	3,437	190,441	221.3	266,942	70.3	29.7	41	79.5	1,462	15.2
Westchester	7	-10.0	61	0.1	4.1	645,915	10,646	72,483	7.0	60,487	72.6	27.4	2	89.6	D	1.7
Wyoming	235	4.0	322	1.7	167.3	1,115,529	3,463	283,473	307.5	421,838	21.1	78.9	14	73.8	2,817	30.0
Yates	115	-9.5	133	0.6	83.0	692,852	5,227	138,824	114.7	132,246	41.2	58.8	119	40.0	825	9.5
NORTH CAROLINA	8,431	0.2	182	143.4	5,000.7	843,154	4,642	112,477	12,900.7	277,924	29.0	71.0	465	75.2	107,565	21.6
Alamance	80	-4.2	111	0.7	33.8	667,068	6,000	64,708	41.8	57,986	35.3	64.7	23	76.4	147	8.6
Alexander	54	-7.7	100	0.3	22.7	560,533	5,632	101,446	176.3	324,158	4.8	95.2	NA	71.1	170	5.5
Alleghany	71	-22.4	158	D	26.2	777,876	4,937	87,835	31.4	70,092	57.9	42.1	6	72.1	32	5.6
Anson	85	2.1	207	0.3	33.6	846,181	4,086	116,392	303.7	737,248	4.3	95.7	NA	69.7	817	27.2
Ashe	110	-2.4	127	0.1	36.4	668,101	5,258	71,937	57.1	66,135	76.9	23.1	6	74.1	76	1.9
Avery	29	1.6	82	0.0	11.9	530,636	6,494	63,220	20.1	57,222	96.1	3.9	6	74.1	37	3.1
Beaufort	139	-5.9	450	2.0	118.6	1,538,781	3,420	265,851	112.0	361,413	65.4	34.6	NA	73.5	4,556	58.4
Bertie	148	0.9	459	3.2	112.3	1,390,119	3,032	238,427	260.5	806,412	30.9	69.1	NA	69.0	4,249	63.2
Bladen	180	53.7	352	6.0	76.8	1,174,444	3,334	225,098	446.4	871,873	15.8	84.2	1	77.7	3,178	35.0
Brunswick	45	-1.6	193	0.5	22.8	758,353	3,920	114,405	46.1	199,437	34.2	65.8	NA	83.1	338	15.2
Buncombe	72	1.1	67	0.8	17.8	670,235	9,949	55,669	48.0	44,747	77.4	22.6	16	78.5	357	12.3
Burke	39	12.4	76	1.8	17.5	433,663	5,701	76,589	81.5	160,366	24.3	75.7	3	75.4	167	5.1
Cabarrus	64	-3.9	101	D	32.8	881,469	8,709	83,381	57.8	91,967	30.7	69.3	NA	75.2	304	10.8
Caldwell	38	18.5	92	0.6	14.4	419,469	4,538	59,705	48.1	116,922	22.9	77.1	3	77.4	152	5.6
Camden	59	20.1	731	D	53.8	2,327,456	3,182	421,303	39.9	492,988	98.3	1.7	NA	64.2	1,262	45.7
Carteret	63	-0.1	397	0.1	44.7	1,801,801	4,536	94,673	23.8	150,506	97.9	2.1	NA	75.3	137	10.1
Caswell	105	8.1	213	1.4	32.3	689,530	3,241	65,751	37.9	76,929	55.7	44.3	13	72.8	164	19.3
Catawba	64	-5.3	100	0.7	34.2	651,547	6,543	87,564	77.3	121,130	28.2	71.8	1	75.4	620	8.5
Chatham	106	-5.2	95	0.3	30.9	522,890	5,505	66,667	171.2	153,360	6.5	93.5	19	78.7	103	8.7
Cherokee	26	22.3	95	0.1	7.6	464,663	4,906	79,138	D	D	D	D	11	81.6	303	18.1

Table B. States and Counties — Water Use, Wholesale Trade, Retail Trade, and Real Estate

STATE County	Water use, 2015 Public supply water withdrawn (mil gal/ day)	Public supply gallons withdrawn per person per day	Wholesale Trade[1], 2012 Number of establish- ments	Number of employees	Sales (mil dol)	Average payroll (mil dol)	Retail Trade[2], 2012 Number of establish- ments	Number of employees	Sales (mil dol)	Average payroll (mil dol)	Real estate and rental and leasing,[2] 2012 Number of establish- ments	Number of employees	Sales (mil dol)	Average payroll (mil dol)
	133	134	135	136	137	138	139	140	141	142	143	144	145	146
NEW YORK— Cont'd														
Genesee	3.74	63.5	76	1,165	1,187.1	51.6	219	2,561	785.8	59.1	29	150	25.2	5.1
Greene	3.07	64.5	27	1,007	724.6	63.0	198	2,329	610.4	53.8	43	181	27.1	7.7
Hamilton	0.75	159.2	NA	NA	NA	NA	33	169	41.6	4.3	7	8	0.9	0.2
Herkimer	28.84	457.1	30	545	162.1	25.3	187	2,016	543.9	44.9	34	113	15.0	2.4
Jefferson	9.29	79.0	67	870	345.2	34.7	476	6,849	1,937.9	161.4	119	588	103.9	17.8
Kings	0.00	0.0	3,457	28,586	16,522.9	1,176.8	9,931	65,979	20,533.1	1,623.7	4,327	15,248	3,765.5	530.6
Lewis	1.81	67.1	7	D	D	D	74	792	258.7	19.8	12	D	D	D
Livingston	3.78	58.4	51	560	458.9	24.0	219	2,501	633.6	55.0	40	206	22.9	5.8
Madison	1.22	17.0	36	434	151.0	16.9	222	2,688	745.5	61.9	43	148	12.1	3.5
Monroe	53.54	71.4	788	10,459	6,131.6	562.0	2,349	40,491	9,494.1	902.0	835	6,237	1,091.2	233.4
Montgomery	2.61	52.6	44	D	D	D	179	2,461	673.3	55.4	22	80	10.2	1.9
Nassau	194.47	142.9	2,856	28,767	27,959.1	1,860.3	6,145	77,488	24,105.6	2,206.3	2,331	9,580	3,054.1	532.1
New York	0.00	0.0	7,678	84,273	128,760.9	6,385.0	11,691	148,493	44,040.0	5,027.8	9,627	70,399	33,323.0	4,826.9
Niagara	49.46	232.6	179	2,187	1,506.4	95.0	735	10,233	2,521.6	212.7	144	563	81.8	16.1
Oneida	32.82	141.2	175	2,081	1,087.5	90.9	830	11,889	3,012.2	263.6	170	686	111.9	20.0
Onondaga	58.04	123.9	591	10,750	17,113.3	559.0	1,682	28,932	6,916.0	639.1	588	3,756	662.3	150.5
Ontario	46.53	424.7	113	1,285	660.2	65.9	527	9,194	2,021.4	193.8	94	423	53.8	10.1
Orange	33.04	87.5	455	6,661	8,298.4	304.8	1,512	23,117	6,221.1	530.6	374	1,407	407.3	51.5
Orleans	1.64	39.4	17	281	130.4	14.3	95	1,097	252.4	22.6	20	61	9.4	1.3
Oswego	34.87	290.2	58	504	368.3	21.8	353	4,392	1,258.4	101.6	69	205	29.6	5.0
Otsego	3.10	51.1	46	460	308.8	19.6	290	3,373	917.0	78.7	53	215	32.7	6.9
Putnam	2.82	28.5	101	905	516.3	50.3	329	3,037	952.2	79.7	89	209	33.9	7.9
Queens	0.00	0.0	2,971	24,171	16,059.4	1,250.3	7,388	59,829	17,003.2	1,542.4	2,840	11,679	3,100.3	509.9
Rensselaer	21.61	134.8	101	1,200	2,270.2	67.3	424	5,814	1,572.2	138.4	101	464	103.0	15.5
Richmond	0.00	0.0	342	1,416	1,460.0	75.0	1,273	15,926	3,816.0	353.5	312	1,151	377.5	43.8
Rockland	33.18	101.8	504	4,697	3,892.0	282.0	1,154	14,253	4,153.7	382.2	443	1,498	281.1	55.0
St. Lawrence	6.95	62.6	46	446	175.0	19.9	414	5,139	1,446.6	116.3	57	167	32.7	5.0
Saratoga	26.12	115.4	176	3,133	2,332.0	181.5	724	10,871	2,980.0	250.5	213	975	233.2	33.5
Schenectady	23.51	152.1	78	774	519.3	37.3	480	7,256	1,821.1	167.3	111	510	112.4	19.5
Schoharie	173.82	5,548.0	19	118	54.9	4.4	95	1,049	319.0	23.9	15	46	7.2	1.5
Schuyler	0.83	45.6	3	D	D	D	59	633	141.4	12.9	5	D	D	D
Seneca	4.41	126.6	27	410	202.5	13.1	183	2,360	489.9	43.9	19	77	26.0	1.9
Steuben	7.50	76.8	40	277	122.4	9.3	326	4,238	1,074.0	95.9	51	232	32.5	8.7
Suffolk	246.12	163.9	2,838	37,819	32,383.0	2,260.5	6,524	79,498	23,693.4	2,182.4	1,677	6,519	1,868.5	303.8
Sullivan	89.77	1,198.9	43	584	363.6	21.5	291	2,673	771.5	66.5	111	398	55.5	9.6
Tioga	3.45	69.8	25	331	396.9	14.3	132	1,367	372.9	32.4	12	23	3.3	0.6
Tompkins	7.87	75.0	36	454	259.0	21.6	349	5,071	1,112.0	105.5	112	609	121.6	20.5
Ulster	394.23	2,188.4	159	1,504	810.4	71.3	733	8,606	2,324.9	211.8	195	732	116.6	22.0
Warren	11.56	178.7	59	575	190.4	21.0	447	6,436	1,549.1	149.5	74	240	45.0	8.9
Washington	2.59	41.6	30	D	D	D	186	1,759	498.8	42.4	17	46	4.8	1.0
Wayne	7.84	85.7	62	607	245.7	22.7	267	3,276	822.6	75.5	58	223	24.7	4.2
Westchester	65.43	67.0	1,286	16,494	20,313.9	1,493.5	3,802	48,739	14,514.2	1,395.5	1,966	8,041	2,436.5	399.2
Wyoming	3.26	79.5	26	219	121.9	9.8	128	1,479	376.0	33.0	18	99	11.3	2.8
Yates	1.10	43.9	10	127	41.0	3.4	92	814	208.9	17.8	22	79	10.2	2.5
NORTH CAROLINA	938.01	93.4	9,713	136,174	105,275.6	7,853.7	34,288	446,373	120,691.0	10,421.2	10,140	47,155	9,301.7	1,942.6
Alamance	15.35	97.0	143	1,642	627.2	70.0	624	8,756	2,108.4	178.0	119	607	142.0	24.4
Alexander	0.03	0.8	17	111	47.8	4.5	86	834	194.8	17.6	10	18	1.6	0.3
Alleghany	0.31	28.6	3	4	1.1	0.7	41	296	67.9	5.9	10	19	1.7	0.3
Anson	8.80	341.6	11	203	109.4	10.3	73	726	181.3	14.7	9	D	D	D
Ashe	0.67	24.8	22	214	101.9	7.0	106	1,020	273.0	22.4	24	48	7.9	1.8
Avery	1.57	88.8	18	D	D	D	82	742	195.5	15.6	32	D	D	D
Beaufort	4.31	90.4	51	477	360.7	20.7	189	2,300	548.4	51.4	36	133	16.6	2.8
Bertie	1.68	83.2	14	126	145.6	4.7	50	357	95.9	6.7	4	5	0.2	0.1
Bladen	37.35	1,088.4	22	174	226.7	6.9	91	823	199.5	15.9	14	27	5.2	0.7
Brunswick	2.80	22.8	69	544	237.1	21.6	371	4,423	1,125.8	100.7	128	556	85.0	20.2
Buncombe	21.12	83.4	265	2,532	1,286.7	110.6	1,135	16,104	3,884.2	381.4	393	1,287	238.0	43.0
Burke	23.00	258.9	48	431	226.2	17.4	260	2,541	680.5	54.9	50	128	15.0	3.0
Cabarrus	17.54	89.1	191	2,454	1,600.3	115.7	708	11,637	2,920.3	247.7	171	645	115.6	18.8
Caldwell	7.16	88.1	64	411	202.3	16.4	256	2,740	701.0	58.2	58	137	16.7	3.4
Camden	0.71	68.9	3	17	4.1	0.4	17	94	24.9	1.7	4	4	1.2	0.1
Carteret	6.97	101.2	47	272	85.7	9.8	363	3,885	972.8	89.3	118	529	63.7	13.5
Caswell	0.43	18.7	5	D	D	D	49	309	63.9	6.5	1	D	D	D
Catawba	4.29	27.7	238	5,320	4,053.8	244.5	715	9,502	2,607.3	222.3	187	534	130.5	17.0
Chatham	25.42	358.4	52	311	115.0	12.6	175	2,089	583.0	43.6	36	80	15.0	2.5
Cherokee	1.73	63.7	15	149	84.4	4.4	130	1,302	363.6	28.6	26	67	15.4	1.8

1 Merchant wholesalers, except manufacturers' sales branches and offices.   2. Employer establishments.

Table B. States and Counties — Professional Services, Manufacturing, and Accommodation and Food Services

STATE County	Professional, scientific, and technical services, 2012				Manufacturing, 2012				Accommodation and food services, 2012			
	Number of establish-ments	Number of employees	Sales (mil dol)	Average payroll (mil dol)	Number of establish-ments	Number of employees	Receipts (mil dol)	Annual payroll (mil dol)	Number of establis-hments	Number of employees	Receipts (mil dol)	Annual payroll (mil dol)
	147	148	149	150	151	152	153	154	155	156	157	158
NEW YORK— Cont'd												
Genesee	76	322	28.3	11.5	95	2,632	983.0	125.8	144	1,910	89.9	25.2
Greene	76	258	27.5	9.9	29	735	339.8	D	191	2,675	99.2	29.4
Hamilton	2	D	D	D	3	8	D	D	57	234	22.8	4.8
Herkimer	61	184	18.3	5.9	60	2,561	666.2	119.4	168	1,469	71.3	19.9
Jefferson	142	1,092	115.9	45.4	66	2,247	770.5	102.6	335	4,117	198.8	57.0
Kings	4,346	23,391	3,467.9	1,312.8	1,756	18,296	3,644.1	731.0	4,809	34,099	2,453.4	615.5
Lewis	23	82	9.5	2.5	25	1,371	532.7	58.1	64	480	19.1	5.5
Livingston	98	374	31.7	10.9	55	2,106	635.9	91.1	142	2,123	80.4	23.4
Madison	121	681	66.5	27.7	58	2,407	885.5	109.2	164	2,024	86.4	23.8
Monroe	1,973	21,387	3,187.1	1,263.9	887	38,958	14,610.3	2,315.5	1,662	26,555	1,300.3	370.6
Montgomery	61	252	25.1	7.5	74	3,578	839.0	134.3	117	948	49.2	12.0
Nassau	6,835	43,568	6,915.5	2,542.9	1,043	16,580	5,196.7	893.7	3,483	43,996	2,938.8	818.0
New York	17,504	289,103	88,609.6	31,491.6	2,063	21,220	4,970.9	899.1	9,634	206,517	20,382.6	6,032.2
Niagara	325	1,810	234.9	86.1	273	7,987	3,134.9	463.1	521	9,841	1,055.9	183.3
Oneida	408	3,645	555.6	210.0	236	9,807	3,481.3	462.0	559	10,870	791.3	199.6
Onondaga	1,179	13,456	2,065.5	767.9	436	18,565	7,576.0	1,034.6	1,146	18,791	918.7	265.5
Ontario	239	1,469	195.5	79.9	167	6,718	2,671.0	332.4	302	4,879	237.3	72.3
Orange	872	5,909	648.5	248.4	318	7,105	2,592.4	336.9	847	9,601	575.2	150.4
Orleans	35	168	15.0	5.2	36	2,026	764.6	96.5	57	692	28.4	7.9
Oswego	135	546	55.0	19.7	85	2,669	2,131.1	139.6	290	3,599	153.2	41.2
Otsego	116	623	54.1	19.6	58	877	203.8	37.7	210	2,560	148.5	37.6
Putnam	311	1,246	208.6	74.9	87	1,478	308.6	74.3	195	1,604	100.4	26.3
Queens	3,248	13,293	1,585.1	669.1	1,294	22,240	4,438.1	972.5	4,558	40,510	3,139.1	749.9
Rensselaer	280	3,464	460.4	193.0	95	3,383	D	176.2	348	4,009	209.2	58.6
Richmond	873	3,535	663.0	169.2	136	999	285.3	44.8	770	7,805	472.6	109.8
Rockland	1,272	5,270	1,616.3	341.6	251	8,416	9,613.2	601.3	769	7,762	501.2	140.1
St. Lawrence	107	611	55.8	21.1	77	2,639	1,302.9	149.6	256	2,904	131.6	34.0
Saratoga	605	3,852	608.6	210.2	138	5,259	1,977.4	331.6	524	8,089	446.4	128.6
Schenectady	276	3,772	207.5	284.3	110	4,490	1,709.3	283.0	339	3,846	191.7	54.9
Schoharie	36	208	18.4	6.5	21	239	D	9.5	62	459	23.1	6.5
Schuyler	15	38	2.5	0.7	35	574	D	30.4	62	572	34.9	9.2
Seneca	35	139	14.4	3.8	40	1,318	674.2	68.8	72	744	35.3	11.0
Steuben	133	1,707	89.4	157.7	77	4,314	1,237.0	212.9	223	2,562	132.2	34.0
Suffolk	5,622	43,771	6,531.9	2,657.2	2,067	51,967	15,887.4	2,800.5	3,624	45,646	2,990.4	810.8
Sullivan	167	D	D	D	51	1,224	354.0	41.0	243	1,572	139.6	34.7
Tioga	55	D	D	D	44	1,228	438.2	48.6	89	829	36.2	10.6
Tompkins	274	2,312	356.6	124.1	93	2,766	861.1	150.4	334	4,408	231.7	65.4
Ulster	443	1,601	189.3	69.1	170	3,518	D	170.2	546	6,655	367.3	117.4
Warren	168	876	106.7	40.0	76	3,767	928.9	206.4	413	3,992	306.1	85.9
Washington	61	235	35.1	9.2	87	2,942	1,206.2	152.3	127	758	38.0	9.7
Wayne	105	589	116.2	26.9	137	5,702	1,656.8	241.8	165	1,732	71.7	19.1
Westchester	4,205	28,162	4,976.7	2,187.8	601	11,776	4,492.9	584.9	2,460	26,862	2,020.0	562.8
Wyoming	62	351	41.9	10.8	44	1,878	473.7	76.3	81	747	31.7	9.0
Yates	31	118	10.6	3.9	44	836	188.5	33.3	55	382	22.7	6.4
NORTH CAROLINA	22,855	196,287	31,947.9	12,940.3	8,953	403,593	202,344.6	18,191.2	19,496	358,602	18,622.3	5,040.6
Alamance	218	1,375	133.0	55.8	200	9,268	3,138.4	399.3	293	5,761	254.4	71.8
Alexander	37	123	11.5	4.2	69	3,284	591.5	107.7	38	D	D	D
Alleghany	12	40	3.1	0.9	17	444	D	15.6	22	211	10.8	3.3
Anson	27	116	10.0	3.2	20	1,428	393.3	54.5	29	401	16.8	4.7
Ashe	24	58	3.5	1.3	20	1,122	232.7	36.1	46	573	23.7	6.7
Avery	29	66	7.2	2.1	13	174	20.5	5.2	59	593	45.6	12.9
Beaufort	88	341	26.2	9.5	64	2,661	1,462.1	152.1	73	1,141	50.1	12.5
Bertie	11	51	4.9	1.5	11	D	D	42.4	15	166	6.5	1.6
Bladen	33	143	17.7	5.0	28	5,565	1,904.3	178.5	46	448	25.6	6.3
Brunswick	196	637	57.7	22.2	71	1,520	1,983.0	101.4	271	3,436	180.8	48.7
Buncombe	873	4,336	473.4	206.2	287	13,805	2,839.5	590.9	735	14,976	880.1	254.3
Burke	110	464	44.3	16.3	126	7,475	2,804.6	288.8	127	2,102	97.2	25.2
Cabarrus	338	1,505	193.8	73.3	162	5,427	1,757.9	237.4	346	8,214	428.0	113.7
Caldwell	79	324	31.9	10.5	121	6,098	1,158.1	197.1	117	D	D	D
Camden	7	28	3.0	1.5	NA	NA	NA	NA	3	28	1.5	0.4
Carteret	122	447	49.2	18.9	61	981	343.7	32.9	229	3,318	164.4	48.3
Caswell	13	37	3.5	1.4	9	172	33.3	5.6	13	D	D	D
Catawba	322	1,627	654.5	71.2	411	20,830	5,850.9	809.8	342	6,737	290.7	83.7
Chatham	145	468	59.6	22.2	72	1,538	487.4	66.7	103	1,674	91.3	25.5
Cherokee	37	250	15.7	8.3	26	1,168	317.1	41.8	61	817	41.0	11.3

Health Care and Social Assistance, Other Services, Nonemployer Businesses, and Residential Construction

STATE County	Health care and social assistance, 2012				Other services, 2012				Nonemployer businesses, 2016		Value of residential construction authorized by building permits, 2018	
	Number of establish-ments	Number of employees	Receipts (mil dol)	Annual payroll (mil dol)	Number of establish-ments	Number of employees	Receipts (mil dol)	Annual payroll (mil dol)	Number	Receipts (mil dol)	New construction ($1,000)	Number of housing units
	159	160	161	162	163	164	165	166	167	168	169	170
NEW YORK— Cont'd												
Genesee	141	3,053	221.6	98.7	100	626	51.8	15.0	3,013	132.6	18,364	93
Greene	94	1,254	88.1	38.8	83	373	32.7	8.2	3,433	139.0	12,359	65
Hamilton	6	25	1.7	0.8	7	D	D	D	482	20.9	5,303	26
Herkimer	109	2,334	184.1	70.5	94	552	32.1	8.3	3,273	132.0	9,733	63
Jefferson	277	6,183	536.8	247.5	187	912	83.3	21.0	5,280	209.8	14,606	138
Kings	6,394	184,851	16,419.6	7,123.6	4,675	18,153	1,622.5	431.4	269,471	12,253.3	1,108,153	8,445
Lewis	49	1,071	83.2	41.4	43	164	21.1	4.7	1,682	75.2	7,391	60
Livingston	143	2,019	140.2	61.2	88	337	39.3	8.6	3,487	148.6	10,980	113
Madison	166	3,027	272.9	110.7	98	349	30.6	7.1	4,240	168.5	18,797	86
Monroe	1,949	63,159	5,819.8	2,425.3	1,151	7,580	772.3	209.4	44,256	2,044.6	213,389	1,433
Montgomery	177	3,970	356.9	149.6	87	558	57.5	15.4	2,384	95.1	7,642	36
Nassau	5,771	111,832	13,166.2	5,522.1	4,068	21,377	2,140.6	587.0	139,758	9,845.5	394,251	984
New York	8,106	251,513	34,680.5	13,322.5	9,778	92,777	21,846.1	4,572.6	226,631	18,653.8	468,326	3,584
Niagara	512	10,096	789.4	345.9	341	1,593	109.0	31.0	9,673	376.0	46,250	204
Oneida	615	19,043	1,636.6	730.7	407	3,677	219.0	74.3	12,032	485.3	43,801	212
Onondaga	1,294	38,389	4,379.2	1,717.8	876	5,965	613.6	178.1	27,919	1,306.6	102,850	519
Ontario	274	8,001	685.0	340.7	211	1,252	98.6	30.5	7,023	318.8	83,663	451
Orange	961	20,593	2,176.8	957.3	749	3,963	460.3	108.4	25,033	1,190.6	164,494	1,084
Orleans	78	1,544	96.0	46.2	63	209	20.6	4.7	1,777	73.9	2,140	17
Oswego	206	4,897	347.9	156.5	183	699	57.4	13.7	5,403	190.4	22,610	133
Otsego	170	6,049	675.4	281.4	103	617	51.3	11.6	4,264	163.9	8,399	53
Putnam	261	5,055	559.1	239.5	233	1,035	118.0	32.3	9,352	482.2	13,396	51
Queens	5,047	122,646	12,103.5	5,098.2	4,645	19,428	1,863.4	500.0	250,998	9,713.9	616,634	4,577
Rensselaer	354	9,708	732.3	349.1	244	1,361	122.5	48.0	8,771	355.9	43,727	242
Richmond	1,308	30,614	2,960.7	1,274.1	869	3,779	342.3	85.5	36,460	1,695.7	117,076	606
Rockland	1,164	22,289	2,083.5	900.8	731	4,364	350.9	106.5	27,661	1,697.1	67,002	324
St. Lawrence	260	6,640	581.7	259.6	170	706	64.8	14.5	4,919	169.4	15,417	149
Saratoga	544	8,412	761.2	317.9	321	1,668	145.3	45.5	16,001	762.3	260,336	1,097
Schenectady	435	11,854	1,005.7	439.2	205	D	D	D	8,276	330.5	25,659	183
Schoharie	62	1,039	69.9	30.7	31	D	D	D	1,863	72.3	7,574	38
Schuyler	39	836	57.5	27.4	34	D	D	D	1,154	36.6	8,506	57
Seneca	63	1,335	82.0	40.4	49	233	19.1	4.6	1,797	82.7	7,661	50
Steuben	238	5,701	488.2	227.8	148	663	59.6	14.5	5,254	205.0	16,017	93
Suffolk	4,736	95,248	10,416.2	4,491.2	3,945	19,049	2,048.8	520.1	128,110	7,264.0	585,410	1,002
Sullivan	250	5,491	412.0	186.4	160	456	66.6	12.0	5,616	236.6	66,370	352
Tioga	68	1,045	54.3	26.7	65	205	20.3	4.8	2,765	104.7	5,291	32
Tompkins	271	5,283	483.0	199.8	152	966	122.9	23.9	7,546	281.5	111,786	805
Ulster	514	8,991	741.4	312.4	322	1,229	114.9	28.6	16,264	679.0	70,760	252
Warren	283	6,574	569.0	261.1	140	817	84.1	26.0	4,811	233.4	33,850	137
Washington	105	1,535	96.2	44.5	78	271	28.6	7.7	3,686	145.9	20,656	90
Wayne	151	3,061	215.0	102.9	133	434	36.2	9.0	4,678	194.7	21,262	120
Westchester	3,592	79,057	9,638.2	4,111.1	2,819	15,205	2,013.8	539.3	97,354	6,578.1	365,102	1,672
Wyoming	68	1,183	94.2	40.9	62	246	21.7	5.7	2,043	80.2	24,707	191
Yates	50	975	64.1	28.0	45	147	12.3	2.7	2,046	97.2	7,826	72
NORTH CAROLINA	22,977	529,570	55,227.5	21,757.0	13,716	80,710	9,141.5	2,321.3	742,858	31,126.5	13,581,958	71,691
Alamance	379	8,367	801.9	369.4	190	1,097	100.7	29.2	10,041	369.4	195,976	1,419
Alexander	43	559	33.5	14.6	36	139	9.8	2.1	2,286	81.4	25,050	97
Alleghany	27	517	31.1	13.8	10	D	D	D	950	36.0	9,947	39
Anson	45	826	50.7	24.7	21	D	D	D	1,314	42.9	6,744	45
Ashe	51	1,136	73.3	35.1	32	118	10.4	2.8	2,425	95.5	20,505	94
Avery	41	746	72.2	25.4	25	180	20.4	5.1	1,659	61.2	54,331	118
Beaufort	120	2,392	186.5	77.6	80	384	32.1	8.6	3,302	127.7	25,927	140
Bertie	57	1,344	63.4	28.5	18	62	5.3	1.4	922	26.9	2,941	11
Bladen	56	998	52.7	19.8	29	D	D	D	1,761	59.5	5,347	31
Brunswick	221	3,576	326.6	127.5	119	463	45.3	12.0	10,579	444.8	703,161	2,926
Buncombe	844	20,510	2,518.2	1,012.7	456	2,461	261.7	69.8	27,219	1,167.3	452,471	1,667
Burke	187	4,495	461.5	183.6	99	434	41.1	11.1	5,159	198.3	44,747	285
Cabarrus	343	6,008	568.1	244.2	266	1,435	119.0	31.6	14,985	574.3	329,239	2,021
Caldwell	132	2,924	234.4	88.5	79	397	39.0	10.9	4,951	189.4	41,428	212
Camden	5	24	1.4	0.6	7	D	D	D	691	18.6	22,696	81
Carteret	191	3,165	283.7	120.4	143	598	51.3	15.5	6,439	279.5	98,906	378
Caswell	29	467	23.7	11.6	14	D	D	D	1,092	33.6	12,407	58
Catawba	382	11,445	1,153.6	446.6	223	1,410	109.8	31.8	10,701	496.7	126,048	742
Chatham	127	2,581	179.1	67.4	83	306	36.8	8.7	6,048	273.3	197,681	710
Cherokee	76	1,217	96.7	41.9	35	103	7.6	2.2	2,151	78.2	29,810	198

Table B. States and Counties — Government Employment and Payroll, and Local Government Finances

	Government employment and payroll, 2012									Local government finances, 2012				
			March payroll (percent of total)							General revenue				
												Taxes		
													Per capita[1] (dollars)	
STATE County	Full-time equivalent employees	March payroll (dollars)	Adminis-tration, judicial, and legal	Police and corrections	Fire protection	Highways and transpor-tation	Health and welfare	Natural resources and utilities	Education and libraries	Total (mil dol)	Inter-govern-mental (mil dol)	Total (mil dol)	Total	Property
	171	172	173	174	175	176	177	178	179	180	181	182	183	184
NEW YORK— Cont'd														
Genesee	3,495	13,011,030	5.1	5.8	1.6	4.1	10.0	1.1	70.6	378.8	154.3	137.4	2,290	1,468
Greene	2,313	9,425,632	7.2	6.0	0.0	7.6	11.6	1.6	64.8	291.0	101.2	151.7	3,117	2,471
Hamilton	511	1,883,521	13.9	3.7	0.5	18.0	10.6	5.4	45.2	54.6	10.1	40.8	8,548	7,863
Herkimer	3,357	17,320,913	6.2	16.3	10.9	9.4	4.5	5.4	45.2	354.3	171.8	137.0	2,124	1,648
Jefferson	5,239	20,682,670	6.0	6.1	2.2	6.7	6.7	3.0	66.9	631.5	312.9	217.3	1,807	1,154
Kings	(2)	(2)	(2)	(2)	(2)	(2)	(2)	(2)	(2)	(2)	(2)	(2)	(2)	(2)
Lewis	1,643	6,393,465	5.3	4.0	0.1	9.3	34.1	0.3	46.2	221.0	80.0	54.5	2,001	1,591
Livingston	2,962	11,287,932	7.2	8.2	0.0	6.5	18.2	2.0	56.7	340.1	136.2	132.2	2,039	1,556
Madison	2,860	10,880,867	5.6	7.3	1.1	8.0	7.4	2.2	66.8	324.2	144.9	143.1	1,977	1,638
Monroe	32,909	147,986,255	4.0	10.2	3.5	2.4	4.8	4.9	68.8	4,246.2	1,878.0	1,825.1	2,441	1,824
Montgomery	2,237	9,439,506	8.2	8.8	2.4	6.9	5.7	2.1	64.3	270.8	126.1	103.0	2,062	1,500
Nassau	60,368	360,394,360	4.0	11.4	0.7	2.4	9.9	3.6	66.2	10,545.3	2,263.0	7,088.6	5,254	4,380
New York	(2)411,393	(2)36,392,993	(2) 3.2	(2)18.6	(2) 5.3	(2)14.2	(2)17.3	(2) 4.7	(2)33.2	(2) 89,561.8	(2) 30,794.6	(2) 42,487.9	(2)5,096	(2)2,183
Niagara	8,942	40,897,207	4.2	9.3	3.5	3.3	5.7	3.9	65.8	1,197.2	504.4	461.1	2,144	1,505
Oneida	10,265	43,288,880	5.1	9.3	3.3	5.7	6.1	4.4	65.3	1,243.2	607.6	466.1	1,996	1,316
Onondaga	21,333	98,896,686	3.5	9.2	2.8	3.6	6.0	5.0	68.2	2,768.2	1,213.5	1,131.6	2,424	1,706
Ontario	5,314	22,633,286	7.3	8.2	1.0	4.3	6.4	3.2	68.2	617.9	231.6	291.0	2,682	1,907
Orange	15,475	79,024,558	5.0	9.7	1.3	3.8	7.6	2.1	69.2	2,388.1	851.1	1,242.0	3,316	2,623
Orleans	1,883	7,322,413	5.8	7.3	1.3	4.6	12.9	1.4	65.5	215.9	108.4	76.5	1,785	1,393
Oswego	5,833	24,108,601	4.0	4.7	1.8	4.8	6.7	1.2	74.7	720.3	332.9	266.4	2,189	1,640
Otsego	2,867	10,320,001	6.5	5.1	1.5	9.1	12.9	1.2	62.0	319.5	134.0	135.1	2,189	1,567
Putnam	3,780	21,486,132	6.3	9.6	0.0	4.8	5.6	1.1	71.4	620.4	156.8	423.9	4,256	3,653
Queens	(2)	(2)	(2)	(2)	(2)	(2)	(2)	(2)	(2)	(2)	(2)	(2)	(2)	(2)
Rensselaer	7,740	35,240,411	5.4	10.0	1.8	3.0	10.0	3.2	65.6	935.0	383.9	372.9	2,333	1,782
Richmond	(2)	(2)	(2)	(2)	(2)	(2)	(2)	(2)	(2)	(2)	(2)	(2)	(2)	(2)
Rockland	12,621	72,071,900	6.2	11.8	0.2	3.4	10.5	3.3	63.3	2,081.2	511.7	1,307.8	4,116	3,491
St. Lawrence	5,029	19,319,273	5.7	6.1	1.0	8.5	20.0	3.1	54.2	629.7	288.6	207.1	1,845	1,390
Saratoga	8,393	36,185,319	5.4	6.8	1.4	6.5	7.0	2.5	68.7	1,010.7	328.4	547.9	2,467	1,874
Schenectady	6,336	30,200,971	4.8	10.8	2.9	3.7	8.4	3.1	64.2	840.2	334.0	398.5	2,569	1,914
Schoharie	1,588	6,242,263	7.0	4.8	0.1	8.7	8.1	2.1	67.7	198.0	92.7	86.5	2,696	2,164
Schuyler	713	2,598,532	9.7	8.4	0.0	8.0	12.3	2.8	55.9	92.6	40.4	41.0	2,213	1,616
Seneca	1,397	5,203,170	7.6	6.3	0.0	6.3	10.3	4.6	63.8	187.5	82.2	75.2	2,129	1,460
Steuben	5,430	22,838,751	6.3	4.7	1.6	6.5	9.0	2.5	68.7	603.0	285.7	219.9	2,220	1,686
Suffolk	63,444	372,480,221	4.1	12.0	1.0	2.5	5.0	2.8	71.0	10,433.2	3,062.8	6,438.8	4,295	3,385
Sullivan	3,903	18,183,844	6.0	6.2	4.1	7.1	11.7	2.9	59.7	571.4	182.8	285.0	3,711	3,207
Tioga	2,377	8,831,267	4.9	6.4	0.5	4.3	7.4	1.1	72.8	263.8	126.3	98.9	1,959	1,427
Tompkins	4,530	19,870,493	5.0	6.2	2.8	4.4	7.3	3.5	68.0	531.9	184.0	252.8	2,465	1,857
Ulster	8,282	38,442,668	5.7	7.7	1.3	4.8	8.8	1.7	68.0	1,095.2	330.4	630.3	3,467	2,848
Warren	3,395	12,916,351	7.7	10.3	0.3	8.0	7.0	4.0	60.4	411.0	122.0	230.3	3,513	2,589
Washington	3,303	11,817,292	4.2	5.9	0.6	5.8	10.6	1.3	70.1	334.5	150.3	129.8	2,063	1,703
Wayne	4,573	16,899,070	5.7	6.6	0.1	4.5	9.5	2.2	70.0	506.8	227.4	194.1	2,088	1,627
Westchester	42,725	278,687,815	4.6	13.0	4.0	2.1	14.4	4.1	55.6	8,694.6	1,905.2	4,937.7	5,135	4,223
Wyoming	1,997	7,253,253	6.6	6.7	0.7	6.2	29.3	3.6	45.9	224.2	78.4	71.1	1,698	1,279
Yates	984	3,705,476	8.7	13.4	0.2	8.3	6.2	2.9	58.0	114.7	43.0	58.3	2,300	1,770
NORTH CAROLINA	X	X	X	X	X	X	X	X	X	X	X	X	X	X
Alamance	1,005,835	17,822,770	4.1	10.8	2.8	1.7	7.8	5.8	64.0	420.3	210.4	147.7	960	694
Alexander	1,147	3,312,277	3.5	5.4	1.2	0.1	15.0	1.1	71.6	79.1	47.9	22.9	622	467
Alleghany	425	1,164,658	3.2	4.3	0.0	1.2	5.7	2.7	76.9	29.9	16.8	10.5	964	802
Anson	1,315	3,876,045	2.9	6.4	2.5	0.6	7.2	4.8	74.4	91.7	58.9	20.0	760	612
Ashe	790	2,611,411	5.6	7.1	0.0	1.1	16.3	2.1	65.4	64.2	34.4	23.7	876	672
Avery	815	1,974,739	6.6	9.8	1.1	1.1	14.1	2.6	59.8	51.3	22.8	24.5	1,387	1,109
Beaufort	2,278	5,974,850	4.5	7.2	2.1	0.6	8.3	10.0	62.5	173.8	99.8	49.9	1,050	812
Bertie	997	3,093,286	5.9	4.6	0.1	0.6	4.8	2.9	80.8	51.4	32.6	12.0	580	454
Bladen	1,399	4,935,403	2.7	6.3	0.5	0.4	11.2	2.6	74.0	133.3	64.5	29.1	834	667
Brunswick	3,900	12,967,182	6.8	10.3	1.5	1.3	19.2	7.5	47.9	393.3	118.2	177.6	1,582	1,215
Buncombe	8,896	30,002,974	4.8	8.2	3.6	1.6	11.7	7.3	59.6	751.0	306.2	322.9	1,321	936
Burke	3,144	9,746,027	4.9	6.5	1.0	0.9	9.1	5.9	70.6	228.4	129.8	66.9	739	594
Cabarrus	7,505	25,676,197	3.6	8.3	4.5	1.2	14.4	6.7	58.7	601.3	252.6	258.8	1,403	1,100
Caldwell	3,445	10,357,515	2.9	6.0	2.1	0.6	13.9	3.0	69.5	257.1	164.6	64.8	791	595
Camden	352	1,014,214	1.0	5.8	0.0	0.0	0.0	4.2	71.8	30.3	17.1	11.7	1,163	952
Carteret	2,554	7,543,452	5.4	9.0	4.8	1.2	10.1	4.3	60.9	338.2	84.6	98.9	1,462	1,061
Caswell	710	2,061,989	3.0	5.5	0.0	0.0	17.8	1.7	67.9	51.5	32.9	13.2	569	464
Catawba	7,515	27,058,433	3.4	5.6	2.5	1.6	35.0	3.0	45.2	716.3	255.5	171.8	1,113	804
Chatham	1,616	6,230,991	4.0	6.8	0.3	0.8	10.6	4.0	68.1	164.8	66.0	78.0	1,182	977
Cherokee	1,091	3,381,536	5.0	8.1	0.0	1.1	13.2	8.0	61.9	84.3	45.8	26.1	966	704

1. Based on the resident population estimated as of July 1 of the year shown. 2. Bronx, Kings, Queens, and Richmond counties are included with New York county.

Items 171—184

STATE County	Local government finances, 2012 (cont.)										Government employment, 2017			Individual income tax returns, 2016		
	Direct general expenditure								Debt outstanding							
			Percent of total for:												Mean adjusted gross income	Mean income tax
	Total (mil dol)	Per capita[1] (dollars)	Education	Health and hospitals	Police protection	Public welfare	Highways	Total (mil dol)	Per capita[1] (dollars)	Federal civilian	Federal military	State and local	Number of returns		
	185	186	187	188	189	190	191	192	193	194	195	196	197	198	199
NEW YORK— Cont'd															
Genesee	380.9	6,350	48.2	3.3	2.6	11.4	6.0	207.2	3,454	584	88	4,891	28,110	49,466	4,855
Greene	302.4	6,212	48.5	5.4	2.1	9.8	9.4	211.7	4,350	87	69	4,255	22,240	56,723	6,562
Hamilton	53.0	11,093	36.6	5.7	1.7	2.5	16.4	24.5	5,123	15	7	853	2,600	50,621	5,147
Herkimer	352.7	5,467	56.7	3.1	1.8	9.3	8.9	252.1	3,907	111	95	4,237	27,820	47,740	4,677
Jefferson	631.0	5,247	49.6	3.4	2.6	9.2	6.9	554.7	4,612	3,069	15,058	8,256	50,570	48,723	4,844
Kings	(2)	(2)	(2)	(2)	(2)	(2)	(2)	(2)	(2)	8,037	4,277	91,926	1,224,210	57,660	8,128
Lewis	250.8	9,211	33.2	34.9	1.3	6.5	7.0	120.5	4,427	60	41	2,283	11,700	46,051	4,126
Livingston	328.9	5,074	44.9	5.5	2.8	18.2	7.8	282.5	4,359	132	90	6,073	27,960	54,992	5,855
Madison	345.6	4,774	52.0	4.3	2.3	7.4	8.1	456.5	6,307	136	104	4,239	31,260	64,149	7,902
Monroe	4,348.7	5,815	50.1	4.2	4.3	10.9	3.2	3,397.3	4,543	2,925	1,217	44,804	361,750	61,646	7,796
Montgomery	305.0	6,106	50.5	2.2	2.0	7.7	5.3	285.4	5,714	104	75	2,630	22,590	46,573	4,559
Nassau	11,105.9	8,231	48.3	7.2	8.7	5.9	3.1	9,302.1	6,894	5,287	2,559	74,476	715,150	111,677	20,437
New York	(2) 84,366.2	(2) 10,120	(2)26.6	(2)10.0	(2) 6.0	(2)15.1	(2) 1.9	(2)168,630.0	(2) 20,227	23,064	2,716	248,441	878,470	193,111	44,131
Niagara	1,203.8	5,596	48.1	2.7	3.7	8.2	5.8	966.3	4,492	1,014	360	12,466	104,580	51,542	5,438
Oneida	1,300.4	5,568	52.4	2.6	3.1	11.0	5.5	1,381.4	5,915	2,315	398	23,275	104,950	52,105	5,740
Onondaga	3,043.0	6,518	47.4	3.2	3.3	10.4	4.6	3,160.9	6,771	4,589	836	35,967	221,690	63,604	8,169
Ontario	612.2	5,642	54.1	2.3	2.9	8.5	6.6	594.8	5,481	1,531	168	7,102	54,850	66,666	8,977
Orange	2,555.9	6,825	54.6	4.6	3.7	10.5	3.3	1,906.2	5,090	4,579	6,700	21,845	181,300	67,670	8,459
Orleans	216.3	5,050	53.5	3.8	2.2	13.7	6.1	184.0	4,295	79	60	3,768	18,370	45,211	4,085
Oswego	722.5	5,936	55.7	2.6	2.1	8.4	6.2	668.5	5,493	255	203	8,808	52,650	50,009	4,940
Otsego	326.6	5,293	47.1	2.7	1.6	14.9	9.2	292.6	4,742	135	86	4,383	26,360	51,666	5,596
Putnam	630.2	6,327	61.1	2.1	4.6	3.9	5.1	400.1	4,017	144	151	4,565	50,060	88,368	12,812
Queens	(2)	(2)	(2)	(2)	(2)	(2)	(2)	(2)	(2)	14,075	3,712	85,333	1,156,710	49,766	5,567
Rensselaer	989.2	6,189	51.6	3.4	3.1	13.0	3.7	809.6	5,065	365	255	11,201	78,450	59,459	6,853
Richmond	(2)	(2)	(2)	(2)	(2)	(2)	(2)	(2)	(2)	1,012	1,168	17,932	223,490	68,734	8,645
Rockland	2,333.3	7,343	45.2	11.3	4.7	6.4	4.3	1,968.4	6,195	484	502	17,446	148,610	86,608	13,297
St. Lawrence	626.2	5,579	45.3	11.0	2.3	10.4	8.4	441.9	3,937	598	260	9,870	42,790	49,223	4,868
Saratoga	1,019.1	4,588	54.8	5.8	3.1	8.2	5.3	814.5	3,667	426	2,039	11,723	117,890	108,861	18,822
Schenectady	849.4	5,476	48.9	2.4	3.7	14.9	3.5	691.5	4,458	606	244	9,382	76,610	60,594	7,085
Schoharie	201.5	6,278	47.0	3.9	1.2	7.5	15.0	132.3	4,121	70	47	2,545	13,940	51,333	5,416
Schuyler	91.9	4,963	40.6	6.3	1.9	11.2	10.5	63.1	3,409	48	28	1,098	8,630	48,139	4,722
Seneca	180.7	5,118	46.5	4.6	2.7	8.7	6.0	331.8	9,398	86	49	2,840	15,300	48,423	4,858
Steuben	616.7	6,226	58.5	3.7	1.6	11.1	8.0	529.5	5,345	1,016	170	6,743	43,510	54,358	6,305
Suffolk	11,000.9	7,338	53.4	3.5	5.3	5.4	3.3	9,786.8	6,528	11,214	2,549	94,163	779,210	86,615	13,609
Sullivan	549.1	7,150	46.8	4.4	2.6	12.2	8.2	363.9	4,739	185	112	5,696	33,880	52,258	5,883
Tioga	265.1	5,251	53.3	3.7	1.7	7.4	7.4	230.5	4,566	160	81	2,428	23,330	52,662	5,450
Tompkins	541.1	5,276	48.3	4.4	2.7	8.0	5.5	696.7	6,794	268	164	5,861	40,530	66,266	8,483
Ulster	1,119.8	6,160	51.1	2.0	2.8	12.1	5.4	695.1	3,823	443	283	12,598	86,480	60,325	7,320
Warren	406.2	6,198	44.0	4.8	3.3	10.1	9.1	365.7	5,580	201	103	4,467	34,240	58,221	7,082
Washington	349.4	5,552	55.7	4.3	1.6	11.5	6.6	209.9	3,336	123	91	4,914	28,300	47,469	4,535
Wayne	528.4	5,684	56.8	4.2	2.3	10.7	5.9	364.9	3,926	179	141	7,069	44,340	51,309	5,047
Westchester	8,708.4	9,055	42.2	12.9	4.6	6.4	1.7	6,138.8	6,383	4,373	1,489	58,110	486,460	143,043	29,230
Wyoming	218.6	5,217	34.6	26.6	2.8	7.6	9.3	135.9	3,244	91	58	4,134	18,190	49,916	4,802
Yates	112.7	4,445	44.0	5.8	4.2	8.7	10.8	161.3	6,365	59	37	1,196	11,080	48,516	4,851
NORTH CAROLINA	X	X	X	X	X	X	X	X	X	72,433	129,581	658,361	4,511,350	60,065	7,592
Alamance	427.7	2,779	50.9	3.4	8.3	5.8	1.6	182.0	1,183	243	357	6,881	72,210	50,942	5,363
Alexander	79.9	2,168	57.3	6.5	5.6	7.5	0.5	21.9	594	53	81	1,843	15,250	47,418	4,667
Alleghany	28.9	2,648	55.4	5.1	5.7	7.6	0.2	8.2	749	44	25	573	4,590	44,991	4,797
Anson	92.1	3,494	62.0	2.8	6.7	6.7	1.0	5.0	191	49	51	2,080	9,650	36,035	2,700
Ashe	66.1	2,439	50.5	2.7	5.8	13.7	1.2	26.9	992	64	60	1,085	11,220	43,667	4,319
Avery	52.4	2,970	45.9	4.8	9.0	7.8	1.8	12.6	717	38	34	1,497	7,170	43,686	4,209
Beaufort	192.0	4,042	45.1	2.4	4.2	6.6	1.0	78.5	1,653	122	105	2,638	20,540	48,629	4,958
Bertie	49.9	2,417	57.0	0.9	7.9	10.3	1.0	16.3	788	91	41	1,260	7,870	37,224	3,021
Bladen	137.6	3,942	46.1	22.2	4.7	6.1	1.2	40.6	1,164	110	75	2,242	12,730	41,611	3,859
Brunswick	396.3	3,530	32.7	9.9	9.3	4.9	1.6	543.6	4,843	462	359	4,898	60,090	64,423	8,144
Buncombe	800.5	3,274	41.8	1.9	10.0	8.4	2.1	617.7	2,527	2,956	629	13,097	125,940	58,399	7,438
Burke	231.0	2,553	56.9	2.9	7.1	6.7	0.9	69.8	771	143	196	6,874	37,740	44,175	4,020
Cabarrus	593.1	3,214	47.0	1.8	6.9	5.0	1.7	669.7	3,630	317	464	14,102	92,380	63,814	7,783
Caldwell	274.4	3,349	49.9	21.1	4.8	6.2	1.3	60.2	735	145	183	4,090	33,790	43,940	4,157
Camden	29.0	2,871	58.0	0.3	6.4	4.2	0.0	8.6	849	11	24	462	4,540	58,402	5,710
Carteret	311.1	4,600	29.2	39.1	5.8	4.1	1.4	132.7	1,963	278	387	4,610	32,410	57,738	6,830
Caswell	54.4	2,344	50.3	5.5	16.1	11.3	0.1	23.2	1,000	40	48	1,229	9,210	42,273	3,579
Catawba	685.5	4,441	36.4	32.8	4.4	5.5	1.4	324.5	2,102	309	353	9,490	72,680	56,175	6,913
Chatham	177.4	2,689	45.4	4.2	15.7	6.3	0.6	171.9	2,605	102	159	2,421	33,620	83,972	12,486
Cherokee	85.8	3,180	51.5	5.7	5.1	7.8	0.4	29.5	1,092	105	62	1,526	11,440	40,146	3,485

1. Based on the resident population estimated as of July 1 of the year shown.   2. Bronx, Kings, Queens, and Richmond counties are included with New York county

Table B. States and Counties — **Land Area and Population**

State / county code	CBSA code[1]	County code[2]	STATE County	Population, 2018				Population and population characteristics, 2018										
								Race alone or in combination, not Hispanic or Latino (percent)					Age (percent)					
				Land area[3] (sq. mi)	Total persons 2018	Rank	Per square mile	White	Black	American Indian, Alaska Native	Asian and Pacific Islancer	Percent Hispanic or Latino[4]	Under 5 years	5 to 17 years	18 to 24 years	25 to 34 years	35 to 44 years	45 to 54 years
				1	2	3	4	5	6	7	8	9	10	11	12	13	14	15
			NORTH CAROLINA—Cont'd															
37041		6	Chowan	172.7	14,029	2,160	81.2	61.1	34.7	0.7	1.1	3.7	4.7	15.4	7.0	10.4	10.5	11.3
37043		9	Clay	215.0	11,139	2,343	51.8	94.2	1.8	1.2	0.7	3.6	4.3	13.0	5.7	8.3	9.5	11.8
37045	43,140	4	Cleveland	464.2	97,645	612	210.4	74.4	21.8	0.6	1.3	3.7	5.6	16.4	8.9	11.8	10.8	13.9
37047		6	Columbus	938.1	55,655	919	59.3	60.5	30.9	4.0	0.8	5.5	5.2	15.7	8.4	12.3	11.7	12.9
37049	35,100	3	Craven	706.6	102,912	588	145.6	67.8	22.3	1.1	4.2	7.4	6.3	15.3	12.1	13.5	10.8	10.3
37051	22,180	2	Cumberland	652.6	332,330	209	509.2	45.9	39.6	2.6	4.5	11.9	7.6	17.1	12.9	17.1	11.9	10.8
37053	47,260	1	Currituck	261.9	27,072	1,523	103.4	89.0	6.4	1.1	1.3	4.0	5.7	16.7	6.7	12.3	11.8	14.6
37055	28,620	4	Dare	383.2	36,501	1,265	95.3	89.1	3.2	0.9	1.2	7.3	4.5	14.4	6.1	10.1	11.9	13.7
37057	49,180	2	Davidson	553.2	166,614	393	301.2	81.1	10.3	0.9	1.9	7.3	5.6	16.4	7.6	11.5	11.6	14.7
37059	49,180	2	Davie	263.7	42,733	1,122	162.1	85.6	7.4	0.7	1.0	7.0	4.9	16.1	7.5	9.7	11.1	14.8
37061		6	Duplin	814.7	58,856	878	72.2	52.2	24.8	0.7	0.6	22.7	6.1	17.6	8.0	11.3	11.7	12.6
37063	20,500	2	Durham	286.5	316,739	221	1,105.5	44.2	37.2	1.0	6.1	13.7	6.4	14.3	10.0	18.2	14.0	12.2
37065	40,580	3	Edgecombe	505.4	52,005	961	102.9	37.1	57.8	0.7	0.6	4.8	5.6	16.9	8.0	11.8	10.8	12.1
37067	49,180	2	Forsyth	407.8	379,099	185	929.6	58.1	27.0	0.8	3.0	13.0	5.9	17.0	9.6	13.3	12.0	13.1
37069	39,580	1	Franklin	491.8	67,560	789	137.4	64.9	26.3	1.1	1.0	8.5	5.6	16.3	8.2	11.7	12.1	14.5
37071	16,740	1	Gaston	355.7	222,846	305	626.5	73.6	18.2	0.9	2.0	7.3	5.9	16.6	8.1	13.4	12.3	14.5
37073	47,260	1	Gates	340.6	11,573	2,321	34.0	65.5	32.2	1.3	0.9	2.3	4.6	15.7	7.1	10.7	10.0	14.7
37075		9	Graham	292.0	8,484	2,543	29.1	87.9	1.2	8.5	0.7	3.8	4.8	15.2	7.0	10.5	10.9	13.1
37077	37,080	4	Granville	532.0	60,115	869	113.0	59.2	32.3	0.9	1.0	8.2	5.0	15.4	8.4	11.9	12.1	15.4
37079		8	Greene	266.7	21,012	1,776	78.8	47.7	36.3	0.9	0.7	15.5	4.8	15.2	8.5	14.1	13.6	12.9
37081	24,660	2	Guilford	645.9	533,670	131	826.2	51.5	35.6	1.1	6.0	8.2	5.9	16.4	10.8	13.8	12.2	13.2
37083	40,260	4	Halifax	723.7	50,574	982	69.9	39.1	53.9	4.1	1.1	3.1	5.5	15.9	7.4	11.8	10.6	13.0
37085	20,380	4	Harnett	595.0	134,214	478	225.6	63.5	22.6	1.8	2.2	13.0	7.4	18.6	9.0	15.7	13.6	12.3
37087	11,700	2	Haywood	553.6	61,971	850	111.9	93.6	1.6	1.1	0.8	4.1	4.8	13.4	6.3	11.4	10.9	13.2
37089	11,700	2	Henderson	372.9	116,748	534	313.1	84.6	4.0	1.0	1.8	10.4	4.8	14.1	6.5	10.4	11.0	12.7
37091		6	Hertford	353.2	23,659	1,658	67.0	34.0	60.9	1.6	1.0	3.8	4.6	14.3	11.1	12.1	10.9	11.9
37093	22,180	2	Hoke	390.1	54,764	932	140.4	42.2	35.9	9.6	2.6	13.6	8.4	18.9	8.0	17.7	14.2	11.8
37095		9	Hyde	612.3	5,230	2,816	8.5	61.2	29.0	1.0	0.9	9.2	3.9	12.8	6.9	13.3	13.4	13.0
37097	16,740	1	Iredell	574.2	178,435	374	310.8	77.3	12.8	0.7	3.1	7.8	5.6	17.4	8.0	11.8	12.6	15.0
37099	19,000	6	Jackson	491.2	43,327	1,106	88.2	82.8	2.7	9.1	1.4	5.9	4.4	12.2	18.3	11.5	10.0	10.9
37101	39,580	1	Johnston	791.2	202,675	331	256.2	68.8	16.9	1.0	1.3	14.0	6.4	19.1	7.8	12.3	13.9	15.1
37103	35,100	3	Jones	471.4	9,637	2,453	20.4	63.7	30.7	1.4	0.8	5.1	4.9	13.7	6.8	11.1	10.4	13.0
37105	41,820	4	Lee	255.1	61,452	857	240.9	59.4	20.3	1.0	1.8	19.5	6.4	17.6	8.3	12.7	12.0	13.4
37107	28,820	4	Lenoir	399.1	55,976	912	140.3	50.3	41.8	0.7	1.1	7.5	5.7	16.8	8.0	11.2	10.9	12.5
37109	16,740	1	Lincoln	295.8	83,770	682	283.2	86.3	6.2	0.8	1.0	7.2	5.2	15.9	7.2	11.2	12.1	15.6
37111	32,000	6	McDowell	440.0	45,507	1,063	103.4	88.6	4.4	0.9	1.1	6.3	5.1	15.0	7.4	11.7	11.6	13.9
37113		7	Macon	515.6	35,285	1,296	68.4	89.9	1.7	1.0	1.2	7.2	5.0	13.7	6.5	9.9	9.6	11.5
37115	11,700	2	Madison	449.6	21,763	1,737	48.4	95.1	1.9	1.2	0.8	2.4	4.7	13.2	10.0	11.0	11.3	12.8
37117		6	Martin	456.4	22,671	1,695	49.7	53.1	42.5	0.7	0.8	4.2	5.4	14.9	7.1	10.8	9.7	13.1
37119	16,740	1	Mecklenburg	523.6	1,093,901	40	2,089.2	48.1	32.7	0.9	7.0	13.6	6.6	16.9	9.0	17.0	14.6	13.5
37121		7	Mitchell	221.3	15,000	2,096	67.8	92.7	0.9	0.8	0.8	5.8	4.7	13.5	6.5	10.9	10.5	13.3
37123		6	Montgomery	491.5	27,271	1,516	55.5	64.2	19.1	0.9	1.7	15.4	5.3	16.7	8.0	10.9	11.0	12.9
37125	38,240	4	Moore	697.7	98,682	606	141.4	78.8	12.9	1.3	2.1	6.8	5.8	15.5	6.3	11.6	11.7	11.7
37127	40,580	3	Nash	540.4	94,016	631	174.0	50.7	41.6	1.2	1.2	7.1	5.5	16.4	8.8	11.8	11.4	13.4
37129	48,900	2	New Hanover	192.2	232,274	286	1,208.5	79.0	14.2	1.0	2.2	5.6	4.9	13.5	12.8	13.4	12.3	12.4
37131	40,260	9	Northampton	536.6	19,676	1,845	36.7	39.9	57.7	1.0	0.5	2.3	4.6	12.8	6.9	10.5	9.6	12.2
37133	27,340	2	Onslow	761.9	197,683	339	259.5	69.3	16.9	1.4	3.8	12.8	8.8	15.7	21.4	18.5	10.4	7.9
37135	20,500	2	Orange	397.5	146,027	449	367.4	71.3	12.3	1.0	9.2	8.6	4.5	15.1	17.3	12.6	11.6	12.7
37137	35,100	3	Pamlico	336.5	12,670	2,245	37.7	75.6	19.7	1.1	1.0	4.1	3.5	11.3	6.1	10.4	9.3	11.4
37139	21,020	4	Pasquotank	226.9	39,639	1,188	174.7	56.3	37.2	0.9	2.2	5.7	6.2	16.0	9.2	13.9	11.8	12.1
37141	48,900	2	Pender	871.3	62,162	848	71.3	76.7	15.6	1.1	1.0	7.4	5.7	16.5	6.8	11.1	12.8	14.2
37143	21,020	8	Perquimans	247.1	13,422	2,197	54.3	73.6	23.6	0.9	0.8	2.6	4.5	13.8	6.2	10.0	9.7	12.2
37145	20,500	2	Person	392.3	39,507	1,192	100.7	67.6	28.0	1.1	0.7	4.4	5.4	15.5	7.5	11.3	11.1	14.0
37147	24,780	3	Pitt	652.4	179,914	367	275.8	55.9	36.3	0.7	2.8	6.3	5.7	15.6	17.5	14.0	11.7	11.1
37149		8	Polk	237.7	20,611	1,791	86.7	88.8	4.9	0.8	0.8	6.1	3.7	12.4	6.3	8.2	8.9	12.6
37151	24,660	2	Randolph	782.3	143,351	455	183.2	80.1	7.0	1.0	1.7	11.7	5.6	16.9	8.0	11.8	11.5	14.4
37153	40,460	5	Richmond	473.7	44,887	1,079	94.8	58.4	32.4	3.4	1.3	6.7	6.0	16.9	8.8	12.4	11.5	13.1
37155	31,300	4	Robeson	947.3	131,831	484	139.2	26.8	24.5	41.2	1.0	9.0	6.6	18.2	10.2	12.7	11.8	12.4
37157	24,660	2	Rockingham	565.6	90,690	648	160.3	74.0	19.8	0.9	1.0	6.2	5.1	15.1	7.4	11.1	10.8	14.2
37159	16,740	1	Rowan	511.5	141,262	460	276.2	73.1	17.1	0.8	1.5	9.2	5.8	16.5	8.5	12.5	11.6	13.6
37161	22,580	4	Rutherford	565.4	66,826	799	118.2	84.7	10.9	0.8	1.0	4.6	5.1	15.5	7.3	10.7	10.8	14.0
37163		6	Sampson	945.7	63,626	838	67.3	51.7	26.2	2.5	0.9	20.4	6.4	17.9	8.6	11.2	11.9	13.1
37165	29,900	6	Scotland	319.1	34,810	1,308	109.1	45.3	39.8	13.1	1.4	3.1	6.3	16.3	9.6	12.5	11.3	12.5
37167	10,620	6	Stanly	395.1	62,075	849	157.1	81.9	12.1	0.7	2.3	4.4	5.8	15.8	8.3	12.6	11.2	13.8
37169	49,180	2	Stokes	449.0	45,467	1,064	101.3	92.3	4.4	0.8	0.6	3.1	4.5	14.3	7.3	10.4	10.8	15.2
37171	34,340	2	Surry	533.7	71,948	753	134.8	84.6	4.3	0.7	0.8	10.8	5.3	15.8	7.8	10.8	11.3	14.3

1. CBSA = Core Based Statistical Area. See Appendix A for explanation. See Appendix B for list of metropolitan areas with component counties. 2. County type code from the Economic Research Service of USDA Rural-Urban Continuum Codes. See Appendix A for definition. 3. Dry land or land partially or temporarily covered by water. 4. May be of any race.

Table B. States and Counties — Population and Households

STATE County	55 to 64 years	65 to 74 years	75 years and over	Percent female	Total persons 2000	Total persons 2010	Percent change 2000-2010	Percent change 2010-2018	Births	Deaths	Net Migration	Number	Persons per household	Family households	Female family householder[1]	One person
	16	17	18	19	20	21	22	23	24	25	26	27	28	29	30	31
NORTH CAROLINA— Cont'd																
Chowan	15.9	14.1	10.5	52.4	14,526	14,793	1.8	-5.2	1,171	1,521	-416	5,903	2.39	69.3	16.3	26.8
Clay	16.4	18.8	12.3	51.2	8,775	10,590	20.7	5.2	710	1,166	1,008	5,049	2.12	65.8	7.2	30.7
Cleveland	14.0	11.1	7.5	51.9	96,287	98,032	1.8	-0.4	8,807	9,654	531	37,782	2.52	67.4	14.7	28.6
Columbus	13.8	11.8	8.3	50.5	54,749	58,110	6.1	-4.2	5,054	5,740	-1,748	22,462	2.39	65.5	17.5	31.6
Craven	12.7	11.0	8.0	49.4	91,436	103,503	13.2	-0.6	12,500	8,416	-4,710	40,571	2.42	68.0	11.5	27.1
Cumberland	10.7	7.1	4.9	50.5	302,963	319,433	5.4	4.0	46,109	20,040	-14,264	124,500	2.55	63.4	16.4	31.5
Currituck	16.0	10.4	5.8	50.5	18,190	23,547	29.5	15.0	2,058	1,810	3,255	9,766	2.57	73.8	7.7	19.9
Dare	17.8	14.0	7.4	50.7	29,967	33,920	13.2	7.6	2,889	2,627	2,316	15,264	2.31	66.6	9.3	26.2
Davidson	14.3	10.7	7.5	51.1	147,246	162,841	10.6	2.3	14,302	14,083	3,709	64,727	2.50	69.8	12.4	24.9
Davie	14.8	11.9	9.3	51.2	34,835	41,221	18.3	3.7	3,174	3,552	1,909	15,895	2.60	71.3	9.3	24.8
Duplin	14.0	10.8	7.9	51.3	49,063	58,399	19.0	0.8	6,061	4,403	-1,198	21,669	2.71	68.4	15.1	26.7
Durham	11.7	8.1	5.0	52.3	223,314	269,999	20.9	17.3	35,335	15,778	26,840	120,936	2.37	57.9	14.5	33.2
Edgecombe	15.1	11.8	7.9	53.8	55,606	56,546	1.7	-8.0	5,188	5,054	-4,718	21,431	2.48	67.4	24.1	27.8
Forsyth	13.1	9.4	6.6	52.6	306,067	350,649	14.6	8.1	37,202	26,142	17,545	145,102	2.47	63.0	13.8	31.6
Franklin	14.8	10.3	6.5	50.6	47,260	60,553	28.1	11.6	5,652	4,521	5,848	24,287	2.56	72.3	14.6	23.4
Gaston	13.2	9.6	6.5	51.8	190,365	206,094	8.3	8.1	20,882	18,424	14,370	80,682	2.62	67.1	14.6	27.6
Gates	17.0	11.8	8.4	50.5	10,516	12,184	15.9	-5.0	873	996	-495	4,439	2.60	70.4	12.6	26.7
Graham	14.8	12.9	10.9	49.0	7,993	8,861	10.9	-4.3	719	881	-213	3,303	2.57	68.2	10.1	27.7
Granville	14.7	10.4	6.7	49.0	48,498	57,531	18.6	4.5	4,689	4,211	2,131	20,945	2.62	71.0	14.9	25.6
Greene	14.3	10.1	6.4	45.4	18,974	21,353	12.5	-1.6	1,776	1,581	-561	7,348	2.56	67.6	19.3	27.4
Guilford	12.4	8.9	6.2	52.7	421,048	488,421	16.0	9.3	50,528	34,147	29,141	200,998	2.49	62.9	15.1	30.4
Halifax	15.1	11.9	8.8	52.0	57,370	54,627	-4.8	-7.4	4,766	5,523	-3,305	21,207	2.40	65.3	21.8	30.8
Harnett	11.0	7.6	4.9	50.5	91,025	114,681	26.0	17.0	15,128	7,809	12,037	44,657	2.81	71.7	14.1	24.1
Haywood	15.3	14.1	10.5	51.7	54,033	59,031	9.2	5.0	4,745	6,044	4,248	26,288	2.26	65.5	11.3	30.3
Henderson	14.7	14.5	11.3	52.0	89,173	106,713	19.7	9.4	8,845	11,099	12,184	47,804	2.32	64.7	9.1	30.4
Hertford	15.3	11.3	8.5	50.9	22,601	24,677	9.2	-4.1	1,910	2,210	-717	8,880	2.41	63.8	20.6	32.2
Hoke	10.9	6.6	3.5	50.6	33,646	46,890	39.4	16.8	7,692	2,571	2,662	17,373	2.94	72.7	17.1	23.6
Hyde	16.1	12.2	8.5	45.3	5,826	5,817	-0.2	-10.1	374	477	-491	1,835	2.63	73.6	18.2	23.7
Iredell	13.7	9.6	6.2	50.8	122,660	159,451	30.0	11.9	15,036	12,350	16,293	63,447	2.66	71.9	12.6	23.4
Jackson	13.0	12.0	7.6	50.9	33,121	40,261	21.6	7.6	3,210	2,909	2,756	16,218	2.35	60.1	11.8	29.7
Johnston	12.1	8.5	4.8	51.0	121,965	168,877	38.5	20.0	18,735	11,166	26,017	65,401	2.82	74.2	13.9	21.4
Jones	17.4	13.4	9.2	51.0	10,381	10,167	-2.1	-5.2	796	1,023	-302	4,148	2.33	68.8	13.2	27.6
Lee	13.2	9.6	6.8	51.1	49,040	57,858	18.0	6.2	6,535	4,496	1,572	21,691	2.71	69.4	14.3	27.3
Lenoir	15.1	11.4	8.4	52.4	59,648	59,511	-0.2	-5.9	5,372	5,897	-3,002	23,263	2.43	65.7	17.6	30.1
Lincoln	15.2	10.9	6.8	50.3	63,780	77,985	22.3	7.4	6,502	6,326	5,626	31,250	2.55	73.3	11.3	21.5
McDowell	14.8	12.0	8.5	50.1	42,151	44,996	6.7	1.1	3,772	4,127	911	17,970	2.44	71.9	12.6	23.3
Macon	15.3	16.2	12.3	51.5	29,811	33,925	13.8	4.0	2,769	3,566	2,183	15,513	2.18	64.4	9.2	31.1
Madison	14.6	13.4	8.9	50.7	19,635	20,784	5.9	4.7	1,591	1,906	1,292	8,346	2.42	65.9	9.8	28.2
Martin	16.0	13.6	9.6	53.0	25,593	24,515	-4.2	-7.5	2,002	2,610	-1,235	9,624	2.40	66.7	15.5	28.7
Mecklenburg	11.0	6.9	4.3	51.9	695,454	919,668	32.2	18.9	117,854	47,835	103,271	395,503	2.58	61.8	13.7	30.4
Mitchell	15.5	14.1	10.8	50.7	15,687	15,576	-0.7	-3.7	1,165	1,810	80	6,390	2.32	64.7	8.5	30.5
Montgomery	14.6	12.3	8.2	51.2	26,822	27,784	3.6	-1.8	2,583	2,308	-775	10,855	2.43	66.7	13.6	30.4
Moore	13.5	12.7	11.3	51.8	74,769	88,242	18.0	11.8	8,525	8,941	10,761	38,185	2.43	65.6	9.3	30.0
Nash	14.3	11.3	7.3	52.1	87,420	95,829	9.6	-1.9	8,849	8,339	-2,303	36,878	2.50	65.9	16.4	29.9
New Hanover	12.9	10.8	7.0	52.3	160,307	202,683	26.4	14.6	18,565	15,048	25,745	91,673	2.32	57.2	11.1	33.0
Northampton	17.5	14.7	11.1	51.2	22,086	22,106	0.1	-11.0	1,542	2,281	-1,699	8,819	2.22	65.3	17.6	30.4
Onslow	8.0	5.5	3.8	44.8	150,355	177,799	18.3	11.2	34,729	8,256	-7,895	63,093	2.73	71.3	12.4	22.6
Orange	12.1	8.9	5.1	52.2	118,227	133,702	13.1	9.2	10,015	6,448	8,772	52,160	2.52	61.1	9.4	28.1
Pamlico	18.0	17.5	12.4	49.4	12,934	13,143	1.6	-3.6	730	1,292	90	5,395	2.25	68.7	10.6	28.0
Pasquotank	13.8	10.1	6.8	51.1	34,897	40,661	16.5	-2.5	4,070	3,373	-1,748	14,629	2.54	67.1	14.6	28.6
Pender	15.0	11.2	6.8	50.1	41,082	52,198	27.1	19.1	5,085	4,264	9,050	21,053	2.68	66.0	9.1	30.2
Perquimans	16.7	15.3	11.6	51.9	11,368	13,453	18.3	-0.2	1,040	1,273	209	5,882	2.28	68.3	12.9	25.5
Person	15.8	11.6	7.9	51.6	35,623	39,478	10.8	0.1	3,397	3,564	225	15,772	2.46	67.6	17.6	28.4
Pitt	11.2	8.0	5.2	53.0	133,798	168,167	25.7	7.0	17,335	10,216	4,662	68,805	2.47	60.0	15.8	29.5
Polk	16.9	16.4	14.7	52.0	18,324	20,521	12.0	0.4	1,164	2,358	1,298	8,913	2.26	63.7	7.7	31.9
Randolph	14.1	10.6	7.2	50.7	130,454	141,823	8.7	1.1	13,112	11,807	347	55,679	2.54	69.1	11.7	26.4
Richmond	13.5	10.7	7.3	51.0	46,564	46,647	0.2	-3.8	4,492	4,515	-1,723	18,371	2.40	64.8	19.2	31.5
Robeson	12.9	9.4	5.8	51.8	123,339	134,229	8.8	-1.8	15,142	10,753	-6,745	46,163	2.84	68.0	21.9	28.2
Rockingham	15.7	11.8	8.6	51.8	91,928	93,641	1.9	-3.2	7,627	9,203	-1,307	37,162	2.42	65.9	14.2	30.1
Rowan	14.0	10.3	7.3	50.6	130,340	138,532	6.3	2.0	12,956	12,834	2,696	51,798	2.60	68.9	13.3	26.8
Rutherford	15.0	12.7	8.9	51.8	62,899	67,816	7.8	-1.5	5,565	6,949	461	26,497	2.47	65.2	12.4	31.0
Sampson	13.1	10.3	7.5	50.6	60,161	63,473	5.5	0.2	6,926	5,413	-1,335	23,431	2.68	65.9	15.0	29.7
Scotland	13.2	11.0	7.3	50.4	35,998	36,160	0.5	-3.7	3,733	3,266	-1,827	13,273	2.48	67.3	22.3	28.8
Stanly	13.7	11.1	7.8	50.1	58,100	60,586	4.3	2.5	5,553	5,591	1,575	23,859	2.46	70.2	12.1	26.2
Stokes	16.3	12.2	9.1	50.8	44,711	47,417	6.1	-4.1	3,282	4,301	-915	19,273	2.37	69.4	11.3	28.0
Surry	14.2	11.7	8.8	51.4	71,219	73,743	3.5	-2.4	6,210	7,114	-842	29,256	2.44	69.0	10.8	27.7

1. No spouse present.

Table B. States and Counties — Population, Vital Statistics, Health, and Crime

STATE County	Persons in group quarters, 2018	Daytime Population, 2013-2017		Births, 2018		Deaths, 2018		Persons under 65 with no health insurance, 2016		Medicare, 2018			Serious crimes known to police[2], 2016 Total	
		Number	Employment/ residence ratio	Total	Rate[1]	Number	Rate[1]	Number	Percent	Total beneficiaries	Enrolled in Original Medicare	Enrolled in Medicare Advantage	Number	Rate[3]
	32	33	34	35	36	37	38	39	40	41	42	43	44	45
NORTH CAROLINA— Cont'd														
Chowan	257	13,446	0.83	118	8.4	193	13.8	1,311	12.1	4,022	3,431	591	370	2,583
Clay	113	9,325	0.66	96	8.6	161	14.5	1,147	15.1	3,734	2,813	921	304	2,834
Cleveland	1,943	91,962	0.87	1,038	10.6	1,206	12.4	9,372	12.0	23,431	16,262	7,169	1,154	1,255
Columbus	3,085	53,036	0.82	565	10.2	758	13.6	6,341	14.9	13,224	10,146	3,078	1,749	3,180
Craven	5,437	106,022	1.06	1,354	13.2	1,008	9.8	9,529	11.9	23,112	19,959	3,153	2,703	2,652
Cumberland	15,292	359,688	1.18	5,298	15.9	2,645	8.0	30,261	10.8	51,495	36,912	14,583	13,850	4,266
Currituck	134	19,587	0.53	269	9.9	235	8.7	2,552	11.7	4,902	4,230	672	393	1,535
Dare	150	37,695	1.13	317	8.7	351	9.6	3,685	12.9	8,597	7,515	1,082	1,421	3,946
Davidson	1,607	138,661	0.64	1,733	10.4	1,796	10.8	17,556	13.0	35,962	15,621	20,341	3,794	2,300
Davie	365	34,890	0.63	398	9.3	387	9.1	4,131	12.3	9,986	4,809	5,177	665	1,627
Duplin	374	56,623	0.89	645	11.0	576	9.8	9,679	20.1	10,590	8,329	2,261	1,196	2,051
Durham	13,909	353,152	1.35	4,209	13.3	2,204	7.0	33,038	12.8	45,279	30,722	14,557	11,969	3,909
Edgecombe	909	50,827	0.85	571	11.0	630	12.1	5,104	12.0	11,928	9,140	2,788	1,713	3,308
Forsyth	10,802	392,641	1.15	4,399	11.6	3,284	8.7	37,955	12.4	70,318	32,110	38,208	17,422	4,675
Franklin	1,524	51,505	0.55	703	10.4	612	9.1	6,878	13.1	11,967	8,079	3,888	1,211	1,883
Gaston	3,413	194,105	0.79	2,545	11.4	2,379	10.7	20,736	11.5	43,613	25,788	17,825	5,947	2,929
Gates	60	8,651	0.41	103	8.9	142	12.3	1,055	11.3	2,446	1,978	468	NA	NA
Graham	94	7,741	0.71	76	9.0	98	11.6	1,096	16.7	2,143	1,519	624	164	1,914
Granville	4,100	54,408	0.84	579	9.6	590	9.8	5,419	11.8	11,484	7,778	3,706	1,532	2,602
Greene	2,605	18,003	0.61	202	9.6	222	10.6	2,791	18.2	3,637	2,951	686	NA	NA
Guilford	19,211	563,878	1.19	6,139	11.5	4,567	8.6	49,069	11.4	93,180	42,963	50,217	17,277	3,300
Halifax	1,401	49,878	0.87	550	10.9	726	14.4	5,495	13.7	13,836	10,551	3,285	2,004	4,089
Harnett	3,388	104,741	0.55	1,851	13.8	1,085	8.1	14,048	12.5	19,543	14,287	5,256	2,552	2,110
Haywood	680	54,663	0.79	604	9.7	756	12.2	5,223	11.4	17,820	11,770	6,050	1,876	3,124
Henderson	1,265	106,412	0.88	1,073	9.2	1,420	12.2	12,077	14.2	32,385	22,639	9,746	1,773	1,558
Hertford	2,496	24,989	1.08	215	9.1	295	12.5	1,998	11.7	5,258	4,225	1,033	629	2,692
Hoke	939	42,709	0.52	891	16.3	351	6.4	7,693	16.2	6,721	4,780	1,941	651	1,210
Hyde	672	5,470	0.98	33	6.3	56	10.7	541	14.3	1,071	810	261	NA	NA
Iredell	1,236	168,640	0.99	1,895	10.6	1,653	9.3	17,695	12.1	32,910	20,376	12,534	4,016	2,335
Jackson	4,014	43,612	1.11	377	8.7	365	8.4	5,437	17.6	8,333	5,933	2,400	1,166	2,813
Johnston	1,714	155,995	0.64	2,353	11.6	1,580	7.8	21,382	12.9	32,183	22,110	10,073	3,927	2,141
Jones	91	7,895	0.50	90	9.3	110	11.4	1,034	13.8	2,418	1,983	435	NA	NA
Lee	1,059	62,586	1.10	776	12.6	548	8.9	7,231	14.7	12,076	8,746	3,330	574	976
Lenoir	1,137	61,842	1.17	611	10.9	775	13.8	6,385	14.0	14,065	11,345	2,720	2,338	4,093
Lincoln	706	69,183	0.69	797	9.5	882	10.5	7,455	11.1	16,639	11,217	5,422	1,541	1,889
McDowell	1,497	43,839	0.93	442	9.7	498	10.9	4,846	13.7	11,422	7,461	3,961	1,390	3,154
Macon	306	33,697	0.97	334	9.5	409	11.6	4,120	16.6	11,303	8,928	2,375	757	2,210
Madison	1,147	18,234	0.66	185	8.5	236	10.8	1,966	12.3	5,600	3,781	1,819	208	1,052
Martin	145	21,761	0.84	233	10.3	304	13.4	2,070	11.6	5,831	4,629	1,202	535	2,312
Mecklenburg	17,480	1,177,322	1.27	14,736	13.5	6,750	6.2	112,129	12.1	134,525	85,303	49,222	48,240	4,560
Mitchell	197	14,827	0.95	136	9.1	229	15.3	1,507	13.3	4,335	2,975	1,360	NA	NA
Montgomery	1,061	26,972	0.95	280	10.3	269	9.9	3,245	15.4	5,650	3,901	1,749	652	2,370
Moore	794	92,262	0.95	1,127	11.4	1,163	11.8	8,367	11.5	25,377	17,626	7,751	1,287	1,395
Nash	2,124	94,787	1.02	1,036	11.0	1,043	11.1	8,957	11.8	20,783	15,930	4,853	2,349	2,715
New Hanover	8,512	237,861	1.17	2,226	9.6	1,992	8.6	19,802	10.9	44,614	35,407	9,207	8,048	3,628
Northampton	745	18,853	0.77	190	9.7	301	15.3	1,739	12.0	5,469	4,329	1,140	310	2,032
Onslow	21,384	194,338	1.02	3,909	19.8	1,087	5.5	14,932	9.6	24,325	20,518	3,807	4,152	2,212
Orange	8,210	151,122	1.13	1,160	7.9	835	5.7	11,942	10.2	21,921	13,723	8,198	3,157	2,210
Pamlico	711	11,711	0.78	79	6.2	152	12.0	1,144	13.4	3,955	3,338	617	213	1,799
Pasquotank	1,858	40,052	1.03	469	11.8	373	9.4	3,743	12.0	8,225	6,724	1,501	1,301	3,280
Pender	1,090	46,527	0.55	666	10.7	556	8.9	6,380	13.4	12,378	9,591	2,787	1,224	2,099
Perquimans	81	11,182	0.55	120	8.9	145	10.8	1,221	12.4	3,770	3,181	589	144	1,122
Person	450	34,172	0.69	411	10.4	450	11.4	3,982	12.5	9,115	5,507	3,608	746	1,902
Pitt	6,710	178,387	1.02	1,998	11.1	1,424	7.9	18,356	12.3	28,991	22,420	6,571	5,829	3,343
Polk	339	17,770	0.69	149	7.2	310	15.0	1,767	12.4	6,217	4,723	1,494	307	1,562
Randolph	1,259	128,136	0.77	1,548	10.8	1,560	10.9	18,029	15.3	29,985	12,826	17,159	NA	NA
Richmond	1,150	43,495	0.89	527	11.7	556	12.4	4,944	13.7	10,685	8,165	2,520	2,153	4,762
Robeson	4,305	130,575	0.92	1,701	12.9	1,373	10.4	20,165	18.4	24,002	17,074	6,928	5,042	3,857
Rockingham	1,029	83,736	0.80	874	9.6	1,167	12.9	9,937	13.6	22,951	10,075	12,876	2,718	3,008
Rowan	4,350	131,210	0.87	1,596	11.3	1,547	11.0	14,309	12.7	30,626	17,145	13,481	3,535	2,623
Rutherford	1,220	61,598	0.81	660	9.9	849	12.7	7,246	13.9	16,297	11,814	4,483	1,854	2,996
Sampson	987	58,884	0.82	812	12.8	691	10.9	9,629	18.8	12,856	8,982	3,874	1,541	2,455
Scotland	2,549	36,779	1.12	443	12.7	422	12.1	3,575	13.4	8,470	6,267	2,203	1,620	4,682
Stanly	2,032	55,404	0.80	699	11.3	711	11.5	5,803	12.0	13,670	9,137	4,533	1,351	2,726
Stokes	459	36,180	0.51	387	8.5	554	12.2	4,280	11.7	10,705	4,303	6,402	1,055	2,285
Surry	817	72,036	0.99	721	10.0	870	12.1	8,631	15.0	17,662	9,066	8,596	2,191	3,019

1. Per 1,000 estimated resident population.   2. Data for serious crimes have not been adjusted for underreporting; this may affect comparability between geographic areas and over time.   3. Per 100,000 population estimated by the FBI.

Table B. States and Counties — Crime, Education, Money Income, and Poverty

STATE County	Serious crimes known to police[2], 2016 (cont.)[1] Rate		School enrollment and attainment, 2013-2017 Enrollment[3]		Attainment[4] (percent)		Local government expenditures,[5] 2014-2015		Money income, 2013-2017		Households		Income and poverty, 2017 Percent below poverty level		
	Violent	Property	Total	Percent private	High school graduate or less	Bachelor's degree or more	Total current spending (mil dol)	Current spending per student (dollars)	Per capita income[6]	Median income (dollars)	Percent with income of less than $50,000	Percent with income of $200,000 or more	Median household income (dollars)	All persons	Children under 18 years	Children 5 to 17 years in families
	46	47	48	49	50	51	52	53	54	55	56	57	58	59	60	61

NORTH CAROLINA— Cont'd

STATE County	46	47	48	49	50	51	52	53	54	55	56	57	58	59	60	61
Chowan	600	1,982	3,016	8.2	51.2	19.0	23.9	10,549	23,542	41,979	58.2	1.7	43,182	17.6	29.2	27.6
Clay	242	2,591	1,892	8.6	44.3	23.1	13.8	10,122	25,433	37,070	66.4	2.0	43,684	15.4	27.4	25.1
Cleveland	153	1,101	22,907	11.2	51.1	16.5	143.3	8,962	21,664	40,002	61.0	1.5	39,911	18.8	26.6	25.1
Columbus	293	2,888	11,873	6.9	52.5	12.5	87.0	8,998	21,849	36,261	63.0	1.9	37,639	23.1	34.7	33.2
Craven	263	2,389	23,916	14.4	38.2	24.3	118.2	8,141	26,830	49,391	50.6	2.8	51,390	16.3	26.4	25.7
Cumberland	579	3,687	94,380	17.2	35.5	24.3	431.3	8,220	23,627	44,737	55.5	2.0	44,065	18.6	25.1	23.9
Currituck	145	1,391	5,959	18.1	40.8	22.9	35.9	9,114	29,340	65,758	37.1	3.0	62,397	10.7	15	13.8
Dare	222	3,724	7,230	11.7	32.4	29.8	54.7	10,757	30,898	55,640	44.7	3.6	57,316	9.4	16.3	14.8
Davidson	175	2,124	38,497	12.3	50.2	18.1	204.6	8,035	24,231	45,806	54.0	2.0	47,595	15.2	21.5	19.8
Davie	142	1,485	9,302	12.4	44.3	23.0	54.9	8,665	29,234	53,493	46.8	5.2	58,147	12.2	17.1	16.4
Duplin	220	1,832	14,088	6.2	59.4	10.8	86.2	8,507	18,529	36,679	63.7	0.9	39,470	20.7	30.5	28
Durham	680	3,229	79,416	26.9	29.3	47.3	402.6	10,166	33,151	56,393	44.2	6.0	60,045	15.7	24.3	24.5
Edgecombe	490	2,817	12,018	5.4	58.5	11.6	65.1	8,893	18,946	32,929	65.4	1.1	35,130	25.5	38.5	33.3
Forsyth	594	4,081	96,329	19.5	36.8	33.8	497.5	8,660	28,640	48,369	51.3	4.5	50,803	16.6	25.1	23.7
Franklin	135	1,748	15,128	18.5	45.8	21.0	76.9	8,644	23,862	48,344	52.1	1.8	53,076	15.7	23.9	23.2
Gaston	396	2,533	48,793	15.2	46.7	20.5	270.5	7,874	24,937	46,626	53.2	2.5	50,016	15.1	21.7	21.2
Gates	NA	NA	2,684	18.0	49.7	15.7	18.5	10,920	24,335	52,481	45.7	1.8	50,164	15.7	22.6	20
Graham	245	1,669	1,869	6.5	55.5	14.2	13.8	11,185	19,095	36,030	65.6	1.3	37,748	18.1	28	25.1
Granville	287	2,315	13,428	12.8	47.8	21.0	73.4	8,390	24,859	52,089	47.4	2.4	53,142	12.6	17	16.3
Greene	NA	NA	4,764	8.2	56.1	9.8	32.5	10,227	18,662	36,989	60.9	1.7	40,131	27.6	43.7	41.2
Guilford	515	2,785	140,310	14.8	35.2	34.9	716.0	9,165	28,582	49,253	50.7	4.5	52,284	14.5	19.7	18.1
Halifax	424	3,665	11,710	10.8	60.3	14.0	76.1	10,539	20,406	33,573	65.2	1.0	34,027	28.1	40.2	37.9
Harnett	225	1,885	37,662	18.7	44.2	20.3	159.9	7,729	22,351	50,323	49.6	2.2	51,406	16.4	22.9	22
Haywood	308	2,816	11,454	12.3	40.4	24.3	67.1	9,009	27,166	45,538	53.5	2.7	47,872	14.5	22.5	21.2
Henderson	117	1,441	22,892	15.4	35.2	31.2	114.2	8,199	28,290	50,454	49.4	3.0	51,314	10.7	17.5	16.4
Hertford	282	2,410	5,933	22.9	52.4	15.3	32.4	10,420	18,383	35,806	65.0	1.2	38,786	24.4	36.7	32.3
Hoke	82	1,129	14,656	14.3	43.3	18.3	70.6	8,164	19,654	45,713	54.5	1.2	50,777	15.9	23.2	23.3
Hyde	NA	NA	1,130	7.2	59.4	7.2	10.1	16,581	19,181	40,532	55.0	1.1	41,214	21.9	30.8	28.8
Iredell	226	2,109	41,202	13.0	39.9	26.9	242.6	7,987	30,393	55,957	44.6	5.4	56,559	11.3	16.4	15
Jackson	193	2,620	12,367	6.6	38.4	30.5	37.2	9,505	23,674	45,078	54.7	2.7	46,113	17	22.5	20.6
Johnston	174	1,967	49,881	10.9	43.8	21.7	288.8	8,177	24,872	54,610	45.5	2.4	58,647	15.1	21.4	19.5
Jones	NA	NA	1,986	13.9	47.1	14.2	14.9	12,272	21,058	37,256	61.1	1.0	41,523	22.3	32.6	31.6
Lee	82	895	15,367	11.3	43.7	21.2	82.2	8,018	23,613	49,272	50.6	2.2	53,297	14.8	22.9	21.8
Lenoir	663	3,429	14,137	9.9	51.8	13.5	81.5	8,597	21,594	37,515	61.9	1.7	39,411	24.7	37.7	34.1
Lincoln	147	1,742	17,028	10.2	46.5	20.2	103.7	7,656	27,359	50,782	49.1	4.3	57,042	12.5	15.1	14.5
McDowell	163	2,991	9,526	9.8	50.6	15.9	58.0	9,156	20,439	38,776	61.8	1.2	42,853	16.2	25.9	24.4
Macon	76	2,134	5,854	10.0	43.7	22.2	39.3	8,849	27,282	40,659	59.1	3.4	42,456	16.2	26.5	25.7
Madison	35	1,016	4,800	29.9	47.3	25.9	23.6	9,485	22,653	40,563	59.8	2.0	41,891	17.6	24.3	22.6
Martin	311	2,000	5,058	11.5	52.6	15.8	38.2	10,128	22,161	35,969	64.9	2.4	37,225	20.5	30.7	28.6
Mecklenburg	642	3,918	272,915	18.0	28.0	44.1	1,343.5	8,582	35,669	61,695	40.9	8.3	65,750	11.4	16.8	15.5
Mitchell	NA	NA	3,135	15.2	50.2	18.1	20.4	10,444	22,302	42,534	58.6	1.0	40,589	16.7	25.6	23
Montgomery	244	2,126	6,040	9.9	55.2	14.0	42.2	10,054	20,900	38,254	60.6	1.8	43,695	17.8	27.3	26.1
Moore	137	1,258	21,025	16.0	32.7	36.0	115.3	8,477	31,554	54,468	45.9	5.0	62,781	10.7	14.8	14
Nash	438	2,277	23,009	14.3	48.6	20.3	148.4	8,517	25,232	46,187	54.0	3.1	47,597	15.8	23.9	21.9
New Hanover	430	3,198	55,501	11.0	29.6	38.9	243.9	9,057	31,708	51,457	48.4	5.2	53,692	15.5	21	19.3
Northampton	223	1,809	3,905	12.1	59.0	12.8	32.7	10,352	19,126	33,508	66.7	0.6	36,190	24.3	40.1	38.8
Onslow	194	2,018	46,998	12.4	37.8	20.2	207.1	7,982	23,141	48,162	51.9	1.7	49,634	13.5	18.3	17.2
Orange	171	2,038	51,342	10.6	22.6	57.6	220.2	10,885	38,348	65,522	39.3	12.4	69,422	13.4	11.2	10.1
Pamlico	51	1,749	2,128	13.3	44.2	19.4	19.5	10,965	25,461	45,211	54.3	2.4	48,410	17.4	30.5	28.9
Pasquotank	419	2,862	10,246	9.3	46.1	20.4	52.4	8,822	23,714	47,264	54.4	1.8	46,709	20.2	30.7	29.6
Pender	111	1,988	12,949	12.4	42.1	25.6	75.3	8,292	25,997	49,357	50.6	3.4	52,187	12.6	17.5	16.4
Perquimans	125	997	2,867	9.4	45.4	19.7	18.3	10,386	25,848	44,039	58.1	1.9	45,011	18	28	26.6
Person	265	1,636	8,441	11.7	51.5	15.3	49.9	8,644	24,477	44,921	55.1	1.5	50,269	15.1	21.9	19.6
Pitt	412	2,931	61,513	8.2	34.5	30.9	202.3	8,325	25,462	43,526	55.2	3.1	46,229	21.7	29.6	27.3
Polk	86	1,475	3,937	11.6	35.9	31.9	27.3	11,490	29,728	48,412	51.6	2.9	45,587	12.5	21.3	19
Randolph	NA	NA	32,727	11.3	53.7	15.3	186.5	8,023	22,349	43,598	55.7	1.3	44,207	15.8	23.4	20.5
Richmond	568	4,194	10,676	8.0	56.0	14.3	67.1	8,670	19,966	33,607	66.4	1.3	36,401	24.8	37.1	33.6
Robeson	470	3,387	34,963	4.4	57.7	12.8	204.4	8,372	17,161	32,407	67.9	1.2	33,714	29	44.4	42.8
Rockingham	290	2,718	19,031	10.9	53.3	14.7	114.5	8,544	22,521	41,700	57.4	1.3	46,247	16.3	23.9	21.8
Rowan	397	2,226	32,680	16.7	48.6	18.4	164.9	8,200	23,838	46,978	52.6	2.1	47,541	15.3	22.4	21.6
Rutherford	259	2,738	13,978	8.9	51.0	17.3	92.1	8,962	21,092	38,573	63.0	2.1	40,758	16.1	24.4	22.6
Sampson	242	2,213	15,348	7.0	56.6	12.5	101.2	8,474	20,872	37,765	62.7	2.1	41,951	20.7	31.1	28
Scotland	746	3,937	8,730	8.8	54.6	15.9	62.4	10,151	17,103	32,739	65.8	0.5	37,947	26.4	39.3	37.9
Stanly	274	2,452	13,453	15.8	48.7	16.5	74.7	8,209	23,398	46,017	53.8	1.9	49,871	12.4	19.6	19.1
Stokes	154	2,132	9,237	7.1	57.3	13.9	59.6	9,085	23,500	44,490	55.7	0.7	48,748	14.1	20.6	18
Surry	171	2,849	14,592	7.9	51.7	16.5	91.1	7,601	22,533	39,071	60.8	1.9	43,023	16.1	23.1	21.3

1. Data for serious crimes have not been adjusted for underreporting; this may affect comparability between geographic areas and over time.   2. Per 100,000 population estimated by the FBI.   3. All persons 3 years old and over enrolled in nursery school through college.   4. Persons 25 years old and over.   5. Elementary and secondary education expenditures.   6. Based on population estimated by the American Community Survey, 2013–2017.

Table B. States and Counties — Personal Income and Earnings

| | Personal income, 2017 | | | | | | | | | | Earnings, 2017 | | |
STATE County	Total (mil dol)	Percent change 2016-2017	Per capita[1] Dollars	Per capita Rank	Wages and salaries (mil dol)	Supplements to wages and salaries, employer contributions (mil dol) Pension and insurance	Government social insurance	Proprietors' income (mil dol)	Dividends, interest, and rent (mil dol)	Personal transfer reecipts (mil dol)	Total (mil dol)	Contributions for government social insurance (mil dol) From employee and self-employed	From employer
	62	63	64	65	66	67	68	69	70	71	72	73	74
NORTH CAROLINA— Cont'd													
Chowan	552	5.9	39,125	1,700	189	32	14	28	125	177	263	20	14
Clay	361	5.0	32,610	2,675	66	13	5	16	85	133	100	11	5
Cleveland	3,531	4.3	36,281	2,153	1,494	252	113	181	551	1,121	2,041	144	113
Columbus	1,787	3.7	31,955	2,755	585	109	43	75	286	683	813	63	43
Craven	4,346	1.5	42,367	1,221	2,224	507	181	166	998	1,074	3,078	185	181
Cumberland	12,439	3.5	37,406	1,969	8,830	2,106	783	448	2,785	3,303	12,167	628	783
Currituck	1,162	5.1	44,149	1,006	261	40	20	64	189	212	386	28	20
Dare	1,928	4.4	53,415	331	714	109	58	251	478	312	1,132	74	58
Davidson	6,273	4.4	37,913	1,898	1,940	304	146	339	921	1,563	2,729	202	146
Davie	1,937	4.9	45,625	836	505	78	39	101	365	409	722	54	39
Duplin	1,974	4.5	33,440	2,563	704	127	53	276	298	520	1,160	66	53
Durham	14,904	4.7	47,825	639	14,700	1,906	1,046	1,419	2,831	2,231	19,071	1,125	1,046
Edgecombe	1,781	3.2	33,761	2,513	653	128	49	28	349	645	857	63	49
Forsyth	17,645	5.1	46,888	720	10,406	1,400	741	1,388	3,513	3,237	13,936	876	741
Franklin	2,270	5.3	34,302	2,447	566	96	42	127	290	542	831	60	42
Gaston	8,714	5.0	39,578	1,624	3,144	493	238	465	1,288	2,117	4,339	301	238
Gates	409	4.5	35,404	2,285	55	11	4	12	62	107	83	8	4
Graham	266	5.5	31,087	2,846	78	14	6	19	43	94	117	9	6
Granville	2,199	4.5	36,924	2,055	1,023	238	77	89	338	492	1,427	91	77
Greene	677	5.1	32,234	2,723	165	37	12	75	84	181	289	17	12
Guilford	23,731	4.7	45,034	897	14,832	2,105	1,075	1,855	4,697	4,318	19,866	1,231	1,075
Halifax	1,801	3.4	35,105	2,337	590	112	44	49	292	681	795	64	44
Harnett	4,374	4.9	32,947	2,623	1,002	176	76	215	724	1,037	1,470	106	76
Haywood	2,375	4.4	38,873	1,742	682	114	51	166	476	711	1,014	82	51
Henderson	4,765	4.8	41,179	1,381	1,631	258	122	357	1,147	1,228	2,368	175	122
Hertford	767	4.2	32,102	2,740	360	65	27	42	116	262	494	33	27
Hoke	1,623	5.2	29,997	2,930	342	68	26	61	247	434	497	34	26
Hyde	221	4.9	41,283	1,368	79	15	6	33	45	47	134	7	6
Iredell	8,541	4.9	48,606	579	3,745	514	265	571	1,480	1,415	5,095	328	265
Jackson	1,366	5.0	31,782	2,783	704	131	52	66	331	345	952	63	52
Johnston	7,530	5.8	38,278	1,831	2,077	354	153	497	924	1,481	3,080	209	153
Jones	374	2.7	38,924	1,733	67	13	5	26	61	119	112	9	5
Lee	2,335	4.5	38,638	1,785	1,145	194	87	116	430	600	1,542	100	87
Lenoir	2,255	5.7	39,636	1,615	1,155	216	86	164	387	686	1,621	105	86
Lincoln	3,581	4.8	43,453	1,083	988	159	74	190	522	705	1,411	99	74
McDowell	1,475	5.0	32,673	2,661	645	126	50	63	204	483	883	63	50
Macon	1,338	4.6	38,516	1,800	421	68	32	98	372	407	619	50	32
Madison	706	4.6	32,453	2,694	141	27	11	52	118	225	231	21	11
Martin	784	3.5	34,415	2,425	296	51	22	19	124	302	388	30	22
Mecklenburg	61,776	5.7	57,368	214	49,011	5,778	3,391	8,160	10,533	6,823	66,339	3,911	3,391
Mitchell	519	3.7	34,415	2,425	187	35	14	20	89	172	256	20	14
Montgomery	924	5.0	33,662	2,534	379	67	29	73	177	262	548	36	29
Moore	4,794	4.2	49,286	512	1,511	216	111	364	1,337	1,048	2,202	156	111
Nash	3,788	3.0	40,299	1,503	1,730	297	130	216	653	985	2,373	157	130
New Hanover	10,050	4.5	44,236	991	5,507	815	396	653	2,580	1,971	7,372	474	396
Northampton	660	4.4	33,205	2,594	203	36	16	23	109	258	277	23	16
Onslow	8,720	-1.3	44,972	902	4,488	1,178	424	353	1,708	1,516	6,443	296	424
Orange	9,016	5.0	62,202	135	4,205	860	287	598	2,622	912	5,950	341	287
Pamlico	516	2.8	40,637	1,451	110	22	8	29	118	161	169	15	8
Pasquotank	1,517	3.8	38,174	1,851	707	140	55	77	266	393	979	62	55
Pender	2,171	6.2	35,619	2,254	463	79	34	162	367	550	738	55	34
Perquimans	532	5.3	39,512	1,637	80	15	6	27	102	160	128	12	6
Person	1,446	4.0	36,722	2,090	435	77	33	66	200	410	610	45	33
Pitt	7,144	4.4	39,900	1,568	3,674	696	263	443	1,331	1,497	5,076	308	263
Polk	890	3.5	43,278	1,108	180	32	14	64	277	237	290	24	14
Randolph	5,207	4.2	36,339	2,144	1,770	300	133	423	744	1,342	2,626	183	133
Richmond	1,545	3.5	34,494	2,413	541	101	44	106	206	554	792	57	44
Robeson	3,832	3.7	28,895	2,990	1,443	268	108	238	490	1,486	2,056	144	108
Rockingham	3,304	3.7	36,323	2,148	1,010	171	76	167	504	1,003	1,424	111	76
Rowan	5,203	4.5	36,994	2,036	2,249	399	172	276	839	1,419	3,096	210	172
Rutherford	2,101	3.2	31,572	2,799	688	123	53	107	344	715	970	77	53
Sampson	2,286	3.5	36,035	2,197	732	124	55	314	350	643	1,225	70	55
Scotland	1,112	3.6	31,680	2,788	469	83	36	58	170	430	646	47	36
Stanly	2,336	5.7	37,989	1,886	745	133	55	200	369	614	1,133	80	55
Stokes	1,627	4.0	35,584	2,260	265	50	20	74	214	455	409	38	20
Surry	2,734	3.9	37,856	1,904	1,130	190	84	201	462	795	1,606	110	84

1. Based on the resident population estimated as of July 1 of the year shown.

Table B. States and Counties — Earnings, Social Security, and Housing

STATE County	Earnings, 2017 (cont.)									Social Security beneficiaries, December 2017		Supplemental Security Income recipients, 2017	Housing units, 2018	
	Percent by selected industries													
	Farm	Mining, quarrying, and extractions	Construction	Manu-facturing	Information; professional, scientific, technical services	Retail trade	Finance, insurance, real estate, and leasing	Health care and social assistance	Govern-ment	Number	Rate[1]		Total	Percent change, 2010-2018
	75	76	77	78	79	80	81	82	83	84	85	86	87	88

STATE County	75	76	77	78	79	80	81	82	83	84	85	86	87	88
NORTH CAROLINA— Cont'd														
Chowan	1.6	0.1	5.2	9.9	6.9	6.7	5.2	D	16.5	4,395	312	538	7,306	0.2
Clay	-3.7	0.1	16.3	D	D	12	5.3	12.6	26.9	3,960	358	284	7,360	3.1
Cleveland	1.5	D	7.3	22.4	4.9	6.8	3.4	12.6	15.8	26,225	269	3,371	43,658	0.7
Columbus	3.3	0	4.4	16.6	2.8	7.5	5.5	13.9	24	14,845	265	2,952	26,362	1.2
Craven	0.1	0.1	3.2	8.9	4.8	5.4	3.3	9	49.8	24,440	238	2,631	47,450	5.4
Cumberland	0.2	0	3.4	4	4.4	4.6	2.3	5.6	63.2	57,565	173	10,580	147,109	8.5
Currituck	-0.7	D	13.4	0.8	6.2	11.2	11.3	D	18.8	5,265	200	309	16,051	11.1
Dare	0	D	12.8	2.8	D	11.8	14.1	5.5	17.2	8,910	247	304	35,012	4.5
Davidson	0.7	0.1	7.1	22.5	3.3	6.4	3.4	8	13.6	38,970	236	3,247	75,582	4
Davie	0.2	0.4	7.9	25.9	D	7.2	4.8	9.7	12.6	10,715	252	600	18,897	3.6
Duplin	20	0	4.9	22.7	D	4.8	1.4	4.2	16.3	11,590	196	1,598	25,943	1
Durham	0.1	D	2.7	17	18.5	2.8	8.4	15.5	9.5	45,600	146	6,342	138,954	15.6
Edgecombe	0.7	D	4.5	19.8	D	10.5	D	D	26.8	13,200	250	2,899	25,028	0.8
Forsyth	0.1	0.1	4.7	10.3	8.5	6.7	11.3	19.2	9	73,935	196	8,585	166,917	6.4
Franklin	4.6	D	11.5	23.7	4.7	5.3	3.2	5.3	16.6	12,930	195	1,391	29,025	9.3
Gaston	0	D	5.9	23.6	4.5	8.1	4.4	15.9	13.8	48,015	218	5,606	93,881	5.8
Gates	4.3	0.2	D	D	3.5	5.6	D	D	30.5	2,650	230	308	5,443	4.6
Graham	1.8	D	28.5	1.6	D	5.9	4.4	4.3	22.5	2,425	284	263	6,059	2.2
Granville	0.9	D	4.8	28.5	D	3.9	1.6	D	40.9	12,560	211	1,368	24,651	8
Greene	23.4	0	6.1	4.4	1.6	3.5	3.7	8.3	35.4	3,910	186	539	8,367	1.9
Guilford	0.2	0	5.6	14.6	9.2	5.9	10.6	11.8	11	97,550	185	11,769	230,471	5.7
Halifax	-0.2	0	5	15.7	2.3	9.3	4.2	10.8	28.6	15,385	300	3,736	25,959	0.8
Harnett	2.5	D	11.4	8	4.1	10.7	4.3	7.6	22.8	21,575	163	2,801	52,548	12.5
Haywood	0.1	D	7.2	21.6	4.8	11	5	15.6	15.4	18,850	309	1,632	35,567	1.8
Henderson	1.4	D	8.4	16	5	8.6	4.7	14.7	15.4	33,595	290	1,809	58,097	6.2
Hertford	5.4	0	4.7	16.8	D	8.9	D	D	23.6	5,720	239	1,161	10,657	0.2
Hoke	6.4	D	7.7	20.1	D	4.4	3.9	9.9	28.9	7,725	143	1,165	21,167	16.3
Hyde	25.3	0	5.7	2.5	D	5.5	2.1	D	26.3	1,170	218	147	3,408	1.8
Iredell	0.8	0.1	7.7	15.9	D	7.1	4.5	8.6	10.3	35,410	202	2,649	75,599	9.5
Jackson	0.4	D	4.8	1.8	D	5.9	2.7	11.6	49.7	8,985	209	715	27,432	5.9
Johnston	2	0.1	11.4	18.2	D	8.5	4.7	6.2	18.3	34,875	177	3,693	77,352	14.3
Jones	16.4	0	10.6	1.7	D	3.2	D	D	27.8	2,665	278	373	5,002	3.2
Lee	0.8	0.3	6.6	34.3	3.1	7.2	2.9	10	12.6	13,115	217	1,644	24,655	2.2
Lenoir	3.2	D	8	25.6	3.3	5.4	5.7	8.3	20.5	15,475	272	2,863	27,649	0.8
Lincoln	2	D	10.8	22.7	5.6	7.5	3.8	4.8	16.3	17,345	210	1,473	36,767	9.7
McDowell	1	0.6	4.6	42.5	D	7.4	1.9	7.1	15.5	12,575	278	1,379	21,460	3.2
Macon	0.6	0.1	13.4	3.4	11.4	11.6	5.6	11.1	16.3	11,975	345	798	25,653	1.5
Madison	1	D	13.2	8.6	D	5.8	3.2	D	20.9	5,990	275	704	11,038	4.1
Martin	2.2	0	3.9	24.7	2.6	8.4	6.8	D	19.9	6,825	299	1,036	11,574	-1.1
Mecklenburg	0.1	0	6.1	5	15.9	4.6	18.6	5.9	9.7	139,890	130	17,955	454,062	13.9
Mitchell	-0.2	D	6.3	D	2.7	8.2	3.9	14.8	19.6	4,720	313	454	8,837	1.4
Montgomery	6.6	0.1	6.4	31	D	6.9	D	D	16.9	6,135	224	736	16,275	2.3
Moore	2.6	D	8.5	4.4	D	7	5.9	28.6	11.6	26,185	269	1,445	47,928	9.1
Nash	1.4	D	6.8	21.5	5.8	7.1	5.6	8.9	15.5	22,610	241	3,510	43,143	2
New Hanover	0.1	D	7.1	6	16.7	7.9	7.9	11	19.5	46,215	203	4,137	113,215	11.6
Northampton	2.4	0.3	7.7	10.1	D	3	D	D	22	5,950	300	1,137	11,695	0.1
Onslow	1.7	D	2.5	0.8	2.2	4.5	2.2	3.1	72.5	27,325	141	3,251	80,259	17.6
Orange	0.4	D	3.5	2.1	11.4	4.3	4.8	6.6	53.4	20,585	142	1,471	59,184	6.6
Pamlico	3.6	0.1	7.4	4.2	4.3	10.9	3.7	D	28.4	4,180	329	257	7,784	3.3
Pasquotank	1.3	0	4.5	3.9	D	8.4	4.4	14.2	35	9,020	227	1,254	17,254	2.5
Pender	7.9	D	12.6	5.7	D	7.1	4.5	8.1	22	13,505	222	1,170	29,625	10.9
Perquimans	8.8	0.1	7.6	1.7	4.2	4	3.3	D	26.2	4,065	302	393	7,188	2.9
Person	2.8	0.1	8.4	18.9	4	7.7	3.5	11	16.5	10,055	255	1,090	18,534	1.8
Pitt	1	D	5.4	10.3	5	6.2	5.5	10.8	37.2	30,610	171	5,804	80,265	7
Polk	3.3	0	10.3	4.5	6.9	4.7	3.4	23.3	17.6	6,505	316	306	11,803	3.2
Randolph	3.1	0.1	8.6	31.4	2.7	5.9	3.6	8.7	12.9	33,720	235	3,441	62,635	2.6
Richmond	7	D	4.7	19.3	2.9	8.3	3.8	11.4	20.3	11,510	257	2,197	21,707	4.7
Robeson	2.8	0	7.5	16.2	2.2	7.5	3.5	16.9	23.2	28,125	212	7,568	53,185	0.8
Rockingham	0.9	D	7.3	22.9	3.2	8.8	3.6	12	15.3	25,230	277	3,059	44,301	1.4
Rowan	1.1	0.5	7	17.2	D	5.6	3	9.4	20.8	33,140	236	2,810	61,982	2.9
Rutherford	0.9	D	8.5	17.2	7.8	8.7	3	12.9	18.5	18,115	272	1,964	34,466	1.7
Sampson	23	0	5.9	14.1	2.2	6.3	2.7	D	18.4	14,265	225	2,085	27,813	2.1
Scotland	2	0	4	21	1.8	8.3	3	17.8	20.3	9,305	265	1,753	15,304	0.7
Stanly	1.6	D	10.1	20.5	3	9.4	3.8	6.4	22.8	14,995	244	1,374	27,988	3.2
Stokes	2.4	0	12.7	11.2	D	9.2	D	10.8	23.2	12,385	271	1,004	22,313	1.7
Surry	3.7	D	17.2	12.5	D	9	4	D	16.1	18,725	259	2,040	34,264	1.6

1. Per 1,000 resident population estimated as of July 1 of the year shown.

Table B. States and Counties — **Housing, Labor Force, and Employment**

STATE County	Housing units, 2013-2017								Civilian labor force, 2018				Civilian employment[6], 2013-2017		
	Occupied units							Sub-standard units[4] (percent)		Percent change, 2017-2018	Unemployment			Percent	
	Owner-occupied			Median owner cost as a percent of income		Renter-occupied									Management, business, science, and arts	Construction, production, and maintenance occupations
	Total	Percent	Median value[1]	With a mort-gage	Without a mort-gage[2]	Median rent[3]	Median rent as a percent of income[2]		Total		Total	Rate[5]	Total		
	89	90	91	92	93	94	95	96	97	98	99	100	101	102	103

NORTH CAROLINA— Cont'd

STATE County	89	90	91	92	93	94	95	96	97	98	99	100	101	102	103
Chowan	5,903	73.0	128,300	24.9	16	737	31.9	3.2	5,582	-0.4	247	4.4	5,439	29.6	25.2
Clay	5,049	77.7	154,600	24.4	11.2	692	27.2	2.9	4,111	4	178	4.3	4,275	34.5	22.1
Cleveland	37,782	67.4	110,500	21.2	11.6	679	31.8	2.5	47,966	1	1,895	4	40,429	29.6	30.6
Columbus	22,462	70.9	85,200	22.6	13.2	607	31	3.2	22,338	0.2	1,115	5	20,496	26.0	30.4
Craven	40,571	63.3	156,500	22.6	11.4	871	28.9	2.6	41,528	-0.6	1,744	4.2	40,286	33.1	24.6
Cumberland	124,500	51.0	131,200	22.3	12	887	31	1.9	127,957	0.2	6,578	5.1	123,968	33.0	20.6
Currituck	9,766	82.5	244,500	23.9	10	947	32.9	2.2	13,633	0.3	492	3.6	12,138	30.3	25.2
Dare	15,264	69.4	285,000	27.7	13.3	1,056	28.9	2.2	19,851	-1.3	1,015	5.1	18,411	30.8	21.4
Davidson	64,727	71.6	134,800	20.1	10.5	687	28.6	2.9	80,112	0.6	2,926	3.7	73,207	27.7	32.6
Davie	15,895	77.5	170,000	20.2	10.3	693	26.5	2.7	20,474	0.6	700	3.4	19,212	32.7	26.8
Duplin	21,669	69.7	88,800	23.3	13.8	640	28.9	6.1	24,946	-2	1,080	4.3	24,678	24.2	39.1
Durham	120,936	53.5	195,900	19.3	10	966	29.4	3	167,606	1.4	5,835	3.5	154,374	49.0	15.1
Edgecombe	21,431	59.1	84,000	23.9	14.2	659	30.2	3.5	21,741	-0.9	1,470	6.8	21,693	24.1	33.1
Forsyth	145,102	62.5	151,400	20.2	10	771	30.4	2.6	186,122	0.7	7,109	3.8	167,780	39.5	19.7
Franklin	24,287	73.1	140,300	22.1	13.5	763	29.4	2.3	30,642	1.7	1,221	4	28,158	31.5	27.7
Gaston	80,682	65.4	130,700	20.0	11.8	768	29.3	3.1	109,604	1.6	4,245	3.9	96,263	30.4	27.9
Gates	4,439	80.4	142,500	22.4	12.7	798	31	2.3	5,309	0.5	212	4	5,012	29.2	34.9
Graham	3,303	81.8	124,800	18.8	11.5	610	21.7	1.2	3,179	1.6	186	5.9	3,025	26.7	25.0
Granville	20,945	73.4	146,100	20.8	10.7	776	29.5	2.2	29,943	-0.3	1,014	3.4	25,650	33.3	27.3
Greene	7,348	69.3	85,700	23.4	14.1	652	30.6	4.6	9,558	0	368	3.9	8,125	26.8	39.1
Guilford	200,998	58.9	160,200	20.6	10.4	817	30.4	2.6	260,591	-0.1	10,771	4.1	246,145	38.1	19.9
Halifax	21,207	63.1	86,500	22.6	14.8	689	34	2.2	20,243	-1.6	1,229	6.1	19,523	25.4	31.7
Harnett	44,657	65.1	144,700	21.4	11.5	836	28.7	2.8	52,791	0.4	2,450	4.6	49,216	33.9	25.3
Haywood	26,288	71.7	175,900	21.7	10.4	721	30.2	2.1	29,465	1.7	993	3.4	25,518	31.7	26.5
Henderson	47,804	72.3	193,200	21.5	10	818	30.2	2.4	54,476	1.8	1,764	3.2	50,174	34.0	25.2
Hertford	8,880	67.2	86,800	23.1	13.9	709	29.8	2.7	9,120	-0.8	458	5	9,163	29.7	27.1
Hoke	17,373	67.0	137,700	23.5	12.7	792	31.1	2.8	19,920	0	1,002	5	17,925	29.4	28.8
Hyde	1,835	76.3	81,000	21.9	12.7	839	26.6	4.3	2,008	-4.4	166	8.3	2,038	26.9	32.5
Iredell	63,447	72.0	173,600	20.2	10	829	26.8	2.6	87,984	1.7	3,143	3.6	80,746	34.5	27.2
Jackson	16,218	65.1	177,200	22.5	10	717	28.9	2.4	19,484	2.1	802	4.1	18,103	33.1	17.8
Johnston	65,401	71.7	150,700	20.3	10.5	827	30.5	2.2	96,136	1.8	3,454	3.6	86,189	35.6	23.9
Jones	4,148	72.5	92,700	23.5	12.6	621	35.1	2.2	4,379	-0.7	184	4.2	3,912	30.8	32.1
Lee	21,691	67.3	138,400	20.7	11.8	723	28	2.9	26,420	-0.6	1,144	4.3	26,983	29.9	31.9
Lenoir	23,263	60.1	93,500	21.8	13.6	690	28.7	2.7	27,857	-0.6	1,104	4	23,873	28.0	30.1
Lincoln	31,250	76.5	158,700	20.6	10.8	698	27.7	2.2	42,654	1.7	1,454	3.4	37,100	29.4	30.2
McDowell	17,970	71.3	110,400	20.6	10	613	24.7	3.5	21,145	0.8	712	3.4	18,193	25.5	35.3
Macon	15,513	73.7	162,000	23.0	10	726	28.9	2.3	15,316	0.5	599	3.9	13,584	28.9	22.9
Madison	8,346	74.6	172,200	26.5	10	644	30	1.9	10,144	1.7	367	3.6	9,464	31.1	29.1
Martin	9,624	68.9	83,100	26.1	14.2	637	30.6	1	9,295	-3.1	463	5	9,311	28.3	28.5
Mecklenburg	395,503	56.7	203,900	19.6	10.8	1,032	28.5	2.5	611,673	1.8	22,686	3.7	537,798	43.4	16.2
Mitchell	6,390	79.5	140,600	22.7	10	559	28.4	0.8	6,025	-1.2	270	4.5	6,199	33.2	32.1
Montgomery	10,855	70.0	105,900	20.8	10.6	568	31.2	3.5	11,588	-1.4	459	4	10,541	24.7	40.2
Moore	38,185	74.4	207,300	20.7	11	838	26.7	2	41,079	3	1,556	3.8	38,668	39.6	18.9
Nash	36,878	65.3	123,100	21.0	12.8	734	31.2	3.3	43,288	-0.9	2,191	5.1	42,367	31.2	27.7
New Hanover	91,673	57.4	225,600	22.9	12.4	938	31.8	1.9	120,980	1.3	4,487	3.7	107,369	39.7	15.8
Northampton	8,819	69.2	81,900	24.0	14.6	694	33.9	1.5	7,628	-1.5	392	5.1	7,083	28.3	29.9
Onslow	63,093	52.5	154,400	24.0	10	987	29.6	1.9	64,341	-0.4	3,040	4.7	61,901	29.5	21.3
Orange	52,160	61.8	283,000	20.2	10.8	1,026	29.3	2.2	77,797	1.4	2,534	3.3	72,255	54.3	10.5
Pamlico	5,395	74.9	150,600	23.4	11.7	716	30.7	2.8	5,348	-0.8	219	4.1	5,015	29.3	28.3
Pasquotank	14,629	60.5	158,900	21.9	12.8	859	32	2.6	17,062	-1.7	813	4.8	16,333	32.6	23.4
Pender	21,053	79.1	167,200	23.5	13.6	828	31.7	2.5	28,265	1	1,158	4.1	24,768	32.0	26.5
Perquimans	5,882	72.8	165,500	24.0	12.6	824	45.4	3.2	5,046	-1.8	242	4.8	5,209	34.5	24.4
Person	15,772	72.0	118,500	20.5	10	649	33.7	4.1	18,261	1.3	748	4.1	16,908	29.5	31.4
Pitt	68,805	52.3	138,700	19.9	11.4	761	34.1	2.2	89,961	0.7	3,811	4.2	82,142	37.4	18.8
Polk	8,913	73.1	205,500	23.3	10	825	26.8	1.3	8,969	0.5	336	3.7	8,710	34.4	21.7
Randolph	55,679	71.5	119,500	20.5	10.5	655	27.9	3.1	66,526	-0.2	2,484	3.7	64,228	26.7	35.3
Richmond	18,371	65.5	80,000	21.5	12.5	617	34.9	2.2	16,519	-1.2	902	5.5	17,354	25.7	33.0
Robeson	46,163	64.7	72,100	22.2	12.8	614	30	4	49,653	-1.1	2,915	5.9	48,024	25.6	34.8
Rockingham	37,162	68.4	109,600	20.7	10.2	635	28.4	2.6	40,499	-0.2	1,829	4.5	39,294	24.7	32.2
Rowan	51,798	68.1	130,400	20.1	10	742	27.1	2.7	65,775	1.5	2,576	3.9	59,529	29.0	32.0
Rutherford	26,497	71.5	109,000	21.5	10.5	614	28.4	2.9	24,757	0.6	1,256	5.1	25,992	28.9	34.4
Sampson	23,431	69.6	87,700	21.3	12.2	647	33.8	3.5	29,207	-0.7	1,168	4	26,794	25.2	37.9
Scotland	13,273	62.0	85,200	22.5	12.7	640	37.2	4	11,457	-0.4	843	7.4	11,660	27.3	28.0
Stanly	23,859	72.5	133,000	21.4	10.8	681	28.9	3.6	29,882	0.3	1,065	3.6	27,689	28.8	29.6
Stokes	19,273	77.6	123,900	20.7	10	640	30.7	2.2	21,781	0.6	793	3.6	20,624	29.6	33.3
Surry	29,256	73.0	120,900	21.0	11	626	28	3	34,033	1.2	1,206	3.5	30,352	30.2	31.5

1. Specified owner-occupied units.   2. A value of 10.0 represents 10 percent or less; a value of 50.0 represents 50 percent or more.   3. Specified renter-occupied units.   4. Overcrowded or lacking complete plumbing facilities.   5. Percent of civilian labor force.   6. Civilian employed persons 16 years old and over.

Nonfarm Employment and Agriculture

STATE County	Private nonfarm establishments, employment and payroll, 2016									Agriculture, 2017			
	Employment							Annual payroll		Farms			Farm producers whose primary occupation is farming (percent)
							Professional, scientific, and technical services				Percent with:		
	Number of establishments	Total	Health care and social assistance	Manufacturing	Retail trade	Finance and insurance		Total (mil dol)	Average per employee (dollars)	Number	Fewer than 50 acres	1000 acres or more	
	104	105	106	107	108	109	110	111	112	113	114	115	116

NORTH CAROLINA—Cont'd

STATE County	104	105	106	107	108	109	110	111	112	113	114	115	116
Chowan	349	3,751	1,008	636	408	81	113	128	34,104	97	35.1	23.7	64.2
Clay	206	1,623	280	228	434	39	28	45	27,521	164	56.7	0.6	51.1
Cleveland	1,905	28,663	5,120	5,778	3,994	492	1,034	1,039	36,237	1,005	43.0	0.9	36.8
Columbus	990	11,463	2,801	1,902	2,367	888	314	399	34,771	514	33.9	8.4	47.7
Craven	2,100	28,007	6,478	3,396	4,548	807	1,998	1,059	37,816	245	36.3	8.6	48.1
Cumberland	5,599	93,911	19,134	5,957	17,281	1,951	5,248	3,190	33,972	336	48.5	4.5	37.7
Currituck	631	4,413	235	37	916	89	127	151	34,232	89	48.3	11.2	43.8
Dare	1,878	14,227	960	489	3,578	426	425	489	34,338	32	65.6	9.4	37.1
Davidson	2,797	50,068	16,484	9,112	5,060	861	938	1,959	39,134	1,003	57.2	0.9	39.0
Davie	796	9,295	1,305	1,481	1,465	165	231	302	32,484	591	46.9	2.2	41.2
Duplin	835	13,375	1,724	5,881	1,788	196	151	417	31,155	820	35.1	6.6	61.3
Durham	7,340	185,285	26,942	12,918	15,989	8,744	30,709	12,204	65,864	241	68.0	0.8	44.9
Edgecombe	745	12,576	2,405	2,932	1,531	160	141	399	31,701	249	29.3	16.1	40.9
Forsyth	8,449	162,073	24,857	16,112	21,567	10,076	6,939	7,943	49,010	557	68.6	0.4	37.1
Franklin	1,011	9,834	840	2,873	1,505	178	213	440	44,784	538	43.9	4.5	38.0
Gaston	4,060	66,598	12,158	14,326	9,457	1,136	1,346	2,421	36,349	522	58.6	0.4	32.4
Gates	121	845	88	D	165	35	27	23	26,870	141	40.4	11.3	46.6
Graham	160	1,484	228	59	252	52	22	55	37,073	123	65.9	NA	39.2
Granville	869	12,744	2,283	4,240	1,428	243	238	497	39,016	557	32.5	3.4	34.9
Greene	256	2,090	644	192	282	48	46	60	28,491	207	34.8	12.6	54.4
Guilford	13,350	255,000	35,837	31,527	29,183	12,112	11,268	11,602	45,497	854	58.0	0.6	39.9
Halifax	951	12,633	2,950	2,015	2,429	297	200	379	29,970	336	23.5	18.5	42.0
Harnett	1,656	20,573	3,407	1,935	3,974	547	478	658	31,984	643	54.9	3.7	40.8
Haywood	1,359	14,921	3,150	1,810	3,155	419	451	501	33,608	541	60.3	1.3	33.8
Henderson	2,616	33,337	6,794	6,157	5,628	682	939	1,231	36,918	455	70.1	1.1	43.6
Hertford	476	7,494	2,169	976	1,213	159	112	257	34,335	126	38.1	19.8	58.7
Hoke	445	5,393	1,523	1,417	824	68	146	160	29,639	189	45.0	7.4	32.2
Hyde	157	812	90	86	147	48	10	25	31,096	138	26.1	26.8	50.4
Iredell	4,633	67,228	9,013	11,445	9,024	1,439	2,942	2,978	44,293	1,055	47.3	1.7	42.9
Jackson	956	13,197	2,293	274	1,816	178	289	444	33,618	215	56.7	0.5	52.1
Johnston	3,224	41,461	5,792	7,487	8,473	843	1,035	1,469	35,433	1,063	51.3	3.7	41.2
Jones	128	835	187	42	101	16	20	25	29,568	177	39.5	9.6	51.0
Lee	1,306	23,380	3,039	8,526	3,155	327	326	876	37,458	250	49.6	3.2	38.3
Lenoir	1,213	23,709	4,332	5,896	2,871	581	615	785	33,110	386	37.8	8.3	53.6
Lincoln	1,621	18,007	2,480	3,673	3,269	394	476	635	35,254	614	58.6	0.8	31.9
McDowell	710	13,591	1,727	6,080	1,728	187	194	433	31,882	333	63.1	NA	41.6
Macon	1,077	9,279	1,294	409	2,005	355	207	299	32,260	340	69.7	NA	34.4
Madison	325	2,716	577	315	469	39	43	82	30,192	639	50.1	1.3	40.5
Martin	432	5,299	1,149	1,050	978	145	147	141	26,570	332	27.4	16.6	54.3
Mecklenburg	30,988	607,555	68,037	26,862	61,441	67,684	51,007	36,810	60,587	216	74.5	NA	36.7
Mitchell	363	3,849	806	564	757	83	88	113	29,381	250	63.6	NA	29.2
Montgomery	482	7,047	1,037	2,581	809	164	62	230	32,682	240	40.4	0.4	51.0
Moore	2,233	30,613	9,395	1,496	4,657	763	1,281	1,166	38,101	733	51.7	2.6	42.9
Nash	2,028	36,538	5,868	7,816	5,055	1,456	931	1,355	37,086	425	45.4	7.8	51.9
New Hanover	7,275	95,838	17,463	5,795	15,694	3,139	5,706	4,046	42,219	59	93.2	NA	43.9
Northampton	258	4,213	575	405	412	20	21	141	33,564	272	21.7	19.9	51.5
Onslow	2,752	35,716	5,416	1,009	8,514	921	1,723	994	27,844	340	50.3	3.5	55.9
Orange	3,277	43,930	16,033	925	5,902	1,616	2,296	1,805	41,086	686	51.7	0.6	44.1
Pamlico	263	2,670	566	102	526	40	49	75	28,249	100	44.0	12.0	39.3
Pasquotank	915	11,235	2,354	528	2,496	656	358	393	34,967	126	31.7	25.4	55.9
Pender	1,016	8,388	1,359	771	1,794	113	262	257	30,686	336	52.1	3.9	48.3
Perquimans	200	1,325	115	60	232	42	28	43	32,573	149	33.6	20.1	77.6
Person	680	8,415	1,304	1,553	1,635	179	176	304	36,131	393	41.7	4.8	50.9
Pitt	3,593	61,227	15,485	5,752	9,250	2,198	2,230	2,335	38,135	478	35.8	12.6	55.0
Polk	487	3,899	1,536	351	428	111	143	115	29,555	281	57.7	0.4	44.6
Randolph	2,481	39,126	5,020	14,755	4,303	1,041	657	1,355	34,632	1,368	45.5	0.7	41.6
Richmond	810	12,059	1,824	3,971	2,002	211	165	369	30,587	237	27.4	3.0	44.4
Robeson	1,804	31,657	7,341	6,993	5,260	1,128	583	958	30,248	722	43.4	11.5	46.0
Rockingham	1,656	22,166	3,090	6,124	3,701	482	453	755	34,071	844	37.3	2.5	40.1
Rowan	2,595	44,279	9,007	8,745	4,786	651	898	1,875	42,345	925	51.1	1.6	37.3
Rutherford	1,244	15,846	2,784	3,354	2,593	292	263	520	32,838	620	46.6	0.3	44.2
Sampson	984	13,928	2,420	3,550	2,348	229	254	465	33,352	960	33.2	7.1	52.2
Scotland	594	9,785	2,306	1,929	1,566	183	87	318	32,535	108	26.9	11.1	55.1
Stanly	1,299	16,036	2,856	3,503	2,772	353	297	537	33,479	672	54.0	2.8	32.6
Stokes	620	5,602	1,183	920	925	105	161	168	30,017	856	39.6	0.9	40.1
Surry	1,649	27,591	4,001	3,898	4,311	716	363	1,029	37,279	1,064	41.8	1.6	42.3

Table B. States and Counties — **Agriculture**

	Agriculture, 2017 (cont.)														
	Land in farms				Value of land and buildings (dollars)		Value of machinery and equiopmnet, average per farm (dollars)	Value of products sold:				Organic farms (number)	Farms with internet access (percent)	Government payments	
			Acres							Percent from:					
STATE County	Acreage (1,000)	Percent change, 2012-2017	Average size of farm	Total irrigated (1,000)	Total cropland (1,000)	Average per farm	Average per acre		Total (mil dol)	Average per farm (acres)	Crops	Livestock and poultry products			Total ($1,000)	Percent of farms
	117	118	119	120	121	122	123	124	125	126	127	128	129	130	131	132
NORTH CAROLINA— Cont'd																
Chowan	54	-7.9	552	4.2	43.9	1,928,100	3,494	396,748	46.6	480,258	82.7	17.3	3	79.4	2,814	66.0
Clay	13	6.6	76	0.2	4.7	479,404	6,277	42,034	2.9	17,860	69.8	30.2	NA	65.2	129	14.0
Cleveland	113	-2.8	113	0.4	45.6	526,049	4,664	66,770	133.8	133,133	11.9	88.1	6	75.4	1,076	29.3
Columbus	141	-11.4	274	2.1	113.0	895,784	3,264	156,073	162.0	315,191	36.1	63.9	1	66.9	2,708	45.3
Craven	81	15.2	332	0.9	61.9	1,307,554	3,937	175,519	71.6	292,273	51.4	48.6	2	77.1	1,461	47.8
Cumberland	66	-19.8	196	1.2	35.5	1,014,731	5,166	123,059	95.8	285,116	26.5	73.5	NA	79.8	355	25.6
Currituck	45	26.8	504	0.1	36.4	2,471,600	4,906	200,095	18.2	204,730	99.6	0.4	NA	87.6	1,247	42.7
Dare	5	D	167	0.1	4.7	702,379	4,207	83,082	1.6	48,969	64.6	35.4	NA	78.1	225	9.4
Davidson	92	5.8	92	0.4	45.5	533,839	5,797	62,547	47.1	46,929	34.5	65.5	5	76.8	523	9.3
Davie	77	29.0	130	0.3	37.5	662,441	5,089	71,003	26.9	45,569	46.0	54.0	NA	72.1	279	9.8
Duplin	243	5.3	296	8.0	165.1	1,422,426	4,798	220,716	1,261.7	1,538,648	7.8	92.2	9	79.5	3,021	30.4
Durham	19	-10.8	77	0.1	6.8	822,548	10,656	57,642	10.1	41,921	89.2	10.8	1	77.6	27	9.1
Edgecombe	149	17.6	598	2.5	106.8	1,823,586	3,049	277,862	176.2	707,614	52.5	47.5	3	61.4	3,812	61.4
Forsyth	35	-14.0	62	0.1	15.7	581,509	9,307	46,871	10.9	19,575	85.1	14.9	NA	70.7	70	5.7
Franklin	108	-7.6	201	1.8	42.8	713,579	3,556	101,007	58.5	108,669	59.4	40.6	7	72.1	575	27.0
Gaston	38	-10.1	72	0.2	15.4	443,484	6,141	50,169	23.2	44,375	24.4	75.6	8	77.8	271	14.8
Gates	58	-8.4	411	3.6	45.5	1,490,928	3,625	231,965	72.9	516,901	32.7	67.3	NA	82.3	1,997	61.7
Graham	11	60.9	89	0.0	3.0	428,116	4,788	78,974	1.4	11,089	28.5	71.5	NA	65.0	66	11.4
Granville	125	23.8	224	1.8	42.7	780,700	3,484	76,280	D	D	D	D	15	79.2	274	28.7
Greene	83	-17.7	403	1.6	69.4	1,588,126	3,945	235,131	242.5	1,171,415	28.9	71.1	NA	77.3	1,055	63.3
Guilford	76	-15.9	89	1.3	40.9	731,162	8,178	69,898	52.2	61,108	62.9	37.1	7	75.3	331	11.0
Halifax	209	6.7	622	2.5	138.1	1,596,584	2,566	245,400	133.2	396,411	62.4	37.6	10	68.8	5,417	64.3
Harnett	106	-11.3	165	2.8	69.7	921,279	5,575	128,788	204.6	318,138	35.0	65.0	5	76.5	536	25.7
Haywood	52	6.7	97	0.3	11.0	623,971	6,461	61,440	18.2	33,567	43.1	56.9	6	71.7	525	22.2
Henderson	41	15.0	90	2.5	25.0	700,622	7,756	96,176	67.2	147,780	96.1	3.9	3	71.4	385	11.9
Hertford	81	-2.6	642	2.1	60.0	2,053,706	3,199	275,035	139.3	1,105,683	32.9	67.1	NA	75.4	1,790	62.7
Hoke	54	-8.4	284	2.2	32.9	1,249,580	4,402	131,728	76.8	406,328	16.5	83.5	NA	79.9	339	31.7
Hyde	125	16.1	905	D	93.1	2,690,902	2,974	326,488	D	D	D	D	1	64.5	2,515	71.0
Iredell	133	-12.5	126	0.3	68.8	687,281	5,438	80,370	112.9	106,988	16.7	83.3	6	70.4	1,627	7.1
Jackson	16	-2.9	73	0.1	5.3	599,496	8,195	62,010	11.6	54,126	96.2	3.8	NA	75.3	86	15.8
Johnston	183	-5.9	172	2.1	129.8	817,375	4,741	117,962	267.8	251,888	55.0	45.0	12	77.0	1,938	28.2
Jones	66	10.6	371	0.5	49.2	1,503,580	4,054	228,303	213.6	1,206,910	13.8	86.2	2	87.0	1,039	45.8
Lee	35	-10.0	141	1.4	19.5	810,854	5,764	108,487	54.4	217,568	34.5	65.5	9	80.4	124	12.8
Lenoir	114	-6.9	295	2.7	85.2	1,172,512	3,980	256,044	311.4	806,666	23.5	76.5	1	77.2	1,589	50.3
Lincoln	54	-2.7	88	0.2	30.1	504,795	5,731	60,532	53.8	87,577	15.7	84.3	NA	75.2	518	16.8
McDowell	23	-7.7	69	0.3	6.2	363,086	5,258	63,862	24.6	73,880	56.6	43.4	3	73.3	73	14.7
Macon	20	-12.8	58	0.0	5.2	463,306	7,966	42,489	7.8	23,065	21.4	78.6	NA	68.2	132	20.0
Madison	57	0.9	89	0.1	11.1	440,456	4,959	34,914	D	D	D	D	12	71.0	194	17.2
Martin	141	10.8	425	D	105.4	1,137,286	2,678	206,716	92.7	279,238	84.5	15.5	NA	69.6	5,810	84.9
Mecklenburg	12	-24.4	54	0.5	5.6	1,853,146	34,288	183,007	D	D	D	100.0	NA	77.3	D	6.5
Mitchell	15	-23.4	59	0.0	4.2	344,314	5,815	50,043	2.4	9,400	74.9	25.1	NA	77.2	38	4.0
Montgomery	34	-4.4	140	1.5	9.4	662,440	4,743	110,080	143.3	597,100	5.7	94.3	2	75.0	86	8.3
Moore	89	8.4	122	2.5	29.0	621,977	5,101	82,084	150.3	205,115	12.2	87.8	11	79.1	685	9.4
Nash	129	-7.9	305	2.2	96.8	1,409,586	4,627	247,776	191.7	450,993	65.8	34.2	14	71.8	1,092	34.8
New Hanover	1	-69.5	15	0.1	0.2	507,127	34,039	106,406	D	D	D	100.0	NA	81.4	D	3.4
Northampton	170	4.6	626	2.9	110.6	1,749,629	2,797	235,146	114.4	420,706	51.4	48.6	NA	73.5	4,683	79.4
Onslow	52	-9.0	154	0.4	35.6	969,753	6,284	93,973	171.6	504,629	13.7	86.3	NA	75.0	862	25.6
Orange	70	23.4	102	0.9	32.1	681,306	6,686	68,490	37.7	54,974	67.3	32.7	28	88.3	428	18.7
Pamlico	43	-7.5	433	3.4	37.4	1,579,956	3,652	266,792	23.4	233,730	98.3	1.7	NA	86.0	1,079	64.0
Pasquotank	72	-0.1	573	0.3	68.8	2,282,057	3,984	346,522	48.8	387,452	99.1	0.9	1	76.2	2,408	59.5
Pender	64	15.6	192	1.8	41.2	1,026,573	5,349	98,925	200.3	596,100	19.2	80.8	9	78.9	583	20.2
Perquimans	80	0.3	539	D	74.5	1,919,310	3,560	300,322	70.6	473,671	57.9	42.1	3	78.5	2,646	69.8
Person	82	-13.8	209	1.6	45.6	790,145	3,778	107,022	39.3	100,000	87.6	12.4	10	72.8	345	22.4
Pitt	186	8.5	390	2.8	149.8	1,499,480	3,845	183,107	242.5	507,234	41.6	58.4	4	81.8	3,291	45.6
Polk	29	20.8	104	0.1	7.9	667,163	6,442	50,460	6.6	23,491	74.8	25.2	NA	85.4	104	13.9
Randolph	148	-5.8	108	1.2	61.7	545,745	5,052	77,013	281.9	206,035	9.9	90.1	20	75.8	360	9.3
Richmond	59	24.4	250	0.5	18.9	1,089,872	4,365	114,969	189.2	798,186	3.8	96.2	NA	72.6	473	23.6
Robeson	264	-0.7	365	11.5	212.8	1,211,105	3,315	182,661	385.8	534,294	27.0	73.0	1	72.6	3,535	43.4
Rockingham	125	11.1	148	3.0	51.3	571,868	3,873	69,782	39.1	46,294	75.1	24.9	13	71.4	580	15.5
Rowan	119	-1.8	129	0.8	67.9	752,022	5,850	103,875	81.8	88,412	58.8	41.2	NA	73.9	1,162	14.3
Rutherford	60	0.6	97	0.1	18.6	462,120	4,782	47,498	45.4	73,289	8.5	91.5	1	76.6	392	16.0
Sampson	301	3.3	314	17.9	209.6	1,534,742	4,891	269,485	1,249.1	1,301,188	16.3	83.7	18	78.1	2,424	32.5
Scotland	55	-20.4	508	D	28.6	1,828,369	3,600	196,309	112.2	1,038,500	10.3	89.7	1	72.2	500	33.3
Stanly	96	3.0	143	0.1	54.2	656,070	4,599	91,390	90.3	134,391	24.9	75.1	NA	72.9	909	20.8
Stokes	93	1.5	109	0.4	34.4	443,265	4,084	60,719	42.4	49,558	29.3	70.7	3	75.5	148	12.0
Surry	152	20.1	143	0.6	73.0	640,586	4,471	96,475	230.1	216,264	21.5	78.5	8	75.5	483	17.7

Water Use, Wholesale Trade, Retail Trade, and Real Estate

STATE County	Water use, 2015		Wholesale Trade[1], 2012				Retail Trade[2], 2012				Real estate and rental and leasing,[2] 2012			
	Public supply water withdrawn (mil gal/ day)	Public supply gallons withdrawn per person per day	Number of establishments	Number of employees	Sales (mil dol)	Average payroll (mil dol)	Number of establishments	Number of employees	Sales (mil dol)	Average payroll (mil dol)	Number of establishments	Number of employees	Sales (mil dol)	Average payroll (mil dol)
	133	134	135	136	137	138	139	140	141	142	143	144	145	146
NORTH CAROLINA— Cont'd														
Chowan	1.39	96.6	20	231	196.7	9.0	56	479	119.2	9.5	12	29	3.8	0.6
Clay	0.21	19.6	1	D	D	D	45	422	134.4	10.7	5	9	0.8	0.1
Cleveland	12.26	126.5	77	1,223	1,309.4	43.4	373	3,656	962.1	83.5	78	253	39.2	7.0
Columbus	2.02	35.6	37	357	295.2	17.4	217	2,125	553.1	47.2	35	85	14.3	2.1
Craven	10.76	104.0	75	D	D	D	394	4,358	1,213.6	103.3	99	336	43.4	9.9
Cumberland	35.85	110.7	164	2,628	1,028.8	103.2	1,049	15,587	4,374.2	365.3	326	D	D	D
Currituck	3.29	130.2	17	103	58.7	3.9	127	879	275.2	23.9	47	D	D	D
Dare	7.28	204.1	33	D	D	D	420	3,372	863.9	89.5	131	D	D	D
Davidson	14.90	90.5	148	1,904	1,032.2	77.9	466	4,824	1,301.8	108.6	91	D	D	D
Davie	3.58	85.7	33	349	160.1	15.9	112	1,258	360.2	28.9	29	D	D	D
Duplin	4.76	80.5	34	441	473.1	15.2	180	1,762	466.4	37.5	25	84	5.5	2.1
Durham	27.74	92.2	198	8,508	6,468.7	981.8	939	14,512	3,402.1	329.8	295	1,661	367.1	70.6
Edgecombe	3.29	60.8	17	359	206.0	11.2	141	1,416	372.1	29.9	39	90	24.4	3.3
Forsyth	48.46	131.3	380	6,070	4,220.3	285.3	1,361	19,642	5,569.4	479.4	373	1,791	313.9	65.9
Franklin	0.95	14.9	35	414	150.2	17.7	129	1,385	353.7	29.3	30	88	16.8	4.2
Gaston	25.08	117.5	198	2,756	2,037.7	120.2	637	9,035	2,329.5	203.3	148	742	151.2	26.1
Gates	0.85	74.4	7	30	23.0	1.1	26	191	43.6	3.8	1	D	D	D
Graham	0.67	77.8	2	D	D	D	33	226	44.5	4.6	3	3	0.3	0.0
Granville	2.99	51.0	24	D	D	D	132	1,306	350.0	29.0	34	87	11.3	1.9
Greene	1.07	50.6	4	D	D	D	45	303	83.5	5.3	2	D	D	D
Guilford	48.12	93.0	957	14,160	14,111.4	788.0	1,851	26,619	6,979.7	664.7	656	4,338	711.8	171.7
Halifax	7.60	144.9	25	D	D	D	236	2,448	607.0	50.9	39	138	13.6	2.7
Harnett	20.57	160.5	53	D	D	D	268	3,037	869.4	66.8	69	226	19.6	5.3
Haywood	5.92	98.9	36	195	109.1	10.7	254	2,768	811.0	66.3	68	170	24.1	4.2
Henderson	11.05	98.1	111	1,236	740.5	46.8	407	4,653	1,330.8	114.2	109	282	52.3	9.0
Hertford	2.09	86.4	17	96	38.7	3.2	101	1,122	254.9	22.8	12	32	5.4	0.8
Hoke	4.42	83.9	9	83	49.6	3.3	79	806	257.7	16.7	19	D	D	D
Hyde	1.08	195.4	12	89	84.8	2.4	36	166	30.4	2.8	6	53	4.5	1.5
Iredell	11.54	67.9	231	1,803	1,233.0	92.9	619	7,783	2,249.9	181.9	167	469	85.5	16.7
Jackson	1.94	47.0	16	D	D	D	157	1,519	403.7	34.0	54	184	21.5	5.4
Johnston	15.77	84.9	95	1,051	897.6	56.0	548	7,446	2,134.2	159.1	89	377	64.5	11.3
Jones	0.72	71.9	7	D	D	D	26	112	33.7	2.5	NA	NA	NA	NA
Lee	7.41	124.2	41	D	D	D	238	3,021	832.2	67.6	51	165	28.6	5.7
Lenoir	8.81	151.6	64	847	478.3	34.6	239	2,746	728.9	67.1	42	161	27.8	4.9
Lincoln	6.63	81.8	72	848	332.9	38.0	237	2,945	789.8	68.7	52	94	16.1	3.0
McDowell	1.95	43.3	30	209	393.2	9.6	125	1,597	457.8	35.9	24	54	5.5	1.2
Macon	2.07	60.5	20	94	33.8	2.8	222	1,757	432.5	43.8	56	93	14.4	2.6
Madison	0.93	44.0	5	21	6.8	0.3	41	408	111.5	7.6	15	17	2.2	0.6
Martin	0.56	24.0	21	163	77.3	5.6	75	914	249.1	19.9	10	28	4.8	0.7
Mecklenburg	112.24	108.5	1,811	28,413	21,895.9	1,802.7	3,378	52,469	14,756.9	1,291.7	1,678	9,686	2,279.5	533.3
Mitchell	1.07	70.2	9	28	25.0	1.1	61	679	182.1	14.4	16	42	5.3	1.4
Montgomery	2.25	81.7	23	185	62.7	7.9	83	719	189.8	15.7	12	18	2.3	0.3
Moore	6.78	71.9	61	360	224.4	16.0	352	4,380	1,094.9	97.0	97	230	32.6	7.1
Nash	9.13	97.2	111	2,045	2,693.9	98.1	410	5,059	1,234.5	110.3	87	374	49.0	11.3
New Hanover	6.25	28.4	282	2,531	1,189.4	122.7	1,027	13,512	3,871.7	336.5	378	2,111	355.7	76.9
Northampton	1.11	54.3	16	D	D	D	49	415	131.2	9.3	4	12	0.4	0.1
Onslow	17.87	95.9	50	304	139.1	11.9	545	7,716	2,213.0	177.9	187	664	127.0	20.7
Orange	8.78	62.1	83	678	510.4	33.2	386	5,621	1,385.3	151.1	153	558	95.7	20.0
Pamlico	1.25	97.8	9	D	D	D	41	412	100.1	9.3	12	40	2.7	0.8
Pasquotank	2.67	67.0	34	496	176.3	17.1	193	2,504	698.3	58.1	36	166	26.2	4.8
Pender	2.77	48.1	33	306	179.4	13.3	147	1,484	386.7	30.6	47	203	39.8	9.4
Perquimans	0.75	55.8	8	63	36.8	2.1	32	232	66.4	4.6	7	55	4.7	3.5
Person	2.53	64.4	22	320	176.0	14.5	126	1,409	378.4	29.3	19	52	7.9	1.1
Pitt	13.64	77.6	144	1,597	1,028.7	69.5	633	8,597	2,354.8	193.0	176	681	115.5	22.7
Polk	0.91	44.7	10	D	D	D	67	467	100.8	8.9	21	85	4.5	1.4
Randolph	16.76	117.4	148	1,753	836.6	80.9	395	4,137	1,107.9	89.7	79	235	46.2	6.7
Richmond	9.87	217.2	22	D	D	D	192	1,899	449.8	41.6	36	115	10.1	2.0
Robeson	21.28	158.6	71	1,050	604.4	34.3	390	4,921	1,395.6	117.3	60	211	27.1	4.3
Rockingham	11.41	124.3	52	769	397.6	24.6	324	3,530	866.3	77.0	56	153	15.9	3.4
Rowan	9.64	69.3	124	1,679	888.2	59.3	402	4,221	1,194.6	95.6	85	312	36.6	8.0
Rutherford	7.68	115.7	41	511	166.0	23.5	233	2,511	600.1	54.2	41	86	10.8	2.5
Sampson	3.67	57.6	43	788	450.6	35.7	191	2,219	593.0	50.2	33	94	17.0	3.0
Scotland	3.10	87.3	18	311	564.5	9.0	139	1,461	351.7	30.0	23	39	9.5	1.3
Stanly	6.40	105.4	49	328	177.7	16.4	232	2,609	618.1	55.4	36	145	22.4	4.3
Stokes	0.30	6.5	18	69	12.8	2.3	104	881	222.1	18.2	23	D	D	D
Surry	4.41	60.6	63	732	396.1	23.7	336	3,903	1,067.1	88.3	68	220	27.2	5.6

1 Merchant wholesalers, except manufacturers' sales branches and offices.   2. Employer establishments.

Professional Services, Manufacturing, and Accommodation and Food Services

STATE County	Professional, scientific, and technical services, 2012				Manufacturing, 2012				Accommodation and food services, 2012			
	Number of establish-ments	Number of employees	Sales (mil dol)	Average payroll (mil dol)	Number of establish-ments	Number of employees	Receipts (mil dol)	Annual payroll (mil dol)	Number of establis-hments	Number of employees	Receipts (mil dol)	Annual payroll (mil dol)
	147	148	149	150	151	152	153	154	155	156	157	158
NORTH CAROLINA—Cont'd												
Chowan	26	138	13.5	4.5	18	493	451.2	20.5	28	430	19.1	5.1
Clay	13	40	3.4	1.4	8	156	D	5.6	18	166	8.6	2.4
Cleveland	131	747	104.7	29.5	118	5,325	1,821.2	232.2	159	2,262	109.1	28.6
Columbus	60	205	20.4	7.0	35	1,943	900.9	94.6	95	1,005	52.2	12.6
Craven	221	1,813	213.8	95.0	66	3,377	1,261.4	158.0	197	D	D	D
Cumberland	547	6,670	904.9	371.3	102	6,182	3,827.0	312.8	633	13,451	629.4	172.7
Currituck	40	115	14.2	4.9	15	43	D	1.4	70	D	D	D
Dare	130	D	D	D	36	398	47.8	13.9	325	D	D	D
Davidson	202	805	81.5	29.4	247	8,405	2,470.2	317.9	230	3,780	163.2	46.6
Davie	78	273	20.5	7.4	43	1,237	448.7	50.2	65	1,005	43.1	11.5
Duplin	53	168	15.4	5.7	32	5,482	2,056.7	169.6	63	921	44.1	10.7
Durham	1,123	32,330	5,726.0	2,810.4	171	11,001	8,955.5	782.2	709	14,103	832.5	226.9
Edgecombe	47	174	11.9	5.2	34	3,000	1,028.9	120.2	53	766	38.1	9.5
Forsyth	928	6,669	942.7	397.4	315	14,325	14,759.1	732.1	728	14,604	713.6	201.7
Franklin	69	247	30.4	12.8	53	2,327	1,047.3	126.8	51	633	27.8	7.6
Gaston	296	1,292	125.0	48.8	276	12,709	5,021.4	544.8	329	6,015	297.4	74.4
Gates	8	32	2.5	0.7	7	133	D	5.7	4	D	D	D
Graham	8	25	2.2	0.8	8	D	D	D	22	214	14.6	4.2
Granville	59	257	24.2	9.4	47	4,229	3,020.6	197.2	73	979	52.4	12.1
Greene	10	44	3.4	1.6	13	103	D	5.3	15	D	D	D
Guilford	1,439	D	D	D	641	32,428	26,932.2	1,690.3	1,143	22,863	1,158.5	319.5
Halifax	53	246	14.8	6.0	33	1,583	486.3	81.2	100	1,968	86.6	20.8
Harnett	116	437	47.8	18.4	63	1,566	358.4	58.5	135	2,305	99.1	26.0
Haywood	117	461	48.3	15.5	34	1,811	D	100.7	160	2,114	102.7	30.0
Henderson	222	821	87.6	30.9	123	5,858	2,625.0	281.7	207	2,925	170.0	48.1
Hertford	19	103	8.5	3.5	16	883	D	55.2	50	748	29.0	7.3
Hoke	30	143	7.0	2.9	13	2,011	1,654.1	66.7	24	477	16.5	4.3
Hyde	5	D	D	D	6	34	D	D	29	D	D	D
Iredell	381	2,671	438.4	124.9	280	9,940	3,628.9	459.9	345	6,011	289.6	76.9
Jackson	84	378	34.8	11.9	17	166	64.5	9.0	104	3,553	548.5	88.6
Johnston	255	845	91.4	31.6	109	6,399	3,712.6	323.3	262	4,949	243.0	61.2
Jones	6	20	1.9	0.5	5	28	D	1.2	6	D	D	D
Lee	80	304	26.5	90.5	73	8,039	2,751.5	340.9	106	1,816	84.2	23.0
Lenoir	64	498	112.4	23.8	46	3,374	D	135.8	99	1,776	78.4	20.9
Lincoln	117	471	53.2	18.2	109	3,974	1,884.9	165.4	101	1,649	75.4	20.2
McDowell	36	162	13.8	6.1	53	5,206	1,324.2	192.5	72	1,006	46.5	12.3
Macon	69	206	16.1	6.1	25	676	181.2	25.5	105	1,194	63.3	20.6
Madison	21	34	3.3	0.9	17	357	D	14.1	25	273	12.2	4.0
Martin	19	133	8.8	2.9	15	786	557.4	30.1	44	673	25.7	7.0
Mecklenburg	3,935	47,897	8,741.1	3,404.2	796	24,964	11,150.0	1,364.6	2,333	49,178	2,845.1	776.0
Mitchell	16	66	4.9	2.0	25	347	56.5	14.1	35	391	19.4	5.0
Montgomery	18	65	5.9	1.7	57	2,275	803.2	77.4	39	D	D	D
Moore	215	1,331	176.2	65.3	84	1,777	781.5	74.4	204	4,650	236.7	69.4
Nash	154	892	97.2	37.3	85	6,582	3,184.4	335.6	191	3,948	166.7	46.5
New Hanover	860	5,650	1,071.2	288.7	170	4,515	2,449.5	321.5	657	12,919	623.3	171.5
Northampton	11	29	2.2	0.8	9	444	246.4	19.2	14	123	4.6	1.3
Onslow	246	1,748	198.1	69.5	40	1,049	271.0	34.2	347	6,640	353.1	86.9
Orange	538	2,132	316.3	130.1	73	862	161.4	41.8	311	5,585	283.0	81.1
Pamlico	23	51	4.9	1.4	14	130	D	5.1	31	D	D	D
Pasquotank	63	334	35.3	13.4	27	726	D	37.4	92	1,774	76.9	19.4
Pender	77	202	19.3	6.7	37	753	191.4	28.0	89	1,032	50.5	14.0
Perquimans	13	33	1.8	0.8	5	D	D	D	13	218	8.6	2.2
Person	32	126	10.3	3.4	34	1,717	841.2	67.2	56	905	41.3	10.5
Pitt	311	1,893	247.9	84.4	87	4,905	2,160.8	248.8	362	8,055	357.6	96.7
Polk	37	135	12.4	4.2	20	304	78.2	9.3	34	352	14.4	4.4
Randolph	165	624	55.8	18.6	293	14,850	4,557.3	510.6	202	3,190	158.6	41.6
Richmond	45	171	12.8	4.0	42	2,775	794.4	87.6	66	949	42.3	10.5
Robeson	110	D	D	D	61	6,421	3,081.4	227.0	173	3,039	139.1	34.2
Rockingham	113	D	D	D	85	6,311	4,268.3	267.6	149	2,132	91.1	24.2
Rowan	177	851	87.9	29.4	186	7,529	3,856.6	327.2	219	3,619	163.2	44.5
Rutherford	78	250	21.3	7.4	71	2,639	672.5	115.4	123	1,590	71.8	19.7
Sampson	55	289	22.9	8.3	47	3,413	821.8	106.9	79	D	D	D
Scotland	27	117	9.4	3.8	30	1,662	984.2	74.8	58	923	43.8	11.3
Stanly	69	315	41.5	11.6	92	3,066	832.9	119.2	119	1,687	70.6	19.7
Stokes	39	141	11.8	4.4	25	896	489.7	33.1	52	721	35.1	9.1
Surry	96	355	33.4	11.2	93	3,511	967.8	122.4	160	2,403	105.4	28.7

Table B. States and Counties — Health Care and Social Assistance, Other Services, Nonemployer Businesses, and Residential Construction

STATE County	Health care and social assistance, 2012				Other services, 2012				Nonemployer businesses, 2016		Value of residential construction authorized by building permits, 2018	
	Number of establishments	Number of employees	Receipts (mil dol)	Annual payroll (mil dol)	Number of establishments	Number of employees	Receipts (mil dol)	Annual payroll (mil dol)	Number	Receipts (mil dol)	New construction ($1,000)	Number of housing units
	159	160	161	162	163	164	165	166	167	168	169	170
NORTH CAROLINA— Cont'd												
Chowan	62	1,194	94.1	39.2	16	80	5.9	1.9	949	35.8	4,184	20
Clay	23	270	14.9	6.5	11	D	D	D	1,058	39.0	17,770	73
Cleveland	227	5,245	496.8	195.7	121	607	58.8	16.3	5,501	174.6	29,779	169
Columbus	169	3,353	246.5	97.1	51	D	D	D	3,473	121.8	5,625	47
Craven	241	7,319	715.4	300.9	143	711	58.2	15.6	5,937	228.4	54,790	330
Cumberland	778	20,384	2,106.5	958.1	417	2,403	221.4	59.4	17,923	669.4	106,824	575
Currituck	27	248	18.0	7.6	43	201	22.2	5.6	2,111	104.7	105,035	425
Dare	92	D	D	D	95	404	33.6	9.7	5,282	292.4	109,137	337
Davidson	196	13,615	1,634.9	566.3	185	709	73.9	18.1	11,182	434.7	162,046	585
Davie	63	1,122	79.5	34.5	53	189	15.7	3.9	3,113	135.6	43,657	443
Duplin	105	1,969	133.2	60.1	52	203	17.4	5.0	3,176	133.3	9,200	52
Durham	772	25,680	3,785.0	1,271.4	433	4,298	708.8	175.8	23,845	846.6	495,816	3,359
Edgecombe	105	2,502	203.1	73.3	46	D	D	D	2,571	71.3	5,306	39
Forsyth	793	22,194	2,115.1	861.5	528	3,078	369.2	86.2	26,573	1,094.5	385,753	2,345
Franklin	81	1,162	86.9	34.7	60	219	19.9	5.2	4,181	164.3	120,665	736
Gaston	471	11,455	1,177.4	486.2	285	1,432	113.7	34.0	13,546	527.2	343,562	1,230
Gates	13	137	7.0	3.7	10	44	3.9	0.8	544	18.0	15,729	46
Graham	10	D	D	D	7	D	D	D	726	25.3	7,701	15
Granville	93	2,089	149.3	62.5	44	118	13.6	3.7	3,142	112.6	51,921	253
Greene	43	671	35.2	15.8	13	D	D	D	1,059	39.2	3,738	26
Guilford	1,289	33,134	3,512.8	1,373.9	804	5,091	830.0	155.1	41,067	1,818.1	381,471	1,662
Halifax	130	3,022	223.0	97.1	71	D	D	D	2,560	77.6	15,143	124
Harnett	175	3,533	302.4	114.4	97	383	35.6	8.8	6,918	259.8	73,887	597
Haywood	141	3,047	314.1	128.9	96	417	36.4	10.8	4,842	173.2	46,047	201
Henderson	292	6,339	581.9	236.3	174	860	84.3	24.7	9,151	374.8	150,676	834
Hertford	82	2,189	155.8	64.7	36	D	D	D	1,004	32.5	0	0
Hoke	65	946	49.5	20.8	24	101	7.5	1.9	2,471	69.9	56,945	244
Hyde	10	D	D	D	3	D	D	D	602	24.2	2,107	11
Iredell	455	6,805	758.7	298.5	272	1,696	149.9	39.2	13,551	632.8	461,234	1,991
Jackson	91	1,900	201.6	84.4	54	205	26.5	6.2	3,148	120.9	134,752	421
Johnston	300	5,165	457.1	177.1	200	868	74.2	21.3	12,818	582.2	425,975	2,550
Jones	15	188	47.7	9.3	5	12	1.1	0.3	587	19.7	2,286	22
Lee	160	2,732	249.7	93.8	84	393	27.9	9.2	3,727	163.6	32,116	158
Lenoir	176	4,333	305.5	133.8	81	522	45.7	13.1	3,254	120.7	9,259	93
Lincoln	137	2,343	223.5	86.8	130	491	41.6	12.3	5,803	250.4	157,737	792
McDowell	91	1,630	119.4	44.9	40	293	21.8	6.7	2,559	86.9	41,426	122
Macon	91	1,546	134.1	53.4	93	354	31.1	8.7	3,262	128.0	27,108	95
Madison	30	652	37.9	16.2	11	38	4.2	0.9	1,964	77.9	22,069	103
Martin	74	1,462	95.3	37.7	19	D	D	D	1,225	39.7	4,209	22
Mecklenburg	2,576	61,634	8,163.9	3,031.5	1,698	12,608	1,767.5	413.7	94,780	4,403.1	2,112,945	14,049
Mitchell	38	886	97.6	29.3	27	84	6.1	1.7	1,134	38.1	6,233	40
Montgomery	55	1,031	61.4	29.7	34	200	11.5	4.7	1,474	56.0	12,940	72
Moore	275	8,294	913.4	374.0	137	709	56.7	16.8	7,731	359.9	168,249	762
Nash	243	4,050	349.4	143.4	138	D	D	D	5,752	230.9	30,955	196
New Hanover	756	12,485	1,277.4	511.7	440	2,566	226.8	65.5	20,563	973.1	533,232	1,918
Northampton	32	693	26.4	12.8	17	D	D	D	867	28.0	6,764	23
Onslow	257	5,765	491.7	197.5	210	1,172	89.9	26.6	9,889	354.5	153,308	1,036
Orange	391	12,581	1,389.9	600.6	196	1,699	271.2	59.1	13,302	564.2	256,380	1,242
Pamlico	37	557	43.0	20.8	19	109	11.4	2.6	1,040	43.4	9,324	37
Pasquotank	138	2,540	225.1	97.3	62	D	D	D	2,653	82.7	20,746	136
Pender	89	1,305	97.3	38.5	55	193	17.4	5.1	4,452	185.7	74,873	532
Perquimans	16	183	8.9	4.5	11	D	D	D	917	33.3	7,810	38
Person	83	1,278	98.9	35.2	43	158	17.0	4.4	2,154	80.1	24,116	105
Pitt	510	16,075	1,880.0	681.9	183	1,104	93.9	25.1	10,594	399.3	178,255	1,150
Polk	58	1,457	104.4	43.8	26	D	D	D	1,955	76.2	18,354	79
Randolph	238	5,136	363.9	164.1	170	709	77.9	19.7	9,661	397.1	71,240	354
Richmond	98	2,042	177.2	73.2	56	272	16.2	4.8	1,949	67.1	9,465	230
Robeson	286	8,151	581.0	256.4	80	358	26.9	7.7	7,322	232.6	21,337	106
Rockingham	170	3,440	287.5	110.4	121	525	39.6	11.1	4,865	183.6	47,640	208
Rowan	263	8,202	837.0	406.4	142	682	58.0	18.0	9,054	334.9	146,069	541
Rutherford	132	2,951	245.8	90.6	68	377	27.7	9.1	4,023	166.3	27,752	150
Sampson	130	2,719	179.4	76.3	64	292	25.4	7.5	3,493	141.6	19,140	120
Scotland	114	2,358	236.0	97.2	32	117	10.2	2.3	1,765	55.6	3,615	20
Stanly	174	3,190	251.4	98.7	81	390	32.2	10.2	3,827	160.1	48,904	272
Stokes	51	1,156	107.1	36.4	47	D	D	D	2,837	104.6	29,479	69
Surry	171	5,086	411.6	173.2	96	487	39.4	11.2	4,860	208.0	26,534	159

Table B. States and Counties — Government Employment and Payroll, and Local Government Finances

	Government employment and payroll, 2012									Local government finances, 2012				
			March payroll (percent of total)							General revenue				
												Taxes		
STATE County	Full-time equivalent employees	March payroll (dollars)	Administration, judicial, and legal	Police and corrections	Fire protection	Highways and transportation	Health and welfare	Natural resources and utilities	Education and libraries	Total (mil dol)	Intergovernmental (mil dol)	Total (mil dol)	Per capita[1] (dollars) Total	Property
	171	172	173	174	175	176	177	178	179	180	181	182	183	184
NORTH CAROLINA— Cont'd														
Chowan	470	1,457,821	1.5	4.5	1.5	0.7	1.5	4.7	79.9	47.9	24.9	15.3	1,036	830
Clay	374	1,096,838	4.9	8.6	0.1	2.1	18.6	3.2	58.6	30.3	17.7	10.0	938	759
Cleveland	5,555	17,029,077	1.4	2.7	1.1	0.6	40.8	3.7	48.8	997.0	173.6	81.7	838	665
Columbus	2,576	8,631,036	7.0	13.2	4.0	1.6	9.8	5.6	57.3	181.2	110.5	43.2	750	595
Craven	5,760	21,786,606	3.1	4.6	1.8	1.3	49.5	4.0	34.0	683.8	247.7	93.3	890	647
Cumberland	18,665	65,054,561	1.3	6.1	1.9	0.8	41.4	3.9	38.6	1,026.5	546.0	340.9	1,052	756
Currituck	1,085	3,605,883	4.2	9.0	1.4	0.2	12.9	4.4	63.7	101.1	28.3	49.2	2,044	1,156
Dare	1,891	6,914,953	10.6	12.1	4.0	0.9	18.7	6.6	40.2	195.1	51.6	121.3	3,507	2,197
Davidson	5,783	17,327,794	4.1	6.9	2.6	0.9	8.4	4.1	68.7	408.7	228.5	125.0	765	602
Davie	1,001,378	4,164,460	3.3	9.1	0.2	0.6	15.6	2.8	66.1	100.6	51.4	36.9	892	723
Duplin	2,002,596	7,169,108	4.4	6.0	0.9	1.1	11.3	3.0	71.0	166.7	96.1	42.2	702	533
Durham	9,926	33,408,797	6.2	5.0	0.4	2.0	10.8	7.2	66.1	1,014.8	394.0	460.1	1,645	1,286
Edgecombe	2,085	7,168,867	2.6	6.9	1.2	0.7	10.7	5.5	70.6	170.1	100.0	37.8	676	569
Forsyth	13,925	45,845,272	4.9	9.9	5.3	1.5	7.4	5.9	62.7	1,198.2	555.3	456.5	1,275	995
Franklin	1,848	5,584,621	4.4	7.9	0.4	0.3	14.6	2.9	65.1	141.2	69.1	51.6	840	681
Gaston	7,249	25,015,194	7.4	6.7	2.8	2.9	12.2	6.4	59.7	643.2	307.9	230.9	1,110	864
Gates	371	1,271,812	3.9	2.8	0.0	1.1	5.8	2.3	82.4	29.7	19.3	7.6	641	522
Graham	358	999,021	5.0	6.3	0.1	2.3	19.0	2.4	60.3	29.4	18.8	7.3	834	661
Granville	1,871	5,604,572	7.1	8.1	0.7	1.1	4.5	5.4	70.7	198.6	73.9	47.4	785	648
Greene	792	2,460,297	7.1	5.1	0.0	2.0	11.7	8.9	63.9	57.2	35.0	8.8	409	388
Guilford	18,710	71,857,919	4.6	10.1	4.0	2.3	6.6	6.4	63.8	1,781.8	770.6	726.5	1,450	1,146
Halifax	5,002,529	8,099,327	3.1	5.7	1.4	1.3	12.8	5.1	68.3	190.1	109.1	47.9	886	669
Harnett	3,872	13,569,140	4.6	12.1	0.4	1.1	9.2	4.4	66.9	288.8	164.5	83.5	684	544
Haywood	3,238	11,027,848	3.6	5.3	0.5	0.6	44.4	2.8	39.6	310.3	118.9	68.8	1,168	882
Henderson	4,495	15,113,386	3.5	6.2	0.7	0.5	37.6	2.5	46.9	628.0	121.4	105.7	976	755
Hertford	1,107	3,318,864	2.9	8.6	0.6	0.6	10.8	4.2	66.9	79.7	46.0	21.1	863	629
Hoke	1,946	6,883,544	2.2	5.4	0.2	1.0	6.2	1.3	80.3	121.2	74.9	31.7	626	463
Hyde	303	895,248	4.8	5.1	0.0	0.0	17.4	6.5	63.4	29.6	15.5	8.8	1,500	1,122
Iredell	5,871	18,788,013	4.4	8.0	3.5	0.6	9.3	4.8	66.7	482.4	216.0	188.6	1,159	907
Jackson	1,418	4,256,176	4.4	6.6	0.0	1.0	11.8	4.0	65.6	109.9	53.3	43.4	1,072	832
Johnston	7,756	24,977,350	2.3	4.6	1.2	0.6	24.0	3.4	62.5	698.3	273.2	164.7	942	743
Jones	494	1,149,556	4.9	6.6	0.0	0.2	13.5	4.3	66.8	28.8	17.3	6.8	664	556
Lee	3,038	10,911,112	3.3	6.5	2.0	1.2	5.3	3.7	57.7	206.8	113.6	67.5	1,130	854
Lenoir	2,634	8,323,127	3.5	7.1	2.0	2.2	10.0	8.6	63.7	209.1	121.6	56.5	955	735
Lincoln	2,462	7,572,141	4.1	8.7	1.3	1.3	14.4	4.8	63.7	182.3	86.5	68.9	868	682
McDowell	1,584	3,817,801	1.8	2.8	0.5	0.8	1.5	2.4	89.3	105.4	60.6	31.8	708	497
Macon	1,378	3,815,292	6.5	9.2	0.5	1.5	16.3	5.7	56.3	100.9	48.1	36.6	1,081	971
Madison	876	2,682,447	3.6	4.9	0.2	0.3	14.0	3.1	71.6	52.3	29.4	15.8	761	620
Martin	1,141	3,472,186	4.5	5.3	2.4	1.3	15.0	4.7	65.2	85.6	46.7	22.7	948	699
Mecklenburg	60,489	285,037,206	2.7	6.4	2.0	1.6	56.6	3.0	26.7	8,195.0	1,390.6	1,863.3	1,923	1,419
Mitchell	1,336	2,250,773	2.5	3.7	0.0	0.0	5.6	2.2	79.0	52.4	33.1	13.0	844	617
Montgomery	1,174	3,454,946	3.3	6.9	0.0	0.7	9.4	3.4	74.1	81.0	47.9	21.9	792	630
Moore	3,494	11,423,864	5.9	7.9	2.5	1.7	12.6	3.7	62.8	269.6	121.4	108.4	1,201	948
Nash	6,656	23,448,806	3.3	5.8	2.6	2.0	39.4	6.2	39.5	555.5	191.0	99.1	1,035	775
New Hanover	11,962	45,527,134	2.5	6.8	2.5	1.2	49.3	4.7	29.7	1,468.2	274.1	326.8	1,562	1,109
Northampton	777	2,301,803	10.7	8.8	0.0	0.6	20.3	6.4	49.8	67.1	36.8	21.0	982	870
Onslow	5,873	18,455,158	3.9	7.0	1.9	1.2	10.7	4.8	66.2	585.4	209.5	152.5	832	536
Orange	5,385	18,675,410	6.4	8.5	3.1	3.3	8.9	7.6	55.3	495.0	178.9	247.0	1,791	1,537
Pamlico	537	1,656,218	4.6	6.6	0.2	0.4	9.9	5.9	70.1	42.4	25.2	12.6	965	785
Pasquotank	3,546	11,505,340	5.8	3.9	1.2	1.0	34.4	2.5	33.1	251.3	70.2	38.8	955	676
Pender	1,621	5,227,407	6.3	8.7	1.1	0.4	9.8	2.7	65.8	149.8	76.0	58.2	1,074	864
Perquimans	396	1,289,198	8.5	2.8	0.0	0.0	8.3	6.7	68.4	34.0	18.9	10.8	795	634
Person	1,548	5,009,176	3.6	7.9	2.5	1.2	11.6	4.6	65.6	119.0	63.0	39.6	1,007	800
Pitt	6,107	20,619,861	3.8	8.9	3.2	2.0	4.2	10.9	60.2	555.7	265.7	167.7	972	677
Polk	5,000,658	2,004,992	5.0	7.0	0.0	2.3	8.7	5.2	70.0	53.2	24.8	21.2	1,045	877
Randolph	4,527	16,669,167	4.3	8.3	2.7	1.2	7.8	3.4	68.3	345.4	185.5	117.9	828	644
Richmond	2,132	5,122,800	4.4	8.9	2.0	1.6	14.1	4.9	62.7	142.5	82.7	39.5	848	648
Robeson	1,006,145	18,365,522	4.4	13.6	1.4	1.1	12.5	5.8	59.7	414.1	250.9	103.1	761	522
Rockingham	3,543	11,125,272	5.5	9.4	2.7	1.5	10.3	3.0	62.8	267.2	141.9	84.2	908	715
Rowan	5,594	16,509,444	3.8	6.2	1.8	1.2	7.6	4.3	71.8	395.5	204.5	128.5	930	719
Rutherford	3,135	8,814,742	3.6	6.0	1.3	1.0	9.8	3.6	57.5	200.1	101.7	53.6	796	593
Sampson	2,002,770	7,777,872	2.8	6.0	0.4	0.4	11.9	2.4	71.5	212.9	127.6	48.5	759	539
Scotland	1,728	5,628,337	3.5	5.7	0.4	0.9	9.5	5.0	72.9	112.7	68.9	30.4	843	662
Stanly	2,443	7,501,977	4.3	7.7	2.6	2.1	13.1	6.3	62.1	184.7	101.2	51.9	857	641
Stokes	1,636	4,531,305	4.4	6.7	2.3	0.1	12.8	2.1	70.0	122.3	78.2	33.7	720	593
Surry	3,820	12,472,258	2.4	4.5	0.8	0.5	33.1	2.1	53.9	321.4	128.8	65.4	889	603

1. Based on the resident population estimated as of July 1 of the year shown.

Local Government Finances, Government Employment, and Income Taxes

STATE County	Total (mil dol) 185	Per capita[1] (dollars) 186	Education 187	Health and hospitals 188	Police protection 189	Public welfare 190	Highways 191	Total (mil dol) 192	Per capita[1] (dollars) 193	Federal civilian 194	Federal military 195	State and local 196	Number of returns 197	Mean adjusted gross income 198	Mean income tax 199
NORTH CAROLINA— Cont'd															
Chowan	47.4	3,208	53.9	0.4	10.6	6.8	2.3	21.8	1,475	29	31	803	6,290	49,893	5,091
Clay	30.1	2,831	45.1	6.7	10.1	14.8	0.1	11.8	1,114	20	25	496	4,600	43,891	4,309
Cleveland	561.2	5,758	30.2	48.9	3.5	3.9	0.5	167.5	1,719	177	215	5,423	41,720	44,380	4,060
Columbus	177.1	3,072	58.4	4.6	6.2	8.6	0.7	63.1	1,095	131	119	3,487	21,540	40,032	3,665
Craven	658.5	6,288	21.8	54.9	3.8	3.5	0.8	179.3	1,712	5,796	7,827	7,090	46,070	52,567	5,680
Cumberland	1,088.1	3,358	50.4	3.7	7.9	6.3	1.3	508.0	1,568	15,208	46,433	22,788	139,980	45,398	4,351
Currituck	92.8	3,854	37.2	6.0	8.8	4.4	0.1	60.9	2,529	37	59	1,199	12,040	56,676	5,818
Dare	214.0	6,189	25.3	7.8	9.4	3.9	1.4	229.3	6,632	228	184	2,807	19,880	56,814	7,029
Davidson	418.5	2,563	60.4	2.9	6.7	5.2	1.1	214.7	1,315	186	369	6,404	72,980	49,084	4,934
Davie	101.9	2,459	54.9	7.3	7.9	6.1	0.9	31.0	749	64	98	1,547	19,180	61,160	7,356
Duplin	161.0	2,681	57.6	5.6	6.5	7.2	1.1	40.0	667	125	132	3,283	21,930	38,674	3,144
Durham	1,130.0	4,041	36.7	5.4	7.7	4.9	2.8	1,199.0	4,288	6,350	810	15,132	143,240	63,814	8,214
Edgecombe	174.9	3,125	52.2	4.1	6.7	12.0	1.1	31.7	567	201	117	3,930	21,910	37,501	2,998
Forsyth	1,295.8	3,618	44.3	6.0	8.5	3.9	2.2	1,426.9	3,984	1,616	867	18,483	169,560	61,777	8,177
Franklin	146.8	2,389	50.6	6.0	5.3	7.7	1.0	126.9	2,064	84	146	2,287	27,130	49,088	4,633
Gaston	705.2	3,389	45.5	9.1	9.5	5.7	2.2	453.5	2,180	370	491	9,493	97,100	51,045	5,410
Gates	29.2	2,457	67.6	0.6	4.9	6.5	0.1	8.9	752	17	26	498	4,670	46,807	4,016
Graham	26.4	3,040	48.5	6.1	10.0	8.9	1.3	9.5	1,093	31	19	482	3,410	36,903	2,991
Granville	202.2	3,345	38.7	26.8	6.4	4.7	0.7	131.9	2,182	1,485	125	6,567	25,400	51,826	5,072
Greene	57.7	2,693	65.9	4.7	3.8	7.2	0.7	25.4	1,185	35	42	1,774	7,690	37,699	2,975
Guilford	1,919.4	3,832	43.8	4.5	7.5	4.2	2.9	2,139.4	4,271	4,043	1,207	29,457	237,800	59,853	7,883
Halifax	185.9	3,442	51.7	6.0	5.5	8.7	1.6	112.0	2,073	132	113	3,937	21,280	38,915	3,503
Harnett	319.1	2,613	48.6	4.3	6.4	3.5	1.3	272.9	2,234	137	303	5,438	51,160	48,059	4,439
Haywood	325.8	5,531	28.2	47.8	4.0	5.8	1.3	100.5	1,706	120	136	2,791	27,770	48,278	4,787
Henderson	411.4	3,800	31.5	38.2	5.0	4.9	1.3	200.9	1,856	233	258	5,544	53,330	54,639	5,947
Hertford	78.3	3,203	52.5	7.5	6.9	8.5	1.0	105.4	4,314	68	48	2,083	8,340	39,365	3,371
Hoke	115.8	2,291	61.0	2.2	4.8	7.7	0.8	96.8	1,915	59	120	2,402	20,020	41,505	3,036
Hyde	31.1	5,313	35.0	17.4	4.4	5.8	0.0	21.2	3,614	41	10	586	2,070	40,795	3,678
Iredell	484.3	2,977	49.9	1.9	7.8	5.0	2.0	564.7	3,470	284	393	8,474	80,550	67,584	9,491
Jackson	117.6	2,908	51.0	4.9	4.2	6.3	0.6	47.1	1,164	57	89	8,263	15,940	47,313	5,092
Johnston	707.4	4,044	42.4	30.3	4.0	3.6	1.0	672.2	3,843	247	440	9,444	84,460	54,539	5,641
Jones	28.7	2,798	50.8	6.3	6.8	10.5	0.5	4.3	418	23	21	552	4,310	40,813	3,645
Lee	211.6	3,544	60.3	1.6	7.1	4.8	1.1	152.3	2,550	160	134	3,326	26,470	48,661	4,780
Lenoir	226.0	3,816	45.8	3.1	5.0	6.3	0.8	200.6	3,387	203	125	5,750	24,510	42,048	4,368
Lincoln	184.5	2,326	52.4	5.8	7.2	7.4	0.6	203.5	2,566	112	184	3,619	36,320	62,656	7,669
McDowell	115.5	2,567	60.9	1.8	4.8	9.3	1.1	20.1	447	80	99	2,479	18,560	41,686	3,542
Macon	106.3	3,138	46.9	3.4	10.5	5.7	2.0	49.0	1,446	175	78	1,701	15,740	52,705	6,463
Madison	53.5	2,579	46.9	5.8	7.8	10.1	0.9	10.7	515	66	46	874	8,860	42,980	3,830
Martin	89.4	3,730	50.1	10.1	7.7	7.3	1.2	36.3	1,513	48	51	1,520	9,980	38,459	3,226
Mecklenburg	7,529.3	7,770	17.3	51.9	4.4	2.3	1.8	7,935.0	8,189	5,994	2,509	73,105	500,480	78,805	12,587
Mitchell	54.4	3,537	64.7	2.0	5.5	8.9	0.2	3.0	192	41	33	1,008	6,070	41,707	3,375
Montgomery	78.0	2,820	58.5	5.5	7.0	5.5	1.1	28.8	1,042	56	60	1,691	11,040	44,981	4,532
Moore	304.5	3,372	46.2	2.7	12.1	4.3	1.8	140.3	1,553	175	232	4,425	43,930	66,436	8,473
Nash	589.1	6,155	29.3	42.9	4.8	3.1	1.6	113.0	1,181	186	207	6,054	43,300	51,298	5,626
New Hanover	1,459.0	6,973	21.3	49.4	4.8	2.5	1.1	1,476.2	7,055	992	697	19,986	104,290	65,864	9,323
Northampton	68.1	3,176	37.6	9.0	6.4	10.1	1.8	37.7	1,759	47	43	1,103	7,770	38,764	3,127
Onslow	563.2	3,073	38.6	24.7	6.7	6.5	1.0	439.4	2,398	6,503	47,081	8,095	78,650	43,168	3,605
Orange	485.2	3,518	44.0	6.5	6.9	6.2	1.4	328.7	2,383	289	354	40,354	61,340	92,694	15,007
Pamlico	43.2	3,303	51.1	3.1	4.3	7.4	0.9	13.7	1,044	29	49	856	5,440	52,062	5,477
Pasquotank	254.1	6,261	28.0	49.1	4.4	3.4	1.2	135.3	3,334	714	972	3,612	17,440	45,077	4,057
Pender	152.0	2,804	46.6	4.9	6.0	6.5	0.6	184.1	3,396	107	171	2,509	25,220	53,831	5,593
Perquimans	34.1	2,515	51.3	2.5	8.3	7.0	1.1	30.1	2,218	40	30	629	5,780	49,724	4,737
Person	126.4	3,218	53.5	5.5	6.7	8.5	0.7	200.1	5,097	56	88	1,788	17,140	46,968	4,402
Pitt	557.6	3,232	46.8	1.8	9.9	5.2	2.1	400.7	2,322	715	431	25,861	71,820	52,775	6,226
Polk	49.0	2,420	52.7	2.7	8.4	8.4	1.3	16.1	796	47	70	885	9,070	56,426	6,942
Randolph	349.0	2,450	59.5	2.6	7.6	5.8	1.4	147.2	1,033	209	320	5,878	62,250	46,179	4,476
Richmond	150.1	3,220	56.1	3.4	6.8	7.0	1.1	48.8	1,047	110	98	2,962	18,060	37,829	3,086
Robeson	429.7	3,171	54.2	4.0	5.7	7.6	1.3	103.7	765	305	291	8,283	48,400	35,890	2,795
Rockingham	263.7	2,844	53.2	2.0	6.8	7.4	2.1	167.2	1,803	149	203	3,834	39,350	45,122	4,223
Rowan	420.9	3,046	54.8	2.5	6.5	5.4	1.5	263.4	1,906	2,683	307	6,552	62,180	46,985	4,631
Rutherford	191.7	2,848	53.0	6.6	6.5	6.8	1.1	113.5	1,685	117	147	3,322	26,060	42,643	4,071
Sampson	232.7	3,639	52.4	12.4	4.0	6.9	0.7	122.1	1,909	109	141	3,961	26,410	42,853	4,277
Scotland	112.8	3,125	56.5	1.8	7.2	8.7	1.5	27.4	758	48	73	2,244	13,430	38,748	3,153
Stanly	179.1	2,956	54.3	4.3	6.6	5.6	1.2	61.7	1,019	152	134	4,220	26,110	49,162	4,861
Stokes	117.6	2,514	64.2	4.7	5.2	6.5	0.4	62.1	1,328	71	102	1,757	19,750	46,604	4,297
Surry	324.4	4,410	40.1	37.5	3.8	3.5	0.8	112.5	1,530	177	161	4,639	30,360	45,486	4,515

1. Based on the resident population estimated as of July 1 of the year shown.

State / county code	CBSA code[1]	County code[2]	STATE County	Land area[3] (sq. mi)	Total persons 2018	Rank	Per square mile	White	Black	American Indian, Alaska Native	Asian and Pacific Islander	Percent Hispanic or Latino[4]	Under 5 years	5 to 17 years	18 to 24 years	25 to 34 years	35 to 44 years	45 to 54 years
				1	2	3	4	5	6	7	8	9	10	11	12	13	14	15
			NORTH CAROLINA—Cont'd															
37173		8	Swain	527.7	14,245	2,148	27.0	65.4	2.0	30.4	1.2	5.5	6.8	15.3	8.3	12.6	11.5	12.6
37175	14,820	6	Transylvania..........	378.4	34,215	1,320	90.4	91.8	4.5	1.1	1.0	3.5	4.1	11.5	7.5	9.5	9.8	11.1
37177	28,620	9	Tyrrell...............	390.8	4,131	2,892	10.6	51.2	38.4	0.8	2.5	9.0	5.4	13.2	7.5	14.9	13.1	12.4
37179	16,740	1	Union................	632.7	235,908	285	372.9	73.2	12.6	0.8	3.8	11.4	5.7	21.2	9.0	9.7	13.5	16.3
37181	25,780	4	Vance................	252.4	44,582	1,086	176.6	40.3	51.4	0.7	1.1	8.0	6.2	17.4	8.6	12.0	10.6	12.9
37183	39,580	1	Wake................	834.8	1,092,305	41	1,308.5	61.7	21.1	0.8	8.4	10.3	6.2	17.7	9.1	14.7	14.9	14.3
37185		8	Warren	429.1	19,807	1,837	46.2	39.6	51.8	6.0	0.7	3.8	4.8	13.6	6.9	10.8	10.1	11.7
37187		7	Washington..........	346.5	11,859	2,304	34.2	45.5	48.8	0.6	0.6	5.8	5.2	14.9	7.7	10.2	9.1	12.2
37189	14,380	5	Watauga.............	312.4	55,945	913	179.1	92.9	2.2	1.0	1.6	3.7	3.3	9.5	28.4	11.2	9.4	10.2
37191	24,140	3	Wayne...............	553.9	123,248	514	222.5	54.8	32.2	0.9	2.0	12.3	6.6	17.0	9.8	13.5	11.2	12.2
37193	35,900	6	Wilkes...............	754.5	68,557	780	90.9	88.1	5.1	0.6	0.8	6.8	5.0	15.4	7.5	10.8	11.0	13.7
37195	48,980	4	Wilson...............	367.6	81,455	696	221.6	48.1	40.4	0.7	1.5	10.8	5.9	17.0	8.5	12.0	11.4	12.9
37197	49,180	2	Yadkin	334.9	37,543	1,236	112.1	85.1	3.7	0.6	0.5	11.2	5.2	15.6	7.8	10.9	10.8	14.9
37199		8	Yancey...............	312.6	17,903	1,926	57.3	92.9	1.3	0.8	0.5	5.5	4.6	13.7	6.7	10.6	10.5	13.3
38000		0	NORTH DAKOTA..........	68,999.4	760,077	X	11.0	85.9	3.9	6.2	2.3	3.9	7.2	16.3	11.1	15.1	11.9	10.5
38001		9	Adams................	987.6	2,294	3,020	2.3	93.9	1.2	1.5	3.7	1.4	5.1	13.9	5.4	10.8	10.0	10.3
38003		6	Barnes...............	1,491.6	10,542	2,389	7.1	94.2	2.0	1.8	1.4	2.1	5.3	14.8	9.8	10.4	10.6	11.4
38005		6	Benson...............	1,388.6	6,962	2,675	5.0	42.8	0.8	54.2	0.5	3.5	11.0	24.4	8.0	11.7	9.3	9.6
38007		9	Billings..............	1,148.8	919	3,109	0.8	92.9	0.4	0.7	4.6	2.0	7.5	12.8	4.9	13.3	12.6	11.9
38009		9	Bottineau............	1,668.4	6,411	2,718	3.8	93.5	1.3	4.3	0.8	2.2	5.4	15.5	8.5	10.2	10.1	10.6
38011		9	Bowman..............	1,161.9	3,076	2,961	2.6	93.0	0.5	1.6	0.3	5.4	6.2	18.3	6.7	10.5	11.3	9.6
38013		9	Burke................	1,103.6	2,100	3,040	1.9	95.0	1.2	2.1	1.0	2.5	8.3	16.7	6.1	11.2	11.1	9.9
38015	13,900	3	Burleigh..............	1,632.5	95,273	624	58.4	90.2	2.9	4.8	1.3	2.6	6.9	16.4	9.0	14.5	13.0	11.2
38017	22,020	2	Cass.................	1,765.0	181,516	360	102.8	86.0	6.9	1.9	4.3	2.8	7.1	14.2	17.5	13.1	10.3	
38019		9	Cavalier..............	1,489.0	3,829	2,914	2.6	95.7	0.8	2.5	0.8	1.8	7.1	15.4	6.7	9.5	8.6	10.6
38021		9	Dickey...............	1,131.5	4,903	2,840	4.3	94.4	1.1	1.5	1.0	3.5	6.6	18.0	9.5	9.8	10.4	10.8
38023		9	Divide...............	1,260.7	2,283	3,021	1.8	92.1	2.4	1.5	2.9	2.6	6.3	16.1	4.9	10.1	9.7	10.9
38025		9	Dunn	2,008.5	4,332	2,873	2.2	83.2	1.8	9.9	1.7	5.5	7.5	16.3	6.9	14.6	11.2	11.0
38027		9	Eddy................	630.2	2,313	3,018	3.7	91.6	0.9	4.9	0.7	3.8	7.0	16.5	6.3	10.2	10.0	10.4
38029		8	Emmons..............	1,509.7	3,295	2,952	2.2	96.5	0.7	1.8	1.2	1.1	5.2	14.6	7.6	8.0	8.6	11.4
38031		9	Foster...............	635.5	3,216	2,956	5.1	95.5	0.7	1.8	1.1	2.1	6.4	14.8	7.5	10.7	10.2	11.4
38033		9	Golden Valley.........	1,001.5	1,769	3,068	1.8	95.0	1.0	1.8	0.4	2.9	6.0	16.2	5.7	9.0	12.7	10.2
38035	24,220	3	Grand Forks..........	1,436.1	70,770	765	49.3	85.2	5.4	3.5	4.1	4.4	6.6	14.1	20.0	16.3	10.4	8.8
38037		8	Grant................	1,659.2	2,374	3,014	1.4	96.1	0.8	2.8	0.8	1.6	6.2	14.3	5.4	9.1	8.9	10.4
38039		9	Griggs...............	708.8	2,232	3,027	3.1	97.3	0.5	0.8	0.2	1.4	5.2	15.2	6.3	7.8	9.4	10.1
38041		9	Hettinger............	1,132.2	2,514	3,002	2.2	92.7	1.4	4.2	1.2	2.4	7.1	17.1	6.1	12.2	10.1	10.5
38043		8	Kidder...............	1,351.2	2,450	3,009	1.8	94.7	0.4	0.6	0.7	4.0	6.1	15.0	5.7	10.2	10.2	11.0
38045		9	LaMoure..............	1,145.9	4,062	2,896	3.5	97.6	0.6	0.9	0.2	1.5	5.6	15.8	6.1	9.0	9.1	10.3
38047		9	Logan................	992.8	1,903	3,057	1.9	96.3	0.7	1.3	0.9	2.4	6.7	16.3	7.2	8.6	8.8	10.7
38049	33,500	9	McHenry..............	1,874.0	5,816	2,766	3.1	96.3	0.7	1.5	0.5	2.1	6.2	17.8	5.8	10.9	11.5	12.4
38051		9	McIntosh.............	974.7	2,585	2,999	2.7	94.9	0.9	1.2	1.5	2.4	4.7	14.0	6.2	8.7	8.0	10.3
38053		9	McKenzie.............	2,760.5	13,632	2,189	4.9	80.1	2.0	10.8	1.2	8.7	9.9	21.6	8.1	17.6	12.2	10.6
38055		8	McLean...............	2,110.3	9,541	2,459	4.5	90.7	0.7	7.5	0.4	2.5	6.3	15.4	6.1	10.5	10.8	10.8
38057		7	Mercer...............	1,042.7	8,267	2,568	7.9	93.8	1.1	2.8	0.8	3.0	6.3	16.8	6.2	11.1	11.2	11.3
38059	13,900	3	Morton...............	1,926.2	31,095	1,405	16.1	91.3	1.6	4.4	0.9	3.7	7.2	15.9	7.2	15.3	12.9	11.3
38061		9	Mountrail............	1,825.3	10,218	2,408	5.6	62.6	1.5	29.9	0.7	8.1	8.5	18.4	9.1	16.4	12.2	11.2
38063		8	Nelson...............	981.8	2,869	2,978	2.9	94.8	1.4	2.3	0.6	2.7	5.2	14.2	6.1	8.8	9.6	10.4
38065	13,900	3	Oliver................	722.5	1,952	3,053	2.7	94.6	0.9	3.5	0.6	2.0	6.6	18.6	5.2	9.9	10.2	11.4
38067		9	Pembina..............	1,118.7	6,947	2,679	6.2	93.3	1.2	4.5	1.0	3.4	5.7	15.1	6.1	11.6	11.2	10.3
38069		7	Pierce...............	1,018.5	4,081	2,894	4.0	92.7	1.2	5.1	0.2	2.0	5.4	17.0	7.0	9.8	11.2	11.0
38071		7	Ramsey...............	1,186.9	11,481	2,327	9.7	86.0	1.2	12.1	1.2	2.7	7.1	16.6	8.3	11.8	10.4	11.2
38073		8	Ransom...............	862.4	5,237	2,814	6.1	95.5	1.1	1.5	1.3	1.9	6.1	16.4	7.6	9.6	11.3	12.8
38075	33,500	9	Renville..............	877.1	2,374	3,014	2.7	96.2	1.1	1.1	0.8	2.3	6.1	16.6	6.5	10.7	10.5	12.8
38077	47,420	6	Richland.............	1,435.8	16,229	2,026	11.3	92.7	1.5	3.0	1.1	3.4	6.3	15.6	13.7	11.3	10.3	10.2
38079		9	Rolette..............	903.1	14,301	2,144	15.8	20.6	0.8	79.0	0.4	2.0	9.1	24.8	8.6	12.1	11.0	10.6
38081		9	Sargent	858.5	3,870	2,911	4.5	93.0	2.3	2.1	1.1	3.2	5.7	15.0	7.1	11.4	10.9	12.3
38083		9	Sheridan.............	972.4	1,349	3,091	1.4	97.0	0.6	2.4	0.7	1.3	5.6	13.3	5.0	8.5	6.9	11.9
38085	13,900	3	Sioux................	1,094.1	4,358	2,870	4.0	16.3	1.4	80.7	0.7	4.6	10.3	25.4	10.3	13.3	11.3	11.5
38087		9	Slope................	1,214.9	763	3,121	0.6	93.8	1.3	1.7	0.3	3.8	5.6	14.7	6.6	9.0	10.0	10.5
38089	19,860	7	Stark................	1,334.8	30,997	1,408	23.2	88.3	3.7	2.2	2.0	5.5	8.6	18.3	7.6	17.1	12.5	10.3
38091		8	Steele...............	712.2	1,903	3,057	2.7	95.5	0.6	2.1	0.4	2.3	7.1	14.6	7.1	10.0	9.2	10.9
38093	27,420	7	Stutsman.............	2,221.7	20,917	1,778	9.4	93.0	2.0	2.4	1.4	2.7	5.4	14.7	10.6	12.3	11.6	11.4
38095		9	Towner...............	1,024.6	2,192	3,032	2.1	92.3	1.0	5.9	0.5	2.0	5.6	15.6	6.2	8.1	8.4	12.7
38097		8	Traill................	861.9	8,037	2,588	9.3	93.4	1.6	2.1	1.1	3.8	6.2	16.6	8.9	11.5	10.7	12.0
38099		6	Walsh................	1,281.7	10,667	2,383	8.3	85.1	0.9	2.4	1.3	11.6	6.8	15.9	7.1	10.7	10.5	11.9

1. CBSA = Core Based Statistical Area. See Appendix A for explanation. See Appendix B for list of metropolitan areas with component counties. Service of USDA Rural-Urban Continuum Codes. See Appendix A for definition.   2. County type code from the Economic Research   3. Dry land or land partially or temporarily covered by water.   4. May be of any race.

Table B. States and Counties — Population and Households

STATE County	55 to 64 years	65 to 74 years	75 years and over	Percent female	Total persons 2000	Total persons 2010	2000-2010	2010-2018	Births	Deaths	Net Migration	Number	Persons per household	Family households	Female family householder[1]	One person
	16	17	18	19	20	21	22	23	24	25	26	27	28	29	30	31
NORTH CAROLINA—Cont'd																
Swain	13.7	11.2	7.9	51.8	12,968	13,984	7.8	1.9	1,560	1,549	254	5,464	2.55	63.4	11.0	33.4
Transylvania	15.8	16.4	14.1	51.7	29,334	33,091	12.8	3.4	2,192	3,315	2,254	14,125	2.27	68.5	10.1	27.2
Tyrrell	14.1	10.1	9.2	44.5	4,149	4,407	6.2	-6.3	357	368	-275	1,539	2.26	65.7	11.9	32.2
Union	11.9	7.8	4.8	50.8	123,677	201,334	62.8	17.2	19,570	10,926	25,824	73,709	2.98	79.9	10.6	16.3
Vance	13.8	11.0	7.5	53.3	42,954	45,419	5.7	-1.8	4,635	4,134	-1,337	17,029	2.56	62.9	21.1	31.5
Wake	11.4	7.2	4.4	51.3	627,846	901,058	43.5	21.2	104,247	42,154	127,891	381,971	2.62	66.8	11.2	25.9
Warren	16.6	14.8	10.6	50.6	19,972	21,028	5.3	-5.8	1,512	1,998	-725	8,157	2.35	60.3	14.8	35.7
Washington	16.3	14.1	10.3	52.5	13,723	13,209	-3.7	-10.2	1,045	1,276	-1,130	5,223	2.33	57.1	17.6	37.3
Watauga	12.1	9.7	6.1	50.1	42,695	51,057	19.6	9.6	2,979	2,842	4,700	20,331	2.35	53.7	6.8	28.1
Wayne	13.1	9.7	6.8	51.4	113,329	122,673	8.2	0.5	13,793	9,771	-3,435	47,587	2.55	67.1	17.4	28.0
Wilkes	14.9	12.4	9.2	50.8	65,632	69,310	5.6	-1.1	5,592	6,468	187	27,765	2.44	68.2	9.6	28.4
Wilson	13.9	10.7	7.5	52.7	73,814	81,218	10.0	0.3	7,901	6,922	-688	32,068	2.49	66.3	18.9	29.5
Yadkin	14.7	11.3	8.8	50.8	36,348	38,409	5.7	-2.3	3,235	3,419	-658	15,521	2.42	69.2	10.8	28.5
Yancey	14.9	14.7	11.1	50.8	17,774	17,818	0.2	0.5	1,380	1,810	528	7,493	2.33	67.1	9.0	29.3
NORTH DAKOTA	12.5	8.4	6.9	48.8	642,200	672,576	4.7	13.0	87,442	50,698	49,192	311,525	2.31	60.0	7.5	31.1
Adams	16.6	13.6	14.3	50.5	2,593	2,343	-9.6	-2.1	196	238	-9	1,052	2.19	67.1	3.6	26.5
Barnes	15.0	12.0	10.8	49.6	11,775	11,064	-6.0	-4.7	922	1,070	-372	5,113	2.03	59.7	4.4	32.7
Benson	12.1	8.4	5.5	48.9	6,964	6,660	-4.4	4.5	1,277	612	-364	2,292	2.99	71.6	19.1	23.5
Billings	14.6	12.3	10.1	45.5	888	784	-11.7	17.2	108	31	54	401	2.37	72.6	3.0	25.2
Bottineau	15.9	13.9	9.9	48.3	7,149	6,429	-10.1	-0.3	564	652	61	3,096	2.05	61.3	4.6	33.3
Bowman	16.0	10.8	10.6	49.7	3,242	3,151	-2.8	-2.4	340	344	-73	1,432	2.20	64.9	5.1	30.7
Burke	15.9	12.7	8.0	47.9	2,242	1,968	-12.2	6.7	283	182	19	950	2.37	61.8	4.9	34.7
Burleigh	13.0	9.0	7.1	49.9	69,416	81,308	17.1	17.2	10,412	5,720	9,099	38,901	2.29	62.0	9.2	29.9
Cass	10.4	7.0	5.0	49.4	123,138	149,778	21.6	21.2	20,428	8,278	19,352	73,039	2.27	55.9	8.6	31.9
Cavalier	15.3	13.5	13.4	48.9	4,831	3,994	-17.3	-4.1	389	400	-153	1,787	2.08	62.5	3.4	33.7
Dickey	14.4	9.9	10.5	50.3	5,757	5,287	-8.2	-7.3	489	593	-280	2,192	2.18	65.1	4.6	27.4
Divide	16.9	13.4	11.9	47.7	2,283	2,071	-9.3	10.2	211	215	205	1,053	2.16	58.4	4.1	38.9
Dunn	16.6	8.7	7.3	46.8	3,600	3,536	-1.8	22.5	485	281	563	1,601	2.63	71.8	4.6	24.5
Eddy	16.5	11.8	11.2	50.4	2,757	2,385	-13.5	-3.0	234	369	62	1,048	2.12	58.7	8.6	33.6
Emmons	16.8	13.5	14.4	49.3	4,331	3,545	-18.1	-7.1	241	400	-90	1,565	2.13	61.6	3.5	32.7
Foster	16.6	11.1	11.4	50.4	3,759	3,337	-11.2	-3.6	294	339	-76	1,502	2.15	67.0	4.7	29.7
Golden Valley	15.7	12.9	11.5	50.3	1,924	1,680	-12.7	5.3	186	136	34	863	2.09	49.4	3.0	43.0
Grand Forks	10.8	7.3	5.4	48.4	66,109	66,864	1.1	5.8	8,250	3,964	-400	29,716	2.20	54.2	7.3	33.5
Grant	15.7	16.0	13.9	50.1	2,841	2,394	-15.7	-0.8	226	228	-19	1,110	2.11	59.0	2.3	36.2
Griggs	15.9	16.4	13.8	48.5	2,754	2,421	-12.1	-7.8	168	315	-42	1,039	2.10	63.2	2.8	35.7
Hettinger	14.4	10.6	11.9	51.6	2,715	2,478	-8.7	1.5	271	268	34	1,078	2.26	67.9	6.2	29.8
Kidder	17.3	12.7	11.8	48.2	2,753	2,435	-11.6	0.6	226	144	-64	1,053	2.33	74.1	4.1	23.0
LaMoure	17.1	13.0	14.0	48.4	4,701	4,141	-11.9	-1.9	352	355	-73	1,811	2.23	65.2	2.4	31.4
Logan	15.7	12.0	14.0	48.3	2,308	1,988	-13.9	-4.3	169	219	-34	879	2.10	64.4	3.1	29.2
McHenry	15.2	11.1	9.3	48.2	5,987	5,392	-9.9	7.9	565	493	341	2,663	2.21	62.7	5.3	30.6
McIntosh	17.4	12.1	18.5	51.2	3,390	2,813	-17.0	-8.1	200	416	-16	1,325	1.94	62.3	7.1	33.0
McKenzie	10.8	5.6	3.6	46.6	5,737	6,359	10.8	114.4	1,526	508	6,080	3,651	3.14	67.3	9.1	22.6
McLean	16.6	14.0	9.6	49.0	9,311	8,962	-3.7	6.5	954	870	482	4,313	2.19	66.4	5.1	30.3
Mercer	18.0	10.7	8.6	48.4	8,644	8,424	-2.5	-1.9	828	671	-319	3,649	2.33	70.8	5.8	25.6
Morton	13.4	9.1	7.6	49.4	25,303	27,469	8.6	13.2	3,730	2,268	2,115	13,246	2.22	61.8	5.7	27.3
Mountrail	12.6	7.3	4.3	46.3	6,631	7,663	15.6	33.3	1,334	691	1,837	3,213	3.07	67.6	10.8	28.6
Nelson	19.0	13.9	13.0	48.7	3,715	3,129	-15.8	-8.3	247	470	-35	1,492	1.94	57.5	5.0	36.1
Oliver	15.9	14.4	7.7	47.7	2,065	1,848	-10.5	5.6	179	97	20	788	2.31	73.2	2.5	25.0
Pembina	16.9	12.5	10.7	47.2	8,585	7,403	-13.8	-6.2	664	671	-453	3,218	2.13	63.7	6.0	29.8
Pierce	15.0	11.4	12.2	48.8	4,675	4,359	-6.8	-6.4	374	493	-160	1,995	2.05	56.9	8.9	35.4
Ramsey	14.8	10.6	9.3	49.6	12,066	11,451	-5.1	0.3	1,330	1,101	-194	4,931	2.24	57.2	6.7	35.6
Ransom	15.5	10.4	10.3	48.0	5,890	5,457	-7.4	-4.0	503	645	-80	2,333	2.25	62.8	6.0	31.3
Renville	16.6	10.6	9.7	47.7	2,610	2,470	-5.4	-3.9	252	223	-129	1,011	2.46	65.7	7.3	29.6
Richland	14.7	9.4	8.5	48.5	17,998	16,321	-9.3	-0.5	1,502	1,139	-437	6,829	2.21	62.8	5.7	28.5
Rolette	12.1	7.2	4.5	50.2	13,674	13,939	1.9	2.6	2,388	1,216	-810	4,740	3.06	68.3	22.5	27.6
Sargent	15.0	13.0	9.5	46.3	4,366	3,829	-12.3	1.1	321	277	-6	1,819	2.11	62.9	4.1	29.7
Sheridan	16.3	14.2	18.2	49.8	1,710	1,321	-22.7	2.1	107	89	10	684	2.05	64.3	5.3	32.9
Sioux	9.9	4.7	3.4	50.1	4,044	4,154	2.7	4.9	785	394	-189	1,114	3.91	76.7	31.9	18.9
Slope	20.7	13.4	9.6	47.7	767	727	-5.2	5.0	73	27	-10	309	2.18	63.8	4.9	34.6
Stark	11.9	6.9	6.6	48.2	22,636	24,199	6.9	28.1	3,860	1,892	4,641	11,962	2.46	64.0	7.9	30.8
Steele	16.9	13.8	10.4	47.7	2,258	1,975	-12.5	-3.6	188	150	-111	916	2.09	62.8	1.1	35.0
Stutsman	14.9	10.4	8.7	48.6	21,908	21,100	-3.7	-0.9	1,898	1,987	-80	9,199	2.11	57.1	6.9	37.3
Towner	18.3	12.5	12.6	49.5	2,876	2,246	-21.9	-2.4	197	221	-31	1,033	2.16	63.6	7.2	35.1
Traill	14.5	9.8	9.8	49.2	8,477	8,121	-4.2	-1.0	798	765	-121	3,349	2.29	61.8	5.2	34.1
Walsh	15.8	10.9	10.3	48.8	12,389	11,123	-10.2	-4.1	1,153	1,160	-446	4,838	2.17	61.9	6.5	34.6

1. No spouse present.

Table B. States and Counties — Population, Vital Statistics, Health, and Crime

STATE County	Persons in group quarters, 2018	Daytime Population, 2013-2017 Number	Daytime Population, 2013-2017 Employment/ residence ratio	Births, 2018 Total	Births, 2018 Rate[1]	Deaths, 2018 Number	Deaths, 2018 Rate[1]	Persons under 65 with no health insurance, 2016 Number	Persons under 65 with no health insurance, 2016 Percent	Medicare, 2018 Total beneficiaries	Medicare, 2018 Enrolled in Original Medicare	Medicare, 2018 Enrolled in Medicare Advantage	Serious crimes known to police[2], 2016 Total Number	Serious crimes known to police[2], 2016 Total Rate[3]
	32	33	34	35	36	37	38	39	40	41	42	43	44	45
NORTH CAROLINA— Cont'd														
Swain	246	15,052	1.16	158	11.1	227	15.9	2,074	18.1	3,852	3,112	740	225	1,723
Transylvania	1,044	31,845	0.89	257	7.5	392	11.5	3,200	14.0	10,078	7,122	2,956	555	1,669
Tyrrell	628	3,974	0.92	44	10.7	53	12.8	472	17.4	827	655	172	48	1,199
Union	2,664	190,592	0.70	2,396	10.2	1,466	6.2	19,618	9.9	32,109	21,542	10,567	5,027	2,213
Vance	786	44,265	0.99	541	12.1	535	12.0	4,452	12.4	10,401	6,820	3,581	1,813	4,081
Wake	21,803	1,054,191	1.06	12,787	11.7	6,042	5.5	84,547	9.2	138,520	90,205	48,315	NA	NA
Warren	893	17,482	0.62	175	8.8	266	13.4	2,396	16.6	4,623	3,138	1,485	352	1,859
Washington	148	12,212	0.97	126	10.6	159	13.4	1,180	12.7	3,369	2,723	646	NA	NA
Watauga	5,899	56,612	1.13	381	6.8	398	7.1	5,337	13.2	9,090	6,286	2,804	872	1,641
Wayne	2,306	122,564	0.96	1,578	12.8	1,405	11.4	15,016	14.7	23,471	17,817	5,654	4,339	3,570
Wilkes	973	66,058	0.91	652	9.5	815	11.9	8,009	14.9	17,582	9,440	8,142	1,303	1,906
Wilson	1,505	85,526	1.12	936	11.5	938	11.5	8,978	13.6	18,732	14,981	3,751	2,879	3,619
Yadkin	297	33,630	0.73	390	10.4	420	11.2	4,354	14.4	8,724	3,775	4,949	770	2,162
Yancey	157	15,612	0.71	157	8.8	207	11.6	1,896	14.4	5,564	3,774	1,790	125	712
NORTH DAKOTA	25,084	780,992	1.09	10,869	14.3	6,213	8.2	47,683	7.6	127,621	104,277	23,344	19,305	2,547
Adams	53	2,239	0.90	25	10.9	24	10.5	149	8.7	668	587	81	6	260
Barnes	534	10,917	0.99	98	9.3	121	11.5	681	8.3	2,638	2,164	474	260	2,397
Benson	16	6,859	0.99	163	23.4	70	10.1	839	14.5	1,079	993	86	45	681
Billings	9	994	1.02	14	15.2	7	7.6	85	11.2	177	158	19	11	1,157
Bottineau	232	6,385	0.92	60	9.4	88	13.7	482	9.8	1,614	1,575	39	75	1,133
Bowman	56	3,341	1.07	35	11.4	31	10.1	224	8.6	709	635	74	32	985
Burke	2	2,114	0.88	33	15.7	19	9.0	167	9.3	481	D	D	8	343
Burleigh	3,720	95,792	1.07	1,261	13.2	750	7.9	4,671	6.0	16,572	12,569	4,003	2,979	3,196
Cass	5,694	186,275	1.16	2,608	14.4	1,120	6.2	9,179	6.1	24,008	18,575	5,433	5,188	3,016
Cavalier	70	3,719	0.95	57	14.9	52	13.6	248	8.9	1,056	946	110	33	889
Dickey	204	4,927	0.96	60	12.2	64	13.1	355	9.1	1,084	930	154	17	343
Divide	66	2,504	1.11	19	8.3	15	6.6	187	10.2	517	D	D	2	81
Dunn	130	5,036	1.33	62	14.3	22	5.1	466	12.4	698	598	100	43	898
Eddy	81	2,132	0.84	33	14.3	40	17.3	174	9.8	619	532	87	36	1,560
Emmons	56	3,347	0.97	30	9.1	40	12.1	277	11.4	948	705	243	41	1,244
Foster	55	3,522	1.12	38	11.8	34	10.6	186	7.2	739	598	141	14	427
Golden Valley	52	1,837	0.94	25	14.1	8	4.5	112	7.9	398	D	D	3	163
Grand Forks	3,519	73,668	1.09	989	14.0	505	7.1	3,947	6.7	10,256	8,417	1,839	2,278	3,251
Grant	24	2,373	0.99	30	12.6	20	8.4	262	15.3	696	548	148	9	386
Griggs	40	2,265	0.99	21	9.4	35	15.7	148	9.3	687	563	124	13	580
Hettinger	163	2,491	0.91	35	13.9	15	6.0	168	8.9	650	544	106	25	930
Kidder	0	2,264	0.85	26	10.6	19	7.8	191	10.1	615	417	198	22	933
LaMoure	67	3,974	0.93	46	11.3	36	8.9	302	9.8	1,059	811	248	4	99
Logan	53	1,960	1.03	21	11.0	21	11.0	222	15.7	510	385	125	8	426
McHenry	46	4,718	0.58	70	12.0	61	10.5	405	8.4	1,276	1,074	202	50	841
McIntosh	93	2,743	1.05	24	9.3	49	19.0	196	10.8	876	689	187	8	298
McKenzie	148	15,288	1.62	253	18.6	65	4.8	1,111	9.5	1,124	1,105	19	369	2,562
McLean	135	9,610	1.00	118	12.4	102	10.7	689	9.2	2,374	1,996	378	148	1,530
Mercer	121	9,242	1.14	94	11.4	84	10.2	448	6.3	1,723	1,437	286	76	870
Morton	820	25,236	0.72	478	15.4	272	8.7	1,679	6.5	5,701	4,097	1,604	1,002	3,321
Mountrail	540	12,397	1.51	183	17.9	91	8.9	1,188	13.0	1,418	1,403	15	121	1,131
Nelson	79	2,784	0.88	27	9.4	50	17.4	189	9.0	919	832	87	51	1,776
Oliver	2	1,694	0.86	22	11.3	5	2.6	102	6.8	429	336	93	7	388
Pembina	148	7,533	1.14	83	11.9	83	11.9	481	8.9	1,734	1,492	242	98	1,427
Pierce	239	4,338	1.03	39	9.6	48	11.8	306	9.8	1,024	724	300	82	1,951
Ramsey	440	11,793	1.04	159	13.8	120	10.5	759	8.4	2,580	2,391	189	360	3,160
Ransom	155	5,326	0.97	53	10.1	75	14.3	291	6.8	1,229	1,080	149	59	1,108
Renville	54	2,427	0.90	27	11.4	23	9.7	146	7.1	514	D	D	14	553
Richland	973	16,521	1.02	200	12.3	137	8.4	882	6.9	3,112	2,316	796	349	2,176
Rolette	122	14,646	1.00	261	18.3	194	13.6	2,178	17.0	2,112	2,037	75	91	630
Sargent	39	4,948	1.52	39	10.1	36	9.3	238	7.8	911	830	81	19	500
Sheridan	4	1,199	0.66	15	11.1	7	5.2	115	12.2	415	349	66	22	1,720
Sioux	60	4,901	1.37	85	19.5	65	14.9	543	13.6	443	407	36	2	46
Slope	0	620	0.82	12	15.7	1	1.3	47	7.8	160	136	24	1	132
Stark	545	32,005	1.10	502	16.2	230	7.4	1,931	7.1	4,512	3,924	588	593	1,811
Steele	1	1,798	0.89	26	13.7	12	6.3	134	9.1	459	383	76	2	105
Stutsman	1,642	21,499	1.04	218	10.4	242	11.6	1,217	7.6	4,783	3,303	1,480	617	2,994
Towner	34	2,182	0.92	24	10.9	20	9.1	188	11.0	614	582	32	7	314
Traill	312	7,429	0.85	101	12.6	89	11.1	415	6.6	1,650	1,406	244	78	999
Walsh	329	11,137	1.04	143	13.4	125	11.7	852	10.0	2,514	2,152	362	220	2,074

1. Per 1,000 estimated resident population.   2. Data for serious crimes have not been adjusted for underreporting; this may affect comparability between geographic areas and over time.   3. Per 100,000 population estimated by the FBI.

Table B. States and Counties — Crime, Education, Money Income, and Poverty

STATE County	Serious crimes known to police[2], 2016 (cont.)[1] Rate Violent	Property	School enrollment and attainment, 2013-2017 Enrollment[3] Total	Percent private	Attainment[4] (percent) High school graduate or less	Bachelor's degree or more	Local government expenditures,[5] 2014-2015 Total current spending (mil dol)	Current spending per student (dollars)	Money income, 2013-2017 Per capita income[6]	Households Median income (dollars)	Percent with income of less than $50,000	Percent with income of $200,000 or more	Income and poverty, 2017 Median household income (dollars)	Percent below poverty level All persons	Children under 18 years	Children 5 to 17 years in families
	46	47	48	49	50	51	52	53	54	55	56	57	58	59	60	61
NORTH CAROLINA— Cont'd																
Swain	153	1,570	2,982	9.2	52.2	15.0	23.1	10,082	20,918	35,271	65.4	1.8	41,407	15.8	24.0	24.1
Transylvania	120	1,549	6,373	20.9	39.7	29.9	38.6	10,155	26,037	44,559	54.7	2.1	47,587	15.2	24.3	23.7
Tyrrell	200	999	649	0.3	67.3	7.6	8.7	14,581	17,736	32,411	64.7	0.7	35,223	24.4	35.0	35.0
Union	207	2,006	65,144	17.4	35.5	34.0	349.1	8,106	32,754	70,858	34.7	8.7	77,875	9.1	11.6	10.8
Vance	515	3,565	10,262	7.9	59.1	12.1	71.8	9,131	21,188	35,246	65.1	1.6	39,847	23.4	38.0	36.3
Wake	NA	NA	287,671	16.6	23.3	51.0	1,347.6	8,145	37,315	73,577	33.4	9.0	77,641	8.9	11.6	11.2
Warren	180	1,680	3,781	13.3	54.5	15.8	27.9	10,512	21,543	35,443	63.9	1.9	36,831	20.9	33.0	31.9
Washington	NA	NA	2,603	6.5	58.6	9.1	20.6	11,092	21,117	34,557	66.2	1.3	36,171	24.8	40.7	39.0
Watauga	128	1,513	20,932	7.5	31.3	41.7	46.0	9,967	24,545	41,541	57.1	3.8	48,417	20.5	16.8	15.3
Wayne	443	3,127	30,922	14.1	46.5	19.7	160.6	8,104	23,163	41,766	57.4	2.2	44,592	20.3	31.1	29.0
Wilkes	212	1,694	14,304	8.0	53.6	15.4	89.4	8,569	21,798	37,173	61.5	1.9	42,453	18.5	24.7	23.3
Wilson	397	3,222	19,712	13.0	52.3	18.8	110.0	8,109	23,383	42,095	57.1	2.0	44,825	18.1	28.7	26.5
Yadkin	227	1,934	7,661	7.2	55.3	12.0	47.8	8,478	23,038	41,126	59.3	1.7	46,885	13.4	22.0	20.0
Yancey	57	655	3,386	12.6	50.3	19.7	22.5	10,078	21,947	37,610	61.0	1.0	41,053	16.5	25.5	24.2
NORTH DAKOTA	251	2,296	181,666	10.5	34.8	28.9	1,417.6	13,301	34,256	61,285	41.3	5.2	62,400	10.2	11.4	10.4
Adams	43	217	464	15.5	38.1	27.4	4.0	13,132	35,933	54,700	47.4	7.3	50,847	9.5	12.6	11.8
Barnes	129	2,268	2,309	5.9	39.0	25.8	19.9	14,199	32,517	56,237	46.1	3.8	56,696	10.7	12.0	10.4
Benson	45	635	1,948	0.9	46.2	15.4	17.6	16,146	21,658	44,500	54.6	3.4	41,941	28.4	39.5	36.7
Billings	105	1,052	173	0.0	44.0	23.1	2.3	24,316	44,683	91,518	31.9	11.2	74,312	9.2	11.3	12.7
Bottineau	60	1,073	1,352	8.9	38.8	21.9	14.3	16,233	35,698	58,767	41.4	4.9	55,775	10	12.2	10.6
Bowman	154	831	537	8.8	40.7	24.5	8.8	14,434	36,318	65,435	37.4	5.6	59,451	8.4	9.9	9.2
Burke	0	343	502	6.8	38.3	20.1	6.4	17,388	35,674	71,667	36.3	6.7	62,629	9.1	11.3	11.6
Burleigh	254	2,942	21,211	23.0	29.7	35.1	147.8	11,744	36,483	67,308	37.2	6.0	70,075	7.3	7.4	6.4
Cass	322	2,694	48,064	9.7	25.8	38.3	281.5	12,303	34,193	58,026	42.9	5.9	64,428	8.6	8.5	7.9
Cavalier	81	809	661	4.1	37.9	18.8	7.2	16,096	43,144	65,505	38.5	6.5	59,794	9.6	12.5	11.9
Dickey	40	303	1,135	15.8	38.9	27.6	9.5	11,590	30,510	58,357	42.1	3.6	53,564	10.5	13.3	12.1
Divide	0	81	342	0.0	50.2	19.4	5.0	13,975	39,171	54,223	44.6	11.0	55,867	10	13.3	12.8
Dunn	104	793	959	12.6	41.1	23.0	9.8	18,289	42,438	68,594	34.7	9.7	67,337	10.5	13.4	12.7
Eddy	303	1,257	428	1.9	42.2	23.3	6.0	17,997	35,444	55,294	46.3	4.7	49,725	10.6	12.8	11.8
Emmons	91	1,153	597	4.0	50.7	15.5	8.7	16,147	29,622	46,581	52.5	3.4	46,681	13.9	17.5	15.7
Foster	0	427	619	3.4	38.8	23.7	6.3	12,180	32,665	59,500	43.1	3.1	58,752	8	8.8	8.5
Golden Valley	54	109	369	11.4	37.6	22.0	5.7	18,523	28,840	44,018	53.2	4.2	63,054	10.6	15.0	14.5
Grand Forks	270	2,982	22,084	5.2	29.1	34.0	112.2	12,641	30,465	51,410	48.5	3.6	50,933	14.8	12.0	10.3
Grant	86	300	439	6.6	47.4	18.2	4.1	18,368	33,537	50,875	49.4	5.7	48,189	15.3	25.1	23.2
Griggs	0	580	369	1.1	41.0	22.6	6.4	16,209	33,416	50,272	49.8	4.4	51,823	8.7	11.6	10.9
Hettinger	74	855	452	15.5	48.4	14.5	7.5	15,428	32,544	56,118	44.1	4.8	51,827	11.8	14.6	13.3
Kidder	0	933	441	5.7	45.6	19.2	5.4	14,584	34,455	60,225	41.3	6.6	46,708	13.1	16.9	16.3
LaMoure	50	50	797	16.1	44.0	23.2	12.8	16,535	36,653	57,463	42.9	6.2	57,808	10.3	12.8	11.5
Logan	53	373	321	3.1	54.5	13.7	5.6	15,681	31,952	57,379	42.3	4.1	46,948	13.1	17.6	16.9
McHenry	50	790	1,167	5.7	44.4	19.6	14.3	14,702	36,874	61,788	40.6	4.9	53,060	11.1	12.3	10.7
McIntosh	0	298	399	1.3	50.7	17.2	6.2	16,424	31,133	46,012	54.0	3.0	43,804	12	17.1	16.3
McKenzie	312	2,250	2,680	14.8	39.7	25.3	27.1	15,077	38,324	79,316	25.1	10.6	75,408	8.5	11.3	9.9
McLean	124	1,406	1,868	5.5	44.1	18.7	23.3	13,799	36,953	63,926	38.7	4.3	61,121	9.1	12.3	11.4
Mercer	172	698	1,835	6.9	35.8	22.7	16.8	12,931	36,720	80,337	33.6	4.6	82,991	6.2	6.2	5.6
Morton	199	3,122	5,880	12.5	38.3	26.1	56.6	12,436	37,335	65,385	38.0	4.2	63,279	8.3	10.6	10.4
Mountrail	75	1,056	2,531	2.4	39.1	21.7	24.7	13,795	40,113	69,622	37.1	10.7	64,247	9.7	13.4	12.5
Nelson	139	1,637	485	7.2	39.4	20.5	7.5	17,025	33,599	52,417	48.1	5.1	47,708	10.9	13.8	12.4
Oliver	0	388	359	17.0	39.4	19.6	3.7	17,370	38,604	71,500	33.9	3.7	68,151	9.4	13.9	13.0
Pembina	44	1,383	1,334	10.9	45.2	20.2	15.4	15,437	34,824	61,393	40.9	4.8	56,164	8.3	11.5	10.6
Pierce	190	1,760	716	7.0	43.2	15.8	8.4	13,817	26,619	45,996	52.5	3.0	48,380	11.8	15.1	13.0
Ramsey	97	3,063	2,568	6.3	38.1	24.7	28.8	16,021	33,884	55,927	45.4	3.7	56,464	12.3	16.2	14.6
Ransom	150	958	1,131	7.0	47.7	19.1	11.1	11,396	33,574	62,524	38.4	3.9	62,465	7.6	9.9	9.1
Renville	79	474	532	2.8	40.4	16.2	8.7	13,878	30,888	66,023	35.8	3.8	60,178	7.9	8.3	7.6
Richland	118	2,058	4,264	6.1	37.8	22.2	35.1	15,314	29,818	60,551	42.1	2.0	61,361	10	10.3	9.3
Rolette	55	575	3,833	1.5	37.4	20.7	43.9	14,798	18,075	36,170	61.1	2.0	40,777	27.1	32.2	27.8
Sargent	132	368	697	2.3	41.9	18.6	9.6	15,291	36,207	60,824	39.5	4.6	62,940	7.7	11.4	10.9
Sheridan	78	1,642	182	8.2	48.6	14.1	2.3	21,990	34,172	49,750	50.4	5.0	40,786	16.3	25.3	23.1
Sioux	0	46	1,479	9.1	45.7	17.3	10.0	22,365	15,944	40,795	58.0	2.3	34,705	35.9	42.7	35.1
Slope	0	132	103	7.8	37.8	26.8	0.6	19,241	35,118	61,250	39.8	3.2	55,326	12.1	17.4	17.0
Stark	116	1,695	6,760	13.6	41.3	23.8	49.7	11,611	37,978	77,328	33.1	7.1	66,925	9	8.4	8.0
Steele	52	52	323	2.5	34.6	25.6	4.3	20,479	40,479	65,437	32.8	4.9	66,210	7.8	12.1	12.2
Stutsman	340	2,654	4,497	24.9	44.4	24.0	37.5	14,208	31,182	56,088	42.6	3.1	57,265	9.7	12.2	10.9
Towner	0	314	446	5.2	41.3	18.1	3.5	11,693	36,099	54,625	45.6	5.6	51,382	10.1	15.0	13.9
Traill	51	948	1,984	6.0	34.4	26.1	19.8	14,540	31,774	60,225	40.9	3.5	63,204	7.7	8.6	7.9
Walsh	189	1,886	2,186	5.5	47.6	16.8	28.7	15,664	30,693	50,781	49.3	3.5	50,807	10.3	13.4	12.5

1. Data for serious crimes have not been adjusted for underreporting; this may affect comparability between geographic areas and over time. 2. Per 100,000 population estimated by the FBI. 3. All persons 3 years old and over enrolled in nursery school through college. 4. Persons 25 years old and over. 5. Elementary and secondary education expenditures. 6. Based on population estimated by the American Community Survey, 2013–2017.

Table B. States and Counties — Personal Income and Earnings

STATE County	Personal income, 2017										Earnings, 2017		
	Total (mil dol)	Percent change 2016-2017	Per capita[1] Dollars	Rank	Wages and salaries (mil dol)	Supplements to wages and salaries, employer contributions (mil dol) Pension and insurance	Government social insurance	Proprietors' income (mil dol)	Dividends, interest, and rent (mil dol)	Personal transfer receipts (mil dol)	Total (mil dol)	Contributions for government social insurance (mil dol) From employee and self-employed	From employer
	62	63	64	65	66	67	68	69	70	71	72	73	74
NORTH CAROLINA—Cont'd													
Swain	530	4.1	37,110	2,011	252	40	19	32	92	161	344	24	19
Transylvania	1,367	4.8	40,264	1,509	353	57	27	121	399	383	558	44	27
Tyrrell	125	1.9	30,876	2,859	41	9	3	10	20	39	64	4	3
Union	11,487	6.2	49,648	487	3,059	454	225	755	1,754	1,414	4,492	287	225
Vance	1,515	3.0	34,271	2,451	565	95	42	79	275	526	781	58	42
Wake	60,217	5.2	56,162	244	34,224	4,346	2,411	4,273	11,524	6,093	45,255	2,719	2,411
Warren	586	2.4	29,453	2,957	112	25	8	22	100	216	167	15	8
Washington	422	3.2	35,133	2,328	108	21	9	10	72	167	148	13	9
Watauga	1,959	5.6	35,542	2,267	925	164	67	194	507	381	1,350	85	67
Wayne	4,610	4.0	37,126	2,009	1,954	391	154	301	824	1,217	2,798	170	154
Wilkes	2,451	4.8	35,736	2,240	891	157	64	177	467	770	1,289	94	64
Wilson	3,210	3.6	39,301	1,672	1,747	273	127	220	531	893	2,367	155	127
Yadkin	1,369	4.4	36,233	2,165	381	62	28	87	203	384	559	42	28
Yancey	611	4.0	34,449	2,419	137	25	11	46	119	211	218	19	11
NORTH DAKOTA	39,484	-0.7	52,284	X	22,133	3,571	1,960	2,995	9,063	5,642	30,659	1,841	1,960
Adams	131	12.6	56,404	237	41	7	4	29	24	26	81	4	4
Barnes	522	-9.0	48,674	573	190	36	18	38	148	111	282	18	18
Benson	209	-5.5	30,142	2,918	83	20	7	0	46	68	110	7	7
Billings	63	0.5	67,237	83	20	4	2	6	25	5	32	2	2
Bottineau	325	0.3	49,720	477	110	22	10	13	94	66	156	11	10
Bowman	172	-3.5	54,364	302	67	11	6	18	49	27	102	6	6
Burke	135	-0.8	63,237	125	39	9	3	10	39	18	61	4	3
Burleigh	5,460	1.5	57,452	212	2,992	460	255	424	1,173	693	4,130	249	255
Cass	9,635	1.6	54,196	306	6,026	903	504	775	2,267	1,041	8,208	487	504
Cavalier	217	-6.6	57,615	209	67	12	6	42	61	40	126	7	6
Dickey	231	-9.3	47,457	667	75	13	7	7	80	53	102	7	7
Divide	96	-18.0	41,783	1,290	45	8	4	-9	41	21	48	4	4
Dunn	228	-4.9	53,267	336	144	23	13	22	62	28	201	12	13
Eddy	113	1.6	48,703	565	28	5	3	11	25	28	47	3	3
Emmons	138	-16.4	41,663	1,307	36	8	3	15	40	36	62	5	3
Foster	179	-13.9	54,870	287	77	12	7	43	39	30	139	8	7
Golden Valley	69	-11.5	38,766	1,762	26	5	2	5	26	13	38	3	2
Grand Forks	3,510	2.6	49,577	494	2,025	375	178	270	759	484	2,848	164	178
Grant	83	-15.7	34,818	2,370	22	4	2	5	24	26	34	3	2
Griggs	115	-11.5	51,105	410	36	7	3	19	33	27	65	4	3
Hettinger	107	8.0	42,991	1,143	36	7	3		33	25	45	4	3
Kidder	106	-3.6	42,882	1,152	26	5	2	14	28	24	47	3	2
LaMoure	163	-26.0	39,972	1,556	58	12	5	-12	67	39	63	6	5
Logan	100	-4.6	52,234	369	21	4	2	26	28	21	54	3	2
McHenry	269	-3.9	45,582	840	61	12	6	30	49	53	108	7	6
McIntosh	141	5.0	54,121	309	40	8	4	27	36	37	79	5	4
McKenzie	711	1.9	55,843	253	680	92	60	56	193	56	887	51	60
McLean	455	-8.1	46,987	714	208	41	18	1	119	97	269	19	18
Mercer	495	-0.9	58,454	194	375	73	37	15	88	72	501	29	37
Morton	1,546	-0.3	50,216	447	583	102	57	82	273	246	824	55	57
Mountrail	517	-4.4	50,331	443	376	57	34	6	161	68	472	30	34
Nelson	168	1.2	57,077	221	36	7	3	26	43	43	72	4	3
Oliver	91	2.4	46,781	729	54	11	5	6	20	15	76	4	5
Pembina	341	-1.6	48,913	545	171	30	16	8	104	67	225	15	16
Pierce	179	2.2	43,745	1,047	78	14	7	19	38	43	117	8	7
Ramsey	527	-3.3	45,791	820	243	44	22	40	126	115	349	22	22
Ransom	259	-2.2	48,808	557	87	16	8	25	58	57	137	9	8
Renville	119	-15.5	48,186	609	33	6	3	1	33	24	44	3	3
Richland	785	-1.4	48,024	624	335	59	30	86	191	130	510	30	30
Rolette	490	-0.4	33,731	2,524	177	50	15	35	78	164	278	16	15
Sargent	218	-8.3	56,426	236	133	28	12	41	62	33	214	11	12
Sheridan	38	-29.2	27,861	3,033	8	2	1	-5	14	15	6	1	1
Sioux	119	-5.4	27,185	3,056	70	19	6	8	21	44	103	6	6
Slope	23	-41.4	30,462	2,888	9	2	1	-3	12	6	8	1	1
Stark	1,786	-4.1	59,106	181	1,144	160	104	139	330	199	1,547	93	104
Steele	111	-12.0	57,998	205	34	6	3	21	36	15	64	3	3
Stutsman	1,041	-3.3	49,366	503	482	85	42	101	235	195	710	43	42
Towner	99	-3.4	43,767	1,045	28	6	2	7	31	26	43	3	2
Traill	384	-2.0	47,890	632	152	28	14	32	93	74	225	14	14
Walsh	489	0.8	45,094	889	201	37	19	35	127	109	293	18	19

1. Based on the resident population estimated as of July 1 of the year shown.

Table B. States and Counties — Earnings, Social Security, and Housing

| | Earnings, 2017 (cont.) | | | | | | | | | Social Security beneficiaries, December 2017 | | | Housing units, 2018 | |
| | Percent by selected industries | | | | | | | | | | | | | |
STATE County	Farm	Mining, quarrying, and extractions	Construction	Manu-facturing	Information; professional, scientific, technical services	Retail trade	Finance, insurance, real estate, and leasing	Health care and social assistance	Govern-ment	Number	Rate[1]	Supple-mental Security Income recipients, 2017	Total	Percent change, 2010-2018
	75	76	77	78	79	80	81	82	83	84	85	86	87	88
NORTH CAROLINA— Cont'd														
Swain	0.1	0.1	D	7.1	1.5	5.5	1.9	D	45.1	4,310	302	336	9,065	3.9
Transylvania	3.3	0.1	11.1	7.6	7.5	8	6.8	14	14.8	10,375	306	621	19,723	2.9
Tyrrell	9.9	0.5	5.3	8.1	D	6.7	D	D	37.3	910	225	131	2,092	1.2
Union	2.1	D	16.3	18.5	6.9	6.9	3.8	4.7	13	33,765	146	2,373	82,557	13.3
Vance	0.9	D	3.9	12.4	4.6	9.7	5.5	14	17.7	11,470	259	2,307	20,160	0.4
Wake	0.1	0.1	7	7.4	21.6	5.6	8.4	9.9	13.4	139,310	130	11,984	441,817	18.8
Warren	6.4	0	4	10.7	D	6.3	2.9	D	40.3	4,915	247	888	12,022	1.7
Washington	-0.3	0.1	2.9	14.6	D	7.3	3.9	12.1	26.8	3,655	304	684	6,458	-0.4
Watauga	0.7	0.2	6.4	1.8	5.2	9.2	6.9	15.9	28.1	9,365	170	607	34,016	5.9
Wayne	4.8	D	4.6	11.4	2.9	7	4.5	12.1	32.7	26,070	210	4,236	54,474	2.8
Wilkes	2.8	D	5.4	18.4	D	7.3	4.8	7.4	18.5	19,570	285	1,937	33,649	1.7
Wilson	2.3	D	9	22.7	6.2	6.4	7.2	9.3	12.3	20,845	255	3,008	36,323	2.3
Yadkin	4.7	0	11.2	25.4	4.8	5.2	3.1	D	14.7	9,510	252	790	17,411	0.4
Yancey	5.3	D	13	8.9	3.9	9.2	2.7	D	23.6	5,955	336	593	11,259	1.9
NORTH DAKOTA	0.2	7.3	9	5.6	6.7	6.3	8.2	12.6	18.3	130,831	173	8,453	377,649	18.9
Adams	24.7	D	4.9	1.9	2.8	6.9	3.9	24.4	8.9	660	285	15	1,435	4.2
Barnes	4.1	D	10.5	9.9	4.6	6.4	4.4	D	22.4	2,730	254	122	6,028	5.7
Benson	-5.9	0	D	D	D	1.3	D	1.9	73.4	1,230	177	164	3,037	2.9
Billings	-5	D	D	D	D	3.4	D	0.8	32	160	170	0	570	17.5
Bottineau	-8.7	14.4	8.3	4	4.4	7	8.6	D	25.2	1,650	253	45	4,506	3.8
Bowman	6.7	4.2	12.2	1	4.1	7.2	D	12	14.4	715	226	27	1,772	5.3
Burke	5.1	D	1.9	0.2	D	4.5	D	0.9	35.7	490	230	12	1,452	8.4
Burleigh	0.3	0.8	7.5	2.1	8.6	7.5	7.6	20	21.1	16,860	177	866	43,152	20.7
Cass	-0.1	0	9	7.1	10.8	6.7	12.5	15.5	12.7	24,275	137	2,083	83,894	23.5
Cavalier	20	D	7.8	0.4	D	5.3	D	7.6	12.7	1,080	287	20	2,372	2.7
Dickey	-4	0.1	4.7	9.7	D	7.6	D	D	15.8	1,120	230	68	2,681	1.7
Divide	-28.6	D	D	D	D	6.2	4.4	D	28.3	530	232	21	1,521	14.9
Dunn	0.6	32.9	D	D	D	2.6	D	2.2	9.9	680	159	23	2,497	17.1
Eddy	7.3	D	9.3	D	D	4.6	D	19.3	18.7	615	266	42	1,371	3.6
Emmons	-0.3	0.1	D	D	D	7.4	D	D	21.8	1,005	304	37	2,155	3.5
Foster	4.2	0.3	7.2	D	D	6.2	6	11.9	10.5	775	238	32	1,838	2.2
Golden Valley	-25.5	D	D	D	D	7.3	7	17.8	22.1	375	210	9	1,049	8.5
Grand Forks	0.6	0.5	8.1	5.7	5.4	8.4	6.6	16.7	28.2	10,565	149	756	33,390	13.8
Grant	-8.8	0.1	6.3	3.3	D	4	7.1	20.8	22.6	680	286	27	1,740	3.1
Griggs	5.5	0.2	6.1	9.6	D	6.1	D	10.2	14.3	680	301	22	1,471	0.6
Hettinger	-13.1	0.1	11.8	3.4	D	5.2	8.3	8.1	24.7	665	268	22	1,433	1.3
Kidder	14.4	D	D	D	D	6.1	D	3.5	17.9	630	254	22	1,723	2.9
LaMoure	-34.8	0.1	8	5.6	D	3.5	D	D	32.8	1,030	252	59	2,271	1.5
Logan	33.9	0.1	8.7	D	D	3.3	D	8.4	14.9	520	271	24	1,159	1.4
McHenry	4	D	D	D	3	3.5	7.3	3.9	19.3	1,310	222	42	3,184	8.1
McIntosh	21	0.1	6.7	2.3	D	5.4	5.4	18.4	12.5	910	349	21	1,861	0.1
McKenzie	-0.6	19.2	15.4	0	4.3	2.2	7.9	D	16.8	1,145	90	56	6,846	121.6
McLean	-9.4	D	8.4	2.2	D	2.8	6.4	6.1	19.1	2,550	263	93	6,262	12
Mercer	-0.4	15.2	22.5	0.1	2.6	2.8	D	D	6.2	1,900	224	48	4,779	7.4
Morton	-2.8	1.2	13	11.3	10.2	7	7.2	8.9	13.2	5,795	188	290	15,280	26.5
Mountrail	-6.7	D	D	D	7.2	4.1	3.8	3	11.4	1,455	142	72	5,070	23.1
Nelson	24	0.1	8	0.8	D	2.5	D	13.7	17.6	965	329	33	1,960	1.6
Oliver	8.1	D	5.4	1.4	D	0.1	D	D	7.4	455	235	0	961	6.1
Pembina	-4.6	0.6	12.7	19.3	D	4.9	D	5.6	26.7	1,825	262	59	3,898	1.1
Pierce	-5.6	D	14.1	5.7	2.8	6.7	D	D	13.3	1,080	263	33	2,254	2.5
Ramsey	0.2	D	7.6	3.6	4.8	10.3	9.1	D	25	2,685	233	212	5,891	4.9
Ransom	1.4	D	5.7	11.9	D	6.8	7.2	11.9	19.9	1,250	236	45	2,701	1.7
Renville	-9.6	6.3	D	D	5.5	10.7	D	9.5	29.9	550	223	12	1,436	3.6
Richland	6.5	D	7.1	24.1	4.1	6	6	6.2	20.7	3,230	198	163	7,788	3.8
Rolette	4	D	5.2	D	0.7	6.1	D	D	64.2	2,320	160	799	5,583	3.9
Sargent	15.2	D	D	D	D	2.1	D	1.3	7.4	955	248	28	2,162	7.9
Sheridan	-143.2	0.5	29.8	D	D	D	D	D	75.6	415	307	22	923	3.2
Sioux	3.1	0	D	-0.1	D	D	D	D	85.1	520	119	187	1,353	3.1
Slope	-75.1	88.8	D	0.6	3	D	1.5	1.6	16.4	155	201	0	450	3.2
Stark	-1.9	22.8	9.9	7.6	4.9	6.1	5.1	7.3	10.1	4,595	152	224	14,727	37.2
Steele	26.5	0.1	13.3	8.3	D	4.9	D	D	10.4	470	245	0	1,210	3.3
Stutsman	4.5	0	5.4	13.3	4.8	7.4	7.8	12.3	18	4,840	230	364	10,276	4.2
Towner	-3.8	0.1	D	D	D	3.8	D	D	19.3	655	291	18	1,456	0.5
Traill	2.1	D	6.3	12.6	2.7	4.1	6.8	D	19.8	1,690	211	51	3,855	2
Walsh	5.9	D	5.7	9.3	4.6	5	6.6	D	22.1	2,625	242	110	5,609	2

1. Per 1,000 resident population estimated as of July 1 of the year shown.

Table B. States and Counties — Housing, Labor Force, and Employment

	Housing units, 2013-2017								Civilian labor force, 2018				Civilian employment[6], 2013-2017		
	Occupied units										Unemployment			Percent	
			Owner-occupied			Renter-occupied									
STATE County	Total	Percent	Median value[1]	Median owner cost as a percent of income		Median rent[3]	Median rent as a percent of income[2]	Sub-standard units[4] (percent)	Total	Percent change, 2017-2018	Total	Rate[5]	Total	Management, business, science, and arts	Construction, production, and maintenance occupations
				With a mort-gage	Without a mort-gage[2]										
	89	90	91	92	93	94	95	96	97	98	99	100	101	102	103
NORTH CAROLINA—Cont'd															
Swain	5,464	71.8	122,300	23.6	10.0	613	26.4	3.5	6,912	0.9	299	4.3	5,578	27.9	22.1
Transylvania	14,125	75.9	202,100	20.5	10.0	680	31.8	2.3	14,275	0.4	538	3.8	13,342	29.9	23.7
Tyrrell	1,539	75.6	113,100	25.3	20.1	756	22	2.2	1,457	-2.5	92	6.3	1,555	16.8	30.1
Union	73,709	80.5	215,200	20.7	10.1	956	28.7	2.6	121,250	1.7	4,151	3.4	106,916	39.3	21.5
Vance	17,029	58.6	95,500	24.0	12.6	652	30.5	3.1	17,444	-2.5	1,003	5.7	18,129	22.4	33.7
Wake	381,971	64.1	250,700	19.2	10.0	1,043	27.7	2.7	584,548	1.9	19,586	3.4	536,376	50.1	12.7
Warren	8,157	72.0	93,900	25.9	14.4	604	27.8	1.3	6,574	-3.7	391	5.9	7,346	28.6	27.1
Washington	5,223	60.6	86,000	22.5	14.7	619	39.8	2.8	4,628	-3	275	5.9	4,548	15.8	37.6
Watauga	20,331	58.9	240,700	22.6	10.3	822	42.1	2.3	28,832	0.9	1,000	3.5	24,564	36.3	14.3
Wayne	47,587	60.9	117,000	20.1	11.9	743	30	2.7	52,731	-1.3	2,271	4.3	51,308	29.1	30.2
Wilkes	27,765	74.5	123,700	21.2	12.0	611	29.9	2.2	30,230	-2.3	1,128	3.7	28,169	27.2	32.8
Wilson	32,068	60.5	119,200	21.9	13.2	735	30.7	3	35,342	-1.8	2,167	6.1	35,115	30.6	29.1
Yadkin	15,521	75.9	127,300	21.2	10.4	600	28.3	3.8	17,791	0.5	600	3.4	15,725	27.1	36.3
Yancey	7,493	73.3	139,800	23.2	10.3	599	32.2	1.9	8,245	11	295	3.6	7,013	31.3	29.7
NORTH DAKOTA	311,525	63.3	174,100	18.4	10.0	775	24.9	2.3	404,299	-1.5	10,544	2.6	400,454	36.1	25.1
Adams	1,052	73.1	144,900	14.3	10.9	491	17.1	0.7	1,065	-4.5	22	2.1	1,275	44.6	29.6
Barnes	5,113	67.0	117,200	17.4	10.0	675	20.6	0.6	5,279	-2.6	142	2.7	5,780	35.1	28.3
Benson	2,292	62.8	68,900	15.1	10.0	444	21.5	9.8	2,300	-3.7	89	3.9	2,432	36.5	25.0
Billings	401	73.8	185,300	17.7	10.0	856	11.3	1	428	-2.5	12	2.8	498	34.9	34.1
Bottineau	3,096	75.7	140,500	19.0	10.0	693	19.5	1	2,992	-3.8	100	3.3	3,283	36.8	24.6
Bowman	1,432	74.2	149,600	16.2	10.0	607	20.5	2.2	1,647	-6	31	1.9	1,796	36.7	29.8
Burke	950	74.4	115,300	13.6	10.0	704	19.4	2	1,078	-1.1	26	2.4	1,129	35.2	34.5
Burleigh	38,901	68.9	237,000	19.0	10.0	822	26.3	2.5	49,251	-2.4	1,297	2.6	51,229	39.6	21.1
Cass	73,039	52.2	198,100	19.2	10.0	770	25.9	1.7	100,944	-0.9	2,315	2.3	99,839	38.7	20.5
Cavalier	1,787	82.0	95,500	16.6	10.0	548	25.7	0.8	1,971	-4.1	51	2.6	1,927	39.4	29.1
Dickey	2,192	70.1	110,400	15.6	10.0	608	20.8	1.9	2,390	-4.6	43	1.8	2,658	32.8	27.1
Divide	1,053	77.7	150,800	14.0	10.4	823	19.7	0	1,536	-2.9	20	1.3	1,201	36.0	31.9
Dunn	1,601	77.9	168,800	15.8	10.0	887	19.7	3	3,021	-4.5	49	1.6	2,080	34.5	34.4
Eddy	1,048	70.8	74,200	14.3	10.0	473	27.7	0.8	1,246	-1.8	61	4.9	1,180	39.6	27.7
Emmons	1,565	84.5	92,200	15.8	12.5	420	23.2	1	1,481	-4.4	71	4.8	1,528	41.4	20.7
Foster	1,502	74.3	125,600	18.0	10.0	536	22.6	2	1,605	-3.1	42	2.6	1,769	37.4	27.4
Golden Valley	863	67.2	119,900	18.7	10.0	638	24.9	1.3	898	-3.6	18	2	1,012	31.7	26.7
Grand Forks	29,716	49.1	181,600	18.9	10.0	796	30.3	2.6	37,913	-2.6	859	2.3	38,387	35.5	20.0
Grant	1,110	84.9	79,800	20.0	10.0	525	27.1	2.9	1,211	-5.2	32	2.6	1,158	49.6	24.0
Griggs	1,039	71.5	91,800	16.9	10.0	405	20.2	0.5	1,060	-5.6	24	2.3	1,180	35.6	28.3
Hettinger	1,078	82.3	108,200	14.4	10.0	583	34.5	2.4	1,395	-5.4	28	2	1,181	36.2	26.0
Kidder	1,053	76.0	104,400	15.9	10.0	504	18.3	2.8	1,310	-3.8	58	4.4	1,276	37.6	25.2
LaMoure	1,811	77.2	91,100	15.3	10.0	567	21.3	0.4	2,126	-6.2	41	1.9	2,019	40.0	29.2
Logan	879	85.2	79,000	15.5	10.0	610	19.8	2.5	896	-5.3	23	2.6	1,030	39.7	28.2
McHenry	2,663	83.8	116,700	17.9	10.0	522	20	0.4	3,155	-4.1	123	3.9	3,005	34.6	32.9
McIntosh	1,325	78.4	72,300	17.7	10.0	530	24.1	0.7	1,157	-5.5	31	2.7	1,364	37.8	25.8
McKenzie	3,651	58.4	213,600	13.3	10.0	1,037	18.5	6.7	8,962	10	150	1.7	5,984	33.6	35.2
McLean	4,313	81.2	159,300	17.3	10.0	595	20.3	1.9	4,795	-4.2	160	3.3	4,670	34.1	33.3
Mercer	3,649	82.2	166,200	15.5	10.0	692	21.3	2.4	3,969	-10.6	167	4.2	4,474	27.4	35.4
Morton	13,246	72.5	187,600	19.4	10.0	839	24.4	1.5	16,169	-2.7	528	3.3	17,262	33.9	27.9
Mountrail	3,213	69.7	169,800	17.9	10.0	718	16.9	4.6	7,078	1.1	112	1.6	4,807	32.5	28.9
Nelson	1,492	75.5	78,700	17.2	10.0	488	17	2.5	1,425	-4.2	48	3.4	1,550	35.4	28.6
Oliver	788	87.1	171,800	18.1	10.0	573	20.2	1.4	873	-4.3	36	4.1	910	40.2	31.5
Pembina	3,218	77.1	85,500	14.9	10.0	563	18.4	1.1	3,375	-4.1	133	3.9	3,519	32.7	30.0
Pierce	1,995	71.9	110,400	19.1	11.5	644	26.2	2.4	1,794	-4.6	57	3.2	2,003	41.9	20.7
Ramsey	4,931	60.6	130,400	16.0	10.0	546	22.2	2.6	5,649	-3.6	161	2.9	6,141	33.8	18.3
Ransom	2,333	69.8	120,600	17.8	10.0	581	19.8	0.5	2,840	1	55	1.9	2,794	31.4	35.7
Renville	1,011	79.3	125,900	18.0	10.0	661	21.5	1.8	1,227	-3.3	30	2.4	1,212	35.3	30.4
Richland	6,829	71.0	116,000	16.9	10.0	560	23.8	1.5	8,730	-0.9	230	2.6	8,842	33.9	32.5
Rolette	4,740	69.0	73,700	17.1	10.0	356	23.4	6.1	4,691	-2.8	442	9.4	5,112	38.3	22.2
Sargent	1,819	74.4	96,400	16.1	10.0	604	17.8	2.1	2,538	6.6	48	1.9	2,124	30.2	42.6
Sheridan	684	78.5	84,900	18.5	10.0	330	25	1.8	687	-6.1	32	4.7	610	39.2	28.2
Sioux	1,114	44.2	76,300	16.7	10.0	486	14.5	14.5	1,250	-3.3	51	4.1	1,332	40.4	10.4
Slope	309	79.6	89,300	14.1	10.0	663	16	0	399	-6.6	9	2.3	307	52.8	22.5
Stark	11,962	66.5	228,200	17.8	10.0	926	23.3	3.6	18,051	0.4	440	2.4	16,457	31.8	31.3
Steele	916	84.6	72,000	12.7	10.0	545	14.3	0.9	1,001	-5.1	20	2	1,056	38.8	28.6
Stutsman	9,199	65.0	130,900	18.2	10.0	673	23.4	0.6	10,536	-3.8	264	2.5	11,038	36.7	23.3
Towner	1,033	78.7	73,000	16.6	10.0	520	24.8	3	1,196	-3.9	31	2.6	993	41.0	20.9
Traill	3,349	73.5	127,200	17.7	10.0	575	23.6	0.9	4,444	-3.1	117	2.6	4,187	35.8	30.3
Walsh	4,838	74.7	83,700	17.7	10.0	613	23.7	1.4	5,328	-4.5	168	3.2	5,545	30.9	35.3

1. Specified owner-occupied units. 2. A value of 10.0 represents 10 percent or less; a value of 50.0 represents 50 percent or more. 3. Specified renter-occupied units. 4. Overcrowded or lacking complete plumbing facilities. 5. Percent of civilian labor force. 6. Civilian employed persons 16 years old and over.

Table B. States and Counties — **Nonfarm Employment and Agriculture**

STATE County	Private nonfarm establishments, employment and payroll, 2016									Agriculture, 2017			
		Employment						Annual payroll		Farms			Farm producers whose primary occupation is farming (percent)
											Percent with:		
	Number of establishments	Total	Health care and social assistance	Manufacturing	Retail trade	Finance and insurance	Professional, scientific, and technical services	Total (mil dol)	Average per employee (dollars)	Number	Fewer than 50 acres	1000 acres or more	
	104	105	106	107	108	109	110	111	112	113	114	115	116
NORTH CAROLINA— Cont'd													
Swain	354	3,681	917	D	585	83	46	115	31,323	99	71.7	1.0	51.4
Transylvania	798	7,598	1,509	618	1,543	175	272	235	30,865	215	69.8	0.9	39.7
Tyrrell	77	462	21	41	156	29	D	14	29,877	68	25.0	22.1	46.5
Union	4,526	53,792	5,649	11,572	7,560	927	1,571	2,108	39,192	957	56.9	4.1	44.7
Vance	832	13,025	2,404	1,500	2,312	238	309	438	33,648	238	30.7	6.7	40.1
Wake	28,325	453,333	60,406	13,731	59,262	24,689	53,509	23,438	51,701	691	64.5	1.9	34.5
Warren	258	2,217	540	374	369	44	41	59	26,754	267	41.9	3.7	38.8
Washington	228	2,931	611	842	417	60	53	110	37,651	141	24.8	19.1	60.4
Watauga	1,603	17,694	2,768	717	3,704	382	701	556	31,408	520	58.1	1.0	35.3
Wayne	2,137	34,226	7,229	5,688	6,276	1,111	830	1,155	33,733	551	39.7	8.5	55.4
Wilkes	1,163	18,842	3,153	4,527	2,552	357	496	770	40,869	932	45.0	1.0	47.2
Wilson	1,750	31,868	5,219	7,332	3,748	2,993	777	1,263	39,635	276	43.8	12.3	51.2
Yadkin	593	8,630	1,015	2,525	818	192	188	270	31,253	818	55.4	1.8	42.5
Yancey	313	3,427	490	1,033	565	81	104	115	33,498	369	51.5	0.3	39.3
NORTH DAKOTA	24,601	346,947	61,322	23,984	50,760	17,843	15,817	15,817	45,588	26,364	11.7	40.0	54.3
Adams	99	803	328	D	164	38	23	28	35,192	380	9.5	36.3	49.6
Barnes	366	3,956	1,140	531	491	142	78	130	32,750	749	14.4	34.3	54.3
Benson	88	1,043	25	55	56	54	D	34	32,891	473	7.6	41.0	58.1
Billings	62	285	NA	NA	15	D	D	18	62,912	204	7.4	53.9	58.0
Bottineau	261	1,742	265	84	375	123	80	72	41,424	684	8.6	39.5	55.6
Bowman	160	1,200	257	34	229	94	47	46	38,565	341	7.0	42.5	46.9
Burke	81	411	10	NA	87	36	49	18	43,754	356	8.7	38.5	47.5
Burleigh	3,011	47,091	10,705	1,141	7,551	1,898	2,544	2,057	43,671	785	29.9	23.7	34.4
Cass	5,523	103,392	17,951	8,595	13,488	8,272	6,030	4,692	45,383	784	20.0	46.9	61.9
Cavalier	158	1,186	220	23	201	92	14	48	40,420	523	5.9	54.7	64.6
Dickey	215	1,749	400	183	316	53	32	53	30,575	419	6.0	42.5	61.8
Divide	97	544	D	D	68	24	11	21	38,441	416	3.4	45.4	52.0
Dunn	164	2,584	D	402	153	32	123	142	54,827	524	9.2	51.9	64.0
Eddy	78	530	204	D	62	21	11	17	32,634	291	3.1	40.2	46.3
Emmons	125	707	184	D	100	51	12	23	32,669	516	6.8	43.8	53.5
Foster	150	1,419	254	D	278	62	8	56	39,485	230	14.3	56.1	61.9
Golden Valley	73	442	128	D	92	32	18	16	35,676	287	10.8	42.9	51.5
Grand Forks	1,918	34,179	7,350	2,337	6,312	900	1,611	1,333	39,003	889	14.5	24.5	48.5
Grant	74	418	189	17	34	31	D	12	29,761	412	7.5	51.7	52.4
Griggs	90	636	D	135	57	24	34	21	33,311	393	8.1	36.6	55.4
Hettinger	95	459	92	D	67	49	15	18	38,259	482	8.9	36.7	44.1
Kidder	68	537	90	D	78	35	26	18	34,361	476	8.2	47.5	49.8
LaMoure	151	1,021	186	83	125	116	NA	36	34,981	571	8.8	41.5	66.2
Logan	67	461	118	D	61	34	D	13	28,694	351	10.3	52.1	59.2
McHenry	123	779	121	D	206	43	14	32	40,673	750	11.2	33.9	48.5
McIntosh	113	817	343	36	131	49	21	25	30,864	363	13.5	36.1	53.7
McKenzie	492	5,435	343	D	458	124	224	372	68,481	539	11.3	51.6	68.0
McLean	256	2,589	447	69	346	116	19	150	57,842	762	9.8	35.7	50.1
Mercer	248	4,349	491	24	480	115	50	294	67,504	317	12.0	40.7	49.3
Morton	838	10,111	1,881	873	1,408	416	1,302	448	44,351	781	12.0	41.5	54.7
Mountrail	389	4,111	242	126	704	113	219	233	56,792	584	6.8	49.0	54.7
Nelson	122	779	274	D	88	64	7	24	30,669	489	8.4	30.7	48.8
Oliver	42	547	17	19	D	D	D	43	79,185	234	14.5	33.3	52.1
Pembina	272	2,396	362	642	356	112	34	100	41,940	481	10.6	38.3	66.4
Pierce	171	1,484	D	D	256	87	54	56	37,455	446	13.2	37.9	55.6
Ramsey	434	4,668	816	88	1,056	300	57	164	35,079	515	13.0	35.9	47.5
Ransom	199	1,493	394	224	179	78	56	51	34,478	507	12.4	30.6	53.0
Renville	113	552	97	22	114	34	10	20	35,527	269	12.6	60.2	71.7
Richland	533	6,087	623	1,809	804	182	158	224	36,857	846	18.8	33.7	60.5
Rolette	195	2,375	563	79	472	99	38	71	29,710	453	8.6	35.8	58.7
Sargent	113	2,339	74	D	144	44	19	117	50,195	501	12.6	33.7	56.9
Sheridan	39	155	28	D	18	10	D	4	27,865	260	2.3	54.6	60.7
Sioux	29	668	D	D	63	D	D	17	25,876	187	16.0	53.5	49.5
Slope	18	76	D	NA	D	NA	NA	4	47,368	215	0.9	54.0	65.7
Stark	1,202	14,757	2,171	1,049	2,295	421	553	745	50,506	678	19.8	29.6	43.4
Steele	60	479	D	126	66	48	5	22	45,537	358	16.8	37.2	56.1
Stutsman	690	9,659	2,772	865	1,530	451	224	357	36,934	939	12.6	37.7	56.7
Towner	78	520	D	D	39	56	24	16	30,292	454	6.8	44.3	51.9
Traill	299	2,778	623	415	348	158	40	111	40,064	415	18.3	45.1	53.3
Walsh	400	3,311	649	575	465	167	94	120	36,277	763	12.1	32.2	47.6

Table B. States and Counties — **Agriculture**

STATE County	Land in farms					Value of land and buildings (dollars)		Value of machinery and equiopmnet, average per farm (dollars)	Value of products sold:				Organic farms (number)	Farms with internet access (percent)	Government payments	
	Acreage (1,000)	Percent change, 2012-2017	Acres			Average per farm	Average per acre				Percent from:				Total ($1,000)	Percent of farms
			Average size of farm	Total irrigated (1,000)	Total cropland (1,000)				Total (mil dol)	Average per farm (acres)	Crops	Livestock and poultry products				
	117	118	119	120	121	122	123	124	125	126	127	128	129	130	131	132
NORTH CAROLINA— Cont'd																
Swain	10	D	102	0.2	1.1	374,350	3,658	43,804	2.2	21,717	58.7	41.3	NA	72.7	42	12.1
Transylvania	15	-18.1	68	0.6	4.5	528,315	7,735	58,576	9.8	45,460	68.8	31.2	5	74.4	74	10.2
Tyrrell	53	-18.0	779	D	51.0	3,229,747	4,148	436,706	D	D	D	D	NA	60.3	1,312	75.0
Union	187	-7.5	195	0.2	142.3	1,040,504	5,336	130,984	482.0	503,637	17.9	82.1	4	76.0	2,529	12.6
Vance	66	20.5	278	1.2	20.6	827,874	2,978	114,092	17.2	72,315	97.6	2.4	9	78.6	164	34.5
Wake	77	-8.6	111	1.2	46.3	1,299,196	11,658	82,844	63.7	92,122	88.8	11.2	2	82.6	557	13.5
Warren	61	-7.5	228	1.2	29.2	662,147	2,909	78,681	40.1	150,176	30.7	69.3	2	69.7	428	33.0
Washington	80	-12.8	565	1.9	71.3	2,072,945	3,668	358,266	49.0	347,844	88.5	11.5	NA	78.7	3,085	68.8
Watauga	50	-11.0	95	0.0	14.4	614,311	6,439	58,217	16.7	32,162	53.4	46.6	16	76.2	351	13.3
Wayne	165	-13.5	300	4.8	130.5	1,497,288	4,990	222,201	592.1	1,074,539	18.1	81.9	13	79.9	3,611	46.1
Wilkes	107	-4.0	114	0.1	41.4	586,674	5,124	106,608	335.1	359,575	4.4	95.6	8	69.6	81	4.2
Wilson	123	10.4	445	1.1	100.3	1,685,619	3,784	304,394	210.7	763,399	77.2	22.8	6	76.4	1,129	49.6
Yadkin	88	-12.9	107	0.9	48.3	585,403	5,471	74,938	139.7	170,722	19.5	80.5	7	70.8	489	13.7
Yancey	31	-0.6	84	0.1	10.2	454,909	5,446	40,731	6.8	18,491	83.1	16.9	1	66.7	157	27.1
NORTH DAKOTA	39,342	0.2	1,492	263.9	27,951.7	2,546,783	1,707	375,872	8,234.1	312,324	81.1	18.9	129	78.9	467,034	77.8
Adams	600	-0.3	1,578	NA	388.0	1,682,952	1,067	297,071	60.4	158,937	50.4	49.6	NA	73.2	8,748	82.1
Barnes	952	1.6	1,271	2.5	819.8	2,937,290	2,311	395,596	278.7	372,143	92.4	7.6	3	80.0	8,226	78.2
Benson	751	-6.4	1,587	2.0	586.7	2,172,369	1,368	384,343	164.3	347,393	89.9	10.1	1	79.5	9,813	78.9
Billings	735	1.7	3,602	D	125.7	3,308,786	919	237,105	28.8	140,951	19.7	80.3	6	71.1	2,338	69.6
Bottineau	958	6.6	1,401	0.0	865.6	2,166,705	1,546	354,320	215.5	315,058	92.5	7.5	1	82.5	18,721	81.4
Bowman	711	-2.6	2,086	0.9	334.9	2,144,932	1,028	254,275	74.1	217,240	26.4	73.6	NA	79.2	5,354	80.1
Burke	519	-12.7	1,459	NA	393.4	1,537,171	1,054	303,368	71.6	201,062	85.4	14.6	NA	67.7	7,985	88.2
Burleigh	824	-13.3	1,050	4.0	423.4	1,994,601	1,900	200,722	134.1	170,866	48.8	51.2	NA	80.5	6,674	52.9
Cass	1,126	1.7	1,436	13.9	1,085.4	5,339,580	3,718	557,103	439.5	560,528	94.9	5.1	7	85.1	8,418	71.3
Cavalier	928	-1.3	1,775	0.3	877.2	3,691,559	2,080	546,736	280.6	536,507	98.5	1.5	2	82.8	25,654	90.4
Dickey	679	7.2	1,620	14.8	541.9	3,847,791	2,375	510,138	225.1	537,212	80.8	19.2	6	79.5	6,323	81.1
Divide	704	24.6	1,693	2.3	538.7	1,808,767	1,069	358,232	71.5	171,755	86.1	13.9	7	75.0	9,797	91.3
Dunn	1,017	-1.4	1,941	0.8	417.8	2,225,966	1,147	297,360	77.6	148,101	35.7	64.3	5	84.0	6,276	66.0
Eddy	377	-4.7	1,296	NA	285.6	1,886,332	1,455	312,599	82.2	282,584	77.3	22.7	NA	84.5	4,439	89.0
Emmons	812	9.1	1,573	10.1	500.4	2,493,059	1,585	357,337	162.1	314,151	69.0	31.0	3	79.7	7,581	81.8
Foster	394	5.3	1,713	2.8	342.9	3,438,653	2,008	609,701	118.7	516,230	76.5	23.5	2	89.1	5,532	85.7
Golden Valley	626	11.4	2,182	1.1	274.1	2,296,429	1,052	313,468	45.2	157,390	46.2	53.8	NA	79.1	5,890	76.0
Grand Forks	798	-2.2	898	27.5	744.1	3,064,078	3,411	359,812	318.4	358,112	92.6	7.4	1	74.6	14,911	87.5
Grant	959	-8.6	2,329	2.1	429.0	2,494,937	1,071	264,216	83.0	201,502	35.0	65.0	NA	76.9	8,094	87.4
Griggs	454	1.8	1,154	1.5	364.8	2,051,720	1,777	339,861	114.6	291,659	91.7	8.3	NA	75.1	7,670	88.3
Hettinger	705	-1.5	1,462	NA	586.0	2,055,386	1,405	264,427	66.6	138,077	80.1	19.9	NA	76.8	13,029	86.7
Kidder	748	-4.1	1,572	23.7	423.9	1,978,460	1,258	264,631	113.6	238,626	64.1	35.9	28	77.5	6,882	82.6
LaMoure	727	0.1	1,273	5.5	632.9	3,230,939	2,539	417,666	226.0	395,781	85.2	14.8	9	79.0	4,860	78.5
Logan	632	10.5	1,800	2.4	347.7	2,144,519	1,191	326,130	155.4	442,675	35.6	64.4	7	76.6	4,218	84.9
McHenry	1,040	-2.0	1,387	6.2	629.4	1,510,122	1,089	241,112	146.3	195,129	56.2	43.8	3	78.3	10,874	77.6
McIntosh	488	-17.3	1,343	0.7	298.3	1,832,362	1,364	275,666	94.8	261,157	56.6	43.4	6	79.6	3,200	76.6
McKenzie	1,119	5.2	2,077	26.7	433.3	2,130,024	1,026	372,024	104.7	194,230	47.9	52.1	NA	82.7	7,119	63.8
McLean	1,045	-6.0	1,372	8.1	807.3	2,448,520	1,785	327,473	176.9	232,180	85.2	14.8	NA	82.8	17,822	81.4
Mercer	518	3.0	1,635	2.4	232.8	2,236,333	1,368	291,683	57.2	180,341	43.8	56.2	2	77.6	4,684	65.3
Morton	1,226	0.5	1,570	4.7	562.8	2,203,330	1,404	275,670	146.0	186,936	43.5	56.5	3	81.8	7,594	65.7
Mountrail	1,081	12.2	1,852	0.0	697.2	2,367,371	1,278	415,245	135.7	232,435	78.0	22.0	NA	80.8	14,849	76.5
Nelson	553	-1.4	1,131	2.9	475.4	1,537,488	1,360	341,693	120.9	247,213	93.1	6.9	NA	67.5	9,416	93.5
Oliver	314	-20.5	1,340	2.7	148.5	1,932,910	1,443	292,694	47.3	202,248	46.3	53.7	NA	76.1	2,639	71.4
Pembina	691	-0.1	1,438	1.4	640.8	3,962,790	2,757	514,306	282.7	587,653	97.4	2.6	NA	78.4	11,608	78.0
Pierce	540	-9.7	1,212	0.8	435.3	1,707,184	1,409	337,405	98.8	221,466	84.3	15.7	1	80.0	8,501	86.3
Ramsey	697	-0.3	1,353	D	626.4	2,446,528	1,809	474,152	190.2	369,297	86.2	13.8	NA	77.3	12,149	84.9
Ransom	549	9.5	1,083	28.9	389.1	2,179,084	2,012	345,733	173.6	342,454	79.3	20.7	3	77.5	6,098	74.0
Renville	554	10.8	2,060	0.0	523.4	3,306,195	1,605	672,748	125.5	466,498	97.7	2.3	NA	86.2	10,660	84.0
Richland	875	0.8	1,035	6.1	823.0	3,300,158	3,189	467,825	390.8	461,935	90.8	9.2	3	78.3	6,568	77.9
Rolette	512	-4.1	1,131	1.0	373.1	1,447,711	1,280	327,186	91.5	202,079	84.3	15.7	NA	72.6	9,446	70.6
Sargent	548	6.9	1,094	16.8	489.2	3,049,460	2,787	399,455	214.1	427,433	88.1	11.9	NA	76.0	5,981	79.0
Sheridan	551	7.4	2,121	NA	397.9	2,328,439	1,098	314,736	92.0	354,015	80.2	19.8	7	78.8	5,366	80.4
Sioux	588	2.6	3,145	D	226.1	3,909,369	1,243	390,741	61.9	331,048	35.1	64.9	NA	77.0	2,912	68.4
Slope	728	7.9	3,385	NA	286.5	3,579,166	1,057	418,177	47.9	222,809	41.3	58.7	NA	77.7	4,683	83.7
Stark	736	-11.3	1,085	0.5	493.6	1,444,094	1,331	222,178	68.5	100,997	63.6	36.4	NA	77.6	7,576	59.6
Steele	421	-1.1	1,177	6.6	398.6	2,584,785	2,197	525,062	149.9	418,782	97.3	2.7	NA	77.7	5,812	80.4
Stutsman	1,316	1.0	1,401	4.2	1,048.2	2,808,671	2,005	370,108	335.6	357,428	85.2	14.8	2	79.2	10,869	74.8
Towner	631	-2.3	1,389	NA	552.4	1,923,869	1,385	399,244	166.1	365,965	84.8	15.2	NA	74.2	14,647	85.2
Traill	539	-1.6	1,298	D	526.1	4,004,597	3,084	592,272	225.9	544,410	99.0	1.0	NA	81.2	4,053	80.0
Walsh	805	0.3	1,054	1.7	720.3	2,649,975	2,513	446,123	335.6	439,840	96.4	3.6	5	76.5	13,679	86.1

Table B. States and Counties — Water Use, Wholesale Trade, Retail Trade, and Real Estate

STATE County	Water use, 2015 Public supply water withdrawn (mil gal/day)	Public supply gallons withdrawn per person per day	Wholesale Trade[1], 2012 Number of establishments	Number of employees	Sales (mil dol)	Average payroll (mil dol)	Retail Trade[2], 2012 Number of establishments	Number of employees	Sales (mil dol)	Average payroll (mil dol)	Real estate and rental and leasing,[2] 2012 Number of establishments	Number of employees	Sales (mil dol)	Average payroll (mil dol)
	133	134	135	136	137	138	139	140	141	142	143	144	145	146
NORTH CAROLINA— Cont'd														
Swain	0.50	34.6	4	D	D	D	96	472	107.1	9.1	7	23	2.0	0.4
Transylvania	1.81	54.5	15	D	D	D	125	1,352	311.3	30.2	48	91	13.4	2.7
Tyrrell	0.48	117.9	1	D	D	D	20	135	36.0	2.3	2	D	D	D
Union	6.57	29.5	266	2,658	1,449.1	126.9	492	6,803	1,943.6	156.4	144	304	60.2	11.2
Vance	5.95	133.5	31	D	D	D	179	2,186	527.9	49.0	51	211	27.5	5.1
Wake	56.66	55.3	1,082	18,108	18,602.6	1,401.0	3,161	51,026	14,359.3	1,264.2	1,320	7,360	1,683.3	391.9
Warren	0.05	2.5	9	21	10.2	0.6	44	314	72.4	6.0	9	D	D	D
Washington	0.79	63.8	12	185	174.1	4.1	48	465	127.7	8.7	4	D	D	D
Watauga	3.30	62.4	37	299	140.2	14.7	318	3,471	762.9	70.2	100	382	55.2	10.0
Wayne	11.27	90.8	95	1,822	1,244.8	74.4	464	5,709	1,557.5	125.8	63	257	29.3	7.1
Wilkes	6.61	96.5	47	D	D	D	223	2,500	1,365.2	53.5	44	185	46.8	7.0
Wilson	9.62	117.7	99	D	D	D	319	3,606	992.7	83.6	76	247	43.1	6.3
Yadkin	1.36	36.2	29	222	87.7	7.8	108	760	242.9	16.0	14	D	D	D
Yancey	0.70	39.8	7	24	3.7	0.4	61	522	144.9	12.3	17	D	D	D
NORTH DAKOTA	84.18	111.2	1,430	18,880	28,150.8	1,078.2	3,185	47,186	15,519.8	1,204.4	912	5,157	1,445.1	247.5
Adams	0.00	0.0	10	49	120.6	1.7	16	169	43.1	4.1	2	D	D	D
Barnes	1.15	103.6	22	192	329.6	9.2	48	479	121.7	10.3	11	86	4.5	1.8
Benson	0.07	10.4	14	86	228.9	4.1	9	55	12.3	1.4	2	D	D	D
Billings	0.00	0.0	1	D	D	D	10	D	D	D	1	D	D	D
Bottineau	0.48	71.5	16	120	99.0	5.6	34	337	95.5	6.8	8	16	1.1	0.1
Bowman	0.22	66.8	13	123	96.6	7.6	19	251	93.2	5.5	3	2	0.2	0.0
Burke	0.26	112.7	6	60	454.5	3.6	10	96	38.5	2.5	3	2	0.7	0.1
Burleigh	11.90	128.0	132	2,094	1,483.2	113.2	373	6,905	1,995.1	177.7	132	404	107.3	13.9
Cass	14.11	82.3	333	6,020	5,497.7	335.9	645	12,500	3,790.4	302.8	277	1,716	302.9	64.8
Cavalier	0.50	130.6	15	D	D	D	29	213	125.7	5.2	1	D	D	D
Dickey	0.83	162.6	16	152	450.1	7.0	41	324	96.3	7.2	1	D	D	D
Divide	0.00	0.0	2	D	D	D	9	86	21.1	1.8	1	D	D	D
Dunn	0.00	0.0	8	50	86.8	2.7	13	161	69.1	3.5	1	D	D	D
Eddy	0.98	414.4	4	D	D	D	10	72	16.7	1.7	2	D	D	D
Emmons	0.43	126.4	14	95	236.9	3.5	20	106	30.7	2.3	NA	NA	NA	NA
Foster	0.43	128.1	19	119	210.8	6.6	28	247	133.0	7.2	2	D	D	D
Golden Valley	0.00	0.0	5	68	87.3	3.2	15	134	72.7	2.8	NA	NA	NA	NA
Grand Forks	8.78	123.8	92	1,235	1,214.9	65.6	314	5,860	1,562.2	130.9	79	504	86.1	14.7
Grant	0.00	0.0	8	50	98.4	2.4	10	31	7.2	0.7	1	D	D	D
Griggs	0.38	164.2	6	104	66.5	5.2	12	60	18.1	1.4	1	D	D	D
Hettinger	0.00	0.0	4	D	D	D	14	87	128.6	2.7	2	D	D	D
Kidder	0.09	37.2	6	17	27.9	0.7	8	66	48.4	1.7	2	D	D	D
LaMoure	0.01	2.4	23	213	391.6	9.9	16	142	133.1	3.8	2	D	D	D
Logan	0.09	46.5	6	D	D	D	11	46	30.5	1.7	1	D	D	D
McHenry	0.97	162.5	5	D	D	D	17	122	26.5	2.5	5	D	D	D
McIntosh	0.26	94.2	11	103	277.1	3.5	19	140	52.1	3.6	3	9	0.8	0.1
McKenzie	0.79	61.6	14	172	263.6	25.7	24	301	166.1	10.6	15	69	27.6	5.0
McLean	0.61	62.6	20	216	528.9	9.4	38	293	132.5	7.2	2	D	D	D
Mercer	6.67	753.4	6	28	21.5	1.5	39	420	125.2	9.6	5	5	0.3	0.1
Morton	2.80	92.4	34	D	D	D	99	1,230	586.1	40.3	43	118	16.8	3.3
Mountrail	0.52	50.3	12	140	406.4	9.1	41	475	274.0	15.4	6	16	1.1	0.3
Nelson	1.33	448.1	13	107	449.2	6.2	19	103	31.5	1.6	4	4	0.1	0.0
Oliver	0.00	0.0	1	D	D	D	2	D	D	D	NA	NA	NA	NA
Pembina	1.10	155.1	35	352	847.9	13.4	45	403	82.9	7.8	3	1	0.3	0.0
Pierce	0.75	173.9	11	112	201.5	5.3	22	263	92.6	6.2	2	D	D	D
Ramsey	0.00	0.0	29	207	622.1	11.0	80	962	311.7	27.1	6	192	7.4	4.6
Ransom	1.02	187.2	13	187	292.1	10.4	30	252	66.2	4.8	4	4	0.7	0.1
Renville	0.00	0.0	12	89	250.5	4.3	13	142	81.1	3.7	2	D	D	D
Richland	2.08	126.8	34	D	D	D	75	899	277.3	19.6	18	50	5.6	1.1
Rolette	1.59	108.5	7	48	103.6	2.9	45	496	132.9	9.7	2	D	D	D
Sargent	0.28	72.2	12	74	145.1	2.9	17	124	20.9	1.8	4	D	D	D
Sheridan	0.01	7.6	3	D	D	D	6	20	5.5	0.2	2	D	D	D
Sioux	0.02	4.6	NA	NA	NA	NA	8	D	D	D	NA	NA	NA	NA
Slope	0.03	39.1	NA	NA	NA	NA	1	D	D	D	NA	NA	NA	NA
Stark	0.00	0.0	53	745	1,186.8	44.7	160	2,050	883.4	62.8	43	211	72.4	12.0
Steele	0.67	342.5	6	D	D	D	10	61	34.4	1.7	1	D	D	D
Stutsman	3.32	157.3	39	470	875.5	24.3	101	1,328	379.1	32.3	28	79	20.9	2.0
Towner	0.19	83.6	8	64	193.8	3.4	13	51	30.4	1.3	2	D	D	D
Traill	0.92	114.8	30	334	1,733.4	16.3	42	313	97.2	7.1	7	9	0.7	0.2
Walsh	1.14	104.6	35	374	599.7	18.9	58	535	123.1	10.4	11	13	1.0	0.3

1 Merchant wholesalers, except manufacturers' sales branches and offices. 2. Employer establishments.

— **Professional Services, Manufacturing, and Accommodation and Food Services**

STATE County	Professional, scientific, and technical services, 2012				Manufacturing, 2012				Accommodation and food services, 2012			
	Number of establish-ments	Number of employees	Sales (mil dol)	Average payroll (mil dol)	Number of establish-ments	Number of employees	Receipts (mil dol)	Annual payroll (mil dol)	Number of establis-hments	Number of employees	Receipts (mil dol)	Annual payroll (mil dol)
	147	148	149	150	151	152	153	154	155	156	157	158
NORTH CAROLINA—Cont'd												
Swain	11	D	D	D	11	414	D	17.1	82	765	50.0	12.4
Transylvania	67	D	D	D	24	440	61.1	18.3	83	1,106	68.5	21.3
Tyrrell	3	D	D	D	3	105	9.6	2.3	6	D	D	D
Union	395	1,221	156.5	54.2	231	9,760	3,645.4	444.3	264	4,159	192.9	50.8
Vance	46	196	16.4	6.9	41	1,581	756.2	66.1	67	1,239	57.0	15.0
Wake	4,332	40,850	7,315.9	3,072.9	576	12,902	13,105.2	696.6	2,102	42,326	2,165.2	606.3
Warren	14	52	3.8	0.9	9	494	128.9	14.7	23	207	8.9	2.3
Washington	12	66	7.5	1.8	12	780	394.6	47.0	27	D	D	D
Watauga	149	723	47.9	20.0	47	667	108.0	23.6	174	3,416	142.1	43.2
Wayne	147	816	76.0	27.4	83	5,833	1,691.3	243.8	186	3,284	161.7	42.0
Wilkes	83	418	36.5	15.0	73	4,288	1,156.1	138.7	105	1,568	65.7	17.9
Wilson	112	769	95.4	36.3	91	7,809	13,159.9	393.6	138	2,749	139.3	34.2
Yadkin	41	230	20.6	8.1	41	2,064	748.3	79.1	58	875	34.4	9.6
Yancey	17	75	5.0	1.5	12	686	145.0	28.9	21	282	11.6	3.4
NORTH DAKOTA	1,722	13,715	1,846.9	735.7	745	23,541	14,427.4	1,042.8	1,935	35,698	2,045.1	521.3
Adams	4	D	D	D	NA	NA	NA	NA	11	D	D	D
Barnes	15	79	9.6	3.6	10	500	D	23.1	31	356	14.1	3.4
Benson	6	14	1.9	0.9	4	102	D	D	16	D	D	D
Billings	3	5	1.0	0.3	3	13	D	D	14	131	19.0	5.4
Bottineau	20	67	6.4	2.9	10	92	D	4.6	28	237	11.0	2.7
Bowman	4	D	D	D	7	35	D	1.0	17	118	5.1	1.2
Burke	4	D	D	D	NA	NA	NA	NA	12	48	4.4	0.5
Burleigh	308	1,969	314.8	118.4	68	900	D	39.3	173	4,980	242.1	70.7
Cass	481	D	D	D	186	8,566	3,451.1	395.7	388	9,671	446.8	130.9
Cavalier	6	16	1.3	0.6	5	14	3.1	0.6	18	D	D	D
Dickey	9	37	2.6	0.9	13	225	60.0	9.4	19	145	4.6	1.1
Divide	6	15	1.6	0.4	3	6	D	D	7	D	D	D
Dunn	4	16	2.2	0.9	5	D	D	D	9	165	24.6	3.5
Eddy	4	10	1.1	0.2	NA	NA	NA	NA	11	30	1.4	0.3
Emmons	9	12	0.9	0.3	3	6	D	D	10	88	2.8	0.8
Foster	7	10	3.4	0.5	3	D	D	D	10	125	5.2	1.5
Golden Valley	5	18	1.8	0.5	NA	NA	NA	NA	4	D	D	D
Grand Forks	130	1,473	167.2	79.1	55	2,166	590.7	78.4	196	4,191	177.6	52.5
Grant	3	7	0.6	0.1	3	27	D	D	6	D	D	D
Griggs	9	43	4.7	1.6	5	155	21.4	5.1	11	D	D	D
Hettinger	5	15	0.9	0.4	3	5	D	D	5	35	1.3	0.2
Kidder	4	D	D	D	3	6	D	D	8	43	2.0	0.6
LaMoure	2	D	D	D	7	52	D	1.9	16	D	D	D
Logan	2	D	D	D	NA	NA	NA	NA	9	57	1.3	0.3
McHenry	6	14	2.1	0.6	4	D	D	D	7	24	1.3	0.3
McIntosh	6	24	1.6	0.6	4	109	D	3.3	10	D	D	D
McKenzie	32	134	46.7	13.9	5	17	1.6	0.4	28	460	31.8	6.5
McLean	7	20	1.6	0.5	5	67	D	3.2	28	181	9.8	2.1
Mercer	11	69	7.2	2.2	7	35	5.7	0.9	30	348	12.4	3.5
Morton	61	D	D	D	36	913	D	56.0	52	D	D	D
Mountrail	18	44	8.9	2.3	3	D	D	D	30	167	18.8	3.1
Nelson	5	12	0.8	0.3	3	57	D	1.4	15	106	3.4	0.8
Oliver	3	D	D	D	5	D	D	D	3	9	0.3	0.1
Pembina	14	27	2.8	0.6	15	520	477.1	22.5	20	D	D	D
Pierce	13	58	4.4	1.1	NA	NA	NA	NA	12	171	5.6	1.5
Ramsey	19	61	7.9	2.4	9	219	D	9.8	47	681	29.6	7.9
Ransom	15	52	4.7	1.3	8	405	D	12.3	19	129	4.8	1.2
Renville	7	14	1.1	0.3	NA	NA	NA	NA	10	30	1.4	0.2
Richland	32	D	D	D	35	1,871	1,276.7	87.2	47	821	89.6	16.1
Rolette	6	8	0.9	0.3	8	231	D	7.4	25	582	43.1	12.5
Sargent	9	34	3.5	1.5	6	D	D	D	14	D	D	D
Sheridan	4	D	D	D	3	43	D	D	2	D	D	D
Sioux	2	D	D	D	NA	NA	NA	NA	6	D	D	D
Slope	NA	NA	NA	NA	NA	NA	NA	NA	1	D	D	D
Stark	71	430	75.9	23.3	28	898	431.8	44.6	80	1,431	111.6	25.8
Steele	3	3	0.3	0.1	8	158	D	4.9	5	20	1.0	0.1
Stutsman	34	174	16.4	6.4	24	902	500.6	37.7	60	926	40.2	11.9
Towner	8	21	1.9	0.5	4	49	D	1.0	9	32	1.3	0.3
Traill	10	31	3.1	1.4	15	311	D	12.3	26	203	7.7	2.0
Walsh	24	88	8.5	3.0	10	522	111.2	17.8	36	259	12.0	2.7

Health Care and Social Assistance, Other Services, Nonemployer Businesses, and Residential Construction

STATE County	Health care and social assistance, 2012				Other services, 2012				Nonemployer businesses, 2016		Value of residential construction authorized by building permits, 2018	
	Number of establish-ments	Number of employees	Receipts (mil dol)	Annual payroll (mil dol)	Number of establish-ments	Number of employees	Receipts (mil dol)	Annual payroll (mil dol)	Number	Receipts (mil dol)	New construction ($1,000)	Number of housing units
	159	160	161	162	163	164	165	166	167	168	169	170
NORTH CAROLINA—Cont'd												
Swain	31	736	89.3	26.7	18	D	D	D	1,400	55.8	13,576	65
Transylvania	70	1,589	148.7	57.5	46	248	21.0	6.0	3,205	137.6	50,263	128
Tyrrell	8	D	D	D	7	44	4.2	1.4	278	9.2	429	3
Union	292	5,038	533.9	201.5	281	1,255	109.2	32.8	17,861	827.6	363,433	1,634
Vance	101	2,512	205.0	83.0	48	225	22.7	6.1	2,292	97.2	7,893	44
Wake	2,688	47,097	5,110.4	2,066.2	1,699	12,705	1,463.3	420.1	87,890	4,070.4	2,318,720	12,664
Warren	23	446	20.0	9.7	12	D	D	D	1,011	29.2	8,791	55
Washington	34	665	34.7	15.0	11	D	D	D	621	17.9	1,207	5
Watauga	140	3,419	624.9	144.3	82	349	28.4	7.6	4,839	208.2	94,124	331
Wayne	254	6,896	606.6	265.8	142	939	69.3	20.3	6,376	231.9	50,728	275
Wilkes	147	2,783	233.7	91.5	72	338	23.2	8.4	4,446	179.6	21,808	94
Wilson	200	5,103	408.7	169.3	114	619	54.4	15.0	4,680	173.1	36,397	234
Yadkin	52	982	60.4	24.8	35	D	D	D	2,340	97.4	13,134	57
Yancey	32	D	D	D	24	86	7.5	2.2	1,626	55.4	7,754	39
NORTH DAKOTA	1,856	56,639	5,418.4	2,414.4	1,716	9,232	1,064.0	253.7	54,064	2,622.7	607,898	3,211
Adams	13	D	D	D	9	D	D	D	210	8.0	0	0
Barnes	37	1,156	53.4	26.8	28	147	10.5	2.9	883	44.2	1,685	7
Benson	6	50	1.5	0.8	3	10	1.8	0.2	287	10.4	0	0
Billings	NA	NA	NA	NA	4	14	1.7	0.4	115	5.5	1,321	7
Bottineau	6	256	14.3	6.8	9	D	D	D	611	24.0	1,950	9
Bowman	11	226	16.7	8.3	14	D	D	D	268	9.6	250	1
Burke	5	D	D	D	2	D	D	D	205	7.5	642	4
Burleigh	271	10,591	1,080.5	488.2	254	1,691	208.8	53.8	7,329	376.6	72,867	367
Cass	439	15,347	1,909.7	815.0	380	2,549	278.0	71.4	12,258	724.2	325,993	1,917
Cavalier	10	242	15.7	5.7	11	D	D	D	388	13.7	1,112	4
Dickey	23	409	31.5	13.0	20	67	5.9	1.6	432	14.6	550	2
Divide	6	D	D	D	5	D	D	D	200	7.9	82	1
Dunn	4	D	D	D	11	D	D	D	366	19.6	5,794	10
Eddy	9	223	11.3	6.5	7	D	D	D	204	8.7	0	0
Emmons	11	213	10.1	5.7	7	12	0.7	0.1	285	8.8	1,800	5
Foster	11	302	22.9	10.1	7	17	1.2	0.3	302	12.1	508	5
Golden Valley	5	114	7.0	3.3	7	28	1.2	0.4	178	8.5	825	5
Grand Forks	160	6,865	668.9	301.2	148	827	103.2	21.7	4,071	196.1	49,245	260
Grant	7	224	12.1	5.3	5	D	D	D	220	7.7	959	6
Griggs	5	D	D	D	7	D	D	D	211	7.8	220	2
Hettinger	10	110	5.1	2.6	8	D	D	D	215	7.9	0	0
Kidder	6	47	1.7	0.8	3	D	D	D	228	10.1	0	0
LaMoure	13	D	D	D	13	49	4.4	0.9	334	11.5	300	1
Logan	7	148	4.6	2.5	7	D	D	D	180	8.3	0	0
McHenry	6	D	D	D	7	D	D	D	434	17.6	1,019	6
McIntosh	10	308	17.0	8.9	7	19	1.0	0.2	238	10.2	0	0
McKenzie	9	184	15.1	6.1	27	112	10.6	2.6	851	45.9	2,624	10
McLean	19	443	23.8	12.0	19	D	D	D	685	28.0	7,331	34
Mercer	18	445	26.7	12.7	16	44	4.0	0.9	626	17.8	584	3
Morton	64	1,627	99.3	48.3	58	D	D	D	2,344	116.8	34,314	159
Mountrail	13	196	12.5	6.2	19	83	10.1	2.5	694	33.4	3,394	20
Nelson	10	256	11.5	5.6	12	D	D	D	285	11.5	0	0
Oliver	4	D	D	D	2	D	D	D	122	6.3	1,276	7
Pembina	16	336	19.1	7.2	18	D	D	D	585	19.7	0	0
Pierce	9	D	D	D	14	D	D	D	358	12.9	1,481	5
Ramsey	41	888	56.7	26.1	28	131	10.9	2.2	903	36.9	1,420	10
Ransom	25	420	26.5	11.9	22	75	6.5	1.3	384	15.4	503	4
Renville	7	D	D	D	3	D	D	D	185	6.9	140	1
Richland	45	578	35.6	18.7	38	143	11.2	3.0	1,197	58.3	6,768	32
Rolette	25	549	54.7	24.7	9	D	D	D	683	16.6	0	0
Sargent	7	65	3.0	1.8	8	31	5.1	0.8	294	12.3	3,906	21
Sheridan	2	D	D	D	5	D	D	D	109	3.9	258	2
Sioux	1	D	D	D	2	D	D	D	110	4.1	0	0
Slope	NA	NA	NA	NA	1	D	D	D	62	3.6	0	0
Stark	91	1,927	131.4	60.4	79	585	78.6	16.0	2,518	117.4	21,448	73
Steele	1	D	D	D	4	7	1.2	0.2	149	8.6	0	0
Stutsman	62	2,423	154.8	88.7	54	299	23.6	6.9	1,461	59.5	2,768	11
Towner	3	D	D	D	6	30	2.5	0.4	228	9.0	0	0
Traill	20	595	34.4	17.5	23	80	15.9	2.2	611	24.7	4,931	16
Walsh	39	726	45.8	21.7	38	101	7.0	1.9	797	33.9	1,960	6

Table B. States and Counties — Government Employment and Payroll, and Local Government Finances

STATE County	Government employment and payroll, 2012									Local government finances, 2012				
			March payroll (percent of total)							General revenue				
												Taxes		
			Adminis-tration, judicial, and legal	Police and corrections	Fire protection	Highways and transpor-tation	Health and welfare	Natural resources and utilities	Education and libraries		Inter-govern-mental		Per capita[1] (dollars)	
	Full-time equivalent employees	March payroll (dollars)								Total (mil dol)	(mil dol)	Total (mil dol)	Total	Property
	171	172	173	174	175	176	177	178	179	180	181	182	183	184
NORTH CAROLINA—Cont'd														
Swain	570	1,634,935	2.8	6.9	0.0	0.2	15.2	3.5	58.7	39.0	24.0	8.3	586	366
Transylvania	1,211	3,349,488	5.1	9.9	0.5	1.7	16.3	4.8	52.7	82.0	34.9	38.2	1,162	930
Tyrrell	212	788,126	5.4	5.1	0.0	0.3	6.1	4.4	76.8	19.0	12.0	4.7	1,091	930
Union	6,960	22,437,486	4.7	8.5	1.4	0.7	5.2	5.8	72.3	593.9	274.3	239.3	1,148	942
Vance	2,151	6,716,262	3.1	6.3	2.9	1.8	9.0	3.0	71.8	166.4	101.2	37.4	828	618
Wake	31,235	120,436,016	3.6	9.3	3.7	3.7	7.3	6.6	61.6	3,180.9	1,227.2	1,366.9	1,436	1,077
Warren	682	2,143,055	2.8	7.9	0.0	0.0	10.7	3.8	61.2	57.4	29.8	20.1	976	845
Washington	551	1,546,357	6.0	8.2	0.0	0.4	15.3	5.7	59.9	40.0	25.2	10.3	805	588
Watauga	1,481	4,632,704	6.0	11.0	2.1	4.5	13.2	7.1	47.6	137.3	56.5	63.0	1,214	855
Wayne	5,237	14,176,474	3.0	6.2	2.1	1.3	9.2	6.0	66.2	346.7	199.6	101.5	817	585
Wilkes	3,431	10,259,077	2.0	4.8	0.3	0.9	32.4	1.6	56.6	184.5	95.3	58.2	840	635
Wilson	3,417	11,244,041	5.5	9.5	3.3	2.4	11.6	11.2	53.8	288.2	140.0	90.5	1,105	863
Yadkin	1,268	3,737,818	3.9	5.9	0.1	0.5	11.5	3.0	70.9	88.3	50.5	29.0	763	624
Yancey	773	2,283,963	4.6	6.2	0.2	1.0	23.0	3.1	60.9	45.5	25.0	17.2	973	798
NORTH DAKOTA	X	X	X	X	X	X	X	X	X	X	X	X	X	X
Adams	92	255,672	10.2	8.6	0.0	6.4	7.5	3.3	62.1	8.2	3.6	3.0	1,313	1,054
Barnes	418	1,392,699	15.6	9.1	0.5	3.9	5.1	9.8	55.6	66.9	40.2	17.6	1,597	1,448
Benson	305	941,315	6.1	1.3	0.6	5.7	5.8	1.7	78.6	27.9	19.5	4.6	683	672
Billings	71	278,902	16.6	9.9	1.1	28.8	4.2	4.9	31.5	14.4	10.4	1.7	1,884	1,457
Bottineau	258	801,858	8.7	5.1	0.1	7.5	5.5	8.6	64.2	29.2	15.4	8.8	1,337	1,194
Bowman	154	498,076	10.9	6.0	0.1	7.5	7.8	4.7	63.1	25.9	15.6	5.2	1,630	1,395
Burke	132	476,712	12.0	4.9	0.0	8.5	2.8	2.4	67.3	11.4	4.8	4.8	2,215	1,096
Burleigh	2,640	9,881,026	4.2	8.2	4.2	3.6	6.6	9.1	61.0	347.2	171.6	100.7	1,174	925
Cass	4,659	18,693,995	4.8	9.4	2.9	4.9	9.6	7.5	60.1	694.2	293.1	246.4	1,578	1,145
Cavalier	150	482,792	10.3	7.1	0.0	7.2	5.9	7.5	58.4	17.1	7.4	6.7	1,688	1,662
Dickey	177	602,013	11.3	6.4	0.0	5.8	12.2	3.2	59.7	28.7	12.8	9.2	1,751	1,617
Divide	112	399,142	14.1	7.5	0.0	19.6	4.6	5.6	47.0	17.6	9.2	3.7	1,673	1,505
Dunn	163	514,670	8.7	4.7	0.8	11.8	6.5	2.4	65.0	27.2	19.0	3.9	992	865
Eddy	101	291,076	9.8	5.2	0.0	6.4	5.8	4.1	67.8	12.9	6.6	3.2	1,370	1,257
Emmons	160	461,725	8.9	3.7	0.1	7.4	1.9	9.4	68.6	16.2	7.3	6.2	1,777	1,711
Foster	109	345,480	14.5	2.4	0.1	5.2	6.9	1.6	67.7	14.4	6.3	5.0	1,462	1,302
Golden Valley	168	598,525	4.4	2.4	0.0	4.3	3.1	1.4	83.6	12.6	6.8	3.5	1,923	1,846
Grand Forks	2,414	9,092,121	5.6	9.8	3.4	6.3	6.5	11.9	54.2	280.6	106.1	94.4	1,399	1,054
Grant	103	251,784	10.0	5.5	0.0	9.2	10.7	3.2	60.2	8.5	3.8	3.4	1,448	1,414
Griggs	112	363,293	9.3	4.3	0.0	8.1	9.0	2.0	65.6	13.5	5.4	5.3	2,241	2,176
Hettinger	147	439,881	7.5	2.1	0.1	8.1	4.0	22.4	54.8	15.0	6.5	5.4	2,133	1,985
Kidder	100	305,849	4.8	4.8	0.0	1.6	8.6	4.8	75.3	16.0	7.8	3.7	1,533	1,484
LaMoure	228	740,715	7.4	3.3	0.0	6.3	2.2	19.6	60.3	63.8	47.3	9.5	2,316	2,252
Logan	83	243,512	4.2	4.7	0.0	5.7	6.1	5.0	73.3	10.5	5.6	3.9	2,040	2,023
McHenry	239	766,397	8.6	2.6	0.1	4.2	4.4	4.0	74.9	20.6	10.3	7.3	1,263	1,225
McIntosh	139	432,649	7.6	5.1	0.1	10.8	4.4	16.0	55.9	10.7	5.5	3.7	1,328	1,289
McKenzie	313	1,128,904	9.9	9.8	0.0	9.8	6.5	4.0	57.4	54.1	24.6	7.4	930	751
McLean	438	1,374,148	6.7	7.0	0.0	5.7	12.1	3.3	64.5	43.6	23.1	11.4	1,229	1,093
Mercer	347	1,135,199	9.4	9.5	0.0	9.4	2.8	4.7	62.2	34.8	17.4	9.3	1,093	917
Morton	946	3,200,962	5.4	9.1	1.2	7.7	8.1	5.9	61.5	106.1	48.2	35.2	1,253	1,139
Mountrail	385	1,261,569	8.3	7.4	0.0	8.6	6.2	3.5	65.1	85.8	57.9	12.5	1,434	1,307
Nelson	146	457,045	9.7	3.0	0.0	8.5	4.7	8.9	63.6	17.3	8.0	6.7	2,183	2,144
Oliver	76	233,042	14.9	6.8	0.0	9.6	2.9	7.5	56.4	9.0	3.8	3.7	2,018	1,749
Pembina	393	1,633,628	6.4	4.3	0.0	3.1	4.1	45.4	36.2	40.0	15.7	16.1	2,221	2,125
Pierce	154	464,990	7.2	8.4	0.0	4.1	5.0	3.6	69.5	21.3	8.8	5.5	1,245	1,151
Ramsey	543	1,755,199	7.3	12.7	1.3	4.3	10.4	5.8	57.4	84.1	57.8	15.4	1,331	1,034
Ransom	223	692,010	8.7	4.1	0.8	4.5	6.6	5.2	68.5	23.4	12.3	7.8	1,436	1,220
Renville	140	452,741	8.2	6.0	0.0	8.7	3.5	2.3	70.0	19.2	9.5	5.9	2,288	2,255
Richland	582	2,019,868	4.8	9.7	0.0	6.5	9.5	7.4	61.0	75.6	33.2	29.0	1,787	1,613
Rolette	726	2,856,302	1.9	2.3	0.2	1.2	3.8	2.8	87.6	53.9	43.3	5.9	409	382
Sargent	167	536,100	9.7	3.9	0.0	3.3	5.4	6.8	70.4	21.4	9.5	8.1	2,073	2,002
Sheridan	59	160,666	12.8	0.0	0.0	8.5	0.2	3.7	73.9	5.6	2.2	2.9	2,255	2,229
Sioux	129	394,909	4.4	0.8	1.7	4.0	0.3	1.7	86.3	11.5	9.3	1.5	349	348
Slope	36	114,876	15.1	4.2	0.0	6.9	0.2	2.1	68.6	5.2	3.3	1.0	1,297	1,208
Stark	970	3,430,314	4.3	17.8	1.0	4.4	10.3	9.5	51.8	103.5	43.2	33.0	1,232	836
Steele	76	279,013	12.8	4.5	0.1	2.6	1.4	2.1	76.4	12.4	4.6	4.9	2,441	2,369
Stutsman	738	2,551,998	5.2	10.8	0.9	5.8	9.7	7.6	58.2	88.6	38.8	29.6	1,413	1,195
Towner	120	341,158	12.4	5.1	0.0	10.5	3.7	3.7	63.4	10.1	3.9	3.9	1,695	1,626
Traill	299	1,042,936	6.6	4.5	0.0	5.7	5.6	2.7	74.1	35.7	16.3	11.8	1,468	1,367
Walsh	425	1,396,845	7.5	5.6	0.0	5.1	6.2	9.3	63.8	46.8	22.8	16.0	1,451	1,295

1. Based on the resident population estimated as of July 1 of the year shown.

Table B. States and Counties — Local Government Finances, Government Employment, and Income Taxes

	Local government finances, 2012 (cont.)									Government employment, 2017			Individual income tax returns, 2016		
	Direct general expenditure							Debt outstanding							
			Percent of total for:											Mean adjusted gross income	Mean income tax
STATE County	Total (mil dol)	Per capita[1] (dollars)	Education	Health and hospitals	Police protection	Public welfare	Highways	Total (mil dol)	Per capita[1] (dollars)	Federal civilian	Federal military	State and local	Number of returns		
	185	186	187	188	189	190	191	192	193	194	195	196	197	198	199
NORTH CAROLINA— Cont'd															
Swain	40.3	2,852	47.4	5.4	7.2	14.3	0.2	10.7	758	153	32	2,483	7,910	41,387	3,989
Transylvania	80.6	2,453	45.7	4.8	9.9	7.4	1.1	13.0	395	134	74	1,324	14,580	53,377	5,802
Tyrrell	18.9	4,355	54.4	1.2	9.5	7.3	0.7	10.3	2,385	20	8	439	1,670	34,007	2,684
Union	614.4	2,946	53.1	2.0	6.1	4.7	1.0	748.0	3,587	297	517	9,092	97,460	81,303	11,498
Vance	164.7	3,650	56.0	9.8	6.5	7.1	0.6	48.5	1,074	96	98	2,547	18,730	39,577	3,669
Wake	3,282.9	3,448	42.3	4.0	6.5	3.3	2.2	9,085.4	9,542	5,620	3,034	79,874	490,660	82,847	12,015
Warren	54.2	2,635	50.1	5.1	10.5	10.6	0.3	7.2	348	31	43	1,233	7,720	38,097	3,043
Washington	43.9	3,443	43.6	0.4	7.2	13.8	1.5	7.6	594	29	27	782	5,120	37,556	3,108
Watauga	128.3	2,473	32.3	4.5	9.1	5.1	3.7	134.7	2,596	109	118	6,425	19,680	55,262	6,789
Wayne	344.7	2,774	55.1	4.8	6.3	6.3	1.4	151.3	1,217	1,225	4,485	8,044	51,490	47,797	5,049
Wilkes	183.3	2,645	60.4	4.2	5.5	7.8	0.6	49.6	715	187	152	4,185	27,500	44,481	4,222
Wilson	278.4	3,401	41.7	5.4	8.2	8.1	1.5	192.4	2,351	132	181	4,943	35,530	45,643	4,578
Yadkin	87.9	2,308	57.4	4.6	6.9	10.0	0.9	50.3	1,322	75	85	1,426	16,220	46,731	4,445
Yancey	44.5	2,522	51.4	2.5	6.4	10.3	0.6	14.3	810	44	40	840	7,450	41,962	3,664
NORTH DAKOTA	X	X	X	X	X	X	X	X	X	9,429	11,679	67,481	360,090	66,360	8,996
Adams	8.2	3,529	45.9	0.0	4.8	3.9	18.8	0.1	33	17	14	127	1,100	47,526	5,482
Barnes	64.0	5,811	34.3	4.3	8.8	3.5	21.8	18.2	1,650	78	64	1,071	5,180	57,711	6,749
Benson	27.4	4,053	65.7	0.2	1.4	3.3	17.2	0.6	85	119	43	1,399	2,500	40,268	4,088
Billings	17.0	18,828	14.4	6.5	9.0	0.0	56.2	0.1	133	39	6	123	460	65,737	9,317
Bottineau	32.3	4,914	41.2	2.2	4.2	0.0	32.5	11.5	1,748	73	39	620	3,170	58,966	7,448
Bowman	21.3	6,655	38.7	2.4	2.9	1.6	30.5	1.3	409	22	19	245	1,540	60,858	8,241
Burke	10.7	4,949	47.9	0.4	2.6	2.0	26.1	0.1	67	91	13	180	1,080	63,829	8,406
Burleigh	313.0	3,649	41.6	1.2	5.7	1.7	12.7	181.5	2,116	1,126	576	10,675	46,120	73,417	10,131
Cass	703.9	4,508	39.9	0.1	5.6	3.0	13.2	1,204.5	7,713	2,449	1,100	12,399	86,020	73,335	10,850
Cavalier	16.8	4,263	40.9	2.0	4.3	4.3	23.7	11.4	2,878	39	23	214	1,880	62,067	7,845
Dickey	36.5	6,935	38.3	1.4	3.0	1.6	13.3	34.3	6,520	26	29	295	2,450	51,368	5,687
Divide	23.6	10,577	21.6	1.5	4.6	0.7	33.8	0.9	389	32	14	152	1,130	60,982	8,282
Dunn	24.7	6,221	37.5	0.0	3.7	1.5	33.1	0.3	74	18	26	296	1,970	66,906	9,520
Eddy	13.4	5,660	43.4	0.1	4.4	2.5	14.8	1.6	686	20	14	166	1,170	47,853	5,897
Emmons	14.9	4,274	52.4	1.3	1.9	2.0	14.2	3.8	1,081	22	20	235	1,580	43,546	5,020
Foster	13.8	4,065	45.3	1.9	3.7	2.8	14.1	10.6	3,116	24	20	215	1,640	68,393	7,839
Golden Valley	12.7	7,062	41.7	1.5	3.3	2.2	17.1	4.6	2,568	9	11	164	800	54,303	6,683
Grand Forks	251.5	3,728	47.0	1.0	5.1	1.4	4.7	705.5	10,456	1,030	2,022	9,293	32,840	63,912	8,667
Grant	8.1	3,453	49.5	18.0	2.5	2.6	12.7	1.2	524	22	15	130	1,050	35,234	4,570
Griggs	13.1	5,527	43.9	3.5	2.8	2.9	21.9	3.7	1,562	20	14	177	1,170	54,854	5,903
Hettinger	16.2	6,357	49.8	0.0	2.6	2.3	14.4	1.9	738	18	14	190	1,140	50,926	6,386
Kidder	15.9	6,560	32.7	24.9	1.7	1.4	20.1	2.4	973	21	15	152	1,150	50,403	5,826
LaMoure	23.0	5,581	54.0	0.0	2.5	2.6	15.6	7.0	1,691	39	25	310	1,960	55,648	6,949
Logan	8.8	4,566	63.4	1.0	2.8	0.2	13.9	1.7	867	16	12	137	890	30,663	4,174
McHenry	20.8	3,592	61.0	0.0	2.3	2.7	13.3	1.0	180	43	37	319	2,700	51,730	5,747
McIntosh	10.1	3,663	56.1	1.5	2.9	2.7	15.9	1.7	619	17	16	182	1,350	41,437	4,796
McKenzie	61.8	7,738	29.9	3.0	3.5	1.3	31.4	15.2	1,897	68	79	2,266	4,760	99,408	17,864
McLean	38.0	4,086	53.6	1.4	4.7	3.8	12.0	18.4	1,973	117	60	733	4,690	61,027	7,495
Mercer	37.5	4,418	49.3	0.5	5.7	1.3	17.4	59.3	6,990	36	52	551	4,100	71,846	9,074
Morton	106.7	3,797	49.8	2.5	5.2	2.3	6.9	103.5	3,685	104	188	1,685	15,450	62,516	7,772
Mountrail	86.5	9,907	36.3	0.5	1.9	1.2	37.1	26.9	3,081	46	61	748	4,400	76,095	11,136
Nelson	16.3	5,277	44.9	2.6	2.2	1.3	18.7	14.3	4,644	19	18	226	1,530	54,243	7,437
Oliver	7.8	4,256	42.5	0.0	3.8	0.0	8.3	20.2	10,993	7	12	111	850	60,667	6,792
Pembina	37.7	5,190	45.2	0.5	3.9	2.4	8.5	14.9	2,043	231	82	531	3,480	60,618	7,736
Pierce	24.3	5,462	53.5	2.7	4.5	1.9	9.5	4.3	974	20	24	254	1,980	53,188	5,816
Ramsey	75.8	6,569	35.0	0.9	2.9	2.1	20.4	33.0	2,865	136	69	1,377	5,640	55,938	6,586
Ransom	25.2	4,634	45.6	1.6	2.9	1.7	12.3	21.6	3,965	40	32	483	2,660	55,525	6,017
Renville	20.6	8,041	40.3	0.1	2.1	0.0	28.2	3.6	1,387	26	15	203	1,210	57,339	6,431
Richland	75.3	4,645	43.3	4.4	4.5	1.9	13.1	88.9	5,482	62	101	1,850	7,700	60,776	7,265
Rolette	53.3	3,703	79.0	1.4	2.2	2.2	5.1	6.0	419	934	90	1,893	5,180	42,783	3,940
Sargent	19.0	4,886	48.6	1.5	1.7	2.4	13.8	11.5	2,940	40	24	255	1,990	55,840	6,537
Sheridan	5.5	4,306	39.7	1.2	1.7	1.0	20.2	0.2	179	9	8	102	600	45,363	4,590
Sioux	11.0	2,521	85.3	0.0	0.5	4.1	5.3	3.0	686	236	27	1,228	1,280	27,740	2,280
Slope	3.6	4,734	14.2	2.9	4.4	0.0	33.2	0.4	538	0	5	35	330	59,891	7,406
Stark	96.5	3,605	41.6	0.9	4.4	3.4	11.2	19.1	712	197	185	2,272	15,090	68,840	8,964
Steele	11.3	5,664	42.7	0.0	2.8	4.2	26.4	5.7	2,876	11	12	109	940	61,855	7,611
Stutsman	83.3	3,978	42.4	3.2	5.0	2.2	13.9	57.9	2,766	163	121	1,870	10,290	57,224	7,137
Towner	8.9	3,844	45.7	5.0	3.3	2.3	18.6	2.2	931	19	14	131	1,140	52,783	5,900
Traill	35.4	4,390	54.9	0.9	3.8	2.9	12.5	42.5	5,269	38	48	852	3,760	67,467	8,539
Walsh	51.9	4,703	54.4	1.3	4.4	2.5	9.7	23.8	2,156	52	66	1,082	5,240	54,743	6,308

1. Based on the resident population estimated as of July 1 of the year shown.

Table B. States and Counties — **Land Area and Population**

State / county code	CBSA code[1]	County code[2]	STATE County	Land area[3] (sq. mi)	Total persons 2018	Rank	Per square mile	White	Black	American Indian, Alaska Native	Asian and Pacific Islancer	Percent Hispanic or Latino[4]	Under 5 years	5 to 17 years	18 to 24 years	25 to 34 years	35 to 44 years	45 to 54 years
				1	2	3	4	5	6	7	8	9	10	11	12	13	14	15
			NORTH DAKOTA— Cont'd															
38101	33,500	5	Ward	2,013.0	67,744	787	33.7	85.0	5.6	3.2	2.9	6.3	7.7	15.9	12.7	18.2	12.2	9.7
38103		9	Wells	1,270.6	3,957	2,904	3.1	97.1	0.8	1.5	0.7	1.2	5.8	15.2	5.5	9.7	8.0	11.4
38105	48,780	7	Williams	2,077.9	35,350	1,294	17.0	82.8	5.0	6.1	1.6	7.9	9.6	19.0	8.6	19.1	12.8	10.5
39000		0	OHIO	40,860.8	11,689,442	X	286.1	80.6	14.0	0.7	3.0	3.9	5.9	16.2	9.1	13.2	11.9	12.7
39001		6	Adams	583.9	27,724	1,505	47.5	97.6	1.0	1.3	0.5	1.0	6.0	17.8	7.4	11.1	11.7	13.4
39003	30,620	3	Allen	402.5	102,663	593	255.1	83.4	14.5	0.7	1.2	3.2	6.2	16.9	9.7	12.3	11.7	11.9
39005	11,740	4	Ashland	423.0	53,745	942	127.1	96.7	1.4	0.6	1.1	1.5	5.8	16.7	10.9	11.1	10.8	12.1
39007	11,780	4	Ashtabula	702.1	97,493	614	138.9	91.3	4.9	0.8	0.8	4.3	5.7	16.4	7.6	11.6	11.2	13.5
39009	11,900	4	Athens	503.6	65,818	811	130.7	91.4	3.7	1.1	4.2	1.9	3.9	10.7	28.2	12.6	10.2	10.2
39011	47,540	4	Auglaize	401.4	45,804	1,055	114.1	96.8	1.2	0.5	0.9	1.8	6.4	17.7	7.9	11.4	11.4	12.6
39013	48,540	3	Belmont	532.1	67,505	791	126.9	94.1	5.2	0.6	0.7	1.0	4.8	14.1	7.5	12.6	11.7	12.8
39015	17,140	1	Brown	490.0	43,602	1,101	89.0	97.4	1.4	0.8	0.5	1.1	5.7	17.1	7.4	11.3	11.8	13.6
39017	17,140	1	Butler	466.6	382,378	182	819.5	82.6	9.9	0.6	4.3	4.9	6.0	17.4	12.2	11.9	12.1	12.7
39019	15,940	2	Carroll	394.6	27,081	1,522	68.6	97.2	1.2	0.9	0.6	1.4	5.1	16.0	7.0	10.3	10.9	13.2
39021	46,500	6	Champaign	429.0	38,754	1,208	90.3	95.3	3.4	1.0	0.8	1.6	5.3	16.8	8.4	11.5	11.2	14.0
39023	44,220	3	Clark	396.9	134,585	474	339.1	86.6	10.7	0.9	1.2	3.5	5.9	16.5	9.1	11.7	10.8	12.7
39025	17,140	1	Clermont	452.1	205,466	328	454.5	94.8	2.3	0.7	1.8	2.0	5.7	17.3	7.7	12.5	12.4	13.5
39027	48,940	6	Clinton	408.7	42,057	1,135	102.9	95.4	3.4	0.8	0.9	1.5	6.0	17.1	9.5	11.5	11.7	12.8
39029	41,400	4	Columbiana	531.9	102,665	592	193.0	95.2	3.1	0.6	0.6	1.9	5.1	15.2	7.3	11.4	11.7	13.1
39031	18,740	6	Coshocton	563.9	36,629	1,261	65.0	97.1	2.0	0.7	0.6	1.0	6.5	17.3	7.3	11.4	11.2	12.7
39033	15,340	4	Crawford	401.8	41,550	1,143	103.4	96.3	1.7	0.6	0.9	1.8	5.7	15.9	7.6	11.1	11.4	12.9
39035	17,460	1	Cuyahoga	457.2	1,243,857	35	2,720.6	60.5	30.9	0.6	3.9	6.2	5.7	15.0	8.7	14.2	11.5	12.4
39037	24,820	6	Darke	598.1	51,323	969	85.8	97.0	1.2	0.6	0.7	1.7	6.1	17.5	7.7	10.7	11.2	12.9
39039	19,580	4	Defiance	411.5	38,165	1,221	92.7	87.3	2.4	0.7	0.7	10.3	5.7	17.2	8.9	11.8	11.8	11.9
39041	18,140	1	Delaware	443.2	204,826	329	462.2	86.3	4.5	0.5	8.0	2.7	6.1	20.2	7.8	9.8	15.1	15.2
39043	41,780	4	Erie	251.4	74,615	740	296.8	85.8	10.6	0.8	1.1	4.6	5.3	14.9	7.8	11.5	10.5	12.6
39045	18,140	1	Fairfield	504.4	155,782	425	308.8	87.6	9.2	0.8	2.3	2.3	6.0	18.1	8.3	11.9	12.9	13.9
39047	47,920	6	Fayette	406.4	28,666	1,471	70.5	94.3	3.6	0.8	1.2	2.3	5.9	17.4	7.7	12.0	11.9	13.3
39049	18,140	1	Franklin	532.4	1,310,300	31	2,461.1	65.2	24.9	0.9	6.5	5.7	7.1	16.2	9.8	18.3	13.4	11.9
39051	45,780	2	Fulton	405.4	42,276	1,132	104.3	89.8	1.1	0.6	0.7	8.9	6.0	17.5	8.3	11.2	11.7	12.9
39053	38,580	6	Gallia	466.5	29,979	1,432	64.3	94.8	3.3	1.0	1.3	1.5	6.2	16.5	8.6	11.4	11.3	12.5
39055	17,460	1	Geauga	400.3	94,031	630	234.9	96.4	1.6	0.4	1.0	1.6	5.3	17.6	8.3	8.8	10.4	13.7
39057	19,380	2	Greene	413.6	167,995	389	406.2	86.3	8.6	1.0	4.2	2.9	5.7	15.0	11.9	13.3	11.4	11.9
39059	15,740	6	Guernsey	522.3	39,022	1,203	74.7	96.4	2.6	0.9	0.8	1.2	5.9	16.3	7.8	11.8	10.9	13.1
39061	17,140	1	Hamilton	405.9	816,684	75	2,012.0	67.1	27.8	0.7	3.5	3.5	6.5	16.5	9.3	15.3	11.9	11.9
39063	22,300	4	Hancock	531.3	75,930	731	142.9	90.5	2.7	0.6	2.3	5.6	6.0	16.2	9.0	13.7	11.6	12.4
39065		6	Hardin	470.4	31,480	1,394	66.9	96.3	1.6	0.7	1.0	1.8	6.2	17.1	15.2	10.4	10.7	11.8
39067		6	Harrison	402.3	15,174	2,082	37.7	96.2	3.0	0.6	0.4	1.3	5.4	15.6	6.8	10.6	10.5	13.3
39069		6	Henry	416.0	27,086	1,521	65.1	90.7	1.1	0.7	0.7	7.8	5.7	17.5	7.7	11.4	12.0	12.5
39071		6	Highland	553.1	43,058	1,115	77.8	96.6	2.5	0.8	0.6	1.2	6.4	17.5	7.4	11.5	11.7	13.2
39073	18,140	1	Hocking	421.3	28,385	1,483	67.4	97.5	1.2	1.0	0.6	1.1	5.6	16.4	7.5	11.2	11.6	13.5
39075		7	Holmes	422.6	43,892	1,095	103.9	98.3	0.6	0.3	0.4	1.0	8.1	22.9	9.9	12.8	10.9	10.6
39077	35,940	4	Huron	491.5	58,504	884	119.0	91.3	2.0	0.8	0.6	6.9	6.5	17.6	8.3	11.8	11.5	13.2
39079	27,160	7	Jackson	420.3	32,384	1,371	77.0	97.4	1.3	1.2	0.5	1.1	6.4	17.2	7.6	12.6	12.1	13.0
39081	48,260	3	Jefferson	408.1	65,767	812	161.2	92.3	6.7	0.7	0.9	1.5	5.0	14.1	9.5	10.9	10.4	12.8
39083	34,540	4	Knox	525.5	61,893	851	117.8	96.6	1.7	0.6	1.0	1.5	6.1	16.6	11.4	11.0	10.7	12.1
39085	17,460	1	Lake	229.3	230,514	291	1,005.3	89.2	5.3	0.5	2.0	4.7	4.9	15.1	7.7	12.1	11.4	13.4
39087	26,580	2	Lawrence	453.4	59,866	871	132.0	96.1	3.1	0.7	0.7	1.0	5.5	16.2	7.4	12.0	12.2	13.8
39089	18,140	1	Licking	682.4	175,769	376	257.6	91.8	5.2	0.8	2.3	2.0	6.0	17.1	9.0	11.9	12.0	13.5
39091	13,340	6	Logan	458.4	45,358	1,066	98.9	95.4	3.2	0.8	1.2	1.6	5.8	17.1	7.8	11.5	11.7	13.1
39093	17,460	1	Lorain	491.2	309,461	225	630.0	80.3	9.6	0.8	1.8	10.2	5.6	16.4	8.6	11.3	12.0	13.4
39095	45,780	2	Lucas	340.7	429,899	164	1,261.8	71.0	21.6	0.8	2.3	7.3	6.4	16.6	8.8	14.3	11.5	12.3
39097	18,140	1	Madison	465.8	44,413	1,089	95.3	89.8	7.2	0.8	1.7	2.1	5.1	15.5	8.0	13.6	14.3	14.7
39099	49,660	2	Mahoning	411.5	229,642	295	558.1	77.3	16.4	0.7	1.3	6.4	5.3	14.7	8.4	12.0	11.1	12.3
39101	32,020	4	Marion	403.8	65,256	820	161.6	90.0	7.6	0.7	0.9	2.8	5.7	15.2	8.1	13.4	12.3	13.4
39103	17,460	1	Medina	421.4	179,146	370	425.1	95.0	2.0	0.5	1.6	2.1	5.4	17.0	7.5	10.8	12.4	14.5
39105		6	Meigs	430.1	23,106	1,675	53.7	97.8	1.5	0.8	0.4	0.8	5.3	16.1	6.8	11.0	12.1	13.6
39107	16,380	7	Mercer	462.4	40,959	1,152	88.6	96.0	1.0	0.5	1.5	2.1	7.5	18.2	7.9	11.8	10.9	11.4
39109	19,380	2	Miami	406.5	106,222	571	261.3	93.9	3.6	0.6	2.1	1.7	6.0	16.9	7.2	12.0	12.1	13.1
39111		8	Monroe	455.7	13,790	2,175	30.3	98.4	1.1	0.9	0.4	0.6	5.0	15.2	6.6	10.5	10.6	13.3
39113	19,380	2	Montgomery	461.5	532,331	132	1,153.5	73.0	22.8	0.9	3.1	3.1	6.1	16.0	9.2	13.7	11.4	12.2
39115		6	Morgan	416.4	14,604	2,120	35.1	95.2	5.4	1.5	0.8	1.0	5.1	15.8	7.3	10.7	11.2	13.0
39117	18,140	1	Morrow	406.1	35,112	1,302	86.5	97.2	1.2	0.8	0.6	1.5	5.3	17.5	7.1	11.0	12.3	14.1
39119	49,780	4	Muskingum	664.5	86,183	670	129.7	94.1	5.8	0.9	0.9	1.2	6.0	16.6	8.9	12.2	11.6	12.9
39121		7	Noble	398.0	14,354	2,135	36.1	96.0	3.2	0.8	0.5	0.7	4.7	13.6	5.8	9.1	8.2	11.5

1. CBSA = Core Based Statistical Area. See Appendix A for explanation. See Appendix B for list of metropolitan areas with component counties.   2. County type code from the Economic Research Service of USDA Rural-Urban Continuum Codes. See Appendix A for definition.   3. Dry land or land partially or temporarily covered by water.   4. May be of any race.

Items 1—15

Table B. States and Counties — Population and Households

STATE County	Age (percent) (cont.) 55 to 64 years	65 to 74 years	75 years and over	Percent female	Population change, 2000-2018 Total persons 2000	2010	Percent change 2000-2010	2010-2018	Components of change, 2010-2018 Births	Deaths	Net Migration	Households, 2013-2017 Number	Persons per household	Family house-holds	Percent Female family house-holder[1]	One person
	16	17	18	19	20	21	22	23	24	25	26	27	28	29	30	31
NORTH DAKOTA— Cont'd																
Ward	10.8	6.9	5.9	47.6	58,795	61,675	4.9	9.8	9,641	3,972	226	27,449	2.44	60.1	6.3	30.9
Wells	16.5	13.2	14.6	49.3	5,102	4,207	-17.5	-5.9	356	549	-59	1,988	2.01	61.6	3.3	34.4
Williams	10.8	5.4	4.2	46.1	19,761	22,399	13.3	57.8	4,768	1,890	9,692	12,895	2.50	61.8	5.5	28.1
OHIO	13.8	9.8	7.2	51.0	11,353,140	11,536,757	1.6	1.3	1,138,227	946,276	-35,269	4,633,145	2.44	63.8	12.7	30.0
Adams	14.7	10.5	7.4	50.4	27,330	28,559	4.5	-2.9	2,776	2,757	-847	10,829	2.54	67.7	13.0	28.1
Allen	13.7	10.0	7.6	49.6	108,473	106,315	-2.0	-3.4	10,445	8,979	-5,125	40,319	2.48	65.7	13.8	29.0
Ashland	13.8	10.4	8.3	50.8	52,523	53,140	1.2	1.1	5,037	4,550	132	20,504	2.49	67.8	9.7	26.7
Ashtabula	15.0	11.0	8.1	49.6	102,728	101,490	-1.2	-3.9	9,157	9,593	-3,557	38,381	2.48	65.1	12.6	29.3
Athens	11.2	8.1	5.0	50.2	62,223	64,764	4.1	1.6	4,439	3,994	504	22,509	2.48	55.1	9.8	32.0
Auglaize	14.2	10.2	8.1	50.0	46,611	45,949	-1.4	-0.3	4,539	3,955	-721	18,342	2.47	69.7	9.1	25.6
Belmont	15.7	11.9	8.9	48.9	70,226	70,405	0.3	-4.1	5,586	7,320	-1,100	26,910	2.41	65.3	11.0	30.6
Brown	15.0	10.3	7.7	50.4	42,285	44,828	6.0	-2.7	4,097	4,060	-1,256	17,333	2.49	71.6	12.2	23.6
Butler	13.0	8.7	6.0	50.9	332,807	368,135	10.6	3.9	37,216	26,244	3,494	136,416	2.67	69.0	12.1	24.3
Carroll	16.4	12.2	9.0	49.9	28,836	28,835	0.0	-6.1	2,279	2,558	-1,472	10,917	2.51	71.5	8.2	23.7
Champaign	14.5	10.5	7.7	50.2	38,890	40,099	3.1	-3.4	3,310	3,234	-1,422	15,274	2.50	70.4	11.4	24.1
Clark	13.9	11.1	8.3	51.6	144,742	138,341	-4.4	-2.7	13,123	14,039	-2,772	54,836	2.41	65.5	14.1	28.3
Clermont	14.6	9.9	6.4	50.7	177,977	197,365	10.9	4.1	19,253	13,810	2,844	76,143	2.63	71.4	10.5	23.6
Clinton	14.3	10.0	7.0	50.7	40,543	42,035	3.7	0.1	4,144	3,594	-519	16,309	2.49	68.0	11.7	26.9
Columbiana	15.7	11.8	8.7	49.4	112,075	107,852	-3.8	-4.8	8,911	10,078	-3,989	41,582	2.42	68.6	12.7	27.2
Coshocton	14.3	10.9	8.6	50.4	36,655	36,898	0.7	-0.7	3,747	3,251	-748	14,367	2.52	67.5	9.7	27.8
Crawford	14.4	11.6	9.4	51.1	46,966	43,783	-6.8	-5.1	3,927	4,441	-1,716	17,833	2.34	64.9	11.7	30.5
Cuyahoga	14.3	10.1	8.1	52.3	1,393,978	1,280,115	-8.2	-2.8	122,180	112,767	-45,648	537,621	2.29	56.7	15.8	37.3
Darke	14.3	10.7	9.0	50.4	53,309	52,969	-0.6	-3.1	5,107	4,801	-1,947	20,803	2.46	69.0	9.0	26.2
Defiance	14.1	10.6	8.0	50.4	39,500	39,030	-1.2	-2.2	3,633	3,211	-1,294	15,309	2.46	69.4	11.7	24.3
Delaware	12.1	8.5	5.2	50.4	109,989	174,172	58.4	17.6	17,685	8,486	21,367	67,701	2.81	76.4	7.1	19.7
Erie	15.5	12.5	9.4	51.2	79,551	77,066	-3.1	-3.2	6,472	7,662	-1,220	31,577	2.34	63.0	12.9	30.2
Fairfield	13.2	9.3	6.5	50.2	122,759	146,182	19.1	6.6	13,873	10,097	5,941	55,549	2.68	72.3	10.6	23.0
Fayette	14.0	10.4	7.3	50.8	28,433	29,035	2.1	-1.3	2,827	2,936	-245	11,729	2.41	68.3	13.8	26.8
Franklin	11.4	7.3	4.7	51.1	1,068,978	1,163,532	8.8	12.6	153,483	75,442	69,013	496,337	2.47	58.7	14.1	32.0
Fulton	14.7	10.3	7.5	50.3	42,084	42,698	1.5	-1.0	4,012	3,399	-1,038	16,404	2.55	73.3	9.6	22.9
Gallia	14.5	10.7	8.4	50.5	31,069	30,942	-0.4	-3.1	3,092	3,025	-1,039	11,520	2.55	68.3	10.3	27.5
Geauga	15.6	11.7	8.7	50.4	90,895	93,409	2.8	0.7	7,556	6,644	-272	35,121	2.65	74.8	7.0	20.3
Greene	13.7	10.0	7.2	50.7	147,886	161,576	9.3	4.0	14,728	11,413	3,132	64,702	2.41	65.8	10.0	28.4
Guernsey	14.7	11.3	8.2	50.1	40,792	40,091	-1.7	-2.7	3,772	3,758	-1,063	16,065	2.42	66.0	13.0	27.4
Hamilton	13.3	8.8	6.5	51.7	845,303	802,372	-5.1	1.8	89,630	64,407	-10,576	338,267	2.34	57.9	14.9	34.9
Hancock	13.8	9.8	7.5	50.5	71,295	74,789	4.9	1.5	7,496	5,970	-353	32,049	2.30	62.3	8.1	30.0
Hardin	12.6	9.2	6.8	50.2	31,945	32,060	0.4	-1.8	3,138	2,593	-1,128	11,430	2.56	66.4	9.8	27.9
Harrison	16.6	12.2	9.1	50.2	15,856	15,860	0.0	-4.3	1,297	1,647	-323	6,192	2.44	69.7	9.4	26.0
Henry	14.6	10.2	8.5	50.6	29,210	28,215	-3.4	-4.0	2,605	2,278	-1,469	11,094	2.44	70.3	11.3	25.0
Highland	13.9	10.6	7.8	50.9	40,875	43,602	6.7	-1.2	4,443	3,964	-1,011	16,731	2.54	66.4	12.2	27.8
Hocking	15.1	11.1	8.0	50.4	28,241	29,373	4.0	-3.4	2,589	2,474	-1,102	11,268	2.47	68.6	9.8	25.9
Holmes	11.0	7.7	6.0	49.9	38,943	42,363	8.8	3.6	6,232	2,519	-2,181	12,520	3.43	81.5	6.9	16.0
Huron	14.1	10.2	7.0	50.6	59,487	59,623	0.2	-1.9	6,083	4,786	-2,432	22,876	2.52	68.6	13.1	25.9
Jackson	13.8	10.6	6.7	51.0	32,641	33,225	1.8	-2.5	3,456	3,329	-961	12,964	2.49	68.8	12.7	27.4
Jefferson	15.7	12.3	9.2	51.4	73,894	69,711	-5.7	-5.7	5,412	7,826	-1,473	27,571	2.35	63.7	12.4	30.5
Knox	13.9	10.5	7.6	51.0	54,500	60,932	11.8	1.6	6,011	5,060	40	23,229	2.47	65.7	8.9	27.3
Lake	15.5	11.3	8.7	51.2	227,511	230,050	1.1	0.2	18,571	19,886	1,979	95,238	2.38	65.1	10.3	29.2
Lawrence	14.0	10.9	8.0	51.3	62,319	62,448	0.2	-4.1	5,632	6,188	-1,992	23,731	2.54	66.4	13.1	28.6
Licking	14.0	9.7	6.7	50.9	145,491	166,482	14.4	5.6	16,254	12,788	5,973	64,434	2.59	70.0	12.0	24.5
Logan	15.0	10.9	7.3	50.5	46,005	45,851	-0.3	-1.1	4,446	3,985	-933	18,627	2.41	68.9	11.9	25.8
Lorain	14.4	10.6	7.7	50.8	284,664	301,371	5.9	2.7	27,575	24,500	5,266	118,594	2.50	67.6	13.7	27.5
Lucas	13.8	9.6	6.7	51.5	455,054	441,815	-2.9	-2.7	46,264	36,253	-22,044	178,971	2.37	59.8	15.4	33.4
Madison	13.5	9.0	6.5	45.8	40,213	43,438	8.0	2.2	3,468	3,349	836	14,916	2.59	69.8	11.5	23.8
Mahoning	15.1	11.6	9.4	51.0	257,555	238,788	-7.3	-3.8	19,818	24,941	-3,904	98,035	2.29	61.1	14.5	34.0
Marion	14.0	10.3	7.4	46.9	66,217	66,501	0.4	-1.9	6,260	5,908	-1,570	24,699	2.42	65.7	12.6	29.4
Medina	14.6	10.7	7.2	50.5	151,095	172,333	14.1	4.0	14,581	11,745	4,140	67,192	2.60	71.4	8.3	24.6
Meigs	15.4	11.6	8.3	50.7	23,072	23,767	3.0	-2.8	2,038	2,272	-413	9,285	2.48	68.3	11.7	26.9
Mercer	14.6	10.0	7.8	49.6	40,924	40,814	-0.3	0.4	4,695	3,355	-1,190	16,142	2.49	70.1	7.1	26.3
Miami	14.0	10.8	7.8	50.7	98,868	102,501	3.7	3.6	9,682	8,560	2,699	40,900	2.52	66.0	8.6	27.7
Monroe	15.2	13.3	10.2	49.7	15,180	14,631	-3.6	-5.7	1,187	1,427	-598	5,984	2.35	70.6	11.4	26.8
Montgomery	13.5	10.1	7.9	51.8	559,062	535,191	-4.3	-0.5	54,914	48,801	-8,709	223,495	2.30	60.5	15.0	33.5
Morgan	15.6	11.9	9.5	50.1	14,897	15,053	1.0	-3.0	1,202	1,412	-232	6,116	2.39	70.1	10.6	25.8
Morrow	15.4	10.2	7.1	50.2	31,628	34,829	10.1	0.8	3,107	2,630	-179	12,781	2.71	73.1	9.8	21.8
Muskingum	14.0	10.1	7.7	51.5	84,585	86,086	1.8	0.1	8,496	7,953	-385	34,348	2.45	65.5	12.8	29.2
Noble	19.6	16.7	10.8	41.7	14,058	14,656	4.3	-2.1	1,150	1,069	-374	5,012	2.39	67.7	6.9	29.8

1. No spouse present.

STATE County	Persons in group quarters, 2018	Daytime Population, 2013-2017 Number	Daytime Population, 2013-2017 Employment/ residence ratio	Births, 2018 Total	Births, 2018 Rate[1]	Deaths, 2018 Number	Deaths, 2018 Rate[1]	Persons under 65 with no health insurance, 2016 Number	Persons under 65 with no health insurance, 2016 Percent	Medicare, 2018 Total beneficiaries	Medicare, 2018 Enrolled in Original Medicare	Medicare, 2018 Enrolled in Medicare Advantage	Serious crimes known to police[2], 2016 Total Number	Serious crimes known to police[2], 2016 Total Rate[3]
	32	33	34	35	36	37	38	39	40	41	42	43	44	45
NORTH DAKOTA— Cont'd														
Ward	2,528	70,614	1.02	1,124	16.6	490	7.2	4,641	7.8	9,725	8,217	1,508	1,800	2,515
Wells	85	4,259	1.08	49	12.4	57	14.4	236	8.0	1,174	1,087	87	45	1,107
Williams	494	41,170	1.47	651	18.4	224	6.3	2,354	7.6	3,645	3,353	292	1,041	2,762
OHIO	315,594	11,630,622	1.00	134,734	11.5	117,359	10.0	632,536	6.7	2,293,632	1,340,210	953,422	334,234	2,878
Adams	338	25,370	0.74	332	12.0	332	12.0	1,979	8.7	6,452	4,512	1,940	280	1,004
Allen	5,863	110,457	1.13	1,212	11.8	1,076	10.5	5,868	7.2	21,754	14,716	7,038	4,050	4,031
Ashland	2,349	48,303	0.80	588	10.9	556	10.3	3,064	7.3	11,209	6,919	4,290	710	1,358
Ashtabula	3,436	90,977	0.81	1,087	11.1	1,133	11.6	6,682	8.6	22,893	16,719	6,174	NA	NA
Athens	9,543	66,246	1.03	514	7.8	493	7.5	4,492	9.3	10,286	7,398	2,888	1,425	2,212
Auglaize	526	43,574	0.90	563	12.3	469	10.2	2,002	5.3	9,269	6,823	2,446	427	1,000
Belmont	3,829	64,585	0.85	580	8.6	854	12.7	3,383	6.5	15,896	8,666	7,230	662	1,125
Brown	575	33,988	0.48	475	10.9	507	11.6	2,695	7.6	9,555	5,711	3,844	570	1,347
Butler	11,767	350,079	0.86	4,399	11.5	3,457	9.0	18,734	5.9	65,858	37,766	28,092	12,685	3,498
Carroll	405	23,654	0.66	264	9.7	323	11.9	1,719	7.9	6,467	3,475	2,992	NA	NA
Champaign	680	33,870	0.71	396	10.2	389	10.0	2,059	6.5	7,994	4,602	3,392	863	2,228
Clark	3,716	126,134	0.84	1,534	11.4	1,675	12.4	7,244	6.8	30,399	15,700	14,699	5,724	4,480
Clermont	1,718	165,994	0.64	2,262	11.0	1,792	8.7	10,133	5.9	38,918	21,018	17,900	4,114	2,031
Clinton	1,119	42,328	1.02	482	11.5	459	10.9	2,118	6.2	8,726	5,492	3,234	778	1,858
Columbiana	3,967	92,549	0.73	1,021	9.9	1,197	11.7	5,671	7.0	24,248	13,574	10,674	602	775
Coshocton	428	34,159	0.84	452	12.3	379	10.3	2,369	8.0	8,209	5,813	2,396	564	1,547
Crawford	579	38,848	0.82	459	11.0	529	12.7	2,217	6.7	10,503	7,692	2,811	1,124	2,739
Cuyahoga	29,963	1,389,762	1.23	14,287	11.5	13,658	11.0	64,178	6.3	253,609	142,397	111,212	40,035	3,740
Darke	607	46,696	0.78	619	12.1	574	11.2	2,868	6.9	11,471	8,263	3,208	417	874
Defiance	736	36,390	0.90	433	11.3	407	10.7	2,059	6.7	8,626	6,046	2,580	534	1,538
Delaware	2,210	177,478	0.84	2,054	10.0	1,175	5.7	6,603	3.9	29,990	18,077	11,913	2,921	1,717
Erie	1,679	76,422	1.03	772	10.3	933	12.5	3,704	6.3	18,468	12,816	5,652	1,748	2,603
Fairfield	2,891	125,053	0.62	1,704	10.9	1,359	8.7	7,744	6.1	28,445	14,721	13,724	3,972	2,617
Fayette	593	28,837	1.01	307	10.7	328	11.4	1,657	7.1	6,258	3,929	2,329	1,192	4,171
Franklin	30,780	1,362,173	1.17	18,799	14.3	9,918	7.6	86,877	7.9	178,620	98,340	80,280	49,905	4,032
Fulton	392	40,201	0.90	471	11.1	447	10.6	2,036	5.8	8,833	5,956	2,877	593	1,507
Gallia	883	30,706	1.04	364	12.1	361	12.0	1,852	7.7	6,780	4,995	1,785	802	2,692
Geauga	864	85,028	0.81	924	9.8	831	8.8	6,357	8.4	20,093	12,594	7,499	674	717
Greene	8,225	171,708	1.09	1,753	10.4	1,466	8.7	7,088	5.4	31,206	19,347	11,859	3,948	2,459
Guernsey	510	39,636	1.01	436	11.2	467	12.0	2,250	7.1	9,180	6,621	2,559	NA	NA
Hamilton	22,425	935,339	1.33	10,603	13.0	8,002	9.8	42,157	6.2	145,211	84,509	60,702	31,649	4,174
Hancock	1,521	85,104	1.26	892	11.7	719	9.5	3,732	6.0	14,657	10,623	4,034	1,667	2,252
Hardin	1,890	28,039	0.74	380	12.1	313	9.9	1,824	7.4	6,062	4,634	1,428	650	2,060
Harrison	232	14,075	0.80	146	9.6	192	12.7	873	7.2	3,645	2,405	1,240	167	1,147
Henry	346	25,126	0.82	292	10.8	248	9.2	1,365	6.1	5,948	4,550	1,398	394	1,490
Highland	484	38,842	0.76	524	12.2	489	11.4	2,848	8.1	9,455	6,516	2,939	802	1,882
Hocking	308	24,732	0.69	309	10.9	319	11.2	1,563	6.8	6,462	4,524	1,938	641	2,311
Holmes	765	47,194	1.18	716	16.3	333	7.6	7,458	19.8	4,908	3,149	1,759	304	693
Huron	578	54,857	0.86	734	12.5	589	10.1	3,931	8.1	12,358	9,224	3,134	NA	NA
Jackson	325	30,430	0.83	388	12.0	388	12.0	1,985	7.4	7,290	5,437	1,853	639	1,999
Jefferson	2,447	63,129	0.84	634	9.6	939	14.3	3,011	5.9	16,552	10,725	5,827	1,385	2,374
Knox	3,576	57,090	0.86	731	11.8	622	10.0	3,441	7.3	12,717	8,635	4,082	1,295	2,124
Lake	2,810	211,400	0.84	2,165	9.4	2,508	10.9	10,392	5.6	51,442	30,395	21,047	3,183	1,734
Lawrence	669	50,909	0.58	604	10.1	756	12.6	3,464	7.0	14,448	11,267	3,181	1,071	1,833
Licking	3,600	154,988	0.81	1,976	11.2	1,637	9.3	8,426	5.9	33,701	19,057	14,644	2,604	1,792
Logan	450	44,380	0.95	502	11.1	492	10.8	2,462	6.6	9,780	7,314	2,466	863	2,005
Lorain	8,624	274,310	0.78	3,183	10.3	3,054	9.9	15,807	6.4	65,013	37,963	27,050	4,076	1,530
Lucas	9,824	449,815	1.08	5,370	12.5	4,422	10.3	23,468	6.6	84,053	46,020	38,033	17,927	4,347
Madison	4,828	42,701	0.94	422	9.5	408	9.2	1,937	5.9	7,731	4,129	3,602	883	2,015
Mahoning	9,138	231,964	1.00	2,426	10.6	2,891	12.6	11,111	6.2	55,586	26,258	29,328	6,425	2,842
Marion	6,018	65,979	1.02	735	11.3	720	11.0	3,068	6.3	13,946	8,764	5,182	2,647	4,069
Medina	1,199	150,092	0.71	1,752	9.8	1,517	8.5	7,175	4.9	35,348	19,669	15,679	1,476	845
Meigs	212	18,876	0.50	246	10.6	262	11.3	1,512	8.1	5,364	3,799	1,565	299	1,293
Mercer	439	38,609	0.90	605	14.8	375	9.2	1,891	5.6	8,322	6,287	2,035	NA	NA
Miami	1,056	97,122	0.86	1,172	11.0	1,021	9.6	5,873	6.9	22,441	13,407	9,034	2,339	2,346
Monroe	165	13,589	0.88	116	8.4	185	13.4	843	7.8	3,855	2,219	1,636	73	508
Montgomery	15,402	551,153	1.08	6,551	12.3	6,034	11.3	31,824	7.5	109,886	57,070	52,816	19,199	3,726
Morgan	188	12,457	0.59	143	9.8	168	11.5	816	7.0	3,303	2,119	1,184	231	1,571
Morrow	366	25,624	0.44	354	10.1	327	9.3	2,058	7.1	6,856	4,474	2,382	NA	NA
Muskingum	1,621	84,472	0.96	1,004	11.6	958	11.1	4,538	6.5	19,832	13,127	6,705	2,585	2,999
Noble	2,673	14,068	0.89	131	9.1	140	9.8	684	7.4	2,597	1,831	766	88	700

1. Per 1,000 estimated resident population.   2. Data for serious crimes have not been adjusted for underreporting; this may affect comparability between geographic areas and over time.   3. Per 100,000 population estimated by the FBI.

Table B. States and Counties — Crime, Education, Money Income, and Poverty

STATE County	Serious crimes known to police[2], 2016 (cont.)[1] Rate Violent	Property	Education School enrollment and attainment, 2013-2017 Enrollment[3] Total	Percent private	Attainment[4] (percent) High school graduate or less	Bachelor's degree or more	Local government expenditures[5] 2014-2015 Total current spending (mil dol)	Current spending per student (dollars)	Money income, 2013-2017 Per capita income[6]	Households Median income (dollars)	Percent with income of less than $50,000	with income of $200,000 or more	Income and poverty, 2017 Median household income (dollars)	Percent below poverty level All persons	Children under 18 years	Children 5 to 17 years in families
	46	47	48	49	50	51	52	53	54	55	56	57	58	59	60	61
NORTH DAKOTA— Cont'd																
Ward	242	2,274	16,849	9.5	37.2	27.9	128.8	12,497	33,414	64,159	38.7	4.4	62,932	10.1	10.7	9.8
Wells	221	886	589	9.7	46.6	22.9	8.4	15,106	33,580	54,464	45.6	2.1	54,556	10.8	11.5	10.6
Williams	252	2,510	7,416	10.7	36.8	22.6	68.1	13,693	44,474	89,874	27.1	10.0	80,161	6.6	8.4	8.1
OHIO	300	2,577	2,880,662	18.1	43.8	27.2	19,865.5	11,518	29,011	52,407	47.7	4.0	54,077	13.9	19.8	18.2
Adams	61	943	5,991	12.4	66.6	12.1	48.4	9,966	20,248	36,320	63.1	1.3	41,644	18.6	27.6	25.4
Allen	398	3,633	26,903	17.6	48.9	17.7	160.4	10,706	24,551	47,905	51.4	2.2	51,325	15.2	23	20.6
Ashland	132	1,226	13,724	28.9	54.1	20.2	88.4	10,540	24,612	50,893	48.8	2.2	51,103	11.4	17.1	15.5
Ashtabula	NA	NA	21,345	14.4	59.0	13.4	147.7	10,679	21,936	43,017	56.8	1.4	45,157	19.3	28.4	26
Athens	116	2,096	27,079	3.9	44.4	29.6	99.1	13,260	20,062	37,191	60.7	2.0	42,955	28.8	28.5	27.4
Auglaize	52	949	10,959	10.0	50.5	18.5	79.5	10,136	28,340	59,516	42.0	2.4	63,336	8.7	11.5	10.1
Belmont	129	995	13,550	12.3	51.8	16.1	86.1	9,777	25,326	46,484	53.4	2.4	52,221	11.1	17.2	16.4
Brown	71	1,276	9,227	7.4	61.4	12.8	73.9	10,270	24,525	49,188	50.6	2.2	48,207	16.9	22.6	20.1
Butler	249	3,250	104,740	13.7	42.8	29.6	597.3	10,429	29,745	62,188	40.3	5.2	64,026	10.7	13.1	12
Carroll	NA	NA	5,619	16.1	60.2	12.3	32.4	9,939	26,908	51,748	48.5	2.7	51,296	13	19.9	17.4
Champaign	90	2,138	9,299	16.9	57.3	16.1	78.3	11,006	25,528	54,495	44.5	1.3	54,335	11	16.7	14.8
Clark	360	4,120	31,962	17.9	49.7	18.6	218.4	10,476	25,270	46,275	53.2	2.1	47,654	15.4	22	21.3
Clermont	109	1,922	47,375	18.9	42.6	28.3	263.6	9,802	31,812	64,183	38.5	5.3	66,193	8.7	12.2	10.9
Clinton	67	1,791	9,919	18.7	52.4	17.5	71.2	9,049	25,238	49,997	50.0	1.9	50,794	13	20	17.4
Columbiana	50	725	21,319	10.2	57.7	13.9	163.5	10,835	24,758	45,498	54.5	1.9	43,123	15.1	23.7	21.8
Coshocton	115	1,432	7,746	18.6	63.4	12.6	53.4	10,899	21,520	43,251	57.6	1.1	44,471	15.7	23.9	23.1
Crawford	136	2,603	8,798	14.1	55.5	14.7	66.0	9,976	24,386	41,726	57.8	1.7	45,395	15.5	25.3	24.4
Cuyahoga	721	3,020	306,268	26.2	39.2	31.5	2,419.3	13,888	30,441	46,720	52.5	4.6	46,918	18.1	27.1	24.9
Darke	105	769	11,983	9.0	58.4	14.2	82.1	9,683	24,768	50,064	49.9	1.4	53,954	9.2	12.5	11.9
Defiance	141	1,397	9,547	18.9	54.0	16.2	60.3	9,604	26,941	55,295	44.8	2.4	59,538	9.5	14.5	13.1
Delaware	109	1,608	56,151	19.9	22.7	53.8	302.4	10,119	45,116	100,229	23.4	15.0	107,676	4.8	5.3	4.4
Erie	98	2,504	16,548	14.7	46.4	22.4	165.8	13,683	30,223	51,033	48.9	3.3	54,849	12.4	18.2	17.5
Fairfield	170	2,447	38,032	15.6	41.8	26.6	252.3	10,234	29,582	63,424	39.5	4.3	67,276	9	12.3	10.9
Fayette	220	3,951	6,382	6.0	60.7	15.8	43.8	9,031	24,013	44,289	55.8	2.4	46,067	15.6	24.3	22.5
Franklin	416	3,617	335,027	16.8	34.4	38.7	2,469.3	11,890	31,199	56,319	44.4	4.9	59,214	16	22.5	21.7
Fulton	94	1,413	10,420	12.3	50.0	17.3	100.2	13,120	27,922	57,774	43.3	2.0	59,214	8.2	10.9	9.7
Gallia	118	2,575	6,687	11.6	59.0	16.2	60.6	14,393	22,293	42,002	56.5	1.3	43,149	19	27.2	24.9
Geauga	35	682	21,311	27.4	35.2	38.0	142.8	13,303	39,513	77,104	31.5	9.2	82,744	6.4	7.2	6.4
Greene	126	2,333	48,416	21.3	32.0	38.8	235.6	10,850	33,138	65,032	38.7	5.6	68,040	9.8	11.7	11.1
Guernsey	NA	NA	8,756	11.9	58.4	13.9	58.6	12,602	22,864	42,744	56.8	1.7	43,733	18.2	27	24.6
Hamilton	471	3,703	207,119	23.6	36.2	36.3	1,369.4	12,492	32,638	52,389	47.9	5.8	55,178	16.2	25.4	23.9
Hancock	176	2,077	18,719	27.9	43.2	27.1	124.7	10,382	29,608	52,831	46.4	3.8	54,386	9.7	12.4	11.8
Hardin	92	1,968	8,920	30.5	58.6	15.5	45.9	10,790	21,099	46,404	53.9	0.7	47,185	15.8	21.2	20
Harrison	89	1,057	2,975	6.7	62.2	10.9	16.0	9,874	22,965	46,223	54.0	1.3	48,160	12.8	21.1	19.6
Henry	121	1,369	6,655	15.5	50.7	17.4	62.8	14,376	27,325	58,070	43.4	2.2	57,678	8.2	11.1	10
Highland	103	1,779	9,746	8.9	60.9	12.3	70.4	9,454	22,079	42,333	57.9	2.0	43,840	16.8	25.4	23.4
Hocking	108	2,203	6,556	8.1	55.5	14.1	38.2	9,727	23,192	48,073	52.1	1.4	48,397	14.5	22.1	20.6
Holmes	18	675	9,380	39.4	76.9	8.5	41.0	10,027	21,143	58,728	41.9	3.1	61,593	9	13.6	13
Huron	NA	NA	13,424	14.1	59.0	13.7	105.2	9,849	24,193	49,710	50.3	1.6	48,244	14.8	23.8	20.3
Jackson	175	1,824	7,283	9.7	58.1	15.8	51.1	9,862	21,730	43,397	59.5	0.6	44,671	17.9	26.4	26.4
Jefferson	156	2,218	15,141	25.8	52.5	14.9	91.7	10,344	24,028	43,161	56.9	1.4	43,520	17.6	26.2	24.3
Knox	108	2,015	15,777	30.5	50.6	22.7	88.6	11,578	24,523	51,211	48.7	1.9	52,061	10.7	16.2	15
Lake	214	1,520	52,373	19.0	40.8	27.2	376.0	11,777	32,125	61,137	41.0	4.2	60,521	8.7	12.4	11.5
Lawrence	171	1,662	13,538	9.0	56.4	14.5	124.7	12,824	22,844	45,466	53.6	1.3	43,108	19.5	26.9	25.7
Licking	65	1,727	43,060	20.6	45.4	24.6	277.8	10,339	29,093	59,747	42.3	4.0	62,658	8.9	12.4	11.3
Logan	93	1,912	9,825	14.5	59.1	15.1	78.6	12,130	26,525	53,051	46.8	1.8	54,782	11.1	16.7	15.1
Lorain	151	1,379	76,604	20.0	42.6	23.7	469.7	10,650	28,555	54,987	45.0	3.7	55,443	13.5	20.1	17.5
Lucas	859	3,488	111,328	17.5	41.3	25.6	794.7	10,660	27,111	44,820	54.1	3.3	47,562	17.9	25.6	24.5
Madison	71	1,944	9,838	15.6	54.4	16.7	76.7	11,209	27,798	62,897	38.1	4.4	69,937	9.6	13.1	11.8
Mahoning	265	2,577	52,896	14.4	47.7	23.2	384.7	11,863	25,901	43,251	56.3	2.7	43,904	18.4	28.9	25.5
Marion	224	3,844	14,010	7.1	55.4	13.5	118.9	10,391	22,579	44,708	54.7	1.5	46,450	16.5	23.6	22.9
Medina	53	793	43,053	16.5	37.7	32.1	268.4	10,080	34,174	71,595	33.2	5.6	72,926	6	7.6	6.7
Meigs	177	1,115	4,798	9.9	59.6	13.0	35.7	10,762	22,396	42,105	58.3	1.2	42,200	19.9	32.2	29
Mercer	NA	NA	9,780	5.1	55.7	16.6	88.7	10,992	27,540	57,052	43.5	2.6	60,055	6.9	9.7	9.5
Miami	106	2,240	24,789	11.5	47.8	21.0	176.5	11,476	28,051	54,568	45.0	2.7	60,800	9	12	11.6
Monroe	77	432	2,798	17.8	64.0	11.4	25.0	10,829	23,154	43,299	57.7	1.5	44,868	15.2	24.2	22.4
Montgomery	430	3,296	136,325	23.3	38.2	26.8	905.5	11,857	27,602	47,045	52.6	3.0	48,039	15.9	23	21
Morgan	197	1,374	2,926	8.4	58.2	13.0	21.4	10,792	22,122	40,276	61.6	1.8	41,375	20.5	27.3	24.4
Morrow	NA	NA	8,139	9.2	57.9	13.6	53.0	9,932	24,864	52,767	44.9	1.9	55,466	11.2	17.9	16.1
Muskingum	175	2,824	20,402	13.8	54.4	15.7	181.1	12,226	22,877	43,325	56.4	1.6	44,884	14.8	21.5	20.7
Noble	0	700	2,629	6.3	65.1	10.6	20.6	12,141	23,119	42,171	56.6	2.0	44,835	16.2	19.8	17.5

1. Data for serious crimes have not been adjusted for underreporting; this may affect comparability between geographic areas and over time.   2. Per 100,000 population estimated by the FBI.   3. All persons 3 years old and over enrolled in nursery school through college.   4. Persons 25 years old and over.   5. Elementary and secondary education expenditures.   6. Based on population estimated by the American Community Survey, 2013–2017.

Table B. States and Counties — Personal Income and Earnings

STATE County	Personal income, 2017										Earnings, 2017		
			Per capita[1]			Supplements to wages and salaries, employer contributions (mil dol)						Contributions for government social insurance (mil dol)	
	Total (mil dol)	Percent change 2016-2017	Dollars	Rank	Wages and salaries (mil dol)	Pension and insurance	Government social insurance	Proprietors' income (mil dol)	Dividends, interest, and rent (mil dol)	Personal transfer receipts (mil dol)	Total (mil dol)	From employee and self-employed	From employer
	62	63	64	65	66	67	68	69	70	71	72	73	74
NORTH DAKOTA— Cont'd													
Ward	3,548		51,462	397	1,935	345	182	219	748	463	2,680	153	182
Wells	215	2.2	53,428	330	68	12	7	32	64	49	118	7	7
Williams	2,214	1.1	66,397	89	2,041	246	194	137	472	178	2,618	153	194
OHIO	544,829	3.8	46,710	X	281,206	47,753	20,637	41,027	93,109	106,869	390,623	22,559	20,637
Adams	923	3.0	33,284	2,582	256	59	18	78	108	320	410	27	18
Allen	4,223	4.1	40,925	1,412	2,420	451	183	299	632	1,023	3,354	197	183
Ashland	1,977	4.3	36,857	2,062	783	145	60	127	290	456	1,115	70	60
Ashtabula	3,616	3.4	36,974	2,041	1,247	252	98	235	467	1,137	1,832	121	98
Athens	2,172	4.0	32,610	2,675	998	299	53	130	391	545	1,480	62	53
Auglaize	2,103	4.3	45,932	803	983	180	75	132	365	370	1,370	82	75
Belmont	2,697	7.2	39,646	1,612	1,058	187	76	108	437	712	1,430	94	76
Brown	1,541	3.3	35,361	2,292	328	80	23	88	187	439	519	37	23
Butler	17,089	4.1	44,900	911	8,349	1,353	611	1,360	2,457	3,080	11,673	676	611
Carroll	1,012	2.8	36,959	2,045	307	55	25	88	143	266	475	32	25
Champaign	1,531	4.5	39,425	1,655	484	96	36	83	210	350	699	44	36
Clark	5,287	3.2	39,289	1,674	2,120	392	160	232	816	1,474	2,905	186	160
Clermont	10,211	3.2	50,003	464	2,822	455	212	1,368	1,308	1,672	4,858	288	212
Clinton	1,810	3.1	43,080	1,133	857	164	64	298	267	387	1,383	79	64
Columbiana	3,725	1.6	36,142	2,182	1,197	243	92	203	531	1,102	1,735	117	92
Coshocton	1,216	3.1	33,268	2,585	427	92	34	97	172	377	649	43	34
Crawford	1,545	3.7	37,012	2,031	553	114	42	67	239	456	777	53	42
Cuyahoga	65,901	3.9	52,783	349	44,218	6,793	3,213	5,371	13,573	12,875	59,594	3,399	3,213
Darke	2,050	4.8	39,773	1,595	803	151	64	111	349	459	1,129	74	64
Defiance	1,498	1.4	39,250	1,682	722	126	56	101	202	361	1,005	63	56
Delaware	14,298	5.9	71,325	61	5,241	742	375	1,142	2,351	1,104	7,500	425	375
Erie	4,800	5.2	64,157	111	1,593	303	123	1,633	655	782	3,652	192	123
Fairfield	6,836	4.9	44,179	999	1,874	334	138	412	953	1,217	2,759	170	138
Fayette	1,064	3.8	37,005	2,033	451	82	35	56	154	301	624	39	35
Franklin	63,885	4.4	49,448	500	45,495	7,650	3,139	4,884	11,338	9,724	61,168	3,185	3,139
Fulton	1,825	1.7	43,149	1,123	822	152	64	148	261	362	1,186	71	64
Gallia	1,108	2.4	36,965	2,043	439	106	32	73	172	378	651	40	32
Geauga	6,219	3.9	66,214	92	1,608	268	125	716	1,366	724	2,717	160	125
Greene	8,016	4.5	48,073	620	4,572	1,011	353	392	1,548	1,363	6,327	346	353
Guernsey	1,464	2.4	37,455	1,959	693	134	52	87	214	448	965	60	52
Hamilton	46,332	4.1	56,931	224	33,261	4,837	2,425	3,528	10,888	7,309	44,051	2,515	2,425
Hancock	3,686	-7.1	48,664	575	2,438	391	180	497	541	590	3,506	203	180
Hardin	974	1.8	31,048	2,850	339	73	26	43	140	265	480	32	26
Harrison	568	8.2	37,302	1,989	202	41	16	30	71	165	289	19	16
Henry	1,164	1.0	42,829	1,162	496	95	38	77	177	254	707	42	38
Highland	1,481	3.0	34,472	2,415	395	92	29	128	205	443	644	42	29
Hocking	1,038	3.9	36,443	2,125	246	58	17	72	132	303	393	26	17
Holmes	1,817	6.2	41,334	1,359	813	136	65	586	232	221	1,599	83	65
Huron	2,271	3.7	38,826	1,751	1,016	178	90	131	328	547	1,416	89	90
Jackson	1,128	2.9	34,760	2,378	393	78	29	75	158	363	575	38	29
Jefferson	2,445	3.5	36,847	2,068	914	183	70	108	336	800	1,275	86	70
Knox	2,489	4.1	40,632	1,453	927	170	72	209	403	593	1,377	86	72
Lake	11,205	4.1	48,695	568	4,639	828	351	557	1,749	2,113	6,374	385	351
Lawrence	2,197	2.4	36,466	2,121	486	108	36	97	257	735	727	53	36
Licking	7,669	4.2	44,212	995	2,425	440	180	495	1,111	1,431	3,540	216	180
Logan	1,831	3.1	40,406	1,489	948	166	73	112	250	413	1,298	79	73
Lorain	13,682	3.9	44,433	965	4,568	861	346	644	2,062	2,850	6,420	397	346
Lucas	19,356	2.5	44,921	907	10,698	1,877	794	1,685	2,940	4,477	15,053	854	794
Madison	1,761	4.1	39,993	1,552	793	163	57	138	246	327	1,151	62	57
Mahoning	9,584	2.0	41,706	1,299	4,125	768	313	599	1,683	2,619	5,805	361	313
Marion	2,360	3.9	36,328	2,147	1,084	227	82	188	325	660	1,581	94	82
Medina	9,548	4.1	53,528	327	2,854	494	214	653	1,373	1,347	4,214	257	214
Meigs	761	2.7	32,964	2,620	128	32	9	33	92	255	202	16	9
Mercer	1,886	2.4	46,149	779	852	163	64	168	326	316	1,248	73	64
Miami	4,766	4.6	45,340	863	1,849	329	141	251	740	920	2,570	158	141
Monroe	440	4.0	31,564	2,801	105	27	7	19	76	155	158	13	7
Montgomery	23,940	4.0	45,039	896	13,181	2,221	997	1,529	4,453	5,311	17,927	1,054	997
Morgan	467	4.5	31,752	2,785	114	26	8	23	59	150	171	13	8
Morrow	1,297	3.1	37,077	2,020	214	52	15	79	161	304	361	25	15
Muskingum	3,389	3.4	39,338	1,665	1,466	273	109	193	466	909	2,041	128	109
Noble	369	3.1	25,592	3,085	122	33	8	26	57	108	189	11	8

1. Based on the resident population estimated as of July 1 of the year shown.

STATE County	Earnings, 2017 (cont.)									Social Security beneficiaries, December 2017			Housing units, 2018	
	Percent by selected industries											Supplemental Security Income recipients, 2017		
	Farm	Mining, quarrying, and extractions	Construction	Manu-facturing	Information; professional, scientific, technical services	Retail trade	Finance, insurance, real estate, and leasing	Health care and social assistance	Govern-ment	Number	Rate[1]		Total	Percent change, 2010-2018
	75	76	77	78	79	80	81	82	83	84	85	86	87	88
NORTH DAKOTA— Cont'd														
Ward	-0.9	6.6	7	1	4.3	6.8	7.9	13.8	31.2	9,855	143	667	33,204	24.2
Wells	16	D	5.9	2	D	6.4	6	D	11.9	1,160	288	47	2,512	1.2
Williams	-0.6	38.9	11.8	1.4	3.7	4.1	5.7	4	6.5	3,750	112	228	19,641	87.7
OHIO	0	0.5	6.1	14.2	9.1	5.8	7.7	13.1	14.9	2,337,114	200	310,489	5,217,423	1.8
Adams	-0.2	D	10.7	16.3	D	9.3	4.2	9.6	22.1	6,750	243	1,733	12,932	-0.4
Allen	-0.2	0.3	4.8	24.8	3.7	6.1	3.5	21.3	12.6	22,915	222	3,013	45,186	0.4
Ashland	-0.4	D	8	20.6	8.7	7.1	3.1	D	14.2	11,685	218	777	22,343	0.9
Ashtabula	-0.2	0.1	10.1	25.8	4.7	6	2.9	14.6	15.3	23,445	240	3,102	46,190	0.2
Athens	-0.1	D	3.8	D	4.3	6.3	3.4	12.9	51.1	9,840	148	2,636	26,678	1.1
Auglaize	-0.1	0.1	5.4	45.8	3.3	5.4	5.4	8.3	10.4	9,410	206	458	20,082	2.5
Belmont	-0.4	14.1	9.7	D	5.1	9.3	6	12.2	16.4	16,880	248	1,999	32,155	-0.9
Brown	-2.7	D	10.7	9.6	D	7.4	3.5	10.8	24.3	10,345	237	1,159	20,391	5.7
Butler	0	0.1	7.5	19.4	4.3	7.3	9.3	9.8	12.3	67,775	178	7,370	152,718	3
Carroll	1.7	1.6	29.6	15.8	2.7	5.6	3.1	6.4	12.2	6,675	244	434	13,626	-0.5
Champaign	2.2	D	7.1	38.3	D	4.7	3	6.2	16.6	8,400	216	652	16,830	0.4
Clark	-0.2	0.6	4.3	16.4	3.1	6.5	8.6	15.8	15.7	31,160	232	4,008	61,289	-0.2
Clermont	0	D	7.7	9.7	D	7.5	7.2	7.7	11	40,280	197	3,344	83,793	3.9
Clinton	-0.7	D	3.7	18.3	4.6	4.7	5.5	D	11.1	9,145	218	1,083	18,211	0.5
Columbiana	0.5	0.8	7.2	20.2	2.8	8.6	2.9	14.1	18.6	25,795	250	3,101	46,844	-0.5
Coshocton	0.4	1	6.9	27.6	D	5.8	3	11.1	14.5	8,800	241	904	16,431	-0.7
Crawford	-0.1	D	5.5	20.3	4	6.5	8.1	D	15.2	11,190	268	1,206	20,025	-0.7
Cuyahoga	0	1.3	3.7	9.6	13	4.2	9.9	15.4	13.4	253,985	203	50,563	617,889	-0.6
Darke	-3.3	D	9.8	28.1	D	6.6	5.1	10.9	12	12,070	234	790	22,942	0.9
Defiance	-0.9	0	4	31	3.5	10.6	6.3	D	13	9,275	243	775	16,819	0.5
Delaware	0.2	D	5.4	7.4	11.9	6.7	13.3	7.9	8.3	27,950	139	1,314	74,520	12.3
Erie	0.5	D	2.6	13.2	2.1	4.6	2.6	8.9	10.2	19,020	254	1,626	37,908	0.2
Fairfield	0.1	0.1	9.3	10.5	4.6	8.2	4.4	17.1	17.5	28,835	186	2,537	61,548	4.9
Fayette	-0.1	0	5.6	18.4	D	11.5	5.7	D	16.7	6,615	230	980	12,793	0.8
Franklin	0	0	5.1	5.6	12.3	4.8	10.7	11.9	19.3	175,300	136	33,560	559,903	6.2
Fulton	-0.2	D	9.5	39.1	D	5.6	3.3	D	12.5	9,190	217	549	17,574	1
Gallia	-0.5	D	7.8	6.3	D	7.9	5.2	D	16.8	7,205	240	1,648	13,897	-0.2
Geauga	0.3	D	16.6	19.2	6	7.1	3.7	9.5	9.4	19,340	206	737	37,334	2.1
Greene	-0.1	D	3.1	4.5	16.8	5.8	3.2	7.1	45.8	30,150	181	2,566	70,844	3.8
Guernsey	-0.6	4.6	12.3	21.5	4.1	6.1	3.4	14.9	15.4	9,745	249	1,459	19,341	0.8
Hamilton	0	0	5.4	11.8	12.7	4	11.2	14.1	10	145,840	179	24,278	380,064	0.7
Hancock	-0.4	D	3.1	25.9	4.2	5	3	10.5	6.3	15,260	201	1,057	34,366	3.6
Hardin	-1.7	0	4.3	26	2.5	6.8	4.4	D	17.5	6,450	206	661	13,254	1.2
Harrison	0	D	13.9	17.6	D	3	D	7.1	15.4	3,880	255	535	8,081	-1.1
Henry	0.3	D	10.7	34.4	2.4	5.5	3.9	9.4	17.1	6,260	230	355	12,125	1.4
Highland	0.2	0.3	10.1	17.4	2.1	9.5	5.8	10.7	21.6	10,220	238	1,466	19,336	-0.3
Hocking	-0.2	D	12.4	13.1	D	8.9	4.3	8.8	29	6,930	243	1,034	13,408	0
Holmes	0.8	0.4	20.4	32.5	1.9	10.7	2.8	D	6.2	4,900	111	374	13,613	-0.4
Huron	1.8	D	13.1	25.7	D	5.2	4.2	11.2	11	12,805	219	1,262	25,298	0.4
Jackson	-0.3	0.5	7.3	27.2	2.3	8.8	3.3	D	17.1	7,710	238	1,521	14,896	2.1
Jefferson	-0.2	0.4	7.2	9	D	7.9	3.2	D	15.1	17,715	267	2,498	32,468	-1.1
Knox	0	0.4	12.6	27.4	2.8	5.8	3.3	12	11.7	13,115	214	1,160	25,922	3.2
Lake	0.8	D	6.5	28.1	5.9	7.2	3.7	10	12.5	51,685	225	2,946	103,281	2.1
Lawrence	-0.1	D	11	D	3.3	8.5	3.9	18.3	24.5	15,150	251	3,516	27,501	-0.4
Licking	0.3	0.2	8	14.6	6.6	9.5	8.5	11.9	16.2	34,780	201	3,174	71,047	2.5
Logan	0.2	0.3	5.1	35.7	D	4.9	3	8.4	11.1	10,130	223	829	23,485	1.3
Lorain	0.8	D	6	21.5	4.7	6.9	4.3	12	17.7	65,865	214	7,098	131,916	3.8
Lucas	0.1	0.1	5.7	14.7	7.6	6.9	7.8	17	14.9	86,275	200	17,487	203,467	0.4
Madison	1.4	0	6.1	24.1	D	7.7	1.9	D	21.4	7,800	177	713	16,118	1.1
Mahoning	0.1	0.2	7.5	9.3	5.8	8.1	4.7	19.5	17.2	57,665	251	8,886	111,312	-0.5
Marion	0.3	D	4	26.4	2.6	6	8.1	15.7	16.9	14,650	225	2,246	27,904	0.3
Medina	0.1	0	13.3	15.9	5.6	7.3	4.6	8.5	11.5	35,345	198	1,498	73,048	5.6
Meigs	-0.8	2.2	10	3.3	D	11.3	4.8	D	30.8	5,605	243	1,149	11,182	-0.1
Mercer	-2.2	D	9.3	34	3	6.5	6.7	D	13.3	8,480	207	414	18,119	2.8
Miami	0	0.2	6.7	29.2	D	7.2	3.8	9.2	12.8	23,070	219	1,734	44,351	0.2
Monroe		4.5	9.9	D	D	6.1	7.2	D	28.8	4,065	291	378	7,500	-0.9
Montgomery	0.1	0	5	12.4	11.1	5	6.9	20	15.2	111,790	210	15,932	254,811	0
Morgan	-0.8	D	8.9	17.6	3.5	6.3	2.5	9.8	22.4	3,485	237	509	8,013	1.5
Morrow	-0.5	0.2	12.8	19.6	D	6.6	3	8.7	25.5	7,290	208	579	14,338	1.3
Muskingum	0	1.9	5.7	9.6	5.6	9.5	4.1	D	15.5	20,955	243	3,453	37,944	-0.4
Noble	-1.4	4.7	6.5	7	6.7	5.1	D	6.4	36.3	2,725	189	268	6,193	2.3

1. Per 1,000 resident population estimated as of July 1 of the year shown.

Table B. States and Counties — Housing, Labor Force, and Employment

	Housing units, 2013-2017								Civilian labor force, 2018				Civilian employment[6], 2013-2017		
	Occupied units										Unemployment			Percent	
			Owner-occupied			Renter-occupied									
STATE County	Total	Percent	Median value[1]	Median owner cost as a percent of income — With a mort-gage	Without a mort-gage[2]	Median rent[3]	Median rent as a percent of income[2]	Sub-standard units[4] (percent)	Total	Percent change, 2017-2018	Total	Rate[5]	Total	Management, business, science, and arts	Construction, production, and maintenance occupations
	89	90	91	92	93	94	95	96	97	98	99	100	101	102	103
NORTH DAKOTA— Cont'd															
Ward	27,449	59.6	211,900	18.8	10.0	986	26.8	2.4	32,013	-1.5	920	2.9	36,497	32.1	25.8
Wells	1,988	80.1	84,200	18.1	10.0	514	24.3	1.1	2,017	-5.7	61	3	2,033	33.4	24.7
Williams	12,895	61.8	238,900	16.6	10.0	922	19.3	4.8	23,910	5.2	468	2	17,779	31.3	38.0
OHIO	4,633,145	66.1	135,100	19.9	11.8	764	28.6	1.7	5,754,931	-0.3	263,346	4.6	5,488,180	36.0	23.4
Adams	10,829	68.4	98,000	21.1	12.9	571	35.9	3.8	10,851	-0.3	767	7.1	10,124	28.3	36.1
Allen	40,319	66.1	110,900	19.3	11.6	663	29.4	1.5	47,855	-1.4	2,147	4.5	48,351	28.2	31.6
Ashland	20,504	72.6	122,000	19.5	11.6	707	23.6	2.9	26,004	-0.8	1,191	4.6	25,070	29.2	33.1
Ashtabula	38,381	70.3	106,300	20.7	11.7	648	31.3	2.5	44,247	0.3	2,330	5.3	40,003	26.1	34.1
Athens	22,509	56.8	116,500	19.8	12.1	754	34.8	2.9	27,741	-2	1,600	5.8	27,434	36.5	17.2
Auglaize	18,342	75.8	143,100	18.5	10.2	688	23.7	1.9	24,540	-0.5	810	3.3	23,229	29.8	35.0
Belmont	26,910	75.9	94,800	18.3	10.8	607	27	0.8	30,588	0.9	1,674	5.5	29,211	28.3	28.9
Brown	17,333	74.3	118,600	20.2	12.6	668	28	1.7	19,478	0	1,044	5.4	19,122	25.6	32.0
Butler	136,416	68.4	162,300	19.6	10.8	839	28.6	1.6	193,092	0.4	7,977	4.1	180,865	38.5	20.7
Carroll	10,917	80.0	116,700	20.1	11.2	682	23.8	2.7	13,091	-1.1	688	5.3	12,637	25.3	34.9
Champaign	15,274	72.7	126,700	19.9	11.8	720	24.5	1.7	19,762	-0.6	759	3.8	18,119	24.5	38.7
Clark	54,836	65.6	107,300	19.7	11.1	706	28.9	1.7	62,963		2,870	4.6	60,438	29.1	29.2
Clermont	76,143	74.3	160,600	19.8	11.2	800	27.1	1.2	105,585	0.4	4,324	4.1	100,348	36.4	22.4
Clinton	16,309	65.1	123,700	20.0	11.0	719	27.6	2.3	17,507	0.6	920	5.3	19,223	27.4	31.8
Columbiana	41,582	73.2	104,300	19.2	11.4	643	27.9	2.1	47,087	-1.1	2,436	5.2	45,737	25.7	34.1
Coshocton	14,367	75.3	95,500	19.8	10.9	594	25.6	2.8	14,392	-1.8	886	6.2	15,613	22.0	39.8
Crawford	17,833	69.3	85,600	19.8	11.5	637	25.3	1	18,330	-2.5	952	5.2	18,534	27.5	33.4
Cuyahoga	537,621	58.8	123,900	20.8	13.3	766	30.2	1.5	612,216	-0.2	32,050	5.2	587,730	39.6	18.2
Darke	20,803	72.5	113,200	19.5	11.1	645	24.9	1.4	25,814	-1.7	1,011	3.9	24,632	25.1	38.8
Defiance	15,309	76.2	112,700	19.3	11.6	703	24.1	1.2	18,126	-1.4	801	4.4	18,654	25.9	35.5
Delaware	67,701	81.2	279,800	20.1	11.4	1,001	26	0.9	107,617	0.6	3,621	3.4	99,215	53.2	10.9
Erie	31,577	69.2	132,400	19.3	12.1	716	27.3	0.8	37,757	-0.9	2,116	5.6	35,825	30.7	27.4
Fairfield	55,549	71.6	168,500	19.6	11.1	836	29.1	1.8	77,307	0.4	3,128	4	71,254	36.5	21.5
Fayette	11,729	62.1	108,900	20.6	11.7	709	27.8	1.9	14,079	-2	582	4.1	12,510	26.7	32.4
Franklin	496,337	53.6	158,400	20.3	12.3	903	28.2	2.4	685,914	0.6	26,122	3.8	650,022	42.4	16.6
Fulton	16,404	77.2	134,700	19.1	10.3	683	27.2	2.3	22,228	-0.9	981	4.4	20,729	27.8	35.0
Gallia	11,520	75.4	103,200	19.6	12.4	646	26.6	3.1	12,102	-1.3	741	6.1	11,930	27.8	30.2
Geauga	35,121	85.8	228,000	20.0	11.1	813	25.9	2.4	48,790	-0.4	2,114	4.3	47,123	40.8	21.1
Greene	64,702	66.9	163,500	19.3	10.1	866	26.4	1.2	82,136	-0.3	3,326	4	77,038	45.2	15.9
Guernsey	16,065	71.6	103,100	18.9	10.9	626	32.2	2.9	18,655	-1.4	1,032	5.5	16,454	27.3	32.5
Hamilton	338,267	57.7	145,800	20.0	12.4	749	29	2	412,156	0.5	16,941	4.1	394,387	41.4	17.3
Hancock	32,049	69.3	132,600	18.7	11.4	721	25.5	0.9	41,318	-0.6	1,410	3.4	37,928	32.8	30.8
Hardin	11,430	70.3	95,400	19.5	11.4	640	25.4	3	14,002	-2.3	611	4.4	14,190	27.2	35.6
Harrison	6,192	79.1	88,600	18.5	11.8	625	25.6	2.4	6,875	-3.5	361	5.3	6,707	24.5	37.4
Henry	11,094	78.4	116,200	18.6	11.6	669	23.8	0.9	13,272	-1.7	655	4.9	13,527	30.2	37.0
Highland	16,731	70.2	107,800	22.0	12.6	668	29.7	2.4	17,038	-0.5	945	5.5	17,468	27.4	37.7
Hocking	11,268	74.7	118,400	19.7	11.5	585	26.3	2.6	13,112	0.4	663	5.1	12,571	29.5	29.1
Holmes	12,520	76.7	183,800	20.0	10.0	602	23.2	5.2	20,592	-0.9	673	3.3	19,857	20.8	46.8
Huron	22,876	69.9	118,800	20.1	11.3	650	26.2	1.6	27,814	-1.1	1,641	5.9	27,061	23.8	40.2
Jackson	12,964	68.5	93,900	21.4	12.8	673	27.4	2.2	12,727	-1.1	835	6.6	13,511	31.1	31.0
Jefferson	27,571	69.0	88,700	18.0	12.4	622	28.4	1.2	27,538	-0.9	1,745	6.3	27,679	28.8	25.9
Knox	23,229	71.3	138,900	21.7	11.9	712	27	2	31,155	-0.4	1,353	4.3	28,489	32.3	28.9
Lake	95,238	74.7	150,100	20.2	11.4	865	27.2	1.2	125,471	-0.1	5,886	4.7	117,678	36.9	22.3
Lawrence	23,731	71.8	101,500	19.1	12.4	682	28.8	2.4	23,690	-1.3	1,335	5.6	24,607	29.5	26.2
Licking	64,434	72.4	157,800	19.7	11.7	792	28.8	1.8	89,021	0.3	3,519	4	83,030	36.1	22.9
Logan	18,627	73.8	127,200	18.6	11.9	717	26	2.7	23,070	-1.8	859	3.7	21,218	27.4	40.5
Lorain	118,594	71.4	140,300	20.3	12.2	751	30.9	1.2	152,368	-0.5	8,220	5.4	140,834	33.6	24.5
Lucas	178,971	60.0	109,000	20.0	12.5	699	29.4	1.4	209,136	-0.5	10,992	5.3	197,953	33.7	23.9
Madison	14,916	71.3	156,700	19.4	11.8	776	22.7	2.1	20,584	0	778	3.8	18,838	32.1	30.1
Mahoning	98,035	68.7	99,300	19.9	11.8	649	30.3	1.1	103,437	-1.5	6,144	5.9	103,418	32.0	24.1
Marion	24,699	68.4	93,700	19.0	11.4	712	30.6	2.1	28,395	1.3	1,256	4.4	25,920	28.0	34.2
Medina	67,192	79.9	185,800	19.8	11.0	846	26.5	1.5	96,495	-0.2	4,111	4.3	91,690	40.0	20.8
Meigs	9,285	78.1	87,400	21.1	11.2	584	29.8	2.5	8,876	-0.9	644	7.3	8,891	27.5	31.9
Mercer	16,142	77.4	137,900	19.0	10.6	646	23.3	1.1	23,528	0.2	649	2.8	20,716	27.0	40.0
Miami	40,900	69.7	138,900	19.5	10.2	756	25.4	1.1	53,197	-0.4	2,082	3.9	50,203	31.7	30.6
Monroe	5,984	78.2	97,400	19.1	10.0	570	30.6	2.3	5,169	0.3	403	7.8	5,341	24.2	38.7
Montgomery	223,495	61.2	112,100	20.4	12.7	754	29.3	1.5	250,717	-0.3	11,350	4.5	241,114	37.1	20.9
Morgan	6,116	78.1	90,500	21.0	12.3	550	28	2.9	6,676	-0.2	403	6	5,835	31.2	36.2
Morrow	12,781	82.3	139,400	20.0	12.8	646	28.4	2.6	16,734	0.1	760	4.5	16,936	27.4	33.6
Muskingum	34,348	67.3	112,500	19.6	12.4	665	29.8	1.8	39,379	-0.9	2,092	5.3	38,123	26.7	29.3
Noble	5,012	84.3	91,300	22.4	10.0	634	28	1.3	4,743	-0.4	318	6.7	4,146	22.3	34.9

1. Specified owner-occupied units.   2. A value of 10.0 represents 10 percent or less; a value of 50.0 represents 50 percent or more.   3. Specified renter-occupied units.   4. Overcrowded or lacking complete plumbing facilities.   5. Percent of civilian labor force.   6. Civilian employed persons 16 years old and over.

Table B. States and Counties — Nonfarm Employment and Agriculture

STATE County	Private nonfarm establishments, employment and payroll, 2016									Agriculture, 2017			
	Number of establish-ments	Employment						Annual payroll		Farms			Farm producers whose primary occupation is farming (percent)
		Total	Health care and social assistance	Manufac-turing	Retail trade	Finance and insurance	Professional, scientific, and technical services	Total (mil dol)	Average per employee (dollars)	Number	Percent with:		
											Fewer than 50 acres	1000 acres or more	
	104	105	106	107	108	109	110	111	112	113	114	115	116

STATE County	104	105	106	107	108	109	110	111	112	113	114	115	116
NORTH DAKOTA— Cont'd													
Ward	2,089	27,110	4,672	490	5,841	1,054	938	1,211	44,664	718	14.5	43.6	55.8
Wells	184	1,285	407	50	243	74	18	42	32,896	435	5.5	47.4	62.2
Williams	1,491	20,466	1,319	333	2,165	404	614	1,349	65,906	569	12.3	46.2	54.1
OHIO	252,201	4,790,178	840,716	662,428	573,837	255,131	250,766	218,467	45,607	77,805	47.4	3.5	37.3
Adams	393	4,354	1,114	683	906	104	88	147	33,728	1,194	44.0	1.3	34.2
Allen	2,412	46,975	12,050	7,882	5,880	1,173	943	1,917	40,801	855	43.5	4.1	36.5
Ashland	1,031	16,447	2,968	3,987	2,098	313	1,064	585	35,548	1,122	44.8	1.8	44.5
Ashtabula	1,914	24,841	5,141	6,515	3,594	575	728	878	35,333	1,212	51.7	1.7	36.1
Athens	1,054	12,856	3,102	283	2,772	398	583	390	30,350	687	35.1	0.9	33.0
Auglaize	975	20,464	2,618	9,353	2,114	338	454	822	40,191	976	39.3	3.7	38.8
Belmont	1,445	19,935	4,780	840	4,411	904	582	669	33,534	750	30.7	1.6	38.6
Brown	531	6,051	1,313	864	951	184	117	190	31,376	1,237	42.3	3.3	38.8
Butler	7,111	134,993	17,026	18,979	18,649	8,092	3,740	5,969	44,216	997	57.1	2.5	34.0
Carroll	465	5,454	787	1,471	751	81	103	173	31,776	888	44.6	1.5	40.2
Champaign	566	9,619	1,016	4,073	948	212	252	382	39,741	860	46.4	5.5	40.7
Clark	2,287	41,915	8,325	6,070	5,144	2,583	1,167	1,493	35,621	742	56.7	7.0	36.2
Clermont	3,585	51,395	6,333	5,441	9,565	2,441	2,959	2,100	40,851	928	66.4	2.2	35.3
Clinton	732	14,678	1,760	3,109	1,620	454	648	643	43,810	747	47.8	8.0	39.8
Columbiana	2,036	26,666	5,504	6,043	4,027	538	426	865	32,454	1,227	51.9	1.5	36.8
Coshocton	632	8,786	2,044	2,192	1,343	204	154	297	33,819	1,191	39.0	2.2	36.7
Crawford	802	12,389	2,694	3,550	1,387	599	530	427	34,437	719	36.7	7.9	46.1
Cuyahoga	32,984	666,446	139,174	66,858	62,576	44,565	43,120	34,524	51,803	111	92.8	NA	49.2
Darke	1,151	16,443	2,201	5,787	2,021	582	293	631	38,400	1,658	45.2	4.4	38.9
Defiance	803	13,765	2,261	3,203	2,350	664	227	575	41,754	907	39.1	6.7	33.2
Delaware	4,447	79,055	7,900	5,680	12,355	14,701	3,887	4,066	51,438	803	63.4	3.9	35.7
Erie	1,851	31,553	4,841	6,923	5,226	633	679	1,179	37,361	382	49.5	4.7	41.5
Fairfield	2,649	35,298	7,205	4,135	7,082	838	1,014	1,220	34,549	1,117	57.6	3.8	37.6
Fayette	599	9,784	1,152	1,559	2,535	159	59	315	32,192	491	46.2	12.8	45.6
Franklin	28,237	632,751	115,540	32,342	67,000	57,615	42,234	31,889	50,398	408	67.6	2.5	35.1
Fulton	949	15,587	1,990	7,188	1,762	367	244	642	41,202	785	44.6	6.5	39.8
Gallia	555	9,487	2,683	520	1,511	345	76	367	38,706	990	36.1	0.7	33.2
Geauga	2,712	29,890	4,623	7,982	3,894	680	1,082	1,276	42,696	1,049	66.7	0.6	31.2
Greene	3,097	52,846	6,887	3,568	9,627	1,344	10,702	2,138	40,461	817	59.0	6.1	38.4
Guernsey	867	13,748	3,056	3,076	1,927	254	300	506	36,836	1,103	35.7	0.9	37.5
Hamilton	21,003	472,410	87,766	39,510	46,064	33,429	40,255	26,762	56,651	318	74.2	0.3	35.1
Hancock	1,709	43,153	5,494	12,117	4,333	691	1,116	1,979	45,855	887	40.2	7.0	34.8
Hardin	451	7,233	664	2,104	869	207	81	235	32,424	726	36.0	8.8	45.5
Harrison	267	3,171	533	380	343	55	30	116	36,558	458	27.1	4.1	46.0
Henry	561	8,363	1,327	3,001	914	240	196	351	41,915	841	38.9	5.6	39.8
Highland	682	8,544	1,637	1,767	1,656	573	115	290	33,982	1,254	37.6	6.0	38.2
Hocking	490	5,309	1,080	851	849	129	101	152	28,682	377	44.8	0.3	32.9
Holmes	1,244	18,650	1,529	6,856	2,170	388	274	638	34,199	1,673	43.5	0.7	39.1
Huron	1,131	17,302	2,785	5,018	2,240	421	411	687	39,723	810	43.1	7.3	44.9
Jackson	611	8,446	1,276	3,004	1,454	269	164	265	31,430	508	38.8	1.4	36.3
Jefferson	1,257	18,853	4,162	1,235	3,189	341	317	681	36,108	599	31.6	NA	35.2
Knox	1,072	19,198	3,103	4,498	2,299	447	351	738	38,423	1,338	50.8	2.5	35.7
Lake	5,986	86,697	11,160	19,472	13,258	1,878	3,128	3,999	46,130	214	70.6	0.5	41.4
Lawrence	793	10,533	2,885	758	1,989	280	305	327	31,073	531	30.1	0.2	32.7
Licking	3,001	49,497	7,743	9,012	6,807	3,449	1,816	1,933	39,054	1,583	57.6	2.7	35.3
Logan	853	16,253	2,008	4,383	1,781	310	818	687	42,278	1,009	51.3	5.5	37.6
Lorain	5,598	86,528	15,925	15,522	13,364	1,885	3,396	3,505	40,503	1,001	63.1	2.2	34.4
Lucas	9,583	207,410	40,867	22,670	24,460	6,142	10,135	8,794	42,401	386	65.8	3.1	43.5
Madison	683	14,224	1,334	3,949	1,890	148	592	573	40,273	789	46.8	9.0	44.0
Mahoning	5,455	87,023	22,138	8,443	12,843	2,387	2,410	3,100	35,618	774	57.9	0.9	38.0
Marion	1,140	21,324	4,326	5,891	2,806	388	275	801	37,569	615	44.1	8.3	41.5
Medina	3,967	52,677	7,003	8,947	8,738	2,524	2,020	2,173	41,256	1,149	71.6	1.6	36.7
Meigs	306	2,592	589	66	653	130	55	69	26,499	515	30.7	1.0	37.5
Mercer	997	16,439	2,153	4,454	2,074	588	312	604	36,731	1,231	40.4	4.4	38.9
Miami	2,093	35,619	4,533	10,921	4,873	684	939	1,402	39,372	1,037	57.7	3.9	34.7
Monroe	243	2,315	309	80	357	160	46	96	41,648	808	27.5	0.5	35.7
Montgomery	11,338	234,459	51,940	28,704	26,913	10,932	13,366	11,094	47,319	781	63.9	2.4	38.0
Morgan	156	2,146	438	730	315	92	53	68	31,548	530	29.4	1.3	39.4
Morrow	380	3,931	1,022	914	475	61	171	132	33,646	865	53.8	5.0	38.2
Muskingum	1,727	28,579	6,516	2,822	4,704	762	444	1,136	39,765	1,263	39.6	1.6	32.0
Noble	221	1,966	354	227	303	89	84	53	26,744	593	32.7	1.0	36.6

Table B. States and Counties — **Agriculture**

	Agriculture, 2017 (cont.)															
	Land in farms					Value of land and buildings (dollars)		Value of machinery and equiopmnet, average per farm (dollars)	Value of products sold:				Organic farms (number)	Farms with internet access (percent)	Government payments	
			Acres								Percent from:					
STATE County	Acreage (1,000)	Percent change, 2012-2017	Average size of farm	Total irrigated (1,000)	Total cropland (1,000)	Average per farm	Average per acre		Total (mil dol)	Average per farm (acres)	Crops	Livestock and poultry products			Total ($1,000)	Percent of farms
	117	118	119	120	121	122	123	124	125	126	127	128	129	130	131	132
NORTH DAKOTA— Cont'd																
Ward	1,153	7.5	1,607	0.5	967.5	2,623,383	1,633	373,715	206.0	286,890	91.5	8.5	2	88.9	20,719	76.3
Wells	786	6.4	1,806	1.0	664.8	3,089,877	1,711	628,953	208.2	478,733	88.8	11.2	4	80.9	10,874	80.2
Williams	999	-6.0	1,756	21.1	754.4	1,925,239	1,096	457,175	131.8	231,601	89.1	10.9	NA	75.0	9,204	58.2
OHIO	13,965	0.0	179	50.7	10,960.7	1,112,700	6,199	129,614	9,341.2	120,059	58.1	41.9	872	74.6	351,125	36.7
Adams	166	-3.7	139	0.3	89.2	539,592	3,882	76,734	40.1	33,599	62.5	37.5	6	67.5	1,814	38.1
Allen	187	1.9	218	0.4	172.7	1,583,677	7,256	163,584	139.9	163,639	61.4	38.6	2	77.8	5,704	67.7
Ashland	161	5.1	143	0.2	120.8	870,121	6,075	100,864	113.8	101,381	38.9	61.1	57	74.8	3,821	29.9
Ashtabula	154	-7.4	127	0.3	101.1	554,349	4,373	92,598	57.9	47,762	66.2	33.8	12	69.1	592	11.2
Athens	99	9.1	144	0.1	30.4	461,747	3,213	56,167	11.4	16,640	50.4	49.6	3	76.1	394	13.7
Auglaize	210	0.0	215	1.2	194.6	1,751,762	8,141	189,133	206.9	211,992	47.4	52.6	3	82.8	8,649	72.7
Belmont	129	14.2	172	0.1	41.4	660,470	3,829	94,858	25.4	33,809	23.2	76.8	4	73.1	50	3.1
Brown	208	0.7	168	0.1	154.7	741,026	4,408	124,535	71.7	57,969	88.0	12.0	8	73.2	4,162	38.1
Butler	124	-15.2	124	0.2	92.1	1,026,003	8,255	89,736	54.9	55,068	74.3	25.7	4	80.0	2,683	25.2
Carroll	111	4.2	125	0.3	64.3	587,003	4,710	97,626	48.6	54,760	39.0	61.0	4	65.9	877	14.0
Champaign	189	-0.6	220	3.8	168.7	1,575,686	7,170	159,256	119.6	139,053	82.9	17.1	4	82.0	7,634	51.2
Clark	171	-1.9	230	1.8	151.4	1,738,039	7,542	165,061	126.5	170,443	79.2	20.8	NA	80.5	6,001	43.3
Clermont	97	-19.6	105	0.1	65.5	587,976	5,605	86,038	31.8	34,234	89.5	10.5	12	79.1	2,588	12.9
Clinton	213	2.2	285	0.0	190.7	1,697,120	5,958	185,154	116.9	156,456	92.1	7.9	4	79.5	8,430	53.4
Columbiana	142	11.4	116	0.3	95.9	669,684	5,769	98,981	106.7	86,932	32.4	67.6	3	74.2	1,687	19.4
Coshocton	183	7.5	153	1.2	97.2	809,143	5,279	97,607	99.1	83,219	33.6	66.4	29	64.7	2,541	26.4
Crawford	238	-0.7	331	0.1	220.9	2,135,734	6,446	242,518	234.0	325,403	49.6	50.4	1	71.9	11,326	68.3
Cuyahoga	2	-13.8	20	0.1	0.6	330,393	16,314	57,328	6.2	56,072	98.6	1.4	4	89.2	14	3.6
Darke	344	1.1	207	0.2	316.1	1,724,791	8,319	194,900	516.2	311,335	31.3	68.7	6	77.1	8,950	60.6
Defiance	228	1.4	252	1.0	205.8	1,444,799	5,736	147,092	107.3	118,279	74.8	25.2	6	78.4	5,649	80.6
Delaware	133	-5.7	165	0.9	117.5	1,294,690	7,824	130,793	86.9	108,172	89.2	10.8	7	85.2	3,590	35.5
Erie	86	3.7	226	D	77.1	1,480,849	6,544	176,619	94.2	246,610	92.3	7.7	6	82.2	3,052	42.1
Fairfield	188	-8.8	169	0.1	153.6	1,299,166	7,702	121,720	99.8	89,303	77.6	22.4	5	83.0	7,261	41.6
Fayette	204	3.9	416	0.1	189.9	2,971,045	7,142	259,936	127.2	259,059	83.3	16.7	3	76.4	6,900	61.9
Franklin	52	-15.6	128	0.4	45.0	1,031,825	8,041	106,842	52.2	127,841	85.1	14.9	9	89.5	1,272	25.7
Fulton	196	0.5	250	0.9	182.2	1,746,704	6,985	191,817	173.1	220,513	71.0	29.0	2	78.3	7,158	59.6
Gallia	119	2.4	120	0.2	37.6	376,628	3,143	67,632	19.0	19,167	49.0	51.0	NA	62.3	511	8.8
Geauga	70	4.6	67	0.6	33.6	482,798	7,245	60,589	36.1	34,417	48.4	51.6	22	61.7	370	4.3
Greene	168	15.0	205	0.4	149.6	1,465,595	7,140	162,563	97.1	118,832	90.8	9.2	10	82.4	7,461	41.0
Guernsey	152	5.6	138	0.1	59.1	512,427	3,722	71,042	26.8	24,287	39.6	60.4	11	66.8	520	10.1
Hamilton	18	-16.9	57	0.2	8.4	751,176	13,293	54,805	23.0	72,443	60.8	39.2	3	79.2	189	3.8
Hancock	240	4.2	271	D	226.7	1,634,840	6,042	184,379	135.8	153,091	80.1	19.9	4	78.4	9,965	67.0
Hardin	262	5.6	361	0.5	244.0	2,122,858	5,888	210,499	222.9	306,978	48.1	51.9	13	77.8	7,663	65.0
Harrison	99	4.1	217	0.0	41.0	717,980	3,310	97,439	18.6	40,688	42.0	58.0	NA	71.4	397	7.2
Henry	235	-0.4	279	0.5	225.2	1,829,400	6,550	211,986	133.4	158,595	87.7	12.3	1	79.3	7,048	73.6
Highland	288	8.9	230	0.2	224.7	1,153,001	5,021	136,788	122.9	98,008	77.1	22.9	20	70.7	10,846	56.1
Hocking	38	0.7	102	0.1	14.1	460,593	4,527	55,840	5.1	13,504	80.6	19.4	NA	77.5	655	13.8
Holmes	174	-21.3	104	0.3	104.2	804,801	7,741	82,807	182.1	108,839	18.4	81.6	134	38.0	1,509	9.0
Huron	241	0.9	297	D	213.9	1,806,321	6,083	226,973	200.0	246,863	67.5	32.5	6	73.1	8,556	48.4
Jackson	67	-5.9	133	0.1	27.3	373,579	2,814	62,710	11.0	21,734	47.1	52.9	1	67.1	632	23.4
Jefferson	77	12.7	129	0.0	33.0	702,325	5,464	80,469	9.2	15,351	46.0	54.0	NA	75.6	188	8.2
Knox	194	4.5	145	0.1	140.0	878,830	6,047	110,224	135.1	101,004	46.0	54.0	37	71.1	3,456	31.1
Lake	13	-23.5	61	1.6	8.3	499,558	8,162	101,442	73.6	344,028	98.7	1.3	NA	79.9	173	7.9
Lawrence	62	-4.0	117	0.1	16.0	383,896	3,287	57,780	4.0	7,597	59.8	40.2	NA	68.7	238	10.5
Licking	220	-1.6	139	0.3	160.7	921,506	6,616	120,427	185.4	117,118	45.1	54.9	13	84.5	4,217	20.2
Logan	211	-0.8	209	0.1	183.9	1,266,978	6,051	136,955	121.7	120,638	70.7	29.3	16	76.5	6,395	45.4
Lorain	126	2.5	126	0.6	105.1	939,911	7,484	118,302	133.9	133,767	87.1	12.9	11	80.8	2,362	27.9
Lucas	66	4.0	170	1.2	61.9	1,405,729	8,277	157,847	50.7	131,288	93.1	6.9	7	81.9	2,319	42.7
Madison	252	-4.1	320	0.1	235.3	2,218,215	6,934	215,221	159.3	201,844	78.8	21.2	25	84.7	7,372	56.1
Mahoning	75	-0.5	96	0.6	56.4	638,290	6,626	101,413	68.6	88,630	35.8	64.2	7	77.8	1,277	16.9
Marion	204	7.7	331	0.2	190.3	1,935,205	5,838	231,900	135.9	221,015	63.5	36.5	7	82.9	7,767	63.6
Medina	99	4.6	86	0.9	78.6	677,096	7,833	80,359	51.5	44,842	74.1	25.9	19	78.7	1,563	14.7
Meigs	78	3.5	152	0.1	31.4	528,124	3,467	92,831	16.6	32,254	64.5	35.5	1	75.3	372	10.9
Mercer	269	-1.5	218	0.1	248.5	2,113,330	9,673	229,931	631.6	513,089	19.5	80.5	6	82.3	8,719	67.9
Miami	173	-6.0	167	1.9	158.3	1,239,097	7,421	114,326	106.7	102,889	86.2	13.8	8	83.6	4,405	53.6
Monroe	108	-3.1	133	0.1	31.1	435,691	3,268	79,164	14.0	17,280	35.0	65.0	3	66.3	69	1.2
Montgomery	113	-8.9	145	0.5	91.4	1,044,818	7,214	118,999	78.7	100,784	88.0	12.0	4	78.0	3,063	37.8
Morgan	99	4.2	187	0.1	40.3	647,339	3,458	88,037	18.0	33,972	39.8	60.2	3	73.2	244	14.5
Morrow	165	-1.5	191	0.3	139.1	1,146,537	6,002	132,894	84.2	97,334	73.1	26.9	12	79.7	3,800	35.6
Muskingum	189	9.1	150	0.4	88.1	613,803	4,101	90,918	70.1	55,482	41.1	58.9	4	70.5	2,539	16.9
Noble	80	-7.0	135	0.1	24.4	415,865	3,078	63,887	7.3	12,304	36.3	63.7	5	62.4	27	2.2

STATE County	Water use, 2015		Wholesale Trade[1], 2012				Retail Trade[2], 2012				Real estate and rental and leasing,[2] 2012			
	Public supply water withdrawn (mil gal/day)	Public supply gallons withdrawn per person per day	Number of establishments	Number of employees	Sales (mil dol)	Average payroll (mil dol)	Number of establishments	Number of employees	Sales (mil dol)	Average payroll (mil dol)	Number of establishments	Number of employees	Sales (mil dol)	Average payroll (mil dol)
	133	134	135	136	137	138	139	140	141	142	143	144	145	146
NORTH DAKOTA— Cont'd														
Ward	6.87	96.4	102	1,621	2,898.0	100.1	297	5,634	1,902.3	162.9	79	735	195.1	37.9
Wells	0.36	86.4	19	D	D	D	36	209	80.4	4.5	3	D	D	D
Williams	9.17	259.8	91	1,527	1,868.5	119.2	114	1,833	797.5	62.2	77	819	573.6	82.4
OHIO	1,306.28	112.5	11,744	182,791	155,426.0	9,627.2	36,531	549,152	153,554.0	13,099.3	9,932	60,966	16,132.7	2,441.8
Adams	2.05	73.2	9	114	77.9	3.9	77	853	224.9	18.0	8	27	3.0	0.8
Allen	18.17	174.0	124	2,287	1,388.8	91.6	417	6,072	1,641.5	134.3	85	376	55.2	11.0
Ashland	2.99	56.2	39	D	D	D	156	2,036	486.1	46.1	31	156	12.8	3.4
Ashtabula	7.20	73.0	48	385	220.1	14.2	327	3,635	1,081.1	80.6	70	199	26.7	5.3
Athens	7.51	114.0	28	D	D	D	192	2,783	695.1	58.7	61	213	24.8	4.5
Auglaize	5.27	114.9	35	D	D	D	165	2,096	491.8	43.1	31	193	14.4	5.9
Belmont	7.61	110.0	38	D	D	D	299	3,837	1,042.5	82.2	54	320	44.1	8.0
Brown	3.06	69.8	23	138	72.3	4.5	102	979	256.4	21.6	14	51	6.0	1.0
Butler	50.69	134.7	435	9,727	8,239.8	545.4	1,011	17,718	7,072.0	482.8	264	1,283	289.6	45.7
Carroll	0.84	30.2	17	D	D	D	65	671	204.9	16.8	12	57	6.7	1.5
Champaign	2.49	63.9	25	D	D	D	95	980	271.3	21.4	22	56	10.3	1.5
Clark	16.17	118.9	88	2,274	2,697.8	111.4	403	5,708	1,541.5	128.0	95	468	56.8	12.5
Clermont	18.46	91.4	148	1,560	1,051.1	83.5	520	9,185	2,659.3	227.7	140	608	105.3	19.7
Clinton	0.88	21.0	29	383	425.2	17.4	127	1,531	443.1	37.0	27	186	37.4	5.4
Columbiana	9.18	87.6	88	1,108	584.6	49.7	338	3,922	1,126.4	88.9	55	215	25.7	5.9
Coshocton	6.59	180.2	16	D	D	D	107	1,219	307.3	25.5	18	D	D	D
Crawford	2.41	57.0	35	D	D	D	135	1,330	349.8	30.4	27	64	7.3	1.3
Cuyahoga	222.45	177.1	1,930	31,718	21,584.9	1,742.5	4,302	59,458	15,072.5	1,412.8	1,534	13,977	4,931.1	691.5
Darke	3.00	57.6	56	628	528.3	25.4	170	1,956	480.6	43.3	36	131	14.3	3.9
Defiance	3.40	88.7	33	445	422.8	19.7	150	2,344	593.9	54.0	25	95	13.5	2.2
Delaware	19.66	101.9	151	D	D	D	587	11,363	3,178.6	273.5	162	697	146.6	28.0
Erie	11.99	158.7	65	743	1,145.5	35.5	309	4,531	1,072.4	96.7	74	282	41.0	9.2
Fairfield	9.20	60.8	75	D	D	D	412	6,930	1,678.8	151.1	130	491	63.7	10.5
Fayette	1.99	69.4	25	D	D	D	183	2,411	675.2	44.9	15	58	20.8	1.5
Franklin	155.82	124.5	1,274	25,263	20,890.3	1,441.5	3,613	65,130	21,384.9	1,810.6	1,394	9,626	2,688.7	420.3
Fulton	2.54	59.7	42	429	382.8	15.7	157	1,651	433.7	37.4	19	70	6.1	1.6
Gallia	3.47	115.1	17	209	68.3	6.3	120	1,320	336.3	28.7	22	65	9.0	1.6
Geauga	1.45	15.4	135	1,382	592.0	74.1	283	3,696	1,007.8	87.6	65	299	30.3	10.1
Greene	8.98	54.6	79	979	1,101.9	46.9	505	9,080	2,121.3	192.5	128	472	96.7	13.6
Guernsey	5.45	138.8	23	D	D	D	144	1,667	547.0	37.8	34	99	25.3	2.6
Hamilton	114.75	142.1	1,112	18,946	15,311.6	1,065.9	2,821	44,091	11,558.5	1,077.1	979	6,913	1,634.4	313.1
Hancock	11.28	149.3	72	964	953.4	47.8	263	4,090	1,103.7	90.6	60	432	55.4	14.2
Hardin	2.23	70.4	16	115	216.4	4.8	90	930	200.0	18.0	13	49	8.0	0.8
Harrison	0.60	38.8	8	D	D	D	33	281	70.9	5.1	5	D	D	D
Henry	2.96	106.4	26	221	305.7	9.6	79	943	290.7	19.0	19	75	24.6	2.2
Highland	2.30	53.5	14	131	95.8	4.4	139	1,532	393.0	34.1	26	65	10.1	1.7
Hocking	1.67	58.6	5	D	D	D	67	799	213.2	17.5	28	110	10.2	2.5
Holmes	1.80	41.0	60	631	332.2	22.7	157	1,976	456.7	45.1	15	40	10.3	1.2
Huron	5.54	94.8	46	607	601.6	27.7	174	1,993	538.4	43.5	47	151	23.3	4.0
Jackson	1.47	45.1	20	123	60.4	4.3	117	1,410	339.5	29.9	24	79	10.4	2.1
Jefferson	8.77	130.2	45	D	D	D	216	3,082	723.2	65.7	43	196	23.1	6.0
Knox	5.47	89.6	43	D	D	D	177	2,051	585.2	47.6	38	137	16.7	3.2
Lake	22.82	99.5	296	2,993	1,406.6	149.5	789	12,537	3,505.0	293.4	189	711	150.6	23.6
Lawrence	5.43	88.9	20	180	100.3	6.3	154	1,870	553.8	42.4	22	59	8.1	1.5
Licking	12.57	73.7	96	1,574	1,634.8	76.6	444	6,954	2,454.9	167.9	110	357	69.0	10.3
Logan	2.80	61.7	28	1,381	748.8	63.3	148	1,685	442.3	38.2	32	153	28.4	4.0
Lorain	42.42	139.0	246	2,943	1,826.6	130.4	814	12,995	3,707.3	310.4	192	1,116	116.2	26.5
Lucas	81.45	187.8	440	6,310	5,058.6	327.0	1,459	23,721	5,977.9	561.0	411	2,688	2,530.9	161.2
Madison	2.05	46.5	23	D	D	D	103	1,719	1,116.1	44.8	30	87	13.6	1.9
Mahoning	4.30	18.5	279	3,666	1,814.7	178.6	893	12,319	3,104.3	262.6	177	2,348	184.5	59.3
Marion	6.14	93.9	36	541	620.1	25.7	181	2,822	745.3	69.5	44	191	28.9	6.0
Medina	3.01	17.1	233	3,012	1,536.8	162.5	486	8,741	2,651.4	199.7	131	487	85.4	13.7
Meigs	1.75	75.2	7	68	13.2	1.7	63	510	155.5	10.1	8	16	1.8	0.2
Mercer	2.88	70.3	49	1,039	790.3	39.4	168	1,930	496.5	46.4	28	69	10.2	1.7
Miami	10.89	104.5	84	820	740.7	35.7	307	4,558	1,239.3	108.0	73	300	44.1	8.8
Monroe	1.07	74.3	6	D	D	D	47	360	74.4	6.5	1	D	D	D
Montgomery	81.14	152.4	521	7,997	15,523.2	450.6	1,675	26,113	6,490.7	605.1	534	3,167	524.5	110.7
Morgan	0.64	43.3	6	D	D	D	26	268	54.5	4.8	3	D	D	D
Morrow	0.55	15.7	14	D	D	D	51	475	164.1	9.7	6	11	2.2	0.2
Muskingum	9.89	114.6	54	868	707.1	33.6	338	4,448	1,117.8	94.1	56	265	41.2	8.3
Noble	1.04	72.6	5	28	16.7	1.1	34	327	105.0	6.7	3	2	0.7	0.1

1 Merchant wholesalers, except manufacturers' sales branches and offices.   2. Employer establishments.

Professional Services, Manufacturing, and Accommodation and Food Services

STATE County	Professional, scientific, and technical services, 2012				Manufacturing, 2012				Accommodation and food services, 2012			
	Number of establishments	Number of employees	Sales (mil dol)	Average payroll (mil dol)	Number of establishments	Number of employees	Receipts (mil dol)	Annual payroll (mil dol)	Number of establishments	Number of employees	Receipts (mil dol)	Annual payroll (mil dol)
	147	148	149	150	151	152	153	154	155	156	157	158
NORTH DAKOTA— Cont'd												
Ward	144	763	116.9	49.4	54	561	D	21.8	173	3,932	211.6	59.1
Wells	9	25	2.0	0.8	7	51	30.0	1.9	17	114	4.8	1.0
Williams	99	558	123.8	37.5	33	250	125.1	12.4	94	2,152	259.1	44.0
OHIO	23,961	233,876	35,970.8	14,219.9	14,482	627,124	313,630.0	33,135.4	23,432	437,293	20,652.8	5,742.7
Adams	26	D	D	D	24	542	103.7	29.8	35	508	21.4	5.8
Allen	164	952	75.8	33.0	124	7,318	15,270.4	448.1	234	4,521	211.3	54.3
Ashland	69	962	127.1	42.8	83	3,655	1,069.9	156.6	91	1,500	61.9	17.2
Ashtabula	118	D	D	D	147	6,167	2,449.5	313.9	229	2,706	121.5	30.8
Athens	71	580	86.0	23.6	38	176	D	6.4	143	2,860	107.2	29.1
Auglaize	70	434	56.8	17.2	83	7,339	2,961.6	363.5	90	1,341	50.5	14.2
Belmont	81	551	55.9	20.1	45	893	D	37.5	127	2,374	112.2	31.4
Brown	28	131	9.2	3.5	32	526	95.1	21.4	67	825	33.0	9.3
Butler	590	3,574	441.6	174.1	402	17,369	10,342.8	997.0	640	12,799	611.8	166.0
Carroll	25	118	9.6	3.5	40	1,366	368.6	55.1	41	485	17.9	5.3
Champaign	47	271	14.6	14.2	41	3,393	1,387.0	170.0	48	701	29.9	7.6
Clark	166	1,172	141.2	58.3	158	6,116	2,832.4	275.0	235	4,288	197.0	53.2
Clermont	385	2,826	469.6	154.5	169	5,182	1,248.5	262.3	280	6,030	285.3	81.9
Clinton	49	D	D	D	41	2,604	1,029.1	128.4	74	1,371	75.2	17.6
Columbiana	106	435	36.3	13.8	171	5,294	1,443.2	213.0	174	2,587	102.9	28.0
Coshocton	29	132	10.8	3.1	52	2,358	1,195.1	113.0	51	717	32.8	9.2
Crawford	45	357	74.1	13.2	80	3,374	1,045.9	149.9	84	987	41.6	10.9
Cuyahoga	4,016	41,345	6,848.8	2,750.9	1,890	69,606	24,399.4	4,048.8	2,959	53,954	2,738.6	758.7
Darke	69	280	30.3	8.8	72	4,475	1,855.5	216.8	88	1,015	43.0	11.0
Defiance	45	221	20.5	7.4	43	3,278	1,018.0	203.5	81	1,228	50.1	13.2
Delaware	534	3,692	667.1	222.2	135	5,463	3,012.0	303.4	421	9,496	460.2	134.1
Erie	117	D	D	D	103	5,465	2,021.6	291.7	263	5,848	305.9	77.6
Fairfield	196	910	76.3	28.9	107	4,219	1,277.9	207.0	244	4,767	203.0	59.6
Fayette	21	72	8.3	2.1	25	1,670	1,343.7	75.9	59	1,053	46.9	12.5
Franklin	3,472	40,628	7,092.6	2,737.0	814	28,991	12,574.1	1,461.7	2,797	57,229	2,980.8	843.3
Fulton	47	D	D	D	93	6,102	3,394.5	290.9	73	936	35.3	10.3
Gallia	29	87	8.7	2.4	22	452	D	22.4	53	886	43.4	11.5
Geauga	349	1,109	207.7	58.4	195	7,259	2,787.3	353.1	171	2,404	98.7	28.5
Greene	437	8,729	1,756.2	651.4	102	3,221	877.9	170.4	311	6,674	319.9	86.5
Guernsey	43	235	30.7	11.1	55	2,634	1,562.7	120.8	89	1,465	71.0	18.0
Hamilton	2,536	40,955	6,599.1	2,839.3	990	45,901	23,167.3	2,800.1	1,853	39,506	2,004.4	569.6
Hancock	136	758	97.8	38.6	94	9,903	4,821.3	491.4	181	4,063	169.8	48.3
Hardin	25	85	7.0	2.4	30	1,722	475.3	73.3	51	868	37.2	12.1
Harrison	13	27	2.4	0.7	12	368	92.3	13.6	27	198	7.9	2.3
Henry	24	91	9.8	3.3	45	3,100	2,313.6	158.0	49	D	D	D
Highland	40	132	11.0	2.9	27	1,698	585.9	68.6	63	878	36.4	9.6
Hocking	26	D	D	D	24	847	287.1	39.3	57	885	45.8	12.6
Holmes	30	267	35.1	11.2	253	6,028	1,483.4	200.9	67	1,374	61.0	17.9
Huron	80	410	33.1	14.4	87	5,436	2,336.8	232.4	107	1,474	60.9	15.5
Jackson	36	153	11.6	3.3	32	3,492	D	117.6	53	884	35.8	9.8
Jefferson	87	D	D	D	35	1,333	D	76.0	142	1,808	76.2	20.0
Knox	54	335	33.4	12.1	69	4,976	2,166.3	300.4	91	1,438	60.7	16.5
Lake	555	3,056	413.5	170.9	617	19,183	6,045.2	970.0	529	9,279	406.8	111.6
Lawrence	42	271	18.0	7.8	34	915	D	30.6	66	1,124	58.9	14.3
Licking	229	1,795	144.3	114.4	151	7,809	2,958.9	358.2	280	4,975	212.7	61.7
Logan	54	766	62.7	27.2	48	4,584	6,790.1	305.7	98	1,214	56.5	15.0
Lorain	448	3,297	276.1	111.4	379	16,010	7,328.0	892.4	514	8,536	397.0	104.6
Lucas	864	8,875	1,182.6	474.5	460	18,286	27,736.6	1,154.6	1,025	19,099	823.0	237.3
Madison	42	D	D	D	44	2,895	1,157.9	135.8	46	844	36.0	10.6
Mahoning	447	3,570	307.8	142.2	326	8,756	1,978.7	398.9	490	9,022	397.2	105.6
Marion	71	303	29.8	9.6	71	5,966	3,681.7	276.5	106	1,893	86.9	22.1
Medina	407	2,028	230.8	83.7	277	8,543	2,970.4	405.6	288	4,897	223.0	61.9
Meigs	11	D	D	D	7	D	D	1.6	28	372	16.4	4.6
Mercer	44	295	31.7	10.6	82	3,807	1,136.9	172.5	85	1,192	44.8	11.9
Miami	159	1,000	112.6	41.6	216	10,888	3,923.9	542.3	188	3,816	159.8	45.7
Monroe	11	D	D	D	9	D	D	D	18	163	5.9	1.6
Montgomery	1,121	12,095	1,713.7	727.6	730	26,188	8,239.2	1,466.6	1,112	22,321	1,028.7	296.6
Morgan	8	D	D	D	9	582	D	27.8	16	159	5.1	1.5
Morrow	33	D	D	D	26	844	D	45.6	29	350	17.6	4.6
Muskingum	106	452	55.6	17.1	72	2,699	867.7	126.2	167	3,102	139.5	39.7
Noble	12	D	D	D	13	299	101.9	D	17	D	D	D

Health Care and Social Assistance, Other Services, Nonemployer Businesses, and Residential Construction

STATE County	Health care and social assistance, 2012				Other services, 2012				Nonemployer businesses, 2016		Value of residential construction authorized by building permits, 2018	
	Number of establish-ments	Number of employees	Receipts (mil dol)	Annual payroll (mil dol)	Number of establish-ments	Number of employees	Receipts (mil dol)	Annual payroll (mil dol)	Number	Receipts (mil dol)	New construction ($1,000)	Number of housing units
	159	160	161	162	163	164	165	166	167	168	169	170
NORTH DAKOTA— Cont'd												
Ward	152	D	D	D	134	751	69.7	19.7	4,318	192.8	21,991	89
Wells	17	461	21.8	10.8	16	D	D	D	367	15.6	215	1
Williams	65	1,485	131.6	57.6	78	467	82.0	17.0	2,486	129.5	23,466	88
OHIO	28,237	798,770	80,915.7	33,141.0	18,851	127,366	13,221.5	3,491.3	768,858	34,053.4	5,189,339	24,221
Adams	48	1,057	67.1	28.3	25	64	26.1	2.2	1,772	68.2	3,227	16
Allen	307	11,307	1,256.5	501.7	197	1,264	92.0	25.5	5,318	221.3	18,996	86
Ashland	112	2,220	188.6	71.4	91	563	44.3	14.7	3,434	154.9	9,150	54
Ashtabula	217	5,453	420.3	171.9	158	646	47.5	10.9	6,074	255.9	20,967	114
Athens	144	3,058	287.7	101.6	80	417	27.6	7.5	3,172	109.6	730	6
Auglaize	97	2,259	169.4	60.0	89	529	38.2	11.9	2,731	104.9	25,895	110
Belmont	208	4,715	311.7	127.6	124	654	41.0	12.0	3,130	123.7	14,397	115
Brown	58	1,461	112.6	42.2	42	180	13.1	3.8	2,734	109.0	23,309	92
Butler	730	15,022	1,491.8	566.6	520	4,178	373.1	108.0	22,228	994.9	166,272	791
Carroll	39	753	41.6	17.4	46	224	16.8	4.0	1,847	84.0	190	1
Champaign	49	1,362	89.1	35.5	48	165	14.0	3.1	2,231	89.5	8,564	46
Clark	313	10,029	912.0	334.8	212	1,363	134.3	40.5	6,613	250.0	18,048	68
Clermont	291	5,950	527.0	211.9	289	1,688	147.8	43.8	13,363	584.0	115,232	579
Clinton	90	1,751	176.2	64.2	60	260	21.5	6.2	2,742	115.7	12,128	54
Columbiana	291	5,444	415.4	161.9	184	857	69.0	18.4	5,874	236.2	5,881	52
Coshocton	84	1,783	143.5	56.0	60	267	22.0	5.0	2,336	93.7	1,556	9
Crawford	98	2,313	176.8	70.1	73	310	27.1	6.3	2,126	83.1	1,355	8
Cuyahoga	3,593	137,744	14,792.8	6,409.1	2,495	18,586	2,072.3	568.0	92,595	4,192.1	190,263	682
Darke	77	2,284	186.6	74.3	106	405	24.9	7.0	3,523	147.1	17,716	68
Defiance	85	2,403	194.0	80.8	70	386	31.2	7.1	2,149	88.5	7,240	39
Delaware	395	6,795	541.6	243.4	270	2,266	458.8	94.2	17,311	968.7	336,802	1,629
Erie	208	5,406	489.8	224.1	138	710	47.5	14.3	4,765	183.4	18,556	71
Fairfield	303	6,114	564.4	241.0	171	1,031	101.5	30.4	10,667	464.1	152,815	682
Fayette	53	1,432	114.4	45.8	40	193	10.7	3.2	1,523	62.5	6,451	34
Franklin	3,325	104,976	11,693.1	4,509.2	1,912	17,718	2,309.3	597.1	95,968	4,397.2	899,797	5,575
Fulton	93	2,330	197.1	76.4	71	254	25.9	6.0	2,886	136.6	12,947	60
Gallia	70	2,473	227.0	97.3	37	241	17.9	5.4	1,653	74.0	660	7
Geauga	237	3,833	360.2	157.2	176	1,179	108.6	36.7	10,997	643.1	50,454	147
Greene	341	5,861	608.5	219.4	212	1,244	99.7	27.9	10,219	418.8	220,070	589
Guernsey	123	2,653	221.2	74.6	60	276	31.0	6.1	2,218	96.8	8,431	39
Hamilton	2,371	80,058	10,054.4	4,272.5	1,488	11,624	1,292.3	344.2	57,758	2,731.1	267,706	1,473
Hancock	183	5,107	523.6	192.3	137	892	99.6	22.9	4,377	195.9	34,029	126
Hardin	48	645	48.9	18.9	32	117	8.9	2.3	1,486	61.4	1,690	13
Harrison	27	513	39.9	15.0	19	61	5.7	1.2	863	43.4	0	0
Henry	52	1,371	81.3	36.0	42	304	19.7	5.2	1,644	64.8	3,819	19
Highland	97	1,650	128.4	50.9	42	154	13.1	2.9	2,890	131.9	1,116	12
Hocking	47	1,075	74.7	29.9	35	199	22.2	4.2	1,897	76.1	529	4
Holmes	60	1,397	153.1	41.2	53	184	21.5	5.0	5,393	335.6	75	1
Huron	102	2,711	269.6	111.4	105	544	41.3	11.6	3,082	139.5	9,191	39
Jackson	74	1,372	120.4	42.5	40	157	16.7	3.6	1,526	63.3	14,481	62
Jefferson	155	4,577	438.1	164.5	101	590	41.0	11.9	3,066	106.8	1,418	6
Knox	130	2,971	231.6	93.2	77	499	42.7	11.7	4,788	217.1	29,489	133
Lake	608	11,077	944.7	408.2	470	2,718	214.6	66.8	15,885	707.7	92,074	409
Lawrence	123	D	D	D	55	281	28.2	6.3	2,762	91.8	1,381	9
Licking	262	7,491	625.0	254.5	203	1,190	103.1	27.8	11,878	513.0	66,161	261
Logan	94	2,122	180.1	69.5	67	505	79.3	13.1	2,868	117.7	10,384	55
Lorain	616	13,559	1,290.7	534.4	454	2,641	260.3	62.6	17,368	695.4	225,076	1,114
Lucas	1,275	38,102	4,107.7	1,677.1	731	5,136	444.5	130.0	24,216	1,069.8	133,226	735
Madison	73	D	D	D	46	159	11.9	3.3	2,697	113.0	40,318	135
Mahoning	767	19,562	1,823.7	717.0	382	2,612	216.7	58.4	15,467	629.2	36,812	162
Marion	157	4,315	369.2	151.5	95	648	40.1	11.0	2,951	110.1	4,617	35
Medina	369	7,484	580.7	238.2	300	1,639	128.9	41.0	13,448	634.9	155,104	629
Meigs	41	473	30.4	11.9	17	53	6.7	1.4	1,101	35.1	1,593	10
Mercer	76	2,104	132.6	57.7	86	436	43.3	10.9	2,738	125.8	19,979	138
Miami	197	4,449	374.8	135.0	178	900	81.3	20.7	6,716	285.5	62,269	227
Monroe	18	D	D	D	23	D	D	D	1,026	32.6	0	0
Montgomery	1,466	48,822	5,573.6	2,243.7	852	6,243	682.6	157.5	31,314	1,312.9	129,787	761
Morgan	16	340	20.2	7.7	13	D	D	D	808	28.3	6,997	30
Morrow	47	D	D	D	24	80	7.3	2.0	2,562	125.7	14,253	78
Muskingum	194	6,011	603.1	266.2	159	1,093	86.6	23.9	5,070	204.8	5,163	33
Noble	20	D	D	D	20	D	D	D	741	29.8	4,988	22

Table B. States and Counties — Government Employment and Payroll, and Local Government Finances

	Government employment and payroll, 2012									Local government finances, 2012				
			March payroll (percent of total)							General revenue				
												Taxes		
											Inter-govern-mental (mil dol)		Per capita[1] (dollars)	
STATE County	Full-time equivalent employees	March payroll (dollars)	Adminis-tration, judicial, and legal	Police and corrections	Fire protection	Highways and transpor-tation	Health and welfare	Natural resources and utilities	Education and libraries	Total (mil dol)		Total (mil dol)	Total	Property
	171	172	173	174	175	176	177	178	179	180	181	182	183	184
NORTH DAKOTA— Cont'd														
Ward	2,136	7,851,589	4.3	7.5	2.8	4.2	5.4	5.7	68.4	241.7	117.3	80.2	1,238	819
Wells	201	657,258	11.8	3.8	0.0	9.3	11.4	5.1	54.7	18.7	8.8	6.5	1,519	1,436
Williams	864	3,064,820	7.6	11.5	0.1	4.9	6.8	4.6	59.1	140.3	49.9	59.7	2,236	1,126
OHIO	X	X	X	X	X	X	X	X	X	X	X	X	X	X
Adams	1,309	4,554,288	8.6	6.3	1.2	4.8	20.7	12.5	44.5	95.0	57.8	28.2	996	856
Allen	4,029	14,917,726	8.3	9.1	4.8	3.4	9.8	5.8	55.9	394.8	197.5	125.6	1,195	774
Ashland	1,952	6,407,247	7.9	9.8	3.4	8.4	11.1	4.1	54.7	148.8	65.0	62.1	1,172	812
Ashtabula	3,445	13,283,345	8.6	8.3	6.3	6.3	10.0	5.8	52.9	379.5	210.8	114.5	1,141	880
Athens	2,322	8,135,468	7.7	8.6	2.5	4.0	14.9	8.3	53.4	218.6	106.3	74.7	1,161	793
Auglaize	1,848	6,837,964	8.1	11.1	3.6	6.2	9.8	11.2	48.9	165.8	68.7	63.4	1,383	791
Belmont	2,607	9,128,313	8.1	10.6	2.1	10.5	11.9	10.3	46.0	191.0	101.3	63.6	913	616
Brown	1,467	5,037,757	10.7	6.4	1.0	3.0	3.9	4.5	68.2	139.2	79.2	35.6	803	573
Butler	12,086	48,616,602	7.6	9.8	5.5	2.6	6.4	6.6	59.8	1,333.8	510.2	553.1	1,493	1,108
Carroll	814	2,533,284	12.9	4.6	0.1	10.7	12.6	3.6	53.6	67.3	39.5	18.9	663	541
Champaign	1,507	5,457,874	8.0	11.9	3.0	4.5	7.3	4.2	60.0	133.3	67.8	46.2	1,167	749
Clark	5,386	19,627,638	7.6	10.0	4.2	2.3	8.2	4.4	57.6	501.3	270.1	168.3	1,227	774
Clermont	5,289	20,437,759	7.0	10.5	7.4	2.9	8.3	2.8	59.9	577.6	246.3	251.2	1,262	1,074
Clinton	1,809	5,888,599	9.0	8.5	2.2	3.7	8.2	6.6	60.3	157.7	71.7	54.0	1,288	849
Columbiana	3,495	11,243,471	8.0	8.4	2.1	5.7	10.5	5.6	58.7	309.6	171.8	94.5	887	570
Coshocton	1,280	4,337,624	6.8	5.0	9.6	5.4	10.8	3.0	57.6	122.4	67.8	38.8	1,056	791
Crawford	1,254	4,325,266	5.9	4.7	3.6	1.8	1.1	5.5	77.2	151.9	72.7	51.8	1,209	747
Cuyahoga	62,490	287,120,691	6.2	10.3	5.0	6.7	17.9	8.2	44.0	8,188.0	2,777.4	3,498.3	2,765	1,595
Darke	1,735	6,310,491	7.2	9.5	3.5	3.8	9.0	4.8	60.8	161.4	77.3	60.1	1,145	652
Defiance	1,658	5,904,403	6.0	5.9	1.8	3.6	22.5	5.1	51.1	159.4	60.4	46.4	1,200	722
Delaware	5,621	21,810,855	6.5	8.3	8.6	3.5	6.9	3.8	60.6	594.5	125.1	379.4	2,096	1,582
Erie	3,210	12,237,910	9.9	7.7	6.1	3.6	6.5	6.6	58.0	347.1	131.6	140.7	1,841	1,302
Fairfield	4,930	17,614,468	7.6	7.4	6.0	3.4	7.0	5.5	62.0	533.2	218.0	227.0	1,539	972
Fayette	1,569	5,994,441	8.4	7.6	3.1	4.0	30.8	6.0	35.4	151.4	51.3	42.0	1,454	900
Franklin	43,936	204,420,126	7.5	12.0	8.0	4.8	6.8	5.9	53.0	6,852.6	2,645.8	3,248.5	2,717	1,632
Fulton	1,714	6,275,872	9.2	6.4	2.8	7.9	4.5	5.4	60.4	175.3	77.4	66.6	1,566	1,017
Gallia	1,230	4,310,190	10.5	5.0	0.3	10.5	8.6	3.8	60.0	121.8	67.0	35.1	1,144	879
Geauga	2,853	10,934,381	6.8	10.3	1.9	6.2	6.6	5.0	60.8	321.0	103.8	177.1	1,890	1,605
Greene	5,165	20,150,214	7.8	10.0	5.1	2.9	8.5	4.8	58.8	586.4	206.6	277.8	1,698	1,294
Guernsey	1,477	4,435,295	10.2	6.1	1.9	6.0	6.7	6.6	52.4	132.8	73.2	38.5	968	624
Hamilton	30,330	130,350,382	7.8	13.0	8.0	5.1	7.5	8.7	47.8	4,236.2	1,499.4	1,927.5	2,403	1,479
Hancock	2,432	8,819,684	8.0	8.9	4.5	4.6	9.6	8.0	55.4	271.6	110.7	109.9	1,453	890
Hardin	1,423	4,258,899	9.1	8.7	1.2	4.7	11.9	3.6	57.1	110.9	55.5	32.7	1,034	564
Harrison	710	1,856,484	14.6	4.5	0.0	15.6	8.0	4.7	51.0	49.7	28.0	13.6	864	670
Henry	1,481	5,408,211	10.0	3.9	0.9	3.5	8.5	11.1	57.7	117.5	56.0	44.6	1,592	1,074
Highland	2,293	6,286,414	5.2	4.7	1.8	3.3	31.1	2.7	50.4	172.7	76.0	41.2	959	563
Hocking	914	2,885,727	10.2	5.6	1.4	5.5	5.2	3.2	67.0	114.8	42.6	28.6	978	747
Holmes	1,321	4,844,879	5.9	5.2	1.1	8.0	34.0	1.8	43.4	120.7	39.0	36.0	838	671
Huron	2,467	10,437,634	6.6	7.8	2.4	4.1	4.3	21.4	48.4	200.0	86.9	77.4	1,306	715
Jackson	1,363	4,190,837	9.9	7.6	2.0	7.6	8.5	6.5	56.1	108.3	64.9	23.7	718	505
Jefferson	2,754	8,388,400	8.2	12.7	2.8	7.2	11.7	7.8	48.7	279.5	143.1	76.7	1,121	730
Knox	2,080	6,852,809	7.4	6.9	4.1	5.9	8.2	4.9	60.0	183.1	81.3	75.5	1,244	918
Lake	9,604	40,201,055	7.4	10.0	6.0	4.6	9.6	6.7	54.4	980.1	328.7	481.4	2,097	1,489
Lawrence	2,540	8,380,560	7.9	7.5	1.5	3.4	6.7	4.8	67.2	216.7	128.7	37.7	607	431
Licking	5,717	20,737,584	8.7	10.0	5.7	3.6	5.5	4.6	60.9	579.7	236.0	255.6	1,525	1,041
Logan	1,959	6,311,962	5.8	5.7	2.0	5.4	16.7	4.0	58.9	181.6	83.8	65.2	1,434	1,028
Lorain	11,564	45,174,817	6.2	9.7	3.8	2.9	8.7	7.0	60.5	1,201.2	540.9	467.7	1,551	1,088
Lucas	14,739	62,111,336	9.0	11.4	8.7	4.8	10.1	5.0	50.5	2,086.3	910.4	780.9	1,783	1,087
Madison	1,659	6,453,004	10.2	8.0	6.0	3.9	8.2	4.3	57.6	145.7	58.9	62.4	1,448	1,020
Mahoning	8,773	31,345,985	6.1	10.6	3.5	4.0	7.9	7.9	58.9	868.3	433.7	320.4	1,363	887
Marion	2,295	8,158,244	7.0	10.0	5.7	2.9	9.1	2.6	60.7	238.0	129.7	65.6	990	651
Medina	5,924	23,018,921	7.1	9.8	2.3	4.3	7.5	6.6	61.1	592.1	209.5	282.6	1,627	1,274
Meigs	1,067	3,103,267	7.9	7.6	0.0	6.4	10.2	11.3	53.7	74.8	52.2	14.0	593	473
Mercer	1,924	6,814,130	6.9	4.9	1.1	2.5	23.6	3.3	56.9	205.3	75.3	58.0	1,418	907
Miami	3,473	13,601,040	7.3	8.3	2.8	3.5	7.7	7.6	59.9	385.2	159.1	157.7	1,531	850
Monroe	802	1,932,268	10.9	3.9	0.2	9.0	13.4	7.6	53.8	74.7	47.7	17.9	1,229	1,062
Montgomery	22,502	93,151,363	7.9	9.7	4.7	6.0	8.0	8.2	54.1	2,605.5	1,042.9	1,055.0	1,974	1,302
Morgan	442	1,318,311	13.5	4.8	0.0	6.2	1.1	3.1	69.8	48.1	33.5	10.1	676	539
Morrow	1,452	4,922,890	11.2	5.3	0.3	5.8	24.4	1.2	49.4	129.7	48.6	32.8	939	663
Muskingum	3,889	12,275,435	6.0	8.2	2.0	4.2	10.5	5.2	60.2	370.0	202.8	113.8	1,324	918
Noble	445	1,384,468	17.5	1.9	0.0	7.5	11.4	15.2	45.8	48.2	22.3	17.2	1,183	1,099

1. Based on the resident population estimated as of July 1 of the year shown.

STATE County	Local government finances, 2012 (cont.)							Debt outstanding		Government employment, 2017			Individual income tax returns, 2016		
	Direct general expenditure														
			Percent of total for:												
	Total (mil dol)	Per capita[1] (dollars)	Education	Health and hospitals	Police protection	Public welfare	Highways	Total (mil dol)	Per capita[1] (dollars)	Federal civilian	Federal military	State and local	Number of returns	Mean adjusted gross income	Mean income tax
	185	186	187	188	189	190	191	192	193	194	195	196	197	198	199
NORTH DAKOTA— Cont'd															
Ward	230.0	3,550	57.5	0.3	5.1	2.2	10.8	95.7	1,477	1,256	5,855	4,485	33,030	62,137	7,861
Wells	18.0	4,209	46.4	1.9	3.5	4.3	18.7	9.3	2,176	25	25	253	2,090	56,157	6,970
Williams	130.1	4,872	37.2	3.2	4.7	0.9	16.5	127.0	4,757	107	205	2,430	16,870	78,278	11,627
OHIO	X	X	X	X	X	X	X	X	X	78,517	35,792	691,621	5,572,450	58,489	7,378
Adams	85.9	3,030	56.6	4.4	3.7	6.7	8.9	48.9	1,726	66	70	1,497	10,970	42,110	3,662
Allen	385.4	3,665	49.5	5.4	6.9	4.3	6.7	180.7	1,719	324	253	5,741	47,640	51,095	5,771
Ashland	147.7	2,789	50.7	9.1	6.1	3.4	7.9	51.1	966	100	131	2,317	24,710	47,124	4,703
Ashtabula	389.2	3,877	53.0	7.0	3.8	6.1	7.1	243.8	2,429	195	261	4,361	44,230	43,059	4,027
Athens	231.8	3,605	47.4	7.2	2.6	14.9	4.9	68.3	1,062	230	157	11,814	22,050	47,574	4,988
Auglaize	176.4	3,848	52.8	1.4	5.8	4.8	6.3	154.1	3,362	95	116	2,266	23,520	55,815	6,176
Belmont	186.0	2,669	48.0	6.2	2.5	6.5	6.8	55.5	797	160	164	3,639	30,390	51,900	5,976
Brown	134.7	3,035	63.4	3.5	6.0	3.2	5.5	58.8	1,325	97	110	1,975	19,270	44,621	3,955
Butler	1,326.8	3,580	50.2	3.7	7.9	4.7	5.8	1,987.8	5,364	564	959	20,759	175,200	60,805	7,350
Carroll	59.8	2,092	47.0	8.7	3.5	6.9	10.6	17.3	605	47	69	990	12,580	47,633	4,744
Champaign	144.3	3,648	59.7	3.7	3.5	3.9	6.6	60.2	1,522	68	98	1,857	18,490	47,746	4,484
Clark	474.6	3,459	49.3	5.8	5.9	6.2	3.3	206.0	1,502	574	339	6,402	62,720	47,399	4,745
Clermont	582.2	2,924	49.6	6.2	6.8	6.0	5.4	332.6	1,671	380	519	7,381	98,450	63,160	7,822
Clinton	150.9	3,602	49.6	3.5	5.9	5.2	7.7	60.1	1,434	131	105	2,246	19,410	52,168	6,260
Columbiana	314.7	2,954	56.2	3.2	5.1	8.9	6.3	123.5	1,160	618	254	4,346	46,790	44,844	4,321
Coshocton	116.3	3,163	50.7	9.0	6.0	6.2	9.6	60.1	1,634	77	92	1,473	16,180	42,884	3,915
Crawford	163.0	3,804	50.5	4.3	4.1	5.0	8.0	99.7	2,328	84	105	1,759	20,220	41,953	3,645
Cuyahoga	8,005.7	6,328	36.6	14.5	5.9	3.6	2.9	11,286.9	8,922	16,521	3,538	78,861	619,030	61,059	8,570
Darke	165.9	3,160	56.8	4.8	5.9	4.6	7.2	76.5	1,457	102	130	2,102	25,090	46,917	4,525
Defiance	164.9	4,263	38.1	17.8	4.2	3.1	5.7	96.2	2,486	83	96	1,986	18,940	49,799	5,160
Delaware	580.7	3,207	51.8	3.6	4.6	2.2	6.9	734.5	4,057	241	540	7,699	94,430	104,857	17,381
Erie	360.9	4,724	52.1	2.5	5.2	3.9	4.2	232.7	3,046	241	189	5,087	39,600	54,861	6,635
Fairfield	537.8	3,647	55.2	5.3	4.9	3.9	3.7	791.1	5,364	242	410	6,753	71,780	59,401	6,744
Fayette	143.4	4,966	32.8	26.1	3.8	3.7	4.5	83.9	2,906	49	72	1,638	13,380	43,247	4,250
Franklin	6,511.1	5,446	38.1	3.0	6.3	6.0	4.2	8,029.0	6,716	13,409	3,694	121,784	622,650	61,515	8,170
Fulton	197.2	4,637	67.2	2.5	4.2	2.4	4.5	104.1	2,450	95	107	2,467	21,230	52,424	5,360
Gallia	123.5	4,023	57.7	2.3	5.6	5.4	6.2	74.2	2,416	64	75	1,877	11,860	46,605	4,602
Geauga	314.3	3,355	48.5	9.3	6.8	2.6	8.8	302.2	3,225	105	238	3,892	47,400	89,617	14,505
Greene	655.1	4,004	53.0	4.0	6.4	4.0	4.8	524.5	3,206	14,333	3,139	10,883	77,220	66,404	8,505
Guernsey	125.8	3,159	48.1	3.5	4.9	8.6	7.9	38.7	973	120	99	2,182	17,910	44,669	4,560
Hamilton	4,409.2	5,497	37.9	6.8	6.8	4.4	3.4	5,717.7	7,129	8,535	2,174	49,287	401,000	70,590	10,721
Hancock	295.5	3,905	53.3	7.9	3.8	2.7	4.3	240.6	3,180	151	190	3,185	37,210	58,670	7,231
Hardin	110.3	3,489	43.3	1.9	7.5	10.6	8.3	59.1	1,869	68	75	1,408	13,200	43,988	3,964
Harrison	46.0	2,927	48.6	1.1	3.7	9.2	14.1	4.8	305	52	38	745	6,570	48,704	5,039
Henry	116.8	4,166	57.4	9.8	4.3	0.3	7.0	51.0	1,819	69	69	1,884	14,070	51,926	5,605
Highland	157.5	3,663	45.3	24.8	5.4	4.0	5.4	55.6	1,293	99	109	2,206	18,300	41,862	3,582
Hocking	118.1	4,036	34.2	34.9	4.9	5.2	5.5	21.9	748	47	72	1,712	12,440	43,803	3,926
Holmes	122.6	2,851	35.9	29.5	3.5	5.1	8.0	35.7	830	63	111	1,552	17,460	50,289	5,277
Huron	227.6	3,839	59.2	1.8	3.8	5.5	5.6	177.4	2,992	143	148	2,333	28,780	46,767	4,690
Jackson	103.5	3,142	55.6	4.5	4.9	6.5	7.1	74.9	2,274	70	82	1,490	13,450	43,861	3,919
Jefferson	274.2	4,010	48.3	6.7	5.3	3.8	7.4	154.1	2,253	170	164	3,158	29,790	45,717	4,539
Knox	190.4	3,137	48.2	3.8	2.8	3.7	12.6	94.4	1,554	106	148	2,651	27,370	50,905	5,145
Lake	960.6	4,184	51.1	7.4	6.8	2.5	5.5	411.1	1,790	472	604	10,988	123,190	57,549	6,866
Lawrence	214.4	3,452	60.9	5.7	3.5	4.9	4.0	51.1	822	134	153	2,866	25,230	45,582	4,335
Licking	578.6	3,453	56.4	0.8	6.3	6.5	4.5	386.9	2,309	368	445	7,832	82,590	57,046	6,412
Logan	185.1	4,071	51.9	5.6	4.3	4.6	6.6	117.8	2,592	128	119	2,180	22,440	49,453	5,145
Lorain	1,206.9	4,003	55.2	4.3	5.8	3.9	4.7	1,730.7	5,741	1,100	785	14,449	149,330	57,411	6,820
Lucas	1,896.4	4,330	37.6	9.4	7.1	4.9	3.8	2,289.2	5,226	1,860	1,172	28,381	200,860	53,755	6,535
Madison	152.8	3,549	60.2	4.9	4.6	3.8	5.7	137.1	3,184	81	100	3,153	19,270	56,898	6,570
Mahoning	851.8	3,622	47.9	5.8	7.8	3.8	4.3	531.9	2,262	1,210	579	13,755	110,860	50,317	5,982
Marion	232.6	3,512	58.7	1.2	4.1	2.2	4.0	316.2	4,773	112	175	3,835	27,740	44,736	4,255
Medina	715.8	4,121	54.5	3.6	4.6	2.1	11.9	431.2	2,483	353	479	6,787	92,400	69,326	9,097
Meigs	70.8	3,002	53.3	2.8	2.8	10.1	10.2	25.4	1,075	60	59	1,031	9,150	42,370	3,566
Mercer	196.0	4,794	46.2	26.1	3.3	3.1	7.9	89.2	2,183	93	104	2,683	21,120	53,300	5,946
Miami	405.1	3,930	56.7	3.4	6.0	3.1	5.3	280.3	2,720	191	268	4,685	51,640	57,594	6,769
Monroe	83.7	5,754	66.8	2.8	2.6	8.8	8.9	2.9	200	51	35	776	6,190	51,782	6,073
Montgomery	2,652.7	4,965	44.5	3.0	6.4	8.6	5.3	2,338.6	4,377	4,337	3,812	27,179	255,360	53,930	6,435
Morgan	43.8	2,938	48.1	4.6	5.2	8.6	11.1	11.3	760	43	37	621	6,090	39,757	3,210
Morrow	139.5	3,994	47.5	22.8	1.4	3.0	5.3	60.5	1,733	48	89	1,580	15,580	48,644	4,591
Muskingum	340.0	3,956	54.4	3.3	4.9	6.1	6.4	122.4	1,424	223	216	5,107	39,590	46,448	4,793
Noble	36.8	2,523	50.8	2.9	4.1	7.6	14.3	3.0	208	22	30	974	5,380	48,080	4,942

1. Based on the resident population estimated as of July 1 of the year shown.

Table B. States and Counties — **Land Area and Population**

State / county code	CBSA code[1]	County code[2]	STATE County	Land area[3] (sq. mi)	Total persons 2018	Rank	Per square mile	White	Black	American Indian, Alaska Native	Asian and Pacific Islander	Percent Hispanic or Latino[4]	Under 5 years	5 to 17 years	18 to 24 years	25 to 34 years	35 to 44 years	45 to 54 years
				1	2	3	4	5	6	7	8	9	10	11	12	13	14	15
			OHIO— Cont'd															
39123	38,840	4	Ottawa	254.7	40,769	1,158	160.1	93.3	1.5	0.6	0.6	5.2	4.3	14.3	6.7	9.6	10.0	12.7
39125		6	Paulding	416.4	18,760	1,886	45.1	93.5	1.6	0.8	0.6	4.8	5.8	17.7	7.6	11.1	11.6	12.9
39127	18,140	1	Perry	407.9	36,033	1,273	88.3	98.0	1.0	1.1	0.4	0.9	6.0	17.4	7.6	12.0	12.0	13.8
39129	18,140	1	Pickaway	501.2	58,086	889	115.9	94.0	4.6	0.8	0.8	1.4	5.4	16.0	8.9	13.4	13.4	14.2
39131		7	Pike	440.3	28,067	1,496	63.7	96.8	1.9	1.4	0.7	1.1	6.2	17.4	7.7	11.3	12.1	13.4
39133	10,420	2	Portage	487.4	162,927	404	334.3	91.1	5.6	0.7	2.7	1.9	4.6	14.1	16.1	11.5	10.6	12.6
39135		6	Preble	424.2	40,997	1,150	96.6	97.5	1.2	0.8	0.9	0.9	5.4	17.0	7.4	11.0	11.8	13.3
39137		6	Putnam	482.5	33,780	1,334	70.0	93.0	0.7	0.3	0.4	6.2	6.8	18.7	7.8	11.0	11.2	12.3
39139	31,900	3	Richland	495.2	121,099	519	244.5	87.5	10.8	0.7	1.2	2.0	5.6	16.0	8.3	12.6	11.8	12.3
39141	17,060	4	Ross	689.2	76,931	721	111.6	92.0	7.2	1.1	1.0	1.3	5.5	15.6	7.9	12.5	13.1	14.2
39143	23,380	4	Sandusky	408.5	58,799	881	143.9	86.3	4.5	0.7	0.7	10.0	5.6	16.7	7.6	11.5	11.8	13.0
39145	39,020	4	Scioto	610.2	75,502	732	123.7	95.1	3.5	1.3	0.7	1.4	5.8	15.8	8.7	12.7	12.0	12.8
39147	45,660	4	Seneca	551.0	55,207	926	100.2	91.2	3.8	0.6	1.0	5.3	5.4	16.5	10.5	11.6	11.6	11.9
39149	43,380	4	Shelby	407.7	48,627	1,012	119.3	94.6	3.7	0.6	1.6	1.6	6.4	18.4	8.2	11.7	11.4	13.2
39151	15,940	2	Stark	575.3	371,574	188	645.9	88.7	9.6	0.8	1.3	2.2	5.6	15.8	8.5	11.9	11.3	12.8
39153	10,420	2	Summit	412.8	541,918	128	1,312.8	78.8	16.3	0.8	4.4	2.2	5.6	15.3	8.5	13.4	11.7	13.1
39155	49,660	2	Trumbull	618.0	198,627	338	321.4	89.1	9.5	0.7	0.9	1.9	5.3	15.2	7.7	11.4	10.8	12.8
39157	35,420	4	Tuscarawas	567.4	92,176	640	162.5	95.6	1.5	0.6	0.7	2.9	6.2	16.7	7.8	11.6	11.6	12.3
39159	18,140	1	Union	431.8	57,835	893	133.9	90.6	3.3	0.6	5.2	1.8	6.3	18.4	7.9	13.3	14.9	14.6
39161	46,780	6	Van Wert	409.2	28,281	1,490	69.1	94.9	1.9	0.5	0.5	3.5	6.3	17.0	7.8	11.4	11.9	12.4
39163		8	Vinton	412.4	13,139	2,222	31.9	97.9	1.1	1.2	0.5	0.9	5.6	16.3	7.4	11.4	12.2	13.5
39165	17,140	1	Warren	401.3	232,173	287	578.6	87.3	4.2	0.5	6.8	2.8	5.8	18.9	8.0	11.2	13.6	14.9
39167	31,930	4	Washington	632.0	60,155	868	95.2	96.6	2.0	1.0	1.2	1.1	4.9	14.8	8.7	11.2	11.2	12.8
39169	49,300	4	Wayne	554.9	115,967	536	209.0	95.0	2.5	0.6	1.5	2.1	6.6	17.7	9.7	11.8	11.1	11.8
39171		6	Williams	420.7	36,804	1,255	87.5	93.3	1.7	0.6	0.8	4.6	5.9	16.9	7.8	11.7	11.7	12.3
39173	45,780	2	Wood	617.2	130,696	489	211.8	89.6	3.5	0.7	2.3	5.7	5.4	15.0	17.3	12.2	11.1	11.4
39175		7	Wyandot	406.9	21,935	1,727	53.9	95.7	0.8	0.6	0.9	3.0	5.6	17.0	7.5	11.1	12.2	12.9
40000		0	OKLAHOMA	68,596.0	3,943,079	X	57.5	70.5	8.9	12.5	3.1	10.9	6.6	17.7	9.6	13.8	12.4	11.7
40001		6	Adair	573.7	22,082	1,717	38.5	49.5	1.2	51.7	1.1	6.8	7.4	19.2	8.3	12.1	11.9	12.7
40003		9	Alfalfa	866.5	5,754	2,774	6.6	85.5	5.3	5.3	0.7	5.6	5.3	14.4	6.0	10.5	15.5	14.8
40005		9	Atoka	975.5	13,838	2,172	14.2	78.1	5.1	19.9	1.2	3.5	6.0	16.5	7.5	13.2	11.8	11.9
40007		9	Beaver	1,814.7	5,319	2,807	2.9	73.1	1.3	2.4	0.5	24.6	5.8	20.1	7.1	10.5	11.0	12.4
40009	21,120	7	Beckham	901.8	21,709	1,741	24.1	77.3	4.8	4.2	1.3	14.9	6.8	17.7	8.7	15.6	13.1	11.4
40011		6	Blaine	928.4	9,485	2,463	10.2	76.2	4.8	11.7	1.0	11.4	7.2	18.9	7.3	10.4	10.5	11.5
40013	20,460	6	Bryan	904.5	47,192	1,034	52.2	77.5	2.8	20.1	0.9	6.1	6.5	17.0	9.4	14.2	11.5	11.6
40015		6	Caddo	1,277.8	28,977	1,459	22.7	61.8	4.1	25.8	1.0	12.9	6.9	18.3	8.2	13.4	11.7	12.0
40017	36,420	1	Canadian	896.6	144,447	453	161.1	79.6	4.3	7.2	3.9	9.3	6.8	19.3	7.6	14.7	14.5	12.2
40019	11,620	5	Carter	822.2	48,177	1,019	58.6	74.8	8.6	13.8	1.7	7.6	6.8	18.2	8.1	12.7	12.2	12.0
40021	45,140	6	Cherokee	749.3	48,675	1,010	65.0	56.0	2.2	42.7	1.2	7.3	5.7	16.2	15.0	12.2	11.3	10.8
40023		7	Choctaw	770.4	14,668	2,116	19.0	66.8	12.3	22.5	0.9	4.5	6.7	17.4	7.2	10.9	10.8	11.7
40025		9	Cimarron	1,834.8	2,153	3,033	1.2	75.8	1.5	2.3	0.7	22.4	6.5	18.4	6.5	9.9	9.7	11.1
40027	36,420	1	Cleveland	538.9	281,669	246	522.7	76.3	6.6	7.9	5.9	9.0	5.4	16.1	14.5	14.8	13.1	11.3
40029		9	Coal	516.7	5,520	2,791	10.7	76.2	1.8	25.1	0.8	4.5	7.0	17.2	7.5	11.2	11.1	11.1
40031	30,020	3	Comanche	1,069.3	120,422	521	112.6	60.9	19.2	8.0	5.0	13.4	6.9	16.6	12.6	16.5	12.3	10.9
40033	30,020	3	Cotton	632.7	5,776	2,771	9.1	80.8	3.3	11.7	1.0	8.3	5.6	16.9	7.1	11.3	11.0	13.1
40035		6	Craig	761.4	14,306	2,143	18.8	71.5	4.3	28.3	1.4	3.7	5.7	16.3	8.0	12.1	11.5	13.1
40037	46,140	2	Creek	950.2	71,604	756	75.4	82.1	3.4	16.1	1.2	4.3	6.3	17.7	7.8	12.0	12.0	12.7
40039	48,220	7	Custer	988.8	29,036	1,457	29.4	70.6	3.8	8.6	1.7	18.9	7.1	17.8	16.6	12.8	11.2	9.6
40041		6	Delaware	738.1	42,733	1,122	57.9	71.4	0.8	30.4	1.5	3.7	5.0	15.0	7.2	10.2	10.0	12.1
40043		9	Dewey	999.5	4,894	2,842	4.9	84.8	1.9	8.2	1.5	7.4	6.8	20.2	7.1	11.7	11.6	10.6
40045		9	Ellis	1,231.5	3,952	2,905	3.2	88.5	1.4	4.0	0.7	7.5	5.7	17.4	6.7	9.7	12.4	10.8
40047	21,420	5	Garfield	1,058.5	60,913	864	57.5	77.5	4.4	4.3	4.7	12.9	7.4	18.5	8.6	14.1	12.2	10.4
40049		6	Garvin	802.1	27,811	1,503	34.7	79.8	3.2	12.1	0.9	9.2	6.6	18.1	8.0	11.9	12.4	11.7
40051	36,420	1	Grady	1,100.5	55,551	922	50.5	85.6	3.2	9.1	0.9	5.9	5.7	18.4	7.8	11.8	13.1	12.6
40053		9	Grant	1,000.4	4,326	2,874	4.3	90.3	2.5	4.2	0.6	5.2	6.0	17.8	6.7	11.0	10.4	11.3
40055		7	Greer	639.3	5,821	2,765	9.1	76.5	9.1	4.5	0.6	12.0	4.9	15.3	8.0	15.9	13.8	12.9
40057		9	Harmon	537.2	2,664	2,990	5.0	59.6	9.1	3.7	1.8	29.8	6.3	19.0	7.1	11.0	11.1	12.7
40059		9	Harper	1,039.0	3,797	2,918	3.7	73.6	0.8	2.3	0.4	24.6	6.7	20.1	6.8	10.7	12.3	11.1
40061		6	Haskell	576.5	12,668	2,246	22.0	76.9	1.3	23.2	1.2	4.5	6.0	17.5	7.5	11.4	12.0	11.6
40063		6	Hughes	804.6	13,335	2,209	16.6	68.8	6.7	24.8	0.8	6.0	6.1	15.7	8.6	13.7	12.6	12.0
40065	11,060	7	Jackson	802.7	24,949	1,607	31.1	65.0	8.1	3.3	2.2	24.6	7.6	17.7	10.3	15.0	11.9	10.8
40067		8	Jefferson	758.8	6,123	2,739	8.1	81.5	2.2	9.0	1.0	10.7	6.4	17.8	6.9	11.5	10.6	11.1
40069		9	Johnston	642.9	10,949	2,356	17.0	76.6	3.6	20.9	0.9	5.6	6.1	17.4	9.0	11.7	11.5	11.7
40071	38,620	5	Kay	919.6	44,161	1,092	48.0	79.0	3.1	13.6	1.3	8.2	6.8	18.3	8.3	12.1	11.5	10.7
40073		6	Kingfisher	898.1	15,816	2,049	17.6	78.8	1.9	5.4	0.6	16.1	6.8	20.3	8.0	11.8	12.1	11.8

1. CBSA = Core Based Statistical Area. See Appendix A for explanation. See Appendix B for list of metropolitan areas with component counties.   2. County type code from the Economic Research Service of USDA Rural-Urban Continuum Codes. See Appendix A for definition.   3. Dry land or land partially or temporarily covered by water.   4. May be of any race.

Table B. States and Counties — Population and Households

STATE County	Population, 2018 (cont.) Age (percent) (cont.) 55 to 64 years	65 to 74 years	75 years and over	Percent female	Population change, 2000-2018 Total persons 2000	2010	Percent change 2000-2010	2010-2018	Components of change, 2010-2018 Births	Deaths	Net Migration	Households, 2013-2017 Number	Persons per household	Family households	Female family householder[1]	One person
	16	17	18	19	20	21	22	23	24	25	26	27	28	29	30	31
OHIO— Cont'd																
Ottawa	17.4	14.5	10.5	50.4	40,985	41,433	1.1	-1.6	2,796	3,974	552	17,495	2.28	67.7	9.7	27.9
Paulding	14.8	10.9	7.7	50.1	20,293	19,610	-3.4	-4.3	1,801	1,596	-1,065	7,589	2.49	69.1	8.4	27.3
Perry	14.6	10.2	6.3	49.9	34,078	36,039	5.8	0.0	3,514	2,876	-634	13,576	2.63	74.1	11.9	21.1
Pickaway	13.0	9.0	6.7	47.5	52,727	55,680	5.6	4.3	4,959	4,440	1,921	19,465	2.69	72.5	10.7	22.0
Pike	14.1	10.2	7.7	50.3	27,695	28,705	3.6	-2.2	2,839	2,782	-684	11,033	2.52	68.0	11.5	27.0
Portage	14.1	9.8	6.6	50.9	152,061	161,425	6.2	0.9	11,849	11,552	1,280	62,208	2.49	63.6	10.5	28.3
Preble	14.8	11.4	7.8	50.5	42,337	42,258	-0.2	-3.0	3,604	3,836	-1,021	16,126	2.54	71.0	9.5	24.0
Putnam	14.8	9.5	7.9	50.1	34,726	34,496	-0.7	-2.1	3,668	2,488	-1,918	13,159	2.56	74.6	7.7	22.1
Richland	13.9	10.7	8.8	49.2	128,852	124,474	-3.4	-2.7	11,378	11,405	-3,332	47,987	2.38	63.2	12.1	31.4
Ross	14.4	9.7	7.0	47.6	73,345	78,078	6.5	-1.5	6,908	6,761	-1,267	28,526	2.49	70.1	14.9	25.0
Sandusky	14.9	10.9	7.9	50.5	61,792	60,946	-1.4	-3.5	5,505	5,256	-2,395	23,721	2.46	66.3	11.5	27.1
Scioto	13.9	10.3	8.0	50.6	79,195	79,493	0.4	-5.0	7,292	7,941	-3,336	30,204	2.43	63.0	11.7	31.0
Seneca	14.3	10.3	7.8	50.0	58,683	56,742	-0.3	-2.7	4,807	4,852	-1,486	21,507	2.44	66.7	12.1	27.2
Shelby	14.1	9.6	7.0	49.8	47,910	49,418	3.1	-1.6	5,048	3,631	-2,230	18,665	2.60	70.9	10.2	24.5
Stark	14.5	11.0	8.5	51.4	378,098	375,590	-0.7	-1.1	34,138	33,961	-3,872	152,037	2.40	65.7	12.6	28.6
Summit	14.5	10.4	7.6	51.5	542,899	541,778	-0.2	0.0	49,974	46,819	-2,677	223,021	2.39	62.2	13.1	31.7
Trumbull	15.1	12.3	9.3	51.3	225,116	210,325	-6.6	-5.6	17,221	20,862	-8,003	86,709	2.30	63.8	13.3	31.4
Tuscarawas	14.3	10.9	8.7	50.7	90,914	92,587	1.8	-0.4	9,377	8,391	-1,339	36,548	2.50	67.0	10.2	27.7
Union	12.2	7.5	4.8	52.1	40,909	52,280	27.8	10.6	5,208	2,896	3,245	19,038	2.70	74.6	7.7	20.0
Van Wert	14.2	10.5	8.5	50.5	29,659	28,759	-3.0	-1.7	2,766	2,596	-640	11,503	2.43	71.0	10.6	25.0
Vinton	15.7	10.8	7.0	49.9	12,806	13,430	4.9	-2.2	1,195	1,171	-317	5,053	2.58	67.9	12.4	27.6
Warren	13.2	8.6	5.9	49.7	158,383	212,820	34.4	9.1	19,773	13,260	13,030	80,704	2.69	75.0	8.3	20.4
Washington	15.3	11.8	9.2	50.9	63,251	61,781	-2.3	-2.6	5,011	6,023	-561	25,378	2.33	65.2	9.6	30.0
Wayne	13.6	10.1	7.8	50.3	111,564	114,516	2.6	1.3	12,603	8,935	-2,164	43,353	2.59	70.3	9.4	26.0
Williams	14.9	10.3	8.5	50.2	39,188	37,648	-3.9	-2.2	3,526	3,252	-1,118	15,263	2.35	64.2	9.7	30.3
Wood	12.3	9.0	6.3	50.7	121,065	125,489	3.7	4.1	11,252	8,740	2,692	50,187	2.44	62.7	8.7	28.0
Wyandot	14.2	10.5	8.9	50.3	22,908	22,617	-1.3	-3.0	2,077	2,007	-748	9,157	2.39	66.6	10.0	26.0
OKLAHOMA	12.5	9.1	6.6	50.5	3,450,654	3,751,583	8.7	5.1	433,393	318,855	76,774	1,468,971	2.58	66.1	12.3	28.2
Adair	12.6	9.4	6.5	50.1	21,038	22,683	7.8	-2.6	2,537	2,018	-1,121	7,796	2.83	72.7	16.0	22.6
Alfalfa	13.9	10.2	9.5	40.3	6,105	5,640	-7.6	2.0	485	536	160	1,978	2.44	69.2	7.1	26.8
Atoka	13.3	11.4	8.5	48.0	13,879	14,165	2.1	-2.3	1,337	1,263	-401	5,284	2.32	69.0	13.8	27.6
Beaver	13.4	10.7	9.0	49.5	5,857	5,636	-3.8	-5.6	464	379	-407	2,103	2.55	74.3	7.1	21.6
Beckham	12.3	8.1	6.2	46.3	19,799	22,119	11.7	-1.9	2,844	1,968	-1,319	7,573	2.80	69.9	10.5	24.8
Blaine	14.6	10.7	8.9	50.8	11,976	11,942	-0.3	-20.6	1,235	1,005	-2,962	3,819	2.14	65.5	12.1	30.9
Bryan	11.9	10.2	7.8	51.1	36,534	42,416	16.1	11.3	4,833	4,058	3,980	16,911	2.60	64.8	12.7	29.0
Caddo	12.7	9.4	7.5	47.5	30,150	29,599	-1.8	-2.1	3,430	2,955	-1,092	10,273	2.76	67.8	13.8	27.8
Canadian	11.8	7.9	5.1	50.4	87,697	115,540	31.7	25.0	14,115	7,628	22,136	43,878	2.98	73.8	10.3	22.5
Carter	13.1	9.4	7.4	51.3	45,621	47,733	4.6	0.9	5,459	5,044	61	18,278	2.60	66.2	11.7	29.7
Cherokee	12.1	9.8	6.9	51.1	42,521	46,982	10.5	3.6	4,934	4,062	838	16,360	2.84	64.4	12.0	30.7
Choctaw	14.6	11.8	8.8	52.0	15,342	15,199	-0.9	-3.5	1,643	1,796	-370	5,962	2.48	63.5	16.0	32.4
Cimarron	12.4	13.6	11.8	48.8	3,148	2,475	-21.4	-13.0	213	233	-307	990	2.22	65.7	10.1	33.2
Cleveland	11.4	8.1	5.3	50.1	208,016	256,009	23.1	10.0	24,880	15,748	16,415	103,028	2.54	65.7	10.6	25.5
Coal	14.5	11.4	8.9	50.2	6,031	5,925	-1.8	-6.8	575	677	-308	2,240	2.50	66.7	12.8	29.6
Comanche	11.6	7.2	5.4	48.2	114,996	124,098	7.9	-3.0	15,656	8,388	-11,140	42,957	2.66	64.9	14.5	28.9
Cotton	15.6	11.0	8.4	50.8	6,614	6,190	-6.4	-6.7	533	666	-282	2,265	2.59	71.4	13.3	25.7
Craig	13.8	10.4	9.2	48.8	14,950	15,025	0.5	-4.8	1,340	1,715	-339	5,413	2.49	67.8	11.0	29.5
Creek	13.9	10.1	7.5	50.5	67,367	69,971	3.9	2.3	7,189	7,057	1,543	26,398	2.65	71.0	12.8	25.0
Custer	11.0	7.6	6.2	50.2	26,142	27,469	5.1	5.7	3,700	2,384	232	10,458	2.63	68.2	10.8	22.4
Delaware	15.4	14.7	10.3	50.7	37,077	41,491	11.9	3.0	3,325	4,392	2,326	16,571	2.50	67.7	11.4	28.0
Dewey	13.4	9.8	8.7	50.7	4,743	4,810	1.4	1.7	493	570	162	1,727	2.78	69.1	6.0	28.3
Ellis	14.8	12.9	9.6	50.9	4,075	4,151	1.9	-4.8	362	451	-113	1,625	2.49	65.2	8.0	31.9
Garfield	12.5	8.8	7.6	50.2	57,813	60,580	4.8	0.5	7,857	5,681	-1,827	23,798	2.55	68.2	10.3	27.9
Garvin	13.3	10.0	7.9	50.6	27,210	27,571	1.3	0.9	3,053	3,030	230	10,473	2.62	67.3	9.5	28.3
Grady	14.3	9.6	6.6	50.0	45,516	52,428	15.2	6.0	4,987	4,431	2,602	19,743	2.72	73.9	10.4	22.0
Grant	14.8	11.4	10.6	50.4	5,144	4,530	-11.9	-4.5	423	501	-126	1,883	2.32	66.2	7.5	30.9
Greer	11.4	8.8	9.0	42.5	6,061	6,239	2.9	-6.7	522	623	-321	2,152	2.31	60.7	10.3	38.0
Harmon	13.1	10.7	9.0	52.2	3,283	2,922	-11.0	-8.8	259	260	-261	1,185	2.24	67.2	11.3	25.7
Harper	14.2	9.3	8.7	50.0	3,562	3,685	3.5	3.0	423	366	52	1,348	2.81	67.1	5.6	32.3
Haskell	13.6	11.5	8.8	50.0	11,792	12,767	8.3	-0.8	1,226	1,252	-67	4,849	2.61	71.4	11.3	24.1
Hughes	12.5	10.6	8.2	46.1	14,154	14,003	-1.1	-4.8	1,235	1,559	-340	4,258	2.77	68.8	12.0	29.1
Jackson	11.8	8.2	6.7	50.3	28,439	26,446	-7.0	-5.7	3,535	2,086	-2,983	9,958	2.50	66.1	11.3	29.5
Jefferson	14.5	12.0	9.3	50.0	6,818	6,472	-5.1	-5.4	577	756	-171	2,392	2.56	65.5	10.3	30.4
Johnston	13.1	11.3	8.1	50.5	10,513	10,957	4.2	-0.1	1,052	1,149	88	4,256	2.53	66.6	12.2	31.2
Kay	12.9	10.5	8.8	50.3	48,080	46,562	-3.2	-5.2	5,143	4,703	-2,847	17,890	2.47	62.7	11.8	31.7
Kingfisher	13.2	8.7	7.2	50.2	13,926	15,025	7.9	5.3	1,628	1,236	406	5,691	2.70	69.6	8.6	27.5

1. No spouse present.

Table B. States and Counties — **Population, Vital Statistics, Health, and Crime**

STATE County	Persons in group quarters, 2018	Daytime Population, 2013-2017		Births, 2018		Deaths, 2018		Persons under 65 with no health insurance, 2016		Medicare, 2018			Serious crimes known to police[2], 2016 Total	
		Number	Employment/ residence ratio	Total	Rate[1]	Number	Rate[1]	Number	Percent	Total beneficiaries	Enrolled in Original Medicare	Enrolled in Medicare Advantage	Number	Rate[3]
	32	33	34	35	36	37	38	39	40	41	42	43	44	45
OHIO— Cont'd														
Ottawa	495	36,978	0.80	315	7.7	507	12.4	2,009	6.5	11,448	7,521	3,927	517	1,530
Paulding	85	15,639	0.61	205	10.9	184	9.8	1,028	6.7	4,158	2,843	1,315	156	1,083
Perry	307	28,580	0.49	406	11.3	373	10.4	2,282	7.6	7,370	4,969	2,401	409	1,181
Pickaway	4,722	49,193	0.67	575	9.9	606	10.4	2,746	6.2	10,829	5,628	5,201	1,562	2,732
Pike	496	29,209	1.09	327	11.7	373	13.3	1,810	7.8	6,337	4,626	1,711	457	1,628
Portage	7,465	144,361	0.78	1,370	8.4	1,434	8.8	9,091	7.0	30,772	15,629	15,143	2,638	1,751
Preble	386	35,005	0.67	428	10.4	462	11.3	2,439	7.3	8,959	5,489	3,470	357	1,146
Putnam	303	28,800	0.70	416	12.3	319	9.4	1,512	5.3	6,595	5,043	1,552	142	437
Richland	7,327	124,619	1.06	1,300	10.7	1,406	11.6	6,481	7.1	27,818	19,526	8,292	4,747	3,951
Ross	5,692	76,703	0.99	819	10.6	805	10.5	3,898	6.6	15,881	10,439	5,442	3,289	4,278
Sandusky	902	58,454	0.96	633	10.8	621	10.6	2,660	5.5	13,091	9,403	3,688	1,297	2,401
Scioto	3,235	74,872	0.93	851	11.3	943	12.5	3,933	6.6	16,468	12,626	3,842	2,442	3,298
Seneca	2,596	50,146	0.78	576	10.4	584	10.6	2,857	6.5	11,968	9,365	2,603	856	1,662
Shelby	589	53,970	1.21	604	12.4	453	9.3	2,180	5.3	9,261	6,795	2,466	1,244	2,650
Stark	8,838	366,865	0.96	4,016	10.8	4,135	11.1	17,591	5.9	84,058	39,117	44,941	9,985	2,932
Summit	10,350	561,400	1.08	5,842	10.8	5,795	10.7	30,012	6.8	110,571	52,989	57,582	16,657	3,157
Trumbull	3,136	193,170	0.88	2,040	10.3	2,515	12.7	10,524	6.7	50,655	25,507	25,148	4,250	2,551
Tuscarawas	1,251	87,898	0.89	1,126	12.2	1,044	11.3	5,969	8.0	20,206	11,265	8,941	892	992
Union	2,739	62,628	1.30	665	11.5	366	6.3	2,229	4.8	8,170	4,972	3,198	433	828
Van Wert	396	26,099	0.84	359	12.7	299	10.6	1,349	5.9	6,250	4,308	1,942	599	2,101
Vinton	68	10,723	0.53	135	10.3	146	11.1	850	8.0	2,613	1,930	683	159	1,227
Warren	5,494	209,765	0.87	2,312	10.0	1,834	7.9	8,753	4.6	36,991	21,208	15,783	2,924	1,309
Washington	1,725	61,287	1.02	591	9.8	743	12.4	3,478	7.4	14,604	11,145	3,459	736	1,265
Wayne	3,592	114,092	0.97	1,470	12.7	1,113	9.6	8,758	9.4	22,988	13,194	9,794	1,675	1,561
Williams	990	37,582	1.03	410	11.1	396	10.8	1,880	6.4	8,232	5,914	2,318	NA	NA
Wood	6,814	134,427	1.08	1,360	10.4	1,083	8.3	5,861	5.6	23,503	14,208	9,295	1,754	1,585
Wyandot	251	20,487	0.84	234	10.7	248	11.3	1,117	6.2	4,854	3,753	1,101	190	891
OKLAHOMA	110,099	3,890,998	1.00	50,778	12.9	40,050	10.2	517,631	16.0	721,972	581,550	140,422	134,685	3,433
Adair	92	20,135	0.75	323	14.6	283	12.8	4,176	22.5	4,336	3,981	355	591	2,717
Alfalfa	1,053	5,932	1.03	55	9.6	56	9.7	547	14.4	1,125	1,081	44	45	764
Atoka	749	13,086	0.82	155	11.2	129	9.3	2,238	21.3	3,178	2,969	209	208	1,523
Beaver	43	4,956	0.80	58	10.9	51	9.6	814	18.6	1,036	1,002	34	43	802
Beckham	1,925	25,598	1.28	285	13.1	251	11.6	2,823	16.0	3,772	3,508	264	553	2,303
Blaine	107	9,803	1.04	141	14.9	107	11.3	1,270	16.3	2,026	1,914	112	113	1,234
Bryan	1,137	44,915	0.99	595	12.6	551	11.7	6,457	17.6	9,061	8,304	757	NA	NA
Caddo	1,927	26,948	0.78	405	14.0	379	13.1	4,712	20.6	5,810	5,438	372	613	2,104
Canadian	2,482	105,293	0.58	1,797	12.4	1,055	7.3	13,452	11.4	20,952	15,152	5,800	4,026	2,952
Carter	913	51,799	1.17	642	13.3	642	13.3	6,530	16.3	10,376	9,551	825	1,912	3,932
Cherokee	2,013	46,164	0.88	562	11.5	505	10.4	8,465	21.5	9,208	8,156	1,052	912	1,881
Choctaw	172	14,788	0.96	204	13.9	220	15.0	2,457	20.9	3,666	3,363	303	175	1,176
Cimarron	7	2,192	0.97	27	12.5	16	7.4	378	23.2	598	583	15	11	509
Cleveland	10,550	230,254	0.68	2,939	10.4	2,069	7.3	27,064	11.5	43,194	33,847	9,347	9,898	3,577
Coal	61	5,207	0.79	74	13.4	74	13.4	874	19.6	1,150	1,077	73	65	1,166
Comanche	10,320	125,536	1.04	1,704	14.2	1,109	9.2	14,345	14.7	18,421	17,042	1,379	4,867	3,966
Cotton	48	5,591	0.83	64	11.1	86	14.9	787	16.4	1,304	1,221	83	79	1,332
Craig	1,050	14,780	1.04	148	10.3	229	16.0	2,077	18.8	3,647	3,213	434	186	1,266
Creek	1,062	60,970	0.67	870	12.2	916	12.8	9,309	16.0	15,553	10,562	4,991	1,468	2,077
Custer	1,523	30,009	1.06	408	14.1	265	9.1	4,861	20.2	4,636	4,267	369	519	1,726
Delaware	356	38,514	0.78	431	10.1	585	13.7	6,743	21.6	10,481	8,760	1,721	629	1,525
Dewey	93	4,899	1.00	57	11.6	75	15.3	654	17.0	1,082	1,021	61	42	839
Ellis	46	3,933	0.90	44	11.1	51	12.9	486	15.1	893	863	30	48	1,136
Garfield	1,831	62,901	1.02	882	14.5	643	10.6	8,114	15.7	11,710	10,805	905	2,455	3,846
Garvin	317	28,918	1.11	345	12.4	337	12.1	4,081	17.9	6,008	5,296	712	846	3,059
Grady	1,075	45,980	0.65	579	10.4	517	9.3	6,426	14.1	10,058	8,294	1,764	1,212	2,211
Grant	73	4,279	0.91	51	11.8	49	11.3	478	13.7	1,048	1,003	45	47	1,045
Greer	1,137	5,503	0.75	45	7.7	58	10.0	561	14.6	1,216	1,179	37	46	765
Harmon	100	2,676	0.93	25	9.4	33	12.4	425	20.5	608	582	26	98	3,565
Harper	41	3,510	0.79	46	12.1	63	16.6	672	22.3	754	726	28	9	240
Haskell	78	12,332	0.91	138	10.9	139	11.0	2,122	21.1	3,125	2,815	310	183	1,429
Hughes	1,557	12,896	0.85	153	11.5	168	12.6	1,828	19.2	3,115	2,746	369	270	1,984
Jackson	687	25,967	1.03	414	16.6	205	8.2	3,430	16.2	4,249	4,054	195	766	3,031
Jefferson	144	5,516	0.66	60	9.8	76	12.4	856	17.6	1,430	1,333	97	89	1,433
Johnston	292	10,176	0.79	125	11.4	170	15.5	1,545	17.7	2,455	2,291	164	194	1,776
Kay	1,274	45,722	1.03	591	13.4	554	12.5	5,844	16.4	10,183	9,087	1,096	1,504	3,347
Kingfisher	155	15,757	1.04	184	11.6	132	8.3	2,116	16.1	2,933	2,658	275	163	1,044

1. Per 1,000 estimated resident population.   2. Data for serious crimes have not been adjusted for underreporting; this may affect comparability between geographic areas and over time.   3. Per 100,000 population estimated by the FBI.

Table B. States and Counties — Crime, Education, Money Income, and Poverty

STATE County	Serious crimes known to police[2], 2016 (cont.)[1] Rate — Violent	Property	Education — Enrollment[3] Total	Percent private	Attainment[4] (percent) High school graduate or less	Bachelor's degree or more	Local government expenditures[5] 2014-2015 Total current spending (mil dol)	Current spending per student (dollars)	Money income, 2013-2017 Per capita income[6]	Median income (dollars)	Households Percent with income of less than $50,000	with income of $200,000 or more	Income and poverty, 2017 Median household income (dollars)	Percent below poverty level All persons	Children under 18 years	Children 5 to 17 years in families
	46	47	48	49	50	51	52	53	54	55	56	57	58	59	60	61
OHIO— Cont'd																
Ottawa	98	1,432	8,221	9.1	43.8	22.3	70.3	10,863	31,574	56,193	44.3	3.9	55,968	8.9	12.9	11.9
Paulding	97	986	4,281	11.2	60.4	14.0	37.2	12,067	24,319	49,866	50.2	1.4	52,534	10.2	15.6	13.9
Perry	92	1,088	8,427	10.1	60.6	11.7	65.3	11,148	21,557	46,477	53.0	1.1	51,702	15.7	24.9	21.7
Pickaway	122	2,609	12,672	10.8	56.0	17.3	96.9	10,534	25,460	60,314	42.1	2.6	62,445	12	16.6	15.1
Pike	89	1,539	6,346	6.2	60.8	13.3	54.5	11,280	21,983	43,562	55.0	1.3	43,499	20	30.5	27.1
Portage	102	1,650	46,733	10.7	45.3	27.5	257.2	11,579	27,985	53,816	46.8	3.2	59,490	11.8	13.9	12.1
Preble	61	1,085	9,376	11.2	55.4	14.4	65.6	10,405	25,374	52,661	46.5	1.7	52,300	9.9	13.9	12.6
Putnam	59	379	8,508	10.9	50.8	19.0	63.6	10,768	28,568	61,161	39.7	2.8	62,944	6.4	7.3	6.8
Richland	248	3,703	26,933	19.2	53.4	17.2	193.7	11,860	23,439	44,138	55.4	1.9	47,141	13.4	20.4	19.5
Ross	278	3,999	16,881	10.6	56.7	16.0	130.4	11,866	22,714	45,792	53.7	2.3	50,387	16.3	23.2	22.4
Sandusky	165	2,236	13,708	13.0	52.8	15.2	93.1	11,131	25,219	50,370	49.6	1.6	53,058	11.1	15.6	14.7
Scioto	182	3,116	18,391	8.6	57.0	15.2	134.7	10,997	22,586	38,978	60.0	2.1	41,843	21.4	30.2	27.3
Seneca	175	1,487	14,360	24.8	54.7	15.3	68.0	11,818	25,004	49,153	50.7	1.7	47,805	13.6	17.3	15.7
Shelby	130	2,520	11,803	11.1	51.9	17.1	79.2	9,304	28,410	57,673	42.8	2.5	60,148	8.1	11.7	10.9
Stark	328	2,604	90,444	17.6	47.0	22.8	593.6	10,365	27,401	50,117	49.9	2.7	51,214	14.3	22.3	20.2
Summit	314	2,842	131,193	16.4	40.1	31.6	857.9	11,578	30,803	53,291	47.0	4.6	55,531	12.9	18.7	16.5
Trumbull	243	2,309	41,596	10.1	55.8	18.7	321.8	11,303	25,542	45,380	54.6	2.1	46,340	15.4	24.1	22.5
Tuscarawas	43	949	20,423	12.7	60.2	15.1	168.9	10,504	25,054	49,460	50.4	2.0	51,408	12.8	17.4	16.3
Union	50	778	14,321	14.3	43.1	30.8	76.1	10,048	33,066	78,848	32.2	7.4	86,609	5.2	5.9	5.2
Van Wert	133	1,968	6,566	14.8	55.2	16.4	54.8	11,039	26,130	50,974	48.8	1.8	49,120	11.4	13.7	12.6
Vinton	170	1,057	2,801	8.1	66.5	10.3	24.3	10,949	19,876	41,541	58.1	0.7	40,927	19.8	29.0	26.4
Warren	69	1,239	59,253	18.4	32.8	41.9	367.1	9,984	37,479	79,397	28.3	10.6	85,532	4.7	5.6	4.5
Washington	105	1,160	12,747	18.9	50.2	18.7	86.6	10,886	26,608	46,021	54.0	2.4	46,417	14.6	20.8	19.1
Wayne	121	1,440	28,064	22.7	54.7	21.0	170.0	10,916	25,762	54,037	45.8	2.7	56,172	12.9	17.4	16.1
Williams	NA	NA	8,534	15.7	54.9	14.6	58.1	10,557	24,160	47,593	53.7	1.6	50,347	10.7	13.9	12.5
Wood	77	1,509	41,126	11.7	36.9	32.2	239.2	12,936	30,042	58,033	43.6	4.4	61,774	10.8	9.5	9.1
Wyandot	66	826	5,065	12.4	56.0	15.0	33.3	9,711	25,431	49,767	50.3	2.3	47,527	8.8	10.5	10.0
OKLAHOMA	450	2,983	1,002,485	10.9	44.0	24.8	5,532.7	8,036	26,461	49,767	50.2	3.6	50,051	15.8	21.3	20.1
Adair	519	2,197	5,500	3.2	63.8	13.6	43.0	9,332	16,576	33,366	66.3	0.8	33,187	27.2	37.5	37.1
Alfalfa	153	611	1,109	5.5	51.6	20.9	14.0	14,654	28,007	57,432	41.4	3.9	52,017	15.8	19.5	18.5
Atoka	95	1,428	2,973	5.5	58.3	14.6	21.3	8,936	19,439	37,106	63.9	1.9	38,595	19.1	28.4	23.0
Beaver	19	784	1,287	4.4	52.5	19.9	12.8	11,427	25,935	52,571	45.9	2.4	53,242	12.4	16.6	14.3
Beckham	196	2,108	5,347	5.2	54.6	16.7	33.8	7,930	23,883	49,625	50.2	4.0	49,784	17.3	22.3	21.4
Blaine	98	1,135	1,845	4.3	51.1	17.0	20.0	10,251	22,823	46,362	51.8	2.0	46,253	17.7	26.1	23.7
Bryan	NA	NA	11,431	8.0	46.8	22.5	66.7	8,760	22,171	41,197	58.3	2.2	41,563	18.2	24.3	24.0
Caddo	268	1,837	7,033	3.3	54.7	17.0	52.6	8,798	21,071	41,626	57.4	2.2	41,085	21.1	28.5	25.8
Canadian	446	2,506	35,883	10.6	37.3	26.2	196.5	7,548	29,852	69,220	33.8	4.4	73,878	7.5	9.3	8.7
Carter	409	3,523	12,769	7.9	50.6	20.4	77.6	8,338	24,965	47,754	52.0	3.2	45,755	17	22.7	21.8
Cherokee	212	1,669	13,500	5.9	46.8	24.0	69.1	8,902	19,799	39,187	59.9	1.7	40,051	21.2	27.5	26.0
Choctaw	188	988	3,271	2.4	58.7	12.5	23.6	8,749	19,446	30,298	67.2	1.8	30,501	26.3	37.1	38.3
Cimarron	139	370	463	5.2	52.0	21.2	5.5	12,223	28,461	44,667	54.8	3.9	40,370	17.4	27.3	27.2
Cleveland	371	3,205	85,243	9.1	33.9	32.1	324.1	7,208	29,231	60,632	40.3	4.3	61,364	11.6	12.7	11.8
Coal	108	1,058	1,308	4.1	57.3	16.6	12.7	10,730	24,004	39,931	56.4	2.9	37,874	22.1	31.2	29.9
Comanche	663	3,303	31,646	8.5	42.8	21.9	176.5	8,087	25,186	49,569	50.4	2.4	50,530	16.8	23.8	22.6
Cotton	34	1,298	1,391	5.7	55.1	15.8	8.7	7,888	21,887	49,962	50.1	0.2	42,518	18.5	23.7	21.7
Craig	109	1,157	3,180	7.4	53.2	14.7	24.0	8,570	20,666	40,465	60.5	1.2	39,320	19.8	25.7	23.6
Creek	218	1,859	16,196	7.3	54.8	15.6	109.7	8,423	24,056	47,147	51.9	2.2	47,397	16.3	25.0	21.7
Custer	143	1,583	9,061	2.6	46.3	26.5	43.5	7,966	24,621	48,520	50.9	2.8	47,244	14.9	19.2	18.8
Delaware	179	1,346	8,652	10.1	52.6	16.5	59.3	9,041	22,175	38,234	61.8	2.2	37,173	18.4	28.3	25.9
Dewey	60	779	1,145	20.3	51.1	21.8	13.2	11,916	25,821	52,930	48.1	5.3	48,939	13.5	18.2	16.7
Ellis	95	1,041	850	5.6	49.6	21.6	12.3	14,136	27,272	50,594	49.1	4.0	48,001	13.5	19.6	17.9
Garfield	367	3,480	14,560	11.5	48.0	22.5	91.6	7,922	25,787	50,724	49.3	2.6	49,116	14	19.8	19.3
Garvin	315	2,744	5,937	4.0	58.6	15.5	44.6	8,012	22,433	42,567	56.3	2.5	41,990	17.1	23.2	21.9
Grady	332	1,879	13,398	6.1	51.9	18.9	70.8	7,472	27,334	55,527	45.2	4.1	54,887	13.2	17.2	15.6
Grant	67	978	965	4.8	43.5	25.9	11.1	13,794	29,002	54,460	43.5	2.0	45,025	12.7	18.5	17.2
Greer	116	648	1,208	1.7	51.6	14.3	8.7	8,521	20,073	35,898	66.0	3.8	34,254	25.9	31.0	29.7
Harmon	364	3,201	731	3.8	45.0	22.5	4.8	8,972	21,620	38,264	60.5	0.0	35,144	24.4	34.8	33.2
Harper	0	240	986	6.6	53.7	23.8	7.5	9,713	23,536	46,915	53.3	1.9	50,101	11.1	17.6	17.0
Haskell	172	1,258	2,936	2.0	58.1	12.9	20.1	8,453	20,009	38,017	59.6	1.3	36,551	20.4	28.8	26.2
Hughes	162	1,822	2,853	3.9	58.0	12.4	20.4	8,982	18,004	38,425	61.3	1.3	35,875	23.6	31.8	30.3
Jackson	301	2,730	6,430	6.5	43.7	21.1	38.0	7,951	22,988	45,189	54.5	1.5	44,733	17.4	23.7	23.1
Jefferson	193	1,240	1,336	3.7	59.5	12.5	11.2	9,533	19,130	35,933	64.0	1.9	36,169	23	32.7	31.9
Johnston	165	1,611	2,855	3.8	52.5	16.6	17.4	8,818	21,022	38,636	61.0	2.3	40,129	18	26.1	23.0
Kay	619	2,729	10,943	9.9	45.6	20.1	68.6	8,166	24,057	44,067	55.0	2.3	45,447	16.6	23.9	22.9
Kingfisher	109	935	3,856	9.2	47.9	23.7	30.4	8,502	31,885	62,829	39.6	6.1	61,728	9.8	13.6	12.6

1. Data for serious crimes have not been adjusted for underreporting; this may affect comparability between geographic areas and over time.   2. Per 100,000 population estimated by the FBI.   3. All persons 3 years old and over enrolled in nursery school through college.   4. Persons 25 years old and over.   5. Elementary and secondary education expenditures.   6. Based on population estimated by the American Community Survey, 2013–2017.

STATE County	Personal income, 2017										Earnings, 2017		
	Total (mil dol)	Percent change 2016-2017	Per capita[1]		Wages and salaries (mil dol)	Supplements to wages and salaries, employer contributions (mil dol)		Proprietors' income (mil dol)	Dividends, interest, and rent (mil dol)	Personal transfer reecipts (mil dol)	Total (mil dol)	Contributions for government social insurance (mil dol)	
			Dollars	Rank		Pension and insurance	Government social insurance					From employee and self-employed	From employer
	62	63	64	65	66	67	68	69	70	71	72	73	74

OHIO— Cont'd

STATE County													
Ottawa	1,984	2.5	48,804	558	627	128	48	99	366	459	902	60	48
Paulding	709	2.9	37,644	1,927	189	43	15	33	117	174	280	18	15
Perry	1,294	4.3	35,920	2,209	271	58	19	106	135	360	454	31	19
Pickaway	2,259	4.0	39,071	1,708	661	154	44	174	311	484	1,033	56	44
Pike	995	3.4	35,201	2,311	512	79	37	92	124	343	720	45	37
Portage	6,813	3.4	41,983	1,267	2,670	562	183	346	1,075	1,331	3,762	209	183
Preble	1,578	2.0	38,372	1,814	438	91	33	104	212	385	666	44	33
Putnam	1,554	2.3	45,866	809	487	96	38	102	251	265	722	45	38
Richland	4,580	3.6	37,977	1,892	2,118	419	161	231	717	1,224	2,929	180	161
Ross	2,720	3.2	35,177	2,318	1,324	283	100	137	352	770	1,843	107	100
Sandusky	2,344	2.9	39,596	1,621	1,151	242	93	87	335	557	1,572	96	93
Scioto	2,769	2.1	36,466	2,121	992	223	74	223	355	969	1,513	92	74
Seneca	2,111	0.7	38,221	1,841	789	160	61	122	323	542	1,133	72	61
Shelby	2,133	3.6	43,739	1,048	1,436	249	111	210	304	383	2,005	115	111
Stark	16,129	3.3	43,293	1,102	7,181	1,250	552	948	2,631	3,692	9,932	615	552
Summit	26,611	4.3	49,168	521	14,207	2,305	1,046	1,724	4,602	5,003	19,282	1,134	1,046
Trumbull	7,969	3.0	39,771	1,596	2,936	546	230	728	1,252	2,256	4,441	287	230
Tuscarawas	3,790	2.9	41,058	1,401	1,675	308	127	383	577	854	2,494	150	127
Union	2,858	5.7	50,362	439	2,096	319	155	170	353	341	2,740	152	155
Van Wert	1,116	3.1	39,537	1,631	460	93	35	63	157	260	650	40	35
Vinton	418	3.4	31,896	2,765	88	23	6	19	56	142	136	9	6
Warren	13,002	4.5	56,808	226	5,058	755	368	692	1,855	1,523	6,873	403	368
Washington	2,423	2.4	40,096	1,535	1,239	227	95	148	399	621	1,709	107	95
Wayne	4,861	3.9	41,891	1,274	2,360	424	175	497	765	924	3,457	201	175
Williams	1,460	2.0	39,684	1,607	750	146	59	104	215	339	1,059	64	59
Wood	5,884	2.6	45,093	890	3,263	605	247	346	940	962	4,461	249	247
Wyandot	922	3.2	41,861	1,282	415	80	31	49	134	190	574	34	31
OKLAHOMA	174,435	5.6	44,356	X	77,912	13,389	5,966	23,786	32,423	33,295	121,053	6,779	5,966
Adair	630	2.7	28,755	2,997	165	36	14	65	92	218	280	18	14
Alfalfa	226	0.5	38,309	1,824	71	15	5	32	66	42	123	6	5
Atoka	444	6.0	31,951	2,757	127	25	10	57	61	140	219	14	10
Beaver	256	6.7	48,213	608	79	15	6	64	44	39	164	7	6
Beckham	794	4.8	36,421	2,128	515	76	39	56	151	167	686	42	39
Blaine	362	4.9	38,097	1,864	145	26	11	53	85	90	234	14	11
Bryan	1,553	5.0	33,533	2,552	721	129	54	110	269	433	1,015	64	54
Caddo	989	9.0	33,886	2,495	339	72	27	61	160	268	498	32	27
Canadian	5,969	3.9	42,657	1,192	1,582	254	122	347	834	874	2,305	143	122
Carter	1,963	1.7	40,727	1,439	1,072	189	81	109	389	476	1,450	90	81
Cherokee	1,524	3.1	31,175	2,841	567	111	43	107	271	438	827	51	43
Choctaw	462	1.6	31,085	2,847	149	32	12	33	62	183	226	16	12
Cimarron	129	1.2	60,048	158	28	5	2	46	20	23	81	3	2
Cleveland	12,106	3.2	43,292	1,103	3,517	659	266	877	2,320	1,954	5,320	315	266
Coal	180	3.7	31,948	2,758	43	9	3	16	35	57	72	5	3
Comanche	4,868	2.6	40,053	1,541	2,447	561	210	219	901	1,074	3,437	183	210
Cotton	222	-2.1	38,155	1,852	60	14	5	5	36	55	84	6	5
Craig	501	1.2	34,984	2,352	206	43	16	35	82	168	300	20	16
Creek	2,850	3.8	39,746	1,600	828	144	65	214	478	691	1,251	84	65
Custer	1,147	7.6	39,818	1,586	568	101	42	136	222	213	848	47	42
Delaware	1,314	4.9	30,839	2,867	332	61	26	112	266	417	530	39	26
Dewey	203	-0.3	41,543	1,324	76	14	6	28	49	40	124	7	6
Ellis	194	3.5	48,799	560	53	10	4	48	40	32	115	5	4
Garfield	2,625	-4	42,622	1,194	1,234	211	99	205	569	544	1,749	104	99
Garvin	1,011	3.9	36,226	2,166	470	91	36	76	178	282	673	42	36
Grady	2,051	2.4	37,334	1,981	508	92	40	134	329	438	774	51	40
Grant	200	0.9	45,441	851	78	14	6	27	51	42	125	7	6
Greer	163	1.0	27,922	3,031	40	10	3	2	31	60	56	5	3
Harmon	105	8.5	39,100	1,702	26	6	2	18	17	28	52	3	2
Harper	171	0.6	44,822	925	37	9	3	38	31	28	86	4	3
Haskell	416	2.2	32,615	2,673	115	22	9	59	60	145	205	13	9
Hughes	405	3.4	30,462	2,888	101	22	8	41	70	142	171	11	8
Jackson	1,010	5.9	40,193	1,521	469	113	40	94	190	223	716	38	40
Jefferson	191	-6	30,860	2,863	39	8	3	19	30	67	68	5	3
Johnston	385	7.1	34,801	2,373	129	32	10	27	50	122	198	13	10
Kay	1,772	2.7	39,780	1,593	814	135	63	127	340	452	1,140	73	63
Kingfisher	707	0.9	45,150	883	317	54	24	52	169	122	447	27	24

1. Based on the resident population estimated as of July 1 of the year shown.

Table B. States and Counties — **Earnings, Social Security, and Housing**

STATE County	Farm	Mining, quarrying, and extractions	Construction	Manufacturing	Information; professional, scientific, technical services	Retail trade	Finance, insurance, real estate, and leasing	Health care and social assistance	Government	Number	Rate[1]	Supplemental Security Income recipients, 2017	Total	Percent change, 2010-2018
	75	76	77	78	79	80	81	82	83	84	85	86	87	88
OHIO— Cont'd														
Ottawa	-0.8	1	7.6	16.3	3.3	6.2	4.4	D	17.9	11,615	286	597	28,600	2.5
Paulding	4.5	D	6.7	29	3.1	5.6	3.2	D	22.1	4,525	240	324	8,795	0.5
Perry	-0.4	2.3	27.9	11.6	2.5	5.3	2.8	D	20.2	7,995	222	1,287	15,349	0.9
Pickaway	3	D	11.4	18.2	D	5.7	2.9	D	28.9	11,185	193	1,167	21,566	1.4
Pike	0.5	D	8.1	6.9	D	4.7	2.6	D	12.5	6,655	235	1,522	12,956	3.8
Portage	0	0.7	7.1	19.7	5.2	6.4	2.9	7.1	24.9	30,780	190	2,438	69,326	2.7
Preble	1.7	D	8	33.8	D	7.1	3.1	7.1	15.8	9,405	229	718	17,913	0.2
Putnam	-1.4	D	12	33.6	3.8	5.8	4.7	D	13.1	6,880	203	337	13,968	1.7
Richland	-0.1	D	7.5	22.9	3.8	8.2	3.4	14.3	17.9	29,245	243	3,495	54,166	-0.8
Ross	0	0.1	4	19.3	2.5	7.5	2.3	18.5	27.7	16,565	214	2,904	32,068	-0.3
Sandusky	-0.7	D	5.4	43.3	2.2	6.1	3.9	D	12.5	13,675	231	1,046	26,366	-0.1
Scioto	-0.2	D	3.9	13.8	4	7	3.8	27.9	22.2	16,930	223	5,372	34,517	1.1
Seneca	-0.5	0.9	8.1	25.1	D	7.2	4.2	10	14.5	12,595	228	1,207	24,172	0.2
Shelby	0.3	0	10.9	51.6	D	3.7	2.9	5.4	7.9	9,740	200	743	20,492	1.6
Stark	0.2	0.4	7.7	18.7	6	7.2	6.4	16.3	12.7	87,265	234	9,868	166,991	1.1
Summit	0	0.1	5.5	11.2	8.9	8	6.6	14.8	11.3	110,965	205	14,931	246,173	0.4
Trumbull	-0.2	0.1	7.5	21.1	2.7	8.3	7.3	13	14.4	53,350	266	6,155	95,695	-0.5
Tuscarawas	0.3	4.8	15.4	20.9	3.9	7.2	3.9	10.2	12.7	21,145	229	1,929	40,236	0.1
Union	0.2	0.3	4.1	31.7	D	3.8	2.3	3.3	10.1	8,175	144	459	21,569	11
Van Wert	0.9	D	6	27.4	D	5.6	10.9	13.4	13.5	6,680	237	441	12,716	0.8
Vinton	-0.1	D	4.9	24	D	2.8	D	9	28.6	2,805	214	629	6,271	-0.3
Warren	0	0	7.1	14	9.2	7.9	6.7	9.1	10.5	36,935	161	1,817	88,441	9.5
Washington	-0.1	2.8	8.2	19.3	4.3	6.1	5.6	21.5	10.9	15,510	257	1,832	28,235	-0.5
Wayne	0.1	2.9	8.4	33.6	3.4	6.5	4.4	7.2	12.6	23,180	200	1,863	46,747	2
Williams	0.5	D	4.6	40.1	D	8.6	3.3	9.9	12	8,555	233	572	16,667	0
Wood	-0.1	0.1	10.6	23.8	5.6	4.7	4.2	7.3	16.3	22,690	174	1,399	54,069	1.3
Wyandot	0.6	2	13	37.4	1.7	5.2	4.3	D	15.9	5,005	227	344	9,962	0.9
OKLAHOMA	0.8	8.7	5.9	8.1	7.2	5.7	5.4	10.5	18.9	778,970	198	96,804	1,743,069	4.7
Adair	7.4	D	10.3	21.2	1.7	7.5	2.5	8.8	19	4,960	226	920	9,388	2.7
Alfalfa	20.6	5.1	7.7	1.6	D	3.6	D	5.4	26.4	1,175	199	93	2,722	-1.4
Atoka	-1.7	8	9.1	2.1	D	9	6.1	D	24.8	3,485	251	555	6,479	2.8
Beaver	30.3	9.7	18.5	D	D	D	D	0.4	14.3	1,090	205	45	2,677	0.3
Beckham	-0.8	32.5	10.1	3.3	D	7.6	5.8	D	10	4,170	191	518	10,038	4.1
Blaine	4.3	5.6	12.5	16.3	2.9	3.5	D	4.5	15.5	2,235	235	222	5,192	0
Bryan	-0.1	0.6	6.8	8.4	3.5	6.2	3.1	10.7	39.8	10,065	217	1,598	20,424	4.3
Caddo	1.8	4.8	11.9	1	9.4	5.5	D	D	29.8	6,500	223	1,002	13,237	0.7
Canadian	0.3	13.8	8.6	12.2	3.9	6.7	6.2	6.4	16.6	21,780	156	1,114	48,961	6.9
Carter	-0.4	7.5	8.6	18.6	4.9	6.3	4.4	12.6	12.4	11,585	240	1,565	21,783	3
Cherokee	2.7	0.5	4.7	1.3	2.8	7	3.8	6.8	54.1	10,230	209	1,534	22,287	3.9
Choctaw	0.6	2.8	4.8	2.7	4	6.6	D	D	29.3	4,060	273	828	7,600	1.1
Cimarron	43.5	D	1.5	D	D	5.3	D	D	14.2	640	297	28	1,576	-0.7
Cleveland	0	0.8	9.2	4.8	8	8.5	5.8	9.7	30.4	45,430	162	3,620	116,905	11.3
Coal	0.8	14.6	8.5	4.7	D	5.1	D	13.8	24.6	1,310	232	210	2,809	0
Comanche	0	0.3	3.6	8.5	5.8	5.2	3.8	5.4	53	20,545	169	3,164	51,688	1.9
Cotton	-2.2	0.5	12.2	D	D	4	3.3	3.5	51.7	1,470	252	159	2,999	-0.5
Craig	2	D	3.6	3	D	7.9	4.9	10.9	28.7	4,090	285	695	6,761	0.2
Creek	-0.2	3.6	12.5	21.3	D	5	4	9.5	14.5	16,880	235	1,711	30,786	3.4
Custer	4.3	13.2	6.1	6.1	5.5	6.4	5.7	7.3	17.8	4,900	170	533	12,635	3.5
Delaware	9.5	D	8.7	7.3	D	8.3	4.6	D	24.1	11,405	268	1,215	25,664	3.4
Dewey	2.4	19	10.4	4.7	1.6	5.6	D	3.4	16.8	1,155	237	73	2,443	-0.1
Ellis	33.1	D	3	0.4	D	4.8	D	D	16.1	930	234	54	2,268	-0.7
Garfield	0.3	6.2	8.4	9.5	D	7	5.5	11.5	19.1	12,490	203	1,294	26,798	-0.1
Garvin	-0.5	11.3	10.4	17.3	4.1	7.6	3.5	D	11.7	6,760	242	851	12,860	0.3
Grady	3.4	7.4	11.3	9.9	4.1	6.7	5.9	8.1	18.4	11,070	201	1,243	23,018	3.6
Grant	13.1	29.1	8.1	1.5	D	2.1	D	D	13.9	1,050	239	61	2,466	-0.9
Greer	-1.8	D	2.5	D	D	7.3	D	20.2	49.6	1,355	232	210	2,708	-1.1
Harmon	29.3	0	D	D	D	D	D	4.5	26.8	695	258	138	1,533	-0.7
Harper	39.6	6.9	D	D	D	3.8	D	2.6	23.3	805	211	44	1,884	-1.3
Haskell	14	6.8	5.8	3	D	7.4	1.9	23.2	15.3	3,525	276	509	6,173	2.4
Hughes	15.3	7.1	5	3.7	D	6.8	D		26.9	3,485	262	475	6,244	1
Jackson	2.3	D	2.5	7	D	5.8	3.7	4.5	50.5	4,625	184	622	12,151	0.6
Jefferson	19.2	1.5	D	D	D	7.1	D	D	24.2	1,660	268	252	3,393	0.4
Johnston	-0.6	7.1	4.8	15.3	D	4.1	D	D	23.9	2,735	247	435	5,195	1.3
Kay	-0.4	2.7	8.5	13.1	D	6.6	3.4	10	18.2	11,145	250	1,154	21,474	-1.1
Kingfisher	0.6	17.9	9.1	8.3	D	7.3	6.5	6.4	9.8	3,095	198	192	6,549	2.2

1. Per 1,000 resident population estimated as of July 1 of the year shown.

STATE County	Housing units, 2013-2017								Civilian labor force, 2018				Civilian employment[6], 2013-2017		
	Occupied units										Unemployment			Percent	
			Owner-occupied			Renter-occupied									
				Median owner cost as a percent of income			Median rent as a percent of income[2]	Sub-standard units[4] (percent)		Percent change, 2017-2018				Management, business, science, and arts	Construction, production, and maintenance occupations
				With a mort-gage	Without a mort-gage[2]	Median rent[3]									
	Total	Percent	Median value[1]						Total		Total	Rate[5]	Total		
	89	90	91	92	93	94	95	96	97	98	99	100	101	102	103
OHIO— Cont'd															
Ottawa	17,495	78.2	145,400	19.3	11.6	699	27.3	0.8	20,986	-0.9	1,323	6.3	19,348	31.3	30.4
Paulding	7,589	76.9	92,500	17.2	12.5	633	24.1	3.1	8,708	-1.9	358	4.1	8,721	25.5	40.4
Perry	13,576	73.7	102,500	20.3	12.3	635	29.9	1.8	15,880	0	884	5.6	15,036	26.6	36.0
Pickaway	19,465	73.8	152,000	20.4	11.3	779	26.1	1.7	26,268	0	1,123	4.3	24,736	32.4	27.3
Pike	11,033	68.7	100,100	18.4	12.1	665	30.3	3.5	10,817	-0.3	708	6.5	10,317	31.2	32.2
Portage	62,208	68.7	152,000	20.4	12.2	824	31.8	1	86,523		3,963	4.6	82,049	32.2	25.1
Preble	16,126	76.3	116,900	20.2	11.5	706	26.9	1.9	21,138	-0.1	863	4.1	19,437	29.0	32.6
Putnam	13,159	80.3	147,200	18.2	10.6	677	24.4	0.8	18,615	-1.3	627	3.4	17,698	31.7	35.0
Richland	47,987	67.7	103,700	19.8	11.2	638	28	1.7	52,743	-0.8	2,583	4.9	50,232	27.9	29.2
Ross	28,526	70.4	114,600	19.5	11.3	721	30.5	2.3	34,678	1.5	1,578	4.6	30,592	29.5	28.0
Sandusky	23,721	71.4	111,900	19.4	11.9	666	26.6	0.8	30,748	-1.7	1,396	4.5	28,434	25.3	38.2
Scioto	30,204	67.8	93,000	19.6	12.2	585	31	2	28,964	-2	1,957	6.8	28,163	33.8	23.9
Seneca	21,507	72.2	98,600	19.0	11.5	672	25.9	0.8	27,129	-0.8	1,193	4.4	25,833	26.8	37.1
Shelby	18,665	70.8	137,800	19.3	10.3	706	22.5	2	23,906	-0.4	899	3.8	24,430	27.4	37.6
Stark	152,037	68.4	127,100	19.1	10.9	711	27.5	1.4	186,227	-0.4	9,140	4.9	177,307	32.2	25.2
Summit	223,021	65.6	137,000	19.8	11.6	783	29.1	1.1	270,717	-0.8	12,634	4.7	264,003	37.5	19.4
Trumbull	86,709	70.6	101,600	19.5	11.3	649	29.3	1.4	87,662	-1.5	5,469	6.2	88,092	28.0	30.2
Tuscarawas	36,548	70.7	117,100	19.2	11.4	725	26.9	1.7	44,390	-2.1	2,030	4.6	43,425	25.9	35.4
Union	19,038	78.1	186,000	19.7	12.5	876	24.5	1.3	28,329	-0.1	980	3.5	26,776	39.6	25.5
Van Wert	11,503	74.8	99,000	18.2	10.0	678	26.7	1	14,362	-0.8	506	3.5	13,522	25.5	38.5
Vinton	5,053	73.4	85,700	20.7	12.5	585	33.1	2.4	5,454	0	340	6.2	5,241	22.5	39.2
Warren	80,704	77.6	200,100	19.4	11.3	998	25.3	0.7	116,814	0.5	4,504	3.9	109,115	48.2	17.2
Washington	25,378	73.9	119,400	19.5	10.2	639	28.2	1.4	27,011	-0.9	1,522	5.6	26,853	30.2	28.1
Wayne	43,353	73.0	140,100	19.7	10.7	700	25.9	3.2	60,780	-1.3	2,198	3.6	55,764	31.1	32.6
Williams	15,263	76.4	94,200	20.1	11.1	665	28.4	1.5	18,898	-0.4	684	3.6	17,586	25.1	40.1
Wood	50,187	65.7	154,700	19.5	11.9	767	28.4	0.9	70,361	-0.3	2,843	4	67,528	37.1	23.6
Wyandot	9,157	72.3	110,600	19.0	10.6	638	22.3	1.3	12,693	0.5	410	3.2	10,902	26.0	40.9
OKLAHOMA	1,468,971	65.7	125,800	19.8	10.3	766	27.6	3.2	1,841,872	0.3	62,502	3.4	1,746,419	34.1	24.7
Adair	7,796	69.8	81,200	19.8	10.6	549	25.2	6.6	8,151	-1.1	340	4.2	8,130	23.9	39.2
Alfalfa	1,978	76.0	74,500	15.3	10.0	677	21.4	2	2,940	-0.7	64	2.2	2,238	31.6	33.7
Atoka	5,284	73.2	98,400	19.6	11.1	578	29.1	2.9	5,121	-1.5	211	4.1	4,664	28.9	30.0
Beaver	2,103	78.1	106,500	19.3	10.0	667	21.4	1.4	2,958	-2.7	60	2	2,492	33.8	34.4
Beckham	7,573	65.6	117,100	19.8	10.9	740	25.3	2.9	11,352	0.4	296	2.6	9,296	25.6	32.4
Blaine	3,819	76.1	83,800	17.8	10.0	517	23.3	2.7	4,428	-4.3	90	2	3,470	35.0	27.3
Bryan	16,911	63.0	98,900	19.3	11.2	703	28.6	4.2	21,001	2.9	658	3.1	18,781	30.6	27.1
Caddo	10,273	70.4	81,900	17.8	10.0	568	21.9	4	12,201	-1.6	435	3.6	11,207	29.1	31.6
Canadian	43,878	76.3	155,400	20.0	10.0	934	24.9	2.5	72,033	1.2	2,003	2.8	67,192	36.7	22.6
Carter	18,278	69.2	109,000	19.6	10.0	717	25.9	3.7	22,149	-1.6	778	3.5	20,543	28.7	29.6
Cherokee	16,360	66.5	111,300	19.8	10.7	621	28.9	3.8	18,796	-2.1	795	4.2	19,399	31.2	22.4
Choctaw	5,962	68.6	88,800	22.3	11.5	548	32.9	3.6	5,756	0.4	286	5	5,061	27.4	30.7
Cimarron	990	72.9	57,400	23.0	10.0	448	17.2	3.6	1,386	-2.4	26	1.9	1,027	35.2	33.7
Cleveland	103,028	64.5	155,500	20.1	10.3	876	27.9	2.7	142,102	1.5	4,088	2.9	137,715	40.1	17.7
Coal	2,240	71.9	87,800	19.3	10.0	609	25.9	2.9	2,278	0	87	3.8	2,243	34.1	31.5
Comanche	42,957	53.7	125,600	20.2	10.0	807	27.4	2.5	48,566	-0.9	1,898	3.9	49,415	34.1	22.6
Cotton	2,265	78.3	77,600	18.5	10.4	619	22.4	3.8	2,748	-2	86	3.1	2,435	32.9	26.3
Craig	5,413	73.5	96,100	22.3	10.0	677	28.7	2	6,115	0.2	211	3.5	5,783	27.8	27.7
Creek	26,398	74.1	112,100	19.7	10.8	755	26.5	4	31,623	0.2	1,204	3.8	30,227	29.6	31.0
Custer	10,458	59.3	127,600	17.3	10.0	697	24.9	3.7	15,694	1.6	379	2.4	13,819	29.6	29.8
Delaware	16,571	76.0	110,000	24.9	11.8	655	29	3.9	18,065	-2.9	705	3.9	15,709	27.1	29.2
Dewey	1,727	73.1	86,700	19.7	10.0	644	22.2	1.4	2,778	10	53	1.9	2,086	30.4	34.6
Ellis	1,625	73.2	83,700	16.3	10.0	646	23.1	1	2,207	-0.9	48	2.2	1,794	33.3	32.1
Garfield	23,798	65.4	104,000	19.4	10.0	806	23.1	3.5	27,330	-1.9	832	3	27,796	28.7	33.2
Garvin	10,473	67.6	93,400	18.1	10.0	631	23.7	3.3	12,710	0.4	417	3.3	10,697	29.4	33.1
Grady	19,743	77.3	117,200	18.5	10.0	682	26.5	2.5	26,292	0.7	803	3.1	24,472	31.8	29.4
Grant	1,883	75.8	76,400	16.2	10.0	649	25.1	1.1	2,742	-5.2	57	2.1	2,055	36.8	33.8
Greer	2,152	72.5	65,800	18.7	11.9	517	26.6	1.3	1,964	-4.8	78	4	2,137	30.3	25.9
Harmon	1,185	72.4	49,700	16.7	11.6	538	18.5	3.2	1,200	-5.9	35	2.9	1,190	35.5	28.5
Harper	1,348	80.6	76,300	14.3	10.6	652	23	3	1,800	-4.1	41	2.3	1,645	27.8	28.8
Haskell	4,849	74.6	87,500	22.0	10.0	591	30.9	4.7	4,222	-3.5	215	5.1	4,659	28.7	35.3
Hughes	4,258	74.8	69,400	19.3	11.6	565	25.9	2.2	5,366	-0.9	224	4.2	4,310	29.0	29.9
Jackson	9,958	57.3	97,800	19.0	11.1	698	27.7	2.6	10,724	-1.3	327	3	10,668	27.1	30.6
Jefferson	2,392	71.9	59,700	19.1	10.9	513	24.4	2.5	2,570	2.8	88	3.4	2,280	22.9	38.2
Johnston	4,256	71.2	79,500	18.9	10.8	576	27.3	2.8	5,319	5.4	154	2.9	4,094	32.7	34.0
Kay	17,890	68.9	84,100	19.2	11.5	653	23.8	3.2	18,989	-1.3	886	4.7	19,325	28.2	29.7
Kingfisher	5,691	80.1	136,200	18.6	10.0	714	22.6	2.1	8,888	1.9	187	2.1	7,046	36.1	28.8

1. Specified owner-occupied units.   2. A value of 10.0 represents 10 percent or less; a value of 50.0 represents 50 percent or more.   3. Specified renter-occupied units.   4. Overcrowded or lacking complete plumbing facilities.   5. Percent of civilian labor force.   6. Civilian employed persons 16 years old and over.

Table B. States and Counties — **Nonfarm Employment and Agriculture**

STATE County	Private nonfarm establishments, employment and payroll, 2016									Agriculture, 2017			
	Number of establish-ments	Employment						Annual payroll		Farms			Farm producers whose primary occupation is farming (percent)
		Total	Health care and social assistance	Manufac-turing	Retail trade	Finance and insurance	Professional, scientific, and technical services	Total (mil dol)	Average per employee (dollars)		Percent with:		
										Number	Fewer than 50 acres	1000 acres or more	
	104	105	106	107	108	109	110	111	112	113	114	115	116

STATE County	104	105	106	107	108	109	110	111	112	113	114	115	116
OHIO— Cont'd													
Ottawa	1,030	10,295	1,795	2,101	1,379	289	179	448	43,488	551	47.2	4.2	36.3
Paulding	297	3,554	565	1,231	368	107	72	117	32,982	622	33.3	10.6	44.5
Perry	421	4,175	878	720	691	137	166	137	32,766	762	44.4	1.4	29.4
Pickaway	781	10,804	1,971	2,261	1,526	302	204	424	39,208	805	43.0	10.9	49.0
Pike	418	7,735	1,593	758	1,027	223	2,047	359	46,387	511	31.3	2.2	29.9
Portage	2,999	46,810	6,049	10,051	8,365	722	1,387	1,758	37,558	1,118	68.4	0.9	29.9
Preble	655	8,985	1,080	3,310	1,236	244	253	321	35,678	1,055	48.6	4.8	39.9
Putnam	723	10,082	1,076	3,705	1,059	241	222	370	36,690	1,335	33.7	4.0	34.1
Richland	2,597	40,569	5,551	8,493	6,538	1,068	910	1,359	33,495	1,160	49.1	1.5	41.8
Ross	1,213	22,985	6,346	3,925	3,887	449	394	1,033	44,951	1,121	40.3	4.6	38.9
Sandusky	1,307	23,452	3,146	9,673	2,573	460	432	861	36,696	768	39.6	5.5	38.4
Scioto	1,286	19,155	7,450	1,445	3,122	502	661	624	32,557	688	42.0	0.9	36.5
Seneca	1,106	17,058	2,402	4,192	2,200	401	360	577	33,805	1,156	40.1	4.5	35.3
Shelby	970	24,701	2,098	12,483	1,969	318	372	1,167	47,229	947	39.7	3.6	36.6
Stark	8,183	142,975	28,749	24,632	19,922	5,650	4,191	5,500	38,466	1,547	67.7	1.2	32.4
Summit	13,391	251,233	47,528	29,016	31,039	11,093	14,617	11,624	46,269	392	77.6	0.8	39.6
Trumbull	4,043	67,053	10,522	17,486	9,903	1,612	1,354	2,640	39,372	1,036	52.0	1.7	33.4
Tuscarawas	2,175	31,127	5,269	7,494	4,472	647	935	1,119	35,938	1,155	47.3	1.6	34.4
Union	1,017	24,207	1,587	6,429	2,274	368	3,651	1,407	58,127	997	50.6	5.3	36.3
Van Wert	544	9,868	1,385	3,225	1,151	796	372	353	35,736	772	40.5	10.1	42.9
Vinton	137	1,704	350	592	161	86	12	50	29,516	227	33.5	0.9	29.3
Warren	4,219	78,842	10,424	11,266	10,149	4,425	5,101	4,036	51,195	925	73.2	2.4	29.1
Washington	1,393	22,761	5,458	3,302	2,990	776	629	962	42,260	1,106	32.5	0.8	34.6
Wayne	2,483	40,184	5,813	12,782	5,039	1,058	1,304	1,641	40,834	2,034	54.7	1.2	42.3
Williams	806	16,035	1,862	7,284	1,345	276	246	585	36,511	881	40.3	5.6	33.8
Wood	2,744	54,283	4,971	12,644	6,582	848	2,055	2,330	42,930	1,069	46.7	6.9	35.8
Wyandot	518	8,264	792	3,466	809	273	84	321	38,883	649	40.4	10.3	42.9
OKLAHOMA	93,232	1,360,379	221,349	129,975	186,499	60,301	73,514	57,194	42,042	78,531	29.6	10.3	37.5
Adair	226	3,102	515	1,020	550	131	75	93	30,070	1,031	28.9	3.1	40.7
Alfalfa	146	1,215	144	24	183	82	28	53	43,525	581	8.8	32.0	52.0
Atoka	280	2,224	340	138	534	146	52	65	29,348	1,057	21.6	6.4	38.1
Beaver	154	1,283	78	D	117	48	30	54	41,719	805	5.0	31.3	37.2
Beckham	795	8,460	1,057	289	1,590	346	248	359	42,412	896	18.8	14.7	33.0
Blaine	269	2,204	364	403	320	155	54	81	36,971	731	13.5	27.4	45.4
Bryan	763	10,542	2,155	1,299	1,662	490	491	325	30,837	1,609	27.8	4.5	39.8
Caddo	449	4,402	619	70	819	167	399	150	33,998	1,396	15.5	16.1	44.2
Canadian	2,593	26,056	2,848	2,996	4,311	825	1,453	904	34,690	1,324	37.8	11.9	35.5
Carter	1,618	20,982	3,632	3,330	3,095	679	678	835	39,783	1,431	34.5	5.6	30.2
Cherokee	741	9,297	2,706	129	1,762	341	119	277	29,767	1,200	33.2	2.6	36.8
Choctaw	282	3,084	1,160	91	493	110	85	92	29,690	851	20.4	9.2	42.4
Cimarron	72	340	D	D	80	39	10	10	28,929	447	4.7	38.3	42.0
Cleveland	5,757	69,262	13,179	3,026	12,714	2,655	3,236	2,384	34,414	1,182	59.4	1.4	31.7
Coal	88	812	213	75	169	53	13	25	31,216	590	16.8	11.2	45.9
Comanche	2,197	32,846	6,156	3,412	5,456	1,523	1,390	1,093	33,284	1,055	30.6	13.2	37.2
Cotton	76	1,228	92	D	100	44	20	38	31,254	448	13.2	29.0	41.0
Craig	346	4,028	1,361	180	680	210	90	136	33,770	1,179	24.8	7.0	41.6
Creek	1,361	16,450	2,181	4,008	2,042	426	331	629	38,226	1,893	46.5	2.0	29.9
Custer	921	10,000	1,482	1,106	1,790	375	291	378	37,795	773	16.4	23.4	40.5
Delaware	745	7,580	1,229	632	1,524	331	189	226	29,814	1,377	33.7	3.3	43.3
Dewey	149	1,022	100	68	245	66	18	38	37,662	728	8.2	25.8	42.6
Ellis	125	846	146	D	127	54	26	30	35,668	677	7.2	29.1	37.5
Garfield	1,657	21,265	4,015	2,111	3,619	800	589	790	37,147	936	22.1	20.6	44.8
Garvin	708	7,936	951	1,121	1,344	265	164	323	40,728	1,500	27.8	6.8	36.0
Grady	1,124	11,093	1,817	1,672	1,578	406	372	368	33,192	1,625	33.8	9.2	36.6
Grant	127	919	127	11	171	48	14	42	46,223	659	10.5	26.7	47.3
Greer	84	657	242	D	135	43	10	19	28,216	432	8.6	20.8	35.8
Harmon	57	442	123	D	90	39	4	15	33,007	374	2.7	31.3	48.3
Harper	91	523	128	NA	118	41	33	17	32,172	438	7.5	37.4	41.1
Haskell	213	2,468	796	D	481	63	49	72	29,031	812	23.3	4.7	37.4
Hughes	224	2,273	744	93	391	70	32	58	25,621	928	19.4	8.1	43.9
Jackson	513	6,463	1,246	931	1,253	364	120	211	32,656	634	20.2	24.6	35.2
Jefferson	97	778	105	24	142	107	35	29	37,744	424	14.4	28.1	50.3
Johnston	181	2,042	513	499	284	36	29	75	36,968	606	21.5	8.3	35.7
Kay	1,102	14,892	2,307	2,560	2,235	426	543	564	37,897	864	28.2	18.5	46.1
Kingfisher	484	5,297	528	347	637	199	183	247	46,706	928	18.5	20.0	44.9

Table B. States and Counties — **Agriculture**

STATE County	Acreage (1,000) 117	Percent change, 2012-2017 118	Average size of farm 119	Total irrigated (1,000) 120	Total cropland (1,000) 121	Average per farm 122	Average per acre 123	Value of machinery and equipment, average per farm (dollars) 124	Total (mil dol) 125	Average per farm (acres) 126	Crops 127	Livestock and poultry products 128	Organic farms (number) 129	Farms with internet access (percent) 130	Total ($1,000) 131	Percent of farms 132
OHIO— Cont'd																
Ottawa	121	7.8	221	1.2	115.1	1,192,630	5,409	173,655	59.2	107,477	92.9	7.1	2	77.3	3,064	70.8
Paulding	220	-0.6	353	0.4	208.2	2,210,654	6,260	220,491	173.5	278,860	46.3	53.7	4	76.2	4,880	83.6
Perry	101	-5.7	133	0.0	58.9	607,087	4,574	75,495	33.8	44,398	68.3	31.7	3	74.0	1,427	18.8
Pickaway	297	1.1	369	2.6	275.0	2,225,570	6,033	220,849	162.7	202,050	91.4	8.6	2	81.7	10,838	61.5
Pike	98	0.4	191	0.6	54.3	795,490	4,156	87,790	55.1	107,771	41.2	58.8	9	68.3	1,495	23.3
Portage	86	3.1	77	0.3	59.5	500,149	6,511	74,045	34.5	30,849	71.0	29.0	5	78.4	1,224	10.4
Preble	213	-4.8	202	0.3	188.3	1,294,416	6,397	133,405	146.3	138,647	67.1	32.9	7	75.3	5,681	51.3
Putnam	305	-0.2	228	0.8	291.2	1,528,572	6,694	186,197	214.5	160,661	65.0	35.0	NA	78.4	7,728	73.5
Richland	156	-3.0	134	0.2	113.1	1,008,273	7,505	108,319	135.1	116,504	37.1	62.9	20	65.4	2,687	21.0
Ross	248	11.8	221	0.7	168.2	1,013,522	4,583	105,244	77.7	69,354	85.8	14.2	8	69.8	10,095	45.2
Sandusky	179	-1.5	233	1.1	166.4	1,379,300	5,926	177,118	101.0	131,561	90.9	9.1	4	80.7	5,305	69.3
Scioto	91	-3.1	133	0.1	45.1	416,922	3,138	89,131	17.8	25,932	78.1	21.9	1	75.3	1,081	15.0
Seneca	267	-8.1	231	0.3	242.8	1,359,558	5,889	176,787	140.9	121,866	82.0	18.0	3	74.4	8,588	72.1
Shelby	215	4.2	227	D	197.3	1,745,226	7,688	179,829	178.2	188,214	52.0	48.0	5	83.7	7,162	68.0
Stark	133	-2.1	86	0.8	101.7	794,143	9,244	89,768	95.8	61,954	42.4	57.6	10	76.3	3,035	13.7
Summit	19	13.3	48	0.2	10.7	639,318	13,365	54,610	12.6	32,156	68.5	31.5	2	86.7	275	7.1
Trumbull	124	8.6	119	0.1	82.0	516,981	4,331	108,297	56.1	54,110	64.4	35.6	12	71.7	1,345	20.9
Tuscarawas	144	4.2	125	0.1	80.1	691,723	5,555	100,450	125.2	108,384	17.2	82.8	26	61.1	1,454	18.5
Union	218	-10.1	218	0.4	196.1	1,386,021	6,350	191,902	209.3	209,954	49.4	50.6	13	86.7	7,490	52.2
Van Wert	248	9.3	322	D	240.8	2,410,706	7,494	215,085	191.3	247,791	64.6	35.4	2	83.4	4,699	68.9
Vinton	31	-5.8	139	0.0	14.0	438,779	3,166	63,613	5.7	25,079	80.3	19.7	3	66.1	261	27.8
Warren	90	-15.3	98	0.5	71.2	763,996	7,824	86,177	47.7	51,536	93.8	6.2	4	81.8	2,580	15.7
Washington	144	3.9	131	0.6	57.0	416,318	3,189	70,252	42.0	38,019	55.5	44.5	NA	71.2	684	17.4
Wayne	252	-7.2	124	0.9	204.0	1,107,599	8,940	116,845	327.9	161,205	24.8	75.2	98	66.3	5,140	21.1
Williams	211	1.2	239	3.8	189.9	1,233,691	5,161	145,441	122.8	139,367	66.1	33.9	3	73.4	7,092	64.4
Wood	269	0.3	251	2.3	253.8	1,674,194	6,659	171,875	159.3	148,985	79.4	20.6	6	76.5	8,030	70.8
Wyandot	225	1.7	346	0.0	205.1	1,974,814	5,706	226,523	157.3	242,385	62.0	38.0	3	74.0	8,100	75.2
OKLAHOMA	34,156	-0.6	435	573.8	11,715.7	754,099	1,734	90,442	7,465.5	95,065	20.3	79.7	54	72.9	232,018	26.3
Adair	239	-5.3	232	0.4	47.6	554,052	2,392	76,599	163.1	158,242	2.0	98.0	1	68.1	216	8.7
Alfalfa	524	-3.9	902	1.4	343.2	1,535,433	1,703	241,428	103.0	177,248	40.3	59.7	NA	74.5	4,482	75.9
Atoka	357	1.2	338	1.5	66.8	619,842	1,834	65,617	39.0	36,901	8.6	91.4	1	67.3	743	32.0
Beaver	1,037	-7.1	1,288	21.5	296.1	1,157,188	898	104,629	155.7	193,388	12.5	87.5	NA	66.2	7,620	67.0
Beckham	498	-12.3	556	10.5	175.7	740,737	1,332	103,007	52.0	58,029	50.7	49.3	NA	70.1	4,317	41.2
Blaine	593	13.6	811	4.3	320.9	1,321,168	1,628	197,612	109.2	149,409	22.8	77.2	NA	74.3	2,599	47.2
Bryan	433	-1.9	269	6.4	104.5	610,009	2,267	69,072	61.4	38,161	33.9	66.1	NA	70.0	2,133	36.1
Caddo	756	6.8	541	37.3	326.7	937,747	1,732	122,802	132.1	94,609	37.4	62.6	5	69.8	12,419	46.6
Canadian	498	-0.5	376	5.4	255.6	884,268	2,349	129,048	135.8	102,535	20.8	79.2	NA	75.8	5,299	38.3
Carter	396	-13.2	277	1.6	64.3	562,555	2,030	59,722	39.4	27,541	16.2	83.8	NA	76.5	932	7.1
Cherokee	217	-8.0	181	0.6	41.4	449,283	2,483	66,353	67.6	56,327	44.5	55.5	2	67.8	838	24.1
Choctaw	338	2.2	397	1.6	66.2	704,003	1,774	82,113	47.0	55,197	11.3	88.7	1	75.0	1,740	15.0
Cimarron	1,097	-5.2	2,455	42.0	402.7	2,026,541	825	215,397	342.4	765,922	16.5	83.5	NA	70.0	8,980	76.1
Cleveland	123	-8.1	104	2.6	31.6	504,329	4,851	52,819	16.6	14,066	44.8	55.2	3	79.4	179	3.4
Coal	273	-0.1	463	0.5	54.4	843,799	1,821	79,114	37.9	64,205	10.6	89.4	NA	61.9	788	33.4
Comanche	467	0.9	443	D	157.7	853,568	1,928	85,581	81.0	76,787	19.0	81.0	2	75.7	3,300	33.6
Cotton	405	1.2	903	0.1	202.7	1,227,562	1,359	137,210	49.8	111,170	21.9	78.1	NA	75.2	5,750	69.9
Craig	423	-8.4	359	D	100.7	755,777	2,105	82,441	99.7	84,545	10.5	89.5	6	74.1	1,567	18.6
Creek	327	-5.7	173	0.7	62.7	379,152	2,193	54,643	18.1	9,587	16.7	83.3	3	70.5	404	3.4
Custer	638	2.5	826	7.5	253.6	1,199,008	1,452	159,557	104.5	135,208	26.5	73.5	NA	72.8	5,809	45.8
Delaware	292	2.9	212	0.1	69.4	577,810	2,729	85,609	244.0	177,207	2.6	97.4	2	73.6	453	7.3
Dewey	652	4.4	896	2.8	185.4	1,228,171	1,371	125,050	41.2	56,651	18.7	81.3	NA	76.4	2,425	56.7
Ellis	724	-4.5	1,070	8.4	127.3	1,062,853	994	79,899	115.7	170,870	4.1	95.9	NA	64.5	2,328	64.1
Garfield	675	1.3	721	3.2	442.9	1,251,739	1,736	180,572	130.4	139,318	48.1	51.9	NA	80.0	6,660	61.3
Garvin	483	4.4	322	2.0	122.1	617,731	1,917	81,615	66.9	44,607	25.3	74.7	1	70.9	2,139	25.6
Grady	593	1.2	365	12.7	200.9	766,106	2,098	116,307	152.7	93,954	14.6	85.4	NA	70.3	4,232	30.3
Grant	575	-1.3	872	1.5	414.8	1,400,015	1,605	206,900	85.3	129,398	72.2	27.8	1	75.7	6,156	78.1
Greer	328	-18.3	760	4.4	132.3	877,992	1,156	98,008	32.3	74,785	45.2	54.8	NA	74.5	4,332	63.7
Harmon	342	0.3	914	24.5	167.3	1,143,452	1,252	143,175	66.2	176,952	43.7	56.3	NA	70.1	5,079	69.0
Harper	668	8.0	1,524	4.3	180.7	1,678,361	1,101	133,044	217.1	495,710	2.8	97.2	NA	71.9	3,424	63.7
Haskell	238	-7.2	293	0.5	45.9	556,633	1,902	91,479	104.2	128,365	2.5	97.5	1	73.4	879	15.9
Hughes	414	-5.1	446	2.9	63.2	710,946	1,595	76,477	306.3	330,044	1.0	99.0	NA	67.0	1,393	19.8
Jackson	511	6.7	806	50.8	335.5	1,125,890	1,398	197,700	115.7	182,442	85.5	14.5	NA	77.4	12,582	58.8
Jefferson	472	-0.7	1,113	0.7	92.6	1,721,210	1,546	113,136	89.7	211,564	4.2	95.8	NA	70.3	3,447	49.8
Johnston	289	1.8	477	0.7	44.0	892,334	1,872	72,388	32.9	54,211	10.6	89.4	1	70.8	1,206	44.9
Kay	498	2.8	576	1.2	346.7	947,482	1,645	131,856	88.2	102,078	68.1	31.9	NA	77.2	5,685	51.7
Kingfisher	575	1.3	620	5.6	353.5	1,191,810	1,923	162,597	145.0	156,278	21.6	78.4	2	74.9	5,382	59.3

Table B. States and Counties — Water Use, Wholesale Trade, Retail Trade, and Real Estate

STATE County	Water use, 2015 Public supply water withdrawn (mil gal/ day)	Public supply gallons withdrawn per person per day	Wholesale Trade[1], 2012 Number of establishments	Number of employees	Sales (mil dol)	Average payroll (mil dol)	Retail Trade[2], 2012 Number of establishments	Number of employees	Sales (mil dol)	Average payroll (mil dol)	Real estate and rental and leasing,[2] 2012 Number of establishments	Number of employees	Sales (mil dol)	Average payroll (mil dol)
	133	134	135	136	137	138	139	140	141	142	143	144	145	146
OHIO— Cont'd														
Ottawa	4.58	112.0	27	156	127.5	6.4	144	1,433	427.7	38.2	44	120	15.1	3.4
Paulding	1.31	69.0	15	201	120.1	7.7	48	385	113.0	7.6	6	D	D	D
Perry	0.96	26.7	15	D	D	D	70	626	173.4	13.1	10	16	2.7	0.4
Pickaway	3.66	64.2	38	D	D	D	124	1,402	437.9	32.6	25	85	12.7	2.1
Pike	2.58	91.4	14	133	46.9	4.5	79	890	219.1	18.4	10	71	11.1	2.1
Portage	43.85	270.2	138	2,930	2,204.2	174.6	438	7,363	1,944.3	159.4	105	621	108.5	25.6
Preble	2.56	61.9	26	221	159.9	8.8	106	1,319	415.5	29.3	13	70	13.3	2.3
Putnam	2.52	74.0	35	354	297.1	13.6	110	1,054	274.8	21.6	10	28	2.5	0.8
Richland	14.45	118.7	104	1,993	939.2	78.9	438	6,528	1,501.2	139.9	102	417	49.2	9.1
Ross	9.48	122.8	44	D	D	D	236	3,582	938.9	77.8	51	198	34.7	6.2
Sandusky	7.89	132.2	47	662	764.0	28.1	199	2,366	629.2	54.7	34	172	17.8	3.5
Scioto	8.60	111.9	25	D	D	D	253	3,085	784.0	70.0	45	246	30.4	5.6
Seneca	1.85	33.3	49	646	504.3	27.0	159	2,064	586.5	49.8	29	71	10.6	1.6
Shelby	3.49	71.4	43	979	543.0	35.6	142	1,754	490.0	39.2	37	132	15.4	3.6
Stark	30.44	81.1	329	4,584	2,551.8	212.6	1,261	19,983	5,330.3	453.5	284	1,295	215.7	41.5
Summit	11.08	20.4	821	13,158	7,841.2	752.5	1,755	29,142	8,439.7	745.7	476	2,570	473.6	92.7
Trumbull	33.85	166.1	170	2,528	2,288.6	124.1	685	9,608	2,495.3	201.1	135	1,323	200.4	47.1
Tuscarawas	17.67	190.2	81	758	321.3	28.6	361	4,334	1,180.3	95.1	61	267	38.0	7.4
Union	1.17	21.6	55	689	2,150.6	38.2	121	1,911	631.1	50.4	42	158	24.2	4.2
Van Wert	1.87	65.5	28	D	D	D	87	1,202	282.7	24.6	13	56	16.5	3.1
Vinton	0.18	13.8	1	D	D	D	30	209	43.7	3.4	1	D	D	D
Warren	15.07	67.1	167	3,371	3,109.6	221.0	532	9,726	2,924.2	246.2	151	664	124.7	20.3
Washington	7.63	124.9	68	D	D	D	227	2,724	756.3	62.9	39	D	D	D
Wayne	8.06	69.4	124	D	D	D	366	4,524	1,060.0	100.6	62	217	46.9	7.0
Williams	2.67	71.9	46	680	413.0	25.1	125	1,266	326.6	25.4	23	80	13.3	2.5
Wood	5.21	40.2	167	2,958	2,057.6	137.0	385	6,264	1,813.4	134.2	117	527	127.2	20.7
Wyandot	0.95	42.7	27	342	270.2	13.8	66	786	228.8	16.2	8	D	D	D
OKLAHOMA	611.24	156.3	3,909	50,660	71,892.9	2,718.6	13,051	168,839	50,256.2	4,055.1	4,000	21,261	4,269.6	898.0
Adair	6.91	314.0	8	63	27.9	1.7	58	549	123.4	9.4	7	12	1.4	0.4
Alfalfa	0.70	119.3	9	D	D	D	24	163	57.1	3.4	1	D	D	D
Atoka	40.42	2,930.5	9	35	34.0	1.2	45	438	129.8	9.8	7	D	D	D
Beaver	0.48	88.4	6	D	D	D	19	106	37.5	1.8	5	5	1.6	0.1
Beckham	3.25	136.7	36	547	305.4	29.2	141	1,657	715.4	41.0	40	421	138.4	27.2
Blaine	1.07	108.8	13	D	D	D	47	272	89.7	4.5	4	D	D	D
Bryan	5.53	123.2	28	D	D	D	124	1,441	432.8	31.5	26	70	12.2	2.4
Caddo	7.15	243.7	17	237	191.5	9.4	89	767	283.9	19.1	9	39	12.1	1.4
Canadian	4.24	31.8	102	877	512.8	42.6	255	3,567	1,306.8	88.1	123	721	212.0	41.9
Carter	5.08	104.3	64	866	872.1	32.3	247	2,700	889.7	65.6	70	345	83.0	16.6
Cherokee	7.40	152.7	16	738	111.3	16.4	143	1,710	390.6	33.7	35	146	25.8	3.5
Choctaw	2.69	179.4	6	31	27.6	1.1	43	481	118.8	9.5	3	8	0.5	0.1
Cimarron	0.34	153.4	6	17	30.3	1.0	11	81	38.5	1.7	NA	NA	NA	NA
Cleveland	23.37	85.1	140	1,360	737.9	70.9	710	10,983	3,168.9	262.2	335	1,479	231.0	52.6
Coal	0.46	81.4	2	D	D	D	20	153	41.9	3.1	1	D	D	D
Comanche	20.98	168.3	62	D	D	D	409	5,286	1,407.8	117.9	125	D	D	D
Cotton	0.51	85.1	2	D	D	D	15	124	36.9	1.6	1	D	D	D
Craig	0.10	6.7	16	135	73.4	5.8	62	720	204.9	15.7	5	9	1.3	0.2
Creek	5.89	83.1	64	1,061	579.7	49.4	181	1,877	570.5	43.7	34	103	14.2	2.9
Custer	3.65	122.7	36	338	442.9	21.7	149	1,655	530.9	37.2	45	383	96.6	34.7
Delaware	35.69	860.9	19	100	26.0	3.4	141	1,428	369.2	30.7	36	279	45.2	11.6
Dewey	0.11	22.0	8	25	17.5	1.0	33	246	74.9	3.8	2	D	D	D
Ellis	0.65	153.6	5	69	39.6	3.9	25	269	53.0	3.0	1	D	D	D
Garfield	2.87	45.1	73	D	D	D	267	3,387	926.8	84.3	80	328	57.5	12.4
Garvin	1.99	71.7	25	177	105.5	7.2	110	1,117	433.7	30.3	12	36	15.6	2.2
Grady	2.40	43.9	42	525	324.9	25.9	152	1,602	491.7	34.7	33	164	38.8	8.1
Grant	1.26	278.6	10	40	69.6	1.5	19	D	D	D	1	D	D	D
Greer	1.46	240.5	4	26	7.8	0.7	13	145	30.2	2.7	2	D	D	D
Harmon	0.73	261.8	1	D	D	D	13	D	D	D	1	D	D	D
Harper	0.60	159.8	3	D	D	D	17	127	26.5	2.4	3	D	D	D
Haskell	1.17	91.1	4	60	18.9	1.5	33	473	142.9	10.2	4	6	0.7	0.1
Hughes	2.57	187.1	5	D	D	D	47	427	111.5	7.8	8	34	3.2	1.2
Jackson	0.21	8.2	24	D	D	D	99	1,241	358.3	27.0	20	146	20.1	3.1
Jefferson	13.79	2,197.3	3	D	D	D	25	149	46.0	2.4	1	D	D	D
Johnston	1.98	180.3	9	68	36.1	2.3	34	229	61.1	4.7	3	5	0.4	0.1
Kay	18.13	399.6	43	D	D	D	183	2,126	631.8	48.2	40	132	22.6	4.0
Kingfisher	1.66	106.5	22	331	450.2	16.1	53	556	198.9	14.1	4	4	2.3	0.5

1 Merchant wholesalers, except manufacturers' sales branches and offices.   2. Employer establishments.

Table B. States and Counties — Professional Services, Manufacturing, and Accommodation and Food Services

STATE County	Professional, scientific, and technical services, 2012				Manufacturing, 2012				Accommodation and food services, 2012			
	Number of establishments	Number of employees	Sales (mil dol)	Average payroll (mil dol)	Number of establishments	Number of employees	Receipts (mil dol)	Annual payroll (mil dol)	Number of establishments	Number of employees	Receipts (mil dol)	Annual payroll (mil dol)
	147	148	149	150	151	152	153	154	155	156	157	158
OHIO— Cont'd												
Ottawa	54	D	D	D	53	2,150	811.8	117.7	165	1,703	115.1	30.4
Paulding	12	52	3.2	1.2	38	1,132	282.8	44.9	25	296	11.0	2.7
Perry	21	D	D	D	22	738	D	28.4	47	355	16.6	4.1
Pickaway	56	429	28.7	9.9	35	2,221	900.0	125.1	70	1,254	51.4	14.0
Pike	21	D	D	D	22	1,388	D	88.8	36	597	28.7	7.2
Portage	224	D	D	D	244	9,585	3,010.8	468.2	304	4,925	250.5	61.7
Preble	38	188	11.4	4.9	55	2,761	1,141.7	148.9	56	882	37.4	10.6
Putnam	35	171	18.0	6.0	53	3,209	2,677.9	145.8	60	D	D	D
Richland	187	925	113.1	36.0	168	8,064	3,122.7	385.9	239	4,556	190.1	54.1
Ross	74	645	37.1	15.7	33	4,270	3,928.5	276.6	123	2,486	115.2	30.7
Sandusky	85	431	39.1	12.2	108	8,458	3,878.0	388.4	117	1,844	76.4	19.8
Scioto	80	792	74.0	37.4	43	1,439	1,190.6	64.3	142	2,485	112.8	29.9
Seneca	69	377	29.3	11.9	79	3,498	1,262.6	152.8	106	1,481	53.4	14.5
Shelby	52	364	48.0	18.6	122	10,052	7,166.1	536.9	80	1,300	58.2	14.4
Stark	675	D	D	D	506	22,667	12,182.9	1,061.2	769	13,844	630.1	174.7
Summit	1,500	14,776	2,443.4	856.7	837	27,965	9,557.1	1,402.7	1,195	21,494	974.7	268.9
Trumbull	306	1,436	175.5	49.5	218	15,764	9,668.4	1,095.3	396	11,386	516.3	156.0
Tuscarawas	140	D	D	D	211	7,401	2,276.1	346.3	194	2,700	112.1	30.6
Union	93	2,362	706.6	211.2	53	6,143	10,102.7	424.9	80	1,335	63.9	17.5
Van Wert	36	141	14.7	6.3	39	3,323	1,505.7	130.2	45	798	31.2	7.8
Vinton	7	D	D	D	15	453	98.2	27.5	13	D	D	D
Warren	473	3,934	567.7	234.9	198	9,523	3,803.4	493.3	350	7,767	386.6	107.1
Washington	96	D	D	D	88	3,628	D	222.3	112	D	D	D
Wayne	153	1,668	117.3	88.3	254	10,257	3,203.8	471.4	171	2,937	125.6	36.6
Williams	40	301	23.3	11.2	113	6,337	2,466.3	274.4	71	927	35.0	9.7
Wood	216	1,658	195.1	93.1	179	11,030	4,256.0	623.3	322	6,468	263.9	73.2
Wyandot	23	76	7.9	2.0	41	3,055	958.8	130.8	49	568	22.6	5.5
OKLAHOMA	9,470	71,997	10,991.3	4,115.2	3,610	133,064	74,295.4	6,416.0	7,403	143,561	7,121.2	1,908.3
Adair	17	D	D	D	16	1,075	485.0	38.3	20	198	7.2	2.2
Alfalfa	9	D	D	D	NA	NA	NA	NA	8	44	3.1	0.7
Atoka	10	D	D	D	17	178	47.0	6.6	25	D	D	D
Beaver	18	D	D	D	3	29	D	D	9	D	D	D
Beckham	80	273	47.2	14.3	17	D	D	D	72	999	51.9	10.7
Blaine	21	183	17.1	7.0	7	391	D	16.8	16	129	6.0	1.5
Bryan	63	382	39.7	15.0	35	1,076	243.2	35.3	76	1,573	73.5	21.1
Caddo	34	D	D	D	10	46	D	1.6	36	339	14.1	3.6
Canadian	232	846	172.5	59.6	79	2,979	1,035.6	114.1	171	3,310	160.6	41.7
Carter	134	722	61.5	33.7	43	2,984	4,853.5	178.2	116	2,397	106.7	29.4
Cherokee	45	129	10.4	2.8	21	107	15.1	3.5	88	1,226	53.1	13.5
Choctaw	18	D	D	D	11	133	D	2.7	24	542	18.1	8.1
Cimarron	4	D	D	D	NA	NA	NA	NA	10	82	4.1	1.0
Cleveland	676	3,166	396.5	131.5	132	3,659	1,495.7	158.7	506	11,290	512.4	140.7
Coal	2	D	D	D	5	73	D	2.9	6	D	D	D
Comanche	162	1,129	114.8	49.8	45	3,487	D	183.7	227	4,863	220.5	66.2
Cotton	6	14	1.0	0.4	4	8	D	D	7	64	2.7	0.6
Craig	24	D	D	D	14	440	89.9	16.8	25	345	14.4	3.7
Creek	104	299	35.1	10.4	124	4,057	1,649.9	212.4	90	D	D	D
Custer	74	D	D	D	32	1,184	429.8	57.3	68	1,284	61.3	14.4
Delaware	54	D	D	D	27	693	87.1	22.0	63	1,816	165.8	40.2
Dewey	4	D	D	D	4	28	D	1.4	6	64	1.9	0.6
Ellis	9	29	6.1	0.8	NA	NA	NA	NA	8	D	D	D
Garfield	118	D	D	D	61	2,451	1,668.7	96.5	125	2,198	112.7	26.8
Garvin	61	D	D	D	31	1,067	2,819.8	53.9	49	660	33.1	7.9
Grady	105	300	35.7	11.5	64	1,505	564.1	57.0	62	1,240	53.2	13.6
Grant	6	D	D	D	3	12	2.1	0.3	5	D	D	D
Greer	9	D	D	D	NA	NA	NA	NA	6	55	1.8	0.5
Harmon	4	D	D	D	NA	NA	NA	NA	2	D	D	D
Harper	7	D	D	D	NA	NA	NA	NA	6	D	D	D
Haskell	23	D	D	D	7	70	D	D	13	D	D	D
Hughes	9	D	D	D	6	29	D	1.0	19	202	7.2	2.1
Jackson	41	D	D	D	13	821	225.6	D	56	1,103	42.0	11.4
Jefferson	5	D	D	D	7	28	D	0.9	8	78	3.0	0.8
Johnston	12	D	D	D	9	285	D	9.4	9	D	D	D
Kay	90	509	52.8	21.7	65	2,983	D	171.0	90	1,350	65.2	15.9
Kingfisher	27	277	41.3	18.4	18	470	130.2	22.5	34	370	16.7	4.4

Items 147—158

Table B. States and Counties — **Health Care and Social Assistance, Other Services, Nonemployer Businesses, and Residential Construction**

STATE County	Health care and social assistance, 2012				Other services, 2012				Nonemployer businesses, 2016		Value of residential construction authorized by building permits, 2018	
	Number of establishments	Number of employees	Receipts (mil dol)	Annual payroll (mil dol)	Number of establishments	Number of employees	Receipts (mil dol)	Annual payroll (mil dol)	Number	Receipts (mil dol)	New construction ($1,000)	Number of housing units
	159	160	161	162	163	164	165	166	167	168	169	170
OHIO— Cont'd												
Ottawa	76	1,771	123.0	49.8	79	311	28.6	8.4	3,029	124.6	40,428	168
Paulding	32	604	36.0	15.8	17	61	6.0	1.2	1,038	39.0	6,804	33
Perry	61	709	40.0	18.5	28	158	11.4	2.4	2,019	76.9	5,740	38
Pickaway	86	2,266	189.6	73.5	51	179	18.2	4.3	3,362	135.5	40,006	175
Pike	60	1,610	118.0	44.4	21	69	6.6	1.4	1,456	55.8	14,864	66
Portage	267	5,974	418.5	181.0	227	1,518	120.6	40.8	10,292	450.2	100,159	504
Preble	61	975	60.4	21.6	59	235	20.8	5.4	2,442	95.5	7,043	45
Putnam	54	990	49.0	20.9	55	274	30.3	6.4	2,062	86.3	14,321	54
Richland	316	7,570	674.5	274.6	209	1,186	108.4	25.3	6,793	281.7	18,939	80
Ross	158	6,268	754.2	373.1	85	490	35.3	9.7	3,856	152.8	2,236	13
Sandusky	160	3,660	283.4	113.3	99	635	42.3	14.1	3,102	104.8	8,731	44
Scioto	214	6,155	591.9	206.7	89	336	30.4	6.8	3,712	125.1	380	4
Seneca	145	2,536	180.6	69.9	104	505	32.0	8.2	2,878	111.8	3,994	26
Shelby	98	1,929	169.1	64.1	69	342	36.3	9.7	2,698	119.8	15,075	53
Stark	996	28,010	2,455.5	1,090.0	694	4,770	460.7	131.2	23,426	976.1	115,707	527
Summit	1,519	45,181	4,649.6	1,869.0	1,084	7,398	853.5	202.2	37,425	1,635.1	314,309	706
Trumbull	578	10,720	991.1	378.8	313	1,771	128.1	36.8	12,527	532.9	16,217	94
Tuscarawas	200	5,156	397.5	157.3	190	1,096	125.2	27.8	6,070	271.2	11,373	66
Union	78	1,732	166.1	63.3	68	354	29.6	8.9	3,681	167.8	208,489	863
Van Wert	60	1,505	113.3	41.8	45	234	20.2	3.6	1,660	69.4	4,199	18
Vinton	22	D	D	D	8	D	D	D	656	23.6	0	0
Warren	433	9,527	853.7	325.5	244	1,944	175.3	56.3	16,282	799.4	361,976	1,472
Washington	139	5,586	453.2	195.2	110	D	D	D	3,755	152.9	1,910	13
Wayne	235	5,274	415.5	178.6	169	891	97.0	20.4	8,957	414.6	48,138	253
Williams	65	2,006	169.7	71.6	66	372	30.3	7.1	2,135	87.8	6,368	29
Wood	243	4,906	384.2	164.5	210	1,433	126.7	38.6	7,626	329.9	72,708	301
Wyandot	37	772	55.6	21.1	56	240	21.5	5.6	1,334	51.2	7,401	22
OKLAHOMA	10,654	213,226	22,795.4	8,289.9	5,411	32,388	4,037.3	939.7	280,292	12,711.8	2,181,297	10,502
Adair	17	562	33.0	16.5	11	28	1.9	0.4	1,382	47.4	623	4
Alfalfa	11	111	6.6	2.9	6	D	D	D	400	12.4	0	0
Atoka	22	466	26.2	9.8	15	D	D	D	925	44.0	155	9
Beaver	6	75	7.1	2.3	11	D	D	D	475	19.4	0	0
Beckham	87	1,235	111.5	39.4	39	247	33.4	7.6	1,808	86.9	2,127	9
Blaine	27	365	21.3	10.0	14	28	3.5	0.4	681	29.2	0	0
Bryan	124	2,092	204.5	66.4	34	159	12.8	3.6	2,945	138.4	20,055	194
Caddo	34	618	29.7	13.1	19	88	12.4	3.3	1,547	60.8	1,168	9
Canadian	233	2,849	228.1	88.7	159	1,006	184.0	32.9	10,528	475.8	94,858	485
Carter	217	3,790	323.6	121.1	93	974	148.1	46.4	3,380	142.2	11,675	77
Cherokee	114	2,633	244.7	106.7	41	279	20.4	5.8	2,825	119.8	10,515	103
Choctaw	40	975	59.7	27.0	13	D	D	D	965	41.8	1,200	10
Cimarron	4	D	D	D	4	D	D	D	220	11.5	0	0
Cleveland	755	12,359	1,158.1	435.8	308	1,761	301.9	44.6	21,279	962.0	165,665	681
Coal	11	242	10.4	5.5	4	D	D	D	425	18.0	110	11
Comanche	275	6,918	704.6	271.8	136	830	69.0	20.9	4,867	210.9	13,326	67
Cotton	7	42	5.1	1.4	5	16	1.6	0.3	316	9.2	256	1
Craig	74	1,329	83.1	43.5	16	43	4.4	1.2	919	43.4	0	0
Creek	113	2,166	147.1	56.4	82	306	35.9	8.1	4,784	201.4	28,859	240
Custer	92	1,668	158.5	59.7	51	302	30.3	8.3	2,238	98.2	11,070	55
Delaware	84	1,440	133.1	47.2	54	241	21.8	5.3	2,754	117.6	5,661	29
Dewey	9	D	D	D	9	42	8.4	1.1	498	20.6	NA	NA
Ellis	10	192	15.5	6.9	5	D	D	D	311	11.4	0	0
Garfield	208	4,158	427.0	151.8	118	586	58.8	14.5	4,316	176.2	8,124	43
Garvin	64	1,277	78.3	30.7	26	129	23.9	4.8	2,164	92.1	1,314	12
Grady	87	D	D	D	65	328	37.1	8.2	3,801	162.3	15,861	92
Grant	7	119	5.1	2.5	4	D	D	D	376	15.7	937	4
Greer	17	D	D	D	7	15	1.5	0.2	297	11.7	263	1
Harmon	6	122	8.5	3.8	2	D	D	D	151	6.7	NA	NA
Harper	9	127	7.5	3.5	6	D	D	D	316	10.5	0	0
Haskell	29	819	53.7	22.3	11	31	2.4	0.4	983	40.7	1,749	14
Hughes	40	D	D	D	10	D	D	D	744	27.1	290	2
Jackson	48	1,389	111.1	47.6	34	151	10.6	2.7	1,428	61.3	3,912	22
Jefferson	7	D	D	D	3	D	D	D	428	15.0	NA	NA
Johnston	30	586	31.8	15.3	10	32	3.3	0.8	675	27.4	777	4
Kay	143	2,252	176.8	65.7	75	335	31.6	8.3	2,500	95.1	1,304	6
Kingfisher	39	479	33.3	13.6	29	D	D	D	1,501	77.2	7,606	32

Table B. States and Counties — Government Employment and Payroll, and Local Government Finances

STATE County	Government employment and payroll, 2012									Local government finances, 2012				
			March payroll (percent of total)							General revenue				
												Taxes		
													Per capita[1] (dollars)	
	Full-time equivalent employees	March payroll (dollars)	Administration, judicial, and legal	Police and corrections	Fire protection	Highways and transportation	Health and welfare	Natural resources and utilities	Education and libraries	Total (mil dol)	Inter-governmental (mil dol)	Total (mil dol)	Total	Property
	171	172	173	174	175	176	177	178	179	180	181	182	183	184
OHIO— Cont'd														
Ottawa	1,807	6,970,433	8.9	9.2	2.9	11.6	10.2	7.2	48.1	169.9	58.3	72.2	1,746	1,408
Paulding	840	2,899,437	7.0	5.4	0.3	5.0	30.9	2.1	47.9	78.4	30.7	20.4	1,057	705
Perry	1,584	4,562,693	8.5	5.7	0.8	9.1	10.2	4.3	60.2	119.5	77.0	27.9	775	640
Pickaway	2,330	14,643,979	43.7	3.1	0.9	1.5	14.8	1.6	34.2	261.8	90.0	68.3	1,211	848
Pike	1,231	4,378,557	9.2	6.9	1.1	6.4	9.9	6.4	59.2	142.7	70.7	26.2	920	694
Portage	6,776	25,510,983	5.9	7.0	4.0	6.3	23.8	3.4	48.7	675.5	218.5	230.1	1,425	1,010
Preble	1,714	6,190,256	11.3	8.4	1.2	8.8	6.9	4.8	52.3	137.6	66.2	50.4	1,204	713
Putnam	1,034	3,725,218	9.3	7.5	0.0	5.3	1.5	3.8	72.3	126.1	61.7	46.9	1,371	814
Richland	5,091	18,513,991	8.5	9.4	5.0	4.1	11.2	8.3	52.0	473.0	237.7	163.9	1,336	864
Ross	2,848	9,604,595	8.8	6.4	2.9	4.7	10.0	4.2	62.4	240.8	134.0	79.9	1,032	625
Sandusky	2,171	7,625,048	7.2	8.4	1.7	3.5	12.3	6.5	58.8	231.5	116.4	82.4	1,362	773
Scioto	2,809	9,457,558	7.1	6.9	2.7	3.9	7.6	6.7	64.1	259.9	167.7	61.3	781	581
Seneca	1,825	6,110,506	9.4	11.2	4.5	4.6	9.9	4.4	55.0	195.7	93.8	60.1	1,073	657
Shelby	1,460	5,397,171	6.3	6.1	4.3	3.0	5.5	5.6	68.3	184.8	82.0	67.4	1,370	761
Stark	11,531	42,201,589	4.3	6.8	4.8	4.1	1.9	6.1	71.3	1,313.7	628.2	474.7	1,266	949
Summit	20,065	81,863,137	7.5	10.7	5.8	4.7	7.7	7.2	54.5	2,401.2	877.7	1,094.2	2,023	1,303
Trumbull	7,911	27,957,859	8.3	9.9	5.3	3.3	10.3	6.6	55.2	724.1	366.6	245.2	1,182	844
Tuscarawas	3,307	11,310,698	8.3	7.0	2.8	5.4	6.0	9.0	58.9	309.5	126.6	106.5	1,152	825
Union	2,131	8,121,953	6.0	5.6	3.5	2.1	30.6	3.2	47.7	262.5	68.5	90.7	1,720	1,149
Van Wert	1,050	4,217,502	8.6	7.4	2.1	8.6	3.4	13.7	52.1	118.7	67.2	36.2	1,260	753
Vinton	591	1,697,854	7.1	2.3	0.0	6.1	13.7	1.9	66.2	47.0	34.8	7.8	590	511
Warren	5,863	22,314,741	4.2	7.3	6.2	2.1	0.6	3.3	75.2	748.9	233.0	383.6	1,766	1,359
Washington	2,326	7,490,510	7.9	9.4	3.2	6.0	8.9	3.7	59.9	189.5	93.8	66.4	1,080	769
Wayne	4,495	16,994,820	7.3	7.8	2.6	5.0	22.5	5.7	48.6	484.9	177.5	144.9	1,261	926
Williams	1,758	5,321,575	7.9	5.7	0.7	4.6	15.8	10.1	54.0	135.0	55.5	50.2	1,339	733
Wood	4,470	17,275,956	8.6	10.8	3.6	3.3	9.2	6.1	56.1	532.6	184.0	232.7	1,815	1,163
Wyandot	1,084	3,936,981	8.9	7.2	0.8	3.5	33.2	5.1	40.6	97.2	30.4	25.4	1,124	531
OKLAHOMA	X	X	X	X	X	X	X	X	X	X	X	X	X	X
Adair	986	2,539,434	3.7	4.1	0.2	2.8	2.6	7.8	77.6	58.2	42.9	7.8	352	205
Alfalfa	248	605,307	12.0	6.9	0.5	12.8	1.7	4.7	59.3	13.7	4.5	6.9	1,225	981
Atoka	901	3,031,357	2.1	2.9	0.0	0.7	13.5	14.8	65.5	69.1	37.2	9.2	658	295
Beaver	349	1,030,481	7.5	3.5	0.0	11.8	12.7	7.2	56.4	23.3	11.7	9.1	1,626	1,124
Beckham	996	2,808,433	5.1	8.4	3.6	5.8	2.7	8.0	63.2	78.3	28.3	36.4	1,577	607
Blaine	619	1,556,580	6.7	6.5	0.9	6.6	23.9	4.9	49.9	45.9	14.5	14.0	1,429	639
Bryan	1,434	4,012,582	7.3	9.9	3.7	4.8	3.9	6.2	62.9	108.1	53.8	36.2	833	407
Caddo	1,563	4,548,760	3.7	5.7	1.7	6.2	8.5	8.8	64.8	96.6	61.1	21.0	708	392
Canadian	3,819	11,398,884	4.8	10.1	3.4	2.2	6.5	2.2	69.3	291.7	123.9	127.1	1,037	614
Carter	1,811	5,386,589	5.3	10.5	3.1	4.9	1.1	6.3	67.9	152.0	61.4	59.3	1,233	591
Cherokee	2,005	6,302,718	3.9	5.1	1.3	3.4	35.5	5.3	44.2	165.4	56.2	22.0	457	230
Choctaw	795	2,289,614	6.3	3.7	1.7	3.9	19.7	5.9	57.8	37.7	23.4	8.9	588	233
Cimarron	196	450,099	9.5	5.4	0.0	14.3	1.7	5.6	54.3	9.9	3.7	3.1	1,291	950
Cleveland	9,950	35,955,536	3.3	6.4	4.0	1.7	32.0	2.8	48.9	893.3	214.7	278.1	1,047	619
Coal	319	840,600	8.4	5.3	4.4	7.5	6.5	3.4	64.6	24.3	13.0	8.5	1,425	897
Comanche	6,240	22,060,234	3.6	5.7	3.0	2.1	37.2	3.2	44.6	505.2	159.3	103.2	817	354
Cotton	263	656,798	7.9	5.3	1.5	6.9	1.4	7.9	66.9	18.1	12.3	3.0	492	352
Craig	859	2,734,367	4.9	5.6	1.6	5.0	35.0	3.8	42.2	46.2	23.2	13.9	943	509
Creek	2,475	7,871,373	5.1	6.6	4.0	2.5	1.9	5.1	74.1	169.5	81.2	61.8	874	489
Custer	1,316	3,555,785	5.3	7.5	2.4	3.8	17.0	5.5	56.6	88.8	32.3	37.3	1,306	656
Delaware	1,264	3,298,724	6.6	7.0	0.4	4.1	1.2	4.6	74.6	80.2	42.1	28.6	690	467
Dewey	334	940,532	8.5	5.7	0.5	11.7	14.3	4.1	54.3	35.1	7.3	21.9	4,581	2,207
Ellis	243	705,922	9.0	9.1	0.0	18.9	2.9	2.2	56.6	31.4	7.5	8.4	2,051	1,616
Garfield	2,242	6,971,075	5.4	9.4	5.9	4.5	1.4	5.0	66.7	176.9	68.5	75.4	1,232	577
Garvin	1,260	3,212,232	6.5	6.6	2.1	5.0	14.9	6.4	57.8	92.3	43.7	25.1	920	451
Grady	1,921	5,776,643	3.4	5.2	3.6	3.2	26.9	2.4	54.3	157.9	56.1	41.4	779	442
Grant	233	634,768	12.0	7.0	0.1	21.2	0.0	6.1	53.1	15.2	6.4	5.9	1,313	1,043
Greer	288	950,821	5.8	5.3	2.0	1.0	29.5	6.4	48.4	16.6	9.5	2.9	481	285
Harmon	242	611,023	7.5	4.4	0.0	5.4	40.8	2.6	38.3	7.4	4.3	1.9	648	388
Harper	266	708,452	8.7	5.5	0.0	9.6	26.4	4.5	45.3	14.8	7.0	5.9	1,592	1,096
Haskell	614	1,704,293	4.5	5.0	0.0	5.1	27.6	1.6	53.4	31.8	20.1	7.0	543	274
Hughes	768	2,037,752	4.4	2.9	0.8	3.3	28.1	3.9	55.8	38.4	20.3	12.6	908	604
Jackson	1,759	6,015,452	3.3	4.6	2.2	1.8	47.3	5.6	33.9	146.2	38.1	20.7	788	304
Jefferson	350	958,729	7.0	3.6	0.7	3.6	15.4	11.0	58.0	49.9	41.2	3.0	470	281
Johnston	410	1,050,719	7.1	6.5	0.6	3.4	2.9	5.1	73.6	22.7	13.6	6.2	561	357
Kay	2,026	5,686,908	6.0	8.0	6.7	4.3	2.5	9.9	60.6	149.2	58.1	50.8	1,108	557
Kingfisher	634	1,825,978	7.8	7.8	3.3	9.1	1.5	4.9	65.1	48.4	22.2	18.8	1,254	825

1. Based on the resident population estimated as of July 1 of the year shown.

Table B. States and Counties — Local Government Finances, Government Employment, and Income Taxes

STATE County	Local government finances, 2012 (cont.) Direct general expenditure Total (mil dol)	Per capita[1] (dollars)	Education	Health and hospitals	Police protection	Public welfare	Highways	Debt outstanding Total (mil dol)	Per capita[1] (dollars)	Government employment, 2017 Federal civilian	Federal military	State and local	Individual income tax returns, 2016 Number of returns	Mean adjusted gross income	Mean income tax
	185	186	187	188	189	190	191	192	193	194	195	196	197	198	199
OHIO— Cont'd															
Ottawa	183.7	4,444	50.5	4.7	6.9	9.8	7.3	162.5	3,930	263	144	2,125	21,700	56,389	6,409
Paulding	83.9	4,350	53.2	21.6	2.3	1.9	7.4	20.8	1,079	52	48	1,045	9,030	44,240	4,163
Perry	127.1	3,530	59.9	5.5	4.7	7.4	7.0	19.6	543	64	91	1,546	15,210	45,088	4,113
Pickaway	245.9	4,360	42.1	29.7	3.7	2.8	4.2	155.1	2,750	93	136	3,906	24,940	53,371	5,371
Pike	136.0	4,775	54.3	20.5	2.3	3.4	5.2	25.3	889	63	71	1,388	11,260	43,783	3,926
Portage	676.4	4,190	37.6	28.6	4.0	3.4	4.1	295.0	1,827	345	407	14,769	75,930	56,647	6,726
Preble	135.2	3,229	56.4	4.3	5.3	6.0	7.0	22.8	546	70	104	1,755	19,310	46,354	4,225
Putnam	148.9	4,353	62.5	3.1	4.2	4.4	6.0	72.4	2,117	65	86	1,521	17,400	56,919	6,459
Richland	480.9	3,920	52.3	8.7	5.0	4.8	5.5	209.0	1,703	644	292	6,962	56,810	45,832	4,681
Ross	234.3	3,026	58.4	0.5	5.1	7.8	4.6	264.6	3,418	1,668	183	5,091	32,430	47,035	4,687
Sandusky	231.1	3,819	59.9	4.6	7.5	4.6	4.8	105.5	1,744	111	149	2,916	30,090	47,234	4,648
Scioto	262.2	3,341	61.1	5.0	1.9	4.1	4.6	211.5	2,694	164	187	5,198	28,770	46,103	4,553
Seneca	196.2	3,502	52.9	6.1	6.7	3.7	7.6	729.9	13,029	127	135	2,532	26,570	45,066	4,252
Shelby	185.3	3,769	51.8	0.7	3.4	11.7	9.7	191.1	3,887	72	123	2,327	24,000	55,299	6,376
Stark	1,278.7	3,411	55.1	4.6	5.7	5.0	5.4	444.1	1,185	989	962	18,293	182,820	52,927	6,202
Summit	2,276.4	4,209	43.9	4.8	5.6	4.3	3.4	4,224.1	7,811	1,797	1,379	27,961	268,200	60,955	8,117
Trumbull	736.8	3,552	53.3	5.9	6.4	5.6	3.7	248.1	1,196	534	535	9,086	98,640	45,862	4,777
Tuscarawas	292.0	3,160	50.0	4.4	5.1	6.3	5.1	119.9	1,297	260	233	4,928	44,320	49,009	5,107
Union	256.7	4,870	31.4	31.2	3.9	1.4	6.7	364.0	6,906	76	138	3,560	25,880	73,226	9,526
Van Wert	130.4	4,536	67.9	0.9	3.8	2.9	7.3	64.6	2,247	49	71	1,454	14,030	47,229	4,559
Vinton	47.0	3,548	53.9	4.2	3.0	10.0	10.2	7.8	588	16	33	631	5,110	41,028	3,279
Warren	743.8	3,424	50.7	0.4	7.2	6.1	4.8	599.3	2,759	311	596	9,799	109,880	83,530	12,295
Washington	192.0	3,124	48.4	9.0	6.4	6.0	9.1	94.7	1,541	201	150	2,781	28,770	49,128	5,229
Wayne	466.4	4,061	44.9	24.0	3.9	6.3	4.1	103.7	903	262	288	6,689	53,810	52,329	5,604
Williams	124.0	3,304	51.6	1.0	5.4	10.9	7.1	67.6	1,801	84	92	2,069	18,260	46,088	4,417
Wood	538.0	4,197	50.7	2.8	4.6	11.9	5.6	402.7	3,142	209	333	11,297	61,300	61,466	7,508
Wyandot	101.5	4,489	33.1	34.8	4.5	8.4	7.7	18.8	830	54	56	1,485	11,160	49,087	5,032
OKLAHOMA	X	X	X	X	X	X	X	X	X	48,620	33,461	287,440	1,616,290	57,178	6,893
Adair	58.1	2,606	75.3	1.7	3.3	0.0	6.3	8.0	359	42	81	1,058	7,810	35,400	2,454
Alfalfa	13.7	2,424	57.6	1.3	4.0	0.0	1.2	6.6	1,158	31	18	575	2,040	60,884	8,178
Atoka	56.5	4,036	38.0	13.0	4.0	0.0	9.5	27.1	1,931	34	49	1,052	5,160	40,135	3,219
Beaver	21.3	3,811	59.5	6.4	2.9	0.1	14.8	3.5	632	26	20	462	2,240	41,617	4,367
Beckham	65.5	2,839	44.5	3.2	6.9	0.0	8.4	42.2	1,830	51	74	1,272	8,280	49,768	5,333
Blaine	43.3	4,420	45.4	22.1	2.7	0.0	10.7	12.1	1,232	51	35	722	3,860	63,489	7,761
Bryan	107.3	2,473	57.5	3.2	6.5	0.0	4.5	150.1	3,458	85	167	7,863	17,480	45,171	4,415
Caddo	102.4	3,449	54.1	1.6	3.8	0.0	12.2	21.8	736	527	101	2,213	10,580	42,534	3,775
Canadian	275.3	2,246	65.8	0.4	5.8	0.0	4.1	217.3	1,773	591	547	5,752	60,620	63,713	6,966
Carter	138.7	2,885	55.4	3.2	6.9	0.0	8.9	72.9	1,517	103	176	3,287	20,460	49,970	5,447
Cherokee	168.8	3,505	38.7	45.6	2.0	0.0	2.6	38.5	800	215	175	7,638	17,720	42,831	3,756
Choctaw	38.5	2,537	57.0	7.0	5.1	0.5	14.4	11.0	728	39	54	1,373	5,570	37,175	3,059
Cimarron	9.8	4,126	56.2	20.2	2.6	0.0	5.2	1.3	527	14	8	251	1,120	34,254	3,088
Cleveland	909.8	3,425	38.7	32.5	4.4	0.0	4.9	703.2	2,647	711	1,040	23,257	120,250	62,445	7,798
Coal	24.2	4,050	54.5	2.2	3.3	0.0	16.0	1.2	199	15	21	358	2,040	40,951	3,368
Comanche	515.7	4,080	36.9	40.3	4.3	0.0	3.0	244.6	1,935	3,867	11,484	9,960	47,510	46,081	4,279
Cotton	18.1	2,940	59.1	0.3	2.7	0.0	14.7	9.2	1,490	25	21	925	2,380	41,477	3,585
Craig	47.8	3,238	66.7	1.2	4.4	0.0	10.2	13.5	915	54	49	1,491	5,530	40,840	3,526
Creek	169.8	2,404	59.1	3.0	5.7	0.0	7.1	161.0	2,279	295	262	2,957	29,260	57,363	6,295
Custer	81.3	2,850	57.0	0.1	7.9	0.0	10.2	57.0	1,999	205	101	2,605	11,370	51,554	5,639
Delaware	80.1	1,934	71.5	1.7	5.9	0.0	2.4	56.3	1,357	76	156	2,673	15,750	45,201	4,438
Dewey	31.7	6,636	49.7	0.2	2.9	9.2	14.3	8.2	1,718	28	18	394	2,070	55,222	6,071
Ellis	30.2	7,367	36.1	47.3	0.6	0.0	4.4	13.0	3,179	21	15	344	1,670	50,777	5,078
Garfield	196.4	3,209	47.9	2.4	5.3	0.1	7.4	189.6	3,098	487	1,365	3,301	26,360	54,931	6,352
Garvin	89.3	3,271	48.3	13.4	4.7	0.0	8.8	23.0	841	80	102	1,493	10,790	46,110	4,409
Grady	154.9	2,916	45.5	28.8	4.1	0.0	7.2	30.5	575	90	199	2,638	21,460	56,468	5,881
Grant	14.3	3,176	61.0	1.3	3.6	0.0	8.2	4.8	1,069	27	16	319	1,910	47,987	5,425
Greer	17.2	2,824	46.1	10.9	6.9	0.0	14.6	3.8	617	26	17	526	1,810	37,030	2,906
Harmon	8.0	2,738	65.6	4.3	8.1	0.0	0.4	0.3	109	21	10	280	920	36,015	3,887
Harper	17.7	4,809	42.7	7.9	3.9	0.0	26.2	2.4	653	23	14	395	1,540	44,655	4,125
Haskell	31.5	2,434	63.9	0.9	4.0	0.2	11.6	2.2	171	55	47	569	4,520	36,686	2,977
Hughes	38.5	2,780	61.1	4.7	3.7	0.0	13.2	24.3	1,755	34	43	935	4,640	35,981	3,148
Jackson	175.1	6,672	28.3	40.8	3.6	0.0	5.4	32.6	1,243	1,390	1,383	2,230	10,430	49,553	5,130
Jefferson	21.5	3,367	52.8	2.1	2.8	0.0	12.1	30.4	4,768	26	22	317	2,080	35,806	3,034
Johnston	21.5	1,952	72.5	4.2	4.8	0.0	3.1	3.8	343	48	40	950	4,140	41,425	3,381
Kay	166.0	3,621	41.7	1.9	7.4	0.0	9.5	127.9	2,790	106	160	4,291	18,280	50,009	5,321
Kingfisher	52.9	3,526	63.6	1.6	4.5	0.0	9.8	16.6	1,106	44	57	874	6,760	73,312	9,993

1. Based on the resident population estimated as of July 1 of the year shown.

Table B. States and Counties — Land Area and Population

State / county code	CBSA code[1]	County code[2]	STATE County	Land area[3] (sq. mi)	Total persons 2018	Rank	Per square mile	White	Black	American Indian, Alaska Native	Asian and Pacific Islancer	Percent Hispanic or Latino[4]	Under 5 years	5 to 17 years	18 to 24 years	25 to 34 years	35 to 44 years	45 to 54 years
				1	2	3	4	5	6	7	8	9	10	11	12	13	14	15
			OKLAHOMA— Cont'd															
40075		6	Kiowa	1,015.1	8,729	2,526	8.6	77.6	5.2	8.6	0.8	11.6	6.2	17.3	7.7	11.0	10.9	11.9
40077		7	Latimer	722.0	10,231	2,405	14.2	72.2	2.0	29.0	0.9	4.0	5.9	15.6	9.8	11.1	10.2	11.6
40079	22,900	2	Le Flore	1,589.3	49,980	990	31.4	76.7	2.7	18.1	1.2	7.1	6.4	17.6	8.2	12.2	11.9	12.3
40081	36,420	1	Lincoln	952.3	34,920	1,305	36.7	87.1	2.7	11.1	0.9	3.5	5.9	17.9	7.5	11.4	11.4	12.8
40083	36,420	1	Logan	743.8	47,291	1,031	63.6	81.2	9.3	6.1	1.1	6.5	5.8	17.2	10.5	11.2	12.9	12.5
40085		9	Love	514.0	10,134	2,420	19.7	75.1	3.3	9.6	0.8	15.5	6.4	17.9	8.3	12.6	11.2	11.7
40087	36,420	1	McClain	570.7	39,985	1,180	70.1	83.8	1.4	10.8	1.0	8.2	6.0	19.7	7.6	11.6	13.7	12.5
40089		7	McCurtain	1,850.6	32,703	1,363	17.7	68.4	9.5	20.9	2.0	6.0	6.9	18.2	8.3	12.2	11.2	12.2
40091		6	McIntosh	618.5	19,815	1,835	32.0	74.9	4.5	24.8	1.0	2.8	5.6	14.7	6.9	9.7	10.2	11.9
40093		9	Major	955.0	7,644	2,621	8.0	86.8	1.5	3.5	1.2	9.5	6.6	18.7	6.7	10.5	11.5	11.0
40095		6	Marshall	371.6	16,806	1,989	45.2	70.1	2.4	14.3	0.7	18.1	5.9	17.2	7.7	10.1	11.3	11.8
40097		6	Mayes	655.4	41,107	1,149	62.7	73.6	1.1	30.1	0.7	3.7	5.9	17.4	8.1	11.9	12.0	12.4
40099		7	Murray	416.3	13,953	2,165	33.5	77.6	2.5	18.5	0.9	7.2	5.6	17.5	7.5	11.3	11.5	12.6
40101	34,780	4	Muskogee	810.4	68,362	782	84.4	63.0	12.8	25.4	1.0	6.3	6.5	17.8	9.0	12.9	12.3	11.7
40103		6	Noble	731.9	11,289	2,332	15.4	85.1	2.7	11.7	1.1	3.9	6.0	17.5	7.2	11.7	11.4	12.6
40105		6	Nowata	565.8	10,218	2,408	18.1	75.3	3.5	26.2	0.8	3.1	5.9	16.9	7.3	12.0	11.3	12.6
40107		6	Okfuskee	618.6	12,098	2,285	19.6	67.1	8.2	26.2	0.9	3.9	5.6	16.9	8.2	12.9	12.5	13.0
40109	36,420	1	Oklahoma	708.8	792,582	80	1,118.2	59.6	17.3	5.7	4.6	17.8	7.5	18.2	9.0	15.6	12.9	11.3
40111	46,140	2	Okmulgee	697.3	38,335	1,218	55.0	69.3	10.4	23.7	1.0	4.3	6.0	17.5	9.4	12.0	11.1	11.6
40113	46,140	2	Osage	2,246.6	47,014	1,036	20.9	69.9	12.5	20.6	0.7	3.7	5.0	16.8	7.5	11.5	11.5	12.7
40115	33,060	6	Ottawa	470.8	31,175	1,401	66.2	72.1	1.7	25.9	2.1	5.8	6.4	18.1	9.8	11.9	11.1	11.6
40117	46,140	2	Pawnee	568.2	16,390	2,016	28.8	81.9	1.7	18.1	0.9	3.2	5.9	17.8	7.5	11.0	11.5	12.9
40119	44,660	4	Payne	684.7	82,040	692	119.8	81.6	5.1	8.3	5.6	4.9	5.3	14.0	26.6	13.5	10.3	8.4
40121	32,540	5	Pittsburg	1,305.5	43,877	1,096	33.6	76.2	4.4	20.9	0.9	5.3	5.9	16.3	7.5	13.1	12.1	11.8
40123	10,220	7	Pontotoc	720.4	38,247	1,220	53.1	72.3	3.9	25.0	1.5	5.4	6.8	17.4	10.8	14.1	11.5	10.8
40125	43,060	4	Pottawatomie	787.7	72,679	749	92.3	78.2	4.4	17.6	1.4	5.2	6.0	17.6	9.6	12.9	12.5	12.3
40127		9	Pushmataha	1,395.8	11,179	2,339	8.0	75.8	1.7	23.6	0.8	4.2	6.0	16.1	7.0	11.2	10.6	12.3
40129		9	Roger Mills	1,141.1	3,656	2,926	3.2	85.7	1.8	7.1	0.6	7.4	6.6	18.6	6.9	9.5	12.1	11.2
40131	46,140	2	Rogers	675.6	91,984	644	136.2	79.4	1.8	20.3	2.0	4.9	5.8	17.5	8.7	12.5	12.1	13.2
40133		7	Seminole	632.8	24,578	1,626	38.8	70.9	6.3	24.4	1.0	5.2	6.5	18.3	9.1	11.1	11.6	11.9
40135	22,900	2	Sequoyah	673.3	41,179	1,148	61.2	71.8	2.6	29.9	1.1	4.3	6.3	16.6	8.2	11.8	11.7	13.1
40137	20,340	4	Stephens	870.2	43,265	1,107	49.7	83.8	2.9	8.7	1.1	8.0	5.9	17.2	7.5	11.6	11.7	11.6
40139	25,100	7	Texas	2,041.3	20,455	1,798	10.0	45.6	4.9	1.6	3.1	46.1	8.4	19.4	11.1	14.1	12.8	11.7
40141		6	Tillman	871.1	7,348	2,635	8.4	61.4	8.6	5.2	0.8	27.4	5.8	17.3	7.9	11.1	11.1	12.5
40143	46,140	2	Tulsa	570.3	648,360	104	1,136.9	66.6	12.1	9.9	4.3	13.0	7.1	18.2	8.8	14.7	12.9	11.9
40145	46,140	2	Wagoner	561.6	80,110	702	142.6	77.9	4.8	15.9	2.4	6.4	5.9	18.4	7.5	12.9	13.0	12.7
40147	12,780	4	Washington	415.5	51,843	964	124.8	78.7	3.9	15.3	2.9	6.1	6.3	17.6	7.7	12.5	11.6	11.2
40149		7	Washita	1,003.2	11,127	2,344	11.1	85.4	2.0	4.7	0.6	10.2	6.9	18.5	6.9	11.9	11.8	10.8
40151		7	Woods	1,286.5	8,897	2,510	6.9	85.2	4.4	4.0	1.7	7.6	6.3	14.1	16.5	14.8	10.3	9.5
40153	49,260	7	Woodward	1,242.4	20,222	1,810	16.3	81.2	2.4	4.3	1.0	13.1	6.6	17.9	8.4	13.9	13.7	11.4
41000		0	OREGON	95,987.7	4,190,713	X	43.7	78.4	2.8	2.4	6.7	13.3	5.6	15.3	8.7	14.2	13.4	12.2
41001		7	Baker	3,068.0	16,006	2,037	5.2	92.6	1.2	2.6	1.7	4.4	5.2	14.4	6.1	10.7	10.3	11.2
41003	18,700	3	Benton	675.2	92,101	641	136.4	83.3	1.8	1.6	9.5	7.6	4.1	12.1	22.9	13.2	10.2	9.8
41005	38,900	1	Clackamas	1,870.7	416,075	169	222.4	84.5	1.7	1.6	6.7	8.9	5.4	16.2	7.5	12.3	13.3	13.3
41007	11,820	4	Clatsop	828.1	39,764	1,186	48.0	87.6	1.3	2.2	3.0	8.7	5.2	13.9	7.5	12.1	11.9	11.3
41009	38,900	1	Columbia	658.1	52,377	959	79.6	91.3	1.2	3.0	2.7	5.4	5.4	15.7	7.4	11.6	12.3	13.6
41011	18,300	5	Coos	1,596.0	64,389	826	40.3	88.7	1.0	5.1	2.6	6.7	5.0	13.4	6.6	11.0	10.7	11.1
41013	39,260	6	Crook	2,978.9	23,867	1,651	8.0	89.8	0.7	2.5	1.2	7.8	5.5	14.2	6.4	10.4	11.2	11.3
41015	15,060	7	Curry	1,628.4	22,813	1,689	14.0	89.1	0.9	4.4	1.6	7.3	4.0	10.5	4.9	8.8	8.4	10.8
41017	13,460	3	Deschutes	3,017.6	191,996	345	63.6	89.3	0.9	1.7	2.4	8.1	5.1	15.0	6.9	13.0	13.2	12.7
41019	40,700	4	Douglas	5,035.6	110,283	551	21.9	90.5	0.9	3.6	2.2	6.0	5.2	14.2	6.5	11.1	10.6	11.3
41021		9	Gilliam	1,204.7	1,894	3,060	1.6	90.0	1.2	2.4	1.5	6.9	4.5	14.9	6.3	7.7	10.5	10.2
41023		9	Grant	4,527.8	7,176	2,648	1.6	93.5	0.8	3.0	1.3	3.9	4.4	13.3	5.6	9.7	9.8	10.0
41025		7	Harney	10,134.4	7,329	2,637	0.7	89.7	1.5	5.5	1.3	4.9	6.0	14.5	7.2	10.9	11.1	10.9
41027	26,220	6	Hood River	522.1	23,428	1,665	44.9	65.0	0.9	1.5	2.7	32.1	6.2	17.8	8.3	12.5	13.4	12.7
41029	32,780	3	Jackson	2,783.3	219,564	309	78.9	83.2	1.4	2.4	2.9	13.2	5.6	15.1	7.6	12.7	11.8	11.5
41031		6	Jefferson	1,782.2	24,192	1,637	13.6	62.4	1.4	17.0	1.6	20.2	6.4	17.1	7.6	12.7	11.1	12.0
41033	24,420	3	Josephine	1,638.7	87,393	662	53.3	89.3	1.0	2.9	2.1	7.6	5.2	14.4	6.5	10.8	10.3	11.3
41035	28,900	5	Klamath	5,942.7	67,653	788	11.4	80.7	1.5	5.9	2.1	13.4	6.2	15.5	8.2	12.7	10.7	11.4
41037		7	Lake	8,138.6	7,879	2,604	1.0	87.4	1.3	4.0	2.2	8.4	5.1	14.1	6.1	10.0	11.4	11.9
41039	21,660	2	Lane	4,556.6	379,611	184	83.3	85.2	2.0	2.8	5.1	9.1	4.9	13.5	12.6	13.1	12.1	11.2
41041	35,440	5	Lincoln	980.4	49,388	1,001	50.4	85.1	1.1	5.3	2.4	9.5	4.5	12.4	5.8	9.5	10.4	10.9
41043	10,540	3	Linn	2,287.1	127,335	501	55.7	87.5	1.2	2.8	2.3	9.3	6.1	16.4	7.8	13.5	11.9	11.8
41045	36,620	6	Malheur	9,887.7	30,725	1,417	3.1	62.0	1.6	1.6	2.1	34.4	7.2	18.9	9.6	13.4	11.9	11.2
41047	41,420	2	Marion	1,180.6	346,868	205	293.8	67.5	1.8	2.2	4.4	27.0	6.7	17.9	9.1	14.1	12.8	11.7

1. CBSA = Core Based Statistical Area. See Appendix A for explanation. See Appendix B for list of metropolitan areas with component counties. 2. County type code from the Economic Research Service of USDA Rural-Urban Continuum Codes. See Appendix A for definition. 3. Dry land or land partially or temporarily covered by water. 4. May be of any race.

Table B. States and Counties — **Population and Households**

STATE County	Age (percent) (cont.)				Population change, 2000-2018							Households, 2013-2017				
	55 to 64 years	65 to 74 years	75 years and over	Percent female	Total persons 2000	Total persons 2010	Percent change 2000-2010	Percent change 2010-2018	Births	Deaths	Net Migration	Number	Persons per household	Family households	Female family householder[1]	One person
	16	17	18	19	20	21	22	23	24	25	26	27	28	29	30	31
OKLAHOMA— Cont'd																
Kiowa	15.2	11.1	8.7	50.3	10,227	9,446	-7.6	-7.6	917	1,095	-540	3,839	2.33	64.1	11.7	30.6
Latimer	13.6	11.3	10.9	49.3	10,692	11,154	4.3	-8.3	1,016	1,040	-905	4,019	2.55	69.5	14.4	26.5
Le Flore	13.2	10.6	7.5	49.7	48,109	50,384	4.7	-0.8	4,981	4,971	-391	18,354	2.64	70.7	12.3	24.4
Lincoln	14.8	10.5	7.8	50.2	32,080	34,274	6.8	1.9	3,243	3,074	491	12,923	2.66	70.3	9.2	26.5
Logan	14.2	9.5	6.3	50.4	33,924	41,854	23.4	13.0	4,148	2,957	4,214	15,651	2.78	72.8	9.9	23.9
Love	12.8	11.1	8.0	50.1	8,831	9,416	6.6	7.6	1,038	939	620	3,104	3.13	73.2	9.9	23.6
McClain	13.4	9.3	6.2	50.4	27,740	34,508	24.4	15.9	3,535	2,800	4,705	13,838	2.72	75.4	9.1	21.2
McCurtain	12.8	10.3	7.9	50.9	34,402	33,154	-3.6	-1.4	3,795	3,403	-823	12,980	2.51	69.1	14.3	27.3
McIntosh	15.8	14.0	11.3	50.6	19,456	20,252	4.1	-2.2	1,766	2,595	406	8,349	2.34	67.3	10.2	29.2
Major	14.1	10.9	10.0	51.0	7,545	7,527	-0.2	1.6	838	700	-19	3,030	2.52	70.7	6.3	23.5
Marshall	14.2	11.9	9.8	51.0	13,184	15,836	20.1	6.1	1,554	1,582	1,001	6,241	2.56	69.2	11.0	26.2
Mayes	13.8	10.9	7.6	50.0	38,369	41,263	7.5	-0.4	4,071	4,108	-89	15,730	2.57	71.0	10.1	24.9
Murray	14.3	11.1	8.6	49.7	12,623	13,488	6.9	3.4	1,269	1,548	745	5,275	2.54	68.1	10.4	27.1
Muskogee	13.0	9.6	7.1	51.3	69,451	70,988	2.2	-3.7	7,597	7,627	-2,582	26,097	2.52	67.2	14.9	29.2
Noble	14.1	10.8	8.6	50.3	11,411	11,561	1.3	-2.4	1,084	1,104	-249	4,598	2.43	72.8	8.7	24.3
Nowata	14.8	10.5	8.7	50.1	10,569	10,536	-0.3	-3.0	950	1,162	-98	4,064	2.52	70.0	12.5	27.8
Okfuskee	13.1	10.1	7.6	46.1	11,814	12,191	3.2	-0.8	1,277	1,400	548	3,987	2.71	69.4	11.1	27.2
Oklahoma	11.8	8.1	5.5	51.0	660,448	718,377	8.8	10.3	100,792	57,411	30,826	296,818	2.55	62.1	13.7	31.1
Okmulgee	13.5	10.6	8.3	50.5	39,685	40,069	1.0	-4.3	4,048	4,269	-1,505	14,852	2.54	64.3	15.6	31.1
Osage	15.1	11.7	8.3	49.9	44,437	47,476	6.8	-1.0	3,627	3,853	-215	18,314	2.51	69.4	10.8	27.2
Ottawa	12.7	10.4	8.0	50.9	33,194	31,848	-4.1	-2.1	3,495	3,659	-499	12,020	2.55	67.8	13.2	27.8
Pawnee	14.1	11.0	8.3	50.4	16,612	16,579	-0.2	-1.1	1,613	1,717	-84	6,211	2.61	72.4	11.4	24.2
Payne	9.3	7.1	5.5	48.9	68,190	77,350	13.4	6.1	7,438	4,604	1,880	30,404	2.39	54.5	8.0	31.4
Pittsburg	13.2	11.2	8.8	49.0	43,953	45,837	4.3	-4.3	4,299	5,044	-1,184	17,828	2.38	66.0	11.2	28.9
Pontotoc	12.0	9.1	7.4	51.4	35,143	37,490	6.7	2.0	4,523	3,652	-84	14,512	2.54	65.2	12.7	27.9
Pottawatomie	12.8	9.5	6.8	52.1	65,521	69,443	6.0	4.7	7,544	6,661	2,386	25,925	2.64	69.1	13.0	26.7
Pushmataha	13.8	12.7	10.3	50.9	11,667	11,578	-0.8	-3.4	1,068	1,349	-118	4,550	2.42	64.5	9.5	32.0
Roger Mills	14.3	11.1	9.7	50.3	3,436	3,647	6.1	0.2	394	285	-100	1,350	2.75	65.2	11.3	28.0
Rogers	13.7	9.6	6.8	50.1	70,641	86,918	23.0	5.8	8,183	6,852	3,816	34,109	2.60	74.9	10.4	21.4
Seminole	13.4	10.0	8.0	50.9	24,894	25,482	2.4	-3.5	2,761	2,810	-841	9,240	2.66	67.7	14.0	27.8
Sequoyah	13.4	11.0	8.0	50.8	38,972	42,439	8.9	-3.0	3,789	4,207	-827	15,412	2.66	73.1	14.7	23.2
Stephens	14.4	11.0	8.9	51.7	43,182	45,048	4.3	-4.0	4,451	4,595	-1,617	17,252	2.53	67.2	11.0	28.8
Texas	10.7	6.8	4.9	46.5	20,107	20,640	2.7	-0.9	2,978	1,249	-1,957	6,989	2.99	66.5	8.9	28.4
Tillman	14.3	11.2	8.8	49.6	9,287	7,991	-14.0	-8.0	780	758	-671	3,012	2.40	67.8	14.9	26.2
Tulsa	12.1	8.5	5.9	51.2	563,299	603,437	7.1	7.4	77,817	47,248	14,676	250,071	2.52	63.3	13.4	30.4
Wagoner	13.2	10.0	6.3	50.5	57,491	73,082	27.1	9.6	7,311	5,242	4,966	28,309	2.70	74.8	11.0	20.8
Washington	13.6	10.2	9.3	51.3	48,996	50,977	4.0	1.7	5,280	5,068	694	20,688	2.47	67.2	11.4	28.4
Washita	15.2	9.7	8.3	50.4	11,508	11,629	1.1	-4.3	1,263	1,163	-607	4,484	2.52	71.2	11.2	25.4
Woods	11.4	8.7	8.4	46.7	9,089	8,878	-2.3	0.2	873	792	-75	3,413	2.43	61.1	10.0	28.8
Woodward	12.4	8.5	7.2	47.4	18,486	20,081	8.6	0.7	2,485	1,636	-737	7,366	2.72	71.5	10.4	24.2
OREGON	13.0	10.7	6.9	50.4	3,421,399	3,831,075	12.0	9.4	374,486	283,146	267,949	1,571,631	2.50	63.3	10.3	27.7
Baker	15.6	15.0	11.4	49.1	16,741	16,131	-3.6	-0.8	1,355	1,680	215	7,033	2.19	62.9	7.6	32.9
Benton	11.6	10.0	6.3	49.8	78,153	85,582	9.5	5.1	6,093	4,644	5,051	34,775	2.38	55.9	6.2	27.9
Clackamas	14.0	11.1	7.0	50.7	338,391	375,996	11.1	10.7	33,541	26,820	33,368	153,822	2.58	68.5	9.2	24.5
Clatsop	15.6	14.5	8.0	50.6	35,630	37,026	3.9	7.4	3,424	3,238	2,546	15,976	2.33	60.6	9.5	32.2
Columbia	15.4	11.6	7.2	50.0	43,560	49,353	13.3	6.1	4,169	3,542	2,394	19,213	2.59	67.4	9.6	26.1
Coos	16.3	15.1	10.7	50.7	62,779	63,054	0.4	2.1	5,111	7,270	3,524	26,473	2.34	62.5	9.5	32.1
Crook	16.0	15.4	9.5	50.3	19,182	20,978	9.4	13.8	1,728	1,993	3,127	9,330	2.31	65.1	8.4	28.6
Curry	18.4	20.4	13.8	50.8	21,137	22,365	5.8	2.0	1,478	3,038	1,996	10,382	2.13	55.8	7.1	36.3
Deschutes	14.1	12.7	7.3	50.5	115,367	157,730	36.7	21.7	14,534	11,384	30,773	69,631	2.50	67.3	9.3	24.5
Douglas	15.4	14.8	11.0	50.7	100,399	107,684	7.3	2.4	8,972	11,714	5,430	44,828	2.36	65.5	11.6	26.6
Gilliam	18.0	15.2	12.6	48.9	1,915	1,873	-2.2	1.1	147	160	31	805	2.35	63.6	8.6	31.2
Grant	16.7	16.7	13.7	50.0	7,935	7,444	-6.2	-3.6	507	684	-90	3,176	2.21	63.0	7.6	30.6
Harney	14.9	13.9	10.6	49.0	7,609	7,422	-2.5	-1.3	676	680	-89	3,079	2.28	66.1	8.6	24.3
Hood River	13.4	9.3	6.4	50.0	20,411	22,346	9.5	4.8	2,312	1,454	231	8,543	2.57	64.7	7.4	26.4
Jackson	14.0	13.0	8.9	51.2	181,269	203,205	12.1	8.1	19,165	18,868	16,066	86,195	2.42	63.8	11.5	28.7
Jefferson	13.7	12.0	7.4	48.4	19,009	21,723	14.3	11.4	2,367	1,695	1,790	7,628	2.87	70.8	15.0	23.5
Josephine	15.5	15.1	10.9	51.2	75,726	82,718	9.2	5.7	6,978	9,741	7,434	35,614	2.34	63.8	10.9	28.4
Klamath	14.2	12.9	8.3	50.0	63,775	66,380	4.1	1.9	6,659	6,256	902	27,171	2.39	64.7	10.9	26.9
Lake	16.2	14.6	10.7	46.7	7,422	7,885	6.2	-0.1	609	704	92	3,522	2.06	60.5	10.5	34.8
Lane	13.3	11.7	7.6	50.8	322,959	351,704	8.9	7.9	29,371	28,191	26,875	148,752	2.39	59.1	10.1	29.6
Lincoln	17.9	18.1	10.4	51.8	44,479	46,033	3.5	7.3	3,563	4,815	4,578	20,674	2.26	59.8	9.3	31.9
Linn	13.8	11.1	7.5	50.6	103,069	116,676	13.2	9.1	12,160	10,073	8,595	46,265	2.59	68.1	12.0	24.7
Malheur	11.4	9.2	7.3	45.7	31,615	31,316	-0.9	-1.9	3,581	2,459	-1,729	10,262	2.61	68.0	14.8	26.9
Marion	12.0	9.3	6.4	50.2	284,834	315,343	10.7	10.0	36,639	22,323	17,384	116,077	2.76	68.2	13.0	25.5

1. No spouse present.

STATE County	Persons in group quarters, 2018	Daytime Population, 2013-2017 Number	Employment/ residence ratio	Births, 2018 Total	Rate[1]	Deaths, 2018 Number	Rate[1]	Persons under 65 with no health insurance, 2016 Number	Percent	Medicare, 2018 Total beneficiaries	Enrolled in Original Medicare	Enrolled in Medicare Advantage	Serious crimes known to police[2], 2016 Total Number	Rate[3]
	32	33	34	35	36	37	38	39	40	41	42	43	44	45
OKLAHOMA— Cont'd														
Kiowa	171	8,622	0.87	94	10.8	112	12.8	1,191	16.7	2,195	2,009	186	140	1,548
Latimer	574	10,364	0.93	119	11.6	107	10.5	1,421	17.9	2,446	2,225	221	126	1,223
Le Flore	1,613	45,850	0.78	622	12.4	689	13.8	8,839	22.3	10,733	9,072	1,661	1,290	2,623
Lincoln	386	29,030	0.60	371	10.6	356	10.2	4,865	17.0	7,131	5,636	1,495	569	1,625
Logan	2,156	34,935	0.50	519	11.0	374	7.9	5,238	13.9	8,129	6,258	1,871	925	1,985
Love	88	11,576	1.44	133	13.1	119	11.7	1,329	16.4	2,236	2,074	162	109	1,100
McClain	194	31,772	0.65	447	11.2	368	9.2	4,775	14.6	7,207	6,138	1,069	902	2,338
McCurtain	454	32,777	0.98	454	13.9	455	13.9	5,532	20.8	7,248	6,715	533	1,110	3,378
McIntosh	345	18,019	0.73	215	10.9	312	15.7	3,029	20.7	5,928	5,223	705	495	2,496
Major	77	7,505	0.93	92	12.0	70	9.2	964	15.5	1,658	1,583	75	81	1,040
Marshall	329	15,194	0.84	198	11.8	159	9.5	2,751	21.9	3,837	3,472	365	364	2,243
Mayes	565	39,641	0.92	470	11.4	554	13.5	5,665	17.0	8,826	7,248	1,578	680	1,675
Murray	313	13,077	0.88	140	10.0	198	14.2	1,770	16.0	3,145	2,952	193	265	1,899
Muskogee	3,505	73,675	1.16	845	12.4	884	12.9	10,496	19.2	15,204	13,237	1,967	2,320	3,359
Noble	273	11,628	1.04	126	11.2	128	11.3	1,334	14.5	2,494	2,348	146	216	1,879
Nowata	157	8,556	0.55	113	11.1	150	14.7	1,535	18.6	2,478	2,206	272	165	1,573
Okfuskee	1,227	11,177	0.74	121	10.0	158	13.1	1,707	18.7	2,589	2,327	262	298	2,460
Oklahoma	15,000	882,973	1.30	11,753	14.8	7,065	8.9	105,836	15.8	125,655	93,286	32,369	32,112	4,093
Okmulgee	1,376	36,240	0.80	432	11.3	530	13.8	5,418	17.5	9,023	7,359	1,664	1,188	3,061
Osage	1,500	38,287	0.52	409	8.7	537	11.4	5,536	15.0	9,522	7,265	2,257	1,243	2,604
Ottawa	969	31,633	0.99	374	12.0	499	16.0	4,639	18.5	7,925	6,658	1,267	NA	NA
Pawnee	194	14,015	0.62	188	11.5	196	12.0	2,214	16.6	3,794	3,337	457	217	1,329
Payne	7,794	83,056	1.07	844	10.3	600	7.3	10,092	15.7	11,731	11,251	480	2,757	3,398
Pittsburg	2,419	45,501	1.05	489	11.1	597	13.6	5,580	16.5	9,828	8,692	1,136	1,444	3,270
Pontotoc	1,703	39,940	1.10	541	14.1	513	13.4	5,423	17.6	7,800	7,331	469	930	2,439
Pottawatomie	3,049	68,555	0.90	867	11.9	810	11.1	9,558	16.5	14,785	11,414	3,371	2,487	3,456
Pushmataha	110	10,222	0.78	118	10.6	154	13.8	1,681	19.9	3,060	2,827	233	115	1,041
Roger Mills	11	3,705	0.98	40	10.9	23	6.3	450	15.4	739	710	29	59	1,553
Rogers	1,216	76,825	0.69	970	10.5	839	9.1	9,881	12.9	17,621	13,707	3,914	1,822	2,000
Seminole	581	24,390	0.91	319	13.0	331	13.5	3,814	18.9	5,348	4,610	738	653	2,567
Sequoyah	463	36,340	0.67	516	12.5	564	13.7	6,673	19.9	9,571	7,906	1,665	1,205	2,961
Stephens	540	43,896	0.98	497	11.5	546	12.6	5,740	16.2	10,276	9,027	1,249	1,407	3,179
Texas	574	20,953	0.96	367	17.9	130	6.4	3,950	21.8	2,622	2,522	100	319	1,482
Tillman	267	7,089	0.83	77	10.5	75	10.2	1,105	19.0	1,658	1,577	81	222	3,005
Tulsa	9,862	700,800	1.21	9,246	14.3	6,122	9.4	87,035	15.9	109,778	74,332	35,446	34,067	5,298
Wagoner	319	54,537	0.37	897	11.2	721	9.0	9,236	14.1	14,311	9,634	4,677	1,798	2,341
Washington	798	53,796	1.09	619	11.9	651	12.6	6,350	15.2	11,657	10,584	1,073	1,352	3,358
Washita	206	9,672	0.61	144	12.9	144	12.9	1,602	17.0	2,207	2,099	108	196	1,688
Woods	999	9,931	1.17	102	11.5	99	11.1	919	13.6	1,649	1,596	53	114	1,220
Woodward	1,232	21,809	1.07	264	13.1	263	13.0	2,441	14.7	3,544	3,365	179	497	2,282
OREGON	88,353	4,073,449	1.03	45,166	10.8	36,052	8.6	248,573	7.4	836,419	458,736	377,683	132,175	3,229
Baker	429	15,802	0.97	157	9.8	209	13.1	920	8.0	4,824	4,504	320	430	2,674
Benton	5,325	89,803	1.04	750	8.1	587	6.4	4,728	6.6	16,050	8,454	7,596	2,376	2,684
Clackamas	2,917	363,729	0.81	4,194	10.1	3,471	8.3	19,633	5.8	81,722	31,815	49,907	8,815	2,272
Clatsop	841	39,228	1.07	392	9.9	416	10.5	2,296	7.6	10,033	7,990	2,043	1,423	3,724
Columbia	458	40,627	0.54	537	10.3	480	9.2	2,622	6.3	11,652	5,778	5,874	684	1,369
Coos	1,230	63,052	1.01	617	9.6	933	14.5	3,878	8.3	19,828	17,456	2,372	2,681	4,394
Crook	246	20,385	0.84	259	10.9	254	10.6	1,281	7.7	6,778	5,190	1,588	588	2,683
Curry	302	22,261	0.98	174	7.6	357	15.6	1,319	8.8	8,877	7,824	1,053	NA	NA
Deschutes	1,381	176,612	1.02	1,871	9.7	1,498	7.8	11,449	7.9	42,608	30,382	12,226	4,217	2,342
Douglas	1,816	106,443	0.97	1,075	9.7	1,470	13.3	6,018	7.5	33,026	21,657	11,369	3,103	2,864
Gilliam	28	2,024	1.15	15	7.9	22	11.6	72	5.4	521	479	42	NA	NA
Grant	109	7,039	0.94	59	8.2	83	11.6	433	8.6	2,228	1,884	344	136	1,895
Harney	140	7,210	1.01	83	11.3	65	8.9	443	8.1	1,971	1,812	159	228	3,165
Hood River	789	24,392	1.13	266	11.4	175	7.5	2,084	10.6	4,126	3,207	919	273	1,166
Jackson	3,630	212,258	1.00	2,293	10.4	2,343	10.7	13,352	8.0	55,159	37,173	17,986	9,958	4,616
Jefferson	945	21,982	0.91	281	11.6	222	9.2	2,101	11.9	5,391	3,973	1,418	461	2,004
Josephine	1,628	83,378	0.96	891	10.2	1,157	13.2	4,947	7.9	26,096	15,736	10,360	2,671	3,119
Klamath	1,033	65,320	0.97	816	12.1	817	12.1	4,867	9.5	17,138	12,768	4,370	NA	NA
Lake	470	7,797	1.00	67	8.5	74	9.4	486	8.9	2,202	2,049	153	NA	NA
Lane	8,786	364,420	1.01	3,577	9.4	3,589	9.5	23,734	8.1	85,230	41,827	43,403	13,360	3,669
Lincoln	822	47,830	1.03	429	8.7	618	12.5	3,371	9.8	15,858	12,737	3,121	585	1,572
Linn	1,084	117,515	0.93	1,523	12.0	1,302	10.2	7,159	7.2	28,686	13,799	14,887	3,429	2,810
Malheur	3,306	34,046	1.34	435	14.2	268	8.7	2,220	10.1	6,070	5,302	768	932	3,068
Marion	10,760	335,727	1.04	4,556	13.1	2,858	8.2	25,002	9.1	63,227	26,597	36,630	10,709	3,189

1. Per 1,000 estimated resident population.   2. Data for serious crimes have not been adjusted for underreporting; this may affect comparability between geographic areas and over time.   3. Per 100,000 population estimated by the FBI.

STATE County	Serious crimes known to police[2], 2016 (cont.)[1] Rate		Education						Money income, 2013-2017					Income and poverty, 2017			
			School enrollment and attainment, 2013-2017				Local government expenditures,[5] 2014-2015				Households				Percent below poverty level		
			Enrollment[3]		Attainment[4] (percent)							Percent					
	Violent	Property	Total	Percent private	High school graduate or less	Bachelor's degree or more	Total current spending (mil dol)	Current spending per student (dollars)	Per capita income[6]	Median income (dollars)	with income of less than $50,000	with income of $200,000 or more	Median household income (dollars)	All persons	Children under 18 years	Children 5 to 17 years in families
	46	47	48	49	50	51	52	53	54	55	56	57	58	59	60	61
OKLAHOMA— Cont'd																
Kiowa	66	1,482	2,019	3.3	52.8	17.1	15.0	9,056	23,076	38,191	62.4	1.7	36,003	25.3	35.4	32.9
Latimer	136	1,087	2,503	4.2	50.2	16.3	12.7	8,370	24,233	40,539	59.2	3.0	37,358	17.4	25.0	23.3
Le Flore	297	2,326	11,518	4.0	59.0	14.9	79.1	8,042	20,264	39,253	61.1	1.7	38,576	22.4	31.4	29.6
Lincoln	228	1,397	8,144	8.5	53.8	14.3	44.7	7,981	23,911	47,539	52.2	2.2	47,011	16.2	22.6	20.8
Logan	200	1,786	12,206	11.9	41.9	28.0	36.8	7,831	28,265	59,133	43.3	5.3	60,628	12.4	14.9	14.5
Love	121	979	2,365	10.4	59.7	14.8	14.8	8,054	20,965	49,409	50.4	1.1	48,312	13.4	20.0	19.2
McClain	163	2,175	10,065	10.0	45.0	24.1	52.9	6,909	28,353	62,081	40.9	4.1	63,787	10.4	14.1	13.6
McCurtain	262	3,117	7,614	5.8	60.2	13.5	60.1	8,730	19,040	34,250	65.4	1.1	32,092	26	34.4	32.3
McIntosh	328	2,168	3,783	8.0	56.9	13.6	26.0	8,640	22,241	38,163	62.2	2.0	37,210	19.9	31.4	30.2
Major	51	989	1,665	8.1	54.1	16.7	11.1	9,464	28,294	52,056	46.6	3.8	49,929	11.9	17.3	16.0
Marshall	154	2,089	3,666	2.7	53.6	14.6	23.8	8,033	22,431	45,671	54.6	1.7	45,133	15.8	23.1	22.4
Mayes	229	1,446	9,349	7.5	52.7	15.4	60.6	8,317	22,575	45,302	54.1	1.7	45,343	17.2	24.3	22.3
Murray	265	1,634	2,955	2.7	55.9	19.8	18.9	6,872	24,804	51,844	46.9	2.2	46,602	15.5	19.6	18.0
Muskogee	698	2,661	16,892	7.1	51.2	18.9	108.1	7,871	21,800	41,329	57.2	1.7	38,692	24.8	35.8	35.5
Noble	165	1,714	2,618	2.5	46.3	23.9	21.0	9,605	28,054	52,372	48.4	3.2	57,383	12.8	17.1	15.6
Nowata	181	1,392	2,338	8.9	57.7	11.5	15.7	8,399	21,491	41,282	60.1	0.9	41,183	17	24.9	22.0
Okfuskee	281	2,180	2,659	8.8	59.4	12.1	20.0	9,671	17,656	38,346	62.1	1.1	37,551	24.2	30.0	28.1
Oklahoma	601	3,492	202,472	14.2	38.5	31.2	1,032.6	7,608	29,127	50,762	49.2	5.0	51,389	15.9	22.8	22.0
Okmulgee	371	2,690	9,444	6.0	48.6	14.6	56.2	8,189	21,436	39,567	60.6	1.6	42,811	18.1	22.6	21.7
Osage	320	2,283	10,775	11.2	51.2	18.0	35.2	9,145	24,195	47,683	51.5	1.8	47,084	16.8	24.5	23.4
Ottawa	NA	NA	7,820	6.5	52.3	14.0	48.2	7,899	19,415	38,472	62.4	1.3	38,168	19.9	28.2	28.2
Pawnee	300	1,029	3,702	6.9	55.7	15.7	21.4	8,191	22,965	46,460	53.0	1.8	46,570	18.5	25.3	25.3
Payne	296	3,102	32,425	3.5	35.5	36.8	90.9	8,371	22,785	39,149	60.1	3.4	40,237	23.8	19.0	17.7
Pittsburg	303	2,966	9,432	7.1	50.6	16.3	69.6	8,798	24,408	44,941	54.3	2.3	44,194	17.7	23.6	22.2
Pontotoc	212	2,227	10,251	6.8	44.9	28.1	60.0	8,301	23,862	46,689	52.7	2.2	44,913	17.9	21.0	19.5
Pottawatomie	488	2,968	18,433	13.3	48.7	18.0	103.7	7,714	22,284	46,159	53.9	2.3	48,103	15.2	19.5	18.3
Pushmataha	172	869	2,306	4.9	55.7	15.2	21.4	9,671	22,596	35,414	64.6	3.1	35,695	20	31.1	30.3
Roger Mills	211	1,342	926	5.9	45.6	20.8	11.3	14,651	27,797	51,286	48.7	6.6	51,695	16.6	23.3	23.6
Rogers	210	1,790	23,091	13.7	41.8	23.5	108.4	7,693	29,824	61,320	40.0	3.9	61,731	10.1	12.8	12.1
Seminole	326	2,241	6,402	4.9	51.1	13.9	45.0	8,645	19,605	37,741	62.4	1.9	36,780	22.1	30.0	29.4
Sequoyah	354	2,607	9,305	5.2	56.8	13.8	67.2	7,980	19,253	37,455	62.0	1.0	37,755	20.5	29.1	29.0
Stephens	192	2,987	9,745	7.2	53.8	17.4	65.0	7,808	25,177	44,805	53.8	2.7	47,637	15	22.0	19.7
Texas	177	1,306	5,848	3.2	56.8	20.8	37.6	8,068	23,324	49,469	50.2	1.6	48,412	16.8	23.7	21.4
Tillman	244	2,762	1,702	4.8	59.0	15.2	15.5	10,215	21,422	40,728	58.5	2.4	39,581	23	31.2	29.8
Tulsa	777	4,521	165,366	18.0	36.6	30.9	966.7	8,050	29,797	52,017	48.1	4.9	52,579	14.4	19.7	18.1
Wagoner	212	2,128	19,195	12.0	43.5	22.7	45.9	6,975	27,337	59,210	41.8	3.2	59,466	10	13.0	12.3
Washington	301	3,058	11,995	10.7	45.2	27.0	71.5	7,710	28,913	50,388	49.6	4.7	51,691	14.3	19.9	17.5
Washita	353	1,335	2,485	3.5	52.5	21.5	19.5	8,772	26,409	51,900	48.4	2.7	44,970	16.2	23.9	22.6
Woods	86	1,135	2,273	11.4	42.3	31.2	16.6	11,539	28,322	57,097	45.4	2.8	49,979	14.6	17.7	17.9
Woodward	188	2,093	4,842	3.2	50.4	19.9	36.1	8,951	27,413	57,602	43.8	2.7	52,345	13.9	18.4	17.7
OREGON	265	2,964	953,282	15.1	33.2	32.3	5,955.9	10,437	30,410	56,119	44.8	5.0	60,123	13.2	16.5	14.9
Baker	75	2,599	3,154	15.7	42.7	22.6	23.2	8,639	25,820	43,765	56.4	2.0	43,929	17.7	27.1	25.3
Benton	129	2,555	32,974	5.6	18.5	53.8	89.0	10,043	30,873	54,682	46.4	6.0	60,572	16	12.0	10.1
Clackamas	160	2,112	94,517	16.4	28.6	35.4	559.0	9,502	37,551	72,408	33.3	8.3	79,404	8.3	9.9	8.8
Clatsop	141	3,582	7,864	10.2	33.3	24.5	55.3	11,091	28,115	49,828	50.2	2.5	52,706	12.2	17.4	16.2
Columbia	164	1,205	10,926	13.0	42.4	18.6	71.9	9,340	28,460	57,449	42.9	2.3	61,453	12.3	16.6	14.8
Coos	197	4,197	11,632	9.6	41.6	18.6	89.2	9,206	26,007	40,848	59.2	2.5	42,464	19.9	27.3	24.4
Crook	488	2,195	3,884	9.8	46.1	17.9	27.8	8,405	24,239	41,777	56.8	1.3	47,940	13.3	20.9	19.3
Curry	NA	NA	3,147	11.9	39.3	23.5	24.0	10,607	26,925	42,519	57.1	1.9	40,580	15.5	24.5	23.0
Deschutes	156	2,186	38,276	13.3	30.4	33.7	258.2	10,105	31,575	59,152	42.7	4.6	65,506	9.7	12.4	11.4
Douglas	226	2,638	20,214	13.1	42.9	17.0	153.9	10,807	25,002	44,023	55.4	2.3	47,157	14.9	22.6	20.3
Gilliam	NA	NA	396	4.8	47.0	19.2	6.9	25,835	24,178	39,831	59.3	1.1	53,792	11.2	17.7	16.5
Grant	98	1,798	1,151	7.3	41.1	20.5	15.4	17,504	25,154	44,826	55.3	1.5	46,329	15.3	24.5	22.6
Harney	389	2,777	1,568	18.9	43.1	19.2	17.1	15,455	24,398	39,504	58.5	2.7	42,883	15.7	22.9	23.3
Hood River	111	1,055	5,093	11.2	42.9	30.2	45.6	10,987	29,595	57,269	42.3	4.8	63,951	10.6	14.6	13.9
Jackson	349	4,266	44,872	12.6	37.2	26.8	291.4	10,053	27,081	48,866	51.3	3.0	51,364	14.3	21.0	18.3
Jefferson	252	1,752	5,019	4.0	45.0	16.9	45.7	12,325	22,957	48,464	51.8	2.1	49,616	17.2	26.3	25.0
Josephine	223	2,896	16,784	12.6	42.8	17.6	107.8	10,022	24,349	40,705	58.6	2.7	43,492	17.8	26.7	22.8
Klamath	NA	NA	14,974	9.1	43.2	18.9	99.0	10,259	23,793	42,531	57.8	2.0	41,875	19.2	25.8	24.2
Lake	NA	NA	1,282	5.9	50.5	14.8	15.4	12,677	21,005	32,769	65.9	2.0	43,627	18.9	23.6	21.9
Lane	325	3,344	91,349	10.4	32.4	29.6	472.9	10,444	27,032	47,710	52.1	3.1	50,711	16.6	18.4	16.6
Lincoln	161	1,411	7,570	11.3	39.2	24.1	52.1	9,954	25,782	43,291	56.4	2.1	45,435	16.2	25.8	23.0
Linn	115	2,695	27,809	11.0	40.0	18.6	192.9	8,560	24,448	49,515	50.4	1.8	51,888	14.3	18.2	16.3
Malheur	155	2,914	7,519	11.0	49.5	13.2	60.5	11,955	17,567	37,112	59.9	1.7	41,786	22.2	29.8	27.8
Marion	226	2,963	84,367	15.2	42.5	22.6	641.7	10,504	24,791	53,828	46.4	2.7	56,148	15.2	20.4	18.6

1. Data for serious crimes have not been adjusted for underreporting; this may affect comparability between geographic areas and over time.   2. Per 100,000 population estimated by the FBI.   3. All persons 3 years old and over enrolled in nursery school through college.   4. Persons 25 years old and over.   5. Elementary and secondary education expenditures.   6. Based on population estimated by the American Community Survey, 2013–2017.

Table B. States and Counties — Personal Income and Earnings

STATE County	Personal income, 2017										Earnings, 2017		
	Total (mil dol)	Percent change 2016-2017	Per capita[1] Dollars	Rank	Wages and salaries (mil dol)	Supplements to wages and salaries, employer contributions (mil dol) Pension and insurance	Government social insurance	Proprietors' income (mil dol)	Dividends, interest, and rent (mil dol)	Personal transfer receipts (mil dol)	Total (mil dol)	Contributions for government social insurance (mil dol) From employee and self-employed	From employer
	62	63	64	65	66	67	68	69	70	71	72	73	74
OKLAHOMA— Cont'd													
Kiowa	301	1.3	33,857	2,501	79	17	6	26	52	96	127	9	6
Latimer	340	-1.3	32,633	2,670	118	28	9	19	57	119	175	12	9
Le Flore	1,623	5.4	32,635	2,667	506	97	40	196	218	523	839	52	40
Lincoln	1,205	2.5	34,279	2,449	266	50	20	101	172	313	436	31	20
Logan	1,831	4.5	39,147	1,696	290	49	23	113	275	344	475	34	23
Love	369	2.5	36,756	2,086	221	54	17	18	60	99	311	18	17
McClain	1,704	5.4	43,323	1,099	374	63	29	135	242	314	602	38	29
McCurtain	1,045	3.7	31,857	2,772	439	80	35	73	133	355	627	41	35
McIntosh	650	1.3	32,909	2,626	130	25	10	38	108	259	204	18	10
Major	308	3.0	40,013	1,549	101	19	8	36	58	62	164	10	8
Marshall	534	5.0	32,465	2,691	164	31	13	42	84	172	250	18	13
Mayes	1,395	2.2	34,098	2,474	563	100	44	102	212	410	809	53	44
Murray	565	2.8	40,808	1,431	214	47	16	36	90	138	314	19	16
Muskogee	2,474	2.8	35,810	2,226	1,296	270	105	182	427	769	1,852	114	105
Noble	450	0.9	39,876	1,577	224	45	17	20	87	104	306	19	17
Nowata	355	1.8	34,428	2,422	65	13	5	20	55	104	104	8	5
Okfuskee	352	1.8	29,033	2,984	78	19	6	32	58	124	135	10	6
Oklahoma	40,303	8.0	51,149	407	25,448	4,168	1,919	6,747	8,046	6,189	38,282	2,043	1,919
Okmulgee	1,270	2.2	32,635	2,667	381	76	29	61	188	426	547	40	29
Osage	1,587	1.3	33,591	2,540	278	56	22	115	250	381	471	34	22
Ottawa	1,095	2.5	34,963	2,355	423	85	33	89	181	355	630	41	33
Pawnee	554	2.2	33,659	2,536	142	31	12	31	80	171	215	16	12
Payne	2,941	3.7	36,054	2,193	1,447	318	107	242	609	541	2,114	118	107
Pittsburg	1,631	3.5	36,903	2,057	774	162	61	64	314	444	1,061	68	61
Pontotoc	1,573	4.2	41,155	1,385	823	166	62	104	283	376	1,155	68	62
Pottawatomie	2,585	1.9	35,794	2,229	873	157	67	229	428	671	1,327	85	67
Pushmataha	351	1.1	31,381	2,820	91	20	7	28	53	134	146	11	7
Roger Mills	177	8.9	47,500	664	40	9	3	31	50	27	83	5	3
Rogers	3,981	3.6	43,539	1,074	1,276	216	100	266	608	745	1,859	117	100
Seminole	806	2.4	32,382	2,705	285	58	22	52	125	267	416	28	22
Sequoyah	1,342	2.1	32,540	2,683	286	62	23	79	225	438	449	35	23
Stephens	1,688	-0.8	38,961	1,727	610	101	48	129	383	442	888	59	48
Texas	938	6.5	44,861	918	388	70	29	228	125	114	715	30	29
Tillman	318	7.6	42,809	1,169	76	16	6	84	43	72	182	8	6
Tulsa	38,120	9.5	58,985	185	18,907	2,796	1,434	9,094	7,800	5,039	32,231	1,642	1,434
Wagoner	2,996	3.8	38,091	1,870	403	69	32	178	375	582	681	51	32
Washington	2,973	12.4	57,255	219	1,058	201	77	824	474	483	2,160	107	77
Washita	391	10.4	35,075	2,341	88	18	7	46	64	95	159	10	7
Woods	369	-4.2	40,899	1,415	163	34	12	21	123	66	230	14	12
Woodward	849	0.3	41,481	1,334	460	75	35	103	158	146	673	37	35
OREGON	199,422	5.2	48,093	X	101,076	15,949	8,838	17,954	40,569	37,700	143,816	9,096	8,838
Baker	627	2.5	39,026	1,718	213	46	20	22	157	196	301	23	20
Benton	4,118	5.6	45,273	872	2,005	401	171	310	1,073	581	2,887	176	171
Clackamas	23,220	6.6	56,268	242	8,969	1,229	786	1,918	4,742	3,034	12,902	837	786
Clatsop	1,676	5.0	42,774	1,176	752	131	71	195	348	424	1,148	76	71
Columbia	2,180	5.1	42,092	1,254	481	93	45	107	324	517	726	55	45
Coos	2,671	4.0	41,802	1,287	947	199	89	232	520	882	1,467	106	89
Crook	887	4.0	38,366	1,815	311	54	27	65	185	273	457	35	27
Curry	932	3.4	41,099	1,397	252	51	24	75	235	326	402	34	24
Deschutes	9,522	5.7	50,955	415	3,800	582	348	1,452	2,284	1,746	6,182	404	348
Douglas	4,240	4.0	38,752	1,766	1,625	309	154	273	799	1,395	2,361	175	154
Gilliam	88	2.5	47,614	658	38	8	4	8	19	21	58	3	4
Grant	286	0.9	39,797	1,589	101	29	10	12	68	85	152	11	10
Harney	278	1.7	38,177	1,850	96	27	9	23	61	83	155	10	9
Hood River	1,218	7.2	52,100	371	548	85	53	167	283	183	854	50	53
Jackson	9,647	4.7	44,360	976	3,870	643	357	1,041	2,173	2,391	5,911	404	357
Jefferson	749	3.6	31,543	2,803	274	62	26	21	137	267	383	28	26
Josephine	3,359	4.4	38,896	1,737	1,033	182	97	363	669	1,143	1,675	130	97
Klamath	2,573	4.6	38,446	1,808	972	191	94	177	479	812	1,435	101	94
Lake	300	1.7	38,091	1,870	106	30	10	13	76	88	159	11	10
Lane	16,275	4.6	43,430	1,087	7,083	1,245	644	1,556	3,420	3,736	10,528	695	644
Lincoln	2,028	4.3	41,448	1,339	743	137	69	188	468	573	1,137	84	69
Linn	5,049	5.4	40,380	1,492	2,031	355	193	383	796	1,434	2,963	201	193
Malheur	921	3.3	30,231	2,909	500	114	47	59	177	331	720	45	47
Marion	14,024	5.4	41,093	1,398	7,220	1,548	650	1,337	2,465	3,402	10,755	647	650

1. Based on the resident population estimated as of July 1 of the year shown.

Table B. States and Counties — Earnings, Social Security, and Housing

STATE County	Earnings, 2017 (cont.)									Social Security beneficiaries, December 2017			Housing units, 2018	
	Percent by selected industries											Supple-mental Security Income recipients, 2017		
	Farm	Mining, quarrying, and extractions	Construction	Manu-facturing	Information; professional, scientific, technical services	Retail trade	Finance, insurance, real estate, and leasing	Health care and social assistance	Govern-ment	Number	Rate[1]		Total	Percent change, 2010-2018
	75	76	77	78	79	80	81	82	83	84	85	86	87	88
OKLAHOMA— Cont'd														
Kiowa	2.1	14.9	D	D	D	6.9	6.6	9.8	26	2,410	271	352	5,145	-1.4
Latimer	0.8	11.4	12.1	D	D	3.9	D	4.4	27.9	2,805	269	406	5,016	0.7
Le Flore	10.5	5.4	2.7	5.7	D	5.6	3.1	D	33.5	12,030	242	1,943	22,154	3.3
Lincoln	-2.4	3.8	15.8	7	3.4	6.5	10.2	D	19.8	8,305	236	767	15,412	1.3
Logan	0	4.8	14.7	5.2	D	8.4	4.4	10.7	15.1	8,630	184	646	17,609	2.4
Love	-0.4	0.8	2.6	1.5	D	3.2	1	D	59.2	2,445	244	241	4,582	1
McClain	0.5	8.2	18.3	5	5.2	8.5	5.2	6.5	16.3	7,895	201	605	15,946	13.9
McCurtain	4.1	D	5.5	24.6	D	8	3	D	19.4	8,270	252	1,462	15,703	1.1
McIntosh	-1.2	D	7.2	1.2	D	15.8	5.4	11.6	26.2	6,445	326	765	13,804	3.4
Major	9	19.2	12.3	7.2	D	4.5	2.7	6.9	10.8	1,770	230	88	3,691	0.5
Marshall	0.2	0.6	3.4	34.2	D	7.2	5.1	8.3	15.3	4,240	258	462	10,337	3.3
Mayes	0.2	D	13.7	25.2	D	8.4	3.1	D	20.2	9,905	242	1,155	19,567	1.7
Murray	0.9	4	7.9	9	D	6.5	2.6	D	39.2	3,415	247	332	6,901	2.3
Muskogee	0	0.2	6.3	13.5	4.2	6.1	4	11.6	34.7	16,995	246	2,992	30,971	0.2
Noble	1.1	1.6	D	D	D	3.4	D	D	21	2,705	240	249	5,337	-0.1
Nowata	0	0.8	8.2	12.4	D	5.7	D	13.7	25.8	2,780	270	271	4,884	1.2
Okfuskee	0.8	2.8	12.1	4.9	D	4.7	3.5	D	38.6	2,920	241	601	5,319	0.7
Oklahoma	0	11.1	5	4.7	D	5.2	6.6	12.6	18.7	131,565	167	19,592	341,523	6.9
Okmulgee	-0.3	0.9	5.1	17.7	3.7	8.9	4	D	34.2	10,085	259	1,503	17,847	-0.2
Osage	7.8	5.6	11.4	6.7	D	5.6	3.7	5.2	31.6	10,525	223	826	21,944	3.8
Ottawa	3.9	0.7	4.3	11.5	2	6	3	D	40	8,765	280	1,502	14,070	0.1
Pawnee	-1.2	D	9.7	1.7	D	7.5	3.7	9.8	28.4	4,345	264	435	7,841	1.2
Payne	-0.3	4.2	7.1	5.1	5.9	6.7	4.1	5.6	42.7	12,575	154	1,350	36,818	8.3
Pittsburg	-0.5	8.9	6.2	8.8	D	6.3	3.7	7.2	38.9	11,095	251	1,518	23,197	2.5
Pontotoc	0.3	2	4.5	7.7	6.2	4.7	4.5	11	41.6	8,580	224	1,242	16,897	1.8
Pottawatomie	0.2	2.5	4.8	12.8	5.4	7	4	D	23.3	16,110	223	1,939	30,009	3
Pushmataha	-0.8	D	11.8	6.4	3.9	6	5	22.3	30.4	3,415	306	576	6,169	0.9
Roger Mills	-7.8	10.4	D	D	D	2.5	D	0.7	27.2	730	196	70	1,902	-0.2
Rogers	0	0.5	14.3	20.1	D	6.7	3.7	6.9	21.9	18,870	206	1,308	38,553	9.6
Seminole	3.6	D	5.2	13.2	2.5	6.1	3.6	D	23.9	6,080	244	1,005	11,704	0.5
Sequoyah	0	1	7.7	3.8	D	10.1	4.1	D	34.2	10,765	261	1,896	19,355	3.7
Stephens	-0.5	D	5.7	11.9	D	6.9	6.8	D	12	11,145	257	1,076	20,674	0.1
Texas	24.7	2.7	4.6	19.3	6.1	4.6	2.7	2.4	12.3	2,780	133	166	8,239	0.4
Tillman	41.6	D	D	D	D	1.8	D	2.3	17.1	1,805	243	290	3,997	-1.9
Tulsa	0	10.3	4.1	8.6	8.2	5.1	5.6	11.3	6.7	115,090	178	15,295	284,578	6
Wagoner	0.3	0.2	17.6	20.2	3.7	7	3.2	D	14.8	15,295	194	1,200	32,870	10.7
Washington	0.1	24	2.7	14.7	D	4.2	3.9	6.4	5.8	12,735	245	1,133	23,867	1.8
Washita	13.4	7	5.6	2.7	8.8	4.4	D	4.9	24	2,475	222	261	5,424	
Woods	1.2	24.5	5.3	5.2	D	7	5.9	D	25.1	1,685	187	89	4,411	-1.5
Woodward	9.9	23	7.8	6.5	D	5.7	4.8	6.8	12.4	3,905	191	259	9,034	2.2
OREGON	1	0.1	6.8	11.5	10.4	6.4	7.2	12.4	16.5	853,498	206	88,659	1,788,681	6.8
Baker	2	0.3	4.6	10.9	4.8	8.3	4.6	D	26	5,095	317	447	9,059	2.7
Benton	1.2	0.1	3.7	10.1	10.4	4.8	4.9	16.4	30.4	15,725	173	1,025	38,451	6.1
Clackamas	1.5	0	9.3	12.4	12.2	7.1	8.3	12.7	10	82,210	199	5,274	169,240	7.8
Clatsop	0.3	D	6.6	11.6	3.8	10.1	4.9	13.7	18.9	10,545	269	795	22,635	5.1
Columbia	1.9	1.1	9.2	16.1	D	8.1	5.2	8.7	20.3	12,465	241	1,040	21,413	3.4
Coos	1.1	0.1	6.2	7.4	3.8	8.3	4.6	12.8	28.9	20,990	329	2,398	31,177	1.9
Crook	0.9	D	10.3	6.3	10.3	4.3	3.2	8.7	20.5	7,160	310	498	10,924	7.1
Curry	1.9	D	7.5	9.3	6.1	9	5.4	8.3	23.7	9,255	408	669	13,022	3.2
Deschutes	-0.1	0.1	13.7	5.7	11.9	8.2	8.6	17.3	11.9	43,715	234	2,383	91,041	13.6
Douglas	0.4	0.4	6.1	13.2	4	6.5	4.9	14.4	22.9	35,110	321	3,534	50,563	3.4
Gilliam	14.4	0	D	D	D	2.8	D	2.9	22.6	545	294	43	1,181	2.1
Grant	1.8	0.1	2.5	5	5.1	5.3	D	D	49.6	2,345	326	166	4,430	2
Harney	5.7	0	4.6	0.3	D	8.3	1.9	D	47.6	2,095	287	238	3,908	1.9
Hood River	6.1	0	5.4	12.2	13.9	6	6.9	12.6	11.2	4,295	184	261	10,011	8
Jackson	0.5	0.1	6.9	8.6	6.7	10.2	6.9	19.6	14.1	56,945	262	4,827	96,241	5.8
Jefferson		D	3.3	16.6	2.3	6	2.8	D	39.8	5,665	238	595	10,190	3.8
Josephine	0.3	D	6.9	10.1	4.5	12.2	7.4	19.5	14	27,485	318	2,876	39,352	3.5
Klamath	1.4	D	5.4	8	4.2	8.3	6.6	16.2	24.9	17,970	268	2,168	33,681	2.8
Lake	3.9	D	4	6	2.7	5	D	D	52.8	2,300	293	245	4,541	2.4
Lane	0.5	0.2	5.9	9.3	7.9	7.9	7.5	16.1	18.6	86,650	231	9,634	163,472	4.7
Lincoln	0.4	D	7.1	6.8	3.9	9.7	4.4	12.1	25	16,230	332	1,272	31,701	3.6
Linn	1.5	D	8.1	20.6	3.8	8.4	4.4	11.2	15.7	30,455	244	3,616	50,883	4.2
Malheur	3.5	D	2.5	7.4	D	9.5	3.6	11.8	32.4	6,465	212	988	11,911	1.8
Marion	2.6	0.2	7.7	6	4.8	6.4	6.5	14.9	30.9	65,880	193	7,659	127,332	5.3

1. Per 1,000 resident population estimated as of July 1 of the year shown.

Table B. States and Counties — Housing, Labor Force, and Employment

STATE County	Housing units, 2013-2017								Civilian labor force, 2018				Civilian employment⁶, 2013-2017		
	Occupied units							Sub-standard units⁴ (percent)			Unemployment			Percent	
	Owner-occupied					Renter-occupied									
				Median owner cost as a percent of income		Median rent³	Median rent as a percent of income²			Percent change, 2017-2018				Management, business, science, and arts	Construction, production, and maintenance occupations
	Total	Percent	Median value¹	With a mortgage	Without a mortgage²				Total		Total	Rate⁵	Total		
	89	90	91	92	93	94	95	96	97	98	99	100	101	102	103
OKLAHOMA— Cont'd															
Kiowa	3,839	69.2	62,500	18.9	10.0	601	27.9	2.5	3,526	-10.4	149	4.2	3,911	31.2	32.2
Latimer	4,019	68.1	81,100	19.0	10.0	544	25.1	4.2	3,219	-5.3	193	6	3,863	33.0	31.6
Le Flore	18,354	73.2	87,200	19.7	11.3	610	27.4	2.9	19,120	-1.3	880	4.6	18,689	26.0	33.7
Lincoln	12,923	79.2	103,400	20.0	10.0	651	26.3	3.3	15,952	1	559	3.5	14,416	29.1	31.3
Logan	15,651	79.5	153,100	19.4	10.0	748	27.6	4.3	21,953	1.2	663	3	20,909	35.0	24.2
Love	3,104	78.4	94,600	19.2	10.0	694	24	2.7	6,451	-2.1	137	2.1	3,982	24.2	29.6
McClain	13,838	78.2	166,400	21.2	10.0	704	24.2	1.9	19,424	0.9	537	2.8	17,629	35.7	25.0
McCurtain	12,980	69.7	78,000	19.6	11.1	582	26.9	5.6	14,211	-3.8	776	5.5	12,423	23.3	38.0
McIntosh	8,349	77.1	95,300	20.0	10.5	576	24.9	5.7	6,865	-1.3	402	5.9	7,053	26.3	33.0
Major	3,030	77.8	94,000	14.8	10.0	662	18.2	3.5	4,005	-0.5	85	2.1	3,343	28.4	35.7
Marshall	6,241	75.5	86,600	19.2	10.0	648	21	4.1	6,705	1.8	252	3.8	6,347	24.0	34.8
Mayes	15,730	73.4	106,700	20.3	10.5	691	24.4	4.2	19,694	2.2	666	3.4	17,137	27.4	32.8
Murray	5,275	67.8	107,100	18.6	10.0	679	19.6	4.2	6,525	1.8	187	2.9	6,064	28.1	28.2
Muskogee	26,097	66.5	97,700	19.3	10.7	658	31.2	2.4	29,238	-1.2	1,181	4	26,861	29.7	27.3
Noble	4,598	73.4	94,800	18.8	10.0	716	23.3	1.5	5,742	-0.4	149	2.6	5,169	36.4	29.8
Nowata	4,064	75.7	81,600	19.4	11.0	642	26.9	2.4	4,633	0.2	194	4.2	4,250	22.8	35.8
Okfuskee	3,987	72.8	79,100	20.6	10.0	547	25.6	5	4,459	-0.2	213	4.8	3,875	26.5	32.9
Oklahoma	296,818	58.9	142,700	20.7	10.5	819	28.6	3.1	383,860	1.4	12,620	3.3	363,998	36.5	21.3
Okmulgee	14,852	70.7	80,300	19.5	11.5	630	28	2.5	15,918	-0.3	776	4.9	15,019	29.1	27.8
Osage	18,314	77.1	110,100	20.1	10.5	707	26.9	3.2	20,848	0.3	891	4.3	19,310	31.9	28.8
Ottawa	12,020	68.6	84,300	21.2	10.7	661	28.4	4.7	14,389	-0.8	498	3.5	12,898	28.1	28.7
Pawnee	6,211	75.9	87,500	19.4	10.4	694	24.7	3.8	7,411	0	306	4.1	6,606	27.8	36.1
Payne	30,404	49.5	147,400	20.5	10.0	765	39.4	3.5	38,700	-0.6	1,135	2.9	36,377	39.4	19.4
Pittsburg	17,828	72.7	98,400	20.1	10.1	689	26.4	2.9	17,838	0.3	693	3.9	18,265	29.1	28.6
Pontotoc	14,512	64.0	120,300	19.3	10.0	659	26.3	2.5	18,656	0.2	574	3.1	17,199	34.9	22.5
Pottawatomie	25,925	68.8	108,400	19.5	10.0	674	27.1	2.8	32,624	-1.4	1,203	3.7	29,570	31.4	25.1
Pushmataha	4,550	73.8	73,400	18.4	10.6	511	26.6	4.4	4,517	-4.7	233	5.2	4,237	29.5	31.8
Roger Mills	1,350	71.7	106,100	18.2	10.0	563	20.2	0.7	1,879	-0.3	45	2.4	1,696	29.6	28.7
Rogers	34,109	78.1	150,900	19.8	10.0	817	25.8	2.9	44,792	0.3	1,483	3.3	43,166	34.8	25.7
Seminole	9,240	70.1	71,200	20.5	10.2	600	26.5	4.7	9,514	0.6	451	4.7	9,310	26.7	32.3
Sequoyah	15,412	71.2	92,500	21.1	11.0	655	30.1	5.7	16,406	-1.2	707	4.3	15,611	28.0	29.6
Stephens	17,252	71.4	104,000	19.1	10.4	677	26.1	2.2	18,519	1.6	730	3.9	18,448	27.4	31.7
Texas	6,989	64.8	109,300	19.7	10.8	707	22.5	7.9	9,145	-2.5	252	2.8	11,355	26.5	42.1
Tillman	3,012	76.9	54,100	18.8	11.1	598	21.3	4.5	3,105	-5.2	116	3.7	3,129	30.9	34.7
Tulsa	250,071	59.1	145,800	19.6	10.7	818	27.9	3.1	322,030	0.6	10,765	3.3	309,735	37.3	21.1
Wagoner	28,309	79.2	150,400	19.8	10.3	835	25.7	3.1	37,252	0.4	1,244	3.3	35,839	32.7	26.0
Washington	20,688	69.9	112,600	18.1	10.0	687	26.1	2.2	23,014	-1.1	897	3.9	22,746	35.6	21.7
Washita	4,484	72.9	80,200	16.7	10.0	661	18.6	2	5,255	-2.3	161	3.1	4,933	31.6	30.5
Woods	3,413	67.0	93,100	15.3	10.0	646	21.4	1	4,632	-6	100	2.2	4,638	31.6	25.9
Woodward	7,366	71.6	123,000	15.8	10.0	768	24.4	2.4	9,286	-1.8	256	2.8	9,313	26.3	37.2
OREGON	1,571,631	61.7	265,700	23.4	12.1	988	31.3	3.5	2,104,516	0.7	87,361	4.2	1,885,983	38.1	20.7
Baker	7,033	68.3	145,600	21.0	11.7	658	28	2.9	6,976	-0.5	383	5.5	6,354	33.6	30.4
Benton	34,775	56.9	288,700	21.2	10.5	962	37.6	2.5	48,345	0	1,535	3.2	41,703	50.2	13.6
Clackamas	153,822	69.6	341,600	23.1	12.3	1,145	29.8	2.7	218,998	0.6	8,248	3.8	197,975	39.4	20.2
Clatsop	15,976	61.1	253,900	22.6	12.9	889	29.9	2.5	19,344	0.6	795	4.1	17,121	30.0	21.2
Columbia	19,213	73.0	223,300	22.3	11.4	877	31.3	1.8	24,387	0.5	1,239	5.1	21,362	28.6	31.4
Coos	26,473	65.2	177,300	23.7	13.2	754	31	3.3	26,460	-0.1	1,433	5.4	24,254	29.9	25.8
Crook	9,330	67.4	187,200	23.7	11.9	821	28.2	4.9	9,464	0.4	566	6	8,828	24.0	24.3
Curry	10,382	67.5	221,300	27.4	12.7	856	33.6	2.7	8,948	-0.3	549	6.1	7,745	34.4	20.8
Deschutes	69,631	65.3	298,200	24.3	12.3	1,061	31.4	2.4	95,367	2.2	4,020	4.2	83,721	36.9	18.9
Douglas	44,828	68.0	174,200	24.3	12.7	772	30	2.8	46,374	0.3	2,505	5.4	40,971	28.6	28.5
Gilliam	805	64.0	110,900	24.2	12.9	814	25.4	2	844	-1.4	33	3.9	751	31.0	33.2
Grant	3,176	73.1	155,400	22.9	11.7	643	25.6	4.4	3,099	-1.2	225	7.3	2,983	38.8	24.9
Harney	3,079	69.9	111,900	22.1	10.0	586	26.4	2.7	3,417	0.1	212	6.2	2,881	38.4	21.3
Hood River	8,543	63.8	339,400	24.9	10.0	983	28.4	5.3	14,533	1.2	485	3.3	11,263	35.6	32.8
Jackson	86,195	62.9	240,900	25.1	13.6	931	34	3.1	104,763	1.4	5,023	4.8	92,422	32.7	21.9
Jefferson	7,628	68.7	178,300	22.5	10.9	818	28.3	4.9	10,241	2.6	559	5.5	8,073	30.1	29.0
Josephine	35,614	66.4	235,600	26.6	12.1	847	35.2	4.2	35,929	2.1	1,990	5.5	30,300	30.2	24.7
Klamath	27,171	65.0	156,900	21.8	11.4	740	31.7	3.8	29,499	-0.3	1,897	6.4	26,034	29.0	25.2
Lake	3,522	59.5	123,100	23.7	12.2	647	28.5	2.4	3,496	-0.5	200	5.7	3,039	30.5	30.1
Lane	148,752	58.8	232,800	24.1	12.3	921	34.4	2.6	181,761	0.1	8,165	4.5	167,083	35.3	20.1
Lincoln	20,674	63.6	227,700	26.3	13.2	862	30.5	3.1	21,215	0.5	1,031	4.9	18,891	27.4	20.8
Linn	46,265	64.1	184,900	23.0	12.1	888	31.5	2.8	58,551	1.2	2,771	4.7	51,079	29.6	29.3
Malheur	10,262	58.0	127,700	23.7	10.7	668	32.3	5.7	12,493	-0.5	575	4.6	10,824	26.5	32.8
Marion	116,077	59.8	205,600	23.2	11.8	879	29.8	5	161,676	0.9	6,960	4.3	146,632	30.5	26.4

1. Specified owner-occupied units. 2. A value of 10.0 represents 10 percent or less; a value of 50.0 represents 50 percent or more. 3. Specified renter-occupied units. 4. Overcrowded or lacking complete plumbing facilities. 5. Percent of civilian labor force. 6. Civilian employed persons 16 years old and over.

Table B. States and Counties — **Nonfarm Employment and Agriculture**

	Private nonfarm establishments, employment and payroll, 2016									Agriculture, 2017			
		Employment						Annual payroll		Farms			Farm producers whose primary occupation is farming (percent)
											Percent with:		
STATE County	Number of establishments	Total	Health care and social assistance	Manufacturing	Retail trade	Finance and insurance	Professional, scientific, and technical services	Total (mil dol)	Average per employee (dollars)	Number	Fewer than 50 acres	1000 acres or more	
	104	105	106	107	108	109	110	111	112	113	114	115	116

STATE County	104	105	106	107	108	109	110	111	112	113	114	115	116
OKLAHOMA— Cont'd													
Kiowa	178	1,427	505	4	282	111	33	40	28,179	579	10.7	29.5	43.8
Latimer	167	1,644	327	D	248	70	63	62	37,521	707	30.8	5.4	38.0
Le Flore	751	8,236	2,771	350	1,558	395	284	269	32,691	1,672	33.4	3.8	40.4
Lincoln	562	5,048	484	652	770	427	128	179	35,440	2,231	32.9	3.5	33.0
Logan	842	6,312	941	414	1,151	258	197	208	32,940	1,262	33.4	8.0	33.6
Love	138	5,333	124	171	115	54	47	164	30,686	725	31.7	5.9	35.5
McClain	843	7,975	1,306	395	1,541	247	283	255	32,018	1,296	45.2	4.9	31.4
McCurtain	603	8,957	1,466	2,522	1,316	248	87	287	32,081	1,479	34.8	3.0	40.0
McIntosh	346	3,130	807	48	946	157	127	101	32,224	1,013	28.8	2.4	38.9
Major	262	1,873	237	58	270	74	62	74	39,584	801	18.2	17.6	35.7
Marshall	272	3,791	618	1,331	635	171	90	126	33,232	588	34.4	6.6	31.2
Mayes	785	10,181	1,049	2,865	1,832	313	409	402	39,495	1,552	41.2	2.8	35.7
Murray	284	3,556	563	326	647	141	71	121	33,941	473	34.7	9.3	34.1
Muskogee	1,419	23,234	5,675	3,340	3,501	578	549	864	37,199	1,586	39.3	3.2	40.8
Noble	212	3,883	361	D	324	171	47	172	44,353	835	20.1	13.9	37.2
Nowata	150	1,317	334	198	161	74	24	36	27,546	883	22.4	7.0	41.5
Okfuskee	165	2,543	1,687	119	226	79	20	82	32,127	934	17.8	7.1	38.3
Oklahoma	23,805	374,642	59,486	19,452	46,956	20,270	25,445	17,249	46,042	1,103	60.7	1.8	35.8
Okmulgee	668	6,795	1,505	1,357	1,290	325	195	211	31,057	1,404	36.9	4.2	33.3
Osage	572	5,397	733	315	821	163	147	184	34,000	1,395	31.6	12.5	36.2
Ottawa	596	9,493	1,466	1,614	1,029	347	318	286	30,144	947	36.4	4.1	38.5
Pawnee	257	2,642	476	209	461	86	D	121	45,661	818	21.5	8.7	34.8
Payne	1,837	22,905	3,510	1,513	4,306	904	1,086	725	31,657	1,541	39.1	5.1	31.9
Pittsburg	939	10,878	2,516	1,006	2,102	394	386	371	34,124	1,623	28.3	6.2	34.8
Pontotoc	951	12,525	3,445	1,240	1,700	465	856	444	35,464	1,438	37.0	3.9	28.9
Pottawatomie	1,328	18,613	3,039	2,801	3,044	666	665	571	30,672	1,856	40.8	3.7	35.1
Pushmataha	198	2,175	908	186	375	117	113	57	26,148	695	17.1	7.1	41.7
Roger Mills	86	462	D	D	84	D	12	16	35,364	612	4.1	31.5	47.7
Rogers	1,733	27,747	2,903	6,725	3,044	825	919	1,207	43,512	1,776	53.9	3.3	33.8
Seminole	442	5,219	950	824	796	217	186	175	33,581	1,143	28.2	3.3	36.8
Sequoyah	578	7,324	2,410	310	1,247	382	117	176	24,035	1,205	40.2	3.2	36.7
Stephens	1,070	11,904	2,300	1,182	2,019	677	504	424	35,591	1,226	22.5	8.3	33.7
Texas	497	8,076	452	D	910	256	101	362	44,850	828	7.1	33.1	37.1
Tillman	140	1,097	204	D	133	80	18	35	32,061	456	10.3	30.9	39.0
Tulsa	18,879	335,082	53,965	38,037	41,617	15,470	20,437	15,609	46,582	1,053	63.1	1.7	33.2
Wagoner	933	8,548	833	1,912	1,514	286	271	302	35,349	1,059	53.2	3.2	35.4
Washington	1,159	20,107	2,886	1,028	2,567	738	1,622	995	49,508	899	40.0	4.7	33.2
Washita	253	1,389	257	97	278	100	29	44	31,734	864	13.7	26.5	42.0
Woods	283	2,898	363	40	492	153	49	140	48,445	710	10.3	32.5	42.8
Woodward	753	7,242	1,092	499	1,336	298	164	318	43,890	843	17.4	25.7	35.2
OREGON	114,551	1,551,192	245,776	163,707	208,523	60,828	91,071	74,063	47,746	37,616	67.1	6.2	40.3
Baker	526	4,208	646	513	801	114	228	141	33,541	705	38.7	16.6	53.9
Benton	2,119	27,066	6,058	2,870	3,857	611	1,814	1,263	46,651	964	72.3	2.9	36.6
Clackamas	11,799	142,880	20,846	18,178	19,873	5,789	8,347	6,898	48,281	4,297	85.9	0.2	33.1
Clatsop	1,434	14,797	2,173	1,818	2,733	257	380	520	35,128	226	66.4	0.4	37.3
Columbia	904	8,237	1,439	1,482	1,513	286	276	283	34,384	789	75.8	0.5	30.0
Coos	1,557	17,908	3,960	1,435	2,907	417	420	658	36,769	559	45.1	4.7	48.9
Crook	514	4,037	516	726	607	98	119	138	34,302	620	57.1	12.1	40.2
Curry	687	5,235	1,056	716	1,034	163	121	169	32,311	200	39.5	8.5	54.1
Deschutes	6,889	64,536	10,752	4,739	10,796	2,123	3,179	2,617	40,554	1,484	85.4	0.8	34.7
Douglas	2,500	29,777	5,772	3,848	4,958	1,089	797	1,157	38,862	2,009	56.6	3.7	44.2
Gilliam	71	791	65	NA	109	14	D	33	41,650	153	6.5	69.9	49.2
Grant	228	1,482	408	D	229	88	69	52	35,230	383	34.5	23.8	47.0
Harney	198	1,419	402	9	294	36	71	45	31,952	532	21.4	30.8	50.6
Hood River	1,041	10,388	1,544	1,591	1,418	177	453	354	34,046	578	75.4	0.5	46.4
Jackson	6,107	72,083	13,909	6,515	12,152	2,074	2,323	2,741	38,033	2,136	78.6	1.1	39.9
Jefferson	383	4,017	589	1,191	533	62	71	136	33,898	397	45.8	12.3	51.0
Josephine	1,934	22,347	4,685	2,869	4,386	623	846	759	33,948	746	85.0	0.3	43.6
Klamath	1,507	17,435	3,210	2,107	3,027	1,023	687	683	39,158	1,005	41.9	9.0	51.5
Lake	190	1,175	286	206	155	34	56	45	38,340	381	25.7	29.4	61.9
Lane	9,819	125,284	23,710	14,334	20,136	4,732	5,472	4,998	39,890	2,646	78.2	1.1	35.9
Lincoln	1,536	14,146	1,784	948	2,862	284	314	469	33,178	384	66.4	0.3	37.2
Linn	2,564	36,488	5,526	7,367	5,427	941	909	1,429	39,153	2,222	71.2	3.1	41.6
Malheur	704	8,535	1,635	1,086	1,981	205	225	259	30,318	964	33.7	17.4	56.4
Marion	8,023	104,786	19,451	10,586	17,312	3,026	3,687	3,975	37,933	2,761	75.8	2.2	41.5

Table B. States and Counties — Agriculture

		Land in farms				Value of land and buildings (dollars)		Value of machinery and equipment, average per farm (dollars)	Value of products sold:				Organic farms (number)	Farms with internet access (percent)	Government payments	
STATE County			Acres								Percent from:					
	Acreage (1,000)	Percent change, 2012-2017	Average size of farm	Total irrigated (1,000)	Total cropland (1,000)	Average per farm	Average per acre		Total (mil dol)	Average per farm (acres)	Crops	Livestock and poultry products			Total ($1,000)	Percent of farms
	117	118	119	120	121	122	123	124	125	126	127	128	129	130	131	132
OKLAHOMA— Cont'd																
Kiowa	583	-1.8	1,006	0.6	302.0	1,262,052	1,254	189,899	98.2	169,539	39.3	60.7	1	76.3	7,426	57.7
Latimer	214	-3.1	302	0.3	38.8	542,932	1,796	63,905	35.4	50,122	4.7	95.3	NA	73.3	273	4.1
Le Flore	381	-3.6	228	1.8	116.2	492,429	2,162	72,515	273.6	163,654	4.2	95.8	NA	72.5	1,040	9.4
Lincoln	482	6.0	216	0.4	132.2	483,860	2,241	65,793	45.5	20,379	21.5	78.5	NA	75.9	733	9.2
Logan	393	6.9	311	0.6	154.8	696,903	2,240	77,436	44.8	35,496	36.2	63.8	NA	77.7	1,801	27.4
Love	203	-7.7	279	1.2	42.0	685,961	2,455	65,841	22.1	30,510	17.1	82.9	NA	68.0	763	14.3
McClain	286	1.2	221	0.4	85.4	582,207	2,636	67,571	42.7	32,955	24.6	75.4	NA	77.5	1,093	12.8
McCurtain	342	8.1	231	2.6	84.9	495,237	2,141	75,986	198.1	133,921	5.7	94.3	NA	70.1	1,705	8.4
McIntosh	226	-4.4	223	1.5	54.2	423,234	1,901	58,461	21.3	20,986	8.8	91.2	NA	64.8	881	14.8
Major	525	-2.2	655	17.9	218.6	972,803	1,484	137,306	107.3	133,939	24.0	76.0	1	77.2	3,562	47.8
Marshall	174	-9.1	297	1.4	31.9	718,380	2,422	59,885	12.1	20,634	16.1	83.9	NA	69.9	348	11.2
Mayes	271	-4.9	175	0.1	90.6	485,811	2,780	62,555	79.4	51,154	9.4	90.6	NA	73.8	722	8.1
Murray	209	0.6	443	0.3	28.3	946,663	2,138	84,584	16.6	35,197	9.6	90.4	NA	72.7	997	25.4
Muskogee	312	-11.0	197	8.8	95.8	443,351	2,256	60,372	47.4	29,912	28.7	71.3	1	72.5	1,872	25.7
Noble	449	1.4	538	9.1	193.6	956,821	1,779	113,383	61.4	73,519	40.7	59.3	NA	69.8	4,528	49.5
Nowata	347	18.6	392	0.1	60.5	809,467	2,063	73,048	54.0	61,142	11.1	88.9	NA	75.0	993	16.2
Okfuskee	347	8.6	372	1.6	75.1	637,122	1,713	75,997	33.3	35,617	17.2	82.8	NA	70.0	654	13.5
Oklahoma	133	-7.5	121	1.4	38.9	783,977	6,480	58,975	21.5	19,447	68.1	31.9	5	78.5	261	7.0
Okmulgee	296	-1.4	211	0.4	72.4	466,316	2,212	58,324	31.0	22,078	20.3	79.7	NA	72.4	337	5.0
Osage	1,101	-9.5	789	1.0	100.0	1,257,014	1,592	62,815	111.9	80,201	8.5	91.5	NA	72.7	3,951	13.7
Ottawa	206	6.6	217	0.2	92.8	603,803	2,776	82,877	139.7	147,558	49.8	50.2	NA	72.4	1,974	23.4
Pawnee	322	12.6	394	0.3	66.9	701,747	1,783	75,890	34.8	42,484	16.8	83.2	NA	68.1	1,780	25.2
Payne	341	-2.6	221	0.7	95.5	535,511	2,421	65,835	41.4	26,870	11.2	88.8	2	75.9	1,060	13.6
Pittsburg	519	-1.0	320	0.3	92.0	559,812	1,752	67,533	42.7	26,302	10.4	89.6	NA	68.6	573	6.8
Pontotoc	320	-1.3	223	0.4	69.3	482,701	2,168	54,476	26.1	18,182	16.5	83.5	NA	71.3	431	11.9
Pottawatomie	346	3.3	186	0.7	83.7	420,405	2,254	62,144	32.6	17,566	22.2	77.8	NA	76.8	1,272	8.9
Pushmataha	263	-11.4	379	0.6	34.0	584,413	1,542	55,456	16.4	23,535	5.7	94.3	NA	69.5	377	8.6
Roger Mills	730	1.5	1,193	3.0	123.4	1,529,868	1,282	106,486	58.5	95,533	17.8	82.2	NA	69.8	2,259	54.7
Rogers	299	-0.8	169	1.2	70.5	490,477	2,910	57,314	52.1	29,346	14.2	85.8	NA	80.0	1,091	6.6
Seminole	266	9.2	232	0.4	50.7	423,540	1,823	58,027	21.6	18,891	11.8	88.2	NA	69.9	657	20.2
Sequoyah	217	0.7	180	7.1	68.0	393,733	2,191	72,790	57.7	47,909	24.9	75.1	4	71.0	446	4.4
Stephens	462	-3.8	377	D	85.1	663,214	1,759	66,173	49.2	40,144	8.9	91.1	1	67.9	2,866	18.4
Texas	1,278	-0.7	1,544	168.8	680.0	1,563,361	1,013	210,974	1,135.7	1,371,593	11.0	89.0	NA	70.9	16,336	72.2
Tillman	557	2.9	1,221	33.0	353.5	1,621,033	1,327	240,298	138.0	302,697	57.3	42.7	NA	78.9	10,974	71.5
Tulsa	113	6.6	108	3.9	45.9	626,847	5,829	51,688	20.9	19,803	78.4	21.6	NA	77.7	178	5.3
Wagoner	194	-2.2	184	9.5	100.6	520,155	2,833	75,163	45.9	43,381	65.8	34.2	NA	75.8	1,580	24.6
Washington	219	-5.0	244	0.5	50.5	574,708	2,354	62,352	35.7	39,665	18.3	81.7	2	77.4	583	8.9
Washita	643	1.5	744	6.2	379.1	1,105,614	1,486	162,962	119.7	138,559	39.1	60.9	NA	78.0	9,041	58.1
Woods	830	2.7	1,169	3.0	285.0	1,549,585	1,326	155,030	79.8	112,376	23.3	76.7	NA	72.7	4,795	53.8
Woodward	788	10.2	935	5.5	173.6	1,136,597	1,216	95,455	70.5	83,625	8.0	92.0	5	74.1	1,892	50.5
OREGON	15,962	-2.1	424	1,664.9	4,726.1	1,032,545	2,433	100,328	5,006.8	133,103	65.6	34.4	659	85.7	92,406	10.7
Baker	755	6.2	1,070	108.5	130.5	1,337,390	1,250	146,937	79.2	112,346	41.8	58.2	4	82.0	3,466	28.1
Benton	128	2.9	132	27.2	69.0	852,300	6,438	80,922	76.5	79,401	82.6	17.4	32	86.7	1,144	6.7
Clackamas	157	-3.2	37	20.5	83.7	788,181	21,514	61,085	376.3	87,575	81.9	18.1	42	87.2	282	1.6
Clatsop	15	-8.0	67	1.9	4.4	476,979	7,153	73,613	9.7	42,743	13.5	86.5	1	85.4	11	3.5
Columbia	43	-23.5	55	2.2	12.6	475,785	8,654	47,057	D	D	D	D	3	84.0	135	1.9
Coos	138	-12.3	247	10.9	16.3	753,383	3,048	74,373	45.2	80,877	18.3	81.7	19	78.9	79	4.8
Crook	800	-2.8	1,290	67.6	49.2	1,231,591	955	98,369	44.6	71,877	27.1	72.9	NA	85.5	869	4.2
Curry	70	11.0	352	3.2	6.3	1,245,333	3,541	82,278	15.8	79,000	55.1	44.9	2	73.5	307	12.5
Deschutes	135	2.7	91	36.0	31.0	786,080	8,667	51,257	28.8	19,386	57.5	42.5	9	93.2	90	0.8
Douglas	400	4.7	199	14.7	52.3	680,086	3,414	54,494	72.5	36,092	37.8	62.2	18	82.9	866	4.4
Gilliam	612	-15.4	3,999	7.7	249.7	2,878,695	720	320,066	26.7	174,242	69.8	30.2	NA	81.0	7,680	83.7
Grant	629	-4.2	1,642	34.5	63.0	1,699,233	1,035	103,621	24.1	63,000	13.6	86.4	6	77.3	1,295	21.1
Harney	1,557	3.4	2,927	166.5	233.5	1,996,031	682	152,672	82.3	154,692	36.0	64.0	7	77.3	2,706	30.5
Hood River	28	10.2	49	16.6	19.3	685,502	13,926	95,942	126.1	218,152	99.2	0.8	25	89.6	365	5.9
Jackson	170	-20.5	80	37.5	40.7	677,191	8,494	44,300	71.0	33,262	74.7	25.3	43	86.6	55	0.8
Jefferson	793	-3.0	1,997	44.5	77.8	1,707,699	855	196,826	67.4	169,866	81.2	18.8	6	84.9	2,162	23.2
Josephine	28	-1.4	37	8.0	8.4	672,056	17,992	38,200	17.5	23,456	49.2	50.8	27	85.1	1	1.1
Klamath	483	-25.7	481	165.5	147.5	1,052,207	2,189	151,621	192.6	191,640	52.7	47.3	83	84.7	2,033	13.3
Lake	756	15.0	1,983	140.3	166.7	2,143,381	1,081	255,011	93.9	246,441	47.7	52.3	21	86.4	829	18.9
Lane	203	-7.5	77	22.3	98.0	656,860	8,556	59,094	158.4	59,873	58.0	42.0	65	83.8	659	2.9
Lincoln	29	-4.0	76	0.4	3.6	415,466	5,498	38,118	D	D	D	D	4	86.5	239	1.3
Linn	315	-4.9	142	36.9	242.6	1,005,264	7,092	100,759	243.0	109,375	74.6	25.4	39	85.8	856	4.8
Malheur	1,093	1.5	1,134	174.0	210.8	1,687,999	1,488	241,602	353.3	366,521	47.9	52.1	8	86.0	4,477	33.1
Marion	289	0.9	105	102.6	237.4	1,292,998	12,367	142,613	701.6	254,104	86.0	14.0	46	84.9	1,995	6.0

Table B. States and Counties — Water Use, Wholesale Trade, Retail Trade, and Real Estate

STATE County	Water use, 2015		Wholesale Trade[1], 2012				Retail Trade[2], 2012				Real estate and rental and leasing,[2] 2012			
	Public supply water withdrawn (mil gal/day)	Public supply gallons withdrawn per person per day	Number of establishments	Number of employees	Sales (mil dol)	Average payroll (mil dol)	Number of establishments	Number of employees	Sales (mil dol)	Average payroll (mil dol)	Number of establishments	Number of employees	Sales (mil dol)	Average payroll (mil dol)
	133	134	135	136	137	138	139	140	141	142	143	144	145	146
OKLAHOMA— Cont'd														
Kiowa	6.38	697.7	8	D	D	D	40	286	58.3	5.5	4	11	1.1	0.2
Latimer	1.40	133.5	5	54	73.5	3.9	24	259	52.5	5.1	4	D	D	D
Le Flore	7.10	143.1	21	D	D	D	145	1,490	406.8	30.3	22	44	5.9	0.9
Lincoln	1.03	29.4	27	183	117.3	8.1	87	814	239.1	17.3	19	69	9.9	2.1
Logan	2.61	56.7	15	63	26.3	2.4	87	1,001	343.9	22.2	40	155	30.2	4.5
Love	0.83	84.1	5	12	9.4	0.5	26	176	77.4	3.8	6	D	D	D
McClain	1.38	36.3	18	103	38.7	3.8	118	1,389	463.6	37.5	27	66	39.7	4.5
McCurtain	5.60	169.5	27	97	86.7	3.7	100	1,156	275.2	24.4	19	78	8.0	1.8
McIntosh	4.59	229.6	6	28	14.6	1.6	68	847	289.7	18.7	12	D	D	D
Major	5.52	710.3	16	100	55.5	3.9	32	264	93.7	5.3	6	D	D	D
Marshall	2.29	141.1	5	64	19.0	4.0	52	542	159.8	12.2	9	31	2.5	0.6
Mayes	47.12	1,152.4	34	344	382.6	18.1	137	1,663	466.8	35.2	20	41	5.4	0.7
Murray	7.77	557.5	7	D	D	D	48	578	196.9	14.2	11	D	D	D
Muskogee	1.15	16.5	57	1,022	509.1	45.7	258	3,194	927.9	75.8	56	211	29.6	5.7
Noble	0.28	24.2	8	81	30.9	2.3	32	326	127.6	7.5	7	17	2.1	0.2
Nowata	1.16	110.1	9	79	33.6	2.1	18	129	36.8	2.7	7	22	1.3	0.5
Okfuskee	0.99	81.3	4	15	2.3	0.2	28	210	88.7	4.8	2	D	D	D
Oklahoma	104.31	134.3	1,128	18,305	43,903.7	1,065.3	2,909	42,001	13,117.1	1,116.5	1,136	6,497	1,502.8	293.8
Okmulgee	5.82	148.5	21	D	D	D	123	1,315	341.0	26.3	16	36	4.7	0.9
Osage	16.58	346.2	15	D	D	D	88	869	216.3	16.8	17	95	21.2	4.7
Ottawa	2.70	84.4	21	180	44.6	6.4	100	993	232.9	20.8	19	46	6.8	1.2
Pawnee	1.02	62.1	5	D	D	D	39	423	115.7	8.8	6	37	8.9	1.9
Payne	2.64	32.7	50	D	D	D	297	4,027	1,021.0	84.7	85	298	53.0	8.3
Pittsburg	5.90	132.3	39	D	D	D	176	2,047	603.8	46.3	44	181	34.5	6.8
Pontotoc	4.35	113.9	41	407	438.3	18.7	167	1,809	437.4	37.8	42	293	65.5	12.6
Pottawatomie	7.51	104.5	38	305	180.3	12.6	238	2,904	755.0	63.6	47	162	23.5	4.5
Pushmataha	0.53	47.4	2	D	D	D	36	328	70.6	5.0	7	22	6.2	0.7
Roger Mills	0.56	147.8	2	D	D	D	16	92	31.6	1.7	1	D	D	D
Rogers	72.73	801.0	73	957	1,885.4	53.1	205	2,530	777.3	62.6	77	222	48.4	7.5
Seminole	3.20	125.3	23	386	161.7	14.2	75	862	233.5	17.6	14	31	6.7	1.4
Sequoyah	4.46	108.4	14	D	D	D	118	1,179	387.7	24.9	14	37	3.8	0.6
Stephens	1.08	24.2	48	D	D	D	194	1,961	550.4	43.9	26	106	23.9	3.8
Texas	4.75	221.0	33	D	D	D	76	890	226.5	18.4	15	42	4.3	0.8
Tillman	1.11	147.7	11	100	83.8	3.7	21	177	27.8	2.7	NA	NA	NA	NA
Tulsa	0.00	0.0	996	14,271	13,182.2	854.3	2,315	36,091	10,454.5	894.5	919	6,119	981.5	242.8
Wagoner	31.31	409.0	36	244	117.8	11.4	115	1,360	389.7	29.0	28	41	4.3	1.0
Washington	1.85	35.6	29	173	194.6	7.4	181	2,270	652.2	53.8	42	195	29.5	5.9
Washita	7.10	608.9	7	131	49.9	5.6	46	283	86.0	5.5	8	69	9.5	2.3
Woods	0.74	79.5	21	186	218.8	9.0	46	465	168.6	10.2	6	10	2.0	0.2
Woodward	6.30	292.2	42	D	D	D	114	1,224	435.2	30.3	33	148	31.4	7.2
OREGON	567.04	140.7	4,393	59,523	48,325.3	3,233.0	13,879	187,402	49,481.1	4,831.5	5,644	26,016	4,649.6	902.8
Baker	3.27	204.3	15	84	30.5	3.0	86	797	198.9	17.6	10	39	4.1	1.7
Benton	11.95	136.5	44	346	452.5	22.6	262	3,455	731.0	82.5	105	453	53.3	10.2
Clackamas	134.35	334.6	563	8,015	5,388.6	456.3	1,188	18,541	5,125.3	486.9	564	2,440	451.9	96.8
Clatsop	10.00	264.3	22	210	110.4	9.1	284	2,756	704.1	67.4	75	239	30.4	6.0
Columbia	4.70	94.8	16	D	D	D	120	1,349	318.1	31.5	37	108	12.8	2.6
Coos	5.05	80.0	42	399	287.8	15.3	262	2,930	745.8	73.8	58	215	26.4	5.1
Crook	2.11	97.5	13	D	D	D	70	583	184.2	14.6	24	33	6.5	0.8
Curry	2.85	126.8	12	35	14.6	0.7	97	988	244.6	23.8	45	81	10.1	1.5
Deschutes	38.00	216.8	215	1,262	794.9	57.1	755	9,365	2,476.6	244.0	388	1,252	186.1	40.0
Douglas	14.20	131.9	54	D	D	D	378	4,419	1,103.4	102.1	120	329	43.4	7.6
Gilliam	0.55	295.9	5	D	D	D	11	52	10.5	1.1	NA	NA	NA	NA
Grant	0.97	135.0	7	D	D	D	38	241	67.4	5.6	10	20	1.2	0.4
Harney	1.72	238.9	3	D	D	D	27	279	107.3	7.2	8	22	2.1	0.4
Hood River	6.30	272.3	24	360	110.5	14.7	157	1,287	315.4	33.5	31	71	10.0	2.0
Jackson	39.04	183.7	206	1,771	828.4	76.8	865	11,223	3,202.7	297.5	306	1,043	164.1	26.3
Jefferson	4.38	193.2	20	194	156.4	9.5	47	506	133.1	11.3	24	65	6.0	1.6
Josephine	7.18	84.7	49	D	D	D	312	4,150	987.9	105.1	106	354	44.8	8.5
Klamath	9.45	143.1	49	533	210.9	21.0	237	2,902	757.5	69.9	72	199	23.5	5.2
Lake	1.56	199.3	8	D	D	D	30	200	74.9	4.8	5	D	D	D
Lane	43.68	120.4	384	4,860	2,852.0	229.0	1,270	18,265	4,291.5	449.9	505	2,115	314.3	58.4
Lincoln	8.65	183.9	27	D	D	D	307	2,758	580.8	62.2	74	320	40.2	7.0
Linn	9.57	79.4	110	1,396	1,066.7	61.3	343	4,753	1,181.6	112.6	112	360	48.5	10.2
Malheur	6.76	222.5	36	584	340.7	17.6	120	1,834	534.5	45.8	29	55	9.0	1.4
Marion	71.92	217.5	264	3,694	3,190.0	177.6	1,103	15,497	3,862.2	377.0	417	1,991	269.7	58.6

1 Merchant wholesalers, except manufacturers' sales branches and offices.   2. Employer establishments.

Professional Services, Manufacturing, and Accommodation and Food Services

STATE County	Professional, scientific, and technical services, 2012				Manufacturing, 2012				Accommodation and food services, 2012			
	Number of establish-ments	Number of employees	Sales (mil dol)	Average payroll (mil dol)	Number of establish-ments	Number of employees	Receipts (mil dol)	Annual payroll (mil dol)	Number of establi-shments	Number of employees	Receipts (mil dol)	Annual payroll (mil dol)
	147	148	149	150	151	152	153	154	155	156	157	158
OKLAHOMA— Cont'd												
Kiowa	16	D	D	D	5	D	D	D	15	D	D	D
Latimer	17	D	D	D	NA	NA	NA	NA	8	D	D	D
Le Flore	86	307	22.1	6.9	30	492	D	17.9	47	D	D	D
Lincoln	40	129	16.7	4.0	29	790	231.5	31.3	44	564	22.6	6.2
Logan	60	160	18.5	5.2	23	363	97.6	14.7	60	837	37.3	9.8
Love	14	D	D	D	5	111	D	4.6	29	579	53.8	10.4
McClain	72	269	40.4	10.4	22	385	103.5	13.9	62	1,110	46.3	12.8
McCurtain	34	D	D	D	29	2,477	1,342.0	91.7	53	691	37.0	7.5
McIntosh	37	D	D	D	14	62	9.5	2.2	34	465	20.8	5.4
Major	17	D	D	D	8	44	D	1.5	11	D	D	D
Marshall	23	D	D	D	20	1,097	245.2	43.8	28	289	17.4	4.1
Mayes	60	D	D	D	58	2,608	1,224.7	130.6	72	940	40.2	10.4
Murray	27	D	D	D	16	451	D	21.5	30	339	17.6	4.8
Muskogee	93	D	D	D	55	3,660	1,489.7	181.3	133	2,384	104.4	27.7
Noble	14	D	D	D	9	1,451	D	80.4	22	D	D	D
Nowata	8	D	D	D	11	254	D	11.3	9	D	D	D
Okfuskee	6	D	D	D	7	132	D	4.5	7	D	D	D
Oklahoma	2,947	22,906	3,372.4	1,360.6	701	21,353	7,681.0	948.9	1,780	39,515	1,909.4	525.0
Okmulgee	44	192	15.1	4.9	34	1,438	533.8	66.3	49	737	32.1	8.0
Osage	45	D	D	D	28	270	D	11.7	43	554	24.7	7.6
Ottawa	50	333	32.3	11.5	43	1,495	D	57.2	58	2,101	228.3	40.2
Pawnee	26	124	36.3	5.4	17	250	D	10.5	22	D	D	D
Payne	150	1,195	131.6	50.4	64	1,538	473.0	62.3	181	3,661	155.0	41.9
Pittsburg	98	422	46.8	18.0	31	999	332.7	50.2	96	1,560	74.2	18.2
Pontotoc	80	342	35.6	12.4	32	1,114	270.3	41.1	69	1,374	62.1	16.7
Pottawatomie	106	681	95.3	29.4	57	2,911	1,112.5	134.5	120	2,528	107.9	29.7
Pushmataha	14	D	D	D	7	85	D	2.7	15	124	4.4	1.2
Roger Mills	6	D	D	D	NA	NA	NA	NA	4	D	D	D
Rogers	135	782	110.8	44.2	150	6,775	3,040.1	365.1	109	3,258	308.2	77.7
Seminole	27	D	D	D	24	738	129.7	29.1	35	553	23.6	6.0
Sequoyah	41	126	10.5	3.2	22	104	D	4.4	59	D	D	D
Stephens	82	427	49.8	15.7	62	2,512	1,935.5	132.0	77	1,098	50.1	12.8
Texas	31	D	D	D	11	D	D	D	50	670	29.2	7.2
Tillman	8	D	D	D	5	D	D	D	10	86	3.5	0.9
Tulsa	2,382	19,526	3,446.4	1,198.9	903	37,197	18,770.2	1,997.1	1,519	30,477	1,425.3	414.5
Wagoner	72	199	18.0	6.1	61	2,163	746.5	111.5	69	D	D	D
Washington	89	D	D	D	36	965	253.2	53.4	111	1,831	91.0	23.2
Washita	20	D	D	D	10	39	D	1.4	14	D	D	D
Woods	23	D	D	D	5	40	D	1.9	33	332	19.2	3.8
Woodward	53	D	D	D	24	498	448.4	32.2	55	862	50.9	11.6
OREGON	11,663	84,493	11,386.1	5,841.1	5,289	D	D	D	10,610	150,482	8,466.8	2,438.5
Baker	40	172	18.4	5.4	29	494	105.1	18.0	56	557	27.5	8.2
Benton	284	1,996	332.6	125.1	93	1,613	412.7	71.4	209	3,087	142.8	41.6
Clackamas	1,231	7,805	1,215.9	525.9	553	15,789	5,371.5	901.1	777	11,638	637.5	188.3
Clatsop	87	326	22.1	7.2	47	1,671	905.8	103.1	248	3,138	210.1	59.7
Columbia	78	275	23.3	8.6	52	1,350	458.3	64.6	85	964	42.9	12.3
Coos	115	439	44.3	16.2	70	1,352	315.7	48.4	165	2,129	126.2	34.9
Crook	34	109	12.2	3.7	30	728	150.8	25.4	44	479	23.7	8.0
Curry	36	105	16.6	2.8	20	578	176.0	27.4	107	880	46.5	12.2
Deschutes	708	2,631	332.0	120.7	279	3,672	801.8	165.8	498	7,635	435.6	133.5
Douglas	157	777	64.4	26.5	126	3,640	1,017.3	158.4	262	3,391	217.2	57.2
Gilliam	3	D	D	D	NA	NA	NA	NA	9	68	1.5	0.6
Grant	18	D	D	D	4	D	D	D	24	135	6.0	1.8
Harney	11	45	2.8	1.2	4	D	D	D	32	186	11.5	2.9
Hood River	125	423	84.4	18.2	63	1,055	304.3	44.5	96	1,306	62.1	19.3
Jackson	506	D	D	D	308	5,370	1,624.6	217.4	586	7,381	382.2	112.5
Jefferson	21	55	3.8	1.3	19	838	168.3	32.4	45	404	21.3	5.9
Josephine	140	563	40.6	13.5	106	2,190	434.8	89.6	199	2,483	124.5	35.8
Klamath	125	625	107.1	24.7	56	1,662	449.9	63.8	171	1,978	110.7	30.1
Lake	12	D	D	D	11	190	34.5	7.2	31	144	6.6	1.6
Lane	948	5,301	583.9	226.2	529	12,345	4,039.3	581.3	937	13,627	711.8	203.7
Lincoln	95	289	27.6	9.8	50	965	579.4	61.0	274	3,593	216.4	63.4
Linn	164	802	84.8	27.8	181	6,318	2,253.6	355.2	216	2,796	130.4	35.5
Malheur	46	185	17.2	7.1	35	1,078	D	34.2	84	1,008	50.8	13.6
Marion	664	3,815	448.4	170.5	352	9,155	2,540.3	347.6	667	D	D	D

Health Care and Social Assistance, Other Services, Nonemployer Businesses, and Residential Construction

STATE County	Health care and social assistance, 2012				Other services, 2012				Nonemployer businesses, 2016		Value of residential construction authorized by building permits, 2018	
	Number of establishments	Number of employees	Receipts (mil dol)	Annual payroll (mil dol)	Number of establishments	Number of employees	Receipts (mil dol)	Annual payroll (mil dol)	Number	Receipts (mil dol)	New construction ($1,000)	Number of housing units
	159	160	161	162	163	164	165	166	167	168	169	170
OKLAHOMA— Cont'd												
Kiowa	24	577	30.6	13.8	8	28	3.5	0.8	585	23.5	250	1
Latimer	25	357	23.0	9.2	8	D	D	D	773	30.5	22	1
Le Flore	95	2,706	202.8	86.1	44	D	D	D	3,038	119.9	6,718	61
Lincoln	57	D	D	D	21	D	D	D	2,488	109.2	1,572	8
Logan	61	D	D	D	52	176	19.8	3.9	3,664	160.5	1,334	9
Love	10	133	5.5	2.6	6	62	3.1	1.3	615	26.2	0	0
McClain	68	D	D	D	48	D	D	D	3,431	160.8	75,522	385
McCurtain	60	1,634	79.5	37.0	37	146	11.1	3.8	2,355	103.5	2,939	26
McIntosh	49	916	71.0	25.3	23	102	13.1	3.1	1,393	59.2	1,400	7
Major	14	231	13.3	6.4	11	D	D	D	699	30.6	1,333	6
Marshall	26	590	70.0	23.2	14	50	4.2	1.1	1,061	42.6	1,983	11
Mayes	86	955	101.6	35.3	46	132	10.6	2.6	2,616	107.2	2,712	19
Murray	31	595	42.3	16.4	11	32	2.8	0.6	919	35.5	1,429	7
Muskogee	230	5,700	616.6	250.4	84	587	57.9	14.6	3,905	169.8	4,559	24
Noble	18	395	24.3	9.8	13	66	5.4	1.2	822	28.8	0	0
Nowata	16	D	D	D	10	30	2.2	0.6	652	23.5	321	5
Okfuskee	43	1,619	104.4	30.0	10	9	3.0	0.7	735	29.0	755	5
Oklahoma	2,873	56,884	7,921.4	2,618.1	1,414	9,503	1,063.4	285.5	62,829	3,104.5	931,810	4,070
Okmulgee	124	2,032	117.5	50.5	39	174	12.7	2.9	2,281	89.3	910	7
Osage	42	732	37.4	15.8	24	76	9.5	1.9	2,926	115.0	27,420	126
Ottawa	72	1,402	110.0	47.6	33	138	12.5	2.8	1,762	71.9	632	10
Pawnee	29	459	27.8	11.4	9	29	2.8	0.8	975	36.1	585	2
Payne	160	3,570	305.4	118.4	109	763	167.3	20.9	5,325	224.0	23,610	129
Pittsburg	116	2,560	218.9	87.2	54	340	24.5	7.3	2,608	112.6	1,974	13
Pontotoc	130	3,418	350.1	128.5	46	194	18.0	4.5	2,757	121.3	3,027	29
Pottawatomie	167	2,451	257.4	100.5	72	350	27.9	8.2	4,302	194.5	14,205	88
Pushmataha	24	732	43.3	16.6	7	28	2.5	0.7	833	32.5	2,400	20
Roger Mills	5	D	D	D	3	D	D	D	367	16.9	0	0
Rogers	193	2,953	268.3	108.2	83	392	43.2	11.7	6,813	300.7	96,931	523
Seminole	43	1,079	81.4	28.1	21	D	D	D	1,393	50.0	1,631	16
Sequoyah	79	2,345	105.4	46.6	29	D	D	D	2,834	129.5	8,465	73
Stephens	101	2,121	177.1	63.3	69	361	68.5	11.3	3,072	134.6	4,520	44
Texas	39	500	44.8	18.0	28	110	12.3	2.2	1,160	52.4	195	1
Tillman	18	298	18.3	7.2	7	D	D	D	433	12.5	0	0
Tulsa	2,063	48,166	5,808.5	2,135.3	1,184	8,068	1,123.9	251.1	49,980	2,417.9	470,583	2,167
Wagoner	76	816	52.8	21.9	58	172	25.9	4.9	5,511	230.8	73,769	347
Washington	172	3,091	284.1	113.0	78	473	38.5	11.9	3,169	140.8	3,249	23
Washita	14	297	13.9	7.4	10	27	3.3	0.6	832	31.0	0	0
Woods	20	D	D	D	18	D	D	D	770	26.8	625	11
Woodward	81	1,029	96.4	34.9	41	262	34.3	8.7	1,457	65.0	2,449	12
OREGON	12,475	217,584	24,956.8	9,689.3	6,894	37,941	4,435.0	1,149.1	286,538	13,632.4	21,269	176
Baker	53	664	54.6	22.9	37	D	D	D	1,099	37.5	5,336	23
Benton	271	5,258	588.1	258.8	147	891	153.8	30.3	5,956	249.6	94,239	622
Clackamas	1,136	17,962	2,424.2	896.7	677	D	D	D	31,469	1,710.0	470,328	1,754
Clatsop	137	2,163	213.9	89.8	91	D	D	D	3,001	137.0	45,023	150
Columbia	114	1,239	62.2	25.8	64	D	D	D	2,781	110.6	29,089	146
Coos	193	3,539	350.3	143.7	86	D	D	D	3,602	154.2	10,904	54
Crook	35	D	D	D	41	D	D	D	1,459	67.6	90,263	305
Curry	89	885	79.9	31.4	28	D	D	D	1,812	81.1	11,997	45
Deschutes	608	9,398	1,114.0	442.5	329	1,526	156.8	41.9	17,623	914.1	499,609	1,983
Douglas	312	4,830	544.3	244.2	135	657	134.1	17.3	5,748	251.8	72,571	284
Gilliam	9	D	D	D	5	D	D	D	109	4.0	NA	NA
Grant	22	D	D	D	14	D	D	D	476	15.7	NA	NA
Harney	22	309	29.8	10.8	14	D	D	D	527	16.5	2,064	7
Hood River	96	1,759	130.8	59.4	55	244	20.7	6.1	2,064	101.3	36,971	140
Jackson	674	12,116	1,443.8	510.7	315	1,836	157.3	51.0	16,943	784.8	192,604	933
Jefferson	40	622	51.2	24.1	22	D	D	D	1,053	48.1	31,241	110
Josephine	269	4,376	418.5	151.1	103	D	D	D	5,805	251.4	55,015	227
Klamath	203	3,067	323.5	122.2	102	D	D	D	3,441	147.7	36,057	146
Lake	21	292	28.6	12.1	10	D	D	D	487	16.3	3,079	14
Lane	1,135	20,576	2,247.4	828.6	611	3,480	443.9	97.7	23,925	1,079.9	267,980	1,389
Lincoln	119	1,657	169.4	73.8	111	D	D	D	3,489	201.9	43,853	234
Linn	216	4,660	422.3	174.0	142	D	D	D	5,973	247.9	122,677	540
Malheur	112	1,563	133.1	53.6	57	D	D	D	1,364	60.8	5,568	22
Marion	971	17,456	1,787.0	758.3	484	2,394	215.7	66.8	16,969	801.0	308,762	1,373

Table B. States and Counties — Government Employment and Payroll, and Local Government Finances

	Government employment and payroll, 2012									Local government finances, 2012				
			March payroll (percent of total)							General revenue				
												Taxes		
STATE County	Full-time equivalent employees	March payroll (dollars)	Administration, judicial, and legal	Police and corrections	Fire protection	Highways and transportation	Health and welfare	Natural resources and utilities	Education and libraries	Total (mil dol)	Inter-governmental (mil dol)	Total (mil dol)	Per capita[1] (dollars)	
													Total	Property
	171	172	173	174	175	176	177	178	179	180	181	182	183	184
OKLAHOMA— Cont'd														
Kiowa	554	1,581,546	4.8	5.3	0.8	4.5	36.0	6.1	41.7	28.0	15.7	7.6	812	529
Latimer	754	2,593,866	3.2	2.1	0.0	3.7	15.7	2.1	72.9	31.9	13.6	7.0	636	318
Le Flore	1,864	5,014,735	3.3	6.0	0.4	3.5	3.6	5.5	75.8	125.0	71.3	28.8	578	300
Lincoln	1,059	2,802,834	6.5	7.7	1.4	5.3	0.3	7.8	70.0	71.7	38.3	21.4	627	358
Logan	875	2,347,456	7.2	7.5	3.8	5.0	0.6	6.6	67.9	60.0	30.1	18.4	421	259
Love	481	1,481,165	6.9	3.8	0.0	3.5	40.8	1.2	43.6	19.3	11.3	5.6	581	387
McClain	1,466	3,975,638	5.5	7.7	3.1	4.0	13.2	3.3	60.7	113.4	39.8	57.3	1,609	1,149
McCurtain	1,454	3,983,530	2.5	5.7	1.1	5.2	4.9	5.0	74.7	93.6	55.4	21.0	632	354
McIntosh	617	1,761,398	8.2	6.9	0.0	2.0	1.7	6.5	74.4	51.2	28.1	16.0	778	358
Major	407	1,118,428	9.8	3.5	0.5	9.3	27.6	2.4	45.6	26.8	10.8	7.7	1,002	610
Marshall	530	1,477,680	5.8	6.2	1.0	4.3	3.0	4.0	74.8	36.0	20.4	10.5	660	446
Mayes	1,472	4,043,970	8.9	5.6	0.7	3.0	3.2	7.1	70.0	95.9	51.9	32.6	792	421
Murray	655	1,707,493	6.8	7.5	3.1	2.3	19.7	11.8	48.5	44.1	24.1	10.4	762	306
Muskogee	3,141	8,727,804	4.0	8.5	4.5	4.3	6.8	5.1	65.6	275.3	85.7	75.6	1,071	547
Noble	622	1,661,200	5.9	6.7	2.5	6.0	18.5	6.1	53.2	44.6	16.7	14.0	1,213	863
Nowata	422	1,000,994	6.4	5.5	1.0	6.4	3.0	5.6	71.4	24.0	14.4	5.9	556	321
Okfuskee	460	1,098,562	3.9	6.1	0.0	6.2	0.9	3.6	76.5	34.2	24.4	6.6	531	326
Oklahoma	24,286	88,713,472	5.8	14.1	10.2	3.4	2.9	6.5	56.5	2,544.3	761.2	1,182.3	1,594	722
Okmulgee	1,552	4,277,777	5.1	5.1	2.9	3.2	3.2	5.9	73.4	89.1	52.5	23.2	586	272
Osage	1,130	2,941,818	9.3	7.0	1.1	14.2	11.3	6.8	48.8	74.5	39.5	19.7	410	229
Ottawa	1,421	4,097,793	5.8	5.3	2.3	2.7	1.7	8.0	73.0	80.7	44.3	21.1	654	269
Pawnee	597	1,604,091	5.8	5.4	1.0	3.9	18.9	7.0	56.7	35.2	20.6	8.5	514	277
Payne	3,634	11,234,115	4.8	7.5	4.2	1.9	31.7	8.2	40.1	192.3	66.9	89.1	1,137	592
Pittsburg	2,380	5,927,369	5.7	11.0	5.4	4.2	4.8	9.9	55.6	254.4	76.4	76.1	1,689	1,039
Pontotoc	1,436	4,130,846	4.3	6.5	3.1	5.4	2.1	5.4	70.4	103.9	50.5	34.4	905	337
Pottawatomie	2,336	6,720,266	6.0	7.2	4.0	2.8	0.1	7.4	71.9	167.8	93.6	52.1	737	301
Pushmataha	607	1,521,960	2.8	3.2	1.8	5.1	17.4	5.2	63.2	38.1	21.2	5.6	504	248
Roger Mills	256	746,029	12.5	6.7	0.0	25.4	12.9	5.1	34.8	20.6	10.5	6.4	1,687	1,138
Rogers	2,835	7,580,674	6.2	6.2	5.0	5.0	1.0	15.1	60.3	197.1	79.1	87.2	986	621
Seminole	1,164	2,881,448	5.7	5.9	2.6	4.0	1.0	5.8	73.2	80.4	47.5	19.7	772	340
Sequoyah	1,722	4,751,418	4.1	6.5	0.8	2.8	13.0	2.9	69.8	115.2	65.1	22.1	534	266
Stephens	1,530	4,875,145	5.7	8.9	3.8	3.6	0.3	5.9	70.1	109.2	51.3	39.9	891	426
Texas	1,138	3,387,767	5.5	7.8	2.0	6.4	23.7	3.4	50.3	93.1	28.0	34.4	1,601	1,035
Tillman	545	1,405,251	6.0	9.3	2.4	4.7	24.1	6.9	45.0	21.8	14.4	3.8	490	335
Tulsa	23,532	78,482,436	5.7	10.6	6.5	3.9	2.1	5.2	62.5	2,206.7	679.3	1,020.7	1,663	890
Wagoner	1,330	3,590,004	7.0	7.2	2.6	4.0	2.4	9.2	64.5	85.8	39.9	34.9	465	232
Washington	1,747	5,123,970	4.5	9.2	5.9	3.5	2.6	6.6	65.7	123.9	52.2	47.3	915	518
Washita	621	1,807,048	6.4	5.9	0.7	7.4	8.9	3.3	66.3	43.9	25.8	12.0	1,030	518
Woods	575	1,537,398	8.0	4.6	2.6	8.1	31.6	4.9	39.0	38.5	13.1	16.6	1,883	804
Woodward	891	2,568,486	5.9	8.6	3.5	5.0	7.2	4.7	61.8	69.5	25.7	32.5	1,583	708
OREGON	X	X	X	X	X	X	X	X	X	X	X	X	X	X
Baker	487	1,718,138	10.0	12.3	6.0	4.4	2.9	7.2	54.6	56.2	31.8	15.5	977	900
Benton	1,834	7,923,562	9.3	13.4	6.2	3.8	7.4	9.4	45.7	259.6	93.0	115.4	1,335	1,185
Clackamas	10,411	44,609,746	8.2	11.7	6.1	3.3	4.7	6.1	57.9	1,431.7	520.8	623.0	1,623	1,458
Clatsop	1,540	5,672,121	8.9	12.5	2.7	5.7	8.3	8.9	49.7	172.7	53.4	71.3	1,912	1,596
Columbia	1,444	6,022,192	7.2	9.3	8.1	2.1	0.4	16.3	52.3	192.4	87.9	59.7	1,211	1,123
Coos	3,079	13,113,856	2.7	5.5	1.8	2.4	45.7	3.7	37.5	386.2	116.4	74.2	1,187	1,048
Crook	584	2,274,092	9.3	15.0	2.6	3.8	3.7	7.2	51.7	72.1	28.3	22.8	1,099	940
Curry	803	3,143,734	7.1	10.1	0.4	5.5	38.6	5.6	31.1	90.5	25.4	26.9	1,211	1,076
Deschutes	4,773	21,188,503	8.1	12.1	5.4	2.6	5.0	7.0	55.3	649.0	217.1	283.8	1,749	1,579
Douglas	3,555	13,196,754	6.3	8.9	6.6	3.1	10.3	6.1	57.1	374.6	196.1	94.6	883	829
Gilliam	145	510,580	18.3	7.1	1.3	10.8	8.3	8.3	45.2	24.4	3.8	15.2	7,770	6,077
Grant	485	1,961,339	5.0	4.3	0.1	3.5	41.5	3.5	38.1	55.0	23.8	7.9	1,083	1,049
Harney	427	1,530,704	6.7	5.9	0.4	3.5	37.4	2.0	42.0	51.3	21.5	7.2	998	925
Hood River	639	2,757,629	6.9	8.8	4.6	6.5	3.0	12.1	54.2	95.2	38.6	26.4	1,171	1,023
Jackson	4,931	20,369,335	9.1	14.6	6.5	6.1	5.2	6.8	50.0	668.0	291.3	260.8	1,263	1,068
Jefferson	1,028	3,923,905	4.1	6.5	1.3	1.7	29.3	8.4	46.4	112.4	50.4	24.0	1,101	997
Josephine	2,192	8,995,230	6.6	12.9	2.5	3.4	1.3	3.1	68.4	243.6	119.9	70.8	854	781
Klamath	1,819	7,192,100	5.9	8.2	6.2	6.2	7.0	7.1	56.2	234.1	125.3	59.4	901	796
Lake	460	1,602,079	5.2	5.5	1.6	6.9	38.3	7.3	33.1	51.6	18.7	10.7	1,372	1,263
Lane	11,647	50,155,119	7.2	10.9	5.2	6.9	4.1	11.4	48.1	1,390.4	585.1	463.2	1,306	1,120
Lincoln	1,465	6,826,571	10.2	14.7	2.9	4.9	8.2	27.9	29.0	200.9	55.6	104.1	2,255	1,881
Linn	3,984	16,207,525	6.1	11.2	5.6	4.0	5.1	4.9	61.9	447.9	223.4	146.4	1,237	1,133
Malheur	1,459	4,992,780	4.9	8.6	1.3	2.7	8.2	7.2	66.0	146.8	85.7	25.2	821	712
Marion	12,046	53,396,211	5.2	8.9	3.6	3.2	3.6	3.7	69.6	1,311.4	678.7	400.1	1,250	1,131

1. Based on the resident population estimated as of July 1 of the year shown.

STATE County	Local government finances, 2012 (cont.) Direct general expenditure Total (mil dol)	Per capita[1] (dollars)	Education	Health and hospitals	Police protection	Public welfare	Highways	Debt outstanding Total (mil dol)	Per capita[1] (dollars)	Government employment, 2017 Federal civilian	Federal military	State and local	Individual income tax returns, 2016 Number of returns	Mean adjusted gross income	Mean income tax
	185	186	187	188	189	190	191	192	193	194	195	196	197	198	199
OKLAHOMA— Cont'd															
Kiowa	28.9	3,103	50.8	1.7	5.1	0.0	11.2	18.6	1,994	45	32	653	3,380	36,354	3,021
Latimer	33.5	3,038	45.3	21.6	2.5	0.0	11.1	4.0	365	28	36	975	3,960	42,507	3,595
Le Flore	128.2	2,571	63.3	5.2	3.9	0.1	7.2	41.9	840	148	178	4,858	17,620	40,044	3,265
Lincoln	69.8	2,043	62.1	1.0	6.3	0.0	9.1	22.4	656	76	129	1,659	13,530	45,076	4,007
Logan	60.7	1,390	56.3	2.5	8.0	0.0	8.8	34.1	782	60	165	1,318	18,250	60,895	7,232
Love	22.3	2,329	73.8	2.7	1.9	0.0	7.2	4.8	506	22	37	3,526	4,290	43,810	3,923
McClain	115.0	3,229	69.2	1.7	5.3	0.0	6.8	54.5	1,531	68	145	1,676	16,950	59,832	6,631
McCurtain	89.7	2,703	65.8	3.0	3.2	0.0	7.5	40.6	1,222	128	120	2,310	12,360	37,334	3,029
McIntosh	48.8	2,370	65.3	1.5	5.7	0.0	9.6	27.7	1,344	35	72	1,089	7,360	40,588	3,533
Major	27.0	3,519	43.6	21.9	3.4	0.2	15.4	8.4	1,096	30	28	366	3,340	50,313	4,814
Marshall	35.6	2,234	67.7	3.5	3.9	0.0	4.1	8.2	513	21	60	722	6,310	45,183	4,378
Mayes	94.4	2,293	68.5	1.3	6.4	0.0	6.3	46.9	1,140	66	149	2,412	15,920	48,582	4,615
Murray	43.2	3,162	41.5	28.0	3.6	0.0	4.3	20.9	1,532	66	50	2,417	5,760	47,249	4,828
Muskogee	284.3	4,027	38.4	31.9	3.5	0.0	3.0	95.6	1,354	2,989	243	6,702	26,440	46,139	4,501
Noble	44.7	3,877	46.3	20.3	3.8	0.0	12.0	32.4	2,812	37	41	1,271	4,680	51,039	5,030
Nowata	24.4	2,295	64.3	0.0	4.0	0.0	11.1	7.8	734	34	38	545	4,130	44,087	3,806
Okfuskee	34.0	2,753	77.0	0.0	2.3	0.0	10.3	17.9	1,449	25	40	1,044	3,940	37,389	2,707
Oklahoma	2,264.8	3,053	44.4	0.4	10.3	0.2	5.6	2,878.7	3,881	27,371	8,490	56,577	336,450	64,636	9,093
Okmulgee	89.9	2,270	65.7	0.5	4.7	0.0	7.2	96.2	2,428	115	139	3,440	14,600	42,538	3,618
Osage	73.9	1,543	50.5	8.5	2.4	0.8	12.7	17.6	367	160	176	2,581	17,700	52,323	5,439
Ottawa	87.3	2,709	53.9	2.6	5.3	0.0	11.8	33.9	1,051	97	112	5,502	12,630	38,623	3,183
Pawnee	33.0	2,003	61.8	3.2	3.7	0.0	10.4	20.5	1,247	213	60	962	6,220	47,874	4,478
Payne	185.3	2,363	48.5	0.4	11.8	0.1	8.4	115.8	1,477	236	283	14,862	29,230	54,953	6,443
Pittsburg	209.1	4,642	32.4	36.3	4.6	0.0	4.1	129.8	2,882	1,909	158	3,912	17,500	45,555	4,220
Pontotoc	100.3	2,643	61.6	0.6	5.6	0.0	7.3	22.3	586	158	135	6,792	15,850	49,599	5,247
Pottawatomie	171.7	2,427	59.2	0.4	6.1	0.0	8.2	62.2	879	143	258	6,253	28,580	46,507	4,438
Pushmataha	38.0	3,395	55.0	22.5	3.5	0.2	8.3	9.5	847	26	41	880	4,220	40,020	3,437
Roger Mills	21.1	5,590	33.6	1.3	3.6	0.0	42.2	0.7	196	37	14	368	1,500	48,057	4,782
Rogers	198.7	2,249	54.8	0.9	4.1	0.0	9.8	136.5	1,544	488	334	6,256	39,610	64,928	7,649
Seminole	79.1	3,109	54.5	1.3	3.6	0.0	6.2	27.2	1,070	159	90	1,845	8,970	39,385	3,376
Sequoyah	115.1	2,781	61.2	12.8	4.0	0.7	4.6	67.9	1,639	130	168	3,032	15,550	41,925	3,733
Stephens	108.9	2,432	55.9	0.5	5.5	0.0	9.4	48.1	1,074	80	158	1,938	17,280	52,645	5,777
Texas	98.3	4,570	36.3	26.0	2.2	0.1	7.6	39.3	1,829	74	75	1,695	9,430	47,152	4,481
Tillman	23.0	2,944	65.1	1.9	5.6	0.0	12.8	6.9	884	31	27	591	2,760	36,043	2,872
Tulsa	2,175.2	3,544	44.8	4.4	6.3	0.8	7.9	3,349.1	5,456	3,426	2,401	31,371	282,180	66,627	9,119
Wagoner	88.4	1,178	62.5	2.4	6.7	0.0	8.5	84.6	1,128	70	302	1,759	32,810	57,815	5,973
Washington	127.7	2,473	49.2	0.7	6.0	0.0	8.3	98.7	1,911	95	189	2,270	22,430	61,992	7,809
Washita	39.5	3,402	50.0	0.3	4.5	0.0	20.5	17.5	1,502	46	40	699	4,440	41,095	3,446
Woods	34.4	3,894	39.3	5.7	3.4	0.0	14.9	7.3	829	27	30	1,124	3,650	56,876	7,490
Woodward	71.3	3,469	43.9	1.0	6.2	0.0	7.9	53.7	2,613	88	71	1,588	8,300	49,306	5,332
OREGON	X	X	X	X	X	X	X	X	X	28,273	11,427	248,389	1,898,860	65,037	8,225
Baker	54.2	3,408	42.8	7.5	5.5	1.6	8.5	12.0	754	206	38	901	7,020	44,442	4,114
Benton	259.2	2,999	46.3	7.4	9.6	0.0	4.2	233.8	2,705	499	247	8,971	39,150	69,630	8,817
Clackamas	1,519.2	3,958	45.7	4.4	7.2	1.0	4.3	2,524.7	6,577	1,052	1,088	14,673	197,240	83,506	12,177
Clatsop	169.8	4,551	35.4	2.0	7.8	5.6	4.9	220.8	5,921	206	500	2,496	18,540	52,374	5,542
Columbia	192.3	3,902	51.6	1.9	4.3	0.2	3.0	214.6	4,353	71	125	1,875	23,110	58,869	6,081
Coos	396.6	6,341	32.9	41.8	2.9	0.1	2.5	240.2	3,841	325	384	5,097	27,260	47,310	4,793
Crook	64.9	3,132	41.4	3.3	7.3	0.2	6.7	59.1	2,852	281	56	878	10,170	51,094	5,356
Curry	101.4	4,557	23.1	33.1	4.3	2.7	5.0	92.8	4,173	79	100	1,129	10,630	47,869	5,161
Deschutes	663.5	4,089	49.1	3.5	7.4	0.4	5.0	1,093.2	6,736	921	455	8,161	91,090	70,581	9,459
Douglas	388.7	3,627	47.5	11.2	5.7	0.2	5.6	258.0	2,407	1,457	307	5,823	45,940	48,070	4,821
Gilliam	26.0	13,296	30.4	4.8	3.1	0.9	11.5	62.9	32,197	13	4	230	830	53,959	5,781
Grant	58.7	8,019	29.3	28.9	3.0	0.6	14.1	17.9	2,444	285	17	723	3,060	44,322	4,391
Harney	51.9	7,203	32.1	38.3	1.6	0.5	8.2	34.0	4,719	232	17	779	3,060	37,878	3,256
Hood River	99.3	4,399	46.3	2.2	2.8	0.6	8.1	98.9	4,381	116	55	1,137	11,960	62,765	7,582
Jackson	678.0	3,285	42.6	5.3	8.6	0.0	6.1	887.0	4,297	1,762	522	8,619	100,910	55,034	6,282
Jefferson	108.0	4,966	39.6	27.4	3.8	0.4	3.9	71.9	3,306	130	56	2,186	9,680	42,608	3,752
Josephine	253.3	3,055	59.6	2.9	7.1	0.1	5.0	145.0	1,748	263	207	2,869	37,020	47,889	5,061
Klamath	233.2	3,538	47.7	4.6	6.8	0.2	7.6	72.7	1,103	909	254	3,765	28,110	46,060	4,675
Lake	52.0	6,689	27.7	39.5	2.5	0.3	10.2	44.6	5,745	263	18	821	3,220	43,890	4,250
Lane	1,390.2	3,921	44.2	5.1	6.9	2.2	4.3	1,580.1	4,457	1,782	996	22,225	168,290	57,772	6,950
Lincoln	229.9	4,981	36.4	6.6	7.4	0.1	6.6	316.8	6,864	329	214	3,370	22,420	50,028	5,132
Linn	449.1	3,794	51.6	3.6	6.2	0.4	4.4	449.9	3,801	314	303	6,266	54,530	50,656	4,799
Malheur	157.2	5,132	62.3	4.3	3.4	0.2	3.8	62.8	2,050	208	66	2,928	10,720	38,856	3,216
Marion	1325.2	4,141	57.0	3.6	5.0	0.2	4.6	1,931.4	6,036	1,265	822	39,160	147,670	54,096	5,642

1. Based on the resident population estimated as of July 1 of the year shown.

Table B. States and Counties — **Land Area and Population**

State / county code	CBSA code[1]	County code[2]	STATE County	Land area[3] (sq. mi)	Population, 2018			Population and population characteristics, 2018										
								Race alone or in combination, not Hispanic or Latino (percent)					Age (percent)					
					Total persons 2018	Rank	Per square mile	White	Black	American Indian, Alaska Native	Asian and Pacific Islander	Percent Hispanic or Latino[4]	Under 5 years	5 to 17 years	18 to 24 years	25 to 34 years	35 to 44 years	45 to 54 years
				1	2	3	4	5	6	7	8	9	10	11	12	13	14	15
			OREGON— Cont'd															
41049	25,840	6	Morrow	2,030.5	11,372	2,328	5.6	60.0	1.0	2.2	1.3	37.3	7.4	20.2	8.8	10.6	11.6	11.4
41051	38,900	1	Multnomah	431.1	811,880	77	1,883.3	72.9	7.1	1.9	10.7	11.7	5.4	13.4	7.8	18.7	16.6	13.1
41053	41,420	2	Polk	740.9	85,234	673	115.0	80.5	1.7	3.1	3.8	14.3	5.8	17.0	12.5	12.2	11.7	11.0
41055		9	Sherman	823.6	1,708	3,072	2.1	89.6	1.2	2.7	1.6	7.4	5.3	12.6	5.6	10.2	11.2	11.7
41057		6	Tillamook	1,102.4	26,787	1,534	24.3	86.1	1.0	2.5	2.4	10.7	4.9	14.0	6.3	10.7	10.5	11.4
41059	25,840	4	Umatilla	3,215.4	77,516	717	24.1	67.4	1.4	4.3	1.8	27.3	6.6	18.7	8.9	14.0	12.6	11.8
41061	29,260	7	Union	2,036.9	26,461	1,548	13.0	90.8	1.3	2.2	3.5	4.9	6.0	16.5	11.2	11.7	11.2	9.8
41063		9	Wallowa	3,145.9	7,081	2,658	2.3	94.7	1.0	1.8	1.2	3.4	4.8	13.8	4.5	9.8	10.3	10.0
41065	45,520	6	Wasco	2,381.1	26,505	1,547	11.1	75.9	0.9	4.0	2.5	18.7	6.4	15.7	7.5	13.5	11.5	10.8
41067	38,900	1	Washington	724.3	597,695	111	825.2	68.5	3.0	1.3	14.2	17.0	6.0	16.8	8.2	15.7	15.0	13.2
41069		9	Wheeler	1,716.0	1,366	3,088	0.8	90.3	1.2	4.4	1.8	6.4	4.9	10.5	4.9	8.3	8.1	10.7
41071	38,900	1	Yamhill	715.9	107,002	566	149.5	79.2	1.5	2.4	3.4	16.2	5.7	16.4	10.2	12.7	12.9	12.1
42000		0	PENNSYLVANIA	44,743.2	12,807,060	X	286.2	77.6	11.9	0.5	4.2	7.6	5.5	15.2	9.1	13.3	11.7	12.9
42001	23,900	3	Adams	518.8	102,811	590	198.2	90.2	2.3	0.5	1.2	7.1	5.0	15.0	9.3	10.9	10.5	13.8
42003	38,300	1	Allegheny	730.1	1,218,452	36	1,668.9	80.2	14.6	0.5	4.7	2.2	5.2	13.4	8.8	15.4	11.8	12.0
42005	38,300	1	Armstrong	653.2	65,263	819	99.9	97.9	1.4	0.4	0.5	0.8	4.9	14.3	6.9	10.7	11.1	13.6
42007	38,300	1	Beaver	434.7	164,742	397	379.0	91.3	7.7	0.5	0.9	1.6	5.1	14.3	7.3	11.7	11.3	12.8
42009		6	Bedford	1,012.3	48,176	1,020	47.6	97.5	1.1	0.5	0.6	1.2	5.0	14.4	7.1	10.4	10.6	13.9
42011	39,740	2	Berks	856.4	420,152	168	490.6	72.2	5.1	0.4	1.8	21.9	5.7	16.6	9.6	12.4	11.5	13.3
42013	11,020	3	Blair	525.8	122,492	515	233.0	95.9	2.8	0.4	1.0	1.3	5.3	15.1	7.7	12.3	11.4	12.8
42015	42,380	6	Bradford	1,147.4	60,833	865	53.0	96.9	1.1	0.7	0.9	1.5	5.9	16.1	7.2	10.9	10.3	12.8
42017	37,980	1	Bucks	604.4	628,195	106	1,039.4	85.2	4.7	0.5	5.7	5.5	4.9	15.5	7.9	11.2	11.7	14.3
42019	38,300	1	Butler	788.6	187,888	352	238.3	95.6	1.7	0.4	1.9	1.6	5.2	14.8	8.6	11.3	11.8	14.1
42021	27,780	3	Cambria	688.4	131,730	485	191.4	94.1	4.5	0.3	0.9	1.7	5.0	14.2	9.1	10.4	10.7	12.6
42023		7	Cameron	396.2	4,492	2,859	11.3	97.1	1.6	0.8	0.6	1.2	4.7	12.7	6.2	8.9	9.3	12.8
42025	10,900	2	Carbon	381.5	64,227	830	168.4	92.3	2.3	0.6	0.8	5.1	4.8	14.5	6.7	11.1	11.2	14.4
42027	44,300	3	Centre	1,109.9	162,805	405	146.7	86.6	4.1	0.4	7.4	3.0	3.9	11.2	23.7	13.9	10.7	11.1
42029	37,980	1	Chester	750.5	522,046	133	695.6	80.7	6.7	0.5	6.4	7.6	5.5	17.1	9.1	11.6	12.3	14.0
42031		6	Clarion	600.8	38,779	1,207	64.5	96.8	1.7	0.5	1.0	1.0	5.2	13.5	13.4	11.6	10.0	12.5
42033	20,180	4	Clearfield	1,144.7	79,388	705	69.4	93.7	2.8	0.4	0.9	3.0	4.6	13.6	7.8	12.1	11.9	14.3
42035	30,820	4	Clinton	888.0	38,684	1,210	43.6	96.0	1.9	0.4	1.0	1.6	5.3	14.9	14.4	11.2	10.3	11.7
42037	14,100	3	Columbia	483.1	65,456	817	135.5	94.0	2.2	0.5	1.4	2.9	4.5	13.2	15.3	10.8	10.3	12.3
42039	32,740	4	Crawford	1,012.3	85,063	677	84.0	95.8	2.6	0.5	0.9	1.4	5.4	15.3	9.1	11.0	10.7	13.0
42041	25,420	2	Cumberland	545.5	251,423	275	460.9	87.0	5.1	0.5	5.3	4.1	5.4	14.8	9.6	13.1	12.2	12.9
42043	25,420	2	Dauphin	524.9	277,097	247	527.9	67.7	19.5	0.7	5.5	9.6	6.2	16.3	8.0	13.9	11.9	12.7
42045	37,980	1	Delaware	183.8	564,751	119	3,072.6	68.0	22.9	0.6	6.8	3.9	5.9	16.0	9.8	13.1	12.1	12.7
42047	41,260	7	Elk	827.4	30,169	1,428	36.5	98.0	0.8	0.5	0.7	0.8	5.0	14.4	7.1	9.8	10.1	14.7
42049	21,500	2	Erie	799.1	272,061	253	340.5	86.2	8.8	0.5	2.3	4.4	5.6	15.7	9.7	13.1	11.3	12.4
42051	38,300	1	Fayette	790.3	130,441	491	165.1	93.2	5.8	0.5	0.9	1.2	5.1	14.1	7.3	12.0	11.3	13.7
42053		9	Forest	427.3	7,279	2,642	17.0	72.5	20.6	0.5	0.3	6.6	2.1	8.6	11.1	17.7	11.5	12.6
42055	16,540	3	Franklin	772.2	154,835	428	200.5	89.3	4.5	0.6	1.5	5.9	6.0	16.2	7.6	12.0	11.6	13.3
42057		8	Fulton	437.6	14,523	2,124	33.2	97.1	1.8	0.7	0.4	1.3	5.2	14.9	7.4	10.5	11.3	14.4
42059		6	Greene	575.9	36,506	1,264	63.4	94.5	3.8	0.7	0.6	1.6	5.2	14.2	9.4	12.3	11.9	13.5
42061	26,500	6	Huntingdon	874.7	45,168	1,071	51.6	91.6	6.1	0.4	1.0	2.0	4.4	13.6	9.5	12.5	11.7	13.4
42063	26,860	4	Indiana	827.5	84,501	678	102.1	94.8	3.1	0.4	1.4	1.3	4.8	13.3	15.9	10.8	9.9	11.7
42065		7	Jefferson	652.4	43,641	1,099	66.9	98.0	0.9	0.6	0.5	0.9	5.5	15.6	7.3	11.5	10.9	12.8
42067		6	Juniata	391.4	24,704	1,621	63.1	94.7	1.0	0.4	0.7	4.0	5.7	16.7	7.5	11.1	11.1	13.2
42069	42,540	2	Lackawanna	458.8	210,793	317	459.4	85.7	3.8	0.4	3.5	8.1	5.4	15.1	8.7	12.5	11.3	12.9
42071	29,540	2	Lancaster	943.9	543,557	126	575.9	83.0	4.6	0.4	2.8	10.8	6.5	17.1	8.9	13.2	11.4	11.9
42073	35,260	4	Lawrence	358.2	86,184	669	240.6	93.7	5.5	0.4	0.8	1.5	5.2	14.6	8.2	10.9	10.7	12.8
42075	30,140	3	Lebanon	361.8	141,314	459	390.6	82.5	2.7	0.4	1.8	13.8	5.9	16.9	8.5	11.7	11.7	12.4
42077	10,900	2	Lehigh	345.2	368,100	192	1,066.1	64.9	6.8	0.4	4.1	25.4	5.9	16.7	9.1	13.2	12.4	12.8
42079	42,540	2	Luzerne	890.3	317,646	219	356.8	81.6	4.9	0.4	1.6	12.9	5.2	14.5	8.7	12.7	11.4	13.5
42081	48,700	3	Lycoming	1,228.8	113,664	540	92.5	92.5	6.0	0.6	1.0	2.1	5.3	15.1	8.9	13.1	11.1	12.6
42083	14,620	7	McKean	979.2	40,968	1,151	41.8	94.5	2.9	0.7	1.0	2.2	4.7	15.0	9.1	11.9	11.4	13.3
42085	49,660	2	Mercer	672.6	110,683	548	164.6	91.7	6.9	0.5	1.1	1.6	5.0	14.4	9.7	10.5	10.5	13.0
42087	30,380	4	Mifflin	411.0	46,222	1,047	112.5	96.7	1.4	0.4	0.9	1.7	6.1	16.1	7.3	11.3	10.4	13.2
42089	20,700	3	Monroe	608.3	169,507	385	278.7	66.8	14.8	0.8	3.2	16.6	4.5	15.1	10.7	11.3	10.7	14.5
42091	37,980	1	Montgomery	483.0	828,604	73	1,715.5	77.1	10.5	0.4	8.8	5.3	5.5	16.0	8.0	12.5	12.5	13.6
42093	14,100	3	Montour	130.2	18,240	1,913	140.1	91.9	2.2	0.4	3.6	2.9	5.7	14.7	6.4	13.6	11.3	11.9
42095	10,900	2	Northampton	369.6	304,807	230	824.7	77.5	6.5	0.5	3.5	13.8	4.8	15.1	9.8	12.1	11.5	13.3
42097	44,980	4	Northumberland	458.0	91,083	647	198.9	93.3	3.0	0.4	0.7	3.6	5.1	14.4	7.2	12.2	11.5	13.3
42099	25,420	2	Perry	551.4	46,139	1,050	83.7	96.2	1.5	0.6	0.8	2.1	5.7	15.7	7.1	11.9	11.6	14.3
42101	37,980	1	Philadelphia	134.2	1,584,138	23	11,804.3	35.9	42.1	0.8	8.3	15.2	6.6	15.1	9.9	19.1	12.5	11.5
42103	35,620	1	Pike	545.0	55,933	914	102.6	81.1	6.3	0.8	1.9	11.4	3.9	14.1	7.8	9.4	10.4	14.8

1. CBSA = Core Based Statistical Area. See Appendix A for explanation. See Appendix B for list of metropolitan areas with component counties. Service of USDA Rural-Urban Continuum Codes. See Appendix A for definition. 3. Dry land or land partially or temporarily covered by water. 2. County type code from the Economic Research 4. May be of any race.

Table B. States and Counties — **Population and Households**

STATE County	55 to 64 years (16)	65 to 74 years (17)	75 years and over (18)	Percent female (19)	2000 (20)	2010 (21)	2000-2010 (22)	2010-2018 (23)	Births (24)	Deaths (25)	Net Migration (26)	Number (27)	Persons per household (28)	Family house-holds (29)	Female family house-holder[1] (30)	One person (31)
OREGON— Cont'd																
Morrow	13.5	10.1	6.4	48.6	10,995	11,177	1.7	1.7	1,338	627	-529	3,936	2.82	75.3	8.9	20.7
Multnomah	11.4	8.5	4.9	50.5	660,486	735,148	11.3	10.4	76,562	46,463	46,042	318,173	2.42	54.7	10.3	32.3
Polk	11.9	10.5	7.4	51.1	62,380	75,407	20.9	13.0	7,348	5,496	7,980	29,128	2.68	67.9	9.0	24.0
Sherman	16.7	13.6	12.9	48.5	1,934	1,766	-8.7	-3.3	135	131	-64	779	2.08	59.1	5.9	32.5
Tillamook	16.3	16.2	9.6	49.4	24,262	25,254	4.1	6.1	2,040	2,413	1,904	10,454	2.41	62.1	8.5	30.8
Umatilla	11.8	9.2	6.5	47.8	70,548	75,885	7.6	2.1	8,617	5,292	-1,665	26,976	2.67	67.8	13.4	26.0
Union	13.4	11.5	8.7	50.3	24,530	25,744	4.9	2.8	2,501	2,169	397	10,291	2.43	63.7	9.4	26.5
Wallowa	17.5	17.1	12.1	50.6	7,226	7,008	-3.0	1.0	497	689	263	3,126	2.15	62.6	7.7	33.5
Wasco	14.0	12.2	8.4	49.7	23,791	25,211	6.0	5.1	2,568	2,548	1,281	10,135	2.42	65.0	10.1	28.7
Washington	11.6	8.2	5.3	50.5	445,342	529,860	19.0	12.8	58,329	26,411	36,033	212,778	2.66	67.9	9.9	24.2
Wheeler	17.7	17.8	17.0	50.4	1,547	1,439	-7.0	-5.1	89	152	-13	677	2.06	59.7	5.8	35.3
Yamhill	12.9	10.1	7.0	49.9	84,992	99,209	16.7	7.9	9,323	7,329	5,826	35,952	2.70	70.5	11.4	23.2
PENNSYLVANIA	14.1	10.2	8.0	51.0	12,281,054	12,702,873	3.4	0.8	1,160,725	1,071,084	22,862	5,007,442	2.47	64.2	11.8	29.7
Adams	15.1	11.7	8.7	50.8	91,292	101,424	11.1	1.4	8,292	8,132	1,301	38,818	2.51	71.5	9.7	23.8
Allegheny	14.4	10.5	8.5	51.7	1,281,666	1,223,323	-4.6	-0.4	108,175	113,111	946	536,439	2.23	56.8	11.1	35.9
Armstrong	16.6	12.3	9.7	50.2	72,392	68,944	-4.8	-5.3	5,415	6,972	-2,084	28,242	2.34	67.9	10.2	27.8
Beaver	16.1	11.8	9.7	51.4	181,412	170,549	-6.0	-3.4	13,835	17,375	-2,097	70,384	2.35	64.9	11.6	30.1
Bedford	15.8	12.2	10.7	50.2	49,984	49,763	-0.4	-3.2	3,986	4,633	-901	19,666	2.46	68.1	7.4	27.4
Berks	13.6	9.7	7.6	50.8	373,638	411,556	10.1	2.1	39,838	31,550	450	153,876	2.61	68.9	12.7	25.0
Blair	14.6	11.5	9.3	51.0	129,144	127,116	-1.6	-3.6	10,714	13,230	-2,001	51,638	2.35	63.6	11.2	31.0
Bradford	15.5	12.0	9.3	50.4	62,761	62,704	-0.1	-3.0	5,956	5,664	-2,159	24,851	2.44	67.7	9.7	26.9
Bucks	15.9	10.6	8.1	50.9	597,635	625,266	4.6	0.5	48,064	47,362	2,575	235,909	2.61	71.0	9.2	24.3
Butler	15.4	10.7	8.2	50.4	174,083	183,856	5.6	2.2	14,981	15,715	4,933	75,596	2.38	67.8	8.1	26.5
Cambria	15.4	12.5	10.1	50.8	152,598	143,681	-5.8	-8.3	11,137	15,137	-7,980	57,154	2.24	63.4	11.1	31.8
Cameron	18.2	15.2	12.0	50.0	5,974	5,085	-14.9	-11.7	365	516	-444	2,196	2.12	56.3	7.7	39.3
Carbon	16.1	12.3	8.9	50.1	58,802	65,252	11.0	-1.6	4,891	6,598	740	25,978	2.43	65.6	11.2	26.5
Centre	11.4	8.1	6.2	47.4	135,758	154,001	13.4	5.7	10,163	7,965	6,621	57,710	2.48	57.0	6.1	29.0
Chester	14.1	9.5	6.9	50.7	433,501	499,133	15.1	4.6	45,306	31,527	9,563	188,613	2.65	70.5	8.9	23.3
Clarion	14.2	10.8	8.8	51.0	41,765	39,991	-4.2	-3.0	3,307	3,528	-1,002	15,925	2.35	62.6	7.3	28.8
Clearfield	15.1	11.3	9.2	47.5	83,382	81,616	-2.1	-2.7	6,166	7,691	-639	31,152	2.41	66.4	9.7	29.0
Clinton	13.6	10.2	8.5	50.8	37,914	39,240	3.5	-1.4	3,493	3,302	-736	14,675	2.55	66.0	9.0	26.8
Columbia	14.1	11.0	8.5	51.8	64,151	67,303	4.9	-2.7	4,941	5,706	-1,036	26,564	2.34	63.7	10.8	27.2
Crawford	15.0	12.2	8.4	51.0	90,366	88,750	-1.8	-4.2	7,635	8,263	-3,028	35,102	2.38	66.8	10.6	26.8
Cumberland	13.4	10.4	8.1	50.5	213,674	235,405	10.2	6.8	21,146	18,637	13,679	97,919	2.38	64.2	8.6	29.7
Dauphin	14.0	10.0	7.0	51.6	251,798	268,123	6.5	3.3	28,251	20,464	1,328	111,489	2.39	62.7	14.0	30.8
Delaware	13.9	9.1	7.3	51.9	550,864	558,759	1.4	1.1	55,056	45,156	-3,719	204,870	2.64	67.1	14.4	28.5
Elk	16.8	11.8	10.2	49.8	35,112	31,946	-9.0	-5.6	2,540	3,207	-1,101	13,447	2.26	64.0	8.7	32.1
Erie	14.2	10.3	7.7	50.6	280,843	280,584	-0.1	-3.0	25,889	23,332	-11,067	110,377	2.40	62.7	12.8	30.6
Fayette	15.4	12.0	9.2	50.5	148,644	136,595	-8.1	-4.5	11,221	14,797	-2,461	54,043	2.38	63.0	12.5	31.8
Forest	13.7	13.0	9.6	31.5	4,946	7,710	55.9	-5.6	270	700	3	1,473	1.97	58.8	5.3	38.2
Franklin	13.6	10.8	8.8	50.9	129,313	149,619	15.7	3.5	15,367	12,228	2,248	60,102	2.51	68.3	10.2	26.8
Fulton	14.8	12.2	9.3	49.4	14,261	14,844	4.1	-2.2	1,108	1,247	-172	5,947	2.45	68.6	8.2	26.5
Greene	14.6	11.4	7.5	48.2	40,672	38,689	-4.9	-5.6	3,249	3,609	-1,818	14,484	2.34	66.4	11.8	27.7
Huntingdon	14.2	11.8	9.0	46.8	45,586	46,009	0.9	-1.8	3,275	3,834	-246	16,935	2.39	68.6	8.9	26.8
Indiana	14.2	10.9	8.6	49.9	89,605	88,889	-0.8	-4.9	6,880	7,436	-3,825	34,030	2.37	62.7	8.1	28.7
Jefferson	15.4	11.5	9.6	50.2	45,932	45,189	-1.6	-3.4	4,081	4,612	-991	18,452	2.36	66.2	9.0	29.3
Juniata	14.5	11.2	8.9	49.9	22,821	24,635	7.9	0.3	2,298	2,098	-116	9,361	2.58	70.1	7.7	25.5
Lackawanna	14.2	11.0	9.0	51.5	213,295	214,439	0.5	-1.7	18,212	21,919	193	85,907	2.37	60.7	11.5	33.2
Lancaster	13.1	9.7	8.2	51.0	470,658	519,446	10.4	4.6	57,772	40,023	6,810	198,565	2.64	70.1	9.5	24.0
Lawrence	15.6	11.9	10.1	51.6	94,643	91,140	-3.7	-5.4	7,265	9,388	-2,797	36,742	2.34	66.6	12.5	29.3
Lebanon	13.5	10.6	8.8	50.9	120,327	133,577	11.0	5.8	13,497	11,922	6,292	52,792	2.55	69.6	10.9	25.4
Lehigh	13.1	9.3	7.4	51.0	312,090	349,676	12.0	5.3	34,195	27,572	12,032	137,239	2.56	67.1	13.8	26.7
Luzerne	14.1	10.9	9.0	50.5	319,250	320,895	0.5	-1.0	26,091	32,959	3,911	128,247	2.38	63.9	13.3	31.2
Lycoming	14.6	10.8	8.5	51.0	120,044	116,114	-3.3	-2.1	10,254	10,423	-2,245	45,991	2.38	64.8	10.1	29.3
McKean	15.2	10.7	8.7	48.6	45,936	43,459	-5.4	-5.7	3,450	4,284	-1,642	17,199	2.27	63.7	11.7	29.8
Mercer	15.1	11.7	10.0	50.6	120,293	116,668	-3.0	-5.1	9,273	11,500	-3,710	45,805	2.32	65.2	11.3	29.9
Mifflin	13.9	11.5	10.2	51.0	46,486	46,679	0.4	-1.0	4,680	4,374	-722	18,939	2.42	67.6	12.1	26.0
Monroe	16.0	10.5	6.7	50.5	138,687	169,832	22.5	-0.2	11,567	11,649	-254	57,526	2.87	71.6	11.4	22.3
Montgomery	14.1	9.7	8.0	51.3	750,097	799,872	6.6	3.6	73,471	61,225	17,253	312,805	2.55	68.6	9.5	26.2
Montour	15.3	10.8	10.3	51.7	18,236	18,258	0.1	-0.1	1,829	1,817	-17	7,423	2.37	61.2	9.4	31.8
Northampton	14.3	10.5	8.5	50.8	267,066	297,694	11.5	2.4	23,482	23,915	7,840	113,827	2.55	68.9	11.0	25.0
Northumberland	15.0	11.8	9.6	49.7	94,556	94,483	-0.1	-3.6	7,811	9,592	-1,552	39,281	2.26	63.6	10.8	31.0
Perry	15.2	11.5	7.0	49.4	43,602	45,940	5.4	0.4	4,470	3,689	-558	17,936	2.52	70.5	8.5	24.3
Philadelphia	11.6	7.8	5.8	52.7	1,517,550	1,526,009	0.6	3.8	184,831	118,899	-6,770	591,280	2.57	52.7	19.7	39.4
Pike	16.9	13.3	9.5	49.3	46,302	57,346	23.9	-2.5	2,908	3,602	-722	21,379	2.59	71.5	8.2	24.0

1. No spouse present.

Table B. States and Counties — **Population, Vital Statistics, Health, and Crime**

STATE County	Persons in group quarters, 2018	Daytime Population, 2013-2017		Births, 2018		Deaths, 2018		Persons under 65 with no health insurance, 2016		Medicare, 2018			Serious crimes known to police[2], 2016 Total	
		Number	Employment/ residence ratio	Total	Rate[1]	Number	Rate[1]	Number	Percent	Total beneficiaries	Enrolled in Original Medicare	Enrolled in Medicare Advantage	Number	Rate[3]
	32	33	34	35	36	37	38	39	40	41	42	43	44	45
OREGON— Cont'd														
Morrow	23	12,662	1.32	165	14.5	79	6.9	1,028	10.9	2,055	1,865	190	310	2,754
Multnomah	19,036	889,912	1.25	8,807	10.8	5,994	7.4	49,888	7.3	123,257	50,693	72,564	42,504	5,384
Polk	1,835	66,969	0.63	951	11.2	696	8.2	4,627	7.0	17,515	7,252	10,263	2,212	2,742
Sherman	0	1,711	1.11	15	8.8	11	6.4	106	8.3	512	426	86	NA	NA
Tillamook	487	25,678	0.98	241	9.0	300	11.2	1,637	8.5	7,932	6,129	1,803	449	1,734
Umatilla	4,186	75,278	0.95	959	12.4	650	8.4	6,166	10.1	14,085	12,874	1,211	1,869	2,425
Union	662	25,751	0.99	305	11.5	273	10.3	1,481	7.3	6,298	5,675	623	640	2,466
Wallowa	105	6,880	1.01	61	8.6	68	9.6	339	6.9	2,364	2,218	146	NA	NA
Wasco	741	25,560	0.99	329	12.4	297	11.2	2,160	10.7	6,225	4,976	1,249	638	2,451
Washington	7,348	578,410	1.02	6,844	11.5	3,478	5.8	30,568	6.0	85,752	35,703	50,049	9,957	1,703
Wheeler	24	1,358	0.88	14	10.2	15	11.0	81	9.5	482	410	72	7	519
Yamhill	5,431	94,400	0.82	1,158	10.8	923	8.6	6,077	7.4	20,643	10,122	10,521	1,951	1,876
PENNSYLVANIA	421,994	12,729,288	0.99	135,905	10.6	133,562	10.4	691,654	6.8	2,681,839	1,566,739	1,115,100	263,242	2,059
Adams	4,039	87,230	0.71	906	8.8	1,001	9.7	5,625	7.1	23,880	16,665	7,215	1,004	983
Allegheny	35,097	1,315,785	1.14	12,795	10.5	13,840	11.4	48,393	4.9	259,608	98,553	161,055	28,974	2,359
Armstrong	650	56,125	0.64	637	9.8	876	13.4	3,147	6.1	16,743	5,944	10,799	515	788
Beaver	3,173	146,902	0.74	1,601	9.7	2,102	12.8	7,330	5.6	41,859	15,123	26,736	3,541	2,163
Bedford	551	44,499	0.80	491	10.2	568	11.8	2,857	7.6	12,741	6,426	6,315	417	889
Berks	11,401	395,093	0.90	4,702	11.2	3,887	9.3	25,190	7.5	83,171	53,970	29,201	7,910	1,907
Blair	3,710	130,492	1.10	1,217	9.9	1,620	13.2	5,664	5.8	30,742	14,991	15,751	1,964	1,572
Bradford	666	61,824	1.01	672	11.0	727	12.0	3,514	7.3	14,719	10,705	4,014	1,025	1,685
Bucks	8,038	571,148	0.83	5,864	9.3	6,071	9.7	25,077	4.9	133,394	89,194	44,200	9,583	1,531
Butler	5,446	187,900	1.02	1,788	9.5	1,956	10.4	6,485	4.3	41,208	16,282	24,926	2,419	1,295
Cambria	5,980	132,394	0.94	1,291	9.8	1,751	13.3	6,099	6.0	36,046	13,534	22,512	2,122	1,576
Cameron	92	4,998	1.12	34	7.6	70	15.6	213	6.1	1,438	962	476	78	1,676
Carbon	700	51,489	0.56	592	9.2	798	12.4	3,165	6.3	15,745	12,161	3,584	1,357	2,136
Centre	19,621	167,865	1.10	1,155	7.1	1,090	6.7	8,764	7.2	23,905	12,430	11,475	1,872	1,160
Chester	13,495	508,875	0.98	5,261	10.1	4,141	7.9	27,100	6.3	91,626	69,393	22,233	6,859	1,329
Clarion	1,925	36,351	0.86	370	9.5	447	11.5	2,225	7.4	9,152	5,758	3,394	489	1,244
Clearfield	5,497	79,487	0.97	732	9.2	947	11.9	4,035	6.8	19,579	11,518	8,061	1,429	1,772
Clinton	2,060	37,386	0.89	396	10.2	400	10.3	2,392	8.0	8,551	4,797	3,754	495	1,257
Columbia	3,684	64,586	0.93	552	8.4	728	11.1	3,553	7.0	14,515	8,787	5,728	993	1,514
Crawford	3,836	84,068	0.93	882	10.4	975	11.5	5,369	8.1	21,092	13,555	7,537	1,192	1,389
Cumberland	12,253	255,509	1.08	2,632	10.5	2,295	9.1	11,365	5.9	51,781	31,204	20,577	2,974	1,200
Dauphin	6,789	324,122	1.38	3,373	12.2	2,564	9.3	15,431	6.8	54,552	27,810	26,742	6,311	2,324
Delaware	22,693	510,452	0.80	6,424	11.4	5,532	9.8	27,150	5.9	105,623	75,985	29,638	12,383	2,199
Elk	355	30,358	0.97	294	9.7	362	12.0	1,241	5.2	7,986	6,101	1,885	532	1,739
Erie	12,129	282,377	1.04	2,912	10.7	2,816	10.4	13,605	6.2	58,439	30,705	27,734	5,924	2,141
Fayette	4,340	119,990	0.75	1,280	9.8	1,838	14.1	6,867	6.7	34,336	14,923	19,413	2,958	2,244
Forest	2,634	8,687	2.81	22	3.0	78	10.7	225	7.1	1,683	985	698	97	1,323
Franklin	2,613	144,045	0.87	1,833	11.8	1,621	10.5	11,636	9.4	34,974	26,225	8,749	2,502	1,625
Fulton	122	13,479	0.82	140	9.6	149	10.3	909	7.9	3,677	2,775	902	181	1,245
Greene	2,971	38,587	1.09	358	9.8	436	11.9	1,564	5.6	8,208	3,705	4,503	591	1,589
Huntingdon	4,889	42,215	0.81	357	7.9	531	11.8	2,078	6.5	10,509	6,442	4,067	496	1,161
Indiana	4,839	86,455	1.00	829	9.8	891	10.5	5,084	7.7	18,754	7,218	11,536	1,364	1,580
Jefferson	775	42,779	0.92	428	9.8	517	11.8	2,561	7.4	10,942	6,326	4,616	385	872
Juniata	292	21,009	0.69	274	11.1	247	10.0	1,618	8.2	5,400	2,924	2,476	196	814
Lackawanna	7,495	214,796	1.03	2,182	10.4	2,553	12.1	10,242	6.2	51,311	36,504	14,807	3,839	1,874
Lancaster	12,722	524,667	0.96	6,864	12.6	5,135	9.4	47,029	10.7	108,513	65,878	42,635	8,354	1,552
Lawrence	2,092	81,396	0.82	838	9.7	1,121	13.0	4,129	6.1	22,215	8,912	13,303	1,511	1,745
Lebanon	3,671	127,500	0.84	1,579	11.2	1,494	10.6	8,168	7.4	31,306	18,529	12,777	2,151	1,633
Lehigh	9,137	378,176	1.10	4,209	11.4	3,326	9.0	21,100	7.1	72,206	47,468	24,738	8,313	2,298
Luzerne	11,904	319,991	1.01	3,145	9.9	3,993	12.6	15,920	6.5	73,679	53,697	19,982	6,574	2,089
Lycoming	5,261	117,465	1.04	1,152	10.1	1,313	11.6	5,161	5.8	26,290	17,341	8,949	1,991	1,721
McKean	3,052	40,708	0.92	352	8.6	506	12.4	1,873	6.0	10,053	7,506	2,547	626	1,519
Mercer	6,355	115,098	1.03	1,116	10.1	1,446	13.1	5,851	7.0	28,639	14,476	14,163	2,094	1,870
Mifflin	560	44,104	0.89	546	11.8	524	11.3	3,098	8.5	11,423	6,577	4,846	739	1,595
Monroe	4,506	153,865	0.82	1,478	8.7	1,603	9.5	10,153	7.5	32,796	25,204	7,592	3,546	2,146
Montgomery	21,657	888,750	1.17	8,564	10.3	7,821	9.4	31,145	4.6	159,479	114,342	45,137	13,585	1,656
Montour	844	26,412	1.95	218	12.0	221	12.1	700	4.9	4,261	2,118	2,143	249	1,342
Northampton	11,245	277,906	0.84	2,826	9.3	2,975	9.8	16,104	6.7	66,679	46,726	19,953	5,098	1,697
Northumberland	3,732	84,174	0.78	897	9.8	1,109	12.2	4,456	6.3	22,672	14,301	8,371	1,421	1,532
Perry	659	33,357	0.45	508	11.0	463	10.0	3,077	8.2	9,944	5,308	4,636	495	1,136
Philadelphia	56,535	1,673,770	1.16	20,991	13.3	15,585	9.8	126,800	9.7	255,966	143,699	112,267	64,761	4,123
Pike	478	44,849	0.55	429	7.7	504	9.0	3,315	7.7	13,907	11,880	2,027	678	1,221

1. Per 1,000 estimated resident population.   2. Data for serious crimes have not been adjusted for underreporting; this may affect comparability between geographic areas and over time.   3. Per 100,000 population estimated by the FBI.

Table B. States and Counties — Crime, Education, Money Income, and Poverty

STATE County	Serious crimes known to police[2], 2016 (cont.)[1] Rate — Violent	Property	Enrollment[3] Total	Percent private	Attainment[4] (percent) High school graduate or less	Bachelor's degree or more	Local government expenditures,[5] 2014-2015 Total current spending (mil dol)	Current spending per student (dollars)	Per capita income[6]	Households Median income (dollars)	Percent with income of less than $50,000	Percent with income of $200,000 or more	Median household income (dollars)	Percent below poverty level All persons	Children under 18 years	Children 5 to 17 years in families
	46	47	48	49	50	51	52	53	54	55	56	57	58	59	60	61
OREGON— Cont'd																
Morrow	480	2,275	2,836	4.4	58.5	9.8	26.4	10,890	21,743	54,386	44.8	1.4	51,673	14.2	18.6	16.3
Multnomah	482	4,902	184,990	20.5	26.6	43.8	1,081.9	11,470	34,848	60,369	42.1	6.9	63,587	14.4	17.3	16.0
Polk	239	2,503	22,076	10.9	33.7	30.6	66.0	9,694	25,928	56,032	43.7	2.8	56,917	14.7	16.4	15.3
Sherman	NA	NA	242	7.4	42.9	17.6	3.6	14,426	34,226	42,074	56.5	6.2	56,096	12.2	17.4	16.9
Tillamook	81	1,653	4,644	13.6	42.7	20.7	40.5	12,299	25,458	45,061	54.8	2.2	48,470	13.9	21.5	17.7
Umatilla	231	2,194	18,786	7.5	46.4	15.9	157.6	11,517	22,153	50,071	49.9	2	51,586	15.6	19.5	17.5
Union	146	2,319	6,525	13.5	40.8	24.0	38.3	10,072	26,586	46,228	53.7	4	46,753	13.3	17.6	16.0
Wallowa	NA	NA	1,148	11.5	37.6	25.8	14.5	17,118	26,898	44,877	55.7	0.7	47,822	13.5	20.2	17.7
Wasco	188	2,262	5,249	11.9	42.5	19.8	41.6	11,508	24,727	48,510	51.8	2.2	49,735	13.8	20.8	19.8
Washington	183	1,520	144,628	11.0	26.8	42.4	899.3	10,390	35,369	74,033	33.2	7.8	80,845	8	9.4	8.4
Wheeler	148	371	230	13.5	45.6	15.8	4.9	13,116	21,268	33,563	65.4	0.6	40,047	20.6	40.2	40.4
Yamhill	133	1,744	25,587	24.6	38.2	25.4	165.6	9,955	28,540	58,392	43.1	4.6	62,759	11	12.8	11.4
PENNSYLVANIA	316	1,743	2,997,324	23.8	45.7	30.1	25,036.3	14,535	31,476	56,951	44.2	5.5	59,165	12.5	16.9	15.7
Adams	163	819	23,748	26.2	52.9	22.1	275.7	19,820	29,685	62,661	39.2	3.8	62,997	8.2	11.4	9.9
Allegheny	388	1,971	283,183	24.9	34.3	40.0	2,418.9	16,405	35,280	56,333	44.9	6	58,547	11.2	15.1	13.9
Armstrong	112	676	12,465	15.2	59.3	15.2	115.5	15,779	25,502	47,527	52.0	1.9	46,227	12.9	18.0	15.6
Beaver	245	1,918	34,997	16.8	46.1	24.0	439.7	13,646	29,162	53,981	46.6	2.7	54,739	11.1	15.1	14.4
Bedford	70	818	8,975	11.9	64.6	13.8	88.0	12,387	24,219	48,703	51.2	1.3	47,760	12.3	17.5	16.5
Berks	272	1,635	101,771	17.0	51.7	23.9	943.2	13,897	29,041	59,580	42.1	4.1	61,022	11.7	17.0	15.6
Blair	214	1,358	26,358	14.0	55.4	20.3	224.9	12,715	25,531	45,664	53.8	2.3	46,072	14.5	18.8	17.2
Bradford	181	1,504	12,530	13.8	58.3	18.0	128.3	13,629	26,937	50,900	49.1	2.7	47,457	13.3	20.2	19.0
Bucks	100	1,431	146,109	24.3	35.7	39.4	1,404.2	16,275	41,924	82,031	29.5	11.7	84,784	6.1	7.5	6.6
Butler	107	1,188	43,366	16.8	39.3	34.6	329.0	12,229	35,101	66,037	37.5	6.5	68,709	8.4	9.5	8.3
Cambria	165	1,411	30,240	22.6	54.2	20.9	227.5	12,743	24,838	44,943	54.6	1.9	46,007	15	23.4	21.0
Cameron	150	1,526	796	13.2	58.1	15.9	9.1	15,157	24,933	40,402	60.1	1.2	41,335	15.1	23.4	22.8
Carbon	285	1,851	12,359	12.7	56.7	16.0	114.4	13,227	25,680	51,236	48.7	1.6	51,395	12.5	18.3	16.2
Centre	95	1,064	57,894	8.8	37.0	43.7	197.0	15,018	28,545	56,466	45.2	5.2	56,366	17.2	11.5	10.4
Chester	137	1,191	135,486	23.1	29.0	51.0	1,275.3	15,958	46,256	92,417	26.6	15.8	96,803	6.3	6.5	6.1
Clarion	117	1,127	9,272	9.7	56.9	21.8	93.9	16,479	23,595	44,373	56.1	1.7	45,657	16.1	20.3	19.1
Clearfield	272	1,500	14,378	12.3	62.9	14.1	155.8	14,069	22,568	45,188	54.6	1.7	47,818	15	21.6	19.3
Clinton	145	1,113	9,620	13.1	58.6	18.0	64.2	14,432	22,794	47,990	52.0	1.3	45,036	16.2	20.2	19.1
Columbia	168	1,346	17,703	8.0	54.8	21.6	84.2	13,553	24,908	48,395	51.3	2.6	51,302	13.5	16.1	15.2
Crawford	94	1,295	18,914	25.9	57.3	20.4	120.5	13,476	24,716	47,179	52.6	2.4	49,044	14.6	21.8	19.7
Cumberland	75	1,125	58,582	21.8	41.3	34.7	369.9	14,209	34,246	65,544	37.0	5.1	69,222	7.3	9.6	9
Dauphin	435	1,888	61,050	17.7	44.5	29.8	585.0	13,155	31,152	57,071	43.2	4.4	61,229	12.1	18.6	18.4
Delaware	377	1,822	148,468	32.5	38.4	37.7	1,340.2	16,290	36,747	69,839	36.7	9.4	73,637	9.8	13.1	12.1
Elk	144	1,595	5,846	23.1	56.3	18.5	45.0	12,528	27,163	49,876	50.1	1.7	51,711	9.9	13.5	12.6
Erie	222	1,919	68,668	24.4	48.6	27.4	506.1	12,796	26,361	48,192	51.6	3	50,419	15.7	24.1	21.4
Fayette	226	2,018	25,032	11.8	61.8	15.4	224.6	13,481	24,247	41,632	56.4	1.7	42,892	17.9	28.0	26.9
Forest	477	846	758	30.9	75.0	7.0	10.0	21,649	14,989	37,106	69.9	0.6	40,564	22	34.4	26.9
Franklin	144	1,482	32,973	16.7	55.3	20.6	255.0	11,169	28,985	58,267	42.4	2.8	60,077	9.7	13.9	13.2
Fulton	172	1,073	2,890	10.4	65.1	13.5	28.4	13,398	25,273	50,007	50.0	1.7	50,716	12.6	18.1	16.8
Greene	129	1,460	7,741	22.4	59.2	18.0	76.3	15,311	25,574	50,972	49.3	2.6	48,590	14.7	21.7	19.3
Huntingdon	164	997	9,495	26.7	61.5	15.3	65.6	11,552	22,908	46,765	53.0	1	49,655	14.9	21.3	19.3
Indiana	268	1,312	23,033	11.2	54.1	22.7	170.8	17,706	25,014	46,306	53.5	2.5	46,084	14.7	20.4	19.4
Jefferson	163	709	8,533	15.8	60.8	15.8	69.9	14,705	23,895	45,342	54.8	1.4	43,911	14.2	20.5	18.4
Juniata	83	731	4,705	24.2	67.9	14.0	30.5	10,420	24,068	50,571	49.5	1.5	48,334	12.2	18.7	17.7
Lackawanna	232	1,642	48,508	32.0	46.9	27.0	371.3	13,180	27,258	48,380	51.5	3	49,082	14.3	20.4	19.0
Lancaster	176	1,376	123,851	26.7	51.9	26.5	974.3	14,519	29,280	61,492	39.7	4	63,402	9.9	13.7	12.7
Lawrence	247	1,498	18,322	17.4	54.2	20.8	161.4	13,482	26,918	47,188	52.4	2.7	48,666	13.3	19.8	18.7
Lebanon	154	1,479	29,777	23.9	56.6	20.4	225.8	11,821	27,916	57,698	41.7	2.7	57,389	10.8	15.0	13.3
Lehigh	234	2,064	87,292	22.2	44.8	29.1	733.4	14,429	30,988	60,116	42.0	5.4	60,706	12.4	18.2	17.2
Luzerne	265	1,824	68,694	22.4	49.6	22.8	578.4	13,052	26,809	49,290	50.5	2.7	50,982	13.8	24.7	22.2
Lycoming	206	1,515	25,061	16.7	49.8	22.1	228.5	14,275	26,265	50,634	49.4	2.2	50,292	12.9	18.1	16.4
McKean	272	1,247	9,192	12.3	57.6	17.4	96.3	15,459	24,868	45,866	54.7	2.3	45,031	17.3	24.9	21.4
Mercer	210	1,660	25,464	23.4	54.1	22.3	248.9	15,781	25,499	47,340	52.3	2.2	46,851	12.4	18.9	18.6
Mifflin	125	1,470	8,836	19.4	67.1	12.2	86.6	16,710	23,568	46,286	53.8	1.3	50,449	12.7	21.5	19.6
Monroe	252	1,894	40,825	12.5	46.9	24.0	437.0	16,578	27,439	61,430	40.7	4.3	61,296	9.3	14.9	13.9
Montgomery	123	1,533	202,460	30.8	29.9	48.2	1,877.5	17,363	45,048	84,791	29.0	13.2	87,338	5.8	6.8	6.2
Montour	253	1,089	3,553	19.1	51.1	30.5	29.3	12,579	31,818	56,250	45.5	5.5	62,595	9.9	15.2	14.2
Northampton	256	1,440	72,348	28.9	44.3	28.8	653.1	14,773	32,608	65,390	38.3	5.8	65,872	10	14.2	13.2
Northumberland	265	1,267	16,663	17.8	64.0	15.4	185.6	15,805	24,278	44,534	54.9	1.7	45,352	14.3	19.6	18.0
Perry	168	969	9,091	19.6	58.1	16.6	80.1	13,014	28,900	60,847	40.5	2.9	61,225	9.5	14.7	14.0
Philadelphia	981	3,142	403,818	33.6	50.6	27.1	2,617.3	13,148	24,811	40,649	58.0	3.5	40,193	25.3	31.9	31.0
Pike	150	1,072	12,019	12.8	62.4	26.5	126.0	15,941	31,156	63,417	38.7	4.6	67,317	9.1	14.3	13.0

1. Data for serious crimes have not been adjusted for underreporting; this may affect comparability between geographic areas and over time.   2. Per 100,000 population estimated by the FBI.   3. All persons 3 years old and over enrolled in nursery school through college.   4. Persons 25 years old and over.   5. Elementary and secondary education expenditures.   6. Based on population estimated by the American Community Survey, 2013–2017.

Table B. States and Counties — Personal Income and Earnings

STATE County	Personal income, 2017										Earnings, 2017		
			Per capita[1]			Supplements to wages and salaries, employer contributions (mil dol)						Contributions for government social insurance (mil dol)	
	Total (mil dol)	Percent change 2016-2017	Dollars	Rank	Wages and salaries (mil dol)	Pension and insurance	Government social insurance	Proprietors' income (mil dol)	Dividends, interest, and rent (mil dol)	Personal transfer receipts (mil dol)	Total (mil dol)	From employee and self-employed	From employer
	62	63	64	65	66	67	68	69	70	71	72	73	74
OREGON— Cont'd													
Morrow	450	0.4	40,309	1,499	321	57	31	52	65	100	462	24	31
Multnomah	43,874	5.1	54,329	303	30,770	4,645	2,669	4,142	8,993	6,241	42,226	2,525	2,669
Polk	3,344	6	39,958	1,558	796	163	75	201	624	738	1,234	89	75
Sherman	85	0.5	48,609	578	43	10	4	12	17	23	69	4	4
Tillamook	1,112	4.8	41,677	1,306	386	74	36	116	261	315	612	42	36
Umatilla	2,923	3.6	37,964	1,893	1,286	259	128	185	480	749	1,858	118	128
Union	1,004	4.1	38,301	1,827	423	86	41	51	195	292	600	42	41
Wallowa	303	2.6	42,926	1,147	97	22	9	21	84	89	150	11	9
Wasco	1,112	3.6	42,069	1,256	487	87	45	99	202	289	717	45	45
Washington	33,766	5.3	57,331	215	20,956	2,515	1,653	2,679	6,841	3,973	27,802	1,705	1,653
Wheeler	47	1.4	34,414	2,427	11	3	1	1	12	18	16	1	1
Yamhill	4,534	5	42,882	1,152	1,529	278	147	398	836	953	2,352	149	147
PENNSYLVANIA	682,534	3.9	53,363	X	324,818	56,336	25,548	71,906	117,784	129,731	478,607	28,254	25,548
Adams	4,817	4.7	47,067	707	1,485	287	126	379	861	915	2,277	144	126
Allegheny	71,115	4.6	58,146	201	44,537	6,759	3,433	6,621	12,521	12,361	61,350	3,590	3,433
Armstrong	2,741	3.2	41,756	1,293	703	159	58	187	389	760	1,108	81	58
Beaver	7,618	3.1	45,851	814	2,460	509	209	451	980	1,938	3,628	244	209
Bedford	1,946	4.5	40,149	1,531	606	128	53	278	257	520	1,065	68	53
Berks	19,765	4.2	47,302	687	8,888	1,710	724	1,462	3,185	4,007	12,785	765	724
Blair	5,407	2.7	43,793	1,042	2,569	529	225	469	851	1,439	3,793	237	225
Bradford	2,365	3.3	38,869	1,744	1,119	221	92	194	411	614	1,626	103	92
Bucks	43,588	3.8	69,370	73	14,782	2,338	1,183	3,358	7,597	5,738	21,661	1,292	1,183
Butler	10,391	4.2	55,534	262	4,652	850	373	683	1,635	1,711	6,558	396	373
Cambria	5,453	2	40,985	1,408	2,091	459	178	272	844	1,725	3,000	206	178
Cameron	210	0.9	45,774	821	81	19	7	12	38	65	120	8	7
Carbon	3,130	4.2	49,020	535	643	145	55	653	404	676	1,495	87	55
Centre	7,182	4.9	44,152	1,005	3,888	1,437	295	529	1,423	1,078	6,149	313	295
Chester	40,227	4.4	77,465	44	18,970	2,712	1,366	3,616	8,145	3,990	26,665	1,513	1,366
Clarion	1,520	2.6	39,516	1,636	504	135	43	155	262	424	837	52	43
Clearfield	3,330	2.6	41,786	1,289	1,217	269	103	198	456	863	1,786	118	103
Clinton	1,481	4	37,986	1,888	593	147	50	107	218	384	896	56	50
Columbia	2,659	3.2	40,337	1,494	1,064	259	89	171	411	637	1,583	99	89
Crawford	3,290	1.9	38,191	1,846	1,254	271	107	357	477	927	1,988	127	107
Cumberland	12,945	3.4	51,767	385	7,277	1,286	589	917	2,387	2,116	10,069	594	589
Dauphin	13,427	4.2	48,699	567	10,545	2,166	822	1,085	2,092	2,679	14,617	825	822
Delaware	35,260	3.7	62,440	129	14,223	2,208	1,080	2,639	6,817	5,619	20,150	1,194	1,080
Elk	1,393	3	46,147	780	652	140	56	77	221	343	924	59	56
Erie	11,500	1.1	41,887	1,275	5,377	1,112	442	745	1,968	2,924	7,676	473	442
Fayette	5,253	2	39,948	1,560	1,621	355	138	313	739	1,657	2,427	172	138
Forest	159	0.2	21,795	3,107	101	34	8	9	43	68	152	10	8
Franklin	6,766	3.7	43,866	1,033	2,615	529	221	542	1,087	1,413	3,907	243	221
Fulton	608	6.4	41,701	1,301	245	55	22	73	89	150	395	24	22
Greene	1,514	4.5	41,168	1,382	794	158	64	100	248	403	1,115	71	64
Huntingdon	1,632	3.7	35,882	2,214	515	131	43	144	250	457	833	55	43
Indiana	3,161	2.8	37,206	1,999	1,432	361	116	256	521	843	2,165	132	116
Jefferson	1,817	3.9	41,477	1,336	636	135	56	191	293	489	1,019	66	56
Juniata	1,060	9.6	43,244	1,113	245	52	21	188	142	221	506	30	21
Lackawanna	9,551	3	45,319	866	4,337	834	363	627	1,691	2,342	6,161	389	363
Lancaster	26,715	4.7	49,207	519	11,657	2,011	942	3,976	4,468	4,558	18,586	1,065	942
Lawrence	3,593	2.7	41,264	1,371	1,212	245	103	218	488	1,055	1,778	123	103
Lebanon	6,379	4.6	45,645	833	2,178	480	182	588	1,071	1,320	3,428	210	182
Lehigh	18,801	4.7	51,298	402	10,754	1,754	842	1,916	2,943	3,444	15,265	892	842
Luzerne	13,706	3.2	43,189	1,119	6,548	1,301	552	753	2,242	3,457	9,154	576	552
Lycoming	4,707	2.6	41,346	1,355	2,331	504	192	223	788	1,159	3,250	204	192
McKean	1,772	2.7	42,882	1,152	659	158	55	148	323	459	1,021	65	55
Mercer	4,476	2	40,050	1,542	2,040	408	171	342	704	1,308	2,960	192	171
Mifflin	1,738	3.9	37,469	1,956	638	133	54	211	225	501	1,036	67	54
Monroe	6,841	4.3	40,706	1,441	2,549	565	210	495	936	1,487	3,819	236	210
Montgomery	63,779	5.3	77,207	45	36,849	5,009	2,733	2,180	17,620	7,213	46,772	2,930	2,733
Montour	1,004	3.6	54,960	281	1,105	176	74	43	143	189	1,399	82	74
Northampton	15,619	4.3	51,479	395	5,809	1,052	476	1,141	2,477	2,965	8,479	526	476
Northumberland	3,634	3.1	39,485	1,642	1,204	261	105	178	553	1,008	1,747	121	105
Perry	1,951	4.8	42,306	1,229	283	72	25	196	270	410	576	39	25
Philadelphia	88,082	3.1	55,718	256	46,892	7,654	3,607	25,599	10,435	19,832	83,752	4,355	3,607
Pike	2,532	4.6	45,465	848	416	100	35	181	420	581	731	54	35

1. Based on the resident population estimated as of July 1 of the year shown.

Table B. States and Counties — Earnings, Social Security, and Housing

STATE County	Earnings, 2017 (cont.)									Social Security beneficiaries, December 2017		Supplemental Security Income recipients, 2017	Housing units, 2018	
					Percent by selected industries									
	Farm	Mining, quarrying, and extractions	Construction	Manu-facturing	Information; professional, scientific, technical services	Retail trade	Finance, insurance, real estate, and leasing	Health care and social assistance	Govern-ment	Number	Rate[1]		Total	Percent change, 2010-2018
	75	76	77	78	79	80	81	82	83	84	85	86	87	88

STATE County	75	76	77	78	79	80	81	82	83	84	85	86	87	88
OREGON— Cont'd														
Morrow	17.3	D	2.8	23	D	2	2.1	2.2	15.1	2,170	194	230	4,638	4.4
Multnomah	0.1	0	6	6.1	15.7	4.9	8.3	11.4	17.3	120,575	149	21,433	353,842	9
Polk	3.4	D	7.2	10.2	3.9	5.4	5.1	12.4	28.3	18,180	217	1,501	32,513	7.3
Sherman	12.5	0.2	8.7	D	0.3	3.1	D	D	38.7	525	299	42	940	2.3
Tillamook	5.8	0	7.5	14.9	3.7	6.7	4	12.1	21.9	8,315	312	544	19,148	4.3
Umatilla	2.7	0.2	5.1	10.1	3	6.6	4.2	11.7	27.4	14,550	189	1,729	30,672	3.3
Union	-0.3	D	6.2	14.4	3.7	8.3	4.3	18	24.5	6,470	247	645	11,833	3
Wallowa	4	0	10.8	3.8	4.9	7.3	4.4	10.2	29.8	2,480	352	149	4,249	3.4
Wasco	7.9	D	6.6	5.5	7.8	9.4	2.8	20.3	21.5	6,425	243	688	11,729	2.1
Washington	0.5	0.1	6.1	23.5	10.2	5.4	7.1	8	6.9	84,450	143	7,341	232,451	9.4
Wheeler	12.7	0.2	D	D	D	8.9	3.1	D	39.1	515	380	35	911	1.9
Yamhill	6.1	0.3	7.5	19.4	5.2	6.5	6	12.3	14	21,250	201	1,671	39,396	6.1
PENNSYLVANIA	0.3	0.6	6	9.6	15.8	5.2	7.7	13.8	12.7	2,795,950	218	361,250	5,713,150	2.6
Adams	2.8	1	9.1	19.7	3.9	6	3.5	D	14.7	24,460	239	1,131	42,563	4.3
Allegheny	0	0.5	5.3	5.4	15.3	4.6	11.1	14.8	9.6	267,740	219	33,780	602,414	2.2
Armstrong	0.8	10.5	6.8	10.9	4.6	7	3.3	15.1	17.1	18,370	280	2,018	32,782	0.8
Beaver	0.1	0.3	9.8	13.5	5.4	6.3	3.5	15.9	14.9	44,290	267	4,614	79,659	1.8
Bedford	2.7	D	12.1	12.3	2.6	8.7	3.6	D	13.4	13,720	283	1,259	24,397	1.8
Berks	0.5	0.1	6.9	19.1	7.3	5.9	5.2	14.2	13	87,295	209	10,821	167,366	1.5
Blair	0.6	0.4	5.6	12.6	5.3	8.1	4	19.4	15.2	30,775	249	4,540	56,945	1.2
Bradford	1.6	6	6.6	15.2	3.2	5.6	3.8	22.3	13	16,025	263	1,807	30,713	2.5
Bucks	0.1	0.1	10	10	12.9	6.9	6.9	14.7	9.7	133,165	212	7,013	251,515	2.3
Butler	0.1	1.4	7.4	15.5	9.2	6.4	4.4	12.5	13.9	43,345	232	3,146	84,252	7.8
Cambria	0.3	0.4	4.8	9	7.2	7.4	5.2	22.6	17.9	38,635	290	4,787	66,022	0.6
Cameron	0	D	D	50	D	2.6	D	5.1	20.2	1,605	350	146	4,426	-0.6
Carbon	0.1	0.1	4.3	8	40.2	5.1	2.5	11.6	12.1	17,180	269	1,338	34,817	1.5
Centre	0.3	0.3	4.6	4.8	7.9	4.4	4.4	10.1	50.3	24,640	151	1,435	67,144	6.1
Chester	0.3	0	5.7	7.3	20.3	6.9	16.7	7.8	8.1	90,085	173	4,138	201,353	4.6
Clarion	1.4	1.2	7.9	10.6	2.5	7.9	3.9	15.4	25.8	9,950	259	1,259	20,555	3
Clearfield	0.2	2	4.2	8.3	3.3	8	3.7	21.6	19	21,270	267	2,385	39,263	1.7
Clinton	2.2	D	6.9	24.3	D	6.6	2.3	D	23.7	9,200	236	1,062	19,274	1
Columbia	-0.3	D	5.9	18.4	4.2	7.2	3.8	11.5	21.4	15,695	238	1,424	30,323	2.8
Crawford	1.6	1.5	6.5	24.9	4.3	6.4	3	16.1	14.6	22,605	262	2,910	44,950	0.6
Cumberland	0.4	0.1	4.6	5.7	12.5	5.5	9.1	12	15.9	52,405	210	2,754	106,899	6.9
Dauphin	0.2	D	3.9	7.6	8.6	3.6	8.6	15.8	23.1	56,850	206	7,853	124,805	3.6
Delaware	0	D	7.6	9.1	9.7	5.1	11.6	13.3	10.4	106,760	189	12,707	224,871	0.9
Elk	0.1	0.4	4.8	48.1	2.9	4.9	2.6	10.8	9.1	8,680	287	593	17,816	1.3
Erie	0.1	0	4.8	18.3	4.8	6.8	8.3	18.3	16.2	63,295	231	10,624	121,617	2.1
Fayette	0.3	3.9	4.1	9.8	4.2	8	3.1	16.3	19.5	37,660	286	7,874	63,962	1.9
Forest	0.3	D	D	D	D	1.6	D	11.5	59.9	1,825	250	161	8,717	-0.4
Franklin	2	0.1	5.9	16.7	4.7	6.8	3.5	15.4	16.4	36,280	235	2,505	65,791	4.1
Fulton	5	D	11.3	38.2	1.3	3.3	1.7	9.6	12	3,995	274	362	7,255	1.9
Greene	0.4	D	8.8	1.9	3.8	5	3.3	D	18.1	8,970	244	1,685	16,739	1.7
Huntingdon	2.5	1	6	8.2	3.2	5.7	4.3	D	28.5	11,450	252	1,109	22,734	1.7
Indiana	0.6	5.9	7.6	6.4	3.9	6.4	5	12.3	24.7	20,550	242	2,729	39,020	2
Jefferson	1.1	5.8	6.4	23	5.4	4.9	2.2	16.2	12.3	11,980	273	1,326	22,730	1.3
Juniata	3.1	D	8.7	29.5	D	5.7	3.7	5.1	10.4	5,795	236	471	11,253	2.5
Lackawanna	0	0	6.7	10.1	7.8	6.9	8.1	18.5	13.4	53,950	256	6,854	100,718	4
Lancaster	1	0.1	11.7	15.2	7.1	7.5	5.7	13	8.5	111,820	206	9,385	212,205	4.6
Lawrence	0.6	0.5	9.8	14	4.9	7.1	5.7	16.2	14.6	24,105	277	3,338	41,328	0.9
Lebanon	2	0	6.2	17.5	5.7	7.7	3.1	12.2	19.5	32,860	235	2,627	58,005	4.3
Lehigh	0.1	D	4.9	13.1	7.7	4.6	5.6	20.9	8.9	75,815	207	9,930	146,707	2.9
Luzerne	0	0.3	5	11.6	5.8	6.9	5.4	16.1	15.6	79,155	249	10,038	150,302	1.1
Lycoming	0.2	3.4	6.8	16.6	5.4	6.7	4.1	16.7	19.1	28,375	249	3,253	53,540	2
McKean	0.3	7.9	6.4	21.2	2.7	5.7	2	14	16.9	11,200	271	1,571	21,286	0.3
Mercer	0.3	0.9	5.9	20	3.5	7.5	6	17.9	12.8	30,950	277	3,788	52,322	1.1
Mifflin	1.8	0	6.6	25.2	2	7.8	3	18	11	12,310	265	1,372	21,919	1.8
Monroe	0.1	0.2	5.1	13.5	3.1	8	3.1	12.3	24.3	35,910	214	3,096	81,663	1.6
Montgomery	0	0	7.7	10.2	23.2	5.1	8.7	12.6	6.9	158,485	192	8,541	336,193	3.2
Montour	0.1	D	1.1	2.7	D	1.6	7.4	D	7.6	4,580	251	413	8,234	3.4
Northampton	0	D	6.2	14.4	7.5	6	6.6	9.4	13.5	70,420	232	6,441	123,436	2.6
Northumberland	1.5	0.6	7.4	16.8	D	6	2.8	12.8	17	24,370	265	2,764	45,480	0.8
Perry	4	D	14.8	5.3	4.4	7.3	5	6.9	21.9	10,570	229	722	20,941	2.6
Philadelphia	0	D	2.1	2.1	36.3	2.2	6.8	13	12.9	259,120	164	107,290	688,833	2.8
Pike	0.1	0.5	9.5	1.6	6.7	8.2	3.9	8.6	27.1	14,985	269	686	39,134	2.1

1. Per 1,000 resident population estimated as of July 1 of the year shown.

Table B. States and Counties — Housing, Labor Force, and Employment

STATE County	Housing units, 2013-2017								Civilian labor force, 2018				Civilian employment[6], 2013-2017		
	Occupied units							Sub-standard units[4] (percent)		Percent change, 2017-2018	Unemployment			Percent	
			Owner-occupied			Renter-occupied									
				Median owner cost as a percent of income		Median rent[3]	Median rent as a percent of income[2]							Management, business, science, and arts	Construction, production, and maintenance occupations
	Total	Percent	Median value[1]	With a mort-gage	Without a mort-gage[2]				Total		Total	Rate[5]	Total		
	89	90	91	92	93	94	95	96	97	98	99	100	101	102	103

STATE County	89	90	91	92	93	94	95	96	97	98	99	100	101	102	103
OREGON— Cont'd															
Morrow	3,936	70.9	131,600	19.3	10.0	739	23	9.2	5,732	-0.5	248	4.3	4,795	26.8	43.9
Multnomah	318,173	54.3	330,900	23.5	13.1	1,094	32.1	4.2	456,886	0.7	16,843	3.7	416,325	45.2	16.0
Polk	29,128	64.6	224,700	22.7	11.1	870	31.5	2.2	39,695	0.9	1,736	4.4	34,825	35.1	21.8
Sherman	779	63.8	144,000	20.1	13.8	765	28.6	1.8	898	-0.1	37	4.1	753	32.8	32.5
Tillamook	10,454	69.2	233,500	24.6	12.0	831	32.3	3.4	11,857	0.8	525	4.4	10,070	27.0	33.2
Umatilla	26,976	62.9	147,900	21.3	10.4	699	26	6.1	36,813	0.2	1,819	4.9	32,063	26.6	33.4
Union	10,291	63.3	172,100	20.2	10.7	746	27.9	3.9	11,935	-0.4	644	5.4	11,256	28.3	26.2
Wallowa	3,126	67.9	217,600	24.0	13.5	676	28.3	2.6	3,318	-0.1	203	6.1	3,034	34.6	24.2
Wasco	10,135	64.1	191,400	24.0	12.2	743	27.9	2.8	13,384	-3.1	578	4.3	11,254	29.7	26.8
Washington	212,778	60.8	331,900	22.4	10.5	1,183	29.3	3.8	322,574	0.6	11,257	3.5	292,979	45.2	16.3
Wheeler	677	74.0	138,300	32.3	17.2	592	24.1	1.2	723	-1.5	25	3.5	498	38.0	32.3
Yamhill	35,952	67.9	254,000	23.7	12.4	963	31.8	3.8	54,524	0.9	2,051	3.8	45,842	33.0	26.9
PENNSYLVANIA	5,007,442	69.0	170,500	21.1	12.9	885	29.6	1.7	6,424,421	0	275,786	4.3	6,096,977	37.7	21.6
Adams	38,818	77.8	197,400	21.9	13.4	871	29.5	1.8	55,121	-0.5	1,805	3.3	50,561	30.1	31.6
Allegheny	536,439	64.9	140,600	18.9	12.4	835	28.2	1.1	645,169	-0.1	26,059	4	622,670	45.0	14.4
Armstrong	28,242	75.8	98,600	19.8	12.3	639	24.8	1.5	32,148	-0.6	1,615	5	29,713	28.3	31.5
Beaver	70,384	73.3	129,200	19.4	12.8	663	27.1	1.4	84,057	-0.5	3,823	4.5	81,802	33.8	23.4
Bedford	19,666	79.5	126,800	20.2	11.5	658	28.4	2.4	23,661	-0.2	1,066	4.5	22,161	25.7	34.8
Berks	153,876	72.2	170,900	22.3	14.1	885	31.2	1.7	212,528	0	8,842	4.2	201,177	31.8	28.1
Blair	51,638	70.1	117,300	19.3	12.3	676	29.5	1.4	59,555		2,505	4.2	56,657	31.2	24.8
Bradford	24,851	74.8	145,600	19.6	11.8	720	27.5	2.1	28,864	-1.5	1,259	4.4	26,598	28.4	35.6
Bucks	235,909	76.6	315,700	22.8	14.0	1,171	30.9	1.1	341,069	0.2	12,783	3.7	326,994	43.1	17.7
Butler	75,596	76.2	190,000	19.3	11.5	790	27.6	1.1	98,563	-0.1	3,844	3.9	93,194	38.8	21.4
Cambria	57,154	74.3	88,900	18.8	12.7	604	28	1.2	58,344	-2.2	3,031	5.2	57,361	33.1	24.2
Cameron	2,196	72.1	73,800	18.9	11.6	591	28.6	0.9	2,143	-2.3	108	5	2,127	23.1	41.2
Carbon	25,978	77.3	141,200	22.9	14.4	807	30.1	2.2	31,526	0.2	1,597	5.1	29,256	27.5	31.5
Centre	57,710	61.4	212,300	20.6	11.3	942	34.3	2.5	79,859	1	2,585	3.2	76,433	46.8	15.3
Chester	188,613	75.2	338,200	21.8	13.0	1,256	29.2	1.6	281,572	0.2	8,931	3.2	267,812	49.7	14.7
Clarion	15,925	69.4	109,900	19.6	11.1	623	28.4	2	17,388	-1.9	822	4.7	17,280	30.1	27.8
Clearfield	31,152	76.9	90,300	20.0	12.4	620	29.1	1.8	35,744	-0.3	1,784	5	33,591	26.7	32.4
Clinton	14,675	70.7	124,700	20.4	13.1	695	27.1	1.3	18,328	-0.1	975	5.3	17,572	26.2	31.0
Columbia	26,564	69.0	143,300	20.2	13.2	745	29.5	0.8	33,495	-0.6	1,595	4.8	30,035	32.2	27.8
Crawford	35,102	72.8	108,200	19.5	12.5	654	26.7	2.8	38,953	-1.2	1,826	4.7	38,270	29.8	31.6
Cumberland	97,919	70.7	194,100	20.5	11.6	940	27.2	1.2	130,339	0.1	4,334	3.3	123,566	40.6	19.0
Dauphin	111,489	63.5	163,300	20.4	11.7	893	28.6	1.8	142,393	0	5,663	4	134,706	38.4	18.4
Delaware	204,870	69.6	235,200	22.4	14.2	1,032	30.9	1.6	295,898	0.3	11,880	4	275,010	43.0	15.6
Elk	13,447	78.8	97,100	17.1	11.3	547	25.3	1	15,830	-1.1	611	3.9	15,169	26.3	41.2
Erie	110,377	66.1	124,100	19.8	12.4	723	29.4	1.8	129,260	-1.1	6,087	4.7	126,958	33.7	22.5
Fayette	54,043	73.0	94,600	19.4	12.7	624	28.5	2.4	57,081	-0.6	3,327	5.8	54,222	27.7	29.9
Forest	1,473	85.4	91,000	23.6	12.3	572	25.9	1.4	1,817	-0.9	113	6.2	751	24.5	28.1
Franklin	60,102	70.6	175,800	21.3	11.3	840	26.1	1.7	77,064	0.6	2,846	3.7	72,456	30.8	29.0
Fulton	5,947	78.5	156,000	21.7	11.3	663	24.8	1.2	7,884	8.8	311	3.9	6,609	25.7	37.4
Greene	14,484	73.7	108,600	17.9	10.8	637	23.9	1.7	16,593	-1.2	811	4.9	14,775	30.7	30.3
Huntingdon	16,935	75.1	121,900	20.7	11.8	579	25.7	1.4	19,810	0.1	1,047	5.3	18,540	28.4	30.1
Indiana	34,030	70.1	111,200	19.8	12.4	702	31.8	2.9	38,781	-1.2	1,906	4.9	38,523	30.0	27.8
Jefferson	18,452	74.9	96,700	19.6	11.1	608	26.5	2.4	20,503	-0.3	953	4.6	19,833	26.3	36.7
Juniata	9,361	75.7	143,600	20.3	10.0	627	24.5	2.9	12,459	0.7	499	4	11,180	26.2	38.9
Lackawanna	85,907	65.6	149,100	21.3	14.5	748	28.4	1.7	105,330	-0.5	4,828	4.6	97,184	35.1	22.9
Lancaster	198,565	68.2	193,200	21.9	12.1	957	29.6	2.4	281,433	0.9	9,542	3.4	267,348	33.3	27.7
Lawrence	36,742	74.1	102,300	19.6	12.9	653	30.8	1.8	40,823	0.5	2,082	5.1	39,309	30.6	27.3
Lebanon	52,792	69.5	166,600	21.2	12.6	810	26.7	2.6	71,222	0.7	2,677	3.8	65,970	30.1	27.5
Lehigh	137,239	65.3	196,000	22.3	14.1	993	31.8	2.3	190,147	0.3	8,768	4.6	174,705	35.1	23.7
Luzerne	128,247	68.4	124,100	20.3	13.7	742	28.3	1.5	157,784	-0.5	8,529	5.4	148,463	31.0	25.2
Lycoming	45,991	69.9	147,400	20.6	13.2	769	29.6	0.9	57,134	-1.2	2,740	4.8	53,885	30.4	25.7
McKean	17,199	73.8	77,100	18.7	10.9	623	27.9	1	17,869	-1.6	860	4.8	18,316	29.4	31.6
Mercer	45,805	73.2	114,100	19.2	12.0	667	27	2.3	50,087	-1.2	2,360	4.7	50,193	30.6	25.5
Mifflin	18,939	70.2	103,700	20.4	13.7	655	25.1	2.7	20,787	0.6	972	4.7	20,884	25.2	36.7
Monroe	57,526	78.2	167,200	26.5	15.9	1,071	31.3	1.7	82,004	-0.2	4,392	5.4	78,341	32.5	22.8
Montgomery	312,805	72.2	299,300	21.8	12.9	1,211	29.2	1.4	449,387	0.3	15,422	3.4	427,012	49.8	14.1
Montour	7,423	71.3	173,800	19.2	12.4	701	25.4	1.6	9,050	-0.6	317	3.5	8,662	38.0	22.2
Northampton	113,827	71.6	209,800	22.5	14.4	997	31	1.4	158,900	0.2	7,045	4.4	148,278	35.4	22.6
Northumberland	39,281	71.3	112,300	20.0	13.3	636	27.7	1.9	43,057	-1.4	2,258	5.2	41,505	27.9	30.0
Perry	17,936	80.1	164,000	21.7	12.0	760	23.9	1.8	24,295	0	907	3.7	22,983	30.4	32.0
Philadelphia	591,280	52.2	151,500	23.4	14.3	970	33.5	2.9	709,586	0.7	39,322	5.5	665,765	37.7	16.8
Pike	21,379	84.1	183,400	23.6	14.3	1,138	36.2	1.2	24,698	0	1,329	5.4	24,832	32.5	23.2

1. Specified owner-occupied units.   2. A value of 10.0 represents 10 percent or less; a value of 50.0 represents 50 percent or more.   3. Specified renter-occupied units.   4. Overcrowded or lacking complete plumbing facilities.   5. Percent of civilian labor force.   6. Civilian employed persons 16 years old and over.

Table B. States and Counties — **Nonfarm Employment and Agriculture**

STATE County	Private nonfarm establishments, employment and payroll, 2016									Agriculture, 2017			
	Number of establish-ments	Employment						Annual payroll		Farms			Farm producers whose primary occupation is farming (percent)
		Total	Health care and social assistance	Manufac-turing	Retail trade	Finance and insurance	Professional, scientific, and technical services	Total (mil dol)	Average per employee (dollars)	Number	Percent with:		
											Fewer than 50 acres	1000 acres or more	
	104	105	106	107	108	109	110	111	112	113	114	115	116

STATE County	104	105	106	107	108	109	110	111	112	113	114	115	116
OREGON— Cont'd													
Morrow	193	3,966	348	1,435	134	93	D	177	44,626	375	30.7	42.7	50.3
Multnomah	27,246	434,205	67,739	34,471	43,904	20,972	34,295	22,673	52,217	653	89.3	0.6	32.0
Polk	1,436	14,220	2,811	1,830	1,627	269	417	478	33,597	1,243	67.3	2.4	41.6
Sherman	64	473	9	D	117	D	D	16	33,869	190	7.4	62.6	47.4
Tillamook	731	7,190	973	1,553	1,089	142	114	254	35,264	293	51.2	0.7	53.4
Umatilla	1,550	22,570	3,036	3,151	3,025	461	638	800	35,433	1,724	59.6	15.7	38.7
Union	727	7,197	1,468	1,217	1,420	220	228	256	35,602	820	54.6	10.2	37.6
Wallowa	379	1,886	425	76	317	65	95	63	33,248	539	40.3	21.2	42.4
Wasco	681	6,987	1,887	273	1,538	246	260	255	36,465	595	33.4	20.2	43.9
Washington	15,316	265,790	31,081	28,593	32,410	11,876	22,091	17,178	64,629	1,755	81.1	1.0	35.5
Wheeler	30	140	D	D	38	D	NA	4	26,000	150	21.3	46.0	40.7
Yamhill	2,475	29,340	4,855	5,856	3,794	672	622	1,100	37,489	2,138	78.0	1.1	32.7
PENNSYLVANIA	301,484	5,354,964	1,005,144	540,072	667,206	273,515	324,440	261,082	48,755	53,157	42.1	1.4	45.7
Adams	1,956	30,027	4,608	6,227	3,450	481	600	1,035	34,481	1,146	50.2	2.2	43.4
Allegheny	33,962	695,456	127,772	33,838	73,083	50,114	58,114	36,409	52,352	389	60.7	0.5	40.2
Armstrong	1,322	13,905	3,542	1,352	2,083	656	375	465	33,464	668	28.4	4.2	43.6
Beaver	3,369	47,967	10,232	6,144	7,432	923	2,001	1,877	39,129	613	46.8	0.2	40.1
Bedford	1,074	12,856	1,718	1,878	2,239	323	241	437	34,018	1,159	29.2	3.1	50.3
Berks	8,406	156,856	25,628	31,471	20,744	5,848	6,585	7,191	45,846	1,809	49.0	0.9	52.9
Blair	3,185	53,686	13,387	6,809	8,887	1,544	1,790	1,964	36,589	496	34.9	1.6	52.7
Bradford	1,345	18,343	5,038	3,218	2,932	546	513	760	41,436	1,449	24.4	1.6	46.4
Bucks	19,217	247,491	43,800	24,794	38,596	8,386	16,648	11,366	45,926	824	72.1	1.5	43.7
Butler	4,866	82,520	13,403	11,755	11,551	1,958	6,611	3,608	43,727	955	40.4	1.4	42.2
Cambria	3,171	46,970	11,781	4,594	6,871	2,142	2,228	1,645	35,031	557	37.0	2.3	36.1
Cameron	108	1,586	191	937	148	17	14	56	35,253	37	16.2	NA	32.8
Carbon	1,126	13,977	3,436	1,516	2,133	292	345	419	29,963	200	53.0	1.0	30.3
Centre	3,347	45,292	8,884	3,906	8,030	1,252	2,974	1,733	38,267	1,023	41.3	1.4	47.0
Chester	14,314	248,421	37,180	16,077	28,205	24,500	24,038	17,300	69,642	1,646	60.6	1.2	52.3
Clarion	922	11,237	2,976	1,641	1,780	291	231	349	31,072	594	25.3	1.9	38.8
Clearfield	1,988	26,413	5,810	2,655	4,835	622	549	902	34,163	497	35.8	0.6	35.4
Clinton	761	10,586	1,302	2,939	1,939	186	207	381	35,951	267	35.6	1.9	50.9
Columbia	1,424	22,707	4,096	4,771	3,412	679	819	796	35,039	779	43.8	1.7	38.1
Crawford	1,969	27,681	5,433	7,462	3,680	574	770	957	34,567	1,091	36.8	2.1	44.3
Cumberland	6,051	119,834	17,295	7,930	17,437	7,873	8,637	5,365	44,774	1,260	45.1	1.5	51.4
Dauphin	6,858	146,996	33,097	8,194	15,788	9,627	7,874	7,182	48,862	692	52.6	1.4	46.9
Delaware	12,864	210,978	42,077	12,753	26,530	13,479	11,281	11,295	53,535	61	77.0	NA	43.0
Elk	889	14,030	1,599	6,931	1,477	240	341	550	39,237	232	43.5	NA	32.1
Erie	6,191	114,476	24,667	20,308	16,123	5,163	3,819	4,372	38,187	1,162	39.6	1.4	46.8
Fayette	2,604	35,982	7,419	3,064	6,525	587	1,011	1,187	33,002	834	38.6	1.8	35.6
Forest	109	1,099	348	230	108	13	D	35	32,064	36	25.0	NA	71.4
Franklin	3,091	49,814	8,290	7,984	7,555	1,159	1,919	1,856	37,256	1,581	37.3	1.6	55.5
Fulton	263	5,704	690	D	353	74	32	267	46,837	545	31.4	1.8	36.1
Greene	752	11,721	1,649	305	2,359	321	250	486	41,470	722	25.2	1.2	39.3
Huntingdon	813	9,566	2,000	1,130	1,477	408	349	301	31,504	714	30.5	1.4	40.4
Indiana	1,864	25,543	4,942	2,202	4,401	1,327	1,057	960	37,593	951	36.9	1.6	37.9
Jefferson	1,125	13,812	3,011	3,489	1,554	239	419	490	35,463	468	23.9	2.1	44.4
Juniata	477	5,877	808	2,369	598	248	59	187	31,853	670	43.9	1.2	49.3
Lackawanna	5,338	95,435	22,124	8,831	12,823	5,255	3,038	3,474	36,404	263	24.3	1.5	35.1
Lancaster	12,874	228,355	35,600	33,465	31,129	7,496	11,719	9,617	42,116	5,108	50.0	0.4	56.9
Lawrence	1,929	26,381	6,499	3,514	3,671	1,150	751	937	35,515	587	38.0	1.7	39.3
Lebanon	2,709	44,345	8,079	9,310	7,018	932	1,149	1,638	36,944	1,149	54.6	0.2	50.5
Lehigh	8,555	174,230	40,076	18,896	22,291	6,542	6,448	8,991	51,604	381	55.4	4.5	52.8
Luzerne	7,241	133,636	25,168	16,953	18,310	5,285	6,086	5,239	39,203	451	39.0	1.6	40.6
Lycoming	2,745	45,232	8,956	7,543	7,555	1,503	1,419	1,705	37,700	1,043	32.2	1.3	38.6
McKean	1,010	12,600	2,629	2,987	1,793	276	201	460	36,525	259	29.3	0.8	35.6
Mercer	2,763	44,900	9,865	7,790	7,495	1,488	784	1,524	33,940	1,168	38.5	1.5	41.5
Mifflin	963	14,218	3,456	3,916	2,257	388	166	538	37,822	711	40.4	0.6	49.7
Monroe	3,372	47,216	7,039	5,420	9,581	983	1,564	1,687	35,721	233	55.4	1.7	40.4
Montgomery	26,220	494,756	82,115	40,518	59,003	37,018	44,839	31,091	62,841	565	76.3	0.7	40.1
Montour	490	14,333	7,514	579	662	1,364	465	969	67,582	356	43.5	0.8	42.5
Northampton	6,320	103,761	14,670	11,972	13,812	3,935	4,113	4,563	43,980	459	64.5	2.8	43.5
Northumberland	1,667	23,822	4,959	4,166	3,460	635	568	846	35,520	728	42.7	2.9	49.3
Perry	790	6,247	977	624	1,208	258	171	171	27,398	759	38.3	1.2	45.6
Philadelphia	27,929	621,865	153,198	21,116	52,151	30,967	47,937	35,402	56,929	43	95.3	NA	25.9
Pike	918	8,469	1,091	340	1,877	168	206	241	28,425	53	56.6	1.9	22.3

Table B. States and Counties — **Agriculture**

STATE County	Acreage (1,000)	Percent change, 2012-2017	Average size of farm	Total irrigated (1,000)	Total cropland (1,000)	Value of land and buildings (dollars) Average per farm	Average per acre	Value of machinery and equiopmnet, average per farm (dollars)	Total (mil dol)	Average per farm (acres)	Crops	Livestock and poultry products	Organic farms (number)	Farms with internet access (percent)	Government payments Total ($1,000)	Percent of farms
	117	118	119	120	121	122	123	124	125	126	127	128	129	130	131	132
OREGON— Cont'd																
Morrow	1,126	-3.3	3,003	111.5	511.9	3,385,469	1,127	416,278	596.5	1,590,632	32.0	68.0	6	86.4	11,659	57.6
Multnomah	25	-15.2	39	5.7	15.6	813,249	20,879	54,930	74.6	114,210	95.8	4.2	24	91.3	84	3.2
Polk	149	2.9	120	20.4	107.6	852,419	7,116	93,564	134.8	108,408	77.2	22.8	26	85.9	776	8.0
Sherman	525	2.2	2,762	1.1	340.9	2,349,030	850	240,036	33.8	177,879	93.7	6.3	3	77.4	9,823	86.8
Tillamook	33	-9.9	112	3.6	12.0	876,306	7,796	168,856	125.3	427,604	1.6	98.4	5	91.1	120	4.4
Umatilla	1,352	3.4	784	108.6	816.0	1,430,953	1,824	155,916	374.7	217,314	78.5	21.5	11	84.7	20,070	30.5
Union	385	-6.4	470	44.3	121.1	851,017	1,812	123,048	57.1	69,662	73.5	26.5	2	83.2	2,731	26.6
Wallowa	520	14.9	965	42.6	94.7	1,575,439	1,632	138,191	38.9	72,217	40.3	59.7	3	82.4	3,206	36.2
Wasco	1,389	-2.7	2,334	21.5	237.7	2,127,529	911	115,183	93.9	157,736	85.3	14.7	9	83.5	7,274	44.2
Washington	105	-22.9	60	18.0	75.7	1,020,247	17,099	88,896	201.6	114,874	96.2	3.8	21	89.5	1,485	9.2
Wheeler	557	-14.2	3,713	8.6	25.4	3,360,966	905	77,154	11.1	74,020	33.3	66.7	NA	80.7	921	23.3
Yamhill	169	-4.5	79	29.1	113.4	806,192	10,178	88,958	314.3	147,017	80.7	19.3	39	88.2	1,658	8.5
PENNSYLVANIA	7,279	-5.5	137	32.1	4,651.2	897,125	6,552	109,024	7,758.9	145,962	35.8	64.2	1,142	69.3	74,182	20.5
Adams	166	-3.0	145	2.2	128.4	998,833	6,886	132,547	207.6	181,122	54.2	45.8	17	77.7	1,503	18.4
Allegheny	29	-16.8	74	0.4	15.5	652,804	8,766	79,400	13.7	35,329	90.0	10.0	7	81.7	D	4.1
Armstrong	127	-1.9	190	0.2	73.7	690,965	3,644	111,565	39.8	59,533	57.8	42.2	6	77.2	654	20.7
Beaver	54	-3.5	88	0.3	30.1	531,298	6,050	80,548	23.7	38,586	61.2	38.8	3	72.6	177	8.0
Bedford	222	5.9	192	0.4	119.5	781,610	4,076	115,752	115.3	99,459	31.8	68.2	19	69.5	1,759	19.4
Berks	225	-3.9	124	1.5	184.5	1,392,373	11,209	138,139	554.7	306,609	43.8	56.2	72	68.4	3,038	22.1
Blair	79	-12.4	159	0.2	55.8	1,073,542	6,747	130,550	107.2	216,087	15.8	84.2	9	61.7	1,064	25.6
Bradford	304	-1.4	210	0.3	183.3	759,047	3,623	106,595	132.6	91,539	28.3	71.7	40	77.0	3,408	36.1
Bucks	77	20.7	94	1.0	60.0	882,088	9,408	85,710	75.8	91,938	72.5	27.5	15	84.2	635	10.1
Butler	134	-1.7	140	0.5	86.2	742,206	5,291	113,631	49.5	51,855	64.9	35.1	6	76.5	840	22.6
Cambria	79	3.2	142	0.1	50.5	659,661	4,631	100,086	30.1	53,982	60.1	39.9	2	68.8	979	30.3
Cameron	5	-15.1	143	NA	1.5	405,700	2,844	77,509	0.5	14,135	69.4	30.6	NA	59.5	61	37.8
Carbon	19	-7.9	97	0.0	13.1	645,238	6,619	106,544	13.0	65,145	87.7	12.3	1	83.5	185	25.0
Centre	150	-7.5	146	0.4	88.3	981,430	6,700	92,395	91.5	89,421	35.3	64.7	23	68.5	2,266	24.0
Chester	151	-8.5	91	1.2	105.8	1,110,075	12,140	130,513	712.5	432,848	80.1	19.9	46	74.5	1,775	10.0
Clarion	100	-13.5	169	0.0	52.5	542,206	3,210	96,875	27.7	46,582	47.9	52.1	9	74.4	835	27.6
Clearfield	61	-12.0	123	0.1	31.0	442,517	3,608	66,449	28.7	57,684	26.4	73.6	2	62.4	478	17.5
Clinton	40	-24.0	150	0.3	26.5	980,810	6,538	125,749	45.6	170,640	28.7	71.3	18	55.8	515	23.2
Columbia	107	-13.0	137	0.8	78.9	826,216	6,029	92,892	67.3	86,376	56.2	43.8	9	71.2	2,290	39.0
Crawford	194	-14.6	178	0.3	121.0	595,435	3,341	124,042	107.3	98,323	39.8	60.2	5	70.4	679	15.4
Cumberland	170	9.5	135	1.4	140.8	1,025,011	7,613	130,622	219.2	173,950	28.7	71.3	22	61.1	2,132	22.1
Dauphin	81	-37.2	117	0.4	63.4	1,032,232	8,791	106,338	93.1	134,499	29.2	70.8	43	68.4	779	21.0
Delaware	2	-49.5	39	0.1	0.7	562,808	14,395	69,987	9.5	155,656	97.7	2.3	NA	98.4	NA	NA
Elk	23	-2.2	99	0.1	9.3	415,868	4,198	65,859	4.0	17,349	50.2	49.8	4	71.1	50	9.9
Erie	153	-9.0	132	1.3	93.5	595,515	4,511	112,026	82.0	70,602	76.4	23.6	3	78.1	907	15.7
Fayette	112	-0.5	135	0.3	59.1	557,551	4,141	75,770	28.8	34,576	56.1	43.9	1	73.3	1,113	15.8
Forest	4	-49.7	116	0.0	1.7	567,562	4,900	71,350	2.1	57,194	14.7	85.3	NA	94.4	D	2.8
Franklin	270	1.9	170	2.8	213.9	1,283,405	7,528	162,878	476.5	301,372	19.2	80.8	44	59.6	3,264	23.0
Fulton	100	-10.5	184	0.0	52.9	769,540	4,175	95,703	75.8	139,110	16.2	83.8	7	72.5	686	29.2
Greene	114	1.5	158	0.0	37.5	575,776	3,644	85,505	16.4	22,763	51.3	48.7	NA	78.4	84	4.4
Huntingdon	120	-24.1	168	0.6	67.5	810,060	4,814	115,139	92.1	129,036	22.0	78.0	11	74.4	1,706	32.1
Indiana	148	-3.6	156	0.4	95.2	561,399	3,600	110,847	72.0	75,693	58.1	41.9	5	63.3	2,432	23.3
Jefferson	80	-11.9	172	0.2	46.6	569,456	3,314	82,484	22.4	47,912	50.3	49.7	3	70.7	519	19.0
Juniata	86	-5.9	128	0.2	55.7	833,587	6,522	106,123	126.8	189,194	17.5	82.5	64	63.3	904	22.8
Lackawanna	37	11.6	139	0.1	20.3	736,770	5,301	108,490	16.5	62,620	60.4	39.6	NA	77.2	119	16.7
Lancaster	394	-10.4	77	4.9	314.9	1,410,238	18,285	120,108	1,507.2	295,068	15.3	84.7	246	48.9	4,834	11.8
Lawrence	82	2.1	140	0.3	55.1	613,904	4,388	96,349	34.8	59,239	54.4	45.6	2	74.4	655	27.3
Lebanon	108	-11.4	94	0.7	86.7	1,348,192	14,400	132,813	350.8	305,312	10.6	89.4	54	71.4	1,021	13.7
Lehigh	75	-2.4	196	0.4	63.1	1,534,921	7,849	136,146	79.2	207,916	72.3	27.7	8	79.3	1,063	18.4
Luzerne	49	-19.4	109	0.3	27.6	659,902	6,063	64,776	17.8	39,452	74.7	25.3	NA	70.3	733	33.9
Lycoming	186	17.5	178	0.2	79.0	913,565	5,119	69,673	63.7	61,086	48.1	51.9	8	67.0	2,683	40.6
McKean	43	18.7	166	0.1	17.5	473,804	2,848	55,905	5.5	21,297	51.4	48.6	1	73.4	315	26.6
Mercer	156	-4.1	134	0.2	98.4	535,249	3,997	103,659	65.7	56,291	53.9	46.1	20	73.6	1,526	26.3
Mifflin	81	-10.6	114	0.1	49.9	703,683	6,179	92,455	140.0	196,896	12.0	88.0	18	65.8	818	17.0
Monroe	28	4.2	118	0.2	13.4	698,127	5,892	85,598	9.9	42,627	64.6	35.4	NA	79.4	190	9.4
Montgomery	31	0.4	55	0.6	20.5	1,058,678	19,360	62,127	35.4	62,609	73.9	26.1	2	83.5	179	4.8
Montour	39	-11.2	109	0.1	29.4	699,083	6,442	103,791	60.2	169,171	42.4	57.6	4	64.9	643	32.9
Northampton	59	-10.0	129	0.3	51.6	967,696	7,504	159,760	36.1	78,558	76.5	23.5	4	80.2	1,204	16.6
Northumberland	124	-4.1	171	0.9	92.7	1,001,321	5,872	143,549	154.6	212,339	38.0	62.0	18	67.7	2,710	35.0
Perry	115	-15.1	151	0.4	77.2	1,002,216	6,629	125,814	172.8	227,613	18.3	81.7	33	68.2	1,251	22.8
Philadelphia	0	-0.4	7	0.0	0.1	387,767	58,711	16,642	0.3	7,605	81.0	19.0	2	90.7	NA	NA
Pike	25	-12.6	466	0.0	1.4	1,037,171	2,226	74,827	0.9	16,830	50.0	50.0	NA	96.2	NA	NA

Table B. States and Counties — Water Use, Wholesale Trade, Retail Trade, and Real Estate

STATE County	Water use, 2015		Wholesale Trade[1], 2012				Retail Trade[2], 2012				Real estate and rental and leasing,[2] 2012			
	Public supply water withdrawn (mil gal/ day)	Public supply gallons withdrawn per person per day	Number of establishments	Number of employees	Sales (mil dol)	Average payroll (mil dol)	Number of establishments	Number of employees	Sales (mil dol)	Average payroll (mil dol)	Number of establishments	Number of employees	Sales (mil dol)	Average payroll (mil dol)
	133	134	135	136	137	138	139	140	141	142	143	144	145	146
OREGON— Cont'd														
Morrow	5.61	501.3	11	60	51.2	3.8	13	79	19.6	2.1	10	11	1.4	0.2
Multnomah	14.72	18.6	1,233	21,805	21,267.8	1,275.5	2,888	37,805	9,982.9	1,016.1	1,373	8,734	1,569.3	369.5
Polk	4.96	62.5	29	264	100.9	10.4	125	1,546	360.7	36.9	59	167	19.4	3.0
Sherman	0.47	279.8	4	D	D	D	7	D	D	D	NA	NA	NA	NA
Tillamook	4.57	178.1	9	105	42.3	3.2	114	1,032	248.9	24.4	27	91	8.0	1.7
Umatilla	28.17	368.1	65	953	738.7	45.4	224	2,922	802.8	70.8	60	148	21.1	4.0
Union	4.58	177.6	22	209	140.3	8.4	103	1,313	318.5	31.6	17	70	9.6	1.8
Wallowa	1.37	199.8	2	D	D	D	51	284	63.6	7.0	18	D	D	D
Wasco	5.34	207.2	25	628	213.6	14.6	123	1,506	389.4	37.1	42	102	10.9	2.6
Washington	50.04	87.1	734	9,915	8,667.6	618.5	1,573	28,336	8,389.7	790.3	809	4,492	1,207.1	158.0
Wheeler	0.17	125.2	1	D	D	D	6	D	D	D	2	D	D	D
Yamhill	8.83	86.0	70	D	D	D	283	3,325	886.6	84.9	102	263	36.4	6.1
PENNSYLVANIA	1,391.70	108.7	12,568	195,004	191,170.1	11,203.8	43,952	643,903	178,794.9	15,330.6	9,438	58,585	13,364.0	2,617.5
Adams	12.39	121.1	61	D	D	D	333	3,231	801.2	74.4	47	210	35.8	7.0
Allegheny	178.17	144.8	1,497	21,265	27,237.9	1,195.1	4,423	72,737	20,553.7	1,730.3	1,291	9,005	2,208.0	414.5
Armstrong	6.65	99.2	35	525	217.2	24.2	215	2,105	551.2	42.1	27	270	33.8	10.0
Beaver	22.14	131.1	112	1,508	1,179.5	74.3	517	7,307	1,590.2	149.3	92	398	83.2	14.2
Bedford	9.99	205.6	39	382	350.6	21.8	183	2,088	576.2	43.0	11	86	21.2	4.9
Berks	31.85	76.7	354	6,912	4,277.4	362.2	1,256	20,219	5,719.4	494.3	246	1,249	213.0	41.4
Blair	13.07	104.1	119	1,832	2,258.4	80.7	561	8,383	2,286.7	189.4	87	349	72.9	11.3
Bradford	3.02	49.3	49	D	D	D	252	3,127	903.7	72.7	30	223	52.6	9.9
Bucks	98.64	157.2	1,152	14,950	12,999.7	854.9	2,408	38,063	10,185.1	975.9	589	3,494	855.9	147.2
Butler	7.66	41.0	253	4,444	3,353.8	249.0	680	11,085	2,902.2	245.0	148	714	160.4	23.9
Cambria	14.93	109.4	115	1,365	664.9	51.0	561	6,927	1,733.8	148.6	86	408	48.3	12.2
Cameron	0.34	71.9	2	D	D	D	17	174	30.9	3.3	1	D	D	D
Carbon	23.34	364.9	19	D	D	D	194	2,142	562.6	49.3	36	121	21.1	3.4
Centre	17.87	111.3	90	873	538.9	42.5	481	7,570	1,748.7	155.7	133	1,036	255.5	34.7
Chester	42.15	81.7	711	12,642	19,155.1	1,204.8	1,517	27,549	12,474.9	984.2	457	2,360	781.2	143.1
Clarion	2.73	69.1	30	385	167.3	14.2	185	1,879	460.4	40.7	21	104	11.0	3.4
Clearfield	5.84	72.1	68	771	703.6	30.4	350	4,731	1,331.3	105.4	43	344	35.9	8.7
Clinton	4.02	101.9	18	D	D	D	121	1,773	582.6	39.5	37	165	26.6	4.3
Columbia	5.02	75.3	46	419	118.4	15.8	236	3,413	904.8	70.4	43	205	33.9	6.4
Crawford	5.67	65.6	57	372	136.3	12.8	317	3,577	973.5	85.5	51	176	24.5	4.3
Cumberland	13.36	54.2	189	2,607	2,666.3	124.9	858	16,016	4,812.9	376.3	222	1,366	316.8	66.3
Dauphin	31.47	115.3	295	6,839	6,655.5	390.2	981	15,280	3,943.9	348.2	218	1,608	505.1	90.5
Delaware	20.79	36.9	522	6,961	5,482.3	536.3	1,700	24,271	6,468.8	602.2	409	2,945	776.4	169.8
Elk	5.32	172.3	26	D	D	D	124	1,496	314.5	28.8	11	46	6.3	1.2
Erie	33.34	119.9	264	3,127	1,242.5	145.7	958	15,221	3,752.8	326.4	182	1,042	158.5	32.3
Fayette	45.89	343.4	107	1,002	496.6	37.7	487	6,040	1,638.8	129.7	69	299	50.9	9.9
Forest	0.41	55.3	1	D	D	D	18	101	24.8	2.0	1	D	D	D
Franklin	8.47	55.1	108	D	D	D	486	7,106	1,809.5	157.6	87	328	54.9	10.4
Fulton	0.37	25.3	12	142	139.8	4.6	42	374	102.9	7.3	3	12	1.2	0.5
Greene	7.19	191.6	26	350	302.8	17.5	138	2,444	883.7	63.3	12	47	6.7	1.1
Huntingdon	2.85	62.4	29	344	94.9	11.6	141	1,424	354.3	28.8	10	28	9.8	1.0
Indiana	4.11	47.3	67	D	D	D	309	5,016	1,318.8	112.7	45	163	26.2	3.8
Jefferson	2.14	48.2	39	441	245.5	17.9	176	1,857	556.2	37.7	24	128	32.2	4.6
Juniata	0.82	33.1	18	133	54.5	5.0	69	601	204.4	13.1	6	12	1.3	0.2
Lackawanna	38.70	182.6	251	3,800	4,374.5	168.9	916	13,197	3,186.3	278.2	138	690	128.5	21.1
Lancaster	54.45	101.5	582	10,776	8,764.0	496.7	1,917	29,783	6,899.6	669.6	342	2,009	396.6	79.1
Lawrence	10.07	114.3	86	D	D	D	292	3,391	838.7	75.6	44	279	29.7	7.0
Lebanon	3.55	25.9	99	2,679	3,913.7	112.7	431	6,597	1,695.7	158.6	70	309	40.5	7.8
Lehigh	34.58	95.9	408	9,182	8,062.4	577.2	1,239	20,261	5,550.4	467.5	315	1,587	324.0	58.2
Luzerne	22.82	71.7	300	5,656	3,435.9	242.3	1,247	18,177	8,097.0	413.8	210	923	214.7	34.0
Lycoming	8.78	75.7	108	2,110	1,271.2	82.6	503	7,404	1,878.1	154.7	89	618	120.0	24.4
McKean	6.77	159.6	31	D	D	D	158	1,551	401.8	34.7	16	62	6.4	1.4
Mercer	13.74	120.3	89	1,099	644.7	42.4	516	7,109	1,527.3	147.2	72	275	101.6	7.8
Mifflin	2.69	57.8	35	D	D	D	162	2,063	539.4	46.9	23	71	11.0	1.7
Monroe	11.35	68.2	97	D	D	D	634	8,710	2,140.4	187.8	123	507	86.8	15.2
Montgomery	63.31	77.3	1,237	19,422	17,692.1	1,444.8	3,261	56,471	16,036.3	1,489.8	931	7,713	1,767.3	412.8
Montour	0.03	1.6	13	149	190.2	6.1	54	662	167.2	13.6	6	18	2.9	0.6
Northampton	9.53	31.7	250	3,917	9,979.8	192.8	873	13,238	3,627.4	316.9	178	726	260.6	27.4
Northumberland	11.05	118.5	56	945	1,152.0	46.6	280	3,188	909.7	76.7	38	182	37.4	7.7
Perry	0.71	15.5	16	144	81.4	6.1	134	1,166	317.8	25.6	10	23	3.4	0.7
Philadelphia	249.54	159.2	1,047	16,940	13,181.9	973.0	4,506	50,185	12,241.3	1,165.5	1,079	8,856	1,951.0	443.5
Pike	3.05	54.5	15	98	31.8	5.4	134	1,862	471.4	40.0	40	442	41.9	10.9

1   Merchant wholesalers, except manufacturers' sales branches and offices.   2. Employer establishments.

Professional Services, Manufacturing, and Accommodation and Food Services

STATE County	Professional, scientific, and technical services, 2012				Manufacturing, 2012				Accommodation and food services, 2012			
	Number of establish-ments	Number of employees	Sales (mil dol)	Average payroll (mil dol)	Number of establish-ments	Number of employees	Receipts (mil dol)	Annual payroll (mil dol)	Number of establis-hments	Number of employees	Receipts (mil dol)	Annual payroll (mil dol)
	147	148	149	150	151	152	153	154	155	156	157	158
OREGON— Cont'd												
Morrow	3	6	1.2	0.2	11	1,120	753.5	46.9	19	125	6.8	2.0
Multnomah	3,682	31,457	5,611.6	2,186.1	1,095	32,206	10,278.1	1,633.4	2,799	42,709	2,506.2	736.3
Polk	117	407	36.2	12.6	60	1,801	424.7	68.1	142	D	D	D
Sherman	1	D	D	D	NA	NA	NA	NA	7	60	4.6	1.2
Tillamook	41	D	D	D	30	1,224	708.3	55.8	120	950	51.2	14.5
Umatilla	102	844	74.3	36.3	70	2,522	858.1	90.3	163	2,903	194.5	47.1
Union	47	225	19.2	7.9	28	1,097	275.9	43.1	65	806	33.8	9.4
Wallowa	24	82	7.5	2.6	15	85	D	2.9	47	139	9.7	2.3
Wasco	48	267	25.0	10.0	30	273	93.6	10.8	85	1,288	66.7	20.8
Washington	1,750	21,129	1,788.4	2,119.1	708	D	D	D	1,141	17,404	970.6	277.9
Wheeler	NA	NA	NA	NA	NA	NA	NA	NA	5	18	0.9	0.2
Yamhill	200	638	67.4	24.7	225	5,407	1,893.6	280.4	195	2,486	129.3	40.0
PENNSYLVANIA	29,297	316,658	54,833.8	22,621.5	13,988	543,641	231,396.2	28,057.8	27,646	439,159	23,504.2	6,377.4
Adams	126	D	D	D	113	5,745	2,148.7	240.8	222	3,521	185.7	53.0
Allegheny	3,864	59,880	11,007.2	4,362.7	1,086	36,428	16,279.5	2,073.3	3,170	57,039	2,940.6	827.4
Armstrong	77	361	37.8	11.5	65	1,468	324.1	62.6	95	1,153	42.7	11.0
Beaver	254	3,560	262.0	143.0	175	7,556	4,615.0	397.5	309	4,456	191.8	51.1
Bedford	45	194	18.5	4.7	64	2,065	863.0	83.5	107	1,607	78.6	24.7
Berks	703	D	D	D	498	29,439	10,905.1	1,547.9	754	12,294	548.8	155.6
Blair	221	1,789	208.3	74.8	135	6,943	2,115.6	298.8	280	4,634	199.4	56.5
Bradford	88	549	64.0	21.4	61	3,921	1,975.5	185.0	125	1,576	76.2	20.4
Bucks	2,331	18,164	3,140.0	1,196.9	1,045	27,061	9,681.4	1,428.8	1,385	21,398	1,136.1	302.9
Butler	426	7,354	2,293.3	622.6	266	12,782	4,630.0	687.1	363	6,841	326.6	89.7
Cambria	228	3,359	380.3	168.2	127	5,232	1,798.8	241.6	300	4,070	179.0	47.8
Cameron	6	D	D	D	23	858	D	38.2	13	D	D	D
Carbon	60	241	19.8	9.7	55	1,678	415.0	68.8	116	1,939	112.0	29.9
Centre	365	3,204	432.1	191.2	145	3,960	1,053.5	181.9	311	6,352	289.0	79.7
Chester	2,239	20,472	4,199.5	1,774.2	533	16,067	6,633.5	961.4	932	15,867	846.1	251.0
Clarion	38	238	22.1	9.9	33	1,293	471.2	52.1	95	1,400	57.4	14.2
Clearfield	106	610	56.1	19.7	108	2,613	962.4	99.9	179	2,407	99.5	27.1
Clinton	48	235	24.0	7.9	47	2,836	1,676.8	130.3	83	1,266	58.0	15.3
Columbia	92	677	54.0	22.0	73	5,484	1,613.4	224.9	159	2,484	109.3	29.6
Crawford	115	800	84.1	32.2	277	7,093	1,759.2	318.1	185	2,349	102.8	27.4
Cumberland	649	7,932	1,161.1	522.0	186	7,550	3,776.4	353.2	506	9,403	465.0	129.1
Dauphin	712	7,608	1,178.0	481.8	186	7,679	3,228.9	404.2	679	12,533	718.3	199.6
Delaware	1,525	12,084	2,383.7	903.0	367	12,929	7,364.9	974.8	1,105	16,283	878.1	236.0
Elk	40	1,020	26.4	17.0	135	6,587	1,732.6	295.0	72	763	28.3	7.1
Erie	412	3,028	375.8	135.3	476	21,490	9,437.7	1,179.0	630	10,877	485.4	128.2
Fayette	137	961	143.0	40.5	111	3,088	1,324.2	157.8	285	4,101	211.8	62.0
Forest	2	D	D	D	5	D	D	D	21	125	7.5	1.8
Franklin	223	2,067	234.8	100.3	196	8,182	3,180.0	403.9	270	D	D	D
Fulton	12	31	1.8	0.5	15	D	D	D	18	255	10.5	3.1
Greene	39	230	23.1	7.4	24	370	101.5	15.8	59	1,087	53.3	14.4
Huntingdon	54	256	17.5	7.6	43	1,884	667.4	75.8	84	964	50.3	13.6
Indiana	125	D	D	D	89	2,570	509.6	101.4	178	2,955	117.6	30.0
Jefferson	69	380	42.1	13.9	101	3,475	887.6	151.7	94	942	41.6	10.2
Juniata	22	60	4.3	1.1	59	1,977	337.1	64.7	31	371	15.4	4.4
Lackawanna	488	2,922	363.3	132.4	237	8,611	D	370.4	590	8,685	411.7	107.9
Lancaster	957	12,486	1,249.1	1,037.2	856	33,212	13,655.7	1,638.7	998	17,833	878.4	246.9
Lawrence	138	D	D	D	140	3,465	1,819.4	192.3	163	2,163	89.0	23.9
Lebanon	197	1,083	151.2	48.6	205	8,099	2,743.8	336.5	232	3,320	146.1	40.5
Lehigh	754	D	D	D	378	15,977	9,889.5	867.6	735	12,283	633.0	175.9
Luzerne	575	5,266	528.3	207.3	314	16,701	6,628.0	728.6	740	10,730	515.6	134.1
Lycoming	200	2,151	184.5	74.5	160	8,162	3,186.7	371.5	296	4,696	237.9	62.6
McKean	60	202	16.3	6.2	51	3,290	1,615.8	170.4	102	954	44.6	11.3
Mercer	164	801	77.1	26.6	186	7,405	3,309.4	351.2	254	4,138	188.3	47.6
Mifflin	38	164	11.7	3.6	86	3,696	1,163.0	184.0	84	1,107	45.2	12.3
Monroe	306	D	D	D	111	4,449	D	358.1	387	8,392	724.8	155.1
Montgomery	3,696	45,260	7,823.6	3,663.3	987	39,566	14,574.7	2,433.5	1,901	29,320	1,723.2	489.4
Montour	37	449	134.9	25.4	18	424	140.7	13.9	39	708	38.7	9.9
Northampton	590	4,342	588.8	252.6	328	11,374	4,081.2	571.4	678	11,011	941.1	198.3
Northumberland	104	534	45.0	17.4	78	3,710	1,194.3	150.7	172	1,549	66.2	17.8
Perry	50	218	18.1	6.6	36	665	102.6	22.0	71	449	21.1	5.2
Philadelphia	2,845	47,158	10,464.6	4,249.2	765	22,558	19,718.6	1,198.5	3,669	53,533	3,551.7	982.4
Pike	77	243	30.6	8.6	20	150	27.1	6.2	103	1,826	127.2	36.3

Table B. States and Counties — Health Care and Social Assistance, Other Services, Nonemployer Businesses, and Residential Construction

STATE County	Health care and social assistance, 2012				Other services, 2012				Nonemployer businesses, 2016		Value of residential construction authorized by building permits, 2018	
	Number of establish-ments	Number of employees	Receipts (mil dol)	Annual payroll (mil dol)	Number of establish-ments	Number of employees	Receipts (mil dol)	Annual payroll (mil dol)	Number	Receipts (mil dol)	New construction ($1,000)	Number of housing units
	159	160	161	162	163	164	165	166	167	168	169	170
OREGON— Cont'd												
Morrow	15	139	9.8	3.6	12	31	2.8	0.8	489	22.9	16,871	140
Multnomah	2,950	62,033	7,703.7	2,988.1	1,867	12,391	1,810.6	423.2	71,087	3,411.4	973,771	6,238
Polk	191	2,531	168.6	75.0	87	332	25.7	7.5	4,316	177.1	74,453	311
Sherman	4	23	0.3	0.1	2	D	D	D	125	5.9	NA	NA
Tillamook	52	810	87.3	36.0	44	D	D	D	1,900	89.4	36,349	141
Umatilla	207	2,923	312.6	115.8	104	500	58.4	17.3	3,336	160.3	32,113	164
Union	103	1,388	127.5	55.3	54	D	D	D	1,576	59.3	13,877	52
Wallowa	35	412	33.9	13.4	19	D	D	D	802	38.3	5,046	28
Wasco	74	1,769	148.2	78.4	48	173	13.4	4.1	1,417	55.4	NA	NA
Washington	1,722	25,903	3,238.1	1,205.9	843	5,106	530.2	179.2	37,958	1,840.7	457,005	1,889
Wheeler	5	D	D	D	1	D	D	D	148	6.4	NA	NA
Yamhill	260	4,241	433.6	151.6	133	D	D	D	6,209	274.3	114,909	492
PENNSYLVANIA	36,552	955,479	96,329.2	39,326.6	25,231	154,319	17,736.7	4,366.6	831,951	39,990.9	4,684,321	23,325
Adams	182	4,634	448.2	167.1	150	909	75.1	19.8	6,527	285.6	49,540	224
Allegheny	4,423	123,336	12,756.2	5,392.7	2,872	19,874	2,346.4	604.4	82,344	3,784.0	509,410	2,222
Armstrong	188	3,504	246.4	106.5	113	499	38.4	10.5	3,572	140.7	3,385	11
Beaver	470	9,380	779.6	351.2	316	1,324	113.6	30.6	8,721	353.1	35,534	201
Bedford	120	1,769	148.9	54.8	95	373	27.1	6.8	3,286	149.8	12,828	70
Berks	827	25,605	2,588.9	1,067.0	767	4,046	363.5	101.5	24,485	1,137.4	103,485	600
Blair	438	11,356	1,149.5	472.4	283	1,573	118.4	36.7	6,276	296.2	20,721	101
Bradford	148	4,744	561.0	228.0	120	558	43.9	11.3	3,578	146.8	13,457	56
Bucks	2,014	40,065	3,735.6	1,582.5	1,424	8,400	746.1	234.1	53,177	3,043.8	226,448	907
Butler	608	12,564	1,198.6	493.0	388	2,309	203.4	54.3	12,195	592.5	174,304	714
Cambria	540	11,708	1,047.3	444.7	312	1,690	133.9	34.2	6,241	244.0	16,414	66
Cameron	11	D	D	D	11	62	3.5	0.6	211	7.1	0	0
Carbon	160	3,302	219.0	97.4	91	310	28.7	6.8	3,397	146.8	17,204	87
Centre	363	7,882	767.4	316.6	249	1,471	131.7	37.0	10,130	457.9	83,405	328
Chester	1,440	34,065	3,442.7	1,431.8	1,042	8,068	1,969.8	300.6	42,998	2,555.5	349,174	1,939
Clarion	137	3,052	197.3	84.0	72	494	53.1	11.3	2,413	108.8	10,006	56
Clearfield	260	6,187	576.4	238.7	165	1,169	90.7	26.1	4,192	168.1	14,076	72
Clinton	71	1,241	98.3	39.3	66	315	30.9	5.5	1,917	82.7	6,440	27
Columbia	164	D	D	D	114	493	48.6	9.8	3,202	139.2	24,615	147
Crawford	238	5,129	424.6	183.6	174	816	70.2	16.4	5,393	230.6	11,339	52
Cumberland	662	15,684	1,650.9	675.6	535	4,185	521.6	130.0	15,795	779.4	208,514	1,179
Dauphin	820	26,291	2,182.0	899.1	685	4,728	580.5	175.7	16,189	728.9	119,507	740
Delaware	1,608	39,002	3,952.6	1,724.6	1,116	6,740	863.0	212.3	42,745	2,139.9	71,609	286
Elk	108	2,117	146.6	66.5	78	340	21.9	5.4	1,502	62.6	5,955	27
Erie	850	24,899	2,216.5	923.1	563	3,591	322.7	80.2	13,838	589.7	46,085	305
Fayette	408	7,929	619.8	259.5	240	1,181	118.1	28.1	6,354	269.5	40,882	163
Forest	10	456	35.9	14.2	6	13	1.2	0.2	274	10.0	0	0
Franklin	305	8,178	820.5	349.3	287	1,558	131.5	32.7	8,944	373.6	82,570	423
Fulton	25	D	D	D	27	97	9.7	2.1	916	40.5	6,970	32
Greene	105	1,588	141.3	52.5	72	369	46.9	10.3	1,551	59.6	6,787	33
Huntingdon	95	1,859	147.4	61.7	79	301	27.3	5.5	2,474	107.6	10,705	49
Indiana	252	4,406	360.6	149.4	151	954	109.1	25.6	4,926	208.7	10,942	46
Jefferson	150	2,991	236.6	100.0	103	426	32.6	7.9	2,931	136.0	6,135	40
Juniata	34	561	37.3	14.2	32	108	9.9	2.5	1,852	94.2	7,377	42
Lackawanna	730	19,120	1,805.5	768.9	401	2,181	180.8	53.0	12,063	595.0	45,757	212
Lancaster	1,110	34,977	3,387.5	1,411.1	1,031	6,339	588.6	161.3	41,920	2,209.2	239,895	1,251
Lawrence	291	6,467	501.7	214.0	174	853	71.5	19.5	5,077	202.0	10,316	46
Lebanon	279	8,165	772.4	341.9	233	1,086	110.1	27.5	8,236	395.7	57,617	299
Lehigh	1,170	40,184	4,351.2	1,715.9	719	4,730	428.3	127.0	22,663	1,040.3	115,700	476
Luzerne	967	23,680	2,273.1	934.5	559	2,803	292.8	71.8	16,868	823.1	67,521	312
Lycoming	287	8,233	825.8	345.7	240	1,546	152.8	35.4	6,249	278.7	30,510	140
McKean	151	2,764	209.7	88.5	95	472	37.9	9.1	2,120	83.0	2,822	15
Mercer	410	10,413	866.4	358.8	251	1,144	97.7	22.7	6,290	289.9	29,028	118
Mifflin	127	3,113	251.0	104.4	67	249	21.1	5.2	2,770	113.3	8,022	42
Monroe	393	7,031	643.1	276.0	309	1,571	115.7	37.0	10,441	477.3	46,920	186
Montgomery	3,023	71,373	7,980.2	3,199.4	1,908	11,847	1,609.1	359.9	71,522	4,456.7	507,069	2,530
Montour	100	D	D	D	35	234	62.0	8.7	1,037	48.1	8,639	47
Northampton	776	13,343	1,137.2	468.0	547	2,875	233.2	71.8	18,366	884.4	104,878	575
Northumberland	206	5,305	340.8	149.5	146	772	46.7	13.8	4,461	209.2	41,616	167
Perry	80	1,007	49.6	23.6	65	245	22.9	4.8	2,931	134.3	23,977	94
Philadelphia	3,920	152,972	17,972.6	6,847.5	2,493	17,972	2,408.7	632.4	95,065	3,505.9	521,128	3,239
Pike	86	961	64.2	26.0	97	950	70.1	19.4	4,008	190.2	25,387	97

Table B. States and Counties — Government Employment and Payroll, and Local Government Finances

	Government employment and payroll, 2012									Local government finances, 2012				
			March payroll (percent of total)							General revenue				
												Taxes		
STATE County	Full-time equivalent employees	March payroll (dollars)	Adminis-tration, judicial, and legal	Police and corrections	Fire protection	Highways and transpor-tation	Health and welfare	Natural resources and utilities	Education and libraries	Total (mil dol)	Inter-govern-mental (mil dol)	Total (mil dol)	Per capita[1] (dollars) Total	Per capita[1] (dollars) Property
	171	172	173	174	175	176	177	178	179	180	181	182	183	184
OREGON— Cont'd														
Morrow	611	2,174,057	7.8	9.3	1.6	5.2	17.4	6.6	45.7	79.1	31.3	21.7	1,928	1,801
Multnomah	29,478	148,927,675	7.5	11.9	4.2	13.6	6.4	9.0	42.8	4,680.8	1,700.4	1,856.1	2,445	1,660
Polk	1,230	4,842,625	12.3	13.6	2.4	1.9	8.6	6.6	52.1	138.5	77.6	42.1	552	500
Sherman	121	446,146	20.7	9.6	8.8	9.9	11.4	7.5	29.5	23.4	4.3	6.6	3,808	3,775
Tillamook	1,081	4,310,792	8.6	7.5	1.5	5.0	4.7	26.1	44.4	116.8	36.6	46.1	1,822	1,701
Umatilla	2,519	9,346,604	6.6	11.0	3.9	3.0	1.9	7.4	65.3	307.6	163.2	86.2	1,122	1,020
Union	750	2,655,712	8.7	12.0	2.8	4.4	0.9	8.8	60.1	87.0	50.9	20.7	802	722
Wallowa	382	1,406,470	6.1	5.5	0.3	3.8	43.8	3.1	36.5	46.2	14.1	8.6	1,262	1,113
Wasco	982	3,676,060	6.9	6.4	4.7	3.8	3.2	15.2	58.1	115.4	52.3	37.4	1,468	1,319
Washington	14,620	63,993,061	6.8	11.2	6.7	2.5	2.0	7.5	60.1	1,882.7	665.8	834.1	1,523	1,366
Wheeler	106	329,289	21.3	2.9	0.0	9.3	0.0	7.4	57.6	8.1	5.1	1.6	1,126	1,092
Yamhill	2,820	11,200,226	7.7	9.1	4.6	1.7	6.0	8.9	59.7	320.3	146.1	104.5	1,043	942
PENNSYLVANIA	X	X	X	X	X	X	X	X	X	X	X	X	X	X
Adams	2,548	9,790,732	7.8	9.5	0.9	2.6	2.1	3.4	73.2	374.0	165.8	167.3	1,648	1,256
Allegheny	43,945	195,375,705	6.5	12.8	2.4	11.5	5.4	5.9	53.8	6,769.1	2,823.5	2,739.2	2,228	1,525
Armstrong	2,222	7,529,691	6.9	7.0	0.0	4.1	6.8	5.5	68.9	227.1	114.7	81.0	1,185	1,004
Beaver	5,422	21,094,763	6.4	10.1	0.3	4.8	6.7	6.8	64.1	785.3	350.5	233.6	1,372	1,124
Bedford	1,369	4,444,835	5.3	5.6	0.8	4.2	1.7	5.0	77.4	128.7	70.2	45.3	918	675
Berks	14,566	69,528,665	6.1	16.3	5.1	2.6	4.7	5.3	58.7	2,039.3	792.5	835.6	2,021	1,642
Blair	4,030	13,533,958	4.8	8.4	2.3	5.0	8.5	7.0	62.6	402.4	214.5	126.2	993	707
Bradford	2,246	8,350,493	7.8	4.9	0.5	5.3	11.4	1.9	67.4	247.1	119.2	78.6	1,252	972
Bucks	18,333	88,124,851	6.0	11.7	0.6	4.0	4.0	3.9	68.9	2,731.2	688.4	1,517.1	2,419	2,074
Butler	4,890	20,031,417	6.5	6.1	0.5	3.3	5.6	4.7	72.2	629.8	252.7	262.6	1,420	1,090
Cambria	4,484	15,273,184	8.2	8.3	1.4	5.9	5.7	6.0	63.9	555.1	293.7	143.3	1,012	781
Cameron	214	664,238	8.3	4.9	0.0	5.0	7.5	2.5	70.2	17.3	9.0	6.0	1,223	1,052
Carbon	2,113	7,282,054	7.7	9.6	0.0	3.5	11.6	5.7	60.5	211.1	71.9	108.6	1,671	1,438
Centre	3,965	14,048,206	7.5	8.6	0.0	7.9	9.9	5.8	58.3	455.2	154.4	216.4	1,394	1,018
Chester	13,231	61,935,244	7.1	9.3	0.2	2.2	4.5	2.8	71.3	2,107.9	567.4	1,254.5	2,476	2,063
Clarion	1,226	4,224,897	6.3	6.9	0.0	3.1	1.8	3.0	78.3	155.3	103.3	39.4	993	773
Clearfield	2,608	9,251,789	4.9	5.4	0.0	3.3	1.6	4.7	78.9	261.5	141.7	88.1	1,086	853
Clinton	1,129	4,364,621	9.8	5.9	2.2	2.6	11.0	7.0	59.8	138.0	54.0	44.3	1,121	835
Columbia	1,917	7,059,353	6.5	11.0	0.0	3.3	2.0	3.1	73.5	197.2	86.4	83.5	1,248	914
Crawford	2,501	8,880,019	8.6	8.3	1.6	5.0	10.3	5.8	59.4	270.2	125.4	98.7	1,127	906
Cumberland	7,023	27,433,306	6.6	8.7	0.0	2.7	6.7	4.9	68.9	914.8	308.3	434.2	1,820	1,330
Dauphin	10,041	42,265,280	7.7	13.4	1.0	4.7	1.7	5.4	64.3	1,441.8	522.5	527.9	1,958	1,407
Delaware	18,047	76,207,314	10.5	9.6	1.0	2.0	6.2	4.1	65.6	2,712.5	932.9	1,199.8	2,138	1,938
Elk	1,009	3,366,414	8.9	6.3	0.0	12.9	2.6	6.2	61.7	108.1	52.0	37.3	1,181	901
Erie	8,523	32,472,819	5.3	9.7	2.6	5.6	3.9	6.0	65.7	1,197.6	616.5	364.0	1,297	1,046
Fayette	3,546	14,568,652	6.8	9.1	0.4	5.2	7.7	9.3	61.2	411.7	262.1	104.7	772	570
Forest	197	632,875	20.3	3.4	0.0	3.6	5.7	3.9	62.0	19.5	9.4	7.5	980	863
Franklin	3,820	13,644,359	7.7	8.8	1.7	2.3	9.1	6.1	63.5	415.1	130.8	191.4	1,265	978
Fulton	454	1,468,178	11.3	2.6	0.0	2.5	0.0	2.1	81.0	47.4	25.7	16.4	1,112	912
Greene	1,301	4,613,569	10.4	5.2	0.0	6.2	4.1	7.8	65.3	144.0	67.6	57.8	1,518	1,258
Huntingdon	1,125	3,453,282	9.3	7.1	0.0	3.2	3.8	5.2	70.1	118.4	66.3	38.4	837	613
Indiana	2,289	9,093,274	6.9	6.4	0.1	4.5	4.9	5.1	70.9	313.8	170.3	97.7	1,107	879
Jefferson	1,211	4,334,856	6.6	7.0	0.0	4.9	1.4	6.4	72.3	125.7	68.4	38.4	858	661
Juniata	563	1,993,044	11.0	5.3	1.3	2.6	0.1	1.9	75.5	49.2	23.8	21.6	867	690
Lackawanna	6,361	25,493,690	6.8	11.8	3.2	4.1	6.5	6.5	59.1	757.3	291.3	324.8	1,515	1,101
Lancaster	12,622	54,624,168	5.9	11.7	0.8	2.8	3.4	3.5	70.9	1,833.2	668.6	843.7	1,601	1,327
Lawrence	2,433	9,509,559	8.0	8.4	1.5	4.9	1.0	3.8	71.8	318.9	174.0	106.5	1,185	905
Lebanon	4,116	14,939,586	6.1	9.0	1.7	2.8	9.0	5.5	65.4	485.8	160.6	191.5	1,416	1,136
Lehigh	11,303	49,829,858	7.3	10.7	1.9	4.5	9.3	4.5	60.4	1,670.5	674.3	669.0	1,883	1,523
Luzerne	9,404	36,055,331	7.5	12.5	3.5	3.7	4.7	5.2	62.1	1,080.5	466.5	439.6	1,369	1,039
Lycoming	3,615	14,906,594	7.7	7.9	1.8	4.3	2.7	6.0	68.7	451.3	198.0	155.7	1,329	953
McKean	1,616	5,647,554	6.9	7.4	1.5	4.5	8.7	8.2	62.2	167.7	97.2	44.6	1,033	829
Mercer	3,570	12,446,506	8.5	9.8	1.2	3.2	1.2	4.2	70.1	402.4	216.5	133.0	1,150	861
Mifflin	1,135	4,324,228	8.8	6.8	1.1	5.0	2.7	9.1	64.8	153.4	81.3	46.8	1,002	733
Monroe	5,957	25,067,544	5.7	4.3	0.0	5.4	1.6	1.5	80.9	719.0	225.3	441.5	2,616	2,404
Montgomery	23,690	112,151,487	6.4	12.2	0.4	2.4	5.0	4.0	68.6	3,430.1	888.0	2,054.1	2,541	2,087
Montour	515	1,746,307	6.4	6.4	0.0	4.4	0.9	6.3	73.4	92.9	26.6	26.3	1,431	915
Northampton	10,782	47,706,434	7.1	11.9	1.8	2.5	7.7	4.9	61.8	1,411.9	496.8	671.7	2,244	1,804
Northumberland	3,162	10,304,053	9.0	7.6	0.0	3.1	16.2	4.4	59.0	273.2	137.2	88.2	934	631
Perry	1,241	4,130,390	6.3	5.0	0.0	3.3	5.0	1.5	77.8	139.6	62.3	60.0	1,312	977
Philadelphia	60,937	311,591,353	8.6	18.6	4.6	16.9	6.0	8.1	36.4	11,133.9	5,530.3	4,080.0	2,636	743
Pike	1,166	4,430,795	9.4	13.5	0.0	2.5	4.3	1.7	67.0	128.4	48.7	71.2	1,252	1,185

1. Based on the resident population estimated as of July 1 of the year shown.

Local Government Finances, Government Employment, and Income Taxes

STATE County	Local government finances, 2012 (cont.)									Government employment, 2017			Individual income tax returns, 2016		
	Direct general expenditure							Debt outstanding							
			Percent of total for:											Mean	
	Total (mil dol)	Per capita[1] (dollars)	Education	Health and hospitals	Police protection	Public welfare	Highways	Total (mil dol)	Per capita[1] (dollars)	Federal civilian	Federal military	State and local	Number of returns	adjusted gross income	Mean income tax
	185	186	187	188	189	190	191	192	193	194	195	196	197	198	199
OREGON— Cont'd															
Morrow	78.1	6,947	32.8	11.0	4.6	0.3	5.8	136.8	12,168	61	34	873	4,630	50,041	4,522
Multnomah	4,425.0	5,828	31.5	4.6	5.2	4.0	6.5	7,864.7	10,358	12,489	2,244	59,865	394,010	70,675	9,890
Polk	140.8	1,844	43.0	8.4	8.3	1.0	5.6	271.5	3,556	106	200	4,967	35,800	58,706	6,139
Sherman	18.9	10,932	20.7	4.0	4.0	1.4	11.8	3.5	2,023	137	4	183	790	58,977	6,371
Tillamook	118.4	4,684	38.3	7.8	3.6	0.3	5.5	166.8	6,595	104	104	1,696	12,340	50,983	5,293
Umatilla	311.2	4,051	58.5	1.4	4.4	0.0	4.1	422.0	5,493	495	178	6,456	31,850	49,820	4,834
Union	90.0	3,495	44.0	3.4	5.7	0.4	5.1	30.5	1,185	238	62	1,812	11,330	49,558	4,810
Wallowa	44.0	6,453	31.6	33.8	3.6	0.8	8.6	38.3	5,620	87	17	524	3,430	45,617	4,374
Wasco	106.5	4,180	48.5	2.2	4.8	0.4	4.4	159.3	6,251	292	63	1,696	11,620	49,591	4,934
Washington	1,940.6	3,543	44.5	2.9	7.1	0.0	5.6	2,532.1	4,623	818	1,423	21,353	275,230	79,585	10,684
Wheeler	9.5	6,659	47.9	0.8	2.6	1.5	12.0	2.0	1,419	5	3	106	570	29,668	2,904
Yamhill	320.3	3,195	49.5	5.9	5.8	0.1	3.1	445.1	4,439	473	244	3,776	45,820	61,324	6,753
PENNSYLVANIA	X	X	X	X	X	X	X	X	X	97,388	35,191	640,542	6,188,330	65,443	8,999
Adams	458.0	4,513	68.9	3.6	1.4	3.2	2.7	405.6	3,997	688	254	3,291	51,650	59,662	6,886
Allegheny	6,640.6	5,402	42.9	7.9	4.6	4.6	3.0	13,494.2	10,977	13,046	3,532	51,783	624,460	69,600	10,230
Armstrong	246.9	3,609	57.6	1.5	1.2	7.5	5.0	239.3	3,498	194	168	2,448	32,030	47,205	4,672
Beaver	789.6	4,638	46.6	3.5	3.0	14.1	3.9	1,928.6	11,328	304	423	7,043	85,040	53,262	5,796
Bedford	155.3	3,148	66.4	0.0	0.4	2.0	4.8	224.7	4,556	108	124	2,118	22,950	45,950	4,434
Berks	2,024.3	4,896	54.5	3.4	4.1	7.2	2.8	3,478.7	8,413	944	1,055	21,427	203,120	58,467	7,047
Blair	409.0	3,217	49.0	3.1	3.0	8.6	3.9	474.2	3,730	1,055	311	7,382	59,120	50,748	5,896
Bradford	244.7	3,898	54.4	2.0	1.6	7.3	6.2	751.2	11,963	215	156	2,809	28,270	49,075	5,117
Bucks	2,875.9	4,586	57.6	0.8	5.5	7.0	4.5	3,960.3	6,316	1,153	1,622	21,386	331,440	90,450	14,670
Butler	656.7	3,550	51.5	4.2	2.4	9.5	4.4	1,305.0	7,055	2,989	474	8,432	94,560	71,707	9,963
Cambria	571.5	4,037	49.2	3.2	5.7	14.0	3.6	641.5	4,531	1,013	352	6,796	62,990	47,456	5,026
Cameron	19.1	3,864	59.4	3.8	1.2	2.5	5.9	30.2	6,117	13	12	356	2,370	41,098	3,746
Carbon	219.0	3,370	60.5	0.1	2.6	4.4	3.4	265.0	4,076	112	163	2,497	31,190	52,032	5,679
Centre	453.5	2,923	51.0	2.2	3.5	7.9	6.1	486.7	3,136	477	449	49,688	59,660	67,532	8,800
Chester	2,204.4	4,352	57.7	5.2	3.8	3.4	3.3	2,995.8	5,914	2,406	1,308	23,477	253,910	111,289	19,689
Clarion	168.8	4,258	67.2	3.0	1.9	2.5	3.4	87.7	2,213	101	110	3,229	16,980	46,552	4,536
Clearfield	261.5	3,221	66.6	0.0	3.5	3.1	4.8	310.5	3,824	243	193	4,450	36,650	45,202	4,509
Clinton	137.3	3,474	41.4	0.3	1.3	4.6	4.0	99.3	2,514	150	98	2,940	16,930	46,975	4,592
Columbia	207.5	3,102	63.6	0.0	3.1	3.7	4.7	212.5	3,176	149	160	5,126	29,620	50,634	5,449
Crawford	281.4	3,212	48.8	2.8	1.9	9.1	5.8	238.2	2,719	253	214	3,684	38,460	46,005	4,566
Cumberland	1,033.3	4,330	58.9	3.0	2.8	6.7	2.5	1,275.7	5,346	4,518	1,318	12,513	125,280	67,710	8,854
Dauphin	1,554.4	5,764	46.5	4.7	3.9	9.1	2.6	2,450.3	9,087	2,729	749	38,473	141,800	56,807	6,977
Delaware	2,744.1	4,891	50.1	2.1	4.9	11.1	2.0	4,601.2	8,200	2,069	1,436	23,249	276,360	82,960	13,128
Elk	92.2	2,921	46.8	0.2	2.8	1.8	8.2	287.8	9,123	88	77	1,135	16,360	51,682	5,832
Erie	1,203.4	4,288	44.0	5.6	2.7	14.2	3.5	1,705.3	6,076	1,559	722	15,527	128,020	51,633	6,031
Fayette	427.6	3,152	56.8	10.4	1.2	3.1	3.6	909.8	6,706	360	330	5,857	61,010	45,914	4,675
Forest	20.2	2,638	52.6	4.6	0.8	4.0	10.1	11.6	1,515	71	12	954	2,170	41,418	3,671
Franklin	452.7	2,992	54.1	4.1	1.9	5.5	4.8	619.1	4,092	2,223	396	5,723	76,500	53,257	5,567
Fulton	47.5	3,214	61.6	0.0	3.7	4.3	4.1	65.3	4,419	27	37	706	7,010	47,383	4,488
Greene	138.0	3,624	59.6	4.6	1.0	1.6	6.1	149.4	3,923	114	87	2,470	15,560	58,928	7,502
Huntingdon	134.9	2,937	57.1	1.3	1.8	2.3	5.0	147.7	3,216	109	105	2,959	19,200	46,691	4,441
Indiana	303.7	3,442	61.2	0.1	1.0	6.1	4.2	387.8	4,396	191	212	7,202	35,580	49,403	5,299
Jefferson	139.0	3,104	60.2	0.0	1.5	3.9	5.0	213.5	4,770	115	111	1,772	20,910	45,634	4,631
Juniata	46.0	1,848	65.2	0.1	0.9	2.6	5.4	13.7	550	64	63	721	11,310	46,937	4,332
Lackawanna	820.1	3,824	47.2	0.3	3.9	6.6	3.0	968.6	4,516	938	533	9,592	102,590	53,000	6,386
Lancaster	2,018.4	3,831	55.1	5.4	4.3	5.1	3.3	3,447.0	6,543	1,281	1,371	19,544	266,240	60,654	7,408
Lawrence	334.2	3,719	50.8	2.1	3.0	11.6	4.1	469.7	5,226	206	240	3,259	41,280	48,881	5,240
Lebanon	507.4	3,752	47.7	2.2	2.9	15.0	5.1	705.4	5,215	3,189	353	4,938	69,400	54,998	5,972
Lehigh	1,756.6	4,945	46.2	3.6	3.3	11.2	2.9	3,948.1	11,114	867	939	16,218	183,160	61,850	8,198
Luzerne	1,193.5	3,718	54.0	0.4	3.0	3.8	4.8	1,386.1	4,318	3,310	807	14,664	157,090	50,250	5,798
Lycoming	560.5	4,783	43.8	0.0	2.2	3.1	4.4	997.6	8,514	367	283	8,666	53,770	49,639	5,239
McKean	182.4	4,229	57.8	3.7	2.0	4.1	3.6	130.5	3,026	431	99	1,968	18,790	47,589	4,895
Mercer	435.3	3,764	63.5	2.3	3.0	2.6	3.9	444.6	3,844	247	272	4,927	52,600	47,826	5,069
Mifflin	166.3	3,555	61.5	4.0	1.7	0.4	3.1	218.1	4,664	86	118	1,579	21,230	43,714	4,005
Monroe	739.9	4,384	67.9	0.1	3.0	3.9	2.5	1,201.0	7,115	3,164	449	8,101	79,080	52,850	5,791
Montgomery	3,494.4	4,322	56.9	1.9	5.0	6.2	3.6	4,364.3	5,398	2,546	2,281	32,632	420,680	105,000	18,332
Montour	79.5	4,333	44.5	0.0	1.9	1.3	3.9	895.8	48,800	39	46	1,461	9,030	68,598	9,943
Northampton	1,501.3	5,017	49.8	3.1	4.0	11.6	2.7	2,550.6	8,523	1,084	781	13,511	153,240	64,956	8,445
Northumberland	266.3	2,820	54.3	3.8	5.1	7.1	3.9	255.4	2,704	157	228	4,032	43,050	45,456	4,416
Perry	128.6	2,813	61.7	2.5	0.8	7.4	4.3	107.1	2,343	83	118	1,761	22,680	50,746	4,887
Philadelphia	9,802.9	6,334	34.2	13.8	6.2	5.8	1.1	18,737.5	12,107	30,089	5,110	73,519	673,540	50,287	6,210
Pike	135.9	2,388	49.0	0.4	1.9	5.8	3.9	42.8	752	212	143	2,326	27,280	58,330	6,779

1. Based on the resident population estimated as of July 1 of the year shown.

Table B. States and Counties — Land Area and Population

State / county code	CBSA code[1]	County code[2]	STATE County	Land area[3] (sq. mi)	Total persons 2018	Rank	Per square mile	White	Black	American Indian, Alaska Native	Asian and Pacific Islancer	Percent Hispanic or Latino[4]	Under 5 years	5 to 17 years	18 to 24 years	25 to 34 years	35 to 44 years	45 to 54 years
				1	2	3	4	5	6	7	8	9	10	11	12	13	14	15
			PENNSYLVANIA—Cont'd															
42105		9	Potter	1,081.3	16,622	2,004	15.4	97.2	1.0	0.7	0.6	1.4	5.2	15.2	6.8	9.9	10.0	12.9
42107	39,060	4	Schuylkill	778.6	142,067	458	182.5	91.5	3.5	0.4	0.8	4.8	4.9	14.8	7.0	12.0	11.8	14.3
42109	42,780	7	Snyder	328.8	40,540	1,167	123.3	95.6	1.5	0.4	1.0	2.4	5.4	15.6	11.6	11.2	10.8	12.8
42111	43,740	4	Somerset	1,074.4	73,952	743	68.8	94.8	3.2	0.4	0.8	1.6	4.6	13.3	7.1	11.6	11.6	13.8
42113		8	Sullivan	449.9	6,071	2,744	13.5	93.4	4.0	0.9	0.6	1.9	2.9	7.7	8.3	9.6	10.0	12.9
42115		6	Susquehanna	823.5	40,589	1,163	49.3	97.1	0.9	0.6	0.7	1.7	4.6	13.9	6.8	10.2	10.0	13.4
42117		6	Tioga	1,133.8	40,763	1,159	36.0	97.1	1.3	0.6	0.8	1.3	5.3	14.7	8.6	11.1	10.4	12.7
42119	30,260	4	Union	316.0	44,785	1,081	141.7	85.6	6.7	0.6	2.4	6.0	4.7	13.5	13.5	13.2	12.6	12.3
42121	36,340	4	Venango	674.3	51,266	971	76.0	97.1	1.8	0.6	0.7	1.1	4.9	14.5	6.8	10.5	10.7	13.0
42123	47,620	6	Warren	884.1	39,498	1,193	44.7	97.5	0.8	0.6	0.8	1.2	5.0	14.3	6.9	10.5	10.3	13.4
42125	38,300	1	Washington	857.0	207,346	322	241.9	93.7	4.4	0.5	1.5	1.8	5.0	14.4	8.4	11.3	11.4	13.4
42127		6	Wayne	725.6	51,276	970	70.7	91.3	3.6	0.5	1.0	4.7	4.3	12.4	6.9	11.2	11.0	13.7
42129	38,300	1	Westmoreland	1,028.0	350,611	202	341.1	95.1	3.4	0.4	1.3	1.2	4.5	13.8	7.5	10.6	10.8	13.8
42131	42,540	2	Wyoming	397.3	27,046	1,525	68.1	96.4	1.3	0.6	0.7	1.9	4.7	14.6	8.4	11.1	10.7	13.4
42133	49,620	2	York	904.2	448,273	156	495.8	84.6	6.9	0.5	2.0	7.9	5.7	16.4	8.1	12.4	12.0	13.7
44000		0	RHODE ISLAND	1,033.9	1,057,315	X	1,022.6	73.8	7.2	1.0	4.3	15.9	5.1	14.3	10.5	13.8	11.7	13.2
44001	39,300	1	Bristol	24.1	48,649	1,011	2,018.6	93.0	1.9	0.6	3.0	3.2	4.0	14.7	10.9	10.0	10.9	14.1
44003	39,300	1	Kent	168.6	163,861	401	971.9	89.7	2.7	0.8	3.4	5.3	4.9	13.8	7.1	13.3	12.2	14.2
44005	39,300	1	Newport	102.4	82,542	688	806.1	87.8	5.0	1.0	2.9	6.0	4.2	12.7	9.4	12.1	11.1	13.0
44007	39,300	1	Providence	409.5	636,084	105	1,553.3	62.8	10.1	1.1	5.1	23.4	5.7	14.8	10.7	15.4	12.2	12.9
44009	39,300	1	Washington	329.3	126,179	507	383.2	92.5	2.1	1.4	2.7	3.3	3.8	12.8	14.6	9.5	9.4	13.0
45000		0	SOUTH CAROLINA	30,063.8	5,084,127	X	169.1	65.2	27.7	0.9	2.3	5.8	5.8	16.0	9.2	13.3	12.0	12.7
45001	24,940	6	Abbeville	491.4	24,541	1,628	49.9	70.1	28.3	0.7	0.6	1.5	4.7	15.4	9.3	10.8	10.4	13.1
45003	12,260	2	Aiken	1,070.6	169,401	386	158.2	67.6	25.8	1.1	1.6	5.9	5.8	16.0	7.8	12.7	11.5	12.5
45005		6	Allendale	408.1	8,903	2,509	21.8	22.9	72.9	0.5	0.8	3.6	4.7	14.2	8.6	14.2	11.1	13.9
45007	24,860	2	Anderson	713.9	200,482	336	280.8	78.8	17.1	0.6	1.3	3.9	5.9	16.9	8.2	12.2	11.8	13.3
45009		7	Bamberg	393.4	14,275	2,146	36.3	36.9	60.4	0.7	0.7	2.2	4.6	14.5	12.5	10.3	9.7	12.2
45011		6	Barnwell	548.4	21,112	1,769	38.5	52.1	44.5	1.0	1.2	2.6	6.1	17.8	8.2	11.6	10.9	12.7
45013	25,940	3	Beaufort	576.2	188,715	351	327.5	69.6	18.5	0.6	1.9	11.2	5.1	13.4	9.0	11.0	10.0	10.5
45015	16,700	2	Berkeley	1,103.6	221,091	307	200.3	65.8	25.2	1.2	3.7	6.9	6.5	17.4	9.3	14.8	13.2	12.8
45017	17,900	2	Calhoun	381.2	14,520	2,127	38.1	55.2	40.6	0.8	0.6	3.9	4.5	14.4	7.1	10.4	11.1	13.0
45019	16,700	2	Charleston	917.9	405,905	175	442.2	66.3	27.2	0.7	2.4	5.1	5.9	13.8	8.7	16.9	13.1	12.0
45021	23,500	4	Cherokee	393.3	57,078	902	145.1	74.2	21.4	0.7	0.8	4.5	5.8	17.2	9.1	12.7	11.6	13.7
45023	16,740	1	Chester	580.7	32,251	1,373	55.5	60.1	37.8	1.0	0.8	2.1	5.7	16.8	7.6	12.1	10.9	13.7
45025		6	Chesterfield	799.0	45,754	1,056	57.3	61.8	33.7	1.1	0.8	4.3	5.6	16.3	8.2	11.7	11.3	14.2
45027		6	Clarendon	607.0	33,700	1,336	55.5	48.8	47.4	0.6	0.9	3.2	4.6	14.6	8.8	11.2	10.1	12.2
45029		6	Colleton	1,056.5	37,660	1,233	35.6	58.3	37.7	1.3	0.8	3.4	6.0	16.3	7.8	11.8	10.7	12.7
45031	22,500	3	Darlington	560.6	66,802	800	119.2	55.8	42.0	0.7	0.7	2.1	5.8	16.4	8.6	11.7	11.3	13.0
45033		6	Dillon	405.1	30,599	1,421	75.5	46.9	48.1	3.2	0.8	2.9	6.5	18.8	8.3	12.5	11.7	12.0
45035	16,700	2	Dorchester	568.6	160,647	412	282.5	66.3	26.7	1.3	3.0	5.6	6.1	18.3	7.9	13.9	13.4	13.6
45037	12,260	2	Edgefield	500.8	27,052	1,524	54.0	57.8	35.9	0.8	0.8	6.0	4.0	14.1	8.2	13.3	13.0	13.9
45039	17,900	2	Fairfield	686.3	22,402	1,706	32.6	39.6	58.0	0.8	1.0	2.2	4.5	14.7	7.4	10.9	10.4	13.3
45041	22,500	3	Florence	800.5	138,159	466	172.6	52.5	43.5	0.7	1.9	2.7	6.0	17.6	8.7	12.7	12.2	12.9
45043	23,860	4	Georgetown	813.9	62,249	845	76.5	65.2	31.2	0.6	0.8	3.2	4.5	13.9	6.9	9.3	9.7	12.0
45045	24,860	2	Greenville	785.1	514,213	136	655.0	69.3	19.0	0.6	3.2	9.3	6.2	16.8	8.8	14.0	12.7	13.1
45047	24,940	4	Greenwood	454.7	70,741	766	155.6	60.3	32.5	0.5	1.6	6.3	6.0	16.6	9.5	12.6	11.3	12.6
45049		6	Hampton	560.0	19,351	1,860	34.6	42.1	53.6	0.8	0.8	4.1	5.3	16.0	8.0	13.1	12.7	12.8
45051	34,820	4	Horry	1,133.7	344,147	206	303.6	79.2	13.8	1.0	1.9	6.1	4.6	13.3	7.3	11.7	11.0	12.4
45053	25,940	3	Jasper	655.2	28,971	1,460	44.2	44.4	41.8	0.8	1.1	13.2	5.7	14.6	8.5	13.5	11.0	12.4
45055	17,900	2	Kershaw	726.5	65,592	815	90.3	70.2	25.2	0.7	1.1	4.4	5.9	17.2	7.4	11.7	12.0	13.1
45057	16,740	1	Lancaster	549.1	95,380	623	173.7	71.3	22.1	0.6	1.8	5.6	6.1	15.7	6.5	12.1	13.1	12.9
45059	24,860	2	Laurens	713.8	66,994	797	93.9	69.1	25.8	0.6	0.8	5.1	5.7	16.1	8.9	12.3	11.0	13.3
45061		6	Lee	410.2	17,142	1,972	41.8	32.9	64.2	0.7	0.7	2.5	5.1	15.1	9.3	13.9	11.5	12.4
45063	17,900	2	Lexington	699.0	295,032	232	422.1	76.0	15.9	0.9	2.7	6.3	5.8	17.4	7.6	13.5	13.0	13.6
45065		8	McCormick	359.1	9,410	2,469	26.2	52.7	45.7	0.5	0.8	1.4	2.8	9.1	5.1	10.1	9.1	12.1
45067		6	Marion	489.3	31,039	1,406	63.4	39.3	57.1	0.9	1.0	2.9	5.9	16.9	7.9	11.3	11.6	12.3
45069	13,500	6	Marlboro	479.9	26,398	1,552	55.0	40.9	51.7	5.4	0.8	3.3	5.3	14.7	8.1	14.3	12.8	13.2
45071	35,140	6	Newberry	630.0	38,520	1,213	61.1	61.4	30.9	0.6	0.8	7.6	6.0	15.8	9.7	11.3	10.6	12.7
45073	42,860	4	Oconee	626.4	78,374	714	125.1	85.6	8.3	0.7	1.2	5.7	4.9	15.0	7.1	11.3	10.4	12.6
45075	36,700	4	Orangeburg	1,106.3	86,934	667	78.6	34.2	62.4	1.1	1.3	2.4	5.5	16.4	10.0	12.1	10.2	12.1
45077	24,860	2	Pickens	496.9	124,937	509	251.4	87.1	7.7	0.7	2.5	3.8	5.1	13.9	17.5	12.1	10.6	11.9
45079	17,900	2	Richland	757.3	414,576	171	547.4	43.9	48.7	0.8	3.8	5.2	5.8	15.6	15.7	15.0	12.3	11.6
45081	17,900	2	Saluda	452.9	20,544	1,793	45.4	58.9	24.9	0.7	0.6	16.2	6.0	15.6	7.5	12.2	11.4	13.0
45083	43,900	2	Spartanburg	807.7	313,888	224	388.6	69.6	21.6	0.7	2.9	7.1	6.1	17.0	9.1	13.8	11.9	13.3

1. CBSA = Core Based Statistical Area. See Appendix A for explanation. See Appendix B for list of metropolitan areas with component counties. 2. County type code from the Economic Research Service of USDA Rural-Urban Continuum Codes. See Appendix A for definition. 3. Dry land or land partially or temporarily covered by water. 4. May be of any race.

Table B. States and Counties — **Population and Households**

STATE County	Age (percent) (cont.) 55 to 64 years	65 to 74 years	75 years and over	Percent female	Total persons 2000	2010	Percent change 2000-2010	2010-2018	Components of change, 2010-2018 Births	Deaths	Net Migration	Households, 2013-2017 Number	Persons per household	Family house-holds	Female family house-holder[1]	One person
	16	17	18	19	20	21	22	23	24	25	26	27	28	29	30	31
PENNSYLVANIA— Cont'd																
Potter	15.9	13.5	10.6	50.2	18,080	17,449	-3.5	-4.7	1,548	1,697	-674	6,536	2.57	65.3	9.6	30.1
Schuylkill	14.8	11.4	9.0	48.8	150,336	148,291	-1.4	-4.2	11,530	15,910	-1,748	58,758	2.33	65.0	11.6	30.3
Snyder	13.7	10.4	8.6	50.4	37,546	39,719	5.8	2.1	3,444	2,915	327	14,576	2.63	72.1	9.3	23.5
Somerset	15.6	12.3	10.0	47.7	80,023	77,737	-2.9	-4.9	5,568	7,942	-1,355	29,918	2.36	68.5	8.5	27.6
Sullivan	20.3	15.8	12.5	47.7	6,556	6,429	-1.9	-5.6	412	874	105	2,648	2.17	58.4	5.9	35.2
Susquehanna	17.5	13.5	10.2	49.6	42,238	43,328	2.6	-6.3	3,033	3,725	-2,035	17,404	2.38	67.9	8.8	26.6
Tioga	15.3	12.2	9.8	50.4	41,373	41,902	1.3	-2.7	3,532	3,682	-988	16,121	2.53	67.7	8.7	26.2
Union	12.1	9.4	8.7	45.6	41,624	44,963	8.0	-0.4	3,327	3,140	-372	14,702	2.42	67.5	8.1	28.3
Venango	17.2	12.9	9.6	50.6	57,565	54,992	-4.5	-6.8	4,467	5,375	-2,808	21,925	2.36	67.8	10.8	27.6
Warren	16.7	12.6	10.3	49.9	43,863	41,811	-4.7	-5.5	3,231	4,151	-1,379	17,095	2.32	64.2	8.6	31.0
Washington	15.5	11.7	8.8	50.9	202,897	207,841	2.4	-0.2	16,452	20,720	3,990	83,897	2.41	66.6	10.2	28.2
Wayne	16.5	14.4	9.8	47.0	47,722	52,850	10.7	-3.0	3,426	5,020	58	19,202	2.49	67.1	8.9	28.0
Westmoreland	16.3	12.7	10.0	51.1	369,993	365,194	-1.3	-4.0	25,519	36,731	-3,058	151,892	2.30	66.5	9.6	29.0
Wyoming	15.9	12.6	8.5	49.8	28,080	28,283	0.7	-4.4	2,297	2,497	-1,029	10,801	2.50	67.4	11.2	26.2
York	14.2	10.1	7.4	50.6	381,751	435,008	14.0	3.0	40,590	32,619	5,722	169,667	2.55	69.5	11.1	24.3
RHODE ISLAND	14.1	9.7	7.5	51.4	1,048,319	1,052,957	0.4	0.4	89,601	80,297	-4,624	412,028	2.46	62.7	13.5	30.6
Bristol	15.6	10.6	9.1	51.7	50,648	49,847	-1.6	-2.4	2,827	4,179	161	19,521	2.33	63.6	8.7	30.4
Kent	15.7	10.8	8.1	51.7	167,090	166,113	-0.6	-1.4	13,070	14,301	-907	69,013	2.36	62.5	9.9	30.9
Newport	15.3	12.5	9.7	50.6	85,433	83,141	-2.7	-0.7	5,654	5,832	-364	35,421	2.24	62.1	10.5	30.0
Providence	13.0	8.5	6.8	51.3	621,602	626,762	0.8	1.5	60,537	46,862	-4,303	238,465	2.55	62.1	16.4	31.4
Washington	16.2	12.2	8.5	51.6	123,546	127,094	2.9	-0.7	7,513	9,123	789	49,608	2.41	65.9	9.1	26.6
SOUTH CAROLINA	13.3	10.8	6.9	51.5	4,012,012	4,625,381	15.3	9.9	471,964	375,950	359,822	1,871,307	2.54	66.2	14.6	28.5
Abbeville	14.6	12.8	8.9	51.6	26,167	25,399	-2.9	-3.4	1,968	2,354	-463	9,392	2.54	65.3	13.9	31.2
Aiken	14.3	11.6	7.9	51.7	142,552	160,114	12.3	5.8	15,749	13,804	7,416	65,703	2.48	68.1	14.6	27.7
Allendale	13.2	12.8	7.3	47.3	11,211	10,419	-7.1	-14.6	751	912	-1,375	3,285	2.50	59.1	20.3	36.7
Anderson	13.4	10.6	7.5	51.9	165,740	186,943	12.8	7.2	18,652	17,143	12,111	76,234	2.51	68.7	13.9	27.0
Bamberg	14.5	12.6	9.1	51.9	16,658	15,972	-4.1	-10.6	1,189	1,504	-1,399	5,587	2.45	64.5	17.3	33.2
Barnwell	14.5	11.2	7.1	52.3	23,478	22,621	-3.7	-6.7	2,262	2,160	-1,623	8,426	2.55	66.2	21.9	30.2
Beaufort	13.7	16.2	11.0	51.0	120,937	162,231	34.1	16.3	16,663	12,219	21,791	68,790	2.53	67.9	9.7	27.1
Berkeley	12.3	8.8	4.9	50.3	142,651	178,316	25.0	24.0	21,876	11,133	31,654	73,168	2.75	71.0	14.3	23.3
Calhoun	16.3	14.0	9.3	52.2	15,185	15,176	-0.1	-4.3	1,132	1,412	-379	6,150	2.38	62.8	13.9	33.7
Charleston	13.2	10.2	6.2	51.6	309,969	350,150	13.0	15.9	40,026	25,518	40,437	154,049	2.44	58.6	12.9	32.6
Cherokee	13.0	10.2	6.6	51.3	52,537	55,488	5.6	2.9	5,540	5,025	1,120	20,480	2.72	59.6	12.4	37.5
Chester	14.5	11.1	7.6	51.8	34,068	33,147	-2.7	-2.7	3,150	3,240	-794	12,384	2.60	63.6	15.7	33.9
Chesterfield	14.3	11.4	7.0	51.4	42,768	46,729	9.3	-2.1	4,147	4,244	-860	18,303	2.48	70.9	17.5	25.5
Clarendon	15.0	14.0	9.5	50.9	32,502	34,951	7.5	-3.6	2,757	3,159	-840	13,573	2.40	66.4	18.1	29.6
Colleton	14.6	12.4	7.8	51.9	38,264	38,893	1.6	-3.2	3,721	4,189	-759	15,134	2.44	66.5	17.9	30.2
Darlington	14.2	11.4	7.5	52.8	67,394	68,609	1.8	-2.6	6,480	6,773	-1,475	26,861	2.47	65.3	19.6	29.5
Dillon	13.6	10.0	6.7	52.6	30,722	32,059	4.4	-4.6	3,431	3,089	-1,814	10,945	2.80	66.4	21.7	30.0
Dorchester	12.6	9.0	5.1	51.4	96,413	136,173	41.2	18.0	14,953	8,400	17,735	54,028	2.77	69.3	14.6	26.0
Edgefield	14.7	11.4	7.4	46.3	24,595	26,975	9.7	0.3	1,625	1,852	314	9,054	2.63	71.7	16.1	25.6
Fairfield	17.0	13.7	8.1	52.2	23,454	23,960	2.2	-6.5	1,788	2,404	-941	8,878	2.53	63.1	17.2	33.2
Florence	13.0	10.4	6.6	53.3	125,761	136,962	8.9	0.9	14,216	12,202	-686	52,092	2.60	67.6	19.0	28.8
Georgetown	15.9	17.2	10.6	52.7	55,797	60,328	8.1	3.2	4,757	6,103	3,294	24,840	2.43	70.7	14.8	26.5
Greenville	12.6	9.4	6.3	51.5	379,616	451,184	18.9	14.0	51,270	33,576	45,048	185,837	2.58	66.7	12.7	28.1
Greenwood	12.9	10.3	8.2	53.4	66,271	69,711	5.2	1.5	7,013	5,967	23	27,022	2.50	65.9	18.2	29.5
Hampton	13.7	11.0	7.4	48.8	21,386	21,090	-1.4	-8.2	1,790	1,808	-1,737	7,129	2.62	61.3	16.5	36.4
Horry	15.7	15.7	8.2	51.8	196,629	269,126	36.9	27.9	25,457	25,896	74,340	125,168	2.45	65.4	12.0	27.9
Jasper	14.9	12.8	6.6	49.5	20,678	24,779	19.8	16.9	2,780	1,920	3,281	9,715	2.77	71.7	19.3	24.4
Kershaw	14.4	11.2	7.2	51.8	52,647	61,592	17.0	6.5	6,117	5,477	3,391	24,711	2.56	69.6	16.0	25.9
Lancaster	12.6	12.8	8.3	51.5	61,351	76,653	24.9	24.4	8,063	6,951	17,403	31,445	2.69	69.1	14.2	27.5
Laurens	14.2	10.8	7.7	51.7	69,567	66,535	-4.4	0.7	6,319	6,622	805	25,543	2.51	69.0	16.9	26.0
Lee	14.4	11.4	6.9	48.6	20,119	19,213	-4.5	-10.8	1,481	1,936	-1,634	6,501	2.50	65.4	21.4	32.4
Lexington	13.4	9.6	6.2	51.3	216,014	262,429	21.5	12.4	26,808	19,138	24,879	109,251	2.55	68.1	13.1	25.9
McCormick	16.7	21.1	13.8	46.3	9,958	10,233	2.8	-8.0	464	1,051	-230	4,077	2.07	66.4	16.1	28.9
Marion	14.3	12.4	7.5	54.2	35,466	33,062	-6.8	-6.1	3,196	3,531	-1,692	11,911	2.65	65.3	23.0	31.8
Marlboro	13.7	11.3	6.7	47.8	28,818	28,935	0.4	-8.8	2,438	2,774	-2,215	9,703	2.52	67.1	21.2	29.2
Newberry	14.3	11.6	8.0	51.2	36,108	37,508	3.9	2.7	3,685	3,563	919	14,893	2.47	69.3	17.0	27.2
Oconee	15.4	14.0	9.2	50.8	66,215	74,275	12.2	5.5	6,388	7,141	4,866	31,354	2.40	67.7	11.4	28.1
Orangeburg	14.0	11.6	8.0	53.4	91,582	92,509	1.0	-6.0	8,603	8,744	-5,455	33,029	2.62	60.6	17.6	36.7
Pickens	12.4	9.6	7.0	50.2	110,757	119,373	7.8	4.7	10,020	9,403	4,971	46,428	2.48	63.8	10.3	26.1
Richland	11.4	8.0	4.8	51.7	320,677	384,450	19.9	7.8	39,719	24,115	14,761	149,161	2.51	60.0	16.9	32.5
Saluda	14.4	11.0	8.8	49.3	19,181	19,869	3.6	3.4	2,015	1,715	389	7,052	2.82	73.1	14.8	24.2
Spartanburg	12.7	9.6	6.5	51.5	253,791	284,317	12.0	10.4	29,775	24,258	24,105	113,191	2.56	68.2	15.0	27.5

1. No spouse present.

Table B. States and Counties — Population, Vital Statistics, Health, and Crime

STATE County	Persons in group quarters, 2018	Daytime Population, 2013-2017		Births, 2018		Deaths, 2018		Persons under 65 with no health insurance, 2016		Medicare, 2018			Serious crimes known to police[2], 2016 Total	
		Number	Employment/residence ratio	Total	Rate[1]	Number	Rate[1]	Number	Percent	Total beneficiaries	Enrolled in Original Medicare	Enrolled in Medicare Advantage	Number	Rate[3]
	32	33	34	35	36	37	38	39	40	41	42	43	44	45
PENNSYLVANIA— Cont'd														
Potter	217	16,961	0.98	162	9.7	216	13.0	1,072	8.3	4,502	3,072	1,430	203	1,236
Schuylkill	6,795	134,167	0.84	1,317	9.3	1,801	12.7	6,672	6.1	35,120	24,766	10,354	2,628	1,867
Snyder	2,657	39,567	0.95	417	10.3	378	9.3	2,800	9.0	8,284	4,711	3,573	586	1,509
Somerset	4,973	70,307	0.84	635	8.6	947	12.8	4,238	7.7	19,122	8,230	10,892	840	1,140
Sullivan	440	5,731	0.82	39	6.4	98	16.1	364	8.3	1,813	1,270	543	59	937
Susquehanna	282	35,847	0.68	337	8.3	463	11.4	2,422	7.6	10,104	7,579	2,525	500	1,286
Tioga	1,321	40,485	0.94	390	9.6	477	11.7	2,378	7.6	10,415	7,441	2,974	460	1,102
Union	8,468	47,167	1.12	407	9.1	424	9.5	2,261	7.7	8,234	5,171	3,063	360	803
Venango	1,302	50,823	0.91	500	9.8	675	13.2	2,950	7.2	14,039	7,914	6,125	672	1,277
Warren	760	39,468	0.95	385	9.7	527	13.3	2,007	6.5	10,250	7,350	2,900	656	1,727
Washington	5,490	203,482	0.96	1,991	9.6	2,511	12.1	8,473	5.2	50,195	19,578	30,617	3,528	1,727
Wayne	3,727	48,532	0.85	408	8.0	626	12.2	2,589	7.2	13,463	10,744	2,719	631	1,244
Westmoreland	6,994	332,029	0.85	2,829	8.1	4,453	12.7	13,023	4.7	91,177	32,667	58,510	5,065	1,442
Wyoming	617	27,483	0.98	241	8.9	321	11.9	1,309	6.1	6,524	4,485	2,039	368	1,349
York	8,691	405,694	0.83	4,859	10.8	4,081	9.1	23,244	6.4	90,689	57,225	33,464	8,051	1,817
RHODE ISLAND	41,231	1,035,604	0.96	10,575	10.0	9,830	9.3	43,275	5.1	216,219	120,608	95,611	22,582	2,138
Bristol	2,771	40,139	0.63	324	6.7	514	10.6	1,348	3.5	11,162	6,235	4,927	478	977
Kent	1,161	152,114	0.86	1,526	9.3	1,705	10.4	4,674	3.5	38,279	20,919	17,360	2,486	1,511
Newport	3,866	85,386	1.05	682	8.3	740	9.0	2,438	3.9	19,266	13,091	6,175	1,358	1,651
Providence	26,386	637,176	1.01	7,137	11.2	5,695	9.0	31,511	6.1	117,958	61,494	56,464	15,492	2,442
Washington	7,047	120,789	0.91	906	7.2	1,176	9.3	3,304	3.4	29,554	18,868	10,686	1,480	1,171
SOUTH CAROLINA	135,823	4,857,707	0.98	56,238	11.1	49,776	9.8	484,799	12.1	1,039,803	752,577	287,226	185,824	3,746
Abbeville	925	21,572	0.65	202	8.2	275	11.2	2,295	12.1	6,222	4,064	2,158	642	2,798
Aiken	2,295	160,119	0.92	1,906	11.3	1,800	10.6	15,802	11.8	37,558	27,995	9,563	6,984	4,176
Allendale	1,143	9,629	1.09	73	8.2	104	11.7	689	11.2	2,090	1,234	856	NA	NA
Anderson	2,946	182,799	0.86	2,304	11.5	2,189	10.9	18,515	11.6	43,954	28,653	15,301	10,564	5,374
Bamberg	1,013	13,881	0.82	125	8.8	189	13.2	1,335	12.4	3,366	2,177	1,189	505	3,491
Barnwell	286	20,494	0.83	235	11.1	289	13.7	1,904	10.9	4,425	3,026	1,399	863	3,996
Beaufort	5,534	182,265	1.04	1,919	10.2	1,684	8.9	18,431	14.1	49,304	39,490	9,814	4,363	2,378
Berkeley	3,837	172,296	0.66	2,761	12.5	1,626	7.4	20,180	11.2	34,796	26,261	8,535	5,927	2,852
Calhoun	158	11,866	0.53	120	8.3	189	13.0	1,433	12.5	3,639	2,500	1,139	337	2,285
Charleston	10,855	452,366	1.33	4,874	12.0	3,555	8.8	40,835	12.5	71,661	55,767	15,894	13,569	3,418
Cherokee	1,138	54,349	0.90	640	11.2	615	10.8	5,518	11.9	12,382	7,755	4,627	2,194	3,888
Chester	218	28,912	0.72	343	10.6	428	13.3	3,076	11.8	7,495	5,239	2,256	1,220	3,793
Chesterfield	874	45,461	0.96	463	10.1	562	12.3	5,224	13.9	9,640	7,436	2,204	1,692	3,679
Clarendon	1,472	31,115	0.74	294	8.7	408	12.1	3,477	14.0	8,656	6,075	2,581	1,161	3,454
Colleton	389	35,219	0.85	437	11.6	574	15.2	4,016	13.4	9,699	6,728	2,971	1,602	4,264
Darlington	1,392	64,122	0.87	747	11.2	841	12.6	6,656	12.4	15,157	12,036	3,121	3,622	5,368
Dillon	481	29,792	0.88	374	12.2	375	12.3	3,647	14.5	6,417	4,653	1,764	1,918	6,163
Dorchester	1,799	122,543	0.59	1,778	11.1	1,174	7.3	13,211	10.0	26,289	20,046	6,243	5,686	3,688
Edgefield	2,844	23,639	0.71	193	7.1	291	10.8	2,424	12.6	5,377	3,772	1,605	274	1,042
Fairfield	397	22,782	0.99	200	8.9	301	13.4	2,171	12.2	5,434	3,646	1,788	919	4,070
Florence	3,164	147,750	1.16	1,582	11.5	1,548	11.2	11,668	10.3	28,873	23,264	5,609	6,492	4,695
Georgetown	554	61,773	1.03	558	9.0	855	13.7	6,228	13.9	19,301	14,425	4,876	2,150	3,487
Greenville	10,941	521,028	1.13	6,243	12.1	4,403	8.6	51,503	12.4	94,653	61,682	32,971	16,942	3,381
Greenwood	2,621	70,981	1.03	763	10.8	792	11.2	7,474	13.5	15,713	11,261	4,452	3,136	4,480
Hampton	1,397	19,659	0.95	192	9.9	237	12.2	1,752	11.8	4,321	2,983	1,338	662	3,710
Horry	3,831	310,173	1.00	3,064	8.9	3,680	10.7	39,291	16.0	92,512	72,373	20,139	16,328	5,131
Jasper	1,235	24,410	0.74	337	11.6	270	9.3	3,895	18.1	5,873	4,074	1,799	958	3,361
Kershaw	400	56,403	0.72	774	11.8	778	11.9	6,276	11.9	14,149	10,793	3,356	1,662	2,592
Lancaster	1,976	77,622	0.75	1,057	11.1	985	10.3	7,205	10.3	21,652	17,000	4,652	1,966	2,493
Laurens	2,294	62,243	0.84	758	11.3	837	12.5	6,315	12.0	15,834	10,392	5,442	2,152	3,223
Lee	1,603	15,760	0.64	180	10.5	284	16.6	1,619	12.7	4,094	2,905	1,189	577	3,264
Lexington	2,340	265,671	0.88	3,232	11.0	2,501	8.5	26,350	10.9	52,534	40,642	11,892	8,346	2,916
McCormick	976	9,212	0.82	48	5.1	148	15.7	604	11.2	3,674	2,349	1,325	200	2,078
Marion	201	28,668	0.73	347	11.2	447	14.4	3,347	13.2	7,535	5,685	1,850	1,848	5,893
Marlboro	2,703	25,489	0.79	260	9.8	312	11.8	2,678	13.8	6,208	4,437	1,771	1,276	4,678
Newberry	1,309	36,860	0.93	448	11.6	451	11.7	4,003	13.5	8,951	6,402	2,549	908	2,379
Oconee	792	73,665	0.93	727	9.3	942	12.0	8,331	14.2	21,099	15,296	5,803	2,218	2,913
Orangeburg	3,017	88,678	0.99	910	10.5	1,151	13.2	8,866	13.0	20,033	12,819	7,214	3,223	3,683
Pickens	7,130	111,288	0.80	1,201	9.6	1,180	9.4	12,359	12.8	25,406	16,039	9,367	4,491	3,668
Richland	31,195	442,878	1.19	4,675	11.3	3,169	7.6	31,317	9.5	63,886	48,913	14,973	21,715	5,268
Saluda	287	17,812	0.71	229	11.1	202	9.8	2,805	17.4	4,388	3,114	1,274	334	1,660
Spartanburg	8,265	308,329	1.08	3,693	11.8	3,131	10.0	31,050	12.6	63,552	38,234	25,318	10,270	3,418

1. Per 1,000 estimated resident population.   2. Data for serious crimes have not been adjusted for underreporting; this may affect comparability between geographic areas and over time.   3. Per 100,000 population estimated by the FBI.

Table B. States and Counties — Crime, Education, Money Income, and Poverty

STATE County	Serious crimes known to police[2], 2016 (cont.)[1] Rate		Education School enrollment and attainment, 2013-2017 Enrollment[3]		Attainment[4] (percent)		Local government expenditures,[5] 2014-2015		Money income, 2013-2017	Households			Income and poverty, 2017	Percent below poverty level		
	Violent	Property	Total	Percent private	High school graduate or less	Bachelor's degree or more	Total current spending (mil dol)	Current spending per student (dollars)	Per capita income[6]	Median income (dollars)	Percent with income of less than $50,000	Percent with income of $200,000 or more	Median household income (dollars)	All persons	Children under 18 years	Children 5 to 17 years in families
	46	47	48	49	50	51	52	53	54	55	56	57	58	59	60	61
PENNSYLVANIA— Cont'd																
Potter	262	974	3,366	11.3	59.8	15.0	32.9	13,953	23,213	41,406	57.6	1.3	41,309	16.5	27.8	23.1
Schuylkill	483	1,384	28,506	13.5	58.9	16.0	234.9	13,532	25,224	47,642	51.6	1.9	49,360	12.1	18.4	16.0
Snyder	209	1,300	9,359	34.3	61.5	17.5	58.0	11,881	24,961	54,182	45.6	3.4	54,336	11.3	16.2	15.1
Somerset	125	1,016	13,146	14.6	62.1	15.7	124.2	13,229	23,877	46,132	53.6	1.8	47,950	12.6	20.1	18.9
Sullivan	79	858	829	13.0	60.0	16.5	11.8	18,859	26,720	45,519	54.5	1.4	43,800	13.9	19.4	18.7
Susquehanna	157	1,129	7,707	15.5	57.4	17.5	98.3	15,484	27,823	52,014	48.2	2.8	50,612	13.1	21.7	19.2
Tioga	139	963	8,239	12.3	54.8	20.2	72.0	13,451	25,353	50,017	50.0	2.0	47,500	15.1	19.0	17.6
Union	60	743	11,226	50.1	53.8	23.8	53.6	13,567	25,089	53,768	44.7	5.0	58,310	12.2	13.6	12.3
Venango	144	1,133	10,043	12.5	59.4	17.2	107.9	13,186	25,190	46,487	53.8	1.7	47,593	14.2	22.6	20.0
Warren	221	1,506	7,542	13.0	54.5	18.9	62.5	12,997	26,558	45,781	53.6	1.6	49,788	13.9	24.5	22.9
Washington	184	1,543	44,998	17.6	46.2	29.0	398.0	14,412	32,828	59,309	42.6	5.4	60,332	9.4	12.2	10.8
Wayne	120	1,124	9,089	15.5	53.9	20.4	77.7	16,543	25,569	52,161	47.3	2.2	49,985	12.9	17.4	16.1
Westmoreland	172	1,270	72,962	18.5	44.3	28.0	614.9	12,886	31,827	56,702	43.8	4.0	60,308	9.9	12.6	12.2
Wyoming	194	1,155	5,697	19.6	55.6	18.8	56.8	15,857	28,046	55,965	45.1	2.9	55,820	11.9	17.8	16.1
York	234	1,583	100,903	19.0	51.2	23.7	841.9	12,615	30,178	61,707	39.3	3.7	63,493	9.4	13.2	11.4
RHODE ISLAND	239	1,899	263,952	26.3	40.6	33.0	2,199.7	15,519	33,315	61,043	42.2	6.0	62,923	12.3	18.2	17.1
Bristol	70	908	13,169	39.5	30.5	46.8	98.8	14,862	42,360	74,630	34.3	11.4	72,614	7.7	8.1	7.1
Kent	103	1,409	35,325	20.6	36.4	32.1	357.6	16,425	37,157	69,047	36.6	5.8	72,765	8.5	11.3	10.5
Newport	141	1,510	18,356	31.8	29.4	46.5	151.0	15,834	43,603	75,463	34.0	8.8	77,186	9	12.3	10.9
Providence	328	2,114	162,437	28.7	46.4	27.8	1,328.7	15,059	29,025	52,530	47.6	4.6	55,848	14.7	22.4	21.4
Washington	71	1,100	34,665	13.3	28.9	45.0	263.6	16,949	39,568	77,862	32.9	9.2	78,599	8.9	10.6	9.5
SOUTH CAROLINA	502	3,244	1,200,892	14.5	42.9	27.0	7,478.3	9,885	26,645	48,781	51.0	3.6	50,675	15.4	22.3	21.3
Abbeville	340	2,458	5,679	17.6	55.8	14.7	29.9	9,791	19,234	35,254	65.3	0.9	41,118	20.3	27.9	24.6
Aiken	536	3,641	37,976	14.1	45.5	25.8	211.3	8,613	26,222	47,713	51.5	2.5	51,583	14.8	23.1	22.2
Allendale	NA	NA	1,969	9.7	65.9	9.4	18.3	13,869	13,439	23,331	75.1	0.0	28,135	36.7	48.6	43.7
Anderson	653	4,721	46,401	14.9	47.1	20.8	292.1	9,197	24,485	45,551	54.4	2.4	48,846	14.4	20.5	18.1
Bamberg	422	3,070	4,220	12.9	52.9	19.1	26.1	12,473	19,256	32,330	64.6	1.1	32,693	26.5	36.2	35.3
Barnwell	722	3,274	5,011	8.1	55.2	11.7	43.0	10,778	20,018	34,035	64.4	1.0	36,568	27.7	39.8	41.5
Beaufort	312	2,066	36,235	18.4	29.6	39.8	229.1	10,729	34,966	60,603	41.1	6.3	60,319	10.7	18.3	18.0
Berkeley	367	2,485	50,738	15.9	41.6	23.3	289.6	8,892	27,010	56,697	42.7	3.5	57,399	11.7	17.8	16.6
Calhoun	258	2,028	3,125	20.4	53.3	18.2	19.6	10,869	24,766	44,010	54.9	2.4	45,149	18.2	26.6	24.4
Charleston	434	2,985	93,275	16.0	31.6	41.9	533.2	11,395	35,587	57,882	43.7	7.9	60,144	13.3	20.4	20.4
Cherokee	416	3,471	13,881	14.7	58.3	15.0	86.8	9,534	20,516	35,286	64.7	1.6	34,962	20.2	26.9	24.2
Chester	672	3,122	7,341	8.8	58.6	14.3	53.7	10,094	20,518	37,421	61.9	1.3	40,850	19.3	30.1	28.2
Chesterfield	478	3,201	10,230	9.5	64.3	11.3	69.0	9,400	19,768	38,469	61.0	0.9	38,881	22.1	32.6	30.4
Clarendon	396	3,059	7,101	10.4	57.4	14.9	48.9	9,695	20,616	35,838	64.6	1.5	36,647	23.2	34.8	33.3
Colleton	751	3,513	8,119	7.8	55.1	15.4	55.8	9,287	21,059	34,996	66.4	1.7	36,139	22.4	37.1	36.7
Darlington	676	4,692	16,277	16.8	54.1	17.8	104.3	9,785	21,225	36,217	62.5	1.8	38,886	21.9	33.0	32.5
Dillon	951	5,212	7,920	6.9	63.4	11.2	50.6	8,445	15,638	30,866	69.0	0.4	32,229	29.8	42.1	38.5
Dorchester	508	3,181	40,554	14.4	37.9	27.4	206.5	7,547	27,317	58,685	41.6	3.3	63,269	10	13.9	13.4
Edgefield	80	962	5,841	13.5	54.5	19.5	36.5	10,511	23,804	47,500	52.8	2.1	48,059	17.3	23.5	21.9
Fairfield	775	3,295	4,475	13.6	56.3	17.6	42.8	14,599	21,972	35,551	63.3	1.6	40,285	19.3	31.1	28.5
Florence	620	4,074	36,510	11.8	48.8	22.5	233.6	9,920	23,797	43,310	55.2	2.4	43,727	18.6	27.9	27.9
Georgetown	496	2,991	12,858	10.2	42.2	27.1	102.0	10,529	28,748	46,967	52.1	4.2	48,373	17.1	31.5	29.7
Greenville	483	2,898	120,415	22.9	37.6	33.3	647.0	8,963	29,132	53,739	46.3	4.6	56,311	12.4	17.5	17.5
Greenwood	649	3,832	18,067	12.0	47.4	23.3	105.6	8,963	22,636	39,196	59.8	2.6	42,740	18.3	28.6	25.6
Hampton	829	2,881	4,143	10.7	61.9	11.7	36.6	11,215	17,676	32,147	68.4	0.8	36,834	25.1	34.6	30.4
Horry	600	4,531	64,146	8.7	43.5	23.0	549.1	9,268	25,804	46,475	53.8	2.4	45,979	16.1	28.4	26.1
Jasper	358	3,004	5,943	22.6	56.1	14.8	36.5	12,619	20,067	39,740	64.7	1.3	40,960	19.9	33.7	32.5
Kershaw	379	2,213	14,438	10.3	50.5	20.4	96.6	9,146	23,530	46,565	53.2	2.4	50,627	14.4	20.5	18.8
Lancaster	320	2,173	18,423	9.8	47.3	25.1	108.9	8,849	26,425	50,557	49.6	3.4	57,667	13.6	19.1	18.2
Laurens	518	2,705	15,502	16.1	54.7	14.6	90.2	9,788	20,748	40,580	60.8	1.3	41,695	21.9	29.3	27.8
Lee	566	2,698	3,953	12.0	64.7	11.6	25.7	11,966	16,972	31,963	68.9	1.5	33,756	25.8	37.0	36.3
Lexington	351	2,564	68,997	11.5	39.5	30.1	416.9	10,649	29,311	57,482	42.8	3.9	60,329	11.7	17.3	17.1
McCormick	364	1,714	1,430	11.6	51.5	19.3	11.0	12,677	22,836	40,622	58.0	2.1	44,644	18.5	33.8	32.0
Marion	784	5,108	7,893	14.5	57.0	16.4	48.7	9,689	18,556	31,129	69.9	0.8	31,438	27.5	39.4	36.7
Marlboro	876	3,802	5,885	7.0	67.2	8.9	42.2	9,932	16,561	33,921	68.3	1.4	33,412	28	39.4	28.6
Newberry	291	2,088	8,578	18.1	56.9	17.1	62.7	10,216	22,190	39,600	59.1	1.6	42,538	19	30.1	28.6
Oconee	293	2,620	16,347	9.6	46.8	24.2	114.5	10,851	26,798	43,978	55.6	3.6	51,087	16	22.9	19.9
Orangeburg	468	3,214	23,864	16.4	48.1	20.1	156.6	11,335	19,489	34,943	64.7	1.3	36,358	24.4	35.2	33.5
Pickens	368	3,301	37,884	10.6	45.6	23.6	134.0	8,060	23,501	45,332	55.3	2.1	48,133	15.3	15.8	15.6
Richland	788	4,480	122,085	15.2	31.7	37.7	857.2	12,296	28,018	52,082	48.0	4.2	52,187	16.9	20.1	19.1
Saluda	383	1,277	4,094	9.4	57.5	16.3	21.3	9,664	20,390	41,885	59.3	1.0	44,487	18	27.2	26.0
Spartanburg	458	2,961	75,160	15.8	44.2	23.8	478.9	10,077	24,786	47,575	52.0	2.6	51,035	13.7	19.7	18.3

1. Data for serious crimes have not been adjusted for underreporting; this may affect comparability between geographic areas and over time.　2. Per 100,000 population estimated by the FBI.　3. All persons 3 years old and over enrolled in nursery school through college.　4. Persons 25 years old and over.　5. Elementary and secondary education expenditures.　6. Based on population estimated by the American Community Survey, 2013–2017.

Table B. States and Counties — **Personal Income and Earnings**

STATE County	Personal income, 2017										Earnings, 2017		
	Total (mil dol)	Percent change 2016-2017	Per capita¹ Dollars	Per capita¹ Rank	Wages and salaries (mil dol)	Supplements to wages and salaries, employer contributions (mil dol) Pension and insurance	Supplements... Government social insurance	Proprietors' income (mil dol)	Dividends, interest, and rent (mil dol)	Personal transfer reecipts (mil dol)	Total (mil dol)	Contributions for government social insurance (mil dol) From employee and self-employed	From employer
	62	63	64	65	66	67	68	69	70	71	72	73	74
PENNSYLVANIA— Cont'd													
Potter	669	5.4	39,830	1,584	239	56	20	102	104	192	417	26	20
Schuylkill	5,784	3.4	40,568	1,462	2,122	459	183	357	922	1,571	3,120	207	183
Snyder	1,629	4.1	39,916	1,566	664	132	56	179	234	422	1,031	63	56
Somerset	2,930	2.7	39,334	1,667	975	231	83	271	492	800	1,560	103	83
Sullivan	269	3.9	44,236	991	59	16	5	26	65	76	106	8	5
Susquehanna	1,702	3.7	41,527	1,325	398	91	33	166	356	402	687	48	33
Tioga	1,599	2.5	39,202	1,690	537	132	45	163	282	430	877	56	45
Union	1,750	4.4	39,232	1,685	826	172	70	210	290	326	1,277	74	70
Venango	2,047	1.6	39,540	1,630	725	181	60	118	330	683	1,085	74	60
Warren	1,575	1.4	39,714	1,605	613	143	51	132	286	443	939	61	51
Washington	11,238	2.8	54,210	305	5,316	876	409	1,092	1,764	2,216	7,693	468	409
Wayne	2,125	4.1	41,503	1,330	632	146	52	226	409	557	1,056	70	52
Westmoreland	17,293	3.0	49,040	532	6,323	1,169	527	1,040	2,749	3,913	9,059	596	527
Wyoming	1,159	2.3	42,406	1,214	491	91	41	123	195	267	745	46	41
York	21,156	4.1	47,427	672	9,056	1,658	744	1,256	3,248	3,989	12,714	783	744
RHODE ISLAND	55,934	4.1	52,943	X	27,036	4,226	2,182	3,598	10,511	11,206	37,041	2,529	2,182
Bristol	3,725	4.5	76,148	50	654	108	55	232	1,029	445	1,049	77	55
Kent	9,334	4.2	56,996	222	3,953	595	328	541	1,485	1,738	5,417	382	328
Newport	5,391	4.0	64,599	106	2,465	463	213	415	1,489	839	3,556	231	213
Providence	29,618	4.1	46,470	755	17,274	2,540	1,361	1,698	4,754	6,970	22,873	1,559	1,361
Washington	7,866	3.9	62,357	130	2,690	519	225	711	1,755	1,214	4,146	279	225
SOUTH CAROLINA	209,180	4.6	41,659	X	98,906	16,419	7,486	14,827	38,116	45,646	137,638	8,877	7,486
Abbeville	817	4.0	33,044	2,609	231	50	18	56	109	266	355	28	18
Aiken	6,837	4.2	40,656	1,449	3,215	446	236	297	1,164	1,606	4,194	288	236
Allendale	279	4.2	30,946	2,855	123	29	9	15	43	102	177	12	9
Anderson	7,607	4.9	38,271	1,833	2,844	504	215	378	1,115	1,918	3,941	277	215
Bamberg	458	0.8	31,881	2,768	150	33	12	19	66	164	213	16	12
Barnwell	692	2.0	32,428	2,702	204	42	16	18	102	223	279	21	16
Beaufort	9,858	4.1	52,763	350	3,387	582	272	689	3,558	1,838	4,930	323	272
Berkeley	8,169	6.7	37,483	1,950	2,903	428	209	503	1,209	1,562	4,043	269	209
Calhoun	541	4.0	36,787	2,080	215	42	16	26	90	154	298	21	16
Charleston	22,995	4.7	57,281	217	14,050	2,306	1,073	2,829	5,701	3,166	20,257	1,174	1,073
Cherokee	1,788	3.9	31,313	2,831	788	132	61	89	234	546	1,071	76	61
Chester	1,055	3.9	32,667	2,664	411	73	31	42	142	347	557	41	31
Chesterfield	1,358	3.5	29,559	2,955	619	111	47	64	170	442	841	59	47
Clarendon	1,091	3.1	32,037	2,749	242	53	19	61	160	391	374	32	19
Colleton	1,292	3.4	34,345	2,435	411	76	32	67	211	441	585	46	32
Darlington	2,406	4.2	35,764	2,235	1,037	179	78	84	347	729	1,377	97	78
Dillon	831	2.4	27,111	3,058	321	58	25	10	105	321	414	33	25
Dorchester	5,921	5.4	37,847	1,906	1,466	258	112	280	823	1,244	2,115	150	112
Edgefield	932	4.4	34,913	2,361	222	49	17	56	132	235	344	25	17
Fairfield	818	3.2	36,198	2,174	666	107	47	33	115	253	853	54	47
Florence	5,600	3.8	40,411	1,487	3,090	533	230	278	924	1,438	4,130	267	230
Georgetown	2,759	4.6	44,782	932	1,021	169	76	194	741	768	1,461	107	76
Greenville	23,348	4.4	46,066	787	14,292	2,035	1,069	1,779	3,891	4,045	19,175	1,190	1,069
Greenwood	2,521	3.6	35,829	2,221	1,301	257	99	109	443	729	1,765	118	99
Hampton	605	2.6	30,861	2,862	204	43	15	11	93	205	274	21	15
Horry	11,838	5.8	35,520	2,271	4,971	757	391	908	2,391	3,386	7,027	510	391
Jasper	790	3.5	27,762	3,036	387	63	29	65	119	249	544	38	29
Kershaw	2,591	4.4	39,842	1,582	762	142	58	158	360	651	1,119	78	58
Lancaster	4,397	12.4	47,505	663	1,273	199	92	956	545	884	2,520	161	92
Laurens	2,232	3.7	33,390	2,572	1,001	177	76	81	311	752	1,334	96	76
Lee	549	3.2	31,616	2,795	145	29	11	30	69	202	215	17	11
Lexington	12,933	3.5	44,497	962	5,516	926	411	924	1,994	2,296	7,777	493	411
McCormick	339	5.0	35,465	2,278	68	17	5	15	80	135	106	11	5
Marion	944	2.6	30,157	2,915	241	48	19	28	123	363	336	29	19
Marlboro	801	3.3	29,861	2,939	331	61	26	12	101	284	429	33	26
Newberry	1,418	3.9	36,846	2,070	552	104	42	40	223	389	738	53	42
Oconee	3,201	5.1	41,424	1,345	1,220	238	91	166	649	826	1,715	122	91
Orangeburg	2,858	2.2	32,668	2,663	1,221	230	94	96	415	969	1,641	118	94
Pickens	4,561	3.9	36,936	2,051	1,593	314	118	227	801	1,085	2,253	157	118
Richland	18,054	4.0	43,863	1,035	11,741	2,135	892	1,429	3,141	3,374	16,197	944	892
Saluda	678	3.2	33,164	2,598	163	34	12	32	94	191	241	18	12
Spartanburg	12,799	4.4	41,709	1,297	7,037	1,108	525	794	2,557	2,741	9,464	609	525

1. Based on the resident population estimated as of July 1 of the year shown.

Table B. States and Counties — Earnings, Social Security, and Housing

STATE County	Farm	Mining, quarrying, and extractions	Construction	Manufacturing	Information; professional, scientific, technical services	Retail trade	Finance, insurance, real estate, and leasing	Health care and social assistance	Government	Number	Rate[1]	Supplemental Security Income recipients, 2017	Total	Percent change, 2010-2018
	75	76	77	78	79	80	81	82	83	84	85	86	87	88
PENNSYLVANIA— Cont'd														
Potter	2.3	0.6	7.2	9.3	D	4	2.3	D	15.5	4,935	294	473	12,976	0.4
Schuylkill	0.4	1.2	4.6	24.2	3.9	6	3.3	13.1	17.4	38,305	269	3,844	69,941	0.9
Snyder	1.9	D	16.3	22	3.3	9.3	2.7	D	14.9	8,990	220	606	16,506	3
Somerset	1.7	3.8	6.6	10.8	4.2	6.5	4.2	13.2	20.8	20,520	275	2,136	38,496	1
Sullivan	1.5	D	11.6	D	D	6.2	D	D	24.6	1,955	321	131	6,379	1.2
Susquehanna	1.6	8.3	13.5	3.9	8	6.6	3.1	D	19	10,920	266	862	23,381	1.9
Tioga	3.9	4.4	5.9	13.3	5.7	7	4.1	D	20.2	11,270	276	1,046	21,826	2.1
Union	2.6	D	6	7.5	2.4	5.8	3.3	D	21	8,715	195	535	17,449	2.6
Venango	0	0.8	4.7	22.3	2.8	7.1	3.6	15.7	21.2	15,575	301	1,995	27,607	0.5
Warren	0.6	1.1	4.1	18.7	3.6	7.4	7.1	14.8	15.5	11,280	284	905	23,616	0.3
Washington	0.1	8.6	11	9.5	9.5	4.8	6.3	10.7	9.3	53,815	260	4,809	96,212	3.5
Wayne	1.4	0.3	12.7	3.1	4.7	8.9	5.1	14.1	24.5	14,680	287	1,084	32,403	2.3
Westmoreland	0.1	1.2	9	14.5	7.2	7.9	4.5	12.9	12.8	96,135	273	7,949	170,776	1.5
Wyoming	2.3	5.2	7.6	25.7	D	5.9	2.3	D	10.3	7,190	263	625	13,525	2
York	0	0.2	9.4	18.7	6	5.7	4.5	13.9	13.3	96,140	216	8,375	184,869	3.5
RHODE ISLAND	0.1	D	D	8.4	9.8	6	10.5	13.8	16.5	222,851	210	33,124	469,157	1.2
Bristol	0.1	0	D	D	10	4.8	5.8	12.6	15.3	11,120	227	703	21,056	1.1
Kent	0	D	5.8	10.2	10.9	8.8	8.2	15.2	12.7	39,900	244	3,626	74,514	1.1
Newport	0.1	D	5.3	D	12.2	5.7	5.4	7.2	34.9	19,085	229	1,391	42,666	2.1
Providence	0	0	5.4	6.6	9.5	4.7	13.1	15.1	14	123,280	193	25,796	266,574	0.6
Washington	0.3	D	6.9	17.2	7.5	9.7	4.5	10.7	19.8	29,465	234	1,608	64,347	3.4
SOUTH CAROLINA	0.1	0.1	6.7	13.7	9.8	6.7	7.5	9.4	20	1,115,313	222	116,683	2,318,271	8.4
Abbeville	0.5	0	10.3	32.9	4	3.6	D	2.8	24.5	6,685	270	570	12,175	0.9
Aiken	-0.1	0.2	9.1	14.9	10.6	6.1	5	7.7	12	40,175	239	3,819	77,687	7.5
Allendale	4.3	0	0.8	34.9	D	2.7	1.1	4.3	32.5	2,320	258	604	4,488	0
Anderson	0.1	0.2	5	25.7	5	8.3	3.6	8.2	21.1	48,145	242	4,295	89,000	5.1
Bamberg	-0.2	0	1.8	22	D	6.5	D	8.9	23	3,770	262	713	7,710	0
Barnwell	D	D	6.4	30.1	D	8.2	2	D	27.6	5,010	235	1,081	10,578	0.9
Beaufort	0.2	0	7.4	0.9	11.1	7.6	8.1	8.3	29.9	48,780	261	1,945	101,247	8.8
Berkeley	0	D	10.3	13.5	21.7	6.7	5.2	3.4	15.9	37,375	171	3,275	85,956	16.8
Calhoun	0.3	0	13.9	34.9	D	2.2	D	D	13.6	4,035	274	390	7,498	2.2
Charleston	0	0	7.4	7.8	12.3	6.2	8.8	10.9	23.2	73,055	182	7,130	191,891	12.9
Cherokee	0.3	D	D	36.9	1.8	7	3.3	D	13.5	14,035	246	1,581	24,638	2.6
Chester	1.3	0	7.4	34.3	D	4.9	D	D	17.5	8,510	263	1,145	14,795	0.6
Chesterfield	0.6	D	5.6	38.6	D	4.7	1.9	8	13.4	10,910	237	1,550	21,687	1
Clarendon	2.9	0	5.8	5.5	5.6	12.6	3.7	7.5	33.4	9,535	280	1,549	17,850	2.2
Colleton	D	D	7.8	8.3	D	8.3	4.3	14.6	19.8	10,710	285	1,691	20,101	1
Darlington	-0.3	0	6.2	26	2.2	5.7	2.5	10.2	13.1	17,020	253	2,764	30,880	2
Dillon	-4.8	0	1.5	23.7	D	10.1	3.8	D	19.5	7,285	238	1,520	13,777	0.3
Dorchester	-0.1	D	9.8	18.7	5.7	8.1	4.4	6.9	18.6	28,515	182	2,869	61,647	12
Edgefield	4.7	D	7.6	17.3	2.8	5	2.4	D	32.6	5,915	222	816	11,047	4.6
Fairfield	0.8	D	34.9	6.9	D	3.7	0.6	2.4	9.6	5,895	261	803	11,946	2.3
Florence	0	0	3.6	12.5	7.3	7.5	12.6	13.7	20.5	31,710	229	5,819	61,116	4.1
Georgetown	0.4	D	6.6	12.6	6.4	7.5	8.8	11.9	22.3	20,680	336	1,792	35,874	6.3
Greenville	0	0	7	13.3	12.5	6	9.1	10	11.7	99,880	197	9,623	214,128	9.6
Greenwood	0	D	4	26.4	2.9	6.7	3.7	12.2	24.9	17,095	243	1,793	31,541	1.5
Hampton	-2.7	0	5.3	8.9	D	6.4	D	D	34.7	4,905	250	973	9,169	0.3
Horry	0.2	0.1	7.9	2.8	6.8	11.8	10.4	11.2	16	96,915	291	5,910	210,698	13.3
Jasper	0.5	0	15.7	4.6	D	16.1	3	13.6	15	6,345	223	677	12,072	17.2
Kershaw	2.9	D	7.8	21.7	5.4	9	6.5	7.8	17.2	15,475	238	1,518	29,381	6.9
Lancaster	0.7	D	2.9	9	43	4.4	6.4	8.1	8.9	22,860	247	1,730	38,541	17.9
Laurens	0.2	D	4.2	41.8	D	4.1	1.7	D	16.4	17,785	266	2,070	31,503	2.6
Lee	9.2	0	2.6	14.4	D	6.6	D	D	27.5	4,600	265	863	7,775	0.1
Lexington	-0.2	0.1	7.5	13.1	6.3	7.9	5.7	6.4	19.9	56,050	193	4,545	126,190	10.7
McCormick	0.3	0	D	12.5	D	3.2	D	D	44.7	3,750	393	315	5,671	4
Marion	-0.5	D	3.4	12	2.3	9.4	6.3	D	23.1	8,680	277	1,621	14,956	0
Marlboro	-1.6	D	1	38.5	D	7.2	2.1	D	27.2	7,085	264	1,458	12,009	-0.5
Newberry	0.4	D	6.8	39.1	D	5.9	1.9	D	19.4	9,930	258	987	18,325	2.2
Oconee	0.2	D	6.1	28.3	4	6.9	3.5	6.7	15	22,635	293	1,489	40,806	5.3
Orangeburg	-0.3	D	4.4	22.3	3.1	7.8	3.5	8.1	27.5	22,535	258	3,947	42,785	0.7
Pickens	-0.1	D	5.6	17.2	4.6	7.9	4	8.1	34.7	27,505	223	2,235	55,074	7.4
Richland	0	0.1	4.3	5.5	11.3	5.2	12	11.7	29.7	68,765	167	8,642	175,070	8.3
Saluda	5.9	D	4.5	36.3	D	4.1	D	D	22.5	4,855	237	503	9,434	1.6
Spartanburg	0	0.1	7	25.5	5.2	6.1	5.1	7	16.1	68,505	223	7,253	131,451	7.2

1. Per 1,000 resident population estimated as of July 1 of the year shown.

Table B. States and Counties — Housing, Labor Force, and Employment

	Housing units, 2013-2017								Civilian labor force, 2018		Unemployment		Civilian employment[6], 2013-2017		
	Occupied units													Percent	
			Owner-occupied			Renter-occupied									
				Median owner cost as a percent of income			Median rent as a percent of income[2]								Construction, production, and maintenance occupations
STATE County				With a mortgage	Without a mortgage[2]	Median rent[3]		Substandard units[4] (percent)		Percent change, 2017-2018				Management, business, science, and arts	
	Total	Percent	Median value[1]						Total		Total	Rate[5]	Total		
	89	90	91	92	93	94	95	96	97	98	99	100	101	102	103
PENNSYLVANIA— Cont'd															
Potter	6,536	77.2	103,700	21.3	13.9	653	29.4	1.6	7,189	-1.1	383	5.3	6,745	29.5	35.7
Schuylkill	58,758	74.8	96,200	20.1	13.7	662	27.8	1.3	66,090	-0.2	3,420	5.2	62,886	27.9	33.3
Snyder	14,576	72.7	154,800	19.9	11.8	714	25	2.7	20,324	-1.9	802	3.9	20,054	26.5	32.2
Somerset	29,918	77.9	103,100	20.0	13.0	607	27.3	1.4	33,553	-0.2	1,713	5.1	32,886	28.3	31.3
Sullivan	2,648	81.5	148,500	22.3	13.8	647	22.5	1.1	2,693	0.1	134	5	2,612	25.0	38.9
Susquehanna	17,404	77.1	159,100	21.6	12.7	738	29.1	1.8	20,483	-0.5	824	4	18,522	27.2	34.1
Tioga	16,121	73.9	139,400	21.3	13.1	709	26.8	1.2	18,812	-1.6	972	5.2	18,203	29.4	31.5
Union	14,702	70.8	172,200	19.9	12.6	733	26.7	2.1	19,640	-0.2	730	3.7	18,397	34.9	25.6
Venango	21,925	74.8	85,000	18.3	10.6	604	26.5	1.5	22,421	-2.3	1,104	4.9	22,971	28.9	28.5
Warren	17,095	76.2	92,200	18.4	11.6	588	25.7	1.7	19,058	-1.2	849	4.5	18,231	30.7	32.3
Washington	83,897	75.6	158,600	18.8	10.9	708	26.4	1.1	106,001	-0.3	4,589	4.3	99,129	35.8	23.8
Wayne	19,202	79.2	174,600	24.5	12.8	832	29.9	1.3	22,367	-0.2	1,057	4.7	21,209	29.9	28.1
Westmoreland	151,892	77.6	144,900	19.1	11.4	674	26.8	1	180,515	-0.1	7,976	4.4	172,844	36.2	23.7
Wyoming	10,801	77.9	163,500	20.9	12.3	764	27.9	1.5	13,746	-0.7	618	4.5	13,053	25.2	33.1
York	169,667	74.4	170,300	22.1	13.5	915	30.3	1.6	234,141	-0.3	9,024	3.9	222,038	33.3	27.0
RHODE ISLAND	412,028	60.0	242,200	23.7	14.5	957	29.9	2	555,807	0.4	22,636	4.1	526,071	38.1	18.6
Bristol	19,521	69.0	341,300	23.0	14.9	1,021	29.8	0.9	26,082	0.4	902	3.5	25,027	47.2	13.6
Kent	69,013	70.5	212,600	23.3	14.6	986	29.5	1.6	90,476	0.4	3,346	3.7	87,822	38.4	18.3
Newport	35,421	62.0	362,800	24.0	14.5	1,193	28.8	1.1	44,657	0.4	1,584	3.5	41,471	44.0	15.1
Providence	238,465	53.2	214,400	24.1	14.6	923	30.1	2.5	325,587	0.4	14,328	4.4	307,175	35.0	20.3
Washington	49,608	73.3	320,600	23.0	13.6	1,086	30.3	1.2	69,005	0.2	2,476	3.6	64,576	44.8	15.5
SOUTH CAROLINA	1,871,307	68.6	148,600	20.8	10.5	836	30.3	2.2	2,323,209	0.7	79,553	3.4	2,181,046	33.7	23.8
Abbeville	9,392	77.0	92,600	22.6	12.7	616	36.3	0.9	10,058	1.1	400	4	9,505	27.2	31.3
Aiken	65,703	72.3	135,900	19.7	10.9	767	30.1	1.9	73,944	0.1	2,474	3.3	70,753	34.0	26.2
Allendale	3,285	66.1	52,100	26.4	15.0	617	38.5	2.8	2,740	1.6	159	5.8	2,668	20.3	36.8
Anderson	76,234	70.6	133,900	19.5	10.0	716	29.4	2.3	89,580	0.3	2,917	3.3	85,591	32.3	27.5
Bamberg	5,587	76.0	65,800	18.9	13.8	754	40.2	2.7	4,990	-2.8	325	6.5	5,592	32.1	31.1
Barnwell	8,426	69.1	76,200	21.5	13.0	603	33.1	2.5	8,343	4.3	399	4.8	8,004	23.9	32.6
Beaufort	68,790	70.5	283,800	25.5	11.5	1,105	30.6	1.9	75,517	1.8	2,435	3.2	74,171	34.7	18.4
Berkeley	73,168	70.0	164,900	21.2	10.3	1,014	29.2	2.2	101,127	1.4	3,069	3	93,092	33.1	25.2
Calhoun	6,150	79.3	103,900	21.9	11.6	710	33.4	2.7	6,665		283	4.2	6,362	28.5	33.3
Charleston	154,049	60.6	273,100	22.8	12.2	1,084	32	1.8	206,317	1.4	5,719	2.8	195,823	41.7	16.1
Cherokee	20,480	70.5	94,300	19.7	10.4	663	30.4	1.4	25,268	6.2	917	3.6	21,599	25.6	33.6
Chester	12,384	75.0	88,900	19.3	10.0	613	31.6	1.7	13,302	0.1	641	4.8	12,706	22.7	36.7
Chesterfield	18,303	71.8	81,200	20.6	10.4	589	28.2	4.5	21,952	2.3	715	3.3	19,051	22.7	38.9
Clarendon	13,573	74.9	89,900	23.3	12.1	593	29.2	3.6	12,548	1.5	589	4.7	11,777	29.0	30.5
Colleton	15,134	72.8	84,600	23.5	11.8	703	29.4	2	16,750	1	671	4	15,638	23.7	31.7
Darlington	26,861	68.6	84,800	19.3	10.3	647	31.9	2.4	30,086	0.8	1,227	4.1	26,757	31.1	27.6
Dillon	10,945	66.0	67,200	19.9	13.1	543	32.6	3.5	12,702	2.2	606	4.8	11,332	21.8	34.4
Dorchester	54,028	71.1	177,500	22.8	10.9	1,003	30.7	2	75,077	1.4	2,269	3	70,522	36.5	20.8
Edgefield	9,054	74.8	123,000	20.4	10.6	591	32.6	3	10,538	-0.3	366	3.5	10,410	28.8	33.3
Fairfield	8,878	74.4	101,100	20.3	13.1	700	41	1.7	9,786	-1.2	602	6.2	8,726	24.2	31.6
Florence	52,092	65.8	128,400	19.6	10.4	722	28.7	2.3	65,996	1.1	2,412	3.7	59,365	34.7	22.1
Georgetown	24,840	76.5	178,600	25.1	11.9	918	31.3	1.7	25,520	2.7	1,158	4.5	24,152	31.0	23.1
Greenville	185,837	66.1	165,600	19.3	10.0	831	28.5	2.2	248,725	0.3	7,294	2.9	233,417	37.9	21.9
Greenwood	27,022	64.3	116,300	19.7	10.0	664	32.1	2.5	30,954	0.9	1,129	3.6	29,541	29.5	29.0
Hampton	7,129	75.7	75,400	22.4	13.3	550	25	1.5	8,234	1.7	289	3.5	7,429	23.8	31.0
Horry	125,168	69.9	166,500	23.7	11.0	883	31.2	2	145,798	1.7	6,108	4.2	138,429	27.6	18.6
Jasper	9,715	69.3	130,700	28.2	11.8	838	33.5	3.6	12,214	1.8	369	3	12,055	17.9	33.3
Kershaw	24,711	81.4	121,200	21.8	10.7	726	25.4	1	28,930	-0.9	1,026	3.5	26,909	31.9	27.6
Lancaster	31,445	78.9	169,000	19.9	11.2	729	30.9	1.8	39,543	0.6	1,500	3.8	36,001	31.6	26.7
Laurens	25,543	71.4	87,400	21.2	10.0	719	29.6	2.5	29,857	0.2	1,071	3.6	28,011	25.8	34.3
Lee	6,501	74.8	69,800	20.8	12.1	645	39.5	2.6	6,586	3.1	302	4.6	6,005	23.4	34.4
Lexington	109,251	73.7	148,400	19.4	10.0	881	29.4	2.2	147,320	-0.7	4,225	2.9	136,891	37.0	22.3
McCormick	4,077	76.1	116,600	26.0	12.0	660	27.9	0.5	3,406	1.3	121	3.6	2,720	24.2	31.1
Marion	11,911	68.9	75,800	21.7	13.1	535	30.2	1.7	12,945	4	713	5.5	11,778	25.7	31.2
Marlboro	9,703	66.3	60,500	20.2	12.3	566	27.9	2.9	9,157	0.3	468	5.1	9,731	23.2	38.2
Newberry	14,893	72.8	99,700	21.2	10.8	738	29.3	3.1	18,656	1.5	585	3.1	16,259	25.1	34.8
Oconee	31,354	72.9	153,300	20.1	10.0	707	32.2	2.5	34,900	2.6	1,159	3.3	31,227	30.3	29.1
Orangeburg	33,029	68.6	92,700	22.8	13.0	668	32.7	2.2	34,534	-0.1	1,987	5.8	34,712	28.0	30.4
Pickens	46,428	68.0	132,300	19.6	10.0	730	31.2	2.4	56,262	0.2	1,894	3.4	53,267	33.9	26.1
Richland	149,161	59.0	154,100	20.8	10.1	922	31	1.9	196,988	-0.8	6,772	3.4	191,869	38.9	15.8
Saluda	7,052	71.9	93,100	23.3	10.0	658	29.9	2.3	8,808	-0.6	273	3.1	8,421	24.6	39.4
Spartanburg	113,191	69.0	128,000	19.4	10.0	746	29.2	2.8	147,900	1.1	4,604	3.1	135,522	31.2	29.6

1. Specified owner-occupied units.   2. A value of 10.0 represents 10 percent or less; a value of 50.0 represents 50 percent or more.   3. Specified renter-occupied units.   4. Overcrowded or lacking complete plumbing facilities.   5. Percent of civilian labor force.   6. Civilian employed persons 16 years old and over.

Table B. States and Counties — Nonfarm Employment and Agriculture

	Private nonfarm establishments, employment and payroll, 2016									Agriculture, 2017			
		Employment						Annual payroll		Farms			Farm producers whose primary occupation is farming (percent)
STATE County	Number of establishments	Total	Health care and social assistance	Manufacturing	Retail trade	Finance and insurance	Professional, scientific, and technical services	Total (mil dol)	Average per employee (dollars)	Number	Percent with:		
											Fewer than 50 acres	1000 acres or more	
	104	105	106	107	108	109	110	111	112	113	114	115	116

STATE County	104	105	106	107	108	109	110	111	112	113	114	115	116
PENNSYLVANIA— Cont'd													
Potter	365	4,308	932	590	554	69	129	158	36,712	447	25.3	4.0	43.5
Schuylkill	2,738	41,126	7,501	10,019	5,741	885	990	1,524	37,065	685	44.5	1.0	44.0
Snyder	870	15,282	1,704	4,150	2,941	286	179	438	28,655	864	49.0	0.9	49.1
Somerset	1,686	18,295	3,597	2,745	2,728	744	609	623	34,053	1,152	28.6	2.1	46.0
Sullivan	155	1,204	438	72	220	28	21	31	25,974	190	21.6	2.6	42.1
Susquehanna	876	6,997	1,203	573	1,206	176	302	218	31,167	909	29.6	0.8	45.7
Tioga	875	10,619	1,829	2,146	1,922	392	237	383	36,048	1,056	24.1	1.7	44.4
Union	925	16,689	4,115	1,592	1,761	446	450	606	36,331	574	38.0	0.7	53.1
Venango	1,172	15,564	3,270	3,803	2,668	317	299	527	33,853	409	40.6	2.0	36.2
Warren	913	14,063	2,944	3,013	2,386	892	244	505	35,907	452	33.0	1.3	46.1
Washington	5,127	82,440	13,712	8,457	8,768	1,521	3,730	4,364	52,934	1,760	37.7	0.1	41.8
Wayne	1,321	12,420	2,431	615	2,861	441	292	429	34,508	640	27.3	0.9	42.3
Westmoreland	8,600	125,776	20,661	17,374	19,344	2,783	6,454	5,037	40,046	1,099	42.0	2.1	38.6
Wyoming	654	10,490	551	2,252	1,307	195	450	534	50,868	410	32.0	1.2	39.7
York	8,646	164,632	25,020	30,464	22,078	3,726	5,947	6,975	42,367	2,067	62.0	2.0	39.3
RHODE ISLAND	28,685	435,148	88,587	40,132	48,978	27,255	23,771	20,151	46,308	1,043	72.5	0.4	38.6
Bristol	1,254	14,525	2,648	2,147	1,403	244	428	487	33,498	40	67.5	NA	41.7
Kent	4,694	70,605	12,616	5,688	11,529	4,891	4,354	3,077	43,582	111	72.1	1.8	29.4
Newport	2,745	31,346	4,930	1,825	4,303	1,343	3,297	1,340	42,760	196	71.4	NA	44.0
Providence	15,908	269,673	59,768	22,992	24,943	18,891	12,954	12,971	48,100	377	73.2	NA	32.5
Washington	3,794	43,531	8,452	7,479	6,795	1,002	1,607	1,974	45,343	319	73.0	0.6	47.0
SOUTH CAROLINA	105,959	1,716,496	230,608	228,268	244,946	69,856	89,194	69,051	40,228	24,791	49.8	3.8	36.1
Abbeville	334	4,772	543	2,064	464	140	44	151	31,644	576	39.6	1.2	30.8
Aiken	2,732	50,307	6,377	7,851	7,513	1,203	1,878	2,115	42,036	1,249	57.1	2.1	38.9
Allendale	122	1,671	300	781	162	54	30	73	43,550	165	21.8	9.1	40.7
Anderson	3,694	57,568	8,773	11,923	9,347	1,139	2,210	2,172	37,721	1,742	54.5	1.5	33.0
Bamberg	261	3,105	530	979	497	91	56	94	30,400	355	29.0	6.2	30.8
Barnwell	354	4,162	440	1,539	728	125	89	134	32,150	369	42.5	4.1	34.3
Beaufort	5,154	54,701	8,209	600	10,121	1,886	2,482	1,855	33,905	161	67.7	9.3	28.4
Berkeley	2,980	46,709	2,684	4,699	7,355	976	3,589	2,258	48,339	339	56.0	5.3	31.9
Calhoun	237	3,694	420	1,365	342	33	18	145	39,239	480	36.9	9.6	42.6
Charleston	13,321	202,114	31,767	15,573	28,565	6,226	15,626	8,777	43,424	403	68.2	1.0	39.3
Cherokee	950	17,671	1,272	5,907	2,927	327	211	591	33,456	415	47.0	2.2	33.0
Chester	511	7,000	615	2,486	943	143	136	280	40,059	517	40.6	4.3	38.8
Chesterfield	684	13,219	1,597	5,771	1,310	206	85	499	37,745	636	47.8	4.4	38.5
Clarendon	465	5,544	1,531	674	1,212	232	76	160	28,844	381	36.2	8.9	50.1
Colleton	738	7,808	1,397	899	1,570	250	211	250	32,068	459	44.4	7.0	32.9
Darlington	1,075	17,022	2,432	2,886	2,482	404	235	755	44,338	322	45.7	12.7	48.1
Dillon	482	7,264	1,160	1,764	1,347	184	392	196	27,030	182	22.0	14.8	54.9
Dorchester	2,282	26,739	3,165	4,426	4,546	693	1,067	950	35,523	358	55.3	4.2	38.7
Edgefield	322	4,962	522	1,011	501	57	63	177	35,753	397	43.1	4.5	35.1
Fairfield	313	7,790	612	1,102	565	57	D	536	68,769	228	25.4	8.3	27.0
Florence	3,136	57,006	13,403	7,075	9,239	3,641	2,372	2,128	37,336	540	42.4	6.7	38.1
Georgetown	1,800	19,471	3,743	2,029	3,180	464	770	717	36,816	166	36.7	8.4	32.9
Greenville	12,909	224,945	27,336	28,166	27,213	9,256	17,050	9,941	44,193	1,036	69.5	0.3	30.4
Greenwood	1,311	22,493	4,478	5,537	3,762	501	714	809	35,983	466	44.2	1.1	31.4
Hampton	325	3,228	670	393	541	128	99	117	36,295	242	24.4	12.0	42.4
Horry	8,629	107,915	11,133	2,819	23,452	3,570	3,641	3,239	30,018	767	47.3	5.7	46.6
Jasper	615	7,512	887	292	2,029	95	190	297	39,576	135	55.6	11.9	45.5
Kershaw	1,109	15,568	2,007	3,514	2,368	515	417	559	35,885	466	50.9	3.6	39.3
Lancaster	1,359	19,564	2,486	2,096	3,151	1,168	930	864	44,140	534	48.5	2.1	31.3
Laurens	927	17,026	2,032	6,545	1,692	295	396	632	37,142	840	44.9	2.1	32.6
Lee	185	1,618	214	117	387	62	40	46	28,639	334	42.2	9.6	38.4
Lexington	6,389	100,083	13,359	9,227	16,935	3,087	3,321	3,788	37,850	1,137	63.5	0.9	32.3
McCormick	84	908	200	269	108	14	17	27	29,254	92	34.8	5.4	51.4
Marion	486	5,081	589	783	1,131	305	87	141	27,708	197	43.7	6.1	41.2
Marlboro	319	4,984	1,080	2,095	749	115	44	167	33,424	201	38.8	10.0	38.8
Newberry	725	12,191	1,423	4,931	1,471	177	152	414	33,953	607	40.4	1.6	35.7
Oconee	1,497	20,436	2,161	5,339	3,116	478	526	852	41,671	815	58.9	0.2	36.7
Orangeburg	1,593	25,314	4,186	6,431	4,003	611	459	887	35,047	978	38.8	8.0	46.5
Pickens	1,990	27,859	3,548	5,235	5,321	612	782	875	31,425	740	73.6	0.1	28.6
Richland	8,918	161,532	27,806	9,041	19,808	18,143	11,455	6,923	42,859	440	62.7	1.4	42.7
Saluda	241	3,829	418	2,133	311	39	122	115	30,141	574	35.0	3.7	39.1
Spartanburg	6,225	126,940	16,246	29,203	14,622	2,017	3,737	5,554	43,750	1,433	67.9	0.3	30.0

Table B. States and Counties — Agriculture

STATE County	Land in farms					Value of land and buildings (dollars)		Value of machinery and equiopmnet, average per farm (dollars)	Value of products sold:				Organic farms (number)	Farms with internet access (percent)	Government payments	
	Acreage (1,000)	Percent change, 2012-2017	Acres			Average per farm	Average per acre		Total (mil dol)	Average per farm (acres)	Percent from:				Total ($1,000)	Percent of farms
			Average size of farm	Total irrigated (1,000)	Total cropland (1,000)						Crops	Livestock and poultry products				
	117	118	119	120	121	122	123	124	125	126	127	128	129	130	131	132
PENNSYLVANIA— Cont'd																
Potter	98	1.1	219	0.0	45.5	750,104	3,429	110,415	39.2	87,756	27.4	72.6	7	74.3	1,139	44.7
Schuylkill	97	-8.4	141	0.4	69.7	939,868	6,645	133,965	143.4	209,400	46.5	53.5	15	74.2	1,655	42.2
Snyder	99	8.6	115	0.7	71.4	839,894	7,332	109,041	200.4	231,888	16.1	83.9	39	64.4	1,125	17.4
Somerset	219	2.1	190	0.2	136.3	612,870	3,223	111,459	115.4	100,216	31.5	68.5	40	62.6	1,265	17.5
Sullivan	43	15.9	229	0.0	20.9	934,952	4,091	109,248	12.2	64,121	31.4	68.6	NA	72.1	495	34.7
Susquehanna	154	-7.2	170	0.2	71.7	805,158	4,740	101,463	49.8	54,758	29.5	70.5	11	76.2	500	24.2
Tioga	213	3.7	202	0.5	123.2	765,228	3,797	98,872	92.3	87,363	27.9	72.1	20	71.8	1,925	39.8
Union	66	-29.5	114	0.2	49.8	1,098,979	9,599	114,872	147.4	256,829	12.7	87.3	24	52.1	800	19.2
Venango	53	-13.3	130	0.1	30.1	495,109	3,797	82,682	14.8	36,137	58.9	41.1	NA	76.3	357	14.7
Warren	68	-17.3	151	0.1	30.4	521,904	3,461	71,238	21.3	47,029	26.3	73.7	1	68.6	157	13.9
Washington	190	-7.5	108	1.0	90.9	704,588	6,511	85,650	37.0	21,022	64.3	35.7	6	74.2	399	8.5
Wayne	101	-10.9	157	0.1	46.3	675,611	4,294	82,875	29.4	45,892	31.6	68.4	4	78.4	211	10.2
Westmoreland	144	0.8	131	0.2	93.4	775,756	5,909	108,523	66.3	60,346	50.7	49.3	13	72.2	1,265	19.1
Wyoming	61	-10.8	150	0.1	29.5	619,664	4,144	78,912	13.2	32,300	49.6	50.4	1	73.9	407	23.7
York	253	-3.6	122	0.7	199.2	1,002,707	8,201	105,570	260.9	126,235	51.7	48.3	25	74.5	4,781	17.8
RHODE ISLAND	57	-18.3	55	3.0	17.7	897,835	16,468	62,786	58.0	55,607	70.5	29.5	22	84.1	1,037	7.0
Bristol	1	D	33	0.0	0.7	1,500,196	45,085	66,112	1.0	25,125	37.2	62.8	NA	75.0	D	2.5
Kent	10	D	87	0.1	1.1	1,227,510	14,155	49,665	3.1	27,856	74.9	25.1	NA	81.1	D	5.4
Newport	10	-16.0	50	0.4	5.3	1,209,495	24,407	80,755	19.3	98,367	62.7	37.3	1	81.1	158	7.1
Providence	16	D	43	0.4	4.2	617,448	14,256	46,482	12.4	32,979	72.7	27.3	7	82.5	218	6.6
Washington	20	-27.2	62	2.0	6.3	847,467	13,608	75,161	22.2	69,561	77.0	23.0	14	90.0	632	8.5
SOUTH CAROLINA	4,745	-4.6	191	210.4	2,035.3	683,873	3,573	83,077	3,008.7	121,364	36.4	63.6	75	72.6	55,192	21.4
Abbeville	89	-3.8	154	0.3	18.8	475,695	3,096	45,030	9.2	15,891	15.7	84.3	1	78.0	643	22.9
Aiken	163	5.4	130	8.5	62.9	490,520	3,767	74,216	137.4	109,990	21.2	78.8	NA	77.3	440	8.7
Allendale	87	-30.4	525	5.9	35.3	1,157,218	2,206	131,114	15.3	92,739	82.0	18.0	NA	50.9	2,259	72.1
Anderson	184	15.5	105	0.6	69.9	598,456	5,675	59,960	75.2	43,144	13.4	86.6	NA	72.1	1,896	15.6
Bamberg	103	10.9	289	9.4	53.5	847,270	2,932	106,214	36.9	104,048	62.1	37.9	NA	74.6	2,126	54.4
Barnwell	74	-15.4	201	4.9	33.3	561,132	2,785	85,317	35.3	95,745	43.2	56.8	NA	69.9	1,556	30.4
Beaufort	56	32.7	348	2.0	7.1	1,258,884	3,622	58,947	20.3	126,006	94.7	5.3	3	78.3	80	9.9
Berkeley	100	33.6	296	0.7	18.1	790,654	2,673	80,348	5.0	14,885	85.4	14.6	NA	66.1	403	12.7
Calhoun	149	25.6	310	24.5	79.9	945,231	3,051	152,649	80.8	168,329	73.0	27.0	1	80.0	3,859	40.6
Charleston	38	6.0	93	0.6	9.7	873,600	9,369	63,570	22.4	55,536	83.6	16.4	1	76.7	D	2.0
Cherokee	61	-5.0	148	D	20.9	497,342	3,364	69,235	33.4	80,407	26.8	73.2	1	66.7	504	17.1
Chester	96	0.5	186	0.2	25.0	616,832	3,323	58,274	31.1	60,077	22.4	77.6	NA	68.1	671	22.8
Chesterfield	126	-4.0	198	1.6	50.7	583,564	2,952	81,283	128.1	201,390	15.2	84.8	NA	69.5	784	21.5
Clarendon	137	-21.3	359	8.9	102.8	816,645	2,274	128,382	108.6	284,979	47.3	52.7	2	65.9	1,608	49.6
Colleton	168	-10.5	366	2.4	40.7	1,109,808	3,030	86,861	20.3	44,266	76.9	23.1	6	71.9	724	16.1
Darlington	144	-18.5	447	6.1	97.1	1,161,402	2,596	170,002	88.2	274,019	55.6	44.4	8	74.8	1,167	27.6
Dillon	91	-14.4	502	0.4	71.8	1,150,361	2,291	197,314	113.1	621,159	28.5	71.5	NA	74.2	1,230	62.6
Dorchester	74	-0.9	206	1.7	32.4	579,913	2,811	100,333	39.9	111,589	36.6	63.4	NA	68.4	901	23.7
Edgefield	79	-3.6	198	8.9	23.2	697,738	3,527	66,385	37.7	94,967	66.6	33.4	NA	76.3	689	17.4
Fairfield	73	64.2	321	0.2	10.8	918,819	2,867	54,829	16.7	73,417	10.2	89.8	NA	64.0	98	10.1
Florence	146	-6.5	270	1.3	103.5	855,509	3,166	102,599	45.3	83,848	97.6	2.4	NA	67.6	1,563	36.5
Georgetown	80	21.0	484	0.2	13.4	988,048	2,043	84,996	9.3	55,861	98.2	1.8	2	74.7	693	42.8
Greenville	59	-18.5	57	1.5	17.0	526,644	9,188	40,726	13.3	12,861	75.6	24.4	9	74.1	290	6.7
Greenwood	72	-15.5	155	0.2	15.1	529,780	3,416	53,938	9.8	20,961	17.6	82.4	NA	79.8	367	13.7
Hampton	107	-23.3	441	8.5	42.3	1,074,779	2,439	129,432	30.5	125,959	98.9	1.1	1	63.6	2,346	57.4
Horry	171	-4.0	222	2.3	117.5	1,002,891	4,510	128,399	87.8	114,536	80.9	19.1	8	71.1	2,287	37.2
Jasper	63	-8.0	468	D	11.9	1,712,283	3,661	101,313	D	D	D	D	NA	73.3	123	15.6
Kershaw	79	-4.6	170	0.4	19.8	523,961	3,089	58,053	137.5	295,155	2.3	97.7	NA	65.5	269	8.6
Lancaster	63	-3.1	118	0.5	17.2	466,819	3,952	63,920	57.1	106,919	6.1	93.9	NA	76.4	91	5.4
Laurens	122	-0.3	146	0.4	40.9	558,251	3,834	65,424	70.9	84,400	13.0	87.0	5	77.9	957	17.9
Lee	110	-22.6	330	15.6	75.2	797,300	2,416	156,323	95.3	285,278	38.4	61.6	NA	65.0	2,612	44.9
Lexington	103	-4.7	90	13.2	47.8	499,227	5,533	77,434	222.2	195,412	32.5	67.5	9	79.6	600	9.3
McCormick	41	35.5	442	D	3.9	886,483	2,004	87,978	D	D	D	D	NA	72.8	D	19.6
Marion	50	-37.2	256	0.5	27.9	596,308	2,331	120,416	22.4	113,761	55.1	44.9	1	74.1	867	46.7
Marlboro	90	-20.3	449	3.5	55.8	865,333	1,927	162,975	79.8	397,060	38.1	61.9	2	70.1	1,856	43.8
Newberry	95	-9.3	156	1.2	31.6	517,675	3,314	74,874	143.0	235,506	4.3	95.7	3	68.4	850	27.0
Oconee	62	-7.9	77	0.4	18.9	489,668	6,385	71,668	159.4	195,610	2.9	97.1	3	74.8	635	16.4
Orangeburg	294	3.8	300	38.0	165.5	906,458	3,018	139,771	213.9	218,724	50.1	49.9	NA	69.5	9,879	30.6
Pickens	39	-12.5	53	0.2	12.2	374,709	7,050	43,935	6.6	8,972	56.2	43.8	NA	75.3	194	5.7
Richland	52	-13.9	119	1.6	22.2	571,315	4,797	67,954	32.3	73,314	44.5	55.5	3	75.7	960	13.4
Saluda	119	10.7	208	5.4	33.3	643,937	3,093	108,040	159.5	277,916	11.8	88.2	1	68.5	540	18.6
Spartanburg	96	-5.9	67	1.8	34.3	550,282	8,231	45,163	30.5	21,292	70.4	29.6	NA	78.4	481	7.9

Table B. States and Counties — Water Use, Wholesale Trade, Retail Trade, and Real Estate

	Water use, 2015		Wholesale Trade[1], 2012				Retail Trade[2], 2012				Real estate and rental and leasing,[2] 2012			
STATE County	Public supply water withdrawn (mil gal/day)	Public supply gallons withdrawn per person per day	Number of establish-ments	Number of employees	Sales (mil dol)	Average payroll (mil dol)	Number of establish-ments	Number of employees	Sales (mil dol)	Average payroll (mil dol)	Number of establish-ments	Number of employees	Sales (mil dol)	Average payroll (mil dol)
	133	134	135	136	137	138	139	140	141	142	143	144	145	146
PENNSYLVANIA— Cont'd														
Potter	0.91	53.2	6	D	D	D	68	546	152.7	13.6	5	16	1.0	0.2
Schuylkill	23.38	161.7	99	1,562	916.6	55.0	504	5,677	1,381.9	119.1	60	240	40.7	6.6
Snyder	1.60	39.6	26	D	D	D	198	2,867	630.2	54.9	13	47	11.1	1.7
Somerset	22.61	299.4	65	894	443.1	34.6	253	2,643	781.1	60.2	46	151	43.6	5.8
Sullivan	0.65	102.7	2	D	D	D	30	279	64.7	4.5	4	D	D	D
Susquehanna	1.41	33.8	34	267	569.9	8.6	146	1,269	533.6	28.0	15	88	24.5	4.7
Tioga	2.03	48.5	28	394	237.7	17.5	155	2,002	563.9	44.5	23	56	8.9	1.6
Union	2.87	63.8	30	D	D	D	130	1,561	479.2	37.0	28	158	19.0	3.4
Venango	4.68	88.1	43	D	D	D	204	2,565	636.9	53.9	26	79	12.6	1.9
Warren	3.07	76.0	27	211	142.0	8.8	130	2,394	674.6	55.4	18	71	7.3	1.4
Washington	39.71	190.7	227	3,257	2,869.3	186.9	691	8,657	2,342.1	194.5	145	772	221.8	38.3
Wayne	2.38	46.5	24	D	D	D	223	2,560	711.1	60.4	27	62	11.5	2.0
Westmoreland	24.18	67.6	330	5,958	7,333.3	308.5	1,258	18,183	4,671.7	416.7	262	1,106	240.4	38.0
Wyoming	0.66	23.7	18	389	106.5	14.5	114	1,334	393.5	28.0	9	27	10.4	2.0
York	34.82	78.6	359	6,685	4,340.8	301.4	1,297	21,024	5,192.4	463.9	258	1,470	263.7	51.8
RHODE ISLAND	97.46	92.3	1,158	15,697	22,310.4	1,000.2	3,795	47,688	12,063.9	1,206.6	1,058	5,615	1,119.8	218.5
Bristol	0.01	0.2	48	385	204.9	21.5	145	1,355	288.1	32.2	43	127	24.2	3.8
Kent	1.04	6.3	213	2,683	1,670.6	156.9	676	11,126	2,984.2	285.3	177	1,298	261.8	49.5
Newport	7.20	87.4	69	390	331.1	22.0	430	4,211	1,116.5	116.3	112	769	100.9	23.1
Providence	80.06	126.4	701	11,014	19,000.6	720.6	1,996	24,365	5,999.4	594.4	598	3,063	659.5	130.0
Washington	9.15	72.3	127	1,225	1,103.3	79.3	548	6,631	1,675.7	178.4	128	358	73.5	12.2
SOUTH CAROLINA	633.39	129.4	4,337	54,949	45,520.9	2,806.2	17,586	220,438	58,093.8	4,954.6	4,692	23,189	4,334.4	825.9
Abbeville	1.97	79.0	6	52	22.1	2.1	62	439	91.4	7.6	2	D	D	D
Aiken	32.01	193.0	69	505	399.4	20.0	508	6,601	1,749.5	139.6	106	331	53.6	9.8
Allendale	1.19	126.2	8	46	55.2	1.8	26	136	33.9	2.7	4	D	D	D
Anderson	19.00	97.6	167	2,514	2,641.3	105.6	697	8,472	2,189.6	188.1	125	422	91.7	13.1
Bamberg	0.92	61.8	6	D	D	D	56	462	95.3	9.6	2	D	D	D
Barnwell	1.54	70.9	4	D	D	D	74	782	167.1	14.9	10	18	2.2	0.4
Beaufort	12.76	71.1	113	470	295.6	21.4	734	9,080	2,090.5	203.1	379	1,718	267.1	62.8
Berkeley	70.34	346.9	151	2,343	3,248.3	125.6	396	6,173	1,730.6	141.6	130	699	132.4	26.1
Calhoun	1.11	75.1	9	D	D	D	35	224	65.9	3.6	3	D	D	D
Charleston	4.52	11.6	468	5,049	2,875.4	264.4	1,935	26,034	6,707.7	628.9	695	3,295	599.2	118.4
Cherokee	8.98	159.8	22	432	131.6	14.6	235	2,648	800.6	49.4	39	153	24.2	2.6
Chester	3.18	98.6	12	175	302.1	10.0	100	828	234.1	17.1	14	D	D	D
Chesterfield	5.83	126.7	27	305	96.4	10.0	135	1,271	317.7	22.8	16	37	4.1	0.8
Clarendon	2.31	68.4	16	113	74.2	3.8	124	1,247	336.3	24.9	16	34	3.9	1.0
Colleton	2.07	54.9	28	195	107.2	7.3	157	1,635	408.3	32.5	44	144	22.5	3.7
Darlington	6.41	94.9	73	592	859.7	25.3	235	2,246	536.6	45.2	37	102	46.5	2.7
Dillon	4.56	146.0	20	443	391.7	15.4	121	1,159	394.2	22.2	21	62	4.9	1.1
Dorchester	33.04	216.7	73	562	215.3	27.5	297	3,697	973.2	78.7	104	332	65.0	11.3
Edgefield	4.54	171.2	8	125	62.7	6.1	54	405	152.1	9.5	8	22	1.7	0.5
Fairfield	1.88	82.6	10	D	D	D	54	539	224.9	12.1	11	D	D	D
Florence	15.70	113.0	158	2,493	1,585.7	105.5	701	8,277	2,149.6	178.9	130	555	104.3	19.7
Georgetown	8.91	145.4	40	280	135.3	10.2	303	2,776	703.3	62.9	86	417	54.8	13.0
Greenville	45.87	93.3	711	9,278	10,153.0	521.9	1,757	24,790	6,380.5	593.2	534	2,681	838.1	113.6
Greenwood	4.85	69.4	49	421	837.9	19.1	275	3,224	758.9	67.6	44	D	D	D
Hampton	1.47	73.3	10	182	118.2	10.0	92	678	164.8	13.2	7	23	2.1	0.8
Horry	50.13	162.1	238	1,605	734.3	65.4	1,666	20,687	5,240.2	455.3	590	4,496	506.6	131.1
Jasper	27.30	981.2	27	258	146.8	12.6	104	1,425	574.8	40.5	18	69	13.6	3.2
Kershaw	5.33	83.8	16	70	43.5	4.8	178	2,122	586.3	44.0	32	83	14.0	3.2
Lancaster	20.99	244.5	47	1,106	719.7	38.8	238	2,673	732.9	60.3	43	D	D	D
Laurens	4.91	73.7	32	227	115.2	10.6	180	1,680	412.1	32.8	20	50	6.3	1.0
Lee	2.54	141.9	11	80	138.2	3.8	42	381	86.0	7.3	2	D	D	D
Lexington	52.21	185.3	302	5,744	3,889.3	292.0	1,046	15,123	3,974.5	338.3	243	1,277	227.9	43.8
McCormick	0.96	98.9	1	D	D	D	22	122	31.9	2.1	2	D	D	D
Marion	3.41	107.4	21	338	208.4	16.5	128	1,042	239.0	21.0	10	30	3.5	0.9
Marlboro	3.90	141.8	13	114	43.5	4.2	98	704	185.5	14.9	13	29	4.3	0.6
Newberry	6.58	173.1	26	238	160.5	10.0	133	1,389	428.1	29.2	17	65	14.9	2.2
Oconee	10.82	142.9	39	388	201.2	13.4	254	2,920	741.0	63.9	64	153	26.0	5.5
Orangeburg	8.96	100.4	66	529	387.8	21.6	370	4,070	1,016.6	80.2	53	241	25.7	7.9
Pickens	33.01	271.3	66	403	301.3	21.5	324	4,215	1,163.1	97.9	68	345	44.5	9.4
Richland	31.44	77.2	417	5,489	4,191.3	303.2	1,254	18,443	4,780.7	433.4	408	2,792	736.4	133.1
Saluda	0.03	1.5	8	45	14.4	1.4	49	414	115.1	8.5	4	D	D	D
Spartanburg	34.72	116.8	414	5,813	5,340.5	297.1	1,069	13,459	3,966.7	316.7	227	999	180.6	37.3

1 Merchant wholesalers, except manufacturers' sales branches and offices. 2. Employer establishments.

Professional Services, Manufacturing, and Accommodation and Food Services

STATE County	Professional, scientific, and technical services, 2012				Manufacturing, 2012				Accommodation and food services, 2012			
	Number of establish-ments	Number of employees	Sales (mil dol)	Average payroll (mil dol)	Number of establish-ments	Number of employees	Receipts (mil dol)	Annual payroll (mil dol)	Number of establis-hments	Number of employees	Receipts (mil dol)	Annual payroll (mil dol)
	147	148	149	150	151	152	153	154	155	156	157	158
PENNSYLVANIA— Cont'd												
Potter	23	113	12.9	4.9	23	513	69.5	19.0	40	254	12.3	2.9
Schuylkill	157	1,040	113.9	49.6	177	8,882	3,400.0	397.6	271	2,671	124.4	31.5
Snyder	44	204	17.3	7.0	62	3,627	678.7	139.7	85	1,743	79.9	20.6
Somerset	96	D	D	D	107	2,854	836.1	130.8	165	3,112	137.2	39.2
Sullivan	10	16	1.7	0.7	5	D	D	D	26	D	D	D
Susquehanna	46	213	26.1	8.5	61	659	124.0	23.8	83	752	44.1	10.8
Tioga	53	306	29.4	11.8	42	2,316	591.7	90.9	104	1,451	65.5	16.9
Union	68	345	25.1	10.0	38	1,343	353.3	55.9	92	2,165	89.3	24.1
Venango	69	365	46.7	14.4	80	4,048	1,388.1	219.2	112	1,325	55.0	15.2
Warren	52	277	25.3	12.6	61	2,652	3,515.5	136.9	78	904	42.3	10.8
Washington	408	3,276	608.1	189.3	247	9,931	3,561.9	514.0	396	6,603	318.0	81.4
Wayne	84	305	30.9	11.0	53	523	104.1	20.1	158	1,490	144.6	39.6
Westmoreland	705	5,812	1,053.4	328.6	556	18,854	7,681.5	920.2	756	12,356	516.6	143.6
Wyoming	48	292	33.6	12.7	30	2,541	D	156.9	60	763	33.7	7.9
York	705	5,671	635.2	279.4	568	31,890	11,489.4	1,602.6	791	13,391	593.3	165.9
RHODE ISLAND	2,997	21,165	3,338.2	1,310.1	1,509	39,608	11,262.2	2,076.5	2,973	44,063	2,481.3	705.9
Bristol	109	381	52.9	19.8	92	1,633	325.1	70.6	124	1,496	72.8	19.9
Kent	503	2,948	418.3	160.4	218	7,609	2,643.0	439.1	467	8,013	412.0	118.5
Newport	326	3,168	545.6	229.0	74	1,860	284.1	148.0	358	5,945	411.2	121.4
Providence	1,719	13,021	2,040.1	803.1	962	21,885	6,126.4	1,026.7	1,563	23,354	1,242.9	351.4
Washington	340	1,647	281.3	97.9	163	6,621	1,883.6	392.1	461	5,255	342.4	94.7
SOUTH CAROLINA	9,721	79,824	12,721.7	4,817.3	3,854	207,396	99,160.8	10,082.1	9,828	185,282	9,763.8	2,650.5
Abbeville	17	43	3.4	0.9	34	1,686	598.8	71.9	26	332	12.5	3.8
Aiken	243	4,751	1,548.2	471.3	82	6,845	4,639.3	390.4	253	D	D	D
Allendale	6	D	D	D	6	719	447.0	35.3	6	D	D	D
Anderson	278	1,822	209.0	74.8	196	10,223	5,435.0	439.9	383	6,019	272.2	75.5
Bamberg	17	66	7.5	1.9	21	823	177.0	32.6	21	235	9.7	2.5
Barnwell	24	D	D	D	20	1,918	564.1	83.1	32	419	16.9	4.3
Beaufort	554	2,876	339.1	144.8	71	524	82.2	20.2	501	10,502	656.6	193.0
Berkeley	246	2,735	477.7	164.5	88	5,106	6,261.6	332.3	241	4,605	195.9	52.6
Calhoun	13	D	D	D	22	1,278	D	80.6	10	D	D	D
Charleston	1,561	15,343	2,760.7	1,096.9	288	13,984	5,668.1	818.4	1,192	26,575	1,640.0	455.0
Cherokee	48	179	16.2	6.0	58	5,455	3,050.6	220.7	86	1,758	73.4	20.5
Chester	32	157	19.9	6.8	40	2,245	1,140.7	105.3	41	536	25.5	6.6
Chesterfield	27	81	7.0	2.0	49	4,375	1,345.2	188.7	63	848	37.8	9.7
Clarendon	18	77	9.5	4.7	18	403	235.2	13.6	58	624	28.3	7.1
Colleton	45	229	34.3	9.3	26	620	137.8	20.1	70	1,205	65.6	18.5
Darlington	60	255	26.5	8.0	50	3,092	1,693.0	171.0	88	1,188	53.2	13.7
Dillon	24	302	8.4	4.0	16	2,214	470.1	54.2	56	872	34.8	9.4
Dorchester	194	796	102.4	34.6	89	4,439	2,026.4	228.4	183	2,879	132.4	36.2
Edgefield	17	42	4.4	1.1	20	1,213	389.5	41.5	22	D	D	D
Fairfield	15	D	D	D	18	754	232.3	30.9	24	234	9.1	2.5
Florence	208	2,429	267.8	104.8	98	5,860	2,633.5	308.5	296	5,423	272.5	71.9
Georgetown	168	837	129.0	34.9	45	2,010	1,032.6	115.9	171	2,819	152.0	44.5
Greenville	1,529	14,537	2,095.5	888.9	555	26,782	9,628.1	1,280.1	1,073	19,791	999.9	271.7
Greenwood	119	1,166	140.8	58.2	62	5,498	2,478.9	251.8	135	2,387	102.5	26.1
Hampton	16	D	D	D	15	621	156.6	26.5	31	347	16.6	3.6
Horry	670	3,059	342.9	121.5	145	2,693	759.8	121.4	1,218	25,903	1,716.7	451.1
Jasper	25	123	13.6	5.4	19	190	46.2	7.3	54	687	32.3	8.9
Kershaw	77	D	D	D	58	3,122	1,419.7	149.0	91	1,308	55.5	14.8
Lancaster	88	559	73.8	28.6	47	1,916	1,292.5	87.0	95	1,491	65.9	16.5
Laurens	46	186	13.3	6.6	78	5,398	1,728.2	230.9	84	1,275	56.6	14.7
Lee	11	D	D	D	11	214	D	11.1	18	234	10.1	2.7
Lexington	579	3,175	367.3	140.1	206	8,527	3,620.3	402.0	513	10,122	455.2	127.3
McCormick	6	D	D	D	5	298	D	12.5	7	D	D	D
Marion	22	69	4.9	1.8	19	714	214.1	26.9	44	708	32.0	8.2
Marlboro	14	55	4.6	1.4	20	1,912	881.9	76.8	27	317	14.7	4.0
Newberry	42	153	12.3	4.4	44	4,831	1,651.5	185.2	61	826	36.6	9.0
Oconee	117	469	42.1	16.8	76	5,151	2,135.2	242.5	119	1,672	81.5	19.2
Orangeburg	80	334	42.9	16.1	70	6,332	2,470.4	275.8	175	3,222	152.1	37.5
Pickens	157	846	92.1	34.2	113	4,713	1,500.8	200.3	235	4,212	186.9	48.9
Richland	1,213	13,037	2,328.9	859.4	204	9,355	5,375.0	536.0	844	17,706	862.2	238.3
Saluda	14	D	D	D	8	1,953	D	52.0	18	D	D	D
Spartanburg	452	4,804	692.5	263.5	397	23,972	15,038.1	1,288.2	550	10,059	477.9	128.0

Health Care and Social Assistance, Other Services, Nonemployer Businesses, and Residential Construction

STATE County	Health care and social assistance, 2012				Other services, 2012				Nonemployer businesses, 2016		Value of residential construction authorized by building permits, 2018	
	Number of establishments	Number of employees	Receipts (mil dol)	Annual payroll (mil dol)	Number of establishments	Number of employees	Receipts (mil dol)	Annual payroll (mil dol)	Number	Receipts (mil dol)	New construction ($1,000)	Number of housing units
	159	160	161	162	163	164	165	166	167	168	169	170
PENNSYLVANIA— Cont'd												
Potter	33	907	88.3	36.1	27	115	8.9	1.9	1,269	50.9	2,869	14
Schuylkill	336	7,975	597.1	259.1	250	1,103	83.9	24.3	6,717	322.6	22,002	105
Snyder	83	1,134	104.6	39.4	69	286	27.4	6.1	2,865	140.6	7,523	36
Somerset	193	3,627	292.2	119.0	143	654	52.9	12.9	4,552	184.7	18,373	94
Sullivan	16	D	D	D	13	61	2.3	0.6	470	21.2	2,743	10
Susquehanna	65	1,136	77.9	34.3	70	291	24.5	5.5	3,093	156.0	10,844	48
Tioga	104	1,901	153.8	62.4	69	255	27.8	6.0	2,555	100.3	7,528	37
Union	144	3,740	315.4	142.1	66	306	23.5	5.9	2,735	134.5	12,090	45
Venango	170	3,475	226.6	114.7	107	419	35.6	8.4	2,794	108.4	6,828	34
Warren	107	3,221	254.0	114.2	85	529	31.4	7.4	2,139	78.3	2,879	18
Washington	690	13,512	1,301.5	518.0	421	2,455	227.6	63.9	12,863	641.9	119,153	442
Wayne	125	2,510	188.0	80.0	103	706	55.4	15.5	3,833	180.5	32,675	122
Westmoreland	1,155	20,603	1,809.4	737.8	805	4,447	477.2	105.5	21,564	944.4	72,412	284
Wyoming	67	687	42.1	18.8	52	237	24.5	6.5	1,760	75.5	6,628	29
York	924	24,161	2,604.4	1,031.9	783	5,242	651.3	139.7	26,109	1,244.4	167,151	916
RHODE ISLAND	3,236	84,067	8,223.0	3,556.0	2,276	13,046	1,444.6	390.9	78,381	3,568.7	260,274	1,294
Bristol	126	2,848	133.7	70.6	121	449	34.9	10.8	4,422	211.5	24,467	189
Kent	570	11,802	1,113.1	455.6	369	2,083	219.7	60.9	11,780	565.4	28,876	192
Newport	250	4,845	375.1	154.4	208	1,133	120.4	35.0	7,891	390.0	46,656	140
Providence	1,898	57,002	5,943.2	2,600.1	1,310	8,075	940.3	249.7	42,458	1,824.0	64,874	376
Washington	392	7,570	658.1	275.4	268	1,306	129.3	34.6	11,830	577.8	95,402	397
SOUTH CAROLINA	9,848	212,444	22,941.3	8,687.3	6,666	44,374	4,464.9	1,302.3	339,739	14,604.2	8,143,578	35,487
Abbeville	27	486	37.9	15.6	23	67	6.7	1.4	1,361	46.1	7,983	38
Aiken	310	6,330	519.8	199.6	169	950	79.6	20.4	10,529	388.4	188,621	879
Allendale	12	283	22.5	8.5	8	D	D	D	463	12.3	1,229	7
Anderson	365	8,273	928.6	343.8	235	3,448	371.8	169.8	12,134	491.1	177,462	1,000
Bamberg	41	693	36.4	20.5	23	D	D	D	833	20.2	2,541	14
Barnwell	34	723	48.5	20.6	26	131	16.9	4.0	1,296	33.7	826	10
Beaufort	426	5,819	661.3	222.0	309	2,700	244.6	82.6	15,908	846.0	700,621	1,889
Berkeley	210	2,318	154.7	65.5	187	1,068	86.9	26.2	13,417	533.7	508,976	2,337
Calhoun	22	D	D	D	16	D	D	D	918	36.3	4,853	29
Charleston	1,250	30,476	4,338.2	1,412.0	768	5,340	579.2	155.9	38,443	2,009.8	859,834	3,969
Cherokee	75	1,180	84.5	36.1	70	319	32.0	7.8	2,500	83.9	17,754	172
Chester	49	707	75.3	27.2	36	141	12.3	3.4	1,598	57.0	5,984	31
Chesterfield	90	1,624	125.4	47.2	40	119	8.7	2.3	2,292	79.2	12,276	73
Clarendon	41	1,456	95.5	41.2	33	194	13.2	4.1	2,152	80.1	7,955	46
Colleton	71	1,443	158.5	60.6	35	145	9.6	2.4	3,007	117.2	19,389	58
Darlington	96	2,444	218.8	83.4	79	345	29.9	7.6	3,725	128.3	17,179	99
Dillon	47	1,170	87.2	37.1	37	83	7.3	1.6	1,632	49.8	2,928	28
Dorchester	209	3,170	271.0	100.7	165	832	67.7	23.0	10,109	385.5	198,710	696
Edgefield	20	526	34.3	14.1	24	65	5.9	1.5	1,417	47.4	26,032	114
Fairfield	27	D	D	D	12	D	D	D	1,396	43.2	11,539	51
Florence	354	13,444	1,565.1	585.4	196	1,348	135.8	32.3	8,670	343.6	63,022	463
Georgetown	215	3,742	467.2	164.1	115	619	44.0	12.7	5,427	248.1	103,242	368
Greenville	1,120	21,857	2,261.7	996.1	706	5,185	651.9	157.1	38,559	1,778.9	1,393,236	4,669
Greenwood	144	4,752	585.2	207.9	78	548	33.4	10.1	3,807	139.8	17,121	115
Hampton	28	520	39.8	17.1	23	105	7.8	1.8	1,154	37.7	1,221	6
Horry	657	10,903	1,274.1	443.5	504	2,720	279.6	65.9	25,202	1,191.4	765,472	4,520
Jasper	44	975	89.8	27.6	42	162	14.1	3.5	1,676	81.1	108,508	447
Kershaw	96	D	D	D	82	373	29.3	8.4	4,209	167.9	41,778	292
Lancaster	136	2,266	229.0	88.2	97	495	50.3	27.5	5,406	208.9	363,463	1,228
Laurens	90	2,033	179.0	68.5	60	278	24.4	7.3	3,204	118.6	25,297	161
Lee	25	323	18.9	8.3	14	D	D	D	858	22.2	1,582	11
Lexington	527	12,620	1,058.8	436.7	491	2,905	277.8	88.1	19,684	863.0	472,822	1,896
McCormick	9	214	12.1	5.0	7	D	D	D	526	15.7	15,025	65
Marion	60	711	51.2	24.2	36	112	9.6	2.2	1,796	53.7	7,650	77
Marlboro	43	971	73.1	27.9	22	45	4.0	1.1	1,028	31.7	2,529	13
Newberry	58	1,175	107.3	42.0	55	232	20.0	5.9	1,921	63.2	17,354	77
Oconee	139	2,882	274.5	107.9	94	542	40.5	12.6	4,777	180.6	114,127	437
Orangeburg	220	3,904	381.9	158.5	98	474	37.5	10.6	4,934	165.7	8,372	59
Pickens	195	3,459	296.7	121.6	137	692	117.3	17.6	7,547	325.2	140,946	600
Richland	944	26,658	3,202.5	1,277.0	609	4,986	475.4	141.8	27,505	1,178.5	332,327	2,644
Saluda	21	D	D	D	14	D	D	D	960	33.8	8,507	40
Spartanburg	583	D	D	D	413	2,940	326.3	80.2	19,694	896.8	440,474	2,659

Table B. States and Counties — Government Employment and Payroll, and Local Government Finances

| | Government employment and payroll, 2012 | | | | | | | | | Local government finances, 2012 | | | | |
STATE County	Full-time equivalent employees	March payroll (dollars)	March payroll (percent of total) Adminis- tration, judicial, and legal	Police and corrections	Fire protection	Highways and transpor- tation	Health and welfare	Natural resources and utilities	Education and libraries	General revenue Total (mil dol)	Inter- govern- mental (mil dol)	Taxes Total (mil dol)	Taxes Per capita[1] (dollars) Total	Taxes Per capita[1] (dollars) Property
	171	172	173	174	175	176	177	178	179	180	181	182	183	184
PENNSYLVANIA— Cont'd														
Potter	590	2,437,639	12.0	6.7	1.0	7.4	0.9	10.0	61.5	73.9	41.6	21.8	1,241	1,052
Schuylkill	4,186	15,090,961	8.1	8.5	0.1	3.8	7.3	7.1	64.1	485.2	233.0	166.2	1,130	842
Snyder	1,018	3,558,017	6.3	8.1	0.0	2.9	3.5	3.8	74.2	107.4	42.7	49.5	1,247	859
Somerset	2,210	7,165,165	8.8	4.3	0.0	5.7	1.8	4.2	70.6	225.8	112.7	81.2	1,055	857
Sullivan	201	742,784	15.2	1.7	1.1	5.2	3.8	5.3	67.2	22.1	7.8	11.8	1,822	1,657
Susquehanna	1,464	5,097,993	5.6	5.6	0.6	4.5	1.7	2.4	79.2	139.9	73.6	54.2	1,268	1,138
Tioga	1,450	4,927,182	7.0	6.0	0.6	3.5	10.4	7.0	64.2	150.3	76.5	54.9	1,290	1,005
Union	883	3,323,742	9.7	6.0	0.0	3.9	4.3	8.9	66.1	157.6	75.7	51.5	1,145	812
Venango	2,052	6,987,537	7.7	7.9	3.0	3.8	5.2	5.7	65.4	196.8	112.6	57.2	1,053	811
Warren	1,409	4,668,630	8.7	7.2	1.1	5.4	17.0	2.6	57.5	113.1	58.7	41.3	1,004	762
Washington	5,853	22,585,416	6.8	9.1	1.4	4.1	7.0	4.9	65.0	790.8	371.8	291.3	1,396	1,069
Wayne	2,592	9,809,084	4.6	4.1	0.0	2.0	28.2	1.9	57.7	212.3	71.7	119.1	2,293	2,175
Westmoreland	10,354	41,162,785	6.1	8.6	0.9	4.3	6.4	9.3	63.6	1,302.8	557.8	500.8	1,378	1,099
Wyoming	947	3,123,745	15.3	5.7	0.0	2.7	0.3	2.0	71.4	97.3	46.7	41.6	1,479	1,225
York	12,293	50,416,660	6.7	12.2	1.5	2.7	6.3	3.6	64.5	1,771.5	572.5	787.5	1,799	1,467
RHODE ISLAND	X	X	X	X	X	X	X	X	X	X	X	X	X	X
Bristol	1,397	7,178,253	3.0	7.9	2.0	3.0	1.9	4.4	77.5	205.0	41.5	148.0	3,011	2,942
Kent	4,694	24,743,968	2.8	9.9	10.7	2.0	1.3	3.7	68.1	624.4	144.3	407.2	2,470	2,403
Newport	2,527	11,716,139	5.0	10.6	9.2	2.6	0.2	5.5	65.4	364.6	76.1	229.2	2,793	2,650
Providence	17,322	86,400,418	3.8	11.7	9.5	2.0	0.4	5.9	66.0	2,313.9	791.5	1,215.6	1,935	1,896
Washington	4,199	20,282,486	4.3	9.4	3.8	3.0	1.3	3.8	73.7	552.3	102.2	401.4	3,187	3,138
SOUTH CAROLINA	X	X	X	X	X	X	X	X	X	X	X	X	X	X
Abbeville	815	2,384,457	7.4	9.5	1.1	1.8	7.5	8.4	63.9	60.8	30.4	21.1	840	689
Aiken	4,376	15,335,939	9.0	9.9	1.0	4.3	3.0	6.2	65.7	401.1	181.9	160.3	984	738
Allendale	625	1,746,281	7.6	6.7	0.0	2.9	29.6	2.5	49.5	29.1	16.4	9.0	902	790
Anderson	5,484	17,493,225	6.4	10.0	1.2	2.0	1.3	5.3	72.7	476.2	210.0	176.3	931	827
Bamberg	819	2,552,389	7.1	5.8	0.6	1.4	37.3	0.9	45.9	39.6	22.1	13.7	867	775
Barnwell	1,118	3,299,448	5.3	8.6	0.4	1.1	16.7	7.6	59.3	70.5	38.2	23.1	1,038	893
Beaufort	5,616	22,420,841	6.5	9.3	6.0	1.7	27.9	4.2	42.3	768.1	132.7	391.8	2,332	1,843
Berkeley	4,857	15,229,373	6.7	8.6	2.0	1.9	2.3	2.1	74.3	476.5	201.9	143.2	755	670
Calhoun	495	1,790,689	3.0	5.0	0.5	1.8	4.1	1.1	81.6	33.4	14.6	15.0	1,004	980
Charleston	13,396	47,281,757	9.0	15.4	8.8	3.6	4.8	11.4	43.8	1,612.3	402.2	924.2	2,531	1,581
Cherokee	1,933	5,953,218	3.7	7.2	1.7	1.1	6.9	7.7	68.8	146.3	65.3	61.5	1,104	806
Chester	1,174	3,574,024	8.6	9.3	2.2	0.6	4.9	8.2	64.8	79.0	35.9	29.6	909	770
Chesterfield	1,558	4,244,462	5.6	8.8	0.8	1.2	1.7	2.9	77.8	100.3	53.6	36.7	796	594
Clarendon	1,529	4,986,545	5.1	7.6	1.8	1.2	37.8	2.0	42.4	136.5	40.9	33.6	977	747
Colleton	1,758	4,967,648	10.1	9.9	7.4	1.9	2.9	2.2	63.4	116.4	49.6	49.9	1,307	1,182
Darlington	2,194	6,310,138	4.5	9.9	1.9	2.4	4.0	4.0	70.6	151.5	78.7	44.0	646	554
Dillon	1,167	2,987,274	6.2	10.5	1.5	1.1	5.2	3.0	70.1	74.9	42.2	21.2	675	561
Dorchester	4,560	14,338,815	6.9	8.6	2.2	1.2	2.7	4.6	73.0	360.3	155.5	139.0	976	789
Edgefield	1,053	2,997,459	5.4	8.0	0.1	1.3	20.4	4.5	59.7	56.1	29.4	18.1	688	606
Fairfield	1,055	3,207,938	8.3	8.3	1.2	2.5	4.8	5.3	67.8	73.7	26.6	41.9	1,793	1,684
Florence	4,772	15,317,333	6.1	8.9	1.8	2.8	7.2	5.8	66.2	387.1	172.1	134.7	976	696
Georgetown	2,430	7,765,625	7.3	7.7	6.1	2.1	3.9	7.3	63.7	209.0	63.2	106.1	1,762	1,609
Greenville	21,594	81,147,575	3.3	5.4	3.5	1.1	44.4	4.7	36.9	2,639.7	456.3	485.5	1,038	884
Greenwood	2,547	7,901,666	5.9	7.9	1.9	1.7	4.3	10.3	62.2	563.0	100.6	69.9	1,002	786
Hampton	938	2,724,640	7.1	11.8	1.3	1.6	5.2	2.5	69.3	58.5	31.0	21.3	1,028	897
Horry	9,820	34,724,743	8.4	11.7	5.0	3.5	2.7	7.6	58.9	1,161.7	254.9	609.6	2,160	1,278
Jasper	809	2,603,546	11.5	13.8	11.9	2.4	1.3	2.1	56.6	69.7	25.2	37.2	1,441	1,298
Kershaw	2,730	9,680,043	3.3	4.0	1.9	0.5	41.5	2.8	45.5	255.3	130.9	56.4	904	774
Lancaster	2,327	7,452,417	5.3	8.0	1.9	1.0	4.2	8.2	68.9	189.5	79.8	80.0	1,012	782
Laurens	2,310	7,353,314	3.4	6.7	2.3	0.9	31.0	8.0	45.9	214.0	83.0	50.0	755	651
Lee	612	1,602,678	12.0	8.7	1.3	2.9	9.6	3.4	62.1	41.4	23.3	12.5	672	517
Lexington	14,886	59,502,218	2.4	4.2	1.3	0.5	41.6	2.7	46.6	1,461.3	374.4	370.5	1,370	1,163
McCormick	304	811,090	7.2	12.7	0.0	1.9	8.7	11.9	53.4	21.6	7.9	10.9	1,095	1,058
Marion	1,230	3,302,618	5.6	10.1	1.2	1.8	3.5	3.5	72.9	78.2	42.6	22.7	700	520
Marlboro	985	2,122,399	9.2	11.9	1.6	1.6	3.1	6.4	62.6	68.7	37.5	16.6	591	514
Newberry	1,757	5,725,610	5.0	8.2	1.1	1.3	25.7	9.1	48.9	109.3	44.6	46.1	1,227	1,069
Oconee	2,527	8,134,083	7.1	8.0	2.1	2.9	2.0	10.1	66.8	184.8	66.5	95.0	1,272	1,175
Orangeburg	4,563	16,266,007	3.4	5.4	0.2	1.1	46.5	2.7	38.9	425.4	101.6	103.8	1,135	920
Pickens	3,247	10,077,389	5.7	8.6	2.0	3.3	4.7	5.9	66.7	262.7	109.4	112.3	939	722
Richland	13,444	45,241,826	6.4	9.8	3.8	1.6	2.7	7.7	65.0	1,390.8	394.8	589.3	1,496	1,309
Saluda	474	1,331,037	7.6	11.4	2.9	2.3	1.5	2.7	69.2	35.8	16.8	14.0	705	629
Spartanburg	14,164	55,750,441	3.2	4.9	1.6	0.6	47.1	3.9	37.9	1,488.8	350.6	322.9	1,118	988

1. Based on the resident population estimated as of July 1 of the year shown.

Table B. States and Counties — Local Government Finances, Government Employment, and Income Taxes

STATE County	Direct general expenditure Total (mil dol) 185	Per capita¹ (dollars) 186	Education 187	Health and hospitals 188	Police protection 189	Public welfare 190	Highways 191	Debt outstanding Total (mil dol) 192	Per capita¹ (dollars) 193	Federal civilian 194	Federal military 195	State and local 196	Number of returns 197	Mean adjusted gross income 198	Mean income tax 199
PENNSYLVANIA— Cont'd															
Potter	70.3	3,999	50.7	1.3	1.0	9.1	10.6	81.5	4,636	45	43	996	7,580	44,760	4,449
Schuylkill	520.8	3,541	55.0	1.5	2.5	6.8	4.7	555.0	3,774	606	352	6,954	67,180	49,928	5,614
Snyder	122.1	3,077	62.0	2.4	4.4	0.0	4.2	222.5	5,610	87	100	2,109	18,240	47,674	4,532
Somerset	213.0	2,768	61.0	0.1	2.5	5.7	5.5	286.3	3,720	188	180	4,208	34,440	46,104	4,480
Sullivan	25.1	3,889	63.1	2.1	0.7	2.7	8.5	9.0	1,396	17	15	369	2,890	48,521	5,082
Susquehanna	148.2	3,471	72.6	0.9	1.4	2.1	5.8	59.8	1,401	105	105	1,772	19,560	51,070	5,554
Tioga	137.5	3,229	52.4	0.0	1.2	10.9	7.3	119.5	2,807	143	103	2,649	18,450	48,456	4,902
Union	203.9	4,535	63.4	1.3	1.3	2.6	2.9	249.6	5,553	1,585	98	1,368	17,140	62,991	7,986
Venango	206.3	3,800	58.4	2.1	1.5	7.2	5.3	271.4	5,001	108	130	3,175	24,570	45,290	4,487
Warren	109.9	2,672	58.9	0.5	2.9	0.7	5.6	93.3	2,267	167	101	1,810	19,100	47,589	5,101
Washington	804.7	3,855	54.3	1.5	2.6	11.8	4.2	903.0	4,326	463	546	9,444	102,710	69,690	9,756
Wayne	210.9	4,059	64.5	2.4	0.7	4.4	3.0	262.7	5,056	551	123	2,549	24,710	52,062	5,834
Westmoreland	1,328.7	3,656	53.4	2.5	2.9	10.3	4.0	1,848.5	5,087	847	911	13,902	181,760	59,309	7,322
Wyoming	92.1	3,276	63.0	0.1	3.2	5.3	6.8	54.9	1,953	56	69	1,043	13,460	50,402	5,308
York	1,790.5	4,089	47.4	3.5	3.3	9.2	2.6	2,454.1	5,605	4,274	1,311	15,873	223,680	59,059	6,869
RHODE ISLAND	X	X	X	X	X	X	X	X	X	10,910	6,752	54,770	529,360	64,164	8,521
Bristol	201.6	4,102	66.6	0.2	4.1	0.1	4.2	147.6	3,004	93	214	1,825	24,240	99,070	16,911
Kent	593.7	3,601	58.4	0.1	6.4	0.5	2.8	449.3	2,725	732	742	7,470	88,410	68,232	9,155
Newport	357.9	4,363	48.4	2.1	8.0	0.4	3.0	203.9	2,486	4,923	2,435	3,491	43,130	81,225	12,003
Providence	2,229.9	3,549	53.2	0.2	8.2	0.1	2.8	1,836.7	2,923	4,524	2,799	30,036	308,450	54,667	6,593
Washington	532.3	4,226	67.5	0.5	5.4	0.4	3.5	302.1	2,398	638	562	11,948	65,160	79,291	11,359
SOUTH CAROLINA	X	X	X	X	X	X	X	X	X	33,770	52,804	323,013	2,203,640	56,479	6,796
Abbeville	59.7	2,377	50.1	3.0	7.7	0.0	1.3	24.7	985	40	91	1,442	9,620	42,732	3,614
Aiken	373.4	2,294	57.5	1.3	7.7	0.1	2.4	155.5	955	681	634	6,961	72,840	55,796	6,069
Allendale	27.5	2,758	69.3	1.7	5.0	0.0	1.5	14.8	1,477	19	30	1,074	3,210	34,014	2,533
Anderson	483.1	2,551	63.5	0.3	6.2	0.2	2.1	1,327.5	7,010	348	750	12,231	85,170	51,575	5,417
Bamberg	61.7	3,917	76.9	0.2	5.2	0.0	0.8	38.4	2,439	34	51	963	5,360	38,456	3,313
Barnwell	71.5	3,218	57.8	0.4	6.7	0.2	2.1	37.0	1,667	48	80	1,427	8,510	39,734	3,201
Beaufort	752.2	4,476	32.2	19.6	6.0	1.1	2.3	1,451.5	8,637	2,209	10,723	8,003	84,950	77,709	11,411
Berkeley	500.4	2,637	57.1	1.2	5.3	0.4	2.8	2,158.7	11,375	868	830	8,242	95,300	55,710	6,313
Calhoun	36.1	2,418	56.3	3.7	6.6	1.8	1.0	42.7	2,864	24	56	778	6,300	49,293	4,541
Charleston	1,363.0	3,733	36.6	1.0	11.9	0.2	4.7	2,857.4	7,825	9,792	11,240	37,297	190,370	78,092	12,470
Cherokee	132.3	2,378	65.3	1.5	6.6	5.1	2.3	1,423.8	25,579	101	221	2,336	23,020	41,375	3,675
Chester	89.7	2,756	62.9	3.1	5.0	0.0	0.4	59.0	1,811	57	122	1,569	14,030	39,411	3,256
Chesterfield	104.7	2,271	63.2	0.0	8.7	0.0	2.6	194.8	4,224	89	172	1,983	17,990	39,167	3,279
Clarendon	138.9	4,044	34.7	40.8	4.1	0.0	1.0	88.7	2,583	63	124	2,046	13,280	37,259	3,084
Colleton	127.8	3,350	47.8	0.7	8.0	0.8	3.0	141.2	3,701	96	153	1,957	16,840	40,220	3,935
Darlington	148.0	2,173	64.2	0.4	7.0	0.0	2.0	103.9	1,525	153	251	3,065	27,910	44,115	4,481
Dillon	76.7	2,441	64.6	0.3	6.0	3.0	2.1	10.2	324	77	115	1,438	12,020	34,007	2,517
Dorchester	349.2	2,451	64.0	1.4	6.0	0.0	7.4	507.4	3,561	223	592	6,554	70,750	53,697	5,310
Edgefield	58.3	2,211	67.5	2.4	6.3	0.5	2.0	25.9	981	426	91	1,216	10,370	50,116	5,005
Fairfield	86.5	3,704	53.6	6.2	5.9	0.0	1.7	21.4	917	40	85	1,344	10,010	43,021	4,224
Florence	382.5	2,773	59.5	5.9	6.5	0.2	1.7	270.2	1,958	529	544	12,502	59,340	49,819	5,536
Georgetown	194.2	3,227	56.8	1.4	5.1	0.6	2.7	502.9	8,355	125	267	4,710	30,000	59,314	7,974
Greenville	2,628.6	5,621	23.1	51.4	2.7	0.2	1.1	3,479.0	7,440	2,090	1,954	30,422	226,010	65,198	8,507
Greenwood	506.5	7,261	23.9	58.7	2.1	0.0	0.7	466.2	6,684	141	259	6,966	29,430	46,345	4,622
Hampton	68.8	3,318	69.0	2.5	7.3	0.9	1.8	31.5	1,522	342	69	1,110	7,810	38,450	3,553
Horry	1,100.1	3,897	39.1	12.4	5.6	0.1	5.5	1,603.2	5,679	699	1,261	16,243	158,360	48,377	5,536
Jasper	67.2	2,600	51.4	0.2	8.9	0.4	1.9	79.1	3,062	59	103	1,261	11,320	43,619	4,206
Kershaw	253.6	4,068	36.7	41.9	2.8	0.2	1.0	291.1	4,669	101	247	3,081	28,250	49,428	4,833
Lancaster	185.7	2,347	54.7	4.0	5.6	0.0	2.8	219.5	2,775	103	346	3,742	38,990	58,954	6,526
Laurens	231.7	3,499	34.1	32.5	3.9	0.1	2.1	194.1	2,931	101	249	3,716	27,070	41,233	3,441
Lee	37.3	1,999	57.1	4.7	6.6	0.1	2.1	54.1	2,902	27	60	1,026	6,850	33,632	2,427
Lexington	1,529.8	5,658	44.1	37.4	3.3	0.0	0.9	1,531.8	5,665	656	1,101	20,516	129,130	59,085	6,940
McCormick	18.6	1,873	57.9	5.8	5.0	0.0	2.0	32.0	3,218	85	32	745	3,930	49,212	4,770
Marion	79.9	2,460	61.3	1.8	8.6	0.0	2.4	5.2	159	68	123	1,363	13,100	31,253	2,321
Marlboro	80.0	2,841	65.4	1.7	6.2	2.2	0.0	67.2	2,386	370	92	1,342	10,400	32,883	2,362
Newberry	116.7	3,107	49.9	1.3	5.2	0.5	1.6	134.2	3,573	114	142	2,336	16,510	46,346	4,351
Oconee	188.2	2,522	59.7	0.5	7.2	0.2	3.1	171.5	2,298	174	292	3,952	32,630	57,197	6,610
Orangeburg	436.4	4,771	34.3	43.8	4.1	0.1	3.6	296.9	3,246	214	329	6,629	36,580	39,017	3,533
Pickens	329.4	2,752	64.3	1.5	5.1	0.1	3.3	469.0	3,919	201	458	9,945	49,310	53,178	6,007
Richland	1,388.2	3,525	44.0	0.2	4.6	0.1	1.1	5,237.8	13,300	9,513	10,771	46,783	179,350	57,892	7,245
Saluda	34.3	1,725	55.3	2.1	7.5	0.1	2.3	31.1	1,565	33	77	986	8,160	43,468	3,873
Spartanburg	1501.9	5,202	32.3	48.4	2.8	0.4	1.0	1,018.7	3,528	546	1,145	20,423	134,430	53,501	5,946

1. Based on the resident population estimated as of July 1 of the year shown.

Table B. States and Counties — Land Area and Population

State / county code	CBSA code[1]	County code[2]	STATE County	Land area[3] (sq. mi)	Population, 2018 Total persons 2018	Rank	Per square mile	Race alone or in combination, not Hispanic or Latino (percent) White	Black	American Indian, Alaska Native	Asian and Pacific Islancer	Percent Hispanic or Latino[4]	Age (percent) Under 5 years	5 to 17 years	18 to 24 years	25 to 34 years	35 to 44 years	45 to 54 years
				1	2	3	4	5	6	7	8	9	10	11	12	13	14	15
			SOUTH CAROLINA— Cont'd															
45085	44,940	3	Sumter	665.1	106,512	568	160.1	46.5	48.3	0.9	2.3	4.1	6.7	17.1	10.0	14.2	11.2	11.7
45087	43,900	2	Union	514.2	27,410	1,513	53.3	65.8	33.1	0.6	0.6	1.7	5.8	15.4	7.6	11.2	11.0	13.8
45089		6	Williamsburg	934.2	30,606	1,420	32.8	32.2	64.9	0.6	1.0	2.1	5.1	15.6	7.8	12.0	11.1	12.5
45091	16,740	1	York	680.7	274,118	251	402.7	72.0	20.1	1.3	3.0	5.7	6.1	18.2	8.3	12.5	13.8	14.2
46000		0	SOUTH DAKOTA	75,810.0	882,235	X	11.6	83.4	3.0	9.5	2.2	4.1	7.0	17.6	9.5	13.2	11.8	11.0
46003		9	Aurora	708.5	2,801	2,985	4.0	89.6	1.0	3.1	1.0	6.4	6.4	18.4	7.6	11.2	10.6	11.0
46005	26,700	7	Beadle	1,258.7	18,883	1,879	15.0	75.3	1.9	1.7	11.7	11.1	8.8	18.8	7.6	12.1	11.4	10.6
46007		9	Bennett	1,184.6	3,468	2,941	2.9	36.8	1.3	60.6	0.8	5.6	9.7	24.2	10.0	12.8	9.2	10.5
46009		9	Bon Homme	563.5	6,980	2,671	12.4	86.7	1.6	9.0	0.5	3.5	5.3	15.0	8.6	13.3	12.2	11.8
46011	15,100	5	Brookings	792.2	35,232	1,298	44.5	90.9	1.9	1.6	3.5	3.4	6.3	14.2	25.6	13.7	10.1	8.7
46013	10,100	5	Brown	1,713.0	39,316	1,196	23.0	87.7	3.0	4.3	3.7	3.3	6.8	17.2	9.4	13.7	11.6	11.0
46015		9	Brule	817.2	5,229	2,817	6.4	87.2	1.1	11.4	0.8	2.9	6.6	19.5	7.5	9.9	11.0	11.6
46017		9	Buffalo	471.4	2,036	3,046	4.3	17.0	1.5	78.2	0.4	4.9	12.2	27.2	9.2	13.7	11.9	8.9
46019		6	Butte	2,250.0	10,222	2,407	4.5	93.3	1.0	3.8	0.9	3.6	6.4	17.8	6.5	11.6	11.0	11.1
46021		9	Campbell	733.7	1,377	3,087	1.9	96.4	0.5	1.4	0.5	2.0	4.3	11.6	6.5	7.8	8.4	11.5
46023		9	Charles Mix	1,097.5	9,338	2,477	8.5	65.6	1.0	32.3	0.9	3.5	8.8	20.9	8.4	10.3	9.8	10.3
46025		9	Clark	957.6	3,739	2,923	3.9	94.2	2.2	0.5	0.7	3.2	10.5	15.4	7.5	11.6	9.4	9.6
46027	46,820	6	Clay	412.0	14,041	2,158	34.1	88.8	2.4	4.7	3.4	3.0	5.3	12.2	31.8	12.4	8.8	8.2
46029	47,980	8	Codington	687.6	28,015	1,499	40.7	93.8	0.9	3.1	1.1	2.5	6.3	17.7	7.9	12.5	12.0	11.9
46031		9	Corson	2,469.7	4,165	2,890	1.7	31.6	0.9	64.4	1.0	5.3	10.3	26.6	8.0	12.2	10.3	9.6
46033	39,660	3	Custer	1,556.9	8,726	2,528	5.6	92.3	0.8	4.9	0.8	3.1	4.0	11.4	4.2	7.8	9.6	12.3
46035	33,580	7	Davison	435.6	19,790	1,839	45.4	92.2	1.4	4.1	1.2	3.1	6.3	16.6	9.7	12.7	11.5	10.5
46037		9	Day	1,028.5	5,505	2,795	5.4	87.4	0.8	10.0	1.2	2.4	5.0	17.5	6.2	9.0	10.4	10.0
46039		9	Deuel	622.7	4,337	2,872	7.0	95.5	1.2	1.1	0.4	2.8	6.4	17.4	6.6	10.5	10.7	11.4
46041		9	Dewey	2,302.5	5,904	2,757	2.6	24.0	0.9	73.8	0.5	4.8	13.0	24.8	9.0	12.4	10.5	10.1
46043		9	Douglas	431.8	2,935	2,971	6.8	95.0	0.9	3.1	0.3	1.9	7.6	18.1	6.1	9.7	8.6	10.2
46045	10,100	9	Edmunds	1,126.0	3,875	2,910	3.4	95.7	0.6	1.5	1.2	2.0	7.0	16.9	6.8	9.5	9.9	12.0
46047		6	Fall River	1,739.9	6,758	2,693	3.9	87.6	1.6	8.0	1.8	4.0	4.1	13.0	6.3	8.4	9.3	11.9
46049		9	Faulk	981.7	2,330	3,017	2.4	97.3	0.6	0.6	0.7	1.3	8.3	17.0	6.3	10.1	9.7	9.9
46051		7	Grant	681.4	7,147	2,651	10.5	92.9	0.9	1.8	0.6	4.9	6.2	16.3	7.3	9.4	11.0	12.2
46053		9	Gregory	1,015.0	4,212	2,885	4.1	90.2	1.0	9.4	0.8	1.6	6.6	17.0	6.9	8.2	10.4	10.3
46055		8	Haakon	1,810.5	1,918	3,056	1.1	94.6	1.0	4.4	1.2	2.1	6.0	17.4	6.8	9.1	10.6	8.2
46057		9	Hamlin	507.2	6,111	2,742	12.0	93.8	0.7	1.1	0.4	4.8	9.0	22.5	8.4	10.4	10.9	10.2
46059		9	Hand	1,436.7	3,262	2,953	2.3	97.5	0.4	1.1	0.7	1.4	5.9	16.1	6.7	9.7	10.0	10.6
46061	33,580	8	Hanson	434.6	3,376	2,945	7.8	97.2	0.7	1.0	0.6	1.5	7.6	23.0	7.4	9.3	12.5	12.1
46063		9	Harding	2,671.6	1,249	3,096	0.5	94.0	1.3	3.4	0.5	2.6	6.6	16.7	6.6	12.2	10.7	12.1
46065	38,180	7	Hughes	741.5	17,650	1,941	23.8	84.0	1.2	12.9	1.2	3.2	6.7	17.4	7.5	13.5	11.9	11.6
46067		8	Hutchinson	813.0	7,380	2,634	9.1	94.8	1.4	1.6	0.4	2.9	9.3	16.2	7.3	9.5	10.0	10.9
46069		9	Hyde	860.6	1,282	3,094	1.5	89.6	1.4	9.4	0.5	1.4	6.1	14.6	6.0	10.9	10.5	10.0
46071		8	Jackson	1,863.9	3,307	2,951	1.8	44.1	2.0	53.6	0.6	4.6	10.7	22.7	10.5	11.5	9.1	10.6
46073		9	Jerauld	526.1	2,043	3,043	3.9	93.9	0.3	1.3	0.6	5.0	6.4	17.1	4.8	9.7	11.6	9.3
46075		9	Jones	969.7	928	3,108	1.0	92.7	1.7	6.6	0.6	2.4	6.1	16.1	5.4	9.9	8.2	12.4
46077		9	Kingsbury	832.2	4,919	2,838	5.9	95.9	0.8	1.8	0.9	2.1	6.6	16.3	6.8	9.8	10.7	10.7
46079		6	Lake	562.9	13,057	2,226	23.2	94.1	1.4	1.9	1.3	2.6	5.4	14.7	10.4	9.0	10.2	10.4
46081	43,940	6	Lawrence	800.1	25,741	1,572	32.2	92.2	1.1	3.3	1.8	3.3	4.4	13.5	11.4	12.1	10.8	10.6
46083	43,620	3	Lincoln	577.3	58,807	880	101.9	94.3	2.2	1.1	1.8	2.2	7.3	20.7	7.3	14.5	14.8	11.7
46085		9	Lyman	1,642.1	3,821	2,917	2.3	58.9	1.2	39.6	0.9	2.7	9.2	20.2	8.3	11.4	10.7	9.6
46087	43,620	3	McCook	574.2	5,546	2,788	9.7	93.9	1.1	1.4	0.5	4.3	7.4	20.2	7.1	9.8	11.7	11.3
46089		9	McPherson	1,136.6	2,407	3,012	2.1	97.3	0.8	0.9	0.5	1.4	6.5	18.1	5.7	8.4	9.8	9.7
46091		9	Marshall	838.1	5,112	2,824	6.1	80.6	0.7	7.4	0.3	12.1	8.5	14.8	7.8	14.0	10.1	10.4
46093	39,660	3	Meade	3,470.9	28,294	1,488	8.2	89.6	2.6	4.2	1.9	4.5	5.4	17.5	10.9	14.5	12.6	10.7
46095		9	Mellette	1,307.3	2,042	3,044	1.6	43.4	1.2	56.6	0.7	3.7	10.3	20.4	9.6	11.9	8.6	10.4
46097		8	Miner	570.2	2,213	3,028	3.9	94.8	1.6	1.0	0.6	3.3	6.0	17.7	7.4	9.6	9.4	11.0
46099	43,620	3	Minnehaha	806.8	192,876	344	239.1	83.5	7.6	3.2	3.0	5.0	7.7	17.7	8.8	15.9	13.2	11.5
46101		8	Moody	519.4	6,579	2,703	12.7	78.7	1.9	14.4	3.4	4.7	7.7	18.4	7.8	9.6	11.6	11.3
46102		0	Oglala Lakota	2,093.6	14,309	2,141	6.8	5.9	0.5	90.6	0.4	3.9	10.2	27.0	11.1	15.3	10.7	10.0
46103	39,660	3	Pennington	2,776.8	111,729	546	40.2	83.1	2.2	11.0	2.2	5.2	6.5	16.5	8.3	13.5	11.7	11.0
46105		8	Perkins	2,870.5	2,922	2,973	1.0	95.8	0.8	2.6	0.7	1.5	6.0	14.7	7.3	8.4	10.5	11.0
46107		9	Potter	861.1	2,207	3,030	2.6	94.6	0.9	3.1	1.0	2.0	5.5	16.2	6.1	8.6	9.0	10.1
46109		9	Roberts	1,101.0	10,447	2,394	9.5	58.6	1.1	38.6	0.7	4.1	8.9	19.7	8.6	10.1	10.3	10.8
46111		9	Sanborn	569.2	2,429	3,011	4.3	95.3	0.5	1.5	0.4	3.7	7.7	17.6	6.5	11.7	11.8	9.4
46115		9	Spink	1,503.5	6,495	2,709	4.3	94.5	0.9	2.0	0.3	3.2	6.0	17.0	7.3	11.3	10.8	11.1
46117	38,180	9	Stanley	1,444.4	3,022	2,966	2.1	89.7	1.3	8.3	0.7	2.6	6.2	18.0	6.1	10.9	12.4	12.2
46119	38,180	9	Sully	1,006.7	1,392	3,083	1.4	94.9	0.8	3.3	0.1	2.4	5.6	15.4	5.5	10.0	10.6	11.0
46121		9	Todd	1,388.6	10,283	2,401	7.4	10.0	0.9	84.2	2.8	4.2	13.0	29.0	9.9	13.8	10.2	8.5

1. CBSA = Core Based Statistical Area. See Appendix A for explanation. See Appendix B for list of metropolitan areas with component counties.   2. County type code from the Economic Research Service of USDA Rural-Urban Continuum Codes. See Appendix A for definition.   3. Dry land or land partially or temporarily covered by water.   4. May be of any race.

Table B. States and Counties — **Population and Households**

STATE County	Age (percent) (cont.)				Population change, 2000-2018							Households, 2013-2017				
	55 to 64 years	65 to 74 years	75 years and over	Percent female	Total persons		Percent change		Components of change, 2010-2018				Persons per household	Family house-holds	Female family house-holder[1]	One person
					2000	2010	2000-2010	2010-2018	Births	Deaths	Net Migration	Number				
	16	17	18	19	20	21	22	23	24	25	26	27	28	29	30	31
SOUTH CAROLINA— Cont'd																
Sumter	12.7	9.5	6.9	51.9	104,646	107,490	2.7	-0.9	12,090	8,732	-4,323	41,417	2.54	68.0	19.9	27.8
Union	15.0	12.1	8.2	52.6	29,881	28,972	-3.0	-5.4	2,571	3,165	-965	11,564	2.36	66.7	16.5	31.2
Williamsburg	14.8	12.8	8.3	52.6	37,217	34,415	-7.5	-11.1	2,750	3,392	-3,199	12,310	2.47	67.4	20.8	30.4
York	12.6	8.9	5.4	51.8	164,614	226,046	37.3	21.3	24,319	16,236	39,627	95,539	2.59	70.8	13.2	24.3
SOUTH DAKOTA	13.3	9.6	7.0	49.5	754,844	814,198	7.9	8.4	99,830	61,308	29,312	339,458	2.42	63.7	9.3	30.0
Aurora	14.2	10.9	9.7	46.8	3,058	2,710	-11.4	3.4	309	217	-2	1,179	2.19	61.3	6.5	33.2
Beadle	13.7	9.0	8.0	49.1	17,023	17,399	2.2	8.5	2,621	1,592	445	7,651	2.28	60.8	8.3	33.5
Bennett	11.2	6.8	5.7	51.1	3,574	3,431	-4.0	1.1	563	285	-244	955	3.56	74.5	20.9	22.6
Bon Homme	13.5	10.1	10.3	40.8	7,260	7,067	-2.7	-1.2	541	613	-13	2,554	2.18	62.3	4.4	33.3
Brookings	9.6	6.8	5.1	48.1	28,220	31,962	13.3	10.2	3,423	1,590	1,444	12,602	2.38	54.9	5.1	32.7
Brown	13.2	9.2	8.0	50.9	35,460	36,532	3.0	7.6	4,148	3,063	1,703	16,328	2.28	61.6	9.3	33.1
Brule	15.0	9.8	9.2	50.0	5,364	5,255	-2.0	-0.5	620	450	-200	2,170	2.30	68.8	7.0	27.4
Buffalo	9.1	4.9	2.9	50.3	2,032	1,913	-5.9	6.4	411	171	-117	530	3.86	78.5	28.9	20.2
Butte	15.6	12.1	8.0	49.4	9,094	10,112	11.2	1.1	1,047	870	-64	4,172	2.41	64.4	8.4	27.3
Campbell	21.6	12.5	15.8	48.0	1,782	1,466	-17.7	-6.1	91	114	-68	690	2.09	56.2	0.9	38.8
Charles Mix	13.1	9.1	9.3	50.0	9,350	9,131	-2.3	2.3	1,316	827	-279	3,184	2.82	64.2	12.0	32.0
Clark	14.9	11.8	9.4	48.5	4,143	3,691	-10.9	1.3	466	374	-43	1,510	2.28	58.8	4.7	36.8
Clay	9.0	7.2	5.0	50.0	13,537	13,868	2.4	1.2	1,230	814	-252	5,302	2.20	49.0	7.5	30.0
Codington	14.0	9.5	8.2	49.7	25,897	27,225	5.1	2.9	3,070	1,989	-278	12,011	2.28	61.4	9.7	29.8
Corson	11.5	6.7	4.6	49.8	4,181	4,048	-3.2	2.9	743	397	-234	1,239	3.37	74.0	23.5	22.4
Custer	20.7	19.2	10.9	50.3	7,275	8,218	13.0	6.2	609	718	612	3,901	2.07	70.7	6.4	23.1
Davison	13.8	9.6	9.3	50.0	18,741	19,504	4.1	1.5	2,092	1,722	-75	8,696	2.16	60.4	9.0	32.9
Day	16.4	13.7	11.7	49.0	6,267	5,710	-8.9	-3.6	502	625	-82	2,567	2.09	65.8	9.0	31.2
Deuel	15.1	12.1	9.8	48.3	4,498	4,364	-3.0	-0.6	414	349	-92	1,835	2.30	65.2	3.4	30.4
Dewey	10.6	5.6	3.8	50.4	5,972	5,301	-11.2	11.4	1,218	542	-71	1,648	3.43	68.6	21.3	26.4
Douglas	15.6	11.9	12.2	50.5	3,458	3,000	-13.2	-2.2	324	338	-48	1,271	2.23	68.8	2.1	24.8
Edmunds	16.5	11.0	10.5	50.0	4,367	4,071	-6.8	-4.8	367	368	-195	1,579	2.40	70.8	5.4	26.3
Fall River	18.0	17.4	11.6	49.4	7,453	7,094	-4.8	-4.7	480	944	125	3,115	2.08	60.8	10.2	36.0
Faulk	15.4	10.7	12.6	50.4	2,640	2,364	-10.5	-1.4	248	225	-57	944	2.12	56.9	3.9	37.7
Grant	16.8	11.5	9.3	47.4	7,847	7,358	-6.2	-2.9	675	677	-215	3,203	2.19	68.6	5.4	26.8
Gregory	15.1	13.2	12.3	48.6	4,792	4,271	-10.9	-1.4	418	499	25	1,943	2.14	63.0	10.3	34.2
Haakon	17.4	12.0	12.4	50.3	2,196	1,937	-11.8	-1.0	176	199	2	893	2.29	69.8	4.1	26.4
Hamlin	13.0	8.4	7.2	48.6	5,540	5,903	6.6	3.5	953	536	-210	2,193	2.60	73.9	5.2	18.9
Hand	15.8	10.9	14.4	50.1	3,741	3,430	-8.3	-4.9	307	353	-126	1,498	2.17	62.1	6.0	35.0
Hanson	12.6	11.4	4.0	49.9	3,139	3,332	6.1	1.3	372	180	-147	1,061	3.15	74.6	3.2	23.4
Harding	17.4	10.5	7.3	47.4	1,353	1,255	-7.2	-0.5	134	68	-77	533	2.26	63.4	4.5	32.5
Hughes	14.2	10.1	7.2	50.8	16,481	17,022	3.3	3.7	1,946	1,180	-137	7,391	2.21	55.5	5.4	40.0
Hutchinson	14.0	10.7	12.3	51.2	8,075	7,343	-9.1	0.5	848	902	93	2,881	2.38	67.4	6.9	31.2
Hyde	16.6	10.8	14.5	48.0	1,671	1,420	-15.0	-9.7	125	150	-116	582	2.29	62.9	6.9	34.7
Jackson	11.5	7.5	5.9	49.7	2,930	3,030	3.4	9.1	615	279	-59	984	3.20	69.9	17.7	28.5
Jerauld	14.1	14.3	12.6	49.5	2,295	2,071	-9.8	-1.4	186	212	-4	911	2.19	60.6	4.9	31.4
Jones	18.6	12.8	10.5	50.6	1,193	1,006	-15.7	-7.8	90	80	-89	405	1.83	53.8	3.0	44.2
Kingsbury	16.0	12.4	10.8	48.7	5,815	5,147	-11.5	-4.4	521	566	-190	2,327	2.11	64.9	5.3	30.0
Lake	17.8	15.1	6.9	47.8	11,276	11,202	-0.7	16.6	1,083	930	1,678	4,817	2.42	66.0	5.3	30.5
Lawrence	15.4	13.4	8.5	50.0	21,802	24,090	10.5	6.9	1,945	1,860	1,548	10,902	2.17	57.5	6.2	33.0
Lincoln	10.8	8.0	4.9	50.5	24,131	44,823	85.7	31.2	6,569	1,826	9,098	18,736	2.81	74.3	7.7	20.9
Lyman	14.8	8.8	7.0	47.7	3,895	3,755	-3.6	1.8	581	267	-249	1,383	2.78	69.9	13.4	23.4
McCook	13.5	9.8	9.2	49.9	5,832	5,618	-3.7	-1.3	626	614	-83	2,182	2.41	71.1	5.1	22.0
McPherson	13.7	12.6	15.5	50.5	2,904	2,459	-15.3	-2.1	199	289	39	1,019	2.03	59.5	3.6	38.5
Marshall	14.2	12.0	8.3	46.2	4,576	4,656	1.7	9.8	548	425	335	1,813	2.55	63.5	7.0	30.1
Meade	13.3	9.5	5.7	48.0	24,253	25,443	4.9	11.2	2,481	1,535	1,896	11,022	2.38	70.4	7.5	24.1
Mellette	13.3	9.4	6.1	48.1	2,083	2,043	-1.9	0.0	307	213	-98	683	2.97	70.9	17.4	26.4
Miner	18.0	10.3	10.7	48.1	2,884	2,389	-17.2	-7.4	192	257	-115	990	2.23	64.9	4.5	31.2
Minnehaha	12.2	8.0	5.0	49.5	148,281	169,474	14.3	13.8	23,775	10,936	10,603	73,762	2.41	61.9	10.2	30.9
Moody	14.9	10.4	8.4	50.3	6,595	6,493	-1.5	1.3	733	430	-220	2,664	2.30	67.8	9.0	27.9
Oglala Lakota	8.5	4.8	2.5	51.0	12,466	13,586	9.0	5.3	2,698	1,194	-784	2,920	4.79	81.2	40.6	16.7
Pennington	14.6	11.0	6.9	49.6	88,565	100,957	14.0	10.7	12,527	6,984	5,202	43,110	2.42	63.3	11.2	30.9
Perkins	17.0	13.2	11.9	49.9	3,363	2,983	-11.3	-2.0	290	344	-9	1,311	2.18	63.8	6.3	33.2
Potter	15.6	15.0	13.9	50.4	2,693	2,334	-13.3	-5.4	193	289	-31	1,025	2.18	59.9	5.3	37.2
Roberts	13.1	10.9	8.6	49.7	10,016	10,147	1.3	3.0	1,449	919	-226	3,756	2.67	68.8	15.7	28.1
Sanborn	15.7	11.6	8.0	47.9	2,675	2,355	-12.0	3.1	281	217	12	1,050	2.21	70.2	7.7	23.7
Spink	15.8	10.6	10.2	49.9	7,454	6,415	-13.9	1.2	642	610	45	2,626	2.39	63.3	9.4	30.8
Stanley	13.9	11.8	8.6	48.7	2,772	2,966	7.0	1.9	305	156	-93	1,309	2.29	76.1	10.3	15.7
Sully	17.0	14.4	10.6	47.4	1,556	1,368	-12.1	1.8	137	74	-42	601	2.30	64.6	5.3	33.8
Todd	8.3	4.6	2.8	51.3	9,050	9,610	6.2	7.0	2,219	825	-726	2,768	3.61	72.1	35.8	23.8

1. No spouse present.

Table B. States and Counties — **Population, Vital Statistics, Health, and Crime**

STATE County	Persons in group quarters, 2018	Daytime Population, 2013-2017		Births, 2018		Deaths, 2018		Persons under 65 with no health insurance, 2016		Medicare, 2018			Serious crimes known to police[2], 2016 Total	
		Number	Employment/ residence ratio	Total	Rate[1]	Number	Rate[1]	Number	Percent	Total beneficiaries	Enrolled in Original Medicare	Enrolled in Medicare Advantage	Number	Rate[3]
	32	33	34	35	36	37	38	39	40	41	42	43	44	45
SOUTH CAROLINA— Cont'd														
Sumter	2,521	107,324	1.00	1,321	12.4	1,070	10.0	10,544	12.0	21,482	16,728	4,754	4,183	3,885
Union	492	25,532	0.80	309	11.3	384	14.0	2,504	11.4	7,362	4,407	2,955	1,339	4,850
Williamsburg	884	30,817	0.87	292	9.5	395	12.9	2,977	12.3	7,862	5,019	2,843	1,154	3,579
York	3,699	232,461	0.84	3,050	11.1	2,155	7.9	22,999	10.4	45,296	32,788	12,508	6,737	2,623
SOUTH DAKOTA	34,043	857,437	1.00	11,943	13.5	7,293	8.3	73,089	10.4	170,864	135,312	35,552	20,762	2,399
Aurora	96	2,534	0.86	43	15.4	24	8.6	266	12.7	595	473	122	5	183
Beadle	621	17,990	0.98	305	16.2	177	9.4	1,898	13.0	3,616	2,765	851	311	1,679
Bennett	37	3,233	0.82	60	17.3	38	11.0	605	20.9	498	478	20	90	2,639
Bon Homme	1,537	6,307	0.76	67	9.6	71	10.2	457	10.7	1,563	1,261	302	1	14
Brookings	3,611	34,545	1.05	417	11.8	189	5.4	2,291	8.4	4,538	3,623	915	530	1,549
Brown	1,370	39,857	1.06	525	13.4	348	8.9	2,987	9.3	7,367	6,447	920	806	2,142
Brule	132	5,262	0.99	73	14.0	42	8.0	646	15.4	982	788	194	NA	NA
Buffalo	3	2,029	0.97	49	24.1	29	14.2	321	17.9	227	D	D	NA	NA
Butte	111	8,790	0.72	133	13.0	107	10.5	988	12.2	2,227	1,624	603	177	1,720
Campbell	0	1,353	0.88	10	7.3	8	5.8	98	9.5	374	295	79	7	507
Charles Mix	589	9,729	1.11	163	17.5	108	11.6	1,250	16.9	1,789	1,609	180	71	872
Clark	489	3,500	0.92	66	17.7	34	9.1	367	12.7	804	514	290	36	988
Clay	2,254	13,122	0.89	143	10.2	86	6.1	1,246	12.0	1,980	1,636	344	308	2,206
Codington	381	29,288	1.09	342	12.2	233	8.3	2,112	9.0	5,530	3,369	2,161	734	2,619
Corson	1	4,188	1.01	99	23.8	59	14.2	657	18.7	571	532	39	33	783
Custer	252	7,528	0.75	72	8.3	83	9.5	652	10.7	2,572	2,117	455	46	544
Davison	771	21,259	1.15	230	11.6	184	9.3	1,376	8.7	4,105	3,318	787	700	3,520
Day	139	5,193	0.88	53	9.6	87	15.8	620	15.1	1,509	1,107	402	NA	NA
Deuel	50	3,902	0.83	59	13.6	43	9.9	348	10.5	1,046	695	351	28	648
Dewey	19	5,922	1.11	156	26.4	81	13.7	946	18.9	759	739	20	1	17
Douglas	178	2,848	0.94	49	16.7	27	9.2	241	11.1	753	598	155	6	202
Edmunds	420	3,380	0.70	43	11.1	41	10.6	293	9.5	857	767	90	4	101
Fall River	221	6,827	1.01	52	7.7	101	14.9	491	10.2	2,414	2,097	317	NA	NA
Faulk	497	2,328	1.00	31	13.3	17	7.3	146	8.1	553	488	65	14	602
Grant	104	7,534	1.11	87	12.2	73	10.2	540	9.6	1,771	986	785	NA	NA
Gregory	44	4,083	0.94	55	13.1	47	11.2	475	15.3	1,123	939	184	NA	NA
Haakon	36	2,142	1.06	22	11.5	13	6.8	177	12.2	449	409	40	NA	NA
Hamlin	245	5,274	0.77	115	18.8	55	9.0	460	9.3	1,096	739	357	23	380
Hand	61	3,231	0.96	43	13.2	29	8.9	208	8.4	836	754	82	20	602
Hanson	520	2,553	0.47	43	12.7	18	5.3	258	8.9	1,332	1,103	229	10	295
Harding	29	1,284	1.00	16	12.8	7	5.6	121	11.6	231	200	31	2	158
Hughes	771	18,174	1.06	222	12.6	163	9.2	1,363	9.6	3,329	3,034	295	747	4,240
Hutchinson	832	7,077	0.94	118	16.0	92	12.5	598	10.6	1,885	1,405	480	17	234
Hyde	38	1,472	1.15	16	12.5	13	10.1	95	9.3	319	D	D	NA	NA
Jackson	42	3,237	0.97	78	23.6	34	10.3	587	21.2	465	414	51	NA	NA
Jerauld	176	2,432	1.42	18	8.8	21	10.3	136	9.1	643	562	81	0	0
Jones	0	746	1.01	13	14.0	10	10.8	112	15.6	223	195	28	NA	NA
Kingsbury	203	4,538	0.82	64	13.0	56	11.4	318	8.3	1,283	1,052	231	NA	NA
Lake	878	11,736	0.90	128	9.8	113	8.7	798	8.3	2,706	2,161	545	NA	NA
Lawrence	1,074	25,167	1.01	236	9.2	226	8.8	1,866	9.5	6,005	4,556	1,449	639	2,566
Lincoln	284	42,836	0.64	823	14.0	255	4.3	2,582	5.3	7,516	5,432	2,084	1,313	2,413
Lyman	38	3,776	0.94	68	17.8	16	4.2	569	17.7	655	577	78	NA	NA
McCook	312	4,471	0.63	79	14.2	60	10.8	432	9.7	1,194	928	266	35	627
McPherson	347	2,341	0.98	22	9.1	22	9.1	180	10.2	726	662	64	15	624
Marshall	373	4,521	0.90	79	15.5	41	8.0	625	16.4	1,040	888	152	56	1,171
Meade	791	20,618	0.56	263	9.3	204	7.2	2,349	10.3	5,420	4,310	1,110	351	1,289
Mellette	49	1,931	0.81	46	22.5	31	15.2	317	18.8	345	331	14	NA	NA
Miner	80	2,141	0.90	22	9.9	18	8.1	154	8.7	569	509	60	6	272
Minnehaha	6,274	199,604	1.16	2,861	14.8	1,366	7.1	15,523	9.8	34,611	26,247	8,364	6,030	3,208
Moody	164	5,722	0.76	83	12.6	51	7.8	782	14.6	1,331	1,048	283	87	1,358
Oglala Lakota	92	14,963	1.22	286	20.0	180	12.6	1,983	15.5	1,319	1,304	15	NA	NA
Pennington	2,571	115,142	1.13	1,434	12.8	916	8.2	9,220	10.4	24,784	19,832	4,952	4,151	3,774
Perkins	65	3,066	1.07	37	12.7	24	8.2	311	13.8	765	656	109	6	199
Potter	63	2,280	0.97	22	10.0	29	13.1	159	9.9	684	620	64	NA	NA
Roberts	281	9,937	0.93	162	15.5	102	9.8	1,458	18.0	2,189	1,701	488	37	359
Sanborn	174	1,944	0.67	37	15.2	12	4.9	178	9.2	498	412	86	37	1,574
Spink	405	6,296	0.94	82	12.6	68	10.5	501	10.1	1,540	1,319	221	40	612
Stanley	0	2,594	0.77	32	10.6	12	4.0	223	9.1	650	586	64	15	510
Sully	0	1,438	1.07	18	12.9	8	5.7	124	10.9	369	345	24	2	140
Todd	28	10,167	1.06	246	23.9	120	11.7	1,503	16.9	958	945	13	NA	NA

1. Per 1,000 estimated resident population.   2. Data for serious crimes have not been adjusted for underreporting; this may affect comparability between geographic areas and over time.   3. Per 100,000 population estimated by the FBI.

Table B. States and Counties — Crime, Education, Money Income, and Poverty

STATE County	Serious crimes known to police[2], 2016 (cont.)[1] Rate Violent	Property	Education — School enrollment and attainment, 2013-2017 — Enrollment[3] Total	Percent private	High school graduate or less	Bachelor's degree or more	Local government expenditures,[5] 2014-2015 Total current spending (mil dol)	Current spending per student (dollars)	Money income, 2013-2017 Per capita income[6]	Households Median income (dollars)	Percent with income of less than $50,000	Percent with income of $200,000 or more	Income and poverty, 2017 Median household income (dollars)	Percent below poverty level All persons	Children under 18 years	Children 5 to 17 years in families
	46	47	48	49	50	51	52	53	54	55	56	57	58	59	60	61
SOUTH CAROLINA— Cont'd																
Sumter	591	3,294	28,324	17.9	47.7	19.5	158.0	9,339	21,733	41,946	57.8	1.8	44,375	19.1	28.7	28.5
Union	822	4,028	6,153	8.2	58.4	12.5	36.2	8,701	21,183	37,493	63.4	1.4	41,327	18	27.8	27.2
Williamsburg	540	3,039	7,646	12.7	60.8	12.6	51.1	11,549	17,440	30,976	68.1	1.4	32,421	26.8	40.8	37.9
York	370	2,253	65,786	9.6	37.5	31.1	410.0	9,702	30,387	59,394	42.5	5.5	62,620	11.2	15.3	14.3
SOUTH DAKOTA	418	1,981	215,415	13.1	39.1	27.8	1,187.2	8,929	28,761	54,126	46.2	3.8	56,871	12.8	16.3	15.2
Aurora	0	183	636	10.5	46.6	20.2	7.4	12,797	30,872	57,257	40.1	4.2	49,406	10.9	14.7	13.8
Beadle	216	1,463	4,054	19.0	49.0	19.6	25.6	9,289	24,950	48,995	50.8	1.4	45,878	15.7	20.9	20.1
Bennett	586	2,052	1,226	7.7	52.0	17.3	5.7	11,287	15,287	45,725	54.3	0.0	35,529	34.9	51.6	47.7
Bon Homme	14	0	1,276	4.9	48.0	19.0	11.2	10,287	24,858	52,923	47.9	2.6	48,110	13.1	17.0	16.6
Brookings	129	1,421	13,733	5.0	31.4	40.4	39.4	8,501	27,197	53,473	46.5	3.5	56,947	13	8.7	8.2
Brown	380	1,762	9,523	20.2	38.5	28.8	43.3	7,906	31,493	53,807	46.1	4.3	55,572	10.9	12.8	11.6
Brule	NA	NA	1,109	18.1	41.4	25.4	11.7	9,687	26,074	50,870	48.9	3.8	50,165	14.3	19.4	17.3
Buffalo	NA	NA	733	10.4	61.5	8.9	NA	NA	10,960	30,500	67.4	0.0	22,679	43.3	48.6	46.8
Butte	136	1,584	2,310	9.2	50.8	20.8	14.3	8,417	26,178	44,786	55.0	3.8	44,135	13.7	19.4	18.4
Campbell	72	435	263	3.0	50.0	23.6	1.4	11,875	36,158	51,548	48.1	4.2	49,459	9.8	13.3	14.3
Charles Mix	197	676	2,454	9.3	50.3	17.2	18.2	10,199	21,805	44,104	55.3	3.2	42,196	24.9	35.2	32.9
Clark	137	851	696	3.6	49.9	18.0	5.9	9,321	26,759	47,500	51.5	2.6	48,207	11.4	18.1	18.4
Clay	208	1,999	6,368	4.4	27.4	49.3	10.9	8,887	24,541	41,773	55.9	3.1	44,943	20.2	17.2	15.6
Codington	350	2,270	6,823	10.8	45.2	21.6	37.0	8,020	29,249	52,025	47.7	3.6	56,913	11.2	12.8	11.3
Corson	24	759	1,199	1.5	52.4	17.7	13.2	15,095	15,160	32,260	68.8	2.4	30,446	42.4	55.3	49.9
Custer	47	496	1,319	14.1	37.7	24.5	9.2	9,600	31,015	56,449	45.6	3.9	56,894	11.3	19.3	19.0
Davison	483	3,037	4,916	26.4	37.7	24.0	27.0	8,425	28,086	48,665	51.1	2.8	52,171	12.8	15.0	13.7
Day	NA	NA	1,045	6.7	48.9	18.6	6.5	9,292	30,841	50,870	55.6	3.7	48,656	15.7	19.1	16.4
Deuel	23	625	856	7.2	51.3	20.1	4.2	7,931	29,204	57,969	40.4	2.3	55,326	9.2	12.0	11.2
Dewey	0	17	1,707	1.7	51.6	14.6	5.1	14,264	17,267	41,190	58.0	2.5	37,621	34.9	41.9	43.6
Douglas	67	135	573	22.2	47.6	18.9	3.4	10,575	27,603	52,543	47.0	3.3	50,666	12.1	14.7	14.7
Edmunds	50	50	794	7.7	45.3	25.0	6.7	10,486	31,836	65,380	40.7	4.5	56,083	10.7	15.2	15.0
Fall River	NA	NA	1,105	15.5	37.8	23.0	11.7	10,758	26,584	48,862	51.3	0.6	45,273	14	20.4	19.4
Faulk	0	602	454	4.0	42.3	26.7	2.9	8,760	29,714	46,750	51.4	1.8	47,700	14.2	20.0	20.0
Grant	NA	NA	1,333	11.1	51.4	14.9	10.9	9,873	29,363	56,276	42.4	2.8	58,575	10	11.9	11.7
Gregory	NA	NA	882	7.0	47.6	21.1	7.7	10,426	26,169	42,672	55.9	2.6	38,420	16.5	21.4	18.7
Haakon	NA	NA	450	5.6	49.1	17.8	2.6	8,997	22,863	38,873	61.9	2.8	46,694	12	15.6	14.5
Hamlin	99	281	1,518	6.9	49.9	21.6	12.2	9,197	27,060	61,784	35.1	2.6	61,935	9	11.5	11.3
Hand	60	541	648	9.0	39.1	24.6	4.2	9,442	33,109	50,720	48.9	4.1	51,252	10.5	13.7	12.4
Hanson	0	295	997	13.5	43.9	21.8	3.3	7,337	24,805	62,448	38.0	3.0	62,790	9.2	15.2	14.0
Harding	158	0	269	2.6	37.1	30.8	3.0	16,799	30,464	55,972	45.2	3.6	53,035	10.9	13.6	14.0
Hughes	471	3,769	3,516	9.0	36.6	34.4	20.8	7,865	32,000	59,741	42.3	2.1	63,049	10.3	12.8	12.1
Hutchinson	41	192	1,560	7.8	47.4	23.7	13.6	10,120	29,869	49,583	50.4	4.4	53,170	11.5	17.2	17.6
Hyde	NA	NA	232	1.3	53.9	19.6	3.0	10,668	30,277	53,696	45.0	2.9	50,134	10.2	11.6	11.4
Jackson	NA	NA	834	3.2	46.5	21.8	4.7	12,835	16,939	38,041	61.5	3.7	32,023	36.2	48.3	47.0
Jerauld	0	0	366	12.0	53.3	19.3	4.0	11,748	38,776	49,882	50.3	5.4	45,021	12.9	19.8	18.8
Jones	NA	NA	119	35.3	51.6	15.9	2.0	11,483	26,526	39,432	60.0	0.0	41,679	13.7	23.0	22.7
Kingsbury	NA	NA	883	5.3	46.3	22.2	10.4	10,251	33,333	58,794	43.7	4.0	54,274	10.3	12.9	13.3
Lake	NA	NA	3,308	6.1	39.7	31.7	17.4	8,272	31,145	58,467	40.3	4.9	59,743	10.1	11.2	10.7
Lawrence	173	2,394	6,355	11.9	37.7	30.9	27.2	9,005	28,606	49,275	50.7	2.7	52,141	13.6	15.1	13.1
Lincoln	305	2,108	14,571	18.6	25.6	41.0	55.3	7,834	39,404	81,849	26.6	9.7	89,458	3.5	3.8	3.3
Lyman	NA	NA	929	9.4	48.5	17.9	5.1	12,539	21,155	47,113	51.9	2.4	43,798	22.2	30.2	30.3
McCook	54	573	1,269	9.1	45.2	21.5	11.8	10,222	29,254	60,808	38.5	2.6	58,271	9.4	12.9	12.7
McPherson	42	583	399	10.8	50.2	15.3	4.4	13,566	25,975	41,674	55.8	2.5	40,867	15.6	24.4	22.4
Marshall	188	982	936	3.6	41.6	23.6	6.0	9,051	28,861	60,948	41.1	2.8	58,651	12.1	18.7	18.6
Meade	158	1,131	6,643	11.2	38.2	24.7	23.1	8,069	26,896	54,286	46.5	2.6	59,563	9.1	11.1	10.1
Mellette	NA	NA	586	6.5	56.2	15.2	5.4	12,858	14,264	31,165	73.8	1.0	32,358	38	49.0	47.7
Miner	0	272	515	9.9	48.5	20.1	3.7	10,165	28,633	50,165	48.5	2.7	51,405	12	15.7	14.5
Minnehaha	432	2,776	44,401	18.3	35.7	30.9	259.2	8,175	29,551	57,322	43.7	3.7	61,182	9	10.0	9.9
Moody	281	1,077	1,563	5.2	42.7	23.9	7.8	8,539	27,774	56,233	42.8	3.6	57,740	10.7	13.2	12.8
Oglala Lakota	NA	NA	5,268	12.3	49.4	12.4	23.0	15,668	9,334	27,804	71.7	1.0	34,411	41.5	45.8	41.7
Pennington	623	3,151	26,913	14.0	34.1	29.6	148.3	8,409	28,910	52,245	47.0	3.6	55,104	12.9	16.6	15.3
Perkins	0	199	597	15.1	46.9	19.4	4.9	11,740	30,120	51,040	49.7	4.8	46,997	12.8	18.8	18.1
Potter	NA	NA	452	5.5	47.3	22.2	4.2	11,191	32,853	51,597	48.9	5.3	53,386	9.4	14.2	13.2
Roberts	126	233	2,346	4.2	49.0	17.5	16.8	11,074	25,767	51,228	48.5	3.5	44,020	17.6	25.4	25.7
Sanborn	340	1,234	397	4.5	46.6	18.5	4.3	10,165	31,965	54,671	43.3	3.6	48,923	13.5	21.8	22.3
Spink	31	582	1,400	10.5	45.4	21.9	12.6	9,795	31,957	52,000	47.6	5.1	50,965	10.3	15.5	13.7
Stanley	136	374	590	7.1	43.2	27.9	4.3	10,025	32,862	63,233	37.4	7.2	66,343	7.6	10.5	9.7
Sully	70	70	360	6.1	38.2	24.9	3.3	12,404	39,888	60,694	38.4	6.0	55,421	8.3	8.2	8.1
Todd	NA	NA	3,435	9.6	50.3	16.2	24.7	12,062	11,665	26,285	72.7	1.8	29,046	50.4	55.8	50.1

1. Data for serious crimes have not been adjusted for underreporting; this may affect comparability between geographic areas and over time.　2. Per 100,000 population estimated by the FBI.　3. All persons 3 years old and over enrolled in nursery school through college.　4. Persons 25 years old and over.　5. Elementary and secondary education expenditures.　6. Based on population estimated by the American Community Survey, 2013–2017.

Table B. States and Counties — Personal Income and Earnings

STATE County	Personal income, 2017										Earnings, 2017		
	Total (mil dol)	Percent change 2016-2017	Per capita[1]		Wages and salaries (mil dol)	Supplements to wages and salaries, employer contributions (mil dol)		Proprietors' income (mil dol)	Dividends, interest, and rent (mil dol)	Personal transfer receipts (mil dol)	Total (mil dol)	Contributions for government social insurance (mil dol)	
			Dollars	Rank		Pension and insurance	Government social insurance					From employee and self-employed	From employer
	62	63	64	65	66	67	68	69	70	71	72	73	74
SOUTH CAROLINA—Cont'd													
Sumter	3,941	3.0	36,887	2,059	1,927	400	159	188	671	1,113	2,674	164	159
Union	877	3.5	31,858	2,771	304	59	23	36	115	324	423	34	23
Williamsburg	988	2.6	31,735	2,786	336	73	26	34	133	370	469	36	26
York	11,815	6.5	44,343	981	4,704	713	351	623	1,534	1,928	6,391	411	351
SOUTH DAKOTA	42,455	1.6	48,616	X	19,003	3,166	1,400	5,297	10,302	6,536	28,866	1,724	1,400
Aurora	119	7.0	43,282	1,107	29	5	2	25	28	20	61	3	2
Beadle	862	-2.4	47,499	665	354	63	26	127	220	139	570	34	26
Bennett	101	8.3	29,283	2,971	31	8	2	9	20	32	50	3	2
Bon Homme	250	4.8	35,797	2,228	64	14	5	38	61	53	122	8	5
Brookings	1,534	1.6	44,774	933	819	174	61	143	390	173	1,197	67	61
Brown	1,943	-1.2	49,593	491	913	157	69	217	504	279	1,355	84	69
Brule	215	0.4	40,543	1,464	69	13	5	36	58	39	122	7	5
Buffalo	47	10.1	23,395	3,101	21	6	2	3	9	19	32	2	2
Butte	366	3.3	36,251	2,158	101	19	8	49	83	77	176	12	8
Campbell	63	-2.7	45,381	857	19	3	1	8	20	11	32	2	1
Charles Mix	380	1.1	40,270	1,508	120	26	9	83	91	83	238	12	9
Clark	159	-5.9	43,269	1,109	36	7	3	18	64	26	64	4	3
Clay	523	-0.1	37,400	1,970	232	54	17	54	129	90	357	20	17
Codington	1,285	3.6	45,720	828	643	111	48	106	335	202	909	56	48
Corson	111	3.5	26,327	3,076	34	8	3	8	23	34	53	3	3
Custer	399	3.7	45,967	799	87	17	7	34	112	80	145	11	7
Davison	963	1.8	48,894	547	500	80	37	117	262	156	734	45	37
Day	230	3.7	41,634	1,314	69	14	5	21	74	54	109	7	5
Deuel	213	-3.4	49,703	478	59	12	5	49	51	35	125	6	5
Dewey	206	-2.0	35,386	2,287	88	22	7	18	40	52	135	7	7
Douglas	163	0.4	55,445	264	42	8	3	52	34	26	106	5	3
Edmunds	168	-1.5	42,976	1,144	49	10	4	10	55	29	72	5	4
Fall River	303	2.6	45,345	862	108	25	10	35	74	89	178	12	10
Faulk	85	8.4	36,489	2,117	24	4	2	3	33	21	33	3	2
Grant	376	-8.8	53,216	337	159	26	12	75	86	61	271	17	12
Gregory	193	6.8	45,771	822	49	10	4	45	47	41	108	6	4
Haakon	91	8.1	46,718	737	34	6	3	16	27	14	59	3	3
Hamlin	241	-2.5	40,601	1,457	72	13	5	28	59	39	119	7	5
Hand	134	-10.5	40,806	1,432	53	9	4	-7	50	26	59	5	4
Hanson	209	8.6	61,173	143	25	5	2	40	61	39	73	4	2
Harding	61	-3.0	48,773	562	20	4	2	16	15	7	42	2	2
Hughes	896	1.5	50,721	421	486	92	35	57	226	121	670	41	35
Hutchinson	354	1.2	48,086	618	97	18	7	80	87	62	201	11	7
Hyde	60	6.1	45,190	879	22	4	2	7	20	11	35	2	2
Jackson	82	10.0	24,857	3,094	26	7	2	4	18	25	39	3	2
Jerauld	98	-0.2	48,313	601	57	9	4	19	25	21	89	5	4
Jones	45	7.3	48,243	604	15	3	1	6	15	7	25	2	1
Kingsbury	222	-4.7	44,895	912	66	13	5	13	64	44	96	7	5
Lake	662	-1.3	51,667	389	207	40	15	89	194	125	351	23	15
Lawrence	1,194	3.8	46,936	716	434	70	32	101	348	198	638	42	32
Lincoln	3,642	2.8	64,275	109	1,132	153	81	325	828	252	1,691	100	81
Lyman	150	-3.3	38,324	1,820	47	10	4	24	37	30	84	4	4
McCook	266	2.9	48,430	594	51	9	4	54	53	43	118	6	4
McPherson	81	8.4	33,556	2,548	21	4	2	5	29	21	32	3	2
Marshall	204	-3.0	42,479	1,205	62	11	5	42	55	34	120	6	5
Meade	1,163	4.1	41,511	1,328	329	76	26	102	239	189	533	34	26
Mellette	56	12.7	26,857	3,063	10	3	1	4	11	18	17	1	1
Miner	111	17.3	49,877	469	26	5	2	31	27	19	63	3	2
Minnehaha	10,085	2.3	53,469	328	6,239	892	449	1,512	2,066	1,309	9,093	536	449
Moody	314	-2.1	47,690	647	85	18	7	45	82	46	155	8	7
Oglala Lakota	342	3.3	23,848	3,100	163	41	13	16	40	144	233	13	13
Pennington	5,351	2.9	48,587	582	2,652	437	201	470	1,424	953	3,761	232	201
Perkins	129	14.6	43,467	1,078	45	10	3	25	29	25	83	5	3
Potter	130	-9.8	58,461	193	32	6	2	23	50	23	64	5	2
Roberts	348	0.9	33,829	2,503	127	27	10	23	89	86	187	13	10
Sanborn	111	8.8	45,272	873	20	4	2	30	21	17	56	2	2
Spink	298	-7.8	46,460	758	93	19	7	13	95	81	132	10	7
Stanley	201	4.5	66,677	88	49	8	4	36	58	20	96	5	4
Sully	79	-0.3	56,447	235	23	3	2	16	27	10	44	2	2
Todd	252	3.6	25,032	3,089	113	27	8	12	37	93	160	9	8

1. Based on the resident population estimated as of July 1 of the year shown.

Table B. States and Counties — Earnings, Social Security, and Housing

STATE County	Earnings, 2017 (cont.)									Social Security beneficiaries, December 2017			Housing units, 2018	
	Percent by selected industries											Supplemental Security Income recipients, 2017		
	Farm	Mining, quarrying, and extractions	Construction	Manufacturing	Information; professional, scientific, technical services	Retail trade	Finance, insurance, real estate, and leasing	Health care and social assistance	Government	Number	Rate[1]		Total	Percent change, 2010-2018
	75	76	77	78	79	80	81	82	83	84	85	86	87	88
SOUTH CAROLINA— Cont'd														
Sumter	0.4	0	7.3	16.4	3.6	5.8	3	12.5	33.7	23,890	224	4,197	48,284	4.9
Union	1.5	D	3	26.2	D	6.1	2.8	D	23.2	8,365	304	992	14,095	-0.4
Williamsburg	0.3	0	7.1	19.6	D	5.3	D	D	27	8,800	283	1,773	15,481	0.8
York	0.6	0.1	5.8	13.9	12.1	6.6	8.2	9	12.6	48,035	180	3,848	110,237	17
SOUTH DAKOTA	3.1	0.3	7	10	5.7	7.4	11.2	15.4	16.8	175,389	202	14,888	397,526	9.4
Aurora	26.8	0.1	6	1.2	D	4.4	5.4	14.3	12.9	610	223	23	1,375	3.9
Beadle	3	D	6.5	22.8	2.5	6.6	8	D	14.6	3,630	200	420	8,569	3.2
Bennett	7.2	0	10.2	D	D	7.7	D	2.9	44.1	505	146	149	1,269	0.5
Bon Homme	10.2	0	8.8	5.4	3.1	4.9	6.4	D	24.8	1,595	228	81	2,992	2.1
Brookings	4.2	D	4.9	28.2	3.9	5.5	5.7	3.7	25.5	4,665	136	281	14,763	12.4
Brown	-1.3	D	7.2	15.5	4.7	8.1	9.5	16	14	7,535	192	544	18,155	8.7
Brule	17.5	D	6.4	0.6	3.9	7.7	6.6	11	17.6	985	185	122	2,576	5.9
Buffalo	10.6	0	D	0	D	D	D	4	76.4	270	135	90	610	0
Butte	5.2	D	8.7	5.4	7.1	11.7	4.6	6.7	16.9	2,360	234	199	4,876	5.5
Campbell	17.5	0	D	D	D	6.5	D	2.3	10	390	283	15	983	0.3
Charles Mix	22.1	0.1	6.8	3.1	2.5	6.5	5	D	28.5	1,845	196	272	3,922	1.9
Clark	15	0.3	8.9	10.4	D	6	D	D	17.4	780	213	93	1,839	7.5
Clay	7.6	0	3.8	3.4	D	5.8	4	D	48.3	2,030	145	181	6,030	6.9
Codington	2.5	0.1	6.7	20.6	3.8	9.8	7.9	13.4	14.5	5,785	206	398	13,203	6.5
Corson	9.3	0.3	2.9	-0.1	2.5	3	D	D	59.6	615	146	244	1,539	0.1
Custer	2.9	D	7.7	1	D	7.9	4.8	11.3	24.2	2,535	292	85	5,285	14.2
Davison	0.5	D	8.2	17.6	5.6	10	6.2	15.2	10.7	4,260	216	367	9,596	8.4
Day	10.9	0.1	6.4	12.5	2.1	7.3	7.2	D	19.1	1,575	285	89	3,811	5
Deuel	25.1	0.1	11.2	11.3	D	4.1	D	D	8.8	1,125	263	40	2,215	0.5
Dewey	9.9	D	2.9	0.5	D	3.5	2.6	D	65.6	875	150	350	2,024	1.1
Douglas	35.4	D	7.6	5.4	D	4.1	3	8.6	8.7	735	251	43	1,478	2.8
Edmunds	-17.1	0.1	8.8	8.1	D	8.3	18	D	23.2	870	222	44	2,085	6.1
Fall River	12.3	0.5	4.6	0.5	3.3	4.6	2.6	D	39.5	2,360	353	183	4,239	1.2
Faulk	-10.3	0.5	D	3.2	2.8	5.8	15.8	D	18.8	525	225	55	1,190	4.8
Grant	-1.9	D	10.1	23.6	2.3	17.9	5.7	7.1	6.7	1,840	261	80	3,641	3.2
Gregory	28.8	D	6.3	1.8	2.1	7.3	7.5	12.5	12.1	1,170	277	107	2,546	1.7
Haakon	10.5	D	7.5	7.2	D	6.8	7.8	D	11.9	440	226	12	1,021	0.8
Hamlin	7.5	0	18.4	D	2.6	5.9	D	4	18.1	1,130	190	54	2,962	7.3
Hand	-33.1	0.9	8.3	4.3	D	10.7	D	D	18.7	845	258	36	1,854	2.2
Hanson	31.8	D	13.9	11.4	D	2.4	D	D	11.7	1,305	381	38	1,210	2.7
Harding	26.2	7.4	13.9	-0.1	D	7.4	D	4.6	14.7	230	185	0	753	3
Hughes	0.1	0	4.6	0.7	6.7	7.4	9.4	12.1	41.7	3,475	197	241	8,071	5.9
Hutchinson	23	D	5.7	6.9	D	4.7	4.9	D	10.2	1,850	251	93	3,393	1.3
Hyde	16.5	0	4.9	1.9	D	6.5	D	D	24.9	325	247	11	701	
Jackson	0.4	0	D	D	D	7.4	D	D	51.9	500	152	140	1,204	0.9
Jerauld	10.6	D	D	D	D	2.6	D	D	6.4	635	313	27	1,081	1
Jones	4.1	0	D	0	D	14.3	4.6	2.2	24.4	235	251	0	650	10.4
Kingsbury	-7.1	0	11.5	15.4	D	6.3	14.3	9.3	15.3	1,315	266	75	2,817	3.6
Lake	5	D	6.8	17.2	7	7.3	5.6	9.3	17.7	3,930	307	146	5,835	4.9
Lawrence	0.1	D	8.5	4.3	6.8	10	6.2	13.3	16.6	6,135	241	342	14,208	11.4
Lincoln	0.5	0	10.5	8.4	8	7.3	19.1	15.7	5.7	7,335	129	233	21,099	18
Lyman	19.8	0.3	3.3	D	D	8.8	D	D	38.3	730	187	71	1,757	3.1
McCook	30.1	D	8.6	2	4.5	5.6	4.4	9.6	11.8	1,225	223	73	2,596	4.2
McPherson	-4.2	0.4	8	4.8	D	D	19.5	D	24.5	700	289	41	1,436	1.3
Marshall	28.8	D	6.7	16.7	3.6	4.6	D	D	14	1,055	220	63	2,656	4.8
Meade	3	D	12.5	2.9	3.4	7.2	4.6	4.8	41.2	5,670	202	274	12,265	11.5
Mellette	-3.8	0	D	0.1	D	D	D	D	54	360	172	131	852	1.8
Miner	35.2	0	6.2	2.5	D	4.9	5.2	6.3	12.2	560	251	32	1,356	3.7
Minnehaha	0.3	D	6.3	8	7.6	7.4	17.8	20.5	9.3	34,665	184	3,009	83,991	17.4
Moody	21.1	0	12.7	10	D	2.2	D	6.2	23.5	1,360	207	50	2,906	2.8
Oglala Lakota	4.6	0	1.1	D	D	D	D	1.8	77.7	1,525	106	1,076	3,643	1.4
Pennington	0.2	0.1	8.1	4	6.1	7.8	8.2	21.3	20.7	25,290	230	2,009	49,240	9.5
Perkins	17.9	0	8	D	D	5.9	D	11.6	14.9	765	257	43	1,740	0
Potter	-36	0	6.7	4.9	2.2	61.8	11	D	13.1	690	309	16	1,516	1
Roberts	2.4	D	4.2	9.8	2.7	6	D	D	43.4	2,345	228	245	5,074	3.5
Sanborn	47	0	D	D	D	2	2.4	D	12.9	515	210	24	1,212	3.4
Spink	-8.8	0.3	6.8	7.5	2.8	8.2	13.1	D	35.4	1,540	240	145	3,263	4
Stanley	26.9	D	23.6	-0.5	D	7.7	3.2	D	11.7	660	219	20	1,528	10.2
Sully	14.5	0.3	D	D	D	7.8	21.3	D	11.7	365	259	5	905	7.2
Todd	5.7	0	0.8	D	D	3.6	D	3.8	74.2	1,145	114	615	3,168	0.9

1. Per 1,000 resident population estimated as of July 1 of the year shown.

Table B. States and Counties — Housing, Labor Force, and Employment

	Housing units, 2013-2017								Civilian labor force, 2018				Civilian employment[6], 2013-2017		
STATE County	Occupied units							Sub-standard units[4] (percent)			Unemployment			Percent	
			Owner-occupied			Renter-occupied									
				Median owner cost as a percent of income			Median rent as a percent of income[2]			Percent change, 2017-2018		Rate[5]		Management, business, science, and arts	Construction, production, and maintenance occupations
	Total	Percent	Median value[1]	With a mort-gage	Without a mort-gage[2]	Median rent[3]			Total		Total		Total		
	89	90	91	92	93	94	95	96	97	98	99	100	101	102	103
SOUTH CAROLINA— Cont'd															
Sumter	41,417	64.9	113,200	20.4	10.3	762	31.9	2.8	44,120	0.5	1,776	4	42,439	28.1	30.5
Union	11,564	70.2	75,600	20.5	11.3	602	25.9	1.5	11,582	0.7	480	4.1	11,655	23.7	40.4
Williamsburg	12,310	73.7	68,400	23.5	14.7	615	29.2	3.5	12,294	1.4	668	5.4	11,370	22.9	32.3
York	95,539	71.0	173,600	19.2	10.0	893	30.1	1.8	134,695	0.7	4,389	3.3	121,792	36.4	21.9
SOUTH DAKOTA	339,458	67.9	152,700	19.8	10.5	696	25.8	2.9	459,459	0.7	13,860	3	438,339	35.2	24.2
Aurora	1,179	77.6	72,300	18.0	10.0	598	21.3	1.9	1,557	2.2	45	2.9	1,462	35.6	30.8
Beadle	7,651	67.0	104,800	18.1	10.0	579	23.9	7.1	9,519	1.4	247	2.6	9,105	29.7	33.8
Bennett	955	60.8	69,000	15.6	12.0	557	20.8	14.1	1,074	-3.4	48	4.5	1,212	37.0	22.7
Bon Homme	2,554	75.4	80,400	18.1	10.0	489	19.7	3.1	2,878	-1.3	73	2.5	2,897	40.5	26.4
Brookings	12,602	59.6	165,100	19.4	10.0	698	30.4	1.2	19,019	1.1	538	2.8	19,080	36.6	23.7
Brown	16,328	65.9	152,900	19.4	10.5	651	25.4	1.7	20,891	-0.2	591	2.8	20,738	33.2	26.8
Brule	2,170	68.0	117,100	20.8	11.1	568	18.3	4.3	2,536	2.3	69	2.7	2,691	37.9	21.3
Buffalo	530	41.9	51,400	22.8	15.0	505	24.1	15.5	709	0.1	42	5.9	594	31.5	16.8
Butte	4,172	74.5	123,900	20.1	13.9	652	27.7	1.5	5,050	0.5	165	3.3	5,096	28.5	31.8
Campbell	690	85.2	65,900	14.9	10.0	511	18.8	0.6	792	-4.8	31	3.9	757	49.8	16.9
Charles Mix	3,184	67.9	89,900	17.7	10.2	500	22.7	3.7	3,872	-0.4	125	3.2	3,829	34.6	23.2
Clark	1,510	77.8	81,100	19.4	10.0	555	19.6	2.4	1,892	0.4	75	4	1,773	37.3	28.9
Clay	5,302	51.6	146,400	19.5	10.0	716	35.5	0.4	7,250	1.7	209	2.9	7,624	40.8	15.8
Codington	12,011	65.1	166,500	20.4	10.0	680	26.8	4.1	15,356	0.9	466	3	15,522	27.4	29.0
Corson	1,239	53.4	53,300	20.1	11.6	421	23.9	11.8	1,379	-3	57	4.1	1,260	43.1	26.0
Custer	3,901	82.8	202,600	23.5	13.2	849	25	2.6	4,051	0.4	163	4	3,961	37.5	24.2
Davison	8,696	60.8	141,000	18.8	10.9	711	24.2	1.5	10,996	-0.3	290	2.6	10,389	33.1	31.3
Day	2,567	73.0	86,000	20.2	10.5	530	26.4	0.3	2,803	-0.8	119	4.2	2,776	35.4	28.0
Deuel	1,835	82.2	112,700	19.7	10.0	438	16.5	2.6	2,159	-1.7	96	4.4	2,307	36.8	34.5
Dewey	1,648	58.4	65,700	14.9	11.0	542	21.3	11.3	2,213	-1.5	195	8.8	1,950	43.2	19.7
Douglas	1,271	76.9	80,800	17.1	10.0	518	22	3	1,576	-1.3	42	2.7	1,477	36.6	25.5
Edmunds	1,579	83.9	114,000	17.2	10.0	603	18.4	0.3	2,100	-0.6	56	2.7	2,006	36.6	29.4
Fall River	3,115	72.7	116,700	23.6	12.1	615	26.6	4.6	3,011	1.1	116	3.9	3,208	32.7	24.7
Faulk	944	77.1	85,700	17.6	11.0	620	19.6	0.5	1,098	-0.2	33	3	1,120	41.3	22.9
Grant	3,203	83.7	115,800	20.4	10.0	621	23.9	1.1	4,449	-0.1	141	3.2	3,718	28.5	30.8
Gregory	1,943	69.7	68,600	19.4	10.0	526	26.8	2	2,048	-0.3	67	3.3	2,017	35.2	25.3
Haakon	893	78.5	78,100	26.1	14.9	550	22.1	0.6	1,080	-2.1	28	2.6	902	37.4	30.8
Hamlin	2,193	81.4	117,400	19.7	10.0	587	18.1	2.7	3,243	3	100	3.1	2,874	31.7	36.2
Hand	1,498	69.5	115,100	17.5	10.0	509	22.3	0	1,827	0.2	42	2.3	1,697	39.7	26.3
Hanson	1,061	88.3	121,300	20.9	11.4	731	21.9	2.3	1,777	0.3	82	4.6	1,638	35.8	30.0
Harding	533	71.1	82,300	13.8	11.1	618	15.7	0.4	731	0.6	18	2.5	660	38.0	32.4
Hughes	7,391	64.7	173,400	17.8	10.2	621	22.1	2.5	9,890	-1.3	255	2.6	9,402	43.1	18.3
Hutchinson	2,881	76.4	81,300	18.8	10.0	505	26.8	3	3,580	-0.9	102	2.8	3,592	35.0	28.6
Hyde	582	80.8	88,100	19.6	11.8	612	18	4.3	688	0.4	21	3.1	683	41.3	26.1
Jackson	984	62.8	55,800	20.0	11.1	501	20	13.2	1,278	-3.4	63	4.9	1,105	45.3	20.1
Jerauld	911	73.7	77,700	16.8	11.8	486	15.5	1.3	1,120	-1.8	28	2.5	987	30.2	35.3
Jones	405	75.8	77,700	19.5	14.1	423	17.7	0.7	556	-0.9	15	2.7	430	44.7	30.5
Kingsbury	2,327	79.7	105,900	16.6	10.2	411	20.9	1.7	2,675	-0.1	78	2.9	2,662	38.8	31.4
Lake	4,817	74.5	155,200	18.6	11.4	552	25.9	0.9	6,662	2.5	227	3.4	6,498	33.9	25.8
Lawrence	10,902	64.2	189,200	23.5	11.2	687	26.6	1.9	13,076	0.2	384	2.9	13,067	31.3	22.8
Lincoln	18,736	78.9	209,700	19.3	10.0	895	23.4	1.2	33,445	1.5	768	2.3	29,254	44.5	17.6
Lyman	1,383	69.9	81,700	18.7	12.2	537	19.2	6.9	1,712	-2	71	4.1	1,756	35.9	24.0
McCook	2,182	75.0	120,700	19.2	10.0	586	18.5	1.1	3,083	0.8	77	2.5	2,882	33.2	26.3
McPherson	1,019	79.4	54,500	17.2	10.7	548	24.3	0.9	1,034	-1.5	39	3.8	1,040	35.7	25.9
Marshall	1,813	71.8	106,700	19.3	10.0	539	20.1	2.3	2,380	-0.8	91	3.8	2,471	36.0	33.9
Meade	11,022	73.6	168,400	22.9	11.8	837	27.2	3.5	14,107	1.1	464	3.3	13,830	31.9	27.5
Mellette	683	67.6	45,300	16.9	11.3	475	22.7	11.7	758	-0.8	37	4.9	680	42.9	26.6
Miner	990	78.5	82,000	17.1	10.8	497	23.2	3.2	1,199	0.3	33	2.8	1,116	36.5	29.2
Minnehaha	73,762	63.6	166,600	19.6	10.0	757	26.6	2.5	110,908	1.5	2,891	2.6	102,646	34.6	23.0
Moody	2,664	75.8	118,900	19.0	12.4	550	17	3	4,012	0.7	121	3	3,307	33.8	30.3
Oglala Lakota	2,920	52.6	18,700	13.1	13.1	488	20.1	38	3,581	-1.1	370	10.3	3,219	33.4	17.8
Pennington	43,110	67.7	172,400	22.4	12.2	790	29.6	2.4	56,253	1	1,720	3.1	54,142	32.1	20.6
Perkins	1,311	74.1	74,300	19.5	10.0	556	24.8	0.6	1,468	-7.8	42	2.9	1,529	39.9	28.1
Potter	1,025	82.6	81,600	18.1	11.8	645	16.7	0.4	1,105	-1.5	39	3.5	1,159	33.9	28.6
Roberts	3,756	67.9	95,700	20.7	10.6	572	21.6	3.4	4,856	0.7	209	4.3	4,585	37.3	26.2
Sanborn	1,050	73.7	72,800	17.4	10.0	549	21.6	0.9	1,160	-1.3	34	2.9	1,300	34.8	31.8
Spink	2,626	73.5	77,300	17.7	10.0	579	20.2	2.4	3,238	0.2	113	3.5	3,204	36.4	26.2
Stanley	1,309	78.8	158,300	20.5	10.6	664	31.8	3.1	1,829	-1.9	48	2.6	1,794	38.1	24.9
Sully	601	76.9	122,300	18.4	10.0	545	14.7	0	817	-2.2	21	2.6	728	42.3	29.7
Todd	2,768	41.6	38,500	20.5	10.5	421	21.9	15.9	3,140	0.1	194	6.2	2,784	37.9	17.2

1. Specified owner-occupied units. 2. A value of 10.0 represents 10 percent or less; a value of 50.0 represents 50 percent or more. 3. Specified renter-occupied units. 4. Overcrowded or lacking complete plumbing facilities. 5. Percent of civilian labor force. 6. Civilian employed persons 16 years old and over.

Table B. States and Counties — **Nonfarm Employment and Agriculture**

STATE County	Private nonfarm establishments, employment and payroll, 2016									Agriculture, 2017			
		Employment						Annual payroll		Farms			Farm producers whose primary occupation is farming (percent)
												Percent with:	
	Number of establishments	Total	Health care and social assistance	Manufacturing	Retail trade	Finance and insurance	Professional, scientific, and technical services	Total (mil dol)	Average per employee (dollars)	Number	Fewer than 50 acres	1000 acres or more	
	104	105	106	107	108	109	110	111	112	113	114	115	116
SOUTH CAROLINA— Cont'd													
Sumter	1,773	32,672	5,179	6,207	4,800	808	849	1,123	34,372	524	55.7	7.3	45.7
Union	414	7,012	940	1,580	855	199	82	220	31,337	241	30.3	2.5	35.3
Williamsburg	497	7,074	886	2,333	883	160	86	251	35,520	552	26.6	8.9	34.7
York	4,893	77,441	9,671	10,577	11,231	5,744	2,925	3,271	42,235	1,000	49.4	1.5	30.2
SOUTH DAKOTA	26,743	357,950	67,218	44,429	54,400	26,276	12,163	14,183	39,623	29,968	19.3	32.0	52.4
Aurora	79	626	182	D	92	41	76	20	32,422	392	17.1	24.2	46.2
Beadle	587	7,089	1,319	1,592	1,127	455	118	243	34,223	744	20.6	30.5	53.9
Bennett	63	697	D	D	128	D	D	19	27,504	213	5.6	65.3	65.1
Bon Homme	161	1,103	309	137	133	92	23	33	29,865	583	22.0	15.4	52.0
Brookings	899	14,005	1,384	5,029	1,859	552	606	521	37,223	886	31.0	14.3	38.9
Brown	1,294	18,667	3,301	3,253	3,038	1,016	477	713	38,220	1,034	24.3	27.4	50.5
Brule	217	1,850	409	30	249	79	45	60	32,338	394	17.3	37.8	54.4
Buffalo	11	180	40	D	D	D	D	5	25,628	68	14.7	64.7	76.6
Butte	321	2,294	284	199	450	82	108	73	31,730	565	17.7	30.4	48.8
Campbell	55	306	22	51	31	D	18	10	31,248	249	7.2	48.2	57.5
Charles Mix	275	2,363	539	91	430	128	42	64	27,175	671	12.8	32.5	53.3
Clark	127	682	103	105	112	29	18	22	32,412	553	10.7	33.1	52.8
Clay	303	3,502	774	199	809	78	140	91	26,029	472	26.3	16.7	50.5
Codington	1,129	14,196	1,881	3,423	2,818	844	255	496	34,905	601	34.4	19.6	44.9
Corson	36	188	9	NA	61	16	NA	7	36,245	322	5.9	67.4	73.0
Custer	268	1,303	242	20	246	37	49	50	38,684	441	24.5	22.4	43.1
Davison	734	11,459	2,175	1,837	2,060	338	772	396	34,532	463	30.7	16.6	43.4
Day	186	1,520	304	209	285	80	42	47	30,637	581	13.9	29.1	52.2
Deuel	130	1,470	169	D	118	42	23	70	47,426	634	24.8	18.3	45.4
Dewey	80	624	128	D	76	D	D	22	34,622	310	12.3	61.3	57.6
Douglas	109	850	224	105	133	35	8	26	31,033	392	21.7	22.7	53.4
Edmunds	124	866	180	69	135	49	22	33	37,811	348	7.8	53.2	59.0
Fall River	218	2,552	D	9	266	37	41	139	54,298	314	14.0	45.5	53.8
Faulk	71	445	D	D	60	25	D	14	31,811	291	7.2	56.4	72.2
Grant	284	3,260	429	626	531	116	62	123	37,737	554	24.5	26.2	52.9
Gregory	188	1,125	312	50	261	70	39	34	30,325	495	9.1	31.1	57.4
Haakon	86	651	D	D	92	46	13	23	35,194	293	8.2	67.2	62.1
Hamlin	188	1,184	146	225	145	63	43	45	37,617	476	27.7	18.1	47.4
Hand	129	1,187	238	67	174	65	47	37	31,497	405	12.8	50.1	70.0
Hanson	77	366	14	101	36	25	12	13	35,967	333	18.3	26.7	47.3
Harding	42	379	90	NA	38	D	D	18	46,314	265	6.4	79.6	70.3
Hughes	667	7,027	1,496	75	1,493	513	329	239	34,004	315	23.2	37.8	41.3
Hutchinson	242	2,243	652	324	313	128	25	74	33,067	775	20.8	19.0	49.8
Hyde	43	470	D	NA	64	D	D	16	34,013	174	6.9	52.9	59.5
Jackson	49	237	D	D	107	D	D	6	27,173	314	4.8	65.9	70.2
Jerauld	74	1,147	128	D	43	31	16	41	35,431	244	13.1	27.9	46.1
Jones	48	275	D	NA	92	11	D	9	31,098	192	4.7	60.4	60.9
Kingsbury	171	1,317	194	375	180	125	13	52	39,465	518	15.3	31.9	56.0
Lake	364	3,697	632	703	484	165	188	135	36,466	463	26.8	19.4	45.8
Lawrence	1,017	9,633	1,438	461	1,485	256	261	295	30,659	275	30.2	14.5	39.6
Lincoln	1,458	15,814	3,152	2,014	2,080	1,355	544	666	42,119	756	36.1	12.0	44.1
Lyman	74	642	D	D	267	34	D	16	25,201	414	5.1	43.5	51.2
McCook	189	1,064	253	7	172	42	30	33	31,295	512	23.0	26.2	47.6
McPherson	76	348	43	56	67	45	D	11	30,259	382	5.0	45.0	59.8
Marshall	144	1,173	158	335	204	47	23	42	35,812	503	12.7	27.0	49.2
Meade	709	5,438	1,440	304	797	179	208	247	45,505	835	19.9	44.3	55.2
Mellette	18	146	D	NA	52	D	D	3	22,329	219	1.4	64.8	68.6
Miner	80	518	119	28	62	23	23	18	35,243	408	15.9	26.0	39.2
Minnehaha	5,735	121,431	24,238	11,857	16,206	12,595	4,447	5,375	44,268	1,023	42.1	11.4	39.9
Moody	160	1,673	213	344	176	21	25	58	34,409	490	33.7	16.1	47.3
Oglala Lakota	72	1,857	282	NA	218	41	D	58	31,462	190	3.7	54.7	54.3
Pennington	3,779	49,590	9,639	2,793	9,040	2,796	1,872	1,864	37,583	656	24.2	28.4	42.6
Perkins	139	785	117	D	133	48	15	24	31,045	421	5.9	65.1	69.4
Potter	102	769	109	D	91	D	10	31	40,178	221	5.4	49.3	60.4
Roberts	235	2,255	476	305	409	110	31	66	29,188	782	15.0	25.2	50.3
Sanborn	59	402	66	D	47	25	18	12	30,236	351	12.5	31.3	52.5
Spink	184	1,417	313	97	200	84	36	50	35,246	556	10.6	48.4	64.5
Stanley	113	1,018	29	D	121	41	28	35	34,401	172	8.7	59.3	58.1
Sully	65	339	7	D	102	22	D	13	38,484	201	10.0	52.7	70.2
Todd	54	975	267	D	275	D	D	32	32,689	223	3.6	58.7	68.3

Table B. States and Counties — **Agriculture**

STATE County	Land in farms — Acreage (1,000) [117]	Percent change, 2012-2017 [118]	Acres — Average size of farm [119]	Acres — Total irrigated (1,000) [120]	Acres — Total cropland (1,000) [121]	Value of land and buildings (dollars) — Average per farm [122]	Average per acre [123]	Value of machinery and equipment, average per farm (dollars) [124]	Value of products sold: Total (mil dol) [125]	Average per farm (acres) [126]	Percent from: Crops [127]	Livestock and poultry products [128]	Organic farms (number) [129]	Farms with internet access (percent) [130]	Government payments Total ($1,000) [131]	Percent of farms [132]
SOUTH CAROLINA—Cont'd																
Sumter	168	-4.7	320	19.1	91.4	958,464	2,995	134,000	153.4	292,763	32.6	67.4	5	79.6	1,534	30.7
Union	44	-7.5	182	0.0	7.3	460,174	2,534	64,867	10.3	42,859	10.4	89.6	NA	62.7	426	25.3
Williamsburg	209	-7.1	378	2.6	107.7	848,443	2,245	118,529	47.2	85,562	86.7	13.3	NA	60.1	2,191	55.3
York	120	-3.0	120	1.2	37.9	838,682	6,979	63,006	100.5	100,504	63.2	36.8	NA	67.7	876	17.5
SOUTH DAKOTA	43,244	0.0	1,443	492.5	19,813.5	2,984,426	2,068	282,162	9,721.5	324,397	53.1	46.9	87	81.0	419,508	72.1
Aurora	355	-19.8	904	NA	228.8	2,400,283	2,654	297,809	138.2	352,541	46.7	53.3	NA	82.1	4,879	82.9
Beadle	811	2.1	1,090	20.1	548.5	2,934,337	2,693	331,767	295.3	396,867	56.6	43.4	NA	84.9	12,672	73.7
Bennett	637	5.0	2,990	8.5	214.3	2,846,734	952	251,150	65.9	309,545	40.6	59.4	NA	72.3	3,641	71.8
Bon Homme	305	-13.3	523	8.6	228.4	2,083,627	3,984	274,056	152.9	262,182	51.0	49.0	2	79.9	6,300	86.6
Brookings	460	2.3	519	20.5	345.4	2,386,912	4,602	248,257	316.3	357,034	39.9	60.1	3	84.4	6,331	59.5
Brown	1,083	0.4	1,047	4.4	884.6	3,521,412	3,362	360,625	377.4	365,032	77.8	22.2	2	78.8	11,893	62.9
Brule	518	0.7	1,314	5.4	277.9	3,386,122	2,578	312,852	153.6	389,759	32.5	67.5	NA	78.4	5,948	77.2
Buffalo	300	1.3	4,410	9.3	85.4	6,815,539	1,545	502,785	39.5	581,059	42.2	57.8	NA	86.8	2,436	79.4
Butte	1,155	1.8	2,044	46.7	150.2	1,959,536	959	127,586	68.0	120,312	12.5	87.5	NA	78.1	5,104	52.4
Campbell	434	20.4	1,742	4.6	250.8	3,190,052	1,831	339,855	96.2	386,333	57.6	42.4	NA	73.9	3,925	87.1
Charles Mix	686	-0.9	1,022	13.4	451.0	2,850,723	2,788	350,312	262.1	390,633	45.8	54.2	1	85.5	9,733	88.5
Clark	602	-1.1	1,089	17.6	444.8	3,428,717	3,150	290,526	267.6	483,870	55.6	44.4	NA	81.7	7,415	82.3
Clay	239	-7.6	506	28.1	221.2	2,380,474	4,702	299,816	113.1	239,606	88.1	11.9	3	79.2	4,754	81.4
Codington	383	3.8	638	8.2	268.0	2,210,441	3,467	217,944	155.9	259,364	57.1	42.9	2	80.5	7,928	58.6
Corson	1,288	3.6	3,998	D	398.6	3,675,545	919	325,133	117.0	363,205	28.6	71.4	2	80.7	6,905	80.1
Custer	612	-1.8	1,387	3.9	49.4	2,213,944	1,596	86,361	26.6	60,392	7.3	92.7	NA	76.9	1,641	37.9
Davison	270	-1.8	584	2.7	212.4	1,983,497	3,398	224,120	107.7	232,538	61.4	38.6	NA	68.7	4,987	60.3
Day	611	7.1	1,051	1.3	456.5	2,779,344	2,645	275,390	184.0	316,661	82.9	17.1	NA	68.7	13,431	79.3
Deuel	335	-1.9	529	0.5	223.8	1,823,780	3,448	207,041	184.9	291,655	37.9	62.1	3	79.5	4,029	73.8
Dewey	1,137	-3.8	3,666	D	195.6	3,555,413	970	259,622	58.7	189,394	23.3	76.7	7	73.2	5,510	83.2
Douglas	275	1.9	701	1.8	214.7	2,607,726	3,721	327,367	144.6	368,954	44.4	55.6	NA	78.3	4,604	76.3
Edmunds	739	6.0	2,124	5.8	569.5	5,223,055	2,460	551,208	237.7	683,029	64.6	35.4	1	85.3	6,569	83.3
Fall River	898	-17.5	2,860	9.3	68.7	2,048,121	716	113,245	87.1	277,347	3.7	96.3	2	81.8	2,368	49.7
Faulk	627	1.9	2,155	D	408.4	5,489,770	2,547	421,205	164.0	563,416	65.9	34.1	2	86.6	12,360	82.8
Grant	426	-0.7	768	5.2	307.7	2,864,773	3,729	336,697	235.4	424,986	50.3	49.7	1	78.5	4,192	69.7
Gregory	562	-11.5	1,136	0.3	226.1	2,134,179	1,879	208,369	93.1	188,004	45.9	54.1	NA	82.6	4,617	80.6
Haakon	1,158	2.1	3,951	D	323.9	3,646,592	923	257,669	77.3	263,949	33.1	66.9	NA	87.0	7,822	84.0
Hamlin	310	-0.3	651	9.0	249.6	2,557,064	3,926	304,618	179.8	377,664	54.1	45.9	1	84.5	3,100	69.3
Hand	895	-1.1	2,211	2.6	578.0	4,545,489	2,056	456,429	224.5	554,210	63.5	36.5	1	82.0	12,357	83.5
Hanson	271	-1.1	814	5.1	226.0	3,516,095	4,322	370,625	132.8	398,778	61.8	38.2	NA	73.9	5,966	76.3
Harding	1,468	0.0	5,539	1.1	184.6	3,683,948	665	228,551	63.4	239,125	12.0	88.0	NA	86.4	6,699	67.2
Hughes	435	1.0	1,381	11.5	263.0	2,611,187	1,891	265,639	70.3	223,095	62.0	38.0	5	84.4	6,354	63.5
Hutchinson	456	-11.2	588	7.3	363.8	2,642,567	4,495	304,494	270.0	348,405	48.6	51.4	3	77.3	9,766	82.5
Hyde	506	-1.7	2,906	D	219.9	4,438,942	1,527	351,062	64.9	372,983	58.6	41.4	NA	87.4	4,401	75.9
Jackson	1,166	0.7	3,714	0.3	185.5	3,248,165	875	164,945	52.4	167,003	14.5	85.5	1	79.3	4,724	67.2
Jerauld	342	2.6	1,400	3.0	219.8	3,348,353	2,391	378,327	112.5	461,242	45.2	54.8	NA	76.6	3,271	80.3
Jones	618	1.0	3,221	D	233.8	3,680,881	1,143	323,434	57.9	301,516	55.6	44.4	NA	81.8	3,245	83.3
Kingsbury	536	2.8	1,035	2.6	391.2	3,941,833	3,810	367,554	257.9	497,790	56.0	44.0	2	82.8	3,492	70.5
Lake	273	4.1	589	8.2	225.6	3,014,550	5,121	299,337	161.9	349,624	61.4	38.6	2	84.0	2,755	76.2
Lawrence	165	3.9	600	4.4	33.6	1,073,421	1,789	103,416	13.1	47,575	14.8	85.2	NA	80.0	452	18.5
Lincoln	295	-19.4	390	2.1	267.9	2,692,014	6,906	189,954	204.8	270,886	59.8	40.2	2	77.5	6,210	70.0
Lyman	951	-7.6	2,297	D	419.2	3,792,074	1,651	300,717	97.0	234,401	56.0	44.0	1	77.1	12,929	89.6
McCook	367	1.2	717	0.0	294.3	3,131,091	4,367	271,011	195.9	382,695	62.6	37.4	NA	82.4	5,726	84.2
McPherson	723	26.2	1,893	1.3	383.9	4,077,571	2,154	363,067	140.2	367,047	45.2	54.8	6	75.7	4,087	85.3
Marshall	525	-1.3	1,045	0.7	343.4	2,939,925	2,814	321,438	270.7	538,147	39.9	60.1	2	83.7	8,489	81.3
Meade	1,999	-1.7	2,394	5.3	394.8	2,277,231	951	169,003	99.2	118,764	11.4	88.6	3	79.2	11,199	52.3
Mellette	753	7.7	3,436	0.7	131.1	3,314,464	965	216,199	45.4	207,411	18.4	81.6	5	81.7	2,321	77.6
Miner	351	-1.7	861	D	239.8	3,042,444	3,533	239,023	126.1	308,963	56.6	43.4	NA	79.7	6,404	79.2
Minnehaha	375	-8.1	366	5.2	318.0	2,362,080	6,449	232,537	253.8	248,073	58.9	41.1	2	87.4	2,507	56.0
Moody	265	4.2	541	3.3	223.5	3,147,674	5,820	296,266	216.1	440,976	47.8	52.2	2	83.9	3,759	59.0
Oglala Lakota	1,116	1.4	5,875	D	88.9	3,960,426	674	147,320	38.7	203,926	20.0	80.0	NA	82.6	3,643	55.8
Pennington	1,147	6.7	1,748	10.7	207.2	1,849,403	1,058	126,171	60.5	92,155	28.0	72.0	NA	83.1	6,415	42.7
Perkins	1,640	0.5	3,895	NA	347.7	3,236,529	831	232,943	84.9	201,646	14.6	85.4	NA	84.3	9,976	79.8
Potter	548	1.9	2,481	1.6	386.5	5,246,162	2,114	546,151	101.9	461,045	82.0	18.0	NA	79.6	7,893	92.3
Roberts	595	-4.5	761	2.4	451.7	2,288,827	3,007	260,731	204.4	261,366	78.1	21.9	7	79.7	8,289	74.9
Sanborn	364	0.9	1,036	0.0	200.4	2,959,610	2,857	265,179	112.1	319,262	46.4	53.6	NA	80.1	2,914	67.2
Spink	961	1.7	1,729	22.3	832.8	5,413,741	3,132	510,061	382.5	687,917	73.7	26.3	1	82.9	20,072	89.6
Stanley	812	2.7	4,722	NA	195.7	4,349,277	921	241,233	50.6	294,256	35.7	64.3	NA	77.9	3,863	76.7
Sully	633	0.7	3,149	23.7	505.7	6,783,106	2,154	612,046	137.2	682,781	74.2	25.8	NA	88.6	10,351	80.1
Todd	880	2.3	3,946	7.8	113.7	3,355,405	850	254,915	53.7	240,619	11.4	88.6	1	82.5	686	57.0

Items 117—132

Table B. States and Counties — Water Use, Wholesale Trade, Retail Trade, and Real Estate

STATE County	Water use, 2015		Wholesale Trade[1], 2012				Retail Trade[2], 2012				Real estate and rental and leasing,[2] 2012			
	Public supply water withdrawn (mil gal/day)	Public supply gallons withdrawn per person per day	Number of establishments	Number of employees	Sales (mil dol)	Average payroll (mil dol)	Number of establishments	Number of employees	Sales (mil dol)	Average payroll (mil dol)	Number of establishments	Number of employees	Sales (mil dol)	Average payroll (mil dol)
	133	134	135	136	137	138	139	140	141	142	143	144	145	146
SOUTH CAROLINA— Cont'd														
Sumter	14.60	135.8	69	635	342.0	28.8	398	4,416	1,096.8	85.4	78	258	28.9	6.4
Union	2.94	105.8	14	102	43.4	4.4	99	905	195.7	16.9	14	134	8.2	3.1
Williamsburg	3.02	92.8	19	249	145.1	8.6	115	927	225.2	18.0	17	45	4.5	1.0
York	20.63	82.1	233	4,335	3,237.0	292.2	656	9,498	2,845.2	218.4	202	717	125.3	25.3
SOUTH DAKOTA	71.95	81.7	1,317	15,827	20,411.1	756.9	3,843	49,867	13,791.8	1,127.3	962	3,526	582.8	105.7
Aurora	0.19	69.5	6	48	65.4	1.5	8	59	10.8	1.1	2	D	D	D
Beadle	2.29	124.6	28	351	615.6	17.8	79	1,084	257.8	23.7	31	155	14.0	2.5
Bennett	0.17	49.7	NA	NA	NA	NA	15	126	32.3	2.4	NA	NA	NA	NA
Bon Homme	0.56	80.2	11	101	76.2	2.9	32	206	47.1	3.7	4	7	0.4	0.1
Brookings	2.77	81.7	29	252	451.6	12.5	121	1,679	375.9	34.7	45	169	21.1	4.4
Brown	3.47	89.5	80	1,048	1,914.6	48.7	201	2,956	809.5	75.0	57	251	31.3	7.0
Brule	0.52	98.5	12	104	102.0	4.3	41	299	99.1	6.4	4	4	0.2	0.1
Buffalo	0.10	47.7	NA	NA	NA	NA	2	D	D	D	NA	NA	NA	NA
Butte	0.52	50.6	6	D	D	D	49	429	157.4	11.4	8	16	1.2	0.4
Campbell	0.08	57.3	5	D	D	D	6	25	10.9	0.4	1	D	D	D
Charles Mix	0.55	58.6	14	182	180.8	5.8	52	445	99.8	7.5	3	D	D	D
Clark	0.16	43.7	8	D	D	D	14	91	34.8	2.0	1	D	D	D
Clay	1.02	73.0	8	44	30.2	1.8	45	665	122.8	11.3	11	20	3.2	0.4
Codington	3.74	133.9	58	773	580.6	36.0	184	2,667	649.1	56.0	50	126	20.3	3.1
Corson	0.18	42.9	4	D	D	D	6	43	15.1	1.1	NA	NA	NA	NA
Custer	0.28	33.2	1	D	D	D	31	261	68.1	4.8	9	16	6.3	0.3
Davison	1.92	96.7	35	D	D	D	130	2,030	530.4	47.3	26	D	D	D
Day	0.44	79.4	9	139	212.7	4.8	29	264	62.2	4.6	2	D	D	D
Deuel	0.17	39.2	6	30	37.6	1.1	23	116	46.1	3.0	1	D	D	D
Dewey	0.33	58.0	5	73	50.1	2.0	14	97	22.0	1.2	4	22	0.9	0.2
Douglas	0.18	60.5	6	D	D	D	18	119	36.4	1.9	2	D	D	D
Edmunds	0.26	65.0	13	202	472.5	8.8	16	126	44.4	2.7	4	6	0.2	0.0
Fall River	0.66	96.1	3	D	D	D	31	239	68.5	4.1	7	11	1.1	0.2
Faulk	0.15	64.2	10	48	113.5	2.4	13	95	29.6	2.2	1	D	D	D
Grant	0.63	88.2	13	129	193.2	6.2	46	501	127.5	10.9	9	18	2.2	0.3
Gregory	0.26	61.9	6	27	39.7	1.0	29	221	67.0	4.5	2	D	D	D
Haakon	0.11	59.1	8	102	232.1	2.7	16	99	29.0	2.0	1	D	D	D
Hamlin	0.41	67.8	11	142	149.8	7.7	18	117	38.5	2.6	2	D	D	D
Hand	0.21	62.7	11	158	89.1	5.0	21	186	36.2	2.8	1	D	D	D
Hanson	0.09	26.6	7	D	D	D	4	32	6.2	0.5	1	D	D	D
Harding	0.03	23.7	NA	NA	NA	NA	7	33	11.4	0.6	NA	NA	NA	NA
Hughes	2.67	152.1	23	D	D	D	105	1,393	347.2	30.6	30	D	D	D
Hutchinson	0.39	53.4	28	336	480.0	12.5	41	321	81.1	6.2	2	D	D	D
Hyde	0.11	78.7	5	58	173.1	2.9	8	97	21.3	1.3	1	D	D	D
Jackson	0.13	39.1	2	D	D	D	14	118	33.6	1.8	NA	NA	NA	NA
Jerauld	0.54	270.4	5	D	D	D	9	65	21.3	1.5	2	D	D	D
Jones	0.05	54.1	2	D	D	D	12	87	32.8	2.0	NA	NA	NA	NA
Kingsbury	0.22	44.1	8	112	240.5	5.2	23	141	34.1	2.5	2	D	D	D
Lake	0.81	64.2	17	198	371.4	11.5	46	491	162.3	12.2	12	28	2.3	0.4
Lawrence	2.35	94.7	19	52	38.8	2.1	142	1,380	434.0	35.2	63	184	22.2	4.6
Lincoln	1.02	19.3	55	390	667.6	19.5	126	1,571	490.6	45.9	54	268	39.2	8.8
Lyman	0.22	56.8	4	D	D	D	16	301	54.5	5.0	1	D	D	D
McCook	0.71	126.8	10	73	100.0	3.4	24	161	52.1	2.9	6	D	D	D
McPherson	0.13	53.8	2	D	D	D	10	61	14.2	1.1	1	D	D	D
Marshall	0.22	46.1	10	60	69.1	2.5	24	194	74.3	4.6	1	D	D	D
Meade	1.42	52.6	21	D	D	D	78	615	211.0	16.2	23	75	11.6	1.9
Mellette	0.09	43.9	NA	NA	NA	NA	7	56	11.6	0.8	1	D	D	D
Miner	0.11	49.2	4	D	D	D	13	65	17.8	1.3	2	D	D	D
Minnehaha	19.65	94.7	359	5,704	3,841.7	291.7	798	14,467	4,264.7	332.8	229	1,189	254.0	44.9
Moody	0.49	76.2	4	31	18.8	1.6	20	188	50.5	3.0	5	5	0.5	0.1
Oglala Lakota	1.10	76.5	1	D	D	D	10	189	51.4	3.2	NA	NA	NA	NA
Pennington	10.62	97.7	158	1,858	1,248.7	83.0	574	8,278	2,250.8	198.6	160	554	97.2	15.8
Perkins	0.16	53.0	5	D	D	D	19	108	24.8	2.2	3	D	D	D
Potter	0.20	86.2	7	94	577.3	5.3	17	123	21.8	1.6	2	D	D	D
Roberts	0.58	56.3	14	101	421.8	4.8	41	359	112.5	6.6	2	D	D	D
Sanborn	0.13	55.2	4	19	25.5	0.8	5	D	D	D	NA	NA	NA	NA
Spink	0.52	79.7	18	202	491.8	11.6	23	184	46.1	3.6	3	4	0.6	0.1
Stanley	0.32	108.3	3	D	D	D	15	133	53.2	3.8	4	D	D	D
Sully	0.00	0.0	5	D	D	D	11	88	42.6	2.4	3	D	D	D
Todd	0.42	42.2	1	D	D	D	15	196	43.0	3.0	3	D	D	D

1 Merchant wholesalers, except manufacturers' sales branches and offices.   2. Employer establishments.

Table B. States and Counties — Professional Services, Manufacturing, and Accommodation and Food Services

STATE County	Professional, scientific, and technical services, 2012				Manufacturing, 2012				Accommodation and food services, 2012			
	Number of establish-ments	Number of employees	Sales (mil dol)	Average payroll (mil dol)	Number of establish-ments	Number of employees	Receipts (mil dol)	Annual payroll (mil dol)	Number of establis-hments	Number of employees	Receipts (mil dol)	Annual payroll (mil dol)
	147	148	149	150	151	152	153	154	155	156	157	158
SOUTH CAROLINA—Cont'd												
Sumter	126	714	75.8	23.2	71	5,524	1,817.5	214.6	158	2,951	127.0	34.9
Union	22	100	5.7	1.8	28	1,483	524.5	63.7	36	485	21.0	6.0
Williamsburg	26	95	10.5	2.8	35	2,110	1,778.0	97.2	27	D	D	D
York	455	2,240	297.2	102.9	213	8,310	3,111.1	439.6	392	7,094	336.9	89.6
SOUTH DAKOTA	1,822	11,144	1,315.4	482.3	1,025	41,931	16,882.6	1,764.7	2,363	37,974	1,873.7	514.2
Aurora	8	D	D	D	5	44	D	1.5	14	35	1.6	0.4
Beadle	28	114	11.0	4.0	31	1,646	495.1	55.7	48	525	21.7	5.4
Bennett	4	5	0.3	0.1	NA	NA	NA	NA	5	46	1.6	0.4
Bon Homme	6	20	1.8	0.5	13	320	D	11.6	14	65	2.4	0.5
Brookings	71	348	43.3	16.2	40	4,565	2,282.1	206.1	84	1,540	55.9	16.0
Brown	80	430	54.7	18.4	40	2,827	D	114.8	108	1,951	81.1	23.8
Brule	22	41	3.3	1.2	3	12	4.6	0.5	24	209	11.4	2.7
Buffalo	1	D	D	D	NA	NA	NA	NA	1	D	D	D
Butte	21	84	6.5	2.5	16	123	60.9	5.2	30	257	11.4	3.3
Campbell	4	7	0.3	0.1	3	48	D	D	7	D	D	D
Charles Mix	10	52	4.5	1.4	8	86	D	3.1	21	438	19.8	7.2
Clark	6	18	2.4	0.4	8	121	D	3.6	9	20	1.3	0.4
Clay	14	50	2.8	1.1	10	275	D	11.5	43	837	28.4	7.5
Codington	72	294	46.2	10.6	78	3,388	1,029.9	140.7	92	1,884	82.6	22.6
Corson	NA	NA	NA	NA	NA	NA	NA	NA	3	D	D	D
Custer	19	D	D	D	12	43	D	1.2	54	366	31.1	7.9
Davison	48	D	D	D	39	1,676	D	75.4	67	1,365	55.9	15.2
Day	5	24	2.2	0.7	13	219	61.5	9.4	17	168	5.2	1.4
Deuel	5	D	D	D	4	D	D	D	13	88	4.3	1.0
Dewey	4	11	0.4	0.1	NA	NA	NA	NA	6	18	1.7	0.2
Douglas	5	10	0.8	0.2	9	105	14.4	3.1	5	D	D	D
Edmunds	6	21	2.6	0.7	5	63	D	2.5	9	72	2.3	0.7
Fall River	13	49	3.1	1.1	8	24	5.5	0.8	37	336	13.5	3.5
Faulk	3	D	D	D	3	13	D	D	13	49	2.5	0.3
Grant	14	46	4.7	1.6	14	580	844.6	25.9	25	286	10.5	2.3
Gregory	8	26	2.3	0.6	6	59	D	D	19	95	3.8	0.8
Haakon	5	14	1.7	0.5	4	62	D	D	7	36	1.6	0.3
Hamlin	3	D	D	D	8	233	D	8.9	11	33	1.4	0.2
Hand	9	30	3.5	1.1	6	40	D	1.6	13	95	3.0	0.6
Hanson	2	D	D	D	3	54	D	D	4	15	0.7	0.1
Harding	NA	NA	NA	NA	NA	NA	NA	NA	3	23	1.0	0.2
Hughes	53	279	35.9	12.3	6	44	D	2.1	51	984	40.9	11.7
Hutchinson	11	30	2.8	1.0	11	214	76.8	8.2	18	D	D	D
Hyde	2	D	D	D	NA	NA	NA	NA	1	D	D	D
Jackson	1	D	D	D	NA	NA	NA	NA	10	39	4.5	1.0
Jerauld	6	8	1.9	0.2	NA	NA	NA	NA	6	42	2.6	0.7
Jones	2	D	D	D	NA	NA	NA	NA	14	78	4.3	1.2
Kingsbury	7	20	2.2	0.5	12	401	75.1	14.3	13	101	3.5	0.9
Lake	29	126	18.1	4.6	21	872	374.0	32.1	36	463	14.3	4.0
Lawrence	69	263	24.8	8.5	41	445	130.9	17.1	137	2,704	197.1	46.4
Lincoln	82	D	D	D	69	2,313	D	97.6	53	D	D	D
Lyman	1	D	D	D	NA	NA	NA	NA	14	173	9.7	2.5
McCook	10	D	D	D	4	8	D	0.2	18	D	D	D
McPherson	4	D	D	D	7	47	4.7	1.6	5	20	0.7	0.2
Marshall	11	21	2.1	0.6	8	355	174.7	16.3	13	115	3.7	1.0
Meade	50	D	D	D	35	225	D	8.3	74	671	43.6	10.9
Mellette	1	D	D	D	NA	NA	NA	NA	4	10	0.4	0.1
Miner	3	16	1.1	0.4	4	32	D	1.3	8	D	D	D
Minnehaha	480	4,148	476.7	201.5	176	10,763	3,612.6	479.0	444	10,517	493.8	147.2
Moody	9	16	1.1	0.4	11	326	88.5	14.1	15	D	D	D
Oglala Lakota	2	D	D	D	NA	NA	NA	NA	10	305	20.3	5.9
Pennington	303	1,928	223.8	76.8	117	2,115	524.3	85.9	352	6,418	351.8	98.3
Perkins	5	11	0.8	0.2	4	D	D	D	8	D	D	D
Potter	3	D	D	D	4	44	D	1.6	12	65	4.8	1.0
Roberts	15	31	3.7	1.0	11	272	D	7.3	18	171	4.6	1.0
Sanborn	7	20	1.9	0.4	NA	NA	NA	NA	6	25	1.2	0.2
Spink	8	36	4.8	1.4	7	72	D	3.3	13	126	4.8	1.2
Stanley	4	D	D	D	3	D	D	D	13	D	D	D
Sully	2	D	D	D	NA	NA	NA	NA	8	D	D	D
Todd	2	D	D	D	3	37	7.0	1.4	3	19	0.6	0.2

Table B. States and Counties — Health Care and Social Assistance, Other Services, Nonemployer Businesses, and Residential Construction

STATE County	Health care and social assistance, 2012				Other services, 2012				Nonemployer businesses, 2016		Value of residential construction authorized by building permits, 2018	
	Number of establish-ments	Number of employees	Receipts (mil dol)	Annual payroll (mil dol)	Number of establish-ments	Number of employees	Receipts (mil dol)	Annual payroll (mil dol)	Number	Receipts (mil dol)	New construction ($1,000)	Number of housing units
	159	160	161	162	163	164	165	166	167	168	169	170
SOUTH CAROLINA—Cont'd												
Sumter	188	5,504	471.1	184.1	130	996	77.4	27.8	6,047	207.7	35,594	279
Union	30	D	D	D	30	132	8.0	2.3	1,094	34.5	5,132	26
Williamsburg	55	797	55.3	22.5	35	D	D	D	1,696	49.8	13,939	103
York	445	8,980	897.0	307.6	283	2,070	188.3	61.7	17,228	677.0	872,144	2,692
SOUTH DAKOTA	2,298	63,494	6,211.7	2,558.4	1,805	8,371	939.5	214.1	65,222	3,046.0	854,338	4,963
Aurora	10	D	D	D	6	D	D	D	240	8.7	1,707	7
Beadle	50	1,409	87.8	40.4	51	175	16.5	4.2	1,038	47.5	3,373	17
Bennett	5	156	9.1	5.1	2	D	D	D	192	5.6	175	3
Bon Homme	21	367	22.0	9.1	14	D	D	D	479	19.5	1,856	10
Brookings	75	1,396	99.0	43.4	66	354	64.9	9.1	2,103	96.5	30,362	244
Brown	112	2,867	240.5	116.1	79	D	D	D	2,877	137.7	5,601	69
Brule	24	457	24.7	10.8	17	69	8.8	1.9	481	23.1	1,625	15
Buffalo	3	D	D	D	1	D	D	D	35	0.5	0	0
Butte	31	282	18.8	8.1	22	D	D	D	867	37.4	9,045	22
Campbell	4	25	0.8	0.5	2	D	D	D	138	5.5	0	0
Charles Mix	22	524	31.9	14.5	26	D	D	D	692	26.0	3,427	16
Clark	10	140	6.1	2.4	11	D	D	D	283	13.3	3,179	10
Clay	30	721	50.5	17.8	24	113	12.1	2.5	856	38.3	40,194	273
Codington	89	1,691	191.5	65.1	79	327	31.2	7.8	2,129	90.1	22,074	179
Corson	6	19	1.0	0.6	NA	NA	NA	NA	135	4.5	0	0
Custer	20	D	D	D	16	78	6.6	2.1	886	39.6	14,043	64
Davison	79	D	D	D	52	D	D	D	1,472	68.3	7,836	40
Day	19	291	18.1	6.3	14	D	D	D	493	17.9	3,133	18
Deuel	5	161	10.6	4.2	5	D	D	D	380	16.5	300	1
Dewey	9	149	18.7	7.2	6	D	D	D	253	11.1	0	0
Douglas	7	265	13.6	6.7	11	28	4.3	0.7	264	11.3	1,467	9
Edmunds	11	197	8.8	3.8	6	D	D	D	381	21.9	2,536	14
Fall River	22	D	D	D	16	67	4.5	1.1	609	18.5	1,109	10
Faulk	4	D	D	D	5	D	D	D	216	10.8	2,705	11
Grant	24	415	30.1	11.4	18	72	7.3	1.5	641	24.5	1,685	10
Gregory	15	317	18.1	7.4	12	D	D	D	525	16.7	742	3
Haakon	7	D	D	D	4	17	1.6	0.5	233	11.7	0	0
Hamlin	12	198	6.5	2.9	7	16	2.3	0.4	442	18.7	8,577	47
Hand	8	229	13.5	6.8	11	19	1.5	0.2	328	17.3	450	1
Hanson	2	D	D	D	1	D	D	D	294	11.3	1,857	13
Harding	4	D	D	D	1	D	D	D	161	7.4	233	2
Hughes	58	1,269	110.1	45.7	76	347	50.8	11.6	1,501	60.8	4,860	22
Hutchinson	17	651	40.2	18.8	14	D	D	D	589	19.2	1,542	6
Hyde	3	D	D	D	2	D	D	D	127	6.6	0	0
Jackson	1	D	D	D	5	10	0.8	0.1	200	6.3	0	0
Jerauld	4	131	9.6	3.8	7	16	1.4	0.3	161	7.4	430	2
Jones	2	D	D	D	2	D	D	D	107	5.4	0	6
Kingsbury	14	240	13.2	5.3	13	33	3.0	0.6	510	21.8	2,898	18
Lake	33	694	40.7	18.5	20	D	D	D	1,110	52.1	10,416	38
Lawrence	87	1,401	126.3	54.9	58	233	21.0	5.3	2,454	109.8	62,413	208
Lincoln	132	3,237	232.2	96.7	80	D	D	D	4,887	262.7	36,528	202
Lyman	2	D	D	D	3	D	D	D	246	10.7	565	3
McCook	17	251	13.5	5.2	13	D	D	D	517	22.6	4,911	22
McPherson	7	53	3.2	1.1	6	D	D	D	205	10.0	600	8
Marshall	13	175	10.7	4.0	7	27	3.7	0.8	348	16.4	2,526	12
Meade	45	D	D	D	50	151	20.8	4.1	2,218	90.2	28,879	148
Mellette	2	D	D	D	1	D	D	D	103	4.3	254	2
Miner	9	156	7.2	3.3	4	12	1.3	0.4	202	7.9	262	3
Minnehaha	462	20,372	2,348.8	970.6	375	2,326	256.5	67.7	13,344	706.7	342,658	2,133
Moody	15	203	13.9	6.0	6	D	D	D	427	20.5	1,582	6
Oglala Lakota	13	285	30.3	10.4	3	11	0.8	0.2	NA	NA	NA	NA
Pennington	343	D	D	D	268	1,572	193.3	39.2	8,071	372.9	99,753	622
Perkins	16	142	7.8	3.4	16	38	3.3	0.9	256	9.0	0	0
Potter	13	70	6.4	2.8	8	D	D	D	243	14.9	0	0
Roberts	23	532	32.7	14.8	16	42	3.2	0.8	643	22.7	6,660	30
Sanborn	4	D	D	D	4	D	D	D	181	7.6	500	3
Spink	17	359	18.3	8.3	12	D	D	D	569	25.3	2,835	12
Stanley	3	D	D	D	11	D	D	D	310	17.4	3,765	12
Sully	3	D	D	D	2	D	D	D	192	9.4	3,380	12
Todd	7	283	37.6	16.2	3	7	0.4	0.1	208	4.7	50	1

Table B. States and Counties — Government Employment and Payroll, and Local Government Finances

STATE County	Government employment and payroll, 2012									Local government finances, 2012				
			March payroll (percent of total)							General revenue				
												Taxes		
													Per capita[1] (dollars)	
	Full-time equivalent employees	March payroll (dollars)	Adminis-tration, judicial, and legal	Police and corrections	Fire protection	Highways and transpor-tation	Health and welfare	Natural resources and utilities	Education and libraries	Total (mil dol)	Inter-govern-mental (mil dol)	Total (mil dol)	Total	Property
	171	172	173	174	175	176	177	178	179	180	181	182	183	184
SOUTH CAROLINA— Cont'd														
Sumter	6,341	17,021,292	4.2	6.1	1.7	1.8	1.6	3.3	80.4	271.8	124.5	114.5	1,060	719
Union	1,425	4,994,326	5.2	7.0	0.2	1.0	39.3	5.0	41.2	156.7	60.9	39.0	1,380	1,287
Williamsburg	1,213	3,312,602	4.2	7.9	1.6	5.2	5.0	3.6	71.8	89.9	50.4	26.4	785	649
York	6,735	24,865,548	7.3	9.2	2.7	1.3	1.7	7.5	67.9	705.5	262.8	328.3	1,399	1,188
SOUTH DAKOTA	X	X	X	X	X	X	X	X	X	X	X	X	X	X
Aurora	140	322,496	9.8	3.3	0.0	8.6	1.1	1.5	66.8	11.3	4.4	5.5	2,022	1,782
Beadle	584	1,871,207	6.9	12.0	1.9	6.5	2.6	6.6	60.1	58.6	17.5	28.6	1,609	1,176
Bennett	147	346,133	7.8	7.3	0.0	5.0	1.7	2.9	72.7	11.6	7.6	3.2	943	754
Bon Homme	246	662,539	7.1	6.3	0.0	9.5	0.7	8.4	67.8	20.1	7.9	9.7	1,383	1,174
Brookings	1,332	4,813,095	7.8	6.0	0.3	3.2	25.9	9.5	35.5	157.9	19.7	49.9	1,530	1,086
Brown	1,246	3,689,884	7.8	11.6	5.1	6.3	2.4	10.7	55.2	123.6	32.4	67.9	1,819	1,288
Brule	271	673,549	6.8	6.7	0.0	5.9	4.3	5.0	71.0	23.2	8.9	9.4	1,779	1,325
Buffalo	8	22,528	50.6	21.1	0.0	22.9	5.5	0.0	0.0	0.8	0.4	0.4	192	185
Butte	371	1,001,042	7.3	7.8	0.0	4.9	3.0	11.2	62.8	30.3	11.5	12.6	1,233	945
Campbell	48	126,932	22.4	4.9	0.0	20.2	1.5	5.8	43.7	4.7	1.5	2.4	1,718	1,442
Charles Mix	442	1,244,510	5.7	6.5	0.0	4.7	3.0	7.5	71.5	43.1	25.6	13.6	1,477	1,206
Clark	179	456,728	7.7	2.5	0.0	10.5	1.0	1.7	74.5	13.4	3.7	8.2	2,276	2,032
Clay	330	1,043,813	10.4	13.3	0.4	5.7	5.0	14.2	48.1	31.3	7.5	16.6	1,174	904
Codington	1,090	3,894,294	3.6	7.6	3.8	3.8	1.7	14.6	62.8	104.2	32.6	43.8	1,587	1,028
Corson	271	904,657	3.0	2.6	0.0	2.6	0.1	2.2	88.7	21.6	17.7	2.5	623	555
Custer	232	684,633	12.9	6.8	0.0	6.7	2.7	5.5	65.3	24.6	3.9	16.5	1,973	1,606
Davison	843	2,644,986	5.7	9.5	3.2	6.0	2.9	7.3	64.6	80.5	25.5	35.2	1,779	1,145
Day	198	482,927	10.0	8.0	0.0	11.7	0.7	5.9	61.4	17.2	6.4	8.5	1,510	1,240
Deuel	127	393,062	16.5	8.2	0.0	17.0	0.4	1.9	51.5	10.7	2.3	7.0	1,607	1,351
Dewey	249	617,513	9.8	3.1	0.0	5.4	0.5	3.0	76.8	18.8	15.2	2.6	474	405
Douglas	103	390,547	16.4	4.6	0.0	12.5	2.5	2.3	56.5	11.6	4.6	5.2	1,737	1,444
Edmunds	292	715,008	7.1	3.1	0.0	7.8	38.4	2.4	38.6	22.4	5.8	9.6	2,374	2,086
Fall River	314	938,839	8.8	7.6	0.0	7.0	1.0	10.3	60.3	26.8	9.4	11.3	1,614	1,321
Faulk	160	527,286	5.6	4.5	0.5	2.3	56.7	2.0	27.9	16.8	4.1	5.1	2,160	1,927
Grant	245	716,131	9.0	6.4	0.0	8.2	1.2	3.8	68.1	23.2	5.9	13.7	1,887	1,505
Gregory	203	581,904	10.2	4.7	0.0	9.2	1.1	2.4	71.6	14.3	5.6	7.1	1,664	1,354
Haakon	81	213,827	13.1	5.5	0.0	16.5	0.4	2.6	58.3	6.5	2.3	3.6	1,879	1,523
Hamlin	251	731,928	6.3	2.3	0.0	5.0	20.2	5.1	60.7	25.7	8.6	10.9	1,835	1,641
Hand	128	359,355	11.0	4.7	0.0	11.4	0.2	8.6	63.0	11.0	2.9	6.5	1,921	1,624
Hanson	122	328,179	9.5	3.1	0.0	9.0	0.2	1.6	71.2	10.7	3.6	5.8	1,710	1,577
Harding	80	208,002	15.2	4.0	0.0	10.1	0.3	2.9	63.3	10.2	6.4	3.1	2,343	2,124
Hughes	626	1,983,352	7.7	12.8	0.3	6.2	2.7	9.5	57.1	62.6	25.1	25.5	1,463	989
Hutchinson	312	1,009,609	5.2	3.1	0.0	6.2	0.4	1.3	82.1	25.8	8.2	14.2	1,970	1,677
Hyde	72	227,594	10.2	2.5	0.0	8.4	0.0	1.6	77.3	7.5	1.8	4.3	2,988	2,608
Jackson	115	288,915	10.3	3.2	0.0	5.1	1.0	2.8	74.9	7.4	4.2	2.7	835	680
Jerauld	90	237,116	13.3	5.9	0.0	10.4	1.6	8.1	58.2	8.7	2.5	4.4	2,169	1,851
Jones	52	131,432	19.8	7.6	0.0	10.4	0.0	7.8	54.5	4.5	1.4	2.5	2,475	1,992
Kingsbury	244	603,141	5.3	3.1	0.0	8.6	0.5	3.3	72.9	19.8	5.2	12.1	2,312	2,048
Lake	462	1,563,214	5.5	6.2	2.0	5.6	2.5	13.5	62.4	39.3	10.2	19.2	1,628	1,310
Lawrence	692	2,469,903	12.9	15.3	0.3	6.8	1.3	10.2	51.2	81.2	20.9	45.9	1,883	1,338
Lincoln	1,033	2,768,370	9.1	4.4	0.0	3.8	0.9	2.0	77.7	90.9	26.1	51.6	1,069	947
Lyman	133	337,375	11.7	3.3	0.0	7.7	3.0	3.7	67.3	10.3	4.3	4.8	1,278	913
McCook	186	538,315	9.8	4.8	0.0	8.7	1.8	2.2	71.0	17.3	5.5	9.8	1,740	1,508
McPherson	123	336,878	14.7	3.6	0.0	5.4	0.4	2.0	72.6	9.5	2.9	5.6	2,295	1,958
Marshall	176	472,048	9.8	7.5	0.0	9.0	0.7	2.0	69.8	18.3	6.1	9.2	1,978	1,696
Meade	671	2,100,253	11.4	12.6	0.3	4.8	2.3	5.9	59.2	71.1	19.6	32.1	1,233	1,036
Mellette	114	303,196	8.5	5.7	0.0	4.1	0.4	0.8	78.5	7.4	5.3	1.6	750	650
Miner	106	326,794	11.4	7.0	0.0	13.4	1.2	6.7	59.0	10.3	2.7	6.3	2,717	2,393
Minnehaha	5,678	21,221,355	6.2	10.8	4.4	3.8	2.4	6.0	65.2	616.7	171.2	329.3	1,882	1,201
Moody	202	536,978	10.4	8.8	0.0	7.4	2.5	6.9	57.6	17.4	5.8	9.2	1,422	1,220
Oglala Lakota	423	1,199,764	0.8	0.3	0.0	0.8	0.1	0.1	98.0	32.0	30.4	0.8	60	34
Pennington	4,148	12,984,488	4.9	10.8	1.8	2.6	2.5	4.4	67.5	388.6	116.3	197.4	1,891	1,300
Perkins	118	328,373	10.9	5.6	0.1	9.6	2.5	6.3	62.1	12.4	5.3	5.7	1,878	1,506
Potter	120	307,306	11.7	3.9	0.0	9.7	0.1	2.7	67.9	9.5	3.0	5.6	2,367	2,004
Roberts	404	1,039,666	5.9	3.7	0.0	5.7	2.4	2.0	77.9	33.8	13.8	12.6	1,220	986
Sanborn	116	293,325	10.3	3.6	0.0	17.9	1.1	1.1	64.9	9.9	3.4	5.4	2,323	2,120
Spink	406	1,160,424	5.6	3.5	0.0	5.0	32.9	2.4	50.2	35.9	9.8	13.7	2,078	1,808
Stanley	129	372,565	10.6	5.4	0.0	9.7	1.2	9.7	61.3	12.9	5.5	6.2	2,082	1,623
Sully	83	220,042	14.4	4.9	0.0	19.2	0.0	3.4	56.8	8.2	1.3	6.2	4,370	3,985
Todd	452	1,136,660	0.9	0.9	0.0	1.9	0.0	0.5	95.5	33.5	29.5	2.7	275	165

1. Based on the resident population estimated as of July 1 of the year shown.

Table B. States and Counties — **Local Government Finances, Government Employment, and Income Taxes**

STATE County	Local government finances, 2012 (cont.)									Government employment, 2017			Individual income tax returns, 2016		
	Direct general expenditure							Debt outstanding							
			Percent of total for:												
	Total (mil dol)	Per capita[1] (dollars)	Education	Health and hospitals	Police protection	Public welfare	Highways	Total (mil dol)	Per capita[1] (dollars)	Federal civilian	Federal military	State and local	Number of returns	Mean adjusted gross income	Mean income tax
	185	186	187	188	189	190	191	192	193	194	195	196	197	198	199
SOUTH CAROLINA— Cont'd															
Sumter	256.2	2,371	55.2	1.2	7.1	0.3	2.5	245.3	2,270	1,207	5,251	5,342	46,710	42,219	3,876
Union	153.8	5,444	47.1	30.4	4.0	0.0	1.3	64.7	2,291	53	103	1,821	11,080	37,341	2,888
Williamsburg	98.8	2,939	50.1	2.9	6.6	0.2	2.4	85.8	2,551	364	115	1,769	12,870	31,516	2,387
York	690.0	2,941	56.4	0.2	5.6	0.3	5.3	1,179.4	5,026	467	1,003	12,356	118,350	65,656	8,064
SOUTH DAKOTA	X	X	X	X	X	X	X	X	X	11,380	8,112	66,292	415,760	61,436	8,224
Aurora	10.8	3,945	58.5	0.4	3.0	0.2	16.5	1.6	575	14	15	168	1,360	43,231	4,115
Beadle	52.6	2,962	43.9	0.4	4.7	0.5	16.7	29.0	1,634	285	101	1,041	8,630	50,617	5,507
Bennett	9.4	2,748	64.2	0.1	4.4	0.1	6.8	1.2	356	34	20	354	1,180	30,956	2,845
Bon Homme	17.7	2,516	62.3	1.6	3.0	0.2	15.6	31.0	4,403	27	32	574	2,750	45,912	4,866
Brookings	154.9	4,746	25.5	21.6	2.6	0.2	6.1	90.0	2,758	134	183	5,817	13,920	62,560	8,026
Brown	117.1	3,136	36.3	1.3	5.8	0.9	19.9	125.1	3,352	469	219	2,742	19,100	61,411	8,316
Brule	20.0	3,782	59.2	3.2	3.6	0.4	11.2	7.8	1,479	36	30	366	2,540	45,098	5,245
Buffalo	0.8	373	0.0	0.1	9.4	0.1	48.9	0.0	0	151	12	278	670	23,576	1,281
Butte	26.8	2,623	51.6	0.6	5.1	0.1	7.2	14.4	1,409	46	58	593	4,770	45,445	4,545
Campbell	4.2	2,981	36.0	0.6	4.6	0.0	22.5	0.4	298	3	8	72	740	44,711	5,108
Charles Mix	36.8	3,989	58.4	1.9	2.5	0.1	9.6	8.3	898	196	51	1,100	3,720	47,909	5,794
Clark	12.5	3,493	42.0	1.9	2.9	0.4	29.1	4.5	1,242	25	18	239	1,660	51,080	6,108
Clay	28.7	2,034	37.0	1.5	8.1	0.3	17.6	30.7	2,172	27	71	3,423	5,310	51,707	5,743
Codington	112.1	4,060	54.8	0.3	6.8	0.1	7.1	80.3	2,910	190	160	2,044	13,900	56,410	6,983
Corson	23.4	5,738	86.2	0.1	2.0	0.0	5.0	0.0	0	76	24	558	1,280	29,974	2,101
Custer	27.8	3,331	34.7	5.4	4.4	0.4	11.1	31.7	3,801	163	49	401	4,290	58,247	6,257
Davison	79.9	4,042	50.0	4.3	4.8	0.5	9.4	39.7	2,006	117	109	1,252	9,820	54,250	6,583
Day	17.9	3,188	37.1	0.7	3.2	0.3	29.6	10.3	1,840	62	31	391	2,750	46,569	5,437
Deuel	11.0	2,511	38.7	3.1	3.5	0.4	20.6	3.8	861	23	24	233	2,060	50,601	5,888
Dewey	20.6	3,719	81.8	0.2	1.5	0.0	11.1	1.0	189	405	34	1,147	2,470	35,775	3,483
Douglas	13.1	4,408	29.4	0.6	2.1	0.1	14.6	4.2	1,429	25	16	191	1,380	46,209	4,949
Edmunds	19.8	4,926	31.7	14.2	1.7	12.6	18.5	5.7	1,415	22	20	335	1,770	62,245	9,112
Fall River	27.6	3,962	45.4	2.5	5.3	0.5	9.0	13.8	1,973	485	37	602	3,440	46,564	4,567
Faulk	15.6	6,550	19.0	49.2	1.5	0.1	14.5	9.5	4,005	17	11	127	980	52,587	6,149
Grant	24.5	3,375	44.5	0.6	3.4	0.2	18.1	33.2	4,576	30	40	342	3,680	52,789	5,994
Gregory	13.6	3,189	55.3	0.9	3.5	0.2	17.9	4.1	966	27	24	245	2,020	43,832	4,745
Haakon	5.9	3,054	42.6	5.8	5.5	0.1	21.5	1.1	586	19	11	99	980	45,205	5,473
Hamlin	22.8	3,851	49.4	1.4	2.0	13.5	15.0	12.1	2,042	16	33	468	2,640	53,964	6,250
Hand	10.6	3,130	41.2	0.5	4.5	0.1	26.1	19.0	5,596	18	19	216	1,660	51,866	6,516
Hanson	11.6	3,434	65.3	0.5	1.6	0.3	16.2	6.0	1,773	4	17	196	1,970	56,515	6,277
Harding	10.1	7,661	50.7	0.5	2.4	0.4	25.4	8.7	6,600	23	7	96	590	54,778	4,998
Hughes	62.3	3,568	31.3	0.8	5.8	0.2	8.1	67.4	3,862	270	99	3,741	8,970	59,968	7,263
Hutchinson	27.0	3,751	58.0	0.4	2.3	0.4	18.5	16.9	2,349	40	38	425	3,380	51,019	5,375
Hyde	6.9	4,834	48.1	0.3	2.2	0.2	22.1	3.4	2,354	7	7	176	650	47,538	5,651
Jackson	6.7	2,101	64.9	0.5	3.6	0.1	11.3	0.1	43	104	19	250	1,090	31,672	2,293
Jerauld	8.5	4,170	41.2	4.0	3.2	0.4	21.3	7.5	3,682	11	11	123	870	46,753	4,630
Jones	4.6	4,509	46.3	0.5	2.9	0.0	21.7	0.2	192	9	5	124	490	37,673	4,443
Kingsbury	18.6	3,559	52.1	0.8	2.8	0.4	20.1	7.7	1,482	34	27	276	2,590	53,549	6,565
Lake	36.5	3,105	51.8	0.5	4.3	0.3	14.7	90.9	7,721	58	69	1,158	6,770	64,591	8,238
Lawrence	77.3	3,170	35.3	0.4	7.0	0.2	6.3	116.0	4,753	171	141	1,861	12,610	62,096	8,121
Lincoln	90.3	1,871	58.4	0.4	3.1	0.3	11.9	267.9	5,547	56	364	1,638	27,880	94,073	15,825
Lyman	9.2	2,439	55.2	0.9	3.3	0.2	15.6	1.7	440	81	22	604	1,620	39,812	4,442
McCook	15.8	2,821	51.5	2.0	4.3	1.1	18.5	9.6	1,716	24	30	277	2,690	56,003	6,452
McPherson	9.4	3,852	48.9	0.7	3.2	0.2	24.6	1.4	581	11	12	161	980	47,435	4,607
Marshall	17.1	3,652	35.5	1.2	4.5	1.6	22.5	18.4	3,939	23	26	339	2,080	47,369	5,298
Meade	75.4	2,895	52.2	1.6	5.1	0.0	8.9	43.4	1,666	1,515	161	1,363	13,550	52,825	5,580
Mellette	6.7	3,182	72.5	0.9	4.5	0.0	7.6	0.1	43	11	12	217	720	27,953	2,521
Miner	10.4	4,490	36.7	2.2	3.5	0.3	27.2	3.8	1,655	17	12	147	1,100	49,656	5,042
Minnehaha	640.2	3,657	45.9	1.7	5.7	0.6	9.2	652.2	3,726	2,650	1,075	8,932	96,930	68,277	9,672
Moody	17.2	2,661	47.1	1.8	6.6	1.5	18.2	8.8	1,373	111	37	673	2,950	53,367	6,334
Oglala Lakota	33.5	2,386	97.4	0.1	0.3	0.0	1.0	0.0	1	622	82	2,460	4,100	29,419	1,815
Pennington	412.8	3,956	45.6	1.3	6.0	0.5	8.9	401.2	3,844	1,480	3,831	6,551	55,440	59,858	7,806
Perkins	12.2	4,029	44.2	1.4	4.2	1.5	18.1	0.6	203	25	17	229	1,380	40,679	4,481
Potter	9.5	4,047	43.5	2.0	3.4	0.0	20.1	1.6	667	16	13	161	1,200	54,792	7,777
Roberts	30.3	2,938	57.6	0.5	2.8	0.1	10.2	9.6	930	194	58	1,351	4,360	45,460	4,736
Sanborn	8.5	3,645	45.3	1.1	3.6	0.1	31.4	2.8	1,215	12	13	163	1,110	44,451	4,279
Spink	34.6	5,228	34.4	27.8	3.5	0.4	14.0	21.8	3,298	36	35	926	2,950	53,845	6,735
Stanley	13.1	4,413	38.6	0.8	6.2	0.1	30.5	9.4	3,157	11	17	198	1,600	61,336	8,723
Sully	7.0	4,938	44.2	0.2	5.0	0.4	25.5	3.3	2,332	10	8	114	730	29,067	10,345
Todd	28.4	2,854	92.0	0.1	0.7	0.0	2.9	1.4	137	252	58	2,121	2,800	30,932	2,095

1. Based on the resident population estimated as of July 1 of the year shown.

Table B. States and Counties — **Land Area and Population**

State / county code	CBSA code[1]	County code[2]	STATE County	Land area[3] (sq. mi)	Total persons 2018	Rank	Per square mile	White	Black	American Indian, Alaska Native	Asian and Pacific Islander	Percent Hispanic or Latino[4]	Under 5 years	5 to 17 years	18 to 24 years	25 to 34 years	35 to 44 years	45 to 54 years
				1	2	3	4	5	6	7	8	9	10	11	12	13	14	15
			SOUTH DAKOTA— Cont'd															
46123		7	Tripp	1,612.5	5,478	2,796	3.4	83.4	0.9	15.5	0.6	2.2	7.1	15.9	7.5	11.0	9.3	11.8
46125	43,620	3	Turner	617.1	8,424	2,549	13.7	95.7	0.8	1.3	0.5	2.8	6.2	18.2	6.2	10.6	12.0	11.6
46127	43,580	3	Union	460.7	15,619	2,059	33.9	93.3	1.6	1.4	2.0	3.2	6.2	18.0	7.1	11.8	12.5	12.5
46129		7	Walworth	708.6	5,587	2,785	7.9	80.2	0.9	16.0	3.8	2.2	7.1	16.6	7.3	10.9	10.3	10.1
46135	49,460	7	Yankton	521.2	22,869	1,687	43.9	89.3	2.5	3.7	1.3	5.0	6.0	15.2	8.8	12.6	11.8	12.4
46137		8	Ziebach	1,961.2	2,742	2,987	1.4	27.6	1.5	69.4	0.7	4.5	5.8	22.4	12.1	10.8	14.8	11.7
47000		0	TENNESSEE	41,236.8	6,770,010	X	164.2	75.3	17.7	0.8	2.4	5.6	6.0	16.2	9.1	13.8	12.4	13.0
47001	28,940	2	Anderson	337.2	76,482	727	226.8	91.0	5.1	1.0	1.9	3.1	5.2	15.8	7.4	12.1	11.6	13.3
47003	43,180	4	Bedford	473.6	49,038	1,005	103.5	78.5	9.0	0.8	1.2	12.6	6.7	18.7	8.2	13.3	12.5	13.2
47005		7	Benton	394.3	16,184	2,030	41.0	93.8	3.1	1.2	0.8	2.5	5.0	15.0	6.7	10.0	10.8	13.8
47007		8	Bledsoe	406.4	14,755	2,110	36.3	89.6	7.7	1.0	0.5	2.5	4.1	11.2	7.1	13.8	14.8	15.2
47009	28,940	2	Blount	558.8	131,349	487	235.1	92.4	3.7	0.9	1.3	3.5	5.0	15.2	7.8	11.8	11.5	14.0
47011	17,420	3	Bradley	328.8	106,727	567	324.6	87.3	5.8	0.9	1.5	6.3	5.7	16.0	9.6	12.8	12.3	13.5
47013	28,940	2	Campbell	480.2	39,583	1,189	82.4	97.5	0.8	1.0	0.5	1.3	5.5	15.1	7.3	11.6	11.6	14.2
47015	34,980	1	Cannon	265.6	14,462	2,131	54.5	95.2	2.2	1.1	0.6	2.5	6.0	15.4	7.4	12.8	11.3	14.5
47017		6	Carroll	597.7	28,020	1,498	46.9	86.3	11.3	1.0	0.6	2.8	5.6	15.8	10.0	11.2	10.4	13.1
47019	27,740	3	Carter	341.3	56,351	906	165.1	95.8	2.1	0.8	0.6	1.9	4.5	13.9	7.0	12.4	11.3	14.3
47021	34,980	1	Cheatham	302.5	40,439	1,171	133.7	94.0	2.5	1.0	0.9	3.2	5.8	16.4	7.4	12.8	12.6	15.1
47023	27,180	3	Chester	285.7	17,276	1,962	60.5	86.7	10.5	1.0	1.0	2.8	5.5	16.6	13.2	11.4	11.7	12.1
47025		6	Claiborne	434.6	31,756	1,384	73.1	96.5	1.6	1.0	1.0	1.3	5.0	14.1	9.0	12.6	11.5	13.6
47027		9	Clay	236.5	7,717	2,614	32.6	95.4	2.3	0.7	0.3	2.6	4.8	15.4	6.2	10.0	10.1	14.3
47029	35,460	6	Cocke	435.8	35,774	1,281	82.1	94.5	2.9	1.1	0.6	2.5	5.3	15.1	7.0	11.0	11.0	14.1
47031	46,100	4	Coffee	429.0	55,700	918	129.8	90.4	4.9	0.9	1.4	4.4	6.3	17.6	7.9	12.3	12.1	13.0
47033	27,180	3	Crockett	265.5	14,328	2,138	54.0	74.8	14.8	0.6	0.4	10.9	5.8	17.7	7.5	12.0	11.7	12.7
47035	18,900	4	Cumberland	681.0	59,673	875	87.6	95.3	0.9	1.0	0.8	3.1	4.5	13.0	6.0	9.9	9.0	11.6
47037	34,980	1	Davidson	503.5	692,587	97	1,375.5	58.1	28.3	0.8	4.7	10.4	6.6	14.2	9.8	20.3	13.8	11.7
47039		9	Decatur	333.9	11,706	2,313	35.1	93.0	3.3	0.8	0.8	3.3	5.4	15.6	6.6	9.8	11.3	12.6
47041		6	DeKalb	304.4	20,138	1,816	66.2	88.6	1.9	0.9	1.2	8.6	5.6	16.0	7.3	12.1	12.1	14.0
47043	34,980	1	Dickson	489.9	53,446	948	109.1	91.3	5.1	0.9	0.9	3.7	6.0	17.1	7.6	12.9	12.5	13.9
47045	20,540	5	Dyer	512.3	37,320	1,242	72.8	81.3	15.1	0.7	1.0	3.6	6.2	17.7	8.2	12.3	11.7	13.3
47047	32,820	1	Fayette	704.8	40,507	1,168	57.5	68.6	27.8	0.6	1.0	2.9	5.0	14.0	6.8	11.1	11.0	13.9
47049		9	Fentress	498.6	18,217	1,915	36.5	97.3	0.7	0.9	0.5	1.6	5.3	15.7	7.2	10.1	10.7	13.9
47051	46,100	6	Franklin	554.5	41,890	1,137	75.5	89.9	5.9	1.1	1.3	3.6	5.0	15.0	11.5	10.6	11.0	12.3
47053		4	Gibson	602.7	49,045	1,004	81.4	78.7	18.9	0.6	0.5	2.8	6.4	18.0	7.6	11.8	12.4	12.6
47055		6	Giles	610.9	29,503	1,444	48.3	86.1	11.4	1.0	0.8	2.8	5.6	15.5	8.2	11.6	10.7	13.3
47057	28,940	2	Grainger	280.6	23,145	1,673	82.5	95.1	1.3	0.9	0.4	3.5	5.0	15.3	7.1	10.8	11.4	14.9
47059	24,620	4	Greene	622.2	69,087	778	111.0	94.1	2.7	0.8	0.7	3.0	4.9	14.5	8.0	11.0	11.4	13.9
47061		8	Grundy	360.4	13,346	2,203	37.0	97.1	0.9	1.4	0.5	1.4	5.6	15.9	7.5	11.1	11.9	13.2
47063	34,100	3	Hamblen	161.2	64,569	824	400.6	82.8	4.8	0.7	1.5	12.0	5.9	17.2	7.8	12.1	11.9	13.6
47065	16,860	2	Hamilton	542.3	364,286	195	671.7	72.6	20.0	0.8	2.6	5.9	5.8	15.0	8.7	14.6	12.3	12.7
47067		8	Hancock	222.3	6,549	2,707	29.5	98.2	0.9	1.2	0.5	0.7	5.4	15.4	6.7	11.2	11.5	12.8
47069		6	Hardeman	667.7	25,220	1,597	37.8	55.3	42.7	0.6	1.0	1.8	5.2	14.4	8.7	14.7	12.7	12.9
47071		6	Hardin	577.3	25,776	1,571	44.6	92.9	4.0	1.1	0.7	2.8	5.3	15.2	7.0	10.7	10.8	13.1
47073	28,700	2	Hawkins	487.1	56,530	905	116.1	96.1	1.9	0.9	0.6	1.7	4.8	15.1	7.2	11.3	11.0	14.7
47075	15,140	6	Haywood	533.1	17,335	1,956	32.5	44.8	51.0	0.5	0.4	4.4	5.5	16.7	7.9	11.5	11.7	12.6
47077		6	Henderson	520.0	27,847	1,501	53.6	89.4	9.1	0.7	0.5	2.3	5.8	17.0	7.5	11.8	12.4	13.3
47079	37,540	7	Henry	561.8	32,358	1,372	57.6	88.8	8.5	0.9	0.7	2.8	5.2	15.3	6.9	10.5	10.8	12.9
47081	34,980	1	Hickman	612.5	25,063	1,605	40.9	91.5	5.6	1.2	0.5	2.6	5.5	15.2	8.0	13.1	12.5	14.1
47083		8	Houston	200.3	8,263	2,569	41.3	93.6	3.9	1.2	0.8	2.5	5.2	16.6	7.3	11.5	11.6	13.1
47085		6	Humphreys	530.8	18,486	1,902	34.8	93.6	3.4	1.1	0.8	2.7	5.5	16.1	7.2	11.6	11.3	13.6
47087	18,260	8	Jackson	308.6	11,758	2,309	38.1	96.4	1.1	1.3	0.4	2.2	4.7	13.2	6.9	10.9	10.9	13.9
47089	34,100	3	Jefferson	274.9	54,012	939	196.5	93.2	2.5	0.9	0.8	3.9	4.8	14.8	8.7	11.1	11.3	14.4
47091		6	Johnson	298.4	17,778	1,935	59.6	94.8	2.7	0.9	0.5	2.2	4.2	12.5	7.1	12.1	12.2	14.7
47093	28,940	2	Knox	508.3	465,289	153	915.4	84.2	9.8	0.8	2.9	4.4	5.7	15.3	11.9	13.7	12.5	12.6
47095		9	Lake	165.8	7,411	2,633	44.7	68.3	29.6	1.0	0.4	2.4	3.9	10.3	10.4	18.6	14.6	14.0
47097		6	Lauderdale	472.0	25,825	1,570	54.7	61.8	35.3	1.0	0.8	2.6	5.8	16.8	9.0	13.4	12.9	13.2
47099	29,980	6	Lawrence	617.1	43,734	1,097	70.9	95.0	2.4	1.1	0.8	2.2	6.6	18.4	7.4	12.3	11.3	13.2
47101		6	Lewis	282.1	12,086	2,287	42.8	94.5	2.6	1.1	0.8	2.4	5.6	15.9	7.5	11.2	11.4	12.5
47103		6	Lincoln	570.3	34,117	1,326	59.8	88.3	7.6	1.5	0.7	3.8	5.5	16.6	7.2	11.4	11.4	13.5
47105	28,940	2	Loudon	229.3	53,054	952	231.4	88.5	1.8	0.8	1.1	9.0	5.2	14.2	6.7	10.0	9.8	12.4
47107	11,940	4	McMinn	430.1	53,285	949	123.9	91.0	4.6	1.2	1.0	4.2	5.5	15.7	8.2	11.4	11.4	13.7
47109		6	McNairy	562.8	25,832	1,569	45.9	91.2	6.8	1.0	0.5	2.2	5.2	16.6	7.4	11.0	11.7	13.5
47111	34,980	1	Macon	307.1	24,265	1,633	79.0	92.6	1.4	0.9	0.8	5.4	7.1	17.6	8.3	13.0	11.7	13.7
47113	27,180	3	Madison	557.1	97,605	613	175.2	57.2	38.5	0.5	1.5	4.0	6.2	16.2	10.5	12.7	11.4	12.5
47115	16,860	2	Marion	498.3	28,575	1,476	57.3	93.1	4.8	1.0	0.8	1.8	5.7	15.4	7.4	11.6	11.5	13.6

1. CBSA = Core Based Statistical Area. See Appendix A for explanation. See Appendix B for list of metropolitan areas with component counties. Service of USDA Rural-Urban Continuum Codes. See Appendix A for definition. 3. Dry land or land partially or temporarily covered by water. 2. County type code from the Economic Research 4. May be of any race.

Table B. States and Counties — Population and Households

STATE County	55 to 64 years	65 to 74 years	75 years and over	Percent female	Total persons 2000	Total persons 2010	Percent change 2000-2010	Percent change 2010-2018	Births	Deaths	Net Migration	Number	Persons per household	Family house-holds	Female family house-holder[1]	One person
	16	17	18	19	20	21	22	23	24	25	26	27	28	29	30	31
SOUTH DAKOTA— Cont'd																
Tripp	14.9	11.5	11.0	49.6	6,430	5,649	-12.1	-3.0	584	575	-179	2,424	2.20	60.8	5.9	33.3
Turner	14.4	10.9	9.8	49.7	8,849	8,347	-5.7	0.9	731	855	205	3,523	2.29	67.8	6.0	26.9
Union	13.8	10.9	7.2	49.6	12,584	14,398	14.4	8.5	1,379	975	812	6,285	2.36	66.4	6.0	28.6
Walworth	14.3	12.0	11.4	50.3	5,974	5,438	-9.0	2.7	595	657	211	2,292	2.27	56.2	6.1	36.2
Yankton	14.4	10.1	8.7	48.0	21,652	22,438	3.6	1.9	2,259	1,848	35	9,283	2.25	62.3	8.0	31.9
Ziebach	12.8	5.5	4.1	50.1	2,519	2,801	11.2	-2.1	283	126	-217	764	3.71	78.4	29.3	19.2
TENNESSEE	13.1	9.8	6.6	51.2	5,689,283	6,346,286	11.5	6.7	662,136	529,573	290,164	2,547,194	2.53	66.3	13.3	28.1
Anderson	14.5	11.5	8.6	51.3	71,330	75,089	5.3	1.9	6,556	7,646	2,554	30,518	2.44	65.8	13.0	29.0
Bedford	12.3	9.2	5.9	50.9	37,586	45,057	19.9	8.8	5,136	3,848	2,698	17,058	2.71	73.7	12.7	20.5
Benton	15.1	13.9	9.7	51.0	16,537	16,491	-0.3	-1.9	1,295	2,031	436	6,693	2.39	59.9	10.5	35.2
Bledsoe	15.4	11.1	7.3	41.1	12,367	12,874	4.1	14.6	1,016	1,104	1,911	4,664	2.84	74.4	9.2	21.8
Blount	14.4	11.9	8.4	51.5	105,823	123,098	16.3	6.7	10,363	10,947	8,878	49,939	2.51	68.1	10.0	26.7
Bradley	12.9	9.9	7.2	51.4	87,965	98,930	12.5	7.9	9,781	8,203	6,237	39,615	2.54	69.0	11.6	26.0
Campbell	13.9	11.9	8.8	50.9	39,854	40,723	2.2	-2.8	3,530	4,614	-14	15,843	2.48	69.9	14.8	26.7
Cannon	14.2	10.7	7.7	50.3	12,826	13,813	7.7	4.7	1,265	1,411	793	5,456	2.50	69.8	12.1	26.1
Carroll	13.7	11.7	8.6	51.1	29,475	28,486	-3.4	-1.6	2,570	3,418	388	11,321	2.40	67.0	11.0	29.1
Carter	14.8	12.5	9.5	51.1	56,742	57,388	1.1	-1.8	4,261	5,620	363	23,798	2.30	66.1	12.1	30.1
Cheatham	14.9	9.7	5.3	50.3	35,912	39,106	8.9	3.4	3,703	3,157	802	14,671	2.68	72.5	11.3	21.8
Chester	12.4	9.8	7.4	51.9	15,540	17,145	10.3	0.8	1,535	1,453	55	5,998	2.65	75.8	16.1	19.8
Claiborne	14.3	12.1	7.8	51.1	29,862	32,212	7.9	-1.4	2,548	3,552	566	12,996	2.33	67.9	11.1	29.2
Clay	14.8	13.4	10.9	50.8	7,976	7,858	-1.5	-1.8	623	950	188	3,171	2.39	68.4	8.6	27.7
Cocke	15.6	12.9	8.2	51.7	33,565	35,642	6.2	0.4	3,144	4,086	1,102	14,592	2.39	64.3	15.0	30.3
Coffee	13.4	9.8	7.4	51.2	48,014	52,803	10.0	5.5	5,472	5,439	2,894	21,576	2.47	67.2	10.0	28.7
Crockett	13.8	10.5	8.3	52.2	14,532	14,576	0.3	-1.7	1,382	1,477	-145	5,400	2.66	63.6	12.3	31.0
Cumberland	15.4	17.5	13.2	51.3	46,802	56,062	19.8	6.4	4,506	6,538	5,601	25,114	2.29	69.4	9.7	26.4
Davidson	11.5	7.4	4.8	51.7	569,891	626,560	9.9	10.5	81,883	42,918	26,651	273,497	2.40	56.3	14.2	34.0
Decatur	15.3	12.9	10.5	50.9	11,731	11,750	0.2	-0.4	958	1,417	426	4,721	2.43	68.8	11.4	27.8
DeKalb	14.5	11.3	7.1	50.0	17,423	18,717	7.4	7.6	1,830	2,009	1,605	7,362	2.59	69.0	11.1	26.7
Dickson	13.8	9.8	6.4	50.9	43,156	49,650	15.0	7.6	5,007	4,364	3,164	19,032	2.66	68.8	12.1	27.1
Dyer	13.0	10.5	7.1	51.8	37,279	38,330	2.8	-2.6	3,901	3,674	-1,234	15,327	2.43	69.7	14.3	24.6
Fayette	16.8	13.0	8.4	50.8	28,806	38,439	33.4	5.4	3,484	3,178	1,764	15,084	2.57	74.5	10.8	21.9
Fentress	15.1	13.8	8.2	51.2	16,625	17,960	8.0	1.4	1,555	1,998	712	7,385	2.41	68.8	10.3	27.4
Franklin	14.5	11.7	8.3	51.2	39,270	41,064	4.6	2.0	3,252	4,046	1,635	16,325	2.42	68.1	9.6	27.4
Gibson	13.3	10.0	8.0	52.1	48,152	49,687	3.2	-1.3	5,009	5,515	-102	19,280	2.49	68.3	16.8	27.8
Giles	15.0	11.7	8.3	51.5	29,447	29,483	0.1	0.1	2,583	2,951	395	11,599	2.43	68.6	12.7	25.3
Grainger	15.0	12.7	7.8	49.6	20,659	22,656	9.7	2.2	1,870	2,275	902	9,112	2.50	72.4	9.1	23.3
Greene	14.8	12.6	9.0	50.8	62,909	68,825	9.4	0.4	5,258	7,234	2,283	27,319	2.44	66.6	11.8	29.8
Grundy	13.9	12.4	8.6	50.5	14,332	13,726	-4.2	-2.8	1,288	1,671	9	4,894	2.69	70.9	15.6	25.7
Hamblen	13.0	10.5	7.9	51.2	58,128	62,531	7.6	3.3	6,354	6,097	1,835	24,343	2.57	69.0	11.8	26.7
Hamilton	13.4	10.2	7.4	51.7	307,896	336,486	9.3	8.3	34,535	28,263	21,440	139,037	2.47	61.8	12.0	32.9
Hancock	15.7	13.4	7.9	50.7	6,786	6,815	0.4	-3.9	560	831	11	2,704	2.38	65.5	11.1	30.5
Hardeman	13.2	10.9	7.2	45.4	28,105	27,247	-3.1	-7.4	2,201	2,395	-1,855	8,680	2.52	67.9	18.3	28.7
Hardin	14.7	13.2	9.9	51.2	25,578	26,012	1.7	-0.9	2,297	3,003	488	10,118	2.51	70.2	12.1	26.6
Hawkins	14.8	12.6	8.5	50.9	53,563	56,829	6.1	-0.5	4,464	5,694	977	23,375	2.39	67.4	12.6	29.3
Haywood	15.1	11.4	7.7	53.4	19,797	18,807	-5.0	-7.8	1,753	1,604	-1,634	7,104	2.49	65.6	18.6	31.8
Henderson	13.8	10.8	7.6	51.5	25,522	27,780	8.8	0.2	2,669	2,659	79	10,827	2.54	67.9	11.4	28.1
Henry	15.1	13.6	9.7	51.5	31,115	32,349	4.0	0.0	2,746	3,781	1,071	13,483	2.36	67.2	12.8	28.1
Hickman	13.9	10.5	7.0	47.4	22,295	24,690	10.7	1.5	2,223	2,258	405	8,930	2.57	67.0	10.5	29.7
Houston	14.2	11.9	8.6	50.9	8,088	8,429	4.2	-2.0	689	873	16	2,999	2.66	68.7	8.7	28.4
Humphreys	14.7	11.6	8.4	50.3	17,929	18,535	3.4	-0.3	1,670	1,992	278	7,064	2.56	63.5	9.0	33.3
Jackson	17.0	13.6	8.9	50.3	10,984	11,632	5.9	1.1	832	1,245	537	4,566	2.49	66.8	12.7	30.0
Jefferson	14.9	11.8	8.2	50.8	44,294	51,668	16.6	4.5	4,240	4,913	3,025	20,088	2.54	71.3	10.4	25.0
Johnson	14.4	13.4	9.4	46.2	17,499	18,240	4.2	-2.5	1,258	1,822	111	6,936	2.29	67.1	9.1	29.5
Knox	12.5	9.3	6.5	51.4	382,032	432,269	13.1	7.6	43,039	34,925	24,936	182,315	2.42	62.1	11.0	30.2
Lake	12.5	8.9	6.8	35.7	7,954	7,832	-1.5	-5.4	545	791	-175	2,164	2.25	66.2	18.1	29.4
Lauderdale	13.1	9.6	6.2	48.5	27,101	27,822	2.7	-7.2	2,511	2,376	-2,164	9,725	2.43	69.7	20.6	25.9
Lawrence	13.0	10.2	7.6	50.9	39,926	41,851	4.8	4.5	4,646	4,291	1,542	16,101	2.62	71.5	12.8	25.5
Lewis	14.9	12.3	8.7	51.2	11,367	12,171	7.1	-0.7	1,084	1,182	14	4,663	2.51	70.1	10.3	26.8
Lincoln	15.0	11.0	8.4	50.9	31,340	33,354	6.4	2.3	2,911	3,343	1,225	13,653	2.43	67.9	12.8	28.7
Loudon	15.2	15.5	10.9	50.8	39,086	48,550	24.2	9.3	4,395	5,101	5,166	20,090	2.52	73.7	9.1	22.5
McMinn	14.5	11.2	8.4	51.3	49,015	52,279	6.7	1.9	4,698	5,425	1,774	20,352	2.53	66.1	10.4	30.5
McNairy	13.9	12.2	8.6	50.9	24,653	26,077	5.8	-0.9	2,297	2,892	368	10,095	2.54	66.3	14.1	30.6
Macon	13.0	9.5	6.2	51.1	20,386	22,226	9.0	9.2	2,640	2,214	1,617	9,158	2.50	69.4	10.5	25.1
Madison	13.6	10.1	7.0	52.6	91,837	98,301	7.0	-0.7	10,220	8,027	-2,850	37,110	2.53	66.7	16.7	27.9
Marion	14.9	12.2	7.9	51.1	27,776	28,222	1.6	1.3	2,560	3,016	828	11,393	2.46	72.9	13.6	24.2

1. No spouse present.

Population, Vital Statistics, Health, and Crime

STATE County	Persons in group quarters, 2018	Daytime Population, 2013-2017		Births, 2018		Deaths, 2018		Persons under 65 with no health insurance, 2016		Medicare, 2018			Serious crimes known to police[2], 2016 Total	
		Number	Employment/ residence ratio	Total	Rate[1]	Number	Rate[1]	Number	Percent	Total beneficiaries	Enrolled in Original Medicare	Enrolled in Medicare Advantage	Number	Rate[3]
	32	33	34	35	36	37	38	39	40	41	42	43	44	45
SOUTH DAKOTA— Cont'd														
Tripp	131	5,523	1.02	80	14.6	65	11.9	621	14.9	1,329	1,186	143	45	836
Turner	153	6,677	0.63	86	10.2	99	11.8	596	9.1	1,841	1,316	525	64	784
Union	89	15,834	1.12	176	11.3	116	7.4	797	6.3	3,153	2,471	682	137	1,045
Walworth	152	5,319	0.93	70	12.5	56	10.0	522	12.5	1,489	1,362	127	68	1,417
Yankton	2,295	24,055	1.12	293	12.8	211	9.2	1,510	9.0	4,804	3,787	1,017	555	2,445
Ziebach	0	2,647	0.80	22	8.0	24	8.8	456	18.2	161	D	D	1	36
TENNESSEE	156,592	6,643,847	1.02	79,474	11.7	67,259	9.9	581,927	10.6	1,324,333	817,210	507,123	231,932	3,487
Anderson	1,184	90,863	1.49	769	10.1	949	12.4	5,550	9.2	18,265	10,541	7,724	2,403	3,168
Bedford	544	43,707	0.85	646	13.2	468	9.5	5,173	13.0	9,022	5,696	3,326	1,225	2,573
Benton	162	14,974	0.79	148	9.1	261	16.1	1,431	11.8	4,638	3,402	1,236	337	2,099
Bledsoe	2,632	12,683	0.66	119	8.1	152	10.3	1,331	14.0	2,888	1,897	991	200	1,346
Blount	2,084	118,381	0.85	1,212	9.2	1,355	10.3	10,388	10.1	30,774	17,799	12,975	3,095	2,416
Bradley	2,762	103,327	0.99	1,205	11.3	1,075	10.1	11,037	13.0	22,402	13,021	9,381	4,269	4,062
Campbell	519	35,542	0.71	440	11.1	595	15.0	3,616	11.6	10,460	4,956	5,504	1,555	3,931
Cannon	164	10,526	0.45	168	11.6	151	10.4	1,339	11.8	3,177	2,056	1,121	189	1,365
Carroll	1,303	25,338	0.74	298	10.6	404	14.4	2,102	9.9	7,453	5,525	1,928	527	1,896
Carter	915	46,737	0.56	470	8.3	728	12.9	5,004	11.4	14,831	6,841	7,990	1,523	2,705
Cheatham	283	30,310	0.50	470	11.6	402	9.9	3,197	9.4	7,588	4,160	3,428	878	2,203
Chester	1,094	14,871	0.68	180	10.4	152	8.8	1,538	11.6	3,817	2,756	1,061	248	1,415
Claiborne	1,263	29,772	0.84	306	9.6	424	13.4	2,461	10.1	8,520	4,163	4,357	654	2,069
Clay	96	6,929	0.70	66	8.6	109	14.1	714	12.4	2,079	1,602	477	96	1,238
Cocke	294	30,991	0.70	362	10.1	507	14.2	3,002	10.9	10,073	5,062	5,011	1,424	4,062
Coffee	557	56,687	1.12	657	11.8	669	12.0	4,851	10.8	12,270	8,608	3,662	1,659	3,040
Crockett	194	12,728	0.69	149	10.4	193	13.5	1,620	13.9	3,242	2,544	698	263	1,801
Cumberland	636	58,365	1.01	501	8.4	847	14.2	5,013	12.3	21,451	15,202	6,249	1,480	2,524
Davidson	26,433	784,137	1.30	9,837	14.2	5,552	8.0	73,272	12.6	95,069	53,892	41,177	33,786	4,857
Decatur	213	10,757	0.79	111	9.5	169	14.4	1,084	12.1	3,514	2,578	936	275	2,362
DeKalb	298	18,278	0.86	202	10.0	235	11.7	2,007	12.9	4,521	2,438	2,083	394	2,044
Dickson	617	46,682	0.79	598	11.2	525	9.8	4,878	11.2	10,383	6,190	4,193	1,781	3,435
Dyer	516	37,873	1.01	457	12.2	458	12.3	3,029	9.9	8,425	6,469	1,956	1,868	4,941
Fayette	423	30,405	0.48	406	10.0	422	10.4	2,904	9.3	9,730	6,981	2,749	693	1,763
Fentress	132	16,858	0.83	181	9.9	253	13.9	1,728	12.4	5,318	4,074	1,244	319	1,781
Franklin	2,094	39,486	0.89	407	9.7	471	11.2	3,434	10.9	10,206	7,143	3,063	1,057	2,544
Gibson	992	43,930	0.74	579	11.8	645	13.2	3,673	9.2	11,611	8,728	2,883	1,355	2,747
Giles	670	28,089	0.92	319	10.8	379	12.8	2,662	11.6	7,145	5,275	1,870	661	2,291
Grainger	151	18,353	0.50	225	9.7	289	12.5	2,230	12.1	5,936	2,781	3,155	357	1,561
Greene	1,825	67,734	0.97	649	9.4	926	13.4	5,761	10.9	18,854	10,141	8,713	1,810	2,641
Grundy	180	12,064	0.69	156	11.7	193	14.5	1,434	13.9	3,634	2,139	1,495	313	2,338
Hamblen	919	68,375	1.19	745	11.5	744	11.5	6,756	13.1	14,818	8,107	6,711	2,142	3,370
Hamilton	9,820	399,421	1.27	4,201	11.5	3,700	10.2	28,689	9.9	71,442	43,068	28,374	15,831	4,428
Hancock	149	5,611	0.54	67	10.2	97	14.8	603	11.8	1,475	738	737	133	2,039
Hardeman	3,797	24,966	0.90	251	10.0	301	11.9	1,886	10.9	5,844	4,158	1,686	683	2,686
Hardin	371	25,363	0.95	266	10.3	364	14.1	2,293	11.6	7,307	5,606	1,701	1,044	4,063
Hawkins	456	48,067	0.61	523	9.3	726	12.8	4,742	10.6	15,707	6,425	9,282	1,193	2,116
Haywood	174	15,903	0.73	189	10.9	219	12.6	1,510	10.4	4,067	2,740	1,327	808	4,520
Henderson	218	25,507	0.79	311	11.2	324	11.6	2,513	11.1	6,127	4,149	1,978	684	2,438
Henry	490	32,000	0.98	318	9.8	470	14.5	2,868	11.7	9,010	6,867	2,143	1,143	3,561
Hickman	1,541	20,003	0.52	258	10.3	271	10.8	2,373	12.4	5,110	3,029	2,081	636	2,617
Houston	177	6,929	0.57	84	10.2	94	11.4	736	11.5	1,912	1,382	530	93	1,149
Humphreys	205	17,809	0.93	195	10.5	253	13.7	1,424	9.8	4,393	3,242	1,151	410	2,272
Jackson	177	9,404	0.45	104	8.8	159	13.5	1,166	13.1	3,111	2,226	885	156	1,357
Jefferson	1,501	46,249	0.70	481	8.9	678	12.6	4,519	10.9	13,240	7,163	6,077	991	1,850
Johnson	1,771	16,821	0.82	143	8.0	235	13.2	1,483	12.2	5,069	2,673	2,396	360	2,030
Knox	12,383	478,609	1.12	5,193	11.2	4,438	9.5	34,810	9.2	86,605	48,911	37,694	17,460	3,837
Lake	2,475	7,663	1.04	61	8.2	95	12.8	452	11.2	1,284	1,031	253	102	1,355
Lauderdale	1,984	25,917	0.93	311	12.0	283	11.0	2,257	11.2	5,275	3,775	1,500	893	3,335
Lawrence	407	38,538	0.74	548	12.5	530	12.1	4,018	11.5	10,100	7,610	2,490	1,238	2,901
Lewis	217	10,270	0.65	135	11.2	147	12.2	1,090	11.6	2,894	1,929	965	419	3,552
Lincoln	283	29,676	0.72	353	10.3	398	11.7	3,011	11.2	8,141	5,299	2,842	931	2,754
Loudon	480	47,759	0.84	525	9.9	620	11.7	4,702	12.3	15,729	9,302	6,427	1,063	2,059
McMinn	965	50,870	0.92	574	10.8	645	12.1	4,359	10.4	12,758	8,253	4,505	2,217	4,205
McNairy	313	23,401	0.72	275	10.6	354	13.7	2,419	11.9	6,983	5,342	1,641	654	2,509
Macon	269	19,572	0.61	317	13.1	265	10.9	2,815	14.5	4,932	3,218	1,714	501	2,144
Madison	4,421	113,695	1.37	1,184	12.1	1,027	10.5	7,113	9.1	20,094	14,730	5,364	4,286	4,397
Marion	250	25,243	0.74	312	10.9	360	12.6	2,228	9.8	7,092	4,163	2,929	717	2,513

1. Per 1,000 estimated resident population.   2. Data for serious crimes have not been adjusted for underreporting; this may affect comparability between geographic areas and over time.   3. Per 100,000 population estimated by the FBI.

Table B. States and Counties — Crime, Education, Money Income, and Poverty

STATE County	Serious crimes known to police[2], 2016 (cont.)[1] Rate Violent	Property	Education — School enrollment and attainment, 2013-2017 Enrollment[3] Total	Percent private	Attainment[4] (percent) High school graduate or less	Bachelor's degree or more	Local government expenditures[5] 2014-2015 Total current spending (mil dol)	Current spending per student (dollars)	Money income, 2013-2017 Per capita income[6]	Median income (dollars)	Households Percent with income of less than $50,000	with income of $200,000 or more	Income and poverty, 2017 Median household income (dollars)	Percent below poverty level All persons	Children under 18 years	Children 5 to 17 years in families
	46	47	48	49	50	51	52	53	54	55	56	57	58	59	60	61
SOUTH DAKOTA— Cont'd																
Tripp	167	669	1,121	4.6	49.7	22.1	8.5	9,203	27,613	48,409	52.3	3.5	42,724	19	26.6	25.7
Turner	159	625	1,761	8.1	41.9	22.6	13.5	8,747	27,844	54,294	47.0	2.2	56,203	10.2	11.0	10.8
Union	137	908	3,436	11.3	38.0	30.6	26.0	8,840	37,093	65,434	37.5	8.9	82,100	6.1	6.6	5.9
Walworth	396	1,021	1,171	11.4	50.2	22.3	7.6	8,801	29,457	46,623	52.2	2.9	46,550	12.3	20.9	19.8
Yankton	282	2,163	5,061	16.8	40.9	27.5	24.0	7,778	30,395	50,029	50.0	4.5	55,907	11.4	12.4	11.5
Ziebach	0	36	853	0.4	55.9	14.9	10.5	14,755	13,461	35,000	66.1	0.3	29,985	56.7	74.7	57.4
TENNESSEE	633	2,854	1,577,392	17.4	46.1	26.1	8,678.7	8,718	27,277	48,708	51.1	3.9	51,319	15	21.1	19.8
Anderson	477	2,690	16,106	13.3	47.5	23.8	118.7	9,880	26,972	47,206	52.1	2.9	48,679	15.3	21.9	20.0
Bedford	500	2,073	10,745	9.5	59.5	15.7	60.1	7,098	22,953	47,117	53.0	2.5	50,904	16.8	22.9	20.8
Benton	112	1,987	3,185	7.3	65.1	12.8	20.6	9,165	21,282	33,702	65.3	1.7	36,034	18.8	29.7	28.7
Bledsoe	202	1,144	2,460	19.2	67.1	12.4	16.2	8,394	21,402	40,450	59.9	3.1	38,261	23.1	30.1	29.1
Blount	432	1,985	26,363	16.5	46.4	23.4	161.1	8,789	28,334	51,172	48.9	3.4	51,391	12.1	17.1	15.7
Bradley	562	3,500	25,930	22.8	48.1	21.8	130.4	8,178	25,144	46,381	53.3	2.5	48,663	16.9	20.6	18.7
Campbell	468	3,463	7,954	12.8	65.9	11.8	42.9	7,447	21,282	35,377	64.8	1.6	40,866	19.2	32.4	28.2
Cannon	173	1,192	2,789	12.2	63.1	12.2	16.9	8,120	24,595	47,457	52.5	2.0	51,795	15	22.7	21.7
Carroll	255	1,640	6,386	20.9	60.4	15.8	39.0	8,523	20,557	38,201	61.6	1.5	41,492	19.5	25.8	26.9
Carter	307	2,397	11,574	14.4	58.1	15.5	71.2	8,793	21,001	34,625	66.0	1.0	39,725	20.7	29.0	27.8
Cheatham	251	1,952	9,380	15.3	52.1	19.4	50.7	7,868	25,673	56,150	44.0	2.2	59,103	11	14.6	13.4
Chester	251	1,164	4,710	23.9	56.4	16.5	20.7	7,279	20,497	43,740	53.8	1.5	45,261	16.9	21.6	20.4
Claiborne	240	1,829	6,984	27.1	61.9	13.0	38.7	8,525	20,184	35,428	65.3	1.6	37,886	22.5	31.2	27.0
Clay	322	915	1,337	4.6	68.3	12.8	9.5	8,597	17,667	30,801	67.5	0.1	34,035	24.8	32.8	31.2
Cocke	693	3,369	6,431	7.6	65.9	11.4	45.9	8,386	20,189	32,027	66.9	0.9	35,788	23	37.3	34.9
Coffee	449	2,591	12,514	7.8	51.3	18.9	86.7	9,205	24,748	46,614	54.2	2.5	48,188	14.9	21.5	20.2
Crockett	315	1,486	3,474	7.8	62.2	13.0	23.3	7,525	21,056	39,692	61.4	1.6	40,480	17.7	24.8	23.2
Cumberland	247	2,277	9,633	10.6	53.4	18.6	59.6	7,960	23,668	40,994	59.9	1.7	45,118	14.1	25.1	24.5
Davidson	1,092	3,765	164,117	31.0	34.9	39.1	946.2	10,358	32,347	53,419	46.3	5.2	58,264	14.6	22.5	22.6
Decatur	283	2,078	2,284	3.1	61.0	11.5	13.0	7,741	21,098	36,427	62.3	1.4	38,988	19.4	25.4	23.3
DeKalb	337	1,707	4,010	7.7	64.3	13.6	22.9	7,663	25,443	40,690	58.7	2.6	42,080	17.1	25.2	24.6
Dickson	534	2,901	11,255	13.2	60.1	14.7	66.7	7,849	25,211	47,398	53.1	3.3	49,518	11.3	17.2	15.9
Dyer	807	4,134	8,587	5.1	55.4	18.1	56.1	8,321	24,695	44,386	55.6	2.1	44,549	17.3	25.0	23.7
Fayette	242	1,521	7,873	28.5	47.2	22.4	28.2	7,946	30,471	57,919	43.5	5.6	60,112	13.9	20.7	19.0
Fentress	134	1,647	3,767	7.5	66.7	11.7	18.9	6,508	18,171	32,616	72.8	1.2	32,895	23.4	31.2	29.5
Franklin	416	2,128	9,625	24.8	52.9	20.6	46.6	8,199	25,637	46,882	53.9	3.1	49,596	14.9	20.3	18.4
Gibson	557	2,189	12,055	8.0	53.7	17.8	74.4	8,105	21,858	41,315	58.4	1.4	42,859	16.4	21.5	20.1
Giles	340	1,951	5,786	17.6	60.1	14.8	34.2	8,493	22,994	43,925	54.6	1.4	47,838	15.2	21.1	19.1
Grainger	240	1,320	4,245	9.4	64.2	11.1	28.4	7,857	20,966	40,088	59.0	1.8	43,190	18.3	25.7	22.8
Greene	304	2,338	14,044	11.5	60.0	15.0	83.2	8,407	21,960	38,266	62.2	1.2	40,145	17.7	24.6	22.1
Grundy	463	1,875	2,746	10.1	67.7	11.0	18.8	8,199	15,824	31,919	70.8	0.7	34,454	23	31.1	29.4
Hamblen	477	2,893	13,879	10.4	58.9	16.4	82.0	7,928	21,962	42,042	57.7	1.7	44,181	16.7	24.7	22.1
Hamilton	683	3,745	82,948	21.5	39.1	30.5	400.1	9,135	29,711	50,273	49.8	4.8	52,096	12.5	17.5	17.5
Hancock	46	1,993	1,306	13.7	65.4	10.2	9.5	9,968	19,396	29,619	69.0	1.7	29,689	28.4	41.6	35.4
Hardeman	559	2,128	4,859	12.0	69.2	10.9	35.2	8,915	16,938	36,686	65.3	0.8	38,426	23	30.1	29.6
Hardin	634	3,429	5,206	11.2	62.7	12.9	30.8	8,384	23,328	39,092	60.1	2.5	39,318	18.7	28.4	27.0
Hawkins	250	1,866	11,402	9.1	60.1	13.2	66.8	8,559	22,141	38,728	61.6	1.3	41,397	16.7	26.0	23.5
Haywood	1,113	3,407	4,130	7.6	64.3	12.4	28.8	9,152	21,453	36,118	63.7	1.8	34,556	20.6	30.8	29.2
Henderson	449	1,989	6,143	8.9	59.2	14.4	40.9	8,172	21,344	42,711	56.3	1.3	43,806	15.2	21.4	20.1
Henry	349	3,212	6,661	7.9	61.7	15.9	40.5	8,264	22,952	40,415	61.4	1.6	41,756	18.3	28.8	27.7
Hickman	395	2,222	5,031	13.5	64.9	11.0	29.4	8,136	20,936	39,333	62.3	1.3	42,824	17	23.8	22.8
Houston	198	952	1,747	4.3	69.1	10.7	11.5	8,246	20,819	41,820	61.1	2.0	42,018	15.7	24.9	22.8
Humphreys	310	1,962	3,892	11.2	61.3	12.5	25.0	8,256	23,498	40,998	59.8	2.1	45,866	13.6	20.8	19.9
Jackson	130	1,227	2,013	4.0	68.9	8.1	13.3	8,461	18,643	33,933	67.1	0.8	36,815	18	27.1	26.9
Jefferson	215	1,635	11,641	17.4	54.9	16.2	61.4	8,175	23,724	45,641	53.9	1.7	45,556	14.1	20.5	19.9
Johnson	677	1,353	3,026	13.6	63.9	10.9	21.3	9,537	19,183	32,994	68.7	2.5	36,331	24.3	32.8	30.9
Knox	528	3,309	115,849	16.6	35.0	36.5	509.1	8,499	30,541	52,458	47.9	4.9	55,299	13.9	17.1	17.0
Lake	239	1,116	1,392	16.5	72.7	9.4	7.9	8,775	14,232	31,993	63.1	1.7	31,144	39.9	46.3	43.0
Lauderdale	541	2,793	6,018	7.3	69.3	8.6	37.5	8,250	17,178	35,551	64.3	0.9	38,718	20.8	28.0	24.1
Lawrence	415	2,486	9,849	15.2	62.7	12.2	55.4	8,096	19,879	41,522	59.5	1.2	41,505	15.6	21.9	19.9
Lewis	585	2,967	2,308	12.0	59.7	12.0	14.3	7,694	20,099	37,092	62.2	1.1	37,959	17.5	24.1	22.9
Lincoln	535	2,219	7,114	9.8	58.3	18.3	43.3	7,753	24,029	42,153	57.6	2.0	49,295	13	19.3	17.8
Loudon	207	1,852	9,368	16.9	48.3	26.2	58.8	8,006	30,177	55,431	43.9	4.1	57,641	12.6	19.2	17.5
McMinn	537	3,668	11,121	15.8	59.5	15.4	64.0	8,098	21,583	39,990	59.5	1.0	39,860	22.4	28.4	25.4
McNairy	361	2,148	5,331	13.6	63.9	12.2	34.6	7,973	19,745	34,353	64.6	1.6	39,407	17.1	23.5	21.6
Macon	351	1,793	5,163	15.8	68.5	9.6	28.6	7,438	20,666	35,533	63.6	1.3	41,266	17.2	25.8	24.3
Madison	782	3,615	25,125	31.5	45.5	26.1	112.1	8,556	24,600	44,496	54.9	3.3	46,424	17.5	24.6	22.5
Marion	322	2,190	5,908	10.1	57.1	13.0	36.9	8,125	23,807	45,366	54.5	2.1	47,331	15.7	23.6	22.5

1. Data for serious crimes have not been adjusted for underreporting; this may affect comparability between geographic areas and over time.   2. Per 100,000 population estimated by the FBI.   3. All persons 3 years old and over enrolled in nursery school through college.   4. Persons 25 years old and over.   5. Elementary and secondary education expenditures.   6. Based on population estimated by the American Community Survey, 2013–2017.

Table B. States and Counties — Personal Income and Earnings

STATE County	Personal income, 2017										Earnings, 2017		
			Per capita[1]			Supplements to wages and salaries, employer contributions (mil dol)						Contributions for government social insurance (mil dol)	
	Total (mil dol)	Percent change 2016-2017	Dollars	Rank	Wages and salaries (mil dol)	Pension and insurance	Government social insurance	Proprietors' income (mil dol)	Dividends, interest, and rent (mil dol)	Personal transfer receipts (mil dol)	Total (mil dol)	From employee and self-employed	From employer
	62	63	64	65	66	67	68	69	70	71	72	73	74
SOUTH DAKOTA— Cont'd													
Tripp	240	1.6	44,033	1,018	80	14	6	33	59	53	134	8	6
Turner	502	-12.7	60,365	150	80	16	6	190	74	65	292	13	6
Union	1,448	1.2	96,345	15	550	72	36	258	440	105	916	51	36
Walworth	235	-0.2	42,389	1,216	81	15	6	15	76	52	117	9	6
Yankton	1,053	2.6	46,470	755	545	93	40	134	230	172	812	49	40
Ziebach	57	-1.7	20,764	3,108	13	3	1	10	12	16	27	1	1
TENNESSEE	305,691	4.6	45,566	X	148,899	23,473	10,295	43,415	45,009	60,246	226,082	13,438	10,295
Anderson	3,115	3.3	40,847	1,426	2,322	335	160	299	450	777	3,116	192	160
Bedford	1,753	4.8	36,427	2,126	724	139	51	186	243	408	1,100	68	51
Benton	530	4.5	33,164	2,598	144	32	10	34	74	205	220	18	10
Bledsoe	378	6.4	25,705	3,083	67	20	5	36	45	128	128	10	5
Blount	5,356	4.2	41,224	1,375	2,380	383	168	415	826	1,189	3,346	218	168
Bradley	4,092	4.1	38,766	1,762	1,821	325	131	401	622	969	2,678	168	131
Campbell	1,310	2.8	33,042	2,610	358	76	27	82	175	501	543	43	27
Cannon	505	5.5	35,489	2,276	87	20	6	36	67	142	149	12	6
Carroll	991	2.3	35,572	2,262	298	61	22	44	122	369	425	34	22
Carter	1,893	3.4	33,506	2,554	426	84	30	147	288	636	687	56	30
Cheatham	1,704	5.3	42,250	1,236	373	83	28	206	194	318	691	44	28
Chester	568	3.3	33,194	2,595	143	32	11	50	75	166	236	17	11
Claiborne	1,095	3.5	34,635	2,397	347	69	25	79	130	378	520	39	25
Clay	240	4.9	31,134	2,842	64	16	5	26	32	89	109	8	5
Cocke	1,115	4.2	31,362	2,824	293	60	21	67	133	412	441	37	21
Coffee	2,103	4.0	38,205	1,845	1,144	200	81	214	300	571	1,639	102	81
Crockett	515	1.8	35,555	2,265	166	34	12	38	64	162	250	18	12
Cumberland	2,129	3.7	36,038	2,196	658	117	48	238	392	770	1,061	84	48
Davidson	43,592	6.7	63,063	127	29,584	3,830	2,005	12,320	6,824	4,997	47,740	2,572	2,005
Decatur	492	1.1	41,882	1,277	145	29	10	32	60	168	217	16	10
DeKalb	769	4.4	38,720	1,771	235	49	18	93	97	189	395	25	18
Dickson	2,064	5.6	39,055	1,713	708	125	50	250	238	473	1,133	72	50
Dyer	1,473	3.1	39,328	1,668	624	126	46	159	204	429	955	61	46
Fayette	2,160	4.4	53,942	315	399	65	27	272	283	368	764	51	27
Fentress	571	3.5	31,462	2,811	171	36	12	63	71	229	282	22	12
Franklin	1,564	4.0	37,556	1,936	464	92	34	150	230	431	740	52	34
Gibson	1,840	2.7	37,464	1,957	547	113	40	130	232	596	830	59	40
Giles	1,123	4.4	38,181	1,849	452	85	32	75	164	318	644	44	32
Grainger	748	4.9	32,317	2,710	156	31	11	69	87	234	267	22	11
Greene	2,681	3.6	38,967	1,725	1,066	200	77	141	325	1,054	1,484	104	77
Grundy	406	3.0	30,407	2,895	66	17	5	46	51	163	134	12	5
Hamblen	2,315	2.7	36,017	2,199	1,276	240	90	252	310	640	1,857	116	90
Hamilton	18,151	4.6	50,196	451	10,550	1,710	736	2,659	2,970	3,243	15,655	905	736
Hancock	174	2.1	26,422	3,072	28	9	2	3	26	74	42	4	2
Hardeman	731	2.6	28,730	3,000	266	59	19	38	97	270	382	28	19
Hardin	986	3.4	38,149	1,855	354	68	24	61	150	342	507	37	24
Hawkins	1,888	3.3	33,439	2,564	594	117	43	93	245	627	847	67	43
Haywood	559	-0.7	31,794	2,782	213	48	16	-4	86	192	272	22	16
Henderson	956	2.9	34,453	2,418	316	58	22	86	121	275	483	33	22
Henry	1,325	3.9	40,839	1,428	457	93	33	215	207	386	798	51	33
Hickman	782	4.5	31,460	2,813	142	32	10	79	87	237	264	20	10
Houston	265	5.2	32,297	2,715	51	13	4	21	34	99	88	7	4
Humphreys	715	4.6	38,686	1,779	318	64	24	57	96	212	462	30	24
Jackson	355	3.8	30,370	2,900	53	13	4	23	43	137	94	9	4
Jefferson	1,849	4.1	34,362	2,433	594	108	42	131	259	549	875	64	42
Johnson	557	2.8	31,464	2,810	189	41	13	28	84	201	270	21	13
Knox	22,243	4.7	48,160	610	12,099	1,855	838	2,913	3,664	3,663	17,705	1,036	838
Lake	173	1.9	23,175	3,103	51	13	4	4	27	88	72	6	4
Lauderdale	711	2.3	28,141	3,024	238	55	17	25	101	263	336	25	17
Lawrence	1,469	4.7	33,845	2,502	383	80	27	170	180	446	660	47	27
Lewis	401	4.2	33,294	2,579	95	22	7	47	44	125	171	12	7
Lincoln	1,365	4.3	40,431	1,484	395	83	28	127	195	346	633	43	28
Loudon	2,409	4.0	46,183	778	692	115	49	184	476	573	1,041	75	49
McMinn	1,855	3.9	35,084	2,340	820	147	60	139	230	553	1,166	79	60
McNairy	830	2.8	31,901	2,763	199	51	15	67	102	309	332	27	15
Macon	796	7.3	33,041	2,611	184	41	14	103	98	230	341	22	14
Madison	4,045	3.5	41,430	1,344	2,600	474	182	381	625	956	3,636	217	182
Marion	1,065	3.5	37,473	1,952	307	57	22	77	143	296	463	34	22

1. Based on the resident population estimated as of July 1 of the year shown.

STATE County					Earnings, 2017 (cont.)					Social Security beneficiaries, December 2017			Housing units, 2018	
					Percent by selected industries							Supplemental Security Income recipients, 2017		
	Farm	Mining, quarrying, and extractions	Construction	Manu-facturing	Information; professional, scientific, technical services	Retail trade	Finance, insurance, real estate, and leasing	Health care and social assistance	Govern-ment	Number	Rate[1]		Total	Percent change, 2010-2018
	75	76	77	78	79	80	81	82	83	84	85	86	87	88
SOUTH DAKOTA— Cont'd														
Tripp	11.4	D	6.1	2.4	6.2	9.1	D	15.4	16	1,340	245	152	3,101	0.9
Turner	18.3	D	5.7	33.9	3.4	2.2	D	D	6.4	1,890	227	86	4,046	2.7
Union	4.6	0.1	3.9	12.2	5.5	3.4	11.6	20.7	4.5	3,155	210	83	7,277	15.9
Walworth	-3.4	D	7.2	1.2	D	9.7	8.5	D	17.8	1,525	275	123	3,063	2
Yankton	5	D	4.9	26.1	3.2	6.3	6.3	15.9	14.4	4,970	219	404	10,273	6.4
Ziebach	33	0	D	D	D	D	D	D	35.2	190	69	88	992	0.5
TENNESSEE	0	0.1	6.7	12	8.8	6.7	7.7	16	12.9	1,431,690	213	179,147	2,992,279	6.4
Anderson	-0.1	D	3.1	31.5	16.7	4.3	4.1	9.6	12.8	19,700	258	2,122	35,022	0.9
Bedford	0.7	D	8.8	30.3	D	6.7	4.3	D	12.2	10,110	210	1,080	19,271	5
Benton		D	5.8	15.9	D	10.1	8.8	D	24.9	5,195	325	598	9,144	1.9
Bledsoe	9.4	0.1	10.6	1.9	D	4.5	2.5	5	45.9	3,335	227	408	5,794	1.3
Blount	-0.2	D	9.5	20	7.4	8.5	6.5	9.4	14.1	32,845	253	2,545	58,673	6.1
Bradley	0.9	D	7.1	24.4	D	7.5	3.4	14	11.1	24,685	234	2,652	44,156	6.7
Campbell	-0.5	D	10.8	15.6	D	8.4	5.2	D	20.2	11,600	293	2,293	21,172	6
Cannon	-3.6	D	14.7	10.7	2.7	5.7	D	11.6	22.5	3,480	245	368	6,161	2
Carroll	-5.4	D	5.6	12.8	3.2	6.7	7.6	D	23.1	8,240	296	1,070	13,260	0.7
Carter	-0.4	D	9.6	11.4	4.4	9.3	5.6	D	19.6	16,230	287	1,869	28,289	2
Cheatham	-0.3	D	16.4	26.6	D	6.3	2.8	D	13.5	8,335	207	654	16,506	5.4
Chester	-1.1	0	D	14	D	8.9	3.1	D	25.4	4,215	246	434	7,158	2.5
Claiborne	-0.7	2.5	5.7	23.2	2.7	6.8	4.7	D	17.3	9,540	302	1,805	15,540	4.6
Clay	4.9	D	4.1	10.9	D	4.9	2.3	13.6	26.3	2,330	302	281	4,359	1.8
Cocke	1.6	0.7	6.9	21.8	2.5	10.5	2.9	D	24	11,200	315	2,009	17,629	1
Coffee	0.2	0	4.6	20.1	19.3	6.8	3.3	11	14.5	13,585	247	1,484	24,283	3.6
Crockett	-12.3	0	6.6	33.5	3.1	14.9	2.7	D	18.6	3,610	249	462	6,420	0
Cumberland	0.6	0.9	7.6	11.7	5.3	10.8	4.6	14.2	12.8	22,610	383	1,621	29,821	5.9
Davidson	0	0.1	6.1	3.3	13.7	5.4	8.7	23.4	7.7	98,770	143	15,059	319,529	12.5
Decatur		D	7.2	14.4	2.2	5.7	D	D	18.8	3,875	330	471	6,920	0.7
DeKalb	3.3	0	5.1	33.4	13.8	4.9	2.1	D	14.9	5,045	254	678	9,644	2.6
Dickson	-0.6	D	15.2	20.2	3.4	8.4	4.2	14.5	13.9	11,365	215	1,184	22,084	6.1
Dyer	-1.1	0	8.2	27.6	D	8	5.4	13.5	14.5	9,470	253	1,465	16,935	1.4
Fayette	-2	D	14.3	35	D	4.7	4.3	5.9	10	10,250	256	1,207	17,419	11.1
Fentress	1.3	D	6	5.3	3.4	8.9	D	D	17.5	5,945	328	1,058	9,053	1
Franklin	-0.3	0.8	7.5	18.2	D	8.4	3.6	D	15.3	10,965	263	979	19,504	4.3
Gibson	-1.8	0	9.8	20.9	D	11	4.7	D	19.8	12,955	264	1,621	22,622	2.8
Giles	-1.7	D	6	38.3	D	6.9	3.7	D	12.6	7,935	270	810	14,127	2.1
Grainger	1.2	D	13.9	25	D	5	D	3.8	18.3	6,585	285	1,009	11,130	2.2
Greene	0.1	D	4.1	26.3	2.6	6.9	3.5	D	15.4	20,870	303	2,537	32,680	2
Grundy	0.4	D	9.8	9.1	D	8.7	2.5	D	26.7	4,210	315	756	6,456	0.8
Hamblen	0.4	D	4.8	31.7	2.9	8.4	3.1	12.5	12.8	16,400	255	2,145	27,251	1.1
Hamilton	0	0	6.3	12.6	7.2	5.4	13.3	12.7	15.5	75,705	209	8,501	160,770	6.4
Hancock	-5.3	D	3.6	D	D	10	D	15.6	51.8	1,605	243	444	3,602	-0.6
Hardeman	-1.9	0	4.9	31.6	D	5.2	D	D	24.2	6,580	259	1,293	11,027	1.6
Hardin	-0.6	D	3.9	32.3	2.6	10.7	4.1	D	19.4	8,135	315	1,087	14,149	1.5
Hawkins	-0.4	D	9.6	34	D	4.8	2.2	D	17.4	17,270	306	1,937	27,330	1.7
Haywood	-15.6	0	7.4	35.8	D	7.1	5.4	6.7	24.7	4,640	264	911	8,418	1.1
Henderson	-0.5	0	6.7	15.3	2.6	6.8	13	D	16.9	6,865	247	914	13,015	1.8
Henry	4.6	D	8.4	20	3.2	8.9	5.2	7.5	20.6	9,920	306	938	17,254	1.1
Hickman	-1.4	D	D	11	3.3	8.2	D	D	23.2	5,740	231	679	10,554	2.3
Houston	-1.6	0	D	12.5	D	5.7	D	14.1	28	2,045	249	276	4,241	1.3
Humphreys		D	7.5	35.1	7.4	6	2.5	D	17.8	5,035	272	493	8,992	1.5
Jackson	-2.4	0	D	7.6	D	4.9	D	D	27.9	3,405	292	393	5,898	1
Jefferson	0.1	D	D	15.9	D	7.4	2.9	D	15.5	14,515	270	1,453	24,301	3.3
Johnson	0	D	D	24.8	3.1	4.4	3.3	8.6	19.4	5,590	316	851	9,039	0.9
Knox	0	0	6.2	5	11.3	8.4	7.6	18	13.8	90,585	196	10,267	206,043	5.7
Lake	-5.6	0	D	D	D	6.8	2.1	D	49.6	1,425	191	365	2,600	0.1
Lauderdale	-5.1	0	3.4	23.6	D	6.5	8.1	8.8	32	6,035	239	1,262	11,319	0.5
Lawrence	1	D	9.4	18.5	3.7	10.5	3.8	10.8	18.1	11,390	262	1,332	18,258	0.5
Lewis	-0.6	0	6.9	12.3	2.9	11.3	2.8	D	22.3	3,170	263	316	5,550	1.4
Lincoln	-1.2	D	7.6	31.3	4.2	8.3	3.6	4	19	8,880	263	876	15,606	2.4
Loudon	2.4	D	9.2	23.4	3.8	7.6	4.8	8.7	13.6	16,195	311	1,046	23,371	7.6
McMinn	0	D	6.2	40.8	2.3	6.2	4.1	D	11.2	13,900	263	1,666	23,439	0.4
McNairy	-2.2	0	7.1	22.3	D	6.4	3.2	10.6	22.1	7,950	306	1,152	12,084	1.3
Macon	9.3	0	7	12.8	4.7	10.3	6.2	D	18.2	5,625	234	686	10,422	5.8
Madison		D	7.1	17.3	4.2	7.1	4.6	14.8	22.6	21,890	224	3,454	43,378	3.6
Marion	-0.2	D	7	28.5	D	8.4	2.5	7.6	16.3	7,760	273	986	13,497	4.2

1. Per 1,000 resident population estimated as of July 1 of the year shown.

Table B. States and Counties — Housing, Labor Force, and Employment

STATE County	Housing units, 2013-2017								Civilian labor force, 2018				Civilian employment[6], 2013-2017		
	Occupied units										Unemployment			Percent	
			Owner-occupied			Renter-occupied									
				Median owner cost as a percent of income			Median rent as a percent of income[2]	Sub-standard units[4] (percent)		Percent change, 2017-2018				Management, business, science, and arts	Construction, production, and maintenance occupations
	Total	Percent	Median value[1]	With a mortgage	Without a mortgage[2]	Median rent[3]			Total		Total	Rate[5]	Total		
	89	90	91	92	93	94	95	96	97	98	99	100	101	102	103
SOUTH DAKOTA— Cont'd															
Tripp	2,424	69.2	85,800	18.9	11.1	562	27.5	0.6	3,078	1.4	79	2.6	2,859	42.6	26.8
Turner	3,523	78.1	110,400	19.3	11.0	660	24.8	0.9	4,695	0.5	127	2.7	4,307	34.6	28.6
Union	6,285	73.2	161,300	17.1	10.5	781	21.8	1.1	8,149	1.3	261	3.2	7,933	38.9	24.8
Walworth	2,292	71.2	82,400	18.3	10.0	614	23.6	1.6	2,235	0	109	4.9	2,741	36.9	21.8
Yankton	9,283	65.3	140,400	19.5	10.0	609	26	0.6	11,826	1.9	312	2.6	11,340	35.9	25.1
Ziebach	764	53.4	57,100	18.0	12.4	537	28.8	15.1	933	-0.5	48	5.1	967	51.3	17.2
TENNESSEE	2,547,194	66.3	151,700	20.9	10.2	808	29.4	2.4	3,244,921	1.7	113,261	3.5	2,996,610	34.4	24.4
Anderson	30,518	67.4	134,100	20.1	10.0	719	27.7	2.2	34,283	1.3	1,288	3.8	32,213	33.6	23.8
Bedford	17,058	68.2	129,700	21.6	10.2	734	27.4	4.6	20,592	0.4	772	3.7	21,387	24.7	39.0
Benton	6,693	75.7	88,700	22.8	11.7	606	32.6	3.4	6,848	2	336	4.9	5,721	23.2	36.1
Bledsoe	4,664	75.8	129,600	20.8	11.4	602	24.3	5.8	4,303	0.2	250	5.8	5,270	25.5	40.6
Blount	49,939	74.8	169,500	20.7	10.0	744	28.2	1.5	62,275	1.2	2,009	3.2	58,333	32.8	25.1
Bradley	39,615	65.9	150,100	20.9	10.0	746	28.3	2.9	50,258	-1.1	1,803	3.6	46,406	31.9	28.9
Campbell	15,843	69.3	92,700	20.8	12.2	571	27	1.3	14,752	1	702	4.8	15,080	23.5	35.4
Cannon	5,456	73.6	151,800	20.5	10.0	633	25.7	3	6,368	2.8	201	3.2	6,072	28.9	34.7
Carroll	11,321	72.5	86,800	19.3	10.6	589	29.5	2	11,940	0.2	591	4.9	11,050	28.0	33.4
Carter	23,798	70.0	114,600	21.7	11.2	606	32	2.2	24,002	0.6	992	4.1	22,819	27.4	28.6
Cheatham	14,671	79.1	170,500	22.3	10.0	948	32.5	2.2	21,459	3.1	587	2.7	19,170	32.3	29.7
Chester	5,998	75.0	113,800	19.6	10.0	690	29.3	2.4	8,422	1.2	318	3.8	7,009	33.0	27.4
Claiborne	12,996	71.1	102,700	21.9	10.0	588	30.3	2.1	12,973	2.2	549	4.2	11,893	29.0	35.9
Clay	3,171	74.4	90,300	23.5	12.4	501	29.4	2.6	2,857	-5.7	142	5	2,568	27.6	35.6
Cocke	14,592	68.3	107,200	23.2	10.1	547	28.4	2	14,847	1.8	696	4.7	14,192	22.4	31.3
Coffee	21,576	67.8	118,000	19.4	10.1	690	25.2	3.2	25,484	2.3	872	3.4	23,291	28.2	35.8
Crockett	5,400	69.8	96,700	20.0	12.6	668	30.1	4.1	7,019	1	271	3.9	6,048	30.0	31.1
Cumberland	25,114	78.2	140,800	22.0	10.0	666	30	1.9	23,336	-0.1	1,017	4.4	20,741	27.3	30.9
Davidson	273,497	54.4	194,800	21.7	10.7	971	29.1	3.2	396,574	3.2	10,438	2.6	364,089	40.6	18.4
Decatur	4,721	73.6	91,800	19.2	11.2	550	30.2	0.6	4,734	1.5	226	4.8	4,497	30.0	30.6
DeKalb	7,362	66.5	131,100	21.6	10.0	624	22.1	2.9	7,730	1	343	4.4	8,003	33.1	39.0
Dickson	19,032	71.3	146,300	20.5	10.0	736	29.2	2.6	26,257	3	793	3	22,454	28.9	30.4
Dyer	15,327	61.5	98,100	18.7	10.8	654	26.2	3.2	16,239	1	742	4.6	16,155	30.5	31.7
Fayette	15,084	79.7	185,000	21.4	10.0	661	30.8	1.3	18,769	1.1	700	3.7	17,508	33.9	28.1
Fentress	7,385	75.6	103,700	20.8	11.7	490	26.6	3	7,162	1.1	299	4.2	6,577	21.2	35.2
Franklin	16,325	73.6	120,600	20.9	10.4	622	26.4	2	19,948	0.7	672	3.4	17,632	29.5	32.8
Gibson	19,280	69.7	94,800	21.6	11.0	660	30.4	2.3	21,436	0.9	955	4.5	20,523	29.4	27.3
Giles	11,599	69.7	120,400	21.1	10.6	627	28.4	3	15,194	-2.1	557	3.7	12,368	25.7	37.5
Grainger	9,112	77.5	110,600	21.4	10.2	604	26.9	3	9,417	1.2	372	4	9,482	24.9	40.1
Greene	27,319	72.7	114,600	21.0	10.2	572	28.3	2	29,829	-1.6	1,376	4.6	28,001	27.7	31.6
Grundy	4,894	75.0	82,400	23.1	11.8	573	29.7	4	4,886	1.3	216	4.4	4,172	21.5	41.0
Hamblen	24,343	66.1	131,200	19.9	10.1	686	30.9	2.9	27,421	0.6	1,050	3.8	26,084	27.6	35.4
Hamilton	139,037	64.5	166,100	19.9	10.4	795	29.9	1.5	179,683	1.9	6,107	3.4	167,211	38.3	20.2
Hancock	2,704	77.4	83,500	21.0	11.3	401	30.1	3.7	2,031	-0.6	103	5.1	2,268	24.5	38.2
Hardeman	8,680	69.6	85,400	23.8	12.4	621	28.3	1.3	9,196	-0.1	459	5	8,181	27.6	34.5
Hardin	10,118	75.1	107,400	21.9	10.0	609	27.8	3.5	10,387	0	455	4.4	9,716	24.2	33.9
Hawkins	23,375	74.0	115,400	20.5	10.4	613	28.6	2.7	23,706	0.3	946	4	21,867	23.9	33.9
Haywood	7,104	59.9	104,300	22.5	12.7	613	32	2	7,738	-0.6	414	5.4	7,686	22.8	35.1
Henderson	10,827	72.3	92,700	17.5	10.3	632	34.8	2.8	11,981	0.9	563	4.7	11,255	29.3	34.8
Henry	13,483	75.5	97,000	21.6	10.4	611	30	1.8	14,231	1.9	595	4.2	12,680	27.1	31.9
Hickman	8,930	78.4	104,800	21.6	10.8	666	33.6	2.8	11,160	3.1	358	3.2	9,659	25.4	37.3
Houston	2,999	77.2	94,900	23.5	11.5	654	24.2	1.3	3,222	0.8	178	5.5	3,049	17.5	43.1
Humphreys	7,064	76.9	103,000	20.4	10.3	632	32.8	1.9	8,813	0.4	379	4.3	7,202	30.5	35.6
Jackson	4,566	76.0	107,700	25.1	11.7	533	26	2.4	4,602	0.2	217	4.7	4,106	24.7	37.6
Jefferson	20,088	73.4	136,700	20.9	10.7	669	26.8	3.4	24,009	0.6	917	3.8	23,110	26.2	31.1
Johnson	6,936	76.5	114,100	24.3	10.7	491	29.9	3.8	7,613	0.4	263	3.5	5,595	25.8	32.2
Knox	182,315	64.1	169,400	19.9	10.0	839	29.2	1.6	240,034	1.2	7,048	2.9	222,748	40.5	16.8
Lake	2,164	59.3	75,100	19.4	11.6	524	26.2	3	1,804	-1.8	93	5.2	1,906	24.4	29.5
Lauderdale	9,725	57.5	81,000	21.9	11.6	634	31.1	3.5	9,619	2.4	554	5.8	9,096	24.2	33.7
Lawrence	16,101	73.8	98,800	20.8	10.0	621	29.6	4.2	18,309	3.1	739	4	16,277	25.7	39.3
Lewis	4,663	78.8	88,300	21.6	11.3	492	29	3.2	5,072	2.7	225	4.4	4,772	27.3	32.2
Lincoln	13,653	72.5	117,500	22.0	11.3	666	31.8	2.8	16,408	0.9	506	3.1	14,216	26.5	37.9
Loudon	20,090	76.1	193,000	20.2	10.0	740	26.9	3.3	22,857	1.1	779	3.4	20,363	27.4	30.0
McMinn	20,352	74.3	123,700	20.8	10.2	624	32.3	1.9	22,719	0.3	928	4.1	20,840	27.0	35.7
McNairy	10,095	73.6	87,500	19.9	11.7	574	29.1	2.1	8,477	-0.7	457	5.4	9,313	27.9	34.9
Macon	9,158	73.4	111,700	22.8	12.2	585	27	2.2	10,991	2.7	353	3.2	9,856	24.8	38.1
Madison	37,110	63.4	126,100	21.7	10.8	837	33.2	1.3	48,664	1.3	1,832	3.8	43,003	32.8	22.8
Marion	11,393	74.7	121,200	21.6	10.0	665	28.7	2.7	12,265	2	575	4.7	11,940	28.0	34.0

1. Specified owner-occupied units.   2. A value of 10.0 represents 10 percent or less; a value of 50.0 represents 50 percent or more.   3. Specified renter-occupied units.   4. Overcrowded or lacking complete plumbing facilities.   5. Percent of civilian labor force.   6. Civilian employed persons 16 years old and over.

Table B. States and Counties — Nonfarm Employment and Agriculture

STATE County	Private nonfarm establishments, employment and payroll, 2016									Agriculture, 2017			
		Employment						Annual payroll		Farms			Farm producers whose primary occupation is farming (percent)
							Professional, scientific, and technical services				Percent with:		
	Number of establishments	Total	Health care and social assistance	Manufacturing	Retail trade	Finance and insurance		Total (mil dol)	Average per employee (dollars)	Number	Fewer than 50 acres	1000 acres or more	
	104	105	106	107	108	109	110	111	112	113	114	115	116
SOUTH DAKOTA— Cont'd													
Tripp	200	1,567	450	40	364	70	51	49	31,243	648	13.7	42.4	58.5
Turner	263	1,488	380	177	218	68	55	52	35,267	757	30.3	16.2	46.6
Union	489	9,110	1,117	1,746	510	1,061	222	462	50,726	557	29.1	18.3	50.7
Walworth	213	2,019	367	D	378	74	68	63	31,405	256	11.3	39.8	52.9
Yankton	737	11,123	1,978	3,014	1,780	694	221	421	37,823	610	23.8	17.4	51.7
Ziebach	51	317	86	D	90	D	D	10	29,968	213	1.4	74.6	70.6
TENNESSEE	135,352	2,592,600	411,490	319,674	329,760	122,885	117,580	114,896	44,317	69,983	45.2	2.3	35.8
Anderson	1,554	39,443	3,895	10,905	3,411	915	8,324	2,345	59,463	538	54.3	0.2	30.5
Bedford	766	14,417	1,123	4,604	1,602	520	218	565	39,178	1,430	41.9	2.4	40.3
Benton	297	3,511	710	745	698	157	37	100	28,363	399	30.8	2.0	29.2
Bledsoe	92	438	78	52	82	49	8	14	31,676	614	36.0	2.0	39.4
Blount	2,312	45,006	6,385	7,053	5,809	2,119	3,667	2,043	45,392	1,073	60.7	1.1	39.6
Bradley	1,904	39,192	5,143	8,087	5,148	1,830	744	1,495	38,151	778	52.6	0.4	42.1
Campbell	595	7,627	1,924	1,685	1,594	241	101	225	29,438	343	47.5	NA	32.2
Cannon	196	1,522	324	258	211	49	39	50	32,575	728	46.7	1.1	30.6
Carroll	435	6,153	1,552	868	797	286	81	183	29,807	662	36.3	5.6	27.8
Carter	705	8,995	1,707	1,103	1,918	328	157	261	28,963	469	58.0	NA	33.7
Cheatham	608	6,377	671	1,825	862	149	170	244	38,249	543	48.4	1.8	34.8
Chester	234	3,181	399	586	437	108	46	87	27,212	380	28.9	4.2	31.0
Claiborne	431	7,485	1,081	2,084	856	258	137	252	33,623	966	42.1	0.6	41.5
Clay	111	1,096	301	285	167	34	7	31	27,864	404	32.9	2.0	42.1
Cocke	474	6,004	902	1,572	1,426	223	92	194	32,315	645	47.6	0.5	40.7
Coffee	1,244	19,894	2,822	4,344	3,139	780	2,350	774	38,901	872	51.1	4.0	34.5
Crockett	220	1,901	450	264	313	74	38	64	33,600	322	39.8	14.9	36.8
Cumberland	1,059	14,841	2,631	2,554	2,726	454	275	491	33,092	886	48.4	1.6	30.7
Davidson	19,470	439,335	83,672	18,834	41,711	28,049	26,963	23,468	53,418	414	56.8	0.2	29.7
Decatur	208	2,754	1,006	450	349	99	41	101	36,645	374	24.1	1.9	33.0
DeKalb	283	4,399	570	2,163	462	83	87	160	36,412	654	43.3	1.5	39.8
Dickson	936	14,087	2,173	3,296	2,475	387	235	481	34,151	1,225	45.0	0.2	30.1
Dyer	792	13,370	2,113	3,762	2,048	502	163	479	35,795	451	35.9	21.1	39.4
Fayette	578	6,941	531	1,875	929	210	100	293	42,167	892	37.6	8.1	33.4
Fentress	243	3,842	909	293	663	177	47	117	30,327	620	41.9	2.3	37.6
Franklin	707	11,392	1,520	3,368	1,483	243	192	460	40,419	818	51.1	1.8	34.0
Gibson	928	11,351	2,015	2,321	2,119	328	209	376	33,089	777	49.3	10.3	37.6
Giles	530	8,553	974	3,582	1,328	275	111	325	38,050	1,599	34.8	1.7	38.0
Grainger	227	2,609	177	1,031	508	38	59	80	30,825	923	46.6	0.3	34.2
Greene	1,109	22,375	4,162	6,328	2,989	570	299	756	33,795	2,562	56.2	0.5	36.7
Grundy	158	1,361	317	275	297	84	25	35	25,521	261	38.7	1.5	41.6
Hamblen	1,296	28,998	3,815	9,460	4,309	467	332	1,036	35,725	559	61.2	0.7	40.1
Hamilton	8,848	185,060	28,522	23,179	21,500	12,520	8,389	7,776	42,018	547	56.7	0.5	37.4
Hancock	47	424	151	D	100	14	D	13	29,637	408	21.6	2.9	46.0
Hardeman	333	5,498	1,192	1,834	610	150	31	189	34,416	613	32.0	6.9	30.2
Hardin	481	6,519	1,188	1,748	1,362	226	66	258	39,609	583	32.1	5.0	34.5
Hawkins	588	9,232	1,334	3,383	1,313	223	113	326	35,319	1,484	47.4	0.5	37.7
Haywood	312	5,099	443	2,229	605	155	66	177	34,618	361	35.7	16.3	41.5
Henderson	488	6,599	982	1,522	1,022	466	109	210	31,898	786	25.1	1.8	35.0
Henry	695	8,664	1,388	1,486	1,710	317	291	288	33,244	710	34.5	6.2	33.6
Hickman	263	2,300	639	487	291	51	35	79	34,221	706	32.2	1.8	38.8
Houston	102	1,086	322	200	162	40	33	30	27,750	326	29.4	1.2	38.1
Humphreys	328	4,213	674	1,244	619	83	74	189	44,763	657	35.5	2.3	31.1
Jackson	99	1,073	126	D	103	24	41	40	37,461	538	33.3	1.3	31.1
Jefferson	700	11,366	1,171	1,738	1,908	254	197	390	34,331	973	50.1	0.4	39.2
Johnson	232	3,194	632	655	369	111	53	127	39,677	517	53.2	0.4	38.6
Knox	11,401	218,158	35,815	10,729	31,297	11,190	10,166	9,197	42,156	1,037	63.6	NA	35.5
Lake	73	587	145	D	136	16	D	18	30,750	52	15.4	48.1	68.8
Lauderdale	295	4,694	655	1,045	721	180	42	151	32,149	404	37.4	8.7	35.5
Lawrence	706	8,385	1,333	1,781	1,548	231	241	256	30,577	1,394	40.0	2.3	35.8
Lewis	212	2,112	530	431	440	77	44	58	27,265	272	32.7	1.1	33.7
Lincoln	563	8,480	855	3,314	1,479	216	144	283	33,402	1,654	37.7	1.7	36.5
Loudon	927	13,330	1,581	2,688	2,001	335	563	521	39,101	691	55.6	0.6	36.0
McMinn	897	16,142	2,158	6,327	2,321	453	299	605	37,471	1,054	49.1	1.4	35.4
McNairy	403	4,714	800	1,045	569	140	76	133	28,295	654	34.9	3.1	33.0
Macon	310	3,556	554	1,024	760	239	62	108	30,450	912	38.3	2.1	35.5
Madison	2,502	52,687	12,464	9,419	7,164	1,329	1,100	1,995	37,858	549	37.9	4.9	34.3
Marion	424	6,067	686	1,774	1,294	142	79	212	34,919	308	36.4	1.9	37.7

Table B. States and Counties — **Agriculture**

STATE County	Acreage (1,000) [117]	Percent change, 2012-2017 [118]	Average size of farm [119]	Total irrigated (1,000) [120]	Total cropland (1,000) [121]	Average per farm [122]	Average per acre [123]	Value of machinery and equipment, average per farm (dollars) [124]	Total (mil dol) [125]	Average per farm (acres) [126]	Crops [127]	Livestock and poultry products [128]	Organic farms (number) [129]	Farms with internet access (percent) [130]	Total ($1,000) [131]	Percent of farms [132]
SOUTH DAKOTA— Cont'd																
Tripp	1,037	1.7	1,600	5.1	438.1	2,591,113	1,620	271,919	202.6	312,627	24.8	75.2	2	83.5	9,317	85.0
Turner	393	2.2	519	26.9	350.3	2,604,252	5,019	265,081	265.7	351,004	61.3	38.7	2	78.2	9,119	72.4
Union	290	0.5	521	40.7	266.7	3,059,199	5,875	315,383	187.0	335,772	71.8	28.2	1	83.3	4,214	81.7
Walworth	453	1.9	1,771	2.8	273.8	3,506,300	1,980	356,021	87.1	340,066	70.1	29.9	2	87.9	6,182	76.6
Yankton	330	0.6	540	38.0	252.6	2,389,517	4,422	258,025	162.4	266,193	65.2	34.8	2	80.5	7,994	76.4
Ziebach	1,099	-0.8	5,162	NA	256.8	4,412,411	855	352,110	59.9	281,272	35.4	64.6	NA	78.4	6,373	87.8
TENNESSEE	10,874	0.1	155	184.9	5,286.3	608,739	3,918	80,447	3,798.9	54,284	57.4	42.6	122	72.7	115,945	26.5
Anderson	43	21.2	81	0.1	14.7	441,499	5,465	59,863	4.3	8,015	31.4	68.6	NA	74.0	205	13.4
Bedford	238	2.4	166	1.2	92.6	693,089	4,167	86,121	151.6	106,013	14.3	85.7	NA	76.9	2,460	28.3
Benton	69	-22.0	172	D	30.3	427,822	2,489	82,014	9.5	23,797	63.2	36.8	NA	74.4	625	30.3
Bledsoe	94	-7.9	153	0.5	34.7	528,198	3,445	85,821	39.9	64,951	26.7	73.3	NA	77.7	628	32.4
Blount	95	-6.1	88	0.1	40.6	567,289	6,436	60,767	16.5	15,347	34.7	65.3	10	77.4	488	11.6
Bradley	85	-2.0	109	0.1	28.3	661,318	6,065	66,853	105.9	136,067	12.6	87.4	3	71.6	872	16.7
Campbell	28	-17.7	80	0.1	10.2	332,638	4,138	55,393	2.9	8,437	43.5	56.5	1	57.1	114	19.0
Cannon	89	-7.4	122	0.0	38.9	438,958	3,587	60,409	22.6	31,021	60.7	39.3	NA	76.6	1,013	20.2
Carroll	170	-4.7	256	4.9	106.2	700,403	2,735	101,405	52.6	79,492	94.7	5.3	NA	69.3	3,582	43.8
Carter	34	-14.9	73	0.1	12.0	379,965	5,199	57,459	7.7	16,377	33.4	66.6	3	71.9	D	2.3
Cheatham	67	28.4	124	0.1	31.8	564,719	4,557	75,846	16.3	30,072	84.6	15.4	5	76.1	313	19.2
Chester	80	31.3	210	D	42.4	534,584	2,540	79,023	16.1	42,347	89.3	10.7	NA	71.1	1,198	37.9
Claiborne	120	-1.3	124	0.0	35.4	388,110	3,128	55,041	17.4	17,971	17.9	82.1	1	58.7	1,282	42.3
Clay	75	-5.6	186	0.0	24.8	620,853	3,333	63,718	60.0	148,634	9.2	90.8	NA	69.1	438	42.1
Cocke	65	7.0	101	D	23.4	448,496	4,427	69,868	36.5	56,563	32.6	67.4	1	64.2	324	19.8
Coffee	139	-4.3	159	1.8	79.9	652,277	4,105	92,203	60.6	69,450	66.5	33.5	NA	79.2	2,149	26.4
Crockett	149	14.3	463	10.4	134.1	1,559,863	3,365	278,689	81.6	253,388	97.0	3.0	NA	64.3	2,486	61.2
Cumberland	129	0.1	146	0.0	46.3	589,663	4,043	73,047	46.7	52,746	47.0	53.0	NA	73.5	790	19.2
Davidson	34	-1.1	83	0.3	13.0	747,014	8,978	62,082	11.1	26,829	78.4	21.6	4	78.5	160	10.9
Decatur	74	-4.4	197	D	24.8	436,208	2,209	78,589	7.4	19,826	56.5	43.5	NA	67.6	583	23.0
DeKalb	88	-1.5	135	0.5	29.7	456,211	3,384	63,777	26.0	39,719	78.4	21.6	NA	72.0	633	32.9
Dickson	140	-5.6	114	0.2	46.9	480,574	4,201	64,723	18.6	15,208	56.6	43.4	2	75.7	412	15.8
Dyer	284	34.1	629	25.5	257.6	2,117,443	3,364	273,302	134.2	297,483	96.8	3.2	NA	80.3	2,700	59.6
Fayette	306	33.8	344	13.3	185.7	1,158,789	3,373	120,662	89.9	100,784	87.0	13.0	NA	71.0	3,742	39.3
Fentress	94	3.5	152	0.0	25.7	526,303	3,472	72,186	37.6	60,584	12.9	87.1	NA	74.4	549	33.4
Franklin	112	-10.4	137	1.5	61.5	563,293	4,101	83,705	72.5	88,641	44.5	55.5	1	72.1	1,795	30.6
Gibson	287	0.4	370	9.9	248.8	1,309,546	3,541	174,608	137.1	176,459	94.6	5.4	NA	73.7	6,511	51.4
Giles	251	-7.1	157	2.1	78.8	514,156	3,275	69,966	48.9	30,551	38.3	61.7	NA	74.2	4,230	37.3
Grainger	87	2.2	94	0.3	25.8	358,497	3,798	60,980	19.5	21,085	55.5	44.5	6	64.1	1,666	31.5
Greene	222	-1.9	86	D	97.2	388,623	4,493	64,414	61.5	24,014	30.8	69.2	1	67.1	1,112	15.8
Grundy	34	1.8	129	0.1	13.3	446,403	3,459	70,611	29.6	113,586	37.2	62.8	NA	68.6	258	19.2
Hamblen	50	-15.0	89	0.0	24.4	492,840	5,507	67,616	15.8	28,188	24.4	75.6	1	68.0	387	25.8
Hamilton	44	-16.5	80	0.1	14.0	786,833	9,850	59,900	20.6	37,649	12.7	87.3	3	77.7	201	12.2
Hancock	73	12.9	178	D	16.5	474,077	2,662	57,539	6.7	16,341	18.3	81.7	NA	62.5	646	40.7
Hardeman	173	12.4	282	2.3	83.9	645,321	2,289	75,727	31.5	51,408	90.7	9.3	NA	63.5	2,859	39.2
Hardin	162	28.5	278	2.2	76.2	620,402	2,232	101,400	29.7	50,871	81.5	18.5	NA	64.5	2,154	43.6
Hawkins	141	6.0	95	0.0	47.8	355,038	3,727	58,427	18.8	12,648	28.5	71.5	NA	62.9	1,252	24.7
Haywood	201	-8.5	556	21.6	178.6	1,845,293	3,319	211,930	97.8	270,925	99.2	0.8	2	71.2	3,391	63.7
Henderson	153	-5.5	195	0.0	63.7	492,153	2,522	89,292	29.2	37,104	60.2	39.8	NA	72.8	1,940	35.4
Henry	204	-0.3	287	4.1	127.5	954,925	3,324	139,412	94.1	132,530	62.2	37.8	1	81.5	2,783	42.4
Hickman	123	2.1	175	0.0	43.9	551,572	3,154	72,096	17.1	24,183	50.6	49.4	2	78.2	1,053	22.2
Houston	50	0.1	154	0.0	11.7	499,292	3,233	71,786	D	D	D	D	NA	81.9	76	10.4
Humphreys	115	-6.5	176	1.5	33.4	489,160	2,783	82,009	11.2	17,078	46.2	53.8	NA	74.0	261	6.5
Jackson	81	9.6	150	0.0	18.6	466,297	3,105	58,481	4.9	9,130	36.1	63.9	8	78.4	270	31.6
Jefferson	89	-6.9	91	0.3	37.2	470,695	5,149	61,911	24.1	24,780	21.8	78.2	NA	67.7	1,260	25.7
Johnson	47	-1.6	90	0.0	16.4	358,093	3,973	62,699	7.7	14,797	29.9	70.1	2	68.9	112	5.8
Knox	67	3.1	65	0.2	26.7	639,694	9,845	53,723	18.7	17,987	61.6	38.4	8	79.7	618	15.5
Lake	88	10.7	1,698	15.0	82.0	5,959,437	3,511	793,852	45.8	880,788	99.8	0.2	NA	84.6	2,175	76.9
Lauderdale	156	-22.5	385	6.1	134.3	1,304,233	3,385	186,207	69.6	172,260	96.0	4.0	NA	63.4	2,608	55.4
Lawrence	230	-2.3	165	D	105.7	544,725	3,296	77,410	71.1	51,024	55.6	44.4	NA	66.9	2,770	37.2
Lewis	41	32.7	150	0.0	10.4	428,585	2,859	53,189	3.0	10,996	35.2	64.8	2	72.8	161	11.4
Lincoln	271	2.0	164	3.4	102.6	600,890	3,663	90,043	124.9	75,524	30.9	69.1	NA	73.1	1,905	19.4
Loudon	59	-15.2	85	0.1	28.4	484,550	5,690	74,092	D	D	D	D	1	73.7	284	20.3
McMinn	129	5.6	123	0.1	49.9	571,882	4,666	65,080	50.1	47,555	16.2	83.8	1	69.2	1,162	24.1
McNairy	139	7.0	213	0.3	65.5	468,203	2,203	70,549	22.4	34,229	86.0	14.0	2	69.7	1,212	40.7
Macon	132	8.0	144	D	51.9	543,237	3,763	72,506	61.5	67,451	44.8	55.2	2	74.2	1,078	32.8
Madison	151	-8.9	275	6.8	107.6	898,835	3,263	136,092	49.5	90,117	93.7	6.3	NA	70.3	3,371	52.6
Marion	55	8.5	179	0.0	23.1	581,773	3,254	86,733	17.1	55,406	33.9	66.1	NA	72.7	500	11.0

Table B. States and Counties — Water Use, Wholesale Trade, Retail Trade, and Real Estate

STATE County	Water use, 2015		Wholesale Trade[1], 2012				Retail Trade[2], 2012				Real estate and rental and leasing,[2] 2012			
	Public supply water withdrawn (mil gal/ day)	Public supply gallons withdrawn per person per day	Number of establish-ments	Number of employees	Sales (mil dol)	Average payroll (mil dol)	Number of establish-ments	Number of employees	Sales (mil dol)	Average payroll (mil dol)	Number of establish-ments	Number of employees	Sales (mil dol)	Average payroll (mil dol)
	133	134	135	136	137	138	139	140	141	142	143	144	145	146
SOUTH DAKOTA— Cont'd														
Tripp	0.49	90.2	14	132	130.1	5.2	47	384	104.3	8.4	4	2	0.4	0.0
Turner	0.47	57.3	16	107	250.4	4.9	33	269	46.6	4.1	4	D	D	D
Union	1.59	106.6	35	641	1,135.3	39.1	46	422	153.2	7.8	21	40	9.1	1.9
Walworth	0.42	77.2	9	73	351.0	3.3	41	366	88.8	6.6	6	D	D	D
Yankton	1.11	48.9	32	240	213.8	10.3	121	1,554	368.6	34.5	21	51	7.6	1.4
Ziebach	0.04	14.3	4	D	D	D	8	62	15.8	0.9	2	D	D	D
TENNESSEE	849.69	128.7	5,828	92,537	111,718.4	4,863.3	22,615	306,078	91,641.6	7,420.3	5,470	30,593	6,178.4	1,220.0
Anderson	10.69	141.1	41	449	591.5	19.5	242	3,510	916.1	76.6	57	184	38.5	6.9
Bedford	6.03	127.8	24	D	D	D	150	1,502	407.6	34.3	31	154	27.4	5.1
Benton	1.25	77.5	11	D	D	D	59	631	150.9	13.5	4	9	1.5	0.2
Bledsoe	2.19	151.0	3	D	D	D	19	127	53.2	3.8	4	6	0.9	0.2
Blount	13.94	109.5	86	D	D	D	360	5,651	1,441.2	144.2	84	334	70.7	10.9
Bradley	13.74	132.0	60	D	D	D	363	4,676	1,335.0	111.7	62	D	D	D
Campbell	3.33	83.8	13	58	46.9	2.5	132	1,492	401.5	33.0	24	62	8.1	1.5
Cannon	5.28	381.5	5	D	D	D	34	213	61.2	4.7	2	D	D	D
Carroll	2.48	88.9	14	D	D	D	98	846	204.4	16.6	13	57	7.1	0.9
Carter	7.07	125.2	12	D	D	D	131	1,692	431.2	35.0	23	61	9.5	1.6
Cheatham	2.93	73.7	10	D	D	D	76	797	225.8	18.0	17	37	7.4	0.9
Chester	0.93	53.2	8	38	35.3	1.1	57	440	132.9	10.0	8	15	2.8	0.3
Claiborne	2.98	94.0	10	D	D	D	86	768	170.1	16.5	19	48	5.3	1.2
Clay	0.86	110.7	2	D	D	D	26	159	37.7	2.8	6	25	1.5	0.2
Cocke	4.72	134.2	5	D	D	D	112	1,271	341.0	28.7	17	113	5.9	1.5
Coffee	5.76	106.1	38	456	269.6	20.1	255	2,834	827.6	67.1	39	144	20.9	4.2
Crockett	1.56	106.8	15	272	352.2	16.4	39	266	78.5	5.1	5	12	3.8	0.2
Cumberland	5.71	98.1	38	D	D	D	229	2,632	750.3	61.1	39	139	19.1	3.6
Davidson	134.11	197.5	923	17,595	17,607.0	1,115.0	2,575	37,506	10,138.3	989.0	897	6,348	1,410.7	284.0
Decatur	1.37	117.5	4	D	D	D	45	335	76.5	7.1	4	7	0.5	0.1
DeKalb	2.17	113.1	9	D	D	D	51	493	107.3	10.0	10	15	1.7	0.5
Dickson	5.24	101.8	28	525	513.7	22.7	179	2,198	714.7	49.8	32	74	10.8	1.8
Dyer	2.71	71.5	40	D	D	D	169	2,053	580.8	50.8	25	72	12.8	3.2
Fayette	1.47	37.5	24	D	D	D	86	924	216.1	19.8	14	24	4.4	0.6
Fentress	1.65	92.1	5	10	5.4	0.3	50	599	145.6	12.4	6	92	10.0	2.8
Franklin	4.27	103.0	12	D	D	D	144	1,379	410.4	32.4	16	D	D	D
Gibson	3.80	76.9	32	367	310.4	15.7	192	1,992	505.8	42.5	26	71	18.0	2.2
Giles	3.00	103.6	25	273	189.1	12.4	124	1,342	317.1	27.8	9	37	2.6	0.9
Grainger	0.00	0.0	1	D	D	D	51	351	89.9	7.3	10	7	1.4	0.2
Greene	8.92	130.1	31	365	181.8	12.3	205	2,642	686.2	56.2	34	129	18.4	2.6
Grundy	1.63	121.3	3	4	0.6	0.1	47	306	72.1	5.9	1	D	D	D
Hamblen	9.18	144.8	50	D	D	D	265	3,888	978.7	93.5	53	165	33.2	4.6
Hamilton	60.03	169.5	437	5,317	2,904.0	266.3	1,410	19,752	5,236.5	485.2	375	2,092	418.4	97.5
Hancock	0.21	32.0	2	D	D	D	16	107	24.7	1.8	3	D	D	D
Hardeman	2.20	85.6	11	76	69.5	3.0	77	629	147.9	12.6	6	22	1.5	0.5
Hardin	2.63	102.1	15	98	228.0	4.2	113	1,269	396.7	30.6	20	55	8.3	2.0
Hawkins	3.42	60.6	19	167	89.1	6.2	113	1,233	303.1	25.1	24	91	11.3	2.6
Haywood	1.49	82.7	10	107	68.1	3.5	59	630	207.6	12.7	9	30	3.2	0.9
Henderson	0.31	11.1	15	224	56.5	5.8	103	1,094	296.9	23.5	8	D	D	D
Henry	2.11	65.6	25	581	159.4	18.4	139	1,604	489.5	40.5	26	84	15.2	2.2
Hickman	2.38	97.7	13	58	45.3	2.1	48	293	71.4	5.9	5	16	0.8	0.2
Houston	1.00	122.7	1	D	D	D	21	154	35.3	3.2	2	D	D	D
Humphreys	2.22	122.4	13	86	111.3	5.4	65	585	185.7	12.0	8	19	1.3	0.3
Jackson	0.56	48.7	4	D	D	D	22	102	30.9	1.8	1	D	D	D
Jefferson	5.28	99.2	18	D	D	D	126	1,786	640.4	38.4	26	132	28.8	4.3
Johnson	1.70	95.3	4	D	D	D	55	453	108.8	8.3	14	34	3.5	0.4
Knox	64.33	142.5	655	9,371	5,382.5	494.3	1,764	29,577	7,926.7	733.1	559	3,312	618.3	123.8
Lake	1.11	146.5	6	D	D	D	21	154	29.8	2.6	3	8	1.0	0.2
Lauderdale	2.53	93.9	19	818	1,545.9	35.0	78	688	161.7	14.5	17	56	18.0	2.1
Lawrence	4.06	95.4	33	258	157.6	9.2	172	1,512	384.2	34.2	18	61	8.2	1.4
Lewis	1.31	110.5	5	D	D	D	41	394	179.5	10.1	3	6	0.7	0.1
Lincoln	4.33	128.3	22	248	385.1	11.7	128	1,240	316.8	30.7	19	122	8.5	2.8
Loudon	13.14	257.0	41	D	D	D	150	1,857	484.0	41.7	32	131	14.8	3.5
McMinn	3.81	72.4	29	D	D	D	172	1,940	542.4	42.9	33	132	18.2	3.3
McNairy	2.54	97.4	15	130	44.2	6.3	83	615	154.8	14.0	8	30	3.9	0.7
Macon	2.09	90.2	10	78	18.7	2.0	70	666	177.4	14.7	16	50	3.4	0.5
Madison	15.74	161.3	141	1,485	808.6	65.7	469	7,050	1,902.6	162.4	104	546	86.8	16.9
Marion	3.42	120.1	19	159	69.1	6.2	99	1,112	336.2	25.4	5	21	2.6	0.5

1 Merchant wholesalers, except manufacturers' sales branches and offices.   2. Employer establishments.

Table B. States and Counties — Professional Services, Manufacturing, and Accommodation and Food Services

STATE County	Professional, scientific, and technical services, 2012				Manufacturing, 2012				Accommodation and food services, 2012			
	Number of establish-ments	Number of employees	Sales (mil dol)	Average payroll (mil dol)	Number of establish-ments	Number of employees	Receipts (mil dol)	Annual payroll (mil dol)	Number of establis-hments	Number of employees	Receipts (mil dol)	Annual payroll (mil dol)
	147	148	149	150	151	152	153	154	155	156	157	158
SOUTH DAKOTA— Cont'd												
Tripp	15	51	6.4	1.7	6	68	D	D	23	166	8.0	2.0
Turner	15	43	9.0	1.6	11	172	D	7.6	20	86	3.5	0.7
Union	49	188	30.9	9.8	23	1,502	D	63.3	40	416	18.5	4.6
Walworth	18	90	9.6	2.8	4	103	D	D	28	428	27.1	6.7
Yankton	45	228	28.4	9.1	29	2,808	849.2	114.8	65	1,013	44.8	12.3
Ziebach	2	D	D	D	NA	NA	NA	NA	4	D	D	D
TENNESSEE	10,863	104,552	14,199.5	6,129.5	5,823	293,646	139,960.5	14,180.5	12,004	241,348	12,499.0	3,546.5
Anderson	201	9,551	871.7	742.0	94	9,177	2,224.0	598.3	132	2,690	127.1	35.0
Bedford	48	218	18.8	6.0	52	3,882	1,121.4	138.4	54	833	40.2	10.9
Benton	14	56	4.2	1.3	19	596	96.3	19.1	30	D	D	D
Bledsoe	6	8	0.6	0.2	7	D	9.9	D	4	D	D	D
Blount	175	D	D	D	107	5,417	3,761.4	306.1	210	4,526	229.8	68.3
Bradley	142	853	76.2	32.0	113	7,961	D	339.8	178	3,538	168.3	44.5
Campbell	26	D	D	D	34	980	235.9	38.6	55	D	D	D
Cannon	12	27	1.9	0.6	14	290	26.1	8.8	10	D	D	D
Carroll	29	114	9.2	3.6	26	727	612.5	35.5	32	398	19.5	4.3
Carter	44	141	12.2	3.7	35	1,007	188.4	40.2	65	1,203	48.5	15.4
Cheatham	37	140	21.8	4.9	39	1,905	820.2	83.4	40	545	26.0	6.7
Chester	13	D	D	D	20	388	76.1	16.7	25	D	D	D
Claiborne	29	D	D	D	32	1,860	327.9	56.7	29	463	23.6	5.7
Clay	4	9	0.7	0.1	9	274	D	7.0	10	D	D	D
Cocke	27	102	7.5	2.4	30	1,486	659.6	69.1	65	915	48.2	13.1
Coffee	83	3,159	361.0	174.2	79	4,443	D	211.8	108	1,893	89.8	23.6
Crockett	10	D	D	D	14	238	127.9	13.7	10	D	D	D
Cumberland	68	248	30.5	7.7	58	2,099	678.0	79.4	97	1,570	101.2	24.9
Davidson	1,930	24,182	4,021.7	1,641.1	552	18,154	7,319.4	851.8	1,714	40,106	2,573.8	759.3
Decatur	16	D	D	D	22	443	117.0	19.0	20	159	7.9	1.7
DeKalb	24	105	7.8	2.9	20	2,359	672.0	80.2	22	284	13.1	3.8
Dickson	53	199	20.5	7.7	47	3,214	775.7	132.0	92	1,396	67.1	19.0
Dyer	45	191	18.5	5.9	40	3,705	1,455.6	146.6	58	949	42.4	10.8
Fayette	32	338	15.5	8.1	46	1,831	814.3	85.5	42	557	22.5	5.4
Fentress	14	43	3.7	0.8	20	298	39.1	10.6	19	D	D	D
Franklin	37	D	D	D	45	D	3,643.1	D	55	D	D	D
Gibson	47	219	14.3	4.8	58	2,620	737.8	116.9	65	985	45.0	11.0
Giles	36	151	12.8	5.2	43	2,376	1,040.2	107.9	46	639	24.8	6.4
Grainger	10	D	D	D	25	867	138.8	25.7	14	D	D	D
Greene	81	279	31.2	9.3	96	5,209	1,771.1	226.8	117	1,658	77.8	21.5
Grundy	7	D	D	D	16	359	D	8.6	13	157	7.2	1.9
Hamblen	70	281	24.8	10.1	101	8,609	3,235.8	357.6	110	1,995	99.2	26.1
Hamilton	787	7,803	1,053.0	390.3	411	25,092	12,127.5	1,323.1	830	17,426	903.3	256.9
Hancock	1	D	D	D	NA	NA	NA	NA	3	38	1.8	0.5
Hardeman	13	44	3.0	0.6	22	1,566	D	57.3	25	229	13.1	3.1
Hardin	31	94	7.5	2.1	34	1,674	743.9	91.7	54	653	31.7	8.2
Hawkins	34	90	11.5	3.1	41	3,475	1,328.3	151.3	67	911	38.1	10.8
Haywood	15	80	4.6	2.0	17	1,798	597.8	73.5	32	288	14.5	3.5
Henderson	32	D	D	D	35	1,202	362.4	48.2	37	656	26.2	6.2
Henry	40	264	18.3	8.4	39	1,358	277.8	51.4	65	798	33.1	9.2
Hickman	9	34	2.4	0.9	24	544	124.4	18.5	22	D	D	D
Houston	5	21	2.3	0.5	7	207	23.2	6.8	16	D	D	D
Humphreys	14	66	4.7	2.0	23	1,353	2,099.1	95.2	40	385	18.1	5.0
Jackson	5	D	D	D	NA	NA	NA	NA	5	D	D	D
Jefferson	40	157	23.9	4.1	43	1,596	988.3	60.5	68	1,070	53.1	14.5
Johnson	14	44	7.4	1.3	18	758	165.4	32.6	22	254	9.3	2.7
Knox	1,153	D	D	D	360	11,934	4,816.9	645.3	934	21,794	1,039.3	315.2
Lake	2	D	D	D	NA	NA	NA	NA	11	135	5.2	1.4
Lauderdale	13	33	3.4	0.8	12	953	209.1	36.4	19	D	D	D
Lawrence	42	177	19.9	5.5	50	1,683	397.6	64.6	49	851	44.6	10.8
Lewis	15	36	2.6	0.8	20	259	46.0	8.1	17	D	D	D
Lincoln	38	154	14.3	4.9	31	2,363	D	79.7	48	545	26.7	6.6
Loudon	53	D	D	D	50	2,804	1,424.2	136.8	77	1,366	64.6	19.3
McMinn	52	350	17.4	5.5	62	4,642	2,196.6	248.2	92	1,539	69.6	18.3
McNairy	19	68	6.2	1.6	49	1,328	352.1	47.6	31	435	15.4	4.4
Macon	25	53	6.3	1.7	35	771	214.2	27.3	24	221	12.0	2.6
Madison	171	1,810	129.4	70.3	101	8,726	4,374.7	406.6	221	4,750	222.5	62.9
Marion	20	77	6.1	2.7	27	1,374	D	59.6	51	D	D	D

Table B. States and Counties — Health Care and Social Assistance, Other Services, Nonemployer Businesses, and Residential Construction

STATE County	Health care and social assistance, 2012				Other services, 2012				Nonemployer businesses, 2016		Value of residential construction authorized by building permits, 2018	
	Number of establishments	Number of employees	Receipts (mil dol)	Annual payroll (mil dol)	Number of establishments	Number of employees	Receipts (mil dol)	Annual payroll (mil dol)	Number	Receipts (mil dol)	New construction ($1,000)	Number of housing units
	159	160	161	162	163	164	165	166	167	168	169	170
SOUTH DAKOTA— Cont'd												
Tripp	19	434	31.6	13.2	16	75	6.4	1.3	542	25.6	385	3
Turner	25	412	21.1	10.4	10	D	D	D	766	35.7	7,545	31
Union	57	1,070	143.3	54.5	30	D	D	D	1,418	90.1	38,645	162
Walworth	12	397	26.0	12.1	20	106	6.6	1.9	467	18.6	1,914	13
Yankton	72	2,028	193.2	83.9	58	243	21.8	5.0	1,544	62.7	18,294	115
Ziebach	8	D	D	D	1	D	D	D	76	2.7	NA	NA
TENNESSEE	14,897	380,453	42,383.7	16,227.9	8,117	55,990	6,525.8	1,711.4	508,596	23,840.0	7,048,088	37,169
Anderson	189	4,140	424.7	164.7	111	491	44.8	13.1	4,650	211.8	37,540	198
Bedford	96	986	86.8	32.6	38	257	19.5	6.2	2,982	126.7	60,648	258
Benton	38	672	51.6	18.0	19	D	D	D	1,003	35.4	273	15
Bledsoe	9	D	D	D	2	D	D	D	789	31.5	0	0
Blount	247	6,554	561.5	249.4	161	896	85.3	28.8	8,840	401.1	170,186	868
Bradley	230	4,659	622.9	188.2	94	851	70.9	21.4	6,980	373.5	76,609	484
Campbell	69	2,191	172.8	68.3	32	D	D	D	2,409	98.7	27,082	264
Cannon	17	377	24.8	11.3	10	D	D	D	1,032	43.1	813	7
Carroll	67	1,721	111.5	49.8	23	D	D	D	1,595	59.3	490	3
Carter	81	1,782	147.9	59.7	40	D	D	D	3,202	111.8	16,963	127
Cheatham	46	567	44.5	17.2	26	D	D	D	3,524	166.9	52,545	292
Chester	28	455	26.9	12.4	10	D	D	D	1,044	47.0	2,013	21
Claiborne	52	1,227	84.4	37.9	32	D	D	D	1,831	75.7	9,793	93
Clay	9	373	13.0	6.0	3	D	D	D	665	21.4	2,762	18
Cocke	40	1,017	102.7	37.5	26	D	D	D	2,114	65.1	0	0
Coffee	197	3,056	305.8	107.0	70	278	21.4	5.9	3,610	152.8	44,706	262
Crockett	29	515	31.6	13.3	10	D	D	D	901	34.2	3,833	25
Cumberland	138	3,018	386.0	91.9	66	580	33.4	12.8	4,484	192.4	107,779	914
Davidson	1,819	62,989	8,547.7	3,158.0	1,225	11,665	1,369.2	407.5	72,148	3,904.1	1,153,064	6,934
Decatur	27	1,019	67.4	39.5	10	D	D	D	797	37.1	0	0
DeKalb	29	533	40.9	15.7	16	D	D	D	1,326	56.5	15,660	101
Dickson	122	2,129	260.3	85.4	45	D	D	D	3,912	179.9	73,027	356
Dyer	108	2,005	200.6	71.7	45	207	20.8	5.2	2,335	87.5	11,235	79
Fayette	54	611	44.1	20.0	29	113	9.7	2.7	3,384	154.7	92,771	328
Fentress	29	D	D	D	15	D	D	D	1,493	77.8	0	0
Franklin	84	1,577	149.7	53.3	50	273	30.7	6.5	2,539	95.3	38,485	211
Gibson	111	2,106	139.7	56.2	53	D	D	D	2,889	111.6	22,108	109
Giles	57	889	77.5	28.3	28	D	D	D	1,737	83.3	13,220	107
Grainger	15	232	11.9	5.6	14	D	D	D	1,438	61.9	10,626	58
Greene	136	4,034	298.1	127.4	60	356	27.9	8.0	3,991	152.0	32,957	171
Grundy	18	379	24.4	11.7	8	D	D	D	1,154	45.8	1,212	4
Hamblen	164	4,246	358.7	147.7	73	349	28.6	8.9	3,486	169.8	25,119	145
Hamilton	1,038	26,382	3,179.1	1,255.6	580	D	D	D	26,421	1,358.3	312,014	1,687
Hancock	12	182	16.6	5.7	2	D	D	D	424	12.4	0	0
Hardeman	40	1,149	76.9	36.5	16	D	D	D	1,482	49.8	632	24
Hardin	59	1,155	100.4	40.4	23	D	D	D	1,774	76.0	1,739	22
Hawkins	54	1,433	102.5	41.7	44	D	D	D	2,936	102.7	14,413	126
Haywood	27	470	37.7	15.4	21	D	D	D	1,155	41.7	2,698	15
Henderson	56	886	60.1	22.9	34	D	D	D	1,758	66.1	2,719	17
Henry	83	1,466	142.0	53.3	52	D	D	D	2,286	98.7	1,888	21
Hickman	23	D	D	D	15	D	D	D	1,746	69.6	12,299	73
Houston	15	408	28.5	12.6	5	D	D	D	516	19.3	0	0
Humphreys	30	595	47.3	15.1	22	D	D	D	1,154	46.0	1,435	11
Jackson	9	D	D	D	4	D	D	D	765	30.0	0	0
Jefferson	66	1,434	132.5	42.1	41	177	13.8	4.1	3,033	133.0	43,073	157
Johnson	23	575	42.8	17.1	9	D	D	D	1,016	35.2	200	1
Knox	1,244	36,221	4,262.2	1,514.8	730	5,946	547.5	191.1	35,445	1,910.3	441,392	2,398
Lake	11	D	D	D	4	D	D	D	327	8.7	171	2
Lauderdale	30	611	62.9	17.6	13	D	D	D	1,270	53.2	3,756	27
Lawrence	76	1,311	107.0	38.8	40	119	10.7	3.2	2,877	130.3	1,839	11
Lewis	26	492	23.9	10.7	10	D	D	D	885	35.6	1,012	83
Lincoln	54	843	59.4	25.7	37	D	D	D	2,304	94.1	2,893	16
Loudon	97	1,796	142.9	55.0	46	216	27.6	6.0	3,402	169.2	104,136	424
McMinn	108	1,805	177.0	62.4	48	219	18.9	5.0	3,031	132.9	2,458	24
McNairy	47	799	63.9	24.5	20	D	D	D	1,700	65.1	835	6
Macon	37	657	50.7	19.2	22	D	D	D	1,655	79.1	30,219	139
Madison	313	11,842	1,172.9	484.4	131	D	D	D	6,518	289.7	48,061	234
Marion	44	D	D	D	31	D	D	D	1,757	72.3	28,968	131

Table B. States and Counties — Government Employment and Payroll, and Local Government Finances

		Government employment and payroll, 2012								Local government finances, 2012				
			March payroll (percent of total)							General revenue				
												Taxes		
											Inter-govern-mental (mil dol)		Per capita[1] (dollars)	
STATE County	Full-time equivalent employees	March payroll (dollars)	Adminis-tration, judicial, and legal	Police and corrections	Fire protection	Highways and transpor-tation	Health and welfare	Natural resources and utilities	Education and libraries	Total (mil dol)		Total (mil dol)	Total	Property
	171	172	173	174	175	176	177	178	179	180	181	182	183	184

SOUTH DAKOTA— Cont'd														
Tripp	313	855,393	8.1	15.4	0.0	7.0	3.8	9.9	55.0	19.6	5.9	10.3	1,882	1,410
Turner	279	817,829	8.0	3.7	0.0	8.8	0.3	5.1	73.1	26.4	8.0	14.2	1,711	1,477
Union	512	1,673,489	7.8	8.7	0.3	5.6	0.6	5.0	68.1	61.5	22.0	30.6	2,059	1,752
Walworth	221	589,011	7.5	16.1	0.1	6.5	1.9	2.6	64.6	20.6	9.1	7.9	1,440	1,024
Yankton	681	2,403,085	7.3	8.7	0.5	6.7	3.4	8.0	64.3	65.0	16.6	35.8	1,586	1,147
Ziebach	95	280,194	7.1	2.1	0.0	3.4	0.6	0.4	86.0	6.0	4.4	1.4	474	432
TENNESSEE	X	X	X	X	X	X	X	X	X	X	X	X	X	X
Anderson	3,051	10,709,572	8.9	7.5	4.2	3.4	1.7	10.8	62.8	221.7	89.4	94.0	1,246	741
Bedford	2,341	6,860,633	3.8	5.9	2.6	2.3	32.4	8.2	44.3	114.2	59.7	38.4	842	542
Benton	474	1,606,363	5.8	8.8	0.2	3.6	4.0	12.7	63.7	37.9	21.5	12.7	775	443
Bledsoe	594	1,386,704	5.7	6.0	0.0	3.7	3.2	3.2	63.4	34.4	25.2	6.2	483	381
Blount	6,070	20,455,931	4.4	6.6	1.8	2.2	37.0	5.4	41.5	528.9	111.3	129.7	1,044	749
Bradley	3,454	10,166,787	4.0	11.4	6.6	3.1	10.6	1.9	61.3	246.4	112.5	81.3	804	494
Campbell	1,510	4,358,532	4.9	7.7	2.4	5.5	4.9	19.0	54.0	98.1	55.2	27.6	684	390
Cannon	555	1,372,374	3.7	6.2	1.4	2.5	4.5	3.9	73.3	29.2	18.5	7.5	546	395
Carroll	1,139	3,140,304	5.3	9.1	1.3	4.5	0.7	12.9	62.8	71.5	41.1	18.0	635	428
Carter	1,973	5,071,600	5.5	8.9	2.0	4.0	1.2	9.8	68.0	111.1	63.2	34.7	606	404
Cheatham	1,170	3,416,461	8.9	8.5	1.2	3.8	4.2	5.4	66.2	87.0	44.5	32.3	824	545
Chester	583	1,479,520	6.9	10.4	1.3	4.6	3.5	4.5	63.6	35.4	21.8	9.2	537	327
Claiborne	1,693	4,650,708	4.4	4.7	0.0	1.8	36.9	4.7	46.4	101.7	41.7	19.7	620	402
Clay	346	836,185	8.5	6.7	0.0	5.7	8.6	7.4	60.8	19.6	11.9	5.0	642	405
Cocke	1,225	3,330,780	5.4	6.8	3.2	4.8	1.6	3.4	73.7	82.1	45.4	25.0	704	410
Coffee	2,224	6,075,717	5.2	8.5	3.3	2.4	3.8	13.4	59.9	153.4	61.5	58.5	1,099	624
Crockett	563	1,474,498	6.0	8.0	0.1	3.9	5.1	5.6	69.5	39.4	25.3	9.5	647	455
Cumberland	1,971	4,871,298	10.5	9.2	1.5	7.6	3.6	6.6	59.6	116.9	58.5	44.1	773	397
Davidson	22,627	87,554,648	6.2	13.1	7.2	2.6	9.0	12.5	47.7	2,674.3	751.4	1,227.6	1,894	1,220
Decatur	576	1,686,615	5.4	7.1	0.0	3.3	24.4	5.4	52.2	40.6	17.7	8.4	718	421
DeKalb	735	1,938,173	2.6	5.5	0.0	2.8	3.4	27.2	58.1	43.2	24.6	12.8	677	446
Dickson	1,972	5,546,728	7.3	6.8	2.6	2.4	3.9	17.9	57.6	141.4	60.1	55.8	1,108	644
Dyer	1,460	4,541,888	6.2	11.6	5.0	4.0	2.4	8.4	60.7	128.0	69.8	34.0	890	593
Fayette	1,075	2,824,788	9.0	14.5	2.4	0.3	4.2	5.6	62.7	63.0	30.1	24.0	622	428
Fentress	636	1,503,203	9.4	7.6	0.0	4.8	9.5	5.6	62.4	35.7	20.4	10.5	583	350
Franklin	1,139	3,326,510	2.9	9.5	1.7	3.7	1.6	11.4	69.2	91.2	43.8	33.8	829	597
Gibson	1,945	5,303,575	3.3	10.5	3.0	4.3	1.1	8.6	68.2	134.8	75.7	35.9	723	550
Giles	1,369	3,634,496	12.1	7.4	0.5	8.8	4.0	4.5	61.5	61.4	31.0	24.0	827	523
Grainger	662	1,667,581	3.5	8.8	0.0	0.6	5.1	2.8	78.1	45.9	30.1	11.3	496	384
Greene	2,317	6,964,692	4.1	9.6	2.3	3.1	6.4	13.2	60.6	142.8	69.9	48.8	709	420
Grundy	608	1,426,124	5.2	4.3	0.0	3.5	2.0	5.6	77.2	32.3	23.7	6.9	507	359
Hamblen	1,973	6,233,306	5.6	9.2	4.7	2.5	1.7	12.8	60.0	162.1	67.7	63.4	1,011	537
Hamilton	14,734	56,385,621	6.4	7.3	3.0	3.5	37.2	11.3	30.7	1,780.1	395.6	494.7	1,432	1,127
Hancock	347	800,025	10.1	7.0	0.2	6.6	20.3	2.7	53.2	20.3	13.2	2.7	407	312
Hardeman	1,079	2,839,972	5.5	9.2	1.0	3.5	5.9	11.2	62.9	64.6	37.7	18.1	684	425
Hardin	1,366	3,651,007	4.5	6.1	0.3	2.3	39.7	2.3	43.0	104.2	34.3	23.2	893	480
Hawkins	2,067	6,744,656	3.8	5.3	0.4	2.2	8.6	5.8	73.1	111.4	61.3	40.6	717	506
Haywood	942	2,633,709	7.9	9.5	3.1	3.5	5.1	9.8	55.4	60.5	32.7	17.9	982	679
Henderson	1,113	2,867,377	7.3	13.1	1.5	3.4	1.2	16.3	56.3	63.0	35.8	20.0	714	394
Henry	1,119	3,290,953	5.3	9.3	2.1	1.8	1.8	14.7	63.3	150.2	42.7	24.7	765	442
Hickman	1,002	2,269,272	16.1	6.3	0.5	2.3	4.1	5.8	61.1	54.5	34.7	13.4	554	369
Houston	381	990,105	9.2	11.3	0.4	5.4	8.2	5.2	59.0	21.6	14.5	4.9	585	382
Humphreys	1,002	3,913,409	14.1	4.3	0.1	2.3	9.0	4.1	63.2	46.8	26.1	15.5	851	526
Jackson	425	1,046,407	9.7	7.7	0.0	7.2	3.9	4.7	66.8	24.4	16.5	5.7	497	349
Jefferson	1,433	4,289,878	5.4	8.6	1.0	4.2	5.2	9.0	66.5	126.4	54.0	43.3	829	545
Johnson	620	1,243,277	8.2	8.9	0.0	5.0	2.1	6.1	68.5	37.2	23.2	8.9	494	360
Knox	13,135	45,220,953	5.5	12.5	2.9	3.2	3.7	15.3	55.2	1,270.2	389.9	630.9	1,430	810
Lake	321	873,740	15.6	15.9	0.2	6.0	4.5	10.1	47.6	18.1	11.6	3.5	457	287
Lauderdale	1,033	2,753,225	7.4	11.7	2.0	4.8	4.6	4.1	64.7	70.8	41.8	18.4	664	441
Lawrence	1,270	4,176,846	6.6	9.0	1.9	3.7	3.6	13.3	60.8	96.9	50.8	33.0	783	468
Lewis	515	1,074,509	10.9	12.0	0.6	6.6	1.4	6.6	61.8	31.6	21.1	6.6	554	298
Lincoln	1,457	3,836,126	5.1	6.7	1.8	3.0	1.0	26.5	54.5	110.1	39.6	20.1	599	348
Loudon	1,628	5,601,296	4.4	6.8	2.4	2.3	1.4	30.5	50.4	114.9	46.7	47.0	944	641
McMinn	2,013	6,789,227	4.8	5.9	1.4	2.2	24.9	7.7	47.8	109.5	59.5	34.1	651	417
McNairy	1,044	2,736,738	6.7	5.8	0.7	3.7	0.6	11.6	68.0	61.0	40.2	14.3	547	361
Macon	840	2,132,533	7.7	8.1	1.0	0.1	5.9	5.3	70.4	49.3	29.8	13.4	597	355
Madison	7,853	28,936,219	2.2	6.4	2.6	1.2	64.3	4.4	18.6	921.0	113.3	137.5	1,393	781
Marion	942	2,790,775	7.6	7.6	0.6	2.9	2.4	9.1	69.0	67.8	35.6	24.6	870	523

1. Based on the resident population estimated as of July 1 of the year shown.

Table B. States and Counties — Local Government Finances, Government Employment, and Income Taxes

STATE County	Local government finances, 2012 (cont.) Direct general expenditure — Total (mil dol)	Per capita[1] (dollars)	Percent of total for: Education	Health and hospitals	Police protection	Public welfare	Highways	Debt outstanding Total (mil dol)	Per capita[1] (dollars)	Government employment, 2017 Federal civilian	Federal military	State and local	Individual income tax returns, 2016 Number of returns	Mean adjusted gross income	Mean income tax
	185	186	187	188	189	190	191	192	193	194	195	196	197	198	199
SOUTH DAKOTA— Cont'd															
Tripp	20.4	3,717	42.1	1.5	4.2	0.3	17.5	16.4	2,990	28	31	382	2,630	42,565	4,610
Turner	25.7	3,093	49.0	0.7	4.4	0.2	18.6	21.3	2,563	27	47	404	4,030	51,597	5,633
Union	61.7	4,151	39.7	0.2	4.0	0.0	10.5	55.2	3,718	53	86	761	7,640	118,133	23,362
Walworth	18.8	3,440	49.6	0.6	5.7	0.1	11.1	8.2	1,510	32	31	397	2,700	54,538	6,860
Yankton	61.7	2,730	45.1	1.7	5.7	0.5	12.7	62.1	2,746	203	118	1,707	10,920	56,023	6,693
Ziebach	6.0	2,081	73.9	0.5	2.6	0.0	10.9	0.0	0	7	16	172	500	28,702	2,372
TENNESSEE	X	X	X	X	X	X	X	X	X	49,579	20,615	375,577	2,990,850	58,315	7,723
Anderson	264.4	3,506	58.7	2.4	7.0	0.0	3.3	316.3	4,194	883	220	4,278	34,290	52,707	5,871
Bedford	117.2	2,572	51.0	2.6	5.8	0.2	4.7	126.0	2,764	69	138	2,262	20,920	46,422	5,083
Benton	36.9	2,254	60.4	2.4	7.0	0.3	8.6	25.4	1,550	60	46	908	6,610	40,730	3,670
Bledsoe	29.7	2,318	58.9	3.4	3.8	0.3	6.6	28.6	2,232	19	35	1,028	4,560	39,224	3,140
Blount	501.3	4,037	31.7	37.6	3.9	0.0	2.2	1,376.5	11,085	255	391	7,364	59,550	55,981	6,516
Bradley	234.0	2,314	53.1	8.4	7.2	0.1	4.8	222.5	2,200	211	298	4,841	45,690	47,891	5,018
Campbell	109.0	2,696	46.6	2.9	5.5	0.1	5.8	125.9	3,115	80	113	2,001	14,830	41,343	3,913
Cannon	28.5	2,064	58.3	3.3	7.4	0.4	8.5	13.9	1,008	30	41	602	6,140	44,350	3,968
Carroll	72.3	2,547	58.4	0.4	6.1	0.2	7.2	63.9	2,250	72	77	1,728	11,460	42,072	3,653
Carter	118.2	2,060	67.1	0.7	5.7	0.0	4.3	105.8	1,845	80	161	2,447	22,900	39,812	3,535
Cheatham	93.0	2,367	69.6	2.1	5.4	0.3	4.2	61.6	1,568	77	116	1,554	19,180	54,467	5,934
Chester	35.0	2,039	59.3	1.0	5.7	0.4	11.6	19.6	1,140	36	46	1,137	6,660	42,488	3,563
Claiborne	96.3	3,036	42.5	32.9	3.7	0.0	3.6	69.4	2,188	63	88	1,703	12,180	40,953	3,721
Clay	20.9	2,663	48.6	6.1	6.2	0.2	10.9	14.3	1,818	47	22	499	3,040	34,902	2,825
Cocke	89.1	2,504	59.3	1.2	4.9	0.0	6.9	71.6	2,014	58	102	1,927	14,900	35,761	2,902
Coffee	162.9	3,060	57.5	2.0	5.5	0.1	4.0	222.3	4,176	510	204	3,117	24,470	48,127	5,142
Crockett	40.8	2,791	61.9	3.1	4.8	0.9	7.7	29.0	1,982	35	41	840	6,090	42,360	4,351
Cumberland	113.1	1,983	49.3	6.2	5.6	0.0	4.0	134.0	2,349	120	169	2,360	26,540	47,789	5,014
Davidson	2,727.2	4,207	31.0	8.4	7.3	1.2	1.6	6,313.0	9,738	8,354	2,371	37,062	338,340	69,418	11,293
Decatur	37.9	3,249	38.3	26.2	3.3	0.3	5.7	26.0	2,228	27	33	844	4,580	40,802	3,473
DeKalb	40.9	2,165	55.5	3.0	7.5	0.1	5.8	23.6	1,246	38	57	1,069	7,990	42,925	4,520
Dickson	126.9	2,520	53.8	2.4	7.4	0.0	4.2	145.3	2,885	87	152	2,643	23,600	50,336	5,501
Dyer	131.4	3,436	50.7	0.2	7.3	0.6	6.4	99.2	2,594	101	107	2,414	15,690	46,215	4,852
Fayette	62.3	1,611	54.0	3.2	7.9	0.0	9.2	51.2	1,325	59	115	1,272	19,030	67,763	9,662
Fentress	35.1	1,954	57.6	4.3	4.7	0.6	7.7	14.5	810	39	52	896	6,800	39,115	3,894
Franklin	85.2	2,091	56.5	0.5	7.5	0.1	5.2	83.2	2,040	127	114	1,907	18,110	49,808	5,273
Gibson	141.6	2,854	58.9	2.2	5.8	0.4	6.0	112.6	2,270	146	139	2,783	21,170	43,633	4,026
Giles	61.6	2,118	59.8	4.3	3.0	0.1	8.6	25.0	859	69	83	1,429	12,900	45,023	4,331
Grainger	44.5	1,960	64.7	3.7	4.6	0.0	7.6	29.5	1,301	61	67	829	9,250	42,380	3,753
Greene	138.3	2,009	61.2	3.2	5.4	0.0	7.0	106.4	1,546	230	194	3,506	29,200	41,960	3,905
Grundy	31.5	2,310	69.9	0.6	3.4	0.2	7.5	12.0	880	22	38	703	5,560	36,777	2,891
Hamblen	158.5	2,526	53.0	0.6	6.2	0.2	4.7	224.6	3,579	175	184	3,915	26,810	45,220	4,569
Hamilton	1,693.1	4,900	23.2	34.8	4.9	0.9	2.5	1,512.3	4,377	5,155	1,077	23,489	164,170	68,522	9,921
Hancock	20.0	2,979	49.9	15.8	3.9	0.2	7.0	17.1	2,543	10	19	472	2,270	32,252	2,154
Hardeman	62.6	2,361	60.6	2.7	6.6	0.1	7.3	28.4	1,071	56	63	1,677	9,750	37,218	2,875
Hardin	104.9	4,042	36.7	35.8	2.7	2.7	4.6	72.4	2,789	109	74	1,772	10,580	43,895	4,424
Hawkins	108.4	1,915	66.6	0.9	4.8	0.3	4.8	126.4	2,234	136	162	2,410	23,170	43,428	3,945
Haywood	64.2	3,520	54.9	2.6	5.5	0.0	5.8	26.7	1,465	94	50	1,029	8,050	36,754	3,093
Henderson	60.8	2,170	65.5	0.2	6.4	0.1	5.4	92.9	3,314	56	80	1,372	11,460	42,489	3,758
Henry	154.5	4,776	27.8	50.9	2.8	0.0	4.3	81.7	2,525	110	119	2,553	14,080	44,304	4,968
Hickman	52.0	2,151	60.6	3.4	4.7	0.0	9.9	46.4	1,921	52	68	1,129	9,570	43,692	3,848
Houston	20.6	2,448	57.1	4.4	4.1	0.4	9.8	13.7	1,623	19	23	537	3,330	43,067	3,725
Humphreys	43.2	2,363	55.4	1.0	7.3	0.0	8.5	7.4	405	193	53	1,044	7,980	47,877	4,896
Jackson	23.3	2,034	61.8	2.9	4.3	0.2	9.2	4.9	428	25	33	520	4,550	37,639	3,030
Jefferson	135.7	2,600	53.6	3.3	4.7	9.4	4.4	112.4	2,153	121	154	2,367	22,450	45,714	4,502
Johnson	35.0	1,933	61.4	0.7	5.0	0.2	7.3	18.8	1,038	37	46	932	6,210	39,950	3,565
Knox	1,174.3	2,661	40.8	2.1	7.9	0.2	2.6	2,290.6	5,191	3,571	1,383	30,395	207,730	68,705	10,625
Lake	17.1	2,221	49.1	3.9	6.9	0.5	10.4	23.7	3,088	15	14	651	2,100	35,856	2,937
Lauderdale	69.4	2,504	56.8	2.7	7.3	0.6	7.8	45.4	1,639	50	70	1,935	9,490	37,371	3,301
Lawrence	93.3	2,217	57.9	3.0	6.7	0.0	7.8	110.6	2,628	114	124	1,914	17,020	42,849	3,740
Lewis	31.4	2,639	46.3	0.6	5.1	0.1	5.8	17.0	1,431	25	34	735	4,940	40,713	3,449
Lincoln	111.8	3,338	38.2	35.1	4.0	0.0	4.7	92.5	2,760	49	97	2,101	15,050	47,915	4,821
Loudon	111.4	2,238	57.9	0.6	7.1	0.2	4.5	662.5	13,305	146	149	2,040	24,540	63,368	7,834
McMinn	110.6	2,110	58.7	0.9	5.3	0.0	5.6	28.0	534	105	150	2,014	22,070	45,757	4,394
McNairy	55.7	2,129	62.1	0.2	4.9	0.0	6.8	28.4	1,086	82	74	1,335	10,290	42,107	3,569
Macon	53.2	2,366	60.7	4.0	6.0	0.1	7.6	27.7	1,232	38	69	1,209	9,560	42,636	4,752
Madison	890.5	9,027	13.8	63.1	3.2	0.0	1.8	1,017.8	10,317	424	272	11,573	44,130	51,801	6,326
Marion	61.4	2,169	58.5	0.8	8.3	0.0	5.6	57.5	2,034	73	81	1,215	12,140	48,213	5,152

1. Based on the resident population estimated as of July 1 of the year shown.

Table B. States and Counties — Land Area and Population

State / county code	CBSA code[1]	County code[2]	STATE County	Land area[3] (sq. mi)	Total persons 2018	Rank	Per square mile	White	Black	American Indian, Alaska Native	Asian and Pacific Islancer	Percent Hispanic or Latino[4]	Under 5 years	5 to 17 years	18 to 24 years	25 to 34 years	35 to 44 years	45 to 54 years
				1	2	3	4	5	6	7	8	9	10	11	12	13	14	15
			TENNESSEE— Cont'd															
47117	30,280	6	Marshall	375.5	33,683	1,337	89.7	87.1	7.5	0.8	1.0	5.4	6.2	17.3	7.5	12.9	12.6	13.9
47119	34,980	1	Maury	613.1	94,340	627	153.9	80.8	12.9	0.8	1.3	6.1	6.6	16.8	7.4	13.8	13.0	12.6
47121		8	Meigs	195.1	12,306	2,268	63.1	95.1	2.0	1.3	0.5	2.3	5.3	15.1	7.2	10.5	11.8	14.5
47123		6	Monroe	635.7	46,357	1,044	72.9	92.4	2.6	1.4	0.7	4.7	5.4	15.6	7.5	11.4	10.9	13.5
47125	17,300	2	Montgomery	539.2	205,950	326	382.0	66.4	22.2	1.3	4.2	10.3	8.2	18.5	11.2	19.1	13.3	10.9
47127	46,100	9	Moore	129.2	6,411	2,718	49.6	94.2	3.4	0.9	1.0	2.0	4.2	14.7	7.5	10.7	11.8	13.7
47129	28,940	2	Morgan	522.2	21,579	1,747	41.3	94.1	4.0	1.2	0.5	1.4	4.8	14.4	8.5	12.9	12.9	14.9
47131	46,460	7	Obion	544.9	30,267	1,425	55.5	84.1	11.5	0.6	0.6	4.6	5.7	16.0	7.7	11.4	11.7	13.0
47133	18,260	7	Overton	433.5	22,068	1,718	50.9	97.1	1.1	0.9	0.5	1.6	5.2	16.0	7.7	11.3	11.6	13.8
47135		8	Perry	414.7	8,064	2,585	19.4	93.4	3.4	1.7	0.8	2.8	6.3	15.8	7.7	11.4	11.1	12.5
47137		9	Pickett	163.0	5,082	2,825	31.2	97.4	0.6	0.7	0.2	2.0	4.6	13.1	6.6	8.2	10.5	13.5
47139	17,420	3	Polk	434.6	16,898	1,981	38.9	96.3	1.1	1.4	0.6	2.2	5.0	14.5	7.4	10.6	11.5	14.9
47141	18,260	4	Putnam	401.1	78,843	710	196.6	89.5	2.9	0.8	1.8	6.5	5.7	15.1	14.5	13.0	11.2	11.8
47143	19,420	6	Rhea	315.4	33,044	1,356	104.8	91.6	2.9	1.1	0.8	5.4	5.9	16.8	9.0	11.7	11.3	13.4
47145	28,940	2	Roane	360.7	53,140	950	147.3	94.3	3.4	1.2	1.0	2.0	4.5	14.3	7.1	10.4	10.7	14.0
47147	34,980	1	Robertson	476.3	71,012	759	149.1	84.4	8.1	0.8	0.9	7.3	6.2	17.6	7.7	12.8	13.0	13.9
47149	34,980	1	Rutherford	619.2	324,890	215	524.7	72.2	16.9	0.8	4.2	8.5	6.6	18.1	12.2	14.8	14.1	13.0
47151		6	Scott	532.3	22,039	1,720	41.4	98.1	0.5	0.9	0.5	1.0	6.3	18.0	7.7	12.1	12.8	13.3
47153	16,860	2	Sequatchie	265.9	14,876	2,105	55.9	94.9	1.2	1.2	0.7	3.5	5.1	15.7	7.2	11.0	11.8	13.6
47155	42,940	4	Sevier	592.5	97,892	611	165.2	90.9	1.6	0.9	1.6	6.3	5.4	15.2	7.5	11.9	11.5	13.9
47157	32,820	1	Shelby	763.6	935,764	56	1,225.5	36.7	54.5	0.5	3.2	6.5	7.0	17.9	9.3	14.9	12.5	12.5
47159	34,980	1	Smith	314.3	19,942	1,830	63.4	94.0	2.9	1.1	0.5	2.9	6.2	16.5	7.9	12.1	11.9	13.9
47161		8	Stewart	459.8	13,561	2,194	29.5	93.4	2.3	1.6	1.4	3.1	5.5	15.4	7.3	10.5	11.5	14.4
47163	28,700	2	Sullivan	413.4	157,668	421	381.4	94.7	3.0	0.8	1.1	1.9	4.8	14.4	7.4	11.7	11.2	14.0
47165	34,980	1	Sumner	529.4	187,149	354	353.5	85.4	8.6	0.8	2.0	5.1	6.1	17.4	7.7	12.4	13.2	14.0
47167	32,820	1	Tipton	458.4	61,581	854	134.3	77.5	19.3	1.0	1.3	2.8	6.0	18.6	8.4	12.8	12.6	13.6
47169	34,980	1	Trousdale	114.3	11,012	2,352	96.3	85.3	12.6	0.7	0.7	2.4	4.9	12.7	11.1	21.4	13.0	13.3
47171	27,740	3	Unicoi	186.1	17,761	1,937	95.4	93.8	0.8	0.9	0.4	5.1	4.5	14.1	7.2	10.7	11.2	13.6
47173	28,940	2	Union	223.6	19,688	1,843	88.1	97.2	0.8	1.2	0.4	1.7	5.3	16.4	7.2	11.9	11.5	13.8
47175		9	Van Buren	273.4	5,765	2,772	21.1	97.0	1.3	1.2	0.4	1.6	5.6	13.6	6.7	10.1	11.3	13.1
47177	32,660	6	Warren	432.7	40,878	1,153	94.5	86.4	4.0	0.9	1.0	9.3	6.0	17.5	7.7	11.9	12.8	13.0
47179	27,740	3	Washington	326.5	128,607	496	393.9	90.1	5.3	0.8	2.1	3.6	5.0	14.1	12.3	12.5	11.5	13.1
47181		8	Wayne	734.1	16,558	2,006	22.6	90.8	6.7	0.9	0.5	2.1	4.3	12.7	7.8	14.4	13.0	14.5
47183	32,280	7	Weakley	580.4	33,415	1,343	57.6	88.2	8.4	0.8	1.5	2.7	5.1	14.2	16.0	11.2	10.2	12.0
47185		7	White	376.7	27,107	1,520	72.0	94.5	2.6	1.0	0.6	2.8	5.9	16.0	7.1	12.1	11.5	13.4
47187	34,980	1	Williamson	582.9	231,729	289	397.5	85.8	4.9	0.6	5.5	4.9	6.0	21.3	7.7	9.3	14.5	15.3
47189	34,980	1	Wilson	571.1	140,625	462	246.2	86.3	8.0	0.9	2.2	4.5	6.0	17.7	7.3	12.0	13.7	14.2
48000		0	**TEXAS**	261,257.3	28,701,845	X	109.9	42.8	12.7	0.7	5.7	39.6	7.1	18.7	9.7	14.8	13.5	12.4
48001	37,300	7	Anderson	1,062.6	58,057	890	54.6	59.9	21.8	0.8	1.0	18.0	5.2	13.9	7.9	16.1	16.0	14.4
48003	11,380	6	Andrews	1,500.7	18,128	1,919	12.1	40.7	4.8	1.0	0.8	56.6	8.7	22.1	8.9	14.8	13.3	11.3
48005	31,260	5	Angelina	797.8	87,092	664	109.2	61.3	15.5	0.6	1.2	22.5	6.8	18.7	8.7	12.8	11.8	12.4
48007	18,580	2	Aransas	252.0	23,792	1,653	94.4	68.7	1.7	1.4	2.1	27.4	4.8	12.7	6.5	9.2	9.3	11.5
48009	48,660	3	Archer	903.3	8,786	2,517	9.7	89.5	1.5	1.4	0.9	8.2	5.2	16.2	7.6	10.6	11.1	13.1
48011	11,100	2	Armstrong	909.1	1,892	3,061	2.1	89.7	1.2	1.4	0.5	8.0	5.7	17.4	6.0	9.3	11.8	10.3
48013	41,700	1	Atascosa	1,219.5	50,310	983	41.3	33.7	1.0	0.7	0.6	64.7	7.3	20.0	9.0	12.9	12.6	11.9
48015	26,420	1	Austin	646.5	29,989	1,431	46.4	62.7	9.3	0.7	0.9	27.6	5.9	17.9	8.0	11.3	11.1	12.2
48017		7	Bailey	827.0	7,027	2,667	8.5	33.6	1.6	0.7	0.8	64.1	8.2	23.2	9.3	11.5	12.1	10.1
48019	41,700	1	Bandera	791.0	22,824	1,688	28.9	78.3	1.3	1.4	0.8	19.4	4.2	12.5	6.1	8.8	9.4	12.7
48021	12,420	1	Bastrop	888.2	86,976	666	97.9	53.3	7.3	1.0	1.1	38.7	6.8	18.6	8.4	12.1	12.1	12.8
48023		8	Baylor	867.5	3,582	2,933	4.1	83.0	3.6	0.8	0.7	13.7	5.9	17.1	6.4	10.6	11.0	11.5
48025	13,300	6	Bee	880.2	32,587	1,368	37.0	31.5	8.6	0.5	0.8	59.3	5.8	15.2	11.3	17.5	15.2	12.5
48027	28,660	2	Bell	1,051.3	355,642	199	338.3	47.8	24.3	1.1	5.3	25.3	8.4	19.3	11.3	16.7	13.0	10.7
48029	41,700	1	Bexar	1,240.2	1,986,049	16	1,601.4	28.6	8.0	0.6	3.9	60.5	7.1	18.4	10.3	16.0	13.5	12.0
48031		8	Blanco	709.3	11,702	2,314	16.5	77.4	1.5	1.0	1.3	19.8	4.4	13.9	6.9	8.7	10.3	13.1
48033		8	Borden	897.4	648	3,132	0.7	79.5	1.7	1.2	0.2	18.7	5.1	15.1	6.0	7.3	10.3	17.4
48035		6	Bosque	983.0	18,691	1,892	19.0	78.3	2.3	1.0	0.6	19.0	5.5	16.1	6.8	9.7	10.3	11.8
48037	45,500	3	Bowie	885.0	94,324	628	106.6	65.0	26.1	1.4	1.9	7.8	6.5	17.3	8.4	13.8	12.8	12.2
48039	26,420	1	Brazoria	1,362.3	370,200	190	271.7	47.6	14.7	0.7	7.5	31.1	7.0	19.5	8.1	14.1	14.7	13.2
48041	17,780	3	Brazos	585.5	226,758	299	387.3	56.7	11.0	0.6	7.2	26.0	6.1	14.5	25.7	16.0	11.2	9.0
48043		7	Brewster	6,183.8	9,267	2,480	1.5	51.7	1.9	1.3	1.6	45.0	5.3	13.6	7.2	13.2	12.6	11.1
48045		9	Briscoe	900.0	1,516	3,078	1.7	70.9	4.3	1.3	0.6	24.8	4.3	14.4	7.5	10.6	11.7	11.9
48047		7	Brooks	943.4	7,114	2,654	7.5	6.8	0.7	0.2	1.0	91.6	8.3	20.0	9.1	12.5	10.8	9.5
48049	15,220	5	Brown	944.5	37,924	1,228	40.2	72.4	4.3	1.1	1.0	22.7	5.4	16.7	8.8	11.9	11.4	12.2
48051	17,780	3	Burleson	659.0	18,389	1,905	27.9	65.8	13.4	0.9	0.6	20.8	6.2	16.0	7.2	11.4	10.5	12.6
48053		6	Burnet	994.3	47,542	1,024	47.8	74.0	2.2	1.1	1.2	22.7	5.6	15.8	7.4	10.9	10.9	11.7

1. CBSA = Core Based Statistical Area. See Appendix A for explanation. See Appendix B for list of metropolitan areas with component counties.
Service of USDA Rural-Urban Continuum Codes. See Appendix A for definition.   3. Dry land or land partially or temporarily covered by water.   2. County type code from the Economic Research   4. May be of any race.

Table B. States and Counties — Population and Households

STATE County	Population, 2018 (cont.) Age (percent) (cont.) 55 to 64 years	65 to 74 years	75 years and over	Percent female	Population change, 2000-2018 Total persons 2000	Total persons 2010	Percent change 2000-2010	Percent change 2010-2018	Components of change, 2010-2018 Births	Deaths	Net Migration	Households, 2013-2017 Number	Persons per household	Family house-holds	Female family house-holder[1]	One person
	16	17	18	19	20	21	22	23	24	25	26	27	28	29	30	31
TENNESSEE— Cont'd																
Marshall	13.5	10.0	6.1	51.0	26,767	30,608	14.3	10.0	3,091	2,628	2,624	12,008	2.61	70.2	13.5	25.6
Maury	13.8	9.8	6.1	51.8	69,498	80,932	16.5	16.6	9,395	7,031	10,947	33,332	2.59	70.5	13.4	24.7
Meigs	14.3	13.6	7.6	50.4	11,086	11,768	6.2	4.6	990	1,256	805	4,818	2.43	70.9	11.1	25.2
Monroe	14.5	13.0	8.2	50.2	38,961	44,504	14.2	4.2	4,058	4,295	2,106	17,416	2.59	73.4	11.6	24.3
Montgomery	9.5	5.7	3.5	50.2	134,768	172,363	27.9	19.5	27,647	9,682	15,274	68,904	2.74	71.7	14.1	22.4
Moore	15.8	12.2	9.4	50.0	5,740	6,342	10.5	1.1	418	536	188	2,613	2.38	74.1	7.8	23.0
Morgan	13.8	10.8	7.0	45.3	19,757	21,986	11.3	-1.9	1,645	1,906	-145	7,384	2.54	74.6	12.0	21.1
Obion	14.2	11.7	8.7	51.6	32,450	31,807	-2.0	-4.8	2,859	3,155	-1,238	12,795	2.36	68.7	14.9	25.9
Overton	13.9	12.2	8.4	50.4	20,118	22,080	9.8	-0.1	1,912	2,411	500	8,937	2.43	68.4	11.3	28.6
Perry	14.0	12.3	8.9	49.5	7,631	7,928	3.9	1.7	821	915	234	3,295	2.35	73.4	8.5	24.0
Pickett	15.9	15.7	11.8	50.0	4,945	5,083	2.8	0.0	342	558	213	2,180	2.29	76.2	11.6	21.5
Polk	15.0	12.2	8.8	50.7	16,050	16,824	4.8	0.4	1,317	1,824	585	7,023	2.35	72.7	11.2	23.7
Putnam	11.9	9.6	7.0	50.2	62,315	72,349	16.1	9.0	7,308	6,371	5,581	30,624	2.36	62.1	12.4	29.5
Rhea	13.3	11.1	7.5	50.4	28,400	31,800	12.0	3.9	3,183	3,172	1,248	12,607	2.50	65.9	13.0	30.6
Roane	16.2	13.2	9.6	51.2	51,910	54,199	4.4	-2.0	3,892	5,812	907	21,619	2.42	65.8	9.4	29.6
Robertson	14.0	9.1	5.7	50.6	54,433	66,332	21.9	7.1	7,274	5,311	2,744	25,065	2.70	75.9	12.9	19.8
Rutherford	10.8	6.6	3.9	50.8	182,023	262,582	44.3	23.7	32,016	14,529	44,352	106,673	2.75	70.1	12.5	21.6
Scott	13.0	10.1	6.7	50.9	21,127	22,232	5.2	-0.9	2,225	2,257	-147	8,519	2.53	67.4	12.1	27.2
Sequatchie	15.2	12.3	8.0	50.5	11,370	14,121	24.2	5.3	1,267	1,286	775	5,505	2.62	77.3	11.8	19.7
Sevier	14.7	12.2	7.6	51.1	71,170	89,719	26.1	9.1	8,636	8,092	7,591	36,901	2.56	69.6	11.2	24.7
Shelby	12.5	8.3	5.2	52.5	897,472	927,682	3.4	0.9	111,562	65,101	-38,355	349,207	2.64	63.0	20.3	31.5
Smith	14.5	10.6	6.4	50.3	17,712	19,149	8.1	4.1	1,889	1,731	636	7,535	2.53	71.6	12.1	25.5
Stewart	15.0	12.3	8.1	50.1	12,370	13,313	7.6	1.9	1,106	1,296	439	5,315	2.47	69.4	9.0	28.1
Sullivan	14.5	12.3	9.6	51.4	153,048	156,800	2.5	0.6	12,712	16,615	4,914	66,388	2.32	65.9	11.6	30.1
Sumner	13.3	9.6	6.3	51.2	130,449	160,634	23.1	16.5	16,767	11,965	21,559	64,600	2.70	73.0	11.6	23.5
Tipton	13.6	8.9	5.6	50.6	51,271	61,006	19.0	0.9	6,018	4,653	-778	21,445	2.83	76.9	16.9	19.6
Trousdale	10.6	7.9	5.0	40.8	7,259	7,864	8.3	40.0	792	752	3,076	2,944	2.94	64.7	11.6	30.8
Unicoi	15.4	13.0	10.2	50.9	17,667	18,311	3.6	-3.0	1,302	2,197	360	7,613	2.27	63.6	11.4	32.3
Union	15.5	11.3	7.0	50.7	17,808	19,107	7.3	3.0	1,698	1,753	642	7,268	2.61	74.8	12.7	21.3
Van Buren	15.9	15.2	8.5	49.9	5,508	5,558	0.9	3.7	500	539	241	2,156	2.58	74.6	11.8	22.7
Warren	13.5	10.2	7.5	50.5	38,276	39,824	4.0	2.6	3,930	3,950	1,106	15,755	2.51	65.4	12.3	29.8
Washington	13.3	10.7	7.7	51.1	107,198	123,058	14.8	4.5	10,846	11,244	5,966	52,684	2.31	62.7	11.5	30.1
Wayne	13.8	11.2	8.3	44.8	16,842	17,027	1.1	-2.8	1,165	1,679	59	5,860	2.51	72.0	11.7	26.1
Weakley	12.6	10.6	8.1	51.0	34,895	35,015	0.3	-4.6	2,873	3,063	-1,415	13,607	2.29	63.2	10.7	29.3
White	13.8	11.7	8.5	51.1	23,102	25,837	11.8	4.9	2,476	2,977	1,776	9,793	2.65	70.0	9.7	27.1
Williamson	12.8	8.2	5.0	50.9	126,638	183,265	44.7	26.4	17,752	9,023	39,493	73,160	2.89	80.4	7.4	16.0
Wilson	13.4	9.8	5.9	50.8	88,809	114,073	28.4	23.3	11,851	8,251	22,719	47,213	2.70	74.7	10.9	21.8
TEXAS	11.3	7.5	5.0	50.3	20,851,820	25,146,114	20.6	14.1	3,221,263	1,511,232	1,832,775	9,430,419	2.84	69.6	14.0	24.9
Anderson	11.8	8.7	6.1	38.8	55,109	58,459	6.1	-0.7	4,867	5,318	80	16,567	2.68	70.1	10.6	26.8
Andrews	10.6	6.0	4.4	48.8	13,004	14,786	13.7	22.6	2,477	1,024	1,839	5,413	3.23	76.8	9.4	19.0
Angelina	12.4	9.3	7.1	51.2	80,130	86,771	8.3	0.4	9,863	7,223	-2,262	30,931	2.73	72.4	15.7	24.4
Aransas	16.3	16.6	13.1	50.6	22,497	23,158	2.9	2.7	2,057	2,840	1,359	9,529	2.56	65.9	7.1	28.4
Archer	16.2	10.9	9.1	50.8	8,854	9,055	2.3	-3.0	620	650	-247	3,351	2.60	71.4	6.4	25.8
Armstrong	15.6	13.6	10.4	51.5	2,148	1,901	-11.5	-0.5	174	225	39	702	2.65	76.9	6.0	19.4
Atascosa	11.7	8.6	6.1	50.1	38,628	44,911	16.3	12.0	5,546	3,267	3,110	15,509	3.08	76.2	16.8	20.3
Austin	14.6	11.2	7.8	50.1	23,590	28,412	20.4	5.6	2,813	2,241	1,019	11,021	2.63	73.8	9.9	23.0
Bailey	11.1	7.8	6.8	50.2	6,594	7,165	8.7	-1.9	1,024	480	-695	2,230	3.10	76.4	13.3	22.7
Bandera	19.4	16.8	10.2	50.4	17,645	20,489	16.1	11.4	1,394	1,750	2,680	8,278	2.51	68.8	9.6	27.2
Bastrop	13.9	9.8	5.4	49.1	57,733	74,202	28.5	17.2	8,170	5,337	9,858	26,015	3.00	73.0	11.4	22.2
Baylor	13.7	11.5	12.3	51.3	4,093	3,726	-9.0	-3.9	314	499	41	1,644	2.14	59.1	8.2	37.6
Bee	10.2	7.1	5.2	39.2	32,359	31,861	-1.5	2.3	3,078	2,064	-288	8,531	2.93	71.8	17.4	24.5
Bell	9.8	6.5	4.3	50.3	237,974	310,159	30.3	14.7	51,754	16,981	10,481	116,397	2.81	70.5	14.8	25.1
Bexar	10.6	7.2	4.9	50.6	1,392,931	1,714,772	23.1	15.8	223,861	103,580	150,104	627,889	2.96	67.4	16.2	26.8
Blanco	18.5	15.2	9.1	49.8	8,418	10,495	24.7	11.5	772	962	1,387	4,230	2.59	72.5	9.2	22.6
Borden	14.0	11.9	12.8	48.0	729	641	-12.1	1.1	53	40	-8	248	2.43	72.2	6.5	26.6
Bosque	15.2	13.9	10.8	50.5	17,204	18,217	5.9	2.6	1,568	2,036	944	7,027	2.50	74.1	8.8	22.8
Bowie	12.5	9.5	7.0	49.7	89,306	92,564	3.6	1.9	10,036	8,270	61	33,171	2.66	68.9	16.0	27.6
Brazoria	11.5	7.4	4.4	49.5	241,767	313,123	29.5	18.2	39,071	18,218	36,049	117,088	2.86	74.8	11.2	21.1
Brazos	8.3	5.4	3.7	49.5	152,415	194,861	27.8	16.4	22,445	7,913	17,293	77,480	2.56	55.8	12.0	27.7
Brewster	14.0	13.8	9.3	49.5	8,866	9,232	4.1	0.4	875	627	-221	3,932	2.32	54.6	8.1	40.0
Briscoe	13.3	14.1	12.1	50.6	1,790	1,637	-8.5	-7.4	105	151	-77	664	2.40	65.5	11.1	29.8
Brooks	11.5	10.0	8.3	49.5	7,976	7,223	-9.4	-1.5	981	652	-443	2,022	3.31	71.4	24.5	27.4
Brown	13.7	11.1	8.8	50.5	37,674	38,106	1.1	-0.5	3,439	4,041	445	13,835	2.61	68.1	8.5	27.7
Burleson	15.7	11.9	8.6	50.8	16,470	17,187	4.4	7.0	1,667	1,715	1,253	6,565	2.65	70.0	10.9	26.5
Burnet	15.3	13.4	8.9	51.0	34,147	42,706	25.1	11.3	3,980	3,873	4,706	16,545	2.69	73.0	8.4	23.4

1. No spouse present.

Table B. States and Counties — Population, Vital Statistics, Health, and Crime

STATE County	Persons in group quarters, 2018	Daytime Population, 2013-2017		Births, 2018		Deaths, 2018		Persons under 65 with no health insurance, 2016		Medicare, 2018			Serious crimes known to police[2], 2016 Total	
		Number	Employment/ residence ratio	Total	Rate[1]	Number	Rate[1]	Number	Percent	Total beneficiaries	Enrolled in Original Medicare	Enrolled in Medicare Advantage	Number	Rate[3]
	32	33	34	35	36	37	38	39	40	41	42	43	44	45

TENNESSEE— Cont'd														
Marshall	359	28,716	0.77	400	11.9	335	9.9	3,028	11.4	6,486	4,042	2,444	507	1,598
Maury	1,008	82,189	0.86	1,217	12.9	949	10.1	7,117	9.4	18,736	12,304	6,432	2,128	2,388
Meigs	128	9,530	0.45	125	10.2	147	11.9	1,123	11.9	3,115	1,922	1,193	373	3,151
Monroe	549	44,470	0.92	473	10.2	540	11.6	4,468	12.4	12,050	6,736	5,314	1,946	4,231
Montgomery	3,844	167,621	0.72	3,390	16.5	1,317	6.4	15,343	8.8	24,787	18,643	6,144	5,615	2,838
Moore	104	5,587	0.74	50	7.8	55	8.6	454	9.1	1,357	1,029	328	74	1,172
Morgan	2,298	18,254	0.51	194	9.0	238	11.0	1,839	11.7	5,097	2,447	2,650	398	1,860
Obion	461	30,398	0.98	336	11.1	396	13.1	2,681	11.1	7,813	5,311	2,502	1,119	3,680
Overton	286	19,389	0.70	218	9.9	309	14.0	2,074	12.0	5,622	4,271	1,351	334	1,509
Perry	123	7,897	1.01	102	12.6	102	12.6	716	11.7	2,054	1,343	711	163	2,056
Pickett	74	4,520	0.74	39	7.7	58	11.4	396	10.6	1,578	1,241	337	68	1,318
Polk	244	13,405	0.50	171	10.1	233	13.8	1,428	10.8	4,294	2,886	1,408	472	2,816
Putnam	2,568	82,525	1.22	873	11.1	757	9.6	7,444	12.2	16,350	12,217	4,133	2,541	3,391
Rhea	830	33,916	1.11	391	11.8	396	12.0	3,210	12.5	7,542	5,059	2,483	701	2,147
Roane	646	47,564	0.74	457	8.6	723	13.6	4,027	9.9	14,296	8,302	5,994	1,403	2,674
Robertson	703	59,466	0.72	865	12.2	663	9.3	6,192	10.5	12,850	7,196	5,654	1,253	1,815
Rutherford	5,098	283,045	0.90	4,111	12.7	2,036	6.3	24,067	8.8	40,401	24,617	15,784	9,081	2,967
Scott	264	20,776	0.86	265	12.0	291	13.2	2,017	11.2	5,083	2,784	2,299	366	1,672
Sequatchie	188	12,111	0.56	157	10.6	163	11.0	1,224	10.4	4,239	2,744	1,495	411	2,749
Sevier	980	97,646	1.05	1,051	10.7	1,033	10.6	11,903	15.4	22,747	12,435	10,312	3,195	3,289
Shelby	18,241	1,012,903	1.18	12,785	13.7	8,361	8.9	92,483	11.6	148,477	102,571	45,906	55,631	5,919
Smith	159	16,785	0.70	242	12.1	202	10.1	1,668	10.3	4,014	2,667	1,347	300	1,552
Stewart	92	11,616	0.68	143	10.5	162	11.9	1,178	11.2	3,339	2,551	788	241	1,820
Sullivan	2,630	167,173	1.16	1,473	9.3	1,971	12.5	12,070	9.9	42,206	17,607	24,599	5,325	3,397
Sumner	1,250	150,145	0.70	2,132	11.4	1,682	9.0	13,249	8.7	33,951	18,808	15,143	2,768	1,601
Tipton	962	46,193	0.44	688	11.2	598	9.7	5,161	9.9	10,918	8,138	2,780	1,834	2,958
Trousdale	2,579	7,423	0.64	100	9.1	84	7.6	846	12.2	1,786	1,095	691	240	2,971
Unicoi	405	16,941	0.87	157	8.8	272	15.3	1,582	11.7	5,161	2,596	2,565	315	1,772
Union	152	15,221	0.44	199	10.1	217	11.0	1,956	12.5	4,548	1,967	2,581	507	2,652
Van Buren	94	4,893	0.65	61	10.6	47	8.2	511	11.8	1,636	1,209	427	85	1,491
Warren	580	39,162	0.94	475	11.6	464	11.4	4,490	13.6	9,259	6,438	2,821	1,104	2,723
Washington	4,529	134,006	1.13	1,241	9.6	1,397	10.9	9,940	9.8	28,931	15,110	13,821	3,765	2,967
Wayne	2,146	15,686	0.82	133	8.0	210	12.7	1,404	12.2	3,851	2,671	1,180	150	898
Weakley	1,651	31,786	0.86	326	9.8	351	10.5	2,501	9.6	7,250	5,472	1,778	646	1,914
White	382	23,917	0.75	303	11.2	344	12.7	2,325	11.1	6,997	4,869	2,128	661	2,480
Williamson	1,153	235,438	1.22	2,357	10.2	1,287	5.6	11,006	5.7	32,548	20,778	11,770	2,683	1,233
Wilson	1,389	114,516	0.77	1,557	11.1	1,114	7.9	8,508	7.6	25,157	15,341	9,816	2,568	1,946
TEXAS	600,251	27,420,251	1.00	391,451	13.6	200,500	7.0	4,444,791	18.6	4,016,438	2,478,637	1,537,801	889,989	3,194
Anderson	14,357	58,430	1.04	580	10.0	686	11.8	6,394	17.6	10,192	6,988	3,204	1,145	2,001
Andrews	80	17,523	0.99	274	15.1	139	7.7	2,897	18.2	2,079	1,507	572	485	2,582
Angelina	2,751	88,707	1.03	1,139	13.1	939	10.8	14,196	19.8	17,210	11,593	5,617	2,445	2,770
Aransas	453	23,090	0.83	230	9.7	362	15.2	3,902	21.3	7,011	4,061	2,950	1,120	4,353
Archer	51	6,336	0.43	75	8.5	73	8.3	1,263	17.9	1,821	1,491	330	NA	NA
Armstrong	54	1,582	0.64	24	12.7	21	11.1	229	15.6	452	357	95	13	666
Atascosa	373	45,974	0.89	698	13.9	422	8.4	7,590	18.3	8,520	4,394	4,126	1,401	2,858
Austin	198	26,837	0.82	336	11.2	276	9.2	4,429	18.3	6,158	4,322	1,836	466	1,568
Bailey	106	6,858	0.92	131	18.6	36	5.1	1,596	26.4	1,078	903	175	129	1,791
Bandera	308	17,904	0.60	189	8.3	240	10.5	2,865	18.0	6,175	4,366	1,809	284	1,330
Bastrop	2,348	66,142	0.57	1,130	13.0	714	8.2	14,519	21.1	14,528	9,947	4,581	2,101	2,575
Baylor	64	3,598	1.00	34	9.5	50	14.0	461	16.8	993	798	195	68	1,895
Bee	7,786	31,873	0.91	339	10.4	234	7.2	3,916	18.2	4,570	2,608	1,962	576	1,747
Bell	9,482	346,256	1.06	6,047	17.0	2,232	6.3	40,741	13.7	48,923	32,770	16,153	10,265	3,043
Bexar	42,261	1,935,267	1.05	27,700	13.9	13,794	6.9	276,390	16.6	285,187	153,664	131,523	101,848	5,280
Blanco	23	9,729	0.72	98	8.4	115	9.8	1,935	22.4	2,930	2,181	749	95	858
Borden	0	557	0.82	6	9.3	6	9.3	69	13.6	130	106	24	11	1,700
Bosque	330	15,309	0.64	205	11.0	247	13.2	3,068	22.7	4,893	3,131	1,762	152	1,000
Bowie	6,203	100,530	1.19	1,187	12.6	1,045	11.1	11,463	15.7	19,051	14,275	4,776	3,193	3,424
Brazoria	10,445	298,320	0.70	4,817	13.0	2,503	6.8	45,562	15.0	48,024	28,992	19,032	6,370	1,810
Brazos	14,246	219,936	1.06	2,736	12.1	1,069	4.7	30,850	16.5	22,557	17,232	5,325	6,373	2,917
Brewster	44	9,102	0.97	96	10.4	71	7.7	1,276	17.7	2,133	1,522	611	131	1,441
Briscoe	0	1,443	0.79	12	7.9	10	6.6	345	31.1	429	329	100	13	880
Brooks	52	7,473	1.09	105	14.8	75	10.5	1,045	18.0	1,596	939	657	166	2,301
Brown	1,670	38,387	1.04	396	10.4	466	12.3	5,028	17.1	8,990	6,830	2,160	959	2,541
Burleson	180	14,706	0.61	214	11.6	223	12.1	2,713	19.1	4,239	2,947	1,292	189	1,176
Burnet	1,161	42,559	0.87	506	10.6	486	10.2	6,937	19.8	12,121	8,434	3,687	851	1,903

1. Per 1,000 estimated resident population. 2. Data for serious crimes have not been adjusted for underreporting; this may affect comparability between geographic areas and over time. 3. Per 100,000 population estimated by the FBI.

Table B. States and Counties — Crime, Education, Money Income, and Poverty

STATE County	Serious crimes known to police[2], 2016 (cont.)[1] Rate		Education School enrollment and attainment, 2013-2017 Enrollment[3]		Attainment[4] (percent)		Local government expenditures,[5] 2014-2015		Money income, 2013-2017		Households Percent		Income and poverty, 2017		Percent below poverty level	
	Violent	Property	Total	Percent private	High school graduate or less	Bachelor's degree or more	Total current spending (mil dol)	Current spending per student (dollars)	Per capita income[6]	Median income (dollars)	with income of less than $50,000	with income of $200,000 or more	Median household income (dollars)	All persons	Children under 18 years	Children 5 to 17 years in families
	46	47	48	49	50	51	52	53	54	55	56	57	58	59	60	61
TENNESSEE— Cont'd																
Marshall	451	1,147	6,888	11.5	58.1	13.4	43.1	8,003	23,920	46,837	52.4	2.1	52,415	11.7	15.8	15.4
Maury	482	1,905	19,252	19.7	46.9	20.7	101.6	8,286	25,872	52,080	48.1	2.8	56,999	10.4	15.5	13.6
Meigs	473	2,678	2,249	10.7	63.5	9.8	15.2	8,257	22,542	39,786	60.5	1.8	45,695	17.4	26.5	24.5
Monroe	580	3,650	8,500	9.7	63.1	11.7	55.6	7,793	20,353	36,931	61.9	1.0	43,749	17.6	26.6	24.4
Montgomery	535	2,304	56,051	11.1	37.6	26.2	263.0	8,203	24,827	53,737	45.7	2.2	57,431	12.8	16.2	17.4
Moore	111	1,061	1,272	11.7	53.9	19.5	8.9	9,598	31,479	51,671	47.4	3.6	55,448	9.9	15.6	14.6
Morgan	229	1,631	3,903	9.7	69.2	7.7	26.9	8,420	18,649	40,707	59.3	1.5	40,667	20.3	24.8	22.9
Obion	490	3,190	6,781	8.0	59.3	15.6	43.4	8,350	21,939	38,063	60.8	1.7	38,160	20.7	29.4	27.5
Overton	181	1,328	4,796	8.7	66.2	13.0	26.8	8,239	19,961	36,052	62.9	1.0	37,154	17.8	23.0	20.8
Perry	290	1,766	1,475	17.8	63.4	10.8	10.2	8,929	20,204	31,503	65.8	2.0	37,135	21.1	28.9	29.9
Pickett	329	988	783	0.6	67.0	7.0	6.0	7,754	21,300	39,313	66.5	0.0	39,858	16.9	26.2	24.6
Polk	251	2,565	3,117	10.7	60.0	10.8	20.3	7,944	24,247	42,307	58.6	2.2	41,191	15.7	22.9	21.5
Putnam	420	2,970	19,976	7.5	52.3	24.8	92.8	8,275	23,337	37,802	60.7	2.7	42,437	19	23.8	21.7
Rhea	276	1,871	7,367	12.0	59.4	14.2	41.9	7,969	22,031	39,368	60.0	2.4	43,426	16	24.1	23.2
Roane	326	2,348	10,436	12.0	51.0	19.3	60.6	8,652	25,555	45,407	54.2	2.3	48,391	15.2	21.3	19.4
Robertson	372	1,443	15,951	18.6	52.8	18.1	89.2	7,668	26,441	57,424	42.8	2.8	59,771	11.6	16.6	14.7
Rutherford	585	2,382	84,459	11.3	37.7	31.8	407.3	8,170	27,932	62,149	38.9	3.4	68,082	10.1	12.6	10.9
Scott	242	1,430	5,093	7.8	67.2	8.3	34.0	7,767	18,748	31,875	65.4	0.6	34,828	22.8	29.8	27.1
Sequatchie	408	2,341	3,243	12.2	57.7	14.5	17.2	7,361	22,744	51,312	49.2	1.0	45,100	16.7	26.3	25.0
Sevier	318	2,971	19,409	11.7	53.0	18.0	130.5	8,932	23,298	44,473	55.0	2.3	48,482	12.6	19.6	19.2
Shelby	1,384	4,535	247,687	19.6	39.5	30.6	1,408.4	9,610	28,117	48,415	51.1	5.0	49,563	18.9	29.2	26.9
Smith	202	1,351	4,375	10.0	64.1	11.2	24.8	7,818	23,015	44,275	55.3	1.7	47,653	13	18.5	17.5
Stewart	476	1,344	2,886	5.7	55.1	15.1	16.8	7,944	22,680	44,090	55.7	1.1	48,175	16.1	23.9	21.6
Sullivan	536	2,861	31,924	14.7	49.7	22.0	196.2	8,972	25,946	42,251	56.6	2.8	45,224	15.7	23.7	22.9
Sumner	247	1,354	42,366	15.4	41.8	26.5	240.9	8,335	30,669	61,584	40.0	4.8	65,174	8.8	11.5	10.6
Tipton	610	2,348	15,720	10.0	53.7	15.3	89.5	7,749	26,110	57,212	44.3	2.9	56,511	14	18.7	17.7
Trousdale	508	2,464	2,032	19.8	60.1	15.2	9.4	7,662	22,863	41,776	54.1	0.9	49,711	17.5	20.7	19.1
Unicoi	225	1,547	3,505	8.6	57.8	14.9	21.2	8,484	21,374	36,576	64.6	1.0	41,188	16.4	25.4	22.2
Union	277	2,374	4,009	16.2	69.4	8.8	35.0	8,051	20,478	40,132	60.3	2.2	40,357	19	28.7	27.4
Van Buren	316	1,175	1,054	16.6	67.2	9.9	7.1	9,077	20,672	43,631	57.5	1.7	38,478	17.5	27.4	28.3
Warren	481	2,242	8,901	6.8	63.3	14.4	53.0	7,883	21,339	36,765	62.4	2.0	37,692	21.6	28.7	26.6
Washington	348	2,620	32,832	12.0	40.9	31.9	142.2	8,519	27,334	44,180	55.6	3.4	43,194	14.9	18.6	16.8
Wayne	317	581	3,168	9.5	65.7	11.1	20.8	8,637	18,702	34,299	65.4	1.3	36,612	21.2	27.9	24.7
Weakley	204	1,710	10,170	7.1	55.2	20.8	34.5	7,800	19,699	36,550	64.6	1.0	39,424	22.1	27.4	22.3
White	266	2,213	5,650	10.0	62.2	12.3	30.4	7,332	19,867	37,654	65.1	1.3	39,642	16	24.2	22.6
Williamson	158	1,075	61,713	23.4	18.9	58.1	346.5	8,813	48,482	103,543	21.5	18.8	111,427	3.9	3.8	3.3
Wilson	282	1,664	31,620	19.7	39.0	29.7	159.0	7,614	31,155	66,123	36.6	5.6	70,674	8.4	10.9	10.7
TEXAS	434	2,760	7,550,309	11.1	42.3	28.7	46,147.9	8,817	28,985	57,051	44.1	6.3	59,195	14.7	21.0	19.9
Anderson	536	1,464	12,888	3.7	55.5	12.4	75.6	9,106	17,466	42,313	56.5	1.8	42,412	18.8	23.4	22.5
Andrews	452	2,129	4,586	5.1	62.7	9.8	37.7	9,391	29,903	70,753	38.7	5.5	63,451	13	17.5	16.9
Angelina	283	2,487	22,482	6.4	50.1	16.7	147.6	8,356	21,974	46,472	52.9	2.1	45,318	20	25.4	24.7
Aransas	525	3,829	4,279	10.8	44.9	19.5	31.0	9,514	29,999	44,601	53.3	4.8	46,970	18.1	32.2	30.8
Archer	NA	NA	1,985	8.3	42.2	23.6	16.6	9,003	31,103	63,192	41.4	3.9	58,311	10.1	13.8	13.2
Armstrong	154	513	386	2.1	34.7	23.6	4.0	11,322	31,219	68,750	32.6	2.7	55,337	10.6	15.1	14.5
Atascosa	222	2,636	12,298	6.9	61.7	14.3	86.4	9,405	23,973	55,194	44.6	3.6	48,636	16.9	25.4	24.4
Austin	202	1,366	6,555	12.9	47.6	22.3	48.5	8,357	30,101	62,614	42.0	4.1	61,111	10.7	16.4	15.5
Bailey	153	1,638	1,720	5.8	57.3	14.4	13.6	9,577	18,662	43,523	60.5	1.6	42,045	17.2	26.3	24.4
Bandera	178	1,152	3,785	13.7	44.1	23.8	22.4	8,789	29,177	56,413	45.1	4.6	55,578	11.9	22.6	20.9
Bastrop	491	2,084	20,072	10.4	48.2	20.3	152.1	9,406	25,172	59,185	42.4	2.8	62,992	11.5	18.7	18.1
Baylor	223	1,672	633	3.8	44.4	24.8	5.9	9,953	30,820	36,157	65.0	5.9	37,013	17.7	27.6	26.3
Bee	321	1,425	6,908	7.3	62.5	9.2	45.1	8,515	17,504	45,415	56.6	3.2	41,392	26.6	33.7	31.2
Bell	430	2,612	97,887	11.3	36.0	24.2	593.5	8,381	25,017	52,583	46.7	3.1	52,164	13.8	20.5	19.1
Bexar	609	4,671	533,711	13.2	41.7	27.3	3,174.8	9,064	26,158	53,999	46.1	4.7	54,163	15.6	22.2	20.8
Blanco	181	677	2,254	16.2	40.1	28.5	18.8	11,170	31,249	58,500	44.3	5.5	62,115	10.6	17.1	15.3
Borden	618	1,082	108	2.8	32.4	38.8	4.5	17,996	38,923	77,708	26.2	3.2	59,039	11	15.8	17.0
Bosque	46	954	3,684	7.8	51.5	18.4	23.1	10,101	25,763	48,677	51.0	3.0	49,139	16	26.2	23.8
Bowie	475	2,949	22,422	7.8	48.2	19.2	158.9	8,871	24,761	46,283	53.6	3.7	49,153	15.9	23.0	23.0
Brazoria	187	1,623	93,995	11.1	37.9	29.7	543.9	8,177	32,343	76,426	32.3	7.8	80,840	9	11.9	11.9
Brazos	347	2,570	89,833	5.9	34.1	39.6	257.5	8,641	25,337	43,907	54.3	4.4	46,083	23.9	20.5	19.6
Brewster	154	1,287	2,068	12.6	37.5	35.7	15.3	13,039	26,073	38,906	62.9	3.7	44,617	14	20.7	20.7
Briscoe	0	880	336	2.1	49.9	21.9	4.3	11,551	23,199	42,500	56.6	2.9	42,678	15.3	26.0	24.7
Brooks	208	2,093	1,929	5.7	60.1	14.7	16.7	10,845	13,549	24,794	70.8	0.7	28,106	35	52.5	55.0
Brown	329	2,213	8,736	13.0	52.3	17.8	60.2	8,926	24,040	43,062	55.9	3.3	41,538	16.8	24.8	22.2
Burleson	205	971	3,655	12.0	59.4	14.8	24.7	8,961	27,112	52,510	46.6	3.6	47,409	16.6	25.4	24.5
Burnet	235	1,668	9,304	10.7	43.6	24.1	64.3	8,925	29,247	57,173	44.7	4.8	59,009	10.4	17.7	16.8

1. Data for serious crimes have not been adjusted for underreporting; this may affect comparability between geographic areas and over time.　2. Per 100,000 population estimated by the FBI.　3. All persons 3 years old and over enrolled in nursery school through college.　4. Persons 25 years old and over.　5. Elementary and secondary education expenditures.　6. Based on population estimated by the American Community Survey, 2013–2017.

Table B. States and Counties — **Personal Income and Earnings**

STATE County	Personal income, 2017										Earnings, 2017		
			Per capita[1]			Supplements to wages and salaries, employer contributions (mil dol)						Contributions for government social insurance (mil dol)	
	Total (mil dol)	Percent change 2016-2017	Dollars	Rank	Wages and salaries (mil dol)	Pension and insurance	Government social insurance	Proprietors' income (mil dol)	Dividends, interest, and rent (mil dol)	Personal transfer receipts (mil dol)	Total (mil dol)	From employee and self-employed	From employer
	62	63	64	65	66	67	68	69	70	71	72	73	74
TENNESSEE— Cont'd													
Marshall	1,210	6.3	36,759	2,083	444	88	32	97	154	279	661	43	32
Maury	3,807	6.1	41,302	1,365	1,690	292	122	376	462	814	2,481	152	122
Meigs	402	4.9	33,347	2,577	89	22	7	23	55	132	141	11	7
Monroe	1,493	3.0	32,283	2,716	575	117	42	113	199	484	847	61	42
Montgomery	8,134	5.0	40,633	1,452	2,163	414	155	590	1,307	1,584	3,321	200	155
Moore	250	2.3	39,185	1,691	96	26	7	17	38	61	145	9	7
Morgan	621	2.5	28,699	3,003	101	28	7	37	71	213	173	16	7
Obion	1,177	4.0	38,750	1,767	378	72	27	105	211	349	582	40	27
Overton	714	3.8	32,445	2,696	185	43	13	84	85	226	325	24	13
Perry	269	4.8	33,670	2,532	70	16	5	26	41	102	117	9	5
Pickett	199	6.2	39,171	1,694	41	9	3	42	27	65	95	7	3
Polk	558	3.5	33,290	2,580	81	20	6	38	69	172	145	13	6
Putnam	3,005	5.2	38,688	1,778	1,429	291	101	422	542	713	2,243	134	101
Rhea	1,120	4.8	34,267	2,452	506	112	38	69	134	353	724	48	38
Roane	2,109	3.4	39,763	1,598	1,232	162	84	125	288	636	1,603	108	84
Robertson	2,840	4.5	40,463	1,480	969	202	72	295	315	585	1,537	93	72
Rutherford	12,676	6.4	39,968	1,557	6,406	1,070	452	1,530	1,440	1,829	9,458	537	452
Scott	632	3.5	28,721	3,001	191	47	15	42	71	252	294	22	15
Sequatchie	541	3.3	36,691	2,092	104	23	7	37	76	171	172	14	7
Sevier	3,721	3.9	38,114	1,862	1,560	236	118	602	537	887	2,516	160	118
Shelby	44,651	2.9	47,655	649	28,692	4,177	1,918	4,491	7,217	7,929	39,278	2,277	1,918
Smith	722	4.8	36,759	2,083	219	46	15	62	111	178	342	23	15
Stewart	528	3.5	39,523	1,634	137	34	11	28	78	153	209	15	11
Sullivan	6,511	3.8	41,431	1,343	3,373	597	236	577	1,030	1,723	4,783	309	236
Sumner	8,626	6.3	46,998	713	2,478	420	176	1,144	1,061	1,433	4,218	255	176
Tipton	2,302	3.3	37,515	1,942	443	91	31	128	269	525	693	51	31
Trousdale	322	8.1	31,893	2,766	58	14	4	43	34	84	118	8	4
Unicoi	653	3.6	36,779	2,081	234	47	18	36	85	244	336	25	18
Union	597	3.4	30,686	2,876	99	22	7	51	66	189	179	16	7
Van Buren	177	1.5	30,793	2,869	33	9	2	12	26	68	57	5	2
Warren	1,361	1.8	33,483	2,557	554	107	40	119	186	423	820	54	40
Washington	5,368	3.9	42,002	1,265	2,676	524	189	510	849	1,220	3,899	238	189
Wayne	453	3.8	27,306	3,052	133	31	10	32	61	177	205	16	10
Weakley	1,209	4.5	36,265	2,155	471	114	33	121	188	355	740	45	33
White	862	3.6	32,207	2,725	276	56	20	77	127	290	429	32	20
Williamson	21,571	5.9	95,339	16	8,761	1,038	573	6,265	2,901	1,153	16,637	857	573
Wilson	6,458	6.5	47,335	682	2,057	309	142	675	799	1,024	3,183	197	142
TEXAS	1,340,568	4.1	47,332	X	700,181	100,593	48,267	150,349	238,805	206,050	999,391	53,478	48,267
Anderson	1,926	0.8	33,362	2,575	915	169	65	77	297	522	1,225	72	65
Andrews	764	4.8	43,105	1,129	468	71	31	44	84	110	615	33	31
Angelina	3,298	0.2	37,555	1,937	1,479	255	104	265	609	922	2,103	123	104
Aransas	1,146	3.5	44,820	926	237	39	17	77	269	313	370	28	17
Archer	415	2.1	47,110	706	78	16	6	41	79	78	140	8	6
Armstrong	85	-0.1	45,262	874	15	3	1	5	16	21	25	2	1
Atascosa	1,684	1.9	34,372	2,431	629	106	44	73	274	422	852	53	44
Austin	1,467	0.9	49,262	514	501	73	36	105	338	268	715	42	36
Bailey	316	12.4	44,659	944	98	19	8	83	49	60	207	8	8
Bandera	946	4.6	42,330	1,226	128	23	9	55	227	222	215	18	9
Bastrop	2,964	6.1	34,969	2,353	739	139	52	246	441	632	1,176	73	52
Baylor	142	3.8	39,650	1,610	46	10	3	13	28	50	72	5	3
Bee	882	1.6	27,078	3,060	336	80	22	39	155	265	477	26	22
Bell	14,617	4.5	42,024	1,261	7,989	1,714	659	865	2,508	3,008	11,226	556	659
Bexar	85,782	4.1	43,798	1,041	47,454	7,568	3,408	9,816	15,775	15,052	68,246	3,646	3,408
Blanco	569	4.4	48,978	540	164	25	12	46	179	103	248	15	12
Borden	35	-0.3	51,776	384	8	2	1	2	14	5	12	1	1
Bosque	746	3.3	40,704	1,442	152	33	11	62	134	206	257	17	11
Bowie	3,648	2.4	38,807	1,754	1,808	349	133	255	696	938	2,545	148	133
Brazoria	16,646	2.8	45,925	804	6,423	1,028	429	745	1,893	2,398	8,624	483	429
Brazos	8,323	5.0	37,352	1,977	4,328	908	275	797	1,736	1,146	6,307	297	275
Brewster	415	3.4	44,418	968	158	34	11	33	139	82	237	13	11
Briscoe	52	14.8	34,165	2,463	12	3	1		14	15	15	1	1
Brooks	242	1.4	33,466	2,558	108	25	8	7	31	110	149	9	8
Brown	1,410	3.4	37,041	2,027	620	117	44	82	216	452	864	54	44
Burleson	729	2.3	40,482	1,476	201	34	15	41	133	181	290	20	15
Burnet	2,123	4.1	45,350	861	630	102	43	174	642	467	949	62	43

1. Based on the resident population estimated as of July 1 of the year shown.

Table B. States and Counties — Earnings, Social Security, and Housing

STATE County	Earnings, 2017 (cont.)									Social Security beneficiaries, December 2017			Housing units, 2018	
	Percent by selected industries											Supplemental Security Income recipients, 2017		
	Farm	Mining, quarrying, and extractions	Construction	Manu-facturing	Information; professional, scientific, technical services	Retail trade	Finance, insurance, real estate, and leasing	Health care and social assistance	Govern-ment	Number	Rate[1]		Total	Percent change, 2010-2018
	75	76	77	78	79	80	81	82	83	84	85	86	87	88

STATE County	75	76	77	78	79	80	81	82	83	84	85	86	87	88
TENNESSEE— Cont'd														
Marshall	-0.7	D	7.4	43.4	D	7.1	2.9	3.9	15.7	7,305	222	690	13,764	4.9
Maury	-0.1	D	8.3	22	4.5	6.2	11	9.4	17.1	20,155	219	1,871	38,351	8.8
Meigs	-1.4	0.1	6.4	40.5	D	3.4	D	8.6	20.8	3,465	287	495	5,922	5.1
Monroe	-0.5	D	4.8	40.4	2.7	8.1	3.5	8.5	12.6	13,265	287	1,663	21,311	2.5
Montgomery	0	0.7	9	10.4	5.8	10.5	5.6	12.4	22.8	28,560	143	3,497	82,598	17.8
Moore	0.6	D	6	D	D	1.5	0.9	D	29.5	1,505	236	80	3,065	5.4
Morgan	0.6	D	9.9	8.7	D	4.6	2.5	7	40.8	5,800	268	876	9,023	1.2
Obion	4.7	0.1	6.5	15.2	D	12.8	5.9	9.4	17.5	8,825	290	1,094	14,625	-0.2
Overton	-1.3	0.9	9.1	17	4	9.3	5.6	13.5	19.4	6,275	285	636	10,409	1.1
Perry	-1.6	D	8.1	23.3	D	8.9	D	D	21.7	2,340	293	263	4,672	1.5
Pickett	0.2	1	16	D	D	11.6	3.4	8.8	15.5	1,705	336	154	3,499	1.1
Polk	5.8	D	7.2	7.6	D	8	3.1	D	29.7	4,650	277	486	9,052	13.2
Putnam	-0.2	0.1	7.1	14.4	5.6	9.1	5.1	11.3	23.1	17,965	231	2,182	34,969	9.7
Rhea	0.7	D	5	26.7	D	4.8	2.3	D	39.9	8,350	255	1,211	14,771	2.8
Roane	-0.3	D	3.7	4.1	D	4	1.6	6.3	13.8	15,640	295	1,520	25,600	-0.5
Robertson	0.6	D	12.3	29.2	2.9	6.6	4	5.9	14.2	14,115	201	1,226	27,756	6.3
Rutherford	0	D	7.9	24.8	5.9	6.8	6.2	8.9	14.1	43,760	138	3,844	121,805	18.3
Scott	-0.6	D	9.3	23.3	D	7.8	2.8	D	24.9	5,845	266	1,401	10,025	1.1
Sequatchie	0.2	D	5.4	12.2	D	11.3	7.8	D	24	4,320	293	495	6,504	2.1
Sevier	-0.1	D	7.6	4.1	3.6	12	7.1	5.9	12.9	25,000	256	1,941	58,281	4.4
Shelby	0	0	5.2	10.1	5.3	6.1	8.7	13.8	13.1	158,165	169	33,854	406,215	2
Smith	-0.4	D	11.8	26.3	2	6.8	4.6	7.4	18.2	4,585	233	518	8,808	3.3
Stewart	0.2	0	14.1	14.6	D	4.6	D	4	47.3	3,775	283	406	6,892	1.7
Sullivan	-0.2	-0.1	8.4	24.7	5	7.2	4.1	17.9	9.9	46,065	293	4,762	75,729	2.7
Sumner	0.1	D	12.7	13.5	9.1	7.9	6.4	11.9	11.8	36,120	197	2,589	73,725	11.8
Tipton	-2.7	D	13.5	14.5	3.6	7.5	3.7	D	24	12,175	198	1,460	23,971	3.4
Trousdale	-0.6	0.1	D	13.2	4	10.4	3.7	D	22.6	1,965	195	248	3,667	8.9
Unicoi	0.4	D	4.9	38.8	D	4.6	1.9	8.4	15	5,295	298	615	8,910	0.9
Union	-1.8	D	D	16.9	D	6.3	D	D	25.7	5,075	261	724	9,471	5.7
Van Buren		0.1	D	20.8	D	4.7	D	D	45.1	1,805	314	173	2,693	1.1
Warren	2.2	0	6.1	31.4	D	6.9	3.7	11	15.1	10,375	255	1,583	18,007	1.1
Washington	0.1	D	3.7	8.4	6.8	8.1	7	22.2	22.3	31,180	244	3,380	60,849	6.2
Wayne	0.4	D	4.4	9.9	D	5.9	D	14.2	29.9	4,305	260	428	7,359	1
Weakley	6.1	1.5	3.2	12	D	5.6	14.7	D	26	8,005	240	889	15,632	0.9
White	-1.6	D	6.5	23.9	D	7.8	3.6	11.6	15.6	7,865	294	989	11,988	4.1
Williamson	0	D	6.5	1.8	15.1	5.5	12	28.1	4.8	32,140	142	1,033	85,029	24.1
Wilson	-0.3	D	11.2	9.6	6.5	11.6	6.4	8	10.2	26,610	195	1,559	55,163	21
TEXAS	0.3	4.6	8.2	8.2	11.9	5.8	8.9	9.7	14.8	4,126,055	146	657,999	11,100,779	11.3
Anderson	-0.1	3.4	4.9	6.6	D	5.9	4.9	10.6	27.3	10,645	184	1,461	20,479	1.8
Andrews	0.2	31.2	12.6	2.9	4.4	4.3	4.5	D	14.9	2,255	127	276	6,274	7.9
Angelina	0.5	2.9	5.3	8.5	4.5	7.6	4.5	20.6	18.9	18,635	212	3,144	36,984	3.9
Aransas	-0.5	3	11.4	1.1	8.7	12.7	6.7	D	17.5	7,610	298	572	15,962	4
Archer	6.3	12.1	7.7	3.5	D	7.7	D	3.4	22.4	1,910	217	125	4,173	1.6
Armstrong	-4.6	1	27.3	D	9.8	D	D	10.6	24.9	465	247	20	914	1.1
Atascosa	-0.4	20.6	5.7	3.3	4.1	7.3	7.6	7.7	17.2	8,990	184	1,395	18,482	4.8
Austin	2.3	4.9	8.5	13.7	8.3	12.6	7.3	4.6	11.9	6,215	209	551	13,288	2.8
Bailey	36.6	0.1	2.3	5.2	D	3.2	2.8	4.3	11.1	1,150	162	141	2,770	-0.5
Bandera	0.8	D	19.1	1.2	6.9	5.9	5.6	11	19.2	6,335	283	374	11,990	3.7
Bastrop	-0.6	2.3	16.7	6	5.7	10.2	4	7.9	23.2	15,235	180	1,839	30,168	2.9
Baylor	2.2	D	D	D	D	5.7	D	D	18.5	1,075	300	130	2,646	-0.7
Bee	0.1	7.4	2.1	2.3	4.3	8.1	3.8	D	41.9	4,870	150	1,008	10,730	0.8
Bell	0.2	0.2	5.5	3.7	4	5.4	3.7	15	47.2	52,865	152	8,594	142,422	13.5
Bexar	0	4.9	6.8	3.9	9.6	5.9	12.4	11.4	21.8	297,890	152	53,473	700,132	5.6
Blanco	1.7	D	25.8	5.2	D	5.9	4.2	D	13.2	2,890	249	129	5,851	5.7
Borden	18.3	D	D	0.5	D	D	D	D	42.1	130	193	0	390	1.3
Bosque	12.3	D	10.4	11.3	4.1	4.9	3.9	D	26.1	5,005	273	401	9,763	1.5
Bowie	0.4	0.2	5	4	3.7	8	7.7	19.4	27.7	19,965	212	3,984	40,028	4
Brazoria	0.2	2.6	16.3	22.7	5.8	5.9	4	8.3	14.7	50,110	138	5,700	139,490	17.9
Brazos	0.2	2.2	7.8	4.3	8.9	6.2	5.5	10.2	36.6	22,450	101	3,418	92,697	19.3
Brewster	0.5	D	10.9	0.7	9.3	5	3.9	D	38.1	2,120	227	199	5,548	3.1
Briscoe	-1.9	0.4	D	D	2.3	5.6	11.4	D	38.5	425	278	34	954	0.1
Brooks	4.2	10.7	3	0	D	4.9	D	7.1	50.1	1,755	243	500	3,243	0.1
Brown	-1.2	0.9	7.1	25.9	D	8.1	4	D	19.9	9,445	248	1,236	19,083	4.3
Burleson	-2	9.5	17.3	6.3	4.4	10	7.2	D	15.3	4,255	236	490	9,213	4.3
Burnet	-0.7	0.5	14.6	7	7.6	9.4	4.5	13.5	16.7	12,195	261	685	23,316	11.9

1. Per 1,000 resident population estimated as of July 1 of the year shown.

Table B. States and Counties — Housing, Labor Force, and Employment

STATE County	Housing units, 2013-2017								Civilian labor force, 2018				Civilian employment[6], 2013-2017		
	Occupied units							Sub-standard units[4] (percent)		Percent change, 2017-2018	Unemployment			Percent	
	Owner-occupied					Renter-occupied									
	Total	Percent	Median value[1]	With a mortgage	Without a mortgage[2]	Median rent[3]	Median rent as a percent of income[2]		Total		Total	Rate[5]	Total	Management, business, science, and arts	Construction, production, and maintenance occupations
	89	90	91	92	93	94	95	96	97	98	99	100	101	102	103

TENNESSEE— Cont'd

STATE County	89	90	91	92	93	94	95	96	97	98	99	100	101	102	103
Marshall	12,008	71.7	119,300	20.2	10.5	690	26.6	2.6	15,332	1.7	528	3.4	13,998	25.4	36.9
Maury	33,332	68.7	156,000	20.9	10.4	796	28.8	2.3	47,485	3.3	1,536	3.2	40,562	32.4	26.1
Meigs	4,818	79.2	118,400	20.4	10.8	651	29.1	2.9	5,061	1.4	228	4.5	4,300	22.3	42.7
Monroe	17,416	75.8	115,200	21.5	10.6	627	28.9	3.4	19,943	1.6	740	3.7	16,551	23.4	39.6
Montgomery	68,904	59.0	153,700	21.1	10.0	931	27.8	2	83,866	2.4	3,187	3.8	77,722	32.6	25.3
Moore	2,613	84.0	166,000	21.3	10.1	632	18.5	1.8	3,536	1.8	107	3	2,807	24.3	39.9
Morgan	7,384	81.2	91,600	21.1	11.5	669	29.7	3.9	7,860	0.8	351	4.5	7,120	23.1	29.4
Obion	12,795	67.5	87,600	18.7	12.3	584	27.3	2	12,291	0.7	608	4.9	12,515	29.3	31.0
Overton	8,937	78.6	114,700	22.5	10.8	500	27.7	2.2	9,818	3.2	369	3.8	8,736	27.8	34.4
Perry	3,295	81.9	84,200	26.1	10.5	554	29	4.6	3,233	0	139	4.3	2,745	21.5	43.0
Pickett	2,180	81.2	129,700	16.4	10.9	457	25.6	1.6	2,446	0.1	93	3.8	2,220	28.9	29.9
Polk	7,023	76.2	110,900	19.6	10.0	672	25.8	3	7,281	-1.4	305	4.2	6,762	26.4	37.1
Putnam	30,624	60.5	152,800	22.2	10.3	652	32.5	2.3	34,330	1.1	1,219	3.6	32,396	33.1	22.9
Rhea	12,607	70.5	114,200	18.7	10.5	637	31.9	2.2	13,026	-1.4	731	5.6	13,341	26.4	35.4
Roane	21,619	75.3	135,900	21.3	10.5	674	29	2.2	23,153	1.1	952	4.1	21,209	31.8	26.3
Robertson	25,065	74.8	163,100	21.1	10.6	851	28.8	3.3	36,975	2.9	1,160	3.1	32,726	31.7	29.6
Rutherford	106,673	65.6	174,200	19.9	10.0	958	28.1	2.6	176,691	3.1	4,750	2.7	154,929	35.0	23.6
Scott	8,519	69.7	86,700	21.2	12.5	517	28.2	1.3	8,481	4	365	4.3	8,347	22.2	42.6
Sequatchie	5,505	75.4	138,100	21.2	10.0	683	24.8	4.4	6,041	1.4	262	4.3	5,947	30.3	28.8
Sevier	36,901	67.4	164,000	21.7	10.0	734	29.1	3.4	53,097	1.9	1,855	3.5	45,945	25.7	20.9
Shelby	349,207	55.9	135,700	22.0	11.6	894	32.3	2.8	442,379	1.3	18,374	4.2	430,218	35.1	22.1
Smith	7,535	74.8	120,700	23.6	10.0	577	25.9	2.6	9,145	2.7	279	3.1	8,427	27.7	33.4
Stewart	5,315	70.9	130,400	21.1	11.9	628	25.7	1	5,176	-0.1	259	5	5,181	26.9	32.0
Sullivan	66,388	72.6	130,300	19.8	10.0	633	28	2	70,100	0.3	2,591	3.7	66,637	33.2	22.9
Sumner	64,600	73.5	194,900	21.4	10.0	930	28.9	2.1	98,706	3.2	2,746	2.8	87,498	35.0	22.5
Tipton	21,445	69.2	142,400	19.0	10.0	768	26.9	1.9	27,895	1.2	1,176	4.2	27,671	28.4	30.2
Trousdale	2,944	71.4	128,000	21.8	12.2	613	27.7	0.9	4,888	3	159	3.3	3,834	25.2	28.4
Unicoi	7,613	72.4	121,200	23.9	11.2	599	31.3	1.9	7,065	0.3	346	4.9	7,017	25.3	34.0
Union	7,268	75.6	114,200	21.4	10.0	594	31.2	4.3	7,463	1.3	304	4.1	7,240	20.8	36.6
Van Buren	2,156	87.6	95,000	23.4	10.0	402	20.9	2.2	2,046	-1.9	97	4.7	2,308	28.0	27.7
Warren	15,755	68.5	108,600	20.6	10.0	619	26.9	2.1	16,736	-2.3	661	3.9	17,029	26.9	37.9
Washington	52,684	64.7	152,800	20.4	10.0	713	29.3	1.8	59,859	0.7	2,112	3.5	59,101	38.5	19.3
Wayne	5,860	80.5	96,400	21.6	11.5	503	22.5	1.6	6,109	-0.1	298	4.9	5,815	24.7	31.9
Weakley	13,607	66.6	94,300	19.7	10.4	590	30.3	0.8	16,008	1.6	675	4.2	14,098	31.3	27.3
White	9,793	78.4	97,700	21.8	10.8	628	33.1	1.6	11,907	0.1	439	3.7	9,994	24.9	34.0
Williamson	73,160	80.6	388,400	19.2	10.0	1,364	27.7	1.4	123,205	3.2	3,056	2.5	105,734	54.4	9.7
Wilson	47,213	77.0	227,100	20.8	10.0	950	28	1.7	73,090	3.1	2,031	2.8	63,207	37.7	20.1
TEXAS	9,430,419	62.0	151,500	21.1	11.4	952	29.1	5.3	13,848,080	1.9	533,877	3.9	12,689,069	35.9	22.7
Anderson	16,567	70.9	91,800	23.0	13.0	748	29	4.3	23,561	1.2	728	3.1	19,102	24.4	28.7
Andrews	5,413	73.5	126,000	15.8	10.5	997	23.9	6.8	9,382	4.1	225	2.4	8,054	21.3	41.5
Angelina	30,931	66.0	97,300	19.5	11.4	774	29.6	5.5	36,211	-1.3	1,589	4.4	36,164	28.2	26.9
Aransas	9,529	73.9	158,900	20.4	14.5	822	33.7	2.8	10,314	-0.3	589	5.7	10,387	28.2	26.4
Archer	3,351	82.1	125,600	19.5	10.4	621	25.4	2.4	4,184	0.9	129	3.1	4,344	34.2	27.1
Armstrong	702	81.1	128,600	16.5	10.0	732	18.2	0.9	926	0.8	26	2.8	968	32.9	33.9
Atascosa	15,509	74.4	96,100	17.9	10.1	797	22.9	8.4	21,247	1.3	800	3.8	20,208	25.8	33.3
Austin	11,021	74.2	175,200	20.1	10.5	802	34.2	6.4	14,015	1.4	509	3.6	13,509	30.9	29.9
Bailey	2,230	72.2	68,000	24.4	10.7	811	23.4	11	2,655	-0.4	116	4.4	3,157	22.9	39.0
Bandera	8,278	84.6	165,900	21.4	10.7	874	28.6	3.1	9,920	1.7	338	3.4	8,682	35.7	24.2
Bastrop	26,015	76.5	150,300	22.0	11.1	932	26.5	6.2	41,491	3.1	1,395	3.4	33,500	33.3	28.8
Baylor	1,644	77.4	67,200	22.4	13.5	472	20.7	0.7	1,566	-1.6	51	3.3	1,434	34.2	20.7
Bee	8,531	63.0	78,500	19.4	11.3	872	29.6	5.9	9,977	0	507	5.1	10,125	20.9	28.8
Bell	116,397	54.8	137,100	20.8	10.7	886	27.7	3.7	142,270	0	5,860	4.1	135,361	33.1	21.1
Bexar	627,889	58.7	142,300	21.4	11.1	942	29.7	4.7	940,900	1.7	31,319	3.3	867,502	34.8	19.7
Blanco	4,230	76.6	230,800	25.6	10.0	790	25.5	4.7	6,250	0.2	164	2.6	5,106	33.6	27.1
Borden	248	73.8	106,900	13.6	10.0	675	20	0	349	8	11	3.2	255	47.8	23.1
Bosque	7,027	77.3	106,700	19.0	11.4	685	25.4	4.3	8,220	0.2	304	3.7	7,475	29.3	32.4
Bowie	33,171	65.1	109,400	19.7	11.1	729	30.7	3.1	39,495	0.5	1,953	4.9	36,668	31.9	25.4
Brazoria	117,088	71.9	164,300	19.2	10.0	1,012	26	4.5	175,989	1.5	7,964	4.5	162,270	41.7	24.1
Brazos	77,480	45.5	170,500	21.3	10.6	895	36.8	3.8	116,882	3.3	3,319	2.8	103,649	41.1	18.0
Brewster	3,932	54.8	113,400	21.0	10.0	617	23.7	4.4	4,062	2.3	137	3.4	4,151	35.8	19.9
Briscoe	664	75.9	65,700	19.8	10.2	613	22	4.2	559	0.7	22	3.9	729	31.4	29.9
Brooks	2,022	61.5	61,900	36.0	12.7	602	34.4	8.1	2,444	0.4	158	6.5	2,489	25.1	24.0
Brown	13,835	72.6	95,100	20.7	12.4	691	26.5	1.6	16,152	0.3	603	3.7	15,238	33.5	26.8
Burleson	6,565	78.1	99,500	21.1	10.0	748	24.8	5.5	8,223	2.8	295	3.6	7,697	25.6	36.1
Burnet	16,545	76.2	171,100	22.1	12.4	842	29.2	3.2	23,033	3.3	660	2.9	19,567	30.2	28.5

1. Specified owner-occupied units. 2. A value of 10.0 represents 10 percent or less; a value of 50.0 represents 50 percent or more. 3. Specified renter-occupied units. 4. Overcrowded or lacking complete plumbing facilities. 5. Percent of civilian labor force. 6. Civilian employed persons 16 years old and over.

Table B. States and Counties — Nonfarm Employment and Agriculture

	Private nonfarm establishments, employment and payroll, 2016									Agriculture, 2017			
		Employment						Annual payroll		Farms			Farm producers whose primary occupation is farming (percent)
											Percent with:		
STATE County	Number of establishments	Total	Health care and social assistance	Manufacturing	Retail trade	Finance and insurance	Professional, scientific, and technical services	Total (mil dol)	Average per employee (dollars)	Number	Fewer than 50 acres	1000 acres or more	
	104	105	106	107	108	109	110	111	112	113	114	115	116
TENNESSEE— Cont'd													
Marshall	475	8,248	725	3,662	1,103	198	119	317	38,475	1,096	43.2	0.7	37.1
Maury	1,746	27,893	5,199	4,756	4,550	1,741	665	1,248	44,743	1,583	46.3	2.1	35.2
Meigs	107	1,500	125	839	243	23	D	53	35,045	351	38.2	2.0	40.9
Monroe	702	11,580	1,320	4,953	1,758	351	170	404	34,862	838	50.6	2.6	38.8
Montgomery	2,827	43,389	7,868	5,415	8,964	1,285	1,819	1,429	32,937	787	45.0	2.3	36.2
Moore	74	1,110	120	D	118	9	16	59	52,852	375	32.0	1.1	32.7
Morgan	158	1,334	299	233	265	48	17	43	31,894	443	35.2	2.7	33.7
Obion	641	9,135	1,107	2,585	1,744	392	121	297	32,485	553	38.9	11.0	41.1
Overton	318	3,621	622	781	534	142	94	124	34,221	1,004	45.5	1.0	28.9
Perry	112	1,670	422	748	222	56	9	50	29,911	287	31.4	4.5	30.6
Pickett	81	720	133	51	91	45	8	23	32,188	287	38.3	1.0	30.9
Polk	212	1,334	287	125	292	62	10	41	30,723	287	52.3	1.4	36.6
Putnam	1,780	29,439	5,776	4,462	5,001	1,035	550	1,012	34,371	1,003	50.8	1.4	31.0
Rhea	481	8,269	1,076	3,557	1,179	220	80	262	31,705	498	50.4	0.4	34.1
Roane	720	8,546	2,139	1,013	1,705	222	505	248	29,002	617	54.1	0.5	32.8
Robertson	1,155	18,705	2,045	6,393	2,468	378	243	716	38,277	1,202	52.7	2.8	37.2
Rutherford	5,103	106,987	12,783	17,722	14,401	4,167	2,914	4,595	42,947	1,414	56.4	1.3	35.8
Scott	322	3,637	695	1,074	726	137	27	104	28,537	288	39.9	0.3	39.3
Sequatchie	178	2,031	528	150	458	190	53	57	28,171	235	48.5	1.7	34.4
Sevier	2,748	39,789	2,523	1,602	8,728	910	777	1,091	27,413	547	43.9	NA	39.7
Shelby	19,463	435,457	71,358	26,674	48,373	16,164	18,117	21,959	50,427	399	58.1	4.0	36.1
Smith	266	3,811	485	1,347	676	111	65	137	35,935	885	33.8	1.2	38.8
Stewart	146	1,253	194	323	257	56	D	37	29,193	389	28.0	3.9	33.4
Sullivan	3,371	62,013	11,718	12,314	8,901	1,974	2,570	2,912	46,964	1,183	62.3	0.3	30.0
Sumner	3,132	46,408	7,003	8,854	6,422	1,700	1,767	1,837	39,578	1,428	53.0	1.5	32.9
Tipton	699	8,734	1,404	1,532	1,669	303	166	307	35,145	527	47.1	8.5	43.6
Trousdale	113	1,234	199	185	214	64	48	38	30,982	317	40.7	NA	32.6
Unicoi	240	3,777	422	1,731	502	81	15	155	41,144	100	57.0	NA	32.9
Union	193	1,708	138	564	365	39	41	52	30,520	505	44.4	0.2	34.2
Van Buren	33	438	D	D	39	D	D	15	34,596	329	37.7	0.6	47.9
Warren	720	11,198	1,542	4,204	1,578	317	151	388	34,675	1,133	45.3	1.9	38.9
Washington	2,836	52,484	13,991	4,557	8,891	3,037	1,497	2,035	38,771	1,428	63.5	0.6	36.8
Wayne	209	2,541	594	578	321	145	18	79	30,922	685	25.4	2.2	34.2
Weakley	568	7,763	1,498	1,632	1,194	328	88	233	30,021	788	44.8	6.3	40.0
White	395	5,428	812	2,104	801	128	49	189	34,884	971	46.9	0.4	38.4
Williamson	6,821	118,657	15,882	2,255	14,075	12,188	9,787	7,097	59,813	1,224	51.0	1.3	31.2
Wilson	2,620	39,311	3,900	4,092	6,129	1,004	1,638	1,536	39,066	1,626	44.6	0.4	34.5
TEXAS	579,168	10,429,924	1,509,548	768,921	1,304,467	535,456	708,331	526,783	50,507	248,416	44.1	8.3	35.8
Anderson	919	11,120	2,265	304	2,069	274	174	409	36,784	1,754	37.6	2.1	38.3
Andrews	401	5,228	582	287	546	115	112	268	51,291	156	43.6	26.9	41.8
Angelina	1,876	29,773	7,828	3,731	4,877	861	821	1,024	34,394	1,028	55.7	0.4	34.1
Aransas	517	4,237	512	56	1,043	163	109	127	29,922	97	68.0	4.1	35.7
Archer	215	1,161	50	94	110	23	41	44	37,546	532	19.4	24.2	34.3
Armstrong	37	279	65	NA	D	D	5	9	31,473	216	7.4	36.6	42.4
Atascosa	780	10,399	1,314	232	1,882	270	281	437	41,978	1,681	39.1	7.4	36.8
Austin	610	7,553	648	938	1,081	277	241	298	39,496	2,113	44.7	2.9	32.9
Bailey	148	1,521	222	381	185	77	38	42	27,529	449	11.1	31.2	44.4
Bandera	387	3,175	339	35	313	79	87	92	28,932	897	37.1	12.7	42.7
Bastrop	1,294	14,402	2,007	1,150	3,489	445	399	461	32,013	2,120	46.8	2.1	34.3
Baylor	115	962	495	D	108	42	28	22	22,405	223	17.9	35.4	38.2
Bee	485	4,980	944	142	1,161	185	124	163	32,770	943	35.8	8.9	35.2
Bell	5,043	92,113	24,863	6,198	15,194	3,380	3,186	3,593	39,009	2,436	61.9	2.4	28.6
Bexar	35,653	741,051	117,976	32,950	93,175	67,664	44,071	32,751	44,195	2,520	62.9	1.4	36.3
Blanco	289	2,123	169	229	252	104	86	91	42,960	1,032	36.7	8.3	38.0
Borden	7	19	NA	NA	D	NA	D	1	28,474	127	3.1	47.2	52.6
Bosque	273	2,433	505	531	386	122	59	83	34,244	1,305	32.0	9.2	37.5
Bowie	2,215	32,982	7,494	2,035	6,605	1,361	1,682	1,134	34,381	1,506	47.1	3.1	34.9
Brazoria	5,518	87,449	9,255	12,921	15,701	2,100	3,316	4,373	50,009	2,851	68.6	2.5	29.7
Brazos	4,251	66,287	9,258	5,496	11,119	1,672	3,338	2,312	34,883	1,363	48.1	4.4	30.8
Brewster	282	2,648	501	47	442	184	40	69	25,924	174	20.7	56.3	54.1
Briscoe	36	103	D	D	21	23	D	3	33,243	249	4.4	35.7	37.0
Brooks	120	1,463	485	NA	238	85	11	36	24,541	437	25.6	7.8	31.5
Brown	882	13,201	3,475	2,660	2,037	453	188	419	31,704	1,838	41.3	6.1	37.9
Burleson	332	3,066	348	368	656	104	142	117	38,015	1,648	33.7	3.2	39.4
Burnet	1,210	11,422	2,132	807	2,140	367	442	419	36,691	1,623	39.4	5.9	31.8

Table B. States and Counties — **Agriculture**

STATE County	Land in farms Acreage (1,000)	Percent change, 2012-2017	Average size of farm	Total irrigated (1,000)	Total cropland (1,000)	Value of land and buildings (dollars) Average per farm	Average per acre	Value of machinery and equipment, average per farm (dollars)	Value of products sold: Total (mil dol)	Average per farm (acres)	Crops	Livestock and poultry products	Organic farms (number)	Farms with internet access (percent)	Government payments Total ($1,000)	Percent of farms
	117	118	119	120	121	122	123	124	125	126	127	128	129	130	131	132
TENNESSEE— Cont'd																
Marshall	153	-5.8	139	0.1	57.0	487,523	3,498	60,310	43.4	39,626	24.3	75.7	6	75.0	518	17.2
Maury	227	-6.3	144	0.7	80.2	579,318	4,037	62,386	45.6	28,788	48.3	51.7	2	71.4	2,408	26.0
Meigs	56	5.5	159	0.1	16.3	528,608	3,327	68,874	7.7	22,009	38.2	61.8	NA	62.4	375	28.2
Monroe	108	-2.2	129	0.0	50.4	548,896	4,252	89,599	42.1	50,186	28.6	71.4	2	67.9	1,842	23.0
Montgomery	133	-9.6	169	0.8	65.8	832,256	4,917	98,150	49.8	63,321	77.1	22.9	3	73.7	1,146	28.2
Moore	58	-0.5	156	D	17.5	563,666	3,621	97,990	20.2	53,883	5.7	94.3	NA	78.9	371	17.6
Morgan	60	7.4	135	0.0	16.9	411,449	3,058	62,700	13.1	29,596	18.1	81.9	NA	75.2	321	25.1
Obion	225	-11.1	406	17.1	186.7	1,462,228	3,599	219,944	137.4	248,488	72.1	27.9	NA	73.8	4,910	54.2
Overton	135	9.5	134	0.0	33.7	452,984	3,374	64,496	31.5	31,382	56.6	43.4	NA	77.8	1,026	35.3
Perry	62	29.7	215	0.0	15.7	477,584	2,216	52,838	4.6	16,056	68.5	31.5	NA	66.9	237	18.8
Pickett	35	-17.4	120	D	11.6	421,319	3,501	68,361	14.3	49,728	7.7	92.3	1	79.8	189	40.1
Polk	35	-0.7	123	0.1	16.6	506,140	4,113	74,965	36.5	127,087	11.8	88.2	5	74.2	451	26.8
Putnam	110	14.9	110	0.0	35.1	509,659	4,649	61,327	15.8	15,728	34.0	66.0	1	77.7	691	26.3
Rhea	46	-20.2	92	0.2	16.8	398,311	4,311	58,673	11.8	23,606	31.4	68.6	NA	70.9	308	23.3
Roane	47	0.9	77	0.0	15.2	404,495	5,266	52,781	6.1	9,877	30.2	69.8	6	79.7	259	20.4
Robertson	192	-8.1	160	1.3	132.1	844,471	5,285	123,828	138.7	115,384	83.2	16.8	3	77.2	1,397	25.6
Rutherford	153	-13.2	108	0.5	60.7	796,242	7,361	58,477	27.2	19,242	57.6	42.4	2	76.2	1,051	16.8
Scott	32	-18.1	111	0.0	10.2	297,351	2,671	48,364	1.8	6,403	45.9	54.1	2	78.8	72	19.4
Sequatchie	31	2.0	133	0.0	9.5	514,760	3,864	83,769	6.9	29,174	22.2	77.8	NA	73.2	71	9.4
Sevier	50	-10.6	91	0.0	17.0	554,793	6,114	57,122	6.1	11,168	35.9	64.1	NA	65.6	265	18.1
Shelby	75	-7.9	189	2.8	49.9	989,747	5,237	98,686	27.4	68,769	94.4	5.6	3	78.2	1,668	15.8
Smith	139	7.0	157	0.1	44.9	540,943	3,451	71,841	26.5	29,977	56.1	43.9	1	80.0	1,169	39.2
Stewart	73	20.7	188	0.0	23.0	498,744	2,650	63,795	7.8	20,149	68.1	31.9	1	78.9	265	8.5
Sullivan	84	-1.2	71	0.1	31.8	500,710	7,065	48,527	22.0	18,596	15.2	84.8	NA	77.2	250	2.3
Sumner	161	-3.8	113	0.1	70.6	598,510	5,312	66,130	44.1	30,891	55.3	44.7	1	75.5	1,402	24.1
Tipton	173	11.5	329	7.8	147.6	1,082,305	3,290	147,688	77.4	146,924	97.3	2.7	NA	77.4	2,301	27.7
Trousdale	43	3.2	134	0.1	10.8	461,107	3,432	59,710	6.4	20,256	18.8	81.2	NA	70.7	447	41.6
Unicoi	6	10.3	60	0.0	2.6	427,336	7,145	53,353	D	D	D	D	1	80.0	D	1.0
Union	44	-2.3	87	0.0	12.5	357,911	4,092	55,794	3.2	6,267	32.0	68.0	2	61.4	370	28.1
Van Buren	53	43.8	162	0.1	14.7	541,592	3,350	77,245	8.3	25,088	21.0	79.0	NA	66.0	317	30.4
Warren	154	-5.9	136	2.6	83.9	469,029	3,456	89,059	126.0	111,236	73.4	26.6	NA	80.3	1,238	30.1
Washington	106	-5.0	74	0.7	53.9	584,921	7,871	74,250	42.5	29,779	40.2	59.8	3	72.1	416	7.3
Wayne	142	6.2	207	0.0	34.7	489,765	2,367	71,722	37.9	55,288	12.8	87.2	NA	60.1	1,102	43.5
Weakley	217	-14.6	276	6.8	171.1	996,358	3,616	140,623	139.3	176,788	57.9	42.1	NA	71.1	3,829	46.7
White	119	-2.6	122	0.0	41.8	466,043	3,816	73,121	30.5	31,441	23.3	76.7	2	75.8	929	32.9
Williamson	142	2.2	116	0.5	54.8	702,557	6,061	64,432	30.9	25,239	59.2	40.8	NA	79.0	1,087	12.7
Wilson	188	0.0	116	0.0	55.7	568,298	4,911	58,928	22.2	13,631	27.4	72.6	2	74.7	1,371	25.8
TEXAS	127,036	-2.4	511	4,363.3	29,360.2	980,409	1,917	83,627	24,924.0	100,332	27.7	72.3	466	72.6	749,231	14.4
Anderson	401	6.8	228	3.1	63.8	647,610	2,836	66,640	92.9	52,989	16.7	83.3	NA	72.6	235	1.5
Andrews	887	17.9	5,684	12.8	78.3	4,473,490	787	116,341	10.6	68,045	48.3	51.7	NA	78.8	2,325	34.0
Angelina	104	-11.1	101	0.5	21.6	368,428	3,644	63,521	61.4	59,736	4.2	95.8	NA	76.1	69	1.1
Aransas	54	35.3	556	D	1.6	935,727	1,684	63,828	1.9	19,969	3.8	96.2	NA	66.0	NA	NA
Archer	560	3.5	1,053	0.2	124.1	1,564,565	1,486	96,119	72.4	136,164	8.0	92.0	NA	77.8	2,826	31.8
Armstrong	443	1.9	2,050	7.3	105.7	1,903,678	929	144,216	49.3	228,315	22.4	77.6	NA	78.2	2,848	59.7
Atascosa	746	12.1	444	25.1	107.1	1,012,562	2,283	78,838	74.3	44,192	27.6	72.4	3	66.2	1,132	4.6
Austin	330	-10.7	156	4.0	74.1	610,855	3,906	61,808	33.1	15,687	31.7	68.3	2	70.0	886	4.2
Bailey	499	5.8	1,111	54.2	332.9	947,108	852	229,500	357.0	795,140	15.4	84.6	6	75.1	11,628	83.7
Bandera	403	0.2	450	1.2	15.4	1,138,137	2,531	44,993	6.9	7,737	11.9	88.1	1	78.9	266	3.1
Bastrop	340	-12.4	160	3.4	49.9	659,245	4,114	53,044	44.7	21,061	30.6	69.4	9	73.3	347	4.6
Baylor	555	2.1	2,490	3.3	175.1	2,568,040	1,032	154,639	53.7	241,018	12.5	87.5	1	72.2	4,551	61.9
Bee	483	-10.4	512	5.5	77.2	1,047,910	2,047	58,599	37.7	39,982	65.1	34.9	2	63.9	1,511	12.0
Bell	487	15.6	200	2.3	152.6	656,224	3,282	62,850	77.0	31,622	49.4	50.6	NA	75.5	3,755	9.6
Bexar	332	-3.2	132	7.3	91.0	782,155	5,939	48,334	67.9	26,935	74.5	25.5	1	68.6	950	4.6
Blanco	337	-7.5	326	0.6	18.4	972,845	2,982	49,514	17.0	16,461	51.6	48.4	NA	76.1	190	3.9
Borden	494	6.5	3,893	2.2	90.8	3,439,101	883	194,541	28.8	226,677	59.2	40.8	1	75.6	1,211	53.5
Bosque	626	9.9	480	1.4	81.2	1,191,428	2,483	64,216	45.1	34,528	15.4	84.6	5	73.8	848	9.6
Bowie	294	7.8	196	7.8	75.1	587,246	3,003	73,633	60.1	39,921	20.8	79.2	NA	74.5	3,834	21.2
Brazoria	460	-27.1	161	20.0	131.8	755,243	4,681	63,949	79.5	27,894	53.7	46.3	NA	74.5	7,201	5.7
Brazos	291	-2.9	213	12.1	50.0	1,212,705	5,689	68,510	91.6	67,232	17.0	83.0	2	76.7	817	2.8
Brewster	2,019	5.5	11,601	4.7	57.1	7,904,621	681	90,298	16.3	93,730	6.3	93.7	NA	84.5	221	6.9
Briscoe	553	5.5	2,222	22.1	151.7	1,984,315	893	151,887	36.6	147,020	73.0	27.0	NA	64.3	5,624	84.7
Brooks	459	-19.9	1,050	0.9	11.6	1,629,772	1,552	50,945	26.2	60,048	1.0	99.0	NA	54.9	322	9.8
Brown	547	-8.2	297	4.1	76.6	717,128	2,411	54,661	46.0	25,011	20.1	79.9	1	73.8	1,071	9.0
Burleson	333	-0.6	202	17.9	67.9	693,069	3,427	66,851	58.6	35,553	38.1	61.9	NA	67.8	446	2.8
Burnet	433	-10.8	267	3.4	25.2	790,719	2,964	53,217	14.1	8,690	24.6	75.4	2	76.2	135	2.6

Table B. States and Counties — Water Use, Wholesale Trade, Retail Trade, and Real Estate

STATE County	Water use, 2015		Wholesale Trade[1], 2012				Retail Trade[2], 2012				Real estate and rental and leasing,[2] 2012			
	Public supply water withdrawn (mil gal/day)	Public supply gallons withdrawn per person per day	Number of establish-ments	Number of employees	Sales (mil dol)	Average payroll (mil dol)	Number of establish-ments	Number of employees	Sales (mil dol)	Average payroll (mil dol)	Number of establish-ments	Number of employees	Sales (mil dol)	Average payroll (mil dol)
	133	134	135	136	137	138	139	140	141	142	143	144	145	146
TENNESSEE— Cont'd														
Marshall	2.69	85.3	14	D	D	D	102	1,033	289.1	23.3	16	35	4.7	0.8
Maury	12.33	140.5	61	977	474.0	46.8	327	4,023	1,132.0	94.1	68	238	46.4	7.6
Meigs	0.66	55.8	1	D	D	D	29	198	51.9	3.9	4	6	0.3	0.1
Monroe	5.62	122.8	23	133	36.7	4.6	141	1,630	412.1	36.4	27	44	6.6	1.0
Montgomery	22.40	115.8	77	1,020	587.5	46.0	533	8,205	2,146.2	199.1	145	623	103.9	19.2
Moore	0.54	85.4	2	D	D	D	15	80	16.3	1.3	1	D	D	D
Morgan	1.35	62.8	3	D	D	D	33	253	54.2	4.2	1	D	D	D
Obion	4.62	150.8	33	423	301.5	14.5	142	1,826	457.7	40.1	22	60	7.3	1.3
Overton	2.33	105.3	8	D	D	D	63	498	164.1	10.9	8	D	D	D
Perry	0.91	114.8	1	D	D	D	29	188	40.2	3.6	3	3	0.4	0.1
Pickett	0.81	157.4	1	D	D	D	26	121	30.0	2.7	1	D	D	D
Polk	0.87	51.9	5	D	D	D	46	370	84.3	7.1	4	D	D	D
Putnam	12.46	167.1	65	1,150	427.2	52.2	349	4,782	1,282.9	104.4	63	172	34.2	4.5
Rhea	3.91	120.2	7	D	D	D	107	1,150	281.1	22.7	21	97	8.4	1.7
Roane	4.86	92.1	20	D	D	D	151	1,746	472.3	39.4	20	65	11.1	1.9
Robertson	4.83	70.4	39	739	724.1	23.5	172	2,313	675.2	58.2	35	95	12.2	2.1
Rutherford	32.98	110.4	219	6,361	14,847.0	287.0	829	12,376	3,515.3	281.7	188	990	314.0	44.2
Scott	2.53	115.3	4	15	9.8	0.6	67	633	153.3	13.8	10	13	2.5	0.4
Sequatchie	0.81	54.7	9	55	83.4	1.4	37	391	104.0	9.1	7	21	4.1	0.5
Sevier	11.48	119.7	38	D	D	D	645	7,349	1,561.1	150.9	146	1,185	143.2	32.0
Shelby	142.33	151.7	1,180	24,270	35,454.3	1,374.8	3,056	46,778	22,058.5	1,261.1	923	6,988	1,437.0	306.3
Smith	0.57	29.5	7	D	D	D	60	579	158.9	14.4	9	21	2.6	0.5
Stewart	0.71	53.5	3	8	1.4	0.2	37	289	86.6	6.3	4	18	1.3	0.2
Sullivan	23.76	151.5	174	1,733	1,006.2	67.9	547	8,149	2,095.9	187.4	110	443	77.7	13.2
Sumner	24.90	141.5	117	1,572	2,117.7	72.8	449	5,756	1,503.6	136.8	131	785	152.0	41.4
Tipton	3.35	54.1	18	D	D	D	145	1,667	393.6	33.3	25	80	10.5	2.2
Trousdale	0.93	115.6	3	D	D	D	30	234	56.2	4.4	1	D	D	D
Unicoi	1.46	81.7	8	D	D	D	37	505	129.5	11.1	6	19	2.4	0.7
Union	0.78	40.8	7	D	D	D	40	346	87.6	6.8	4	D	D	D
Van Buren	0.00	0.0	1	D	D	D	10	60	9.4	0.8	2	D	D	D
Warren	4.77	118.0	26	D	D	D	157	1,618	376.4	34.6	22	51	11.8	1.5
Washington	19.08	151.1	118	1,259	791.3	52.2	520	8,260	2,011.5	174.7	114	588	91.7	18.0
Wayne	1.07	63.9	5	D	D	D	45	335	65.0	5.8	5	D	D	D
Weakley	2.26	66.5	27	295	243.0	13.6	123	1,178	297.4	24.5	20	57	9.3	1.1
White	2.81	106.0	15	D	D	D	82	811	209.4	18.6	14	32	2.4	0.6
Williamson	1.42	6.7	237	2,762	10,285.7	186.4	766	12,866	3,968.6	354.4	249	1,397	500.8	77.0
Wilson	15.58	120.9	88	1,646	1,362.9	88.5	403	5,471	1,432.6	123.7	106	542	94.8	18.5
TEXAS	2,885.33	105.0	27,752	408,692	691,242.6	24,826.1	78,281	1,150,148	356,116.4	28,835.5	26,639	169,941	38,757.4	7,751.8
Anderson	9.06	157.3	33	D	D	D	164	1,913	572.1	47.1	34	124	34.7	5.8
Andrews	2.36	130.4	15	D	D	D	30	344	169.8	12.5	15	114	26.7	8.5
Angelina	11.30	128.0	62	808	360.6	35.2	324	4,580	1,274.7	109.4	79	329	54.4	10.8
Aransas	0.21	8.3	8	63	10.5	1.1	73	920	288.9	25.0	36	79	13.3	1.9
Archer	4.59	526.7	13	D	D	D	14	102	25.5	1.8	3	D	D	D
Armstrong	0.23	118.1	3	D	D	D	4	D	D	D	1	D	D	D
Atascosa	5.34	110.3	38	D	D	D	115	1,709	564.7	38.8	35	226	66.5	11.6
Austin	2.03	68.7	23	679	728.8	34.1	83	939	272.4	22.4	20	47	9.5	1.5
Bailey	6.18	857.1	19	D	D	D	21	229	49.0	4.3	NA	NA	NA	NA
Bandera	0.63	29.6	5	28	8.1	1.1	49	299	81.2	5.7	8	18	2.8	0.6
Bastrop	10.60	131.6	34	D	D	D	175	2,462	867.8	59.6	44	132	24.8	3.7
Baylor	2.47	682.7	6	35	30.9	1.4	16	99	24.0	1.7	1	D	D	D
Bee	1.07	32.5	12	D	D	D	78	1,050	330.6	26.1	27	98	17.8	3.7
Bell	16.31	48.7	126	2,616	3,630.5	135.2	922	13,098	3,626.1	293.2	299	1,486	217.9	50.4
Bexar	212.33	111.9	1,464	D	D	D	4,845	80,840	26,480.6	1,994.5	1,718	13,472	3,054.2	601.3
Blanco	0.78	70.9	8	D	D	D	32	209	68.7	4.7	4	9	1.1	0.2
Borden	0.06	92.6	NA	NA	NA	NA	1	D	D	D	NA	NA	NA	NA
Bosque	2.33	130.2	10	77	22.0	2.9	53	417	90.7	8.1	10	23	2.1	0.5
Bowie	16.94	181.4	90	D	D	D	413	6,170	1,611.3	146.2	102	455	93.3	17.3
Brazoria	21.13	61.0	228	1,865	1,636.4	102.3	797	13,282	3,686.3	314.0	248	1,566	392.8	77.3
Brazos	31.46	146.3	140	1,704	1,191.8	86.6	629	9,807	2,672.0	207.8	231	1,299	260.8	43.5
Brewster	1.02	111.5	11	D	D	D	49	405	87.7	8.0	21	148	5.4	1.2
Briscoe	0.19	126.2	4	D	D	D	6	23	6.3	0.4	1	D	D	D
Brooks	1.10	152.1	2	D	D	D	18	297	85.8	6.7	4	10	2.1	0.3
Brown	0.06	1.6	35	D	D	D	181	1,872	509.0	41.5	36	132	20.0	3.9
Burleson	1.76	100.8	18	D	D	D	58	653	293.2	17.9	6	14	3.1	0.6
Burnet	4.09	90.0	41	336	163.1	14.8	182	2,015	617.7	52.1	46	148	25.8	5.2

1 Merchant wholesalers, except manufacturers' sales branches and offices. 2. Employer establishments.

Professional Services, Manufacturing, and Accommodation and Food Services

STATE County	Professional, scientific, and technical services, 2012				Manufacturing, 2012				Accommodation and food services, 2012			
	Number of establish-ments	Number of employees	Sales (mil dol)	Average payroll (mil dol)	Number of establish-ments	Number of employees	Receipts (mil dol)	Annual payroll (mil dol)	Number of establis-hments	Number of employees	Receipts (mil dol)	Annual payroll (mil dol)
	147	148	149	150	151	152	153	154	155	156	157	158
TENNESSEE— Cont'd												
Marshall	30	88	7.7	2.2	45	2,656	1,085.2	128.0	45	512	25.5	6.4
Maury	104	620	57.8	23.4	76	3,582	1,902.1	201.5	158	2,859	123.1	35.4
Meigs	3	D	D	D	11	753	233.0	28.2	15	D	D	D
Monroe	42	197	16.2	6.1	60	4,333	1,509.3	171.6	82	918	41.7	10.6
Montgomery	177	1,677	235.5	78.7	68	5,519	2,256.0	258.2	338	6,157	296.8	81.1
Moore	4	D	D	D	5	D	D	D	8	D	D	D
Morgan	6	D	D	D	20	330	63.3	12.8	8	D	D	D
Obion	32	119	14.1	4.3	39	2,439	1,195.0	82.2	57	822	33.4	8.4
Overton	22	D	D	D	28	D	D	D	25	D	D	D
Perry	4	D	D	D	11	515	D	17.2	8	D	D	D
Pickett	3	5	0.4	0.1	8	86	14.8	2.2	12	D	D	D
Polk	8	14	2.2	0.5	9	108	D	5.4	18	296	9.3	2.5
Putnam	141	584	70.8	25.4	99	4,301	1,214.4	162.2	159	3,666	158.8	45.1
Rhea	29	79	6.0	2.0	29	3,544	848.6	121.0	48	792	30.7	8.0
Roane	56	D	D	D	23	1,096	270.1	40.5	68	1,359	52.0	15.1
Robertson	64	208	21.2	7.3	78	5,788	1,793.0	218.1	91	1,536	65.6	18.4
Rutherford	340	2,304	265.6	117.2	200	14,761	11,539.0	818.0	469	11,020	502.7	146.5
Scott	13	41	3.8	2.1	31	738	113.7	22.2	24	387	14.4	3.9
Sequatchie	13	42	4.0	1.7	8	111	D	5.1	15	D	D	D
Sevier	151	779	69.9	25.3	69	939	263.2	41.2	508	11,751	832.7	221.2
Shelby	1,762	17,349	2,496.2	1,055.5	580	24,360	22,412.7	1,417.0	1,659	36,739	1,889.7	529.1
Smith	16	D	D	D	17	959	D	41.9	21	D	D	D
Stewart	4	D	D	D	9	194	37.1	6.2	19	D	D	D
Sullivan	266	1,875	232.4	89.4	143	15,287	6,361.4	1,030.5	317	6,340	286.4	82.4
Sumner	210	1,837	213.7	92.7	173	6,127	2,158.4	271.7	231	4,416	195.6	58.1
Tipton	33	131	11.1	3.3	26	1,591	446.3	56.2	63	882	39.5	10.1
Trousdale	8	35	2.5	0.8	6	195	D	6.8	9	108	4.3	1.1
Unicoi	7	16	2.0	0.6	19	1,698	440.7	90.4	32	344	15.9	4.1
Union	11	D	D	D	14	544	125.9	19.2	9	161	7.4	2.0
Van Buren	1	D	D	D	6	D	D	D	1	D	D	D
Warren	40	117	10.4	3.4	57	3,276	1,311.7	141.4	51	770	32.3	8.2
Washington	222	2,751	218.3	102.0	116	4,536	1,503.7	179.2	283	6,344	278.5	80.8
Wayne	10	19	1.4	0.4	21	530	79.9	16.4	17	170	7.1	2.0
Weakley	23	91	8.3	2.4	25	1,033	D	34.7	58	816	35.5	8.8
White	18	32	3.4	0.7	40	1,910	561.1	82.2	28	D	D	D
Williamson	792	7,610	1,465.0	580.1	119	2,237	558.3	92.9	437	9,418	485.2	138.0
Wilson	185	D	D	D	108	2,851	1,281.6	143.6	212	4,345	190.0	56.8
TEXAS	62,322	639,561	122,086.2	47,256.4	19,782	767,024	702,603.1	42,529.8	48,721	976,390	54,480.8	14,743.8
Anderson	81	238	32.0	10.6	24	245	D	10.8	68	D	D	D
Andrews	24	D	D	D	7	387	135.9	15.3	26	372	21.4	5.1
Angelina	147	768	91.7	33.6	65	4,602	1,451.6	177.8	144	3,162	141.5	40.1
Aransas	37	153	20.8	4.9	7	26	D	0.8	74	1,032	50.5	13.4
Archer	9	D	D	D	11	D	D	D	8	D	D	D
Armstrong	1	D	D	D	NA	NA	NA	NA	1	D	D	D
Atascosa	44	240	34.2	10.8	21	216	D	8.3	62	951	52.3	13.6
Austin	49	235	23.8	10.9	33	2,085	D	117.2	49	521	28.7	7.5
Bailey	12	38	4.2	1.5	7	148	D	5.2	14	212	7.9	2.3
Bandera	35	104	10.5	3.4	11	35	D	1.0	49	559	26.6	8.6
Bastrop	101	416	46.1	14.6	59	990	284.4	42.0	109	2,273	138.0	39.8
Baylor	7	24	1.4	0.8	4	44	D	1.1	9	71	5.5	0.7
Bee	38	D	D	D	9	92	D	4.3	56	725	40.5	10.5
Bell	365	3,505	407.6	164.2	136	5,724	1,962.5	237.3	584	11,467	552.0	149.9
Bexar	3,963	40,811	6,684.3	2,557.1	873	30,474	14,766.1	1,478.3	3,612	88,432	5,006.7	1,365.3
Blanco	26	D	D	D	13	109	26.4	4.6	27	277	11.5	3.6
Borden	1	D	D	D	NA	NA	NA	NA	NA	NA	NA	NA
Bosque	22	48	5.7	2.3	16	431	115.2	19.2	22	172	10.1	2.3
Bowie	156	846	86.5	29.2	56	1,840	462.7	78.9	184	4,141	193.8	55.7
Brazoria	456	2,433	316.1	126.5	212	12,119	32,864.6	1,016.8	474	9,303	462.5	127.2
Brazos	401	2,690	523.0	134.3	100	4,480	1,063.6	178.3	436	9,491	446.5	121.5
Brewster	17	49	5.6	1.6	11	27	5.9	0.9	40	617	31.5	8.5
Briscoe	1	D	D	D	NA	NA	NA	NA	3	10	0.3	0.1
Brooks	9	25	2.3	0.5	NA	NA	NA	NA	21	289	15.6	4.3
Brown	54	D	D	D	31	2,292	1,222.0	107.5	81	1,270	59.9	16.4
Burleson	23	149	12.4	4.2	15	353	D	16.9	40	266	14.1	3.3
Burnet	84	473	33.5	14.6	52	687	259.9	33.2	110	1,545	89.0	25.6

Table B. States and Counties — Health Care and Social Assistance, Other Services, Nonemployer Businesses, and Residential Construction

STATE County	Health care and social assistance, 2012				Other services, 2012				Nonemployer businesses, 2016		Value of residential construction authorized by building permits, 2018	
	Number of establishments	Number of employees	Receipts (mil dol)	Annual payroll (mil dol)	Number of establishments	Number of employees	Receipts (mil dol)	Annual payroll (mil dol)	Number	Receipts (mil dol)	New construction ($1,000)	Number of housing units
	159	160	161	162	163	164	165	166	167	168	169	170
TENNESSEE— Cont'd												
Marshall	56	724	57.3	19.8	25	111	11.9	2.8	2,084	91.1	30,524	162
Maury	213	5,384	539.7	208.3	107	661	60.5	18.1	6,485	290.2	275,582	1,566
Meigs	10	D	D	D	7	D	D	D	672	25.2	6,000	40
Monroe	72	1,480	118.5	42.1	40	D	D	D	2,740	119.8	22,433	109
Montgomery	331	7,170	662.2	251.9	184	975	76.1	21.2	10,391	475.2	249,109	1,723
Moore	6	187	12.5	7.5	5	9	0.6	0.1	443	21.3	5,095	21
Morgan	15	370	33.2	13.1	7	D	D	D	1,060	40.3	0	0
Obion	86	D	D	D	39	D	D	D	1,851	71.4	4,661	28
Overton	35	D	D	D	18	D	D	D	1,803	77.0	375	5
Perry	14	396	26.1	10.8	8	D	D	D	639	29.6	1,366	7
Pickett	5	D	D	D	4	D	D	D	450	25.9	NA	NA
Polk	18	395	30.9	12.7	8	22	2.0	0.4	1,009	37.4	34,584	192
Putnam	228	5,719	511.9	214.5	115	D	D	D	5,910	278.4	78,244	496
Rhea	68	968	68.2	28.4	26	89	7.6	2.1	1,777	71.4	17,618	101
Roane	91	1,892	128.6	53.5	46	192	20.3	5.0	2,984	114.7	24,190	103
Robertson	122	1,908	176.3	70.4	69	209	21.7	5.5	5,288	255.7	72,818	387
Rutherford	524	13,614	1,376.6	586.1	301	2,632	282.7	78.4	21,720	990.9	771,569	3,971
Scott	41	1,002	65.2	23.7	16	D	D	D	1,336	65.1	978	9
Sequatchie	22	D	D	D	8	21	1.8	0.4	1,040	35.0	1,112	10
Sevier	150	2,281	198.9	67.3	144	846	78.6	22.3	7,944	394.3	171,010	1,040
Shelby	2,338	68,016	8,166.7	3,140.9	1,202	10,502	1,938.8	366.1	81,318	3,023.8	381,841	2,251
Smith	26	D	D	D	12	D	D	D	1,375	55.3	13,181	77
Stewart	15	195	18.2	8.1	11	D	D	D	787	31.9	974	6
Sullivan	444	12,341	1,521.5	567.3	220	D	D	D	9,869	416.4	59,741	333
Sumner	334	5,369	599.5	219.1	197	944	98.6	24.6	15,341	787.5	326,865	1,728
Tipton	84	1,314	141.3	45.5	41	160	20.1	4.9	3,811	133.5	34,466	183
Trousdale	23	233	19.3	6.1	6	D	D	D	588	25.5	14,029	125
Unicoi	26	747	44.7	18.3	19	D	D	D	822	32.7	616	7
Union	20	177	11.6	4.8	15	47	4.9	1.3	1,248	48.3	17,372	100
Van Buren	2	D	D	D	2	D	D	D	398	15.0	200	2
Warren	98	1,428	114.7	43.6	48	D	D	D	2,883	121.4	13,750	88
Washington	351	14,010	1,641.3	737.0	175	910	69.9	22.6	8,212	383.3	91,836	501
Wayne	31	402	34.3	12.7	12	39	4.7	1.0	851	33.1	0	0
Weakley	81	1,582	134.6	50.9	37	168	15.2	4.2	1,644	72.4	8,504	55
White	38	856	68.3	24.3	27	D	D	D	1,876	77.0	14,363	138
Williamson	634	11,192	1,456.1	591.2	323	2,109	200.2	60.5	26,569	1,855.6	755,998	2,121
Wilson	268	3,941	392.5	151.2	149	1,091	95.2	31.3	11,457	572.8	384,720	1,383
TEXAS	61,342	1,345,664	145,035.1	54,570.6	34,116	259,128	30,172.2	8,454.5	2,251,787	106,276.4	34,689,871	192,878
Anderson	141	2,214	216.2	78.4	60	308	22.3	7.8	2,865	117.6	5,460	33
Andrews	26	475	64.0	22.8	23	D	D	D	1,374	68.1	4,294	22
Angelina	285	7,839	588.4	240.8	119	818	152.6	32.8	5,434	246.4	11,275	93
Aransas	44	518	46.2	14.8	47	150	14.1	3.4	2,427	99.1	43,760	189
Archer	12	D	D	D	10	D	D	D	885	43.3	2,791	17
Armstrong	4	93	3.1	1.6	2	D	D	D	176	7.7	1,891	8
Atascosa	80	1,309	115.4	43.0	48	217	23.8	5.2	3,465	137.1	7,108	40
Austin	44	D	D	D	31	114	11.6	2.8	2,746	122.3	3,862	21
Bailey	15	251	16.9	6.6	12	37	3.9	0.8	404	23.1	0	0
Bandera	24	339	21.4	8.4	32	105	11.4	2.8	2,281	104.6	0	0
Bastrop	108	1,983	155.1	62.7	78	330	31.1	8.6	6,202	288.9	23,478	156
Baylor	13	511	19.3	8.6	15	D	D	D	275	12.4	0	0
Bee	50	D	D	D	38	187	18.3	4.7	1,476	45.3	1,075	9
Bell	524	22,484	2,849.6	1,245.3	409	2,898	202.5	72.7	17,547	725.6	368,913	2,170
Bexar	4,314	110,407	12,143.6	4,363.8	2,461	17,571	1,645.4	478.9	137,240	6,291.4	1,148,153	7,278
Blanco	18	159	7.8	3.6	15	44	7.4	1.4	1,422	69.6	786	5
Borden	NA	NA	NA	NA	NA	NA	NA	NA	64	2.1	NA	NA
Bosque	20	606	42.2	16.4	21	69	5.4	1.4	1,495	64.6	392	5
Bowie	289	7,151	798.4	295.4	154	979	87.0	26.4	5,248	236.8	13,811	154
Brazoria	627	8,038	646.5	273.7	369	2,558	237.6	75.3	24,040	956.5	777,802	3,367
Brazos	399	8,166	1,040.0	376.0	266	1,939	374.6	53.6	13,859	637.4	256,091	1,766
Brewster	24	548	30.0	12.1	20	D	D	D	1,023	35.2	1,130	9
Briscoe	3	4	0.2	0.1	1	D	D	D	135	4.2	NA	NA
Brooks	20	339	10.7	5.3	11	31	3.3	0.7	574	11.1	110	1
Brown	136	3,126	206.2	77.2	69	381	24.3	6.9	2,491	97.5	22,975	157
Burleson	16	D	D	D	26	115	11.4	3.7	1,404	58.4	991	6
Burnet	106	1,302	145.3	51.5	71	303	24.0	6.9	5,106	294.6	113,954	613

Table B. States and Counties — Government Employment and Payroll, and Local Government Finances

	Government employment and payroll, 2012									Local government finances, 2012				
			March payroll (percent of total)							General revenue				
												Taxes		
STATE County	Full-time equivalent employees	March payroll (dollars)	Administration, judicial, and legal	Police and corrections	Fire protection	Highways and transportation	Health and welfare	Natural resources and utilities	Education and libraries	Total (mil dol)	Inter-govern-mental (mil dol)	Total (mil dol)	Per capita[1] (dollars) Total	Per capita[1] (dollars) Property
	171	172	173	174	175	176	177	178	179	180	181	182	183	184
TENNESSEE— Cont'd														
Marshall	1,203	3,538,766	7.5	9.0	3.9	2.6	5.0	17.4	52.4	86.1	36.7	29.2	947	612
Maury	4,616	17,056,047	3.2	6.1	2.9	2.0	47.4	6.3	30.7	499.9	86.1	89.0	1,086	702
Meigs	438	942,766	9.9	10.0	0.1	7.3	3.2	2.3	67.2	24.7	17.0	5.2	441	333
Monroe	1,373	3,993,045	7.7	8.8	1.3	3.3	4.4	9.7	64.2	96.5	51.5	31.4	696	447
Montgomery	6,061	19,419,026	4.6	11.0	3.6	3.7	5.7	6.1	63.4	519.4	202.5	207.0	1,122	681
Moore	237	724,102	2.2	14.7	0.1	9.4	3.2	8.5	61.9	15.5	8.0	5.6	884	707
Morgan	796	1,965,391	7.2	7.4	0.0	4.6	5.8	5.4	68.9	42.3	28.2	10.4	475	387
Obion	1,057	3,471,219	8.5	14.0	3.5	4.1	0.4	7.6	60.8	80.5	42.6	24.7	789	436
Overton	829	2,041,789	5.5	9.1	0.7	4.4	6.6	7.0	65.6	46.5	30.0	11.5	520	304
Perry	339	836,675	10.6	3.6	0.0	5.3	3.5	5.7	67.5	22.6	13.7	5.6	716	537
Pickett	180	540,892	11.1	15.0	0.6	9.3	3.5	4.7	55.8	13.0	8.2	3.4	670	349
Polk	595	1,517,421	15.7	1.5	0.0	7.2	2.1	5.6	67.4	36.3	22.3	11.2	674	514
Putnam	4,261	15,613,316	2.1	4.8	1.2	1.6	55.8	4.6	27.7	418.9	71.7	81.6	1,114	597
Rhea	1,269	3,661,964	5.1	6.0	0.8	2.6	18.6	8.5	54.3	86.8	39.8	20.0	621	367
Roane	1,700	6,055,393	5.5	6.7	3.8	2.6	1.3	17.4	61.6	147.3	59.5	50.7	948	593
Robertson	2,143	5,842,234	11.7	12.9	2.0	4.7	1.8	7.6	58.5	164.1	73.4	70.3	1,050	658
Rutherford	8,751	29,120,491	7.0	11.2	3.9	1.2	3.2	8.8	62.0	738.4	270.4	325.5	1,186	718
Scott	1,044	2,569,027	6.5	7.4	0.9	5.4	5.6	10.3	62.6	56.6	33.7	12.4	560	370
Sequatchie	429	1,170,657	6.1	8.5	0.0	0.5	5.6	7.1	71.3	32.3	19.5	9.3	645	457
Sevier	3,747	12,103,289	4.1	9.3	3.0	4.0	3.5	8.2	62.6	359.9	83.9	186.0	2,010	703
Shelby	39,378	138,123,866	7.0	15.4	7.3	4.6	11.4	14.4	38.1	4,311.3	1,448.6	1,719.3	1,828	1,235
Smith	725	1,800,266	8.4	11.3	0.6	6.1	2.0	7.1	61.0	45.3	25.5	13.2	693	395
Stewart	498	1,358,521	8.2	10.6	0.2	5.1	5.7	3.5	65.2	36.1	23.5	9.2	693	470
Sullivan	5,719	18,566,959	5.4	9.7	3.3	4.6	4.4	5.7	64.8	404.7	154.7	177.3	1,131	800
Sumner	5,626	16,827,689	5.9	10.4	4.6	1.7	3.7	8.6	63.7	406.0	171.8	163.0	981	658
Tipton	2,180	6,476,685	4.4	8.2	2.1	2.7	0.9	8.0	72.1	146.0	87.1	41.2	668	453
Trousdale	275	758,540	10.0	16.9	0.0	0.0	4.0	1.1	68.0	18.5	11.4	4.6	596	490
Unicoi	819	2,543,400	3.6	3.8	1.5	4.4	24.1	4.2	48.7	63.6	21.5	9.0	495	392
Union	593	1,652,593	8.9	6.9	0.0	4.2	0.9	6.7	72.2	47.6	34.6	8.9	466	312
Van Buren	275	698,479	8.3	7.1	1.3	19.0	5.9	2.5	55.9	13.1	8.7	3.1	554	397
Warren	1,148	3,625,874	6.8	9.9	2.3	1.1	6.3	13.7	58.4	97.8	53.6	31.0	779	452
Washington	4,114	12,590,200	5.8	10.1	3.4	7.7	2.2	15.3	53.6	294.8	106.3	133.5	1,068	712
Wayne	611	1,515,515	5.5	10.2	0.2	4.9	1.5	4.4	71.7	45.0	23.8	10.1	595	364
Weakley	1,333	3,550,802	5.6	11.2	2.3	5.4	9.1	13.8	50.6	73.0	37.4	20.2	579	318
White	908	2,433,483	6.9	8.8	0.8	3.2	3.5	9.7	65.1	53.2	31.7	14.3	548	338
Williamson	8,184	27,964,745	5.4	6.5	3.3	2.0	20.1	5.4	55.8	754.7	175.6	348.2	1,805	1,175
Wilson	3,881	11,949,351	7.0	10.1	4.4	3.3	1.0	8.4	64.6	281.9	110.9	131.1	1,102	707
TEXAS	X	X	X	X	X	X	X	X	X	X	X	X	X	X
Anderson	1,888	5,360,452	8.0	11.5	3.0	3.1	0.6	3.8	69.2	124.5	47.1	61.2	1,052	867
Andrews	1,090	4,021,801	5.8	6.7	0.0	2.3	33.8	5.1	46.1	121.7	9.4	81.6	5,063	4,756
Angelina	4,483	13,382,100	4.8	8.0	2.7	2.0	11.2	3.8	66.5	300.9	135.8	97.6	1,114	832
Aransas	888	2,584,176	9.4	13.5	0.0	5.1	2.4	5.8	61.2	78.8	13.5	50.4	2,117	1,856
Archer	436	1,231,876	8.0	6.2	0.0	2.7	1.6	4.3	76.7	26.8	10.9	12.0	1,378	1,224
Armstrong	112	284,475	10.7	2.6	0.0	2.6	2.2	3.2	77.2	9.5	3.3	3.2	1,666	1,480
Atascosa	2,208	6,519,286	5.0	7.2	0.0	2.0	13.3	3.4	67.8	191.3	123.7	49.0	1,056	822
Austin	1,209	3,635,522	7.8	10.5	0.0	3.4	2.6	5.7	69.1	87.7	23.7	51.5	1,801	1,613
Bailey	547	1,435,208	5.2	6.9	0.0	2.6	29.6	1.9	53.0	36.8	12.6	9.8	1,375	1,158
Bandera	640	2,084,125	8.5	10.8	0.2	3.9	4.1	2.5	68.5	46.4	8.5	32.2	1,567	1,462
Bastrop	2,838	9,520,485	5.2	12.2	0.0	2.3	0.8	3.0	76.0	243.4	86.4	112.0	1,498	1,314
Baylor	318	889,487	6.6	4.2	0.0	2.8	45.1	5.7	34.2	22.6	4.9	3.9	1,085	880
Bee	1,435	4,453,164	5.0	5.5	1.3	2.9	4.8	5.0	74.6	114.4	63.6	30.2	930	752
Bell	16,055	50,764,685	4.5	8.6	3.4	1.9	2.7	4.5	73.5	1,144.1	497.9	378.1	1,171	912
Bexar	76,821	296,304,428	4.1	8.7	3.4	4.0	10.0	11.6	57.2	7,217.6	2,547.6	2,991.4	1,675	1,345
Blanco	357	1,339,398	8.8	7.8	0.0	1.9	0.2	3.3	77.7	39.5	6.7	29.4	2,761	2,644
Borden	74	200,651	18.7	3.1	0.0	8.2	0.0	0.5	68.4	14.0	2.2	11.3	18,268	18,188
Bosque	689	2,029,654	8.4	7.1	0.0	2.6	0.4	2.1	77.7	47.1	20.0	22.7	1,253	1,100
Bowie	4,233	13,543,434	5.4	7.5	2.7	2.3	0.7	7.1	73.2	292.7	128.5	118.6	1,273	993
Brazoria	12,753	42,706,512	5.9	10.5	0.7	2.7	5.3	4.6	69.2	1,184.7	316.7	617.5	1,901	1,646
Brazos	7,250	22,942,099	8.3	13.0	5.1	4.6	3.7	12.3	47.5	549.9	134.9	310.5	1,547	1,241
Brewster	439	1,264,854	9.4	14.2	0.0	3.7	0.7	6.1	63.5	31.3	14.9	12.8	1,373	1,071
Briscoe	68	181,356	19.1	3.9	0.0	5.1	1.2	13.9	56.0	4.9	1.8	2.3	1,491	1,329
Brooks	470	1,100,857	8.0	8.1	0.4	3.7	1.2	7.4	70.9	40.5	15.5	18.6	2,598	2,321
Brown	1,839	5,391,982	6.8	9.8	2.3	3.3	10.4	7.5	59.2	125.8	54.0	52.8	1,397	1,099
Burleson	707	1,886,727	9.3	7.8	0.0	4.3	0.7	3.5	74.3	46.7	14.9	26.1	1,507	1,240
Burnet	1,778	6,073,530	9.9	14.7	4.3	2.7	0.2	7.3	59.5	155.5	24.4	99.6	2,293	2,003

1. Based on the resident population estimated as of July 1 of the year shown.

Table B. States and Counties — Local Government Finances, Government Employment, and Income Taxes

STATE County	Local government finances, 2012 (cont.)										Government employment, 2017			Individual income tax returns, 2016		
	Direct general expenditure							Debt outstanding								
			Percent of total for:												Mean	
	Total (mil dol)	Per capita[1] (dollars)	Education	Health and hospitals	Police protection	Public welfare	Highways	Total (mil dol)	Per capita[1] (dollars)	Federal civilian	Federal military	State and local	Number of returns	adjusted gross income	Mean income tax
	185	186	187	188	189	190	191	192	193	194	195	196	197	198	199
TENNESSEE— Cont'd															
Marshall	82.9	2,684	52.1	3.0	8.4	0.2	5.3	93.9	3,039	65	94	1,769	14,820	46,765	4,596
Maury	491.1	5,990	19.6	56.1	3.7	0.0	3.1	294.5	3,592	176	265	6,682	43,550	52,544	5,616
Meigs	23.1	1,979	63.8	2.5	5.7	0.5	8.0	7.5	637	27	35	482	5,120	44,363	3,984
Monroe	104.4	2,314	64.5	4.7	5.5	0.1	5.1	101.6	2,250	96	132	1,925	18,780	45,439	4,456
Montgomery	461.9	2,504	57.1	3.0	7.0	0.0	4.1	4,359.0	23,630	1,430	607	9,926	83,700	46,810	4,432
Moore	15.3	2,419	59.1	2.9	4.2	0.1	11.9	10.0	1,582	6	18	943	2,820	53,463	5,485
Morgan	41.9	1,911	64.0	5.8	4.0	0.4	6.2	30.5	1,389	38	56	1,311	7,390	42,660	3,591
Obion	81.3	2,595	55.8	0.3	6.3	3.1	8.4	30.1	960	114	87	1,679	13,620	42,624	4,079
Overton	44.3	1,997	60.0	3.6	4.9	0.1	6.9	44.2	1,992	46	63	1,302	8,930	40,344	3,483
Perry	21.2	2,699	47.8	5.5	4.8	0.0	8.5	8.1	1,031	17	23	448	3,180	41,222	3,760
Pickett	13.0	2,545	48.4	5.3	3.9	0.0	10.4	3.4	663	10	14	304	2,120	45,022	4,532
Polk	34.7	2,079	61.1	2.7	6.5	0.1	8.0	19.5	1,171	72	48	693	7,040	43,289	4,013
Putnam	420.4	5,740	22.0	57.2	3.4	0.0	2.3	286.9	3,919	241	221	8,063	32,020	51,196	6,328
Rhea	100.3	3,111	50.3	17.1	4.9	0.0	5.3	141.2	4,378	1,075	92	1,832	13,430	43,912	4,156
Roane	135.7	2,538	58.0	2.9	4.6	0.2	4.6	117.8	2,203	411	152	3,264	23,100	54,719	6,067
Robertson	151.2	2,259	56.5	3.0	9.4	0.0	4.9	198.9	2,971	92	201	3,570	33,320	51,491	5,408
Rutherford	715.7	2,608	53.2	2.1	8.2	1.5	4.4	983.5	3,583	2,813	923	16,558	143,830	55,171	6,101
Scott	55.5	2,502	62.9	3.9	4.5	2.5	6.6	69.2	3,121	94	63	1,385	7,770	36,868	2,869
Sequatchie	28.3	1,960	60.8	3.3	6.5	0.0	5.5	20.7	1,434	11	42	837	6,180	46,883	4,679
Sevier	377.1	4,076	36.1	2.9	5.4	0.1	6.1	1,420.7	15,357	352	280	4,782	46,400	43,533	4,665
Shelby	4,592.5	4,882	44.5	8.2	8.9	1.1	2.0	5,549.0	5,898	13,372	3,485	51,304	431,650	59,000	8,348
Smith	46.3	2,421	56.5	3.9	7.0	0.1	6.8	37.3	1,955	125	56	977	8,480	50,066	4,358
Stewart	34.1	2,565	59.2	4.6	6.3	0.0	7.3	35.9	2,697	426	38	650	5,550	44,382	3,858
Sullivan	439.1	2,801	49.3	2.5	6.5	0.0	4.1	464.0	2,959	478	447	7,383	70,200	52,023	6,023
Sumner	387.5	2,333	56.0	2.5	7.6	0.1	4.7	365.1	2,198	480	527	7,875	85,000	67,338	9,352
Tipton	139.6	2,263	63.6	0.7	6.7	0.1	6.6	67.3	1,091	96	175	2,707	26,370	49,496	4,787
Trousdale	20.8	2,672	57.7	2.4	6.2	0.2	9.5	0.0	0	32	24	439	3,860	43,833	4,126
Unicoi	70.8	3,884	31.1	44.7	3.2	0.3	5.1	50.1	2,748	65	50	834	7,490	42,501	3,812
Union	45.7	2,387	70.7	3.8	4.1	0.2	4.9	34.2	1,787	18	56	812	7,420	41,350	3,632
Van Buren	17.4	3,085	70.1	3.3	3.6	0.0	8.9	9.0	1,604	12	16	440	2,320	39,203	3,156
Warren	107.0	2,687	60.0	3.5	4.8	0.0	5.4	47.1	1,181	90	116	2,029	16,840	39,632	3,581
Washington	308.7	2,467	44.9	1.3	7.5	0.5	5.7	609.5	4,872	2,787	398	9,890	56,270	54,690	6,734
Wayne	44.4	2,612	47.4	0.4	4.4	17.6	6.9	31.8	1,874	30	42	1,133	5,730	42,036	3,411
Weakley	68.4	1,967	54.8	0.5	6.6	11.4	8.3	23.7	682	126	97	3,395	12,850	43,842	4,166
White	50.7	1,943	60.1	2.7	5.8	0.3	5.6	21.8	835	51	76	1,369	11,030	39,733	3,254
Williamson	720.3	3,734	44.7	20.8	4.0	0.0	4.3	886.6	4,596	885	653	11,445	103,130	127,037	23,931
Wilson	304.2	2,557	61.0	0.4	7.4	0.0	4.9	398.5	3,350	215	391	4,852	64,160	66,336	8,271
TEXAS	X	X	X	X	X	X	X	X	X	200,710	172,334	1,685,472	12,114,850	64,281	9,069
Anderson	133.7	2,297	64.2	0.2	4.5	0.4	4.2	165.8	2,850	148	89	5,451	19,400	44,531	4,308
Andrews	109.9	6,817	50.8	29.4	3.5	0.0	1.1	185.6	11,518	13	36	1,320	6,970	63,929	7,954
Angelina	307.3	3,509	57.1	10.2	4.5	0.3	4.2	395.7	4,517	334	171	6,660	35,820	48,551	5,184
Aransas	80.8	3,391	53.6	1.1	9.5	1.2	4.4	116.6	4,897	19	51	1,056	10,710	54,661	6,809
Archer	26.8	3,072	60.0	1.1	6.2	0.4	7.7	257.0	29,423	19	85	478	3,870	57,377	6,849
Armstrong	8.5	4,369	44.7	28.9	3.6	0.2	4.8	4.2	2,172	4	4	127	860	49,688	5,644
Atascosa	210.7	4,536	43.4	9.8	2.8	0.8	23.3	433.1	9,325	59	105	2,433	20,410	48,084	4,903
Austin	84.2	2,944	55.5	4.8	7.5	0.0	7.6	104.0	3,635	74	60	1,360	13,800	60,941	7,927
Bailey	34.7	4,873	39.4	36.7	4.8	0.0	3.9	50.9	7,137	22	14	410	2,740	41,666	3,950
Bandera	43.7	2,128	59.1	2.9	6.1	0.5	5.8	35.4	1,721	12	44	711	9,860	59,150	7,612
Bastrop	242.4	3,242	50.0	11.5	5.2	0.6	5.9	413.3	5,529	369	182	3,792	36,070	51,286	5,353
Baylor	20.8	5,731	29.9	49.2	3.4	0.6	3.5	3.0	829	18	7	242	1,470	43,554	5,254
Bee	111.6	3,432	71.0	1.4	3.1	1.8	2.5	62.7	1,928	31	114	3,551	10,530	42,661	3,948
Bell	1,144.2	3,542	60.4	2.5	4.9	0.5	2.7	1,912.0	5,919	10,643	34,767	20,194	147,100	48,093	4,892
Bexar	7,362.8	4,123	44.0	14.4	5.4	2.0	2.3	18,461.5	10,338	35,257	36,242	110,369	862,020	56,317	7,176
Blanco	38.6	3,621	55.5	0.1	3.6	0.0	9.2	37.3	3,505	53	23	506	5,360	76,215	11,499
Borden	23.8	38,584	84.8	0.0	0.6	0.1	3.3	22.5	36,494	1	1	77	260	86,823	14,777
Bosque	45.2	2,493	68.1	0.1	4.3	0.7	4.0	30.9	1,705	65	36	1,205	7,760	49,012	5,265
Bowie	279.8	3,004	63.0	0.3	4.7	0.4	5.3	243.0	2,609	3,807	195	6,306	39,750	51,275	6,047
Brazoria	1,133.2	3,489	48.6	5.5	5.0	0.2	6.1	3,469.8	10,684	509	776	18,988	149,790	70,430	8,864
Brazos	577.4	2,877	45.4	2.3	6.2	0.4	5.6	1,281.3	6,385	742	497	36,907	80,270	62,205	8,476
Brewster	31.8	3,412	50.6	3.2	7.7	0.4	6.8	9.3	995	261	19	1,076	4,410	53,903	6,790
Briscoe	3.7	2,339	51.9	0.1	4.3	0.0	11.3	7.8	4,998	11	3	114	630	43,681	4,600
Brooks	42.3	5,904	45.4	2.3	10.2	0.3	5.0	40.3	5,626	336	14	544	2,800	31,535	2,138
Brown	120.7	3,191	51.3	7.8	5.5	0.5	4.3	150.8	3,986	127	73	2,838	15,900	45,941	4,731
Burleson	42.2	2,441	59.8	0.6	4.9	0.0	11.0	23.6	1,367	49	36	786	8,070	48,405	5,164
Burnet	148.6	3,420	46.0	1.6	5.8	0.4	3.8	219.9	5,061	79	92	2,573	22,080	66,790	9,420

1. Based on the resident population estimated as of July 1 of the year shown.

Table B. States and Counties — **Land Area and Population**

State / county code	CBSA code[1]	County code[2]	STATE County	Land area[3] (sq. mi)	Total persons 2018	Rank	Per square mile	White	Black	American Indian, Alaska Native	Asian and Pacific Islander	Percent Hispanic or Latino[4]	Under 5 years	5 to 17 years	18 to 24 years	25 to 34 years	35 to 44 years	45 to 54 years
				1	2	3	4	5	6	7	8	9	10	11	12	13	14	15
			TEXAS— Cont'd															
48055	12,420	1	Caldwell	545.2	43,247	1,108	79.3	40.0	6.3	0.7	1.1	53.0	6.4	17.4	11.4	13.5	12.4	12.3
48057	38,920	6	Calhoun	506.8	21,561	1,748	42.5	42.6	3.0	0.7	5.6	49.1	6.6	17.6	8.6	12.6	11.6	11.9
48059	10,180	3	Callahan	899.4	13,994	2,163	15.6	87.2	2.1	1.3	1.1	9.9	6.0	16.5	6.6	11.2	11.8	12.0
48061	15,180	2	Cameron	891.0	423,908	167	475.8	9.0	0.5	0.2	0.8	89.8	8.1	22.2	10.6	12.4	12.2	11.2
48063		6	Camp	195.8	13,033	2,228	66.6	57.1	17.3	0.8	1.2	25.7	7.5	19.1	9.0	10.9	10.4	11.7
48065	11,100	2	Carson	920.2	6,005	2,754	6.5	86.7	1.7	2.2	0.8	10.5	5.4	18.7	7.4	10.8	12.2	11.5
48067		6	Cass	937.0	30,119	1,429	32.1	77.5	17.4	1.0	0.8	4.7	6.0	16.6	7.3	10.2	10.9	12.7
48069		6	Castro	894.4	7,665	2,619	8.6	31.3	2.3	0.7	0.7	65.5	7.3	21.3	10.5	11.2	11.4	10.0
48071	26,420	1	Chambers	597.2	42,454	1,130	71.1	67.4	8.6	0.8	1.6	22.8	7.1	20.9	8.7	13.3	14.2	12.9
48073	27,380	6	Cherokee	1,053.0	52,592	955	49.9	61.6	14.7	0.9	0.7	23.6	7.1	18.3	9.3	12.0	11.4	12.1
48075		7	Childress	696.5	7,291	2,640	10.5	56.4	10.8	1.1	0.9	32.0	4.8	14.9	12.9	20.2	12.4	9.1
48077	48,660	3	Clay	1,088.8	10,456	2,393	9.6	91.0	1.3	2.0	0.9	6.5	4.6	15.4	6.8	9.3	11.3	12.6
48079		9	Cochran	775.1	2,836	2,983	3.7	35.7	3.7	1.0	0.5	59.9	7.2	20.5	7.4	13.6	10.5	11.6
48081		8	Coke	911.6	3,370	2,946	3.7	76.7	1.2	2.0	0.4	21.5	5.8	15.2	7.0	10.3	9.4	10.8
48083		6	Coleman	1,262.9	8,397	2,554	6.6	77.8	3.5	1.3	1.4	17.5	5.2	15.8	6.7	9.2	10.4	11.5
48085	19,100	1	Collin	841.3	1,005,146	45	1,194.8	58.1	10.9	0.9	17.2	15.4	6.2	19.7	8.2	12.8	15.8	15.1
48087		9	Collingsworth	918.4	2,962	2,970	3.2	59.2	5.8	2.0	0.7	33.9	6.0	20.3	8.9	11.1	11.0	11.0
48089		6	Colorado	960.3	21,217	1,764	22.1	56.7	12.3	0.5	0.8	30.6	6.4	16.4	8.0	10.7	10.3	11.3
48091	41,700	1	Comal	559.5	148,373	445	265.2	68.3	2.6	0.9	1.8	27.8	5.8	16.9	7.6	11.5	12.1	13.4
48093		7	Comanche	937.8	13,534	2,195	14.4	70.1	0.9	1.1	0.7	28.3	5.6	16.6	7.5	9.9	10.1	12.6
48095		8	Concho	983.8	4,276	2,881	4.3	40.9	2.2	0.5	1.7	55.3	2.7	9.2	7.2	16.9	19.9	14.8
48097	23,620	6	Cooke	874.8	40,574	1,164	46.4	76.2	3.8	1.5	1.3	18.8	6.8	17.0	8.4	12.2	10.9	11.8
48099	28,660	2	Coryell	1,052.2	74,808	739	71.1	61.1	18.5	1.4	4.3	18.7	6.8	16.0	12.6	19.4	14.8	11.3
48101		9	Cottle	900.6	1,389	3,084	1.5	65.0	10.7	0.6	0.5	24.6	5.4	17.7	5.8	9.7	10.9	10.2
48103		6	Crane	785.1	4,794	2,847	6.1	31.1	2.9	1.0	0.5	65.2	8.0	21.4	9.4	13.0	12.6	11.5
48105		7	Crockett	2,807.3	3,499	2,938	1.2	31.8	0.7	1.0	0.7	66.3	6.7	17.8	7.7	11.0	12.5	12.7
48107	31,180	2	Crosby	900.2	5,779	2,770	6.4	40.5	3.4	0.8	0.5	55.8	6.7	19.9	8.2	11.4	11.5	10.7
48109		9	Culberson	3,812.2	2,204	3,031	0.6	24.4	1.4	1.3	2.2	72.1	7.0	15.7	8.6	11.6	9.6	12.3
48111		7	Dallam	1,503.1	7,200	2,645	4.8	49.0	2.3	1.2	1.2	47.4	9.7	21.9	8.5	14.4	11.2	12.8
48113	19,100	1	Dallas	872.1	2,637,772	8	3,024.6	29.8	23.3	0.7	7.2	40.5	7.5	18.7	9.5	16.5	13.7	12.4
48115	29,500	7	Dawson	900.3	12,619	2,248	14.0	35.6	5.6	0.5	1.0	58.1	6.9	18.7	10.1	16.0	12.4	9.9
48117	25,820	6	Deaf Smith	1,496.8	18,760	1,886	12.5	24.6	1.2	0.6	0.7	73.5	8.6	22.4	10.1	13.2	11.7	11.0
48119		8	Delta	256.8	5,349	2,805	20.8	82.7	7.6	2.8	1.2	8.5	6.8	16.3	7.1	10.9	11.3	12.5
48121	19,100	1	Denton	878.6	859,064	67	977.8	60.3	11.0	1.0	10.5	19.5	6.3	18.4	9.3	14.8	15.4	14.5
48123		6	DeWitt	909.0	20,187	1,812	22.2	55.4	8.9	0.5	0.4	35.5	6.3	16.1	6.8	11.9	12.7	12.4
48125		8	Dickens	901.7	2,249	3,024	2.5	61.8	5.0	1.3	1.3	31.6	5.2	13.7	8.4	13.7	12.9	9.7
48127		6	Dimmit	1,328.9	10,308	2,400	7.8	10.8	1.2	0.2	0.7	87.4	7.5	21.5	9.0	12.3	11.8	10.4
48129		8	Donley	926.9	3,319	2,948	3.6	81.1	6.4	1.3	0.8	11.9	5.2	14.6	13.6	8.3	10.9	9.5
48131		7	Duval	1,793.5	11,212	2,337	6.3	9.2	1.2	0.3	0.4	89.1	7.0	17.9	10.3	12.7	11.6	11.3
48133		6	Eastland	926.5	18,322	1,911	19.8	80.0	2.3	1.2	1.0	16.8	6.1	15.4	10.0	10.4	10.7	11.0
48135	36,220	3	Ector	897.8	162,124	407	180.6	32.6	4.8	0.7	1.4	61.3	9.0	21.2	10.1	16.9	13.0	10.4
48137		9	Edwards	2,117.9	1,928	3,055	0.9	43.2	0.8	1.0	0.4	55.3	6.5	16.1	5.9	8.9	9.2	10.3
48139	19,100	1	Ellis	935.7	179,436	368	191.8	61.2	11.4	1.0	1.2	26.6	6.8	19.9	8.8	13.0	13.2	13.2
48141	21,340	2	El Paso	1,013.2	840,758	70	829.8	12.4	3.4	0.5	1.7	83.0	7.5	19.6	11.2	15.0	12.5	11.5
48143	44,500	4	Erath	1,083.2	42,446	1,131	39.2	75.2	2.2	1.1	1.0	21.7	5.7	14.8	21.2	12.7	10.2	10.0
48145	47,380	2	Falls	765.5	17,335	1,956	22.6	52.1	23.9	0.9	0.9	23.7	6.0	14.8	8.6	14.5	12.1	12.6
48147	14,300	6	Fannin	890.8	35,286	1,295	39.6	80.2	7.1	1.9	1.0	11.6	5.3	16.2	8.1	12.8	12.3	13.0
48149		6	Fayette	949.9	25,349	1,591	26.7	71.5	6.6	0.6	0.6	21.6	5.0	15.2	7.1	9.6	10.5	11.3
48151		8	Fisher	899.0	3,839	2,913	4.3	66.8	4.0	1.1	0.6	28.6	5.5	15.7	7.0	11.1	9.7	11.7
48153		6	Floyd	992.1	5,837	2,763	5.9	36.5	3.5	0.6	0.5	59.5	6.5	20.5	8.9	11.1	11.2	11.2
48155		9	Foard	704.4	1,200	3,100	1.7	75.3	5.4	0.8	0.8	18.8	3.8	16.8	6.9	9.1	8.7	13.8
48157	26,420	1	Fort Bend	861.6	787,858	82	914.4	34.1	21.0	0.6	21.6	24.7	6.9	20.5	8.3	12.0	15.3	14.0
48159		7	Franklin	284.4	10,766	2,369	37.9	80.0	4.4	1.2	1.2	14.8	5.4	18.1	7.0	10.9	10.5	12.1
48161		7	Freestone	877.7	19,808	1,836	22.6	67.9	15.7	1.1	0.8	15.8	5.8	17.1	6.9	11.1	13.3	12.7
48163		6	Frio	1,133.5	19,816	1,834	17.5	15.0	3.2	0.4	2.5	79.3	6.4	16.7	13.5	18.9	12.7	10.6
48165		7	Gaines	1,502.4	20,901	1,779	13.9	55.3	1.9	0.6	0.5	42.4	10.3	25.5	9.3	13.8	12.0	10.4
48167	26,420	1	Galveston	378.9	337,890	208	891.8	58.5	13.3	0.8	4.1	25.0	6.4	17.9	8.4	13.4	13.2	13.0
48169		6	Garza	893.4	6,578	2,704	7.4	40.4	6.9	0.8	0.4	52.4	4.6	12.4	14.0	21.4	11.5	13.9
48171	23,240	7	Gillespie	1,058.2	26,804	1,532	25.3	75.0	0.6	0.7	0.7	23.7	5.0	15.0	6.6	8.8	9.5	10.4
48173	13,700	8	Glasscock	900.2	1,388	3,085	1.5	59.4	1.7	0.4	0.4	38.5	6.5	19.7	8.9	12.0	13.3	12.4
48175	47,020	3	Goliad	852.0	7,584	2,623	8.9	58.6	4.7	0.8	0.5	36.4	5.6	15.8	7.0	10.3	10.8	12.0
48177		6	Gonzales	1,066.7	20,826	1,782	19.5	41.8	6.4	0.5	0.6	51.5	7.3	19.7	8.5	12.1	11.2	11.5
48179	37,420	6	Gray	926.0	21,895	1,730	23.6	64.8	5.4	1.5	0.8	29.2	6.9	18.8	7.7	13.3	13.0	12.1
48181	43,300	3	Grayson	932.8	133,991	479	143.6	77.2	7.0	2.3	2.1	13.8	6.4	17.3	8.4	12.4	11.6	12.3
48183	30,980	3	Gregg	273.4	123,707	513	452.5	58.6	21.2	0.9	1.8	19.2	7.1	18.7	9.3	13.7	12.0	11.4
48185		6	Grimes	787.5	28,360	1,485	36.0	59.6	15.6	1.0	0.6	24.6	6.0	16.5	7.9	12.9	12.1	13.0

1. CBSA = Core Based Statistical Area. See Appendix A for explanation. See Appendix B for list of metropolitan areas with component counties. 2. County type code from the Economic Research Service of USDA Rural-Urban Continuum Codes. See Appendix A for definition. 3. Dry land or land partially or temporarily covered by water. 4. May be of any race.

Table B. States and Counties — Population and Households

STATE County	|	Population, 2018 (cont.) Age (percent) (cont.)				Population change, 2000-2018							Households, 2013-2017				
						Total persons		Percent change		Components of change, 2010-2018						Percent	
		55 to 64 years	65 to 74 years	75 years and over	Percent female	2000	2010	2000-2010	2010-2018	Births	Deaths	Net Migration	Number	Persons per household	Family house-holds	Female family house-holder[1]	One person
		16	17	18	19	20	21	22	23	24	25	26	27	28	29	30	31

TEXAS— Cont'd

STATE County	16	17	18	19	20	21	22	23	24	25	26	27	28	29	30	31
Caldwell	12.3	8.6	5.8	49.5	32,194	38,057	18.2	13.6	4,224	2,583	3,559	12,894	2.85	69.6	15.8	23.3
Calhoun	13.2	10.5	7.4	48.6	20,647	21,382	3.6	0.8	2,391	1,692	-513	7,733	2.79	70.0	11.5	26.2
Callahan	15.5	11.7	8.8	50.5	12,905	13,546	5.0	3.3	1,175	1,431	712	5,291	2.57	61.8	7.4	35.1
Cameron	9.7	7.6	5.9	51.3	335,227	406,215	21.2	4.4	59,248	21,145	-20,487	122,188	3.41	78.8	20.2	18.8
Camp	12.8	10.9	7.6	51.4	11,549	12,401	7.4	5.1	1,521	1,171	285	4,730	2.66	71.4	14.7	24.9
Carson	14.5	11.0	8.5	49.9	6,516	6,186	-5.1	-2.9	483	541	-124	2,292	2.61	70.3	9.8	25.4
Cass	14.2	12.3	9.9	51.6	30,438	30,464	0.1	-1.1	2,873	3,381	177	11,811	2.51	69.8	12.6	27.7
Castro	12.6	8.1	7.7	48.5	8,285	8,063	-2.7	-4.9	994	462	-952	2,462	3.17	72.3	11.3	23.8
Chambers	11.2	7.6	4.2	49.3	26,031	35,099	34.8	21.0	4,128	2,209	5,392	13,320	2.93	78.3	8.4	20.2
Cherokee	12.2	10.2	7.4	49.0	46,659	50,834	8.9	3.5	6,231	4,348	-83	17,885	2.72	73.8	13.6	22.0
Childress	10.2	8.3	7.1	39.2	7,688	7,041	-8.4	3.6	638	574	178	2,282	2.52	64.5	12.4	32.0
Clay	17.1	13.1	9.6	50.2	11,006	10,754	-2.3	-2.8	726	974	-52	4,076	2.53	70.5	7.4	25.7
Cochran	12.9	8.4	7.9	49.8	3,730	3,127	-16.2	-9.3	364	212	-452	1,000	2.81	71.8	15.7	26.9
Coke	14.1	14.5	12.7	50.6	3,864	3,317	-14.2	1.6	269	415	199	1,574	1.99	61.4	8.4	33.7
Coleman	16.2	14.3	10.6	49.5	9,235	8,893	-3.7	-5.6	699	1,067	-125	3,470	2.41	68.7	11.7	27.7
Collin	11.1	6.9	4.1	50.8	491,675	782,220	59.1	28.5	88,953	31,772	164,434	323,905	2.81	74.2	10.1	21.3
Collingsworth	12.9	10.5	8.4	51.1	3,206	3,057	-4.6	-3.1	318	300	-116	1,099	2.69	73.0	8.2	25.6
Colorado	14.8	12.2	9.9	49.7	20,390	20,872	2.4	1.7	2,126	2,192	425	7,603	2.70	70.3	11.9	26.3
Comal	14.7	11.3	6.8	50.6	78,021	108,485	39.0	36.8	11,716	8,826	36,510	47,253	2.71	74.9	9.6	20.6
Comanche	13.6	13.4	11.0	50.2	14,026	13,960	-0.5	-3.1	1,263	1,423	-262	5,107	2.60	68.7	11.3	29.2
Concho	11.6	10.1	7.6	29.4	3,966	4,087	3.1	4.6	205	260	242	791	3.27	70.0	7.2	27.9
Cooke	14.2	10.9	7.7	50.1	36,363	38,439	5.7	5.6	4,489	3,329	981	15,185	2.53	72.1	11.4	22.1
Coryell	8.9	6.1	4.1	50.3	74,978	75,474	0.7	-0.9	8,257	3,629	-5,429	22,424	2.74	72.7	12.6	22.8
Cottle	15.9	12.9	11.4	51.5	1,904	1,506	-20.9	-7.8	119	192	-43	664	2.26	69.6	11.9	30.1
Crane	12.1	6.4	5.5	49.6	3,996	4,375	9.5	9.6	604	291	98	1,479	3.20	73.8	7.4	22.2
Crockett	13.8	10.2	7.5	50.1	4,099	3,719	-9.3	-5.9	414	286	-349	1,411	2.66	74.4	10.2	25.6
Crosby	12.9	9.8	8.9	50.6	7,072	6,056	-14.4	-4.6	631	570	-341	2,064	2.81	71.3	14.5	26.8
Culberson	13.7	12.0	9.4	50.6	2,975	2,398	-19.4	-8.1	249	127	-323	735	3.02	69.0	17.1	30.5
Dallam	10.2	7.0	4.5	47.9	6,222	6,700	7.7	7.5	1,193	351	-344	2,432	2.95	73.0	10.9	22.0
Dallas	10.9	6.6	4.2	50.6	2,218,899	2,366,683	6.7	11.5	326,208	127,538	73,764	906,179	2.78	65.2	16.0	28.4
Dawson	11.0	8.0	6.9	45.1	14,985	13,833	-7.7	-8.8	1,516	1,128	-1,642	4,339	2.61	68.2	15.0	28.5
Deaf Smith	10.2	7.2	5.4	50.1	18,561	19,372	4.4	-3.2	2,807	1,205	-2,246	6,118	3.04	71.2	9.7	26.2
Delta	14.2	11.9	8.9	50.3	5,327	5,231	-1.8	2.3	526	615	204	2,035	2.51	69.5	11.4	27.7
Denton	11.2	6.6	3.6	50.8	432,976	662,554	53.0	29.7	80,194	27,248	141,751	275,164	2.79	71.1	11.0	22.3
DeWitt	13.7	10.8	9.1	47.5	20,013	20,097	0.4	0.4	2,089	2,083	92	7,260	2.56	72.3	10.4	23.8
Dickens	13.5	11.9	10.9	44.6	2,762	2,441	-11.6	-7.9	166	209	-153	832	2.50	65.0	9.6	32.5
Dimmit	10.7	9.4	7.4	50.8	10,248	9,996	-2.5	3.1	1,369	717	-354	3,476	3.08	66.0	20.4	31.8
Donley	14.0	13.0	10.9	50.9	3,828	3,726	-2.7	-10.9	276	410	-277	1,230	2.54	64.1	10.5	32.2
Duval	11.2	9.4	8.5	48.4	13,120	11,784	-10.2	-4.9	1,373	1,091	-867	3,845	2.84	71.0	21.0	22.8
Eastland	14.6	12.0	9.9	50.1	18,297	18,582	1.6	-1.4	1,702	2,092	141	6,437	2.69	57.0	9.7	40.1
Ector	9.7	5.8	4.0	49.1	121,123	137,136	13.2	18.2	23,002	9,736	11,351	51,475	2.99	70.4	16.7	24.3
Edwards	13.9	17.6	11.5	47.1	2,162	2,002	-7.4	-3.7	191	166	-102	634	3.31	63.7	4.4	35.2
Ellis	12.3	8.0	4.8	50.7	111,360	149,604	34.3	19.9	17,268	9,585	22,087	54,725	2.97	78.7	11.6	17.8
El Paso	10.5	7.0	5.3	50.7	679,622	800,653	17.8	5.0	110,306	41,787	-28,701	263,200	3.11	74.3	19.2	22.6
Erath	11.1	8.3	5.9	51.0	33,001	37,900	14.8	12.0	4,007	2,695	3,175	13,827	2.82	64.4	8.5	24.9
Falls	13.3	10.1	8.1	52.5	18,576	17,867	-3.8	-3.0	1,723	1,517	-741	5,405	2.87	65.8	12.7	30.8
Fannin	13.8	10.6	7.9	46.9	31,242	33,910	8.5	4.1	2,835	3,445	2,013	12,027	2.55	70.8	12.1	24.3
Fayette	16.1	13.8	11.6	50.9	21,804	24,556	12.6	3.2	1,977	2,546	1,378	9,298	2.63	72.3	6.9	23.9
Fisher	14.8	12.4	12.1	50.4	4,344	3,978	-8.4	-3.5	312	406	-46	1,696	2.26	61.5	7.0	33.9
Floyd	12.0	9.4	9.3	49.6	7,771	6,446	-17.1	-9.4	658	522	-757	2,320	2.55	74.3	13.3	22.7
Foard	14.6	12.7	13.7	51.4	1,622	1,336	-17.6	-10.2	98	159	-78	562	2.45	64.8	7.8	32.4
Fort Bend	11.8	7.3	3.7	50.9	354,452	584,690	65.0	34.7	74,264	23,657	151,039	222,331	3.17	82.1	12.3	15.1
Franklin	14.3	12.4	9.5	50.3	9,458	10,603	12.1	1.5	889	936	210	3,931	2.68	69.9	8.8	25.9
Freestone	13.2	11.2	8.7	48.1	17,867	19,817	10.9	0.0	1,781	1,741	-37	7,232	2.49	73.6	13.1	24.1
Frio	8.9	7.2	5.0	40.7	16,252	17,217	5.9	15.1	2,066	1,075	1,596	4,530	3.52	74.3	15.5	24.2
Gaines	9.8	5.1	3.8	49.3	14,467	17,526	21.1	19.3	3,340	944	977	5,716	3.46	77.6	8.2	20.0
Galveston	13.4	8.9	5.5	50.8	250,158	291,307	16.4	16.0	33,346	21,057	34,041	117,455	2.68	69.7	13.6	25.2
Garza	11.2	5.6	5.5	33.8	4,872	6,461	32.6	1.8	524	414	524	1,715	2.79	82.6	20.9	12.8
Gillespie	15.0	15.7	14.1	51.3	20,814	24,836	19.3	7.9	2,079	2,865	2,753	10,795	2.37	70.0	9.0	27.9
Glasscock	12.0	8.6	6.6	44.9	1,406	1,226	-12.8	13.2	122	53	90	475	2.99	87.6	3.8	8.8
Goliad	15.7	13.5	9.4	50.5	6,928	7,210	4.1	5.2	583	647	435	2,755	2.69	76.5	11.7	21.3
Gonzales	13.0	9.1	7.6	49.5	18,628	19,811	6.4	5.1	2,426	1,661	256	7,018	2.88	72.0	12.9	26.3
Gray	11.9	8.6	7.6	47.0	22,744	22,537	-0.9	-2.8	2,639	2,142	-1,165	7,971	2.68	65.6	9.7	29.8
Grayson	13.9	10.3	7.3	51.2	110,595	120,875	9.3	10.9	12,704	11,389	11,842	47,550	2.60	69.0	12.5	26.4
Gregg	12.3	8.6	6.8	51.4	111,379	121,745	9.3	1.6	15,226	10,441	-2,764	45,615	2.60	66.7	16.2	28.4
Grimes	14.3	10.7	6.7	45.6	23,552	26,581	12.9	6.7	2,651	2,289	1,428	8,980	2.65	69.6	15.7	26.4

1. No spouse present.

Table B. States and Counties — Population, Vital Statistics, Health, and Crime

STATE County	Persons in group quarters, 2018	Daytime Population, 2013-2017 Number	Employment/ residence ratio	Births, 2018 Total	Births, 2018 Rate[1]	Deaths, 2018 Number	Deaths, 2018 Rate[1]	Persons under 65 with no health insurance, 2016 Number	Persons under 65 with no health insurance, 2016 Percent	Medicare, 2018 Total beneficiaries	Medicare, 2018 Enrolled in Original Medicare	Medicare, 2018 Enrolled in Medicare Advantage	Serious crimes known to police[2], 2016 Total Number	Serious crimes known to police[2], 2016 Total Rate[3]
	32	33	34	35	36	37	38	39	40	41	42	43	44	45
TEXAS— Cont'd														
Caldwell	3,348	32,649	0.56	568	13.1	344	8.0	7,105	20.9	7,189	4,816	2,373	674	1,648
Calhoun	249	25,134	1.35	272	12.6	219	10.2	3,335	18.4	4,096	3,229	867	728	3,690
Callahan	73	11,026	0.48	159	11.4	183	13.1	2,088	18.9	3,182	2,311	871	165	1,220
Cameron	3,376	415,117	0.97	6,547	15.4	2,769	6.5	106,485	29.5	61,988	32,673	29,315	13,708	3,234
Camp	65	10,951	0.67	175	13.4	125	9.6	2,168	20.6	2,783	1,890	893	257	2,024
Carson	25	5,660	0.87	48	8.0	69	11.5	761	15.0	1,171	866	305	82	1,387
Cass	354	27,480	0.78	316	10.5	435	14.4	3,637	15.5	7,736	5,253	2,483	747	2,506
Castro	70	7,497	0.88	104	13.6	50	6.5	1,792	27.6	1,178	954	224	171	2,266
Chambers	228	37,152	0.87	565	13.3	264	6.2	5,524	15.7	5,882	3,855	2,027	1,168	2,959
Cherokee	2,851	47,928	0.82	734	14.0	564	10.7	9,108	22.5	10,256	6,804	3,452	1,236	2,706
Childress	1,690	7,179	1.05	79	10.8	55	7.5	766	16.7	1,319	964	355	NA	NA
Clay	70	7,922	0.42	88	8.4	127	12.1	1,411	17.5	2,527	1,993	534	114	1,112
Cochran	78	2,639	0.75	37	13.0	6	2.1	686	28.4	545	391	154	83	2,853
Coke	35	2,836	0.72	37	11.0	48	14.2	414	17.2	879	652	227	30	934
Coleman	53	7,580	0.74	78	9.3	119	14.2	1,303	20.4	2,407	1,911	496	NA	NA
Collin	4,394	876,280	0.92	11,160	11.1	4,741	4.7	90,995	10.8	111,370	77,764	33,606	16,097	1,715
Collingsworth	54	2,868	0.88	30	10.1	23	7.8	726	29.7	608	510	98	21	692
Colorado	329	20,229	0.93	270	12.7	261	12.3	3,218	19.6	5,157	4,032	1,125	279	1,341
Comal	1,186	127,702	0.98	1,549	10.4	1,179	7.9	15,496	14.1	31,405	21,519	9,886	2,674	2,010
Comanche	150	12,328	0.78	139	10.3	184	13.6	2,493	24.5	3,523	2,678	845	307	2,311
Concho	1,629	4,051	1.19	20	4.7	34	8.0	372	18.4	732	526	206	15	369
Cooke	631	37,666	0.92	563	13.9	411	10.1	6,491	20.4	7,971	5,847	2,124	844	2,192
Coryell	12,095	66,200	0.69	927	12.4	469	6.3	7,510	13.4	9,854	7,008	2,846	1,403	1,864
Cottle	0	1,521	1.04	14	10.1	13	9.4	280	26.3	414	305	109	11	782
Crane	87	4,746	0.95	69	14.4	24	5.0	834	19.8	668	464	204	38	734
Crockett	40	3,892	1.03	32	9.1	28	8.0	633	20.7	691	536	155	40	1,081
Crosby	62	5,153	0.70	69	11.9	60	10.4	1,041	21.6	1,264	829	435	30	629
Culberson	12	2,268	1.01	32	14.5	14	6.4	447	25.3	497	396	101	0	0
Dallam	39	7,810	1.17	151	21.0	40	5.6	1,659	26.0	943	758	185	260	3,622
Dallas	32,325	2,874,663	1.26	40,055	15.2	17,009	6.4	492,034	21.6	313,250	193,868	119,382	94,170	3,645
Dawson	1,347	13,177	1.02	175	13.9	132	10.5	2,131	21.8	2,277	1,676	601	478	3,593
Deaf Smith	348	19,388	1.05	333	17.8	162	8.6	3,901	24.0	2,718	2,041	677	511	2,718
Delta	53	4,129	0.45	67	12.5	56	10.5	739	18.2	1,315	993	322	28	539
Denton	11,477	641,856	0.66	10,227	11.9	4,106	4.8	83,638	11.6	91,462	61,716	29,746	14,351	1,787
DeWitt	1,833	21,336	1.11	231	11.4	222	11.0	2,576	16.9	4,406	3,388	1,018	452	2,164
Dickens	315	2,309	1.12	20	8.9	17	7.6	337	24.0	532	390	142	37	1,717
Dimmit	94	15,222	2.17	131	12.7	74	7.2	1,650	18.2	1,870	1,156	714	185	1,659
Donley	226	3,191	0.83	33	9.9	43	13.0	536	22.2	879	671	208	48	1,394
Duval	663	11,331	0.97	143	12.8	145	12.9	1,654	18.7	2,339	1,436	903	286	2,533
Eastland	816	18,004	0.96	215	11.7	247	13.5	2,837	20.8	4,525	3,252	1,273	344	1,999
Ector	2,805	156,371	1.01	2,713	16.7	1,253	7.7	29,226	20.9	19,100	13,946	5,154	7,306	4,459
Edwards	5	2,121	1.01	19	9.9	15	7.8	344	24.5	550	417	133	22	1,178
Ellis	1,656	142,186	0.72	2,276	12.7	1,352	7.5	25,255	17.3	26,732	17,881	8,851	3,043	1,834
El Paso	16,458	833,389	1.00	12,426	14.8	5,500	6.5	152,482	21.2	125,853	51,527	74,326	17,420	2,078
Erath	3,894	39,804	0.94	489	11.5	362	8.5	7,032	21.8	6,471	4,773	1,698	777	1,864
Falls	1,940	15,569	0.70	211	12.2	165	9.5	2,429	19.7	3,408	2,139	1,269	129	868
Fannin	3,091	30,145	0.72	363	10.3	435	12.3	5,286	21.1	7,546	5,662	1,884	379	1,224
Fayette	402	24,725	0.98	223	8.8	319	12.6	3,651	19.3	6,680	5,168	1,512	353	1,403
Fisher	22	3,334	0.68	37	9.6	43	11.2	524	17.7	935	689	246	66	1,741
Floyd	34	5,899	0.98	79	13.5	44	7.5	1,087	22.8	1,239	853	386	128	2,211
Foard	31	1,314	0.83	11	9.2	13	10.8	212	24.1	329	264	65	0	0
Fort Bend	5,117	564,486	0.56	9,935	12.6	3,627	4.6	79,016	12.0	88,043	51,824	36,219	12,644	1,705
Franklin	94	10,207	0.90	107	9.9	123	11.4	1,477	17.7	2,484	1,751	733	136	1,280
Freestone	1,615	18,117	0.79	201	10.1	196	9.9	2,926	20.3	4,048	2,840	1,208	261	1,331
Frio	3,381	21,310	1.33	245	12.4	144	7.3	2,674	20.1	2,635	1,678	957	376	1,973
Gaines	80	19,121	0.90	439	21.0	112	5.4	5,733	30.9	1,996	1,542	454	255	1,242
Galveston	4,990	285,689	0.76	4,121	12.2	2,943	8.7	43,977	15.7	54,148	34,760	19,388	9,711	2,965
Garza	2,129	6,811	1.03	59	9.0	40	6.1	797	22.3	816	536	280	63	987
Gillespie	309	26,297	1.03	263	9.8	380	14.2	4,392	23.6	8,257	6,552	1,705	284	1,088
Glasscock	0	1,624	1.31	15	10.8	8	5.8	232	20.2	203	177	26	17	1,279
Goliad	90	6,276	0.58	76	10.0	63	8.3	835	14.2	1,635	1,190	445	108	1,426
Gonzales	312	20,564	1.00	289	13.9	210	10.1	4,298	24.9	3,908	2,922	986	463	2,240
Gray	1,788	22,655	0.97	274	12.5	257	11.7	3,881	22.4	3,961	3,142	819	1,068	4,585
Grayson	2,300	120,853	0.91	1,595	11.9	1,434	10.7	20,325	19.4	27,371	19,829	7,542	2,752	2,221
Gregg	4,074	143,312	1.37	1,666	13.5	1,324	10.7	19,949	19.5	23,911	16,378	7,533	5,083	4,094
Grimes	2,911	25,370	0.81	329	11.6	245	8.6	4,279	21.0	5,592	3,830	1,762	541	1,959

1. Per 1,000 estimated resident population.   2. Data for serious crimes have not been adjusted for underreporting; this may affect comparability between geographic areas and over time.   3. Per 100,000 population estimated by the FBI.

Table B. States and Counties — Crime, Education, Money Income, and Poverty

STATE County	Serious crimes known to police[2], 2016 (cont.)[1] Rate Violent	Property	Education School enrollment and attainment, 2013-2017 Enrollment[3] Total	Percent private	Attainment[4] (percent) High school graduate or less	Bachelor's degree or more	Local government expenditures[5] 2014-2015 Total current spending (mil dol)	Current spending per student (dollars)	Money income, 2013-2017 Per capita income[6]	Median income (dollars)	Households Percent with income of less than $50,000	with income of $200,000 or more	Income and poverty, 2017 Median household income (dollars)	Percent below poverty level All persons	Children under 18 years	Children 5 to 17 years in families
	46	47	48	49	50	51	52	53	54	55	56	57	58	59	60	61
TEXAS— Cont'd																
Caldwell	237	1,411	10,168	8.3	58.5	14.3	58.9	8,521	23,366	51,346	48.6	2.3	51,895	14.5	21.3	20.9
Calhoun	654	3,036	5,103	5.2	52.1	16.2	35.8	8,472	26,909	58,788	42.8	2.3	55,240	16.3	24.2	23.0
Callahan	67	1,153	2,973	9.8	52.8	16.0	23.2	9,173	22,205	40,945	57.2	1.6	45,843	14	23.3	23.0
Cameron	379	2,855	127,140	4.1	58.9	17.2	944.9	9,433	16,085	36,095	62.2	1.8	36,624	27.7	38.4	37.2
Camp	244	1,780	3,061	11.3	54.6	16.7	29.5	12,089	21,069	41,811	57.9	0.7	41,932	20.3	31.3	31.1
Carson	490	896	1,518	10.5	35.4	29.2	14.0	11,082	31,788	67,010	34.7	5.0	60,668	8.5	11.3	10.4
Cass	376	2,131	6,448	5.2	59.7	15.3	50.4	8,975	22,145	41,432	57.7	1.7	40,104	19	29.5	30.9
Castro	93	2,173	2,197	2.6	59.4	13.4	17.2	10,090	22,292	44,643	56.8	1.1	41,746	17.2	25.1	23.5
Chambers	415	2,543	10,379	6.9	44.3	20.5	76.7	10,162	31,412	74,368	36.9	8.1	81,018	9.5	12.9	12.0
Cherokee	412	2,294	13,140	9.7	52.0	18.1	91.8	8,253	21,102	44,294	55.4	2.4	47,147	17.2	25.2	23.2
Childress	NA	NA	1,221	10.0	53.6	18.5	10.3	8,924	18,694	40,432	59.1	0.1	40,925	20.3	26.7	23.8
Clay	137	975	2,270	13.2	51.1	17.9	17.3	9,919	27,593	46,863	52.6	3.9	53,438	11.8	17.3	16.0
Cochran	241	2,613	700	7.0	63.2	10.5	12.0	15,121	19,195	37,500	60.3	1.5	40,796	24.8	38.3	38.0
Coke	31	903	719	6.3	50.5	20.6	6.0	10,929	24,623	42,500	60.0	1.2	42,314	13.3	21.2	20.2
Coleman	NA	NA	1,499	7.6	55.4	14.4	12.9	9,638	26,436	40,804	64.1	5.2	35,596	25.2	41.2	37.6
Collin	154	1,561	260,518	12.4	21.5	50.9	1,576.9	8,259	41,609	90,124	25.9	12.6	95,394	5.9	6.2	5.3
Collingsworth	297	396	646	6.8	54.8	15.6	5.4	9,020	21,356	46,348	53.8	2.1	39,809	18	28.1	25.0
Colorado	255	1,086	4,365	11.7	54.5	18.9	32.2	9,152	26,689	50,241	49.7	3.2	49,100	14.9	23.0	22.0
Comal	250	1,760	29,302	13.5	33.0	36.0	230.2	7,996	35,841	73,655	33.9	9.1	72,562	8.9	13.1	12.6
Comanche	196	2,115	2,737	6.9	55.5	18.6	21.3	9,372	22,751	42,419	57.8	1.1	46,161	15	25.1	22.9
Concho	25	344	756	0.5	67.2	11.3	5.0	10,978	17,513	46,696	53.0	4.2	42,723	15.4	28.2	25.8
Cooke	343	1,849	9,244	13.5	43.1	22.7	55.1	8,632	29,067	60,027	43.3	4.1	57,382	13	20.6	19.1
Coryell	279	1,585	21,127	9.6	40.3	15.4	94.1	8,476	21,171	50,865	48.9	1.6	51,486	13.6	19.0	18.8
Cottle	71	711	330	11.2	57.5	16.7	2.6	12,546	20,566	33,534	64.5	1.5	36,201	21.2	39.4	35.1
Crane	77	656	1,448	3.5	54.6	11.7	15.5	13,327	24,582	63,935	37.2	4.1	56,356	11.7	16.4	16.0
Crockett	81	1,000	760	1.8	59.5	8.9	10.0	11,587	23,296	52,310	47.0	0.4	44,991	16.8	26.3	25.5
Crosby	63	566	1,430	7.6	61.0	13.0	15.5	12,552	20,057	38,674	64.4	2.1	36,942	22.3	37.8	35.9
Culberson	0	0	420	3.6	70.4	9.0	5.1	11,891	16,763	33,125	67.2	1.4	37,825	22.1	35.6	33.9
Dallam	669	2,953	1,857	10.4	61.0	12.4	17.8	9,137	25,221	45,580	53.9	3.4	47,838	11.5	16.3	16.2
Dallas	515	3,130	685,116	12.5	44.2	30.1	4,398.4	8,876	29,810	53,626	46.4	6.4	56,732	14.8	22.1	21.8
Dawson	466	3,127	3,300	8.1	63.5	12.7	28.6	10,547	21,360	43,201	57.1	3.5	42,127	21.7	30.7	28.6
Deaf Smith	319	2,399	5,921	5.8	59.0	14.2	38.5	8,845	21,209	51,543	48.2	2.0	42,698	17.7	26.7	26.0
Delta	0	539	1,176	6.5	49.8	17.4	7.1	8,843	22,732	42,642	55.4	2.6	41,644	17.5	27.7	27.3
Denton	173	1,614	228,173	11.6	26.4	43.4	1,188.4	8,397	37,928	80,290	29.8	10.3	86,462	7.1	7.8	6.6
DeWitt	464	1,700	3,920	8.8	60.3	13.6	32.9	10,817	28,116	50,960	49.3	7.2	47,657	18.8	27.4	26.3
Dickens	557	1,160	446	6.3	50.8	15.2	5.3	13,955	24,171	43,088	57.3	3.0	38,702	21.2	28.8	26.9
Dimmit	27	1,633	3,073	3.4	66.4	10.1	22.9	9,363	17,939	31,384	68.1	2.8	35,696	31.2	42.6	39.7
Donley	87	1,307	923	8.5	43.1	18.9	6.1	10,309	23,212	44,429	54.3	3.0	41,867	19.9	32.8	31.0
Duval	585	1,949	2,681	4.0	65.4	8.7	28.9	11,129	19,085	35,443	64.1	2.3	33,495	28.6	40.1	38.7
Eastland	227	1,772	3,885	6.6	51.9	12.7	27.9	9,557	20,433	32,135	69.0	2.0	39,620	16.8	29.0	27.9
Ector	713	3,746	43,805	10.0	54.5	15.0	253.0	7,703	27,728	59,528	41.9	4.6	54,422	13.5	17.9	17.8
Edwards	214	964	205	0.0	54.6	20.6	6.6	11,937	28,968	48,462	51.3	4.4	35,164	22.6	38.2	38.1
Ellis	168	1,666	45,559	12.8	44.0	22.1	279.8	8,442	28,612	67,371	35.3	5.4	71,512	8.5	12.4	11.1
El Paso	364	1,713	258,209	7.7	47.2	22.2	1,611.6	9,134	19,950	43,244	56.6	2.3	44,120	21	29.6	29.0
Erath	151	1,713	14,227	7.2	39.3	27.8	48.2	8,456	23,511	47,013	53.1	2.2	48,230	15.8	19.3	18.6
Falls	128	740	3,584	5.0	60.5	12.1	23.6	10,575	17,755	38,834	61.8	1.0	35,988	27.6	32.9	32.0
Fannin	142	1,082	7,434	9.4	49.5	16.2	51.3	9,304	23,212	47,875	51.5	2.5	50,598	12.9	18.0	16.5
Fayette	258	1,145	5,058	11.4	55.3	18.1	35.5	9,580	30,405	56,941	44.7	5.7	56,320	10.8	16.7	16.1
Fisher	343	1,398	712	10.8	47.9	18.0	6.1	11,425	27,750	45,294	54.3	1.5	47,292	14.7	21.0	20.1
Floyd	466	1,745	1,453	4.5	52.0	17.4	14.1	11,257	24,347	48,767	51.6	2.2	41,390	20.2	34.0	30.7
Foard	0	0	316	1.6	54.6	16.7	2.7	12,613	26,034	50,000	50.0	3.0	35,007	18	30.7	28.0
Fort Bend	225	1,480	216,477	13.1	27.4	45.7	1,525.2	8,469	38,382	93,645	24.8	15.1	91,661	8	10.2	9.7
Franklin	273	1,007	2,426	16.1	45.1	19.8	15.1	9,113	23,642	43,967	55.1	3.5	44,358	14.8	24.2	21.7
Freestone	143	1,188	4,108	5.0	53.3	11.7	38.1	10,291	24,060	45,890	53.1	3.3	47,616	16.1	21.4	20.9
Frio	178	1,794	4,461	10.2	69.8	7.2	33.2	9,733	16,833	37,382	60.6	2.1	37,853	27.9	34.7	34.1
Gaines	97	1,145	5,088	24.4	68.4	11.2	44.7	12,579	22,656	58,167	43.0	3.0	52,138	15	22.0	21.8
Galveston	304	2,661	86,408	10.9	37.2	29.5	665.3	8,129	33,870	65,702	39.5	8.6	69,674	12	16.9	15.2
Garza	157	830	1,109	10.4	69.6	10.2	12.4	11,775	20,635	53,832	42.3	4.3	46,587	25.3	26.5	25.3
Gillespie	50	1,038	4,825	20.1	40.0	33.4	36.2	9,944	32,557	56,267	44.9	5.4	58,412	10.9	17.6	16.2
Glasscock	0	1,279	394	3.6	48.6	25.3	5.8	18,812	32,885	64,886	43.2	11.8	78,088	9.4	11.5	11.2
Goliad	211	1,215	1,634	3.4	45.5	17.6	13.8	9,830	30,075	56,737	45.2	4.9	52,403	15.2	24.7	24.3
Gonzales	542	1,698	4,760	7.5	62.6	13.2	41.9	9,969	23,635	47,516	52.2	3.0	45,052	16.7	26.2	26.7
Gray	502	4,082	5,220	9.1	52.3	12.8	37.5	8,830	23,457	48,314	50.9	1.8	46,599	17	24.0	21.9
Grayson	270	1,950	30,846	11.8	43.2	20.2	195.3	8,935	26,535	52,683	47.7	3.1	54,431	13.4	19.2	19.3
Gregg	466	3,628	31,185	12.4	44.4	20.4	222.3	9,172	25,144	47,970	52.1	3.1	47,208	16.5	23.6	22.8
Grimes	290	1,669	6,334	6.4	56.5	13.7	39.9	8,920	23,585	49,745	50.3	2.9	48,023	18	25.7	24.2

1. Data for serious crimes have not been adjusted for underreporting; this may affect comparability between geographic areas and over time. 2. Per 100,000 population estimated by the FBI. 3. All persons 3 years old and over enrolled in nursery school through college. 4. Persons 25 years old and over. 5. Elementary and secondary education expenditures. 6. Based on population estimated by the American Community Survey, 2013–2017.

STATE County	Personal income, 2017										Earnings, 2017		
	Total (mil dol)	Percent change 2016-2017	Per capita[1] Dollars	Rank	Wages and salaries (mil dol)	Supplements to wages and salaries, employer contributions (mil dol) Pension and insurance	Government social insurance	Proprietors' income (mil dol)	Dividends, interest, and rent (mil dol)	Personal transfer receipts (mil dol)	Total (mil dol)	Contributions for government social insurance (mil dol) From employee and self-employed	From employer
	62	63	64	65	66	67	68	69	70	71	72	73	74

TEXAS— Cont'd

STATE County	62	63	64	65	66	67	68	69	70	71	72	73	74
Caldwell	1,392	6.4	32,889	2,630	340	62	25	110	201	356	537	34	25
Calhoun	796	1.2	36,587	2,107	702	123	47	18	114	218	890	51	47
Callahan	530	3.7	38,029	1,879	98	18	7	26	92	143	148	12	7
Cameron	11,754	1.7	27,741	3,037	4,831	1,015	350	957	1,561	3,831	7,153	406	350
Camp	495	3.3	38,491	1,804	149	28	10	60	76	139	248	14	10
Carson	268	3.1	44,364	975	376	40	26	33	38	49	474	26	26
Cass	1,080	2.6	35,996	2,203	300	59	22	72	164	391	453	31	22
Castro	394	7.6	50,209	449	107	18	9	123	51	68	258	7	9
Chambers	2,148	3.6	51,832	381	900	139	60	74	232	279	1,173	66	60
Cherokee	1,790	1.9	34,257	2,454	564	121	40	139	297	540	864	50	40
Childress	212	3.6	29,965	2,933	98	24	6	9	38	64	138	7	6
Clay	443	2.8	42,522	1,200	57	13	4	21	70	106	95	7	4
Cochran	116	8.7	40,614	1,455	32	7	2	21	19	30	62	2	2
Coke	128	-0.1	38,586	1,792	27	6	2	2	24	41	37	3	2
Coleman	327	3.2	38,788	1,760	75	17	5	17	70	118	114	9	5
Collin	62,078	5.7	64,025	114	27,536	3,183	1,860	6,648	9,048	4,471	39,227	2,074	1,860
Collingsworth	114	8.4	38,186	1,848	38	7	3	2	22	36	50	3	3
Colorado	952	4.9	44,836	922	341	53	24	99	204	245	517	31	24
Comal	7,892	6.1	55,965	250	2,473	342	174	722	1,435	1,230	3,712	219	174
Comanche	541	6.2	39,842	1,582	131	26	10	71	96	157	238	14	10
Concho	88	0.7	32,328	2,709	34	6	3	2	22	34	45	3	3
Cooke	1,889	3.3	47,339	681	671	118	47	188	426	377	1,024	59	47
Coryell	2,465	2.9	32,904	2,628	795	158	52	88	487	581	1,093	62	52
Cottle	84	12.5	60,247	153	17	3	1	10	32	19	31	2	1
Crane	188	5.1	39,596	1,621	69	14	4	14	19	34	101	5	4
Crockett	131	-0.7	36,757	2,085	65	14	5	3	31	30	86	5	5
Crosby	204	23.7	34,530	2,411	60	11	5	8	32	78	84	5	5
Culberson	105	9.4	47,127	704	57	11	4	3	13	26	74	4	4
Dallam	393	5.3	54,562	294	179	24	14	117	45	55	334	15	14
Dallas	146,248	3.8	55,859	252	119,808	14,028	8,154	20,966	34,315	17,103	162,956	8,616	8,154
Dawson	472	14.8	36,857	2,062	172	37	12	69	80	129	289	14	12
Deaf Smith	784	2.1	41,634	1,314	300	50	22	203	101	163	575	22	22
Delta	184	-0.2	34,737	2,381	32	9	2	2	23	64	45	4	2
Denton	45,112	6.1	53,948	313	13,007	1,786	906	3,225	5,824	4,049	18,924	1,020	906
DeWitt	1,050	1.5	51,896	378	363	67	24	60	362	239	514	30	24
Dickens	71	6.3	32,006	2,751	22	5	2	1	15	26	29	2	2
Dimmit	334	-2.5	32,067	2,746	286	51	22	26	56	113	384	21	22
Donley	146	6.4	44,176	1,001	32	8	2	23	28	39	65	3	2
Duval	390	-0.7	34,579	2,404	130	30	9	-2	50	165	168	11	9
Eastland	1,036	13.6	56,294	241	359	64	26	108	372	235	557	32	26
Ector	6,417	7.4	40,851	1,425	4,223	563	291	439	855	1,054	5,516	301	291
Edwards	67	3.1	34,266	2,453	17	4	1	-3	24	24	19	2	1
Ellis	7,377	5.7	42,490	1,201	2,265	359	161	485	869	1,212	3,271	191	161
El Paso	29,063	3.0	34,582	2,402	13,931	2,932	1,062	2,007	4,794	6,760	19,933	1,062	1,062
Erath	1,579	6.1	37,624	1,930	615	121	43	228	292	329	1,006	49	43
Falls	565	2.8	32,392	2,704	136	36	9	22	93	195	203	14	9
Fannin	1,268	4.4	36,826	2,074	321	71	23	64	175	377	480	33	23
Fayette	1,234	4.0	48,833	554	383	67	27	82	320	288	559	36	27
Fisher	141	-0.7	36,259	2,156	39	9	3	-7	31	46	43	4	3
Floyd	229	18.2	39,067	1,710	67	14	5	35	34	69	122	6	5
Foard	46	3.6	37,809	1,911	12	3	1		10	19	15	1	1
Fort Bend	41,690	3.1	54,510	297	9,766	1,317	668	3,124	5,475	3,645	14,876	815	668
Franklin	413	5.6	38,351	1,817	130	20	10	63	72	109	223	13	10
Freestone	700	0.7	35,681	2,247	238	48	18	31	124	190	335	22	18
Frio	518	0.9	26,421	3,073	357	58	26	25	85	158	466	26	26
Gaines	758	11.4	36,750	2,087	331	57	24	169	90	115	580	28	24
Galveston	16,443	2.9	49,079	529	5,663	1,141	371	736	2,517	2,728	7,911	427	371
Garza	173		26,482	3,068	74	13	6	14	41	47	106	6	6
Gillespie	1,529	3.2	57,382	213	432	67	31	121	622	303	652	43	31
Glasscock	105	13.6	78,012	42	24	5	2	16	46	7	47	2	2
Goliad	309	0.0	40,890	1,419	51	11	3	5	70	79	71	6	3
Gonzales	860	6.5	41,154	1,386	294	55	21	160	189	203	530	24	21
Gray	936	5.5	41,781	1,291	392	70	27	95	210	201	584	31	27
Grayson	5,409	4.5	41,250	1,373	2,086	330	149	294	904	1,334	2,860	177	149
Gregg	5,437	0.8	44,073	1,013	3,635	509	272	400	1,042	1,279	4,817	276	272
Grimes	945	3.7	33,661	2,535	351	65	25	62	164	246	504	31	25

1. Based on the resident population estimated as of July 1 of the year shown.

Table B. States and Counties — Earnings, Social Security, and Housing

STATE County	Earnings, 2017 (cont.) Percent by selected industries									Social Security beneficiaries, December 2017		Supplemental Security Income recipients, 2017	Housing units, 2018	
	Farm	Mining, quarrying, and extractions	Construction	Manu-facturing	Information; professional, scientific, technical services	Retail trade	Finance, insurance, real estate, and leasing	Health care and social assistance	Govern-ment	Number	Rate[1]		Total	Percent change, 2010-2018
	75	76	77	78	79	80	81	82	83	84	85	86	87	88

TEXAS— Cont'd

STATE County	75	76	77	78	79	80	81	82	83	84	85	86	87	88
Caldwell	-0.2	2.8	14.6	5.3	D	8.5	4.4	12.6	19.3	7,480	177	1,079	15,098	9.7
Calhoun	-0.3	D	16.5	46	6.5	4.9	2.9	3.8	9.5	4,410	203	532	12,048	5.6
Callahan	-4.6	2.8	19	4.5	4.5	16.6	5.8	6.2	24.1	3,365	241	312	6,706	2.4
Cameron	0.9	0.1	4.3	4.7	3.8	8.4	4.9	20.3	27.8	65,705	155	22,537	152,353	7.4
Camp	8.2	D	19.6	D	D	6.3	6.4	9	13.1	2,985	232	473	5,790	2.4
Carson	4.4	D	4.4	D	1.4	1.5	D	D	4.8	1,175	195	52	2,800	0.6
Cass	3.4	1.4	8	22.9	D	5.5	3.7	D	19.5	8,285	276	1,126	14,626	1.7
Castro	53.6	0.8	0.9	1.1	D	2.4	4.3	0.9	12.7	1,250	159	133	3,176	0.3
Chambers	0.8	2.1	16.9	26.8	D	3.7	2.1	2.9	12.5	6,405	155	512	16,151	21.5
Cherokee	8.2	0.3	6.5	12.6	D	5.5	5	D	26.4	11,020	211	1,445	21,333	2.3
Childress	0.8	D	D	D	7.3	7.8	6	4.6	48.8	1,335	189	164	2,838	-1.6
Clay	2.7	2.5	7.4	4.7	D	7.8	D	D	29	2,660	255	160	5,262	2.1
Cochran	36.9	D	D	D	D	3.1	2	3.1	27	585	205	114	1,359	-0.1
Coke	-10.8	8.2	12.1	D	D	7.8	D	2.4	38.8	960	290	76	2,722	2.3
Coleman	-4.9	2.3	11.7	3.8	D	8.4	10.1	D	26.3	2,540	301	264	5,520	-0.4
Collin	0	1	6.3	8	19.1	7.3	14.7	10.2	9	106,265	110	8,063	377,338	25.4
Collingsworth	-3.4	D	D	D	5.1	6.1	D	D	22.8	630	211	69	1,594	-1.4
Colorado	2.1	3.4	16.2	22.3	D	6.1	4.4	D	12.3	5,270	248	482	10,696	1.6
Comal	-0.2	1.3	15.3	5	8	10.1	6.8	10	11.2	30,845	219	1,461	60,948	29.4
Comanche	16.4	0.3	6.1	3.1	4.5	8.3	4.6	D	16.9	3,670	270	343	7,359	2
Concho	-2.3	D	D	D	D	3.3	D	12.5	30.3	720	265	62	1,657	1.2
Cooke	-0.4	16.2	6	21.6	4	6.7	9.2	D	17	8,130	204	598	17,033	2.6
Coryell	-0.8	0.1	7.9	3.5	11.3	8.3	8.8	6.4	36.4	10,930	146	1,286	26,859	6.5
Cottle	28.4	0.5	D	0.1	D	6.1	D	4.6	22.1	440	317	46	946	-2.4
Crane	0.5	34	D	D	D	4.6	4.1	2.4	24.3	720	152	81	1,677	2.8
Crockett	-3.7	31.9	D	D	D	5.8	11	0.6	23.5	730	205	54	1,892	1.4
Crosby	9.5	D	D	D	D	15.9	D	8.3	27.4	1,350	229	172	2,902	0
Culberson	0.9	5.3	D	D	D	9.5	D	D	30.1	530	238	119	1,176	3.4
Dallam	14.1	0	13	13.5	4.1	6	6.9	D	5.2	970	135	85	2,950	4.4
Dallas	0	2.2	6.5	6.9	17.8	4.7	13.9	9.8	9.2	317,775	121	63,915	1,027,837	9
Dawson	16	12.1	3.4	1.5	2.1	12.3	4.7	D	27.1	2,460	192	396	5,163	-1.1
Deaf Smith	34	D	3.3	15	2	6.4	3.3	2.3	12.9	2,890	153	400	7,041	-0.5
Delta	-9.9	0.2	10.4	D	D	2.3	3.2	32.1	34.3	1,405	265	192	2,489	1.3
Denton	0.1	0.5	9.3	6.9	12.6	7	9.1	9.1	14.3	90,080	108	7,077	319,948	24.9
DeWitt	-1.4	14.6	7.8	12	D	5.5	7.5	4.4	24.5	4,600	227	490	9,240	0.7
Dickens		D	3.6	D	D	8.2	4.6	0.9	27	585	265	46	1,281	0
Dimmit	1.4	34	4.5	0.7	D	3.4	4.2	D	23.7	2,050	197	560	4,427	1.8
Donley	26.2	D	D	D	D	4.9	4.7	2.5	31.4	910	275	69	2,150	0.6
Duval	-4.8	19.3	D	D	D	2.6	1.2	11.4	37.7	2,565	228	642	5,626	1.9
Eastland		28	9.2	5.6	2.6	4.5	5.5	D	18.4	4,805	261	580	10,298	0.4
Ector	-0.1	21.1	12.4	6.8	3.7	6.2	5.3	5.9	13	20,425	130	3,419	58,680	10.6
Edwards	-30.9	D	D	D	D	12.2	D	6	43.5	565	289	71	1,626	1.3
Ellis	0.1	0.4	12.5	23.1	4.8	6.9	4.9	7.7	14.4	27,505	158	2,885	63,512	16.8
El Paso	0.1	0	5.3	5.4	4.9	7.6	5.4	10.5	36.7	130,330	155	29,700	299,638	10.8
Erath	10.3	1.2	9.9	10.1	D	8	4.9	8.6	21.2	6,590	157	569	18,407	8.3
Falls	-4	D	7	4.7	4.7	9.2	D	8.7	43.4	3,525	202	722	7,754	0.4
Fannin	-1.3	1.5	9.2	9.5	3.4	8.4	6	D	36.5	7,930	230	839	14,495	2.2
Fayette	-0.9	7.2	8.9	7.3	4.9	10	9.5	D	18.4	6,775	268	412	13,964	0.7
Fisher	-32.8	4.1	D	D	D	6.9	D	6.8	38.6	980	253	101	2,208	-0.3
Floyd	27.3	D	3.6	1.9	D	5.1	D	3.5	23.1	1,215	208	160	2,968	-1.2
Foard	-0.9	0.5	D	D	D	7.3	D	D	32.7	345	282	34	784	-0.6
Fort Bend	0	3.9	12.5	11.7	11.7	8.4	6.4	10	12	83,825	110	11,003	260,754	32.5
Franklin	12.6	D	6.7	D	D	3.7	4.1	19.5	10.8	2,480	230	179	5,868	1.7
Freestone	-0.7	21.2	5	2.5	5.2	5.3	3.3	D	22.3	4,245	216	431	9,476	2.3
Frio	2.5	23.7	9.2	2.2	D	4.4	2.6	D	19.9	2,865	146	708	5,983	2.3
Gaines	1.4	20.3	22.8	2.3	1.6	8.9	2.3	D	14	2,145	104	313	6,483	2.9
Galveston	0	1.4	8.1	11.6	6.3	6.7	7.4	6.7	29.9	55,810	167	6,759	148,274	11.9
Garza	-2	29.5	D	D	D	3.9	1.6	D	18.9	855	131	96	2,200	-1.7
Gillespie	-2.2	1.6	15.2	7.9	7.7	9.7	7.6	17.6	11.4	8,080	303	275	13,229	3.5
Glasscock	13.9	D	D	D	D	D	D	0.9	16.6	195	145	0	587	1.2
Goliad	-12.4	12	17	D	D	4.6	4.6	D	33.7	1,730	229	186	3,798	2.4
Gonzales	21.9	4.7	3.9	11.7	2.9	5.4	4.7	D	17.2	4,100	196	519	8,987	2.2
Gray	8.7	14	4.6	18.6	D	6	3.4	8.1	15.1	4,300	192	361	9,984	-1.7
Grayson	0.4	0.8	9.7	14.5	4.3	7.8	8.5	18.2	14.2	28,295	216	3,024	56,731	5.6
Gregg	-0.1	7.5	11.8	11.3	6.5	7.4	6	14.6	9.3	25,305	205	4,660	52,103	5.2
Grimes	-2.3	1.3	10.6	20.7	3.7	4.2	5.3	D	23.2	5,775	206	736	11,350	4

1. Per 1,000 resident population estimated as of July 1 of the year shown.

Items 75—88

Table B. States and Counties — Housing, Labor Force, and Employment

STATE County	Total	Percent	Median value[1]	With a mortgage	Without a mortgage[2]	Median rent[3]	Median rent as a percent of income[2]	Sub-standard units[4] (percent)	Total	Percent change, 2017-2018	Total	Rate[5]	Total	Management, business, science, and arts	Construction, production, and maintenance occupations
	89	90	91	92	93	94	95	96	97	98	99	100	101	102	103
TEXAS— Cont'd															
Caldwell	12,894	67.3	124,300	19.9	11.8	813	29.5	6.1	19,092	3	691	3.6	18,238	25.3	31.0
Calhoun	7,733	70.6	114,900	19.5	10.0	766	24.7	9.3	11,213	6.7	464	4.1	9,676	24.8	39.3
Callahan	5,291	82.3	76,500	19.1	12.1	720	22.5	2	6,023	1.8	202	3.4	5,128	24.9	35.1
Cameron	122,188	67.2	82,500	22.5	12.5	683	32.4	11.9	166,001	-0.3	10,235	6.2	153,938	28.2	21.1
Camp	4,730	70.7	83,600	18.8	12.0	695	29.5	4.3	4,990	-0.9	245	4.9	5,274	22.5	37.0
Carson	2,292	85.0	107,800	18.5	10.0	711	21.6	0.9	3,040	0.2	86	2.8	2,896	37.8	29.0
Cass	11,811	77.9	86,200	22.2	11.4	585	26.2	4.2	12,335	1.1	624	5.1	11,991	22.9	33.2
Castro	2,462	64.3	80,300	18.5	10.0	644	22.5	5.7	3,525	3.7	101	2.9	3,289	24.7	34.4
Chambers	13,320	82.8	171,500	18.2	12.9	889	23	3.6	19,157	1.1	1,036	5.4	16,713	36.1	34.7
Cherokee	17,885	73.6	98,200	20.4	12.4	684	26.8	6.9	20,979	0.9	863	4.1	20,526	28.9	30.2
Childress	2,282	55.0	81,000	26.0	13.7	749	25.7	0.3	2,950	1.3	75	2.5	2,515	31.8	32.0
Clay	4,076	85.4	87,200	19.2	11.6	669	27.6	2.7	4,945	0.7	157	3.2	4,373	30.6	28.6
Cochran	1,000	76.1	33,300	16.1	10.0	492	36.6	10	1,115	-1.7	47	4.2	1,189	25.7	49.4
Coke	1,574	71.2	81,800	19.9	12.3	548	32.6	1.3	1,454	3.7	49	3.4	1,462	41.3	29.5
Coleman	3,470	71.1	65,900	19.8	13.6	663	27.9	1.8	2,960	-3.6	118	4	3,310	33.0	35.9
Collin	323,905	65.6	265,300	20.4	11.3	1,225	26.6	2.5	545,243	2.4	18,052	3.3	474,671	52.7	10.9
Collingsworth	1,099	80.3	55,800	16.7	10.0	620	29.4	5	1,185	1.5	38	3.2	1,386	20.9	37.6
Colorado	7,603	82.1	116,700	18.7	11.7	690	24.7	4.5	9,680	-0.8	322	3.3	9,491	29.4	29.2
Comal	47,253	75.3	244,100	20.9	10.0	1,078	28.3	3.1	70,132	1.8	2,254	3.2	59,833	39.0	19.0
Comanche	5,107	78.4	89,600	19.8	12.3	517	22.2	5.3	5,385	1.4	196	3.6	5,454	29.6	34.2
Concho	791	71.3	109,800	18.4	12.5	654	28.8	2.3	1,120	-7.7	40	3.6	1,023	30.8	30.7
Cooke	15,185	68.9	144,700	19.1	11.5	782	27.1	4.5	19,182	1.6	591	3.1	18,724	29.2	28.8
Coryell	22,424	57.6	107,700	20.1	10.5	928	27.5	2.9	24,402	-0.1	1,010	4.1	23,306	29.8	21.4
Cottle	664	65.4	44,700	19.9	12.6	288	28.5	1.8	529	1.7	23	4.3	651	26.0	27.2
Crane	1,479	78.3	81,500	13.4	10.0	702	25.4	5.2	1,796	12.6	69	3.8	2,023	19.1	48.1
Crockett	1,411	72.8	80,600	15.5	10.0	526	24.5	6.3	1,645	-2.1	49	3	1,733	26.4	37.5
Crosby	2,064	68.6	57,500	18.1	12.8	614	24.7	6.3	2,566	0.7	116	4.5	2,519	30.0	30.1
Culberson	735	66.7	57,000	19.5	13.4	586	33.3	5.3	979	5.8	31	3.2	974	19.3	26.8
Dallam	2,432	59.6	77,000	20.5	10.0	693	19.1	4.2	4,075	0.3	83	2	3,501	20.9	39.8
Dallas	906,179	50.5	148,300	22.5	12.1	984	28.9	7.1	1,359,225	2.3	50,682	3.7	1,252,101	34.0	24.2
Dawson	4,339	71.1	66,400	17.9	11.6	571	26	3.1	4,590		198	4.3	4,968	25.0	36.2
Deaf Smith	6,118	65.0	88,000	19.6	10.4	763	22.5	4.8	8,474	1.4	238	2.8	8,619	27.7	41.0
Delta	2,035	77.2	73,100	20.9	11.1	565	33.7	1.3	2,460	-3.5	84	3.4	1,980	31.0	30.5
Denton	275,164	64.5	232,000	20.4	11.3	1,109	28.4	2.7	482,610	2.3	15,321	3.2	419,189	46.0	14.5
DeWitt	7,260	75.3	100,000	18.1	10.0	728	28.7	6.3	9,784	2	308	3.1	7,965	30.5	31.4
Dickens	832	71.5	54,200	17.5	12.5	488	16.9	4	672	-1.3	28	4.2	747	37.1	24.8
Dimmit	3,476	70.4	65,200	20.6	14.0	733	25	9.1	7,414	14.1	224	3	3,805	23.1	22.5
Donley	1,230	74.4	65,100	17.5	11.8	612	24.9	2.9	1,574	4.6	53	3.4	1,421	30.5	25.1
Duval	3,845	67.2	48,500	16.1	10.6	679	24	10.7	5,049	5	267	5.3	3,950	19.6	34.8
Eastland	6,437	74.8	59,800	21.0	12.6	566	20.5	2.3	8,724	9.7	294	3.4	6,910	28.7	30.3
Ector	51,475	66.0	120,800	19.3	10.0	971	24.6	6.8	85,132	8.2	2,289	2.7	72,576	23.4	35.0
Edwards	634	86.9	72,800	13.1	12.1	463	18.8	6.2	892	-1.7	25	2.8	888	14.0	26.8
Ellis	54,725	73.1	158,200	20.4	11.5	960	29.1	3.7	89,935	2.3	2,964	3.3	78,597	33.2	27.6
El Paso	263,200	61.6	116,600	22.8	11.4	790	29.8	6.1	359,136	1.3	15,221	4.2	341,350	30.1	22.0
Erath	13,827	63.7	128,300	20.6	10.4	785	32.2	3.9	20,784	0.4	639	3.1	19,076	32.1	26.9
Falls	5,405	72.7	63,000	20.0	12.6	517	29	5.3	6,668	0.2	257	3.9	5,774	23.0	37.7
Fannin	12,027	74.6	98,200	19.2	12.3	732	27.6	2.9	16,471	3.1	504	3.1	13,407	31.7	29.3
Fayette	9,298	81.2	158,700	17.9	11.3	742	21.7	2.9	12,606	0.1	356	2.8	11,626	22.3	32.7
Fisher	1,696	72.3	60,500	18.8	10.1	592	21.4	2.9	1,666	-2.3	55	3.3	1,728	32.8	30.8
Floyd	2,320	72.7	60,500	17.3	10.0	698	25.5	6	2,693	-0.4	141	5.2	2,444	30.0	37.3
Foard	562	80.2	47,400	24.1	11.5	517	16.2	2.8	591	-2.9	17	2.9	591	22.2	31.6
Fort Bend	222,331	78.1	233,300	21.1	11.1	1,297	27.9	3.5	382,102	1.6	15,180	4	339,159	50.4	14.5
Franklin	3,931	74.5	130,300	25.8	12.4	746	27.8	3.1	4,579	0.7	189	4.1	4,397	24.3	34.3
Freestone	7,232	74.8	86,100	20.5	11.5	672	23.2	2.8	6,573	-2.8	384	5.8	7,422	26.4	29.4
Frio	4,530	70.1	75,900	22.2	13.3	747	22.8	10.2	10,071	7.4	289	2.9	6,859	19.2	41.0
Gaines	5,716	76.3	111,000	19.6	10.0	697	19.6	5.9	9,439	2	241	2.6	8,134	28.6	41.0
Galveston	117,455	66.3	171,600	19.8	11.4	971	29.7	3.3	164,757	1.6	7,576	4.6	149,076	41.1	19.3
Garza	1,715	65.0	77,500	18.3	10.0	741	23.5	1.7	2,133	0.5	63	3	2,445	30.3	31.9
Gillespie	10,795	76.3	269,900	23.8	11.6	869	31.7	5.3	13,417	2	341	2.5	11,800	33.6	23.6
Glasscock	475	71.8	193,600	16.4	10.0	906	21.6	2.9	857	20.7	17	2	669	45.3	27.7
Goliad	2,755	81.9	130,900	15.1	10.0	648	24.4	3.6	3,305	0.8	126	3.8	2,994	29.4	33.9
Gonzales	7,018	68.7	92,900	19.2	10.0	638	27.1	11	9,552	1.8	290	3	8,939	19.5	39.8
Gray	7,971	75.2	71,700	17.0	10.4	746	27.2	3.3	8,181	-0.7	323	3.9	9,498	23.1	34.5
Grayson	47,550	67.0	116,600	20.3	12.0	814	27.2	3.6	63,488	2.4	2,061	3.2	57,373	31.1	25.6
Gregg	45,615	58.8	130,000	20.3	10.5	814	30.8	3.8	57,815	0.6	2,381	4.1	55,237	27.8	28.4
Grimes	8,980	77.8	110,100	21.4	10.3	657	26.9	5.6	11,108	1.9	459	4.1	10,403	23.3	36.4

1. Specified owner-occupied units.   2. A value of 10.0 represents 10 percent or less; a value of 50.0 represents 50 percent or more.   3. Specified renter-occupied units.   4. Overcrowded or lacking complete plumbing facilities.   5. Percent of civilian labor force.   6. Civilian employed persons 16 years old and over.

Table B. States and Counties — **Nonfarm Employment and Agriculture**

STATE County	Private nonfarm establishments, employment and payroll, 2016									Agriculture, 2017			
	Number of establishments	Employment						Annual payroll		Farms			Farm producers whose primary occupation is farming (percent)
		Total	Health care and social assistance	Manufacturing	Retail trade	Finance and insurance	Professional, scientific, and technical services	Total (mil dol)	Average per employee (dollars)	Number	Percent with:		
											Fewer than 50 acres	1000 acres or more	
	104	105	106	107	108	109	110	111	112	113	114	115	116

TEXAS— Cont'd

STATE County	104	105	106	107	108	109	110	111	112	113	114	115	116
Caldwell	604	6,878	1,969	723	1,058	189	114	203	29,502	1,517	47.9	2.8	37.2
Calhoun	453	8,339	806	3,079	1,061	176	586	510	61,128	290	44.1	16.6	45.7
Callahan	211	1,462	137	140	362	56	51	51	34,600	961	37.4	10.0	38.2
Cameron	6,376	108,580	35,817	4,259	18,647	3,399	3,413	2,906	26,761	1,418	74.3	6.3	34.1
Camp	222	2,521	388	198	437	114	30	106	41,964	484	45.5	1.4	42.1
Carson	127	781	23	D	184	37	23	30	38,312	331	19.3	34.7	45.1
Cass	502	5,770	854	1,666	824	226	110	210	36,480	1,081	39.1	2.0	39.7
Castro	159	1,043	D	44	176	57	89	36	34,730	411	7.3	38.9	54.1
Chambers	612	12,115	747	2,347	1,160	119	272	751	62,022	562	55.5	7.8	33.6
Cherokee	746	10,890	2,285	2,384	1,432	357	205	370	33,937	1,587	40.3	2.0	35.4
Childress	155	1,339	113	D	428	56	36	36	27,243	285	7.7	20.0	41.6
Clay	125	695	94	D	213	42	9	21	29,837	851	20.9	18.3	39.9
Cochran	46	254	101	D	61	D	D	8	30,756	286	5.6	41.6	45.9
Coke	55	262	NA	D	88	29	D	6	21,538	449	10.9	22.9	32.6
Coleman	201	1,451	345	100	262	84	35	40	27,467	976	14.3	16.1	40.7
Collin	22,620	388,842	50,360	18,243	51,551	48,319	39,109	23,771	61,134	2,706	74.3	1.4	28.2
Collingsworth	60	498	128	D	78	D	18	18	36,773	301	4.7	28.2	39.5
Colorado	544	5,956	850	1,552	946	179	139	228	38,281	1,773	37.2	5.4	32.9
Comal	3,475	46,645	5,954	3,030	7,113	965	1,825	1,832	39,272	1,068	54.4	5.3	32.6
Comanche	249	2,306	494	119	513	150	60	73	31,798	1,427	32.6	8.8	40.8
Concho	51	708	175	D	73	D	D	26	36,218	396	9.1	32.1	44.9
Cooke	900	12,684	1,040	3,116	1,982	412	236	535	42,185	2,284	49.7	4.1	35.4
Coryell	720	9,764	1,176	508	1,887	409	750	256	26,235	1,479	38.2	5.7	36.4
Cottle	26	109	D	D	51	21	D	3	28,679	154	2.6	29.9	31.9
Crane	86	970	150	D	122	12	11	53	54,991	30	30.0	53.3	34.7
Crockett	129	1,142	21	D	166	D	12	60	52,412	219	1.4	59.4	52.3
Crosby	97	615	161	D	125	26	8	30	48,205	343	5.2	36.2	44.6
Culberson	54	629	84	D	175	D	D	26	41,304	66	15.2	63.6	48.4
Dallam	220	1,809	43	61	282	79	67	63	34,826	340	2.4	50.9	52.0
Dallas	65,781	1,456,092	178,969	96,299	127,241	96,627	140,389	88,127	60,523	775	69.5	1.2	25.9
Dawson	274	2,475	268	112	674	125	64	89	35,965	386	11.7	34.2	50.8
Deaf Smith	395	5,467	528	1,648	844	198	187	221	40,340	562	13.5	43.4	49.0
Delta	54	788	632	NA	41	17	9	11	13,591	571	45.4	4.4	36.0
Denton	14,284	211,883	26,462	14,553	32,205	14,382	9,783	9,210	43,469	3,295	80.2	2.4	29.2
DeWitt	448	5,364	985	624	831	255	108	207	38,598	1,768	27.3	4.8	41.9
Dickens	42	243	15	NA	60	D	10	9	35,453	393	11.7	23.7	28.0
Dimmit	246	4,509	451	49	492	32	31	205	45,368	328	21.0	25.9	32.9
Donley	81	425	43	D	108	18	26	9	22,344	283	8.1	25.8	39.4
Duval	151	2,045	386	D	182	54	30	78	38,303	1,367	11.1	11.7	29.8
Eastland	425	5,476	784	579	831	147	1,039	221	40,424	1,198	22.5	7.4	36.5
Ector	3,584	57,465	6,976	3,311	8,324	1,506	1,389	2,780	48,383	275	68.7	14.5	28.2
Edwards	38	184	13	D	79	D	D	5	27,245	380	3.7	34.5	43.8
Ellis	2,825	42,063	4,061	9,938	6,008	910	890	1,660	39,458	2,551	57.5	3.7	31.8
El Paso	14,393	235,714	45,424	13,758	39,863	6,680	10,889	7,494	31,793	656	88.7	3.4	36.6
Erath	957	11,860	1,584	2,031	2,062	318	368	396	33,370	2,402	39.5	5.8	40.4
Falls	222	1,711	330	131	468	71	53	52	30,143	1,103	36.2	8.2	39.5
Fannin	470	4,992	1,263	622	964	163	112	175	35,149	2,255	45.8	3.3	33.0
Fayette	768	7,370	1,078	1,137	1,406	295	201	252	34,228	3,166	36.9	2.1	36.7
Fisher	72	541	111	D	73	46	18	22	41,030	486	9.7	25.7	36.1
Floyd	150	949	229	40	110	53	7	32	33,358	440	8.4	35.5	39.4
Foard	25	129	D	D	28	D	D	3	26,922	172	12.2	36.0	40.8
Fort Bend	12,668	160,048	26,424	13,004	27,699	5,186	10,273	6,902	43,127	1,155	52.6	5.5	35.4
Franklin	158	5,732	3,582	71	276	97	31	105	18,266	493	32.7	2.8	34.5
Freestone	341	3,504	580	174	469	127	90	140	39,851	1,459	36.5	6.1	40.9
Frio	320	5,340	634	63	722	153	63	232	43,410	663	25.5	18.4	38.0
Gaines	418	3,909	319	194	490	94	60	206	52,765	507	11.0	43.4	51.3
Galveston	5,761	85,769	15,271	6,006	13,750	4,097	4,548	3,397	39,612	633	70.8	2.4	30.0
Garza	125	1,237	164	D	184	27	8	44	35,491	237	13.1	31.6	34.2
Gillespie	977	9,292	1,691	728	1,612	314	352	310	33,322	2,079	38.4	8.9	32.2
Glasscock	30	206	NA	D	D	D	D	12	58,471	175	6.3	54.3	57.1
Goliad	117	755	93	D	87	22	28	31	41,121	1,255	32.3	5.4	34.5
Gonzales	408	4,999	739	1,277	757	170	102	188	37,627	1,612	26.9	8.7	42.4
Gray	567	5,965	821	649	1,048	186	193	245	41,118	348	23.0	26.4	31.1
Grayson	2,526	38,357	8,095	7,031	6,279	1,810	988	1,389	36,220	2,845	61.4	2.4	32.3
Gregg	4,057	64,947	10,903	8,735	9,509	2,108	2,722	2,680	41,270	541	65.6	2.8	28.2
Grimes	417	5,286	323	1,698	666	137	137	227	42,924	1,771	46.6	3.1	37.6

Table B. States and Counties — **Agriculture**

							Agriculture, 2017 (cont.)								
	Land in farms				Value of land and buildings (dollars)		Value of machinery and equiopmnet, average per farm (dollars)	Value of products sold:				Organic farms (number)	Farms with internet access (percent)	Government payments	
		Acres								Percent from:					
STATE County	Acreage (1,000)	Percent change, 2012-2017	Average size of farm	Total irrigated (1,000)	Total cropland (1,000)	Average per farm	Average per acre		Total (mil dol)	Average per farm (acres)	Crops	Livestock and poultry products			Total ($1,000)	Percent of farms
	117	118	119	120	121	122	123	124	125	126	127	128	129	130	131	132

TEXAS— Cont'd

STATE County	117	118	119	120	121	122	123	124	125	126	127	128	129	130	131	132
Caldwell	285	-8.1	188	0.7	67.9	718,250	3,821	57,287	53.6	35,358	27.0	73.0	4	75.2	1,191	5.7
Calhoun	190	2.9	654	2.3	48.2	1,401,219	2,144	113,299	32.1	110,845	66.3	33.7	6	80.3	1,781	37.9
Callahan	478	-15.2	497	0.2	85.5	861,252	1,732	60,872	31.2	32,508	9.7	90.3	NA	75.0	711	20.8
Cameron	271	-12.3	191	100.9	212.5	681,492	3,560	73,661	122.6	86,428	96.2	3.8	10	64.3	6,669	26.0
Camp	77	-1.3	160	0.6	20.8	525,814	3,294	76,458	114.2	235,934	1.4	98.6	NA	73.6	235	16.3
Carson	521	7.5	1,574	64.4	322.6	2,139,551	1,359	305,633	91.8	277,426	89.5	10.5	NA	78.2	9,238	65.3
Cass	177	5.7	164	0.2	35.1	384,391	2,345	60,321	53.4	49,439	7.7	92.3	2	70.3	424	13.9
Castro	555	1.2	1,350	121.8	394.6	1,863,235	1,380	600,576	1,121.6	2,728,944	8.2	91.8	NA	76.4	15,189	84.9
Chambers	205	-19.1	365	21.0	99.0	865,025	2,367	102,607	19.3	34,256	57.5	42.5	7	71.4	5,885	16.0
Cherokee	276	-8.6	174	1.0	58.3	539,484	3,107	74,929	115.7	72,900	57.5	42.5	2	72.1	49	1.1
Childress	444	0.1	1,559	8.7	121.4	1,442,095	925	112,358	27.2	95,565	72.4	27.6	NA	65.6	2,721	72.3
Clay	648	2.4	761	0.3	100.8	1,464,315	1,924	80,343	55.7	65,394	10.7	89.3	NA	75.6	2,054	29.7
Cochran	486	8.3	1,700	113.2	373.6	1,574,348	926	320,452	87.6	306,367	94.7	5.3	2	68.2	9,199	91.3
Coke	469	-3.1	1,045	0.7	43.0	1,005,986	962	63,144	7.8	17,459	16.0	84.0	NA	65.3	644	15.8
Coleman	672	-7.4	689	0.7	146.3	1,131,892	1,643	68,996	41.2	42,215	32.4	67.6	NA	73.2	2,521	35.7
Collin	281	-10.2	104	1.0	140.3	1,032,094	9,946	57,985	66.8	24,697	44.2	55.8	NA	82.0	2,401	4.8
Collingsworth	407	-17.7	1,353	25.8	168.0	1,370,944	1,014	183,807	39.7	131,980	78.0	22.0	1	70.8	8,813	74.8
Colorado	563	16.0	317	34.1	132.3	954,840	3,009	79,375	71.0	40,040	54.7	45.3	21	64.6	8,199	11.1
Comal	206	0.7	193	0.3	23.6	660,324	3,415	45,101	9.6	8,999	9.7	90.3	2	80.0	190	3.2
Comanche	487	-5.8	341	17.4	137.6	900,640	2,639	82,769	173.3	121,419	13.5	86.5	4	73.2	2,533	16.0
Concho	561	11.8	1,417	4.3	108.5	2,089,817	1,475	123,623	28.1	71,008	47.6	52.4	NA	71.5	2,775	57.3
Cooke	492	-2.3	216	0.9	135.6	712,860	3,307	67,174	53.8	23,568	23.8	76.2	4	78.2	2,342	14.8
Coryell	457	-1.3	309	1.4	92.1	805,175	2,606	70,764	36.3	24,527	22.5	77.5	2	76.3	1,112	11.1
Cottle	579	2.5	3,759	2.3	104.4	4,174,361	1,110	133,366	27.7	180,104	35.5	64.5	NA	66.9	1,829	80.5
Crane	244	2.1	8,137	D	0.2	6,902,732	848	106,427	D	D	D	D	NA	93.3	9	10.0
Crockett	1,534	-0.8	7,005	0.0	6.3	5,686,480	812	84,106	D	D	D	D	6	73.5	208	9.1
Crosby	551	-1.4	1,605	86.5	272.9	1,556,556	970	262,721	86.9	253,364	93.4	6.6	1	69.1	5,844	79.9
Culberson	1,504	-7.0	22,791	5.7	13.5	16,763,487	736	245,880	15.9	240,864	59.5	40.5	NA	72.7	313	15.2
Dallam	895	5.1	2,633	149.9	393.6	2,986,690	1,134	451,440	634.9	1,867,426	14.6	85.4	NA	77.4	15,216	82.4
Dallas	64	-23.6	83	0.5	26.1	668,126	8,097	54,512	29.8	38,427	87.0	13.0	NA	72.0	404	3.6
Dawson	536	-4.0	1,388	54.8	408.6	1,442,556	1,040	333,933	121.3	314,236	97.6	2.4	18	73.3	11,958	79.8
Deaf Smith	967	4.8	1,722	122.4	617.3	1,942,201	1,128	349,244	1,638.8	2,916,004	5.7	94.3	4	82.6	29,893	74.9
Delta	144	9.7	252	D	80.5	495,901	1,968	78,856	36.3	63,620	69.9	30.1	NA	71.5	1,843	30.6
Denton	359	-6.3	109	2.9	144.0	1,041,728	9,550	55,272	123.2	37,393	19.7	80.3	8	82.0	1,877	6.5
DeWitt	484	-9.8	274	3.5	50.8	840,718	3,072	74,495	38.7	21,881	17.4	82.6	NA	68.3	186	1.4
Dickens	543	-5.1	1,382	8.9	166.1	1,472,068	1,065	97,078	26.9	68,336	49.5	50.5	NA	70.7	2,200	54.7
Dimmit	484	-28.5	1,476	3.5	68.0	2,080,509	1,410	95,610	28.5	86,756	8.3	91.7	NA	61.0	84	4.6
Donley	593	1.4	2,096	17.1	57.2	1,813,922	865	112,440	94.2	332,707	14.6	85.4	NA	70.7	2,234	52.7
Duval	836	-12.9	612	2.0	45.4	1,037,873	1,697	39,468	11.0	8,045	5.9	94.1	NA	47.4	1,741	17.5
Eastland	490	-2.8	409	1.9	80.1	802,949	1,964	63,040	23.5	19,632	21.1	78.9	NA	68.4	1,837	14.6
Ector	558	30.1	2,029	0.9	1.9	2,350,073	1,158	63,273	3.4	12,298	7.6	92.4	NA	75.6	57	1.5
Edwards	1,013	4.5	2,667	0.4	12.5	3,121,016	1,170	65,091	10.9	28,768	3.0	97.0	NA	66.6	1,609	22.6
Ellis	473	-0.1	186	2.4	221.5	595,894	3,211	76,740	73.1	28,673	73.1	26.9	1	75.3	5,962	17.4
El Paso	143	-31.9	217	31.6	39.9	873,269	4,015	87,385	46.7	71,248	86.4	13.6	4	76.7	286	1.5
Erath	626	3.0	260	14.3	134.3	824,386	3,166	96,022	312.3	130,007	6.1	93.9	10	77.7	1,229	3.6
Falls	392	2.4	355	4.0	203.8	893,002	2,513	124,859	157.9	143,191	26.8	73.2	NA	73.2	3,201	21.8
Fannin	482	-6.2	214	4.9	212.4	614,054	2,873	70,196	86.3	38,267	50.8	49.2	NA	74.9	7,452	24.1
Fayette	522	6.0	165	1.5	99.8	664,110	4,032	55,919	47.4	14,966	22.5	77.5	NA	70.3	446	6.3
Fisher	478	-3.4	983	10.5	248.7	1,112,312	1,131	132,231	35.7	73,537	75.5	24.5	NA	65.8	2,874	65.0
Floyd	639	9.8	1,452	120.1	437.7	1,460,850	1,006	263,008	D	D	D	D	NA	68.2	12,373	91.4
Foard	440	19.5	2,557	1.1	92.4	2,854,518	1,116	110,669	14.9	86,860	24.8	75.2	NA	65.7	2,360	64.5
Fort Bend	279	-17.6	242	9.6	140.7	750,749	3,103	102,575	85.0	73,603	82.6	17.4	1	71.7	4,623	22.3
Franklin	103	-9.2	208	0.9	28.4	645,217	3,100	87,557	134.1	272,000	2.1	97.9	NA	74.8	208	5.5
Freestone	414	-1.7	284	1.3	55.7	727,956	2,565	71,717	68.1	46,697	6.8	93.2	NA	66.2	61	1.0
Frio	678	-4.9	1,023	48.6	90.9	1,889,823	1,848	103,474	124.4	187,703	56.1	43.9	NA	69.7	1,214	11.6
Gaines	858	10.7	1,692	197.0	680.0	1,955,071	1,155	389,035	188.8	372,373	93.9	6.1	33	73.6	31,166	82.6
Galveston	73	-18.3	116	1.1	17.0	612,200	5,299	53,747	9.2	14,586	48.6	51.4	2	69.0	722	3.8
Garza	416	-8.7	1,754	8.9	68.3	1,763,789	1,005	117,857	22.1	93,338	75.6	24.4	NA	67.1	1,005	46.0
Gillespie	680	4.3	327	2.8	73.9	993,949	3,039	49,491	31.2	15,013	22.5	77.5	1	75.6	1,244	11.3
Glasscock	496	14.4	2,836	39.7	180.3	2,604,656	919	515,993	50.6	289,400	93.7	6.3	NA	85.7	1,233	60.0
Goliad	380	-23.2	303	0.1	36.2	804,567	2,658	53,417	17.7	14,072	25.9	74.1	NA	70.3	991	5.7
Gonzales	614	0.7	381	1.5	58.5	1,211,682	3,180	96,128	560.8	347,909	6.9	93.1	1	68.5	478	4.0
Gray	483	-6.2	1,389	16.9	124.8	1,588,481	1,144	111,560	154.6	444,313	15.8	84.2	10	73.9	4,042	40.8
Grayson	430	-0.3	151	2.3	207.0	1,023,106	6,770	68,105	66.2	23,259	60.8	39.2	1	81.0	4,729	9.9
Gregg	58	20.1	107	0.3	14.5	602,572	5,649	51,338	4.1	7,584	21.7	78.3	NA	73.8	D	0.4
Grimes	341	-18.3	192	4.0	54.3	740,438	3,847	68,597	47.5	26,826	29.6	70.4	NA	74.5	79	1.1

Table B. States and Counties — Water Use, Wholesale Trade, Retail Trade, and Real Estate

STATE County	Water use, 2015		Wholesale Trade[1], 2012				Retail Trade[2], 2012				Real estate and rental and leasing,[2] 2012			
	Public supply water withdrawn (mil gal/day)	Public supply gallons withdrawn per person per day	Number of establishments	Number of employees	Sales (mil dol)	Average payroll (mil dol)	Number of establishments	Number of employees	Sales (mil dol)	Average payroll (mil dol)	Number of establishments	Number of employees	Sales (mil dol)	Average payroll (mil dol)
	133	134	135	136	137	138	139	140	141	142	143	144	145	146
TEXAS— Cont'd														
Caldwell	3.70	91.3	18	D	D	D	81	1,035	345.2	26.7	21	55	7.4	1.3
Calhoun	0.25	11.4	16	D	D	D	63	927	435.3	31.4	20	146	35.2	5.9
Callahan	0.25	18.4	7	32	11.7	1.0	38	330	157.0	10.5	8	D	D	D
Cameron	24.18	57.3	317	D	D	D	1,119	16,624	4,124.8	353.2	312	1,338	185.5	32.2
Camp	1.10	86.7	9	82	34.0	2.9	50	371	111.2	8.4	7	D	D	D
Carson	9.00	1,507.8	7	D	D	D	20	150	57.4	2.7	1	D	D	D
Cass	1.05	34.6	18	D	D	D	88	883	218.4	18.4	18	33	5.0	0.7
Castro	1.06	138.5	12	142	117.2	6.2	33	185	55.0	3.6	8	16	2.9	0.3
Chambers	1.59	40.9	32	407	138.9	18.5	85	588	283.2	13.7	22	68	37.5	3.4
Cherokee	6.31	122.4	31	D	D	D	132	1,438	383.2	31.8	29	60	8.8	1.6
Childress	0.00	0.0	3	D	D	D	29	370	90.4	7.3	4	D	D	D
Clay	6.30	608.1	3	D	D	D	28	226	88.8	6.4	5	D	D	D
Cochran	0.40	135.5	3	D	D	D	12	68	50.2	1.7	NA	NA	NA	NA
Coke	0.37	114.3	2	D	D	D	14	66	32.4	1.6	NA	NA	NA	NA
Coleman	1.31	157.1	7	48	23.3	2.1	32	259	68.2	5.0	10	15	1.6	0.4
Collin	3.04	3.3	817	13,530	18,366.8	1,074.2	2,433	44,931	14,623.9	1,209.9	928	6,910	1,363.0	316.6
Collingsworth	0.52	170.8	5	D	D	D	14	74	15.8	1.6	NA	NA	NA	NA
Colorado	2.94	140.9	32	262	151.7	9.7	101	905	256.5	21.3	18	194	49.0	7.9
Comal	16.70	129.4	123	D	D	D	380	5,498	1,894.5	147.7	165	800	131.4	29.0
Comanche	0.04	3.0	22	D	D	D	49	430	138.1	10.2	9	27	1.9	0.7
Concho	0.33	80.9	1	D	D	D	12	73	17.1	1.1	1	D	D	D
Cooke	4.19	106.8	46	D	D	D	145	1,787	543.4	43.4	30	102	21.5	3.1
Coryell	0.21	2.8	11	D	D	D	120	1,704	493.6	36.2	37	112	14.3	3.0
Cottle	0.21	147.3	NA	NA	NA	NA	5	44	11.6	1.0	NA	NA	NA	NA
Crane	1.41	279.3	4	23	16.9	1.3	12	109	30.2	2.0	2	D	D	D
Crockett	0.96	258.8	4	36	36.3	2.3	19	181	72.9	4.7	3	D	D	D
Crosby	1.51	252.6	8	D	D	D	19	133	35.8	2.8	2	D	D	D
Culberson	0.81	362.3	1	D	D	D	17	247	136.7	4.1	2	D	D	D
Dallam	2.05	287.9	20	354	394.1	14.3	23	203	89.8	5.8	5	D	D	D
Dallas	334.54	131.0	3,657	67,700	80,605.0	4,255.0	7,518	112,656	35,957.9	3,151.9	3,490	32,478	7,691.3	1,679.2
Dawson	0.51	37.7	21	104	78.5	4.8	43	659	316.8	19.0	7	D	D	D
Deaf Smith	4.25	224.3	34	D	D	D	66	747	275.8	17.7	14	53	4.5	1.0
Delta	5.37	1,029.3	3	17	16.3	0.6	14	33	11.7	0.6	2	D	D	D
Denton	31.52	40.4	513	8,395	16,900.0	539.7	1,625	26,041	8,274.0	645.1	582	3,180	655.5	129.7
DeWitt	2.81	135.1	14	213	124.9	11.4	61	667	220.2	16.2	13	195	52.1	10.3
Dickens	0.10	45.3	NA	NA	NA	NA	9	57	11.9	1.0	2	D	D	D
Dimmit	1.69	153.9	6	191	174.6	13.1	28	446	142.6	11.2	9	35	3.5	0.9
Donley	0.38	108.6	1	D	D	D	20	113	27.9	1.9	6	9	1.7	0.4
Duval	1.21	106.3	9	74	24.8	2.5	29	240	78.6	4.7	3	29	6.0	1.0
Eastland	0.68	37.4	12	D	D	D	81	807	314.0	19.2	19	34	4.6	0.9
Ector	0.64	4.0	298	4,659	3,608.8	330.5	451	7,286	2,711.7	218.7	176	1,482	604.9	101.9
Edwards	0.20	105.6	NA	NA	NA	NA	7	83	21.7	2.2	2	D	D	D
Ellis	15.24	93.1	113	D	D	D	360	5,007	1,459.4	115.4	122	381	66.0	10.7
El Paso	114.33	136.8	952	D	D	D	2,322	34,934	9,180.6	753.5	699	3,143	617.3	108.0
Erath	2.21	53.7	35	D	D	D	172	1,831	535.2	41.5	40	111	15.8	2.8
Falls	2.29	133.6	9	D	D	D	52	419	97.5	8.4	5	19	3.9	0.9
Fannin	2.60	77.2	11	D	D	D	80	924	281.9	24.3	12	121	8.9	3.1
Fayette	2.56	102.0	34	D	D	D	125	1,134	368.6	28.5	32	109	20.4	3.3
Fisher	0.02	5.2	2	D	D	D	13	70	15.6	1.4	1	D	D	D
Floyd	0.41	69.5	12	D	D	D	22	131	31.5	2.5	1	D	D	D
Foard	0.01	8.2	1	D	D	D	7	31	7.4	0.5	NA	NA	NA	NA
Fort Bend	55.86	78.0	579	5,593	6,110.2	302.2	1,423	23,132	7,147.2	561.9	457	1,521	428.0	61.4
Franklin	2.77	260.1	4	16	5.1	0.7	27	269	105.9	6.1	9	16	2.1	0.3
Freestone	2.10	106.6	13	168	127.5	9.6	63	498	221.3	11.3	12	102	22.6	5.2
Frio	2.72	144.7	13	D	D	D	54	619	250.4	12.7	11	30	6.4	1.2
Gaines	8.21	409.5	27	374	362.2	25.9	45	498	108.9	10.3	12	22	3.8	0.7
Galveston	0.23	0.7	197	1,701	1,933.8	83.5	876	11,165	3,523.0	294.5	283	1,422	252.3	50.3
Garza	4.70	732.7	4	D	D	D	21	203	58.5	3.4	5	13	4.1	0.6
Gillespie	2.13	82.0	33	D	D	D	167	1,490	327.8	33.7	39	182	24.1	6.5
Glasscock	0.00	0.0	2	D	D	D	1	D	D	D	NA	NA	NA	NA
Goliad	0.34	45.1	3	13	3.3	0.3	15	128	41.0	2.0	2	D	D	D
Gonzales	29.05	1,412.0	20	277	228.2	13.1	72	770	238.6	15.7	9	15	3.4	0.5
Gray	1.24	53.4	31	447	1,065.5	31.3	100	1,082	314.8	25.0	30	118	23.7	4.8
Grayson	21.61	172.2	100	905	906.6	36.6	417	5,685	1,620.2	137.9	109	327	48.9	8.6
Gregg	7.13	57.4	252	3,592	2,395.6	194.3	664	9,190	2,639.8	233.0	199	1,220	411.8	62.5
Grimes	2.22	80.7	19	195	189.0	9.5	67	713	213.1	16.7	14	44	5.1	1.2

1   Merchant wholesalers, except manufacturers' sales branches and offices.   2. Employer establishments.

Table B. States and Counties — Professional Services, Manufacturing, and Accommodation and Food Services

STATE County	Professional, scientific, and technical services, 2012				Manufacturing, 2012				Accommodation and food services, 2012			
	Number of establishments	Number of employees	Sales (mil dol)	Average payroll (mil dol)	Number of establishments	Number of employees	Receipts (mil dol)	Annual payroll (mil dol)	Number of establishments	Number of employees	Receipts (mil dol)	Annual payroll (mil dol)
	147	148	149	150	151	152	153	154	155	156	157	158
TEXAS— Cont'd												
Caldwell	32	108	6.7	2.2	19	699	153.4	24.3	59	740	41.1	10.5
Calhoun	27	D	D	D	19	3,274	11,074.5	304.2	61	619	32.9	8.2
Callahan	11	49	6.8	2.1	10	126	D	4.9	19	D	D	D
Cameron	488	2,359	258.4	81.1	204	4,414	1,709.6	D	660	12,582	635.1	171.7
Camp	9	25	4.5	1.4	8	202	D	8.3	8	D	D	D
Carson	6	D	D	D	3	D	D	D	10	D	D	D
Cass	28	135	10.1	3.9	23	1,257	D	66.0	43	495	18.8	4.9
Castro	12	107	10.4	4.1	7	42	D	1.9	12	77	3.1	0.8
Chambers	32	190	29.1	10.1	30	2,135	D	184.1	54	876	48.7	12.2
Cherokee	56	277	48.0	12.9	66	2,711	458.5	93.6	58	828	39.4	10.4
Childress	11	43	5.0	1.2	NA	NA	NA	NA	26	344	16.6	4.0
Clay	6	D	D	D	NA	NA	NA	NA	7	D	D	D
Cochran	4	5	0.5	0.1	NA	NA	NA	NA	2	D	D	D
Coke	3	D	D	D	NA	NA	NA	NA	6	D	D	D
Coleman	20	35	4.3	1.0	10	168	D	7.2	20	D	D	D
Collin	3,138	D	D	D	419	18,588	8,652.9	1,309.7	1,620	34,192	1,892.3	540.8
Collingsworth	5	D	D	D	NA	NA	NA	NA	4	35	1.2	0.3
Colorado	37	88	11.5	3.5	37	1,597	556.6	78.7	44	578	33.4	7.4
Comal	304	1,340	188.4	58.3	110	3,244	960.3	134.7	318	5,723	304.9	80.1
Comanche	24	85	10.6	3.7	7	131	D	5.3	19	D	D	D
Concho	2	D	D	D	4	27	D	D	5	D	D	D
Cooke	65	223	25.4	8.9	57	2,953	999.7	133.0	71	1,325	61.6	16.6
Coryell	69	780	88.1	36.5	21	293	D	12.4	80	1,316	60.7	15.5
Cottle	NA	NA	NA	NA	NA	NA	NA	NA	4	D	D	D
Crane	5	24	2.3	1.0	NA	NA	NA	NA	6	D	D	D
Crockett	5	14	0.8	0.3	NA	NA	NA	NA	19	269	14.2	2.8
Crosby	3	D	D	D	3	28	D	1.0	5	D	D	D
Culberson	1	D	D	D	NA	NA	NA	NA	15	174	9.5	2.4
Dallam	14	D	D	D	7	57	D	2.4	20	249	13.8	3.2
Dallas	8,837	125,146	23,867.3	10,053.0	2,347	94,078	37,035.6	4,801.6	5,059	107,611	6,753.1	1,887.8
Dawson	18	D	D	D	15	121	22.0	5.7	27	335	17.8	4.1
Deaf Smith	28	224	25.1	9.5	25	1,469	1,084.2	59.8	27	D	D	D
Delta	4	D	D	D	NA	NA	NA	NA	4	D	D	D
Denton	1,626	8,428	1,246.8	446.6	366	12,933	6,886.9	651.8	1,117	22,142	1,138.8	307.1
DeWitt	37	121	14.8	4.8	18	594	D	16.1	51	440	27.3	6.2
Dickens	4	D	D	D	NA	NA	NA	NA	5	36	1.7	0.4
Dimmit	8	D	D	D	4	84	11.2	2.7	30	399	32.8	5.5
Donley	10	D	D	D	NA	NA	NA	NA	9	103	4.1	1.2
Duval	7	56	6.4	1.4	NA	NA	NA	NA	17	75	5.7	1.0
Eastland	28	365	51.8	21.6	20	511	D	20.9	46	530	24.9	6.6
Ector	227	1,832	205.4	80.1	251	4,756	1,706.3	265.7	261	6,150	389.0	94.0
Edwards	2	D	D	D	NA	NA	NA	NA	5	D	D	D
Ellis	179	D	D	D	160	8,301	4,129.7	407.5	207	3,753	177.7	49.5
El Paso	1,201	D	D	D	504	D	13,643.2	D	1,476	28,733	1,384.4	375.2
Erath	68	324	32.8	11.9	40	2,463	D	114.6	98	1,682	71.4	18.8
Falls	8	24	6.4	0.9	8	90	D	5.1	15	D	D	D
Fannin	30	130	10.3	3.3	27	606	135.7	20.3	38	D	D	D
Fayette	64	201	21.8	7.0	39	951	314.0	38.6	74	925	44.5	11.8
Fisher	4	D	D	D	NA	NA	NA	NA	6	D	D	D
Floyd	7	17	1.1	0.4	7	38	11.4	1.8	10	46	2.0	0.4
Foard	1	D	D	D	NA	NA	NA	NA	3	11	0.6	0.1
Fort Bend	1,505	10,000	1,749.9	911.6	342	13,045	4,791.5	722.0	889	16,733	885.3	244.6
Franklin	13	29	2.5	0.8	NA	NA	NA	NA	14	D	D	D
Freestone	28	68	8.2	2.7	12	222	D	7.9	30	549	25.0	6.5
Frio	13	68	4.0	1.7	3	50	D	2.2	40	449	34.2	6.5
Gaines	15	72	7.0	2.8	17	158	31.9	7.8	27	D	D	D
Galveston	541	6,889	778.8	347.9	154	6,236	41,294.9	613.6	646	14,121	763.3	212.4
Garza	6	9	0.8	0.2	NA	NA	NA	NA	9	D	D	D
Gillespie	71	D	D	D	56	544	114.7	20.7	104	1,472	72.7	22.9
Glasscock	2	D	D	D	NA	NA	NA	NA	1	D	D	D
Goliad	14	25	3.3	1.5	4	69	D	D	16	109	5.7	1.6
Gonzales	39	106	10.9	3.6	23	1,456	554.5	52.5	38	473	24.6	5.5
Gray	46	413	65.2	27.6	21	927	453.0	52.5	40	816	35.0	8.9
Grayson	227	844	99.0	32.7	112	6,886	2,574.9	288.3	224	4,305	200.2	57.1
Gregg	382	2,759	357.5	143.4	176	9,075	3,582.7	486.9	322	6,608	307.4	86.3
Grimes	26	142	16.1	5.5	37	2,617	1,501.4	138.9	34	323	20.3	4.7

Table B. States and Counties — Health Care and Social Assistance, Other Services, Nonemployer Businesses, and Residential Construction

STATE County	Health care and social assistance, 2012				Other services, 2012				Nonemployer businesses, 2016		Value of residential construction authorized by building permits, 2018	
	Number of establish-ments	Number of employees	Receipts (mil dol)	Annual payroll (mil dol)	Number of establish-ments	Number of employees	Receipts (mil dol)	Annual payroll (mil dol)	Number	Receipts (mil dol)	New construction ($1,000)	Number of housing units
	159	160	161	162	163	164	165	166	167	168	169	170
TEXAS— Cont'd												
Caldwell	65	1,279	93.7	46.7	33	106	11.9	3.0	2,869	123.1	77,335	478
Calhoun	34	582	44.8	17.9	34	244	28.4	8.8	1,355	53.4	12,616	57
Callahan	11	118	6.0	2.5	8	40	2.8	0.9	1,206	46.6	1,407	16
Cameron	1,003	31,018	1,911.3	844.7	402	2,159	163.6	44.6	31,083	1,156.6	173,151	1,487
Camp	22	459	41.0	13.1	9	D	D	D	817	33.6	1,005	13
Carson	4	D	D	D	8	D	D	D	423	12.8	383	2
Cass	46	1,096	63.5	29.2	37	186	16.9	4.8	1,877	77.5	1,217	15
Castro	5	165	14.0	5.2	14	49	7.4	1.4	462	22.2	280	1
Chambers	31	D	D	D	28	104	9.1	2.5	2,647	108.0	97,396	593
Cherokee	83	2,521	179.2	87.3	42	171	15.1	3.9	3,140	130.1	1,670	16
Childress	20	360	33.3	12.4	11	27	2.9	0.6	378	14.8	0	0
Clay	11	D	D	D	7	D	D	D	847	38.2	5,393	52
Cochran	9	96	6.9	2.8	3	D	D	D	161	5.8	0	0
Coke	1	D	D	D	4	D	D	D	261	7.8	0	0
Coleman	14	344	22.6	8.2	14	D	D	D	756	36.0	0	0
Collin	2,690	35,757	4,766.3	1,665.7	1,036	7,810	1,154.4	276.8	89,459	4,997.5	3,921,637	15,786
Collingsworth	5	D	D	D	5	16	0.8	0.1	226	6.8	0	0
Colorado	43	1,165	92.4	37.7	35	128	10.9	2.8	1,797	74.2	2,305	23
Comal	305	5,472	497.2	202.0	218	1,821	94.9	50.8	13,751	737.2	520,086	2,811
Comanche	19	466	32.6	13.3	19	46	3.3	0.9	1,046	42.3	550	13
Concho	6	141	10.5	4.7	2	D	D	D	222	7.4	0	0
Cooke	84	1,135	100.8	41.5	55	411	37.5	13.7	3,407	173.1	12,531	55
Coryell	57	1,136	70.1	30.9	75	360	29.2	7.8	2,963	118.3	31,992	248
Cottle	4	46	1.3	0.7	1	D	D	D	138	3.2	0	0
Crane	9	167	13.4	6.2	3	D	D	D	337	12.0	30	1
Crockett	6	35	2.6	1.3	5	25	2.1	0.5	322	11.5	NA	NA
Crosby	10	157	9.6	4.0	6	D	D	D	347	11.9	15	1
Culberson	4	D	D	D	2	D	D	D	208	10.2	650	7
Dallam	10	D	D	D	21	D	D	D	545	39.1	2,427	18
Dallas	6,754	155,579	19,683.2	7,652.7	3,427	32,368	4,510.7	1,244.5	233,530	12,770.6	2,915,649	18,123
Dawson	14	378	42.6	10.5	23	79	6.2	1.7	650	28.3	0	0
Deaf Smith	21	505	39.5	16.0	37	174	17.5	3.8	1,290	60.3	390	2
Delta	6	299	6.7	3.1	5	16	1.3	0.2	380	11.7	699	3
Denton	1,462	21,835	2,473.8	893.3	743	4,951	497.3	145.7	71,031	3,520.0	2,224,738	8,479
DeWitt	39	D	D	D	34	191	31.9	6.0	1,475	61.7	950	9
Dickens	5	D	D	D	3	D	D	D	167	5.2	NA	NA
Dimmit	24	419	45.1	13.0	19	D	D	D	695	23.3	0	0
Donley	9	99	4.8	2.3	8	20	2.5	0.6	304	10.7	0	0
Duval	19	351	14.5	9.0	6	D	D	D	832	20.5	NA	NA
Eastland	53	885	45.2	21.2	37	132	11.4	3.1	1,422	57.4	1,440	11
Ector	293	7,384	823.7	297.6	250	2,276	340.1	83.5	11,316	541.5	145,006	740
Edwards	3	13	0.6	0.1	3	D	D	D	225	10.1	NA	NA
Ellis	259	3,610	326.6	125.6	170	786	71.1	18.6	14,234	693.1	487,926	2,458
El Paso	1,523	D	D	D	907	5,672	464.4	129.3	59,033	2,522.9	494,196	2,416
Erath	75	1,839	152.9	56.8	73	381	40.5	9.2	3,330	160.9	12,207	199
Falls	27	470	42.9	13.7	18	44	2.8	0.9	913	42.7	407	4
Fannin	49	1,211	128.3	49.1	34	122	12.5	2.5	2,422	102.4	4,171	43
Fayette	64	D	D	D	51	278	22.1	6.8	2,433	98.3	1,609	16
Fisher	8	129	9.4	4.2	7	18	2.1	0.4	241	6.5	NA	NA
Floyd	15	265	18.3	7.7	14	37	3.9	0.9	379	11.8	0	0
Foard	5	D	D	D	3	D	D	D	117	4.6	NA	NA
Fort Bend	1,490	18,644	1,809.7	648.0	566	3,481	366.9	101.0	65,167	3,016.7	722,396	9,023
Franklin	21	3,787	85.5	42.1	18	109	7.1	1.7	818	40.3	1,171	6
Freestone	29	631	45.3	15.7	26	88	10.2	1.9	1,248	47.2	253	5
Frio	31	786	42.6	16.4	16	D	D	D	1,037	33.9	873	11
Gaines	15	300	29.9	10.0	31	D	D	D	1,879	137.6	650	1
Galveston	556	12,280	1,211.2	495.9	419	2,455	368.2	73.9	23,029	948.5	521,940	2,201
Garza	11	177	9.3	4.4	4	11	2.0	0.2	373	16.2	195	1
Gillespie	84	1,611	138.5	66.4	53	269	26.4	6.4	3,645	175.6	11,905	60
Glasscock	NA	NA	NA	NA	1	D	D	D	133	5.8	NA	NA
Goliad	10	107	4.5	1.8	7	10	0.4	0.1	573	19.4	0	0
Gonzales	31	734	49.2	22.2	30	89	8.6	2.2	1,301	55.4	3,904	20
Gray	58	879	87.3	31.7	45	170	19.9	5.0	1,354	55.7	675	2
Grayson	381	9,105	809.1	337.4	139	834	81.0	27.5	9,935	497.1	123,504	757
Gregg	435	10,345	1,323.8	420.7	246	1,979	256.7	80.9	9,684	465.4	33,814	243
Grimes	23	D	D	D	18	D	D	D	2,112	90.5	13,250	106

Table B. States and Counties — Government Employment and Payroll, and Local Government Finances

STATE County	\[Government employment and payroll, 2012\] Full-time equivalent employees	March payroll (dollars)	March payroll (percent of total) Administration, judicial, and legal	Police and corrections	Fire protection	Highways and transportation	Health and welfare	Natural resources and utilities	Education and libraries	\[Local government finances, 2012 — General revenue\] Total (mil dol)	Intergovernmental (mil dol)	Taxes Total (mil dol)	Per capita[1] (dollars) Total	Property
	171	172	173	174	175	176	177	178	179	180	181	182	183	184
TEXAS— Cont'd														
Caldwell	1,295	4,627,444	7.7	8.7	1.9	2.0	2.0	4.0	73.2	94.8	42.5	38.1	983	834
Calhoun	989	2,883,600	7.4	10.3	2.1	7.4	2.5	3.0	65.2	113.6	11.0	59.8	2,767	2,477
Callahan	610	1,550,184	5.1	6.1	0.1	2.1	0.9	3.3	80.5	36.2	16.2	14.8	1,095	992
Cameron	21,552	67,816,703	3.9	8.4	2.8	2.4	1.6	5.2	74.0	1,662.8	982.8	420.5	1,012	795
Camp	508	1,428,009	4.7	3.7	0.0	2.7	0.0	6.7	81.7	31.5	14.9	13.1	1,056	885
Carson	384	1,061,435	13.7	2.8	0.0	2.8	2.7	4.8	64.8	23.9	6.1	15.1	2,453	2,374
Cass	1,554	4,198,540	6.2	6.2	1.2	1.7	13.0	3.1	67.7	95.7	40.0	32.1	1,064	938
Castro	547	1,382,117	5.7	6.3	0.0	3.1	22.6	2.8	59.3	40.7	18.5	9.6	1,182	1,099
Chambers	1,626	5,773,846	8.8	6.1	0.0	3.1	10.0	6.3	64.8	164.5	34.4	100.6	2,780	2,551
Cherokee	1,869	5,488,563	6.6	9.7	2.3	2.5	5.7	2.1	69.7	129.7	67.3	48.0	938	770
Childress	583	1,738,210	4.7	11.1	1.6	1.8	46.8	4.4	29.0	62.7	9.4	6.1	867	753
Clay	559	1,694,976	3.7	2.8	0.0	4.0	14.3	8.9	63.3	47.0	12.1	16.9	1,605	1,445
Cochran	322	904,022	9.5	5.0	0.0	3.0	15.4	3.4	63.0	25.0	7.6	15.4	5,071	4,948
Coke	281	838,152	5.9	2.3	0.0	2.1	28.4	5.7	54.6	19.7	5.9	9.5	2,954	2,830
Coleman	629	1,691,631	4.4	5.0	0.9	13.7	19.1	6.3	48.7	34.6	18.7	11.3	1,301	1,096
Collin	28,433	113,769,771	4.6	8.7	4.4	3.5	1.7	4.9	69.6	3,611.2	681.0	1,995.2	2,390	2,038
Collingsworth	212	542,831	8.4	5.4	0.0	4.5	10.4	2.8	67.4	13.8	5.2	4.4	1,449	1,266
Colorado	861	2,596,959	7.5	9.0	0.0	6.1	1.1	3.8	71.4	68.4	17.2	35.5	1,716	1,501
Comal	4,722	16,455,274	5.9	10.7	5.6	2.4	1.7	4.9	65.1	413.5	81.4	279.4	2,443	2,055
Comanche	808	2,419,843	5.0	9.4	3.7	2.4	31.9	1.8	45.5	44.9	19.7	15.0	1,088	940
Concho	164	494,362	12.1	5.4	0.0	4.2	27.0	5.6	44.3	14.7	3.5	6.1	1,522	1,335
Cooke	2,150	7,756,968	4.6	7.0	2.3	2.2	22.1	3.1	58.0	192.9	53.2	71.4	1,846	1,489
Coryell	2,637	8,819,482	4.6	7.6	1.9	0.9	12.3	2.8	67.6	181.4	80.4	52.0	674	538
Cottle	98	244,407	17.9	5.3	0.0	6.5	0.0	11.3	51.6	5.8	2.0	2.8	1,867	1,769
Crane	326	1,145,731	9.6	10.7	0.0	1.4	1.7	18.9	57.2	40.3	6.9	31.6	6,922	6,690
Crockett	357	1,200,438	6.5	5.5	0.5	4.8	18.8	4.6	54.0	42.3	5.4	32.0	8,555	8,552
Crosby	396	1,113,076	6.6	6.1	0.0	1.6	0.7	8.5	76.2	24.3	14.0	7.8	1,271	1,153
Culberson	191	571,285	13.3	8.3	0.0	6.0	1.7	9.4	60.5	20.8	4.5	8.8	3,852	3,344
Dallam	459	1,265,633	7.6	10.7	0.5	2.5	1.7	3.2	73.1	27.7	8.8	15.1	2,154	1,701
Dallas	105,099	440,691,940	4.7	11.6	5.3	7.3	14.2	4.5	50.8	12,510.2	3,260.1	5,736.3	2,338	1,792
Dawson	1,027	2,968,415	3.1	5.5	0.8	1.9	24.1	9.3	55.0	56.2	16.2	34.3	2,514	2,311
Deaf Smith	1,045	3,343,534	6.0	8.2	0.3	2.5	18.1	3.3	61.2	124.1	26.6	28.5	1,470	1,181
Delta	249	617,205	10.2	5.7	0.1	0.9	0.0	6.2	76.6	18.1	9.8	6.9	1,304	1,174
Denton	21,018	80,654,351	6.5	9.2	4.5	1.3	2.5	6.0	68.8	2,022.8	459.3	1,266.0	1,790	1,527
DeWitt	1,484	4,135,234	4.5	4.4	0.5	2.2	24.6	3.4	59.6	97.2	42.1	29.7	1,450	1,280
Dickens	132	357,360	9.4	5.8	0.0	5.1	0.0	3.9	70.5	10.8	3.0	6.0	2,586	2,419
Dimmit	818	1,945,120	7.2	5.4	0.0	1.0	23.0	4.5	58.2	46.5	21.1	19.9	1,904	1,452
Donley	386	1,127,365	14.0	2.9	0.0	2.0	12.1	7.2	61.3	18.4	8.5	4.9	1,371	1,208
Duval	1,069	2,869,544	5.5	8.4	0.0	5.8	26.4	3.4	49.4	84.6	22.4	23.2	1,983	1,875
Eastland	1,310	3,783,362	4.4	5.2	0.7	1.4	13.7	3.5	70.8	84.5	34.9	24.4	1,322	1,079
Ector	6,915	26,339,816	4.0	7.3	3.2	1.3	27.3	2.1	53.3	690.5	140.4	269.5	1,867	1,389
Edwards	196	461,967	5.6	6.6	0.5	3.6	2.2	2.7	77.7	11.0	3.0	7.2	3,657	3,565
Ellis	6,187	19,866,741	5.2	9.5	4.1	1.8	0.8	3.8	73.5	481.2	162.1	262.5	1,705	1,483
El Paso	38,262	139,590,880	4.5	10.3	3.7	3.1	8.1	3.0	65.5	3,339.7	1,610.5	1,090.4	1,318	1,018
Erath	1,440	4,169,914	6.4	10.7	3.0	2.6	13.7	4.5	57.7	97.3	38.9	48.4	1,230	1,006
Falls	755	2,249,164	5.5	10.4	1.3	2.6	0.2	6.9	72.4	45.7	26.5	12.5	711	588
Fannin	1,308	3,305,390	7.2	6.5	4.5	3.2	0.4	4.6	72.9	79.2	36.7	29.9	885	758
Fayette	1,047	3,070,054	8.5	11.9	0.0	5.3	5.8	7.8	59.5	68.3	15.9	38.4	1,557	1,347
Fisher	274	819,484	9.8	4.3	0.0	4.0	33.9	2.2	42.7	20.3	6.0	7.5	1,949	1,549
Floyd	494	1,401,943	6.0	6.3	0.0	3.0	29.3	3.2	52.2	29.3	12.8	7.3	1,148	1,016
Foard	109	252,340	7.9	2.2	0.0	27.8	2.3	4.6	52.5	6.5	3.6	2.6	1,980	1,699
Fort Bend	16,162	56,081,173	6.1	10.9	2.4	2.1	1.2	2.8	73.5	1,700.0	419.7	1,031.0	1,644	1,484
Franklin	376	1,062,026	10.1	8.0	0.0	4.2	0.1	6.2	71.2	29.0	7.2	17.8	1,676	1,502
Freestone	870	2,743,049	6.9	7.9	0.0	2.8	1.7	3.3	77.1	162.3	33.5	110.1	5,642	5,300
Frio	734	2,179,421	2.5	6.3	0.0	4.5	0.2	6.1	79.7	65.4	34.3	19.5	1,102	928
Gaines	1,152	3,808,818	1.9	4.1	0.0	3.9	20.6	2.9	66.0	125.0	15.5	87.9	4,775	4,628
Galveston	16,441	61,971,543	4.8	11.2	1.9	2.4	3.8	5.1	69.9	1,645.6	615.8	806.4	2,684	2,330
Garza	293	892,400	9.4	14.2	0.0	2.3	1.8	3.0	68.2	25.0	4.6	15.2	2,373	2,062
Gillespie	1,151	3,952,390	6.0	8.2	0.8	2.5	3.0	27.3	49.9	76.0	11.8	50.4	2,005	1,655
Glasscock	71	223,571	6.0	3.1	0.0	7.3	0.0	3.2	74.8	20.5	1.8	16.3	12,932	12,861
Goliad	327	1,001,812	9.8	6.6	0.0	4.9	0.3	2.6	69.7	27.2	7.6	18.0	2,453	2,250
Gonzales	1,193	3,267,421	6.8	6.0	0.5	2.5	24.1	5.5	54.2	101.3	40.1	26.2	1,309	1,024
Gray	994	2,974,220	9.1	9.3	4.4	4.3	1.5	4.0	66.4	72.0	21.7	36.7	1,599	1,291
Grayson	5,248	18,290,717	5.6	9.2	3.5	2.7	4.2	4.8	69.0	414.8	144.6	188.3	1,544	1,271
Gregg	5,913	19,287,172	4.5	10.7	5.5	1.7	6.6	4.4	64.2	499.5	162.8	256.1	2,088	1,490
Grimes	917	2,789,960	7.3	9.4	0.7	2.4	1.2	2.1	74.4	77.3	25.0	42.7	1,594	1,464

1. Based on the resident population estimated as of July 1 of the year shown.

Table B. States and Counties — Local Government Finances, Government Employment, and Income Taxes

STATE County	Total (mil dol) [185]	Per capita¹ (dollars) [186]	Education [187]	Health and hospitals [188]	Police protection [189]	Public welfare [190]	Highways [191]	Total (mil dol) [192]	Per capita¹ (dollars) [193]	Federal civilian [194]	Federal military [195]	State and local [196]	Number of returns [197]	Mean adjusted gross income [198]	Mean income tax [199]
TEXAS— Cont'd															
Caldwell	103.3	2,667	49.6	3.3	5.2	0.3	3.5	64.6	1,669	63	79	1,677	17,920	43,937	4,179
Calhoun	106.7	4,938	37.9	23.7	4.3	0.2	4.4	73.3	3,392	39	100	1,324	9,200	50,423	5,430
Callahan	33.7	2,494	68.1	0.5	5.7	0.0	2.9	34.4	2,546	45	28	617	5,850	46,170	4,466
Cameron	1,613.4	3,883	61.9	0.8	4.4	0.5	3.7	1,801.3	4,335	3,391	949	26,768	163,580	37,740	3,268
Camp	30.6	2,461	71.8	0.2	3.9	0.1	5.5	43.1	3,459	29	26	577	5,190	44,135	4,189
Carson	23.0	3,741	59.9	1.1	2.8	0.0	5.0	34.1	5,539	14	12	423	2,580	57,854	6,275
Cass	91.1	3,021	59.3	15.9	3.7	0.3	2.8	50.0	1,659	64	60	1,616	12,470	45,061	4,323
Castro	33.2	4,069	51.2	27.7	4.5	0.0	3.7	20.0	2,445	17	16	619	2,880	36,435	4,340
Chambers	168.5	4,656	51.2	9.0	4.2	0.4	4.6	360.8	9,968	58	83	2,088	18,650	76,424	9,744
Cherokee	167.4	3,268	66.5	4.9	3.9	0.1	4.5	85.5	1,669	73	100	4,063	20,360	46,302	4,993
Childress	54.2	7,712	18.8	64.6	2.7	0.0	2.7	6.3	898	17	11	1,089	2,470	42,555	3,938
Clay	46.1	4,377	39.2	17.7	2.7	0.1	5.6	119.9	11,385	22	21	521	4,600	53,500	4,975
Cochran	27.0	8,873	69.4	12.8	3.0	0.0	3.8	0.1	27	12	6	309	1,120	41,465	4,005
Coke	16.5	5,122	42.6	0.1	3.0	32.6	4.0	24.2	7,483	11	7	340	1,390	46,173	4,443
Coleman	34.1	3,930	44.6	22.9	4.1	0.1	3.7	15.9	1,837	39	17	539	3,460	40,096	4,539
Collin	4,140.4	4,961	43.1	0.7	3.6	0.1	8.6	16,872.8	20,216	1,921	2,036	47,823	431,270	97,472	16,071
Collingsworth	16.5	5,436	37.3	43.5	4.4	0.0	1.5	12.6	4,138	14	6	214	1,170	41,111	4,484
Colorado	71.5	3,453	50.2	14.9	5.5	0.1	5.4	63.0	3,042	51	42	1,060	9,440	56,429	7,221
Comal	446.0	3,899	56.1	0.9	6.3	0.6	5.0	943.7	8,251	211	282	5,852	66,530	80,738	12,079
Comanche	42.2	3,069	50.8	15.3	4.6	0.2	5.8	30.9	2,246	47	27	798	5,550	40,339	3,767
Concho	12.3	3,067	36.9	29.2	4.3	0.0	4.1	3.9	977	14	5	227	1,010	41,992	4,203
Cooke	191.9	4,961	48.0	22.9	5.0	0.1	3.7	159.4	4,119	63	79	2,818	18,160	54,952	6,267
Coryell	215.6	2,792	43.6	12.0	4.0	0.3	22.6	217.4	2,815	175	481	6,051	26,840	42,608	3,438
Cottle	5.4	3,651	50.1	1.6	2.9	0.1	3.3	1.4	940	9	3	130	600	31,063	2,762
Crane	40.9	8,956	77.6	0.0	3.1	0.0	1.6	6.3	1,384	6	9	376	1,960	53,518	5,069
Crockett	42.8	11,437	63.2	0.7	1.7	0.8	5.5	6.0	1,614	4	7	395	1,500	54,084	6,248
Crosby	24.1	3,941	70.8	0.1	3.8	1.1	3.7	0.5	83	16	12	461	2,390	36,924	3,067
Culberson	18.7	8,167	29.9	32.6	5.7	0.0	3.2	2.8	1,224	83	4	226	1,040	37,712	3,124
Dallam	28.3	4,044	60.6	0.3	5.2	0.0	6.8	30.2	4,320	19	14	276	3,370	49,274	6,149
Dallas	11,949.9	4,870	37.6	17.2	5.8	0.7	2.6	27,138.7	11,060	25,384	5,799	150,522	1,173,930	70,904	11,700
Dawson	56.4	4,132	73.5	0.6	3.9	0.1	3.1	165.8	12,154	66	23	1,304	4,790	48,541	5,457
Deaf Smith	135.2	6,983	26.5	25.1	2.4	0.1	2.8	2,436.8	125,866	49	37	1,284	7,900	36,046	3,248
Delta	15.4	2,898	62.3	0.0	6.5	0.3	5.4	19.5	3,660	15	11	298	2,070	39,588	3,603
Denton	2,006.9	2,837	52.0	1.7	5.6	0.1	6.2	6,231.1	8,810	1,956	1,726	34,308	373,390	83,118	12,525
DeWitt	94.1	4,596	46.6	28.3	3.1	0.2	3.8	56.7	2,773	35	37	2,200	8,000	72,821	13,170
Dickens	13.9	5,980	66.7	0.3	4.5	0.0	7.7	7.5	3,235	12	4	160	710	44,854	4,145
Dimmit	42.2	4,036	66.0	0.3	4.0	0.0	3.8	95.0	9,081	253	21	1,081	3,970	41,918	4,298
Donley	19.7	5,489	76.6	0.0	1.8	2.7	1.6	21.5	5,966	12	6	415	1,410	36,162	3,304
Duval	69.0	5,890	36.6	35.9	4.0	0.7	3.7	59.2	5,053	121	21	942	4,360	37,375	3,207
Eastland	81.8	4,441	62.6	14.7	2.7	0.2	2.9	42.9	2,328	49	379	1,402	7,360	41,171	4,716
Ector	691.3	4,790	36.3	40.0	3.5	0.0	2.4	385.4	2,670	198	312	10,119	65,870	53,440	5,948
Edwards	10.4	5,270	76.7	0.0	6.7	0.0	2.3	2.5	1,271	18	4	127	790	40,371	3,957
Ellis	446.9	2,903	57.1	0.3	6.0	0.3	3.9	1,320.0	8,573	241	347	7,394	77,350	60,665	7,053
El Paso	3,257.4	3,937	52.3	15.6	4.9	0.4	0.9	4,034.1	4,876	12,695	27,097	56,036	362,040	41,774	4,032
Erath	86.0	2,188	55.2	1.6	7.4	0.4	5.3	109.6	2,786	70	84	4,282	15,750	47,877	5,747
Falls	44.4	2,519	65.6	1.1	5.3	0.8	6.2	13.4	762	404	31	1,199	6,340	38,699	3,661
Fannin	76.7	2,268	61.1	2.7	7.1	0.7	5.8	54.2	1,601	739	63	1,893	13,680	48,500	5,007
Fayette	68.1	2,756	56.7	3.7	5.9	0.8	7.7	47.6	1,928	71	50	1,498	11,440	60,116	8,046
Fisher	21.3	5,529	41.6	30.6	4.6	0.1	5.1	3.0	779	16	8	301	1,550	48,020	4,556
Floyd	29.6	4,646	49.4	29.9	3.4	0.0	1.0	5.9	923	29	12	518	2,430	42,142	4,306
Foard	4.6	3,531	56.3	4.7	6.8	0.2	7.6	0.1	79	8	2	103	500	37,046	3,098
Fort Bend	1,722.6	2,746	46.9	0.7	4.7	0.3	7.2	5,183.8	8,264	784	1,535	23,922	314,700	87,805	13,505
Franklin	25.1	2,364	51.5	0.1	5.6	0.4	9.6	29.4	2,760	17	22	431	4,310	46,781	5,067
Freestone	159.6	8,177	39.9	10.8	11.9	0.0	12.6	91.4	4,681	41	36	1,290	7,830	47,577	5,260
Frio	58.9	3,327	54.3	3.8	5.2	0.0	3.8	93.0	5,256	159	33	1,354	6,390	38,775	3,401
Gaines	132.6	7,199	63.4	14.7	1.8	0.0	4.5	120.9	6,566	27	42	1,374	7,500	48,900	5,243
Galveston	1,667.3	5,549	43.5	4.3	5.0	0.5	5.1	3,060.4	10,185	973	1,079	28,275	147,420	70,274	9,740
Garza	22.3	3,480	59.5	0.1	9.6	0.7	5.7	14.9	2,330	10	14	356	1,800	53,159	6,406
Gillespie	76.0	3,023	58.0	2.8	9.2	0.3	5.1	26.7	1,061	49	53	1,165	13,420	72,329	11,128
Glasscock	21.4	16,992	83.0	6.7	0.3	0.0	0.7	8.1	6,411	6	3	138	610	134,146	31,764
Goliad	22.9	3,113	65.5	4.1	7.2	0.8	7.3	16.0	2,182	15	15	396	3,120	56,752	6,900
Gonzales	101.6	5,069	39.0	28.7	5.0	0.0	3.6	43.0	2,146	64	42	1,493	8,870	50,586	6,379
Gray	70.1	3,049	52.0	0.4	5.0	0.2	5.4	80.6	3,506	42	41	1,536	8,620	46,225	4,957
Grayson	423.3	3,471	54.8	3.3	5.1	0.0	6.0	717.6	5,885	334	260	6,576	57,330	56,567	6,664
Gregg	514.7	4,196	54.4	5.9	5.3	0.0	4.4	916.0	7,468	350	241	7,222	54,580	51,861	6,237
Grimes	84.3	3,146	51.8	0.3	3.8	0.0	6.3	95.1	3,549	52	51	1,780	11,420	48,051	5,335

1. Based on the resident population estimated as of July 1 of the year shown.

Table B. States and Counties — Land Area and Population

State / county code	CBSA code[1]	County code[2]	STATE County	Land area[3] (sq. mi)	Total persons 2018	Rank	Per square mile	White	Black	American Indian, Alaska Native	Asian and Pacific Islander	Percent Hispanic or Latino[4]	Under 5 years	5 to 17 years	18 to 24 years	25 to 34 years	35 to 44 years	45 to 54 years
				1	2	3	4	5	6	7	8	9	10	11	12	13	14	15
			TEXAS— Cont'd															
48187	41,700	1	Guadalupe	711.3	163,694	402	230.1	51.6	8.5	0.8	2.9	38.3	6.3	18.8	8.9	12.9	14.3	13.3
48189	38,380	4	Hale	1,004.7	33,830	1,333	33.7	34.3	5.4	0.7	0.8	59.7	6.7	20.4	11.4	14.0	11.8	11.4
48191		9	Hall	883.5	3,028	2,963	3.4	56.8	8.8	1.0	0.3	34.2	4.7	18.2	8.2	10.0	10.2	11.2
48193		6	Hamilton	835.9	8,484	2,543	10.1	85.1	1.1	1.0	0.9	13.0	6.1	16.0	6.6	11.1	9.9	10.8
48195		7	Hansford	919.8	5,463	2,797	5.9	50.4	1.0	0.6	0.5	48.3	7.6	21.6	8.7	12.7	11.2	11.7
48197		9	Hardeman	695.1	3,922	2,908	5.6	69.9	5.9	1.2	1.0	23.8	5.1	16.2	7.5	10.4	11.9	12.7
48199	13,140	2	Hardin	890.6	57,207	901	64.2	87.5	6.0	0.9	1.0	5.9	6.5	18.1	7.5	12.6	12.5	12.6
48201	26,420	1	Harris	1,705.2	4,698,619	3	2,755.5	30.3	19.4	0.5	7.9	43.3	7.6	19.1	9.3	16.1	14.3	12.4
48203	32,220	4	Harrison	900.0	66,726	803	74.1	64.4	21.4	1.0	1.0	13.6	6.4	18.8	8.6	11.9	11.9	12.1
48205		7	Hartley	1,462.0	5,619	2,783	3.8	65.2	6.8	0.9	0.9	27.1	5.4	15.7	6.9	14.4	15.9	15.5
48207		6	Haskell	903.1	5,813	2,767	6.4	64.8	4.7	1.0	1.5	29.7	3.9	14.8	9.7	14.0	11.4	10.4
48209	12,420	1	Hays	678.0	222,631	306	328.4	54.7	4.3	0.8	2.3	39.6	6.2	16.7	16.5	14.4	13.5	11.3
48211		7	Hemphill	906.3	3,825	2,916	4.2	63.5	0.7	1.3	1.3	34.2	6.7	24.0	7.6	10.6	13.8	11.2
48213	11,980	4	Henderson	873.8	82,299	690	94.2	79.1	6.8	1.4	0.9	13.3	5.6	15.9	7.7	11.1	10.5	12.2
48215	32,580	2	Hidalgo	1,570.9	865,939	66	551.2	6.2	0.5	0.1	1.0	92.4	8.9	23.6	10.9	13.5	12.6	11.0
48217		6	Hill	958.9	36,354	1,267	37.9	71.1	7.1	0.9	0.9	21.4	5.9	17.4	8.1	11.3	10.8	11.9
48219	30,220	6	Hockley	908.4	22,980	1,682	25.3	46.9	3.9	0.8	0.6	48.7	6.6	19.1	11.5	13.6	11.8	10.8
48221	19,100	1	Hood	420.7	60,537	867	143.9	84.6	1.3	1.2	1.1	12.9	5.6	15.7	6.4	10.6	10.4	11.5
48223	44,860	6	Hopkins	767.3	36,810	1,254	48.0	74.2	7.8	1.1	1.0	17.4	6.5	18.2	8.1	12.2	11.2	12.4
48225		7	Houston	1,231.0	23,169	1,671	18.8	62.4	25.5	0.8	1.0	11.5	5.2	14.6	6.6	11.7	12.8	13.2
48227	13,700	4	Howard	900.8	36,459	1,266	40.5	49.0	6.6	1.1	1.3	43.1	6.2	15.2	9.6	16.1	13.0	15.2
48229	21,340	2	Hudspeth	4,570.5	4,795	2,846	1.0	17.7	3.3	0.8	1.3	78.0	6.0	15.2	9.8	19.8	15.0	9.0
48231	19,100	1	Hunt	840.3	96,493	618	114.8	72.6	8.7	1.5	2.0	17.0	6.5	17.6	9.8	12.5	11.7	12.9
48233	14,420	6	Hutchinson	887.4	21,198	1,766	23.9	71.2	3.3	2.4	0.9	24.0	6.8	18.9	8.1	12.5	12.6	11.2
48235	41,660	3	Irion	1,051.5	1,522	3,077	1.4	71.6	1.5	1.6	0.4	26.3	5.5	16.5	6.9	12.3	9.7	11.9
48237		6	Jack	910.9	8,843	2,511	9.7	77.8	4.3	1.0	0.8	17.3	5.5	16.3	9.5	14.0	12.0	13.1
48239		6	Jackson	829.4	14,874	2,106	17.9	58.6	6.3	0.8	1.3	34.0	6.9	18.6	7.8	12.5	11.9	11.3
48241		6	Jasper	938.7	35,872	1,277	38.2	76.1	16.7	1.0	0.8	6.9	6.2	17.8	7.5	11.5	11.0	12.2
48243		9	Jeff Davis	2,264.6	2,252	3,023	1.0	64.7	1.4	1.5	1.6	32.8	1.6	6.2	4.6	9.5	9.1	12.7
48245	13,140	2	Jefferson	876.4	255,001	269	291.0	40.9	33.9	0.7	4.3	21.5	7.0	17.0	9.5	14.7	12.9	11.9
48247		6	Jim Hogg	1,136.2	5,248	2,812	4.6	5.8	0.8	0.5	0.5	92.8	8.1	22.7	8.3	11.5	11.8	9.9
48249	10,860	4	Jim Wells	865.2	40,822	1,155	47.2	18.2	0.9	0.5	0.5	80.4	7.5	20.3	9.2	13.1	12.1	11.2
48251	19,100	1	Johnson	724.8	171,361	382	236.4	72.7	4.1	1.1	1.8	22.0	6.7	19.3	8.5	13.1	12.9	12.9
48253	10,180	3	Jones	928.6	19,817	1,833	21.3	59.2	12.5	0.8	0.7	27.8	4.4	12.8	9.9	17.0	14.9	13.5
48255		6	Karnes	747.5	15,650	2,057	20.9	35.6	8.7	0.4	0.4	55.3	6.0	15.4	10.5	18.1	14.0	10.9
48257	19,100	1	Kaufman	780.7	128,622	495	164.8	63.7	12.9	1.1	1.7	22.4	7.4	20.4	8.0	13.6	14.1	12.9
48259	41,700	1	Kendall	662.5	45,641	1,059	68.9	72.8	1.4	1.0	1.7	24.4	5.1	17.9	7.8	9.9	12.5	13.5
48261	28,780	9	Kenedy	1,458.5	442	3,139	0.3	22.4	2.9	2.0	0.9	73.3	3.8	23.3	10.2	11.3	10.0	13.1
48263		9	Kent	902.5	726	3,126	0.8	78.0	1.8	2.1	0.1	19.7	5.1	16.0	5.6	8.1	9.2	12.5
48265	28,500	4	Kerr	1,103.3	52,405	958	47.5	69.5	1.8	1.1	1.3	27.5	5.2	14.0	8.0	10.6	9.2	10.9
48267		7	Kimble	1,251.0	4,362	2,869	3.5	73.1	0.6	0.8	0.9	24.9	4.4	13.2	6.6	9.1	9.4	11.4
48269		9	King	910.9	277	3,140	0.3	83.4	1.1	1.8	0.7	15.5	4.7	20.6	5.4	11.2	10.8	14.8
48271		7	Kinney	1,360.1	3,767	2,919	2.8	37.6	1.7	1.4	0.5	60.2	4.0	14.8	9.2	12.3	12.8	11.2
48273	28,780	4	Kleberg	881.3	31,129	1,403	35.3	20.6	3.8	0.5	2.7	73.4	6.8	17.4	20.3	14.1	10.4	9.3
48275		9	Knox	850.6	3,653	2,927	4.3	58.8	6.2	1.2	0.5	34.9	7.0	19.4	7.2	12.1	10.4	10.6
48277	37,580	5	Lamar	907.2	49,728	993	54.8	76.5	14.4	2.6	1.3	8.1	6.7	17.1	8.0	12.5	11.0	12.5
48279		6	Lamb	1,016.2	13,158	2,220	12.9	40.0	3.9	0.8	0.4	55.9	7.4	20.4	8.6	11.8	11.6	10.8
48281	28,660	2	Lampasas	712.8	21,229	1,762	29.8	74.2	4.3	1.7	2.4	19.8	5.4	16.7	7.3	10.4	12.1	13.8
48283		6	La Salle	1,486.7	7,531	2,625	5.1	11.6	0.7	0.5	0.4	87.1	5.6	14.1	17.1	18.3	12.3	10.9
48285		6	Lavaca	969.7	20,110	1,818	20.7	74.1	6.4	0.5	0.7	19.2	5.9	17.7	7.4	10.2	10.3	11.4
48287		6	Lee	629.0	17,144	1,971	27.3	64.5	11.2	0.9	0.8	23.9	5.8	16.1	7.9	11.6	11.9	12.3
48289		8	Leon	1,073.2	17,270	1,963	16.1	76.8	7.4	1.0	0.9	15.0	6.1	16.4	6.8	9.6	10.6	10.9
48291	26,420	1	Liberty	1,158.4	86,323	668	74.5	62.7	10.1	0.9	0.9	26.8	7.2	19.3	9.0	14.2	12.6	12.8
48293		6	Limestone	905.4	23,519	1,663	26.0	59.5	17.6	0.8	1.0	22.7	6.3	16.1	8.5	12.7	11.6	11.5
48295		9	Lipscomb	932.2	3,355	2,947	3.6	62.8	1.7	1.9	1.1	34.5	5.9	19.9	7.5	12.1	12.2	10.5
48297		8	Live Oak	1,039.7	12,166	2,280	11.7	54.1	4.5	1.0	0.9	40.4	5.4	14.5	7.6	14.3	12.5	11.0
48299		7	Llano	934.1	21,646	1,743	23.2	86.8	1.4	1.2	0.8	10.9	4.4	11.1	5.3	7.8	7.7	10.5
48301		9	Loving	668.8	152	3,141	0.2	78.3	4.6	0.7	0.0	16.4	7.2	27.0	9.2	17.8	9.9	5.9
48303	31,180	2	Lubbock	895.6	307,412	228	343.2	54.2	7.6	0.7	2.9	35.9	6.7	17.1	16.7	14.7	11.8	10.0
48305	31,180	2	Lynn	891.9	5,877	2,760	6.6	49.9	2.7	0.6	0.3	47.2	7.0	19.8	7.8	12.1	12.2	11.1
48307		7	McCulloch	1,065.6	7,987	2,595	7.5	64.1	2.4	1.0	1.0	32.9	5.3	16.9	8.1	10.9	10.9	11.5
48309	47,380	2	McLennan	1,037.1	254,607	270	245.5	57.1	14.9	0.7	2.3	26.7	7.0	17.7	14.3	13.2	11.5	10.7
48311		9	McMullen	1,139.8	749	3,123	0.7	53.5	2.7	1.1	0.5	43.0	4.4	14.3	7.2	12.7	8.9	14.6
48313		6	Madison	466.1	14,422	2,134	30.9	56.2	20.0	0.8	1.0	23.4	5.4	15.8	11.5	17.8	12.8	10.7
48315		8	Marion	380.9	9,928	2,433	26.1	72.6	22.0	1.9	1.4	4.3	4.5	13.6	6.2	9.4	9.8	12.7
48317	33,260	3	Martin	915.0	5,753	2,775	6.3	49.8	2.1	0.6	0.7	47.4	8.8	22.3	8.4	14.2	11.4	12.0

1. CBSA = Core Based Statistical Area. See Appendix A for explanation. See Appendix B for list of metropolitan areas with component counties.   2. County type code from the Economic Research Service of USDA Rural-Urban Continuum Codes. See Appendix A for definition.   3. Dry land or land partially or temporarily covered by water.   4. May be of any race.

Table B. States and Counties — Population and Households

STATE County	55 to 64 years	65 to 74 years	75 years and over	Percent female	2000	2010	2000-2010	2010-2018	Births	Deaths	Net Migration	Number	Persons per household	Family households	Female family householder[1]	One person
	16	17	18	19	20	21	22	23	24	25	26	27	28	29	30	31
TEXAS— Cont'd																
Guadalupe	11.7	8.3	5.5	50.5	89,023	131,534	47.8	24.4	14,627	8,092	25,324	51,990	2.87	75.8	12.7	20.7
Hale	11.0	7.3	6.1	47.8	36,602	36,206	-1.1	-6.6	4,085	2,522	-3,999	11,217	2.87	71.9	15.1	24.9
Hall	14.3	11.8	11.4	50.5	3,782	3,353	-11.3	-9.7	231	386	-172	1,244	2.43	66.2	13.5	30.9
Hamilton	14.6	12.5	12.4	50.3	8,229	8,512	3.4	-0.3	742	1,134	366	3,157	2.51	70.2	8.5	28.0
Hansford	11.8	7.8	7.0	49.0	5,369	5,613	4.5	-2.7	633	412	-378	1,924	2.83	74.3	5.9	23.5
Hardeman	13.7	12.3	10.2	49.4	4,724	4,139	-12.4	-5.2	330	365	-185	1,533	2.58	65.4	9.2	31.1
Hardin	13.6	9.8	6.9	50.7	48,073	54,635	13.7	4.7	5,751	4,582	1,452	20,739	2.68	72.9	11.9	24.2
Harris	10.7	6.6	3.9	50.3	3,400,578	4,093,188	20.4	14.8	573,962	203,745	235,934	1,562,813	2.87	68.3	15.6	26.1
Harrison	13.3	10.1	6.9	51.1	62,110	65,644	5.7	1.6	6,918	5,237	-567	23,363	2.79	73.2	13.3	23.0
Hartley	10.9	7.6	7.6	40.1	5,537	6,062	9.5	-7.3	499	314	-647	1,754	2.44	73.4	5.4	22.6
Haskell	13.9	12.0	9.9	46.5	6,093	5,902	-3.1	-1.5	379	669	196	2,128	2.34	67.4	11.0	28.5
Hays	10.2	7.2	3.8	50.3	97,589	157,099	61.0	41.7	19,157	7,813	53,262	68,045	2.76	65.0	10.2	22.6
Hemphill	11.6	8.8	5.7	49.8	3,351	3,807	13.6	0.5	510	287	-213	1,358	3.03	79.4	7.3	16.3
Henderson	14.9	12.6	9.4	51.1	73,277	78,534	7.2	4.8	7,457	8,568	4,907	30,459	2.57	71.3	11.2	24.1
Hidalgo	8.3	6.2	4.9	51.0	569,463	774,768	36.1	11.8	129,815	33,426	-4,910	232,523	3.57	82.0	21.8	15.4
Hill	13.8	11.7	9.0	50.2	32,321	35,088	8.6	3.6	3,377	3,407	1,315	12,674	2.69	70.7	11.0	24.4
Hockley	11.9	8.3	6.4	50.1	22,716	22,927	0.9	0.2	2,597	1,743	-799	8,065	2.79	71.4	12.2	25.5
Hood	15.2	14.1	10.4	51.1	41,100	51,163	24.5	18.3	4,939	5,382	9,751	21,527	2.54	69.4	8.5	26.8
Hopkins	13.2	10.4	7.9	50.8	31,960	35,161	10.0	4.7	3,787	3,200	1,074	13,287	2.67	74.0	12.7	21.6
Houston	13.8	11.9	10.1	46.5	23,185	23,731	2.4	-2.4	1,939	2,484	-12	8,328	2.36	65.4	13.8	31.5
Howard	11.7	7.3	5.6	42.5	33,627	35,012	4.1	4.1	3,771	3,167	819	11,032	2.82	66.8	13.4	28.3
Hudspeth	9.9	9.0	6.4	47.0	3,344	3,476	3.9	37.9	347	148	1,102	890	3.50	73.6	13.3	23.0
Hunt	13.2	9.2	6.6	50.7	76,596	86,162	12.5	12.0	9,228	7,432	8,540	31,781	2.76	69.0	10.8	25.6
Hutchinson	13.4	9.5	7.0	49.7	23,857	22,249	-6.7	-4.7	2,445	1,977	-1,531	7,799	2.77	66.3	12.0	30.9
Irion	15.8	12.0	9.5	48.7	1,771	1,597	-9.8	-4.7	124	110	-91	648	2.46	73.8	6.0	24.1
Jack	12.5	10.0	7.1	43.6	8,763	9,044	3.2	-2.2	804	728	-276	3,075	2.49	70.7	9.3	25.7
Jackson	13.1	9.6	8.4	50.2	14,391	14,075	-2.2	5.7	1,645	1,199	352	5,232	2.77	70.1	11.4	25.4
Jasper	14.2	11.4	8.2	50.5	35,604	35,710	0.3	0.5	3,629	3,432	-36	11,974	2.88	68.2	11.2	29.7
Jeff Davis	21.4	21.4	13.5	48.8	2,207	2,342	6.1	-3.8	121	145	-71	1,007	2.16	58.9	1.3	35.9
Jefferson	12.6	8.3	6.2	48.7	252,051	252,277	0.1	1.1	29,260	20,361	-6,192	94,020	2.54	63.5	16.3	31.6
Jim Hogg	10.1	10.1	7.5	48.7	5,281	5,300	0.4	-1.0	719	424	-349	1,587	3.30	71.2	19.7	26.8
Jim Wells	11.3	8.9	6.5	50.4	39,326	40,836	3.8	0.0	5,215	3,291	-1,943	13,614	3.00	74.0	19.6	22.6
Johnson	12.4	8.6	5.5	50.1	126,811	150,940	19.0	13.5	16,781	10,760	14,451	55,467	2.83	76.0	11.5	19.9
Jones	11.9	8.8	6.8	37.3	20,785	20,192	-2.9	-1.9	1,387	1,560	-223	5,635	2.25	70.4	11.2	25.0
Karnes	11.1	7.6	6.5	41.2	15,446	14,828	-4.0	5.5	1,414	1,193	583	4,303	2.82	67.8	12.3	29.8
Kaufman	11.7	7.4	4.6	50.7	71,313	103,363	44.9	24.4	12,730	7,318	19,729	36,525	3.10	77.4	12.4	18.9
Kendall	14.3	11.1	8.0	51.0	23,743	33,411	40.7	36.6	2,929	2,870	12,042	13,691	2.91	75.0	9.2	21.6
Kenedy	12.7	8.6	7.0	48.4	414	413	-0.2	7.0	32	17	10	152	3.68	69.7	25.0	30.3
Kent	16.3	12.4	14.7	50.3	859	808	-5.9	-10.1	60	101	-44	275	2.30	58.9	4.4	39.3
Kerr	14.5	14.9	12.8	51.9	43,653	49,625	13.7	5.6	4,300	5,911	4,390	20,580	2.38	66.6	11.8	29.8
Kimble	16.6	16.5	12.9	51.1	4,468	4,605	3.1	-5.3	338	444	-137	1,941	2.25	69.7	9.5	29.2
King	14.8	8.3	9.4	49.5	356	285	-19.9	-2.8	20	10	-19	101	2.86	61.4	3.0	23.8
Kinney	11.5	11.7	12.3	44.9	3,379	3,598	6.5	4.7	275	291	182	1,200	2.77	56.7	3.8	39.3
Kleberg	8.8	7.2	5.7	48.8	31,549	32,061	1.6	-2.9	3,739	2,109	-2,606	10,958	2.70	62.3	12.5	28.9
Knox	13.4	10.8	9.1	50.5	4,253	3,719	-12.6	-1.8	387	450	-5	1,376	2.62	71.2	8.2	28.0
Lamar	13.1	10.8	8.4	51.8	48,499	49,789	2.7	-0.1	5,477	5,047	-471	19,085	2.55	68.8	13.9	27.1
Lamb	12.5	8.5	8.4	50.4	14,709	13,976	-5.0	-5.9	1,600	1,251	-1,183	4,790	2.75	69.9	14.1	26.6
Lampasas	14.7	11.4	8.2	50.7	17,762	19,680	10.8	7.9	1,885	1,642	1,305	7,748	2.61	74.0	9.6	22.9
La Salle	8.1	7.8	5.9	40.8	5,866	6,886	17.4	9.4	771	432	293	2,286	2.85	64.3	9.1	33.2
Lavaca	13.9	12.6	10.7	51.2	19,210	19,263	0.3	4.4	1,851	2,065	1,071	7,684	2.52	72.1	10.1	25.9
Lee	15.9	10.5	8.0	49.8	15,657	16,610	6.1	3.2	1,648	1,346	241	6,118	2.67	73.8	10.2	23.1
Leon	15.2	13.8	10.7	50.3	15,335	16,801	9.6	2.8	1,723	1,779	531	6,245	2.70	70.0	14.1	25.9
Liberty	12.0	8.1	4.7	50.4	70,154	75,641	7.8	14.1	8,944	6,320	8,063	25,974	2.81	72.8	12.0	23.5
Limestone	13.8	11.4	8.1	48.4	22,051	23,388	6.1	0.6	2,514	2,141	-228	8,100	2.77	69.9	13.2	28.0
Lipscomb	13.8	9.5	8.6	48.3	3,057	3,302	8.0	1.6	373	224	-102	1,276	2.70	70.7	8.7	26.7
Live Oak	14.2	11.3	9.3	45.2	12,309	11,533	-6.3	5.5	1,035	997	586	3,586	2.93	66.3	7.6	29.9
Llano	17.0	19.8	16.3	51.6	17,044	19,301	13.2	12.1	1,331	2,495	3,472	8,681	2.30	67.8	5.2	28.8
Loving	13.2	7.9	2.0	44.1	67	82	22.4	85.4	17	10	61	31	2.39	61.3	9.7	32.3
Lubbock	10.4	7.1	5.3	50.7	242,628	278,918	15.0	10.2	33,860	19,476	14,079	110,275	2.59	62.4	13.8	27.8
Lynn	13.1	8.7	8.2	49.0	6,550	5,915	-9.7	-0.6	637	436	-243	2,147	2.68	76.2	16.0	21.1
McCulloch	14.1	12.6	9.7	49.8	8,205	8,284	1.0	-3.6	755	901	-153	3,143	2.54	68.9	13.5	27.8
McLennan	11.2	8.2	6.2	51.1	213,517	234,899	10.0	8.4	28,667	17,146	8,326	88,208	2.68	66.5	15.3	26.8
McMullen	13.9	11.1	13.0	45.1	851	707	-16.9	5.9	70	70	36	194	3.09	78.9	13.9	17.0
Madison	10.4	8.6	7.2	42.6	12,940	13,667	5.6	5.5	1,290	1,050	519	4,174	2.35	67.9	11.7	27.7
Marion	17.5	15.3	11.0	51.2	10,941	10,536	-3.7	-5.8	774	1,363	-15	4,457	2.25	61.9	8.8	33.6
Martin	11.7	6.6	4.7	49.4	4,746	4,799	1.1	19.9	764	342	521	1,635	3.35	75.9	12.4	20.9

1. No spouse present.

Table B. States and Counties — Population, Vital Statistics, Health, and Crime

STATE County	Persons in group quarters, 2018	Daytime Population, 2013-2017		Births, 2018		Deaths, 2018		Persons under 65 with no health insurance, 2016		Medicare, 2018			Serious crimes known to police[2], 2016 Total	
		Number	Employment/ residence ratio	Total	Rate[1]	Number	Rate[1]	Number	Percent	Total beneficiaries	Enrolled in Original Medicare	Enrolled in Medicare Advantage	Number	Rate[3]
	32	33	34	35	36	37	38	39	40	41	42	43	44	45
TEXAS— Cont'd														
Guadalupe	1,915	124,288	0.62	1,868	11.4	1,094	6.7	19,985	15.0	25,279	17,428	7,851	3,343	2,159
Hale	2,754	33,694	0.94	420	12.4	291	8.6	6,218	23.0	5,423	3,826	1,597	982	3,086
Hall	43	3,237	1.12	18	5.9	35	11.6	705	29.5	778	595	183	42	1,360
Hamilton	216	7,970	0.93	90	10.6	123	14.5	1,400	22.9	2,305	1,461	844	135	1,999
Hansford	70	5,341	0.92	67	12.3	39	7.1	1,253	26.7	917	784	133	19	340
Hardeman	21	3,702	0.83	32	8.2	38	9.7	756	24.2	973	756	217	46	1,220
Hardin	411	44,210	0.51	714	12.5	571	10.0	6,950	14.7	10,992	6,422	4,570	832	1,488
Harris	48,643	4,838,418	1.15	70,034	14.9	27,998	6.0	847,947	20.7	525,196	279,073	246,123	194,894	4,223
Harrison	1,250	62,587	0.85	797	11.9	679	10.2	9,562	17.4	12,776	8,555	4,221	1,573	2,356
Hartley	1,122	6,120	1.15	65	11.6	23	4.1	818	21.2	636	511	125	155	2,499
Haskell	524	5,709	0.95	42	7.2	62	10.7	882	22.3	1,357	988	369	60	1,054
Hays	7,788	172,880	0.78	2,668	12.0	1,115	5.0	27,423	15.6	27,783	18,415	9,368	4,417	2,182
Hemphill	13	4,820	1.35	45	11.8	35	9.2	716	20.3	569	482	87	49	1,126
Henderson	1,238	70,214	0.69	910	11.1	1,123	13.6	13,038	21.2	20,358	13,386	6,972	2,016	2,543
Hidalgo	7,384	827,240	0.96	14,568	16.8	4,583	5.3	220,267	29.7	101,694	48,664	53,030	26,543	3,134
Hill	751	31,732	0.76	404	11.1	407	11.2	6,194	22.6	8,519	5,691	2,828	685	1,974
Hockley	807	22,668	0.94	276	12.0	214	9.3	3,768	19.7	3,830	2,540	1,290	737	3,139
Hood	691	51,818	0.84	625	10.3	680	11.2	7,634	17.9	15,954	10,913	5,041	955	1,728
Hopkins	443	33,838	0.86	441	12.0	416	11.3	6,293	21.2	7,735	6,106	1,629	392	1,079
Houston	2,769	22,655	0.97	244	10.5	309	13.3	2,947	19.1	5,207	3,648	1,559	467	2,072
Howard	6,066	37,165	1.05	443	12.2	354	9.7	4,477	17.0	5,200	3,988	1,212	1,842	4,905
Hudspeth	86	3,900	1.19	37	7.7	21	4.4	1,023	31.0	744	424	320	16	477
Hunt	2,521	85,058	0.86	1,201	12.4	989	10.2	14,815	19.6	17,653	13,628	4,025	2,038	2,331
Hutchinson	259	22,602	1.10	286	13.5	217	10.2	3,498	19.5	3,963	3,177	786	655	3,321
Irion	0	2,285	1.96	15	9.9	8	5.3	177	14.1	354	282	72	30	1,951
Jack	1,121	8,639	0.94	94	10.6	68	7.7	1,311	20.9	1,645	1,255	390	147	1,666
Jackson	233	14,198	0.92	210	14.1	136	9.1	2,272	18.7	2,929	2,201	728	240	1,608
Jasper	940	33,844	0.87	420	11.7	413	11.5	4,522	16.1	8,059	5,414	2,645	858	2,428
Jeff Davis	87	2,239	1.00	17	7.5	20	8.9	406	28.9	685	513	172	10	473
Jefferson	16,256	279,202	1.24	3,494	13.7	2,612	10.2	40,948	20.0	42,225	23,739	18,486	10,245	4,035
Jim Hogg	16	5,030	0.86	75	14.3	52	9.9	837	19.8	959	620	339	11	213
Jim Wells	354	42,503	1.07	549	13.4	390	9.6	6,645	19.1	7,691	4,013	3,678	1,879	4,543
Johnson	2,660	135,588	0.66	2,161	12.6	1,409	8.2	24,831	17.9	29,038	15,344	13,694	2,882	1,787
Jones	5,174	19,375	0.88	164	8.3	172	8.7	2,344	19.6	3,311	2,426	885	427	2,150
Karnes	3,012	18,800	1.70	179	11.4	142	9.1	1,583	15.6	2,714	1,944	770	397	2,655
Kaufman	1,302	94,745	0.62	1,745	13.6	996	7.7	18,042	17.5	19,423	12,850	6,573	2,111	1,810
Kendall	548	38,212	0.88	394	8.6	386	8.5	4,763	14.0	10,031	7,166	2,865	573	1,372
Kenedy	0	794	2.28	4	9.0	0	0.0	69	20.1	47	34	13	13	3,218
Kent	53	762	1.27	6	8.3	12	16.5	107	20.2	197	136	61	13	1,724
Kerr	1,971	51,181	1.02	546	10.4	733	14.0	7,275	20.2	15,714	12,471	3,243	1,066	2,087
Kimble	41	4,217	0.89	43	9.9	58	13.3	703	22.3	1,276	996	280	32	738
King	0	278	0.94	3	10.8	0	0.0	49	20.3	26	D	D	0	0
Kinney	334	3,791	1.12	34	9.0	34	9.0	489	20.6	901	623	278	NA	NA
Kleberg	1,691	31,086	0.97	402	12.9	261	8.4	5,426	21.0	4,881	2,467	2,414	1,206	3,802
Knox	99	3,646	0.93	37	10.1	48	13.1	675	22.5	838	644	194	88	2,270
Lamar	681	50,724	1.06	645	13.0	662	13.3	7,814	19.6	11,344	9,392	1,952	1,508	3,064
Lamb	185	12,745	0.89	177	13.5	126	9.6	2,648	24.3	2,652	1,860	792	287	2,331
Lampasas	227	17,431	0.65	217	10.2	194	9.1	3,233	19.3	5,109	3,534	1,575	260	1,385
La Salle	1,634	10,287	2.10	85	11.3	42	5.6	833	17.0	1,134	685	449	62	799
Lavaca	415	17,787	0.76	234	11.6	256	12.7	2,616	17.1	5,101	4,043	1,058	240	1,206
Lee	497	16,281	0.93	197	11.5	146	8.5	2,531	18.6	3,501	2,460	1,041	281	1,662
Leon	104	17,020	1.01	209	12.1	207	12.0	2,954	22.5	5,075	3,499	1,576	257	1,616
Liberty	5,093	71,455	0.70	1,128	13.1	821	9.5	13,595	20.6	13,175	7,374	5,801	2,005	2,500
Limestone	1,598	23,448	1.00	288	12.2	261	11.1	3,686	20.7	5,010	3,375	1,635	585	2,519
Lipscomb	39	3,222	0.83	40	11.9	30	8.9	715	24.4	592	502	90	16	442
Live Oak	1,120	13,264	1.28	130	10.7	113	9.3	1,668	19.5	2,042	1,323	719	240	1,946
Llano	137	19,100	0.85	175	8.1	334	15.4	2,572	19.4	7,131	5,039	2,092	188	1,141
Loving	0	419	9.85	4	26.3	0	0.0	22	21.2	15	15	0	11	9,091
Lubbock	11,731	300,474	1.02	4,160	13.5	2,601	8.5	39,443	15.4	44,944	28,226	16,718	16,911	5,626
Lynn	42	4,936	0.64	84	14.3	48	8.2	967	20.6	1,084	776	308	71	1,424
McCulloch	99	8,279	1.04	84	10.5	111	13.9	1,310	20.8	2,031	1,609	422	132	1,583
McLennan	8,432	251,895	1.06	3,455	13.6	2,221	8.7	37,861	18.4	42,916	27,411	15,505	8,183	3,360
McMullen	0	1,589	6.53	6	8.0	10	13.4	101	16.1	178	118	60	27	3,210
Madison	2,603	15,128	1.27	160	11.1	118	8.2	2,096	22.0	2,403	1,638	765	331	2,349
Marion	154	8,732	0.61	80	8.1	149	15.0	1,309	17.4	2,854	1,963	891	259	2,574
Martin	48	5,279	0.89	88	15.3	42	7.3	1,054	21.1	758	605	153	120	2,067

1. Per 1,000 estimated resident population.   2. Data for serious crimes have not been adjusted for underreporting; this may affect comparability between geographic areas and over time.   3. Per 100,000 population estimated by the FBI.

Crime, Education, Money Income, and Poverty

STATE County	Serious crimes known to police[2], 2016 (cont.)[1] Rate		Education — School enrollment and attainment, 2013-2017 Enrollment[3]		Attainment[4] (percent)		Local government expenditures,[5] 2014-2015		Money income, 2013-2017 Per capita income[6]	Households Median income (dollars)	Percent		Income and poverty, 2017 Median household income (dollars)	Percent below poverty level		
	Violent	Property	Total	Percent private	High school graduate or less	Bachelor's degree or more	Total current spending (mil dol)	Current spending per student (dollars)			with income of less than $50,000	with income of $200,000 or more		All persons	Children under 18 years	Children 5 to 17 years in families
	46	47	48	49	50	51	52	53	54	55	56	57	58	59	60	61
TEXAS— Cont'd																
Guadalupe	204	1,955	41,292	11.5	41.8	26.8	193.3	7,652	29,300	66,187	35.7	4.4	66,886	9.3	12	12.1
Hale	248	2,838	9,754	10.1	58.3	16.1	67.5	9,167	19,205	46,012	55.0	1.4	43,570	19.9	27.7	25.4
Hall	356	1,004	763	2.1	54.2	12.7	5.6	10,442	20,022	31,324	69.8	1.1	32,980	24	41.4	37.6
Hamilton	296	1,703	1,677	7.7	50.3	22.8	13.3	8,749	26,522	46,611	51.6	3.8	44,230	16.1	25.8	24.7
Hansford	143	197	1,431	3.6	56.4	15.9	16.3	11,262	21,989	40,678	60.4	1.2	55,761	11.9	17.1	15.6
Hardeman	53	1,167	883	3.6	56.5	14.4	9.3	12,634	21,517	37,995	60.2	2.7	39,022	18	29	28.5
Hardin	150	1,338	13,385	14.0	50.4	16.8	86.4	8,065	29,693	56,131	44.4	5.3	58,829	12.7	16.7	15.1
Harris	742	3,480	1,264,758	11.8	42.8	30.5	7,077.5	8,654	30,856	57,791	43.5	7.8	58,664	15.9	23.2	21.9
Harrison	312	2,045	16,340	11.3	49.8	18.8	112.3	8,512	25,123	48,644	51.2	2.8	50,584	17.3	22.7	21.4
Hartley	387	2,112	1,064	22.4	58.2	17.0	4.3	11,464	20,676	64,427	40.3	3.0	69,000	8.9	9.4	9
Haskell	141	914	924	8.7	63.4	12.3	10.9	12,513	21,120	43,529	56.9	2.2	35,075	20.6	32.8	30.7
Hays	236	1,947	64,275	7.8	33.1	36.6	274.1	8,141	29,253	62,815	40.4	5.8	66,525	12.2	11.8	11.1
Hemphill	276	850	1,278	1.9	49.5	22.7	10.5	10,043	29,470	68,679	38.7	5.5	64,338	10	15.5	13.9
Henderson	366	2,177	16,879	5.9	50.6	18.1	88.2	8,668	24,315	44,888	54.0	2.6	44,500	17.2	26.2	24.1
Hidalgo	294	2,840	272,122	6.2	59.5	17.8	2,186.4	9,531	15,883	37,097	60.9	2.0	36,978	29.5	41.3	39.7
Hill	184	1,790	8,421	5.6	52.6	16.4	63.8	9,871	23,342	45,970	53.3	3.0	47,162	14.9	22.2	21.1
Hockley	473	2,666	6,785	5.1	51.2	13.6	53.6	10,764	22,673	49,184	50.7	3.0	48,449	16.2	23.3	22.6
Hood	181	1,547	10,515	11.5	40.6	26.3	66.8	8,402	32,578	60,275	42.9	5.7	64,687	10.6	17.2	16.9
Hopkins	143	936	8,518	7.1	53.4	17.3	59.2	8,800	24,236	47,832	52.2	3.1	44,925	13.7	21.1	19.7
Houston	240	1,832	4,094	8.2	55.4	14.5	30.1	9,633	17,884	33,552	66.5	1.2	37,723	22.3	31.8	29.9
Howard	530	4,375	7,910	5.9	54.8	12.9	55.8	9,468	22,994	50,855	48.9	3.0	46,899	18.1	23.1	22.8
Hudspeth	119	358	817	2.0	75.8	7.6	8.1	12,429	12,543	26,346	75.7	0.7	39,683	18.3	25.4	27.2
Hunt	329	2,002	24,024	6.7	50.0	19.1	122.4	8,332	23,942	49,319	50.6	2.6	53,421	16.9	22.7	22.5
Hutchinson	304	3,016	5,275	6.1	47.2	13.7	39.3	9,273	25,154	50,035	50.0	2.6	53,465	12.9	17.2	15.3
Irion	65	1,886	380	1.8	46.8	14.8	3.9	11,722	32,307	63,021	39.2	6.0	63,827	9.3	13.2	12.1
Jack	261	1,405	1,699	10.4	62.3	11.4	16.6	10,304	25,553	52,829	46.8	3.7	47,824	17.4	23.6	21.1
Jackson	241	1,367	3,565	6.4	48.2	18.3	32.1	8,984	26,809	58,504	40.7	4.4	49,350	16	20.2	19.7
Jasper	356	2,071	7,534	6.7	58.9	11.6	56.9	8,922	21,402	41,960	55.1	1.9	43,368	20	28.3	27.2
Jeff Davis	95	378	440	11.8	35.1	36.3	3.7	14,496	25,167	46,534	51.6	0.1	38,537	12.8	34.8	41
Jefferson	763	3,272	59,845	6.3	49.2	18.9	368.8	8,794	25,370	46,315	53.2	3.6	47,852	18.6	27	27
Jim Hogg	39	174	1,452	0.3	61.5	11.3	11.1	9,816	17,761	31,403	67.5	2.5	32,319	27.3	40.2	38.4
Jim Wells	522	4,021	10,807	4.6	63.3	11.3	76.4	9,086	20,631	41,103	55.0	1.9	40,681	23.7	36.3	36.5
Johnson	218	1,569	37,375	12.6	48.9	18.5	276.1	8,445	26,574	60,458	40.2	3.3	61,813	10.4	15.4	14.4
Jones	222	1,928	3,514	6.3	62.3	10.9	27.8	10,340	17,960	48,601	51.0	3.5	44,132	20.9	24.9	24.1
Karnes	301	2,354	2,899	10.3	60.8	13.7	26.5	10,496	27,011	53,051	48.5	6.4	48,708	22.1	25.8	24.4
Kaufman	242	1,568	31,444	12.3	47.4	20.7	211.1	8,057	26,631	63,926	38.9	3.6	65,942	9.3	12.8	12.4
Kendall	84	1,288	9,787	15.3	29.1	39.0	73.7	8,452	39,517	81,023	30.1	12.4	89,637	7.3	10.9	9.6
Kenedy	1,485	1,733	136	13.2	84.8	6.5	2.0	25,705	13,705	24,800	71.7	0.0	38,031	15.2	18.8	14.3
Kent	398	1,326	104	0.0	47.2	23.8	3.0	23,292	27,515	52,250	48.4	5.8	45,330	13.3	18.1	17.8
Kerr	243	1,845	10,019	15.1	39.5	25.9	57.4	8,383	28,484	48,698	51.0	3.1	49,748	13.3	23.5	21.3
Kimble	92	646	681	2.3	50.8	19.3	6.2	9,347	26,982	41,095	60.7	3.2	41,081	18.6	36.8	33.8
King	0	0	64	0.0	53.1	19.8	3.2	27,617	29,918	56,964	44.6	9.9	56,346	13.9	24.4	20.9
Kinney	NA	NA	818	20.3	59.7	11.5	6.8	10,657	21,395	34,926	59.8	1.1	42,650	20.1	26.7	25
Kleberg	299	3,502	11,035	7.5	45.0	24.1	50.1	9,684	19,806	41,700	58.2	1.9	41,257	25.5	34.1	32.7
Knox	361	1,909	872	3.9	52.9	20.5	9.4	11,643	21,046	46,319	53.6	0.9	37,749	20.6	32.9	30.2
Lamar	408	2,655	11,390	7.1	49.5	17.1	76.8	8,971	23,625	42,198	56.7	2.9	47,212	16.2	24	23.8
Lamb	447	1,884	3,447	2.2	58.4	16.4	30.0	9,752	21,760	43,712	56.9	3.4	41,099	20	29.6	26.7
Lampasas	37	1,347	4,995	10.7	38.4	20.1	30.4	8,359	26,405	54,467	45.4	3.0	55,759	13.2	20.7	18.9
La Salle	90	708	1,517	16.4	71.0	15.1	16.0	11,811	26,268	44,601	59.8	6.1	41,518	29.2	36.1	36.1
Lavaca	146	1,060	4,734	17.5	57.3	17.4	41.0	10,373	29,946	51,708	48.4	4.6	51,191	12.1	17.4	16.1
Lee	237	1,425	3,987	9.5	54.2	17.6	27.8	8,910	26,740	55,741	45.0	3.7	54,164	12.7	19.1	18.9
Leon	176	1,440	3,496	3.5	56.9	15.9	31.6	10,130	27,096	44,875	53.7	2.6	43,189	16.1	23.6	21.6
Liberty	382	2,119	18,144	8.5	62.7	9.3	126.8	8,445	22,153	48,344	51.0	2.9	50,420	15.5	22.2	21.1
Limestone	379	2,140	4,886	7.1	53.7	13.8	37.9	9,154	21,093	40,356	59.4	1.2	41,434	19.1	28.7	27.5
Lipscomb	111	332	791	4.0	52.6	18.8	10.6	12,116	29,995	59,583	42.6	4.2	54,091	13.4	19.1	17.8
Live Oak	284	1,662	2,220	4.5	56.2	11.3	19.5	10,534	22,847	51,480	47.9	3.6	50,430	17.4	25.1	24.1
Llano	121	1,020	2,538	7.8	40.0	26.6	18.6	10,350	35,680	50,524	49.5	6.4	51,078	12.9	25.5	24.8
Loving	0	9,091	7	0.0	53.1	4.7	NA	NA	35,530	80,938	29.0	9.7	65,203	9.7	23.9	16.2
Lubbock	959	4,667	99,824	9.5	40.4	28.7	430.8	8,684	26,196	49,078	50.8	4.4	47,460	18.9	22.4	21.6
Lynn	160	1,263	1,436	9.6	55.6	17.0	15.0	10,898	26,758	44,922	53.8	4.7	44,567	18.1	28.1	27
McCulloch	48	1,535	1,623	2.6	53.0	16.0	16.5	10,480	23,398	42,367	55.2	2.4	40,157	19.4	29.4	26.8
McLennan	444	2,916	74,556	22.6	44.0	22.9	461.1	8,807	24,273	46,262	53.3	3.5	47,306	17.3	22.5	21
McMullen	119	3,092	165	12.7	55.4	20.7	4.7	17,962	33,472	71,389	40.2	13.4	68,133	11.6	16.6	14.5
Madison	355	1,994	2,433	3.8	60.0	13.0	22.9	8,532	17,436	44,004	55.7	2.0	42,058	18.3	24.2	23.2
Marion	606	1,967	1,837	7.9	56.7	14.1	11.2	9,681	25,933	36,938	63.5	3.5	36,936	22.8	37.2	35.8
Martin	155	1,912	1,524	6.8	54.6	20.6	14.5	12,114	28,560	71,115	36.5	9.7	59,907	13.3	20.4	19.2

1. Data for serious crimes have not been adjusted for underreporting; this may affect comparability between geographic areas and over time.   2. Per 100,000 population estimated by the FBI.   3. All persons 3 years old and over enrolled in nursery school through college.   4. Persons 25 years old and over.   5. Elementary and secondary education expenditures.   6. Based on population estimated by the American Community Survey, 2013–2017.

Table B. States and Counties — Personal Income and Earnings

STATE County	Personal income, 2017										Earnings, 2017		
	Total (mil dol)	Percent change 2016-2017	Per capita Dollars[1]	Per capita Rank	Wages and salaries (mil dol)	Supplements to wages and salaries, employer contributions (mil dol) Pension and insurance	Government social insurance	Proprietors' income (mil dol)	Dividends, interest, and rent (mil dol)	Personal transfer reecipts (mil dol)	Total (mil dol)	Contributions for government social insurance (mil dol) From employee and self-employed	From employer
	62	63	64	65	66	67	68	69	70	71	72	73	74
TEXAS— Cont'd													
Guadalupe	6,868	5.2	43,019	1,141	1,835	300	129	378	1,076	1,253	2,642	159	129
Hale	1,085	5.6	31,778	2,784	465	84	35	105	175	307	688	37	35
Hall	92	9.8	30,033	2,927	26	6	2	0	21	40	35	3	2
Hamilton	479	2.9	56,845	225	95	20	7	25	224	103	146	10	7
Hansford	331	9.3	60,759	147	127	25	8	120	51	41	281	9	8
Hardeman	152	0.9	38,151	1,853	47	10	3	9	30	51	70	4	3
Hardin	2,540	3.6	44,456	964	567	89	42	73	298	559	771	54	42
Harris	247,482	4.7	53,188	339	165,462	20,885	10,976	44,989	42,447	30,033	242,312	12,462	10,976
Harrison	2,671	1.3	40,068	1,538	1,168	204	83	172	451	639	1,627	97	83
Hartley	354	14.0	62,274	133	113	20	9	161	58	24	304	7	9
Haskell	199	2.0	34,682	2,392	60	13	4	14	35	68	92	6	4
Hays	8,987	7.7	41,902	1,273	2,798	479	192	852	1,569	1,192	4,321	230	192
Hemphill	212	-10.7	52,632	354	136	24	9	30	71	23	200	10	9
Henderson	3,098	3.4	38,216	1,843	652	124	46	240	522	955	1,062	77	46
Hidalgo	22,047	2.3	25,617	3,084	9,157	1,896	645	2,344	2,607	6,509	14,042	758	645
Hill	1,345	4.3	37,502	1,944	375	69	26	94	215	388	564	38	26
Hockley	859	-1.2	37,199	2,002	497	86	34	31	126	226	647	37	34
Hood	2,760	3.9	47,368	678	678	101	49	192	573	615	1,021	71	49
Hopkins	1,382	3.7	37,868	1,903	524	85	37	138	216	364	785	46	37
Houston	841	3.6	36,552	2,111	352	62	23	21	153	270	458	30	23
Howard	1,311	3.7	36,367	2,139	653	142	46	60	224	295	901	50	46
Hudspeth	147	6.2	33,241	2,588	68	17	6	5	18	28	95	5	6
Hunt	3,447	4.5	36,725	2,089	1,601	293	112	191	428	878	2,196	128	112
Hutchinson	899	1.0	42,053	1,257	529	112	36	48	129	196	726	40	36
Irion	84	-3.3	55,231	269	59	11	4	6	26	13	80	4	4
Jack	345	7.2	39,070	1,709	164	27	11	25	78	74	228	14	11
Jackson	592	3.7	39,981	1,553	262	45	19	26	97	151	351	21	19
Jasper	1,391	2.3	39,105	1,701	433	76	31	61	175	425	602	40	31
Jeff Davis	90	0.8	39,627	1,617	27	6	2	9	29	20	44	3	2
Jefferson	10,851	1.9	42,338	1,225	7,285	1,320	512	842	1,554	2,593	9,958	543	512
Jim Hogg	157	-0.9	30,088	2,922	69	18	5	1	24	58	94	6	5
Jim Wells	1,549	0.1	37,906	1,900	726	110	52	67	204	507	955	58	52
Johnson	6,682	5.4	39,941	1,562	2,124	344	151	429	834	1,381	3,049	185	151
Jones	599	2.9	29,969	2,932	177	48	11	44	92	182	280	15	11
Karnes	683	5.3	44,986	901	311	58	21	28	264	150	417	24	21
Kaufman	5,055	6.7	41,140	1,389	1,385	235	97	294	563	876	2,010	119	97
Kendall	3,690	6.5	83,808	29	803	110	55	443	992	371	1,411	78	55
Kenedy	17	-2.6	41,297	1,366	36	6	3	5	4	2	49	2	3
Kent	37	5.4	48,558	586	10	3	1	9	7	10	23	1	1
Kerr	2,446	2.7	47,288	689	788	131	56	235	803	584	1,211	79	56
Kimble	181	-.6	41,007	1,406	45	10	3	8	53	54	67	5	3
King	11	-26.1	37,689	1,924	4	1	0	2	3	1	8	0	0
Kinney	108	1.9	28,964	2,987	39	11	3		27	35	52	4	3
Kleberg	1,154	2.3	37,123	2,010	492	123	36	48	189	308	699	37	36
Knox	136	0.0	36,564	2,109	46	10	3	9	23	49	69	4	3
Lamar	2,014	4.2	40,610	1,456	958	161	68	151	294	589	1,339	81	68
Lamb	508	11.7	38,465	1,805	161	31	12	104	59	136	308	13	12
Lampasas	1,011	3.3	48,098	615	165	31	12	61	215	262	269	19	12
La Salle	263	-0.4	34,696	2,389	222	35	16	12	98	58	284	16	16
Lavaca	961	2.5	47,880	633	245	43	17	82	215	243	387	25	17
Lee	773	5.4	44,991	900	370	57	26	72	148	164	525	30	26
Leon	655	2.2	37,988	1,887	244	39	18	64	124	211	364	24	18
Liberty	2,998	3.6	35,840	2,217	792	142	55	143	295	755	1,133	71	55
Limestone	799	2.4	33,945	2,489	325	77	21	23	124	288	447	27	21
Lipscomb	185	7.9	54,838	288	71	12	5	57	34	23	146	7	5
Live Oak	392	0.7	32,196	2,727	223	46	16	7	103	101	292	17	16
Llano	993	4.3	46,826	727	192	31	13	110	337	258	347	26	13
Loving	6	11.2	45,858	810	3	1	0	0	3	0	4	0	0
Lubbock	12,646	3.7	41,433	1,342	6,250	1,081	422	978	2,294	2,359	8,731	464	422
Lynn	203	12.7	34,704	2,387	71	15	5		30	55	90	6	5
McCulloch	298	4.8	37,492	1,947	127	25	9	14	61	101	174	11	9
McLennan	9,985	4.4	39,740	1,601	5,383	865	383	740	1,628	2,141	7,371	417	383
McMullen	46	-18.6	58,513	192	31	6	2	-4	31		35	2	2
Madison	426	3.3	29,957	2,935	166	32	12	31	86	132	242	14	12
Marion	367	2.4	36,419	2,130	73	14	6	15	61	141	109	9	6
Martin	263	3.8	46,781	729	108	20	8	14	61	45	150	8	8

1. Based on the resident population estimated as of July 1 of the year shown.

Table B. States and Counties — Earnings, Social Security, and Housing

STATE County	Earnings, 2017 (cont.)									Social Security beneficiaries, December 2017			Housing units, 2018	
	Percent by selected industries											Supplemental Security Income recipients, 2017		
	Farm	Mining, quarrying, and extractions	Construction	Manufacturing	Information; professional, scientific, technical services	Retail trade	Finance, insurance, real estate, and leasing	Health care and social assistance	Government	Number	Rate[1]		Total	Percent change, 2010-2018
	75	76	77	78	79	80	81	82	83	84	85	86	87	88
TEXAS— Cont'd														
Guadalupe	0	0.5	10.4	21.1	4.3	7.1	4.3	6.8	16	26,370	165	1,920	60,135	20.2
Hale	9.7	0.8	5.8	5.4	3.1	7.4	4.4	D	19.7	5,840	171	909	13,377	-1.1
Hall	-2.6	0.6	2.5	4	D	9.1	7.6	8.4	36	825	269	84	1,915	-1.4
Hamilton	-0.2	0.1	11.8	7.2	5.2	9.1	4	9.4	28.4	2,355	280	179	4,568	0.1
Hansford	43.2	20.1	2.5	0.8	D	1.6	3.3	0.3	12	925	170	36	2,343	0.2
Hardeman	10.8	D	D	D	D	6.4	3.9	D	32.1	1,030	258	128	2,380	-1.5
Hardin	-0.4	3.4	15	8.3	5.8	11.1	3.6	15.4	16	11,820	207	1,219	25,004	10.7
Harris	0	6.8	8.3	7.9	13.1	4.3	8	7.5	9.5	533,250	115	107,185	1,788,240	11.8
Harrison	0.1	8.5	7.3	27.9	D	4.8	6.4	D	11.1	13,705	206	1,856	28,726	3.7
Hartley	53.3	D	D	D	D	2.1	D	D	15.1	590	104	8	2,017	3.6
Haskell	8	5.5	5.5	1.4	D	13.3	D	6.9	26.8	1,395	243	170	3,445	0
Hays	-0.1	0.7	13.9	7.8	7.5	9.4	5.5	8.6	20.6	27,555	128	2,275	82,002	38
Hemphill	6.4	30.5	15.2	2.3	2	2.4	3.1	0.6	14.1	555	138	21	1,690	3.8
Henderson	0.3	4.9	10	11.8	5.7	9.9	4.3	12.5	18.1	21,625	267	2,565	41,478	4.8
Hidalgo	0.4	1	4.4	2.6	4.6	10	5.2	19.3	27.3	108,345	126	41,737	281,639	13.4
Hill	-2.2	1.9	20.4	10	4.4	9.9	3.9	D	20.6	8,910	249	981	16,388	1.7
Hockley	-1.6	40	6.1	1.9	D	3.9	3.7	D	15.9	4,105	178	506	9,370	0.9
Hood	-0.3	14.3	11	4.6	D	9.4	8.6	12.5	12	16,015	275	844	26,776	7.3
Hopkins	7.4	1.5	6.2	13.3	D	8.3	5.5	9	13.5	8,205	225	920	15,451	2.8
Houston	-2.4	3.4	6.6	13.1	D	5.3	12.7	6.8	20.8	5,510	239	884	11,712	1.6
Howard	-0.7	10.9	6.5	12.1	4.5	5.8	3.8	D	27.9	5,730	159	825	13,197	0.6
Hudspeth	1.7	0.3	D	D	D	0.8	D	1.3	61.3	785	178	180	1,581	3.5
Hunt	0	D	6.1	38.9	4.2	5.9	2.2	7	20.6	18,740	200	2,459	38,084	3.7
Hutchinson	0.2	26.3	15.2	19.1	2.5	4.6	2.3	D	12.3	4,290	201	337	10,668	0.4
Irion	-0.8	68.5	D	D	D	D	D	0.9	7.7	360	237	19	862	0.8
Jack	-3.7	37.4	18	1.4	D	1.5	3.6	D	15.9	1,775	201	114	4,161	1.6
Jackson	1.2	7.6	16.3	D	5.3	4.5	3.2	D	18.2	3,095	209	308	6,742	2.3
Jasper	0.1	1.4	12.4	21.6	4.1	7.4	3.8	D	18.7	8,735	246	1,258	17,280	2.9
Jeff Davis	-0.5	D	D	D	D	3.8	D	8.6	34.8	665	292	37	1,641	1.7
Jefferson	0	0.6	13	23.8	7.2	5.8	3.6	10.9	12.7	46,175	180	8,797	108,771	4.2
Jim Hogg	-2.9	8	3.7	2.8	D	5.9	D	D	51.2	1,025	197	279	2,473	1.3
Jim Wells	0.5	31.5	3	2.8	2.7	5.4	6.3	D	12.7	8,570	210	1,791	16,418	1.7
Johnson	0	4.4	13.8	15.3	4	9.2	4.1	8.6	15.4	29,935	179	3,046	62,793	10.7
Jones	5.3	3.2	6	3.7	D	4.7	4.5	3.5	46.9	3,555	178	390	7,437	0.3
Karnes	-2.9	17.8	3.6	5.7	D	5	4.3	2.7	25.4	2,795	184	439	6,041	6.9
Kaufman	-0.6	0.2	15.2	14.3	D	7.9	4.4	7.1	20.2	20,150	164	2,048	42,480	10.8
Kendall	-0.2	3	16.2	3.9	15.9	13.1	9.7	8.2	9.2	9,580	218	313	16,563	17.8
Kenedy	15	D	0.6	0	D	D	D	D	9.9	50	120	7	233	0.4
Kent	-1.6	D	D	0.5	D	9.4	D	8.5	34	185	242	14	558	1.1
Kerr	-0.1	0.2	13.3	6.7	7.3	8.8	6.1	D	17.7	15,865	307	977	24,706	3.7
Kimble	-6.3	1.1	15.4	5.5	D	9.4	6.2	4.3	29.8	1,355	307	116	3,398	0.9
King	8.7	2.3	D	0.1	D	5.9	4.1	D	46.6	30	101	0	187	1.1
Kinney	-3.5	0.1	D	D	0.1	3.1	D	1.2	61.7	945	252	100	1,968	1.4
Kleberg	0.5	2.4	3.6	2.9	D	7	3.7	D	50.2	5,150	166	1,045	13,296	4
Knox	11.6	12.8	D	D	D	8	D	D	32.9	880	237	110	2,037	-0.3
Lamar	-0.3	D	8.9	26.1	D	7.6	4	14.5	12.8	12,220	246	1,946	22,785	1.4
Lamb	34.4	0	4	1	D	4.3	D	3.3	17.2	2,765	209	435	6,058	-1.1
Lampasas	-4	D	14	9.2	4.8	18.7	9.1	D	21.4	5,340	254	453	9,453	8.4
La Salle	0.5	50.4	5.9	0.1	D	2.3	D	1.7	20.8	1,215	160	314	2,968	8.1
Lavaca	-1.3	4.5	16.6	19.1	4.3	6.2	5.7	D	13.9	5,190	259	419	10,465	1.2
Lee	-0.4	4.2	45.7	5	3.8	3.3	5.9	D	14.2	3,615	210	310	7,795	4
Leon	3.8	10.8	19.9	21.2	2.7	4.1	5.3	1.8	13.5	5,320	309	456	9,813	3.2
Liberty	-0.2	7	13.1	7.6	3.5	8.7	4	6.7	24.5	14,565	174	2,628	31,735	10.4
Limestone	-2.2	9.3	3.8	5.6	D	6	3.4	8.2	38.6	5,325	226	786	10,692	1.5
Lipscomb	1.6	7.1	D	D	D	4.8	D	2.5	13.3	590	175	32	1,509	-0.2
Live Oak	-3.5	19.8	7.1	14.8	7.1	4.2	6.7	2	20.9	2,100	172	199	6,255	3.1
Llano	-2.2	0.5	10.6	3.5	6.2	5.5	9.2	7	14.8	6,995	330	340	15,542	8.8
Loving	-4.6	D	D	D	D	0	0	0	22.2	15	112	0	51	2
Lubbock	0.1	0.5	7.1	3.2	7.3	8.5	7.9	16	25	46,335	152	6,436	129,655	12.7
Lynn	-7.9	9.5	8.7	1.3	D	3.6	D	D	33.1	1,130	193	159	2,671	-0.2
McCulloch	-3.6	19.4	6.5	5.3	2.6	8.2	3.9	7	20.3	2,130	268	280	4,342	0.9
McLennan	-0.1	0.3	8.2	17.9	5.5	6.5	9.6	10.7	15.6	44,820	178	7,281	102,452	7.7
McMullen	-2.6	33.1	0.3	D	D	3.6	D	D	26.7	190	244	10	497	2.5
Madison	4.3	D	14.1	5.5	D	12.8	3.1	D	29.4	2,555	180	295	5,301	4
Marion	-0.3	D	2.5	19.1	D	7.2	2.6	D	19.6	3,060	304	411	6,391	2.9
Martin	4	D	19.2	D	D	5.7	D	3.4	23.4	810	144	102	1,897	2.4

1. Per 1,000 resident population estimated as of July 1 of the year shown.

STATE County	Housing units, 2013-2017								Civilian labor force, 2018				Civilian employment[6], 2013-2017		
	Occupied units										Unemployment			Percent	
			Owner-occupied			Renter-occupied									
				Median owner cost as a percent of income			Median rent as a percent of income[2]	Sub-standard units[4] (percent)		Percent change, 2017-2018				Management, business, science, and arts	Construction, production, and maintenance occupations
				With a mort-gage	Without a mort-gage[2]	Median rent[3]									
	Total	Percent	Median value[1]						Total		Total	Rate[5]	Total		
	89	90	91	92	93	94	95	96	97	98	99	100	101	102	103

STATE County	89	90	91	92	93	94	95	96	97	98	99	100	101	102	103
TEXAS— Cont'd															
Guadalupe	51,990	75.4	175,000	20.7	10.6	1,018	25.9	3.6	79,824	1.7	2,497	3.1	70,169	33.4	25.2
Hale	11,217	60.4	80,200	18.8	10.0	644	24.9	6.7	12,540	0.1	604	4.8	14,267	25.6	31.6
Hall	1,244	62.6	48,700	23.6	12.2	547	24.4	4.4	1,128	-0.2	49	4.3	1,125	20.4	30.4
Hamilton	3,157	75.7	108,500	21.2	12.3	607	26.9	4.7	3,648	0.6	121	3.3	3,584	29.0	32.1
Hansford	1,924	73.0	93,500	19.1	15.2	716	28.6	4.2	2,879	0.5	67	2.3	2,394	32.8	39.1
Hardeman	1,533	75.0	38,400	16.5	13.2	523	22.8	3.6	1,678	1.1	61	3.6	1,695	30.4	30.2
Hardin	20,739	80.8	113,100	18.2	10.0	781	25	3.3	25,465	0.5	1,324	5.2	24,056	31.9	29.6
Harris	1,562,813	54.7	154,100	21.2	10.9	976	29.6	6	2,304,397	1.6	100,473	4.4	2,180,392	35.4	24.3
Harrison	23,363	74.2	115,100	19.2	11.6	743	27.2	4.2	30,028	1.8	1,308	4.4	27,603	32.4	31.5
Hartley	1,754	60.8	146,900	19.9	11.1	742	22.2	4.8	2,890	-1.8	53	1.8	2,049	38.0	29.9
Haskell	2,128	77.8	49,200	20.6	10.5	555	37.8	4.8	2,356	-3.4	90	3.8	2,180	22.9	35.3
Hays	68,045	62.1	204,700	22.6	11.7	1,047	34.4	4.5	114,386	3.2	3,385	3	99,069	37.5	18.1
Hemphill	1,358	68.4	130,700	18.0	10.0	814	21.1	4.5	2,285	-1.4	48	2.1	1,898	31.3	27.5
Henderson	30,459	75.4	99,000	21.6	12.8	778	29.7	3.5	36,389	2	1,364	3.7	31,087	29.1	28.4
Hidalgo	232,523	67.5	82,400	23.4	12.6	699	31.9	13.6	348,672	1.6	22,881	6.6	313,678	27.0	23.9
Hill	12,674	73.8	93,700	20.8	12.1	690	28.6	5.5	16,326	0.9	592	3.6	14,579	26.2	32.3
Hockley	8,065	68.6	82,300	19.1	10.0	673	26.4	5.3	11,562	2.6	359	3.1	10,337	26.2	32.3
Hood	21,527	76.1	170,800	20.5	10.7	896	30.5	3.6	26,510	2.2	984	3.7	22,905	32.6	29.3
Hopkins	13,287	69.3	97,200	19.7	10.5	746	27.4	5.2	17,354	1	584	3.4	15,408	28.4	31.5
Houston	8,328	68.7	80,200	22.1	13.7	650	44.4	3.3	10,162	-2.3	380	3.7	7,642	24.7	31.0
Howard	11,032	68.1	85,700	18.7	10.0	837	26.9	3.6	13,648	3.1	446	3.3	14,393	29.0	29.5
Hudspeth	890	74.7	44,100	22.9	15.5	597	17	14.6	1,666	0	79	4.7	1,083	17.8	29.6
Hunt	31,781	69.7	105,000	21.8	11.9	826	31.3	4.6	42,373	2.3	1,605	3.8	38,753	31.7	26.7
Hutchinson	7,799	79.5	75,500	17.1	10.0	726	26.6	3.6	9,065	-3.7	453	5	9,149	22.0	36.1
Irion	648	79.3	146,400	23.7	10.0	858	20.9	4.5	771	1.8	24	3.1	718	37.2	32.2
Jack	3,075	82.1	81,400	14.7	11.2	704	23.8	2.8	4,444	12.3	111	2.5	3,160	24.9	38.1
Jackson	5,232	69.8	96,700	16.4	10.0	815	22.8	5.9	7,412	0.4	243	3.3	6,760	26.6	38.3
Jasper	11,974	75.1	97,400	20.0	12.0	724	31.7	2.7	13,377	-0.6	864	6.5	12,541	23.7	32.8
Jeff Davis	1,007	80.3	111,300	16.1	11.6	676	17.1	5.9	1,082	1.3	32	3	911	32.1	31.6
Jefferson	94,020	61.9	101,300	20.8	11.4	808	29.6	3.1	108,181	0.4	6,859	6.3	105,319	28.9	28.4
Jim Hogg	1,587	75.9	61,800	19.0	11.3	500	33.2	7.5	1,875	-1.7	107	5.7	1,646	26.4	36.5
Jim Wells	13,614	69.4	73,800	19.5	11.2	742	32.6	7.3	17,059	2.3	926	5.4	16,282	28.6	32.3
Johnson	55,467	73.9	132,000	19.6	11.5	934	27.9	3.5	79,949	2.3	2,749	3.4	72,273	30.6	33.2
Jones	5,635	73.9	73,100	17.4	12.2	713	21.8	2.1	5,721	1.2	274	4.8	5,057	31.9	24.6
Karnes	4,303	74.4	94,100	15.3	10.0	698	24.9	6.8	6,845	6.1	193	2.8	5,433	27.4	29.6
Kaufman	36,525	77.1	154,000	22.2	12.1	933	29.4	3.3	61,846	2.4	2,146	3.5	53,146	33.4	25.5
Kendall	13,691	72.9	297,700	21.0	11.4	1,123	26.8	1.8	21,491	1.8	628	2.9	18,640	44.8	16.1
Kenedy	152	28.3	21,300	0.0	16.6	474	26.8	11.2	242	0	9	3.7	183	19.1	28.4
Kent	275	73.5	70,500	12.8	10.0	475	35	4.7	458	0.9	11	2.4	304	40.1	22.0
Kerr	20,580	71.2	164,000	21.4	11.3	802	28.5	3.8	21,848	2.3	705	3.2	21,475	30.3	22.5
Kimble	1,941	75.1	107,200	23.3	12.1	589	30.7	1.5	1,890	-0.2	58	3.1	2,027	26.0	27.3
King	101	19.8	38,800	0.0	10.0	700	13.8	10.9	214	29.7	6	2.8	173	38.2	38.7
Kinney	1,200	77.3	64,200	21.6	10.0	513	25.3	2.2	1,257	7.7	59	4.7	1,351	24.2	26.5
Kleberg	10,958	53.0	86,800	18.4	11.5	800	29.5	6.8	13,333	-0.6	662	5	13,683	31.1	27.8
Knox	1,376	80.7	44,400	13.1	10.0	494	23.5	3.9	1,466	-1.3	53	3.6	1,504	32.6	38.1
Lamar	19,085	64.3	88,100	18.4	11.4	670	28.7	3.1	23,954	0.7	905	3.8	21,134	27.1	30.5
Lamb	4,790	71.0	62,700	20.1	12.3	644	21.8	4.1	5,247	1	232	4.4	5,671	34.8	31.3
Lampasas	7,748	74.3	136,800	20.1	12.4	823	26.5	1.8	9,243	0.2	343	3.7	8,612	32.4	26.9
La Salle	2,286	70.3	70,800	18.6	12.2	549	19.4	10.6	4,599	9.2	112	2.4	2,716	29.6	36.4
Lavaca	7,684	75.5	143,300	18.5	10.0	663	21.9	8	8,784	0.5	277	3.2	8,843	32.8	32.5
Lee	6,118	77.5	138,300	22.2	12.0	855	28.9	4.9	9,425	-1.3	293	3.1	7,894	26.5	27.8
Leon	6,245	78.4	102,300	20.5	10.0	633	25.5	3.5	6,155	-0.6	309	5	6,574	26.9	36.0
Liberty	25,974	74.8	93,200	20.0	12.2	806	28.1	5	32,303	0.9	1,889	5.8	28,685	24.7	38.4
Limestone	8,100	75.4	84,800	24.4	12.7	680	28.4	3.8	8,399	0.9	393	4.7	8,824	27.3	30.8
Lipscomb	1,276	73.3	92,400	18.3	10.0	705	16.4	3.4	1,657	1.8	45	2.7	1,653	31.6	40.3
Live Oak	3,586	82.5	84,900	17.1	10.7	765	29.5	3.7	5,233	-3.5	197	3.8	4,301	25.2	33.0
Llano	8,681	76.6	184,500	21.7	11.4	819	28.9	4.1	8,543	2	313	3.7	7,660	31.3	22.3
Loving	31	51.6	0	0.0	10.0	930	22.5	0	102	2	4	3.9	39	33.3	53.8
Lubbock	110,275	55.9	122,700	20.4	11.2	882	32.3	3.5	157,225	0.7	4,811	3.1	145,154	35.0	19.7
Lynn	2,147	68.7	76,800	23.4	10.1	663	27.4	2.7	2,772	-0.1	90	3.2	2,419	31.1	29.8
McCulloch	3,143	76.3	82,000	20.9	12.1	721	32	3.1	3,753	1.8	125	3.3	3,658	23.2	33.6
McLennan	88,208	58.0	125,200	21.3	12.1	805	31.5	3.3	118,786	0.5	4,242	3.6	112,592	32.8	23.9
McMullen	194	73.7	74,700	27.5	10.0	529	10	13.9	740	-1.2	14	1.9	202	30.7	26.7
Madison	4,174	73.5	101,700	27.8	10.6	790	25.2	8	4,582	-2.3	201	4.4	4,249	28.6	28.5
Marion	4,457	79.2	88,600	22.3	10.0	674	34.8	3.1	4,260	-1.9	195	4.6	3,635	28.7	30.5
Martin	1,635	77.1	120,500	17.7	10.0	800	21	8.3	2,807	11	68	2.4	2,527	29.3	37.4

1. Specified owner-occupied units. 2. A value of 10.0 represents 10 percent or less; a value of 50.0 represents 50 percent or more. 3. Specified renter-occupied units. 4. Overcrowded or lacking complete plumbing facilities. 5. Percent of civilian labor force. 6. Civilian employed persons 16 years old and over.

Table B. States and Counties — Nonfarm Employment and Agriculture

	Private nonfarm establishments, employment and payroll, 2016									Agriculture, 2017			
	Employment						Annual payroll		Farms			Farm producers whose primary occupation is farming (percent)
STATE County	Number of establishments	Total	Health care and social assistance	Manufacturing	Retail trade	Finance and insurance	Professional, scientific, and technical services	Total (mil dol)	Average per employee (dollars)	Number	Percent with:		
											Fewer than 50 acres	1000 acres or more	
	104	105	106	107	108	109	110	111	112	113	114	115	116
TEXAS— Cont'd													
Guadalupe	2,026	32,126	3,166	6,804	5,048	631	864	1,272	39,590	2,543	52.4	2.2	34.3
Hale	689	9,036	1,091	604	1,401	243	162	311	34,409	671	18.6	27.6	42.5
Hall	66	646	72	24	91	57	D	21	32,850	327	4.3	35.8	35.6
Hamilton	201	1,585	241	195	392	32	51	52	32,601	1,163	19.4	9.7	38.9
Hansford	146	1,174	288	19	165	91	37	46	39,420	181	6.1	55.2	63.8
Hardeman	83	705	142	D	108	D	D	28	39,321	275	6.2	24.0	38.9
Hardin	803	9,270	1,024	830	2,326	223	306	350	37,768	661	64.6	1.7	29.8
Harris	100,884	2,045,435	262,449	151,272	213,643	79,522	174,681	129,246	63,188	1,891	80.7	1.7	31.9
Harrison	1,286	19,404	1,610	4,837	2,031	833	1,019	776	39,993	1,134	51.5	2.4	32.2
Hartley	115	1,309	328	NA	196	30	14	48	36,851	206	7.3	45.1	65.4
Haskell	139	1,114	149	D	394	49	37	34	30,181	488	16.0	21.9	39.3
Hays	4,034	53,431	7,241	4,140	12,280	1,010	2,188	1,784	33,384	1,128	53.9	5.9	31.0
Hemphill	145	1,383	203	24	204	21	23	64	46,491	230	7.8	38.3	49.5
Henderson	1,295	13,096	2,137	1,485	2,732	413	693	432	32,957	1,988	51.3	2.2	36.7
Hidalgo	11,937	194,826	62,411	6,296	38,238	6,786	6,155	5,356	27,490	2,436	73.6	6.4	32.0
Hill	639	7,337	1,122	1,107	1,526	198	142	237	32,277	2,003	40.8	4.6	39.3
Hockley	504	6,520	878	207	885	243	92	298	45,774	661	24.2	23.3	35.1
Hood	1,282	14,301	2,182	483	3,079	467	392	546	38,209	1,176	64.0	3.5	35.4
Hopkins	750	10,743	1,432	1,774	1,671	498	245	371	34,561	2,200	36.4	3.2	41.7
Houston	343	3,278	322	552	665	144	101	119	36,450	1,422	27.8	5.2	43.9
Howard	725	8,951	1,677	699	1,483	270	186	346	38,606	373	26.8	22.5	34.5
Hudspeth	31	323	D	D	56	D	D	15	46,207	134	13.4	49.3	54.1
Hunt	1,414	23,535	3,102	8,430	3,710	379	600	1,168	49,616	4,110	63.6	1.8	31.6
Hutchinson	464	6,470	575	1,542	939	187	202	352	54,459	149	26.8	37.6	45.5
Irion	58	465	D	NA	24	D	12	21	44,542	175	18.3	40.6	42.4
Jack	222	2,057	72	48	152	32	56	85	41,513	870	22.9	10.5	39.1
Jackson	304	4,621	309	D	528	133	152	202	43,816	788	30.7	12.6	37.4
Jasper	605	8,434	2,273	1,391	1,529	253	187	301	35,678	896	66.2	1.5	35.8
Jeff Davis	63	388	80	NA	63	30	28	11	28,822	77	28.6	49.4	43.2
Jefferson	5,652	103,217	17,467	14,629	14,284	2,687	5,071	5,265	51,005	729	62.3	7.5	44.6
Jim Hogg	84	1,035	542	60	193	45	D	25	24,359	244	14.8	29.5	33.1
Jim Wells	875	13,161	4,423	429	1,658	333	296	443	33,627	1,224	42.2	6.5	36.4
Johnson	2,742	36,603	3,698	5,718	5,974	761	893	1,427	38,978	3,140	67.1	2.3	33.5
Jones	294	2,258	434	211	245	106	45	93	41,089	915	31.1	14.0	35.5
Karnes	334	4,766	449	265	554	109	56	260	54,646	1,213	19.5	6.8	40.6
Kaufman	1,856	24,260	3,409	3,599	4,261	646	583	906	37,333	2,778	64.7	2.4	35.0
Kendall	1,269	12,356	1,764	858	2,680	432	1,021	517	41,810	1,349	48.2	6.4	31.1
Kenedy	20	173	NA	NA	NA	NA	NA	13	73,179	30	3.3	56.7	67.3
Kent	12	78	D	NA	18	D	NA	6	71,179	164	3.0	34.1	31.4
Kerr	1,394	16,027	3,747	755	2,987	483	732	591	36,872	1,128	34.2	11.5	38.3
Kimble	131	937	144	66	296	41	11	26	27,556	670	19.3	26.0	35.6
King	1	D	NA	NA	NA	NA	NA	D	D	43	NA	39.5	21.5
Kinney	38	510	13	NA	30	NA	NA	15	29,769	236	17.4	37.7	37.4
Kleberg	571	6,976	1,732	101	1,614	308	151	213	30,474	459	60.3	3.7	29.8
Knox	87	625	121	NA	121	47	2	22	34,984	216	17.6	22.7	43.9
Lamar	1,180	17,023	3,491	4,582	2,570	498	378	629	36,964	1,946	38.4	3.9	33.3
Lamb	240	2,106	409	73	357	141	61	80	38,204	777	13.4	22.9	42.5
Lampasas	400	3,717	511	644	651	102	106	108	28,997	1,151	42.1	8.1	41.5
La Salle	147	2,782	136	NA	356	D	D	151	54,269	383	11.5	32.4	38.3
Lavaca	483	5,541	1,225	1,233	814	271	136	202	36,478	2,900	34.4	1.9	34.5
Lee	408	5,654	266	404	661	244	164	266	47,034	1,809	41.5	2.3	33.7
Leon	334	4,408	77	681	590	112	49	225	51,070	1,951	34.8	3.3	41.9
Liberty	1,057	12,556	1,651	798	2,693	324	752	472	37,588	1,538	59.5	3.0	33.8
Limestone	388	5,046	1,198	779	961	266	60	179	35,542	1,284	33.9	6.5	40.0
Lipscomb	89	829	D	D	117	65	28	35	42,730	299	6.7	40.5	36.9
Live Oak	279	3,009	139	D	422	96	103	161	53,484	856	21.8	12.0	37.1
Llano	462	3,673	503	82	562	169	150	106	28,791	835	30.5	15.1	37.8
Loving	4	10	NA	NA	NA	D	NA	1	62,700	8	NA	100.0	45.8
Lubbock	7,120	113,615	24,285	5,094	18,172	5,755	4,350	4,040	35,562	1,033	48.2	14.4	37.3
Lynn	87	678	D	78	67	64	D	29	43,316	434	15.4	33.4	47.0
McCulloch	205	2,225	149	152	480	96	133	86	38,430	682	17.4	19.1	41.2
McLennan	5,169	104,732	18,119	13,986	12,074	5,210	5,125	3,850	36,760	3,366	60.2	3.2	30.5
McMullen	45	632	D	D	73	D	D	59	93,242	191	6.8	45.0	46.7
Madison	252	2,920	262	31	727	93	70	89	30,409	977	35.7	4.4	42.3
Marion	153	1,703	481	362	214	34	19	49	28,956	280	39.3	5.7	27.5
Martin	109	1,225	258	D	154	32	D	63	51,444	356	15.2	30.9	42.5

Table B. States and Counties — Agriculture

			Land in farms			Value of land and buildings (dollars)		Value of machinery and equiopmnet, average per farm (dollars)	Value of products sold:				Organic farms (number)	Farms with internet access (percent)	Government payments	
				Acres							Percent from:					
STATE County	Acreage (1,000)	Percent change, 2012-2017	Average size of farm	Total irrigated (1,000)	Total cropland (1,000)	Average per farm	Average per acre		Total (mil dol)	Average per farm (acres)	Crops	Livestock and poultry products			Total ($1,000)	Percent of farms
	117	118	119	120	121	122	123	124	125	126	127	128	129	130	131	132
TEXAS— Cont'd																
Guadalupe	359	-6.2	141	2.2	102.5	550,283	3,893	54,175	73.6	28,937	28.1	71.9	3	73.4	1,652	6.9
Hale	584	-8.8	870	189.3	458.9	1,131,985	1,301	249,333	411.7	613,568	33.3	66.7	NA	70.6	14,493	73.0
Hall	494	-2.9	1,511	29.7	236.5	1,389,562	919	222,564	56.4	172,502	81.0	19.0	NA	67.9	5,295	77.1
Hamilton	484	8.5	416	1.5	86.1	1,044,354	2,510	67,913	62.0	53,333	10.3	89.7	1	74.6	1,045	17.5
Hansford	587	3.6	3,243	93.7	301.1	4,353,971	1,342	539,803	737.4	4,074,127	12.5	87.5	NA	71.3	7,750	73.5
Hardeman	295	-16.9	1,072	0.9	114.2	1,118,742	1,044	91,771	18.0	65,436	29.9	70.1	NA	69.8	2,537	73.8
Hardin	65	-5.0	98	1.1	13.1	307,897	3,127	74,026	4.7	7,101	50.4	49.6	1	72.9	201	1.1
Harris	219	-7.5	116	7.3	52.7	998,511	8,635	58,260	50.6	26,765	73.4	26.6	10	75.0	1,448	2.7
Harrison	190	-4.7	168	1.7	38.5	440,839	2,628	66,104	15.8	13,964	26.1	73.9	2	75.4	421	4.7
Hartley	835	-7.6	4,052	153.0	296.4	5,028,050	1,241	997,785	1,221.7	5,930,437	12.8	87.2	6	74.3	6,780	59.7
Haskell	565	-0.4	1,158	14.8	293.0	1,218,046	1,052	175,284	54.3	111,307	68.3	31.7	2	69.5	6,906	73.0
Hays	263	7.4	233	0.6	53.0	2,280,804	9,773	53,651	21.8	19,282	52.6	47.4	4	79.9	324	3.6
Hemphill	528	-8.3	2,296	2.3	32.1	2,558,235	1,114	122,556	138.9	603,870	1.7	98.3	NA	62.6	1,699	46.1
Henderson	310	-10.2	156	1.6	86.6	497,751	3,188	64,795	40.2	20,213	29.0	71.0	1	78.6	58	1.2
Hidalgo	624	-21.5	256	162.5	356.9	1,106,061	4,319	92,928	311.0	127,681	94.3	5.7	26	61.8	6,631	10.5
Hill	523	3.8	261	1.2	256.4	660,515	2,529	89,657	114.0	56,915	56.6	43.4	1	70.0	7,927	22.8
Hockley	525	8.5	794	106.4	394.1	800,066	1,008	176,801	92.0	139,215	96.6	3.4	NA	69.9	6,956	65.2
Hood	205	-8.4	175	2.7	39.7	598,809	3,428	53,816	18.9	16,109	40.6	59.4	1	83.3	25	0.9
Hopkins	395	-6.6	179	2.5	127.9	523,841	2,918	78,642	253.7	115,335	4.1	95.9	NA	73.5	1,644	14.7
Houston	395	-15.7	277	3.5	70.8	774,459	2,791	75,170	64.5	45,371	10.5	89.5	NA	68.7	358	3.0
Howard	521	4.5	1,397	6.9	148.3	1,291,868	925	132,948	26.9	72,027	75.4	24.6	NA	70.2	3,272	46.6
Hudspeth	2,276	1.1	16,985	9.7	20.5	15,341,351	903	151,528	17.4	129,881	56.4	43.6	NA	61.9	171	6.0
Hunt	483	6.2	117	3.5	155.0	363,446	3,094	54,517	55.3	13,458	46.7	53.3	5	75.8	4,192	11.5
Hutchinson	548	5.2	3,679	26.7	81.7	3,561,262	968	227,673	44.9	301,416	55.5	44.5	NA	70.5	3,068	30.9
Irion	613	23.5	3,501	0.9	4.3	3,482,288	995	81,488	9.3	53,000	3.2	96.8	NA	81.1	318	10.9
Jack	468	-11.4	537	0.8	34.2	1,253,848	2,333	62,108	23.2	26,639	6.1	93.9	1	71.7	414	5.5
Jackson	382	-13.5	485	6.4	176.9	1,411,888	2,910	146,609	85.0	107,854	79.0	21.0	1	66.6	7,988	24.0
Jasper	91	3.8	102	0.3	13.4	327,242	3,207	58,063	9.1	10,200	43.8	56.2	3	73.1	9	0.8
Jeff Davis	1,378	9.8	17,896	0.1	0.6	12,302,948	687	125,618	D	D	D	D	NA	67.5	192	10.4
Jefferson	359	1.4	492	24.9	137.3	1,159,300	2,355	96,054	32.3	44,331	54.7	45.3	9	68.7	9,154	22.8
Jim Hogg	692	7.3	2,836	0.3	10.4	4,926,365	1,737	76,129	10.4	42,816	2.0	98.0	NA	59.4	529	9.0
Jim Wells	426	-15.4	348	2.4	158.1	720,153	2,069	70,377	121.6	99,379	30.2	69.8	NA	65.8	3,855	11.0
Johnson	411	-4.2	131	3.7	136.7	517,349	3,951	57,125	57.9	18,424	29.6	70.4	1	79.3	3,814	4.1
Jones	517	-8.2	564	4.6	313.8	644,140	1,141	91,000	41.5	45,344	72.0	28.0	NA	74.5	4,470	37.4
Karnes	432	-7.1	356	0.7	75.0	870,685	2,446	81,068	29.4	24,267	37.4	62.6	NA	61.7	508	5.0
Kaufman	455	1.3	164	1.7	133.6	493,007	3,010	59,513	57.1	20,541	27.0	73.0	NA	72.4	1,551	2.2
Kendall	394	6.5	292	0.7	32.4	904,088	3,096	41,444	12.4	9,222	9.7	90.3	NA	77.8	1,207	6.6
Kenedy	869	-5.2	28,961	0.7	1.9	21,350,824	737	105,455	D	D	D	D	NA	83.3	D	6.7
Kent	578	2.6	3,522	D	45.2	3,017,965	857	73,840	9.9	60,159	10.4	89.6	NA	66.5	1,025	47.6
Kerr	518	-11.1	459	0.8	16.0	1,145,687	2,497	48,881	9.3	8,268	16.9	83.1	1	73.9	225	3.0
Kimble	746	7.5	1,114	2.2	11.3	2,218,386	1,992	49,335	10.9	16,197	8.2	91.8	NA	74.6	743	6.9
King	417	-0.1	9,700	D	10.0	6,723,919	693	95,161	13.8	320,140	0.9	99.1	NA	67.4	320	60.5
Kinney	587	1.8	2,487	2.3	15.8	3,086,936	1,241	69,026	5.0	21,377	10.3	89.7	3	60.6	386	11.4
Kleberg	483	-0.3	1,051	0.0	65.6	1,387,563	1,320	100,068	52.8	114,996	41.6	58.4	1	67.1	1,537	15.0
Knox	489	8.5	2,263	11.2	207.4	2,520,181	1,114	211,879	60.5	280,222	22.4	77.6	NA	76.9	3,982	70.8
Lamar	464	-6.6	238	5.0	170.7	597,545	2,507	80,089	73.4	37,738	34.0	66.0	NA	73.0	8,480	34.2
Lamb	569	-7.6	733	173.9	489.3	912,685	1,246	268,352	537.3	691,529	22.1	77.9	3	64.7	16,363	81.5
Lampasas	469	5.5	407	0.4	40.4	1,152,472	2,828	61,081	18.4	16,021	10.9	89.1	2	72.5	381	6.7
La Salle	533	-16.1	1,391	2.1	19.8	2,203,808	1,584	120,717	6.3	16,444	8.5	91.5	NA	58.2	165	3.1
Lavaca	507	-7.3	175	2.6	74.2	613,235	3,511	58,515	50.5	17,430	14.8	85.2	3	65.1	856	7.0
Lee	329	3.3	182	0.8	41.4	667,815	3,676	54,124	56.9	31,478	26.7	73.3	NA	67.6	608	6.1
Leon	488	-18.0	250	2.0	71.2	759,052	3,037	71,907	169.4	86,829	5.9	94.1	1	70.3	144	0.8
Liberty	252	-12.0	164	5.2	68.3	493,738	3,008	74,395	30.0	19,473	40.3	59.7	NA	75.0	3,962	4.1
Limestone	493	1.2	384	0.5	73.0	706,578	1,842	71,310	66.3	51,602	15.1	84.9	NA	68.5	678	6.2
Lipscomb	586	-0.9	1,961	23.8	115.7	2,204,190	1,124	137,377	79.3	265,204	21.5	78.5	NA	72.2	4,833	65.2
Live Oak	455	-15.9	531	2.4	47.4	1,147,237	2,159	84,738	19.5	22,723	25.8	74.2	NA	74.2	717	10.3
Llano	523	-0.9	627	0.5	21.6	1,642,693	2,620	54,170	15.7	18,832	9.5	90.5	NA	76.8	355	4.9
Loving	468	23.3	58,518	D	D	11,163,974	191	146,059	D	D	NA	D	NA	62.5	D	37.5
Lubbock	531	5.6	514	166.7	451.4	874,304	1,702	186,233	219.5	212,458	58.0	42.0	2	82.0	4,685	41.7
Lynn	499	5.7	1,150	83.1	456.3	1,158,640	1,007	318,081	111.4	256,758	95.7	4.3	10	70.5	6,493	73.3
McCulloch	563	-8.3	826	1.9	83.7	1,627,004	1,971	73,710	22.5	32,978	30.5	69.5	NA	77.9	2,261	31.5
McLennan	573	3.6	170	2.2	262.5	614,516	3,608	67,948	179.7	53,377	33.1	66.9	4	72.5	5,860	11.7
McMullen	452	-12.7	2,365	D	26.7	4,293,308	1,816	111,599	8.3	43,586	7.5	92.5	NA	77.0	360	5.8
Madison	246	-15.7	251	1.3	34.0	752,922	2,996	87,971	D	D	D	D	1	71.0	60	1.4
Marion	50	24.5	178	D	13.6	357,305	2,003	53,364	5.9	21,021	9.2	90.8	NA	71.1	151	7.1
Martin	445	-2.0	1,249	12.2	298.9	1,111,299	890	191,065	54.3	152,522	96.7	3.3	NA	79.8	5,464	68.5

Table B. States and Counties — Water Use, Wholesale Trade, Retail Trade, and Real Estate

STATE County	Water use, 2015		Wholesale Trade[1], 2012				Retail Trade[2], 2012				Real estate and rental and leasing,[2] 2012			
	Public supply water withdrawn (mil gal/day)	Public supply gallons withdrawn per person per day	Number of establishments	Number of employees	Sales (mil dol)	Average payroll (mil dol)	Number of establishments	Number of employees	Sales (mil dol)	Average payroll (mil dol)	Number of establishments	Number of employees	Sales (mil dol)	Average payroll (mil dol)
	133	134	135	136	137	138	139	140	141	142	143	144	145	146
TEXAS— Cont'd														
Guadalupe	6.85	45.3	92	D	D	D	270	3,756	1,166.8	90.5	89	373	70.1	14.2
Hale..............................	1.44	41.9	45	D	D	D	114	1,464	346.9	29.0	31	103	15.9	2.4
Hall..............................	0.04	12.7	2	D	D	D	15	94	48.3	1.7	1	D	D	D
Hamilton.......................	0.16	19.6	6	85	32.9	3.7	52	366	87.1	7.8	1	D	D	D
Hansford	0.96	171.1	18	98	148.0	3.7	24	213	74.2	5.3	4	4	0.9	0.1
Hardeman	0.07	18.2	7	D	D	D	15	135	33.4	2.3	NA	NA	NA	NA
Hardin	4.03	72.1	19	D	D	D	155	2,033	712.6	51.4	26	54	7.3	1.4
Harris...........................	287.29	63.3	6,363	100,988	340,775.7	6,909.3	12,644	189,299	61,669.4	4,940.5	4,930	37,842	9,174.7	1,850.8
Harrison	8.53	127.8	58	D	D	D	192	2,069	647.6	49.5	62	288	45.3	10.9
Hartley..........................	1.02	164.7	10	78	85.2	4.2	13	D	D	D	5	13	4.2	1.0
Haskell	0.14	24.4	1	D	D	D	27	298	89.8	7.0	NA	NA	NA	NA
Hays.............................	8.21	42.2	117	D	D	D	619	10,400	2,471.3	208.4	177	680	161.8	21.6
Hemphill	0.50	117.3	13	D	D	D	23	148	64.8	3.9	9	96	24.4	5.6
Henderson	4.55	57.2	34	D	D	D	230	2,599	671.8	58.0	56	201	26.4	5.8
Hidalgo.........................	64.64	76.7	841	D	D	D	2,219	33,566	9,296.8	733.9	497	2,209	445.0	61.9
Hill...............................	2.97	85.2	21	D	D	D	151	1,427	409.7	28.1	28	86	12.0	2.1
Hockley.........................	0.50	21.3	23	D	D	D	61	850	221.0	18.8	12	63	13.4	4.7
Hood............................	4.85	87.5	55	396	222.5	19.5	195	2,394	747.6	60.6	70	376	50.0	11.9
Hopkins	11.05	305.1	31	904	1,176.6	42.2	147	1,659	496.7	37.5	28	116	15.8	2.7
Houston........................	2.34	102.7	11	D	D	D	60	640	160.7	13.6	9	45	4.8	1.2
Howard.........................	0.03	0.8	27	D	D	D	108	D	D	D	41	156	30.1	4.5
Hudspeth......................	0.24	71.0	NA	NA	NA	NA	10	41	11.3	0.6	NA	NA	NA	NA
Hunt.............................	4.87	54.2	51	D	D	D	247	3,428	966.3	90.9	66	182	28.5	4.8
Hutchinson	5.30	243.9	19	D	D	D	79	867	205.2	17.7	11	93	17.0	2.2
Irion.............................	0.08	51.5	2	D	D	D	4	17	1.6	0.2	NA	NA	NA	NA
Jack.............................	0.55	62.0	7	D	D	D	26	187	38.7	3.9	7	12	2.4	0.3
Jackson........................	0.90	60.7	15	124	230.1	7.4	38	511	165.6	10.8	10	D	D	D
Jasper..........................	2.97	83.6	29	D	D	D	127	1,457	425.7	32.5	23	78	14.0	2.3
Jeff Davis	1.12	519.5	1	D	D	D	6	51	7.9	0.8	4	9	2.4	0.4
Jefferson.......................	23.95	94.2	273	2,964	2,451.0	156.3	992	13,877	3,968.3	348.1	264	1,759	372.3	73.9
Jim Hogg.......................	0.67	128.8	4	D	D	D	20	209	72.8	4.6	3	D	D	D
Jim Wells.......................	3.95	95.5	39	D	D	D	142	1,708	641.6	43.8	46	527	128.1	30.9
Johnson........................	10.33	64.6	124	1,160	604.6	52.8	381	4,843	1,513.4	119.0	108	610	125.6	28.9
Jones............................	8.07	404.1	23	108	538.5	4.4	34	216	158.4	5.9	6	D	D	D
Karnes..........................	2.75	183.6	13	69	45.3	2.7	39	479	192.0	11.9	11	8	2.1	0.5
Kaufman........................	0.85	7.4	62	D	D	D	291	3,480	1,021.0	84.9	50	150	27.6	4.8
Kendall.........................	1.66	41.1	51	D	D	D	152	2,107	941.0	66.1	47	116	24.3	4.2
Kenedy	0.07	172.0	NA	NA	NA	NA	NA	NA	NA	NA	1	D	D	D
Kent..............................	0.08	104.7	NA	NA	NA	NA	3	D	D	D	NA	NA	NA	NA
Kerr..............................	5.58	109.5	44	D	D	D	215	3,006	791.7	72.0	84	229	31.7	8.2
Kimble	0.45	102.6	NA	NA	NA	NA	34	239	97.5	6.0	3	7	1.6	0.4
King..............................	0.19	673.8	NA	NA	NA	NA	NA	NA	NA	NA	NA	NA	NA	NA
Kinney	0.82	231.1	2	D	D	D	8	58	9.8	0.8	2	D	D	D
Kleberg.........................	3.31	103.9	5	D	D	D	110	1,490	524.3	33.8	27	D	D	D
Knox.............................	0.14	36.3	11	D	D	D	15	139	31.6	2.1	3	4	0.2	0.1
Lamar...........................	14.84	300.2	43	D	D	D	212	2,426	678.6	57.3	48	161	22.4	4.9
Lamb............................	1.35	100.9	19	172	123.6	8.4	40	374	93.0	7.8	1	D	D	D
Lampasas	2.71	131.6	6	D	D	D	51	604	208.9	15.1	14	42	9.5	2.0
La Salle.........................	1.36	178.2	6	72	33.9	3.3	22	238	134.4	4.9	5	D	D	D
Lavaca..........................	1.44	72.6	15	D	D	D	90	772	178.8	15.3	12	39	8.5	1.2
Lee..............................	3.97	234.9	19	D	D	D	62	618	151.6	12.8	14	111	39.9	5.5
Leon.............................	1.90	111.2	13	D	D	D	66	558	156.8	10.9	13	51	9.3	2.4
Liberty	6.42	80.6	45	500	239.1	25.8	197	2,468	796.6	60.9	32	192	33.0	8.3
Limestone	1.95	83.6	10	D	D	D	93	966	263.8	20.6	14	47	6.1	1.1
Lipscomb.......................	0.81	227.0	4	D	D	D	20	120	98.1	3.6	1	D	D	D
Live Oak........................	2.76	225.7	15	D	D	D	39	347	263.0	9.5	10	40	20.1	1.8
Llano............................	2.87	145.0	15	236	79.0	10.1	68	480	135.3	11.0	22	39	9.1	1.4
Loving	0.01	89.3	NA	NA	NA	NA	NA	NA	NA	NA	NA	NA	NA	NA
Lubbock	1.32	4.4	377	5,273	4,815.9	259.1	1,046	16,460	4,796.6	405.0	394	1,559	270.4	49.7
Lynn..............................	0.15	26.2	4	D	D	D	8	76	18.5	1.7	3	D	D	D
McCulloch......................	2.69	322.5	9	180	57.7	10.5	39	481	139.0	10.6	5	8	0.9	0.2
McLennan......................	41.41	168.6	239	2,976	1,634.7	123.0	846	11,099	3,223.8	250.4	223	1,512	286.8	63.8
McMullen.......................	0.10	122.0	NA	NA	NA	NA	4	D	D	D	2	D	D	D
Madison	2.37	168.5	6	D	D	D	37	655	244.8	17.9	13	47	14.6	1.2
Marion..........................	0.35	34.4	2	D	D	D	28	192	61.3	4.6	7	8	1.4	0.2
Martin...........................	1.48	262.4	7	D	D	D	12	144	88.7	4.6	1	D	D	D

1   Merchant wholesalers, except manufacturers' sales branches and offices.   2. Employer establishments.

Table B. States and Counties — Professional Services, Manufacturing, and Accommodation and Food Services

STATE County	Professional, scientific, and technical services, 2012				Manufacturing, 2012				Accommodation and food services, 2012			
	Number of establish-ments	Number of employees	Sales (mil dol)	Average payroll (mil dol)	Number of establish-ments	Number of employees	Receipts (mil dol)	Annual payroll (mil dol)	Number of establis-hments	Number of employees	Receipts (mil dol)	Annual payroll (mil dol)
	147	148	149	150	151	152	153	154	155	156	157	158
TEXAS— Cont'd												
Guadalupe	132	568	54.5	19.5	111	5,290	2,542.7	231.0	176	3,082	153.7	39.8
Hale	47	D	D	D	23	2,631	2,414.6	90.2	53	985	44.5	12.2
Hall	3	D	D	D	3	35	D	D	12	D	D	D
Hamilton	13	37	4.2	1.0	15	234	38.2	6.6	17	179	8.7	2.4
Hansford	9	39	4.8	1.8	3	16	2.1	0.6	12	D	D	D
Hardeman	3	D	D	D	NA	NA	NA	NA	8	D	D	D
Hardin	49	258	29.6	15.8	24	658	D	33.6	75	1,188	50.7	13.9
Harris	12,925	192,436	44,873.8	17,280.7	4,082	164,479	200,035.4	10,303.2	7,946	166,626	10,106.1	2,710.0
Harrison	115	825	141.8	53.9	77	4,454	2,856.9	183.1	106	1,784	78.2	23.1
Hartley	7	D	D	D	NA	NA	NA	NA	4	14	0.9	0.1
Haskell	7	D	D	D	NA	NA	NA	NA	17	120	5.6	1.2
Hays	381	1,870	198.0	77.7	136	3,908	1,179.0	203.9	361	7,110	348.3	99.3
Hemphill	10	35	15.3	1.4	4	21	D	1.0	12	91	8.0	1.8
Henderson	93	3,061	264.5	68.9	62	1,665	265.1	63.7	135	1,755	77.9	20.5
Hidalgo	886	5,381	566.0	169.6	268	5,713	1,675.4	216.0	1,014	19,468	985.9	247.1
Hill	38	139	15.7	5.2	40	850	265.3	34.0	69	954	43.9	12.5
Hockley	28	D	D	D	15	199	D	8.5	39	547	25.8	7.1
Hood	124	369	47.5	15.2	32	400	D	15.4	101	1,452	66.1	19.0
Hopkins	49	250	66.4	11.5	44	1,840	910.7	69.6	52	791	39.2	12.0
Houston	27	95	8.6	2.1	20	511	160.0	24.5	32	380	16.9	4.2
Howard	45	D	D	D	23	640	D	41.8	76	D	D	D
Hudspeth	1	D	D	D	NA	NA	NA	NA	5	24	1.1	0.3
Hunt	84	424	61.9	14.4	70	7,508	3,089.7	556.3	116	2,052	98.6	26.0
Hutchinson	33	208	25.2	10.5	22	1,712	D	156.7	46	709	31.3	8.8
Irion	4	4	0.7	0.1	NA	NA	NA	NA	1	D	D	D
Jack	10	D	D	D	5	50	D	2.1	17	D	D	D
Jackson	22	134	10.0	3.9	11	D	D	D	20	258	11.9	3.3
Jasper	43	151	18.2	4.1	19	1,335	771.2	90.0	56	777	31.7	8.5
Jeff Davis	5	D	D	D	NA	NA	NA	NA	13	159	8.9	2.4
Jefferson	510	5,909	985.5	383.2	202	13,123	80,760.5	1,106.7	478	10,150	485.5	132.2
Jim Hogg	1	D	D	D	6	69	D	4.1	10	82	3.5	0.8
Jim Wells	62	273	66.6	12.9	20	620	454.7	35.9	84	1,345	74.2	17.4
Johnson	199	1,032	131.0	45.3	161	4,977	1,498.0	245.1	230	3,690	170.9	47.6
Jones	14	44	4.4	1.7	11	182	D	5.5	16	D	D	D
Karnes	17	113	15.3	3.9	8	284	D	14.6	32	427	29.0	5.4
Kaufman	116	556	66.8	21.0	95	3,210	1,100.1	165.3	161	2,618	127.0	34.3
Kendall	136	793	131.1	46.6	36	1,003	D	41.1	96	1,486	64.7	20.7
Kenedy	NA	NA	NA	NA	NA	NA	NA	NA	1	D	D	D
Kent	NA	NA	NA	NA	NA	NA	NA	NA	1	D	D	D
Kerr	134	684	70.6	27.3	44	586	D	23.4	131	1,991	122.8	35.7
Kimble	10	D	D	D	6	68	D	2.8	15	D	D	D
King	NA	NA	NA	NA	NA	NA	NA	NA	NA	NA	NA	NA
Kinney	NA	NA	NA	NA	NA	NA	NA	NA	4	20	0.8	0.2
Kleberg	32	D	D	D	16	98	D	5.1	76	D	D	D
Knox	2	D	D	D	NA	NA	NA	NA	5	D	D	D
Lamar	53	D	D	D	56	3,525	2,152.6	177.8	105	1,568	73.1	20.4
Lamb	17	48	4.6	1.1	6	D	D	17.8	16	D	D	D
Lampasas	40	98	8.5	3.1	23	539	D	18.4	33	458	19.8	5.3
La Salle	1	D	D	D	NA	NA	NA	NA	18	D	D	D
Lavaca	40	136	17.1	5.8	35	1,554	377.5	54.6	31	371	19.5	4.9
Lee	26	117	15.9	4.6	19	418	108.6	20.8	38	316	15.9	4.0
Leon	20	D	D	D	20	751	D	48.8	42	346	18.0	3.9
Liberty	88	333	38.0	11.4	35	1,262	D	78.8	95	1,403	67.5	17.4
Limestone	25	71	7.3	2.4	11	818	193.2	33.5	40	430	22.1	5.2
Lipscomb	4	D	D	D	NA	NA	NA	NA	5	D	D	D
Live Oak	21	D	D	D	6	D	D	D	33	312	27.6	5.4
Llano	38	104	10.6	3.9	17	62	D	2.3	51	1,047	64.2	21.1
Loving	NA	NA	NA	NA	NA	NA	NA	NA	NA	NA	NA	NA
Lubbock	631	3,860	482.3	175.9	240	4,984	1,572.9	216.1	627	D	D	D
Lynn	6	D	D	D	3	63	D	1.9	6	D	D	D
McCulloch	20	D	D	D	12	435	D	16.8	23	265	11.5	2.9
McLennan	369	2,583	331.4	139.6	232	14,194	D	677.1	487	D	D	D
McMullen	3	D	D	D	NA	NA	NA	NA	3	6	0.5	0.1
Madison	19	73	8.4	2.3	8	33	6.8	1.5	36	386	23.0	4.9
Marion	10	D	D	D	9	182	D	7.4	21	211	11.2	2.8
Martin	4	12	1.3	0.7	NA	NA	NA	NA	6	D	D	D

Health Care and Social Assistance, Other Services, Nonemployer Businesses, and Residential Construction

STATE County	Health care and social assistance, 2012				Other services, 2012				Nonemployer businesses, 2016		Value of residential construction authorized by building permits, 2018	
	Number of establish-ments	Number of employees	Receipts (mil dol)	Annual payroll (mil dol)	Number of establish-ments	Number of employees	Receipts (mil dol)	Annual payroll (mil dol)	Number	Receipts (mil dol)	New construction ($1,000)	Number of housing units
	159	160	161	162	163	164	165	166	167	168	169	170
TEXAS— Cont'd												
Guadalupe	189	3,077	275.1	107.5	141	923	76.9	22.3	10,777	448.3	228,150	967
Hale	84	1,058	104.5	36.0	49	345	24.7	7.5	2,215	90.7	2,625	12
Hall	7	87	4.3	2.1	6	46	4.0	1.3	220	5.3	0	0
Hamilton	24	531	35.7	16.5	22	38	5.4	1.5	748	33.8	480	6
Hansford	7	D	D	D	12	42	4.9	1.3	483	20.9	0	0
Hardeman	13	210	18.3	7.7	10	51	3.1	0.9	257	8.8	0	0
Hardin	65	D	D	D	52	D	D	D	3,584	138.5	45,698	230
Harris	10,433	232,131	29,549.4	10,842.4	5,820	58,629	7,505.2	2,234.1	390,881	17,813.0	5,548,381	34,149
Harrison	123	1,881	203.6	66.2	77	923	89.0	32.8	4,857	202.6	5,780	30
Hartley	7	D	D	D	12	D	D	D	334	20.4	NA	NA
Haskell	11	D	D	D	15	55	5.7	1.0	416	15.2	113	3
Hays	309	5,778	603.3	220.8	203	1,170	114.0	35.3	17,132	802.0	596,398	2,890
Hemphill	10	169	12.7	5.7	8	D	D	D	402	17.8	0	0
Henderson	126	2,180	215.6	84.3	69	295	24.9	7.0	6,203	301.5	21,206	138
Hidalgo	2,048	54,356	3,479.0	1,471.2	571	3,701	350.3	84.2	70,258	2,728.5	559,362	4,642
Hill	50	1,168	79.0	33.0	38	178	11.6	3.2	2,371	99.6	727	11
Hockley	46	1,089	74.8	28.8	27	D	D	D	1,384	57.3	2,206	17
Hood	131	2,352	242.5	89.9	82	534	38.1	11.7	5,616	272.0	61,842	272
Hopkins	76	1,416	120.2	47.4	48	221	17.4	4.8	2,808	147.3	6,531	46
Houston	37	768	53.9	21.6	27	144	13.4	3.9	1,355	46.5	0	0
Howard	67	1,699	163.7	51.4	40	D	D	D	1,644	65.0	6,781	38
Hudspeth	2	D	D	D	3	4	0.1	0.0	243	8.6	NA	NA
Hunt	175	3,165	308.8	118.2	93	409	32.2	10.3	6,775	343.6	28,239	207
Hutchinson	44	486	49.7	16.7	34	223	25.8	6.9	1,011	35.3	0	0
Irion	1	D	D	D	3	D	D	D	183	9.1	0	0
Jack	13	D	D	D	12	87	16.2	2.7	748	36.8	615	3
Jackson	16	303	24.9	9.9	26	63	6.5	1.4	1,003	39.6	590	4
Jasper	80	2,341	107.3	47.8	35	137	11.5	2.9	2,344	82.3	74	1
Jeff Davis	4	D	D	D	5	D	D	D	279	9.0	NA	NA
Jefferson	810	17,453	1,760.8	625.3	362	2,712	286.6	81.2	15,181	629.4	106,846	609
Jim Hogg	11	645	13.9	8.0	4	9	0.7	0.2	420	11.9	NA	NA
Jim Wells	114	4,355	211.2	96.0	69	381	63.0	15.8	2,992	96.1	977	6
Johnson	240	D	D	D	183	1,110	118.5	42.2	13,130	614.0	140,308	687
Jones	20	632	32.3	15.2	16	54	3.8	1.1	1,207	47.4	0	0
Karnes	27	437	30.7	12.6	15	57	3.4	0.8	912	34.3	9,900	55
Kaufman	160	3,412	235.5	100.1	112	557	63.1	22.3	10,420	490.6	184,324	1,112
Kendall	129	1,548	125.3	44.9	69	365	30.6	8.4	5,395	332.0	81,417	313
Kenedy	NA	NA	NA	NA	4	D	D	D	23	0.7	NA	NA
Kent	2	D	D	D	NA	NA	NA	NA	55	2.2	NA	NA
Kerr	176	3,826	370.5	164.1	101	537	61.7	15.2	5,376	280.8	25,032	137
Kimble	8	141	8.6	4.1	6	19	1.4	0.4	655	22.0	0	0
King	NA	NA	NA	NA	NA	NA	NA	NA	30	1.0	NA	NA
Kinney	2	D	D	D	3	D	D	D	204	5.9	195	1
Kleberg	67	1,599	115.8	45.5	46	D	D	D	1,621	49.1	605	6
Knox	8	166	10.7	4.5	10	D	D	D	265	11.6	0	0
Lamar	177	3,747	326.1	121.7	86	425	39.7	10.4	3,953	173.3	7,048	48
Lamb	27	429	23.8	10.9	17	D	D	D	735	28.6	0	0
Lampasas	25	747	45.7	19.3	22	153	16.7	4.2	1,540	69.1	6,365	42
La Salle	9	D	D	D	4	14	1.5	0.4	562	15.4	390	2
Lavaca	38	981	65.3	24.5	47	140	13.3	2.6	1,673	66.6	739	6
Lee	29	325	20.8	8.3	25	85	9.3	2.2	1,405	56.4	2,100	12
Leon	19	291	11.6	5.5	25	114	6.9	2.0	1,512	66.5	0	0
Liberty	102	D	D	D	71	491	55.1	16.8	5,180	197.8	92,243	724
Limestone	49	1,120	84.0	31.2	21	D	D	D	1,321	47.8	240	2
Lipscomb	3	10	0.5	0.2	7	12	1.8	0.2	293	9.9	500	1
Live Oak	12	250	8.7	3.6	14	D	D	D	989	42.3	180	3
Llano	31	605	46.5	19.3	22	63	6.9	1.7	2,139	107.9	49,745	266
Loving	NA	NA	NA	NA	NA	NA	NA	NA	20	0.5	NA	NA
Lubbock	848	22,202	2,519.2	866.0	460	D	D	D	21,665	1,104.3	325,530	1,479
Lynn	6	131	9.2	3.1	6	D	D	D	360	13.8	60	1
McCulloch	16	267	19.9	8.2	19	78	6.3	1.8	701	27.5	150	1
McLennan	547	16,602	1,484.1	627.5	361	2,364	233.2	64.5	15,601	723.7	169,225	846
McMullen	1	D	D	D	NA	NA	NA	NA	131	4.5	NA	NA
Madison	19	306	24.8	11.3	15	D	D	D	1,012	41.2	2,147	11
Marion	13	354	15.7	9.7	13	D	D	D	671	27.3	161	5
Martin	7	135	11.6	4.7	8	21	3.2	0.6	429	19.0	1,570	5

Table B. States and Counties — Government Employment and Payroll, and Local Government Finances

STATE County	Government employment and payroll, 2012									Local government finances, 2012				
			March payroll (percent of total)							General revenue				
												Taxes		
			Adminis-tration, judicial, and legal	Police and corrections	Fire protection	Highways and transpor-tation	Health and welfare	Natural resources and utilities	Education and libraries	Total (mil dol)	Inter-govern-mental (mil dol)	Total (mil dol)	Per capita[1] (dollars)	
	Full-time equivalent employees	March payroll (dollars)											Total	Property
	171	172	173	174	175	176	177	178	179	180	181	182	183	184
TEXAS— Cont'd														
Guadalupe	4,848	17,546,517	6.1	10.0	2.4	1.9	15.8	3.7	58.3	422.8	109.1	182.6	1,306	1,097
Hale	1,782	7,262,318	4.1	6.3	2.1	1.0	6.9	2.2	76.9	114.8	52.3	44.9	1,233	1,018
Hall	222	559,195	7.2	8.3	0.0	3.6	2.3	5.4	72.7	14.8	8.2	4.0	1,202	1,007
Hamilton	539	1,700,689	4.8	3.1	0.0	3.4	41.0	2.4	45.4	45.9	10.7	12.7	1,528	1,340
Hansford	494	1,557,868	4.9	2.9	0.1	2.2	32.4	1.8	53.8	31.7	6.9	19.4	3,509	3,267
Hardeman	417	1,303,943	5.8	4.2	0.7	1.9	46.4	3.2	37.5	42.6	8.4	16.1	3,932	3,714
Hardin	2,150	6,172,176	6.7	7.8	0.0	2.1	0.7	3.2	78.4	141.1	61.5	64.0	1,160	1,008
Harris	166,045	659,443,824	4.4	11.0	3.4	5.0	8.8	2.9	62.2	19,260.3	5,471.7	9,235.2	2,171	1,765
Harrison	2,833	8,500,249	3.8	8.6	2.9	1.9	0.3	3.6	77.3	193.7	50.6	119.6	1,773	1,592
Hartley	92	266,990	18.2	0.7	0.0	0.0	0.4	1.3	72.8	11.2	1.1	8.7	1,410	1,297
Haskell	331	767,433	9.1	5.5	0.1	3.6	22.4	5.8	53.3	22.1	9.1	7.4	1,260	1,097
Hays	7,053	24,108,223	5.6	10.9	2.6	1.5	6.6	5.7	64.1	545.5	162.4	287.7	1,703	1,398
Hemphill	358	1,141,524	8.4	5.9	0.0	4.6	27.8	4.3	48.3	47.6	3.4	36.2	8,863	8,415
Henderson	2,818	8,513,766	7.2	8.3	1.6	1.5	0.2	3.2	76.9	203.3	68.1	103.6	1,309	1,130
Hidalgo	39,042	129,583,687	3.7	6.7	1.7	1.6	2.9	3.9	78.6	3,159.2	1,926.2	864.1	1,071	868
Hill	1,782	5,391,972	5.2	8.8	1.2	2.0	0.1	2.7	79.5	122.0	52.4	48.3	1,376	1,175
Hockley	1,746	5,964,084	3.8	4.6	0.6	1.5	0.5	1.6	86.7	146.0	48.8	70.9	3,073	2,862
Hood	1,577	5,364,527	10.6	11.6	0.3	2.2	0.8	4.5	68.5	134.0	27.6	93.9	1,804	1,536
Hopkins	1,924	6,315,574	4.5	5.5	2.0	2.2	35.9	2.7	46.4	157.4	43.9	43.8	1,235	1,002
Houston	827	2,210,644	8.8	8.8	0.6	3.0	1.9	5.5	70.3	60.8	24.7	26.3	1,135	940
Howard	2,006	6,202,628	4.2	6.9	2.7	2.0	15.7	7.1	59.9	146.9	52.2	61.9	1,747	1,467
Hudspeth	286	780,976	7.7	13.3	0.0	2.9	1.1	7.6	67.2	19.0	10.0	7.0	2,108	2,025
Hunt	4,073	13,501,049	5.0	7.3	2.3	1.6	26.3	8.0	48.4	331.7	94.9	108.8	1,250	1,039
Hutchinson	1,204	3,868,672	7.3	8.9	2.7	2.5	1.7	5.0	70.3	90.0	30.2	42.4	1,935	1,693
Irion	111	320,492	16.7	8.2	0.0	4.3	0.8	7.7	60.9	14.0	1.4	12.0	7,598	7,380
Jack	453	1,551,359	5.7	9.9	0.3	1.9	21.3	3.8	56.6	35.4	3.7	28.0	3,118	2,834
Jackson	834	2,725,347	5.8	6.2	1.3	2.4	17.9	11.4	54.8	75.0	21.3	27.7	1,942	1,729
Jasper	1,516	4,363,997	5.7	7.7	0.0	3.0	2.1	6.7	72.0	103.2	47.1	43.9	1,222	1,064
Jeff Davis	113	390,447	7.2	8.1	0.0	0.0	1.2	1.2	81.3	9.9	6.7	3.0	1,289	1,181
Jefferson	10,830	41,244,326	6.6	14.9	6.1	3.8	6.0	8.0	53.1	1,149.2	304.3	568.5	2,258	1,850
Jim Hogg	316	819,818	7.4	11.3	0.9	0.2	7.1	5.0	62.8	22.9	9.1	11.0	2,095	1,786
Jim Wells	1,854	5,562,478	7.3	10.0	2.6	4.3	1.8	3.2	68.8	136.7	63.1	61.1	1,463	914
Johnson	6,428	20,663,672	6.4	10.8	3.7	2.3	0.9	4.4	69.6	540.8	136.3	306.3	1,996	1,658
Jones	1,148	3,124,966	5.6	5.9	0.0	1.6	32.6	5.2	48.8	55.2	25.7	15.1	754	677
Karnes	676	1,956,116	5.9	7.8	0.1	2.4	17.7	3.7	62.1	49.9	22.4	22.9	1,501	1,339
Kaufman	4,535	15,218,689	4.8	9.9	1.3	2.3	10.1	6.4	64.2	385.5	158.1	186.8	1,750	1,528
Kendall	1,662	5,537,436	9.0	8.0	1.1	3.0	1.6	5.5	70.6	133.9	20.6	100.2	2,786	2,470
Kenedy	35	84,678	6.2	3.9	0.0	0.0	0.5	0.4	86.0	11.6	0.2	10.5	24,369	24,346
Kent	75	243,441	11.6	3.7	0.1	21.1	0.0	2.6	60.8	8.5	1.3	6.8	8,151	8,082
Kerr	1,700	5,612,578	8.7	13.7	6.0	3.2	1.3	4.7	60.4	120.6	27.6	78.6	1,580	1,286
Kimble	171	555,031	11.3	14.1	0.0	6.0	2.2	4.9	60.8	13.0	3.2	6.7	1,472	1,379
King	59	195,445	17.5	2.0	0.0	2.6	0.0	0.5	77.5	9.5	1.7	7.1	25,620	25,616
Kinney	195	518,153	13.2	15.7	0.0	1.2	4.8	4.1	59.5	14.4	8.6	3.8	1,046	948
Kleberg	1,554	3,973,033	8.5	14.3	3.3	6.7	4.0	5.3	56.2	170.5	58.0	63.5	1,984	1,710
Knox	325	851,631	7.1	3.5	0.0	2.7	26.8	6.9	52.1	19.7	7.7	5.6	1,486	1,218
Lamar	2,237	7,154,454	5.0	8.6	0.2	1.3	0.9	4.5	77.8	165.7	68.1	68.9	1,384	1,087
Lamb	779	2,277,980	7.5	10.4	1.2	3.2	3.0	4.3	70.1	61.1	24.1	21.0	1,499	1,349
Lampasas	821	2,377,321	5.2	9.7	1.6	2.7	0.6	3.2	72.8	53.7	20.4	26.9	1,339	1,135
La Salle	315	950,554	9.0	9.5	0.0	3.2	0.2	4.1	71.9	22.1	6.6	13.4	1,887	1,739
Lavaca	808	2,421,042	9.6	8.5	3.3	4.6	17.2	10.0	41.0	73.1	14.0	28.2	1,446	1,296
Lee	700	2,033,290	5.6	8.6	0.0	3.2	0.0	4.3	74.9	49.3	14.2	29.5	1,776	1,564
Leon	757	2,170,423	7.7	7.0	0.0	3.1	1.2	2.4	78.4	47.5	14.0	28.8	1,714	1,601
Liberty	2,976	8,829,594	6.7	8.2	1.1	2.8	0.4	3.1	76.8	210.0	86.8	98.0	1,280	1,101
Limestone	1,302	3,748,599	6.3	12.5	1.9	3.5	15.2	4.0	56.2	116.3	27.5	51.1	2,165	1,970
Lipscomb	247	785,351	10.0	5.2	0.0	6.1	4.3	3.8	69.9	21.9	4.9	15.8	4,530	4,351
Live Oak	529	1,441,098	7.4	10.9	0.0	3.7	1.5	5.4	67.2	34.0	9.9	21.0	1,801	1,538
Llano	637	1,790,590	16.6	12.9	0.0	4.0	0.3	8.5	56.3	64.8	6.8	51.0	2,670	2,571
Loving	12	46,971	59.5	22.6	0.0	14.3	0.0	3.6	0.0	4.4	0.6	3.4	48,366	47,718
Lubbock	12,902	47,474,349	4.7	10.5	4.4	1.1	28.6	5.7	43.9	1,264.7	335.5	406.2	1,421	1,107
Lynn	453	1,252,881	5.2	5.1	0.0	1.3	20.1	4.2	62.8	30.1	12.7	8.8	1,516	1,374
McCulloch	585	1,662,784	6.4	5.5	1.5	2.1	23.0	8.4	50.7	33.3	13.2	11.4	1,371	1,168
McLennan	10,401	35,092,132	5.7	11.4	3.1	2.0	4.5	8.6	63.6	1,172.8	436.4	367.8	1,541	1,222
McMullen	82	296,876	20.7	8.4	0.0	8.2	1.7	1.9	58.1	10.8	0.8	9.1	12,590	12,296
Madison	473	1,465,387	9.1	5.4	0.0	2.2	0.6	3.0	77.1	37.7	16.3	14.6	1,066	920
Marion	304	892,993	8.9	7.6	0.0	4.1	0.5	2.4	76.0	19.4	6.6	11.1	1,074	952
Martin	332	1,249,120	9.9	4.5	0.0	9.6	23.0	3.5	48.5	39.6	3.4	28.7	5,722	5,575

1. Based on the resident population estimated as of July 1 of the year shown.

— **Local Government Finances, Government Employment, and Income Taxes**

STATE County	Local government finances, 2012 (cont.)										Government employment, 2017			Individual income tax returns, 2016		
	Direct general expenditure							Debt outstanding								
			Percent of total for:													
	Total (mil dol)	Per capita[1] (dollars)	Education	Health and hospitals	Police protection	Public welfare	Highways	Total (mil dol)	Per capita[1] (dollars)	Federal civilian	Federal military	State and local	Number of returns	Mean adjusted gross income	Mean income tax
	185	186	187	188	189	190	191	192	193	194	195	196	197	198	199
TEXAS— Cont'd															
Guadalupe	411.4	2,942	44.3	19.5	5.0	0.8	3.8	852.5	6,096	229	318	6,276	73,350	58,101	6,312
Hale	116.3	3,196	62.2	9.1	7.7	0.6	2.8	79.2	2,177	79	63	2,324	13,110	38,265	3,408
Hall	13.5	4,104	66.2	1.9	3.1	0.1	5.0	0.2	72	17	6	250	1,220	33,938	2,707
Hamilton	41.2	4,960	31.5	48.5	2.0	0.3	2.3	24.5	2,949	29	17	745	3,620	49,888	6,619
Hansford	29.9	5,415	58.4	21.3	2.2	0.0	2.5	26.3	4,772	16	11	632	2,280	49,192	6,745
Hardeman	52.1	12,765	19.2	41.9	2.9	17.5	2.7	3.2	781	18	8	410	1,610	34,453	3,345
Hardin	129.3	2,342	65.3	0.6	6.8	0.5	3.7	120.4	2,181	70	115	2,253	23,910	61,261	6,848
Harris	18,773.0	4,413	44.4	10.5	5.7	0.1	4.8	54,673.5	12,853	25,414	10,314	253,696	1,959,360	64,889	9,873
Harrison	211.9	3,142	59.8	0.1	4.4	0.4	3.4	272.1	4,034	124	132	3,103	28,140	49,966	5,334
Hartley	10.5	1,709	39.9	0.0	7.7	0.2	15.4	0.2	32	7	9	784	1,750	52,437	8,445
Haskell	22.2	3,760	53.2	17.8	3.7	0.0	7.7	2.3	395	26	11	438	2,130	40,387	4,335
Hays	604.2	3,575	42.7	5.8	5.4	0.3	6.3	1,700.9	10,065	251	457	13,242	91,900	64,694	8,527
Hemphill	40.3	9,878	51.7	16.2	2.1	0.1	5.1	11.9	2,915	11	8	488	1,650	65,090	9,441
Henderson	213.8	2,703	68.0	1.9	5.3	0.0	3.7	147.7	1,868	85	161	3,382	33,040	50,420	5,714
Hidalgo	3,161.8	3,920	67.1	2.0	3.8	0.5	2.9	3,738.4	4,635	4,415	1,764	54,144	312,950	37,838	3,300
Hill	125.8	3,583	69.5	0.2	4.8	0.9	4.9	161.8	4,607	98	71	2,175	14,860	44,696	4,361
Hockley	161.5	7,000	72.9	0.5	2.3	0.2	2.4	78.0	3,383	41	45	1,974	9,320	48,640	5,253
Hood	131.2	2,521	60.0	0.3	6.6	0.1	3.8	144.0	2,767	101	116	1,942	26,170	68,628	8,967
Hopkins	166.2	4,685	40.6	33.8	3.5	0.0	3.4	140.0	3,947	72	73	1,923	15,390	44,782	4,634
Houston	60.7	2,619	51.0	8.0	6.2	0.1	5.3	62.1	2,682	69	41	1,699	8,240	40,333	3,774
Howard	188.2	5,315	65.7	10.8	3.1	0.2	2.0	576.8	16,289	965	60	2,557	12,770	59,276	7,913
Hudspeth	19.7	5,893	49.6	0.3	7.1	0.2	7.3	2.3	676	293	9	284	2,070	40,337	3,287
Hunt	326.3	3,747	36.3	30.6	4.6	0.2	2.6	436.0	5,007	264	258	7,492	38,850	50,344	5,207
Hutchinson	107.0	4,880	47.7	23.7	4.7	0.1	2.3	102.9	4,693	72	43	1,535	8,890	58,961	7,105
Irion	11.6	7,395	70.4	0.2	3.8	0.0	4.9	6.1	3,865	3	3	114	710	76,639	11,807
Jack	45.5	5,070	74.2	0.0	3.7	0.0	2.4	80.2	8,928	18	16	658	3,260	43,472	4,628
Jackson	78.6	5,513	49.1	25.8	3.2	0.1	3.9	106.4	7,462	33	29	1,099	6,410	53,956	6,210
Jasper	96.3	2,680	59.7	2.7	8.6	0.0	5.7	89.0	2,478	77	70	2,008	13,840	49,352	4,803
Jeff Davis	9.6	4,176	59.9	0.4	3.0	0.1	0.2	0.3	132	24	4	214	1,030	53,162	5,936
Jefferson	1,153.5	4,581	41.4	4.2	7.0	0.6	5.6	5,050.2	20,055	1,813	694	15,446	105,380	54,032	6,319
Jim Hogg	22.0	4,186	44.7	0.9	5.9	2.1	11.8	5.1	979	209	10	381	1,950	37,259	3,171
Jim Wells	136.5	3,268	62.9	0.3	5.4	0.2	3.5	108.5	2,599	89	82	2,122	16,490	42,016	4,092
Johnson	466.6	3,041	55.2	0.5	6.0	0.3	3.6	1,105.1	7,202	290	333	7,387	73,780	54,816	6,005
Jones	52.9	2,651	52.3	25.3	1.5	0.0	3.3	40.8	2,041	50	34	2,218	6,440	41,773	3,911
Karnes	43.7	2,867	55.3	6.6	2.9	0.5	5.2	10.2	671	74	25	1,767	5,620	74,710	13,683
Kaufman	387.6	3,631	51.9	6.6	4.1	0.3	7.0	686.1	6,427	188	245	6,525	54,630	58,032	6,359
Kendall	128.4	3,571	58.1	1.2	6.7	0.2	4.5	314.6	8,750	61	88	1,707	21,290	116,681	21,500
Kenedy	11.2	25,935	97.1	0.0	0.4	0.0	0.5	2.3	5,397	1	1	85	150	36,093	2,573
Kent	8.2	9,762	93.8	0.1	0.5	0.0	0.6	0.0	11	6	1	181	350	43,720	4,380
Kerr	109.6	2,202	53.6	0.5	9.0	0.7	3.7	92.9	1,865	495	101	2,593	24,470	58,671	7,692
Kimble	12.1	2,660	49.4	6.6	3.6	0.0	5.0	15.9	3,427	14	9	361	2,030	44,507	4,960
King	6.3	22,880	69.2	0.0	1.3	0.0	7.6	6.0	21,884	3	1	55	120	44,917	3,442
Kinney	13.4	3,722	44.0	4.4	9.1	0.6	3.6	2.9	792	126	7	279	1,310	47,383	4,626
Kleberg	174.6	5,453	30.3	33.2	3.9	0.0	12.4	115.3	3,599	888	439	3,826	12,730	44,758	4,581
Knox	18.2	4,797	47.6	28.6	3.0	0.3	3.7	1.1	293	27	7	427	1,430	36,897	3,025
Lamar	164.5	3,303	65.4	1.9	5.1	1.8	4.5	148.6	2,982	139	100	2,894	20,910	45,999	4,941
Lamb	58.4	4,171	54.5	18.7	5.0	0.0	4.5	16.0	1,139	39	26	980	5,350	38,855	3,788
Lampasas	51.3	2,552	61.5	0.3	7.0	0.3	5.8	67.4	3,353	44	42	999	9,160	53,079	5,655
La Salle	18.2	2,554	68.9	0.1	1.4	0.3	5.5	31.9	4,493	110	12	740	2,450	66,820	12,777
Lavaca	68.8	3,532	36.2	22.8	5.2	0.2	7.3	31.6	1,625	55	40	948	9,240	54,801	6,667
Lee	48.0	2,889	56.5	0.5	6.1	0.7	6.6	75.0	4,518	26	34	1,258	7,770	54,640	5,362
Leon	49.2	2,929	78.9	0.0	2.9	0.1	4.5	50.5	3,005	44	35	833	7,510	46,184	4,852
Liberty	200.4	2,617	61.0	0.6	5.8	0.5	5.2	218.2	2,850	109	159	4,681	31,730	51,528	5,432
Limestone	124.3	5,268	41.5	12.6	11.7	0.3	4.7	91.4	3,877	48	44	2,990	9,110	43,058	4,095
Lipscomb	21.7	6,247	73.2	0.5	3.5	0.1	5.7	7.8	2,241	27	7	363	1,410	47,006	5,650
Live Oak	41.2	3,535	63.8	0.2	3.3	0.0	5.5	61.8	5,297	261	22	583	4,660	59,332	8,002
Llano	64.4	3,376	59.1	0.1	6.5	0.0	4.8	33.0	1,727	29	43	805	8,990	62,483	8,773
Loving	1.8	25,817	0.0	0.0	11.2	0.0	10.5	0.0	0	0	0	15	40	75,775	7,950
Lubbock	1,336.0	4,675	34.3	32.4	4.8	0.0	2.2	2,306.4	8,071	1,342	622	28,645	127,980	56,334	7,304
Lynn	28.7	4,967	57.9	19.6	4.2	0.0	3.2	5.0	865	19	12	561	2,440	51,543	5,525
McCulloch	37.3	4,484	41.7	24.2	3.9	0.0	4.2	38.1	4,581	27	16	634	3,530	42,382	4,260
McLennan	1,142.6	4,787	41.4	2.5	5.0	0.6	1.6	11,590.0	48,553	2,732	596	14,607	106,390	52,267	6,095
McMullen	9.6	13,263	74.2	0.8	4.8	0.2	7.4	23.3	32,058	6	2	149	410	88,076	16,054
Madison	33.7	2,466	63.1	0.8	7.5	2.9	5.7	33.0	2,410	19	23	1,226	5,120	42,593	4,148
Marion	19.4	1,875	65.3	1.5	8.2	0.0	7.5	15.3	1,483	37	20	387	3,950	40,771	3,639
Martin	116.9	23,298	19.8	76.2	0.5	0.0	0.4	67.3	13,408	16	11	518	2,140	78,750	12,525

1. Based on the resident population estimated as of July 1 of the year shown.

State / county code	CBSA code[1]	County code[2]	STATE County	Land area[3] (sq. mi)	Total persons 2018	Rank	Per square mile	White	Black	American Indian, Alaska Native	Asian and Pacific Islancer	Percent Hispanic or Latino[4]	Under 5 years	5 to 17 years	18 to 24 years	25 to 34 years	35 to 44 years	45 to 54 years
				1	2	3	4	5	6	7	8	9	10	11	12	13	14	15
			TEXAS— Cont'd															
48319		9	Mason	928.8	4,280	2,879	4.6	72.8	0.7	0.7	0.4	26.1	5.7	15.2	6.5	8.6	9.7	11.1
48321	13,060	4	Matagorda	1,092.9	36,552	1,263	33.4	44.5	10.8	0.7	2.0	42.9	7.2	18.3	8.3	12.6	11.4	11.4
48323	20,580	5	Maverick	1,279.5	58,485	885	45.7	2.9	0.3	1.2	0.6	95.2	9.2	22.0	11.7	13.7	11.5	11.0
48325	41,700	1	Medina	1,325.4	50,921	977	38.4	43.9	2.8	0.8	1.0	52.4	6.0	17.1	9.7	12.3	11.6	13.2
48327		9	Menard	902.0	2,139	3,035	2.4	61.5	1.6	0.7	0.4	36.5	4.3	13.4	6.1	8.6	8.6	10.2
48329	33,260	3	Midland	900.3	172,578	380	191.7	46.0	6.7	0.8	2.4	45.3	8.8	19.7	8.7	18.1	13.5	10.3
48331		6	Milam	1,016.9	25,131	1,598	24.7	63.0	9.4	0.8	1.1	26.9	6.3	18.3	7.7	10.7	11.0	11.6
48333		9	Mills	748.2	4,921	2,837	6.6	80.2	1.2	0.8	0.6	18.4	4.5	16.0	6.8	8.2	9.4	12.0
48335		7	Mitchell	911.1	8,145	2,582	8.9	49.4	9.6	1.2	0.7	40.2	5.8	15.7	11.2	16.6	12.9	11.8
48337		6	Montague	930.9	19,596	1,847	21.1	86.9	1.1	1.6	0.7	11.3	6.0	16.7	7.0	11.2	10.6	12.1
48339	26,420	1	Montgomery	1,042.6	590,925	114	566.8	66.6	5.7	0.8	3.8	24.8	6.8	19.6	8.2	12.7	13.7	13.5
48341	20,300	7	Moore	899.7	21,485	1,756	23.9	32.2	3.7	1.0	7.7	56.3	10.0	22.0	9.1	14.0	12.7	10.8
48343		6	Morris	252.0	12,339	2,263	49.0	66.3	23.7	1.4	1.1	10.0	5.7	17.1	7.2	11.0	11.3	11.2
48345		9	Motley	989.6	1,234	3,098	1.2	78.3	2.8	1.1	0.2	18.3	4.7	15.2	7.1	9.7	7.9	10.5
48347	34,860	5	Nacogdoches	946.6	65,711	813	69.4	60.6	18.5	0.9	1.9	19.7	6.5	16.7	19.2	11.5	10.3	10.0
48349	18,620	4	Navarro	1,009.6	49,565	997	49.1	56.8	13.6	0.8	2.3	28.0	7.5	19.0	8.7	11.7	11.2	12.0
48351	13,140	2	Newton	933.7	13,746	2,182	14.7	74.7	21.1	1.3	0.9	3.7	5.0	15.3	8.4	11.9	10.9	13.2
48353	45,020	6	Nolan	912.0	14,751	2,111	16.2	56.3	5.1	0.9	0.9	38.1	7.2	18.9	8.8	11.7	11.4	11.3
48355	18,580	2	Nueces	838.3	362,265	196	432.1	29.9	3.9	0.6	2.6	64.2	6.7	17.8	10.0	14.3	12.8	11.7
48357		7	Ochiltree	917.7	9,947	2,431	10.8	42.8	1.0	1.2	0.6	55.4	8.6	23.1	9.2	12.7	12.5	11.3
48359	11,100	2	Oldham	1,500.5	2,131	3,037	1.4	78.5	3.6	1.3	1.6	16.3	4.6	20.1	7.2	11.3	14.0	13.4
48361	13,140	2	Orange	333.8	83,572	683	250.4	81.7	9.1	1.1	1.6	8.0	6.9	18.0	7.9	13.2	12.2	12.4
48363	33,420	6	Palo Pinto	952.5	28,875	1,463	30.3	76.0	3.0	1.1	1.1	20.2	6.1	17.1	8.3	12.0	10.4	12.0
48365		6	Panola	811.4	23,148	1,672	28.5	74.2	16.2	1.0	1.1	8.8	5.9	17.4	8.4	11.2	12.0	11.7
48367	19,100	1	Parker	903.5	138,371	465	153.1	84.3	1.9	1.4	1.1	12.8	6.3	18.5	7.1	11.7	12.7	13.7
48369		7	Parmer	880.8	9,864	2,439	11.2	33.7	1.2	0.4	0.8	64.3	8.0	20.6	9.2	12.9	11.9	11.7
48371		7	Pecos	4,763.8	15,673	2,056	3.3	25.8	4.3	0.8	1.2	68.8	6.5	17.8	8.4	15.7	14.6	12.7
48373		6	Polk	1,057.0	50,031	989	47.3	72.0	10.4	2.4	1.1	15.5	5.4	14.7	7.5	12.1	11.8	12.7
48375	11,100	2	Potter	908.4	119,648	522	131.7	44.8	10.9	0.9	6.3	38.7	7.8	19.7	9.0	15.2	13.1	11.7
48377		7	Presidio	3,855.3	6,948	2,678	1.8	13.0	1.2	0.8	2.7	83.0	8.0	18.4	8.0	10.6	11.0	10.5
48379		8	Rains	229.5	12,159	2,282	53.0	86.3	2.9	1.6	1.4	9.2	4.8	15.2	6.4	10.4	10.3	11.9
48381	11,100	2	Randall	911.9	136,271	471	149.4	72.3	3.8	1.0	2.2	22.3	6.5	17.4	9.9	14.7	13.2	11.2
48383		9	Reagan	1,175.3	3,741	2,922	3.2	27.9	3.0	0.7	0.7	68.9	7.8	21.4	9.6	12.6	14.6	11.5
48385		9	Real	699.2	3,478	2,939	5.0	70.0	1.5	1.4	0.9	27.8	4.4	12.4	6.2	8.6	9.1	12.1
48387		6	Red River	1,043.9	12,175	2,278	11.7	74.8	17.0	1.7	0.6	7.5	5.2	14.7	6.8	10.2	10.4	12.6
48389	37,780	7	Reeves	2,635.4	15,695	2,055	6.0	18.6	4.8	0.4	1.6	75.0	6.5	15.9	11.8	17.2	15.6	12.1
48391		6	Refugio	770.5	7,032	2,666	9.1	43.0	6.0	0.8	1.0	50.3	6.4	16.3	7.6	10.9	10.5	11.9
48393		9	Roberts	924.1	903	3,111	1.0	87.5	1.1	1.3	0.6	11.2	6.4	17.9	5.8	10.9	13.3	10.4
48395	17,780	3	Robertson	855.1	17,284	1,961	20.2	58.1	19.8	0.8	1.0	21.5	6.6	17.5	7.4	12.1	11.6	12.1
48397	19,100	1	Rockwall	127.1	100,657	598	792.0	71.8	7.2	0.9	3.9	18.0	6.3	20.7	8.0	11.1	14.9	14.3
48399		6	Runnels	1,051.1	10,234	2,404	9.7	61.8	2.3	0.9	1.6	34.2	5.5	17.3	7.9	11.6	10.9	12.3
48401	30,980	3	Rusk	924.0	54,450	935	58.9	64.4	18.0	0.9	0.9	17.3	5.6	16.6	8.9	13.5	13.4	12.5
48403		8	Sabine	491.7	10,589	2,386	21.5	87.2	7.6	1.3	0.7	4.9	4.9	13.8	6.1	8.9	8.4	10.8
48405		9	San Augustine	530.7	8,232	2,576	15.5	70.4	22.5	0.8	0.5	7.1	5.1	14.7	6.1	10.3	8.9	12.0
48407		8	San Jacinto	569.2	28,719	1,467	50.5	76.2	10.2	1.3	1.0	13.2	5.6	16.0	7.4	10.5	10.4	11.8
48409	18,580	2	San Patricio	693.4	66,893	798	96.5	38.6	1.8	0.6	1.5	58.4	7.3	19.4	8.7	13.3	12.8	11.8
48411		7	San Saba	1,135.3	6,054	2,747	5.3	64.5	4.0	1.1	0.9	30.7	5.2	15.0	9.6	14.8	8.5	10.6
48413		8	Schleicher	1,310.6	2,895	2,975	2.2	44.9	1.7	0.4	0.5	53.3	5.2	20.5	7.6	12.0	11.7	11.6
48415	43,660	7	Scurry	905.4	16,866	1,984	18.6	53.7	5.4	0.7	0.8	40.6	6.9	18.3	9.5	13.3	13.3	11.7
48417		8	Shackelford	914.3	3,253	2,954	3.6	87.2	1.8	0.7	0.8	10.9	5.3	17.7	7.3	11.2	10.3	11.1
48419		7	Shelby	795.6	25,418	1,586	31.9	62.3	17.9	0.7	1.7	18.6	7.1	18.7	8.1	12.0	11.6	12.0
48421		9	Sherman	923.0	3,079	2,960	3.3	53.9	1.6	0.7	0.6	43.9	6.8	21.4	8.3	11.4	10.9	13.9
48423	46,340	3	Smith	921.5	230,221	292	249.8	60.7	18.1	0.8	2.2	19.9	6.9	17.7	9.6	13.7	11.8	11.7
48425	19,100	1	Somervell	186.5	9,016	2,499	48.3	79.0	1.6	1.4	1.3	18.3	5.0	17.4	7.8	10.9	11.9	13.7
48427	40,100	4	Starr	1,223.2	64,525	825	52.8	3.3	0.2	0.0	0.2	96.4	9.7	23.1	11.3	13.3	11.7	11.1
48429		7	Stephens	896.7	9,433	2,466	10.5	71.8	2.8	1.2	1.2	23.9	5.4	16.3	9.1	12.6	12.2	10.9
48431		8	Sterling	923.4	1,311	3,092	1.4	56.2	2.6	1.4	0.8	40.7	8.3	20.1	7.6	11.5	13.7	11.2
48433		9	Stonewall	916.3	1,362	3,089	1.5	75.6	3.5	1.2	2.3	18.9	5.8	16.4	5.8	8.7	10.3	12.0
48435		7	Sutton	1,453.9	3,758	2,920	2.6	36.0	0.7	0.2	0.3	63.1	6.4	17.5	7.7	11.7	10.4	13.5
48437		6	Swisher	890.2	7,462	2,628	8.4	46.7	8.2	1.0	0.7	44.5	6.2	18.9	9.6	14.0	11.3	11.3
48439	19,100	1	Tarrant	863.6	2,084,931	15	2,414.2	47.7	17.6	0.9	6.7	29.2	7.0	19.3	9.3	15.0	13.7	13.0
48441	10,180	3	Taylor	915.5	137,640	467	150.3	64.9	8.5	0.9	3.1	24.8	7.3	17.4	14.2	14.7	11.4	9.7
48443		9	Terrell	2,358.0	823	3,116	0.3	42.4	1.7	1.6	1.7	54.3	5.1	14.7	7.3	8.7	11.5	11.1
48445		6	Terry	888.8	12,287	2,271	13.8	39.3	4.5	0.6	0.6	55.9	8.0	19.5	9.4	14.0	11.4	11.1
48447		9	Throckmorton	912.6	1,515	3,079	1.7	83.2	1.3	1.3	0.6	14.5	4.8	14.9	6.2	8.4	10.2	12.1
48449	34,420	7	Titus	406.1	33,033	1,357	81.3	45.3	9.6	0.7	1.4	44.1	8.0	21.0	9.8	12.2	11.7	12.2

1. CBSA = Core Based Statistical Area. See Appendix A for explanation. See Appendix B for list of metropolitan areas with component counties. Service of USDA Rural-Urban Continuum Codes. See Appendix A for definition. 3. Dry land or land partially or temporarily covered by water. 2. County type code from the Economic Research 4. May be of any race.

Table B. States and Counties — **Population and Households**

	Population, 2018 (cont.)				Population change, 2000-2018							Households, 2013-2017				
	Age (percent) (cont.)				Total persons		Percent change		Components of change, 2010-2018						Percent	
STATE County	55 to 64 years	65 to 74 years	75 years and over	Percent female	2000	2010	2000-2010	2010-2018	Births	Deaths	Net Migration	Number	Persons per household	Family house-holds	Female family house-holder[1]	One person
	16	17	18	19	20	21	22	23	24	25	26	27	28	29	30	31
TEXAS— Cont'd																
Mason	14.6	15.5	13.0	49.9	3,738	4,013	7.4	6.7	311	378	336	1,622	2.53	63.3	10.9	32.7
Matagorda	13.9	10.0	7.0	49.6	37,957	36,702	-3.3	-0.4	4,425	3,103	-1,467	13,811	2.63	66.2	12.0	31.3
Maverick	9.0	6.8	5.0	50.1	47,297	54,258	14.7	7.8	8,982	3,063	-1,689	16,416	3.47	81.0	17.7	16.7
Medina	13.5	10.0	6.7	48.4	39,304	46,006	17.1	10.7	4,627	3,290	3,591	15,154	3.03	73.6	10.7	21.3
Menard	17.1	16.4	15.3	50.4	2,360	2,242	-5.0	-4.6	148	278	23	964	2.15	60.4	8.6	37.1
Midland	10.6	5.8	4.5	49.5	116,009	136,872	18.0	26.1	22,260	8,710	21,718	55,045	2.87	69.7	12.7	24.4
Milam	14.0	11.5	8.8	50.7	24,238	24,756	2.1	1.5	2,532	2,389	232	9,437	2.54	66.1	12.5	30.9
Mills	14.6	15.3	13.2	50.1	5,151	4,941	-4.1	-0.4	346	520	154	1,833	2.57	65.4	8.3	33.1
Mitchell	10.8	8.8	6.4	41.7	9,698	9,403	-3.0	-13.4	816	788	-1,308	2,639	2.41	72.0	10.1	21.5
Montague	14.4	12.5	9.5	50.9	19,117	19,720	3.2	-0.6	1,906	2,214	196	8,044	2.37	67.6	7.3	29.0
Montgomery	12.3	8.2	4.9	50.5	293,768	455,750	55.1	29.7	56,794	28,230	105,423	186,861	2.85	74.6	10.4	21.2
Moore	10.5	6.3	4.6	48.1	20,121	21,904	8.9	-1.9	3,463	1,159	-2,773	6,725	3.25	76.0	11.3	20.4
Morris	14.6	11.9	10.0	51.9	13,048	12,934	-0.9	-4.6	1,262	1,400	-452	5,024	2.46	72.1	11.5	26.4
Motley	14.6	16.8	13.5	48.6	1,426	1,205	-15.5	2.4	73	138	91	469	2.38	65.7	13.9	32.2
Nacogdoches	11.1	8.7	6.0	52.1	59,203	64,524	9.0	1.8	7,163	4,638	-1,358	23,825	2.52	64.3	11.8	28.4
Navarro	12.9	9.9	7.1	50.9	45,124	47,840	6.0	3.6	5,773	4,303	280	17,326	2.73	74.6	14.5	21.7
Newton	14.8	11.8	8.8	48.6	15,072	14,445	-4.2	-4.8	1,134	1,317	-516	4,781	2.93	66.1	10.4	30.9
Nolan	12.4	10.2	8.1	50.0	15,802	15,215	-3.7	-3.0	1,673	1,470	-666	5,552	2.64	68.5	13.7	28.5
Nueces	12.2	8.5	5.9	50.6	313,645	340,223	8.5	6.5	39,739	23,284	5,675	128,857	2.72	68.2	15.7	25.0
Ochiltree	11.4	6.6	4.5	49.4	9,006	10,223	13.5	-2.7	1,478	683	-1,086	3,549	2.94	77.5	8.0	19.5
Oldham	14.5	9.2	5.8	48.0	2,185	2,052	-6.1	3.8	186	120	9	581	2.58	72.5	4.0	22.7
Orange	13.3	9.3	6.8	50.4	84,966	81,837	-3.7	2.1	9,252	7,818	362	32,272	2.57	70.8	12.8	25.2
Palo Pinto	14.5	11.7	7.9	50.7	27,026	28,122	4.1	2.7	2,958	2,683	490	10,441	2.67	68.9	11.5	25.7
Panola	14.2	11.2	7.9	50.5	22,756	23,796	4.6	-2.7	2,360	2,268	-734	9,032	2.56	70.4	12.0	25.3
Parker	13.9	9.4	5.9	50.2	88,495	116,957	32.2	18.3	11,703	8,594	18,219	43,942	2.82	76.2	8.7	20.3
Parmer	11.9	7.5	6.3	48.1	10,016	10,269	2.5	-3.9	1,284	605	-1,105	3,222	3.04	77.6	12.8	17.9
Pecos	10.8	7.7	5.7	43.1	16,809	15,507	-7.7	1.1	1,743	946	-622	4,420	3.09	67.5	7.6	30.1
Polk	16.9	13.1	5.7	46.2	41,133	45,415	10.4	10.2	4,186	5,202	5,542	17,632	2.46	69.7	14.9	26.3
Potter	11.1	7.2	5.3	48.5	113,546	121,078	6.6	-1.2	16,342	9,800	-8,051	43,453	2.63	65.1	15.9	29.9
Presidio	10.3	11.1	12.0	48.8	7,304	7,817	7.0	-11.1	974	379	-1,497	2,589	2.78	66.0	11.0	33.1
Rains	16.5	15.1	9.5	50.3	9,139	10,916	19.4	11.4	824	1,137	1,546	4,333	2.58	70.6	10.1	26.4
Randall	12.1	8.8	6.2	50.8	104,312	120,720	15.7	12.9	13,570	8,340	10,291	49,118	2.61	69.2	11.3	25.0
Reagan	11.3	6.5	4.8	46.5	3,326	3,367	1.2	11.1	500	203	68	1,171	3.16	76.6	9.1	19.9
Real	17.7	17.2	12.2	50.2	3,047	3,309	8.6	5.1	286	416	293	1,123	2.89	61.7	15.7	37.0
Red River	15.4	13.4	11.2	51.4	14,314	12,864	-10.1	-5.4	1,060	1,449	-295	5,218	2.33	63.9	15.3	34.1
Reeves	8.8	6.4	5.6	38.6	13,137	13,783	4.9	13.9	1,542	845	1,206	3,731	3.31	69.4	9.9	27.6
Refugio	13.8	12.6	10.0	50.9	7,828	7,383	-5.7	-4.8	720	739	-335	2,694	2.64	68.9	13.8	29.0
Roberts	14.4	12.8	8.1	50.4	887	929	4.7	-2.8	79	70	-36	326	2.73	77.0	8.9	16.9
Robertson	13.4	11.1	8.3	50.4	16,000	16,620	3.9	4.0	1,735	1,562	496	6,298	2.62	70.1	14.5	25.0
Rockwall	12.1	7.6	4.9	50.6	43,080	78,330	81.8	28.5	8,270	4,401	18,298	30,365	2.96	80.8	9.9	15.8
Runnels	13.8	11.1	9.6	49.2	11,495	10,506	-8.6	-2.6	892	1,131	-35	3,781	2.65	71.4	11.2	25.2
Rusk	12.9	9.7	6.9	46.1	47,372	53,307	12.5	2.1	5,198	4,501	449	17,982	2.68	72.8	13.9	23.4
Sabine	16.5	17.0	13.5	50.8	10,469	10,838	3.5	-2.3	785	1,388	353	3,811	2.71	66.0	9.2	32.8
San Augustine	16.5	13.9	12.6	50.8	8,946	8,861	-1.0	-7.1	771	1,110	-291	3,202	2.54	66.8	13.2	31.0
San Jacinto	16.4	13.1	8.8	50.4	22,246	26,377	18.6	8.9	2,348	2,429	2,415	9,414	2.90	70.0	9.3	26.4
San Patricio	11.7	8.9	6.0	49.7	67,138	64,802	-3.5	3.2	8,038	5,161	-802	23,246	2.84	74.4	14.6	21.7
San Saba	12.5	13.2	10.6	45.4	6,186	6,130	-0.9	-1.2	528	553	-54	2,135	2.41	58.8	6.4	32.4
Schleicher	11.8	12.2	7.4	50.4	2,935	3,461	17.9	-16.4	269	196	-648	1,102	2.83	73.3	10.2	22.2
Scurry	11.9	8.0	7.1	45.8	16,361	16,919	3.4	-0.3	2,056	1,413	-700	5,838	2.65	67.0	9.2	29.6
Shackelford	16.7	10.9	9.6	50.3	3,302	3,380	2.4	-3.8	270	255	-145	1,257	2.64	67.4	9.6	28.9
Shelby	12.9	9.9	7.6	50.3	25,224	25,448	0.9	-0.1	3,022	2,372	-690	9,218	2.76	69.1	15.1	29.5
Sherman	12.3	8.1	6.8	47.9	3,186	3,034	-4.8	1.5	316	224	-50	1,063	2.85	76.9	7.3	19.8
Smith	12.2	9.2	7.3	51.7	174,706	209,725	20.0	9.8	25,372	16,735	11,910	77,801	2.79	68.6	12.7	26.7
Somervell	14.4	11.2	7.8	50.7	6,809	8,491	24.7	6.2	700	704	532	3,234	2.57	75.6	15.6	20.7
Starr	8.3	6.4	4.9	51.3	53,597	60,968	13.8	5.8	10,905	3,274	-4,112	16,320	3.85	81.6	25.3	17.4
Stephens	13.8	11.0	8.7	47.1	9,674	9,630	-0.5	-2.0	829	917	-115	3,361	2.62	69.0	10.8	27.9
Sterling	13.1	7.0	7.4	49.0	1,393	1,143	-17.9	14.7	129	109	143	462	2.38	72.3	6.7	25.1
Stonewall	14.5	13.7	12.8	51.2	1,693	1,490	-12.0	-8.6	116	175	-75	458	2.25	60.3	4.1	39.7
Sutton	14.5	10.7	7.7	48.9	4,077	4,128	1.3	-9.0	430	267	-545	1,573	2.46	73.3	11.4	24.2
Swisher	11.0	9.4	8.3	46.7	8,378	7,859	-6.2	-5.1	833	658	-578	2,602	2.64	74.0	17.1	22.6
Tarrant	11.5	6.9	4.4	51.1	1,446,219	1,810,655	25.2	15.1	231,821	100,220	142,869	689,921	2.84	69.8	14.1	24.8
Taylor	10.9	7.8	6.6	51.2	126,555	131,508	3.9	4.7	17,007	10,668	-133	49,443	2.60	66.2	13.2	26.2
Terrell	11.9	17.0	12.6	48.8	1,081	984	-9.0	-16.4	92	92	-166	343	2.10	53.1	12.8	44.3
Terry	11.5	8.1	7.0	47.8	12,761	12,651	-0.9	-2.9	1,592	1,034	-924	4,142	2.80	72.1	15.7	25.9
Throckmorton	15.4	14.2	13.9	53.3	1,850	1,641	-11.3	-7.7	121	161	-88	712	2.15	65.2	11.4	33.8
Titus	10.9	8.5	5.7	51.0	28,118	32,334	15.0	2.2	4,191	2,244	-1,251	10,675	3.03	77.8	14.3	19.4

1. No spouse present.

Table B. States and Counties — Population, Vital Statistics, Health, and Crime

STATE County	Persons in group quarters, 2018	Daytime Population, 2013-2017		Births, 2018		Deaths, 2018		Persons under 65 with no health insurance, 2016		Medicare, 2018			Serious crimes known to police[2], 2016 Total	
		Number	Employment/ residence ratio	Total	Rate[1]	Number	Rate[1]	Number	Percent	Total beneficiaries	Enrolled in Original Medicare	Enrolled in Medicare Advantage	Number	Rate[3]
	32	33	34	35	36	37	38	39	40	41	42	43	44	45
TEXAS— Cont'd														
Mason	3	4,031	0.96	37	8.6	49	11.4	781	26.7	1,236	929	307	45	1,118
Matagorda	367	35,433	0.92	543	14.9	381	10.4	6,171	20.0	6,894	4,755	2,139	1,363	3,717
Maverick	1,045	53,717	0.82	1,069	18.3	380	6.5	13,611	27.5	9,893	6,378	3,515	1,276	2,192
Medina	2,382	40,212	0.59	608	11.9	441	8.7	6,524	16.6	9,250	5,589	3,661	1,048	2,204
Menard	41	1,846	0.72	18	8.4	23	10.8	385	26.3	634	492	142	4	187
Midland	1,603	176,679	1.21	2,847	16.5	1,106	6.4	25,409	17.5	18,564	14,291	4,273	4,676	2,819
Milam	421	22,388	0.78	294	11.7	281	11.2	3,828	19.5	5,778	3,553	2,225	502	2,057
Mills	146	4,924	1.02	39	7.9	62	12.6	846	24.0	1,401	935	466	28	574
Mitchell	1,428	8,391	0.86	103	12.6	69	8.5	1,134	20.1	1,422	1,015	407	117	1,304
Montague	180	17,769	0.79	227	11.6	277	14.1	3,251	21.5	5,024	4,038	986	436	2,407
Montgomery	3,202	490,714	0.82	7,408	12.5	4,140	7.0	81,793	16.9	84,348	49,524	34,824	9,259	1,674
Moore	151	22,777	1.07	403	18.8	135	6.3	5,063	25.8	2,485	2,052	433	384	1,727
Morris	144	11,450	0.78	141	11.4	162	13.1	1,942	19.8	3,545	2,264	1,281	345	2,782
Motley	0	1,029	0.83	12	9.7	16	13.0	210	25.7	362	277	85	14	1,236
Nacogdoches	5,035	64,363	0.96	788	12.0	585	8.9	11,001	21.2	11,325	8,231	3,094	1,391	2,118
Navarro	738	46,473	0.91	713	14.4	565	11.4	8,612	21.5	10,106	7,276	2,830	1,254	2,685
Newton	725	11,622	0.48	123	8.9	182	13.2	1,827	17.0	2,571	1,709	862	NA	NA
Nolan	413	15,753	1.12	195	13.2	178	12.1	2,097	17.4	3,161	2,363	798	676	4,930
Nueces	6,634	369,023	1.06	4,554	12.6	3,024	8.3	55,992	18.3	57,960	27,133	30,827	16,004	4,413
Ochiltree	28	11,570	1.24	163	16.4	71	7.1	2,438	26.6	1,264	1,078	186	145	1,338
Oldham	278	2,481	1.52	27	12.7	11	5.2	229	15.0	406	307	99	11	532
Orange	675	75,562	0.77	1,116	13.4	1,005	12.0	9,875	13.8	16,424	9,857	6,567	2,185	2,603
Palo Pinto	268	26,261	0.84	349	12.1	353	12.2	4,851	21.5	6,108	4,780	1,328	797	2,869
Panola	374	22,715	0.91	260	11.2	264	11.4	3,283	17.3	5,053	3,475	1,578	661	2,790
Parker	1,240	106,131	0.66	1,582	11.4	1,138	8.2	17,019	15.7	23,889	16,963	6,926	1,804	1,415
Parmer	67	11,042	1.27	159	16.1	56	5.7	2,121	25.1	1,418	1,211	207	99	1,029
Pecos	2,077	16,205	1.07	183	11.7	102	6.5	2,577	21.6	2,259	1,691	568	335	2,056
Polk	4,327	45,321	0.91	507	10.1	644	12.9	7,577	21.9	18,152	12,244	5,908	911	1,933
Potter	6,885	147,719	1.51	1,791	15.0	1,125	9.4	23,015	23.1	18,473	13,810	4,663	6,120	5,036
Presidio	0	7,157	0.99	105	15.1	53	7.6	1,568	28.9	1,819	1,397	422	48	719
Rains	59	9,739	0.66	110	9.0	134	11.0	1,817	21.2	2,976	2,187	789	131	1,172
Randall	2,519	101,944	0.58	1,587	11.6	1,060	7.8	14,461	12.9	22,009	16,601	5,408	5,752	4,365
Reagan	33	4,888	1.67	66	17.6	13	3.5	696	21.7	436	339	97	71	1,832
Real	71	3,303	0.96	35	10.1	51	14.7	578	24.5	1,205	900	305	45	1,366
Red River	176	10,358	0.58	120	9.9	176	14.5	1,887	20.5	3,441	2,656	785	125	1,013
Reeves	3,133	18,053	1.65	193	12.3	96	6.1	2,088	20.8	2,114	1,690	424	361	2,426
Refugio	128	6,996	0.90	78	11.1	56	8.0	977	17.0	1,698	1,212	486	97	1,337
Roberts	0	791	0.75	8	8.9	6	6.6	76	10.2	185	144	41	8	878
Robertson	198	15,167	0.78	213	12.3	183	10.6	2,653	19.6	3,617	2,590	1,027	240	1,443
Rockwall	694	79,188	0.74	1,058	10.5	614	6.1	10,894	13.3	13,962	9,762	4,200	1,251	1,343
Runnels	183	9,668	0.85	106	10.4	124	12.1	1,624	20.0	2,534	2,115	419	246	2,336
Rusk	6,206	47,311	0.72	587	10.8	569	10.4	8,256	20.7	9,797	6,501	3,296	1,571	2,972
Sabine	129	9,899	0.83	102	9.6	148	14.0	1,389	19.2	3,407	2,596	811	195	2,066
San Augustine	179	8,059	0.86	84	10.2	119	14.5	1,122	18.4	2,434	1,755	679	130	1,552
San Jacinto	127	21,429	0.40	300	10.4	302	10.5	4,689	21.5	6,165	3,537	2,628	409	1,486
San Patricio	614	61,146	0.80	974	14.6	605	9.0	10,600	18.5	12,600	5,856	6,744	1,966	2,902
San Saba	698	5,685	0.93	56	9.3	67	11.1	1,044	26.4	1,506	1,076	430	32	548
Schleicher	1	2,917	0.86	22	7.6	19	6.6	577	22.7	595	457	138	54	1,715
Scurry	1,691	18,064	1.11	229	13.6	169	10.0	2,342	17.6	2,842	2,100	742	392	2,215
Shackelford	11	3,188	0.89	30	9.2	36	11.1	557	20.7	705	532	173	34	1,019
Shelby	158	24,803	0.91	353	13.9	300	11.8	5,362	25.2	5,124	3,621	1,503	492	2,035
Sherman	29	2,654	0.74	36	11.7	22	7.1	719	27.6	385	321	64	14	456
Smith	4,800	229,410	1.07	3,109	13.5	2,152	9.3	33,998	18.4	44,072	30,468	13,604	7,207	3,233
Somervell	283	9,995	1.38	86	9.5	97	10.8	1,323	18.7	1,824	1,218	606	83	947
Starr	833	59,749	0.82	1,227	19.0	418	6.5	15,589	28.2	9,359	5,963	3,396	900	1,403
Stephens	688	9,143	0.94	89	9.4	97	10.3	1,588	22.8	2,042	1,545	497	180	1,919
Sterling	35	1,296	1.31	15	11.4	20	15.3	216	19.0	219	176	43	1	72
Stonewall	25	1,040	0.90	12	8.8	15	11.0	195	18.4	363	292	71	7	504
Sutton	14	3,885	1.00	47	12.5	28	7.5	656	20.7	743	637	106	46	1,188
Swisher	644	7,000	0.79	86	11.5	76	10.2	1,258	22.9	1,496	1,203	293	169	2,271
Tarrant	24,353	1,974,219	0.99	28,566	13.7	13,659	6.6	303,048	17.0	262,026	145,222	116,804	65,230	3,243
Taylor	5,083	138,284	1.04	2,058	15.0	1,384	10.1	18,571	16.4	24,084	17,550	6,534	4,948	3,625
Terrell	0	730	1.03	8	9.7	7	8.5	130	21.6	247	175	72	14	1,739
Terry	955	12,597	0.96	182	14.8	132	10.7	2,378	24.2	2,052	1,317	735	262	2,060
Throckmorton	13	1,543	1.00	12	7.9	14	9.2	239	21.0	392	322	70	0	0
Titus	437	36,143	1.25	519	15.7	267	8.1	6,705	24.3	5,243	3,540	1,703	882	2,708

1. Per 1,000 estimated resident population.   2. Data for serious crimes have not been adjusted for underreporting; this may affect comparability between geographic areas and over time.   3. Per 100,000 population estimated by the FBI.

Table B. States and Counties — Crime, Education, Money Income, and Poverty

STATE County	Serious crimes known to police[2], 2016 (cont.)[1] Rate Violent	Property	Education — School enrollment and attainment, 2013-2017 Enrollment[3] Total	Percent private	Attainment[4] (percent) High school graduate or less	Bachelor's degree or more	Local government expenditures[5] 2014-2015 Total current spending (mil dol)	Current spending per student (dollars)	Money income, 2013-2017 Per capita income[6]	Households Median income (dollars)	Percent with income of less than $50,000	Percent with income of $200,000 or more	Income and poverty, 2017 Median household income (dollars)	Percent below poverty level All persons	Children under 18 years	Children 5 to 17 years in families
	46	47	48	49	50	51	52	53	54	55	56	57	58	59	60	61
TEXAS— Cont'd																
Mason	50	1,069	639	7.0	45.6	20.3	7.1	10,817	24,519	40,949	59.0	1.4	47,213	12.5	21.1	20.1
Matagorda	368	3,348	8,578	9.7	55.4	14.7	71.3	10,010	23,294	44,896	54.1	2.6	46,801	18	26.4	25.1
Maverick	180	2,012	16,303	5.0	61.8	11.8	133.3	8,840	16,658	37,734	59.9	1.5	33,507	27	33.3	32.7
Medina	278	1,926	12,607	12.0	49.4	20.0	84.2	8,605	25,572	59,305	43.3	4.8	56,173	14.7	21.7	20.0
Menard	0	187	392	2.0	57.1	15.8	4.3	14,098	23,613	37,917	63.3	1.1	34,033	20.6	36.3	35.0
Midland	303	2,516	40,804	15.3	41.8	26.8	245.9	9,120	38,545	75,815	32.3	10.8	76,307	10.7	15.5	15.1
Milam	225	1,831	5,799	7.7	55.8	15.0	45.3	9,655	22,911	41,768	57.0	1.7	44,855	19.3	32.6	31.9
Mills	41	533	1,327	4.9	45.1	23.0	12.5	12,875	24,858	46,318	52.9	3.7	42,463	15.8	22.7	20.4
Mitchell	100	1,204	2,048	6.7	61.1	11.8	16.7	11,186	19,741	52,194	45.5	2.7	41,512	20.6	26.5	26.1
Montague	171	2,236	4,108	10.3	53.6	16.2	32.2	9,562	26,278	46,592	53.5	3.4	47,590	15.3	22.2	20.8
Montgomery	172	1,502	141,480	13.6	36.5	33.7	809.4	8,071	38,012	74,323	33.5	12.2	77,149	8.9	12.5	11.9
Moore	175	1,551	6,179	2.3	59.0	13.4	46.2	9,073	21,372	52,469	47.0	1.9	51,444	11.7	16.7	17.0
Morris	306	2,476	2,774	6.8	50.8	16.0	19.1	9,166	22,803	40,227	59.5	1.2	39,627	18.4	29.5	28.2
Motley	0	1,236	270	2.2	43.0	15.6	2.6	15,449	25,908	40,598	61.0	3.6	36,782	17.7	32.1	30.2
Nacogdoches	294	1,824	21,922	5.0	45.9	25.2	95.4	8,527	22,589	41,482	57.7	3.5	42,367	23.9	33.7	34.9
Navarro	381	2,304	11,753	5.3	52.2	15.6	83.6	8,474	22,152	45,103	54.8	2.5	41,944	16.9	25.3	23.1
Newton	NA	NA	2,913	3.3	60.5	8.8	20.1	10,264	20,800	40,180	57.3	1.1	41,736	20.8	28.5	26.1
Nolan	394	4,536	3,588	8.2	53.7	13.3	32.9	10,402	23,686	42,019	56.2	2.0	42,662	19.3	29.4	27.3
Nueces	723	3,690	92,459	6.2	47.0	20.9	556.8	8,926	26,780	53,317	47.0	3.9	51,910	16.1	22.8	20.8
Ochiltree	388	951	2,979	4.9	54.3	18.3	21.4	8,826	24,157	50,120	49.9	3.0	58,962	12.3	18.6	18.2
Oldham	145	387	733	3.8	41.2	26.5	13.7	16,135	25,461	62,426	40.1	7.9	55,451	12.8	30.3	24.8
Orange	342	2,261	20,179	8.9	49.5	15.7	128.5	8,435	27,938	53,667	47.2	3.3	57,257	13.7	20.3	19.3
Palo Pinto	209	2,660	5,936	8.4	51.5	16.6	40.8	8,755	24,840	45,067	54.5	2.9	45,869	16.8	28.0	26.4
Panola	215	2,575	5,497	7.5	47.8	14.7	40.2	9,949	26,205	49,704	50.4	3.9	48,971	15	21.4	20.7
Parker	136	1,279	30,870	14.1	38.2	26.9	169.7	8,440	33,367	70,608	35.3	8.3	74,076	8	11.8	11.0
Parmer	83	946	2,632	9.9	62.5	16.1	23.6	9,916	21,876	50,410	49.4	2.0	48,189	13.3	18.4	17.9
Pecos	331	1,725	3,570	4.6	67.0	9.6	31.4	9,777	19,088	50,543	49.5	1.2	44,352	20.6	26.2	25.3
Polk	242	1,691	8,649	7.8	59.1	12.3	63.7	9,295	23,023	43,267	56.0	3.0	44,596	18	28.7	26.6
Potter	658	4,379	32,609	7.5	53.8	14.8	323.5	8,583	21,941	41,852	57.9	2.6	43,778	18.5	25.2	25.3
Presidio	60	659	1,832	1.7	65.7	20.2	20.2	11,685	15,329	26,486	73.4	0.3	29,761	23.4	32.3	35.8
Rains	125	1,047	2,322	8.5	58.2	10.8	14.3	8,722	23,976	48,308	51.3	1.9	43,403	17	26.1	23.5
Randall	560	3,805	36,393	9.5	30.6	30.9	93.0	9,874	32,922	65,564	37.3	4.7	63,077	8.8	10.5	9.9
Reagan	103	1,729	938	2.9	61.8	11.0	10.6	11,908	25,273	59,760	37.5	4.0	58,168	11.4	17.8	18.5
Real	182	1,184	574	3.3	45.7	21.9	5.9	12,512	20,873	36,493	63.6	1.1	36,146	12.3	36.6	37.0
Red River	89	924	2,354	6.2	55.8	13.8	22.9	10,428	21,177	35,356	65.3	1.5	35,643	19.5	27.9	26.5
Reeves	423	2,003	3,159	5.5	65.4	9.5	29.9	11,544	18,992	49,390	50.5	1.9	40,694	25.1	28.0	27.9
Refugio	427	910	1,571	3.6	54.3	12.1	18.7	12,929	23,959	50,338	49.6	2.1	42,898	16.9	26.4	25.8
Roberts	0	878	234	6.4	36.5	31.2	3.1	14,880	34,555	79,167	24.8	2.1	67,688	7	7.6	7.2
Robertson	247	1,197	4,082	8.5	53.7	15.0	37.2	11,381	23,337	52,189	47.8	1.3	44,355	17.4	26.4	25.3
Rockwall	104	1,239	25,829	12.4	28.6	40.0	163.8	8,163	38,933	93,269	24.8	11.6	98,442	5.3	6.8	6.3
Runnels	209	2,127	2,252	6.0	57.5	19.1	21.0	10,255	22,190	41,226	57.3	2.2	41,830	17.3	26.1	23.8
Rusk	460	2,512	11,072	7.2	51.3	15.5	71.6	8,635	23,521	49,270	50.6	2.9	49,872	15.2	21.6	20.0
Sabine	307	1,759	1,766	8.3	56.7	14.4	14.2	9,035	20,876	33,561	66.6	2.7	37,770	20.2	31.0	28.4
San Augustine	466	1,086	1,499	2.3	59.3	12.1	8.2	10,691	21,066	32,394	64.1	1.4	39,133	21.6	34.9	33.9
San Jacinto	171	1,315	5,780	9.0	65.6	10.1	31.4	9,106	22,308	43,421	54.0	2.3	44,707	18.2	28.4	26.8
San Patricio	332	2,570	16,513	6.7	54.2	14.3	131.7	8,925	24,613	53,332	47.0	2.8	50,752	19	26.9	24.3
San Saba	68	479	1,322	12.6	56.3	15.1	9.9	10,550	22,481	40,301	57.8	1.4	43,112	17.1	26.3	25.7
Schleicher	0	1,715	825	3.2	46.9	20.3	6.5	10,848	28,112	63,432	41.6	4.4	45,821	16.2	25.0	21.7
Scurry	113	2,102	4,679	6.5	54.1	16.6	32.0	9,458	24,140	54,565	46.4	3.1	51,772	17.2	24.3	23.7
Shackelford	60	959	882	8.5	40.1	27.4	7.0	11,947	24,296	46,685	51.9	2.4	61,155	14.2	21.6	19.7
Shelby	244	1,791	6,479	6.8	58.5	15.3	54.3	9,635	20,686	38,121	62.8	3.2	39,745	20.8	33.0	30.6
Sherman	195	260	678	5.5	51.9	21.4	7.7	9,788	25,358	54,961	45.5	3.6	49,349	12.5	16.4	14.7
Smith	328	2,905	59,288	11.9	39.7	25.2	293.8	8,473	26,270	50,742	49.3	4.2	54,044	15.6	20.0	18.7
Somervell	148	799	2,072	6.3	45.2	20.0	21.0	10,979	27,095	52,346	48.1	6.0	62,803	10.4	16.6	15.1
Starr	254	1,149	19,067	2.6	74.9	9.7	186.2	10,592	13,167	27,133	71.6	1.0	28,377	32	40.2	38.8
Stephens	203	1,716	1,936	5.8	55.5	16.8	12.3	8,335	23,044	45,862	55.4	2.9	41,977	19.5	30.1	28.1
Sterling	0	72	194	0.0	59.2	21.4	3.7	11,233	25,675	50,000	50.0	2.2	55,690	12.2	17.7	16.8
Stonewall	144	360	249	1.6	59.1	12.5	4.1	16,432	28,063	46,786	52.0	3.7	43,702	15.3	20.3	20.1
Sutton	52	1,136	870	0.0	52.3	19.8	11.4	12,415	31,603	60,996	39.9	4.2	57,986	14.3	23.6	23.4
Swisher	672	1,599	1,868	2.2	57.4	13.0	15.8	10,110	18,878	37,883	64.7	1.8	41,264	19.9	29.6	28.1
Tarrant	405	2,838	556,646	13.1	38.4	31.1	3,020.3	8,491	30,857	62,532	39.5	6.8	65,021	11.6	17.1	16.0
Taylor	411	3,214	37,956	26.8	42.5	24.1	204.5	8,593	25,419	49,161	50.5	3.3	50,338	15.2	20.8	20.4
Terrell	248	1,491	158	10.8	47.6	17.3	2.5	17,556	21,204	26,063	71.4	0.6	39,033	19.3	23.3	21.4
Terry	252	1,809	3,223	7.5	61.7	12.8	24.8	10,263	21,938	42,441	56.3	2.2	40,899	21.5	30.2	28.5
Throckmorton	0	0	280	3.9	48.3	20.0	3.8	11,146	27,732	37,279	56.9	2.5	38,162	15.4	27.1	25.0
Titus	362	2,346	8,897	4.2	56.1	15.8	61.4	8,631	21,090	46,980	52.9	2.6	47,097	16.3	24.8	23.4

1. Data for serious crimes have not been adjusted for underreporting; this may affect comparability between geographic areas and over time. 2. Per 100,000 population estimated by the FBI. 3. All persons 3 years old and over enrolled in nursery school through college. 4. Persons 25 years old and over. 5. Elementary and secondary education expenditures. 6. Based on population estimated by the American Community Survey, 2013–2017.

Table B. States and Counties — Personal Income and Earnings

	Personal income, 2017										Earnings, 2017		
			Per capita[1]			Supplements to wages and salaries, employer contributions (mil dol)						Contributions for government social insurance (mil dol)	
STATE County	Total (mil dol)	Percent change 2016-2017	Dollars	Rank	Wages and salaries (mil dol)	Pension and insurance	Government social insurance	Proprietors' income (mil dol)	Dividends, interest, and rent (mil dol)	Personal transfer receipts (mil dol)	Total (mil dol)	From employee and self-employed	From employer
	62	63	64	65	66	67	68	69	70	71	72	73	74
TEXAS— Cont'd													
Mason	178	7.3	42,113	1,253	41	9	3	20	57	43	73	5	3
Matagorda	1,504	2.2	40,827	1,429	616	118	41	95	220	377	870	49	41
Maverick	1,667	3.1	28,636	3,008	616	151	43	127	164	541	937	54	43
Medina	1,912	4.3	38,189	1,847	387	80	26	117	328	442	611	39	26
Menard	75	-3.9	35,475	2,277	13	4	1	6	21	27	23	2	1
Midland	12,379	-1.1	75,002	52	6,603	864	432	2,401	2,700	973	10,300	522	432
Milam	920	2.4	36,731	2,088	257	45	19	76	153	296	398	26	19
Mills	181	2.1	36,789	2,079	48	10	3	10	47	61	71	5	3
Mitchell	254	2.0	30,037	2,926	91	25	6	-3	48	82	118	7	6
Montague	764	3.3	39,085	1,705	205	38	14	53	157	237	311	22	14
Montgomery	32,877	5.6	57,585	211	10,218	1,351	691	2,998	4,959	3,653	15,257	842	691
Moore	894	5.1	40,454	1,483	499	99	35	131	103	136	764	35	35
Morris	527	4.6	42,249	1,237	172	33	14	96	73	178	315	19	14
Motley	35	2.4	28,447	3,016	11	2	1	2	8	13	16	1	1
Nacogdoches	2,387	3.3	36,398	2,134	880	172	61	287	413	618	1,400	74	61
Navarro	1,800	2.6	36,960	2,044	645	121	46	77	324	529	889	56	46
Newton	437	0.9	31,306	2,832	48	13	3	7	50	141	71	7	3
Nolan	595	2.8	40,256	1,510	268	50	19	36	100	170	372	22	19
Nueces	15,125	2.9	41,873	1,278	8,224	1,437	600	1,264	2,466	3,342	11,526	627	600
Ochiltree	506	-1.8	50,251	445	235	40	16	119	77	61	410	17	16
Oldham	102	-2.2	48,409	595	39	7	3	24	16	16	73	3	3
Orange	3,692	2.6	43,412	1,088	1,241	209	86	125	400	926	1,661	106	86
Palo Pinto	1,057	3.2	36,987	2,037	401	70	27	54	214	293	552	35	27
Panola	939	3.9	40,411	1,487	410	66	30	50	168	253	557	34	30
Parker	6,931	6.1	51,930	376	1,531	236	108	511	1,222	983	2,386	143	108
Parmer	465	12.8	47,274	690	230	36	19	155	49	72	439	15	19
Pecos	523	1.6	33,461	2,559	268	54	18	18	79	127	358	19	18
Polk	1,878	3.0	38,210	1,844	453	84	31	80	447	758	649	57	31
Potter	4,873	-0.4	40,456	1,482	3,723	632	272	775	818	1,098	5,401	282	272
Presidio	280	-1.7	39,183	1,692	91	23	7	38	57	66	158	8	7
Rains	381	3.0	32,379	2,706	66	13	5	19	62	124	102	9	5
Randall	6,281	3.1	46,718	737	1,425	200	93	594	1,082	871	2,313	135	93
Reagan	150	3.9	40,496	1,474	114	22	8	3	28	23	146	8	8
Real	117	3.7	34,198	2,461	22	5	2	11	32	48	39	3	2
Red River	482	0.5	39,414	1,656	101	22	7	11	79	181	141	12	7
Reeves	502	10.2	32,859	2,638	282	49	20	35	84	114	386	21	20
Refugio	300	5.9	41,496	1,332	95	20	6	8	65	91	129	8	6
Roberts	37	4.8	39,397	1,658	11	3	1	-3	12	7	11	1	1
Robertson	677	3.5	39,350	1,662	207	38	15	35	120	186	295	19	15
Rockwall	5,683	7.0	58,717	189	1,321	192	93	568	825	560	2,173	118	93
Runnels	403	2.5	39,215	1,689	109	23	8	32	67	124	172	11	8
Rusk	1,876	2.5	35,508	2,275	609	108	43	127	289	497	887	55	43
Sabine	370	4.1	35,371	2,290	89	19	7	23	77	165	138	11	7
San Augustine	316	5.7	38,277	1,832	68	15	5	29	50	135	117	8	5
San Jacinto	953	3.1	33,712	2,526	83	20	5	37	134	292	145	15	5
San Patricio	2,880	2.8	42,852	1,160	1,074	185	82	95	385	690	1,436	86	82
San Saba	218	0.5	36,596	2,104	70	18	5	8	50	65	102	7	5
Schleicher	108	-12.1	35,836	2,219	38	8	3	4	19	27	53	3	3
Scurry	640	-3.1	37,542	1,938	366	65	24	20	125	150	475	27	24
Shackelford	259	-7.0	77,918	43	69	12	5	107	54	33	192	9	5
Shelby	984	6.8	38,554	1,796	310	57	23	144	151	285	533	27	23
Sherman	199	15.2	64,897	103	40	7	3	97	18	17	147	3	3
Smith	10,749	2.0	47,200	696	4,800	737	339	1,892	1,995	2,103	7,767	419	339
Somervell	397	5.8	44,871	916	223	46	15	35	65	80	319	17	15
Starr	1,610	1.3	24,981	3,091	499	149	35	98	152	613	781	45	35
Stephens	347	-3.8	37,189	2,003	125	27	9	15	68	107	175	11	9
Sterling	67	-3.0	52,080	372	24	6	2	5	24	11	36	2	2
Stonewall	68	2.8	48,863	550	27	5	2	0	20	20	34	2	2
Sutton	221	4.9	58,599	191	129	19	8	13	42	36	169	9	8
Swisher	335	13.8	44,632	947	72	17	5	109	47	73	204	6	5
Tarrant	97,639	2.8	47,525	662	50,684	7,198	3,654	7,606	17,987	13,126	69,143	3,775	3,654
Taylor	5,905	2.0	43,329	1,098	2,866	504	213	433	1,259	1,279	4,016	220	213
Terrell	39	-7.9	48,058	621	15	4	1	-2	15	10	18	1	1
Terry	415	11.9	32,649	2,665	183	31	13	39	57	129	267	15	13
Throckmorton	52	-6.9	33,732	2,523	15	4	1	-2	12	21	18	1	1
Titus	1,099	3.2	33,406	2,568	605	119	42	90	176	286	856	46	42

1. Based on the resident population estimated as of July 1 of the year shown.

Earnings, Social Security, and Housing

STATE County	Farm	Mining, quarrying, and extractions	Construction	Manu-facturing	Information; professional, scientific, technical services	Retail trade	Finance, insurance, real estate, and leasing	Health care and social assistance	Govern-ment	Social Security beneficiaries, December 2017 Number	Rate[1]	Supplemental Security Income recipients, 2017	Housing units, 2018 Total	Percent change, 2010-2018
	75	76	77	78	79	80	81	82	83	84	85	86	87	88
TEXAS— Cont'd														
Mason	2.2	D	15.4	1.3	D	4.8	13.3	3.5	20.4	1,190	282	77	2,762	1
Matagorda	3.7	2.7	7.4	1.9	D	5.5	3.3	6.6	16.6	7,360	200	1,056	19,548	4
Maverick	0.3	1.7	5.4	3.2	3.5	8.8	3.5	D	41.2	10,715	184	3,406	18,589	6.5
Medina	1.6	6.7	12.6	0.8	5.3	9.2	6.5	D	29.6	9,590	192	1,093	18,708	4
Menard	-0.4	D	D	D	D	7.6	9.9	D	40.4	635	299	51	1,726	1.4
Midland	0	48.6	4.6	1.8	5.2	3.6	5.4	4.6	6.4	19,200	116	1,990	61,859	13.8
Milam	0.2	0.8	17.7	5	D	5.8	5.4	D	17.1	6,080	243	793	11,482	1.6
Mills	-2.3	D	8.3	5.6	D	12.8	5.9	7.1	28.4	1,425	290	122	2,870	0.8
Mitchell	-8.8	17.3	D	D	2.3	6.4	D	D	53	1,505	178	204	4,073	0.2
Montague	-1.9	18.6	8.2	6.6	6.4	7.2	6.2	D	19.9	5,280	270	475	10,310	1.7
Montgomery	0	7.2	12.1	6.3	12.2	6.5	7.2	9.3	11.7	84,620	148	7,458	222,592	25.3
Moore	13.1	4.3	D	D	D	4	2.1	D	13.7	2,630	119	276	8,051	2.2
Morris	4.8	0.4	2	35.2	22.8	3.1	D	2.9	10.5	3,845	308	547	6,063	0.6
Motley	4.6	0.4	D	D	D	10.1	D	8.3	33.2	360	293	24	773	-0.6
Nacogdoches	5.9	0.5	7.2	11.2	4	7.8	5.8	14.4	24.5	12,065	184	2,020	28,488	3.9
Navarro	-1.9	0.6	9.2	18.6	3.5	7.2	6.1	D	20.8	10,785	221	1,696	21,117	4.3
Newton	-4.4	D	D	D	D	6.2	D	7.9	41.5	2,785	200	544	7,336	2.7
Nolan	-1.8	6	6.6	15.6	2.8	8.8	5.4	D	24.6	3,310	224	503	7,041	-1.6
Nueces	0.8	4.1	13.8	7.5	7.4	5.7	5.4	14.8	19.3	60,645	168	12,019	149,950	6.3
Ochiltree	19.2	31.1	9.8	0.6	2.3	3.7	2.7	D	11.6	1,340	133	101	4,155	2.3
Oldham	32.1	D	D	D	D	1.7	D	D	23.5	420	199	24	859	2.1
Orange	-0.4	0.5	13.1	33.1	3.8	6.3	4.3	5.1	14.8	18,470	217	2,449	37,735	6.9
Palo Pinto	-0.2	10.6	6.5	25	D	8.8	3.4	D	19.8	6,510	228	719	15,525	2
Panola	2.5	D	24.9	8.5	D	4.9	2.9	5.1	14	5,420	233	649	11,236	2.9
Parker	0.1	7.8	13.4	7.9	6.7	10.2	5.7	8.8	14.1	24,290	182	1,361	50,820	9
Parmer	40.5	0.1	D	D	D	1.7	D	1.8	10	1,475	150	128	3,791	-0.2
Pecos	-0.5	15.5	5.7	2	D	6.2	4.1	2.9	32.9	2,380	152	364	5,749	2.9
Polk	-1.1	0.8	8.8	11.9	D	8.5	6.1	D	25.6	19,160	390	1,746	26,043	14.8
Potter	0	2.6	5.8	10.6	7.5	6.3	8	15.8	19.4	19,275	160	3,009	50,175	6.1
Presidio	13.8	0.2	D	D	D	4.8	D	2.2	46.4	1,755	245	591	3,904	2.1
Rains	-4.1	D	16.3	5.1	D	11.3	D	4.8	23.7	3,120	265	263	5,411	2.7
Randall	4.2	0.4	12.7	4.1	6.4	10.5	7.1	10.3	11.2	21,625	161	1,358	55,241	7.1
Reagan	-1.2	33.5	3.2	0	0.6	3.6	D	D	17.7	455	123	46	1,417	3.3
Real	-1.9	D	13	4.9	D	10.8	D	11	24.3	1,215	354	120	2,651	2.1
Red River	-1.9	D	12.4	15.2	4.4	3.8	3.9	10.5	24.3	3,670	300	498	6,940	1.7
Reeves	1.3	10.9	15.1	7.3	D	7.2	5.1	1.6	27.1	2,245	147	413	4,625	-0.3
Refugio	-0.2	22.8	D	D	D	6	5.5	D	30.4	1,825	253	224	3,711	-0.4
Roberts	-35.5	D	D	1	D	D	D	D	49.7	180	192	0	438	-0.2
Robertson	1.9	6.6	10.2	2.4	3.4	4.5	3.1	D	19.2	3,775	219	608	8,923	5.2
Rockwall	-0.1	0.4	12	6.2	10.6	9.3	7.6	16.5	11.5	13,860	143	787	35,836	28.3
Runnels	5.4	2.4	7.2	14.5	1.6	10.8	D	7	25.6	2,670	260	293	5,250	
Rusk	2.7	13.2	8.1	10.7	5.4	4.7	6.4	7.9	15.8	10,645	201	1,207	21,604	2
Sabine	3	8.5	7.2	18	D	6.5	D	12.1	21.2	3,700	354	314	8,323	4.2
San Augustine	17.2	D	10.8	D	D	6.6	1.8	13.5	18.2	2,585	313	410	5,477	2.6
San Jacinto	-5.4	0.4	18	3.6	6.8	4.6	4.2	4.9	34.7	6,480	229	760	14,238	8
San Patricio	0.6	3.2	29.9	6.9	4.5	6.4	3.1	4.3	25.5	13,550	202	2,230	28,483	7.4
San Saba	-6.5	2.9	5	2.4	D	5.1	D	3.6	27.8	1,525	256	139	3,191	0.5
Schleicher	-2	10.7	28.5	D	D	1.9	D	6.2	24	585	195	58	1,505	1.1
Scurry	-1.3	30	3	2.6	2.5	5.6	4.1	D	21.6	3,000	176	330	7,184	3.2
Shackelford	-0.1	73	2	4.1	D	1.4	1.9	D	6.7	725	218	58	1,767	0.6
Shelby	21.3	1.9	3.2	18.3	D	6.4	5	D	14.6	5,610	220	1,008	12,239	3.1
Sherman	67.7	D	D	D	D	2.5	D	D	10	390	127	19	1,333	6.5
Smith	0.3	12.2	5.8	5.3	7.2	10.1	7.4	19.9	11.8	45,425	199	5,476	91,101	4.3
Somervell	0.7	D	7.3	2.6	D	1.8	2.8	D	15.5	1,845	209	122	3,886	5.7
Starr	0.9	2.5	1.9	0.3	1.4	8.4	2	D	50.1	10,005	155	4,825	19,851	1.7
Stephens	-2.4	17.6	10.4	14.5	D	6.6	5.7	6.4	22.1	2,150	230	208	4,952	0.3
Sterling	-5.2	38.1	4.6	0.2	D	2.9	D	D	22.6	255	197	25	623	1.3
Stonewall	-17.5	20.1	28.5	1.2	D	7.5	D	D	37.2	390	281	22	933	0.5
Sutton	-0.2	26.5	6.2	4.2	D	3	2.6	D	14.1	800	212	57	2,062	1.5
Swisher	54.6	D	1.3	2.6	D	2	D	D	20.4	1,565	208	167	3,177	-1.4
Tarrant	0	2.3	9	11	7.8	6.2	7.8	10.9	12.8	265,690	129	36,831	778,975	8.9
Taylor	0.9	2.6	6.5	3.6	5.9	7.2	7.1	17.1	24.7	25,080	184	3,786	57,787	3.7
Terrell	-7.9	0.2	3.2	0.2	D	4.1	D	D	65.4	215	265	24	704	0.6
Terry	5.7	23.5	4	3.9	2.6	10.3	D	D	22.5	2,205	173	346	4,850	0.5
Throckmorton	-18	11	D	D	D	6.1	D	3.7	45.9	395	259	24	1,079	0
Titus	2.3	1.9	4	33.4	2.1	6.3	4.2	7.2	19.7	5,635	171	803	12,420	3

1. Per 1,000 resident population estimated as of July 1 of the year shown.

STATE County	Total	Percent	Median value[1]	With a mort-gage	Without a mort-gage[2]	Median rent[3]	Median rent as a percent of income[2]	Sub-standard units[4] (percent)	Total	Percent change, 2017-2018	Total	Rate[5]	Total	Management, business, science, and arts	Construction, production, and maintenance occupations
	89	90	91	92	93	94	95	96	97	98	99	100	101	102	103
TEXAS— Cont'd															
Mason	1,622	73.1	156,400	27.2	11.4	804	31.7	0.5	1,779	-2	55	3.1	2,173	21.0	31.4
Matagorda	13,811	67.8	102,200	18.7	12.5	773	24.5	5	16,912	-0.1	1,036	6.1	16,009	23.9	35.4
Maverick	16,416	68.0	95,100	22.8	13.0	628	24.5	13.7	23,789	-0.7	1,926	8.1	21,113	21.1	29.8
Medina	15,154	82.1	134,400	19.9	10.2	732	22.7	4.4	21,595	1.4	746	3.5	20,958	31.1	28.0
Menard	964	66.7	60,800	18.0	13.6	604	26.2	7	841	4.2	34	4	1,014	30.9	38.8
Midland	55,045	66.8	187,400	19.3	10.0	1,180	26.5	6.6	102,277	12.6	2,147	2.1	80,471	34.4	27.7
Milam	9,437	68.3	88,500	19.7	11.1	642	28.8	4.3	9,904	-2	544	5.5	9,527	28.9	32.8
Mills	1,833	84.7	111,200	24.2	11.8	534	28	2.7	1,879	-1.8	66	3.5	2,055	29.8	26.4
Mitchell	2,639	76.0	65,700	13.9	10.2	634	18.9	2.8	2,338	-6.5	103	4.4	2,801	32.3	28.7
Montague	8,044	71.9	107,100	19.5	12.1	776	31	2.5	9,130	0.4	293	3.2	7,938	26.0	36.2
Montgomery	186,861	71.2	206,400	20.7	10.7	1,127	27.2	4.3	275,152	1.7	10,334	3.8	249,640	39.8	21.0
Moore	6,725	63.9	106,400	19.9	10.0	740	21.7	10.2	11,039	-0.4	297	2.7	10,591	22.1	47.1
Morris	5,024	74.3	82,300	19.3	12.4	673	28.2	4.9	4,749	1.4	312	6.6	5,044	25.4	34.8
Motley	469	71.6	57,300	24.1	12.5	601	26.4	6.8	467	-5.7	17	3.6	513	35.9	35.7
Nacogdoches	23,825	55.9	117,700	20.5	10.2	763	32.1	3.9	28,799	0.7	1,124	3.9	28,199	32.1	26.7
Navarro	17,326	68.6	88,900	21.6	11.9	761	29.1	4.8	23,633	3.5	873	3.7	20,325	27.8	31.5
Newton	4,781	82.8	73,300	22.0	11.3	652	21.9	0.6	5,283	0	351	6.6	4,971	21.6	37.0
Nolan	5,552	69.3	66,100	18.8	11.3	627	24.3	4.1	6,718		222	3.3	6,316	27.9	35.2
Nueces	128,857	57.8	122,400	20.8	11.5	948	29.1	5.6	168,149	0	7,849	4.7	165,116	29.4	24.8
Ochiltree	3,549	72.2	102,400	20.4	10.7	734	19.8	7	4,487	-0.9	127	2.8	4,679	22.9	40.1
Oldham	581	73.8	87,000	19.8	10.0	725	17.9	4.5	908	0.6	24	2.6	776	35.3	25.5
Orange	32,272	75.3	104,700	18.9	10.0	778	25.6	3.4	37,295	0.3	2,137	5.7	36,743	29.4	31.6
Palo Pinto	10,441	70.2	88,600	19.7	12.1	742	33.1	6.1	13,504	0.7	454	3.4	11,724	24.3	33.6
Panola	9,032	77.4	97,200	19.5	10.0	721	24.6	3	10,684	2.5	451	4.2	9,855	24.0	34.4
Parker	43,942	77.5	180,900	19.6	10.9	949	27.9	3.5	64,740	2.3	2,013	3.1	58,626	38.3	23.3
Parmer	3,222	68.9	86,200	22.4	10.3	667	24.4	10.1	4,905	-0.4	114	2.3	4,411	26.2	43.6
Pecos	4,420	69.6	68,600	17.1	10.0	819	24.1	4.6	6,486	3.3	233	3.6	6,103	21.3	37.9
Polk	17,632	76.7	84,900	21.2	11.3	675	27.1	4.5	17,894	2	900	5	17,988	22.8	30.7
Potter	43,453	57.3	89,000	20.9	10.8	747	29.4	6.8	55,816	0.6	1,628	2.9	52,859	24.2	30.1
Presidio	2,589	59.6	50,700	26.5	11.1	523	24	8.7	3,050	0.2	213	7	2,426	28.0	27.9
Rains	4,333	77.2	114,000	22.6	13.6	695	24.9	4.1	5,903	3.4	205	3.5	4,601	27.0	33.3
Randall	49,118	69.8	157,600	19.5	10.6	882	26.5	2.4	71,375	0.5	1,873	2.6	68,640	37.3	19.0
Reagan	1,171	70.3	88,400	21.0	10.0	763	21.1	2.4	1,896	5.6	47	2.5	1,752	19.7	45.4
Real	1,123	76.8	105,100	25.0	13.5	797	25.7	2.8	1,060	0.5	53	5	1,281	28.9	17.9
Red River	5,218	75.8	65,200	23.4	11.7	602	25.9	1.5	5,094	-2.1	277	5.4	4,770	26.5	34.8
Reeves	3,731	71.7	52,900	15.3	10.0	781	21.9	6.2	9,126	30.3	193	2.1	5,140	22.5	36.4
Refugio	2,694	72.3	80,800	18.5	10.2	673	28.3	4.7	3,160	-2.6	148	4.7	2,961	24.1	33.9
Roberts	326	74.2	135,700	16.8	10.0	875	16.6	0.6	436	-1.4	13	3	409	46.2	24.4
Robertson	6,298	74.5	93,900	18.2	10.0	668	30.1	4.2	7,655	2.7	317	4.1	7,180	30.1	32.6
Rockwall	30,365	80.4	225,400	20.4	12.8	1,283	28.1	2.1	50,192	2.4	1,616	3.2	44,335	47.5	15.2
Runnels	3,781	71.8	76,500	17.1	13.1	600	21.7	3.3	4,628	1	145	3.1	4,184	31.1	31.9
Rusk	17,982	76.1	111,200	19.0	10.9	730	25.7	3	22,296	0.7	913	4.1	20,340	26.7	34.4
Sabine	3,811	88.0	92,100	20.5	13.0	549	44.8	2.1	3,568	-0.3	281	7.9	3,379	18.7	32.3
San Augustine	3,202	79.2	81,900	19.2	13.2	538	27.4	6.1	2,987	4	195	6.5	2,493	28.1	33.5
San Jacinto	9,414	83.0	95,900	22.2	13.1	719	31.7	3.8	11,518	0.4	573	5	10,221	22.0	36.8
San Patricio	23,246	66.9	105,400	20.0	12.4	886	26.9	6.7	30,351	-0.8	1,916	6.3	28,869	26.0	32.2
San Saba	2,135	67.4	97,000	23.6	12.2	657	33.4	2.8	2,521	4.2	76	3	2,475	29.0	39.4
Schleicher	1,102	76.9	72,900	15.5	10.0	483	18.8	7.2	1,363	2	40	2.9	1,475	29.2	37.9
Scurry	5,838	74.1	89,800	20.5	10.0	737	23.8	4.4	6,969	-0.4	238	3.4	6,772	23.7	35.7
Shackelford	1,257	78.9	78,900	21.1	14.7	628	30.4	4.5	1,978	4.6	46	2.3	1,508	33.4	22.9
Shelby	9,218	71.4	73,100	21.8	10.2	568	32.7	3.9	11,089	2.8	480	4.3	9,432	26.8	39.5
Sherman	1,063	80.9	86,800	21.9	10.0	675	30	2.8	1,336	3.5	36	2.7	1,604	29.2	43.3
Smith	77,801	65.9	144,800	21.0	11.6	873	30.4	3.5	107,543	1.3	3,909	3.6	98,488	33.0	24.8
Somervell	3,234	73.9	172,200	20.9	10.3	851	29.1	9.1	4,287	2.3	178	4.2	3,671	34.8	28.6
Starr	16,320	74.4	67,200	26.2	11.5	525	33.8	13.4	25,217	-3.5	2,548	10.1	21,423	22.3	29.6
Stephens	3,361	78.9	73,400	21.8	12.3	574	22.6	4.2	3,987	-0.5	145	3.6	3,730	25.1	36.1
Sterling	462	85.1	66,100	22.1	10.0	919	21.3	2.2	582	-2	19	3.3	515	32.2	29.3
Stonewall	458	76.0	53,700	14.5	11.2	508	28	4.8	596	-2.9	21	3.5	442	34.8	32.4
Sutton	1,573	68.2	95,500	18.6	10.9	631	16.2	6.7	1,469	-2.7	56	3.8	1,827	31.6	36.8
Swisher	2,602	69.7	70,800	20.6	12.2	651	29	4.6	2,684	-0.4	115	4.3	2,704	30.3	28.5
Tarrant	689,921	60.7	158,200	21.1	11.6	987	29	4.8	1,062,733	2.4	37,114	3.5	974,947	36.6	22.0
Taylor	49,443	59.0	112,400	19.2	11.4	846	29.4	2.7	65,309	1.6	2,072	3.2	62,872	30.6	22.1
Terrell	343	76.7	66,600	23.0	17.7	722	39.4	0	382	-3	13	3.4	260	33.1	31.2
Terry	4,142	69.9	68,000	16.7	10.7	724	24.9	6.4	5,228	-0.4	215	4.1	4,556	31.1	33.9
Throckmorton	712	73.0	68,600	13.8	12.7	425	22.6	2.8	705	1.9	24	3.4	661	35.1	28.9
Titus	10,675	67.1	96,300	20.3	10.0	676	25.9	9	12,947	-0.1	652	5	14,307	22.8	38.5

1. Specified owner-occupied units. 2. A value of 10.0 represents 10 percent or less; a value of 50.0 represents 50 percent or more. 3. Specified renter-occupied units. 4. Overcrowded or lacking complete plumbing facilities. 5. Percent of civilian labor force. 6. Civilian employed persons 16 years old and over.

Nonfarm Employment and Agriculture

STATE County	Number of establishments	Total	Health care and social assistance	Manufacturing	Retail trade	Finance and insurance	Professional, scientific, and technical services	Total (mil dol)	Average per employee (dollars)	Number	Fewer than 50 acres	1000 acres or more	Farm producers whose primary occupation is farming (percent)
	104	105	106	107	108	109	110	111	112	113	114	115	116
TEXAS— Cont'd													
Mason	141	821	130	44	155	55	37	22	26,408	680	15.4	22.5	39.3
Matagorda	722	8,100	1,309	633	1,396	201	291	455	56,116	858	36.2	14.8	40.4
Maverick	791	12,636	4,195	593	2,781	379	209	308	24,409	339	53.1	15.0	34.8
Medina	724	7,196	946	329	1,452	310	426	228	31,623	2,281	39.9	7.9	35.1
Menard	47	192	D	D	47	23	7	5	25,313	346	13.0	29.8	40.7
Midland	5,195	81,103	7,340	2,595	9,279	1,991	2,773	4,953	61,065	410	59.8	11.5	24.4
Milam	412	4,579	1,320	188	627	213	124	216	47,217	2,053	41.7	4.1	38.2
Mills	107	840	143	83	195	59	17	24	28,581	896	22.1	10.8	38.2
Mitchell	125	1,236	D	D	257	39	27	41	33,366	362	23.5	18.2	27.7
Montague	426	3,743	401	261	638	199	114	164	43,693	1,615	32.1	6.3	37.4
Montgomery	11,152	155,450	20,652	8,658	25,039	5,582	9,488	8,526	54,845	1,614	69.1	1.8	30.4
Moore	441	7,656	609	3,509	897	136	95	322	42,122	250	28.4	32.4	48.1
Morris	223	3,286	180	1,687	329	127	73	106	32,226	449	39.2	2.0	35.7
Motley	26	188	D	D	D	D	D	4	23,707	237	6.3	40.9	36.2
Nacogdoches	1,280	17,923	3,158	3,582	2,899	550	479	581	32,421	1,123	33.6	2.4	37.8
Navarro	959	13,374	2,452	2,944	2,303	370	264	421	31,499	2,471	44.7	4.0	35.9
Newton	124	984	278	73	162	21	97	25	25,763	430	58.6	0.2	34.0
Nolan	359	4,365	589	859	828	135	93	164	37,459	410	18.0	20.0	35.2
Nueces	7,974	146,343	29,955	7,187	19,073	4,015	6,778	5,849	39,965	646	61.8	13.3	33.4
Ochiltree	362	3,701	317	34	418	134	124	176	47,565	282	12.1	41.8	48.6
Oldham	45	590	D	D	72	D	D	19	32,122	132	3.8	49.2	46.7
Orange	1,317	19,316	1,517	4,704	3,199	561	484	944	48,892	663	81.1	1.2	31.6
Palo Pinto	605	5,879	775	1,152	1,063	147	144	214	36,374	1,265	49.2	8.6	36.0
Panola	467	6,761	682	1,023	857	177	229	288	42,608	978	30.9	3.0	37.0
Parker	2,590	28,520	3,462	2,863	5,672	672	959	1,055	37,003	4,626	73.1	1.8	29.3
Parmer	193	3,452	183	D	174	78	44	134	38,832	464	10.3	36.6	52.5
Pecos	344	3,896	568	28	752	152	58	157	40,381	309	9.1	61.2	45.6
Polk	756	8,422	1,334	1,262	1,858	347	217	288	34,244	742	40.2	1.6	36.1
Potter	3,579	61,381	12,598	6,505	8,603	4,147	2,228	2,492	40,593	239	38.5	17.6	42.5
Presidio	118	934	46	D	270	57	D	21	22,961	142	5.6	58.5	53.7
Rains	163	1,334	104	70	419	53	218	36	26,963	787	57.6	2.2	34.1
Randall	2,560	32,352	3,403	4,824	5,845	1,308	868	1,352	41,805	781	41.4	17.4	35.2
Reagan	130	1,505	113	D	133	11	18	71	47,148	112	10.7	56.3	50.3
Real	77	717	121	31	93	D	7	18	24,676	198	16.2	27.8	41.7
Red River	160	1,280	146	362	275	86	20	42	32,682	1,126	26.1	8.6	41.2
Reeves	275	3,468	398	9	472	37	56	170	49,080	224	19.2	27.7	43.6
Refugio	155	1,742	243	D	287	40	24	70	40,296	238	31.9	23.5	37.4
Roberts	17	138	NA	NA	D	D	D	6	45,174	104	10.6	48.1	58.2
Robertson	277	2,796	339	166	395	84	290	111	39,786	1,471	34.2	5.2	40.6
Rockwall	2,103	25,646	4,397	1,442	5,405	743	1,357	925	36,054	403	74.9	1.5	24.4
Runnels	216	2,173	277	457	404	127	33	75	34,593	833	18.7	17.0	38.8
Rusk	813	10,430	1,331	1,278	1,393	470	387	416	39,869	1,441	33.2	1.8	35.1
Sabine	155	1,528	301	D	323	54	34	49	32,266	200	43.5	2.5	33.5
San Augustine	120	1,151	366	51	193	42	7	40	34,784	293	30.0	1.7	40.9
San Jacinto	192	1,080	108	127	217	36	34	32	29,961	786	56.6	1.0	31.6
San Patricio	1,052	15,696	1,623	3,409	2,636	382	1,247	720	45,866	656	52.4	13.1	38.8
San Saba	165	893	156	46	210	22	39	24	27,274	773	16.4	22.1	43.6
Schleicher	55	439	D	D	60	25	16	19	42,975	327	12.5	44.6	42.2
Scurry	416	4,919	569	65	750	124	102	250	50,826	560	21.8	17.5	33.5
Shackelford	123	1,038	43	162	95	50	5	44	42,803	223	15.7	30.9	37.1
Shelby	484	6,244	475	2,123	994	588	117	209	33,541	995	30.8	1.6	39.1
Sherman	63	370	D	D	120	27	D	15	39,692	245	6.9	41.2	47.5
Smith	5,775	91,444	22,480	6,924	13,229	4,603	4,959	3,780	41,337	2,928	58.8	1.1	31.7
Somervell	215	3,356	499	48	198	43	91	192	57,114	352	53.7	5.1	29.5
Starr	553	8,781	4,597	53	1,811	318	144	185	21,026	1,345	31.7	8.8	34.1
Stephens	243	2,019	232	188	354	136	41	78	38,818	575	13.7	20.2	34.9
Sterling	54	333	D	NA	45	14	14	15	44,631	76	5.3	51.3	50.0
Stonewall	48	422	D	NA	48	D	7	17	40,912	314	5.1	29.6	33.1
Sutton	130	1,042	68	D	141	33	25	50	48,299	261	9.2	52.1	47.1
Swisher	141	1,013	190	121	145	42	25	29	29,080	432	4.9	34.3	46.8
Tarrant	41,261	771,088	101,940	76,574	102,779	46,884	38,138	37,257	48,317	1,173	82.5	1.8	31.1
Taylor	3,445	55,579	12,482	2,489	8,370	2,439	1,789	1,896	34,111	1,394	36.7	9.0	29.6
Terrell	13	45	D	NA	17	D	D	2	39,156	85	NA	74.1	50.4
Terry	227	2,469	448	59	445	100	57	90	36,615	558	13.4	22.4	46.2
Throckmorton	51	269	D	D	20	D	8	8	27,911	274	4.7	27.4	38.3
Titus	625	13,634	2,037	5,906	1,788	489	90	473	34,710	812	43.2	3.0	38.4

Table B. States and Counties — Agriculture

STATE County	Acreage (1,000) [117]	Percent change, 2012-2017 [118]	Average size of farm [119]	Total irrigated (1,000) [120]	Total cropland (1,000) [121]	Average per farm [122]	Average per acre [123]	Value of machinery and equipment, average per farm (dollars) [124]	Total (mil dol) [125]	Average per farm (acres) [126]	Crops [127]	Livestock and poultry products [128]	Organic farms (number) [129]	Farms with internet access (percent) [130]	Total ($1,000) [131]	Percent of farms [132]
TEXAS— Cont'd																
Mason	539	-2.2	793	3.9	21.8	1,838,623	2,318	72,646	21.7	31,881	10.7	89.3	NA	70.3	1,416	15.0
Matagorda	551	-2.9	643	25.6	176.2	1,540,205	2,397	146,410	124.2	144,773	58.8	41.2	16	70.6	9,559	26.7
Maverick	434	-19.7	1,282	14.6	21.3	1,801,266	1,405	56,810	43.0	126,737	5.8	94.2	NA	59.3	752	8.0
Medina	782	-6.1	343	39.4	153.5	917,319	2,674	63,914	93.9	41,170	48.8	51.2	1	73.4	2,804	10.9
Menard	508	-5.4	1,467	1.2	10.5	2,174,290	1,482	68,492	9.1	26,220	6.3	93.8	NA	74.6	596	17.3
Midland	345	-14.7	841	7.4	75.8	1,353,752	1,609	99,126	16.3	39,851	79.6	20.4	NA	79.5	910	17.3
Milam	497	-5.8	242	2.7	168.0	766,554	3,163	79,326	129.5	63,087	25.7	74.3	2	70.3	3,149	8.7
Mills	441	-6.4	492	3.1	44.6	1,235,360	2,509	65,340	30.9	34,484	7.9	92.1	NA	76.9	580	14.2
Mitchell	583	1.7	1,611	3.0	153.1	1,604,910	997	96,432	21.7	60,061	62.5	37.5	NA	65.2	2,422	50.8
Montague	498	2.0	309	1.5	82.9	842,695	2,732	67,799	33.4	20,691	16.0	84.0	1	72.6	1,075	12.0
Montgomery	145	-6.8	90	0.7	25.3	1,024,558	11,414	54,308	25.8	15,963	26.5	73.5	1	82.5	201	1.4
Moore	478	-8.8	1,911	84.8	207.6	2,167,617	1,134	373,450	478.1	1,912,300	14.9	85.1	NA	71.2	8,544	58.4
Morris	74	-19.6	165	0.2	16.1	375,751	2,283	58,729	44.2	98,354	2.5	97.5	4	67.0	436	16.7
Motley	580	-2.7	2,446	4.4	100.3	2,072,503	847	112,229	15.2	64,249	15.9	84.1	NA	75.9	2,016	54.4
Nacogdoches	265	0.0	236	0.3	29.5	682,387	2,895	92,115	370.7	330,135	0.9	99.1	4	68.3	144	1.5
Navarro	559	0.2	226	1.7	178.6	531,307	2,349	68,964	73.3	29,667	45.9	54.1	4	65.9	2,195	7.2
Newton	59	0.0	137	0.1	5.5	303,605	2,221	54,042	1.6	3,691	30.6	69.4	4	63.3	24	2.8
Nolan	466	0.3	1,137	3.5	161.9	1,253,213	1,102	107,278	36.6	89,290	70.4	29.6	NA	72.4	1,351	44.1
Nueces	475	-9.4	735	1.2	332.3	2,243,539	3,052	220,795	161.0	249,260	96.2	3.8	4	63.6	8,905	27.4
Ochiltree	569	4.4	2,016	59.0	343.8	2,484,158	1,232	353,856	349.1	1,237,791	20.0	80.0	2	79.4	7,773	72.0
Oldham	945	13.8	7,157	1.8	105.3	5,834,781	815	158,947	156.0	1,181,909	3.5	96.5	NA	81.8	3,798	78.8
Orange	53	0.2	80	0.3	4.7	368,662	4,619	55,345	5.0	7,492	30.0	70.0	NA	78.4	142	0.8
Palo Pinto	573	-3.4	453	4.4	73.0	1,104,960	2,440	58,278	43.2	34,165	23.8	76.2	NA	72.4	249	3.3
Panola	206	-9.4	211	0.8	39.8	562,292	2,670	78,393	100.7	102,986	4.6	95.4	NA	70.4	96	1.6
Parker	522	5.5	113	1.7	95.1	484,457	4,296	48,756	65.0	14,060	18.7	81.3	2	81.3	250	1.0
Parmer	549	-0.9	1,183	110.1	399.2	1,330,531	1,125	346,434	893.3	1,925,302	10.3	89.7	NA	75.9	17,933	81.9
Pecos	2,868	-2.7	9,281	12.9	50.8	6,420,541	692	136,293	46.2	149,398	52.8	47.2	NA	73.1	1,560	23.6
Polk	125	-10.1	169	0.3	22.6	507,818	3,011	58,728	6.8	9,206	33.5	66.5	NA	70.1	166	0.7
Potter	424	-25.5	1,773	3.6	49.6	1,802,406	1,016	76,318	24.8	103,891	10.5	89.5	NA	67.4	1,962	20.1
Presidio	1,841	11.2	12,967	1.8	18.0	10,152,603	783	122,932	D	D	D	D	NA	77.5	644	12.0
Rains	111	-4.6	142	0.3	27.7	492,612	3,479	61,364	22.8	28,919	37.8	62.2	NA	69.4	213	3.9
Randall	560	-1.9	718	16.2	233.9	1,135,115	1,582	108,685	479.5	613,910	5.0	95.0	NA	79.9	9,464	40.1
Reagan	736	5.4	6,574	8.1	55.6	5,510,283	838	242,344	18.2	162,527	65.6	34.4	NA	76.8	768	42.0
Real	317	-1.1	1,601	0.4	1.3	3,074,966	1,921	47,687	1.3	6,379	4.9	95.1	NA	87.4	19	4.0
Red River	458	2.2	407	5.1	103.1	784,848	1,927	85,573	94.0	83,515	10.9	89.1	1	70.2	3,425	34.1
Reeves	1,064	-13.9	4,750	8.1	54.7	2,500,484	526	80,186	10.9	48,621	47.5	52.5	1	72.8	790	24.1
Refugio	489	2.9	2,053	0.5	56.3	2,565,852	1,250	170,947	35.9	150,891	69.2	30.8	NA	73.5	1,986	27.7
Roberts	553	-1.7	5,318	7.4	36.1	4,045,126	761	140,728	18.3	175,971	20.7	79.3	NA	76.0	1,450	52.9
Robertson	475	1.5	323	20.4	107.3	932,356	2,889	72,519	158.1	107,507	15.6	84.4	2	70.0	2,496	4.6
Rockwall	40	-11.0	100	0.1	21.0	554,781	5,536	52,992	7.8	19,429	79.0	21.0	3	80.4	439	3.7
Runnels	672	1.0	807	5.6	256.2	1,116,037	1,383	111,613	53.4	64,146	59.7	40.3	NA	70.9	6,275	52.1
Rusk	243	-11.5	168	0.5	46.1	431,457	2,561	71,067	100.2	69,505	5.9	94.1	NA	69.6	313	1.1
Sabine	38	31.9	192	0.1	5.6	432,114	2,256	85,329	17.7	88,575	2.5	97.5	NA	73.0	36	2.5
San Augustine	62	-15.2	211	0.0	9.2	594,832	2,820	83,472	56.7	193,433	2.3	97.7	NA	72.0	D	1.0
San Jacinto	84	-24.5	107	1.0	16.9	440,438	4,100	75,877	7.2	9,148	34.5	65.5	NA	70.2	130	0.5
San Patricio	371	-0.9	565	4.1	235.8	1,497,600	2,650	192,771	131.3	200,216	88.4	11.6	NA	78.4	6,745	25.8
San Saba	660	-1.7	854	4.8	81.3	2,091,365	2,449	87,070	35.8	46,343	18.1	81.9	2	79.8	1,777	18.2
Schleicher	811	-2.7	2,480	1.4	30.6	2,929,781	1,181	90,424	17.8	54,404	19.3	80.7	NA	74.6	1,449	22.6
Scurry	531	7.4	948	5.5	201.7	991,118	1,046	124,077	45.2	80,629	54.0	46.0	5	70.4	2,730	52.1
Shackelford	537	6.3	2,407	0.3	49.4	3,105,956	1,290	75,451	16.6	74,480	4.9	95.1	NA	76.2	610	35.4
Shelby	179	-9.2	180	0.4	28.6	631,226	3,507	88,864	467.6	469,907	0.6	99.4	NA	70.7	50	0.6
Sherman	590	1.2	2,409	184.7	355.2	3,446,896	1,431	645,756	838.1	3,420,641	17.5	82.5	3	75.9	11,501	78.0
Smith	272	-10.1	93	1.9	64.3	487,136	5,248	52,759	53.6	18,308	68.6	31.4	NA	71.8	94	1.2
Somervell	83	-9.2	236	0.3	15.7	738,349	3,133	58,179	4.1	11,648	28.1	71.9	NA	75.3	40	3.4
Starr	571	-14.5	425	3.4	74.1	779,096	1,834	49,858	47.2	35,115	19.9	80.1	NA	42.4	1,977	8.7
Stephens	470	-9.0	818	0.3	37.1	1,430,192	1,749	65,383	10.6	18,477	5.3	94.7	NA	66.8	641	21.7
Sterling	584	-0.1	7,688	0.4	9.4	5,208,932	678	107,859	D	D	D	D	NA	86.8	165	9.2
Stonewall	469	-0.8	1,493	0.8	113.4	1,365,112	914	80,900	15.5	49,500	44.3	55.7	NA	62.7	1,995	63.1
Sutton	901	-1.1	3,452	0.3	12.4	4,384,828	1,270	67,361	10.4	39,655	1.3	98.7	NA	74.3	331	9.2
Swisher	563	3.3	1,304	71.5	399.8	1,364,672	1,046	292,743	623.9	1,444,259	11.0	89.0	NA	76.4	13,019	86.1
Tarrant	191	30.9	163	1.3	43.5	992,283	6,104	53,767	29.4	25,058	59.4	40.6	NA	79.7	170	2.2
Taylor	484	-16.4	347	1.2	159.2	713,098	2,053	64,361	31.5	22,626	35.4	64.6	NA	73.7	2,520	23.2
Terrell	835	-24.1	9,825	0.6	9.4	7,373,840	751	95,965	4.2	49,306	13.1	86.9	NA	76.5	193	10.6
Terry	496	12.1	889	104.4	436.8	905,405	1,019	245,583	136.9	245,418	83.2	16.8	13	64.3	16,544	80.3
Throckmorton	507	-0.2	1,850	0.4	157.2	2,604,134	1,408	111,148	27.3	99,489	20.2	79.8	3	73.0	2,844	52.9
Titus	159	8.4	196	2.1	33.8	493,023	2,520	74,641	149.3	183,858	2.7	97.3	NA	69.2	501	17.0

Table B. States and Counties — Water Use, Wholesale Trade, Retail Trade, and Real Estate

STATE County	Water use, 2015		Wholesale Trade[1], 2012				Retail Trade[2], 2012				Real estate and rental and leasing,[2] 2012			
	Public supply water withdrawn (mil gal/day)	Public supply gallons withdrawn per person per day	Number of establishments	Number of employees	Sales (mil dol)	Average payroll (mil dol)	Number of establishments	Number of employees	Sales (mil dol)	Average payroll (mil dol)	Number of establishments	Number of employees	Sales (mil dol)	Average payroll (mil dol)
	133	134	135	136	137	138	139	140	141	142	143	144	145	146
TEXAS— Cont'd														
Mason	0.44	109.1	8	D	D	D	25	140	36.4	2.6	4	5	2.0	0.2
Matagorda	4.44	120.8	31	123	104.9	4.5	128	1,241	324.6	25.7	33	170	32.1	7.5
Maverick	6.95	120.4	44	D	D	D	166	2,511	585.6	49.4	26	71	12.5	1.9
Medina	6.65	137.3	24	D	D	D	100	1,112	436.7	30.3	25	42	5.3	0.9
Menard	0.37	171.0	4	D	D	D	9	49	11.9	0.8	NA	NA	NA	NA
Midland	1.04	6.5	265	4,659	3,749.7	289.5	503	7,463	2,930.6	216.9	266	D	D	D
Milam	10.89	444.3	16	138	110.5	5.3	64	681	186.9	14.6	16	38	5.0	0.9
Mills	0.28	57.1	1	D	D	D	23	203	65.2	5.3	2	D	D	D
Mitchell	1.28	141.2	4	10	4.3	0.6	30	284	71.3	6.2	2	D	D	D
Montague	1.07	55.5	22	68	35.2	3.0	69	686	192.6	15.3	9	12	3.1	0.4
Montgomery	57.29	106.6	501	4,711	9,996.3	290.2	1,313	21,292	6,297.8	535.2	482	2,134	489.6	108.6
Moore	5.07	227.8	29	D	D	D	75	898	276.4	19.4	13	31	5.0	0.8
Morris	0.23	18.4	12	631	212.7	35.0	39	316	63.6	6.1	7	33	4.8	0.8
Motley	0.15	130.7	3	D	D	D	4	24	3.3	0.4	NA	NA	NA	NA
Nacogdoches	11.20	170.6	45	D	D	D	241	2,944	880.8	70.7	54	168	29.3	4.5
Navarro	2.33	48.2	29	D	D	D	163	2,039	539.2	46.1	48	136	19.4	3.3
Newton	0.97	69.4	4	D	D	D	32	177	73.3	3.5	NA	NA	NA	NA
Nolan	2.28	150.9	19	D	D	D	53	691	210.1	14.5	10	47	5.3	0.7
Nueces	72.38	201.2	361	4,987	5,153.6	264.8	1,128	17,030	5,138.3	418.1	414	2,868	667.2	132.2
Ochiltree	1.76	163.8	30	D	D	D	37	448	127.2	11.0	16	90	44.2	5.5
Oldham	0.56	270.7	2	D	D	D	7	D	D	D	NA	NA	NA	NA
Orange	8.40	99.7	36	D	D	D	269	3,130	909.6	71.8	59	272	58.3	8.7
Palo Pinto	1.98	71.0	23	267	121.4	11.8	118	1,089	281.8	23.1	28	91	16.9	3.2
Panola	1.15	48.4	23	D	D	D	81	939	228.7	20.7	26	155	24.8	6.1
Parker	7.51	59.6	97	1,053	779.1	41.6	316	4,515	1,772.7	128.0	88	302	55.0	9.5
Parmer	0.86	88.2	26	201	426.9	6.7	25	167	43.9	3.3	4	4	0.6	0.1
Pecos	4.33	267.2	16	166	135.6	8.0	58	645	185.9	14.4	9	64	11.8	2.2
Polk	561.79	11,960.1	19	99	45.9	4.3	128	1,738	474.6	40.9	30	87	17.6	3.0
Potter	5.46	44.8	169	D	D	D	555	D	D	D	167	827	162.2	29.0
Presidio	2.54	369.4	2	D	D	D	27	212	51.3	3.6	2	D	D	D
Rains	1.25	112.0	5	D	D	D	27	408	149.0	11.2	5	10	1.5	0.2
Randall	2.23	17.1	79	D	D	D	352	5,343	1,805.1	142.0	142	D	D	D
Reagan	0.00	0.0	5	D	D	D	9	60	29.2	1.6	1	D	D	D
Real	0.35	105.8	3	4	1.0	0.1	12	45	14.6	1.0	4	6	0.9	0.1
Red River	0.92	73.9	5	D	D	D	40	249	54.8	4.2	5	5	0.7	0.1
Reeves	3.65	247.8	7	D	D	D	29	425	162.0	9.0	8	29	8.1	1.1
Refugio	0.65	89.2	5	D	D	D	22	252	101.1	5.0	7	29	3.9	0.7
Roberts	0.13	141.9	NA	NA	NA	NA	2	D	D	D	NA	NA	NA	NA
Robertson	2.25	135.1	2	D	D	D	49	370	148.6	8.1	7	39	7.7	2.1
Rockwall	0.00	0.0	66	D	D	D	251	4,179	1,444.8	108.4	76	289	56.0	9.1
Runnels	3.82	362.1	5	D	D	D	47	473	139.8	10.3	2	D	D	D
Rusk	5.77	108.7	27	255	152.4	11.8	126	1,410	442.1	34.2	22	68	12.7	2.7
Sabine	0.76	73.3	1	D	D	D	31	310	65.6	5.4	4	2	0.1	0.0
San Augustine	0.81	95.6	4	12	2.9	0.4	24	215	58.2	4.8	6	10	0.6	0.2
San Jacinto	2.13	77.7	7	D	D	D	29	229	59.6	4.5	13	D	D	D
San Patricio	1.25	18.6	38	D	D	D	150	2,298	712.2	52.4	54	162	26.4	4.2
San Saba	1.43	242.3	9	61	14.1	1.1	35	198	45.3	3.7	3	3	0.2	0.1
Schleicher	0.38	118.3	3	D	D	D	10	56	12.3	1.2	NA	NA	NA	NA
Scurry	0.13	7.4	25	D	D	D	63	739	242.3	18.1	14	88	16.6	4.4
Shackelford	0.00	0.0	8	53	24.1	2.8	14	100	16.1	2.0	5	8	0.7	0.2
Shelby	4.78	188.2	10	D	D	D	93	1,087	302.1	24.3	22	91	9.8	2.5
Sherman	0.44	143.2	6	D	D	D	10	92	28.5	2.7	1	D	D	D
Smith	42.89	192.4	215	D	D	D	829	11,883	3,388.9	293.6	281	1,477	301.0	61.6
Somervell	1.18	135.0	6	46	25.8	1.9	30	218	47.8	4.3	10	17	2.4	0.3
Starr	7.81	122.4	24	D	D	D	135	1,735	435.4	33.6	14	45	5.6	0.9
Stephens	9.32	987.3	6	D	D	D	36	380	84.0	8.4	6	D	D	D
Sterling	0.19	140.5	2	D	D	D	3	D	D	D	1	D	D	D
Stonewall	0.00	0.0	2	D	D	D	6	35	8.9	0.6	1	D	D	D
Sutton	0.81	207.0	8	D	D	D	20	139	49.5	3.0	3	D	D	D
Swisher	0.59	78.3	13	55	23.4	1.8	20	152	51.5	2.9	3	6	0.4	0.1
Tarrant	26.52	13.4	1,944	34,600	30,173.3	1,974.7	5,705	91,200	28,908.8	2,381.7	1,826	12,190	2,647.1	528.7
Taylor	0.46	3.4	146	1,803	2,007.0	90.0	563	7,825	2,223.5	185.7	166	885	150.3	27.1
Terrell	0.13	155.3	NA	NA	NA	NA	4	19	5.0	0.4	NA	NA	NA	NA
Terry	0.17	13.3	18	D	D	D	43	453	131.5	10.1	8	D	D	D
Throckmorton	0.05	31.7	6	17	5.9	0.5	5	19	7.1	0.4	NA	NA	NA	NA
Titus	5.35	164.0	31	D	D	D	133	1,732	477.8	41.7	25	65	10.4	1.6

1 Merchant wholesalers, except manufacturers' sales branches and offices.   2. Employer establishments.

Professional Services, Manufacturing, and Accommodation and Food Services

STATE County	Professional, scientific, and technical services, 2012				Manufacturing, 2012				Accommodation and food services, 2012			
	Number of establish-ments	Number of employees	Sales (mil dol)	Average payroll (mil dol)	Number of establish-ments	Number of employees	Receipts (mil dol)	Annual payroll (mil dol)	Number of establis-hments	Number of employees	Receipts (mil dol)	Annual payroll (mil dol)
	147	148	149	150	151	152	153	154	155	156	157	158
TEXAS— Cont'd												
Mason	14	D	D	D	6	29	5.3	1.2	14	D	D	D
Matagorda	43	162	11.8	4.2	28	513	1,657.5	41.4	84	1,045	51.5	14.0
Maverick	40	D	D	D	14	339	49.0	9.0	72	2,103	211.4	34.6
Medina	62	380	32.8	11.7	21	247	D	9.2	73	872	41.7	11.1
Menard	2	D	D	D	NA	NA	NA	NA	3	24	1.1	0.3
Midland	495	4,727	1,004.8	266.6	142	D	D	D	298	D	D	D
Milam	41	117	9.1	3.3	14	278	D	14.9	44	381	16.7	4.1
Mills	7	D	D	D	8	59	D	1.6	10	100	4.0	1.1
Mitchell	10	35	4.6	1.2	NA	NA	NA	NA	15	D	D	D
Montague	39	112	18.6	4.6	15	270	D	8.2	30	418	16.2	4.5
Montgomery	1,341	8,823	1,351.7	629.7	407	10,599	D	571.8	782	16,697	944.9	253.2
Moore	21	D	D	D	14	D	D	165.0	47	685	32.6	8.7
Morris	15	D	D	D	15	1,945	1,327.1	136.4	20	275	12.1	3.1
Motley	1	D	D	D	NA	NA	NA	NA	3	10	0.3	0.1
Nacogdoches	94	D	D	D	59	3,883	1,258.7	113.2	115	2,516	99.7	27.7
Navarro	59	298	24.0	8.0	55	2,834	1,046.9	115.2	63	1,017	50.7	13.0
Newton	9	58	4.1	1.5	6	81	D	1.3	3	27	0.4	0.2
Nolan	28	D	D	D	11	665	203.7	38.3	39	506	26.2	6.2
Nueces	812	5,789	849.1	309.6	193	7,063	41,840.9	514.2	849	17,049	892.8	242.4
Ochiltree	23	167	30.6	11.5	9	40	7.3	1.3	19	270	16.3	3.6
Oldham	NA	NA	NA	NA	NA	NA	NA	NA	9	54	2.0	0.5
Orange	92	501	57.9	23.0	74	5,287	6,340.3	426.6	140	2,002	101.2	25.5
Palo Pinto	39	211	33.7	8.6	33	1,325	460.4	55.2	73	1,023	47.1	13.2
Panola	39	206	25.3	8.0	16	905	281.9	29.6	30	419	17.8	4.8
Parker	208	892	115.3	37.7	127	2,360	582.9	109.6	190	3,237	152.0	42.0
Parmer	9	23	1.8	0.4	6	14	D	D	6	D	D	D
Pecos	16	60	2.4	1.8	4	14	D	D	43	627	36.6	7.8
Polk	73	340	30.5	10.1	25	1,227	362.5	58.1	57	940	44.5	11.9
Potter	322	1,967	414.6	115.3	125	11,535	D	716.9	366	D	D	D
Presidio	5	14	0.5	0.2	3	13	D	D	23	185	9.5	2.5
Rains	13	D	D	D	7	85	D	3.0	20	154	7.1	1.8
Randall	199	2,294	123.3	66.7	72	1,297	D	65.8	184	3,387	164.3	43.0
Reagan	7	26	1.8	0.6	NA	NA	NA	NA	7	D	D	D
Real	5	D	D	D	5	23	D	0.9	13	74	4.9	1.1
Red River	8	25	3.2	1.1	14	242	D	8.6	15	D	D	D
Reeves	16	D	D	D	3	6	2.0	D	32	434	33.9	6.4
Refugio	4	20	2.1	0.8	4	5	0.3	0.1	21	D	D	D
Roberts	1	D	D	D	NA	NA	NA	NA	1	D	D	D
Robertson	17	38	4.4	1.0	8	70	D	3.0	26	327	15.8	4.9
Rockwall	226	D	D	D	55	1,081	285.0	56.3	169	3,686	194.1	56.5
Runnels	13	D	D	D	14	505	297.9	18.8	17	D	D	D
Rusk	75	793	150.0	53.9	34	1,297	333.1	51.7	67	D	D	D
Sabine	16	D	D	D	4	309	D	D	15	77	3.9	0.7
San Augustine	7	D	D	D	5	85	D	2.3	7	D	D	D
San Jacinto	22	D	D	D	14	137	D	7.4	11	111	4.4	1.4
San Patricio	78	436	58.0	23.8	38	3,861	D	260.3	125	2,052	103.0	24.1
San Saba	16	39	4.2	1.2	7	30	D	1.4	18	D	D	D
Schleicher	4	D	D	D	NA	NA	NA	NA	1	D	D	D
Scurry	23	D	D	D	16	119	43.0	5.1	49	591	29.4	7.1
Shackelford	5	D	D	D	6	148	D	6.6	9	D	D	D
Shelby	32	133	19.7	4.5	23	2,465	577.3	72.1	34	D	D	D
Sherman	1	D	D	D	NA	NA	NA	NA	2	D	D	D
Smith	596	4,265	689.9	244.8	189	6,739	5,066.1	318.0	405	9,236	427.1	124.3
Somervell	14	59	9.7	3.8	6	33	D	1.1	28	455	23.0	7.4
Starr	30	D	D	D	6	29	2.3	0.6	51	648	35.5	8.2
Stephens	20	92	8.2	2.6	15	348	D	13.7	18	D	D	D
Sterling	2	D	D	D	NA	NA	NA	NA	3	D	D	D
Stonewall	3	D	D	D	NA	NA	NA	NA	5	22	0.8	0.2
Sutton	10	21	1.6	0.4	4	D	D	D	15	203	12.0	2.7
Swisher	7	25	1.5	0.7	8	75	D	3.1	13	D	D	D
Tarrant	4,314	39,363	6,258.9	2,258.2	1,568	70,421	45,771.0	3,894.9	3,474	77,362	4,483.6	1,188.2
Taylor	274	1,775	183.3	72.7	95	2,098	913.9	87.8	301	6,435	303.2	85.3
Terrell	2	D	D	D	NA	NA	NA	NA	5	11	0.4	0.0
Terry	15	61	4.7	1.2	5	22	D	0.8	23	280	15.4	3.4
Throckmorton	2	D	D	D	NA	NA	NA	NA	4	D	D	D
Titus	29	D	D	D	40	5,865	1,341.0	162.5	62	1,229	54.8	15.2

Health Care and Social Assistance, Other Services, Nonemployer Businesses, and Residential Construction

STATE County	Health care and social assistance, 2012				Other services, 2012				Nonemployer businesses, 2016		Value of residential construction authorized by building permits, 2018	
	Number of establish-ments	Number of employees	Receipts (mil dol)	Annual payroll (mil dol)	Number of establish-ments	Number of employees	Receipts (mil dol)	Annual payroll (mil dol)	Number	Receipts (mil dol)	New construction ($1,000)	Number of housing units
	159	160	161	162	163	164	165	166	167	168	169	170
TEXAS— Cont'd												
Mason	11	98	5.1	2.7	8	19	2.5	0.4	617	27.2	5,481	49
Matagorda	79	1,418	151.0	48.1	60	282	31.9	9.3	2,587	95.0	28,920	168
Maverick	96	4,039	213.0	84.4	37	145	9.5	2.5	4,622	156.8	18,124	72
Medina	69	935	55.0	25.4	40	200	18.0	4.4	3,357	154.2	5,459	31
Menard	2	D	D	D	2	D	D	D	280	10.6	NA	NA
Midland	398	7,196	817.7	299.7	264	2,138	337.4	73.6	16,518	1,041.4	307,846	1,222
Milam	38	791	51.8	22.9	32	117	10.7	2.6	1,652	70.8	2,088	9
Mills	13	156	7.9	3.7	7	D	D	D	446	16.6	NA	NA
Mitchell	8	D	D	D	5	17	1.2	0.3	451	14.6	620	41
Montague	40	643	46.1	19.4	37	122	11.1	2.7	1,925	85.4	750	8
Montgomery	1,015	15,877	2,147.8	724.1	579	4,253	353.2	111.7	45,333	2,369.6	1,397,142	7,062
Moore	43	680	49.6	21.7	27	109	11.9	2.6	1,153	64.7	1,993	9
Morris	23	257	11.9	5.8	17	78	9.9	2.0	808	28.3	0	0
Motley	1	D	D	D	2	D	D	D	124	4.3	NA	NA
Nacogdoches	202	3,339	353.7	119.6	85	427	37.1	9.6	4,108	177.8	357	4
Navarro	130	2,338	163.0	65.3	63	214	21.0	5.1	3,337	142.3	28,611	154
Newton	9	D	D	D	5	D	D	D	570	18.7	NA	NA
Nolan	32	D	D	D	15	D	D	D	1,057	35.9	1,248	9
Nueces	1,045	28,174	2,640.5	984.5	522	4,501	525.5	143.9	22,491	912.6	213,451	1,167
Ochiltree	20	D	D	D	24	101	11.6	2.8	820	37.0	690	2
Oldham	2	D	D	D	2	D	D	D	193	9.2	0	0
Orange	141	1,419	119.6	43.3	85	D	D	D	4,652	169.1	38,789	565
Palo Pinto	49	670	89.0	31.5	37	145	16.9	3.9	2,274	103.3	1,295	11
Panola	43	653	56.1	19.7	27	126	12.7	3.2	1,710	69.7	1,200	6
Parker	207	D	D	D	150	914	79.0	23.9	13,003	698.7	114,950	698
Parmer	9	140	14.3	4.9	19	D	D	D	502	27.5	90	1
Pecos	17	470	51.9	17.6	23	114	10.6	3.1	926	33.6	1,346	5
Polk	72	1,413	121.7	45.6	43	268	19.6	5.5	3,705	152.1	52,943	300
Potter	460	D	D	D	237	1,916	253.5	60.9	8,307	431.5	149,628	656
Presidio	4	41	2.6	1.3	4	14	0.5	0.2	863	26.9	2,928	15
Rains	12	144	7.8	3.1	12	D	D	D	883	40.9	1,016	7
Randall	235	D	D	D	162	D	D	D	10,523	499.9	20,382	84
Reagan	5	D	D	D	8	D	D	D	398	12.1	218	1
Real	10	199	8.5	4.3	2	D	D	D	474	21.3	0	0
Red River	16	395	29.8	12.2	7	D	D	D	907	39.3	195	1
Reeves	10	D	D	D	11	D	D	D	692	32.4	7,113	45
Refugio	8	257	23.0	7.3	7	23	1.9	0.6	449	13.7	3,208	19
Roberts	NA	NA	NA	NA	NA	NA	NA	NA	86	3.7	NA	NA
Robertson	18	D	D	D	24	139	19.2	5.5	1,269	54.5	16,189	84
Rockwall	234	3,578	472.7	146.0	96	741	53.4	16.9	9,603	576.5	463,011	1,517
Runnels	19	387	24.8	12.0	14	D	D	D	847	31.2	1,273	6
Rusk	73	1,596	104.0	41.2	41	275	23.2	7.6	3,182	132.6	1,279	11
Sabine	14	320	12.7	6.3	14	45	3.7	0.9	689	26.8	150	1
San Augustine	17	393	20.8	8.4	5	D	D	D	503	18.5	0	0
San Jacinto	11	138	7.4	3.1	12	40	4.6	1.0	1,902	69.4	82,979	376
San Patricio	97	1,722	113.9	50.0	64	342	42.4	11.4	4,442	157.3	41,847	371
San Saba	17	194	15.3	4.6	6	D	D	D	607	20.8	315	2
Schleicher	3	D	D	D	1	D	D	D	287	8.1	10	1
Scurry	22	538	60.3	19.5	29	251	38.3	9.4	1,121	43.0	619	12
Shackelford	4	D	D	D	7	8	1.0	0.2	478	22.8	NA	NA
Shelby	40	820	49.2	19.4	30	D	D	D	1,655	80.3	0	0
Sherman	2	D	D	D	4	7	0.5	0.1	235	12.1	1,479	18
Smith	640	21,211	2,527.9	969.6	347	2,613	252.8	87.5	18,574	909.1	160,273	660
Somervell	15	D	D	D	12	D	D	D	759	33.4	2,340	12
Starr	100	5,009	170.5	85.9	21	D	D	D	6,812	169.5	157	2
Stephens	19	314	19.5	9.6	17	56	4.5	1.1	877	43.1	40	1
Sterling	2	D	D	D	2	D	D	D	163	6.7	NA	NA
Stonewall	6	D	D	D	3	6	0.5	0.1	145	6.8	NA	NA
Sutton	4	61	7.4	2.9	9	13	2.1	0.5	408	11.6	0	0
Swisher	10	206	15.7	5.9	15	D	D	D	489	15.6	0	0
Tarrant	4,575	91,404	11,276.2	4,009.1	2,390	19,504	2,118.4	563.0	170,222	7,982.7	2,723,194	14,459
Taylor	389	11,883	1,026.5	403.9	224	1,763	145.6	40.3	9,921	466.1	73,460	341
Terrell	1	D	D	D	2	D	D	D	83	2.2	NA	NA
Terry	21	446	31.9	12.1	22	63	5.1	1.6	687	28.6	0	0
Throckmorton	3	D	D	D	4	8	0.6	0.1	228	7.5	NA	NA
Titus	88	D	D	D	41	204	19.9	4.8	1,873	80.8	3,462	26

Government Employment and Payroll, and Local Government Finances

STATE County	Full-time equivalent employees	March payroll (dollars)	March payroll (percent of total) Administration, judicial, and legal	Police and corrections	Fire protection	Highways and transportation	Health and welfare	Natural resources and utilities	Education and libraries	General revenue Total (mil dol)	Intergovernmental (mil dol)	Taxes Total (mil dol)	Per capita (dollars) Total	Per capita (dollars) Property
	171	172	173	174	175	176	177	178	179	180	181	182	183	184
TEXAS— Cont'd														
Mason	187	574,614	8.5	5.1	0.0	5.6	6.2	8.5	64.4	12.7	4.9	6.2	1,550	1,351
Matagorda	1,950	6,092,071	4.5	8.9	0.0	2.4	17.9	4.6	60.5	272.8	55.1	91.7	2,509	2,321
Maverick	3,274	9,420,323	4.8	5.7	1.7	2.4	2.2	3.5	79.0	215.5	121.7	45.7	826	606
Medina	2,042	6,076,041	4.7	6.4	0.0	2.1	11.3	4.7	68.9	144.1	64.8	47.3	1,012	893
Menard	160	407,534	7.5	8.8	0.0	1.5	18.9	3.1	58.6	9.7	3.2	4.0	1,788	1,631
Midland	6,743	26,604,150	5.0	7.8	4.1	1.5	30.2	1.5	47.9	761.2	127.7	334.2	2,279	1,657
Milam	1,010	3,486,020	6.1	8.9	0.2	4.0	1.5	3.6	74.9	75.2	30.4	35.9	1,485	1,337
Mills	267	764,983	7.7	3.6	0.0	3.0	2.7	4.7	78.1	16.6	9.4	5.5	1,135	994
Mitchell	583	1,683,044	7.8	5.5	0.2	3.5	33.1	3.1	46.1	46.4	10.5	19.0	2,033	1,894
Montague	1,080	3,133,643	3.8	5.6	1.7	2.8	25.9	4.1	52.2	89.9	35.1	30.6	1,565	1,349
Montgomery	15,517	53,618,969	5.3	8.9	4.3	1.6	4.2	3.6	70.3	1,469.3	416.6	880.8	1,816	1,602
Moore	1,387	4,297,575	5.7	7.6	1.6	2.0	18.7	4.0	59.3	101.2	21.6	47.4	2,125	1,879
Morris	525	1,489,068	7.2	8.0	0.0	2.6	0.2	4.5	77.3	33.3	11.9	17.9	1,399	1,218
Motley	53	139,031	14.8	3.4	0.0	11.8	4.1	2.8	61.5	4.2	1.7	2.0	1,659	1,542
Nacogdoches	3,209	11,081,415	3.8	5.6	2.6	0.8	27.6	2.8	56.3	249.0	82.9	70.1	1,062	894
Navarro	2,582	8,615,927	4.3	7.4	1.8	2.3	3.2	3.1	74.7	198.0	85.4	69.3	1,444	1,208
Newton	492	1,402,695	9.9	5.3	0.0	3.1	1.3	4.5	74.9	46.4	14.2	18.8	1,321	1,309
Nolan	1,074	3,200,019	5.7	6.5	2.3	1.6	30.0	3.7	48.4	92.2	25.3	33.8	2,265	1,854
Nueces	15,002	50,012,628	4.7	10.3	4.3	5.0	3.5	5.4	62.9	1,333.3	434.9	623.4	1,793	1,377
Ochiltree	750	1,938,537	5.3	7.0	1.8	3.2	23.4	3.9	53.5	38.3	10.0	24.3	2,264	1,986
Oldham	268	808,206	6.5	4.6	0.0	1.8	0.0	1.4	85.2	17.9	9.3	4.2	2,028	1,796
Orange	3,533	11,142,459	7.8	12.4	2.2	3.6	1.2	10.2	61.9	284.3	105.6	118.8	1,432	1,208
Palo Pinto	1,439	4,512,709	5.6	7.4	0.8	3.8	30.1	2.6	48.2	125.0	32.7	53.6	1,926	1,663
Panola	1,035	3,674,945	5.9	7.4	0.6	4.5	0.6	2.7	77.7	119.5	26.6	78.0	3,248	3,005
Parker	3,910	13,841,811	8.1	6.9	2.5	2.7	2.3	3.6	72.3	342.4	84.3	203.7	1,701	1,506
Parmer	674	1,770,342	9.3	9.6	0.0	4.1	7.1	4.4	65.0	56.5	17.4	22.7	2,231	2,142
Pecos	928	3,033,599	8.3	7.8	0.0	4.3	11.7	7.2	58.4	127.5	16.7	76.1	4,873	4,588
Polk	1,509	6,360,260	11.3	19.6	0.1	3.8	2.1	6.1	56.0	118.9	38.8	47.9	1,049	878
Potter	8,893	30,669,359	4.8	10.2	6.1	3.0	6.5	3.7	64.1	740.4	307.7	290.5	2,375	1,650
Presidio	514	1,310,951	9.3	7.0	0.0	3.7	6.0	5.4	67.8	35.4	22.2	7.8	1,041	903
Rains	490	1,074,762	8.2	7.5	0.0	2.1	0.3	4.6	75.7	30.7	11.0	16.4	1,498	1,297
Randall	1,728	5,466,299	10.7	21.4	1.0	1.7	0.6	1.5	61.9	119.8	28.9	76.8	614	566
Reagan	366	1,075,023	9.6	7.2	0.4	4.0	23.8	3.8	50.1	44.4	3.9	33.4	9,618	8,897
Real	97	286,334	19.1	8.8	0.0	5.7	12.5	1.5	51.9	7.4	1.1	5.5	1,637	1,475
Red River	579	1,522,449	5.6	7.7	1.5	3.4	0.0	3.7	77.9	37.1	22.5	10.9	857	736
Reeves	1,448	3,858,596	5.2	36.7	1.3	1.5	16.8	4.5	33.4	149.1	13.2	27.3	1,981	1,689
Refugio	551	1,642,349	7.4	7.5	0.7	4.5	25.8	3.6	49.3	40.3	10.7	21.9	3,017	2,809
Roberts	81	227,300	16.9	8.7	0.0	5.2	2.4	7.8	59.0	9.8	1.4	7.9	9,265	8,938
Robertson	905	2,580,494	9.2	10.0	0.0	3.8	0.5	5.5	69.4	85.5	23.3	56.6	3,421	3,199
Rockwall	3,263	11,181,638	8.8	10.5	1.2	0.8	0.1	2.9	74.8	283.0	72.7	179.3	2,159	1,870
Runnels	671	2,087,986	8.8	8.8	0.6	3.6	22.7	8.6	45.9	42.1	20.2	12.8	1,230	1,099
Rusk	1,692	6,115,196	8.9	12.8	1.3	2.9	0.5	7.7	64.0	130.2	38.5	76.0	1,407	1,267
Sabine	470	1,232,799	8.2	5.9	0.0	2.1	12.7	6.2	63.1	31.3	14.1	9.8	938	790
San Augustine	376	978,889	9.7	7.9	0.0	4.2	0.9	5.0	71.7	33.0	20.0	10.7	1,214	1,066
San Jacinto	778	2,008,317	6.5	5.3	0.1	3.0	0.8	1.6	81.9	49.7	19.2	26.2	965	899
San Patricio	3,506	9,765,866	4.9	8.3	1.0	2.9	7.6	7.3	67.8	239.0	100.4	101.3	1,544	1,330
San Saba	434	1,149,764	5.8	3.1	0.0	36.7	1.6	5.8	45.2	25.2	16.5	6.7	1,112	1,001
Schleicher	239	526,633	7.5	4.0	0.0	5.0	19.5	5.6	57.3	13.1	4.2	6.5	2,000	1,918
Scurry	995	3,410,030	6.1	6.6	1.3	2.1	20.3	2.2	60.2	121.2	28.5	57.3	3,345	2,945
Shackelford	207	556,026	10.6	6.6	0.0	5.6	3.6	4.5	68.0	12.7	3.6	7.4	2,193	1,913
Shelby	1,249	3,791,323	5.4	6.0	0.5	2.4	0.0	3.4	81.5	78.9	40.8	30.6	1,176	971
Sherman	266	825,372	8.9	3.5	0.0	4.4	16.5	9.6	54.1	17.5	2.5	11.5	3,752	3,455
Smith	8,764	29,028,100	7.6	10.8	2.8	1.5	6.8	3.6	65.8	648.3	207.0	325.4	1,515	1,170
Somervell	476	1,533,907	6.3	9.3	0.2	6.9	1.2	3.4	65.6	85.7	11.9	48.2	5,603	5,421
Starr	4,112	12,165,296	5.7	7.0	1.5	2.0	8.1	2.5	71.6	268.0	173.1	50.8	825	734
Stephens	543	1,467,714	8.2	6.9	1.9	2.5	26.7	3.6	48.8	27.8	5.2	19.3	2,044	1,781
Sterling	86	271,999	21.3	6.6	0.0	4.1	0.0	5.7	60.3	15.5	4.1	9.5	8,008	7,790
Stonewall	209	553,406	6.8	2.8	0.0	10.2	50.6	1.9	26.7	13.8	2.1	5.9	3,967	3,683
Sutton	312	1,080,664	8.3	4.9	0.0	4.6	23.3	3.3	51.3	24.7	7.3	14.2	3,596	3,274
Swisher	403	1,118,598	6.5	7.0	0.0	2.6	0.9	4.3	77.3	36.9	14.7	7.6	964	823
Tarrant	76,274	291,509,259	6.4	12.5	4.8	1.5	9.8	4.8	58.6	7,673.3	2,064.9	3,815.1	2,029	1,629
Taylor	5,091	16,346,681	6.1	13.5	5.9	1.9	5.4	4.7	60.8	427.2	176.5	186.9	1,401	997
Terrell	108	366,799	22.2	0.0	0.0	7.7	5.5	4.7	44.6	12.5	1.9	9.9	10,751	10,482
Terry	926	2,466,610	5.9	8.0	1.0	2.6	26.1	3.6	51.2	56.3	12.9	26.6	2,108	1,903
Throckmorton	113	346,336	4.5	0.0	0.0	1.3	25.5	5.9	62.6	9.8	3.2	3.9	2,462	2,280
Titus	2,456	7,751,640	2.6	4.2	1.3	1.2	29.0	2.5	58.4	124.8	50.8	52.8	1,617	1,410

1. Based on the resident population estimated as of July 1 of the year shown.

Table B. States and Counties — Local Government Finances, Government Employment, and Income Taxes

STATE County	Local government finances, 2012 (cont.)									Government employment, 2017			Individual income tax returns, 2016		
	Direct general expenditure							Debt outstanding							
			Percent of total for:												
	Total (mil dol)	Per capita[1] (dollars)	Education	Health and hospitals	Police protection	Public welfare	Highways	Total (mil dol)	Per capita[1] (dollars)	Federal civilian	Federal military	State and local	Number of returns	Mean adjusted gross income	Mean income tax
	185	186	187	188	189	190	191	192	193	194	195	196	197	198	199
TEXAS— Cont'd															
Mason	11.2	2,787	63.4	2.7	6.9	0.1	5.9	3.4	853	16	9	274	1,950	49,430	6,334
Matagorda	250.1	6,844	32.2	45.6	2.8	0.0	2.5	242.4	6,631	79	74	2,390	15,790	53,176	5,892
Maverick	219.2	3,958	56.6	2.8	3.8	0.0	8.5	215.3	3,888	822	115	5,340	24,940	34,695	2,141
Medina	151.4	3,238	58.2	13.0	3.7	0.4	3.0	135.1	2,888	68	96	3,086	20,110	54,700	6,195
Menard	9.9	4,437	46.2	0.0	6.1	23.8	3.2	1.6	696	7	4	190	900	37,571	4,120
Midland	747.6	5,098	34.2	40.2	3.6	0.0	1.3	587.4	4,005	557	330	8,808	73,490	109,372	19,745
Milam	70.4	2,914	62.9	2.6	4.1	0.6	7.3	71.3	2,950	52	50	1,243	10,440	44,681	4,754
Mills	17.5	3,633	61.9	2.4	3.5	0.4	4.0	5.4	1,116	14	10	363	2,110	43,523	4,534
Mitchell	47.8	5,118	43.4	36.9	2.7	0.1	3.9	37.5	4,017	21	14	1,118	2,790	45,625	4,365
Montague	91.2	4,662	32.2	41.0	3.2	0.2	3.8	35.2	1,798	50	39	1,093	8,420	48,294	4,771
Montgomery	1,474.0	3,039	50.5	6.5	5.6	0.1	4.0	4,045.0	8,339	1,001	1,148	27,280	240,260	86,629	14,010
Moore	95.6	4,283	47.6	26.8	5.1	0.1	0.9	47.9	2,146	69	44	1,628	9,470	43,450	4,148
Morris	30.0	2,343	68.2	0.1	4.2	0.6	3.3	10.3	804	29	25	613	5,320	41,255	4,298
Motley	4.0	3,301	70.6	4.0	1.7	0.1	5.8	0.1	49	9	6	98	510	35,265	2,757
Nacogdoches	257.8	3,903	37.6	34.4	3.9	0.9	1.9	196.8	2,981	142	128	5,362	25,010	48,051	5,537
Navarro	194.1	4,045	64.8	2.1	5.7	0.3	4.2	235.6	4,910	90	97	3,178	20,390	44,606	4,410
Newton	45.7	3,222	44.4	0.0	8.1	1.7	3.7	33.4	2,356	23	27	575	4,700	46,592	3,948
Nolan	90.3	6,050	47.2	28.5	3.6	0.0	3.1	76.3	5,116	40	29	1,492	6,250	48,067	5,400
Nueces	1,384.5	3,982	48.2	4.5	6.3	0.1	3.8	2,805.4	8,069	5,653	3,117	22,375	150,780	50,796	5,794
Ochiltree	30.1	2,806	68.7	0.5	3.5	0.0	4.9	31.4	2,924	21	20	828	4,250	55,006	6,475
Oldham	17.7	8,594	83.4	0.0	4.2	0.0	2.0	4.6	2,220	7	4	296	950	48,488	4,728
Orange	269.5	3,248	46.6	0.7	7.3	0.2	3.2	736.8	8,880	109	170	4,040	35,910	56,410	6,055
Palo Pinto	119.5	4,289	40.7	32.3	3.8	0.0	3.5	91.1	3,271	54	57	1,766	11,940	47,654	5,315
Panola	120.9	5,033	70.2	0.4	3.5	0.2	6.0	54.6	2,272	71	46	1,274	9,660	51,646	5,406
Parker	370.5	3,095	53.1	7.2	4.5	0.0	11.8	720.3	6,017	181	268	5,299	59,840	75,146	10,848
Parmer	51.6	5,067	48.1	20.9	4.1	4.3	4.2	28.1	2,758	67	20	818	4,040	39,626	3,535
Pecos	125.4	8,031	44.7	24.0	3.2	0.0	4.0	74.8	4,792	50	27	1,841	5,950	49,939	5,755
Polk	109.6	2,400	62.3	0.6	6.0	0.2	7.5	278.0	6,089	82	90	2,878	23,250	53,178	5,782
Potter	749.2	6,124	53.7	5.1	5.8	0.0	2.4	762.3	6,231	2,009	305	12,971	50,300	46,693	5,628
Presidio	41.0	5,442	67.0	0.7	1.8	0.0	1.4	21.5	2,854	311	14	615	3,560	38,794	3,572
Rains	31.1	2,840	44.9	2.6	3.6	0.5	6.4	25.3	2,316	18	24	486	4,580	49,463	5,143
Randall	116.9	935	49.6	1.1	7.6	0.1	3.1	128.5	1,027	188	272	4,262	60,960	64,251	8,393
Reagan	38.8	11,153	53.5	17.4	3.8	0.3	7.7	32.0	9,222	11	7	418	1,530	61,573	8,246
Real	6.9	2,039	48.7	0.5	9.4	2.4	11.7	0.3	75	5	7	207	1,540	45,140	4,318
Red River	37.7	2,968	74.1	0.1	2.9	1.4	1.5	18.4	1,453	36	24	694	5,180	40,341	3,385
Reeves	138.8	10,063	21.0	12.8	3.3	0.0	1.6	136.0	9,859	68	25	1,600	4,970	58,716	8,584
Refugio	40.6	5,594	55.7	13.7	4.6	0.0	5.7	20.5	2,822	31	14	667	3,130	47,426	4,666
Roberts	9.1	10,678	90.1	0.4	2.2	0.0	2.1	0.7	768	5	2	104	420	54,695	6,350
Robertson	89.0	5,381	81.1	0.1	3.4	0.3	3.2	84.0	5,080	41	34	998	7,470	43,279	4,210
Rockwall	297.5	3,584	49.5	0.4	5.7	0.2	5.2	881.6	10,619	132	194	3,820	42,760	93,472	14,652
Runnels	43.0	4,112	51.2	23.8	1.8	0.0	4.7	11.5	1,101	40	20	810	4,510	42,189	3,951
Rusk	130.1	2,408	66.3	0.4	4.6	0.1	6.1	181.9	3,368	70	97	2,473	20,290	49,591	5,214
Sabine	29.1	2,787	50.7	22.5	5.3	0.0	6.3	11.3	1,081	47	21	497	4,150	49,683	5,378
San Augustine	28.0	3,179	73.4	1.6	6.1	0.0	0.7	34.8	3,949	19	16	400	3,300	38,918	3,212
San Jacinto	46.2	1,704	66.1	0.2	5.1	0.5	6.7	34.4	1,269	26	57	901	10,350	50,139	5,353
San Patricio	237.2	3,616	57.1	6.5	5.8	0.3	3.2	231.1	3,524	93	1,563	4,000	30,630	50,470	5,366
San Saba	18.5	3,087	57.6	1.7	4.5	1.1	6.8	15.9	2,642	20	11	498	2,370	43,838	4,462
Schleicher	13.7	4,190	45.0	27.0	0.7	0.0	3.4	34.9	10,699	11	6	247	1,140	47,068	4,575
Scurry	113.5	6,628	57.4	17.4	3.7	0.1	3.7	74.5	4,348	35	31	1,695	6,560	54,297	6,180
Shackelford	11.4	3,400	61.4	4.1	6.5	0.0	5.6	0.9	262	13	7	220	1,430	67,936	7,534
Shelby	75.6	2,905	71.6	0.6	5.1	0.0	6.1	42.1	1,619	76	51	1,326	10,020	41,392	3,822
Sherman	18.7	6,099	54.0	15.6	4.5	0.0	6.0	3.1	1,017	8	6	265	1,100	48,361	5,077
Smith	645.1	3,003	55.0	5.1	5.6	0.2	3.4	1,145.0	5,330	643	483	13,505	98,700	59,423	7,889
Somervell	86.1	10,008	49.0	29.8	3.5	0.5	3.8	65.4	7,610	14	17	846	3,870	65,187	7,842
Starr	254.5	4,130	66.2	11.4	3.9	0.0	3.6	277.9	4,510	801	128	5,388	24,440	31,811	1,741
Stephens	27.4	2,898	46.7	2.5	5.2	0.1	3.9	19.2	2,029	17	17	671	3,540	41,771	4,005
Sterling	17.5	14,668	64.5	1.9	2.1	15.3	2.0	10.2	8,554	5	3	155	620	62,616	9,027
Stonewall	23.1	15,635	13.2	76.1	1.3	0.0	2.7	0.1	57	13	3	229	600	49,233	5,002
Sutton	22.3	5,656	62.2	17.0	3.3	0.1	3.4	1.6	405	5	8	403	1,700	54,461	6,450
Swisher	30.7	3,895	48.7	32.1	4.0	0.0	0.8	3.2	409	22	14	752	2,820	40,860	3,820
Tarrant	7,651.9	4,070	42.5	12.1	6.9	0.1	3.7	19,647.2	10,450	15,315	5,550	98,238	921,690	67,048	9,540
Taylor	402.0	3,012	53.5	4.7	7.8	0.6	3.1	263.9	1,977	1,177	4,562	8,773	59,810	53,545	6,352
Terrell	12.1	13,215	63.5	3.9	7.6	0.0	8.3	21.1	22,972	43	2	104	340	45,444	4,747
Terry	59.1	4,683	48.8	27.3	3.7	0.4	3.1	17.6	1,397	25	23	1,053	4,630	39,838	3,600
Throckmorton	9.9	6,177	38.7	32.3	0.8	0.0	11.7	0.2	137	7	3	183	660	47,180	6,564
Titus	127.0	3,889	67.0	0.4	4.2	0.1	6.4	228.1	6,985	94	65	2,855	13,500	43,844	4,126

1. Based on the resident population estimated as of July 1 of the year shown.

Table B. States and Counties — **Land Area and Population**

State / county code	CBSA code[1]	County code[2]	STATE County	Land area[3] (sq. mi)	Total persons 2018	Rank	Per square mile	White	Black	American Indian, Alaska Native	Asian and Pacific Islander	Percent Hispanic or Latino[4]	Under 5 years	5 to 17 years	18 to 24 years	25 to 34 years	35 to 44 years	45 to 54 years
				1	2	3	4	5	6	7	8	9	10	11	12	13	14	15
			TEXAS— Cont'd															
48451	41,660	3	Tom Green	1,522.0	118,189	526	77.7	54.1	4.3	0.8	1.9	40.5	6.8	17.1	11.7	15.5	11.6	10.3
48453	12,420	1	Travis	991.8	1,248,743	34	1,259.1	50.6	8.7	0.7	8.2	33.9	6.3	15.4	9.2	20.1	16.0	12.7
48455	26,660	7	Trinity	693.8	14,740	2,112	21.2	79.2	9.9	1.3	0.9	10.5	5.3	14.7	6.2	9.7	9.8	11.6
48457		6	Tyler	924.4	21,696	1,742	23.5	79.8	11.4	1.2	0.8	8.1	4.8	14.5	8.5	13.6	11.4	11.3
48459	30,980	3	Upshur	583.0	41,260	1,145	70.8	82.0	8.7	1.4	0.7	9.0	5.9	17.9	7.5	11.5	11.6	12.1
48461		8	Upton	1,241.3	3,671	2,925	3.0	42.7	2.7	1.3	0.5	53.7	8.1	21.4	7.2	13.8	12.6	10.5
48463	46,620	6	Uvalde	1,551.9	26,846	1,531	17.3	26.3	0.8	0.4	0.9	72.1	7.3	19.7	10.5	13.2	11.1	10.8
48465	19,620	5	Val Verde	3,144.8	49,208	1,002	15.6	15.2	1.6	0.4	1.0	82.5	8.7	19.9	11.1	14.6	11.7	10.9
48467		6	Van Zandt	842.6	56,019	911	66.5	84.8	3.3	1.4	0.8	11.2	5.9	17.2	7.6	10.7	11.3	12.8
48469	47,020	3	Victoria	882.1	92,035	642	104.3	45.2	6.3	0.5	1.6	47.4	6.9	18.5	9.2	14.0	12.1	11.0
48471	26,660	4	Walker	784.2	72,480	750	92.4	57.4	23.5	0.7	1.5	18.1	4.3	10.8	18.7	15.1	13.1	13.7
48473	26,420	1	Waller	513.3	53,126	951	103.5	44.0	24.2	0.7	1.4	30.8	6.6	17.6	20.2	11.2	10.6	10.8
48475		6	Ward	835.6	11,720	2,312	14.0	40.6	4.7	1.0	0.7	54.3	7.6	21.1	8.5	13.9	12.7	10.9
48477	14,780	6	Washington	604.2	35,108	1,303	58.1	64.8	17.3	0.6	2.1	16.4	5.8	15.9	10.3	10.5	10.5	11.1
48479	29,700	2	Webb	3,361.5	275,910	248	82.1	3.7	0.3	0.1	0.6	95.5	9.4	23.5	11.3	13.5	12.6	11.5
48481	20,900	4	Wharton	1,086.2	41,619	1,140	38.3	44.5	13.1	0.4	0.6	42.0	6.8	19.0	8.9	12.3	11.4	11.5
48483		9	Wheeler	914.5	5,191	2,819	5.7	70.3	3.5	1.2	1.2	25.6	6.6	18.4	7.5	11.0	11.6	10.9
48485	48,660	3	Wichita	627.6	132,064	483	210.4	66.9	11.7	1.4	3.1	19.4	6.3	16.1	13.2	15.1	11.6	10.7
48487	46,900	6	Wilbarger	970.9	12,820	2,236	13.2	59.3	8.4	1.6	3.1	29.5	5.9	16.4	8.9	13.6	11.6	11.6
48489	39,700	6	Willacy	590.6	21,515	1,754	36.4	8.9	2.0	0.2	0.7	88.4	6.4	17.2	13.0	16.1	13.2	10.5
48491	12,420	1	Williamson	1,118.3	566,719	118	506.8	60.7	7.4	0.8	8.7	24.8	6.5	19.1	7.9	13.9	16.3	13.5
48493	41,700	1	Wilson	803.7	50,224	986	62.5	57.6	1.8	0.8	0.8	40.0	6.0	18.0	8.3	11.4	12.2	14.1
48495		6	Winkler	841.3	7,720	2,613	9.2	35.8	2.6	0.8	1.0	60.8	7.6	22.0	9.5	13.4	12.8	11.7
48497	19,100	1	Wise	904.4	68,305	783	75.5	77.6	1.7	1.4	0.9	19.7	6.3	18.5	7.8	12.3	12.5	13.6
48499		6	Wood	645.2	45,129	1,074	69.9	83.4	5.7	1.2	0.8	10.3	4.9	14.3	8.1	9.6	9.3	11.4
48501		7	Yoakum	799.7	8,591	2,540	10.7	31.3	1.3	0.7	0.6	66.9	8.9	23.7	9.7	12.6	12.1	10.1
48503		7	Young	914.5	18,045	1,920	19.7	78.3	1.8	1.0	1.0	19.1	6.1	17.9	7.3	11.6	11.1	11.6
48505	49,820	6	Zapata	998.4	14,190	2,150	14.2	4.9	0.2	0.2	0.2	94.6	9.1	24.1	10.2	12.5	12.0	10.4
48507		7	Zavala	1,297.4	11,983	2,292	9.2	5.2	0.7	0.2	0.2	93.9	7.7	21.6	11.7	13.6	11.2	10.4
49000		0	UTAH	82,195.8	3,161,105	X	38.5	80.0	1.7	1.4	5.0	14.2	8.0	21.5	11.3	14.7	13.7	10.2
49001		7	Beaver	2,582.9	6,580	2,702	2.5	86.0	0.6	1.6	1.7	11.7	8.7	23.5	8.6	11.4	12.3	9.3
49003	36,260	2	Box Elder	5,745.6	54,950	929	9.6	88.4	0.7	1.2	1.7	9.5	8.2	23.5	8.5	12.7	13.5	9.7
49005	30,860	3	Cache	1,164.7	127,068	504	109.1	84.8	1.2	1.0	3.8	10.9	8.5	21.8	19.0	13.9	11.7	8.0
49007	39,220	7	Carbon	1,479.2	20,269	1,809	13.7	84.4	1.0	1.6	1.3	13.3	6.1	19.7	9.2	11.8	12.6	10.0
49009		9	Daggett	697.0	980	3,107	1.4	94.3	0.5	1.7	1.5	4.1	4.9	17.2	6.1	7.4	10.4	11.8
49011	36,260	2	Davis	299.0	351,713	201	1,176.3	85.6	1.8	0.8	4.3	9.9	8.4	23.7	9.2	14.0	14.8	10.3
49013		7	Duchesne	3,235.3	19,964	1,828	6.2	87.1	0.8	4.9	1.3	8.3	9.1	24.5	7.7	13.0	13.9	9.4
49015		7	Emery	4,462.3	10,014	2,426	2.2	91.9	0.7	1.2	1.1	6.3	6.0	22.7	7.8	10.2	12.9	10.0
49017		9	Garfield	5,175.1	5,080	2,826	1.0	89.3	0.9	2.5	2.4	6.3	5.9	17.4	6.9	11.1	11.2	10.2
49019		7	Grand	3,672.7	9,764	2,445	2.7	83.1	1.1	4.5	2.0	10.9	6.1	15.3	6.8	12.8	13.6	11.8
49021	16,260	4	Iron	3,296.3	52,775	954	16.0	87.5	1.0	2.4	2.1	8.8	7.8	21.2	14.4	13.2	11.9	9.0
49023	39,340	2	Juab	3,391.7	11,555	2,322	3.4	93.0	0.7	1.5	0.9	5.1	9.0	25.4	9.5	11.9	13.3	10.1
49025		6	Kane	3,989.9	7,709	2,616	1.9	92.1	0.9	2.3	1.3	4.8	6.0	17.5	6.7	11.4	10.9	10.1
49027		7	Millard	6,605.0	13,006	2,230	2.0	83.9	0.7	1.7	2.0	13.2	7.8	22.9	8.5	10.3	11.6	9.7
49029	36,260	2	Morgan	609.2	12,045	2,290	19.8	95.5	0.8	0.7	0.9	3.1	7.4	28.0	8.6	9.3	14.0	10.9
49031		9	Piute	758.4	1,445	3,081	1.9	91.1	1.2	0.8	0.8	7.5	3.3	19.7	6.6	7.5	10.4	9.6
49033		8	Rich	1,028.8	2,464	3,008	2.4	91.6	0.9	0.9	0.5	7.1	7.6	21.4	8.7	10.8	11.3	10.7
49035	41,620	1	Salt Lake	742.1	1,152,633	37	1,553.2	72.8	2.4	1.1	7.6	18.6	7.5	19.6	9.6	16.5	14.7	11.2
49037		7	San Juan	7,819.8	15,449	2,071	2.0	45.4	0.7	48.7	1.3	5.8	7.7	22.8	10.2	12.2	10.7	10.8
49039		6	Sanpete	1,589.9	30,623	1,419	19.3	86.7	1.3	1.5	2.2	9.7	6.2	19.4	14.5	12.9	12.7	10.2
49041		7	Sevier	1,910.4	21,539	1,749	11.3	92.4	0.8	1.5	1.0	5.4	7.4	22.0	8.4	11.1	13.3	9.9
49043	44,920	4	Summit	1,870.6	41,933	1,136	22.4	85.5	1.2	0.6	2.6	11.4	5.4	19.0	8.0	12.0	12.9	15.0
49045	41,620	1	Tooele	6,941.9	69,907	773	10.1	84.4	1.2	1.3	2.2	12.6	8.1	24.6	8.9	13.4	15.5	11.2
49047	46,860	7	Uintah	4,482.4	35,438	1,292	7.9	83.1	0.8	7.9	1.6	8.6	8.6	24.6	7.8	14.0	14.6	9.5
49049	39,340	2	Utah	2,003.6	622,213	107	310.5	84.2	1.0	0.9	4.4	12.0	9.5	23.9	16.8	14.4	12.6	8.4
49051	25,720	6	Wasatch	1,177.0	33,240	1,352	28.2	84.2	0.8	0.7	1.7	13.8	7.7	23.8	8.5	11.1	14.8	11.4
49053	41,100	3	Washington	2,427.4	171,700	381	70.7	85.9	1.1	1.5	2.9	10.6	6.7	19.4	8.8	11.5	11.9	9.3
49055		9	Wayne	2,461.0	2,690	2,988	1.1	91.2	0.9	0.9	1.3	6.9	6.1	18.4	8.0	10.3	10.2	10.7
49057	36,260	2	Weber	576.3	256,359	267	444.8	77.6	1.9	1.1	2.9	18.7	7.7	20.6	9.6	15.3	13.8	10.7
50000		0	VERMONT	9,217.9	626,299	X	67.9	94.3	1.9	1.2	2.6	2.0	4.7	13.8	10.7	11.8	11.3	12.9
50001		6	Addison	766.3	36,973	1,248	48.2	94.2	1.9	0.8	2.8	2.3	4.3	12.6	13.8	10.2	10.7	13.1
50003	13,540	6	Bennington	675.0	35,631	1,287	52.8	95.2	1.7	0.8	1.7	2.2	4.7	14.3	9.1	9.8	9.9	13.0
50005		7	Caledonia	649.0	30,302	1,424	46.7	96.1	1.2	1.3	1.2	1.7	4.8	14.5	9.3	10.5	11.2	13.0

1. CBSA = Core Based Statistical Area. See Appendix A for explanation. See Appendix B for list of metropolitan areas with component counties.   2. County type code from the Economic Research Service of USDA Rural-Urban Continuum Codes. See Appendix A for definition.   3. Dry land or land partially or temporarily covered by water.   4. May be of any race.

Table B. States and Counties — Population and Households

STATE County	Age (percent) (cont.)				Population change, 2000-2018							Households, 2013-2017				
					Total persons		Percent change		Components of change, 2010-2018						Percent	
	55 to 64 years	65 to 74 years	75 years and over	Percent female	2000	2010	2000-2010	2010-2018	Births	Deaths	Net Migration	Number	Persons per household	Family house-holds	Female family house-holder[1]	One person
	16	17	18	19	20	21	22	23	24	25	26	27	28	29	30	31
TEXAS— Cont'd																
Tom Green	11.6	8.7	6.8	50.3	104,010	110,228	6.0	7.2	13,032	8,487	3,396	43,081	2.57	63.0	11.2	30.4
Travis	10.5	6.4	3.5	49.4	812,280	1,024,462	26.1	21.9	130,938	43,019	134,002	447,561	2.58	56.9	10.2	31.1
Trinity	16.0	15.4	11.2	51.8	13,779	14,675	6.5	0.4	1,178	1,835	719	5,934	2.42	66.5	12.3	29.4
Tyler	13.6	12.3	10.0	46.1	20,871	21,760	4.3	-0.3	1,767	2,184	370	7,312	2.56	71.4	12.1	26.4
Upshur	15.0	10.9	7.5	50.6	35,291	39,315	11.4	4.9	3,959	3,724	1,731	14,061	2.84	70.4	9.9	25.7
Upton	12.4	7.4	6.7	48.8	3,404	3,349	-1.6	9.6	439	259	134	1,308	2.68	66.1	10.5	32.0
Uvalde	10.5	9.2	7.6	50.8	25,926	26,405	1.8	1.7	3,326	2,035	-827	8,624	3.08	67.9	14.9	28.8
Val Verde	8.9	7.8	6.5	48.9	44,856	48,879	9.0	0.7	7,158	2,969	-3,905	15,189	3.12	76.0	12.9	21.2
Van Zandt	14.4	11.6	8.6	51.2	48,140	52,560	9.2	6.6	4,891	5,314	3,903	19,354	2.73	70.9	9.9	23.8
Victoria	12.3	9.1	7.0	51.0	84,088	86,793	3.2	6.0	10,616	6,537	1,166	32,734	2.75	70.2	13.6	24.0
Walker	11.1	7.9	5.3	41.8	61,758	67,861	9.9	6.8	5,189	4,223	3,639	21,294	2.45	58.1	11.7	30.9
Waller	11.1	7.3	4.5	50.2	32,663	43,277	32.5	22.8	5,075	2,449	7,150	14,698	2.96	73.2	12.8	19.4
Ward	11.4	7.9	6.0	49.7	10,909	10,658	-2.3	10.0	1,419	925	553	3,954	2.88	67.6	9.7	28.0
Washington	14.1	11.5	10.2	50.9	30,373	33,695	10.9	4.2	3,362	3,114	1,180	12,205	2.65	69.2	11.2	28.0
Webb	8.7	5.6	3.9	50.9	193,117	250,304	29.6	10.2	44,093	10,774	-7,690	72,379	3.68	80.6	22.2	16.7
Wharton	12.9	9.5	7.6	50.7	41,188	41,280	0.2	0.8	4,590	3,475	-757	15,224	2.68	70.5	13.8	26.4
Wheeler	14.6	10.7	8.6	49.7	5,284	5,406	2.3	-4.0	620	550	-295	2,287	2.42	67.7	10.5	27.0
Wichita	12.2	8.1	6.6	48.3	131,664	131,665	0.0	0.3	14,348	11,059	-2,877	48,528	2.40	63.4	14.2	31.0
Wilbarger	13.8	10.2	8.2	50.5	14,676	13,535	-7.8	-5.3	1,352	1,261	-816	5,155	2.39	64.4	12.3	33.0
Willacy	9.6	7.8	6.2	44.7	20,082	22,136	10.2	-2.8	2,494	1,370	-1,755	5,737	3.51	81.7	23.9	16.6
Williamson	10.5	7.6	4.6	50.8	249,967	422,501	69.0	34.1	52,135	19,733	110,250	170,051	2.96	72.3	9.8	22.6
Wilson	14.1	9.7	6.3	49.9	32,408	42,913	32.4	17.0	4,233	3,111	6,140	15,755	2.96	78.5	9.6	18.0
Winkler	10.7	7.3	5.0	48.7	7,173	7,110	-0.9	8.6	986	519	129	2,524	3.04	70.2	12.8	26.3
Wise	14.1	9.0	5.9	50.0	48,793	59,100	21.1	15.6	6,389	4,511	7,326	21,691	2.87	75.1	11.4	20.2
Wood	15.5	15.5	11.4	50.4	36,752	41,959	14.2	7.6	3,392	5,068	4,813	16,122	2.59	72.3	9.8	24.2
Yoakum	11.1	6.7	5.1	49.0	7,322	7,879	7.6	9.0	1,259	484	-66	2,652	3.20	76.8	8.7	20.2
Young	14.1	11.3	9.0	50.5	17,943	18,550	3.4	-2.7	1,858	2,127	-230	7,066	2.53	74.1	11.5	22.5
Zapata	8.8	7.2	5.8	50.1	12,182	14,018	15.1	1.2	2,312	728	-1,416	4,457	3.23	76.3	18.7	20.2
Zavala	9.7	8.4	5.9	49.4	11,600	11,677	0.7	2.6	1,574	775	-491	3,536	3.37	72.7	26.4	22.4
UTAH	9.5	6.6	4.4	49.6	2,233,169	2,763,891	23.8	14.4	420,885	136,102	113,137	938,365	3.14	75.1	9.3	19.2
Beaver	11.8	8.6	5.8	48.9	6,005	6,629	10.4	-0.7	906	452	-516	2,313	2.74	69.3	8.2	29.4
Box Elder	11.0	7.4	5.6	49.3	42,745	49,978	16.9	9.9	7,182	3,000	794	17,035	3.04	79.3	6.1	18.7
Cache	7.6	5.5	4.0	49.4	91,391	112,656	23.3	12.8	19,436	4,241	-786	36,829	3.19	74.4	7.7	16.6
Carbon	13.2	10.6	6.8	50.3	20,422	21,403	4.8	-5.3	2,308	1,830	-1,631	7,841	2.55	65.0	10.5	29.0
Daggett	16.4	16.3	9.3	43.3	921	1,061	15.2	-7.6	84	70	-101	168	3.38	82.7	0.6	14.9
Davis	9.5	6.0	4.0	49.5	238,994	306,492	28.2	14.8	47,534	13,419	11,245	101,422	3.28	81.6	8.9	15.0
Duchesne	10.3	6.9	5.1	49.4	14,371	18,605	29.5	7.3	3,331	1,118	-870	6,650	2.99	79.1	8.8	17.1
Emery	13.1	10.1	7.2	49.0	10,860	10,976	1.1	-8.8	1,189	732	-1,436	3,564	2.90	77.6	6.5	20.2
Garfield	14.1	14.3	8.9	47.9	4,735	5,172	9.2	-1.8	497	375	-221	1,756	2.72	73.6	7.5	20.4
Grand	15.0	11.7	6.9	49.5	8,485	9,224	8.7	5.9	1,001	649	190	3,873	2.44	67.8	10.4	28.7
Iron	9.8	7.9	4.8	50.0	33,779	46,163	36.7	14.3	6,998	2,478	2,076	15,575	3.07	72.2	9.7	21.3
Juab	8.7	7.5	4.6	48.7	8,238	10,246	24.4	12.8	1,534	591	366	3,287	3.20	80.5	11.6	17.7
Kane	14.2	14.4	8.9	49.5	6,046	7,125	17.8	8.2	670	595	489	2,514	2.84	59.5	3.2	31.2
Millard	12.1	9.5	7.6	48.3	12,405	12,503	0.8	4.0	1,611	823	-292	4,235	2.94	79.7	6.8	17.3
Morgan	10.3	6.7	4.8	48.3	7,129	9,469	32.8	27.2	1,346	450	1,674	3,236	3.40	89.7	3.0	9.1
Piute	14.2	16.6	12.2	48.4	1,435	1,557	8.5	-7.2	106	119	-100	516	3.54	73.8	6.8	25.4
Rich	12.4	10.6	7.4	48.5	1,961	2,264	15.5	8.8	281	119	36	601	3.83	77.5	6.2	20.5
Salt Lake	10.1	6.6	4.2	49.8	898,387	1,029,590	14.6	12.0	146,335	51,790	29,219	363,058	3.01	70.5	10.5	22.6
San Juan	11.4	8.3	5.8	50.0	14,413	14,745	2.3	4.8	1,950	831	-417	4,019	3.68	75.5	15.1	21.9
Sanpete	10.2	8.3	5.6	47.4	22,763	27,822	22.2	10.1	3,224	1,522	1,097	8,366	3.07	78.2	5.8	17.4
Sevier	11.8	9.2	6.9	49.2	18,842	20,801	10.4	3.5	2,568	1,603	-226	7,171	2.87	76.6	8.9	20.4
Summit	15.0	8.8	3.8	48.8	29,736	36,324	22.2	15.4	3,592	1,172	3,194	14,781	2.67	73.9	6.4	19.2
Tooele	9.3	5.8	3.4	49.4	40,735	58,218	42.9	20.1	8,170	2,803	6,333	19,562	3.22	80.0	9.9	17.4
Uintah	10.1	6.5	4.4	49.2	25,224	32,588	29.2	8.7	5,420	1,826	-827	10,616	3.39	72.7	10.6	22.2
Utah	6.7	4.6	3.2	49.4	368,536	516,639	40.2	20.4	98,968	18,591	25,396	155,664	3.61	81.9	7.8	11.9
Wasatch	11.2	7.7	3.8	49.2	15,215	23,525	54.6	41.3	3,528	1,048	7,146	9,040	3.22	78.5	6.9	16.5
Washington	11.0	11.8	9.6	50.5	90,354	138,115	52.9	24.3	18,481	9,929	24,835	52,385	2.93	75.3	8.7	20.5
Wayne	14.6	14.7	7.1	48.7	2,509	2,778	10.7	-3.2	255	202	-142	990	2.67	67.7	2.6	30.9
Weber	10.6	7.0	4.6	49.7	196,533	231,223	17.7	10.9	32,380	13,724	6,612	81,298	2.96	73.1	10.7	21.8
VERMONT	15.4	11.6	7.7	50.6	608,827	625,744	2.8	0.1	48,976	46,463	-1,566	258,535	2.32	61.3	8.9	29.6
Addison	15.5	12.3	7.6	50.0	35,974	36,821	2.4	0.4	2,584	2,558	147	14,701	2.31	64.1	8.7	29.3
Bennington	16.4	12.9	10.0	51.3	36,994	37,125	0.4	-4.0	2,761	3,622	-617	15,280	2.26	63.9	12.2	29.4
Caledonia	15.8	13.0	7.9	50.0	29,702	31,231	5.1	-3.0	2,352	2,527	-746	12,094	2.43	60.6	7.9	30.8

1. No spouse present.

Table B. States and Counties — Population, Vital Statistics, Health, and Crime

STATE County	Persons in group quarters, 2018	Daytime Population, 2013-2017 Number	Daytime Population, 2013-2017 Employment/residence ratio	Births, 2018 Total	Births, 2018 Rate[1]	Deaths, 2018 Number	Deaths, 2018 Rate[1]	Persons under 65 with no health insurance, 2016 Number	Persons under 65 with no health insurance, 2016 Percent	Medicare, 2018 Total beneficiaries	Medicare, 2018 Enrolled in Original Medicare	Medicare, 2018 Enrolled in Medicare Advantage	Serious crimes known to police[2], 2016 Total Number	Serious crimes known to police[2], 2016 Total Rate[3]
	32	33	34	35	36	37	38	39	40	41	42	43	44	45
TEXAS— Cont'd														
Tom Green	5,315	116,454	0.99	1,530	12.9	1,098	9.3	16,506	17.2	21,294	15,575	5,719	5,900	4,946
Travis	22,843	1,296,857	1.19	15,703	12.6	6,015	4.8	162,725	15.2	131,114	89,714	41,400	41,981	3,485
Trinity	138	12,603	0.61	141	9.6	222	15.1	2,327	21.7	4,220	2,789	1,431	190	1,644
Tyler	2,440	19,887	0.76	200	9.2	246	11.3	2,459	16.5	4,928	3,439	1,489	327	1,542
Upshur	445	32,772	0.52	479	11.6	471	11.4	6,134	18.3	8,550	5,703	2,847	743	1,879
Upton	62	4,178	1.43	57	15.5	19	5.2	647	20.5	567	405	162	20	540
Uvalde	631	27,095	1.01	390	14.5	255	9.5	5,022	22.5	5,356	3,588	1,768	840	3,074
Val Verde	1,914	48,072	0.95	820	16.7	400	8.1	9,023	22.5	8,458	5,749	2,709	1,102	2,256
Van Zandt	571	46,455	0.68	643	11.5	672	12.0	9,532	22.1	12,521	8,498	4,023	594	1,109
Victoria	1,871	93,586	1.05	1,218	13.2	850	9.2	14,481	18.8	17,126	11,611	5,515	3,198	3,429
Walker	16,932	71,737	1.04	627	8.7	590	8.1	8,314	17.9	9,796	5,879	3,917	1,299	1,830
Waller	4,191	46,599	0.91	669	12.6	322	6.1	9,537	23.9	6,622	4,134	2,488	879	1,771
Ward	119	11,411	0.98	160	13.7	92	7.8	1,911	19.4	1,860	1,365	495	357	2,994
Washington	2,082	36,803	1.14	402	11.5	376	10.7	4,677	17.9	8,337	6,181	2,156	591	1,695
Webb	3,593	269,342	1.00	5,026	18.2	1,395	5.1	66,407	27.5	31,967	22,717	9,250	9,174	3,364
Wharton	488	39,513	0.90	560	13.5	423	10.2	7,434	21.5	8,047	5,834	2,213	1,270	3,068
Wheeler	40	6,261	1.26	66	12.7	66	12.7	961	21.3	1,086	904	182	82	1,440
Wichita	12,562	136,294	1.07	1,619	12.3	1,411	10.7	15,908	15.7	23,944	19,522	4,422	4,862	3,703
Wilbarger	647	13,420	1.07	146	11.4	137	10.7	2,012	19.3	2,703	1,988	715	429	3,327
Willacy	3,298	20,935	0.86	277	12.9	188	8.7	3,523	22.8	3,482	1,853	1,629	734	3,370
Williamson	4,260	442,911	0.74	6,638	11.7	2,837	5.0	50,361	10.9	73,627	49,418	24,209	9,879	1,881
Wilson	521	37,140	0.51	539	10.7	428	8.5	6,225	15.3	8,550	5,324	3,226	575	1,190
Winkler	97	7,874	1.03	103	13.3	53	6.9	1,317	19.1	1,075	831	244	87	1,064
Wise	805	57,556	0.79	768	11.2	613	9.0	9,540	17.6	11,323	7,710	3,613	770	1,211
Wood	1,721	40,348	0.81	410	9.1	648	14.4	6,178	20.0	13,928	9,649	4,279	569	1,308
Yoakum	56	9,049	1.15	150	17.5	47	5.5	1,754	23.6	1,178	884	294	125	1,442
Young	248	18,494	1.04	215	11.9	239	13.2	3,059	21.2	4,304	3,681	623	259	1,426
Zapata	31	14,001	0.91	243	17.1	105	7.4	3,611	28.9	1,920	1,413	507	NA	NA
Zavala	413	11,739	0.91	165	13.8	99	8.3	1,994	20.1	1,971	1,153	818	198	1,609
UTAH	48,109	2,994,499	1.00	50,124	15.9	17,156	5.4	259,941	9.7	385,977	246,021	139,956	97,465	3,194
Beaver	10	6,649	1.09	102	15.5	53	8.1	656	12.0	1,170	1,095	75	120	2,201
Box Elder	337	48,660	0.84	854	15.5	396	7.2	3,848	8.4	8,138	5,006	3,132	1,168	2,250
Cache	3,835	119,949	0.99	2,253	17.7	531	4.2	10,011	9.3	13,461	7,178	6,283	1,451	1,183
Carbon	474	20,876	1.04	213	10.5	186	9.2	1,551	9.4	4,340	3,958	382	536	2,859
Daggett	0	690	0.96	6	6.1	9	9.2	75	9.7	231	185	46	0	0
Davis	3,066	298,572	0.77	5,616	16.0	1,716	4.9	20,715	6.7	39,167	24,949	14,218	6,563	1,914
Duchesne	297	20,818	1.07	324	16.2	128	6.4	2,431	13.7	3,047	2,389	658	775	3,621
Emery	43	9,867	0.86	108	10.8	90	9.0	741	8.7	1,988	1,704	284	122	1,187
Garfield	174	4,934	0.96	62	12.2	39	7.7	550	14.7	1,124	1,057	67	NA	NA
Grand	144	10,023	1.10	105	10.8	78	8.0	1,090	13.9	1,975	1,932	43	154	1,606
Iron	851	47,555	0.95	832	15.8	320	6.1	5,090	11.9	7,790	6,171	1,619	1,064	2,174
Juab	122	9,816	0.80	194	16.8	82	7.1	975	10.2	1,620	1,552	68	246	2,300
Kane	258	7,666	1.13	83	10.8	59	7.7	464	8.6	1,836	1,775	61	104	1,454
Millard	177	12,537	0.98	201	15.5	94	7.2	1,366	13.1	2,336	2,280	56	248	1,952
Morgan	0	8,369	0.43	173	14.4	49	4.1	668	6.5	1,515	1,003	512	NA	NA
Piute	37	1,656	0.67	10	6.9	10	6.9	131	12.8	421	407	14	15	991
Rich	1	2,350	1.06	35	14.2	14	5.7	192	10.2	415	331	84	34	1,459
Salt Lake	14,845	1,188,980	1.15	17,266	15.0	6,596	5.7	108,324	10.9	137,875	78,219	59,656	57,457	5,105
San Juan	359	15,295	1.02	209	13.5	120	7.8	2,466	17.1	2,072	2,036	36	166	1,037
Sanpete	2,958	27,389	0.86	387	12.6	186	6.1	2,891	12.7	4,663	4,025	638	264	1,023
Sevier	307	21,247	1.03	310	14.4	194	9.0	1,850	10.6	4,047	3,591	456	555	2,633
Summit	114	43,801	1.19	435	10.4	145	3.5	3,453	9.5	5,565	3,846	1,719	823	2,037
Tooele	319	53,223	0.63	1,022	14.6	345	4.9	4,744	8.1	7,579	5,412	2,167	1,941	3,030
Uintah	192	36,373	1.00	545	15.4	231	6.5	4,213	12.9	4,138	3,120	1,018	693	1,766
Utah	13,972	557,875	0.93	12,121	19.5	2,356	3.8	42,480	7.9	53,562	31,007	22,555	10,853	1,844
Wasatch	250	24,513	0.66	480	14.4	139	4.2	3,389	12.4	3,907	2,415	1,492	287	941
Washington	2,237	155,599	1.00	2,282	13.3	1,338	7.8	14,457	11.6	36,615	26,586	10,029	2,954	1,884
Wayne	9	2,641	0.95	25	9.3	21	7.8	288	13.6	618	590	28	NA	NA
Weber	2,721	236,576	0.93	3,871	15.1	1,631	6.4	20,832	9.6	34,762	22,204	12,558	7,813	3,167
VERMONT	25,709	623,111	1.00	5,599	8.9	5,587	8.9	23,063	4.7	143,440	128,568	14,872	11,591	1,856
Addison	2,871	34,230	0.87	311	8.4	323	8.7	1,270	4.6	8,108	6,937	1,171	348	941
Bennington	1,427	37,774	1.10	308	8.6	436	12.2	1,346	5.0	9,614	8,616	998	636	1,763
Caledonia	1,358	28,669	0.87	279	9.2	273	9.0	1,155	4.9	7,437	6,787	650	565	1,845

1. Per 1,000 estimated resident population.   2. Data for serious crimes have not been adjusted for underreporting; this may affect comparability between geographic areas and over time.   3. Per 100,000 population estimated by the FBI.

Table B. States and Counties — Crime, Education, Money Income, and Poverty

	Serious crimes known to police[2], 2016 (cont.)[1]		Education						Money income, 2013-2017				Income and poverty, 2017			
	Rate		School enrollment and attainment, 2013-2017				Local government expenditures,[5] 2014-2015			Households			Percent below poverty level			
			Enrollment[3]		Attainment[4] (percent)							Percent					
STATE County	Violent	Property	Total	Percent private	High school graduate or less	Bachelor's degree or more	Total current spending (mil dol)	Current spending per student (dollars)	Per capita income[6]	Median income (dollars)	with income of less than $50,000	with income of $200,000 or more	Median household income (dollars)	All persons	Children under 18 years	Children 5 to 17 years in families
	46	47	48	49	50	51	52	53	54	55	56	57	58	59	60	61

TEXAS— Cont'd

STATE County	Violent	Property	Total	Percent private	High school graduate or less	Bachelor's degree or more	Total current spending (mil dol)	Current spending per student (dollars)	Per capita income	Median income	with income of less than $50,000	with income of $200,000 or more	Median household income	All persons	Children under 18 years	Children 5 to 17 years in families
Tom Green	337	4,609	29,864	10.2	44.7	23.8	177.3	8,763	27,513	49,662	50.3	3.9	49,462	13.5	19.9	19.6
Travis	384	3,101	311,399	14.0	28.3	47.5	1,530.3	9,390	38,820	68,350	36.6	9.9	72,785	11.5	14.7	14.3
Trinity	173	1,471	2,701	6.1	54.5	11.7	22.6	9,851	20,369	37,398	65.9	0.6	34,741	21	35.0	34.3
Tyler	368	1,174	3,426	7.8	57.2	12.1	34.4	9,765	21,172	44,396	54.4	2.0	43,394	19.6	26.7	25.4
Upshur	268	1,611	9,463	10.9	50.3	16.9	66.7	9,368	24,088	48,796	51.1	2.8	47,517	16.4	23.7	21.3
Upton	135	405	994	1.5	59.4	11.1	13.4	16,236	25,290	52,750	46.9	5.3	56,448	14	21.1	20.7
Uvalde	220	2,854	7,086	4.6	53.3	15.1	57.2	9,696	19,146	40,781	58.7	1.9	39,610	20.5	33.4	32.8
Val Verde	143	2,113	12,576	7.5	58.2	18.1	96.7	8,894	20,160	44,609	55.4	2.9	41,441	21.4	30.6	30.6
Van Zandt	50	1,058	11,904	9.6	50.4	16.6	84.5	8,566	25,394	50,061	49.9	2.6	50,308	13.1	18.9	17.6
Victoria	406	3,023	22,926	12.6	48.0	19.5	141.3	9,105	28,181	55,740	45.0	4.2	52,161	15.7	23.2	22.0
Walker	370	1,459	20,555	4.3	53.9	20.3	74.0	9,567	17,194	41,456	57.8	2.1	42,304	23.1	23.9	24.1
Waller	330	1,441	16,922	5.3	52.6	19.2	88.5	8,900	23,888	53,506	47.3	5.7	55,224	15.5	22.4	20.3
Ward	612	2,382	2,763	3.3	57.6	13.5	21.4	8,883	26,860	63,333	39.0	4.0	53,242	15.1	21.2	19.7
Washington	201	1,494	8,373	9.0	45.1	23.9	46.9	8,885	28,517	55,793	45.9	4.7	51,276	12.9	18.6	18.5
Webb	362	3,002	88,808	6.0	60.2	17.4	611.3	8,884	16,316	40,442	58.7	2.7	41,979	27.3	36.2	35.3
Wharton	418	2,650	10,073	6.9	53.6	15.0	74.1	8,815	25,867	50,145	49.8	2.8	46,194	16	24.8	23.6
Wheeler	176	1,264	1,287	10.2	51.5	14.6	15.7	12,864	25,809	50,910	48.4	2.0	45,356	14.5	22.9	22.3
Wichita	388	3,315	32,925	7.5	45.6	22.4	184.2	8,872	23,263	45,776	53.9	2.4	44,593	16.8	21.0	20.3
Wilbarger	473	2,854	3,145	7.0	51.3	15.2	21.3	8,654	21,938	43,913	53.2	1.2	40,353	16.4	22.9	22.2
Willacy	652	2,718	5,393	3.7	71.3	9.0	47.3	10,720	13,369	29,104	68.1	0.7	30,392	35	44.4	43.5
Williamson	173	1,708	141,422	13.6	27.5	40.2	926.0	8,221	34,575	79,123	28.8	7.9	82,131	6.1	7.2	6.3
Wilson	122	1,068	11,676	9.3	50.4	19.5	70.9	8,054	29,862	71,942	34.9	5.8	70,829	9.1	13.6	12.4
Winkler	49	1,015	1,821	0.9	58.9	10.7	24.0	12,884	23,483	55,000	49.0	3.9	51,965	14.7	21.9	21.5
Wise	173	1,038	14,891	8.9	49.7	17.2	84.5	9,483	27,447	59,081	41.8	4.0	60,675	11.1	15.3	14.7
Wood	159	1,149	8,709	11.4	49.4	16.0	54.5	8,960	25,955	48,038	51.6	2.9	49,739	15.2	24.8	22.7
Yoakum	196	1,246	2,292	1.9	57.7	15.1	23.1	10,424	23,681	62,500	39.1	3.0	58,363	12	17.3	16.9
Young	138	1,288	4,242	6.3	51.9	19.6	31.5	9,179	25,661	46,351	52.4	1.7	44,909	15.8	24.5	22.9
Zapata	NA	NA	4,133	2.8	69.7	11.4	39.6	10,704	17,817	34,550	64.8	1.7	32,172	30	45.6	43.3
Zavala	276	1,333	3,378	1.4	69.6	7.6	28.2	11,033	13,105	25,988	73.2	1.0	28,867	31.6	43.3	41.6
UTAH	243	2,952	958,707	13.8	31.1	32.5	4,158.6	6,543	26,907	65,325	36.7	5.1	68,395	9.7	10.6	9.5
Beaver	18	2,182	1,846	4.0	48.0	18.5	13.6	8,817	21,128	47,878	52.8	0.6	51,187	9.2	12.6	12.0
Box Elder	143	2,108	15,858	7.8	38.0	22.7	73.2	6,127	22,808	58,835	41.6	1.8	63,624	7.9	10.1	8.4
Cache	70	1,113	46,613	6.1	28.1	36.9	163.1	6,486	21,752	53,812	46.7	2.9	55,036	15	11.7	10.8
Carbon	139	2,720	5,505	5.5	38.0	15.7	31.6	7,820	22,536	46,994	52.8	2.1	47,627	15.3	19.0	16.9
Daggett	0	0	138	5.1	48.2	9.3	3.2	15,257	28,533	85,000	36.3	0.0	55,521	6.7	9.7	9.1
Davis	102	1,812	109,515	10.2	25.5	36.2	501.2	6,232	28,293	75,961	27.9	5.2	80,433	5.4	6.3	5.8
Duchesne	425	3,196	5,894	7.1	48.5	14.5	36.7	6,939	23,323	63,000	39.1	1.9	60,569	13.3	16.6	15.3
Emery	156	1,031	2,863	5.4	39.2	15.0	24.3	10,263	21,465	51,852	46.6	0.9	52,877	13.2	17.2	15.6
Garfield	NA	NA	1,086	4.6	42.2	21.1	9.6	9,803	23,228	51,700	49.0	2.1	50,945	9.9	14.8	13.9
Grand	376	1,231	1,846	7.7	36.0	27.8	14.3	8,807	25,662	46,658	54.3	0.9	48,920	10.8	17.8	17.4
Iron	274	1,900	16,265	9.5	32.3	28.7	62.1	6,136	19,791	45,422	53.2	2.1	48,168	15.6	18.4	17.9
Juab	94	2,207	3,334	9.9	44.6	16.8	18.2	6,939	20,457	57,590	40.4	1.9	60,078	10.2	13.4	13.0
Kane	350	1,105	1,579	19.2	32.1	27.0	12.8	10,542	24,836	50,266	49.8	1.6	49,982	10.9	15.3	14.5
Millard	307	1,645	3,550	4.8	42.3	21.4	26.1	8,700	23,283	59,312	42.3	1.5	56,215	12.4	17.7	15.8
Morgan	NA	NA	3,888	16.3	20.4	40.0	15.0	5,322	30,457	86,071	23.9	10.2	96,201	4.1	4.5	4.1
Piute	132	859	428	8.2	52.5	22.7	4.6	14,137	17,455	41,750	55.6	0.0	41,334	16.7	31.8	27.2
Rich	86	1,373	655	11.3	33.3	22.8	6.5	13,332	19,512	52,917	47.1	4.5	58,807	9.2	13.5	12.8
Salt Lake	412	4,692	324,448	12.4	32.6	33.6	1,415.0	6,696	30,134	67,922	35.1	6.5	71,396	9.2	10.8	9.7
San Juan	81	955	4,711	5.8	47.4	17.3	34.8	11,053	17,385	42,581	57.4	1.3	43,962	25.9	32.7	28.4
Sanpete	97	926	9,237	10.0	38.2	19.2	43.4	7,485	17,426	50,928	48.9	1.4	52,251	14.2	15.6	15.1
Sevier	114	2,519	6,238	5.5	42.0	16.8	32.1	6,685	21,196	50,850	49.2	1.5	52,668	12.4	15.7	14.3
Summit	126	1,911	10,047	12.7	20.7	53.5	80.8	9,927	52,671	94,952	23.4	19.2	100,879	4.9	5.7	5.2
Tooele	306	2,724	20,271	10.5	38.3	22.6	96.8	6,335	24,069	66,542	33.5	2.0	72,198	6.8	8.4	7.3
Uintah	117	1,649	10,740	12.5	49.2	14.3	55.0	6,750	25,001	67,012	37.5	3.9	57,355	12.7	15.7	14.5
Utah	78	1,766	226,961	23.8	22.0	39.4	799.5	5,831	23,207	67,042	35.3	4.9	70,461	10.5	9.1	7.8
Wasatch	92	849	8,856	13.5	25.8	38.7	48.0	7,546	30,086	74,552	30.9	7.0	83,344	5.2	7.0	6.4
Washington	169	1,715	44,937	11.5	31.0	28.1	199.9	6,398	25,415	55,175	44.7	3.8	55,518	11.2	14.3	12.5
Wayne	NA	NA	684	3.4	35.2	26.0	5.9	11,168	22,195	42,444	56.9	0.4	43,805	13.7	22.4	21.0
Weber	236	2,931	70,714	8.6	39.1	24.0	331.0	6,686	25,275	62,036	39.1	2.9	62,937	10.8	12.5	11.8
VERMONT	158	1,697	146,742	20.8	37.3	36.8	1,557.4	18,035	31,917	57,808	43.3	4.5	58,271	10.8	12.8	11.6
Addison	62	879	9,391	37.7	38.5	36.7	89.4	19,198	31,051	61,875	40.6	4.1	59,467	8.3	10.0	8.4
Bennington	177	1,586	7,888	26.9	39.3	34.3	84.8	16,263	31,313	52,251	47.7	4.4	52,770	12.3	16.8	15.7
Caledonia	118	1,727	6,837	21.4	46.8	27.9	63.8	15,396	25,896	47,371	52.8	2.3	46,299	15	20.1	17.8

1. Data for serious crimes have not been adjusted for underreporting; this may affect comparability between geographic areas and over time.   2. Per 100,000 population estimated by the FBI.   3. All persons 3 years old and over enrolled in nursery school through college.   4. Persons 25 years old and over.   5. Elementary and secondary education expenditures.   6. Based on population estimated by the American Community Survey, 2011–2015.

Table B. States and Counties — **Personal Income and Earnings**

STATE County	Personal income, 2017										Earnings, 2017		
	Total (mil dol)	Percent change 2016-2017	Per capita[1] Dollars	Per capita[1] Rank	Wages and salaries (mil dol)	Supplements to wages and salaries, employer contributions (mil dol) Pension and insurance	Supplements to wages and salaries, employer contributions (mil dol) Government social insurance	Proprietors' income (mil dol)	Dividends, interest, and rent (mil dol)	Personal transfer receipts (mil dol)	Total (mil dol)	Contributions for government social insurance (mil dol) From employee and self-employed	Contributions for government social insurance (mil dol) From employer
	62	63	64	65	66	67	68	69	70	71	72	73	74

STATE County	62	63	64	65	66	67	68	69	70	71	72	73	74
TEXAS— Cont'd													
Tom Green	5,038	1.9	42,688	1,187	2,198	399	161	382	1,164	1,054	3,140	175	161
Travis	76,306	6.0	62,205	134	49,638	6,328	3,306	10,032	18,572	6,320	69,303	3,529	3,306
Trinity	504	2.2	34,383	2,430	85	17	6	27	67	190	135	12	6
Tyler	680	1.3	31,551	2,802	144	36	9	27	100	233	217	16	9
Upshur	1,436	2.4	34,783	2,376	287	57	20	83	179	411	447	32	20
Upton	144	2.6	39,222	1,686	109	21	7	8	30	28	145	8	7
Uvalde	998	0.5	36,797	2,077	363	79	26	69	223	301	537	31	26
Val Verde	1,709	1.5	34,732	2,382	772	187	63	101	278	418	1,123	63	63
Van Zandt	2,022	3.8	36,649	2,098	411	75	30	140	279	576	656	46	30
Victoria	3,912	0.7	42,484	1,203	1,839	300	129	262	793	888	2,530	146	129
Walker	1,972	1.8	27,302	3,053	1,022	273	59	70	422	482	1,424	68	59
Waller	1,924	2.6	37,508	1,943	777	142	53	122	264	353	1,094	58	53
Ward	477	9.7	41,579	1,320	277	42	19	22	63	95	359	21	19
Washington	1,673	-0.4	47,741	643	619	112	43	115	397	403	888	53	43
Webb	8,246	1.8	30,008	2,929	3,789	768	271	856	1,242	1,994	5,685	299	271
Wharton	1,701	3.0	40,535	1,467	619	107	45	130	268	422	902	50	45
Wheeler	209	1.1	38,978	1,724	90	18	6	18	53	61	131	7	6
Wichita	5,284	0.4	40,034	1,545	2,523	499	191	342	1,142	1,279	3,555	196	191
Wilbarger	505	1.0	39,542	1,628	223	56	15	25	99	148	318	17	15
Willacy	649	10.6	30,047	2,925	131	29	10	157	55	234	326	13	10
Williamson	26,332	7.1	48,091	616	9,670	1,213	649	2,058	3,727	2,900	13,589	763	649
Wilson	2,082	4.3	42,219	1,241	333	67	22	102	304	392	525	35	22
Winkler	325	7.6	42,940	1,146	170	28	11	18	54	64	228	13	11
Wise	2,735	4.2	41,321	1,362	928	167	64	215	392	495	1,374	78	64
Wood	1,658	3.5	37,426	1,963	398	76	29	123	293	587	625	48	29
Yoakum	341	15.7	39,807	1,588	226	38	15	39	40	63	318	16	15
Young	816	-1.9	45,405	855	299	57	21	97	170	212	474	28	21
Zapata	391	5.4	27,325	3,051	183	36	13	6	55	123	238	14	13
Zavala	331	2.3	27,695	3,040	121	23	9	10	49	129	163	10	9
UTAH	134,804	5.0	43,441	X	72,321	12,056	5,635	10,682	28,356	17,392	100,695	5,966	5,635
Beaver	188	2.7	29,364	2,962	113	21	12	-20	40	51	125	9	12
Box Elder	1,923	5.6	35,552	2,266	892	157	73	95	323	324	1,218	76	73
Cache	4,585	5.7	36,847	2,068	2,150	449	170	540	896	640	3,309	186	170
Carbon	722	2.3	35,573	2,261	349	69	28	31	123	195	477	32	28
Daggett	40	0.4	39,087	1,704	15	4	1	1	12	8	20	1	1
Davis	15,333	5.3	44,106	1,010	6,254	1,252	513	869	2,896	1,693	8,887	517	513
Duchesne	678	1.9	33,878	2,497	379	79	30	27	122	127	515	31	30
Emery	304	-0.4	30,131	2,920	144	34	12	9	53	83	199	13	12
Garfield	183	5.9	35,988	2,205	84	16	8	6	44	40	114	8	8
Grand	480	7.9	49,593	491	203	34	17	50	154	78	304	20	17
Iron	1,535	5.3	30,088	2,922	657	138	53	49	320	351	897	58	53
Juab	383	5.9	34,089	2,476	133	26	11	25	49	73	196	12	11
Kane	287	4.7	37,981	1,890	126	22	10	18	74	62	177	12	10
Millard	452	3.4	35,174	2,320	209	45	17	34	81	95	305	17	17
Morgan	582	6.8	49,013	537	101	17	8	36	101	56	161	10	8
Piute	46	4.8	32,046	2,748	9	2	1	4	9	16	16	1	1
Rich	82	2.9	34,121	2,471	26	5	2	10	24	15	44	2	2
Salt Lake	56,153	4.5	49,445	501	38,509	6,059	2,935	5,279	11,943	6,565	52,782	3,080	2,935
San Juan	382	3.8	24,905	3,093	169	39	14	14	72	107	236	15	14
Sanpete	832	4.9	27,710	3,039	268	64	22	80	145	199	435	26	22
Sevier	675	5.0	31,677	2,790	335	68	27	30	126	168	461	30	27
Summit	5,012	6.7	121,932	6	1,309	156	102	432	2,174	198	1,999	115	102
Tooele	2,372	7.6	35,166	2,322	728	137	59	65	305	330	989	63	59
Uintah	1,053	2.3	29,962	2,934	602	112	48	20	214	180	783	48	48
Utah	23,134	5.0	38,149	1,855	11,065	1,690	858	1,959	4,317	2,715	15,572	916	858
Wasatch	1,576	8.4	49,092	528	374	60	29	67	416	140	529	34	29
Washington	5,825	5.8	35,161	2,325	2,450	418	196	415	1,444	1,293	3,480	237	196
Wayne	96	6.3	35,126	2,330	36	8	3	4	26	21	51	4	3
Weber	9,891	5.1	39,286	1,676	4,631	876	375	532	1,852	1,570	6,414	392	375
VERMONT	32,570	3.2	52,152	X	14,846	2,769	1,264	2,722	6,752	6,562	21,601	1,437	1,264
Addison	1,826	3.5	49,645	488	743	131	64	187	393	316	1,126	74	64
Bennington	1,850	3.9	51,980	375	757	139	67	170	464	421	1,133	79	67
Caledonia	1,206	2.6	39,977	1,554	449	94	39	95	228	309	676	49	39

1. Based on the resident population estimated as of July 1 of the year shown.

Table B. States and Counties — Earnings, Social Security, and Housing

STATE County	Earnings, 2017 (cont.) Percent by selected industries									Social Security beneficiaries, December 2017		Supplemental Security Income recipients, 2017	Housing units, 2018	
	Farm	Mining, quarrying, and extractions	Construction	Manufacturing	Information; professional, scientific, technical services	Retail trade	Finance, insurance, real estate, and leasing	Health care and social assistance	Government	Number	Rate[1]		Total	Percent change, 2010-2018
	75	76	77	78	79	80	81	82	83	84	85	86	87	88
TEXAS— Cont'd														
Tom Green	1.1	3.7	5.9	8.8	5.6	7.7	7.3	15.5	25	22,320	189	2,907	48,620	4.4
Travis	0	3.4	7.5	6.8	22.5	4.7	9.2	7.9	15	126,985	104	16,957	527,803	19.6
Trinity	-3.1	D	5.3	9.5	D	4.8	D	D	25.1	4,525	309	606	9,054	3.9
Tyler	3	1.1	4.4	4.2	D	8.1	D	D	43.3	5,390	250	666	10,860	2.7
Upshur	2.6	1.9	15.5	4.6	12.9	5.1	3.9	D	21.9	9,300	225	1,111	17,112	3
Upton	-2	42.6	7.6	0.2	D	D	D	0.5	20.7	595	162	74	1,559	0.8
Uvalde	0.3	1.3	4.9	4.2	D	9	5.5	D	33.7	5,635	208	1,106	11,168	3.3
Val Verde	0.1	0.8	3.5	7.4	D	8.3	3.6	9.3	46.6	8,655	176	2,131	19,280	3.4
Van Zandt	3.6	0.7	16.9	8.8	D	9.9	3.9	6.7	19.1	13,210	239	1,276	23,464	2.9
Victoria	0	8.5	8.1	8	4.3	8.4	5.4	15.5	16.5	18,120	197	2,556	37,072	4.7
Walker	0.4	0.2	3.3	5.1	3.3	6.3	3.8	8	59.1	10,015	139	1,330	26,408	9.8
Waller	2.2	3.6	9.8	24.8	D	3.8	2.9	3.2	24.6	6,830	133	926	17,241	8.7
Ward	-0.2	38.7	6.8	3	3.4	3.8	4.6	0.9	13.9	2,000	174	258	4,808	2.4
Washington	-0.4	0.8	7	18.2	5.9	8	10.7	8.4	19.7	8,410	240	952	16,340	5.4
Webb	0	3.6	3.8	0.6	4.7	7.5	5.5	11.2	28.5	34,010	124	12,364	84,455	14.9
Wharton	8.5	6.9	6.1	9.1	D	10.8	5.6	8.8	17.7	8,490	202	1,148	17,636	3
Wheeler	4.5	28	5.4	0.6	D	5.1	4.7	3.4	24.7	1,135	212	78	2,715	-0.5
Wichita	-0.3	3.6	4.5	9.9	4	7.6	6	15.6	30.7	25,510	193	4,154	56,002	0.8
Wilbarger	-0.6	0.7	2.3	17	D	7.6	4.1	4.3	39.8	2,855	224	417	6,229	-1.4
Willacy	41.3	D	1.5	0.6	D	3.4	3.1	6.4	20.9	3,820	177	1,267	7,372	4.7
Williamson	0	0.5	11.3	12.6	11.3	8.7	6.9	8.5	11.2	72,095	132	4,594	198,630	22.1
Wilson	0.7	3.5	14.6	7.1	5.3	10.2	4.1	D	26.3	8,900	181	662	17,759	5.9
Winkler	-0.3	D	20.7	0.6	D	3.3	2.9	D	15.3	1,215	160	218	3,100	2.4
Wise	-0.3	11.8	10.4	9.6	5.1	7.4	4.7	7	20.3	11,790	178	774	24,927	4.9
Wood	3.8	3.9	10.5	12.4	6.4	8.3	6.2	D	16.6	14,340	324	1,066	21,339	2.3
Yoakum	3.5	39	7.8	1.7	1.1	3.4	5.3	D	15.1	1,310	153	131	3,056	2.6
Young	-1.5	11	7	20.4	4.2	5.5	13.2	7.8	15.7	4,455	248	475	8,723	1.2
Zapata	-3.2	40.2	5.2	1.9	D	3.1	D	3.5	29.2	2,145	150	638	6,463	4.2
Zavala	0.2	3	D	D	D	2.9	D	7.7	26.7	2,185	183	744	4,367	2
UTAH	0.3	0.6	8.2	9.6	12.7	7.7	9.6	8.6	16.2	395,718	128	31,756	1,108,763	13.2
Beaver	22.6	-24.5	6.1	4.9	1.9	8.2	D	D	31.1	1,185	186	69	3,046	4.7
Box Elder	2.4	0.1	8.2	38.2	2.8	5.3	3	6.2	12.2	8,660	160	587	19,085	10.1
Cache	1.1	0	4.9	21.2	9.1	6.8	9.8	9.5	19.2	13,865	111	873	42,243	14.1
Carbon	0	D	5.1	4.8	3	7.4	3.9	D	22.1	4,760	235	505	9,836	3
Daggett	0.8	D	D	D	D	D	D	1.6	59.7	245	238	0	1,209	5.9
Davis	0.1	0.1	9.4	10.2	9.8	7	5.4	7.8	29	39,730	114	2,414	110,412	13.2
Duchesne	1.8	27.8	6.3	1.7	D	5.6	3.7	D	22.2	3,370	168	322	10,392	9.5
Emery	0.7	10.9	9.9	0.9	D	6.5	D	D	21.3	2,250	223	130	4,618	2.9
Garfield	1.8	D	2.7	2	D	4.6	2.1	D	28	1,220	240	32	3,915	5.1
Grand	0.2	D	7.7	2.5	D	12	10	7.9	19.8	2,015	208	124	5,566	15.6
Iron	1.6	0.4	6.9	10.6	3.7	9	6.8	10.6	27.8	8,235	161	697	21,593	9.8
Juab	1.3	0.6	9.1	24.9	D	4	D	D	19.1	1,760	156	123	3,824	9.2
Kane	0.5	D	4.2	4.5	2.9	7.2	3.4	3.3	23.7	1,970	260	62	6,082	4.6
Millard	11.4	2.7	3.2	5	D	5.7	D	D	18.5	2,495	194	136	5,112	3.5
Morgan	2.6	D	22.8	9.3	8.5	5.3	9	4.2	15.8	1,515	128	40	3,658	21.7
Piute	13.8	-0.6	D	D	D	D	D	D	40.1	465	327	21	991	10.2
Rich	19.4	D	8.8	D	D	6.2	D	2.6	24.3	435	182	0	3,123	10.2
Salt Lake	0	0.3	7.2	8.4	13.9	7.4	12.5	7.7	14.5	140,125	123	13,757	403,666	10.9
San Juan	-0.3	10.3	5.2	1.5	D	3.1	1.7	17.3	38.9	2,240	146	590	6,019	5
Sanpete	11.2	0.2	6.7	10.8	D	5.5	3.1	7.7	30.8	5,020	167	350	10,803	4.1
Sevier	2.6	10.7	4	5.5	3.7	10	3.8	D	18.9	4,360	205	320	8,900	5.4
Summit	0.2	0.3	9.1	3.4	13.4	7.2	13.7	5.2	8.8	5,230	127	109	28,302	6.6
Tooele	1.2	0.5	5.7	10.5	D	6	3.4	7.4	28.5	7,965	118	698	22,462	15.5
Uintah	0.3	22.3	7.2	0.8	2.8	7.9	4.4	6.1	22.3	4,480	127	394	13,757	14.9
Utah	0.4	0	11	9.1	19.1	10.1	5.3	9.2	10.7	56,000	92	4,211	180,062	21.3
Wasatch	0.1	D	19.8	4.2	11.1	8.1	3.3	9.1	18.3	3,890	121	117	13,830	30.8
Washington	0	0.2	10.7	5.4	7.5	9.8	8.7	17.4	13.6	36,865	223	1,430	71,363	23.6
Wayne	1.5	D	16.9	0.6	D	5.8	D	10.3	29.1	640	235	21	1,680	5.6
Weber	0.2	0.1	7.7	16.6	6.3	6.9	7.5	12.7	19.9	34,730	138	3,612	93,214	8.2
VERMONT	0.9	0.2	7.7	10.4	9.9	7.3	5.8	14.8	18.7	147,683	237	15,374	337,110	4.5
Addison	3.8	0.2	8.4	13.4	6.6	8.2	3.6	D	11.6	8,135	221	551	17,614	5.1
Bennington	0.5	0	6.6	12.6	D	9.7	4.8	18.2	13.3	10,055	282	1,207	21,173	1.2
Caledonia	1.2	D	9.4	11.6	6.3	8.7	3.5	16.8	18.9	7,860	261	932	16,439	3.1

1. Per 1,000 resident population estimated as of July 1 of the year shown.

Table B. States and Counties — Housing, Labor Force, and Employment

STATE County	Housing units, 2013-2017								Civilian labor force, 2018				Civilian employment[6], 2013-2017		
	Occupied units							Sub-standard units[4] (percent)			Unemployment			Percent	
			Owner-occupied			Renter-occupied					Percent change, 2017-2018				
				Median owner cost as a percent of income			Median rent as a percent of income[2]								Construction, production, and maintenance occupations
	Total	Percent	Median value[1]	With a mortgage	Without a mortgage[2]	Median rent[3]			Total		Total	Rate[5]	Total	Management, business, science, and arts	
	89	90	91	92	93	94	95	96	97	98	99	100	101	102	103

TEXAS— Cont'd

STATE County	89	90	91	92	93	94	95	96	97	98	99	100	101	102	103
Tom Green	43,081	63.1	122,600	20.5	10.5	832	29.2	3.4	54,959	1.4	1,738	3.2	53,414	32.2	24.7
Travis	447,561	52.3	275,800	21.9	12.1	1,172	29.5	4.8	721,786	3.2	20,404	2.8	645,807	47.4	14.7
Trinity	5,934	77.8	75,300	20.5	13.7	723	31	3.8	5,346	-0.7	275	5.1	4,946	27.5	26.0
Tyler	7,312	84.3	81,500	19.1	11.1	722	36	5.2	7,009		462	6.6	6,746	23.6	32.9
Upshur	14,061	77.0	111,600	19.2	11.3	749	24.8	5.2	17,841	0.6	746	4.2	16,720	29.1	30.1
Upton	1,308	72.9	62,900	18.6	10.0	643	21	4.3	1,580	2	54	3.4	1,398	27.4	41.8
Uvalde	8,624	72.9	77,800	22.3	12.5	629	28	6.3	11,506	-1.8	495	4.3	11,605	24.1	31.6
Val Verde	15,189	63.2	94,500	19.6	11.4	688	24.3	7.5	20,445	1.7	876	4.3	18,667	25.5	29.9
Van Zandt	19,354	77.1	112,600	21.1	12.7	774	24.9	3	25,908	1.9	904	3.5	22,384	30.0	27.6
Victoria	32,734	65.6	129,100	20.0	10.0	864	28.6	5	43,370	0.9	1,653	3.8	43,077	30.0	27.3
Walker	21,294	52.8	132,200	20.0	10.7	838	33.8	3.1	23,970	1.1	1,009	4.2	24,044	31.7	18.5
Waller	14,698	68.6	157,600	22.2	10.9	853	32.2	6.9	22,763	1.6	977	4.3	21,837	26.5	26.9
Ward	3,954	70.0	85,600	16.9	10.0	801	18.1	4.6	6,678	19.4	172	2.6	4,823	28.6	37.8
Washington	12,205	77.0	163,400	21.0	11.2	854	28.7	3.4	14,966	0.5	547	3.7	14,897	32.7	27.4
Webb	72,379	63.0	115,500	24.4	13.5	784	33.8	14.6	116,573	1.2	4,383	3.8	102,713	26.2	22.8
Wharton	15,224	67.5	115,700	19.4	10.9	727	24.7	5	21,416	1.4	796	3.7	18,767	25.4	34.2
Wheeler	2,287	63.9	86,500	20.4	10.0	630	23	5.6	2,474	5.1	78	3.2	2,551	25.5	33.6
Wichita	48,528	61.3	93,200	20.5	12.1	770	29.7	3	56,739	1.1	1,937	3.4	55,552	33.2	22.2
Wilbarger	5,155	64.8	69,900	19.9	12.2	638	20	3.5	4,993	0.5	207	4.1	6,329	26.5	26.5
Willacy	5,737	77.8	49,100	23.0	13.5	576	27	10.3	6,381	0.8	634	9.9	6,415	21.5	31.3
Williamson	170,051	68.9	227,100	21.0	11.3	1,172	28.2	2.6	300,336	3.2	9,168	3.1	254,840	45.6	15.1
Wilson	15,755	83.5	170,600	21.4	11.0	895	26	5.1	24,556	1.4	750	3.1	21,002	31.8	26.6
Winkler	2,524	78.2	58,200	15.6	10.0	820	18.4	5.3	4,030	23.5	113	2.8	3,267	23.5	40.8
Wise	21,691	76.7	141,700	21.3	11.8	945	29.1	4.1	30,816	2	1,063	3.4	27,736	29.6	31.4
Wood	16,122	80.4	117,000	22.8	11.7	755	30	2.7	17,343	-0.1	736	4.2	15,960	28.7	29.6
Yoakum	2,652	77.5	81,900	19.4	10.0	735	25.1	8.8	3,736	-2.4	106	2.8	3,755	21.8	42.2
Young	7,066	78.3	87,500	17.6	11.6	625	21.5	4.4	8,187	1.3	265	3.2	8,248	31.5	28.7
Zapata	4,457	72.3	60,700	22.9	10.0	523	30.2	15.6	5,376	-0.4	299	5.6	5,146	17.7	37.0
Zavala	3,536	69.3	39,900	28.7	11.6	541	38.9	12	3,593	-3.8	343	9.5	4,397	29.0	32.0
UTAH	938,365	69.6	238,300	21.5	10.0	948	28	3.7	1,572,136	1.5	48,978	3.1	1,412,214	37.7	21.2
Beaver	2,313	71.0	147,300	18.3	10.5	687	23.8	6.6	3,014		106	3.5	2,653	23.9	32.4
Box Elder	17,035	76.2	179,600	21.5	10.0	709	25.4	1.9	25,435	0.4	773	3	22,319	31.5	33.1
Cache	36,829	63.1	202,400	21.3	10.0	745	29.2	3.2	63,262	1	1,699	2.7	56,905	37.9	23.7
Carbon	7,841	72.8	129,900	19.4	10.0	651	27.1	2.7	8,477	2.3	385	4.5	8,906	27.9	29.5
Daggett	168	93.5	202,900	15.2	10.0	0	0	0.6	410	-4.4	18	4.4	293	19.8	29.0
Davis	101,422	77.3	246,500	20.9	10.0	986	26.5	2.4	170,592	1.1	5,005	2.9	155,828	40.6	18.8
Duchesne	6,650	74.3	178,100	20.9	10.0	848	24.9	4.9	7,724	-3.2	355	4.6	8,026	30.7	36.9
Emery	3,564	79.9	136,200	18.4	10.0	607	21.7	3.5	4,342	3.6	208	4.8	4,030	29.0	31.6
Garfield	1,756	80.0	166,300	22.2	10.0	788	19.8	3.2	2,789	-3.9	217	7.8	2,212	26.4	21.7
Grand	3,873	70.0	230,900	19.2	10.0	777	32.5	3.9	6,084	2.5	289	4.8	4,859	28.0	21.1
Iron	15,575	64.4	183,100	22.1	10.0	716	29.9	2.7	22,815	2.5	814	3.6	20,960	31.5	23.3
Juab	3,287	80.8	175,800	21.2	10.0	728	23	5	5,574	2.8	166	3	4,602	27.9	32.6
Kane	2,514	81.0	190,200	21.7	10.2	918	21.4	1	3,798	1.4	122	3.2	3,152	30.6	20.2
Millard	4,235	78.6	150,300	18.0	10.0	678	21.6	2.8	6,239	-3	204	3.3	5,546	29.4	36.1
Morgan	3,236	84.5	311,000	21.5	10.0	1,156	24	1.5	5,446	1	152	2.8	4,701	41.7	23.3
Piute	516	88.2	143,800	20.8	10.7	725	22.8	2.5	482	-0.4	26	5.4	636	38.7	16.0
Rich	601	76.7	160,400	17.4	10.0	597	30	3.3	1,176	3.1	39	3.3	671	29.2	35.2
Salt Lake	363,058	66.5	260,700	21.4	10.0	1,015	28.1	3.7	620,909	1	18,786	3	564,689	38.8	19.9
San Juan	4,019	80.5	136,600	20.9	10.5	629	23.2	11.7	5,755	1	359	6.2	5,247	33.2	26.2
Sanpete	8,366	74.0	169,400	22.1	10.5	714	24	6.3	12,476	3.8	465	3.7	10,784	34.2	28.2
Sevier	7,171	76.7	152,800	20.2	10.0	740	27.5	1.9	9,879	0.9	354	3.6	8,634	27.0	32.8
Summit	14,781	73.7	558,300	21.0	10.0	1,230	25.6	2.2	24,320	-0.1	739	3	21,711	46.8	15.5
Tooele	19,562	79.2	196,300	21.8	10.0	871	26	2.3	32,612	0.9	1,126	3.5	28,406	32.1	27.9
Uintah	10,616	76.3	194,800	21.2	10.0	952	24.2	3.9	13,595	-0.7	641	4.7	15,087	28.6	34.1
Utah	155,664	67.3	256,900	21.9	10.0	954	29.1	4.8	299,868	3.1	8,477	2.8	257,679	41.0	17.4
Wasatch	9,040	69.8	357,300	23.1	10.5	1,257	27.5	4.5	15,108	3.4	475	3.1	14,397	36.7	18.0
Washington	52,385	70.1	240,300	24.4	10.0	983	29.7	5	73,929	4.5	2,517	3.4	62,920	30.9	21.2
Wayne	990	76.6	175,800	20.0	10.0	574	26.2	3.7	1,435	-1.8	86	6	1,215	30.0	27.8
Weber	81,298	71.8	183,100	21.0	10.0	825	27.7	3.2	124,592	1	4,375	3.5	115,146	32.9	27.8
VERMONT	258,535	70.5	220,600	23.7	15.9	945	30.6	2.3	346,061	0	9,223	2.7	327,264	40.7	20.7
Addison	14,701	72.4	237,000	24.6	16.2	955	28	1.6	20,782	-0.1	534	2.6	19,872	40.8	24.6
Bennington	15,280	72.9	208,600	24.8	16.9	858	29.3	1.5	18,308	0.1	576	3.1	17,605	36.1	23.5
Caledonia	12,094	73.2	164,500	23.8	17.0	737	30.4	2.8	14,770	0.4	481	3.3	14,475	34.8	24.9

1. Specified owner-occupied units. 2. A value of 10.0 represents 10 percent or less; a value of 50.0 represents 50 percent or more. 3. Specified renter-occupied units. 4. Overcrowded or lacking complete plumbing facilities. 5. Percent of civilian labor force. 6. Civilian employed persons 16 years old and over.

Table B. States and Counties — Nonfarm Employment and Agriculture

STATE County	Private nonfarm establishments, employment and payroll, 2016									Agriculture, 2017			Farm producers whose primary occupation is farming (percent)
	Number of establish-ments	Employment						Annual payroll		Farms			
		Total	Health care and social assistance	Manufac-turing	Retail trade	Finance and insurance	Professional, scientific, and technical services	Total (mil dol)	Average per employee (dollars)	Number	Percent with:		
											Fewer than 50 acres	1000 acres or more	
	104	105	106	107	108	109	110	111	112	113	114	115	116

STATE County	104	105	106	107	108	109	110	111	112	113	114	115	116
TEXAS— Cont'd													
Tom Green	2,769	39,784	7,400	3,210	6,854	1,565	1,399	1,502	37,746	1,303	56.3	10.3	29.4
Travis	34,547	582,889	69,113	26,202	63,280	27,843	79,605	34,479	59,153	1,099	57.0	4.7	39.5
Trinity	162	1,638	265	185	255	57	68	51	30,947	601	43.3	2.3	39.6
Tyler	261	2,259	494	236	629	72	48	68	30,169	778	61.2	2.3	35.0
Upshur	493	4,586	395	381	799	238	431	155	33,746	1,652	51.2	0.9	32.5
Upton	86	1,235	D	NA	77	20	D	66	53,096	98	13.3	62.2	48.7
Uvalde	626	8,753	2,982	388	1,523	245	188	242	27,682	592	30.9	15.4	35.4
Val Verde	765	10,677	3,086	435	2,148	464	251	271	25,346	528	46.4	25.6	38.3
Van Zandt	862	8,025	1,066	765	1,517	237	303	272	33,896	3,405	56.0	1.5	35.2
Victoria	2,358	34,326	7,268	1,981	6,308	929	1,140	1,392	40,565	1,286	51.5	6.3	30.1
Walker	973	12,091	2,111	834	2,792	398	400	355	29,345	1,441	58.3	2.8	34.2
Waller	748	10,720	1,229	2,569	1,034	119	254	446	41,579	1,881	64.5	2.6	34.3
Ward	291	3,466	240	42	337	87	67	174	50,306	102	32.4	32.4	18.9
Washington	878	12,604	1,982	2,691	2,118	817	359	428	33,919	2,607	48.7	0.8	33.3
Webb	5,298	77,269	16,139	652	13,530	2,639	1,820	2,219	28,720	656	19.1	22.6	36.3
Wharton	978	11,394	1,895	1,388	2,255	412	263	370	32,452	1,500	42.3	10.0	37.7
Wheeler	188	1,646	283	D	266	56	48	50	30,662	510	9.6	24.9	35.4
Wichita	3,071	44,908	11,294	4,381	7,430	1,638	1,663	1,589	35,382	614	47.9	12.5	33.7
Wilbarger	294	3,416	304	D	703	135	57	116	34,002	395	18.7	23.8	39.6
Willacy	194	2,027	500	D	296	87	28	61	30,037	351	54.1	16.5	43.8
Williamson	10,280	151,143	21,700	8,081	25,280	7,945	19,790	7,297	48,280	2,634	57.3	4.6	31.4
Wilson	679	6,351	1,182	368	1,435	182	226	206	32,420	2,621	45.6	2.4	36.0
Winkler	171	1,764	86	NA	259	62	7	112	63,240	46	17.4	60.9	63.3
Wise	1,296	18,065	3,015	1,835	2,310	370	342	802	44,392	3,697	63.2	2.4	32.6
Wood	809	8,930	1,287	940	1,470	355	916	287	32,110	1,587	48.0	1.6	39.8
Yoakum	194	2,458	D	127	262	96	12	138	56,151	291	14.8	41.6	46.1
Young	581	5,629	1,212	836	823	248	122	214	37,976	853	22.2	13.7	36.2
Zapata	147	1,568	267	16	288	89	D	50	31,893	412	12.1	27.9	31.2
Zavala	107	1,595	619	D	193	45	21	37	23,307	281	14.2	35.2	44.6
UTAH	77,504	1,239,348	138,929	120,947	156,070	65,259	88,760	54,331	43,839	18,409	62.1	6.9	32.1
Beaver	170	1,801	285	109	455	39	15	51	28,049	272	41.5	9.6	45.8
Box Elder	1,115	17,316	1,600	7,231	1,776	278	246	841	48,582	1,187	50.5	15.4	37.8
Cache	3,344	42,345	5,266	11,825	6,331	1,271	3,364	1,409	33,273	1,397	58.3	3.8	30.3
Carbon	493	5,787	1,026	411	1,119	216	107	215	37,190	309	69.9	13.3	26.4
Daggett	22	121	NA	NA	39	NA	D	3	28,438	52	40.4	11.5	29.2
Davis	7,060	87,062	10,442	11,029	15,385	3,091	8,879	3,389	38,931	528	90.3	1.3	30.8
Duchesne	630	5,734	1,073	189	763	93	226	257	44,743	1,063	49.6	5.3	28.9
Emery	184	2,106	143	14	478	34	63	105	49,702	504	51.6	6.9	34.5
Garfield	171	1,426	D	25	137	19	18	46	32,360	286	51.7	7.0	36.5
Grand	459	4,445	364	90	758	64	134	125	28,159	102	49.0	8.8	37.4
Iron	1,349	12,402	2,088	1,626	2,263	474	422	378	30,517	486	37.9	16.7	42.1
Juab	204	2,459	479	588	316	30	267	81	32,811	292	27.7	14.7	26.4
Kane	250	2,631	217	101	389	96	33	81	30,903	182	41.2	17.0	33.3
Millard	257	2,973	239	528	590	66	97	134	45,191	654	28.0	18.3	39.0
Morgan	278	1,661	216	149	197	56	104	73	43,983	372	63.4	7.3	26.5
Piute	28	58	D	D	21	D	NA	2	29,345	104	31.7	16.3	36.1
Rich	93	453	D	D	28	D	28	22	37,302	160	31.9	32.5	44.5
Salt Lake	31,598	580,855	63,360	50,712	65,558	42,521	47,255	28,788	49,561	592	87.2	2.0	31.6
San Juan	256	2,676	659	149	362	105	22	90	33,771	823	52.5	13.0	64.9
Sanpete	431	5,007	885	813	968	124	598	148	29,512	1,003	52.9	6.3	35.4
Sevier	520	6,529	880	263	1,457	138	144	225	34,392	691	67.6	2.9	30.3
Summit	2,363	27,584	1,363	550	4,161	1,191	1,140	958	34,724	626	67.6	5.4	26.5
Tooele	835	10,716	1,282	1,676	1,872	222	442	391	36,449	540	63.3	7.6	29.1
Uintah	1,046	9,069	740	227	1,729	200	388	379	41,804	1,114	56.7	6.3	30.3
Utah	12,852	203,985	24,822	16,977	26,846	5,626	14,788	8,362	40,995	2,589	82.2	1.9	23.6
Wasatch	919	6,690	715	256	1,197	134	448	226	33,713	475	82.3	1.9	23.2
Washington	4,795	49,056	9,298	2,574	9,117	1,436	2,076	1,638	33,389	537	60.5	5.8	26.8
Wayne	86	630	D	2	134	NA	6	18	29,343	209	51.2	5.3	36.4
Weber	5,212	77,637	11,020	12,832	11,601	4,318	3,899	3,032	39,054	1,260	85.0	0.8	24.2
VERMONT	21,174	262,705	48,818	29,913	39,998	9,539	12,916	10,828	41,219	6,808	41.1	2.3	42.1
Addison	1,164	14,006	2,084	1,680	2,030	323	635	556	39,694	720	40.0	5.1	46.6
Bennington	1,387	14,924	3,324	2,214	2,910	313	380	551	36,928	250	56.4	2.4	35.4
Caledonia	895	8,689	1,840	1,245	1,603	276	249	320	36,851	585	40.9	0.5	37.8

682 TX(Tom Green)—VT(Caledonia)

Table B. States and Counties — **Agriculture**

STATE County	Land in farms Acreage (1,000)	Percent change, 2012-2017	Acres Average size of farm	Total irrigated (1,000)	Total cropland (1,000)	Value of land and buildings (dollars) Average per farm	Average per acre	Value of machinery and equiopmnet, average per farm (dollars)	Value of products sold: Total (mil dol)	Average per farm (acres)	Percent from: Crops	Livestock and poultry products	Organic farms (number)	Farms with internet access (percent)	Government payments Total ($1,000)	Percent of farms
	117	118	119	120	121	122	123	124	125	126	127	128	129	130	131	132
TEXAS— Cont'd																
Tom Green	813	-15.0	624	19.6	125.0	980,735	1,572	76,726	100.0	76,769	29.9	70.1	1	75.4	2,964	13.4
Travis	222	-12.2	202	2.0	55.1	1,263,065	6,256	62,118	28.1	25,578	71.3	28.7	8	78.3	884	11.9
Trinity	99	-11.1	165	0.3	20.1	435,080	2,644	70,677	8.2	13,691	25.6	74.4	NA	66.6	42	1.5
Tyler	91	0.5	117	0.8	18.8	399,746	3,412	61,078	14.9	19,134	64.8	35.2	NA	77.6	96	2.7
Upshur	185	-8.4	112	0.4	36.9	386,205	3,443	51,583	40.7	24,645	8.5	91.5	8	75.1	347	7.2
Upton	725	5.7	7,399	15.8	74.9	5,980,038	808	270,042	19.1	194,520	72.8	27.2	NA	79.6	568	29.6
Uvalde.............................	987	1.0	1,668	32.6	111.3	2,165,457	1,299	108,251	87.1	147,130	43.3	56.7	NA	73.3	2,202	14.7
Val Verde.........................	1,471	-1.7	2,787	0.7	7.2	2,808,164	1,008	52,049	9.4	17,890	1.9	98.1	NA	54.9	416	2.8
Van Zandt........................	380	2.5	112	2.1	99.0	409,609	3,673	55,302	104.6	30,720	40.6	59.4	3	73.5	295	1.7
Victoria............................	426	-2.7	331	8.1	83.2	967,562	2,920	76,948	58.4	45,392	58.6	41.4	NA	69.8	2,630	12.1
Walker..............................	227	-19.0	158	0.6	27.5	580,115	3,679	58,302	33.8	23,452	56.7	43.3	2	75.8	143	0.9
Waller...............................	253	-19.6	135	11.6	71.4	628,544	4,670	69,415	102.4	54,423	74.5	25.5	1	75.3	5,198	4.6
Ward	406	3.6	3,978	3.3	6.5	4,234,789	1,064	84,959	D	D	D	100.0	NA	48.0	D	20.6
Washington	320	-13.2	123	2.3	68.7	587,144	4,781	57,676	35.6	13,661	15.3	84.7	NA	64.7	417	3.2
Webb................................	1,845	-12.1	2,812	3.3	35.0	4,817,630	1,713	69,020	28.4	43,287	1.5	98.5	NA	47.6	525	3.2
Wharton	535	-19.0	357	56.7	325.8	1,035,627	2,902	149,677	208.5	139,027	86.0	14.0	17	67.4	14,777	36.7
Wheeler............................	529	1.9	1,038	12.3	121.7	1,129,454	1,089	95,512	70.6	138,424	12.0	88.0	NA	71.6	3,608	46.5
Wichita	370	1.0	603	10.2	153.0	889,018	1,474	88,165	33.8	54,992	43.3	56.7	NA	79.5	3,583	23.8
Wilbarger	620	5.7	1,571	13.7	235.1	2,009,636	1,279	187,858	51.9	131,380	68.7	31.3	NA	80.8	5,709	64.6
Willacy	318	-5.4	906	19.0	197.4	1,591,245	1,757	197,576	88.1	250,943	95.1	4.9	NA	59.0	4,971	46.2
Williamson........................	559	0.1	212	1.6	231.5	790,257	3,722	72,687	114.9	43,631	57.5	42.5	12	78.9	6,359	18.0
Wilson	434	-1.4	165	11.7	87.9	525,222	3,174	62,753	68.6	26,185	18.5	81.5	2	65.2	1,923	8.9
Winkler	489	-8.3	10,635	D	D	11,922,788	1,121	108,111	D	D	D	D	NA	89.1	NA	NA
Wise	514	5.5	139	4.5	110.6	541,645	3,896	58,259	46.3	12,515	25.0	75.0	4	78.1	932	5.4
Wood	210	-7.6	132	1.2	60.5	445,231	3,362	69,250	127.5	80,366	6.8	93.2	6	76.8	77	1.2
Yoakum	518	6.0	1,779	92.8	318.0	1,670,162	939	315,408	100.2	344,333	96.0	4.0	4	78.4	11,936	74.6
Young	575	9.8	674	1.9	114.5	1,139,664	1,691	59,190	21.7	25,433	12.0	88.0	6	76.1	1,277	18.2
Zapata	438	-22.2	1,063	1.5	18.9	1,500,482	1,412	68,908	6.3	15,408	6.9	93.1	NA	53.9	441	8.3
Zavala	729	5.2	2,595	43.8	76.0	4,517,368	1,741	205,052	66.6	237,103	35.2	64.8	1	61.6	1,796	14.6
UTAH	10,812	-1.5	587	1,097.2	1,654.4	1,067,323	1,817	97,789	1,838.6	99,876	30.5	69.5	95	77.7	27,868	12.0
Beaver..............................	157	-17.4	577	40.2	44.4	1,284,918	2,226	217,327	258.0	948,559	7.8	92.2	NA	76.8	699	26.1
Box Elder	1,221	4.3	1,028	103.8	308.3	1,577,010	1,533	147,150	134.1	112,947	42.4	57.6	14	83.2	8,193	34.1
Cache..............................	276	2.9	198	90.1	159.4	955,825	4,833	120,832	162.7	116,490	25.4	74.6	8	81.1	3,439	25.8
Carbon	231	-4.0	747	9.3	15.8	924,915	1,238	68,983	6.5	20,906	35.9	64.1	2	84.8	101	5.5
Daggett	18	D	340	7.2	6.6	943,662	2,777	98,797	2.4	46,212	14.1	85.9	NA	80.8	220	7.7
Davis................................	52	-5.9	98	10.0	7.7	914,737	9,325	58,022	23.8	45,074	85.0	15.0	NA	76.1	50	2.8
Duchesne.........................	1,057	-2.9	995	96.5	77.3	970,628	976	100,563	57.9	54,461	27.9	72.1	NA	82.0	584	5.0
Emery	134	-14.4	265	32.8	36.9	557,310	2,101	74,404	15.4	30,464	31.8	68.2	2	84.5	460	14.3
Garfield	83	-9.7	289	21.2	16.3	903,654	3,127	91,968	21.8	76,175	16.5	83.5	5	72.4	D	3.8
Grand	231	D	2,268	11.5	14.6	1,868,935	824	139,177	7.2	70,294	65.5	34.5	5	81.4	D	3.9
Iron..................................	513	-3.7	1,055	64.4	83.4	2,063,886	1,955	179,494	133.5	274,716	40.6	59.4	NA	75.7	530	12.1
Juab.................................	265	8.9	906	23.7	56.6	1,202,491	1,327	122,499	53.7	183,832	57.3	42.7	NA	80.5	933	34.2
Kane.................................	129	2.6	707	6.9	4.9	1,282,578	1,814	80,345	6.3	34,440	11.8	88.2	NA	83.0	56	2.7
Millard	482	-16.6	736	122.7	146.0	1,504,464	2,043	236,249	180.0	275,168	47.5	52.5	6	81.5	3,031	39.8
Morgan............................	243	6.1	652	9.0	16.6	1,434,803	2,200	70,446	17.1	46,046	14.4	85.6	NA	80.9	392	4.3
Piute................................	54	43.9	524	15.3	14.9	1,089,630	2,081	125,352	40.6	390,433	8.5	91.5	NA	81.7	68	7.7
Rich.................................	375	-8.4	2,343	42.4	70.6	2,046,056	873	136,133	22.1	137,963	16.1	83.9	NA	76.3	633	13.1
Salt Lake	62	-20.7	105	7.4	10.9	1,013,467	9,682	52,551	19.9	33,617	85.7	14.3	10	78.7	188	2.4
San Juan..........................	1,657	3.0	2,014	7.6	130.2	738,348	367	48,406	16.8	20,383	51.3	48.7	21	33.2	1,636	14.5
Sanpete............................	302	6.1	301	76.5	71.7	848,242	2,820	109,542	171.8	171,243	12.1	87.9	2	76.7	854	14.6
Sevier...............................	109	-10.9	158	49.4	50.5	675,452	4,282	118,445	88.5	128,140	24.3	75.7	2	78.3	432	10.1
Summit.............................	296	9.5	472	21.3	26.3	1,541,565	3,265	71,386	25.5	40,799	16.0	84.0	3	79.9	833	5.0
Tooele	349	0.6	646	21.9	21.7	888,625	1,375	89,898	40.8	75,469	15.9	84.1	1	80.6	406	2.6
Uintah	1,825	D	1,638	65.3	70.7	1,032,638	630	88,260	42.3	37,943	38.6	61.4	NA	75.9	1,402	6.4
Utah	304	-11.4	117	72.7	118.1	1,024,882	8,734	74,291	202.6	78,246	39.4	60.6	6	81.8	1,679	5.7
Wasatch	97	-34.9	204	11.3	8.8	1,135,964	5,557	62,791	8.8	18,531	21.5	78.5	NA	82.3	102	2.1
Washington	155	4.8	289	13.0	22.3	1,078,856	3,737	61,328	16.5	30,648	39.3	60.7	3	76.9	190	3.2
Wayne..............................	43	0.9	205	16.6	14.6	928,420	4,539	89,480	12.9	61,646	15.7	84.3	NA	90.9	87	22.0
Weber	94	-19.6	75	27.2	28.3	697,872	9,319	59,112	49.4	39,240	50.0	50.0	5	75.0	497	3.1
VERMONT	1,193	-4.7	175	3.0	479.7	620,691	3,541	100,672	781.0	114,713	24.0	76.0	679	86.4	5,698	10.0
Addison	170	-18.5	236	0.4	107.8	786,959	3,335	150,113	173.4	240,889	14.7	85.3	81	92.4	1,362	17.2
Bennington.......................	33	-20.1	132	0.5	11.0	630,681	4,766	80,601	17.6	70,200	62.2	37.8	13	88.0	63	4.8
Caledonia.........................	87	6.3	149	0.1	31.3	474,564	3,191	77,061	42.2	72,077	16.6	83.4	46	87.4	263	6.5

Items 117—132

Table B. States and Counties — Water Use, Wholesale Trade, Retail Trade, and Real Estate

STATE County	Water use, 2015		Wholesale Trade[1], 2012				Retail Trade[2], 2012				Real estate and rental and leasing,[2] 2012			
	Public supply water withdrawn (mil gal/day)	Public supply gallons withdrawn per person per day	Number of establish-ments	Number of employees	Sales (mil dol)	Average payroll (mil dol)	Number of establish-ments	Number of employees	Sales (mil dol)	Average payroll (mil dol)	Number of establish-ments	Number of employees	Sales (mil dol)	Average payroll (mil dol)
	133	134	135	136	137	138	139	140	141	142	143	144	145	146
TEXAS— Cont'd														
Tom Green	1.16	9.8	113	D	D	D	418	5,963	1,821.7	149.8	134	595	92.7	16.5
Travis	122.10	103.8	1,166	21,735	56,614.8	1,470.9	3,469	54,094	15,583.7	1,443.3	1,771	10,798	2,455.1	539.0
Trinity	0.96	66.7	3	D	D	D	38	291	62.0	4.9	2	D	D	D
Tyler	2.84	133.0	7	47	39.7	3.6	53	531	115.8	10.0	4	21	1.0	0.2
Upshur	4.29	105.7	11	103	54.1	3.7	76	763	203.4	16.6	10	15	2.6	0.4
Upton	0.00	0.0	6	D	D	D	8	73	22.3	1.4	1	D	D	D
Uvalde	3.63	133.2	29	D	D	D	105	1,249	424.2	27.6	32	97	15.5	2.9
Val Verde	7.18	146.6	24	D	D	D	148	2,019	583.5	44.1	35	122	17.5	2.8
Van Zandt	3.38	63.1	29	263	72.3	11.3	147	1,406	430.7	31.2	29	83	6.2	1.4
Victoria	12.06	130.5	112	1,703	1,247.7	91.4	382	5,501	1,657.7	141.3	127	D	D	D
Walker	2.67	37.8	25	D	D	D	165	2,397	759.7	51.0	57	D	D	D
Waller	4.82	99.1	51	1,043	684.4	47.2	90	934	303.5	21.3	23	104	10.7	2.4
Ward	5.20	443.6	8	116	36.6	4.6	30	359	105.4	7.5	10	151	55.2	16.0
Washington	0.89	25.6	35	508	516.6	24.2	140	1,945	569.2	46.4	48	160	47.0	8.9
Webb	36.08	133.8	357	2,839	2,410.1	97.0	784	12,356	3,217.6	257.8	199	692	132.4	22.0
Wharton	3.69	88.9	49	890	572.2	37.2	163	1,999	563.8	49.1	39	168	29.4	7.5
Wheeler	1.14	201.5	9	D	D	D	33	239	71.6	5.1	6	8	1.1	0.2
Wichita	0.81	6.2	147	1,191	660.1	55.3	502	7,397	1,991.0	166.2	162	807	167.8	29.9
Wilbarger	1.85	142.0	12	D	D	D	48	664	254.6	14.3	10	22	2.7	0.6
Willacy	0.43	19.6	7	D	D	D	32	420	118.4	9.4	9	17	3.5	0.4
Williamson	35.49	69.8	306	D	D	D	1,277	21,844	8,585.0	593.3	408	1,550	348.9	65.5
Wilson	5.69	119.7	19	D	D	D	73	1,151	452.4	25.3	15	28	4.9	0.7
Winkler	1.45	181.1	7	D	D	D	20	195	53.6	4.4	7	D	D	D
Wise	2.23	35.4	57	609	658.0	31.9	154	2,174	757.1	62.1	46	291	61.3	13.8
Wood	4.21	97.1	31	257	169.8	7.6	129	1,345	393.7	33.4	30	133	31.0	4.9
Yoakum	0.97	113.5	11	135	43.6	8.9	28	211	61.6	5.2	6	D	D	D
Young	2.76	151.1	28	D	D	D	68	827	215.5	18.4	20	51	43.4	2.1
Zapata	2.20	153.1	1	D	D	D	32	263	75.7	5.3	4	26	5.7	0.7
Zavala	2.27	185.5	2	D	D	D	17	181	45.6	3.8	NA	NA	NA	NA
UTAH	785.91	262.3	3,015	43,523	30,927.9	2,364.4	9,095	133,535	38,024.5	3,334.9	4,446	16,197	3,226.1	604.8
Beaver	2.25	354.1	1	D	D	D	38	383	115.5	6.6	1	D	D	D
Box Elder	11.70	224.6	32	D	D	D	134	1,605	482.7	33.4	41	43	6.4	0.9
Cache	25.91	214.5	109	D	D	D	402	5,469	1,154.2	108.7	181	483	69.1	16.5
Carbon	4.35	212.4	30	D	D	D	86	1,084	311.3	26.0	15	57	17.9	1.9
Daggett	0.18	162.3	NA	NA	NA	NA	3	D	D	D	2	D	D	D
Davis	46.73	139.1	241	2,363	1,300.8	94.8	827	12,937	3,448.8	309.8	396	1,002	220.0	35.1
Duchesne	7.03	337.0	18	198	90.3	8.2	66	758	264.9	18.2	34	116	76.8	6.9
Emery	1.73	166.8	5	D	D	D	36	478	105.1	10.2	NA	NA	NA	NA
Garfield	1.42	283.5	4	D	D	D	23	116	29.9	2.2	2	D	D	D
Grand	6.05	635.8	13	D	D	D	79	678	170.1	16.0	31	131	14.0	2.7
Iron	10.64	220.0	33	261	246.0	9.7	172	1,892	567.8	43.3	72	165	28.7	4.8
Juab	4.59	433.3	9	62	36.3	2.2	33	313	114.5	5.0	2	D	D	D
Kane	2.33	326.7	4	7	1.3	0.2	41	337	77.1	6.4	16	26	3.6	0.7
Millard	3.91	309.2	13	D	D	D	61	549	122.1	9.1	3	4	0.3	0.1
Morgan	5.37	485.3	4	D	D	D	26	213	52.1	4.6	9	15	1.9	0.3
Piute	0.77	507.6	1	D	D	D	7	D	D	D	NA	NA	NA	NA
Rich	1.22	527.9	1	D	D	D	10	49	9.6	0.7	10	23	5.1	1.1
Salt Lake	394.81	356.5	1,653	27,748	19,734.9	1,640.3	3,395	55,808	17,178.4	1,536.0	1,931	8,980	1,927.6	378.3
San Juan	1.03	65.3	4	D	D	D	36	291	68.7	4.7	2	D	D	D
Sanpete	6.37	221.3	9	45	35.0	1.2	80	861	169.5	15.8	15	42	4.6	0.7
Sevier	5.19	247.3	13	90	211.9	3.4	88	1,255	331.8	29.2	14	85	17.7	2.9
Summit	8.80	222.0	43	551	378.7	32.0	295	4,105	1,013.6	101.5	245	900	124.1	27.6
Tooele	18.35	291.5	13	63	31.9	2.9	104	1,688	496.8	37.1	30	76	10.3	1.6
Uintah	4.93	130.0	45	D	D	D	135	1,575	503.2	43.4	79	453	104.1	21.8
Utah	127.67	222.0	368	5,770	3,112.6	298.4	1,520	22,096	6,039.4	529.6	684	D	D	D
Wasatch	4.34	148.8	17	35	11.0	1.0	88	1,021	267.4	20.7	44	105	27.3	3.4
Washington	49.38	317.3	149	1,284	1,514.7	47.4	574	7,375	1,900.8	168.4	306	702	95.2	18.7
Wayne	1.18	438.3	NA	NA	NA	NA	15	104	32.1	1.9	1	D	D	D
Weber	27.68	113.6	183	2,924	2,655.6	129.1	721	10,462	2,991.6	245.8	280	905	130.9	24.9
VERMONT	42.66	68.1	696	9,464	6,450.1	464.4	3,509	38,910	9,933.8	967.1	741	3,092	509.9	103.6
Addison	3.45	93.2	31	D	D	D	184	1,886	536.9	51.6	37	94	11.0	2.4
Bennington	3.30	90.9	27	D	D	D	271	3,051	806.2	79.8	53	222	29.9	6.7
Caledonia	1.77	57.5	29	D	D	D	173	1,687	451.4	43.1	30	D	D	D

1 Merchant wholesalers, except manufacturers' sales branches and offices.   2. Employer establishments.

Professional Services, Manufacturing, and Accommodation and Food Services

STATE County	Professional, scientific, and technical services, 2012				Manufacturing, 2012				Accommodation and food services, 2012			
	Number of establish-ments	Number of employees	Sales (mil dol)	Average payroll (mil dol)	Number of establish-ments	Number of employees	Receipts (mil dol)	Annual payroll (mil dol)	Number of establis-hments	Number of employees	Receipts (mil dol)	Annual payroll (mil dol)
	147	148	149	150	151	152	153	154	155	156	157	158
TEXAS— Cont'd												
Tom Green	209	1,358	159.0	58.5	101	3,434	D	135.1	230	D	D	D
Travis	5,624	59,846	12,138.9	4,870.9	788	23,903	12,281.9	1,501.1	2,731	59,496	3,726.8	1,033.0
Trinity	11	42	3.3	1.0	9	158	79.9	8.8	15	223	14.7	3.2
Tyler	23	50	6.0	1.6	13	71	D	2.7	21	218	9.6	2.4
Upshur	51	446	47.0	16.6	23	285	113.3	13.4	37	D	D	D
Upton	3	D	D	D	NA	NA	NA	NA	11	D	D	D
Uvalde	41	D	D	D	17	409	149.5	12.1	80	1,063	58.1	13.3
Val Verde	45	D	D	D	22	321	D	11.0	94	1,647	77.8	19.8
Van Zandt	63	258	33.9	11.9	35	690	142.8	37.9	77	975	44.8	13.7
Victoria	159	874	115.1	41.1	73	2,021	D	D	188	3,593	187.0	49.2
Walker	90	473	42.9	14.2	41	761	352.7	37.3	103	1,875	92.1	24.8
Waller	62	490	72.7	40.2	70	2,744	919.4	160.1	46	647	33.2	7.8
Ward	18	62	7.4	2.6	4	38	D	2.1	28	326	22.3	5.0
Washington	59	339	48.1	13.8	45	2,967	883.6	128.4	86	1,084	54.9	14.8
Webb	317	1,803	186.1	58.6	69	635	339.6	22.0	389	8,216	423.7	106.2
Wharton	59	267	31.5	9.6	40	1,513	400.8	55.0	68	948	47.5	12.8
Wheeler	17	102	13.7	5.1	NA	NA	NA	NA	23	284	19.7	3.9
Wichita	235	D	D	D	129	4,885	1,400.8	230.7	271	D	D	D
Wilbarger	17	D	D	D	11	D	D	D	38	484	20.8	5.1
Willacy	10	D	D	D	3	12	D	D	23	253	13.1	2.9
Williamson	1,118	7,490	1,158.6	451.6	299	7,485	1,886.3	386.1	793	15,477	817.0	224.2
Wilson	37	166	22.8	11.9	24	327	121.9	15.2	62	763	36.8	9.6
Winkler	12	18	4.1	0.7	NA	NA	NA	NA	10	D	D	D
Wise	85	289	40.3	11.2	75	1,892	550.2	94.0	105	1,568	75.9	19.4
Wood	73	643	28.0	12.5	38	822	575.7	35.6	76	864	40.6	11.3
Yoakum	7	14	1.7	0.4	7	98	D	4.8	24	168	8.1	1.8
Young	34	102	13.7	5.2	22	881	252.2	42.5	42	474	21.9	6.0
Zapata	4	D	D	D	NA	NA	NA	NA	19	D	D	D
Zavala	7	27	1.0	0.2	3	D	D	D	17	200	8.8	2.1
UTAH	9,009	76,345	10,555.1	3,909.0	3,163	108,264	50,046.4	5,762.6	5,108	95,933	4,789.3	1,362.9
Beaver	5	11	1.0	0.2	6	79	D	2.9	29	244	12.0	3.1
Box Elder	53	213	23.6	7.1	72	6,206	D	469.2	69	1,174	47.5	14.8
Cache	368	2,487	245.2	87.2	207	10,515	4,516.6	434.4	162	2,969	125.1	33.8
Carbon	29	108	14.5	4.2	21	426	121.5	19.0	37	640	25.6	7.3
Daggett	1	D	D	D	NA	NA	NA	NA	7	64	5.1	1.5
Davis	868	6,369	974.4	320.4	265	9,506	5,982.0	459.4	420	8,178	350.5	96.9
Duchesne	50	168	27.0	6.9	22	209	D	9.9	33	396	21.7	4.8
Emery	14	149	7.8	3.5	4	17	D	0.9	20	192	8.2	2.0
Garfield	9	D	D	D	5	21	2.1	0.6	51	556	62.9	15.6
Grand	30	148	12.7	4.2	6	71	D	3.8	90	1,513	86.7	24.9
Iron	107	425	59.4	15.5	65	1,273	656.4	54.4	101	1,475	64.3	17.2
Juab	18	313	34.2	17.0	12	364	136.4	13.2	21	203	7.9	2.3
Kane	17	20	2.4	0.5	5	73	D	D	52	564	47.9	12.7
Millard	10	88	6.3	3.2	12	485	D	24.0	29	308	12.4	3.2
Morgan	23	86	7.8	2.6	12	143	D	9.2	8	111	4.5	1.7
Piute	NA	NA	NA	NA	NA	NA	NA	NA	5	22	0.8	0.3
Rich	6	10	1.3	0.5	NA	NA	NA	NA	14	79	9.5	2.7
Salt Lake	4,145	D	D	D	1,360	46,402	22,060.4	2,669.6	2,080	41,574	2,170.9	634.1
San Juan	13	23	1.6	0.7	7	230	D	10.8	52	744	65.0	14.3
Sanpete	22	92	7.2	2.3	25	657	174.7	22.5	36	390	10.5	3.1
Sevier	32	109	11.0	4.7	20	202	45.1	8.3	52	725	26.9	7.4
Summit	339	900	218.6	55.3	39	465	D	24.3	169	5,803	323.2	103.6
Tooele	68	D	D	D	34	1,705	884.3	92.3	69	1,028	46.4	12.4
Uintah	102	542	73.3	25.3	33	309	52.1	12.8	68	1,079	57.5	13.1
Utah	1,636	16,643	1,707.6	639.2	513	15,599	5,945.7	794.0	688	13,046	569.4	159.2
Wasatch	109	337	45.5	13.7	33	204	41.5	7.6	56	1,066	63.1	16.8
Washington	433	D	D	D	133	1,838	415.3	76.1	307	5,140	282.3	74.4
Wayne	3	D	D	D	4	D	1.7	D	25	157	12.8	2.4
Weber	499	4,180	401.7	195.7	247	11,260	4,799.0	540.7	358	6,493	268.6	77.3
VERMONT	2,113	15,948	1,782.0	739.9	1,013	31,487	9,315.5	1,594.3	1,920	31,365	1,564.3	494.0
Addison	123	D	D	D	57	1,472	D	82.1	86	873	55.2	18.8
Bennington	125	409	43.7	16.2	69	2,472	764.5	108.4	143	1,821	95.0	33.9
Caledonia	70	D	D	D	57	1,361	256.5	61.5	72	661	37.7	10.2

Health Care and Social Assistance, Other Services, Nonemployer Businesses, and Residential Construction

STATE County	Health care and social assistance, 2012				Other services, 2012				Nonemployer businesses, 2016		Value of residential construction authorized by building permits, 2018	
	Number of establishments	Number of employees	Receipts (mil dol)	Annual payroll (mil dol)	Number of establishments	Number of employees	Receipts (mil dol)	Annual payroll (mil dol)	Number	Receipts (mil dol)	New construction ($1,000)	Number of housing units
	159	160	161	162	163	164	165	166	167	168	169	170
TEXAS— Cont'd												
Tom Green	269	D	D	D	210	D	D	D	8,589	331.6	56,755	262
Travis	2,969	57,586	6,996.8	2,731.1	2,084	18,611	2,448.4	703.7	118,984	6,531.3	3,023,092	19,520
Trinity	22	320	24.4	9.7	17	64	4.1	0.8	972	34.0	515	3
Tyler	23	523	33.6	15.3	13	D	D	D	1,113	42.2	250	5
Upshur	35	634	40.6	17.7	24	95	8.2	2.5	2,963	126.4	308	5
Upton	5	D	D	D	NA	NA	NA	NA	279	14.4	525	3
Uvalde	73	1,731	130.7	45.8	33	D	D	D	2,759	126.3	1,401	18
Val Verde	92	2,819	89.9	45.2	47	255	15.1	4.4	3,381	110.4	16,479	81
Van Zandt	68	1,201	72.1	33.4	56	272	27.4	7.2	4,386	192.9	4,351	31
Victoria	304	6,591	679.7	274.5	151	1,165	162.8	46.8	6,013	243.2	14,816	70
Walker	97	2,179	180.2	75.2	54	297	23.6	6.1	4,321	149.3	89,641	552
Waller	38	D	D	D	43	195	25.2	5.7	3,735	184.7	11,289	148
Ward	12	229	15.9	8.7	13	168	21.6	6.8	677	31.0	95	1
Washington	98	1,906	98.3	43.0	53	212	17.4	5.1	3,182	141.4	14,078	139
Webb	536	14,678	926.2	373.6	203	1,129	101.1	27.1	25,100	1,169.5	167,410	1,375
Wharton	67	2,374	131.4	51.3	71	274	18.5	5.0	3,153	115.4	18,812	100
Wheeler	13	271	17.8	7.4	12	D	D	D	543	23.3	0	0
Wichita	391	10,832	1,051.7	391.7	225	1,212	118.8	31.1	7,825	356.7	36,960	251
Wilbarger	34	513	34.2	15.1	26	D	D	D	715	20.5	270	1
Willacy	33	547	27.1	12.8	12	39	2.4	0.5	1,259	37.6	4,997	43
Williamson	982	16,410	1,861.9	721.8	608	4,107	378.7	122.0	43,039	1,924.1	1,495,370	6,991
Wilson	55	1,158	69.5	29.3	46	140	11.8	2.7	3,567	165.3	11,513	57
Winkler	6	86	8.0	3.0	7	65	13.7	2.5	590	22.3	80	1
Wise	113	D	D	D	66	D	D	D	5,532	295.1	15,552	83
Wood	86	1,421	99.9	43.5	47	186	16.5	4.3	3,635	167.0	1,908	13
Yoakum	10	D	D	D	9	37	6.5	1.9	486	20.9	770	4
Young	58	1,032	77.3	31.7	37	147	13.3	3.6	2,086	117.2	586	3
Zapata	18	264	9.1	4.1	5	D	D	D	1,504	41.5	NA	NA
Zavala	12	D	D	D	2	D	D	D	811	20.8	0	0
UTAH	7,285	126,175	14,521.9	5,020.8	4,259	26,026	2,544.5	723.2	225,383	10,422.5	5,610,557	25,574
Beaver	21	D	D	D	10	26	3.6	0.8	466	16.1	3,951	15
Box Elder	116	D	D	D	66	D	D	D	3,250	126.8	63,231	294
Cache	348	5,106	494.3	161.6	172	810	60.7	17.8	8,713	335.1	230,726	1,163
Carbon	71	862	100.7	28.9	44	D	D	D	1,053	34.6	7,175	23
Daggett	NA	NA	NA	NA	NA	NA	NA	NA	90	2.6	1,677	9
Davis	667	9,466	888.6	340.7	395	2,471	182.9	54.0	23,555	1,048.7	460,667	2,169
Duchesne	50	D	D	D	34	D	D	D	1,481	57.7	25,585	147
Emery	17	D	D	D	15	D	D	D	637	16.8	3,206	15
Garfield	6	D	D	D	3	D	D	D	484	15.5	545	3
Grand	25	287	37.5	12.4	22	D	D	D	1,040	44.3	31,699	158
Iron	138	1,641	130.9	43.9	74	343	24.8	6.5	3,625	132.8	109,045	499
Juab	22	415	44.2	14.5	7	19	1.6	0.5	759	35.2	18,805	72
Kane	12	268	18.3	8.2	16	D	D	D	730	29.7	28,666	119
Millard	21	D	D	D	17	D	D	D	815	33.1	5,932	33
Morgan	21	D	D	D	8	D	D	D	1,057	45.2	29,193	74
Piute	1	D	D	D	1	D	D	D	103	5.5	4,948	32
Rich	2	D	D	D	6	D	D	D	268	9.1	15,828	51
Salt Lake	2,933	60,445	7,609.2	2,669.6	1,872	12,731	1,328.0	396.5	85,158	4,287.9	1,616,469	8,030
San Juan	34	701	76.0	28.2	11	D	D	D	799	24.6	5,180	33
Sanpete	47	856	58.7	23.0	25	D	D	D	1,797	72.2	12,028	62
Sevier	58	804	71.3	24.1	29	D	D	D	1,467	61.6	16,952	70
Summit	134	D	D	D	106	769	115.4	27.0	6,160	413.5	159,550	388
Tooele	92	1,267	125.5	45.5	58	239	20.9	5.5	3,069	103.6	153,974	720
Uintah	63	D	D	D	73	436	60.3	13.7	1,842	67.2	10,935	53
Utah	1,197	20,831	2,184.1	761.6	627	3,379	271.1	73.4	46,086	2,021.0	1,665,050	6,769
Wasatch	58	D	D	D	38	D	D	D	3,048	155.2	122,854	525
Washington	500	7,443	830.8	271.4	188	1,043	87.9	24.3	13,717	649.4	535,219	2,889
Wayne	4	D	D	D	2	D	D	D	348	12.4	6,300	24
Weber	627	10,695	1,335.5	418.8	340	1,964	166.7	47.1	13,766	565.2	265,171	1,135
VERMONT	2,096	44,198	4,458.0	1,789.2	1,588	7,211	755.4	199.3	60,226	2,607.1	365,383	2,080
Addison	120	2,091	159.6	72.5	88	330	55.0	10.1	3,837	146.0	20,913	89
Bennington	158	2,704	274.8	116.3	97	395	30.7	7.8	3,676	162.3	13,981	52
Caledonia	94	1,732	146.3	63.4	76	234	21.2	5.7	2,925	117.3	9,684	56

Table B. States and Counties — Government Employment and Payroll, and Local Government Finances

	Government employment and payroll, 2012									Local government finances, 2012				
			March payroll (percent of total)							General revenue				
STATE County	Full-time equivalent employees	March payroll (dollars)	Administration, judicial, and legal	Police and corrections	Fire protection	Highways and transportation	Health and welfare	Natural resources and utilities	Education and libraries	Total (mil dol)	Intergovernmental (mil dol)	Taxes Total (mil dol)	Per capita[1] (dollars) Total	Per capita[1] (dollars) Property
	171	172	173	174	175	176	177	178	179	180	181	182	183	184

TEXAS— Cont'd														
Tom Green	4,430	11,842,865	8.7	16.5	6.7	1.4	3.6	6.1	55.2	321.7	125.9	138.0	1,218	917
Travis	45,034	190,376,191	8.0	14.8	5.4	4.1	5.1	18.3	42.4	4,794.7	942.7	2,689.4	2,455	2,026
Trinity	657	1,816,086	6.2	7.0	0.0	3.0	19.3	2.2	60.4	42.8	22.8	13.7	954	889
Tyler	945	2,527,612	9.2	3.5	0.0	3.0	16.0	2.8	65.4	63.8	23.6	34.9	1,625	1,538
Upshur	1,527	4,228,679	4.9	8.6	0.6	1.7	0.1	2.3	81.6	91.7	43.7	38.4	961	866
Upton	396	1,316,616	8.8	8.6	0.0	3.5	31.5	4.4	42.2	64.5	4.8	53.2	16,191	16,022
Uvalde	2,058	6,807,776	3.6	5.1	0.2	1.9	25.8	2.2	60.5	171.9	70.8	36.8	1,374	1,094
Val Verde	2,194	5,580,787	14.3	6.2	5.3	3.0	2.4	6.1	61.0	177.1	111.3	44.7	918	690
Van Zandt	1,960	5,471,112	4.9	6.7	0.3	1.8	0.4	2.9	82.3	133.5	67.2	50.0	953	821
Victoria	5,364	18,189,328	3.7	10.4	3.1	1.8	31.4	3.0	46.0	455.8	105.2	155.9	1,746	1,294
Walker	1,980	6,982,834	14.0	12.7	0.8	2.6	1.0	18.0	43.7	157.3	53.4	61.8	904	699
Waller	1,643	5,642,929	7.6	7.4	0.3	2.5	0.1	3.3	77.2	129.4	49.0	69.2	1,560	1,448
Ward	559	1,720,115	12.0	13.3	0.1	4.4	3.1	7.7	57.1	58.5	9.0	35.1	3,231	2,922
Washington	2,307	7,486,978	4.8	5.4	0.9	1.6	2.0	4.0	80.0	171.2	48.3	57.0	1,671	1,323
Webb	14,741	48,977,584	5.1	9.2	5.1	3.0	3.0	3.7	70.4	1,245.0	614.2	391.8	1,512	1,216
Wharton	3,171	11,435,949	2.9	4.7	1.0	2.5	19.8	1.5	66.6	188.9	70.3	71.4	1,729	1,485
Wheeler	514	1,406,670	6.6	3.2	0.0	2.3	33.3	2.8	49.5	54.5	8.1	36.6	6,498	6,236
Wichita	5,729	18,326,731	6.5	14.8	7.0	2.9	9.1	5.0	51.8	380.0	131.8	178.0	1,353	1,020
Wilbarger	1,195	3,537,696	3.1	4.1	2.6	1.8	21.1	2.8	64.1	75.4	29.4	23.4	1,765	1,490
Willacy	988	3,020,755	5.5	5.6	0.0	2.6	0.6	4.5	80.4	77.1	48.6	20.8	941	793
Williamson	16,819	59,733,376	3.1	6.7	3.0	0.5	4.4	2.8	78.5	1,670.1	418.9	1,031.8	2,262	1,950
Wilson	1,799	5,521,367	3.9	4.2	0.0	1.3	11.3	8.0	71.0	127.9	49.4	47.4	1,067	977
Winkler	465	1,871,237	6.8	7.5	0.0	1.6	15.1	4.2	63.8	57.9	10.9	36.9	5,029	4,658
Wise	2,052	6,283,194	8.7	7.9	0.7	4.7	0.0	3.9	72.0	189.8	35.2	132.2	2,187	1,913
Wood	1,347	3,686,462	6.7	10.8	0.5	4.1	1.5	3.8	72.4	92.1	31.3	50.5	1,202	1,071
Yoakum	719	2,354,261	7.1	8.7	0.1	3.1	26.1	3.9	50.3	97.6	9.0	68.0	8,426	8,230
Young	1,189	3,441,113	4.9	6.9	1.2	1.6	33.2	3.4	47.6	89.6	22.2	26.3	1,434	1,181
Zapata	901	2,905,195	13.0	4.2	3.8	4.8	1.0	3.6	68.4	76.6	24.7	47.2	3,300	3,261
Zavala	676	1,796,547	3.7	8.4	0.0	2.9	3.4	5.7	71.6	42.2	30.7	7.7	641	557
UTAH	X	X	X	X	X	X	X	X	X	X	X	X	X	X
Beaver	339	1,182,302	5.5	2.7	0.0	0.6	31.1	8.3	50.7	51.1	10.9	13.4	2,054	1,709
Box Elder	1,701	4,888,324	8.2	9.3	0.8	3.1	2.0	5.8	69.8	163.1	71.5	66.7	1,329	1,068
Cache	3,328	10,972,734	7.5	7.4	2.7	3.6	8.3	6.1	61.3	309.3	134.5	108.6	940	578
Carbon	959	3,089,135	8.6	9.2	0.6	4.8	13.4	11.0	49.4	77.6	27.1	32.7	1,540	1,152
Daggett	101	367,263	17.3	30.4	0.1	4.2	2.7	2.2	42.0	12.0	5.2	2.8	2,550	2,139
Davis	10,391	37,610,946	5.6	7.5	2.5	1.4	4.5	5.5	72.1	900.2	374.8	329.2	1,042	745
Duchesne	667	2,048,894	10.0	11.8	0.7	5.0	1.5	5.8	63.0	84.8	40.2	33.0	1,715	1,314
Emery	466	1,718,363	11.2	10.6	0.0	4.9	2.1	8.1	62.3	62.8	21.5	29.4	2,685	2,355
Garfield	208	742,442	11.2	13.2	0.0	8.1	3.9	3.0	59.1	29.9	14.5	10.4	2,048	1,146
Grand	491	1,568,944	14.6	13.1	0.9	6.9	12.1	8.6	39.6	48.0	15.0	23.4	2,503	1,486
Iron	1,282	4,462,404	8.5	11.6	1.0	3.6	3.5	5.1	64.5	132.5	51.2	58.7	1,257	954
Juab	437	1,313,251	9.2	9.3	0.0	4.6	1.1	6.7	66.9	40.9	23.8	12.2	1,178	963
Kane	440	1,479,423	9.0	11.3	0.3	3.4	34.0	2.0	37.7	48.6	12.0	21.3	2,951	1,982
Millard	516	1,988,139	9.7	11.9	0.0	5.8	2.6	6.2	62.0	68.1	23.0	25.6	2,037	1,792
Morgan	299	975,455	9.6	3.4	0.9	2.2	0.0	4.1	79.3	26.9	11.8	11.1	1,126	946
Piute	89	242,632	8.4	6.3	0.0	5.8	1.4	1.1	68.5	7.9	5.5	1.6	1,026	813
Rich	110	395,515	10.7	7.4	1.1	3.8	1.8	4.6	67.9	13.2	5.2	6.2	2,714	2,297
Salt Lake	34,230	125,577,298	7.2	10.3	5.3	9.8	5.0	8.9	51.0	3,731.7	1,299.6	1,519.3	1,428	1,028
San Juan	708	2,586,369	5.3	6.4	0.5	6.1	20.5	1.9	57.4	84.2	52.5	14.9	994	908
Sanpete	1,157	3,481,157	6.7	6.0	0.2	1.8	18.6	4.4	59.7	95.1	43.9	20.5	734	527
Sevier	746	2,317,397	8.0	11.6	0.2	2.5	2.9	7.4	65.4	75.7	42.9	22.0	1,059	746
Summit	1,737	6,591,640	8.6	7.7	9.0	7.8	2.4	12.1	48.0	236.3	39.4	155.2	4,084	3,100
Tooele	2,049	6,240,915	9.0	10.6	1.0	2.9	5.1	6.2	64.3	202.7	99.2	53.2	888	639
Uintah	1,239	3,713,017	11.2	10.8	0.4	5.2	9.6	10.8	46.9	155.8	52.9	70.7	2,048	1,456
Utah	14,037	52,266,547	6.3	8.0	2.5	1.4	4.9	8.4	66.6	1,574.6	646.3	574.1	1,062	718
Wasatch	952	3,521,146	10.0	7.9	0.0	2.6	6.3	11.3	55.4	122.6	39.4	52.8	2,091	1,673
Washington	4,130	14,492,173	7.3	10.1	1.7	2.6	6.5	13.4	56.5	453.7	154.1	197.8	1,366	972
Wayne	114	391,098	6.2	5.1	0.5	6.5	3.8	4.8	70.9	13.2	9.5	2.6	961	721
Weber	7,494	26,228,893	6.1	11.2	4.3	1.7	7.0	6.9	60.7	668.4	249.5	273.1	1,154	796
VERMONT	X	X	X	X	X	X	X	X	X	X	X	X	X	X
Addison	1,255	4,519,763	4.3	2.9	0.0	5.3	0.9	2.2	84.0	127.5	92.7	23.2	632	604
Bennington	948	3,568,427	6.0	7.7	0.1	5.9	0.6	5.2	74.2	128.5	92.0	25.4	692	657
Caledonia	1,032	3,333,702	5.5	3.4	1.1	8.2	0.9	4.6	76.0	108.5	81.8	18.1	580	578

1. Based on the resident population estimated as of July 1 of the year shown.

Table B. States and Counties — Local Government Finances, Government Employment, and Income Taxes

STATE County	Direct general expenditure — Total (mil dol)	Per capita[1] (dollars)	Percent of total for: Education	Health and hospitals	Police protection	Public welfare	Highways	Debt outstanding — Total (mil dol)	Per capita[1] (dollars)	Gov. empl. 2017 Federal civilian	Federal military	State and local	Individual income tax returns, 2016 — Number of returns	Mean adjusted gross income	Mean income tax
	185	186	187	188	189	190	191	192	193	194	195	196	197	198	199
TEXAS— Cont'd															
Tom Green	347.3	3,066	51.9	3.4	5.7	0.2	2.7	583.9	5,155	1,205	3,364	7,780	51,660	53,997	6,971
Travis	4,740.6	4,327	38.8	6.7	7.4	0.8	6.5	15,845.5	14,463	11,542	2,598	115,642	574,730	88,533	15,294
Trinity	41.5	2,899	53.9	9.1	1.8	0.5	4.9	18.1	1,265	23	29	619	5,840	40,198	3,729
Tyler	60.2	2,805	57.5	0.1	4.6	0.3	5.4	43.0	2,002	43	39	1,677	7,260	47,264	4,485
Upshur	91.6	2,291	72.4	0.0	4.3	0.1	3.6	89.1	2,229	62	82	1,717	16,070	46,766	4,566
Upton	68.5	20,851	78.3	16.8	0.3	0.1	0.7	15.4	4,703	5	7	490	1,380	65,543	9,384
Uvalde	177.9	6,652	45.7	29.2	4.7	0.7	3.6	95.4	3,566	212	54	2,649	11,770	42,182	4,434
Val Verde	202.3	4,154	44.6	1.1	4.3	0.6	18.1	196.2	4,027	2,147	1,311	2,897	20,800	41,148	3,417
Van Zandt	133.6	2,548	65.3	0.2	3.7	0.1	5.1	143.4	2,735	90	110	2,328	22,640	48,809	5,010
Victoria	447.8	5,016	35.0	30.9	5.7	0.0	7.0	427.6	4,790	193	190	6,504	40,340	57,596	7,194
Walker	336.2	4,914	20.8	2.8	2.4	0.0	2.2	2,119.8	30,987	141	140	12,930	23,830	45,991	4,651
Waller	122.5	2,761	63.3	0.0	5.3	0.2	5.2	201.4	4,540	60	101	4,452	19,490	57,668	7,299
Ward	50.2	4,618	39.7	22.1	5.2	0.5	5.1	27.1	2,491	13	23	800	4,770	54,075	6,363
Washington	177.9	5,218	67.6	1.5	3.7	0.2	9.5	209.7	6,151	76	67	2,890	16,000	54,796	6,689
Webb	1,204.4	4,647	58.3	1.3	6.0	0.4	1.5	1,569.6	6,056	3,370	547	18,825	110,380	39,262	3,586
Wharton	212.0	5,136	49.9	27.3	4.1	0.3	4.0	112.7	2,730	84	84	2,824	18,990	48,240	5,211
Wheeler	47.3	8,406	62.3	25.4	2.4	0.0	1.9	10.4	1,840	24	11	591	2,270	47,455	5,022
Wichita	367.1	2,790	48.2	3.9	7.6	0.8	4.0	311.8	2,370	1,850	6,224	9,348	53,450	50,912	5,714
Wilbarger	85.1	6,421	56.2	22.2	2.7	0.1	3.2	25.5	1,920	38	24	2,418	5,560	44,359	4,448
Willacy	71.7	3,250	69.9	2.0	3.8	0.0	3.5	245.2	11,115	31	37	1,193	7,420	32,294	2,346
Williamson	1,761.9	3,862	55.5	3.1	4.1	0.1	8.7	4,547.8	9,968	774	1,131	23,107	246,490	74,711	9,796
Wilson	123.3	2,779	58.0	17.0	2.5	0.0	3.5	291.4	6,568	88	98	2,345	20,870	63,483	7,511
Winkler	63.1	8,609	59.5	14.6	3.7	0.3	1.7	83.7	11,417	9	15	590	3,050	54,350	5,710
Wise	185.9	3,076	52.9	1.7	4.7	0.4	8.7	328.2	5,430	120	133	4,120	28,200	58,101	6,593
Wood	83.7	1,992	65.3	0.6	6.3	0.2	7.2	54.2	1,291	92	86	1,787	18,550	49,834	5,320
Yoakum	112.1	13,883	63.5	19.3	2.1	0.0	3.3	58.6	7,256	15	17	845	3,510	55,761	5,781
Young	85.3	4,653	35.5	36.5	4.0	0.1	3.6	63.6	3,466	41	36	1,348	7,640	53,839	7,279
Zapata	71.8	5,023	53.0	1.7	6.5	2.5	10.2	53.7	3,754	138	29	909	4,920	33,422	2,392
Zavala	39.0	3,260	64.7	0.8	4.7	0.6	3.1	27.4	2,292	9	23	910	4,290	34,677	2,387
UTAH	X	X	X	X	X	X	X	X	X	36,130	16,396	202,758	1,288,730	64,981	7,838
Beaver	56.0	8,618	45.5	16.6	4.4	0.1	4.4	64.4	9,900	37	26	689	2,670	46,601	3,534
Box Elder	160.8	3,204	53.7	1.5	5.9	0.0	5.0	153.6	3,061	185	217	2,617	22,210	53,567	4,599
Cache	279.8	2,422	51.7	4.7	6.0	0.3	5.2	189.4	1,640	343	492	10,782	48,290	61,487	6,669
Carbon	97.8	4,605	33.6	5.7	8.9	1.4	15.4	82.2	3,869	144	80	1,869	7,860	48,576	4,417
Daggett	10.8	9,932	41.8	0.6	12.0	0.0	4.4	7.7	7,049	54	4	133	430	48,074	4,002
Davis	883.2	2,797	54.5	3.5	5.9	0.7	2.9	783.9	2,482	13,492	5,134	14,843	143,770	70,382	8,081
Duchesne	87.6	4,553	62.9	1.4	3.7	0.6	5.4	67.8	3,525	70	79	2,160	7,250	51,544	4,901
Emery	55.4	5,071	43.3	1.6	9.6	0.2	10.6	197.2	18,039	53	40	803	3,780	48,434	3,834
Garfield	23.9	4,686	43.6	2.6	4.9	0.2	12.7	15.3	3,013	137	20	394	2,160	43,242	3,617
Grand	44.6	4,784	31.4	1.2	9.8	0.7	9.0	75.2	8,066	227	38	723	4,890	52,974	6,066
Iron	125.1	2,675	48.9	0.6	7.6	0.2	7.1	124.1	2,655	281	203	3,975	18,950	45,716	3,703
Juab	41.3	3,997	42.5	0.6	7.1	0.0	6.0	46.1	4,459	25	45	802	4,330	56,612	5,377
Kane	51.0	7,056	25.3	22.9	3.7	0.0	6.3	44.9	6,214	83	29	646	3,100	48,889	4,582
Millard	53.8	4,280	54.0	3.6	7.9	0.0	7.1	9.5	752	90	51	966	5,080	46,596	3,926
Morgan	30.5	3,110	65.1	1.3	3.6	0.0	3.2	31.7	3,228	17	48	501	4,650	89,311	11,697
Piute	8.4	5,526	63.5	0.9	6.3	0.0	8.4	7.6	5,012	3	6	129	510	35,896	2,353
Rich	11.4	5,038	56.3	0.8	5.5	2.9	8.5	10.7	4,710	9	10	194	920	46,973	3,923
Salt Lake	3,568.5	3,354	42.8	1.1	5.6	2.0	5.4	7,237.3	6,803	11,394	4,763	93,651	507,440	67,178	8,702
San Juan	80.3	5,367	48.8	16.3	2.8	0.1	14.7	21.4	1,432	158	60	1,548	4,530	41,557	3,197
Sanpete	90.3	3,237	50.5	20.9	4.6	0.0	3.0	121.5	4,352	85	109	2,646	9,590	44,590	3,640
Sevier	69.0	3,318	48.6	2.0	9.0	0.0	7.7	54.0	2,596	181	85	1,483	8,190	49,184	4,388
Summit	247.7	6,518	32.0	2.0	5.3	0.0	14.4	271.7	7,150	55	165	2,821	22,330	134,787	27,001
Tooele	205.1	3,426	44.3	2.1	5.5	2.9	3.0	186.1	3,109	1,229	299	2,760	26,800	55,968	4,767
Uintah	172.6	4,998	36.6	3.9	4.3	4.9	15.3	199.3	5,772	394	141	2,658	12,470	52,390	4,719
Utah	1,425.3	2,637	52.2	4.1	6.0	0.1	5.2	2,402.3	4,445	1,015	2,408	29,322	226,840	65,333	7,656
Wasatch	116.2	4,598	37.8	2.6	4.5	0.1	8.0	196.8	7,787	54	128	1,552	13,080	78,643	11,001
Washington	401.3	2,771	50.1	0.8	7.7	0.0	6.0	585.2	4,041	584	659	7,842	67,010	57,070	6,228
Wayne	11.3	4,138	49.8	0.3	9.5	0.0	14.9	0.8	300	84	11	177	1,100	42,695	3,819
Weber	687.2	2,904	45.7	2.1	6.6	3.6	2.8	686.2	2,900	5,647	1,046	14,072	108,650	55,790	5,544
VERMONT	X	X	X	X	X	X	X	X	X	6,969	3,989	46,928	325,840	59,267	7,111
Addison	134.4	3,658	71.2	0.1	2.3	0.1	11.8	60.1	1,636	109	217	1,895	18,950	57,679	6,254
Bennington	140.1	3,818	69.0	0.2	4.4	0.3	12.1	38.6	1,051	173	218	2,116	18,720	55,090	6,651
Caledonia	107.7	3,461	66.7	0.1	3.0	0.0	14.0	33.2	1,066	92	184	1,974	14,670	46,155	4,495

1. Based on the resident population estimated as of July 1 of the year shown.

Table B. States and Counties — **Land Area and Population**

State / county code	CBSA code[1]	County code[2]	STATE County	Land area[3] (sq. mi)	Total persons 2018	Rank	Per square mile	White	Black	American Indian, Alaska Native	Asian and Pacific Islander	Percent Hispanic or Latino[4]	Under 5 years	5 to 17 years	18 to 24 years	25 to 34 years	35 to 44 years	45 to 54 years
				1	2	3	4	5	6	7	8	9	10	11	12	13	14	15
			VERMONT— Cont'd															
50007	15,540	3	Chittenden	536.6	164,572	398	306.7	90.2	3.2	0.8	5.6	2.4	4.7	13.0	16.4	14.1	11.6	12.0
50009	13,620	9	Essex	663.6	6,250	2,730	9.4	96.8	1.0	1.5	1.0	1.3	4.8	12.9	6.0	8.8	9.7	14.1
50011	15,540	3	Franklin	634.1	49,421	1,000	77.9	95.7	1.2	2.4	1.3	1.7	5.9	16.3	7.6	12.7	12.5	13.9
50013	15,540	3	Grand Isle	81.8	7,090	2,657	86.7	95.0	1.4	3.3	0.9	2.1	4.1	13.9	6.3	11.0	11.0	13.7
50015		8	Lamoille	458.9	25,300	1,596	55.1	96.1	1.5	1.3	1.0	1.8	5.2	15.1	9.2	12.5	12.6	13.5
50017	17,200	9	Orange	687.0	28,999	1,458	42.2	96.9	1.1	1.2	0.9	1.4	4.7	13.6	8.1	10.5	11.4	13.3
50019		7	Orleans	693.6	26,907	1,529	38.8	96.6	1.3	1.6	0.8	1.6	4.9	14.5	7.4	10.9	11.1	13.0
50021	40,860	4	Rutland	929.8	58,672	882	63.1	96.5	1.1	0.9	1.4	1.6	4.6	13.2	9.1	10.8	10.1	13.2
50023	12,740	4	Washington	687.0	58,140	888	84.6	95.9	1.5	1.1	1.5	2.0	4.8	14.0	9.3	11.3	12.0	13.6
50025		7	Windham	785.5	42,756	1,121	54.4	94.5	2.0	1.2	1.9	2.4	4.4	13.4	7.9	10.8	10.8	12.5
50027	17,200	7	Windsor	969.6	55,286	925	57.0	96.1	1.3	1.1	1.5	1.7	4.5	13.6	6.5	11.0	11.1	12.8
51000		0	VIRGINIA	39,481.9	8,517,685	X	215.7	63.8	20.5	0.8	8.1	9.6	6.0	16.0	9.5	14.0	13.0	13.2
51001		8	Accomack	449.3	32,412	1,370	72.1	61.4	28.9	0.9	1.1	9.3	5.6	15.0	6.2	11.2	10.2	12.0
51003	16,820	3	Albemarle	720.5	108,718	559	150.9	78.7	10.6	0.6	6.6	5.9	5.3	14.5	12.0	12.9	11.6	11.8
51005		6	Alleghany	446.6	14,910	2,102	33.4	93.2	5.9	0.7	0.6	1.5	4.3	14.3	7.3	9.8	9.8	14.2
51007	40,060	1	Amelia	355.3	13,013	2,229	36.6	75.8	21.5	0.9	0.8	2.9	5.0	15.5	7.2	11.4	10.6	13.6
51009	31,340	2	Amherst	474.0	31,666	1,387	66.8	76.8	20.4	1.5	1.1	2.6	5.2	14.4	8.3	11.3	10.5	13.9
51011	31,340	2	Appomattox	334.2	15,841	2,048	47.4	78.8	20.5	0.7	0.6	1.6	5.8	15.3	7.4	12.1	11.3	12.7
51013	47,900	1	Arlington	26.0	237,521	281	9,135.4	63.8	9.9	0.7	12.9	15.8	6.0	12.1	8.2	24.1	16.6	12.5
51015	44,420	3	Augusta	967.1	75,457	734	78.0	91.8	5.1	0.6	1.0	2.9	4.6	14.5	7.5	11.7	11.5	14.0
51017		8	Bath	529.2	4,292	2,877	8.1	92.3	5.5	0.4	0.8	2.4	4.4	10.7	6.5	10.4	9.4	14.3
51019	31,340	2	Bedford	760.1	78,747	712	103.6	89.1	7.8	0.8	1.6	2.3	4.6	15.3	7.3	10.2	10.4	14.4
51021		8	Bland	357.7	6,293	2,725	17.6	94.5	4.4	0.4	0.7	0.8	3.8	11.5	6.5	12.3	12.8	15.6
51023	40,220	2	Botetourt	541.3	33,277	1,351	61.5	93.9	3.8	0.7	1.2	1.8	4.2	14.6	7.0	9.6	10.4	15.0
51025		6	Brunswick	566.2	16,384	2,017	28.9	41.7	55.4	0.6	1.2	2.4	4.1	12.2	8.8	14.1	11.9	12.6
51027		9	Buchanan	502.9	21,221	1,763	42.2	95.6	3.4	0.4	0.6	0.7	4.0	13.3	6.7	11.3	11.7	14.6
51029	16,820	3	Buckingham	579.6	16,999	1,977	29.3	63.0	35.1	0.7	0.6	2.5	4.0	13.7	7.2	13.9	13.0	14.1
51031	31,340	2	Campbell	503.2	54,973	928	109.2	81.3	15.7	0.8	1.5	2.8	4.8	14.6	8.0	13.2	11.2	13.5
51033	40,060	1	Caroline	527.6	30,772	1,415	58.3	66.2	28.8	1.4	1.8	5.0	6.6	16.4	7.0	13.9	12.5	13.3
51035		7	Carroll	474.7	29,636	1,441	62.4	95.1	1.2	0.5	0.4	3.7	4.4	13.8	6.6	10.0	10.6	14.3
51036	40,060	1	Charles City	182.8	6,941	2,680	38.0	45.5	46.9	7.8	1.5	1.8	3.7	11.5	6.3	10.7	9.5	14.9
51037		8	Charlotte	475.3	11,938	2,296	25.1	69.5	28.7	0.8	0.6	2.1	5.5	15.4	7.5	10.3	9.9	13.2
51041	40,060	1	Chesterfield	423.6	348,556	204	822.8	63.3	24.8	0.8	4.6	9.2	6.0	17.8	8.8	12.0	13.4	13.9
51043	47,900	1	Clarke	175.9	14,523	2,124	82.6	87.4	5.7	1.1	1.9	6.3	4.7	15.2	7.2	9.1	10.6	15.3
51045	40,220	2	Craig	328.1	5,064	2,827	15.4	97.7	0.7	0.5	0.4	1.5	3.9	13.7	7.0	10.1	10.2	15.2
51047	47,900	1	Culpeper	379.2	51,859	963	136.8	72.6	15.8	0.8	2.3	11.3	6.5	18.3	7.6	12.0	12.8	13.6
51049		8	Cumberland	297.5	9,809	2,442	33.0	65.6	31.7	1.0	0.9	3.0	4.8	14.6	7.5	11.8	10.3	13.8
51051	13,720	9	Dickenson	330.5	14,523	2,124	43.9	98.1	0.7	0.5	0.4	1.0	4.8	15.0	6.5	11.2	12.6	12.9
51053	40,060	1	Dinwiddie	503.9	28,529	1,480	56.6	63.0	32.6	0.7	1.4	3.9	4.7	15.2	8.0	12.9	11.3	15.0
51057		6	Essex	257.1	10,919	2,357	42.5	56.7	39.1	1.1	1.6	3.9	4.7	13.8	7.0	11.8	9.8	13.6
51059	47,900	1	Fairfax	391.0	1,150,795	38	2,943.2	53.3	10.8	0.6	22.4	16.4	6.3	17.1	8.4	13.4	14.4	14.2
51061	47,900	1	Fauquier	648.0	70,675	767	109.1	81.6	8.8	0.8	2.4	8.9	5.9	17.5	7.8	11.1	11.7	14.7
51063	13,980	3	Floyd	380.9	15,795	2,050	41.5	94.0	2.5	0.6	0.9	3.3	4.8	14.9	6.6	9.7	11.4	13.7
51065	16,820	3	Fluvanna	287.1	26,783	1,535	93.3	80.1	16.4	0.8	1.5	3.6	4.8	14.9	7.2	11.7	12.8	13.8
51067	40,220	2	Franklin	690.6	56,195	908	81.4	88.5	8.7	0.5	0.7	2.9	4.7	14.4	7.6	10.0	9.8	13.7
51069	49,020	3	Frederick	413.2	88,355	658	213.8	84.5	5.5	0.7	2.3	9.1	6.1	16.9	7.6	12.1	12.3	14.0
51071	13,980	3	Giles	357.2	16,844	1,986	47.2	95.7	2.2	0.6	0.8	1.9	5.4	15.3	7.1	10.9	11.2	14.5
51073	47,260	1	Gloucester	217.8	37,349	1,241	171.5	86.7	9.1	1.2	1.7	3.8	5.1	15.0	7.0	11.8	11.6	13.8
51075	40,060	1	Goochland	280.6	23,244	1,670	82.8	79.1	16.6	0.7	2.1	3.0	3.8	13.9	6.6	9.8	10.7	15.0
51077		9	Grayson	441.8	15,631	2,058	35.4	90.3	6.1	0.6	0.3	3.6	4.2	12.5	7.1	10.5	10.9	14.3
51079	16,820	3	Greene	155.9	19,779	1,841	126.9	84.8	8.3	0.7	2.5	6.1	6.3	17.7	6.8	12.1	12.1	13.8
51081		6	Greensville	295.2	11,627	2,317	39.4	37.2	59.5	0.5	1.1	2.6	5.1	12.2	8.4	16.0	14.7	15.6
51083		6	Halifax	817.7	34,120	1,325	41.7	60.8	36.8	0.6	0.9	2.1	5.2	15.1	7.3	10.4	9.9	12.6
51085	40,060	1	Hanover	467.9	107,239	565	229.2	85.4	10.0	0.8	2.5	3.2	5.1	16.9	8.6	10.4	11.8	14.4
51087	40,060	1	Henrico	233.7	329,261	212	1,408.9	54.6	31.4	0.8	9.9	5.8	5.9	16.6	7.7	14.4	13.3	13.4
51089	32,300	4	Henry	382.4	50,953	975	133.2	71.3	23.4	0.6	0.9	5.6	4.6	14.8	6.9	10.4	10.1	13.8
51091		8	Highland	415.2	2,210	3,029	5.3	97.2	1.0	0.3	0.7	1.0	4.5	8.6	4.2	8.6	7.7	9.6
51093	47,260	1	Isle of Wight	315.7	36,953	1,250	117.1	72.2	24.0	1.0	1.8	3.3	5.3	15.5	7.4	10.9	11.3	13.9
51095	47,260	1	James City	142.4	76,397	729	536.5	77.7	14.4	0.9	3.8	5.9	4.9	15.1	7.0	10.2	10.9	12.6
51097		8	King and Queen	315.2	7,042	2,662	22.3	68.0	28.1	2.3	0.9	3.3	4.3	13.2	7.2	11.4	9.8	14.1
51099		6	King George	179.6	26,575	1,543	148.0	76.2	17.5	1.3	2.7	5.7	6.0	18.9	8.5	12.5	13.8	13.9
51101	40,060	1	King William	273.9	16,939	1,978	61.8	79.1	16.7	2.2	1.8	2.7	6.0	17.0	7.1	13.2	12.3	14.3
51103		9	Lancaster	133.3	10,783	2,366	80.9	68.0	29.6	0.5	0.9	2.3	4.5	11.5	5.2	8.2	7.4	9.8
51105		8	Lee	435.4	23,541	1,661	54.1	93.9	3.9	0.8	0.5	1.9	4.6	14.2	6.6	12.5	12.2	13.6
51107	47,900	1	Loudoun	515.8	406,850	174	788.8	58.5	8.7	0.6	22.1	13.8	7.1	21.2	7.5	11.8	17.1	15.7

1. CBSA = Core Based Statistical Area. See Appendix A for explanation. See Appendix B for list of metropolitan areas with component counties.   2. County type code from the Economic Research Service of USDA Rural-Urban Continuum Codes. See Appendix A for definition.   3. Dry land or land partially or temporarily covered by water.   4. May be of any race.

Items 1—15

STATE County	55 to 64 years	65 to 74 years	75 years and over	Percent female	Total persons 2000	2010	Percent change 2000-2010	2010-2018	Births	Deaths	Net Migration	Number	Persons per household	Family households	Female family householder[1]	One person
	16	17	18	19	20	21	22	23	24	25	26	27	28	29	30	31
VERMONT— Cont'd																
Chittenden	13.1	8.7	6.3	51.0	146,571	156,540	6.8	5.1	12,820	8,817	4,171	64,906	2.33	57.6	8.1	28.8
Essex	18.1	15.1	10.4	49.9	6,459	6,306	-2.4	-0.9	429	499	15	2,720	2.27	63.5	9.9	31.3
Franklin	15.1	9.9	6.1	50.2	45,417	47,752	5.1	3.5	4,740	3,323	292	18,649	2.59	68.6	9.4	25.1
Grand Isle	19.2	14.4	6.4	49.5	6,901	6,970	1.0	1.7	471	490	142	2,952	2.35	70.9	7.8	24.1
Lamoille	14.5	10.5	6.8	50.0	23,233	24,475	5.3	3.4	2,147	1,644	334	10,401	2.36	60.7	8.1	30.5
Orange	17.2	13.3	7.9	49.9	28,226	28,941	2.5	0.2	2,218	2,079	-54	12,275	2.30	64.9	9.3	27.4
Orleans	15.6	13.6	9.1	49.8	26,277	27,234	3.6	-1.2	2,179	2,531	54	11,498	2.27	64.0	9.5	29.3
Rutland	16.8	13.3	8.7	50.7	63,400	61,653	-2.8	-4.8	4,403	5,534	-1,836	25,160	2.28	60.0	8.0	32.3
Washington	15.3	11.8	7.8	50.5	58,039	59,522	2.6	-2.3	4,665	4,433	-1,586	24,719	2.28	61.8	9.9	30.1
Windham	17.3	14.1	8.7	51.1	44,216	44,513	0.7	-3.9	3,228	3,639	-1,335	19,059	2.18	58.5	9.0	33.0
Windsor	17.2	13.9	9.4	51.3	57,418	56,661	-1.3	-2.4	3,979	4,767	-547	24,121	2.26	61.8	8.7	30.5
VIRGINIA	13.0	9.1	6.3	50.8	7,078,515	8,001,055	13.0	6.5	843,184	528,521	200,978	3,105,636	2.62	66.9	12.1	26.8
Accomack	16.3	13.7	9.8	51.2	38,305	33,162	-13.4	-2.3	3,225	3,681	-263	13,528	2.35	66.2	13.2	27.9
Albemarle	13.2	10.5	8.1	52.2	79,236	98,988	24.9	9.8	9,116	6,558	7,227	40,015	2.44	63.7	9.1	28.6
Alleghany	15.7	13.8	10.9	51.1	17,215	16,261	-5.5	-8.3	1,152	1,878	-622	6,866	2.21	63.0	10.1	31.9
Amelia	17.0	11.4	8.4	50.7	11,400	12,695	11.4	2.5	1,087	1,115	351	4,699	2.69	72.5	9.8	20.3
Amherst	15.2	12.0	9.2	51.5	31,894	32,354	1.4	-2.1	2,684	2,828	-550	12,110	2.53	68.7	12.8	27.8
Appomattox	14.6	11.8	8.9	51.4	13,705	15,029	9.7	5.4	1,441	1,393	768	5,948	2.59	75.3	14.8	22.3
Arlington	9.8	6.5	4.1	49.9	189,453	207,687	9.6	14.4	26,043	7,960	11,450	102,310	2.21	46.6	5.7	39.2
Augusta	15.3	12.0	9.0	49.3	65,615	73,753	12.4	2.3	5,500	5,820	2,063	28,790	2.46	71.7	8.7	24.5
Bath	16.7	15.7	12.0	49.7	5,048	4,727	-6.4	-9.2	311	502	-242	1,847	2.34	61.6	3.3	30.0
Bedford	16.5	12.7	8.6	50.7	60,371	74,936	24.1	5.1	5,845	6,318	4,324	30,927	2.48	72.8	8.5	23.2
Bland	14.5	13.2	9.8	45.3	6,871	6,824	-0.7	-7.8	380	710	-197	2,561	2.24	71.8	8.5	27.4
Botetourt	16.4	13.7	9.0	50.4	30,496	33,150	8.7	0.4	2,052	2,687	785	13,238	2.48	72.5	8.2	22.9
Brunswick	14.7	12.5	9.0	46.5	18,419	17,422	-5.4	-6.0	1,176	1,647	-556	6,048	2.36	62.9	19.9	34.0
Buchanan	16.3	13.0	9.1	49.4	26,978	24,100	-10.7	-11.9	1,605	2,486	-2,015	9,022	2.40	68.1	13.5	28.0
Buckingham	14.5	11.8	7.8	44.9	15,623	17,140	9.7	-0.8	1,215	1,316	-44	5,705	2.64	66.5	13.3	28.8
Campbell	14.8	11.3	8.6	51.4	51,078	54,807	7.3	0.3	4,482	4,443	170	22,608	2.42	68.5	12.2	27.3
Caroline	13.9	9.9	6.5	50.6	22,121	28,558	29.1	7.8	3,223	2,157	1,147	10,815	2.57	71.5	16.0	22.6
Carroll	15.8	14.2	10.3	50.5	29,245	30,076	2.8	-1.5	2,060	3,059	587	12,517	2.37	66.0	10.1	28.7
Charles City	18.9	15.2	9.4	51.8	6,926	7,256	4.8	-4.3	441	672	-81	2,899	2.42	65.2	14.0	29.9
Charlotte	16.1	12.3	9.9	50.6	12,472	12,591	1.0	-5.2	1,112	1,280	-476	4,493	2.67	63.0	12.8	32.0
Chesterfield	13.3	9.5	5.5	51.8	259,903	316,239	21.7	10.2	31,356	18,495	19,735	120,907	2.74	72.2	12.3	22.8
Clarke	16.8	12.6	8.5	50.2	12,652	14,025	10.9	3.6	1,060	1,260	696	5,568	2.54	67.2	11.2	27.8
Craig	16.6	14.1	9.3	50.5	5,091	5,175	1.6	-2.1	312	429	4	2,344	2.18	59.0	5.6	35.5
Culpeper	13.3	9.5	6.2	50.0	34,262	46,691	36.3	11.1	5,229	3,275	3,225	16,837	2.87	74.5	10.6	20.4
Cumberland	14.9	13.4	9.0	51.7	9,017	10,039	11.3	-2.3	815	786	-258	3,972	2.46	67.6	13.7	26.8
Dickenson	15.1	12.9	9.1	49.3	16,395	15,877	-3.2	-8.5	1,268	1,750	-872	6,096	2.42	68.7	12.0	28.7
Dinwiddie	15.5	10.4	7.1	51.1	24,533	28,014	14.2	1.8	2,162	2,083	456	10,347	2.64	69.9	16.3	26.0
Essex	16.2	13.8	9.4	53.2	9,989	11,149	11.6	-2.1	964	1,057	-127	4,470	2.44	63.6	11.2	32.6
Fairfax	12.7	8.2	5.3	50.4	969,749	1,081,667	11.5	6.4	122,532	41,681	-12,208	393,380	2.88	71.5	9.2	22.4
Fauquier	14.9	9.9	6.5	50.5	55,139	65,236	18.3	8.3	6,254	4,431	3,658	23,981	2.84	74.1	8.4	21.1
Floyd	16.1	13.3	9.5	49.7	13,874	15,292	10.2	3.3	1,211	1,264	564	6,434	2.41	69.3	8.3	26.6
Fluvanna	14.6	11.9	8.3	54.3	20,047	25,744	28.4	4.0	2,107	1,690	632	9,794	2.54	72.7	7.9	21.8
Franklin	16.2	14.2	9.4	50.8	47,286	56,135	18.7	0.1	4,243	4,876	752	23,203	2.36	70.2	10.5	26.2
Frederick	13.6	10.1	7.2	50.2	59,209	78,283	32.2	12.9	7,965	5,324	7,439	30,495	2.71	74.3	10.2	20.8
Giles	13.7	12.7	9.1	50.7	16,657	17,286	3.8	-2.6	1,464	1,813	-82	7,088	2.36	65.5	10.6	27.7
Gloucester	16.7	11.3	7.8	50.8	34,780	36,859	6.0	1.3	2,980	3,061	596	14,746	2.49	70.0	8.6	24.1
Goochland	17.8	13.9	8.4	51.0	16,863	21,692	28.6	7.2	1,350	1,468	1,640	8,257	2.54	77.3	6.7	20.0
Grayson	15.9	13.9	10.6	48.5	17,917	15,554	-13.2	0.5	1,121	1,741	667	6,653	2.25	63.3	10.1	33.3
Greene	13.9	10.7	6.6	51.3	15,244	18,389	20.6	7.6	1,825	1,236	812	7,260	2.63	72.5	11.0	21.3
Greensville	12.8	9.4	5.7	37.3	11,560	12,245	5.9	-5.0	974	1,092	-529	3,649	2.33	67.0	13.0	29.7
Halifax	15.1	13.9	10.5	52.1	37,355	36,243	-3.0	-5.9	2,988	3,921	-1,164	14,084	2.43	65.7	14.7	30.3
Hanover	15.1	10.5	7.3	51.1	86,320	99,850	15.7	7.4	7,614	7,074	6,910	38,208	2.65	75.8	9.2	19.7
Henrico	13.0	9.0	6.5	52.6	262,300	306,810	17.0	7.3	32,791	21,750	11,641	126,115	2.55	63.7	14.9	29.9
Henry	15.5	12.8	11.1	51.9	57,930	54,182	-6.5	-6.0	3,966	5,751	-1,421	22,161	2.31	66.7	14.6	29.6
Highland	22.3	20.8	13.6	50.2	2,536	2,319	-8.6	-4.7	138	224	-21	1,163	1.90	59.5	7.8	33.8
Isle of Wight	16.5	11.4	7.8	51.0	29,728	35,274	18.7	4.8	2,879	2,869	1,693	14,157	2.53	72.1	10.9	23.2
James City	14.2	14.0	11.3	51.7	48,102	67,385	40.1	13.4	5,673	5,572	8,873	28,410	2.53	70.9	9.5	24.9
King and Queen	17.1	13.5	9.4	49.3	6,630	6,942	4.7	1.4	501	618	219	2,811	2.51	66.2	12.7	27.5
King George	13.3	8.0	5.1	49.4	16,803	23,578	40.3	12.7	2,533	1,316	1,773	8,972	2.83	74.8	9.6	20.4
King William	14.0	10.1	6.0	51.1	13,146	15,927	21.2	6.4	1,611	1,181	585	6,079	2.68	79.6	13.6	17.6
Lancaster	17.3	18.6	17.5	52.9	11,567	11,390	-1.5	-5.3	726	1,648	330	5,081	2.11	60.0	9.0	35.1
Lee	14.9	12.5	8.8	48.0	23,589	25,583	8.5	-8.0	1,910	2,429	-1,521	9,278	2.47	68.1	12.4	29.0
Loudoun	10.4	5.6	3.7	50.5	169,599	312,348	84.2	30.3	42,470	10,200	61,576	121,299	3.07	77.7	8.4	17.3

1. No spouse present.

Table B. States and Counties — Population, Vital Statistics, Health, and Crime

STATE County	Persons in group quarters, 2018	Daytime Population, 2013-2017 Number	Daytime Population Employment/residence ratio	Births, 2018 Total	Births Rate[1]	Deaths, 2018 Number	Deaths Rate[1]	Persons under 65 with no health insurance, 2016 Number	Percent	Medicare, 2018 Total beneficiaries	Enrolled in Original Medicare	Enrolled in Medicare Advantage	Serious crimes known to police[2], 2016 Total Number	Total Rate[3]
	32	33	34	35	36	37	38	39	40	41	42	43	44	45
VERMONT— Cont'd														
Chittenden	10,143	174,593	1.15	1,490	9.1	1,133	6.9	5,451	4.2	29,686	26,267	3,419	3,666	2,264
Essex	16	4,928	0.52	45	7.2	69	11.0	307	6.6	1,906	1,763	143	15	245
Franklin	568	43,265	0.78	540	10.9	402	8.1	1,793	4.3	8,917	8,051	866	824	1,686
Grand Isle	0	4,921	0.45	49	6.9	59	8.3	274	4.9	1,918	1,690	228	45	659
Lamoille	775	24,446	0.94	249	9.8	197	7.8	1,143	5.5	5,133	4,667	466	189	747
Orange	729	23,439	0.63	261	9.0	247	8.5	1,139	5.0	6,805	6,308	497	83	288
Orleans	773	26,518	0.96	240	8.9	283	10.5	1,217	5.9	7,341	6,687	654	353	1,307
Rutland	2,274	59,135	0.98	500	8.5	667	11.4	2,081	4.6	16,370	14,656	1,714	840	1,418
Washington	2,405	62,262	1.11	518	8.9	537	9.2	1,979	4.3	13,602	12,502	1,100	1,085	1,862
Windham	1,547	45,412	1.10	350	8.2	430	10.1	1,810	5.5	11,260	10,089	1,171	799	1,855
Windsor	823	53,519	0.93	459	8.3	531	9.6	2,098	4.9	15,342	13,547	1,795	573	1,034
VIRGINIA	244,557	8,269,501	0.98	99,570	11.7	68,820	8.1	692,343	9.9	1,469,195	1,175,741	293,454	174,714	2,077
Accomack	430	32,479	0.97	350	10.8	481	14.8	4,488	17.9	8,750	7,303	1,447	568	1,755
Albemarle	6,686	112,118	1.14	1,107	10.2	875	8.0	8,710	10.6	20,566	18,340	2,226	1,580	1,484
Alleghany	281	15,289	0.97	119	8.0	249	16.7	1,137	9.8	4,506	3,917	589	168	1,085
Amelia	128	9,524	0.46	117	9.0	142	10.9	1,332	12.9	3,050	2,339	711	149	1,158
Amherst	1,393	26,584	0.63	307	9.7	383	12.1	2,764	11.4	7,799	6,415	1,384	332	1,049
Appomattox	56	12,211	0.52	177	11.2	177	11.2	1,457	11.8	3,842	3,196	646	153	993
Arlington	2,883	275,405	1.32	3,144	13.2	1,107	4.7	14,916	7.2	24,134	20,910	3,224	4,071	1,754
Augusta	2,922	68,229	0.82	635	8.4	782	10.4	6,123	10.7	18,166	15,689	2,477	808	1,091
Bath	53	4,637	1.09	36	8.4	43	10.0	351	10.7	1,264	1,165	99	29	659
Bedford	547	62,182	0.58	657	8.3	864	11.0	5,609	9.1	19,714	16,215	3,499	827	1,062
Bland	680	5,941	0.77	41	6.5	85	13.5	426	9.6	1,788	1,366	422	61	942
Botetourt	287	28,030	0.68	250	7.5	363	10.9	2,128	8.2	8,605	6,623	1,982	274	825
Brunswick	2,184	14,387	0.66	128	7.8	224	13.7	1,456	13.2	3,972	3,291	681	117	711
Buchanan	1,027	23,126	1.08	155	7.3	309	14.6	2,099	12.7	7,290	4,231	3,059	404	1,803
Buckingham	2,214	14,446	0.59	112	6.6	172	10.1	1,597	13.4	3,501	2,957	544	165	975
Campbell	458	49,817	0.80	473	8.6	554	10.1	4,788	10.8	12,644	10,448	2,196	871	1,589
Caroline	513	23,189	0.54	363	11.8	287	9.3	2,698	10.9	5,811	4,785	1,026	368	1,223
Carroll	337	25,788	0.69	219	7.4	413	13.9	3,009	13.3	8,091	6,791	1,300	458	1,553
Charles City	0	5,348	0.49	43	6.2	100	14.4	883	16.3	1,914	1,498	416	49	704
Charlotte	175	10,179	0.58	127	10.6	168	14.1	1,377	14.7	3,334	2,778	556	135	1,119
Chesterfield	4,559	292,381	0.75	3,852	11.1	2,467	7.1	23,422	8.1	59,211	45,019	14,192	7,072	2,095
Clarke	180	12,164	0.68	130	9.0	149	10.3	1,179	10.3	3,278	2,879	399	156	1,087
Craig	9	3,501	0.23	31	6.1	69	13.6	385	9.6	1,339	1,046	293	27	520
Culpeper	1,475	43,850	0.74	624	12.0	431	8.3	5,280	12.8	9,364	7,936	1,428	590	1,187
Cumberland	37	6,871	0.36	82	8.4	117	11.9	939	12.4	2,261	1,766	495	86	896
Dickenson	512	14,223	0.79	119	8.2	204	14.0	1,319	11.5	4,749	2,741	2,008	180	1,209
Dinwiddie	862	22,608	0.59	201	7.0	276	9.7	2,558	11.3	5,868	4,665	1,203	385	1,392
Essex	190	9,950	0.78	92	8.4	120	11.0	1,009	11.6	2,923	2,371	552	166	1,500
Fairfax	10,623	1,166,017	1.04	13,962	12.1	5,940	5.2	92,410	9.3	148,830	123,578	25,252	16,466	1,435
Fauquier	389	58,528	0.71	762	10.8	615	8.7	5,409	9.3	12,474	11,124	1,350	711	1,029
Floyd	85	12,401	0.55	138	8.7	160	10.1	1,572	12.8	4,033	3,260	773	133	851
Fluvanna	1,252	18,779	0.38	241	9.0	210	7.8	2,221	11.1	5,833	5,099	734	218	833
Franklin	1,159	48,030	0.67	517	9.2	682	12.1	5,114	12.0	14,568	10,685	3,883	817	1,460
Frederick	1,176	73,666	0.76	997	11.3	705	8.0	7,053	10.1	16,355	14,331	2,024	1,148	1,372
Giles	136	14,849	0.73	170	10.1	218	12.9	1,479	11.1	4,600	3,592	1,008	222	1,346
Gloucester	293	30,286	0.62	352	9.4	443	11.9	2,876	9.5	8,471	7,057	1,414	549	1,485
Goochland	982	25,601	1.33	156	6.7	173	7.4	1,080	6.3	5,742	4,531	1,211	196	881
Grayson	1,068	13,616	0.67	111	7.1	196	12.5	1,435	12.7	4,688	3,890	798	186	1,160
Greene	137	14,276	0.46	227	11.5	144	7.3	2,061	12.8	3,775	3,310	465	206	1,073
Greensville	3,413	11,444	0.96	131	11.3	116	10.0	644	9.8	2,458	1,839	619	109	927
Halifax	757	33,756	0.91	352	10.3	504	14.8	3,100	11.8	9,650	8,143	1,507	700	2,016
Hanover	1,953	96,336	0.87	955	8.9	850	7.9	6,029	7.1	20,680	15,692	4,988	1,407	1,362
Henrico	2,749	333,123	1.05	3,762	11.4	2,752	8.4	26,793	9.7	55,922	41,243	14,679	8,865	2,711
Henry	561	48,156	0.81	441	8.7	757	14.9	5,108	13.0	15,026	10,990	4,036	1,416	2,768
Highland	0	1,992	0.75	18	8.1	28	12.7	263	17.2	779	708	71	28	1,281
Isle of Wight	310	29,985	0.65	367	9.9	396	10.7	2,614	8.8	8,192	6,485	1,707	525	1,446
James City	1,141	69,472	0.89	739	9.7	689	9.0	4,420	7.9	20,337	17,644	2,693	1,237	1,675
King and Queen	0	5,087	0.37	54	7.7	83	11.8	788	14.2	1,761	1,470	291	71	992
King George	301	26,528	1.08	299	11.3	162	6.1	1,564	7.0	3,845	3,468	377	285	1,107
King William	72	12,594	0.54	208	12.3	147	8.7	1,343	9.8	3,378	2,852	526	115	708
Lancaster	183	11,227	1.09	93	8.6	193	17.9	764	11.1	4,320	3,734	586	163	1,506
Lee	1,460	21,667	0.62	205	8.7	325	13.8	2,363	13.4	6,440	3,751	2,689	360	1,472
Loudoun	1,696	343,498	0.84	5,305	13.0	1,562	3.8	24,460	6.9	36,830	30,694	6,136	4,054	1,048

1. Per 1,000 estimated resident population.   2. Data for serious crimes have not been adjusted for underreporting; this may affect comparability between geographic areas and over time.   3. Per 100,000 population estimated by the FBI.

Items 32—45

Table B. States and Counties — Crime, Education, Money Income, and Poverty

STATE County	Serious crimes known to police², 2016 (cont.)¹ — Rate		School enrollment and attainment, 2013-2017				Local government expenditures,⁵ 2014-2015		Money income, 2013-2017				Income and poverty, 2017			
			Enrollment³		Attainment⁴ (percent)				Households					Percent below poverty level		
	Violent	Property	Total	Percent private	High school graduate or less	Bachelor's degree or more	Total current spending (mil dol)	Current spending per student (dollars)	Per capita income⁶	Median income (dollars)	Percent with income of less than $50,000	Percent with income of $200,000 or more	Median household income (dollars)	All persons	Children under 18 years	Children 5 to 17 years in families
	46	47	48	49	50	51	52	53	54	55	56	57	58	59	60	61
VERMONT— Cont'd																
Chittenden..................	163	2,101	46,011	21.9	26.0	49.6	385.2	17,949	36,384	66,906	37.3	7.1	65,851	10.8	9.9	8.9
Essex..........................	16	229	1,106	13.5	61.1	14.7	14.6	21,327	23,022	38,767	60.7	0.8	40,288	14.6	21.9	20.4
Franklin......................	147	1,538	10,419	7.2	46.5	24.7	131.7	15,829	30,624	62,214	37.9	3.6	60,670	8.9	11.9	10.6
Grand Isle..................	15	644	1,336	12.9	33.0	38.3	12.4	13,339	38,635	66,111	34.4	7.2	61,971	8.2	11.9	10.7
Lamoille.....................	63	683	5,862	12.6	33.9	37.6	63.8	17,309	31,390	54,899	46.2	4.7	56,965	11.8	12.9	12.1
Orange.......................	14	274	5,951	14.9	43.2	30.0	67.8	17,066	29,651	56,584	43.9	2.4	56,138	10.4	13.1	12.3
Orleans......................	193	1,115	5,416	14.4	50.7	22.0	73.7	19,033	25,392	45,664	53.2	2.4	44,070	15.2	19.6	17.7
Rutland......................	162	1,256	13,040	15.8	43.0	30.0	151.6	19,983	28,443	52,635	47.8	2.4	53,492	10.8	14.8	13.6
Washington................	127	1,735	13,551	26.6	34.8	40.5	152.5	18,872	32,137	60,602	41.3	3.8	62,203	9.4	10.1	9.1
Windham....................	111	1,744	8,957	27.5	37.4	37.0	107.8	18,149	29,819	50,831	49.1	3.6	47,827	11.6	15.3	14.2
Windsor......................	88	945	10,977	16.0	38.1	36.0	148.5	19,732	34,264	56,828	43.8	5.4	58,403	9.9	11.1	9.8
VIRGINIA....................	218	1,859	2,146,448	17.1	35.3	37.6	14,381.7	D	36,268	68,766	36.6	9.2	71,518	10.7	14.0	13.3
Accomack...................	204	1,551	6,197	12.8	56.8	19.6	53.3	10,145	24,266	42,260	56.3	2.5	44,038	17.8	28.0	27.6
Albemarle..................	101	1,384	30,130	17.1	26.2	52.3	(7) 228.5	(7) 12,669	39,273	72,265	34.2	10.6	77,591	7.9	8.8	8.2
Alleghany...................	265	820	2,940	15.2	52.9	15.8	26.1	11,184	25,952	46,020	52.7	1.0	49,655	14.5	20.7	19.7
Amelia.......................	163	995	2,916	18.3	54.9	14.5	16.7	9,204	26,118	58,535	41.0	0.5	54,979	11.4	14.4	14.0
Amherst.....................	133	916	6,975	30.6	50.3	19.9	43.9	10,292	24,296	49,677	50.2	1.6	48,980	12.7	18.3	17.1
Appomattox................	123	870	3,495	18.3	51.1	20.6	20.3	8,827	26,347	54,875	45.6	2.6	50,148	11.9	17.5	16.6
Arlington....................	161	1,594	47,449	29.1	14.1	74.1	428.0	17,428	67,061	112,138	19.1	21.8	114,705	5.7	7.3	7.6
Augusta......................	100	991	14,753	20.7	51.4	23.4	105.0	9,980	30,088	59,544	40.9	3.7	58,368	8.9	11.5	11.0
Bath...........................	227	432	1,032	14.8	54.4	15.9	10.2	16,729	28,195	44,483	58.4	0.8	48,753	10.1	14.2	14.3
Bedford	68	994	17,352	22.3	41.0	28.3	92.1	9,126	30,633	59,405	40.9	4.2	65,172	9	12.5	11.5
Bland.........................	31	911	1,188	12.8	52.2	14.2	8.0	9,653	23,505	46,927	55.3	1.7	45,564	13.7	17.2	15.1
Botetourt....................	111	714	7,288	19.9	40.4	28.3	49.8	10,240	34,733	64,733	38.3	5.4	70,388	6.4	8.3	7.7
Brunswick..................	128	583	3,702	17.0	59.7	13.1	20.5	11,034	20,278	40,871	58.0	1.6	42,569	21.5	30.1	27.4
Buchanan...................	254	1,549	4,248	15.0	64.8	10.8	36.6	11,702	19,241	30,828	67.4	1.4	32,993	27.9	40.3	35.4
Buckingham...............	118	857	3,549	16.9	64.6	11.4	22.9	10,669	19,702	46,610	52.3	0.6	41,763	17.5	22.7	21.9
Campbell....................	224	1,365	12,183	25.7	47.2	21.5	75.3	9,254	26,417	48,823	50.9	2.5	50,849	11.3	15.8	14.7
Caroline.....................	150	1,073	6,421	18.4	53.4	19.2	40.0	9,173	28,039	60,925	39.5	3.0	62,207	9.6	15.0	14.4
Carroll.......................	85	1,468	5,499	9.5	53.4	14.5	41.6	10,681	23,690	41,145	60.1	0.9	42,262	16.8	22.7	20.0
Charles City	58	647	1,133	15.4	62.1	12.8	9.6	13,490	32,689	55,069	46.3	3.1	54,504	12	17.5	17.4
Charlotte	232	887	2,458	5.5	60.5	11.9	22.7	11,554	19,830	38,350	64.9	2.0	40,864	17.4	26.2	26.1
Chesterfield...............	143	1,951	89,999	15.3	31.9	38.4	549.7	9,203	35,370	76,969	30.1	7.3	80,573	6.7	8.7	8.0
Clarke........................	118	969	3,014	19.3	41.5	31.5	21.9	10,967	38,658	72,129	33.9	9.4	76,359	6.7	8.1	7.1
Craig.........................	58	463	963	11.1	50.8	19.2	7.3	11,266	26,753	53,526	48.3	0.0	50,210	11.7	19.3	18.4
Culpeper....................	171	1,016	11,949	17.6	46.8	23.4	78.4	9,715	29,979	69,693	34.3	5.7	69,318	9.9	13.2	12.6
Cumberland................	219	677	1,940	24.6	56.2	16.7	15.1	10,543	23,488	43,020	55.6	0.8	44,699	15.3	23.7	22.9
Dickenson..................	228	981	2,794	8.2	62.9	9.3	24.4	10,377	21,082	29,916	70.7	1.0	33,383	25	30.7	29.1
Dinwiddie...................	235	1,157	5,944	12.3	55.7	16.6	42.7	9,610	25,981	54,640	45.7	2.9	57,284	10.1	16.0	15.3
Essex........................	208	1,292	2,236	15.7	52.8	18.9	16.6	10,854	25,730	50,629	49.0	2.0	50,112	13.6	23.4	24.7
Fairfax.......................	100	1,335	309,068	18.9	20.8	60.7	(10)2,551.5	(10) 13,752	52,976	117,515	17.0	22.8	117,989	6.7	8.6	7.6
Fauquier....................	75	954	16,839	18.1	35.9	35.3	132.6	11,878	43,067	94,775	24.5	13.9	96,835	5.7	6.6	6.0
Floyd.........................	192	659	2,749	21.1	49.0	19.4	19.1	9,594	25,446	48,396	51.7	1.9	48,341	12.4	17.7	16.8
Fluvanna....................	122	710	6,121	15.9	34.3	32.3	36.1	9,949	31,952	67,964	34.1	5.0	71,863	6.7	9.0	8.1
Franklin.....................	172	1,288	12,084	23.1	46.8	20.7	76.0	10,144	27,282	51,208	49.1	3.0	51,031	13.3	18.4	16.9
Frederick...................	102	1,270	19,549	18.1	44.2	27.7	(9) 196.6	(9) 11,267	32,554	71,037	32.0	5.0	72,139	6.7	8.8	8.4
Giles.........................	115	1,231	3,327	11.4	51.1	17.0	24.0	9,903	25,004	49,734	50.3	1.9	52,808	11.4	16.2	15.1
Gloucester.................	114	1,371	8,022	15.4	42.9	22.8	55.1	9,966	32,271	63,881	36.3	4.5	63,902	9.8	13.8	13.4
Goochland..................	103	778	4,619	30.3	34.0	38.9	27.7	11,343	47,610	86,652	27.5	15.4	100,686	6.1	7.9	7.4
Grayson.....................	119	1,042	2,887	10.0	57.7	12.8	20.8	11,780	20,525	32,048	67.7	0.9	37,247	19.1	26.6	26.6
Greene.......................	120	953	4,668	18.7	46.0	26.7	30.6	9,613	30,215	62,952	37.9	2.6	65,394	8.3	12.3	11.9
Greensville................	85	842	2,246	10.5	68.0	7.5	(8)26.2	(8) 10,338	16,835	42,121	58.4	0.6	47,097	23.9	25.6	25.9
Halifax.......................	216	1,800	6,802	12.6	56.2	15.9	53.0	9,596	21,155	39,233	59.5	0.9	42,552	17.9	24.4	23.8
Hanover.....................	128	1,234	26,884	17.9	33.3	37.9	171.2	9,488	37,924	84,955	26.9	8.4	89,723	5.4	5.9	5.4
Henrico......................	193	2,518	80,526	16.5	30.9	42.1	470.9	9,238	36,497	66,447	37.3	8.0	67,434	9.5	13.9	13.6
Henry.........................	225	2,543	10,188	8.8	54.1	12.8	68.0	9,151	21,473	36,779	64.4	1.2	41,206	16.2	24.9	23.4
Highland....................	183	1,098	218	37.2	51.1	25.0	3.7	18,460	32,648	45,094	57.0	4.6	43,939	12.5	18.0	17.6
Isle of Wight..............	132	1,313	8,661	21.2	40.3	26.9	54.6	9,793	33,172	67,767	36.6	4.8	70,842	8.5	11.2	10.3
James City................	120	1,554	17,409	14.8	25.1	47.9	(11) 129.4	(11) 11,365	42,047	80,772	29.7	10.2	88,149	6.8	9.1	8.6
King and Queen..........	252	741	1,434	20.2	56.4	18.9	9.7	10,910	25,831	51,495	49.0	1.4	51,055	12.3	18.1	17.0
King George..............	97	1,009	6,600	17.6	33.4	34.2	37.8	8,631	35,676	84,770	26.4	7.3	86,878	6.8	8.5	7.8
King William..............	99	610	4,039	15.7	47.6	19.0	31.8	10,593	31,192	67,423	31.7	4.6	69,806	6.8	9.8	9.1
Lancaster..................	185	1,321	1,762	7.6	40.7	31.9	15.3	12,510	33,997	51,495	49.5	5.2	50,793	12.9	23.7	23.2
Lee............................	78	1,395	4,709	5.4	59.0	11.1	34.5	10,504	18,514	32,590	65.8	1.6	32,152	28.2	33.0	29.7
Loudoun.....................	119	929	112,112	16.9	19.4	59.8	933.9	12,720	50,456	129,588	14.1	24.8	136,191	3	3.0	2.6

1. Data for serious crimes have not been adjusted for underreporting; this may affect comparability between geographic areas and over time.   2. Per 100,000 population estimated by the FBI.   3. All persons 3 years old and over enrolled in nursery school through college.   4. Persons 25 years old and over.   5. Elementary and secondary education expenditures.   6. Based on population estimated by the American Community Survey, 2013–2017.   7. Charlottesville city is included with Albemarle county.   8. Emporia city is included with Greensville county.   9. Winchester city is included with Frederick county.   10. Fairfax city is included with Fairfax county   11. Williamsburg city is included with James city county

Table B. States and Counties — **Personal Income and Earnings**

	Personal income, 2017										Earnings, 2017		
			Per capita[1]			Supplements to wages and salaries, employer contributions (mil dol)						Contributions for government social insurance (mil dol)	
STATE County	Total (mil dol)	Percent change 2016-2017	Dollars	Rank	Wages and salaries (mil dol)	Pension and insurance	Government social insurance	Proprietors' income (mil dol)	Dividends, interest, and rent (mil dol)	Personal transfer receipts (mil dol)	Total (mil dol)	From employee and self-employed	From employer
	62	63	64	65	66	67	68	69	70	71	72	73	74

VERMONT— Cont'd													
Chittenden	9,610	3.4	59,184	178	5,636	984	469	814	2,027	1,385	7,903	498	469
Essex	218	4.1	34,997	2,349	39	11	4	21	36	65	75	7	4
Franklin	2,173	3.0	44,320	984	845	186	74	139	323	414	1,244	81	74
Grand Isle	401	3.9	57,258	218	45	10	4	36	87	64	94	8	4
Lamoille	1,306	2.4	51,558	394	499	89	45	136	336	228	768	52	45
Orange	1,312	3.3	45,275	871	324	70	28	120	239	276	543	39	28
Orleans	1,137	3.3	42,350	1,224	428	91	40	101	196	337	659	47	40
Rutland	2,953	2.1	49,974	467	1,218	239	107	178	491	948	1,743	123	107
Washington	3,437	3.8	58,968	186	1,785	331	143	258	686	693	2,517	164	143
Windham	2,110	2.2	49,220	517	966	176	85	222	478	492	1,450	100	85
Windsor	3,032	3.0	55,034	278	1,112	219	96	244	768	612	1,670	117	96
VIRGINIA	466,743	4.0	55,137	X	240,108	37,975	17,382	27,567	95,567	64,529	323,031	19,522	17,382
Accomack	1,325	3.2	40,701	1,443	559	114	42	83	291	365	797	53	42
Albemarle	[2]10,531	[2]5.5	[2]67,630	[2]82	[2]5,693	[2]1,068	[2]399	[2]879	[2]3,642	[2]1,041	[2]8,038	[2]461	[2]399
Alleghany	[3]787	[3]2.5	[3]38,094	[3]1,867	[3]370	[3]65	[3]28	[3]16	[3]135	[3]258	[3]478	[3]36	[3]28
Amelia	560	4.1	43,032	1,138	100	19	7	46	83	125	172	12	7
Amherst	1,137	3.4	35,992	2,204	337	68	25	31	187	314	461	36	25
Appomattox	575	3.3	36,663	2,097	114	24	8	14	86	163	161	14	8
Arlington	21,026	4.0	89,487	20	17,868	2,614	1,295	1,258	4,598	1,005	23,034	1,289	1,295
Augusta	[10]5,177	[10]4.4	[10]42,436	[10]1,211	[10]2,130	[10]386	[10]155	[10]331	[10]1,007	[10]1,121	[10]3,002	[10]201	[10]155
Bath	253	3.1	58,876	187	102	17	7	8	90	50	133	9	7
Bedford	3,417	3.2	43,826	1,039	796	137	59	131	661	731	1,123	89	59
Bland	223	3.3	35,046	2,344	91	23	7	7	41	69	128	9	7
Botetourt	1,598	2.2	48,152	611	466	79	34	60	294	316	639	47	34
Brunswick	527	2.7	32,432	2,701	154	32	11	8	87	186	205	17	11
Buchanan	741	5.3	34,420	2,423	316	64	23	25	104	313	428	34	23
Buckingham	502	3.9	29,397	2,961	140	33	10	23	80	149	206	16	10
Campbell	[7]4,945	[7]3.1	[7]36,356	[7]2,142	[7]3,425	[7]517	[7]247	[7]158	[7]930	[7]1,391	[7]4,346	[7]280	[7]247
Caroline	1,234	4.5	40,509	1,470	254	56	19	29	190	247	358	27	19
Carroll	[6]1,269	[6]4.2	[6]34,940	[6]2,360	[6]431	[6]85	[6]33	[6]62	[6]206	[6]435	[6]611	[6]47	[6]33
Charles City	300	2.8	42,788	1,171	85	14	6	5	58	71	111	9	6
Charlotte	412	1.3	33,975	2,486	113	26	8	17	77	134	163	14	8
Chesterfield	17,783	4.8	51,755	386	7,006	1,098	505	741	2,978	2,514	9,350	588	505
Clarke	922	4.5	63,577	120	197	30	14	53	238	113	294	20	14
Craig	179	1.0	35,458	2,279	29	6	2	4	34	50	42	4	2
Culpeper	2,274	4.3	44,336	982	729	128	53	146	385	382	1,056	69	53
Cumberland	364	4.2	37,106	2,012	54	12	4	24	57	97	95	8	4
Dickenson	454	2.9	30,687	2,875	142	32	10	8	63	200	192	17	10
Dinwiddie	[9]3,083	[9]4.7	[9]39,637	[9]1,614	[9]1,350	[9]239	[9]99	[9]79	[9]559	[9]917	[9]1,768	[9]119	[9]99
Essex	443	2.7	40,170	1,527	140	25	10	16	93	119	191	15	10
Fairfax	[5]93,042	[5]3.3	[5]78,376	[5]40	[5]60,685	[5]7,021	[5]4,144	[5]5,489	[5]21,597	[5]6,392	[5]77,339	[5]4,632	[5]4,144
Fauquier	4,637	4.3	66,756	87	1,185	187	85	291	1,105	486	1,748	111	85
Floyd	577	2.6	36,640	2,099	111	22	8	23	109	151	165	15	8
Fluvanna	1,141	5.8	43,145	1,124	184	40	13	51	217	210	289	23	13
Franklin	2,185	2.7	38,707	1,774	562	102	42	118	450	549	825	65	42
Frederick	[12]5,550	[12]5.0	[12]48,509	[12]590	[12]2,824	[12]469	[12]205	[12]404	[12]967	[12]839	[12]3,902	[12]239	[12]205
Giles	640	2.6	38,015	1,882	198	39	15	20	103	183	273	21	15
Gloucester	1,788	3.7	47,935	629	356	71	26	59	339	340	511	39	26
Goochland	2,108	5.6	92,911	18	1,678	166	103	92	677	206	2,039	125	103
Grayson	498	2.4	31,820	2,777	97	26	7	13	92	172	143	15	7
Greene	844	5.7	43,055	1,137	146	27	11	67	135	150	251	18	11
Greensville	[4]544	[4]6.6	[4]32,071	[4]2,745	[4]320	[4]64	[4]23	[4]14	[4]79	[4]177	[4]421	[4]27	[4]23
Halifax	1,236	2.7	35,761	2,237	488	98	36	45	225	407	668	50	36
Hanover	6,166	4.6	58,214	199	2,483	350	177	406	1,072	788	3,417	215	177
Henrico	20,865	4.8	63,634	118	11,552	1,513	813	3,807	3,726	2,414	17,685	1,031	813
Henry	[8]2,435	[8]2.8	[8]37,827	[8]1,908	[8]912	[8]170	[8]68	[8]105	[8]456	[8]830	[8]1,255	[8]96	[8]68
Highland	95	1.7	42,873	1,155	18	5	1	7	38	25	31	2	1
Isle of Wight	1,943	3.9	53,168	340	547	82	37	61	304	335	727	51	37
James City	[11]5,646	[11]4.4	[11]62,350	[11]131	[11]1,875	[11]323	[11]135	[11]265	[11]1,574	[11]843	[11]2,598	[11]171	[11]135
King and Queen	291	4.4	41,599	1,319	48	9	4	12	47	71	73	6	4
King George	1,342	4.0	50,971	413	956	239	78	72	254	168	1,344	75	78
King William	757	5.1	45,300	868	190	31	14	29	112	138	264	19	14
Lancaster	598	4.6	55,403	265	186	30	13	37	227	151	266	21	13
Lee	696	2.5	29,295	2,967	167	45	13	16	107	289	241	22	13
Loudoun	29,790	5.9	74,834	54	11,483	1,480	786	1,548	3,981	1,490	15,296	891	786

1. Based on the resident population estimated as of July 1 of the year shown.　2. Charlottesville city is included with Albemarle county.　3. Covington city is included with Alleghany county.　4. Emporia city is included with Greensville county.　5. Fairfax city and Falls Church city are included with Fairfax county.　6. Galax city is included with Carroll county.　7. Lynchburg city is included with Campbell county.　8. Martinsville city is included with Henry county.　9. Petersburg and Colonial Heights cities are included with Dinwiddie county　10. Staunton and Waynesboro cities are included with Augusta county.　11. Williamsburg city is included with James City county.　12. Winchester city is included with Frederick county.

Table B. States and Counties — Earnings, Social Security, and Housing

STATE County	Earnings, 2017 (cont.)									Social Security beneficiaries, December 2017			Housing units, 2018	
	Percent by selected industries											Supplemental Security Income recipients, 2017		
	Farm	Mining, quarrying, and extractions	Construction	Manufacturing	Information; professional, scientific, technical services	Retail trade	Finance, insurance, real estate, and leasing	Health care and social assistance	Government	Number	Rate[1]		Total	Percent change, 2010-2018
	75	76	77	78	79	80	81	82	83	84	85	86	87	88
VERMONT— Cont'd														
Chittenden	0.3	0	6.6	10.5	15	6.8	6.4	15.1	17.5	29,210	180	3,114	70,352	7
Essex	4.6	D	10.8	8.9	D	D	D	D	34.1	2,120	340	236	5,197	3.5
Franklin	2.6	0.2	5.8	16.3	3.7	7.3	2.3	13.2	29.8	9,860	201	1,277	22,714	5.2
Grand Isle	3.9	D	17.5	2	D	D	D	D	17.7	1,970	282	137	5,332	5.6
Lamoille	0.6	D	11.1	4.7	8.9	7.7	3.9	15.3	14.4	5,305	209	486	13,815	6.5
Orange	3.6	0.2	14.6	6.6	D	5.9	D	17.8	20.9	7,070	244	624	15,522	4.5
Orleans	3	D	10	12.2	D	10.2	3.7	16	20	7,680	286	943	17,743	9.8
Rutland	0.4	1.9	8.3	13.2	4.7	8.2	3.4	18.2	15.3	17,370	294	2,001	34,541	2.3
Washington	0.4	0.2	5.9	6.1	7.3	6.4	12.9	12.8	24.8	13,975	240	1,398	30,872	3.1
Windham	0.6	D	8.8	12.6	5.8	7.3	4.3	15	12.3	11,550	269	1,232	30,764	3.5
Windsor	0.5	0.1	9.2	7	11	6.6	4	12.2	24.2	15,525	282	1,236	35,032	2.7
VIRGINIA	0.1	0.1	5.6	5.5	19.6	4.9	7.2	9.3	23.5	1,501,543	177	157,658	3,538,847	5.2
Accomack	3.1	0	4.8	18.4	12.1	5.1	3.3	D	27.1	9,560	294	1,109	21,290	1.4
Albemarle	[2] 0.1	[2] 0.1	[2] 4.2	[2] D	[2] 12.6	[2] 4.6	[2] 8.0	[2] 10.5	[2] 35.3	19,800	184	978	46,076	9.4
Alleghany	[3] -0.7	[3] D	[3] 6.5	[3] D	[3] D	[3] 5.8	[3] D	[3] D	[3] 18.3	4,605	305	303	8,017	-0.8
Amelia	12.8	D	15.3	7.8	3.2	4.6	2.8	D	17.7	3,315	255	309	5,621	4.8
Amherst	0	0	8.9	22.3	D	7.8	2.4	D	27.1	8,405	266	804	14,227	1.8
Appomattox	-4	D	10.9	3.2	D	13.8	2.7	D	28.3	4,150	265	496	7,370	6.1
Arlington	0	0	1.4	D	34.4	1.8	5.1	3.5	29.9	20,170	86	2,213	116,532	10.5
Augusta	[10] 1.3	[10] D	[10] D	[10] 17.9	[10] 3.7	6.5	[10] 4.3	[10] D	[10] 17.6	18,815	250	642	32,732	4.9
Bath	-0.6	-0.1	6.1	1.7	14.1	1.4	1.7	D	15.8	1,365	318	80	3,297	0.9
Bedford	-1.3	-0.1	8.7	13.6	8.9	7.2	6	11.4	15.7	20,640	265	1,164	36,997	6.1
Bland	-3.4	D	3.7	34.2	1.3	D	D	D	26.7	1,955	308	135	3,331	2
Botetourt	-0.9	D	9	18.6	4.2	4.4	3.8	6.4	14	8,700	262	730	14,927	2.5
Brunswick	-0.2	D	7	8.9	D	4.1	3	D	25.9	4,350	268	652	8,244	1
Buchanan	-0.1	28.1	7.2	4.8	D	5.5	3	8.3	19.4	8,400	390	1,595	11,560	-0.1
Buckingham	1	D	10.4	3	3.7	4.7	1.9	9.9	37.5	3,805	223	426	7,443	2.8
Campbell	[7] 0.0	[7] D	[7] D	[7] 19.7	[7] 10.2	[7] 6.2	[7] 6.5	[7] 17.4	[7] 10.2	13,765	250	1,081	26,082	5.4
Caroline	-1.2	D	8.4	5.6	D	4.8	1.9	D	32.8	6,265	206	481	12,328	5.1
Carroll	[6] 0.7	[6] D	[6] D	[6] 17.3	[6] 4.0	[6] 10.0	[6] 2.6	[6] 17.9	[6] 21.5	8,835	297	568	16,720	0.8
Charles City	-2.3	D	25.1	15.2	D	2.4	D	D	17.5	2,060	294	137	3,378	4.6
Charlotte	-4.1	0	5.4	16	D	4.9	2.3	D	29.2	3,675	303	574	6,334	0.9
Chesterfield	0	D	8	8.5	10.4	7.9	7.4	10.8	16.4	61,275	178	4,474	132,356	8
Clarke	2.3	D	11.1	13.8	13.4	3.2	5.3	6.2	14.3	3,205	221	137	6,382	2.4
Craig	-6.7	-0.1	9	D	D	8.8	7.8	D	30	1,475	291	99	2,909	3.7
Culpeper	-0.7	0.5	11.1	8.5	12.2	8.6	3.8	12.5	20.9	9,645	188	914	18,946	7.3
Cumberland	10.5	-0.1	22.1	7.6	D	5.9	D	D	26.1	2,465	251	231	4,737	2.4
Dickenson	-1.3	35.1	6.7	0.7	D	6.2	D	6.2	24	5,470	370	898	7,562	-0.1
Dinwiddie	[9] 0.4	[9] D	[9] D	[9] 7.8	[9] 2.9	[9] 8.3	[9] 5.0	[9] D	[9] 22.1	6,340	225	469	11,799	3.2
Essex	-1.6	0	6.1	7.7	3.3	15	6.2	21.6	16.5	3,110	282	355	5,869	1.9
Fairfax	[5] 0.0	[5] 0.0	[5] 4.4	[5] 0.6	[5] 37.5	[5] 3.8	[5] 8.5	[5] 6.6	[5] 16.5	129,285	113	11,055	415,461	1.8
Fauquier	-1.1	D	14.6	3.3	15.7	7.1	8	9.7	20.5	12,330	177	600	27,140	5.9
Floyd	-3	D	10.8	12.7	D	6.8	4.9	14.5	21.9	4,285	272	289	8,075	3.6
Fluvanna	-1.2	-0.3	16.5	3.2	4.6	3.8	2.8	6.5	29.3	6,020	228	237	11,047	6.2
Franklin	0.1	D	13	18.6	4.1	8.5	3.7	9.4	16.5	15,315	271	1,237	30,021	2.4
Frederick	[12] 0.2	[12] D	[12] D	[12] 13.7	[12] D	[12] 8.1	[12] 7.6	[12] 17.6	[12] 17.9	16,895	195	915	34,843	11.2
Giles	-1.2	0	D	26.3	9.4	8.2	2.5	D	17.1	5,000	297	551	8,359	0.5
Gloucester	0	D	9.8	2.3	4.8	12.7	4.3	16.7	27	8,900	239	649	16,755	5.7
Goochland	-0.3	0.4	5.1	2	3.1	1.1	53.6	1.8	4.3	5,650	249	243	9,452	9.8
Grayson	-5.7	D	6.2	15.5	D	2.8	7	D	37.7	5,035	321	344	9,238	0.8
Greene	-0.1	D	15.2	1.9	12.7	10.2	2.3	D	20.8	3,930	200	238	8,344	11.2
Greensville	[4] 2.7	[4] D	[4] D	[4] D	[4] D	[4] 5.3	[4] D	[4] 14.0	[4] 26.4	2,500	214	54	4,199	2.7
Halifax	-0.7	D	6.8	18	2.8	5.7	2.9	17.5	17.5	10,590	306	1,492	18,193	1
Hanover	-0.2	0.1	12.3	7.5	6.6	9	4.1	12	9.7	21,090	199	935	41,872	9.2
Henrico	0	0	4	3.3	13.2	5.1	15.5	13.7	7.9	57,460	175	5,042	138,177	4.1
Henry	[8] 0.3	[8] 0.0	[8] D	[8] 20.8	[8] D	[8] 9.9	[8] 3.9	[8] D	[8] 17.9	17,105	334	2,438	26,182	-0.4
Highland	12.8	-0.1	8.7	4.2	D	3.5	D	D	29	845	382	23	1,883	2.7
Isle of Wight	0.4	0	5.2	25.1	D	3.1	3.5	D	12.9	8,555	234	508	15,889	8.6
James City	[11] -0.1	[11] D	[11] 5.5	[11] 5.9	[11] D	[11] 6.7	[11] 6.8	[11] 11.7	[11] 23.5	19,695	261	821	33,763	12.3
King and Queen	-1.1	D	16	13.3	D	D	D	D	21.9	1,895	271	151	3,512	2.9
King George	-0.2	D	1.7	3.5	18.7	2	1.5	1.3	65.3	3,885	148	288	10,165	7.3
King William	-1.2	D	8.3	26.7	D	5.8	4.8	D	16.8	3,665	219	199	7,155	9.8
Lancaster	-0.8	-0.1	10.6	2	8.4	9.4	13.5	D	12	4,365	405	290	7,655	3.5
Lee	-3.7	2.6	6.6	1.9	2	9.2	3	12.2	45.1	7,270	306	1,622	11,778	0.3
Loudoun	-0.1	D	10.7	5.6	28.2	4.7	3.6	5.9	13.8	33,865	85	2,091	136,506	24.7

1. Per 1,000 resident population estimated as of July 1 of the year shown.   2. Charlottesville city is included with Albemarle county.   3. Covington city is included with Alleghany county.   4. Emporia city is included with Greensville county.   5. Fairfax city and Falls Church city are included with Fairfax county.   6. Galax city is included with Carroll county.   7. Lynchburg city is included with Campbell county.   8. Martinsville city is included with Henry county.   9. Petersburg and Colonial Heights cities are included with Dinwiddie county   10. Staunton and Waynesboro cities are included with Augusta county.   11. Williamsburg city is included with James City county.   12. Winchester city is included with Frederick county.

Table B. States and Counties — Housing, Labor Force, and Employment

STATE County	Housing units, 2013-2017 Owner-occupied Total	Percent	Median value[1]	Median owner cost as a percent of income With a mortgage	Without a mortgage[2]	Renter-occupied Median rent[3]	Median rent as a percent of income[2]	Substandard units[4] (percent)	Civilian labor force, 2018 Total	Percent change, 2017-2018	Unemployment Total	Rate[5]	Civilian employment[6], 2013-2017 Total	Percent Management, business, science, and arts	Construction, production, and maintenance occupations
	89	90	91	92	93	94	95	96	97	98	99	100	101	102	103
VERMONT— Cont'd															
Chittenden	64,906	63.1	280,000	22.9	14.2	1,186	32.7	1.8	96,716	-0.2	1,984	2.1	90,054	47.6	15.2
Essex	2,720	79.0	128,900	23.6	17.1	688	28	2.4	2,698	0	98	3.6	2,784	27.8	30.0
Franklin	18,649	74.3	209,100	22.7	15.7	930	27.1	2.1	27,610	-0.2	697	2.5	25,865	36.2	25.9
Grand Isle	2,952	80.0	274,700	24.3	16.7	1,028	30.3	0.9	4,054	-0.3	129	3.2	3,766	37.5	22.4
Lamoille	10,401	71.4	225,200	25.1	18.6	894	29.1	2.2	14,071	-0.2	495	3.5	13,437	37.6	20.7
Orange	12,275	80.7	188,300	24.9	15.7	847	30.4	2.7	15,980	0.2	426	2.7	15,343	38.4	25.0
Orleans	11,498	77.8	161,100	24.7	16.4	736	30.3	2.1	13,612	-0.1	604	4.4	12,227	33.5	27.4
Rutland	25,160	72.1	177,600	23.6	16.2	821	30.7	4.4	31,142	0	975	3.1	30,152	34.2	23.3
Washington	24,719	71.6	217,200	22.8	16.0	880	28.9	1.9	34,497	0.6	896	2.6	31,703	44.7	17.5
Windham	19,059	67.7	212,000	25.5	17.2	862	32.4	2.8	22,643	-0.9	646	2.9	21,882	40.2	20.8
Windsor	24,121	71.7	216,300	24.3	16.3	892	30.4	1.9	29,178	0.3	682	2.3	28,099	39.1	21.0
VIRGINIA	3,105,636	66.2	255,800	21.9	10.1	1,166	29.5	2.3	4,331,380	0.5	128,579	3	4,084,035	43.3	17.8
Accomack	13,528	70.0	157,200	21.4	11.0	771	29.9	2.5	16,762	0.8	639	3.8	13,837	31.1	32.4
Albemarle	40,015	63.6	329,600	20.2	10.0	1,189	28.5	1.1	55,903	1.1	1,495	2.7	50,689	54.0	11.8
Alleghany	6,866	76.1	113,600	17.7	10.0	653	28.8	1.1	6,948	-0.8	261	3.8	6,225	28.3	32.9
Amelia	4,699	83.6	185,100	22.3	10.0	729	33.1	3.4	6,240	0.5	201	3.2	6,166	25.8	28.3
Amherst	12,110	76.9	151,500	20.1	10.0	731	30	2.5	14,984	-0.1	488	3.3	14,506	27.9	27.1
Appomattox	5,948	81.0	151,700	18.4	10.0	683	31.6	1.6	7,083	0	258	3.6	6,890	33.2	26.8
Arlington	102,310	44.5	643,300	20.3	10.0	1,895	26.4	3	151,720	1.3	3,028	2	143,798	69.0	6.7
Augusta	28,790	79.1	206,300	21.6	10.0	857	26.6	1.1	36,922	0.6	993	2.7	34,960	32.8	27.6
Bath	1,847	73.9	151,100	22.3	10.0	478	11.5	6.1	2,502	-2.3	63	2.5	2,073	21.6	28.0
Bedford	30,927	81.4	198,100	20.2	10.0	816	25.1	0.9	38,097	0.1	1,163	3.1	36,735	34.9	24.6
Bland	2,561	82.6	109,300	15.7	10.5	639	38.2	2.6	2,834	-1.2	90	3.2	2,578	23.7	25.2
Botetourt	13,238	85.2	220,000	21.1	10.0	898	26.5	1	17,222	-0.2	464	2.7	16,102	38.4	25.0
Brunswick	6,048	73.9	110,900	20.9	13.5	693	33.7	1.4	5,990	-2.1	292	4.9	6,258	26.3	28.6
Buchanan	9,022	78.9	71,900	23.4	11.5	611	30.8	1.1	6,952	-0.5	380	5.5	6,679	25.9	34.9
Buckingham	5,705	75.3	132,500	21.8	10.6	721	32.5	2.1	6,357	0.7	280	4.4	6,543	27.8	29.3
Campbell	22,608	75.0	154,300	19.6	10.0	747	28	1.3	26,036	0	871	3.3	26,478	32.6	27.1
Caroline	10,815	80.1	193,200	22.6	10.5	996	24.9	1.9	15,067	0.4	520	3.5	13,227	28.8	26.7
Carroll	12,517	78.0	107,300	22.2	10.0	563	25.4	1.4	13,341	-1.2	478	3.6	13,125	27.1	32.9
Charles City	2,899	83.3	163,000	22.9	10.6	885	24.8	1.4	3,692	0.3	145	3.9	3,348	23.0	33.6
Charlotte	4,493	71.2	107,500	22.2	12.4	600	32.4	2.2	5,225	-1.7	191	3.7	4,929	27.1	26.4
Chesterfield	120,907	75.3	224,200	20.4	10.0	1,180	28.9	1.4	184,434	0.5	5,379	2.9	171,886	42.1	17.6
Clarke	5,568	75.0	333,100	23.5	10.0	1,031	36	0.5	7,545	1.3	216	2.9	7,087	41.0	21.6
Craig	2,344	74.0	164,800	19.6	10.0	527	23.4	0	2,286	0	81	3.5	2,219	25.5	33.5
Culpeper	16,837	72.9	266,400	24.0	10.0	1,092	30.4	3.4	24,178	1.2	688	2.8	23,377	36.1	24.0
Cumberland	3,972	72.3	146,600	22.3	14.3	818	30.8	3.5	4,636		151	3.3	4,810	30.1	31.2
Dickenson	6,096	76.0	77,500	22.8	11.4	569	37.7	1.9	4,495	-2.9	234	5.2	4,577	26.5	27.5
Dinwiddie	10,347	77.1	160,100	20.7	12.4	945	29.7	1.7	13,470	0.4	473	3.5	13,375	27.0	28.2
Essex	4,470	70.5	177,200	25.8	10.1	864	32.8	2.1	5,493	-1.7	212	3.9	5,272	26.9	27.4
Fairfax	393,380	67.8	534,800	21.3	10.0	1,823	28.2	3.6	630,229	1.2	15,320	2.4	609,859	56.6	10.3
Fauquier	23,981	78.4	370,000	22.7	10.0	1,229	27.3	1.2	36,319	1.2	944	2.6	34,893	42.8	19.8
Floyd	6,434	80.8	153,800	21.4	10.0	611	23.2	0.9	8,105	0.4	221	2.7	7,210	30.7	34.6
Fluvanna	9,794	80.8	228,100	22.3	11.0	1,252	26.5	1.2	13,553	1.1	339	2.5	12,127	45.0	18.0
Franklin	23,203	79.3	176,900	21.9	10.0	660	26	2.1	26,271	-0.1	807	3.1	25,460	32.8	27.7
Frederick	30,495	77.5	239,100	21.1	10.0	1,121	26.2	2.7	46,803	1	1,212	2.6	42,721	37.3	25.2
Giles	7,088	74.8	114,500	19.8	10.0	683	22.9	1.7	7,845	-0.2	261	3.3	7,545	25.2	33.6
Gloucester	14,746	77.2	224,100	21.2	10.0	923	27.9	1.4	19,445	0.5	521	2.7	17,770	30.4	28.9
Goochland	8,257	87.0	327,700	19.0	10.0	1,096	21.8	1.5	10,913	0.9	323	3	10,561	43.3	18.3
Grayson	6,653	78.7	95,700	20.4	11.6	513	28.1	1.1	7,643	-0.3	234	3.1	6,509	23.1	35.5
Greene	7,260	80.6	242,500	23.8	10.0	957	27.3	1.6	10,261	1.2	258	2.5	9,209	38.7	19.0
Greensville	3,649	75.5	89,400	21.3	13.7	769	27.9	2.1	4,388	-0.8	161	3.7	4,012	19.9	30.5
Halifax	14,084	72.6	110,800	20.7	11.1	595	28.8	1.7	15,201	-2.2	623	4.1	14,426	27.6	30.9
Hanover	38,208	81.3	267,600	20.3	10.0	1,113	26.2	1.1	58,367	0.5	1,523	2.6	54,324	45.4	16.0
Henrico	126,115	62.9	223,900	21.2	10.0	1,095	29	1.7	180,933	0.5	5,387	3	168,806	44.4	14.1
Henry	22,161	73.2	94,300	20.4	11.5	586	28	2.3	23,565	-0.7	883	3.7	20,659	26.6	30.4
Highland	1,163	85.5	184,000	20.4	10.0	555	19.9	1	1,253	-3	34	2.7	905	28.4	29.8
Isle of Wight	14,157	77.3	249,100	22.6	11.4	1,018	28.1	1.5	19,135	0.3	568	3	17,338	36.9	25.4
James City	28,410	74.3	328,700	21.4	10.0	1,202	32.4	1.3	36,069	0.5	1,046	2.9	33,064	44.9	13.6
King and Queen	2,811	78.7	170,000	21.3	10.0	845	25.8	3.9	3,849	1.4	117	3	3,157	27.7	34.3
King George	8,972	75.6	294,300	21.6	10.0	1,178	25.9	0.9	13,155	1.7	387	2.9	12,525	41.7	19.0
King William	6,079	86.1	199,700	23.1	10.0	1,094	27.9	1.8	9,004	0.9	263	2.9	8,284	34.9	31.0
Lancaster	5,081	73.2	226,900	26.3	10.0	817	26.9	0.5	5,291	-0.7	230	4.3	4,384	30.5	19.3
Lee	9,278	71.9	81,700	19.7	10.0	530	33.2	2.5	8,322	-2.6	342	4.1	7,559	29.6	29.1
Loudoun	121,299	77.9	475,500	21.6	10.0	1,764	28.1	2.1	216,433	1.1	5,305	2.5	201,528	57.3	9.6

1. Specified owner-occupied units.   2. A value of 10.0 represents 10 percent or less; a value of 50.0 represents 50 percent or more.   3. Specified renter-occupied units.   4. Overcrowded or lacking complete plumbing facilities.   5. Percent of civilian labor force.   6. Civilian employed persons 16 years old and over.

Table B. States and Counties — Nonfarm Employment and Agriculture

STATE County	Private nonfarm establishments, employment and payroll, 2016									Agriculture, 2017			
	Number of establish-ments	Employment						Annual payroll		Farms			Farm producers whose primary occupation is farming (percent)
		Total	Health care and social assistance	Manufac-turing	Retail trade	Finance and insurance	Professional, scientific, and technical services	Total (mil dol)	Average per employee (dollars)	Number	Percent with:		
											Fewer than 50 acres	1000 acres or more	
	104	105	106	107	108	109	110	111	112	113	114	115	116

STATE County	104	105	106	107	108	109	110	111	112	113	114	115	116
VERMONT— Cont'd													
Chittenden	5,680	90,777	15,920	9,211	13,179	3,168	7,052	4,086	45,016	585	54.4	1.0	39.7
Essex	110	455	78	125	72	11	18	15	34,033	106	31.1	3.8	50.9
Franklin	1,012	12,724	2,795	2,771	2,302	290	247	507	39,812	729	31.3	4.0	49.1
Grand Isle	187	652	52	59	151	20	44	23	35,713	119	42.0	2.5	47.4
Lamoille	965	11,332	1,815	487	1,465	241	282	357	31,520	329	39.8	1.8	35.8
Orange	750	6,340	1,529	749	1,034	145	318	252	39,820	569	35.5	1.4	43.6
Orleans	793	8,337	1,719	1,373	1,297	216	168	276	33,137	558	33.2	2.9	47.8
Rutland	2,130	23,965	4,564	3,174	4,165	535	608	920	38,370	614	38.8	2.0	44.6
Washington	2,233	27,659	4,881	2,679	4,415	2,482	931	1,229	44,429	553	47.2	0.9	35.6
Windham	1,694	21,105	3,537	2,070	2,365	591	549	813	38,503	414	53.6	0.2	46.4
Windsor	1,985	19,856	4,030	2,076	3,005	500	1,104	811	40,824	677	38.7	2.7	33.6
VIRGINIA	199,548	3,254,172	438,562	240,375	430,293	153,431	460,280	170,160	52,290	43,225	42.2	3.1	40.1
Accomack	733	8,679	1,178	3,047	1,388	166	313	247	28,513	239	53.6	8.8	54.9
Albemarle	2,715	39,777	7,316	3,013	6,274	2,837	3,551	1,936	48,669	913	40.7	4.3	38.6
Alleghany	235	2,213	778	250	246	51	33	75	33,835	165	35.2	3.0	40.9
Amelia	268	1,822	392	183	185	37	53	56	30,849	370	36.8	6.5	44.6
Amherst	573	6,340	723	1,265	1,276	134	275	210	33,092	369	32.5	3.8	40.3
Appomattox	289	2,474	482	125	685	84	146	63	25,383	412	28.6	2.7	34.1
Arlington	6,344	132,629	9,578	236	9,312	3,330	42,468	10,760	81,131	5	100.0	NA	NA
Augusta	1,417	20,634	4,132	5,152	2,108	266	441	861	41,713	1,665	45.7	2.6	44.6
Bath	126	2,240	242	44	70	22	129	81	36,096	110	8.2	10.0	47.7
Bedford	1,383	11,768	1,261	2,167	1,953	321	830	453	38,503	1,418	38.7	2.2	36.3
Bland	75	1,437	159	568	63	D	D	61	42,321	339	24.2	2.7	43.5
Botetourt	731	10,077	906	2,446	804	209	239	416	41,260	551	35.2	1.8	38.6
Brunswick	249	2,323	191	215	326	51	39	79	34,037	242	26.0	4.1	43.3
Buchanan	406	5,016	646	196	787	179	229	218	43,551	89	52.8	NA	50.0
Buckingham	256	1,985	343	131	281	25	73	70	35,024	408	28.7	2.5	37.9
Campbell	1,191	17,042	1,171	4,909	2,284	399	783	746	43,782	702	30.6	2.1	37.1
Caroline	381	3,745	302	248	584	D	195	134	35,858	222	47.7	8.6	40.7
Carroll	409	4,630	720	1,243	758	93	111	119	25,781	900	38.9	0.9	35.0
Charles City	146	1,516	D	286	97	D	27	63	41,715	77	49.4	15.6	40.4
Charlotte	214	1,713	327	373	252	50	35	53	30,684	460	20.9	4.1	40.3
Chesterfield	7,264	114,688	13,517	9,055	18,967	4,225	10,965	4,825	42,067	210	62.9	1.0	36.2
Clarke	363	3,007	429	513	248	115	147	137	45,595	427	47.8	3.7	43.5
Craig	58	332	42	D	120	21	10	11	32,087	179	20.1	1.1	43.4
Culpeper	992	12,944	2,011	1,391	2,399	207	759	521	40,229	682	49.1	4.7	39.4
Cumberland	134	864	77	D	177	16	D	25	29,417	264	36.4	3.4	41.7
Dickenson	202	1,847	353	24	423	67	197	62	33,682	128	50.0	1.6	37.0
Dinwiddie	344	4,428	387	668	499	117	61	186	42,056	358	33.5	6.4	40.4
Essex	297	3,603	588	618	877	111	101	104	28,891	88	31.8	21.6	40.3
Fairfax	30,921	586,050	57,442	5,994	51,264	29,851	194,461	45,380	77,434	117	78.6	NA	31.8
Fauquier	1,828	17,743	2,460	972	2,882	678	1,931	780	43,964	1,154	50.3	4.0	39.3
Floyd	316	2,222	452	387	328	85	64	67	30,349	741	37.4	0.9	36.6
Fluvanna	377	2,487	223	146	330	47	62	86	34,756	273	44.7	0.7	42.5
Franklin	1,168	12,622	1,467	2,593	1,875	253	282	367	29,087	1,019	35.0	1.7	38.0
Frederick	1,506	25,894	1,857	4,761	3,790	1,984	1,899	1,050	40,561	762	55.2	2.0	34.6
Giles	288	3,608	514	844	689	75	399	145	40,153	389	40.4	3.3	32.9
Gloucester	855	7,292	1,332	206	2,037	239	316	211	28,939	166	64.5	4.8	37.7
Goochland	647	14,586	518	145	562	3,555	314	1,367	93,690	355	47.3	2.0	40.4
Grayson	152	1,692	172	853	167	95	19	49	28,878	716	39.5	1.8	38.4
Greene	347	2,592	185	59	792	44	166	79	30,637	214	39.3	0.5	39.8
Greensville	101	2,175	D	D	253	D	D	64	29,459	150	27.3	8.7	40.7
Halifax	697	9,771	1,569	2,075	1,374	195	142	347	35,560	895	21.7	3.1	39.0
Hanover	3,143	46,459	5,732	3,965	6,540	657	1,415	1,787	38,454	567	61.7	4.6	42.5
Henrico	9,260	174,122	24,680	5,467	23,060	23,038	15,312	8,868	50,928	99	70.7	2.0	37.0
Henry	796	11,642	741	3,466	1,622	285	473	375	32,188	212	30.2	5.7	30.6
Highland	89	343	60	17	36	D	5	9	26,910	275	16.7	6.2	48.6
Isle of Wight	636	9,129	666	3,609	855	199	331	416	45,539	237	47.3	13.1	52.8
James City	1,703	26,998	3,884	2,591	3,852	626	1,587	1,025	37,951	72	59.7	2.8	25.8
King and Queen	100	530	10	53	33	D	18	19	35,828	151	41.7	8.6	43.7
King George	510	6,162	335	129	861	152	2,736	351	57,009	141	36.2	4.3	33.3
King William	330	3,403	302	718	434	91	106	161	47,176	90	51.1	15.6	36.8
Lancaster	456	4,026	1,115	111	788	303	299	154	38,141	80	41.3	5.0	24.4
Lee	273	2,656	547	107	759	169	66	72	27,271	830	40.5	0.6	38.4
Loudoun	10,175	151,257	12,022	5,693	19,613	3,065	27,497	8,908	58,893	1,259	69.5	1.3	33.3

Table B. States and Counties — **Agriculture**

STATE County	Acreage (1,000) 117	Percent change, 2012-2017 118	Average size of farm 119	Total irrigated (1,000) 120	Total cropland (1,000) 121	Average per farm 122	Average per acre 123	Value of machinery and equipment, average per farm (dollars) 124	Total (mil dol) 125	Average per farm (acres) 126	Crops 127	Livestock and poultry products 128	Organic farms (number) 129	Farms with internet access (percent) 130	Total ($1,000) 131	Percent of farms 132
VERMONT— Cont'd																
Chittenden	64	-12.7	110	0.5	26.8	701,224	6,387	84,797	43.6	74,492	51.2	48.8	68	90.8	545	12.1
Essex	43	67.9	404	0.0	8.0	789,828	1,956	137,512	12.7	119,887	39.7	60.3	10	83.0	41	15.1
Franklin	190	1.8	260	0.3	83.2	811,688	3,119	165,431	185.6	254,615	20.8	79.2	125	84.8	965	11.7
Grand Isle	19	-1.2	158	0.0	12.6	679,940	4,304	122,915	17.9	150,723	16.9	83.1	11	88.2	354	19.3
Lamoille	53	2.0	162	0.2	14.6	563,296	3,486	72,199	27.7	84,319	36.3	63.7	48	86.6	74	9.1
Orange	86	-18.6	150	0.2	32.6	553,914	3,681	90,079	55.1	96,749	22.8	77.2	59	80.8	389	8.4
Orleans	128	-1.6	230	0.1	58.6	623,033	2,708	119,211	92.0	164,875	13.7	86.3	52	81.9	234	3.6
Rutland	99	-8.9	161	0.2	34.6	444,531	2,761	70,922	28.8	46,932	35.9	64.1	24	81.9	657	16.9
Washington	64	-4.3	117	0.1	21.6	499,088	4,283	86,311	30.7	55,566	29.8	70.2	78	86.8	153	4.0
Windham	45	-11.7	108	0.4	14.4	542,832	5,011	71,071	28.6	69,048	39.8	60.2	28	93.0	457	8.5
Windsor	113	11.1	166	0.1	22.6	643,087	3,865	74,480	25.1	37,013	34.4	65.6	36	84.8	141	8.0
VIRGINIA	7,798	-6.1	180	63.4	3,084.1	834,254	4,624	86,136	3,960.5	91,625	34.4	65.6	252	74.0	60,805	13.9
Accomack	77	-0.8	321	5.1	57.7	1,370,847	4,268	217,830	163.3	683,134	28.7	71.3	1	81.2	2,399	30.5
Albemarle	183	8.2	200	0.8	51.8	1,980,339	9,892	68,432	29.6	32,472	63.6	36.4	9	81.3	477	6.8
Alleghany	31	-16.5	187	NA	8.9	788,210	4,215	66,701	2.7	16,618	29.5	70.5	NA	81.8	16	5.5
Amelia	103	16.3	278	0.2	34.8	858,640	3,094	108,375	86.6	233,992	10.7	89.3	NA	70.5	545	34.1
Amherst	79	-20.4	214	0.2	17.3	993,967	4,654	60,527	8.1	22,068	43.2	56.8	NA	71.5	24	5.1
Appomattox	76	-21.4	184	0.0	20.9	568,840	3,094	72,238	10.0	24,218	33.3	66.7	3	66.5	329	12.1
Arlington	0	-86.1	1	NA	NA	298,000	298,000	30,686	NA	NA	NA	100.0	NA	100.0	NA	NA
Augusta	291	11.8	175	2.5	116.8	1,222,854	6,999	101,481	292.5	175,704	12.8	87.2	5	71.5	1,049	15.7
Bath	48	15.8	435	D	15.3	1,599,416	3,677	100,025	6.7	61,345	24.8	75.2	1	66.4	91	10.0
Bedford	211	2.2	149	0.1	65.9	654,822	4,399	68,521	26.5	18,667	31.9	68.1	1	76.0	658	10.4
Bland	70	-9.2	207	0.8	17.3	714,594	3,446	73,919	8.8	25,906	25.7	74.3	NA	67.3	79	11.2
Botetourt	89	-0.5	161	0.0	27.0	676,797	4,198	72,657	14.1	25,506	28.8	71.2	1	76.6	152	9.3
Brunswick	66	-26.1	274	2.1	24.4	689,842	2,514	118,499	23.1	95,438	71.7	28.3	1	69.4	378	50.8
Buchanan	11	15.5	124	D	1.2	300,008	2,418	33,157	0.4	4,876	54.8	45.2	NA	51.7	NA	NA
Buckingham	79	-5.6	194	0.1	30.5	724,596	3,731	81,081	43.4	106,480	15.7	84.3	1	73.0	555	12.7
Campbell	132	-12.6	188	0.3	42.9	578,961	3,086	78,302	25.4	36,179	25.7	74.3	NA	76.4	204	13.1
Caroline	62	9.7	279	3.4	42.4	1,029,270	3,696	134,498	22.9	103,189	95.8	4.2	4	88.3	739	19.8
Carroll	119	-15.3	132	0.6	32.2	425,568	3,219	63,111	44.5	49,488	30.7	69.3	7	65.1	113	7.9
Charles City	31	0.7	408	1.4	20.6	1,375,102	3,373	187,684	D	D	D	D	1	96.1	1,156	22.1
Charlotte	122	-18.5	264	0.5	46.1	693,206	2,621	92,853	26.0	56,470	37.8	62.2	6	67.6	950	27.6
Chesterfield	18	-9.8	86	0.1	7.2	790,553	9,216	72,007	4.5	21,481	64.3	35.7	3	81.0	122	15.7
Clarke	67	-0.5	156	0.1	24.7	1,099,589	7,046	72,761	16.4	38,375	41.2	58.8	NA	85.0	75	7.5
Craig	43	-6.9	243	0.1	12.0	725,533	2,990	80,837	4.7	26,022	18.1	81.9	5	84.4	143	14.5
Culpeper	124	-1.6	182	0.6	60.1	1,048,206	5,747	87,179	48.5	71,176	64.7	35.3	5	81.5	568	11.0
Cumberland	53	-7.9	199	0.2	15.4	758,741	3,806	71,848	39.8	150,780	10.2	89.8	NA	68.2	196	15.9
Dickenson	11	-25.8	87	NA	1.8	246,038	2,820	74,934	0.6	4,375	17.7	82.3	NA	72.7	216	10.2
Dinwiddie	93	4.0	259	1.6	42.8	795,681	3,068	105,397	25.7	71,799	85.4	14.6	NA	64.2	1,534	34.6
Essex	59	3.5	667	D	42.3	2,130,482	3,194	333,241	21.0	239,159	94.3	5.7	NA	78.4	1,341	51.1
Fairfax	6	-24.4	51	0.1	0.8	852,783	16,806	45,082	1.2	10,624	81.3	18.7	2	90.6	21	6.8
Fauquier	217	-5.1	188	0.5	83.8	1,381,646	7,359	83,383	54.8	47,497	40.0	60.0	4	85.6	403	5.6
Floyd	110	-23.8	149	0.2	32.3	565,896	3,802	62,225	33.7	45,511	48.3	51.7	11	74.8	73	3.9
Fluvanna	44	-5.7	163	0.1	13.3	702,048	4,315	66,495	6.1	22,436	63.6	36.4	2	81.3	170	11.7
Franklin	156	-5.0	153	0.4	72.8	552,387	3,602	81,393	69.2	67,909	24.6	75.4	4	66.7	705	8.0
Frederick	110	9.1	144	0.0	45.2	1,041,790	7,223	67,981	33.8	44,324	72.9	27.1	6	77.7	78	3.7
Giles	65	-0.3	168	0.0	13.0	516,470	3,073	66,106	9.7	24,871	13.7	86.3	NA	74.6	58	2.3
Gloucester	26	28.1	157	0.0	14.2	739,196	4,717	108,605	11.7	70,482	80.0	20.0	6	81.9	580	12.0
Goochland	57	13.2	160	0.1	24.0	867,877	5,430	89,076	11.7	33,070	38.6	61.4	NA	78.3	144	7.6
Grayson	119	-9.5	167	0.2	34.4	692,467	4,155	68,462	40.8	57,011	26.1	73.9	2	73.9	157	8.7
Greene	29	4.6	133	0.0	10.0	870,295	6,531	60,814	7.6	35,579	23.6	76.4	NA	78.0	211	16.4
Greensville	55	-6.4	364	D	33.5	986,245	2,712	147,447	19.4	129,653	98.1	1.9	NA	72.0	1,707	58.7
Halifax	209	-1.2	233	1.1	57.5	619,060	2,651	70,488	31.9	35,617	51.3	48.7	15	66.9	429	20.0
Hanover	89	-5.4	157	3.6	61.3	791,920	5,035	102,289	49.3	86,868	83.7	16.3	NA	81.3	768	9.3
Henrico	10	-23.8	99	D	7.3	601,700	6,066	59,847	7.3	73,606	97.5	2.5	1	75.8	36	14.1
Henry	46	6.0	215	0.0	11.7	635,840	2,961	55,004	14.1	66,618	16.1	83.9	6	72.6	34	5.2
Highland	93	-0.1	338	D	15.6	1,080,848	3,198	65,010	26.1	94,982	6.6	93.4	1	68.0	279	11.3
Isle of Wight	81	6.6	340	0.9	51.5	1,264,037	3,714	173,573	64.2	270,687	61.9	38.1	NA	89.5	2,755	36.7
James City	7	19.6	92	0.0	3.6	931,231	10,113	129,707	2.0	28,458	92.6	7.4	NA	93.1	78	15.3
King and Queen	48	14.9	320	1.2	33.6	1,078,959	3,377	158,462	18.4	121,682	75.6	24.4	NA	79.5	817	37.1
King George	26	8.4	187	D	13.0	954,694	5,111	99,089	11.9	84,546	95.1	4.9	NA	73.8	134	27.7
King William	47	-11.4	527	1.6	26.3	2,133,522	4,046	250,259	14.2	157,411	88.1	11.9	NA	87.8	713	28.9
Lancaster	16	51.8	203	0.0	11.3	860,073	4,237	123,923	5.6	69,388	91.9	8.1	3	90.0	659	37.5
Lee	95	-19.0	114	0.0	25.2	302,584	2,646	71,083	15.3	18,393	26.0	74.0	5	61.8	1,658	9.8
Loudoun	122	-9.5	97	0.4	60.2	950,622	9,816	59,142	44.0	34,940	70.2	29.8	11	88.6	190	3.9

Table B. States and Counties — **Water Use, Wholesale Trade, Retail Trade, and Real Estate**

STATE County	Water use, 2015 Public supply water withdrawn (mil gal/day)	Public supply gallons withdrawn per person per day	Wholesale Trade[1], 2012 Number of establish-ments	Number of employees	Sales (mil dol)	Average payroll (mil dol)	Retail Trade[2], 2012 Number of establish-ments	Number of employees	Sales (mil dol)	Average payroll (mil dol)	Real estate and rental and leasing,[2] 2012 Number of establish-ments	Number of employees	Sales (mil dol)	Average payroll (mil dol)
	133	134	135	136	137	138	139	140	141	142	143	144	145	146
VERMONT— Cont'd														
Chittenden	13.89	86.1	246	4,085	3,133.9	239.1	839	12,464	2,959.4	308.4	232	1,297	275.2	49.5
Essex	0.25	40.6	3	2	0.4	0.0	20	93	19.0	1.3	2	D	D	D
Franklin	3.00	61.5	46	794	1,257.8	32.1	195	2,139	628.6	50.7	26	74	7.4	1.8
Grand Isle	0.50	72.9	5	6	3.4	0.2	30	165	50.0	3.6	7	6	1.5	0.2
Lamoille	1.29	51.1	23	D	D	D	163	1,508	360.4	36.5	32	103	13.7	3.3
Orange	2.16	74.7	24	182	78.4	7.8	102	1,001	245.4	23.6	19	34	4.9	1.1
Orleans	1.63	60.1	23	D	D	D	147	1,285	350.3	31.3	21	94	14.2	2.7
Rutland	4.37	73.2	73	D	D	D	411	4,139	1,082.8	97.7	67	276	30.8	7.8
Washington	1.85	31.6	70	D	D	D	380	4,258	1,112.6	105.1	65	277	45.6	7.9
Windham	2.10	48.4	43	D	D	D	283	2,540	604.4	63.9	69	258	32.0	8.6
Windsor	3.10	55.6	53	670	276.6	32.1	311	2,694	726.3	70.5	81	265	30.9	8.7
VIRGINIA	695.63	83.0	6,232	88,353	86,613.6	4,983.1	27,415	410,918	110,002.4	10,007.9	8,862	54,246	11,758.9	2,378.3
Accomack	0.88	26.7	28	159	78.9	5.1	169	1,402	348.2	28.8	38	103	13.0	2.5
Albemarle	13.29	125.7	66	1,102	574.5	67.1	325	5,511	1,497.5	147.8	151	766	129.5	25.7
Alleghany	0.91	58.0	5	30	7.7	1.0	38	280	75.1	6.3	4	16	2.1	0.3
Amelia	0.10	7.8	6	D	D	D	30	227	71.1	4.9	6	7	0.5	0.1
Amherst	12.03	377.0	11	D	D	D	94	1,137	273.4	22.7	17	38	3.7	0.7
Appomattox	0.00	0.0	7	75	9.9	2.4	56	631	143.8	12.9	12	19	5.1	0.4
Arlington	0.00	0.0	85	1,090	935.3	88.8	613	9,610	2,608.8	265.6	404	5,188	1,493.4	219.8
Augusta	7.50	100.9	52	737	249.6	33.1	208	1,941	621.3	46.5	61	185	18.9	4.1
Bath	0.29	64.9	2	D	D	D	21	94	17.2	1.4	8	37	3.6	1.9
Bedford	1.54	19.8	53	503	342.0	20.4	216	2,512	652.3	57.9	79	143	24.1	4.4
Bland	0.04	6.1	7	D	D	D	12	64	33.8	1.2	2	D	D	D
Botetourt	5.46	163.7	37	D	D	D	85	873	321.4	18.5	19	D	D	D
Brunswick	24.34	1,457.7	6	45	27.1	1.6	45	326	103.6	6.3	5	D	D	D
Buchanan	0.00	0.0	21	231	265.3	13.2	79	834	173.0	14.5	12	29	4.8	0.9
Buckingham	0.36	21.1	8	D	D	D	38	293	83.0	6.0	3	D	D	D
Campbell	4.46	81.0	38	D	D	D	188	1,904	601.0	43.3	52	126	18.2	3.2
Caroline	0.83	27.7	8	D	D	D	49	655	404.2	15.5	12	24	4.3	0.5
Carroll	1.70	57.2	15	121	40.2	2.8	89	748	285.7	14.6	14	43	5.2	0.9
Charles City	0.00	0.0	8	D	D	D	10	57	14.7	2.0	6	20	3.8	0.6
Charlotte	0.24	19.7	9	68	29.6	2.2	32	230	56.5	4.3	5	12	0.7	0.2
Chesterfield	39.86	118.7	290	3,411	1,729.4	182.3	933	17,142	4,657.3	410.9	281	1,511	331.7	65.3
Clarke	0.50	34.8	9	D	D	D	35	229	81.5	4.6	17	D	D	D
Craig	0.00	0.0	3	D	D	D	11	110	18.6	1.7	2	D	D	D
Culpeper	2.33	47.1	24	448	296.8	16.5	157	2,120	550.1	52.5	43	239	31.2	9.2
Cumberland	0.00	0.0	1	D	D	D	34	204	40.4	3.9	3	D	D	D
Dickenson	4.96	328.2	7	20	5.3	0.4	44	451	102.3	9.4	4	5	0.4	0.1
Dinwiddie	0.03	1.1	8	D	D	D	56	541	144.9	9.8	7	52	7.5	1.8
Essex	0.02	1.8	7	D	D	D	60	826	236.6	20.3	10	73	7.1	2.6
Fairfax	0.06	0.1	750	11,158	25,177.2	930.7	2,735	50,244	14,589.5	1,418.8	1,447	10,962	2,918.3	687.9
Fauquier	3.10	45.1	38	445	159.7	20.1	223	2,632	920.8	75.7	77	203	34.6	8.1
Floyd	0.11	7.0	11	D	D	D	42	321	70.7	5.9	5	5	1.9	0.2
Fluvanna	0.77	29.4	11	117	76.0	5.4	39	308	75.3	6.3	15	20	3.6	0.7
Franklin	1.76	31.3	39	424	291.4	26.7	190	1,857	459.0	42.0	46	103	17.8	3.2
Frederick	5.27	63.3	84	D	D	D	197	3,512	1,346.1	91.3	54	143	30.4	6.0
Giles	1.12	67.0	8	D	D	D	62	694	184.0	14.8	11	22	3.1	0.7
Gloucester	0.66	17.8	23	87	22.7	2.9	141	1,905	496.2	45.7	43	110	11.6	2.6
Goochland	0.08	3.6	32	D	D	D	62	491	215.5	13.9	13	102	13.4	5.3
Grayson	0.11	6.9	6	D	D	D	24	161	40.5	2.8	5	3	0.8	0.1
Greene	0.63	32.9	9	60	14.6	2.8	52	764	183.9	16.9	9	D	D	D
Greensville	0.03	2.5	9	24	1.8	0.7	25	209	130.8	3.7	4	18	2.0	0.4
Halifax	2.10	59.8	20	244	99.2	8.8	133	1,436	358.1	30.3	21	69	12.1	1.6
Hanover	4.08	39.5	216	4,016	3,161.4	205.6	358	5,917	1,752.1	151.6	106	466	176.3	22.0
Henrico	20.15	62.0	405	7,312	7,293.9	446.7	1,277	22,637	5,519.9	538.8	447	3,659	718.5	164.4
Henry	2.86	55.1	44	D	D	D	167	1,715	581.5	41.4	25	110	16.1	2.9
Highland	0.10	45.2	2	D	D	D	17	44	8.6	0.6	1	D	D	D
Isle of Wight	1.55	42.7	16	75	51.2	3.4	104	950	246.9	16.8	29	80	11.3	2.5
James City	5.36	73.3	47	335	131.6	14.4	281	3,679	630.2	66.6	82	502	102.7	19.9
King and Queen	0.00	0.0	4	D	D	D	11	31	12.4	0.6	4	4	0.4	0.1
King George	0.93	36.4	8	D	D	D	54	721	232.4	15.4	16	46	8.7	1.3
King William	0.56	34.4	7	35	12.0	1.3	49	437	133.3	10.1	11	26	2.3	0.7
Lancaster	0.12	10.9	15	114	83.9	3.3	79	805	161.5	18.1	17	38	5.4	0.8
Lee	2.34	94.6	12	68	33.4	2.1	68	828	208.1	16.6	10	26	2.5	0.5
Loudoun	6.86	18.3	243	3,225	2,319.4	236.1	952	17,774	5,140.4	481.0	341	1,877	528.1	82.5

1   Merchant wholesalers, except manufacturers' sales branches and offices.   2. Employer establishments.

Table B. States and Counties — Professional Services, Manufacturing, and Accommodation and Food Services

STATE County	Professional, scientific, and technical services, 2012				Manufacturing, 2012				Accommodation and food services, 2012			
	Number of establish-ments	Number of employees	Sales (mil dol)	Average payroll (mil dol)	Number of establish-ments	Number of employees	Receipts (mil dol)	Annual payroll (mil dol)	Number of establis-hments	Number of employees	Receipts (mil dol)	Annual payroll (mil dol)
	147	148	149	150	151	152	153	154	155	156	157	158
VERMONT— Cont'd												
Chittenden	752	6,327	941.2	403.6	189	9,861	3,388.0	556.6	433	8,124	459.9	133.8
Essex	5	25	2.8	1.4	7	129	11.4	4.2	13	58	2.4	0.7
Franklin	62	236	26.7	11.9	55	2,770	D	132.8	88	771	44.6	13.6
Grand Isle	21	48	4.4	1.6	7	40	D	1.1	25	111	9.4	2.9
Lamoille	88	394	71.3	20.3	49	406	D	18.4	112	4,203	183.7	73.0
Orange	73	352	60.4	18.7	49	673	133.0	28.6	59	589	40.0	12.5
Orleans	48	169	16.5	6.5	41	1,108	D	36.8	68	1,446	54.1	20.4
Rutland	178	D	D	D	105	3,126	613.1	164.0	247	2,795	130.1	37.8
Washington	251	D	D	D	126	3,959	819.8	225.4	163	2,923	123.9	41.2
Windham	124	476	49.9	20.9	92	2,049	421.4	87.5	212	3,498	151.5	44.2
Windsor	193	5,011	265.8	108.4	110	2,062	442.6	86.8	199	3,492	176.8	50.9
VIRGINIA	29,368	429,690	92,775.9	36,364.7	5,101	228,197	96,389.9	11,586.1	16,832	320,514	17,795.9	4,908.6
Accomack	64	410	79.3	19.9	18	3,001	667.9	78.1	101	993	53.6	13.9
Albemarle	353	3,204	501.5	204.2	68	2,855	786.4	172.2	182	3,780	230.6	67.5
Alleghany	11	24	2.4	0.6	8	468	D	19.7	26	299	14.0	3.7
Amelia	14	46	3.1	1.0	19	247	98.4	7.6	11	93	5.0	1.1
Amherst	43	253	32.2	13.5	39	1,314	572.0	67.7	44	D	D	D
Appomattox	14	D	D	D	13	71	D	2.4	14	D	D	D
Arlington	1,829	42,070	11,167.3	4,296.3	34	220	54.1	7.4	647	17,342	1,362.4	363.6
Augusta	93	413	39.9	15.0	73	4,382	1,884.2	221.4	79	1,229	56.5	15.9
Bath	9	D	D	D	4	47	D	D	18	1,021	63.5	26.8
Bedford	166	630	76.4	23.0	71	3,393	D	181.0	106	1,231	50.8	14.2
Bland	2	D	D	D	8	488	D	25.5	6	46	2.3	0.6
Botetourt	63	D	D	D	30	D	812.0	114.2	49	D	D	D
Brunswick	13	36	3.3	1.0	17	217	69.1	10.5	11	D	D	D
Buchanan	35	277	20.9	7.4	10	238	91.7	13.8	22	317	15.3	4.2
Buckingham	15	100	12.9	5.2	11	116	D	3.5	7	D	D	D
Campbell	85	741	84.8	52.2	70	2,632	1,555.4	128.0	82	1,511	64.3	16.9
Caroline	30	206	19.9	8.7	17	279	76.1	10.8	30	332	18.5	4.9
Carroll	26	89	6.6	2.8	20	1,109	D	31.0	38	613	34.4	7.6
Charles City	3	D	D	D	18	292	D	10.6	4	D	D	D
Charlotte	9	40	2.3	0.8	15	419	74.8	13.3	10	91	4.5	1.3
Chesterfield	813	6,640	891.7	359.6	168	8,594	3,845.3	536.1	528	10,919	514.5	142.1
Clarke	44	113	16.4	6.6	14	706	89.8	27.0	21	D	D	D
Craig	7	D	D	D	NA	NA	NA	NA	4	D	D	D
Culpeper	92	674	96.9	31.4	39	1,382	563.6	63.6	77	1,193	59.3	14.7
Cumberland	5	D	D	D	3	D	D	D	4	44	1.4	0.4
Dickenson	11	163	8.9	3.7	6	43	D	1.9	13	D	D	D
Dinwiddie	24	64	4.1	1.7	10	652	D	D	18	270	15.4	3.6
Essex	23	93	6.4	2.7	14	609	90.7	16.7	30	459	19.6	5.8
Fairfax	8,232	197,134	48,404.9	18,643.4	357	6,199	1,408.8	349.1	2,158	39,514	2,795.4	731.2
Fauquier	267	1,590	287.5	115.2	58	872	137.8	39.7	110	2,008	108.1	29.8
Floyd	22	48	4.1	1.5	30	331	D	12.6	18	230	7.6	2.5
Fluvanna	29	71	7.6	2.0	10	89	D	3.0	22	D	D	D
Franklin	83	299	25.8	9.0	53	2,440	D	D	68	958	44.7	12.3
Frederick	114	D	D	D	84	4,514	2,537.6	220.9	129	2,381	117.5	30.6
Giles	15	264	19.2	10.1	13	994	D	60.1	35	429	18.3	4.9
Gloucester	74	283	24.2	9.8	15	181	22.1	6.5	65	934	40.4	12.1
Goochland	65	275	36.7	12.1	19	154	27.1	7.0	42	372	25.6	7.7
Grayson	11	20	2.1	0.6	17	819	D	27.4	14	110	4.4	1.4
Greene	30	336	23.7	20.0	11	48	D	1.9	27	299	14.9	4.0
Greensville	1	D	D	D	6	818	261.5	27.8	15	191	11.4	2.2
Halifax	35	157	17.6	4.9	37	1,685	573.4	73.0	62	914	36.0	10.1
Hanover	270	1,418	191.6	66.3	147	3,629	917.2	155.3	200	3,482	164.7	44.1
Henrico	1,142	11,253	1,505.7	630.6	175	5,104	1,808.2	262.6	720	16,249	832.8	238.8
Henry	33	270	13.4	6.6	69	2,885	834.7	115.5	55	1,003	41.3	10.9
Highland	5	7	0.9	0.3	NA	NA	NA	NA	5	D	D	D
Isle of Wight	60	296	30.2	11.8	15	D	D	83.1	50	766	34.1	9.8
James City	222	D	D	D	31	1,661	1,621.3	96.9	117	3,412	264.1	84.6
King and Queen	8	20	2.4	0.9	5	32	D	D	2	D	D	D
King George	108	2,415	459.4	194.9	8	82	D	3.3	37	369	21.8	5.4
King William	29	137	9.4	3.3	11	465	209.2	22.8	20	232	10.6	2.6
Lancaster	54	319	33.4	17.1	15	152	D	7.5	32	510	18.9	8.1
Lee	19	49	4.0	1.2	8	85	D	2.2	17	D	D	D
Loudoun	2,266	19,300	3,985.2	1,741.2	158	4,462	1,636.9	345.1	611	13,152	877.0	245.2

Health Care and Social Assistance, Other Services, Nonemployer Businesses, and Residential Construction

STATE County	Health care and social assistance, 2012				Other services, 2012				Nonemployer businesses, 2016		Value of residential construction authorized by building permits, 2018	
	Number of establish-ments	Number of employees	Receipts (mil dol)	Annual payroll (mil dol)	Number of establish-ments	Number of employees	Receipts (mil dol)	Annual payroll (mil dol)	Number	Receipts (mil dol)	New construction ($1,000)	Number of housing units
	159	160	161	162	163	164	165	166	167	168	169	170
VERMONT— Cont'd												
Chittenden	565	14,159	1,652.4	588.8	414	2,291	223.5	65.9	14,420	730.9	152,833	987
Essex	9	64	3.5	1.9	9	45	3.6	0.5	517	19.9	3,765	16
Franklin	108	D	D	D	69	264	25.9	6.1	3,659	156.4	32,556	148
Grand Isle	12	D	D	D	10	17	3.2	0.4	713	26.5	6,958	29
Lamoille	84	1,532	133.6	57.6	65	289	45.0	7.3	2,756	127.3	19,844	96
Orange	82	1,466	153.7	54.2	42	135	13.6	3.8	2,933	111.8	3,287	14
Orleans	75	1,714	152.5	67.2	69	217	18.9	4.3	2,569	101.0	13,847	153
Rutland	207	4,898	440.4	179.6	154	715	58.7	16.8	4,903	180.0	9,757	47
Washington	232	4,359	408.5	162.1	220	1,030	128.7	37.2	6,105	249.0	29,792	143
Windham	183	3,103	278.5	124.6	129	489	44.7	11.4	5,150	215.6	32,355	141
Windsor	167	3,691	436.7	204.6	146	760	82.6	21.9	6,063	263.0	15,811	109
VIRGINIA	18,774	411,108	47,705.0	18,628.8	14,726	112,430	17,079.4	4,471.2	597,409	26,318.0	5,830,512	31,977
Accomack	57	1,101	62.7	28.0	60	332	22.1	7.0	2,310	86.9	16,649	92
Albemarle	314	6,428	950.1	372.5	151	1,445	308.7	75.0	9,503	453.2	222,140	1,097
Alleghany	34	867	85.7	33.7	22	117	10.6	2.6	681	21.3	2,155	15
Amelia	24	369	21.6	9.9	20	D	D	D	850	33.5	8,343	49
Amherst	41	D	D	D	55	152	12.2	3.2	1,598	50.5	14,001	66
Appomattox	25	D	D	D	19	74	6.9	1.9	907	30.8	11,519	66
Arlington	484	8,987	1,450.6	465.6	642	10,355	2,577.8	721.4	20,234	1,054.5	363,417	2,756
Augusta	110	3,916	512.2	177.0	100	472	43.7	14.1	4,622	217.7	43,011	222
Bath	4	D	D	D	6	D	D	D	345	10.6	2,355	6
Bedford	145	1,295	82.4	34.3	118	601	62.3	17.6	4,957	207.9	10,145	82
Bland	7	81	7.6	3.2	6	D	D	D	261	8.6	2,010	25
Botetourt	48	D	D	D	57	D	D	D	2,373	87.3	23,890	114
Brunswick	12	189	10.4	4.7	20	D	D	D	702	25.9	0	0
Buchanan	43	655	53.4	23.0	26	D	D	D	816	27.5	788	4
Buckingham	15	375	17.4	11.2	16	70	7.9	2.2	738	27.7	3,841	23
Campbell	93	D	D	D	87	332	25.0	7.0	3,000	96.3	14,670	78
Caroline	19	283	18.2	9.2	30	172	15.1	3.8	1,702	58.9	21,782	104
Carroll	41	569	39.1	17.3	25	D	D	D	1,682	59.4	250	1
Charles City	3	D	D	D	7	D	D	D	401	14.0	2,787	17
Charlotte	23	284	13.2	7.7	17	D	D	D	678	27.9	4,675	23
Chesterfield	757	11,169	1,338.3	518.8	479	3,341	368.3	87.3	22,976	970.5	375,002	2,260
Clarke	25	D	D	D	30	79	10.1	3.0	1,403	61.8	10,967	35
Craig	5	D	D	D	3	D	D	D	288	11.7	1,170	5
Culpeper	74	2,007	204.3	84.8	75	539	47.4	17.3	3,631	166.2	85,296	342
Cumberland	10	115	3.3	2.1	9	D	D	D	532	21.0	3,345	25
Dickenson	27	402	24.7	12.2	19	D	D	D	463	12.5	248	2
Dinwiddie	26	263	15.5	6.7	32	D	D	D	1,340	49.6	11,555	75
Essex	35	623	68.4	19.7	23	D	D	D	764	31.4	6,036	40
Fairfax	2,860	52,008	6,870.2	2,622.2	1,950	17,487	2,708.3	760.6	108,810	5,574.1	314,132	1,557
Fauquier	125	2,571	274.8	114.2	128	875	82.3	28.9	6,338	330.0	122,205	337
Floyd	23	320	45.0	8.4	24	D	D	D	1,317	40.3	8,869	44
Fluvanna	22	199	11.7	5.5	22	138	9.4	3.0	1,724	59.9	32,757	121
Franklin	74	D	D	D	91	287	25.6	6.5	3,698	137.9	38,290	122
Frederick	88	1,551	114.1	45.9	104	591	55.8	17.4	5,530	221.2	149,017	716
Giles	29	500	46.1	16.5	26	D	D	D	867	32.4	6,455	31
Gloucester	69	1,282	128.1	45.2	75	323	22.5	7.2	2,351	84.6	43,649	158
Goochland	28	D	D	D	38	D	D	D	2,145	129.2	56,272	190
Grayson	17	197	11.3	4.5	9	D	D	D	1,026	36.0	5,621	29
Greene	15	D	D	D	20	103	9.2	2.5	1,348	47.1	23,840	149
Greensville	3	D	D	D	3	D	D	D	367	9.3	2,207	13
Halifax	82	1,767	159.9	73.5	50	173	16.1	3.9	1,777	63.4	7,562	42
Hanover	258	4,764	706.4	221.0	258	1,649	150.5	44.8	8,292	377.9	98,255	487
Henrico	977	24,726	2,887.9	1,138.2	635	4,883	735.9	163.0	24,009	1,052.0	185,826	1,478
Henry	55	1,005	51.9	23.4	47	257	20.5	6.3	2,303	71.7	5,157	21
Highland	5	58	3.3	1.4	9	D	D	D	248	5.8	1,886	14
Isle of Wight	50	648	44.0	21.2	64	309	29.2	9.7	2,264	89.4	36,349	178
James City	159	3,572	305.5	138.8	108	D	D	D	5,450	236.9	107,218	454
King and Queen	3	D	D	D	5	D	D	D	409	13.4	2,349	15
King George	21	321	21.3	8.8	29	D	D	D	1,434	49.1	25,745	132
King William	23	327	17.5	8.8	29	111	8.9	2.3	1,047	46.3	19,294	129
Lancaster	35	1,088	87.0	41.1	42	177	13.5	4.4	1,055	45.8	13,999	51
Lee	32	786	53.3	24.8	17	D	D	D	1,142	36.3	1,535	15
Loudoun	759	9,585	1,188.5	459.1	566	4,756	597.3	217.1	33,911	1,712.6	644,907	3,715

— **Government Employment and Payroll, and Local Government Finances**

STATE County	Full-time equivalent employees	March payroll (dollars)	Adminis-tration, judicial, and legal	Police and corrections	Fire protection	Highways and transpor-tation	Health and welfare	Natural resources and utilities	Education and libraries	Total (mil dol)	Inter-govern-mental (mil dol)	Total (mil dol)	Per capita[1] (dollars) Total	Per capita[1] (dollars) Property
					March payroll (percent of total)						General revenue / Taxes			
	171	172	173	174	175	176	177	178	179	180	181	182	183	184
VERMONT— Cont'd														
Chittenden	6,092	25,796,817	4.3	6.7	2.8	6.4	0.8	8.4	68.8	648.3	401.0	117.0	738	613
Essex	227	673,088	8.5	1.1	0.0	5.4	1.1	1.2	82.3	22.3	16.5	3.7	588	586
Franklin	1,780	6,015,525	5.6	3.3	0.4	4.9	1.2	3.1	80.8	156.8	118.8	21.4	443	432
Grand Isle	201	726,392	10.7	0.0	0.0	6.8	2.7	2.1	76.7	25.5	17.3	7.2	1,026	1,022
Lamoille	1,075	3,560,151	5.3	4.1	0.1	5.4	1.5	5.9	77.1	94.8	63.4	20.8	832	792
Orange	1,252	3,813,072	7.2	1.2	0.1	5.8	0.2	0.5	84.5	109.1	85.0	17.9	618	616
Orleans	1,359	3,619,393	5.7	2.4	0.1	7.1	0.3	1.7	82.4	103.1	75.1	19.7	725	721
Rutland	2,343	8,318,234	5.3	3.7	1.6	7.2	0.7	4.0	76.9	234.3	164.7	46.5	764	726
Washington	2,492	8,165,965	5.6	4.3	2.3	5.1	1.2	3.5	77.0	224.6	150.4	42.0	707	701
Windham	1,877	6,583,583	5.5	4.5	2.2	6.1	1.0	3.8	75.7	202.3	137.1	44.4	1,010	989
Windsor	2,421	8,862,072	5.4	5.6	2.7	6.6	1.1	3.8	74.2	247.7	169.7	49.6	883	878
VIRGINIA	X	X	X	X	X	X	X	X	X	X	X	X	X	X
Accomack	1,352	3,776,224	8.2	7.7	0.6	0.7	9.6	1.0	70.7	104.5	55.5	39.6	1,188	876
Albemarle	3,014	10,671,438	7.3	10.3	3.1	1.0	4.5	4.6	65.3	368.6	114.7	187.5	1,833	1,375
Alleghany	689	2,172,894	9.7	10.5	0.3	0.7	8.8	8.3	59.0	58.7	31.2	19.1	1,178	989
Amelia	422	1,273,101	3.9	5.8	0.0	0.0	1.9	1.5	85.8	26.8	15.3	8.2	645	518
Amherst	989	3,067,237	5.7	5.9	0.0	0.0	5.8	6.4	73.5	75.6	42.9	26.1	807	633
Appomattox	535	1,345,618	8.3	5.6	2.3	0.0	7.7	3.3	71.1	37.2	20.5	13.3	878	716
Arlington	9,317	49,809,798	6.9	10.3	4.2	20.3	7.8	5.4	41.2	2,574.1	624.2	861.8	3,899	3,016
Augusta	2,388	6,901,173	5.3	10.5	2.9	0.7	5.8	1.4	72.4	160.8	85.2	60.8	826	604
Bath	219	806,860	8.1	6.7	0.0	0.0	0.7	2.2	80.7	19.6	4.6	14.0	3,000	2,445
Bedford	2,625	7,051,188	4.0	20.1	0.0	0.0	9.1	1.8	63.5	181.5	95.3	61.4	882	750
Bland	206	534,449	5.2	7.3	0.0	0.0	2.6	3.3	70.3	17.5	11.4	4.6	690	588
Botetourt	1,128	3,464,230	7.8	10.1	0.0	0.0	5.0	2.6	72.5	84.1	39.8	37.2	1,122	904
Brunswick	651	1,620,721	7.3	12.5	0.0	0.2	9.0	1.7	67.5	39.3	24.2	10.4	610	490
Buchanan	834	2,368,397	7.1	6.9	0.7	1.0	4.4	1.1	76.6	101.0	43.8	50.0	2,095	742
Buckingham	544	1,683,523	4.7	32.1	0.0	0.0	2.0	2.6	57.1	44.0	28.4	13.4	782	682
Campbell	1,839	5,409,816	5.0	6.0	1.2	0.4	4.4	1.8	78.6	131.1	70.6	44.2	801	613
Caroline	918	2,716,780	8.5	9.8	2.1	0.0	5.6	2.6	68.0	76.7	35.1	35.8	1,236	1,010
Carroll	1,015	2,970,573	6.2	5.3	1.8	0.4	12.0	2.7	68.4	74.0	35.3	24.9	836	659
Charles City	243	709,888	11.5	6.6	0.0	0.0	0.0	4.7	70.0	21.2	9.1	8.1	1,137	1,012
Charlotte	499	1,413,313	6.4	8.9	0.0	0.1	7.7	2.4	72.2	35.7	24.5	8.0	646	537
Chesterfield	12,105	41,117,167	7.5	9.1	5.5	0.2	7.4	4.0	62.3	1,045.1	437.5	443.8	1,370	1,103
Clarke	531	1,954,739	5.8	7.2	0.0	1.3	3.8	2.9	72.3	48.5	15.8	21.7	1,516	1,292
Craig	169	483,380	9.9	7.8	0.0	0.0	5.9	2.1	74.4	13.0	8.1	3.8	730	626
Culpeper	1,841	5,945,989	8.3	10.6	0.9	1.1	9.5	4.7	63.2	142.8	61.0	63.9	1,333	1,025
Cumberland	297	961,120	9.9	8.2	0.0	0.0	1.6	1.1	72.0	23.9	13.9	8.8	889	758
Dickenson	610	1,668,965	6.7	7.4	0.0	0.0	4.2	7.9	70.6	68.6	37.7	20.1	1,282	855
Dinwiddie	890	2,870,612	6.8	7.8	0.3	0.0	11.1	3.2	67.5	79.3	43.7	31.3	1,119	925
Essex	422	1,333,678	8.5	8.1	3.2	2.6	2.1	8.3	64.6	32.1	12.9	16.4	1,462	1,109
Fairfax	43,275	208,710,868	5.3	8.1	5.1	0.4	7.2	5.9	62.9	5,025.9	1,140.8	3,142.7	2,810	2,292
Fauquier	2,840	9,833,163	6.6	9.0	2.5	0.7	3.2	5.4	69.2	232.3	78.6	133.9	2,012	1,727
Floyd	421	1,524,813	5.3	6.1	0.0	0.0	3.6	2.2	81.6	27.7	14.4	11.9	771	609
Fluvanna	723	2,499,361	7.1	4.3	0.0	0.0	3.5	1.7	78.2	61.3	29.5	28.7	1,105	989
Franklin	1,773	5,802,144	5.5	5.8	2.1	0.7	4.3	1.4	79.1	131.8	64.9	58.9	1,044	833
Frederick	3,183	9,479,873	6.7	10.3	3.6	0.6	2.4	2.0	72.9	235.3	97.7	114.5	1,425	1,069
Giles	586	1,588,082	11.1	11.9	0.0	1.6	2.9	6.0	64.6	54.9	29.9	17.0	1,002	801
Gloucester	1,208	3,733,992	8.5	8.9	0.0	0.0	3.3	3.6	71.8	99.1	42.2	45.2	1,224	938
Goochland	541	1,850,764	13.7	7.7	3.4	0.0	1.5	3.0	67.1	56.0	13.5	37.7	1,768	1,342
Grayson	541	1,324,989	8.4	7.8	0.0	0.3	3.4	2.6	76.5	36.9	21.4	11.7	771	658
Greene	657	1,764,870	6.8	4.8	0.0	2.2	0.6	0.4	80.2	51.3	25.0	19.5	1,040	871
Greensville	571	1,743,841	9.5	15.1	0.0	0.0	1.0	4.8	67.5	48.9	30.7	8.1	686	540
Halifax	1,547	3,858,184	6.4	5.9	1.6	1.0	5.8	2.5	75.9	111.3	60.8	33.7	940	669
Hanover	4,522	15,814,948	6.9	13.8	4.2	0.4	5.6	3.8	63.1	349.4	131.9	160.0	1,590	1,262
Henrico	11,822	42,600,655	5.0	12.2	6.3	3.6	7.0	2.9	59.3	1,060.7	406.5	484.0	1,537	1,115
Henry	1,709	4,761,002	6.5	7.7	0.9	0.0	9.6	0.7	71.0	124.5	75.9	32.9	620	403
Highland	101	285,647	13.1	13.3	0.0	0.0	5.6	0.9	63.7	8.1	4.2	3.1	1,401	1,221
Isle of Wight	1,226	4,460,998	6.8	4.8	1.2	1.8	1.9	2.5	75.6	106.3	46.2	51.6	1,459	1,145
James City	3,104	11,075,839	5.4	9.6	5.6	1.6	3.8	10.2	60.5	257.6	89.5	138.2	2,003	1,605
King and Queen	300	906,918	6.2	30.6	0.0	0.0	0.5	0.0	57.6	23.5	13.1	6.2	884	787
King George	1,018	3,118,233	7.1	5.5	4.7	0.0	3.5	3.8	73.7	80.3	31.9	31.4	1,282	770
King William	608	1,988,526	5.8	6.3	0.6	0.6	2.4	1.7	79.0	49.7	22.6	23.3	1,459	1,282
Lancaster	380	818,567	17.4	17.6	0.0	0.5	6.5	2.5	53.6	32.1	11.5	18.8	1,669	1,337
Lee	981	2,345,408	5.5	6.0	0.0	0.7	1.6	1.9	83.8	61.5	44.1	13.2	519	363
Loudoun	13,775	59,560,641	6.5	6.9	4.6	0.5	5.4	3.9	70.0	1,546.1	373.1	1,012.0	3,004	2,472

1. Based on the resident population estimated as of July 1 of the year shown.

Table B. States and Counties — Local Government Finances, Government Employment, and Income Taxes

STATE County	Total (mil dol)	Per capita[1] (dollars)	Education	Health and hospitals	Police protection	Public welfare	Highways	Total (mil dol)	Per capita[1] (dollars)	Federal civilian	Federal military	State and local	Number of returns	Mean adjusted gross income	Mean income tax
	185	186	187	188	189	190	191	192	193	194	195	196	197	198	199
VERMONT— Cont'd															
Chittenden	643.2	4,058	61.0	0.2	5.1	0.1	5.6	564.9	3,564	2,406	1,093	14,600	84,470	72,379	9,731
Essex	23.3	3,739	69.1	0.2	1.7	0.1	14.9	1.6	258	78	40	298	2,870	38,314	3,158
Franklin	162.7	3,374	75.1	0.6	4.0	0.0	8.1	53.3	1,106	1,549	309	2,931	24,590	53,187	5,519
Grand Isle	24.7	3,541	70.6	0.0	3.4	0.1	10.5	14.7	2,098	18	45	268	3,880	66,204	8,341
Lamoille	96.7	3,874	66.5	0.9	8.2	0.2	8.6	76.2	3,054	58	157	1,632	13,590	64,852	8,437
Orange	114.2	3,950	75.9	0.6	1.8	0.1	10.2	35.3	1,220	71	180	1,800	14,880	52,488	5,568
Orleans	106.7	3,935	76.0	0.3	1.8	0.0	9.3	33.0	1,219	235	166	1,828	13,670	42,602	4,218
Rutland	244.1	4,010	70.6	0.1	3.7	0.0	7.9	67.5	1,108	279	362	3,703	31,270	50,019	5,485
Washington	229.0	3,852	62.5	0.9	3.6	0.1	11.1	117.9	1,983	237	399	7,643	30,940	63,528	7,871
Windham	233.0	5,297	58.8	0.2	2.3	0.2	13.5	108.8	2,474	142	264	2,750	23,180	49,437	5,325
Windsor	275.6	4,903	62.8	0.8	3.4	0.0	12.6	98.2	1,746	1,522	355	3,490	30,220	59,600	7,130
VIRGINIA	X	X	X	X	X	X	X	X	X	197,619	137,423	543,882	3,910,050	74,819	10,458
Accomack	93.0	2,789	51.9	1.1	4.4	4.8	1.7	62.8	1,884	665	258	2,269	15,940	44,229	4,098
Albemarle	356.2	3,484	49.8	9.7	4.8	4.1	0.2	444.7	4,349	(2)1,293	(2) 936	(2) 31,396	49,310	98,833	16,234
Alleghany	59.6	3,670	51.9	0.6	5.0	6.2	1.3	32.8	2,020	(3)64	(3)66	(3)1,552	6,850	48,906	4,692
Amelia	26.9	2,108	60.3	2.6	6.3	6.1	1.7	4.0	313	30	42	471	6,150	51,202	4,873
Amherst	71.6	2,212	62.9	0.8	7.1	6.1	0.1	27.2	840	49	98	2,064	14,180	47,145	4,230
Appomattox	35.6	2,351	57.9	1.0	6.3	6.5	0.0	34.6	2,285	46	51	763	7,010	47,011	4,194
Arlington	2,639.2	11,940	16.7	1.1	2.2	3.0	2.0	8,672.6	39,235	27,407	8,438	13,382	123,520	116,880	21,366
Augusta	170.0	2,308	65.1	0.6	3.9	8.2	0.9	103.4	1,404	(10) 275	(10) 382	(10)8,420	34,850	54,128	5,508
Bath	17.3	3,728	54.1	1.3	5.9	4.2	0.0	9.3	1,990	27	14	352	2,260	50,609	5,347
Bedford	182.3	2,619	49.8	0.5	3.6	8.7	0.1	152.7	2,194	131	250	2,990	36,090	62,134	7,172
Bland	15.8	2,338	54.4	0.9	6.4	8.4	6.8	5.0	743	15	25	586	2,530	46,955	4,376
Botetourt	82.4	2,486	63.3	0.6	6.0	3.8	0.0	55.7	1,681	56	106	1,455	16,020	66,615	7,876
Brunswick	41.2	2,421	57.0	0.6	6.4	7.4	0.2	19.3	1,133	38	46	954	6,460	40,416	3,416
Buchanan	84.4	3,538	45.9	0.7	4.7	11.2	11.3	12.4	520	63	66	1,477	7,290	42,195	3,997
Buckingham	45.4	2,658	45.9	1.1	3.9	6.2	0.1	68.7	4,022	30	52	1,276	6,380	42,892	3,841
Campbell	128.3	2,326	59.4	5.8	4.7	7.0	2.3	58.2	1,055	(7) 337	(7) 445	(7)7,012	25,160	47,812	4,382
Caroline	67.8	2,338	54.8	0.4	8.4	6.1	3.4	132.8	4,584	409	133	1,234	14,100	52,054	4,871
Carroll	84.4	2,829	57.3	7.7	4.7	6.3	0.7	59.6	1,996	(6)90	(6) 115	(6)2,250	12,250	40,381	3,252
Charles City	20.4	2,844	63.8	0.5	3.9	5.3	0.0	2.7	382	20	23	295	3,580	53,705	6,028
Charlotte	37.5	3,022	59.8	2.5	5.0	11.4	0.1	6.2	500	40	39	864	5,130	39,460	3,212
Chesterfield	985.4	3,043	54.6	5.0	6.6	4.1	1.2	716.3	2,212	3,261	1,151	17,657	165,150	71,096	8,990
Clarke	61.0	4,259	55.3	0.7	3.6	3.6	0.4	147.7	10,315	28	46	724	7,210	80,558	11,290
Craig	12.6	2,425	55.8	1.3	6.8	12.8	0.3	4.1	793	13	16	235	2,200	47,600	4,212
Culpeper	140.4	2,931	53.3	0.9	7.6	9.8	2.8	122.9	2,566	220	161	3,144	22,600	62,026	6,960
Cumberland	23.1	2,345	63.3	1.2	6.5	4.8	0.0	44.0	4,466	12	32	462	4,300	42,557	3,672
Dickenson	61.5	3,918	45.4	5.6	3.7	9.6	1.7	13.6	869	35	46	900	4,810	40,151	3,273
Dinwiddie	72.2	2,580	60.9	3.9	5.4	4.8	0.1	113.2	4,044	(9) 241	(9) 257	(9)5,729	12,930	49,917	4,681
Essex	34.5	3,071	57.7	0.0	5.0	9.0	1.4	48.6	4,329	17	35	532	5,310	50,535	5,504
Fairfax	4,854.2	4,340	51.6	4.1	4.6	6.0	2.1	5,037.1	4,503	(5) 45,826	(5) 10,212	(5) 61,328	547,290	115,992	20,088
Fauquier	242.3	3,641	59.7	0.4	7.0	4.2	1.2	187.2	2,813	616	223	3,731	34,160	90,532	13,132
Floyd	26.9	1,751	66.1	2.5	5.5	3.9	0.0	15.6	1,013	53	51	622	6,800	47,333	4,563
Fluvanna	74.8	2,882	70.0	0.8	3.4	6.6	0.3	91.0	3,506	31	82	1,315	12,240	60,572	6,304
Franklin	130.9	2,320	61.7	0.5	4.3	7.9	1.1	36.2	641	98	178	2,284	24,040	52,701	5,669
Frederick	220.1	2,740	72.6	0.5	5.1	2.7	0.1	196.2	2,443	(12)2,146	(12) 379	(12)6,847	40,940	64,055	7,447
Giles	49.2	2,909	47.4	0.4	7.2	7.5	2.9	61.0	3,603	32	54	882	7,410	46,856	4,321
Gloucester	94.6	2,564	65.7	1.1	5.1	5.2	0.1	62.6	1,698	89	119	2,052	18,360	57,906	5,921
Goochland	45.4	2,128	55.2	1.1	5.8	4.2	0.5	133.0	6,229	40	70	1,376	11,190	128,785	24,705
Grayson	35.4	2,329	60.0	0.4	6.1	6.7	0.3	38.8	2,555	25	47	1,031	6,250	38,366	2,943
Greene	53.8	2,869	65.7	0.8	5.7	5.5	1.9	57.6	3,067	33	63	846	9,050	58,467	6,061
Greensville	52.0	4,385	49.3	0.3	4.8	5.4	0.4	56.1	4,732	(4)35	(4)43	(4)1,769	3,640	40,162	3,401
Halifax	113.2	3,157	52.4	10.5	5.0	6.6	2.0	72.1	2,012	90	109	2,084	14,820	44,388	4,249
Hanover	342.5	3,403	52.1	0.4	6.9	6.6	1.7	364.1	3,617	171	347	5,055	52,600	77,696	10,127
Henrico	1,095.4	3,478	45.2	3.0	6.3	2.5	4.7	980.8	3,114	2,329	1,051	17,477	161,170	71,118	9,826
Henry	127.8	2,414	68.2	0.9	4.2	6.1	0.0	28.3	534	(8) 133	(8) 223	(8)3,815	21,930	40,113	3,413
Highland	7.7	3,440	49.1	2.3	7.9	4.4	7.0	0.7	311	6	7	169	1,050	48,546	4,960
Isle of Wight	103.6	2,926	49.8	4.9	5.6	3.1	1.0	149.3	4,218	84	117	1,356	17,990	66,078	7,417
James City	260.7	3,781	54.2	6.4	4.7	1.9	0.0	269.9	3,914	(11) 230	(11) 424	(11)8,275	37,300	87,929	12,450
King and Queen	25.3	3,591	43.8	0.8	5.0	7.9	0.0	5.0	707	9	23	286	3,220	47,806	4,477
King George	72.4	2,957	53.1	0.9	9.0	6.0	0.1	190.9	7,793	4,801	645	1,120	11,750	70,887	8,085
King William	48.1	3,007	64.8	0.3	6.0	3.6	0.6	39.7	2,483	26	54	723	8,220	56,439	5,554
Lancaster	31.1	2,771	52.2	1.4	6.6	6.9	0.5	18.4	1,636	33	36	539	5,680	66,121	7,889
Lee	59.5	2,335	64.3	1.3	5.4	10.3	0.9	7.4	290	442	72	1,144	7,560	38,067	3,084
Loudoun	1488.4	4,418	60.1	2.4	5.3	2.4	1.9	1,679.5	4,985	4,230	1,283	20,370	181,490	115,453	18,531

1. Based on the resident population estimated as of July 1 of the year shown. 2. Charlottesville city is included with Albemarle county. 3. Covington city is included with Alleghany county. 4. Emporia city is included with Greensville county. 5. Fairfax city and Falls Church city are included with Fairfax county. 6. Galax city is included with Carroll county. 7. Lynchburg city is included with Campbell county. 8. Martinsville city is included with Henry county. 9. Petersburg and Colonial Heights cities are included with Dinwiddie county. 10. Staunton and Waynesboro cities are included with Augusta county. 11. Williamsburg city is included with James City county. 12. Winchester city is included with Frederick county.

Table B. States and Counties — Land Area and Population

State / county code	CBSA code[1]	County code[2]	STATE County	Land area[3] (sq. mi)	Total persons 2018	Rank	Per square mile	White	Black	American Indian, Alaska Native	Asian and Pacific Islancer	Percent Hispanic or Latino[4]	Under 5 years	5 to 17 years	18 to 24 years	25 to 34 years	35 to 44 years	45 to 54 years
				1	2	3	4	5	6	7	8	9	10	11	12	13	14	15
			VIRGINIA— Cont'd															
51109		8	Louisa	496.1	36,778	1,258	74.1	79.9	17.1	1.0	1.1	3.1	5.4	14.8	6.5	11.8	11.1	13.9
51111		9	Lunenburg	431.7	12,086	2,287	28.0	60.9	34.5	0.9	0.6	4.8	4.9	13.7	6.4	12.2	12.3	12.8
51113		8	Madison	320.6	13,295	2,211	41.5	86.9	10.6	1.0	1.1	3.1	4.9	15.4	6.6	10.9	10.3	13.0
51115	47,260	1	Mathews	85.9	8,802	2,515	102.5	87.2	9.4	1.2	1.6	2.8	3.6	11.8	6.9	8.3	8.7	12.8
51117		7	Mecklenburg	625.3	30,650	1,418	49.0	61.4	35.2	0.8	1.2	3.1	4.8	13.7	6.9	10.1	10.0	12.6
51119		8	Middlesex	130.3	10,769	2,368	82.6	79.6	17.8	1.2	0.9	2.8	4.7	11.7	5.9	8.9	8.3	11.7
51121	13,980	3	Montgomery	386.8	98,985	602	255.9	85.7	4.9	0.6	7.9	3.3	4.3	11.2	27.2	14.4	9.9	10.3
51125	16,820	3	Nelson	470.7	14,836	2,108	31.5	83.1	12.3	1.0	1.0	4.5	4.2	13.6	6.3	9.4	10.2	12.4
51127	40,060	1	New Kent	210.0	22,391	1,708	106.6	80.3	14.4	2.0	2.0	3.7	5.1	15.0	7.0	12.8	12.4	14.6
51131		8	Northampton	211.7	11,735	2,311	55.4	55.9	34.3	0.8	1.3	9.3	4.7	14.9	6.3	9.9	9.4	10.9
51133		9	Northumberland	191.4	12,147	2,283	63.5	70.6	25.7	0.8	0.8	3.8	3.4	11.1	5.3	7.8	7.7	10.3
51135		6	Nottoway	314.4	15,420	2,075	49.0	55.4	39.5	1.0	1.1	4.7	5.0	14.1	8.4	14.1	12.3	13.3
51137		6	Orange	341.1	36,644	1,260	107.4	80.1	14.5	1.0	1.9	5.3	5.6	15.5	7.4	11.8	11.5	13.3
51139		6	Page	310.0	23,933	1,646	77.2	95.0	2.6	0.7	0.8	2.1	5.2	14.6	6.8	11.4	11.3	14.1
51141		6	Patrick	483.0	17,673	1,940	36.6	90.6	6.1	0.7	0.5	3.2	4.1	13.3	6.6	8.6	10.2	14.2
51143	19,260	4	Pittsylvania	969.0	60,949	862	62.9	75.0	22.1	0.6	0.8	2.7	4.3	14.6	7.3	10.3	10.6	14.1
51145	40,060	1	Powhatan	260.2	29,189	1,451	112.2	87.0	10.0	0.7	1.1	2.4	4.4	13.8	7.3	10.6	12.8	16.6
51147		6	Prince Edward	350.0	22,950	1,683	65.6	62.6	33.9	0.7	2.0	2.7	4.9	11.5	25.5	11.0	8.8	10.0
51149	40,060	1	Prince George	265.3	38,082	1,223	143.5	56.9	33.1	1.2	3.5	8.5	5.6	16.0	8.4	16.1	15.1	12.6
51153	47,900	1	Prince William	335.7	468,011	149	1,394.1	45.4	22.6	0.9	11.1	24.2	7.5	17.7	8.7	13.4	15.2	14.3
51155	13,980	3	Pulaski	319.8	34,066	1,328	106.5	92.3	6.0	0.6	0.8	1.8	4.8	12.9	7.0	11.7	10.8	14.7
51157	47,900	1	Rappahannock	266.4	7,252	2,644	27.2	90.5	5.4	1.0	1.3	3.8	3.4	12.9	6.8	9.6	9.2	13.2
51159		9	Richmond	191.5	9,038	2,495	47.2	62.3	30.7	0.8	1.1	7.2	4.5	12.7	7.0	14.0	13.5	13.5
51161	40,220	2	Roanoke	250.5	94,073	629	375.5	87.0	6.9	0.5	4.1	3.1	4.4	15.4	7.8	11.4	11.7	13.7
51163		6	Rockbridge	596.5	22,752	1,691	38.1	93.3	4.0	1.2	1.0	2.1	4.2	13.3	7.6	10.2	9.9	12.8
51165	25,500	3	Rockingham	849.8	81,244	698	95.6	89.5	2.7	0.5	1.2	7.3	5.6	16.3	8.9	11.8	11.6	12.8
51167		7	Russell	473.5	26,748	1,537	56.5	97.2	1.2	0.5	0.4	1.4	4.8	14.1	6.8	10.8	11.8	13.7
51169	28,700	2	Scott	535.8	21,534	1,751	40.2	97.3	1.2	0.6	0.4	1.4	4.0	13.7	6.7	10.7	11.4	13.8
51171		6	Shenandoah	508.1	43,497	1,105	85.6	88.8	3.3	0.7	1.4	7.3	5.7	15.5	7.0	11.4	10.9	13.2
51173		7	Smyth	451.4	30,472	1,422	67.5	94.8	2.9	0.6	0.7	2.2	4.6	14.7	7.2	11.3	11.4	14.1
51175		6	Southampton	599.2	17,586	1,946	29.3	62.5	35.5	0.9	0.9	1.8	3.8	14.4	6.8	10.9	10.8	15.9
51177	47,900	1	Spotsylvania	401.5	134,238	477	334.3	70.2	18.0	0.9	4.0	10.3	6.1	18.6	8.3	12.5	12.7	14.3
51179	47,900	1	Stafford	269.2	149,960	444	557.1	63.7	20.4	1.1	5.3	13.6	6.4	19.7	9.6	13.4	13.9	14.7
51181		8	Surry	278.9	6,474	2,713	23.2	54.6	42.8	1.1	0.9	2.5	4.1	12.7	6.8	11.0	8.9	14.2
51183	40,060	1	Sussex	490.2	11,237	2,335	22.9	40.0	56.8	0.7	0.6	3.1	4.2	11.2	9.1	18.2	12.2	13.7
51185	14,140	5	Tazewell	518.8	40,855	1,154	78.7	94.8	3.8	0.5	0.9	1.1	5.0	14.3	7.4	11.1	12.0	12.9
51187	47,900	1	Warren	214.5	40,003	1,179	186.5	88.7	5.9	0.9	1.9	4.9	6.0	16.0	8.2	12.9	11.5	14.1
51191	28,700	2	Washington	561.2	54,402	936	96.9	96.1	1.9	0.5	0.8	1.6	4.7	13.8	8.0	10.4	11.4	13.6
51193		6	Westmoreland	229.3	17,830	1,930	77.8	66.2	27.0	1.3	1.4	6.7	5.4	13.4	6.5	11.4	9.7	11.8
51195	13,720	7	Wise	403.4	38,012	1,225	94.2	92.4	6.3	0.5	0.7	1.2	5.2	14.5	9.2	13.5	12.3	13.2
51197		6	Wythe	461.9	28,754	1,466	62.3	94.9	3.7	0.7	0.9	1.4	4.9	14.8	6.6	11.1	11.5	14.7
51199	47,260	1	York	104.6	67,846	786	648.6	73.5	14.7	1.0	7.9	6.6	5.6	18.2	8.7	11.6	13.1	13.0
			Independent Cities															
51510	47,900	1	Alexandria city	14.9	160,530	413	10,773.8	54.1	23.2	0.7	8.2	16.7	7.1	11.2	6.0	21.5	18.4	13.3
51520	28,700	2	Bristol city	12.9	16,482	2,010	1,277.7	89.7	7.6	0.7	1.4	2.6	5.2	15.0	6.7	13.0	12.4	13.1
51530		6	Buena Vista city	6.4	6,237	2,731	974.5	89.4	6.6	1.7	1.7	2.7	2.6	14.8	15.1	12.8	10.5	11.9
51540	16,820	3	Charlottesville city	10.2	48,117	1,021	4,717.4	68.4	19.2	0.6	8.8	5.7	5.7	10.2	19.4	20.4	12.5	10.2
51550	47,260	1	Chesapeake city	338.5	242,634	280	716.8	59.6	31.2	1.0	5.1	6.5	6.3	17.8	8.4	14.3	13.7	13.0
51570	40,060	1	Colonial Heights city	7.5	17,833	1,929	2,377.7	73.2	17.1	1.0	5.0	6.3	7.0	17.1	7.8	12.8	11.1	11.9
51580		6	Covington city	5.5	5,460	2,799	992.7	82.9	14.5	0.9	1.6	2.3	2.4	15.6	8.3	12.8	11.0	13.5
51590	19,260	4	Danville city	42.8	40,693	1,160	950.8	43.1	51.4	0.6	1.7	4.6	5.8	15.9	8.7	12.7	9.9	11.7
51595		6	Emporia city	6.9	5,121	2,823	742.2	29.2	63.7	0.4	1.4	6.4	3.0	18.2	7.7	13.2	11.1	12.7
51600	47,900	1	Fairfax city	6.2	24,574	1,627	3,963.5	57.5	6.6	0.8	20.7	17.4	10.7	14.3	8.5	13.7	12.8	13.1
51610	47,900	1	Falls Church city	2.0	14,772	2,109	7,386.0	74.2	5.4	0.8	12.0	11.1	7.4	19.0	7.1	12.0	13.8	15.0
51620		6	Franklin city	8.3	8,013	2,592	965.4	38.4	58.5	0.8	1.4	2.6	5.6	18.1	7.2	12.7	10.0	11.8
51630	47,900	1	Fredericksburg city	10.5	29,144	1,453	2,775.6	62.2	25.5	0.9	4.4	11.0	6.9	14.0	19.7	15.8	11.6	10.7
51640		7	Galax city	8.2	6,423	2,716	783.3	77.2	7.2	0.5	1.2	15.8	4.8	17.0	8.4	12.1	10.4	13.9
51650	47,260	1	Hampton city	51.4	134,313	476	2,613.1	40.7	52.2	1.4	3.8	6.0	6.0	15.0	11.9	15.6	11.3	11.2
51660	25,500	3	Harrisonburg city	17.3	54,033	938	3,123.3	67.2	8.5	0.5	5.4	20.6	5.7	11.3	31.9	14.3	10.9	8.7
51670	40,060	1	Hopewell city	10.4	22,596	1,703	2,172.7	48.1	43.4	1.1	2.3	8.3	7.7	18.3	8.0	14.5	11.5	12.1
51678		6	Lexington city	2.5	7,136	2,653	2,854.4	84.1	9.4	0.9	4.6	3.4	1.4	8.0	45.4	8.2	6.9	6.6
51680	31,340	2	Lynchburg city	49.0	82,126	691	1,676.0	64.3	29.4	0.7	3.5	4.4	6.2	13.2	24.8	14.2	8.7	8.9
51683	47,900	1	Manassas city	9.9	41,641	1,139	4,206.2	42.3	14.9	0.7	6.9	37.8	8.5	18.5	8.7	15.2	14.3	12.7
51685	47,900	1	Manassas Park city	2.5	17,307	1,959	6,922.8	34.2	14.8	0.9	12.5	40.1	3.9	18.8	9.5	17.1	16.8	15.6

1. CBSA = Core Based Statistical Area. See Appendix A for explanation. See Appendix B for list of metropolitan areas with component counties.   2. County type code from the Economic Research Service of USDA Rural-Urban Continuum Codes. See Appendix A for definition.   3. Dry land or land partially or temporarily covered by water.   4. May be of any race.

Table B. States and Counties — **Population and Households**

STATE County	Population, 2018 (cont.) Age (percent) (cont.)				Population change, 2000-2018							Households, 2013-2017				
	55 to 64 years	65 to 74 years	75 years and over	Percent female	Total persons 2000	2010	Percent change 2000-2010	2010-2018	Components of change, 2010-2018 Births	Deaths	Net Migration	Number	Persons per household	Family house-holds	Percent Female family house-holder[1]	One person
	16	17	18	19	20	21	22	23	24	25	26	27	28	29	30	31

STATE County																
VIRGINIA— Cont'd																
Louisa	16.8	12.5	7.3	50.6	25,627	33,168	29.4	10.9	3,107	2,546	3,033	13,451	2.58	71.0	9.4	23.2
Lunenburg	15.4	13.2	9.1	47.0	13,146	12,916	-1.7	-6.4	958	1,231	-562	4,480	2.55	67.8	13.4	28.5
Madison	16.6	12.8	9.4	51.7	12,520	13,309	6.3	-0.1	1,033	1,126	86	5,107	2.52	71.7	12.5	23.8
Mathews	16.8	17.1	13.9	51.9	9,207	8,976	-2.5	-1.9	478	984	339	3,766	2.32	67.4	8.4	27.1
Mecklenburg	16.2	14.7	10.9	51.4	32,380	32,720	1.1	-6.3	2,411	3,668	-818	11,785	2.54	63.5	13.9	33.9
Middlesex	17.7	17.4	13.7	51.3	9,932	10,959	10.3	-1.7	727	1,246	336	4,522	2.28	64.7	9.5	31.1
Montgomery	10.1	7.3	5.3	48.0	83,629	94,422	12.9	4.8	7,186	5,050	2,444	35,577	2.49	54.5	7.2	27.6
Nelson	16.7	17.1	10.2	51.7	14,445	15,015	3.9	-1.2	1,059	1,498	268	6,523	2.26	66.5	14.6	25.9
New Kent	15.9	11.8	5.5	48.9	13,462	18,432	36.9	21.5	1,628	1,218	3,507	7,555	2.64	78.6	9.5	18.9
Northampton	17.6	15.1	11.3	52.3	13,093	12,391	-5.4	-5.3	1,047	1,550	-148	5,177	2.26	64.2	17.2	30.9
Northumberland	17.6	20.5	16.2	51.0	12,259	12,331	0.6	-1.5	738	1,430	514	5,774	2.12	69.0	11.1	26.4
Nottoway	13.8	10.7	8.5	45.9	15,725	15,852	0.8	-2.7	1,348	1,642	-135	5,633	2.44	66.6	19.2	30.5
Orange	14.6	11.5	8.8	51.2	25,881	33,557	29.7	9.2	3,146	2,998	2,933	13,470	2.58	71.7	11.8	24.6
Page	15.2	12.1	9.2	50.6	23,177	24,052	3.8	-0.5	1,944	2,370	327	9,467	2.48	68.7	12.6	24.4
Patrick	16.6	14.7	11.7	50.6	19,407	18,500	-4.7	-4.5	1,191	2,125	124	7,713	2.29	67.2	9.3	30.5
Pittsylvania	16.2	13.2	9.5	50.7	61,745	63,473	2.8	-4.0	4,332	5,833	-1,007	26,687	2.28	68.8	13.4	28.1
Powhatan	16.3	11.7	6.6	48.2	22,377	28,064	25.4	4.0	1,939	1,666	853	9,974	2.58	79.9	9.3	17.2
Prince Edward	11.8	8.8	7.7	49.9	19,720	23,357	18.4	-1.7	1,746	1,834	-414	7,281	2.52	62.3	12.9	28.0
Prince George	12.2	8.5	5.5	45.9	33,047	35,719	8.1	6.6	3,074	1,910	1,164	11,298	2.98	77.1	11.0	18.7
Prince William	11.3	6.3	3.5	50.0	280,813	401,997	43.2	16.4	55,281	14,505	24,997	139,306	3.21	77.4	11.5	18.5
Pulaski	15.2	13.6	9.4	50.0	35,127	34,859	-0.8	-2.3	2,651	3,574	160	14,577	2.28	67.5	12.1	27.8
Rappahannock	17.7	16.2	11.1	50.9	6,983	7,503	7.4	-3.3	440	585	-105	3,131	2.34	68.8	7.2	27.9
Richmond	13.8	10.5	10.6	43.7	8,809	9,254	5.1	-2.3	628	881	27	3,250	2.20	67.2	11.8	28.3
Roanoke	14.2	12.0	9.4	51.8	85,778	92,462	7.8	1.7	6,524	8,033	3,199	38,434	2.37	67.7	10.8	27.8
Rockbridge	16.1	14.4	11.6	50.5	20,808	22,358	7.4	1.8	1,447	2,032	997	9,160	2.43	66.4	7.7	27.0
Rockingham	13.9	10.5	8.6	50.8	67,725	76,321	12.7	6.5	6,976	5,815	3,843	30,503	2.52	71.6	9.5	23.4
Russell	16.4	12.7	8.9	51.1	30,308	28,902	-4.6	-7.5	2,113	2,974	-1,287	11,102	2.45	66.3	8.9	31.0
Scott	15.4	13.5	10.7	49.7	23,403	23,170	-1.0	-7.1	1,509	2,598	-535	8,976	2.40	67.1	9.0	29.5
Shenandoah	14.5	12.2	9.5	51.1	35,075	41,996	19.7	3.6	3,902	3,854	1,485	17,262	2.46	67.7	9.1	28.0
Smyth	14.7	12.2	9.8	51.0	33,081	32,214	-2.6	-5.4	2,453	3,545	-627	12,829	2.39	66.2	11.7	29.7
Southampton	17.3	11.7	8.5	48.0	17,482	18,571	6.2	-5.3	1,230	1,534	-689	6,664	2.49	73.9	14.9	23.3
Spotsylvania	13.2	8.8	5.5	50.9	90,395	122,449	35.5	9.6	12,949	6,925	5,845	43,279	3.00	76.9	11.6	18.8
Stafford	11.8	6.6	3.9	49.6	92,446	128,984	39.5	16.3	14,019	5,628	12,594	45,345	3.04	81.6	11.4	14.4
Surry	19.7	13.6	9.0	50.6	6,829	7,064	3.4	-8.4	491	604	-480	2,773	2.41	74.9	17.9	20.7
Sussex	13.6	10.3	7.5	40.7	12,504	12,070	-3.5	-6.9	829	1,117	-556	3,388	2.05	63.2	15.6	31.1
Tazewell	15.1	13.2	9.1	50.5	44,598	45,068	1.1	-9.3	3,576	5,133	-2,655	17,330	2.38	66.5	10.4	30.0
Warren	15.2	9.8	6.2	50.2	31,584	37,435	18.5	6.9	3,878	2,973	1,558	14,190	2.69	70.6	14.3	24.1
Washington	15.4	13.1	9.6	50.7	51,103	54,964	7.6	-1.0	4,132	5,097	432	22,388	2.36	67.1	10.9	29.7
Westmoreland	16.5	14.8	10.6	51.2	16,718	17,460	4.4	2.1	1,571	1,785	590	7,412	2.36	61.1	7.4	31.7
Wise	13.9	11.1	7.1	48.0	40,123	41,450	3.3	-8.3	3,564	4,143	-2,887	15,104	2.42	67.9	14.4	26.7
Wythe	14.8	12.4	9.3	51.2	27,599	29,235	5.9	-1.6	2,355	3,053	244	11,892	2.42	65.8	7.3	29.8
York	13.7	9.3	6.8	51.0	56,297	65,239	15.9	4.0	5,318	3,469	739	24,333	2.72	78.8	10.3	16.8
Independent Cities																
Alexandria city	11.0	7.1	4.4	51.9	128,283	140,008	9.1	14.7	22,818	6,103	3,796	68,663	2.23	48.3	8.3	41.9
Bristol city	13.5	11.6	9.5	52.6	17,367	17,739	2.1	-7.1	1,439	2,240	-451	7,418	2.25	62.9	15.5	31.9
Buena Vista city	12.7	10.9	8.6	53.1	6,349	6,607	4.1	-5.6	415	619	-172	2,606	2.31	68.4	11.2	27.2
Charlottesville city	10.1	7.3	4.3	51.5	45,049	43,425	-3.6	10.8	4,606	2,298	2,389	18,408	2.38	45.8	10.8	34.6
Chesapeake city	13.2	8.1	5.2	51.2	199,184	222,306	11.6	9.1	23,591	14,037	10,866	83,031	2.76	75.0	15.3	21.2
Colonial Heights city	12.7	10.0	9.6	54.2	16,897	17,410	3.0	2.4	1,907	1,886	411	7,092	2.45	62.9	16.2	32.3
Covington city	15.2	12.1	9.1	51.7	6,303	5,954	-5.5	-8.3	298	693	-95	2,399	2.33	59.6	14.8	35.8
Danville city	14.3	11.4	9.5	54.0	48,411	43,077	-11.0	-5.5	4,146	5,586	-918	18,517	2.18	58.1	20.4	36.0
Emporia city	13.9	9.6	10.6	53.7	5,665	5,925	4.6	-13.6	340	628	-518	2,119	2.48	68.9	26.0	29.5
Fairfax city	12.6	8.2	6.1	50.3	21,498	22,554	4.9	9.0	3,610	1,644	34	8,499	2.70	66.8	10.1	22.0
Falls Church city	12.4	8.4	4.8	50.9	10,377	12,279	18.3	20.3	1,569	612	1,509	5,308	2.60	65.2	11.2	30.1
Franklin city	14.9	11.2	8.5	54.9	8,346	8,580	2.8	-6.6	784	1,024	-328	3,470	2.36	65.3	25.6	32.2
Fredericksburg city	10.0	6.6	4.5	53.8	19,279	24,178	25.4	20.5	3,333	1,571	3,102	10,419	2.44	54.7	16.5	36.3
Galax city	13.3	10.2	10.0	53.6	6,837	6,989	2.2	-8.1	663	1,002	-230	2,837	2.25	63.8	14.0	35.0
Hampton city	13.7	9.1	6.4	51.9	146,437	137,384	-6.2	-2.2	14,705	10,056	-7,738	53,555	2.46	60.4	17.4	32.3
Harrisonburg city	7.8	5.2	4.2	51.9	40,468	48,900	20.8	10.5	4,902	2,217	2,398	16,848	2.71	52.4	13.2	28.9
Hopewell city	12.2	8.8	6.9	53.4	22,354	22,591	1.1	0.0	2,855	2,353	-497	9,123	2.42	61.1	20.8	32.4
Lexington city	7.5	8.4	7.8	43.8	6,867	7,034	2.4	1.5	201	535	432	1,935	1.85	40.6	8.8	50.1
Lynchburg city	9.7	7.6	6.8	53.1	65,269	75,533	15.7	8.7	8,773	6,374	4,196	28,150	2.43	58.3	16.9	32.3
Manassas city	11.8	6.7	3.6	49.9	35,135	37,819	7.6	10.1	5,798	1,623	-407	12,540	3.29	75.8	12.0	19.4
Manassas Park city	10.3	5.0	3.0	48.5	10,290	14,241	38.4	21.5	1,261	303	2,062	4,778	3.37	73.1	9.3	20.4

1. No spouse present.

STATE County	Persons in group quarters, 2018	Daytime Population, 2013-2017		Births, 2018		Deaths, 2018		Persons under 65 with no health insurance, 2016		Medicare, 2018			Serious crimes known to police[2], 2016 Total	
		Number	Employment/residence ratio	Total	Rate[1]	Number	Rate[1]	Number	Percent	Total beneficiaries	Enrolled in Original Medicare	Enrolled in Medicare Advantage	Number	Rate[3]
	32	33	34	35	36	37	38	39	40	41	42	43	44	45
VIRGINIA— Cont'd														
Louisa	211	28,831	0.63	382	10.4	367	10.0	3,619	12.7	8,019	6,546	1,473	483	1,393
Lunenburg	1,002	10,469	0.58	99	8.2	164	13.6	1,234	14.3	3,028	2,632	396	97	801
Madison	193	11,006	0.65	135	10.2	114	8.6	1,388	13.6	2,981	2,553	428	115	883
Mathews	86	6,797	0.50	56	6.4	125	14.2	552	9.0	2,843	2,386	457	79	898
Mecklenburg	925	32,238	1.10	298	9.7	481	15.7	2,850	12.6	9,128	7,410	1,718	476	1,556
Middlesex	377	9,814	0.79	91	8.5	137	12.7	820	11.4	3,590	3,048	542	139	1,327
Montgomery	9,835	103,620	1.13	818	8.3	662	6.7	7,708	9.9	13,871	11,393	2,478	1,618	1,656
Nelson	102	12,784	0.70	114	7.7	152	10.2	1,449	13.1	4,612	3,979	633	198	1,350
New Kent	552	14,267	0.38	229	10.2	154	6.9	1,547	9.0	4,468	3,658	810	304	1,471
Northampton	255	12,155	1.03	98	8.4	199	17.0	1,256	14.2	3,637	3,018	619	131	1,088
Northumberland	0	10,614	0.64	81	6.7	192	15.8	993	12.6	4,615	3,979	636	134	1,104
Nottoway	2,247	17,218	1.31	145	9.4	212	13.7	1,318	12.5	3,660	3,079	581	267	1,717
Orange	601	29,270	0.62	385	10.5	332	9.1	3,236	11.6	8,766	7,611	1,155	352	989
Page	194	19,936	0.64	233	9.7	295	12.3	2,508	13.5	6,183	5,341	842	394	1,674
Patrick	295	15,796	0.70	153	8.7	242	13.7	1,860	14.2	5,146	3,927	1,219	257	1,439
Pittsylvania	1,067	50,305	0.58	507	8.3	759	12.5	5,632	11.9	16,205	12,324	3,881	462	750
Powhatan	1,118	23,277	0.60	237	8.1	253	8.7	2,047	9.2	5,888	4,682	1,206	231	829
Prince Edward	4,051	25,109	1.25	206	9.0	231	10.1	1,936	12.6	4,672	3,925	747	379	1,666
Prince George	4,273	42,666	1.31	327	8.6	265	7.0	2,285	8.1	5,894	5,093	801	431	1,131
Prince William	2,701	366,831	0.64	6,689	14.3	2,069	4.4	42,693	10.4	47,798	39,074	8,724	6,276	1,368
Pulaski	1,094	34,461	1.01	314	9.2	446	13.1	2,374	9.2	9,077	7,259	1,818	994	2,919
Rappahannock	35	6,115	0.65	35	4.8	80	11.0	742	13.7	2,018	1,824	194	28	383
Richmond	1,666	9,399	1.16	93	10.3	100	11.1	709	12.8	2,032	1,641	391	65	740
Roanoke	2,347	84,294	0.80	714	7.6	978	10.4	5,687	7.8	23,538	18,208	5,330	1,589	1,685
Rockbridge	501	19,318	0.69	145	6.4	239	10.5	1,956	11.8	5,988	5,117	871	296	1,331
Rockingham	1,633	75,496	0.92	845	10.4	753	9.3	8,529	13.5	17,370	14,899	2,471	788	1,002
Russell	433	25,528	0.78	234	8.7	368	13.8	2,460	11.4	7,861	4,889	2,972	427	1,550
Scott	793	19,567	0.67	164	7.6	305	14.2	1,875	11.5	6,636	3,222	3,414	262	1,201
Shenandoah	427	37,442	0.73	489	11.2	464	10.7	3,915	11.6	10,478	9,153	1,325	569	1,318
Smyth	769	30,656	0.95	272	8.9	475	15.6	2,628	10.9	8,808	6,504	2,304	658	2,112
Southampton	1,576	14,519	0.54	107	6.1	211	12.0	1,471	11.2	4,099	3,467	632	204	1,139
Spotsylvania	524	104,050	0.59	1,526	11.4	982	7.3	11,146	9.8	20,704	18,122	2,582	1,928	1,469
Stafford	3,455	114,191	0.62	1,725	11.5	771	5.1	9,481	7.5	17,185	15,387	1,798	2,129	1,481
Surry	0	6,129	0.82	54	8.3	60	9.3	548	10.6	1,590	1,254	336	69	1,045
Sussex	2,598	12,178	1.22	94	8.4	136	12.1	844	11.9	2,391	1,866	525	128	1,104
Tazewell	1,765	42,786	1.01	389	9.5	635	15.5	3,747	11.7	12,014	8,134	3,880	938	2,221
Warren	680	34,145	0.74	478	11.9	385	9.6	3,359	10.3	7,515	6,670	845	619	1,580
Washington	1,785	54,243	0.99	518	9.5	665	12.2	4,370	10.6	15,005	9,642	5,363	1,047	1,931
Westmoreland	70	13,816	0.50	189	10.6	221	12.4	1,750	13.2	4,963	4,359	604	210	1,195
Wise	2,907	42,676	1.24	408	10.7	475	12.5	3,553	11.9	10,678	6,503	4,175	674	1,722
Wythe	260	29,289	1.02	288	10.0	381	13.3	2,615	11.4	7,652	5,824	1,828	429	1,483
York	646	58,348	0.73	652	9.6	527	7.8	4,004	7.0	11,818	10,232	1,586	1,399	2,057
Independent Cities														
Alexandria city	1,834	159,529	1.05	2,780	17.3	843	5.3	16,008	11.6	17,759	15,066	2,693	3,128	2,014
Bristol city	224	20,093	1.43	140	8.5	238	14.4	1,338	10.1	4,531	2,567	1,964	471	2,786
Buena Vista city	491	5,833	0.76	2	0.3	79	12.7	467	9.6	1,452	1,205	247	58	882
Charlottesville city	2,422	63,255	1.69	622	12.9	330	6.9	4,749	11.8	6,243	5,588	655	1,477	3,144
Chesapeake city	4,307	218,684	0.85	2,829	11.7	1,896	7.8	17,909	8.8	37,644	29,883	7,761	7,008	2,962
Colonial Heights city	171	19,714	1.28	262	14.7	191	10.7	1,447	10.3	4,163	3,495	668	874	4,906
Covington city	87	5,483	0.91	0	0.0	60	11.0	428	9.9	1,651	1,448	203	129	2,316
Danville city	1,579	51,905	1.61	422	10.4	639	15.7	3,444	10.8	11,164	8,656	2,508	1,872	4,491
Emporia city	246	6,867	1.72	0	0.0	75	14.6	504	11.9	1,156	877	279	294	5,463
Fairfax city	521	45,573	2.75	646	26.3	210	8.5	1,875	9.4	3,792	3,081	711	431	1,783
Falls Church city	42	17,704	1.52	248	16.8	86	5.8	464	3.7	2,004	1,692	312	246	1,742
Franklin city	129	8,786	1.13	60	7.5	85	10.6	682	10.3	1,979	1,650	329	334	3,965
Fredericksburg city	2,676	41,850	1.94	375	12.9	238	8.2	2,557	11.2	4,018	3,522	496	1,146	3,976
Galax city	377	8,618	1.64	48	7.5	85	13.2	827	15.8	1,846	1,682	164	241	3,514
Hampton city	5,009	135,707	0.99	1,665	12.4	1,307	9.7	10,079	9.1	24,856	18,633	6,223	5,099	3,763
Harrisonburg city	7,684	63,653	1.42	664	12.3	269	5.0	5,902	14.3	5,364	4,748	616	1,217	2,297
Hopewell city	237	20,250	0.78	344	15.2	269	11.9	2,205	11.7	4,520	3,541	979	748	3,369
Lexington city	2,748	10,412	2.53	6	0.8	45	6.3	342	10.3	1,652	1,495	157	87	1,198
Lynchburg city	11,039	102,607	1.67	1,132	13.8	697	8.5	6,293	10.8	14,632	12,173	2,459	2,114	2,635
Manassas city	46	41,191	0.99	737	17.7	169	4.1	5,635	15.0	4,464	3,621	843	938	2,219
Manassas Park city	6	10,863	0.36	17	1.0	50	2.9	2,310	15.9	1,312	1,003	309	183	1,150

1. Per 1,000 estimated resident population. 2. Data for serious crimes have not been adjusted for underreporting; this may affect comparability between geographic areas and over time. 3. Per 100,000 population estimated by the FBI.

Table B. States and Counties — Crime, Education, Money Income, and Poverty

STATE County	Serious crimes known to police[2], 2016 (cont.)[1] Rate Violent	Property	School enrollment and attainment, 2013-2017 Enrollment[3] Total	Percent private	Attainment[4] (percent) High school graduate or less	Bachelor's degree or more	Local government expenditures[5] 2014-2015 Total current spending (mil dol)	Current spending per student (dollars)	Money income, 2013-2017 Per capita income[6]	Households Median income (dollars)	Percent with income of less than $50,000	Percent with income of $200,000 or more	Income and poverty, 2017 Median household income (dollars)	Percent below poverty level All persons	Children under 18 years	Children 5 to 17 years in families
	46	47	48	49	50	51	52	53	54	55	56	57	58	59	60	61
VIRGINIA— Cont'd																
Louisa	182	1,212	7,122	12.7	50.4	23.2	53.1	10,962	30,237	56,946	42.7	4.0	60,641	10.8	14.5	13.6
Lunenburg	165	636	2,449	13.5	60.6	10.6	15.8	9,932	18,555	39,537	61.1	0.1	36,591	20.5	26.9	25.8
Madison	107	775	2,765	16.8	49.0	26.9	19.2	10,293	29,705	52,287	46.7	6.5	58,680	11.3	15.0	14.0
Mathews	68	830	1,245	15.7	41.9	26.9	12.8	11,244	35,252	63,622	39.0	6.7	59,296	9.7	16.2	15.9
Mecklenburg	199	1,356	5,749	9.0	51.7	18.2	42.6	9,301	22,970	41,126	59.3	1.8	42,275	17.5	26.4	25.2
Middlesex	134	1,193	1,857	10.2	44.9	22.1	12.7	10,046	29,871	50,483	49.6	4.5	51,534	13.6	23.6	22.5
Montgomery	138	1,517	40,789	8.5	30.8	46.3	100.8	10,393	28,277	53,424	46.5	5.8	54,297	23.0	15.1	14.0
Nelson	225	1,125	2,735	14.8	46.5	30.8	24.4	12,639	33,597	53,834	45.0	3.3	53,965	13.2	20.6	19.7
New Kent	145	1,326	4,554	16.4	41.5	26.9	28.1	9,285	36,768	78,429	26.6	7.7	89,682	5.5	7.6	7.3
Northampton	125	963	1,961	20.4	52.3	23.2	18.8	11,368	24,835	41,468	57.7	3.3	41,160	18.6	28.8	27.3
Northumberland	247	857	2,000	8.7	41.6	26.4	15.9	11,164	33,364	56,677	43.2	3.8	53,381	14.4	27.8	26.7
Nottoway	122	1,594	2,833	12.1	61.1	13.7	22.0	9,503	19,452	38,410	63.2	1.3	40,911	22.1	25.3	26.7
Orange	101	888	7,879	13.0	45.9	25.6	50.3	9,640	30,660	67,196	35.7	2.7	62,707	9.1	12.6	11.5
Page	140	1,534	4,995	14.2	63.9	13.2	34.3	9,784	24,057	46,140	54.1	1.4	45,691	15.4	22.1	20.2
Patrick	185	1,254	3,206	8.0	55.6	14.3	26.2	9,019	21,785	37,757	61.3	0.8	40,421	14.5	22.3	19.4
Pittsylvania	83	668	13,301	9.8	53.2	14.1	85.0	9,145	23,597	44,356	57.2	1.0	47,411	12.6	18.8	17.4
Powhatan	72	757	6,281	17.8	39.8	28.4	43.6	10,342	33,807	80,441	26.2	7.8	87,756	5.4	6.8	6.3
Prince Edward	158	1,508	8,230	24.6	50.3	24.9	23.7	10,833	19,751	44,147	56.0	1.8	43,761	23.4	27.1	26.0
Prince George	108	1,023	9,639	11.9	43.4	23.0	59.0	9,129	27,970	68,461	35.8	4.5	68,884	10.7	12.7	10.4
Prince William	195	1,173	132,209	15.3	32.0	39.8	913.7	10,546	38,225	101,059	20.4	14.5	100,431	6.1	8.0	8.1
Pulaski	273	2,646	6,379	6.5	47.8	18.5	45.1	10,179	26,328	49,691	50.3	1.8	48,743	14.8	21.1	19.2
Rappahannock	14	369	1,324	27.9	38.5	33.6	11.8	12,842	38,185	62,541	39.2	10.0	68,166	8.9	15.2	14.5
Richmond	114	626	1,940	4.3	58.4	13.4	14.5	11,823	19,728	47,341	54.0	1.4	48,355	18.4	23.0	21.6
Roanoke	200	1,485	21,586	16.9	33.8	34.7	133.8	9,304	33,717	62,134	38.4	4.2	65,171	7.3	8.6	7.9
Rockbridge	139	1,191	3,760	23.6	49.4	25.8	30.7	10,887	31,534	53,918	46.6	4.3	53,606	12.6	17.0	15.6
Rockingham	123	879	18,202	23.2	52.5	24.8	(9) 190.0	(9) 10,852	28,884	57,651	42.8	3.6	59,492	8.4	11.5	10.3
Russell	211	1,339	5,426	13.7	56.9	13.6	38.1	9,129	21,673	40,083	59.5	0.9	39,219	20.2	25.0	23.2
Scott	105	1,096	4,340	5.8	57.6	13.3	34.4	9,095	20,969	38,725	61.5	0.8	39,640	17.6	23.1	20.6
Shenandoah	176	1,142	9,254	14.7	52.4	19.2	62.2	10,041	27,016	53,934	47.3	2.2	56,733	9.5	13.9	13.3
Smyth	254	1,858	6,019	9.1	54.9	14.5	44.3	9,468	22,319	40,544	59.9	1.1	42,008	17.7	25.1	22.0
Southampton	128	1,011	4,061	13.5	48.9	19.0	29.4	10,601	25,784	53,681	47.4	2.4	49,512	14.7	20.5	18.5
Spotsylvania	174	1,294	34,791	12.6	40.6	30.4	241.6	10,113	33,859	81,434	27.2	8.7	85,743	6.9	10.0	9.6
Stafford	215	1,266	41,563	11.4	28.6	38.7	261.5	9,484	39,158	103,005	19.7	14.9	111,184	4.6	5.8	5.5
Surry	242	803	1,251	15.7	47.6	19.1	15.2	17,587	27,162	54,656	44.5	1.4	49,064	12.8	19.7	19.0
Sussex	121	983	2,381	10.5	67.3	11.7	17.8	16,009	15,882	44,608	57.0	0.4	41,594	22.4	29.3	28.7
Tazewell	204	2,018	8,130	12.5	56.1	15.2	56.3	9,037	24,325	40,309	60.1	2.5	38,855	18.1	25.6	23.0
Warren	166	1,414	8,783	25.4	50.0	20.9	52.1	9,659	30,009	65,353	37.5	3.9	63,785	9.3	12.7	12.3
Washington	166	1,765	11,797	21.0	47.8	23.4	70.8	9,655	25,640	44,844	54.0	2.9	49,866	13.9	18.5	17.5
Westmoreland	131	1,064	3,191	10.2	47.5	21.1	24.7	10,916	32,265	55,688	44.5	4.3	50,046	15.5	26.3	25.6
Wise	215	1,508	8,732	8.1	56.7	13.9	56.6	9,263	21,694	38,255	61.4	1.9	37,460	23.3	29.5	28.1
Wythe	135	1,348	5,669	9.9	55.0	18.3	41.2	9,553	24,879	46,119	53.3	1.6	46,795	13.8	20.1	18.9
York	182	1,875	18,622	14.0	24.9	43.6	124.8	9,828	38,193	86,781	24.8	8.4	85,292	5.0	5.9	5.3
Independent Cities																
Alexandria city	185	1,828	29,332	27.2	20.5	61.8	244.3	17,188	57,019	93,370	24.7	16.1	99,959	10.1	17.0	18.6
Bristol city	219	2,567	3,609	11.3	49.2	23.0	24.4	10,600	21,589	37,844	61.9	0.7	38,232	19.3	30.8	28.1
Buena Vista city	46	836	1,896	42.6	59.3	16.3	10.5	9,947	17,969	33,672	66.7	1.4	42,924	14.0	20.9	18.3
Charlottesville city	526	2,618	15,749	12.1	29.1	51.4	(7)	(7)	32,860	54,739	46.9	7.6	54,034	20.3	19.4	20.5
Chesapeake city	412	2,550	64,755	15.2	33.7	31.5	427.2	10,760	32,123	72,214	32.7	5.9	75,529	9.3	14.0	13.2
Colonial Heights city	326	4,581	3,883	8.0	42.4	23.6	34.2	12,087	27,608	50,952	49.1	3.5	53,769	9.8	16.4	17.4
Covington city	144	2,172	1,027	8.8	58.5	14.6	10.6	10,618	22,098	35,546	67.1	1.8	38,000	15.9	25.0	21.0
Danville city	804	3,687	10,226	16.3	47.8	18.9	67.8	10,737	21,882	34,951	66.6	1.8	33,626	24.4	38.5	37.9
Emporia city	632	4,831	1,482	14.2	58.8	15.3	(8)	(8)	18,548	27,426	67.6	2.2	35,770	23.4	36.7	33.8
Fairfax city	95	1,688	6,245	14.6	21.8	56.9	(10)	(10)	46,489	106,870	21.8	18.3	99,662	7.7	7.2	8.4
Falls Church city	184	1,558	3,941	24.1	9.1	78.1	44.1	17,902	65,510	114,795	16.7	26.0	123,923	3.4	3.1	2.6
Franklin city	285	3,680	2,363	14.9	45.5	25.3	16.5	13,742	24,820	38,760	58.7	3.4	37,117	20.8	35.1	33.7
Fredericksburg city	361	3,615	8,809	11.6	31.6	42.9	44.0	12,704	32,359	57,258	43.9	6.9	56,580	14.1	20.3	21.0
Galax city	306	3,208	1,351	10.1	59.7	10.3	13.9	10,027	22,572	31,311	66.3	1.2	33,391	21.5	35.4	34.3
Hampton city	323	3,440	37,290	23.2	36.9	25.6	216.4	10,406	27,053	52,021	48.0	2.0	52,894	15.5	23.5	23.6
Harrisonburg city	219	2,078	23,974	7.8	42.1	34.9	(9)	(9)	20,134	43,009	57.2	1.5	44,688	23.3	20.3	20.0
Hopewell city	464	2,905	5,421	7.5	53.8	15.1	43.0	9,873	22,668	40,712	58.2	2.0	40,209	19.9	32.5	30.8
Lexington city	138	1,060	4,484	27.2	39.1	38.5	4.8	9,743	16,668	37,309	60.2	5.1	47,749	24.5	13.1	10.1
Lynchburg city	375	2,260	29,251	56.6	36.8	33.6	98.7	11,476	22,439	41,971	57.3	2.7	44,122	18.8	25.0	25.2
Manassas city	291	1,928	10,982	13.0	43.7	29.7	97.2	12,996	30,572	77,551	29.3	6.8	75,621	8.7	14.2	14.2
Manassas Park city	145	1,006	4,859	11.7	42.5	31.4	36.8	10,954	29,641	79,131	26.2	5.5	80,482	7.1	11.4	9.9

1. Data for serious crimes have not been adjusted for underreporting; this may affect comparability between geographic areas and over time.   2. Per 100,000 population estimated by the FBI.   3. All persons 3 years and over enrolled in nursery school through college.   4. Persons 25 years old and over.   5. Elementary and secondary education expenditures.   6. Based on population estimated by the American Community Survey, 2013–2017.   7. Charlottesville city is included with Albemarle county.   8. Emporia city is included with Greensville county.   9. Harrisonburg city is included with Rockingham county.   10. Fairfax city is included with Fairfax county.

Table B. States and Counties — **Personal Income and Earnings**

| | Personal income, 2017 | | | | | | | | | | Earnings, 2017 | | |
STATE County	Total (mil dol)	Percent change 2016-2017	Per capita[1] Dollars	Per capita[1] Rank	Wages and salaries (mil dol)	Supplements to wages and salaries, employer contributions (mil dol) Pension and insurance	Supplements to wages and salaries, employer contributions (mil dol) Government social insurance	Proprietors' income (mil dol)	Dividends, interest, and rent (mil dol)	Personal transfer receipts (mil dol)	Total (mil dol)	Contributions for government social insurance (mil dol) From employee and self-employed	Contributions for government social insurance (mil dol) From employer
	62	63	64	65	66	67	68	69	70	71	72	73	74
VIRGINIA— Cont'd													
Louisa	1,455	5.6	40,581	1,460	513	96	37	70	244	305	715	49	37
Lunenburg	393	1.6	32,149	2,733	101	22	7	8	82	125	138	12	7
Madison	624	-1.1	47,022	712	126	22	9	51	138	113	209	16	9
Mathews	469	3.6	53,380	332	51	11	4	29	135	103	94	9	4
Mecklenburg	1,105	3.3	36,014	2,200	439	80	32	25	227	370	577	45	32
Middlesex	520	5.4	48,703	565	136	29	10	34	146	137	208	16	10
Montgomery	[19]4,163	[19]4.4	[19]35,822	[19]2,223	[19]2,322	[19]546	[19]168	[19]221	[19]971	[19]695	[19]3,257	[19]189	[19]168
Nelson	721	3.6	48,220	607	150	29	11	45	185	169	235	19	11
New Kent	1,448	6.2	66,794	86	177	33	13	62	198	166	284	21	13
Northampton	543	2.8	45,848	815	157	30	13	45	126	155	244	17	13
Northumberland	601	4.4	48,939	544	109	20	8	24	212	161	162	16	8
Nottoway	520	2.7	33,682	2,530	226	63	18	7	109	184	313	21	18
Orange	1,670	3.2	46,293	767	396	75	29	70	341	330	569	43	29
Page	891	3.8	37,533	1,940	206	43	17	67	166	236	332	25	17
Patrick	582	2.9	32,959	2,622	165	35	13	24	106	199	237	20	13
Pittsylvania	[6]3,794	[6]3.6	[6]37,053	[6]2,025	[6]1,530	[6]277	[6]113	[6]146	[6]653	[6]1,230	[6]2,066	[6]150	[6]113
Powhatan	1,557	5	54,427	300	312	58	22	73	261	214	465	33	22
Prince Edward	697	3.2	30,688	2,874	363	76	27	34	131	205	499	33	27
Prince George	[13]2,291	[13]4.3	[13]37,916	[13]1,896	[13]1,924	[13]495	[13]167	[13]48	[13]464	[13]532	[13]2,634	[13]135	[13]167
Prince William	[15]27,582	[15]4.6	[15]52,929	[15]344	[15]8,938	[15]1,505	[15]665	[15]1,566	[15]4,126	[15]2,702	[15]12,674	[15]735	[15]665
Pulaski	1,318	2.9	38,549	1,797	548	105	41	50	224	377	745	53	41
Rappahannock	446	3.5	60,919	144	95	14	5	37	140	67	151	11	5
Richmond	315	3	35,263	2,304	121	28	9	8	72	81	166	11	9
Roanoke	[20]5,963	[20]2.5	[20]49,860	[20]471	[20]2,836	[20]492	[20]206	[20]406	[20]1,163	[20]1,086	[20]3,940	[20]253	[20]206
Rockbridge	[3]1,407	[3]3.7	[3]38,981	[3]1,723	[3]540	[3]103	[3]42	[3]82	[3]359	[3]341	[3]768	[3]54	[3]42
Rockingham	[12]5,115	[12]5.0	[12]38,045	[12]1,877	[12]2,810	[12]499	[12]203	[12]532	[12]994	[12]899	[12]4,044	[12]240	[12]203
Russell	865	2.3	31,977	2,753	315	57	24	9	137	323	405	35	24
Scott	715	2.8	32,685	2,658	173	36	13	10	121	264	233	23	13
Shenandoah	1,859	4.2	43,015	1,142	561	100	41	127	364	396	830	58	41
Smyth	1,097	-0.1	35,778	2,231	472	103	35	31	183	358	640	47	35
Southampton	[9]1,061	[9]6.8	[9]40,917	[9]1,413	[9]300	[9]68	[9]22	[9]48	[9]210	[9]284	[9]438	[9]30	[9]22
Spotsylvania	[10]7,880	[10]4.3	[10]48,823	[10]555	[10]2,752	[10]438	[10]198	[10]401	[10]1,373	[10]1,163	[10]3,789	[10]238	[10]198
Stafford	7,779	4.9	53,048	341	2,477	477	181	239	1,239	907	3,374	202	181
Surry	277	5.2	42,427	1,213	193	44	14	2	43	67	253	15	14
Sussex	343	3.4	30,151	2,916	151	34	11	9	57	108	204	14	11
Tazewell	1,505	5.4	36,612	2,102	578	119	43	53	266	514	793	61	43
Warren	1,791	4.3	45,257	875	527	92	40	71	290	304	729	49	40
Washington	[2]2,792	[2]7.7	[2]39,221	[2]1,687	[2]1,188	[2]229	[2]88	[2]130	[2]631	[2]769	[2]1,636	[2]116	[2]88
Westmoreland	734	3.5	41,283	1,368	122	27	9	22	193	191	181	16	9
Wise	[16]1,354	[16]3.1	[16]31,849	[16]2,774	[16]593	[16]131	[16]44	[16]36	[16]215	[16]540	[16]804	[16]60	[16]44
Wythe	978	2.5	33,876	2,498	438	89	33	32	168	311	592	43	33
York	[18]4,529	[18]3.4	[18]56,763	[18]228	[18]1,092	[18]204	[18]84	[18]136	[18]982	[18]584	[18]1,516	[18]99	[18]84
Independent Cities													
Alexandria city	13,456	3.8	84,079	28	7,762	1,197	580	847	3,203	844	10,386	595	580
Bristol city	(2)	(2)	(2)	(2)	(2)	(2)	(2)	(2)	(2)	(2)	(2)	(2)	(2)
Buena Vista city	(3)	(3)	(3)	(3)	(3)	(3)	(3)	(3)	(3)	(3)	(3)	(3)	(3)
Charlottesville city	(4)	(4)	(4)	(4)	(4)	(4)	(4)	(4)	(4)	(4)	(4)	(4)	(4)
Chesapeake city	11,676	4.1	48,569	583	4,806	757	349	332	2,015	1,790	6,245	390	349
Colonial Heights city	(17)	(17)	(17)	(17)	(17)	(17)	(17)	(17)	(17)	(17)	(17)	(17)	(17)
Covington city	(5)	(5)	(5)	(5)	(5)	(5)	(5)	(5)	(5)	(5)	(5)	(5)	(5)
Danville city	(6)	(6)	(6)	(6)	(6)	(6)	(6)	(6)	(6)	(6)	(6)	(6)	(6)
Emporia city	(7)	(7)	(7)	(7)	(7)	(7)	(7)	(7)	(7)	(7)	(7)	(7)	(7)
Fairfax city	(8)	(8)	(8)	(8)	(8)	(8)	(8)	(8)	(8)	(8)	(8)	(8)	(8)
Falls Church city	(8)	(8)	(8)	(8)	(8)	(8)	(8)	(8)	(8)	(8)	(8)	(8)	(8)
Franklin city	(9)	(9)	(9)	(9)	(9)	(9)	(9)	(9)	(9)	(9)	(9)	(9)	(9)
Fredericksburg city	(10)	(10)	(10)	(10)	(10)	(10)	(10)	(10)	(10)	(10)	(10)	(10)	(10)
Galax city	(11)	(11)	(11)	(11)	(11)	(11)	(11)	(11)	(11)	(11)	(11)	(11)	(11)
Hampton city	5,674	2.9	42,133	1,249	3,309	736	268	119	1,179	1,282	4,432	257	268
Harrisonburg city	(12)	(12)	(12)	(12)	(12)	(12)	(12)	(12)	(12)	(12)	(12)	(12)	(12)
Hopewell city	(13)	(13)	(13)	(13)	(13)	(13)	(13)	(13)	(13)	(13)	(13)	(13)	(13)
Lexington city	(3)	(3)	(3)	(3)	(3)	(3)	(3)	(3)	(3)	(3)	(3)	(3)	(3)
Lynchburg city	(14)	(14)	(14)	(14)	(14)	(14)	(14)	(14)	(14)	(14)	(14)	(14)	(14)
Manassas city	(15)	(15)	(15)	(15)	(15)	(15)	(15)	(15)	(15)	(15)	(15)	(15)	(15)
Manassas Park city	(15)	(15)	(15)	(15)	(15)	(15)	(15)	(15)	(15)	(15)	(15)	(15)	(15)

1. Based on the resident population estimated as of July 1 of the year shown.   2. Bristol city is included with Washington county.   3. Buena Vista and Lexington cities are included with Rockbridge county.   4. Charlottesville city is included with Albemarle county.   5. Covington city is included with Alleghany county.   6. Danville city is included with Pittsylvania county.   7. Emporia city is included with Greensville county.   8. Fairfax city and Falls Church city are included with Fairfax county.   9. Franklin city is included with Southampton county.   10. Fredericksburg city is included with Spotsylvania county.   11. Galax city is included with Carroll county.   12. Harrisonburg city is included with Rockingham county.   13. Hopewell city is included with Prince George county.   14. Lynchburg city is included with Campbell county.   15. Manassas and Manassas Park cities are included with Prince William county.   16. Norton city is included with Wise county.   17. Petersburg and Colonial Heights cities are included with Dinwiddie county.   18. Poquoson city is included with York county.   19. Radford city is included with Montgomery county.   20. Salem city is included with Roanoke county.

Table B. States and Counties — Earnings, Social Security, and Housing

STATE County	Earnings, 2017 (cont.) — Percent by selected industries									Social Security beneficiaries, December 2017		Supplemental Security Income recipients, 2017	Housing units, 2018	
	Farm	Mining, quarrying, and extractions	Construction	Manufacturing	Information; professional, scientific, technical services	Retail trade	Finance, insurance, real estate, and leasing	Health care and social assistance	Government	Number	Rate[1]		Total	Percent change, 2010-2018
	75	76	77	78	79	80	81	82	83	84	85	86	87	88

VIRGINIA— Cont'd

STATE County	75	76	77	78	79	80	81	82	83	84	85	86	87	88
Louisa	-0.6	D	17.1	13.2	D	5.4	2.2	D	13.3	8,425	235	606	17,643	8.1
Lunenburg	-1.8	0	8.5	12.4	D	4.5	D	D	31.6	3,250	266	359	5,987	0.9
Madison	-3.2	-0.1	13.4	9.6	D	22.6	2.3	D	17.1	3,135	236	189	6,104	2.9
Mathews	-0.3	0	11.9	3.9	D	5.9	8.5	D	24.4	2,955	337	153	5,757	1.6
Mecklenburg		D	4.5	10.4	8.6	8.9	4.2	17.7	18.4	9,965	325	1,178	19,011	2.3
Middlesex	0.1	0	11.3	4.7	D	6.4	6.6	D	27.1	3,750	351	266	7,361	3.2
Montgomery	(19) 0.1	(19) 0.1	(19) D	(19)14.8	(19) D	(19) 5.4	(19) 3.5	(19) D	(19)40.3	14,175	144	1,139	40,707	5.5
Nelson	0.4	D	10.3	10.2	D	3	3.7	7	17.8	4,735	317	397	10,190	2.6
New Kent	-0.4	-0.1	24.4	3.6	6.1	6.6	3.7	D	21.5	4,660	215	245	8,728	19.6
Northampton	12.2	0	5.1	8.5	D	5.4	3.1	13.6	23.5	3,805	321	592	7,426	1.7
Northumberland	-1.9	-0.1	11.4	31.1	D	5.7	4.1	2.1	18.2	4,685	382	251	9,345	3.9
Nottoway	1.3	D	2.9	5.3	2.6	5.8	2.3	D	53.5	3,895	252	610	6,786	2.1
Orange	-0.6	0	8.7	14.4	D	8.3	6.7	3.8	22.8	8,950	248	611	15,239	4
Page	8.1	0	7.9	11.4	6.8	7.2	3.8	9.2	22.9	6,705	283	583	11,779	1.5
Patrick	-0.7	-0.1	6.4	25	6.7	7.7	D	D	19.4	5,660	320	525	10,215	1.3
Pittsylvania	(6) 1.7	(6) D	(6) D	(6)20.4	(6) 3.7	(6) 8.1	(6) 3.8	(6)15.4	(6)18.1	17,695	289	1,506	31,656	1.2
Powhatan	-0.3	D	22.9	3.4	10.3	6.8	5.7	5.2	26.2	6,135	215	263	11,103	10.5
Prince Edward	-0.1	D	4.3	1.2	2.5	8.2	3.9	D	30.4	5,040	222	883	9,485	3.7
Prince George	(13) 0.0	(13) 0.0	(13) D	(13)12.6	(13) D	(13) 2.0	(13) 1.1	(13) D	(13)62.3	6,400	169	348	12,565	4.3
Prince William	(15) 0.0	(15) D	(15) D	(15) 3.5	(15) D	(15) 4.0	(15) D	(15) D	(15)27.8	46,425	100	4,163	150,444	9.7
Pulaski	-0.3	D	4.1	39	D	7.4	2.2	8.6	17.1	9,890	289	881	17,286	0.3
Rappahannock	-2.6	-0.1	12.8	2.9	40.4	4.3	2.3	2.9	13.5	2,020	276	71	3,984	2.3
Richmond	0.2	0	6.8	5.7	D	4.7	3	D	38.9	2,075	232	249	3,965	3
Roanoke	(20) 0.0	(20) D	(20) D	(20)14.0	(20) 8.8	(20) 6.1	(20) 7.8	(20) D	(20)16.7	22,910	244	972	41,023	2.4
Rockbridge	(3)-0.2	(3) D	(3) 6.3	(3) D	(3) D	(3) 7.2	(3) 3.1	(3) 7.9	(3)22.4	6,120	270	318	11,500	2.9
Rockingham	(12) 3.7	(12) D	(12) 7.4	(12)15.8	(12) 6.7	(12) 6.2	(12) 4.8	(12)12.0	(12)17.9	17,955	224	837	35,852	6.5
Russell	-3.2	5.5	8	5	12.4	7	3.6	16.6	21	8,800	325	1,407	13,532	0.4
Scott	-5.4	0	3.8	19.9	D	8.3	2.2	14.3	29.7	7,270	332	1,208	11,944	0.2
Shenandoah	1.9	D	8.1	22	6.3	6.8	3.7	10	15.7	11,065	256	756	21,271	1.9
Smyth	-1.7	D	6.1	29.3	D	5.3	1.8	D	25.3	9,865	322	1,179	15,363	-0.4
Southampton	(9) 5.8	(9)-0.1	(9) 3.0	(9) 7.4	(9) 3.6	(9) 3.2	(9) 4.4	(9)15.0	(9)30.6	4,505	254	365	7,657	2.4
Spotsylvania	(10) 0.0	(10) D	(10) 6.7	(10) D	(10)10.7	(10)11.9	(10) 6.0	(10)19.4	(10)17.5	21,470	161	1,453	48,155	6.6
Stafford	-0.1	D	6.9	1.1	11.8	5.3	D	D	35	17,335	118	1,150	50,449	14.7
Surry	-0.8	0	8.9	D	D	0.5	D	0.1	12.7	1,745	267	161	3,604	4.6
Sussex	1.1	D	3.2	2	D	7.6	1.1	D	39.6	2,675	235	443	4,805	2.5
Tazewell	-0.9	7.6	5.2	9	4.2	11.4	4.2	D	21.3	13,375	325	1,876	20,735	-0.4
Warren	-0.5	0	9.4	10.9	5.1	7	3.2	11.4	18.1	7,805	197	651	16,501	3.3
Washington	(2) 0.0	(2) D	(2) D	(2)17.5	(2) 5.0	(2) 9.9	(2) 4.6	(2)12.4	(2)18.4	16,245	299	1,521	25,992	1.4
Westmoreland	1.9	0	9.3	14.4	D	7.4	3.9	D	28.3	5,120	288	454	10,998	3.5
Wise	(16) 0.2	(16) 3.5	(16) D	(16) 2.7	(16) 7.6	(16) 9.9	(16) 2.7	(16) D	(16)30.5	12,010	311	2,302	17,926	0
Wythe	-2	1.2	5.2	24.2	2.8	10.3	3.9	12	22.3	8,455	293	872	14,379	2.1
York	(18) 0.0	(18) 0.0	(18) 9.3	(18) 1.8	(18) D	(18) 8.7	(18) 4.0	(18) D	(18)31.8	11,775	174	341	27,905	4.5

Independent Cities

STATE County	75	76	77	78	79	80	81	82	83	84	85	86	87	88
Alexandria city	0.0	0.0	2.3	D	26.3	3.8	5.8	4.8	31.7	15,350	96	1,834	76,529	5.7
Bristol city	(2)	(2)	(2)	(2)	(2)	(2)	(2)	(2)	(2)	5,050	301	781	8,730	-0.7
Buena Vista city	(3)	(3)	(3)	(3)	(3)	(3)	(3)	(3)	(3)	1,645	260	285	2,864	-2.0
Charlottesville city	(4)	(4)	(4)	(4)	(4)	(4)	(4)	(4)	(4)	6,295	131	1,026	20,772	8.3
Chesapeake city	0.0	0.1	10.4	5.5	14.5	8.9	7.0	7.3	18.1	39,010	162	3,705	91,765	10.2
Colonial Heights city	(17)	(17)	(17)	(17)	(17)	(17)	(17)	(17)	(17)	4,455	250	539	7,719	-1.4
Covington city	(5)	(5)	(5)	(5)	(5)	(5)	(5)	(5)	(5)	1,950	353	442	2,984	-2.6
Danville city	(6)	(6)	(6)	(6)	(6)	(6)	(6)	(6)	(6)	12,720	309	2,935	22,014	-1.9
Emporia city	(7)	(7)	(7)	(7)	(7)	(7)	(7)	(7)	(7)	1,510	286	616	2,604	1.4
Fairfax city	(8)	(8)	(8)	(8)	(8)	(8)	(8)	(8)	(8)	3,450	143	20	9,095	4.8
Falls Church city	(8)	(8)	(8)	(8)	(8)	(8)	(8)	(8)	(8)	1,625	111	106	6,019	10.0
Franklin city	(9)	(9)	(9)	(9)	(9)	(9)	(9)	(9)	(9)	2,225	272	618	3,833	-1.7
Fredericksburg city	(10)	(10)	(10)	(10)	(10)	(10)	(10)	(10)	(10)	4,095	144	544	11,730	12.4
Galax city	(11)	(11)	(11)	(11)	(11)	(11)	(11)	(11)	(11)	2,220	335	620	3,185	-1.4
Hampton city	0.0	0.0	3.3	4.1	10.3	4.7	2.6	9.8	49.8	26,840	199	3,423	60,111	0.9
Harrisonburg city	(12)	(12)	(12)	(12)	(12)	(12)	(12)	(12)	(12)	5,825	107	1,035	18,313	5.0
Hopewell city	(13)	(13)	(13)	(13)	(13)	(13)	(13)	(13)	(13)	5,005	221	1,145	10,328	2.0
Lexington city	(3)	(3)	(3)	(3)	(3)	(3)	(3)	(3)	(3)	1,685	237	239	2,508	-1.3
Lynchburg city	(14)	(14)	(14)	(14)	(14)	(14)	(14)	(14)	(14)	15,905	196	2,758	32,518	1.7
Manassas city	(15)	(15)	(15)	(15)	(15)	(15)	(15)	(15)	(15)	4,555	110	506	13,887	5.8
Manassas Park city	(15)	(15)	(15)	(15)	(15)	(15)	(15)	(15)	(15)	1,320	80	9	4,875	-0.4

1. Per 1,000 resident population estimated as of July 1 of the year shown.   2. Bristol city is included with Washington county.   3. Buena Vista and Lexington cities are included with Rockbridge county.   4. Charlottesville city is included with Albemarle county.   5. Covington city is included with Alleghany county.   6. Danville city is included with Pittsylvania county.   7. Emporia city is included with Greensville county.   8. Fairfax city and Falls Church city are included with Fairfax county.   9. Franklin city is included with Southampton county.   10. Fredericksburg city is included with Spotsylvania county.   11. Galax city is included with Carroll county.   12. Harrisonburg city is included with Rockingham county.   13. Hopewell city is included with Prince George county.   14. Lynchburg city is included with Campbell county.   15. Manassas and Manassas Park cities are included with Prince William county.   16. Norton city is included with Wise county.   17. Petersburg and Colonial Heights cities are included with Dinwiddie county.   18. Poquoson city is included with York county.   19. Radford city is included with Montgomery county.   20. Salem city is included with Roanoke county.

Table B. States and Counties — Housing, Labor Force, and Employment

	Housing units, 2013-2017								Civilian labor force, 2018				Civilian employment[6], 2013-2017		
	Occupied units										Unemployment			Percent	
			Owner-occupied			Renter-occupied										
STATE County	Total	Percent	Median value[1]	Median owner cost as a percent of income		Median rent[3]	Median rent as a percent of income[2]	Sub-standard units[4] (percent)	Total	Percent change, 2017-2018	Total	Rate[5]	Total	Management, business, science, and arts	Construction, production, and maintenance occupations
				With a mortgage	Without a mortgage[2]										
	89	90	91	92	93	94	95	96	97	98	99	100	101	102	103
VIRGINIA— Cont'd															
Louisa	13,451	79.7	212,900	22.3	12.4	932	29.3	1.8	19,660	0.5	539	2.7	16,325	35.0	24.7
Lunenburg	4,480	72.0	108,400	23.7	10.8	676	27.5	3	5,340	-0.2	173	3.2	4,694	23.1	35.9
Madison	5,107	73.4	256,500	23.8	11.9	742	31.1	2.9	7,261	0	175	2.4	6,097	32.2	25.6
Mathews	3,766	86.2	227,200	19.9	12.4	924	19.9	1.3	4,111	0.5	124	3	4,151	29.9	28.6
Mecklenburg	11,785	72.2	125,300	22.7	11.8	690	26.1	1.6	12,636	-0.7	515	4.1	12,739	32.2	25.4
Middlesex	4,522	80.9	248,400	27.5	11.6	793	26.8	2.5	5,258	0.1	139	2.6	4,385	28.6	25.9
Montgomery	35,577	54.9	213,300	19.3	10.0	936	32.2	2.1	49,715	0.1	1,453	2.9	46,955	47.2	13.3
Nelson	6,523	71.8	231,400	22.8	10.0	688	26.7	2.9	7,399	1.6	226	3.1	7,131	35.1	25.2
New Kent	7,555	81.8	256,600	19.9	10.0	882	24	2.8	12,070	0.8	329	2.7	10,248	35.4	21.3
Northampton	5,177	64.6	165,800	19.9	13.1	713	30.3	1.2	5,382	-2.4	291	5.4	4,892	32.0	24.4
Northumberland	5,774	85.2	277,900	23.5	11.4	754	32.4	2.5	5,556	0	247	4.4	4,733	34.9	20.0
Nottoway	5,633	58.9	134,800	21.1	12.2	780	33.5	4	7,226	1.5	222	3.1	5,577	25.6	30.7
Orange	13,470	77.3	235,200	22.8	11.4	918	29.7	3.5	16,967	0.7	508	3	15,957	33.7	24.8
Page	9,467	68.9	172,200	22.9	11.0	734	28	3.5	11,849	-0.1	492	4.2	10,627	24.7	28.8
Patrick	7,713	77.0	116,000	20.4	10.3	544	31.7	2.6	7,438	-3.2	287	3.9	7,383	24.2	41.1
Pittsylvania	26,687	75.2	113,800	20.5	10.4	667	27.7	1.3	30,546	-0.3	1,085	3.6	27,749	24.9	34.8
Powhatan	9,974	89.8	264,300	21.5	10.0	983	22.1	0.8	13,821	0.7	374	2.7	12,939	41.3	22.4
Prince Edward	7,281	64.9	154,800	23.8	10.0	764	25	1.7	10,330	0.9	394	3.8	8,898	30.2	19.4
Prince George	11,298	68.2	212,100	21.0	10.0	1,295	33.2	1.2	14,955	0.3	541	3.6	14,926	35.7	22.7
Prince William	139,306	72.5	358,300	22.3	10.0	1,620	30.8	3.6	241,651	1	6,581	2.7	231,096	43.4	16.5
Pulaski	14,577	72.8	139,600	19.3	10.5	641	23.1	1.1	16,055	-0.8	555	3.5	15,462	31.2	28.9
Rappahannock	3,131	75.2	358,600	23.1	12.2	1,056	36.1	0.5	3,701	1.6	101	2.7	3,580	39.6	17.9
Richmond	3,250	71.9	163,200	24.6	10.0	816	31.2	1.9	4,040	0	124	3.1	3,240	32.1	30.0
Roanoke	38,434	74.8	192,100	20.1	10.0	907	24.7	1	48,833	-0.1	1,329	2.7	45,305	41.8	17.5
Rockbridge	9,160	76.9	197,200	23.6	10.0	742	30.8	1.3	10,514	-0.5	315	3	10,267	34.3	27.5
Rockingham	30,503	73.3	206,700	21.5	10.0	848	26.5	2.6	40,737	0.4	1,079	2.6	38,878	32.3	27.8
Russell	11,102	77.9	94,900	21.0	10.0	544	27.8	1.4	11,205	-2	478	4.3	10,120	31.8	29.8
Scott	8,976	77.2	90,500	19.1	10.8	529	28.3	3	9,250	-0.5	299	3.2	8,445	23.7	34.0
Shenandoah	17,262	69.7	204,000	22.3	10.4	831	29	2.8	22,092	2.2	627	2.8	20,182	30.0	30.1
Smyth	12,829	70.3	89,600	19.1	10.8	598	28.8	1.8	13,714	-1.1	545	4	12,817	27.3	31.3
Southampton	6,664	71.6	172,800	21.8	10.0	724	29.5	1.7	9,024	-0.1	252	2.8	7,887	29.4	28.7
Spotsylvania	43,279	77.4	265,600	21.7	10.0	1,400	31.7	2	66,032	1	2,006	3	64,416	39.2	18.9
Stafford	45,345	75.8	327,600	20.5	10.0	1,481	30.4	1.1	70,084	1	2,070	3	68,238	47.3	14.4
Surry	2,773	76.1	172,700	22.3	12.4	920	30.3	2.5	3,716	-0.5	129	3.5	3,099	24.0	39.3
Sussex	3,388	70.7	121,600	21.2	12.8	837	31.6	1.2	3,822	0.1	187	4.9	2,684	29.7	28.7
Tazewell	17,330	76.8	96,500	20.0	11.5	622	23.7	1.1	15,905	-1.5	698	4.4	16,237	29.5	29.1
Warren	14,190	76.7	231,000	21.7	10.0	940	29.1	1.6	20,094	1.2	615	3.1	18,753	34.1	27.6
Washington	22,388	75.6	137,200	20.5	10.0	644	27.2	0.8	26,683	-0.5	898	3.4	23,980	34.1	22.9
Westmoreland	7,412	76.8	203,100	23.9	11.0	961	33.2	1.2	9,367	0.2	341	3.6	7,696	33.8	24.3
Wise	15,104	69.2	84,500	19.2	10.3	634	33.4	1.4	13,198	-2.5	656	5	13,321	34.2	25.8
Wythe	11,892	76.0	127,400	20.5	10.0	635	27.5	1.8	13,694	-2.3	508	3.7	13,014	28.8	27.4
York	24,333	72.1	315,400	21.2	10.0	1,458	29	1.5	32,590	0.3	909	2.8	30,172	49.7	13.7
Independent Cities															
Alexandria city	68,663	43.1	537,900	21.9	11.4	1,663	27.8	4.5	100,409	1.1	2,255	2.2	95,344	58.5	9.4
Bristol city	7,418	58.9	114,100	20.7	12.6	685	33.4	1.9	7,316	-0.4	271	3.7	7,139	35.6	21.3
Buena Vista city	2,606	62.3	111,700	26.9	12.6	742	33.1	1.6	3,347	-0.2	104	3.1	2,806	22.8	35.9
Charlottesville city	18,408	44.1	277,800	21.1	10.0	1,089	30.2	1.7	26,014	1.0	662	2.5	24,447	50.5	9.9
Chesapeake city	83,031	70.9	260,900	23.9	11.2	1,201	31.9	1.5	121,125	0.3	3,685	3.0	108,589	40.4	19.6
Colonial Heights city	7,092	63.0	163,300	22.4	10.0	1,001	32.9	1.3	8,779	0.4	289	3.3	7,587	36.4	20.0
Covington city	2,399	75.2	72,200	17.7	12.6	688	33.8	4.5	2,401	-1.8	111	4.6	2,173	18.3	28.6
Danville city	18,517	53.2	90,900	21.2	11.8	628	27.7	3.0	19,579	-1.7	989	5.1	16,814	30.4	25.1
Emporia city	2,119	42.6	115,700	23.0	14.6	738	33.6	4.6	2,342	-0.8	111	4.7	1,893	31.1	31.1
Fairfax city	8,499	70.0	501,900	21.7	10.2	1,803	31.2	2.9	13,113	1.2	300	2.3	12,834	53.0	10.3
Falls Church city	5,308	59.9	742,000	22.7	10.0	1,775	30.2	3.6	8,436	1.4	181	2.1	7,672	67.3	5.0
Franklin city	3,470	49.7	186,100	24.9	14.1	847	31.7	0.3	3,587	0.5	157	4.4	3,488	30.6	23.3
Fredericksburg city	10,419	36.0	341,200	19.5	10.0	1,123	30.7	2.4	13,690	0.8	476	3.5	14,674	45.4	10.6
Galax city	2,837	59.0	105,500	23.5	11.8	580	29.6	2.7	2,946	-1.9	102	3.5	2,901	24.1	34.2
Hampton city	53,555	56.9	186,600	24.2	12.0	1,062	32.8	3.5	64,378	0.0	2,596	4.0	62,042	34.0	23.4
Harrisonburg city	16,848	38.3	196,200	20.1	10.0	857	31.5	3.7	24,736	-0.1	857	3.5	26,008	32.6	20.9
Hopewell city	9,123	51.0	122,400	18.4	14.5	831	28.4	3.1	9,703	-0.3	463	4.8	9,503	25.4	27.1
Lexington city	1,935	59.3	252,500	30.9	13.3	785	33.0	0.0	2,074	-2.2	97	4.7	2,257	48.0	12.6
Lynchburg city	28,150	49.7	153,800	20.2	10.7	835	32.8	1.7	35,927	-0.3	1,437	4.0	35,605	37.9	17.8
Manassas city	12,540	63.6	307,000	23.7	10.1	1,439	33.9	5.2	21,856	1.1	585	2.7	21,846	33.7	22.6
Manassas Park city	4,778	67.5	263,300	26.1	14.5	1,635	25.3	3.8	8,944	1.2	242	2.7	8,326	36.7	23.5

1. Specified owner-occupied units.   2. A value of 10.0 represents 10 percent or less; a value of 50.0 represents 50 percent or more.   3. Specified renter-occupied units.   4. Overcrowded or lacking complete plumbing facilities.   5. Percent of civilian labor force.   6. Civilian employed persons 16 years old and over.

STATE County	Private nonfarm establishments, employment and payroll, 2016									Agriculture, 2017			
	Number of establishments	Employment						Annual payroll		Farms			Farm producers whose primary occupation is farming (percent)
		Total	Health care and social assistance	Manufacturing	Retail trade	Finance and insurance	Professional, scientific, and technical services	Total (mil dol)	Average per employee (dollars)		Percent with:		
										Number	Fewer than 50 acres	1000 acres or more	
	104	105	106	107	108	109	110	111	112	113	114	115	116

VIRGINIA— Cont'd

STATE County	104	105	106	107	108	109	110	111	112	113	114	115	116
Louisa	541	6,815	318	1,130	1,202	90	143	320	47,000	431	38.7	1.6	38.8
Lunenburg	173	1,799	186	534	425	71	53	53	29,282	335	29.3	2.7	43.9
Madison	274	2,525	330	267	665	23	80	91	35,891	533	33.4	3.6	45.6
Mathews	174	1,086	222	49	222	19	44	26	24,018	43	65.1	2.3	31.8
Mecklenburg	789	9,872	1,697	1,400	1,789	280	796	343	34,787	512	25.6	4.9	42.7
Middlesex	334	2,195	376	127	474	59	149	65	29,804	79	50.6	6.3	43.5
Montgomery	1,966	29,453	4,515	4,918	5,284	676	2,194	1,150	39,054	584	41.3	2.4	39.3
Nelson	367	3,124	220	489	266	35	191	90	28,717	409	34.5	1.2	41.7
New Kent	360	2,896	586	132	447	33	116	97	33,458	138	64.5	4.3	39.5
Northampton	313	3,060	856	331	458	47	67	102	33,319	142	47.9	10.6	43.3
Northumberland	314	1,631	114	290	329	64	87	60	36,925	134	58.2	11.9	46.3
Nottoway	317	3,425	1,034	373	648	106	99	108	31,488	311	34.1	2.9	48.2
Orange	645	6,875	409	1,404	1,363	134	264	256	37,169	417	34.1	5.3	40.6
Page	400	4,063	505	547	735	170	245	125	30,868	519	47.0	1.9	46.3
Patrick	284	4,334	608	1,360	527	82	100	116	26,738	483	38.5	1.9	41.2
Pittsylvania	833	8,432	1,232	1,865	874	144	176	278	32,962	1,157	30.2	2.9	41.5
Powhatan	683	4,975	295	139	871	118	222	191	38,390	263	52.5	1.5	47.6
Prince Edward	526	6,579	1,818	122	1,384	171	101	212	32,264	341	27.9	2.3	37.7
Prince George	480	10,821	481	1,099	938	92	971	342	31,625	164	37.8	7.3	43.6
Prince William	8,036	98,094	10,030	1,481	22,591	2,122	10,165	4,196	42,772	304	75.7	1.3	38.0
Pulaski	592	11,262	1,193	4,894	1,623	153	222	425	37,777	394	40.4	3.0	31.9
Rappahannock	201	1,100	42	74	167	14	76	38	34,116	439	49.2	2.5	37.5
Richmond	177	2,031	732	142	228	44	45	59	28,961	98	38.8	9.2	64.3
Roanoke	1,987	28,036	4,414	3,391	3,789	3,268	1,758	1,070	38,180	262	52.3	0.4	43.1
Rockbridge	429	5,214	316	1,050	1,478	92	232	152	29,078	752	36.6	2.4	38.2
Rockingham	1,445	27,349	3,937	7,115	1,950	381	493	1,125	41,119	2,026	46.2	0.6	49.3
Russell	450	5,649	1,163	512	900	219	724	203	35,905	918	36.2	2.7	40.7
Scott	275	3,560	705	853	676	85	109	115	32,247	1,138	41.4	0.5	34.9
Shenandoah	881	12,113	1,501	3,666	1,736	264	324	430	35,528	965	49.4	1.6	42.5
Smyth	511	8,777	1,758	3,210	1,232	209	150	332	37,853	663	41.0	2.9	37.3
Southampton	221	2,126	121	741	265	20	61	83	38,999	257	23.0	20.2	51.4
Spotsylvania	2,443	31,225	4,215	1,260	7,827	501	2,749	1,172	37,528	338	57.4	2.7	40.7
Stafford	2,278	31,902	3,402	878	4,794	4,550	4,204	1,343	42,102	243	75.7	0.8	36.6
Surry	74	1,345	D	92	57	D	19	106	78,895	111	40.5	7.2	40.0
Sussex	182	1,961	336	224	331	28	23	61	31,321	124	28.2	21.0	48.5
Tazewell	1,012	12,724	2,465	1,122	3,078	637	352	411	32,298	512	37.1	8.0	35.1
Warren	790	10,438	1,353	1,024	1,751	231	323	364	34,911	321	62.6	1.2	33.8
Washington	1,152	18,034	2,776	3,801	3,211	495	653	665	36,892	1,506	49.7	1.1	37.8
Westmoreland	315	2,539	224	613	453	77	172	70	27,668	183	34.4	7.7	50.5
Wise	731	8,214	1,693	216	1,989	215	376	255	31,051	147	46.3	5.4	38.1
Wythe	680	9,530	1,209	2,038	2,048	262	170	316	33,209	819	30.9	2.0	43.4
York	1,400	18,284	1,811	279	3,793	440	2,061	621	33,957	40	85.0	NA	23.1
Independent Cities													
Alexandria city	4,711	84,594	7,433	1,207	7,587	3,080	19,115	5,145	60,815	NA	NA	NA	NA
Bristol city	619	10,576	891	1,340	1,842	344	183	367	34,662	NA	NA	NA	NA
Buena Vista city	106	1,834	140	837	87	30	14	64	34,784	NA	NA	NA	NA
Charlottesville city	2,062	33,985	9,432	638	3,771	862	2,489	1,805	53,126	NA	NA	NA	NA
Chesapeake city	5,375	89,955	9,794	4,271	16,169	3,576	8,565	3,762	41,826	248	76.2	5.2	33.8
Colonial Heights city	669	9,665	1,679	D	3,383	268	352	244	25,294	NA	NA	NA	NA
Covington city	219	3,938	168	D	728	94	46	177	45,009	NA	NA	NA	NA
Danville city	1,286	23,789	5,164	4,736	4,327	804	407	803	33,743	NA	NA	NA	NA
Emporia city	235	4,008	1,155	858	662	85	54	136	34,002	NA	NA	NA	NA
Fairfax city	2,280	33,021	4,092	156	6,684	1,279	7,348	1,822	55,180	NA	NA	NA	NA
Falls Church city	875	10,060	2,010	74	1,054	194	1,675	510	50,653	NA	NA	NA	NA
Franklin city	270	3,499	1,261	32	1,008	178	109	99	28,380	NA	NA	NA	NA
Fredericksburg city	1,373	19,093	4,577	275	4,166	629	1,340	801	41,959	NA	NA	NA	NA
Galax city	301	5,088	1,438	799	1,247	123	135	156	30,745	NA	NA	NA	NA
Hampton city	2,371	42,353	7,552	2,120	7,226	836	4,473	1,718	40,557	NA	NA	NA	NA
Harrisonburg city	1,593	25,301	3,054	2,861	5,238	863	1,215	804	31,772	NA	NA	NA	NA
Hopewell city	407	6,237	1,144	1,807	659	109	257	323	51,746	NA	NA	NA	NA
Lexington city	278	3,832	675	23	399	104	150	152	39,670	NA	NA	NA	NA
Lynchburg city	2,199	57,209	9,810	6,481	7,779	2,727	3,630	2,231	39,000	NA	NA	NA	NA
Manassas city	1,501	19,240	3,403	3,513	2,421	482	1,381	1,061	55,164	NA	NA	NA	NA
Manassas Park city	330	3,472	123	299	182	24	140	159	45,887	NA	NA	NA	NA

Table B. States and Counties — **Agriculture**

STATE County	Land in farms — Acreage (1,000)	Land in farms — Percent change, 2012-2017	Acres — Average size of farm	Acres — Total irrigated (1,000)	Acres — Total cropland (1,000)	Value of land and buildings (dollars) — Average per farm	Value of land and buildings (dollars) — Average per acre	Value of machinery and equiopmnet, average per farm (dollars)	Value of products sold: Total (mil dol)	Value of products sold: Average per farm (acres)	Percent from: Crops	Percent from: Livestock and poultry products	Organic farms (number)	Farms with internet access (percent)	Government payments Total ($1,000)	Government payments Percent of farms
	117	118	119	120	121	122	123	124	125	126	127	128	129	130	131	132
VIRGINIA— Cont'd																
Louisa	68	-14.6	159	0.2	24.8	787,124	4,953	76,509	15.0	34,735	48.7	51.3	5	76.3	314	16.5
Lunenburg	73	-11.9	217	1.4	25.7	579,358	2,664	81,398	17.2	51,206	77.7	22.3	7	69.9	354	24.5
Madison	107	-0.1	201	0.1	45.1	1,193,189	5,949	90,957	28.4	53,263	39.6	60.4	2	74.1	1,313	17.3
Mathews	7	41.7	153	0.0	4.2	655,108	4,278	63,683	3.8	87,814	55.4	44.6	NA	81.4	31	18.6
Mecklenburg	141	-3.0	276	4.2	62.9	762,052	2,764	122,271	50.0	97,590	90.1	9.9	21	64.5	334	30.3
Middlesex	20	1.7	247	0.3	14.7	979,876	3,967	154,776	8.8	111,620	96.7	3.3	3	87.3	586	44.3
Montgomery	102	-5.2	174	0.3	28.8	842,923	4,842	78,230	24.3	41,604	30.2	69.8	2	81.8	327	8.2
Nelson	68	-15.2	166	1.0	20.2	841,397	5,073	85,319	26.7	65,328	83.0	17.0	5	72.9	118	9.0
New Kent	18	-7.0	133	0.3	11.1	711,167	5,353	85,624	5.1	37,159	93.2	6.8	NA	83.3	558	18.8
Northampton	48	-13.9	340	5.9	37.8	1,558,831	4,585	281,016	96.0	675,993	70.7	29.3	3	93.0	1,180	29.6
Northumberland	43	0.5	324	NA	33.8	975,400	3,006	226,725	20.1	149,642	85.8	14.2	NA	64.9	1,423	26.1
Nottoway	50	-18.2	162	0.0	20.1	514,211	3,174	76,270	50.5	162,486	7.9	92.1	1	71.4	405	25.7
Orange	95	-9.1	228	0.2	39.8	1,438,347	6,297	115,676	113.1	271,149	77.7	22.3	NA	79.1	292	12.7
Page	72	1.3	139	0.1	30.4	904,349	6,515	90,614	150.1	289,260	4.2	95.8	2	73.0	836	11.8
Patrick	91	15.4	189	0.2	21.6	524,237	2,775	58,469	17.3	35,762	42.5	57.5	NA	73.3	260	12.6
Pittsylvania	246	-14.3	213	1.5	83.4	603,542	2,835	93,701	72.7	62,816	41.1	58.9	6	68.3	1,441	17.2
Powhatan	35	7.8	132	0.1	11.4	696,770	5,299	47,626	11.2	42,772	22.6	77.4	1	75.3	54	9.9
Prince Edward	70	-11.9	204	0.0	20.1	580,742	2,848	65,360	23.8	69,768	11.2	88.8	NA	71.8	198	36.1
Prince George	40	8.1	242	D	22.0	920,064	3,807	88,285	9.3	56,616	94.5	5.5	NA	69.5	933	37.2
Prince William	23	-35.8	75	0.9	14.1	804,671	10,694	78,627	11.6	38,197	61.1	38.9	NA	92.1	227	5.9
Pulaski	78	-19.8	197	0.0	23.8	692,087	3,518	84,261	33.0	83,716	35.9	64.1	NA	77.4	88	7.6
Rappahannock	70	11.7	160	0.1	25.2	1,101,588	6,891	64,028	10.1	23,109	50.4	49.6	2	78.4	90	8.7
Richmond	32	-1.3	326	0.0	26.2	1,289,515	3,955	173,701	16.8	171,571	95.3	4.7	NA	48.0	823	42.9
Roanoke	26	-17.1	100	0.1	6.2	572,455	5,743	55,410	2.5	9,691	67.5	32.5	NA	66.4	D	1.9
Rockbridge	135	-19.9	179	0.1	36.5	881,466	4,918	70,368	31.0	41,201	16.9	83.1	NA	76.3	422	10.0
Rockingham	229	2.9	113	5.5	121.9	997,634	8,844	118,949	795.9	392,852	6.8	93.2	37	65.5	1,852	11.5
Russell	170	-9.2	185	D	32.7	536,112	2,890	53,598	23.2	25,277	11.4	88.6	1	61.9	269	8.8
Scott	125	-20.8	110	0.0	30.5	290,473	2,637	53,894	15.6	13,671	24.7	75.3	2	69.9	79	7.3
Shenandoah	131	-2.1	135	0.9	61.2	796,732	5,884	99,776	142.8	148,006	14.1	85.9	2	76.7	593	7.3
Smyth	123	-26.1	186	0.0	25.7	544,580	2,930	75,941	37.6	56,653	8.5	91.5	1	65.6	782	14.6
Southampton	142	-7.7	552	1.6	97.6	1,704,698	3,087	237,200	75.1	292,070	82.4	17.6	NA	76.3	6,847	72.8
Spotsylvania	42	-1.2	123	0.1	16.7	695,020	5,637	70,042	9.0	26,660	48.5	51.5	2	76.6	199	8.6
Stafford	17	13.1	71	0.0	10.1	930,372	13,104	73,999	6.1	25,206	62.6	37.4	2	85.2	68	6.2
Surry	42	-6.8	379	0.9	25.4	1,280,403	3,379	175,981	D	D	D	D	3	84.7	1,280	39.6
Sussex	66	3.1	534	0.7	44.9	1,482,681	2,775	209,543	D	D	D	D	NA	74.2	1,963	54.0
Tazewell	138	-8.1	269	D	24.7	737,125	2,736	66,474	24.6	48,117	8.5	91.5	NA	68.8	820	9.6
Warren	39	-19.4	121	0.0	13.9	909,921	7,548	68,431	5.9	18,355	36.1	63.9	2	81.0	5	1.2
Washington	176	-8.2	117	0.1	58.3	589,890	5,038	60,654	69.0	45,821	12.1	87.9	2	68.0	596	11.5
Westmoreland	53	-11.4	288	0.9	32.0	1,073,155	3,732	170,589	D	D	D	D	2	74.3	1,175	36.1
Wise	26	1.7	179	0.0	5.0	554,986	3,097	66,109	2.4	16,000	33.5	66.5	NA	66.0	15	2.7
Wythe	152	-13.0	185	0.0	49.1	725,643	3,921	87,090	65.5	80,018	8.4	91.6	NA	75.5	474	19.4
York	1	-67.5	23	0.0	0.1	276,375	12,095	39,402	1.5	37,800	75.1	24.9	NA	97.5	D	2.5
Independent Cities																
Alexandria city	NA	NA	NA	NA	NA	NA	NA	NA	NA	NA	NA	NA	NA	NA	NA	NA
Bristol city	NA	NA	NA	NA	NA	NA	NA	NA	NA	NA	NA	NA	NA	NA	NA	NA
Buena Vista city	NA	NA	NA	NA	NA	NA	NA	NA	NA	NA	NA	NA	NA	NA	NA	NA
Charlottesville city	NA	NA	NA	NA	NA	NA	NA	NA	NA	NA	NA	NA	NA	NA	NA	NA
Chesapeake city	37	-18.4	148	0.1	32.3	867,657	5,848	102,911	31.1	125,552	94.8	5.2	NA	82.3	646	16.1
Colonial Heights city	NA	NA	NA	NA	NA	NA	NA	NA	NA	NA	NA	NA	NA	NA	NA	NA
Covington city	NA	NA	NA	NA	NA	NA	NA	NA	NA	NA	NA	NA	NA	NA	NA	NA
Danville city	NA	NA	NA	NA	NA	NA	NA	NA	NA	NA	NA	NA	NA	NA	NA	NA
Emporia city	NA	NA	NA	NA	NA	NA	NA	NA	NA	NA	NA	NA	NA	NA	NA	NA
Fairfax city	NA	NA	NA	NA	NA	NA	NA	NA	NA	NA	NA	NA	NA	NA	NA	NA
Falls Church city	NA	NA	NA	NA	NA	NA	NA	NA	NA	NA	NA	NA	NA	NA	NA	NA
Franklin city	NA	NA	NA	NA	NA	NA	NA	NA	NA	NA	NA	NA	NA	NA	NA	NA
Fredericksburg city	NA	NA	NA	NA	NA	NA	NA	NA	NA	NA	NA	NA	NA	NA	NA	NA
Galax city	NA	NA	NA	NA	NA	NA	NA	NA	NA	NA	NA	NA	NA	NA	NA	NA
Hampton city	NA	NA	NA	NA	NA	NA	NA	NA	NA	NA	NA	NA	NA	NA	NA	NA
Harrisonburg city	NA	NA	NA	NA	NA	NA	NA	NA	NA	NA	NA	NA	NA	NA	NA	NA
Hopewell city	NA	NA	NA	NA	NA	NA	NA	NA	NA	NA	NA	NA	NA	NA	NA	NA
Lexington city	NA	NA	NA	NA	NA	NA	NA	NA	NA	NA	NA	NA	NA	NA	NA	NA
Lynchburg city	NA	NA	NA	NA	NA	NA	NA	NA	NA	NA	NA	NA	NA	NA	NA	NA
Manassas city	NA	NA	NA	NA	NA	NA	NA	NA	NA	NA	NA	NA	NA	NA	NA	NA
Manassas Park city	NA	NA	NA	NA	NA	NA	NA	NA	NA	NA	NA	NA	NA	NA	NA	NA

Table B. States and Counties — **Water Use, Wholesale Trade, Retail Trade, and Real Estate**

STATE County	Water use, 2015		Wholesale Trade[1], 2012				Retail Trade[2], 2012				Real estate and rental and leasing,[2] 2012			
	Public supply water withdrawn (mil gal/ day)	Public supply gallons withdrawn per person per day	Number of establish-ments	Number of employees	Sales (mil dol)	Average payroll (mil dol)	Number of establish-ments	Number of employees	Sales (mil dol)	Average payroll (mil dol)	Number of establish-ments	Number of employees	Sales (mil dol)	Average payroll (mil dol)
	133	134	135	136	137	138	139	140	141	142	143	144	145	146
VIRGINIA— Cont'd														
Louisa	0.53	15.3	11	100	45.3	6.3	77	1,086	276.4	22.9	20	71	10.4	2.5
Lunenburg	0.48	39.0	6	112	111.2	7.3	36	250	51.3	5.0	1	D	D	D
Madison	0.00	0.0	13	74	16.5	2.6	40	635	186.4	15.0	4	6	1.0	0.1
Mathews	0.00	0.0	5	D	D	D	25	232	54.4	4.5	10	D	D	D
Mecklenburg	1.87	60.2	31	263	159.0	11.1	160	1,677	417.1	35.7	33	131	14.3	3.2
Middlesex	0.07	6.6	12	83	25.7	3.0	56	437	101.3	9.8	13	D	D	D
Montgomery	6.92	70.9	46	808	593.0	35.8	324	4,992	1,280.6	108.9	91	535	103.8	19.0
Nelson	0.20	13.5	4	D	D	D	50	299	115.1	6.3	12	D	D	D
New Kent	19.91	976.4	4	28	13.6	1.2	39	488	155.0	8.8	14	21	2.0	0.5
Northampton	0.40	32.9	18	160	167.1	5.2	72	543	117.9	10.4	13	43	6.8	0.8
Northumberland	0.14	11.4	12	69	31.4	2.6	48	352	85.3	7.6	18	39	5.2	1.6
Nottoway	0.48	30.6	12	98	85.2	3.4	62	607	126.6	12.9	6	14	2.0	0.4
Orange	2.08	58.8	7	D	D	D	107	970	311.6	24.5	23	41	6.1	1.1
Page	1.27	53.5	8	D	D	D	76	772	173.9	17.3	11	35	5.5	0.7
Patrick	0.29	16.1	6	52	21.7	1.9	54	550	204.6	11.0	6	6	0.4	0.1
Pittsylvania	1.62	26.0	29	771	381.0	21.7	133	868	242.8	16.8	24	86	12.8	1.9
Powhatan	0.11	3.9	21	156	51.0	6.3	66	550	264.2	17.5	22	67	12.0	1.9
Prince Edward	1.11	48.4	14	140	41.7	4.8	99	1,488	390.5	35.9	25	99	11.0	1.9
Prince George	0.14	3.7	24	D	D	D	73	977	260.7	22.7	19	41	9.1	0.9
Prince William	79.73	176.5	172	2,387	2,222.7	138.3	1,083	20,117	5,638.2	516.7	306	1,242	339.7	50.4
Pulaski	4.39	127.9	17	114	36.0	3.4	110	1,599	352.7	32.1	21	65	7.8	1.5
Rappahannock	0.03	4.1	5	22	2.4	0.6	26	150	29.3	3.6	4	D	D	D
Richmond	0.36	40.4	7	68	72.2	2.5	38	252	68.2	5.6	7	19	1.6	0.3
Roanoke	25.13	266.2	98	1,168	700.2	66.9	260	3,609	891.0	84.3	104	352	60.4	12.0
Rockbridge	1.74	77.8	9	53	16.5	1.5	74	1,175	360.1	25.8	13	38	3.6	0.8
Rockingham	14.75	187.7	56	946	626.3	48.3	206	1,871	429.8	40.3	44	568	110.4	23.9
Russell	1.18	42.3	14	53	30.0	2.0	81	934	233.2	20.3	13	43	3.5	1.1
Scott	1.12	50.6	10	D	D	D	78	709	210.5	13.5	5	11	1.5	0.3
Shenandoah	2.57	59.5	18	440	519.7	15.5	150	1,705	499.5	36.1	30	D	D	D
Smyth	2.19	69.6	16	D	D	D	114	1,202	272.0	24.0	15	43	7.1	1.4
Southampton	0.84	46.4	10	142	131.2	5.9	30	236	55.7	4.4	8	20	2.5	0.4
Spotsylvania	11.05	84.7	64	678	341.7	31.3	402	6,758	2,160.1	184.4	113	508	77.9	18.1
Stafford	21.98	154.8	47	D	D	D	253	4,489	1,247.9	111.3	89	298	58.1	10.2
Surry	0.15	22.4	1	D	D	D	12	53	14.9	1.0	3	D	D	D
Sussex	0.56	47.8	9	D	D	D	43	332	112.6	6.8	5	13	2.2	0.4
Tazewell	3.79	88.3	60	527	265.7	22.1	212	3,044	804.6	65.9	50	170	24.9	4.6
Warren	9.08	232.3	7	D	D	D	137	1,718	444.6	40.2	22	71	9.9	1.9
Washington	11.77	215.6	38	D	D	D	206	3,207	820.5	67.8	46	127	26.1	5.1
Westmoreland	0.79	44.8	16	48	31.2	1.7	45	415	109.8	8.7	12	22	2.1	0.4
Wise	4.90	123.4	37	345	299.7	16.4	168	2,092	500.9	45.1	23	69	7.3	1.5
Wythe	4.35	149.4	13	D	D	D	137	1,922	905.5	44.0	22	75	21.7	2.5
York	19.05	280.8	34	139	80.0	6.1	220	3,922	884.4	86.9	50	256	28.2	7.9
Independent Cities														
Alexandria city	0.02	0.1	82	1,139	502.8	61.6	480	7,180	2,416.0	222.6	240	1,475	524.1	76.6
Bristol city	0.00	0.0	34	802	370.4	22.5	157	1,732	349.9	33.6	23	69	9.9	2.0
Buena Vista city	1.06	160.2	1	D	D	D	19	156	34.8	3.0	3	4	0.4	0.0
Charlottesville city	0.00	0.0	48	513	183.3	23.7	331	3,925	747.9	82.8	99	502	107.6	19.7
Chesapeake city	7.12	30.2	239	3,447	2,225.2	169.7	789	15,088	4,114.9	336.7	273	1,227	291.6	52.9
Colonial Heights city	0.00	0.0	10	53	19.7	2.0	180	3,498	763.3	65.3	27	151	31.6	4.5
Covington city	2.14	378.2	6	D	D	D	60	734	158.3	15.8	9	24	2.5	0.5
Danville city	5.36	127.4	50	545	285.2	24.5	306	4,165	965.0	87.2	64	339	48.7	9.1
Emporia city	0.69	125.5	3	D	D	D	52	620	136.5	13.5	11	36	4.6	0.8
Fairfax city	0.00	0.0	40	372	408.9	18.2	251	5,526	1,757.5	176.4	60	261	61.3	13.5
Falls Church city	0.00	0.0	18	D	D	D	92	1,010	310.2	35.9	35	192	71.7	9.3
Franklin city	0.87	102.5	7	52	28.3	1.8	63	979	228.3	21.6	11	D	D	D
Fredericksburg city	0.00	0.0	21	224	95.3	11.8	253	4,098	1,075.0	88.1	70	308	63.3	12.5
Galax city	1.74	251.7	5	69	117.5	3.0	64	1,105	259.6	24.3	13	52	9.9	1.6
Hampton city	0.00	0.0	71	886	344.7	39.3	436	6,791	1,512.5	148.3	114	750	117.3	23.7
Harrisonburg city	0.00	0.0	57	1,006	405.9	43.2	334	5,664	1,519.8	144.6	72	351	75.9	10.9
Hopewell city	20.55	918.3	11	84	26.9	3.5	73	586	164.8	13.1	22	97	20.3	3.7
Lexington city	0.00	0.0	NA	NA	NA	NA	44	458	92.7	9.4	17	32	4.4	1.0
Lynchburg city	0.00	0.0	69	877	509.0	39.0	385	7,371	1,995.2	178.2	109	447	79.9	14.5
Manassas city	0.21	5.0	41	D	D	D	194	2,778	895.3	86.1	52	229	64.0	11.4
Manassas Park city	0.00	0.0	23	281	170.8	17.1	31	240	124.7	7.5	9	33	7.3	1.3

1   Merchant wholesalers, except manufacturers' sales branches and offices.   2. Employer establishments.

Professional Services, Manufacturing, and Accommodation and Food Services

STATE County	Professional, scientific, and technical services, 2012				Manufacturing, 2012				Accommodation and food services, 2012			
	Number of establish-ments	Number of employees	Sales (mil dol)	Average payroll (mil dol)	Number of establish-ments	Number of employees	Receipts (mil dol)	Annual payroll (mil dol)	Number of establis-hments	Number of employees	Receipts (mil dol)	Annual payroll (mil dol)
	147	148	149	150	151	152	153	154	155	156	157	158
VIRGINIA— Cont'd												
Louisa	57	188	16.2	5.4	32	1,162	426.8	58.2	30	348	18.2	4.8
Lunenburg	10	44	3.9	1.1	7	429	99.4	12.9	8	D	D	D
Madison	22	51	5.4	1.6	18	250	D	8.5	18	190	9.4	2.8
Mathews	19	D	D	D	3	D	D	D	13	178	6.4	1.7
Mecklenburg	49	264	26.3	9.2	34	1,338	298.0	49.4	67	1,179	46.6	12.7
Middlesex	28	150	8.7	4.7	12	133	D	4.9	26	190	9.5	3.1
Montgomery	267	2,714	265.2	142.7	50	3,054	936.8	159.8	197	4,223	186.5	53.5
Nelson	42	140	14.7	5.5	27	268	D	9.0	20	168	6.4	1.9
New Kent	28	94	7.7	3.4	14	157	D	4.6	29	D	D	D
Northampton	21	56	4.7	1.8	9	397	D	13.8	40	476	29.0	6.9
Northumberland	21	91	20.4	4.5	21	426	D	14.9	20	134	5.7	2.0
Nottoway	19	93	6.8	2.5	12	329	104.3	12.7	27	335	12.7	3.8
Orange	74	302	52.6	14.7	18	836	230.0	34.0	58	850	36.3	10.3
Page	25	164	15.4	5.3	13	552	161.5	15.6	56	652	39.9	11.1
Patrick	18	67	3.4	1.4	35	1,342	189.2	39.9	20	163	7.0	1.7
Pittsylvania	47	149	19.3	4.8	45	1,959	615.9	82.0	38	421	15.5	4.7
Powhatan	62	249	27.4	11.1	19	99	D	D	25	494	17.1	5.4
Prince Edward	34	111	8.6	3.0	14	107	D	2.9	49	1,148	49.9	13.9
Prince George	49	695	89.4	35.1	24	839	602.9	42.3	45	668	39.3	8.8
Prince William	1,067	10,927	1,557.4	753.1	94	1,634	353.1	75.2	633	11,867	673.7	177.6
Pulaski	38	170	17.2	7.8	39	3,797	2,861.3	183.6	74	1,148	53.4	14.1
Rappahannock	29	77	9.1	3.2	7	36	D	0.9	14	D	D	D
Richmond	13	42	4.8	2.4	7	122	D	4.8	13	122	6.2	1.6
Roanoke	217	1,101	124.5	49.8	63	3,134	815.7	164.8	132	2,663	128.3	32.4
Rockbridge	28	89	7.8	2.9	20	1,203	197.6	42.3	52	802	44.3	11.9
Rockingham	76	565	75.6	32.5	88	7,047	5,397.1	323.0	91	2,128	82.7	35.7
Russell	46	634	80.9	42.0	9	345	D	10.7	38	504	19.3	5.7
Scott	22	102	10.6	3.9	9	962	486.8	37.8	24	D	D	D
Shenandoah	63	262	33.2	14.4	35	3,271	796.2	109.7	81	1,365	56.0	17.1
Smyth	37	198	14.7	6.4	40	3,129	833.0	128.8	45	727	29.0	8.1
Southampton	11	D	D	D	12	411	106.4	15.0	13	84	3.8	1.0
Spotsylvania	227	2,219	424.7	190.8	59	1,517	D	67.7	203	3,880	190.4	53.4
Stafford	318	3,786	677.6	268.6	39	768	171.1	31.7	183	3,102	161.4	40.9
Surry	7	21	1.2	0.5	3	108	D	3.7	5	39	1.6	0.4
Sussex	7	D	D	D	9	120	D	6.2	13	239	11.7	3.1
Tazewell	60	443	39.8	16.3	53	1,294	297.8	60.0	71	1,245	59.6	16.1
Warren	77	277	28.3	12.8	25	810	811.8	41.1	79	1,203	61.2	18.0
Washington	94	642	49.0	26.5	66	3,763	1,095.6	153.6	96	D	D	D
Westmoreland	30	235	14.4	8.3	9	560	167.0	12.9	31	D	D	D
Wise	58	423	38.4	18.1	26	303	D	12.4	55	1,130	42.1	12.2
Wythe	43	204	20.8	8.9	40	1,705	1,292.9	71.6	83	1,509	78.3	19.4
York	177	D	D	D	27	D	D	8.9	155	3,804	269.9	56.2
Independent Cities												
Alexandria city	1,238	18,505	3,799.3	1,692.1	72	1,332	273.0	57.9	387	8,051	647.5	180.7
Bristol city	44	239	24.2	13.0	23	1,057	302.3	48.6	82	1,811	86.8	23.8
Buena Vista city	6	20	1.3	0.5	14	894	351.4	39.1	12	D	D	D
Charlottesville city	322	2,555	406.5	164.9	46	455	98.7	21.6	293	5,199	293.3	75.9
Chesapeake city	510	D	D	D	130	3,965	1,504.2	211.6	466	10,267	447.6	121.1
Colonial Heights city	50	491	21.5	8.3	8	129	D	5.4	82	2,180	99.9	27.8
Covington city	19	52	6.5	1.2	6	D	D	D	20	D	D	D
Danville city	74	522	71.0	31.7	46	4,635	1,703.0	223.7	139	2,850	120.4	33.6
Emporia city	18	79	4.7	1.9	9	850	203.7	35.3	26	586	25.1	7.2
Fairfax city	647	6,022	1,368.7	522.1	29	158	18.8	6.3	192	3,608	218.6	60.9
Falls Church city	157	1,798	352.4	136.3	17	74	16.1	3.4	119	1,098	73.5	19.1
Franklin city	20	200	12.5	6.2	6	27	8.5	1.3	28	484	20.3	5.1
Fredericksburg city	180	1,390	227.1	99.5	26	221	57.0	8.3	165	3,718	179.5	55.4
Galax city	26	138	12.8	4.4	12	719	157.9	18.6	39	540	22.7	7.1
Hampton city	279	3,711	648.1	289.6	68	2,189	508.3	114.9	250	5,380	249.0	72.2
Harrisonburg city	139	924	98.8	43.9	46	2,556	832.6	99.4	186	4,468	216.0	58.8
Hopewell city	35	184	16.8	7.5	16	1,338	1,930.8	110.8	52	728	33.5	8.2
Lexington city	29	121	10.5	3.7	5	14	D	D	52	540	34.2	9.3
Lynchburg city	200	3,395	969.0	265.2	83	8,339	2,749.6	504.3	215	5,071	216.4	61.0
Manassas city	213	3,462	612.2	285.9	32	4,012	1,365.7	366.4	109	1,587	91.4	24.7
Manassas Park city	23	153	18.2	10.3	12	237	29.6	8.1	14	89	5.6	1.8

Health Care and Social Assistance, Other Services, Nonemployer Businesses, and Residential Construction

STATE County	Health care and social assistance, 2012				Other services, 2012				Nonemployer businesses, 2016		Value of residential construction authorized by building permits, 2018	
	Number of establishments	Number of employees	Receipts (mil dol)	Annual payroll (mil dol)	Number of establishments	Number of employees	Receipts (mil dol)	Annual payroll (mil dol)	Number	Receipts (mil dol)	New construction ($1,000)	Number of housing units
	159	160	161	162	163	164	165	166	167	168	169	170
VIRGINIA— Cont'd												
Louisa	25	299	24.6	10.4	47	D	D	D	2,309	97.9	62,136	287
Lunenburg	16	326	11.3	5.5	12	D	D	D	548	20.3	1,498	7
Madison	21	286	13.8	6.7	21	D	D	D	1,145	41.6	13,704	60
Mathews	9	D	D	D	12	D	D	D	809	32.1	3,872	19
Mecklenburg	75	1,843	153.7	62.3	68	333	23.7	6.9	1,609	67.8	14,879	68
Middlesex	20	440	23.2	9.5	25	D	D	D	1,000	39.4	6,831	35
Montgomery	224	3,898	489.7	167.8	148	814	165.6	23.1	5,112	207.1	70,000	429
Nelson	20	D	D	D	21	181	13.1	4.9	1,295	51.7	14,302	45
New Kent	25	610	37.2	17.0	29	D	D	D	1,706	70.1	63,583	253
Northampton	40	942	97.8	34.3	20	D	D	D	1,011	42.3	11,064	49
Northumberland	11	84	3.1	1.6	26	D	D	D	1,115	43.7	9,612	42
Nottoway	28	959	48.7	25.9	25	D	D	D	644	18.1	5,034	50
Orange	45	389	23.9	10.0	56	373	36.9	10.8	2,443	99.2	40,994	187
Page	24	479	46.8	17.6	35	D	D	D	1,452	53.8	7,280	59
Patrick	23	673	40.5	17.4	13	D	D	D	1,024	31.6	8,312	43
Pittsylvania	52	1,120	51.6	23.3	72	281	23.5	6.5	3,227	106.7	9,927	50
Powhatan	27	D	D	D	57	344	24.2	7.6	2,043	109.9	45,224	191
Prince Edward	82	1,697	135.0	59.4	35	160	14.5	3.5	997	32.4	7,371	49
Prince George	25	159	18.1	8.3	32	143	12.2	4.4	1,556	48.4	14,155	89
Prince William	718	9,320	993.6	387.7	537	3,703	653.2	116.1	36,693	1,458.2	298,427	1,561
Pulaski	57	1,109	108.8	43.8	43	208	20.8	5.5	1,522	46.3	9,098	49
Rappahannock	10	D	D	D	9	D	D	D	982	47.4	5,495	24
Richmond	15	802	27.2	13.5	12	D	D	D	556	17.7	4,926	28
Roanoke	229	4,773	381.7	174.4	142	695	53.8	17.5	5,602	220.0	32,304	159
Rockbridge	39	356	24.2	9.8	28	D	D	D	1,525	61.6	13,800	60
Rockingham	100	4,573	496.7	202.5	104	474	42.1	13.5	5,596	247.0	113,680	395
Russell	65	1,199	97.1	41.9	27	D	D	D	1,147	35.9	1,033	12
Scott	37	679	39.4	18.5	15	D	D	D	924	27.3	2,904	21
Shenandoah	74	1,273	109.4	46.0	81	379	33.6	9.0	2,907	106.9	19,785	115
Smyth	65	1,756	143.8	66.6	35	179	18.5	4.7	1,405	46.0	3,205	17
Southampton	10	143	7.8	3.9	14	D	D	D	873	26.7	8,064	50
Spotsylvania	198	3,021	262.5	122.9	173	1,021	86.9	26.8	8,786	367.1	281,981	1,588
Stafford	173	3,363	287.0	118.9	199	1,195	107.4	35.2	9,059	359.2	255,778	1,048
Surry	4	11	0.9	0.4	2	D	D	D	356	10.2	5,397	25
Sussex	14	D	D	D	19	D	D	D	459	14.5	3,905	33
Tazewell	140	2,377	209.2	80.2	92	605	71.7	20.8	2,085	72.4	1,996	14
Warren	61	D	D	D	68	517	74.3	13.5	2,774	109.1	35,148	158
Washington	150	2,410	258.4	108.1	62	D	D	D	3,481	131.1	14,365	65
Westmoreland	18	238	13.2	6.7	27	88	4.8	1.4	1,218	38.6	17,648	95
Wise	93	1,598	125.1	46.5	53	D	D	D	1,580	45.5	1,330	6
Wythe	75	1,274	108.6	47.1	55	324	27.2	8.7	1,535	59.6	10,672	61
York	107	1,667	215.8	81.2	116	D	D	D	3,900	150.9	76,031	697
Independent Cities												
Alexandria city	397	7,356	1,041.6	376.9	584	9,997	2,626.4	670.0	16,187	770.1	21,577	112
Bristol city	48	654	54.7	18.6	46	D	D	D	999	38.1	1,505	11
Buena Vista city	12	183	5.1	2.7	9	D	D	D	313	8.9	75	1
Charlottesville city	175	D	D	D	151	1,444	318.3	52.5	4,232	230.8	45,773	180
Chesapeake city	497	9,693	978.2	435.2	399	2,990	313.4	95.8	14,358	541.6	291,400	1,031
Colonial Heights city	108	1,746	139.9	56.8	50	357	25.0	8.8	959	39.2	1,821	12
Covington city	17	178	8.8	2.9	22	D	D	D	240	11.2	100	1
Danville city	194	4,803	441.4	188.5	101	535	49.2	11.2	2,312	72.4	692	3
Emporia city	37	1,078	80.1	34.4	18	D	D	D	245	10.8	405	5
Fairfax city	265	3,637	339.1	135.3	146	1,531	424.5	77.8	3,124	177.1	3,293	17
Falls Church city	108	D	D	D	93	588	69.5	22.6	1,456	98.5	21,784	46
Franklin city	52	1,200	105.1	39.4	26	182	12.3	3.1	438	13.9	0	0
Fredericksburg city	189	5,216	789.2	335.8	104	860	69.9	22.8	2,017	114.0	38,717	410
Galax city	45	D	D	D	24	D	D	D	388	14.7	354	2
Hampton city	265	7,739	888.7	394.2	176	1,056	87.5	25.0	6,913	192.4	11,156	179
Harrisonburg city	163	2,860	211.7	96.1	127	690	67.3	18.2	2,720	127.1	12,514	88
Hopewell city	49	1,450	144.0	60.4	38	200	16.7	5.1	916	27.4	10,924	118
Lexington city	41	669	69.2	23.4	34	229	31.0	7.4	443	15.7	8,925	45
Lynchburg city	268	9,339	1,046.5	427.9	173	1,161	100.6	30.6	4,257	157.0	19,225	138
Manassas city	174	3,297	418.2	176.8	141	848	93.5	26.4	3,552	157.3	19,044	87
Manassas Park city	5	D	D	D	52	D	D	D	1,361	57.4	0	0

Table B. States and Counties — Government Employment and Payroll, and Local Government Finances

STATE County	Full-time equivalent employees	March payroll (dollars)	Administration, judicial, and legal	Police and corrections	Fire protection	Highways and transportation	Health and welfare	Natural resources and utilities	Education and libraries	Total (mil dol)	Intergovern-mental (mil dol)	Taxes Total (mil dol)	Taxes Per capita Total (dollars)	Taxes Per capita Property (dollars)
	171	172	173	174	175	176	177	178	179	180	181	182	183	184
VIRGINIA— Cont'd														
Louisa	1,124	3,411,101	8.2	6.8	4.2	0.0	1.1	4.9	73.3	96.7	33.7	53.8	1,609	1,418
Lunenburg	403	1,190,954	9.0	11.5	0.0	0.0	2.3	2.4	72.9	33.1	20.6	9.9	790	676
Madison	403	1,326,277	10.7	6.4	0.0	0.0	5.8	0.3	69.8	34.3	15.7	16.2	1,227	1,036
Mathews	358	848,780	8.9	7.2	0.0	0.0	5.4	0.0	74.9	23.0	9.7	12.1	1,364	1,166
Mecklenburg	1,375	3,603,811	7.0	12.8	0.2	1.1	10.7	2.6	62.8	94.5	47.2	37.6	1,185	856
Middlesex	280	843,355	10.1	15.3	0.0	0.0	3.5	0.8	70.3	25.5	8.9	15.3	1,409	1,212
Montgomery	2,699	8,781,181	9.0	11.9	0.5	4.6	2.7	5.5	61.5	255.0	103.6	112.5	1,182	829
Nelson	457	1,391,646	8.9	4.1	0.0	0.0	1.6	0.5	80.1	45.2	17.7	23.6	1,590	1,346
New Kent	638	2,123,526	10.3	8.3	5.3	0.3	4.1	7.3	63.1	52.7	21.7	26.8	1,400	1,195
Northampton	850	3,278,000	5.0	9.0	0.0	20.1	6.5	3.2	55.2	101.7	23.0	21.3	1,740	1,417
Northumberland	358	1,244,110	8.2	7.7	0.0	0.0	4.8	0.9	77.1	28.9	10.2	17.4	1,407	1,269
Nottoway	548	1,646,561	8.1	8.7	0.0	2.8	5.9	4.4	67.2	39.4	23.9	10.3	650	454
Orange	1,173	3,380,570	7.0	14.3	3.2	1.7	2.2	2.9	67.7	89.1	37.1	42.7	1,247	997
Page	878	2,456,816	8.1	13.4	0.0	0.6	1.8	3.8	71.0	65.3	32.2	27.2	1,138	890
Patrick	695	1,689,450	5.6	12.0	0.0	0.0	4.5	0.8	75.3	43.9	24.0	14.5	784	617
Pittsylvania	1,563	4,924,209	5.8	7.5	0.1	0.5	1.4	1.2	80.6	127.9	84.1	37.6	599	478
Powhatan	855	2,784,066	7.2	7.7	0.5	0.0	3.4	1.3	77.9	69.7	28.5	38.3	1,361	1,230
Prince Edward	701	2,116,144	10.4	10.6	0.3	3.1	2.0	3.4	66.4	54.6	29.8	19.8	852	490
Prince George	1,519	5,308,620	5.9	28.6	0.9	0.0	2.5	1.5	58.6	118.9	72.6	36.1	976	765
Prince William	15,485	68,447,361	3.7	8.8	4.5	3.3	4.4	3.5	69.0	1,578.6	659.7	752.7	1,749	1,412
Pulaski	1,288	4,175,730	6.1	8.3	0.9	1.1	3.6	5.9	68.5	117.9	56.3	35.2	1,013	707
Rappahannock	256	760,848	9.7	11.1	0.0	0.0	6.5	0.8	68.9	20.6	4.6	14.7	1,978	1,804
Richmond	326	1,099,371	6.8	32.6	0.0	0.0	0.6	2.6	56.3	32.9	20.4	9.1	1,002	790
Roanoke	3,729	13,158,244	7.7	7.6	6.2	0.3	4.8	9.4	62.7	353.7	116.0	158.3	1,704	1,275
Rockbridge	661	1,852,653	7.0	8.7	0.0	0.3	5.5	2.1	74.0	71.1	30.7	29.1	1,299	943
Rockingham	2,706	8,346,966	7.1	8.4	3.0	0.8	4.8	4.5	70.2	227.8	108.4	83.5	1,079	895
Russell	1,094	4,018,658	3.7	6.4	0.2	1.1	0.2	2.5	83.0	73.8	48.1	20.2	710	482
Scott	721	2,170,415	5.9	6.0	0.0	0.8	3.3	2.2	79.1	62.5	41.3	16.4	722	496
Shenandoah	1,504	4,472,709	7.1	9.2	3.6	1.5	4.6	6.2	65.6	123.4	60.3	48.9	1,149	882
Smyth	1,259	3,570,921	6.6	8.1	0.4	1.0	11.3	5.6	65.4	92.2	58.8	22.8	718	494
Southampton	717	2,092,925	8.4	10.2	0.0	0.2	6.0	3.3	70.4	53.2	26.3	21.4	1,162	1,013
Spotsylvania	3,637	13,506,224	7.0	5.7	4.9	0.0	3.5	3.8	72.0	382.7	163.4	188.0	1,496	1,158
Stafford	4,475	17,648,377	6.1	5.1	2.8	0.2	2.7	4.7	77.1	448.6	192.3	213.9	1,592	1,307
Surry	386	1,034,084	6.2	6.4	0.0	0.0	0.8	3.6	77.4	29.5	7.5	21.1	3,078	2,927
Sussex	423	1,312,782	12.9	14.1	0.0	0.2	7.5	2.3	61.1	40.7	22.0	10.1	843	685
Tazewell	1,644	4,416,984	7.8	8.5	0.4	2.1	7.4	4.0	67.6	142.1	75.0	40.0	903	580
Warren	1,201	3,547,039	8.8	13.4	0.9	2.4	2.5	5.2	65.3	103.2	45.3	48.1	1,264	942
Washington	2,294	6,382,778	4.2	19.7	0.0	2.6	2.7	7.4	62.3	154.9	83.7	51.1	926	645
Westmoreland	590	1,733,294	11.3	10.8	0.0	0.5	7.2	2.7	66.0	47.8	21.1	21.6	1,230	999
Wise	1,524	4,814,554	7.6	7.5	0.1	1.5	2.6	6.1	72.2	146.0	82.3	52.0	1,271	712
Wythe	1,424	3,649,638	5.6	26.2	0.3	2.6	1.1	5.5	55.4	100.6	52.2	30.2	1,032	628
York	2,630	9,095,299	7.9	5.3	7.7	0.0	3.3	2.6	66.6	226.0	92.7	107.0	1,618	1,182
Independent Cities														
Alexandria city	5,221	27,072,935	10.0	12.5	7.7	2.6	11.9	7.2	44.7	658.7	76.2	498.6	3,408	2,503
Bristol city	765	2,448,312	7.6	15.4	6.1	3.8	8.9	3.5	53.6	72.5	36.3	26.8	1,519	788
Buena Vista city	329	965,276	10.8	5.3	0.0	3.3	1.3	7.0	71.5	22.5	12.2	6.9	1,023	765
Charlottesville city	2,284	8,528,975	9.8	5.8	3.3	6.0	4.6	8.3	55.8	212.5	76.7	93.0	2,116	1,314
Chesapeake city	11,013	41,054,055	4.1	9.2	5.0	1.7	24.6	3.7	49.6	1,127.4	370.1	422.6	1,850	1,301
Colonial Heights city	802	3,016,516	7.0	9.3	9.1	2.9	0.6	5.1	64.2	74.5	26.0	40.1	2,297	1,225
Covington city	279	921,554	6.6	10.3	0.0	0.0	7.9	9.3	65.9	26.1	10.0	11.0	1,904	1,291
Danville city	2,451	7,816,325	9.2	11.3	5.7	3.0	4.1	10.7	51.6	173.3	85.4	50.7	1,180	635
Emporia city	121	358,410	26.1	32.7	0.8	10.3	9.0	14.9	0.0	22.4	7.1	10.4	1,814	786
Fairfax city	414	2,320,342	17.7	23.1	21.4	10.9	3.8	13.9	0.0	121.0	20.6	87.1	3,711	2,469
Falls Church city	720	3,347,248	12.1	9.0	0.2	2.9	0.5	11.6	62.0	84.9	11.0	58.9	4,454	3,374
Franklin city	602	1,874,981	4.7	34.1	3.4	2.6	4.5	7.4	40.0	43.1	23.9	11.8	1,389	766
Fredericksburg city	1,610	5,694,248	7.8	27.8	4.3	5.6	3.2	3.1	44.2	149.0	48.1	67.8	2,483	1,244
Galax city	414	1,172,160	3.5	10.4	0.0	4.3	9.1	11.5	57.5	25.9	13.1	8.9	1,283	595
Hampton city	6,125	20,173,326	6.9	11.1	6.0	1.0	6.7	5.9	61.4	526.3	220.7	218.7	1,599	1,068
Harrisonburg city	1,474	5,157,943	4.1	7.6	6.7	5.8	3.6	11.7	53.6	162.1	48.7	63.4	1,244	631
Hopewell city	1,107	3,758,446	8.1	8.6	4.7	2.5	4.1	11.7	58.7	102.8	47.0	32.3	1,448	1,059
Lexington city	273	881,406	8.8	24.4	4.0	7.7	2.1	13.4	30.0	22.6	6.6	7.8	1,109	687
Lynchburg city	3,057	9,313,489	8.7	9.6	8.0	2.9	7.1	8.5	52.5	265.1	109.0	117.5	1,524	905
Manassas city	1,551	7,149,920	5.0	8.7	4.1	2.5	2.9	8.2	67.1	180.9	61.7	83.5	2,055	1,564
Manassas Park city	547	2,174,966	6.3	8.6	5.6	0.7	1.8	6.3	67.3	58.7	24.8	25.4	1,608	1,293

1. Based on the resident population estimated as of July 1 of the year shown.

Local Government Finances, Government Employment, and Income Taxes

STATE County	Local government finances, 2012 (cont.)									Government employment, 2017			Individual income tax returns, 2016		
	Direct general expenditure							Debt outstanding							
			Percent of total for:											Mean	
	Total (mil dol)	Per capita[1] (dollars)	Education	Health and hospitals	Police protection	Public welfare	Highways	Total (mil dol)	Per capita[1] (dollars)	Federal civilian	Federal military	State and local	Number of returns	adjusted gross income	Mean income tax
	185	186	187	188	189	190	191	192	193	194	195	196	197	198	199
VIRGINIA— Cont'd															
Louisa	99.6	2,980	58.3	1.2	5.3	6.6	0.3	25.5	763	60	115	1,558	16,380	58,840	6,414
Lunenburg	35.6	2,826	62.6	1.1	5.0	6.7	2.1	26.9	2,134	20	36	768	4,830	41,442	3,516
Madison	32.1	2,431	58.6	4.5	8.2	11.2	0.0	15.3	1,157	64	42	538	6,190	59,639	6,850
Mathews	20.3	2,283	58	0.8	7.8	7.9	0.7	9.8	1,108	18	66	367	4,250	60,871	6,712
Mecklenburg	89.8	2,829	48.3	6.5	7.0	4.6	2.7	33.6	1,059	119	96	1,736	13,470	44,485	4,343
Middlesex	23.8	2,198	52.5	2.0	5.6	6.1	0.0	22.7	2,100	21	33	1,016	5,190	58,531	6,636
Montgomery	258.1	2,711	48.5	0.4	8.4	3.5	4.9	475.3	4,993	(19) 330	(19) 418	(19) 17,961	34,850	61,436	7,540
Nelson	40.8	2,750	59.8	0.5	7.1	4.4	0.7	45.5	3,068	48	48	687	7,340	59,494	6,752
New Kent	49.4	2,579	54.5	1.0	4.6	4.2	0.0	60.4	3,152	49	68	949	10,680	90,257	13,989
Northampton	81.1	6,632	27.6	1.0	3.1	3.3	15.7	159.5	13,045	31	67	931	5,960	49,319	5,668
Northumberland	27.3	2,213	57.8	1.2	7.1	6.9	1.7	42.0	3,401	31	40	462	5,960	61,291	7,139
Nottoway	38.9	2,460	57.3	0.4	7.7	6.1	2.3	16.5	1,044	338	54	2,437	6,060	42,976	3,801
Orange	87.3	2,548	55.7	0.6	6.4	3.0	2.0	124.0	3,620	59	115	2,237	16,990	58,727	6,261
Page	66.1	2,765	55.3	0.9	7.9	5.0	2.0	77.1	3,228	195	76	1,135	10,900	45,275	4,123
Patrick	36.7	1,989	67.6	1.0	5.6	2.7	0.2	44.5	2,411	44	56	842	7,320	42,142	3,730
Pittsylvania	127.3	2,026	65.4	0.5	5.2	7.6	0.3	112.9	1,797	(6) 196	(6) 324	(6) 6,415	26,730	46,360	4,422
Powhatan	65.5	2,328	65.3	0.3	6.2	5.1	0.0	103.3	3,675	50	89	1,899	13,580	78,691	10,323
Prince Edward	54.4	2,342	50	0.5	7.0	7.1	5.6	67.7	2,914	65	61	2,448	7,930	44,279	4,193
Prince George	134.6	3,644	45.1	2.0	4.5	2.6	0.3	173.0	4,684	(13) 4,705	(13) 10,033	(13) 3,226	15,460	57,757	5,782
Prince William	1,678.9	3,902	57.5	1.9	5.9	2.5	1.6	1,440.8	3,349	(15) 7,213	(15) 9,225	(15) 24,530	215,980	76,253	9,419
Pulaski	110.5	3,181	43.4	0.7	5.8	9.2	2.0	71.9	2,069	36	107	2,342	14,730	47,008	4,469
Rappahannock	21	2,817	57.1	0.7	5.0	4.4	0.0	10.8	1,446	17	24	310	3,610	73,989	10,495
Richmond	32.3	3,565	42	0.6	4.9	5.4	0.1	11.6	1,280	28	26	1,073	3,520	47,124	4,187
Roanoke	397.1	4,275	42	6.5	5.5	3.6	0.2	497.3	5,353	(20) 2,159	(20) 373	(20) 6,777	46,310	67,679	8,665
Rockbridge	69.2	3,088	45.1	10.9	3.4	9.5	0.0	67.1	2,995	(3) 87	(3) 150	(3) 2,651	10,080	54,074	5,772
Rockingham	234.6	3,031	52.1	2.8	3.5	11.4	1.3	200.1	2,585	(12) 348	(12) 411	(12) 11,500	37,330	56,468	6,065
Russell	71	2,495	57.5	0.7	4.1	8.4	6.4	22.5	790	62	86	1,416	9,780	43,307	3,760
Scott	60.2	2,640	60.3	0.7	6.9	7.1	1.4	30.5	1,339	51	68	1,217	8,200	41,130	3,388
Shenandoah	116.2	2,729	54.8	0.6	6.7	6.1	3.0	146.9	3,449	132	138	2,049	20,790	52,438	5,496
Smyth	94.6	2,984	50.5	0.9	6.6	10.5	2.3	141.0	4,444	71	97	2,918	12,560	40,177	3,188
Southampton	56	3,044	56.1	0.8	3.6	3.8	0.2	67.3	3,657	(9) 74	(9) 78	(9) 2,333	7,540	50,786	4,663
Spotsylvania	378.7	3,013	60.7	0.4	4.3	4.3	2.1	483.9	3,850	(10) 475	(10) 513	(10) 10,157	61,880	67,971	7,999
Stafford	443.1	3,298	62.9	0.3	5.0	3.4	1.5	601.1	4,474	4,637	644	6,301	65,780	78,177	9,457
Surry	27.8	4,061	61.1	1.2	4.9	7.5	0.0	16.2	2,369	9	21	550	3,250	48,090	4,573
Sussex	39.1	3,269	58.6	0.5	7.2	7.5	0.1	26.7	2,229	48	28	1,223	4,380	40,752	3,482
Tazewell	136.7	3,088	44.7	17.2	6.0	6.5	4.1	52.5	1,186	70	128	3,343	15,510	47,088	4,679
Warren	120.1	3,155	38.6	12.5	13.4	5.4	1.5	214.6	5,637	204	125	1,755	18,910	58,194	6,326
Washington	172.4	3,125	41.6	10.5	5.9	3.9	1.1	101.3	1,835	(2) 222	(2) 227	(2) 4,784	22,500	53,115	6,083
Westmoreland	49.6	2,832	53.8	0.8	8.0	6.1	1.5	23.2	1,322	54	57	884	8,550	54,175	5,926
Wise	142.7	3,487	49.3	6.0	6.1	9.8	4.4	186.8	4,565	(16) 222	(16) 127	(16) 3,985	13,440	42,116	3,782
Wythe	103.2	3,530	39.8	0.1	5.8	6.6	2.0	150.9	5,159	86	93	2,302	12,590	43,625	4,029
York	226.9	3,430	55.6	0.6	4.0	2.9	0.0	176.3	2,665	(18) 1,056	(18) 1,988	(18) 3,734	31,830	74,967	9,269
Independent Cities															
Alexandria city	692.1	4,731	34.7	6.0	9.7	6.4	3.7	714.3	4,882	13,933	1,414	8,283	84,170	103,310	17,669
Bristol city	80.9	4,578	41.9	3.1	10.9	5.1	11.6	60.4	3,418	(2)	(2)	(2)	7,140	39,262	3,478
Buena Vista city	21.2	3,164	51.2	2.1	6.2	6.2	4.2	43.1	6,424	(3)	(3)	(3)	2,750	36,476	2,502
Charlottesville city	227.5	5,176	31.3	8.0	7.2	11.1	6.4	151.8	3,454	(4)	(4)	(4)	20,170	95,591	15,832
Chesapeake city	1,112.4	4,870	42.2	24.6	3.6	2.6	4.4	886.9	3,883	1,157	1,552	14,726	111,730	61,971	6,737
Colonial Heights city	69.5	3,974	51.8	0.0	5.3	0.6	4.6	61.6	3,526	(17)	(17)	(17)	8,870	47,965	4,370
Covington city	33.2	5,752	46	0.3	7.1	5.4	4.1	55.3	9,583	(5)	(5)	(5)	2,790	38,548	3,176
Danville city	179.2	4,169	41.3	2.3	5.5	4.2	5.7	156.0	3,628	(6)	(6)	(6)	18,370	39,943	4,073
Emporia city	22.3	3,882	17.9	1.2	14.0	1.4	4.2	14.6	2,551	(7)	(7)	(7)	2,520	34,706	2,735
Fairfax city	112.7	4,804	34.1	0.9	9.6	1.5	4.8	321.3	13,695	(8)	(8)	(8)	12,250	92,320	13,619
Falls Church city	76.6	5,787	47.6	0.3	8.2	2.3	6.9	97.9	7,399	(8)	(8)	(8)	6,730	141,749	25,843
Franklin city	51.8	6,072	32	0.5	5.3	3.8	4.2	22.8	2,673	(9)	(9)	(9)	3,840	42,587	3,649
Fredericksburg city	158.1	5,789	24.4	0.5	4.5	4.2	4.1	451.1	16,521	(10)	(10)	(10)	12,660	62,942	8,689
Galax city	28.7	4,153	45.2	0.7	8.9	5.8	7.1	10.9	1,575	(11)	(11)	(11)	2,840	38,370	3,301
Hampton city	524.9	3,836	44.8	0.8	5.1	5.6	1.2	438.4	3,204	7,220	7,234	8,374	63,630	46,525	4,306
Harrisonburg city	165.9	3,255	39	0.7	4.7	1.8	11.4	529.2	10,380	(12)	(12)	(12)	17,860	44,823	4,349
Hopewell city	116	5,192	43.8	0.5	4.4	5.9	3.4	114.6	5,128	(13)	(13)	(13)	10,450	37,311	2,944
Lexington city	28.1	4,013	24.4	2.6	5.2	2.6	4.3	34.5	4,926	(3)	(3)	(3)	2,350	67,259	8,453
Lynchburg city	262.8	3,408	36.6	0.8	6.5	7.2	2.8	337.4	4,375	(14)	(14)	(14)	31,900	50,543	5,904
Manassas city	169.8	4,182	54	2.2	7.8	0.7	6.2	130.5	3,213	(15)	(15)	(15)	20,580	58,908	6,344
Manassas Park city	60.1	3,803	52	0.2	7.5	2.3	0.9	123.4	7,811	(15)	(15)	(15)	8,240	54,608	5,379

1. Based on the resident population estimated as of July 1 of the year shown. 2. Bristol city is included with Washington county. 3. Buena Vista and Lexington cities are included with Rockbridge county. 4. Charlottesville city is included with Albemarle county. 5. Covington city is included with Alleghany county. 6. Danville city is included with Pittsylvania county. 7. Emporia city is included with Greensville county. 8. Fairfax city and Falls Church city are included with Fairfax county. 9. Franklin city is included with Southampton county. 10. Fredericksburg city is included with Spotsylvania county. 11. Galax city is included with Carroll county. 12. Harrisonburg city is included with Rockingham county. 13. Hopewell city is included with Prince George county. 14. Lynchburg city is included with Campbell county. 15. Manassas and Manassas Park cities are included with Prince William county. 16. Norton city is included with Wise county. 17. Petersburg and Colonial Heights cities are included with Dinwiddie county. 18. Poquoson city is included with York county. 19. Radford city is included with Montgomery county. 20. Salem city is included with Roanoke county.

State / county code	CBSA code[1]	County code[2]	STATE County	Land area[3] (sq. mi)	Total persons 2018	Rank	Per square mile	White	Black	American Indian, Alaska Native	Asian and Pacific Islancer	Percent Hispanic or Latino[4]	Under 5 years	5 to 17 years	18 to 24 years	25 to 34 years	35 to 44 years	45 to 54 years
					Population, 2018			Population and population characteristics, 2018										
								Race alone or in combination, not Hispanic or Latino (percent)					Age (percent)					
				1	2	3	4	5	6	7	8	9	10	11	12	13	14	15
			VIRGINIA— Cont'd															
51690	32,300	4	Martinsville city	11.0	12,902	2,233	1,172.9	46.0	48.3	0.7	1.4	6.1	7.4	17.4	7.6	11.4	10.3	12.9
51700	47,260	1	Newport News city	69.1	178,626	371	2,585.0	45.6	43.3	1.2	4.9	9.2	7.3	15.8	11.8	17.0	12.1	11.0
51710	47,260	1	Norfolk city	53.3	244,076	277	4,579.3	46.0	42.8	1.3	5.3	8.4	6.5	13.1	17.6	19.5	11.4	9.8
51720	13,720	7	Norton city	7.5	3,968	2,903	529.1	87.2	7.1	0.8	2.3	4.8	5.1	14.9	8.7	15.3	12.1	11.8
51730	40,060	1	Petersburg city	22.7	31,567	1,390	1,390.6	16.6	77.8	1.0	1.8	5.2	8.6	14.0	8.6	16.0	9.8	12.3
51735	47,260	1	Poquoson city	15.4	12,190	2,276	791.6	92.9	1.8	0.8	3.5	3.1	4.8	17.3	7.6	10.4	12.4	13.8
51740	47,260	1	Portsmouth city	33.3	94,632	625	2,841.8	39.5	55.1	1.2	2.5	4.7	7.3	16.0	9.0	16.8	12.3	11.0
51750	13,980	3	Radford city	9.7	18,339	1,909	1,890.6	85.0	11.1	0.7	2.7	3.0	3.5	8.9	39.4	12.4	8.5	9.2
51760	40,060	1	Richmond city	59.9	228,783	298	3,819.4	43.2	48.0	0.8	3.1	7.1	5.9	11.6	12.0	22.1	12.0	10.9
51770	40,220	2	Roanoke city	42.5	99,920	599	2,351.1	60.7	30.9	0.8	4.0	6.5	7.1	15.5	7.5	15.5	12.3	12.5
51775	40,220	2	Salem city	14.5	25,643	1,576	1,768.5	86.7	8.6	0.7	2.4	3.4	5.4	14.5	12.6	11.5	10.7	12.8
51790	44,420	3	Staunton city	19.9	24,922	1,610	1,252.4	83.4	13.5	0.9	2.1	3.2	6.5	12.9	7.8	13.7	12.4	11.9
51800	47,260	1	Suffolk city	399.2	91,185	646	228.4	51.2	43.1	0.9	2.9	4.7	6.8	17.5	7.8	13.5	12.8	13.7
51810	47,260	1	Virginia Beach city	244.7	450,189	155	1,839.8	64.5	21.0	1.0	9.3	8.3	6.3	15.8	9.2	16.5	13.2	12.3
51820	44,420	3	Waynesboro city	15.0	22,628	1,697	1,508.5	77.2	14.7	1.0	2.3	8.3	7.4	16.2	7.5	14.2	12.4	11.6
51830	47,260	1	Williamsburg city	8.9	14,896	2,104	1,673.7	70.8	16.7	1.0	7.9	7.0	3.3	8.2	35.4	11.8	7.4	7.5
51840	49,020	3	Winchester city	9.2	28,108	1,495	3,055.2	68.2	12.7	0.7	3.2	18.4	6.7	15.9	10.9	13.9	12.2	12.1
53000		0	WASHINGTON	66,453.0	7,535,591	X	113.4	71.7	5.2	2.5	12.2	12.9	6.1	15.9	8.7	15.3	13.3	12.4
53001	36,830	6	Adams	1,925.0	19,759	1,842	10.3	33.8	0.9	0.8	1.1	64.3	9.7	25.8	9.9	12.5	11.2	10.1
53003	30,300	3	Asotin	636.1	22,610	1,700	35.5	92.2	1.5	2.8	2.0	4.2	5.2	15.1	6.4	11.6	11.2	11.5
53005	28,420	2	Benton	1,700.0	201,877	333	118.8	72.3	2.3	1.6	4.4	22.3	7.2	19.6	8.4	13.7	12.6	11.4
53007	48,300	3	Chelan	2,921.2	77,036	720	26.4	69.1	0.9	1.7	1.8	28.3	6.3	17.1	7.9	12.5	11.8	11.2
53009	38,820	5	Clallam	1,738.7	76,737	725	44.1	85.7	1.5	6.6	3.4	6.4	4.6	12.4	6.2	10.9	10.0	10.0
53011	38,900	1	Clark	628.5	481,857	145	766.7	81.4	3.2	1.8	7.6	10.0	6.1	17.8	8.1	13.3	13.3	13.1
53013	47,460	3	Columbia	868.6	4,059	2,897	4.7	86.9	1.4	2.4	3.8	7.8	5.1	13.8	5.9	10.1	9.7	11.9
53015	31,020	3	Cowlitz	1,140.6	108,987	558	95.6	86.4	1.6	3.1	3.0	9.2	6.2	16.8	7.5	12.3	11.8	12.2
53017	48,300	3	Douglas	1,819.3	42,907	1,119	23.6	65.4	0.9	1.6	1.8	32.1	6.6	19.2	8.4	12.5	11.9	11.3
53019		9	Ferry	2,203.2	7,649	2,620	3.5	77.2	1.6	19.0	2.2	5.0	4.8	12.6	7.4	8.8	10.0	11.9
53021	28,420	2	Franklin	1,241.6	94,347	626	76.0	41.5	2.7	1.0	3.0	53.5	9.0	23.4	9.5	15.5	13.9	10.6
53023		8	Garfield	710.8	2,247	3,025	3.2	91.1	1.2	1.2	3.2	5.4	7.1	14.2	6.1	8.6	11.7	10.6
53025	34,180	5	Grant	2,679.5	97,331	615	36.3	55.0	1.4	1.6	1.6	42.1	7.7	21.7	9.4	13.7	11.8	10.9
53027	10,140	4	Grays Harbor	1,901.3	73,901	744	38.9	82.4	1.9	6.2	2.9	10.2	5.3	15.2	7.0	11.9	11.4	12.1
53029	36,020	4	Island	208.5	84,460	679	405.1	82.6	4.0	2.0	7.8	8.1	5.7	12.4	8.8	14.1	10.2	10.1
53031		6	Jefferson	1,803.7	31,729	1,386	17.6	91.1	1.4	3.6	3.0	3.7	3.0	8.8	4.7	8.5	8.5	10.4
53033	42,660	1	King	2,115.3	2,233,163	12	1,055.7	62.8	8.0	1.6	22.7	9.8	5.8	14.5	8.1	18.3	15.0	13.2
53035	14,740	2	Kitsap	395.1	269,805	256	682.9	81.2	4.3	2.9	9.7	8.0	5.8	14.7	9.6	14.7	11.9	11.7
53037	21,260	4	Kittitas	2,297.3	47,364	1,028	20.6	86.5	1.7	2.1	3.8	8.9	4.6	12.5	21.3	12.7	10.1	10.2
53039		6	Klickitat	1,871.6	22,107	1,716	11.8	84.4	0.9	3.5	1.8	11.9	5.0	14.4	6.2	10.1	11.7	12.5
53041	16,500	4	Lewis	2,402.8	79,604	704	33.1	86.0	1.4	3.0	2.4	10.3	5.9	15.5	7.5	11.9	11.4	12.0
53043		8	Lincoln	2,310.6	10,740	2,370	4.6	93.5	1.0	3.2	1.4	3.5	5.2	16.5	6.4	8.4	10.5	11.1
53045	43,220	4	Mason	959.4	65,507	816	68.3	83.3	2.0	5.0	3.1	10.4	5.3	14.2	7.0	12.0	10.9	11.7
53047		6	Okanogan	5,266.2	42,132	1,134	8.0	67.1	1.1	12.2	1.6	20.5	6.2	16.9	6.7	11.1	11.1	11.1
53049		7	Pacific	932.8	22,036	1,721	23.6	85.0	1.3	4.2	2.9	9.8	4.2	11.7	5.5	9.3	9.7	10.9
53051	44,060	2	Pend Oreille	1,400.3	13,602	2,190	9.7	90.6	1.2	4.7	2.1	3.8	4.4	14.6	6.2	8.7	9.4	12.1
53053	42,660	1	Pierce	1,667.8	891,099	63	534.4	71.8	9.6	2.6	11.8	11.1	6.7	16.8	8.9	15.7	13.3	12.4
53055		9	San Juan	173.9	17,128	1,974	98.5	90.3	1.1	2.0	2.3	6.7	2.9	10.1	5.2	8.3	9.5	11.1
53057	34,580	3	Skagit	1,730.2	128,206	497	74.1	76.2	1.4	2.8	3.5	18.7	6.1	15.8	7.7	12.6	11.8	11.3
53059	38,900	1	Skamania	1,658.3	11,924	2,299	7.2	90.2	1.2	3.0	2.1	6.3	4.4	14.1	6.3	10.3	11.9	13.4
53061	42,660	1	Snohomish	2,086.5	814,901	76	390.6	72.7	4.6	2.2	14.7	10.4	6.4	16.3	7.7	15.0	14.2	13.6
53063	44,060	1	Spokane	1,763.9	514,631	135	291.8	87.7	3.2	2.7	4.5	5.9	6.1	16.1	9.3	15.0	12.3	11.9
53065	44,060	2	Stevens	2,477.4	45,260	1,070	18.3	89.3	1.0	7.3	1.9	3.8	5.4	16.2	6.6	9.4	10.2	11.9
53067	36,500	2	Thurston	722.5	286,419	243	396.4	79.1	4.7	2.7	9.8	9.2	5.8	15.6	8.1	14.5	13.5	12.2
53069		8	Wahkiakum	262.9	4,426	2,865	16.8	90.8	1.3	3.4	3.0	5.3	3.1	14.2	6.1	8.0	8.5	11.6
53071	47,460	3	Walla Walla	1,270.0	60,922	863	48.0	73.4	2.6	1.7	3.2	21.5	5.5	15.5	12.9	12.9	11.5	11.1
53073	13,380	3	Whatcom	2,107.9	225,685	302	107.1	81.8	1.9	3.8	6.7	9.5	5.3	14.1	13.8	13.8	11.9	11.3
53075	39,420	4	Whitman	2,159.3	49,791	991	23.1	81.8	3.1	1.6	10.8	6.6	4.2	10.7	34.4	14.7	9.1	7.6
53077	49,420	3	Yakima	4,294.5	251,446	274	58.6	44.3	1.3	4.5	2.0	49.9	8.1	21.5	9.5	13.4	11.8	11.0
54000		0	WEST VIRGINIA	24,041.2	1,805,832	X	75.1	93.7	4.5	0.8	1.2	1.7	5.3	14.9	8.7	11.9	12.0	13.0
54001		6	Barbour	341.1	16,535	2,007	48.5	97.1	1.6	1.3	0.5	1.0	5.0	14.7	11.5	11.0	11.1	12.4
54003	25,180	2	Berkeley	321.1	117,123	531	364.8	86.6	9.3	0.7	1.7	4.6	6.1	17.1	7.5	14.1	13.3	14.0
54005	16,620	3	Boone	501.5	21,951	1,724	43.8	98.4	1.1	0.4	0.2	0.6	5.1	16.2	7.0	10.2	12.8	13.7
54007		8	Braxton	510.8	14,089	2,156	27.6	97.8	1.1	0.6	0.5	0.8	5.0	14.4	6.7	11.4	11.1	13.4
54009	48,260	3	Brooke	89.2	22,203	1,713	248.9	97.0	2.2	0.5	0.8	0.9	4.4	13.3	9.0	10.2	10.8	12.6
54011	26,580	2	Cabell	281.0	93,224	634	331.8	92.3	6.2	0.7	1.8	1.4	5.4	14.4	13.3	12.3	11.8	11.7

1. CBSA = Core Based Statistical Area. See Appendix A for explanation. See Appendix B for list of metropolitan areas with component counties. Service of USDA Rural-Urban Continuum Codes. See Appendix A for definition.   3. Dry land or land partially or temporarily covered by water.   2. County type code from the Economic Research Service of USDA Rural-Urban Continuum Codes.   4. May be of any race.

Table B. States and Counties — **Population and Households**

STATE County	Population, 2018 (cont.) Age (percent) (cont.)				Population change, 2000-2018 Total persons		Percent change		Components of change, 2010-2018			Households, 2013-2017		Percent		
	55 to 64 years	65 to 74 years	75 years and over	Percent female	2000	2010	2000-2010	2010-2018	Births	Deaths	Net Migration	Number	Persons per household	Family house-holds	Female family house-holder[1]	One person
	16	17	18	19	20	21	22	23	24	25	26	27	28	29	30	31
VIRGINIA— Cont'd																
Martinsville city	14.0	10.4	8.5	53.7	15,416	13,814	-10.4	-6.6	1,615	1,973	-554	5,740	2.24	57.5	19.9	37.2
Newport News city	12.0	7.5	5.6	51.7	180,150	180,994	0.5	-1.3	23,162	12,200	-13,442	68,665	2.51	61.6	17.5	32.0
Norfolk city	10.9	6.7	4.5	47.9	234,403	242,827	3.6	0.5	30,066	16,092	-12,639	87,249	2.52	57.5	17.8	33.4
Norton city	13.4	10.1	8.6	53.2	3,904	3,993	2.3	-0.6	334	336	-26	1,786	2.23	55.4	13.2	39.0
Petersburg city	13.7	9.8	7.1	54.0	33,740	32,435	-3.9	-2.7	4,704	3,685	-1,894	13,262	2.36	54.0	24.0	39.2
Poquoson city	14.3	10.9	8.4	50.0	11,566	12,157	5.1	0.3	785	873	120	4,583	2.61	73.4	9.7	22.0
Portsmouth city	12.6	8.7	6.2	52.0	100,565	95,527	-5.0	-0.9	12,368	8,642	-4,590	36,616	2.52	60.6	20.3	33.2
Radford city	8.9	5.1	4.0	53.0	15,859	16,395	3.4	11.9	1,092	830	1,646	5,503	2.61	43.9	10.8	37.3
Richmond city	12.3	8.0	5.2	52.6	197,790	204,327	3.3	12.0	24,262	15,704	15,527	89,238	2.35	45.2	17.2	42.8
Roanoke city	13.1	9.8	6.7	52.1	94,911	96,912	2.1	3.1	12,221	9,661	480	42,333	2.30	54.6	16.0	37.5
Salem city	13.6	10.6	8.3	52.4	24,747	24,835	0.4	3.3	2,227	2,570	1,159	9,997	2.31	63.1	15.6	32.4
Staunton city	13.5	12.0	9.3	54.1	23,853	23,745	-0.5	5.0	2,600	2,861	1,424	10,477	2.19	56.1	9.9	36.8
Suffolk city	13.5	8.7	5.8	51.6	63,677	84,572	32.8	7.8	9,426	6,118	3,321	32,331	2.70	73.4	16.8	22.5
Virginia Beach city	12.4	8.4	5.8	50.9	425,257	437,903	3.0	2.8	49,717	24,843	-12,496	167,731	2.62	69.2	13.7	24.3
Waynesboro city	12.8	9.7	8.2	52.3	19,520	20,998	7.6	7.8	2,569	2,122	1,191	9,128	2.35	59.5	14.4	34.5
Williamsburg city	10.1	9.0	7.3	54.0	11,998	13,689	14.1	8.8	824	757	1,129	4,649	2.29	45.8	9.6	43.3
Winchester city	12.3	9.3	6.6	51.3	23,585	26,223	11.2	7.2	3,128	2,193	949	10,520	2.52	58.8	13.0	33.9
WASHINGTON	12.8	9.4	6.0	50.0	5,894,121	6,724,540	14.1	12.1	729,978	435,888	516,914	2,755,697	2.55	64.7	10.0	27.1
Adams	9.9	6.8	4.3	49.3	16,428	18,728	14.0	5.5	3,271	981	-1,278	5,824	3.26	76.0	14.1	20.6
Asotin	15.7	12.8	10.5	51.2	20,551	21,623	5.2	4.6	1,927	1,981	1,040	9,235	2.39	62.8	11.1	29.6
Benton	12.3	9.0	5.9	49.9	142,475	175,169	22.9	15.2	21,713	11,056	16,037	70,363	2.68	69.0	11.0	25.2
Chelan	14.0	11.2	7.8	50.0	66,616	72,460	8.8	6.3	7,675	5,517	2,470	27,383	2.70	66.5	9.0	28.6
Clallam	16.3	17.3	12.3	50.7	64,525	71,404	10.7	7.5	5,531	7,839	7,622	32,280	2.24	60.3	10.6	32.2
Clark	12.8	9.7	5.8	50.6	345,238	425,360	23.2	13.3	45,582	26,797	37,667	167,717	2.70	69.8	10.4	23.6
Columbia	15.6	15.7	12.1	51.2	4,064	4,078	0.3	-0.5	294	447	131	1,759	2.22	61.9	9.8	30.8
Cowlitz	14.2	11.3	7.6	50.5	92,948	102,408	10.2	6.4	10,156	9,106	5,547	40,668	2.52	65.9	11.4	27.4
Douglas	12.6	10.2	7.3	49.3	32,603	38,427	17.9	11.7	4,389	2,514	2,623	14,706	2.74	73.5	11.1	20.9
Ferry	17.2	17.4	9.8	48.9	7,260	7,554	4.0	1.3	579	695	215	3,056	2.41	64.5	9.8	30.0
Franklin	9.0	5.9	3.3	48.3	49,347	78,163	58.4	20.7	13,677	3,096	5,454	25,835	3.36	76.9	17.1	19.0
Garfield	16.3	15.0	10.5	51.1	2,397	2,266	-5.5	-0.8	195	212	-4	1,007	2.19	64.8	5.6	29.5
Grant	11.1	8.3	5.4	49.1	74,698	89,124	19.3	9.2	12,570	5,578	1,263	30,512	3.03	72.5	11.7	21.8
Grays Harbor	15.6	13.4	8.3	48.8	67,194	72,798	8.3	1.5	6,429	6,764	1,436	28,070	2.44	63.3	11.9	29.1
Island	14.2	15.1	9.5	50.1	71,558	78,508	9.7	7.6	7,607	5,666	3,990	34,027	2.30	67.9	8.2	25.4
Jefferson	19.1	23.3	13.6	51.1	25,953	29,872	15.1	6.2	1,563	2,928	3,200	13,903	2.14	62.0	7.2	29.0
King	11.9	7.9	5.3	49.8	1,737,034	1,931,292	11.2	15.6	208,954	104,333	197,023	851,077	2.45	60.2	8.6	29.5
Kitsap	13.8	11.1	6.7	48.9	231,969	251,143	8.3	7.4	24,956	17,497	11,107	100,484	2.51	67.6	9.6	25.6
Kittitas	12.6	9.8	6.2	49.6	33,362	40,909	22.6	15.8	3,384	2,446	5,479	17,648	2.34	54.1	7.6	29.5
Klickitat	16.2	15.0	8.9	49.5	19,161	20,317	6.0	8.8	1,706	1,525	1,599	8,247	2.54	65.1	7.2	27.6
Lewis	14.8	12.5	8.5	50.0	68,600	75,457	10.0	5.5	7,455	6,989	3,696	30,036	2.49	66.5	10.7	26.8
Lincoln	16.4	14.9	10.7	48.9	10,184	10,570	3.8	1.6	821	934	285	4,416	2.31	68.3	7.4	27.2
Mason	16.2	14.2	8.6	48.0	49,405	60,692	22.8	7.9	5,308	5,374	4,898	23,034	2.62	66.0	9.5	27.0
Okanogan	15.2	13.4	8.2	49.7	39,564	41,117	3.9	2.5	4,331	3,595	299	17,075	2.36	67.5	11.4	26.9
Pacific	17.9	19.3	11.4	50.1	20,984	20,919	-0.3	5.3	1,600	2,562	2,065	8,786	2.35	62.0	7.9	31.2
Pend Oreille	18.2	17.0	9.0	49.1	11,732	13,001	10.8	4.6	956	1,229	876	5,637	2.30	68.2	8.4	26.3
Pierce	12.5	8.4	5.4	50.3	700,820	795,217	13.5	12.1	94,117	51,866	54,024	312,839	2.64	66.5	11.6	26.4
San Juan	18.9	22.0	12.1	51.6	14,077	15,769	12.0	8.6	705	1,133	1,782	7,718	2.08	60.8	6.3	30.7
Skagit	14.0	12.4	8.4	50.4	102,979	116,893	13.5	9.7	12,080	9,568	8,835	47,341	2.53	67.5	9.9	25.1
Skamania	18.6	13.3	7.8	49.2	9,872	11,070	12.1	7.7	810	682	726	4,713	2.43	66.1	8.3	27.0
Snohomish	13.4	8.4	5.1	49.8	606,024	713,296	17.7	14.2	78,907	42,082	64,778	284,477	2.68	68.4	9.8	23.9
Spokane	13.1	9.8	6.4	50.4	417,939	471,229	12.8	9.2	49,533	35,888	29,979	194,995	2.43	63.4	10.9	29.0
Stevens	17.2	14.6	8.7	50.1	40,066	43,523	8.6	4.0	3,637	3,681	1,806	17,534	2.48	69.2	9.2	25.1
Thurston	13.0	10.7	6.5	51.1	207,355	252,260	21.7	13.5	25,761	17,225	25,634	106,229	2.50	66.3	10.9	26.4
Wahkiakum	16.5	19.5	12.7	49.8	3,824	3,979	4.1	11.2	225	377	600	1,823	2.22	70.4	10.1	23.6
Walla Walla	12.6	10.2	7.9	48.9	55,180	58,781	6.5	3.6	5,520	4,691	1,335	22,391	2.44	64.2	10.1	29.6
Whatcom	12.4	10.7	6.6	50.5	166,814	201,146	20.6	12.2	18,889	13,017	18,679	83,475	2.48	60.8	8.3	27.2
Whitman	8.8	6.0	4.4	49.0	40,740	44,778	9.9	11.2	3,634	2,166	3,467	17,657	2.31	48.3	6.0	32.0
Yakima	10.8	8.0	5.8	50.0	222,581	243,240	9.3	3.4	33,531	15,851	-9,471	81,720	2.99	71.9	14.8	22.9
WEST VIRGINIA	14.3	11.8	8.1	50.5	1,808,344	1,853,001	2.5	-2.5	163,804	182,973	-27,508	737,671	2.42	65.2	11.4	29.4
Barbour	14.2	11.6	8.5	51.3	15,557	16,589	6.6	-0.3	1,391	1,565	116	6,293	2.58	67.1	11.1	25.7
Berkeley	13.2	9.4	5.2	50.4	75,905	104,172	37.2	12.4	11,230	7,993	9,619	42,456	2.61	69.7	12.2	24.8
Boone	14.9	12.8	7.2	50.2	25,535	24,625	-3.6	-10.9	2,115	2,641	-2,163	9,298	2.49	70.2	13.4	25.0
Braxton	15.0	13.7	9.2	49.4	14,702	14,519	-1.2	-3.0	1,233	1,420	-231	5,498	2.54	74.8	11.8	21.8
Brooke	15.7	13.7	10.1	50.9	25,447	24,067	-5.4	-7.7	1,584	2,754	-675	9,961	2.22	64.1	10.5	30.9
Cabell	12.4	10.8	8.0	51.1	96,784	96,297	-0.5	-3.2	9,239	9,918	-2,324	40,239	2.29	56.4	11.9	34.9

1. No spouse present.

Table B. States and Counties — **Population, Vital Statistics, Health, and Crime**

STATE County	Persons in group quarters, 2018	Daytime Population, 2013-2017 Number	Daytime Population, 2013-2017 Employment/ residence ratio	Births, 2018 Total	Births, 2018 Rate[1]	Deaths, 2018 Number	Deaths, 2018 Rate[1]	Persons under 65 with no health insurance, 2016 Number	Persons under 65 with no health insurance, 2016 Percent	Medicare, 2018 Total beneficiaries	Medicare, 2018 Enrolled in Original Medicare	Medicare, 2018 Enrolled in Medicare Advantage	Serious crimes known to police[2], 2016 Total Number	Serious crimes known to police[2], 2016 Total Rate[3]
	32	33	34	35	36	37	38	39	40	41	42	43	44	45
VIRGINIA— Cont'd														
Martinsville city..................	377	16,734	1.66	200	15.5	181	14.0	1,097	10.6	3,961	3,020	941	392	2,892
Newport News city	7,956	206,340	1.29	2,648	14.8	1,509	8.4	16,931	11.2	27,963	20,844	7,119	6,454	3,552
Norfolk city	34,020	303,468	1.46	3,404	13.9	2,102	8.6	21,989	11.8	32,699	24,520	8,179	11,261	4,583
Norton city	68	3,632	0.74	27	6.8	32	8.1	323	10.1	1,190	786	404	160	4,091
Petersburg city..................	884	33,356	1.10	649	20.6	446	14.1	3,141	12.0	7,171	5,447	1,724	1,312	4,063
Poquoson city	51	8,658	0.44	105	8.6	103	8.4	617	6.3	2,515	2,209	306	191	1,595
Portsmouth city	3,057	104,850	1.21	1,354	14.3	1,042	11.0	7,963	10.2	18,097	13,613	4,484	6,226	6,498
Radford city......................	3,473	17,113	0.96	137	7.5	80	4.4	1,172	8.9	2,042	1,682	360	400	2,285
Richmond city	12,514	288,572	1.63	2,987	13.1	2,193	9.6	22,098	12.0	33,832	23,045	10,787	9,343	4,200
Roanoke city	2,113	124,962	1.55	1,484	14.9	1,166	11.7	10,943	13.3	20,527	14,962	5,565	4,615	4,616
Salem city	1,991	35,624	1.82	292	11.4	314	12.2	1,601	8.3	6,141	4,901	1,240	552	2,174
Staunton city	993	23,904	0.97	359	14.4	302	12.1	1,761	9.5	6,229	5,460	769	576	2,361
Suffolk city.......................	992	81,138	0.83	1,172	12.9	836	9.2	6,705	8.8	16,029	12,744	3,285	2,398	2,714
Virginia Beach city	9,620	421,306	0.88	5,670	12.6	3,344	7.4	33,040	8.6	70,947	58,318	12,629	10,590	2,338
Waynesboro city	192	21,119	0.95	341	15.1	232	10.3	2,153	12.2	4,759	4,130	629	528	2,460
Williamsburg city	4,279	22,429	2.26	87	5.8	99	6.6	1,011	12.1	2,583	2,199	384	255	1,671
Winchester city	1,079	40,699	2.00	386	13.7	255	9.1	3,237	14.5	5,171	4,553	618	NA	NA
WASHINGTON	143,185	7,122,588	0.99	90,495	12.0	57,568	7.6	420,125	6.9	1,319,672	894,410	425,262	276,676	3,796
Adams...............................	162	19,555	1.04	388	19.6	107	5.4	2,111	12.6	2,484	2,163	321	576	2,966
Asotin...............................	174	19,108	0.67	216	9.6	248	11.0	1,134	6.6	6,152	5,208	944	792	3,556
Benton..............................	1,422	192,451	1.02	2,720	13.5	1,437	7.1	12,075	7.3	34,412	33,675	737	4,748	2,448
Chelan..............................	931	78,935	1.11	891	11.6	665	8.6	5,961	9.7	16,986	13,013	3,973	1,909	2,494
Clallam.............................	1,871	72,265	0.96	670	8.7	1,017	13.3	4,592	8.9	26,053	25,315	738	2,141	2,887
Clark.................................	3,425	410,765	0.78	5,694	11.8	3,590	7.5	25,879	6.5	85,476	36,641	48,835	10,346	2,210
Columbia...........................	75	4,086	1.05	38	9.4	47	11.6	193	6.9	1,278	1,240	38	137	3,488
Cowlitz.............................	1,208	102,778	0.98	1,320	12.1	1,177	10.8	6,018	7.2	25,737	12,858	12,879	3,735	3,588
Douglas............................	190	35,070	0.69	541	12.6	317	7.4	3,332	9.8	7,793	6,068	1,725	889	2,163
Ferry................................	252	7,317	0.89	75	9.8	83	10.9	625	11.1	2,246	2,194	52	28	428
Franklin............................	2,901	83,517	0.85	1,622	17.2	442	4.7	9,282	11.8	10,130	9,740	390	2,014	2,207
Garfield............................	36	2,016	0.77	27	12.0	23	10.2	80	4.8	647	634	13	66	2,974
Grant................................	1,225	95,023	1.04	1,468	15.1	699	7.2	9,137	11.5	15,580	13,115	2,465	3,956	4,192
Grays Harbor.....................	2,696	69,359	0.92	742	10.0	860	11.6	4,357	8.0	19,575	18,542	1,033	2,016	2,903
Island...............................	1,941	71,575	0.76	976	11.6	735	8.7	3,839	6.3	22,645	16,744	5,901	1,034	1,289
Jefferson...........................	628	29,990	0.95	179	5.6	373	11.8	1,477	7.5	12,635	12,207	428	536	1,746
King..................................	38,771	2,303,740	1.17	26,097	11.7	13,730	6.1	104,849	5.6	310,781	192,734	118,047	99,598	4,604
Kitsap...............................	9,300	247,842	0.91	3,098	11.5	2,354	8.7	13,378	6.3	53,957	42,490	11,467	7,664	2,915
Kittitas.............................	2,617	41,708	0.90	425	9.0	312	6.6	2,769	7.8	8,480	7,853	627	1,059	2,412
Klickitat............................	198	20,847	0.96	214	9.7	215	9.7	1,363	8.4	5,976	5,829	147	263	1,238
Lewis................................	935	73,347	0.91	955	12.0	882	11.1	4,671	7.8	20,265	13,456	6,809	2,373	3,138
Lincoln..............................	94	9,864	0.88	105	9.8	116	10.8	521	6.8	2,996	2,911	85	175	1,697
Mason...............................	2,791	55,703	0.74	684	10.4	677	10.3	4,503	9.9	17,064	13,696	3,368	1,755	2,862
Okanogan..........................	640	41,963	1.04	510	12.1	484	11.5	4,434	13.8	10,516	9,289	1,227	691	1,656
Pacific..............................	282	20,651	0.96	194	8.8	340	15.4	1,419	9.6	7,863	7,519	344	314	1,501
Pend Oreille	98	12,526	0.87	120	8.8	160	11.8	705	7.2	3,883	3,738	145	308	2,340
Pierce...............................	17,439	792,070	0.86	11,722	13.2	7,181	8.1	47,893	6.5	147,236	98,456	48,780	37,711	4,399
San Juan...........................	187	16,416	1.03	84	4.9	126	7.4	974	8.8	5,698	4,592	1,106	187	1,139
Skagit...............................	1,625	122,330	1.01	1,499	11.7	1,261	9.8	8,328	8.5	30,255	21,794	8,461	4,590	3,722
Skamania..........................	25	9,466	0.56	102	8.6	91	7.6	651	7.0	2,480	2,266	214	78	682
Snohomish........................	9,983	686,675	0.78	10,138	12.4	5,757	7.1	43,348	6.4	123,130	65,960	57,170	23,553	2,991
Spokane............................	14,276	500,611	1.04	6,098	11.8	4,695	9.1	25,701	6.3	102,207	63,206	39,001	28,297	5,697
Stevens............................	266	40,257	0.78	444	9.8	475	10.5	2,677	7.8	12,285	11,647	638	806	1,842
Thurston...........................	4,096	257,293	0.90	3,187	11.1	2,273	7.9	12,634	5.6	58,026	36,998	21,028	8,757	3,196
Wahkiakum	48	4,148	1.04	21	4.7	43	9.7	222	7.9	1,453	1,049	404	51	1,252
Walla Walla	4,819	63,665	1.15	645	10.6	601	9.9	3,719	8.2	12,835	11,508	1,327	2,078	3,414
Whatcom..........................	5,720	209,130	0.96	2,293	10.2	1,675	7.4	15,140	8.6	44,788	28,715	16,073	7,159	3,325
Whitman...........................	6,332	50,526	1.13	427	8.6	248	5.0	2,397	6.4	5,822	5,631	191	997	2,083
Yakima.............................	3,506	248,000	1.00	3,866	15.4	2,052	8.2	27,737	13.2	41,847	33,714	8,133	9,833	3,922
WEST VIRGINIA.............	47,916	1,819,263	0.98	18,010	10.0	22,551	12.5	94,163	6.5	433,710	298,418	135,292	44,044	2,405
Barbour.............................	905	14,228	0.59	160	9.7	190	11.5	912	7.2	3,910	2,903	1,007	240	1,444
Berkeley............................	895	93,615	0.65	1,357	11.6	1,066	9.1	6,179	6.4	20,977	16,389	4,588	2,567	2,277
Boone...............................	135	23,339	1.02	226	10.3	309	14.1	1,176	6.4	5,920	3,427	2,493	391	1,800
Braxton.............................	395	13,788	0.89	121	8.6	171	12.1	787	7.2	3,606	2,410	1,196	189	1,473
Brooke..............................	727	21,566	0.85	190	8.6	293	13.2	889	5.2	5,970	3,711	2,259	191	1,017
Cabell...............................	3,934	110,298	1.37	1,026	11.0	1,189	12.8	4,763	6.3	21,223	13,982	7,241	4,056	4,210

1. Per 1,000 estimated resident population.   2. Data for serious crimes have not been adjusted for underreporting; this may affect comparability between geographic areas and over time.   3. Per 100,000 population estimated by the FBI.

Table B. States and Counties — Crime, Education, Money Income, and Poverty

STATE County	Serious crimes known to police[2], 2016 (cont.)[1] Rate Violent	Property	School enrollment and attainment, 2013-2017 Enrollment Total	Percent private	Attainment[4] (percent) High school graduate or less	Bachelor's degree or more	Local government expenditures,[5] 2014-2015 Total current spending (mil dol)	Current spending per student (dollars)	Per capita income[6]	Households Median income (dollars)	Percent with income of less than $50,000	Percent with income of $200,000 or more	Median household income (dollars)	Percent below poverty level All persons	Children under 18 years	Children 5 to 17 years in families
	46	47	48	49	50	51	52	53	54	55	56	57	58	59	60	61
VIRGINIA— Cont'd																
Martinsville city	207	2,686	3,016	14.9	49.1	20.9	25.7	11,170	22,544	33,545	63.0	2.5	34,463	22.5	34.4	34.1
Newport News city	472	3,080	49,695	12.9	38.6	24.8	310.9	10,522	26,028	51,082	49.0	2.7	49,635	17.2	25.2	26.6
Norfolk city	659	3,923	67,195	12.2	38.5	27.3	350.1	10,844	26,670	47,137	52.8	3.4	48,218	20.9	27.9	27.3
Norton city	409	3,682	880	4.4	41.0	17.0	7.3	8,688	19,297	26,971	69.5	1.3	33,442	22.3	33.5	30.2
Petersburg city	740	3,323	6,516	12.1	52.8	17.5	48.4	11,205	21,992	33,939	66.5	1.2	36,038	21.8	34.5	39.2
Poquoson city	167	1,428	3,088	13.2	28.6	41.5	20.8	9,916	39,305	88,328	27.4	8.7	99,089	5.0	5.7	4.8
Portsmouth city	796	5,702	23,738	13.6	43.3	21.9	159.9	10,601	24,291	48,727	51.2	1.6	48,532	18.5	30.6	29.9
Radford city	474	1,811	9,197	3.1	34.8	34.4	15.6	9,358	19,539	36,082	63.4	2.0	40,941	28.6	17.5	16.2
Richmond city	569	3,632	55,963	17.5	38.5	37.5	317.4	13,024	30,113	42,356	56.3	5.2	46,073	24.0	35.2	37.9
Roanoke city	412	4,204	22,095	13.5	46.8	23.2	166.5	12,202	24,697	41,483	58.2	2.5	43,135	19.3	29.4	29.4
Salem city	95	2,079	6,818	25.4	41.5	27.7	40.3	10,438	30,141	53,990	45.3	4.1	54,989	10.8	13.4	14.1
Staunton city	168	2,193	4,970	29.8	39.4	33.8	31.7	11,195	27,571	46,435	53.3	2.4	51,551	13.1	21.0	21.5
Suffolk city	281	2,434	23,512	18.3	39.4	27.2	136.1	9,473	31,239	68,089	36.5	4.7	68,961	11.3	16.6	16.4
Virginia Beach city	155	2,183	117,625	18.0	28.5	34.8	766.4	10,930	34,607	70,500	33.1	5.9	72,126	8.3	11.2	10.9
Waynesboro city	186	2,274	4,767	10.5	46.9	22.3	32.9	10,179	23,640	42,112	56.6	1.2	44,008	14.9	21.7	21.6
Williamsburg city	164	1,508	7,235	5.1	25.4	55.2	(7)	(7)	26,921	54,606	45.5	7.1	53,737	22.5	23.0	22.6
Winchester city	NA	NA	6,939	29.2	43.6	32.5	(8)	(8)	28,429	49,330	50.7	5.7	49,588	12.6	19.7	18.8
WASHINGTON	302	3,494	1,726,179	14.8	31.7	34.5	11,519.4	10,734	34,869	66,174	37.7	7.3	70,942	11.0	14.2	13.4
Adams	206	2,760	5,565	3.8	60.8	13.6	49.1	10,436	18,415	48,131	51.3	1.5	48,056	15.8	20.5	19.4
Asotin	184	3,372	4,705	6.6	38.7	21.4	35.4	10,731	26,878	47,483	50.7	2.2	50,777	12.9	21.3	18.7
Benton	196	2,252	50,052	12.6	34.6	30.0	341.3	9,642	30,511	63,001	38.9	5.7	64,717	12.0	16.5	15.4
Chelan	161	2,334	17,283	10.4	44.6	26.3	155.7	11,678	27,605	54,975	46.1	3.6	57,284	13.3	17.0	16.8
Clallam	302	2,585	13,661	9.0	35.3	25.0	103.2	9,866	28,857	48,002	52.0	2.7	49,070	16.4	25.5	21.8
Clark	231	1,979	115,324	12.1	32.5	29.0	843.6	10,616	32,162	67,832	36.1	5.7	74,243	10.2	13.6	12.2
Columbia	76	3,411	751	11.5	35.1	26.5	5.8	12,246	28,950	46,250	53.6	5.3	50,322	13.5	20.8	19.4
Cowlitz	269	3,319	23,430	11.0	42.3	16.1	170.1	10,186	25,878	49,804	50.2	2.3	50,617	16.4	21.0	18.7
Douglas	112	2,051	9,890	6.7	47.9	18.3	83.2	10,412	25,060	55,805	43.6	2.2	54,580	13.4	19.3	17.9
Ferry	107	321	1,488	16.2	45.7	17.5	13.0	15,253	21,951	41,081	59.3	0.6	43,665	17.3	26.9	23.6
Franklin	189	2,019	26,359	7.4	52.3	16.3	203.7	10,572	22,125	60,275	41.0	3.0	61,285	13.4	18.2	17.5
Garfield	90	2,884	502	2.4	35.8	23.0	4.3	13,631	24,781	51,399	47.7	0.3	52,682	14.0	22.2	21.6
Grant	268	3,924	25,493	6.6	51.2	16.7	199.9	10,278	22,508	52,382	47.0	2.5	55,807	14.7	20.3	19.1
Grays Harbor	212	2,691	14,589	7.9	44.7	15.2	120.7	11,753	24,081	45,483	53.8	2.0	47,619	18.3	26.1	23.2
Island	112	1,177	15,595	15.6	27.6	32.4	81.5	10,104	33,837	61,516	40.0	4.2	63,529	9.2	12.1	12.0
Jefferson	134	1,612	4,075	14.5	26.3	39.9	32.4	11,905	32,317	51,842	47.8	3.6	53,364	12.7	20.7	18.7
King	347	4,257	493,964	19.1	22.9	50.3	2,906.0	11,167	46,316	83,571	30.1	13.4	89,519	9.3	11.6	11.6
Kitsap	260	2,656	57,423	12.5	28.2	31.8	387.1	10,725	34,412	68,336	35.5	5.7	72,795	8.3	10.8	9.9
Kittitas	112	2,300	14,340	8.5	32.8	35.0	50.1	10,051	26,698	53,163	47.2	2.2	56,393	14.2	14.2	13.1
Klickitat	104	1,135	4,176	17.8	40.3	25.8	37.4	11,973	25,069	51,258	48.0	1.9	55,282	14.5	21.5	20.3
Lewis	180	2,958	16,286	11.6	43.3	15.4	124.7	10,476	23,853	46,387	52.6	1.5	50,086	15.0	21.4	19.3
Lincoln	116	1,581	2,167	9.9	38.9	22.9	29.4	14,216	26,918	49,460	50.7	2.4	53,504	12.6	17.0	15.6
Mason	207	2,655	11,423	7.6	43.6	17.8	87.3	10,925	26,312	53,087	46.7	2.7	55,030	14.5	23.0	19.6
Okanogan	177	1,478	8,442	9.8	48.7	18.3	96.0	9,637	22,755	42,598	58.1	1.4	44,819	20.4	28.6	24.3
Pacific	158	1,343	3,747	6.0	43.3	17.0	36.1	11,967	23,050	39,895	60.1	1.2	45,526	16.9	25.2	24.8
Pend Oreille	198	2,142	2,495	14.8	40.8	20.1	15.9	12,183	26,128	49,184	50.9	2.0	48,574	16.3	26.6	23.0
Pierce	483	3,916	205,480	14.9	36.5	26.0	1,379.8	10,609	31,157	63,881	38.1	4.9	69,027	10.2	12.1	11.9
San Juan	61	1,078	2,366	24.5	20.6	48.3	21.1	10,834	40,784	60,271	42.0	6.7	59,538	10.3	14.8	13.1
Skagit	185	3,537	26,319	10.1	37.2	25.6	231.3	12,066	30,069	59,263	42.1	4.5	65,505	11.3	15.8	14.4
Skamania	70	612	2,247	10.5	38.7	23.2	12.0	10,702	28,644	53,606	47.4	2.4	59,639	12.0	17.8	15.6
Snohomish	225	2,765	184,828	15.2	31.7	31.3	1,345.7	10,291	35,737	78,020	30.2	7.3	82,405	7.3	8.8	7.9
Spokane	360	5,337	123,646	17.3	31.4	29.4	792.3	10,580	28,325	52,159	48.0	3.4	53,438	14.1	17.0	15.5
Stevens	112	1,730	8,873	15.2	44.0	18.6	69.2	11,580	24,707	47,272	52.1	2.3	52,136	14.8	23.6	22.0
Thurston	246	2,949	63,136	14.1	28.3	34.4	452.3	10,954	32,410	66,113	36.4	4.5	71,370	10.5	12.5	11.0
Wahkiakum	221	1,031	720	19.3	41.8	17.1	4.6	10,002	26,964	49,508	50.4	2.4	53,694	12.3	22.9	21.4
Walla Walla	261	3,153	16,043	31.0	32.7	29.1	96.0	10,670	26,651	52,630	47.6	3.7	54,243	13.6	18.0	17.3
Whatcom	199	3,126	57,529	12.7	30.8	33.8	281.6	10,627	29,186	56,419	44.4	3.6	61,026	13.0	13.1	11.8
Whitman	176	1,908	23,679	4.5	21.7	48.4	55.5	11,967	22,154	41,574	58.0	3.1	44,913	21.4	14.2	13.4
Yakima	302	3,620	68,088	8.2	55.1	15.9	561.7	10,469	21,510	47,470	52.5	2.5	47,573	18.1	26.1	24.2
WEST VIRGINIA	358	2,047	398,364	10.3	54.6	19.9	3,159.9	11,273	24,774	44,061	55.3	2.5	43,238	18.5	24.4	22.3
Barbour	451	993	3,861	21.2	60.2	15.3	24.0	9,810	20,762	37,516	65.1	0.7	37,255	21.2	28.1	26.0
Berkeley	179	2,098	27,593	12.7	49.9	20.7	197.3	10,566	27,658	59,480	40.5	2.0	59,071	11.8	16.6	15.8
Boone	207	1,593	4,830	8.3	71.0	7.9	59.8	13,433	20,992	37,955	61.0	1.4	38,584	21.4	29.7	25.9
Braxton	281	1,193	2,694	6.8	66.0	15.7	22.0	10,346	20,633	41,266	57.2	0.8	37,762	22.5	31.0	30.5
Brooke	149	868	5,127	24.4	49.1	19.9	37.6	12,020	25,630	48,835	51.2	1.3	50,775	13.2	19.4	18.1
Cabell	461	3,749	23,856	8.4	45.0	25.7	144.3	10,926	24,646	37,816	60.2	3.0	38,191	26.1	30.4	27.2

1. Data for serious crimes have not been adjusted for underreporting; this may affect comparability between geographic areas and over time.   2. Per 100,000 population estimated by the FBI.   3. All persons 3 years old and over enrolled in nursery school through college.   4. Persons 25 years old and over.   5. Elementary and secondary education expenditures.   6. Based on population estimated by the American Community Survey, 2013–2017.   7. Williamsburg city is included with James City county.   8. Winchester city is included with Frederick county.

Table B. States and Counties — **Personal Income and Earnings**

STATE County	Personal income, 2017										Earnings, 2017		
	Total (mil dol)	Percent change 2016-2017	Per capita[1]		Wages and salaries (mil dol)	Supplements to wages and salaries, employer contributions (mil dol)		Proprietors' income (mil dol)	Dividends, interest, and rent (mil dol)	Personal transfer receipts (mil dol)	Total (mil dol)	Contributions for government social insurance (mil dol)	
			Dollars	Rank		Pension and insurance	Government social insurance					From employee and self-employed	From employer
	62	63	64	65	66	67	68	69	70	71	72	73	74

STATE County	62	63	64	65	66	67	68	69	70	71	72	73	74
VIRGINIA— Cont'd													
Martinsville city	(2)	(2)	(2)	(2)	(2)	(2)	(2)	(2)	(2)	(2)	(2)	(2)	(2)
Newport News city	7,471	2.6	41,646	1,310	6,011	1,145	459	262	1,495	1,515	7,877	448	459
Norfolk city	9,811	2.9	40,094	1,536	11,014	2,467	923	287	2,566	1,963	14,691	765	923
Norton city	(3)	(3)	(3)	(3)	(3)	(3)	(3)	(3)	(3)	(3)	(3)	(3)	(3)
Petersburg city	(4)	(4)	(4)	(4)	(4)	(4)	(4)	(4)	(4)	(4)	(4)	(4)	(4)
Poquoson city	(5)	(5)	(5)	(5)	(5)	(5)	(5)	(5)	(5)	(5)	(5)	(5)	(5)
Portsmouth city	3,785	3.6	40,026	1,547	2,902	781	244	74	748	978	4,002	221	244
Radford city	(6)	(6)	(6)	(6)	(6)	(6)	(6)	(6)	(6)	(6)	(6)	(6)	(6)
Richmond city	12,165	5.0	53,581	321	10,173	1,736	710	1,351	3,170	1,950	13,970	795	710
Roanoke city	4,188	2.7	41,946	1,269	3,444	547	263	291	942	1,055	4,545	279	263
Salem city	(7)	(7)	(7)	(7)	(7)	(7)	(7)	(7)	(7)	(7)	(7)	(7)	(7)
Staunton city	(8)	(8)	(8)	(8)	(8)	(8)	(8)	(8)	(8)	(8)	(8)	(8)	(8)
Suffolk city	4,492	4.2	49,779	473	1,602	281	119	166	811	792	2,168	137	119
Virginia Beach city	24,822	3.2	55,108	276	9,419	1,673	721	1,410	5,746	3,418	13,223	780	721
Waynesboro city	(8)	(8)	(8)	(8)	(8)	(8)	(8)	(8)	(8)	(8)	(8)	(8)	(8)
Williamsburg city	(9)	(9)	(9)	(9)	(9)	(9)	(9)	(9)	(9)	(9)	(9)	(9)	(9)
Winchester city	(10)	(10)	(10)	(10)	(10)	(10)	(10)	(10)	(10)	(10)	(10)	(10)	(10)
WASHINGTON	428,765	6.1	57,743	X	218,077	30,299	18,388	35,590	96,125	61,992	302,354	17,619	18,388
Adams	812	3.6	41,603	1,318	296	54	32	126	192	179	508	23	32
Asotin	1,011	4.7	44,848	920	263	47	25	81	222	275	416	30	25
Benton	9,034	3.8	45,587	839	4,952	680	448	835	1,489	1,627	6,915	398	448
Chelan	3,936	4.5	51,434	398	1,809	298	186	412	978	788	2,705	153	186
Clallam	3,269	4.6	43,316	1,101	1,008	209	96	192	908	977	1,507	112	96
Clark	23,769	5.7	50,078	460	8,532	1,317	768	1,617	4,820	3,880	12,234	758	768
Columbia	186	2.4	45,918	805	56	13	5	24	41	54	99	6	5
Cowlitz	4,585	5.0	42,888	1,151	1,977	308	188	348	733	1,226	2,822	184	188
Douglas	1,637	4.9	39,037	1,717	482	85	51	99	346	362	716	43	51
Ferry	272	2.5	35,771	2,233	73	19	7	10	59	97	109	9	7
Franklin	3,278	3.3	35,587	2,259	1,421	248	151	357	477	666	2,176	113	151
Garfield	94	5.9	42,429	1,212	33	10	3	5	22	28	51	3	3
Grant	3,645	1.6	38,308	1,825	1,616	303	173	459	630	859	2,552	128	173
Grays Harbor	2,792	5.4	38,406	1,810	987	189	94	163	538	898	1,433	99	94
Island	4,339	5.7	52,174	370	1,132	273	111	298	1,199	861	1,814	113	111
Jefferson	1,530	5.7	48,975	541	372	75	35	130	544	420	612	48	35
King	182,495	6.7	83,383	30	115,979	12,694	8,860	16,960	47,716	15,012	154,493	8,842	8,860
Kitsap	13,989	5.8	52,508	358	5,428	1,268	502	733	3,439	2,318	7,931	461	502
Kittitas	1,858	4.9	40,218	1,517	660	129	64	158	458	367	1,011	61	64
Klickitat	985	6.6	45,143	884	396	71	41	87	231	267	594	37	41
Lewis	3,209	6.4	41,041	1,402	1,139	203	111	218	550	931	1,671	112	111
Lincoln	456	1.1	43,145	1,124	113	28	11	54	111	122	206	13	11
Mason	2,580	6.6	40,500	1,473	610	130	57	146	553	709	943	70	57
Okanogan	1,726	3.1	41,344	1,356	612	130	65	166	373	501	973	58	65
Pacific	868	3.9	40,150	1,530	267	55	27	61	204	315	410	31	27
Pend Oreille	524	4.5	39,247	1,683	155	34	14	22	116	171	225	17	14
Pierce	43,149	6.5	49,214	518	18,130	3,182	1,695	3,316	7,639	7,595	26,323	1,514	1,695
San Juan	1,206	5.3	72,153	59	230	37	22	128	635	178	416	29	22
Skagit	6,219	6.0	49,505	496	2,542	473	241	547	1,422	1,284	3,802	227	241
Skamania	519	6.2	43,851	1,037	82	17	8	24	123	106	131	10	8
Snohomish	42,009	6.5	52,405	362	18,051	2,683	1,578	2,929	6,457	5,540	25,241	1,485	1,578
Spokane	22,251	5.2	43,962	1,027	11,305	1,821	1,034	1,469	4,443	4,878	15,629	955	1,034
Stevens	1,677	4.0	37,499	1,946	441	93	43	96	329	525	673	51	43
Thurston	13,705	6.5	48,845	551	5,932	1,123	538	868	2,883	2,537	8,461	504	538
Wahkiakum	176	6.2	41,270	1,370	30	7	3	9	45	53	49	4	3
Walla Walla	2,603	3.0	42,973	1,145	1,224	230	120	241	577	585	1,815	102	120
Whatcom	10,191	5.5	46,028	791	4,396	772	418	1,006	2,332	1,869	6,592	393	418
Whitman	1,839	4.3	37,486	1,949	922	254	84	157	439	317	1,417	73	84
Yakima	10,341	3.8	41,331	1,361	4,426	739	476	1,040	1,854	2,613	6,681	352	476
WEST VIRGINIA	69,873	3.4	38,454	X	30,875	5,495	2,557	3,941	10,769	20,081	42,867	3,018	2,557
Barbour	503	3.4	30,472	2,886	134	25	11	23	69	170	194	17	11
Berkeley	4,540	4.3	39,509	1,639	1,523	303	131	225	565	840	2,181	147	131
Boone	701	1.8	31,368	2,823	237	42	20	30	77	279	329	28	20
Braxton	433	2.1	30,406	2,896	138	26	12	30	62	154	206	17	12
Brooke	886	2.9	39,457	1,650	345	61	29	46	137	260	481	35	29
Cabell	3,735	1.2	39,335	1,666	2,352	394	195	135	645	1,093	3,076	208	195

1. Based on the resident population estimated as of July 1 of the year shown.   2. Martinsville city is included with Henry county.   3. Norton city is included with Wise county.   4. Petersburg and Colonial Heights cities are included with Dinwiddie county.   5. Poquoson city is included with York county.   6. Radford city is included with Montgomery county.   7. Salem city is included with Roanoke county.   8. Staunton and Waynesboro cities are included with Augusta county.   9. Williamsburg city is included with James City county.   10. Winchester city is included with Frederick county.

Table B. States and Counties — Earnings, Social Security, and Housing

STATE County	Earnings, 2017 (cont.) Percent by selected industries									Social Security beneficiaries, December 2017		Supplemental Security Income recipients, 2017	Housing units, 2018	
	Farm	Mining, quarrying, and extractions	Construction	Manu-facturing	Information; professional, scientific, technical services	Retail trade	Finance, insurance, real estate, and leasing	Health care and social assistance	Govern-ment	Number	Rate[1]		Total	Percent change, 2010-2018
	75	76	77	78	79	80	81	82	83	84	85	86	87	88
VIRGINIA— Cont'd														
Martinsville city	(2)	(2)	(2)	(2)	(2)	(2)	(2)	(2)	(2)	4,125	314	44	7,056	-2.0
Newport News city	0.0	0.0	3.4	28.8	7.9	4.1	3.4	10.5	24.5	30,160	168	4,895	78,010	2.2
Norfolk city	0.0	D	2.5	2.8	7.7	2.6	4.2	10.4	51.5	35,170	144	7,700	98,218	3.4
Norton city	(3)	(3)	(3)	(3)	(3)	(3)	(3)	(3)	(3)	1,410	358	370	1,960	-0.5
Petersburg city	(4)	(4)	(4)	(4)	(4)	(4)	(4)	(4)	(4)	8,065	254	3,056	16,349	0.1
Poquoson city	(5)	(5)	(5)	(5)	(5)	(5)	(5)	(5)	(5)	2,550	212	77	4,835	2.2
Portsmouth city	0.0	0.0	4.1	D	3.9	2.4	1.2	9.7	63.3	19,005	201	3,954	40,899	0.2
Radford city	(6)	(6)	(6)	(6)	(6)	(6)	(6)	(6)	(6)	2,320	131	390	6,520	1.5
Richmond city	0.0	D	3.7	3.7	16.4	2.1	9.1	12.1	26.4	35,420	156	9,560	101,065	2.7
Roanoke city	0.0	D	6.4	D	8.2	6.3	8.3	21.1	13.3	21,840	219	4,817	47,008	-0.8
Salem city	(7)	(7)	(7)	(7)	(7)	(7)	(7)	(7)	(7)	6,410	248	591	10,867	0.2
Staunton city	(8)	(8)	(8)	(8)	(8)	(8)	(8)	(8)	(8)	6,870	280	805	11,840	0.9
Suffolk city	0.5	0.0	5.2	7.4	14.7	5.7	3.9	12.7	26.6	16,990	188	2,342	37,338	13.0
Virginia Beach city	0.0	D	7.1	3.2	11.3	6.5	10.7	12.0	27.2	73,190	162	5,676	186,117	4.7
Waynesboro city	(8)	(8)	(8)	(8)	(8)	(8)	(8)	(8)	(8)	5,305	238	737	10,020	3.1
Williamsburg city	(9)	(9)	(9)	(9)	(9)	(9)	(9)	(9)	(9)	2,535	169	12	5,297	7.7
Winchester city	(10)	(10)	(10)	(10)	(10)	(10)	(10)	(10)	(10)	5,465	196	746	11,978	0.8
WASHINGTON	1.3	0.1	6.9	9.1	17.3	8.5	6.1	10.3	17.9	1,319,176	178	150,504	3,148,129	9.1
Adams	23.3	0.0	2.4	14.0	1.3	4.5	3.6	D	20.5	2,640	135	354	6,662	6.7
Asotin	0.5	D	13.3	6.4	4.6	13.8	5.0	D	17.3	6,610	293	745	10,080	2.1
Benton	4.3	D	8.9	5.1	17.5	5.7	3.8	11.0	17.1	35,390	179	3,871	77,371	12.8
Chelan	7.1	D	5.2	4.2	4.5	10.6	4.5	17.6	19.8	17,385	227	1,481	38,074	7.4
Clallam	0.3	0.1	7.3	5.0	D	9.5	3.6	9.1	39.3	26,060	345	1,923	37,336	4.9
Clark	0.2	0.1	10.1	8.4	10.5	7.3	7.1	12.8	17.6	85,905	181	8,341	186,167	11.2
Columbia	15.5	D	10.2	3.0	2.6	2.9	1.8	6.1	36.3	1,305	322	138	2,173	1.7
Cowlitz	0.7	0.9	12.6	20.1	3.6	6.6	3.8	14.4	15.4	27,445	257	3,938	44,968	3.5
Douglas	13.2	0.1	7.8	5.5	D	10.1	2.7	5.5	25.3	8,075	193	554	17,173	7.3
Ferry	1.3	D	D	D	D	3.7	D	D	53.6	2,385	314	248	4,528	2.8
Franklin	11.8	0.3	7.6	9.3	2.2	8.0	2.9	6.9	21.6	10,525	114	1,804	28,647	17.3
Garfield	0.6	0.2	D	0.6	D	4.4	5.2	D	67.4	670	303	57	1,247	1.1
Grant	18.9	D	5.2	12.9	2.7	6.0	3.6	5.6	25.5	16,255	171	2,120	37,967	8.2
Grays Harbor	1.4	D	7.0	12.1	3.8	7.8	3.5	10.6	31.1	20,720	285	3,101	36,433	3.6
Island	0.3	D	6.9	3.4	5.5	5.6	4.2	5.3	51.6	22,345	269	1,026	42,277	5.1
Jefferson	0.8	D	11.0	7.5	8.6	7.1	5.2	6.7	31.1	12,370	396	600	18,814	5.9
King	0.1	0.1	5.7	7.4	27.3	9.7	6.6	8.3	11.1	292,135	133	37,355	952,569	11.9
Kitsap	0.0	D	5.1	2.4	8.1	5.7	3.7	9.7	52.6	52,655	198	4,947	113,733	5.9
Kittitas	3.5	D	9.4	3.3	5.3	7.8	5.1	6.3	34.9	8,575	186	563	24,191	10.5
Klickitat	7.5	D	4.7	29.1	D	2.6	2.7	2.9	19.8	6,225	285	634	10,551	7.8
Lewis	4.2	0.7	6.1	12.9	3.1	9.9	3.2	13.7	20.4	21,840	279	2,736	35,343	3.8
Lincoln	18.0	D	8.1	D	5.9	4.5	D	D	34.5	3,155	298	262	6,083	5.3
Mason	2.7	0.5	6.8	6.5	3.3	8.3	3.3	5.9	42.8	17,830	280	1,627	33,675	3.6
Okanogan	11.1	1.9	5.7	2.2	3.2	8.9	2.5	8.5	34.7	10,940	262	1,284	23,355	5.0
Pacific	5.1	0.5	6.5	9.5	D	5.4	3.4	D	34.4	8,260	382	709	16,265	4.6
Pend Oreille	0.6	D	5.7	9.3	3.6	3.5	2.6	D	48.0	4,260	319	504	8,306	4.7
Pierce	0.2	0.1	8.3	5.2	4.7	7.2	5.8	16.1	30.3	151,605	173	19,759	351,048	7.9
San Juan	0.5	D	17.7	2.7	10.4	9.4	7.0	5.5	13.8	5,415	324	130	14,239	6.9
Skagit	4.8	0.1	10.8	14.1	5.7	8.4	7.4	7.3	23.2	30,455	242	2,435	54,443	5.8
Skamania	1.5	D	8.0	13.8	D	3.4	2.5	D	33.2	2,570	217	203	5,924	5.2
Snohomish	0.4	0.1	10.0	27.9	8.5	6.8	6.3	8.5	14.4	122,095	152	12,127	313,818	9.5
Spokane	0.1	0.1	6.7	7.0	7.3	7.7	8.9	17.5	19.6	103,735	205	14,419	219,880	9.2
Stevens	1.8	0.8	7.7	11.0	3.9	7.1	3.3	14.5	28.0	12,965	290	1,370	21,848	3.3
Thurston	1.2	D	6.1	2.9	D	6.4	4.6	13.2	38.5	59,565	212	5,382	117,872	9.0
Wahkiakum	2.5	0.1	11.5	4.8	8.9	3.7	D	D	31.2	1,530	359	127	2,171	4.9
Walla Walla	9.6	D	4.0	14.8	D	4.6	4.4	15.8	24.5	12,875	213	1,390	24,902	6.2
Whatcom	2.7	D	11.4	13.5	7.2	8.9	5.5	12.0	18.0	44,305	200	4,386	97,855	7.9
Whitman	4.0	D	2.8	17.3	3.0	5.1	2.5	5.5	47.9	5,885	120	499	21,011	8.7
Yakima	14.5	0.0	5.1	8.3	3.0	7.3	3.2	14.2	18.7	44,215	177	7,355	89,130	4.3
WEST VIRGINIA	-0.2	4.6	6.6	8.5	8.2	6.8	4.6	16.6	21.2	473,398	261	73,879	893,778	1.3
Barbour	-1.1	D	5.4	D	D	5.1	2.4	D	19.2	4,245	257	727	7,923	1.0
Berkeley	0.2	D	5.4	4.9	10.9	6.7	3.7	12.9	32.0	22,450	195	2,373	49,425	10.4
Boone	0.0	D	1.3	1.0	D	6.1	D	D	23.7	6,900	309	1,332	11,166	0.9
Braxton	-0.4	1.3	9.2	11.1	3.4	14.3	2.5	13.3	21.2	3,900	274	627	7,427	0.2
Brooke	-0.1	0.0	D	25.3	1.8	7.2	3.9	D	9.7	6,505	290	491	10,798	-1.5
Cabell	0.0	D	5.0	10.6	7.1	8.6	5.3	28.4	16.8	22,555	238	4,427	46,327	0.4

1. Per 1,000 resident population estimated as of July 1 of the year shown.   2. Martinsville city is included with Henry county.   3. Norton city is included with Wise county.   4. Petersburg and Colonial Heights cities are included with Dinwiddie county.   5. Poquoson city is included with York county.   6. Radford city is included with Montgomery county.   7. Salem city is included with Roanoke county.   8. Staunton and Waynesboro cities are included with Augusta county.   9. Williamsburg city is included with James City county.   10. Winchester city is included with Frederick county.

Table B. States and Counties — **Housing, Labor Force, and Employment**

STATE County	Total	Percent	Median value[1]	With a mortgage	Without a mortgage[2]	Median rent[3]	Median rent as a percent of income[2]	Sub-standard units[4] (percent)	Total	Percent change, 2017-2018	Total	Rate[5]	Total	Management, business, science, and arts	Construction, production, and maintenance occupations
	89	90	91	92	93	94	95	96	97	98	99	100	101	102	103
VIRGINIA— Cont'd															
Martinsville city..............	5,740	55.1	90,100	20.7	12.9	642	28.8	1.0	5,456	-0.9	253	4.6	5,359	25.2	31.5
Newport News city............	68,665	50.0	189,300	23.3	11.8	985	31.8	3.0	88,872	0.0	3,207	3.6	81,596	33.9	23.1
Norfolk city......................	87,249	43.4	194,800	25.4	13.5	1,003	33.0	2.5	111,524	0.0	4,028	3.6	104,089	33.6	21.8
Norton city.......................	1,786	48.6	92,500	17.7	12.3	549	33.3	1.8	1,659	-2.4	65	3.9	1,620	26.3	21.5
Petersburg city.................	13,262	41.7	112,900	26.2	13.9	882	35.3	3.4	13,120	-0.2	798	6.1	13,348	25.1	25.2
Poquoson city..................	4,583	79.8	316,800	22.3	14.1	1,173	27.3	0.0	6,288	0.4	169	2.7	5,908	50.1	18.2
Portsmouth city................	36,616	54.4	169,400	25.0	15.0	988	34.2	1.9	44,095	-0.3	1,792	4.1	41,692	29.8	25.5
Radford city.....................	5,503	46.5	160,600	22.5	12.6	779	35.8	2.0	8,301	-0.4	308	3.7	7,455	32.2	15.4
Richmond city	89,238	41.7	209,200	23.2	13.6	942	33.4	2.4	117,259	0.4	4,134	3.5	109,362	41.0	15.6
Roanoke city	42,333	51.9	133,700	22.1	12.3	776	29.8	2.0	48,774	-0.3	1,575	3.2	47,334	31.9	21.8
Salem city........................	9,997	65.5	174,000	21.2	11.3	874	28.0	1.5	12,993	-0.3	383	2.9	12,446	37.0	17.3
Staunton city....................	10,477	57.5	162,500	21.3	10.0	806	28.6	1.7	11,920	0.5	342	2.9	11,848	37.4	17.8
Suffolk city.......................	32,331	69.2	238,200	24.4	11.5	1,083	31.4	1.5	44,014	0.1	1,419	3.2	41,009	39.1	21.1
Virginia Beach city	167,731	63.8	267,300	24.2	11.0	1,296	30.6	1.6	232,342	0.4	6,647	2.9	219,573	40.0	17.0
Waynesboro city	9,128	58.9	161,600	24.2	13.9	835	29.1	1.7	10,461	0.4	338	3.2	9,976	27.6	25.6
Williamsburg city..............	4,649	47.3	307,000	22.9	10.0	1,118	34.3	3.1	6,729	-0.1	271	4.0	6,235	47.2	9.1
Winchester city.................	10,520	45.6	226,200	19.8	11.9	973	29.8	4.1	14,588	0.9	427	2.9	13,358	35.6	19.2
WASHINGTON	2,755,697	62.7	286,800	23.0	11.3	1,120	29.6	3.6	3,793,095	2.0	170,796	4.5	3,418,123	40.3	20.9
Adams.............................	5,824	64.3	150,300	23.1	10.0	691	25.9	13.7	9,479	6.8	511	5.4	7,757	22.8	49.1
Asotin.............................	9,235	70.7	176,700	21.9	11.2	739	26.5	1.9	10,153	-0.7	442	4.4	9,824	30.0	23.2
Benton............................	70,363	68.1	198,600	19.8	10.0	903	28.1	3.8	99,084	2.4	5,160	5.2	85,352	39.4	23.2
Chelan............................	27,383	65.8	256,400	23.3	10.6	830	24.4	4.1	45,580	3.1	2,063	4.5	34,063	30.4	28.6
Clallam............................	32,280	69.6	227,400	24.2	10.8	875	31.7	2.8	28,030	1.1	1,790	6.4	28,027	30.2	22.3
Clark...............................	167,717	65.8	272,400	22.6	10.4	1,094	29.6	3.1	230,353	1.3	11,123	4.8	213,776	36.3	23.0
Columbia..........................	1,759	71.0	161,700	24.9	12.7	745	29.3	2.4	1,789	1.0	100	5.6	1,628	33.8	22.9
Cowlitz	40,668	66.3	186,600	22.4	11.9	796	32.6	2.7	45,923	0.6	2,729	5.9	42,579	27.7	31.6
Douglas	14,706	70.3	229,100	22.8	10.0	836	26.1	7.6	21,603	2.5	1,151	5.3	18,297	26.6	32.2
Ferry...............................	3,056	70.4	165,900	27.2	10.3	646	27.4	6.9	2,488	-0.8	292	11.7	2,465	37.0	26.4
Franklin	25,835	69.0	177,400	20.5	10.0	847	28.2	10.8	41,496	2.1	2,515	6.1	38,844	25.6	38.8
Garfield............................	1,007	69.0	143,800	18.6	11.7	598	28.5	0.6	901	-0.3	52	5.8	934	33.7	22.7
Grant...............................	30,512	62.0	161,700	20.5	10.0	752	24.5	7.0	46,386	2.9	2,894	6.2	39,432	27.8	39.6
Grays Harbor	28,070	66.1	161,800	22.5	11.2	771	29.8	2.8	28,109	1.1	1,892	6.7	27,104	28.5	25.0
Island..............................	34,027	68.1	311,400	25.2	11.6	1,117	29.3	1.6	34,628	2.2	1,810	5.2	32,230	34.6	24.2
Jefferson	13,903	73.4	304,000	25.5	11.7	895	32.6	1.8	12,156	2.2	708	5.8	11,289	35.4	20.4
King................................	851,077	57.4	446,600	22.8	11.9	1,379	28.5	3.9	1,258,687	2.0	43,467	3.5	1,140,353	51.0	14.0
Kitsap.............................	100,484	66.8	277,500	23.2	10.9	1,116	29.8	2.1	122,885	2.3	5,713	4.6	112,032	38.9	20.9
Kittitas	17,648	57.6	256,700	24.6	10.2	894	35.4	2.4	22,541	1.4	1,190	5.3	20,901	33.0	22.9
Klickitat...........................	8,247	67.6	219,200	25.0	10.0	791	31.7	4.6	10,076	2.1	573	5.7	8,242	32.8	29.6
Lewis..............................	30,036	68.8	176,000	23.7	12.4	834	31.7	4.0	33,752	2.1	2,122	6.3	29,789	26.4	29.9
Lincoln............................	4,416	79.0	150,500	21.7	11.7	713	25.6	2.1	5,069	2.6	246	4.9	4,126	37.8	24.0
Mason.............................	23,034	77.2	206,700	25.5	10.9	925	30.6	3.9	24,274	2.2	1,531	6.3	23,051	28.6	29.4
Okanogan	17,075	67.4	169,100	21.8	10.8	657	27.3	6.7	20,808	-0.4	1,331	6.4	16,762	29.1	31.0
Pacific	8,786	76.3	163,400	23.0	13.1	703	28.7	1.6	8,403	0.9	578	6.9	6,916	27.7	30.2
Pend Oreille	5,637	77.8	186,000	22.2	10.0	782	27.6	4.6	4,812	1.9	345	7.2	4,401	33.9	31.1
Pierce.............................	312,839	61.2	255,800	23.8	12.4	1,116	31.0	3.1	424,137	2.1	21,947	5.2	383,286	33.9	23.8
San Juan	7,718	74.1	452,300	27.1	11.3	965	28.9	5.5	8,160	-0.2	321	3.9	7,635	39.7	21.5
Skagit	47,341	67.8	269,100	24.2	12.5	1,007	32.2	5.8	60,278	1.7	3,126	5.2	54,177	31.7	27.5
Skamania.........................	4,713	69.3	248,500	24.1	12.5	747	27.4	2.6	5,335	1.0	299	5.6	4,934	34.8	28.8
Snohomish.......................	284,477	66.6	338,400	23.5	11.6	1,269	29.7	3.3	430,470	1.9	16,181	3.8	390,186	38.9	22.1
Spokane..........................	194,995	62.4	195,500	22.3	10.7	842	31.0	2.2	244,056	2.0	12,754	5.2	221,595	35.9	19.5
Stevens...........................	17,534	77.1	184,600	22.7	10.5	662	30.2	3.6	18,379	1.8	1,309	7.1	16,545	29.3	29.8
Thurston..........................	106,229	63.9	255,500	23.0	10.3	1,134	30.3	2.4	137,697	2.7	6,553	4.8	122,976	41.9	18.1
Wahkiakum	1,823	81.0	202,600	24.3	12.3	717	39.2	2.0	1,317	1.1	86	6.5	1,215	30.1	34.2
Walla Walla	22,391	64.5	196,300	22.1	10.0	843	31.2	3.2	29,270	1.6	1,383	4.7	26,496	36.0	22.1
Whatcom..........................	83,475	61.8	299,800	23.9	12.2	972	34.0	3.4	111,670	1.7	5,295	4.7	102,696	35.3	22.0
Whitman..........................	17,657	44.5	199,400	21.2	10.0	737	35.7	1.6	23,685	1.8	1,025	4.3	22,218	48.2	16.1
Yakima............................	81,720	62.7	163,500	23.3	11.1	797	28.8	8.6	129,176	3.0	8,190	6.3	103,990	24.6	38.9
WEST VIRGINIA...............	737,671	72.7	111,600	18.6	10.0	681	28.7	1.9	783,344	0.5	41,165	5.3	746,958	32.8	24.2
Barbour	6,293	71.6	101,200	17.7	10.0	553	29.7	0.9	6,816	0.1	409	6.0	6,421	26.3	28.4
Berkeley...........................	42,456	73.8	168,200	21.4	10.0	964	28.2	2.9	56,576	0.7	2,312	4.1	52,254	33.9	24.5
Boone..............................	9,298	76.9	71,800	20.7	10.0	603	33.8	2.4	7,452	-1.3	458	6.1	7,030	24.4	31.3
Braxton............................	5,498	77.6	91,100	16.3	10.0	524	26.7	2.7	5,085	-3.1	358	7.0	5,320	28.5	27.2
Brooke.............................	9,961	74.7	91,000	16.2	10.0	589	25.7	2.5	9,822	0.5	603	6.1	10,404	30.9	25.5
Cabell..............................	40239	60.9	119,800	19.3	10.1	707	31.9	1.3	41,287	-0.5	1,955	4.7	39,455	36.5	15.8

1. Specified owner-occupied units. 2. A value of 10.0 represents 10 percent or less; a value of 50.0 represents 50 percent or more. 3. Specified renter-occupied units. 4. Overcrowded or lacking complete plumbing facilities. 5. Percent of civilian labor force. 6. Civilian employed persons 16 years old and over.

Table B. States and Counties — Nonfarm Employment and Agriculture

STATE County	Private nonfarm establishments, employment and payroll, 2016									Agriculture, 2017			
	Number of establishments	Employment						Annual payroll		Farms			Farm producers whose primary occupation is farming (percent)
		Total	Health care and social assistance	Manufacturing	Retail trade	Finance and insurance	Professional, scientific, and technical services	Total (mil dol)	Average per employee (dollars)	Number	Percent with:		
											Fewer than 50 acres	1000 acres or more	
	104	105	106	107	108	109	110	111	112	113	114	115	116
VIRGINIA— Cont'd													
Martinsville city	529	9,203	2,092	1,512	1,454	207	307	282	30,672	NA	NA	NA	NA
Newport News city	3,782	90,485	14,491	29,760	10,461	1,718	5,381	4,510	49,844	NA	NA	NA	NA
Norfolk city	5,341	101,136	18,921	6,568	11,948	4,142	10,614	4,662	46,100	NA	NA	NA	NA
Norton city	234	4,928	1,359	D	790	84	81	199	40,366	NA	NA	NA	NA
Petersburg city	723	12,639	5,116	1,129	1,420	195	219	467	36,976	NA	NA	NA	NA
Poquoson city	199	1,260	181	7	298	41	77	34	27,002	NA	NA	NA	NA
Portsmouth city	1,660	27,032	7,824	1,311	3,179	467	1,477	1,034	38,263	NA	NA	NA	NA
Radford city	311	4,280	513	1,188	594	130	144	155	36,206	NA	NA	NA	NA
Richmond city	6,129	120,124	26,688	4,813	9,168	10,953	11,736	7,099	59,100	NA	NA	NA	NA
Roanoke city	3,112	68,516	14,482	4,324	9,783	3,258	2,741	2,997	43,743	NA	NA	NA	NA
Salem city	1,004	18,508	4,728	3,132	1,999	522	583	871	47,059	NA	NA	NA	NA
Staunton city	748	10,308	2,248	512	1,936	308	290	313	30,358	NA	NA	NA	NA
Suffolk city	1,588	21,887	4,681	1,892	3,931	712	1,014	859	39,263	270	57.4	11.1	38.6
Virginia Beach city	11,095	158,104	20,235	5,601	24,435	11,714	15,992	6,271	39,661	196	67.9	2.0	35.6
Waynesboro city	628	9,588	697	1,622	2,272	395	296	332	34,640	NA	NA	NA	NA
Williamsburg city	543	9,525	820	25	1,789	185	147	274	28,773	NA	NA	NA	NA
Winchester city	1,361	25,540	7,332	2,040	4,273	626	914	987	38,631	NA	NA	NA	NA
WASHINGTON	186,164	2,685,355	407,355	265,401	336,572	98,196	201,766	156,915	58,434	35,793	66.6	7.2	39.9
Adams	367	4,516	803	1,056	710	84	53	184	40,684	586	20.8	32.8	55.2
Asotin	441	4,740	1,008	362	1,097	141	261	170	35,881	205	42.9	35.6	37.8
Benton	4,274	64,268	11,117	3,773	10,296	1,610	7,891	3,234	50,320	1,520	81.1	4.9	34.2
Chelan	2,533	28,923	5,942	1,725	4,620	669	1,237	1,250	43,230	835	72.7	0.5	47.3
Clallam	2,032	17,428	4,043	1,046	3,599	481	644	621	35,605	528	83.9	NA	39.3
Clark	10,614	131,177	21,777	14,181	18,373	5,439	9,174	6,396	48,757	1,978	87.4	0.3	29.9
Columbia	122	790	164	D	103	19	20	29	37,213	257	27.6	17.9	43.2
Cowlitz	2,150	30,646	5,688	6,213	5,083	763	730	1,391	45,389	403	76.9	1.5	33.3
Douglas	745	6,852	834	399	1,741	189	180	231	33,734	729	41.0	25.4	49.7
Ferry	140	1,097	153	177	126	19	27	61	55,763	252	31.3	9.1	53.3
Franklin	1,523	20,033	1,700	3,136	3,332	355	531	837	41,773	772	40.2	18.0	55.9
Garfield	46	310	108	NA	48	11	6	11	36,832	226	22.1	31.9	45.9
Grant	1,846	21,473	2,967	4,142	3,591	536	477	857	39,902	1,384	36.1	18.8	60.0
Grays Harbor	1,622	15,540	2,808	1,945	2,947	557	395	581	37,382	469	65.0	1.9	35.6
Island	1,735	12,552	2,571	824	2,429	368	715	452	36,039	390	83.6	NA	43.0
Jefferson	1,037	6,860	1,434	676	1,094	122	312	248	36,184	221	63.3	NA	39.2
King	68,079	1,167,201	149,502	87,277	107,472	42,299	110,197	87,676	75,116	1,796	93.1	0.1	35.3
Kitsap	5,795	59,446	12,707	2,273	11,273	1,769	4,212	2,291	38,546	698	96.3	NA	29.0
Kittitas	1,220	11,102	1,625	556	1,832	207	287	358	32,290	1,008	71.1	3.0	37.1
Klickitat	524	4,036	843	599	443	68	273	159	39,374	750	46.3	13.3	38.9
Lewis	1,849	20,391	3,546	3,251	3,876	361	535	766	37,553	1,723	70.3	0.6	35.9
Lincoln	246	1,567	414	54	292	58	95	67	42,869	783	15.2	43.2	53.1
Mason	1,037	10,023	1,892	1,177	1,725	298	257	368	36,754	324	82.1	0.6	35.5
Okanogan	1,152	8,610	1,719	643	1,933	215	279	273	31,729	1,192	55.4	8.1	44.6
Pacific	561	4,058	649	578	543	161	108	132	32,481	346	56.1	3.8	37.4
Pend Oreille	216	1,579	385	262	232	48	68	67	42,706	261	47.9	5.7	33.3
Pierce	17,409	251,689	47,628	17,868	36,591	9,625	9,547	11,327	45,006	1,607	87.4	0.2	31.8
San Juan	1,019	4,632	353	210	659	129	248	180	38,881	316	70.6	0.6	36.5
Skagit	3,457	41,928	7,619	5,809	7,553	1,493	1,833	1,874	44,704	1,041	75.7	1.6	40.8
Skamania	196	1,536	138	364	160	21	42	49	31,870	145	80.0	NA	24.4
Snohomish	18,253	251,289	30,078	60,299	36,416	8,775	11,777	13,530	53,843	1,558	85.2	0.4	34.3
Spokane	12,823	187,843	38,221	15,030	26,697	11,003	9,023	8,221	43,764	2,425	63.9	5.8	33.6
Stevens	887	7,207	1,659	1,111	1,289	207	208	267	37,062	1,114	44.9	5.0	41.6
Thurston	6,092	71,359	14,503	2,778	12,566	2,753	4,689	2,856	40,028	1,200	77.8	0.6	35.3
Wahkiakum	76	394	45	50	32	9	18	14	35,376	145	60.7	0.7	49.2
Walla Walla	1,364	19,821	4,113	3,488	2,307	657	479	753	38,000	903	54.2	18.4	41.7
Whatcom	6,550	74,548	10,368	10,326	11,683	2,348	3,460	3,132	42,014	1,712	79.6	0.7	35.4
Whitman	826	10,438	1,846	D	1,371	200	328	420	40,225	1,039	27.0	35.5	50.0
Yakima	4,674	68,496	13,849	9,237	10,404	1,497	1,736	2,677	39,080	2,952	74.1	3.8	44.3
WEST VIRGINIA	36,607	558,905	134,188	47,274	86,580	17,092	25,026	21,638	38,715	23,622	34.7	1.5	36.7
Barbour	213	3,092	790	106	336	72	75	89	28,827	594	28.1	1.3	37.7
Berkeley	1,629	24,785	5,958	2,559	4,385	587	910	958	38,662	946	67.2	0.5	28.8
Boone	263	3,811	825	115	631	120	78	165	43,373	35	17.1	NA	34.5
Braxton	254	3,578	867	299	784	83	45	119	33,199	381	16.8	3.1	40.8
Brooke	375	6,955	2,293	1,591	903	112	74	264	38,006	89	28.1	NA	45.9
Cabell	2,391	46,924	13,868	4,430	7,039	1,274	1,988	1,804	38,456	407	36.9	NA	34.8

STATE County	Land in farms — Acreage (1,000) [117]	Percent change, 2012-2017 [118]	Average size of farm [119]	Total irrigated (1,000) [120]	Total cropland (1,000) [121]	Value of land and buildings — Average per farm [122]	Average per acre [123]	Value of machinery and equipment, average per farm (dollars) [124]	Value of products sold: Total (mil dol) [125]	Average per farm (acres) [126]	Percent from: Crops [127]	Livestock and poultry products [128]	Organic farms (number) [129]	Farms with internet access (percent) [130]	Government payments — Total ($1,000) [131]	Percent of farms [132]
VIRGINIA— Cont'd																
Martinsville city	NA	NA	NA	NA	NA	NA	NA	NA	NA	NA	NA	NA	NA	NA	NA	NA
Newport News city	NA	NA	NA	NA	NA	NA	NA	NA	NA	NA	NA	NA	NA	NA	NA	NA
Norfolk city	NA	NA	NA	NA	NA	NA	NA	NA	NA	NA	NA	NA	NA	NA	NA	NA
Norton city	NA	NA	NA	NA	NA	NA	NA	NA	NA	NA	NA	NA	NA	NA	NA	NA
Petersburg city	NA	NA	NA	NA	NA	NA	NA	NA	NA	NA	NA	NA	NA	NA	NA	NA
Poquoson city	NA	NA	NA	NA	NA	NA	NA	NA	NA	NA	NA	NA	NA	NA	NA	NA
Portsmouth city	NA	NA	NA	NA	NA	NA	NA	NA	NA	NA	NA	NA	NA	NA	NA	NA
Radford city	NA	NA	NA	NA	NA	NA	NA	NA	NA	NA	NA	NA	NA	NA	NA	NA
Richmond city	NA	NA	NA	NA	NA	NA	NA	NA	NA	NA	NA	NA	NA	NA	NA	NA
Roanoke city	NA	NA	NA	NA	NA	NA	NA	NA	NA	NA	NA	NA	NA	NA	NA	NA
Salem city	NA	NA	NA	NA	NA	NA	NA	NA	NA	NA	NA	NA	NA	NA	NA	NA
Staunton city	NA	NA	NA	NA	NA	NA	NA	NA	NA	NA	NA	NA	NA	NA	NA	NA
Suffolk city	79	14.1	293	0.6	57.9	1,208,063	4,127	131,386	53.7	199,041	84.2	15.8	NA	82.6	3,185	56.3
Virginia Beach city	23	-10.8	119	0.3	18.6	1,149,351	9,648	107,202	13.7	69,796	91.1	8.9	3	82.7	382	17.3
Waynesboro city	NA	NA	NA	NA	NA	NA	NA	NA	NA	NA	NA	NA	NA	NA	NA	NA
Williamsburg city	NA	NA	NA	NA	NA	NA	NA	NA	NA	NA	NA	NA	NA	NA	NA	NA
Winchester city	NA	NA	NA	NA	NA	NA	NA	NA	NA	NA	NA	NA	NA	NA	NA	NA
WASHINGTON	14,680	-0.5	410	1,689.4	7,488.6	1,143,889	2,789	121,662	9,634.5	269,172	72.5	27.5	933	84.1	168,990	15.4
Adams	972	-6.3	1,659	127.9	745.9	2,369,294	1,428	320,442	363.9	620,947	71.4	28.6	15	80.0	16,076	67.4
Asotin	251	-4.7	1,224	0.9	79.9	1,618,697	1,323	86,684	12.9	62,961	58.5	41.5	NA	93.7	3,920	48.3
Benton	614	-12.8	404	204.3	473.1	1,573,284	3,898	188,926	1,005.3	661,374	76.5	23.5	25	84.9	6,663	7.0
Chelan	60	-21.2	72	23.8	29.1	1,102,315	15,400	78,413	258.4	309,501	98.9	1.1	54	84.7	1,087	3.6
Clallam	17	-27.3	33	3.5	7.4	415,890	12,769	40,366	12.0	22,777	42.3	57.7	20	83.5	43	3.0
Clark	91	21.4	46	4.9	24.3	410,366	8,946	42,816	47.7	24,116	41.7	58.3	32	82.9	208	1.7
Columbia	243	-18.2	947	3.0	149.5	1,541,289	1,628	155,022	30.7	119,479	86.4	13.6	NA	79.8	4,211	61.5
Cowlitz	29	-26.3	71	3.0	11.0	639,038	8,955	53,997	19.0	47,045	52.8	47.2	NA	80.9	27	1.5
Douglas	823	1.1	1,129	16.3	544.4	1,331,223	1,180	134,210	186.0	255,154	96.5	3.5	23	76.5	14,978	48.7
Ferry	789	-0.5	3,130	2.8	19.4	1,620,480	518	56,595	D	D	D	D	4	71.0	135	7.1
Franklin	615	-1.6	797	188.1	446.8	3,662,394	4,595	365,464	631.6	818,132	74.3	25.7	31	88.0	9,867	24.7
Garfield	290	-6.0	1,283	1.0	182.8	2,017,792	1,573	196,343	37.2	164,385	85.7	14.3	NA	80.1	5,997	70.8
Grant	1,042	8.1	753	448.0	800.9	2,574,272	3,421	447,392	1,938.9	1,400,936	76.3	23.7	89	84.8	13,885	29.1
Grays Harbor	105	-11.9	224	6.3	17.1	537,286	2,395	84,525	33.6	71,635	52.3	47.7	6	81.4	62	2.1
Island	16	3.9	41	1.9	6.9	446,211	10,979	42,783	12.0	30,774	24.9	75.1	19	85.6	85	4.9
Jefferson	14	-11.6	62	1.0	3.7	473,659	7,611	41,419	9.3	41,860	23.3	76.7	10	89.1	30	8.6
King	42	-10.2	23	4.1	18.7	823,790	35,248	38,650	135.5	75,425	66.9	33.1	39	87.6	760	2.6
Kitsap	9	-6.7	13	0.5	2.3	473,099	35,164	33,113	6.6	9,463	73.2	26.8	26	88.3	D	0.6
Kittitas	173	-5.8	171	66.8	71.1	706,325	4,127	90,038	83.0	82,347	76.7	23.3	7	88.1	1,257	6.7
Klickitat	574	4.1	765	24.4	229.5	1,360,462	1,778	103,084	99.2	132,212	81.4	18.6	22	81.9	4,684	33.5
Lewis	123	-7.5	71	10.0	50.5	427,935	6,001	55,899	136.3	79,132	26.1	73.9	50	83.4	442	3.6
Lincoln	1,181	5.9	1,509	29.5	817.0	1,843,885	1,222	233,510	130.2	166,331	91.5	8.5	4	78.2	24,298	79.3
Mason	18	-23.6	56	1.0	3.6	479,276	8,562	52,381	48.5	149,790	5.6	94.4	4	83.0	77	4.3
Okanogan	1,232	2.2	1,033	46.0	98.7	1,247,686	1,207	91,219	338.1	283,631	88.0	12.0	84	81.9	2,307	7.1
Pacific	52	0.4	151	3.7	15.5	524,322	3,464	81,240	38.9	112,361	18.7	81.3	15	88.2	504	5.2
Pend Oreille	58	33.1	223	1.3	19.0	593,012	2,665	48,783	4.7	18,130	47.4	52.6	NA	87.4	74	4.2
Pierce	46	-7.5	28	3.0	12.1	612,026	21,490	43,894	64.9	40,371	45.4	54.6	17	87.4	71	2.2
San Juan	18	17.4	58	0.3	5.8	550,693	9,457	28,800	4.1	13,035	58.6	41.4	12	92.1	55	2.8
Skagit	98	-8.3	94	23.5	65.7	950,360	10,130	129,653	287.1	275,789	66.6	33.4	61	83.0	407	7.8
Skamania	6	-9.3	41	0.4	2.3	489,432	12,082	41,679	5.6	38,828	29.2	70.8	1	90.3	D	2.8
Snohomish	64	-10.1	41	8.4	33.6	790,023	19,332	60,306	157.6	101,133	48.5	51.5	31	89.0	464	4.6
Spokane	549	2.1	226	12.7	378.8	843,187	3,728	78,785	117.0	48,265	83.3	16.7	4	84.6	8,095	19.6
Stevens	518	-1.7	465	7.2	77.1	729,604	1,569	60,364	30.2	27,105	39.8	60.2	47	80.2	734	7.3
Thurston	62	-18.8	52	6.4	22.1	616,274	11,880	58,420	176.1	146,742	32.0	68.0	34	86.8	107	1.9
Wahkiakum	14	44.8	95	0.1	5.1	458,501	4,805	45,757	2.6	17,959	21.4	78.6	1	91.7	52	13.1
Walla Walla	703	8.9	778	101.7	565.8	1,968,909	2,531	208,241	D	D	D	D	13	85.3	16,092	40.1
Whatcom	103	-11.5	60	36.5	75.6	1,005,681	16,794	95,376	372.9	217,786	41.3	58.7	48	83.7	1,047	12.6
Whitman	1,288	1.0	1,240	5.1	1,032.7	2,164,850	1,746	273,129	278.8	268,309	93.1	6.9	1	87.4	24,847	70.8
Yakima	1,781	0.1	603	260.0	344.0	1,662,430	2,755	174,332	1,988.0	673,451	71.3	28.7	84	79.0	5,221	6.5
WEST VIRGINIA	3,662	1.5	155	1.7	947.7	411,482	2,654	56,120	754.3	31,931	20.3	79.7	63	70.0	9,094	7.9
Barbour	95	11.7	159	0.0	26.7	371,966	2,335	56,514	6.0	10,167	33.7	66.3	3	70.9	205	5.1
Berkeley	73	4.3	77	0.1	37.6	413,514	5,349	47,415	25.9	27,387	72.2	27.8	2	68.8	857	8.4
Boone	4	61.7	103	0.0	0.5	241,209	2,339	23,954	0.1	4,114	77.1	22.9	NA	71.4	5	11.4
Braxton	90	0.8	235	0.0	17.9	482,984	2,054	51,405	4.5	11,916	28.5	71.5	NA	61.9	133	11.5
Brooke	14	-2.7	161	D	4.3	454,092	2,825	90,249	1.3	14,135	46.4	53.6	NA	78.7	4	4.5
Cabell	40	-5.0	99	0.0	7.3	352,954	3,564	42,757	2.7	6,595	64.1	35.9	NA	61.9	9	4.2

Table B. States and Counties — Water Use, Wholesale Trade, Retail Trade, and Real Estate

STATE County	Water use, 2015		Wholesale Trade[1], 2012				Retail Trade[2], 2012				Real estate and rental and leasing,[2] 2012			
	Public supply water withdrawn (mil gal/ day)	Public supply gallons withdrawn per person per day	Number of establishments	Number of employees	Sales (mil dol)	Average payroll (mil dol)	Number of establishments	Number of employees	Sales (mil dol)	Average payroll (mil dol)	Number of establishments	Number of employees	Sales (mil dol)	Average payroll (mil dol)
	133	134	135	136	137	138	139	140	141	142	143	144	145	146
VIRGINIA— Cont'd														
Martinsville city	2.00	146.6	16	D	D	D	111	1,578	317.8	34.4	31	104	14.3	2.3
Newport News city	22.20	121.7	110	1,438	851.3	72.7	686	9,879	2,480.8	229.7	254	1,672	276.5	60.3
Norfolk city	0.28	1.1	209	3,287	3,195.3	161.6	867	12,440	2,683.2	281.6	291	2,496	430.8	127.7
Norton city	0.53	134.6	8	123	78.3	7.1	48	786	219.7	19.3	11	42	5.0	1.0
Petersburg city	0.00	0.0	21	570	560.1	16.2	145	1,426	334.5	33.0	32	223	27.2	5.8
Poquoson city	0.00	0.0	4	D	D	D	28	305	63.8	6.1	12	20	3.2	0.6
Portsmouth city	60.83	632.3	48	688	249.5	32.0	273	3,081	699.5	71.1	71	332	52.6	9.7
Radford city	2.48	142.5	8	51	84.6	2.3	39	537	105.8	11.8	21	83	12.5	2.5
Richmond city	70.23	318.8	269	3,767	3,288.5	201.3	808	8,666	1,955.2	206.1	258	1,539	304.3	67.1
Roanoke city	4.99	50.0	180	2,727	1,398.0	130.3	535	9,912	2,461.0	230.1	155	950	141.8	31.0
Salem city	3.84	151.0	77	1,567	1,228.3	89.3	145	1,995	507.8	48.3	35	176	50.4	7.2
Staunton city	0.00	0.0	22	200	76.0	7.1	134	1,862	432.7	42.6	43	D	D	D
Suffolk city	44.45	504.2	54	961	666.0	49.8	226	3,536	958.9	79.1	67	243	37.5	8.1
Virginia Beach city	1.76	3.9	391	6,893	8,187.6	477.1	1,500	22,723	5,671.5	521.6	649	6,165	902.5	210.7
Waynesboro city	0.78	36.3	16	253	113.3	12.7	123	2,123	474.3	45.2	30	D	D	D
Williamsburg city	0.00	0.0	7	49	31.9	3.2	119	1,931	348.7	37.9	24	D	D	D
Winchester city	0.00	0.0	39	677	286.8	26.1	283	4,126	888.5	94.4	59	260	56.4	8.0
WASHINGTON	866.53	120.8	7,733	103,307	83,313.4	5,789.8	21,588	307,089	118,924.0	8,722.5	9,913	45,209	9,695.5	1,895.1
Adams	5.58	289.8	26	D	D	D	51	548	157.8	13.1	10	21	3.4	0.4
Asotin	5.21	235.7	13	D	D	D	59	1,094	285.9	30.3	21	143	11.8	3.1
Benton	34.48	181.2	109	999	1,230.3	44.5	583	9,216	2,463.5	222.7	244	1,004	179.4	30.2
Chelan	11.29	149.3	89	2,118	1,018.7	76.5	379	4,154	1,004.5	106.7	118	399	51.9	11.3
Clallam	6.16	83.8	38	D	D	D	287	3,476	812.0	92.1	87	246	35.3	7.0
Clark	46.57	101.4	414	4,410	4,395.4	253.2	1,011	15,547	4,276.5	419.9	465	D	D	D
Columbia	1.00	253.5	18	D	D	D	18	111	30.5	2.6	7	12	0.8	0.2
Cowlitz	10.31	99.6	85	1,036	2,021.4	53.2	333	4,644	1,188.3	113.8	104	337	50.7	8.5
Douglas	5.45	134.5	38	D	D	D	98	1,547	430.0	40.2	27	76	11.1	2.2
Ferry	0.58	76.5	1	D	D	D	27	167	45.4	3.8	6	20	0.7	0.3
Franklin	16.30	183.5	113	1,513	1,741.6	67.8	189	2,719	918.9	84.7	56	240	41.0	7.1
Garfield	0.57	256.9	9	D	D	D	11	55	10.4	1.0	NA	NA	NA	NA
Grant	23.52	252.2	117	D	D	D	287	3,160	825.6	77.4	81	203	28.2	5.1
Grays Harbor	7.63	107.3	52	D	D	D	264	2,871	761.5	73.3	82	246	24.5	5.6
Island	6.49	80.5	36	145	57.5	6.3	212	2,181	456.3	52.5	82	238	36.8	6.6
Jefferson	2.25	73.9	20	D	D	D	144	1,012	209.9	26.0	49	116	14.5	2.6
King	197.62	93.3	3,235	49,268	42,092.5	3,183.4	6,524	97,959	61,598.2	3,159.6	4,186	23,233	5,825.0	1,180.7
Kitsap	19.63	75.5	147	953	407.9	43.7	731	10,343	2,674.2	276.3	338	979	198.5	32.7
Kittitas	6.90	159.5	41	442	398.7	23.6	159	1,646	516.0	39.0	54	140	25.6	4.1
Klickitat	3.09	147.0	16	D	D	D	47	330	64.5	7.0	21	23	3.6	0.4
Lewis	5.95	78.4	60	D	D	D	314	3,521	912.2	87.0	75	251	34.4	7.7
Lincoln	2.03	196.7	27	D	D	D	46	292	106.9	8.1	5	6	0.5	0.1
Mason	4.96	81.3	33	D	D	D	134	1,557	404.3	40.4	44	233	17.6	5.1
Okanogan	6.05	145.7	39	D	D	D	199	1,836	447.0	44.5	60	154	11.5	2.3
Pacific	2.73	130.9	6	D	D	D	89	555	107.9	14.2	22	52	4.5	1.0
Pend Oreille	0.99	75.6	4	D	D	D	32	249	58.3	5.0	7	14	0.8	0.2
Pierce	110.41	130.8	686	9,171	7,705.6	449.9	2,154	33,111	10,114.4	944.9	947	4,673	837.6	158.6
San Juan	0.88	54.1	14	61	12.7	2.0	111	608	150.6	19.6	52	92	12.9	2.0
Skagit	20.31	166.7	104	1,277	793.5	58.2	553	6,801	1,999.2	186.8	158	467	81.8	14.4
Skamania	1.06	93.5	5	24	10.7	1.0	21	134	25.2	2.7	3	D	D	D
Snohomish	65.52	84.8	731	7,287	5,652.7	407.7	2,184	32,776	9,130.8	903.2	863	3,131	710.2	122.0
Spokane	138.81	282.7	561	8,334	4,946.9	400.8	1,617	24,749	6,560.8	668.0	614	3,053	518.3	102.2
Stevens	6.19	141.4	21	D	D	D	128	1,214	283.2	27.5	23	76	12.1	2.0
Thurston	22.58	83.8	169	1,824	1,252.0	90.8	769	12,317	3,330.8	324.6	325	994	202.1	31.3
Wahkiakum	0.32	79.2	2	D	D	D	9	51	10.1	1.0	6	9	0.4	0.1
Walla Walla	12.72	210.8	70	D	D	D	183	2,322	555.5	56.5	55	175	22.2	5.0
Whatcom	18.13	85.4	289	D	D	D	818	11,310	3,103.6	272.4	317	1,131	230.9	34.3
Whitman	6.26	129.9	61	D	D	D	100	1,331	333.6	28.0	50	194	21.5	4.6
Yakima	30.00	120.6	234	4,373	3,335.1	198.3	713	9,575	2,560.2	246.1	249	974	132.0	26.7
WEST VIRGINIA	184.96	100.3	1,334	16,906	14,295.4	761.9	6,393	85,305	22,637.9	1,908.5	1,405	6,011	1,255.8	203.8
Barbour	1.45	86.8	4	8	1.3	0.2	37	378	89.6	7.0	6	13	0.8	0.3
Berkeley	5.97	53.4	40	840	709.5	39.3	247	3,879	939.2	82.4	67	264	32.9	6.6
Boone	0.19	8.1	10	D	D	D	63	790	227.4	17.7	5	D	D	D
Braxton	1.09	75.6	8	59	23.3	2.1	67	572	171.1	13.5	8	26	3.4	0.6
Brooke	5.21	223.1	13	D	D	D	63	931	236.8	20.4	2	D	D	D
Cabell	12.17	125.7	106	1,754	873.6	82.4	439	6,687	1,570.9	145.2	97	362	69.0	12.4

1 Merchant wholesalers, except manufacturers' sales branches and offices.   2. Employer establishments.

Table B. States and Counties — Professional Services, Manufacturing, and Accommodation and Food Services

STATE County	Professional, scientific, and technical services, 2012				Manufacturing, 2012				Accommodation and food services, 2012			
	Number of establish-ments	Number of employees	Sales (mil dol)	Average payroll (mil dol)	Number of establish-ments	Number of employees	Receipts (mil dol)	Annual payroll (mil dol)	Number of establis-hments	Number of employees	Receipts (mil dol)	Annual payroll (mil dol)
	147	148	149	150	151	152	153	154	155	156	157	158
VIRGINIA— Cont'd												
Martinsville city..............	48	241	21.6	8.9	24	1,041	192.7	33.0	46	718	28.8	7.8
Newport News city	364	4,971	762.0	292.6	91	26,503	5,578.9	1,558.5	386	6,621	323.8	87.6
Norfolk city	708	12,065	2,415.0	1,025.2	130	6,866	1,812.5	328.2	593	11,264	547.1	148.4
Norton city.......................	21	173	12.9	5.7	8	585	109.8	22.2	24	D	D	D
Petersburg city................	36	175	20.5	8.0	28	1,646	D	91.0	79	885	39.1	10.2
Poquoson city	22	85	7.2	3.1	3	D	1.0	D	21	278	10.0	2.9
Portsmouth city	147	D	D	D	56	2,196	447.1	97.6	172	2,624	107.1	29.3
Radford city.....................	25	196	20.1	7.9	18	2,794	712.0	149.8	49	934	36.0	9.3
Richmond city	856	10,406	2,522.3	894.5	187	5,882	16,885.9	386.3	618	11,470	576.5	184.1
Roanoke city	328	2,920	390.6	170.1	100	3,869	1,629.7	174.8	320	6,509	308.1	94.4
Salem city	75	552	66.4	24.2	61	3,558	1,335.7	199.7	92	1,825	75.6	22.7
Staunton city	52	295	30.7	11.9	23	430	87.3	19.1	80	1,433	59.5	18.2
Suffolk city......................	123	D	D	D	46	1,996	1,521.0	103.6	147	2,477	122.9	30.6
Virginia Beach city	1,395	17,405	3,911.2	1,197.5	207	5,616	1,954.2	255.1	1,153	21,910	1,202.7	324.3
Waynesboro city	42	761	21.7	43.4	28	1,856	465.5	79.5	68	1,330	67.9	18.2
Williamsburg city.............	39	154	12.5	4.6	3	D	1.0	0.3	143	4,043	217.5	71.5
Winchester city................	131	1,122	98.6	47.9	23	2,197	866.2	117.6	130	2,518	119.1	33.1
WASHINGTON	20,047	167,512	28,283.6	11,976.5	6,992	248,192	131,530.6	14,461.8	16,333	234,145	14,297.3	4,159.7
Adams..............................	13	D	D	D	10	1,243	D	43.2	37	341	18.7	4.6
Asotin..............................	32	1,182	19.7	11.9	25	277	50.5	10.1	40	581	25.2	8.5
Benton..............................	436	8,899	1,654.5	668.2	144	3,990	1,828.0	217.8	375	5,996	311.6	88.4
Chelan..............................	181	886	100.9	38.8	89	1,702	572.6	83.5	289	3,364	197.2	61.8
Clallam.............................	170	850	77.1	33.7	82	1,215	372.2	57.4	224	2,050	113.3	33.5
Clark................................	1,141	7,197	1,005.6	364.9	409	11,562	D	630.8	721	10,524	550.7	163.9
Columbia..........................	8	21	1.1	0.5	6	57	D	2.7	12	62	3.2	0.8
Cowlitz.............................	140	830	86.5	34.9	116	5,722	3,264.5	385.6	215	2,796	124.2	39.2
Douglas............................	36	184	15.3	6.5	20	304	62.4	16.1	52	810	36.1	11.4
Ferry................................	7	D	D	D	6	141	D	5.2	17	D	D	D
Franklin	75	442	46.6	19.0	53	2,774	993.7	109.3	117	1,740	94.2	26.1
Garfield	4	D	D	D	NA	NA	NA	NA	6	12	0.3	0.1
Grant................................	101	406	40.6	14.5	73	4,074	1,458.5	182.3	189	1,935	117.2	29.7
Grays Harbor	91	427	43.9	18.6	84	2,580	874.2	121.2	232	1,902	104.2	29.5
Island	181	D	D	D	65	705	125.7	25.7	159	D	D	D
Jefferson	108	256	25.2	10.1	70	676	D	30.2	108	939	44.9	14.4
King..................................	9,676	97,576	18,749.2	7,992.6	2,233	79,631	D	4,816.6	5,861	93,388	6,223.8	1,864.5
Kitsap..............................	710	D	D	D	161	1,817	328.2	80.7	468	7,138	426.0	124.0
Kittitas	66	252	23.1	8.9	29	640	D	15.5	161	1,990	101.4	35.4
Klickitat............................	61	298	59.5	11.4	33	638	139.0	26.9	50	298	20.8	5.7
Lewis...............................	118	D	D	D	123	3,270	1,238.1	139.7	188	1,842	93.6	26.6
Lincoln.............................	11	D	D	D	8	36	D	1.5	24	D	D	D
Mason..............................	73	D	D	D	47	942	268.5	40.2	95	D	D	D
Okanogan.........................	76	227	23.8	6.6	35	354	123.7	12.4	124	1,031	54.8	16.6
Pacific	38	104	10.4	4.0	32	566	154.9	21.2	110	698	46.1	11.6
Pend Oreille	15	D	D	D	10	298	D	19.5	27	176	8.7	2.6
Pierce..............................	1,427	9,464	1,043.4	546.3	566	16,027	4,461.0	796.5	1,553	22,535	1,363.0	368.8
San Juan..........................	96	230	35.7	12.2	37	207	D	7.2	100	699	67.8	21.8
Skagit..............................	300	D	D	D	174	5,269	11,529.4	295.7	330	4,195	291.5	79.1
Skamania	17	55	8.5	4.1	16	192	D	8.9	25	517	32.9	10.2
Snohomish........................	1,548	10,150	1,514.0	712.6	785	60,156	D	4,264.2	1,550	19,757	1,168.5	324.6
Spokane...........................	1,259	D	D	D	512	13,940	3,943.1	660.3	1,057	17,949	1,062.6	299.7
Stevens............................	63	208	18.1	7.3	44	987	282.2	43.8	87	567	28.4	7.9
Thurston...........................	593	D	D	D	168	2,883	910.5	123.8	533	7,785	419.2	120.5
Wahkiakum........................	7	D	D	D	6	D	D	D	7	D	D	D
Walla Walla	109	438	44.8	17.1	131	3,394	D	156.8	135	1,936	92.7	27.6
Whatcom..........................	685	D	D	D	330	9,613	14,932.2	552.3	509	8,282	492.9	140.6
Whitman...........................	56	D	D	D	27	2,136	D	128.4	130	1,463	62.1	17.1
Yakima	319	2,023	193.3	80.5	232	8,152	2,622.2	327.3	416	5,364	281.5	79.8
WEST VIRGINIA...............	2,974	24,816	3,104.8	1,143.4	1,245	48,686	24,553.1	2,603.9	3,629	66,302	4,036.3	975.9
Barbour............................	16	116	8.6	3.2	10	101	28.6	D	24	D	D	D
Berkeley...........................	136	963	133.6	48.4	41	2,210	866.6	98.0	171	2,660	127.5	36.5
Boone..............................	18	D	D	D	4	34	D	1.1	20	D	D	D
Braxton............................	12	50	4.5	1.5	12	258	148.2	12.2	27	D	D	D
Brooke.............................	21	D	D	D	22	1,800	1,641.4	102.4	55	D	D	D
Cabell..............................	202	2,070	204.9	77.5	90	4,818	2,345.2	298.5	269	4,968	237.4	64.9

Health Care and Social Assistance, Other Services, Nonemployer Businesses, and Residential Construction

STATE County	Health care and social assistance, 2012				Other services, 2012				Nonemployer businesses, 2016		Value of residential construction authorized by building permits, 2018	
	Number of establish-ments	Number of employees	Receipts (mil dol)	Annual payroll (mil dol)	Number of establish-ments	Number of employees	Receipts (mil dol)	Annual payroll (mil dol)	Number	Receipts (mil dol)	New construction ($1,000)	Number of housing units
	159	160	161	162	163	164	165	166	167	168	169	170
VIRGINIA— Cont'd												
Martinsville city..................	109	2,135	205.5	80.8	46	231	20.6	4.7	739	30.7	0	0
Newport News city............	390	13,476	1,546.8	651.1	289	1,963	210.3	60.0	9,367	324.5	22,907	124
Norfolk city........................	533	18,651	2,391.6	900.9	374	3,245	443.7	110.7	12,413	497.7	74,834	594
Norton city........................	52	1,379	141.0	51.2	15	D	D	D	231	7.6	170	2
Petersburg city..................	126	4,740	437.7	175.4	74	554	43.2	14.7	1,334	48.6	1,204	13
Poquoson city....................	14	204	12.6	5.3	26	D	D	D	818	32.2	9,252	41
Portsmouth city.................	207	7,793	815.7	310.9	148	1,100	134.6	38.1	4,807	129.5	17,058	137
Radford city.......................	39	507	40.4	17.4	29	D	D	D	645	31.2	1,827	13
Richmond city	597	25,804	3,769.4	1,303.8	516	3,904	445.6	125.1	15,655	686.0	80,046	563
Roanoke city	314	12,451	1,582.3	615.0	250	2,083	159.3	47.5	5,820	274.2	13,719	115
Salem city	114	5,223	737.8	266.3	101	563	33.6	12.8	1,449	65.9	0	0
Staunton city	86	2,194	154.1	74.3	85	436	38.3	11.3	1,599	69.9	6,735	50
Suffolk city........................	177	4,087	494.9	192.3	94	593	43.3	13.3	5,292	189.2	101,412	717
Virginia Beach city............	997	18,362	1,959.4	814.7	829	4,778	618.6	119.9	30,920	1,492.7	119,041	779
Waynesboro city	48	875	66.9	24.1	52	364	39.4	11.5	1,065	44.8	4,420	45
Williamsburg city..............	44	D	D	D	29	276	33.3	12.4	868	42.5	4,292	25
Winchester city.................	261	6,460	885.3	355.8	85	506	36.7	10.9	2,054	124.4	22,122	158
WASHINGTON	19,833	374,227	43,966.9	17,833.2	12,425	69,976	13,185.2	2,203.3	459,590	22,726.9	9,807,980	47,746
Adams.............................	27	716	64.2	30.7	28	D	D	D	813	43.9	9,084	47
Asotin..............................	54	995	99.1	36.8	23	D	D	D	1,022	39.4	7,435	34
Benton.............................	544	9,802	1,108.3	436.7	250	1,506	120.3	39.1	9,108	410.8	322,652	1,285
Chelan.............................	221	5,233	642.6	288.8	162	571	67.6	15.7	4,676	232.2	103,677	590
Clallam.............................	273	4,062	329.7	146.7	148	D	D	D	4,602	161.1	75,396	336
Clark................................	1,075	20,893	2,251.1	1,011.9	682	D	D	D	30,532	1,526.1	848,319	3,598
Columbia..........................	11	164	11.9	5.8	8	D	D	D	238	7.4	613	4
Cowlitz.............................	240	5,444	567.0	232.1	148	D	D	D	4,387	187.3	67,853	318
Douglas............................	64	1,042	59.3	25.6	43	149	12.1	3.3	1,719	71.3	56,566	217
Ferry................................	13	165	12.4	4.7	8	D	D	D	341	10.5	114	1
Franklin............................	118	1,737	201.5	83.8	95	462	41.3	11.1	3,502	177.4	175,331	616
Garfield	4	D	D	D	1	D	D	D	137	4.3	432	2
Grant...............................	146	2,710	255.6	104.2	125	D	D	D	3,723	188.7	93,757	451
Grays Harbor	202	2,882	263.9	107.1	104	D	D	D	3,140	126.4	66,558	463
Island	172	2,326	228.3	94.4	96	401	28.1	9.1	5,893	240.6	96,860	391
Jefferson	108	1,370	127.3	54.3	88	D	D	D	3,138	116.6	34,956	143
King.................................	7,309	135,353	17,719.2	7,109.5	4,537	29,268	9,324.7	1,074.5	172,297	9,588.4	3,389,593	18,460
Kitsap..............................	685	11,861	1,272.8	484.3	382	1,789	149.7	48.6	14,639	655.4	327,676	1,149
Kittitas	96	1,613	114.9	48.7	76	D	D	D	2,719	124.0	151,554	629
Klickitat...........................	40	599	63.7	26.3	33	103	7.3	2.2	1,502	65.0	24,764	127
Lewis...............................	202	3,432	350.3	140.9	116	D	D	D	3,600	150.8	45,363	275
Lincoln.............................	16	441	42.4	19.2	11	D	D	D	676	25.5	11,840	58
Mason..............................	94	1,658	161.5	65.4	80	D	D	D	2,870	103.3	66,754	276
Okanogan	116	1,704	143.8	64.2	68	D	D	D	2,291	90.6	27,484	153
Pacific.............................	44	618	55.6	23.5	39	D	D	D	1,424	57.9	22,763	131
Pend Oreille	19	D	D	D	15	32	4.9	0.8	730	22.9	12,470	48
Pierce..............................	1,915	43,245	5,369.3	2,118.8	1,328	8,133	760.7	241.0	43,855	2,080.0	1,131,706	5,449
San Juan..........................	61	352	26.5	10.4	62	D	D	D	2,727	120.9	29,831	156
Skagit..............................	330	7,152	700.3	296.6	252	1,128	106.0	31.3	7,844	388.2	132,101	585
Skamania	15	128	5.6	3.0	11	22	2.2	0.5	695	33.7	13,523	63
Snohomish.......................	1,770	28,491	2,931.5	1,217.9	1,223	6,446	572.5	178.0	46,983	2,154.4	993,275	4,277
Spokane...........................	1,497	33,772	3,968.0	1,576.7	813	4,742	415.5	126.4	29,885	1,379.7	581,447	2,926
Stevens............................	82	1,627	128.4	54.5	60	D	D	D	2,502	91.2	43,806	200
Thurston...........................	790	13,079	1,584.8	619.1	483	2,769	331.1	98.1	15,022	652.7	332,518	1,750
Wahkiakum........................	7	D	D	D	2	D	D	D	316	14.5	2,845	11
Walla Walla	160	4,194	443.5	198.7	80	D	D	D	3,172	134.9	56,864	221
Whatcom..........................	659	9,901	1,026.2	422.5	404	2,282	239.2	70.4	15,486	729.5	280,020	1,464
Whitman...........................	97	D	D	D	60	D	D	D	2,123	71.2	45,121	264
Yakima............................	557	12,903	1,431.4	574.7	281	1,449	130.9	34.3	9,261	447.9	125,061	578
WEST VIRGINIA.............	4,939	129,075	12,259.4	4,824.5	2,661	16,583	1,773.3	443.6	87,671	3,296.7	500,078	2,887
Barbour............................	31	842	43.7	18.2	17	D	D	D	645	18.1	862	4
Berkeley...........................	197	5,667	629.5	296.9	116	635	55.2	15.7	5,757	226.4	208,951	1,083
Boone..............................	37	835	45.1	22.0	23	D	D	D	726	18.3	640	6
Braxton............................	19	842	48.3	17.5	17	D	D	D	531	16.5	0	0
Brooke.............................	65	1,959	171.3	66.2	32	165	9.7	3.2	956	38.9	1,451	5
Cabell..............................	372	12,905	1,426.9	570.0	170	1,053	161.2	32.3	4,713	177.5	15,463	99

STATE County	Government employment and payroll, 2012									Local government finances, 2012				
			March payroll (percent of total)							General revenue				
												Taxes		
	Full-time equivalent employees	March payroll (dollars)	Administration, judicial, and legal	Police and corrections	Fire protection	Highways and transportation	Health and welfare	Natural resources and utilities	Education and libraries	Total (mil dol)	Inter-governmental (mil dol)	Total (mil dol)	Per capita[1] (dollars)	
													Total	Property
	171	172	173	174	175	176	177	178	179	180	181	182	183	184
VIRGINIA— Cont'd														
Martinsville city	769	2,241,998	9.4	13.6	4.4	3.9	2.0	9.5	54.3	58.0	32.0	15.8	1,148	628
Newport News city	8,482	34,753,223	6.1	10.1	4.5	2.1	4.5	9.1	62.7	786.5	332.1	322.2	1,783	1,269
Norfolk city	14,612	55,628,038	4.8	10.3	4.2	8.7	8.6	7.9	54.2	1,422.2	577.3	416.3	1,694	1,029
Norton city	226	662,054	8.5	13.0	0.5	4.4	8.7	6.7	55.1	22.2	11.9	7.7	1,884	632
Petersburg city	1,476	4,759,064	5.8	19.4	8.6	4.3	5.8	7.7	45.6	126.3	70.3	45.2	1,415	1,044
Poquoson city	447	1,474,638	7.0	6.8	6.8	3.3	0.8	2.3	70.5	38.2	15.0	19.1	1,576	1,340
Portsmouth city	4,358	16,114,476	6.2	15.8	6.6	0.8	6.9	6.3	55.4	449.4	234.6	161.2	1,671	1,219
Radford city	450	1,533,350	9.5	10.2	2.3	3.6	4.7	13.6	53.1	37.9	20.4	11.1	664	455
Richmond city	8,977	34,059,020	8.8	19.1	5.9	2.9	6.0	10.3	41.5	1,102.8	456.7	412.6	1,962	1,249
Roanoke city	3,900	14,209,461	8.0	12.7	8.2	3.3	6.2	4.1	55.6	398.1	176.5	172.9	1,774	1,086
Salem city	1,239	4,093,202	12.6	9.6	6.7	6.7	2.4	12.1	49.5	108.5	42.3	49.5	1,982	1,301
Staunton city	1,131	3,120,624	7.9	23.4	4.4	2.5	1.7	5.3	51.1	82.8	39.3	32.3	1,349	839
Suffolk city	3,558	11,946,187	10.3	7.7	9.6	2.9	4.4	6.4	58.0	305.1	145.8	134.5	1,579	1,162
Virginia Beach city	19,058	68,439,433	3.5	9.0	3.4	0.3	6.4	12.4	57.0	1,816.6	615.1	810.1	1,812	1,218
Waynesboro city	795	2,593,698	8.5	8.2	4.6	3.4	1.3	8.3	60.2	77.5	33.4	33.2	1,574	946
Williamsburg city	407	1,404,121	11.0	37.6	9.6	3.3	4.2	10.1	21.2	46.8	11.2	29.9	1,971	766
Winchester city	1,491	5,190,139	6.6	22.4	6.4	2.6	4.2	6.7	49.4	137.9	46.7	61.6	2,292	1,298
WASHINGTON	X	X	X	X	X	X	X	X	X	X	X	X	X	X
Adams	1,040	3,937,847	5.7	6.6	0.8	5.5	21.8	10.0	47.7	141.3	72.5	24.1	1,269	906
Asotin	728	2,891,078	6.7	8.1	3.6	6.7	12.3	6.0	54.9	69.3	39.9	19.3	881	674
Benton	7,559	41,657,634	4.9	6.8	3.2	4.4	13.0	32.6	34.0	876.0	367.1	242.6	1,330	745
Chelan	3,427	16,843,859	4.7	6.8	2.3	5.4	9.3	32.8	36.9	368.1	151.3	114.2	1,550	1,003
Clallam	3,439	16,962,339	5.9	7.8	3.5	5.3	38.0	11.5	26.0	416.5	135.2	89.7	1,249	834
Clark	11,478	56,406,570	6.0	8.5	5.1	6.1	1.9	9.2	59.4	1,575.0	717.2	576.6	1,316	967
Columbia	318	1,186,883	10.8	5.9	1.0	8.9	38.0	7.4	25.7	32.7	11.4	6.7	1,687	1,352
Cowlitz	3,301	15,112,407	7.8	11.6	3.0	7.2	3.7	14.2	51.3	420.9	170.2	127.1	1,246	848
Douglas	1,297	6,128,626	5.0	6.0	1.5	6.7	0.5	26.3	52.5	145.0	88.5	39.7	1,008	759
Ferry	420	1,474,156	7.4	5.9	0.4	5.7	31.9	8.5	39.8	44.5	24.8	5.0	651	505
Franklin	2,593	11,637,558	6.0	7.6	3.3	4.6	0.0	14.4	62.8	318.4	176.1	82.9	965	615
Garfield	229	842,190	7.7	6.5	0.9	9.8	47.5	1.7	24.6	29.1	16.3	3.5	1,591	960
Grant	4,837	22,986,238	4.1	5.2	1.2	2.7	20.7	28.8	35.5	555.0	232.9	128.7	1,403	1,005
Grays Harbor	2,841	12,751,235	7.3	9.1	6.2	10.1	5.9	14.9	44.7	305.6	124.6	95.4	1,330	817
Island	2,321	11,320,614	5.9	5.9	5.9	8.0	32.6	3.6	36.8	280.9	92.9	87.2	1,101	776
Jefferson	1,311	6,130,951	7.9	5.4	5.8	9.2	41.3	2.8	26.6	158.5	38.9	46.4	1,556	1,102
King	65,821	388,288,446	8.0	10.3	5.9	13.1	13.5	13.9	33.3	12,411.3	3,474.5	5,105.6	2,543	1,381
Kitsap	6,732	32,797,634	7.2	7.7	9.1	6.6	1.0	9.5	56.8	1,053.2	532.7	344.8	1,352	960
Kittitas	1,664	7,365,807	8.8	8.2	3.6	3.8	32.4	9.0	32.4	197.1	81.5	58.9	1,412	1,006
Klickitat	1,119	4,905,212	5.9	6.8	0.4	4.5	31.9	13.1	35.6	136.0	44.1	27.2	1,316	1,015
Lewis	2,603	11,808,449	7.8	9.5	3.2	6.0	10.1	11.8	47.1	268.0	123.6	81.1	1,072	750
Lincoln	806	3,420,386	7.1	4.6	0.1	8.4	38.7	1.4	38.6	95.2	44.6	15.2	1,458	1,199
Mason	2,164	10,240,656	6.6	6.6	4.0	5.9	26.0	11.1	37.8	268.3	97.3	72.6	1,193	869
Okanogan	1,848	8,014,386	6.5	8.2	0.5	3.7	30.9	10.5	38.5	228.9	90.9	42.6	1,031	722
Pacific	1,032	5,269,056	8.5	7.3	3.7	6.5	27.8	11.0	33.1	126.6	42.8	31.2	1,518	1,146
Pend Oreille	786	3,517,534	6.4	5.1	0.4	3.4	34.6	21.7	26.3	81.4	36.0	10.4	799	627
Pierce	23,934	131,701,698	8.7	9.5	9.2	8.4	2.7	12.1	47.1	3,300.2	1,329.7	1,234.7	1,521	1,076
San Juan	551	2,448,595	14.0	7.8	3.9	9.0	9.8	11.9	39.1	76.6	25.1	34.7	2,196	1,573
Skagit	5,963	27,675,332	5.4	5.4	2.0	4.5	41.5	4.7	33.8	852.8	275.6	199.6	1,688	1,157
Skamania	390	1,668,143	14.8	12.9	0.3	6.4	8.7	12.8	38.8	36.0	20.0	8.7	781	588
Snohomish	19,389	108,720,406	6.9	9.4	6.5	8.0	5.4	13.4	47.9	2,865.2	1,091.9	1,077.6	1,470	1,030
Spokane	13,368	67,439,060	9.4	11.5	7.6	7.3	3.7	7.0	51.9	1,818.7	806.0	639.3	1,344	862
Stevens	1,254	5,040,095	8.1	7.4	1.3	6.3	7.8	4.7	61.9	143.8	97.8	31.2	717	541
Thurston	7,290	36,403,899	10.9	9.6	5.9	9.3	2.0	8.9	51.8	946.4	372.7	391.6	1,516	997
Wahkiakum	161	658,898	16.0	9.8	0.1	7.0	12.6	16.9	31.8	27.2	18.9	3.6	909	651
Walla Walla	1,801	7,900,373	8.1	11.4	5.9	6.2	5.5	3.9	55.3	236.4	107.1	76.1	1,281	877
Whatcom	5,120	25,193,563	10.0	10.9	7.5	8.7	1.8	7.1	50.4	696.1	261.3	292.4	1,424	871
Whitman	1,636	7,215,336	5.6	5.7	3.5	8.0	37.2	2.3	36.4	210.9	64.2	44.8	961	644
Yakima	8,019	34,900,911	7.0	10.7	3.2	2.8	3.3	5.9	66.0	970.4	601.4	232.4	941	607
WEST VIRGINIA	X	X	X	X	X	X	X	X	X	X	X	X	X	X
Barbour	525	1,593,938	6.5	3.2	0.0	1.0	6.3	5.7	74.1	35.3	22.1	6.7	408	324
Berkeley	3,583	11,743,879	4.1	3.5	2.1	0.6	1.2	4.4	82.8	263.0	125.8	97.1	907	806
Boone	1,129	3,935,149	4.3	3.0	1.1	0.8	17.5	1.2	69.9	102.4	38.1	37.4	1,528	1,483
Braxton	464	1,418,168	6.8	3.5	5.0	0.8	1.9	4.6	76.8	34.7	20.6	7.6	528	481
Brooke	700	2,209,915	5.0	5.9	0.0	2.9	3.5	5.7	73.7	55.0	24.1	20.4	854	747
Cabell	2866	9,646,891	2.5	7.4	3.4	4.5	2.0	4.8	70.4	298.6	122.6	110.8	1,142	895

1. Based on the resident population estimated as of July 1 of the year shown.

Table B. States and Counties — Local Government Finances, Government Employment, and Income Taxes

STATE County	Total (mil dol) [185]	Per capita¹ (dollars) [186]	Education [187]	Health and hospitals [188]	Police protection [189]	Public welfare [190]	Highways [191]	Total (mil dol) [192]	Per capita¹ (dollars) [193]	Federal civilian [194]	Federal military [195]	State and local [196]	Number of returns [197]	Mean adjusted gross income [198]	Mean income tax [199]
VIRGINIA— Cont'd															
Martinsville city	59.6	4,339	42.2	0.5	6.3	0.5	5.7	35.1	2,555	(2)	(2)	(2)	6,030	42,015	4,189
Newport News city	820.9	4,542	41.6	8.3	5.6	5.0	3.9	1,041.2	5,761	5,282	6,321	11,335	84,080	47,333	4,771
Norfolk city	1,457.9	5,932	43.5	5.0	4.7	5.2	3.6	2,294.3	9,335	20,502	39,633	20,220	100,840	47,922	5,250
Norton city	20.8	5,109	39.7	0.5	9.9	6.6	7.9	19.6	4,823	(3)	(3)	(3)	1,640	40,800	3,670
Petersburg city	134.0	4,190	38.8	1.0	8.8	11.1	4.6	60.3	1,887	(4)	(4)	(4)	15,880	33,027	2,480
Poquoson city	38.6	3,191	55.1	1.5	6.4	1.1	7.3	56.8	4,694	(5)	(5)	(5)	5,950	83,748	10,883
Portsmouth city	543.5	5,633	31.4	2.0	6.5	4.7	1.3	647.6	6,713	14,112	5,967	5,279	44,100	41,957	3,551
Radford city	44.5	2,667	45.2	0.5	8.1	5.6	5.3	28.4	1,701	(6)	(6)	(6)	5,380	49,344	5,400
Richmond city	1,081.3	5,141	30.1	4.3	8.5	1.5	3.8	1,910.6	9,085	5,837	1,319	38,775	101,380	64,118	10,014
Roanoke city	391.0	4,011	38.2	0.8	5.9	14.8	3.4	597.7	6,132	1,534	347	6,653	45,750	48,805	5,695
Salem city	120.6	4,828	38.5	0.7	5.3	1.5	4.9	167.0	6,689	(7)	(7)	(7)	11,650	57,788	6,787
Staunton city	94.0	3,928	32.9	8.4	5.8	5.6	5.2	98.6	4,122	(8)	(8)	(8)	11,830	49,212	4,964
Suffolk city	324.3	3,808	45.2	0.2	6.3	4.4	6.8	654.0	7,677	1,355	439	5,182	40,740	63,789	7,152
Virginia Beach city	2,062.0	4,613	40.8	2.6	4.3	3.3	4.2	2,582.9	5,778	6,363	17,385	22,368	218,990	67,794	8,957
Waynesboro city	75.1	3,556	42.8	0.6	5.0	4.9	6.7	92.3	4,374	(8)	(8)	(8)	10,830	46,330	4,444
Williamsburg city	53.2	3,510	14.0	0.9	7.4	3.7	3.5	32.4	2,134	(9)	(9)	(9)	5,310	63,798	8,212
Winchester city	131.6	4,897	37.2	0.9	5.5	5.5	4.3	337.1	12,539	(10)	(10)	(10)	13,490	61,779	8,847
WASHINGTON	X	X	X	X	X	X	X	X	X	74,962	74,266	498,971	3,488,880	79,308	11,724
Adams	135.7	7,140	46.3	18.1	2.6	0.0	5.7	62.9	3,309	36	50	1,642	8,430	43,574	3,906
Asotin	68.8	3,142	46.9	7.4	5.3	0.0	7.3	21.9	1,003	51	58	1,165	9,910	58,245	7,084
Benton	835.7	4,582	38.0	28.0	4.0	0.0	3.3	6,728.4	36,888	771	528	12,708	87,460	66,644	8,334
Chelan	345.4	4,688	41.8	14.6	4.2	0.0	5.4	1,594.5	21,638	603	198	6,472	38,150	60,970	8,038
Clallam	403.3	5,612	25.3	39.7	3.3	0.0	3.6	172.3	2,398	459	527	7,345	35,450	55,136	6,040
Clark	1,525.7	3,481	51.0	3.7	4.0	0.5	5.8	2,123.7	4,845	3,388	1,278	22,925	221,240	72,186	9,687
Columbia	29.1	7,286	21.7	37.4	4.2	0.0	7.5	17.2	4,300	69	10	443	1,720	51,404	5,098
Cowlitz	424.6	4,163	38.6	3.9	5.4	0.0	4.9	609.4	5,974	224	276	6,112	47,040	55,031	5,968
Douglas	142.5	3,622	59.9	8.3	5.1	0.0	6.7	350.0	8,893	257	109	2,026	19,230	52,854	5,622
Ferry	39.2	5,090	46.3	22.7	2.6	0.0	9.2	9.5	1,236	160	19	717	2,750	47,943	4,759
Franklin	294.3	3,429	60.6	1.4	3.9	0.0	4.7	315.8	3,679	485	232	6,065	37,220	52,073	5,331
Garfield	32.0	14,354	37.5	23.0	2.9	0.0	17.9	7.7	3,442	138	6	339	890	48,535	4,479
Grant	519.5	5,664	37.4	28.7	3.4	0.6	4.6	1,451.0	15,819	781	245	7,626	40,930	48,901	4,860
Grays Harbor	303.0	4,227	38.5	9.5	5.7	0.2	6.2	405.8	5,660	178	221	6,450	30,250	49,252	5,071
Island	257.0	3,246	28.7	33.0	3.3	0.2	7.4	171.2	2,163	1,345	5,995	3,329	40,820	66,847	8,062
Jefferson	155.4	5,205	19.1	39.9	3.6	0.3	5.2	145.8	4,885	182	91	2,298	16,220	65,391	8,254
King	11,212.0	5,585	28.9	12.4	5.0	1.2	5.5	22,389.4	11,153	20,327	7,305	158,947	1,091,020	113,012	20,038
Kitsap	1,054.5	4,135	42.3	4.6	3.5	0.0	3.5	748.5	2,935	19,368	11,410	13,366	125,870	72,383	9,465
Kittitas	186.9	4,485	26.5	30.6	4.7	0.0	6.5	110.8	2,658	150	125	4,083	19,070	58,283	7,058
Klickitat	118.4	5,721	34.2	32.3	3.9	0.0	8.0	215.9	10,431	91	56	1,647	10,020	64,450	8,400
Lewis	254.6	3,367	47.6	10.3	5.3	0.0	6.3	343.9	4,547	223	201	5,051	34,690	51,024	5,244
Lincoln	96.3	9,226	34.5	30.0	2.8	0.0	10.9	34.2	3,279	63	27	1,152	4,650	53,787	5,477
Mason	257.4	4,232	32.2	26.8	3.0	0.0	4.3	295.3	4,854	70	159	5,680	27,360	54,673	5,678
Okanogan	207.5	5,027	35.7	32.4	4.0	0.1	3.7	126.1	3,056	435	107	4,670	18,470	44,330	4,265
Pacific	123.7	6,010	30.5	32.4	3.3	0.0	4.1	113.3	5,509	59	167	1,828	9,950	49,370	5,262
Pend Oreille	75.9	5,850	25.2	33.2	3.2	0.1	6.9	158.1	12,178	109	35	1,416	5,480	68,883	10,464
Pierce	3,273.5	4,033	43.7	2.1	5.8	0.6	5.6	4,565.2	5,624	12,014	31,445	47,068	409,920	64,671	7,944
San Juan	74.8	4,726	30.2	8.5	3.4	0.3	9.8	34.2	2,159	59	43	772	9,050	84,956	13,906
Skagit	797.6	6,747	26.4	43.2	2.9	0.1	3.4	556.4	4,706	411	323	11,093	59,440	63,826	7,819
Skamania	41.2	3,682	35.3	7.8	6.4	0.2	7.2	16.3	1,455	108	31	502	5,010	66,903	8,231
Snohomish	2,730.6	3,725	42.2	8.8	4.8	0.6	4.4	3,753.7	5,121	2,131	6,193	37,499	380,290	74,186	9,771
Spokane	1,872.4	3,936	45.5	5.1	5.4	0.2	4.0	1,560.2	3,280	4,706	4,215	31,320	231,050	59,523	7,395
Stevens	148.2	3,405	61.9	5.5	3.5	0.0	7.0	45.9	1,055	335	116	2,726	18,570	51,232	5,437
Thurston	952.8	3,688	42.4	5.4	4.0	0.0	7.1	917.5	3,552	879	800	37,763	134,630	63,310	7,597
Wahkiakum	25.9	6,484	20.6	41.0	3.8	0.0	7.9	4.8	1,207	10	11	266	1,850	53,182	5,758
Walla Walla	228.3	3,844	45.7	5.8	5.9	0.0	7.1	249.9	4,207	1,393	151	4,344	25,800	61,701	7,710
Whatcom	644.4	3,139	42.5	4.3	6.1	0.0	5.7	595.5	2,901	1,396	629	14,198	102,600	62,170	7,852
Whitman	199.6	4,282	27.1	40.8	3.9	0.3	4.7	87.2	1,870	248	122	9,086	17,280	53,640	6,025
Yakima	1,052.2	4,260	60.9	3.2	4.2	0.8	4.9	606.3	2,455	1,250	752	16,832	109,230	49,165	5,516
WEST VIRGINIA	X	X	X	X	X	X	X	X	X	23,862	8,662	122,343	766,630	50,054	5,387
Barbour	38.2	2,315	63.0	3.6	3.6	0.0	1.0	23.1	1,402	32	74	683	6,250	40,467	3,271
Berkeley	274.3	2,561	76.5	0.5	4.5	0.0	0.7	319.3	2,981	3,450	589	5,247	53,840	51,560	5,097
Boone	117.1	4,784	50.3	15.4	4.9	0.2	0.5	11.7	479	58	106	1,413	8,080	42,911	3,635
Braxton	39.8	2,754	58.6	1.2	2.1	0.0	0.5	106.5	7,361	60	66	938	5,120	42,656	4,077
Brooke	57.1	2,394	62.3	1.0	9.7	0.1	2.8	99.9	4,186	31	103	903	10,580	47,948	4,854
Cabell	294.4	3,035	46.5	1.1	6.6	0.4	1.3	141.0	1,454	984	568	7,331	39,270	52,579	6,423

1. Based on the resident population estimated as of July 1 of the year shown. 2. Martinsville city is included with Henry county. 3. Norton city is included with Wise county. 4. Petersburg and Colonial Heights cities are included with Dinwiddie county. 5. Poquoson city is included with York county. 6. Radford city is included with Montgomery county. 7. Salem city is included with Roanoke county. 8. Staunton and Waynesboro cities are included with Augusta county. 9. Williamsburg city is included with James City county. 10. Winchester city is included with Frederick county.

Table B. States and Counties — Land Area and Population

State / county code	CBSA code[1]	County code[2]	STATE County	Land area[3] (sq. mi)	Total persons 2018	Rank	Per square mile	White	Black	American Indian, Alaska Native	Asian and Pacific Islancer	Percent Hispanic or Latino[4]	Under 5 years	5 to 17 years	18 to 24 years	25 to 34 years	35 to 44 years	45 to 54 years
				1	2	3	4	5	6	7	8	9	10	11	12	13	14	15
			WEST VIRGINIA—Cont'd															
54013		8	Calhoun	279.3	7,254	2,643	26.0	97.8	0.8	0.8	0.4	1.3	4.8	14.1	5.8	9.4	11.3	13.5
54015	16,620	3	Clay	341.9	8,632	2,538	25.2	98.4	0.6	0.8	0.3	0.9	5.5	16.6	6.9	10.0	11.8	13.2
54017	17,220	9	Doddridge	319.7	8,406	2,553	26.3	96.4	2.6	1.0	0.6	0.8	3.8	11.8	9.2	11.8	12.3	14.4
54019	13,220	3	Fayette	661.6	43,018	1,117	65.0	93.9	5.3	0.8	0.4	1.2	5.3	15.4	7.1	11.0	12.2	12.8
54021		7	Gilmer	338.5	8,026	2,589	23.7	82.4	11.0	1.2	1.2	5.8	3.7	10.7	14.9	14.7	13.6	13.2
54023		7	Grant	477.4	11,626	2,318	24.4	97.4	1.3	0.6	0.3	1.3	5.5	13.9	7.0	10.4	10.6	13.7
54025		6	Greenbrier	1,019.8	34,786	1,309	34.1	94.2	3.8	1.0	0.9	2.1	5.2	14.2	6.8	10.8	11.8	12.7
54027	49,020	3	Hampshire	640.4	23,347	1,668	36.5	96.7	1.7	0.7	0.5	1.6	4.7	14.0	7.0	10.4	11.2	14.5
54029	48,260	3	Hancock	82.6	29,094	1,456	352.2	94.9	3.7	0.6	0.6	1.6	4.5	14.5	6.6	10.4	11.5	13.6
54031		6	Hardy	582.3	13,775	2,176	23.7	91.2	3.7	0.7	1.0	4.8	5.2	15.1	6.6	10.6	11.3	13.9
54033	17,220	5	Harrison	416.0	67,554	790	162.4	95.7	2.6	0.8	0.9	1.7	5.5	15.9	7.3	11.9	12.3	13.2
54035		6	Jackson	464.4	28,706	1,470	61.8	97.8	1.1	0.8	0.5	1.0	5.4	15.9	7.2	10.8	11.6	13.6
54037	47,900	1	Jefferson	209.3	56,811	903	271.4	86.1	7.6	1.0	2.2	5.8	5.3	16.9	8.0	11.4	12.9	15.2
54039	16,620	3	Kanawha	901.6	180,454	364	200.1	90.0	9.1	0.8	1.6	1.1	5.3	14.7	7.6	12.2	12.1	12.5
54041		7	Lewis	386.9	16,024	2,036	41.4	97.5	1.1	0.7	0.6	1.2	5.5	15.7	6.8	11.3	12.0	13.6
54043	26,580	2	Lincoln	437.0	20,599	1,792	47.1	98.6	0.7	0.6	0.3	0.7	5.7	16.4	6.8	10.4	12.5	13.9
54045	30,880	6	Logan	453.8	32,607	1,365	71.9	96.6	2.4	0.5	0.4	1.0	5.4	15.1	7.1	11.2	12.9	13.3
54047		7	McDowell	533.5	18,223	1,914	34.2	90.0	8.9	0.7	0.3	1.4	5.4	15.1	6.1	10.9	11.3	12.8
54049	21,900	4	Marion	308.7	56,097	909	181.7	94.5	4.2	0.8	0.9	1.3	5.5	14.5	11.2	11.7	11.8	12.5
54051	48,540	3	Marshall	305.4	30,785	1,412	100.8	97.7	1.3	0.6	0.5	1.0	4.9	14.4	6.9	11.4	11.1	13.3
54053	38,580	6	Mason	430.8	26,718	1,540	62.0	97.8	1.5	0.7	0.5	0.8	5.3	15.6	6.9	11.0	12.1	12.6
54055	14,140	4	Mercer	419.0	59,131	876	141.1	92.0	7.0	0.6	0.8	1.2	5.7	14.9	8.1	11.7	11.4	12.3
54057	19,060	3	Mineral	327.9	26,940	1,528	82.2	95.2	3.9	0.6	0.9	1.0	5.2	14.7	8.4	11.5	10.9	13.7
54059		7	Mingo	423.1	23,785	1,654	56.2	96.9	2.6	0.6	0.4	0.8	6.0	16.2	6.6	11.1	12.5	13.5
54061	34,060	3	Monongalia	360.1	106,420	569	295.5	90.2	5.1	0.6	4.3	2.1	5.0	11.3	20.9	17.1	12.1	10.4
54063		8	Monroe	472.8	13,280	2,212	28.1	97.7	1.4	1.2	0.4	0.9	4.6	15.2	6.1	10.1	10.7	13.4
54065		8	Morgan	229.1	17,787	1,934	77.6	96.7	1.4	1.1	0.7	1.6	4.1	13.8	7.1	10.1	10.8	14.6
54067		6	Nicholas	646.8	24,842	1,615	38.4	97.9	0.9	1.1	0.5	0.8	5.3	15.3	6.4	11.1	11.3	13.3
54069	48,540	3	Ohio	105.8	41,755	1,138	394.7	94.2	5.0	0.7	1.2	1.2	5.0	14.0	10.2	11.5	11.0	11.8
54071		6	Pendleton	696.0	6,997	2,669	10.1	96.2	2.5	0.8	0.5	1.2	4.9	13.5	5.8	9.7	9.9	12.1
54073		9	Pleasants	130.1	7,507	2,627	57.7	96.9	2.0	0.9	0.5	1.0	5.0	13.6	8.1	12.4	13.1	14.6
54075		9	Pocahontas	940.3	8,414	2,551	8.9	96.8	1.6	1.0	0.5	1.6	4.9	12.5	6.2	11.0	10.8	12.6
54077	34,060	3	Preston	648.8	33,839	1,332	52.2	96.6	1.6	0.7	0.4	1.7	5.1	14.1	6.9	13.5	12.8	13.5
54079	26,580	2	Putnam	345.7	56,682	904	164.0	96.5	1.8	0.7	1.2	1.2	5.3	16.9	7.0	11.1	13.3	13.9
54081	13,220	3	Raleigh	605.4	74,254	741	122.7	89.1	9.0	0.9	1.4	1.7	5.4	15.4	7.3	12.3	12.8	12.3
54083	21,180	7	Randolph	1,039.7	28,823	1,464	27.7	96.4	2.3	0.6	0.8	1.0	5.0	13.8	8.2	12.3	11.3	13.1
54085		8	Ritchie	452.0	9,721	2,449	21.5	98.2	0.7	0.6	0.5	1.0	5.0	15.0	6.2	9.9	11.3	13.9
54087		6	Roane	483.6	13,932	2,167	28.8	97.9	0.7	0.8	0.7	1.2	4.7	15.9	6.5	10.1	11.6	13.2
54089		6	Summers	360.6	12,760	2,239	35.4	93.2	5.1	1.0	0.6	1.8	4.0	12.6	5.9	10.7	12.4	13.2
54091	17,220	6	Taylor	172.8	16,862	1,985	97.6	96.9	1.7	0.6	0.8	1.1	5.3	14.9	6.5	12.3	12.5	13.9
54093		8	Tucker	419.0	6,955	2,677	16.6	98.2	0.9	0.7	0.5	0.8	4.2	11.3	6.6	10.4	11.2	14.3
54095		9	Tyler	256.3	8,746	2,523	34.1	98.5	0.7	0.7	0.4	0.8	5.1	14.6	6.7	10.0	10.6	14.3
54097		7	Upshur	354.6	24,415	1,631	68.9	96.8	1.6	0.7	0.7	1.4	5.4	15.2	10.6	11.3	11.0	12.6
54099	26,580	2	Wayne	506.0	39,944	1,183	78.9	98.0	1.0	0.8	0.5	0.7	5.2	15.3	7.4	11.0	11.9	13.6
54101		9	Webster	553.5	8,285	2,563	15.0	98.4	1.0	0.8	0.5	0.7	4.7	15.3	6.3	10.1	10.7	13.6
54103		6	Wetzel	358.1	15,270	2,077	42.6	98.1	0.9	0.6	0.5	1.0	5.3	14.5	7.6	10.3	10.6	13.4
54105	37,620	3	Wirt	232.5	5,830	2,764	25.1	98.1	1.0	0.8	0.5	0.8	5.0	16.3	6.3	10.4	11.5	13.3
54107	37,620	3	Wood	366.5	84,203	681	229.7	96.6	2.2	0.7	1.0	1.2	5.6	15.3	7.3	11.4	11.9	13.3
54109		6	Wyoming	499.5	20,786	1,785	41.6	98.2	1.2	0.8	0.3	0.7	4.8	15.5	7.1	10.4	12.3	13.1
55000		0	**WISCONSIN**	54,166.3	5,813,568	X	107.3	82.7	7.3	1.4	3.5	6.9	5.8	16.2	9.5	12.7	12.1	12.7
55001		8	Adams	645.7	20,348	1,804	31.5	91.2	3.5	1.4	0.9	4.2	3.4	11.1	5.5	9.6	9.6	12.4
55003		7	Ashland	1,045.0	15,600	2,063	14.9	85.3	1.0	13.0	1.0	3.0	5.6	16.2	9.6	10.4	11.2	11.5
55005		6	Barron	863.0	45,164	1,072	52.3	94.3	2.0	1.4	1.1	2.6	5.5	16.1	7.0	10.7	11.1	12.2
55007		8	Bayfield	1,477.9	15,042	2,092	10.2	87.0	1.2	11.7	1.0	2.0	4.5	12.6	6.0	8.2	9.3	12.6
55009	24,580	2	Brown	530.1	263,378	261	496.8	82.5	3.7	3.3	3.9	8.8	6.4	17.4	9.1	13.6	12.6	12.8
55011		8	Buffalo	675.8	13,125	2,223	19.4	96.4	0.9	0.8	0.7	2.2	5.4	15.4	6.9	10.5	10.7	13.0
55013		8	Burnett	821.6	15,392	2,076	18.7	92.4	1.4	5.7	0.9	2.0	4.4	13.4	5.6	8.1	9.3	12.2
55015	11,540	3	Calumet	318.3	50,159	987	157.6	92.0	1.3	0.8	2.8	4.4	5.4	18.5	7.5	11.1	13.3	14.8
55017	20,740	3	Chippewa	1,008.4	64,135	832	63.6	94.5	2.2	0.9	1.7	1.8	5.5	16.6	7.1	12.3	12.6	13.2
55019		6	Clark	1,209.7	34,709	1,311	28.7	93.5	0.8	0.8	0.8	4.8	8.2	21.3	8.0	9.8	10.6	11.7
55021	31,540	2	Columbia	765.5	57,358	900	74.9	93.5	2.1	0.9	1.2	3.4	5.3	15.9	7.5	11.8	12.4	13.9
55023		7	Crawford	570.6	16,291	2,023	28.6	95.0	2.6	0.7	1.0	1.7	4.8	15.6	7.4	10.3	10.6	12.4
55025	31,540	2	Dane	1,196.5	542,364	127	453.3	81.6	6.5	0.7	7.3	6.4	5.6	14.8	13.5	15.8	13.3	11.7
55027	13,180	4	Dodge	875.7	87,847	660	100.3	90.6	3.7	0.8	1.0	4.9	4.6	15.2	7.8	12.8	12.6	13.9
55029		6	Door	482.0	27,610	1,508	57.3	94.9	1.2	1.2	0.8	3.2	3.9	12.4	5.9	8.6	9.8	11.6

1. CBSA = Core Based Statistical Area. See Appendix A for explanation. See Appendix B for list of metropolitan areas with component counties. 2. County type code from the Economic Research Service of USDA Rural-Urban Continuum Codes. See Appendix A for definition. 3. Dry land or land partially or temporarily covered by water. 4. May be of any race.

Table B. States and Counties — **Population and Households**

	Population, 2018 (cont.)				Population change, 2000-2018							Households, 2013-2017				
	Age (percent) (cont.)				Total persons		Percent change		Components of change, 2010-2018						Percent	
STATE County	55 to 64 years	65 to 74 years	75 years and over	Percent female	2000	2010	2000-2010	2010-2018	Births	Deaths	Net Migration	Number	Persons per household	Family house-holds	Female family house-holder[1]	One person
	16	17	18	19	20	21	22	23	24	25	26	27	28	29	30	31
WEST VIRGINIA— Cont'd																
Calhoun	16.5	14.8	9.7	50.1	7,582	7,627	0.6	-4.9	604	736	-239	2,808	2.64	69.4	9.3	25.7
Clay	15.5	12.0	8.5	49.5	10,330	9,384	-9.2	-8.0	849	910	-699	3,365	2.62	68.0	10.0	23.4
Doddridge	15.1	13.0	8.7	45.0	7,403	8,201	10.8	2.5	557	687	322	2,662	2.98	68.3	7.7	26.1
Fayette	15.1	12.4	8.7	49.7	47,579	46,049	-3.2	-6.6	4,194	5,355	-1,847	17,697	2.42	68.9	12.6	27.6
Gilmer	11.7	9.3	8.2	40.2	7,160	8,695	21.4	-7.7	536	617	-599	2,703	2.45	64.6	8.7	27.2
Grant	14.6	13.8	10.6	50.1	11,299	11,942	5.7	-2.6	1,000	1,092	-218	4,372	2.64	66.2	6.1	27.3
Greenbrier	15.3	13.6	9.7	51.0	34,453	35,483	3.0	-2.0	2,970	3,956	297	15,255	2.29	63.1	10.1	31.4
Hampshire	15.9	13.9	8.5	49.0	20,203	23,969	18.6	-2.6	1,815	2,208	-217	9,676	2.36	57.4	11.1	39.1
Hancock	15.9	13.1	10.0	51.3	32,667	30,672	-6.1	-5.1	2,214	3,334	-425	12,760	2.33	63.7	12.9	31.0
Hardy	15.3	13.1	8.8	49.7	12,669	14,025	10.7	-1.8	1,234	1,238	-250	5,561	2.47	73.2	9.7	23.0
Harrison	14.4	11.1	8.3	50.9	68,652	69,108	0.7	-2.2	6,411	7,029	-881	27,542	2.45	65.5	11.9	29.4
Jackson	15.1	11.2	9.2	50.3	28,000	29,214	4.3	-1.7	2,620	2,876	-228	11,149	2.60	69.2	10.1	27.9
Jefferson	14.1	10.3	5.9	50.4	42,190	53,488	26.8	6.2	4,816	3,825	2,349	20,808	2.60	70.4	11.1	22.9
Kanawha	15.0	12.1	8.6	51.8	200,073	193,051	-3.5	-6.5	17,163	20,307	-9,332	80,267	2.30	62.7	13.4	31.9
Lewis	14.4	12.2	8.4	50.3	16,919	16,372	-3.2	-2.1	1,580	1,839	-75	6,586	2.45	68.8	11.3	25.1
Lincoln	15.0	11.7	7.8	50.5	22,108	21,709	-1.8	-5.1	2,105	2,244	-962	8,046	2.63	69.2	11.6	26.9
Logan	14.9	12.9	7.4	50.6	37,710	36,754	-2.5	-11.3	3,257	4,444	-2,978	13,978	2.42	68.6	11.4	27.3
McDowell	16.5	13.1	8.7	51.1	27,329	22,111	-19.1	-17.6	1,953	2,853	-3,029	7,702	2.34	67.1	14.0	28.3
Marion	13.2	11.2	8.3	50.6	56,598	56,418	-0.3	-0.6	5,337	5,454	-156	22,718	2.43	65.1	10.3	28.6
Marshall	15.6	13.5	8.9	50.4	35,519	33,107	-6.8	-7.0	2,594	3,379	-1,511	12,695	2.49	66.9	10.2	28.3
Mason	15.5	12.0	8.9	51.6	25,957	27,348	5.4	-2.3	2,261	2,800	-68	11,079	2.38	69.5	11.3	27.5
Mercer	14.0	12.9	9.1	52.0	62,980	62,265	-1.1	-5.0	5,982	7,412	-1,664	25,019	2.39	66.0	13.9	29.7
Mineral	14.0	12.9	8.8	50.2	27,078	28,198	4.1	-4.5	2,323	2,741	-823	11,274	2.36	64.6	12.0	31.8
Mingo	15.2	12.3	6.7	50.7	28,253	26,834	-5.0	-11.4	2,675	3,042	-2,704	10,910	2.30	67.9	13.1	28.9
Monongalia	10.6	7.7	4.9	48.4	81,866	96,190	17.5	10.6	8,948	5,552	6,738	38,410	2.54	53.2	8.2	34.2
Monroe	14.9	14.2	10.8	50.0	14,583	13,498	-7.4	-1.6	1,064	1,424	149	5,815	2.30	68.8	11.8	28.9
Morgan	16.4	13.9	9.2	49.9	14,943	17,541	17.4	1.4	1,183	1,828	900	7,118	2.44	63.5	5.2	29.2
Nicholas	15.0	13.5	8.9	50.8	26,562	26,233	-1.2	-5.3	2,295	2,771	-906	10,671	2.38	69.0	9.8	26.2
Ohio	14.8	12.1	9.7	51.7	47,427	44,448	-6.3	-6.1	3,703	4,715	-1,665	17,846	2.27	58.5	11.0	36.1
Pendleton	17.0	14.3	12.7	49.4	8,196	7,695	-6.1	-9.1	572	786	-489	3,032	2.30	67.2	10.3	29.7
Pleasants	14.1	11.3	7.8	45.6	7,514	7,602	1.2	-1.2	557	758	108	2,868	2.43	75.0	10.1	20.6
Pocahontas	16.8	14.5	10.7	48.7	9,131	8,722	-4.5	-3.5	696	861	-144	3,647	2.27	60.0	6.6	33.9
Preston	14.1	12.1	7.9	48.7	29,334	33,520	14.3	1.0	2,796	2,965	499	12,420	2.51	69.5	10.4	25.1
Putnam	14.1	10.9	7.4	50.8	51,589	55,495	7.6	2.1	4,809	4,659	1,076	21,734	2.59	70.9	9.5	25.5
Raleigh	13.8	12.4	8.2	49.9	79,220	78,865	-0.4	-5.8	7,277	8,355	-3,516	31,069	2.38	68.3	14.1	27.1
Randolph	14.4	12.6	9.3	48.2	28,262	29,405	4.0	-2.0	2,505	2,978	-89	11,391	2.37	64.8	9.3	30.4
Ritchie	16.1	13.2	9.4	50.0	10,343	10,448	1.0	-7.0	785	1,031	-479	3,825	2.60	66.5	9.4	29.3
Roane	16.1	13.1	8.8	50.7	15,446	14,927	-3.4	-6.7	1,189	1,586	-591	5,815	2.45	68.3	7.7	27.1
Summers	16.3	14.6	10.3	54.9	12,999	13,926	7.1	-8.4	902	1,589	-479	5,482	2.22	65.9	12.4	31.7
Taylor	14.5	11.7	8.5	49.3	16,089	16,888	5.0	-0.2	1,415	1,615	181	6,616	2.50	64.6	10.1	28.6
Tucker	16.0	15.1	11.1	48.9	7,321	7,141	-2.5	-2.6	543	730	6	2,951	2.32	64.3	7.6	29.7
Tyler	16.1	13.2	9.5	49.7	9,592	9,230	-3.8	-5.2	722	964	-243	3,563	2.49	65.7	11.5	31.4
Upshur	13.5	11.8	8.5	50.4	23,404	24,254	3.6	0.7	2,220	2,239	197	9,341	2.50	66.1	11.2	29.3
Wayne	14.5	12.2	8.9	51.1	42,903	42,495	-1.0	-6.0	3,422	4,108	-1,856	16,305	2.51	68.0	11.2	29.7
Webster	16.1	14.1	9.1	50.0	9,719	9,150	-5.9	-9.5	744	1,002	-608	3,690	2.33	67.2	14.4	28.2
Wetzel	15.1	12.5	10.6	50.9	17,693	16,565	-6.4	-7.8	1,385	1,839	-842	5,979	2.62	64.5	12.5	31.3
Wirt	17.0	12.2	8.1	49.1	5,873	5,715	-2.7	2.0	476	491	134	2,427	2.39	65.0	9.2	27.4
Wood	14.7	11.7	8.8	51.4	87,986	86,953	-1.2	-3.2	7,939	8,698	-1,908	36,110	2.36	64.7	11.6	30.8
Wyoming	15.5	13.6	7.6	50.6	25,708	23,802	-7.4	-12.7	1,815	2,760	-2,086	9,169	2.41	71.2	11.0	25.5
WISCONSIN	14.1	9.8	7.1	50.2	5,363,675	5,687,282	6.0	2.2	551,536	410,971	-11,715	2,328,754	2.41	63.6	9.9	29.0
Adams	19.3	17.3	11.8	46.3	18,643	20,871	12.0	-2.5	1,078	2,089	488	8,163	2.32	64.7	7.4	29.7
Ashland	15.8	11.7	7.8	49.9	16,866	16,157	-4.2	-3.4	1,474	1,530	-504	6,504	2.33	59.7	9.5	32.3
Barron	15.6	12.5	9.4	49.9	44,963	45,867	2.0	-1.5	4,196	4,109	-759	19,133	2.33	65.4	7.6	28.5
Bayfield	19.0	17.1	10.6	49.1	15,013	15,013	0.0	0.2	1,005	1,321	356	6,859	2.17	64.3	6.5	29.9
Brown	13.2	8.8	6.0	50.4	226,778	248,007	9.4	6.2	27,880	15,539	3,268	103,267	2.43	64.6	10.2	28.1
Buffalo	16.0	12.6	9.5	49.1	13,804	13,587	-1.6	-3.4	1,163	1,070	-553	5,723	2.29	68.2	6.7	26.7
Burnett	18.6	17.0	11.6	48.8	15,674	15,458	-1.4	-0.4	1,092	1,467	318	7,284	2.07	64.9	7.3	29.1
Calumet	14.4	9.1	6.0	49.6	40,631	48,973	20.5	2.4	4,401	2,672	-533	19,345	2.56	74.1	8.4	21.5
Chippewa	14.8	10.6	7.4	48.2	55,195	62,506	13.2	2.6	5,861	4,624	448	25,247	2.41	67.4	7.4	26.7
Clark	13.8	9.0	7.6	49.5	33,557	34,691	3.4	0.1	4,724	2,783	-1,938	12,755	2.66	68.9	6.8	26.1
Columbia	15.3	10.6	7.3	48.9	52,468	56,849	8.3	0.9	4,960	4,374	-46	23,317	2.37	67.7	9.0	26.8
Crawford	15.7	13.4	9.9	48.1	17,243	16,644	-3.5	-2.1	1,349	1,436	-257	6,610	2.35	62.1	7.1	32.7
Dane	11.7	8.4	5.3	50.3	426,526	488,067	14.4	11.1	50,397	25,905	29,874	216,930	2.35	57.3	8.2	30.2
Dodge	15.4	9.8	7.8	47.1	85,897	88,759	3.3	-1.0	6,798	7,282	-371	33,987	2.45	66.0	7.7	28.2
Door	18.1	17.8	11.9	50.7	27,961	27,785	-0.6	-0.6	1,747	2,716	814	13,159	2.06	66.9	6.5	26.7

1. No spouse present.

Table B. States and Counties — **Population, Vital Statistics, Health, and Crime**

STATE County	Persons in group quarters, 2018	Daytime Population, 2013-2017		Births, 2018		Deaths, 2018		Persons under 65 with no health insurance, 2016		Medicare, 2018			Serious crimes known to police[2], 2016 Total	
		Number	Employment/residence ratio	Total	Rate[1]	Number	Rate[1]	Number	Percent	Total beneficiaries	Enrolled in Original Medicare	Enrolled in Medicare Advantage	Number	Rate[3]
	32	33	34	35	36	37	38	39	40	41	42	43	44	45
WEST VIRGINIA— Cont'd														
Calhoun	22	6,697	0.66	65	9.0	80	11.0	447	7.9	2,052	1,546	506	56	818
Clay	74	8,019	0.64	84	9.7	114	13.2	499	7.1	2,441	1,547	894	NA	NA
Doddridge	931	7,616	0.66	59	7.0	78	9.3	403	6.8	1,627	1,101	526	61	751
Fayette	1,840	40,136	0.72	415	9.6	646	15.0	2,534	7.5	10,990	7,519	3,471	923	2,262
Gilmer	1,863	8,312	1.00	58	7.2	77	9.6	355	7.1	1,445	987	458	69	819
Grant	126	11,083	0.88	121	10.4	126	10.8	589	6.6	3,202	2,530	672	68	768
Greenbrier	612	37,067	1.11	335	9.6	504	14.5	1,830	6.8	9,480	7,213	2,267	392	1,159
Hampshire	442	19,422	0.56	198	8.5	283	12.1	1,569	8.7	5,731	4,534	1,197	129	568
Hancock	226	28,676	0.90	224	7.7	438	15.1	1,427	6.2	7,756	5,562	2,194	253	890
Hardy	58	14,294	1.08	155	11.3	148	10.7	875	8.0	3,377	2,611	766	158	1,174
Harrison	911	77,033	1.29	695	10.3	854	12.6	3,221	5.8	16,212	11,335	4,877	NA	NA
Jackson	180	26,958	0.80	284	9.9	364	12.7	1,455	6.2	7,160	5,087	2,073	288	991
Jefferson	1,051	47,651	0.70	550	9.7	526	9.3	2,863	6.1	10,577	8,414	2,163	961	1,803
Kanawha	3,338	208,719	1.26	1,845	10.2	2,496	13.8	9,225	6.2	45,735	29,005	16,730	9,032	5,047
Lewis	247	17,095	1.12	160	10.0	234	14.6	860	6.7	4,278	2,746	1,532	145	886
Lincoln	65	17,128	0.41	221	10.7	295	14.3	1,304	7.6	5,306	3,265	2,041	NA	NA
Logan	691	35,454	1.10	341	10.5	525	16.1	1,826	6.8	9,009	6,021	2,988	505	1,624
McDowell	139	20,252	1.14	182	10.0	324	17.8	1,529	10.0	5,869	4,240	1,629	202	1,435
Marion	1,333	51,992	0.82	621	11.1	666	11.9	2,561	5.7	13,154	8,557	4,597	732	1,382
Marshall	540	30,004	0.84	286	9.3	393	12.8	1,370	5.6	7,070	3,785	3,285	547	1,783
Mason	677	24,252	0.69	246	9.2	352	13.2	1,209	5.8	6,718	4,590	2,128	399	1,634
Mercer	1,113	59,992	0.96	649	11.0	916	15.5	3,163	6.7	16,464	11,401	5,063	1,316	2,229
Mineral	566	23,737	0.67	255	9.5	357	13.3	1,259	6.0	6,631	5,441	1,190	301	1,373
Mingo	85	24,310	0.88	269	11.3	383	16.1	1,540	7.6	6,913	4,782	2,131	195	846
Monongalia	6,770	116,002	1.25	1,071	10.1	699	6.6	5,697	6.6	13,798	8,847	4,951	1,719	1,801
Monroe	57	11,037	0.51	115	8.7	168	12.7	771	7.6	3,751	2,765	986	96	715
Morgan	123	14,458	0.56	147	8.3	245	13.8	1,003	7.4	4,500	3,605	895	212	1,299
Nicholas	162	24,346	0.88	253	10.2	351	14.1	1,319	6.6	7,105	4,571	2,534	571	2,446
Ohio	2,385	52,770	1.51	388	9.3	558	13.4	1,658	5.2	10,997	6,358	4,639	1,151	2,793
Pendleton	117	6,428	0.74	68	9.7	80	11.4	395	7.7	2,142	1,583	559	NA	NA
Pleasants	698	7,351	0.94	61	8.1	79	10.5	268	4.9	1,768	1,208	560	37	484
Pocahontas	318	8,419	0.96	82	9.7	113	13.4	433	7.0	2,328	1,751	577	82	1,092
Preston	2,104	28,782	0.62	314	9.3	372	11.0	1,972	7.8	7,566	5,413	2,153	299	1,095
Putnam	249	52,811	0.85	516	9.1	590	10.4	2,393	5.1	12,348	7,671	4,677	736	1,359
Raleigh	3,698	80,698	1.13	746	10.0	1,018	13.7	3,750	6.5	19,766	14,122	5,644	2,711	3,601
Randolph	2,316	29,936	1.07	290	10.1	359	12.5	1,470	7.0	7,209	5,436	1,773	467	2,156
Ritchie	106	10,280	1.07	89	9.2	145	14.9	597	7.7	2,647	1,919	728	54	668
Roane	98	12,962	0.70	123	8.8	186	13.4	874	7.8	4,052	2,752	1,300	154	1,080
Summers	1,103	11,748	0.66	100	7.8	176	13.8	604	6.7	3,482	2,659	823	82	779
Taylor	511	13,339	0.47	148	8.8	189	11.2	851	6.4	3,787	2,795	992	NA	NA
Tucker	198	6,681	0.88	62	8.9	97	13.9	334	6.4	1,936	1,265	671	53	969
Tyler	67	8,216	0.77	82	9.4	102	11.7	451	6.4	2,342	1,510	832	71	1,057
Upshur	1,224	23,753	0.91	253	10.4	286	11.7	1,285	6.9	5,701	3,781	1,920	393	1,591
Wayne	246	36,894	0.71	359	9.0	544	13.6	2,228	6.9	10,103	6,795	3,308	NA	NA
Webster	58	8,076	0.80	70	8.4	117	14.1	498	7.5	2,533	1,662	871	NA	NA
Wetzel	124	16,836	1.20	156	10.2	235	15.4	765	6.3	3,961	2,367	1,594	79	580
Wirt	0	4,641	0.41	51	8.7	49	8.4	325	6.9	1,506	1,087	419	83	1,414
Wood	1,007	89,091	1.09	887	10.5	1,060	12.6	4,262	6.2	21,597	16,039	5,558	2,707	3,155
Wyoming	56	20,975	0.81	181	8.7	336	16.2	1,341	7.7	5,986	3,815	2,171	178	969
WISCONSIN	144,736	5,719,530	0.98	64,939	11.2	50,283	8.6	297,297	6.3	1,141,746	670,341	471,405	129,399	2,239
Adams	1,212	17,171	0.60	123	6.0	252	12.4	1,087	8.3	6,796	4,993	1,803	518	2,593
Ashland	623	16,949	1.16	173	11.1	170	10.9	920	7.5	3,919	2,756	1,163	466	2,958
Barron	610	45,612	1.01	484	10.7	479	10.6	2,581	7.3	11,542	7,187	4,355	561	1,235
Bayfield	116	12,885	0.69	120	8.0	173	11.5	1,052	9.6	4,716	3,162	1,554	213	1,425
Brown	6,524	277,260	1.15	3,286	12.5	1,887	7.2	14,837	6.8	45,907	21,379	24,528	4,793	1,841
Buffalo	80	10,766	0.63	133	10.1	132	10.1	803	7.8	3,183	2,713	470	58	473
Burnett	134	14,080	0.82	129	8.4	183	11.9	972	8.9	5,160	3,342	1,818	414	2,745
Calumet	163	38,113	0.57	481	9.6	353	7.0	1,967	4.6	8,077	2,882	5,195	528	1,060
Chippewa	2,694	59,139	0.86	665	10.4	564	8.8	2,766	5.5	13,395	8,884	4,511	781	1,228
Clark	464	32,205	0.85	572	16.5	325	9.4	5,102	18.0	6,448	3,428	3,020	188	547
Columbia	1,413	48,660	0.73	589	10.3	506	8.8	2,672	5.8	12,174	8,536	3,638	830	1,466
Crawford	762	16,486	1.02	160	9.8	179	11.0	886	7.4	4,318	2,916	1,402	234	1,434
Dane	12,800	562,276	1.14	5,955	11.0	3,269	6.0	21,783	4.8	83,885	62,840	21,045	12,168	2,329
Dodge	6,317	80,204	0.82	780	8.9	862	9.8	3,644	5.4	17,691	11,031	6,660	1,054	1,193
Door	340	27,074	0.97	214	7.8	345	12.5	1,161	6.0	9,410	6,568	2,842	214	779

1. Per 1,000 estimated resident population.　　2. Data for serious crimes have not been adjusted for underreporting; this may affect comparability between geographic areas and over time.　　3. Per 100,000 population estimated by the FBI.

Table B. States and Counties — Crime, Education, Money Income, and Poverty

STATE County	Serious crimes known to police[2], 2016 (cont.)[1] Rate — Violent	Property	School enrollment and attainment, 2013-2017 Enrollment[3] Total	Percent private	Attainment[4] (percent) High school graduate or less	Bachelor's degree or more	Local government expenditures,[5] 2014-2015 Total current spending (mil dol)	Current spending per student (dollars)	Money income, 2013-2017 Per capita income[6]	Median income (dollars)	Households Percent with income of less than $50,000	Percent with income of $200,000 or more	Income and poverty, 2017 Median household income (dollars)	Percent below poverty level All persons	Children under 18 years	Children 5 to 17 years in families
	46	47	48	49	50	51	52	53	54	55	56	57	58	59	60	61
WEST VIRGINIA— Cont'd																
Calhoun	219	599	1,371	11.1	68.3	10.6	11.6	10,843	19,696	36,279	62.0	1.0	33,527	24.8	32.7	28.6
Clay	NA	NA	1,946	3.4	77.5	9.0	20.9	10,586	16,229	34,242	69.5	0.7	34,321	27.3	37.4	35.2
Doddridge	209	542	1,539	7.3	62.9	14.9	17.0	14,655	21,164	44,437	54.3	0.9	44,370	20.1	28.2	26.1
Fayette	274	1,987	8,901	15.9	61.4	14.7	74.6	10,986	20,758	39,297	61.6	1.2	38,063	22.3	30.1	27.7
Gilmer	237	582	2,019	9.0	58.7	16.0	11.3	12,457	18,207	37,175	62.4	1.0	35,429	26.6	27.1	25.5
Grant	260	509	2,073	7.2	64.9	14.5	17.5	9,737	21,705	40,093	59.9	1.5	41,040	14.5	21.7	21.1
Greenbrier	95	1,065	6,489	8.3	55.1	20.3	58.8	11,403	23,777	40,483	60.4	1.6	37,902	18.5	26.7	23.8
Hampshire	145	422	4,534	5.1	65.2	12.6	50.4	14,245	21,771	36,575	62.2	0.4	47,606	16.9	25.8	25.1
Hancock	113	778	6,017	7.4	54.4	17.9	46.8	11,228	25,157	43,634	57.5	2.2	44,623	14.9	20.4	18.2
Hardy	468	706	2,635	9.2	66.5	14.4	22.6	9,596	23,446	42,573	58.8	1.3	44,263	14.4	22.0	20.2
Harrison	NA	NA	14,121	10.6	49.5	22.6	122.3	11,173	27,162	48,315	51.4	3.2	51,711	16.8	21.2	20.7
Jackson	386	606	5,359	8.3	56.3	16.2	54.5	11,124	23,246	41,731	58.2	2.4	45,199	17.0	24.1	23.0
Jefferson	173	1,631	14,332	13.2	43.3	30.5	100.9	11,128	33,241	72,526	33.1	6.8	70,203	10.4	12.4	11.7
Kanawha	667	4,380	37,888	12.0	49.3	25.3	331.1	11,593	28,201	46,859	53.1	3.6	43,598	18.1	25.0	20.4
Lewis	86	801	3,017	8.3	61.4	13.4	28.9	11,238	21,513	39,793	59.2	1.3	41,908	18.4	25.8	24.2
Lincoln	NA	NA	4,061	4.6	66.3	8.9	41.6	11,217	19,321	37,075	62.6	0.2	36,055	25.7	32.3	29.6
Logan	547	1,078	6,679	6.5	64.7	8.7	70.3	11,412	21,074	37,859	59.9	1.4	34,925	29.2	37.7	33.3
McDowell	469	966	3,111	4.2	79.2	4.9	45.3	13,247	13,985	25,595	78.3	0.8	26,491	31.7	46.3	43.1
Marion	378	1,004	13,014	5.4	51.4	22.0	93.0	11,387	25,205	48,158	51.8	2.5	46,514	16.2	20.1	18.4
Marshall	271	1,513	6,355	13.0	55.4	17.1	59.8	12,758	24,043	42,473	55.5	2.4	41,471	19.1	24.8	21.8
Mason	115	1,519	5,284	7.5	63.5	11.0	47.7	11,227	21,094	38,977	59.7	0.5	40,314	20.2	28.0	24.2
Mercer	461	1,768	13,007	9.0	55.6	19.8	103.2	10,912	21,698	37,763	60.9	1.2	36,160	21.0	30.0	29.1
Mineral	242	1,131	5,792	8.3	59.4	12.7	47.7	11,374	21,888	40,749	57.1	0.5	45,144	13.6	21.5	20.6
Mingo	247	598	4,924	3.1	68.2	9.2	51.2	11,777	19,272	31,227	68.2	1.6	30,880	31.0	38.5	35.5
Monongalia	254	1,547	35,840	7.3	37.4	39.8	128.4	11,367	29,285	49,624	50.2	5.6	50,621	17.3	13.9	13.4
Monroe	119	596	2,438	9.2	67.8	14.5	20.4	11,074	22,830	36,684	63.0	2.1	44,230	16.5	25.6	23.2
Morgan	349	950	3,329	12.2	56.1	18.0	27.6	11,031	24,026	46,346	55.4	1.3	44,448	13.0	18.8	17.3
Nicholas	677	1,769	4,864	4.3	63.3	14.7	42.9	10,862	22,101	39,037	61.3	2.2	37,358	20.1	28.1	26.3
Ohio	767	2,026	9,337	20.0	42.5	30.8	63.5	11,643	29,769	45,777	53.4	3.5	47,818	12.7	17.8	17.0
Pendleton	NA	NA	1,158	11.1	69.6	13.9	13.1	13,811	23,697	39,554	63.1	2.7	41,281	15.3	23.8	22.1
Pleasants	157	327	1,475	3.7	61.4	13.8	16.1	13,317	24,605	45,152	51.9	1.8	47,118	13.1	17.6	16.1
Pocahontas	306	786	1,379	7.8	62.8	17.8	14.9	13,869	23,219	37,111	62.7	0.9	35,367	18.9	25.8	25.3
Preston	304	791	6,234	8.0	64.0	15.0	42.6	10,040	22,540	46,673	53.3	1.5	45,215	17.5	23.3	21.2
Putnam	283	1,077	12,527	12.7	46.1	24.9	108.1	11,040	30,690	59,113	43.1	5.0	59,815	10.4	12.2	10.9
Raleigh	507	3,094	15,969	11.2	54.5	18.6	135.9	10,934	23,435	42,386	56.4	1.6	41,286	19.9	26.6	23.4
Randolph	549	1,606	5,473	17.0	63.5	17.7	44.1	10,833	23,642	40,094	60.9	3.0	37,208	19.6	27.3	28.3
Ritchie	62	606	1,821	8.3	67.9	9.3	17.1	11,431	21,533	41,497	59.9	0.8	40,636	18.5	28.5	27.1
Roane	309	771	2,999	6.2	66.1	11.4	23.2	9,770	20,723	37,931	63.4	1.6	37,067	21.2	32.0	28.4
Summers	181	599	2,277	8.2	59.2	14.5	16.7	10,183	20,142	35,218	68.1	0.5	32,375	28.8	43.0	40.9
Taylor	NA	NA	3,191	19.7	57.1	18.6	24.7	10,274	23,683	45,916	53.9	1.7	45,400	16.0	22.1	20.8
Tucker	165	804	1,178	9.8	63.2	14.8	12.3	12,001	22,385	43,294	57.6	0.4	39,539	16.2	22.9	23.1
Tyler	283	775	1,706	3.8	60.1	13.6	17.4	13,309	24,599	40,902	58.8	1.7	43,951	16.0	21.6	21.0
Upshur	81	1,510	5,464	26.4	63.4	18.1	41.6	10,850	21,279	39,434	59.1	1.1	37,896	22.7	27.9	25.3
Wayne	NA	NA	8,907	5.4	61.6	13.0	79.1	10,674	20,582	38,905	60.0	1.5	39,355	20.4	25.9	24.2
Webster	NA	NA	1,489	1.8	70.0	10.5	15.7	10,947	20,314	33,390	66.7	0.9	31,446	28.1	41.9	38.5
Wetzel	95	485	2,980	2.2	66.1	11.8	38.6	14,144	22,088	40,694	60.7	0.9	41,882	20.6	29.3	27.0
Wirt	221	1,192	1,178	7.1	63.6	7.5	11.6	11,135	19,747	38,936	61.3	0.5	42,330	19.2	27.8	25.1
Wood	406	2,749	18,515	11.8	45.8	21.5	140.3	10,579	26,717	45,537	53.8	2.9	44,742	18.2	26.0	23.7
Wyoming	305	664	4,207	4.0	70.0	9.3	49.8	12,024	20,474	37,644	61.6	1.3	34,603	25.7	32.3	29.6
WISCONSIN	306	1,933	1,442,264	16.6	39.6	29.0	9,802.8	11,250	30,557	56,759	44.0	3.9	59,300	11.3	14.6	13.5
Adams	190	2,403	3,049	8.3	55.5	12.5	39.5	11,579	24,874	44,003	56.3	1.8	44,767	14.8	24.8	23.4
Ashland	241	2,717	3,909	19.3	43.6	21.7	32.8	12,291	22,983	41,505	59.4	1.7	43,784	15.1	22.6	21.0
Barron	57	1,178	8,865	10.5	47.6	19.5	91.3	11,693	26,935	49,257	50.7	2.4	50,940	13.1	16.7	15.3
Bayfield	241	1,184	2,681	11.1	33.6	31.0	24.1	16,390	28,272	50,110	49.9	1.8	51,120	12.3	21.5	19.9
Brown	243	1,598	66,348	15.9	38.8	29.5	472.3	10,670	29,874	56,775	43.8	4.1	61,240	9.7	12.7	11.9
Buffalo	41	433	2,844	12.5	49.6	17.9	23.3	11,424	28,286	54,753	45.3	2.1	55,297	9.4	12.5	12.2
Burnett	232	2,513	2,743	10.8	46.6	18.5	27.8	10,894	26,308	45,891	54.9	1.6	47,727	12.7	20.7	19.5
Calumet	124	935	12,822	14.2	38.3	28.6	40.2	10,355	32,713	70,662	33.4	4.2	72,309	5.4	6.5	5.8
Chippewa	116	1,111	13,913	11.0	44.2	20.2	99.2	11,107	27,020	55,240	45.6	2.4	56,678	10.1	13.5	12.7
Clark	73	475	7,492	26.1	60.8	11.4	56.0	11,348	23,437	49,131	50.9	2.0	49,718	11.8	18.7	17.7
Columbia	141	1,324	12,663	10.7	42.0	22.6	94.7	10,908	31,290	63,293	38.5	3.4	65,931	7.6	10.0	9.0
Crawford	116	1,318	3,364	11.7	50.1	16.8	28.5	12,962	24,391	47,331	52.9	1.8	47,341	12.4	18.4	17.5
Dane	225	2,104	150,110	11.3	22.4	50.0	883.8	11,553	37,193	67,631	36.7	6.6	72,385	11.3	9.3	8.8
Dodge	104	1,089	18,638	18.4	51.1	16.1	118.1	10,994	27,000	56,038	44.6	1.8	57,862	8.6	10.0	8.8
Door	44	735	4,760	10.5	37.6	32.7	44.3	12,484	34,253	56,494	42.6	3.7	59,956	7.7	11.7	10.8

1. Data for serious crimes have not been adjusted for underreporting; this may affect comparability between geographic areas and over time. 2. Per 100,000 population estimated by the FBI. 3. All persons 3 years old and over enrolled in nursery school through college. 4. Persons 25 years old and over. 5. Elementary and secondary education expenditures. 6. Based on population estimated by the American Community Survey, 2013–2017.

Table B. States and Counties — **Personal Income and Earnings**

STATE County	Personal income, 2017										Earnings, 2017		
	Total (mil dol)	Percent change 2016-2017	Per capita[1] Dollars	Per capita[1] Rank	Wages and salaries (mil dol)	Supplements to wages and salaries, employer contributions (mil dol) Pension and insurance	Supplements to wages and salaries, employer contributions (mil dol) Government social insurance	Proprietors' income (mil dol)	Dividends, interest, and rent (mil dol)	Personal transfer receipts (mil dol)	Total (mil dol)	Contributions for government social insurance (mil dol) From employee and self-employed	Contributions for government social insurance (mil dol) From employer
	62	63	64	65	66	67	68	69	70	71	72	73	74
WEST VIRGINIA— Cont'd													
Calhoun	207	4.5	28,392	3,018	52	10	4	3	27	89	70	7	4
Clay	251	1.1	28,588	3,011	47	10	4	10	28	97	72	8	4
Doddridge	221	3.3	25,807	3,082	97	18	8	5	43	55	127	9	8
Fayette	1,431	3.1	32,883	2,632	419	79	35	50	187	555	583	48	35
Gilmer	221	1.9	27,579	3,044	80	22	7	4	52	76	112	8	7
Grant	411	0.7	35,250	2,306	153	31	13	26	64	137	223	17	13
Greenbrier	1,279	3.0	36,241	2,161	512	84	45	86	219	443	727	54	45
Hampshire	798	2.9	33,981	2,485	132	28	11	41	117	214	212	20	11
Hancock	1,177	3.6	39,954	1,559	398	78	33	53	157	348	563	42	33
Hardy	441	1.5	32,148	2,734	212	39	19	2	74	119	272	20	19
Harrison	3,008	3.6	44,352	978	1,876	355	155	205	495	729	2,592	166	155
Jackson	1,019	2.0	35,153	2,326	330	57	27	56	126	301	470	37	27
Jefferson	2,736	3.6	48,569	583	750	132	64	112	420	480	1,058	72	64
Kanawha	8,366	1.8	45,642	834	5,099	843	404	688	1,449	2,327	7,035	460	404
Lewis	585	0.5	36,045	2,194	285	50	23	31	104	177	389	28	23
Lincoln	597	1.6	28,665	3,007	107	20	9	19	70	215	154	17	9
Logan	1,107	2.3	33,627	2,539	430	75	36	22	130	499	563	45	36
McDowell	553	4.6	29,939	2,936	204	44	17	14	72	276	279	24	17
Marion	2,238	4.0	39,732	1,602	842	145	70	112	334	603	1,169	84	70
Marshall	1,183	6.3	37,916	1,896	747	123	57	36	190	326	962	65	57
Mason	840	3.2	31,359	2,825	252	53	21	34	106	298	361	29	21
Mercer	2,156	3.2	36,087	2,189	779	138	68	125	295	856	1,110	87	68
Mineral	1,019	2.5	37,443	1,960	332	65	29	32	134	309	458	35	29
Mingo	738	5.2	30,592	2,882	259	47	24	20	93	339	350	30	24
Monongalia	4,488	4.5	42,734	1,179	3,105	546	246	237	826	777	4,133	248	246
Monroe	393	1.6	29,293	2,968	84	21	7	17	59	140	129	13	7
Morgan	585	3.8	33,067	2,605	102	19	9	32	91	191	162	15	9
Nicholas	792	1.5	31,629	2,793	271	48	24	31	129	314	374	32	24
Ohio	2,606	14.4	62,006	136	1,313	205	105	520	527	535	2,143	135	105
Pendleton	235	1.2	33,574	2,542	50	10	4	9	51	85	73	7	4
Pleasants	299	2.0	39,788	1,592	142	30	11	12	41	102	195	13	11
Pocahontas	313	4.3	37,065	2,022	105	20	10	20	57	128	156	12	10
Preston	1,163	4.0	34,542	2,409	319	70	28	49	160	319	466	37	28
Putnam	2,515	3.2	44,279	988	1,111	159	95	131	326	496	1,496	102	95
Raleigh	2,830	4.1	37,726	1,919	1,341	239	113	127	427	962	1,820	130	113
Randolph	1,010	2.3	35,075	2,341	415	78	36	63	155	353	591	43	36
Ritchie	335	2.5	34,252	2,455	143	27	12	17	56	110	199	15	12
Roane	450	2.5	32,066	2,747	116	22	10	17	59	172	165	15	10
Summers	412	4.0	31,679	2,789	88	17	9	13	58	178	127	13	9
Taylor	631	5.6	37,278	1,991	149	27	12	20	83	167	208	17	12
Tucker	277	3.5	40,066	1,539	102	19	9	17	44	87	147	11	9
Tyler	305	3.3	34,645	2,395	107	22	8	9	59	96	147	12	8
Upshur	761	2.0	31,104	2,844	297	51	26	47	117	233	421	32	26
Wayne	1,243	1.7	30,956	2,854	386	91	34	70	153	371	581	46	34
Webster	224	0.1	26,739	3,065	65	13	6	6	32	107	90	9	6
Wetzel	506	6.8	32,801	2,647	161	31	14	17	90	198	224	18	14
Wirt	174	2.3	29,994	2,931	18	4	2	8	23	56	32	4	2
Wood	3,340	1.9	39,244	1,684	1,564	293	131	160	535	980	2,148	151	131
Wyoming	607	2.9	28,635	3,009	196	37	16	14	69	261	265	24	16
WISCONSIN	283,636	3.6	48,970	X	143,412	26,881	10,878	19,078	54,032	48,659	200,250	12,370	10,878
Adams	754	4.2	37,748	1,916	173	42	15	38	132	246	268	23	15
Ashland	614	4.2	39,621	1,619	338	77	27	55	105	179	497	31	27
Barron	2,091	4.1	46,214	775	917	197	74	127	492	470	1,316	85	74
Bayfield	682	5.0	45,438	852	132	41	11	48	166	170	232	18	11
Brown	13,002	3.8	49,618	489	8,245	1,450	610	975	2,455	1,830	11,281	675	610
Buffalo	569	3.3	43,223	1,115	157	38	13	37	107	125	245	17	13
Burnett	626	4.1	40,774	1,436	174	45	14	40	134	189	273	21	14
Calumet	2,399	3.3	47,920	630	571	111	44	128	379	301	854	55	44
Chippewa	2,781	3.7	43,573	1,067	1,056	220	83	227	454	560	1,586	102	83
Clark	1,335	3.6	38,498	1,802	465	106	37	214	232	275	822	47	37
Columbia	2,762	3.2	48,239	605	1,006	214	81	212	494	461	1,514	96	81
Crawford	653	3.0	40,252	1,512	289	60	23	46	118	168	418	28	23
Dane	31,166	4.4	58,100	203	19,060	3,724	1,396	2,194	6,640	3,412	26,373	1,521	1,396
Dodge	3,743	3.1	42,640	1,193	1,672	323	132	237	618	688	2,364	150	132
Door	1,627	3.6	59,196	176	526	110	44	122	513	308	803	55	44

1. Based on the resident population estimated as of July 1 of the year shown.

Table B. States and Counties — Earnings, Social Security, and Housing

STATE County	Earnings, 2017 (cont.)									Social Security beneficiaries, December 2017			Housing units, 2018	
	Percent by selected industries											Supple-mental Security Income recipients, 2017		
	Farm	Mining, quarrying, and extractions	Construction	Manu-facturing	Information; professional, scientific, technical services	Retail trade	Finance, insurance, real estate, and leasing	Health care and social assistance	Govern-ment	Number	Rate[1]		Total	Percent change, 2010-2018
	75	76	77	78	79	80	81	82	83	84	85	86	87	88
WEST VIRGINIA— Cont'd														
Calhoun	-2.8	D	D	D	D	D	D	D	21.8	2,330	319	564	3,994	0.8
Clay	-0.1	D	6.2	D	D	5.8	D	17.2	33.1	2,815	321	681	4,629	1.3
Doddridge	-1.5	23.8	D	D	D	3.7	2.3	3.4	21.9	1,825	213	197	3,908	-0.9
Fayette	-0.2	8.2	3.7	4.8	4.0	8.6	4.0	15.7	26.5	12,425	285	2,536	21,518	-0.5
Gilmer	1.5	D	1.5	7.7	D	3.8	D	D	55.9	1,610	201	319	3,569	3.5
Grant	-1.7	D	12.9	6.2	2.9	7.0	3.2	10.0	22.5	3,515	301	369	6,724	5.6
Greenbrier	0.4	2.3	5.1	7.2	4.1	9.1	4.0	19.3	17.6	10,320	292	1,359	19,376	2.1
Hampshire	-1.9	D	9.2	2.9	3.7	9.0	5.6	D	29.9	6,185	264	707	14,079	2.8
Hancock	0.0	D	D	35.8	6.0	4.7	5.9	8.9	12.2	8,645	294	948	14,332	-1.4
Hardy	-4.2	0.0	2.2	45.3	D	6.7	4.2	D	14.8	3,735	272	405	8,357	3.5
Harrison	-0.3	5.1	7.6	4.7	9.0	6.3	4.1	14.5	26.1	17,330	256	2,737	31,769	1.0
Jackson	-0.6	0.9	4.9	28.1	4.9	8.7	6.0	D	15.6	7,925	274	1,181	13,433	1.0
Jefferson	0.5	D	4.6	5.0	9.1	5.2	3.5	7.1	31.5	10,865	193	836	23,418	6.3
Kanawha	0.0	3.1	5.6	4.6	12.0	5.8	8.8	19.5	18.7	49,985	273	7,031	92,333	-0.3
Lewis	-0.4	21.0	7.7	1.9	D	6.6	1.9	D	18.4	4,700	290	885	7,960	0.0
Lincoln	-0.1	6.9	20.6	0.3	4.7	6.5	1.6	13.1	28.8	5,995	288	1,655	9,949	0.7
Logan	0.0	20.5	1.6	3.4	4.9	9.9	2.0	D	19.5	10,395	316	2,234	16,875	0.8
McDowell	0.0	32.2	D	D	D	4.9	2.1	6.4	35.9	6,745	365	2,656	11,173	-1.3
Marion	-0.3	D	6.2	5.7	9.0	7.8	3.8	9.9	19.9	14,470	257	2,014	26,437	-0.1
Marshall	-0.7	25.7	21.3	12.5	2.0	4.2	1.7	D	10.3	7,795	250	889	15,734	-1.2
Mason	2.0	D	D	11.1	2.8	5.0	2.8	15.5	20.5	7,555	282	1,263	13,089	0.6
Mercer	0.1	0.6	4.8	4.8	5.3	11.2	3.5	18.2	24.3	17,765	297	3,706	30,013	-0.3
Mineral	-0.7	D	5.9	32.0	D	6.7	2.4	D	18.4	6,885	253	774	13,151	0.9
Mingo	0.0	34.3	2.6	2.7	D	3.9	2.3	D	17.2	7,865	326	2,676	12,843	1.1
Monongalia	-0.1	1.3	6.0	10.0	7.9	4.9	2.5	22.3	25.4	14,310	136	1,604	45,074	4.2
Monroe	-5.3	0.0	7.7	26.3	D	D	2.4	7.4	36.8	4,035	301	431	7,657	0.8
Morgan	-0.1	D	9.2	6.2	D	7.5	5.2	D	21.4	4,890	276	323	10,015	2.7
Nicholas	0.0	4.7	5.3	12.1	D	12.2	2.2	D	25.1	7,900	315	1,221	13,170	0.8
Ohio	-0.1	D	D	3.4	27.0	5.4	5.1	19.3	9.6	11,700	278	1,346	20,912	-1.2
Pendleton	-5.0	D	D	D	5.2	7.7	D	D	22.8	2,325	332	188	5,218	1.7
Pleasants	-0.1	D	5.6	28.0	2.2	3.0	D	6.0	15.2	1,985	264	219	3,404	0.4
Pocahontas	0.0	D	5.7	7.7	8.5	6.1	3.4	D	27.4	2,540	300	291	8,940	1.0
Preston	-1.5	0.6	16.6	5.7	3.9	6.3	3.7	D	39.4	8,145	242	1,089	15,175	0.5
Putnam	0.2	0.2	14.5	14.0	6.7	5.7	5.5	10.2	9.5	13,495	238	1,059	24,249	3.5
Raleigh	-0.1	8.9	3.9	2.8	5.7	9.2	3.3	20.6	21.6	22,095	295	3,256	36,172	0.7
Randolph	0.0	4.4	3.0	10.0	3.3	9.6	4.2	D	18.5	7,755	269	1,171	14,248	0.4
Ritchie	-2.0	30.3	6.7	22.4	D	5.8	4.0	4.5	12.1	2,960	303	507	5,901	1.0
Roane	-2.6	D	8.7	5.1	D	9.8	6.3	D	18.1	4,555	324	956	7,437	1.2
Summers	-2.0	0.0	10.1	1.4	D	6.8	4.1	D	24.7	3,590	276	735	7,712	0.4
Taylor	-1.5	D	8.2	D	D	7.4	D	D	27.4	4,020	237	666	7,535	0.0
Tucker	0.3	D	D	11.1	D	3.7	3.2	10.0	19.7	2,090	302	198	5,366	0.4
Tyler	-0.7	D	D	43.6	D	3.2	D	7.4	20.1	2,655	302	297	5,019	0.2
Upshur	-0.4	1.8	13.4	11.3	5.7	9.4	4.0	D	16.1	6,275	256	1,015	11,428	3.0
Wayne	-0.1	D	8.8	11.4	2.1	4.9	1.4	D	41.5	10,665	266	1,955	19,289	0.3
Webster	-0.1	D	8.6	11.4	D	5.8	D	11.5	32.7	2,825	337	661	5,448	0.4
Wetzel	-0.3	D	9.3	3.3	D	12.6	4.8	D	27.3	4,390	284	739	8,175	0.1
Wirt	-2.9	2.9	10.0	D	D	6.4	2.5	12.5	39.8	1,710	295	321	3,332	3.2
Wood	-0.2	0.5	7.2	11.0	5.3	8.9	6.4	16.0	22.6	23,325	274	3,460	40,286	0.2
Wyoming	-0.1	34.9	3.3	1.1	4.5	6.5	1.6	D	22.2	6,930	327	1,572	10,887	-0.7
WISCONSIN	0.9	0.2	6.3	17.6	8.3	5.9	7.9	12.6	14.7	1,212,439	209	118,112	2,710,723	3.3
Adams	7.1	0.0	6.4	7.2	D	5.3	D	8.9	29.7	7,315	366	405	17,795	2.1
Ashland	0.5	0.0	10.1	13.2	D	7.7	2.9	D	22.8	4,280	276	396	9,648	-0.1
Barron	2.1	1.6	6.1	25.1	2.5	8.0	3.0	14.6	17.8	12,515	277	925	24,208	2.5
Bayfield	1.3	0.3	12.1	4.5	D	6.3	2.2	D	35.7	5,025	335	249	13,437	3.4
Brown	0.8	0.1	5.7	16.3	7.5	5.1	10.3	14.0	11.8	48,890	187	4,737	110,388	5.8
Buffalo	2.6	D	7.6	5.7	D	3.3	4.2	D	22.5	3,490	265	198	6,839	2.6
Burnett	1.8	D	7.3	22.3	2.5	6.8	2.2	D	30.3	5,635	367	248	15,729	2.9
Calumet	5.1	D	7.3	28.6	D	7.0	7.0	D	11.4	8,650	173	233	20,933	6.3
Chippewa	1.9	1.2	10.2	24.2	3.8	9.7	2.1	10.2	14.6	14,540	228	1,132	28,615	5.3
Clark	10.7	D	9.7	25.0	1.8	6.1	D	D	15.4	6,960	201	497	15,217	0.9
Columbia	0.7	D	6.3	27.6	3.4	6.3	3.2	11.3	15.8	13,020	227	759	26,912	2.9
Crawford	1.9	D	5.0	25.3	D	13.6	D	D	15.5	4,540	280	300	9,007	2.3
Dane	0.4	0.1	6.0	7.3	16.9	5.6	9.3	9.6	21.9	84,710	158	7,518	236,941	9.7
Dodge	1.3	D	9.9	30.6	2.9	5.0	2.6	10.0	13.6	18,670	213	851	37,903	2.4
Door	1.7	D	9.4	20.0	D	9.8	4.1	11.8	14.9	9,610	350	282	25,052	4.5

1. Per 1,000 resident population estimated as of July 1 of the year shown.

Table B. States and Counties — Housing, Labor Force, and Employment

	Housing units, 2013-2017								Civilian labor force, 2018				Civilian employment[6], 2013-2017		
	Occupied units										Unemployment			Percent	
		Owner-occupied				Renter-occupied									
STATE County	Total	Percent	Median value[1]	Median owner cost as a percent of income — With a mortgage	Without a mortgage[2]	Median rent[3]	Median rent as a percent of income[2]	Sub-standard units[4] (percent)	Total	Percent change, 2017-2018	Total	Rate[5]	Total	Management, business, science, and arts	Construction, production, and maintenance occupations
	89	90	91	92	93	94	95	96	97	98	99	100	101	102	103
WEST VIRGINIA— Cont'd															
Calhoun	2,808	83.9	79,900	17.0	10.0	495	27.4	1.6	2,417	0.5	252	10.4	2,284	31.6	34.8
Clay	3,365	81.4	79,100	21.9	10.0	441	31.8	2.3	3,113	-1.1	263	8.4	2,516	24.6	37.8
Doddridge	2,662	84.0	105,900	18.5	10.0	558	28.4	1.4	3,968	2.1	158	4.0	2,843	25.4	32.2
Fayette	17,697	78.5	86,400	19.1	10.0	573	29.1	1.8	15,785	0.4	1,015	6.4	16,147	28.7	25.7
													2,526	31.9	25.2
Gilmer	2,703	74.3	91,600	15.5	10.0	528	30.1	3.1	2,379	-0.9	150	6.3			
Grant	4,372	79.7	144,600	19.0	10.0	567	24.5	0.9	5,799	-1.6	329	5.7	4,823	25.5	39.1
Greenbrier	15,255	72.6	115,400	19.7	10.0	700	27.9	1.9	15,611	-0.7	800	5.1	13,947	33.1	23.4
Hampshire	9,676	64.5	136,700	21.7	10.0	594	26.6	3.0	10,509	1.8	446	4.2	9,270	25.0	39.8
Hancock	12,760	71.7	89,800	17.7	10.0	648	26.2	1.4	12,846	0.3	758	5.9	13,416	26.6	29.8
Hardy	5,561	72.8	121,900	21.2	10.0	668	23.2	2.6	5,738	-2.8	318	5.5	6,463	20.8	38.0
Harrison	27,542	74.5	110,000	16.8	10.0	700	28.7	1.9	34,132	3.0	1,542	4.5	30,340	33.9	23.1
Jackson	11,149	77.5	113,300	18.4	10.0	630	26.1	1.8	16,374	36.4	649	4.0	11,221	28.7	28.5
Jefferson	20,808	74.1	227,300	20.0	10.0	979	28.7	2.0	29,579	1.0	983	3.3	27,255	41.0	19.3
Kanawha	80,267	69.1	111,200	17.9	10.0	712	26.5	1.4	82,263	-0.9	4,263	5.2	81,941	37.4	16.7
													6,279	24.3	31.2
Lewis	6,586	70.4	98,600	19.7	10.0	622	25.4	3.0	6,560	0.6	373	5.7			
Lincoln	8,046	77.3	82,000	16.2	10.0	536	39.6	3.1	7,112	-0.6	494	6.9	7,139	22.6	29.7
Logan	13,978	74.0	85,800	21.1	10.0	605	29.9	1.9	10,624	-1.4	746	7.0	10,678	27.4	28.9
McDowell	7,702	79.4	34,800	23.4	11.0	529	36.2	2.7	4,470	-4.3	422	9.4	4,081	24.3	28.1
Marion	22,718	75.2	110,100	16.9	10.0	732	28.1	1.8	25,169	-0.7	1,439	5.7	25,174	34.0	24.9
Marshall	12,695	78.2	99,800	16.1	10.8	608	28.9	1.3	14,237	1.9	824	5.8	12,847	28.2	28.8
Mason	11,079	77.5	78,300	18.9	10.0	565	29.4	2.2	9,832	-1.6	693	7.0	9,259	23.5	35.7
Mercer	25,019	71.8	89,400	18.8	10.4	614	30.2	1.1	20,928	-1.8	1,320	6.3	22,634	30.8	21.8
Mineral	11,274	66.8	129,800	18.5	10.0	586	28.2	1.0	12,262	0.5	676	5.5	11,195	27.5	33.7
Mingo	10,910	73.8	71,000	19.3	12.4	600	35.4	1.2	6,881	1.9	520	7.6	7,263	27.1	35.3
													49,725	45.1	15.8
Monongalia	38,410	57.7	178,200	17.8	10.0	788	32.4	3.1	53,305	0.9	2,178	4.1			
Monroe	5,815	80.3	105,700	19.1	10.0	604	25.8	2.6	5,777	-2.0	277	4.8	5,215	28.4	32.3
Morgan	7,118	81.1	170,600	23.8	10.3	751	27.1	2.0	7,943	1.7	341	4.3	7,090	28.5	32.5
Nicholas	10,671	79.4	88,900	19.2	10.1	573	30.4	2.7	9,309	0.6	600	6.4	9,796	22.6	30.1
Ohio	17,846	69.4	114,800	16.4	10.0	625	29.7	1.4	21,331	2.0	982	4.6	20,005	34.9	19.8
Pendleton	3,032	79.8	107,900	24.5	10.0	578	21.4	2.6	3,501	-1.6	132	3.8	2,726	25.2	40.7
Pleasants	2,868	81.6	104,700	17.8	10.0	647	23.9	1.4	2,750	-2.3	176	6.4	2,994	27.7	37.5
Pocahontas	3,647	81.7	117,200	18.6	10.0	612	25.8	1.4	3,768	0.6	235	6.2	3,518	31.8	29.8
Preston	12,420	81.8	106,600	17.8	10.0	630	27.2	1.7	15,341	0.9	802	5.2	13,500	26.6	33.1
Putnam	21,734	81.3	157,500	17.9	10.0	791	24.8	1.2	26,118	-0.4	1,289	4.9	25,834	39.5	21.3
													28,925	29.9	21.7
Raleigh	31,069	73.2	105,700	18.1	10.0	664	27.5	1.4	29,465	0.3	1,557	5.3			
Randolph	11,391	72.3	99,800	19.2	10.0	585	26.1	1.7	11,987	-1.2	663	5.5	11,496	29.6	25.5
Ritchie	3,825	78.6	82,100	17.3	10.0	576	28.8	0.5	4,326	-1.7	230	5.3	3,734	20.2	37.2
Roane	5,815	79.4	92,700	19.9	10.0	481	30.1	2.6	4,924	-2.0	389	7.9	4,752	31.5	30.6
Summers	5,482	74.0	95,100	19.0	10.0	634	30.0	3.2	4,198	-4.1	258	6.1	4,436	30.7	28.0
Taylor	6,616	78.6	100,200	18.9	10.0	577	26.9	0.6	7,794	-0.1	377	4.8	6,905	33.4	27.7
Tucker	2,951	80.9	104,300	19.6	10.0	507	27.4	1.1	3,327	-2.2	182	5.5	2,883	30.5	29.9
Tyler	3,563	77.6	92,400	17.8	10.0	618	29.4	2.1	3,072	-4.4	226	7.4	3,186	26.7	30.9
Upshur	9,341	74.5	111,900	19.4	10.0	662	26.9	2.1	9,373	-0.3	537	5.7	9,824	32.5	27.5
Wayne	16,305	74.7	90,600	18.9	10.0	649	31.8	1.8	15,503	-0.5	931	6.0	14,439	28.9	25.0
													2,963	25.5	30.9
Webster	3,690	71.4	68,400	18.7	10.0	508	37.8	0.4	3,175	-3.7	201	6.3			
Wetzel	5,979	78.9	90,700	16.0	10.0	630	31.9	1.4	6,548	-2.8	473	7.2	5,399	21.0	38.2
Wirt	2,427	83.4	81,400	17.6	10.0	513	31.4	2.7	2,171	-1.1	153	7.0	2,022	26.7	33.7
Wood	36,110	71.1	115,100	18.1	10.0	676	30.1	1.2	35,936	-0.5	1,974	5.5	36,841	34.0	21.8
Wyoming	9,169	81.5	67,900	17.9	10.0	613	26.8	4.1	6,783	-1.2	479	7.1	6,325	29.7	30.0
WISCONSIN	2,328,754	67.0	169,300	21.2	12.9	813	28.1	2.1	3,133,294	-0.2	93,999	3.0	2,939,880	35.5	25.1
Adams	8,163	84.7	127,800	25.4	13.9	720	28.5	1.7	8,209	-0.6	387	4.7	7,530	23.6	31.9
Ashland	6,504	68.5	107,400	21.2	13.6	644	28.7	2.4	7,910	-0.1	338	4.3	7,366	31.2	24.8
Barron	19,133	74.5	145,500	22.2	13.5	686	26.6	2.3	25,058	1.2	848	3.4	22,255	28.9	35.6
Bayfield	6,859	83.5	163,400	22.7	13.8	660	27.0	3.6	7,612	0.1	373	4.9	6,994	36.0	25.1
Brown	103,267	65.1	163,200	19.7	11.9	746	26.7	2.5	143,673	0.4	3,925	2.7	134,015	34.3	24.7
Buffalo	5,723	75.3	150,400	21.3	13.4	698	25.7	2.0	6,652	0.8	229	3.4	6,826	30.5	35.0
Burnett	7,284	80.8	150,800	23.7	13.2	693	28.2	2.2	7,332	-0.5	339	4.6	6,535	29.1	30.5
Calumet	19,345	80.8	168,400	19.1	10.9	744	25.8	1.6	27,919	-0.2	715	2.6	27,483	34.9	28.7
Chippewa	25,247	72.2	154,900	20.2	12.5	764	26.0	2.0	33,580	0.1	1,103	3.3	31,454	30.0	32.8
Clark	12,755	77.8	117,400	21.6	12.9	602	21.9	5.3	18,169	0.8	524	2.9	15,796	27.9	40.3
Columbia	23,317	73.9	180,100	21.7	12.6	767	24.4	1.8	31,806	0.0	856	2.7	30,041	32.6	28.7
Crawford	6,610	76.1	127,000	21.4	13.2	574	27.2	2.9	7,874	-0.4	291	3.7	7,530	27.1	34.3
Dane	216,930	58.3	242,700	21.4	12.1	983	29.1	2.2	320,589	-0.2	7,138	2.2	297,072	49.9	13.5
Dodge	33,987	70.4	156,200	21.9	13.3	769	25.4	1.5	48,227	-0.6	1,265	2.6	44,063	26.3	36.5
Door	13,159	78.3	204,700	22.7	12.2	756	28.6	1.2	15,499	-0.7	559	3.6	13,419	33.1	28.3

1. Specified owner-occupied units.   2. A value of 10.0 represents 10 percent or less; a value of 50.0 represents 50 percent or more.   3. Specified renter-occupied units.   4. Overcrowded or lacking complete plumbing facilities.   5. Percent of civilian labor force.   6. Civilian employed persons 16 years old and over.

Table B. States and Counties — Nonfarm Employment and Agriculture

STATE County	Private nonfarm establishments, employment and payroll, 2016									Agriculture, 2017			
	Number of establish-ments	Employment						Annual payroll		Farms			Farm producers whose primary occupation is farming (percent)
		Total	Health care and social assistance	Manufac-turing	Retail trade	Finance and insurance	Professional, scientific, and technical services	Total (mil dol)	Average per employee (dollars)	Number	Percent with:		
											Fewer than 50 acres	1000 acres or more	
	104	105	106	107	108	109	110	111	112	113	114	115	116
WEST VIRGINIA— Cont'd													
Calhoun	97	798	D	18	100	49	26	35	43,873	296	18.9	2.4	33.6
Clay	85	800	324	D	141	D	D	23	29,260	131	23.7	0.8	37.0
Doddridge	72	1,413	142	D	94	D	D	146	103,110	392	28.6	1.8	36.1
Fayette	735	7,889	2,050	474	1,474	234	162	272	34,436	253	49.8	0.4	34.2
Gilmer	120	1,042	272	193	148	28	12	33	31,697	264	8.3	0.4	37.1
Grant	231	2,663	826	283	398	96	39	103	38,520	522	30.5	2.9	34.9
Greenbrier	916	10,905	2,654	870	2,050	229	230	354	32,437	891	31.9	2.8	39.6
Hampshire	319	2,730	911	108	483	180	86	75	27,374	883	51.4	2.5	35.0
Hancock	570	9,109	1,157	2,706	957	284	433	305	33,476	93	43.0	1.1	35.3
Hardy	256	4,959	481	2,713	612	192	56	147	29,703	580	34.5	5.3	39.3
Harrison	1,800	27,946	6,775	1,478	4,836	627	1,716	1,175	42,056	810	33.2	1.1	35.2
Jackson	480	7,041	1,098	1,647	1,232	214	249	285	40,504	982	31.4	0.6	31.8
Jefferson	859	12,602	1,164	905	1,911	343	385	434	34,411	607	63.9	1.8	39.7
Kanawha	4,880	83,337	20,101	3,114	11,524	3,996	5,307	3,550	42,599	214	34.6	0.5	36.3
Lewis	384	5,289	1,194	68	1,087	101	55	216	40,822	481	21.2	0.8	41.8
Lincoln	187	1,525	584	D	308	56	40	46	30,360	177	17.5	NA	42.4
Logan	597	8,997	1,927	529	1,807	201	233	360	39,985	8	50.0	NA	15.4
McDowell	244	2,603	1,110	D	459	116	39	75	28,958	14	100.0	NA	77.8
Marion	1,183	16,063	2,962	803	2,413	404	1,174	611	38,066	599	41.6	NA	39.5
Marshall	486	9,096	1,673	566	1,277	218	269	382	41,950	638	28.7	0.2	36.9
Mason	323	3,976	991	485	630	107	67	177	44,636	876	32.9	1.5	35.9
Mercer	1,231	17,084	4,669	1,113	3,180	421	543	557	32,622	410	36.3	0.7	38.4
Mineral	444	5,659	1,452	1,082	948	115	158	228	40,203	519	35.6	2.3	35.9
Mingo	387	2,759	604	75	379	144	365	81	29,288	8	62.5	NA	40.0
Monongalia	2,337	46,993	14,542	3,849	6,325	769	2,498	2,060	43,830	542	36.2	0.2	36.7
Monroe	175	1,399	304	D	129	50	38	51	36,673	929	38.2	1.6	38.4
Morgan	231	2,009	537	D	397	84	96	66	32,993	207	50.7	NA	30.1
Nicholas	571	6,150	1,611	690	1,552	129	150	194	31,602	372	43.8	1.3	36.4
Ohio	1,385	27,203	7,179	989	3,304	1,147	1,822	1,023	37,612	208	28.4	NA	39.1
Pendleton	142	1,126	331	145	178	61	15	33	29,346	584	19.3	5.5	42.7
Pleasants	125	2,045	391	487	144	72	39	96	46,953	208	27.9	1.0	26.5
Pocahontas	210	3,088	417	288	290	44	D	71	22,936	500	28.4	4.4	34.2
Preston	531	5,485	1,147	587	934	160	97	191	34,879	1,142	34.1	0.6	39.6
Putnam	1,216	18,180	2,156	2,281	2,545	574	713	795	43,720	514	32.9	0.4	30.5
Raleigh	1,782	26,162	7,141	682	5,022	536	900	929	35,520	365	50.1	1.4	35.8
Randolph	666	9,391	2,772	1,154	1,551	256	206	272	28,988	402	33.6	5.5	36.7
Ritchie	202	2,554	212	925	248	77	65	106	41,368	473	23.9	3.0	38.0
Roane	229	2,165	676	167	484	104	36	75	34,429	604	19.7	1.2	38.4
Summers	160	1,427	443	23	231	50	49	44	31,013	357	28.0	2.5	35.6
Taylor	222	2,434	561	D	461	35	37	102	41,884	413	48.4	1.2	34.7
Tucker	154	2,079	306	240	235	44	14	60	28,644	159	28.3	1.3	40.1
Tyler	106	1,874	491	769	149	79	18	75	39,877	305	19.0	1.0	42.7
Upshur	519	6,050	1,341	792	821	95	227	218	35,980	499	37.3	1.0	36.2
Wayne	488	6,647	2,220	650	1,035	129	145	274	41,253	237	24.1	0.4	41.8
Webster	137	1,262	469	282	165	36	9	38	30,373	83	31.3	NA	57.2
Wetzel	334	4,345	791	905	951	123	167	179	41,222	261	13.0	0.4	35.5
Wirt	51	311	D	D	68	12	6	7	23,447	256	28.5	1.2	37.7
Wood	2,028	31,635	7,097	2,110	6,270	999	910	1,061	33,528	881	38.4	0.2	34.5
Wyoming	274	2,721	811	39	561	73	53	87	32,102	21	52.4	NA	39.5
WISCONSIN	140,859	2,524,329	395,239	452,798	314,425	138,232	107,316	115,817	45,880	64,793	35.3	3.6	45.6
Adams	328	3,201	481	393	489	47	60	98	30,696	308	31.2	7.5	50.3
Ashland	516	6,389	1,283	1,098	972	212	152	237	37,173	263	34.6	3.0	33.9
Barron	1,338	16,800	2,732	5,013	3,054	513	295	643	38,268	1,200	31.6	4.7	45.9
Bayfield	431	2,255	338	177	378	83	33	67	29,901	427	32.6	3.3	36.4
Brown	6,473	143,037	21,347	25,464	15,821	8,417	5,303	6,695	46,804	975	52.3	3.7	45.5
Buffalo	305	3,000	279	279	257	125	74	110	36,733	966	20.5	4.9	47.8
Burnett	395	3,287	763	744	516	84	83	108	32,813	369	22.2	3.8	40.2
Calumet	883	13,021	1,187	3,557	1,835	659	199	530	40,715	684	41.5	4.7	51.4
Chippewa	1,582	21,930	3,259	6,184	3,857	342	568	876	39,952	1,409	31.3	4.7	45.3
Clark	750	9,176	1,006	3,591	1,020	165	156	326	35,475	2,095	22.5	2.2	59.5
Columbia	1,442	20,517	2,822	5,130	3,012	404	464	760	37,035	1,357	41.3	4.5	46.5
Crawford	378	5,772	906	1,518	1,030	120	115	193	33,411	1,034	24.8	2.6	39.7
Dane	14,093	281,349	46,809	25,340	32,249	23,381	22,836	14,743	52,401	2,566	44.4	3.3	43.9
Dodge	1,734	29,770	4,208	9,605	3,373	650	595	1,505	50,555	1,749	35.9	3.5	48.9
Door	1,269	10,404	1,326	2,367	1,784	300	229	379	36,476	626	41.5	2.9	43.8

Table B. States and Counties — **Agriculture**

STATE County	Acreage (1,000)	Percent change, 2012-2017	Average size of farm	Total irrigated (1,000)	Total cropland (1,000)	Average per farm	Average per acre	Value of machinery and equipment, average per farm (dollars)	Total (mil dol)	Average per farm (acres)	Crops	Livestock and poultry products	Organic farms (number)	Farms with internet access (percent)	Total ($1,000)	Percent of farms
	117	118	119	120	121	122	123	124	125	126	127	128	129	130	131	132
WEST VIRGINIA— Cont'd																
Calhoun	61	23.3	206	0.0	12.4	375,391	1,823	62,763	2.4	8,047	39.8	60.2	NA	67.2	82	9.1
Clay	21	6.0	162	NA	3.2	279,733	1,722	39,293	0.6	4,374	45.2	54.8	NA	74.8	20	7.6
Doddridge	67	2.9	172	0.0	11.8	365,169	2,129	60,481	2.0	5,171	41.6	58.4	NA	67.3	10	1.0
Fayette	26	10.9	102	0.0	6.2	295,809	2,913	45,353	1.7	6,779	37.1	62.9	NA	81.8	48	5.5
	65	-7.6	246	D	11.1	324,619	1,317	61,671	2.8	10,538	17.3	82.7	NA	72.7	102	5.3
Gilmer																
Grant	120	6.7	230	0.0	26.2	601,970	2,622	74,196	57.1	109,316	3.0	97.0	NA	64.8	635	13.0
Greenbrier	192	1.2	216	0.0	44.1	562,728	2,606	76,127	69.3	77,797	6.0	94.0	2	74.9	970	18.5
Hampshire	132	-7.2	149	0.1	36.9	448,587	3,004	56,173	38.7	43,847	13.1	86.9	NA	69.4	244	12.3
Hancock	8	-6.1	90	0.0	3.4	410,404	4,574	65,960	0.5	5,667	74.0	26.0	NA	91.4	D	1.1
Hardy	155	-0.4	267	0.0	40.5	857,054	3,213	99,840	190.6	328,583	2.8	97.2	2	73.3	597	14.7
Harrison	112	-4.2	138	0.0	28.0	346,717	2,504	51,626	7.7	9,546	33.2	66.8	NA	78.0	142	5.7
Jackson	128	22.1	130	0.0	33.4	287,864	2,211	41,845	6.9	7,059	38.5	61.5	NA	71.4	162	5.3
Jefferson	66	-1.3	109	0.3	44.5	639,634	5,873	57,139	28.7	47,206	62.2	37.8	7	82.9	476	15.2
Kanawha	24	-9.0	111	0.0	4.1	429,309	3,881	38,062	1.0	4,710	39.1	60.9	1	73.8	27	8.9
	100	21.2	208	D	22.4	449,021	2,160	53,052	6.3	13,035	21.3	78.7	NA	69.6	29	4.6
Lewis																
Lincoln	24	-6.9	135	0.0	4.2	248,623	1,843	54,669	0.8	4,559	55.8	44.2	NA	73.4	23	15.8
Logan	1	11.7	116	D	D	287,031	2,474	22,010	0.0	5,125	82.9	17.1	NA	100.0	D	12.5
McDowell	0	-84.3	12	NA	0.1	72,143	6,196	38,104	0.3	21,214	98.7	1.3	NA	100.0	NA	NA
Marion	52	-3.4	86	0.0	13.5	255,112	2,964	40,156	2.5	4,200	45.7	54.3	1	65.9	22	2.8
Marshall	76	-11.6	119	0.0	22.6	308,256	2,587	65,533	3.8	5,966	51.1	48.9	1	66.5	95	3.9
Mason	125	-10.1	142	0.2	37.6	345,965	2,430	58,830	36.4	41,502	80.8	19.2	2	65.8	829	11.0
Mercer	53	2.6	130	0.0	12.4	326,001	2,515	57,803	6.9	16,763	21.5	78.5	NA	68.8	59	4.4
Mineral	99	30.0	191	0.1	29.6	531,811	2,788	57,610	21.6	41,667	14.8	85.2	1	66.9	134	8.1
Mingo	2	16.4	295	D	D	329,528	1,116	37,841	0.2	19,750	10.8	89.2	NA	100.0	3	50.0
	62	7.1	115	0.0	18.6	518,881	4,530	60,065	5.0	9,273	35.1	64.9	4	71.8	68	5.7
Monongalia																
Monroe	145	0.3	156	0.0	31.9	415,440	2,662	51,310	22.6	24,277	15.9	84.1	15	64.2	363	11.0
Morgan	17	-8.4	81	0.0	7.2	426,092	5,234	40,087	3.3	15,836	78.3	21.7	2	69.1	148	8.7
Nicholas	46	-21.6	122	0.0	11.8	319,996	2,615	47,319	3.1	8,304	33.9	66.1	NA	73.1	330	11.3
Ohio	24	-21.8	113	D	10.9	409,625	3,624	64,696	2.7	13,014	43.2	56.8	NA	78.4	24	7.2
Pendleton	176	3.5	302	0.0	29.6	678,517	2,250	84,763	99.9	171,074	2.7	97.3	2	61.1	324	12.7
Pleasants	24	11.0	115	0.0	5.3	264,777	2,308	44,817	1.1	5,524	43.4	56.6	NA	78.8	D	1.0
Pocahontas	131	10.9	263	0.0	26.4	492,444	1,875	65,758	8.6	17,128	22.7	77.3	2	67.2	372	16.4
Preston	143	-11.1	125	0.0	48.2	343,865	2,747	58,868	16.2	14,145	38.9	61.1	2	68.1	309	6.4
Putnam	52	-13.9	101	0.1	13.7	288,179	2,866	41,740	7.3	14,239	71.0	29.0	1	63.0	126	6.0
	44	19.4	121	0.0	11.2	447,458	3,709	52,892	3.0	8,263	28.2	71.8	1	70.1	12	2.5
Raleigh																
Randolph	98	3.6	243	0.0	26.7	588,534	2,425	65,505	7.9	19,704	32.0	68.0	4	66.7	112	8.7
Ritchie	98	9.8	206	0.0	22.6	372,079	1,805	53,870	9.6	20,334	18.4	81.6	2	72.7	148	3.0
Roane	113	1.9	187	0.0	27.8	361,187	1,930	54,938	6.4	10,675	34.7	65.3	3	72.4	118	7.0
Summers	55	-5.7	153	0.0	12.0	347,761	2,272	46,335	3.5	9,846	38.8	61.2	2	66.9	86	5.3
Taylor	46	-6.9	111	0.0	14.0	340,360	3,075	58,663	3.4	8,324	36.5	63.5	NA	71.4	28	2.9
Tucker	26	-22.1	166	D	6.5	476,151	2,863	57,473	1.9	11,937	30.4	69.6	NA	78.6	11	3.8
Tyler	56	15.4	182	0.0	12.3	348,921	1,913	51,025	2.5	8,079	40.9	59.1	NA	67.9	82	7.9
Upshur	61	-10.8	122	0.1	16.3	323,626	2,645	48,952	4.8	9,615	49.6	50.4	1	72.5	63	3.8
Wayne	39	27.5	163	0.0	5.9	326,612	2,009	46,764	1.7	7,097	44.7	55.3	NA	71.7	56	11.0
	10	32.1	126	0.0	2.4	290,032	2,299	40,787	0.5	5,434	55.7	44.3	NA	65.1	D	8.4
Webster																
Wetzel	41	8.5	158	0.0	8.8	305,112	1,927	45,093	1.3	4,950	54.6	45.4	NA	60.2	11	4.2
Wirt	41	9.0	162	0.0	9.3	292,717	1,808	49,820	2.3	8,949	30.2	69.8	NA	71.5	120	4.7
Wood	90	2.4	102	0.0	25.0	340,345	3,333	43,873	6.3	7,120	44.4	55.6	NA	72.3	187	3.1
Wyoming	1	-51.0	69	D	0.7	231,769	3,347	59,560	0.1	4,429	74.2	25.8	NA	76.2	20	19.0
WISCONSIN	14,319	-1.7	221	454.4	10,085.0	1,083,640	4,904	156,689	11,427.4	176,368	35.6	64.4	1,708	76.1	126,583	42.4
Adams	117	-1.0	381	50.9	84.5	1,708,212	4,489	227,089	D	D	D	D	6	80.8	637	30.2
Ashland	52	14.4	199	0.4	24.7	445,403	2,234	71,332	17.6	66,806	15.0	85.0	3	74.9	273	12.5
Barron	306	-1.3	255	15.3	208.8	870,734	3,419	170,748	266.4	222,001	28.8	71.2	6	81.7	936	36.1
Bayfield	81	12.8	190	0.2	42.6	415,918	2,191	75,186	15.9	37,302	51.6	48.4	9	78.5	100	12.6
Brown	192	6.0	197	0.5	166.6	1,672,996	8,495	205,925	292.7	300,255	13.8	86.2	17	77.7	2,847	37.4
Buffalo	293	-4.0	303	7.6	164.3	1,195,520	3,940	184,155	203.1	210,203	26.7	73.3	36	77.6	3,056	62.2
Burnett	89	6.7	242	0.3	49.0	658,630	2,723	110,503	37.9	102,835	36.0	64.0	4	71.0	360	27.6
Calumet	154	8.1	225	D	131.5	1,771,197	7,874	207,062	203.6	297,601	21.8	78.2	13	81.9	924	52.5
Chippewa	356	-7.4	253	8.6	243.0	899,774	3,559	148,239	215.3	152,830	37.5	62.5	26	74.2	2,197	42.2
Clark	451	-1.6	215	0.5	323.8	873,709	4,058	149,770	404.1	192,889	17.9	82.1	58	54.9	1,430	27.8
Columbia	304	-1.3	224	5.6	243.9	1,305,879	5,828	158,741	222.3	163,808	51.0	49.0	23	78.3	1,602	36.7
Crawford	211	-2.8	204	0.1	99.0	647,573	3,180	82,180	73.4	70,965	43.6	56.4	50	73.6	1,616	43.3
Dane	507	0.4	197	4.9	410.3	1,626,929	8,239	166,567	509.1	198,391	36.3	63.7	58	81.5	10,186	50.9
Dodge	406	1.0	232	0.2	340.5	1,356,553	5,844	210,146	345.7	197,636	42.1	57.9	18	78.0	5,238	49.7
Door	115	-13.2	183	0.6	90.1	870,229	4,757	157,612	78.7	125,786	41.5	58.5	18	77.0	795	40.7

Table B. States and Counties — Water Use, Wholesale Trade, Retail Trade, and Real Estate

STATE County	Water use, 2015 Public supply water withdrawn (mil gal/day)	Public supply gallons withdrawn per person per day	Wholesale Trade[1], 2012 Number of establishments	Number of employees	Sales (mil dol)	Average payroll (mil dol)	Retail Trade[2], 2012 Number of establishments	Number of employees	Sales (mil dol)	Average payroll (mil dol)	Real estate and rental and leasing,[2] 2012 Number of establishments	Number of employees	Sales (mil dol)	Average payroll (mil dol)
	133	134	135	136	137	138	139	140	141	142	143	144	145	146
WEST VIRGINIA— Cont'd														
Calhoun	0.32	42.8	NA	NA	NA	NA	19	128	27.3	2.4	3	6	0.5	0.1
Clay	0.40	44.9	1	D	D	D	17	134	45.7	2.7	1	D	D	D
Doddridge	0.22	26.9	1	D	D	D	10	90	22.8	1.4	1	D	D	D
Fayette	5.37	119.3	25	D	D	D	134	1,683	413.8	37.0	21	56	8.6	1.2
	0.64	75.1	4	D	D	D	22	157	38.3	3.2	2	D	D	D
Gilmer														
Grant	0.97	82.4	2	D	D	D	38	377	115.2	7.7	5	10	0.9	0.2
Greenbrier	3.42	96.3	17	D	D	D	173	2,029	543.4	47.6	42	118	23.3	3.7
Hampshire	0.53	22.7	6	D	D	D	57	480	123.6	9.6	14	29	3.6	0.8
Hancock	1.46	49.0	13	154	105.9	4.9	93	1,000	235.3	19.2	22	D	D	D
Hardy	3.01	217.3	4	D	D	D	45	599	133.3	12.2	7	20	2.2	0.4
Harrison	7.91	115.1	74	867	381.8	37.0	327	4,727	1,314.7	104.5	62	508	161.0	24.8
Jackson	1.81	61.9	18	254	191.4	9.9	96	1,138	348.2	25.9	14	49	24.9	2.1
Jefferson	2.70	47.8	14	58	51.0	2.8	142	1,866	451.4	40.8	43	117	18.0	3.4
Kanawha	32.16	170.8	256	3,709	2,518.9	183.3	760	11,292	3,186.6	274.2	238	1,208	278.6	42.3
	1.08	65.7	14	116	109.9	5.8	75	1,063	301.2	23.6	9	39	5.2	0.8
Lewis														
Lincoln	0.30	14.0	3	D	D	D	38	312	80.3	6.5	2	D	D	D
Logan	4.29	123.6	34	411	138.2	18.1	118	1,726	551.2	42.6	20	86	9.3	2.4
McDowell	2.90	146.2	5	D	D	D	53	650	131.2	12.7	6	29	17.9	3.1
Marion	8.21	144.2	44	D	D	D	189	2,291	743.2	55.4	35	128	24.0	4.4
Marshall	4.67	146.0	16	D	D	D	85	1,224	344.7	27.3	7	D	D	D
Mason	2.33	86.2	5	D	D	D	54	575	143.9	11.9	14	51	6.1	1.2
Mercer	3.58	58.5	52	590	355.8	28.1	251	3,183	929.1	78.2	38	126	61.9	4.6
Mineral	1.57	57.2	12	D	D	D	71	999	237.3	20.4	15	37	4.7	0.8
Mingo	4.02	158.9	14	197	55.0	8.2	62	445	119.7	11.2	15	D	D	D
	10.87	104.3	56	401	340.9	14.5	382	6,325	1,608.6	129.8	132	D	D	D
Monongalia														
Monroe	0.49	36.3	6	16	3.6	0.4	31	145	26.6	2.7	3	4	0.6	0.1
Morgan	0.55	31.4	3	D	D	D	48	397	90.3	8.2	10	29	3.4	0.6
Nicholas	2.78	108.6	17	149	59.3	6.3	109	1,505	432.5	34.7	18	46	9.0	1.5
Ohio	7.70	178.8	72	D	D	D	201	3,486	896.0	79.7	56	D	D	D
Pendleton	0.31	42.9	3	D	D	D	24	204	37.2	3.5	2	D	D	D
Pleasants	0.57	74.3	NA	NA	NA	NA	16	168	45.7	3.7	2	D	D	D
Pocahontas	0.38	44.2	1	D	D	D	33	327	75.7	6.0	11	47	6.2	1.0
Preston	2.21	65.1	15	85	33.3	2.9	94	854	234.5	16.9	20	D	D	D
Putnam	2.61	45.9	74	D	D	D	174	2,359	748.5	55.8	57	316	112.1	18.1
	9.89	127.6	96	D	D	D	346	5,057	1,452.4	124.3	74	287	50.0	9.8
Raleigh														
Randolph	2.75	94.4	24	238	368.9	8.9	142	1,477	352.7	32.6	21	100	14.7	3.3
Ritchie	0.48	48.1	5	D	D	D	34	288	73.2	5.6	4	8	0.5	0.1
Roane	0.85	58.9	9	78	50.8	2.2	41	513	132.6	11.3	10	22	1.8	0.4
Summers	2.49	188.1	6	D	D	D	29	259	68.4	5.6	3	6	0.5	0.1
Taylor	1.82	107.6	7	D	D	D	33	448	110.9	10.3	2	D	D	D
Tucker	0.61	87.6	1	D	D	D	28	223	50.1	4.8	10	52	3.8	1.1
Tyler	0.57	63.5	NA	NA	NA	NA	21	139	44.1	2.7	1	D	D	D
Upshur	2.11	85.2	12	154	171.6	6.6	82	874	264.2	20.4	19	65	8.8	1.7
Wayne	2.91	71.0	15	252	140.5	11.4	107	1,048	254.9	20.8	19	D	D	D
	0.49	56.0	3	D	D	D	21	153	42.9	3.2	3	D	D	D
Webster														
Wetzel	1.78	112.5	12	93	27.6	2.4	77	879	208.7	18.7	13	34	4.4	1.0
Wirt	0.00	0.0	1	D	D	D	13	77	19.8	1.2	1	D	D	D
Wood	7.97	92.2	76	699	332.7	27.9	390	6,018	1,396.6	129.2	84	332	68.8	10.4
Wyoming	1.82	82.2	5	D	D	D	72	677	154.3	12.6	9	28	3.1	0.7
WISCONSIN	479.38	83.1	5,990	97,040	77,066.9	5,253.6	19,272	296,956	78,201.8	6,835.0	4,509	23,762	4,358.9	801.1
Adams	0.81	40.2	6	32	10.3	0.8	44	454	192.3	11.7	13	41	4.8	1.1
Ashland	0.99	62.5	11	90	33.7	3.2	87	897	214.2	20.0	9	38	2.7	0.5
Barron	4.48	98.3	41	319	166.0	11.3	220	3,033	713.3	67.7	33	80	12.8	2.0
Bayfield	0.37	24.7	8	D	D	D	69	391	84.5	6.6	9	18	2.1	0.3
Brown	19.19	74.2	329	6,081	4,360.8	321.1	864	14,521	3,686.2	322.1	203	1,407	203.8	43.4
Buffalo	0.40	30.3	9	117	62.3	5.9	46	281	77.8	5.6	10	24	2.5	0.3
Burnett	0.36	23.7	4	D	D	D	63	588	121.0	10.8	15	18	4.3	0.5
Calumet	10.93	219.6	44	498	222.9	22.9	109	1,796	418.6	37.0	13	50	3.1	0.8
Chippewa	6.96	109.6	62	671	408.4	24.9	213	3,500	1,064.9	82.6	34	95	13.8	2.5
Clark	1.23	35.7	41	331	256.0	16.9	99	820	260.6	18.1	7	15	1.7	0.3
Columbia	3.56	62.7	46	494	342.4	23.0	197	3,292	795.2	76.2	41	D	D	D
Crawford	1.43	87.2	11	D	D	D	78	1,034	216.6	22.0	8	21	2.1	0.3
Dane	43.49	83.1	597	11,599	8,106.6	613.2	1,687	29,330	8,516.2	743.4	620	4,076	952.3	158.3
Dodge	6.30	71.2	71	978	474.7	40.7	234	3,189	833.0	69.8	40	100	18.3	2.9
Door	1.36	49.4	25	144	62.9	6.0	259	1,682	414.1	40.8	46	188	20.7	4.4

1 Merchant wholesalers, except manufacturers' sales branches and offices.   2. Employer establishments.

Table B. States and Counties — Professional Services, Manufacturing, and Accommodation and Food Services

STATE County	Professional, scientific, and technical services, 2012				Manufacturing, 2012				Accommodation and food services, 2012			
	Number of establishments	Number of employees	Sales (mil dol)	Average payroll (mil dol)	Number of establishments	Number of employees	Receipts (mil dol)	Annual payroll (mil dol)	Number of establishments	Number of employees	Receipts (mil dol)	Annual payroll (mil dol)
	147	148	149	150	151	152	153	154	155	156	157	158
WEST VIRGINIA— Cont'd												
Calhoun	5	21	1.8	0.6	6	33	D	0.7	4	22	1.1	0.4
Clay	2	D	D	D	4	43	D	2.4	5	D	D	D
Doddridge	1	D	D	D	NA	NA	NA	NA	3	D	D	D
Fayette	50	222	25.1	9.9	31	583	275.0	31.0	73	989	58.6	16.9
Gilmer	8	55	5.4	2.0	5	214	D	6.4	11	D	D	D
Grant	12	58	4.2	1.6	7	221	68.9	8.8	21	D	D	D
Greenbrier	75	295	24.0	7.7	35	774	D	30.8	88	2,455	190.7	67.3
Hampshire	24	D	D	D	12	153	66.0	7.7	35	310	18.7	5.2
Hancock	47	487	36.2	13.1	20	2,689	D	136.6	79	D	D	D
Hardy	15	48	4.4	1.3	11	2,575	D	71.4	28	309	13.9	3.9
Harrison	139	1,674	270.5	99.6	52	1,752	D	D	155	3,196	155.3	41.2
Jackson	43	236	29.9	11.9	15	1,188	D	78.3	52	852	39.1	10.4
Jefferson	84	360	48.6	18.6	17	816	206.7	35.2	127	D	D	D
Kanawha	565	5,965	884.4	340.3	121	2,985	2,196.6	185.5	458	9,306	552.9	145.9
Lewis	15	56	5.5	1.6	15	124	D	4.6	37	596	34.3	11.0
Lincoln	9	71	8.0	2.6	4	11	2.2	0.5	15	D	D	D
Logan	39	246	17.7	7.5	36	734	157.8	31.1	62	979	48.3	12.7
McDowell	13	D	D	D	4	26	D	0.8	22	D	D	D
Marion	119	1,060	130.7	59.5	50	1,154	469.5	50.6	113	2,043	93.7	23.7
Marshall	33	173	15.7	5.5	19	473	D	24.3	60	792	32.4	8.5
Mason	25	87	9.1	3.0	19	696	D	41.2	33	344	14.2	4.2
Mercer	92	639	71.4	20.2	57	1,246	241.5	50.6	106	2,177	100.9	27.6
Mineral	27	195	11.2	4.5	16	1,821	D	117.3	50	D	D	D
Mingo	47	D	D	D	13	173	D	4.2	31	322	11.2	3.4
Monongalia	205	2,723	394.9	120.9	53	3,668	2,034.3	256.4	281	5,885	253.5	70.4
Monroe	9	30	2.2	0.6	5	411	D	19.0	11	D	D	D
Morgan	13	79	13.2	6.3	6	140	D	D	27	D	D	D
Nicholas	45	246	14.7	7.7	25	709	212.9	30.6	59	844	36.9	10.3
Ohio	154	1,777	215.8	80.0	42	1,520	337.5	55.6	135	2,984	226.7	45.3
Pendleton	5	D	D	D	5	127	D	5.3	11	D	D	D
Pleasants	4	D	D	D	8	565	305.6	32.5	12	D	D	D
Pocahontas	6	D	D	D	6	261	38.1	7.9	24	1,360	51.4	16.8
Preston	29	111	10.4	3.8	25	465	147.1	17.4	36	280	13.6	3.4
Putnam	105	1,037	117.0	42.1	41	1,989	1,948.4	115.1	91	1,535	74.3	19.6
Raleigh	123	864	107.0	41.2	60	1,058	278.6	48.3	149	3,189	177.8	48.3
Randolph	49	226	17.8	6.8	24	1,069	189.4	37.2	54	776	38.4	10.6
Ritchie	14	51	3.8	1.6	13	741	D	31.8	17	D	D	D
Roane	16	46	4.2	1.4	16	226	45.2	8.1	13	D	D	D
Summers	11	70	6.8	2.5	7	19	3.1	0.7	19	247	9.6	2.5
Taylor	10	D	D	D	8	D	D	D	26	D	D	D
Tucker	7	D	D	D	15	224	D	9.9	32	D	D	D
Tyler	8	19	1.4	0.3	4	514	D	46.2	6	D	D	D
Upshur	37	228	15.8	6.4	18	665	285.3	32.5	48	644	30.0	8.5
Wayne	22	158	17.4	5.7	26	523	446.1	26.7	52	D	D	D
Webster	5	D	D	D	7	114	D	3.1	11	D	D	D
Wetzel	19	117	8.9	3.3	10	850	D	70.5	42	606	28.2	6.6
Wirt	4	D	D	D	4	D	D	2.2	8	D	D	D
Wood	161	986	105.9	42.2	59	D	2,261.9	205.7	210	4,070	181.8	53.1
Wyoming	19	55	4.5	1.4	9	51	D	2.5	21	D	D	D
WISCONSIN	11,301	99,162	15,135.0	5,738.3	8,995	436,777	177,728.9	21,879.3	14,137	221,567	10,303.3	2,764.3
Adams	15	57	4.6	1.6	12	377	D	18.3	60	1,117	55.1	17.9
Ashland	29	161	15.2	7.2	23	1,107	219.8	51.9	62	588	28.9	7.9
Barron	66	317	28.2	12.4	92	4,865	1,520.7	199.1	137	1,474	59.1	15.8
Bayfield	9	28	2.0	0.6	21	170	D	5.5	90	515	31.8	9.0
Brown	526	4,885	709.5	255.6	442	24,628	11,068.4	1,230.8	593	11,889	479.2	141.4
Buffalo	18	63	4.8	1.3	20	386	303.2	17.7	41	286	10.5	2.6
Burnett	22	62	7.1	2.3	25	790	286.6	34.5	65	456	20.9	5.8
Calumet	64	206	18.6	7.8	71	3,827	1,616.8	174.4	95	1,502	47.0	12.7
Chippewa	86	383	48.5	17.9	125	5,030	1,930.5	237.5	165	1,801	70.0	17.0
Clark	33	165	13.4	5.1	77	3,513	2,021.0	136.7	57	508	17.8	4.9
Columbia	80	465	41.3	15.9	94	4,732	2,530.5	220.7	167	3,440	158.0	45.2
Crawford	21	227	10.0	4.7	24	1,534	1,054.2	66.7	55	638	27.6	7.0
Dane	1,741	19,907	3,387.5	1,313.8	521	23,154	7,205.3	1,210.9	1,265	24,284	1,111.2	316.1
Dodge	78	467	52.4	19.0	148	10,011	3,727.6	462.8	155	1,801	69.5	18.2
Door	74	237	28.7	9.4	56	1,968	416.7	88.3	238	1,999	147.6	36.9

Table B. States and Counties — Health Care and Social Assistance, Other Services, Nonemployer Businesses, and Residential Construction

STATE County	Health care and social assistance, 2012				Other services, 2012				Nonemployer businesses, 2016		Value of residential construction authorized by building permits, 2018	
	Number of establishments	Number of employees	Receipts (mil dol)	Annual payroll (mil dol)	Number of establishments	Number of employees	Receipts (mil dol)	Annual payroll (mil dol)	Number	Receipts (mil dol)	New construction ($1,000)	Number of housing units
	159	160	161	162	163	164	165	166	167	168	169	170
WEST VIRGINIA— Cont'd												
Calhoun	9	294	17.0	10.0	5	D	D	D	417	8.5	NA	NA
Clay	12	283	10.6	5.2	5	D	D	D	375	11.9	450	18
Doddridge	11	176	4.2	2.4	2	D	D	D	231	7.3	0	0
Fayette	105	2,040	162.6	65.2	56	372	37.0	9.1	1,733	57.7	3,377	24
Gilmer	13	255	14.2	7.1	9	32	2.6	0.6	344	7.0	3,898	36
Grant	28	738	45.9	19.5	19	D	D	D	709	26.3	4,590	65
Greenbrier	145	3,028	238.4	101.2	55	291	26.7	7.9	2,232	77.8	15,644	71
Hampshire	34	752	52.1	21.9	26	107	9.1	2.3	1,392	58.9	9,423	60
Hancock	75	1,251	73.4	31.6	46	198	13.8	3.4	1,238	42.1	3,609	15
Hardy	30	451	28.4	12.1	19	54	5.6	0.9	849	25.7	6,272	40
Harrison	237	6,341	666.5	275.1	134	D	D	D	3,748	157.4	21,499	151
Jackson	62	1,111	71.6	30.1	27	D	D	D	1,345	51.3	105	2
Jefferson	77	1,217	103.1	41.8	72	541	76.6	15.1	3,599	141.8	57,478	217
Kanawha	746	18,799	2,083.3	768.4	388	D	D	D	9,064	394.2	10,914	82
Lewis	35	1,261	112.6	42.7	30	103	8.6	2.2	818	30.7	0	0
Lincoln	18	D	D	D	15	66	4.4	1.3	738	21.5	2,322	18
Logan	96	1,880	186.3	68.7	60	486	87.4	15.9	1,153	40.6	0	0
McDowell	34	867	58.5	21.8	19	D	D	D	500	13.7	302	2
Marion	163	2,878	259.9	99.2	107	761	59.1	20.2	2,559	93.7	2,049	21
Marshall	79	D	D	D	42	208	16.0	4.2	1,120	36.2	0	0
Mason	38	1,034	93.9	37.5	28	111	9.7	2.5	925	27.5	275	5
Mercer	244	4,629	432.9	161.6	94	831	81.3	25.1	2,957	103.5	650	5
Mineral	64	1,382	70.4	28.4	41	180	14.1	3.8	1,373	42.3	6,575	37
Mingo	48	686	71.0	23.7	21	211	19.8	6.8	889	28.3	0	0
Monongalia	233	13,029	1,513.8	539.2	143	1,104	170.3	29.1	5,604	247.2	31,721	259
Monroe	19	338	18.5	7.2	8	29	1.9	0.5	764	22.6	0	0
Morgan	20	558	44.9	16.3	22	66	4.4	1.1	1,126	39.4	6,434	36
Nicholas	58	1,626	100.1	47.2	35	168	19.3	5.1	1,169	43.3	0	0
Ohio	234	D	D	D	125	1,074	117.3	28.9	2,466	108.1	108	1
Pendleton	17	325	18.4	7.9	11	49	5.6	1.3	509	18.7	1,570	10
Pleasants	15	497	21.0	8.8	7	D	D	D	282	8.9	2,280	9
Pocahontas	20	415	24.2	9.9	17	104	7.1	1.8	539	22.3	240	4
Preston	62	1,149	68.3	30.3	34	212	20.4	5.2	1,600	62.4	1,023	7
Putnam	120	D	D	D	64	418	51.5	12.8	2,984	119.9	19,773	85
Raleigh	284	7,414	735.3	289.5	112	796	87.8	23.4	3,493	130.4	11,417	62
Randolph	107	2,872	183.3	82.9	44	217	19.9	5.5	1,435	47.1	1,456	13
Ritchie	18	208	11.7	5.3	11	D	D	D	648	20.7	6,427	54
Roane	22	665	48.6	20.5	8	D	D	D	745	23.8	0	0
Summers	20	426	33.6	12.7	14	D	D	D	464	13.3	2,992	21
Taylor	27	552	47.1	17.7	23	D	D	D	711	23.7	0	0
Tucker	10	284	12.8	6.4	11	101	9.8	2.5	461	13.6	10	1
Tyler	12	544	26.7	13.1	16	53	2.7	0.8	361	9.6	1,680	10
Upshur	77	1,626	100.5	53.6	30	124	11.7	2.5	1,260	49.7	6,980	44
Wayne	72	2,462	312.9	122.2	32	150	14.5	4.2	1,514	49.7	2,478	28
Webster	13	462	25.8	12.5	2	D	D	D	318	12.6	0	0
Wetzel	41	717	52.7	19.7	32	152	9.5	2.6	526	15.0	4,395	50
Wirt	5	73	4.1	1.5	2	D	D	D	257	7.7	1,368	9
Wood	282	7,096	635.4	247.0	150	859	83.5	20.6	4,079	163.1	20,651	116
Wyoming	27	778	36.1	17.6	13	D	D	D	720	22.4	277	2
WISCONSIN	14,659	386,141	40,680.6	16,257.6	10,210	62,054	6,406.7	1,732.2	346,514	16,351.7	4,008,219	19,113
Adams	30	454	31.0	12.0	25	121	10.9	3.4	1,101	42.9	18,836	82
Ashland	62	1,629	143.1	62.5	36	121	9.1	2.7	1,090	46.1	1,705	8
Barron	127	2,646	282.3	112.2	96	316	27.8	7.1	3,140	140.6	36,607	239
Bayfield	21	248	12.4	6.7	24	41	5.2	1.4	1,529	62.8	17,347	99
Brown	593	19,588	2,446.2	907.0	433	2,833	241.9	67.9	13,860	708.3	200,804	1,007
Buffalo	23	293	14.0	6.3	19	D	D	D	1,032	45.1	6,072	27
Burnett	30	587	34.7	16.6	22	63	6.4	1.4	1,152	44.9	18,071	82
Calumet	79	1,175	95.3	37.3	58	261	18.5	5.1	2,595	109.8	45,771	231
Chippewa	175	3,185	260.2	110.4	101	545	58.6	15.3	3,906	204.2	55,744	299
Clark	61	904	54.5	26.0	62	D	D	D	2,303	133.0	11,117	68
Columbia	132	2,563	206.1	91.7	91	398	37.1	9.9	3,741	172.4	43,573	165
Crawford	48	1,129	74.6	35.1	34	107	9.5	2.4	1,139	73.9	6,363	35
Dane	1,217	43,351	5,188.2	2,019.6	1,094	8,233	1,237.6	280.6	38,192	1,900.8	759,024	3,330
Dodge	205	4,611	437.1	170.0	133	452	39.3	10.9	4,468	205.8	28,843	224
Door	78	1,630	131.8	61.6	98	472	53.9	11.6	2,869	119.4	39,838	166

STATE County	Government employment and payroll, 2012									Local government finances, 2012				
			March payroll (percent of total)							General revenue				
	Full-time equivalent employees	March payroll (dollars)	Adminis-tration, judicial, and legal	Police and corrections	Fire protection	Highways and transpor-tation	Health and welfare	Natural resources and utilities	Education and libraries	Total (mil dol)	Inter-govern-mental (mil dol)	Taxes		
												Total (mil dol)	Per capita[1] (dollars)	
													Total	Property
	171	172	173	174	175	176	177	178	179	180	181	182	183	184
WEST VIRGINIA— Cont'd														
Calhoun	235	856,049	5.0	1.6	0.0	0.1	2.0	2.3	88.7	15.2	10.3	3.4	451	395
Clay	380	1,124,468	6.3	1.8	0.0	0.0	5.2	2.2	84.1	27.4	19.9	4.1	442	430
Doddridge	298	898,174	6.8	2.9	0.0	0.0	5.3	2.4	82.0	22.4	10.1	9.7	1,188	1,164
Fayette	1,528	4,553,455	4.1	5.0	0.3	1.5	1.0	5.1	80.2	107.2	57.1	37.1	808	664
Gilmer	243	631,014	10.3	2.7	0.0	0.5	1.7	3.3	80.9	15.5	7.0	5.8	665	612
Grant	680	2,034,759	3.4	1.7	0.0	3.5	45.2	3.2	40.6	59.3	13.0	10.1	852	816
Greenbrier	1,170	3,506,733	7.6	5.7	0.3	0.6	1.5	5.0	78.7	105.9	52.9	33.6	939	809
Hampshire	737	2,045,370	7.4	3.3	0.0	0.4	2.4	3.6	80.9	45.1	25.8	14.3	602	574
Hancock	1,042	3,202,337	5.3	8.5	2.6	2.7	1.3	6.7	66.6	87.7	34.1	29.9	986	818
Hardy	415	1,314,488	8.0	4.5	0.0	1.3	3.9	3.7	78.2	29.6	15.9	10.0	724	691
Harrison	2,683	9,099,926	6.8	6.1	3.8	3.1	1.3	6.8	71.1	209.4	84.1	90.4	1,308	979
Jackson	990	3,308,041	4.4	4.8	0.0	0.8	4.8	4.0	80.4	73.7	39.2	26.2	895	804
Jefferson	1,638	5,678,847	10.1	5.7	0.0	0.8	0.7	3.3	76.3	146.5	52.8	59.7	1,096	978
Kanawha	6,718	23,530,157	5.6	7.2	4.5	3.9	6.5	3.5	65.5	605.2	237.9	258.2	1,344	860
Lewis	544	1,762,505	8.2	4.5	0.7	0.9	5.8	2.3	77.1	39.7	21.5	16.2	990	848
Lincoln	667	2,364,650	4.5	2.3	0.0	1.6	1.0	3.2	85.7	53.6	38.2	11.4	526	507
Logan	1,162	3,939,889	5.9	3.5	0.7	0.2	1.5	5.1	81.4	91.3	48.4	36.2	1,001	949
McDowell	898	2,888,117	9.6	3.1	0.0	0.2	2.7	2.7	81.5	73.1	34.6	20.5	959	873
Marion	1,717	5,814,952	5.2	6.4	2.4	3.4	0.7	6.1	74.1	167.3	77.9	56.2	991	827
Marshall	1,141	3,323,871	5.8	8.5	0.5	1.2	2.2	5.2	75.5	112.7	45.9	46.4	1,420	1,271
Mason	808	2,759,625	5.8	3.8	1.1	0.5	1.8	4.4	81.7	67.3	31.9	24.3	894	820
Mercer	2,791	9,567,647	3.0	2.7	1.1	1.6	34.9	3.3	53.2	241.4	83.0	39.7	634	442
Mineral	785	2,765,305	6.5	4.1	0.0	1.4	1.0	5.1	80.1	68.4	36.1	19.1	682	591
Mingo	985	3,045,535	7.8	3.4	0.6	0.0	0.8	5.9	81.3	90.1	46.0	25.0	959	895
Monongalia	2,739	8,098,611	6.5	7.5	2.5	4.8	3.8	8.2	63.2	216.0	81.0	90.9	906	711
Monroe	414	1,100,622	5.2	1.8	0.0	0.0	1.4	2.7	86.0	27.7	19.5	5.8	431	417
Morgan	518	1,614,401	8.1	3.1	0.0	0.2	3.5	2.2	81.4	35.9	14.8	15.4	884	845
Nicholas	1,289	3,992,571	5.3	3.7	0.0	1.2	46.4	3.6	39.7	111.9	37.5	19.6	748	569
Ohio	2,026	6,205,898	4.8	7.0	5.8	5.4	1.5	21.6	51.3	195.9	55.2	71.7	1,626	865
Pendleton	226	700,064	8.4	1.3	0.0	0.8	2.2	3.9	80.7	15.5	10.2	4.1	537	478
Pleasants	324	1,102,661	10.6	2.5	0.0	0.4	3.5	3.5	79.3	32.6	11.4	12.9	1,701	1,664
Pocahontas	405	1,184,054	6.2	3.0	0.0	0.0	30.8	3.2	53.8	31.5	10.0	9.0	1,038	857
Preston	940	2,685,410	7.1	3.2	0.9	1.2	1.0	4.1	82.2	66.4	36.1	18.3	541	504
Putnam	1,860	6,184,199	4.2	3.8	0.1	0.5	2.8	5.9	81.7	150.7	66.0	58.4	1,035	970
Raleigh	2,440	7,917,866	5.4	5.4	1.7	1.5	2.8	5.6	75.8	223.2	112.9	76.2	964	750
Randolph	999	2,905,572	3.8	2.3	0.5	0.9	3.4	6.7	80.2	72.1	40.5	17.4	593	462
Ritchie	297	909,321	8.7	3.8	0.0	1.0	0.1	2.4	84.1	24.5	12.7	8.6	838	761
Roane	376	1,154,052	6.1	3.9	0.0	1.0	2.1	6.9	79.1	31.0	21.0	6.6	447	384
Summers	287	926,192	9.8	3.8	1.5	1.2	2.4	1.1	80.2	23.4	14.8	6.1	443	343
Taylor	364	895,244	5.7	4.2	1.5	2.1	4.6	11.1	66.9	51.2	18.8	11.0	648	459
Tucker	275	825,484	9.3	1.5	0.0	1.3	7.1	3.8	69.5	25.7	10.2	7.0	1,003	837
Tyler	484	1,507,476	5.2	4.0	0.0	1.0	29.5	1.8	58.1	30.4	11.4	7.0	778	752
Upshur	769	2,460,649	3.9	3.4	0.6	1.2	4.6	5.0	78.3	57.1	29.8	16.0	654	566
Wayne	1,363	3,245,672	6.1	5.2	0.0	0.5	1.6	4.5	81.4	101.8	63.8	27.0	648	573
Webster	358	989,930	7.5	2.5	2.2	1.0	1.1	6.1	78.1	23.4	16.4	3.8	420	365
Wetzel	861	2,789,337	4.5	3.5	0.0	0.7	30.1	6.0	54.4	69.9	21.7	17.0	1,038	859
Wirt	221	579,537	5.0	1.0	0.0	0.0	0.0	1.9	92.1	12.0	8.3	2.5	428	408
Wood	2,923	9,783,040	4.6	5.6	2.1	2.8	2.7	6.6	73.9	223.4	105.4	75.1	866	645
Wyoming	818	2,431,168	7.1	3.1	0.0	0.1	2.6	2.9	82.3	59.6	32.3	21.1	906	862
WISCONSIN	X	X	X	X	X	X	X	X	X	X	X	X	X	X
Adams	752	2,398,694	11.0	12.5	0.7	11.1	19.9	3.2	40.0	75.0	26.6	36.5	1,766	1,664
Ashland	751	2,545,721	7.6	8.1	4.1	10.6	10.7	7.0	49.8	79.8	47.9	22.4	1,398	1,298
Barron	1,838	6,618,589	8.0	8.4	1.3	6.3	10.3	4.0	60.6	190.4	84.2	79.1	1,729	1,625
Bayfield	707	2,315,340	13.5	8.9	0.8	14.7	14.5	4.4	42.0	70.7	26.8	33.0	2,186	2,071
Brown	9,417	41,301,919	3.9	9.3	3.3	3.0	7.6	3.8	67.8	1,182.5	506.0	459.7	1,817	1,685
Buffalo	479	1,597,741	7.7	7.1	0.2	11.0	7.2	3.7	62.0	50.4	28.0	18.4	1,378	1,318
Burnett	687	2,258,798	11.7	9.6	0.3	13.5	8.5	4.2	51.0	63.0	23.4	33.2	2,157	2,077
Calumet	1,110	4,057,590	8.1	8.8	0.2	5.3	10.0	4.7	61.8	111.1	46.0	47.5	956	941
Chippewa	1,941	7,086,033	6.6	8.6	2.6	10.3	6.3	4.1	60.8	196.6	102.1	74.2	1,179	1,086
Clark	1,398	4,771,022	6.3	8.0	0.1	9.4	23.0	4.1	48.3	140.3	73.6	38.4	1,115	1,055
Columbia	2,325	8,247,107	8.1	9.2	0.4	3.5	8.2	3.5	65.9	255.2	98.3	121.8	2,154	2,025
Crawford	593	1,975,908	11.0	8.6	0.2	10.4	5.2	3.1	60.2	77.0	46.6	24.3	1,469	1,348
Dane	19,136	83,118,268	5.7	10.6	3.0	6.3	5.9	6.9	59.9	2,389.4	787.6	1,194.7	2,373	2,225
Dodge	2,529	9,541,340	7.2	13.4	1.1	6.9	16.7	4.2	48.9	269.1	119.0	102.8	1,162	1,082
Door	1,091	4,311,224	10.3	10.3	2.4	7.1	11.5	5.3	51.6	140.6	38.4	81.9	2,946	2,757

1. Based on the resident population estimated as of July 1 of the year shown.

Table B. States and Counties — **Local Government Finances, Government Employment, and Income Taxes**

STATE County	Local government finances, 2012 (cont.) Direct general expenditure Total (mil dol)	Per capita[1] (dollars)	Percent of total for: Education	Health and hospitals	Police protection	Public welfare	Highways	Debt outstanding Total (mil dol)	Per capita[1] (dollars)	Government employment, 2017 Federal civilian	Federal military	State and local	Individual income tax returns, 2016 Number of returns	Mean adjusted gross income	Mean income tax
	185	186	187	188	189	190	191	192	193	194	195	196	197	198	199

WEST VIRGINIA— Cont'd

STATE County	185	186	187	188	189	190	191	192	193	194	195	196	197	198	199
Calhoun	16.5	2,170	67.3	0.0	4.6	0.1	0.1	13.0	1,714	13	35	280	2,450	40,595	3,333
Clay	29.0	3,117	78.1	4.6	7.4	0.0	0.0	1.2	128	12	41	473	3,050	38,785	2,851
Doddridge	22.0	2,695	75.1	2.0	2.2	0.0	0.2	8.1	994	10	36	531	2,820	52,654	5,921
Fayette	113.9	2,482	68.7	0.5	5.7	0.0	1.6	47.9	1,045	244	202	2,709	16,520	39,928	3,405
Gilmer	17.4	1,988	61.7	1.3	6.6	0.0	0.4	4.5	516	316	29	619	2,420	41,412	4,027
Grant	59.2	5,007	30.0	52.8	2.8	0.0	0.1	13.9	1,177	47	55	885	5,230	42,001	3,625
Greenbrier	128.0	3,574	63.2	0.6	4.9	0.1	1.0	116.1	3,241	91	165	2,178	15,010	45,180	4,615
Hampshire	52.8	2,229	71.4	1.4	6.3	0.0	0.5	31.5	1,328	36	110	1,237	9,860	43,950	3,970
Hancock	95.4	3,148	57.0	1.9	5.9	0.4	3.5	88.0	2,903	60	139	1,264	14,230	47,793	4,950
Hardy	30.9	2,227	67.5	1.2	3.9	0.1	1.5	61.4	4,426	50	65	768	6,530	39,262	3,298
Harrison	213.8	3,092	57.6	0.7	4.7	0.0	3.1	154.5	2,234	4,192	322	3,872	30,960	54,018	6,242
Jackson	77.4	2,647	65.9	3.3	6.4	0.0	0.9	34.3	1,172	76	137	1,253	12,040	48,061	4,830
Jefferson	165.6	3,037	64.7	0.4	7.7	0.0	1.5	64.5	1,183	1,275	263	3,022	25,830	66,103	7,707
Kanawha	630.4	3,280	49.5	0.7	6.4	0.0	3.1	316.3	1,646	2,202	873	19,681	84,120	54,501	6,705
Lewis	44.9	2,740	61.9	2.9	2.7	0.3	0.8	5.9	361	55	76	1,340	7,600	45,625	4,440
Lincoln	56.1	2,593	81.6	0.7	1.6	0.1	0.0	11.6	535	38	99	788	7,300	41,065	3,287
Logan	90.2	2,493	72.3	0.9	1.5	0.0	1.1	10.2	281	93	154	1,991	11,520	42,192	3,668
McDowell	77.6	3,641	65.1	0.4	3.6	0.0	1.0	12.9	606	377	87	1,470	5,390	34,783	2,423
Marion	168.8	2,978	58.1	1.2	4.9	0.0	1.1	273.1	4,819	177	278	4,182	25,450	49,096	4,955
Marshall	98.2	3,004	56.7	2.0	5.2	0.2	2.1	187.9	5,751	54	146	1,841	14,180	48,040	4,783
Mason	71.4	2,625	63.5	7.2	3.0	0.1	1.4	29.8	1,097	99	124	1,348	10,220	45,695	4,281
Mercer	244.7	3,914	40.5	39.9	4.2	0.0	1.0	92.7	1,483	158	279	4,830	23,810	41,694	3,801
Mineral	67.8	2,426	67.5	0.9	6.0	0.1	1.0	39.5	1,413	95	127	1,475	12,370	46,421	4,353
Mingo	98.5	3,774	63.6	0.6	2.1	0.1	1.1	29.5	1,128	70	114	1,065	7,790	38,831	3,145
Monongalia	226.2	2,254	54.5	2.7	5.6	0.4	2.1	196.0	1,954	1,173	482	15,331	41,450	64,668	8,841
Monroe	25.2	1,875	79.9	0.7	5.6	0.1	0.8	11.1	828	201	64	512	5,380	41,265	3,514
Morgan	37.8	2,162	73.4	1.3	6.3	0.0	0.5	22.3	1,279	25	84	683	7,980	44,128	3,926
Nicholas	110.3	4,207	42.1	40.3	4.8	0.0	1.0	40.6	1,546	95	118	1,554	9,980	43,141	3,973
Ohio	204.2	4,634	34.0	0.9	7.3	0.2	3.3	309.3	7,017	389	190	3,420	20,220	59,563	7,960
Pendleton	16.3	2,160	74.5	2.0	1.0	0.0	0.2	4.2	549	21	33	322	3,250	41,097	3,696
Pleasants	31.1	4,098	51.5	1.1	2.8	1.2	0.9	168.6	22,201	10	32	620	3,180	50,812	5,118
Pocahontas	32.3	3,712	42.6	29.0	6.8	0.3	0.3	7.5	861	62	39	793	3,710	37,935	3,102
Preston	67.7	2,001	71.9	0.8	3.4	0.0	0.8	71.7	2,120	900	150	1,623	13,900	46,098	4,314
Putnam	187.6	3,324	75.3	0.9	5.2	0.0	0.4	178.8	3,168	233	270	2,049	25,510	63,283	7,643
Raleigh	227.9	2,884	60.0	0.6	7.4	0.1	1.6	109.6	1,387	1,724	347	3,903	30,020	49,098	5,356
Randolph	78.4	2,667	59.6	0.4	4.2	0.1	1.6	33.1	1,126	161	126	1,856	12,080	42,667	4,061
Ritchie	26.4	2,577	64.5	8.2	3.8	0.1	1.0	5.0	492	27	46	487	4,030	46,595	4,759
Roane	32.6	2,218	76.9	1.3	2.2	0.0	1.1	10.7	731	24	66	567	5,280	40,422	3,547
Summers	26.4	1,922	59.2	1.1	4.3	0.0	1.2	7.1	514	38	56	703	4,320	39,328	3,306
Taylor	50.1	2,947	47.3	30.5	3.2	0.0	2.7	25.2	1,485	45	78	1,076	7,170	49,316	4,949
Tucker	25.6	3,656	47.4	5.2	1.8	0.0	0.6	6.1	873	53	32	556	3,240	42,965	3,932
Tyler	31.5	3,490	53.3	28.3	3.8	0.0	0.6	14.5	1,606	13	42	563	3,770	50,479	5,323
Upshur	57.5	2,351	66.4	0.5	2.2	0.1	1.6	23.7	969	123	111	1,169	9,810	44,316	4,129
Wayne	99.1	2,380	75.7	1.2	4.2	0.1	0.6	56.7	1,362	1,456	190	1,707	15,200	44,754	4,002
Webster	23.6	2,613	67.1	0.1	6.5	0.0	0.6	2.3	257	12	40	543	3,020	36,769	3,025
Wetzel	76.4	4,650	43.1	35.0	3.3	0.0	1.3	24.0	1,459	35	73	1,173	6,800	47,236	4,685
Wirt	12.5	2,133	82.9	0.0	0.1	0.0	0.6	1.6	280	12	28	239	2,270	39,783	2,969
Wood	223.9	2,582	63.1	0.1	5.4	0.0	4.0	189.9	2,190	2,479	402	4,297	38,650	50,339	5,541
Wyoming	60.0	2,578	76.4	0.9	3.5	0.1	0.4	21.2	910	96	101	980	6,780	40,676	3,276
WISCONSIN	X	X	X	X	X	X	X	X	X	29,093	15,960	390,612	2,842,590	62,464	7,958
Adams	74.9	3,623	28.9	10.0	7.1	4.2	20.2	54.3	2,624	273	50	808	9,400	43,834	4,199
Ashland	80.3	5,021	41.4	3.1	6.4	7.4	11.1	35.5	2,221	167	40	1,721	7,360	43,324	3,874
Barron	194.8	4,259	48.2	0.6	5.4	8.5	14.2	109.9	2,402	143	119	3,708	22,880	50,847	5,554
Bayfield	74.2	4,916	33.4	7.0	4.7	0.1	19.4	43.1	2,852	112	55	1,451	7,820	52,589	5,818
Brown	1,202.2	4,751	49.8	5.5	6.3	4.1	6.6	1,130.3	4,467	1,242	705	17,697	130,230	65,628	9,008
Buffalo	53.1	3,982	48.0	1.8	3.5	5.5	22.8	23.0	1,723	154	35	678	6,660	45,944	4,298
Burnett	66.0	4,292	45.3	5.0	4.3	3.4	18.5	34.6	2,248	28	40	1,554	7,780	47,034	4,614
Calumet	110.0	2,217	42.6	3.7	6.9	6.6	12.0	109.5	2,206	53	134	1,422	24,540	66,724	7,874
Chippewa	206.5	3,282	53.4	4.8	4.8	2.5	14.8	127.7	2,030	189	164	3,217	30,690	52,484	5,540
Clark	143.7	4,173	42.9	4.9	4.0	14.6	11.4	69.7	2,024	110	90	2,101	14,940	49,673	5,972
Columbia	257.0	4,546	51.3	1.4	5.7	6.8	11.3	215.7	3,815	170	148	3,541	30,130	58,321	6,748
Crawford	74.8	4,519	39.3	3.0	5.3	4.1	18.5	47.8	2,889	59	41	1,004	7,850	43,376	4,324
Dane	2,429.4	4,825	46.4	1.9	6.1	8.3	5.9	2,890.1	5,740	5,181	1,498	75,687	269,600	77,140	11,020
Dodge	312.6	3,536	31.9	3.5	7.1	19.1	11.6	247.2	2,795	172	216	4,654	42,820	54,350	5,805
Door	143.6	5,161	33.0	8.5	5.0	3.5	16.6	112.6	4,047	69	146	1,769	15,780	62,122	7,672

1. Based on the resident population estimated as of July 1 of the year shown.

Table B. States and Counties — **Land Area and Population**

State / county code	CBSA code[1]	County code[2]	STATE County	Population, 2018			Population and population characteristics, 2018										
							Race alone or in combination, not Hispanic or Latino (percent)					Age (percent)					
				Land area[3] (sq. mi)	Total persons 2018	Rank	Per square mile	White	Black	American Indian, Alaska Native	Asian and Pacific Islander	Percent Hispanic or Latino[4]	Under 5 years	5 to 17 years	18 to 24 years	25 to 34 years	35 to 44 years	45 to 54 years
				1	2	3	4	5	6	7	8	9	10	11	12	13	14	15
			WISCONSIN— Cont'd															
55031	20,260	2	Douglas	1,304.3	43,208	1,110	33.1	94.1	2.1	3.3	1.7	1.6	4.8	14.9	8.7	12.4	12.1	12.7
55033	32,860	6	Dunn	850.2	45,131	1,073	53.1	93.8	1.3	0.8	3.4	1.9	5.2	14.5	18.8	11.3	10.9	11.2
55035	20,740	3	Eau Claire	637.9	104,534	578	163.9	91.3	1.9	1.0	5.0	2.6	5.8	14.6	16.1	13.8	11.5	10.7
55037	27,020	9	Florence	488.1	4,321	2,875	8.9	97.2	1.0	1.5	0.9	0.9	3.9	10.9	5.1	8.8	9.3	13.9
55039	22,540	3	Fond du Lac	719.6	103,066	586	143.2	90.4	2.5	0.8	2.3	5.3	5.3	16.1	8.4	11.9	12.1	13.0
55041		9	Forest	1,014.2	8,991	2,502	8.9	81.6	2.0	16.2	1.0	2.3	5.7	13.8	8.5	10.2	9.5	12.6
55043	38,420	6	Grant	1,146.9	51,554	968	45.0	95.6	1.7	0.4	1.2	1.8	5.7	15.2	17.2	10.9	10.2	10.5
55045	31,540	2	Green	584.0	36,929	1,251	63.2	95.2	1.3	0.5	1.0	3.1	5.2	16.9	7.0	10.8	12.0	13.6
55047		6	Green Lake	349.5	18,918	1,876	54.1	92.6	1.3	0.7	1.0	5.2	5.8	16.6	7.2	9.4	10.5	12.1
55049	31,540	2	Iowa	762.7	23,771	1,655	31.2	96.2	1.3	0.6	1.2	1.8	5.7	17.2	6.7	10.7	11.8	13.3
55051		9	Iron	758.2	5,676	2,781	7.5	96.8	0.8	2.1	0.6	1.3	3.0	12.4	5.0	7.1	9.5	12.7
55053		6	Jackson	987.2	20,478	1,795	20.7	87.6	2.6	7.0	1.0	3.4	5.9	15.9	7.4	12.2	11.6	13.1
55055	48,020	4	Jefferson	556.5	85,129	676	153.0	90.5	1.4	0.7	1.3	7.2	5.1	16.0	9.3	11.6	12.6	13.8
55057		7	Juneau	767.0	26,617	1,542	34.7	92.9	2.7	1.8	0.9	2.9	5.4	14.8	6.6	11.3	11.8	13.8
55059	16,980	1	Kenosha	271.9	169,290	387	622.6	77.7	8.2	0.8	2.3	13.4	5.7	17.1	9.7	12.9	12.5	13.9
55061	24,580	2	Kewaunee	342.5	20,383	1,802	59.5	95.3	0.9	1.0	0.8	3.2	5.2	16.3	7.3	10.3	11.6	13.3
55063	29,100	3	La Crosse	451.8	118,230	525	261.7	91.3	2.4	0.8	5.3	2.0	5.1	14.7	16.0	12.7	11.2	11.1
55065		8	Lafayette	633.6	16,665	2,001	26.3	94.6	0.9	0.6	0.7	4.0	6.2	18.2	7.6	10.5	10.7	12.2
55067		6	Langlade	870.7	19,268	1,863	22.1	95.2	1.7	1.8	0.7	2.0	5.1	14.5	6.7	9.4	10.3	12.7
55069	32,980	6	Lincoln	878.7	27,689	1,506	31.5	96.4	1.3	1.0	0.8	1.7	4.6	13.7	6.9	9.6	11.1	14.7
55071	31,820	4	Manitowoc	589.3	79,074	709	134.2	91.5	1.5	1.0	3.2	4.2	5.1	15.4	7.5	10.6	11.3	13.3
55073	48,140	3	Marathon	1,545.3	135,428	473	87.6	89.9	1.4	0.9	6.6	2.8	5.9	16.9	7.6	12.0	12.3	13.1
55075	31,940	6	Marinette	1,399.5	40,434	1,172	28.9	96.3	0.9	1.3	0.9	1.9	4.8	14.4	6.5	9.8	10.4	12.6
55077		8	Marquette	455.7	15,434	2,073	33.9	94.2	1.1	1.2	0.9	3.7	4.9	14.3	5.9	9.1	9.8	12.9
55078	43,020	8	Menominee	357.6	4,658	2,853	13.0	13.8	1.7	78.0	3.5	6.0	10.0	23.9	8.7	11.6	8.8	10.6
55079	33,340	1	Milwaukee	241.5	948,201	53	3,926.3	53.0	27.8	1.2	5.2	15.4	6.9	17.1	9.5	16.3	12.8	11.6
55081		6	Monroe	900.9	46,051	1,051	51.1	91.6	2.2	1.6	1.4	4.8	6.8	18.6	7.1	11.6	12.2	12.4
55083	24,580	2	Oconto	997.5	37,830	1,229	37.9	95.9	0.7	2.0	0.7	1.8	4.9	15.4	6.3	9.9	11.3	14.2
55085		7	Oneida	1,113.9	35,470	1,290	31.8	96.1	1.0	1.9	0.9	1.6	4.4	12.7	6.2	9.6	9.8	12.8
55087	11,540	3	Outagamie	637.6	187,365	353	293.9	88.8	2.1	2.1	4.2	4.4	6.3	17.3	8.5	13.4	13.0	13.2
55089	33,340	1	Ozaukee	233.0	89,147	655	382.6	92.4	2.1	0.6	3.3	3.1	5.1	16.2	8.8	9.7	11.5	13.5
55091		8	Pepin	232.0	7,289	2,641	31.4	97.0	0.7	0.5	0.6	1.9	5.5	15.4	6.9	9.5	10.9	13.0
55093	33,460	1	Pierce	573.9	42,555	1,127	74.2	95.3	1.3	0.9	1.7	2.1	4.8	15.7	16.2	10.9	11.3	12.6
55095		6	Polk	914.1	43,598	1,102	47.7	96.0	0.9	1.5	0.9	2.0	5.0	15.9	6.9	9.7	11.4	13.6
55097	44,620	4	Portage	800.9	70,942	762	88.6	92.2	1.5	0.7	3.6	3.4	5.0	14.3	16.4	11.8	11.0	11.5
55099		9	Price	1,254.1	13,397	2,199	10.7	95.0	1.0	1.4	2.0	2.0	4.5	13.6	6.1	7.5	10.1	13.5
55101	39,540	3	Racine	332.6	196,584	340	591.1	73.6	12.7	0.8	1.7	13.4	6.1	17.0	8.4	12.0	12.0	13.4
55103		6	Richland	586.2	17,377	1,952	29.6	95.6	1.2	0.7	1.1	2.4	5.2	16.5	7.3	9.5	10.7	12.0
55105	27,500	3	Rock	718.1	163,129	403	227.2	84.5	6.2	0.7	1.9	8.9	6.1	17.0	8.6	12.3	12.2	13.2
55107		6	Rusk	913.6	14,147	2,153	15.5	95.6	1.6	1.3	0.9	2.0	5.2	15.0	6.7	8.7	10.2	12.5
55109	33,460	1	St. Croix	722.4	89,694	654	124.2	95.2	1.4	0.7	1.8	2.4	6.2	18.6	7.5	11.5	13.9	14.1
55111	12,660	4	Sauk	831.5	64,249	829	77.3	91.9	1.6	1.5	1.0	5.2	6.1	16.7	7.5	11.8	12.2	12.9
55113		7	Sawyer	1,257.6	16,489	2,009	13.1	79.4	1.1	19.0	0.8	2.8	5.1	14.4	6.2	8.7	9.1	12.1
55115	43,020	6	Shawano	893.2	40,796	1,156	45.7	88.3	0.9	9.1	0.9	2.9	5.3	16.0	6.8	10.3	10.8	13.7
55117	43,100	3	Sheboygan	511.5	115,456	537	225.7	85.2	2.8	0.8	6.2	6.5	5.5	16.6	8.3	11.6	12.0	13.2
55119		6	Taylor	975.0	20,412	1,799	20.9	96.3	0.8	0.8	0.9	2.2	5.8	17.6	6.8	9.8	11.7	12.7
55121		6	Trempealeau	733.0	29,442	1,446	40.2	89.9	0.8	0.6	0.9	8.8	7.0	17.9	6.9	10.9	11.4	13.4
55123		6	Vernon	791.6	30,785	1,412	38.9	97.2	1.0	0.6	0.8	1.6	6.9	19.1	6.9	9.4	10.6	11.9
55125		9	Vilas	857.7	21,938	1,726	25.6	86.2	0.8	10.9	0.9	2.8	4.5	12.5	5.3	7.9	7.9	12.3
55127	48,580	4	Walworth	555.4	103,718	582	186.7	86.4	1.5	0.6	1.4	11.2	4.9	15.7	12.9	10.4	11.0	12.7
55129		7	Washburn	797.1	15,878	2,046	19.9	95.7	0.8	2.6	0.8	1.9	4.7	14.4	5.6	8.7	9.5	12.4
55131	33,340	1	Washington	430.6	135,693	472	315.1	93.7	1.8	0.6	1.8	3.2	5.3	16.6	7.3	10.6	12.2	14.6
55133	33,340	1	Waukesha	549.7	403,072	176	733.3	89.5	2.1	0.5	4.5	4.8	5.2	16.3	7.8	10.5	12.3	13.7
55135		6	Waupaca	747.7	51,128	972	68.4	95.2	0.9	1.1	0.8	3.3	5.0	15.3	7.0	10.5	11.4	13.5
55137		6	Waushara	626.2	24,263	1,634	38.7	90.6	2.4	1.0	0.9	6.3	4.7	13.5	6.2	9.7	10.5	13.3
55139	36,780	3	Winnebago	434.7	171,020	383	393.4	89.9	3.0	1.0	3.6	4.2	5.5	15.0	11.7	13.3	12.0	12.6
55141	49,220	4	Wood	793.0	73,055	748	92.1	93.3	1.5	1.1	2.3	3.1	5.7	15.9	7.2	11.2	11.0	12.8
56000		0	WYOMING	97,088.7	577,737	X	6.0	85.5	1.7	2.9	1.7	10.1	6.2	17.1	9.1	13.5	12.6	11.2
56001	29,660	4	Albany	4,274.3	38,601	1,212	9.0	84.0	2.4	1.3	4.7	9.8	4.8	11.5	27.8	16.0	10.4	8.0
56003		9	Big Horn	3,137.0	11,881	2,301	3.8	88.7	0.8	1.5	0.8	9.2	6.3	19.0	7.3	10.4	11.1	11.2
56005	23,940	5	Campbell	4,802.1	46,140	1,049	9.6	89.1	0.9	1.9	1.3	8.7	7.4	19.9	7.9	15.1	14.3	11.3
56007		7	Carbon	7,897.8	14,971	2,098	1.9	78.7	1.6	1.8	1.2	18.2	6.3	16.5	7.3	14.4	12.9	11.0
56009		6	Converse	4,255.0	13,640	2,188	3.2	89.7	0.8	1.5	0.9	8.5	6.4	18.2	7.1	12.2	12.3	12.4
56011		9	Crook	2,854.5	7,450	2,631	2.6	95.2	1.4	1.6	0.5	2.4	7.2	17.1	5.6	10.3	10.0	12.1
56013	40,180	7	Fremont	9,183.6	39,531	1,191	4.3	72.0	0.8	21.8	1.0	7.0	6.7	18.8	7.7	12.1	11.4	10.9

1. CBSA = Core Based Statistical Area. See Appendix A for explanation. See Appendix B for list of metropolitan areas with component counties.   2. County type code from the Economic Research Service of USDA Rural-Urban Continuum Codes. See Appendix A for definition.   3. Dry land or land partially or temporarily covered by water.   4. May be of any race.

Table B. States and Counties — **Population and Households**

STATE County	55 to 64 years	65 to 74 years	75 years and over	Percent female	2000	2010	2000-2010	2010-2018	Births	Deaths	Net Migration	Number	Persons per household	Family households	Female family householder[1]	One person
	16	17	18	19	20	21	22	23	24	25	26	27	28	29	30	31
WISCONSIN— Cont'd																
Douglas	15.7	11.0	7.6	49.9	43,287	44,159	2.0	-2.2	3,576	3,437	-1,063	18,717	2.26	60.7	10.8	32.2
Dunn	12.5	9.2	6.5	49.8	39,858	43,865	10.1	2.9	3,748	2,653	184	16,652	2.45	62.8	7.1	26.6
Eau Claire	11.9	9.2	6.4	50.6	93,142	98,879	6.2	5.7	9,834	6,683	2,541	40,528	2.42	58.6	7.5	30.7
Florence	22.1	15.7	10.3	48.5	5,088	4,423	-13.1	-2.3	239	440	100	1,979	2.17	66.2	6.5	28.9
Fond du Lac	14.7	10.5	8.1	50.8	97,296	101,627	4.5	1.4	8,936	7,668	216	41,387	2.39	66.5	7.5	27.8
Forest	16.9	13.1	9.8	49.3	10,024	9,304	-7.2	-3.4	889	954	-245	4,040	2.17	64.7	10.3	29.9
Grant	13.1	9.2	8.0	48.1	49,597	51,205	3.2	0.7	4,593	4,045	-211	19,444	2.46	61.6	6.7	28.6
Green	15.8	10.7	8.0	50.3	33,647	36,842	9.5	0.2	3,151	2,811	-232	14,957	2.44	67.2	8.1	26.5
Green Lake	16.2	12.8	9.4	49.8	19,105	19,051	-0.3	-0.7	1,684	1,878	73	7,932	2.33	64.9	6.5	31.1
Iowa	15.9	11.6	7.1	49.9	22,780	23,691	4.0	0.3	2,217	1,714	-411	9,799	2.38	67.7	8.2	25.2
Iron	19.5	17.5	13.3	49.7	6,861	5,916	-13.8	-4.1	293	696	166	2,948	1.91	59.6	7.2	35.2
Jackson	15.0	11.1	7.9	46.4	19,100	20,441	7.0	0.2	1,992	1,679	-260	8,154	2.37	65.3	10.0	28.7
Jefferson	14.6	10.1	6.8	50.0	74,021	83,683	13.1	1.7	7,231	5,388	-341	32,739	2.47	68.2	9.1	25.0
Juneau	16.0	11.8	8.5	46.8	24,316	26,665	9.7	-0.2	2,261	2,326	34	10,149	2.42	62.8	8.0	30.0
Kenosha	14.0	8.2	5.9	50.5	149,577	166,424	11.3	1.7	16,075	11,362	-1,760	63,286	2.58	65.3	12.6	27.8
Kewaunee	15.5	11.5	9.0	49.3	20,187	20,574	1.9	-0.9	1,638	1,516	-306	8,234	2.45	68.9	5.8	26.8
La Crosse	12.7	9.4	7.1	51.2	107,120	114,638	7.0	3.1	10,269	8,085	1,471	46,966	2.39	59.9	8.5	28.2
Lafayette	15.8	10.1	8.6	49.4	16,137	16,836	4.3	-1.0	1,730	1,102	-799	6,714	2.48	68.9	8.1	26.1
Langlade	17.4	13.2	10.8	49.6	20,740	19,977	-3.7	-3.5	1,620	1,930	-396	8,646	2.19	61.6	8.5	32.6
Lincoln	17.9	11.9	9.6	49.3	29,641	28,743	-3.0	-3.7	2,238	2,711	-568	12,560	2.17	66.2	8.0	26.8
Manitowoc	16.4	11.5	9.0	50.0	82,887	81,442	-1.7	-2.9	6,684	7,013	-2,029	34,119	2.30	63.4	7.2	31.7
Marathon	14.5	10.0	7.7	49.7	125,834	134,061	6.5	1.0	13,201	9,534	-2,234	54,820	2.44	66.8	8.2	27.2
Marinette	17.8	13.4	10.4	49.4	43,384	41,749	-3.8	-3.1	3,123	4,134	-274	18,548	2.14	61.5	7.8	32.4
Marquette	18.5	14.4	10.1	49.0	15,832	15,404	-2.7	0.2	1,219	1,486	304	6,389	2.33	63.0	7.1	30.3
Menominee	13.2	8.1	5.1	50.2	4,562	4,232	-7.2	10.1	794	373	-1	1,354	3.28	72.2	29.9	22.1
Milwaukee	12.1	7.9	5.7	51.6	940,164	947,736	0.8	0.0	114,449	67,571	-46,255	382,027	2.44	56.6	16.6	35.2
Monroe	14.3	9.9	7.1	49.4	40,899	44,675	9.2	3.1	5,016	3,430	-182	17,832	2.49	65.6	10.0	28.7
Oconto	17.6	12.4	8.0	48.8	35,634	37,660	5.7	0.5	2,950	2,945	189	15,634	2.38	69.5	7.2	25.0
Oneida	18.6	15.0	11.0	49.8	36,776	36,010	-2.1	-1.5	2,483	3,711	728	14,994	2.32	64.9	6.1	29.7
Outagamie	13.7	8.6	6.1	50.0	160,971	176,691	9.8	6.0	18,901	10,971	2,896	72,288	2.49	66.8	9.1	26.6
Ozaukee	15.5	11.2	8.6	50.8	82,317	86,395	5.0	3.2	6,694	6,110	2,229	35,044	2.47	71.2	7.2	24.1
Pepin	16.5	12.4	10.0	48.9	7,213	7,469	3.5	-2.4	654	594	-244	3,005	2.39	67.4	6.1	27.3
Pierce	13.8	9.0	5.6	50.2	36,804	41,019	11.5	3.7	3,218	2,210	524	15,302	2.52	67.0	6.9	23.5
Polk	16.8	12.0	8.6	49.6	41,319	44,202	7.0	-1.4	3,491	3,548	-539	18,189	2.35	67.4	8.4	26.7
Portage	13.4	9.7	6.9	49.6	67,182	70,021	4.2	1.3	5,730	4,315	-454	28,072	2.39	61.0	7.1	27.8
Price	19.0	14.7	11.0	49.1	15,822	14,159	-10.5	-5.4	926	1,474	-211	6,567	2.03	62.8	6.0	30.0
Racine	14.6	9.6	6.9	50.5	188,831	195,428	3.5	0.6	19,758	14,415	-4,136	75,640	2.51	68.1	12.5	26.4
Richland	15.9	12.8	10.0	49.7	17,924	18,021	0.5	-3.6	1,473	1,481	-635	7,564	2.27	65.3	8.7	28.7
Rock	14.0	9.5	7.0	50.7	152,307	160,335	5.3	1.7	16,054	12,055	-1,113	64,482	2.45	65.6	13.1	28.3
Rusk	17.4	13.9	10.3	49.2	15,347	14,754	-3.9	-4.1	1,169	1,454	-328	6,294	2.23	65.4	9.5	29.2
St. Croix	14.2	8.7	5.4	50.1	63,155	84,347	33.6	6.3	8,612	4,744	1,509	33,389	2.58	72.9	8.4	21.7
Sauk	14.4	10.8	7.7	50.1	55,225	61,965	12.2	3.7	6,354	4,984	975	25,678	2.43	66.3	9.6	27.7
Sawyer	18.5	15.7	10.2	48.9	16,196	16,547	2.2	-0.4	1,371	1,693	277	7,573	2.12	65.2	10.5	27.6
Shawano	15.8	11.8	9.4	50.0	40,664	41,955	3.2	-2.8	3,563	3,767	-928	17,024	2.38	66.1	8.0	28.8
Sheboygan	14.8	10.4	7.6	49.7	112,646	115,510	2.5	0.0	10,402	8,920	-1,499	47,532	2.36	65.6	8.3	29.4
Taylor	16.4	10.2	8.9	49.2	19,680	20,690	5.1	-1.3	1,860	1,504	-646	8,769	2.30	66.3	7.0	28.5
Trempealeau	14.2	10.4	7.7	49.2	27,010	28,816	6.7	2.2	3,342	2,293	-408	11,892	2.44	65.0	9.2	28.2
Vernon	15.5	11.2	8.3	49.7	28,056	29,771	6.1	3.4	3,457	2,448	31	12,095	2.48	68.1	7.7	26.9
Vilas	18.8	17.5	13.3	49.2	21,033	21,430	1.9	2.4	1,472	2,390	1,432	10,758	1.98	62.6	8.0	32.1
Walworth	14.7	10.5	7.2	50.1	93,759	102,228	9.0	1.5	8,382	7,458	620	40,246	2.48	66.5	9.0	25.6
Washburn	18.4	15.8	10.4	50.5	16,036	15,909	-0.8	-0.2	1,239	1,703	441	7,142	2.16	64.5	6.8	29.7
Washington	15.4	10.4	7.6	50.3	117,493	131,885	12.2	2.9	11,061	8,955	1,807	53,756	2.47	71.1	7.5	23.4
Waukesha	15.5	10.7	8.0	50.8	360,767	389,938	8.1	3.4	31,674	26,875	8,634	156,996	2.49	70.0	6.5	25.0
Waupaca	16.5	11.3	9.6	49.3	51,731	52,410	1.3	-2.4	4,205	5,908	460	21,793	2.30	64.4	8.1	29.6
Waushara	17.7	14.2	10.2	47.4	23,154	24,496	5.8	-1.0	1,870	2,206	117	9,851	2.33	66.5	6.3	29.0
Winnebago	13.5	9.2	7.2	49.7	156,763	166,996	6.5	2.4	15,524	11,941	573	69,759	2.31	60.4	9.5	30.4
Wood	15.7	11.2	9.4	50.8	75,555	74,749	-1.1	-2.3	6,822	6,363	-2,143	32,223	2.25	62.7	8.7	31.1
WYOMING	13.8	10.1	6.4	49.0	493,782	563,773	14.2	2.5	61,495	38,474	-9,463	230,237	2.47	64.8	8.2	28.3
Albany	9.8	7.4	4.3	47.8	32,014	36,299	13.4	6.3	3,358	1,547	478	16,009	2.23	48.3	4.6	31.8
Big Horn	13.8	12.1	8.9	49.7	11,461	11,669	1.8	1.8	1,169	1,128	169	4,481	2.60	64.4	6.5	31.5
Campbell	14.0	6.9	3.1	48.5	33,698	46,133	36.9	0.0	6,041	2,068	-4,030	17,588	2.70	69.9	8.0	24.0
Carbon	14.5	10.6	6.5	46.0	15,639	15,884	1.6	-5.7	1,674	1,095	-1,497	6,205	2.39	66.8	9.7	28.2
Converse	14.8	10.1	6.5	49.2	12,052	13,833	14.8	-1.4	1,494	1,032	-678	5,630	2.51	69.7	5.4	26.1
Crook	17.0	12.6	8.0	49.2	5,887	7,083	20.3	5.2	839	513	44	3,010	2.42	71.1	5.1	25.7
Fremont	14.1	11.1	7.2	49.8	35,804	40,123	12.1	-1.5	4,744	3,586	-1,766	15,167	2.60	65.2	10.0	28.0

1. No spouse present.

Table B. States and Counties — Population, Vital Statistics, Health, and Crime

STATE County	Persons in group quarters, 2018	Daytime Population, 2013-2017		Births, 2018		Deaths, 2018		Persons under 65 with no health insurance, 2016		Medicare, 2018			Serious crimes known to police[2], 2016 Total	
		Number	Employment/ residence ratio	Total	Rate[1]	Number	Rate[1]	Number	Percent	Total beneficiaries	Enrolled in Original Medicare	Enrolled in Medicare Advantage	Number	Rate[3]
	32	33	34	35	36	37	38	39	40	41	42	43	44	45
WISCONSIN— Cont'd														
Douglas	1,379	40,275	0.85	415	9.6	401	9.3	2,054	5.9	9,840	5,542	4,298	1,553	3,577
Dunn	3,260	40,988	0.85	451	10.0	335	7.4	2,218	6.4	9,310	6,623	2,687	694	1,558
Eau Claire	4,598	108,463	1.11	1,189	11.4	785	7.5	5,064	6.1	19,532	13,163	6,369	2,239	2,183
Florence	48	3,531	0.56	34	7.9	57	13.2	251	7.8	1,403	996	407	105	2,348
Fond du Lac	3,543	97,869	0.92	1,030	10.0	916	8.9	4,570	5.6	21,291	10,488	10,803	1,563	1,534
Forest	353	8,918	0.97	103	11.5	106	11.8	715	10.4	2,591	1,674	917	147	1,634
Grant	4,436	47,668	0.84	583	11.3	487	9.4	2,712	6.9	10,480	5,879	4,601	722	1,378
Green	387	34,135	0.86	364	9.9	330	8.9	1,735	5.7	7,820	6,307	1,513	398	1,070
Green Lake	180	17,326	0.84	214	11.3	232	12.3	1,293	9.0	4,876	2,251	2,625	215	1,144
Iowa	180	22,561	0.92	274	11.5	197	8.3	1,143	5.9	5,055	3,428	1,627	188	790
Iron	91	5,152	0.76	32	5.6	88	15.5	288	7.2	2,006	1,195	811	112	1,942
Jackson	1,316	19,490	0.89	221	10.8	191	9.3	1,424	9.2	4,412	2,908	1,504	282	1,373
Jefferson	2,987	74,770	0.78	834	9.8	702	8.2	3,983	5.8	16,463	11,420	5,043	1,255	1,483
Juneau	1,619	25,385	0.91	275	10.3	265	10.0	1,643	8.3	6,360	5,008	1,352	437	1,675
Kenosha	4,385	150,310	0.78	1,882	11.1	1,372	8.1	9,148	6.4	28,563	19,564	8,999	3,538	2,099
Kewaunee	158	17,880	0.76	200	9.8	194	9.5	971	6.0	4,405	2,134	2,271	160	788
La Crosse	5,569	126,341	1.14	1,182	10.0	997	8.4	4,732	5.0	22,364	13,657	8,707	3,454	2,910
Lafayette	100	14,474	0.73	200	12.0	144	8.6	1,166	8.5	3,387	2,182	1,205	157	934
Langlade	279	18,541	0.93	204	10.6	221	11.5	996	6.9	5,558	3,157	2,401	628	3,296
Lincoln	596	25,690	0.84	279	10.1	307	11.1	1,312	6.1	7,249	4,268	2,981	518	1,865
Manitowoc	998	75,591	0.90	779	9.9	842	10.6	3,618	5.7	19,006	10,031	8,975	1,507	1,898
Marathon	1,561	137,654	1.03	1,534	11.3	1,140	8.4	7,205	6.4	26,915	14,257	12,658	1,968	1,447
Marinette	608	41,934	1.07	381	9.4	503	12.4	2,085	6.8	11,722	6,834	4,888	656	1,613
Marquette	149	13,035	0.69	134	8.7	167	10.8	877	7.7	4,399	2,893	1,506	162	1,081
Menominee	57	5,581	1.70	92	19.8	66	14.2	424	11.2	877	630	247	45	972
Milwaukee	22,853	987,039	1.07	13,197	13.9	8,251	8.7	62,419	7.8	153,182	79,839	73,343	45,881	4,789
Monroe	814	46,765	1.07	572	12.4	433	9.4	3,372	9.0	9,011	6,529	2,482	620	1,359
Oconto	238	29,188	0.56	358	9.5	392	10.4	1,853	6.2	9,003	3,997	5,006	NA	NA
Oneida	592	35,573	1.01	293	8.3	461	13.0	1,802	6.8	11,504	7,524	3,980	542	1,530
Outagamie	2,970	188,448	1.05	2,246	12.0	1,328	7.1	8,669	5.5	32,404	12,902	19,502	2,955	1,604
Ozaukee	1,882	84,936	0.94	811	9.1	787	8.8	2,674	3.8	19,473	11,696	7,777	855	972
Pepin	103	6,614	0.82	82	11.2	77	10.6	417	7.3	2,008	1,709	299	85	1,173
Pierce	2,777	30,307	0.52	383	9.0	298	7.0	1,766	5.3	7,238	4,203	3,035	505	1,380
Polk	397	38,679	0.78	410	9.4	451	10.3	2,426	7.0	10,531	5,978	4,553	580	1,342
Portage	3,319	71,282	1.02	678	9.6	505	7.1	3,163	5.6	13,553	8,114	5,439	875	1,243
Price	161	13,810	1.04	119	8.9	150	11.2	666	6.7	4,226	2,708	1,518	166	1,227
Racine	4,998	182,625	0.86	2,341	11.9	1,716	8.7	10,251	6.4	39,329	22,589	16,740	4,175	2,144
Richland	299	16,282	0.84	176	10.1	189	10.9	981	7.3	4,213	3,621	592	122	702
Rock	2,694	150,122	0.85	1,945	11.9	1,462	9.0	9,002	6.7	32,385	20,556	11,829	3,940	2,441
Rusk	175	14,067	0.98	142	10.0	156	11.0	896	8.4	3,904	2,435	1,469	166	1,187
St. Croix	741	76,106	0.76	995	11.1	621	6.9	3,583	4.7	14,380	8,247	6,133	997	1,169
Sauk	704	65,717	1.07	771	12.0	614	9.6	3,974	7.6	13,680	9,026	4,654	1,564	2,449
Sawyer	313	16,572	1.03	160	9.7	196	11.9	1,231	10.3	5,320	3,582	1,738	297	1,821
Shawano	672	35,759	0.73	438	10.7	418	10.2	2,679	8.4	9,649	4,142	5,507	706	1,717
Sheboygan	2,794	115,933	1.01	1,212	10.5	1,060	9.2	5,179	5.5	24,086	12,870	11,216	1,829	1,585
Taylor	212	19,799	0.95	217	10.6	184	9.0	1,443	8.8	4,142	2,332	1,810	250	1,226
Trempealeau	461	29,850	1.02	412	14.0	272	9.2	1,937	8.0	6,178	4,139	2,039	254	877
Vernon	321	27,357	0.77	414	13.4	313	10.2	2,306	9.4	6,852	3,766	3,086	226	768
Vilas	200	21,294	0.98	177	8.1	283	12.9	1,622	11.0	8,214	5,710	2,504	303	1,420
Walworth	3,074	98,122	0.91	932	9.0	932	9.0	6,540	7.8	20,495	15,345	5,150	1,514	1,473
Washburn	197	15,589	0.99	149	9.4	209	13.2	843	7.3	5,181	3,250	1,931	268	1,734
Washington	1,027	117,351	0.77	1,287	9.5	1,162	8.6	4,727	4.2	27,022	15,633	11,389	1,748	1,306
Waukesha	5,519	426,034	1.14	3,922	9.7	3,442	8.5	11,850	3.6	83,465	47,732	35,733	4,740	1,194
Waupaca	1,513	48,521	0.88	489	9.6	738	14.4	2,732	6.7	12,679	5,785	6,894	1,149	2,220
Waushara	1,232	20,913	0.68	212	8.7	259	10.7	1,587	9.2	6,592	3,106	3,486	314	1,314
Winnebago	7,617	180,250	1.12	1,845	10.8	1,448	8.5	7,527	5.5	32,105	13,746	18,359	3,138	1,848
Wood	778	76,184	1.08	804	11.0	752	10.3	3,320	5.7	17,243	8,430	8,813	1,421	1,945
WYOMING	14,207	589,507	1.02	6,840	11.8	4,947	8.6	65,310	13.4	106,077	101,788	4,289	12,890	2,202
Albany	2,195	37,525	0.98	382	9.9	194	5.0	3,723	11.7	4,954	4,641	313	595	1,568
Big Horn	183	11,557	0.93	137	11.5	144	12.1	1,673	17.7	2,623	2,580	43	NA	NA
Campbell	422	51,279	1.13	615	13.3	314	6.8	5,161	11.6	5,330	5,271	59	1,017	2,058
Carbon	791	15,869	1.02	188	12.6	147	9.8	1,847	14.7	2,782	2,675	107	353	2,362
Converse	103	14,181	1.00	143	10.5	133	9.8	1,400	11.6	2,498	2,466	32	NA	NA
Crook	34	6,707	0.82	106	14.2	69	9.3	823	13.6	1,577	1,488	89	98	1,393
Fremont	1,039	39,754	0.97	501	12.7	485	12.3	6,914	21.2	8,287	7,684	603	1,093	2,734

1. Per 1,000 estimated resident population.   2. Data for serious crimes have not been adjusted for underreporting; this may affect comparability between geographic areas and over time.   3. Per 100,000 population estimated by the FBI.

Table B. States and Counties — Crime, Education, Money Income, and Poverty

STATE County	Serious crimes known to police[2], 2016 (cont.)[1] Rate Violent	Property	Education — Enrollment[3] Total	Percent private	Attainment[4] (percent) High school graduate or less	Bachelor's degree or more	Local government expenditures[5] 2014-2015 Total current spending (mil dol)	Current spending per student (dollars)	Money income, 2013-2017 Per capita income[6]	Households Median income (dollars)	Percent with income of less than $50,000	Percent with income of $200,000 or more	Income and poverty, 2017 Median household income (dollars)	Percent below poverty level All persons	Children under 18 years	Children 5 to 17 years in families
	46	47	48	49	50	51	52	53	54	55	56	57	58	59	60	61
WISCONSIN— Cont'd																
Douglas	175	3,402	10,076	10.0	38.1	23.9	72.8	11,489	27,844	50,730	49.2	1.9	53,091	11.6	15.1	13.4
Dunn	164	1,394	14,449	5.2	40.6	27.7	64.8	10,532	26,354	54,605	44.8	2.5	58,902	11.6	13.4	12.5
Eau Claire	153	2,030	29,620	7.6	32.7	30.3	155.5	10,956	27,780	52,178	48.1	3.0	55,418	14.5	14.0	13.4
Florence	112	2,237	747	11.6	44.5	16.1	6.5	16,466	28,211	47,827	51.8	2.1	50,284	12.1	19.0	18.3
Fond du Lac	183	1,352	24,201	23.2	45.3	22.9	144.9	10,813	29,431	57,798	42.5	2.3	61,591	8.6	11.6	10.6
Forest	289	1,345	1,851	7.3	50.3	14.5	21.2	13,720	23,936	43,356	55.8	1.5	46,137	15.1	22.7	23.2
Grant	170	1,209	15,681	9.8	46.1	21.5	85.9	12,140	23,753	50,522	49.3	1.8	51,157	13.6	15.4	15.0
Green	78	992	8,346	8.6	44.8	23.2	65.5	11,874	30,208	60,609	41.6	3.0	62,456	8.0	10.8	10.1
Green Lake	32	1,112	3,770	16.8	52.5	18.5	34.9	11,372	26,372	50,276	49.7	1.9	52,917	10.0	17.1	15.8
Iowa	113	676	5,389	11.0	40.7	24.5	43.6	12,338	31,717	60,017	41.2	3.5	63,476	8.7	10.9	10.1
Iron	17	1,925	853	7.0	41.7	19.3	10.1	13,151	26,689	39,855	59.1	1.1	41,251	15.1	22.9	20.5
Jackson	97	1,275	4,233	9.4	53.3	13.8	35.5	11,050	24,740	51,108	48.8	1.9	51,131	13.3	17.4	16.0
Jefferson	177	1,306	21,168	17.0	42.8	23.9	154.9	11,529	28,819	59,215	42.2	2.6	58,759	8.5	10.1	9.3
Juneau	268	1,406	5,183	19.3	54.8	13.3	45.0	12,044	24,376	48,817	51.1	2.0	50,931	14.8	22.4	20.8
Kenosha	260	1,839	44,892	14.0	42.2	25.1	341.7	11,539	28,996	57,269	43.3	4.1	61,312	11.4	16.0	14.4
Kewaunee	148	641	4,521	15.8	49.3	18.2	35.8	10,159	28,767	60,320	42.7	2.2	62,107	8.0	8.6	8.2
La Crosse	152	2,758	34,981	12.8	31.4	33.0	192.1	11,845	29,495	54,127	46.1	3.8	57,145	12.0	10.5	9.7
Lafayette	107	827	3,842	11.9	49.0	17.9	35.2	12,099	27,023	55,859	45.3	2.4	55,586	10.9	16.1	15.6
Langlade	63	3,233	3,629	15.7	51.6	16.6	35.5	12,057	25,142	44,122	55.2	1.5	46,910	14.0	20.5	19.0
Lincoln	212	1,652	5,462	16.9	47.7	17.3	48.5	10,260	28,603	54,203	46.2	1.9	55,564	10.3	14.1	13.6
Manitowoc	219	1,679	17,361	18.2	47.5	19.7	117.9	11,073	27,777	51,053	48.9	1.9	55,741	9.2	13.0	11.9
Marathon	132	1,315	32,052	13.1	43.7	24.5	228.4	11,454	30,151	56,509	44.7	3.3	59,302	10.0	12.5	11.2
Marinette	39	1,574	8,605	10.5	51.2	14.8	68.2	11,253	25,778	44,958	55.1	1.1	47,449	13.3	18.9	16.8
Marquette	53	1,027	2,716	16.2	53.2	13.6	20.7	11,441	26,050	49,052	51.3	1.1	46,901	12.8	19.0	17.0
Menominee	0	972	1,334	4.1	52.0	15.9	15.5	18,259	17,197	38,080	62.8	1.2	36,936	27.6	44.4	42.9
Milwaukee	1,037	3,752	257,495	25.4	40.8	30.1	1,572.1	11,237	26,933	46,784	52.6	3.1	47,795	19.1	26.0	24.8
Monroe	149	1,210	10,687	14.3	46.8	19.5	75.9	10,665	26,724	56,479	43.5	2.1	55,690	11.4	18.3	17.2
Oconto	NA	NA	7,358	7.2	52.7	16.8	51.8	12,408	28,437	55,762	44.4	2.1	57,860	9.0	12.8	11.0
Oneida	138	1,391	6,133	17.2	40.3	27.5	57.6	13,645	30,550	52,945	47.3	3.0	56,170	9.4	14.7	13.8
Outagamie	162	1,442	46,192	15.0	39.2	28.3	358.0	10,154	30,858	61,523	39.9	3.2	65,945	7.1	8.3	7.6
Ozaukee	62	909	22,813	26.0	24.7	47.7	135.9	10,754	45,820	80,526	30.3	11.2	85,098	4.9	4.5	4.0
Pepin	124	1,049	1,432	16.0	49.1	19.1	15.3	13,326	27,901	51,470	48.6	3.0	51,544	10.7	16.4	14.7
Pierce	205	1,175	12,769	9.4	39.8	27.7	80.5	10,580	31,109	66,772	37.0	4.3	69,271	7.8	6.9	6.5
Polk	312	1,029	9,038	9.4	45.0	19.8	84.3	11,431	27,993	53,551	46.6	2.2	55,180	9.3	12.2	10.9
Portage	126	1,117	21,025	8.9	38.0	31.5	100.8	10,730	28,363	54,620	44.8	2.8	53,883	11.9	10.6	8.3
Price	37	1,190	2,317	11.2	50.9	17.0	23.4	11,867	27,161	45,680	54.9	1.4	47,302	11.3	17.2	15.8
Racine	219	1,925	48,334	19.2	42.3	24.4	352.6	11,993	29,582	58,334	42.1	4.0	61,118	10.9	17.9	16.1
Richland	6	697	3,782	15.8	50.7	18.8	20.3	11,484	24,941	48,234	51.7	1.3	49,092	13.1	20.5	18.7
Rock	229	2,211	39,954	14.0	46.7	21.4	305.7	10,916	26,954	53,410	46.9	2.4	55,905	12.1	17.5	16.6
Rusk	236	951	2,690	16.9	55.5	14.8	25.4	13,181	23,574	41,930	58.9	1.7	44,780	14.7	21.9	20.7
St. Croix	64	1,104	22,556	13.4	30.1	34.0	147.3	10,303	36,561	77,768	29.1	6.6	82,253	4.5	5.2	4.5
Sauk	127	2,322	14,178	13.8	44.5	23.4	112.9	11,114	28,331	54,447	45.5	2.5	58,372	9.9	14.1	13.3
Sawyer	184	1,637	3,104	10.1	43.4	22.0	27.1	11,721	29,712	43,565	56.4	3.5	47,183	17.0	29.2	27.2
Shawano	102	1,615	8,769	11.5	52.7	15.8	63.8	11,827	26,627	51,751	48.2	2.3	55,546	11.6	17.6	16.8
Sheboygan	155	1,430	27,250	16.2	44.4	23.8	208.8	10,831	28,849	56,114	44.3	2.4	59,231	7.8	9.8	9.0
Taylor	103	1,123	4,407	13.6	56.9	14.4	34.9	11,075	26,290	49,821	50.2	2.3	51,038	10.4	15.6	14.9
Trempealeau	66	811	6,573	9.8	49.2	19.7	68.2	11,620	26,654	54,009	46.0	1.9	56,051	8.8	11.4	11.2
Vernon	41	727	6,440	23.7	49.1	21.6	48.0	11,850	25,314	49,996	50.0	2.5	44,444	17.0	27.1	27.1
Vilas	47	1,373	3,495	8.6	38.3	27.1	43.4	16,570	29,058	42,720	57.7	3.2	44,740	13.9	24.5	23.4
Walworth	99	1,374	28,324	10.9	40.5	28.5	192.2	11,858	29,192	58,401	43.0	3.8	60,675	10.6	11.8	10.9
Washburn	188	1,547	2,788	11.6	44.7	22.0	33.8	12,667	28,232	46,592	53.2	2.1	48,139	12.8	18.7	17.6
Washington	61	1,245	31,410	23.1	35.8	29.7	211.5	10,545	36,177	73,021	32.2	5.4	76,551	5.3	5.4	4.8
Waukesha	69	1,125	98,092	22.3	27.6	42.9	685.7	11,047	42,094	81,140	29.3	9.4	82,627	4.8	5.0	4.6
Waupaca	236	1,984	10,772	14.4	51.2	18.5	94.8	10,829	29,423	54,071	45.7	2.4	58,474	10.6	16.1	14.5
Waushara	113	1,201	4,309	10.7	55.2	15.2	31.7	12,098	25,838	48,412	51.4	2.0	47,653	12.2	19.3	18.5
Winnebago	166	1,683	42,995	11.5	42.0	27.3	242.0	10,805	29,763	55,128	44.8	3.2	57,529	11.1	12.7	11.4
Wood	31	1,914	15,620	12.6	45.5	21.1	140.7	11,416	29,039	51,603	48.3	2.5	53,346	10.7	13.9	11.9
WYOMING	244	1,957	147,269	9.4	36.0	26.7	1,507.0	16,021	31,214	60,938	41.3	3.8	61,279	10.8	12.9	11.6
Albany	124	1,444	16,268	5.8	19.9	49.8	61.5	15,770	26,034	45,816	54.1	2.4	44,745	19.5	12.8	11.6
Big Horn	NA	NA	2,933	8.8	38.4	19.2	44.9	17,441	23,724	51,716	48.1	1.2	50,380	12.2	15.6	13.6
Campbell	381	1,678	12,131	7.5	44.4	18.5	135.6	14,847	33,200	80,178	30.1	4.2	78,240	9.4	11.8	9.9
Carbon	167	2,195	3,646	13.6	43.0	20.9	43.2	17,596	27,797	57,644	42.7	2.5	60,634	11.9	14.2	12.9
Converse	NA	NA	3,259	16.8	46.1	18.2	40.5	16,479	31,948	62,776	40.4	2.5	65,469	9.2	12.1	10.8
Crook	71	1,322	1,582	4.5	38.1	20.7	20.7	18,235	34,186	66,944	37.5	5.0	61,664	7.7	10.1	10.1
Fremont	180	2,553	10,169	8.6	40.6	23.3	134.0	19,288	27,220	55,013	46.3	3.2	50,134	16.2	21.7	20.3

1. Data for serious crimes have not been adjusted for underreporting; this may affect comparability between geographic areas and over time. 2. Per 100,000 population estimated by the FBI. 3. All persons 3 years old and over enrolled in nursery school through college. 4. Persons 25 years old and over. 5. Elementary and secondary education expenditures. 6. Based on population estimated by the American Community Survey, 2013–2017.

Table B. States and Counties — **Personal Income and Earnings**

STATE County	Personal income, 2017										Earnings, 2017		
			Per capita[1]			Supplements to wages and salaries, employer contributions (mil dol)						Contributions for government social insurance (mil dol)	
	Total (mil dol)	Percent change 2016-2017	Dollars	Rank	Wages and salaries (mil dol)	Pension and insurance	Government social insurance	Proprietors' income (mil dol)	Dividends, interest, and rent (mil dol)	Personal transfer reecipts (mil dol)	Total (mil dol)	From employee and self-employed	From employer
	62	63	64	65	66	67	68	69	70	71	72	73	74
WISCONSIN— Cont'd													
Douglas	1,768	3.9	40,846	1,427	736	170	65	76	288	453	1,046	72	65
Dunn	1,714	4.1	38,345	1,818	784	185	61	84	296	370	1,115	71	61
Eau Claire	4,714	5.2	45,468	846	2,824	535	213	293	954	820	3,864	237	213
Florence	219	-1.6	50,145	454	32	9	3	14	45	52	57	5	3
Fond du Lac	4,692	3.9	45,753	825	2,263	426	178	342	783	866	3,210	200	178
Forest	353	3.3	39,367	1,661	125	37	10	16	78	107	188	13	10
Grant	2,150	3.8	41,349	1,354	758	204	59	272	385	432	1,293	77	59
Green	1,794	2.3	48,687	569	696	145	54	144	359	289	1,039	64	54
Green Lake	826	2.0	44,037	1,016	250	56	20	54	220	182	381	27	20
Iowa	1,104	4.3	46,563	745	446	83	35	99	207	182	663	41	35
Iron	274	3.7	48,393	597	58	14	5	21	67	79	98	8	5
Jackson	887	5.2	43,185	1,121	390	89	31	54	181	179	564	35	31
Jefferson	3,702	3.3	43,637	1,059	1,432	299	111	192	586	667	2,033	130	111
Juneau	959	3.7	36,103	2,187	383	91	30	44	152	256	549	37	30
Kenosha	7,563	4.1	44,879	915	3,078	604	240	392	1,088	1,342	4,313	271	240
Kewaunee	924	3.5	45,183	880	286	62	23	94	149	167	465	27	23
La Crosse	5,575	3.0	47,134	703	3,369	657	262	347	1,131	971	4,636	282	262
Lafayette	718	3.3	42,908	1,150	179	44	14	99	142	128	336	19	14
Langlade	802	4.2	41,836	1,283	287	63	23	71	144	224	443	30	23
Lincoln	1,223	3.4	43,935	1,028	496	103	38	76	182	289	713	48	38
Manitowoc	3,624	2.5	45,767	823	1,578	318	124	290	668	735	2,310	146	124
Marathon	6,463	3.5	47,617	657	3,474	651	260	500	1,090	1,025	4,886	298	260
Marinette	1,705	3.5	42,296	1,230	818	179	65	95	267	476	1,156	77	65
Marquette	602	4.2	39,340	1,664	147	35	12	24	106	161	217	17	12
Menominee	133	1.8	28,761	2,996	77	34	5	4	25	45	120	7	5
Milwaukee	42,938	3.0	45,099	886	27,879	4,803	2,084	2,853	7,938	9,369	37,619	2,308	2,084
Monroe	1,814	5.0	39,766	1,597	948	230	77	124	343	374	1,379	83	77
Oconto	1,658	2.6	44,140	1,008	342	85	28	132	243	339	587	41	28
Oneida	1,688	3.3	47,868	636	706	135	55	136	389	431	1,031	72	55
Outagamie	9,152	3.5	49,191	520	5,540	949	423	632	1,524	1,249	7,543	455	423
Ozaukee	7,008	3.1	79,255	36	2,216	398	165	329	1,915	685	3,108	195	165
Pepin	337	4.0	46,468	757	99	21	8	27	61	80	155	11	8
Pierce	1,870	3.8	44,636	946	429	128	33	107	319	288	697	44	33
Polk	1,941	3.4	44,669	942	649	151	52	123	330	419	975	65	52
Portage	3,080	3.9	43,699	1,053	1,674	331	130	185	553	559	2,320	142	130
Price	594	2.5	44,166	1,002	230	53	18	61	108	171	361	25	18
Racine	9,100	3.6	46,412	763	3,789	747	292	333	1,727	1,748	5,161	334	292
Richland	722	1.3	41,198	1,380	230	56	18	63	128	171	366	23	18
Rock	6,821	3.5	42,026	1,260	3,202	609	247	309	1,237	1,396	4,368	282	247
Rusk	604	4.5	42,704	1,184	212	52	17	37	94	161	318	22	17
St. Croix	4,689	4.5	52,858	346	1,519	298	117	245	758	565	2,179	136	117
Sauk	2,933	3.5	45,847	816	1,545	289	121	308	511	521	2,262	139	121
Sawyer	718	3.9	43,724	1,051	259	60	21	53	172	205	393	28	21
Shawano	1,652	3.4	40,357	1,493	495	113	39	134	275	377	781	53	39
Sheboygan	5,776	4.8	50,081	459	3,096	544	230	570	1,051	910	4,441	273	230
Taylor	779	2.1	38,313	1,821	335	70	27	92	124	163	524	32	27
Trempealeau	1,256	3.0	42,616	1,195	620	129	48	52	202	268	849	54	48
Vernon	1,192	3.2	38,766	1,762	358	86	28	120	198	268	592	39	28
Vilas	1,123	4.8	51,814	382	283	67	23	176	308	282	549	40	23
Walworth	4,818	3.5	46,737	733	1,805	401	140	301	1,029	807	2,647	166	140
Washburn	714	4.6	45,307	867	217	53	17	83	147	207	369	26	17
Washington	7,398	3.8	54,760	290	2,711	486	204	455	1,276	985	3,856	246	204
Waukesha	27,687	3.4	69,111	76	14,319	2,209	1,071	1,779	5,803	3,038	19,379	1,188	1,071
Waupaca	2,254	2.6	44,009	1,020	792	178	62	145	397	538	1,178	79	62
Waushara	952	4.1	39,064	1,711	221	57	18	63	181	238	358	27	18
Winnebago	7,814	3.4	45,852	813	5,114	897	384	417	1,521	1,270	6,812	419	384
Wood	3,261	2.6	44,601	949	1,830	344	138	240	542	700	2,553	162	138
WYOMING	33,221	2.4	57,384	X	13,694	2,621	1,367	3,333	10,525	4,533	21,014	1,217	1,367
Albany	1,545	2.1	40,301	1,502	700	184	69	85	377	227	1,037	58	69
Big Horn	427	1.3	35,888	2,213	188	43	20	19	81	103	271	17	20
Campbell	2,259	-1.9	48,842	552	1,483	244	142	238	379	257	2,106	121	142
Carbon	805	0.9	52,575	357	348	95	36	50	183	116	528	30	36
Converse	681	-0.2	49,290	510	318	64	31	40	162	116	452	27	31
Crook	341	2.5	46,013	793	111	23	11	26	85	55	172	11	11
Fremont	1,672	2.6	42,013	1,264	676	148	68	96	381	380	988	62	68

1. Based on the resident population estimated as of July 1 of the year shown.

Table B. States and Counties — Earnings, Social Security, and Housing

STATE County	Earnings, 2017 (cont.)									Social Security beneficiaries, December 2017		Supplemental Security Income recipients, 2017	Housing units, 2018	
	Percent by selected industries													
	Farm	Mining, quarrying, and extractions	Construction	Manu-facturing	Information; professional, scientific, technical services	Retail trade	Finance, insurance, real estate, and leasing	Health care and social assistance	Govern-ment	Number	Rate[1]		Total	Percent change, 2010-2018
	75	76	77	78	79	80	81	82	83	84	85	86	87	88
WISCONSIN— Cont'd														
Douglas	-0.1	D	7.0	11.2	2.9	6.7	2.9	8.1	21.4	9,935	230	1,107	23,223	1.7
Dunn	0.9	D	6.6	20.7	3.4	5.7	3.7	D	23.9	9,635	216	738	18,588	3.5
Eau Claire	0.1	D	6.6	8.9	6.2	7.0	6.7	22.9	15.1	20,695	200	1,929	44,399	5.3
Florence	0.0	0.1	4.3	15.0	D	D	D	5.3	28.9	1,540	352	67	4,914	2.8
Fond du Lac	2.5	0.4	9.2	24.5	4.4	6.3	4.8	13.3	12.0	22,480	219	1,609	45,361	3.3
Forest	-0.2	D	3.9	8.7	D	3.9	1.9	D	59.8	2,835	316	239	9,215	2.8
Grant	6.5	D	6.1	14.3	3.9	5.7	4.2	9.5	26.6	11,330	218	806	22,179	2.8
Green	2.6	D	6.0	23.9	D	12.2	3.7	12.5	13.1	8,225	223	411	16,075	1.4
Green Lake	0.5	1.4	10.9	15.0	D	7.7	5.3	14.7	17.9	5,200	277	306	10,750	1.3
Iowa	4.7	D	9.0	11.2	2.8	25.9	3.0	D	13.6	5,355	226	331	10,952	2.2
Iron	1.0	D	15.1	D	3.8	6.7	D	17.0	24.0	2,220	391	132	6,110	1.9
Jackson	4.2	3.5	14.2	8.7	D	4.3	3.0	D	25.4	4,780	233	367	9,974	2.6
Jefferson	0.8	D	7.6	30.9	3.7	6.4	3.6	9.1	12.8	17,535	207	957	35,993	2.4
Juneau	2.6	0.0	4.9	25.3	2.3	5.6	2.7	12.5	25.3	7,000	263	654	15,245	3.9
Kenosha	0.2	0.0	4.5	13.8	3.4	7.0	3.6	13.7	16.3	31,150	185	3,694	70,657	2.0
Kewaunee	17.5	D	7.9	23.6	3.1	3.8	3.0	D	15.6	4,725	231	228	9,462	1.7
La Crosse	0.1	D	5.3	11.5	5.9	6.0	7.7	22.6	15.2	23,180	196	2,115	50,569	4.5
Lafayette	18.2	D	10.0	15.1	D	3.1	4.6	2.7	20.9	3,670	219	182	7,322	1.3
Langlade	4.3	0.0	4.8	18.5	D	12.8	5.8	D	15.2	5,975	312	435	12,587	1.8
Lincoln	0.8	D	7.4	25.0	1.8	6.6	15.2	7.3	16.2	8,010	288	450	17,237	2.7
Manitowoc	3.7	0.3	6.0	28.9	3.2	5.4	3.4	10.7	12.6	20,595	260	1,407	37,582	1.1
Marathon	1.4	0.2	5.2	22.3	4.9	6.0	10.5	15.2	11.2	28,575	211	1,960	59,734	3.5
Marinette	2.4	D	4.6	37.7	2.5	5.9	3.0	D	12.9	12,865	319	873	30,872	1.6
Marquette	2.0	D	5.4	36.0	3.0	6.0	2.3	D	21.5	4,815	315	335	10,005	1.1
Menominee	0.0	0.0	0.2	D	D	D	D	0.7	93.8	1,015	220	218	2,296	1.9
Milwaukee	0.0	0.0	3.4	11.5	10.8	4.4	11.0	15.4	13.3	164,270	173	43,119	419,554	0.4
Monroe	1.6	3.1	5.7	18.2	D	4.8	2.6	7.7	30.7	9,550	209	822	20,012	4.2
Oconto	8.6	D	9.5	21.8	D	5.9	2.6	10.8	19.6	9,900	264	598	24,331	3.4
Oneida	0.8	0.0	8.8	11.2	4.7	12.0	5.0	19.9	15.5	12,245	347	622	31,240	3.7
Outagamie	0.7	D	10.0	19.4	6.7	6.1	9.2	12.0	11.3	35,180	189	2,626	77,594	6.1
Ozaukee	0.6	0.1	4.8	24.2	9.7	5.4	10.4	13.9	9.0	19,525	221	576	37,791	4.2
Pepin	3.1	0.0	14.7	5.9	4.0	9.6	3.8	8.8	18.2	2,095	289	106	3,692	3.2
Pierce	2.0	1.2	8.0	13.9	3.7	4.3	4.1	4.9	35.5	7,640	182	390	16,693	3.5
Polk	1.3	D	7.2	22.7	D	6.3	3.2	15.1	17.6	11,440	263	620	24,787	2.2
Portage	2.0	D	4.4	13.1	5.4	6.9	19.3	9.7	16.3	14,340	203	837	31,127	3.6
Price	2.2	0.1	4.6	34.0	6.5	5.1	2.5	D	14.9	4,605	343	299	11,402	2.6
Racine	0.2	0.1	5.4	32.5	4.3	6.1	4.5	12.2	13.7	42,660	218	5,618	82,907	0.9
Richland	7.9	D	6.3	25.4	2.0	7.9	2.8	15.0	17.2	4,460	255	361	8,998	1.5
Rock	0.4	0.4	6.8	17.2	5.0	6.2	4.1	16.0	14.4	35,625	219	3,945	69,227	1.2
Rusk	3.6	D	5.1	29.6	D	5.3	2.2	7.6	22.3	4,335	306	358	9,253	4.2
St. Croix	0.0	D	9.0	21.4	6.1	7.6	5.1	12.7	14.3	15,120	170	579	36,313	6.9
Sauk	0.9	D	11.9	17.6	4.6	7.7	4.6	11.1	15.4	14,300	224	893	30,591	3.0
Sawyer	0.4	0.1	9.2	11.2	3.5	9.8	4.4	D	27.4	5,700	347	362	16,604	4.0
Shawano	5.7	0.0	7.2	17.2	D	7.0	3.6	D	21.1	10,445	255	707	20,943	1.1
Sheboygan	1.1	D	5.3	41.8	3.0	5.1	6.7	11.4	8.9	25,865	224	1,768	51,340	1.1
Taylor	5.5	D	6.9	23.7	D	5.3	3.6	D	12.3	4,495	221	241	10,765	1.7
Trempealeau	-0.9	0.8	5.1	43.0	D	4.2	2.5	D	17.4	6,550	222	408	13,218	4.7
Vernon	5.3	D	8.2	9.0	5.1	7.2	3.5	16.2	18.8	7,550	245	612	14,204	3.5
Vilas	0.6	0.1	13.3	2.8	4.0	7.3	3.1	6.0	24.5	8,490	392	337	26,145	4.1
Walworth	0.6	D	7.0	22.8	4.7	6.5	4.2	7.4	21.2	21,635	210	1,263	52,651	2.2
Washburn	1.7	D	6.4	18.1	D	7.4	3.7	D	21.4	5,415	344	371	13,379	3.1
Washington	0.6	0.2	7.0	27.9	4.9	6.7	7.9	11.2	9.9	28,240	209	959	57,201	4.6
Waukesha	0.1	0.1	8.5	19.2	11.3	6.3	10.1	10.1	7.0	84,930	212	3,031	166,643	3.6
Waupaca	2.3	0.0	6.0	34.8	3.4	6.8	3.2	8.9	18.5	13,850	270	868	25,847	1.8
Waushara	5.6	0.1	7.4	17.5	D	6.2	3.0	D	22.9	7,185	295	415	15,137	2.0
Winnebago	0.3	D	7.3	27.6	7.5	4.7	5.8	9.1	11.8	34,690	204	2,597	76,028	3.7
Wood	0.8	D	5.8	16.3	6.2	5.8	4.0	24.9	12.8	18,920	259	1,524	35,181	3.2
WYOMING	0.7	11.5	7.7	D	5.9	5.6	5.3	7.4	25.6	109,624	189	6,815	278,595	6.4
Albany	1.4	0.7	6.0	2.4	7.6	5.8	5.7	7.7	49.2	4,865	127	307	19,422	8.3
Big Horn	2.5	12.9	9.2	7.3	D	2.9	3.3	D	36.1	2,705	227	168	5,475	1.8
Campbell	-0.4	35.3	7.4	1.8	3.2	4.7	3.8	3.2	17.4	5,770	125	295	20,317	7.2
Carbon	0.7	D	6.1	D	2.7	5.9	2.3	D	25.7	2,815	184	147	8,819	2.8
Converse	0.2	24.2	6.4	2.4	2.5	3.4	5.2	3.7	26.4	2,600	188	148	6,675	4.2
Crook	2.4	11.6	10.3	8.6	D	4.8	3.2	D	27.5	1,645	222	41	3,669	2.1
Fremont	0.9	6.5	6.3	1.4	4.7	6.9	4.9	D	37.5	8,935	224	892	18,023	1.3

1. Per 1,000 resident population estimated as of July 1 of the year shown.

STATE County	Housing units, 2013-2017								Civilian labor force, 2018				Civilian employment[6], 2013-2017		
	Occupied units										Unemployment			Percent	
			Owner-occupied			Renter-occupied									
				Median owner cost as a percent of income			Median rent as a percent of income[2]	Sub-standard units[4] (percent)		Percent change, 2017-2018				Construction, production, and maintenance occupations
				With a mort-gage	Without a mort-gage[2]	Median rent[3]								Management, business, science, and arts	
	Total	Percent	Median value[1]						Total		Total	Rate[5]	Total		
	89	90	91	92	93	94	95	96	97	98	99	100	101	102	103

STATE County	89	90	91	92	93	94	95	96	97	98	99	100	101	102	103
WISCONSIN— Cont'd															
Douglas	18,717	67.2	140,400	20.3	12.9	747	27.3	1.6	23,315	-1.3	928	4.0	21,594	31.7	24.8
Dunn	16,652	68.5	156,700	20.7	12.8	742	26.6	2.0	24,449	-0.3	746	3.1	22,972	32.3	28.3
Eau Claire	40,528	62.9	156,200	19.9	13.2	787	29.4	2.2	59,280	-0.3	1,545	2.6	55,778	34.5	21.9
Florence	1,979	86.5	132,600	22.6	14.0	498	25.7	3.4	2,274	-0.9	88	3.9	1,949	27.9	30.7
Fond du Lac	41,387	71.2	149,400	20.6	12.3	734	27.1	1.8	57,658	0.8	1,519	2.6	53,195	30.2	32.1
Forest	4,040	74.9	131,400	22.7	13.3	507	22.9	3.0	3,998	-1.0	192	4.8	3,658	27.8	31.5
Grant	19,444	69.2	137,200	20.6	12.1	664	26.0	2.3	28,492	0.8	810	2.8	26,480	30.0	29.6
Green	14,957	73.7	163,600	21.5	13.8	712	25.3	1.4	21,282	0.5	543	2.6	20,015	34.1	28.8
Green Lake	7,932	74.2	139,300	21.5	13.4	661	25.8	2.2	9,773	0.4	325	3.3	8,961	27.5	37.4
Iowa	9,799	74.2	171,700	22.0	13.6	730	24.4	1.9	13,933	0.7	363	2.6	12,412	33.4	29.0
Iron	2,948	76.2	107,200	21.5	13.4	517	30.6	2.8	2,584	-1.2	150	5.8	2,536	26.6	30.7
Jackson	8,154	74.5	129,400	21.8	13.6	646	23.3	3.7	10,679	2.2	332	3.1	9,551	26.8	33.3
Jefferson	32,739	69.7	177,500	22.5	13.6	814	26.8	1.8	46,319	1.3	1,328	2.9	44,955	32.0	27.8
Juneau	10,149	77.0	120,100	22.9	14.4	715	26.6	2.3	13,567	-0.4	416	3.1	11,918	23.8	33.3
Kenosha	63,286	65.6	164,100	22.1	14.4	884	30.6	2.3	89,687	-0.2	3,164	3.5	82,194	32.4	25.5
Kewaunee	8,234	78.2	155,900	21.2	12.3	626	23.1	2.1	11,370	1.4	327	2.9	10,520	31.2	36.3
La Crosse	46,966	63.8	161,300	20.8	12.1	792	28.4	1.6	67,261	-0.8	1,766	2.6	62,589	36.6	20.5
Lafayette	6,714	75.7	126,600	21.2	13.0	687	25.0	2.4	10,286	1.0	236	2.3	8,640	31.9	34.1
Langlade	8,646	76.7	106,200	20.8	12.0	609	29.7	3.3	9,522	-1.5	377	4.0	8,872	26.9	31.9
Lincoln	12,560	77.5	135,500	19.1	12.3	627	23.3	2.0	15,363	-1.1	486	3.2	14,327	27.7	32.4
Manitowoc	34,119	75.0	126,200	19.8	12.9	648	24.3	1.2	41,426	-0.9	1,288	3.1	41,085	28.2	34.2
Marathon	54,820	72.8	147,600	19.8	12.1	709	26.3	2.2	74,073	0.0	1,975	2.7	71,112	34.1	27.4
Marinette	18,548	74.4	116,600	19.7	13.1	669	26.0	1.7	19,716	-0.5	791	4.0	18,850	26.1	36.3
Marquette	6,389	80.9	144,000	23.0	14.4	710	23.3	2.6	7,738	1.5	274	3.5	6,984	23.2	38.7
Menominee	1,354	66.3	85,400	22.3	10.0	465	18.3	10.0	1,619	0.5	92	5.7	1,562	22.0	20.7
Milwaukee	382,027	49.7	150,300	22.9	14.6	844	30.9	3.0	472,701	-0.7	17,157	3.6	454,524	36.0	21.3
Monroe	17,832	69.9	144,100	20.8	12.1	798	24.9	2.7	23,664	0.4	644	2.7	21,433	27.8	32.5
Oconto	15,634	83.3	156,700	21.6	12.0	642	25.0	1.9	20,868	0.8	689	3.3	19,216	29.5	36.2
Oneida	14,994	83.7	165,000	21.6	13.2	747	27.5	0.8	18,233	-1.0	655	3.6	16,826	31.7	24.9
Outagamie	72,288	70.5	160,100	19.7	12.0	769	25.1	1.8	103,628	-0.6	2,898	2.8	98,822	34.0	27.4
Ozaukee	35,044	75.2	262,100	20.5	11.7	867	25.5	1.0	49,109	-0.3	1,240	2.5	46,395	47.5	16.7
Pepin	3,005	81.2	143,800	22.1	14.1	599	25.3	1.1	4,252	0.6	139	3.3	3,686	32.8	32.1
Pierce	15,302	72.8	193,800	21.6	12.9	779	26.7	1.5	25,310	0.3	807	3.2	23,358	32.3	29.8
Polk	18,189	78.4	158,300	23.4	13.9	740	26.7	1.6	24,691	-0.9	916	3.7	21,257	29.4	34.4
Portage	28,072	68.6	158,800	19.7	11.2	708	28.2	1.9	39,282	-1.1	1,180	3.0	37,291	34.6	25.0
Price	6,567	78.2	120,000	22.1	13.5	570	24.3	2.2	6,673	-2.0	247	3.7	6,571	26.7	38.6
Racine	75,640	69.0	165,200	21.2	13.7	841	29.4	1.5	99,570	-0.3	3,600	3.6	93,603	32.4	27.2
Richland	7,564	74.2	134,400	23.3	12.8	646	26.2	2.8	9,333	0.2	249	2.7	8,418	28.0	35.8
Rock	64,482	68.7	135,000	21.0	12.5	782	28.7	2.0	85,397	-0.1	2,766	3.2	77,910	30.3	30.4
Rusk	6,294	77.5	106,300	23.7	13.2	669	26.6	2.9	6,994	-0.2	279	4.0	6,463	23.2	41.6
St. Croix	33,389	75.7	223,000	20.1	10.8	929	25.8	1.8	50,379	0.2	1,528	3.0	47,132	38.9	23.5
Sauk	25,678	68.7	172,500	21.7	12.4	757	29.3	2.5	35,680	0.1	915	2.6	33,623	30.9	27.3
Sawyer	7,573	73.0	161,700	22.9	12.2	667	27.8	3.1	8,004	-0.2	345	4.3	7,254	29.8	26.7
Shawano	17,024	76.3	135,800	20.6	13.5	611	22.5	1.7	21,599	0.5	651	3.0	20,189	28.9	33.6
Sheboygan	47,532	69.6	149,800	19.8	12.4	680	24.2	2.3	62,903	0.3	1,571	2.5	59,570	30.0	32.6
Taylor	8,769	76.8	129,300	22.0	13.3	615	27.2	3.0	11,091	-0.5	346	3.1	10,222	26.6	43.2
Trempealeau	11,892	72.1	147,000	21.8	13.7	682	24.9	2.3	16,424	-0.5	469	2.9	15,191	29.3	37.0
Vernon	12,095	77.2	148,900	22.8	13.2	647	28.7	6.8	15,559	-1.4	448	2.9	13,425	31.4	31.5
Vilas	10,758	76.5	206,500	25.2	13.6	673	30.4	1.8	10,182	-0.1	402	3.9	9,038	29.5	22.6
Walworth	40,246	68.4	192,500	23.1	13.9	833	29.3	2.4	58,515	0.7	1,708	2.9	53,327	30.8	27.2
Washburn	7,142	78.4	147,000	22.7	13.3	677	27.5	1.7	7,944	0.1	308	3.9	7,011	30.2	30.1
Washington	53,756	77.5	219,600	21.3	12.7	873	25.3	1.0	77,606	-0.4	1,976	2.5	73,513	36.6	24.4
Waukesha	156,996	76.3	262,700	20.6	12.5	978	26.7	1.2	225,432	-0.5	5,985	2.7	212,647	45.6	17.1
Waupaca	21,793	73.2	142,300	20.4	13.6	681	25.8	1.3	26,377	-1.1	780	3.0	26,033	26.6	35.4
Waushara	9,851	81.5	140,500	23.2	13.3	669	29.5	1.7	11,675	2.0	406	3.5	10,435	25.2	37.6
Winnebago	69,759	64.5	147,300	20.2	12.6	721	26.9	1.3	92,956	-0.9	2,524	2.7	87,905	31.4	27.2
Wood	32,223	72.9	127,700	19.2	11.4	675	27.2	1.0	35,497	1.1	1,227	3.5	36,504	31.5	31.0
WYOMING	230,237	69.2	204,900	20.5	10.0	828	26.0	2.4	289,574	-1.1	11,754	4.1	293,633	33.6	27.9
Albany	16,009	49.6	223,000	21.4	10.0	748	34.0	2.8	20,307	-0.8	668	3.3	21,115	42.1	17.9
Big Horn	4,481	72.6	151,900	20.0	10.0	651	22.0	2.2	5,257	-1.9	246	4.7	5,280	29.5	32.8
Campbell	17,588	71.5	213,900	19.2	10.0	949	24.4	2.8	22,821	-0.9	938	4.1	25,511	26.5	37.6
Carbon	6,205	70.7	158,600	18.9	10.0	851	21.3	3.1	7,786	-1.4	295	3.8	7,519	30.7	33.3
Converse	5,630	73.2	197,200	20.1	10.0	711	22.9	4.3	7,554	1.0	278	3.7	6,902	28.0	34.2
Crook	3,010	79.3	219,000	18.8	10.8	759	17.6	3.2	3,696	0.4	119	3.2	3,613	29.0	39.4
Fremont	15,167	70.5	189,700	21.6	10.0	742	22.0	4.6	18,865	-2.5	985	5.2	18,674	33.5	26.3

1. Specified owner-occupied units.   2. A value of 10.0 represents 10 percent or less; a value of 50.0 represents 50 percent or more.   3. Specified renter-occupied units.   4. Overcrowded or lacking complete plumbing facilities.   5. Percent of civilian labor force.   6. Civilian employed persons 16 years old and over.

Table B. States and Counties — Nonfarm Employment and Agriculture

STATE County	Private nonfarm establishments, employment and payroll, 2016									Agriculture, 2017			
	Employment							Annual payroll		Farms			Farm producers whose primary occupation is farming (percent)
	Number of establishments	Total	Health care and social assistance	Manufac-turing	Retail trade	Finance and insurance	Professional, scientific, and technical services	Total (mil dol)	Average per employee (dollars)	Number	Percent with:		
											Fewer than 50 acres	1000 acres or more	
	104	105	106	107	108	109	110	111	112	113	114	115	116
WISCONSIN— Cont'd													
Douglas	1,030	13,748	1,975	1,642	2,279	329	393	520	37,848	329	24.0	2.7	35.4
Dunn	896	14,447	2,409	2,929	1,960	432	409	554	38,328	1,288	29.1	4.9	43.1
Eau Claire	2,709	51,153	11,109	5,078	7,424	2,620	2,291	2,017	39,440	1,069	33.6	1.0	37.1
Florence	102	581	D	146	68	39	7	17	28,482	101	21.8	NA	34.9
Fond du Lac	2,358	42,959	6,333	8,569	6,026	1,640	1,386	1,746	40,652	1,244	35.9	4.8	53.4
Forest	237	1,681	218	313	255	68	73	50	29,948	140	25.0	2.9	48.9
Grant	1,231	13,980	2,266	2,274	2,575	713	523	476	34,042	2,482	25.7	3.2	48.6
Green	973	13,594	2,077	3,382	1,716	333	381	527	38,761	1,428	43.8	3.4	46.3
Green Lake	459	5,399	1,072	929	1,032	261	76	196	36,259	502	29.3	5.4	53.0
Iowa	569	9,001	1,076	1,187	4,055	193	134	352	39,073	1,576	28.3	3.4	39.9
Iron	193	1,381	310	164	232	30	36	37	27,140	49	28.6	2.0	31.6
Jackson	421	6,557	1,068	563	856	206	107	285	43,437	855	22.3	5.4	44.5
Jefferson	1,952	30,554	4,129	8,501	4,163	641	591	1,193	39,054	1,098	41.5	3.6	41.5
Juneau	563	6,582	1,099	2,212	1,078	169	53	237	35,960	715	32.3	4.3	40.4
Kenosha	3,174	52,787	8,501	7,094	10,953	876	1,332	2,076	39,335	415	55.7	3.6	42.1
Kewaunee	463	4,977	452	1,927	585	140	164	191	38,419	655	33.4	4.1	51.9
La Crosse	3,053	61,882	11,239	7,901	8,916	2,171	1,880	2,529	40,861	667	29.8	2.1	46.2
Lafayette	376	3,200	271	894	389	147	61	107	33,514	1,327	39.5	5.0	52.8
Langlade	560	6,455	928	1,446	1,411	282	131	233	36,159	432	23.8	4.4	49.7
Lincoln	688	8,794	960	2,377	1,361	1,000	115	376	42,793	426	29.8	1.9	41.2
Manitowoc	1,755	30,100	4,392	10,036	3,771	753	540	1,245	41,359	1,171	43.2	4.1	48.4
Marathon	3,353	64,918	10,357	17,196	7,743	4,457	1,523	2,724	41,954	2,237	33.8	2.9	50.2
Marinette	1,065	15,690	2,572	6,178	2,083	415	251	609	38,801	515	32.6	5.2	47.5
Marquette	274	3,554	313	1,255	309	43	72	118	33,342	458	33.8	5.0	40.7
Menominee	24	703	NA	D	39	NA	D	17	23,509	3	33.3	NA	50.0
Milwaukee	19,879	445,787	87,838	45,690	44,228	34,152	22,370	23,225	52,098	86	83.7	NA	38.2
Monroe	954	15,766	2,494	3,811	1,956	423	398	651	41,287	1,555	29.2	2.3	45.2
Oconto	791	6,770	1,355	2,026	928	169	140	229	33,843	834	37.9	5.2	44.0
Oneida	1,378	13,774	2,667	1,361	3,567	321	378	526	38,178	131	39.7	3.8	38.1
Outagamie	5,022	103,022	12,912	18,312	13,048	5,864	3,785	4,554	44,207	1,130	44.8	3.6	45.8
Ozaukee	2,774	40,912	6,238	9,088	5,387	2,239	2,379	1,762	43,057	316	46.2	2.8	49.7
Pepin	223	1,816	261	170	250	89	39	70	38,757	448	27.2	4.0	41.3
Pierce	792	6,967	997	1,431	1,063	281	206	241	34,613	1,229	39.9	3.1	38.9
Polk	1,117	13,229	2,539	4,101	1,951	318	307	448	33,879	1,234	35.4	3.6	44.1
Portage	1,701	30,896	3,741	4,844	3,970	4,953	1,025	1,267	41,001	982	35.0	5.5	48.0
Price	396	4,599	825	1,901	555	141	78	173	37,626	410	25.1	2.0	41.1
Racine	4,024	66,437	11,043	15,606	9,313	2,058	1,996	3,058	46,029	611	51.7	3.8	42.6
Richland	366	4,813	962	1,469	859	149	68	160	33,327	1,103	31.1	3.0	37.0
Rock	3,330	57,883	8,754	10,139	9,147	1,335	2,133	2,451	42,336	1,587	53.7	4.7	40.6
Rusk	321	4,338	826	1,626	633	105	40	149	34,408	501	14.6	5.2	57.6
St. Croix	2,226	29,300	4,253	6,088	4,444	890	1,390	1,158	39,533	1,444	41.6	3.2	40.6
Sauk	1,808	31,298	3,811	6,331	4,267	983	1,008	1,173	37,492	1,412	31.7	2.5	43.8
Sawyer	639	4,974	749	601	1,016	168	153	175	35,276	175	22.3	4.0	45.7
Shawano	872	10,456	1,485	2,176	1,547	285	206	360	34,431	1,139	30.3	2.7	50.7
Sheboygan	2,662	54,987	6,591	17,857	5,997	2,083	1,122	2,430	44,197	958	43.6	3.9	49.6
Taylor	480	7,705	1,065	3,033	909	242	112	298	38,672	893	23.7	3.1	47.4
Trempealeau	639	13,995	1,092	8,106	1,063	302	229	557	39,768	1,229	24.6	4.6	40.0
Vernon	630	7,123	1,774	951	1,218	293	152	242	34,000	1,961	31.1	1.8	48.8
Vilas	940	5,816	581	327	1,084	196	132	169	28,988	67	64.2	1.5	23.6
Walworth	2,668	35,008	3,987	8,357	4,913	655	1,335	1,280	36,561	941	49.5	5.2	44.1
Washburn	516	4,516	975	1,153	734	118	184	137	30,353	372	36.0	4.3	37.2
Washington	3,205	51,435	5,982	14,137	7,111	2,081	1,868	2,171	42,204	578	40.8	3.5	53.7
Waukesha	12,544	239,451	28,207	42,842	26,397	13,370	13,201	12,706	53,061	574	56.8	4.2	39.0
Waupaca	1,211	16,565	2,696	5,987	2,438	511	263	616	37,198	1,031	33.9	3.2	44.5
Waushara	465	4,673	791	888	766	98	159	141	30,114	633	42.8	4.4	39.9
Winnebago	3,564	84,456	12,357	21,609	8,751	3,373	3,021	4,271	50,566	957	49.9	2.2	37.8
Wood	1,785	34,647	8,742	6,126	3,943	1,360	710	1,510	43,592	1,062	32.9	3.9	51.3
WYOMING	20,966	208,440	33,429	9,183	31,157	6,668	9,720	9,304	44,636	11,938	32.7	25.0	43.0
Albany	1,041	9,743	2,034	395	1,844	495	775	327	33,532	451	28.2	30.2	38.6
Big Horn	305	2,536	380	208	376	98	55	103	40,800	586	40.4	12.8	50.7
Campbell	1,460	20,636	1,634	539	2,698	372	692	1,159	56,178	643	25.5	45.4	44.6
Carbon	520	4,374	584	D	821	135	86	201	46,051	345	18.8	42.6	49.1
Converse	448	4,811	630	174	464	129	148	252	52,459	384	23.7	40.9	57.3
Crook	237	1,503	174	150	161	62	54	71	47,023	554	15.7	37.0	45.8
Fremont	1,281	10,507	2,001	263	2,059	298	373	383	36,444	1,152	36.3	12.1	46.1

Table B. States and Counties — **Agriculture**

STATE County	Acreage (1,000) [117]	Percent change, 2012-2017 [118]	Average size of farm [119]	Total irrigated (1,000) [120]	Total cropland (1,000) [121]	Average per farm [122]	Average per acre [123]	Value of machinery and equipment, average per farm (dollars) [124]	Total (mil dol) [125]	Average per farm (acres) [126]	Crops [127]	Livestock and poultry products [128]	Organic farms (number) [129]	Farms with internet access (percent) [130]	Total ($1,000) [131]	Percent of farms [132]
WISCONSIN— Cont'd																
Douglas	70	-1.2	212	0.2	26.8	415,809	1,961	58,358	8.5	25,936	40.4	59.6	2	74.8	36	2.4
Dunn	348	-6.4	270	40.1	240.8	973,838	3,601	148,164	212.9	165,325	47.8	52.2	23	82.3	1,863	41.7
Eau Claire	172	-15.4	161	2.5	114.0	735,990	4,567	92,355	89.9	84,116	49.1	50.9	40	73.3	2,237	45.4
Florence	19	39.0	184	0.0	8.0	465,629	2,527	52,675	1.3	12,723	56.9	43.1	NA	67.3	18	10.9
Fond du Lac	317	0.6	255	1.9	270.4	1,855,960	7,275	227,075	396.7	318,921	24.0	76.0	33	77.7	3,762	56.5
Forest	38	25.9	272	0.4	13.1	660,064	2,426	81,548	4.9	35,064	80.6	19.4	2	75.7	24	11.4
Grant	600	2.2	242	1.0	380.0	1,140,897	4,717	168,735	447.2	180,181	32.3	67.7	71	73.2	6,383	53.8
Green	292	-3.3	205	3.0	239.5	1,111,218	5,427	158,955	221.0	154,796	41.7	58.3	18	82.8	3,648	47.4
Green Lake	127	-18.0	252	5.4	99.7	1,444,204	5,720	196,500	90.6	180,512	49.9	50.1	11	70.7	1,594	45.8
Iowa	360	2.7	229	8.6	216.4	1,111,469	4,864	141,447	206.7	131,149	38.1	61.9	41	80.8	4,969	64.4
Iron	9	-9.9	188	0.6	5.4	638,606	3,401	D	D	D	D	D	2	93.9	D	6.1
Jackson	248	3.5	290	6.3	135.6	1,103,760	3,800	161,242	154.2	180,294	52.2	47.8	41	78.1	1,034	42.6
Jefferson	221	-2.9	202	11.4	183.9	1,240,595	6,154	167,109	305.3	278,041	32.3	67.7	21	76.2	1,264	45.8
Juneau	175	-2.6	245	6.7	114.0	908,759	3,704	149,546	116.8	163,295	55.8	44.2	10	73.1	1,244	39.2
Kenosha	78	1.5	187	1.1	65.2	1,419,789	7,575	170,756	59.9	144,222	67.4	32.6	6	82.4	2,469	36.1
Kewaunee	170	-3.6	260	0.7	146.2	1,462,089	5,620	241,636	314.3	479,771	16.8	83.2	7	75.7	1,879	62.1
La Crosse	144	-9.1	216	1.1	85.9	1,079,187	4,987	124,594	74.6	111,867	37.6	62.4	27	76.8	1,955	51.4
Lafayette	343	-7.1	258	D	265.4	1,542,860	5,977	200,412	301.5	227,199	38.0	62.0	57	74.0	5,322	54.1
Langlade	116	2.2	269	18.3	75.8	881,494	3,272	208,454	102.2	236,655	58.4	41.6	16	76.4	542	32.2
Lincoln	78	1.9	184	0.3	43.0	595,649	3,241	102,719	37.0	86,838	44.7	55.3	12	74.9	206	15.0
Manitowoc	232	0.4	198	1.1	188.0	1,349,733	6,824	168,986	309.1	263,971	14.7	85.3	11	73.0	1,844	51.8
Marathon	473	-1.2	212	7.0	322.9	1,004,890	4,751	161,950	413.6	184,888	24.4	75.6	51	73.0	1,226	29.2
Marinette	133	0.8	258	1.9	88.6	1,001,818	3,877	158,953	116.0	225,266	20.6	79.4	9	79.2	1,466	36.7
Marquette	113	-5.8	247	10.7	82.0	1,031,933	4,176	145,836	71.5	156,059	51.2	48.8	7	72.3	432	25.5
Menominee	D	D	D	NA	D	143,544	1,736	D	D	D	D	D	NA	100.0	NA	NA
Milwaukee	D	D	D	0.1	D	542,871	8,928	68,761	6.8	79,047	96.2	3.8	2	72.1	64	18.6
Monroe	301	-11.0	193	4.9	165.2	767,038	3,967	138,159	202.7	130,380	34.8	65.2	134	72.0	840	34.6
Oconto	190	0.3	228	1.2	142.9	948,545	4,166	161,633	145.9	174,930	29.7	70.3	11	73.6	1,669	46.3
Oneida	35	-0.7	265	1.2	11.5	1,075,764	4,065	90,003	12.6	96,412	91.5	8.5	2	79.4	102	10.7
Outagamie	237	-5.5	210	0.8	206.2	1,511,380	7,207	198,453	263.7	233,388	27.3	72.7	6	79.2	1,606	46.3
Ozaukee	59	-8.8	188	0.4	48.3	1,229,816	6,554	158,401	75.2	238,054	25.2	74.8	7	86.1	355	44.0
Pepin	107	3.2	239	6.6	69.3	924,201	3,874	156,970	72.3	161,413	33.7	66.3	5	79.2	979	62.9
Pierce	233	-5.2	190	1.3	166.3	876,620	4,620	134,135	149.4	121,535	45.9	54.1	28	81.8	2,297	40.5
Polk	256	0.1	208	2.1	165.0	734,098	3,537	113,889	138.3	112,064	37.6	62.4	18	80.4	1,397	34.2
Portage	280	0.6	286	96.2	207.1	1,170,886	4,100	221,156	280.5	285,660	73.4	26.6	20	77.7	1,383	34.7
Price	89	-3.4	218	0.7	34.3	535,028	2,459	66,706	25.8	62,932	16.7	83.3	3	72.9	105	14.9
Racine	127	15.9	209	1.6	109.8	1,602,954	7,682	181,939	86.4	141,475	74.8	25.2	1	82.3	2,502	44.5
Richland	221	-3.1	200	0.3	118.5	671,915	3,356	108,023	136.7	123,890	22.5	77.5	37	67.6	2,493	50.7
Rock	354	-0.1	223	15.6	302.8	1,467,760	6,589	175,571	294.5	185,539	56.0	44.0	20	79.7	4,915	54.7
Rusk	136	1.8	272	0.0	70.7	674,903	2,485	130,623	53.8	107,353	24.8	75.2	12	70.9	689	24.2
St. Croix	279	4.3	193	8.7	216.5	906,467	4,688	141,360	189.1	130,944	44.0	56.0	22	79.4	1,778	49.7
Sauk	299	-10.1	212	13.2	197.7	890,636	4,207	150,164	188.5	133,470	37.2	62.8	27	73.7	2,048	45.5
Sawyer	46	5.6	263	1.5	26.0	681,805	2,593	136,876	21.9	125,091	41.6	58.4	2	72.0	152	18.3
Shawano	247	-5.3	217	0.3	186.2	1,012,006	4,662	173,988	250.4	219,851	20.9	79.1	20	72.7	1,571	50.2
Sheboygan	196	3.0	205	0.3	164.3	1,348,670	6,594	198,128	213.4	222,785	22.6	77.4	14	84.2	1,215	39.5
Taylor	226	4.1	253	0.1	133.7	742,339	2,935	119,424	113.0	126,517	24.6	75.4	20	68.6	650	27.0
Trempealeau	330	2.1	268	8.6	215.6	1,062,452	3,958	181,542	291.1	236,873	24.8	75.2	37	77.1	2,725	56.1
Vernon	337	-2.5	172	1.5	196.6	667,687	3,884	107,179	181.5	92,577	34.1	65.9	297	70.4	1,575	32.6
Vilas	6	-17.9	84	0.9	3.3	498,803	5,913	88,693	7.0	103,851	97.3	2.7	2	94.0	D	9.0
Walworth	192	2.5	204	2.1	167.7	1,417,724	6,933	162,989	167.4	177,865	46.1	53.9	15	83.2	6,423	51.4
Washburn	74	-15.6	198	2.7	34.1	620,384	3,128	85,256	30.3	81,384	32.7	67.3	2	75.5	283	18.3
Washington	126	-5.5	218	0.3	108.9	1,539,370	7,053	216,870	157.4	272,394	43.4	56.6	14	79.2	565	32.5
Waukesha	97	5.7	170	1.1	71.5	935,065	5,507	108,440	51.1	88,944	73.9	26.1	7	79.8	1,122	27.9
Waupaca	202	-6.4	196	7.7	142.6	883,093	4,516	135,842	152.1	147,516	24.8	75.2	6	74.4	1,777	48.2
Waushara	135	-6.8	214	37.6	100.2	904,427	4,221	149,181	126.7	200,161	68.4	31.6	12	75.7	1,253	25.4
Winnebago	162	4.2	169	0.5	136.2	1,180,421	6,971	140,934	122.2	127,711	40.0	60.0	7	76.6	3,326	53.1
Wood	221	-0.8	208	6.8	128.1	688,696	3,311	157,699	141.1	132,857	40.0	60.0	35	80.4	1,105	27.0
WYOMING	29,005	-4.5	2,430	1,567.6	2,587.5	1,892,340	779	126,844	1,472.1	123,313	21.6	78.4	69	80.5	30,218	17.6
Albany	1,407	-28.4	3,119	109.5	106.9	2,280,442	731	96,165	50.8	112,683	12.5	87.5	4	81.2	441	5.3
Big Horn	322	6.5	550	107.4	117.9	874,055	1,589	161,355	74.9	127,852	59.5	40.5	2	78.2	541	16.2
Campbell	2,901	0.8	4,512	5.1	184.3	2,553,745	566	134,546	69.9	108,705	3.7	96.3	NA	79.3	3,119	26.6
Carbon	2,812	18.4	8,150	187.4	143.9	4,486,393	550	145,397	73.2	212,293	8.4	91.6	1	78.6	423	6.1
Converse	2,594	6.0	6,754	65.2	106.7	3,576,045	529	159,841	56.3	146,734	12.2	87.8	NA	75.5	657	9.6
Crook	1,466	-7.6	2,646	9.4	175.5	2,590,429	979	134,976	52.9	95,552	6.8	93.2	NA	70.6	2,959	31.6
Fremont	1,165	-31.9	1,011	135.9	125.9	1,288,331	1,274	122,650	82.4	71,551	40.6	59.4	1	84.9	2,073	13.3

STATE County	Water use, 2015		Wholesale Trade[1], 2012				Retail Trade[2], 2012				Real estate and rental and leasing,[2] 2012			
	Public supply water withdrawn (mil gal/day)	Public supply gallons withdrawn per person per day	Number of establishments	Number of employees	Sales (mil dol)	Average payroll (mil dol)	Number of establishments	Number of employees	Sales (mil dol)	Average payroll (mil dol)	Number of establishments	Number of employees	Sales (mil dol)	Average payroll (mil dol)
	133	134	135	136	137	138	139	140	141	142	143	144	145	146
WISCONSIN— Cont'd														
Douglas	0.03	0.7	44	701	840.6	33.1	150	1,993	577.7	48.7	37	110	14.9	2.5
Dunn	2.39	53.7	36	D	D	D	113	1,755	440.6	35.2	29	D	D	D
Eau Claire	7.40	72.5	95	1,601	1,013.6	69.6	402	6,995	1,658.9	143.1	107	564	77.4	16.0
Florence	0.08	17.9	5	D	D	D	11	61	19.9	1.2	2	D	D	D
Fond du Lac	7.93	77.8	111	1,541	1,372.0	74.4	354	5,462	1,402.4	130.0	64	235	37.7	6.0
Forest	0.40	44.2	4	D	D	D	33	276	72.2	5.3	5	13	0.8	0.2
Grant	3.39	64.9	61	481	213.7	17.9	191	2,379	657.0	51.2	49	118	16.7	3.8
Green	2.66	71.5	41	699	269.3	29.2	150	2,325	1,003.2	71.1	25	D	D	D
Green Lake	0.35	18.6	14	87	77.4	4.4	71	952	253.1	21.9	13	45	3.9	0.8
Iowa	1.01	42.4	25	280	252.3	13.7	89	3,980	1,426.1	151.6	9	D	D	D
Iron	0.21	36.2	9	91	21.3	2.3	30	232	54.3	4.9	8	D	D	D
Jackson	0.96	46.7	15	174	97.9	5.6	66	784	327.5	16.8	7	15	1.6	0.2
Jefferson	5.71	67.5	66	1,356	793.8	55.6	273	3,891	911.0	77.6	60	219	33.6	6.6
Juneau	1.70	64.8	17	205	110.5	5.8	92	1,030	335.5	20.9	11	21	6.8	0.4
Kenosha	14.86	88.2	101	1,639	1,779.7	86.5	491	8,523	2,134.1	213.6	115	460	73.0	11.2
Kewaunee	0.87	42.7	12	151	75.3	5.0	65	561	146.3	11.7	7	7	0.8	0.2
La Crosse	14.23	120.4	121	2,592	6,131.4	115.3	421	8,393	1,891.1	173.4	121	791	99.3	20.6
Lafayette	0.97	57.6	20	260	187.3	9.4	50	433	119.5	8.0	6	D	D	D
Langlade	1.16	60.3	26	352	450.3	17.7	89	1,310	428.7	31.0	13	32	3.3	0.6
Lincoln	1.38	49.3	21	328	143.7	13.0	111	1,222	308.7	26.0	14	68	7.3	2.1
Manitowoc	15.68	196.5	68	837	497.0	38.1	254	3,473	848.6	76.0	43	D	D	D
Marathon	10.98	80.8	180	2,955	1,276.6	126.2	472	9,545	2,572.4	208.5	83	412	79.2	11.9
Marinette	2.57	62.9	22	D	D	D	181	2,109	532.5	43.8	17	D	D	D
Marquette	0.16	10.6	8	D	D	D	35	319	70.9	5.2	8	D	D	D
Menominee	0.32	70.0	NA	NA	NA	NA	5	29	6.6	0.4	NA	NA	NA	NA
Milwaukee	114.35	119.4	848	17,873	12,445.3	1,263.2	2,724	41,381	10,427.9	945.7	795	5,063	1,085.5	208.1
Monroe	3.56	78.2	36	538	510.0	28.7	150	1,865	575.3	40.8	31	106	10.0	2.9
Oconto	1.36	36.3	23	143	54.9	5.4	100	872	261.1	19.8	23	71	4.9	1.2
Oneida	2.03	57.1	29	359	171.1	17.6	221	3,450	959.5	84.1	59	178	26.6	4.5
Outagamie	6.13	33.5	273	4,591	7,397.7	236.8	729	12,738	3,277.8	277.5	138	859	160.7	27.8
Ozaukee	5.11	58.2	150	1,479	1,677.6	75.9	303	4,642	1,228.0	108.0	94	312	59.5	10.0
Pepin	0.39	53.5	12	154	145.0	6.5	41	246	80.2	6.1	3	3	1.8	0.2
Pierce	2.00	48.9	18	D	D	D	102	984	256.5	19.3	23	D	D	D
Polk	2.02	46.5	37	465	183.9	20.1	165	1,889	452.0	38.6	36	59	7.8	1.2
Portage	8.69	123.4	70	D	D	D	230	3,758	933.9	79.2	45	188	21.4	4.3
Price	1.02	74.8	19	122	63.5	6.6	73	536	126.4	11.4	11	25	2.8	0.6
Racine	19.14	98.1	170	2,243	1,702.5	118.6	591	8,542	2,182.0	181.6	100	327	58.9	9.7
Richland	1.18	67.4	13	74	50.3	2.3	66	878	200.3	17.1	12	37	6.8	1.1
Rock	16.71	103.5	149	3,035	3,225.1	155.1	502	8,396	2,215.2	208.2	101	400	148.1	18.7
Rusk	0.48	34.0	6	101	18.9	3.6	52	595	145.3	12.0	5	11	0.6	0.2
St. Croix	4.43	50.6	99	1,072	1,907.3	55.0	263	3,935	1,107.7	90.4	64	D	D	D
Sauk	7.23	113.6	54	1,341	929.1	66.9	322	3,971	990.8	84.9	59	255	45.0	9.5
Sawyer	0.64	39.1	14	159	61.0	5.7	103	946	238.1	22.3	27	63	8.7	1.3
Shawano	2.42	58.6	38	1,219	498.6	54.1	122	1,441	397.1	30.9	13	43	5.0	1.0
Sheboygan	15.80	136.7	86	1,002	593.9	47.9	395	6,124	1,400.0	133.5	73	298	58.2	10.4
Taylor	0.60	29.3	9	82	36.0	3.2	76	838	238.3	17.1	9	26	3.4	0.4
Trempealeau	2.94	99.5	32	253	163.6	9.8	105	1,163	322.8	26.2	7	D	D	D
Vernon	1.09	35.7	18	D	D	D	98	1,138	320.4	25.7	18	29	2.2	0.5
Vilas	0.48	22.4	11	123	68.3	4.8	151	989	269.1	23.0	22	70	7.4	1.6
Walworth	7.35	71.5	107	1,395	1,544.6	67.7	358	4,521	1,234.4	106.2	88	350	54.8	10.4
Washburn	0.63	40.5	10	62	17.2	2.4	78	828	196.0	16.4	18	39	4.2	0.9
Washington	7.91	59.2	167	2,850	2,053.3	159.7	369	7,039	1,813.6	152.1	75	223	35.6	6.4
Waukesha	19.63	49.5	816	12,343	6,986.1	744.7	1,299	24,751	6,616.8	600.8	390	3,505	456.2	119.2
Waupaca	4.94	95.1	35	429	286.6	14.2	191	2,247	541.6	50.7	33	150	15.6	3.3
Waushara	1.14	47.4	19	154	100.6	6.9	73	706	219.5	13.9	11	19	2.6	0.5
Winnebago	13.99	82.5	136	D	D	D	473	7,892	2,064.9	174.5	113	576	219.2	19.9
Wood	4.73	64.4	59	913	626.2	46.6	279	4,815	1,101.7	105.6	59	210	37.8	4.6
WYOMING	101.35	172.9	709	7,003	5,597.9	398.7	2,681	30,088	9,446.0	796.0	1,076	4,546	1,259.1	215.6
Albany	6.45	169.9	23	115	132.8	4.6	141	1,729	479.6	36.8	53	147	22.5	3.2
Big Horn	2.20	183.0	10	57	43.7	2.3	47	403	90.7	8.4	9	15	2.1	0.4
Campbell	5.97	121.3	76	1,403	758.3	81.2	184	2,533	896.0	74.8	76	304	86.9	11.5
Carbon	2.85	183.2	4	D	D	D	86	683	305.5	17.3	25	83	25.0	2.5
Converse	2.04	143.3	9	45	19.3	1.9	57	486	141.5	9.6	21	55	6.1	0.9
Crook	6.44	865.1	8	D	D	D	26	160	39.6	3.4	8	D	D	D
Fremont	4.31	106.9	42	D	D	D	165	2,096	581.8	53.8	71	459	130.6	27.0

1   Merchant wholesalers, except manufacturers' sales branches and offices.   2. Employer establishments.

Professional Services, Manufacturing, and Accommodation and Food Services

STATE County	Professional, scientific, and technical services, 2012				Manufacturing, 2012				Accommodation and food services, 2012			
	Number of establishments	Number of employees	Sales (mil dol)	Average payroll (mil dol)	Number of establishments	Number of employees	Receipts (mil dol)	Annual payroll (mil dol)	Number of establishments	Number of employees	Receipts (mil dol)	Annual payroll (mil dol)
	147	148	149	150	151	152	153	154	155	156	157	158
WISCONSIN— Cont'd												
Douglas	72	343	37.1	15.0	46	1,222	D	78.5	157	1,906	72.1	19.7
Dunn	66	388	38.5	16.9	58	2,369	1,528.6	118.7	89	1,222	42.9	11.9
Eau Claire	179	1,706	203.6	84.9	84	4,938	1,690.9	207.0	275	5,130	206.6	58.5
Florence	7	11	0.5	0.2	9	112	D	3.8	26	154	6.4	1.4
Fond du Lac	154	1,337	154.4	76.3	144	9,140	3,989.9	407.6	240	3,872	140.8	39.8
Forest	10	91	11.2	3.5	19	223	D	7.6	36	D	D	D
Grant	64	518	59.4	26.7	67	2,315	965.2	101.1	122	1,205	47.1	11.7
Green	57	280	73.7	13.7	82	2,934	1,420.7	131.1	84	966	37.9	10.2
Green Lake	22	76	6.8	2.3	37	1,335	390.1	53.5	50	538	21.9	7.5
Iowa	39	128	12.4	4.8	37	846	1,335.1	32.8	51	525	23.3	6.8
Iron	8	28	2.5	0.8	16	191	D	6.3	54	D	D	D
Jackson	22	93	6.0	2.5	29	921	499.5	47.3	59	661	27.9	7.1
Jefferson	129	672	92.1	24.4	152	8,385	3,842.9	415.5	186	2,126	88.3	22.0
Juneau	17	51	4.3	1.7	50	2,136	719.2	92.2	76	604	26.8	6.7
Kenosha	223	1,212	123.1	50.9	168	5,704	2,370.3	260.6	362	5,510	237.8	66.8
Kewaunee	27	135	13.2	5.4	37	1,771	466.7	81.3	50	518	15.4	4.2
La Crosse	250	1,855	177.7	85.7	157	6,805	1,941.7	266.0	330	6,383	243.7	72.1
Lafayette	16	55	6.2	2.0	23	681	270.2	22.8	36	D	D	D
Langlade	22	110	6.5	4.6	47	1,494	330.2	57.0	59	583	26.1	7.0
Lincoln	32	111	7.3	3.4	50	2,329	772.4	103.1	90	681	27.6	7.0
Manitowoc	103	646	92.8	23.7	179	9,968	3,138.3	457.1	174	2,443	87.7	24.9
Marathon	225	1,943	284.9	113.9	238	14,472	4,306.0	654.1	305	4,458	180.7	51.8
Marinette	49	243	22.8	11.0	90	6,302	1,889.6	300.4	161	1,398	61.1	15.5
Marquette	17	54	6.2	1.5	21	1,325	D	53.5	40	282	13.4	3.0
Menominee	3	D	D	D	NA	NA	NA	NA	3	D	D	D
Milwaukee	1,955	23,788	3,849.6	1,598.9	991	48,963	19,176.2	2,974.2	1,900	36,303	1,831.0	496.0
Monroe	72	545	48.6	19.5	59	3,937	1,364.2	163.2	112	1,540	60.0	16.6
Oconto	47	159	14.4	5.2	56	1,897	522.3	72.7	98	669	29.1	7.2
Oneida	81	363	51.2	12.4	46	1,397	330.5	69.2	186	1,503	82.0	22.2
Outagamie	385	3,279	499.0	179.5	357	17,963	7,208.5	888.2	453	8,198	330.0	91.7
Ozaukee	336	2,169	353.2	112.6	206	8,663	2,762.9	473.0	207	3,307	134.8	38.9
Pepin	15	43	4.9	1.6	13	140	D	5.4	28	D	D	D
Pierce	66	177	22.6	7.2	47	1,250	516.5	57.4	99	994	38.2	10.3
Polk	84	352	46.2	12.6	105	3,117	995.3	133.7	118	1,108	42.2	11.0
Portage	100	892	84.9	35.0	75	3,912	1,383.0	165.0	204	2,827	112.4	31.4
Price	20	83	5.2	2.0	44	1,973	502.0	85.5	48	319	11.8	3.1
Racine	310	1,967	234.8	91.7	325	15,444	8,100.1	844.4	382	5,974	251.7	70.5
Richland	18	60	3.6	1.3	30	1,545	682.1	61.8	29	333	11.3	2.9
Rock	208	1,172	129.3	49.5	224	8,850	4,474.2	421.3	363	5,355	236.2	63.7
Rusk	12	59	3.3	1.2	27	1,579	423.5	48.3	29	210	8.9	2.2
St. Croix	221	1,273	228.3	68.9	161	5,838	1,307.7	269.4	184	2,922	122.9	33.9
Sauk	120	982	118.6	49.3	94	5,001	1,669.5	223.1	238	7,576	542.6	133.3
Sawyer	41	136	21.1	5.1	46	561	256.7	27.1	115	1,022	67.2	19.5
Shawano	36	D	D	D	66	D	633.2	84.7	115	D	D	D
Sheboygan	179	1,240	207.9	65.8	230	16,716	7,346.2	825.1	269	4,151	188.8	53.4
Taylor	18	116	10.2	3.8	45	2,483	817.6	85.0	43	495	13.0	5.1
Trempealeau	38	195	15.3	5.9	58	6,418	1,786.7	248.4	81	649	25.4	6.6
Vernon	42	170	11.0	4.6	33	981	275.8	40.7	53	626	19.5	5.8
Vilas	37	91	13.8	3.0	28	257	39.0	8.7	207	1,941	126.0	34.1
Walworth	192	1,000	135.9	43.3	207	7,974	2,705.8	384.6	298	6,109	288.1	81.2
Washburn	28	193	25.2	8.0	29	969	198.9	28.4	81	505	25.0	6.7
Washington	222	1,643	278.9	95.9	318	13,257	3,740.7	676.5	248	4,147	165.4	43.7
Waukesha	1,328	13,383	2,265.1	822.6	950	43,232	15,221.2	2,481.1	824	16,092	725.2	202.0
Waupaca	62	309	29.2	10.8	89	5,784	2,587.2	277.4	151	1,621	64.5	17.6
Waushara	17	153	8.9	3.4	27	873	369.5	33.4	68	582	24.8	6.1
Winnebago	247	2,575	514.5	134.8	300	23,892	11,476.5	1,321.6	367	5,963	234.6	65.3
Wood	89	589	69.7	25.6	117	5,757	2,482.4	285.9	179	1,972	78.6	21.2
WYOMING	2,141	9,134	1,297.4	467.0	553	10,094	10,783.8	630.6	1,799	27,580	1,644.8	468.7
Albany	116	832	115.7	41.0	31	341	D	16.1	113	2,074	79.6	23.3
Big Horn	23	67	6.9	2.2	16	185	D	8.5	27	D	D	D
Campbell	113	757	97.8	37.2	35	632	267.8	38.4	105	1,678	95.1	26.6
Carbon	36	126	14.5	4.5	9	390	D	D	83	718	47.7	13.2
Converse	32	108	13.0	5.0	16	129	D	7.1	45	D	D	D
Crook	14	30	4.0	1.1	7	139	D	5.4	27	156	8.5	1.9
Fremont	129	494	66.2	25.4	35	246	57.0	10.4	128	1,373	66.1	18.5

Table B. States and Counties — Health Care and Social Assistance, Other Services, Nonemployer Businesses, and Residential Construction

STATE County	Health care and social assistance, 2012				Other services, 2012				Nonemployer businesses, 2016		Value of residential construction authorized by building permits, 2018	
	Number of establishments	Number of employees	Receipts (mil dol)	Annual payroll (mil dol)	Number of establishments	Number of employees	Receipts (mil dol)	Annual payroll (mil dol)	Number	Receipts (mil dol)	New construction ($1,000)	Number of housing units
	159	160	161	162	163	164	165	166	167	168	169	170
WISCONSIN— Cont'd												
Douglas	114	2,066	129.1	51.7	77	590	36.4	12.2	2,190	91.1	21,661	100
Dunn	92	2,779	170.5	76.9	71	301	23.1	7.1	2,543	112.5	22,127	104
Eau Claire	364	11,109	1,261.7	552.5	201	1,283	103.5	29.9	5,901	300.0	91,285	463
Florence	3	D	D	D	7	11	1.6	0.3	328	11.8	4,723	19
Fond du Lac	281	5,764	758.8	248.8	191	1,245	114.4	31.3	4,995	236.9	44,500	275
Forest	17	294	10.6	5.9	14	25	2.8	0.8	696	35.4	8,264	45
Grant	113	2,435	145.0	65.9	114	399	45.3	9.6	3,314	154.6	19,192	100
Green	71	2,048	206.9	91.7	77	286	27.5	6.7	2,485	111.8	27,424	93
Green Lake	48	1,111	101.2	44.7	33	108	8.8	3.1	1,399	64.6	13,556	49
Iowa	53	1,116	83.5	36.3	36	117	12.1	2.8	1,991	83.6	17,491	64
Iron	13	321	12.6	7.3	8	D	D	D	531	21.6	6,221	29
Jackson	48	1,012	82.3	37.1	27	D	D	D	1,146	49.9	7,676	37
Jefferson	229	4,021	395.0	134.6	139	607	53.3	15.0	4,977	250.4	53,218	237
Juneau	52	1,138	105.4	43.9	48	184	24.0	5.5	1,457	67.5	21,732	123
Kenosha	415	8,620	831.7	339.9	241	1,485	101.2	31.0	8,512	374.8	79,140	311
Kewaunee	37	495	21.2	10.9	28	61	7.4	1.4	1,248	49.2	10,008	42
La Crosse	282	11,223	1,472.4	520.9	233	1,679	148.1	44.8	6,299	288.2	94,505	548
Lafayette	23	232	19.5	6.2	29	D	D	D	1,313	64.6	5,648	31
Langlade	45	984	114.5	40.4	47	164	13.1	4.1	1,248	53.3	10,000	62
Lincoln	60	D	D	D	59	242	18.3	5.1	1,722	76.5	16,875	132
Manitowoc	175	4,731	382.0	176.8	130	553	54.3	12.0	3,978	170.2	28,289	149
Marathon	367	10,123	1,133.0	459.7	221	1,313	138.5	37.7	7,846	389.5	68,221	308
Marinette	117	2,875	251.2	109.4	77	322	27.1	7.6	2,276	104.1	21,973	125
Marquette	24	273	10.0	4.9	28	D	D	D	1,056	44.0	8,388	41
Menominee	1	D	D	D	3	15	1.0	0.4	102	3.3	1,554	9
Milwaukee	2,847	86,674	9,866.4	3,872.0	1,476	11,203	1,438.2	368.4	48,001	2,040.6	165,706	1,535
Monroe	83	2,640	255.6	138.7	73	427	28.9	8.7	2,614	125.9	19,805	115
Oconto	71	1,578	111.1	46.5	44	125	12.0	2.9	2,268	103.4	34,412	152
Oneida	139	2,895	335.8	115.0	98	387	32.7	8.9	2,952	121.1	45,932	178
Outagamie	464	11,090	1,289.6	521.0	361	2,827	247.8	73.7	10,131	513.7	126,356	756
Ozaukee	289	5,256	623.2	242.1	183	1,178	81.0	27.0	7,081	390.2	89,036	260
Pepin	15	286	26.7	9.3	18	D	D	D	563	24.3	2,702	13
Pierce	63	909	53.8	23.5	60	203	20.9	4.6	2,620	112.4	34,503	137
Polk	99	2,477	227.0	88.9	79	246	18.9	5.3	3,304	135.1	40,418	203
Portage	154	3,797	385.8	155.9	119	759	72.6	19.6	3,789	229.2	42,731	161
Price	43	890	55.9	26.2	29	81	6.2	1.8	1,115	43.5	10,281	62
Racine	459	10,588	764.4	335.7	317	1,839	140.4	44.5	9,668	401.9	94,503	379
Richland	48	898	71.3	31.4	25	D	D	D	1,220	56.3	8,318	75
Rock	320	9,667	1,120.9	438.4	268	1,417	105.0	30.8	8,106	349.3	75,614	340
Rusk	34	780	62.4	27.9	20	D	D	D	1,005	39.7	16,138	70
St. Croix	189	4,427	353.4	151.4	148	696	56.8	15.7	6,450	289.1	130,369	563
Sauk	144	3,910	340.6	147.5	129	541	50.6	16.3	4,499	216.4	50,812	210
Sawyer	39	832	71.5	28.7	40	168	15.1	3.9	1,581	65.5	15,033	95
Shawano	79	D	D	D	61	233	20.2	5.4	2,465	106.9	15,249	69
Sheboygan	299	6,483	597.2	247.8	202	992	67.4	19.5	5,536	245.0	48,926	191
Taylor	49	1,017	81.1	35.5	39	92	6.9	1.9	1,441	73.6	7,199	37
Trempealeau	53	1,344	86.0	38.7	40	110	11.2	2.8	1,967	90.1	25,136	139
Vernon	66	1,768	131.7	55.8	38	97	8.0	1.6	2,425	104.8	17,561	99
Vilas	51	519	46.7	16.1	59	216	15.1	4.5	2,392	103.2	58,073	246
Walworth	219	4,385	342.3	133.0	192	877	80.9	20.6	7,016	338.2	104,543	375
Washburn	49	992	59.8	26.2	37	131	9.6	2.7	1,428	61.1	15,829	77
Washington	263	6,231	482.2	208.8	265	1,450	113.4	34.6	8,340	424.7	112,934	416
Waukesha	1,333	25,812	2,722.5	1,122.9	812	6,537	634.5	206.3	27,878	1,561.5	440,277	1,580
Waupaca	114	2,577	198.7	73.5	91	322	30.0	7.9	3,042	128.5	29,750	202
Waushara	42	806	46.1	20.3	32	D	D	D	1,502	76.7	12,972	65
Winnebago	439	13,580	1,272.0	555.0	257	2,279	221.0	68.1	8,544	388.9	83,546	378
Wood	178	9,523	1,234.5	493.6	133	798	64.2	17.6	3,901	171.6	40,172	377
WYOMING	1,898	31,340	3,291.5	1,361.9	1,373	6,655	884.6	214.9	49,495	2,342.2	593,197	1,812
Albany	127	2,241	178.2	80.9	87	433	33.9	9.7	2,613	91.4	30,945	146
Big Horn	21	373	23.9	12.2	19	48	4.0	0.9	911	29.6	1,150	5
Campbell	97	1,738	264.5	91.6	132	989	146.5	41.5	3,260	137.9	22,038	84
Carbon	49	642	51.4	22.1	37	130	15.8	3.5	1,060	43.5	5,487	26
Converse	29	568	67.3	25.4	37	119	12.6	2.8	1,036	44.6	2,642	12
Crook	15	D	D	D	9	D	D	D	744	29.9	1,729	8
Fremont	161	1,985	181.5	72.1	82	349	37.2	9.5	2,958	107.3	2,346	12

Table B. States and Counties — Government Employment and Payroll, and Local Government Finances

	Government employment and payroll, 2012									Local government finances, 2012				
			March payroll (percent of total)							General revenue				
												Taxes		
													Per capita[1] (dollars)	
STATE County	Full-time equivalent employees	March payroll (dollars)	Adminis-tration, judicial, and legal	Police and corrections	Fire protection	Highways and transpor-tation	Health and welfare	Natural resources and utilities	Education and libraries	Total (mil dol)	Inter-govern-mental (mil dol)	Total (mil dol)	Total	Property
	171	172	173	174	175	176	177	178	179	180	181	182	183	184

WISCONSIN— Cont'd														
Douglas	2,164	7,766,579	6.6	9.7	2.6	4.7	3.9	4.3	66.9	239.4	102.3	103.0	2,352	2,221
Dunn	1,509	5,639,405	7.9	8.3	2.6	8.0	16.0	4.0	50.9	163.0	74.1	60.7	1,377	1,302
Eau Claire	3,593	14,808,173	5.9	7.8	3.1	4.5	5.6	4.3	67.1	406.0	166.9	179.3	1,781	1,647
Florence	185	612,638	17.1	13.9	0.2	11.3	10.7	4.5	42.3	20.9	8.4	9.9	2,211	2,114
Fond du Lac	3,703	15,389,801	4.9	9.2	2.4	4.4	10.7	3.5	63.8	424.7	174.4	182.3	1,790	1,688
Forest	493	1,528,680	11.1	10.4	0.1	9.6	6.8	1.9	59.2	43.8	19.4	21.0	2,284	2,224
Grant	2,070	7,484,129	5.4	5.9	0.1	7.1	11.1	4.5	64.9	195.5	97.7	59.2	1,159	1,089
Green	1,522	5,434,245	4.8	8.5	0.3	10.0	14.6	4.1	57.2	147.1	64.1	57.3	1,551	1,465
Green Lake	764	2,599,596	7.3	12.4	0.1	5.7	12.4	4.5	56.6	82.2	28.8	43.6	2,290	2,188
Iowa	1,004	3,519,446	8.0	6.3	0.3	11.9	9.5	4.0	59.0	96.3	43.2	39.1	1,641	1,551
Iron	343	1,294,139	9.8	10.2	0.3	17.8	25.1	5.0	30.4	30.8	12.7	13.2	2,218	2,077
Jackson	903	2,811,059	8.8	7.7	0.2	16.9	6.6	2.7	55.8	82.1	42.1	26.7	1,304	1,221
Jefferson	2,850	11,172,911	7.2	10.2	3.2	5.1	9.1	5.9	58.7	312.5	124.7	137.1	1,622	1,528
Juneau	1,087	3,617,443	10.2	11.0	0.2	10.0	8.0	7.6	51.7	107.4	51.9	43.2	1,624	1,536
Kenosha	6,796	30,615,896	4.1	10.1	3.6	2.9	5.4	4.3	68.6	855.8	363.2	367.3	2,187	2,088
Kewaunee	848	3,565,289	8.2	10.2	0.1	10.8	12.1	3.4	53.7	87.1	41.2	29.7	1,440	1,419
La Crosse	4,828	18,746,528	5.8	8.4	2.7	4.3	18.1	4.4	55.5	639.3	314.3	218.1	1,873	1,730
Lafayette	850	2,868,337	5.6	5.1	0.3	8.3	23.6	4.4	52.0	87.8	38.3	24.8	1,472	1,414
Langlade	760	2,800,264	10.3	8.9	3.8	7.9	3.0	5.0	60.4	84.0	40.2	32.5	1,656	1,556
Lincoln	1,136	4,470,314	7.0	8.8	2.5	7.1	16.7	4.1	52.4	126.6	51.7	46.2	1,628	1,550
Manitowoc	2,832	11,154,230	5.9	8.4	4.1	9.0	10.6	8.0	52.8	283.3	138.4	103.3	1,281	1,252
Marathon	5,721	22,517,091	4.6	6.0	1.9	5.6	19.3	2.6	59.4	701.3	346.1	232.0	1,722	1,622
Marinette	1,554	5,323,156	6.8	9.6	2.0	8.0	9.0	6.7	56.8	164.4	77.1	65.5	1,576	1,476
Marquette	499	1,734,369	8.4	12.2	0.1	8.1	10.6	1.6	56.1	50.8	18.7	27.4	1,805	1,741
Menominee	308	1,058,752	4.7	7.1	0.5	4.3	17.3	0.5	64.4	30.1	23.2	5.7	1,306	1,299
Milwaukee	34,086	166,779,941	5.4	14.8	5.3	4.3	9.0	4.7	53.9	5,067.2	2,122.5	1,803.2	1,888	1,733
Monroe	1,770	5,806,833	5.3	7.6	0.2	6.8	15.8	3.7	59.6	171.3	88.6	56.7	1,258	1,152
Oconto	1,242	4,597,591	8.0	8.3	1.4	7.3	18.7	4.2	50.7	129.3	64.1	50.5	1,349	1,293
Oneida	1,507	5,601,172	7.6	9.0	2.1	9.2	4.7	4.2	61.9	177.2	45.0	110.8	3,102	2,972
Outagamie	6,670	30,535,826	4.5	7.0	2.4	3.0	7.4	3.1	70.7	783.6	353.3	271.9	1,521	1,483
Ozaukee	2,849	10,891,062	5.8	12.2	1.1	5.8	11.9	5.0	57.3	314.5	88.3	173.0	1,993	1,870
Pepin	383	1,190,672	6.0	7.9	0.0	9.8	16.0	3.3	54.8	32.7	15.7	13.8	1,862	1,799
Pierce	1,550	5,604,968	7.8	8.1	0.6	7.2	7.5	3.9	64.3	161.3	69.8	71.2	1,743	1,678
Polk	1,872	6,676,347	6.7	6.6	0.1	8.1	13.3	2.7	61.5	182.9	73.8	81.7	1,873	1,795
Portage	2,267	8,603,550	8.0	9.1	2.6	7.5	10.8	4.0	57.1	239.8	105.3	94.6	1,343	1,237
Price	681	1,985,878	8.8	8.8	0.2	14.3	8.2	2.4	55.9	60.2	26.4	26.8	1,934	1,859
Racine	6,208	25,453,020	4.3	13.6	5.6	3.5	5.9	4.0	61.9	757.1	345.7	302.7	1,554	1,513
Richland	693	2,209,583	6.2	8.6	0.0	9.2	22.4	9.3	43.6	68.8	31.9	17.8	999	928
Rock	6,252	25,471,665	5.9	9.6	3.9	4.4	7.9	4.5	62.6	723.4	387.9	249.8	1,557	1,471
Rusk	655	2,410,554	18.7	7.8	0.0	7.6	8.7	4.6	51.6	86.0	34.2	18.5	1,293	1,209
St. Croix	2,777	10,535,818	8.9	8.5	0.6	5.0	10.3	3.3	61.9	287.9	124.7	126.4	1,483	1,393
Sauk	2,740	9,073,443	5.8	14.7	0.2	6.1	14.5	4.3	52.3	342.6	171.4	136.3	2,178	1,826
Sawyer	647	2,033,247	11.4	10.0	0.3	11.0	9.7	2.2	53.1	68.2	23.3	37.0	2,229	2,110
Shawano	1,508	5,334,917	7.7	11.2	0.3	6.9	9.6	4.4	58.3	146.4	73.0	52.6	1,264	1,190
Sheboygan	4,469	19,622,392	8.8	8.8	2.1	5.2	8.0	3.0	63.5	489.1	213.6	207.1	1,801	1,746
Taylor	791	2,632,338	8.6	8.5	0.1	7.8	13.4	3.7	56.2	77.9	42.6	26.0	1,270	1,206
Trempealeau	1,609	5,095,842	6.3	7.1	0.0	5.3	19.8	4.5	56.5	151.2	71.4	42.1	1,437	1,369
Vernon	1,200	3,885,090	13.0	10.1	0.0	9.9	7.7	3.8	53.3	116.3	57.2	38.4	1,270	1,203
Vilas	838	2,943,859	11.7	11.7	1.3	12.5	6.2	4.2	50.1	90.0	23.9	58.7	2,751	2,602
Walworth	3,935	15,369,324	8.6	14.6	5.1	5.4	7.1	4.6	53.9	432.3	127.0	247.7	2,409	2,279
Washburn	809	2,970,221	6.5	8.7	0.0	6.2	26.7	4.1	45.5	75.6	23.6	43.2	2,729	2,639
Washington	3,924	16,777,954	5.5	11.3	2.0	3.5	11.1	4.9	60.4	533.8	224.7	238.1	1,795	1,685
Waukesha	12,148	56,004,430	5.2	10.5	3.1	3.9	3.5	4.4	68.1	1,501.6	376.8	897.3	2,287	2,229
Waupaca	2,041	7,209,482	6.6	9.8	1.0	6.0	8.5	3.2	64.1	213.4	94.7	87.0	1,668	1,589
Waushara	768	2,669,797	12.8	9.7	0.0	7.3	14.0	2.2	51.2	79.8	31.6	38.3	1,565	1,495
Winnebago	5,300	21,156,305	4.4	11.7	4.6	5.5	11.2	7.1	54.5	697.9	338.4	249.0	1,475	1,436
Wood	3,170	12,767,826	6.1	9.1	3.2	5.9	6.1	3.5	65.8	337.6	146.1	136.7	1,837	1,741
WYOMING	X	X	X	X	X	X	X	X	X	X	X	X	X	X
Albany	2,004	7,113,079	5.9	6.8	3.8	1.8	26.8	5.7	48.8	203.8	74.7	35.3	948	550
Big Horn	940	3,298,694	4.9	6.2	0.2	2.2	30.5	4.5	51.0	99.0	52.6	18.8	1,595	1,308
Campbell	3,518	15,943,966	6.3	7.1	1.0	2.6	31.3	5.6	43.0	513.4	102.2	227.8	4,757	4,113
Carbon	1,195	4,095,546	7.4	9.7	1.4	3.4	23.3	5.9	44.5	136.5	41.4	57.8	3,691	2,846
Converse	1,098	4,194,426	4.6	6.9	0.0	1.8	33.4	4.4	47.4	123.9	29.5	48.7	3,477	2,778
Crook	486	1,567,725	9.6	7.3	0.1	2.9	16.3	2.3	60.3	47.3	23.8	13.5	1,893	1,459
Fremont	2,549	9,152,411	3.7	7.9	0.4	2.1	3.0	9.4	71.6	264.6	168.1	62.0	1,509	1,270

1. Based on the resident population estimated as of July 1 of the year shown.

Local Government Finances, Government Employment, and Income Taxes

STATE County	Local government finances, 2012 (cont.)								Debt outstanding		Government employment, 2017			Individual income tax returns, 2016		
	Direct general expenditure															
			Percent of total for:													
	Total (mil dol)	Per capita[1] (dollars)	Education	Health and hospitals	Police protection	Public welfare	Highways		Total (mil dol)	Per capita[1] (dollars)	Federal civilian	Federal military	State and local	Number of returns	Mean adjusted gross income	Mean income tax
	185	186	187	188	189	190	191		192	193	194	195	196	197	198	199

WISCONSIN— Cont'd																
Douglas	245.2	5,600	52.1	1.4	5.6	3.7	10.6		236.8	5,408	167	111	3,251	20,520	51,967	5,308
Dunn	163.3	3,704	41.6	2.5	5.7	12.3	12.7		105.8	2,402	86	111	4,553	19,510	51,982	5,612
Eau Claire	470.2	4,671	54.2	3.8	7.3	3.4	9.5		361.0	3,586	347	261	8,261	48,230	63,323	9,034
Florence	21.2	4,727	37.2	8.9	7.2	0.6	19.4		5.9	1,314	14	11	290	2,240	48,946	4,779
Fond du Lac	449.6	4,415	51.8	7.3	5.2	3.9	9.0		580.9	5,704	195	263	5,229	50,870	59,404	7,231
Forest	45.1	4,904	47.2	2.3	5.4	5.0	13.7		7.9	854	98	23	1,755	4,210	52,818	6,103
Grant	214.5	4,199	52.3	3.3	4.2	7.2	12.4		147.8	2,894	144	125	5,672	22,620	45,523	4,470
Green	151.7	4,109	48.0	2.6	6.1	10.5	13.8		103.5	2,805	80	97	2,067	18,840	57,699	6,795
Green Lake	81.9	4,301	48.2	3.2	6.9	5.3	9.5		68.9	3,620	49	49	1,080	9,390	49,635	5,381
Iowa	95.1	3,993	48.5	1.0	5.7	8.7	15.3		45.1	1,896	73	62	1,334	11,870	55,182	5,926
Iron	31.8	5,354	32.4	7.4	7.7	0.5	21.4		22.9	3,853	15	15	330	3,070	46,496	4,643
Jackson	85.1	4,152	52.3	2.5	4.5	6.0	13.4		40.6	1,983	42	55	2,414	9,590	45,983	4,843
Jefferson	322.8	3,820	49.7	5.1	6.2	5.7	8.1		312.0	3,693	171	216	3,838	41,440	55,278	5,759
Juneau	108.2	4,063	46.9	4.1	5.3	3.2	12.3		117.9	4,426	245	66	1,794	12,420	43,839	4,173
Kenosha	850.4	5,064	53.7	3.4	6.5	6.9	5.1		759.4	4,522	265	454	9,669	81,490	57,207	6,562
Kewaunee	102.8	4,983	40.7	9.0	4.0	5.5	16.5		50.3	2,438	70	54	1,168	10,110	52,824	5,364
La Crosse	639.1	5,488	42.3	2.8	3.9	23.8	4.9		409.7	3,518	479	303	10,115	56,350	59,745	7,299
Lafayette	90.2	5,355	43.0	14.6	2.7	11.4	12.9		33.1	1,965	47	44	1,107	8,070	45,929	4,648
Langlade	87.8	4,467	47.1	4.3	4.7	3.7	13.7		55.1	2,802	42	50	1,027	9,630	45,163	4,424
Lincoln	128.6	4,529	40.0	5.5	5.8	12.3	13.4		69.0	2,431	59	72	1,683	14,190	51,163	5,321
Manitowoc	296.5	3,675	42.9	1.3	6.2	6.4	9.3		337.8	4,187	194	232	3,858	40,140	58,368	7,058
Marathon	710.6	5,274	41.9	10.2	3.9	18.8	7.9		440.9	3,273	409	358	7,568	67,740	60,360	7,657
Marinette	165.7	3,988	44.3	5.4	5.8	7.1	14.3		116.0	2,790	164	110	2,151	20,140	46,527	4,673
Marquette	54.9	3,612	43.4	5.5	7.6	3.4	17.9		23.8	1,566	52	40	712	7,760	46,156	4,976
Menominee	30.7	7,067	60.2	0.0	5.9	18.3	5.8		5.7	1,309	5	12	2,077	1,820	34,217	2,416
Milwaukee	5,034.7	5,271	40.9	10.3	8.2	1.9	4.9		6,485.7	6,790	9,495	2,789	51,987	439,410	55,072	6,790
Monroe	165.6	3,672	50.0	1.1	5.0	10.2	11.3		105.8	2,346	2,516	397	2,653	21,660	49,534	4,989
Oconto	134.4	3,590	40.5	9.2	4.7	5.0	18.4		80.7	2,154	92	99	1,795	18,510	54,274	5,621
Oneida	201.2	5,634	52.6	2.8	6.1	3.2	10.2		98.0	2,743	193	92	2,040	19,580	56,178	6,638
Outagamie	855.9	4,786	56.0	2.4	5.0	4.7	8.6		649.4	3,632	635	514	10,781	94,020	68,861	9,145
Ozaukee	321.3	3,701	46.5	2.6	7.4	7.0	10.8		290.2	3,342	153	229	3,605	46,060	108,525	19,248
Pepin	34.1	4,609	48.2	4.5	4.1	3.3	20.4		10.3	1,392	33	19	480	3,530	55,561	6,415
Pierce	163.8	4,014	51.4	3.3	5.2	3.2	16.2		140.8	3,451	84	104	4,145	19,210	63,233	7,186
Polk	186.0	4,265	50.3	5.5	4.6	6.5	13.2		178.6	4,095	124	114	2,683	21,930	51,615	5,211
Portage	238.8	3,391	43.8	5.1	6.1	6.5	12.7		142.9	2,029	167	185	5,940	33,830	57,671	6,761
Price	60.0	4,326	45.1	2.0	5.7	8.2	16.4		25.8	1,862	84	35	872	6,970	46,855	4,557
Racine	764.1	3,923	45.5	3.8	9.7	5.3	7.3		710.7	3,648	354	506	8,563	96,420	58,017	6,788
Richland	68.5	3,844	34.6	2.0	4.7	20.1	12.9		25.0	1,405	52	45	1,065	7,930	45,376	4,589
Rock	729.2	4,546	49.6	7.4	6.2	7.1	5.3		614.8	3,833	299	422	8,530	79,100	52,868	5,678
Rusk	90.1	6,292	32.1	22.9	3.9	8.8	12.1		51.6	3,603	36	37	1,100	6,540	42,138	3,815
St. Croix	287.7	3,375	50.6	2.2	5.7	8.2	13.4		288.4	3,383	158	233	4,557	44,070	76,103	10,016
Sauk	331.0	5,288	35.3	5.0	4.8	22.8	8.1		211.8	3,384	161	168	5,494	33,840	52,423	5,680
Sawyer	72.4	4,365	38.2	6.1	5.3	7.8	21.4		22.8	1,377	78	43	1,837	8,320	49,264	5,239
Shawano	157.1	3,776	42.7	6.0	5.5	4.6	17.3		107.1	2,575	113	106	2,851	19,660	47,736	4,691
Sheboygan	492.9	4,286	55.2	3.6	5.7	6.1	8.2		375.9	3,269	197	318	5,592	58,650	58,998	6,957
Taylor	77.2	3,770	44.9	3.6	5.2	8.1	16.4		38.0	1,857	56	53	1,019	9,150	47,063	4,625
Trempealeau	154.8	5,283	44.9	1.8	4.6	18.1	10.5		112.0	3,824	122	77	2,285	15,110	48,143	4,637
Vernon	117.6	3,887	43.6	1.7	3.8	13.5	14.5		68.6	2,265	116	80	1,793	13,480	47,176	4,597
Vilas	84.7	3,971	43.9	2.5	7.8	5.4	13.1		52.1	2,443	64	89	2,096	11,540	54,286	6,854
Walworth	423.9	4,121	48.5	3.3	9.0	4.8	9.2		448.4	4,360	179	266	8,560	49,780	60,479	7,490
Washburn	75.7	4,781	45.6	1.7	4.0	5.9	18.7		56.9	3,597	83	41	1,198	8,290	48,362	4,910
Washington	537.2	4,049	42.6	2.9	6.1	19.2	7.1		398.2	3,001	249	355	5,174	69,670	71,386	9,007
Waukesha	1,525.8	3,890	54.5	2.7	7.1	2.3	6.8		1,282.0	3,268	775	1,049	16,964	207,850	92,101	14,369
Waupaca	217.6	4,174	48.6	2.1	6.1	7.4	12.8		224.2	4,301	131	132	3,316	25,440	51,353	5,249
Waushara	86.2	3,523	39.0	3.9	8.2	9.2	13.7		34.2	1,400	44	61	1,263	11,390	46,225	4,621
Winnebago	708.5	4,197	35.6	2.5	5.6	20.8	8.3		688.0	4,076	429	436	11,669	83,510	60,508	7,468
Wood	353.7	4,752	52.5	6.5	5.5	4.9	9.8		274.0	3,681	187	191	4,690	37,670	52,116	5,738
WYOMING	X	X	X	X	X	X	X		X	X	7,549	6,074	61,695	269,360	70,105	9,966
Albany	193.6	5,194	32.5	30.5	5.1	0.3	6.1		57.2	1,535	172	203	7,798	15,930	54,805	6,430
Big Horn	99.3	8,416	44.8	21.5	3.8	0.1	2.7		33.3	2,823	94	62	1,386	4,880	45,300	4,978
Campbell	532.9	11,131	37.0	22.6	3.1	1.5	5.4		188.2	3,931	91	244	4,858	21,100	67,893	8,960
Carbon	136.8	8,731	40.1	19.3	4.0	0.4	2.9		63.8	4,069	188	77	1,687	6,930	60,825	7,618
Converse	125.0	8,921	39.9	31.1	4.0	0.2	6.5		11.6	826	67	73	1,501	6,310	65,123	8,431
Crook	47.5	6,641	47.4	16.7	4.3	0.1	7.7		3.6	504	89	39	622	3,340	67,594	9,416
Fremont	258.8	6,295	73.2	1.1	4.0	0.4	3.3		31.2	759	474	206	5,051	17,260	49,476	6,043

1. Based on the resident population estimated as of July 1 of the year shown.

State / county code	CBSA code[1]	County code[2]	STATE County	Land area[3] (sq. mi)	Total persons 2018	Rank	Per square mile	White	Black	American Indian, Alaska Native	Asian and Pacific Islancer	Percent Hispanic or Latino[4]	Under 5 years	5 to 17 years	18 to 24 years	25 to 34 years	35 to 44 years	45 to 54 years
										Race alone or in combination, not Hispanic or Latino (percent)			Age (percent)					
				1	2	3	4	5	6	7	8	9	10	11	12	13	14	15
			WYOMING— Cont'd															
56015		7	Goshen	2,225.6	13,376	2,201	6.0	86.5	1.3	1.5	1.0	10.9	5.8	14.3	9.2	11.7	11.2	11.4
56017		7	Hot Springs	2,004.4	4,555	2,856	2.3	93.3	1.2	2.3	0.8	4.0	5.1	16.0	5.8	9.8	10.2	10.7
56019		7	Johnson	4,154.2	8,460	2,546	2.0	92.8	1.0	2.0	1.0	4.8	4.8	17.1	5.9	9.7	11.6	11.3
56021	16,940	3	Laramie	2,685.9	98,976	603	36.9	80.7	3.4	1.4	2.2	14.8	6.3	17.0	8.9	14.9	12.3	11.6
56023		7	Lincoln	4,075.3	19,434	1,854	4.8	93.5	0.8	1.3	1.0	4.7	6.8	19.7	6.7	9.8	13.0	11.5
56025	16,220	3	Natrona	5,340.5	79,115	708	14.8	88.4	1.9	1.7	1.4	8.6	6.6	17.4	7.8	14.6	13.2	11.2
56027		9	Niobrara	2,626.0	2,388	3,013	0.9	93.7	1.6	2.3	1.0	3.6	5.6	12.2	7.4	13.2	12.3	11.3
56029		7	Park	6,939.0	29,324	1,449	4.2	92.2	1.0	1.4	1.3	5.6	5.4	15.2	7.6	11.1	11.1	10.8
56031		7	Platte	2,081.4	8,566	2,541	4.1	89.2	0.9	1.5	1.5	8.5	5.3	14.9	5.9	10.6	10.3	11.5
56033	43,260	7	Sheridan	2,523.4	30,233	1,427	12.0	92.9	1.1	1.8	1.4	4.3	5.5	15.9	7.9	11.6	11.9	11.4
56035		9	Sublette	4,886.5	9,813	2,441	2.0	90.3	1.1	1.4	1.1	7.5	5.4	17.1	6.0	11.4	13.2	12.8
56037	40,540	5	Sweetwater	10,427.0	43,051	1,116	4.1	80.9	1.6	1.5	1.6	16.1	6.9	19.4	8.5	14.0	14.5	11.3
56039	27,220	7	Teton	3,996.8	23,081	1,676	5.8	82.7	0.9	0.8	2.2	14.9	4.9	13.5	6.1	17.0	16.5	13.5
56041	21,740	7	Uinta	2,081.7	20,299	1,806	9.8	88.8	1.0	1.5	1.0	9.2	7.3	21.5	7.3	11.8	13.4	10.8
56043		7	Washakie	2,238.7	7,885	2,603	3.5	84.0	1.0	1.5	1.2	14.1	5.1	17.6	6.7	9.9	11.8	12.4
56045		7	Weston	2,398.0	6,967	2,674	2.9	91.8	1.3	2.5	2.4	4.1	5.2	15.6	6.1	11.5	12.1	11.6

1. CBSA = Core Based Statistical Area. See Appendix A for explanation. See Appendix B for list of metropolitan areas with component counties. 2. County type code from the Economic Research Service of USDA Rural-Urban Continuum Codes. See Appendix A for definition. 3. Dry land or land partially or temporarily covered by water. 4. May be of any race.

Table B. States and Counties — **Population and Households**

STATE County	Population, 2018 (cont.)				Population change, 2000-2018							Households, 2013-2017				
	Age (percent) (cont.)				Total persons		Percent change		Components of change, 2010-2018						Percent	
	55 to 64 years	65 to 74 years	75 years and over	Percent female	2000	2010	2000-2010	2010-2018	Births	Deaths	Net Migration	Number	Persons per household	Family house-holds	Female family house-holder[1]	One person
	16	17	18	19	20	21	22	23	24	25	26	27	28	29	30	31
WYOMING— Cont'd																
Goshen	14.5	11.7	10.2	47.8	12,538	13,247	5.7	1.0	1,161	1,133	80	5,328	2.40	67.5	6.7	28.8
Hot Springs	16.2	14.1	12.1	49.5	4,882	4,812	-1.4	-5.3	413	594	-76	2,246	2.07	60.2	5.8	36.6
Johnson	16.0	13.9	9.8	49.6	7,075	8,569	21.1	-1.3	727	724	-108	3,778	2.25	64.8	8.4	33.0
Laramie	13.0	9.6	6.4	49.3	81,607	91,885	12.6	7.7	10,547	6,479	3,019	38,447	2.47	66.4	10.3	27.8
Lincoln	15.2	11.3	6.1	48.9	14,573	18,106	24.2	7.3	2,031	1,039	333	7,063	2.65	69.6	5.8	24.4
Natrona	13.7	9.3	6.1	49.6	66,533	75,448	13.4	4.9	9,043	5,832	344	32,984	2.41	62.1	9.8	30.7
Niobrara	15.4	12.4	10.2	54.3	2,407	2,484	3.2	-3.9	216	209	-109	982	2.22	53.7	3.1	40.4
Park	15.6	13.8	9.4	50.2	25,786	28,207	9.4	4.0	2,558	2,268	829	11,811	2.41	68.5	7.5	26.4
Platte	15.8	14.4	11.2	49.7	8,807	8,667	-1.6	-1.2	704	802	-1	3,740	2.30	64.4	4.9	30.8
Sheridan	14.9	12.7	8.3	49.8	26,560	29,119	9.6	3.8	2,729	2,577	978	13,130	2.20	62.6	6.1	31.6
Sublette	14.6	12.1	7.4	46.0	5,920	10,244	73.0	-4.2	1,012	406	-1,065	3,197	3.10	68.0	4.9	28.1
Sweetwater	13.4	8.0	4.1	48.5	37,613	43,806	16.5	-1.7	5,072	2,335	-3,566	16,269	2.70	69.0	9.6	25.8
Teton	13.2	10.0	5.4	48.4	18,251	21,298	16.7	8.4	2,052	667	372	8,795	2.51	59.5	5.3	28.6
Uinta	13.8	9.3	4.8	49.3	19,742	21,121	7.0	-3.9	2,518	1,164	-2,207	7,705	2.66	71.0	10.4	23.8
Washakie	14.8	11.9	9.8	49.4	8,289	8,528	2.9	-7.5	755	713	-687	3,490	2.32	66.8	7.9	26.3
Weston	17.5	11.6	8.9	47.1	6,644	7,208	8.5	-3.3	638	563	-319	3,182	2.12	65.6	7.5	31.0

1. No spouse present.

Table B. States and Counties — **Population, Vital Statistics, Health, and Crime**

STATE County	Persons in group quarters, 2018	Daytime Population, 2013-2017		Births, 2018		Deaths, 2018		Persons under 65 with no health insurance, 2016		Medicare, 2018			Serious crimes known to police[2], 2016 Total	
		Number	Employment/residence ratio	Total	Rate[1]	Number	Rate[1]	Number	Percent	Total beneficiaries	Enrolled in Original Medicare	Enrolled in Medicare Advantage	Number	Rate[3]
	32	33	34	35	36	37	38	39	40	41	42	43	44	45
WYOMING— Cont'd														
Goshen	1,229	13,002	0.92	145	10.8	135	10.1	1,451	15.4	3,094	3,050	44	193	1,455
Hot Springs	86	4,677	0.97	47	10.3	79	17.3	472	13.6	1,390	1,353	37	56	1,195
Johnson	71	7,806	0.82	75	8.9	87	10.3	1,013	15.4	2,162	2,121	41	128	1,504
Laramie	1,962	99,784	1.06	1,270	12.8	831	8.4	8,707	10.7	18,489	17,816	673	3,184	3,273
Lincoln	71	17,650	0.87	237	12.2	131	6.7	2,128	13.3	3,594	3,495	99	127	722
Natrona	1,699	81,825	1.02	986	12.5	736	9.3	9,464	13.8	13,939	13,163	776	2,249	2,714
Niobrara	242	2,497	1.02	31	13.0	16	6.7	274	16.0	608	D	D	NA	NA
Park.................................	762	29,511	1.02	288	9.8	289	9.9	3,289	14.6	7,529	7,329	200	509	1,745
Platte...............................	102	8,785	1.02	80	9.3	90	10.5	857	13.1	2,325	2,276	49	96	1,270
Sheridan...........................	1,042	29,575	0.97	320	10.6	329	10.9	2,861	12.1	7,098	6,724	374	442	1,526
Sublette............................	550	10,453	1.08	97	9.9	60	6.1	1,144	13.6	1,550	1,506	44	82	841
Sweetwater	660	45,855	1.06	546	12.7	303	7.0	4,975	12.8	6,030	5,935	95	870	1,957
Teton	270	26,530	1.25	230	10.0	75	3.2	3,005	15.0	3,436	3,263	173	NA	NA
Uinta................................	220	19,775	0.90	276	13.6	147	7.2	2,255	12.6	3,301	2,986	315	426	2,069
Washakie	140	8,362	1.03	74	9.4	85	10.8	1,072	16.7	1,873	1,855	18	82	998
Weston.............................	334	6,548	0.83	66	9.5	68	9.8	802	14.4	1,607	1,505	102	65	1,071

1. Per 1,000 estimated resident population.   2. Data for serious crimes have not been adjusted for underreporting; this may affect comparability between geographic areas and over time.   3. Per 100,000 population estimated by the FBI.

Table B. States and Counties — **Crime, Education, Money Income, and Poverty**

STATE County	Serious crimes known to police[2], 2016 (cont.)[1] Rate		School enrollment and attainment, 2013-2017 Enrollment[3]		Attainment[4] (percent)		Local government expenditures,[5] 2014-2015		Money income, 2013-2017 Per	Households			Income and poverty, 2017 Median	Percent below poverty level		
	Violent	Property	Total	Percent private	High school graduate or less	Bachelor's degree or more	Total current spending (mil dol)	Current spending per student (dollars)	Per capita income[6]	Median income (dollars)	Percent with income of less than $50,000	with income of $200,000 or more	Median household income (dollars)	All persons	Children under 18 years	Children 5 to 17 years in families
	46	47	48	49	50	51	52	53	54	55	56	57	58	59	60	61
WYOMING— Cont'd																
Goshen	392	1,063	2,938	14.8	37.3	24.4	31.8	18,591	27,253	48,422	51.2	1.7	51,023	12.9	16.1	14.1
Hot Springs	171	1,024	943	20.9	33.8	21.6	12.0	19,370	30,939	48,403	51.0	2.2	47,775	12.1	17.4	16.0
Johnson	141	1,363	1,571	11.0	38.0	26.8	21.7	16,930	32,732	52,415	47.0	3.8	55,412	9.5	12.4	10.8
Laramie	252	3,021	23,925	9.0	32.1	28.7	233.0	15,797	31,554	62,879	38.7	3.1	61,658	9.7	11.6	10.6
Lincoln	148	574	4,972	6.3	38.3	20.5	51.6	15,556	29,516	63,756	38.8	4.4	65,137	7.6	9.1	8.1
Natrona	203	2,511	19,616	9.1	37.2	22.8	195.8	14,574	31,900	59,400	42.9	4.0	61,049	11.1	13.3	11.8
Niobrara	NA	NA	511	7.2	39.0	18.3	12.7	12,990	23,370	36,793	57.8	2.5	45,768	13.4	16.1	16.1
Park	185	1,560	6,337	9.3	32.4	32.2	62.9	15,824	32,557	60,828	39.0	4.1	57,619	9.4	12.2	11.2
Platte	119	1,151	1,654	8.8	40.1	22.6	23.7	19,220	31,242	47,380	52.0	4.3	50,775	10.4	14.6	13.3
Sheridan	152	1,374	6,683	11.2	28.4	31.3	69.6	15,634	31,643	56,455	44.0	2.5	54,482	9.1	11.5	10.2
Sublette	31	810	2,482	12.8	41.0	25.4	29.3	17,645	32,175	84,911	31.9	4.6	74,811	6.6	7.6	7.0
Sweetwater	306	1,651	12,116	9.7	42.3	22.2	121.4	14,370	31,700	71,083	35.9	3.5	75,590	10.0	13.4	11.6
Teton	NA	NA	4,752	19.9	17.8	54.1	47.7	17,713	49,200	80,049	25.8	16.5	90,145	5.8	6.9	6.0
Uinta	92	1,977	5,557	4.9	45.6	17.4	67.9	15,344	27,115	54,672	44.6	2.2	67,404	10.2	11.8	10.2
Washakie	73	925	1,783	6.7	40.4	21.0	26.5	18,365	27,345	51,362	47.7	2.8	57,989	10.7	14.0	13.1
Weston	132	939	1,441	17.6	42.5	19.8	19.1	18,204	30,955	59,605	43.1	3.2	56,214	10.6	14.0	12.6

1. Data for serious crimes have not been adjusted for underreporting; this may affect comparability between geographic areas and over time.   2. Per 100,000 population estimated by the FBI.   3. All persons 3 years old and over enrolled in nursery school through college.   4. Persons 25 years old and over.   5. Elementary and secondary education expenditures.   6. Based on population estimated by the American Community Survey, 2013–2017.

Table B. States and Counties — Personal Income and Earnings

STATE County	Personal income, 2017										Earnings, 2017		
	Total (mil dol)	Percent change 2016-2017	Per capita[1]		Wages and salaries (mil dol)	Supplements to wages and salaries, employer contributions (mil dol)		Proprietors' income (mil dol)	Dividends, interest, and rent (mil dol)	Personal transfer receipts (mil dol)	Total (mil dol)	Contributions for government social insurance (mil dol)	
			Dollars	Rank		Pension and insurance	Government social insurance					From employee and self-employed	From employer
	62	63	64	65	66	67	68	69	70	71	72	73	74
WYOMING— Cont'd													
Goshen	555	2.5	41,492	1,333	182	41	19	57	117	125	299	18	19
Hot Springs	239	-2.6	50,891	418	76	18	8	46	46	59	147	9	8
Johnson	404	-0.2	47,629	654	133	29	13	24	111	73	200	13	13
Laramie	4,972	4.2	50,563	428	2,494	530	255	366	1,106	848	3,646	210	255
Lincoln	793	5.2	41,139	1,390	308	68	30	43	223	136	448	28	30
Natrona	5,332	1.6	67,023	85	1,972	305	196	1,338	1,300	623	3,812	200	196
Niobrara	108	2.4	45,020	898	38	11	4	16	28	24	70	4	4
Park	1,467	1.8	49,600	490	591	119	60	102	458	277	872	55	60
Platte	403	2.5	47,027	711	186	41	20	29	83	91	276	17	20
Sheridan	1,653	2.1	54,727	291	596	118	62	123	563	269	898	56	62
Sublette	491	3.6	50,090	458	250	46	23	23	175	54	343	20	23
Sweetwater	2,171	3.2	49,870	470	1,392	239	127	228	300	282	1,985	115	127
Teton	5,441	4.6	233,860	1	1,033	122	109	304	4,067	130	1,568	89	109
Uinta	795	1.4	38,797	1,758	360	74	37	33	147	153	504	31	37
Washakie	370	2.3	45,933	802	161	33	17	31	94	73	241	15	17
Weston	300	-2.4	43,340	1,097	96	27	10	17	59	62	150	9	10

1. Based on the resident population estimated as of July 1 of the year shown.

Table B. States and Counties — **Earnings, Social Security, and Housing**

STATE County	Earnings, 2017 (cont.)									Social Security beneficiaries, December 2017		Supple- mental Security Income recipients, 2017	Housing units, 2018	
	Percent by selected industries													
	Farm	Mining, quarrying, and extractions	Construction	Manu- facturing	Information; professional, scientific, technical services	Retail trade	Finance, insurance, real estate, and leasing	Health care and social assistance	Govern- ment	Number	Rate[1]		Total	Percent change, 2010-2018
	75	76	77	78	79	80	81	82	83	84	85	86	87	88
WYOMING— Cont'd														
Goshen	9.3	0.0	5.1	4.6	2.6	4.7	5.2	D	30.8	3,165	237	218	6,033	1.0
Hot Springs	0.7	D	3.5	2.1	2.4	D	2.4	8.1	23.9	1,480	315	84	2,588	0.2
Johnson	3.8	9.8	7.0	1.4	6.5	5.8	7.2	3.6	35.9	2,225	263	49	4,629	1.7
Laramie	0.8	1.8	6.3	D	8.0	6.2	6.4	8.2	39.8	18,580	189	1,485	43,894	8.5
Lincoln	0.8	17.8	14.3	1.8	4.6	5.1	4.1	3.2	29.1	3,780	196	152	9,565	6.9
Natrona	0.1	7.2	6.8	3.1	4.5	5.1	5.9	11.8	11.8	14,675	184	1,244	37,181	10.0
Niobrara	3.5	3.5	5.2	D	D	D	2.6	D	43.4	615	257	24	1,369	2.3
Park	1.0	4.4	9.6	4.3	7.8	7.1	5.2	11.4	29.7	7,825	265	287	14,578	7.5
Platte	5.4	2.2	9.7	1.1	4.7	5.0	4.3	D	22.5	2,380	278	84	4,880	4.6
Sheridan	0.6	2.5	10.0	3.5	7.7	7.1	4.5	8.2	31.2	7,055	234	304	15,058	8.0
Sublette	1.2	37.9	9.3	0.6	3.4	3.9	4.2	D	23.2	1,545	158	43	6,053	4.9
Sweetwater	-0.1	34.7	6.8	9.3	2.7	4.6	3.4	3.3	16.4	6,675	153	374	19,836	5.9
Teton	0.2	0.8	12.2	0.2	14.3	6.6	9.2	4.4	14.0	3,110	134	39	14,034	9.5
Uinta	0.0	7.0	11.3	3.4	8.1	7.1	5.1	10.8	26.6	3,525	172	290	9,060	4.0
Washakie	1.8	2.5	6.8	13.2	4.6	5.6	4.6	D	24.8	1,965	244	86	3,870	1.0
Weston	2.2	7.3	6.8	12.1	2.6	5.4	4.8	D	35.1	1,690	244	54	3,567	1.0

1. Per 1,000 resident population estimated as of July 1 of the year shown.

Table B. States and Counties — **Housing, Labor Force, and Employment**

STATE County	Housing units, 2013-2017								Civilian labor force, 2018				Civilian employment[6], 2013-2017		
	Occupied units										Unemployment			Percent	
		Owner-occupied				Renter-occupied									
				Median owner cost as a percent of income			Median rent as a percent of income[2]	Sub-standard units[4] (percent)		Percent change, 2017-2018				Management, business, science, and arts	Construction, production, and maintenance occupations
	Total	Percent	Median value[1]	With a mortgage	Without a mortgage[2]	Median rent[3]			Total		Total	Rate[5]	Total		
	89	90	91	92	93	94	95	96	97	98	99	100	101	102	103
WYOMING— Cont'd															
Goshen	5,328	76.0	154,900	19.4	11.7	715	26.4	1.1	6,830	-1.3	226	3.3	6,122	34.0	28.9
Hot Springs	2,246	76.9	147,700	21.7	10.0	725	25.7	2.7	2,208	-5.3	82	3.7	2,290	40.1	21.4
Johnson	3,778	71.9	255,200	21.3	12.7	886	22.7	0.7	4,211	0.4	168	4.0	4,267	32.8	29.0
Laramie	38,447	69.3	202,800	21.5	10.2	902	28.5	1.3	47,682	-1.1	1,847	3.9	47,243	37.1	23.1
Lincoln	7,063	78.4	205,900	20.9	10.0	836	22.0	2.7	8,711	-0.4	332	3.8	9,124	31.2	33.2
Natrona	32,984	66.6	198,600	20.7	10.0	852	26.2	2.2	39,059	-1.2	1,813	4.6	41,467	31.0	27.8
Niobrara	982	71.6	152,500	19.5	15.1	615	21.7	1.3	1,275	-2.0	36	2.8	1,067	31.6	23.9
Park	11,811	72.3	236,200	21.3	10.0	759	22.3	1.2	15,567	-0.8	681	4.4	15,092	33.6	23.5
Platte	3,740	76.4	169,900	22.8	11.2	679	28.4	0.3	4,680	-2.0	178	3.8	4,289	29.1	35.1
Sheridan	13,130	68.6	240,900	22.3	10.8	810	25.9	1.6	15,593	-1.3	631	4.0	14,663	41.1	21.3
Sublette	3,197	75.7	264,800	19.4	10.0	1,078	17.4	0.9	4,264	0.2	179	4.2	5,396	41.9	30.7
Sweetwater	16,269	73.8	201,000	18.4	10.0	870	23.9	2.8	21,150	-1.9	896	4.2	22,739	27.7	36.2
Teton	8,795	58.5	739,100	21.6	10.0	1,272	26.1	5.8	15,340	-0.5	464	3.0	14,492	39.4	18.2
Uinta	7,705	72.1	178,400	19.0	10.0	652	25.6	2.8	8,931	-1.9	390	4.4	9,528	30.4	32.2
Washakie	3,490	76.1	165,500	20.7	10.0	627	27.0	2.3	4,058	-1.3	172	4.2	3,833	32.1	34.1
Weston	3,182	76.6	180,100	18.9	10.0	769	20.0	2.9	3,731	-0.6	131	3.5	3,407	32.0	37.2

1. Specified owner-occupied units. lacking complete plumbing facilities.   2. A value of 10.0 represents 10 percent or less; a value of 50.0 represents 50 percent or more.   3. Specified renter-occupied units.   4. Overcrowded or
5. Percent of civilian labor force.   6. Civilian employed persons 16 years old and over.

Table B. States and Counties — **Nonfarm Employment and Agriculture**

STATE County	Private nonfarm establishments, employment and payroll, 2016									Agriculture, 2017			Farm producers whose primary occupation is farming (percent)
	Number of establishments	Employment						Annual payroll		Farms			
		Total	Health care and social assistance	Manufacturing	Retail trade	Finance and insurance	Professional, scientific, and technical services	Total (mil dol)	Average per employee (dollars)	Number	Percent with:		
											Fewer than 50 acres	1000 acres or more	
	104	105	106	107	108	109	110	111	112	113	114	115	116
WYOMING— Cont'd													
Goshen	348	2,987	707	209	416	137	128	94	31,442	842	19.1	24.8	48.9
Hot Springs	184	1,587	403	42	182	41	49	55	34,432	223	39.9	18.4	42.7
Johnson	467	2,341	397	67	334	156	172	82	34,877	384	21.1	42.2	46.8
Laramie	3,234	35,366	8,045	1,130	5,765	1,578	2,488	1,413	39,958	999	31.7	21.9	38.8
Lincoln	668	4,467	774	357	667	108	110	216	48,451	698	52.0	10.5	31.0
Natrona	2,953	32,937	5,675	1,382	5,082	965	1,428	1,443	43,825	430	40.0	25.3	39.3
Niobrara	89	413	56	D	104	D	8	12	28,695	242	5.0	69.4	67.9
Park	1,188	9,669	1,954	588	1,634	306	395	396	40,995	1,008	45.6	9.9	40.5
Platte	260	2,191	304	128	434	105	45	94	42,831	505	24.4	33.1	45.4
Sheridan	1,178	10,392	2,175	295	1,694	331	728	372	35,824	833	45.7	17.5	35.1
Sublette	408	2,885	161	49	344	75	92	187	64,932	402	35.3	28.6	34.3
Sweetwater	1,268	16,419	1,456	1,807	2,410	315	469	937	57,083	219	25.6	24.7	38.3
Teton	2,105	17,864	1,316	172	1,925	418	988	781	43,739	142	34.5	13.4	40.6
Uinta	573	6,990	1,410	193	1,095	145	227	339	48,558	403	42.9	19.9	34.8
Washakie	358	2,828	736	316	361	101	113	100	35,519	246	36.2	22.8	49.6
Weston	228	1,621	377	D	286	62	25	59	36,493	247	17.8	45.7	41.8

Table B. States and Counties — **Agriculture**

STATE County	Land in farms					Value of land and buildings (dollars)		Value of machinery and equiopmnet, average per farm (dollars)	Value of products sold:				Organic farms (number)	Farms with internet access (percent)	Government payments	
	Acreage (1,000)	Percent change, 2012-2017	Acres			Average per farm	Average per acre		Total (mil dol)		Percent from:				Total ($1,000)	Percent of farms
			Average size of farm	Total irrigated (1,000)	Total cropland (1,000)					Average per farm (acres)	Crops	Livestock and poultry products				
	117	118	119	120	121	122	123	124	125	126	127	128	129	130	131	132
WYOMING— Cont'd																
Goshen	1,256	-8.3	1,492	118.4	234.3	1,286,023	862	156,103	201.9	239,760	24.0	76.0	3	78.9	4,111	40.5
Hot Springs	528	2.1	2,368	14.8	22.7	1,469,992	621	90,195	15.2	68,278	6.6	93.4	1	77.6	408	13.0
Johnson	1,974	-3.0	5,142	31.7	41.0	3,020,697	588	128,544	44.1	114,966	7.0	93.0	NA	82.6	1,088	21.6
Laramie	1,630	-2.8	1,631	67.1	382.3	1,383,473	848	123,891	184.6	184,762	17.9	82.1	42	77.7	4,856	29.3
Lincoln	365	6.1	523	81.3	94.0	955,622	1,828	82,429	47.9	68,566	23.3	76.7	NA	81.2	182	5.2
Natrona	1,933	14.3	4,496	44.3	55.7	2,039,344	454	109,339	43.2	100,493	12.9	87.1	NA	76.0	318	7.9
Niobrara	1,277	-6.0	5,279	10.5	54.6	3,308,558	627	156,480	49.7	205,306	8.1	91.9	NA	71.5	1,861	37.2
Park	930	14.4	923	127.5	140.5	1,378,458	1,494	124,845	85.2	84,497	53.7	46.3	5	86.9	931	10.0
Platte	1,047	-14.5	2,073	58.9	134.8	1,820,452	878	136,932	94.2	186,598	19.7	80.3	6	82.2	2,872	27.1
Sheridan	1,214	-7.0	1,457	54.6	95.9	1,783,962	1,224	101,776	59.7	71,637	14.5	85.5	1	78.9	1,417	12.2
Sublette	546	-29.7	1,359	158.7	143.5	2,243,832	1,651	128,778	47.9	119,085	12.9	87.1	2	84.3	155	2.7
Sweetwater	1,370	-17.7	6,256	35.4	35.6	1,851,640	296	110,326	16.5	75,132	27.7	72.3	NA	82.6	201	5.9
Teton	68	68.4	476	25.5	15.8	1,929,058	4,049	103,147	17.6	123,817	22.6	77.4	NA	88.7	131	4.2
Uinta	657	1.0	1,630	76.2	84.8	1,747,715	1,072	102,095	26.7	66,159	13.6	86.4	1	80.9	130	1.5
Washakie	316	-7.4	1,285	38.5	53.4	1,502,187	1,169	211,277	43.0	174,874	37.8	62.2	NA	91.1	508	25.2
Weston	1,227	-4.9	4,968	4.2	37.5	3,321,035	669	129,296	34.3	138,761	1.8	98.2	NA	81.0	836	31.2

STATE County	Water use, 2015		Wholesale Trade[1], 2012				Retail Trade[2], 2012				Real estate and rental and leasing,[2] 2012			
	Public supply water withdrawn (mil gal/ day)	Public supply gallons withdrawn per person per day	Number of establish- ments	Number of employees	Sales (mil dol)	Average payroll (mil dol)	Number of establish- ments	Number of employees	Sales (mil dol)	Average payroll (mil dol)	Number of establish- ments	Number of employees	Sales (mil dol)	Average payroll (mil dol)
	133	134	135	136	137	138	139	140	141	142	143	144	145	146
WYOMING— Cont'd														
Goshen	1.85	138.2	20	156	69.8	5.8	51	402	107.4	8.7	14	25	3.5	0.6
Hot Springs	0.67	141.3	4	30	13.1	2.3	26	195	48.2	3.0	6	D	D	D
Johnson	1.61	187.5	6	27	8.6	0.7	52	359	91.4	8.1	17	46	4.8	1.5
Laramie.........................	14.00	144.2	121	1,105	722.2	67.0	370	5,513	1,896.2	161.3	142	461	99.5	16.5
Lincoln...........................	4.05	216.3	8	55	17.8	1.7	79	659	180.6	13.3	13	17	2.2	0.4
Natrona.........................	12.26	149.2	163	1,890	2,052.7	115.2	363	4,796	1,487.5	132.1	166	1,281	502.0	79.4
Niobrara........................	1.00	393.4	2	D	D	D	13	110	28.8	2.3	5	3	1.7	0.2
Park..............................	3.17	108.5	40	270	227.9	12.3	185	1,523	417.5	37.1	57	117	15.1	2.3
Platte............................	1.56	177.0	5	28	22.0	0.8	35	371	87.5	8.0	11	44	15.2	2.2
Sheridan........................	4.55	151.6	34	187	84.7	6.8	151	1,559	475.9	42.5	60	204	28.6	5.9
Sublette.........................	2.21	223.3	8	46	41.6	2.7	41	401	94.7	9.7	31	151	27.9	6.4
Sweetwater	11.37	254.8	61	D	D	D	199	2,461	921.4	69.9	85	377	115.4	21.0
Teton	7.78	336.4	32	D	D	D	241	1,929	512.6	55.6	146	527	128.8	26.0
Uinta.............................	3.90	187.3	20	216	153.9	11.3	92	1,119	389.9	24.3	39	148	29.8	5.1
Washakie	0.09	10.8	8	42	15.8	1.3	46	334	95.4	10.0	17	D	D	D
Weston...........................	1.02	141.0	5	40	27.6	1.7	31	267	76.5	6.1	4	6	1.1	0.2

1   Merchant wholesalers, except manufacturers' sales branches and offices.   2. Employer establishments.

Professional Services, Manufacturing, and Accommodation and Food Services

STATE County	Professional, scientific, and technical services, 2012				Manufacturing, 2012				Accommodation and food services, 2012			
	Number of establish-ments	Number of employees	Sales (mil dol)	Average payroll (mil dol)	Number of establish-ments	Number of employees	Receipts (mil dol)	Annual payroll (mil dol)	Number of establis-hments	Number of employees	Receipts (mil dol)	Annual payroll (mil dol)
	147	148	149	150	151	152	153	154	155	156	157	158
WYOMING— Cont'd												
Goshen	24	158	8.4	4.3	12	308	D	9.9	30	320	15.9	3.8
Hot Springs	15	49	4.2	1.7	4	32	8.0	2.1	26	D	D	D
Johnson	49	149	18.1	6.6	12	64	D	2.8	42	403	23.3	7.2
Laramie	458	1,860	279.8	99.7	67	1,190	2,549.8	76.8	207	3,980	224.8	59.8
Lincoln	62	106	12.6	4.0	18	371	D	22.2	60	406	18.0	4.4
Natrona	278	1,537	222.4	83.2	83	2,428	1,780.3	163.0	200	3,814	198.2	57.4
Niobrara	5	9	0.7	0.1	3	D	1.4	D	13	95	5.1	1.2
Park	99	338	36.9	14.6	44	410	90.4	18.5	124	1,891	170.9	49.7
Platte	16	51	6.2	1.3	14	64	10.8	2.3	36	346	21.3	4.1
Sheridan	127	675	92.3	31.2	28	383	102.3	19.3	92	1,213	68.7	19.2
Sublette	54	139	20.1	6.7	9	31	D	1.5	40	358	24.4	6.9
Sweetwater	121	493	90.2	31.7	35	1,772	1,575.5	148.7	113	1,771	128.9	28.1
Teton	268	744	139.3	46.8	34	254	34.1	8.0	186	4,598	344.0	114.7
Uinta	54	285	33.8	13.8	24	233	204.2	9.8	48	875	35.5	9.9
Washakie	37	104	11.9	4.1	14	387	187.5	18.5	32	284	11.6	3.2
Weston	11	23	2.4	0.7	3	D	D	D	22	190	9.4	2.4

Table B. States and Counties — **Health Care and Social Assistance, Other Services, Nonemployer Businesses, and Residential Construction**

STATE County	Health care and social assistance, 2012				Other services, 2012				Nonemployer businesses, 2016		Value of residential construction authorized by building permits, 2018	
	Number of establish-ments	Number of employees	Receipts (mil dol)	Annual payroll (mil dol)	Number of establish-ments	Number of employees	Receipts (mil dol)	Annual payroll (mil dol)	Number	Receipts (mil dol)	New construction ($1,000)	Number of housing units
	159	160	161	162	163	164	165	166	167	168	169	170
WYOMING— Cont'd												
Goshen	27	803	60.5	25.6	28	89	9.3	2.3	956	40.0	0	0
Hot Springs	19	395	34.2	15.5	14	58	3.9	1.1	401	11.8	100	1
Johnson	32	375	32.1	13.2	22	104	7.6	2.8	1,288	73.3	5,418	19
Laramie	323	6,700	647.9	305.2	189	943	93.6	27.1	8,118	524.1	86,186	539
Lincoln	56	643	58.5	24.1	38	77	9.9	2.2	1,995	82.6	41,390	148
Natrona	305	5,141	687.2	266.3	207	1,333	227.6	49.8	5,984	273.6	34,553	174
Niobrara	7	D	D	D	7	28	6.7	1.3	241	7.0	227	1
Park	116	1,399	146.3	55.5	70	248	24.9	6.5	3,174	130.1	33,605	127
Platte	22	325	27.7	10.9	13	50	3.7	0.9	772	26.7	5,757	26
Sheridan	128	2,705	302.2	125.1	74	334	31.1	8.6	2,971	124.9	42,075	177
Sublette	23	207	13.3	6.8	32	162	25.1	6.3	990	39.4	15,826	56
Sweetwater	104	1,285	150.2	51.2	88	464	58.7	16.1	2,166	85.2	14,739	54
Teton	117	1,120	158.9	60.5	113	450	109.0	17.0	5,161	337.1	241,004	168
Uinta	67	1,265	110.3	53.9	35	D	D	D	1,416	62.3	5,981	29
Washakie	29	787	51.6	23.0	28	94	9.7	1.8	695	19.1	0	0
Weston	24	352	25.3	10.5	12	38	3.1	0.8	585	20.6	0	0

Table B. States and Counties — **Government Employment and Payroll, and Local Government Finances**

STATE County	Government employment and payroll, 2012									Local government finances, 2012				
	Full-time equivalent employees	March payroll (dollars)	March payroll (percent of total)							General revenue				
			Adminis- tration, judicial, and legal	Police and corrections	Fire protection	Highways and transpor- tation	Health and welfare	Natural resources and utilities	Education and libraries	Total (mil dol)	Inter- govern- mental (mil dol)	Taxes		
												Total (mil dol)	Per capita[1] (dollars)	
													Total	Property
	171	172	173	174	175	176	177	178	179	180	181	182	183	184

WYOMING— Cont'd

STATE County	171	172	173	174	175	176	177	178	179	180	181	182	183	184
Goshen	800	2,841,581	5.6	7.0	0.0	2.4	1.3	5.3	77.7	86.6	58.5	10.5	773	552
Hot Springs	363	1,248,475	7.7	7.2	0.0	3.0	30.6	3.5	46.8	44.5	12.8	14.8	3,062	2,366
Johnson	670	2,461,238	5.8	13.9	1.0	2.9	30.1	3.1	42.7	83.0	14.4	44.9	5,208	4,585
Laramie	6,173	27,578,286	2.8	4.6	1.9	1.8	39.8	1.5	46.1	796.0	292.8	103.3	1,094	589
Lincoln	1,211	4,847,475	5.1	5.7	0.0	2.9	30.1	3.4	50.4	146.8	60.4	43.1	2,402	2,075
Natrona	3,954	15,321,295	4.4	7.8	3.5	2.3	2.0	5.1	72.5	442.5	254.7	108.8	1,384	938
Niobrara	300	1,035,735	7.3	4.9	0.0	2.2	34.2	5.3	43.5	21.1	9.3	5.8	2,352	1,687
Park	2,084	8,399,901	4.2	4.7	0.4	2.6	27.2	5.2	52.8	238.1	92.8	47.9	1,668	1,494
Platte	543	2,168,168	5.1	7.9	0.2	2.2	1.5	6.3	74.9	46.5	26.6	13.3	1,519	995
Sheridan	2,207	8,719,701	3.2	4.7	1.0	2.3	30.0	3.0	54.6	234.1	106.6	40.1	1,354	946
Sublette	677	2,840,346	8.1	15.4	0.0	10.5	11.9	4.2	49.3	142.2	33.5	91.3	8,805	8,657
Sweetwater	2,985	12,809,450	6.0	8.4	2.4	2.6	20.2	5.8	52.6	382.6	116.8	165.8	3,662	2,797
Teton	1,475	6,340,874	5.4	7.3	1.5	7.9	37.5	5.7	32.3	225.0	41.2	80.1	3,695	2,344
Uinta	1,240	4,518,508	5.8	7.1	0.8	2.5	1.9	5.2	73.2	117.5	70.3	38.1	1,811	1,505
Washakie	459	1,506,233	5.8	5.8	0.7	2.9	2.6	6.0	75.1	45.2	28.7	12.2	1,442	998
Weston	521	1,865,375	4.5	8.0	0.4	2.9	23.8	5.3	54.7	44.2	22.9	9.7	1,375	1,062

1. Based on the resident population estimated as of July 1 of the year shown.

Table B. States and Counties — Local Government Finances, Government Employment, and Income Taxes

STATE County	Local government finances, 2012 (cont.)							Debt outstanding		Government employment, 2017			Individual income tax returns, 2016		
	Direct general expenditure														
			Percent of total for:											Mean adjusted gross income	Mean income tax
	Total (mil dol)	Per capita[1] (dollars)	Education	Health and hospitals	Police protection	Public welfare	Highways	Total (mil dol)	Per capita[1] (dollars)	Federal civilian	Federal military	State and local	Number of returns		
	185	186	187	188	189	190	191	192	193	194	195	196	197	198	199
WYOMING— Cont'd															
Goshen	86.2	6,325	66.3	1.5	3.7	0.9	7.3	10.3	756	69	65	1,344	5,590	48,822	4,777
Hot Springs	44.9	9,306	33.3	31.7	3.7	0.0	5.2	4.5	931	15	25	528	2,240	43,285	4,209
Johnson	95.5	11,080	33.0	26.7	3.3	0.5	6.3	14.7	1,711	126	45	867	4,210	50,943	6,674
Laramie	781.4	8,270	37.0	40.5	2.5	0.2	3.1	132.4	1,401	2,772	3,523	11,363	47,710	61,049	7,452
Lincoln	144.3	8,033	47.9	26.3	3.6	0.1	4.8	60.9	3,388	114	102	1,719	8,200	70,545	8,998
Natrona	436.0	5,546	59.1	0.4	4.8	0.7	4.1	147.1	1,871	657	414	5,102	37,050	69,220	10,271
Niobrara	27.9	11,371	45.7	24.9	4.4	0.1	4.6	111.4	45,347	12	12	447	1,110	45,065	4,370
Park	277.9	9,682	41.4	36.2	2.5	0.0	2.9	79.0	2,754	755	153	2,842	14,720	66,007	8,582
Platte	48.9	5,582	54.4	2.9	7.4	0.1	4.1	8.7	993	101	92	815	4,180	51,188	5,692
Sheridan	252.8	8,543	49.0	26.5	2.5	0.0	5.2	33.2	1,121	754	155	2,821	14,940	66,891	9,239
Sublette	154.1	14,868	43.1	8.2	4.0	1.8	11.0	9.5	919	125	49	931	4,090	71,262	10,049
Sweetwater	389.7	8,609	48.2	17.5	5.5	0.3	4.3	69.5	1,536	210	228	4,295	19,570	67,432	8,235
Teton	218.0	10,059	24.1	34.3	3.8	0.0	2.4	92.9	4,287	420	122	2,106	14,220	210,905	45,308
Uinta	121.7	5,787	64.9	0.8	5.8	0.9	4.8	14.0	665	69	108	2,108	9,030	60,236	6,726
Washakie	52.1	6,153	68.3	0.8	4.1	0.4	3.0	12.8	1,512	119	42	769	3,670	61,277	8,338
Weston	48.0	6,780	47.5	21.6	4.2	0.6	10.3	2.0	286	56	35	735	3,140	60,679	7,041

1. Based on the resident population estimated as of July 1 of the year shown.

Metropolitan Areas

(For explanation of symbols, see page viii)

Page

775	Metropolitan Area Highlights and Rankings
793	Metropolitan Area Column Headings
797	Table C
797	Abilene, TX—Casper, WY
811	Cedar Rapids, IA—Eugene, OR
825	Evansville, IN-KY—Johnstown, PA
839	Jonesboro, AR—Missoula, MT
853	Mobile, AL—Rapid City, SD
867	Reading, PA—Terre Haute, IN
881	Texarkana, TX-AR—Yuma, AZ

Metropolitan Area Highlights and Rankings

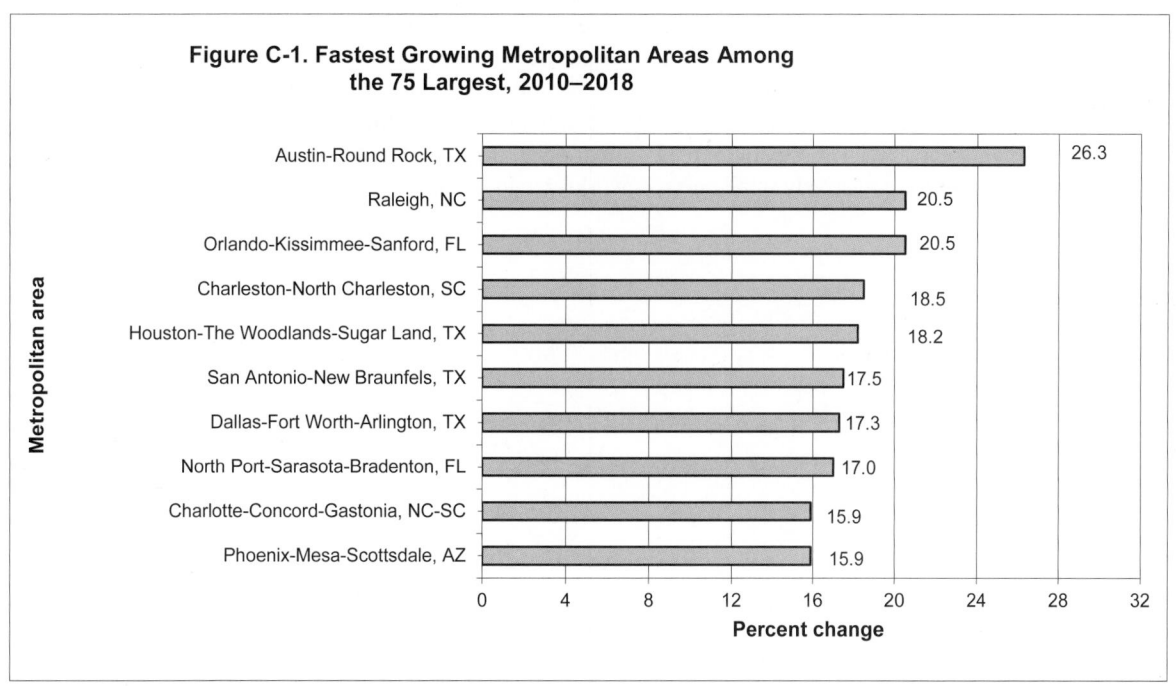

Figure C-1. Fastest Growing Metropolitan Areas Among the 75 Largest, 2010–2018

Metropolitan area	Percent change
Austin-Round Rock, TX	26.3
Raleigh, NC	20.5
Orlando-Kissimmee-Sanford, FL	20.5
Charleston-North Charleston, SC	18.5
Houston-The Woodlands-Sugar Land, TX	18.2
San Antonio-New Braunfels, TX	17.5
Dallas-Fort Worth-Arlington, TX	17.3
North Port-Sarasota-Bradenton, FL	17.0
Charlotte-Concord-Gastonia, NC-SC	15.9
Phoenix-Mesa-Scottsdale, AZ	15.9

In 2018, 86.0 percent of Americans lived in metropolitan areas, but these metropolitan areas made up a mere 28 percent of the nation's land area. After nearly a decade of research and development, the Office of Management and Budget (OMB) first established new rules for defining metropolitan areas and issued a completely new list after the 2000 census. This scheme defines a variety of areas called "Core Based Statistical Areas" (CBSAs). Along with the new definition of metropolitan areas, OMB defined a new type of area—called a micropolitan area—that defines the many American communities with population clusters that are too small to meet the 50,000 minimum that defines a metropolitan area. Appendix C lists these micropolitan areas as of August 2017, but because of size constraints, *County and City Extra* continues to include only metropolitan area data in Table C. In 2013, the Census Bureau released data for new metropolitan and micropolitan areas based on the 2010 census, and these were updated in 2015 and again in 2017. This edition of *County and City Extra* uses the 2015 metropolitan area delineations. Appendix C shows the 2017 list where one micropolitan area became a metropolitan area (Twin Falls, Idaho).

With nearly 20 million people, the New York metropolitan area was the largest, followed by Los Angeles with a population of over 13 million. Chicago ranked third with 9.5 million people. Another 11 metropolitan areas had more than 4 million residents (Dallas, Houston, Washington, Philadelphia, Miami, Atlanta, Boston, San Francisco, Phoenix, Riverside, and Detroit), while 39 other metropolitan areas had between 1 million and 4 million people. Fifty-six percent of the U.S. population lived in these 53 metropolitan areas with one million or more residents.

One hundred eighty-five metropolitan areas grew by 5 percent or more between 2010 and 2018. The Villages, FL had the highest growth rate, increasing by 37.8 percent to a 2018 population of 128,754 residents. Among the 75 largest metropolitan areas, Austin-Round Rock-San Marcos, TX had the largest increase at 26.3 percent followed by Raleigh, NC and Orlando-Kissimmee-Sanford, FL at 20.5 percent. Six of the most populous metropolitan areas lost population since 2010—Pittsburgh, PA; Cleveland-Elyria, OH, New Haven-Milford, CT; Rochester, NY, Hartford-West Hartford-East Hartford, CT and Buffalo-Cheektowaga-Niagara Falls, NY. While many large metropolitan areas in the Midwest lost population or increased only slightly, Columbus, Omaha, Indianapolis, Minneapolis, and Grand Rapids all grew by more than eight percent.

Among metropolitan areas, New York and Los Angeles shared the top spots for density as well as for total population. With 2,739.9 persons per square mile, Los Angeles-Long Beach-Anaheim, CA was the most densely populated metropolitan area in the country. At the other extreme, eight of the largest metropolitan areas had fewer than 200 persons per square mile. These areas typically had large land areas and were located in the west and south.

In 2018, two metropolitan areas had an unemployment rate at 10 percent or higher. In contrast, 131 metropolitan areas had an unemployment rate at 10 percent or higher in 2010. Topping the list are El Centro, CA and Yuma, AZ, two metropolitan areas with large agricultural workforces and unemployment rates at 18.1 percent and 17.0 percent respectively. Eight of the 10 metropolitan areas with the highest unemployment were in California. Among the 75 most populous metropolitan areas, Bakersfield, CA was the only MSA with an unemployment rate at 8 percent or above. Three hundred twenty-three metropolitan areas had unemployment rates below 5 percent in 2018. Many of them were relatively small areas.

Iowa City, IA and Ames, IA had the lowest unemployment rates among all metropolitan areas at 2.0 percent and 1.6 percent respectively followed by Midland, TX at 2.1 percent; and Burlington-South Burlington, VT at 2.2 percent; Forty-four of the 75 largest metropolitan areas had unemployment rates below 4 percent. These were metropolitan areas in different regions of the country, and with different employment patterns. Among them was Grand Rapids-Wyoming, MI with an unemployment rate of 3.0 percent. This metropolitan area had the highest level of manufacturing employment of the 75 largest metropolitan areas, with 22.0 percent of the workforce in manufacturing industries.

75 Largest Metropolitan Areas by 2018 Population
Selected Rankings

Population, 2018			Total land area, 2018			
Population rank	Metropolitan area	Population [col 2]	Population rank	Land area rank	Metropolitan area	Land area (square miles) [col 1]
1	New York-Newark-Jersey City, NY-NJ-PA	19,979,477	13	1	Riverside-San Bernardino-Ontario, CA	27,267
2	Los Angeles-Long Beach-Anaheim, CA	13,291,486	11	2	Phoenix-Mesa-Scottsdale, AZ	14,565
3	Chicago-Naperville-Elgin, IL-IN-WI	9,498,716	60	3	Albuquerque, NM	9,283
4	Dallas-Fort Worth-Arlington, TX	7,539,711	4	4	Dallas-Fort Worth-Arlington, TX	9,279
5	Houston-The Woodlands-Sugar Land, TX	6,997,384	53	5	Tucson, AZ	9,187
6	Washington-Arlington-Alexandria, DC-VA-MD-WV	6,249,950	9	6	Atlanta-Sandy Springs-Roswell, GA	8,686
7	Miami-Fort Lauderdale-West Palm Beach, FL	6,198,782	19	7	Denver-Aurora-Lakewood, CO	8,345
8	Philadelphia-Camden-Wilmington, PA-NJ-DE-MD	6,096,372	1	8	New York-Newark-Jersey City, NY-NJ-PA	8,293
9	Atlanta-Sandy Springs-Roswell, GA	5,949,951	5	9	Houston-The Woodlands-Sugar Land, TX	8,266
10	Boston-Cambridge-Newton, MA-NH	4,875,390	62	10	Bakersfield, CA	8,132
11	Phoenix-Mesa-Scottsdale, AZ	4,857,962	28	11	Las Vegas-Henderson-Paradise, NV	7,892
12	San Francisco-Oakland-Hayward, CA	4,729,484	20	12	St. Louis, MO-IL	7,864
13	Riverside-San Bernardino-Ontario, CA	4,622,361	47	13	Salt Lake City, UT	7,684
14	Detroit-Warren-Dearborn, MI	4,326,442	16	14	Minneapolis-St. Paul-Bloomington, MN	7,636
15	Seattle-Tacoma-Bellevue, WA	3,939,363	24	15	San Antonio-New Braunfels, TX	7,313
16	Minneapolis-St. Paul-Bloomington, MN	3,629,190	31	16	Kansas City, MO-KS	7,257
17	San Diego-Carlsbad, CA	3,343,364	3	17	Chicago-Naperville-Elgin, IL-IN-WI	7,195
18	Tampa-St. Petersburg-Clearwater, FL	3,142,663	25	18	Portland-Vancouver-Hillsboro, OR-WA	6,687
19	Denver-Aurora-Lakewood, CO	2,932,415	36	19	Nashville-Davidson--Murfreesboro--Franklin, TN	6,302
20	St. Louis, MO-IL	2,805,465	55	20	Tulsa, OK	6,270
21	Baltimore-Columbia-Towson, MD	2,802,789	6	21	Washington-Arlington-Alexandria, DC-VA-MD-WV	6,247
22	Orlando-Kissimmee-Sanford, FL	2,572,962	54	22	Fresno, CA	5,958
23	Charlotte-Concord-Gastonia, NC-SC	2,569,213	15	23	Seattle-Tacoma-Bellevue, WA	5,870
24	San Antonio-New Braunfels, TX	2,518,036	68	24	El Paso, TX	5,584
25	Portland-Vancouver-Hillsboro, OR-WA	2,478,810	41	25	Oklahoma City, OK	5,512
26	Sacramento--Roseville--Arden-Arcade, CA	2,345,210	27	26	Pittsburgh, PA	5,282
27	Pittsburgh, PA	2,324,743	49	27	Birmingham-Hoover, AL	5,280
28	Las Vegas-Henderson-Paradise, NV	2,231,647	26	28	Sacramento--Roseville--Arden-Arcade, CA	5,095
29	Cincinnati, OH-KY-IN	2,190,209	7	29	Miami-Fort Lauderdale-West Palm Beach, FL	5,068
30	Austin-Round Rock, TX	2,168,316	23	30	Charlotte-Concord-Gastonia, NC-SC	5,065
31	Kansas City, MO-KS	2,143,651	43	31	Memphis, TN-MS-AR	4,986
32	Columbus, OH	2,106,541	2	32	Los Angeles-Long Beach-Anaheim, CA	4,851
33	Cleveland-Elyria, OH	2,057,009	32	33	Columbus, OH	4,797
34	Indianapolis-Carmel-Anderson, IN	2,048,703	8	34	Philadelphia-Camden-Wilmington, PA-NJ-DE-MD	4,603
35	San Jose-Sunnyvale-Santa Clara, CA	1,999,107	44	35	Richmond, VA	4,576
36	Nashville-Davidson--Murfreesboro--Franklin, TN	1,930,961	59	36	Omaha-Council Bluffs, NE-IA	4,347
37	Virginia Beach-Norfolk-Newport News, VA-NC	1,728,733	34	37	Indianapolis-Carmel-Anderson, IN	4,306
38	Providence-Warwick, RI-MA	1,621,337	30	38	Austin-Round Rock, TX	4,222
39	Milwaukee-Waukesha-West Allis, WI	1,576,113	17	39	San Diego-Carlsbad, CA	4,209
40	Jacksonville, FL	1,534,701	29	40	Cincinnati, OH-KY-IN	4,163
41	Oklahoma City, OK	1,396,445	71	41	Baton Rouge, LA	4,027
42	Raleigh, NC	1,362,540	14	42	Detroit-Warren-Dearborn, MI	3,890
43	Memphis, TN-MS-AR	1,350,620	70	43	Columbia, SC	3,703
44	Richmond, VA	1,306,172	45	44	Louisville/Jefferson County, KY-IN	3,579
45	Louisville/Jefferson County, KY-IN	1,297,301	63	45	Knoxville, TN	3,501
46	New Orleans-Metairie, LA	1,270,399	22	46	Orlando-Kissimmee-Sanford, FL	3,490
47	Salt Lake City, UT	1,222,540	10	47	Boston-Cambridge-Newton, MA-NH	3,487
48	Hartford-West Hartford-East Hartford, CT	1,206,300	51	48	Rochester, NY	3,266
49	Birmingham-Hoover, AL	1,151,801	46	49	New Orleans-Metairie, LA	3,203
50	Buffalo-Cheektowaga-Niagara Falls, NY	1,130,152	40	50	Jacksonville, FL	3,202
51	Rochester, NY	1,071,082	64	51	Albany-Schenectady-Troy, NY	2,812
52	Grand Rapids-Wyoming, MI	1,069,405	61	52	Greenville-Anderson-Mauldin, SC	2,710
53	Tucson, AZ	1,039,073	37	53	Virginia Beach-Norfolk-Newport News, VA-NC	2,683
54	Fresno, CA	994,400	35	54	San Jose-Sunnyvale-Santa Clara, CA	2,680
55	Tulsa, OK	993,797	52	55	Grand Rapids-Wyoming, MI	2,670
56	Urban Honolulu, HI	980,080	21	56	Baltimore-Columbia-Towson, MD	2,602
57	Worcester, MA-CT	947,866	74	57	Charleston-North Charleston, SC	2,590
58	Bridgeport-Stamford-Norwalk, CT	943,823	18	58	Tampa-St. Petersburg-Clearwater, FL	2,515
59	Omaha-Council Bluffs, NE-IA	942,198	12	59	San Francisco-Oakland-Hayward, CA	2,470
60	Albuquerque, NM	915,927	42	60	Raleigh, NC	2,118
61	Greenville-Anderson-Mauldin, SC	906,626	57	61	Worcester, MA-CT	2,024
62	Bakersfield, CA	896,764	33	62	Cleveland-Elyria, OH	1,999
63	Knoxville, TN	883,309	75	63	Greensboro-High Point, NC	1,994
64	Albany-Schenectady-Troy, NY	883,169	67	64	Oxnard-Thousand Oaks-Ventura, CA	1,843
65	McAllen-Edinburg-Mission, TX	865,939	38	65	Providence-Warwick, RI-MA	1,587
66	New Haven-Milford, CT	857,620	65	66	McAllen-Edinburg-Mission, TX	1,571
67	Oxnard-Thousand Oaks-Ventura, CA	850,967	50	67	Buffalo-Cheektowaga-Niagara Falls, NY	1,565
68	El Paso, TX	845,553	48	68	Hartford-West Hartford-East Hartford, CT	1,515
69	Allentown-Bethlehem-Easton, PA-NJ	842,913	39	69	Milwaukee-Waukesha-West Allis, WI	1,455
70	Columbia, SC	832,666	69	70	Allentown-Bethlehem-Easton, PA-NJ	1,453
71	Baton Rouge, LA	831,310	72	71	North Port-Sarasota-Bradenton, FL	1,300
72	North Port-Sarasota-Bradenton, FL	821,573	73	72	Dayton, OH	1,282
73	Dayton, OH	806,548	58	73	Bridgeport-Stamford-Norwalk, CT	625
74	Charleston-North Charleston, SC	787,643	66	74	New Haven-Milford, CT	605
75	Greensboro-High Point, NC	767,711	56	75	Urban Honolulu, HI	601

75 Largest Metropolitan Areas by 2018 Population
Selected Rankings

Population density, 2018

Population rank	Density rank	Metropolitan area	Density (per square kilometer) [col 4]
2	1	Los Angeles-Long Beach-Anaheim, CA	2,739.9
1	2	New York-Newark-Jersey City, NY-NJ-PA	2,409.3
12	3	San Francisco-Oakland-Hayward, CA	1,914.5
56	4	Urban Honolulu, HI	1,631.8
58	5	Bridgeport-Stamford-Norwalk, CT	1,510.1
66	6	New Haven-Milford, CT	1,418.7
10	7	Boston-Cambridge-Newton, MA-NH	1,398.4
8	8	Philadelphia-Camden-Wilmington, PA-NJ-DE-MD	1,324.4
3	9	Chicago-Naperville-Elgin, IL-IN-WI	1,320.2
18	10	Tampa-St. Petersburg-Clearwater, FL	1,249.6
7	11	Miami-Fort Lauderdale-West Palm Beach, FL	1,223.2
14	12	Detroit-Warren-Dearborn, MI	1,112.3
39	13	Milwaukee-Waukesha-West Allis, WI	1,083.3
21	14	Baltimore-Columbia-Towson, MD	1,077.4
33	15	Cleveland-Elyria, OH	1,028.8
38	16	Providence-Warwick, RI-MA	1,021.6
6	17	Washington-Arlington-Alexandria, DC-VA-MD-WV	1,000.5
5	18	Houston-The Woodlands-Sugar Land, TX	846.5
4	19	Dallas-Fort Worth-Arlington, TX	812.5
48	20	Hartford-West Hartford-East Hartford, CT	796.4
17	21	San Diego-Carlsbad, CA	794.4
35	22	San Jose-Sunnyvale-Santa Clara, CA	746.0
22	23	Orlando-Kissimmee-Sanford, FL	737.2
50	24	Buffalo-Cheektowaga-Niagara Falls, NY	722.1
9	25	Atlanta-Sandy Springs-Roswell, GA	685.0
15	26	Seattle-Tacoma-Bellevue, WA	671.1
37	27	Virginia Beach-Norfolk-Newport News, VA-NC	644.4
42	28	Raleigh, NC	643.3
72	29	North Port-Sarasota-Bradenton, FL	632.0
73	30	Dayton, OH	629.3
69	31	Allentown-Bethlehem-Easton, PA-NJ	580.2
65	32	McAllen-Edinburg-Mission, TX	551.2
29	33	Cincinnati, OH-KY-IN	526.2
30	34	Austin-Round Rock, TX	513.6
23	35	Charlotte-Concord-Gastonia, NC-SC	507.2
40	36	Jacksonville, FL	479.2
34	37	Indianapolis-Carmel-Anderson, IN	475.7
16	38	Minneapolis-St. Paul-Bloomington, MN	475.3
57	39	Worcester, MA-CT	468.4
67	40	Oxnard-Thousand Oaks-Ventura, CA	461.9
26	41	Sacramento--Roseville--Arden-Arcade, CA	460.3
27	42	Pittsburgh, PA	440.1
32	43	Columbus, OH	439.2
52	44	Grand Rapids-Wyoming, MI	400.5
46	45	New Orleans-Metairie, LA	396.7
75	46	Greensboro-High Point, NC	385.0
25	47	Portland-Vancouver-Hillsboro, OR-WA	370.7
45	48	Louisville/Jefferson County, KY-IN	362.5
20	49	St. Louis, MO-IL	356.8
19	50	Denver-Aurora-Lakewood, CO	351.4
24	51	San Antonio-New Braunfels, TX	344.3
61	52	Greenville-Anderson-Mauldin, SC	334.6
11	53	Phoenix-Mesa-Scottsdale, AZ	333.5
51	54	Rochester, NY	328.0
64	55	Albany-Schenectady-Troy, NY	314.1
36	56	Nashville-Davidson--Murfreesboro--Franklin, TN	306.4
74	57	Charleston-North Charleston, SC	304.1
31	58	Kansas City, MO-KS	295.4
44	59	Richmond, VA	285.5
28	60	Las Vegas-Henderson-Paradise, NV	282.8
43	61	Memphis, TN-MS-AR	270.9
41	62	Oklahoma City, OK	253.4
63	63	Knoxville, TN	252.3
70	64	Columbia, SC	224.9
49	65	Birmingham-Hoover, AL	218.2
59	66	Omaha-Council Bluffs, NE-IA	216.7
71	67	Baton Rouge, LA	206.4
13	68	Riverside-San Bernardino-Ontario, CA	169.5
54	69	Fresno, CA	166.9
47	70	Salt Lake City, UT	159.1
55	71	Tulsa, OK	158.5
68	72	El Paso, TX	151.4
53	73	Tucson, AZ	113.1
62	74	Bakersfield, CA	110.3
60	75	Albuquerque, NM	98.7

Percent population change, 2010–2018

Population rank	Percent change rank	Metropolitan area	Percent change [col 23]
30	1	Austin-Round Rock, TX	26.3
22	2	Orlando-Kissimmee-Sanford, FL	20.5
42	2	Raleigh, NC	20.5
74	4	Charleston-North Charleston, SC	18.5
5	5	Houston-The Woodlands-Sugar Land, TX	18.2
24	6	San Antonio-New Braunfels, TX	17.5
4	7	Dallas-Fort Worth-Arlington, TX	17.3
72	8	North Port-Sarasota-Bradenton, FL	17.0
11	9	Phoenix-Mesa-Scottsdale, AZ	15.9
23	9	Charlotte-Concord-Gastonia, NC-SC	15.9
36	11	Nashville-Davidson--Murfreesboro--Franklin, TN	15.6
19	12	Denver-Aurora-Lakewood, CO	15.3
15	13	Seattle-Tacoma-Bellevue, WA	14.5
28	14	Las Vegas-Henderson-Paradise, NV	14.4
40	15	Jacksonville, FL	14.1
18	16	Tampa-St. Petersburg-Clearwater, FL	12.9
9	17	Atlanta-Sandy Springs-Roswell, GA	12.5
47	18	Salt Lake City, UT	12.4
65	19	McAllen-Edinburg-Mission, TX	11.8
7	20	Miami-Fort Lauderdale-West Palm Beach, FL	11.4
25	20	Portland-Vancouver-Hillsboro, OR-WA	11.4
41	20	Oklahoma City, OK	11.4
6	23	Washington-Arlington-Alexandria, DC-VA-MD-WV	10.9
32	24	Columbus, OH	10.8
61	25	Greenville-Anderson-Mauldin, SC	10.0
13	26	Riverside-San Bernardino-Ontario, CA	9.4
12	27	San Francisco-Oakland-Hayward, CA	9.1
26	27	Sacramento--Roseville--Arden-Arcade, CA	9.1
59	29	Omaha-Council Bluffs, NE-IA	8.9
35	30	San Jose-Sunnyvale-Santa Clara, CA	8.8
34	31	Indianapolis-Carmel-Anderson, IN	8.5
70	31	Columbia, SC	8.5
16	33	Minneapolis-St. Paul-Bloomington, MN	8.4
44	34	Richmond, VA	8.1
52	34	Grand Rapids-Wyoming, MI	8.1
17	36	San Diego-Carlsbad, CA	8.0
10	37	Boston-Cambridge-Newton, MA-NH	7.1
54	38	Fresno, CA	6.9
46	39	New Orleans-Metairie, LA	6.8
62	39	Bakersfield, CA	6.8
31	41	Kansas City, MO-KS	6.7
75	42	Greensboro-High Point, NC	6.1
53	43	Tucson, AZ	6.0
55	43	Tulsa, OK	6.0
63	45	Knoxville, TN	5.4
68	46	El Paso, TX	5.2
45	47	Louisville/Jefferson County, KY-IN	5.0
2	48	Los Angeles-Long Beach-Anaheim, CA	3.6
29	48	Cincinnati, OH-KY-IN	3.6
71	48	Baton Rouge, LA	3.6
21	51	Baltimore-Columbia-Towson, MD	3.4
57	51	Worcester, MA-CT	3.4
60	53	Albuquerque, NM	3.3
67	53	Oxnard-Thousand Oaks-Ventura, CA	3.3
37	55	Virginia Beach-Norfolk-Newport News, VA-NC	3.1
58	56	Bridgeport-Stamford-Norwalk, CT	2.9
56	57	Urban Honolulu, HI	2.8
69	58	Allentown-Bethlehem-Easton, PA-NJ	2.6
8	59	Philadelphia-Camden-Wilmington, PA-NJ-DE-MD	2.2
1	60	New York-Newark-Jersey City, NY-NJ-PA	2.1
49	60	Birmingham-Hoover, AL	2.1
43	62	Memphis, TN-MS-AR	1.9
64	63	Albany-Schenectady-Troy, NY	1.4
38	64	Providence-Warwick, RI-MA	1.3
39	64	Milwaukee-Waukesha-West Allis, WI	1.3
73	66	Dayton, OH	0.9
14	67	Detroit-Warren-Dearborn, MI	0.7
20	68	St. Louis, MO-IL	0.6
3	69	Chicago-Naperville-Elgin, IL-IN-WI	0.4
48	70	Hartford-West Hartford-East Hartford, CT	-0.5
50	70	Buffalo-Cheektowaga-Niagara Falls, NY	-0.5
66	72	New Haven-Milford, CT	-0.6
51	73	Rochester, NY	-0.8
33	74	Cleveland-Elyria, OH	-1.0
27	75	Pittsburgh, PA	-1.3

75 Largest Metropolitan Areas by 2018 Population
Selected Rankings

	Percent White, not Hispanic or Latino, alone or in combination, 2018				Percent Black, not Hispanic or Latino, alone or in combination, 2018		
Popu-lation rank	White rank	Metropolitan area	Percent White [col 5]	Popu-lation rank	Black rank	Metropolitan area	Percent Black [col 6]
63	1	Knoxville, TN	88.3	43	1	Memphis, TN-MS-AR	48.1
27	2	Pittsburgh, PA	86.9	71	2	Baton Rouge, LA	36.5
64	3	Albany-Schenectady-Troy, NY	81.6	46	3	New Orleans-Metairie, LA	35.7
29	4	Cincinnati, OH-KY-IN	81.0	9	4	Atlanta-Sandy Springs-Roswell, GA	35.3
52	5	Grand Rapids-Wyoming, MI	80.5	70	5	Columbia, SC	34.8
50	6	Buffalo-Cheektowaga-Niagara Falls, NY	78.8	37	6	Virginia Beach-Norfolk-Newport News, VA-NC	32.2
57	7	Worcester, MA-CT	78.5	44	7	Richmond, VA	30.9
72	7	North Port-Sarasota-Bradenton, FL	78.5	21	8	Baltimore-Columbia-Towson, MD	30.6
73	7	Dayton, OH	78.5	49	9	Birmingham-Hoover, AL	29.7
51	10	Rochester, NY	78.1	75	10	Greensboro-High Point, NC	28.4
59	11	Omaha-Council Bluffs, NE-IA	77.9	6	11	Washington-Arlington-Alexandria, DC-VA-MD-WV	26.5
45	12	Louisville/Jefferson County, KY-IN	77.8	74	11	Charleston-North Charleston, SC	26.5
16	13	Minneapolis-St. Paul-Bloomington, MN	77.6	23	13	Charlotte-Concord-Gastonia, NC-SC	23.7
38	14	Providence-Warwick, RI-MA	77.4	14	14	Detroit-Warren-Dearborn, MI	23.2
25	15	Portland-Vancouver-Hillsboro, OR-WA	76.2	40	15	Jacksonville, FL	22.4
20	16	St. Louis, MO-IL	75.4	8	16	Philadelphia-Camden-Wilmington, PA-NJ-DE-MD	21.8
31	17	Kansas City, MO-KS	74.7	7	17	Miami-Fort Lauderdale-West Palm Beach, FL	21.1
32	17	Columbus, OH	74.7	33	18	Cleveland-Elyria, OH	21.0
61	19	Greenville-Anderson-Mauldin, SC	74.1	42	19	Raleigh, NC	20.7
34	20	Indianapolis-Carmel-Anderson, IN	74.0	20	20	St. Louis, MO-IL	19.4
36	21	Nashville-Davidson--Murfreesboro--Franklin, TN	73.9	5	21	Houston-The Woodlands-Sugar Land, TX	17.7
69	22	Allentown-Bethlehem-Easton, PA-NJ	73.7	32	22	Columbus, OH	17.5
47	23	Salt Lake City, UT	73.4	39	22	Milwaukee-Waukesha-West Allis, WI	17.5
10	24	Boston-Cambridge-Newton, MA-NH	71.8	61	22	Greenville-Anderson-Mauldin, SC	17.5
33	25	Cleveland-Elyria, OH	71.3	73	25	Dayton, OH	17.3
55	26	Tulsa, OK	70.3	3	26	Chicago-Naperville-Elgin, IL-IN-WI	17.0
48	27	Hartford-West Hartford-East Hartford, CT	68.3	22	27	Orlando-Kissimmee-Sanford, FL	16.8
41	28	Oklahoma City, OK	68.2	1	28	New York-Newark-Jersey City, NY-NJ-PA	16.7
14	29	Detroit-Warren-Dearborn, MI	68.1	34	28	Indianapolis-Carmel-Anderson, IN	16.7
39	29	Milwaukee-Waukesha-West Allis, WI	68.1	4	30	Dallas-Fort Worth-Arlington, TX	16.6
15	31	Seattle-Tacoma-Bellevue, WA	66.9	36	31	Nashville-Davidson--Murfreesboro--Franklin, TN	16.3
74	32	Charleston-North Charleston, SC	66.2	45	32	Louisville/Jefferson County, KY-IN	15.9
19	33	Denver-Aurora-Lakewood, CO	66.1	66	33	New Haven-Milford, CT	14.0
40	34	Jacksonville, FL	64.8	29	34	Cincinnati, OH-KY-IN	13.7
49	35	Birmingham-Hoover, AL	64.5	31	34	Kansas City, MO-KS	13.7
18	36	Tampa-St. Petersburg-Clearwater, FL	64.1	28	36	Las Vegas-Henderson-Paradise, NV	13.1
66	37	New Haven-Milford, CT	63.9	50	36	Buffalo-Cheektowaga-Niagara Falls, NY	13.1
8	38	Philadelphia-Camden-Wilmington, PA-NJ-DE-MD	63.1	18	38	Tampa-St. Petersburg-Clearwater, FL	12.8
42	39	Raleigh, NC	62.9	51	39	Rochester, NY	12.2
58	40	Bridgeport-Stamford-Norwalk, CT	62.8	41	40	Oklahoma City, OK	12.1
23	41	Charlotte-Concord-Gastonia, NC-SC	62.3	48	41	Hartford-West Hartford-East Hartford, CT	11.9
75	42	Greensboro-High Point, NC	59.5	58	42	Bridgeport-Stamford-Norwalk, CT	11.7
44	43	Richmond, VA	59.1	16	43	Minneapolis-St. Paul-Bloomington, MN	10.1
21	44	Baltimore-Columbia-Towson, MD	58.2	55	44	Tulsa, OK	9.7
70	45	Columbia, SC	57.8	27	45	Pittsburgh, PA	9.6
37	46	Virginia Beach-Norfolk-Newport News, VA-NC	57.7	64	46	Albany-Schenectady-Troy, NY	9.4
71	47	Baton Rouge, LA	57.5	59	47	Omaha-Council Bluffs, NE-IA	8.9
11	48	Phoenix-Mesa-Scottsdale, AZ	57.0	10	48	Boston-Cambridge-Newton, MA-NH	8.7
26	49	Sacramento--Roseville--Arden-Arcade, CA	55.5	26	49	Sacramento--Roseville--Arden-Arcade, CA	8.6
3	50	Chicago-Naperville-Elgin, IL-IN-WI	54.0	12	50	San Francisco-Oakland-Hayward, CA	8.3
30	51	Austin-Round Rock, TX	53.6	13	51	Riverside-San Bernardino-Ontario, CA	8.0
53	52	Tucson, AZ	53.2	30	52	Austin-Round Rock, TX	7.8
46	53	New Orleans-Metairie, LA	52.7	52	52	Grand Rapids-Wyoming, MI	7.8
9	54	Atlanta-Sandy Springs-Roswell, GA	48.3	15	54	Seattle-Tacoma-Bellevue, WA	7.6
17	55	San Diego-Carlsbad, CA	48.1	24	55	San Antonio-New Braunfels, TX	7.2
22	56	Orlando-Kissimmee-Sanford, FL	47.7	2	56	Los Angeles-Long Beach-Anaheim, CA	7.1
1	57	New York-Newark-Jersey City, NY-NJ-PA	47.6	72	56	North Port-Sarasota-Bradenton, FL	7.1
6	58	Washington-Arlington-Alexandria, DC-VA-MD-WV	47.5	38	58	Providence-Warwick, RI-MA	6.7
4	59	Dallas-Fort Worth-Arlington, TX	47.4	63	58	Knoxville, TN	6.7
67	60	Oxnard-Thousand Oaks-Ventura, CA	47.2	19	60	Denver-Aurora-Lakewood, CO	6.5
28	61	Las Vegas-Henderson-Paradise, NV	45.3	11	61	Phoenix-Mesa-Scottsdale, AZ	6.3
43	62	Memphis, TN-MS-AR	44.4	69	62	Allentown-Bethlehem-Easton, PA-NJ	6.2
12	63	San Francisco-Oakland-Hayward, CA	42.6	62	63	Bakersfield, CA	5.9
60	64	Albuquerque, NM	40.4	17	64	San Diego-Carlsbad, CA	5.7
5	65	Houston-The Woodlands-Sugar Land, TX	36.9	54	65	Fresno, CA	5.3
62	66	Bakersfield, CA	35.2	57	65	Worcester, MA-CT	5.3
24	67	San Antonio-New Braunfels, TX	34.7	53	67	Tucson, AZ	4.2
35	68	San Jose-Sunnyvale-Santa Clara, CA	33.8	25	68	Portland-Vancouver-Hillsboro, OR-WA	4.1
13	69	Riverside-San Bernardino-Ontario, CA	33.5	56	69	Urban Honolulu, HI	3.7
56	70	Urban Honolulu, HI	31.8	68	70	El Paso, TX	3.4
2	71	Los Angeles-Long Beach-Anaheim, CA	31.4	35	71	San Jose-Sunnyvale-Santa Clara, CA	2.9
7	72	Miami-Fort Lauderdale-West Palm Beach, FL	30.8	60	71	Albuquerque, NM	2.9
54	73	Fresno, CA	30.7	47	73	Salt Lake City, UT	2.3
68	74	El Paso, TX	12.4	67	73	Oxnard-Thousand Oaks-Ventura, CA	2.3
65	75	McAllen-Edinburg-Mission, TX	6.2	65	75	McAllen-Edinburg-Mission, TX	0.5

75 Largest Metropolitan Areas by 2018 Population
Selected Rankings

	Percent American Indian, Alaska Native, alone or in combination, 2018				Percent Asian and Pacific Islander, alone or in combination, 2018		
Population rank	American Indian Alaska native rank	Metropolitan area	Percent American Indian, Alaska Native [col 7]	Population rank	Asian and Pacific Islander rank	Metropolitan area	Percent Asian and Pacific Islander [col 8]
55	1	Tulsa, OK	13.0	56	1	Urban Honolulu, HI	78.6
41	2	Oklahoma City, OK	6.8	35	2	San Jose-Sunnyvale-Santa Clara, CA	39.4
60	3	Albuquerque, NM	6.1	12	3	San Francisco-Oakland-Hayward, CA	30.7
53	4	Tucson, AZ	3.0	15	4	Seattle-Tacoma-Bellevue, WA	18.6
11	5	Phoenix-Mesa-Scottsdale, AZ	2.5	2	5	Los Angeles-Long Beach-Anaheim, CA	18.1
15	6	Seattle-Tacoma-Bellevue, WA	2.0	26	6	Sacramento--Roseville--Arden-Arcade, CA	17.4
25	7	Portland-Vancouver-Hillsboro, OR-WA	1.7	17	7	San Diego-Carlsbad, CA	14.9
26	8	Sacramento--Roseville--Arden-Arcade, CA	1.5	28	8	Las Vegas-Henderson-Paradise, NV	13.2
56	8	Urban Honolulu, HI	1.5	1	9	New York-Newark-Jersey City, NY-NJ-PA	12.3
16	10	Minneapolis-St. Paul-Bloomington, MN	1.3	6	10	Washington-Arlington-Alexandria, DC-VA-MD-WV	12.2
31	11	Kansas City, MO-KS	1.2	54	11	Fresno, CA	11.5
62	11	Bakersfield, CA	1.2	25	12	Portland-Vancouver-Hillsboro, OR-WA	9.8
19	13	Denver-Aurora-Lakewood, CO	1.1	10	13	Boston-Cambridge-Newton, MA-NH	9.4
28	13	Las Vegas-Henderson-Paradise, NV	1.1	67	14	Oxnard-Thousand Oaks-Ventura, CA	9.2
37	13	Virginia Beach-Norfolk-Newport News, VA-NC	1.1	5	15	Houston-The Woodlands-Sugar Land, TX	8.7
47	13	Salt Lake City, UT	1.1	13	16	Riverside-San Bernardino-Ontario, CA	8.4
50	13	Buffalo-Cheektowaga-Niagara Falls, NY	1.1	4	17	Dallas-Fort Worth-Arlington, TX	8.0
54	13	Fresno, CA	1.1	16	18	Minneapolis-St. Paul-Bloomington, MN	7.9
75	13	Greensboro-High Point, NC	1.1	3	19	Chicago-Naperville-Elgin, IL-IN-WI	7.8
59	20	Omaha-Council Bluffs, NE-IA	1.0	30	20	Austin-Round Rock, TX	7.3
74	20	Charleston-North Charleston, SC	1.0	47	20	Salt Lake City, UT	7.3
4	22	Dallas-Fort Worth-Arlington, TX	0.9	8	22	Philadelphia-Camden-Wilmington, PA-NJ-DE-MD	7.0
13	22	Riverside-San Bernardino-Ontario, CA	0.9	9	22	Atlanta-Sandy Springs-Roswell, GA	7.0
14	22	Detroit-Warren-Dearborn, MI	0.9	42	22	Raleigh, NC	7.0
17	22	San Diego-Carlsbad, CA	0.9	21	25	Baltimore-Columbia-Towson, MD	6.9
23	22	Charlotte-Concord-Gastonia, NC-SC	0.9	58	26	Bridgeport-Stamford-Norwalk, CT	6.5
38	22	Providence-Warwick, RI-MA	0.9	48	27	Hartford-West Hartford-East Hartford, CT	5.9
39	22	Milwaukee-Waukesha-West Allis, WI	0.9	62	28	Bakersfield, CA	5.8
42	22	Raleigh, NC	0.9	19	29	Denver-Aurora-Lakewood, CO	5.7
44	22	Richmond, VA	0.9	37	30	Virginia Beach-Norfolk-Newport News, VA-NC	5.6
46	22	New Orleans-Metairie, LA	0.9	14	31	Detroit-Warren-Dearborn, MI	5.5
52	22	Grand Rapids-Wyoming, MI	0.9	57	31	Worcester, MA-CT	5.5
63	22	Knoxville, TN	0.9	64	31	Albany-Schenectady-Troy, NY	5.5
73	22	Dayton, OH	0.9	22	34	Orlando-Kissimmee-Sanford, FL	5.4
6	35	Washington-Arlington-Alexandria, DC-VA-MD-WV	0.8	32	34	Columbus, OH	5.4
12	35	San Francisco-Oakland-Hayward, CA	0.8	11	36	Phoenix-Mesa-Scottsdale, AZ	5.3
21	35	Baltimore-Columbia-Towson, MD	0.8	40	36	Jacksonville, FL	5.3
30	35	Austin-Round Rock, TX	0.8	44	38	Richmond, VA	4.9
32	35	Columbus, OH	0.8	66	39	New Haven-Milford, CT	4.8
36	35	Nashville-Davidson--Murfreesboro--Franklin, TN	0.8	23	40	Charlotte-Concord-Gastonia, NC-SC	4.6
40	35	Jacksonville, FL	0.8	39	40	Milwaukee-Waukesha-West Allis, WI	4.6
67	35	Oxnard-Thousand Oaks-Ventura, CA	0.8	75	40	Greensboro-High Point, NC	4.6
70	35	Columbia, SC	0.8	18	43	Tampa-St. Petersburg-Clearwater, FL	4.5
9	44	Atlanta-Sandy Springs-Roswell, GA	0.7	41	44	Oklahoma City, OK	4.3
18	44	Tampa-St. Petersburg-Clearwater, FL	0.7	53	45	Tucson, AZ	4.2
20	44	St. Louis, MO-IL	0.7	34	46	Indianapolis-Carmel-Anderson, IN	4.1
35	44	San Jose-Sunnyvale-Santa Clara, CA	0.7	31	47	Kansas City, MO-KS	4.0
45	44	Louisville/Jefferson County, KY-IN	0.7	59	47	Omaha-Council Bluffs, NE-IA	4.0
49	44	Birmingham-Hoover, AL	0.7	38	49	Providence-Warwick, RI-MA	3.9
51	44	Rochester, NY	0.7	50	50	Buffalo-Cheektowaga-Niagara Falls, NY	3.8
2	51	Los Angeles-Long Beach-Anaheim, CA	0.6	36	51	Nashville-Davidson--Murfreesboro--Franklin, TN	3.6
5	51	Houston-The Woodlands-Sugar Land, TX	0.6	51	51	Rochester, NY	3.6
8	51	Philadelphia-Camden-Wilmington, PA-NJ-DE-MD	0.6	69	51	Allentown-Bethlehem-Easton, PA-NJ	3.6
22	51	Orlando-Kissimmee-Sanford, FL	0.6	52	54	Grand Rapids-Wyoming, MI	3.5
24	51	San Antonio-New Braunfels, TX	0.6	20	55	St. Louis, MO-IL	3.4
29	51	Cincinnati, OH-KY-IN	0.6	24	55	San Antonio-New Braunfels, TX	3.4
33	51	Cleveland-Elyria, OH	0.6	29	55	Cincinnati, OH-KY-IN	3.4
34	51	Indianapolis-Carmel-Anderson, IN	0.6	46	55	New Orleans-Metairie, LA	3.4
43	51	Memphis, TN-MS-AR	0.6	55	59	Tulsa, OK	3.3
48	51	Hartford-West Hartford-East Hartford, CT	0.6	7	60	Miami-Fort Lauderdale-West Palm Beach, FL	3.2
57	51	Worcester, MA-CT	0.6	73	60	Dayton, OH	3.2
61	51	Greenville-Anderson-Mauldin, SC	0.6	27	62	Pittsburgh, PA	3.1
64	51	Albany-Schenectady-Troy, NY	0.6	60	62	Albuquerque, NM	3.1
66	51	New Haven-Milford, CT	0.6	33	64	Cleveland-Elyria, OH	3.0
71	51	Baton Rouge, LA	0.6	70	64	Columbia, SC	3.0
72	51	North Port-Sarasota-Bradenton, FL	0.6	74	66	Charleston-North Charleston, SC	2.9
1	67	New York-Newark-Jersey City, NY-NJ-PA	0.5	45	67	Louisville/Jefferson County, KY-IN	2.8
3	67	Chicago-Naperville-Elgin, IL-IN-WI	0.5	43	68	Memphis, TN-MS-AR	2.6
10	67	Boston-Cambridge-Newton, MA-NH	0.5	61	69	Greenville-Anderson-Mauldin, SC	2.5
27	67	Pittsburgh, PA	0.5	71	69	Baton Rouge, LA	2.5
68	67	El Paso, TX	0.5	72	69	North Port-Sarasota-Bradenton, FL	2.5
69	67	Allentown-Bethlehem-Easton, PA-NJ	0.5	63	72	Knoxville, TN	2.1
58	73	Bridgeport-Stamford-Norwalk, CT	0.4	49	73	Birmingham-Hoover, AL	1.9
7	74	Miami-Fort Lauderdale-West Palm Beach, FL	0.3	68	74	El Paso, TX	1.7
65	75	McAllen-Edinburg-Mission, TX	0.1	65	75	McAllen-Edinburg-Mission, TX	1.0

75 Largest Metropolitan Areas by 2018 Population
Selected Rankings

Percent Hispanic or Latino,[1] 2018				Percent under 18 years old, 2018			
Population rank	Hispanic or Latino rank	Metropolitan area	Percent Hispanic or Latino [col 9]	Population rank	Under 18 years old rank	Metropolitan area	Percent Under 18 years old [cols 10 and 11]
65	1	McAllen-Edinburg-Mission, TX	92.4	65	1	McAllen-Edinburg-Mission, TX	32.5
68	2	El Paso, TX	82.9	62	2	Bakersfield, CA	28.9
24	3	San Antonio-New Braunfels, TX	55.6	54	3	Fresno, CA	28.4
62	4	Bakersfield, CA	54.0	47	4	Salt Lake City, UT	27.4
54	5	Fresno, CA	53.5	68	5	El Paso, TX	27.1
13	6	Riverside-San Bernardino-Ontario, CA	51.6	5	6	Houston-The Woodlands-Sugar Land, TX	26.6
60	7	Albuquerque, NM	49.4	4	7	Dallas-Fort Worth-Arlington, TX	25.9
7	8	Miami-Fort Lauderdale-West Palm Beach, FL	45.8	13	8	Riverside-San Bernardino-Ontario, CA	25.7
2	9	Los Angeles-Long Beach-Anaheim, CA	45.2	59	9	Omaha-Council Bluffs, NE-IA	25.6
67	10	Oxnard-Thousand Oaks-Ventura, CA	43.0	24	10	San Antonio-New Braunfels, TX	25.2
5	11	Houston-The Woodlands-Sugar Land, TX	37.6	41	11	Oklahoma City, OK	24.7
53	11	Tucson, AZ	37.6	43	11	Memphis, TN-MS-AR	24.7
17	13	San Diego-Carlsbad, CA	34.0	55	11	Tulsa, OK	24.7
30	14	Austin-Round Rock, TX	32.7	34	14	Indianapolis-Carmel-Anderson, IN	24.6
22	15	Orlando-Kissimmee-Sanford, FL	31.5	9	15	Atlanta-Sandy Springs-Roswell, GA	24.4
28	16	Las Vegas-Henderson-Paradise, NV	31.4	31	16	Kansas City, MO-KS	24.2
11	17	Phoenix-Mesa-Scottsdale, AZ	31.2	42	17	Raleigh, NC	24.1
4	18	Dallas-Fort Worth-Arlington, TX	29.0	52	18	Grand Rapids-Wyoming, MI	23.9
35	19	San Jose-Sunnyvale-Santa Clara, CA	26.4	11	19	Phoenix-Mesa-Scottsdale, AZ	23.8
1	20	New York-Newark-Jersey City, NY-NJ-PA	24.6	16	20	Minneapolis-St. Paul-Bloomington, MN	23.7
19	21	Denver-Aurora-Lakewood, CO	23.2	23	20	Charlotte-Concord-Gastonia, NC-SC	23.7
3	22	Chicago-Naperville-Elgin, IL-IN-WI	22.4	32	22	Columbus, OH	23.5
12	23	San Francisco-Oakland-Hayward, CA	21.9	29	23	Cincinnati, OH-KY-IN	23.4
26	24	Sacramento--Roseville--Arden-Arcade, CA	21.8	71	23	Baton Rouge, LA	23.4
58	25	Bridgeport-Stamford-Norwalk, CT	20.2	28	25	Las Vegas-Henderson-Paradise, NV	23.2
18	26	Tampa-St. Petersburg-Clearwater, FL	20.0	30	26	Austin-Round Rock, TX	23.1
66	27	New Haven-Milford, CT	18.6	36	26	Nashville-Davidson--Murfreesboro--Franklin, TN	23.1
47	28	Salt Lake City, UT	18.2	6	28	Washington-Arlington-Alexandria, DC-VA-MD-WV	23.0
69	29	Allentown-Bethlehem-Easton, PA-NJ	17.7	39	28	Milwaukee-Waukesha-West Allis, WI	23.0
6	30	Washington-Arlington-Alexandria, DC-VA-MD-WV	16.1	49	30	Birmingham-Hoover, AL	22.9
48	31	Hartford-West Hartford-East Hartford, CT	15.2	67	30	Oxnard-Thousand Oaks-Ventura, CA	22.9
41	32	Oklahoma City, OK	13.7	26	32	Sacramento--Roseville--Arden-Arcade, CA	22.8
38	33	Providence-Warwick, RI-MA	13.3	3	33	Chicago-Naperville-Elgin, IL-IN-WI	22.7
72	34	North Port-Sarasota-Bradenton, FL	12.9	19	34	Denver-Aurora-Lakewood, CO	22.5
25	35	Portland-Vancouver-Hillsboro, OR-WA	12.2	45	34	Louisville/Jefferson County, KY-IN	22.5
57	36	Worcester, MA-CT	12.0	58	34	Bridgeport-Stamford-Norwalk, CT	22.5
10	37	Boston-Cambridge-Newton, MA-NH	11.5	40	37	Jacksonville, FL	22.4
9	38	Atlanta-Sandy Springs-Roswell, GA	10.9	61	37	Greenville-Anderson-Mauldin, SC	22.4
39	38	Milwaukee-Waukesha-West Allis, WI	10.9	46	39	New Orleans-Metairie, LA	22.3
42	40	Raleigh, NC	10.8	20	40	St. Louis, MO-IL	22.2
59	41	Omaha-Council Bluffs, NE-IA	10.7	14	41	Detroit-Warren-Dearborn, MI	22.1
23	42	Charlotte-Concord-Gastonia, NC-SC	10.5	35	41	San Jose-Sunnyvale-Santa Clara, CA	22.1
15	43	Seattle-Tacoma-Bellevue, WA	10.2	60	41	Albuquerque, NM	22.1
55	43	Tulsa, OK	10.2	75	41	Greensboro-High Point, NC	22.1
56	45	Urban Honolulu, HI	10.0	37	45	Virginia Beach-Norfolk-Newport News, VA-NC	22.0
8	46	Philadelphia-Camden-Wilmington, PA-NJ-DE-MD	9.7	70	45	Columbia, SC	22.0
52	46	Grand Rapids-Wyoming, MI	9.7	21	47	Baltimore-Columbia-Towson, MD	21.9
31	48	Kansas City, MO-KS	9.2	73	47	Dayton, OH	21.9
40	48	Jacksonville, FL	9.2	2	49	Los Angeles-Long Beach-Anaheim, CA	21.8
46	50	New Orleans-Metairie, LA	9.0	22	49	Orlando-Kissimmee-Sanford, FL	21.8
75	51	Greensboro-High Point, NC	8.6	74	49	Charleston-North Charleston, SC	21.8
51	52	Rochester, NY	7.6	8	52	Philadelphia-Camden-Wilmington, PA-NJ-DE-MD	21.7
36	53	Nashville-Davidson--Murfreesboro--Franklin, TN	7.5	17	53	San Diego-Carlsbad, CA	21.6
37	54	Virginia Beach-Norfolk-Newport News, VA-NC	7.0	44	53	Richmond, VA	21.6
61	54	Greenville-Anderson-Mauldin, SC	7.0	1	55	New York-Newark-Jersey City, NY-NJ-PA	21.4
34	56	Indianapolis-Carmel-Anderson, IN	6.9	15	55	Seattle-Tacoma-Bellevue, WA	21.4
44	57	Richmond, VA	6.5	25	55	Portland-Vancouver-Hillsboro, OR-WA	21.4
21	58	Baltimore-Columbia-Towson, MD	6.1	56	58	Urban Honolulu, HI	21.2
16	59	Minneapolis-St. Paul-Bloomington, MN	6.0	33	59	Cleveland-Elyria, OH	21.1
33	59	Cleveland-Elyria, OH	6.0	69	59	Allentown-Bethlehem-Easton, PA-NJ	21.1
43	61	Memphis, TN-MS-AR	5.7	57	61	Worcester, MA-CT	20.9
70	61	Columbia, SC	5.7	53	62	Tucson, AZ	20.8
74	61	Charleston-North Charleston, SC	5.7	63	63	Knoxville, TN	20.6
64	64	Albany-Schenectady-Troy, NY	5.4	51	64	Rochester, NY	20.5
50	65	Buffalo-Cheektowaga-Niagara Falls, NY	5.2	7	65	Miami-Fort Lauderdale-West Palm Beach, FL	20.2
45	66	Louisville/Jefferson County, KY-IN	5.0	50	65	Buffalo-Cheektowaga-Niagara Falls, NY	20.2
14	67	Detroit-Warren-Dearborn, MI	4.6	66	67	New Haven-Milford, CT	20.1
49	68	Birmingham-Hoover, AL	4.5	48	68	Hartford-West Hartford-East Hartford, CT	20.0
32	69	Columbus, OH	4.3	18	69	Tampa-St. Petersburg-Clearwater, FL	19.9
71	70	Baton Rouge, LA	4.1	10	70	Boston-Cambridge-Newton, MA-NH	19.8
63	71	Knoxville, TN	4.0	38	70	Providence-Warwick, RI-MA	19.8
29	72	Cincinnati, OH-KY-IN	3.4	12	72	San Francisco-Oakland-Hayward, CA	19.7
20	73	St. Louis, MO-IL	3.1	64	73	Albany-Schenectady-Troy, NY	19.6
73	74	Dayton, OH	2.9	27	74	Pittsburgh, PA	18.9
27	75	Pittsburgh, PA	1.8	72	75	North Port-Sarasota-Bradenton, FL	16.2

75 Largest Metropolitan Areas by 2018 Population
Selected Rankings

		Percent 65 years old and over, 2018					Percent female-headed family households, 2017	
Popu-lation rank	65 years old and over rank	Metropolitan area	Percent 65 years old and over [cols 17 + 18]	Popu-lation rank	Female house-holds rank	Metropolitan area	Percent female house-holds [col 30]
72	1	North Port-Sarasota-Bradenton, FL............	32.2	65	1	McAllen-Edinburg-Mission, TX........................	22.4
27	2	Pittsburgh, PA...	20.0	68	2	El Paso, TX..	20.3
18	3	Tampa-St. Petersburg-Clearwater, FL......	19.7	43	3	Memphis, TN-MS-AR.....................................	17.6
53	3	Tucson, AZ...	19.7	54	4	Fresno, CA...	17.1
33	5	Cleveland-Elyria, OH...............................	18.4	71	5	Baton Rouge, LA...	16.5
63	5	Knoxville, TN...	18.4	46	6	New Orleans-Metairie, LA..............................	16.2
7	7	Miami-Fort Lauderdale-West Palm Beach, FL.	18.2	62	6	Bakersfield, CA...	16.2
50	7	Buffalo-Cheektowaga-Niagara Falls, NY..	18.2	70	8	Columbia, SC..	15.6
69	9	Allentown-Bethlehem-Easton, PA-NJ........	18.1	7	9	Miami-Fort Lauderdale-West Palm Beach, FL..	15.3
51	10	Rochester, NY..	17.8	49	10	Birmingham-Hoover, AL.................................	15.0
73	10	Dayton, OH...	17.8	9	11	Atlanta-Sandy Springs-Roswell, GA...............	14.7
56	12	Urban Honolulu, HI.................................	17.7	13	12	Riverside-San Bernardino-Ontario, CA...........	14.6
48	13	Hartford-West Hartford-East Hartford, CT.	17.4	24	12	San Antonio-New Braunfels, TX.....................	14.6
64	13	Albany-Schenectady-Troy, NY..................	17.4	37	12	Virginia Beach-Norfolk-Newport News, VA-NC.	14.6
66	13	New Haven-Milford, CT............................	17.4	1	15	New York-Newark-Jersey City, NY-NJ-PA......	14.4
38	16	Providence-Warwick, RI-MA.....................	17.1	28	16	Las Vegas-Henderson-Paradise, NV..............	14.3
60	17	Albuquerque, NM....................................	16.8	5	17	Houston-The Woodlands-Sugar Land, TX.......	14.1
61	18	Greenville-Anderson-Mauldin, SC............	16.6	21	17	Baltimore-Columbia-Towson, MD...................	14.1
20	19	St. Louis, MO-IL.....................................	16.5	44	17	Richmond, VA...	14.1
14	20	Detroit-Warren-Dearborn, MI....................	16.4	66	17	New Haven-Milford, CT..................................	14.1
75	21	Greensboro-High Point, NC......................	16.3	40	21	Jacksonville, FL..	14.0
49	22	Birmingham-Hoover, AL...........................	16.1	2	22	Los Angeles-Long Beach-Anaheim, CA..........	13.9
8	23	Philadelphia-Camden-Wilmington, PA-NJ-DE-MD	16.0	14	23	Detroit-Warren-Dearborn, MI.........................	13.7
45	23	Louisville/Jefferson County, KY-IN...........	16.0	51	23	Rochester, NY..	13.7
58	25	Bridgeport-Stamford-Norwalk, CT............	15.9	75	23	Greensboro-High Point, NC............................	13.7
40	26	Jacksonville, FL......................................	15.8	22	26	Orlando-Kissimmee-Sanford, FL....................	13.6
46	26	New Orleans-Metairie, LA........................	15.8	33	27	Cleveland-Elyria, OH....................................	13.5
57	26	Worcester, MA-CT...................................	15.8	50	28	Buffalo-Cheektowaga-Niagara Falls, NY........	13.4
1	29	New York-Newark-Jersey City, NY-NJ-PA.	15.7	55	28	Tulsa, OK..	13.4
10	29	Boston-Cambridge-Newton, MA-NH..........	15.7	56	30	Urban Honolulu, HI.......................................	13.2
11	31	Phoenix-Mesa-Scottsdale, AZ..................	15.6	8	31	Philadelphia-Camden-Wilmington, PA-NJ-DE-MD	13.1
21	31	Baltimore-Columbia-Towson, MD.............	15.6	4	32	Dallas-Fort Worth-Arlington, TX....................	13.0
39	31	Milwaukee-Waukesha-West Allis, WI........	15.6	38	32	Providence-Warwick, RI-MA..........................	13.0
67	31	Oxnard-Thousand Oaks-Ventura, CA.........	15.6	61	32	Greenville-Anderson-Mauldin, SC..................	13.0
26	35	Sacramento--Roseville--Arden-Arcade, CA.	15.5	73	32	Dayton, OH..	13.0
44	35	Richmond, VA..	15.5	3	36	Chicago-Naperville-Elgin, IL-IN-WI.................	12.8
55	35	Tulsa, OK...	15.5	74	36	Charleston-North Charleston, SC...................	12.8
12	38	San Francisco-Oakland-Hayward, CA........	15.4	32	38	Columbus, OH..	12.7
29	39	Cincinnati, OH-KY-IN...............................	15.2	45	38	Louisville/Jefferson County, KY-IN.................	12.7
74	39	Charleston-North Charleston, SC.............	15.2	60	38	Albuquerque, NM...	12.7
25	41	Portland-Vancouver-Hillsboro, OR-WA......	14.9	39	41	Milwaukee-Waukesha-West Allis, WI.............	12.6
22	42	Orlando-Kissimmee-Sanford, FL..............	14.8	20	42	St. Louis, MO-IL...	12.4
28	42	Las Vegas-Henderson-Paradise, NV.........	14.8	23	42	Charlotte-Concord-Gastonia, NC-SC..............	12.4
31	42	Kansas City, MO-KS................................	14.8	26	42	Sacramento--Roseville--Arden-Arcade, CA.....	12.4
70	42	Columbia, SC..	14.8	53	42	Tucson, AZ..	12.4
3	46	Chicago-Naperville-Elgin, IL-IN-WI...........	14.6	17	46	San Diego-Carlsbad, CA................................	12.3
37	46	Virginia Beach-Norfolk-Newport News, VA-NC.	14.6	57	46	Worcester, MA-CT..	12.3
52	48	Grand Rapids-Wyoming, MI......................	14.5	18	48	Tampa-St. Petersburg-Clearwater, FL............	12.2
16	49	Minneapolis-St. Paul-Bloomington, MN.....	14.0	48	48	Hartford-West Hartford-East Hartford, CT.......	12.2
17	49	San Diego-Carlsbad, CA..........................	14.0	67	48	Oxnard-Thousand Oaks-Ventura, CA..............	12.2
43	49	Memphis, TN-MS-AR...............................	14.0	29	51	Cincinnati, OH-KY-IN....................................	12.1
71	49	Baton Rouge, LA.....................................	14.0	41	51	Oklahoma City, OK.......................................	12.1
2	53	Los Angeles-Long Beach-Anaheim, CA.....	13.9	6	53	Washington-Arlington-Alexandria, DC-VA-MD-WV	11.9
41	53	Oklahoma City, OK..................................	13.9	11	53	Phoenix-Mesa-Scottsdale, AZ........................	11.9
34	55	Indianapolis-Carmel-Anderson, IN............	13.7	34	53	Indianapolis-Carmel-Anderson, IN..................	11.9
59	55	Omaha-Council Bluffs, NE-IA...................	13.7	36	53	Nashville-Davidson--Murfreesboro--Franklin, TN	11.9
23	57	Charlotte-Concord-Gastonia, NC-SC.........	13.6	63	57	Knoxville, TN...	11.6
15	58	Seattle-Tacoma-Bellevue, WA..................	13.4	69	57	Allentown-Bethlehem-Easton, PA-NJ..............	11.6
35	58	San Jose-Sunnyvale-Santa Clara, CA.......	13.4	42	59	Raleigh, NC...	11.5
32	60	Columbus, OH..	13.3	58	59	Bridgeport-Stamford-Norwalk, CT...................	11.5
36	60	Nashville-Davidson--Murfreesboro--Franklin, TN	13.3	31	61	Kansas City, MO-KS.....................................	11.3
13	62	Riverside-San Bernardino-Ontario, CA......	13.1	10	62	Boston-Cambridge-Newton, MA-NH................	11.2
6	63	Washington-Arlington-Alexandria, DC-VA-MD-WV	13.0	12	63	San Francisco-Oakland-Hayward, CA..............	10.8
19	63	Denver-Aurora-Lakewood, CO..................	13.0	52	64	Grand Rapids-Wyoming, MI...........................	10.3
24	63	San Antonio-New Braunfels, TX...............	13.0	27	65	Pittsburgh, PA...	10.1
54	66	Fresno, CA...	12.3	35	65	San Jose-Sunnyvale-Santa Clara, CA............	10.1
68	66	El Paso, TX..	12.3	59	65	Omaha-Council Bluffs, NE-IA.........................	10.1
9	68	Atlanta-Sandy Springs-Roswell, GA.........	12.2	64	65	Albany-Schenectady-Troy, NY........................	10.1
42	68	Raleigh, NC..	12.2	19	69	Denver-Aurora-Lakewood, CO.......................	10.0
4	70	Dallas-Fort Worth-Arlington, TX...............	11.3	47	69	Salt Lake City, UT..	10.0
5	71	Houston-The Woodlands-Sugar Land, TX..	11.1	16	71	Minneapolis-St. Paul-Bloomington, MN...........	9.5
65	71	McAllen-Edinburg-Mission, TX..................	11.1	25	72	Portland-Vancouver-Hillsboro, OR-WA............	9.4
30	73	Austin-Round Rock, TX...........................	10.9	30	72	Austin-Round Rock, TX.................................	9.4
62	73	Bakersfield, CA.......................................	10.9	15	74	Seattle-Tacoma-Bellevue, WA........................	9.1
47	75	Salt Lake City, UT...................................	10.8	72	75	North Port-Sarasota-Bradenton, FL.................	8.4

75 Largest Metropolitan Areas by 2018 Population
Selected Rankings

Birth rate, 2018				Percent under 65 who have no health insurance, 2017			
Population rank	Birth rate rank	Metropolitan area	Births (per 1,000 population) [col 36]	Population rank	No health insurance rank	Metropolitan area	Percent with no health insurance [col 40]
65	1	McAllen-Edinburg-Mission, TX	16.8	65	1	McAllen-Edinburg-Mission, TX	31.2
47	2	Salt Lake City, UT	15.0	68	2	El Paso, TX	22.6
62	2	Bakersfield, CA	15.0	5	3	Houston-The Woodlands-Sugar Land, TX	20.0
54	4	Fresno, CA	14.9	4	4	Dallas-Fort Worth-Arlington, TX	18.4
68	5	El Paso, TX	14.7	7	4	Miami-Fort Lauderdale-West Palm Beach, FL	18.4
5	6	Houston-The Woodlands-Sugar Land, TX	14.2	24	6	San Antonio-New Braunfels, TX	16.6
59	7	Omaha-Council Bluffs, NE-IA	14.0	72	7	North Port-Sarasota-Bradenton, FL	16.2
4	8	Dallas-Fort Worth-Arlington, TX	13.5	55	8	Tulsa, OK	15.4
24	9	San Antonio-New Braunfels, TX	13.3	41	9	Oklahoma City, OK	15.0
41	10	Oklahoma City, OK	13.2	9	10	Atlanta-Sandy Springs-Roswell, GA	14.9
13	11	Riverside-San Bernardino-Ontario, CA	13.1	22	11	Orlando-Kissimmee-Sanford, FL	14.7
43	11	Memphis, TN-MS-AR	13.1	18	12	Tampa-St. Petersburg-Clearwater, FL	14.5
55	11	Tulsa, OK	13.1	30	13	Austin-Round Rock, TX	14.4
71	14	Baton Rouge, LA	13.0	28	14	Las Vegas-Henderson-Paradise, NV	13.3
32	15	Columbus, OH	12.9	61	15	Greenville-Anderson-Mauldin, SC	13.2
6	16	Washington-Arlington-Alexandria, DC-VA-MD-WV	12.8	74	16	Charleston-North Charleston, SC	12.6
34	16	Indianapolis-Carmel-Anderson, IN	12.8	75	16	Greensboro-High Point, NC	12.6
31	18	Kansas City, MO-KS	12.6	40	18	Jacksonville, FL	12.5
52	18	Grand Rapids-Wyoming, MI	12.6	23	19	Charlotte-Concord-Gastonia, NC-SC	12.1
56	18	Urban Honolulu, HI	12.6	11	20	Phoenix-Mesa-Scottsdale, AZ	12.0
16	21	Minneapolis-St. Paul-Bloomington, MN	12.5	70	21	Columbia, SC	11.7
17	21	San Diego-Carlsbad, CA	12.5	43	22	Memphis, TN-MS-AR	11.5
36	21	Nashville-Davidson--Murfreesboro--Franklin, TN	12.5	36	23	Nashville-Davidson--Murfreesboro--Franklin, TN	11.0
37	24	Virginia Beach-Norfolk-Newport News, VA-NC	12.4	53	24	Tucson, AZ	10.9
30	25	Austin-Round Rock, TX	12.3	42	25	Raleigh, NC	10.8
46	25	New Orleans-Metairie, LA	12.3	47	25	Salt Lake City, UT	10.8
9	27	Atlanta-Sandy Springs-Roswell, GA	12.2	63	27	Knoxville, TN	10.4
15	27	Seattle-Tacoma-Bellevue, WA	12.2	44	28	Richmond, VA	10.3
28	27	Las Vegas-Henderson-Paradise, NV	12.2	46	29	New Orleans-Metairie, LA	10.1
39	27	Milwaukee-Waukesha-West Allis, WI	12.2	31	30	Kansas City, MO-KS	10.0
23	31	Charlotte-Concord-Gastonia, NC-SC	12.1	49	30	Birmingham-Hoover, AL	10.0
29	31	Cincinnati, OH-KY-IN	12.1	60	32	Albuquerque, NM	9.8
40	31	Jacksonville, FL	12.1	2	33	Los Angeles-Long Beach-Anaheim, CA	9.6
49	31	Birmingham-Hoover, AL	12.1	37	33	Virginia Beach-Norfolk-Newport News, VA-NC	9.6
1	35	New York-Newark-Jersey City, NY-NJ-PA	12.0	34	35	Indianapolis-Carmel-Anderson, IN	9.3
11	35	Phoenix-Mesa-Scottsdale, AZ	12.0	67	35	Oxnard-Thousand Oaks-Ventura, CA	9.3
19	35	Denver-Aurora-Lakewood, CO	12.0	58	37	Bridgeport-Stamford-Norwalk, CT	8.9
74	35	Charleston-North Charleston, SC	12.0	3	38	Chicago-Naperville-Elgin, IL-IN-WI	8.7
45	39	Louisville/Jefferson County, KY-IN	11.9	54	38	Fresno, CA	8.7
2	40	Los Angeles-Long Beach-Anaheim, CA	11.8	13	40	Riverside-San Bernardino-Ontario, CA	8.6
3	40	Chicago-Naperville-Elgin, IL-IN-WI	11.8	62	40	Bakersfield, CA	8.6
21	42	Baltimore-Columbia-Towson, MD	11.7	19	42	Denver-Aurora-Lakewood, CO	8.5
73	42	Dayton, OH	11.7	59	42	Omaha-Council Bluffs, NE-IA	8.5
35	44	San Jose-Sunnyvale-Santa Clara, CA	11.6	6	44	Washington-Arlington-Alexandria, DC-VA-MD-WV	8.4
42	44	Raleigh, NC	11.6	17	44	San Diego-Carlsbad, CA	8.4
61	44	Greenville-Anderson-Mauldin, SC	11.6	71	44	Baton Rouge, LA	8.4
20	47	St. Louis, MO-IL	11.5	1	47	New York-Newark-Jersey City, NY-NJ-PA	8.0
26	47	Sacramento--Roseville--Arden-Arcade, CA	11.5	20	47	St. Louis, MO-IL	8.0
14	49	Detroit-Warren-Dearborn, MI	11.4	25	49	Portland-Vancouver-Hillsboro, OR-WA	7.4
22	50	Orlando-Kissimmee-Sanford, FL	11.3	32	50	Columbus, OH	7.3
44	50	Richmond, VA	11.3	73	51	Dayton, OH	7.0
8	52	Philadelphia-Camden-Wilmington, PA-NJ-DE-MD	11.2	69	52	Allentown-Bethlehem-Easton, PA-NJ	6.9
75	52	Greensboro-High Point, NC	11.2	45	53	Louisville/Jefferson County, KY-IN	6.6
70	54	Columbia, SC	11.1	33	54	Cleveland-Elyria, OH	6.5
7	55	Miami-Fort Lauderdale-West Palm Beach, FL	11.0	39	54	Milwaukee-Waukesha-West Allis, WI	6.5
25	55	Portland-Vancouver-Hillsboro, OR-WA	11.0	8	56	Philadelphia-Camden-Wilmington, PA-NJ-DE-MD	6.4
67	55	Oxnard-Thousand Oaks-Ventura, CA	11.0	15	56	Seattle-Tacoma-Bellevue, WA	6.4
12	58	San Francisco-Oakland-Hayward, CA	10.8	29	58	Cincinnati, OH-KY-IN	6.2
33	58	Cleveland-Elyria, OH	10.8	14	59	Detroit-Warren-Dearborn, MI	6.0
53	58	Tucson, AZ	10.8	26	59	Sacramento--Roseville--Arden-Arcade, CA	6.0
60	61	Albuquerque, NM	10.6	52	59	Grand Rapids-Wyoming, MI	6.0
50	62	Buffalo-Cheektowaga-Niagara Falls, NY	10.5	21	62	Baltimore-Columbia-Towson, MD	5.9
10	63	Boston-Cambridge-Newton, MA-NH	10.4	66	63	New Haven-Milford, CT	5.7
63	63	Knoxville, TN	10.4	12	64	San Francisco-Oakland-Hayward, CA	5.6
18	65	Tampa-St. Petersburg-Clearwater, FL	10.3	35	65	San Jose-Sunnyvale-Santa Clara, CA	5.2
58	65	Bridgeport-Stamford-Norwalk, CT	10.3	48	66	Hartford-West Hartford-East Hartford, CT	5.1
69	67	Allentown-Bethlehem-Easton, PA-NJ	10.2	27	67	Pittsburgh, PA	4.9
51	68	Rochester, NY	10.1	16	68	Minneapolis-St. Paul-Bloomington, MN	4.8
57	68	Worcester, MA-CT	10.1	38	68	Providence-Warwick, RI-MA	4.8
66	68	New Haven-Milford, CT	10.1	51	68	Rochester, NY	4.8
38	71	Providence-Warwick, RI-MA	10.0	50	71	Buffalo-Cheektowaga-Niagara Falls, NY	4.6
64	71	Albany-Schenectady-Troy, NY	10.0	64	72	Albany-Schenectady-Troy, NY	4.4
27	73	Pittsburgh, PA	9.9	56	73	Urban Honolulu, HI	4.1
48	74	Hartford-West Hartford-East Hartford, CT	9.6	10	74	Boston-Cambridge-Newton, MA-NH	3.5
72	75	North Port-Sarasota-Bradenton, FL	7.6	57	74	Worcester, MA-CT	3.5

75 Largest Metropolitan Areas by 2018 Population
Selected Rankings

Population rank	Percent college graduates rank	Metropolitan area	Percent college graduates [col 51]	Population rank	Median income rank	Metropolitan area	Median income (dollars) [col 55]
		Percent college graduates (bachelor's degree or more), 2017				Median household income, 2017	
6	1	Washington-Arlington-Alexandria, DC-VA-MD-WV	50.8	35	1	San Jose-Sunnyvale-Santa Clara, CA	153,684
35	1	San Jose-Sunnyvale-Santa Clara, CA	50.8	58	2	Bridgeport-Stamford-Norwalk, CT	148,996
12	3	San Francisco-Oakland-Hayward, CA	49.3	12	3	San Francisco-Oakland-Hayward, CA	140,720
10	4	Boston-Cambridge-Newton, MA-NH	47.6	6	4	Washington-Arlington-Alexandria, DC-VA-MD-WV	128,402
58	5	Bridgeport-Stamford-Norwalk, CT	47.1	10	5	Boston-Cambridge-Newton, MA-NH	116,561
42	6	Raleigh, NC	46.2	1	6	New York-Newark-Jersey City, NY-NJ-PA	110,849
30	7	Austin-Round Rock, TX	44.8	67	7	Oxnard-Thousand Oaks-Ventura, CA	110,266
19	8	Denver-Aurora-Lakewood, CO	43.9	15	8	Seattle-Tacoma-Bellevue, WA	109,619
15	9	Seattle-Tacoma-Bellevue, WA	41.9	56	9	Urban Honolulu, HI	103,713
16	10	Minneapolis-St. Paul-Bloomington, MN	41.7	17	10	San Diego-Carlsbad, CA	103,215
25	11	Portland-Vancouver-Hillsboro, OR-WA	40.3	16	11	Minneapolis-St. Paul-Bloomington, MN	101,405
1	12	New York-Newark-Jersey City, NY-NJ-PA	39.6	19	12	Denver-Aurora-Lakewood, CO	101,249
21	13	Baltimore-Columbia-Towson, MD	39.5	21	13	Baltimore-Columbia-Towson, MD	101,124
17	14	San Diego-Carlsbad, CA	38.8	30	14	Austin-Round Rock, TX	100,282
48	15	Hartford-West Hartford-East Hartford, CT	38.3	2	15	Los Angeles-Long Beach-Anaheim, CA	99,303
9	16	Atlanta-Sandy Springs-Roswell, GA	37.9	48	16	Hartford-West Hartford-East Hartford, CT	96,260
3	17	Chicago-Naperville-Elgin, IL-IN-WI	37.7	8	17	Philadelphia-Camden-Wilmington, PA-NJ-DE-MD	95,595
8	17	Philadelphia-Camden-Wilmington, PA-NJ-DE-MD	37.7	42	18	Raleigh, NC	95,164
64	19	Albany-Schenectady-Troy, NY	37.2	3	19	Chicago-Naperville-Elgin, IL-IN-WI	95,010
44	20	Richmond, VA	36.8	25	20	Portland-Vancouver-Hillsboro, OR-WA	92,750
31	21	Kansas City, MO-KS	36.5	5	21	Houston-The Woodlands-Sugar Land, TX	92,532
59	22	Omaha-Council Bluffs, NE-IA	36.3	4	22	Dallas-Fort Worth-Arlington, TX	92,495
36	23	Nashville-Davidson--Murfreesboro--Franklin, TN	36.0	57	23	Worcester, MA-CT	91,200
32	24	Columbus, OH	35.9	9	24	Atlanta-Sandy Springs-Roswell, GA	90,879
39	25	Milwaukee-Waukesha-West Allis, WI	35.8	26	25	Sacramento--Roseville--Arden-Arcade, CA	90,806
34	26	Indianapolis-Carmel-Anderson, IN	35.6	47	26	Salt Lake City, UT	90,790
23	27	Charlotte-Concord-Gastonia, NC-SC	35.5	66	27	New Haven-Milford, CT	90,654
47	27	Salt Lake City, UT	35.5	44	28	Richmond, VA	89,615
74	29	Charleston-North Charleston, SC	35.2	64	29	Albany-Schenectady-Troy, NY	89,097
27	30	Pittsburgh, PA	35.1	36	30	Nashville-Davidson--Murfreesboro--Franklin, TN	87,562
57	31	Worcester, MA-CT	35.0	38	31	Providence-Warwick, RI-MA	86,816
56	32	Urban Honolulu, HI	34.7	23	32	Charlotte-Concord-Gastonia, NC-SC	85,987
4	33	Dallas-Fort Worth-Arlington, TX	34.6	31	33	Kansas City, MO-KS	85,949
20	33	St. Louis, MO-IL	34.6	59	34	Omaha-Council Bluffs, NE-IA	84,781
2	35	Los Angeles-Long Beach-Anaheim, CA	34.2	69	35	Allentown-Bethlehem-Easton, PA-NJ	84,133
66	35	New Haven-Milford, CT	34.2	32	36	Columbus, OH	83,780
51	37	Rochester, NY	34.1	74	37	Charleston-North Charleston, SC	83,736
52	38	Grand Rapids-Wyoming, MI	33.7	11	38	Phoenix-Mesa-Scottsdale, AZ	83,688
53	39	Tucson, AZ	33.6	29	39	Cincinnati, OH-KY-IN	83,111
67	40	Oxnard-Thousand Oaks-Ventura, CA	33.4	37	40	Virginia Beach-Norfolk-Newport News, VA-NC	82,927
29	41	Cincinnati, OH-KY-IN	33.2	20	41	St. Louis, MO-IL	82,841
72	41	North Port-Sarasota-Bradenton, FL	33.2	72	42	North Port-Sarasota-Bradenton, FL	82,540
26	43	Sacramento--Roseville--Arden-Arcade, CA	32.7	39	43	Milwaukee-Waukesha-West Allis, WI	81,635
50	44	Buffalo-Cheektowaga-Niagara Falls, NY	32.5	7	44	Miami-Fort Lauderdale-West Palm Beach, FL	81,633
5	45	Houston-The Woodlands-Sugar Land, TX	32.4	14	45	Detroit-Warren-Dearborn, MI	81,606
7	46	Miami-Fort Lauderdale-West Palm Beach, FL	32.1	13	46	Riverside-San Bernardino-Ontario, CA	81,378
22	46	Orlando-Kissimmee-Sanford, FL	32.1	34	47	Indianapolis-Carmel-Anderson, IN	81,056
37	46	Virginia Beach-Norfolk-Newport News, VA-NC	32.1	27	48	Pittsburgh, PA	80,012
60	46	Albuquerque, NM	32.1	40	49	Jacksonville, FL	79,596
38	50	Providence-Warwick, RI-MA	31.9	52	50	Grand Rapids-Wyoming, MI	79,512
70	50	Columbia, SC	31.9	28	51	Las Vegas-Henderson-Paradise, NV	78,422
11	52	Phoenix-Mesa-Scottsdale, AZ	31.1	22	52	Orlando-Kissimmee-Sanford, FL	77,135
14	52	Detroit-Warren-Dearborn, MI	31.1	45	53	Louisville/Jefferson County, KY-IN	77,113
41	54	Oklahoma City, OK	31.0	41	54	Oklahoma City, OK	77,056
33	55	Cleveland-Elyria, OH	30.8	24	55	San Antonio-New Braunfels, TX	77,001
40	56	Jacksonville, FL	30.7	71	56	Baton Rouge, LA	76,318
49	57	Birmingham-Hoover, AL	30.5	51	57	Rochester, NY	75,771
18	58	Tampa-St. Petersburg-Clearwater, FL	30.0	49	58	Birmingham-Hoover, AL	74,667
73	59	Dayton, OH	29.8	18	59	Tampa-St. Petersburg-Clearwater, FL	74,499
46	60	New Orleans-Metairie, LA	29.5	33	60	Cleveland-Elyria, OH	74,406
75	60	Greensboro-High Point, NC	29.5	63	61	Knoxville, TN	74,016
69	62	Allentown-Bethlehem-Easton, PA-NJ	28.9	50	62	Buffalo-Cheektowaga-Niagara Falls, NY	73,903
45	63	Louisville/Jefferson County, KY-IN	28.8	43	63	Memphis, TN-MS-AR	73,581
63	63	Knoxville, TN	28.8	54	64	Fresno, CA	73,235
61	65	Greenville-Anderson-Mauldin, SC	28.6	70	65	Columbia, SC	72,572
24	66	San Antonio-New Braunfels, TX	28.1	46	66	New Orleans-Metairie, LA	72,130
43	67	Memphis, TN-MS-AR	27.8	61	67	Greenville-Anderson-Mauldin, SC	72,038
71	67	Baton Rouge, LA	27.8	55	68	Tulsa, OK	71,534
55	69	Tulsa, OK	27.6	53	69	Tucson, AZ	71,284
28	70	Las Vegas-Henderson-Paradise, NV	24.4	73	70	Dayton, OH	70,571
68	71	El Paso, TX	22.8	60	71	Albuquerque, NM	68,453
13	72	Riverside-San Bernardino-Ontario, CA	21.4	75	72	Greensboro-High Point, NC	68,047
54	73	Fresno, CA	20.4	62	73	Bakersfield, CA	67,703
65	74	McAllen-Edinburg-Mission, TX	18.7	68	74	El Paso, TX	61,583
62	75	Bakersfield, CA	16.0	65	75	McAllen-Edinburg-Mission, TX	55,786

75 Largest Metropolitan Areas by 2018 Population
Selected Rankings

Percent of population below the poverty level, 2017				Percent of children under 18 years old below the poverty level, 2017			
Population rank	Poverty rate rank	Metropolitan area	Poverty rate [col 59]	Population rank	Poverty rate rank	Metropolitan area	Poverty rate [col 60]
65	1	McAllen-Edinburg-Mission, TX	30.0	65	1	McAllen-Edinburg-Mission, TX	42.4
62	2	Bakersfield, CA	21.4	68	2	El Paso, TX	30.1
54	3	Fresno, CA	21.1	62	3	Bakersfield, CA	29.8
68	3	El Paso, TX	21.1	54	4	Fresno, CA	28.5
46	5	New Orleans-Metairie, LA	18.6	46	5	New Orleans-Metairie, LA	27.4
43	6	Memphis, TN-MS-AR	17.1	43	6	Memphis, TN-MS-AR	27.1
53	7	Tucson, AZ	16.7	53	7	Tucson, AZ	22.4
71	8	Baton Rouge, LA	16.3	33	8	Cleveland-Elyria, OH	21.7
60	9	Albuquerque, NM	15.5	71	8	Baton Rouge, LA	21.7
70	10	Columbia, SC	15.1	14	10	Detroit-Warren-Dearborn, MI	21.6
75	10	Greensboro-High Point, NC	15.1	51	11	Rochester, NY	21.3
33	12	Cleveland-Elyria, OH	14.8	24	12	San Antonio-New Braunfels, TX	21.2
14	13	Detroit-Warren-Dearborn, MI	14.6	50	13	Buffalo-Cheektowaga-Niagara Falls, NY	20.9
49	13	Birmingham-Hoover, AL	14.6	75	14	Greensboro-High Point, NC	20.8
24	15	San Antonio-New Braunfels, TX	14.5	22	15	Orlando-Kissimmee-Sanford, FL	20.6
13	16	Riverside-San Bernardino-Ontario, CA	14.4	55	16	Tulsa, OK	20.4
7	17	Miami-Fort Lauderdale-West Palm Beach, FL	14.3	28	17	Las Vegas-Henderson-Paradise, NV	20.3
55	17	Tulsa, OK	14.3	5	18	Houston-The Woodlands-Sugar Land, TX	20.2
63	17	Knoxville, TN	14.3	60	18	Albuquerque, NM	20.2
50	20	Buffalo-Cheektowaga-Niagara Falls, NY	14.2	63	20	Knoxville, TN	19.7
61	20	Greenville-Anderson-Mauldin, SC	14.2	2	21	Los Angeles-Long Beach-Anaheim, CA	19.6
2	22	Los Angeles-Long Beach-Anaheim, CA	14.1	18	22	Tampa-St. Petersburg-Clearwater, FL	19.4
22	22	Orlando-Kissimmee-Sanford, FL	14.1	49	22	Birmingham-Hoover, AL	19.4
5	24	Houston-The Woodlands-Sugar Land, TX	13.9	7	24	Miami-Fort Lauderdale-West Palm Beach, FL	19.3
18	24	Tampa-St. Petersburg-Clearwater, FL	13.9	13	24	Riverside-San Bernardino-Ontario, CA	19.3
41	24	Oklahoma City, OK	13.9	61	26	Greenville-Anderson-Mauldin, SC	19.2
51	24	Rochester, NY	13.9	70	26	Columbia, SC	19.2
28	28	Las Vegas-Henderson-Paradise, NV	13.8	41	28	Oklahoma City, OK	19.1
73	28	Dayton, OH	13.8	40	29	Jacksonville, FL	19.0
11	30	Phoenix-Mesa-Scottsdale, AZ	13.3	73	29	Dayton, OH	19.0
39	30	Milwaukee-Waukesha-West Allis, WI	13.3	11	31	Phoenix-Mesa-Scottsdale, AZ	18.8
40	30	Jacksonville, FL	13.3	37	32	Virginia Beach-Norfolk-Newport News, VA-NC	18.7
26	33	Sacramento--Roseville--Arden-Arcade, CA	13.1	32	33	Columbus, OH	18.3
32	33	Columbus, OH	13.1	39	34	Milwaukee-Waukesha-West Allis, WI	18.1
1	35	New York-Newark-Jersey City, NY-NJ-PA	12.8	1	35	New York-Newark-Jersey City, NY-NJ-PA	17.4
8	35	Philadelphia-Camden-Wilmington, PA-NJ-DE-MD	12.8	74	35	Charleston-North Charleston, SC	17.4
37	37	Virginia Beach-Norfolk-Newport News, VA-NC	12.3	23	37	Charlotte-Concord-Gastonia, NC-SC	17.2
45	38	Louisville/Jefferson County, KY-IN	12.2	45	37	Louisville/Jefferson County, KY-IN	17.2
23	39	Charlotte-Concord-Gastonia, NC-SC	12.1	69	37	Allentown-Bethlehem-Easton, PA-NJ	17.2
29	39	Cincinnati, OH-KY-IN	12.1	38	40	Providence-Warwick, RI-MA	17.1
9	41	Atlanta-Sandy Springs-Roswell, GA	12.0	29	41	Cincinnati, OH-KY-IN	17.0
34	42	Indianapolis-Carmel-Anderson, IN	11.9	9	42	Atlanta-Sandy Springs-Roswell, GA	16.7
74	42	Charleston-North Charleston, SC	11.9	34	42	Indianapolis-Carmel-Anderson, IN	16.7
3	44	Chicago-Naperville-Elgin, IL-IN-WI	11.8	4	44	Dallas-Fort Worth-Arlington, TX	16.2
17	44	San Diego-Carlsbad, CA	11.8	8	44	Philadelphia-Camden-Wilmington, PA-NJ-DE-MD	16.2
20	46	St. Louis, MO-IL	11.6	3	46	Chicago-Naperville-Elgin, IL-IN-WI	16.1
38	47	Providence-Warwick, RI-MA	11.4	20	47	St. Louis, MO-IL	16.0
4	48	Dallas-Fort Worth-Arlington, TX	11.3	17	48	San Diego-Carlsbad, CA	15.7
44	49	Richmond, VA	11.2	26	49	Sacramento--Roseville--Arden-Arcade, CA	15.4
69	49	Allentown-Bethlehem-Easton, PA-NJ	11.2	44	49	Richmond, VA	15.4
27	51	Pittsburgh, PA	11.0	42	51	Raleigh, NC	15.2
25	52	Portland-Vancouver-Hillsboro, OR-WA	10.9	36	52	Nashville-Davidson--Murfreesboro--Franklin, TN	15.1
36	52	Nashville-Davidson--Murfreesboro--Franklin, TN	10.9	27	53	Pittsburgh, PA	14.7
66	54	New Haven-Milford, CT	10.7	66	54	New Haven-Milford, CT	14.4
57	55	Worcester, MA-CT	10.6	31	55	Kansas City, MO-KS	14.2
42	56	Raleigh, NC	10.5	25	56	Portland-Vancouver-Hillsboro, OR-WA	13.5
30	57	Austin-Round Rock, TX	10.4	48	57	Hartford-West Hartford-East Hartford, CT	13.2
64	57	Albany-Schenectady-Troy, NY	10.4	67	57	Oxnard-Thousand Oaks-Ventura, CA	13.2
21	59	Baltimore-Columbia-Towson, MD	10.2	52	59	Grand Rapids-Wyoming, MI	13.1
31	60	Kansas City, MO-KS	10.0	57	60	Worcester, MA-CT	13.0
48	60	Hartford-West Hartford-East Hartford, CT	10.0	21	61	Baltimore-Columbia-Towson, MD	12.9
52	60	Grand Rapids-Wyoming, MI	10.0	72	62	North Port-Sarasota-Bradenton, FL	12.8
10	63	Boston-Cambridge-Newton, MA-NH	9.6	59	63	Omaha-Council Bluffs, NE-IA	12.6
59	63	Omaha-Council Bluffs, NE-IA	9.6	30	64	Austin-Round Rock, TX	12.3
72	65	North Port-Sarasota-Bradenton, FL	9.5	64	65	Albany-Schenectady-Troy, NY	12.2
67	66	Oxnard-Thousand Oaks-Ventura, CA	9.3	10	66	Boston-Cambridge-Newton, MA-NH	11.7
15	67	Seattle-Tacoma-Bellevue, WA	9.0	58	67	Bridgeport-Stamford-Norwalk, CT	11.3
47	68	Salt Lake City, UT	8.9	15	68	Seattle-Tacoma-Bellevue, WA	11.0
12	69	San Francisco-Oakland-Hayward, CA	8.8	47	69	Salt Lake City, UT	10.6
58	69	Bridgeport-Stamford-Norwalk, CT	8.8	19	70	Denver-Aurora-Lakewood, CO	10.5
19	71	Denver-Aurora-Lakewood, CO	8.6	16	71	Minneapolis-St. Paul-Bloomington, MN	10.4
56	72	Urban Honolulu, HI	8.4	6	72	Washington-Arlington-Alexandria, DC-VA-MD-WV	10.3
16	73	Minneapolis-St. Paul-Bloomington, MN	8.1	12	73	San Francisco-Oakland-Hayward, CA	10.2
6	74	Washington-Arlington-Alexandria, DC-VA-MD-WV	7.9	56	73	Urban Honolulu, HI	10.2
35	75	San Jose-Sunnyvale-Santa Clara, CA	7.3	35	75	San Jose-Sunnyvale-Santa Clara, CA	7.9

75 Largest Metropolitan Areas by 2018 Population
Selected Rankings

Median value of owner-occupied housing units, 2017				Median gross rent of renter-occupied housing units, 2017			
Population rank	Median value rank	Metropolitan area	Median value (dollars) [col 91]	Population rank	Median gross rent	Metropolitan area	Median rent (dollars) [col 94]
35	1	San Jose-Sunnyvale-Santa Clara, CA	957,700	35	1	San Jose-Sunnyvale-Santa Clara, CA	2,213
12	2	San Francisco-Oakland-Hayward, CA	849,500	12	2	San Francisco-Oakland-Hayward, CA	1,853
56	3	Urban Honolulu, HI	680,200	67	3	Oxnard-Thousand Oaks-Ventura, CA	1,736
2	4	Los Angeles-Long Beach-Anaheim, CA	617,100	56	4	Urban Honolulu, HI	1,712
67	5	Oxnard-Thousand Oaks-Ventura, CA	592,500	6	5	Washington-Arlington-Alexandria, DC-VA-MD-WV	1,629
17	6	San Diego-Carlsbad, CA	563,800	17	6	San Diego-Carlsbad, CA	1,598
10	7	Boston-Cambridge-Newton, MA-NH	441,400	2	7	Los Angeles-Long Beach-Anaheim, CA	1,476
1	8	New York-Newark-Jersey City, NY-NJ-PA	440,900	15	8	Seattle-Tacoma-Bellevue, WA	1,443
15	9	Seattle-Tacoma-Bellevue, WA	439,800	58	9	Bridgeport-Stamford-Norwalk, CT	1,438
58	10	Bridgeport-Stamford-Norwalk, CT	425,900	10	10	Boston-Cambridge-Newton, MA-NH	1,397
6	11	Washington-Arlington-Alexandria, DC-VA-MD-WV	424,600	1	11	New York-Newark-Jersey City, NY-NJ-PA	1,379
26	12	Sacramento--Roseville--Arden-Arcade, CA	390,000	19	12	Denver-Aurora-Lakewood, CO	1,352
19	13	Denver-Aurora-Lakewood, CO	386,800	7	13	Miami-Fort Lauderdale-West Palm Beach, FL	1,316
25	14	Portland-Vancouver-Hillsboro, OR-WA	376,000	13	14	Riverside-San Bernardino-Ontario, CA	1,268
13	15	Riverside-San Bernardino-Ontario, CA	342,300	26	15	Sacramento--Roseville--Arden-Arcade, CA	1,246
21	16	Baltimore-Columbia-Towson, MD	297,300	21	16	Baltimore-Columbia-Towson, MD	1,241
47	17	Salt Lake City, UT	294,800	25	17	Portland-Vancouver-Hillsboro, OR-WA	1,238
30	18	Austin-Round Rock, TX	283,600	30	18	Austin-Round Rock, TX	1,223
7	19	Miami-Fort Lauderdale-West Palm Beach, FL	278,700	72	19	North Port-Sarasota-Bradenton, FL	1,171
38	20	Providence-Warwick, RI-MA	277,400	22	20	Orlando-Kissimmee-Sanford, FL	1,151
57	21	Worcester, MA-CT	269,600	37	21	Virginia Beach-Norfolk-Newport News, VA-NC	1,124
16	22	Minneapolis-St. Paul-Bloomington, MN	254,800	9	22	Atlanta-Sandy Springs-Roswell, GA	1,115
8	23	Philadelphia-Camden-Wilmington, PA-NJ-DE-MD	250,900	66	23	New Haven-Milford, CT	1,107
28	24	Las Vegas-Henderson-Paradise, NV	250,000	74	24	Charleston-North Charleston, SC	1,102
54	25	Fresno, CA	248,700	11	25	Phoenix-Mesa-Scottsdale, AZ	1,091
48	26	Hartford-West Hartford-East Hartford, CT	247,900	4	26	Dallas-Fort Worth-Arlington, TX	1,085
11	27	Phoenix-Mesa-Scottsdale, AZ	246,900	8	27	Philadelphia-Camden-Wilmington, PA-NJ-DE-MD	1,082
37	28	Virginia Beach-Norfolk-Newport News, VA-NC	245,900	28	28	Las Vegas-Henderson-Paradise, NV	1,079
74	29	Charleston-North Charleston, SC	245,500	3	29	Chicago-Naperville-Elgin, IL-IN-WI	1,078
42	30	Raleigh, NC	244,500	42	30	Raleigh, NC	1,073
72	31	North Port-Sarasota-Bradenton, FL	244,400	18	31	Tampa-St. Petersburg-Clearwater, FL	1,070
66	32	New Haven-Milford, CT	243,400	47	32	Salt Lake City, UT	1,068
36	33	Nashville-Davidson--Murfreesboro--Franklin, TN	242,900	48	33	Hartford-West Hartford-East Hartford, CT	1,061
3	34	Chicago-Naperville-Elgin, IL-IN-WI	240,300	44	34	Richmond, VA	1,060
44	35	Richmond, VA	237,900	16	35	Minneapolis-St. Paul-Bloomington, MN	1,057
22	36	Orlando-Kissimmee-Sanford, FL	219,000	5	36	Houston-The Woodlands-Sugar Land, TX	1,041
64	37	Albany-Schenectady-Troy, NY	216,400	40	37	Jacksonville, FL	1,031
9	38	Atlanta-Sandy Springs-Roswell, GA	215,100	36	38	Nashville-Davidson--Murfreesboro--Franklin, TN	1,030
4	39	Dallas-Fort Worth-Arlington, TX	214,900	69	39	Allentown-Bethlehem-Easton, PA-NJ	988
39	40	Milwaukee-Waukesha-West Allis, WI	213,800	23	40	Charlotte-Concord-Gastonia, NC-SC	977
69	41	Allentown-Bethlehem-Easton, PA-NJ	213,400	57	41	Worcester, MA-CT	974
62	42	Bakersfield, CA	205,700	64	42	Albany-Schenectady-Troy, NY	968
40	43	Jacksonville, FL	205,100	46	43	New Orleans-Metairie, LA	965
23	44	Charlotte-Concord-Gastonia, NC-SC	197,100	24	44	San Antonio-New Braunfels, TX	959
46	45	New Orleans-Metairie, LA	193,100	54	45	Fresno, CA	955
5	46	Houston-The Woodlands-Sugar Land, TX	192,900	62	46	Bakersfield, CA	948
60	47	Albuquerque, NM	191,700	31	47	Kansas City, MO-KS	935
18	48	Tampa-St. Petersburg-Clearwater, FL	191,200	32	48	Columbus, OH	916
32	49	Columbus, OH	182,300	38	48	Providence-Warwick, RI-MA	916
53	49	Tucson, AZ	182,300	14	50	Detroit-Warren-Dearborn, MI	898
71	51	Baton Rouge, LA	182,000	71	51	Baton Rouge, LA	894
31	52	Kansas City, MO-KS	180,700	59	52	Omaha-Council Bluffs, NE-IA	891
52	53	Grand Rapids-Wyoming, MI	174,900	70	52	Columbia, SC	891
20	54	St. Louis, MO-IL	172,200	43	54	Memphis, TN-MS-AR	887
14	55	Detroit-Warren-Dearborn, MI	171,600	53	54	Tucson, AZ	887
59	56	Omaha-Council Bluffs, NE-IA	170,200	34	56	Indianapolis-Carmel-Anderson, IN	886
24	57	San Antonio-New Braunfels, TX	170,100	52	57	Grand Rapids-Wyoming, MI	871
63	58	Knoxville, TN	169,200	51	58	Rochester, NY	870
45	59	Louisville/Jefferson County, KY-IN	168,600	39	59	Milwaukee-Waukesha-West Allis, WI	869
29	60	Cincinnati, OH-KY-IN	165,500	20	60	St. Louis, MO-IL	868
34	61	Indianapolis-Carmel-Anderson, IN	162,200	60	61	Albuquerque, NM	860
61	62	Greenville-Anderson-Mauldin, SC	162,100	41	62	Oklahoma City, OK	851
49	63	Birmingham-Hoover, AL	161,400	49	63	Birmingham-Hoover, AL	842
41	64	Oklahoma City, OK	156,800	68	64	El Paso, TX	826
70	65	Columbia, SC	156,600	55	65	Tulsa, OK	823
27	66	Pittsburgh, PA	153,300	45	66	Louisville/Jefferson County, KY-IN	818
55	67	Tulsa, OK	150,700	63	67	Knoxville, TN	803
33	68	Cleveland-Elyria, OH	150,400	61	68	Greenville-Anderson-Mauldin, SC	797
75	69	Greensboro-High Point, NC	150,100	27	69	Pittsburgh, PA	794
50	70	Buffalo-Cheektowaga-Niagara Falls, NY	148,900	75	70	Greensboro-High Point, NC	791
43	71	Memphis, TN-MS-AR	148,800	29	71	Cincinnati, OH-KY-IN	790
51	72	Rochester, NY	144,500	33	72	Cleveland-Elyria, OH	789
73	73	Dayton, OH	133,400	50	73	Buffalo-Cheektowaga-Niagara Falls, NY	772
68	74	El Paso, TX	122,200	73	74	Dayton, OH	764
65	75	McAllen-Edinburg-Mission, TX	86,100	65	75	McAllen-Edinburg-Mission, TX	695

75 Largest Metropolitan Areas by 2018 Population
Selected Rankings

Unemployment rate, 2018

Population rank	Unemployment rate rank	Metropolitan area	Unemployment rate [col 100]
62	1	Bakersfield, CA	8.0
54	2	Fresno, CA	7.5
65	3	McAllen-Edinburg-Mission, TX	6.6
33	4	Cleveland-Elyria, OH	5.1
28	5	Las Vegas-Henderson-Paradise, NV	4.8
60	6	Albuquerque, NM	4.7
46	7	New Orleans-Metairie, LA	4.6
50	7	Buffalo-Cheektowaga-Niagara Falls, NY	4.6
53	9	Tucson, AZ	4.5
69	9	Allentown-Bethlehem-Easton, PA-NJ	4.5
66	11	New Haven-Milford, CT	4.4
71	11	Baton Rouge, LA	4.4
5	13	Houston-The Woodlands-Sugar Land, TX	4.3
14	13	Detroit-Warren-Dearborn, MI	4.3
27	13	Pittsburgh, PA	4.3
73	13	Dayton, OH	4.3
2	17	Los Angeles-Long Beach-Anaheim, CA	4.2
8	17	Philadelphia-Camden-Wilmington, PA-NJ-DE-MD	4.2
11	17	Phoenix-Mesa-Scottsdale, AZ	4.2
13	17	Riverside-San Bernardino-Ontario, CA	4.2
51	17	Rochester, NY	4.2
68	17	El Paso, TX	4.2
38	23	Providence-Warwick, RI-MA	4.1
43	23	Memphis, TN-MS-AR	4.1
48	23	Hartford-West Hartford-East Hartford, CT	4.1
75	23	Greensboro-High Point, NC	4.1
1	27	New York-Newark-Jersey City, NY-NJ-PA	4.0
3	27	Chicago-Naperville-Elgin, IL-IN-WI	4.0
21	27	Baltimore-Columbia-Towson, MD	4.0
29	27	Cincinnati, OH-KY-IN	4.0
58	27	Bridgeport-Stamford-Norwalk, CT	4.0
15	32	Seattle-Tacoma-Bellevue, WA	3.9
25	32	Portland-Vancouver-Hillsboro, OR-WA	3.9
45	32	Louisville/Jefferson County, KY-IN	3.9
9	35	Atlanta-Sandy Springs-Roswell, GA	3.8
32	35	Columbus, OH	3.8
64	35	Albany-Schenectady-Troy, NY	3.8
67	35	Oxnard-Thousand Oaks-Ventura, CA	3.8
26	39	Sacramento--Roseville--Arden-Arcade, CA	3.7
57	39	Worcester, MA-CT	3.7
7	41	Miami-Fort Lauderdale-West Palm Beach, FL	3.6
23	41	Charlotte-Concord-Gastonia, NC-SC	3.6
4	43	Dallas-Fort Worth-Arlington, TX	3.5
18	43	Tampa-St. Petersburg-Clearwater, FL	3.5
49	43	Birmingham-Hoover, AL	3.5
55	43	Tulsa, OK	3.5
20	47	St. Louis, MO-IL	3.4
31	47	Kansas City, MO-KS	3.4
40	47	Jacksonville, FL	3.4
42	47	Raleigh, NC	3.4
72	47	North Port-Sarasota-Bradenton, FL	3.4
6	52	Washington-Arlington-Alexandria, DC-VA-MD-WV	3.3
17	52	San Diego-Carlsbad, CA	3.3
22	52	Orlando-Kissimmee-Sanford, FL	3.3
24	52	San Antonio-New Braunfels, TX	3.3
37	52	Virginia Beach-Norfolk-Newport News, VA-NC	3.3
63	52	Knoxville, TN	3.3
70	52	Columbia, SC	3.3
19	59	Denver-Aurora-Lakewood, CO	3.2
34	59	Indianapolis-Carmel-Anderson, IN	3.2
39	59	Milwaukee-Waukesha-West Allis, WI	3.2
44	59	Richmond, VA	3.2
41	63	Oklahoma City, OK	3.1
61	63	Greenville-Anderson-Mauldin, SC	3.1
10	65	Boston-Cambridge-Newton, MA-NH	3.0
47	65	Salt Lake City, UT	3.0
52	65	Grand Rapids-Wyoming, MI	3.0
30	68	Austin-Round Rock, TX	2.9
59	68	Omaha-Council Bluffs, NE-IA	2.9
74	68	Charleston-North Charleston, SC	2.9
12	71	San Francisco-Oakland-Hayward, CA	2.7
16	71	Minneapolis-St. Paul-Bloomington, MN	2.7
35	71	San Jose-Sunnyvale-Santa Clara, CA	2.7
36	71	Nashville-Davidson--Murfreesboro--Franklin, TN	2.7
56	75	Urban Honolulu, HI	2.3

Mean income tax, 2016

Population rank	Mean income tax rank	Metropolitan area	Mean income tax [col 199]
58	1	Bridgeport-Stamford-Norwalk, CT	$31,256
35	2	San Jose-Sunnyvale-Santa Clara, CA	$27,867
12	3	San Francisco-Oakland-Hayward, CA	$21,775
10	4	Boston-Cambridge-Newton, MA-NH	$17,116
15	5	Seattle-Tacoma-Bellevue, WA	$15,327
1	6	New York-Newark-Jersey City, NY-NJ-PA	$15,321
6	7	Washington-Arlington-Alexandria, DC-VA-MD-WV	$14,199
30	8	Austin-Round Rock, TX	$12,673
72	9	North Port-Sarasota-Bradenton, FL	$12,020
19	10	Denver-Aurora-Lakewood, CO	$11,958
2	11	Los Angeles-Long Beach-Anaheim, CA	$11,832
3	12	Chicago-Naperville-Elgin, IL-IN-WI	$11,803
8	13	Philadelphia-Camden-Wilmington, PA-NJ-DE-MD	$11,751
16	14	Minneapolis-St. Paul-Bloomington, MN	$11,541
4	15	Dallas-Fort Worth-Arlington, TX	$11,314
64	16	Albany-Schenectady-Troy, NY	$11,279
67	17	Oxnard-Thousand Oaks-Ventura, CA	$11,168
48	18	Hartford-West Hartford-East Hartford, CT	$10,923
42	19	Raleigh, NC	$10,789
21	20	Baltimore-Columbia-Towson, MD	$10,666
5	21	Houston-The Woodlands-Sugar Land, TX	$10,476
36	22	Nashville-Davidson--Murfreesboro--Franklin, TN	$10,451
7	23	Miami-Fort Lauderdale-West Palm Beach, FL	$10,428
17	24	San Diego-Carlsbad, CA	$10,382
25	25	Portland-Vancouver-Hillsboro, OR-WA	$10,221
66	26	New Haven-Milford, CT	$9,930
23	27	Charlotte-Concord-Gastonia, NC-SC	$9,887
39	28	Milwaukee-Waukesha-West Allis, WI	$9,809
9	29	Atlanta-Sandy Springs-Roswell, GA	$9,647
20	30	St. Louis, MO-IL	$9,632
14	31	Detroit-Warren-Dearborn, MI	$9,509
74	32	Charleston-North Charleston, SC	$9,402
29	33	Cincinnati, OH-KY-IN	$9,396
31	34	Kansas City, MO-KS	$9,390
57	35	Worcester, MA-CT	$9,333
28	36	Las Vegas-Henderson-Paradise, NV	$9,281
71	37	Baton Rouge, LA	$9,202
44	38	Richmond, VA	$9,130
59	39	Omaha-Council Bluffs, NE-IA	$9,041
27	40	Pittsburgh, PA	$8,964
49	41	Birmingham-Hoover, AL	$8,959
34	42	Indianapolis-Carmel-Anderson, IN	$8,870
11	43	Phoenix-Mesa-Scottsdale, AZ	$8,849
26	44	Sacramento--Roseville--Arden-Arcade, CA	$8,779
40	45	Jacksonville, FL	$8,619
32	46	Columbus, OH	$8,562
46	47	New Orleans-Metairie, LA	$8,521
47	48	Salt Lake City, UT	$8,504
52	49	Grand Rapids-Wyoming, MI	$8,479
63	50	Knoxville, TN	$8,439
33	51	Cleveland-Elyria, OH	$8,433
18	52	Tampa-St. Petersburg-Clearwater, FL	$8,289
38	53	Providence-Warwick, RI-MA	$8,280
41	54	Oklahoma City, OK	$8,245
55	55	Tulsa, OK	$8,128
56	56	Urban Honolulu, HI	$8,105
69	57	Allentown-Bethlehem-Easton, PA-NJ	$8,104
45	58	Louisville/Jefferson County, KY-IN	$7,768
24	59	San Antonio-New Braunfels, TX	$7,644
43	60	Memphis, TN-MS-AR	$7,438
51	61	Rochester, NY	$7,387
50	62	Buffalo-Cheektowaga-Niagara Falls, NY	$7,289
61	63	Greenville-Anderson-Mauldin, SC	$7,156
22	64	Orlando-Kissimmee-Sanford, FL	$7,084
37	65	Virginia Beach-Norfolk-Newport News, VA-NC	$6,977
73	66	Dayton, OH	$6,896
75	67	Greensboro-High Point, NC	$6,834
70	68	Columbia, SC	$6,740
53	69	Tucson, AZ	$6,565
60	70	Albuquerque, NM	$6,360
54	71	Fresno, CA	$5,767
13	72	Riverside-San Bernardino-Ontario, CA	$5,533
62	73	Bakersfield, CA	$5,147
68	74	El Paso, TX	$4,028
65	75	McAllen-Edinburg-Mission, TX	$3,300

75 Largest Metropolitan Areas by 2018 Population
Selected Rankings

Employment in manufacturing as a percent of total nonfarm employment, 2016				Employment in professional, scientific, and technical services as a percent of total nonfarm employment, 2016			
Population rank	Manu-facturing rank	Metropolitan area	Percent employed in manu-facturing [col 107/col 105]	Population rank	Profess-ional services rank	Metropolitan area	Percent employed in services [col 110/col 105]
52	1	Grand Rapids-Wyoming, MI	22.0	6	1	Washington-Arlington-Alexandria, DC-VA-MD-WV	20.5
75	2	Greensboro-High Point, NC	16.6	35	2	San Jose-Sunnyvale-Santa Clara, CA	13.5
61	3	Greenville-Anderson-Mauldin, SC	15.8	30	3	Austin-Round Rock, TX	12.6
39	4	Milwaukee-Waukesha-West Allis, WI	14.4	12	4	San Francisco-Oakland-Hayward, CA	11.8
73	5	Dayton, OH	13.4	21	4	Baltimore-Columbia-Towson, MD	11.8
14	6	Detroit-Warren-Dearborn, MI	13.2	42	6	Raleigh, NC	10.9
55	7	Tulsa, OK	13.1	60	7	Albuquerque, NM	10.8
33	8	Cleveland-Elyria, OH	12.9	10	8	Boston-Cambridge-Newton, MA-NH	10.1
45	8	Louisville/Jefferson County, KY-IN	12.9	14	8	Detroit-Warren-Dearborn, MI	10.1
51	10	Rochester, NY	11.8	17	10	San Diego-Carlsbad, CA	10.0
57	10	Worcester, MA-CT	11.8	1	11	New York-Newark-Jersey City, NY-NJ-PA	9.2
48	12	Hartford-West Hartford-East Hartford, CT	11.6	58	11	Bridgeport-Stamford-Norwalk, CT	9.2
69	13	Allentown-Bethlehem-Easton, PA-NJ	11.1	18	13	Tampa-St. Petersburg-Clearwater, FL	8.9
50	14	Buffalo-Cheektowaga-Niagara Falls, NY	10.9	9	14	Atlanta-Sandy Springs-Roswell, GA	8.7
29	15	Cincinnati, OH-KY-IN	10.8	19	14	Denver-Aurora-Lakewood, CO	8.7
63	16	Knoxville, TN	10.6	67	14	Oxnard-Thousand Oaks-Ventura, CA	8.7
16	17	Minneapolis-St. Paul-Bloomington, MN	10.5	37	17	Virginia Beach-Norfolk-Newport News, VA-NC	8.6
38	17	Providence-Warwick, RI-MA	10.5	31	18	Kansas City, MO-KS	8.5
25	19	Portland-Vancouver-Hillsboro, OR-WA	10.2	64	18	Albany-Schenectady-Troy, NY	8.5
15	20	Seattle-Tacoma-Bellevue, WA	9.9	3	20	Chicago-Naperville-Elgin, IL-IN-WI	8.2
23	21	Charlotte-Concord-Gastonia, NC-SC	9.6	47	21	Salt Lake City, UT	8.1
37	21	Virginia Beach-Norfolk-Newport News, VA-NC	9.6	5	22	Houston-The Woodlands-Sugar Land, TX	7.9
67	21	Oxnard-Thousand Oaks-Ventura, CA	9.6	15	22	Seattle-Tacoma-Bellevue, WA	7.9
54	24	Fresno, CA	9.3	44	22	Richmond, VA	7.9
3	25	Chicago-Naperville-Elgin, IL-IN-WI	9.2	2	25	Los Angeles-Long Beach-Anaheim, CA	7.8
66	25	New Haven-Milford, CT	9.2	8	25	Philadelphia-Camden-Wilmington, PA-NJ-DE-MD	7.8
2	27	Los Angeles-Long Beach-Anaheim, CA	9.1	4	27	Dallas-Fort Worth-Arlington, TX	7.7
70	28	Columbia, SC	9.0	73	27	Dayton, OH	7.7
74	28	Charleston-North Charleston, SC	9.0	7	29	Miami-Fort Lauderdale-West Palm Beach, FL	7.6
47	30	Salt Lake City, UT	8.9	25	30	Portland-Vancouver-Hillsboro, OR-WA	7.4
31	31	Kansas City, MO-KS	8.8	74	30	Charleston-North Charleston, SC	7.4
34	31	Indianapolis-Carmel-Anderson, IN	8.8	26	32	Sacramento--Roseville--Arden-Arcade, CA	7.2
20	33	St. Louis, MO-IL	8.6	27	32	Pittsburgh, PA	7.2
36	33	Nashville-Davidson--Murfreesboro--Franklin, TN	8.6	71	32	Baton Rouge, LA	7.2
13	35	Riverside-San Bernardino-Ontario, CA	8.4	16	35	Minneapolis-St. Paul-Bloomington, MN	7.1
35	36	San Jose-Sunnyvale-Santa Clara, CA	8.3	34	35	Indianapolis-Carmel-Anderson, IN	7.1
49	36	Birmingham-Hoover, AL	8.3	11	37	Phoenix-Mesa-Scottsdale, AZ	6.9
17	38	San Diego-Carlsbad, CA	8.1	63	37	Knoxville, TN	6.9
4	39	Dallas-Fort Worth-Arlington, TX	7.9	20	39	St. Louis, MO-IL	6.7
5	40	Houston-The Woodlands-Sugar Land, TX	7.7	22	40	Orlando-Kissimmee-Sanford, FL	6.5
32	40	Columbus, OH	7.7	46	41	New Orleans-Metairie, LA	6.4
58	40	Bridgeport-Stamford-Norwalk, CT	7.7	50	41	Buffalo-Cheektowaga-Niagara Falls, NY	6.4
27	43	Pittsburgh, PA	7.6	29	43	Cincinnati, OH-KY-IN	6.3
71	44	Baton Rouge, LA	7.4	32	43	Columbus, OH	6.3
59	45	Omaha-Council Bluffs, NE-IA	7.3	40	43	Jacksonville, FL	6.3
53	46	Tucson, AZ	7.2	51	43	Rochester, NY	6.3
43	47	Memphis, TN-MS-AR	7.0	23	47	Charlotte-Concord-Gastonia, NC-SC	6.2
8	48	Philadelphia-Camden-Wilmington, PA-NJ-DE-MD	6.5	41	47	Oklahoma City, OK	6.2
64	49	Albany-Schenectady-Troy, NY	6.4	48	47	Hartford-West Hartford-East Hartford, CT	6.2
72	49	North Port-Sarasota-Bradenton, FL	6.4	61	47	Greenville-Anderson-Mauldin, SC	6.2
9	51	Atlanta-Sandy Springs-Roswell, GA	6.3	70	47	Columbia, SC	6.2
11	52	Phoenix-Mesa-Scottsdale, AZ	6.2	59	52	Omaha-Council Bluffs, NE-IA	6.1
62	52	Bakersfield, CA	6.2	72	52	North Port-Sarasota-Bradenton, FL	6.1
10	54	Boston-Cambridge-Newton, MA-NH	6.0	24	54	San Antonio-New Braunfels, TX	5.7
12	55	San Francisco-Oakland-Hayward, CA	5.8	33	54	Cleveland-Elyria, OH	5.7
68	55	El Paso, TX	5.8	55	54	Tulsa, OK	5.7
41	57	Oklahoma City, OK	5.7	57	57	Worcester, MA-CT	5.6
44	57	Richmond, VA	5.7	62	57	Bakersfield, CA	5.6
24	59	San Antonio-New Braunfels, TX	5.2	36	59	Nashville-Davidson--Murfreesboro--Franklin, TN	5.4
18	60	Tampa-St. Petersburg-Clearwater, FL	5.1	53	59	Tucson, AZ	5.4
60	60	Albuquerque, NM	5.1	28	61	Las Vegas-Henderson-Paradise, NV	5.2
30	62	Austin-Round Rock, TX	5.0	39	62	Milwaukee-Waukesha-West Allis, WI	5.1
46	63	New Orleans-Metairie, LA	4.9	49	62	Birmingham-Hoover, AL	5.1
42	64	Raleigh, NC	4.8	56	62	Urban Honolulu, HI	5.1
26	65	Sacramento--Roseville--Arden-Arcade, CA	4.7	45	65	Louisville/Jefferson County, KY-IN	4.7
40	65	Jacksonville, FL	4.7	38	66	Providence-Warwick, RI-MA	4.6
19	67	Denver-Aurora-Lakewood, CO	4.5	68	66	El Paso, TX	4.6
21	67	Baltimore-Columbia-Towson, MD	4.5	66	68	New Haven-Milford, CT	4.5
1	69	New York-Newark-Jersey City, NY-NJ-PA	4.0	52	69	Grand Rapids-Wyoming, MI	4.2
22	70	Orlando-Kissimmee-Sanford, FL	3.5	54	70	Fresno, CA	4.0
7	71	Miami-Fort Lauderdale-West Palm Beach, FL	3.4	75	71	Greensboro-High Point, NC	3.9
65	72	McAllen-Edinburg-Mission, TX	3.2	69	72	Allentown-Bethlehem-Easton, PA-NJ	3.8
56	73	Urban Honolulu, HI	2.8	43	73	Memphis, TN-MS-AR	3.7
28	74	Las Vegas-Henderson-Paradise, NV	2.3	13	74	Riverside-San Bernardino-Ontario, CA	3.4
6	75	Washington-Arlington-Alexandria, DC-VA-MD-WV	1.9	65	75	McAllen-Edinburg-Mission, TX	3.2

75 Largest Metropolitan Areas by 2018 Population
Selected Rankings

Per capita local government taxes, 2012				Violent crime rate, 2016 (violent crimes known to police)			
Population rank	Local taxes rank	Metropolitan area	Local per capita taxes (dollars) [col 183]	Population rank	Crime rate rank	Metropolitan area	Crime rate (per 100,000 population) [col 46]
1	1	New York-Newark-Jersey City, NY-NJ-PA	4,280	43	1	Memphis, TN-MS-AR	1,082
58	2	Bridgeport-Stamford-Norwalk, CT	3,419	60	2	Albuquerque, NM	901
6	3	Washington-Arlington-Alexandria, DC-VA-MD-WV	3,255	28	3	Las Vegas-Henderson-Paradise, NV	771
3	4	Chicago-Naperville-Elgin, IL-IN-WI	2,701	34	4	Indianapolis-Carmel-Anderson, IN	713
12	5	San Francisco-Oakland-Hayward, CA	2,658	21	5	Baltimore-Columbia-Towson, MD	710
64	6	Albany-Schenectady-Troy, NY	2,620	39	6	Milwaukee-Waukesha-West Allis, WI	656
35	7	San Jose-Sunnyvale-Santa Clara, CA	2,585	36	7	Nashville-Davidson--Murfreesboro--Franklin, TN	622
48	8	Hartford-West Hartford-East Hartford, CT	2,512	54	8	Fresno, CA	613
51	9	Rochester, NY	2,381	70	9	Columbia, SC	590
33	10	Cleveland-Elyria, OH	2,378	55	10	Tulsa, OK	589
10	11	Boston-Cambridge-Newton, MA-NH	2,362	62	11	Bakersfield, CA	580
66	12	New Haven-Milford, CT	2,358	5	12	Houston-The Woodlands-Sugar Land, TX	578
8	13	Philadelphia-Camden-Wilmington, PA-NJ-DE-MD	2,356	46	13	New Orleans-Metairie, LA	559
50	14	Buffalo-Cheektowaga-Niagara Falls, NY	2,326	14	14	Detroit-Warren-Dearborn, MI	556
32	15	Columbus, OH	2,274	24	15	San Antonio-New Braunfels, TX	526
30	16	Austin-Round Rock, TX	2,267	71	16	Baton Rouge, LA	505
19	17	Denver-Aurora-Lakewood, CO	2,240	22	17	Orlando-Kissimmee-Sanford, FL	504
21	18	Baltimore-Columbia-Towson, MD	2,145	53	18	Tucson, AZ	496
4	19	Dallas-Fort Worth-Arlington, TX	2,139	41	19	Oklahoma City, OK	491
7	20	Miami-Fort Lauderdale-West Palm Beach, FL	2,106	7	20	Miami-Fort Lauderdale-West Palm Beach, FL	486
69	20	Allentown-Bethlehem-Easton, PA-NJ	2,106	40	21	Jacksonville, FL	479
15	22	Seattle-Tacoma-Bellevue, WA	2,088	12	22	San Francisco-Oakland-Hayward, CA	478
5	23	Houston-The Woodlands-Sugar Land, TX	2,087	2	23	Los Angeles-Long Beach-Anaheim, CA	477
31	24	Kansas City, MO-KS	2,040	63	24	Knoxville, TN	449
59	25	Omaha-Council Bluffs, NE-IA	2,037	8	25	Philadelphia-Camden-Wilmington, PA-NJ-DE-MD	447
38	26	Providence-Warwick, RI-MA	2,018	33	26	Cleveland-Elyria, OH	446
46	27	New Orleans-Metairie, LA	1,991	3	27	Chicago-Naperville-Elgin, IL-IN-WI	443
39	28	Milwaukee-Waukesha-West Allis, WI	1,986	45	28	Louisville/Jefferson County, KY-IN	438
2	29	Los Angeles-Long Beach-Anaheim, CA	1,870	11	29	Phoenix-Mesa-Scottsdale, AZ	427
73	30	Dayton, OH	1,861	74	30	Charleston-North Charleston, SC	418
20	31	St. Louis, MO-IL	1,841	26	31	Sacramento--Roseville--Arden-Arcade, CA	411
17	32	San Diego-Carlsbad, CA	1,791	47	31	Salt Lake City, UT	411
29	33	Cincinnati, OH-KY-IN	1,786	50	31	Buffalo-Cheektowaga-Niagara Falls, NY	411
27	34	Pittsburgh, PA	1,785	9	34	Atlanta-Sandy Springs-Roswell, GA	403
25	35	Portland-Vancouver-Hillsboro, OR-WA	1,774	13	35	Riverside-San Bernardino-Ontario, CA	397
71	36	Baton Rouge, LA	1,760	19	36	Denver-Aurora-Lakewood, CO	389
9	37	Atlanta-Sandy Springs-Roswell, GA	1,744	68	37	El Paso, TX	365
37	38	Virginia Beach-Norfolk-Newport News, VA-NC	1,733	4	38	Dallas-Fort Worth-Arlington, TX	360
74	39	Charleston-North Charleston, SC	1,730	1	39	New York-Newark-Jersey City, NY-NJ-PA	355
72	40	North Port-Sarasota-Bradenton, FL	1,684	15	40	Seattle-Tacoma-Bellevue, WA	353
24	41	San Antonio-New Braunfels, TX	1,669	37	41	Virginia Beach-Norfolk-Newport News, VA-NC	352
67	42	Oxnard-Thousand Oaks-Ventura, CA	1,650	59	42	Omaha-Council Bluffs, NE-IA	351
57	43	Worcester, MA-CT	1,628	18	43	Tampa-St. Petersburg-Clearwater, FL	341
22	44	Orlando-Kissimmee-Sanford, FL	1,583	72	43	North Port-Sarasota-Bradenton, FL	341
16	45	Minneapolis-St. Paul-Bloomington, MN	1,558	52	45	Grand Rapids-Wyoming, MI	337
43	46	Memphis, TN-MS-AR	1,555	56	46	Urban Honolulu, HI	335
44	47	Richmond, VA	1,521	17	47	San Diego-Carlsbad, CA	330
26	48	Sacramento--Roseville--Arden-Arcade, CA	1,504	66	48	New Haven-Milford, CT	323
23	49	Charlotte-Concord-Gastonia, NC-SC	1,487	30	49	Austin-Round Rock, TX	317
49	50	Birmingham-Hoover, AL	1,483	38	50	Providence-Warwick, RI-MA	315
11	51	Phoenix-Mesa-Scottsdale, AZ	1,447	73	51	Dayton, OH	311
36	52	Nashville-Davidson--Murfreesboro--Franklin, TN	1,445	6	52	Washington-Arlington-Alexandria, DC-VA-MD-WV	301
40	52	Jacksonville, FL	1,445	65	53	McAllen-Edinburg-Mission, TX	296
53	54	Tucson, AZ	1,438	64	54	Albany-Schenectady-Troy, NY	290
34	55	Indianapolis-Carmel-Anderson, IN	1,402	27	55	Pittsburgh, PA	289
47	56	Salt Lake City, UT	1,399	16	56	Minneapolis-St. Paul-Bloomington, MN	288
70	57	Columbia, SC	1,385	32	57	Columbus, OH	285
18	58	Tampa-St. Petersburg-Clearwater, FL	1,381	51	58	Rochester, NY	281
14	59	Detroit-Warren-Dearborn, MI	1,374	35	59	San Jose-Sunnyvale-Santa Clara, CA	280
28	60	Las Vegas-Henderson-Paradise, NV	1,367	25	60	Portland-Vancouver-Hillsboro, OR-WA	276
62	61	Bakersfield, CA	1,365	67	61	Oxnard-Thousand Oaks-Ventura, CA	258
56	62	Urban Honolulu, HI	1,348	29	62	Cincinnati, OH-KY-IN	257
42	63	Raleigh, NC	1,332	48	63	Hartford-West Hartford-East Hartford, CT	238
41	64	Oklahoma City, OK	1,331	58	64	Bridgeport-Stamford-Norwalk, CT	230
13	65	Riverside-San Bernardino-Ontario, CA	1,326	10		Boston-Cambridge-Newton, MA-NH	NA
68	66	El Paso, TX	1,321	20		St. Louis, MO-IL	NA
55	67	Tulsa, OK	1,319	23		Charlotte-Concord-Gastonia, NC-SC	NA
45	68	Louisville/Jefferson County, KY-IN	1,265	31		Kansas City, MO-KS	NA
75	69	Greensboro-High Point, NC	1,262	42		Raleigh, NC	NA
60	70	Albuquerque, NM	1,208	44		Richmond, VA	NA
63	71	Knoxville, TN	1,191	49		Birmingham-Hoover, AL	NA
52	72	Grand Rapids-Wyoming, MI	1,159	57		Worcester, MA-CT	NA
54	73	Fresno, CA	1,131	61		Greenville-Anderson-Mauldin, SC	NA
65	74	McAllen-Edinburg-Mission, TX	1,071	69		Allentown-Bethlehem-Easton, PA-NJ	NA
61	75	Greenville-Anderson-Mauldin, SC	978	75		Greensboro-High Point, NC	NA

75 Largest Metropolitan Areas by 2018 Population
Selected Rankings

Nonemployer businesses, 2016				Value of residential construction authorized by building permits, 2018			
Population rank	Non-employer businesses rank	Metropolitan area	Non-employer businesses [col 167]	Population rank	New construction rank	Metropolitan area	New construction ($1,000) [col 169]
1	1	New York-Newark-Jersey City, NY-NJ-PA	1,902,946	4	1	Dallas-Fort Worth-Arlington, TX	13,110,100
2	2	Los Angeles-Long Beach-Anaheim, CA	1,353,478	1	2	New York-Newark-Jersey City, NY-NJ-PA	8,228,018
7	3	Miami-Fort Lauderdale-West Palm Beach, FL	892,975	5	3	Houston-The Woodlands-Sugar Land, TX	7,880,444
3	4	Chicago-Naperville-Elgin, IL-IN-WI	792,915	2	4	Los Angeles-Long Beach-Anaheim, CA	7,847,474
4	5	Dallas-Fort Worth-Arlington, TX	643,314	9	5	Atlanta-Sandy Springs-Roswell, GA	6,730,191
9	6	Atlanta-Sandy Springs-Roswell, GA	572,951	11	6	Phoenix-Mesa-Scottsdale, AZ	6,502,995
5	7	Houston-The Woodlands-Sugar Land, TX	562,758	15	7	Seattle-Tacoma-Bellevue, WA	6,016,009
6	8	Washington-Arlington-Alexandria, DC-VA-MD-WV	549,377	22	8	Orlando-Kissimmee-Sanford, FL	5,043,464
12	9	San Francisco-Oakland-Hayward, CA	447,000	12	9	San Francisco-Oakland-Hayward, CA	4,793,715
8	10	Philadelphia-Camden-Wilmington, PA-NJ-DE-MD	425,972	6	10	Washington-Arlington-Alexandria, DC-VA-MD-WV	4,569,027
10	11	Boston-Cambridge-Newton, MA-NH	392,720	7	11	Miami-Fort Lauderdale-West Palm Beach, FL	4,566,545
14	12	Detroit-Warren-Dearborn, MI	335,864	19	12	Denver-Aurora-Lakewood, CO	4,479,714
11	13	Phoenix-Mesa-Scottsdale, AZ	329,315	23	13	Charlotte-Concord-Gastonia, NC-SC	4,456,543
13	14	Riverside-San Bernardino-Ontario, CA	308,401	30	14	Austin-Round Rock, TX	4,454,994
17	15	San Diego-Carlsbad, CA	277,207	3	15	Chicago-Naperville-Elgin, IL-IN-WI	4,186,157
16	16	Minneapolis-St. Paul-Bloomington, MN	269,649	18	16	Tampa-St. Petersburg-Clearwater, FL	4,141,302
15	17	Seattle-Tacoma-Bellevue, WA	263,135	36	17	Nashville-Davidson--Murfreesboro--Franklin, TN	4,082,862
19	18	Denver-Aurora-Lakewood, CO	258,376	16	18	Minneapolis-St. Paul-Bloomington, MN	3,569,215
18	19	Tampa-St. Petersburg-Clearwater, FL	246,143	10	19	Boston-Cambridge-Newton, MA-NH	3,256,773
22	20	Orlando-Kissimmee-Sanford, FL	226,474	13	20	Riverside-San Bernardino-Ontario, CA	3,170,580
21	21	Baltimore-Columbia-Towson, MD	210,872	25	21	Portland-Vancouver-Hillsboro, OR-WA	3,122,424
23	22	Charlotte-Concord-Gastonia, NC-SC	193,812	40	22	Jacksonville, FL	2,740,377
30	23	Austin-Round Rock, TX	188,226	42	23	Raleigh, NC	2,632,993
20	24	St. Louis, MO-IL	187,228	17	24	San Diego-Carlsbad, CA	2,432,915
25	25	Portland-Vancouver-Hillsboro, OR-WA	180,731	26	25	Sacramento--Roseville--Arden-Arcade, CA	2,409,421
24	26	San Antonio-New Braunfels, TX	179,833	14	26	Detroit-Warren-Dearborn, MI	2,250,302
36	27	Nashville-Davidson--Murfreesboro--Franklin, TN	172,840	34	27	Indianapolis-Carmel-Anderson, IN	2,190,102
28	28	Las Vegas-Henderson-Paradise, NV	167,624	24	28	San Antonio-New Braunfels, TX	2,130,334
26	29	Sacramento--Roseville--Arden-Arcade, CA	167,269	8	29	Philadelphia-Camden-Wilmington, PA-NJ-DE-MD	2,030,197
32	30	Columbus, OH	152,042	31	30	Kansas City, MO-KS	1,970,930
33	31	Cleveland-Elyria, OH	150,293	35	31	San Jose-Sunnyvale-Santa Clara, CA	1,875,263
27	32	Pittsburgh, PA	147,613	72	32	North Port-Sarasota-Bradenton, FL	1,856,925
35	33	San Jose-Sunnyvale-Santa Clara, CA	147,097	28	33	Las Vegas-Henderson-Paradise, NV	1,844,987
31	34	Kansas City, MO-KS	145,940	61	34	Greenville-Anderson-Mauldin, SC	1,795,415
29	35	Cincinnati, OH-KY-IN	142,037	32	35	Columbus, OH	1,758,539
34	36	Indianapolis-Carmel-Anderson, IN	139,555	20	36	St. Louis, MO-IL	1,647,750
46	37	New Orleans-Metairie, LA	119,932	74	37	Charleston-North Charleston, SC	1,606,852
43	38	Memphis, TN-MS-AR	111,608	47	38	Salt Lake City, UT	1,486,818
38	39	Providence-Warwick, RI-MA	111,009	21	39	Baltimore-Columbia-Towson, MD	1,256,273
40	40	Jacksonville, FL	108,197	29	40	Cincinnati, OH-KY-IN	1,240,838
41	41	Oklahoma City, OK	108,020	41	41	Oklahoma City, OK	1,199,517
42	42	Raleigh, NC	104,889	37	42	Virginia Beach-Norfolk-Newport News, VA-NC	1,107,543
37	43	Virginia Beach-Norfolk-Newport News, VA-NC	103,185	44	43	Richmond, VA	1,104,317
58	44	Bridgeport-Stamford-Norwalk, CT	94,038	53	44	Tucson, AZ	1,025,886
39	45	Milwaukee-Waukesha-West Allis, WI	91,300	45	45	Louisville/Jefferson County, KY-IN	1,022,768
47	46	Salt Lake City, UT	88,227	27	46	Pittsburgh, PA	955,403
44	47	Richmond, VA	87,390	52	47	Grand Rapids-Wyoming, MI	930,596
45	48	Louisville/Jefferson County, KY-IN	87,085	63	48	Knoxville, TN	840,797
49	49	Birmingham-Hoover, AL	82,208	70	49	Columbia, SC	805,323
48	50	Hartford-West Hartford-East Hartford, CT	81,630	59	50	Omaha-Council Bluffs, NE-IA	797,040
55	51	Tulsa, OK	73,270	33	51	Cleveland-Elyria, OH	760,385
52	52	Grand Rapids-Wyoming, MI	72,616	39	52	Milwaukee-Waukesha-West Allis, WI	760,232
72	53	North Port-Sarasota-Bradenton, FL	70,304	71	53	Baton Rouge, LA	743,893
65	54	McAllen-Edinburg-Mission, TX	70,258	55	54	Tulsa, OK	733,732
67	55	Oxnard-Thousand Oaks-Ventura, CA	69,019	43	55	Memphis, TN-MS-AR	724,726
56	56	Urban Honolulu, HI	66,902	58	56	Bridgeport-Stamford-Norwalk, CT	667,495
53	57	Tucson, AZ	65,734	46	57	New Orleans-Metairie, LA	655,895
51	58	Rochester, NY	63,267	49	58	Birmingham-Hoover, AL	654,728
71	59	Baton Rouge, LA	63,014	54	59	Fresno, CA	627,312
74	60	Charleston-North Charleston, SC	61,969	65	60	McAllen-Edinburg-Mission, TX	609,699
63	61	Knoxville, TN	61,476	75	61	Greensboro-High Point, NC	603,220
61	62	Greenville-Anderson-Mauldin, SC	61,444	68	62	El Paso, TX	601,524
66	63	New Haven-Milford, CT	61,104	62	63	Bakersfield, CA	565,821
59	64	Omaha-Council Bluffs, NE-IA	59,958	56	64	Urban Honolulu, HI	504,266
57	65	Worcester, MA-CT	59,570	67	65	Oxnard-Thousand Oaks-Ventura, CA	461,558
68	66	El Paso, TX	59,276	60	66	Albuquerque, NM	448,738
50	67	Buffalo-Cheektowaga-Niagara Falls, NY	57,470	64	67	Albany-Schenectady-Troy, NY	444,376
75	68	Greensboro-High Point, NC	55,593	38	68	Providence-Warwick, RI-MA	412,316
70	69	Columbia, SC	54,672	50	69	Buffalo-Cheektowaga-Niagara Falls, NY	382,666
64	70	Albany-Schenectady-Troy, NY	52,844	73	70	Dayton, OH	369,085
60	71	Albuquerque, NM	52,689	51	71	Rochester, NY	327,536
54	72	Fresno, CA	51,942	57	72	Worcester, MA-CT	324,565
69	73	Allentown-Bethlehem-Easton, PA-NJ	51,564	48	73	Hartford-West Hartford-East Hartford, CT	258,634
73	74	Dayton, OH	48,249	69	74	Allentown-Bethlehem-Easton, PA-NJ	218,124
62	75	Bakersfield, CA	45,491	66	75	New Haven-Milford, CT	124,211

75 Metropolitan Areas with Highest Agricultural Sales
Selected Rankings

Value of agricultural products sold, 2017				Number of farms, 2017		
Value of sales rank	Metropolitan area	Value of sales (millions of dollars) [col 125]	Value of sales rank	Number of farms rank	Metropolitan area	Number of farms [col 113]
1	Fresno, CA	5,743	65	1	Dallas-Fort Worth-Arlington, TX	30,782
2	Visalia-Porterville, CA	4,475	37	2	Kansas City, MO-KS	12,437
3	Salinas, CA	4,116	11	3	Minneapolis-St. Paul-Bloomington, MN	12,423
4	Bakersfield, CA	4,077	35	4	Portland-Vancouver-Hillsboro, OR-WA	11,755
5	Merced, CA	2,938	25	5	St. Louis, MO-IL	11,057
6	Modesto, CA	2,526	32	6	Columbus, OH	8,506
7	Stockton-Lodi, CA	2,176	41	7	Atlanta-Sandy Springs-Roswell, GA	7,760
8	Phoenix-Mesa-Scottsdale, AZ	2,071	63	8	New York-Newark-Jersey City, NY-NJ-P	7,135
9	Greeley, CO	2,047	36	9	Charlotte-Concord-Gastonia, NC-SC	6,969
10	Yakima, WA	1,988	29	10	Madison, WI	6,927
11	Minneapolis-St. Paul-Bloomington, MN	1,882	12	11	Chicago-Naperville-Elgin, IL-IN-WI	6,565
12	Chicago-Naperville-Elgin, IL-IN-WI	1,860	26	12	Philadelphia-Camden-Wilmington, PA-N	6,506
13	El Centro, CA	1,860	20	13	Fayetteville-Springdale-Rogers, AR-M	6,384
14	Salisbury, MD-DE	1,828	40	14	Indianapolis-Carmel-Anderson, IN	5,999
15	Miami-Fort Lauderdale-West Palm Beach, FL	1,764	22	15	Omaha-Council Bluffs, NE-IA	5,843
16	Sioux City, IA-NE-SD	1,651	55	16	Wichita, KS	5,276
17	Hanford-Corcoran, CA	1,649	23	17	Lancaster, PA	5,108
18	Kennewick-Richland, WA	1,637	34	18	Boise City, ID	5,108
19	Oxnard-Thousand Oaks-Ventura, CA	1,633	49	19	San Diego-Carlsbad, CA	5,082
20	Fayetteville-Springdale-Rogers, AR-MO	1,579	1	20	Fresno, CA	4,774
21	Santa Maria-Santa Barbara, CA	1,520	31	21	Sacramento--Roseville--Arden-Arcade,	4,737
22	Omaha-Council Bluffs, NE-IA	1,510	15	22	Miami-Fort Lauderdale-West Palm Beac	4,690
23	Lancaster, PA	1,507	54	23	Des Moines-West Des Moines, IA	4,672
24	Madera, CA	1,493	60	24	Lexington-Fayette, KY	4,619
25	St. Louis, MO-IL	1,376	75	25	Tampa-St. Petersburg-Clearwater, FL	4,325
26	Philadelphia-Camden-Wilmington, PA-NJ-DE-MD	1,359	38	26	Rochester, NY	4,215
27	Twin Falls, ID	1,320	2	27	Visalia-Porterville, CA	4,187
28	Riverside-San Bernardino-Ontario, CA	1,306	9	28	Greeley, CO	4,062
29	Madison, WI	1,159	30	29	Grand Rapids-Wyoming, MI	4,040
30	Grand Rapids-Wyoming, MI	1,090	48	30	Salem, OR	4,004
31	Sacramento--Roseville--Arden-Arcade, CA	1,081	42	31	Rochester, MN	3,960
32	Columbus, OH	1,079	39	32	St. Cloud, MN	3,767
33	Grand Island, NE	1,054	28	33	Riverside-San Bernardino-Ontario, CA	3,729
34	Boise City, ID	1,022	16	34	Sioux City, IA-NE-SD	3,647
35	Portland-Vancouver-Hillsboro, OR-WA	1,020	47	35	Cedar Rapids, IA	3,632
36	Charlotte-Concord-Gastonia, NC-SC	1,002	6	36	Modesto, CA	3,621
37	Kansas City, MO-KS	985	44	37	Santa Rosa, CA	3,594
38	Rochester, NY	957	66	38	Jackson, MS	3,523
39	St. Cloud, MN	955	51	39	Peoria, IL	3,495
40	Indianapolis-Carmel-Anderson, IN	944	45	40	Davenport-Moline-Rock Island, IA-IL	3,434
41	Atlanta-Sandy Springs-Roswell, GA	931	7	41	Stockton-Lodi, CA	3,430
42	Rochester, MN	931	64	42	Columbia, SC	3,325
43	Sioux Falls, SD	920	74	43	Orlando-Kissimmee-Sanford, FL	3,120
44	Santa Rosa, CA	919	43	44	Sioux Falls, SD	3,048
45	Davenport-Moline-Rock Island, IA-IL	894	10	45	Yakima, WA	2,952
46	Iowa City, IA	892	56	46	Waterloo-Cedar Falls, IA	2,691
47	Cedar Rapids, IA	855	8	47	Phoenix-Mesa-Scottsdale, AZ	2,636
48	Salem, OR	836	57	48	Green Bay, WI	2,464
49	San Diego-Carlsbad, CA	831	46	49	Iowa City, IA	2,386
50	Mankato-North Mankato, MN	823	62	50	San Luis Obispo-Paso Robles-Arroyo G	2,349
51	Peoria, IL	818	5	51	Merced, CA	2,337
52	Amarillo, TX	802	18	52	Kennewick-Richland, WA	2,292
53	Harrisonburg, VA	796	33	53	Grand Island, NE	2,268
54	Des Moines-West Des Moines, IA	774	14	54	Salisbury, MD-DE	2,237
55	Wichita, KS	760	59	55	Champaign-Urbana, IL	2,200
56	Waterloo-Cedar Falls, IA	758	58	56	Grand Forks, ND-MN	2,147
57	Green Bay, WI	753	19	57	Oxnard-Thousand Oaks-Ventura, CA	2,135
58	Grand Forks, ND-MN	748	53	58	Harrisonburg, VA	2,026
59	Champaign-Urbana, IL	732	69	59	Yuba City, CA	1,921
60	Lexington-Fayette, KY	723	70	60	Bloomington, IL	1,920
61	Fargo, ND-MN	717	71	61	Napa, CA	1,866
62	San Luis Obispo-Paso Robles-Arroyo Grande, CA	702	73	62	Reading, PA	1,809
63	New York-Newark-Jersey City, NY-NJ-PA	678	4	63	Bakersfield, CA	1,731
64	Columbia, SC	649	52	64	Amarillo, TX	1,699
65	Dallas-Fort Worth-Arlington, TX	635	27	65	Twin Falls, ID	1,697
66	Jackson, MS	616	50	66	Mankato-North Mankato, MN	1,672
67	Santa Cruz-Watsonville, CA	607	72	67	Lafayette-West Lafayette, IN	1,624
68	Goldsboro, NC	592	61	68	Fargo, ND-MN	1,478
69	Yuba City, CA	591	21	69	Santa Maria-Santa Barbara, CA	1,467
70	Bloomington, IL	578	24	70	Madera, CA	1,386
71	Napa, CA	573	3	71	Salinas, CA	1,104
72	Lafayette-West Lafayette, IN	572	17	72	Hanford-Corcoran, CA	963
73	Reading, PA	555	67	73	Santa Cruz-Watsonville, CA	625
74	Orlando-Kissimmee-Sanford, FL	555	68	74	Goldsboro, NC	551
75	Tampa-St. Petersburg-Clearwater, FL	535	13	75	El Centro, CA	396

75 Metropolitan Areas with Highest Agricultural Sales
Selected Rankings

Land in farms, 2017				Average value of agricultural land and buildings per acre, 2017			
Value of sales rank	Land in farms rank	Metropolitan area	Land in farms (1,000 acres) [col 117]	Value of sales rank	Value per Acre rank	Metropolitan area	Value per acre (1,000 acres) [col 123]
65	1	Dallas-Fort Worth-Arlington, TX	4,082	71	1	Napa, CA	44,154
37	2	Kansas City, MO-KS	3,126	19	2	Oxnard-Thousand Oaks-Ventura, CA	25,498
55	3	Wichita, KS	2,913	49	3	San Diego-Carlsbad, CA	23,209
52	4	Amarillo, TX	2,893	44	4	Santa Rosa, CA	22,186
25	5	St. Louis, MO-IL	2,780	67	5	Santa Cruz-Watsonville, CA	21,352
11	6	Minneapolis-St. Paul-Bloomington, MN	2,492	28	6	Riverside-San Bernardino-Ontario, CA	18,504
22	7	Omaha-Council Bluffs, NE-IA	2,363	23	7	Lancaster, PA	18,285
4	8	Bakersfield, CA	2,295	6	8	Modesto, CA	15,619
12	9	Chicago-Naperville-Elgin, IL-IN-WI	2,147	7	9	Stockton-Lodi, CA	15,020
9	10	Greeley, CO	2,099	35	10	Portland-Vancouver-Hillsboro, OR-WA	14,558
58	11	Grand Forks, ND-MN	1,822	5	11	Merced, CA	13,086
10	12	Yakima, WA	1,781	63	12	New York-Newark-Jersey City, NY-NJ-P	12,945
61	13	Fargo, ND-MN	1,703	15	13	Miami-Fort Lauderdale-West Palm Beac	12,654
16	14	Sioux City, IA-NE-SD	1,690	2	14	Visalia-Porterville, CA	11,726
32	15	Columbus, OH	1,666	1	15	Fresno, CA	11,359
1	16	Fresno, CA	1,647	73	16	Reading, PA	11,209
40	17	Indianapolis-Carmel-Anderson, IN	1,603	13	17	El Centro, CA	11,135
8	18	Phoenix-Mesa-Scottsdale, AZ	1,595	24	18	Madera, CA	10,958
29	19	Madison, WI	1,463	17	19	Hanford-Corcoran, CA	10,815
43	20	Sioux Falls, SD	1,429	26	20	Philadelphia-Camden-Wilmington, PA-N	10,688
34	21	Boise City, ID	1,351	48	21	Salem, OR	10,580
3	22	Salinas, CA	1,340	21	22	Santa Maria-Santa Barbara, CA	10,381
54	23	Des Moines-West Des Moines, IA	1,338	75	23	Tampa-St. Petersburg-Clearwater, FL	9,761
2	24	Visalia-Porterville, CA	1,250	70	24	Bloomington, IL	9,508
18	25	Kennewick-Richland, WA	1,229	31	25	Sacramento--Roseville--Arden-Arcade,	9,440
51	26	Peoria, IL	1,215	69	26	Yuba City, CA	9,107
33	27	Grand Island, NE	1,164	59	27	Champaign-Urbana, IL	8,927
45	28	Davenport-Moline-Rock Island, IA-IL	1,146	53	28	Harrisonburg, VA	8,844
42	29	Rochester, MN	1,140	56	29	Waterloo-Cedar Falls, IA	8,630
59	30	Champaign-Urbana, IL	1,109	12	30	Chicago-Naperville-Elgin, IL-IN-WI	8,547
47	31	Cedar Rapids, IA	1,089	51	31	Peoria, IL	8,331
20	32	Fayetteville-Springdale-Rogers, AR-M	1,030	72	32	Lafayette-West Lafayette, IN	8,083
66	33	Jackson, MS	1,017	45	33	Davenport-Moline-Rock Island, IA-IL	7,762
5	34	Merced, CA	946	62	34	San Luis Obispo-Paso Robles-Arroyo G	7,547
62	35	San Luis Obispo-Paso Robles-Arroyo G	931	47	35	Cedar Rapids, IA	7,533
31	36	Sacramento--Roseville--Arden-Arcade,	929	46	36	Iowa City, IA	7,457
38	37	Rochester, NY	900	4	37	Bakersfield, CA	7,380
36	38	Charlotte-Concord-Gastonia, NC-SC	885	3	38	Salinas, CA	7,368
41	39	Atlanta-Sandy Springs-Roswell, GA	872	40	39	Indianapolis-Carmel-Anderson, IN	7,349
56	40	Waterloo-Cedar Falls, IA	862	14	40	Salisbury, MD-DE	7,315
74	41	Orlando-Kissimmee-Sanford, FL	853	60	41	Lexington-Fayette, KY	7,245
39	42	St. Cloud, MN	846	50	42	Mankato-North Mankato, MN	7,121
70	43	Bloomington, IL	806	16	43	Sioux City, IA-NE-SD	6,855
7	44	Stockton-Lodi, CA	773	54	44	Des Moines-West Des Moines, IA	6,828
60	45	Lexington-Fayette, KY	752	32	45	Columbus, OH	6,557
6	46	Modesto, CA	723	29	46	Madison, WI	6,346
21	47	Santa Maria-Santa Barbara, CA	715	22	47	Omaha-Council Bluffs, NE-IA	6,243
30	48	Grand Rapids-Wyoming, MI	714	25	48	St. Louis, MO-IL	6,158
72	49	Lafayette-West Lafayette, IN	697	57	49	Green Bay, WI	6,120
26	50	Philadelphia-Camden-Wilmington, PA-N	656	42	50	Rochester, MN	6,115
50	51	Mankato-North Mankato, MN	648	36	51	Charlotte-Concord-Gastonia, NC-SC	6,009
24	52	Madera, CA	645	11	52	Minneapolis-St. Paul-Bloomington, MN	5,982
27	53	Twin Falls, ID	640	30	53	Grand Rapids-Wyoming, MI	5,943
17	54	Hanford-Corcoran, CA	616	43	54	Sioux Falls, SD	5,616
46	55	Iowa City, IA	615	74	55	Orlando-Kissimmee-Sanford, FL	5,516
35	56	Portland-Vancouver-Hillsboro, OR-WA	597	41	56	Atlanta-Sandy Springs-Roswell, GA	5,337
64	57	Columbia, SC	575	33	57	Grand Island, NE	5,035
15	58	Miami-Fort Lauderdale-West Palm Beac	573	68	58	Goldsboro, NC	4,990
44	59	Santa Rosa, CA	567	39	59	St. Cloud, MN	4,974
69	60	Yuba City, CA	560	27	60	Twin Falls, ID	4,868
57	61	Green Bay, WI	552	65	61	Dallas-Fort Worth-Arlington, TX	4,740
63	62	New York-Newark-Jersey City, NY-NJ-P	532	8	62	Phoenix-Mesa-Scottsdale, AZ	4,689
14	63	Salisbury, MD-DE	523	20	63	Fayetteville-Springdale-Rogers, AR-M	4,456
13	64	El Centro, CA	522	18	64	Kennewick-Richland, WA	4,247
48	65	Salem, OR	438	38	65	Rochester, NY	3,920
75	66	Tampa-St. Petersburg-Clearwater, FL	425	61	66	Fargo, ND-MN	3,795
23	67	Lancaster, PA	394	34	67	Boise City, ID	3,783
28	68	Riverside-San Bernardino-Ontario, CA	332	64	68	Columbia, SC	3,643
19	69	Oxnard-Thousand Oaks-Ventura, CA	260	37	69	Kansas City, MO-KS	3,606
71	70	Napa, CA	256	58	70	Grand Forks, ND-MN	3,338
53	71	Harrisonburg, VA	229	66	71	Jackson, MS	2,900
73	72	Reading, PA	225	10	72	Yakima, WA	2,755
49	73	San Diego-Carlsbad, CA	222	9	73	Greeley, CO	2,586
68	74	Goldsboro, NC	165	55	74	Wichita, KS	2,351
67	75	Santa Cruz-Watsonville, CA	64	52	75	Amarillo, TX	1,109

Table C. Metropolitan Areas — **Land Area and Population**

CBSA/ DIV Code[1]	Area name	Land area[2] (sq mi)	Total persons	Rank	Per square mile	White	Black	American Indian, Alaska Native	Asian and Pacific Islander	Percent Hispanic or Latino[3]	Under 5 years	5 to 17 years	18 to 24 years	25 to 34 years	35 to 44 years	45 to 54 years
			Population, 2018			**Population characteristics, 2018**										
						Race alone or in combination, not Hispanic or Latino (percent)					**Age (percent)**					
		1	2	3	4	5	6	7	8	9	10	11	12	13	14	15

1. CBSA = Core Based Statistical Area. DIV = Metropolitan Division. See Appendix A for explanation. See Appendix B for list of metropolitan areas or temporarily covered by water. 2. Dry land or land partially or temporarily covered by water. 3. May be of any race.

Table C. Metropolitan Areas — **Population and Households**

Area name	55 to 64 years	65 to 74 years	75 years and over	Percent female	2000	2010	2000-2010	2010-2018	Births	Deaths	Net migration	Number	Persons per house-hold	Family house-holds	Female family house-holder[1]	One person
	Age (percent) (cont.)				**Total persons**		**Percent change**		**Components of change, 2010-2018**						**Percent**	
					Population change and components of change, 2000-2018							**Households, 2017**				
	16	17	18	19	20	21	22	23	24	25	26	27	28	29	30	31

1. No spouse present

Table C. Metropolitan Areas — **Population, Vital Statistics, Health, and Crime**

Area name	Persons in group quarters, 2018	Number	Employ-ment/ residence ratio	Total	Rate[1]	Number	Rate[1]	Number	Percent	Total Ben-eficiaries	Enrolled in Original Medicare	Enrolled in Medicare Advantage	Number	Rate[3]
		Daytime population, 2017		**Births, 2018**		**Deaths, 2018**		**Persons under 65 with no health insurance 2017**		**Medicare, 2018**			**Serious crimes known to police[2], 2016**	
													Total	
	32	33	34	35	36	37	38	39	40	41	42	43	44	45

1. Per 1,000 estimated resident population. 2. Data for serious crimes have not been adjusted for underreporting; this may affect comparability between geographic areas and over time. 3. Per 100,000 population estimated by the FBI.

Table C. Metropolitan Areas — **Crime, Education, Money Income, and Poverty**

Area name	Violent	Property	Total	Percent private	High school gradu-ate or less	Bach-elor's degree or more	Total current expendi-tures (mil dol)	Current expen-ditures per student (dollars)	Per capita income[6] (dollars)	Mean house-hold income (dollars)	Median house-hold income	Percent of house-holds with income less than $50,000	Percent of house-holds with income of $200,000 or more	All persons	Chil-dren under 18 years	Age 65 years and older
	Rate		**Enrollment[3]**		**Attainment[4]**		**Local government expenditures,[5] 2014-2015**								**Percent below poverty level**	
			School enrollment and attainment, 2017						**Income and poverty, 2017**							
															Serious crimes known to police[2], 2016 (cont.)	
	46	47	48	49	50	51	52	53	54	55	56	57	58	59	60	61

1. Data for serious crimes have not been adjusted for underreporting; this may affect comparability between geographic areas and over time. 2. Per 100,000 population estimated by the FBI. 3. All persons 3 years old and over enrolled in nursery school through college. 4. Persons 25 years old and over. 5. Elementary and secondary education expenditures. 6. Based on population estimated by the American Community Survey, 2017.

Table C. Metropolitan Areas — **Personal Income and Earnings**

Area name	Personal income, 2017											Earnings, 2017		
	Total (mil dol)	Percent change, 2016-2017	Per capita[1]		Wages and Salaries (mil dol)	Supplements to wages and salaries, employer contributions (mil dol)		Proprietors' income	Dividends, interest, and rent (mil dol)	Personal transfer receipts (mil dol)		Total (mil dol)	Contributrions for government social insurance (mil dol)	
			Dollars	Rank		Pension and insurance	Government social insurance						From employee and self-employed	From employer
	62	63	64	65	66	67	68	69	70	71		72	73	74

1. Based on the resident population estimated as of July 1 of the year shown.

Table C. Metropolitan Areas — **Earnings, Social Security, and Housing**

Area name	Earnings, 2017 (cont.)									Social Security beneficiaries, December 2017		Supplemental Security Income Recipients, December 2017	Housing units, 2018	
	Percent by selected industries													
	Farm	Mining, quarrying, and extracting	Construction	Manufacturing	Information; professional, scientific, and technical serviecs	Retail trade	Finance, insurance, real estate, rental and leasing	Health care and social assistance	Government	Number	Rate[1]		Total	Percent change, 2010-2018
	75	76	77	78	79	80	81	82	83	84	85	86	87	88

1. Per 1,000 resident population estimated as of July 1 of the year shown.

Table C. Metropolitan Areas — **Housing, Labor Force, and Employment**

Area name	Housing units, 2017								Civilian labor force, 2018				Civilian employment[5], 2017		
	Occupied units										Unemployment			Percent	
		Owner-occupied				Renter-occupied									
				Median owner cost as a percent of income			Median rent as a percent of income								
	Total	Percent	Median value[1]	With a mortgage	Without a mortgage[2]	Median rent[3]		Internet access	Total	Percent change 2017-2018	Total	Rate[4]	Total	Management, business, science, and arts	Construction, production, and maintenance occupations
	89	90	91	92	93	94	95	96	97	98	99	100	101	102	103

1. Specified owner-occupied units. 2. A value of 10.0 represents 10 percent or less; a value of 50.0 represents 50 percent or more. 3. Specified renter-occupied units. 4. Overcrowded or
lacking complete plumbing facilities. 5. Percent of civilian labor force. 6. Civilian employed persons 16 years old and over.

Table C. Metropolitan Areas — **Nonfarm Employment and Agriculture**

Area name	Private nonfarm establishments, employment and payroll, 2016									Agriculture, 2017				
		Employment						Annual payroll		Farms			Farm producers whose primary occupation is farming (percent)
											Percent with:		
	Number of establishments	Total	Health care and social assistance	Manufacturing	Retail trade	Finance and insurance	Professional, scientific, and technical services	Total (mil dol)	Average per employee (dollars)	Number	Fewer than 50 acres	1000 acres or more	
	104	105	106	107	108	109	110	111	112	113	114	115	116

794

Table C. Metropolitan Areas — **Agriculture**

Area name	Agriculture, 2017 (cont.)															
	Land in farms					Value of land and buildings (dollars)		Value of machinery and equipmnet, average per farm (dollars)	Value of products sold:				Organic farms (num-ber)	Farms with internet access (percent)	Government payments	
			Acres								Percent from:					
	Acreage (1,000)	Percent change, 2012-2017	Aver-age size of farm	Total irrigated (1,000)	Total cropland (1,000)	Average per farm	Aver-age per acre		Total (mil dol)	Average per farm (acres)	Crops	Live-stock and poultry products			Total ($1,000)	Percent of farms
	117	118	119	120	121	122	123	124	125	126	127	128	129	130	131	132

Table C. Metropolitan Areas — **Water Use, Wholesale Trade, Retail Trade, and Real Estate**

Area name	Water use, 2015		Wholesale Trade[1], 2012				Retail Trade[2], 2012				Real estate and rental and leasing,[2] 2012			
	Public supply water withdrawn (mil gal/day)	Public supply gallons withdrawn per person per day	Number of establish-ments	Number of employees	Sales (mil dol)	Average payroll (mil dol)	Number of establish-ments	Number of employees	Sales (mil dol)	Average payroll (mil dol)	Number of establish-ments	Number of employees	Sales (mil dol)	Average payroll (mil dol)
	133	134	135	136	137	138	139	140	141	142	143	144	145	146

1. Merchant wholesalers, except manufacturers' sales branches and offices. 2. Employer establishments.

Table C. Metropolitan Areas — **Professional Services, Manufacturing, and Accommodation and Food Services**

Area name	Professional, scientific, and technical services, 2012				Manufacturing, 2012				Accommodation and food services, 2012			
	Number of establish-ments	Number of employees	Sales (mil dol)	Average payroll (mil dol)	Number of establish-ments	Number of employees	Receipts (mil dol)	Annual payroll (mil dol)	Number of establish-ments	Number of employees	Receipts (mil dol)	Annual payroll (mil dol)
	147	148	149	150	151	152	153	154	155	156	157	158

Table C. Metropolitan Areas — **Health Care and Social Assistance, Other Services, Nonemployer Businesses, and Residential Construction**

Area name	Health care and social assistance, 2012				Other services, 2012				Nonemployer businesses, 2016		Value of residential construction authorized by building permits, 2018	
	Number of establish-ments	Number of employees	Receipts (mil dol)	Annual payroll (mil dol)	Number of establish-ments	Number of employees	Receipts (mil dol)	Annual payroll (mil dol)	Number	Receipts (mil dol)	New construc-tion ($1,000)	Number of housing units
	159	160	161	162	163	164	165	166	167	168	169	170

Table C. Metropolitan Areas — **Government Employment and Payroll, and Local Government Finances**

Area name	Government employment and payroll, 2012									Local government finances, 2012				
			March payroll (percent of total)							General revenue				
												Taxes		
													Per capita[1] (dollars)	
	Full-time equivalent employees	March payroll (dollars)	Administration, judicial, and legal	Police and corrections	Fire protection	Highways and transportation	Health and welfare	Natural resources and utilities	Education and libraries	Total (mil dol)	Inter-governmental (mil dol)	Total (mil dol)	Total	Property
	171	172	173	174	175	176	177	178	179	180	181	182	183	184

Table C. Metropolitan Areas — **Local Government Finances, Government Employment, and Income Taxes**

Area name	Local government finances, 2012 (cont.)									Government employment, 2017			Individual income tax returns, 2016		
	Direct general expenditure							Debt outstanding							
				Percent of total for:											
	Total (mil dol)	Per capita[1] (dollars)	Education	Health and hospitals	Police protection	Public welfare	Highways	Total (mil dol)	Per capita[1] (dollars)	Federal civilian	Federal military	State and local	Number of returns	Mean adjusted gross income	Mean income tax
	185	186	187	188	189	190	191	192	193	194	195	196	197	198	199

1. Based on the resident population estimated as of July 1 of the year shown.

Table C. Metropolitan Areas — **Land Area and Population**

CBSA/ DIV Code[1]	Area name	Land area[2] (sq mi)	Total persons	Rank	Per square mile	White	Black	American Indian, Alaska Native	Asian and Pacific Islander	Percent Hispanic or Latino[3]	Under 5 years	5 to 17 years	18 to 24 years	25 to 34 years	35 to 44 years	45 to 54 years
		1	2	3	4	5	6	7	8	9	10	11	12	13	14	15
10180	Abilene, TX............................	2,743.5	171,451	246	62.5	66.1	8.4	0.9	2.7	23.9	6.9	16.8	13.1	14.7	11.8	10.3
10420	Akron, OH..............................	900.2	704,845	82	783.0	81.7	13.8	0.7	4.0	2.2	5.4	15.0	10.3	12.9	11.4	13.0
10500	Albany, GA.............................	1,932.9	153,009	270	79.2	41.3	54.9	0.6	1.6	2.9	6.2	17.4	11.5	12.9	11.7	11.9
10540	Albany, OR.............................	2,287.1	127,335	309	55.7	87.5	1.2	2.8	2.3	9.3	6.1	16.4	7.8	13.5	11.9	11.8
10580	Albany-Schenectady-Troy, NY	2,811.7	883,169	64	314.1	81.6	9.4	0.6	5.5	5.4	5.2	14.4	11.0	13.1	11.9	13.2
10740	Albuquerque, NM	9,283.3	915,927	60	98.7	40.4	2.9	6.1	3.1	49.4	5.6	16.5	8.8	14.2	12.7	12.1
10780	Alexandria, LA.......................	1,963.4	153,044	269	77.9	64.9	30.2	1.5	1.7	3.5	6.7	17.5	8.6	13.6	12.4	12.1
10900	Allentown-Bethlehem-Easton, PA-NJ	1,452.8	842,913	69	580.2	73.7	6.2	0.5	3.6	17.7	5.3	15.8	9.1	12.4	11.8	13.4
11020	Altoona, PA............................	525.8	122,492	321	233.0	95.9	2.8	0.4	1.0	1.3	5.3	15.1	7.7	12.3	11.4	12.8
11100	Amarillo, TX...........................	5,150.2	265,947	183	51.6	60.4	6.9	1.0	4.0	29.2	7.0	18.5	9.4	14.7	13.1	11.5
11180	Ames, IA................................	572.7	98,105	358	171.3	84.9	3.4	0.5	9.3	3.6	4.6	13.2	30.9	13.2	9.9	8.3
11260	Anchorage, AK	26,420.2	399,148	134	15.1	69.5	6.1	11.7	12.5	8.2	7.2	17.9	9.4	16.5	13.2	12.1
11460	Ann Arbor, MI	706.0	370,963	144	525.4	73.0	13.6	1.0	11.0	4.8	4.9	13.7	18.8	14.5	11.4	11.6
11500	Anniston-Oxford-Jacksonville, AL	605.9	114,277	334	188.6	73.7	21.8	1.0	1.5	3.9	5.8	15.9	9.1	13.2	11.9	12.5
11540	Appleton, WI..........................	955.9	237,524	193	248.5	89.5	1.9	1.8	3.9	4.4	6.1	17.5	8.2	12.9	13.0	13.5
11700	Asheville, NC.........................	2,032.6	459,585	117	226.1	86.7	5.3	1.0	1.7	7.1	4.9	13.6	7.3	12.6	12.3	12.8
12020	Athens-Clarke County, GA	1,024.9	211,306	211	206.2	67.2	21.1	0.5	4.4	8.7	5.4	14.7	18.7	14.3	11.9	11.1
12060	Atlanta-Sandy Springs-Roswell, GA.................	8,685.7	5,949,951	9	685.0	48.3	35.3	0.7	7.0	10.9	6.3	18.1	9.1	14.3	13.8	14.2
12100	Atlantic City-Hammonton, NJ .	555.5	265,429	185	477.8	57.5	15.6	0.6	9.1	19.2	5.4	15.8	9.0	12.0	11.1	13.7
12220	Auburn-Opelika, AL	607.6	163,941	257	269.8	68.9	23.5	0.7	4.8	3.8	5.9	15.4	18.0	14.2	12.0	11.8
12260	Augusta-Richmond County, GA-SC	3,480.7	604,167	92	173.6	56.4	36.6	0.9	3.0	5.6	6.2	16.9	9.0	14.3	12.2	12.3
12420	Austin-Round Rock, TX.........	4,221.6	2,168,316	30	513.6	53.6	7.8	0.8	7.3	32.7	6.4	16.7	9.6	17.4	15.6	12.8
12540	Bakersfield, CA......................	8,132.3	896,764	62	110.3	35.2	5.9	1.2	5.8	54.0	7.8	21.1	10.1	15.6	12.8	11.2
12580	Baltimore-Columbia-Towson, MD	2,601.5	2,802,789	21	1,077.4	58.2	30.6	0.8	6.9	6.1	6.0	15.9	8.7	14.5	12.7	13.2
12620	Bangor, ME............................	3,397.2	151,096	275	44.5	95.3	1.4	2.1	1.6	1.4	4.7	13.4	10.2	13.2	11.4	13.2
12700	Barnstable Town, MA.............	394.2	213,413	209	541.4	91.3	4.0	1.2	2.2	3.2	3.7	11.4	7.0	8.9	8.7	12.1
12940	Baton Rouge, LA	4,026.9	831,310	71	206.4	57.5	36.5	0.6	2.5	4.1	6.5	16.9	11.0	14.4	12.8	12.1
12980	Battle Creek, MI....................	706.3	134,487	300	190.4	80.2	12.9	1.4	3.5	5.3	6.2	16.7	9.0	12.3	11.7	12.5
13020	Bay City, MI	442.2	103,923	346	235.0	91.7	2.8	1.1	0.9	5.4	5.0	15.2	7.6	12.3	11.4	12.7
13140	Beaumont-Port Arthur, TX	3,034.4	409,526	132	135.0	56.9	24.5	0.8	3.2	16.0	6.8	17.3	8.9	14.0	12.6	12.2
13220	Beckley, WV..........................	1,267.0	117,272	330	92.6	90.9	7.6	0.9	1.0	1.5	5.3	15.4	7.3	11.8	12.6	12.5
13380	Bellingham, WA.....................	2,107.9	225,685	200	107.1	81.8	1.9	3.8	6.7	9.5	5.3	14.1	13.8	13.8	11.9	11.3
13460	Bend-Redmond, OR...............	3,017.6	191,996	226	63.6	89.3	0.9	1.7	2.4	8.1	5.1	15.0	6.9	13.0	13.2	12.7
13740	Billings, MT...........................	5,855.6	171,677	245	29.3	89.0	1.4	5.3	1.5	5.6	6.1	17.0	7.8	13.6	12.5	11.7
13780	Binghamton, NY	1,224.4	240,219	191	196.2	87.5	5.9	0.7	4.5	3.9	5.2	14.4	12.8	11.2	10.5	11.8
13820	Birmingham-Hoover, AL	5,279.5	1,151,801	49	218.2	64.5	29.7	0.7	1.9	4.5	6.2	16.7	8.4	13.7	12.8	12.9
13900	Bismarck, ND	5,375.3	132,678	303	24.7	88.1	2.5	7.2	1.2	2.9	7.1	16.6	8.6	14.6	12.9	11.3
13980	Blacksburg-Christiansburg-Radford, VA.................	1,454.5	184,029	230	126.5	88.5	5.3	0.6	4.8	2.9	4.4	12.0	21.1	13.0	10.2	11.7
14010	Bloomington, IL	1,580.8	188,597	228	119.3	82.6	8.6	0.5	5.7	4.9	5.8	15.7	16.6	12.9	12.0	11.5
14020	Bloomington, IN.....................	779.8	167,762	253	215.1	87.1	4.1	0.8	7.2	3.2	4.5	11.8	24.0	13.9	10.7	10.1
14100	Bloomsburg-Berwick, PA........	613.3	83,696	372	136.5	93.6	2.2	0.5	1.9	2.9	4.8	13.5	13.3	11.4	10.6	12.2
14260	Boise City, ID........................	11,766.6	730,426	80	62.1	82.2	1.5	1.3	3.6	13.8	6.3	18.8	8.8	13.8	13.5	12.3
14460	Boston-Cambridge-Newton, MA-NH	3,486.5	4,875,390	10	1,398.4	71.8	8.7	0.5	9.4	11.5	5.3	14.5	10.1	15.2	12.5	13.4
14460	Boston, MA Div 14454..........	1,113.3	2,030,772	X	1,824.1	66.2	14.2	0.6	9.0	12.0	5.3	14.1	10.7	16.6	12.4	13.0
14460	Cambridge-Newton-Framingham, MA Div 15764	1,310.3	2,405,352	X	1,835.7	72.6	5.4	0.4	10.8	12.7	5.4	14.8	9.7	14.5	12.7	13.5
14460	Rockingham County-Strafford County, NH 40484	1,062.9	439,266	X	413.3	93.2	1.4	0.7	3.3	3.0	4.7	14.5	10.0	12.3	11.4	14.5
14500	Boulder, CO...........................	726.4	326,078	155	448.9	79.8	1.5	0.9	6.3	13.9	4.4	14.6	14.9	14.0	12.5	12.7
14540	Bowling Green, KY.................	1,615.0	177,432	239	109.9	84.0	8.5	0.7	4.0	4.7	6.3	16.3	14.0	13.2	12.2	11.8
14740	Bremerton-Silverdale, WA......	395.1	269,805	180	682.9	81.2	4.3	2.9	9.7	8.0	5.8	14.7	9.6	14.7	11.9	11.7
14860	Bridgeport-Stamford-Norwalk, CT	625.0	943,823	58	1,510.1	62.8	11.7	0.4	6.5	20.2	5.5	17.0	9.1	11.4	12.4	14.7
15180	Brownsville-Harlingen, TX	891.0	423,908	127	475.8	9.0	0.5	0.2	0.8	89.8	8.1	22.2	10.6	12.4	12.2	11.2
15260	Brunswick, GA.......................	1,293.9	118,456	329	91.5	69.3	24.4	0.8	1.7	5.5	5.5	15.1	7.9	11.9	11.2	12.9
15380	Buffalo-Cheektowaga-Niagara Falls, NY................	1,565.1	1,130,152	50	722.1	78.8	13.1	1.1	3.8	5.2	5.4	14.8	9.0	14.0	11.2	12.8
15500	Burlington, NC.......................	423.4	166,436	256	393.1	64.9	21.1	0.9	2.1	12.9	5.8	16.5	10.4	12.5	11.5	13.5
15540	Burlington-South Burlington, VT............................	1,252.5	221,083	202	176.5	91.6	2.7	1.2	4.5	2.2	4.9	13.8	14.1	13.7	11.8	12.5
15680	California-Lexington Park, MD	358.7	112,664	336	314.1	76.8	16.2	0.9	4.2	5.3	6.4	17.8	9.2	14.1	12.4	14.0
15940	Canton-Massillon, OH............	969.9	398,655	135	411.0	89.3	9.0	0.8	1.3	2.1	5.6	15.8	8.4	11.8	11.3	12.9
15980	Cape Coral-Fort Myers, FL.....	782.0	754,610	76	965.0	67.9	8.8	0.5	2.2	21.9	4.6	13.0	6.9	11.0	10.3	11.7
16020	Cape Girardeau, MO-IL..........	1,432.0	96,982	362	67.7	87.6	9.4	0.8	2.0	2.2	5.7	15.7	12.6	12.4	11.2	11.6
16060	Carbondale-Marion, IL............	1,004.3	124,475	317	123.9	84.2	10.5	0.8	3.1	3.6	5.7	14.5	13.6	13.3	11.6	11.3
16180	Carson City, NV	144.7	55,414	383	383.0	68.8	2.4	2.9	3.6	24.5	5.7	14.6	7.9	13.2	11.1	12.6
16220	Casper, WY	5,340.5	79,115	378	14.8	88.4	1.9	1.7	1.4	8.6	6.6	17.4	7.8	14.6	13.2	11.2

1. CBSA = Core Based Statistical Area. DIV = Metropolitan Division. See Appendix A for explanation. See Appendix B for list of metropolitan areas or temporarily covered by water.   2. Dry land or land partially or temporarily covered by water.   3. May be of any race.

Table C. Metropolitan Areas — Population and Households

Area name	55 to 64 years	65 to 74 years	75 years and over	Percent female	Total persons 2000	Total persons 2010	Percent change 2000-2010	Percent change 2010-2018	Births	Deaths	Net migration	Number	Persons per house-hold	Family house-holds	Female family house-holder[1]	One person
	16	17	18	19	20	21	22	23	24	25	26	27	28	29	30	31
Abilene, TX..................	11.4	8.2	6.8	49.5	160,245	165,246	3.1	3.8	19,569	13,659	356	61,603	2.52	67.6	13.3	25.8
Akron, OH...................	14.4	10.3	7.3	51.4	694,960	703,203	1.2	0.2	61,823	58,371	-1,397	289,282	2.37	61.4	12.5	31.5
Albany, GA..................	12.6	9.5	6.2	52.8	157,833	157,493	-0.2	-2.8	17,048	11,992	-9,674	57,607	2.54	67.6	24.3	27.9
Albany, OR..................	13.8	11.1	7.5	50.6	103,069	116,676	13.2	9.1	12,160	10,073	8,595	47,188	2.62	73.6	14.2	21.9
Albany-Schenectady-Troy, NY	14.0	10.1	7.3	51.0	825,875	870,714	5.4	1.4	74,807	64,209	2,350	348,421	2.45	59.2	10.1	32.2
Albuquerque, NM	13.2	10.2	6.6	50.8	729,649	887,064	21.6	3.3	86,296	59,097	2,115	347,357	2.60	61.1	12.7	32.9
Alexandria, LA.............	12.8	9.4	6.8	50.5	145,035	153,918	6.1	-0.6	16,959	13,344	-4,412	55,634	2.64	63.6	16.4	32.7
Allentown-Bethlehem-Easton, PA-NJ	14.1	10.1	8.0	50.9	740,395	821,267	10.9	2.6	70,420	66,081	17,904	320,990	2.55	67.8	11.6	25.2
Altoona, PA.................	14.6	11.5	9.3	51.0	129,144	127,116	-1.6	-3.6	10,714	13,230	-2,001	51,885	2.32	64.2	12.5	29.7
Amarillo, TX...............	11.7	8.2	5.9	49.7	228,707	251,937	10.2	5.6	30,755	19,026	2,164	97,963	2.61	67.1	11.0	27.3
Ames, IA...................	9.2	6.8	5.3	47.8	79,981	89,542	12.0	9.6	7,670	4,128	4,993	37,689	2.28	51.2	4.2	28.4
Anchorage, AK	12.4	7.5	3.8	48.8	319,605	380,821	19.2	4.8	49,597	18,064	-13,566	136,816	2.87	66.7	11.8	25.0
Ann Arbor, MI..............	11.3	8.4	5.4	50.4	322,895	345,104	6.9	7.5	30,655	18,048	13,480	140,729	2.47	56.0	8.0	30.1
Anniston-Oxford-Jacksonville, AL..................	14.0	10.6	7.2	51.9	112,249	118,594	5.7	-3.6	11,052	11,657	-3,673	44,507	2.50	64.8	13.6	28.7
Appleton, WI...............	13.9	8.7	6.1	49.9	201,602	225,664	11.9	5.3	23,302	13,643	2,363	94,400	2.47	67.8	8.0	26.2
Asheville, NC..............	14.3	12.9	9.3	51.9	369,171	424,859	15.1	8.2	36,328	39,665	37,730	190,004	2.35	59.8	8.9	33.4
Athens-Clarke County, GA	10.8	8.0	5.1	51.9	166,079	192,564	15.9	9.7	18,280	11,225	11,557	76,556	2.56	61.8	12.4	26.1
Atlanta-Sandy Springs-Roswell, GA .	11.9	7.7	4.5	51.7	4,263,438	5,286,750	24.0	12.5	600,415	289,971	351,958	2,102,145	2.76	67.8	14.7	26.0
Atlantic City-Hammonton, NJ .	15.0	10.3	7.6	51.6	252,552	274,521	8.7	-3.3	25,415	21,754	-12,869	97,618	2.70	65.0	15.2	28.8
Auburn-Opelika, AL	10.8	7.4	4.5	50.8	115,092	140,300	21.9	16.9	14,978	8,361	16,848	58,555	2.66	60.4	13.4	28.6
Augusta-Richmond County, GA-SC..................	13.1	9.7	6.3	51.4	508,032	564,873	11.2	7.0	61,471	43,498	21,215	211,489	2.76	65.9	14.8	29.6
Austin-Round Rock, TX.......	10.6	7.0	3.9	49.9	1,249,763	1,716,321	37.3	26.3	214,624	78,485	310,931	755,333	2.75	62.4	9.4	27.6
Bakersfield, CA............	10.5	6.6	4.3	48.7	661,645	839,619	26.9	6.8	115,471	47,309	-10,776	269,147	3.21	73.3	16.2	20.7
Baltimore-Columbia-Towson, MD	13.5	9.1	6.5	51.8	2,552,994	2,710,602	6.2	3.4	277,512	198,098	14,554	1,053,386	2.60	64.5	14.1	29.0
Bangor, ME.................	15.2	10.9	7.8	50.5	144,919	153,932	6.2	-1.8	12,048	12,747	-2,043	60,620	2.39	60.7	9.3	29.6
Barnstable Town, MA...........	17.6	17.4	13.2	52.2	222,230	215,875	-2.9	-1.1	12,928	23,732	8,544	92,148	2.29	60.5	7.6	33.6
Baton Rouge, LA	12.2	8.6	5.4	51.1	705,973	802,504	13.7	3.6	91,164	55,624	-6,781	299,655	2.71	66.4	16.5	27.5
Battle Creek, MI...........	13.8	10.2	7.7	51.1	137,985	136,148	-1.3	-1.2	13,638	12,114	-3,178	54,556	2.38	62.2	13.2	33.1
Bay City, MI	15.3	11.6	8.8	50.9	110,157	107,773	-2.2	-3.6	8,770	9,820	-2,745	44,907	2.29	61.5	11.1	33.0
Beaumont-Port Arthur, TX	13.0	8.8	6.5	49.3	400,162	403,194	0.8	1.6	45,397	34,078	-4,894	149,713	2.62	67.1	15.1	27.5
Beckley, WV	14.3	12.4	8.4	49.8	126,799	124,914	-1.5	-6.1	11,471	13,710	-5,363	48,342	2.36	68.1	12.7	27.5
Bellingham, WA.............	12.4	10.7	6.6	50.5	166,814	201,146	20.6	12.2	18,889	13,017	18,679	88,636	2.44	61.5	7.6	25.7
Bend-Redmond, OR...........	14.1	12.7	7.3	50.5	115,367	157,730	36.7	21.7	14,534	11,384	30,773	74,498	2.49	71.4	8.8	21.9
Billings, MT...............	13.8	10.2	7.3	50.7	139,946	158,944	13.6	8.0	17,042	12,691	8,395	70,979	2.38	63.8	9.3	29.3
Binghamton, NY.............	14.7	10.4	9.0	50.7	252,320	251,724	-0.2	-4.6	20,808	20,896	-11,484	99,370	2.33	58.1	11.4	34.2
Birmingham-Hoover, AL	13.2	9.6	6.5	52.0	1,052,238	1,128,058	7.2	2.1	119,160	96,217	1,466	439,543	2.56	65.3	15.0	29.6
Bismarck, ND	13.0	8.9	7.1	49.8	100,828	114,779	13.8	15.6	15,106	8,479	11,045	55,632	2.31	63.3	9.2	29.5
Blacksburg-Christiansburg-Radford, VA...................	11.8	9.3	6.6	49.3	165,146	178,254	7.9	3.2	13,604	12,531	4,732	66,947	2.52	58.9	9.5	29.5
Bloomington, IL	11.9	8.0	5.7	51.3	167,231	186,135	11.3	1.3	18,556	10,993	-5,169	71,476	2.50	60.2	9.4	29.9
Bloomington, IN............	11.1	8.2	5.7	50.3	142,349	159,536	12.1	5.2	12,547	9,413	5,132	64,763	2.36	56.4	10.7	30.0
Bloomsburg-Berwick, PA........	14.3	11.0	8.9	51.8	82,387	85,561	3.9	-2.2	6,770	7,523	-1,053	33,823	2.34	62.1	11.0	31.0
Boise City, ID	11.8	9.0	5.6	50.1	464,840	616,566	32.6	18.5	70,673	36,821	79,539	257,970	2.70	63.4	8.4	30.6
Boston-Cambridge-Newton, MA-NH	13.3	9.0	6.7	51.4	4,391,344	4,552,598	3.7	7.1	424,813	295,701	197,049	1,823,034	2.56	63.6	11.2	28.0
Boston, MA Div 14454......	12.8	8.7	6.5	51.7	1,812,937	1,888,034	4.1	7.6	179,889	122,413	86,521	760,359	2.55	60.8	12.4	29.6
Cambridge-Newton-Framingham, MA Div 15764	13.4	9.0	6.8	51.3	2,188,815	2,246,204	2.6	7.1	213,136	146,237	94,064	893,591	2.59	65.2	10.8	27.2
Rockingham County-Strafford County, NH 40484........	15.6	10.4	6.7	50.6	389,592	418,360	7.4	5.0	31,788	27,051	16,464	169,084	2.50	67.4	8.5	24.3
Boulder, CO...............	12.6	8.8	5.4	49.7	269,814	294,561	9.2	10.7	23,685	14,085	21,827	128,497	2.42	59.2	8.7	26.9
Bowling Green, KY	11.8	8.6	5.8	50.8	134,976	158,608	17.5	11.9	17,235	11,942	13,518	65,444	2.60	67.0	14.3	25.4
Bremerton-Silverdale, WA......	13.8	11.1	6.7	48.9	231,969	251,143	8.3	7.4	24,956	17,497	11,107	104,902	2.47	68.4	10.0	24.4
Bridgeport-Stamford-Norwalk, CT	14.0	8.7	7.2	51.3	882,567	916,864	3.9	2.9	83,244	54,956	-1,185	336,433	2.77	69.0	11.5	25.0
Brownsville-Harlingen, TX	9.7	7.6	5.9	51.3	335,227	406,215	21.2	4.4	59,248	21,145	-20,487	123,024	3.42	76.9	18.0	20.9
Brunswick, GA.............	14.3	12.3	8.1	52.3	93,044	112,371	20.8	5.4	10,773	9,474	4,797	45,891	2.46	61.5	11.5	35.2
Buffalo-Cheektowaga-Niagara Falls, NY...................	14.7	10.2	8.0	51.6	1,170,111	1,135,614	-2.9	-0.5	99,888	99,732	-4,873	475,055	2.32	60.5	13.4	32.8
Burlington, NC.............	13.1	9.5	7.4	52.6	130,800	151,160	15.6	10.1	14,876	13,010	13,430	64,371	2.45	66.5	15.4	28.0
Burlington-South Burlington, VT	13.8	9.2	6.2	50.8	198,889	211,262	6.2	4.6	18,031	12,630	4,605	87,914	2.37	60.4	9.2	28.9
California-Lexington Park, MD	13.0	7.8	5.3	50.2	86,211	105,143	22.0	7.2	11,699	6,290	2,134	40,820	2.67	71.2	13.9	25.6
Canton-Massillon, OH	14.6	11.1	8.5	51.3	406,934	404,425	-0.6	-1.4	36,417	36,519	-5,344	165,473	2.36	65.3	13.0	28.5
Cape Coral-Fort Myers, FL.....	14.1	15.5	13.1	51.1	440,888	618,754	40.3	22.0	53,688	54,928	135,696	266,266	2.74	66.1	9.6	28.2
Cape Girardeau, MO-IL.....	13.2	9.9	7.7	51.3	90,312	96,274	6.6	0.7	9,296	8,090	-481	37,032	2.55	65.2	14.1	27.3
Carbondale-Marion, IL...........	12.6	10.0	7.5	50.3	120,908	126,574	4.7	-1.7	12,018	10,072	-4,116	50,153	2.36	60.0	13.5	31.4
Carson City, NV............	14.6	11.9	8.5	48.7	52,457	55,274	5.4	0.3	4,898	5,693	916	22,773	2.31	62.3	10.4	31.6
Casper, WY	13.7	9.3	6.1	49.6	66,533	75,448	13.4	4.9	9,043	5,832	344	32,556	2.39	63.3	9.2	30.9

1. No spouse present

Table C. Metropolitan Areas — **Population, Vital Statistics, Health, and Crime**

Area name	Persons in group quarters, 2018	Daytime population, 2017 Number	Employ-ment/residence ratio	Births, 2018 Total	Rate[1]	Deaths, 2018 Number	Rate[1]	Persons under 65 with no health insurance 2017 Number	Percent	Medicare, 2018 Total Ben-eficiaries	Enrolled in Original Medicare	Enrolled in Medicare Advantage	Serious crimes known to police[2], 2016 Total Number	Rate[3]
	32	33	34	35	36	37	38	39	40	41	42	43	44	45
Abilene, TX...........................	10,330	168,565	0.98	2,381	13.9	1,739	10.1	23,224	17.0	30,577	22,287	8,290	5,546	3,265
Akron, OH.............................	17,815	707,690	1.01	7,212	10.2	7,229	10.3	38,313	6.7	141,343	68,618	72,725	19,824	2,818
Albany, GA............................	8,206	152,919	1.02	1,844	12.1	1,561	10.2	18,120	14.8	28,907	18,181	10,726	6,874	4,506
Albany, OR............................	1,084	120,392	0.91	1,523	12.0	1,302	10.2	8,084	8.0	28,686	13,799	14,887	3,422	2,804
Albany-Schenectady-Troy, NY	32,694	904,130	1.04	8,836	10.0	8,229	9.3	31,152	4.4	176,700	96,398	80,302	20,191	2,299
Albuquerque, NM	14,835	908,287	0.99	9,738	10.6	7,846	8.6	73,470	9.8	172,626	86,657	85,969	56,149	6,190
Alexandria, LA	7,458	156,071	1.04	1,984	13.0	1,623	10.6	11,890	9.6	31,673	25,482	6,191	8,658	5,621
Allentown-Bethlehem-Easton, PA-NJ	23,057	807,751	0.92	8,569	10.2	8,069	9.6	46,406	6.9	176,410	124,453	51,957	D	D
Altoona, PA...........................	3,710	128,506	1.09	1,217	9.9	1,620	13.2	5,557	5.8	30,742	14,991	15,751	1,964	1,572
Amarillo, TX..........................	9,761	264,278	0.98	3,477	13.1	2,286	8.6	39,589	18.0	42,511	31,941	10,570	11,912	4,526
Ames, IA...............................	11,339	99,964	1.05	900	9.2	525	5.4	4,009	5.3	13,065	11,116	1,949	1,798	1,850
Anchorage, AK	9,687	398,449	0.99	5,747	14.4	2,397	6.0	46,619	13.3	50,430	49,530	900	19,145	6,066
Ann Arbor, MI........................	22,604	406,052	1.21	3,637	9.8	2,395	6.5	13,709	4.6	57,596	38,670	18,926	7,103	1,965
Anniston-Oxford-Jacksonville, AL	2,739	113,620	0.98	1,293	11.3	1,494	13.1	11,021	11.9	27,130	19,623	7,507	4,795	4,177
Appleton, WI.........................	3,133	230,196	0.95	2,727	11.5	1,681	7.1	10,242	5.1	40,481	15,784	24,697	3,464	1,480
Asheville, NC........................	10,774	464,724	1.04	4,317	9.4	5,080	11.1	47,965	13.7	114,456	79,356	35,100	D	D
Athens-Clarke County, GA	10,676	215,136	1.09	2,201	10.4	1,444	6.8	27,310	15.9	32,694	21,316	11,378	6,457	3,150
Atlanta-Sandy Springs-Roswell, GA.	86,517	5,899,631	1.01	72,419	12.2	40,087	6.7	763,108	14.9	816,042	483,018	333,024	196,965	3,402
Atlantic City-Hammonton, NJ .	6,037	271,181	1.01	2,722	10.3	2,805	10.6	22,842	10.5	55,867	45,199	10,668	NA	NA
Auburn-Opelika, AL	4,958	153,178	0.88	1,865	11.4	1,114	6.8	14,323	10.4	23,185	15,272	7,913	5,053	3,157
Augusta-Richmond County, GA-SC.	18,456	601,741	1.00	7,408	12.3	5,716	9.5	65,125	13.3	112,612	74,973	37,639	20,801	3,495
Austin-Round Rock, TX..........	40,587	2,143,016	1.02	26,707	12.3	11,025	5.1	267,150	14.4	254,241	172,310	81,931	59,012	2,872
Bakersfield, CA.....................	32,382	899,000	1.02	13,415	15.0	6,242	7.0	65,273	8.6	115,416	72,084	43,332	37,698	4,262
Baltimore-Columbia-Towson, MD	70,700	2,790,085	0.99	32,718	11.7	26,006	9.3	136,444	5.9	483,463	420,181	63,282	97,949	3,501
Bangor, ME...........................	6,982	153,484	1.02	1,437	9.5	1,573	10.4	12,874	10.9	36,184	26,043	10,141	3,110	2,037
Barnstable Town, MA..............	4,108	207,512	0.94	1,552	7.3	2,907	13.6	5,190	3.5	74,491	63,535	10,956	D	D
Baton Rouge, LA....................	25,594	847,246	1.03	10,769	13.0	7,213	8.7	58,636	8.4	135,276	67,888	67,388	32,517	3,903
Battle Creek, MI....................	4,326	140,896	1.12	1,615	12.0	1,389	10.3	6,066	5.6	30,456	21,500	8,956	5,205	3,887
Bay City, MI	1,439	93,939	0.77	1,026	9.9	1,163	11.2	5,064	6.1	26,067	16,674	9,393	2,339	2,223
Beaumont-Port Arthur, TX	18,067	410,586	1.00	5,447	13.3	4,370	10.7	60,695	18.2	72,212	41,727	30,485	13,527	3,314
Beckley, WV..........................	5,538	118,111	0.99	1,161	9.9	1,664	14.2	6,829	7.6	30,756	21,641	9,115	3,829	3,157
Bellingham, WA.....................	5,720	216,504	0.95	2,293	10.2	1,675	7.4	13,574	7.6	44,788	28,715	16,073	7,480	3,474
Bend-Redmond, OR..............	1,381	189,254	1.03	1,871	9.7	1,498	7.8	11,542	7.7	42,608	30,382	12,226	4,182	2,322
Billings, MT...........................	3,840	174,196	1.02	2,001	11.7	1,584	9.2	12,842	9.2	33,349	25,544	7,805	6,798	3,993
Binghamton, NY	11,435	238,309	0.96	2,416	10.1	2,593	10.8	9,804	5.2	55,341	32,372	22,969	5,881	2,417
Birmingham-Hoover, AL	24,652	1,155,448	1.01	13,915	12.1	12,259	10.6	95,238	10.0	228,742	110,354	118,388	NA	NA
Bismarck, ND	4,602	131,913	0.99	1,846	13.9	1,092	8.2	7,673	7.0	23,145	17,409	5,736	4,056	3,132
Blacksburg-Christiansburg-Radford, VA.	14,623	182,885	1.01	1,577	8.6	1,566	8.5	15,306	10.8	33,623	27,186	6,437	3,410	1,880
Bloomington, IL	10,756	188,560	1.02	2,093	11.1	1,423	7.5	7,898	5.1	29,185	20,808	8,377	3,414	1,806
Bloomington, IN.....................	15,204	174,325	1.08	1,471	8.8	1,195	7.1	12,323	9.4	25,739	20,078	5,661	4,727	2,842
Bloomsburg-Berwick, PA........	4,528	90,501	1.16	770	9.2	949	11.3	3,684	5.7	18,776	10,905	7,871	NA	NA
Boise City, ID........................	14,767	705,627	0.99	8,515	11.7	4,850	6.6	65,345	10.9	121,733	63,620	58,113	13,975	2,015
Boston-Cambridge-Newton, MA-NH	167,079	5,013,772	1.07	50,680	10.4	38,134	7.8	137,888	3.5	853,176	661,145	192,031	D	D
Boston, MA Div 14454	79,102	2,212,031	1.19	21,600	10.6	15,893	7.8	52,127	3.2	343,486	267,073	76,413	D	D
Cambridge-Newton-Framingham, MA Div 15764	76,336	2,384,449	1.00	25,213	10.5	18,752	7.8	64,098	3.3	421,607	318,062	103,545	34,775	1,465
Rockingham County-Strafford County, NH 40484..........	11,641	D	D	3,867	8.8	3,489	7.9	21,663	6.1	88,083	76,010	12,073	6,439	1,494
Boulder, CO..........................	11,627	357,413	1.20	2,663	8.2	1,888	5.8	18,291	6.8	50,110	31,031	19,079	8,267	2,551
Bowling Green, KY	7,644	181,374	1.04	2,144	12.1	1,500	8.5	10,522	7.4	30,307	21,634	8,673	3,944	2,317
Bremerton-Silverdale, WA......	9,300	255,654	0.92	3,098	11.5	2,354	8.7	11,251	5.3	53,957	42,490	11,467	7,673	2,919
Bridgeport-Stamford-Norwalk, CT	19,596	946,359	0.99	9,711	10.3	7,036	7.5	70,340	8.9	154,014	110,533	43,481	15,574	1,664
Brownsville-Harlingen, TX	3,376	418,178	0.97	6,547	15.4	2,769	6.5	104,621	29.0	61,988	32,673	29,315	13,708	3,234
Brunswick, GA.......................	1,756	113,166	0.97	1,253	10.6	1,297	10.9	16,270	17.4	24,812	17,141	7,671	3,954	3,391
Buffalo-Cheektowaga-Niagara Falls, NY...	31,658	1,146,085	1.02	11,824	10.5	12,211	10.8	42,013	4.6	244,416	97,460	146,956	31,895	2,828
Burlington, NC.......................	6,014	154,493	0.90	1,895	11.4	1,623	9.8	18,526	14.1	32,379	14,521	17,858	4,369	2,736
Burlington-South Burlington, VT.	10,711	224,734	1.05	2,079	9.4	1,594	7.2	8,898	5.0	40,521	36,008	4,513	NA	NA
California-Lexington Park, MD	2,791	110,879	0.97	1,365	12.1	851	7.6	5,057	5.2	16,111	15,725	386	2,302	2,057
Canton-Massillon, OH	9,243	389,990	0.95	4,280	10.7	4,458	11.2	23,312	7.3	90,525	42,592	47,933	NA	NA
Cape Coral-Fort Myers, FL.....	8,484	723,170	0.95	6,692	8.9	7,875	10.4	97,648	18.6	186,099	121,317	64,782	14,199	1,970
Cape Girardeau, MO-IL..........	4,136	101,108	1.07	1,038	10.7	940	9.7	8,146	10.6	20,074	17,700	2,374	2,811	2,879
Carbondale-Marion, IL...........	5,587	127,270	1.03	1,349	10.8	1,265	10.2	6,416	6.5	24,560	19,204	5,356	NA	NA
Carson City, NV	2,828	D	D	641	11.6	632	11.4	5,199	12.6	13,443	11,475	1,968	1,152	2,110
Casper, WY...........................	1,699	D	D	986	12.5	736	9.3	9,473	14.2	13,939	13,163	776	2,249	2,714

1. Per 1,000 estimated resident population.   2. Data for serious crimes have not been adjusted for underreporting; this may affect comparability between geographic areas and over time.   3. Per 100,000 population estimated by the FBI.

Table C. Metropolitan Areas — Crime, Education, Money Income, and Poverty

Area name	Serious crimes known to police[2], 2016 (cont.) Rate Violent	Property	Education — School enrollment and attainment, 2017 Enrollment[3] Total	Percent private	Attainment[4] High school graduate or less	Bachelor's degree or more	Local government expenditures,[5] 2014-2015 Total current expenditures (mil dol)	Current expenditures per student (dollars)	Income and poverty, 2017 Per capita income[6] (dollars)	Mean household income[6] (dollars)	Median household income (dollars)	Percent of households with income less than $50,000	Percent of households with income of $200,000 or more	Percent below poverty level All persons	Children under 18 years	Age 65 years and older
	46	47	48	49	50	51	52	53	54	55	56	57	58	59	60	61
Abilene, TX..................	361	2,903	41,485	22.4	46.8	22.2	255.6	8,806	26,048	68,263	51,130	49.2	4.0	15.0	19.1	8.8
Akron, OH..................	253	2,565	170,212	16.8	39.3	32.2	1,115.1	11,578	31,774	75,838	56,106	44.5	4.5	12.5	17.3	5.7
Albany, GA..................	735	3,771	43,436	8.7	47.8	21.2	275.8	10,190	22,192	56,185	43,614	57.7	2.1	24.7	37.4	13.4
Albany, OR..................	114	2,690	25,046	11.7	42.0	17.3	192.9	8,560	25,416	64,798	51,541	48.3	1.6	14.6	15.4	6.5
Albany-Schenectady-Troy, NY	290	2,010	222,303	21.8	33.6	37.2	2,058.4	16,721	36,549	89,097	68,681	37.1	7.0	10.4	12.2	7.1
Albuquerque, NM..................	901	5,289	231,270	11.8	35.1	32.1	1,292.3	9,200	27,536	68,453	50,906	49.0	3.7	15.5	20.2	8.9
Alexandria, LA..................	923	4,698	40,715	17.4	51.2	19.1	258.4	9,607	21,922	57,088	40,585	58.9	2.1	20.1	24.0	14.2
Allentown-Bethlehem-Easton, PA-NJ..................	D	D	200,567	21.6	44.5	28.9	1,805.4	14,939	32,798	84,133	63,944	39.7	6.6	11.2	17.2	7.4
Altoona, PA..................	213	1,359	27,402	16.0	51.5	21	224.9	12,715	25,912	59,821	45,957	54.3	2.3	14.6	17.3	8.1
Amarillo, TX..................	593	3,933	73,061	8.0	42.9	24.2	448.2	9,040	27,948	73,109	53,922	45.5	4.2	12.5	14.0	9.7
Ames, IA..................	163	1,687	43,013	3.9	20.7	53	114.3	10,199	30,490	78,596	60,351	44.8	5.3	19.5	6.9	2.2
Anchorage, AK..................	1,115	4,951	101,533	11.2	33.5	31.6	1,134.3	17,076	35,544	97,769	76,871	29.9	8.1	10.4	14.2	7.8
Ann Arbor, MI..................	317	1,648	128,691	9.0	20.7	54.5	518.7	11,840	38,987	97,065	70,286	35.7	10.0	13.0	11.3	5.6
Anniston-Oxford-Jacksonville, AL	895	3,283	26,916	8.0	48.7	19.3	168.7	9,199	25,961	65,315	46,763	52.8	2.4	17.7	22.4	11.2
Appleton, WI..................	151	1,329	57,037	15.1	35.6	29.9	398.2	10,174	33,406	82,663	65,990	37.9	4.1	6.9	7.9	5.0
Asheville, NC..................	D	240	93,487	19.8	32.7	37.1	489.2	8,921	29,492	67,786	50,015	50.0	3.8	11.0	15.3	7.6
Athens-Clarke County, GA	342	2,808	70,395	11.4	37.0	39.7	294.8	10,850	26,322	68,688	46,521	53.3	3.6	21.0	19.3	10.1
Atlanta-Sandy Springs-Roswell, GA..................	403	2,998	1,587,440	15.5	35.0	37.9	9,226.1	9,263	33,693	90,879	65,381	38.0	7.9	12.0	16.7	8.8
Atlantic City-Hammonton, NJ	NA	NA	67,395	13.2	45.0	28.4	842.3	18,511	30,800	81,145	61,777	44.0	6.1	14.8	22.3	10.4
Auburn-Opelika, AL	572	2,585	57,130	8.6	33.7	33.4	201.5	9,040	26,542	69,475	52,943	48.0	3.4	19.5	23.6	7.8
Augusta-Richmond County, GA-SC..................	343	3,152	152,518	12.4	45.0	25.3	861.5	9,046	25,163	66,326	50,492	49.6	2.7	15.5	23.0	7.9
Austin-Round Rock, TX..............	317	2,555	563,909	13.3	29.3	44.8	2,941.5	8,850	37,823	100,282	73,800	32.7	9.7	10.4	12.3	8.0
Bakersfield, CA..................	580	3,683	261,365	9.0	54.7	16	1,891.9	10,493	21,346	67,703	49,854	50.1	3.6	21.4	29.8	12.6
Baltimore-Columbia-Towson, MD	710	2,790	701,316	20.5	34.6	39.5	5,638.9	14,113	39,217	101,124	77,394	33.0	10.1	10.2	12.9	9.3
Bangor, ME..................	96	1,942	37,623	11.3	41.7	29.1	274.3	12,593	27,409	65,926	50,349	49.6	3.2	14.6	18.4	6.5
Barnstable Town, MA..................	D	1,562	36,962	16.6	28.8	44.6	452.5	17,796	41,708	94,013	71,235	35.3	8.1	6.8	9.0	5.5
Baton Rouge, LA..................	505	3,398	224,887	23.2	43.9	27.8	1,449.8	11,279	28,872	76,318	57,401	44.6	5.2	16.3	21.7	8.8
Battle Creek, MI..................	747	3,140	31,400	10.7	44.2	21.9	251.4	12,503	26,088	61,253	45,386	54.7	2.6	20.7	34.0	9.0
Bay City, MI..................	370	1,854	23,402	10.9	43.9	21.9	164.4	11,440	25,963	59,156	44,770	55.0	2.2	15.1	19.6	9.3
Beaumont-Port Arthur, TX	574	2,740	95,688	7.0	47.3	17.8	603.8	8,645	26,441	69,847	49,875	50.1	4.5	16.6	24.7	10.9
Beckley, WV..................	417	2,740	24,296	16.0	54.7	19.2	210.5	10,953	22,572	54,567	42,493	57.3	0.8	20.0	28.6	10.6
Bellingham, WA..................	224	3,249	59,336	11.7	28.0	35.8	281.6	10,627	31,955	79,237	61,186	41.4	4.8	13.1	11.1	5.7
Bend-Redmond, OR..................	152	2,171	34,160	14.7	30.3	33.7	258.2	10,105	32,756	80,563	66,273	36.5	5.1	9.4	10.7	6.4
Billings, MT..................	377	3,616	37,134	17.6	35.0	32.2	242.8	9,867	32,531	77,523	58,085	43.3	3.5	9.7	12.7	6.0
Binghamton, NY..................	289	2,128	62,344	11.2	41.1	26.8	631.8	17,874	27,830	66,865	50,545	49.5	2.5	15.7	17.4	8.9
Birmingham-Hoover, AL	NA	NA	282,680	14.2	39.3	30.5	1,672.9	9,427	29,908	74,667	53,107	46.7	5.3	14.6	19.4	9.5
Bismarck, ND..................	294	2,839	28,448	19.4	31.6	33	218.2	12,256	35,276	83,730	66,087	37.5	3.5	9.1	10.8	10.8
Blacksburg-Christiansburg-Radford, VA..................	198	1,682	61,909	8.2	39.2	30.4	204.6	10,124	26,553	68,198	52,075	47.1	3.4	21.2	16.9	5.0
Bloomington, IL..................	277	1,528	58,436	8.4	30.2	43.1	320.8	11,154	33,070	84,248	65,936	40.0	6.3	17.6	19.5	13.1
Bloomington, IN..................	313	2,529	62,717	5.8	32.9	40.9	161.3	9,612	27,157	67,459	49,043	50.6	3.7	22.7	23.2	6.0
Bloomsburg-Berwick, PA..............	NA	NA	21,365	9.9	51.7	25.9	113.5	13,288	27,718	68,303	54,137	46.0	3.5	12.3	11.5	8.0
Boise City, ID..................	244	1,771	188,611	13.0	36.4	30.1	794.9	6,608	29,116	76,825	55,324	44.8	4.9	12.9	14.2	9.9
Boston-Cambridge-Newton, MA-NH..................	D	1,399	1,215,997	30.3	30.8	47.6	10,528.1	15,971	45,273	116,561	85,691	30.9	14.6	9.6	11.7	9.2
Boston, MA Div 14454..............	D	1,612	523,476	34.0	32.1	45.5	4,400.1	16,381	44,537	113,877	82,502	32.7	13.7	11.2	13.6	10.6
Cambridge-Newton-Framingham, MA Div 15764..................	235	1,230	594,327	29.5	29.4	50.7	5,290.6	15,937	46,530	121,080	89,426	29.8	16.2	8.8	11.0	8.7
Rockingham County-Strafford County, NH 40484..............	148	1,346	98,194	15.0	32.2	39.6	837.4	14,285	41,775	104,749	82,210	29.3	10.4	6.3	6.6	6.6
Boulder, CO..................	236	2,314	100,205	12.6	15.7	63.2	606.0	9,777	45,752	113,034	80,834	31.5	13.2	13.4	12.0	6.2
Bowling Green, KY..................	165	2,153	51,008	9.4	48.2	23.9	223.9	8,531	26,579	69,412	46,478	52.8	4.4	17.2	22.6	8.2
Bremerton-Silverdale, WA..........	259	2,660	57,746	10.9	28.4	33.5	387.1	10,725	35,908	89,494	73,026	31.7	6.3	7.8	9.8	6.1
Bridgeport-Stamford-Norwalk, CT	230	1,434	252,401	23.1	32.4	47.1	2,693.7	18,477	54,260	148,996	91,198	29.8	20.4	8.8	11.3	7.9
Brownsville-Harlingen, TX	379	2,855	126,318	2.8	59.2	18.1	944.9	9,433	16,392	52,297	36,975	60.4	1.6	27.9	39.2	25.8
Brunswick, GA..................	372	3,019	27,360	13.0	42.3	25.3	178.4	9,745	29,762	71,621	47,047	52.1	4.8	17.0	26.9	8.3
Buffalo-Cheektowaga-Niagara Falls, NY..................	411	2,417	266,393	17.5	36.6	32.5	2,556.9	16,090	31,542	73,903	55,448	45.6	4.3	14.2	20.9	8.7
Burlington, NC..................	391	2,345	40,867	18.4	45.1	23.4	197.9	8,061	26,561	66,251	45,150	53.7	2.9	14.4	21.6	9.7
Burlington-South Burlington, VT..	NA	NA	55,838	16.2	31.2	43	529.4	17,235	36,140	87,439	63,160	38.5	7.7	11.3	12.9	5.3
California-Lexington Park, MD	203	1,854	32,029	15.9	40.9	31.8	218.2	12,201	37,970	102,679	81,495	27.6	9.6	9.0	13.1	6.0
Canton-Massillon, OH	NA	NA	91,331	17.8	47.8	21.6	626.0	10,342	27,327	65,527	51,198	49.1	2.3	14.4	24.1	6.1
Cape Coral-Fort Myers, FL..........	355	1,614	146,205	15.0	43.0	27.3	796.1	8,909	31,114	77,931	53,928	45.2	5.1	11.6	20.8	7.2
Cape Girardeau, MO-IL..............	480	2,399	25,728	17.2	45.0	27.4	117.1	9,015	23,977	60,846	47,927	52.1	1.6	16.3	23.6	6.2
Carbondale-Marion, IL..................	NA	NA	35,560	6.5	35.7	27.1	206.8	11,622	25,046	61,850	43,892	54.6	2.7	22.6	25.9	9.3
Carson City, NV..................	288	1,822	D	D	41.0	23.7	224.1	8,023	30,695	71,066	55,700	45.0	3.7	7.5	8.0	6.4
Casper, WY..................	203	2,511	19,449	6.1	35.7	24.2	195.8	14,574	32,749	75,655	60,546	42.5	4.4	10.9	10.6	9.1

1. Data for serious crimes have not been adjusted for underreporting; this may affect comparability between geographic areas and over time. 2. Per 100,000 population estimated by the FBI. 3. All persons 3 years old and over enrolled in nursery school through college. 4. Persons 25 years old and over. 5. Elementary and secondary education expenditures. 6. Based on population estimated by the American Community Survey, 2017.

Table C. Metropolitan Areas — **Personal Income and Earnings**

| | Personal income, 2017 | | | | | | | | | | Earnings, 2017 | | |
Area name	Total (mil dol)	Percent change, 2016-2017	Per capita[1] Dollars	Per capita[1] Rank	Wages and Salaries (mil dol)	Supplements to wages and salaries, employer contributions (mil dol) Pension and insurance	Supplements to wages and salaries, employer contributions (mil dol) Government social insurance	Proprietors' income	Dividends, interest, and rent (mil dol)	Personal transfer receipts (mil dol)	Total (mil dol)	Contributions for government social insurance (mil dol) From employee and self-employed	Contributions for government social insurance (mil dol) From employer
	62	63	64	65	66	67	68	69	70	71	72	73	74
Abilene, TX..........................	7,035	2.2	41,326	251	3,141	570	231	502	1,443	1,604	4,444	246	231
Akron, OH............................	33,424	4.1	47,511	119	16,878	2,866	1,229	2,070	5,676	6,334	23,044	1,343	1,229
Albany, GA..........................	5,574	2.6	36,805	351	2,649	521	186	235	980	1,487	3,592	219	186
Albany, OR..........................	5,049	5.4	40,380	273	2,031	355	193	383	796	1,434	2,963	201	193
Albany-Schenectady-Troy, NY	49,492	4.5	55,848	39	25,654	5,642	2,079	2,885	9,349	8,845	36,259	1,980	2,079
Albuquerque, NM	37,209	1.8	40,856	264	18,907	3,270	1,487	1,710	7,054	7,975	25,374	1,668	1,487
Alexandria, LA	6,562	2.5	42,613	219	2,657	559	175	669	1,038	1,998	4,059	228	175
Allentown-Bethlehem-Easton, PA-NJ	43,267	4.4	51,474	75	19,006	3,254	1,515	4,125	6,707	8,071	27,899	1,677	1,515
Altoona, PA.........................	5,407	2.7	43,793	190	2,569	529	225	469	851	1,439	3,793	237	225
Amarillo, TX........................	11,609	1.6	43,820	189	5,578	882	395	1,432	1,970	2,054	8,286	447	395
Ames, IA.............................	3,885	2.6	39,848	287	2,317	564	169	229	938	516	3,280	188	169
Anchorage, AK	23,474	1.8	58,555	29	10,949	2,576	837	2,291	4,355	3,561	16,653	885	837
Ann Arbor, MI......................	20,715	4.5	56,348	35	11,788	2,497	835	1,293	4,493	2,497	16,414	934	835
Anniston-Oxford-Jacksonville, AL.................................	4,160	3.7	36,255	357	1,853	402	138	201	752	1,212	2,594	176	138
Appleton, WI........................	11,552	3.5	48,921	101	6,110	1,061	467	760	1,903	1,550	8,398	510	467
Asheville, NC.......................	19,721	4.7	43,235	203	8,421	1,313	628	1,702	4,652	4,542	12,064	822	628
Athens-Clarke County, GA	8,042	4.8	38,428	317	4,215	949	274	538	1,716	1,439	5,976	324	274
Atlanta-Sandy Springs-Roswell, GA.	292,221	5.2	49,657	89	167,692	23,247	11,141	27,450	49,609	37,765	229,529	13,168	11,141
Atlantic City-Hammonton, NJ .	12,567	3.6	46,557	135	6,237	1,053	497	1,100	2,173	2,907	8,885	556	497
Auburn-Opelika, AL	5,970	5.0	36,941	347	2,465	492	176	303	1,133	1,042	3,436	215	176
Augusta-Richmond County, GA-SC..............................	24,187	4.4	40,302	275	12,154	2,360	890	1,287	4,220	5,432	16,691	991	890
Austin-Round Rock, TX..........	115,982	6.4	54,817	46	63,185	8,220	4,223	13,299	24,510	11,400	88,927	4,628	4,223
Bakersfield, CA.....................	34,438	2.8	38,560	314	15,858	3,601	1,160	4,159	5,590	6,842	24,779	1,259	1,160
Baltimore-Columbia-Towson, MD..................................	167,921	3.8	59,797	22	89,688	15,211	6,616	12,958	31,182	26,040	124,473	7,194	6,616
Bangor, ME..........................	6,061	3.5	39,885	284	3,097	590	222	301	929	1,580	4,210	276	222
Barnstable Town, MA..............	15,033	4.3	70,430	10	4,828	879	352	1,499	4,336	2,822	7,559	449	352
Baton Rouge, LA...................	38,184	2.7	45,775	149	21,321	3,793	1,337	2,600	6,286	7,139	29,051	1,561	1,337
Battle Creek, MI....................	5,189	1.9	38,683	312	3,073	546	233	200	832	1,414	4,052	261	233
Bay City, MI.........................	4,276	3.9	41,024	258	1,577	299	118	170	695	1,216	2,164	155	118
Beaumont-Port Arthur, TX	17,520	2.3	42,480	222	9,140	1,631	643	1,047	2,302	4,220	12,461	710	643
Beckley, WV	4,261	3.8	35,948	362	1,760	318	147	178	614	1,517	2,403	178	147
Bellingham, WA....................	10,191	5.5	46,028	144	4,396	772	418	1,006	2,332	1,869	6,592	393	418
Bend-Redmond, OR..............	9,522	5.7	50,955	76	3,800	582	348	1,452	2,284	1,746	6,182	404	348
Billings, MT..........................	8,484	5.0	49,760	86	4,153	602	340	931	1,676	1,441	6,026	389	340
Binghamton, NY	10,427	4.6	43,047	209	4,553	1,128	376	651	1,710	2,648	6,707	395	376
Birmingham-Hoover, AL	55,312	4.6	48,105	110	27,851	4,299	1,956	4,972	10,488	10,211	39,078	2,502	1,956
Bismarck, ND	7,216	1.0	54,606	48	3,699	592	322	520	1,487	998	5,133	314	322
Blacksburg-Christiansburg-Radford, VA........................	6,698	3.7	36,604	355	3,180	713	232	315	1,408	1,405	4,439	278	232
Bloomington, IL	8,913	0.6	47,350	122	5,315	956	330	623	1,522	1,182	7,224	383	330
Bloomington, IN....................	6,656	5.6	39,658	291	3,273	710	234	482	1,381	1,171	4,699	272	234
Bloomsburg-Berwick, PA........	3,664	3.3	43,510	194	2,170	435	163	214	554	826	2,982	181	163
Boise City, ID.......................	30,954	6.2	43,606	192	15,135	2,321	1,268	3,222	6,371	4,961	21,946	1,360	1,268
Boston-Cambridge-Newton, MA-NH	358,021	4.5	74,024	6	211,022	28,447	13,668	34,129	74,247	43,005	287,267	15,519	13,668
Boston, MA Div 14454	152,704	4.2	75,844	X	101,453	13,931	6,403	16,426	32,033	19,638	138,214	7,303	6,403
Cambridge-Newton-Framingham, MA Div 15764	177,284	4.6	74,235	X	97,802	12,834	6,462	14,652	37,672	19,970	131,750	7,151	6,462
Rockingham County-Strafford County, NH 40484	28,032	5.8	64,446	X	11,767	1,682	803	3,051	4,542	3,396	17,303	1,065	803
Boulder, CO.........................	21,940	4.9	68,027	13	12,451	1,506	858	1,650	6,398	1,918	16,465	900	858
Bowling Green, KY	6,231	4.1	35,639	365	3,147	555	242	468	895	1,491	4,411	277	242
Bremerton-Silverdale, WA......	13,989	5.8	52,508	64	5,428	1,268	502	733	3,439	2,318	7,931	461	502
Bridgeport-Stamford-Norwalk, CT	104,590	3.3	110,104	1	38,308	4,826	2,362	13,413	30,677	7,948	58,909	3,144	2,362
Brownsville-Harlingen, TX......	11,755	1.7	27,741	382	4,831	1,015	350	957	1,561	3,831	7,153	406	350
Brunswick, GA......................	4,545	3.3	38,477	316	1,910	357	134	264	1,106	1,064	2,665	171	134
Buffalo-Cheektowaga-Niagara Falls, NY...........................	54,926	4.8	48,314	108	27,010	5,667	2,224	3,555	8,980	12,371	38,457	2,186	2,224
Burlington, NC	6,307	5.2	38,839	307	2,681	386	198	336	1,061	1,418	3,601	246	198
Burlington-South Burlington, VT...................................	12,183	3.4	55,785	40	6,526	1,180	547	989	2,437	1,863	9,242	587	547
California-Lexington Park, MD	6,188	3.8	54,921	45	3,292	703	262	269	1,113	819	4,526	255	262
Canton-Massillon, OH	17,141	3.3	42,860	213	7,488	1,306	577	1,036	2,774	3,958	10,407	647	577
Cape Coral-Fort Myers, FL.....	36,787	5.6	49,764	85	12,480	1,742	848	3,769	13,467	7,347	18,840	1,319	848
Cape Girardeau, MO-IL..........	4,000	3.7	41,333	249	1,879	317	135	481	684	889	2,812	174	135
Carbondale-Marion, IL...........	4,958	2.5	39,468	294	2,440	639	162	296	941	1,098	3,536	185	162
Carson City, NV....................	2,682	9.3	48,997	100	1,516	419	93	335	589	585	2,362	111	93
Casper, WY	5,332	1.6	67,023	14	1,972	305	196	1,338	1,300	623	3,812	200	196

1. Based on the resident population estimated as of July 1 of the year shown.

Table C. Metropolitan Areas — Earnings, Social Security, and Housing

Area name	Earnings, 2017 (cont.)									Social Security beneficiaries, December 2017		Supplemental Security Income Recipients, December 2017	Housing units, 2018	
	Percent by selected industries													
	Farm	Mining, quarrying, and extracting	Construction	Manufacturing	Information; professional, scientific, and technical serviecs	Retail trade	Finance, insurance, real estate, rental and leasing	Health care and social assistance	Government	Number	Rate[1]		Total	Percent change, 2010-2018
	75	76	77	78	79	80	81	82	83	84	85	86	87	88
Abilene, TX...............	1.0	2.6	6.9	3.7	D	7.4	6.8	15.8	26.1	32,000	188	4,488	71,930	3.2
Akron, OH...............	0.0	0.2	5.7	12.6	8.3	7.7	6.0	13.5	13.5	141,745	201	17,369	315,499	0.9
Albany, GA...............	1.4	D	D	9.3	6.1	6.9	D	16.3	23.6	31,925	211	6,975	67,204	1.6
Albany, OR...............	1.5	D	8.1	20.6	3.8	8.4	4.4	11.2	15.7	30,455	244	3,616	50,883	4.2
Albany-Schenectady-Troy, NY	0.1	0.3	5.7	7.8	12.8	5.3	8.2	11.7	26.8	185,020	209	19,993	410,490	4.4
Albuquerque, NM	0.1	0.2	6.7	4.6	D	6.5	D	D	25.2	177,815	195	23,806	392,050	4.7
Alexandria, LA....................	0.7	D	6.7	7.5	4.8	10.0	D	19.9	23.7	33,490	217	7,657	67,818	5.0
Allentown-Bethlehem-Easton, PA-NJ	0.1	D	D	13.1	9.4	5.5	5.5	16.1	11.3	186,290	222	19,262	350,522	2.4
Altoona, PA........................	0.6	0.4	5.6	12.6	5.3	8.1	4.0	19.4	15.2	30,775	249	4,540	56,945	1.2
Amarillo, TX........................	1.7	D	D	12.5	D	D	D	13.4	16.3	42,960	162	4,463	109,989	6.4
Ames, IA........................	-0.3	D	6.0	11.4	8.3	4.9	4.5	8.2	39.9	12,910	132	653	40,766	10.8
Anchorage, AK....................	0.0	4.2	7.6	1.0	9.9	5.9	5.8	14.7	27.1	51,440	128	7,636	160,226	3.8
Ann Arbor, MI....................	0.0	0.0	2.8	7.5	17.8	4.0	4.7	11.0	34.9	58,325	159	5,575	151,550	2.7
Anniston-Oxford-Jacksonville, AL...	0.8	D	3.3	16.1	4.6	7.6	3.5	9.6	32.9	30,330	264	4,628	53,888	1.1
Appleton, WI........................	1.2	0.2	9.7	20.3	D	6.1	8.9	D	11.3	43,830	186	2,859	98,527	6.1
Asheville, NC........................	0.6	0.1	6.9	12.3	D	8.1	6.0	D	14.1	118,375	260	9,716	231,269	8.3
Athens-Clarke County, GA	2.8	0.2	3.7	9.5	D	6.4	6.8	14.6	31.3	34,630	165	4,777	86,439	5.8
Atlanta-Sandy Springs-Roswell, GA...............	0.1	0.2	6.0	6.4	20.9	5.7	9.5	8.7	11.2	854,700	145	115,510	2,330,253	7.2
Atlantic City-Hammonton, NJ .	0.6	0.5	7.1	1.6	6.9	7.4	4.5	16.3	23.6	59,315	220	7,270	128,409	1.4
Auburn-Opelika, AL...............	0.3	0.2	7.5	12.0	5.6	6.7	4.2	5.9	33.3	25,475	158	3,271	70,369	12.8
Augusta-Richmond County, GA-SC...............	0.3	0.1	6.9	10.2	D	5.7	4.8	10.3	28.8	122,550	204	16,758	260,909	7.9
Austin-Round Rock, TX.........	0.0	2.8	8.6	7.7	D	5.6	8.6	8.0	14.8	249,350	118	26,744	853,701	20.8
Bakersfield, CA....................	10.1	5.4	5.4	4.3	4.7	6.3	3.5	8.7	25.3	121,740	136	33,705	300,377	5.6
Baltimore-Columbia-Towson, MD	0.1	0.0	6.2	4.6	D	4.6	9.6	12.2	22.0	482,200	172	70,372	1,164,130	2.8
Bangor, ME....................	0.2	D	5.9	3.9	5.3	9.2	4.7	23.8	20.7	37,695	248	5,545	76,136	3.1
Barnstable Town, MA............	0.0	D	12.7	D	8.6	9.2	6.6	16.2	18.0	71,395	334	3,201	164,321	2.5
Baton Rouge, LA...............	0.1	0.2	16.2	11.8	D	5.9	6.8	10.6	16.9	140,285	168	24,382	358,015	8.6
Battle Creek, MI....................	0.1	D	3.8	24.9	10.1	4.8	2.4	14.0	21.0	32,920	245	4,894	60,864	-0.3
Bay City, MI....................	-1.0	0.0	4.4	15.6	11.0	8.0	4.5	17.1	18.0	29,035	279	3,218	48,336	0.2
Beaumont-Port Arthur, TX	-0.1	D	D	D	D	6.2	D	10.4	13.4	79,250	192	13,009	178,846	5.5
Beckley, WV	-0.1	8.7	3.9	3.3	5.3	9.1	3.5	19.4	22.8	34,520	291	5,792	57,690	0.2
Bellingham, WA....................	2.7	D	11.4	13.5	7.2	8.9	5.5	12.0	18.0	44,305	200	4,386	97,855	7.9
Bend-Redmond, OR...............	-0.1	0.1	13.7	5.7	11.9	8.2	8.6	17.3	11.9	43,715	234	2,383	91,041	13.6
Billings, MT....................	0.5	D	D	D	9.4	D	8.3	D	11.9	34,330	201	2,708	79,448	12.1
Binghamton, NY	0.1	0.9	5.6	15.4	D	6.6	4.9	15.7	24.5	59,820	247	8,164	113,834	0.9
Birmingham-Hoover, AL	0.2	0.3	6.7	7.1	D	5.7	12.1	14.4	14.7	249,865	217	34,776	519,827	4.0
Bismarck, ND....................	0.0	D	D	3.5	D	D	7.3	17.6	20.9	23,630	179	1,343	60,746	21.4
Blacksburg-Christiansburg-Radford, VA...............	-0.2	0.1	4.5	19.5	D	6.0	3.3	8.9	34.3	35,670	195	3,250	80,947	3.3
Bloomington, IL....................	1.1	D	4.1	3.1	D	5.1	36.6	9.0	15.4	30,180	160	2,065	80,260	4.0
Bloomington, IN....................	0.1	0.3	4.7	15.0	D	5.4	4.7	D	30.5	27,220	162	2,205	72,279	4.5
Bloomsburg-Berwick, PA........	-0.1	D	3.7	11.1	D	4.6	5.5	D	15.0	20,275	241	1,837	38,557	2.9
Boise City, ID....................	1.4	0.2	8.5	14.3	D	7.8	D	12.7	14.0	126,360	178	12,254	282,300	14.7
Boston-Cambridge-Newton, MA-NH	0.0	D	D	D	22.8	4.1	12.8	12.1	10.4	813,120	168	105,489	1,973,298	4.8
Boston, MA Div 14454.........	0.0	D	5.1	D	20.1	3.8	20.1	14.2	11.1	325,285	162	53,814	830,457	5.6
Cambridge-Newton-Framingham, MA Div 15764	0.1	0.0	6.0	11.4	26.7	3.9	5.7	10.2	9.5	398,150	167	47,516	955,356	4.0
Rockingham County-Strafford County, NH 40484	0.1	D	D	D	15.1	7.8	7.5	9.9	10.7	89,685	206	4,159	187,485	5.1
Boulder, CO........................	0.1	0.1	3.9	11.2	30.9	4.4	6.5	9.9	15.1	44,915	139	2,472	137,435	8.2
Bowling Green, KY....................	0.9	D	7.4	D	D	6.5	D	14.2	15.2	32,645	187	5,171	76,043	10.4
Bremerton-Silverdale, WA......	0.0	D	5.1	2.4	8.1	5.7	3.7	9.7	52.6	52,655	198	4,947	113,733	5.9
Bridgeport-Stamford-Norwalk, CT	0.0	0.1	5.0	10.3	15.0	5.1	23.6	8.7	7.6	151,240	159	12,492	374,481	3.7
Brownsville-Harlingen, TX	0.9	0.1	4.3	4.7	3.8	8.4	4.9	20.3	27.8	65,705	155	22,537	152,353	7.4
Brunswick, GA....................	0.1	D	4.8	D	5.5	7.6	4.2	14.3	24.7	26,675	226	2,814	61,279	5.6
Buffalo-Cheektowaga-Niagara Falls, NY....................	0.2	D	4.6	11.5	8.7	6.3	8.7	13.2	21.0	259,050	228	33,249	530,328	2.2
Burlington, NC....................	0.0	0.1	6.2	15.6	4.5	8.6	6.0	19.8	11.1	34,775	214	3,545	71,660	7.6
Burlington-South Burlington, VT....................	0.6	D	6.6	11.2	D	6.8	5.8	D	19.2	41,040	188	4,528	98,398	6.5
California-Lexington Park, MD	-0.2	D	4.0	0.9	23.4	4.0	2.8	6.3	46.7	16,275	144	1,663	46,013	11.5
Canton-Massillon, OH	0.3	0.4	8.7	18.6	5.9	7.1	6.2	15.8	12.6	93,940	235	10,302	180,617	1.0
Cape Coral-Fort Myers, FL.....	0.3	0.1	10.0	2.1	10.5	8.9	7.3	10.0	16.7	189,485	256	12,863	399,729	7.7
Cape Girardeau, MO-IL.........	0.7	0.4	5.7	15.8	D	8.0	5.6	23.1	13.9	21,380	221	2,379	44,073	3.7
Carbondale-Marion, IL...........	0.5	3.4	4.8	7.7	D	6.8	4.6	17.6	33.8	25,470	203	3,188	60,406	2.5
Carson City, NV....................	0.2	D	6.3	8.0	8.2	6.4	4.2	14.3	36.4	13,265	242	1,061	24,026	2.1
Casper, WY	0.1	7.2	6.8	3.1	4.5	5.1	5.9	11.8	11.8	14,675	184	1,244	37,181	10.0

1. Per 1,000 resident population estimated as of July 1 of the year shown.

Table C. Metropolitan Areas — Housing, Labor Force, and Employment

Area name	Total	Percent	Median value[1]	With a mort-gage	Without a mort-gage[2]	Median rent[3]	Median rent as a percent of income	Percent with Internet access	Total	Percent change 2017-2018	Total	Rate[4]	Total	Management, business, science, and arts	Construc-tion, produc-tion, and maintenance occupations
	89	90	91	92	93	94	95	96	97	98	99	100	101	102	103
Abilene, TX	61,603	65.0	114,500	19.2	10.8	803	29.5	77.1	77,053	1.6	2,548	3.3	75,968	32.1	21.6
Akron, OH	289,282	66.7	146,800	19.1	11.2	811	28.0	87.5	357,240	-0.9	16,597	4.6	352,693	35.4	21.9
Albany, GA	57,607	52.4	115,900	21.7	10.7	696	28.4	80.2	67,318	-1.2	3,203	4.8	62,311	29.8	27.7
Albany, OR	47,188	63.1	216,100	21.3	10.7	932	37.0	86.7	58,551	1.2	2,771	4.7	54,332	27.6	33.1
Albany-Schenectady-Troy, NY	348,421	64.3	216,400	19.6	11.6	968	27.7	89.1	450,252	0.7	16,972	3.8	447,756	45.0	15.3
Albuquerque, NM	347,357	67.2	191,700	22.1	10.0	860	30.8	86.2	429,850	0.5	20,144	4.7	410,406	40.8	15.5
Alexandria, LA	55,634	62.6	139,700	18.6	10.0	778	32.4	77.5	63,352	-1.3	3,411	5.4	60,313	33.4	22.5
Allentown-Bethlehem-Easton, PA-NJ	320,990	69.0	213,400	21.3	14.0	988	31.2	86.3	435,921	0.2	19,528	4.5	414,094	35.2	23.4
Altoona, PA	51,885	66.0	129,600	19.7	12.0	688	31.4	83.3	59,555	-1.0	2,505	4.2	55,137	29.8	25.4
Amarillo, TX	97,963	64.8	139,900	20.5	11.3	826	26.8	84.4	132,065	0.6	3,637	2.8	128,125	31.9	26.2
Ames, IA	37,689	52.1	200,300	16.8	10.0	885	35.8	92.3	57,756	0.9	916	1.6	49,905	45.9	17.3
Anchorage, AK	136,816	62.6	298,100	22.4	12.4	1,268	28.4	92.3	199,604	-1.2	11,988	6.0	193,326	38.0	19.4
Ann Arbor, MI	140,729	61.8	258,700	20.3	11.1	1,062	28.6	92.8	194,621	0.6	5,928	3.0	192,219	52.0	13.5
Anniston-Oxford-Jacksonville, AL	44,507	69.9	117,700	19.2	10.0	632	25.4	79.1	45,972	0.4	2,139	4.7	48,810	31.1	29.7
Appleton, WI	94,400	72.9	168,300	18.6	10.0	764	25.0	90.3	131,547	-0.5	3,613	2.7	129,835	37.2	27.8
Asheville, NC	190,004	68.0	220,900	22.1	10.0	891	30.0	84.6	233,404	1.9	7,258	3.1	223,039	36.3	21.8
Athens-Clarke County, GA	76,556	54.6	181,600	19.4	10.0	844	31.7	87.7	101,975	1.0	3,756	3.7	97,995	43.0	19.4
Atlanta-Sandy Springs-Roswell, GA	2,102,145	63.0	215,100	19.8	10.0	1,115	29.4	90.0	3,071,572	1.2	115,989	3.8	2,934,502	41.2	19.4
Atlantic City-Hammonton, NJ	97,618	64.5	211,600	24.7	18.9	1,031	34.9	86.6	118,969	0.3	7,001	5.9	128,005	33.9	17.7
Auburn-Opelika, AL	58,555	63.5	160,700	18.4	10.0	804	29.9	87.1	74,654	1.6	2,703	3.6	73,109	37.5	17.7
Augusta-Richmond County, GA-SC	211,489	66.6	144,000	20.1	10.4	814	31.3	83.0	268,009	0.6	11,149	4.2	248,549	34.4	24.1
Austin-Round Rock, TX	755,333	57.7	283,600	21.2	11.7	1,223	28.7	91.7	1,197,091	3.2	35,043	2.9	1,132,219	46.5	15.8
Bakersfield, CA	269,147	57.9	205,700	24.6	11.1	948	32.2	82.2	386,997	0.6	30,865	8.0	341,802	26.2	34.3
Baltimore-Columbia-Towson, MD	1,053,386	66.6	297,300	21.1	11.0	1,241	30.1	89.2	1,493,496	0.2	59,512	4.0	1,421,604	46.7	15.3
Bangor, ME	60,620	71.7	136,300	19.5	12.0	836	28.0	87.3	77,127	0.2	2,920	3.8	74,986	35.1	20.1
Barnstable Town, MA	92,148	79.8	401,100	25.3	14.2	1,287	35.2	90.6	116,225	2.5	4,974	4.3	104,780	39.9	16.7
Baton Rouge, LA	299,655	68.0	182,000	18.6	10.0	894	29.3	85.8	418,946	0.4	18,290	4.4	389,315	34.1	22.7
Battle Creek, MI	54,556	68.2	116,200	19.8	12.1	694	35.2	82.6	62,865	-1.5	2,646	4.2	59,163	28.5	28.5
Bay City, MI	44,907	75.8	102,800	20.1	12.5	613	30.9	81.2	50,352	-0.9	2,410	4.8	45,257	31.8	25.9
Beaumont-Port Arthur, TX	149,713	68.5	108,900	19.2	10.6	791	27.6	78.8	176,224	0.4	10,671	6.1	172,352	28.6	29.1
Beckley, WV	48,342	77.1	98,500	19.1	10.0	561	27.9	80.5	45,250	0.3	2,572	5.7	42,438	29.1	22.8
Bellingham, WA	88,636	61.6	355,500	22.8	12.8	1,078	33.5	91.1	111,670	1.7	5,295	4.7	111,592	36.3	22.7
Bend-Redmond, OR	74,498	65.2	368,600	25.0	13.3	1,176	29.2	92.0	95,367	2.2	4,020	4.2	91,818	36.6	19.7
Billings, MT	70,979	69.0	225,900	20.8	11.8	840	28.4	89.0	87,125	0.0	2,925	3.4	89,355	34.0	23.0
Binghamton, NY	99,370	67.6	113,500	19.9	11.5	742	30.4	83.8	107,364	0.2	5,114	4.8	107,746	38.5	19.4
Birmingham-Hoover, AL	439,543	68.0	161,400	19.1	10.0	842	29.1	84.1	544,863	1.2	19,254	3.5	515,451	38.4	21.0
Bismarck, ND	55,632	67.4	250,200	19.6	10.0	864	30.5	90.5	67,543	-2.5	1,912	2.8	71,477	40.9	20.7
Blacksburg-Christiansburg-Radford, VA	66,947	61.8	190,200	18.9	10.0	856	28.0	86.4	90,021	-0.1	2,798	3.1	86,166	41.0	19.5
Bloomington, IL	71,476	66.5	163,100	18.2	10.6	785	27.3	88.2	95,471	-1.0	4,065	4.3	95,098	43.3	16.3
Bloomington, IN	64,763	56.6	166,200	18.4	10.0	835	33.2	91.0	79,040	1.7	2,917	3.7	82,405	43.7	16.1
Bloomsburg-Berwick, PA	33,823	69.0	156,300	19.1	13.2	753	24.7	85.0	42,545	-0.6	1,912	4.5	40,230	34.8	27.0
Boise City, ID	257,970	68.1	228,800	21.4	10.0	920	28.5	84.5	361,718	4.1	9,718	2.7	339,487	37.2	22.6
Boston-Cambridge-Newton, MA-NH	1,823,034	61.8	441,400	22.3	14.0	1,397	29.6	90.5	2,746,759	3.0	81,805	3.0	2,627,364	48.9	13.9
Boston, MA Div 14454	760,359	57.9	443,300	22.5	13.9	1,453	30.2	90.0	1,134,416	3.4	35,344	3.1	1,089,151	47.5	13.0
Cambridge-Newton-Framingham, MA Div 15764	893,591	63.2	473,600	22.2	14.0	1,389	29.1	90.3	1,353,655	3.1	39,685	2.9	1,292,827	51.1	13.9
Rockingham County-Strafford County, NH 40484	169,084	72.2	297,700	22.1	14.1	1,163	28.9	93.3	258,688	1.2	6,776	2.6	245,386	43.7	18.0
Boulder, CO	128,497	61.4	504,800	19.9	10.0	1,483	34.4	94.7	193,822	3.8	5,519	2.8	177,104	53.3	13.3
Bowling Green, KY	65,444	62.5	150,700	18.3	10.0	762	28.8	85.6	83,443	0.5	3,219	3.9	83,487	31.2	28.5
Bremerton-Silverdale, WA	104,902	66.6	326,200	21.7	11.1	1,179	28.9	94.1	122,885	2.3	5,713	4.6	117,361	40.2	18.9
Bridgeport-Stamford-Norwalk, CT	336,433	66.8	425,900	23.7	15.8	1,438	32.4	90.8	480,767	0.3	19,017	4.0	479,747	45.7	13.6
Brownsville-Harlingen, TX	123,024	65.0	92,000	20.8	13.0	697	32.4	69.8	166,001	-0.3	10,235	6.2	163,181	28.9	22.4
Brunswick, GA	45,891	71.4	148,500	20.6	12.5	864	28.9	80.3	53,766	1.0	2,052	3.8	47,587	35.1	21.4
Buffalo-Cheektowaga-Niagara Falls, NY	475,055	65.5	148,900	18.5	12.3	772	30.2	84.6	542,584	0.0	24,771	4.6	561,299	38.1	18.4
Burlington, NC	64,371	63.8	153,800	18.6	10.4	758	29.2	81.6	80,583	0.7	2,958	3.7	76,369	30.9	29.5
Burlington-South Burlington, VT	87,914	64.2	272,200	22.5	14.8	1,212	32.2	88.6	128,380	-0.2	2,810	2.2	120,403	44.7	18.9
California-Lexington Park, MD	40,820	71.2	294,000	21.7	10.0	1,227	29.8	89.1	55,295	0.6	2,102	3.8	53,418	42.9	18.3
Canton-Massillon, OH	165,473	67.6	132,600	18.3	10.5	723	26.7	86.0	199,318	-0.4	9,828	4.9	186,585	31.6	26.4
Cape Coral-Fort Myers, FL	266,266	71.4	225,300	23.4	12.6	1,116	29.4	91.2	342,684	1.9	11,634	3.4	316,819	29.3	22.4
Cape Girardeau, MO-IL	37,032	72.2	151,200	20.2	10.9	750	27.0	82.3	47,659	0.3	1,471	3.1	44,894	34.9	26.1
Carbondale-Marion, IL	50,153	63.2	120,600	19.0	11.1	690	29.7	82.7	60,010	0.2	2,927	4.9	51,202	33.5	23.7
Carson City, NV	22,773	52.4	256,100	22.8	10.0	1,027	27.2	86.5	25,718	1.4	1,216	4.7	26,575	29.9	23.2
Casper, WY	32,556	72.4	206,200	21.6	10.0	871	28.8	87.0	39,059	-1.2	1,813	4.6	39,307	33.7	25.3

1. Specified owner-occupied units. 2. A value of 10.0 represents 10 percent or less; a value of 50.0 represents 50 percent or more. 3. Specified renter-occupied units. 4. Overcrowded or lacking complete plumbing facilities. 5. Percent of civilian labor force. 6. Civilian employed persons 16 years old and over.

Table C. Metropolitan Areas — **Nonfarm Employment and Agriculture**

Area name	Private nonfarm establishments, employment and payroll, 2016									Agriculture, 2017			
		Employment						Annual payroll		Farms			Farm producers whose primary occupation is farming (percent)
											Percent with:		
	Number of establishments	Total	Health care and social assistance	Manufacturing	Retail trade	Finance and insurance	Professional, scientific, and technical services	Total (mil dol)	Average per employee (dollars)	Number	Fewer than 50 acres	1000 acres or more	
	104	105	106	107	108	109	110	111	112	113	114	115	116
Abilene, TX	3,950	59,299	13,053	2,840	8,977	2,601	1,885	2,039	34,389	3,270	35.4	10.7	33.8
Akron, OH	16,390	298,043	53,577	39,067	39,404	11,815	16,004	13,382	44,901	1,510	70.8	0.9	32.4
Albany, GA	3,123	45,414	9,179	4,005	8,072	1,463	2,735	1,687	37,140	1,188	31.8	15.6	42.9
Albany, OR	2,564	36,488	5,526	7,367	5,427	941	909	1,429	39,153	2,222	71.2	3.1	41.6
Albany-Schenectady-Troy, NY	21,444	352,322	68,306	22,643	48,674	20,136	29,863	16,520	46,890	2,227	40	1.4	46.4
Albuquerque, NM	18,645	307,102	57,005	15,624	43,131	12,726	33,069	12,635	41,144	4,331	73.8	7.3	34.3
Alexandria, LA	3,296	49,291	14,194	4,006	8,439	1,517	1,938	1,859	37,709	1,063	48.1	6.6	41.9
Allentown-Bethlehem-Easton, PA-NJ	18,429	320,006	63,608	35,663	44,109	11,320	12,039	15,195	47,484	1,958	64.5	2.2	40.4
Altoona, PA	3,185	53,686	13,387	6,809	8,887	1,544	1,790	1,964	36,589	496	34.9	1.6	52.7
Amarillo, TX	6,348	95,383	16,435	11,365	14,727	5,505	3,127	3,902	40,906	1,699	29.4	25.7	40.1
Ames, IA	2,030	32,670	5,626	4,951	5,173	720	1,413	1,301	39,836	955	48.2	10.8	37.8
Anchorage, AK	11,002	165,702	29,917	2,131	19,743	5,515	16,278	9,877	59,607	350	64.3	0.9	44.4
Ann Arbor, MI	8,119	150,135	37,479	15,005	17,704	3,911	15,217	8,233	54,838	1,245	59.7	2.7	39.8
Anniston-Oxford-Jacksonville, AL	2,326	35,843	6,020	5,985	6,561	977	926	1,188	33,139	643	43.4	1.4	34.5
Appleton, WI	5,905	116,043	14,099	21,869	14,883	6,523	3,984	5,084	43,815	1,814	43.6	4	47.9
Asheville, NC	12,552	167,634	35,373	20,232	28,208	3,885	6,012	6,378	38,047	2,708	62.3	0.9	38.7
Athens-Clarke County, GA	4,660	62,632	11,669	6,729	10,591	1,624	2,468	2,317	36,999	1,520	47.8	1.6	38.8
Atlanta-Sandy Springs-Roswell, GA	139,929	2,310,613	271,476	145,157	279,538	117,041	200,110	126,682	54,826	7,760	55.7	1	39.4
Atlantic City-Hammonton, NJ	6,302	105,922	19,072	1,800	15,978	2,377	4,368	4,072	38,442	450	75.3	0.9	52.1
Auburn-Opelika, AL	2,726	43,945	6,191	6,940	7,084	1,100	1,608	1,395	31,746	314	43.9	5.7	35.5
Augusta-Richmond County, GA-SC	10,488	187,559	36,742	21,594	27,639	4,597	11,541	7,790	41,534	2,787	48.4	4.6	37
Austin-Round Rock, TX	50,759	808,743	102,030	40,296	105,387	37,432	102,096	44,224	54,683	8,498	52.5	3.8	34.1
Bakersfield, CA	12,724	190,503	30,127	11,832	32,769	5,802	10,631	8,342	43,788	1,731	40.3	17.6	51.1
Baltimore-Columbia-Towson, MD	67,109	1,165,540	200,793	52,291	142,069	54,445	137,789	63,801	54,739	3,704	61.7	2.6	40.3
Bangor, ME	4,144	57,622	15,015	3,066	11,164	1,921	1,789	2,187	37,954	601	41.3	3.2	44.6
Barnstable Town, MA	8,596	76,683	16,339	1,957	15,886	2,276	4,922	3,430	44,724	321	93.5	NA	46.5
Baton Rouge, LA	18,237	341,885	48,618	25,252	45,730	14,683	24,679	16,806	49,158	2,763	54.1	7	40.1
Battle Creek, MI	2,558	53,966	9,228	14,614	6,161	1,015	2,516	2,716	50,327	958	42.6	5.8	44.2
Bay City, MI	2,195	30,973	7,257	4,090	5,450	968	1,550	1,216	39,250	726	36.8	8.8	48.8
Beaumont-Port Arthur, TX	7,896	132,787	20,286	20,236	19,971	3,492	5,958	6,584	49,586	2,483	67.3	3	35.3
Beckley, WV	2,517	34,051	9,191	1,156	6,496	770	1,062	1,201	35,269	618	50	1	35.1
Bellingham, WA	6,550	74,548	10,368	10,326	11,683	2,348	3,460	3,132	42,014	1,712	79.6	0.7	35.4
Bend-Redmond, OR	6,889	64,536	10,752	4,739	10,796	2,123	3,179	2,617	40,554	1,484	85.4	0.8	34.7
Billings, MT	6,037	72,621	14,599	3,324	11,104	4,423	3,511	3,082	42,444	2,196	37.5	20.3	42.9
Binghamton, NY	5,034	78,734	16,898	8,527	12,223	2,254	3,987	3,035	38,547	1,029	32.9	1.7	44.1
Birmingham-Hoover, AL	25,821	447,451	68,974	37,258	59,426	33,991	22,731	21,575	48,218	3,639	45.7	1.7	37.6
Bismarck, ND	3,920	58,417	12,612	2,033	9,045	2,328	3,856	2,566	43,918	1,987	19.8	34.6	46
Blacksburg-Christiansburg-Radford, VA	3,473	50,825	7,187	12,231	8,518	1,119	3,023	1,943	38,229	2,108	39.6	2.2	35.8
Bloomington, IL	3,957	81,675	9,291	4,137	11,100	21,560	2,430	4,193	51,343	1,920	36.7	13.4	45.6
Bloomington, IN	3,333	53,821	10,428	10,113	7,716	1,700	2,092	2,022	37,573	1,139	47.5	2.4	31
Bloomsburg-Berwick, PA	1,914	37,040	11,610	5,350	4,074	2,043	1,284	1,764	47,632	1,135	43.7	1.4	39.5
Boise City, ID	17,870	250,085	40,370	23,600	34,275	10,646	15,248	10,944	43,760	5,108	76.4	4.1	37.5
Boston-Cambridge-Newton, MA-NH	128,936	2,482,491	457,720	148,498	273,074	159,944	250,409	169,185	68,151	2,943	74.4	0.4	43.1
Boston, MA Div 14454	NA	NA	NA	NA	NA	NA	NA	NA	NA	976	76.6	0.7	46.1
Cambridge-Newton-Framingham, MA Div 15764	NA	NA	NA	NA	NA	NA	NA	NA	NA	1,039	75.6	0.2	43.8
Rockingham County-Strafford County, NH 40484	NA	NA	NA	NA	NA	NA	NA	NA	NA	928	70.9	0.2	39.1
Boulder, CO	12,399	150,243	21,226	13,833	18,574	3,781	26,032	8,716	58,010	1,012	79	2.2	33.1
Bowling Green, KY	3,538	58,965	9,934	10,139	8,857	1,796	2,133	2,284	38,741	4,102	41.2	2.2	33.9
Bremerton-Silverdale, WA	5,795	59,446	12,707	2,273	11,273	1,769	4,212	2,291	38,546	698	96.3	NA	29
Bridgeport-Stamford-Norwalk, CT	27,134	427,361	67,963	32,794	50,319	46,775	39,240	35,735	83,617	402	81.8	2.2	49.3
Brownsville-Harlingen, TX	6,376	108,580	35,817	4,259	18,647	3,399	3,413	2,906	26,761	1,418	74.3	6.3	34.1
Brunswick, GA	2,901	33,562	5,110	2,287	5,751	805	1,035	1,153	34,362	320	55	0.6	32.2
Buffalo-Cheektowaga-Niagara Falls, NY	27,379	478,608	85,403	52,228	66,247	29,846	30,820	20,562	42,963	1,630	51.2	3.7	46.3
Burlington, NC	3,215	59,118	12,604	9,922	9,079	1,430	1,320	2,308	39,047	720	45.8	0.7	40.6
Burlington-South Burlington, VT	6,879	104,153	18,767	12,041	15,632	3,478	7,343	4,616	44,322	1,433	41.6	2.7	45
California-Lexington Park, MD	1,937	29,819	4,765	335	4,741	454	8,199	1,484	49,765	615	57.2	1.5	43.7
Canton-Massillon, OH	8,648	148,429	29,536	26,103	20,673	5,731	4,294	5,673	38,220	2,435	59.3	1.3	35.1
Cape Coral-Fort Myers, FL	18,143	209,788	35,633	5,278	40,208	6,018	12,271	8,205	39,111	800	81.6	2.4	38.5
Cape Girardeau, MO-IL	2,752	40,993	11,105	4,066	6,621	1,320	1,297	1,514	36,923	1,993	28.8	5.1	40.6
Carbondale-Marion, IL	2,932	40,926	10,155	3,958	7,681	1,826	1,272	1,458	35,636	1,382	39.6	5.9	35.3
Carson City, NV	1,916	21,862	3,730	2,586	3,523	1,125	1,188	935	42,754	17	70.6	NA	53.3
Casper, WY	2,953	32,937	5,675	1,382	5,082	965	1,428	1,443	43,825	430	40	25.3	39.3

Table C. Metropolitan Areas — **Agriculture**

Area name	Land in farms — Acreage (1,000)	Percent change, 2012-2017	Acres — Average size of farm	Total irrigated (1,000)	Total cropland (1,000)	Value of land and buildings (dollars) — Average per farm	Average per acre	Value of machinery and equipment, average per farm (dollars)	Value of products sold — Total (mil dol)	Average per farm (acres)	Percent from: Crops	Livestock and poultry products	Organic farms (number)	Farms with internet access (percent)	Government payments — Total ($1,000)	Percent of farms
	117	118	119	120	121	122	123	124	125	126	127	128	129	130	131	132
Abilene, TX	1,479	-13.3	452	6	558.5	737,343	1,631	70,790	104.3	31,887	42.2	57.8	NA	74.3	7,701	26.5
Akron, OH	105	4.8	69	0.5	70.1	536,277	7,740	69,000	47.1	31,188	70.3	29.7	7	80.5	1,499	9.5
Albany, GA	668	0	562	144.9	355.5	1,664,513	2,962	244,190	315.1	265,194	81.2	18.8	2	75.2	26,930	56.3
Albany, OR	315	-4.9	142	36.9	242.6	1,005,264	7,092	100,759	243	109,375	74.6	25.4	39	85.8	856	4.8
Albany-Schenectady-Troy, NY	331	-5.2	149	3.1	193.3	581,420	3,911	102,818	218.5	98,131	47.2	52.8	69	81.2	1,939	15.3
Albuquerque, NM	3,084	-19.6	712	43.1	71.8	548,325	770	41,738	113.7	26,245	25.3	74.7	35	65	2,852	4.5
Alexandria, LA	254	-1.9	239	26.3	148.7	847,287	3,545	122,673	155.3	146,070	90.5	9.5	1	73.1	3,988	23.4
Allentown-Bethlehem-Easton, PA-NJ	227	-3.6	116	2.1	174.6	1,051,135	9,064	110,824	221.5	113,135	73.7	26.3	16	80.6	3,404	15
Altoona, PA	79	-12.4	159	0.2	55.8	1,073,542	6,747	130,550	107.2	216,087	15.8	84.2	9	61.7	1,064	25.6
Amarillo, TX	2,893	0.1	1,703	93.3	817.1	1,887,508	1,109	150,924	801.5	471,719	15.6	84.4	NA	77.8	27,310	47.7
Ames, IA	304	-0.6	318	0.4	284.2	3,013,806	9,467	199,884	224.9	235,519	73	27	12	86.4	4,910	51.8
Anchorage, AK	34	-5.5	98	1.1	15.6	809,797	8,242	D	37.5	107,246	45.6	54.4	4	87.7	262	20.6
Ann Arbor, MI	179	5.2	144	4	150.4	1,124,667	7,823	112,400	91.2	73,227	76.3	23.7	29	84.3	3,438	24.6
Anniston-Oxford-Jacksonville, AL	89	9.5	138	1.1	28.5	587,726	4,246	74,079	86.8	135,003	15	85	NA	77.1	913	28.8
Appleton, WI	391	-0.6	215	0.8	337.7	1,609,348	7,470	201,699	467.3	257,601	24.9	75.1	19	80.2	2,530	48.6
Asheville, NC	222	4.7	82	3.7	65.0	611,878	7,451	58,730	133.4	49,267	82.2	17.8	37	74.2	1,461	15.4
Athens-Clarke County, GA	185	-10.2	122	2.6	50.4	675,115	5,541	76,858	524.8	345,272	7	93	6	80.7	1,945	24.5
Atlanta-Sandy Springs-Roswell, GA	872	1.9	112	7.9	208.4	599,404	5,337	63,245	931.1	119,985	10.6	89.4	31	79.1	5,463	12.9
Atlantic City-Hammonton, NJ	29	-1.6	64	11.6	17.8	823,031	12,764	135,393	120.7	268,162	98.7	1.3	10	85.3	198	7.8
Auburn-Opelika, AL	68	14.8	216	0.2	9.0	895,685	4,150	95,631	D	D	D	D	4	79.9	432	26.8
Augusta-Richmond County, GA-SC	562	15.8	202	61.4	231.2	668,247	3,312	101,967	302.2	108,416	41.7	58.3	8	76.7	8,683	17.4
Austin-Round Rock, TX	1,669	-4.8	196	8.2	457.4	1,003,716	5,110	61,144	263.1	30,957	47.8	52.2	37	76.9	9,105	9.8
Bakersfield, CA	2,295	-1.5	1,326	730.7	954.1	9,787,244	7,380	406,230	4,076.8	2,355,161	84.3	15.7	30	82.7	5,101	13.8
Baltimore-Columbia-Towson, MD	520	5.8	140	20.2	379.8	1,325,778	9,451	114,805	449.8	121,442	65.2	34.8	33	83.6	11,036	26.3
Bangor, ME	105	-6.6	175	1.6	41.1	432,699	2,466	93,820	50.9	84,717	35.6	64.4	33	79	603	9.2
Barnstable Town, MA	7	40.4	20	1.1	1.6	624,807	30,555	60,763	23.1	72,019	40.4	59.6	11	90	197	4.7
Baton Rouge, LA	784	0.7	284	6.9	346.5	924,505	3,259	123,586	229.4	83,010	68.1	31.9	5	74.3	6,035	13.6
Battle Creek, MI	214	-4.9	223	13.3	174.6	1,185,546	5,309	138,963	113.9	118,861	61.1	38.9	20	71.5	4,522	36.7
Bay City, MI	210	8.3	289	5.2	197.1	1,460,329	5,052	242,521	116.5	160,519	88.3	11.7	NA	69.3	4,501	67.8
Beaumont-Port Arthur, TX	536	0.3	216	26.4	160.6	573,348	2,657	72,044	43.6	17,545	50.6	49.4	14	71.5	9,521	7.7
Beckley, WV	70	16.1	113	0	17.3	385,375	3,416	49,804	4.7	7,655	31.4	68.6	1	74.9	60	3.7
Bellingham, WA	103	-11.5	60	36.5	75.6	1,005,680	16,794	95,376	372.9	217,786	41.3	58.7	48	83.7	1,047	12.6
Bend-Redmond, OR	135	2.7	91	36	31.0	786,080	8,667	51,257	28.8	19,386	57.5	42.5	9	93.2	90	0.8
Billings, MT	3,102	-2.1	1,412	182.9	542.0	1,491,870	1,056	123,224	252.9	115,169	32.2	67.8	3	81.8	10,052	28.8
Binghamton, NY	176	-6.3	171	0.8	88.3	438,814	2,571	86,513	72.9	70,888	31	69	26	78.6	1,317	20.2
Birmingham-Hoover, AL	510	-0.7	140	5	145.2	506,482	3,617	77,767	396.4	108,918	12.5	87.5	9	75.5	5,937	22.6
Bismarck, ND	2,952	-6	1,486	11.4	1,360.8	2,249,580	1,514	258,895	389.4	195,953	44.3	55.7	3	80.2	19,819	61.6
Blacksburg-Christiansburg-Radford, VA	355	-14.3	168	0.6	97.8	657,109	3,903	71,494	100.7	47,761	36.5	63.5	13	77.2	546	5.5
Bloomington, IL	806	-9.2	420	3.4	777.0	3,991,216	9,508	260,130	577.5	300,758	86.4	13.6	8	80.7	13,699	72
Bloomington, IN	160	7.7	140	0.3	95.8	721,922	5,149	68,376	43.5	38,219	82.3	17.7	19	76.3	2,350	27.6
Bloomsburg-Berwick, PA	145	-12.5	128	0.9	108.3	786,339	6,139	96,310	127.5	112,345	49.7	50.3	13	69.3	2,933	37.1
Boise City, ID	1,351	-1.8	264	420.9	450.1	1,000,490	3,783	131,482	1,021.5	199,985	42.7	57.3	35	86.1	6,139	9
Boston-Cambridge-Newton, MA-NH	171	-10.3	58	15.3	61.1	687,073	11,814	62,502	201.5	68,484	84.2	15.8	97	87.7	1,398	5
Boston, MA Div 14454	68	-7.9	69	12.4	21.3	727,928	10,497	69,057	72.5	74,237	86.5	13.5	31	88.7	380	5.4
Cambridge-Newton-Framingham, MA Div 15764	48	-5.1	46	2.5	23.9	767,516	16,593	64,666	96.2	92,604	87.6	12.4	32	86.6	226	3.8
Rockingham County-Strafford County, NH 40484	55	-16.9	60	0.4	15.8	554,039	9,278	53,184	32.9	35,428	69.1	30.9	34	87.9	792	5.9
Boulder, CO	107	-19.5	106	27.2	38.1	1,329,691	12,571	67,039	43.9	43,378	87.4	12.6	29	90.7	501	5.6
Bowling Green, KY	659	4.7	161	0.6	344.6	641,344	3,990	78,685	275.9	67,255	44.4	55.6	8	71.8	11,581	25.2
Bremerton-Silverdale, WA	9	-6.7	13	0.5	2.3	473,099	35,164	33,113	6.6	9,463	73.2	26.8	26	88.3	D	0.6
Bridgeport-Stamford-Norwalk, CT	52	-3.2	130	0.2	4.6	1,402,826	10,794	57,697	42.1	104,649	52.7	47.3	9	87.1	33	3.5
Brownsville-Harlingen, TX	271	-12.3	191	100.9	212.5	681,492	3,560	73,661	122.6	86,428	96.2	3.8	10	64.3	6,669	26
Brunswick, GA	36	-18	113	1	7.0	388,278	3,436	54,650	0.3	975	26	74	2	75.6	135	14.4
Buffalo-Cheektowaga-Niagara Falls, NY	283	-0.8	174	3.5	212.6	665,840	3,830	147,731	249.6	153,123	55.1	44.9	47	81.9	3,500	20.1
Burlington, NC	80	-4.2	111	0.7	33.8	667,068	6,000	64,708	41.8	57,986	35.3	64.7	23	76.4	147	8.6
Burlington-South Burlington, VT	273	-2.2	190	0.8	122.6	755,652	3,970	128,983	247.1	172,455	25.9	74.1	204	87.5	1,864	12.5
California-Lexington Park, MD	62	-7.9	100	0.7	37.0	999,805	9,949	75,424	26	42,203	78.8	21.2	2	58	970	19.5
Canton-Massillon, OH	244	0.6	100	1.1	166.0	718,603	7,184	92,634	144.5	59,331	41.2	58.8	14	72.5	3,912	13.8
Cape Coral-Fort Myers, FL	87	0.1	109	10.5	22.2	1,330,329	12,206	53,238	104.4	130,449	93.8	6.2	7	76	163	1.8
Cape Girardeau, MO-IL	521	1	261	52.5	329.5	944,908	3,618	104,757	148	74,249	74.2	25.8	NA	67.7	6,795	44.9
Carbondale-Marion, IL	325	2.5	236	1.7	250.0	1,160,781	4,929	125,249	121.9	88,196	82.6	17.4	3	69.9	6,583	44.2
Carson City, NV	1	D	57	0.4	0.6	D	D	D	D	D	D	D	1	100	NA	NA
Casper, WY	1,933	14.3	4,496	44.3	55.7	2,039,344	454	109,340	43.2	100,493	12.9	87.1	NA	76	318	7.9

Table C. Metropolitan Areas — Water Use, Wholesale Trade, Retail Trade, and Real Estate

Area name	Water use, 2015		Wholesale Trade[1], 2012				Retail Trade[2], 2012				Real estate and rental and leasing,[2] 2012			
	Public supply water withdrawn (mil gal/day)	Public supply gallons withdrawn per person per day	Number of establishments	Number of employees	Sales (mil dol)	Average payroll (mil dol)	Number of establishments	Number of employees	Sales (mil dol)	Average payroll (mil dol)	Number of establishments	Number of employees	Sales (mil dol)	Average payroll (mil dol)
	133	134	135	136	137	138	139	140	141	142	143	144	145	146
Abilene, TX	8.78	51.8	176	1,943	2,557.2	95.4	635	8,371	2,538.9	202.1	180	928	155.6	28.5
Akron, OH	54.93	78	959	16,088	10,045.5	927.1	2,193	36,505	10,384.1	905.1	581	3,191	582.1	118.3
Albany, GA	16.04	104.5	166	2,133	1,897.2	109.2	661	7,757	1,874.7	166.1	173	654	113.5	20.4
Albany, OR	9.57	79.4	110	1,396	1,066.7	61.3	343	4,753	1,181.6	112.6	112	360	48.5	10.2
Albany-Schenectady-Troy, NY	290.84	329.8	768	10,035	9,506.1	543.4	3,028	46,426	12,455.2	1,118.7	852	4,632	1,021.3	171.6
Albuquerque, NM	105.54	116.3	858	10,480	5,775.8	508.1	2,448	39,437	11,245.8	996.7	1,062	4,578	876.4	161.5
Alexandria, LA	23.45	151.8	125	1,550	829.5	59.6	611	7,996	2,294.7	193.6	139	605	92.0	18.4
Allentown-Bethlehem-Easton, PA-NJ	74.71	89.8	772	D	D	D	2,695	41,717	11,314.2	976.6	587	2,615	648.7	95.6
Altoona, PA	13.07	104.1	119	1,832	2,258.4	80.7	561	8,383	2,286.7	189.4	87	349	72.9	11.3
Amarillo, TX	17.48	66.7	260	D	D	D	938	13,922	4,425.5	331.7	311	1,431	287.9	48.9
Ames, IA	8.42	87.7	74	D	D	D	288	4,708	1,084.2	98.5	97	465	75.5	16.1
Anchorage, AK	47.18	118	376	5,526	3,282.6	311.4	1,104	18,668	6,005.9	551.5	458	2,584	669.6	118.4
Ann Arbor, MI	18.36	51.2	276	3,580	4,695.9	221.8	1,106	16,577	4,461.1	411.4	306	2,409	727.2	115.9
Anniston-Oxford-Jacksonville, AL	25.25	218.4	97	1,792	1,808.8	73.6	477	5,954	1,463.5	134.1	73	299	48.9	8.0
Appleton, WI	17.06	73.2	317	5,089	7,620.6	259.7	838	14,534	3,696.4	314.4	151	909	163.8	28.6
Asheville, NC	39.02	87.3	417	3,984	2,143.2	168.3	1,837	23,933	6,137.5	569.6	585	1,756	316.6	56.7
Athens-Clarke County, GA	12.62	62.1	148	2,155	2,079.7	100.6	698	9,141	2,257.6	195.6	262	1,199	223.1	41.9
Atlanta-Sandy Springs-Roswell, GA	480.18	84.1	6,996	107,280	102,221.8	6,641.1	16,888	246,883	69,477.9	6,136.7	6,808	39,825	11,502.2	2,232.5
Atlantic City-Hammonton, NJ	30.2	110.1	188	D	D	D	1,227	16,099	4,292.7	394.9	227	1,383	351.1	52.0
Auburn-Opelika, AL	15.83	100.8	75	613	504.3	28.3	477	6,450	1,632.1	141.6	113	544	81.0	16.0
Augusta-Richmond County, GA-SC	95.09	161.1	357	3,678	1,952.8	163.5	1,851	25,118	6,639.8	563.7	437	1,920	386.4	62.5
Austin-Round Rock, TX	180.1	90	1,641	32,902	77,904.9	2,642.0	5,621	89,835	27,852.9	2,331.3	2,421	13,215	2,998.0	631.2
Bakersfield, CA	168.87	191.4	582	7,990	6,987.9	447.4	1,867	27,918	8,640.6	700.7	634	3,492	733.6	141.3
Baltimore-Columbia-Towson, MD	267.62	95.7	2,653	43,211	33,873.6	2,572.3	8,871	136,209	36,505.4	3,449.0	2,795	19,455	6,677.9	965.9
Bangor, ME	4.79	31.4	162	1,794	955.4	82.3	735	10,931	3,203.1	249.6	172	692	123.3	22.9
Barnstable Town, MA	31.84	148.6	178	1,152	563.1	57.0	1,503	14,395	3,856.9	401.4	331	1,361	260.5	53.1
Baton Rouge, LA	103.82	125	845	10,959	7,974.1	590.2	2,873	41,392	11,292.1	987.8	756	4,551	944.6	171.3
Battle Creek, MI	12.53	93.3	94	D	D	D	488	5,858	1,702.3	133.4	87	373	53.9	10.5
Bay City, MI	8.97	84.9	87	D	D	D	419	5,526	1,303.0	124.5	65	212	29.3	4.7
Beaumont-Port Arthur, TX	37.35	91.5	332	D	D	D	1,448	19,217	5,663.9	474.7	349	2,085	437.8	84.0
Beckley, WV	15.26	124.6	121	1,426	797.4	63.4	480	6,740	1,866.3	161.3	95	343	58.6	10.9
Bellingham, WA	18.13	85.4	289	D	D	D	818	11,310	3,103.6	272.4	317	1,131	230.9	34.3
Bend-Redmond, OR	38	216.8	215	1,262	794.9	57.1	755	9,365	2,476.6	244.0	388	1,252	186.1	40.0
Billings, MT	26.89	159.8	322	4,747	3,237.2	233.6	785	10,572	3,334.4	283.3	295	944	166.8	30.7
Binghamton, NY	22.18	90.2	221	4,201	3,365.7	177.8	851	12,657	3,114.1	278.6	172	857	183.5	28.1
Birmingham-Hoover, AL	182.44	159.2	1,513	21,833	21,530.8	1,180.9	4,281	55,841	15,249.7	1,379.9	996	8,182	1,597.3	354.4
Bismarck, ND	14.72	113.7	167	2,362	2,105.2	126.5	482	8,216	2,621.2	219.6	175	522	124.1	17.1
Blacksburg-Christiansburg-Radford, VA	15.02	82.6	90	1,056	758.2	44.7	577	8,143	1,993.7	173.5	149	710	129.1	23.9
Bloomington, IL	11.81	62.4	196	2,867	9,734.4	185.1	632	10,111	2,662.2	218.4	152	748	151.6	23.1
Bloomington, IN	17.18	103.8	92	D	D	D	496	7,814	1,773.2	154.5	170	872	153.9	27.8
Bloomsburg-Berwick, PA	5.05	59.3	59	568	308.6	21.9	290	4,075	1,072.1	84.0	49	223	36.9	7.0
Boise City, ID	90.7	134	717	9,901	8,538.3	497.1	1,977	28,218	8,072.2	735.4	879	3,055	510.1	96.5
Boston-Cambridge-Newton, MA-NH	274.73	57.5	5,066	88,499	106,488.4	6,697.2	16,564	252,652	67,308.1	6,697.1	4,796	35,738	12,052.3	2,087.3
Boston, MA Div 14454	103.97	52.4	2,008	33,191	36,166.3	2,246.6	6,851	101,678	27,541.6	2,754.3	2,231	19,179	5,940.4	1,278.7
Cambridge-Newton-Framingham, MA Div 15764	147.41	62.4	2,486	47,467	61,732.6	3,937.2	7,741	118,530	31,382.5	3,150.4	2,169	14,713	5,717.1	730.1
Rockingham County-Strafford County, NH 40484	23.35	54.5	572	7,841	8,589.5	513.4	1,972	32,444	8,384.0	792.4	396	1,846	394.9	78.5
Boulder, CO	48.3	151.2	392	D	D	D	1,174	16,623	4,498.3	478.9	648	1,954	434.3	74.5
Bowling Green, KY	21.3	126.5	146	2,040	2,960.5	92.7	612	7,922	1,892.4	170.4	138	455	86.7	13.4
Bremerton-Silverdale, WA	19.63	75.5	147	953	407.9	43.7	731	10,343	2,674.2	276.3	338	979	198.5	32.7
Bridgeport-Stamford-Norwalk, CT	87.98	92.8	1,190	18,611	130,674.8	1,622.4	3,459	49,401	15,166.5	1,553.9	1,077	6,971	1,808.6	418.1
Brownsville-Harlingen, TX	24.18	57.3	317	D	D	D	1,119	16,624	4,124.8	353.2	312	1,338	185.5	32.2
Brunswick, GA	10.59	91.3	74	557	307.6	22.2	550	5,299	1,579.2	123.8	151	526	71.9	16.6
Buffalo-Cheektowaga-Niagara Falls, NY	220.89	194.6	1,177	20,641	20,849.6	1,106.2	4,078	62,656	14,627.6	1,352.0	929	6,446	944.0	207.0
Burlington, NC	15.35	97	143	1,642	627.2	70.0	624	8,756	2,108.4	178.0	119	607	142.0	24.4
Burlington-South Burlington, VT	17.39	80.1	297	4,885	4,395.2	271.4	1,064	14,768	3,638.0	362.7	265	1,377	284.2	51.6
California-Lexington Park, MD	4.15	37.2	39	397	189.5	17.6	294	4,835	1,227.0	109.5	83	312	94.7	11.4
Canton-Massillon, OH	31.28	77.6	346	D	D	D	1,326	20,654	5,535.1	470.3	296	1,352	222.3	43.0
Cape Coral-Fort Myers, FL	64.55	92	585	5,144	2,481.0	232.6	2,517	34,453	9,445.3	850.6	1,218	3,992	856.4	135.9
Cape Girardeau, MO-IL	9.63	98.7	147	1,565	935.9	65.4	468	6,306	1,709.0	140.0	117	357	56.4	9.7
Carbondale-Marion, IL	7.18	56.6	86	962	442.8	38.2	496	7,467	2,124.6	170.2	128	537	79.1	12.7
Carson City, NV	11.5	210.9	89	519	276.4	25.2	212	3,139	918.2	92.6	111	304	51.7	9.5
Casper, WY	12.26	149.2	163	1,890	2,052.7	115.2	363	4,796	1,487.5	132.1	166	1,281	502.0	79.4

1. Merchant wholesalers, except manufacturers' sales branches and offices. 2. Employer establishments.

Table C. Metropolitan Areas — Professional Services, Manufacturing, and Accommodation and Food Services

Area name	Professional, scientific, and technical services, 2012				Manufacturing, 2012				Accommodation and food services, 2012			
	Number of establishments	Number of employees	Sales (mil dol)	Average payroll (mil dol)	Number of establishments	Number of employees	Receipts (mil dol)	Annual payroll (mil dol)	Number of establishments	Number of employees	Receipts (mil dol)	Annual payroll (mil dol)
	147	148	149	150	151	152	153	154	155	156	157	158
Abilene, TX............................	299	1,868	194.5	76.5	116	2,406	992.5	98.2	336	6,732	316.9	88.9
Akron, OH.............................	1,724	D	D	D	1,081	37,550	12,567.9	1,871.0	1,499	26,419	1,225.2	330.6
Albany, GA............................	275	D	D	D	94	4,213	3,493.7	214.9	265	4,706	212.9	55.7
Albany, OR............................	164	802	84.8	27.8	181	6,318	2,253.6	355.2	216	2,796	130.4	35.5
Albany-Schenectady-Troy, NY	2,313	26,033	4,405.1	1,717.2	595	20,698	8,060.7	1,223.8	2,284	31,820	1,736.9	489.3
Albuquerque, NM	2,521	19,811	3,610.6	1,150.8	673	16,378	18,058.5	841.3	1,667	37,340	1,989.1	578.5
Alexandria, LA......................	291	2,261	243.0	96.9	83	4,158	3,339.5	228.1	242	4,406	219.3	59.1
Allentown-Bethlehem-Easton, PA-NJ	1,634	D	D	D	869	32,882	16,436.0	1,734.7	1,774	27,527	1,808.3	436.2
Altoona, PA	221	1,789	208.3	74.8	135	6,943	2,115.6	298.8	280	4,634	199.4	56.5
Amarillo, TX..........................	528	4,274	538.8	182.4	202	12,867	D	784.6	570	11,176	558.8	151.3
Ames, IA...............................	203	1,114	118.0	53.3	77	4,821	2,787.2	256.8	229	4,269	172.6	48.0
Anchorage, AK	1,306	14,431	2,646.4	1,004.2	227	2,272	533.7	104.8	988	16,739	1,241.7	373.4
Ann Arbor, MI........................	1,284	13,390	2,329.9	928.1	332	13,232	5,419.9	725.8	766	14,879	764.9	216.3
Anniston-Oxford-Jacksonville, AL..................	167	1,140	137.1	43.1	114	5,957	2,713.2	256.9	212	4,673	199.1	53.0
Appleton, WI.........................	449	3,485	517.6	187.4	428	21,791	8,825.3	1,062.6	548	9,700	377.0	104.3
Asheville, NC........................	1,233	5,652	612.7	253.5	461	21,831	6,553.6	987.3	1,127	20,288	1,165.0	336.4
Athens-Clarke County, GA	490	D	D	D	138	5,949	2,145.1	259.3	423	7,878	354.2	96.4
Atlanta-Sandy Springs-Roswell, GA..................	20,920	192,024	36,037.1	13,725.0	3,762	131,702	60,486.1	6,477.2	10,694	208,494	11,868.4	3,260.4
Atlantic City-Hammonton, NJ .	579	D	D	D	96	1,730	285.4	72.3	860	46,661	4,008.5	1,282.5
Auburn-Opelika, AL	202	1,474	138.0	55.1	111	5,903	2,386.1	248.4	323	5,947	271.6	70.4
Augusta-Richmond County, GA-SC..................	996	10,922	2,764.6	797.1	318	21,316	13,266.7	1,143.5	960	18,609	852.8	232.8
Austin-Round Rock, TX..........	7,256	69,730	13,548.4	5,417.0	1,301	36,984	15,784.9	2,157.4	4,053	85,096	5,071.2	1,406.8
Bakersfield, CA.....................	1,204	11,757	1,641.3	637.3	391	12,257	6,890.7	558.2	1,278	19,829	1,092.2	284.0
Baltimore-Columbia-Towson, MD	9,506	117,982	27,098.7	9,886.3	1,631	53,494	22,199.6	3,275.5	5,570	101,810	6,089.2	1,659.1
Bangor, ME...........................	328	1,831	179.4	84.5	134	3,749	977.7	164.0	315	5,639	313.9	86.7
Barnstable Town, MA.............	733	4,806	932.9	341.7	187	2,157	478.6	119.4	1,143	13,117	1,000.4	291.5
Baton Rouge, LA...................	2,138	19,451	3,087.2	1,126.7	600	24,133	84,643.9	1,778.4	1,507	31,681	1,626.7	447.9
Battle Creek, MI....................	191	1,058	93.0	55.5	148	11,179	5,445.1	599.3	280	6,023	471.2	104.3
Bay City, MI	152	1,360	111.0	57.1	123	3,650	1,149.4	190.6	233	4,039	172.0	47.6
Beaumont-Port Arthur, TX	660	6,726	1,077.1	423.5	306	19,149	87,422.5	1,568.3	696	13,367	637.8	171.8
Beckley, WV	173	1,086	132.0	51.1	91	1,641	553.6	79.4	222	4,178	236.4	65.2
Bellingham, WA.....................	685	D	D	D	330	9,613	14,932.2	552.3	509	8,282	492.9	140.6
Bend-Redmond, OR...............	708	2,631	332.0	120.7	279	3,672	801.8	165.8	498	7,635	435.6	133.5
Billings, MT	633	3,693	634.7	205.6	194	3,225	6,885.5	187.0	459	8,438	477.5	128.8
Binghamton, NY	367	6,531	973.4	425.8	217	8,946	2,639.1	451.7	611	8,814	423.6	115.1
Birmingham-Hoover, AL	2,690	22,265	3,914.9	1,383.4	950	36,531	14,836.4	1,827.0	2,010	38,797	2,033.2	578.4
Bismarck, ND	374	3,124	490.9	182.4	110	1,833	2,998.6	96.0	234	6,184	336.0	92.0
Blacksburg-Christiansburg-Radford, VA..................	367	3,392	325.8	170.0	150	10,969	5,682.6	565.9	373	6,964	301.9	84.2
Bloomington, IL	386	2,942	289.8	127.8	106	4,393	1,771.6	220.2	417	8,625	412.8	114.3
Bloomington, IN	311	2,082	246.1	100.7	121	7,695	1,717.9	331.8	386	8,168	348.3	95.8
Bloomsburg-Berwick, PA........	129	1,126	188.9	47.4	91	5,908	1,754.0	238.8	198	3,192	148.0	39.5
Boise City, ID	1,928	13,673	1,947.4	772.0	589	22,032	7,099.3	1,212.2	1,277	21,430	964.4	276.0
Boston-Cambridge-Newton, MA-NH	17,311	225,723	55,357.8	21,911.7	4,533	156,284	58,110.8	10,067.9	11,697	202,244	13,543.1	3,886.6
Boston, MA Div 14454	7,073	89,222	22,948.5	8,531.9	1,450	39,895	17,097.4	2,241.3	5,103	100,153	7,073.7	2,041.1
Cambridge-Newton-Framingham, MA Div 15764	8,954	126,579	31,082.5	12,822.1	2,521	97,905	35,508.6	6,773.6	5,459	84,611	5,476.4	1,556.1
Rockingham County-Strafford County, NH 40484	1,284	9,922	1,326.8	557.7	562	18,483	5,504.8	1,052.9	1,135	17,480	993.0	289.4
Boulder, CO..........................	2,679	27,395	4,767.9	2,011.5	536	14,305	5,061.5	998.4	866	15,855	842.2	252.2
Bowling Green, KY	234	2,203	185.8	65.7	139	8,810	5,362.6	440.2	302	6,331	297.6	79.1
Bremerton-Silverdale, WA......	710	D	D	D	161	1,817	328.2	80.7	468	7,138	426.0	124.0
Bridgeport-Stamford-Norwalk, CT	3,481	40,694	8,738.6	3,975.9	837	35,507	13,412.5	2,338.2	2,266	30,574	2,153.3	604.6
Brownsville-Harlingen, TX......	488	2,359	258.4	81.1	204	4,414	1,709.6	D	660	12,582	635.1	171.7
Brunswick, GA.......................	292	912	121.5	41.1	69	2,197	1,010.8	131.0	298	7,042	409.6	125.3
Buffalo-Cheektowaga-Niagara Falls, NY..................	2,463	30,722	3,833.2	1,742.2	1,281	50,593	18,970.4	2,713.2	2,800	50,984	2,927.8	734.8
Burlington, NC	218	1,375	133.0	55.8	200	9,268	3,138.4	399.3	293	5,761	254.4	71.8
Burlington-South Burlington, VT	835	6,611	972.3	417.1	251	12,671	4,891.5	690.5	546	9,006	513.9	150.4
California-Lexington Park, MD	309	8,327	1,654.0	640.7	28	225	D	9.6	184	3,670	166.6	48.1
Canton-Massillon, OH	700	D	D	D	546	24,034	12,551.4	1,116.3	810	14,329	648.0	180.0
Cape Coral-Fort Myers, FL.....	1,893	12,312	2,202.7	844.3	366	4,010	812.8	165.1	1,189	25,851	1,346.6	402.6
Cape Girardeau, MO-IL..........	172	D	D	D	113	3,999	D	193.2	192	4,338	177.5	50.6
Carbondale-Marion, IL...........	229	1,325	133.9	48.4	81	2,421	971.3	104.4	288	5,651	235.2	66.8
Carson City, NV.....................	295	1,180	170.1	60.0	122	2,798	634.0	162.7	159	2,740	133.4	41.2
Casper, WY	278	1,537	222.4	83.2	83	2,428	1,780.3	163.0	200	3,814	198.2	57.4

Table C. Metropolitan Areas — Health Care and Social Assistance, Other Services, Nonemployer Businesses, and Residential Construction

Area name	Health care and social assistance, 2012				Other services, 2012				Nonemployer businesses, 2016		Value of residential construction authorized by building permits, 2018	
	Number of establish-ments	Number of employees	Receipts (mil dol)	Annual payroll (mil dol)	Number of establish-ments	Number of employees	Receipts (mil dol)	Annual payroll (mil dol)	Number	Receipts (mil dol)	New construc-tion ($1,000)	Number of housing units
	159	160	161	162	163	164	165	166	167	168	169	170
Abilene, TX..................	420	12,633	1,064.8	421.7	248	1,857	152.3	42.3	12,334	560.1	74,867	357
Akron, OH......................	1,786	51,155	5,068.1	2,050.0	1,311	8,916	974.1	243.0	47,717	2,085.2	414,468	1,210
Albany, GA....................	382	9,907	968.2	368.4	222	1,234	112.6	30.5	11,204	358.9	23,923	188
Albany, OR....................	216	4,660	422.3	174.0	142	D	D	D	5,973	247.9	122,676	540
Albany-Schenectady-Troy, NY	2,412	64,310	6,091.5	2,533.7	1,611	10,243	1,081.3	347.0	52,844	2,481.8	567,036	2,239
Albuquerque, NM	2,205	54,420	5,690.4	2,313.8	1,276	8,132	814.0	238.6	52,689	2,124.8	470,291	2,186
Alexandria, LA	523	14,367	1,529.4	560.2	209	1,068	107.6	28.5	9,203	413.5	65,245	305
Allentown-Bethlehem-Easton, PA-NJ..................	2,401	61,400	6,250.5	2,499.5	1,579	9,010	803.1	234.6	51,564	2,427.8	254,294	1,246
Altoona, PA....................	438	11,356	1,149.5	472.4	283	1,573	118.4	36.7	6,276	296.2	20,721	101
Amarillo, TX....................	705	17,438	1,952.4	701.1	411	2,866	350.5	85.9	19,622	961.1	172,283	750
Ames, IA......................	192	4,855	513.2	206.0	146	1,000	136.1	27.5	5,531	240.7	105,685	626
Anchorage, AK	1,432	29,237	4,067.7	1,509.4	703	4,435	578.7	152.7	28,430	1,361.2	342,010	1,259
Ann Arbor, MI..................	964	36,873	4,710.2	2,219.2	537	3,891	489.6	143.2	29,801	1,313.9	193,830	805
Anniston-Oxford-Jacksonville, AL..................	273	5,785	573.5	221.0	177	785	80.2	23.3	6,412	239.6	10,958	70
Appleton, WI....................	543	12,265	1,384.9	558.4	419	3,088	266.3	78.8	12,726	623.5	172,128	987
Asheville, NC..................	1,307	30,548	3,452.0	1,394.1	737	3,776	386.7	106.2	43,176	1,793.2	671,262	2,805
Athens-Clarke County, GA	602	10,408	1,274.7	512.7	271	1,723	235.1	52.1	15,631	630.0	202,000	1,069
Atlanta-Sandy Springs-Roswell, GA..................	13,077	230,926	28,008.1	10,487.2	8,560	59,105	7,668.8	1,894.6	572,951	23,281.2	7,522,295	39,441
Atlantic City-Hammonton, NJ .	846	17,487	1,969.3	780.4	563	3,588	293.9	85.2	17,231	838.9	131,882	833
Auburn-Opelika, AL	235	5,923	541.5	218.4	172	787	72.8	18.6	10,154	435.4	296,765	1,131
Augusta-Richmond County, GA-SC..................	1,277	35,811	4,187.5	1,602.4	658	3,832	374.8	102.8	37,806	1,372.2	531,846	2,867
Austin-Round Rock, TX..........	4,433	83,036	9,710.8	3,783.2	3,006	24,324	2,984.0	872.5	188,226	9,669.5	5,215,674	30,035
Bakersfield, CA..................	1,550	27,833	3,675.0	1,265.4	835	5,099	567.8	153.6	45,491	2,273.4	488,476	2,452
Baltimore-Columbia-Towson, MD..................	7,428	200,484	23,846.6	9,213.0	4,781	37,448	4,255.3	1,233.4	210,872	9,613.1	1,647,759	9,287
Bangor, ME....................	547	14,740	1,570.2	624.9	273	1,395	142.7	36.9	9,258	359.0	46,343	261
Barnstable Town, MA.............	811	15,781	1,766.8	730.5	590	3,176	320.4	95.6	26,068	1,347.3	281,588	1,005
Baton Rouge, LA..................	1,918	48,310	4,807.8	1,827.7	1,261	11,145	1,308.9	452.0	63,014	2,759.8	761,218	3,922
Battle Creek, MI..................	323	9,313	966.4	421.9	208	1,173	448.4	41.7	6,261	233.3	11,040	54
Bay City, MI....................	329	7,152	682.5	261.2	190	928	70.8	21.3	5,465	210.3	29,838	85
Beaumont-Port Arthur, TX	1,025	20,354	1,951.3	701.4	504	3,670	393.6	111.7	23,987	955.8	191,333	1,404
Beckley, WV....................	389	9,454	898.0	354.7	168	1,168	124.8	32.5	5,226	188.2	14,793	86
Bellingham, WA..................	659	9,901	1,026.2	422.5	404	2,282	239.2	70.4	15,486	729.5	280,020	1,464
Bend-Redmond, OR..............	608	9,398	1,114.0	442.5	329	1,526	156.8	41.9	17,623	914.1	499,609	1,983
Billings, MT....................	592	12,939	1,549.9	590.1	389	2,186	239.0	59.9	12,927	654.9	172,075	1,476
Binghamton, NY	503	15,897	1,582.1	639.3	406	2,142	171.4	48.5	12,589	508.9	35,141	315
Birmingham-Hoover, AL	2,524	70,853	8,979.9	3,315.2	1,607	12,325	1,613.1	398.1	82,208	3,694.7	765,703	3,025
Bismarck, ND	340	12,237	1,180.9	537.1	316	1,975	246.8	63.0	9,905	503.8	108,458	533
Blacksburg-Christiansburg-Radford, VA..................	372	6,334	730.0	254.0	270	1,359	225.8	39.1	9,463	357.2	96,250	566
Bloomington, IL	399	9,128	1,008.2	385.5	286	2,409	221.6	77.3	10,546	423.0	24,386	220
Bloomington, IN..................	352	9,328	950.4	366.4	231	1,973	270.3	56.9	10,720	411.1	85,643	417
Bloomsburg-Berwick, PA.......	264	11,077	1,817.3	664.3	149	727	110.5	18.4	4,239	187.3	33,254	194
Boise City, ID..................	1,829	37,600	3,759.2	1,594.3	1,010	5,254	477.6	141.0	52,697	2,377.7	1,830,749	8,917
Boston-Cambridge-Newton, MA-NH..................	13,000	422,688	48,286.9	20,807.5	10,259	72,079	8,446.7	2,368.1	392,720	22,169.8	3,254,010	14,183
Boston, MA Div 14454	5,263	214,091	25,294.2	10,889.4	4,533	34,135	4,287.4	1,114.9	156,221	8,983.5	NA	NA
Cambridge-Newton-Framingham, MA Div 15764	6,569	186,471	20,460.6	8,918.9	4,846	33,113	3,711.6	1,116.2	201,543	11,057.8	NA	NA
Rockingham County-Strafford County, NH 40484	1,168	22,126	2,532.1	999.2	880	4,831	447.8	137.0	34,956	2,128.6	NA	NA
Boulder, CO....................	1,332	18,386	2,129.6	841.9	717	4,415	670.1	176.7	39,089	1,984.5	623,379	2,954
Bowling Green, KY..............	444	8,799	924.0	349.4	242	1,169	98.7	28.3	12,399	655.6	276,613	2,199
Bremerton-Silverdale, WA......	685	11,861	1,272.8	484.3	382	1,789	149.7	48.6	14,639	655.4	327,677	1,149
Bridgeport-Stamford-Norwalk, CT	2,827	63,963	8,087.6	3,291.8	2,103	13,041	1,654.3	420.8	94,038	6,734.7	531,590	1,097
Brownsville-Harlingen, TX	1,003	31,018	1,911.3	844.7	402	2,159	163.6	44.6	31,083	1,156.6	173,152	1,487
Brunswick, GA..................	291	5,206	657.2	240.4	169	806	89.7	19.1	8,416	343.5	181,669	652
Buffalo-Cheektowaga-Niagara Falls, NY..................	3,187	85,040	8,321.9	3,500.3	2,093	12,616	1,168.9	314.5	57,470	2,567.2	352,089	1,453
Burlington, NC..................	379	8,367	801.9	369.4	190	1,097	100.7	29.2	10,041	369.4	195,976	1,419
Burlington-South Burlington, VT..................	685	16,844	1,869.8	685.4	493	2,572	252.7	72.4	18,792	913.8	192,347	1,164
California-Lexington Park, MD	179	4,110	379.9	172.2	142	865	80.7	30.1	6,914	271.6	178,933	931
Canton-Massillon, OH	1,035	28,763	2,497.1	1,107.4	740	4,994	477.5	135.2	25,273	1,060.1	115,896	528
Cape Coral-Fort Myers, FL.....	1,488	26,009	3,362.1	1,226.1	1,209	6,696	580.1	164.2	63,568	2,979.7	1,869,044	9,721
Cape Girardeau, MO-IL.........	345	11,469	1,176.6	468.0	181	864	84.3	21.1	6,306	273.0	29,490	816
Carbondale-Marion, IL	371	9,440	1,194.8	410.7	186	915	94.1	22.5	7,382	267.8	29,390	238
Carson City, NV..................	224	3,744	510.8	182.9	126	660	62.8	19.0	4,850	398.4	59,901	310
Casper, WY....................	305	5,141	687.2	266.3	207	1,333	227.6	49.8	5,984	273.6	34,552	174

Table C. Metropolitan Areas

Government Employment and Payroll, and Local Government Finances

Area name	Full-time equivalent employees	March payroll (dollars)	Adminis- tration, judicial, and legal	Police and corrections	Fire protection	Highways and transpor- tation	Health and welfare	Natural resources and utilities	Education and libraries	Total (mil dol)	Inter- govern- mental (mil dol)	Total (mil dol)	Per capita Total	Property
	171	172	173	174	175	176	177	178	179	180	181	182	183	184
Abilene, TX.........................	6,849	21,021,831	5.9	11.8	4.6	1.9	9.1	4.7	60.5	518.5	218.5	216.8	1,298	958
Akron, OH..........................	26,841	107,374,120	7.1	9.8	5.3	5.1	11.5	6.3	53.1	3,076.7	1,096.1	1,324.2	1,886	1,236
Albany, GA........................	7,162	21,657,598	7.9	10.7	4.5	3.1	5.4	7.1	58.2	562.0	254.3	209.6	1,331	844
Albany, OR........................	3,984	16,207,525	6.1	11.2	5.6	4.0	5.1	4.9	61.9	447.9	223.4	146.4	1,237	1,133
Albany-Schenectady-Troy, NY	36,516	166,624,101	5.4	11.1	2.5	4.0	8.5	3.7	63.1	4,760.1	1,679.6	2,291.7	2,620	1,927
Albuquerque, NM	30,074	112,231,236	6.2	14.9	5.8	5.5	4.5	5.9	55.8	3,116.0	1,545.5	1,089.1	1,208	691
Alexandria, LA.....................	6,219	18,920,106	10.2	14.7	7.3	3.5	1.6	5.7	54.5	537.9	262.7	207.5	1,343	529
Allentown-Bethlehem-Easton, PA-NJ	28,544	125,365,734	7.1	11.0	1.6	3.5	8.4	4.3	62.3	3,830.4	1,426.8	1,741.8	2,106	1,770
Altoona, PA........................	4,030	13,533,958	4.8	8.4	2.3	5.0	8.5	7.0	62.6	402.4	214.5	126.2	993	707
Amarillo, TX........................	11,385	38,289,774	6.0	11.5	5.0	2.8	5.4	3.4	64.4	911.4	355.4	389.8	1,513	1,141
Ames, IA...........................	2,892	10,932,541	7.4	7.6	2.9	7.7	10.1	9.9	52.8	476.0	102.3	138.3	1,518	1,219
Anchorage, AK	12,850	64,974,760	5.2	7.0	5.6	4.8	2.6	8.4	65.2	1,699.8	812.1	683.6	1,741	1,513
Ann Arbor, MI......................	9,997	45,620,706	8.5	10.1	3.0	4.2	5.2	5.4	62.0	1,472.6	631.4	577.8	1,646	1,596
Anniston-Oxford-Jacksonville, AL...	5,708	17,129,463	3.6	6.8	2.8	2.8	32.2	7.0	43.2	507.7	169.3	112.4	958	366
Appleton, WI.......................	7,780	34,593,416	4.9	7.3	2.2	3.3	7.7	3.3	69.6	894.7	399.3	319.4	1,398	1,365
Asheville, NC.......................	17,505	58,826,655	4.2	7.0	2.1	1.1	24.6	5.0	53.1	1,741.6	575.9	513.1	1,187	868
Athens-Clarke County, GA	7,394	23,449,444	6.9	10.8	3.3	3.2	5.2	6.6	61.6	987.4	199.2	256.9	1,308	933
Atlanta-Sandy Springs-Roswell, GA..	203,403	731,570,783	7.2	9.5	4.1	4.5	5.7	5.0	62.5	20,074.6	5,922.8	9,520.7	1,744	1,190
Atlantic City-Hammonton, NJ .	14,001	71,971,044	5.3	13.7	4.7	1.7	5.3	3.8	63.4	1,749.6	507.4	1,016.6	3,691	3,639
Auburn-Opelika, AL	6,506	23,295,526	2.9	5.8	2.5	1.6	40.7	4.1	41.4	640.1	158.1	164.2	1,115	594
Augusta-Richmond County, GA-SC..	20,099	65,183,308	7.2	9.6	2.7	2.9	4.2	5.7	66.1	1,739.1	746.8	669.1	1,162	761
Austin-Round Rock, TX.........	73,039	288,365,719	6.7	12.6	4.5	3.0	4.9	13.3	53.3	7,348.5	1,653.0	4,159.1	2,267	1,895
Bakersfield, CA....................	32,191	158,787,344	5.1	10.1	4.5	2.2	16.0	4.2	56.8	6,098.2	2,797.6	1,169.0	1,365	1,151
Baltimore-Columbia-Towson, MD ..	99,896	465,911,722	4.8	11.2	4.8	2.5	4.4	5.4	65.0	11,911.4	4,396.6	5,905.6	2,145	1,222
Bangor, ME.........................	5,352	18,128,721	5.6	7.8	5.2	7.6	1.3	6.1	64.9	466.9	185.2	205.7	1,338	1,324
Barnstable Town, MA.............	7,548	35,968,725	7.2	11.5	10.0	4.2	3.5	6.4	53.6	1,003.5	207.7	645.0	2,994	2,809
Baton Rouge, LA..................	30,360	102,896,811	8.5	10.0	4.5	3.6	6.5	7.1	57.0	3,050.2	1,092.8	1,434.7	1,760	767
Battle Creek, MI...................	4,008	16,572,500	10.0	11.0	3.1	3.3	5.9	4.4	61.4	671.0	371.6	175.1	1,296	1,142
Bay City, MI	4,027	15,471,429	6.7	5.7	2.4	4.8	13.5	5.1	61.1	536.8	284.0	123.7	1,157	1,137
Beaumont-Port Arthur, TX	17,005	59,961,656	6.9	13.5	4.6	3.6	4.5	7.9	57.9	1,621.0	485.7	770.1	1,905	1,584
Beckley, WV	3,968	12,471,321	4.9	5.2	1.2	1.5	2.1	5.4	77.4	330.4	170.0	113.2	907	718
Bellingham, WA....................	5,120	25,193,563	10.0	10.9	7.5	8.7	1.8	7.1	50.4	696.1	261.3	292.4	1,424	871
Bend-Redmond, OR..............	4,773	21,188,503	8.1	12.1	5.4	2.6	5.0	7.0	55.3	649.0	217.1	283.8	1,749	1,579
Billings, MT.........................	5,275	20,966,552	5.5	8.5	4.5	5.0	8.4	5.9	55.7	507.5	191.1	179.3	1,101	1,025
Binghamton, NY	11,995	45,564,792	4.9	8.0	2.3	4.3	9.9	2.6	66.0	1,446.5	620.9	619.4	2,492	1,689
Birmingham-Hoover, AL	41,677	145,061,797	5.5	12.3	6.2	3.5	6.2	8.1	54.6	3,941.4	1,461.0	1,685.8	1,483	659
Bismarck, ND	3,791	13,709,939	4.6	8.1	3.4	4.7	6.7	8.1	61.8	473.7	232.8	141.1	1,176	966
Blacksburg-Christiansburg-Radford, VA..	5,444	17,603,156	8.2	10.4	0.7	3.0	3.2	6.1	64.4	493.5	224.5	187.6	1,048	749
Bloomington, IL	7,152	27,482,356	6.5	10.1	4.3	4.2	7.4	5.2	60.3	732.2	198.8	386.9	2,050	1,720
Bloomington, IN....................	4,067	13,951,012	10.1	10.5	4.9	5.1	2.9	7.9	58.1	391.1	166.8	163.4	1,006	789
Bloomsburg-Berwick, PA........	2,432	8,805,660	6.5	10.1	0.0	3.5	1.8	3.7	73.5	290.1	113.0	109.7	1,287	914
Boise City, ID	19,235	61,842,070	8.7	13.8	5.3	3.5	3.2	5.5	58.0	1,734.2	757.9	596.2	935	874
Boston-Cambridge-Newton, MA-NH ..	153,708	758,103,739	4.2	10.4	7.6	2.3	4.2	5.6	63.4	20,238.4	6,374.7	10,961.5	2,362	2,272
Boston, MA Div 14454.........	62,159	318,038,206	3.6	12.1	8.7	2.3	3.8	6.0	61.6	8,478.9	2,834.2	4,659.2	2,419	2,297
Cambridge-Newton-Framingham, MA Div 15764	76,602	380,709,237	4.6	9.0	6.9	2.4	4.4	5.7	64.4	10,119.6	3,073.3	5,273.3	2,300	2,225
Rockingham County-Strafford County, NH 40484	14,947	59,356,296	4.6	10.5	5.5	2.5	4.3	3.2	67.3	1,639.9	467.1	1,028.9	2,439	2,409
Boulder, CO........................	11,666	48,102,144	8.2	10.8	5.0	2.7	5.3	10.3	53.3	1,374.3	334.5	816.3	2,674	1,840
Bowling Green, KY	5,785	16,747,663	3.0	7.9	3.3	1.9	4.2	9.0	67.7	397.4	175.4	150.8	930	466
Bremerton-Silverdale, WA......	6,732	32,797,634	7.2	7.7	9.1	6.6	1.0	9.5	56.8	1,053.2	532.7	344.8	1,352	960
Bridgeport-Stamford-Norwalk, CT ..	32,029	179,963,079	3.5	9.1	5.1	3.1	3.2	3.7	70.6	4,597.7	963.2	3,193.1	3,419	3,370
Brownsville-Harlingen, TX	21,552	67,816,703	3.9	8.4	2.8	2.4	1.6	5.2	74.0	1,662.8	982.8	420.5	1,012	795
Brunswick, GA.....................	6,136	22,282,830	5.0	6.9	2.5	1.3	40.1	3.5	40.2	600.6	116.0	196.4	1,731	1,127
Buffalo-Cheektowaga-Niagara Falls, NY	44,201	202,514,083	3.8	12.1	3.3	3.0	5.4	4.9	65.5	6,495.4	2,759.6	2,637.8	2,326	1,539
Burlington, NC......................	1,005,835	17,822,770	4.1	10.8	2.8	1.7	7.8	5.8	64.0	420.3	210.4	147.7	960	694
Burlington-South Burlington, VT..	8,073	32,538,734	4.7	5.9	2.3	6.1	0.9	7.3	71.2	830.6	537.1	145.5	681	585
California-Lexington Park, MD	3,187	14,069,480	5.9	10.5	0.0	2.3	1.5	4.3	73.2	356.5	125.4	191.8	1,760	923
Canton-Massillon, OH	12,345	44,734,873	4.8	6.7	4.6	4.4	2.5	5.9	70.3	1,381.0	667.7	493.7	1,224	920
Cape Coral-Fort Myers, FL.....	29,739	118,190,826	4.0	7.9	5.4	3.4	39.4	4.7	33.6	3,672.5	586.2	1,065.4	1,651	1,448
Cape Girardeau, MO-IL.........	3,276	8,670,805	6.6	8.7	4.7	6.8	1.2	9.4	60.9	259.7	107.2	113.5	1,169	651
Carbondale-Marion, IL...........	4,224	14,371,667	6.4	9.2	3.2	3.8	4.1	6.6	65.5	411.6	200.9	146.7	1,158	929
Carson City, NV....................	1,396	6,652,347	9.5	13.4	7.3	4.2	3.5	6.4	53.3	189.1	96.1	54.9	1,001	717
Casper, WY	3,954	15,321,295	4.4	7.8	3.5	2.3	2.0	5.1	72.5	442.5	254.7	108.8	1,384	938

1. Based on the resident population estimated as of July 1 of the year shown.

Area name	Local government finances, 2012 (cont.)									Government employment, 2017			Individual income tax returns, 2016		
	Direct general expenditure							Debt outstanding							
			Percent of total for:											Mean adjusted gross income	
	Total (mil dol)	Per capita[1] (dollars)	Educa- tion	Health and hospitals	Police protection	Public welfare	Highways	Total (mil dol)	Per capita[1] (dollars)	Federal civilian	Federal military	State and local	Number of returns		Mean income tax
	185	186	187	188	189	190	191	192	193	194	195	196	197	198	199
Abilene, TX.............................	488.6	2,927	54.4	6.6	7.0	0.5	3.1	339.1	2,031	1,272	4,624	11,608	72,100	51,895	5,981
Akron, OH...............................	2,952.8	4,205	42.5	10.2	5.2	4.1	3.5	4,519.2	6,435	2,142	1,786	42,730	344,130	60,004	7,810
Albany, GA..............................	576.8	3,665	46.3	10.0	6.0	0.1	3.2	314.8	2,000	2,633	705	9,721	62,640	44,783	4,455
Albany, OR..............................	449.1	3,794	51.6	3.6	6.2	0.4	4.4	449.9	3,801	314	303	6,266	54,530	50,656	4,799
Albany-Schenectady-Troy, NY	4,877.2	5,576	47.3	3.9	3.9	11.4	4.6	4,658.9	5,327	6,565	3,264	92,326	439,270	77,239	11,279
Albuquerque, NM.....................	2,976.7	3,301	50.0	1.6	8.3	1.5	5.0	4,360.6	4,836	14,530	5,707	67,399	407,660	54,654	6,360
Alexandria, LA.........................	559.7	3,624	51.4	0.1	8.2	0.1	5.0	528.4	3,421	2,870	578	10,702	63,590	52,333	5,913
Allentown-Bethlehem-Easton, PA-NJ...................................	4,050.8	4,897	50.0	3.0	3.6	9.9	3.0	7,000.9	8,464	2,279	2,092	37,614	421,140	63,055	8,104
Altoona, PA.............................	409.0	3,217	49.0	3.1	3.0	8.6	3.9	474.2	3,730	1,055	311	7,382	59,120	50,748	5,896
Amarillo, TX............................	915.3	3,553	53.8	4.6	5.9	0.0	2.6	933.7	3,625	2,222	597	18,079	115,650	56,234	7,093
Ames, IA.................................	440.2	4,830	30.3	42.8	3.2	0.5	3.7	391.5	4,295	949	345	19,275	36,690	67,234	8,304
Anchorage, AK	1,661.6	4,233	54.5	2.2	8.1	0.0	6.1	2,262.7	5,764	8,729	12,309	24,369	191,630	73,480	10,760
Ann Arbor, MI..........................	1,495.8	4,262	46.0	12.6	6.5	0.9	4.9	2,033.3	5,794	4,135	629	71,379	165,230	80,390	12,655
Anniston-Oxford-Jacksonville, AL..	517.7	4,414	32.7	36.2	5.9	0.0	3.9	358.0	3,052	3,613	536	8,631	47,590	46,197	4,383
Appleton, WI............................	965.9	4,228	54.4	2.6	5.2	4.9	9.0	758.9	3,322	688	648	12,203	118,560	68,419	8,882
Asheville, NC...........................	1,591.2	3,680	36.5	20.8	7.4	7.0	1.7	929.8	2,150	3,375	1,069	22,306	215,900	55,536	6,580
Athens-Clarke County, GA	1,058.7	5,390	28.8	41.0	3.3	0.2	2.0	748.8	3,812	1,076	618	27,734	81,370	57,985	7,202
Atlanta-Sandy Springs-Roswell, GA................	19,663.2	3,603	49.2	7.0	6.1	0.9	3.6	35,894.1	6,577	47,225	16,767	282,204	2,604,850	68,866	9,647
Atlantic City-Hammonton, NJ .	1,718.6	6,240	52.7	0.6	6.1	2.1	1.7	1,314.6	4,773	2,623	826	19,736	132,660	53,739	6,109
Auburn-Opelika, AL.................	638.8	4,338	33.9	39.7	4.1	0.0	2.6	782.4	5,313	298	727	17,243	63,090	57,114	6,654
Augusta-Richmond County, GA-SC................................	1,747.7	3,035	52.5	4.4	5.9	0.3	3.6	1,584.4	2,751	9,214	13,397	42,887	253,570	53,889	5,885
Austin-Round Rock, TX..........	7,452.3	4,063	43.6	5.9	6.4	0.6	7.0	22,572.2	12,306	12,999	4,447	157,460	967,110	80,529	12,673
Bakersfield, CA.......................	5,683.5	6,638	55.4	8.5	3.6	6.7	3.0	3,571.0	4,171	10,558	3,953	54,711	335,910	51,053	5,147
Baltimore-Columbia-Towson, MD......................................	12,715.1	4,618	49.6	1.9	6.8	0.5	4.0	11,152.6	4,051	79,892	26,848	166,561	1,344,440	76,397	10,666
Bangor, ME.............................	527.2	3,429	48.1	1.1	3.8	0.2	4.2	409.3	2,662	1,169	461	12,847	67,980	51,210	5,675
Barnstable Town, MA...............	1,041.6	4,835	45.9	1.1	5.3	0.2	3.5	892.5	4,143	1,645	1,163	13,336	126,520	73,120	10,150
Baton Rouge, LA.....................	3,383.6	4,150	44.3	5.0	6.4	0.2	4.9	3,940.9	4,834	2,970	3,276	67,264	357,000	66,634	9,202
Battle Creek, MI......................	680.5	5,037	45.5	17.6	4.3	2.6	5.4	473.1	3,502	3,060	267	7,959	61,020	49,750	5,298
Bay City, MI............................	521.5	4,877	44.7	20.6	3.3	4.5	4.2	246.5	2,305	252	225	5,545	52,920	47,921	5,087
Beaumont-Port Arthur, TX	1,598.1	3,954	44.3	3.2	7.1	0.5	5.0	5,940.9	14,699	2,015	1,006	22,314	169,900	55,346	6,272
Beckley, WV	341.8	2,737	62.9	0.6	6.8	0.1	1.6	157.5	1,261	1,968	549	6,612	46,540	45,843	4,664
Bellingham, WA.......................	644.4	3,139	42.5	4.3	6.1	0.0	5.7	595.5	2,901	1,396	629	14,198	102,600	62,170	7,852
Bend-Redmond, OR.................	663.5	4,089	49.1	3.5	7.4	0.4	5.0	1,093.2	6,736	921	455	8,161	91,090	70,581	9,459
Billings, MT.............................	545.0	3,346	48.4	6.7	5.9	0.2	6.4	248.2	1,524	1,881	792	7,859	82,830	60,881	7,600
Binghamton, NY	1,497.1	6,024	49.5	3.4	2.7	11.2	4.5	1,460.3	5,875	683	367	20,481	110,780	52,730	5,853
Birmingham-Hoover, AL	3,959.1	3,483	45.9	4.8	7.2	0.1	4.3	8,903.8	7,833	9,134	5,178	71,477	493,630	65,897	8,959
Bismarck, ND..........................	438.5	3,652	44.7	1.5	5.4	1.8	11.0	308.2	2,567	1,473	803	13,699	63,700	69,685	9,356
Blacksburg-Christiansburg-Radford, VA....................	489.3	2,734	47.9	0.6	7.5	5.4	3.8	652.1	3,644	451	630	21,807	69,170	54,475	6,082
Bloomington, IL.......................	735.9	3,900	45.5	3.6	4.9	1.2	5.6	815.8	4,323	500	362	15,919	84,200	69,144	9,180
Bloomington, IN.......................	330.0	2,032	47.5	1.0	4.6	0.4	4.3	424.9	2,617	361	482	23,181	66,430	57,841	7,246
Bloomsburg-Berwick, PA........	287.0	3,367	58.3	0.0	2.7	3.0	4.5	1,108.2	13,001	188	206	6,587	38,650	54,831	6,499
Boise City, ID..........................	1,619.0	2,538	42.6	1.3	9.7	0.9	6.7	1,042.0	1,633	6,445	2,376	40,576	309,490	62,752	7,793
Boston-Cambridge-Newton, MA-NH................................	19,978.0	4,305	50.4	5.7	5.4	0.8	2.6	12,543.9	2,703	36,065	14,259	267,727	2,425,570	99,125	17,116
Boston, MA Div 14454..........	8,442.8	4,384	47.1	3.7	6.6	0.7	2.2	5,428.2	2,818	19,506	5,865	126,415	NA	NA	NA
Cambridge-Newton-Framingham, MA Div 15764......................	9,961.0	4,344	52.0	8.3	4.3	0.2	2.7	6,297.2	2,746	15,199	6,739	116,527	NA	NA	NA
Rockingham County-Strafford County, NH 40484......................	1,574.2	3,731	58.3	0.3	6.2	4.9	4.0	818.5	1,940	1,360	1,655	24,785	NA	NA	NA
Boulder, CO.............................	1,414.6	4,633	43.6	2.5	8.2	2.3	4.6	1,940.0	6,354	2,077	848	32,749	157,470	95,151	15,835
Bowling Green, KY	401.0	2,472	50.4	4.6	5.8	0.1	3.9	1,131.7	6,976	663	518	11,353	71,260	50,750	5,610
Bremerton-Silverdale, WA......	1,054.5	4,135	42.3	4.6	3.5	0.0	3.5	748.5	2,935	19,368	11,410	13,366	125,870	72,383	9,465
Bridgeport-Stamford-Norwalk, CT......................................	4,616.9	4,944	50.9	1.2	6.6	1.0	3.1	4,013.1	4,297	2,862	1,907	44,076	459,130	148,397	31,256
Brownsville-Harlingen, TX......	1,613.4	3,883	61.9	0.8	4.4	0.5	3.7	1,801.3	4,335	3,391	949	26,768	163,580	37,740	3,268
Brunswick, GA.........................	608.7	5,365	32.5	39.7	4.6	0.1	2.6	370.2	3,264	1,921	396	6,653	48,030	53,907	6,338
Buffalo-Cheektowaga-Niagara Falls, NY.............................	6,848.3	6,038	44.7	9.1	3.7	9.2	3.7	6,125.0	5,400	9,439	1,968	78,358	552,690	58,804	7,289
Burlington, NC.........................	427.7	2,779	50.9	3.4	8.3	5.8	1.6	182.0	1,183	243	357	6,881	72,210	50,942	5,363
Burlington-South Burlington, VT.......................................	830.6	3,887	64.1	0.3	4.8	0.1	6.2	632.9	2,962	3,973	1,447	17,799	112,940	67,989	8,766
California-Lexington Park, MD	331.8	3,045	62.8	2.2	6.2	0.9	2.7	197.3	1,810	9,628	2,476	4,597	51,910	74,587	9,057
Canton-Massillon, OH	1,338.5	3,318	54.8	4.8	5.6	5.1	5.6	461.4	1,144	1,036	1,031	19,283	195,400	52,586	6,108
Cape Coral-Fort Myers, FL.....	3,730.8	5,782	25.4	32.3	4.8	0.5	3.9	5,119.6	7,934	2,410	1,385	39,980	334,840	70,174	10,635
Cape Girardeau, MO-IL...........	263.0	2,710	55.0	0.5	5.3	0.1	9.3	203.7	2,098	420	332	6,746	42,070	54,602	6,390
Carbondale-Marion, IL............	466.0	3,677	59.1	1.7	5.1	2.0	4.7	325.9	2,572	1,811	253	15,012	52,110	51,296	5,762
Carson City, NV......................	205.0	3,738	48.3	2.1	8.1	1.2	5.3	391.1	7,131	635	143	9,081	27,420	53,397	6,659
Casper, WY	436.0	5,546	59.1	0.4	4.8	0.7	4.1	147.1	1,871	657	414	5,102	37,050	69,220	10,271

1. Based on the resident population estimated as of July 1 of the year shown.

Table C. Metropolitan Areas — **Land Area and Population**

CBSA/ DIV Code[1]	Area name	Land area[2] (sq mi)	Total persons	Rank	Per square mile	White	Black	American Indian, Alaska Native	Asian and Pacific Islander	Percent Hispanic or Latino[3]	Under 5 years	5 to 17 years	18 to 24 years	25 to 34 years	35 to 44 years	45 to 54 years
		1	2	3	4	5	6	7	8	9	10	11	12	13	14	15
16300	Cedar Rapids, IA..................	2,008.8	272,295	177	135.6	89.3	6.4	0.6	2.9	3.1	6.2	16.9	8.8	13.2	12.8	12.6
16540	Chambersburg-Waynesboro, PA......	772.2	154,835	265	200.5	89.3	4.5	0.6	1.5	5.9	6.0	16.2	7.6	12.0	11.6	13.3
16580	Champaign-Urbana, IL..........	1,920.9	239,643	192	124.8	72.6	12.9	0.5	10.9	5.6	5.5	13.7	21.1	14.0	11.0	9.9
16620	Charleston, WV	1,745.1	211,037	212	120.9	91.2	8.0	0.7	1.4	1.1	5.3	14.9	7.5	11.9	12.2	12.7
16700	Charleston-North Charleston, SC	2,590.1	787,643	74	304.1	66.2	26.5	1.0	2.9	5.7	6.1	15.7	8.7	15.7	13.2	12.6
16740	Charlotte-Concord-Gastonia, NC-SC.........	5,065.1	2,569,213	23	507.2	62.3	23.7	0.9	4.6	10.5	6.2	17.5	8.5	14.2	13.7	14.2
16820	Charlottesville, VA.............	2,224.1	235,232	194	105.8	76.4	14.7	0.7	5.4	5.3	5.2	13.8	11.8	14.1	12.0	12.1
16860	Chattanooga, TN-GA.............	2,089.0	560,793	99	268.5	79.7	14.4	0.8	2.1	4.7	5.7	15.4	8.4	13.6	12.3	13.0
16940	Cheyenne, WY	2,685.9	98,976	356	36.9	80.7	3.4	1.4	2.2	14.8	6.3	17.0	8.9	14.9	12.3	11.6
16980	Chicago-Naperville-Elgin, IL-IN-WI..........	7,195.1	9,498,716	3	1,320.2	54.0	17.0	0.5	7.8	22.4	6.0	16.7	9.0	14.4	13.3	13.1
16980	Chicago-Naperville-Arlington Heights, IL Div 16974...	3,450.3	7,288,849	X	2,112.5	50.9	19.0	0.4	8.6	22.7	6.1	16.4	8.8	15.1	13.5	13.0
16980	Elgin, IL Div 20994	1,150.7	638,359	X	554.8	61.3	6.4	0.4	4.5	28.9	6.2	18.6	10.7	12.2	13.0	13.5
16980	Gary, IN Div 23844	1,878.3	701,386	X	373.4	64.8	17.9	0.6	1.9	16.3	5.8	17.2	8.8	12.2	12.7	12.7
16980	Lake County-Kenosha County, IL-WI Div 29404	715.8	870,122	X	1,215.6	65.5	7.7	0.4	7.8	20.5	5.7	18.1	10.1	11.5	12.5	14.0
17020	Chico, CA	1,636.5	231,256	197	141.3	75.1	2.6	3.0	6.7	16.7	5.5	14.4	14.3	13.1	10.9	10.5
17140	Cincinnati, OH-KY-IN............	4,162.5	2,190,209	29	526.2	81.0	13.7	0.6	3.4	3.4	6.2	17.2	9.3	13.5	12.3	12.9
17300	Clarksville, TN-KY	1,698.2	292,264	166	172.1	68.0	21.8	1.2	3.7	9.3	8.4	18.1	12.3	18.0	12.4	10.4
17420	Cleveland, TN	763.4	123,625	318	161.9	88.5	5.2	1.0	1.4	5.8	5.7	15.8	9.3	12.5	12.2	13.7
17460	Cleveland-Elyria, OH..........	1,999.4	2,057,009	33	1,028.8	71.3	21.0	0.6	3.0	6.0	5.6	15.5	8.5	13.0	11.6	12.9
17660	Coeur d'Alene, ID	1,237.8	161,505	261	130.5	92.6	0.8	2.2	1.9	4.8	6.0	16.8	7.5	12.9	12.0	12.1
17780	College Station-Bryan, TX......	2,099.7	262,431	187	125.0	57.4	11.8	0.6	6.4	25.4	6.2	14.8	23.2	15.4	11.2	9.5
17820	Colorado Springs, CO	2,683.9	738,939	79	275.3	72.9	7.6	1.5	5.0	17.1	6.7	17.2	10.8	15.8	12.6	11.8
17860	Columbia, MO	685.5	180,005	233	262.6	81.1	11.2	1.0	6.3	3.5	5.8	14.5	19.2	15.3	11.8	10.3
17900	Columbia, SC	3,703.1	832,666	70	224.9	57.8	34.8	0.8	3.0	5.7	5.7	16.3	11.6	13.9	12.4	12.6
17980	Columbus, GA-AL	1,936.2	305,451	163	157.8	48.5	42.9	1.0	3.2	7.1	6.8	17.3	9.8	15.6	12.3	12.0
18020	Columbus, IN	406.9	82,753	374	203.4	82.8	3.0	0.6	8.2	6.9	6.6	17.2	8.1	14.5	12.4	12.6
18140	Columbus, OH	4,796.6	2,106,541	32	439.2	74.7	17.5	0.8	5.4	4.3	6.6	16.9	9.2	15.8	13.4	12.8
18580	Corpus Christi, TX	1,783.8	452,950	118	253.9	33.2	3.4	0.6	2.4	61.4	6.7	17.8	9.6	13.9	12.7	11.7
18700	Corvallis, OR	675.2	92,101	365	136.4	83.3	1.8	1.6	9.5	7.6	4.1	12.1	22.9	13.2	10.2	9.8
18880	Crestview-Fort Walton Beach-Destin, FL..........	1,968.0	278,644	173	141.6	79.0	9.8	1.4	4.5	8.8	6.4	15.4	8.1	15.0	12.2	11.8
19060	Cumberland, MD-WV	750.1	97,915	361	130.5	90.4	8.0	0.5	1.3	1.6	4.7	13.3	11.2	12.5	11.3	12.9
19100	Dallas-Fort Worth-Arlington, TX..........	9,279.2	7,539,711	4	812.5	47.4	16.6	0.9	8.0	29.0	6.9	19.0	9.1	14.9	14.1	13.3
19100	Dallas-Plano-Irving, TX Div 19124	5,275.7	5,007,190	X	949.1	44.4	17.4	0.8	9.2	30.0	6.9	18.9	9.1	15.1	14.4	13.4
19100	Fort Worth-Arlington, TX Div 23104	4,003.5	2,532,521	X	632.6	53.2	15.0	0.9	5.7	27.1	6.9	19.2	9.1	14.5	13.5	13.0
19140	Dalton, GA.....................	634.9	143,983	288	226.8	65.5	3.4	0.6	1.4	30.3	6.5	19.0	9.0	13.2	12.5	13.7
19180	Danville, IL...................	898.3	76,806	379	85.5	80.1	15.2	0.6	1.3	5.2	6.4	17.1	7.8	12.0	11.5	11.9
19300	Daphne-Fairhope-Foley, AL....	1,589.8	218,022	206	137.1	84.6	9.5	1.4	1.6	4.6	5.5	16.1	7.2	11.3	11.9	13.2
19340	Davenport-Moline-Rock Island, IA-IL	2,269.7	381,451	140	168.1	80.7	9.2	0.7	3.0	8.9	6.2	16.7	8.2	12.5	12.4	12.2
19380	Dayton, OH....................	1,281.6	806,548	73	629.3	78.5	17.3	0.9	3.2	2.9	6.0	15.9	9.5	13.4	11.5	12.3
19460	Decatur, AL....................	1,270.1	152,046	271	119.7	78.0	13.2	3.4	1.0	7.1	5.9	16.7	7.8	12.2	11.9	13.9
19500	Decatur, IL....................	580.6	104,712	345	180.4	78.8	19.5	0.6	1.7	2.3	6.1	16.0	8.8	11.9	11.5	11.6
19660	Deltona-Daytona Beach-Ormond Beach, FL.......	1,586.4	659,605	86	415.8	73.4	11.2	0.8	2.7	13.9	4.6	13.0	7.8	11.3	10.3	12.2
19740	Denver-Aurora-Lakewood, CO..........	8,344.9	2,932,415	19	351.4	66.1	6.5	1.1	5.7	23.2	6.0	16.5	8.0	16.9	14.7	13.0
19780	Des Moines-West Des Moines, IA..........	2,882.0	655,409	87	227.4	82.1	6.6	0.6	5.2	7.5	7.1	18.2	8.5	14.8	13.8	12.5
19820	Detroit-Warren-Dearborn, MI..	3,889.8	4,326,442	14	1,112.3	68.1	23.2	0.9	5.5	4.6	5.9	16.2	8.3	13.5	11.9	13.7
19820	Detroit-Dearborn-Livonia, MI Div 19804	612.0	1,753,893	X	2,865.8	51.5	39.6	1.1	4.3	6.1	6.5	17.1	8.7	14.2	11.7	13.0
19820	Warren-Troy-Farmington Hills, MI Div 47664	3,277.8	2,572,549	X	784.8	79.5	12.0	0.9	6.3	3.5	5.4	15.6	8.1	12.9	12.1	14.2
20020	Dothan, AL....................	1,716.1	148,245	283	86.4	71.3	24.6	1.1	1.3	3.5	5.9	16.7	7.5	12.5	12.1	13.0
20100	Dover, DE	585.8	178,550	237	304.8	63.7	27.7	1.3	3.5	7.4	6.3	16.6	9.9	13.6	11.6	12.1
20220	Dubuque, IA...................	608.3	96,854	363	159.2	92.1	4.3	0.5	2.2	2.5	6.3	16.5	10.1	12.7	11.1	11.8
20260	Duluth, MN-WI.................	8,413.4	278,799	172	33.1	92.9	2.4	3.8	1.6	1.7	5.1	14.3	11.8	11.8	11.6	11.7
20500	Durham-Chapel Hill, NC.........	1,758.0	575,412	96	327.3	56.4	27.2	0.9	6.1	11.6	5.7	14.7	11.2	15.2	12.9	12.7
20700	East Stroudsburg, PA............	608.3	169,507	250	278.7	66.8	14.8	0.8	3.2	16.6	4.5	15.1	10.7	11.3	10.7	14.5
20740	Eau Claire, WI	1,646.3	168,669	252	102.5	92.5	2.0	0.9	3.8	2.3	5.7	15.4	12.6	13.2	11.9	11.7
20940	El Centro, CA..................	4,176.6	181,827	231	43.5	10.8	2.6	0.9	1.6	84.6	8.2	20.3	10.1	14.8	12.2	11.1
21060	Elizabethtown-Fort Knox, KY .	1,190.4	153,378	267	128.8	82.4	11.4	1.1	3.1	5.3	6.3	17.7	8.9	13.4	13.0	13.1
21140	Elkhart-Goshen, IN.............	463.2	205,560	217	443.4	76.6	7.0	0.7	1.6	16.3	7.5	20.0	8.9	12.8	12.1	12.2
21300	Elmira, NY	407.4	84,254	371	206.8	88.9	8.0	0.7	2.1	3.2	5.6	15.8	8.2	12.4	11.7	12.7
21340	El Paso, TX	5,583.7	845,553	68	151.4	12.4	3.4	0.5	1.7	82.9	7.5	19.6	11.2	15.1	12.5	11.4
21420	Enid, OK.....................	1,058.5	60,913	382	57.5	77.5	4.4	4.3	4.7	12.9	7.4	18.5	8.6	14.1	12.2	10.4
21500	Erie, PA.....................	799.1	272,061	178	340.5	86.2	8.8	0.5	2.3	4.4	5.6	15.7	9.7	13.1	11.3	12.4
21660	Eugene, OR...................	4,556.6	379,611	141	83.3	85.2	2.0	2.8	5.1	9.1	4.9	13.5	12.6	13.1	12.1	11.2

1. CBSA = Core Based Statistical Area. DIV = Metropolitan Division. See Appendix A for explanation. See Appendix B for list of metropolitan areas or temporarily covered by water. 2. Dry land or land partially or temporarily covered by water. 3. May be of any race.

Table C. Metropolitan Areas — **Population and Households**

Area name	Population, 2018 (cont.) Age (percent) (cont.) 55 to 64 years	65 to 74 years	75 years and over	Percent female	Population change and components of change, 2000-2018 Total persons 2000	2010	Percent change 2000-2010	2010-2018	Components of change, 2010-2018 Births	Deaths	Net migration	Households, 2017 Number	Persons per house-hold	Percent Family house-holds	Female family house-holder[1]	One person
	16	17	18	19	20	21	22	23	24	25	26	27	28	29	30	31
Cedar Rapids, IA	13.1	9.3	7.1	50.5	237,230	257,943	8.7	5.6	27,018	17,537	5,072	107,802	2.45	64.1	9.3	29.1
Chambersburg-Waynesboro, PA	13.6	10.8	8.8	50.9	129,313	149,619	15.7	3.5	15,367	12,228	2,248	60,979	2.49	66.0	11.0	28.5
Champaign-Urbana, IL	11.1	7.8	5.8	50.2	210,275	231,887	10.3	3.3	22,302	13,502	-1,168	95,429	2.36	54.1	9.0	34.8
Charleston, WV	15.0	12.2	8.4	51.6	235,938	227,060	-3.8	-7.1	20,127	23,858	-12,194	87,463	2.42	64.6	12.8	29.9
Charleston-North Charleston, SC	12.8	9.6	5.6	51.2	549,033	664,639	21.1	18.5	76,855	45,051	89,826	290,586	2.61	63.5	12.8	30.1
Charlotte-Concord-Gastonia, NC-SC	12.1	8.3	5.3	51.5	1,717,372	2,216,997	29.1	15.9	248,073	147,528	250,067	944,261	2.64	66.9	12.4	27.1
Charlottesville, VA	13.1	10.6	7.3	51.7	189,644	218,701	15.3	7.6	19,928	14,596	11,284	88,632	2.47	60.0	8.8	29.0
Chattanooga, TN-GA	13.6	10.4	7.5	51.5	476,531	528,150	10.8	6.2	51,809	45,093	25,948	220,186	2.45	62.2	10.5	33.1
Cheyenne, WY	13.0	9.6	6.4	49.3	81,607	91,885	12.6	7.7	10,547	6,479	3,019	39,054	2.47	65.4	10.0	28.2
Chicago-Naperville-Elgin, IL-IN-WI	12.8	8.5	6.1	51.0	9,098,316	9,461,539	4.0	0.4	978,809	576,086	-365,909	3,488,312	2.69	64.8	12.8	29.0
Chicago-Naperville-Arlington Heights, IL Div 16974 ...	12.6	8.4	6.1	51.2	7,135,324	7,263,064	1.8	0.4	764,701	442,211	-296,782	2,690,967	2.68	63.2	12.9	30.1
Elgin, IL Div 20994	12.3	8.1	5.4	50.2	493,088	620,538	25.8	2.9	65,706	31,227	-16,629	219,111	2.87	71.4	11.7	23.4
Gary, IN Div 23844	14.0	9.7	6.9	51.2	675,971	708,117	4.8	-1.0	67,580	54,968	-19,181	266,968	2.59	66.7	14.6	28.5
Lake County-Kenosha County, IL-WI Div 29404	13.7	8.4	5.8	50.1	793,933	869,820	9.6	0.0	80,822	47,680	-33,317	311,266	2.73	71.8	11.2	23.1
Chico, CA	12.7	11.0	7.6	50.6	203,171	220,002	8.3	5.1	20,190	18,934	10,103	88,797	2.50	59.0	12.8	30.8
Cincinnati, OH-KY-IN	13.4	9.0	6.2	50.9	1,994,830	2,114,659	6.0	3.6	222,609	156,748	10,873	852,639	2.50	64.2	12.1	29.0
Clarksville, TN-KY	9.7	6.4	4.3	49.3	219,630	260,630	18.7	12.1	41,401	15,992	5,790	105,056	2.62	70.5	13.0	23.5
Cleveland, TN	13.2	10.2	7.4	51.3	104,015	115,754	11.3	6.8	11,098	10,027	6,822	47,923	2.51	69.4	12.4	25.0
Cleveland-Elyria, OH	14.5	10.4	8.0	51.7	2,148,143	2,077,278	-3.3	-1.0	190,463	175,542	-34,535	862,586	2.34	59.7	13.5	33.9
Coeur d'Alene, ID	13.7	11.5	7.5	50.6	108,685	138,466	27.4	16.6	14,532	10,710	19,111	60,383	2.58	69.0	8.7	26.5
College Station-Bryan, TX...	9.2	6.2	4.4	49.6	184,885	228,668	23.7	14.8	25,847	11,190	19,042	91,999	2.63	59.5	14.2	28.5
Colorado Springs, CO	12.1	8.2	4.9	49.5	537,484	645,609	20.1	14.5	78,692	35,546	50,027	268,122	2.64	68.8	10.0	24.2
Columbia, MO	10.8	7.4	4.8	51.5	135,454	162,645	20.1	10.7	17,323	8,572	8,607	70,355	2.41	55.4	10.9	34.3
Columbia, SC	12.6	9.1	5.7	51.5	647,158	767,476	18.6	8.5	77,579	54,261	42,100	309,760	2.55	64.0	15.6	30.4
Columbus, GA-AL	12.2	8.4	5.7	50.8	281,768	295,523	4.9	3.4	37,080	23,106	-4,652	112,937	2.60	62.3	16.7	33.0
Columbus, IN	12.4	9.4	6.9	49.7	71,435	76,786	7.5	7.8	8,710	6,016	3,303	31,498	2.57	68.8	10.3	25.7
Columbus, OH	12.1	8.0	5.3	50.8	1,675,013	1,902,007	13.6	10.8	224,140	125,478	106,381	788,946	2.57	64.2	12.7	28.0
Corpus Christi, TX	12.3	9.0	6.3	50.4	403,280	428,183	6.2	5.8	49,834	31,285	6,232	160,796	2.73	69.1	16.9	25.5
Corvallis, OR	11.6	10.0	6.3	49.8	78,153	85,582	9.5	7.6	6,093	4,644	5,051	35,445	2.39	58.3	8.2	25.2
Crestview-Fort Walton Beach-Destin, FL...............	14.0	10.3	6.9	49.4	211,099	235,868	11.7	18.1	28,336	18,676	32,718	108,474	2.43	65.1	10.5	28.7
Cumberland, MD-WV	13.4	11.5	9.2	48.5	102,008	103,245	1.2	-5.2	7,817	10,211	-2,899	37,611	2.39	60.4	12.6	35.2
Dallas-Fort Worth-Arlington, TX..	11.4	7.0	4.3	50.8	5,204,126	6,426,222	23.5	17.3	815,184	345,465	641,751	2,573,711	2.84	69.7	13.0	24.8
Dallas-Plano-Irving, TX Div 19124	11.1	6.8	4.2	50.7	3,445,899	4,228,916	22.7	18.4	542,851	215,294	448,603	1,720,901	2.82	69.0	12.9	25.4
Fort Worth-Arlington, TX Div 23104	11.8	7.4	4.7	50.9	1,758,227	2,197,306	25.0	15.3	272,333	130,171	193,148	852,810	2.88	71.0	13.2	23.6
Dalton, GA...........................	11.8	8.4	5.9	50.4	120,031	142,221	18.5	1.2	15,622	9,617	-4,197	48,645	2.93	74.2	12.7	21.6
Danville, IL...........................	14.0	10.8	8.6	50.2	83,919	81,625	-2.7	-5.9	8,537	7,908	-5,455	30,241	2.48	61.6	15.2	31.4
Daphne-Fairhope-Foley, AL....	14.4	12.3	8.2	51.5	140,415	182,264	29.8	19.6	18,267	16,586	33,655	79,120	2.65	66.2	9.8	30.0
Davenport-Moline-Rock Island, IA-IL..................	13.7	10.3	7.8	50.7	376,019	379,688	1.0	0.5	39,019	30,567	-6,596	151,284	2.46	62.6	11.0	32.3
Dayton, OH...........................	13.6	10.1	7.7	51.5	805,816	799,268	-0.8	0.9	79,324	68,774	-2,878	329,442	2.35	61.9	13.0	31.9
Decatur, AL...........................	13.9	10.4	7.4	50.9	145,867	153,825	5.5	-1.2	14,721	13,774	-2,644	56,691	2.64	68.8	13.5	26.8
Decatur, IL...........................	14.2	11.0	9.0	52.1	114,706	110,775	-3.4	-5.5	11,087	9,953	-7,220	42,977	2.37	60.2	12.2	36.1
Deltona-Daytona Beach-Ormond Beach, FL.......	15.4	14.4	11.1	51.3	493,175	590,299	19.7	11.7	46,351	64,988	87,461	260,002	2.45	62.6	11.4	30.3
Denver-Aurora-Lakewood, CO......................	12.0	8.1	4.9	50.0	2,179,240	2,543,602	16.7	15.3	287,545	139,237	237,154	1,105,758	2.58	62.9	10.0	27.5
Des Moines-West Des Moines, IA...............	11.7	7.9	5.4	50.7	481,394	569,632	18.3	15.1	72,920	36,469	49,051	250,612	2.53	64.0	9.5	27.2
Detroit-Warren-Dearborn, MI..	14.1	9.6	6.8	51.3	4,452,557	4,296,290	-3.5	0.7	413,334	335,651	-47,656	1,707,501	2.50	64.1	13.7	30.2
Detroit-Dearborn-Livonia, MI Div 19804	13.3	9.0	6.4	51.8	2,061,162	1,820,539	-11.7	-3.7	191,941	149,228	-111,147	683,986	2.53	60.8	18.1	33.7
Warren-Troy-Farmington Hills, MI Div 47664	14.6	10.0	7.1	50.9	2,391,395	2,475,751	3.5	3.9	221,393	186,423	63,491	1,023,515	2.48	66.3	10.8	27.9
Dothan, AL...........................	13.5	11.0	7.8	51.8	130,861	145,641	11.3	1.8	14,589	13,546	1,668	55,442	2.64	67.4	14.0	28.5
Dover, DE	12.8	10.0	7.1	51.8	126,697	162,349	28.1	10.0	18,200	12,606	10,595	63,807	2.69	69.8	15.4	24.7
Dubuque, IA..........................	13.6	9.7	8.3	50.6	89,143	93,643	5.0	3.4	9,861	7,351	770	37,785	2.46	64.2	8.0	29.1
Duluth, MN-WI.......................	15.0	11.0	8.0	49.6	275,486	279,776	1.6	-0.3	23,293	23,568	-450	117,874	2.26	57.3	8.3	34.5
Durham-Chapel Hill, NC.........	12.5	9.3	5.9	52.2	426,493	506,660	18.8	13.6	53,994	31,158	45,535	224,437	2.42	60.9	13.2	30.5
East Stroudsburg, PA.............	16.0	10.5	6.7	50.5	138,687	169,832	22.5	-0.2	11,567	11,649	-254	57,668	2.87	72.1	12.0	22.4
Eau Claire, WI	13.0	9.8	6.8	49.7	148,337	161,385	8.8	4.5	15,695	11,307	2,989	67,079	2.39	62.5	9.0	29.3
El Centro, CA........................	10.4	7.2	5.8	48.7	142,361	174,524	22.6	4.2	25,092	8,202	-9,701	44,478	3.89	77.7	19.0	18.2
Elizabethtown-Fort Knox, KY .	13.3	8.5	5.8	50.1	133,896	148,340	10.8	3.4	16,253	10,606	-811	57,979	2.53	70.9	10.0	24.6
Elkhart-Goshen, IN................	11.8	8.4	6.3	50.6	182,791	197,559	8.1	4.0	25,296	13,544	-3,676	73,363	2.75	75.4	14.5	20.6
Elmira, NY	14.7	10.6	8.3	50.3	91,070	88,849	-2.4	-5.2	8,067	7,715	-4,950	32,247	2.50	65.4	12.4	30.2
El Paso, TX	10.4	7.0	5.3	50.7	682,966	804,129	17.7	5.2	110,653	41,935	-27,599	270,076	3.07	74.3	20.3	22.4
Enid, OK	12.5	8.8	7.6	50.2	57,813	60,580	4.8	0.5	7,857	5,681	-1,827	22,784	2.63	63.1	9.8	33.0
Erie, PA	14.2	11.0	7.7	50.6	280,843	280,584	-0.1	-3.0	25,889	23,332	-11,067	108,458	2.41	61.7	11.3	31.2
Eugene, OR..........................	13.3	11.7	7.6	50.8	322,959	351,704	8.9	7.9	29,371	28,191	26,875	151,675	2.42	58.0	9.0	30.5

1. No spouse present

Table C. Metropolitan Areas — Population, Vital Statistics, Health, and Crime

Area name	Persons in group quarters, 2018	Daytime population, 2017		Births, 2018		Deaths, 2018		Persons under 65 with no health insurance 2017		Medicare, 2018			Serious crimes known to police[2], 2016 Total	
		Number	Employ-ment/residence ratio	Total	Rate[1]	Number	Rate[1]	Number	Percent	Total Ben-eficiaries	Enrolled in Original Medicare	Enrolled in Medicare Advantage	Number	Rate[3]
	32	33	34	35	36	37	38	39	40	41	42	43	44	45
Cedar Rapids, IA...................	6,753	273,919	1.03	3,285	12.1	2,206	8.1	9,607	4.3	49,943	36,026	13,917	D	D
Chambersburg-Waynesboro, PA....	2,613	142,758	0.84	1,833	11.8	1,621	10.5	9,643	7.8	34,974	26,225	8,749	2,502	1,625
Champaign-Urbana, IL..........	16,880	246,322	1.05	2,650	11.1	1,737	7.2	11,517	6.0	35,159	20,402	14,757	7,200	3,010
Charleston, WV	3,547	233,327	1.21	2,155	10.2	2,919	13.8	11,999	7.1	54,096	33,979	20,117	10,397	4,768
Charleston-North Charleston, SC ...	16,491	783,434	1.02	9,413	12.0	6,355	8.1	81,376	12.6	132,746	102,074	30,672	24,887	3,264
Charlotte-Concord-Gastonia, NC-SC...	37,106	2,551,283	1.02	30,966	12.1	19,895	7.7	261,334	12.1	397,071	255,698	141,373	NA	NA
Charlottesville, VA	12,813	243,290	1.10	2,423	10.3	1,883	8.0	20,325	11.1	44,530	39,273	5,257	3,826	1,661
Chattanooga, TN-GA............	13,136	563,495	1.03	6,233	11.1	5,900	10.5	53,403	11.9	114,269	71,343	42,926	20,908	3,792
Cheyenne, WY	1,962	D	D	1,270	12.8	831	8.4	9,326	11.4	18,489	17,816	673	3,184	3,273
Chicago-Naperville-Elgin, IL-IN-WI....	161,113	9,579,018	1.01	111,625	11.8	75,213	7.9	701,620	8.7	1,500,335	1,123,527	376,808	240,415	2,525
Chicago-Naperville-Arlington Heights, IL Div 16974...	114,662	7,439,332	1.03	87,098	11.9	57,860	7.9	549,339	8.9	1,138,857	845,762	293,095	196,058	2,679
Elgin, IL Div 20994	12,456	597,108	0.86	7,577	11.9	4,169	6.5	47,362	8.7	91,213	69,393	21,820	10,168	1,601
Gary, IN Div 23844	10,939	668,497	0.89	7,632	10.9	7,094	10.1	53,217	9.2	133,652	97,269	36,383	19,826	2,830
Lake County-Kenosha County, IL-WI Div 29404	23,056	D	D	9,318	10.7	6,090	7.0	51,702	7.0	136,613	111,103	25,510	14,363	1,653
Chico, CA.........................	5,457	227,987	0.99	2,480	10.7	2,395	10.4	13,164	7.2	49,786	47,629	2,157	8,097	3,599
Cincinnati, OH-KY-IN.............	49,957	2,186,986	1.01	26,444	12.1	20,175	9.2	113,844	6.2	386,036	225,619	160,417	62,168	2,874
Clarksville, TN-KY	10,017	276,379	0.93	4,982	17.0	2,114	7.2	20,001	8.2	39,822	30,194	9,628	7,530	2,641
Cleveland, TN...................	3,006	122,733	0.98	1,376	11.1	1,308	10.6	13,012	13.2	26,696	15,907	10,789	4,726	3,878
Cleveland-Elyria, OH...........	43,460	2,108,664	1.05	22,311	10.8	21,568	10.5	107,946	6.5	425,505	243,018	182,487	58,150	2,829
Coeur d'Alene, ID	1,487	149,871	0.89	1,793	11.1	1,428	8.8	12,970	10.1	36,671	25,565	11,106	3,924	2,553
College Station-Bryan, TX......	14,624	262,546	1.03	3,163	12.1	1,475	5.6	37,451	17.2	30,413	22,769	7,644	6,839	2,708
Colorado Springs, CO	20,436	713,547	0.97	9,831	13.3	4,928	6.7	46,808	7.6	110,608	74,493	36,115	23,012	3,253
Columbia, MO	9,034	181,401	1.03	2,045	11.4	1,127	6.3	14,994	10.1	26,216	18,231	7,985	4,904	2,768
Columbia, SC	34,777	836,883	1.03	9,230	11.1	7,140	8.6	78,573	11.7	144,030	109,608	34,422	33,741	4,115
Columbus, GA-AL	9,931	321,201	1.12	4,036	13.2	3,010	9.9	32,242	12.8	54,542	35,396	19,146	13,723	4,329
Columbus, IN.....................	1,148	91,137	1.23	1,044	12.6	723	8.7	6,762	9.9	15,344	12,269	3,075	2,578	3,148
Columbus, OH....................	52,751	2,113,021	1.03	27,264	12.9	16,488	7.8	129,424	7.3	318,174	178,891	139,283	65,296	3,196
Corpus Christi, TX................	7,701	456,559	1.03	5,758	12.7	3,991	8.8	72,732	19.1	77,571	37,050	40,521	19,280	4,227
Corvallis, OR	5,325	94,796	1.08	750	8.1	587	6.4	4,890	6.8	16,050	8,454	7,596	2,369	2,676
Crestview-Fort Walton Beach-Destin, FL................	6,793	283,343	1.10	3,463	12.4	2,537	9.1	31,844	14.5	54,173	42,780	11,393	7,354	2,741
Cumberland, MD-WV	8,158	100,924	1.05	869	8.9	1,239	12.7	4,446	6.2	23,465	21,367	2,098	2,828	2,864
Dallas-Fort Worth-Arlington, TX....	84,401	7,438,918	1.01	101,510	13.5	47,403	6.3	1,199,409	18.4	937,906	584,839	353,067	204,752	2,836
Dallas-Plano-Irving, TX Div 19124	54,369	5,015,005	1.04	67,722	13.5	29,807	6.0	803,557	18.5	593,852	387,469	206,383	133,044	2,777
Fort Worth-Arlington, TX Div 23104	30,032	2,423,913	0.95	33,788	13.3	17,596	6.9	395,852	18.3	344,054	197,370	146,684	71,708	2,953
Dalton, GA.........................	1,335	148,321	1.06	1,816	12.6	1,236	8.6	27,300	22.3	24,425	19,437	4,988	5,896	4,097
Danville, IL........................	2,900	76,165	0.94	960	12.5	929	12.1	3,920	6.5	17,474	10,943	6,531	3,375	4,303
Daphne-Fairhope-Foley, AL....	2,190	197,799	0.84	2,254	10.3	2,228	10.2	19,119	11.3	50,999	28,779	22,220	NA	NA
Davenport-Moline-Rock Island, IA-IL..................	8,899	385,369	1.02	4,472	11.7	3,699	9.7	17,938	5.8	77,655	53,268	24,387	D	D
Dayton, OH........................	24,683	822,998	1.05	9,476	11.7	8,521	10.6	45,203	7.0	163,533	89,824	73,709	25,925	3,241
Decatur, AL.......................	2,227	146,093	0.91	1,768	11.6	1,744	11.5	14,975	12.1	33,658	23,930	9,728	4,200	2,762
Decatur, IL........................	4,009	112,760	1.15	1,268	12.1	1,174	11.2	4,550	5.5	23,982	20,644	3,338	3,409	3,213
Deltona-Daytona Beach-Ormond Beach, FL.......	15,111	614,213	0.87	5,780	8.8	8,485	12.9	69,372	14.6	179,318	92,721	86,597	20,529	3,252
Denver-Aurora-Lakewood, CO....	35,042	2,892,780	1.00	35,091	12.0	18,793	6.4	212,311	8.5	407,467	209,334	198,133	95,885	3,343
Des Moines-West Des Moines, IA....	12,015	656,394	1.03	9,026	13.8	4,811	7.3	28,622	5.2	99,770	75,617	24,153	D	D
Detroit-Warren-Dearborn, MI..	48,485	4,331,632	1.01	49,115	11.4	42,028	9.7	215,762	6.0	827,342	493,372	333,970	113,621	2,641
Detroit-Dearborn-Livonia, MI Div 19804	22,715	1,814,930	1.09	22,418	12.8	18,489	10.5	99,583	6.8	325,601	185,189	140,412	72,817	4,167
Warren-Troy-Farmington Hills, MI Div 47664	25,770	2,516,702	0.97	26,697	10.4	23,539	9.2	116,179	5.5	501,741	308,183	193,558	40,804	1,597
Dothan, AL........................	1,844	149,162	1.02	1,726	11.6	1,755	11.8	13,971	11.7	34,775	23,374	11,401	D	D
Dover, DE.........................	4,643	170,244	0.92	2,135	12.0	1,733	9.7	9,173	6.4	35,284	30,754	4,530	5,228	2,986
Dubuque, IA.......................	4,286	106,558	1.20	1,150	11.9	907	9.4	3,356	4.3	19,903	9,064	10,839	2,291	2,347
Duluth, MN-WI....................	12,499	281,521	1.02	2,732	9.8	2,821	10.1	11,812	5.4	62,499	28,847	33,652	9,557	3,423
Durham-Chapel Hill, NC.........	23,331	602,776	1.13	6,430	11.2	4,235	7.4	58,751	12.7	94,387	60,910	33,477	NA	NA
East Stroudsburg, PA...........	4,506	152,495	0.81	1,478	8.7	1,603	9.5	10,125	7.5	32,796	25,204	7,592	3,546	2,146
Eau Claire, WI	7,292	170,238	1.03	1,854	11.0	1,349	8.0	8,280	6.2	32,927	22,047	10,880	3,018	1,816
El Centro, CA.....................	9,052	180,432	0.96	2,851	15.7	1,033	5.7	11,751	7.9	30,471	25,338	5,133	6,073	3,373
Elizabethtown-Fort Knox, KY .	3,748	142,518	0.90	1,822	11.9	1,343	8.8	6,789	5.4	28,071	21,771	6,300	1,660	1,120
Elkhart-Goshen, IN................	3,669	236,315	1.33	3,054	14.9	1,665	8.1	24,444	14.2	33,882	23,499	10,383	NA	NA
Elmira, NY........................	3,945	86,513	1.03	905	10.7	942	11.2	2,761	4.2	19,738	11,763	7,975	2,064	2,397
El Paso, TX.......................	16,544	841,097	1.00	12,463	14.7	5,521	6.5	164,137	22.6	126,597	51,951	74,646	17,522	2,079
Enid, OK..........................	1,831	D	D	882	14.5	643	10.6	9,111	18.0	11,710	10,805	905	2,453	3,843
Erie, PA...........................	12,129	279,359	1.04	2,912	10.7	2,816	10.4	13,934	6.4	58,439	30,705	27,734	5,901	2,133
Eugene, OR.......................	8,786	374,455	1.00	3,577	9.4	3,589	9.5	24,351	8.2	85,230	41,827	43,403	13,400	3,648

1. Per 1,000 estimated resident population. 2. Data for serious crimes have not been adjusted for underreporting; this may affect comparability between geographic areas and over time. 3. Per 100,000 population estimated by the FBI.

Table C. Metropolitan Areas — Crime, Education, Money Income, and Poverty

Area name	Serious crimes known to police[2], 2016 (cont.) Rate — Violent	Property	School enrollment and attainment, 2016 — Enrollment[3] Total	Percent private	Attainment[4] High school graduate or less	Bachelor's degree or more	Local government expenditures,[5] 2014-2015 Total current expenditures (mil dol)	Current expenditures per student (dollars)	Per capita income[6] (dollars)	Mean household income (dollars)	Median household income	Percent of households with income less than $50,000	Percent of households with income of $200,000 or more	Percent below poverty level — All persons	Children under 18 years	Age 65 years and older
	46	47	48	49	50	51	52	53	54	55	56	57	58	59	60	61
Cedar Rapids, IA	220	D	64,492	17.4	34.2	31	504.2	11,417	31,979	78,464	63,697	38.6	4.2	8.7	12.0	5.6
Chambersburg-Waynesboro, PA.	144	1,482	35,294	12.0	52.7	23.7	255.0	11,169	29,365	72,639	60,459	39.3	2.7	9.8	12.6	8.6
Champaign-Urbana, IL	440	2,570	88,120	7.4	27.7	41.6	384.9	12,744	30,112	73,747	50,999	49.0	5.8	18.7	16.1	6.7
Charleston, WV	615	4,153	44,348	11.7	51.2	23.3	411.9	11,770	25,336	60,327	41,558	56.1	3.2	19.0	27.4	8.8
Charleston-North Charleston, SC	418	2,846	186,345	13.8	35.5	35.2	1,029.2	9,645	33,252	83,736	60,546	41.1	7.3	11.9	17.4	7.5
Charlotte-Concord-Gastonia, NC-SC	NA	NA	633,213	14.9	34.6	35.5	3,349.0	8,458	33,209	85,987	61,156	41.2	6.8	12.1	17.2	8.1
Charlottesville, VA	198	1,462	64,062	15.1	31.5	46	342.6	11,841	37,735	95,564	66,853	37.1	8.9	11.6	12.6	3.7
Chattanooga, TN-GA	541	3,251	121,937	19.8	42.5	27.2	676.8	9,114	29,855	72,046	50,250	49.8	5.1	12.5	17.1	8.1
Cheyenne, WY	252	3,021	23,835	11.1	33.8	27.9	233.0	15,797	32,574	79,176	61,961	38.2	2.3	9.9	9.5	9.7
Chicago-Naperville-Elgin, IL-IN-WI	443	2,082	2,421,077	19.7	35.6	37.7	22,342.9	14,332	36,010	95,010	68,403	37.1	8.8	11.8	16.1	9.3
Chicago-Naperville-Arlington Heights, IL Div 16974	513	2,166	1,832,118	21.4	34.7	39.2	17,142.5	14,836	36,292	95,108	68,006	37.6	8.9	12.1	16.4	10.0
Elgin, IL Div 20994	193	1,409	183,643	14.5	38.8	31.9	1,507.8	12,681	33,367	95,092	73,245	32.7	8.5	10.1	14.2	5.3
Gary, IN Div 23844	272	2,558	171,462	13.6	45.3	23.8	1,138.4	9,602	28,321	71,786	57,453	43.2	3.1	14.2	21.2	8.7
Lake County-Kenosha County, IL-WI Div 29404	175	1,478	233,854	15.0	33.3	41.2	2,554.2	15,382	41,770	114,026	78,791	31.4	13.5	8.1	10.9	6.2
Chico, CA	351	3,248	66,232	6.2	32.3	26.6	335.4	10,820	28,038	70,280	49,061	50.7	5.1	18.3	22.3	8.2
Cincinnati, OH-KY-IN	257	2,617	546,699	18.4	39.1	33.2	3,386.3	10,705	33,048	83,111	61,653	40.6	6.0	12.1	17.0	7.3
Clarksville, TN-KY	428	2,214	77,353	14.9	37.4	24.5	367.6	8,462	26,488	69,258	54,667	45.4	3.2	14.9	19.6	10.4
Cleveland, TN	512	3,366	29,835	19.6	48.4	20.5	150.7	8,145	24,626	62,314	46,822	52.4	2.7	17.9	22.3	13.0
Cleveland-Elyria, OH	446	2,384	486,937	23.2	38.2	30.8	3,676.2	12,783	31,900	74,406	52,489	47.7	4.9	14.8	21.7	8.7
Coeur d'Alene, ID	232	2,321	33,926	17.9	31.9	26	144.1	6,599	27,843	75,775	57,219	41.5	3.5	10.1	17.6	5.0
College Station-Bryan, TX	331	2,376	104,460	5.6	37.6	36.1	319.3	8,916	24,627	64,918	45,515	53.8	3.4	24.6	21.9	9.1
Colorado Springs, CO	405	2,848	191,499	11.4	25.9	39.2	1,039.3	8,511	31,892	83,525	65,593	37.1	5.6	10.7	14.0	6.6
Columbia, MO	380	2,388	60,710	13.0	28.0	45.7	233.1	9,977	29,078	71,990	51,324	48.0	5.2	15.9	12.3	6.2
Columbia, SC	590	3,525	209,185	11.5	38.3	31.9	1,454.4	11,510	28,649	72,572	54,480	46.0	4.5	15.1	19.2	9.7
Columbus, GA-AL	518	3,811	80,911	9.5	42.1	24.3	463.1	9,149	25,224	64,177	43,051	55.5	3.3	22.1	35.3	12.4
Columbus, IN	82	3,067	17,506	10.8	39.9	35.1	119.0	9,613	31,306	78,611	61,533	39.6	4.3	12.4	22.6	5.0
Columbus, OH	285	2,911	525,675	17.3	36.6	35.9	3,708.1	11,311	32,887	83,780	63,764	39.2	6.0	13.1	18.3	7.9
Corpus Christi, TX	659	3,568	113,117	4.4	48.2	19.7	719.5	8,950	26,743	72,496	52,193	48.0	4.7	16.6	23.1	11.0
Corvallis, OR	128	2,549	35,463	6.8	15.9	53.8	89.0	10,043	33,185	83,490	60,260	43.5	6.6	17.5	9.7	4.2
Crestview-Fort Walton Beach-Destin, FL	382	2,359	59,108	11.6	33.3	30.5	353.3	9,094	32,432	78,536	59,619	42.0	5.5	13.2	21.2	6.4
Cumberland, MD-WV	318	2,546	23,461	5.8	53.6	16.6	174.1	13,331	22,911	55,284	42,113	55.8	1.7	14.3	19.1	12.1
Dallas-Fort Worth-Arlington, TX	360	2,476	2,003,434	12.3	37.0	34.6	11,579.1	8,581	33,404	92,495	67,382	36.4	8.1	11.3	16.2	8.7
Dallas-Plano-Irving, TX Div 19124	357	2,420	1,344,984	12.0	35.7	37.1	7,940.7	8,611	34,626	95,459	68,734	35.9	8.7	11.3	15.9	9.1
Fort Worth-Arlington, TX Div 23104	366	2,587	658,450	13.0	39.6	29.7	3,638.3	8,515	30,992	86,514	65,439	37.3	6.8	11.2	16.8	7.8
Dalton, GA	689	3,408	36,335	3.8	66.9	13.5	257.6	8,890	21,863	60,469	41,441	57.7	3.5	18.9	30.8	10.6
Danville, IL	808	3,494	17,618	8.1	53.0	16.8	151.8	11,542	23,298	57,732	42,345	56.0	2.1	19.9	33.0	8.5
Daphne-Fairhope-Foley, AL	NA	NA	45,966	19.7	35.9	33.6	269.9	8,822	29,847	74,963	55,342	43.5	4.0	9.4	10.9	6.0
Davenport-Moline-Rock Island, IA-IL	393	D	92,566	15.4	39.7	26.9	709.5	11,379	29,996	72,402	54,173	44.7	3.8	11.6	16.8	6.3
Dayton, OH	311	2,929	206,399	23.0	38.1	29.8	1,317.6	11,613	29,503	70,571	52,745	47.4	3.7	13.8	19.0	6.9
Decatur, AL	232	2,530	36,215	12.3	49.8	18.5	229.4	9,395	23,976	61,490	47,042	52.1	2.6	15.6	21.7	12.4
Decatur, IL	411	2,802	24,028	13.1	40.9	23.2	206.7	12,453	28,827	69,125	51,970	47.8	4.2	12.8	18.2	6.0
Deltona-Daytona Beach-Ormond Beach, FL	391	2,861	129,974	16.1	43.1	23.1	637.5	8,549	27,007	63,640	47,351	52.2	2.9	15.0	26.3	7.7
Denver-Aurora-Lakewood, CO	389	2,954	699,865	13.2	29.1	43.9	4,299.7	9,241	39,832	101,249	76,643	31.4	9.5	8.6	10.5	7.2
Des Moines-West Des Moines, IA	372	D	166,276	18.2	32.6	36.6	1,177.9	10,867	35,877	90,259	68,649	35.3	6.5	8.3	10.8	5.5
Detroit-Warren-Dearborn, MI	556	2,085	1,035,246	12.5	36.6	31.1	7,413.6	11,202	32,924	81,606	58,411	43.3	6.2	14.6	21.6	9.7
Detroit-Dearborn-Livonia, MI Div 19804	1,034	3,133	437,627	10.1	43.6	23.4	3,162.1	11,190	26,126	64,912	45,135	54.4	3.6	22.7	34.0	13.4
Warren-Troy-Farmington Hills, MI Div 47664	228	1,369	597,619	14.3	32.0	36.2	4,251.5	11,211	37,581	92,763	69,018	35.9	7.9	9.0	12.2	7.4
Dothan, AL	D	2,865	34,643	13.6	47.2	20.2	192.9	8,671	24,740	62,939	45,396	53.9	2.9	17.5	30.1	9.1
Dover, DE	474	2,512	48,634	11.9	43.8	23.3	333.0	12,738	28,214	73,873	57,608	43.4	3.5	13.8	21.3	8.4
Dubuque, IA	243	2,104	26,291	30.7	36.7	33	163.7	11,156	32,863	82,496	61,497	40.4	5.3	9.7	10.2	8.4
Duluth, MN-WI	230	3,193	69,504	11.0	33.5	28.3	426.8	11,336	29,916	68,868	54,162	46.3	3.0	13.6	12.8	7.2
Durham-Chapel Hill, NC	NA	NA	151,777	17.8	30.3	46.9	761.8	10,911	35,901	88,648	61,271	42.1	8.1	14.9	21.6	7.3
East Stroudsburg, PA	252	1,894	37,702	15.1	44.5	24.1	437.0	16,578	29,674	79,766	61,612	39.4	5.5	7.3	10.5	4.6
Eau Claire, WI	138	1,678	44,627	10.6	35.4	28.9	254.7	11,014	28,502	69,893	55,480	45.2	3.9	13.6	13.6	7.1
El Centro, CA	389	2,983	55,501	7.4	56.8	15.1	419.4	11,277	18,521	67,264	47,211	51.1	3.1	20.7	28.1	16.5
Elizabethtown-Fort Knox, KY	122	998	36,773	13.1	42.8	20.5	219.5	8,865	28,022	71,289	52,622	47.1	2.2	12.2	15.2	6.7
Elkhart-Goshen, IN	NA	NA	52,702	15.2	51.5	20.2	351.3	9,633	26,677	73,704	58,960	42.2	3.3	10.3	14.3	5.7
Elmira, NY	200	2,197	18,814	21.4	47.8	23.9	185.7	15,711	25,348	64,774	51,194	49.0	3.3	14.9	24.3	5.1
El Paso, TX	365	1,713	253,736	8.1	45.8	22.8	1,619.8	9,146	21,198	61,583	44,416	56.0	3.0	21.1	30.1	20.2
Enid, OK	365	3,478	15,595	13.6	47.5	23	91.6	7,922	25,144	63,430	47,915	52.1	2.0	12.1	11.5	6.7
Erie, PA	215	1,918	66,998	24.1	47.7	27.1	506.1	12,796	27,295	67,811	50,614	49.4	3.3	16.0	24.9	10.3
Eugene, OR	321	3,327	89,341	10.1	30.0	31.1	472.9	10,444	28,432	68,593	50,654	49.4	3.7	16.8	17.9	10.7

1. Data for serious crimes have not been adjusted for underreporting; this may affect comparability between geographic areas and over time.   2. Per 100,000 population estimated by the FBI.   3. All persons 3 years old and over enrolled in nursery school through college.   4. Persons 25 years old and over.   5. Elementary and secondary education expenditures.   6. Based on population estimated by the American Community Survey, 2015.

Table C. Metropolitan Areas — Personal Income and Earnings

Area name	Personal income, 2017										Earnings, 2017		
	Total (mil dol)	Percent change, 2016-2017	Per capita[1] Dollars	Per capita[1] Rank	Wages and Salaries (mil dol)	Supplements to wages and salaries, employer contributions (mil dol) Pension and insurance	Supplements to wages and salaries, employer contributions (mil dol) Government social insurance	Proprietors' income	Dividends, interest, and rent (mil dol)	Personal transfer receipts (mil dol)	Total (mil dol)	Contributions for government social insurance (mil dol) From employee and self-employed	Contributions for government social insurance (mil dol) From employer
	62	63	64	65	66	67	68	69	70	71	72	73	74
Cedar Rapids, IA..................	13,446	2.9	49,746	88	7,565	1,241	580	744	2,506	2,074	10,131	633	580
Chambersburg-Waynesboro, PA.....	6,766	3.7	43,866	188	2,615	529	221	542	1,087	1,413	3,907	243	221
Champaign-Urbana, IL...........	10,609	0.4	44,365	173	5,318	1,381	324	793	2,210	1,477	7,815	368	324
Charleston, WV	9,317	1.8	43,457	197	5,383	896	428	728	1,555	2,703	7,435	495	428
Charleston-North Charleston, SC	37,085	5.2	47,800	113	18,418	2,992	1,393	3,612	7,733	5,973	26,415	1,594	1,393
Charlotte-Concord-Gastonia, NC-SC	125,654	5.8	49,758	87	72,100	9,318	5,092	12,571	19,871	18,528	99,081	6,060	5,092
Charlottesville, VA	13,739	5.4	58,767	28	6,315	1,197	444	1,063	4,260	1,719	9,018	537	444
Chattanooga, TN-GA.............	24,782	4.4	44,528	172	12,171	2,047	853	3,095	3,851	5,045	18,166	1,089	853
Cheyenne, WY	4,972	4.2	50,563	81	2,494	530	255	366	1,106	848	3,646	210	255
Chicago-Naperville-Elgin, IL-IN-WI....	555,922	3.4	58,315	31	303,830	47,017	20,414	42,109	114,504	74,956	413,371	22,603	20,414
Chicago-Naperville-Arlington Heights, IL Div 16974...	433,285	3.3	59,192	X	247,111	37,364	16,554	34,726	90,299	58,624	335,755	18,250	16,554
Elgin, IL Div 20994	30,252	3.9	47,313	X	13,146	2,547	903	1,774	4,842	3,898	18,370	980	903
Gary, IN Div 23844	31,195	3.9	44,462	X	13,184	2,223	973	1,893	4,499	6,573	18,273	1,149	973
Lake County-Kenosha County, IL-WI Div 29404	61,190	4.1	70,169	X	30,389	4,883	1,985	3,715	14,865	5,860	40,972	2,224	1,985
Chico, CA	9,926	4.5	43,287	202	3,716	835	267	968	2,125	2,508	5,787	347	267
Cincinnati, OH-KY-IN............	112,302	4.0	51,536	74	60,376	9,139	4,426	8,568	20,928	18,017	82,509	4,828	4,426
Clarksville, TN-KY	11,305	4.3	39,661	290	5,385	1,239	465	842	1,941	2,360	7,930	414	465
Cleveland, TN.....................	4,650	4.0	38,016	326	1,902	345	137	439	691	1,141	2,823	181	137
Cleveland-Elyria, OH...........	106,555	3.9	51,755	73	57,887	9,243	4,249	7,941	20,123	19,908	79,320	4,599	4,249
Coeur d'Alene, ID.................	6,656	5.7	42,224	229	2,543	430	229	491	1,502	1,342	3,692	252	229
College Station-Bryan, TX......	9,729	4.7	37,704	332	4,736	979	305	873	1,989	1,514	6,892	336	305
Colorado Springs, CO	33,681	5.2	46,529	136	16,823	2,722	1,315	1,993	6,954	5,712	22,853	1,241	1,315
Columbia, MO	7,986	3.2	44,797	167	4,514	926	302	462	1,570	1,203	6,204	339	302
Columbia, SC	35,615	3.8	43,168	206	19,063	3,386	1,437	2,600	5,794	6,919	26,485	1,610	1,437
Columbus, GA-AL	12,227	3.3	40,247	277	6,626	1,373	496	392	2,948	2,901	8,887	503	496
Columbus, IN......................	3,922	3.7	47,804	112	2,839	470	198	257	638	665	3,764	222	198
Columbus, OH......................	103,195	4.6	49,644	90	59,317	9,970	4,138	7,673	17,090	15,594	81,097	4,349	4,138
Corpus Christi, TX	19,152	2.9	42,184	231	9,535	1,661	699	1,437	3,121	4,345	13,331	741	699
Corvallis, OR	4,118	5.6	45,273	157	2,005	401	171	310	1,073	581	2,887	176	171
Crestview-Fort Walton Beach-Destin, FL........	13,462	5.0	49,611	92	6,332	1,168	493	910	3,946	2,440	8,903	528	493
Cumberland, MD-WV	3,835	2.6	38,803	309	1,625	339	136	168	653	1,243	2,268	154	136
Dallas-Fort Worth-Arlington, TX........	392,146	4.3	52,995	62	223,091	28,169	15,424	41,364	72,943	45,829	308,048	16,535	15,424
Dallas-Plano-Irving, TX Div 19124	275,002	4.8	55,996	X	166,923	20,075	11,383	32,376	51,871	29,148	230,756	12,265	11,383
Fort Worth-Arlington, TX Div 23104	117,144	3.2	47,073	X	56,168	8,094	4,041	8,988	21,072	16,681	77,292	4,270	4,041
Dalton, GA............................	5,073	3.7	35,118	370	3,035	484	220	567	905	1,117	4,307	256	220
Danville, IL............................	2,913	1.4	37,387	336	1,269	295	91	162	468	807	1,817	108	91
Daphne-Fairhope-Foley, AL....	9,373	5.0	44,079	182	2,817	444	206	672	1,856	1,938	4,140	300	206
Davenport-Moline-Rock Island, IA-IL.................	18,182	3.7	47,564	118	9,407	1,682	690	1,260	3,540	3,341	13,039	778	690
Dayton, OH...........................	36,723	4.2	45,708	151	19,601	3,560	1,490	2,172	6,741	7,594	26,823	1,559	1,490
Decatur, AL...........................	5,679	4.1	37,396	335	2,390	433	174	317	900	1,437	3,314	228	174
Decatur, IL............................	4,835	0.2	45,701	152	2,734	494	198	298	885	1,084	3,725	217	198
Deltona-Daytona Beach-Ormond Beach, FL.......	26,703	5.1	41,132	256	8,386	1,253	586	1,166	6,280	7,213	11,391	878	586
Denver-Aurora-Lakewood, CO.......	172,311	6.5	59,660	24	97,836	11,770	6,865	17,231	35,479	19,011	133,701	7,473	6,865
Des Moines-West Des Moines, IA...................	33,781	3.9	52,300	69	20,350	3,063	1,527	2,317	6,087	4,219	27,257	1,658	1,527
Detroit-Warren-Dearborn, MI..	219,372	3.6	50,863	78	120,026	17,249	8,786	16,786	37,144	41,488	162,847	10,088	8,786
Detroit-Dearborn-Livonia, MI Div 19804....................	73,133	2.7	41,704	X	46,289	6,962	3,364	4,190	11,578	19,688	60,806	3,798	3,364
Warren-Troy-Farmington Hills, MI Div 47664.......	146,239	4.0	57,138	X	73,736	10,287	5,422	12,596	25,566	21,799	102,042	6,291	5,422
Dothan, AL............................	5,839	3.8	39,478	293	2,439	436	176	371	1,018	1,517	3,422	235	176
Dover, DE.............................	7,127	4.7	40,304	274	3,197	720	247	405	1,176	1,810	4,569	272	247
Dubuque, IA..........................	4,463	2.7	45,990	145	2,649	448	208	257	976	791	3,562	224	208
Duluth, MN-WI.......................	12,125	3.4	43,492	195	5,999	1,115	478	531	2,139	3,028	8,122	526	478
Durham-Chapel Hill, NC........	29,663	4.8	52,277	70	19,953	2,940	1,411	2,292	6,799	4,228	26,597	1,589	1,411
East Stroudsburg, PA.............	6,841	4.3	40,706	269	2,549	565	210	495	936	1,487	3,819	236	210
Eau Claire, WI	7,494	4.6	44,746	169	3,880	755	296	520	1,408	1,380	5,450	338	296
El Centro, CA.......................	6,620	4.2	36,206	358	2,631	759	197	1,036	912	1,679	4,623	217	197
Elizabethtown-Fort Knox, KY .	6,138	4.1	40,805	266	2,734	611	226	437	1,012	1,407	4,008	235	226
Elkhart-Goshen, IN...............	9,051	6.0	44,143	178	7,330	1,235	542	875	1,303	1,565	9,982	573	542
Elmira, NY	3,643	4.5	42,577	221	1,682	379	139	173	530	1,001	2,374	142	139
El Paso, TX	29,209	3.0	34,575	374	13,999	2,949	1,068	2,012	4,812	6,787	20,028	1,068	1,068
Enid, OK...............................	2,625	-4.0	42,622	218	1,234	211	99	205	569	544	1,749	104	99
Erie, PA................................	11,500	1.1	41,887	236	5,377	1,112	442	745	1,968	2,924	7,676	473	442
Eugene, OR..........................	16,275	4.6	43,430	199	7,083	1,245	644	1,556	3,420	3,736	10,528	695	644

1. Based on the resident population estimated as of July 1 of the year shown.

Items 62—74

Table C. Metropolitan Areas — Earnings, Social Security, and Housing

Area name	Earnings, 2017 (cont.) — Percent by selected industries									Social Security beneficiaries, December 2017		Supplemental Security Income Recipients, December 2017	Housing units, 2018	
	Farm	Mining, quarrying, and extracting	Construction	Manufacturing	Information; professional, scientific, and technical serviecs	Retail trade	Finance, insurance, real estate, rental and leasing	Health care and social assistance	Government	Number	Rate[1]		Total	Percent change, 2010-2018
	75	76	77	78	79	80	81	82	83	84	85	86	87	88
Cedar Rapids, IA	0.2	0.2	7.5	21.7	9.1	5.5	9.2	D	11.2	52,705	195	4,449	118,215	5.3
Chambersburg-Waynesboro, PA	2.0	0.1	5.9	16.7	4.7	6.8	3.5	15.4	16.4	36,280	235	2,505	65,791	4.1
Champaign-Urbana, IL	0.4	D	5.2	6.6	D	6.1	5.3	D	37.4	34,350	144	3,496	107,185	6.0
Charleston, WV	0.0	D	5.4	D	11.8	5.8	D	D	19.0	59,700	278	9,044	108,128	-0.1
Charleston-North Charleston, SC	0.0	0.1	8.1	9.6	13.2	6.4	7.9	9.5	21.7	138,945	179	13,274	339,494	13.7
Charlotte-Concord-Gastonia, NC-SC	0.3	0.1	6.7	8.6	D	5.4	D	D	11.3	421,750	167	42,796	1,049,294	12.1
Charlottesville, VA	0.1	D	5.2	D	D	4.7	7.5	D	34.3	44,585	191	3,302	103,872	7.8
Chattanooga, TN-GA	0.3	0.1	D	13.8	D	5.9	D	D	16.0	122,660	220	13,399	246,062	5.0
Cheyenne, WY	0.8	1.8	6.3	D	8.0	6.2	6.4	8.2	39.8	18,580	189	1,485	43,894	8.5
Chicago-Naperville-Elgin, IL-IN-WI	0.0	0.0	4.7	10.0	D	4.7	11.5	D	12.0	1,498,945	157	202,823	3,858,431	1.6
Chicago-Naperville-Arlington Heights, IL Div 16974	0.0	0.0	4.3	7.8	17.5	4.3	12.8	9.9	11.6	1,125,335	154	169,074	2,989,001	1.3
Elgin, IL Div 20994	-0.1	0.1	8.3	16.3	8.0	5.3	5.5	D	19.1	91,185	143	6,228	230,720	3.4
Gary, IN Div 23844	0.1	D	9.0	19.9	4.7	6.7	4.3	15.1	10.4	145,375	207	15,521	302,903	3.0
Lake County-Kenosha County, IL-WI Div 29404	0.0	D	4.9	20.9	9.2	7.1	6.5	7.2	13.4	137,050	157	12,000	335,807	1.9
Chico, CA	4.3	0.0	6.8	5.0	5.8	8.9	6.0	20.3	21.9	52,370	228	11,063	100,033	4.4
Cincinnati, OH-KY-IN	0.0	D	D	13.2	9.9	5.4	D	12.0	11.1	395,545	182	47,924	937,069	2.9
Clarksville, TN-KY	0.4	D	4.9	9.7	3.8	5.9	3.4	8.3	47.5	45,090	158	6,250	120,570	12.3
Cleveland, TN	1.1	D	7.1	23.5	D	7.5	3.4	D	12.0	29,335	240	3,138	53,208	7.8
Cleveland-Elyria, OH	0.1	D	5.0	12.7	11.2	4.9	8.4	14.1	13.5	426,220	207	62,842	963,468	0.8
Coeur d'Alene, ID	0.1	0.8	9.6	8.0	7.0	10.5	7.0	12.7	19.9	38,230	243	2,632	72,499	14.8
College Station-Bryan, TX	0.2	2.7	8.3	4.3	8.5	6.3	5.5	9.8	35.0	30,480	118	4,516	110,833	16.6
Colorado Springs, CO	0.0	D	7.0	D	13.9	6.0	7.3	D	30.7	111,615	154	9,388	288,745	8.8
Columbia, MO	0.2	0.0	4.4	4.7	7.2	6.5	9.2	11.5	36.1	26,770	150	2,750	78,940	13.5
Columbia, SC	0.2	0.2	6.5	9.1	D	6.0	9.4	9.6	25.4	155,075	188	16,401	359,526	8.5
Columbus, GA-AL	0.2	D	3.5	D	D	4.9	D	10.3	35.5	60,615	200	10,417	134,763	5.1
Columbus, IN	0.3	D	3.8	46.6	4.9	4.4	4.0	7.4	9.1	16,575	202	1,257	34,531	4.3
Columbus, OH	0.1	0.1	5.6	7.7	11.5	5.4	10.0	11.2	18.0	316,240	152	45,824	869,366	5.9
Corpus Christi, TX	0.7	4.0	15.5	7.3	7.1	6.0	5.2	D	19.9	81,805	180	14,821	194,395	6.3
Corvallis, OR	1.2	0.1	3.7	10.1	10.4	4.8	4.9	16.4	30.4	15,725	173	1,025	38,451	6.1
Crestview-Fort Walton Beach-Destin, FL	0.1	D	6.0	3.1	12.0	7.6	5.8	7.8	36.2	57,415	212	4,312	151,330	10.0
Cumberland, MD-WV	-0.2	D	4.2	14.2	D	7.2	4.4	D	23.9	24,370	247	3,124	45,977	-0.8
Dallas-Fort Worth-Arlington, TX	0.0	D	7.5	8.5	14.7	5.7	11.8	D	10.7	943,940	128	130,212	2,853,212	12.9
Dallas-Plano-Irving, TX Div 19124	0.0	1.8	6.9	7.7	17.1	5.5	13.3	9.8	9.8	594,375	121	87,234	1,905,035	15.0
Fort Worth-Arlington, TX Div 23104	0.0	2.9	9.4	10.9	7.5	6.5	7.5	10.6	13.1	349,565	140	42,978	948,177	8.9
Dalton, GA	0.9	0.4	2.4	38.0	D	5.7	5.1	D	10.1	27,360	189	3,706	56,311	0.8
Danville, IL	1.5	D	4.1	21.4	1.9	6.4	4.4	10.0	23.8	18,695	240	2,771	36,129	-0.5
Daphne-Fairhope-Foley, AL	0.4	0.2	10.3	6.4	5.9	11.9	7.9	12.5	13.9	53,970	254	3,531	116,631	12.1
Davenport-Moline-Rock Island, IA-IL	0.3	D	7.1	14.3	D	6.2	5.4	D	15.8	81,065	212	7,487	170,422	2.0
Dayton, OH	0.0	D	4.7	12.1	D	5.4	5.7	15.9	22.2	165,010	205	20,232	370,006	0.7
Decatur, AL	1.1	D	8.2	30.0	4.7	6.5	4.2	D	14.8	37,755	249	4,696	67,748	2.0
Decatur, IL	0.3	D	7.2	30.1	4.5	5.3	4.5	13.1	11.1	25,215	238	3,297	50,393	-0.2
Deltona-Daytona Beach-Ormond Beach, FL	0.7	0.0	7.5	7.1	7.3	9.9	6.1	17.5	14.0	188,935	291	14,225	314,618	3.9
Denver-Aurora-Lakewood, CO	0.0	4.6	7.5	D	16.6	D	10.6	8.6	12.5	389,375	135	36,227	1,195,422	10.8
Des Moines-West Des Moines, IA	0.0	0.1	7.6	5.7	10.2	5.7	22.6	10.4	12.6	102,475	159	9,019	276,151	15.0
Detroit-Warren-Dearborn, MI	0.0	D	5.1	14.7	17.1	5.5	8.6	11.7	9.8	883,865	205	134,652	1,912,679	1.4
Detroit-Dearborn-Livonia, MI Div 19804	0.0	0.1	4.0	14.2	13.4	4.3	5.9	13.5	12.2	357,250	204	84,810	815,803	-0.7
Warren-Troy-Farmington Hills, MI Div 47664	0.0	D	5.8	15.0	19.3	6.1	10.1	10.7	8.4	526,615	206	49,842	1,096,876	3.0
Dothan, AL	1.3	D	4.7	8.3	5.5	9.7	4.6	D	19.3	38,215	258	5,805	69,817	4.4
Dover, DE	2.4	D	6.0	D	D	7.4	3.1	12.4	36.9	37,540	212	3,479	73,093	11.8
Dubuque, IA	0.7	D	5.6	20.2	7.6	6.5	11.2	14.6	8.3	21,110	218	1,611	41,504	6.6
Duluth, MN-WI	0.0	4.2	6.4	6.8	5.7	7.0	5.3	22.0	19.9	65,335	234	6,725	144,316	2.0
Durham-Chapel Hill, NC	0.3	0.0	3.2	13.5	16.3	3.5	7.3	13.3	19.7	94,720	167	9,810	249,685	12.1
East Stroudsburg, PA	0.1	0.2	5.1	13.5	3.1	8.0	3.1	12.3	24.3	35,910	214	3,096	81,663	1.6
Eau Claire, WI	0.6	D	7.7	13.4	5.5	7.8	5.4	19.2	14.9	35,235	210	3,061	73,014	5.3
El Centro, CA	16.9	0.9	2.5	1.7	2.3	7.3	2.4	5.9	36.7	32,605	178	10,455	57,895	3.3
Elizabethtown-Fort Knox, KY	0.2	D	4.0	14.8	D	6.2	4.4	6.3	39.8	31,000	206	4,436	66,008	7.9
Elkhart-Goshen, IN	0.3	0.0	3.5	53.1	2.9	3.8	2.7	6.9	5.0	35,975	175	3,057	79,492	2.2
Elmira, NY	0.0	0.5	5.4	16.6	4.0	7.1	5.5	16.9	23.7	21,575	252	3,102	38,916	1.4
El Paso, TX	0.1	0.0	D	D	D	7.5	D	10.5	36.8	131,115	155	29,880	301,219	10.8
Enid, OK	0.3	6.2	8.4	9.5	D	7.0	5.5	11.5	19.1	12,490	203	1,294	26,798	-0.1
Erie, PA	0.1	0.0	4.8	18.3	4.8	6.8	8.3	18.3	16.2	63,295	231	10,624	121,617	2.1
Eugene, OR	0.5	0.2	5.9	9.3	7.9	7.9	7.5	16.1	18.6	86,650	231	9,634	163,472	4.7

1. Per 1,000 resident population estimated as of July 1 of the year shown.

Table C. Metropolitan Areas — Housing, Labor Force, and Employment

	Housing units, 2017								Civilian labor force, 2018				Civilian employment[5], 2017		
	Occupied units										Unemployment			Percent	
		Owner-occupied				Renter-occupied									
				Median owner cost as a percent of income											
Area name	Total	Percent	Median value[1]	With a mortgage	Without a mortgage[2]	Median rent[3]	Median rent as a percent of income	Internet access	Total	Percent change 2017-2018	Total	Rate[4]	Total	Management, business, science, and arts	Construction, production, and maintenance occupations
	89	90	91	92	93	94	95	96	97	98	99	100	101	102	103
Cedar Rapids, IA	107,802	76.5	156,400	19.5	10.8	728	25.6	88.6	143,364	0.7	3,986	2.8	144,032	37.2	23.2
Chambersburg-Waynesboro, PA	60,979	68.1	182,000	20.1	11.4	860	25.9	85.2	77,064	0.6	2,846	3.7	73,647	31.1	28.0
Champaign-Urbana, IL	95,429	56.3	161,300	18.4	11.7	812	33.3	89.5	120,433	0.3	5,321	4.4	116,299	43.4	18.2
Charleston, WV	87,463	71.1	107,500	17.7	10.6	665	26.5	84.1	92,828	-1.0	4,984	5.4	86,746	34.9	17.4
Charleston-North Charleston, SC	290,586	64.2	245,500	21.2	10.8	1,102	31.8	88.0	382,521	1.4	11,057	2.9	385,368	39.1	19.0
Charlotte-Concord-Gastonia, NC-SC	944,261	65.6	197,100	19.1	10.0	977	27.6	88.2	1,333,081	1.6	48,579	3.6	1,260,210	39.4	21.1
Charlottesville, VA	88,632	62.8	271,900	20.0	10.0	1,141	27.5	86.2	119,487	1.1	3,260	2.7	111,596	50.9	14.8
Chattanooga, TN-GA	220,186	65.2	160,000	19.0	10.0	795	28.7	81.4	270,586	1.6	9,584	3.5	259,379	36.8	23.3
Cheyenne, WY	39,054	71.7	217,500	22.5	10.0	950	28.5	89.3	47,682	-1.1	1,847	3.9	46,520	34.9	22.8
Chicago-Naperville-Elgin, IL-IN-WI	3,488,312	64.4	240,300	22.4	13.9	1,078	29.6	87.7	4,876,393	-0.5	197,067	4.0	4,738,337	39.1	20.2
Chicago-Naperville-Arlington Heights, IL Div 16974	2,690,967	62.3	252,400	22.9	14.3	1,105	29.6	87.4	3,736,153	-1.0	145,136	3.9	3,663,584	40.1	19.4
Elgin, IL Div 20994	219,111	71.5	226,100	21.9	13.0	1,026	30.0	90.8	329,388	1.7	15,892	4.8	319,289	33.9	22.8
Gary, IN Div 23844	266,968	71.0	158,700	19.1	10.1	848	29.1	84.0	342,764	0.9	15,776	4.6	317,900	31.4	28.3
Lake County-Kenosha County, IL-WI Div 29404	311,266	71.8	240,000	21.7	13.8	1,082	28.7	91.6	468,088	1.1	20,263	4.3	437,564	40.2	19.7
Chico, CA	88,797	58.0	268,900	23.6	13.5	1,000	34.1	91.7	102,712	0.5	5,093	5.0	98,494	35.3	19.0
Cincinnati, OH-KY-IN	852,639	65.9	165,500	18.6	11.0	790	26.9	88.5	1,115,797	0.7	44,184	4.0	1,090,591	40.4	19.9
Clarksville, TN-KY	105,056	57.9	159,800	19.9	10.0	907	28.5	86.6	114,720	2.1	4,775	4.2	116,309	31.5	24.8
Cleveland, TN	47,923	65.8	162,000	19.8	10.0	728	28.4	83.8	57,539	-1.1	2,108	3.7	57,689	33.3	31.9
Cleveland-Elyria, OH	862,586	64.4	150,400	19.7	12.3	789	29.6	85.0	1,035,340	-0.3	52,381	5.1	992,192	39.5	19.8
Coeur d'Alene, ID	60,383	73.0	263,500	22.8	11.1	972	27.3	91.1	77,765	2.6	2,700	3.5	70,914	34.4	21.8
College Station-Bryan, TX	91,999	53.0	173,900	22.4	10.1	899	41.1	86.4	132,760	3.2	3,931	3.0	118,319	39.1	21.0
Colorado Springs, CO	268,122	63.7	274,100	21.0	10.0	1,146	31.9	93.7	349,735	3.4	13,737	3.9	331,768	41.0	18.3
Columbia, MO	70,355	56.3	181,900	18.3	10.0	869	31.6	86.1	97,114	-0.4	2,206	2.3	93,725	43.7	15.5
Columbia, SC	309,760	67.7	156,600	19.4	10.0	891	30.6	83.8	398,497	-0.8	13,181	3.3	390,679	35.3	20.6
Columbus, GA-AL	112,937	54.4	137,000	21.5	10.0	807	32.1	81.2	125,266	0.6	5,840	4.7	115,742	33.7	21.5
Columbus, IN	31,498	70.9	148,500	17.8	10.0	871	23.2	84.5	45,295	1.7	1,185	2.6	40,460	40.2	28.1
Columbus, OH	788,946	61.8	182,300	19.1	11.7	916	27.4	89.9	1,080,766	0.5	41,578	3.8	1,057,573	42.0	18.8
Corpus Christi, TX	160,796	60.0	135,900	20.7	11.8	951	29.0	83.6	208,814	-0.1	10,354	5.0	200,708	28.6	27.1
Corvallis, OR	35,445	55.4	351,100	21.0	10.5	1,051	37.2	94.0	48,345	0.0	1,535	3.2	46,403	51.4	12.9
Crestview-Fort Walton Beach-Destin, FL	108,474	65.8	214,100	20.8	10.0	1,037	29.6	89.2	126,914	1.7	3,781	3.0	118,802	37.4	17.5
Cumberland, MD-WV	37,611	67.8	128,700	18.3	11.5	664	26.8	80.6	44,246	-0.3	2,440	5.5	39,381	31.0	24.4
Dallas-Fort Worth-Arlington, TX	2,573,711	59.7	214,900	20.5	11.6	1,085	28.4	89.8	3,900,459	2.4	136,487	3.5	3,714,074	39.3	21.1
Dallas-Plano-Irving, TX Div 19124	1,720,901	57.7	235,200	20.7	11.7	1,106	28.3	89.6	2,631,424	2.3	92,386	3.5	2,494,507	40.8	20.0
Fort Worth-Arlington, TX Div 23104	852,810	63.5	183,800	20.0	11.4	1,033	28.6	90.1	1,269,035	2.4	44,101	3.5	1,219,567	36.3	23.3
Dalton, GA	48,645	61.6	126,400	20.4	10.1	694	22.8	82.0	61,199	0.7	2,996	4.9	61,957	21.9	43.5
Danville, IL	30,241	72.5	77,900	18.6	11.4	669	24.0	79.1	33,578	-1.8	2,074	6.2	31,614	26.3	25.7
Daphne-Fairhope-Foley, AL	79,120	74.0	199,800	19.8	10.0	930	27.4	87.3	93,849	1.9	3,393	3.6	94,170	38.7	20.9
Davenport-Moline-Rock Island, IA-IL	151,284	71.3	134,500	18.7	12.2	743	27.7	85.5	191,911	0.7	8,011	4.2	183,205	33.2	27.0
Dayton, OH	329,442	62.4	133,400	19.2	11.0	764	26.8	88.1	386,050	-0.3	16,758	4.3	373,900	39.7	20.0
Decatur, AL	56,691	72.8	137,100	19.3	10.0	599	29.5	82.1	70,258	2.3	2,566	3.7	62,404	29.1	29.1
Decatur, IL	42,979	73.1	97,000	18.2	11.5	670	27.2	85.3	49,961	1.1	2,795	5.6	46,886	31.2	25.9
Deltona-Daytona Beach-Ormond Beach, FL	260,002	70.8	184,300	22.8	12.9	1,046	33.0	83.0	300,516	1.3	11,376	3.8	267,323	32.1	20.4
Denver-Aurora-Lakewood, CO	1,105,758	64.1	386,800	21.2	10.0	1,352	30.4	92.3	1,646,346	3.4	51,977	3.2	1,582,380	43.8	16.9
Des Moines-West Des Moines, IA	250,612	70.6	187,500	19.0	11.1	873	26.1	88.5	353,613	1.8	8,563	2.4	349,042	40.4	18.3
Detroit-Warren-Dearborn, MI	1,707,501	68.9	171,600	19.4	12.7	898	29.4	87.2	2,130,620	0.7	91,155	4.3	2,021,708	39.3	21.3
Detroit-Dearborn-Livonia, MI Div 19804	683,986	61.6	114,400	19.9	13.6	831	32.0	82.2	794,466	0.4	41,540	5.2	737,289	33.1	24.5
Warren-Troy-Farmington Hills, MI Div 47664	1,023,515	73.8	204,400	19.2	11.9	970	27.3	90.6	1,336,154	0.8	49,615	3.7	1,284,419	42.8	19.4
Dothan, AL	55,442	69.3	134,400	19.0	10.0	711	26.2	77.4	62,767	0.9	2,551	4.1	62,102	28.9	27.4
Dover, DE	63,807	70.4	223,100	23.0	10.0	978	32.0	89.0	78,124	0.8	3,239	4.1	80,743	33.1	23.7
Dubuque, IA	37,785	74.6	167,600	19.6	11.3	766	25.8	87.5	55,213	1.4	1,333	2.4	49,144	36.9	21.2
Duluth, MN-WI	117,874	70.8	158,000	19.5	10.8	753	30.3	85.4	142,927	-0.6	5,412	3.8	134,826	36.2	20.5
Durham-Chapel Hill, NC	224,437	59.0	234,400	18.4	10.0	998	29.8	89.3	298,301	1.4	10,275	3.4	287,348	49.2	15.9
East Stroudsburg, PA	57,668	79.3	164,000	26.0	14.1	1,090	29.1	88.2	82,004	-0.2	4,392	5.4	81,955	32.1	23.9
Eau Claire, WI	67,079	67.0	168,900	19.1	13.3	767	28.7	88.3	92,860	-0.1	2,648	2.9	88,202	35.2	25.3
El Centro, CA	44,478	61.4	200,700	21.9	12.0	827	30.6	81.4	71,055	-1.5	12,855	18.1	59,899	28.8	27.0
Elizabethtown-Fort Knox, KY	57,979	61.0	144,500	18.1	10.0	788	24.6	83.1	67,543	0.8	2,830	4.2	65,765	32.6	26.6
Elkhart-Goshen, IN	73,363	69.7	143,900	17.1	10.0	789	24.1	85.7	116,267	3.4	3,012	2.6	96,434	28.9	38.0
Elmira, NY	32,247	67.0	112,900	18.1	12.2	820	29.4	88.6	35,373	-0.7	1,649	4.7	37,356	35.5	20.4
El Paso, TX	270,076	61.2	122,200	22.9	12.4	826	31.1	84.2	360,802	1.3	15,300	4.2	357,762	30.4	21.6
Enid, OK	22,784	64.6	115,300	17.4	10.0	835	28.4	76.7	27,330	-1.9	832	3.0	27,344	30.9	29.0
Erie, PA	108,458	66.6	138,700	19.1	12.2	719	27.9	84.7	129,260	-1.1	6,087	4.7	123,077	32.3	23.1
Eugene, OR	151,675	59.4	258,300	23.8	13.0	943	33.7	90.4	181,761	0.1	8,165	4.5	174,646	36.4	19.4

1. Specified owner-occupied units.   2. A value of 10.0 represents 10 percent or less; a value of 50.0 represents 50 percent or more.   3. Specified renter-occupied units.   4. Overcrowded or lacking complete plumbing facilities.   5. Percent of civilian labor force.   6. Civilian employed persons 16 years old and over.

Table C. Metropolitan Areas — Nonfarm Employment and Agriculture

	Private nonfarm establishments, employment and payroll, 2016									Agriculture, 2017			
		Employment						Annual payroll		Farms			Farm producers whose primary occupation is farming (percent)
Area name	Number of establishments	Total	Health care and social assistance	Manufacturing	Retail trade	Finance and insurance	Professional, scientific, and technical services	Total (mil dol)	Average per employee (dollars)	Number	Percent with: Fewer than 50 acres	1000 acres or more	
	104	105	106	107	108	109	110	111	112	113	114	115	116
Cedar Rapids, IA	6,523	130,819	18,225	17,869	17,400	11,499	6,421	6,103	46,654	3,632	37.7	8.6	43.7
Chambersburg-Waynesboro, PA	3,091	49,814	8,290	7,984	7,555	1,159	1,919	1,856	37,256	1,581	37.3	1.6	55.5
Champaign-Urbana, IL	4,858	75,956	14,411	7,629	10,969	3,399	2,981	3,078	40,527	2,200	32.8	16.4	50.5
Charleston, WV	5,228	87,948	21,250	3,250	12,296	4,148	5,391	3,739	42,511	380	29.2	0.5	36.3
Charleston-North Charleston, SC	18,583	275,562	37,616	24,698	40,466	7,895	20,282	11,984	43,490	1,100	60.3	3.4	36.9
Charlotte-Concord-Gastonia, NC-SC	59,420	1,023,314	128,146	97,757	123,465	80,202	63,900	53,591	52,370	6,969	52.6	2	36.7
Charlottesville, VA	6,124	83,950	17,719	4,476	11,714	3,850	6,532	4,066	48,439	2,217	37.7	2.6	39.7
Chattanooga, TN-GA	11,242	217,706	32,085	31,315	28,254	13,559	9,076	8,857	40,684	2,162	47.2	1.2	37.1
Cheyenne, WY	3,234	35,366	8,045	1,130	5,765	1,578	2,488	1,413	39,958	999	31.7	21.9	38.8
Chicago-Naperville-Elgin, IL-IN-WI	245,377	4,158,944	597,162	383,614	474,724	269,616	340,278	240,971	57,941	6,565	49.3	9.5	46.8
Chicago-Naperville-Arlington Heights, IL Div 16974	NA	NA	NA	NA	NA	NA	NA	NA	NA	2,666	53.3	8.9	46.9
Elgin, IL Div 20994	NA	NA	NA	NA	NA	NA	NA	NA	NA	1,384	43.1	11.5	51.1
Gary, IN Div 23844	NA	NA	NA	NA	NA	NA	NA	NA	NA	1,798	42	11.2	45.7
Lake County-Kenosha County, IL-WI Div 29404	NA	NA	NA	NA	NA	NA	NA	NA	NA	717	65	3.2	41.5
Chico, CA	4,627	60,432	15,032	4,271	10,238	2,564	2,471	2,302	38,087	1,912	65.2	2.9	51.3
Cincinnati, OH-KY-IN	46,150	924,037	145,609	99,514	109,321	58,872	58,052	46,744	50,587	9,699	49.6	1.7	32.6
Clarksville, TN-KY	4,428	69,651	11,264	12,573	12,662	2,020	2,574	2,356	33,826	2,329	37.4	4.9	39.9
Cleveland, TN	2,116	40,526	5,430	8,212	5,440	1,892	754	1,536	37,907	1,065	52.5	0.7	40.7
Cleveland-Elyria, OH	51,247	922,238	177,885	118,781	101,830	51,532	52,746	45,477	49,312	3,524	68.4	1.3	35
Coeur d'Alene, ID	4,659	50,135	9,532	5,278	8,929	2,194	2,233	1,915	38,196	1,073	68.7	2.1	32.1
College Station-Bryan, TX	4,860	72,149	9,945	6,030	12,170	1,860	3,770	2,540	35,206	4,482	38.3	4.2	37.2
Colorado Springs, CO	17,815	241,394	37,593	11,060	33,205	10,800	22,773	10,715	44,390	1,504	46.1	10.5	35.4
Columbia, MO	4,671	77,527	17,549	4,133	12,833	7,279	3,869	2,946	38,005	1,184	47.1	3	30.5
Columbia, SC	17,207	292,496	44,622	26,382	40,329	21,874	18,107	12,066	41,252	3,325	50.3	3.6	37
Columbus, GA-AL	5,685	96,286	16,791	10,184	14,407	13,035	3,738	3,879	40,287	856	36.7	6.2	37.9
Columbus, IN	1,835	47,791	4,940	13,008	5,023	994	2,923	2,241	46,884	564	47	8.7	36.6
Columbus, OH	42,106	859,251	146,260	66,293	100,949	77,748	53,836	41,933	48,802	8,506	53.3	4.6	37.5
Corpus Christi, TX	9,543	166,276	32,090	10,652	22,752	4,560	8,134	6,695	40,266	1,399	57.8	12.6	36
Corvallis, OR	2,119	27,066	6,058	2,870	3,857	611	1,814	1,263	46,651	964	72.3	2.9	36.6
Crestview-Fort Walton Beach-Destin, FL	7,437	79,095	10,734	2,046	16,671	2,715	7,067	2,949	37,282	1,079	56.4	2.3	38.5
Cumberland, MD-WV	1,986	30,313	7,449	3,451	4,870	978	1,240	1,088	35,881	809	38.6	1.6	35.7
Dallas-Fort Worth-Arlington, TX	160,269	3,044,254	385,556	240,025	350,393	211,203	233,526	167,046	54,872	30,782	68.6	2.2	31.2
Dallas-Plano-Irving, TX Div 19124	NA	NA	NA	NA	NA	NA	NA	NA	NA	16,618	68.4	2.2	30.7
Fort Worth-Arlington, TX Div 23104	NA	NA	NA	NA	NA	NA	NA	NA	NA	14,164	68.7	2.3	31.8
Dalton, GA	2,587	57,127	5,243	21,987	5,868	860	1,413	2,272	39,778	664	49.2	0.9	37.3
Danville, IL	1,411	24,530	5,336	4,861	3,872	1,101	428	973	39,647	1,049	38.9	14.1	47.8
Daphne-Fairhope-Foley, AL	5,235	61,341	7,858	4,120	13,738	1,607	2,120	1,960	31,955	842	53.8	4.5	45
Davenport-Moline-Rock Island, IA-IL	8,873	159,956	24,678	23,582	22,681	6,205	6,449	6,957	43,496	3,434	36.1	9.5	45.3
Dayton, OH	16,528	322,924	63,360	43,193	41,413	12,960	25,007	14,635	45,320	2,635	59.9	4.1	36.8
Decatur, AL	2,960	45,875	6,642	12,092	6,372	1,490	1,602	1,886	41,110	2,416	49	1.8	36.1
Decatur, IL	2,441	45,380	8,176	6,330	5,872	1,569	1,086	1,988	43,810	589	41.8	16	49.9
Deltona-Daytona Beach-Ormond Beach, FL	14,674	161,757	30,599	9,818	30,724	5,345	7,047	5,563	34,391	1,691	81.3	2.5	39.9
Denver-Aurora-Lakewood, CO	82,462	1,248,441	162,701	55,972	143,912	72,023	108,742	70,125	56,170	5,606	59.6	7.3	28.6
Des Moines-West Des Moines, IA	16,122	314,623	41,679	19,086	40,859	50,044	17,999	15,736	50,015	4,672	41.9	8	34.9
Detroit-Warren-Dearborn, MI	99,127	1,741,079	272,645	229,757	208,106	83,748	176,051	94,635	54,354	3,980	58.2	2.7	44.3
Detroit-Dearborn-Livonia, MI Div 19804	NA	NA	NA	NA	NA	NA	NA	NA	NA	248	79.8	NA	47.5
Warren-Troy-Farmington Hills, MI Div 47664	NA	NA	NA	NA	NA	NA	NA	NA	NA	3,732	56.8	2.9	44
Dothan, AL	3,409	50,246	10,416	5,382	9,214	1,412	1,399	1,906	37,939	1,973	35	6	38.4
Dover, DE	3,422	53,196	10,879	4,810	9,317	1,581	2,452	2,040	38,349	822	53.4	6.3	48.5
Dubuque, IA	2,759	55,171	8,317	8,847	7,662	3,948	2,346	2,285	41,419	1,402	30.5	3.4	42.8
Duluth, MN-WI	7,079	110,266	28,830	7,051	16,294	5,169	4,282	4,507	40,874	1,637	26.1	1.7	35.8
Durham-Chapel Hill, NC	12,702	251,653	46,919	17,484	25,779	10,794	33,754	14,782	58,739	2,436	50.3	1.2	42.4
East Stroudsburg, PA	3,372	47,216	7,039	5,420	9,581	983	1,564	1,687	35,721	233	55.4	1.7	40.4
Eau Claire, WI	4,291	73,083	14,368	11,262	11,281	2,962	2,859	2,894	39,594	2,478	32.3	3.1	41.7
El Centro, CA	2,519	33,092	5,105	3,504	8,631	768	854	1,093	33,018	396	24.7	35.1	73.7
Elizabethtown-Fort Knox, KY	2,908	41,533	8,295	7,361	7,098	1,570	1,488	1,486	35,791	2,804	49.8	2.8	34.4
Elkhart-Goshen, IN	4,856	126,911	10,915	68,531	9,552	2,105	2,055	5,716	45,040	1,667	64.1	1.9	34.8
Elmira, NY	1,791	30,971	6,589	5,345	5,300	934	804	1,228	39,640	398	29.1	1.3	37.8
El Paso, TX	14,424	236,037	45,447	13,765	39,919	6,688	10,889	7,509	31,813	790	75.9	11.1	39.6
Enid, OK	NA	NA	NA	NA	NA	NA	NA	NA	NA	936	22.1	20.6	44.8
Erie, PA	6,191	114,476	24,667	20,308	16,123	5,163	3,819	4,372	38,187	1,162	39.6	1.4	46.8
Eugene, OR	9,819	125,284	23,710	14,334	20,136	4,732	5,472	4,998	39,890	2,646	78.2	1.1	35.9

Table C. Metropolitan Areas — Agriculture

	Agriculture, 2017 (cont.)														
	Land in farms				Value of land and buildings (dollars)		Value of machinery and equipment, average per farm (dollars)	Value of products sold:				Organic farms (number)	Farms with internet access (percent)	Government payments	
			Acres							Percent from:					
Area name	Acreage (1,000)	Percent change, 2012-2017	Average size of farm	Total irrigated (1,000)	Total cropland (1,000)	Average per farm	Average per acre		Total (mil dol)	Average per farm (acres)	Crops	Livestock and poultry products			Total ($1,000)	Percent of farms
	117	118	119	120	121	122	123	124	125	126	127	128	129	130	131	132
Cedar Rapids, IA.................	1,089	1.2	300	1	954.7	2,258,419	7,533	212,260	854.5	235,265	62.8	37.2	14	82	23,487	71.1
Chambersburg-Waynesboro, PA..............	270	1.9	170	2.8	213.9	1,283,405	7,528	162,879	476.5	301,372	19.2	80.8	44	59.6	3,264	23
Champaign-Urbana, IL..........	1,109	-6.3	504	16.3	1,080.3	4,499,637	8,927	310,513	731.6	332,534	93.5	6.5	11	81.3	12,800	76.4
Charleston, WV....................	49	0.5	128	NA	7.8	360,418	2,820	37,184	1.7	4,539	44.3	55.7	1	73.9	52	8.7
Charleston-North Charleston, SC..............................	212	14.4	192	3.1	60.1	752,456	3,909	80,705	67.4	61,251	55.9	44.1	1	70.7	1,304	12.4
Charlotte-Concord-Gastonia, NC-SC........................	885	-5.7	127	4.1	442.9	763,308	6,009	84,492	1,001.9	143,770	25.9	74.1	18	73.2	8,049	13.1
Charlottesville, VA	403	-1.1	182	2	125.8	1,274,568	7,015	72,902	113.5	51,217	47.2	52.8	17	77.9	1,531	9.8
Chattanooga, TN-GA............	274	2.8	127	0.4	85.0	630,797	4,977	70,938	248.7	115,034	8	92	7	76.6	2,430	18.9
Cheyenne, WY	1,630	-2.8	1,631	67.1	382.3	1,383,473	848	123,891	184.6	184,762	17.9	82.1	42	77.7	4,856	29.3
Chicago-Naperville-Elgin, IL-IN-WI....................	2,147	-3.8	327	59.4	2,016.0	2,794,684	8,547	216,405	1,859.9	283,303	71.1	28.9	53	82.4	36,682	45.6
Chicago-Naperville-Arlington Heights, IL Div 16974...	810	-2.5	304	10.2	768.8	2,817,586	9,273	196,990	557.9	209,267	88.5	11.5	17	83	8,888	35.5
Elgin, IL Div 20994	542	-4.3	392	1.8	524.5	3,829,259	9,777	268,870	565.5	408,572	68.6	31.4	21	85.6	12,555	60.3
Gary, IN Div 23844	686	-5.8	382	45.8	633.6	2,544,392	6,668	234,527	637.6	354,611	57.6	42.4	1	79.9	12,347	57.1
Lake County-Kenosha County, IL-WI Div 29404	108	1.6	151	1.6	89.1	1,340,176	8,866	141,879	98.9	137,964	74.4	25.6	14	80.5	2,892	25.5
Chico, CA	348	-8.6	182	192.5	214.2	2,193,552	12,042	163,066	524.2	274,140	96.8	3.2	100	80.4	6,677	6.1
Cincinnati, OH-KY-IN............	1,198	-1.5	124	2.1	692.6	642,707	5,202	77,847	353.7	36,464	80.4	19.6	35	75.9	16,157	16.7
Clarksville, TN-KY...............	601	-5.6	258	8.2	387.5	1,211,628	4,696	130,349	313.9	134,783	79.3	20.7	21	63	10,108	36.7
Cleveland, TN	120	-1.6	113	0.2	44.8	619,500	5,491	69,039	142.3	133,647	12.4	87.6	8	72.3	1,323	19.4
Cleveland-Elyria, OH............	310	2	88	3.9	226.3	672,210	7,634	85,806	301.4	85,520	83.3	16.7	56	74.6	4,482	14.6
Coeur d'Alene, ID................	140	12.4	130	13.7	62.2	719,382	5,525	49,847	21.5	20,057	81	19	3	81.7	1,211	9.9
College Station-Bryan, TX....	1,099	-0.3	245	50.4	225.2	929,627	3,792	69,216	308.4	68,802	20.3	79.7	4	71.2	3,759	3.4
Colorado Springs, CO	701	-2.6	466	9.8	57.1	685,392	1,470	45,681	33.1	22,035	42.1	57.9	8	81.1	1,300	6.7
Columbia, MO	213	-11.6	180	3.8	128.5	1,015,840	5,654	74,663	105	88,688	44.2	55.8	4	82.4	1,827	20.6
Columbia, SC	575	10.2	173	45.3	213.9	630,372	3,643	88,055	649	195,201	26.1	73.9	14	74.2	6,326	15.9
Columbus, GA-AL................	216	4.9	252	5.8	60.8	742,168	2,948	78,621	51.9	60,673	40.9	59.1	1	71.3	3,511	30
Columbus, IN.......................	160	-6.5	284	15.5	142.2	1,902,512	6,688	159,738	93	164,929	88.3	11.7	NA	79.3	3,919	55.7
Columbus, OH.....................	1,666	-4.6	196	5.1	1,395.2	1,284,052	6,557	141,978	1,078.5	126,795	69.5	30.5	89	82.9	47,922	36.9
Corpus Christi, TX	900	-4.1	643	5.3	569.8	1,803,086	2,804	196,771	294.3	210,365	92.1	7.9	4	70.7	15,650	24.7
Corvallis, OR	128	2.9	132	27.2	69.0	852,301	6,438	80,922	76.5	79,401	82.6	17.4	32	86.7	1,144	6.7
Crestview-Fort Walton Beach-Destin, FL..................	136	-35.2	126	1.6	36.8	517,386	4,111	42,599	38.9	36,088	30.4	69.6	NA	76.5	1,999	15.7
Cumberland, MD-WV	134	19.4	166	0.1	42.8	585,037	3,525	56,221	25.8	31,879	24.2	75.8	2	64.9	379	13.3
Dallas-Fort Worth-Arlington, TX..............................	4,082	0.2	133	26.4	1,282.7	628,493	4,740	57,011	634.8	20,621	39	61	25	78.5	22,057	5.8
Dallas-Plano-Irving, TX Div 19124	2,156	-2.1	130	12.1	841.4	683,005	5,265	59,441	413.2	24,863	43.7	56.3	17	77.3	16,826	8.2
Fort Worth-Arlington, TX Div 23104	1,926	2.9	136	14.3	441.2	564,536	4,152	54,161	221.6	15,645	30.3	69.7	8	79.9	5,231	3
Dalton, GA...........................	84	-2.7	126	0.9	21.0	700,661	5,556	81,532	259.5	390,855	2.3	97.7	NA	77.9	1,035	32.8
Danville, IL...........................	471	8.5	449	0.8	443.7	3,686,595	8,203	261,347	283	269,783	95.2	4.8	6	77.8	5,125	56.7
Daphne-Fairhope-Foley, AL....	175	-9.1	208	7.4	110.4	1,208,663	5,822	136,496	120.4	142,973	84.4	15.6	NA	78.1	6,316	27.3
Davenport-Moline-Rock Island, IA-IL.................	1,146	4.1	334	21.9	1,022.2	2,590,577	7,762	218,339	894.2	260,397	71.4	28.6	18	79.9	29,119	71.3
Dayton, OH..........................	454	0	172	2.8	399.3	1,251,741	7,266	130,667	282.5	107,208	88.3	11.7	22	81.6	14,929	45
Decatur, AL..........................	349	-12.1	144	6.7	166.7	581,656	4,031	89,976	312.6	129,400	22.3	77.7	2	74	5,769	32.8
Decatur, IL...........................	277	-17.6	471	0.1	268.0	4,356,859	9,250	281,637	180	305,610	97.7	2.3	5	84.6	4,815	69.4
Deltona-Daytona Beach-Ormond Beach, FL.......	194	29.3	114	12.6	30.9	957,517	8,366	53,386	210.7	124,603	93.2	6.8	9	76.1	1,194	6
Denver-Aurora-Lakewood, CO..............................	2,489	-0.1	444	46.4	965.9	1,006,299	2,267	66,978	222.6	39,705	68.1	31.9	27	85.3	10,661	11.3
Des Moines-West Des Moines, IA....................	1,338	-2.5	286	2.1	1,060.8	1,954,793	6,828	161,440	773.9	165,648	65.1	34.9	30	79.9	26,818	52.1
Detroit-Warren-Dearborn, MI..	550	-1.4	138	9.9	448.1	767,746	5,560	115,703	340.6	85,581	81.1	18.9	46	79.5	5,926	16.3
Detroit-Dearborn-Livonia, MI Div 19804	10	-36.3	40	0.6	7.8	467,879	11,561	70,633	23.1	93,274	96.8	3.2	2	88.3	56	4.8
Warren-Troy-Farmington Hills, MI Div 47664	540	-0.3	145	9.4	440.3	787,673	5,448	118,698	317.5	85,069	79.9	20.1	44	78.9	5,870	17.1
Dothan, AL...........................	506	-13.8	256	28.3	241.8	723,587	2,822	111,553	330.2	167,361	33.3	66.7	1	72.8	16,021	53.2
Dover, DE............................	182	5.9	222	57.8	155.7	1,758,029	7,923	179,332	391.3	476,038	27.9	72.1	4	76.6	4,531	34.3
Dubuque, IA.........................	313	7.6	224	0.4	258.5	1,930,243	8,633	188,850	440.1	313,898	29.2	70.8	15	82	5,667	73.5
Duluth, MN-WI......................	302	4	184	0.2	135.2	375,332	2,035	63,851	35.7	21,782	48.9	51.1	17	77.8	280	3.5
Durham-Chapel Hill, NC........	277	-2.8	114	2.9	115.3	640,264	5,637	72,798	258.3	106,020	31	69	58	80.3	903	13.8
East Stroudsburg, PA...........	28	4.2	118	0.2	13.4	698,129	5,892	85,597	9.9	42,627	64.6	35.4	NA	79.4	190	9.4
Eau Claire, WI.....................	528	-10.2	213	11	357.0	829,118	3,888	124,131	305.3	123,187	40.9	59.1	66	73.8	4,434	43.6
El Centro, CA.......................	522	1.2	1,317	456.1	504.0	14,670,311	11,135	884,987	1,859.7	4,696,157	65.7	34.3	45	90.7	3,640	27.5
Elizabethtown-Fort Knox, KY .	451	3.7	161	D	257.6	683,751	4,255	88,940	146.1	52,121	69.8	30.2	1	78.4	4,561	24.4
Elkhart-Goshen, IN...............	175	1.2	105	25	146.5	1,173,020	11,178	98,422	298.3	178,936	23.4	76.6	86	45.5	3,082	16.3
Elmira, NY...........................	67	15.1	168	0.1	35.0	440,269	2,619	91,731	19	47,771	50.6	49.4	5	78.6	384	19.1
El Paso, TX..........................	2,419	-1.7	3,062	41.3	60.4	3,327,349	1,087	98,266	64.1	81,194	78.3	21.7	4	74.2	457	2.3
Enid, OK..............................	675	1.3	721	3.2	442.9	1,251,739	1,736	180,573	130.4	139,318	48.1	51.9	NA	80	6,660	61.3
Erie, PA...............................	153	-9	132	1.3	93.5	595,515	4,511	112,026	82	70,602	76.4	23.6	3	78.1	907	15.7
Eugene, OR..........................	203	-7.5	77	22.3	98.0	656,860	8,556	59,094	158.4	59,873	58	42	65	83.8	659	2.9

Table C. Metropolitan Areas — Water Use, Wholesale Trade, Retail Trade, and Real Estate

Area name	Water use, 2015		Wholesale Trade[1], 2012				Retail Trade[2], 2012				Real estate and rental and leasing,[2] 2012			
	Public supply water withdrawn (mil gal/day)	Public supply gallons withdrawn per person per day	Number of establish-ments	Number of employees	Sales (mil dol)	Average payroll (mil dol)	Number of establish-ments	Number of employees	Sales (mil dol)	Average payroll (mil dol)	Number of establish-ments	Number of employees	Sales (mil dol)	Average payroll (mil dol)
	133	134	135	136	137	138	139	140	141	142	143	144	145	146
Cedar Rapids, IA	44.04	165.5	364	5,483	4,229.0	284.7	882	16,193	4,949.8	393.1	239	1,022	210.4	36.0
Chambersburg-Waynesboro, PA	8.47	55.1	108	D	D	D	486	7,106	1,809.5	157.6	87	328	54.9	10.4
Champaign-Urbana, IL	26.98	112.9	235	3,501	3,586.0	161.9	724	11,239	2,735.2	241.0	213	3,033	562.6	119.0
Charleston, WV	32.75	148.4	267	3,771	2,568.6	186.0	840	12,216	3,459.6	294.5	244	1,220	279.9	42.5
Charleston-North Charleston, SC	107.9	144.9	692	7,954	6,339.0	417.6	2,628	35,904	9,411.5	849.2	929	4,326	796.6	155.8
Charlotte-Concord-Gastonia, NC-SC	234.04	96.5	3,185	46,227	33,695.9	2,696.6	7,467	107,892	29,996.8	2,541.1	2,704	13,096	2,885.5	646.3
Charlottesville, VA	15.25	66.4	146	1,853	868.8	100.8	835	11,100	2,702.8	266.0	289	1,356	248.1	48.0
Chattanooga, TN-GA..............	77.58	141.6	543	6,354	3,413.3	305.2	1,932	25,651	6,903.8	613.2	445	2,309	453.4	103.9
Cheyenne, WY	14	144.2	121	1,105	722.2	67.0	370	5,513	1,896.2	161.3	142	461	99.5	16.5
Chicago-Naperville-Elgin, IL-IN-WI....................	1,142.97	119.7	12,340	204,598	231,996.5	13,565.0	28,181	437,310	127,688.0	11,090.7	9,629	64,763	21,668.7	3,443.4
Chicago-Naperville-Arlington Heights, IL Div 16974 ...	905.71	123.4	9,720	158,870	187,061.2	10,316.5	21,489	331,143	93,728.7	8,416.8	7,713	55,585	19,420.2	3,045.0
Elgin, IL Div 20994	69.39	109.2	801	9,957	9,982.0	598.8	1,767	27,240	6,733.8	599.9	508	2,492	684.0	97.9
Gary, IN Div 23844	93.36	132.8	612	6,761	6,918.2	335.4	2,125	32,702	10,190.7	748.4	548	2,840	496.9	96.3
Lake County-Kenosha County, IL-WI Div 29404	74.51	85.4	1,207	29,010	28,035.2	2,314.3	2,800	46,225	17,034.7	1,325.6	860	3,846	1,067.6	204.2
Chico, CA	28.81	127.8	148	D	D	D	725	9,231	2,576.9	240.4	234	1,160	147.6	28.3
Cincinnati, OH-KY-IN.............	237.83	110.2	2,292	43,770	51,641.2	2,634.6	6,428	104,296	30,586.2	2,564.2	1,911	11,621	2,614.7	482.8
Clarksville, TN-KY	36.68	130.5	147	1,921	1,653.1	79.5	828	11,849	3,261.3	284.6	211	958	146.6	29.3
Cleveland, TN	14.61	120.9	65	D	D	D	409	5,046	1,419.3	118.8	66	294	38.3	8.6
Cleveland-Elyria, OH..............	292.15	141.8	2,840	42,048	26,946.9	2,259.0	6,674	97,427	25,943.9	2,303.9	2,111	16,590	5,313.5	765.5
Coeur d'Alene, ID	34.69	230.7	132	D	D	D	574	7,996	2,501.7	207.0	201	623	122.6	19.1
College Station-Bryan, TX......	35.47	142.4	160	1,805	1,275.7	91.1	736	10,830	3,113.8	233.7	244	1,352	271.6	46.2
Colorado Springs, CO	94.52	135.4	442	4,431	2,576.6	248.6	2,025	29,505	8,137.0	775.0	1,074	3,427	669.1	122.3
Columbia, MO	17.85	102	135	1,461	631.4	73.2	627	11,563	3,741.0	287.7	227	920	160.6	28.8
Columbia, SC	92	113.6	762	11,901	8,591.9	627.6	2,616	36,865	9,747.3	839.7	701	4,198	985.9	181.5
Columbus, GA-AL	53.2	169.6	182	2,405	1,716.5	95.0	1,034	13,671	3,475.8	300.0	289	1,615	285.7	59.6
Columbus, IN	9.49	116.9	77	998	774.4	52.7	306	4,701	1,113.1	99.4	72	303	57.0	9.4
Columbus, OH	207.31	102.5	1,746	30,642	33,473.9	1,742.1	5,592	97,309	31,432.9	2,571.3	1,937	11,638	3,033.5	480.4
Corpus Christi, TX	73.84	163.2	407	D	D	D	1,351	20,248	6,139.4	495.5	504	3,109	706.8	138.3
Corvallis, OR	11.95	136.5	44	346	452.5	22.6	262	3,455	731.0	82.5	105	453	53.3	10.2
Crestview-Fort Walton Beach-Destin, FL...................	32.98	125.8	184	1,624	883.8	79.2	1,194	14,773	3,704.0	346.5	528	2,300	404.8	86.3
Cumberland, MD-WV	2.24	22.4	57	596	234.7	25.5	359	4,853	1,160.1	102.0	67	236	34.0	6.4
Dallas-Fort Worth-Arlington, TX.......................	442.68	62.3	7,562	130,067	150,841.7	8,112.6	19,506	305,066	97,494.7	8,162.1	7,462	57,356	12,829.3	2,748.1
Dallas-Plano-Irving, TX Div 19124	390.06	82.9	5,279	92,203	118,378.4	5,990.3	12,725	199,722	63,747.3	5,406.4	5,314	43,570	9,887.9	2,154.9
Fort Worth-Arlington, TX Div 23104	52.62	22	2,283	37,864	32,463.3	2,122.4	6,781	105,344	33,747.3	2,755.7	2,148	13,786	2,941.5	593.2
Dalton, GA...........................	25.85	179.8	217	3,003	1,320.0	120.1	525	5,401	1,500.4	123.7	75	349	133.7	13.2
Danville, IL	8.95	112.9	77	1,788	3,136.5	84.3	255	3,401	850.3	74.3	45	158	28.7	4.5
Daphne-Fairhope-Foley, AL....	23.67	116.2	175	1,868	1,118.2	84.1	950	12,072	3,145.8	280.0	292	1,760	250.3	53.8
Davenport-Moline-Rock Island, IA-IL	40.06	104.4	496	7,650	7,471.4	414.1	1,314	21,284	5,530.5	501.3	326	1,311	309.0	42.9
Dayton, OH..........................	101.01	126.1	684	9,796	17,365.8	533.2	2,487	39,751	9,851.3	905.5	735	3,939	665.2	133.2
Decatur, AL..........................	33.33	218.3	164	2,144	1,455.9	91.4	583	6,300	1,891.5	144.5	87	351	78.8	12.7
Decatur, IL...........................	20.02	186.6	112	D	D	D	395	5,724	1,494.2	133.7	88	471	105.2	13.8
Deltona-Daytona Beach-Ormond Beach, FL.......	64.62	103.7	474	3,222	1,725.6	154.7	2,104	26,736	6,941.6	642.5	792	2,866	478.1	88.2
Denver-Aurora-Lakewood, CO.......................	453.79	161.2	3,311	48,922	53,628.2	3,061.7	8,302	123,338	35,076.0	3,331.1	4,455	20,864	5,461.1	959.7
Des Moines-West Des Moines, IA	59.77	96	795	12,805	10,596.6	699.5	1,966	35,339	9,452.9	842.5	654	3,714	759.0	160.6
Detroit-Warren-Dearborn, MI..	634.84	147.6	4,655	66,120	60,968.3	4,010.0	15,127	194,583	54,637.0	4,845.5	3,605	25,561	8,298.0	1,035.2
Detroit-Dearborn-Livonia, MI Div 19804	466.55	265.2	1,483	23,525	25,358.3	1,417.5	6,091	65,409	17,409.4	1,539.9	1,070	6,044	4,464.6	225.3
Warren-Troy-Farmington Hills, MI Div 47664	168.29	66.2	3,172	42,595	35,609.9	2,592.5	9,036	129,174	37,227.6	3,305.6	2,535	19,517	3,833.4	810.0
Dothan, AL...........................	22.38	151	196	2,986	8,979.2	154.7	716	8,675	2,426.0	204.9	110	440	74.7	16.4
Dover, DE............................	11.81	68.1	94	D	D	D	561	8,856	2,690.8	214.1	127	459	92.2	17.0
Dubuque, IA.........................	7.71	79.4	158	2,353	2,083.1	107.4	442	7,157	1,659.1	149.1	110	381	72.4	12.2
Duluth, MN-WI	36.82	131.7	267	3,351	2,368.2	158.6	1,168	15,179	3,937.6	340.4	260	1,098	180.2	30.4
Durham-Chapel Hill, NC.........	64.47	116.7	355	9,817	7,270.2	1,042.0	1,626	23,631	5,748.8	553.7	503	2,351	485.6	94.3
East Stroudsburg, PA	11.35	68.2	97	D	D	D	634	8,710	2,140.4	187.8	123	507	86.8	15.2
Eau Claire, WI	14.36	86.7	157	2,272	1,422.0	94.5	615	10,495	2,723.8	225.7	141	659	91.2	18.5
El Centro, CA.......................	24.47	135.8	197	1,801	1,599.1	72.5	446	7,322	1,676.9	160.3	119	574	92.6	15.9
Elizabethtown-Fort Knox, KY .	15.75	106	74	D	D	D	501	6,618	1,900.3	154.9	129	543	68.2	12.9
Elkhart-Goshen, IN...............	12.95	63.6	340	5,803	3,329.9	249.5	678	8,754	2,440.4	206.9	157	768	134.5	25.4
Elmira, NY	8.37	96.1	85	1,193	765.0	51.5	350	5,044	1,174.8	115.8	84	382	106.6	17.0
El Paso, TX	114.57	136.6	952	D	D	D	2,332	34,975	9,192.0	754.1	699	3,143	617.3	108.0
Enid, OK..............................	2.87	45.1												
Erie, PA...............................	33.34	119.9	264	3,127	1,242.5	145.7	958	15,221	3,752.8	326.4	182	1,042	158.5	32.3
Eugene, OR..........................	43.68	120.4	384	4,860	2,852.0	229.0	1,270	18,265	4,291.5	449.9	505	2,115	314.3	58.4

1. Merchant wholesalers, except manufacturers' sales branches and offices. 2. Employer establishments.

Table C. Metropolitan Areas — Professional Services, Manufacturing, and Accommodation and Food Services

Area name	Professional, scientific, and technical services, 2012				Manufacturing, 2012				Accommodation and food services, 2012			
	Number of establishments	Number of employees	Sales (mil dol)	Average payroll (mil dol)	Number of establishments	Number of employees	Receipts (mil dol)	Annual payroll (mil dol)	Number of establishments	Number of employees	Receipts (mil dol)	Annual payroll (mil dol)
	147	148	149	150	151	152	153	154	155	156	157	158
Cedar Rapids, IA..................	564	5,682	747.4	328.4	265	19,213	10,486.4	1,348.3	570	9,449	410.9	119.2
Chambersburg-Waynesboro, PA............	223	2,067	234.8	100.3	196	8,182	3,180.0	403.9	270	D	D	D
Champaign-Urbana, IL...........	485	2,967	381.1	144.2	162	7,807	3,700.2	345.5	579	10,454	459.4	126.4
Charleston, WV................	585	6,079	898.7	344.1	129	3,062	2,207.6	188.9	483	9,649	568.7	150.6
Charleston-North Charleston, SC............	2,001	18,874	3,340.8	1,296.0	465	23,529	13,956.2	1,379.1	1,616	34,059	1,968.3	543.8
Charlotte-Concord-Gastonia, NC-SC............	6,214	58,864	10,186.8	3,891.2	2,340	86,773	36,489.5	4,175.6	4,465	87,966	4,719.8	1,269.1
Charlottesville, VA............	791	6,406	967.0	401.8	173	3,830	977.5	211.2	551	9,857	561.8	153.9
Chattanooga, TN-GA.............	942	D	D	D	557	32,303	14,940.6	1,610.2	1,056	21,292	1,089.7	306.5
Cheyenne, WY	458	1,860	279.8	99.7	67	1,190	2,549.8	76.8	207	3,980	224.8	59.8
Chicago-Naperville-Elgin, IL-IN-WI............	33,178	323,636	64,623.4	26,279.3	10,473	383,870	194,249.9	21,208.1	19,708	355,344	22,899.9	6,279.1
Chicago-Naperville-Arlington Heights, IL Div 16974...	26,911	277,996	58,343.8	23,040.6	8,005	274,717	127,047.1	14,762.8	15,390	281,814	18,925.7	5,214.3
Elgin, IL Div 20994	1,690	10,006	1,667.7	598.1	909	33,826	11,678.1	1,702.8	1,064	18,219	856.3	243.1
Gary, IN Div 23844	1,302	8,302	1,004.9	369.3	545	34,450	41,108.4	2,531.9	1,394	25,099	1,480.8	349.3
Lake County-Kenosha County, IL-WI Div 29404	3,275	27,332	3,606.9	2,271.3	1,014	40,878	14,416.3	2,210.6	1,860	30,212	1,637.1	472.3
Chico, CA	424	2,394	388.0	97.2	177	4,126	1,341.1	168.3	397	7,091	350.5	96.4
Cincinnati, OH-KY-IN.............	D	D	D	D	2,239	100,872	47,994.7	5,697.6	4,151	88,347	4,798.4	1,274.3
Clarksville, TN-KY	297	2,668	337.7	120.4	155	10,702	4,287.4	484.5	470	8,759	408.6	113.4
Cleveland, TN......................	150	867	78.4	32.6	122	8,069	5,718.3	345.2	196	3,834	177.5	47.1
Cleveland-Elyria, OH..............	5,775	50,835	7,976.9	3,175.2	3,358	120,600	43,530.2	6,669.9	4,461	79,070	3,864.1	1,065.2
Coeur d'Alene, ID............	442	D	D	D	241	4,011	D	170.2	362	D	D	D
College Station-Bryan, TX......	441	2,877	539.8	139.6	123	4,903	1,180.0	198.2	502	10,084	476.3	129.7
Colorado Springs, CO	2,505	20,151	3,041.6	1,280.6	479	10,471	3,382.5	562.2	1,371	28,383	1,554.0	427.2
Columbia, MO	414	3,570	424.0	156.7	99	3,994	2,042.1	173.3	419	9,006	373.2	104.7
Columbia, SC	1,911	16,971	2,745.8	1,045.8	516	24,989	13,694.4	1,250.5	1,500	29,589	1,391.3	385.3
Columbus, GA-AL	463	3,050	359.1	133.7	186	11,255	3,755.5	471.4	562	12,474	617.9	173.3
Columbus, IN........................	159	3,550	299.0	234.7	142	11,663	5,636.4	553.6	201	4,243	198.6	54.2
Columbus, OH......................	4,702	50,668	8,800.6	3,360.9	1,411	60,169	33,070.4	3,129.4	4,071	81,490	4,087.9	1,162.2
Corpus Christi, TX.................	927	6,378	928.0	338.3	238	10,950	44,697.1	775.4	1,048	20,133	1,046.4	279.9
Corvallis, OR	284	1,996	332.6	125.1	93	1,613	412.7	71.4	209	3,087	142.8	41.6
Crestview-Fort Walton Beach-Destin, FL............	811	6,485	975.9	407.7	113	2,832	572.2	139.7	666	16,040	940.1	278.4
Cumberland, MD-WV	123	681	53.9	22.8	68	4,367	1,470.3	236.5	231	D	D	D
Dallas-Fort Worth-Arlington, TX......	19,150	210,153	39,787.8	15,548.4	5,481	225,780	109,647.6	12,308.6	12,577	263,818	15,353.0	4,225.5
Dallas-Plano-Irving, TX Div 19124	14,206	168,149	33,185.1	13,176.9	3,512	145,699	61,179.9	7,948.5	8,449	176,054	10,381.6	2,902.0
Fort Worth-Arlington, TX Div 23104	4,944	42,004	6,602.7	2,371.5	1,969	80,081	48,467.8	4,360.1	4,128	87,764	4,971.4	1,323.5
Dalton, GA..........................	188	D	D	D	330	17,966	7,111.9	668.8	213	3,781	196.4	50.1
Danville, IL..........................	84	428	46.7	16.6	96	5,168	2,353.2	256.1	143	2,161	86.0	25.4
Daphne-Fairhope-Foley, AL....	450	1,899	211.5	86.2	146	3,780	1,438.8	166.8	462	10,726	560.6	161.1
Davenport-Moline-Rock Island, IA-IL..................	776	5,712	1,007.7	280.0	402	24,533	16,677.3	1,289.9	872	15,809	832.3	208.7
Dayton, OH.........................	1,717	21,824	3,582.6	1,420.6	1,048	40,297	13,041.0	2,179.3	1,611	32,811	1,508.4	428.8
Decatur, AL..........................	230	1,483	167.8	69.3	202	12,048	10,543.3	718.5	243	4,370	197.9	54.9
Decatur, IL...........................	157	1,216	142.7	54.0	109	8,240	13,379.3	435.3	225	4,331	189.8	55.6
Deltona-Daytona Beach-Ormond Beach, FL.......	1,510	7,316	886.3	301.5	380	8,224	2,024.2	367.4	1,156	22,876	1,134.5	341.5
Denver-Aurora-Lakewood, CO......................	12,927	108,529	22,675.3	8,365.9	2,237	52,525	24,861.3	2,880.5	5,846	115,312	7,069.5	2,014.3
Des Moines-West Des Moines, IA	1,686	15,965	2,633.1	966.8	427	19,669	11,785.8	953.5	1,354	24,834	1,211.0	348.2
Detroit-Warren-Dearborn, MI..	11,419	163,997	24,342.5	12,026.3	5,353	199,394	110,685.0	11,620.7	8,168	153,118	8,567.2	2,275.4
Detroit-Dearborn-Livonia, MI Div 19804	2,848	46,825	7,135.0	3,444.6	1,483	71,526	56,638.5	4,413.5	3,184	61,446	4,238.8	1,050.2
Warren-Troy-Farmington Hills, MI Div 47664	8,571	117,172	17,207.5	8,581.7	3,870	127,869	54,046.5	7,207.2	4,984	91,672	4,328.4	1,225.2
Dothan, AL..........................	261	1,359	162.4	59.6	132	4,834	1,646.4	182.8	280	5,084	231.9	61.9
Dover, DE..........................	278	D	D	D	74	4,797	1,930.8	218.9	272	6,183	475.8	101.1
Dubuque, IA........................	166	2,956	450.9	147.7	144	8,498	6,036.4	434.6	242	4,456	169.5	49.8
Duluth, MN-WI.....................	510	D	D	D	286	6,999	12,135.4	375.2	754	12,463	632.6	155.0
Durham-Chapel Hill, NC.........	1,838	35,056	6,112.3	2,966.1	350	15,118	10,445.6	957.9	1,179	22,267	1,248.1	344.0
East Stroudsburg, PA............	306	D	D	D	111	4,449	D	358.1	387	8,392	724.8	155.1
Eau Claire, WI	265	2,089	252.1	102.8	209	9,968	3,621.4	444.4	440	6,931	276.6	75.5
El Centro, CA.......................	179	787	79.1	30.4	50	2,218	1,466.0	95.4	258	3,516	182.6	47.9
Elizabethtown-Fort Knox, KY .	270	1,809	184.5	69.0	88	5,679	2,366.8	262.1	229	5,034	220.3	61.7
Elkhart-Goshen, IN...............	313	2,004	220.2	81.0	795	53,705	14,833.3	2,288.0	348	6,500	280.7	75.8
Elmira, NY	111	774	83.5	36.1	85	5,495	1,247.0	278.8	202	3,534	154.5	43.3
El Paso, TX	1,202	D	D	D	505	13,129	D	543.2	1,481	28,757	1,385.5	375.5
Enid, OK..............................												
Erie, PA..............................	412	3,028	375.8	135.3	476	21,490	9,437.7	1,179.0	630	10,877	485.4	128.2
Eugene, OR.........................	948	5,301	583.9	226.2	529	12,345	4,039.3	581.3	937	13,627	711.8	203.7

Table C. Metropolitan Areas — Health Care and Social Assistance, Other Services, Nonemployer Businesses, and Residential Construction

Area name	Health care and social assistance, 2012				Other services, 2012				Nonemployer businesses, 2016		Value of residential construction authorized by building permits, 2018	
	Number of establishments	Number of employees	Receipts (mil dol)	Annual payroll (mil dol)	Number of establishments	Number of employees	Receipts (mil dol)	Annual payroll (mil dol)	Number	Receipts (mil dol)	New construction ($1,000)	Number of housing units
	159	160	161	162	163	164	165	166	167	168	169	170
Cedar Rapids, IA	663	16,556	1,557.5	658.3	469	2,866	281.8	83.6	16,684	726.4	114,270	959
Chambersburg-Waynesboro, PA	305	8,178	820.5	349.3	287	1,558	131.5	32.7	8,944	373.6	82,569	423
Champaign-Urbana, IL	420	13,306	1,770.8	610.5	317	2,293	414.2	69.0	14,469	557.9	242,998	1,506
Charleston, WV	795	19,917	2,139.0	795.7	416	3,070	299.4	91.1	10,165	424.4	12,004	106
Charleston-North Charleston, SC	1,669	35,964	4,763.9	1,578.2	1,120	7,240	733.9	205.1	61,969	2,928.9	1,567,520	7,002
Charlotte-Concord-Gastonia, NC-SC	5,167	113,438	13,463.8	5,178.0	3,490	22,305	2,609.7	674.3	193,812	8,493.4	5,155,809	26,209
Charlottesville, VA	561	16,296	2,372.6	999.2	381	3,381	666.6	140.0	18,840	870.5	342,653	1,615
Chattanooga, TN-GA	1,275	31,220	3,602.0	1,420.4	716	5,022	569.2	149.4	38,555	1,890.9	420,924	2,227
Cheyenne, WY	323	6,700	647.9	305.2	189	943	93.6	27.1	8,118	524.1	86,186	539
Chicago-Naperville-Elgin, IL-IN-WI	25,714	569,844	63,927.3	24,944.8	17,586	132,350	17,826.4	4,831.8	792,915	35,670.4	3,516,676	17,681
Chicago-Naperville-Arlington Heights, IL Div 16974	20,277	459,774	51,473.0	20,190.9	13,870	107,796	15,518.3	4,150.1	649,235	28,964.9	NA	NA
Elgin, IL Div 20994	1,382	26,345	2,910.1	1,147.8	968	6,879	664.2	187.5	39,900	1,700.4	NA	NA
Gary, IN Div 23844	1,691	41,436	4,686.3	1,716.8	1,231	8,564	814.5	239.1	40,697	1,601.4	NA	NA
Lake County-Kenosha County, IL-WI Div 29404	2,364	42,289	4,858.0	1,889.3	1,517	9,111	829.4	255.1	63,083	3,403.7	NA	NA
Chico, CA	716	12,868	1,434.5	560.2	321	2,158	190.0	56.0	13,739	663.1	141,164	703
Cincinnati, OH-KY-IN	4,831	134,554	15,421.0	6,374.0	3,255	24,339	2,431.1	681.1	142,037	6,510.3	1,233,661	6,076
Clarksville, TN-KY	510	10,678	986.1	367.7	285	1,577	129.3	36.8	14,812	662.0	259,016	1,803
Cleveland, TN	248	5,054	653.8	200.8	102	873	73.0	21.8	7,989	410.8	111,194	676
Cleveland-Elyria, OH	5,423	173,697	17,969.1	7,747.1	3,895	26,763	2,784.6	775.0	150,293	6,873.2	712,972	2,981
Coeur d'Alene, ID	509	8,630	806.2	308.4	236	D	D	D	12,316	545.7	451,559	2,210
College Station-Bryan, TX	433	8,794	1,080.7	395.8	316	2,193	405.2	62.8	16,532	750.3	273,272	1,856
Colorado Springs, CO	1,955	31,286	3,300.0	1,327.9	1,128	8,548	1,816.7	326.1	52,806	2,126.3	1,830,696	5,734
Columbia, MO	602	16,725	2,033.5	699.4	327	1,985	187.4	53.2	11,783	570.4	127,986	557
Columbia, SC	1,637	42,874	4,546.9	1,828.4	1,224	8,398	794.5	241.2	54,672	2,322.7	871,826	4,952
Columbus, GA-AL	691	16,540	1,625.9	635.9	404	2,693	259.9	74.2	19,000	631.9	187,227	1,004
Columbus, IN	221	4,824	512.8	203.1	111	692	82.5	19.7	4,212	172.2	37,313	170
Columbus, OH	4,677	133,376	14,049.2	5,491.7	2,808	23,334	3,073.2	774.6	152,042	7,038.2	1,764,912	9,440
Corpus Christi, TX	1,186	30,414	2,800.7	1,049.3	633	4,993	581.9	158.7	29,360	1,168.9	299,058	1,727
Corvallis, OR	271	5,258	588.1	258.8	147	891	153.8	30.3	5,956	249.6	94,240	622
Crestview-Fort Walton Beach-Destin, FL	658	11,275	1,378.0	474.1	435	2,145	198.0	56.5	23,968	1,305.8	903,790	2,385
Cumberland, MD-WV	314	7,665	686.5	263.5	180	960	72.1	20.7	4,358	154.5	13,372	67
Dallas-Fort Worth-Arlington, TX	17,015	331,041	40,730.9	15,173.9	8,560	70,090	8,772.4	2,385.7	643,314	33,287.7	13,283,707	63,893
Dallas-Plano-Irving, TX Div 19124	11,734	226,936	28,266.9	10,701.7	5,677	47,622	6,382.3	1,735.2	435,052	23,391.8	NA	NA
Fort Worth-Arlington, TX Div 23104	5,281	104,105	12,464.0	4,472.2	2,883	22,468	2,390.1	650.5	208,262	9,895.9	NA	NA
Dalton, GA	225	4,744	525.2	198.0	141	958	85.2	28.7	7,798	379.1	43,922	321
Danville, IL	143	4,736	514.4	235.4	121	540	47.4	13.3	4,158	129.9	6,270	65
Daphne-Fairhope-Foley, AL	444	7,029	622.5	265.3	269	1,203	110.5	31.9	18,470	898.2	615,245	3,047
Davenport-Moline-Rock Island, IA-IL	1,010	22,953	2,081.4	893.2	684	4,209	364.7	106.2	21,179	894.0	113,867	559
Dayton, OH	2,004	59,132	6,556.8	2,598.1	1,242	8,387	863.6	206.1	48,249	2,017.2	412,127	1,577
Decatur, AL	376	6,469	541.2	207.7	180	1,060	103.0	29.5	9,514	378.1	27,606	152
Decatur, IL	291	8,193	886.2	332.1	176	1,170	239.1	37.3	5,463	181.8	9,198	37
Deltona-Daytona Beach-Ormond Beach, FL	1,542	28,190	3,112.5	1,157.7	1,150	5,517	584.5	186.5	48,778	1,957.1	1,068,116	3,859
Denver-Aurora-Lakewood, CO	7,163	130,863	15,988.2	6,540.4	5,189	35,432	4,395.4	1,161.3	258,376	12,781.9	4,787,475	21,729
Des Moines-West Des Moines, IA	1,414	39,163	4,078.1	1,844.6	1,143	8,007	992.9	271.6	45,034	2,161.8	1,050,270	4,923
Detroit-Warren-Dearborn, MI	12,474	254,643	28,793.7	11,432.0	6,992	44,589	4,734.0	1,273.7	335,864	14,997.0	1,912,103	7,163
Detroit-Dearborn-Livonia, MI Div 19804	4,091	101,848	12,420.4	4,712.3	2,645	16,865	1,763.8	497.5	126,180	4,117.0	NA	NA
Warren-Troy-Farmington Hills, MI Div 47664	8,383	152,795	16,373.3	6,719.7	4,347	27,724	2,970.2	776.2	209,684	10,880.0	NA	NA
Dothan, AL	375	10,243	1,127.1	486.2	221	D	D	D	9,729	421.8	93,865	414
Dover, DE	398	9,405	990.6	379.5	233	1,325	105.5	32.0	10,088	638.0	212,126	1,459
Dubuque, IA	271	7,806	702.0	318.7	201	1,157	109.4	28.1	6,446	284.0	84,021	322
Duluth, MN-WI	931	28,824	2,484.4	1,168.0	525	3,338	297.5	76.6	15,720	620.7	133,591	736
Durham-Chapel Hill, NC	1,373	42,120	5,452.9	1,974.5	755	6,461	1,033.8	248.0	45,349	1,764.2	973,992	5,416
East Stroudsburg, PA	393	7,031	643.1	276.0	309	1,571	115.7	37.0	10,441	477.3	46,920	186
Eau Claire, WI	539	14,294	1,521.9	662.8	302	1,828	162.1	45.1	9,807	504.2	147,030	762
El Centro, CA	268	4,536	511.1	182.9	142	608	53.4	16.5	9,442	348.3	60,416	400
Elizabethtown-Fort Knox, KY	398	8,120	728.7	319.5	182	1,053	95.6	24.0	8,071	313.9	82,663	458
Elkhart-Goshen, IN	362	10,105	1,160.8	413.6	336	2,069	261.0	61.1	12,573	568.5	96,206	351
Elmira, NY	211	6,421	621.6	294.0	128	670	57.3	15.6	3,870	141.5	30,006	186
El Paso, TX	1,525	41,470	4,304.3	1,488.3	910	5,676	464.5	129.4	59,276	2,531.5	494,196	2,416
Enid, OK									4,316	176.2	8,124	43
Erie, PA	850	24,899	2,216.5	923.1	563	3,591	322.7	80.2	13,838	589.7	46,085	305
Eugene, OR	1,135	20,576	2,247.4	828.6	611	3,480	443.9	97.7	23,925	1,079.9	267,980	1,389

Table C. Metropolitan Areas — Government Employment and Payroll, and Local Government Finances

Area name	Government employment and payroll, 2012									Local government finances, 2012				
			March payroll (percent of total)							General revenue				
	Full-time equivalent employees	March payroll (dollars)	Administration, judicial, and legal	Police and corrections	Fire protection	Highways and transportation	Health and welfare	Natural resources and utilities	Education and libraries	Total (mil dol)	Intergovernmental (mil dol)	Taxes		
												Total (mil dol)	Per capita[1] (dollars)	
													Total	Property
	171	172	173	174	175	176	177	178	179	180	181	182	183	184
Cedar Rapids, IA	10,705	42,251,213	4.0	6.0	2.5	6.3	2.3	4.9	72.2	1,343.4	584.3	503.5	1,924	1,486
Chambersburg-Waynesboro, PA	3,820	13,644,359	7.7	8.8	1.7	2.3	9.1	6.1	63.5	415.1	130.8	191.4	1,265	978
Champaign-Urbana, IL	8,553	32,026,460	5.7	8.9	3.4	7.5	6.1	5.5	61.1	891.5	342.7	404.0	1,728	1,506
Charleston, WV	8,227	28,589,774	5.5	6.5	3.8	3.3	7.9	3.1	66.9	735.0	295.9	299.7	1,326	910
Charleston-North Charleston, SC	22,813	76,849,945	8.2	12.8	6.2	2.8	3.9	8.3	55.3	2,449.1	759.7	1,206.4	1,730	1,171
Charlotte-Concord-Gastonia, NC-SC	106,366	436,927,670	3.6	7.0	2.3	1.5	39.9	4.1	40.2	12,067.6	3,110.9	3,416.0	1,487	1,141
Charlottesville, VA	7,679	26,539,813	8.0	9.0	2.3	2.5	3.9	4.9	64.7	782.8	292.5	365.6	1,641	1,221
Chattanooga, TN-GA	19,778	70,912,137	6.7	7.6	2.9	3.3	31.0	10.3	37.0	2,452.8	620.7	669.9	1,245	910
Cheyenne, WY	6,173	27,578,286	2.8	4.6	1.9	1.8	39.8	1.5	46.1	796.0	292.8	103.3	1,094	589
Chicago-Naperville-Elgin, IL-IN-WI	358,119	1,755,095,339	5.6	15.8	4.2	6.1	4.0	6.3	56.6	49,995.8	16,211.6	25,716.1	2,701	2,261
Chicago-Naperville-Arlington Heights, IL Div 16974	272,297	1,388,594,555	5.4	17.5	4.2	7.0	4.3	6.3	54.0	39,231.9	12,680.6	19,977.9	2,730	2,208
Elgin, IL Div 20994	25,482	114,832,272	5.3	10.3	5.2	2.2	1.5	6.6	67.5	3,172.7	934.1	1,826.9	2,913	2,670
Gary, IN Div 23844	25,614	86,646,440	8.5	10.0	3.9	4.2	3.6	7.3	60.8	3,048.3	1,320.8	1,243.6	1,759	1,670
Lake County-Kenosha County, IL-WI Div 29404	34,726	165,022,072	5.5	8.7	3.9	2.4	4.0	6.2	68.5	4,542.9	1,276.0	2,667.7	3,066	2,896
Chico, CA	8,734	37,694,370	6.4	9.6	2.6	2.0	12.6	5.9	58.9	1,079.1	643.7	243.0	1,097	878
Cincinnati, OH-KY-IN	72,643	287,857,130	6.6	10.8	6.5	4.5	6.9	6.8	56.1	8,861.6	3,178.0	3,802.3	1,786	1,197
Clarksville, TN-KY	8,620	27,138,883	4.3	10.6	3.8	3.1	6.5	6.8	62.4	701.2	298.6	267.5	975	569
Cleveland, TN	4,049	11,684,208	5.5	10.1	5.8	3.7	9.5	2.4	62.1	282.7	134.8	92.6	786	497
Cleveland-Elyria, OH	92,435	406,449,865	6.4	10.2	4.7	5.9	15.2	7.7	48.3	11,282.4	3,960.2	4,907.0	2,378	1,483
Coeur d'Alene, ID	6,580	25,436,541	6.0	8.3	3.6	2.4	37.6	3.3	38.1	678.7	158.8	148.1	1,040	972
College Station-Bryan, TX	8,862	27,409,320	8.4	12.4	4.3	4.5	3.2	11.0	51.4	682.0	173.0	393.1	1,676	1,379
Colorado Springs, CO	25,178	98,225,856	5.3	9.9	3.8	2.2	15.3	15.2	45.7	2,631.8	836.0	850.3	1,272	745
Columbia, MO	6,008	20,052,275	7.9	5.3	3.3	2.8	2.7	11.3	63.5	497.3	161.0	228.2	1,354	805
Columbia, SC	33,084	120,753,751	4.2	6.5	2.3	1.0	25.0	4.6	54.7	3,250.3	958.1	1,087.0	1,385	1,204
Columbus, GA-AL	13,084	41,360,235	6.9	10.8	4.0	2.6	6.1	6.8	60.6	1,009.9	422.9	376.5	1,213	848
Columbus, IN	4,371	15,688,309	3.2	6.6	2.9	1.3	44.5	3.1	37.7	469.7	111.3	106.7	1,348	1,076
Columbus, OH	70,274	306,173,279	9.4	10.4	7.0	4.4	8.1	5.2	53.9	9,594.0	3,610.3	4,421.2	2,274	1,428
Corpus Christi, TX	19,396	62,362,670	4.9	10.1	3.6	4.7	4.1	5.7	63.6	1,651.1	548.8	775.1	1,773	1,396
Corvallis, OR	1,834	7,923,562	9.3	13.4	6.2	3.8	7.4	9.4	45.7	259.6	93.0	115.4	1,335	1,185
Crestview-Fort Walton Beach-Destin, FL	8,719	30,209,052	6.5	11.1	6.5	3.5	2.3	6.1	60.8	813.5	261.8	380.6	1,537	1,209
Cumberland, MD-WV	3,611	14,623,810	4.0	5.7	1.6	3.1	0.5	6.1	76.2	340.7	169.2	105.4	1,034	723
Dallas-Fort Worth-Arlington, TX	263,325	1,034,080,549	5.5	11.1	4.7	4.3	9.8	4.8	58.2	28,591.5	7,248.4	14,334.2	2,139	1,724
Dallas-Plano-Irving, TX Div 19124	172,608	694,884,179	5.0	10.6	4.8	5.5	10.3	4.8	57.3	19,625.6	4,888.2	9,734.9	2,199	1,766
Fort Worth-Arlington, TX Div 23104	90,717	339,196,370	6.6	12.1	4.4	1.7	8.6	4.7	60.2	8,965.9	2,360.2	4,599.3	2,022	1,644
Dalton, GA	5,343	18,100,335	4.0	6.7	3.7	3.2	5.9	9.7	65.2	440.0	199.5	149.2	1,045	674
Danville, IL	3,642	12,242,579	7.0	7.8	2.7	3.5	3.6	4.2	67.9	289.5	151.8	91.4	1,132	940
Daphne-Fairhope-Foley, AL	7,374	22,581,577	7.4	8.0	2.9	4.3	20.7	5.6	47.7	640.7	189.9	231.1	1,211	537
Davenport-Moline-Rock Island, IA-IL	14,533	58,873,005	5.4	9.2	3.4	4.7	5.9	5.6	64.3	1,610.6	616.3	675.0	1,764	1,489
Dayton, OH	31,140	126,902,617	7.8	9.6	4.5	5.3	8.1	7.6	55.4	3,577.2	1,408.5	1,490.6	1,861	1,242
Decatur, AL	6,083	20,609,391	3.2	7.4	2.8	2.6	21.3	8.4	53.1	589.6	255.2	134.1	870	438
Decatur, IL	4,204	17,133,160	5.9	11.8	4.5	3.0	2.0	8.2	63.3	407.1	180.7	163.9	1,488	1,260
Deltona-Daytona Beach-Ormond Beach, FL	23,653	83,363,572	6.3	11.3	4.7	2.1	21.7	6.5	45.3	2,404.0	575.9	895.2	1,504	1,170
Denver-Aurora-Lakewood, CO	95,098	432,423,959	6.6	12.7	5.6	6.2	10.7	9.5	46.7	13,355.6	3,846.7	5,924.4	2,240	1,358
Des Moines-West Des Moines, IA	22,853	93,893,961	5.5	8.0	3.0	4.3	8.9	5.3	63.7	2,778.1	968.6	1,212.2	2,058	1,784
Detroit-Warren-Dearborn, MI	115,282	533,695,857	7.4	12.9	5.0	4.6	2.5	4.5	60.8	18,679.3	8,819.4	5,896.0	1,374	1,225
Detroit-Dearborn-Livonia, MI Div 19804	52,078	243,918,311	7.3	16.2	6.7	6.5	2.2	6.4	52.0	9,260.6	4,384.4	2,686.6	1,499	1,195
Warren-Troy-Farmington Hills, MI Div 47664	63,204	289,777,546	7.4	10.1	3.5	3.0	2.7	2.9	68.2	9,418.7	4,435.0	3,209.5	1,284	1,246
Dothan, AL	7,365	24,527,281	3.9	6.4	3.0	2.7	40.1	5.5	36.7	730.7	179.2	156.0	1,057	387
Dover, DE	4,210	17,226,252	4.7	6.0	0.1	0.6	1.6	5.6	79.4	494.8	323.1	88.0	525	459
Dubuque, IA	3,261	12,486,456	6.7	9.6	3.9	7.2	5.0	6.0	60.6	400.9	169.8	165.8	1,743	1,320
Duluth, MN-WI	11,586	52,151,960	6.8	9.8	2.9	6.5	13.3	7.0	48.7	1,488.3	728.3	373.6	1,337	1,215
Durham-Chapel Hill, NC	18,475	63,324,374	5.8	6.4	1.4	2.2	10.3	6.8	63.0	1,793.6	701.9	824.7	1,577	1,277
East Stroudsburg, PA	5,957	25,067,544	5.7	4.3	0.0	5.4	1.6	1.5	80.9	719.0	225.3	441.5	2,616	2,404
Eau Claire, WI	5,534	21,894,206	6.1	8.1	3.0	6.4	5.8	4.3	65.0	602.6	268.9	253.5	1,549	1,431
El Centro, CA	10,122	49,143,599	4.2	6.0	1.7	1.1	19.5	16.2	45.5	1,293.3	740.8	180.2	1,019	733
Elizabethtown-Fort Knox, KY	6,654	21,761,001	1.7	4.2	1.5	1.3	37.6	3.5	49.3	547.6	189.2	112.2	746	448
Elkhart-Goshen, IN	6,985	24,411,992	5.4	8.4	4.1	2.5	1.6	3.6	73.6	630.5	315.1	218.4	1,094	907
Elmira, NY	3,853	14,858,297	5.0	9.7	2.9	4.0	13.2	3.8	59.7	476.3	219.3	175.3	1,971	1,236
El Paso, TX	38,548	140,371,856	4.5	10.4	3.7	3.1	8.1	3.1	65.5	3,358.7	1,620.5	1,097.5	1,321	1,022
Enid, OK														
Erie, PA	8,523	32,472,819	5.3	9.7	2.6	5.6	3.9	6.0	65.7	1,197.6	616.5	364.0	1,297	1,046
Eugene, OR	11,647	50,155,119	7.2	10.9	5.2	6.9	4.1	11.4	48.1	1,390.4	585.1	463.2	1,306	1,120

1. Based on the resident population estimated as of July 1 of the year shown.

Area name	Local government finances, 2012 (cont.)										Government employment, 2017			Individual income tax returns, 2016		
	Direct general expenditure							Debt outstanding								
			Percent of total for:													
	Total (mil dol)	Per capita[1] (dollars)	Educa-tion	Health and hospitals	Police protection	Public welfare	Highways	Total (mil dol)	Per capita[1] (dollars)	Federal civilian	Federal military	State and local	Number of returns	Mean adjusted gross income	Mean income tax
	185	186	187	188	189	190	191	192	193	194	195	196	197	198	199
Cedar Rapids, IA..................	1,498.7	5,725	47.4	3.1	3.7	1.0	5.5	1,735.1	6,629	1,177	974	15,498	128,180	64,456	7,747
Chambersburg-Waynesboro, PA.	452.7	2,992	54.1	4.1	1.9	5.5	4.8	619.1	4,092	2,223	396	5,723	76,500	53,257	5,567
Champaign-Urbana, IL..........	941.0	4,025	49.1	2.4	5.0	2.5	6.1	728.3	3,115	1,339	472	37,662	99,010	62,535	8,036
Charleston, WV	776.4	3,436	50.7	3.1	6.2	0.1	2.6	329.2	1,457	2,272	1,020	21,567	95,250	53,014	6,321
Charleston-North Charleston, SC	2,212.6	3,173	45.5	1.1	9.5	0.2	4.7	5,523.5	7,920	10,883	12,662	52,093	356,420	67,265	9,402
Charlotte-Concord-Gastonia, NC-SC	11,496.9	5,006	29.1	35.1	5.3	2.9	2.0	12,295.6	5,354	10,684	6,336	142,104	1,137,840	69,851	9,887
Charlottesville, VA	798.6	3,583	47.8	6.8	5.5	6.6	2.1	859.4	3,856	1,435	1,181	35,520	104,490	84,050	12,689
Chattanooga, TN-GA.............	2,273.9	4,228	31.4	31.0	4.8	0.8	2.7	1,828.1	3,399	5,440	1,609	31,640	241,450	61,609	8,186
Cheyenne, WY	781.4	8,270	37.0	40.5	2.5	0.2	3.1	132.4	1,401	2,772	3,523	11,363	47,710	61,049	7,452
Chicago-Naperville-Elgin, IL-IN-WI.............................	48,512.9	5,095	44.9	3.1	7.1	1.3	4.3	81,674.3	8,577	54,545	32,390	510,718	4,607,880	76,640	11,803
Chicago-Naperville-Arlington Heights, IL Div 16974 ...	38,566.5	5,270	42.7	3.4	7.4	1.3	4.3	70,331.4	9,610	45,082	15,065	387,622	NA	NA	NA
Elgin, IL Div 20994	3,112.0	4,962	53.7	0.6	6.3	0.5	5.5	4,822.0	7,688	1,854	1,271	42,953	NA	NA	NA
Gary, IN Div 23844	2,464.8	3,487	47.7	2.5	4.8	0.9	2.2	2,682.0	3,795	1,974	2,099	32,706	NA	NA	NA
Lake County-Kenosha County, IL-WI Div 29404	4,369.5	5,022	56.1	2.3	6.1	1.8	4.4	3,838.9	4,412	5,635	13,955	47,437	NA	NA	NA
Chico, CA	1,098.2	4,957	46.2	6.8	4.4	11.8	3.6	480.5	2,169	564	335	16,150	93,910	54,112	6,013
Cincinnati, OH-KY-IN...........	9,065.0	4,259	41.6	5.6	6.4	3.8	4.1	13,076.8	6,143	15,305	5,884	113,543	1,041,490	68,050	9,396
Clarksville, TN-KY	654.4	2,385	56.0	3.0	7.0	0.1	4.1	4,800.5	17,498	5,626	27,763	13,893	118,970	45,869	4,401
Cleveland, TN.....................	268.7	2,281	54.1	7.7	7.1	0.1	5.2	242.0	2,054	283	346	5,534	52,730	47,277	4,884
Cleveland-Elyria, OH............	11,203.3	5,429	41.3	12.0	5.9	3.4	4.1	14,162.1	6,863	18,551	5,644	114,977	1,031,350	62,165	8,433
Coeur d'Alene, ID	637.0	4,475	29.8	40.2	5.8	0.4	3.9	121.1	851	634	513	10,604	74,530	55,358	6,355
College Station-Bryan, TX......	708.6	3,022	50.7	1.9	5.8	0.4	5.6	1,389.0	5,923	832	567	38,691	95,810	59,567	7,864
Colorado Springs, CO	2,586.9	3,871	37.1	21.4	6.1	2.0	8.1	4,453.6	6,663	12,182	37,118	40,157	331,250	61,742	7,350
Columbia, MO	580.4	3,444	44.8	3.1	4.3	0.2	6.2	2,592.5	15,382	2,532	605	29,235	77,800	64,254	8,777
Columbia, SC	3,328.6	4,242	44.0	20.7	4.0	0.1	1.1	7,155.9	9,119	10,367	12,337	73,488	361,200	56,769	6,740
Columbus, GA-AL	1,107.4	3,566	50.3	6.1	5.6	1.9	4.1	1,051.1	3,385	6,640	19,352	17,746	127,320	49,594	5,344
Columbus, IN......................	465.6	5,883	32.7	40.9	1.8	0.5	0.9	364.3	4,603	173	245	6,360	39,530	62,360	7,576
Columbus, OH.....................	9,248.5	4,757	41.8	5.3	5.8	5.4	4.5	10,699.7	5,504	14,669	5,715	159,525	984,770	64,472	8,562
Corpus Christi, TX	1,702.5	3,895	49.7	4.7	6.4	0.2	3.7	3,153.1	7,214	5,765	4,731	27,431	192,120	50,959	5,783
Corvallis, OR	259.2	2,999	46.3	7.4	9.6	0.0	4.2	233.8	2,705	499	247	8,971	39,150	69,630	8,817
Crestview-Fort Walton Beach-Destin, FL.................	907.3	3,663	47.7	3.2	7.3	0.3	4.4	501.5	2,025	8,827	16,256	11,470	130,810	66,243	9,966
Cumberland, MD-WV	335.7	3,292	62.0	0.8	3.9	0.5	4.1	213.3	2,092	585	380	7,015	41,140	47,035	4,532
Dallas-Fort Worth-Arlington, TX.....................................	28,447.6	4,245	42.1	11.3	5.7	0.4	4.3	75,576.3	11,278	46,107	17,022	375,716	3,305,730	73,856	11,314
Dallas-Plano-Irving, TX Div 19124	19,555.5	4,418	41.1	11.5	5.2	0.5	4.4	53,566.2	12,101	30,086	10,605	257,884	NA	NA	NA
Fort Worth-Arlington, TX Div 23104	8,892.1	3,910	44.2	11.0	6.7	0.1	4.1	22,010.2	9,677	16,021	6,417	117,832	NA	NA	NA
Dalton, GA..........................	487.6	3,416	54.9	8.7	3.9	0.4	4.8	143.3	1,004	249	393	6,610	57,290	48,394	5,163
Danville, IL.........................	308.3	3,819	56.4	0.7	6.4	3.5	6.3	102.1	1,265	1,461	151	4,459	33,190	45,952	4,560
Daphne-Fairhope-Foley, AL......	700.0	3,669	34.5	19.2	6.1	0.1	7.7	911.0	4,775	350	971	9,262	95,900	61,610	7,919
Davenport-Moline-Rock Island, IA-IL..................	1,675.1	4,378	48.5	5.0	5.5	1.5	4.6	1,215.2	3,176	5,716	1,416	20,868	182,360	60,175	7,358
Dayton, OH.........................	3,712.9	4,635	47.4	3.3	6.4	7.2	5.2	3,143.4	3,924	18,861	7,219	42,747	384,220	56,930	6,896
Decatur, AL.........................	670.1	4,345	54.9	16.9	4.4	0.3	3.3	924.8	5,996	390	641	7,764	65,430	50,566	5,212
Decatur, IL..........................	452.8	4,112	52.8	2.0	7.8	0.1	8.1	462.5	4,200	319	215	5,450	47,990	56,069	6,776
Deltona-Daytona Beach-Ormond Beach, FL.......	2,484.9	4,174	30.8	22.3	7.3	0.4	3.9	3,027.1	5,085	1,453	1,253	21,800	301,180	51,613	6,298
Denver-Aurora-Lakewood, CO.....................................	12,432.0	4,700	33.7	6.3	6.2	4.2	4.8	24,877.2	9,405	28,722	10,093	179,577	1,402,590	80,053	11,958
Des Moines-West Des Moines, IA	3,004.6	5,101	48.5	8.3	4.2	1.2	5.5	3,647.7	6,193	6,318	2,450	38,204	302,270	72,878	9,829
Detroit-Warren-Dearborn, MI...	19,021.2	4,432	43.4	5.7	6.5	3.0	3.8	31,478.0	7,334	28,177	7,878	166,821	2,094,840	66,026	9,509
Detroit-Dearborn-Livonia, MI Div 19804	9,500.3	5,300	36.3	3.3	7.0	5.2	2.9	21,084.6	11,764	13,918	3,243	74,000	NA	NA	NA
Warren-Troy-Farmington Hills, MI Div 47664	9,520.9	3,809	50.5	8.0	6.0	0.9	4.7	10,393.4	4,158	14,259	4,635	92,821	NA	NA	NA
Dothan, AL..........................	704.8	4,774	29.3	42.3	4.1	0.1	4.1	485.5	3,289	414	664	10,358	61,370	50,657	6,091
Dover, DE...........................	527.3	3,145	73.4	1.1	4.4	0.0	1.5	478.7	2,856	1,680	4,266	17,168	80,670	50,842	5,184
Dubuque, IA........................	405.9	4,268	37.6	4.5	4.7	2.0	7.0	372.4	3,916	266	360	4,468	46,910	61,097	7,592
Duluth, MN-WI.....................	1,639.0	5,865	37.0	6.4	5.3	6.4	9.4	1,391.0	4,977	1,643	1,038	23,787	130,500	55,959	6,180
Durham-Chapel Hill, NC........	1,919.0	3,670	40.5	5.6	8.2	5.6	2.1	1,899.7	3,633	6,797	1,411	59,695	255,340	72,275	10,152
East Stroudsburg, PA............	739.9	4,384	67.9	0.1	3.0	3.9	2.5	1,201.0	7,115	3,164	449	8,101	79,080	52,850	5,791
Eau Claire, WI	676.7	4,137	54.0	4.1	6.5	3.1	11.1	488.8	2,988	536	425	11,478	78,920	59,108	7,675
El Centro, CA......................	1,172.3	6,625	40.7	23.6	4.1	7.5	2.9	1,408.8	7,962	2,111	367	16,532	78,510	40,026	3,307
Elizabethtown-Fort Knox, KY .	515.1	3,425	39.9	37.7	2.7	0.0	2.2	447.0	2,972	5,359	4,858	9,322	67,010	50,293	4,863
Elkhart-Goshen, IN................	609.8	3,055	58.2	1.0	3.9	0.2	3.5	758.8	3,801	278	611	8,288	93,820	61,910	8,238
Elmira, NY	467.0	5,252	42.9	3.0	3.0	18.1	8.9	490.6	5,518	211	128	5,817	38,630	52,861	5,779
El Paso, TX	3,277.0	3,945	52.3	15.5	5.0	0.4	1.0	4,036.3	4,859	12,988	27,106	56,320	364,110	41,766	4,028
Enid, OK.............................										487	1,365	3,301	NA	NA	NA
Erie, PA..............................	1,203.4	4,288	44.0	5.6	2.7	14.2	3.5	1,705.3	6,076	1,559	722	15,527	128,020	51,633	6,031
Eugene, OR.........................	1,390.2	3,921	44.2	5.1	6.9	2.2	4.3	1,580.1	4,457	1,782	996	22,225	168,290	57,772	6,950

1. Based on the resident population estimated as of July 1 of the year shown.

Table C. Metropolitan Areas — **Land Area and Population**

CBSA/ DIV Code[1]	Area name	Population, 2018				Population characteristics, 2018										
						Race alone or in combination, not Hispanic or Latino (percent)					Age (percent)					
		Land area[2] (sq mi)	Total persons	Rank	Per square mile	White	Black	American Indian, Alaska Native	Asian and Pacific Islander	Percent Hispanic or Latino[3]	Under 5 years	5 to 17 years	18 to 24 years	25 to 34 years	35 to 44 years	45 to 54 years
		1	2	3	4	5	6	7	8	9	10	11	12	13	14	15
21780	Evansville, IN-KY..................	1,464.4	314,672	159	214.9	88.7	8.5	0.6	2.0	2.5	5.9	16.4	8.7	13.1	12.1	12.3
21820	Fairbanks, AK........................	7,329.5	98,971	357	13.5	75.0	6.4	10.9	6.0	8.4	7.6	16.5	13.2	18.7	12.5	10.2
22020	Fargo, ND-MN.......................	2,810.2	245,471	189	87.4	86.7	6.3	2.0	3.8	3.2	7.2	15.9	14.3	16.5	13.0	10.3
22140	Farmington, NM....................	5,517.2	125,043	316	22.7	39.8	1.1	39.8	1.0	20.5	6.7	19.8	8.3	13.8	12.5	11.0
22180	Fayetteville, NC....................	1,042.7	387,094	138	371.2	45.3	39.1	3.6	4.2	12.1	7.7	17.4	12.2	17.2	12.2	10.9
22220	Fayetteville-Springdale-Rogers, AR-MO...........	3,163.3	549,128	102	173.6	75.0	3.1	2.6	5.4	16.4	6.9	18.4	10.9	14.7	13.6	11.8
22380	Flagstaff, AZ........................	18,618.7	142,854	289	7.7	56.2	2.0	27.1	3.2	14.3	5.5	15.1	20.1	14.2	11.0	10.1
22420	Flint, MI..............................	637.0	406,892	133	638.8	74.8	21.6	1.3	1.5	3.5	5.9	16.6	8.6	12.3	11.6	13.2
22500	Florence, SC........................	1,361.1	204,961	218	150.6	53.6	43.0	0.7	1.5	2.5	5.9	17.2	8.7	12.4	11.9	12.9
22520	Florence-Muscle Shoals, AL...	1,260.8	147,149	285	116.7	83.8	13.0	1.1	0.9	2.8	5.3	14.7	10.0	12.2	11.0	12.8
22540	Fond du Lac, WI..................	719.6	103,066	347	143.2	90.4	2.5	0.8	2.3	5.3	5.3	16.1	8.4	11.9	12.1	13.0
22660	Fort Collins, CO..................	2,595.8	350,518	150	135.0	84.5	1.6	1.1	3.4	11.7	5.1	14.5	14.1	14.7	12.4	11.0
22900	Fort Smith, AR-OK................	3,385.7	282,318	171	83.4	76.1	5.0	10.0	3.3	10.3	6.4	17.5	8.5	12.9	12.0	12.8
23060	Fort Wayne, IN	1,361.0	437,631	123	321.6	78.9	11.8	0.8	4.4	6.9	6.9	18.6	8.8	13.6	12.2	12.2
23420	Fresno, CA...........................	5,958.1	994,400	54	166.9	30.7	5.3	1.1	11.5	53.5	7.8	20.6	9.9	15.3	12.6	11.1
23460	Gadsden, AL.........................	535.3	102,501	351	191.5	79.2	16.3	1.1	1.0	4.0	5.8	15.7	8.2	12.1	12.0	13.5
23540	Gainesville, FL.....................	1,224.7	288,212	168	235.3	64.6	20.3	0.7	7.0	10.0	5.3	12.9	20.3	15.3	10.9	9.9
23580	Gainesville, GA....................	393.0	202,148	220	514.4	61.4	8.0	0.6	2.4	29.0	6.6	18.8	9.1	13.0	12.5	13.5
23900	Gettysburg, PA.....................	518.8	102,811	348	198.2	90.2	2.3	0.5	1.2	7.1	5.0	15.0	9.3	10.9	10.5	13.8
24020	Glens Falls, NY	1,698.4	125,462	314	73.9	94.1	2.6	0.7	1.1	2.8	4.6	13.9	7.5	12.1	11.2	14.0
24140	Goldsboro, NC......................	553.9	123,248	319	222.5	54.8	32.2	0.9	2.0	12.3	6.6	17.0	9.8	13.5	11.2	12.2
24220	Grand Forks, ND-MN	3,407.2	102,299	352	30.0	86.2	4.7	3.2	3.3	5.1	7.0	15.1	16.5	15.0	10.6	9.6
24260	Grand Island, NE.................	2,143.5	85,088	370	39.7	74.5	2.7	0.7	1.4	21.7	7.4	19.0	8.0	12.5	12.1	11.8
24300	Grand Junction, CO.............	3,328.9	153,207	268	46.0	82.7	1.3	1.4	1.6	14.8	5.7	15.9	9.2	13.1	12.1	11.0
24340	Grand Rapids-Wyoming, MI ...	2,670.0	1,069,405	52	400.5	80.5	7.8	0.9	3.5	9.7	6.5	17.4	10.3	14.4	12.3	12.0
24420	Grants Pass, OR	1,638.7	87,393	368	53.3	89.3	1.0	2.9	2.1	7.6	5.2	14.4	6.5	10.8	10.3	11.3
24500	Great Falls, MT....................	2,698.2	81,643	376	30.3	88.3	2.4	6.4	2.1	4.6	6.7	15.7	9.3	14.4	11.1	10.8
24540	Greeley, CO..........................	3,986.0	314,305	160	78.9	66.9	1.6	1.1	2.4	29.6	7.3	19.0	9.1	15.3	13.7	12.1
24580	Green Bay, WI......................	1,870.0	321,591	157	172.0	84.9	3.2	3.0	3.3	7.6	6.2	17.1	8.7	12.9	12.4	13.0
24660	Greensboro-High Point, NC ...	1,993.8	767,711	75	385.0	59.5	28.4	1.1	4.6	8.6	5.8	16.3	9.9	13.1	11.9	13.6
24780	Greenville, NC......................	652.4	179,914	234	275.8	55.9	36.3	0.7	2.8	6.3	5.7	15.6	17.5	14.0	11.7	11.1
24860	Greenville-Anderson-Mauldin, SC	2,709.6	906,626	61	334.6	74.1	17.5	0.6	2.5	7.0	6.0	16.4	9.9	13.2	12.1	13.0
25060	Gulfport-Biloxi-Pascagoula, MS	1,770.4	397,261	136	224.4	69.4	22.8	1.0	3.2	5.9	6.1	17.2	8.7	13.5	12.3	12.7
25180	Hagerstown-Martinsburg, MD-WV......................	778.9	268,049	181	344.1	83.3	11.7	0.7	2.2	5.1	5.9	16.6	7.8	13.5	12.6	14.1
25220	Hammond, LA.......................	791.3	133,777	302	169.1	64.3	30.8	0.8	1.1	4.4	7.2	17.3	9.9	14.9	12.3	11.6
25260	Hanford-Corcoran, CA...........	1,390.3	151,366	273	108.9	33.7	6.9	1.4	5.3	55.0	7.5	19.6	11.0	17.0	13.8	11.5
25420	Harrisburg-Carlisle, PA.........	1,621.9	574,659	97	354.3	78.4	11.7	0.6	5.0	6.6	5.8	15.6	8.6	13.4	12.0	12.9
25500	Harrisonburg, VA..................	867.1	135,277	298	156.0	80.6	5.0	0.5	2.9	12.6	5.6	14.3	18.1	12.8	11.3	11.1
25540	Hartford-West Hartford-East Hartford, CT	1,514.6	1,206,300	48	796.4	68.3	11.9	0.6	5.9	15.2	5.0	15.0	10.2	12.7	11.9	13.5
25620	Hattiesburg, MS...................	1,609.9	149,414	280	92.8	66.7	29.8	0.6	1.5	2.7	6.5	17.3	11.3	14.6	12.8	11.7
25860	Hickory-Lenoir-Morganton, NC	1,639.5	368,416	146	224.7	82.1	8.0	0.7	3.4	7.6	5.2	15.4	8.2	11.7	11.5	14.4
25940	Hilton Head Island-Bluffton-Beaufort, NC	1,231.3	217,686	207	176.8	66.2	21.6	0.6	1.8	11.4	5.2	13.6	9.0	11.4	10.1	10.7
25980	Hinesville, GA......................	916.9	80,495	377	87.8	46.1	40.8	1.3	3.6	12.4	9.7	18.1	12.7	18.7	11.7	9.9
26140	Homosassa Springs, FL.........	581.9	147,929	284	254.2	89.1	3.5	0.9	2.1	5.9	3.8	11.1	5.2	8.6	7.7	11.0
26300	Hot Springs, AR...................	677.7	99,154	355	146.3	84.0	9.6	1.5	1.3	5.9	5.4	14.7	7.2	11.4	11.0	12.0
26380	Houma-Thibodaux, LA..........	2,298.2	209,136	215	91.0	73.2	17.5	5.4	1.4	4.7	6.7	17.6	8.2	14.1	12.5	12.7
26420	Houston-The Woodlands-Sugar Land, TX...........	8,266.0	6,997,384	5	846.5	36.9	17.7	0.6	8.7	37.6	7.3	19.3	9.0	15.0	14.3	12.8
26580	Huntington-Ashland, WV-KY-OH..............................	2,527.4	352,823	149	139.6	95.4	3.2	0.7	1.0	1.2	5.4	15.7	8.8	11.6	12.3	13.1
26620	Huntsville, AL......................	1,361.5	462,693	116	339.8	69.1	23.3	1.5	3.3	5.3	5.8	16.2	9.1	13.8	12.5	13.7
26820	Idaho Falls, ID	5,196.1	148,904	281	28.7	85.2	0.9	1.3	1.8	12.6	8.4	22.9	8.4	13.3	13.0	10.1
26900	Indianapolis-Carmel-Anderson, IN...........	4,306.4	2,048,703	34	475.7	74.0	16.7	0.6	4.1	6.9	6.6	18.0	8.7	14.4	13.3	12.9
26980	Iowa City, IA........................	1,181.8	173,401	243	146.7	81.5	7.2	0.6	6.9	5.9	6.0	14.6	19.4	14.9	11.9	10.3
27060	Ithaca, NY............................	474.6	102,793	349	216.6	79.6	5.2	0.8	12.1	5.3	3.8	10.8	26.5	12.8	10.4	10.1
27100	Jackson, MI..........................	701.9	158,823	262	226.3	87.1	9.7	1.0	1.3	3.6	5.6	15.8	8.7	12.7	11.6	13.2
27140	Jackson, MS.........................	4,648.6	580,166	95	124.8	46.9	49.6	0.4	1.5	2.6	6.1	17.7	9.5	14.0	13.0	12.3
27180	Jackson, TN	1,108.4	129,209	306	116.6	63.1	32.1	0.6	1.3	4.6	6.0	16.4	10.5	12.4	11.4	12.5
27260	Jacksonville, FL....................	3,202.3	1,534,701	40	479.2	64.8	22.4	0.8	5.3	9.2	6.2	16.2	8.2	14.6	12.7	13.0
27340	Jacksonville, NC...................	761.9	197,683	223	259.5	69.3	16.9	1.4	3.8	12.8	8.8	15.7	21.4	18.5	10.4	7.9
27500	Janesville-Beloit, WI............	718.1	163,129	258	227.2	84.5	6.2	0.7	1.9	8.9	6.1	17.0	8.6	12.3	12.2	13.2
27620	Jefferson City, MO................	2,247.7	151,520	272	67.4	87.9	8.9	0.9	1.4	2.7	5.9	16.3	9.1	13.3	12.7	12.9
27740	Johnson City, TN..................	853.8	202,719	219	237.4	92.0	4.0	0.8	1.5	3.3	4.8	14.0	10.4	12.3	11.4	13.5
27780	Johnstown, PA......................	688.4	131,730	305	191.4	94.1	4.5	0.3	0.9	1.7	5.0	14.2	9.1	10.4	10.7	12.6

1. CBSA = Core Based Statistical Area. DIV = Metropolitan Division. See Appendix A for explanation. See Appendix B for list of metropolitan areas or temporarily covered by water. 2. Dry land or land partially or temporarily covered by water. 3. May be of any race.

Table C. Metropolitan Areas — **Population and Households**

| | Population, 2018 (cont.) | | | | Population change and components of change, 2000-2018 | | | | | | | Households, 2017 | | | | |
| Area name | Age (percent) (cont.) | | | Percent female | Total persons | | Percent change | | Components of change, 2010-2018 | | | | | Percent | | |
	55 to 64 years	65 to 74 years	75 years and over		2000	2010	2000-2010	2010-2018	Births	Deaths	Net migration	Number	Persons per house-hold	Family house-holds	Female family house-holder[1]	One person
	16	17	18	19	20	21	22	23	24	25	26	27	28	29	30	31
Evansville, IN-KY..............	14.2	10.0	7.3	51.3	296,195	311,548	5.2	1.0	30,826	26,431	-1,038	130,667	2.34	63.0	11.7	30.1
Fairbanks, AK...................	11.0	7.2	3.1	46.1	82,840	97,585	17.8	1.4	13,888	3,957	-8,736	35,046	2.71	67.9	10.3	24.3
Fargo, ND-MN...................	10.5	7.0	5.3	49.7	174,367	208,777	19.7	17.6	27,396	12,127	21,211	100,721	2.31	58.7	7.9	29.3
Farmington, NM.................	13.0	8.7	6.2	50.5	113,801	130,045	14.3	-3.8	14,824	8,045	-11,873	41,071	3.05	71.6	16.7	23.9
Fayetteville, NC................	10.7	7.0	4.7	50.5	336,609	366,323	8.8	5.7	53,801	22,611	-11,602	143,306	2.58	61.9	13.9	33.1
Fayetteville-Springdale-Rogers, AR-MO..........	10.7	7.6	5.3	50.1	347,045	463,202	33.5	18.6	59,768	29,435	55,068	194,671	2.69	70.0	9.6	23.0
Flagstaff, AZ....................	11.5	8.0	4.5	50.6	116,320	134,431	15.6	6.3	13,703	6,476	1,169	47,977	2.65	59.7	14.3	28.6
Flint, MI...........................	14.3	10.1	7.4	51.8	436,141	425,789	-2.4	-4.4	40,445	36,323	-23,255	165,719	2.42	63.0	16.2	31.6
Florence, SC.....................	13.4	10.7	6.9	53.2	193,155	205,571	6.4	-0.3	20,696	18,975	-2,161	79,458	2.53	66.3	20.2	29.6
Florence-Muscle Shoals, AL...	13.9	11.4	8.7	52.0	142,950	147,137	2.9	0.0	12,636	14,795	2,294	60,041	2.41	64.9	12.1	30.3
Fond du Lac, WI.................	14.7	10.5	8.1	50.8	97,296	101,627	4.5	1.4	8,936	7,668	216	42,449	2.34	65.7	6.5	27.7
Fort Collins, CO.................	12.5	9.6	6.0	50.1	251,494	299,615	19.1	17.0	28,123	17,275	39,542	134,709	2.48	60.0	6.2	27.1
Fort Smith, AR-OK..............	13.1	9.9	7.1	50.7	255,399	280,532	9.8	0.6	29,066	24,625	-2,528	108,133	2.57	67.3	12.3	27.8
Fort Wayne, IN	12.7	8.9	6.2	51.0	390,156	416,262	6.7	5.1	48,911	29,974	2,769	168,359	2.54	65.0	11.0	28.6
Fresno, CA........................	10.4	7.2	5.1	50.1	799,407	930,496	16.4	6.9	128,424	54,033	-10,112	305,819	3.18	73.2	17.1	21.4
Gadsden, AL.....................	13.7	11.3	7.7	51.6	103,459	104,427	0.9	-1.8	9,766	11,440	-157	37,091	2.74	62.1	12.5	35.2
Gainesville, FL..................	11.1	8.6	5.8	51.5	232,392	264,278	13.7	9.1	25,219	16,659	15,439	104,101	2.59	48.1	9.4	40.4
Gainesville, GA.................	11.8	8.8	6.1	50.3	139,277	179,726	29.0	12.5	21,184	11,473	12,744	62,164	3.18	73.7	14.0	21.7
Gettysburg, PA.................	15.1	11.7	8.7	50.8	91,292	101,424	11.1	1.4	8,292	8,132	1,301	39,527	2.48	69.7	9.3	25.9
Glens Falls, NY.................	15.8	12.1	8.8	49.6	124,345	128,941	3.7	-2.7	9,674	10,674	-2,405	50,135	2.43	61.1	10.8	29.5
Goldsboro, NC..................	13.1	9.7	6.8	51.4	113,329	122,673	8.2	0.5	13,793	9,771	-3,435	47,720	2.54	68.6	18.9	26.7
Grand Forks, ND-MN	11.9	8.0	6.3	48.8	97,478	98,464	1.0	3.9	11,667	6,771	-1,071	42,613	2.26	51.1	6.8	39.1
Grand Island, NE...............	12.8	9.1	7.3	49.6	77,708	81,850	5.3	4.0	10,067	6,295	-502	32,578	2.60	70.5	9.5	23.0
Grand Junction, CO............	14.0	11.1	8.0	50.6	116,255	146,717	26.2	4.4	14,756	11,666	3,456	61,763	2.40	63.9	8.2	29.9
Grand Rapids-Wyoming, MI ...	12.6	8.5	6.0	50.5	930,670	988,940	6.3	8.1	111,657	61,920	31,285	394,268	2.62	68.3	10.3	24.9
Grants Pass, OR	15.5	15.1	10.9	51.2	75,726	82,718	9.2	5.7	6,978	9,741	7,434	36,493	2.34	64.3	8.9	27.7
Great Falls, MT.................	13.5	10.4	8.2	49.4	80,357	81,323	1.2	0.4	9,484	6,875	-2,252	33,346	2.38	61.7	7.1	33.3
Greeley, CO......................	11.5	7.7	4.5	49.6	180,926	252,847	39.8	24.3	33,427	13,595	41,180	104,611	2.85	73.0	10.4	19.6
Green Bay, WI...................	13.9	9.4	6.5	50.2	282,599	306,241	8.4	5.0	32,468	20,000	3,151	129,383	2.41	65.5	9.4	28.1
Greensboro-High Point, NC ...	13.1	9.6	6.7	52.2	643,430	723,885	12.5	6.1	71,267	55,157	28,181	297,140	2.49	63.9	13.7	29.9
Greenville, NC..................	11.2	8.0	5.2	53.0	133,798	168,167	25.7	7.0	17,335	10,216	4,662	68,505	2.52	63.3	16.4	26.9
Greenville-Anderson-Mauldin, SC	12.9	9.8	6.8	51.4	725,680	824,035	13.6	10.0	86,261	66,744	62,935	343,167	2.54	66.3	13.0	27.7
Gulfport-Biloxi-Pascagoula, MS	13.6	9.6	6.3	50.9	363,988	370,787	1.9	7.1	40,078	30,384	16,855	150,780	2.57	65.3	14.9	28.9
Hagerstown-Martinsburg, MD-WV......................	13.4	9.5	6.6	49.7	207,828	251,602	21.1	6.5	25,385	20,304	11,342	98,959	2.59	68.7	12.3	26.3
Hammond, LA...................	12.5	9.0	5.4	51.6	100,588	121,107	20.4	10.5	15,846	9,880	6,704	49,272	2.62	66.4	18.8	26.4
Hanford-Corcoran, CA..........	9.5	5.9	4.3	45.0	129,461	152,982	18.2	-1.1	19,367	6,764	-14,567	43,029	3.19	79.8	18.3	16.0
Harrisburg-Carlisle, PA.........	13.8	10.3	7.5	50.9	509,074	549,468	7.9	4.6	53,867	42,790	14,449	226,354	2.43	65.5	12.1	28.0
Harrisonburg, VA................	11.5	8.4	6.8	51.2	108,193	125,221	15.7	8.0	11,878	8,032	6,241	47,777	2.62	65.1	10.3	26.4
Hartford-West Hartford-East Hartford, CT................	14.2	9.7	7.7	51.2	1,148,618	1,212,453	5.6	-0.5	98,709	86,265	-18,697	470,731	2.47	63.2	12.2	30.0
Hattiesburg, MS..................	11.7	8.2	5.8	52.2	123,812	142,845	15.4	4.6	16,308	10,562	751	54,181	2.63	64.6	13.9	27.8
Hickory-Lenoir-Morganton, NC................................	14.4	11.2	7.9	50.5	341,851	365,830	7.0	0.7	31,065	32,347	4,119	141,250	2.54	68.6	12.1	26.7
Hilton Head Island-Bluffton-Beaufort, NC	13.8	15.8	10.4	50.8	141,615	187,010	32.1	16.4	19,443	14,139	25,072	79,217	2.65	65.4	9.1	30.3
Hinesville, GA...................	9.8	6.0	3.3	49.4	71,914	77,919	8.4	3.3	13,849	3,497	-8,248	29,826	2.65	67.7	14.6	25.4
Homosassa Springs, FL........	16.3	19.5	16.8	51.5	118,085	141,229	19.6	4.7	8,626	20,255	18,293	61,290	2.33	62.2	10.0	31.3
Hot Springs, AR.................	14.5	13.4	10.4	51.9	88,068	96,100	9.0	3.3	9,095	11,248	5,326	38,594	2.50	62.1	10.9	32.0
Houma-Thibodaux, LA..........	13.2	8.7	6.2	50.9	194,477	208,184	7.0	0.5	23,667	15,614	-7,035	77,302	2.68	68.3	13.5	25.5
Houston-The Woodlands-Sugar Land, TX..........	11.2	7.0	4.1	50.4	4,693,161	5,920,487	26.2	18.2	798,397	308,126	584,110	2,324,758	2.93	70.9	14.1	23.9
Huntington-Ashland, WV-KY-OH................................	13.8	11.2	8.1	51.0	362,346	364,884	0.7	-3.3	32,938	35,842	-8,960	139,983	2.49	64.8	10.8	30.3
Huntsville, AL...................	13.9	8.8	6.3	50.9	342,376	417,593	22.0	10.8	42,439	30,240	32,831	180,708	2.46	66.2	13.2	28.9
Idaho Falls, ID...................	10.8	7.8	5.3	49.9	104,576	133,329	27.5	11.7	20,093	8,085	3,601	50,941	2.83	74.3	8.2	23.4
Indianapolis-Carmel-Anderson, IN	12.4	8.2	5.5	51.1	1,658,462	1,888,085	13.8	8.5	219,513	130,925	72,585	773,361	2.57	63.6	11.9	30.1
Iowa City, IA....................	10.3	7.6	5.1	50.4	131,676	152,586	15.9	13.6	17,294	7,610	11,156	67,822	2.41	53.7	6.8	30.0
Ithaca, NY........................	11.2	8.9	5.6	50.8	96,501	101,580	5.3	1.2	7,004	5,514	-343	40,230	2.27	50.9	7.6	31.8
Jackson, MI......................	14.5	10.4	7.4	48.9	158,422	160,245	1.2	-0.9	14,728	13,450	-2,622	62,220	2.39	63.2	10.7	31.8
Jackson, MS.....................	12.7	8.8	5.8	52.0	525,346	567,632	8.0	2.2	61,374	42,153	-6,810	211,178	2.63	67.7	18.2	27.9
Jackson, TN	13.4	10.1	7.2	52.5	121,909	130,022	6.7	-0.6	13,137	10,957	-2,940	47,865	2.59	62.9	12.2	32.1
Jacksonville, FL.................	13.3	9.7	6.1	51.2	1,122,750	1,345,591	19.8	14.1	148,758	100,463	140,382	560,169	2.64	67.3	14.0	26.6
Jacksonville, NC...............	8.0	5.5	3.8	44.8	150,355	177,799	18.3	11.2	34,729	8,256	-7,895	62,941	2.76	70.2	10.7	22.8
Janesville-Beloit, WI...........	14.0	9.5	7.0	50.7	152,307	160,335	5.3	1.7	16,054	12,055	-1,113	64,878	2.46	65.6	12.9	28.6
Jefferson City, MO.............	13.4	9.7	6.8	48.9	140,052	149,797	7.0	1.2	14,690	10,683	-2,214	54,732	2.51	67.1	11.6	26.6
Johnson City, TN...............	13.9	11.4	8.4	51.1	181,607	198,757	9.4	2.0	16,409	19,061	6,689	83,579	2.35	62.3	11.9	30.4
Johnstown, PA...................	15.4	12.5	10.1	50.8	152,598	143,681	-5.8	-8.3	11,137	15,137	-7,980	56,023	2.26	64.7	11.5	31.0

1. No spouse present

Table C. Metropolitan Areas — Population, Vital Statistics, Health, and Crime

Area name	Persons in group quarters, 2018	Daytime population, 2017		Births, 2018		Deaths, 2018		Persons under 65 with no health insurance 2017		Medicare, 2018			Serious crimes known to police[2], 2016 — Total	
		Number	Employ-ment/residence ratio	Total	Rate[1]	Number	Rate[1]	Number	Percent	Total Ben-eficiaries	Enrolled in Original Medicare	Enrolled in Medicare Advantage	Number	Rate[3]
	32	33	34	35	36	37	38	39	40	41	42	43	44	45
Evansville, IN-KY..................	9,211	319,998	1.03	3,581	11.4	3,286	10.4	19,634	7.7	64,474	46,015	18,459	9,788	3,099
Fairbanks, AK.......................	4,816	D	D	1,580	16.0	505	5.1	11,342	13.2	11,598	11,497	101	NA	NA
Fargo, ND-MN......................	8,615	245,615	1.03	3,511	14.3	1,593	6.5	13,340	6.5	33,756	23,397	10,359	6,442	2,742
Farmington, NM....................	1,743	125,713	0.97	1,543	12.3	1,078	8.6	15,066	14.0	20,476	18,531	1,945	4,274	3,681
Fayetteville, NC....................	16,231	400,178	1.08	6,189	16.0	2,996	7.7	37,300	11.5	58,216	41,692	16,524	15,150	4,004
Fayetteville-Springdale-Rogers, AR-MO............	10,650	541,768	1.02	7,538	13.7	3,710	6.8	54,055	11.7	82,656	57,076	25,580	NA	NA
Flagstaff, AZ.........................	12,364	141,070	1.00	1,567	11.0	879	6.2	14,874	13.1	19,462	17,022	2,440	4,709	3,356
Flint, MI...............................	5,860	389,684	0.89	4,653	11.4	4,558	11.2	22,396	6.7	88,552	45,647	42,905	11,645	2,855
Florence, SC........................	4,556	211,848	1.07	2,329	11.4	2,389	11.7	19,480	11.7	44,030	35,300	8,730	10,160	4,908
Florence-Muscle Shoals, AL...	2,560	146,090	0.98	1,476	10.0	1,801	12.2	12,431	10.7	35,485	25,866	9,619	3,636	2,481
Fond du Lac, WI...................	3,543	96,463	0.89	1,030	10.0	916	8.9	4,506	5.5	21,291	10,488	10,803	1,561	1,533
Fort Collins, CO...................	9,369	337,852	0.97	3,395	9.7	2,261	6.5	21,174	7.4	59,706	41,244	18,462	8,236	2,419
Fort Smith, AR-OK................	4,891	281,266	0.99	3,528	12.5	3,170	11.2	33,548	14.5	59,585	42,627	16,958	11,019	3,942
Fort Wayne, IN.....................	7,018	439,868	1.03	5,819	13.3	3,690	8.4	34,784	9.5	77,537	40,494	37,043	12,410	2,876
Fresno, CA...........................	16,963	989,828	1.00	14,814	14.9	7,242	7.3	73,987	8.7	138,674	94,236	44,438	37,858	3,876
Gadsden, AL.........................	2,086	99,050	0.90	1,175	11.5	1,473	14.4	10,219	12.5	25,656	15,386	10,270	4,432	4,322
Gainesville, FL.....................	15,678	296,902	1.09	3,007	10.4	2,204	7.6	27,850	12.1	46,845	35,456	11,389	9,581	3,418
Gainesville, GA.....................	2,756	203,054	1.04	2,566	12.7	1,592	7.9	36,296	21.7	34,879	22,525	12,354	5,538	2,823
Gettysburg, PA.....................	4,039	D	D	906	8.8	1,001	9.7	5,938	7.5	23,880	16,665	7,215	983	962
Glens Falls, NY	3,709	120,536	0.91	1,104	8.8	1,342	10.7	5,257	5.4	30,988	17,414	13,574	1,772	1,410
Goldsboro, NC......................	2,306	120,807	0.94	1,578	12.8	1,405	11.4	15,078	15.0	23,471	17,817	5,654	4,435	3,565
Grand Forks, ND-MN	4,779	104,304	1.04	1,419	13.9	831	8.1	6,067	7.3	16,802	11,511	5,291	2,794	2,752
Grand Island, NE..................	1,416	86,856	1.02	1,208	14.2	764	9.0	8,493	12.1	15,578	14,620	958	2,218	2,593
Grand Junction, CO..............	4,660	150,754	0.99	1,695	11.1	1,474	9.6	11,396	9.5	33,200	22,605	10,595	5,092	3,421
Grand Rapids-Wyoming, MI...	24,268	1,083,172	1.04	13,456	12.6	7,904	7.4	53,608	6.0	181,260	81,965	99,295	20,473	1,953
Grants Pass, OR	1,628	83,651	0.91	891	10.2	1,157	13.2	5,324	8.5	26,096	15,736	10,360	2,607	3,044
Great Falls, MT.....................	2,488	D	D	1,067	13.1	843	10.3	6,557	10.1	17,500	13,061	4,439	3,338	4,047
Greeley, CO..........................	4,949	272,106	0.79	4,427	14.1	1,840	5.9	24,729	9.4	42,137	27,254	14,883	6,647	2,279
Green Bay, WI	6,920	329,761	1.06	3,844	12.0	2,473	7.7	18,637	7.0	59,315	27,510	31,805	5,299	1,666
Greensboro-High Point, NC ...	21,499	786,645	1.07	8,561	11.2	7,294	9.5	78,271	12.6	146,116	65,864	80,252	NA	NA
Greenville, NC......................	6,710	181,802	1.03	1,998	11.1	1,424	7.9	16,127	10.8	28,991	22,420	6,571	NA	NA
Greenville-Anderson-Mauldin, SC	23,311	893,889	1.00	10,506	11.6	8,609	9.5	96,654	13.2	179,847	116,766	63,081	NA	NA
Gulfport-Biloxi-Pascagoula, MS	7,184	396,223	1.01	4,738	11.9	3,829	9.6	49,326	15.1	75,320	56,172	19,148	NA	NA
Hagerstown-Martinsburg, MD-WV.......................	9,209	247,182	0.85	3,001	11.2	2,587	9.7	14,481	6.7	51,605	43,507	8,098	6,206	2,371
Hammond, LA........................	3,643	122,082	0.82	1,933	14.4	1,363	10.2	11,175	10.1	22,480	14,216	8,264	6,824	5,257
Hanford-Corcoran, CA...........	16,066	149,904	1.00	2,225	14.7	900	5.9	10,715	9.0	16,975	13,923	3,052	3,806	2,543
Harrisburg-Carlisle, PA..........	19,701	620,366	1.17	6,513	11.3	5,322	9.3	30,818	6.7	116,277	64,322	51,955	9,824	1,735
Harrisonburg, VA..................	9,317	144,701	1.16	1,509	11.2	1,022	7.6	16,422	15.6	22,734	19,647	3,087	2,008	1,526
Hartford-West Hartford-East Hartford, CT	45,688	1,245,539	1.06	11,638	9.6	10,912	9.0	49,065	5.1	231,620	129,228	102,392	24,996	2,451
Hattiesburg, MS....................	3,347	147,802	1.02	1,864	12.5	1,301	8.7	18,196	14.5	25,169	19,847	5,322	4,366	2,919
Hickory-Lenoir-Morganton, NC	8,338	360,858	0.97	3,673	10.0	4,056	11.0	40,191	13.7	82,609	50,691	31,918	NA	NA
Hilton Head Island-Bluffton-Beaufort, NC	6,769	215,626	1.00	2,256	10.4	1,954	9.0	24,694	16.1	55,177	43,564	11,613	5,302	2,501
Hinesville, GA.......................	2,208	78,856	0.94	1,639	20.4	453	5.6	9,282	13.1	8,649	6,014	2,635	2,194	2,716
Homosassa Springs, FL........	2,250	139,263	0.87	1,072	7.2	2,599	17.6	14,181	15.4	57,065	35,221	21,844	2,317	1,640
Hot Springs, AR....................	2,167	100,662	1.05	1,070	10.8	1,354	13.7	7,267	9.8	28,329	20,970	7,359	5,239	5,384
Houma-Thibodaux, LA...........	3,105	210,160	1.00	2,663	12.7	2,005	9.6	21,220	12.0	38,394	28,340	10,054	7,647	3,600
Houston-The Woodlands-Sugar Land, TX...........	82,107	6,916,202	1.01	99,013	14.2	42,894	6.1	1,209,876	20.0	831,596	463,858	367,738	237,756	3,502
Huntington-Ashland, WV-KY-OH..............................	7,726	351,902	0.97	3,537	10.0	4,444	12.6	19,775	7.0	84,808	58,360	26,448	1,048	292
Huntsville, AL.......................	11,016	472,515	1.08	5,144	11.1	4,049	8.8	37,050	9.8	81,487	57,974	23,513	16,841	3,751
Idaho Falls, ID	1,371	149,528	1.06	2,406	16.2	1,025	6.9	12,781	10.1	22,762	D	D	2,651	1,869
Indianapolis-Carmel-Ander-son, IN............................	38,693	2,047,351	1.02	26,271	12.8	16,497	8.1	160,181	9.3	328,811	220,259	108,552	78,593	3,920
Iowa City, IA.........................	8,815	172,793	1.01	2,086	12.0	944	5.4	7,972	5.6	24,495	20,527	3,968	3,414	2,019
Ithaca, NY............................	13,094	117,540	1.26	769	7.5	630	6.1	4,160	5.3	16,429	11,833	4,596	NA	NA
Jackson, MI..........................	8,665	150,769	0.89	1,737	10.9	1,628	10.3	7,041	5.7	33,884	24,070	9,814	4,377	2,748
Jackson, MS.........................	24,460	586,940	1.03	6,866	11.8	5,367	9.3	60,937	12.7	102,977	76,276	26,701	NA	NA
Jackson, TN	5,709	138,534	1.17	1,513	11.7	1,372	10.6	10,672	10.4	27,153	20,030	7,123	4,782	3,690
Jacksonville, FL....................	28,373	1,517,124	1.02	18,533	12.1	13,738	9.0	156,514	12.5	278,188	184,240	93,948	49,711	3,373
Jacksonville, NC...................	21,384	194,057	1.00	3,909	19.8	1,087	5.5	13,652	8.8	24,325	20,518	3,807	NA	NA
Janesville-Beloit, WI..............	2,694	152,766	0.87	1,945	11.9	1,462	9.0	9,577	7.2	32,385	20,556	11,829	3,940	2,441
Jefferson City, MO................	10,383	152,271	1.07	1,716	11.3	1,386	9.1	12,681	10.8	28,967	23,724	5,243	3,300	2,183
Johnson City, TN	5,849	201,185	0.97	1,868	9.2	2,397	11.8	18,298	11.5	48,923	24,547	24,376	5,247	2,611
Johnstown, PA......................	5,980	129,740	0.94	1,291	9.8	1,751	13.3	5,334	5.4	36,046	13,534	22,512	2,062	1,531

1. Per 1,000 estimated resident population.   2. Data for serious crimes have not been adjusted for underreporting; this may affect comparability between geographic areas and over time.   3. Per 100,000 population estimated by the FBI.

Area name	Serious crimes known to police[2], 2016 (cont.) Rate Violent	Property	Education — School enrollment and attainment, 2016 — Enrollment[3] Total	Percent private	Attainment[4] High school graduate or less	Bachelor's degree or more	Local government expenditures,[5] 2014-2015 Total current expenditures (mil dol)	Current expenditures per student (dollars)	Income and poverty, 2017 Per capita income[6] (dollars)	Mean household income (dollars)	Median household income	Percent of households with income less than $50,000	Percent of households with income of $200,000 or more	Percent below poverty level All persons	Children under 18 years	Age 65 years and older
	46	47	48	49	50	51	52	53	54	55	56	57	58	59	60	61
Evansville, IN-KY	362	2,737	73,738	21.2	39.4	27.3	449.0	10,119	29,637	71,523	51,964	47.9	4.7	15.0	19.4	11.1
Fairbanks, AK	NA	NA	27,354	18.4	30.0	29.6	297.7	19,439	34,883	93,422	76,747	31.9	6.8	6.0	4.9	4.5
Fargo, ND-MN	270	2,472	66,826	10.1	23.8	39.8	377.9	11,558	33,806	81,787	63,353	37.8	6.5	9.7	8.0	4.2
Farmington, NM	947	2,734	35,083	9.1	47.9	14	244.5	9,975	20,719	58,947	45,942	52.9	2.1	24.8	32.7	14.8
Fayetteville, NC	524	3,480	107,183	17.3	37.5	23.6	502.0	8,212	22,856	57,324	44,757	55.4	1.8	18.2	24.6	9.5
Fayetteville-Springdale-Rogers, AR-MO	NA	NA	142,164	11.9	42.3	31.8	832.3	9,364	29,158	78,173	56,038	44.3	5.3	12.1	15.0	7.1
Flagstaff, AZ	365	2,991	46,981	5.6	31.9	37.3	171.8	9,069	26,436	74,035	54,893	47.2	6.0	19.0	20.7	9.5
Flint, MI	628	2,227	98,686	10.4	40.3	20.9	742.4	11,028	26,181	63,052	46,298	53.7	3.0	18.3	26.2	10.9
Florence, SC	641	4,268	48,890	14.2	48.7	24.1	337.9	9,878	23,419	57,430	40,562	58.2	1.9	19.3	29.1	11.5
Florence-Muscle Shoals, AL	293	2,189	34,638	9.7	48.3	22.2	200.4	9,439	25,351	59,651	45,903	52.9	2.3	13.7	16.8	8.3
Fond du Lac, WI	181	1,352	23,923	19.8	42.8	24.7	144.9	10,813	31,118	75,054	61,417	39.6	2.9	8.1	12.3	7.1
Fort Collins, CO	209	2,210	93,442	9.7	24.1	47.9	429.9	9,283	35,923	89,304	69,102	38.0	7.2	11.4	9.0	7.0
Fort Smith, AR-OK	498	3,444	66,840	6.5	51.3	18.1	438.2	8,840	22,430	56,307	46,082	57.2	1.9	20.6	33.7	11.6
Fort Wayne, IN	299	2,577	110,620	24.6	40.6	25.7	602.0	9,500	27,067	67,732	52,908	45.6	3.3	12.3	18.3	7.3
Fresno, CA	613	3,263	292,068	7.8	46.8	20.4	2,127.9	10,858	23,670	73,235	51,800	48.4	4.8	21.1	28.5	12.0
Gadsden, AL	712	3,610	22,726	7.6	49.2	19.3	135.8	8,502	22,866	57,242	41,576	56.1	2.0	18.2	32.0	9.0
Gainesville, FL	540	2,878	98,136	9.5	33.3	38.7	281.9	8,685	26,830	65,397	44,548	54.2	5.0	21.2	18.6	11.0
Gainesville, GA	261	2,562	49,821	10.4	49.5	26.3	312.5	8,904	30,494	89,711	61,977	39.7	7.4	13.1	22.6	5.1
Gettysburg, PA	163	800	22,867	28.0	51.4	22.9	275.7	19,820	30,301	76,008	63,107	39.3	3.8	7.6	10.2	4.9
Glens Falls, NY	165	1,245	24,618	10.9	45.7	25.5	334.2	18,482	30,380	72,738	58,723	43.4	3.4	9.0	11.7	6.3
Goldsboro, NC	439	3,126	30,383	16.7	46.8	20.3	160.6	8,104	25,450	64,283	44,347	55.4	2.3	21.2	34.3	9.1
Grand Forks, ND-MN	240	2,511	29,215	5.8	30.0	33.9	167.9	12,128	29,727	68,203	48,609	51.9	4.1	15.5	13.0	14.9
Grand Island, NE	286	2,306	20,478	9.2	43.6	23	190.8	11,981	29,132	76,901	60,116	41.9	4.1	10.3	16.9	5.7
Grand Junction, CO	349	3,072	37,210	10.1	36.2	25.8	185.2	8,286	28,431	68,315	52,742	47.5	2.7	16.2	20.3	8.5
Grand Rapids-Wyoming, MI	337	1,616	277,603	19.2	35.4	33.7	1,873.8	11,010	30,224	79,512	61,298	40.1	4.5	10.0	13.1	6.0
Grants Pass, OR	222	2,822	16,056	15.8	39.7	18.9	107.8	10,022	25,828	60,929	44,426	54.2	2.9	17.4	24.3	10.1
Great Falls, MT	229	3,818	17,976	17.0	43.6	26.3	114.8	9,779	30,181	69,810	47,713	51.8	3.9	10.3	11.1	8.0
Greeley, CO	258	2,021	82,656	9.3	39.7	27.5	363.2	8,853	29,503	83,706	68,884	36.3	5.2	9.0	8.8	10.2
Green Bay, WI	214	1,452	76,965	16.9	39.5	30.4	559.8	10,775	31,769	77,677	60,456	41.7	4.4	9.4	12.7	7.6
Greensboro-High Point, NC	NA	NA	189,683	14.9	38.8	29.5	1,017.0	8,861	27,490	68,047	50,285	49.6	3.6	15.1	20.8	9.3
Greenville, NC	NA	NA	62,014	5.8	30.3	34.6	202.3	8,325	26,301	66,154	45,849	52.8	3.8	22.0	33.1	7.0
Greenville-Anderson-Mauldin, SC	NA	NA	219,684	18.4	40.9	28.6	1,163.3	8,724	28,361	72,038	51,154	48.7	4.0	14.2	19.2	9.6
Gulfport-Biloxi-Pascagoula, MS	NA	NA	94,669	13.5	40.6	23.4	545.5	8,691	24,795	62,115	47,099	53.0	2.6	17.1	26.5	9.6
Hagerstown-Martinsburg, MD-WV	248	2,122	60,870	14.1	46.7	23	491.0	11,978	28,068	73,082	59,801	42.0	3.3	13.4	20.0	7.1
Hammond, LA	916	4,341	33,320	13.5	56.9	19.1	187.3	9,396	23,410	59,624	44,861	54.4	2.3	20.7	32.8	10.4
Hanford-Corcoran, CA	427	2,116	42,218	15.5	51.3	13.2	288.9	11,145	20,825	68,727	57,555	44.7	2.4	18.2	26.8	11.5
Harrisburg-Carlisle, PA	255	1,479	127,228	18.7	43.5	31.8	1,035.0	13,502	33,090	81,898	65,069	36.9	4.6	9.6	13.9	5.9
Harrisonburg, VA	163	1,363	42,129	20.1	51.6	29	190.0	10,852	26,343	70,235	54,681	46.2	2.6	13.7	12.1	5.0
Hartford-West Hartford-East Hartford, CT	238	2,213	303,902	15.8	36.7	38.3	3,193.0	17,306	38,551	96,260	71,414	35.4	9.1	10.0	13.2	7.7
Hattiesburg, MS	199	2,720	43,882	10.7	38.8	30.5	210.5	8,773	23,334	58,961	46,167	54.6	2.0	21.6	23.9	13.1
Hickory-Lenoir-Morganton, NC	NA	NA	78,427	14.0	49.9	17.9	465.2	8,425	25,996	65,388	48,079	51.7	3.8	14.3	18.7	11.4
Hilton Head Island-Bluffton-Beaufort, NC	315	2,186	43,011	17.7	33.9	37.8	265.6	10,955	33,321	83,477	55,430	45.3	6.7	10.9	18.9	4.1
Hinesville, GA	426	2,290	20,460	10.2	36.5	21.9	124.0	9,298	23,009	60,541	49,364	50.7	0.7	19.1	28.9	6.4
Homosassa Springs, FL	239	1,401	21,667	15.9	50.6	16.8	132.2	8,740	25,074	55,172	43,548	57.8	2.1	13.6	26.1	7.0
Hot Springs, AR	652	4,732	22,966	4.9	42.3	19.5	148.3	9,801	25,876	62,006	46,101	56.1	2.7	15.1	23.2	5.9
Houma-Thibodaux, LA	449	3,151	50,496	21.1	62.3	16	334.1	10,027	24,419	64,256	47,069	51.9	4.1	18.0	22.2	10.9
Houston-The Woodlands-Sugar Land, TX	578	2,924	1,893,312	11.4	39.7	32.4	10,961.8	8,532	32,441	92,532	63,802	38.9	9.0	13.9	20.2	9.9
Huntington-Ashland, WV-KY-OH	292	D	82,360	8.3	52.8	18.9	622.3	10,818	23,899	58,619	40,646	56.6	3.0	20.9	28.2	10.5
Huntsville, AL	557	3,194	119,697	17.4	31.5	38.8	618.5	9,470	33,018	81,282	61,331	42.0	5.9	13.2	20.0	7.9
Idaho Falls, ID	300	1,569	43,299	9.9	32.4	29.6	174.8	5,694	24,152	67,794	54,515	45.1	1.6	8.8	11.7	4.4
Indianapolis-Carmel-Anderson, IN	713	3,207	506,069	17.5	37.8	35.6	3,202.9	9,521	32,086	81,056	59,566	42.1	6.1	11.9	16.7	6.6
Iowa City, IA	292	1,728	60,858	8.4	22.6	51.5	220.2	10,426	31,774	78,361	60,888	40.8	5.6	15.7	9.7	2.0
Ithaca, NY	NA	NA	39,884	44.8	25.0	52.2	225.0	20,066	30,545	77,758	56,672	44.5	7.7	20.5	15.9	7.0
Jackson, MI	533	2,215	37,665	13.4	41.1	22.2	277.3	11,984	28,186	70,530	50,258	49.7	2.5	13.2	22.8	4.6
Jackson, MS	NA	NA	157,368	20.1	38.0	30.5	780.1	8,444	26,655	70,461	52,434	47.2	3.7	15.4	21.8	10.6
Jackson, TN	650	3,039	33,041	28.9	51.6	23.4	156.1	8,197	24,106	61,474	43,570	55.3	2.9	17.8	24.4	9.0
Jacksonville, FL	479	2,894	358,934	18.7	37.9	30.7	1,840.0	8,499	31,303	79,596	58,709	43.1	4.9	13.3	19.0	9.3
Jacksonville, NC	NA	NA	49,391	14.1	36.8	22.3	207.1	7,982	23,335	61,862	49,883	50.2	1.8	12.9	15.6	14.0
Janesville-Beloit, WI	229	2,212	39,444	12.3	46.0	21.4	305.7	10,916	27,042	66,216	55,304	44.1	2.0	12.5	18.7	5.7
Jefferson City, MO	294	1,889	32,188	27.1	47.3	25.8	182.4	8,234	26,847	69,782	52,579	46.4	2.8	12.8	21.3	5.7
Johnson City, TN	291	2,320	46,003	12.7	45.2	26.7	234.6	8,597	25,778	60,060	40,663	58.2	3.3	17.0	21.9	10.3
Johnstown, PA	159	1,372	27,940	21.1	53.8	21.3	227.5	12,743	25,167	58,753	46,598	52.6	1.9	15.1	27.2	8.4

1. Data for serious crimes have not been adjusted for underreporting; this may affect comparability between geographic areas and over time.   2. Per 100,000 population estimated by the FBI.   3. All persons 3 years old and over enrolled in nursery school through college.   4. Persons 25 years old and over.   5. Elementary and secondary education expenditures.   6. Based on population estimated by the American Community Survey, 2015.

Table C. Metropolitan Areas — **Personal Income and Earnings**

| | Personal income, 2017 | | | | | | | | | | Earnings, 2017 | | |
Area name	Total (mil dol)	Percent change, 2016-2017	Per capita[1] Dollars	Per capita Rank	Wages and Salaries (mil dol)	Supplements to wages and salaries, employer contributions (mil dol) Pension and insurance	Government social insurance	Proprietors' income	Dividends, interest, and rent (mil dol)	Personal transfer receipts (mil dol)	Total (mil dol)	Contributions for government social insurance (mil dol) From employee and self-employed	From employer
	62	63	64	65	66	67	68	69	70	71	72	73	74
Evansville, IN-KY..................	14,286	3.9	45,256	158	7,453	1,246	549	927	2,446	2,981	10,176	627	549
Fairbanks, AK......................	5,434	2.2	54,497	52	2,636	749	213	246	1,054	865	3,843	185	213
Fargo, ND-MN	12,243	1.7	50,725	80	6,888	1,061	576	935	2,661	1,562	9,459	568	576
Farmington, NM....................	4,284	1.4	33,751	376	2,318	436	181	110	651	1,042	3,044	199	181
Fayetteville, NC...................	14,063	3.7	36,369	356	9,173	2,174	808	509	3,032	3,737	12,664	662	808
Fayetteville-Springdale-Rogers, AR-MO...........	31,939	5.4	59,425	26	13,470	1,715	931	1,169	13,415	3,594	17,285	1,097	931
Flagstaff, AZ	6,513	5.0	46,266	139	2,872	591	213	494	1,481	1,160	4,170	246	213
Flint, MI...............................	16,147	2.7	39,636	292	6,539	1,151	497	795	2,451	4,753	8,982	614	497
Florence, SC	8,005	3.9	38,892	306	4,127	711	308	362	1,271	2,166	5,508	364	308
Florence-Muscle Shoals, AL...	5,422	3.3	36,876	349	2,237	419	168	298	1,012	1,470	3,122	223	168
Fond du Lac, WI	4,692	3.9	45,753	150	2,263	426	178	342	783	866	3,210	200	178
Fort Collins, CO..................	17,384	6.3	50,539	82	8,538	1,210	588	1,202	4,084	2,280	11,538	636	588
Fort Smith, AR-OK.............	10,146	3.4	35,968	361	4,588	732	352	912	1,574	2,760	6,583	432	352
Fort Wayne, IN	19,177	4.3	44,124	179	10,171	1,707	752	1,513	3,258	3,631	14,143	851	752
Fresno, CA..........................	41,024	4.1	41,470	245	17,888	3,928	1,327	4,207	7,368	9,380	27,350	1,462	1,327
Gadsden, AL........................	3,706	3.7	36,069	360	1,412	249	105	234	560	1,156	1,999	147	105
Gainesville, FL.....................	11,877	4.6	41,718	238	6,677	1,243	459	415	2,617	2,267	8,794	521	459
Gainesville, GA.....................	8,216	4.9	41,219	253	4,378	709	282	682	1,399	1,468	6,051	360	282
Gettysburg, PA	4,817	4.7	47,067	130	1,485	287	126	379	861	915	2,277	144	126
Glens Falls, NY	5,661	5.1	44,894	164	2,435	544	208	415	950	1,366	3,602	213	208
Goldsboro, NC......................	4,610	4.0	37,126	343	1,954	391	154	301	824	1,217	2,798	170	154
Grand Forks, ND-MN	4,934	2.6	48,176	109	2,531	472	220	360	1,007	821	3,582	211	220
Grand Island, NE..................	3,673	3.7	43,187	205	1,844	328	138	363	736	661	2,673	160	138
Grand Junction, CO..............	6,293	5.2	41,503	243	2,835	415	218	471	1,271	1,308	3,939	240	218
Grand Rapids-Wyoming, MI ...	51,538	3.8	48,661	105	27,646	4,562	2,049	3,859	11,366	7,717	38,115	2,294	2,049
Grants Pass, OR	3,359	4.4	38,896	304	1,033	182	97	363	669	1,143	1,675	130	97
Great Falls, MT.....................	3,753	4.1	45,959	146	1,723	300	147	238	840	806	2,409	156	147
Greeley, CO.........................	13,428	4.3	44,080	181	5,539	765	415	1,519	1,933	1,876	8,238	442	415
Green Bay, WI	15,584	3.7	48,692	104	8,873	1,597	661	1,200	2,846	2,335	12,332	742	661
Greensboro-High Point, NC ...	32,241	4.6	42,356	228	17,612	2,575	1,285	2,444	5,945	6,663	23,916	1,526	1,285
Greenville, NC	7,144	4.4	39,900	283	3,674	696	263	443	1,331	1,497	5,076	308	263
Greenville-Anderson-Mauldin, SC	37,747	4.4	42,132	232	19,730	3,030	1,478	2,465	6,118	7,801	26,703	1,720	1,478
Gulfport-Biloxi-Pascagoula, MS..............	14,261	2.4	36,175	359	7,459	1,396	583	772	2,805	3,424	10,210	672	583
Hagerstown-Martinsburg, MD-WV..............	11,408	3.9	42,969	211	4,631	865	366	761	1,703	2,307	6,623	420	366
Hammond, LA........................	5,010	4.2	37,814	331	1,753	396	106	298	619	1,454	2,553	139	106
Hanford-Corcoran, CA...........	5,303	5.8	35,326	367	2,416	678	184	403	985	1,127	3,681	170	184
Harrisburg-Carlisle, PA..........	28,324	3.9	49,525	93	18,105	3,524	1,436	2,197	4,749	5,206	25,262	1,458	1,436
Harrisonburg, VA	5,115	5.0	38,045	325	2,810	499	203	532	994	899	4,044	240	203
Hartford-West Hartford-East Hartford, CT	74,253	2.5	61,353	18	42,371	6,801	3,005	7,115	12,307	11,321	59,292	3,223	3,005
Hattiesburg, MS....................	5,648	2.5	37,938	329	2,617	436	192	508	1,025	1,286	3,752	250	192
Hickory-Lenoir-Morganton, NC................	14,067	5.5	38,379	318	6,599	1,083	496	908	2,398	3,542	9,086	610	496
Hilton Head Island-Bluffton-Beaufort, NC	10,649	4.1	49,459	95	3,774	645	302	754	3,677	2,088	5,475	361	302
Hinesville, GA.......................	2,607	2.9	32,425	379	1,818	516	165	37	514	605	2,537	114	165
Homosassa Springs, FL.........	5,444	4.4	37,379	337	1,341	213	93	300	1,349	2,120	1,947	192	93
Hot Springs, AR....................	3,775	4.3	38,259	320	1,477	214	113	283	731	1,189	2,087	157	113
Houma-Thibodaux, LA...........	8,716	1.1	41,405	246	4,423	766	283	626	1,689	1,927	6,099	350	283
Houston-The Woodlands-Sugar Land, TX...........	363,677	4.4	52,765	63	200,503	26,218	13,341	53,035	58,419	44,113	293,096	15,266	13,341
Huntington-Ashland, WV-KY-OH......................	13,420	2.2	37,646	333	5,980	1,059	491	582	1,847	3,938	8,111	569	491
Huntsville, AL........................	21,738	4.7	47,729	114	13,405	2,265	1,004	1,075	4,114	3,532	17,749	1,084	1,004
Idaho Falls, ID	6,264	5.6	43,006	210	3,023	435	258	874	1,429	1,009	4,590	279	258
Indianapolis-Carmel-Anderson, IN.........................	106,415	4.5	52,457	65	56,572	8,657	4,057	14,814	16,101	15,690	84,100	4,792	4,057
Iowa City, IA........................	8,603	4.0	50,164	83	4,681	1,186	351	646	1,943	976	6,864	381	351
Ithaca, NY...........................	4,441	4.9	42,373	226	2,823	482	230	340	903	725	3,875	210	230
Jackson, MI..........................	6,039	2.4	38,069	324	2,843	553	213	319	954	1,571	3,929	257	213
Jackson, MS.........................	24,969	1.7	43,145	208	12,668	2,013	923	2,066	4,700	5,121	17,671	1,162	923
Jackson, TN	5,128	3.3	39,681	289	2,909	540	205	469	764	1,284	4,122	252	205
Jacksonville, FL....................	71,707	5.7	47,647	116	37,547	5,295	2,619	3,499	15,336	13,090	48,959	3,051	2,619
Jacksonville, NC...................	8,720	-1.3	44,972	161	4,488	1,178	424	353	1,708	1,516	6,443	296	424
Janesville-Beloit, WI..............	6,821	3.5	42,026	234	3,202	609	247	309	1,237	1,396	4,368	282	247
Jefferson City, MO................	6,228	3.5	41,121	257	3,386	724	231	442	1,090	1,230	4,784	273	231
Johnson City, TN	7,914	3.8	39,168	301	3,336	655	238	693	1,222	2,099	4,922	319	238
Johnstown, PA......................	5,453	2.0	40,985	260	2,091	459	178	272	844	1,725	3,000	206	178

1. Based on the resident population estimated as of July 1 of the year shown.

Table C. Metropolitan Areas — Earnings, Social Security, and Housing

Area name	Earnings, 2017 (cont.) Percent by selected industries									Social Security beneficiaries, December 2017		Supplemental Security Income Recipients, December 2017	Housing units, 2018	
	Farm	Mining, quarrying, and extracting	Construction	Manufacturing	Information; professional, scientific, and technical serviecs	Retail trade	Finance, insurance, real estate, rental and leasing	Health care and social assistance	Government	Number	Rate[1]		Total	Percent change, 2010-2018
	75	76	77	78	79	80	81	82	83	84	85	86	87	88
Evansville, IN-KY	0.6	0.4	7.3	20.2	D	6.2	4.8	18.3	9.3	69,875	221	7,208	143,102	3.2
Fairbanks, AK	0.1	3.0	7.9	1.1	4.2	5.5	3.1	10.6	48.7	11,215	112	1,124	44,300	6.0
Fargo, ND-MN	-0.1	D	8.8	7.1	10.0	6.8	11.6	14.9	14.1	34,370	142	3,229	110,698	20.5
Farmington, NM	-0.6	18.6	8.4	2.4	D	8.4	3.3	14.0	22.7	22,745	179	4,020	51,276	3.9
Fayetteville, NC	0.4	D	3.6	4.6	D	4.6	2.4	5.7	61.9	65,290	169	11,745	168,276	9.5
Fayetteville-Springdale-Rogers, AR-MO	1.3	D	6.1	9.5	D	5.6	2.0	8.8	11.6	89,645	167	9,037	221,051	11.5
Flagstaff, AZ	0.2	D	4.0	10.1	4.9	6.8	4.1	15.1	31.1	20,370	145	2,493	66,840	5.6
Flint, MI	0.1	0.0	5.9	11.2	7.4	8.5	6.2	18.8	16.4	99,615	245	16,841	192,637	0.2
Florence, SC	-0.1	0.0	4.3	15.9	6.1	7.0	10.1	12.8	18.7	48,730	237	8,583	91,996	3.4
Florence-Muscle Shoals, AL	0.2	D	7.9	19.6	3.9	9.2	4.7	12.5	19.9	39,335	268	4,575	72,194	3.8
Fond du Lac, WI	2.5	0.4	9.2	24.5	4.4	6.3	4.8	13.3	12.0	22,480	219	1,609	45,361	3.3
Fort Collins, CO	0.5	0.7	9.3	13.0	12.7	6.4	5.9	8.2	21.4	56,480	164	2,580	151,848	14.4
Fort Smith, AR-OK	2.0	1.8	4.8	16.0	4.1	6.7	7.1	14.2	16.0	66,710	236	10,118	125,704	4.0
Fort Wayne, IN	0.2	D	7.2	19.1	D	6.5	8.2	18.7	9.3	84,095	193	8,867	186,086	4.5
Fresno, CA	6.7	0.2	5.8	6.2	5.6	6.5	5.5	14.3	22.3	138,195	140	43,836	333,769	5.8
Gadsden, AL	0.6	D	5.5	15.8	3.7	8.3	5.4	D	15.0	28,885	281	4,557	47,846	0.8
Gainesville, FL	0.8	D	3.8	3.6	8.0	5.6	6.2	17.8	36.8	48,640	171	7,047	126,546	5.4
Gainesville, GA	0.4	D	6.1	19.9	4.5	5.7	6.6	16.4	11.2	36,550	183	3,096	74,423	8.1
Gettysburg, PA	2.8	1.0	9.1	19.7	3.9	6.0	3.5	D	14.7	24,460	239	1,131	42,563	4.3
Glens Falls, NY	1.1	0.7	7.8	13.4	6.6	8.3	4.8	D	21.3	33,630	267	3,164	69,791	3.3
Goldsboro, NC	4.8	D	4.6	11.4	2.9	7.0	4.5	12.1	32.7	26,070	210	4,236	54,474	2.8
Grand Forks, ND-MN	1.0	0.4	8.2	7.8	5.0	8.0	6.1	D	26.8	17,420	170	1,335	48,429	10.2
Grand Island, NE	5.0	0.1	7.5	18.5	D	7.9	6.1	10.3	16.6	16,280	191	1,194	36,169	5.9
Grand Junction, CO	0.4	6.5	11.0	4.1	5.5	7.6	7.6	16.8	16.6	32,865	217	2,590	67,215	7.3
Grand Rapids-Wyoming, MI	0.4	D	6.5	24.3	D	5.5	7.3	D	9.4	193,185	182	19,042	424,687	5.0
Grants Pass, OR	0.3	D	6.9	10.1	4.5	12.2	7.4	19.5	14.0	27,485	318	2,876	39,352	3.5
Great Falls, MT	0.4	0.0	7.9	3.5	6.0	8.2	7.7	17.4	27.2	18,455	226	1,849	39,036	4.7
Greeley, CO	5.2	9.1	14.3	11.2	4.3	5.8	5.7	7.3	11.6	42,050	138	3,306	112,465	16.8
Green Bay, WI	1.8	0.1	6.0	16.8	D	5.1	9.7	D	12.3	63,515	198	5,563	144,181	5.1
Greensboro-High Point, NC	0.5	D	6.0	17.0	8.1	6.1	9.4	11.5	11.5	156,500	206	18,269	337,407	4.5
Greenville, NC	1.0	D	5.4	10.3	5.0	6.2	5.5	10.8	37.2	30,610	171	5,804	80,265	7.0
Greenville-Anderson-Mauldin, SC	0.0	0.1	6.5	16.9	D	6.4	7.5	D	15.3	193,315	216	18,223	389,705	7.6
Gulfport-Biloxi-Pascagoula, MS	-0.1	0.1	6.0	16.6	6.7	6.0	3.6	7.7	29.5	83,335	211	11,016	182,556	9.2
Hagerstown-Martinsburg, MD-WV	0.3	0.1	5.5	9.3	6.7	8.5	9.5	14.2	20.2	54,850	207	6,033	111,063	5.2
Hammond, LA	0.2	0.4	5.0	5.1	6.4	11.5	5.6	10.4	28.9	23,970	181	5,150	56,361	12.6
Hanford-Corcoran, CA	10.4	D	2.3	8.4	1.9	4.8	2.1	9.4	45.4	18,145	121	4,658	46,645	6.3
Harrisburg-Carlisle, PA	0.3	0.0	4.4	6.8	10.1	4.5	8.7	14.1	20.2	119,825	210	11,329	252,645	4.9
Harrisonburg, VA	3.7	D	7.4	15.8	6.7	6.2	4.8	12.0	17.9	23,780	177	1,872	54,165	6.0
Hartford-West Hartford-East Hartford, CT	0.1	D	D	D	11.3	4.7	18.7	11.9	15.2	234,635	194	24,310	517,040	2.0
Hattiesburg, MS	0.3	0.4	6.4	7.8	D	8.6	D	18.3	23.3	28,395	191	4,679	63,656	2.9
Hickory-Lenoir-Morganton, NC	1.3	0.1	4.0	27.3	D	7.1	3.5	11.0	14.8	90,590	247	7,613	165,150	1.5
Hilton Head Island-Bluffton-Beaufort, NC	0.2	0.0	8.3	1.3	D	8.5	7.6	8.9	28.5	55,125	256	2,622	113,319	9.7
Hinesville, GA	0.2	D	D	D	D	D	D	D	74.7	10,085	125	1,525	35,570	8.5
Homosassa Springs, FL	0.1	0.2	12.1	1.6	6.4	11.4	4.8	21.8	12.8	60,020	412	3,441	79,988	2.5
Hot Springs, AR	0.3	0.3	10.2	6.9	4.7	10.5	6.0	22.0	13.3	30,465	309	3,994	51,026	1.0
Houma-Thibodaux, LA	0.3	10.1	7.1	9.1	6.0	5.8	4.7	10.5	13.2	42,110	200	7,918	87,333	5.9
Houston-The Woodlands-Sugar Land, TX	0.0	6.3	9.0	8.7	12.5	4.8	7.7	7.7	10.6	841,630	122	142,722	2,637,765	14.9
Huntington-Ashland, WV-KY-OH	-0.1	-0.6	8.5	D	6.0	7.3	4.4	D	17.3	89,630	251	16,498	165,282	0.5
Huntsville, AL	0.2	0.0	4.3	12.2	24.0	5.3	3.5	7.1	28.5	85,200	187	8,913	200,801	10.7
Idaho Falls, ID	1.8	D	D	D	20.0	13.7	D	11.8	10.1	24,435	168	2,691	54,717	9.9
Indianapolis-Carmel-Anderson, IN	0.1	0.1	5.9	10.8	D	6.2	15.9	D	10.8	352,050	174	37,359	867,936	6.3
Iowa City, IA	0.9	0.1	5.6	6.4	4.4	5.3	4.8	7.5	44.4	24,325	142	2,049	74,816	14.3
Ithaca, NY	0.3	D	D	7.3	11.1	4.6	3.5	D	12.9	16,265	155	1,516	43,879	5.3
Jackson, MI	-0.3	0.1	5.0	19.2	4.6	6.1	4.8	16.0	14.2	37,230	235	4,545	69,685	0.3
Jackson, MS	0.4	1.2	5.2	8.2	D	7.4	7.5	13.8	21.8	112,650	195	20,243	244,500	5.1
Jackson, TN	-1.7	D	D	18.1	D	7.7	4.4	14.0	22.5	29,715	230	4,350	56,956	3.0
Jacksonville, FL	0.1	0.0	6.7	5.4	11.3	6.4	14.0	13.1	14.1	288,425	192	33,351	655,272	9.5
Jacksonville, NC	1.7	D	2.5	0.8	2.2	4.5	2.2	3.1	72.5	27,325	141	3,251	80,259	17.6
Janesville-Beloit, WI	0.4	0.4	6.8	17.2	5.0	6.2	4.1	16.0	14.4	35,625	219	3,945	69,227	1.2
Jefferson City, MO	1.2	D	7.4	9.1	D	5.9	5.5	9.0	32.2	32,470	214	2,528	65,369	2.9
Johnson City, TN	0.0	D	4.6	10.9	D	8.1	6.5	D	21.4	52,705	261	5,864	98,048	4.5
Johnstown, PA	0.3	0.4	4.8	9.0	7.2	7.4	5.2	22.6	17.9	38,635	290	4,787	66,022	0.6

1. Per 1,000 resident population estimated as of July 1 of the year shown.

Table C. Metropolitan Areas — Housing, Labor Force, and Employment

Area name	Housing units, 2017								Civilian labor force, 2018				Civilian employment[5], 2017		
	Occupied units										Unemployment			Percent	
	Owner-occupied					Renter-occupied									
					Median owner cost as a percent of income		Median rent as a percent of income							Management, business, science, and arts	Construction, production, and maintenance occupations
	Total	Percent	Median value[1]	With a mortgage	Without a mortgage[2]	Median rent[3]		Internet access	Total	Percent change 2017-2018	Total	Rate[4]	Total		
	89	90	91	92	93	94	95	96	97	98	99	100	101	102	103
Evansville, IN-KY	130,667	68.9	140,600	18.4	10.9	740	29.5	83.7	164,282	1.4	5,249	3.2	151,314	36.6	25.3
Fairbanks, AK	35,046	59.5	239,000	19.8	10.0	1,210	30.4	87.0	46,101	-0.7	2,675	5.8	43,035	38.3	23.4
Fargo, ND-MN	100,721	58.4	215,600	19.3	10.0	793	26.3	91.0	136,735	-0.6	3,340	2.4	142,377	39.9	18.3
Farmington, NM	41,071	74.0	156,300	20.7	10.0	782	28.8	73.9	52,537	-2.4	3,029	5.8	47,676	30.2	27.3
Fayetteville, NC	143,306	52.1	138,100	21.2	11.4	870	31.9	88.3	147,877	0.1	7,580	5.1	146,480	31.9	23.7
Fayetteville-Springdale-Rogers, AR-MO	194,671	61.0	173,100	18.0	10.0	807	23.7	85.6	274,906	1.4	7,595	2.8	256,913	38.1	24.2
Flagstaff, AZ	47,977	61.3	277,400	20.7	10.0	1,215	32.4	80.0	77,083	2.0	4,233	5.5	66,370	35.7	18.1
Flint, MI	165,719	71.2	110,000	19.4	12.8	730	33.1	81.5	181,781	0.0	8,894	4.9	171,775	32.2	24.3
Florence, SC	79,458	66.3	114,900	18.3	10.4	711	29.0	78.7	96,082	1.0	3,639	3.8	88,125	35.9	22.6
Florence-Muscle Shoals, AL	60,041	67.2	134,600	19.1	10.0	683	26.8	79.5	65,399	0.1	2,840	4.3	63,268	31.9	30.0
Fond du Lac, WI	42,449	69.4	152,100	20.0	10.3	760	22.9	86.4	57,658	0.8	1,519	2.6	54,580	29.0	30.6
Fort Collins, CO	134,709	66.6	359,800	20.7	10.0	1,233	35.4	93.0	202,449	3.6	5,695	2.8	178,403	45.2	18.6
Fort Smith, AR-OK	108,133	66.0	114,800	18.5	10.7	627	28.9	78.6	119,462	-0.6	4,592	3.8	117,098	27.8	31.3
Fort Wayne, IN	168,359	69.5	133,700	17.5	10.0	737	27.3	88.1	216,904	1.9	6,740	3.1	210,522	32.5	27.0
Fresno, CA	305,819	53.4	248,700	22.7	10.9	955	32.9	85.2	448,353	0.7	33,427	7.5	411,529	29.3	28.1
Gadsden, AL	37,091	71.5	115,200	18.4	10.6	618	31.8	79.2	43,096	0.1	1,768	4.1	38,818	30.2	28.0
Gainesville, FL	104,101	57.4	170,700	20.8	10.7	941	38.9	88.7	144,208	1.1	4,751	3.3	134,407	44.9	11.5
Gainesville, GA	62,164	70.5	195,600	19.4	10.0	892	28.2	89.2	102,169	1.8	3,235	3.2	97,520	28.8	32.5
Gettysburg, PA	39,527	76.6	203,500	21.3	13.2	857	28.6	82.9	55,121	-0.5	1,805	3.3	51,121	30.4	30.9
Glens Falls, NY	50,135	74.1	172,300	21.0	12.4	826	34.0	84.7	59,873	0.0	2,638	4.4	60,877	34.0	24.0
Goldsboro, NC	47,720	65.6	117,600	19.1	10.7	739	30.4	84.5	52,731	-1.3	2,271	4.3	54,282	28.6	29.9
Grand Forks, ND-MN	42,613	51.7	198,300	19.2	11.3	728	28.6	82.4	54,699	-2.2	1,474	2.7	53,568	35.7	20.9
Grand Island, NE	32,578	68.0	147,400	17.4	10.0	643	19.1	88.0	43,679	0.3	1,328	3.0	44,514	32.1	35.5
Grand Junction, CO	61,763	68.1	226,400	22.5	10.0	928	29.9	90.8	76,060	3.2	3,111	4.1	70,254	33.4	26.3
Grand Rapids-Wyoming, MI	394,268	73.4	174,900	18.8	10.4	871	28.9	89.1	579,139	1.1	17,445	3.0	544,182	36.1	25.7
Grants Pass, OR	36,493	65.6	278,000	26.7	10.0	861	31.3	85.2	35,929	2.1	1,990	5.5	30,648	31.4	21.0
Great Falls, MT	33,346	68.6	174,300	22.1	10.9	689	26.9	80.9	37,848	0.3	1,362	3.6	37,263	30.6	25.2
Greeley, CO	104,611	74.0	295,100	22.1	10.0	1,003	29.8	87.9	165,290	4.7	4,970	3.0	153,525	33.3	26.8
Green Bay, WI	129,383	66.8	171,600	18.8	11.3	747	24.3	87.7	175,911	0.5	4,941	2.8	168,501	35.7	26.0
Greensboro-High Point, NC	297,140	62.5	150,100	19.5	10.0	791	28.8	82.9	367,616	-0.1	15,084	4.1	362,391	34.8	24.3
Greenville, NC	68,505	53.6	150,800	18.6	10.0	787	38.6	89.7	89,961	0.7	3,811	4.2	84,782	38.9	17.7
Greenville-Anderson-Mauldin, SC	343,167	68.8	162,100	18.6	10.0	797	28.8	84.4	424,424	0.3	13,176	3.1	423,479	36.5	24.4
Gulfport-Biloxi-Pascagoula, MS	150,780	63.0	152,100	21.5	10.1	848	30.3	83.5	164,143	-0.2	8,100	4.9	165,667	32.8	22.9
Hagerstown-Martinsburg, MD-WV	98,959	67.9	199,900	21.1	10.0	923	29.8	82.8	131,318	0.0	5,561	4.2	123,468	35.7	23.2
Hammond, LA	49,272	67.7	157,500	18.2	10.3	802	33.3	79.5	54,353	-0.8	2,979	5.5	59,096	25.5	28.6
Hanford-Corcoran, CA	43,029	55.3	224,500	22.1	10.0	876	29.2	83.2	57,865	0.9	4,481	7.7	56,775	23.4	34.6
Harrisburg-Carlisle, PA	226,354	69.0	186,000	19.9	11.1	916	27.2	86.5	297,027	0.1	10,904	3.7	287,720	39.2	20.9
Harrisonburg, VA	47,777	61.8	216,400	19.9	10.0	866	28.0	83.3	65,473	0.2	1,936	3.0	65,930	33.1	29.6
Hartford-West Hartford-East Hartford, CT	470,731	66.5	247,900	22.0	14.4	1,061	31.3	88.3	659,896	0.6	26,744	4.1	611,699	44.2	16.8
Hattiesburg, MS	54,181	62.3	144,800	18.3	10.0	794	33.6	81.3	68,628	0.3	2,858	4.2	63,530	37.8	20.9
Hickory-Lenoir-Morganton, NC	141,250	71.9	132,900	18.4	10.5	677	24.6	79.8	173,999	0.2	6,179	3.6	167,757	27.6	33.8
Hilton Head Island-Bluffton-Beaufort, NC	79,217	72.5	279,100	24.4	11.9	1,076	36.0	86.7	87,731	1.8	2,804	3.2	86,452	33.9	22.9
Hinesville, GA	29,826	53.9	115,800	21.0	10.0	951	28.9	91.7	33,734	0.8	1,427	4.2	29,783	29.7	26.1
Homosassa Springs, FL	61,290	81.4	128,900	21.1	10.0	779	30.2	86.1	47,799	-0.4	2,485	5.2	49,929	27.5	21.7
Hot Springs, AR	38,594	66.9	140,400	19.2	10.0	694	29.6	79.8	40,797	1.1	1,651	4.0	38,379	32.4	23.5
Houma-Thibodaux, LA	77,302	71.9	153,600	19.1	10.0	789	30.3	79.9	88,248	-0.4	4,304	4.9	84,740	31.3	30.6
Houston-The Woodlands-Sugar Land, TX	2,324,758	60.7	192,900	20.9	10.8	1,041	29.3	89.3	3,390,635	1.6	145,938	4.3	3,257,299	38.0	23.0
Huntington-Ashland, WV-KY-OH	139,983	69.4	118,600	18.1	10.6	682	33.4	77.5	145,268	-0.8	7,970	5.5	136,021	33.6	22.0
Huntsville, AL	180,708	67.8	176,500	17.6	10.0	784	27.8	89.5	222,145	2.2	7,723	3.5	217,599	45.5	17.9
Idaho Falls, ID	50,941	73.0	173,900	20.1	10.0	796	32.4	90.0	70,273	3.3	1,675	2.4	65,926	39.1	26.3
Indianapolis-Carmel-Anderson, IN	773,361	65.4	162,200	18.0	10.0	886	28.9	86.9	1,061,803	1.4	34,240	3.2	1,007,071	40.3	20.4
Iowa City, IA	67,822	62.6	218,500	18.9	10.4	943	33.4	92.9	97,309	-0.1	1,918	2.0	95,682	47.1	14.7
Ithaca, NY	40,230	55.3	205,300	22.9	10.6	1,120	38.9	91.7	50,112	0.6	1,829	3.6	51,062	47.0	12.0
Jackson, MI	62,220	73.7	131,300	20.3	10.4	731	28.6	85.7	74,281	0.2	2,930	3.9	71,504	32.5	25.3
Jackson, MS	211,178	67.3	147,700	19.4	10.0	857	28.4	84.8	270,001	-0.6	11,191	4.1	262,443	38.6	21.8
Jackson, TN	47,865	65.1	121,900	19.1	10.5	834	29.9	78.2	64,105	1.3	2,421	3.8	55,559	33.1	22.2
Jacksonville, FL	560,169	63.6	205,100	20.8	10.2	1,031	30.0	88.8	773,494	1.7	26,270	3.4	707,604	37.8	18.2
Jacksonville, NC	62,941	54.7	158,600	24.8	10.5	1,056	26.5	91.3	64,341	-0.4	3,040	4.7	60,597	31.3	17.6
Janesville-Beloit, WI	64,878	66.0	142,700	20.0	12.2	800	28.3	86.7	85,397	-0.1	2,766	3.2	77,364	28.4	31.9
Jefferson City, MO	54,732	70.1	155,200	18.4	10.0	640	22.3	77.9	73,535	-1.7	1,959	2.7	70,476	32.9	26.7
Johnson City, TN	83,579	66.4	146,500	19.9	10.0	658	29.7	79.8	90,926	0.7	3,450	3.8	91,669	36.6	22.6
Johnstown, PA	56,023	75.6	91,600	17.3	12.9	601	28.9	82.8	58,344	-2.2	3,031	5.2	56,555	32.9	25.2

1. Specified owner-occupied units.   2. A value of 10.0 represents 10 percent or less; a value of 50.0 represents 50 percent or more.   3. Specified renter-occupied units.   4. Overcrowded or lacking complete plumbing facilities.   5. Percent of civilian labor force.   6. Civilian employed persons 16 years old and over.

Table C. Metropolitan Areas — Nonfarm Employment and Agriculture

Area name	Private nonfarm establishments, employment and payroll, 2016									Agriculture, 2017			
	Number of establishments	Employment						Annual payroll		Farms			Farm producers whose primary occupation is farming (percent)
		Total	Health care and social assistance	Manufacturing	Retail trade	Finance and insurance	Professional, scientific, and technical services	Total (mil dol)	Average per employee (dollars)	Number	Percent with:		
											Fewer than 50 acres	1000 acres or more	
	104	105	106	107	108	109	110	111	112	113	114	115	116
Evansville, IN-KY	7,632	142,342	26,411	21,960	17,164	5,927	5,147	6,106	42,900	1,564	45.7	11.1	43.6
Fairbanks, AK	2,466	27,962	6,101	616	5,205	760	1,201	1,430	51,124	274	49.6	8	45
Fargo, ND-MN	6,840	121,307	22,328	9,395	16,389	8,694	6,573	5,297	43,663	1,478	20.1	36.1	58.8
Farmington, NM	2,651	37,010	6,875	1,315	6,193	927	1,226	1,587	42,871	2,965	56.5	21	54.9
Fayetteville, NC	6,044	99,304	20,657	7,374	18,105	2,019	5,394	3,350	33,737	525	47.2	5.5	35.7
Fayetteville-Springdale-Rogers, AR-MO	11,873	211,543	24,580	27,918	27,521	5,387	11,630	10,608	50,147	6,384	37.9	1.7	39.9
Flagstaff, AZ	3,650	51,713	8,356	5,590	8,259	905	1,713	2,002	38,720	2,142	77.8	11.6	55.7
Flint, MI	7,684	120,175	27,279	10,873	19,837	4,072	4,355	5,010	41,686	820	59.4	3.4	46.2
Florence, SC	4,211	74,028	15,835	9,961	11,721	4,045	2,607	2,883	38,946	862	43.6	8.9	42.1
Florence-Muscle Shoals, AL	3,260	48,037	7,488	9,499	8,583	1,638	1,126	1,617	33,671	1,900	45.6	4.9	36.6
Fond du Lac, WI	2,358	42,959	6,333	8,569	6,026	1,640	1,386	1,746	40,652	1,244	35.9	4.8	53.4
Fort Collins, CO	10,577	125,796	20,875	10,965	19,329	3,740	9,143	5,853	46,527	2,043	71	4.4	31.6
Fort Smith, AR-OK	5,758	96,317	17,953	18,143	13,319	2,715	2,033	3,539	36,738	4,382	38.9	3.1	37.7
Fort Wayne, IN	10,424	195,521	36,734	34,250	24,353	9,266	6,271	8,106	41,456	2,825	51.8	7.3	35.1
Fresno, CA	16,619	255,652	44,569	23,821	38,532	9,143	10,242	10,692	41,823	4,774	54.1	6.6	57.1
Gadsden, AL	1,974	30,834	7,349	5,344	4,951	1,039	580	1,018	33,028	817	55.2	0.5	38.2
Gainesville, FL	6,343	95,053	25,808	3,825	14,391	4,172	5,685	3,719	39,121	2,176	70.9	2.4	37.4
Gainesville, GA	4,205	74,898	12,645	20,491	9,097	2,021	1,951	3,324	44,381	551	63.5	0.4	38.1
Gettysburg, PA	1,956	30,027	4,608	6,227	3,450	481	600	1,035	34,481	1,146	50.2	2.2	43.4
Glens Falls, NY	3,369	41,974	8,444	6,262	7,835	1,498	1,088	1,659	39,517	995	38.9	2.6	43.4
Goldsboro, NC	2,137	34,226	7,229	5,688	6,276	1,111	830	1,155	33,733	551	39.7	8.5	55.4
Grand Forks, ND-MN	2,686	43,585	9,549	4,063	7,790	1,143	1,821	1,662	38,135	2,147	14.3	25	53.5
Grand Island, NE	2,595	36,002	5,276	7,688	5,805	1,562	794	1,311	36,413	2,268	28.5	16.4	53
Grand Junction, CO	4,362	51,511	10,232	2,546	8,767	1,984	2,218	2,014	39,103	2,465	80.1	2.6	32.1
Grand Rapids-Wyoming, MI	24,259	490,271	67,606	107,785	49,977	19,335	20,358	21,684	44,228	4,040	51.5	3.7	42.5
Grants Pass, OR	1,934	22,347	4,685	2,869	4,386	623	846	759	33,948	746	85	0.3	43.6
Great Falls, MT	2,410	30,825	7,140	1,453	4,964	1,627	1,199	1,120	36,342	1,027	37.7	22.6	42.1
Greeley, CO	5,922	83,654	8,969	13,027	10,437	3,361	2,858	3,964	47,386	4,062	46.3	10.2	38.1
Green Bay, WI	7,727	154,784	23,154	29,417	17,334	8,726	5,607	7,115	45,967	2,464	42.4	4.3	46.7
Greensboro-High Point, NC	17,487	316,292	43,947	52,406	37,187	13,635	12,378	13,712	43,352	3,066	46.7	1.1	40.7
Greenville, NC	3,593	61,227	15,485	5,752	9,250	2,198	2,230	2,335	38,135	478	35.8	12.6	55
Greenville-Anderson-Mauldin, SC	19,520	327,398	41,689	51,869	43,573	11,302	20,438	13,620	41,602	4,358	59.5	1.1	31.5
Gulfport-Biloxi-Pascagoula, MS	7,175	129,905	20,840	19,532	18,956	3,859	5,486	5,223	40,202	1,082	66.7	0.6	33
Hagerstown-Martinsburg, MD-WV	5,032	85,107	15,802	8,501	14,535	7,321	2,698	3,255	38,242	1,823	59.1	0.8	37.1
Hammond, LA	2,366	35,635	8,434	2,305	6,721	2,251	1,017	1,307	36,674	967	55	1.1	37.4
Hanford-Corcoran, CA	1,596	23,824	4,613	4,169	4,205	520	868	952	39,939	963	48.9	9.2	54.1
Harrisburg-Carlisle, PA	13,699	273,077	51,369	16,748	34,433	17,758	16,682	12,719	46,577	2,711	45.1	1.4	48.6
Harrisonburg, VA	3,038	52,650	6,991	9,976	7,188	1,244	1,708	1,928	36,628	2,026	46.2	0.6	49.3
Hartford-West Hartford-East Hartford, CT	29,461	548,076	107,146	63,574	64,947	56,295	33,907	31,351	57,202	1,747	72.9	0.5	38.6
Hattiesburg, MS	3,342	51,572	11,996	4,501	9,881	1,612	1,870	1,842	35,715	1,173	49.3	1.5	36
Hickory-Lenoir-Morganton, NC	7,355	131,952	20,724	40,585	16,874	2,169	2,862	4,971	37,675	2,101	54	0.8	40.1
Hilton Head Island-Bluffton-Beaufort, NC	5,769	62,213	9,096	892	12,150	1,981	2,672	2,152	34,590	296	62.2	10.5	35.4
Hinesville, GA	889	12,478	2,231	1,726	2,221	369	611	486	38,982	154	53.2	0.6	26.3
Homosassa Springs, FL	2,732	29,803	10,283	303	5,686	673	853	1,004	33,683	609	75.2	2.1	43.4
Hot Springs, AR	2,712	33,063	7,261	2,375	6,152	1,011	1,529	1,060	32,070	357	47.6	0.3	38.5
Houma-Thibodaux, LA	4,680	74,243	11,749	6,002	11,580	1,992	3,308	3,424	46,119	592	54.1	7.4	33.2
Houston-The Woodlands-Sugar Land, TX	139,010	2,577,095	338,326	198,513	301,800	97,326	203,825	154,412	59,917	14,238	63.5	2.9	32.2
Huntington-Ashland, WV-KY-OH	6,933	111,371	28,768	10,392	17,763	3,074	4,067	4,430	39,778	2,653	33.1	0.3	34.4
Huntsville, AL	9,697	175,587	27,337	19,706	23,232	4,104	37,492	8,504	48,431	2,177	54.2	4	35.9
Idaho Falls, ID	3,995	52,238	9,099	4,171	8,713	1,391	7,480	2,181	41,749	2,048	60.5	10.7	37.5
Indianapolis-Carmel-Anderson, IN	46,490	880,174	135,986	77,323	101,756	45,732	62,542	41,644	47,314	5,999	55.1	7.4	37.4
Iowa City, IA	3,973	69,062	18,499	5,844	10,583	2,694	3,160	2,855	41,334	2,386	34.7	4.9	46.3
Ithaca, NY	2,370	49,767	5,710	2,954	4,991	1,119	1,947	1,833	36,841	523	47.6	2.9	39.6
Jackson, MI	2,897	50,505	10,043	9,290	7,378	1,312	2,931	2,310	45,746	923	52.1	3.9	41.5
Jackson, MS	13,146	220,881	48,987	18,811	30,906	11,472	9,992	9,116	41,273	3,523	30.7	6.3	37.1
Jackson, TN	2,956	57,769	13,313	10,269	7,914	1,511	1,184	2,145	37,132	1,251	35.7	7.3	33.9
Jacksonville, FL	37,310	556,603	81,922	26,281	77,222	48,055	35,117	25,335	45,518	1,681	75.1	2	40.6
Jacksonville, NC	2,752	35,716	5,416	1,009	8,514	921	1,723	994	27,844	340	50.3	3.5	55.9
Janesville-Beloit, WI	3,330	57,883	8,754	10,139	9,147	1,335	2,133	2,451	42,336	1,587	53.7	4.7	40.6
Jefferson City, MO	3,597	53,215	9,914	6,094	7,818	2,482	1,929	2,064	38,779	5,019	26.2	2.8	33.9
Johnson City, TN	3,781	65,256	16,120	7,391	11,311	3,446	1,669	2,451	37,556	1,997	61.9	0.4	35.9
Johnstown, PA	3,171	46,970	11,781	4,594	6,871	2,142	2,228	1,645	35,031	557	37	2.3	36.1

Table C. Metropolitan Areas — **Agriculture**

Area name	Acreage (1,000) [117]	Percent change, 2012-2017 [118]	Average size of farm [119]	Total irrigated (1,000) [120]	Total cropland (1,000) [121]	Average per farm [122]	Average per acre [123]	Value of machinery and equipment, average per farm (dollars) [124]	Total (mil dol) [125]	Average per farm (acres) [126]	Crops [127]	Livestock and poultry products [128]	Organic farms (number) [129]	Farms with internet access (percent) [130]	Total ($1,000) [131]	Percent of farms [132]
Evansville, IN-KY	544	-6.4	348	23.5	479.4	2,029,390	5,839	213,324	304.3	194,577	92.2	7.8	2	77.8	16,227	57.6
Fairbanks, AK	102	2.4	372	1.1	63.2	610,606	1,640	NA	10.4	37,927	81.6	18.4	5	86.9	1,124	21.9
Fargo, ND-MN	1,703	-0.9	1,152	16.8	1,623.6	4,372,599	3,795	467,605	717.2	485,254	91.7	8.3	19	84.9	14,177	72.3
Farmington, NM	2,551	-1.1	861	73.6	107.9	345,734	402	39,306	74.1	24,998	91.5	8.5	1	44.9	1,383	8.3
Fayetteville, NC	120	-15.1	228	3.4	68.4	1,099,278	4,824	126,181	172.6	328,752	22.1	77.9	NA	79.8	694	27.8
Fayetteville-Springdale-Rogers, AR-MO	1,030	-4	161	1.4	263.6	718,677	4,456	75,790	1,579.4	247,404	1.6	98.4	25	76.1	2,391	6.6
Flagstaff, AZ	6,139	5.6	2,866	1.3	6.9	607,822	212	34,544	23.9	11,162	4.1	95.9	2	43.9	807	0.8
Flint, MI	124	0.5	151	1.5	104.3	795,230	5,262	103,909	70.4	85,871	86.5	13.5	11	84.8	2,561	25
Florence, SC	290	-12.9	336	7.4	200.6	969,775	2,883	127,777	133.5	154,886	69.8	30.2	8	70.3	2,730	33.2
Florence-Muscle Shoals, AL	361		190	0.9	194.8	612,645	3,226	91,579	132.5	69,754	58.9	41.1	NA	70.7	7,434	40.9
Fond du Lac, WI	317	0.6	255	1.9	270.4	1,855,960	7,275	227,075	396.7	318,921	24	76	33	77.7	3,762	56.5
Fort Collins, CO	482	7.1	236	60.2	98.6	1,095,047	4,637	76,905	150.7	73,772	45.7	54.3	20	85.1	633	5.5
Fort Smith, AR-OK	821	-4	187	11.9	265.4	458,679	2,450	69,894	503.6	114,935	9	91	7	72.8	1,976	6.2
Fort Wayne, IN	683	11.7	242	2	619.0	1,789,285	7,401	161,236	488.9	173,066	66.3	33.7	23	71.7	11,716	53
Fresno, CA	1,647	-4.3	345	972.6	1,142.7	3,917,829	11,359	234,782	5,742.8	1,202,926	71.1	28.9	183	75.6	8,894	7.7
Gadsden, AL	89	3.7	109	0.6	24.8	419,479	3,836	78,982	93.4	114,356	6.7	93.3	NA	73.8	804	21.5
Gainesville, FL	260	-4.2	120	21.2	97.9	842,326	7,039	64,143	189.7	87,158	55.7	44.3	23	77.6	1,123	6.4
Gainesville, GA	41	-21.7	74	0.1	13.8	689,172	9,332	79,541	128.5	233,156	2.3	97.7	1	80.9	789	20.3
Gettysburg, PA	166	-3	145	2.2	128.4	998,832	6,886	132,547	207.6	181,122	54.2	45.8	17	77.7	1,503	18.4
Glens Falls, NY	195	-1.8	196	1	103.9	562,560	2,865	127,784	135.8	136,494	18	82	19	84	1,418	17.4
Goldsboro, NC	165	-13.5	300	4.8	130.5	1,497,289	4,990	222,201	592.1	1,074,539	18.1	81.9	13	79.9	3,611	46.1
Grand Forks, ND-MN	1,822	-4.7	848	33.1	1,682.6	2,831,795	3,338	378,326	748.1	348,455	93.3	6.7	19	75.5	32,024	81.8
Grand Island, NE	1,164	-1.5	513	758.4	938.2	2,584,005	5,035	294,892	1,053.7	464,577	53.3	46.7	15	82.3	42,513	67.3
Grand Junction, CO	343	-11.5	139	76.2	79.8	767,492	5,523	57,249	94.2	38,209	48.7	51.3	12	86.2	730	3.9
Grand Rapids-Wyoming, MI	714	-4.3	177	102.7	581.1	1,050,874	5,943	148,977	1,089.6	269,710	60.2	39.8	33	81.7	10,565	23.2
Grants Pass, OR	28	-1.4	37	8	8.4	672,056	17,992	38,200	17.5	23,456	49.2	50.8	27	85.1	1	1.1
Great Falls, MT	1,270	1.2	1,237	35.7	420.0	1,499,360	1,212	134,128	107.3	104,453	47.7	52.3	9	80.2	7,780	42.7
Greeley, CO	2,099	7.3	517	323.4	923.0	1,335,953	2,586	159,663	2,047.2	503,982	17	83	42	82.9	19,375	26
Green Bay, WI	552	0.9	224	2.4	455.7	1,371,723	6,120	200,427	752.9	305,556	18.1	81.9	35	75.8	6,395	47
Greensboro-High Point, NC	349	-3.1	114	5.4	153.8	604,582	5,315	73,041	373.1	121,694	24.2	75.8	40	74.5	1,271	11.5
Greenville, NC	186	8.5	390	2.8	149.8	1,499,479	3,845	183,107	242.5	507,234	41.6	58.4	4	81.8	3,291	45.6
Greenville-Anderson-Mauldin, SC	405	1.3	93	2.7	140.1	535,642	5,767	53,720	166	38,095	19.9	80.1	14	74.2	3,337	12.2
Gulfport-Biloxi-Pascagoula, MS	85	-2.6	78	0.3	19.8	407,491	5,201	61,546	15.5	14,335	45.5	54.5	6	75.8	202	5.7
Hagerstown-Martinsburg, MD-WV	192	-3.7	106	0.7	119.8	741,647	7,028	82,967	179.6	98,537	31.6	68.4	14	69	1,852	12.9
Hammond, LA	98	-8.1	101	1.2	29.6	513,368	5,061	63,007	42.4	43,845	47.3	52.7	5	67.6	208	5
Hanford-Corcoran, CA	616	-8.6	640	371.7	488.5	6,917,469	10,815	349,654	1,649.3	1,712,640	50.1	49.9	25	80.4	5,849	29.8
Harrisburg-Carlisle, PA	366	-12.8	135	2.1	281.4	1,020,473	7,566	123,077	485	178,904	25.1	74.9	98	65	4,162	22
Harrisonburg, VA	229	2.9	113	5.5	121.9	997,634	8,844	118,949	795.9	392,852	6.8	93.2	37	65.5	1,852	11.5
Hartford-West Hartford-East Hartford, CT	100	-20.6	57	4.3	48.9	779,882	13,635	64,238	204.4	117,004	87	13	22	81.2	731	3.9
Hattiesburg, MS	165	10	141	1	32.3	516,265	3,660	63,667	99.3	84,688	11	89	NA	72.6	1,263	21.7
Hickory-Lenoir-Morganton, NC	194	1.1	92	3.5	88.8	529,900	5,730	83,055	383.1	182,363	15.9	84.1	7	74.7	1,109	6.3
Hilton Head Island-Bluffton-Beaufort, NC	119	7.5	402	2	19.0	1,465,669	3,643	78,267	20.3	68,537	94.7	5.3	3	76	203	12.5
Hinesville, GA	17	0.4	107	0.2	4.0	441,065	4,103	55,760	7.8	50,331	12.1	87.9	NA	81.2	82	10.4
Homosassa Springs, FL	56	37.5	92	0.9	9.6	726,031	7,929	49,552	13.5	22,118	67.3	32.7	NA	81	197	2.6
Hot Springs, AR	34	-4.9	95	0.1	8.2	496,952	5,226	46,232	10	27,972	30.5	69.5	NA	74.5	93	5.9
Houma-Thibodaux, LA	236	-6.1	398	0.3	94.4	1,316,841	3,306	143,334	69.1	116,730	62.4	37.6	NA	73.6	255	3.4
Houston-The Woodlands-Sugar Land, TX	2,218	-17.2	156	80.6	680.3	749,277	4,810	67,839	434.9	30,543	62.4	37.6	24	74.4	30,126	5.9
Huntington-Ashland, WV-KY-OH	310	-4.2	117	0.3	69.6	318,925	2,733	51,126	23.5	8,858	59.1	40.9	3	69.6	589	7
Huntsville, AL	410	-10.2	188	21.1	282.6	877,456	4,662	110,397	201.8	92,678	71	29	2	76.4	6,048	30.9
Idaho Falls, ID	883	3	431	399.3	567.5	1,300,466	3,017	187,303	504.6	246,386	63.3	36.7	14	85.2	13,659	25.9
Indianapolis-Carmel-Anderson, IN	1,603	-5.1	267	10	1,440.5	1,963,457	7,349	158,827	944.4	157,420	89	11	23	82.3	39,946	42.9
Iowa City, IA	615	-4.4	258	1.2	528.6	1,921,071	7,457	191,325	891.5	373,645	31.5	68.5	132	75.6	20,966	68.6
Ithaca, NY	91	0.6	175	0.4	62.1	661,191	3,789	138,310	64.7	123,715	24.6	75.4	45	85.9	1,575	22.6
Jackson, MI	160	-12.4	174	4.7	125.8	866,522	4,986	116,065	70.8	76,714	61.6	38.4	6	78.2	3,526	25.9
Jackson, MS	1,017	-12.1	289	64.5	353.4	837,099	2,900	89,515	616.2	174,916	22.6	77.4	1	64.7	19,073	42
Jackson, TN	380	6.5	304	17.2	284.1	958,336	3,151	155,461	147.2	117,631	95.1	4.9	NA	69	7,055	50.4
Jacksonville, FL	152	-18	91	17.4	36.3	599,377	6,617	58,273	101.9	60,642	69.5	30.5	6	75.4	466	5.1
Jacksonville, NC	52	-9	154	0.4	35.6	969,753	6,284	93,974	171.6	504,629	13.7	86.3	NA	75	862	25.6
Janesville-Beloit, WI	354	-0.1	223	15.6	302.8	1,467,761	6,589	175,570	294.5	185,539	56	44	20	79.7	4,915	54.7
Jefferson City, MO	1,029	1.8	205	10.8	443.2	684,076	3,337	83,549	386.7	77,050	31.2	68.8	17	73.6	7,408	26.5
Johnson City, TN	146	-7	73	0.8	68.4	528,895	7,215	69,260	50.2	25,140	39.2	60.8	7	72.5	416	5.8
Johnstown, PA	79	3.2	142	0.1	50.5	659,661	4,631	100,086	30.1	53,982	60.1	39.9	2	68.8	979	30.3

Table C. Metropolitan Areas — Water Use, Wholesale Trade, Retail Trade, and Real Estate

Area name	Water use, 2015		Wholesale Trade[1], 2012				Retail Trade[2], 2012				Real estate and rental and leasing,[2] 2012			
	Public supply water withdrawn (mil gal/day)	Public supply gallons withdrawn per person per day	Number of establishments	Number of employees	Sales (mil dol)	Average payroll (mil dol)	Number of establishments	Number of employees	Sales (mil dol)	Average payroll (mil dol)	Number of establishments	Number of employees	Sales (mil dol)	Average payroll (mil dol)
	133	134	135	136	137	138	139	140	141	142	143	144	145	146
Evansville, IN-KY..................	29.78	94.3	366	5,873	3,818.1	346.7	1,154	17,133	4,570.3	396.7	289	1,954	297.2	54.7
Fairbanks, AK.....................	14.12	141.7	69	666	413.5	36.5	301	4,758	1,732.5	153.1	144	661	159.6	33.2
Fargo, ND-MN......................	19.03	81.4	401	6,920	6,673.0	383.0	805	15,182	4,455.4	360.4	318	1,876	322.0	68.5
Farmington, NM....................	18.83	158.6	156	1,412	663.0	73.8	450	6,210	1,801.6	157.4	107	750	205.0	36.8
Fayetteville, NC...................	40.27	107	173	2,711	1,078.4	106.5	1,128	16,393	4,631.9	382.0	345	1,903	368.3	63.2
Fayetteville-Springdale-Rogers, AR-MO...........	66.79	130.1	484	5,216	4,145.6	273.4	1,522	22,576	6,183.1	524.0	498	3,276	367.4	100.3
Flagstaff, AZ......................	19.87	142.8	95	738	439.3	33.8	590	7,337	1,896.5	164.8	188	667	137.3	28.1
Flint, MI..........................	4.22	10.3	272	3,969	3,673.6	218.5	1,459	19,368	5,307.9	444.9	318	1,843	255.8	57.1
Florence, SC.......................	22.11	107.1	231	3,085	2,445.4	130.8	936	10,523	2,686.2	224.1	167	657	150.8	22.3
Florence-Muscle Shoals, AL...	20.65	140.5	154	2,097	1,235.0	71.4	647	7,749	2,202.1	181.0	127	522	70.0	14.0
Fond du Lac, WI....................	7.93	77.8	111	1,541	1,372.0	74.4	354	5,462	1,402.4	130.0	64	235	37.7	6.0
Fort Collins, CO...................	30.58	91.7	295	4,294	5,143.6	368.5	1,244	17,307	4,341.3	414.2	526	2,112	307.0	71.4
Fort Smith, AR-OK..................	40.55	144.7	291	3,410	2,259.1	145.2	990	12,490	3,264.4	271.3	246	1,167	176.1	37.3
Fort Wayne, IN	39.52	91.9	556	9,321	14,090.5	435.5	1,465	22,309	5,772.6	520.2	428	2,005	385.3	70.5
Fresno, CA.........................	157.08	161.1	819	12,981	9,266.3	663.0	2,421	32,954	9,117.8	836.0	769	4,299	715.1	139.6
Gadsden, AL........................	16.85	163.5	82	837	549.9	31.2	392	4,675	1,236.5	96.1	62	367	57.2	10.5
Gainesville, FL....................	23.6	85.1	205	1,896	1,356.0	92.7	958	13,245	3,261.2	286.8	325	1,727	232.5	52.3
Gainesville, GA....................	88.18	455.6	235	3,265	9,022.6	173.1	579	7,640	2,231.9	193.5	164	450	116.5	17.1
Gettysburg, PA.....................	12.39	121.1	61	D	D	D	333	3,231	801.2	74.4	47	210	35.8	7.0
Glens Falls, NY	14.15	111.5	89	D	D	D	633	8,195	2,047.9	191.9	91	286	49.8	10.0
Goldsboro, NC......................	11.27	90.8	95	1,822	1,244.8	74.4	464	5,709	1,557.5	125.8	63	257	29.3	7.1
Grand Forks, ND-MN	17.35	169.4	136	1,704	2,175.4	85.6	423	7,237	1,893.8	159.3	88	554	89.2	15.8
Grand Island, NE...................	14.54	170.9	144	1,833	1,868.6	92.9	397	5,589	1,497.8	123.6	89	315	58.5	10.2
Grand Junction, CO.............	17.51	117.9	219	2,076	876.5	96.2	604	7,966	2,173.3	202.6	263	889	170.7	33.7
Grand Rapids-Wyoming, MI ...	101.87	98.1	1,336	26,242	20,615.3	1,444.6	3,218	44,758	12,253.0	1,107.9	882	4,947	859.4	175.3
Grants Pass, OR	7.18	84.7	49	D	D	D	312	4,150	987.9	105.1	106	354	44.8	8.5
Great Falls, MT....................	12.79	155.4	112	D	D	D	352	4,859	1,359.7	117.4	121	349	62.1	9.8
Greeley, CO........................	28.3	99.2	246	3,166	5,349.2	157.4	620	8,154	2,707.6	228.7	212	870	149.0	31.5
Green Bay, WI......................	21.42	67.7	364	6,375	4,491.1	331.5	1,029	15,954	4,093.6	353.6	233	1,485	209.4	44.7
Greensboro-High Point, NC ...	76.29	101.4	1,157	16,682	15,345.7	893.5	2,570	34,286	8,953.9	831.4	791	4,726	773.8	181.8
Greenville, NC.....................	13.64	77.6	144	1,597	1,028.7	69.5	633	8,597	2,354.8	193.0	176	681	115.5	22.7
Greenville-Anderson-Mauldin, SC	102.79	117.5	976	12,422	13,210.8	659.6	2,958	39,157	10,145.3	912.0	747	3,498	980.5	137.0
Gulfport-Biloxi-Pascagoula, MS	39.73	102.1	236	2,165	911.0	90.8	1,357	17,028	4,425.8	382.2	375	1,614	270.2	50.4
Hagerstown-Martinsburg, MD-WV...................	23.24	88.9	177	2,757	2,513.7	128.2	859	13,123	3,396.8	290.0	208	1,019	249.3	36.1
Hammond, LA.......................	15.06	117	86	1,701	1,300.4	68.5	438	6,290	1,769.7	144.7	94	498	86.5	18.5
Hanford-Corcoran, CA...........	29.07	192.6	69	684	746.6	36.3	285	3,961	1,032.0	92.2	97	371	71.0	9.9
Harrisburg-Carlisle, PA..........	45.54	80.6	500	9,590	9,403.2	521.2	1,973	32,462	9,074.5	750.1	450	2,997	825.2	157.6
Harrisonburg, VA	14.75	112.5	113	1,952	1,032.2	91.5	540	7,535	1,949.6	185.0	116	919	186.3	34.8
Hartford-West Hartford-East Hartford, CT	71.46	59	1,192	21,837	17,564.8	1,261.3	4,166	63,342	17,268.0	1,593.2	1,082	6,148	1,269.1	270.7
Hattiesburg, MS....................	19.25	129.3	126	1,168	747.6	46.2	683	9,522	4,784.0	198.8	156	594	111.0	19.8
Hickory-Lenoir-Morganton, NC	34.48	95.1	367	6,273	4,530.1	282.7	1,317	15,617	4,183.6	353.0	305	817	163.8	23.6
Hilton Head Island-Bluffton-Beaufort, NC	40.06	193.1	140	728	442.4	34.0	838	10,505	2,665.3	243.6	397	1,787	280.7	66.0
Hinesville, GA.....................	6.93	86.4	12	217	151.6	12.1	183	1,990	580.2	42.0	51	187	24.9	5.6
Homosassa Springs, FL.........	14.15	100.3	80	D	D	D	455	5,122	1,421.0	121.8	172	415	54.4	10.4
Hot Springs, AR....................	16.07	165.4	79	D	D	D	513	5,877	1,564.0	133.8	133	439	65.0	13.0
Houma-Thibodaux, LA...........	27.54	129.7	257	2,970	1,943.9	160.2	793	11,090	2,895.0	256.2	233	2,023	530.3	113.4
Houston-The Woodlands-Sugar Land, TX...........	436.66	65.6	8,019	117,487	362,243.5	7,813.0	17,508	263,099	83,979.5	6,764.3	6,497	44,896	10,828.1	2,163.8
Huntington-Ashland, WV-KY-OH.......................	38.31	106	292	4,395	3,127.7	208.0	1,237	16,832	4,430.6	367.6	258	1,265	264.5	49.3
Huntsville, AL.....................	78.67	176.9	376	4,558	4,101.6	240.2	1,577	21,457	5,735.1	514.5	461	1,872	370.6	66.3
Idaho Falls, ID	39.12	279.9	197	2,401	3,208.9	103.3	534	7,307	2,094.6	168.7	147	485	83.3	14.3
Indianapolis-Carmel-Anderson, IN....................	202.51	101.8	2,120	36,502	30,286.1	2,075.0	5,917	94,488	28,311.3	2,293.9	2,162	15,619	3,839.4	666.8
Iowa City, IA.......................	11.85	71.2	127	1,695	1,284.8	74.3	612	9,834	2,117.8	218.0	146	560	132.6	21.1
Ithaca, NY.........................	7.87	75	36	454	259.0	21.6	349	5,071	1,112.0	105.5	112	609	121.6	20.5
Jackson, MI........................	10.84	68	137	D	D	D	526	7,003	1,841.7	163.5	99	567	82.0	15.5
Jackson, MS........................	97.6	168.6	676	9,658	9,533.7	490.2	2,142	28,676	7,644.0	665.5	622	3,434	612.3	131.5
Jackson, TN	18.23	140.6	164	1,795	1,196.1	83.2	565	7,756	2,114.1	177.4	117	573	93.4	17.4
Jacksonville, FL...................	147.27	101.6	1,447	21,814	21,129.8	1,212.3	4,889	66,146	18,318.6	1,632.2	1,787	9,036	2,200.0	383.6
Jacksonville, NC...................	17.87	95.9	50	304	139.1	11.9	545	7,716	2,213.0	177.9	187	664	127.0	20.7
Janesville-Beloit, WI.............	16.71	103.5	149	3,035	3,225.1	155.1	502	8,396	2,215.2	208.2	101	400	148.1	18.7
Jefferson City, MO.................	13.8	91.3	115	2,595	1,154.4	77.3	531	7,253	1,924.3	158.9	100	344	54.1	9.2
Johnson City, TN	27.61	137.6	138	1,477	871.3	57.2	688	10,457	2,572.3	220.8	143	668	103.6	20.3
Johnstown, PA......................	14.93	109.4	115	1,365	664.9	51.0	561	6,927	1,733.8	148.6	86	408	48.3	12.2

1. Merchant wholesalers, except manufacturers' sales branches and offices. 2. Employer establishments.

Area name	Professional, scientific, and technical services, 2012				Manufacturing, 2012				Accommodation and food services, 2012			
	Number of establish-ments	Number of employees	Sales (mil dol)	Average payroll (mil dol)	Number of establish-ments	Number of employees	Receipts (mil dol)	Annual payroll (mil dol)	Number of establish-ments	Number of employees	Receipts (mil dol)	Annual payroll (mil dol)
	147	148	149	150	151	152	153	154	155	156	157	158
Evansville, IN-KY..................	640	5,050	D	228.1	398	20,872	15,137.5	1,118.6	656	14,254	694.8	185.7
Fairbanks, AK........................	237	1,683	293.4	86.5	67	641	1,941.2	36.2	213	3,092	255.3	66.4
Fargo, ND-MN.......................	558	D	D	D	224	9,398	3,860.5	D	469	11,495	515.6	151.1
Farmington, NM.....................	256	D	D	D	85	1,318	268.6	62.8	197	4,253	201.8	56.3
Fayetteville, NC.....................	577	6,813	911.9	374.1	115	8,193	5,481.1	379.5	657	13,928	645.9	177.0
Fayetteville-Springdale-Rogers, AR-MO...........	1,226	9,359	1,413.8	541.7	409	25,466	7,229.0	917.4	950	17,956	786.9	224.0
Flagstaff, AZ	331	1,584	178.5	65.3	90	4,025	2,181.3	312.0	545	11,436	765.7	191.8
Flint, MI................................	639	3,544	370.3	143.2	273	10,675	9,418.1	684.4	704	13,207	563.9	157.4
Florence, SC	268	2,684	294.3	112.7	148	8,952	4,326.5	479.5	384	6,611	325.8	85.6
Florence-Muscle Shoals, AL...	246	1,071	110.4	40.5	181	7,761	3,325.2	322.7	268	5,455	231.8	66.1
Fond du Lac, WI....................	154	1,337	154.4	76.3	144	9,140	3,989.9	407.6	240	3,872	140.8	39.8
Fort Collins, CO....................	1,493	8,727	1,031.1	450.9	403	10,163	4,275.7	642.6	847	14,821	756.5	218.0
Fort Smith, AR-OK................	534	2,168	304.8	80.0	298	18,435	6,525.7	709.7	458	8,769	433.6	117.5
Fort Wayne, IN	950	5,721	757.5	266.1	621	32,052	19,526.4	1,658.4	817	16,688	703.1	204.7
Fresno, CA	1,522	10,531	1,367.8	474.3	585	25,269	8,658.3	1,052.9	1,450	24,100	1,226.2	333.9
Gadsden, AL..........................	130	1,250	82.2	35.5	96	4,715	1,355.8	194.1	172	3,231	153.0	40.0
Gainesville, FL......................	841	4,713	553.2	221.0	158	3,270	1,135.7	169.8	578	11,837	553.1	148.7
Gainesville, GA.....................	402	D	D	D	225	17,020	7,629.2	647.1	283	4,742	298.3	67.4
Gettysburg, PA......................	126	D	D	D	113	5,745	2,148.7	240.8	222	3,521	185.7	53.0
Glens Falls, NY	229	1,111	141.8	49.2	163	6,709	2,135.1	358.7	540	4,750	344.1	95.6
Goldsboro, NC.......................	147	816	76.0	27.4	83	5,833	1,691.3	243.8	186	3,284	161.7	42.0
Grand Forks, ND-MN	178	D	D	D	89	3,692	1,778.5	142.3	257	5,362	226.3	67.4
Grand Island, NE..................	143	767	90.3	30.2	114	7,947	7,126.4	313.9	198	2,852	128.6	36.5
Grand Junction, CO...............	561	2,529	289.0	119.8	159	2,388	520.6	95.1	300	6,052	282.6	88.8
Grand Rapids-Wyoming, MI ...	2,215	17,189	2,524.8	982.1	1,735	94,665	30,246.9	4,672.9	1,735	34,865	1,559.5	448.7
Grants Pass, OR	140	563	40.6	13.5	106	2,190	434.8	89.6	199	2,483	124.5	35.8
Great Falls, MT.....................	202	1,159	131.8	50.3	62	964	955.3	45.0	240	3,887	194.7	51.5
Greeley, CO..........................	533	2,362	311.5	113.7	284	11,102	5,991.4	485.8	400	5,794	273.9	76.2
Green Bay, WI	600	5,179	737.1	266.2	535	28,296	12,057.4	1,384.8	741	13,076	523.8	152.8
Greensboro-High Point, NC ...	1,717	D	D	D	1,019	53,589	35,757.7	2,468.5	1,494	28,185	1,408.2	385.3
Greenville, NC	311	1,893	247.9	84.4	87	4,905	2,160.8	248.8	362	8,055	357.6	96.7
Greenville-Anderson-Mauldin, SC	2,010	17,391	2,409.8	1,004.5	942	47,115	18,292.1	2,151.2	1,775	31,297	1,515.6	410.8
Gulfport-Biloxi-Pascagoula, MS..................................	692	6,021	792.9	312.5	215	19,150	20,839.8	1,341.7	789	23,827	1,832.9	459.6
Hagerstown-Martinsburg, MD-WV............................	370	2,689	324.2	120.5	168	7,822	3,601.7	405.2	461	7,743	386.2	110.3
Hammond, LA........................	208	889	93.5	33.6	79	2,389	681.2	84.4	213	4,285	185.8	50.9
Hanford-Corcoran, CA...........	85	461	51.0	18.4	60	4,380	2,904.0	180.5	172	2,824	378.6	42.6
Harrisburg-Carlisle, PA..........	1,411	15,758	2,357.2	1,010.5	408	15,894	7,108.0	779.4	1,256	22,385	1,204.4	333.9
Harrisonburg, VA...................	215	1,489	174.5	76.4	134	9,603	6,229.7	422.4	277	6,596	298.7	94.5
Hartford-West Hartford-East Hartford, CT	2,801	30,314	5,830.7	2,201.0	1,638	69,502	21,474.5	4,621.6	2,685	42,030	2,453.9	706.2
Hattiesburg, MS....................	309	1,777	214.9	80.2	91	4,070	1,202.2	170.7	313	6,850	301.0	82.8
Hickory-Lenoir-Morganton, NC..................................	548	2,538	742.2	102.2	727	37,686	10,405.1	1,403.5	624	10,992	481.6	134.1
Hilton Head Island-Bluffton-Beaufort, NC	579	2,999	352.7	150.2	90	713	128.5	27.5	555	11,189	688.9	202.0
Hinesville, GA.......................	76	776	65.5	25.7	19	1,737	767.7	83.4	105	1,680	81.6	19.0
Homosassa Springs, FL.........	254	891	106.3	35.8	44	203	35.8	7.2	191	2,362	114.6	32.2
Hot Springs, AR....................	217	1,160	91.1	40.4	90	2,180	476.9	95.1	274	5,162	218.0	63.4
Houma-Thibodaux, LA...........	447	4,432	492.2	211.9	202	8,876	2,402.4	462.9	394	7,792	410.5	113.8
Houston-The Woodlands-Sugar Land, TX............	16,999	221,829	49,233.9	19,369.0	5,365	214,702	290,261.2	13,767.5	10,981	226,927	13,340.3	3,592.4
Huntington-Ashland, WV-KY-OH..................................	507	4,535	452.5	174.0	246	11,611	19,017.6	716.9	649	11,746	561.3	151.9
Huntsville, AL........................	1,442	33,281	7,765.6	2,691.5	344	20,108	8,833.7	1,121.3	828	16,350	810.1	224.6
Idaho Falls, ID	406	8,460	1,379.8	585.5	158	3,193	845.8	117.1	280	4,757	207.9	59.7
Indianapolis-Carmel-Anderson, IN	5,276	48,613	7,960.5	3,183.3	1,704	72,434	41,533.8	3,938.9	3,983	84,075	4,306.3	1,207.4
Iowa City, IA.........................	328	2,127	314.1	96.7	125	6,061	3,799.2	276.4	419	8,252	436.6	114.4
Ithaca, NY............................	274	2,312	356.6	124.1	93	2,766	861.1	150.4	334	4,408	231.7	65.4
Jackson, MI...........................	217	2,504	367.1	180.4	268	8,414	2,621.3	409.3	275	4,788	201.5	57.3
Jackson, MS..........................	1,412	9,876	1,571.9	566.0	355	15,987	8,597.5	793.7	1,096	20,707	1,050.9	273.8
Jackson, TN	194	1,874	138.2	72.2	135	9,352	4,578.7	437.0	256	5,191	242.5	68.8
Jacksonville, FL.....................	4,523	35,397	6,308.6	2,429.5	803	25,439	11,888.7	1,444.0	2,849	55,538	2,999.8	853.5
Jacksonville, NC....................	246	1,748	198.1	69.5	40	1,049	271.0	34.2	347	6,640	353.1	86.9
Janesville-Beloit, WI..............	208	1,172	129.3	49.5	224	8,850	4,474.2	421.3	363	5,355	236.2	63.7
Jefferson City, MO................	290	1,937	279.3	93.1	147	5,562	3,774.8	238.7	279	4,545	185.2	54.0
Johnson City, TN	273	2,908	232.5	106.2	170	7,241	2,132.8	309.7	380	7,891	343.0	100.3
Johnstown, PA.......................	228	3,359	380.3	168.2	127	5,232	1,798.8	241.6	300	4,070	179.0	47.8

Table C. Metropolitan Areas — Health Care and Social Assistance, Other Services, Nonemployer Businesses, and Residential Construction

Area name	Health care and social assistance, 2012				Other services, 2012				Nonemployer businesses, 2016		Value of residential construction authorized by building permits, 2018	
	Number of establishments	Number of employees	Receipts (mil dol)	Annual payroll (mil dol)	Number of establishments	Number of employees	Receipts (mil dol)	Annual payroll (mil dol)	Number	Receipts (mil dol)	New construction ($1,000)	Number of housing units
	159	160	161	162	163	164	165	166	167	168	169	170
Evansville, IN-KY..................	852	24,213	2,658.0	999.2	548	3,988	441.5	121.4	17,090	709.6	128,462	596
Fairbanks, AK.........................	290	5,748	746.9	305.5	185	842	88.8	25.6	5,802	227.7	3,483	13
Fargo, ND-MN.......................	606	19,302	2,096.3	901.9	485	3,040	316.3	82.2	16,354	883.7	392,690	2,313
Farmington, NM......................	275	6,819	682.5	291.7	226	1,571	164.1	54.5	5,104	193.9	15,779	71
Fayetteville, NC.....................	843	21,330	2,156.0	978.9	441	2,504	229.0	61.4	20,394	739.3	163,769	819
Fayetteville-Springdale-Rogers, AR-MO............	1,084	22,894	2,307.6	908.9	596	3,738	472.9	101.8	36,893	1,689.0	1,133,798	5,570
Flagstaff, AZ...........................	381	6,995	1,040.7	354.3	230	1,307	105.8	32.7	9,228	383.5	129,939	665
Flint, MI..................................	1,294	25,418	2,787.5	1,148.7	562	3,406	376.2	91.1	27,464	988.5	107,825	630
Florence, SC...........................	450	15,888	1,783.9	668.8	275	1,693	165.6	40.0	12,395	471.9	80,201	562
Florence-Muscle Shoals, AL...	382	6,957	731.4	269.8	186	D	D	D	9,937	436.9	34,107	335
Fond du Lac, WI.....................	281	5,764	758.8	248.8	191	1,245	114.4	31.3	4,995	236.9	44,500	275
Fort Collins, CO.....................	1,021	18,142	1,988.2	783.2	658	3,536	374.1	96.2	31,698	1,420.8	645,800	2,944
Fort Smith, AR-OK.................	681	18,011	1,641.2	658.4	341	1,645	141.9	40.0	18,394	865.7	84,946	598
Fort Wayne, IN.......................	1,069	31,129	3,035.1	1,282.7	791	5,195	491.7	147.2	27,363	1,134.5	403,227	1,884
Fresno, CA.............................	2,204	42,281	5,325.6	1,997.0	1,000	7,367	747.6	200.1	51,942	2,629.2	704,153	2,929
Gadsden, AL............................	316	7,433	701.9	303.4	125	632	98.9	19.0	7,267	316.1	16,901	104
Gainesville, FL......................	757	22,437	2,752.6	1,043.5	392	2,664	465.2	93.2	18,918	693.1	234,939	1,569
Gainesville, GA......................	443	9,275	1,297.8	493.4	246	1,193	123.8	32.4	15,291	699.4	294,876	1,778
Gettysburg, PA.......................	182	4,634	448.2	167.1	150	909	75.1	19.8	6,527	285.6	49,540	224
Glens Falls, NY......................	388	8,109	665.2	305.5	218	1,088	112.7	33.7	8,497	379.3	54,506	227
Goldsboro, NC........................	254	6,896	606.6	265.8	142	939	69.3	20.3	6,376	231.9	50,728	275
Grand Forks, ND-MN..............	250	9,377	823.3	372.6	204	1,128	126.4	27.2	6,301	286.8	71,425	355
Grand Island, NE...................	231	5,479	552.8	199.0	202	1,161	111.3	25.6	5,908	262.5	37,958	205
Grand Junction, CO...............	426	10,176	1,029.0	427.2	293	1,883	182.6	47.8	11,817	501.0	129,423	830
Grand Rapids-Wyoming, MI...	2,285	64,137	6,540.1	2,608.2	1,690	11,582	1,100.9	313.1	72,616	3,630.2	891,817	3,854
Grants Pass, OR	269	4,376	418.5	151.1	103	D	D	D	5,805	251.4	55,015	227
Great Falls, MT.......................	262	6,363	711.9	269.1	155	871	76.6	21.7	4,775	200.1	34,820	144
Greeley, CO............................	435	7,951	893.1	325.4	329	1,537	175.9	44.5	21,999	1,012.3	885,450	4,107
Green Bay, WI........................	701	21,661	2,578.4	964.5	505	3,019	261.3	72.2	17,376	861.0	245,224	1,201
Greensboro-High Point, NC ...	1,697	41,710	4,164.2	1,648.4	1,095	6,325	947.5	185.8	55,593	2,398.7	500,351	2,224
Greenville, NC........................	510	16,075	1,880.0	681.9	183	1,104	93.9	25.1	10,594	399.3	178,255	1,150
Greenville-Anderson-Mauldin, SC.................	1,770	35,622	3,666.0	1,530.0	1,138	9,603	1,165.4	351.8	61,444	2,713.8	1,736,942	6,430
Gulfport-Biloxi-Pascagoula, MS.................	789	18,643	2,454.1	1,001.3	462	2,663	247.4	73.3	27,309	1,057.8	354,563	2,159
Hagerstown-Martinsburg, MD-WV.......................	637	15,877	1,685.9	725.3	377	2,229	191.8	54.1	14,382	611.2	283,423	1,393
Hammond, LA..........................	301	8,143	655.2	261.4	149	966	98.1	25.5	10,120	365.0	186,102	1,322
Hanford-Corcoran, CA............	231	4,770	587.8	203.5	94	382	37.4	9.9	4,520	200.5	84,402	352
Harrisburg-Carlisle, PA..........	1,562	42,982	3,882.5	1,598.3	1,285	9,158	1,124.9	310.5	34,915	1,642.6	351,998	2,013
Harrisonburg, VA....................	263	7,433	708.4	298.6	231	1,164	109.4	31.6	8,316	374.1	126,194	483
Hartford-West Hartford-East Hartford, CT	3,543	99,706	10,449.5	4,596.2	2,462	15,615	1,759.3	537.5	81,630	4,378.0	232,878	1,587
Hattiesburg, MS......................	368	11,108	1,237.7	562.0	168	943	83.1	22.5	10,578	493.2	19,255	106
Hickory-Lenoir-Morganton, NC.................	744	19,423	1,882.9	733.3	437	2,380	199.7	55.8	23,097	965.8	237,273	1,336
Hilton Head Island-Bluffton-Beaufort, NC	470	6,794	751.1	249.6	351	2,862	258.7	86.0	17,584	927.1	809,129	2,336
Hinesville, GA.........................	81	2,055	251.1	101.6	68	435	32.7	9.5	3,512	99.7	86,467	398
Homosassa Springs, FL.........	390	7,932	819.7	307.1	212	744	53.2	15.5	8,987	359.3	178,006	884
Hot Springs, AR.....................	319	7,374	717.5	275.4	161	766	53.3	16.2	7,890	337.6	14,898	91
Houma-Thibodaux, LA...........	478	11,115	1,181.6	466.8	285	2,135	304.2	92.7	15,371	654.4	117,129	505
Houston-The Woodlands-Sugar Land, TX...........	14,336	290,976	35,675.8	13,099.0	7,926	72,280	8,932.1	2,623.8	562,758	25,717.0	9,172,451	57,288
Huntington-Ashland, WV-KY-OH.................	1,054	28,659	3,170.0	1,241.0	457	3,096	360.0	96.4	16,995	620.3	47,982	260
Huntsville, AL.........................	1,053	23,925	2,645.2	1,060.2	556	4,015	617.2	140.6	30,066	1,215.9	458,339	2,941
Idaho Falls, ID	577	8,114	865.6	297.5	194	892	91.4	22.7	11,037	494.7	152,999	1,037
Indianapolis-Carmel-Anderson, IN....................	4,724	131,895	15,661.0	6,100.5	3,192	26,908	4,270.6	900.2	139,555	6,087.4	2,279,674	8,894
Iowa City, IA..........................	450	16,991	2,046.3	803.8	270	1,667	207.7	46.4	11,585	548.7	232,750	1,367
Ithaca, NY..............................	271	5,283	483.0	199.8	152	966	122.9	23.9	7,546	281.5	111,786	805
Jackson, MI............................	351	9,060	936.8	409.4	210	1,361	129.7	37.1	8,958	349.1	32,711	172
Jackson, MS...........................	1,446	44,764	4,786.6	1,894.4	853	5,442	604.1	185.0	49,687	2,193.1	319,823	1,341
Jackson, TN	370	12,812	1,231.3	510.1	151	812	66.4	20.5	8,463	370.9	53,907	280
Jacksonville, FL.....................	3,685	74,724	9,238.6	3,315.2	2,369	13,420	2,219.2	438.7	108,197	4,205.5	3,213,253	15,450
Jacksonville, NC....................	257	5,765	491.7	197.5	210	1,172	89.9	26.6	9,889	354.5	153,308	1,036
Janesville-Beloit, WI..............	320	9,667	1,120.9	438.4	268	1,417	105.0	30.8	8,106	349.3	75,614	340
Jefferson City, MO.................	370	9,486	874.8	358.5	325	1,760	200.3	59.5	9,230	408.9	45,970	249
Johnson City, TN	458	16,539	1,833.8	815.0	234	1,347	100.5	32.1	12,236	527.8	109,415	635
Johnstown, PA........................	540	11,708	1,047.3	444.7	312	1,690	133.9	34.2	6,241	244.0	16,414	66

Table C. Metropolitan Areas — Government Employment and Payroll, and Local Government Finances

	Government employment and payroll, 2012									Local government finances, 2012				
			March payroll (percent of total)							General revenue				
													Taxes	
													Per capita[1] (dollars)	
Area name	Full-time equivalent employees	March payroll (dollars)	Adminis-tration, judicial, and legal	Police and corrections	Fire protection	Highways and transpor-tation	Health and welfare	Natural resources and utilities	Education and libraries	Total (mil dol)	Inter-govern-mental (mil dol)	Total (mil dol)	Total	Property
	171	172	173	174	175	176	177	178	179	180	181	182	183	184
Evansville, IN-KY..................	10,347	34,710,256	6.8	10.9	4.5	3.9	1.7	8.5	62.2	995.2	463.1	341.3	1,089	857
Fairbanks, AK......................	2,949	14,833,210	7.9	3.4	2.6	2.4	1.8	5.3	75.9	380.0	201.2	148.5	1,481	1,335
Fargo, ND-MN......................	6,888	27,847,634	5.1	9.5	2.7	4.4	9.5	7.5	60.2	969.4	445.6	298.8	1,381	1,058
Farmington, NM....................	5,857	21,149,302	4.2	11.0	2.6	2.0	1.9	8.4	68.4	491.8	290.9	126.9	987	702
Fayetteville, NC...................	20,611	71,938,105	1.4	6.0	1.8	0.8	38.1	3.6	42.6	1,147.7	620.9	372.5	995	717
Fayetteville-Springdale-Rogers, AR-MO............	15,951	51,196,846	5.5	9.4	4.3	3.2	1.0	5.4	70.1	1,400.1	793.7	404.4	839	367
Flagstaff, AZ......................	4,575	17,536,070	11.8	13.5	9.2	3.5	4.5	6.4	48.1	469.7	159.1	223.4	1,643	979
Flint, MI...............................	15,234	64,330,939	5.5	5.9	1.4	3.5	24.1	3.5	55.1	2,005.4	1,056.8	353.2	844	786
Florence, SC.......................	6,966	21,627,471	5.6	9.2	1.9	2.7	6.2	5.3	67.5	538.5	250.7	178.7	867	649
Florence-Muscle Shoals, AL...	5,882	19,596,410	3.1	6.8	3.3	3.2	20.6	13.8	47.1	488.1	192.2	137.3	934	418
Fond du Lac, WI..................	3,703	15,389,801	4.9	9.2	2.4	4.4	10.7	3.5	63.8	424.7	174.4	182.3	1,790	1,688
Fort Collins, CO..................	10,782	47,317,101	8.8	11.5	1.1	2.8	7.5	18.4	46.2	1,178.8	292.6	577.8	1,861	1,211
Fort Smith, AR-OK...............	9,950	33,824,806	6.1	6.9	2.1	3.1	5.0	11.1	65.4	795.9	453.2	202.5	722	305
Fort Wayne, IN....................	12,482	46,187,211	6.4	12.8	3.8	4.6	1.3	5.6	63.8	1,286.9	601.6	479.3	1,137	913
Fresno, CA...........................	34,954	165,436,346	4.1	10.3	2.1	3.3	9.7	4.5	65.0	5,127.4	3,047.2	1,071.6	1,131	789
Gadsden, AL........................	3,980	11,900,349	4.3	10.5	6.2	3.7	6.9	8.4	56.6	284.1	137.1	99.7	955	293
Gainesville, FL....................	10,035	36,051,916	10.0	15.5	4.4	4.8	3.2	11.5	46.9	897.9	290.9	376.2	1,402	1,085
Gainesville, GA...................	6,523	22,620,107	6.4	9.1	7.3	1.6	4.4	4.9	65.4	563.5	217.3	266.2	1,436	890
Gettysburg, PA....................	2,548	9,790,732	7.8	9.5	0.9	2.6	2.1	3.4	73.2	374.0	165.8	167.3	1,648	1,256
Glens Falls, NY...................	6,698	24,733,643	6.0	8.2	0.4	6.9	8.7	2.7	65.0	745.4	272.2	360.1	2,803	2,155
Goldsboro, NC.....................	5,237	14,176,474	3.0	6.2	2.1	1.3	9.2	6.0	66.2	346.7	199.6	101.5	817	585
Grand Forks, ND-MN	4,147	14,917,010	5.7	8.3	2.6	5.2	15.5	10.4	50.1	471.6	218.9	130.8	1,323	1,063
Grand Island, NE.................	4,036	14,835,732	5.6	6.7	2.9	4.0	6.4	15.9	57.5	355.7	117.9	148.0	1,773	1,410
Grand Junction, CO..............	5,197	18,735,519	8.2	13.3	5.0	4.1	7.0	9.6	48.8	498.4	180.8	228.0	1,542	966
Grand Rapids-Wyoming, MI...	26,602	112,436,599	7.9	9.0	2.5	4.3	3.1	4.9	66.6	3,718.2	1,877.6	1,165.3	1,159	1,055
Grants Pass, OR	2,192	8,995,230	6.6	12.9	2.5	3.4	1.3	3.1	68.4	243.6	119.9	70.8	854	781
Great Falls, MT....................	2,704	9,771,107	6.8	13.0	3.8	5.6	3.7	6.9	59.0	238.3	103.2	77.2	944	913
Greeley, CO..........................	8,663	35,763,495	8.2	17.4	4.0	5.2	6.6	11.0	45.5	919.9	308.8	411.9	1,562	1,194
Green Bay, WI......................	11,507	49,464,799	4.6	9.3	2.9	4.0	8.9	3.8	65.2	1,398.9	611.3	539.9	1,735	1,620
Greensboro-High Point, NC ...	26,780	99,652,358	4.7	9.7	3.6	2.0	7.2	5.5	64.4	2,394.5	1,098.1	928.6	1,262	995
Greenville, NC.....................	6,107	20,619,861	3.8	8.9	3.2	2.0	4.2	10.9	60.2	555.7	265.7	167.7	972	677
Greenville-Anderson-Mauldin, SC..............................	32,635	116,071,503	4.0	6.4	3.0	1.4	33.6	5.1	45.4	3,592.7	858.8	824.2	978	830
Gulfport-Biloxi-Pascagoula, MS............................	18,635	68,245,147	4.0	7.4	3.9	3.0	36.0	3.0	41.5	2,388.7	948.4	466.4	1,229	1,099
Hagerstown-Martinsburg, MD-WV........................	8,853	33,633,765	4.2	5.9	2.5	1.9	0.9	6.7	76.6	810.6	360.1	325.5	1,270	912
Hammond, LA.......................	6,393	23,444,209	4.2	6.0	1.2	1.7	46.4	1.8	37.5	621.2	213.8	128.9	1,044	366
Hanford-Corcoran, CA............	4,882	22,137,016	6.6	11.1	2.5	1.2	11.7	3.6	60.7	623.0	383.4	130.2	860	727
Harrisburg-Carlisle, PA..........	18,305	73,828,976	7.2	11.2	0.6	3.9	3.7	5.0	66.8	2,496.2	893.1	1,022.1	1,845	1,338
Harrisonburg, VA..................	4,180	13,504,909	5.9	8.1	4.4	2.7	4.3	7.2	63.8	389.9	157.1	146.9	1,145	791
Hartford-West Hartford-East Hartford, CT	41,889	212,590,921	3.4	7.9	3.6	2.6	3.3	4.5	73.1	5,466.8	1,915.2	3,050.0	2,512	2,484
Hattiesburg, MS...................	9,029	27,151,166	3.5	4.9	2.0	2.5	47.7	1.9	36.9	819.4	196.1	154.2	1,050	973
Hickory-Lenoir-Morganton, NC..............................	15,251	50,474,252	3.6	5.9	2.0	1.2	24.3	3.5	56.8	1,280.9	597.8	326.4	898	671
Hilton Head Island-Bluffton-Beaufort, NC	6,425	25,024,387	7.0	9.7	6.6	1.7	25.2	3.9	43.8	837.8	157.8	429.0	2,213	1,771
Hinesville, GA......................	3,104	9,754,876	5.6	9.3	1.5	1.2	15.4	1.8	61.7	272.2	113.4	80.9	993	612
Homosassa Springs, FL.........	3,890	11,674,757	8.6	11.3	0.1	3.6	5.4	3.4	65.1	322.4	98.7	162.1	1,163	1,064
Hot Springs, AR...................	2,929	9,379,603	4.7	8.8	4.0	3.5	3.4	5.5	68.3	270.5	155.0	62.1	640	262
Houma-Thibodaux, LA............	10,111	34,879,997	4.6	9.7	0.6	2.6	31.8	4.0	45.8	1,130.5	411.7	323.8	1,550	688
Houston-The Woodlands-Sugar Land, TX............	234,372	897,703,915	4.7	10.8	3.1	4.2	7.4	3.2	64.5	25,851.7	7,434.4	12,890.3	2,087	1,738
Huntington-Ashland, WV-KY-OH...............................	12,579	40,423,670	4.4	6.3	2.0	2.6	4.4	5.0	73.1	1,054.7	525.7	330.6	907	701
Huntsville, AL......................	20,024	74,872,202	3.7	6.3	3.0	2.8	37.7	7.5	35.8	2,192.6	900.1	428.1	994	510
Idaho Falls, ID.....................	4,554	14,040,874	6.5	10.1	4.5	3.7	7.6	7.0	58.6	341.3	174.7	100.7	740	715
Indianapolis-Carmel-Ander-son, IN............................	70,652	276,197,106	4.2	7.9	5.6	1.8	17.0	11.3	51.5	8,491.3	3,269.0	2,704.9	1,402	1,025
Iowa City, IA........................	3,919	16,365,120	7.2	7.7	1.2	4.7	10.4	5.1	60.1	620.3	195.2	302.5	1,912	1,555
Ithaca, NY............................	4,530	19,870,493	5.0	6.2	2.8	4.4	7.3	3.5	68.0	531.9	184.0	252.8	2,465	1,857
Jackson, MI..........................	4,304	17,626,740	7.6	8.1	2.4	4.2	3.5	3.4	69.5	585.1	325.3	139.2	868	809
Jackson, MS........................	21,103	60,140,323	6.0	10.4	4.8	2.9	1.9	4.3	69.2	1,733.1	846.9	586.9	1,017	965
Jackson, TN.........................	8,999	31,890,237	2.6	6.7	2.4	1.5	58.7	4.5	23.0	995.9	160.4	156.2	1,197	685
Jacksonville, FL....................	42,905	156,841,760	5.8	13.6	6.1	2.2	1.4	6.6	57.0	4,877.5	1,516.3	1,990.7	1,445	1,051
Jacksonville, NC...................	5,873	18,455,158	3.9	7.0	1.9	1.2	10.7	4.8	66.2	585.4	209.5	152.5	832	536
Janesville-Beloit, WI..............	6,252	25,471,665	5.9	9.6	3.9	4.4	7.9	4.5	62.6	723.4	387.9	249.8	1,557	1,471
Jefferson City, MO................	4,566	13,402,962	7.4	8.2	3.3	4.3	4.8	6.3	65.4	359.6	122.3	173.3	1,154	721
Johnson City, TN.................	6,906	20,205,200	5.5	9.0	2.8	6.4	4.7	12.5	56.6	469.5	191.0	177.3	884	595
Johnstown, PA......................	4,484	15,273,184	8.2	8.3	1.4	5.9	5.7	6.0	63.9	555.1	293.7	143.3	1,012	781

1. Based on the resident population estimated as of July 1 of the year shown.

Area name	Local government finances, 2012 (cont.)									Government employment, 2017			Individual income tax returns, 2016		
	Direct general expenditure							Debt outstanding							
			Percent of total for:											Mean	
	Total (mil dol)	Per capita¹ (dollars)	Educa-tion	Health and hospitals	Police protection	Public welfare	Highways	Total (mil dol)	Per capita¹ (dollars)	Federal civilian	Federal military	State and local	Number of returns	adjusted gross income	Mean income tax
	185	186	187	188	189	190	191	192	193	194	195	196	197	198	199
Evansville, IN-KY..................	984.8	3,142	43.4	0.7	5.9	0.3	3.2	1,444.5	4,609	1,331	963	15,437	147,050	58,138	7,250
Fairbanks, AK.......................	342.4	3,415	63.0	1.6	2.3	0.0	6.2	170.2	1,698	3,041	9,791	7,512	46,040	65,853	8,618
Fargo, ND-MN......................	990.1	4,577	37.7	0.6	5.3	4.1	12.4	1,641.6	7,589	2,560	1,315	16,802	114,410	68,935	9,552
Farmington, NM.....................	551.0	4,287	55.6	3.3	6.3	1.2	4.3	2,140.3	16,652	1,510	327	9,635	48,640	48,945	5,153
Fayetteville, NC....................	1,203.8	3,214	51.4	3.6	7.6	6.4	1.2	604.8	1,615	15,267	46,553	25,190	160,000	44,911	4,186
Fayetteville-Springdale-Rogers, AR-MO...........	1,387.0	2,876	60.9	0.3	5.5	0.0	4.9	2,146.7	4,452	2,560	2,078	29,422	224,910	80,076	11,602
Flagstaff, AZ	457.2	3,361	35.9	3.4	6.5	1.6	7.6	377.9	2,779	2,773	306	16,181	59,500	56,172	6,803
Flint, MI................................	2,064.7	4,935	41.9	28.1	3.5	1.1	3.3	995.9	2,380	1,094	649	19,375	190,860	50,338	5,826
Florence, SC.........................	530.6	2,575	60.9	4.4	6.7	0.2	1.8	374.1	1,815	682	795	15,567	87,250	47,995	5,198
Florence-Muscle Shoals, AL...	484.2	3,294	44.6	19.9	4.8	0.1	5.0	444.4	3,023	886	620	8,881	61,940	53,872	6,195
Fond du Lac, WI....................	449.6	4,415	51.8	7.3	5.2	3.9	9.0	580.9	5,704	195	263	5,229	50,870	59,404	7,231
Fort Collins, CO....................	1,080.2	3,479	37.9	4.5	6.4	3.0	9.0	1,388.6	4,472	2,555	869	35,172	165,500	71,345	9,953
Fort Smith, AR-OK.................	802.3	2,860	58.0	2.8	5.0	0.2	6.3	1,030.6	3,674	1,294	1,122	16,918	110,190	47,685	4,974
Fort Wayne, IN.....................	1,126.6	2,673	51.6	0.6	6.1	0.3	3.5	1,205.7	2,861	2,190	1,327	20,091	206,820	56,548	7,102
Fresno, CA...........................	5,031.5	5,308	44.7	7.0	5.6	10.3	3.4	3,847.5	4,059	9,924	1,632	62,586	393,330	52,038	5,767
Gadsden, AL.........................	278.9	2,672	46.7	1.9	11.2	0.2	4.8	218.9	2,097	301	430	5,065	41,770	45,540	4,425
Gainesville, FL......................	944.7	3,522	39.3	3.8	8.2	1.7	4.8	1,953.5	7,283	4,716	571	37,458	118,160	57,276	7,639
Gainesville, GA.....................	566.0	3,053	55.8	6.1	4.5	0.8	2.5	1,522.9	8,213	474	540	10,413	86,160	57,746	6,874
Gettysburg, PA......................	458.0	4,513	68.9	3.6	1.4	3.2	2.7	405.6	3,997	688	254	3,291	51,650	59,662	6,886
Glens Falls, NY.....................	755.6	5,881	49.4	4.6	2.6	10.7	7.9	575.7	4,481	324	194	9,381	62,540	53,355	5,930
Goldsboro, NC.......................	344.7	2,774	55.1	4.8	6.3	6.3	1.4	151.3	1,217	1,225	4,485	8,044	51,490	47,797	5,049
Grand Forks, ND-MN	433.5	4,384	39.7	1.2	4.5	5.2	9.0	875.4	8,852	1,126	2,130	11,933	47,510	61,017	7,724
Grand Island, NE..................	357.6	4,284	52.8	8.0	4.1	0.3	5.6	317.1	3,799	736	291	6,057	40,690	52,679	5,925
Grand Junction, CO...............	517.8	3,502	35.4	1.7	13.1	5.6	9.4	476.5	3,223	1,573	385	8,487	68,820	54,254	6,163
Grand Rapids-Wyoming, MI ...	3,715.2	3,694	53.0	6.3	4.2	1.7	4.7	5,263.1	5,234	3,546	1,782	45,718	498,270	65,221	8,479
Grants Pass, OR	253.3	3,055	59.6	2.9	7.1	0.1	5.0	145.0	1,748	263	207	2,869	37,020	47,889	5,061
Great Falls, MT.....................	242.5	2,968	53.0	1.0	9.7	1.4	5.2	90.0	1,101	1,675	3,472	4,040	39,330	50,718	5,428
Greeley, CO..........................	839.9	3,185	42.6	1.2	7.3	4.0	6.6	868.6	3,294	662	755	15,983	132,160	61,915	7,268
Green Bay, WI.......................	1,439.4	4,627	48.3	6.1	6.0	4.3	8.4	1,261.2	4,054	1,404	858	20,660	158,850	63,490	8,381
Greensboro-High Point, NC ...	2,532.1	3,440	46.9	4.0	7.4	4.8	2.6	2,453.8	3,334	4,401	1,730	39,169	339,400	55,637	6,834
Greenville, NC.......................	557.6	3,232	46.8	1.8	9.9	5.2	2.1	400.7	2,322	715	431	25,861	71,820	52,775	6,226
Greenville-Anderson-Mauldin, SC	3,672.8	4,358	32.8	39.0	3.5	0.2	1.5	5,469.6	6,489	2,740	3,411	56,314	387,560	59,001	7,156
Gulfport-Biloxi-Pascagoula, MS	2,433.4	6,411	24.7	32.2	3.8	0.1	4.4	1,537.8	4,051	8,751	9,819	24,359	165,930	49,529	5,370
Hagerstown-Martinsburg, MD-WV......................	838.7	3,272	65.4	0.7	4.2	0.3	3.3	710.6	2,773	4,034	1,069	13,309	122,930	53,684	5,574
Hammond, LA........................	692.4	5,610	29.5	47.0	3.7	0.0	2.7	361.5	2,929	372	491	10,682	51,830	50,148	5,647
Hanford-Corcoran, CA...........	602.9	3,983	45.9	6.6	4.9	9.6	2.9	261.9	1,730	1,160	4,890	13,623	54,070	46,648	4,207
Harrisburg-Carlisle, PA..........	2,716.3	4,903	51.9	3.9	3.3	8.1	2.6	3,833.1	6,919	7,330	2,185	52,747	289,760	61,047	7,625
Harrisonburg, VA...................	400.5	3,120	46.7	1.9	4.0	7.4	5.5	729.3	5,681	348	411	11,500	55,190	52,700	5,509
Hartford-West Hartford-East Hartford, CT	5,447.0	4,485	58.0	0.9	5.6	0.7	4.2	3,350.1	2,759	6,230	2,460	90,822	597,880	76,536	10,923
Hattiesburg, MS....................	821.7	5,598	26.1	51.6	3.1	0.0	4.2	543.5	3,703	815	1,199	14,082	59,620	54,259	6,785
Hickory-Lenoir-Morganton, NC	1,270.8	3,495	44.3	23.2	5.0	6.0	1.2	476.3	1,310	650	813	22,297	159,460	49,905	5,430
Hilton Head Island-Bluffton-Beaufort, NC	819.4	4,226	33.8	18.0	6.2	1.1	2.3	1,530.6	7,895	2,268	10,826	9,264	96,270	73,701	10,564
Hinesville, GA.......................	286.7	3,516	55.3	16.9	4.8	0.2	3.0	89.3	1,095	3,744	15,516	3,895	31,810	37,817	2,609
Homosassa Springs, FL.........	362.7	2,602	47.4	5.5	9.1	2.5	6.6	493.5	3,541	235	258	4,075	65,200	47,080	5,251
Hot Springs, AR....................	268.9	2,775	57.5	0.3	5.6	0.0	3.6	344.1	3,551	453	382	3,994	42,920	50,162	5,742
Houma-Thibodaux, LA...........	1,104.3	5,286	31.2	30.4	4.8	0.4	2.8	502.1	2,403	419	866	11,750	85,460	53,605	6,892
Houston-The Woodlands-Sugar Land, TX	25,345.7	4,103	45.4	8.8	5.5	0.2	5.0	71,316.9	11,545	28,982	15,255	364,742	2,895,200	69,605	10,476
Huntington-Ashland, WV-KY-OH.......................	1,087.6	2,982	60.9	2.7	4.7	1.1	2.2	804.6	2,206	3,303	1,526	19,186	146,220	51,613	5,658
Huntsville, AL.......................	2,106.9	4,891	33.3	37.0	3.8	0.1	2.7	2,214.6	5,141	19,435	2,632	30,848	206,870	67,070	8,763
Idaho Falls, ID	346.6	2,547	46.8	2.7	7.1	0.3	4.8	344.6	2,532	872	497	7,094	59,730	62,444	7,066
Indianapolis-Carmel-Anderson, IN.........................	8,480.2	4,396	36.1	22.7	4.0	0.2	1.7	17,097.1	8,863	17,058	6,619	116,825	964,260	65,153	8,870
Iowa City, IA.........................	652.2	4,122	35.8	7.3	3.9	0.8	6.6	863.6	5,458	2,140	639	37,202	75,210	69,641	9,199
Ithaca, NY............................	541.1	5,276	48.3	4.4	2.7	8.0	5.5	696.7	6,794	268	164	5,861	40,530	66,266	8,483
Jackson, MI..........................	586.0	3,655	54.4	10.1	2.6	3.6	6.4	539.6	3,366	332	244	7,458	70,940	52,836	5,966
Jackson, MS.........................	1,812.3	3,142	55.0	1.6	6.1	0.3	7.0	2,027.9	3,516	6,324	3,329	52,454	249,750	56,707	7,053
Jackson, TN	966.4	7,408	17.5	58.3	3.3	0.1	2.4	1,066.4	8,174	495	359	13,550	56,880	49,700	5,791
Jacksonville, FL....................	4,951.5	3,594	40.9	2.0	9.1	1.2	4.9	13,946.9	10,122	18,029	13,255	59,848	704,510	63,394	8,619
Jacksonville, NC...................	563.2	3,073	38.6	24.7	6.7	6.5	1.0	439.4	2,398	6,503	47,081	8,095	78,650	43,168	3,605
Janesville-Beloit, WI.............	729.2	4,546	49.6	7.4	6.2	7.1	5.3	614.8	3,833	299	422	8,530	79,100	52,868	5,678
Jefferson City, MO................	363.3	2,419	52.7	3.5	8.9	0.0	8.7	294.3	1,960	807	506	24,455	68,780	53,631	5,905
Johnson City, TN	497.7	2,480	48.2	7.3	6.4	0.4	5.3	765.4	3,814	2,932	609	13,171	86,660	49,705	5,636
Johnstown, PA......................	571.5	4,037	49.2	3.2	5.7	14.0	3.6	641.5	4,531	1,013	352	6,796	62,990	47,456	5,026

1. Based on the resident population estimated as of July 1 of the year shown.

Table C. Metropolitan Areas — **Land Area and Population**

CBSA/DIV Code[1]	Area name	Land area[2] (sq mi)	Total persons	Rank	Per square mile	White	Black	American Indian, Alaska Native	Asian and Pacific Islander	Percent Hispanic or Latino[3]	Under 5 years	5 to 17 years	18 to 24 years	25 to 34 years	35 to 44 years	45 to 54 years
			Population, 2018			Population characteristics, 2018										
						Race alone or in combination, not Hispanic or Latino (percent)					Age (percent)					
		1	2	3	4	5	6	7	8	9	10	11	12	13	14	15
27860	Jonesboro, AR......................	1,465.7	132,532	304	90.4	79.1	15.6	0.8	1.4	4.8	7.0	17.8	10.1	14.9	12.5	11.8
27900	Joplin, MO...........................	1,263.3	178,902	235	141.6	87.3	2.7	3.4	2.3	7.4	6.6	17.9	8.8	13.3	12.1	12.0
27980	Kahului-Wailuku-Lahaina, HI..	1,173.5	167,295	255	142.6	43.9	1.4	1.8	67.7	11.5	5.9	15.8	6.8	12.7	13.4	13.0
28020	Kalamazoo-Portage, MI.........	1,169.9	340,318	152	290.9	80.8	11.6	1.3	3.0	6.5	6.0	16.0	13.8	13.1	11.6	11.5
28100	Kankakee, IL	676.5	110,024	339	162.6	73.5	15.7	0.5	1.4	10.6	5.9	16.8	11.0	12.2	11.7	12.4
28140	Kansas City, MO-KS.............	7,256.5	2,143,651	31	295.4	74.7	13.7	1.2	4.0	9.2	6.5	17.7	8.0	14.3	13.2	12.6
28420	Kennewick-Richland, WA	2,941.6	296,224	164	100.7	62.4	2.4	1.4	3.9	32.2	7.7	20.8	8.7	14.2	13.0	11.2
28660	Killeen-Temple, TX	2,816.3	451,679	119	160.4	51.3	22.4	1.2	5.0	23.9	8.0	18.6	11.3	16.8	13.3	10.9
28700	Kingsport-Bristol-Bristol, TN-VA....	2,010.3	306,616	162	152.5	95.1	2.7	0.7	0.9	1.8	4.8	14.4	7.4	11.4	11.3	14.0
28740	Kingston, NY	1,124.2	178,599	236	158.9	80.9	7.4	0.8	2.8	10.5	4.4	13.3	9.1	12.6	11.6	13.8
28940	Knoxville, TN	3,500.9	883,309	63	252.3	88.3	6.7	0.9	2.1	4.0	5.4	15.2	9.8	12.6	11.9	13.2
29020	Kokomo, IN..........................	293.0	82,366	375	281.1	87.4	9.1	0.9	1.7	3.5	6.0	16.6	8.0	12.0	11.3	12.6
29100	La Crosse-Onalaska, WI-MN .	1,003.8	136,808	296	136.3	92.1	2.2	0.8	4.7	1.9	5.2	14.9	14.7	12.4	11.2	11.3
29180	Lafayette, LA	3,408.4	489,364	109	143.6	68.7	26.0	0.7	2.1	4.1	6.9	17.7	8.6	14.8	12.7	12.1
29200	Lafayette-West Lafayette, IN..	1,277.5	221,828	201	173.6	79.5	5.7	0.6	8.2	8.0	5.9	15.1	21.5	13.8	10.7	10.2
29340	Lake Charles, LA.................	2,349.2	210,080	213	89.4	69.5	25.8	1.1	1.8	3.8	7.1	17.7	8.7	14.7	12.3	11.7
29420	Lake Havasu City-Kingman, AZ.................	13,311.1	209,550	214	15.7	78.6	1.5	2.9	2.0	16.8	4.4	12.7	6.2	10.2	9.0	10.9
29460	Lakeland-Winter Haven, FL....	1,797.2	708,009	81	394.0	59.4	15.6	0.7	2.4	23.6	5.8	16.3	8.4	13.1	11.9	12.0
29540	Lancaster, PA	943.9	543,557	103	575.9	83.0	4.6	0.4	2.8	10.8	6.5	17.1	8.9	13.2	11.4	11.9
29620	Lansing-East Lansing, MI.......	1,697.7	481,893	111	283.9	78.5	10.7	1.2	6.1	6.8	5.6	14.9	14.9	13.6	11.5	11.6
29700	Laredo, TX...........................	3,361.5	275,910	174	82.1	3.7	0.3	0.1	0.6	95.5	9.4	23.5	11.3	13.5	12.6	11.5
29740	Las Cruces, NM....................	3,808.2	217,522	208	57.1	27.8	1.9	1.2	1.5	68.6	6.4	18.1	14.4	13.0	11.0	10.2
29820	Las Vegas-Henderson-Paradise, NV	7,891.7	2,231,647	28	282.8	45.3	13.1	1.1	13.2	31.4	6.3	16.9	8.2	14.9	13.8	13.3
29940	Lawrence, KS	455.8	121,436	322	266.4	81.8	6.0	3.6	6.2	6.4	5.0	13.2	23.3	14.6	11.8	9.6
30020	Lawton, OK..........................	1,701.9	126,198	313	74.2	61.8	18.5	8.2	4.8	13.1	6.8	16.7	12.3	16.3	12.3	11.0
30140	Lebanon, PA........................	361.8	141,314	290	390.6	82.5	2.7	0.4	1.8	13.8	5.9	16.9	8.5	11.7	11.7	12.4
30300	Lewiston, ID-WA...................	1,484.4	63,018	381	42.5	90.2	1.1	5.3	1.8	4.1	5.6	15.2	7.9	12.7	11.3	11.7
30340	Lewiston-Auburn, ME............	467.9	107,679	342	230.1	92.5	5.3	1.1	1.5	2.0	5.8	15.8	8.4	12.4	11.8	13.6
30460	Lexington-Fayette, KY...........	1,469.9	516,697	106	351.5	79.2	12.5	0.6	3.6	6.3	6.1	15.8	12.1	14.3	13.0	12.4
30620	Lima, OH.............................	402.5	102,663	350	255.1	83.4	14.5	0.7	1.2	3.2	6.2	16.9	9.7	12.3	11.7	11.9
30700	Lincoln, NE..........................	1,409.0	334,590	154	237.5	83.9	5.2	1.2	5.4	7.0	6.3	16.6	14.8	13.7	12.5	10.7
30780	Little Rock-North Little Rock-Conway, AR.................	4,084.7	741,104	78	181.4	68.5	24.7	1.1	2.3	5.4	6.4	17.0	9.4	14.2	12.9	12.3
30860	Logan, UT-ID.......................	1,827.8	140,794	291	77.0	85.6	1.2	1.0	3.5	10.5	8.4	22.1	18.0	13.6	11.9	8.3
30980	Longview, TX........................	1,780.4	219,417	205	123.2	64.5	18.1	1.0	1.4	16.8	6.5	18.0	8.9	13.3	12.3	11.8
31020	Longview, WA.......................	1,140.6	108,987	341	95.6	86.4	1.6	3.1	3.0	9.2	6.2	16.8	7.5	12.3	11.8	12.2
31080	Los Angeles-Long Beach-Anaheim, CA.................	4,851.0	13,291,486	2	2,739.9	31.4	7.1	0.6	18.1	45.2	6.0	15.8	9.4	15.8	13.5	13.5
31080	Anaheim-Santa Ana-Irvine, CA Div 11244......	792.8	3,185,968	X	4,018.6	42.6	2.1	0.6	23.4	34.2	5.9	16.0	9.2	14.5	12.9	14.0
31080	Los Angeles-Long Beach-Glendale, CA Div 31084......	4,058.2	10,105,518	X	2,490.1	27.9	8.7	0.6	16.5	48.6	6.0	15.7	9.5	16.2	13.7	13.3
31140	Louisville/Jefferson County, KY-IN	3,578.8	1,297,301	45	362.5	77.8	15.9	0.7	2.8	5.0	6.1	16.4	8.3	13.8	12.7	13.1
31180	Lubbock, TX.........................	2,687.7	319,068	158	118.7	53.8	7.4	0.7	2.8	36.5	6.7	17.2	16.4	14.6	11.9	10.1
31340	Lynchburg, VA	2,120.4	263,353	186	124.2	77.6	18.5	0.8	2.1	3.0	5.3	14.4	13.0	12.3	10.1	12.3
31420	Macon, GA...........................	1,723.6	229,737	199	133.3	49.8	45.8	0.6	2.1	3.1	6.2	17.3	9.4	13.0	11.6	12.6
31460	Madera, CA..........................	2,136.9	157,672	263	73.8	35.0	3.7	1.8	2.7	58.3	7.6	19.9	9.4	14.0	12.6	11.5
31540	Madison, WI.........................	3,308.8	660,422	85	199.6	83.9	5.7	0.7	6.2	5.8	5.6	15.1	12.3	15.0	13.1	12.1
31700	Manchester-Nashua, NH........	876.5	415,247	129	473.8	85.8	3.2	0.7	5.2	7.0	5.2	15.2	8.6	13.7	12.2	14.4
31740	Manhattan, KS......................	1,450.5	97,980	359	67.5	82.5	6.4	1.3	5.3	7.7	6.1	13.6	26.1	16.2	10.8	7.7
31860	Mankato-North Mankato, MN .	1,196.4	101,647	353	85.0	89.4	4.8	0.7	2.9	4.1	5.6	14.9	18.5	13.3	11.6	10.1
31900	Mansfield, OH.......................	495.2	121,099	323	244.5	87.5	10.8	0.7	1.2	2.0	5.6	16.0	8.3	12.6	11.8	12.3
32580	McAllen-Edinburg-Mission, TX	1,570.9	865,939	65	551.2	6.2	0.5	0.1	1.0	92.4	8.9	23.6	10.9	13.5	12.6	11.0
32780	Medford, OR........................	2,783.3	219,564	204	78.9	83.2	1.4	2.4	2.9	13.2	5.6	15.1	7.6	12.7	11.8	11.5
32820	Memphis, TN-MS-AR	4,985.6	1,350,620	43	270.9	44.4	48.1	0.6	2.6	5.7	6.7	18.0	9.1	14.2	12.6	12.8
32900	Merced, CA..........................	1,935.6	274,765	175	142.0	28.7	3.6	0.9	8.5	60.2	7.7	21.6	11.2	14.7	12.3	11.2
33100	Miami-Fort Lauderdale-West Palm Beach, FL..........	5,067.5	6,198,782	7	1,223.2	30.8	21.1	0.3	3.2	45.8	5.6	14.6	8.0	13.5	13.1	14.0
33100	Fort Lauderdale-Pompano Beach-Deerfield Beach, FL 22744.........	1,203.1	1,951,260	X	1,621.9	36.8	29.4	0.4	4.7	30.4	5.8	15.4	7.9	13.5	13.4	14.1
33100	Miami-Miami Beach-Kendall, FL Div 33124	1,898.8	2,761,581	X	1,454.4	13.5	16.0	0.2	2.0	69.1	5.8	14.4	8.4	14.3	13.7	14.7
33100	West Palm Beach-Boca Raton-Delray Beach, FL Div 48424	1,965.6	1,485,941	X	756.0	55.2	19.4	0.4	3.6	22.9	5.1	14.0	7.5	12.0	11.5	12.8
33140	Michigan City-La Porte, IN	598.3	110,007	340	183.9	80.9	12.6	0.7	1.0	6.8	6.0	15.5	8.2	13.3	12.1	13.1
33220	Midland, MI..........................	516.3	83,209	373	161.2	92.9	1.9	1.0	2.9	2.8	5.4	15.9	8.3	12.4	11.8	13.4
33260	Midland, TX..........................	1,815.2	178,331	238	98.2	46.1	6.5	0.8	2.4	45.4	8.8	19.8	8.7	17.9	13.4	10.3
33340	Milwaukee-Waukesha-West Allis, WI............	1,454.9	1,576,113	39	1,083.3	68.1	17.5	0.9	4.6	10.9	6.2	16.8	8.9	14.0	12.6	12.5
33460	Minneapolis-St. Paul-Bloomington, MN.........	7,636.2	3,629,190	16	475.3	77.6	10.1	1.3	7.9	6.0	6.5	17.2	8.5	14.6	13.4	12.9
33540	Missoula, MT	2,593.0	118,791	327	45.8	91.9	1.0	3.9	2.9	3.3	5.1	13.6	14.0	15.6	12.9	10.9

1. CBSA = Core Based Statistical Area. DIV = Metropolitan Division. See Appendix A for explanation. See Appendix B for list of metropolitan areas or temporarily covered by water.   2. Dry land or land partially or temporarily covered by water.   3. May be of any race.

Table C. Metropolitan Areas — Population and Households

Area name	55 to 64 years	65 to 74 years	75 years and over	Percent female	2000	2010	2000-2010	2010-2018	Births	Deaths	Net migration	Number	Persons per house-hold	Family house-holds	Female family house-holder[1]	One person
	16	17	18	19	20	21	22	23	24	25	26	27	28	29	30	31
Jonesboro, AR	11.3	8.4	6.2	51.4	107,762	121,020	12.3	9.5	14,552	10,260	7,201	51,087	2.49	66.0	12.8	25.1
Joplin, MO	12.7	9.4	7.1	50.8	157,322	175,509	11.6	1.9	19,813	14,678	-1,684	69,136	2.53	67.0	10.6	26.5
Kahului-Wailuku-Lahaina, HI	14.2	11.3	7.0	50.3	128,241	154,930	20.8	8.0	16,166	9,562	5,840	53,616	3.05	67.9	11.4	24.2
Kalamazoo-Portage, MI	12.5	9.2	6.4	50.9	314,866	326,591	3.7	4.2	33,247	23,260	3,927	133,112	2.47	61.1	11.2	30.4
Kankakee, IL	13.2	9.5	7.3	50.8	103,833	113,450	9.3	-3.0	11,073	9,119	-5,386	39,628	2.63	64.8	13.3	30.2
Kansas City, MO-KS	12.9	8.7	6.1	50.9	1,811,254	2,009,341	10.9	6.7	227,214	137,685	45,997	829,475	2.53	63.9	11.3	29.6
Kennewick-Richland, WA	11.2	8.0	5.1	49.4	191,822	253,332	32.1	16.9	35,390	14,152	21,491	98,742	2.90	69.1	12.1	23.7
Killeen-Temple, TX	9.9	6.7	4.5	50.3	330,714	405,313	22.6	11.4	61,896	22,252	6,357	149,197	2.81	69.3	14.7	26.2
Kingsport-Bristol-Bristol, TN-VA	14.7	12.5	9.5	51.1	298,484	309,502	3.7	-0.9	24,256	32,244	5,337	129,285	2.32	66.8	12.1	28.9
Kingston, NY	15.5	11.6	8.2	50.4	177,749	182,512	2.7	-2.1	12,978	13,758	-3,069	68,822	2.44	64.0	13.8	28.4
Knoxville, TN	13.6	10.8	7.6	51.1	748,259	837,677	12.0	5.4	76,988	74,979	43,826	347,479	2.47	65.6	11.6	28.3
Kokomo, IN	14.0	11.0	8.5	51.5	84,964	82,752	-2.6	-0.5	8,151	7,894	-584	34,243	2.37	63.2	13.1	33.5
La Crosse-Onalaska, WI-MN	13.3	9.7	7.4	51.0	126,838	133,660	5.4	2.4	11,861	9,511	861	55,940	2.35	60.4	9.0	28.8
Lafayette, LA	13.1	8.4	5.7	51.3	425,020	466,736	9.8	4.8	55,769	34,004	953	179,072	2.70	64.9	13.9	28.5
Lafayette-West Lafayette, IN	10.2	7.3	5.3	49.0	178,541	201,794	13.0	9.9	21,559	11,652	10,197	80,855	2.50	59.4	9.2	28.5
Lake Charles, LA	12.9	8.8	6.1	51.1	193,568	199,641	3.1	5.2	23,711	16,587	3,458	81,266	2.55	63.4	14.3	30.9
Lake Havasu City-Kingman, AZ	16.3	17.2	13.1	49.4	155,032	200,182	29.1	4.7	15,133	23,119	17,225	87,565	2.33	63.3	9.3	30.0
Lakeland-Winter Haven, FL	12.3	11.3	8.9	51.0	483,924	602,098	24.4	17.6	61,773	52,726	96,548	233,058	2.89	70.3	12.9	24.5
Lancaster, PA	13.1	9.7	8.2	51.0	470,658	519,446	10.4	4.6	57,772	40,023	6,810	201,150	2.64	70.5	10.0	23.8
Lansing-East Lansing, MI	12.6	9.2	6.0	51.1	447,728	464,021	3.6	3.9	43,482	29,954	4,360	186,203	2.45	58.6	10.6	32.4
Laredo, TX	8.7	5.6	3.9	50.9	193,117	250,304	29.6	10.2	44,093	10,774	-7,690	74,045	3.67	80.0	22.3	18.0
Las Cruces, NM	11.1	9.1	6.7	50.9	174,682	209,202	19.8	4.0	24,508	12,451	-3,755	75,441	2.77	66.0	16.8	27.4
Las Vegas-Henderson-Paradise, NV	11.8	9.1	5.7	50.1	1,375,765	1,951,271	41.8	14.4	221,151	124,882	183,271	781,796	2.79	64.8	14.3	27.3
Lawrence, KS	10.2	7.5	4.9	50.2	99,962	110,826	10.9	9.6	10,073	5,404	5,987	47,643	2.36	54.8	7.7	30.3
Lawton, OK	11.8	7.4	5.5	48.3	121,610	130,288	7.1	-3.1	16,189	9,054	-11,422	46,009	2.58	64.1	14.4	28.8
Lebanon, PA	13.5	10.6	8.8	50.9	120,327	133,577	11.0	5.8	13,497	11,922	6,292	52,786	2.58	68.9	9.4	26.0
Lewiston, ID-WA	14.3	11.6	9.6	50.8	57,961	60,893	5.1	3.5	5,879	6,074	2,346	25,553	2.41	69.3	10.9	24.5
Lewiston-Auburn, ME	14.4	10.4	7.4	51.1	103,793	107,710	3.8	0.0	10,531	8,762	-1,753	45,979	2.27	56.8	8.4	32.1
Lexington-Fayette, KY	12.2	8.5	5.7	51.0	408,326	472,103	15.6	9.4	52,120	31,807	24,363	202,610	2.45	62.5	12.1	27.7
Lima, OH	13.7	10.0	7.6	49.6	108,473	106,315	-2.0	-3.4	10,445	8,979	-5,125	40,872	2.44	66.9	12.8	29.2
Lincoln, NE	11.3	8.4	5.6	49.8	266,787	302,157	13.3	10.7	34,954	18,210	15,816	129,363	2.45	61.2	9.0	29.2
Little Rock-North Little Rock-Conway, AR	12.5	9.2	6.1	51.6	610,518	699,796	14.6	5.9	79,527	53,354	15,273	283,142	2.56	64.7	14.3	30.6
Logan, UT-ID	7.9	5.7	4.2	49.8	102,720	125,442	22.1	12.2	21,078	5,053	-680	42,764	3.16	71.8	8.8	17.4
Longview, TX	12.9	9.3	7.0	49.9	194,042	214,367	10.5	2.4	24,383	18,666	-584	76,055	2.72	66.7	13.4	29.2
Longview, WA	14.2	11.3	7.6	50.5	92,948	102,408	10.2	6.4	10,156	9,106	5,547	41,611	2.54	61.7	11.8	30.1
Los Angeles-Long Beach-Anaheim, CA	12.2	7.9	6.0	50.7	12,365,627	12,828,946	3.7	3.6	1,357,648	663,733	-226,757	4,348,543	3.02	67.7	13.9	24.9
Anaheim-Santa Ana-Irvine, CA Div 11244	12.7	8.4	6.4	50.6	2,846,289	3,010,274	5.8	5.8	311,831	157,140	23,512	1,037,312	3.03	71.9	11.8	20.8
Los Angeles-Long Beach-Glendale, CA Div 31084	12.0	7.8	5.9	50.7	9,519,338	9,818,672	3.1	2.9	1,045,817	506,593	-250,269	3,311,231	3.02	66.4	14.6	26.2
Louisville/Jefferson County, KY-IN	13.6	9.6	6.4	51.1	1,121,109	1,235,691	10.2	5.0	129,976	100,050	32,465	502,581	2.52	63.9	12.7	29.8
Lubbock, TX	10.5	7.2	5.4	50.7	256,250	290,889	13.5	9.7	35,128	20,482	13,495	116,077	2.64	62.3	12.7	28.1
Lynchburg, VA	13.8	10.7	8.1	51.7	228,616	252,659	10.5	4.2	23,225	21,356	8,908	98,409	2.51	66.2	11.6	28.6
Macon, GA	13.4	9.9	6.8	52.3	222,368	232,287	4.5	-1.1	24,485	19,725	-7,291	84,028	2.64	61.2	17.8	34.7
Madera, CA	11.0	8.4	5.6	51.8	123,109	150,841	22.5	4.5	19,209	8,729	-3,700	46,282	3.22	78.1	9.9	17.5
Madison, WI	12.4	8.8	5.7	50.1	535,421	605,449	13.1	9.1	60,725	34,804	29,185	272,698	2.34	59.3	8.1	29.4
Manchester-Nashua, NH	14.9	9.3	6.4	50.2	380,841	400,699	5.2	3.6	35,319	26,060	5,493	161,414	2.49	66.4	9.9	24.6
Manhattan, KS	8.8	6.2	4.5	48.2	81,052	92,740	14.4	5.7	11,635	4,228	-2,405	35,489	2.47	57.6	9.5	28.8
Mankato-North Mankato, MN	11.4	8.2	6.5	49.6	85,712	96,742	12.9	5.1	9,240	5,724	1,422	38,901	2.42	60.6	7.2	25.6
Mansfield, OH	13.9	10.7	8.8	49.2	128,852	124,474	-3.4	-2.7	11,378	11,405	-3,332	48,998	2.31	61.0	11.9	32.3
McAllen-Edinburg-Mission, TX	8.3	6.2	4.9	51.0	569,463	774,768	36.1	11.8	129,815	33,426	-4,910	239,825	3.55	82.0	22.4	15.4
Medford, OR	14.0	13.0	8.9	51.2	181,269	203,205	12.1	8.1	19,165	18,868	16,066	89,701	2.39	62.0	11.5	30.5
Memphis, TN-MS-AR	12.6	8.6	5.4	52.2	1,213,230	1,324,829	9.2	1.9	153,471	94,819	-32,900	493,068	2.68	64.2	17.6	30.7
Merced, CA	10.1	6.6	4.6	49.5	210,554	255,796	21.5	7.4	34,422	13,707	-1,666	80,969	3.30	74.2	18.1	20.4
Miami-Fort Lauderdale-West Palm Beach, FL	13.0	9.6	8.6	51.4	5,007,564	5,566,294	11.2	11.4	558,369	398,295	472,395	2,105,878	2.88	64.8	15.3	28.8
Fort Lauderdale-Pompano Beach-Deerfield Beach, FL	13.4	9.3	7.3	51.3	1,623,018	1,748,146	7.7	11.6	179,562	122,233	146,904	685,559	2.80	62.5	14.7	30.4
Miami-Miami Beach-Kendall, FL Div 33124	12.5	8.7	7.5	51.5	2,253,362	2,498,013	10.9	10.6	260,128	160,080	162,409	872,495	3.10	68.5	18.1	25.7
West Palm Beach-Boca Raton-Delray Beach, FL Div 48	13.3	11.6	12.3	51.5	1,131,184	1,320,135	16.7	12.6	118,679	115,982	163,082	547,824	2.65	61.8	11.5	31.7
Michigan City-La Porte, IN	14.0	10.7	7.2	48.5	110,106	111,463	1.2	-1.3	10,803	9,750	-2,441	42,385	2.41	63.5	12.1	28.9
Midland, MI	14.5	10.0	8.3	50.7	82,874	83,626	0.9	-0.5	7,000	5,930	-1,474	34,096	2.40	67.5	8.5	26.7
Midland, TX	10.6	5.8	4.5	49.5	120,755	141,671	17.3	25.9	23,024	9,052	22,239	58,490	2.87	71.7	14.3	24.8
Milwaukee-Waukesha-West Allis, WI	13.4	9.0	6.6	51.2	1,500,741	1,555,954	3.7	1.3	163,878	109,511	-33,585	625,495	2.47	60.9	12.6	31.6
Minneapolis-St. Paul-Bloomington, MN	13.0	8.3	5.7	50.4	3,031,918	3,348,862	10.5	8.4	376,747	186,702	92,289	1,376,557	2.57	64.6	9.5	27.8
Missoula, MT	12.2	9.8	5.8	49.9	95,802	109,296	14.1	8.7	10,052	6,985	6,448	48,806	2.34	55.8	6.8	30.4

1. No spouse present

Table C. Metropolitan Areas — **Population, Vital Statistics, Health, and Crime**

Area name	Persons in group quarters, 2018	Daytime population, 2017		Births, 2018		Deaths, 2018		Persons under 65 with no health insurance 2017		Medicare, 2018			Serious crimes known to police[2], 2016 Total	
		Number	Employment/ residence ratio	Total	Rate[1]	Number	Rate[1]	Number	Percent	Total Beneficiaries	Enrolled in Original Medicare	Enrolled in Medicare Advantage	Number	Rate[3]
	32	33	34	35	36	37	38	39	40	41	42	43	44	45
Jonesboro, AR....................	4,095	132,118	1.01	1,775	13.4	1,342	10.1	8,951	8.2	24,210	18,813	5,397	5,203	4,009
Joplin, MO...............	3,367	181,500	1.04	2,302	12.9	1,771	9.9	21,559	14.7	35,065	25,157	9,908	D	D
Kahului-Wailuku-Lahaina, HI..	2,811	D	D	1,850	11.1	1,358	8.1	7,402	5.4	29,470	15,062	14,408	6,191	3,757
Kalamazoo-Portage, MI.........	9,337	333,287	0.97	3,950	11.6	3,002	8.8	17,191	6.1	64,250	36,166	28,084	10,814	3,210
Kankakee, IL	6,272	106,957	0.95	1,302	11.8	1,181	10.7	5,858	6.7	21,515	17,096	4,419	2,971	2,705
Kansas City, MO-KS.............	31,349	2,144,527	1.02	27,031	12.6	17,775	8.3	179,919	10.0	359,851	236,018	123,833	NA	NA
Kennewick-Richland, WA......	4,323	286,010	0.97	4,342	14.7	1,879	6.3	22,063	8.9	44,542	43,415	1,127	6,753	2,368
Killeen-Temple, TX	21,804	432,431	0.95	7,191	15.9	2,895	6.4	51,951	13.9	63,886	43,312	20,574	12,223	2,813
Kingsport-Bristol-Bristol, TN-VA....	5,888	306,112	1.00	2,818	9.2	3,905	12.7	24,802	10.5	84,085	39,463	44,622	8,259	2,698
Kingston, NY	11,815	160,667	0.78	1,451	8.1	1,738	9.7	9,437	6.8	39,967	29,687	10,280	2,628	1,472
Knoxville, TN	19,897	886,984	1.02	9,214	10.4	9,424	10.7	73,662	10.4	191,710	107,006	84,704	27,792	3,209
Kokomo, IN............................	1,281	84,945	1.07	969	11.8	940	11.4	5,447	8.3	19,405	13,952	5,453	2,599	3,156
La Crosse-Onalaska, WI-MN .	5,826	140,630	1.05	1,384	10.1	1,173	8.6	5,505	5.0	26,886	15,877	11,009	3,560	2,591
Lafayette, LA	8,387	492,601	1.00	6,436	13.2	4,581	9.4	42,916	10.3	83,078	67,734	15,344	1,887	382
Lafayette-West Lafayette, IN..	16,056	226,310	1.07	2,640	11.9	1,461	6.6	17,893	10.0	30,590	23,749	6,841	5,335	2,464
Lake Charles, LA.................	3,814	228,402	1.18	3,020	14.4	2,096	10.0	15,550	8.9	37,679	30,540	7,139	10,111	4,907
Lake Havasu City-Kingman, AZ..................	4,635	197,267	0.86	1,754	8.4	3,230	15.4	18,843	13.4	64,238	43,880	20,358	NA	NA
Lakeland-Winter Haven, FL....	13,542	651,892	0.87	7,886	11.1	7,042	9.9	84,052	15.8	150,956	72,421	78,535	17,766	2,687
Lancaster, PA......................	12,722	533,571	0.97	6,864	12.6	5,135	9.4	52,836	12.0	108,513	65,878	42,635	8,355	1,552
Lansing-East Lansing, MI.......	19,594	494,004	1.07	5,301	11.0	3,768	7.8	22,457	5.8	84,824	56,776	28,048	10,902	2,302
Laredo, TX............................	3,593	274,446	1.00	5,026	18.2	1,395	5.1	69,387	28.6	31,967	22,717	9,250	9,174	3,364
Las Cruces, NM.....................	4,394	210,365	0.94	2,750	12.6	1,614	7.4	20,424	11.5	39,562	24,687	14,875	6,899	3,220
Las Vegas-Henderson-Para-dise, NV	22,978	2,207,100	1.00	27,244	12.2	17,506	7.8	246,807	13.3	345,424	202,854	142,570	75,433	3,499
Lawrence, KS	8,822	112,723	0.88	1,146	9.4	663	5.5	9,148	9.2	16,869	14,326	2,543	NA	NA
Lawton, OK..........................	10,368	130,711	1.05	1,768	14.0	1,195	9.5	15,335	15.1	19,725	18,263	1,462	4,970	3,829
Lebanon, PA.........................	3,671	130,478	0.86	1,579	11.2	1,494	10.6	9,594	8.7	31,306	18,529	12,777	2,240	1,631
Lewiston, ID-WA....................	1,237	62,479	0.98	691	11.0	707	11.2	4,518	9.2	15,888	12,765	3,123	2,284	3,642
Lewiston-Auburn, ME............	2,875	108,209	1.01	1,209	11.2	1,062	9.9	8,153	9.4	24,376	14,729	9,647	1,971	1,837
Lexington-Fayette, KY...........	17,050	545,825	1.13	6,287	12.2	4,016	7.8	30,133	7.0	83,201	53,194	30,007	19,503	3,857
Lima, OH..............................	5,863	108,633	1.11	1,212	11.8	1,076	10.5	6,172	7.7	21,754	14,716	7,038	4,134	3,979
Lincoln, NE...........................	16,305	341,830	1.06	4,145	12.4	2,258	6.7	22,558	8.3	51,821	44,454	7,367	10,299	3,146
Little Rock-North Little Rock-Conway, AR	15,272	747,993	1.03	9,175	12.4	6,718	9.1	47,060	7.6	139,750	110,390	29,360	5,602	760
Logan, UT-ID.........................	3,937	134,977	0.95	2,452	17.4	632	4.5	12,350	10.3	15,700	9,119	6,581	1,571	1,156
Longview, TX.........................	10,725	221,644	1.05	2,732	12.5	2,364	10.8	35,825	20.5	42,258	28,582	13,676	NA	NA
Longview, WA........................	1,208	106,496	0.99	1,320	12.1	1,177	10.8	5,662	6.6	25,737	12,858	12,879	3,727	3,581
Los Angeles-Long Beach-Anaheim, CA...............	223,260	13,584,920	1.04	156,304	11.8	90,127	6.8	1,098,314	9.6	1,954,763	990,854	963,909	382,205	2,863
Anaheim-Santa Ana-Irvine, CA Div 11244................	44,926	3,299,971	1.07	37,050	11.6	21,220	6.7	226,030	8.3	491,674	243,918	247,756	73,329	2,306
Los Angeles-Long Beach-Glendale, CA Div 31084........................	178,334	10,284,949	1.03	119,254	11.8	68,907	6.8	872,284	10.1	1,463,089	746,936	716,153	308,876	3,037
Louisville/Jefferson County, KY-IN	27,300	1,312,607	1.03	15,457	11.9	12,340	9.5	70,322	6.6	245,057	166,452	78,605	48,795	3,797
Lubbock, TX	11,835	319,222	1.01	4,313	13.5	2,709	8.5	43,118	16.1	47,292	29,831	17,461	17,114	5,447
Lynchburg, VA	13,493	257,852	0.98	2,746	10.4	2,675	10.2	21,598	10.7	58,631	48,447	10,184	4,269	1,642
Macon, GA............................	7,838	236,272	1.08	2,747	12.0	2,607	11.3	26,390	14.4	46,959	28,417	18,542	10,372	4,521
Madera, CA...........................	7,905	151,328	0.90	2,336	14.8	1,039	6.6	13,143	10.4	23,921	15,829	8,092	4,729	3,056
Madison, WI..........................	14,780	685,962	1.09	7,182	10.9	4,302	6.5	28,642	5.2	108,934	81,111	27,823	13,719	2,119
Manchester-Nashua, NH........	7,759	393,697	0.93	4,193	10.1	3,393	8.2	24,573	7.2	77,050	64,574	12,476	7,324	1,794
Manhattan, KS......................	9,983	94,904	0.94	1,319	13.5	556	5.7	6,680	8.5	11,476	10,641	835	1,864	1,881
Mankato-North Mankato, MN .	6,767	103,753	1.05	1,075	10.6	713	7.0	3,599	4.4	16,840	7,578	9,262	2,031	2,042
Mansfield, OH.......................	7,327	123,738	1.06	1,300	10.7	1,406	11.6	7,557	8.3	27,818	19,526	8,292	4,748	3,922
McAllen-Edinburg-Mission, TX	7,384	847,039	0.96	14,568	16.8	4,583	5.3	233,591	31.2	101,694	48,664	53,030	26,798	3,142
Medford, OR.........................	3,630	218,675	1.01	2,293	10.4	2,343	10.7	15,615	9.3	55,159	37,173	17,986	10,111	4,686
Memphis, TN-MS-AR	24,748	1,360,357	1.02	17,729	13.1	12,257	9.1	130,521	11.5	223,100	160,411	62,689	66,677	4,950
Merced, CA............................	6,696	258,885	0.86	4,042	14.7	1,748	6.4	20,452	8.7	35,326	31,287	4,039	9,146	3,400
Miami-Fort Lauderdale-West Palm Beach, FL..........	80,148	6,178,766	1.01	67,987	11.0	53,351	8.6	918,156	18.4	1,088,390	483,364	605,026	226,253	3,701
Fort Lauderdale-Pompano Beach-Deerfield Beach, FL	16,295	1,850,209	0.91	21,943	11.2	16,035	8.2	271,480	16.9	315,011	139,897	175,114	66,421	3,441
Miami-Miami Beach-Kendall, FL Div 33124	42,228	2,833,692	1.06	31,268	11.3	21,861	7.9	453,444	20.0	457,618	148,960	308,658	111,219	4,063
West Palm Beach-Boca Raton-Delray Beach, FL Div 48	21,625	1,494,865	1.04	14,776	9.9	15,455	10.4	193,232	17.4	315,761	194,507	121,254	48,613	3,361
Michigan City-La Porte, IN	6,347	107,671	0.95	1,252	11.4	1,225	11.1	7,479	8.8	22,671	18,170	4,501	3,276	2,964
Midland, MI...........................	1,274	87,110	1.10	813	9.8	743	8.9	3,395	5.0	17,677	10,732	6,945	994	1,189
Midland, TX...........................	1,651	188,391	1.23	2,935	16.5	1,148	6.4	30,344	19.9	19,322	14,896	4,426	4,796	2,793
Milwaukee-Waukesha-West Allis, WI..........	31,281	1,618,738	1.05	19,217	12.2	13,642	8.7	84,649	6.5	283,142	154,900	128,242	53,203	3,374
Minneapolis-St. Paul-Bloom-ington, MN	64,860	3,617,294	1.01	45,349	12.5	24,241	6.7	147,086	4.8	564,078	228,240	335,838	92,552	2,603
Missoula, MT	3,645	D	D	1,174	9.9	878	7.4	8,389	8.6	21,531	17,288	4,243	4,563	3,960

1. Per 1,000 estimated resident population.   2. Data for serious crimes have not been adjusted for underreporting; this may affect comparability between geographic areas and over time.   3. Per 100,000 population estimated by the FBI.

Items 32—45

Table C. Metropolitan Areas — Crime, Education, Money Income, and Poverty

Area name	Serious crimes known to police[2], 2016 (cont.) Rate Violent	Property	School enrollment and attainment, 2016 — Enrollment[3] Total	Percent private	Attainment[4] High school graduate or less	Bachelor's degree or more	Local government expenditures,[5] 2014-2015 Total current expenditures (mil dol)	Current expenditures per student (dollars)	Per capita income[6] (dollars)	Mean household income (dollars)	Median household income	Percent of households with income less than $50,000	Percent of households with income of $200,000 or more	Percent below poverty level All persons	Children under 18 years	Age 65 years and older
	46	47	48	49	50	51	52	53	54	55	56	57	58	59	60	61
Jonesboro, AR	417	3,592	34,880	5.6	48.4	24	204.3	8,968	26,049	65,681	48,929	51.4	3.0	15.2	18.6	9.9
Joplin, MO	D	4,042	43,672	9.9	44.8	22.7	245.4	8,045	24,062	60,736	48,979	50.7	2.0	15.4	23.8	9.3
Kahului-Wailuku-Lahaina, HI	273	3,484	33,071	20.1	39.4	27	NA	NA	34,843	101,541	80,183	30.7	9.2	9.7	9.3	10.0
Kalamazoo-Portage, MI	527	2,683	96,625	11.9	30.3	35.3	578.0	11,613	31,388	76,971	55,129	45.5	5.2	13.5	15.5	5.1
Kankakee, IL	311	2,395	28,649	22.5	44.0	20.8	226.6	12,114	27,894	72,518	58,539	42.1	4.4	15.4	20.9	10.6
Kansas City, MO-KS	NA	NA	535,098	16.1	34.0	36.5	3,493.8	10,078	34,457	85,949	63,404	39.0	6.3	10.0	14.2	6.9
Kennewick-Richland, WA	193	2,175	81,014	11.7	40.2	25.7	545.0	9,970	28,680	81,725	63,617	38.3	5.7	12.7	18.0	10.5
Killeen-Temple, TX	387	2,426	123,014	13.7	34.5	24.6	718.0	8,393	24,285	66,768	53,303	45.9	2.6	13.7	20.2	8.4
Kingsport-Bristol-Bristol, TN-VA	367	2,331	58,550	13.0	50.7	20.5	392.7	9,111	26,042	61,070	43,516	56.1	2.6	15.3	24.0	8.4
Kingston, NY	164	1,309	38,918	15.0	37.6	32.7	529.3	22,491	32,637	82,278	63,621	39.6	5.3	14.1	19.0	8.2
Knoxville, TN	449	2,760	199,591	12.6	43.0	28.8	1,041.4	8,571	30,333	74,016	51,848	47.9	4.1	14.3	19.7	8.7
Kokomo, IN	634	2,522	19,088	7.2	49.1	20.4	132.1	9,463	25,647	61,216	49,346	50.5	1.1	14.8	22.2	7.3
La Crosse-Onalaska, WI-MN	135	2,456	38,418	9.6	34.8	30.4	238.1	11,656	30,779	74,455	56,552	42.8	4.5	11.5	6.6	7.3
Lafayette, LA	382	D	127,310	21.5	53.8	22.5	720.4	9,861	25,248	65,245	47,848	51.9	3.9	19.6	27.8	13.7
Lafayette-West Lafayette, IN	248	2,217	75,990	7.6	36.0	36.6	262.9	9,606	27,150	69,329	52,224	47.1	4.1	17.8	17.3	4.3
Lake Charles, LA	659	4,249	51,273	12.9	45.7	24.1	380.2	10,818	28,515	71,908	52,314	48.1	4.7	12.9	17.9	7.0
Lake Havasu City-Kingman, AZ	NA	NA	33,876	16.3	49.5	13.5	171.2	7,119	25,212	58,052	42,311	56.9	2.4	16.7	27.0	8.0
Lakeland-Winter Haven, FL	333	2,354	157,004	18.5	48.8	19	879.5	8,820	23,684	64,787	48,475	51.5	3.4	16.0	26.2	10.3
Lancaster, PA	175	1,377	118,218	28.8	50.6	28	974.3	14,519	29,786	79,242	63,407	37.6	4.2	10.0	13.6	6.9
Lansing-East Lansing, MI	459	1,843	139,753	9.6	31.2	35.1	788.6	11,381	30,046	73,938	56,440	44.9	3.7	15.3	18.9	7.6
Laredo, TX	362	3,002	89,411	8.4	60.8	17.1	611.3	8,884	16,587	57,088	43,408	57.0	2.3	28.0	37.0	28.3
Las Cruces, NM	253	2,967	68,946	7.6	42.8	24.9	390.0	9,480	19,974	53,825	37,144	60.8	2.3	28.1	42.3	16.5
Las Vegas-Henderson-Paradise, NV	771	2,728	517,646	11.9	43.1	24.4	2,675.1	8,254	29,479	78,422	57,189	43.2	4.7	13.8	20.3	8.5
Lawrence, KS	NA	NA	40,209	9.3	22.6	47.3	148.5	9,946	30,459	75,162	55,646	45.9	4.3	17.4	12.6	5.8
Lawton, OK	628	3,201	31,873	10.0	39.0	23.7	185.3	8,077	25,971	66,130	50,702	48.9	1.9	16.2	24.1	8.8
Lebanon, PA	154	1,476	29,690	18.0	54.6	22.2	225.8	11,821	27,954	71,305	57,372	42.0	2.6	11.4	15.8	8.0
Lewiston, ID-WA	152	3,490	12,625	7.2	36.1	23.8	85.5	9,633	29,199	70,477	55,116	45.0	3.0	10.1	12.2	5.5
Lewiston-Auburn, ME	136	1,701	25,077	19.9	44.1	24.6	204.0	12,096	26,395	62,221	48,286	51.6	1.8	11.7	10.7	6.2
Lexington-Fayette, KY	264	3,593	136,354	16.8	32.4	37.5	706.9	9,919	32,009	80,041	58,069	44.4	5.8	15.8	19.4	6.7
Lima, OH	390	3,589	25,924	14.9	48.2	19.7	160.4	10,706	25,204	61,942	51,542	48.2	1.9	14.9	24.6	7.0
Lincoln, NE	322	2,824	100,069	21.7	28.3	38.1	514.7	10,976	31,006	78,036	60,057	41.5	4.5	11.2	10.5	5.2
Little Rock-North Little Rock-Conway, AR	760	D	188,105	15.8	38.3	31.1	1,120.1	9,739	29,350	73,068	53,173	47.0	4.3	13.0	15.7	10.7
Logan, UT-ID	66	1,090	58,047	5.7	27.1	38.4	181.6	6,412	21,516	68,565	52,974	48.0	2.7	15.4	12.8	5.8
Longview, TX	NA	NA	51,771	10.1	45.5	18.2	360.6	9,095	25,222	66,538	48,259	52.0	3.4	15.5	20.7	10.4
Longview, WA	268	3,313	25,203	18.3	40.6	17.3	170.1	10,186	25,915	64,312	49,456	50.8	2.3	17.2	20.5	12.2
Los Angeles-Long Beach-Anaheim, CA	477	2,386	3,497,961	15.2	39.3	34.2	21,963.1	10,785	33,996	99,303	69,992	36.8	10.3	14.1	19.6	12.1
Anaheim-Santa Ana-Irvine, CA Div 11244	229	2,078	858,030	15.9	32.3	40.3	4,817.7	9,691	39,038	115,705	86,217	28.6	13.9	11.5	15.8	8.8
Los Angeles-Long Beach-Glendale, CA Div 31084	554	2,483	2,639,931	15.0	41.5	32.3	17,145.4	11,138	32,413	94,165	65,006	39.4	9.1	14.9	20.8	13.2
Louisville/Jefferson County, KY-IN	438	3,359	298,044	22.4	40.5	28.8	1,950.4	10,574	31,055	77,113	57,279	43.9	5.2	12.2	17.2	7.7
Lubbock, TX	924	4,523	105,040	9.0	40.5	29.5	461.3	8,833	25,977	68,417	47,276	52.0	4.3	19.4	22.4	11.2
Lynchburg, VA	204	1,439	68,467	35.7	43.6	25.9	330.4	9,890	26,369	65,821	52,976	47.1	3.4	11.9	14.5	7.6
Macon, GA	382	4,139	58,399	18.1	46.9	22.3	360.7	9,854	24,632	62,745	41,303	57.4	3.7	21.9	32.7	14.7
Madera, CA	662	2,395	46,062	11.0	52.1	15.3	313.5	10,157	20,573	67,518	51,283	48.7	3.1	22.6	32.0	9.6
Madison, WI	203	1,916	177,890	11.0	25.2	45.9	1,087.5	11,542	37,469	89,595	71,301	34.7	6.4	11.0	9.7	6.5
Manchester-Nashua, NH	269	1,526	93,104	23.4	34.4	37.6	771.2	13,354	40,001	100,105	78,769	31.2	9.7	8.2	11.7	4.7
Manhattan, KS	259	1,621	37,341	5.4	27.9	44.4	117.2	10,127	27,515	70,613	50,698	49.0	4.0	20.1	14.8	5.4
Mankato-North Mankato, MN	154	1,888	32,356	19.1	29.0	37.2	145.4	11,167	31,227	79,634	61,241	41.1	4.6	15.0	9.3	6.4
Mansfield, OH	240	3,682	25,814	21.9	52.7	18.8	193.7	11,860	24,576	60,281	46,032	52.7	2.5	12.3	16.6	10.8
McAllen-Edinburg-Mission, TX	296	2,846	273,957	5.9	58.2	18.7	2,186.4	9,531	16,450	55,786	37,106	60.1	2.1	30.0	42.4	22.6
Medford, OR	358	4,329	45,712	12.7	34.8	28.4	291.4	10,053	29,619	70,249	51,409	47.5	4.9	14.1	22.3	6.2
Memphis, TN-MS-AR	1,082	3,868	339,258	17.3	41.5	27.8	1,966.4	10,806	28,349	73,581	50,984	49.0	4.8	17.1	27.1	9.8
Merced, CA	553	2,847	90,516	4.4	56.2	13.4	611.8	10,806	21,866	69,191	47,735	52.2	4.4	23.8	37.1	12.3
Miami-Fort Lauderdale-West Palm Beach, FL	486	3,215	1,467,944	20.6	41.1	32.1	7,252.6	8,912	30,408	81,633	54,284	46.2	6.9	14.3	19.3	14.6
Fort Lauderdale-Pompano Beach-Deerfield Beach, FL	391	3,050	479,823	19.7	38.0	32.7	2,331.4	8,704	31,594	82,449	56,842	44.7	6.9	13.1	17.9	13.4
Miami-Miami Beach-Kendall, FL Div 33124	571	3,492	658,985	21.9	46.1	29.3	3,166.6	8,871	25,996	73,762	49,930	50.1	5.7	16.6	21.8	19.9
West Palm Beach-Boca Raton-Delray Beach, FL Div 48 ...	452	2,910	329,136	19.3	35.7	36.2	1,754.7	9,283	37,100	93,146	60,057	41.8	8.7	11.7	16.5	9.1
Michigan City-La Porte, IN	301	2,662	22,412	15.5	51.8	16.9	177.8	9,971	23,806	62,150	50,736	49.4	1.6	14.3	20.5	6.3
Midland, MI	128	1,061	19,800	20.4	33.7	37.1	133.6	11,093	36,349	88,348	61,624	41.8	7.8	10.8	12.8	7.6
Midland, TX	298	2,496	43,096	13.8	44.1	27.6	260.4	9,247	36,335	100,248	75,266	31.3	8.5	10.6	16.3	9.5
Milwaukee-Waukesha-West Allis, WI	656	2,718	391,958	22.7	35.7	35.8	2,605.3	11,101	33,598	81,635	59,448	42.9	5.7	13.3	18.1	9.0
Minneapolis-St. Paul-Bloomington, MN	288	2,316	925,212	16.2	28.0	41.7	6,738.5	11,925	39,686	101,405	76,856	31.2	9.2	8.1	10.4	6.4
Missoula, MT	413	3,547	30,524	13.1	24.5	46	142.8	10,496	30,464	72,218	54,311	46.7	4.2	15.4	17.7	2.8

1. Data for serious crimes have not been adjusted for underreporting; this may affect comparability between geographic areas and over time. 2. Per 100,000 population estimated by the FBI. 3. All persons 3 years old and over enrolled in nursery school through college. 4. Persons 25 years old and over. 5. Elementary and secondary education expenditures. 6. Based on population estimated by the American Community Survey, 2015.

Table C. Metropolitan Areas — **Personal Income and Earnings**

Area name	Personal income, 2017										Earnings, 2017		
	Total (mil dol)	Percent change, 2016-2017	Per capita[1]		Supplements to wages and salaries, employer contributions (mil dol)			Proprietors' income	Dividends, interest, and rent (mil dol)	Personal transfer receipts (mil dol)	Contributrions for government social insurance (mil dol)		
			Dollars	Rank	Wages and Salaries (mil dol)	Pension and insurance	Government social insurance				Total (mil dol)	From employee and self-employed	From employer
	62	63	64	65	66	67	68	69	70	71	72	73	74
Jonesboro, AR.....................	4,595	3.6	35,005	371	2,348	370	180	343	600	1,231	3,241	212	180
Joplin, MO......................	6,757	2.8	37,850	330	3,373	558	241	614	1,039	1,566	4,786	298	241
Kahului-Wailuku-Lahaina, HI..	7,856	5.4	47,226	126	3,712	618	278	821	1,764	1,249	5,428	337	278
Kalamazoo-Portage, MI.........	15,135	3.1	44,733	170	7,497	1,350	551	965	2,830	2,906	10,363	639	551
Kankakee, IL	4,369	2.3	39,862	286	2,025	423	145	176	641	1,026	2,768	159	145
Kansas City, MO-KS.............	108,374	3.5	50,906	77	60,599	8,626	4,392	9,489	18,777	16,142	83,106	4,965	4,392
Kennewick-Richland, WA.......	12,313	3.7	42,414	224	6,373	928	599	1,192	1,966	2,293	9,091	511	599
Killeen-Temple, TX	18,094	4.2	40,773	267	8,949	1,903	722	1,014	3,210	3,851	12,588	637	722
Kingsport-Bristol-Bristol, TN-VA	11,905	4.5	38,823	308	5,328	980	380	810	2,027	3,382	7,499	514	380
Kingston, NY	8,758	5.5	48,811	103	2,764	685	232	643	1,636	2,025	4,324	258	232
Knoxville, TN	38,507	4.3	43,903	186	19,440	3,006	1,352	4,174	6,103	7,976	27,972	1,725	1,352
Kokomo, IN.....................	3,306	3.1	40,135	280	2,040	347	147	138	498	908	2,673	171	147
La Crosse-Onalaska, WI-MN .	6,495	3.0	47,428	120	3,560	698	278	413	1,307	1,148	4,949	304	278
Lafayette, LA	20,225	2.1	41,145	255	9,496	1,600	615	1,632	3,589	4,391	13,343	759	615
Lafayette-West Lafayette, IN..	8,180	3.6	37,309	339	4,621	884	333	555	1,507	1,374	6,393	371	333
Lake Charles, LA...............	9,725	5.2	46,451	137	6,293	1,102	404	798	1,390	1,935	8,598	471	404
Lake Havasu City-Kingman, AZ.................	6,395	3.7	30,865	380	1,987	330	149	365	1,132	2,277	2,831	248	149
Lakeland-Winter Haven, FL....	23,487	4.9	34,213	375	10,173	1,537	693	1,082	4,554	6,603	13,486	945	693
Lancaster, PA	26,715	4.7	49,207	96	11,657	2,011	942	3,976	4,468	4,558	18,586	1,065	942
Lansing-East Lansing, MI.......	19,177	2.8	40,148	279	10,652	2,110	778	920	3,281	3,882	14,460	884	778
Laredo, TX......................	8,246	1.8	30,008	381	3,789	768	271	856	1,242	1,994	5,685	299	271
Las Cruces, NM.................	7,623	3.2	35,362	366	2,968	618	236	798	1,306	2,006	4,620	298	236
Las Vegas-Henderson-Para- dise, NV	97,457	5.1	44,217	175	49,312	7,433	3,580	5,671	22,989	16,191	65,996	3,761	3,580
Lawrence, KS	4,996	3.9	41,360	247	2,107	426	157	410	1,042	700	3,101	181	157
Lawton, OK.....................	5,090	2.4	39,967	281	2,507	575	214	224	937	1,129	3,520	189	214
Lebanon, PA....................	6,379	4.6	45,645	154	2,178	480	182	588	1,071	1,320	3,428	210	182
Lewiston, ID-WA................	2,727	4.6	43,332	201	1,217	213	108	215	560	662	1,752	117	108
Lewiston-Auburn, ME..........	4,292	4.3	39,873	285	2,210	364	164	226	589	1,132	2,964	200	164
Lexington-Fayette, KY...........	23,223	2.6	45,300	156	13,465	2,287	1,016	1,674	4,659	3,730	18,443	1,074	1,016
Lima, OH.......................	4,223	4.1	40,925	261	2,420	451	183	299	632	1,023	3,354	197	183
Lincoln, NE	15,556	3.7	46,924	133	8,605	1,561	647	1,033	3,262	2,226	11,845	709	647
Little Rock-North Little Rock- Conway, AR	32,250	3.0	43,679	191	17,427	2,678	1,305	1,990	5,517	6,857	23,400	1,479	1,305
Logan, UT-ID	5,057	5.6	36,644	353	2,267	475	180	602	969	727	3,524	198	180
Longview, TX	8,749	1.5	40,229	278	4,531	674	336	610	1,510	2,187	6,151	362	336
Longview, WA...................	4,585	5.0	42,888	212	1,977	308	188	348	733	1,226	2,822	184	188
Los Angeles-Long Beach- Anaheim, CA..................	802,394	3.3	60,087	20	407,541	64,749	27,549	90,102	179,373	116,742	589,941	32,872	27,549
Anaheim-Santa Ana-Irvine, CA Div 11244..............	208,653	4.6	65,400	X	107,138	16,021	7,496	22,182	49,466	22,381	152,837	8,616	7,496
Los Angeles-Long Beach- Glendale, CA Div 31084........................	593,741	2.9	58,419	X	300,403	48,728	20,053	67,920	129,906	94,362	437,104	24,256	20,053
Louisville/Jefferson County, KY-IN	61,197	3.6	47,294	125	33,860	5,062	2,530	4,078	10,476	11,497	45,530	2,821	2,530
Lubbock, TX	13,053	4.1	41,180	254	6,381	1,108	432	985	2,357	2,492	8,905	475	432
Lynchburg, VA	10,074	3.2	38,560	314	4,673	746	338	335	1,864	2,599	6,091	420	338
Macon, GA......................	9,033	3.0	39,460	295	4,594	808	315	604	1,600	2,311	6,321	389	315
Madera, CA	6,087	5.8	38,799	310	2,233	536	168	1,117	1,071	1,252	4,054	188	168
Madison, WI	36,826	4.2	56,289	36	21,209	4,166	1,566	2,648	7,700	4,343	29,589	1,722	1,566
Manchester-Nashua, NH........	24,608	5.2	60,064	21	13,197	1,851	893	2,296	3,844	3,334	18,237	1,110	893
Manhattan, KS..................	4,311	2.0	43,958	185	1,653	355	122	308	909	523	2,438	139	122
Mankato-North Mankato, MN .	4,519	4.5	44,767	168	2,491	441	191	343	888	776	3,465	205	191
Mansfield, OH..................	4,580	3.6	37,977	327	2,118	419	161	231	717	1,224	2,929	180	161
McAllen-Edinburg-Mission, TX	22,047	2.3	25,617	383	9,157	1,896	645	2,344	2,607	6,509	14,042	758	645
Medford, OR....................	9,647	4.7	44,360	174	3,870	643	357	1,041	2,173	2,391	5,911	404	357
Memphis, TN-MS-AR	60,614	3.1	44,958	162	33,419	4,907	2,270	5,603	9,031	11,301	46,199	2,769	2,270
Merced, CA.....................	10,557	6.5	38,716	311	3,563	898	266	1,526	1,735	2,494	6,253	286	266
Miami-Fort Lauderdale-West Palm Beach, FL.............	330,929	5.0	53,732	61	149,264	19,271	9,923	22,446	101,408	54,623	200,903	12,672	9,923
Fort Lauderdale-Pompano Beach-Deerfield Beach, FL	94,239	5.2	48,680	X	46,364	5,900	3,105	5,279	22,363	15,212	60,648	3,790	3,105
Miami-Miami Beach-Kendall, FL Div 33124..............	126,716	4.3	46,048	X	66,925	8,953	4,465	11,197	28,941	25,387	91,540	5,727	4,465
West Palm Beach-Boca Raton-Delray Beach, FL Div 48..............	109,974	5.6	74,754	X	35,975	4,418	2,352	5,970	50,104	14,024	48,715	3,155	2,352
Michigan City-La Porte, IN	4,429	3.4	40,253	276	1,772	317	135	282	686	1,021	2,506	163	135
Midland, MI.....................	4,581	16.6	54,922	44	2,668	377	157	339	863	756	3,541	222	157
Midland, TX.....................	12,642	-1.0	74,072	5	6,711	884	439	2,415	2,761	1,018	10,450	530	439
Milwaukee-Waukesha-West Allis, WI......................	85,032	3.2	53,946	56	47,125	7,896	3,525	5,415	16,932	14,076	63,961	3,937	3,525
Minneapolis-St. Paul-Bloom- ington, MN	215,087	4.7	59,736	23	124,190	17,789	8,910	15,422	41,401	27,608	166,311	9,828	8,910
Missoula, MT	5,500	5.3	46,829	134	2,654	403	223	489	1,534	929	3,769	244	223

1. Based on the resident population estimated as of July 1 of the year shown.

Table C. Metropolitan Areas — Earnings, Social Security, and Housing

| | Earnings, 2017 (cont.) | | | | | | | | | Social Security beneficiaries, December 2017 | | | Housing units, 2018 | |
| | Percent by selected industries | | | | | | | | | | | | | |
Area name	Farm	Mining, quarrying, and extracting	Construction	Manufacturing	Information; professional, scientific, and technical serviecs	Retail trade	Finance, insurance, real estate, rental and leasing	Health care and social assistance	Government	Number	Rate[1]	Supplemental Security Income Recipients, December 2017	Total	Percent change, 2010-2018
	75	76	77	78	79	80	81	82	83	84	85	86	87	88
Jonesboro, AR	0.5	D	6.4	14.2	4.2	7.8	4.6	22.4	16.2	27,195	207	5,459	57,268	11.3
Joplin, MO	1.5	D	5.4	21.3	3.9	7.9	3.9	15.0	10.7	38,310	215	4,499	76,587	2.1
Kahului-Wailuku-Lahaina, HI	1.4	D	9.4	1.2	4.4	7.9	5.6	8.4	16.0	30,565	184	2,061	73,888	4.8
Kalamazoo-Portage, MI	0.8	D	6.8	20.9	6.8	6.0	7.8	D	14.4	69,305	205	8,586	150,181	2.3
Kankakee, IL	1.0	D	4.6	21.2	4.2	6.3	4.9	17.3	16.0	22,720	207	2,693	45,652	0.9
Kansas City, MO-KS	0.1	0.1	6.4	7.5	16.9	5.3	10.9	10.9	13.9	371,075	174	33,954	918,595	5.3
Kennewick-Richland, WA	6.1	D	8.6	6.1	13.8	6.3	3.6	10.0	18.2	45,915	158	5,675	106,018	14.0
Killeen-Temple, TX	0.0	D	5.9	3.8	4.6	5.9	4.2	D	45.7	69,135	156	10,333	178,734	12.1
Kingsport-Bristol-Bristol, TN-VA	-0.3	D	D	24.0	4.7	7.5	4.0	D	13.2	91,900	300	10,209	149,725	1.9
Kingston, NY	0.6	0.2	7.0	6.4	5.9	8.0	4.7	13.7	28.8	41,500	231	4,068	85,421	2.1
Knoxville, TN	0.0	D	D	10.9	13.0	7.6	D	14.6	14.1	204,025	233	22,402	399,505	4.8
Kokomo, IN	0.0	D	3.1	46.2	2.7	6.0	3.8	13.5	9.3	21,590	262	2,187	39,567	2.3
La Crosse-Onalaska, WI-MN	0.2	D	5.7	11.4	D	6.0	7.5	21.8	15.5	27,850	203	2,314	59,346	4.1
Lafayette, LA	0.6	10.9	6.6	8.2	D	7.5	7.0	14.5	12.6	89,265	182	15,567	211,670	8.0
Lafayette-West Lafayette, IN	0.6	0.1	5.0	D	D	5.3	5.2	D	25.7	32,670	149	2,650	90,324	6.9
Lake Charles, LA	0.1	D	27.9	16.6	D	6.4	3.4	9.8	11.2	40,680	194	6,283	96,171	12.3
Lake Havasu City-Kingman, AZ	0.2	D	6.9	6.5	5.6	12.8	5.0	19.1	17.5	67,710	327	4,702	115,269	3.9
Lakeland-Winter Haven, FL	0.6	0.6	6.1	9.0	5.2	8.2	7.7	14.2	13.2	161,690	236	22,069	299,421	6.5
Lancaster, PA	1.0	0.1	11.7	15.2	7.1	7.5	5.7	13.0	8.5	111,820	206	9,385	212,205	4.6
Lansing-East Lansing, MI	-0.1	D	5.0	11.0	D	5.4	9.1	12.6	27.0	91,680	192	10,439	203,760	2.4
Laredo, TX	0.0	3.6	3.8	0.6	4.7	7.5	5.5	11.2	28.5	34,010	124	12,364	84,455	14.9
Las Cruces, NM	4.0	0.1	6.8	3.4	7.1	5.9	4.8	15.9	29.8	41,375	192	8,264	89,049	9.3
Las Vegas-Henderson-Paradise, NV	0.0	0.0	6.4	2.5	9.1	7.2	6.6	9.1	15.5	354,170	161	43,628	913,260	8.7
Lawrence, KS	0.6	0.1	5.5	8.9	9.5	6.5	8.2	7.9	32.3	17,065	141	1,383	51,073	9.3
Lawton, OK	0.0	0.3	3.9	D	D	5.2	3.8	5.4	53.0	22,015	173	3,323	54,687	1.7
Lebanon, PA	2.0	0.0	6.2	17.5	5.7	7.7	3.1	12.2	19.5	32,860	235	2,627	58,005	4.3
Lewiston, ID-WA	0.0	D	7.6	18.3	4.5	9.1	7.7	D	17.7	16,970	270	1,710	27,990	2.5
Lewiston-Auburn, ME	0.4	D	7.4	10.9	7.4	7.9	5.9	21.0	11.7	25,955	241	4,215	50,056	2.0
Lexington-Fayette, KY	2.8	-1.2	6.8	14.4	D	5.9	5.0	11.3	21.2	86,410	169	11,259	222,278	6.3
Lima, OH	-0.2	0.3	4.8	24.8	3.7	6.1	3.5	21.3	12.6	22,915	222	3,013	45,186	0.4
Lincoln, NE	0.8	D	6.2	8.1	D	5.8	10.0	D	21.9	51,140	154	5,102	140,692	10.1
Little Rock-North Little Rock-Conway, AR	0.2	0.4	5.9	6.0	10.4	7.1	D	13.9	22.5	150,405	204	24,559	328,596	7.1
Logan, UT-ID	2.0	D	5.1	20.3	D	7.0	9.5	D	19.3	16,290	118	1,032	47,144	13.5
Longview, TX	0.5	7.9	11.6	10.7	6.8	6.8	5.9	D	11.2	45,250	208	6,978	90,819	4.0
Longview, WA	0.7	0.9	12.6	20.1	3.6	6.6	3.8	14.4	15.4	27,445	257	3,938	44,968	3.5
Los Angeles-Long Beach-Anaheim, CA	0.1	0.1	4.7	8.4	18.1	5.3	11.8	9.6	13.5	1,796,430	135	479,600	4,672,296	4.0
Anaheim-Santa Ana-Irvine, CA Div 11244	0.1	0.1	7.6	10.4	14.2	5.6	14.5	8.9	10.5	450,355	141	73,829	1,111,227	5.9
Los Angeles-Long Beach-Glendale, CA Div 31084	0.1	0.1	3.7	7.7	19.5	5.2	10.9	9.8	14.6	1,346,075	132	405,771	3,561,069	3.4
Louisville/Jefferson County, KY-IN	0.0	-0.1	5.7	14.2	D	5.5	D	12.7	11.4	258,900	200	34,453	562,202	4.0
Lubbock, TX	0.1	D	D	D	D	8.5	7.9	D	25.1	48,815	154	6,767	135,228	12.1
Lynchburg, VA	-0.5	D	D	18.3	D	6.7	6.0	15.5	13.0	62,865	241	6,303	117,194	4.2
Macon, GA	0.7	0.8	D	D	7.5	D	D	D	14.3	50,455	220	9,671	102,807	1.2
Madera, CA	20.4	D	4.4	6.6	2.1	4.6	2.2	14.1	22.2	25,300	161	4,775	50,966	3.7
Madison, WI	0.5	0.1	6.1	9.0	D	6.3	8.6	D	21.1	111,310	170	9,019	290,880	8.2
Manchester-Nashua, NH	0.0	D	D	14.7	14.9	7.4	11.5	11.3	9.5	80,435	196	7,108	172,031	3.6
Manhattan, KS	0.7	D	6.7	7.3	6.8	6.8	9.8	D	31.7	11,740	120	758	41,175	11.8
Mankato-North Mankato, MN	2.1	D	6.2	15.6	D	6.7	5.2	D	17.0	17,185	170	1,347	42,446	8.6
Mansfield, OH	-0.1	D	7.5	22.9	3.8	8.2	3.4	14.3	17.9	29,245	243	3,495	54,166	-0.8
McAllen-Edinburg-Mission, TX	0.4	1.0	4.4	2.6	4.6	10.0	5.2	19.3	27.3	108,345	126	41,737	281,639	13.4
Medford, OR	0.5	0.1	6.9	8.6	6.7	10.2	6.9	19.6	14.1	56,945	262	4,827	96,241	5.8
Memphis, TN-MS-AR	0.0	0.0	5.8	10.5	4.9	6.5	8.0	13.2	13.3	240,625	178	46,520	574,558	3.5
Merced, CA	20.2	D	3.6	9.6	2.1	5.7	2.9	8.9	26.0	37,790	139	11,070	85,756	2.5
Miami-Fort Lauderdale-West Palm Beach, FL	0.3	0.1	6.8	3.3	14.7	7.2	10.1	11.4	12.8	1,062,030	172	234,011	2,548,762	3.4
Fort Lauderdale-Pompano Beach-Deerfield Beach, FL	0.1	0.0	6.9	3.5	14.7	8.1	9.8	10.2	13.7	319,595	165	45,759	826,899	2.0
Miami-Miami Beach-Kendall, FL Div 33124	0.4	0.1	6.9	2.9	14.7	6.8	9.9	11.4	13.3	425,610	155	164,076	1,031,955	4.3
West Palm Beach-Boca Raton-Delray Beach, FL Div 48	0.4	0.2	6.4	3.7	14.8	6.9	10.9	12.7	10.6	316,825	215	24,176	689,908	3.8
Michigan City-La Porte, IN	0.0	0.0	8.5	21.0	3.3	6.8	4.4	13.8	14.7	24,810	225	2,179	49,225	1.6
Midland, MI	-0.3	D	5.2	25.0	3.4	3.6	3.1	10.3	6.3	19,405	233	1,555	37,114	3.2
Midland, TX	0.0	D	4.8	D	D	3.7	D	4.6	6.6	20,010	117	2,092	63,756	13.4
Milwaukee-Waukesha-West Allis, WI	0.1	0.1	5.2	15.4	10.5	5.2	10.5	13.5	10.9	296,965	188	47,685	681,189	1.7
Minneapolis-St. Paul-Bloomington, MN	0.1	0.1	5.6	11.2	D	4.9	11.5	10.8	11.7	563,215	156	60,894	1,460,551	5.3
Missoula, MT	0.1	0.1	7.0	3.2	9.7	8.9	7.4	18.3	18.9	21,760	185	2,097	54,926	9.6

1. Per 1,000 resident population estimated as of July 1 of the year shown.

Table C. Metropolitan Areas — **Housing, Labor Force, and Employment**

Area name	Housing units, 2017								Civilian labor force, 2018		Unemployment		Civilian employment[5], 2017	Percent	
	Occupied units														
			Owner-occupied			Renter-occupied									
				Median owner cost as a percent of income											
	Total	Percent	Median value[1]	With a mortgage	Without a mortgage[2]	Median rent[3]	Median rent as a percent of income	Internet access	Total	Percent change 2017-2018	Total	Rate[4]	Total	Management, business, science, and arts	Construction, production, and maintenance occupations
	89	90	91	92	93	94	95	96	97	98	99	100	101	102	103
Jonesboro, AR	51,087	58.7	127,800	16.0	10.0	733	26.2	87.6	64,389	0.8	2,053	3.2	63,055	29.9	30.1
Joplin, MO	69,136	66.9	119,700	18.3	11.0	715	27.7	83.3	83,856	-0.5	2,376	2.8	85,047	30.0	31.0
Kahului-Wailuku-Lahaina, HI	53,616	58.4	641,500	26.9	10.0	1,421	29.8	88.9	86,137	-0.5	2,109	2.4	84,521	30.9	16.3
Kalamazoo-Portage, MI	133,112	67.3	153,800	18.4	11.7	770	26.1	89.5	168,567	0.2	6,263	3.7	168,338	40.8	22.0
Kankakee, IL	39,628	68.9	151,100	18.8	13.2	792	29.3	81.2	55,920	0.9	3,032	5.4	49,540	29.1	29.4
Kansas City, MO-KS	829,475	64.6	180,700	19.0	11.3	935	27.2	88.8	1,134,500	0.4	38,025	3.4	1,085,801	41.1	20.0
Kennewick-Richland, WA	98,742	67.0	228,500	20.2	10.0	945	26.5	87.2	140,580	2.3	7,675	5.5	132,113	35.7	26.0
Killeen-Temple, TX	149,197	56.9	142,500	20.4	10.3	902	27.7	90.1	175,915	0.0	7,213	4.1	177,500	35.2	21.2
Kingsport-Bristol-Bristol, TN-VA	129,285	73.2	136,700	18.9	10.0	629	27.0	80.3	137,055	0.0	5,005	3.7	129,118	31.7	26.4
Kingston, NY	68,822	70.1	233,000	23.7	14.2	1,077	34.3	92.4	88,712	0.9	3,452	3.9	86,711	39.6	18.0
Knoxville, TN	347,479	67.7	169,200	19.1	10.0	803	27.6	83.5	422,094	1.2	13,805	3.3	414,300	36.4	21.2
Kokomo, IN	34,243	71.5	98,500	16.8	10.0	688	24.1	82.1	37,645	-1.0	1,529	4.1	38,131	29.8	30.2
La Crosse-Onalaska, WI-MN	55,940	62.9	171,500	19.7	11.6	802	25.6	86.3	77,721	-0.7	2,065	2.7	73,376	36.0	21.7
Lafayette, LA	179,072	68.7	160,700	19.3	10.0	742	32.1	81.6	212,523	-0.1	10,483	4.9	215,847	31.8	25.5
Lafayette-West Lafayette, IN	80,855	62.1	145,000	17.5	10.0	784	31.3	92.8	112,531	2.1	3,564	3.2	111,744	40.0	23.0
Lake Charles, LA	81,266	70.3	163,500	17.4	10.0	812	33.2	78.4	113,935	1.4	4,338	3.8	101,327	34.4	23.5
Lake Havasu City-Kingman, AZ	87,565	70.0	157,100	21.4	10.0	783	29.4	83.1	85,442	3.5	4,934	5.8	73,978	23.7	24.1
Lakeland-Winter Haven, FL	233,058	67.8	153,700	21.5	11.1	938	30.2	82.1	298,759	1.5	12,156	4.1	281,545	30.0	25.0
Lancaster, PA	201,150	66.9	204,200	21.6	11.8	977	27.9	83.6	281,433	0.9	9,542	3.4	275,020	33.8	27.6
Lansing-East Lansing, MI	186,203	64.5	152,200	18.5	11.7	843	28.6	87.5	248,507	-0.2	8,763	3.5	232,703	40.3	20.5
Laredo, TX	74,045	60.8	133,200	23.7	12.0	801	31.8	66.2	116,573	1.2	4,383	3.8	109,608	25.6	21.9
Las Cruces, NM	75,441	64.3	145,200	22.2	10.6	716	30.5	77.3	96,769	1.3	5,470	5.7	84,356	34.3	15.8
Las Vegas-Henderson-Paradise, NV	781,796	54.2	250,000	22.2	10.0	1,079	29.6	87.3	1,098,114	2.7	52,643	4.8	1,044,668	28.0	17.8
Lawrence, KS	47,643	51.2	211,600	19.0	12.2	884	31.3	93.0	65,199	0.0	1,995	3.1	67,975	45.0	12.1
Lawton, OK	46,009	54.9	133,400	20.8	10.0	786	28.4	88.6	51,314	-1.0	1,984	3.9	51,921	36.5	22.1
Lebanon, PA	52,786	70.0	172,900	20.8	12.0	816	27.6	83.9	71,222	0.7	2,677	3.8	66,901	31.8	29.5
Lewiston, ID-WA	25,553	75.5	190,700	20.8	10.0	668	27.3	81.1	31,206	-0.6	1,021	3.3	30,083	30.8	26.4
Lewiston-Auburn, ME	45,979	65.7	153,500	20.3	13.2	688	28.3	83.9	55,449	-0.2	1,828	3.3	52,572	32.1	22.2
Lexington-Fayette, KY	202,610	59.6	184,700	18.2	10.0	817	27.9	89.6	271,580	-0.4	9,260	3.4	262,482	40.2	21.1
Lima, OH	40,872	66.6	121,500	17.7	11.6	636	26.8	85.5	47,855	-1.4	2,147	4.5	48,113	33.6	29.8
Lincoln, NE	129,363	62.2	178,600	19.7	11.2	811	25.9	90.7	182,114	1.8	4,633	2.5	180,721	42.8	17.7
Little Rock-North Little Rock-Conway, AR	283,142	63.6	155,200	18.9	10.0	811	28.9	83.8	354,824	0.2	11,930	3.4	346,757	39.9	18.6
Logan, UT-ID	42,764	64.7	215,000	20.0	10.0	797	30.7	92.8	70,182	1.1	1,847	2.6	66,886	37.4	24.7
Longview, TX	76,055	67.9	135,000	20.5	10.3	819	28.8	80.9	97,952	0.6	4,040	4.1	93,985	29.8	28.5
Longview, WA	41,611	65.0	208,900	24.0	12.6	812	30.4	87.1	45,923	0.6	2,729	5.9	43,937	28.1	29.8
Los Angeles-Long Beach-Anaheim, CA	4,348,543	48.4	617,100	27.0	10.8	1,476	33.9	89.5	6,761,767	0.8	287,370	4.2	6,582,282	38.1	19.6
Anaheim-Santa Ana-Irvine, CA Div 11244	1,037,312	57.4	679,400	25.8	10.0	1,786	33.6	93.4	1,625,426	1.0	47,541	2.9	1,607,525	41.6	17.0
Los Angeles-Long Beach-Glendale, CA Div 31084	3,311,231	45.6	588,700	27.4	11.2	1,402	34.0	88.3	5,136,341	0.8	239,829	4.7	4,974,757	37.0	20.4
Louisville/Jefferson County, KY-IN	502,581	66.8	168,600	19.0	10.6	818	26.7	85.9	670,808	1.0	25,893	3.9	638,559	34.8	25.4
Lubbock, TX	116,070	53.4	135,100	19.2	12.1	878	34.6	84.5	162,563	0.7	5,017	3.1	155,813	35.6	18.6
Lynchburg, VA	98,409	70.5	171,500	18.9	10.0	777	28.4	78.4	122,127	-0.1	4,217	3.5	121,463	34.1	22.4
Macon, GA	84,028	60.9	118,600	19.8	11.4	778	30.1	78.1	104,769	-0.5	4,525	4.3	94,032	31.1	19.8
Madera, CA	46,282	68.7	240,800	26.0	10.7	994	37.4	83.5	61,528	0.8	4,316	7.0	59,053	22.2	35.9
Madison, WI	272,698	61.4	247,000	20.2	11.9	1,009	27.6	91.3	387,610	-0.1	8,900	2.3	368,220	48.8	15.5
Manchester-Nashua, NH	161,414	65.5	278,400	21.5	14.1	1,133	28.0	93.7	236,915	1.2	6,223	2.6	225,829	42.7	19.7
Manhattan, KS	35,489	53.1	189,600	20.4	10.6	891	31.5	92.6	47,707	1.0	1,365	2.9	48,803	42.0	15.4
Mankato-North Mankato, MN	38,901	66.3	188,300	19.1	10.0	855	32.5	90.1	61,033	0.6	1,467	2.4	57,824	35.7	24.1
Mansfield, OH	48,998	67.7	107,900	18.7	10.8	596	27.1	80.0	52,743	-0.8	2,583	4.9	52,595	30.9	26.6
McAllen-Edinburg-Mission, TX	239,825	66.4	86,100	22.8	12.2	695	31.2	71.3	348,672	1.6	22,881	6.6	334,478	27.4	23.5
Medford, OR	89,701	63.5	291,600	25.4	13.7	958	32.7	88.1	104,763	1.4	5,023	4.8	96,395	35.9	22.0
Memphis, TN-MS-AR	493,068	60.3	148,800	19.7	10.4	887	29.7	81.6	634,895	1.1	26,297	4.1	622,294	33.8	24.4
Merced, CA	80,969	48.8	253,700	23.1	12.6	1,003	32.4	87.6	115,408	0.0	9,574	8.3	103,680	24.0	36.3
Miami-Fort Lauderdale-West Palm Beach, FL	2,105,878	59.5	278,700	25.7	14.1	1,316	36.9	86.2	3,150,518	0.8	114,247	3.6	2,965,498	34.8	18.7
Fort Lauderdale-Pompano Beach-Deerfield Beach, FL	685,559	62.2	260,700	25.2	13.9	1,328	35.3	89.6	1,036,212	1.1	34,919	3.4	960,761	36.7	18.1
Miami-Miami Beach-Kendall, FL Div 33124	872,495	51.0	288,100	27.1	14.3	1,290	38.4	82.6	1,383,302	0.6	53,279	3.9	1,323,402	32.6	20.2
West Palm Beach-Boca Raton-Delray Beach, FL Div 48	547,824	69.5	282,900	24.6	14.2	1,349	35.5	87.7	731,004	0.9	26,049	3.6	681,335	36.6	16.8
Michigan City-La Porte, IN	42,385	71.5	131,300	18.2	10.1	695	28.2	81.9	48,027	0.4	2,102	4.4	45,603	25.2	31.1
Midland, MI	34,096	77.8	140,200	17.8	10.7	726	31.8	88.3	40,611	0.5	1,618	4.0	37,664	45.0	18.9
Midland, TX	58,490	66.9	197,000	19.2	10.0	1,097	24.6	87.9	105,084	12.5	2,215	2.1	82,538	35.3	25.2
Milwaukee-Waukesha-West Allis, WI	625,495	59.7	213,800	20.7	12.8	869	29.1	85.3	824,848	-0.6	26,358	3.2	790,676	40.2	19.4
Minneapolis-St. Paul-Bloomington, MN	1,376,557	70.2	254,800	19.8	10.2	1,057	28.1	91.6	2,001,280	0.7	53,283	2.7	1,971,465	43.9	18.1
Missoula, MT	48,806	57.9	295,600	21.1	12.7	783	30.7	89.1	63,069	1.2	2,100	3.3	65,844	36.2	18.9

1. Specified owner-occupied units lacking complete plumbing facilities.   2. A value of 10.0 represents 10 percent or less; a value of 50.0 represents 50 percent or more.   3. Specified renter-occupied units.   4. Overcrowded or   5. Percent of civilian labor force.   6. Civilian employed persons 16 years old and over.

Table C. Metropolitan Areas — **Nonfarm Employment and Agriculture**

Area name	Number of establishments	Total	Health care and social assistance	Manufacturing	Retail trade	Finance and insurance	Professional, scientific, and technical services	Total (mil dol)	Average per employee (dollars)	Number	Fewer than 50 acres	1000 acres or more	Farm producers whose primary occupation is farming (percent)
	104	105	106	107	108	109	110	111	112	113	114	115	116
Jonesboro, AR	2,841	46,557	11,562	6,719	8,167	1,190	1,052	1,690	36,290	886	28.6	24.9	50.4
Joplin, MO	4,041	69,595	12,423	12,478	10,477	1,699	1,431	2,635	37,857	2,903	39.3	2.4	38
Kahului-Wailuku-Lahaina, HI..	4,620	64,168	6,280	1,146	9,720	806	1,597	2,510	39,124	1,408	89.6	2.3	43.8
Kalamazoo-Portage, MI	6,864	124,066	22,211	19,945	16,418	6,089	6,002	5,721	46,110	1,660	56.3	3.5	42.7
Kankakee, IL	2,325	36,552	6,840	5,800	6,122	824	775	1,395	38,156	756	36.6	12.3	46.9
Kansas City, MO-KS	53,694	929,192	139,068	81,679	113,547	60,712	79,255	46,544	50,091	12,437	42	5.7	34.5
Kennewick-Richland, WA	5,797	84,301	12,817	6,909	13,628	1,965	8,422	4,071	48,289	2,292	67.3	9.3	41.6
Killeen-Temple, TX	6,163	105,594	26,550	7,350	17,732	3,891	4,042	3,957	37,476	5,066	50.5	4.7	33.8
Kingsport-Bristol-Bristol, TN-VA	6,005	103,415	17,424	21,691	15,943	3,121	3,628	4,385	42,404	5,311	50.1	0.6	35.4
Kingston, NY	4,814	46,586	9,586	3,530	9,247	2,040	1,640	1,649	35,405	421	51.8	0.7	51
Knoxville, TN	18,087	337,761	52,353	35,901	46,955	15,147	23,443	14,754	43,681	6,170	53.4	0.6	34.9
Kokomo, IN	1,776	32,760	5,505	9,968	5,118	733	690	1,385	42,292	422	36.3	10	49.1
La Crosse-Onalaska, WI-MN .	3,479	65,905	12,249	8,377	9,491	2,274	1,978	2,655	40,282	1,558	25	2.2	43.6
Lafayette, LA	13,042	184,397	33,639	12,549	27,639	5,491	9,997	7,748	42,016	3,511	54.1	7.7	36.4
Lafayette-West Lafayette, IN..	4,129	72,177	11,296	18,324	10,017	1,850	2,841	3,020	41,847	1,624	45	13.9	41.6
Lake Charles, LA	4,682	75,798	13,986	8,585	11,532	2,049	4,615	3,375	44,531	1,225	44.1	9.4	29
Lake Havasu City-Kingman, AZ	3,697	41,954	8,666	2,965	9,654	1,002	947	1,362	32,464	317	60.6	17.4	40.7
Lakeland-Winter Haven, FL....	11,530	181,761	28,214	16,638	27,610	11,624	6,072	7,236	39,810	2,080	63.2	4.8	37.6
Lancaster, PA	12,874	228,355	35,600	33,465	31,129	7,496	11,719	9,617	42,116	5,108	50	0.4	56.9
Lansing-East Lansing, MI	9,506	165,890	29,134	18,805	22,124	13,479	7,909	7,432	44,802	2,891	49.3	5.1	41.1
Laredo, TX	5,298	77,269	16,139	652	13,530	2,639	1,820	2,219	28,720	656	19.1	22.6	36.3
Las Cruces, NM	3,615	51,225	14,177	2,241	8,289	1,563	3,885	1,580	30,852	1,946	86.7	1.8	33.1
Las Vegas-Henderson-Paradise, NV	44,564	847,203	86,056	19,629	108,100	26,494	44,256	34,904	41,199	179	77.1	0.6	30.5
Lawrence, KS	2,713	40,244	6,073	3,530	6,512	1,074	4,640	1,226	30,452	998	44.7	5.6	33.5
Lawton, OK	2,273	34,074	6,248	3,416	5,556	1,567	1,410	1,132	33,211	1,503	25.4	17.9	38.3
Lebanon, PA	2,709	44,345	8,079	9,310	7,018	932	1,149	1,638	36,944	1,149	54.6	0.2	50.5
Lewiston, ID-WA	1,549	22,367	4,128	4,622	3,676	1,184	759	849	37,972	651	45.9	27.8	41
Lewiston-Auburn, ME	2,746	46,326	10,236	5,974	6,109	3,420	1,915	1,804	38,944	496	58.7	1	61
Lexington-Fayette, KY	12,526	223,796	37,781	28,439	28,757	6,108	16,072	9,614	42,960	4,619	46.2	2.3	40.6
Lima, OH	2,412	46,975	12,050	7,882	5,880	1,173	943	1,917	40,801	855	43.5	4.1	36.5
Lincoln, NE	8,890	141,994	26,290	13,654	19,353	10,344	8,597	5,786	40,746	2,730	49.5	9.2	36.3
Little Rock-North Little Rock-Conway, AR	17,904	278,783	53,892	20,923	40,178	15,123	14,006	11,731	42,080	3,353	42.8	4.8	37.6
Logan, UT-ID	3,643	44,465	5,574	12,128	6,876	1,331	3,447	1,476	33,201	2,184	53.4	5.2	31.6
Longview, TX	5,363	79,963	12,629	10,394	11,701	2,816	3,540	3,251	40,656	3,634	46.2	1.5	32.9
Longview, WA	2,150	30,646	5,688	6,213	5,083	763	730	1,391	45,389	403	76.9	1.5	33.3
Los Angeles-Long Beach-Anaheim, CA	364,192	5,354,318	700,182	488,003	582,725	251,863	418,379	296,492	55,374	1,228	88.8	1.1	45.6
Anaheim-Santa Ana-Irvine, CA Div 11244	NA	NA	NA	NA	NA	NA	NA	NA	NA	193	83.4	1.6	42.6
Los Angeles-Long Beach-Glendale, CA Div 31084	NA	NA	NA	NA	NA	NA	NA	NA	NA	1,035	89.9	1	46.1
Louisville/Jefferson County, KY-IN	29,330	569,316	85,658	73,569	64,809	36,526	26,780	26,052	45,761	7,635	49.3	2.5	35.3
Lubbock, TX	7,304	114,908	24,624	5,195	18,364	5,845	4,368	4,099	35,675	1,810	32.2	23.1	40.8
Lynchburg, VA	5,928	98,466	14,349	15,549	14,762	3,786	5,752	3,823	38,821	2,901	34.5	2.4	36.7
Macon, GA	5,102	84,402	17,645	5,982	11,813	9,102	2,781	3,290	38,984	790	39.5	5.1	35.1
Madera, CA	1,950	26,668	5,884	3,824	3,750	475	467	1,102	41,325	1,386	41.6	8.7	52.7
Madison, WI	17,077	324,461	52,784	35,039	41,032	24,311	23,815	16,382	50,488	6,927	40	3.6	44
Manchester-Nashua, NH	10,944	184,677	30,117	26,458	29,088	9,189	11,802	10,001	54,153	605	63.3	0.2	42
Manhattan, KS	2,215	29,982	4,799	2,234	6,017	1,197	1,413	999	33,318	1,278	29.1	13.5	33.9
Mankato-North Mankato, MN .	2,614	49,801	11,210	7,874	7,411	1,189	1,530	1,857	37,285	1,672	27.5	9.6	50.3
Mansfield, OH	2,597	40,569	5,551	8,493	6,538	1,068	910	1,359	33,495	1,160	49.1	1.5	41.8
McAllen-Edinburg-Mission, TX	11,937	194,826	62,411	6,296	38,238	6,786	6,155	5,356	27,490	2,436	73.6	6.4	32
Medford, OR	6,107	72,083	13,909	6,515	12,152	2,074	2,323	2,741	38,033	2,136	78.6	1.1	39.9
Memphis, TN-MS-AR	25,428	535,580	83,892	37,547	65,139	18,451	19,789	25,256	47,156	4,081	38.6	9.9	38.7
Merced, CA	3,041	43,152	7,035	9,361	8,589	1,066	830	1,702	39,453	2,337	53.5	7.4	56.3
Miami-Fort Lauderdale-West Palm Beach, FL	191,720	2,178,850	315,756	73,151	332,879	105,672	165,559	102,797	47,179	4,690	92.6	1	46.7
Fort Lauderdale-Pompano Beach-Deerfield Beach, FL	NA	NA	NA	NA	NA	NA	NA	NA	NA	640	97.2	0.2	41.5
Miami-Miami Beach-Kendall, FL Div 33124	NA	NA	NA	NA	NA	NA	NA	NA	NA	2,752	93.2	0.3	47.1
West Palm Beach-Boca Raton-Delray Beach, FL Div 48	NA	NA	NA	NA	NA	NA	NA	NA	NA	1,298	89.1	3	48.3
Michigan City-La Porte, IN	2,295	35,365	6,205	7,407	5,897	896	790	1,337	37,810	740	42.4	9.5	45.4
Midland, MI	2,081	35,682	6,644	6,859	4,066	1,125	978	2,271	63,646	530	51.3	4.2	39.2
Midland, TX	5,304	82,328	7,598	2,607	9,433	2,023	2,782	5,016	60,922	766	39	20.5	32.4
Milwaukee-Waukesha-West Allis, WI	38,402	777,585	128,265	111,757	83,123	51,842	39,818	39,863	51,265	1,554	50.2	3.4	46.8
Minneapolis-St. Paul-Bloomington, MN	96,013	1,789,890	287,626	187,270	192,176	128,119	126,590	99,711	55,708	12,423	45.7	4.2	40.1
Missoula, MT	4,386	49,585	9,849	1,896	8,499	1,955	3,019	1,793	36,152	576	66.1	3.6	32.9

Table C. Metropolitan Areas — **Agriculture**

Area name	Land in farms Acreage (1,000)	Percent change, 2012-2017	Average size of farm	Total irrigated (1,000)	Total cropland (1,000)	Value of land and buildings (dollars) Average per farm	Average per acre	Value of machinery and equipment, average per farm (dollars)	Value of products sold: Total (mil dol)	Average per farm (acres)	Percent from: Crops	Live-stock and poultry products	Organic farms (number)	Farms with internet access (percent)	Government payments Total ($1,000)	Percent of farms
	117	118	119	120	121	122	123	124	125	126	127	128	129	130	131	132
Jonesboro, AR	638	-11.8	720	510	592.3	3,038,718	4,220	385,903	381	430,029	98.8	1.2	NA	75.4	31,077	63.2
Joplin, MO	526	6.4	181	5.8	232.4	621,114	3,429	84,225	343.2	118,235	18.1	81.9	1	74.2	2,415	18.4
Kahului-Wailuku-Lahaina, HI..	249	8.6	177	4.8	56.6	2,027,298	11,466	51,466	82.2	58,385	90.3	9.7	40	83.5	2,174	9.4
Kalamazoo-Portage, MI	290	-8.9	175	78.6	229.9	1,118,184	6,393	174,292	442.5	266,549	77.7	22.3	9	78.4	4,266	17.5
Kankakee, IL	313	-8.7	414	18.4	300.4	3,237,466	7,822	285,392	221.1	292,508	91.3	8.7	3	75.5	2,346	45.4
Kansas City, MO-KS	3,126	0.1	251	26	2,026.9	906,374	3,606	99,443	985.3	79,220	75.1	24.9	39	76.7	29,916	34.7
Kennewick-Richland, WA	1,229	-7.5	536	392.4	919.9	2,276,946	4,247	248,388	1,636.9	714,174	75.7	24.3	56	86	16,530	13
Killeen-Temple, TX	1,413	6.3	279	4.1	285.1	812,458	2,913	64,759	131.7	26,006	36.6	63.4	4	75	5,248	9.4
Kingsport-Bristol-Bristol, TN-VA	527	-7.3	99	0.2	168.3	440,247	4,437	55,882	125.3	23,599	16.7	83.3	4	69	2,177	12.2
Kingston, NY	59	-17.3	140	3.7	24.1	965,682	6,899	95,713	54.3	129,088	88.3	11.7	24	86.9	164	8.1
Knoxville, TN	530	-1.4	86	1	190.9	470,339	5,474	59,663	84.2	13,640	42.6	57.4	34	72.7	4,325	20
Kokomo, IN	146	1.1	345	D	138.0	2,681,235	7,765	219,981	97.1	230,078	83.1	16.9	3	79.9	4,286	68.2
La Crosse-Onalaska, WI-MN .	361	-6.8	232	1.3	211.6	1,059,615	4,568	128,124	190.8	122,458	38.2	61.8	49	77.5	5,327	61.2
Lafayette, LA	923	21.4	263	165.7	606.7	793,548	3,018	142,157	336.8	95,939	77.2	22.8	2	64.8	31,262	40.4
Lafayette-West Lafayette, IN..	697	2.8	429	12.9	656.8	3,471,032	8,083	257,784	571.9	352,154	72	28	9	79.6	12,142	61.3
Lake Charles, LA	542	-5.4	442	18.9	128.4	1,386,167	3,133	80,170	37.7	30,793	49.9	50.1	NA	75	5,190	22.4
Lake Havasu City-Kingman, AZ	745	-40.1	2,351	20.9	30.7	1,972,874	839	96,073	32.3	101,871	71.1	28.9	NA	87.4	390	2.8
Lakeland-Winter Haven, FL....	487	-6.5	234	88.6	131.0	1,420,064	6,064	69,094	297.7	143,136	81	19	5	71.5	2,242	11.5
Lancaster, PA	394	-10.4	77	4.9	314.9	1,410,238	18,285	120,108	1,507.2	295,068	15.3	84.7	246	48.9	4,834	11.8
Lansing-East Lansing, MI	618	-7.4	214	5.1	530.2	1,081,159	5,057	157,795	421.4	145,758	52.1	47.9	52	79.8	12,505	33.4
Laredo, TX	1,845	-12.1	2,812	3.3	35.0	4,817,630	1,713	69,020	28.4	43,287	1.5	98.5	NA	47.6	525	3.2
Las Cruces, NM	528	-20	271	73.7	93.1	674,302	2,484	91,092	370.3	190,284	61.8	38.2	23	73.7	578	4
Las Vegas-Henderson-Para-dise, NV	D	-100	D	3.7	4.0	1,439,603	D	76,922	12.7	70,676	90.2	9.8	1	74.9	16	2.2
Lawrence, KS	230	9.3	231	3.5	159.3	939,826	4,072	94,196	65.9	65,999	76.7	23.3	11	78.3	1,316	38.8
Lawton, OK	872	1	580	0.1	360.4	965,045	1,664	100,970	130.8	87,035	20.1	79.9	2	75.6	9,050	44.4
Lebanon, PA	108	-11.4	94	0.7	86.7	1,348,192	14,400	132,813	350.8	305,312	10.6	89.4	54	71.4	1,021	13.7
Lewiston, ID-WA	632	8	972	2	313.7	1,728,575	1,779	185,061	87.2	133,986	78	22	1	87.1	11,239	44.7
Lewiston-Auburn, ME	56	-6.4	112	1	24.6	395,349	3,526	68,417	40.5	81,726	37.6	62.4	18	85.1	481	10.5
Lexington-Fayette, KY	752		163	1.3	305.4	1,179,163	7,245	87,936	723.3	156,582	15	85	15	82.1	2,574	10.6
Lima, OH	187	1.9	218	0.4	172.7	1,583,677	7,256	163,585	139.9	163,639	61.4	38.6	2	77.8	5,704	67.7
Lincoln, NE	786	-6.8	288	160	673.4	1,627,411	5,650	169,707	439.8	161,095	70.4	29.6	11	83.6	20,112	59.5
Little Rock-North Little Rock-Conway, AR	816	3.5	243	258.9	451.5	885,319	3,640	104,215	302.1	90,088	66.2	33.8	18	76.8	19,878	16.2
Logan, UT-ID	505	-5	231	155.4	291.4	854,536	3,698	123,635	245.5	112,417	27.4	72.6	34	82	6,169	30.8
Longview, TX	486	-7.4	134	1.2	97.5	436,360	3,264	59,272	145	39,894	7.1	92.9	8	72.7	660	3.8
Longview, WA	29	-26.3	71	3	11.0	639,037	8,955	53,998	19	47,045	52.8	47.2	NA	80.9	27	1.5
Los Angeles-Long Beach-Anaheim, CA	90	-40.7	73	18	39.2	1,378,476	18,765	72,823	237.1	193,090	91	9	48	78.9	529	2.3
Anaheim-Santa Ana-Irvine, CA Div 11244	32	-46.4	168	4.2	9.6	3,205,503	19,094	162,435	82.5	427,497	99.5	0.5	7	79.8	6	3.1
Los Angeles-Long Beach-Glendale, CA Div 31084	58	-37	56	13.8	29.6	1,037,785	18,580	56,113	154.6	149,380	86.5	13.5	41	78.7	523	2.1
Louisville/Jefferson County, KY-IN	1,127	5.5	148	6.4	679.0	748,967	5,074	83,352	486.1	63,662	58.4	41.6	13	74.2	13,262	17.9
Lubbock, TX	1,580	3.1	873	336.3	1,180.5	1,071,771	1,228	232,519	417.8	230,832	75.4	24.6	13	76.8	17,022	56.5
Lynchburg, VA	497	-10	171	0.6	147.0	667,392	3,893	70,399	70	24,126	31.1	68.9	4	74.1	1,215	10.6
Macon, GA	169	16.4	213	6.3	41.5	677,035	3,172	83,004	129.7	164,133	16.2	83.8	7	81.1	974	17.1
Madera, CA	645	-1.3	466	300.2	346.1	5,102,429	10,958	229,882	1,492.6	1,076,903	77.4	22.6	74	77.1	2,192	8.4
Madison, WI	1,463	-0.2	211	22	1,110.1	1,340,446	6,346	157,750	1,159.1	167,331	40.5	59.5	140	81	20,405	50.5
Manchester-Nashua, NH	44	-7.3	73	0.6	11.7	568,208	7,775	67,926	18.8	31,030	77.2	22.8	18	93.1	281	7.8
Manhattan, KS	620	-1.2	485	23.4	264.8	1,288,708	2,655	129,736	152.5	119,355	48.7	51.3	3	81.2	3,627	51
Mankato-North Mankato, MN .	648	-0.5	387	4.3	605.0	2,757,805	7,121	290,184	822.8	492,108	41.4	58.6	8	82.8	15,176	64.6
Mansfield, OH	156	-3	134	0.2	113.1	1,008,272	7,505	108,319	135.1	116,504	37.1	62.9	20	65.4	2,687	21
McAllen-Edinburg-Mission, TX	624	-21.5	256	162.5	356.9	1,106,061	4,319	92,928	311	127,681	94.3	5.7	26	61.8	6,631	10.5
Medford, OR	170	-20.5	80	37.5	40.7	677,191	8,494	44,300	71	33,262	74.7	25.3	43	86.6	55	0.8
Memphis, TN-MS-AR	1,623	3.1	398	327.8	1,092.5	1,280,497	3,221	137,309	475.8	116,595	90.9	9.1	4	69.9	32,532	36.5
Merced, CA	946	-3.3	405	493.7	546.5	5,299,308	13,086	334,860	2,938.4	1,257,337	43.9	56.1	68	78.5	8,726	12.5
Miami-Fort Lauderdale-West Palm Beach, FL	573	-6	122	408.2	495.8	1,546,374	12,654	84,442	1,764.3	376,191	98.5	1.5	45	76.4	1,865	1.4
Fort Lauderdale-Pompano Beach-Deerfield Beach, FL	7	-53.5	11	0.7	1.6	348,906	33,140	31,889	24.9	38,883	94.2	5.8	NA	85.5	18	0.6
Miami-Miami Beach-Kendall, FL Div 33124	79	-3.4	29	36.8	55.2	1,068,826	37,450	51,638	837.7	304,409	98.8	1.2	35	70.6	1,733	1.8
West Palm Beach-Boca Raton-Delray Beach, FL Div 48	488	-5.1	376	370.7	438.9	3,149,297	8,379	179,904	901.7	694,699	98.3	1.7	10	84.2	114	1.1
Michigan City-La Porte, IN	249	9.2	336	68.5	230.0	2,473,619	7,355	210,853	166.4	224,842	82.2	17.8	7	79.6	8,644	58.4
Midland, MI	88	-2.1	165	0.6	69.9	916,909	5,542	121,113	46.9	88,483	57.1	42.9	5	80.2	2,366	40
Midland, TX	790	-8	1,031	19.6	374.7	1,241,070	1,204	141,855	70.6	92,215	92.7	7.3	NA	79.6	6,374	41.1
Milwaukee-Waukesha-West Allis, WI	283	-4.2	182	1.9	228.7	1,198,064	6,581	156,733	290.5	186,950	45.3	54.7	30	80.4	2,106	32.4
Minneapolis-St. Paul-Bloom-ington, MN	2,492	-4.1	201	134.9	2,045.3	1,199,988	5,982	154,833	1,881.5	151,453	62.4	37.6	174	80.6	23,920	39.5
Missoula, MT	260	5.3	452	15.5	21.6	1,262,722	2,796	42,356	9.8	17,099	57.3	42.7	5	82.8	417	6.1

Table C. Metropolitan Areas — Water Use, Wholesale Trade, Retail Trade, and Real Estate

Area name	Water use, 2015		Wholesale Trade[1], 2012				Retail Trade[2], 2012				Real estate and rental and leasing,[2] 2012			
	Public supply water withdrawn (mil gal/day)	Public supply gallons withdrawn per person per day	Number of establishments	Number of employees	Sales (mil dol)	Average payroll (mil dol)	Number of establishments	Number of employees	Sales (mil dol)	Average payroll (mil dol)	Number of establishments	Number of employees	Sales (mil dol)	Average payroll (mil dol)
	133	134	135	136	137	138	139	140	141	142	143	144	145	146
Jonesboro, AR	16.3	127	153	1,899	1,854.8	94.1	524	7,142	1,858.9	156.2	124	509	83.2	13.9
Joplin, MO	22.87	129.1	184	2,895	2,647.0	118.9	710	9,859	2,841.3	215.3	143	583	86.0	14.9
Kahului-Wailuku-Lahaina, HI	42.1	255.6	140	1,141	714.6	50.4	759	9,174	2,461.0	258.2	306	2,022	454.4	70.8
Kalamazoo-Portage, MI	27.9	83.2	287	D	D	D	1,115	14,993	3,764.0	338.3	242	2,430	239.0	73.5
Kankakee, IL	13.26	119.6	119	2,196	1,443.3	95.0	370	5,548	1,463.3	120.0	95	371	70.9	10.6
Kansas City, MO-KS	270.8	129.7	2,529	42,419	52,860.3	2,756.7	6,294	104,436	29,998.3	2,579.3	2,430	13,232	3,092.0	568.9
Kennewick-Richland, WA	50.78	181.9	222	2,512	2,971.9	112.3	772	11,935	3,382.4	307.4	300	1,244	220.5	37.3
Killeen-Temple, TX	19.23	44.6	143	2,717	3,687.0	139.5	1,093	15,406	4,328.6	344.5	350	1,640	241.7	55.4
Kingsport-Bristol-Bristol, TN-VA	40.07	130.5	275	3,317	1,816.0	121.0	1,101	15,030	3,779.9	327.2	208	741	126.5	23.1
Kingston, NY	394.23	2,188.4	159	1,504	810.4	71.3	733	8,606	2,324.9	211.8	195	732	116.6	22.0
Knoxville, TN	112.42	130.5	867	12,090	8,194.7	621.5	2,923	44,783	11,873.6	1,086.3	791	4,105	764.5	149.0
Kokomo, IN	8.47	102.6	62	559	512.7	31.6	328	4,927	1,193.3	104.0	71	311	50.4	8.9
La Crosse-Onalaska, WI-MN	15.09	110.2	137	2,724	6,239.4	119.7	491	9,017	2,027.3	185.4	125	801	101.7	20.9
Lafayette, LA	51.43	104.9	708	10,557	5,896.8	547.1	1,856	25,397	7,064.9	625.9	688	6,875	2,269.2	460.8
Lafayette-West Lafayette, IN	14.55	67.9	142	1,637	1,256.9	69.6	611	9,409	2,378.7	200.9	181	892	148.2	30.0
Lake Charles, LA	29.01	141.1	199	2,196	1,971.0	102.7	772	10,240	3,155.4	241.0	216	1,018	235.6	41.5
Lake Havasu City-Kingman, AZ	47.86	233.8	114	816	391.1	30.5	593	8,918	2,712.7	211.4	199	628	83.2	15.6
Lakeland-Winter Haven, FL	67.54	103.9	544	8,056	10,601.3	394.0	1,756	22,988	6,495.3	558.8	651	2,928	510.6	93.1
Lancaster, PA	54.45	101.5	582	10,776	8,764.0	496.7	1,917	29,783	6,899.6	669.6	342	2,009	396.6	79.1
Lansing-East Lansing, MI	29.88	63.3	327	5,044	7,143.8	236.0	1,416	20,926	5,462.7	475.9	385	2,530	349.8	88.0
Laredo, TX	36.08	133.8	357	2,839	2,410.1	97.0	784	12,356	3,217.6	257.8	199	692	132.4	22.0
Las Cruces, NM	33.99	158.6	102	D	D	D	496	7,916	1,965.4	167.7	209	690	116.6	18.9
Las Vegas-Henderson-Paradise, NV	432.47	204.5	1,630	16,747	11,597.1	958.8	5,712	95,369	27,971.7	2,531.6	2,794	17,855	3,700.3	647.4
Lawrence, KS	12.67	107.3	71	610	282.9	24.6	373	6,066	1,354.2	122.6	157	761	97.7	20.9
Lawton, OK	21.49	164.5	64	D	D	D	424	5,410	1,444.7	119.5	126	519	90.6	16.5
Lebanon, PA	3.55	25.9	99	2,679	3,913.7	112.7	431	6,597	1,695.7	158.6	70	309	40.5	7.8
Lewiston, ID-WA	15.28	245.8	55	613	497.2	26.3	259	3,343	968.8	87.2	60	280	37.3	7.6
Lewiston-Auburn, ME	7.92	73.9	102	1,236	473.9	54.6	439	6,018	1,818.1	138.5	111	376	62.9	11.6
Lexington-Fayette, KY	55.56	111	473	9,899	9,127.9	669.6	1,734	27,528	7,438.5	652.4	554	2,474	505.0	85.7
Lima, OH	18.17	174	124	2,287	1,388.8	91.6	417	6,072	1,641.5	134.3	85	376	55.2	11.0
Lincoln, NE	2.91	9	305	4,427	3,667.9	183.4	1,063	17,686	4,428.3	398.8	353	1,726	257.6	56.7
Little Rock-North Little Rock-Conway, AR	76.47	104.5	868	12,971	9,583.7	658.8	2,605	37,471	10,847.9	901.3	836	4,140	765.8	147.3
Logan, UT-ID	37.53	280.4	119	978	613.1	37.7	447	5,980	1,270.6	118.4	190	D	D	D
Longview, TX	17.19	78.9	290	3,950	2,602.1	209.8	866	11,363	3,285.3	283.8	231	1,303	427.0	65.6
Longview, WA	10.31	99.6	85	1,036	2,021.4	53.2	333	4,644	1,188.3	113.8	104	337	50.7	8.5
Los Angeles-Long Beach-Anaheim, CA	1,713.98	128.5	27,704	317,329	297,600.8	18,082.1	37,817	528,453	166,583.0	14,835.1	19,194	120,995	38,846.0	6,397.2
Anaheim-Santa Ana-Irvine, CA Div 11244	457.54	144.3	6,434	79,685	97,796.0	5,200.7	9,390	143,012	45,193.6	4,135.3	5,320	38,952	9,259.7	1,921.2
Los Angeles-Long Beach-Glendale, CA Div 31084	1,256.44	123.5	21,270	237,644	199,804.8	12,881.4	28,427	385,441	121,389.4	10,699.7	13,874	82,043	29,586.3	4,476.1
Louisville/Jefferson County, KY-IN	175.09	137	1,322	19,345	15,452.9	992.4	4,011	59,405	16,279.7	1,413.5	1,250	8,356	3,099.2	326.1
Lubbock, TX	2.98	9.6	389	D	D	D	1,073	16,669	4,850.9	409.5	399	D	D	D
Lynchburg, VA	18.03	69.4	178	2,025	1,098.8	87.6	939	13,555	3,665.7	315.0	269	773	131.2	23.3
Macon, GA	29.29	127.3	224	2,679	1,666.2	128.0	980	11,588	2,932.4	260.9	225	969	179.2	32.4
Madera, CA	15.63	100.8	76	815	508.9	37.8	326	3,455	1,012.9	84.3	75	336	38.4	8.5
Madison, WI	50.72	79.1	709	13,072	8,970.5	679.2	2,123	38,927	11,740.7	1,042.3	695	4,410	992.1	164.6
Manchester-Nashua, NH	38.74	95.3	537	6,822	4,749.3	470.5	1,584	26,984	7,724.7	700.9	387	2,697	565.9	123.8
Manhattan, KS	9.25	93.9	56	725	307.1	30.8	353	6,208	1,242.8	130.0	129	511	74.1	13.2
Mankato-North Mankato, MN	10.45	105.4	123	1,798	1,325.4	85.2	395	6,930	1,645.7	151.2	104	692	75.5	16.9
Mansfield, OH	14.45	118.7	104	1,993	939.2	78.9	438	6,528	1,501.2	139.9	102	417	49.2	9.1
McAllen-Edinburg-Mission, TX	64.64	76.7	841	D	D	D	2,219	33,566	9,296.8	733.9	497	2,209	445.0	61.9
Medford, OR	39.04	183.7	206	1,771	828.4	76.8	865	11,223	3,202.7	297.5	306	1,043	164.1	26.3
Memphis, TN-MS-AR	181.72	135.2	1,435	28,963	41,205.9	1,583.6	4,178	61,787	26,311.6	1,598.5	1,125	7,663	1,573.2	327.6
Merced, CA	50.17	186.9	112	1,635	2,260.2	71.2	528	7,497	1,959.5	173.3	152	532	79.1	14.6
Miami-Fort Lauderdale-West Palm Beach, FL	824.3	137.1	14,077	109,773	124,749.4	5,674.1	22,695	290,852	90,104.2	7,832.7	10,475	48,690	11,005.1	1,996.5
Fort Lauderdale-Pompano Beach-Deerfield Beach, FL	233.65	123.2	3,902	33,141	33,606.6	1,781.8	7,070	97,344	32,042.9	2,675.4	3,237	17,682	3,934.9	701.7
Miami-Miami Beach-Kendall, FL Div 33124	351.92	130.7	8,242	61,377	78,985.4	3,003.6	10,389	123,883	38,361.2	3,252.7	4,776	19,563	4,936.4	811.9
West Palm Beach-Boca Raton-Delray Beach, FL Div 48	238.73	167.8	1,933	15,255	12,157.3	888.7	5,236	69,625	19,700.1	1,904.6	2,462	11,445	2,133.8	482.9
Michigan City-La Porte, IN	9.35	84.3	100	1,161	694.9	46.8	457	5,845	1,367.8	116.2	84	367	95.2	10.6
Midland, MI	0.14	1.7	44	297	703.7	16.7	314	4,050	1,015.7	88.4	63	257	36.8	8.4
Midland, TX	2.52	15.1	272	D	D	D	515	7,607	3,019.3	221.5	267	1,505	491.4	79.1
Milwaukee-Waukesha-West Allis, WI	147	93.3	1,981	34,545	23,162.4	2,243.4	4,695	77,813	20,086.4	1,806.6	1,354	9,103	1,636.8	343.6
Minneapolis-St. Paul-Bloomington, MN	337.29	95.7	4,390	77,536	72,483.1	5,723.3	10,525	179,498	51,537.1	4,494.9	4,636	27,832	6,835.8	1,224.7
Missoula, MT	30.41	266.3	151	1,838	1,220.7	81.5	570	7,931	2,044.0	180.0	206	918	130.6	29.7

1. Merchant wholesalers, except manufacturers' sales branches and offices. 2. Employer establishments.

Table C. Metropolitan Areas — Professional Services, Manufacturing, and Accommodation and Food Services

Area name	Professional, scientific, and technical services, 2012				Manufacturing, 2012				Accommodation and food services, 2012			
	Number of establish-ments	Number of employees	Sales (mil dol)	Average payroll (mil dol)	Number of establish-ments	Number of employees	Receipts (mil dol)	Annual payroll (mil dol)	Number of establish-ments	Number of employees	Receipts (mil dol)	Annual payroll (mil dol)
	147	148	149	150	151	152	153	154	155	156	157	158
Jonesboro, AR	188	916	129.1	47.1	120	5,910	2,325.7	245.4	248	4,784	213.7	57.5
Joplin, MO	250	D	D	D	243	11,659	4,282.8	486.5	358	6,644	297.2	81.6
Kahului-Wailuku-Lahaina, HI	390	1,381	186.4	67.0	99	997	D	41.1	499	19,943	2,307.5	625.7
Kalamazoo-Portage, MI	621	5,037	771.8	268.6	398	18,339	8,609.7	1,051.9	695	13,630	575.0	173.0
Kankakee, IL	152	735	64.1	24.5	100	4,889	4,842.8	269.7	219	3,675	160.3	47.4
Kansas City, MO-KS	6,155	69,705	13,938.8	5,014.4	1,744	74,320	40,520.9	4,025.8	3,910	82,476	4,552.6	1,254.3
Kennewick-Richland, WA	511	9,341	1,701.1	687.2	197	6,764	2,821.7	327.1	492	7,736	405.8	114.5
Killeen-Temple, TX	474	4,383	504.2	203.8	180	6,556	2,110.1	268.1	697	13,241	632.5	170.8
Kingsport-Bristol-Bristol, TN-VA	460	2,948	327.7	135.9	282	24,543	9,574.3	1,421.8	586	10,841	488.5	140.0
Kingston, NY	443	1,601	189.3	69.1	170	3,518	D	170.2	546	6,655	367.3	117.4
Knoxville, TN	1,691	21,671	2,523.0	1,399.6	727	33,148	13,060.5	1,823.5	1,507	32,820	1,566.1	466.9
Kokomo, IN	114	631	61.2	22.6	70	7,671	D	593.4	186	3,866	159.9	46.1
La Crosse-Onalaska, WI-MN	274	1,949	185.4	88.2	179	7,092	1,996.6	277.2	365	6,575	252.0	74.4
Lafayette, LA	1,761	10,784	1,848.4	631.0	582	19,339	9,405.7	1,128.7	969	19,563	1,026.7	290.3
Lafayette-West Lafayette, IN	331	2,418	345.0	108.9	161	16,598	13,028.7	935.4	446	8,493	383.2	104.9
Lake Charles, LA	432	5,212	479.4	222.9	128	8,620	44,186.6	688.2	358	10,817	984.6	210.8
Lake Havasu City-Kingman, AZ	239	931	72.4	30.8	133	2,566	D	109.5	382	5,787	256.7	74.3
Lakeland-Winter Haven, FL	1,036	6,724	768.7	300.4	401	14,200	9,822.2	681.0	788	15,188	797.9	220.1
Lancaster, PA	957	12,486	1,249.1	1,037.2	856	33,212	13,655.7	1,638.7	998	17,833	878.4	246.9
Lansing-East Lansing, MI	1,051	7,399	1,210.3	408.7	341	17,312	16,198.9	1,002.6	913	17,000	708.1	201.7
Laredo, TX	317	1,803	186.1	58.6	69	635	339.6	22.0	389	8,216	423.7	106.2
Las Cruces, NM	339	D	D	D	128	2,520	D	87.1	319	6,813	285.2	80.7
Las Vegas-Henderson-Paradise, NV	5,645	35,253	5,825.0	2,128.2	894	17,390	5,673.8	782.0	4,050	250,601	24,283.8	7,612.3
Lawrence, KS	292	D	D	D	69	3,079	1,217.3	136.1	301	6,511	261.1	72.2
Lawton, OK	168	1,143	115.7	50.2	49	3,495	1,354.6	D	234	4,927	223.2	66.8
Lebanon, PA	197	1,083	151.2	48.6	205	8,099	2,743.8	336.5	232	3,320	146.1	40.5
Lewiston, ID-WA	112	D	D	D	60	3,067	1,175.1	144.0	139	2,677	133.7	38.7
Lewiston-Auburn, ME	183	1,652	359.2	80.1	150	5,205	1,886.9	251.6	209	3,021	153.3	44.5
Lexington-Fayette, KY	1,384	12,042	1,702.3	653.5	423	25,017	17,174.3	1,286.4	1,051	23,086	1,191.8	340.1
Lima, OH	164	952	75.8	33.0	124	7,318	15,270.4	448.1	234	4,521	211.3	54.3
Lincoln, NE	871	9,241	1,313.8	464.2	255	13,208	6,540.1	653.7	702	13,936	616.8	161.3
Little Rock-North Little Rock-Conway, AR	2,012	12,058	1,911.2	627.2	540	21,045	9,263.0	990.1	1,461	29,034	1,362.2	386.9
Logan, UT-ID	385	2,538	251.4	88.6	226	10,761	4,556.5	443.1	178	3,173	130.7	35.4
Longview, TX	508	3,998	554.5	213.9	233	10,657	4,029.0	552.1	426	8,138	374.1	105.1
Longview, WA	140	830	86.5	34.9	116	5,722	3,264.5	385.6	215	2,796	124.2	39.2
Los Angeles-Long Beach-Anaheim, CA	45,444	633,648	90,371.7	35,143.8	17,461	509,552	211,129.0	28,731.8	27,439	499,255	32,015.8	8,990.4
Anaheim-Santa Ana-Irvine, CA Div 11244	14,120	112,581	24,110.2	8,899.6	4,701	150,020	47,299.4	8,879.0	7,141	143,519	9,050.6	2,599.9
Los Angeles-Long Beach-Glendale, CA Div 31084	31,324	521,067	66,261.5	26,244.3	12,760	359,532	163,829.6	19,852.8	20,298	355,736	22,965.1	6,390.6
Louisville/Jefferson County, KY-IN	3,045	26,012	3,734.3	1,286.6	1,223	65,362	37,466.2	3,253.0	2,382	56,076	2,984.5	793.9
Lubbock, TX	640	3,878	483.4	176.3	246	5,075	1,586.2	219.0	638	14,366	721.2	191.8
Lynchburg, VA	508	5,203	1,175.9	359.6	276	15,749	6,265.7	883.3	461	8,653	367.3	101.8
Macon, GA	467	2,857	365.3	128.7	154	5,041	1,729.2	234.4	470	8,864	394.7	109.9
Madera, CA	116	493	66.9	21.6	92	3,298	1,441.1	168.0	193	2,461	150.1	37.1
Madison, WI	1,917	20,780	3,515.0	1,348.2	734	31,666	12,491.6	1,595.6	1,567	29,215	1,330.4	378.2
Manchester-Nashua, NH	1,335	10,986	1,721.0	737.1	554	25,287	7,450.8	1,732.0	897	14,781	762.2	229.8
Manhattan, KS	198	D	D	D	60	1,847	472.0	93.5	201	4,325	164.5	46.5
Mankato-North Mankato, MN	189	1,540	173.9	77.6	138	7,573	4,903.6	321.6	208	4,343	170.1	46.8
Mansfield, OH	187	925	113.1	36.0	168	8,064	3,122.7	385.9	239	4,556	190.1	54.1
McAllen-Edinburg-Mission, TX	886	5,381	566.0	169.6	268	5,713	1,675.4	216.0	1,014	19,468	985.9	247.1
Medford, OR	506	D	D	D	308	5,370	1,624.6	217.4	586	7,381	382.2	112.5
Memphis, TN-MS-AR	2,112	19,494	2,687.2	1,117.7	846	34,515	26,369.2	1,846.8	2,239	55,258	3,253.0	858.2
Merced, CA	142	791	67.1	26.2	116	9,973	4,435.6	405.4	298	4,585	232.9	60.2
Miami-Fort Lauderdale-West Palm Beach, FL	28,955	142,450	26,210.5	9,220.5	4,452	63,174	16,753.9	2,987.1	11,402	234,634	16,293.0	4,445.0
Fort Lauderdale-Pompano Beach-Deerfield Beach, FL	9,583	46,815	8,286.6	2,833.0	1,454	21,057	6,010.6	1,054.7	3,685	72,428	5,129.2	1,322.2
Miami-Miami Beach-Kendall, FL Div 33124	12,008	58,711	11,734.8	4,018.8	2,070	30,387	7,192.9	1,318.2	5,052	104,467	7,696.6	2,078.4
West Palm Beach-Boca Raton-Delray Beach, FL Div 48	7,364	36,924	6,189.1	2,368.7	928	11,731	3,550.4	614.2	2,665	57,739	3,467.3	1,044.3
Michigan City-La Porte, IN	158	1,069	85.0	40.4	172	7,589	2,644.0	350.5	235	4,992	357.0	78.7
Midland, MI	154	785	87.9	34.9	62	6,241	3,591.1	466.1	138	2,861	136.2	40.7
Midland, TX	499	4,739	1,006.1	267.4	143	3,296	1,324.8	165.8	304	6,675	477.6	109.6
Milwaukee-Waukesha-West Allis, WI	3,841	40,983	6,746.8	2,630.0	2,465	114,114	40,901.0	6,604.8	3,179	59,849	2,856.5	780.7
Minneapolis-St. Paul-Bloomington, MN	13,160	111,963	20,342.0	8,273.1	4,641	176,842	71,530.0	10,348.0	6,596	144,111	7,830.5	2,217.4
Missoula, MT	501	2,865	325.4	137.2	102	1,351	310.6	49.1	342	6,106	317.4	84.0

Table C. Metropolitan Areas — Health Care and Social Assistance, Other Services, Nonemployer Businesses, and Residential Construction

Area name	Health care and social assistance, 2012				Other services, 2012				Nonemployer businesses, 2016		Value of residential construction authorized by building permits, 2018	
	Number of establishments	Number of employees	Receipts (mil dol)	Annual payroll (mil dol)	Number of establishments	Number of employees	Receipts (mil dol)	Annual payroll (mil dol)	Number	Receipts (mil dol)	New construction ($1,000)	Number of housing units
	159	160	161	162	163	164	165	166	167	168	169	170
Jonesboro, AR	405	9,349	958.7	378.4	151	D	D	D	9,214	440.3	95,819	843
Joplin, MO	474	12,922	1,236.6	588.5	288	1,496	119.0	35.0	10,429	535.4	82,250	640
Kahului-Wailuku-Lahaina, HI..	393	6,138	741.5	308.2	383	2,185	238.1	62.0	16,792	813.7	240,389	838
Kalamazoo-Portage, MI	760	21,248	2,457.4	946.4	516	3,367	414.5	97.6	20,945	893.4	137,750	579
Kankakee, IL	311	7,349	753.9	294.5	180	956	100.3	25.1	6,066	203.8	29,707	157
Kansas City, MO-KS	5,421	133,626	15,085.9	5,992.9	3,361	22,120	3,219.6	701.1	145,940	6,824.8	2,044,135	10,268
Kennewick-Richland, WA	662	11,539	1,309.8	520.5	345	1,968	161.5	50.3	12,610	588.3	497,984	1,901
Killeen-Temple, TX	606	24,367	2,965.3	1,295.4	506	3,411	248.4	84.7	22,050	912.9	407,270	2,460
Kingsport-Bristol-Bristol, TN-VA	733	17,517	1,976.4	754.1	387	2,119	527.7	56.8	18,209	715.6	92,929	556
Kingston, NY	514	8,991	741.4	312.4	322	1,229	114.9	28.6	16,264	679.0	70,760	252
Knoxville, TN	1,987	53,573	5,749.5	2,129.1	1,162	8,068	755.7	251.4	61,476	3,056.3	832,522	4,413
Kokomo, IN	221	5,417	456.4	182.6	129	922	68.2	18.9	4,238	150.1	46,802	349
La Crosse-Onalaska, WI-MN .	327	12,270	1,508.1	539.7	274	1,785	157.9	46.8	7,695	356.4	101,900	594
Lafayette, LA	1,533	32,257	3,120.9	1,178.7	715	5,199	674.7	168.1	43,177	1,845.4	356,727	1,687
Lafayette-West Lafayette, IN..	424	11,181	1,217.2	433.2	276	1,907	218.4	49.4	11,160	487.0	316,261	1,818
Lake Charles, LA	521	12,330	1,209.9	457.2	244	1,617	178.0	51.1	14,107	642.5	219,461	1,391
Lake Havasu City-Kingman, AZ	478	8,222	995.0	364.2	290	1,394	110.3	29.4	10,781	480.1	203,858	1,018
Lakeland-Winter Haven, FL....	1,048	27,066	3,015.2	1,109.8	673	3,366	328.5	94.6	42,327	1,562.3	1,092,544	5,331
Lancaster, PA	1,110	34,977	3,387.5	1,411.1	1,031	6,339	588.6	161.3	41,920	2,209.2	239,896	1,251
Lansing-East Lansing, MI	1,155	27,524	2,988.8	1,167.0	817	6,682	808.3	240.6	31,388	1,402.8	160,165	825
Laredo, TX	536	14,678	926.2	373.6	203	1,129	101.1	27.1	25,100	1,169.5	167,410	1,375
Las Cruces, NM	496	12,122	1,010.7	418.4	234	1,124	86.4	26.3	12,557	476.8	199,004	965
Las Vegas-Henderson-Paradise, NV	4,426	75,019	9,714.9	3,493.8	2,344	17,926	1,602.8	476.8	167,624	8,150.3	2,246,486	12,044
Lawrence, KS	289	6,580	545.8	211.1	181	1,423	230.7	37.2	8,281	341.6	126,151	823
Lawton, OK	282	6,960	709.7	273.2	141	846	70.7	21.3	5,183	220.1	13,582	68
Lebanon, PA	279	8,165	772.4	341.9	233	1,086	110.1	27.5	8,236	395.7	57,617	299
Lewiston, ID-WA	192	4,024	440.3	159.8	108	561	39.4	12.2	3,145	123.7	28,438	120
Lewiston-Auburn, ME	385	9,531	947.5	402.8	211	1,024	84.6	23.5	6,302	292.1	52,289	300
Lexington-Fayette, KY	1,524	34,868	4,154.5	1,607.9	792	5,378	821.8	163.5	36,371	1,705.0	364,140	2,772
Lima, OH	307	11,307	1,256.5	501.7	197	1,264	92.0	25.5	5,318	221.3	18,995	86
Lincoln, NE	1,007	23,965	2,418.6	963.5	705	4,286	593.7	134.2	22,517	905.5	345,088	1,804
Little Rock-North Little Rock-Conway, AR	2,067	52,656	5,908.8	2,359.2	1,178	8,198	1,001.5	238.3	51,469	2,252.0	391,843	2,174
Logan, UT-ID	373	5,431	519.3	170.7	191	D	D	D	9,740	377.1	239,460	1,211
Longview, TX	543	12,575	1,468.4	479.6	311	2,349	288.1	91.0	15,829	724.4	35,401	259
Longview, WA	240	5,444	567.0	232.1	148	D	D	D	4,387	187.3	67,852	318
Los Angeles-Long Beach-Anaheim, CA	40,695	651,603	87,943.5	31,496.0	20,823	146,211	17,344.3	4,317.7	1,353,478	73,922.4	7,348,035	29,524
Anaheim-Santa Ana-Irvine, CA Div 11244	10,873	152,659	20,682.2	7,379.9	4,980	35,537	3,782.2	1,039.3	307,052	17,934.0	NA	NA
Los Angeles-Long Beach-Glendale, CA Div 31084	29,822	498,944	67,261.3	24,116.1	15,843	110,674	13,562.1	3,278.3	1,046,426	55,988.4	NA	NA
Louisville/Jefferson County, KY-IN	3,410	86,187	9,206.9	3,559.7	1,965	16,301	1,665.5	481.2	87,085	3,967.3	1,175,638	5,513
Lubbock, TX	864	22,490	2,538.0	873.1	472	3,502	313.4	94.4	22,372	1,129.9	325,605	1,481
Lynchburg, VA	572	13,913	1,313.6	539.9	452	2,320	207.0	60.3	14,719	542.5	69,561	430
Macon, GA	642	16,370	1,869.5	686.3	318	1,831	220.9	58.8	17,654	604.6	45,408	397
Madera, CA	204	5,871	761.0	321.0	112	489	45.2	11.8	7,272	354.2	122,117	503
Madison, WI	1,473	49,078	5,684.6	2,239.3	1,298	9,034	1,314.3	300.0	46,409	2,268.7	847,511	3,652
Manchester-Nashua, NH	1,094	28,561	3,089.1	1,339.9	824	5,516	490.3	160.3	28,882	1,698.6	207,435	1,406
Manhattan, KS	230	4,249	391.3	142.5	172	1,252	223.3	48.7	5,262	232.2	66,508	241
Mankato-North Mankato, MN .	301	11,383	823.6	416.8	186	1,230	262.3	31.3	6,314	283.7	90,921	487
Mansfield, OH	316	7,570	674.5	274.6	209	1,186	108.4	25.3	6,793	281.7	18,939	80
McAllen-Edinburg-Mission, TX	2,048	54,356	3,479.0	1,471.2	571	3,701	350.3	84.2	70,258	2,728.5	559,363	4,642
Medford, OR	674	12,116	1,443.8	510.7	315	1,836	157.3	51.0	16,943	784.8	192,604	933
Memphis, TN-MS-AR	2,948	80,010	9,324.5	3,561.1	1,557	12,365	2,119.0	414.4	111,608	4,273.5	811,529	4,492
Merced, CA	427	6,718	788.1	302.8	183	895	72.4	26.3	11,008	558.1	143,449	630
Miami-Fort Lauderdale-West Palm Beach, FL	20,622	297,739	39,497.8	13,743.7	12,231	68,020	7,193.6	1,854.5	892,975	36,268.7	4,292,819	19,553
Fort Lauderdale-Pompano Beach-Deerfield Beach, FL	6,273	89,756	12,193.7	4,272.6	4,124	21,448	2,245.9	602.5	252,396	10,014.7	NA	NA
Miami-Miami Beach-Kendall, FL Div 33124	9,030	132,886	17,547.4	6,100.1	4,903	28,561	3,116.7	758.0	469,992	18,147.3	NA	NA
West Palm Beach-Boca Raton-Delray Beach, FL Div 48	5,319	75,097	9,756.7	3,371.0	3,204	18,011	1,831.0	493.9	170,587	8,106.8	NA	NA
Michigan City-La Porte, IN	228	5,626	611.2	208.3	194	1,090	79.0	22.5	5,937	213.4	32,150	140
Midland, MI	239	6,268	682.2	242.8	147	882	113.0	23.2	5,003	195.3	16,538	88
Midland, TX	405	7,331	829.3	304.4	272	2,159	340.6	74.2	16,947	1,060.4	309,416	1,227
Milwaukee-Waukesha-West Allis, WI	4,732	123,973	13,694.3	5,445.8	2,736	20,368	2,267.0	636.2	91,300	4,416.9	803,520	3,769
Minneapolis-St. Paul-Bloomington, MN	9,429	270,065	26,555.5	11,497.3	6,672	51,085	5,701.2	1,543.4	269,678	12,810.2	4,306,686	18,206
Missoula, MT	489	9,292	965.9	351.1	287	1,889	258.2	56.0	10,111	471.2	120,594	689

Table C. Metropolitan Areas — Government Employment and Payroll, and Local Government Finances

Area name	Government employment and payroll, 2012									Local government finances, 2012				
	Full-time equivalent employees	March payroll (dollars)	March payroll (percent of total)							General revenue				
			Administration, judicial, and legal	Police and corrections	Fire protection	Highways and transportation	Health and welfare	Natural resources and utilities	Education and libraries	Total (mil dol)	Inter-governmental (mil dol)	Taxes		
												Total (mil dol)	Per capita¹ (dollars)	
													Total	Property
	171	172	173	174	175	176	177	178	179	180	181	182	183	184
Jonesboro, AR	4,524	13,523,979	4.9	9.6	2.5	3.7	1.1	9.1	68.6	354.5	215.8	87.8	708	311
Joplin, MO	6,292	18,337,340	4.7	8.3	3.6	3.0	2.0	3.3	74.4	510.9	199.2	185.7	1,065	527
Kahului-Wailuku-Lahaina, HI..	2,328	11,762,934	19.0	23.7	16.4	6.9	6.2	25.4	0.0	252.6	23.1	224.7	1,419	1,316
Kalamazoo-Portage, MI	9,976	43,436,306	7.0	10.5	12.8	2.9	6.0	3.3	56.6	1,340.8	705.4	408.5	1,238	1,210
Kankakee, IL	4,413	16,356,166	7.8	13.5	3.6	3.7	1.5	3.4	65.4	441.9	208.0	169.2	1,496	1,433
Kansas City, MO-KS	86,196	339,122,341	5.7	9.8	5.2	3.5	13.8	6.1	54.6	9,183.3	2,533.9	4,159.3	2,040	1,219
Kennewick-Richland, WA	10,152	53,295,192	5.2	7.0	3.2	4.4	10.2	28.7	40.3	1,194.4	543.2	325.4	1,213	704
Killeen-Temple, TX	19,513	61,961,488	4.6	8.5	3.2	1.8	4.0	4.2	72.6	1,379.2	598.6	457.1	1,087	854
Kingsport-Bristol-Bristol, TN-VA	11,566	36,313,120	5.1	10.8	2.2	3.5	5.1	5.7	66.0	805.9	377.3	312.3	1,011	695
Kingston, NY	8,282	38,442,668	5.7	7.7	1.3	4.8	8.8	1.7	68.0	1,095.2	330.4	630.3	3,467	2,848
Knoxville, TN	29,145	97,687,242	5.6	9.5	2.6	3.1	10.2	13.4	54.2	2,517.0	845.0	1,010.5	1,191	718
Kokomo, IN	4,091	15,459,399	5.0	6.2	3.5	2.0	35.8	3.0	42.2	435.8	136.7	118.7	1,433	1,170
La Crosse-Onalaska, WI-MN .	5,559	21,504,753	6.0	8.2	2.4	4.3	16.8	4.2	57.0	720.4	365.8	237.4	1,755	1,630
Lafayette, LA	17,787	55,296,831	6.7	12.0	3.2	3.4	8.4	8.0	57.3	1,668.5	663.9	685.1	1,444	587
Lafayette-West Lafayette, IN..	5,636	18,225,886	7.4	11.9	4.8	5.8	2.8	5.4	60.9	552.8	259.3	207.6	1,006	798
Lake Charles, LA	9,670	30,588,485	5.1	13.5	3.3	5.8	7.9	5.3	57.2	1,055.7	360.2	475.0	2,361	1,046
Lake Havasu City-Kingman, AZ	5,613	20,393,845	13.0	13.4	11.7	4.5	2.0	5.6	47.4	538.5	183.2	229.9	1,131	849
Lakeland-Winter Haven, FL....	22,910	75,047,946	7.9	12.5	4.2	2.1	2.6	10.6	56.6	1,844.2	710.5	644.8	1,047	726
Lancaster, PA	12,622	54,624,168	5.9	11.7	0.8	2.8	3.4	3.5	70.9	1,833.2	668.6	843.7	1,601	1,327
Lansing-East Lansing, MI	15,249	64,035,635	8.2	8.0	3.0	4.4	9.2	6.8	56.5	1,895.2	923.3	587.0	1,260	1,174
Laredo, TX	14,741	48,977,584	5.1	9.2	5.1	3.0	3.0	3.7	70.4	1,245.0	614.2	391.8	1,512	1,216
Las Cruces, NM	7,916	26,726,295	5.8	10.4	2.7	2.6	2.1	5.9	66.7	732.8	425.3	209.7	978	447
Las Vegas-Henderson-Para-dise, NV	51,796	300,546,553	8.1	16.4	5.9	3.4	8.6	10.1	45.3	8,606.7	3,678.4	2,735.1	1,367	869
Lawrence, KS	4,535	18,551,008	5.6	11.2	5.0	2.9	33.2	7.9	33.4	537.2	114.0	188.6	1,671	1,239
Lawton, OK	6,503	22,717,032	3.8	5.7	3.0	2.2	36.2	3.3	45.2	523.3	171.6	106.3	802	354
Lebanon, PA	4,116	14,939,586	6.1	9.0	1.7	2.8	9.0	5.5	65.4	485.8	160.6	191.5	1,416	1,136
Lewiston, ID-WA	2,076	7,939,079	7.0	11.4	5.6	6.0	7.0	7.6	51.8	188.3	89.3	64.0	1,042	932
Lewiston-Auburn, ME	3,959	13,779,680	4.1	8.3	4.8	4.2	2.0	5.1	70.2	355.6	153.6	163.3	1,517	1,507
Lexington-Fayette, KY	16,579	58,038,313	4.2	11.6	6.9	2.1	7.1	4.3	61.5	1,418.6	398.6	746.8	1,540	758
Lima, OH	4,029	14,917,726	8.3	9.1	4.8	3.4	9.8	5.8	55.9	394.8	197.5	125.6	1,195	774
Lincoln, NE	11,413	48,128,898	5.2	7.7	3.8	4.5	4.1	11.5	61.4	1,034.8	326.0	505.1	1,628	1,186
Little Rock-North Little Rock-Conway, AR	24,915	82,533,612	5.8	10.8	5.3	3.7	2.5	8.9	61.2	2,303.6	1,228.7	601.7	838	423
Logan, UT-ID	3,888	12,693,319	7.2	7.0	2.3	3.6	11.8	5.5	59.8	338.7	155.8	113.9	888	560
Longview, TX	9,132	29,631,047	5.5	10.9	3.9	2.0	4.4	4.8	66.6	721.4	245.0	370.6	1,710	1,319
Longview, WA	3,301	15,112,407	7.8	11.6	3.0	7.2	3.7	14.2	51.3	420.9	170.2	127.1	1,246	848
Los Angeles-Long Beach-Anaheim, CA	471,707	2,757,691,350	8.8	12.1	4.7	5.2	12.5	8.6	45.7	77,422.5	34,902.2	24,415.1	1,870	1,275
Anaheim-Santa Ana-Irvine, CA Div 11244	85,251	527,595,855	5.4	11.0	4.8	3.1	7.4	5.7	58.4	14,543.9	5,867.6	5,580.4	1,806	1,406
Los Angeles-Long Beach-Glendale, CA Div 31084	386,456	2,230,095,495	9.6	12.3	4.7	5.7	13.7	9.3	42.7	62,878.6	29,034.6	18,834.7	1,891	1,234
Louisville/Jefferson County, KY-IN	45,148	162,939,795	3.7	9.1	3.7	3.4	14.2	6.3	58.2	4,084.7	1,333.6	1,583.1	1,265	787
Lubbock, TX	13,751	49,840,306	4.7	10.3	4.2	1.2	27.8	5.7	45.1	1,319.2	362.2	422.7	1,420	1,113
Lynchburg, VA	9,196	26,684,206	6.4	11.2	3.2	1.3	7.0	5.1	63.4	712.1	348.1	270.1	1,058	752
Macon, GA	9,317	31,505,415	6.5	10.3	4.0	2.8	5.6	5.3	64.2	803.6	331.4	347.0	1,491	1,002
Madera, CA	4,578	20,019,402	8.1	8.1	0.2	2.2	10.1	5.2	64.4	627.3	366.3	154.2	1,013	706
Madison, WI	23,987	100,319,066	5.9	10.2	2.5	6.5	6.7	6.3	60.2	2,887.9	993.2	1,412.8	2,276	2,136
Manchester-Nashua, NH	13,991	56,054,764	4.1	10.8	6.0	4.5	3.9	3.8	65.8	1,458.9	470.6	808.2	2,006	1,981
Manhattan, KS	3,088	9,783,062	8.5	11.2	3.9	5.6	3.6	7.1	58.8	275.9	79.3	146.5	1,497	1,108
Mankato-North Mankato, MN .	3,049	12,248,005	8.1	9.4	1.0	5.0	10.7	5.9	57.5	419.6	200.3	109.1	1,113	999
Mansfield, OH	5,091	18,513,991	8.5	9.4	5.0	4.1	11.2	8.3	52.0	473.0	237.7	163.9	1,336	864
McAllen-Edinburg-Mission, TX	39,042	129,583,687	3.7	6.7	1.7	1.6	2.9	3.9	78.6	3,159.2	1,926.2	864.1	1,071	868
Medford, OR	4,931	20,369,335	9.1	14.6	6.5	6.1	5.2	6.8	50.0	668.0	291.3	260.8	1,263	1,068
Memphis, TN-MS-AR	53,881	181,275,652	6.8	14.3	6.6	4.1	9.1	12.2	45.2	5,455.9	2,056.3	2,087.0	1,555	1,086
Merced, CA	10,959	49,202,192	6.5	7.6	1.6	1.1	10.0	6.7	63.4	1,305.5	840.8	219.3	836	680
Miami-Fort Lauderdale-West Palm Beach, FL	222,370	1,025,593,818	5.5	14.7	6.9	4.6	20.6	7.6	34.5	30,329.9	7,063.4	12,134.4	2,106	1,662
Fort Lauderdale-Pompano Beach-Deerfield Beach, FL	73,864	331,154,408	5.1	13.2	6.2	3.7	29.6	6.0	33.6	9,918.0	2,186.8	3,161.3	1,742	1,392
Miami-Miami Beach-Kendall, FL Div 33124	102,308	498,941,928	4.9	14.9	6.0	5.9	20.8	6.6	32.3	14,058.6	3,695.7	5,524.1	2,132	1,564
West Palm Beach-Boca Raton-Delray Beach, FL Div 48	46,198	195,497,482	7.6	16.4	10.2	2.6	5.1	13.1	41.6	6,353.4	1,180.9	3,449.0	2,542	2,211
Michigan City-La Porte, IN	4,264	12,639,630	5.9	11.9	4.3	3.5	3.5	6.6	63.1	369.8	180.5	137.0	1,231	1,055
Midland, MI	2,175	9,622,686	11.4	7.8	3.3	4.0	3.3	5.7	62.5	271.7	113.5	103.5	1,235	1,220
Midland, TX	7,075	27,853,270	5.2	7.7	3.9	1.9	29.9	1.6	47.9	800.8	131.1	362.9	2,393	1,787
Milwaukee-Waukesha-West Allis, WI	53,007	250,453,387	5.4	13.5	4.4	4.2	8.1	4.6	57.7	7,417.1	2,812.4	3,111.6	1,986	1,860
Minneapolis-St. Paul-Bloom-ington, MN	104,532	577,809,573	7.1	9.9	1.7	3.7	7.6	5.5	63.0	15,990.0	6,976.7	5,332.5	1,558	1,450
Missoula, MT	3,035	11,623,602	8.8	11.6	6.2	6.3	5.7	3.6	55.2	333.0	140.7	131.9	1,189	1,156

1. Based on the resident population estimated as of July 1 of the year shown.

Table C. Metropolitan Areas — Local Government Finances, Government Employment, and Income Taxes

Area name	Local government finances, 2012 (cont.)									Government employment, 2017			Individual income tax returns, 2016		
	Direct general expenditure							Debt outstanding							
			Percent of total for:												
	Total (mil dol)	Per capita[1] (dollars)	Education	Health and hospitals	Police protection	Public welfare	Highways	Total (mil dol)	Per capita[1] (dollars)	Federal civilian	Federal military	State and local	Number of returns	Mean adjusted gross income	Mean income tax
	185	186	187	188	189	190	191	192	193	194	195	196	197	198	199
Jonesboro, AR	344.4	2,776	59.5	0.3	5.9	0.1	5.2	518.7	4,182	390	508	9,446	51,060	52,035	6,163
Joplin, MO	524.5	3,009	58.0	8.8	4.8	0.2	5.1	349.6	2,005	435	622	9,000	75,110	50,103	5,592
Kahului-Wailuku-Lahaina, HI	264.1	1,668	0.0	0.0	15.8	6.0	2.7	281.6	1,779	867	1,191	8,384	80,560	56,193	6,478
Kalamazoo-Portage, MI	1,323.6	4,011	48.7	15.6	6.2	1.0	5.0	1,469.4	4,452	846	540	19,001	155,610	60,906	7,898
Kankakee, IL	442.3	3,912	52.1	0.7	6.1	0.1	5.9	327.2	2,894	234	213	5,901	50,220	53,026	5,575
Kansas City, MO-KS	8,722.0	4,278	43.2	9.9	7.0	0.6	5.4	16,793.0	8,237	27,760	11,017	121,691	1,001,700	68,558	9,390
Kennewick-Richland, WA	1,130.0	4,213	43.9	21.1	4.0	0.0	3.7	7,044.2	26,261	1,256	760	18,773	124,680	62,294	7,438
Killeen-Temple, TX	1,411.2	3,357	57.9	3.8	4.8	0.5	5.9	2,196.8	5,226	10,862	35,290	27,244	183,100	47,538	4,717
Kingsport-Bristol-Bristol, TN-VA	860.9	2,786	50.0	3.8	6.6	1.8	4.1	782.5	2,532	887	904	15,794	131,210	49,317	5,363
Kingston, NY	1,119.8	6,160	51.1	2.0	2.8	12.1	5.4	695.1	3,823	443	283	12,598	86,480	60,325	7,320
Knoxville, TN	2,428.1	2,862	44.3	9.6	6.5	0.1	3.1	4,983.9	5,875	5,463	2,587	52,294	388,100	61,477	8,439
Kokomo, IN	406.5	4,907	32.7	36.7	3.9	0.3	1.8	200.3	2,417	185	247	4,896	40,280	49,484	5,092
La Crosse-Onalaska, WI-MN	720.8	5,328	43.6	2.8	4.0	21.7	5.6	467.2	3,453	548	368	11,238	65,820	59,493	7,222
Lafayette, LA	1,702.8	3,589	44.6	7.6	6.9	0.4	5.4	2,036.0	4,292	1,416	1,896	24,114	208,690	57,608	7,646
Lafayette-West Lafayette, IN	486.9	2,359	51.4	0.5	5.8	0.7	6.1	413.5	2,003	523	686	25,039	88,150	56,213	6,684
Lake Charles, LA	995.9	4,950	38.4	7.2	6.5	0.4	6.8	2,332.0	11,591	564	860	14,077	90,490	59,746	7,470
Lake Havasu City-Kingman, AZ	555.1	2,730	33.9	2.7	6.9	0.1	8.7	627.7	3,087	461	459	7,139	81,660	42,857	4,178
Lakeland-Winter Haven, FL	1,992.7	3,234	48.6	3.2	8.2	1.6	5.5	2,776.3	4,506	1,094	1,268	27,113	291,930	46,779	4,849
Lancaster, PA	2,018.4	3,831	55.1	5.4	4.3	5.1	3.3	3,447.0	6,543	1,281	1,371	19,544	266,240	60,654	7,408
Lansing-East Lansing, MI	1,885.3	4,048	47.2	10.6	4.5	3.4	4.3	2,304.1	4,947	2,003	927	47,921	216,200	57,764	7,085
Laredo, TX	1,204.4	4,647	58.3	1.3	6.0	0.4	1.5	1,569.6	6,056	3,370	547	18,825	110,380	39,262	3,586
Las Cruces, NM	719.6	3,356	57.5	1.3	6.7	1.9	4.1	440.1	2,052	3,401	559	16,476	91,660	42,947	4,403
Las Vegas-Henderson-Paradise, NV	9,171.7	4,584	29.1	8.3	9.6	2.7	7.2	21,727.8	10,860	13,093	15,498	88,167	999,150	63,607	9,281
Lawrence, KS	474.7	4,206	28.6	35.1	4.9	0.0	3.3	544.9	4,828	439	451	16,043	50,540	62,339	8,063
Lawton, OK	533.8	4,027	37.6	38.9	4.3	0.0	3.4	253.8	1,915	3,892	11,505	10,885	49,890	45,861	4,246
Lebanon, PA	507.4	3,752	47.7	2.2	2.9	15.0	5.1	705.4	5,215	3,189	353	4,938	69,400	54,998	5,972
Lewiston, ID-WA	188.3	3,065	43.4	3.1	7.2	0.1	7.4	47.1	767	249	190	5,183	28,380	54,227	5,955
Lewiston-Auburn, ME	348.5	3,239	53.0	0.2	4.0	0.4	5.6	353.5	3,285	277	327	5,142	49,530	48,757	4,909
Lexington-Fayette, KY	1,363.2	2,811	49.9	3.2	5.3	0.7	2.2	2,544.8	5,247	4,556	1,569	48,493	225,510	62,461	8,217
Lima, OH	385.4	3,665	49.5	5.4	6.9	4.3	6.7	180.7	1,719	324	253	5,741	47,640	51,095	5,771
Lincoln, NE	1,130.3	3,642	53.2	1.9	4.3	0.9	6.9	2,872.1	9,255	3,349	1,135	31,566	150,960	63,149	7,817
Little Rock-North Little Rock-Conway, AR	2,292.8	3,195	53.1	2.7	6.0	0.0	4.2	3,061.0	4,265	9,544	6,347	59,726	318,740	60,125	7,595
Logan, UT-ID	308.4	2,404	52.6	4.4	6.1	0.3	5.4	194.5	1,516	376	536	11,819	53,700	59,955	6,361
Longview, TX	736.4	3,399	58.8	4.2	5.0	0.0	4.6	1,187.1	5,479	482	420	11,412	90,940	50,454	5,714
Longview, WA	424.6	4,163	38.6	3.9	5.4	0.0	4.9	609.4	5,974	224	276	6,112	47,040	55,031	5,968
Los Angeles-Long Beach-Anaheim, CA	74,228.5	5,687	36.2	9.6	7.8	8.4	3.3	106,636.6	8,170	59,926	22,347	696,323	6,139,220	75,945	11,832
Anaheim-Santa Ana-Irvine, CA Div 11244	13,915.7	4,503	41.4	2.9	7.7	7.3	4.5	22,316.3	7,222	11,375	5,099	147,611	NA	NA	NA
Los Angeles-Long Beach-Glendale, CA Div 31084	60,312.8	6,054	35.0	11.1	7.8	8.7	3.1	84,320.3	8,464	48,551	17,248	548,712	NA	NA	NA
Louisville/Jefferson County, KY-IN	4,180.4	3,341	44.5	11.9	4.0	0.3	2.5	7,079.6	5,658	9,082	4,101	64,362	616,220	60,884	7,768
Lubbock, TX	1,388.9	4,666	35.4	31.5	4.7	0.1	2.3	2,311.9	7,767	1,377	646	29,667	132,810	55,897	7,195
Lynchburg, VA	701.3	2,747	47.7	1.7	5.7	7.2	1.9	641.2	2,511	563	844	12,829	114,340	52,963	5,657
Macon, GA	816.9	3,510	46.8	7.0	6.4	0.3	2.9	577.8	2,483	1,151	609	13,023	96,460	49,893	5,533
Madera, CA	649.2	4,265	45.6	3.7	3.9	8.8	6.2	475.5	3,124	299	222	10,538	58,630	48,338	4,660
Madison, WI	2,933.1	4,725	47.0	1.8	6.0	8.3	7.1	3,254.4	5,243	5,504	1,805	82,629	330,440	73,527	10,206
Manchester-Nashua, NH	1,496.1	3,713	52.0	0.6	6.1	3.8	4.7	1,157.0	2,872	3,985	1,415	17,455	214,430	73,723	10,442
Manhattan, KS	320.7	3,279	52.2	2.1	6.0	0.0	6.6	601.2	6,146	486	364	13,665	36,470	57,219	6,567
Mankato-North Mankato, MN	409.8	4,181	36.2	5.3	4.8	5.7	13.5	455.8	4,650	294	354	8,209	46,680	59,511	7,135
Mansfield, OH	480.9	3,920	52.3	8.7	5.0	4.8	5.5	209.0	1,703	644	292	6,962	56,810	45,832	4,681
McAllen-Edinburg-Mission, TX	3,161.8	3,920	67.1	2.0	3.8	0.5	2.9	3,738.4	4,635	4,415	1,764	54,144	312,950	37,838	3,300
Medford, OR	678.0	3,285	42.6	5.3	8.6	0.0	6.1	887.0	4,297	1,762	522	8,619	100,910	55,034	6,282
Memphis, TN-MS-AR	5,764.4	4,296	46.3	6.7	8.6	0.9	2.8	6,748.2	5,030	14,084	5,473	68,381	613,070	56,527	7,438
Merced, CA	1,403.1	5,349	48.6	3.6	4.1	10.0	2.7	901.0	3,435	773	396	18,522	102,870	44,605	4,014
Miami-Fort Lauderdale-West Palm Beach, FL	31,257.3	5,424	25.8	15.2	8.8	2.5	2.0	39,629.0	6,877	34,211	14,137	276,801	2,907,560	64,493	10,428
Fort Lauderdale-Pompano Beach-Deerfield Beach, FL	10,214.0	5,627	24.6	26.3	10.2	1.2	1.4	8,639.5	4,760	7,001	3,977	98,576	NA	NA	NA
Miami-Miami Beach-Kendall, FL Div 33124	14,468.1	5,584	25.8	12.2	7.5	3.5	2.2	23,549.3	9,089	20,354	7,413	121,855	NA	NA	NA
West Palm Beach-Boca Raton-Delray Beach, FL Div 48	6,575.2	4,847	27.6	4.7	9.3	2.5	2.5	7,440.3	5,485	6,856	2,747	56,370	NA	NA	NA
Michigan City-La Porte, IN	330.9	2,974	53.0	1.0	4.1	0.3	2.3	311.4	2,799	182	334	6,588	51,030	50,455	5,550
Midland, MI	272.5	3,250	51.0	2.8	4.1	2.1	7.6	318.6	3,800	158	132	3,059	40,010	72,793	10,587
Midland, TX	864.5	5,700	32.3	45.1	3.2	0.0	1.2	654.6	4,316	573	341	9,326	75,630	108,505	19,540
Milwaukee-Waukesha-West Allis, WI	7,419.0	4,735	44.0	7.8	7.8	3.4	5.7	8,456.0	5,396	10,672	4,422	77,730	762,990	69,876	9,809
Minneapolis-St. Paul-Bloomington, MN	16,677.1	4,873	39.7	6.9	5.5	5.4	7.0	24,523.9	7,166	21,409	12,898	230,513	1,795,130	79,562	11,541
Missoula, MT	338.7	3,052	44.0	5.5	7.0	0.8	5.2	188.8	1,701	1,399	538	9,148	57,390	59,888	7,493

1. Based on the resident population estimated as of July 1 of the year shown.

Table C. Metropolitan Areas — **Land Area and Population**

CBSA/ DIV Code[1]	Area name	Land area[2] (sq mi)	Total persons	Rank	Per square mile	White	Black	Amer- ican Indian, Alaska Native	Asian and Pacific Islander	Percent Hispanic or Latino[3]	Under 5 years	5 to 17 years	18 to 24 years	25 to 34 years	35 to 44 years	45 to 54 years
		1	2	3	4	5	6	7	8	9	10	11	12	13	14	15
33660	Mobile, AL.................	1,229.4	413,757	130	336.6	58.0	36.6	1.5	2.5	3.1	6.5	16.9	9.0	14.0	12.0	12.2
33700	Modesto, CA.................	1,496.0	549,815	101	367.5	43.4	3.4	1.2	7.9	47.0	7.2	19.8	9.4	14.5	12.7	11.9
33740	Monroe, LA.................	1,487.4	176,805	240	118.9	60.4	36.4	0.6	1.3	2.5	6.8	17.7	9.3	13.9	12.1	11.9
33780	Monroe, MI.................	549.3	150,439	277	273.9	92.8	3.4	0.9	1.1	3.7	5.3	16.1	7.9	11.7	11.6	13.8
33860	Montgomery, AL.................	2,714.1	373,225	143	137.5	49.0	45.7	0.7	2.8	3.3	6.4	16.7	9.2	14.1	12.7	12.8
34060	Morgantown, WV.................	1,008.9	140,259	292	139.0	91.7	4.2	0.6	3.4	2.0	5.0	12.0	17.6	16.2	12.2	11.2
34100	Morristown, TN.................	436.1	118,581	328	271.9	87.5	3.8	0.8	1.2	8.3	5.4	16.1	8.2	11.6	11.6	14.0
34580	Mount Vernon-Anacortes, WA....	1,730.2	128,206	308	74.1	76.2	1.4	2.8	3.5	18.7	6.1	15.8	7.7	12.6	11.8	11.3
34620	Muncie, IN.................	392.1	114,772	333	292.7	88.7	8.3	0.7	2.0	2.6	4.9	13.4	19.6	11.5	10.0	11.4
34740	Muskegon, MI.................	503.9	173,588	242	344.5	78.8	15.4	1.6	1.1	5.8	6.1	17.0	8.2	13.1	12.0	12.3
34820	Myrtle Beach-Conway-North Myrtle Beach, NC-SC......	1,982.9	480,891	112	242.5	80.5	13.0	1.1	1.7	5.7	4.4	12.8	6.7	10.9	10.6	12.1
34900	Napa, CA.................	748.3	139,417	295	186.3	54.1	2.7	1.1	10.1	34.5	5.1	15.6	8.5	12.3	12.6	13.2
34940	Naples-Immokalee-Marco Island, FL.................	1,996.3	378,488	142	189.6	63.2	7.2	0.4	2.0	28.2	4.4	12.7	6.6	9.5	9.7	11.5
34980	Nashville-Davidson-- Murfreesboro--Franklin, TN.................	6,301.8	1,930,961	36	306.4	73.9	16.3	0.8	3.6	7.5	6.4	16.7	9.2	15.4	13.6	13.1
35100	New Bern, NC	1,514.5	125,219	315	82.7	68.3	22.7	1.1	3.6	6.9	5.9	14.8	11.1	13.0	10.6	10.6
35300	New Haven-Milford, CT............	604.5	857,620	66	1,418.7	63.9	14.0	0.6	4.8	18.6	5.1	15.0	10.0	13.4	11.7	13.4
35380	New Orleans-Metairie, LA	3,202.8	1,270,399	46	396.7	52.7	35.7	0.9	3.4	9.0	6.3	16.0	8.0	14.8	12.9	12.5
35620	New York-Newark-Jersey City, NY-NJ-PA.................	8,292.6	19,979,477	1	2,409.3	47.6	16.7	0.5	12.3	24.6	6.0	15.4	8.6	14.7	13.0	13.4
35620	Dutchess County-Putnam County, NY Div 20524......	1,026.0	392,610	X	382.7	74.5	9.5	0.5	4.1	13.3	4.5	14.5	10.1	11.7	11.6	14.7
35620	Nassau County-Suffolk County, NY Div 35004	1,196.4	2,839,436	X	2,373.3	64.6	10.1	0.4	7.8	18.6	5.4	15.9	8.9	11.8	11.9	14.4
35620	Newark, NJ-PA Div 35084	2,482.8	2,504,672	X	1,008.8	52.0	20.0	0.4	8.7	20.5	5.7	16.6	8.5	12.2	13.0	14.7
35620	New York-Jersey City-White Plains, NY-NJ Div 35614 ..	3,587.4	14,242,759	X	3,970.2	42.7	17.6	0.5	14.1	26.9	6.3	15.2	8.6	15.9	13.3	13.0
35660	Niles-Benton Harbor, MI............	567.8	154,141	266	271.5	76.9	15.9	1.2	2.8	5.7	5.7	16.1	8.1	11.8	11.3	12.6
35840	North Port-Sarasota-Bradenton, FL.................	1,300.0	821,573	72	632.0	78.5	7.1	0.6	2.5	12.9	4.1	12.1	6.1	9.4	9.3	11.6
35980	Norwich-New London, CT	665.1	266,784	182	401.1	77.9	7.4	1.8	5.4	10.9	5.0	14.4	10.0	13.1	11.1	13.3
36100	Ocala, FL.................	1,588.4	359,977	148	226.6	71.5	13.4	0.8	2.3	13.6	4.9	13.6	6.6	10.9	9.8	11.4
36140	Ocean City, NJ	251.5	92,560	364	368.0	86.7	5.0	0.5	1.5	7.9	4.6	12.9	7.5	10.4	9.2	12.0
36220	Odessa, TX.................	897.8	162,124	260	180.6	32.6	4.8	0.7	1.4	61.3	9.0	21.2	10.1	16.9	13.0	10.4
36260	Ogden-Clearfield, UT	7,230.1	675,067	83	93.4	83.0	1.7	1.0	3.5	13.1	8.1	22.6	9.3	14.3	14.3	10.4
36420	Oklahoma City, OK.............	5,511.7	1,396,445	41	253.4	68.2	12.1	6.8	4.3	13.7	6.8	17.9	9.9	14.8	13.1	11.6
36500	Olympia-Tumwater, WA.............	722.5	286,419	169	396.4	79.1	4.7	2.7	9.8	9.2	5.8	15.6	8.1	14.5	13.5	12.2
36540	Omaha-Council Bluffs, NE-IA.....	4,347.0	942,198	59	216.7	77.9	8.9	1.0	4.0	10.7	7.2	18.4	8.7	14.4	13.3	12.0
36740	Orlando-Kissimmee-Sanford, FL	3,490.3	2,572,962	22	737.2	47.7	16.8	0.6	5.4	31.5	5.8	16.0	9.3	15.3	13.8	13.1
36780	Oshkosh-Neenah, WI.............	434.7	171,020	247	393.4	89.9	3.0	1.0	3.6	4.2	5.5	15.0	11.7	13.3	12.0	12.6
36980	Owensboro, KY.................	898.6	119,114	326	132.6	90.8	5.7	0.5	1.9	3.0	6.7	17.8	7.9	12.6	11.8	12.5
37100	Oxnard-Thousand Oaks- Ventura, CA.................	1,842.5	850,967	67	461.9	47.2	2.3	0.8	9.2	43.0	5.9	17.0	9.3	13.4	12.4	13.2
37340	Palm Bay-Melbourne-Titusville, FL.................	1,015.2	596,849	94	587.9	76.2	11.1	0.8	3.7	10.7	4.7	13.6	7.2	11.4	10.4	12.7
37460	Panama City, FL.................	1,312.0	201,451	221	153.5	78.7	12.9	1.5	3.4	6.5	5.9	15.0	7.8	14.4	12.1	12.9
37620	Parkersburg-Vienna, WV............	599.0	90,033	366	150.3	96.7	2.1	0.7	1.0	1.1	5.6	15.3	7.2	11.4	11.9	13.3
37860	Pensacola-Ferry Pass-Brent, FL	1,669.3	494,883	108	296.5	73.4	18.0	1.6	4.5	5.8	5.9	15.4	10.1	14.4	11.7	12.3
37900	Peoria, IL.................	2,467.7	368,373	147	149.3	84.1	10.8	0.6	3.0	3.6	6.3	16.9	8.1	12.6	12.4	12.2
37980	Philadelphia-Camden- Wilmington, PA-NJ- DE-MD.................	4,603.0	6,096,372	8	1,324.4	63.1	21.8	0.6	7.0	9.7	5.8	15.9	8.9	14.4	12.3	13.1
37980	Camden, NJ Div 15804	1,342.6	1,243,870	X	926.5	67.0	17.3	0.6	5.9	11.5	5.5	16.3	8.4	13.1	12.5	13.9
37980	Montgomery County-Bucks County-Chester County, PA Div 33874.................	1,837.9	1,978,845	X	1,076.7	80.6	7.6	0.5	7.2	6.0	5.3	16.2	8.2	11.9	12.2	13.9
37980	Philadelphia, PA Div 37964	318.1	2,148,889	X	6,755.4	44.3	37.0	0.7	7.9	12.2	6.4	15.4	9.9	17.5	12.4	11.8
37980	Wilmington, DE-MD-NJ Div 48864	1,104.4	724,768	X	656.3	64.1	22.7	0.7	5.4	9.4	5.7	15.9	9.0	14.0	12.2	13.5
38060	Phoenix-Mesa-Scottsdale, AZ....	14,565.1	4,857,962	11	333.5	57.0	6.3	2.5	5.3	31.2	6.3	17.5	9.1	14.5	13.0	12.4
38220	Pine Bluff, AR.................	2,029.3	89,515	367	44.1	47.6	49.5	0.8	1.0	2.4	5.7	15.6	9.9	13.4	12.0	12.5
38300	Pittsburgh, PA.................	5,282.0	2,324,743	27	440.1	86.9	9.6	0.5	3.1	1.8	5.1	13.8	8.3	13.4	11.5	12.8
38340	Pittsfield, MA.................	926.9	126,348	312	136.3	89.8	4.3	0.6	2.4	5.1	4.2	12.7	9.5	10.7	10.4	13.0
38540	Pocatello, ID.................	1,112.5	87,138	369	78.3	85.5	1.4	3.6	2.8	8.8	7.1	19.1	10.3	14.8	12.7	10.1
38860	Portland-South Portland, ME......	2,080.7	535,420	105	257.3	93.8	2.7	1.0	2.5	2.0	4.8	13.9	8.0	12.9	11.9	13.6
38900	Portland-Vancouver-Hillsboro, OR-WA.................	6,686.8	2,478,810	25	370.7	76.2	4.1	1.7	9.8	12.2	5.7	15.7	8.0	15.4	14.7	13.1
38940	Port St. Lucie, FL.................	1,115.5	482,040	110	432.1	65.1	15.9	0.6	2.4	17.7	4.7	13.9	6.8	10.7	10.4	12.4
39140	Prescott, AZ.................	8,123.5	231,993	196	28.6	81.9	1.1	2.3	1.8	14.7	4.2	12.1	6.5	9.1	8.8	10.6
39300	Providence-Warwick, RI-MA.......	1,587.0	1,621,337	38	1,021.6	77.4	6.7	0.9	3.9	13.3	5.2	14.6	10.0	13.5	11.9	13.5
39340	Provo-Orem, UT.................	5,395.3	633,768	90	117.5	84.4	1.0	0.9	4.4	11.9	9.4	24.0	16.7	14.3	12.7	8.4
39380	Pueblo, CO.................	2,386.1	167,529	254	70.2	53.4	2.3	1.4	1.4	43.1	5.8	16.6	8.9	13.1	11.8	11.8
39460	Punta Gorda, FL.................	681.1	184,998	229	271.6	85.3	6.2	0.7	1.9	7.4	3.0	8.9	5.1	7.8	7.3	10.5
39540	Racine, WI.................	332.6	196,584	224	591.1	73.6	12.7	0.8	1.7	13.4	6.1	17.0	8.4	12.0	12.0	13.4
39580	Raleigh, NC.................	2,117.9	1,362,540	42	643.3	62.9	20.7	0.9	7.0	10.8	6.2	17.9	8.9	14.2	14.6	14.4
39660	Rapid City, SD.................	7,804.7	148,749	282	19.1	84.9	2.2	9.4	2.0	4.9	6.1	16.4	8.5	13.4	11.7	11.0

1. CBSA = Core Based Statistical Area. DIV = Metropolitan Division. See Appendix A for explanation. See Appendix B for list of metropolitan areas or temporarily covered by water.   2. Dry land or land partially or temporarily covered by water.   3. May be of any race.

Table C. Metropolitan Areas — **Population and Households**

Area name	Age (percent) (cont.) 55 to 64 years	65 to 74 years	75 years and over	Percent female	Total persons 2000	2010	Percent change 2000-2010	2010-2018	Components of change, 2010-2018 Births	Deaths	Net migration	Households, 2017 Number	Persons per house-hold	Family house-holds	Female family house-holder[1]	One person
	16	17	18	19	20	21	22	23	24	25	26	27	28	29	30	31
Mobile, AL..................	13.3	9.7	6.5	52.4	399,843	413,145	3.3	0.1	45,785	35,223	-9,729	154,683	2.63	64.1	17.3	31.1
Modesto, CA..................	11.3	7.7	5.4	50.5	446,997	514,451	15.1	6.9	63,394	33,011	5,279	173,573	3.13	75.0	14.5	20.4
Monroe, LA..................	12.7	9.0	6.5	51.9	170,053	176,505	3.8	0.2	20,761	14,769	-5,596	66,881	2.55	65.0	17.0	28.9
Monroe, MI..................	15.5	10.6	7.5	50.6	145,945	152,024	4.2	-1.0	12,611	11,597	-2,597	59,528	2.49	68.5	11.7	27.9
Montgomery, AL..............	12.8	9.0	6.3	52.4	346,528	374,541	8.1	-0.4	39,865	29,068	-12,144	141,960	2.54	65.6	18.0	30.1
Morgantown, WV..............	11.4	8.8	5.6	48.4	111,200	129,710	16.6	8.1	11,744	8,517	7,237	51,043	2.56	53.8	7.2	33.6
Morristown, TN..............	13.8	11.1	8.1	51.0	102,422	114,199	11.5	3.8	10,594	11,010	4,860	43,879	2.63	71.9	10.0	23.8
Mount Vernon-Anacortes, WA	14.0	12.4	8.4	50.4	102,979	116,893	13.5	9.7	12,080	9,568	8,835	49,262	2.51	64.9	10.8	27.3
Muncie, IN..................	12.0	9.5	7.6	51.7	118,769	117,664	-0.9	-2.5	10,028	9,998	-2,889	46,588	2.31	58.5	12.1	31.1
Muskegon, MI................	14.3	10.2	6.8	50.3	170,200	172,194	1.2	0.8	17,385	13,948	-2,065	64,581	2.58	66.3	14.3	28.3
Myrtle Beach-Conway-North Myrtle Beach, NC-SC...	16.4	17.3	8.8	51.9	269,772	376,555	39.6	27.7	33,919	36,696	105,460	184,898	2.48	67.2	10.9	26.8
Napa, CA....................	13.6	10.8	8.3	50.2	124,279	136,578	9.9	2.1	11,958	10,052	1,043	47,848	2.87	68.8	10.0	25.8
Naples-Immokalee-Marco Island, FL	13.4	15.8	16.4	50.7	251,377	321,521	27.9	17.7	26,632	26,056	56,188	144,354	2.55	67.3	8.7	26.6
Nashville-Davidson--Murfreesboro--Franklin, TN	12.3	8.2	5.1	51.1	1,381,287	1,670,876	21.0	15.6	194,457	114,915	178,958	717,370	2.60	67.4	11.9	25.5
New Bern, NC................	13.6	11.9	8.6	49.6	114,751	126,813	10.5	-1.3	14,026	10,731	-4,922	49,667	2.42	67.5	10.8	26.5
New Haven-Milford, CT........	14.0	9.7	7.7	51.8	824,008	862,456	4.7	-0.6	73,479	63,497	-14,814	324,837	2.56	62.6	14.1	31.6
New Orleans-Metairie, LA	13.7	9.6	6.2	51.8	1,337,726	1,189,889	-11.1	6.8	130,891	90,369	38,789	481,828	2.60	60.7	16.2	33.5
New York-Newark-Jersey City, NY-NJ-PA	13.0	8.8	6.9	51.6	18,944,519	19,566,527	3.3	2.1	2,051,037	1,189,313	-448,336	7,204,800	2.76	66.0	14.4	27.8
Dutchess County-Putnam County, NY Div 20524..	15.4	10.0	7.5	50.2	375,895	397,112	5.6	-1.1	28,699	25,751	-7,434	140,592	2.65	66.9	9.2	27.0
Nassau County-Suffolk County, NY Div 35004..	14.5	9.6	7.7	51.0	2,753,913	2,833,032	2.9	0.2	247,644	189,324	-51,151	929,077	3.03	74.5	11.0	21.3
Newark, NJ-PA Div 35084	13.9	8.7	6.7	51.2	2,396,333	2,469,811	3.1	1.4	228,526	152,733	-41,225	891,015	2.79	70.2	13.6	25.4
New York-Jersey City-White Plains, NY-NJ Div 35614	12.5	8.6	6.8	51.8	13,418,378	13,866,572	3.3	2.7	1,546,168	821,505	-348,526	5,244,116	2.72	63.8	15.3	29.3
Niles-Benton Harbor, MI........	14.7	11.2	8.5	51.1	162,453	156,811	-3.5	-1.7	14,784	14,097	-3,322	64,166	2.35	64.9	12.6	29.6
North Port-Sarasota-Bradenton, FL	15.2	16.7	15.5	52.0	589,959	702,314	19.0	17.0	52,011	74,951	140,889	328,943	2.42	61.7	8.4	31.4
Norwich-New London, CT	14.8	10.4	7.8	49.9	259,088	274,068	5.8	-2.7	22,191	19,816	-9,732	107,229	2.39	64.5	12.1	28.6
Ocala, FL...................	13.7	15.6	13.4	52.0	258,916	331,299	28.0	8.7	28,107	39,023	39,511	140,620	2.45	64.5	13.6	29.4
Ocean City, NJ	16.8	15.2	11.3	51.1	102,326	97,261	-4.9	-4.8	7,299	10,708	-1,206	39,526	2.30	68.4	10.7	26.2
Odessa, TX	9.7	5.8	4.0	49.1	121,123	137,136	13.2	18.2	23,002	9,736	11,351	51,388	3.03	69.0	15.8	27.2
Ogden-Clearfield, UT	10.0	6.5	4.4	49.5	485,401	597,162	23.0	13.0	88,442	30,593	20,325	209,577	3.15	76.9	8.4	18.2
Oklahoma City, OK............	12.0	8.3	5.6	50.7	1,095,421	1,252,990	14.4	11.4	155,700	94,049	81,389	511,242	2.64	64.2	12.1	28.6
Olympia-Tumwater, WA........	13.0	10.7	6.5	51.1	207,355	252,260	21.7	13.5	25,761	17,225	25,634	112,075	2.47	67.1	12.8	24.7
Omaha-Council Bluffs, NE-IA.	12.2	8.2	5.5	50.4	767,041	865,347	12.8	8.9	109,755	54,742	22,329	359,372	2.55	65.1	10.1	28.6
Orlando-Kissimmee-Sanford, FL	11.8	8.7	6.1	51.1	1,644,561	2,134,402	29.8	20.5	229,739	136,302	344,022	875,259	2.82	67.1	13.6	25.1
Oshkosh-Neenah, WI............	13.5	9.2	7.2	49.7	156,763	166,996	6.5	2.4	15,524	11,941	573	70,008	2.32	60.1	8.7	29.6
Owensboro, KY...............	13.6	9.8	7.3	50.9	109,875	114,748	4.4	3.8	12,881	10,039	1,628	48,691	2.36	68.0	13.9	27.8
Oxnard-Thousand Oaks-Ventura, CA..................	13.2	9.0	6.6	50.5	753,197	823,393	9.3	3.3	84,239	45,315	-10,891	272,085	3.09	71.8	12.2	22.0
Palm Bay-Melbourne-Titusville, FL	16.4	12.8	10.9	51.1	476,230	543,372	14.1	9.8	42,504	55,817	66,747	228,385	2.55	62.2	10.0	31.3
Panama City, FL..............	14.3	10.2	7.3	49.7	161,549	184,713	14.3	9.1	19,776	16,431	13,302	76,386	2.59	64.2	12.4	27.3
Parkersburg-Vienna, WV.......	14.8	11.7	8.7	51.3	93,859	92,668	-1.3	-2.8	8,415	9,189	-1,774	36,629	2.44	64.5	12.1	30.3
Pensacola-Ferry Pass-Brent, FL	13.7	9.9	6.7	50.0	412,153	448,991	8.9	10.2	47,474	37,730	35,963	184,622	2.52	65.5	14.0	27.4
Peoria, IL...................	13.4	10.1	7.9	51.1	366,899	379,182	3.3	-2.9	39,360	31,426	-18,737	147,367	2.47	64.0	10.3	30.5
Philadelphia-Camden-Wilmington, PA-NJ-DE-MD	13.6	9.1	6.9	51.6	5,687,147	5,965,705	4.9	2.2	589,193	446,059	-8,994	2,282,935	2.60	63.3	13.1	30.8
Camden, NJ Div 15804	14.1	9.3	6.9	51.3	1,186,999	1,251,019	5.4	-0.6	113,623	91,451	-29,153	460,100	2.67	69.5	14.0	25.5
Montgomery County-Bucks County-Chester County, PA.	14.7	9.9	7.7	51.0	1,781,233	1,924,271	8.0	2.8	166,841	140,114	29,391	743,933	2.59	69.1	9.0	25.5
Philadelphia, PA Div 37964 ..	12.2	8.2	6.2	52.5	2,068,414	2,084,768	0.8	3.1	239,887	164,055	-10,489	811,603	2.56	54.1	16.7	39.3
Wilmington, DE-MD-NJ Div 48864	13.8	9.3	6.5	51.3	650,501	705,647	8.5	2.7	68,842	50,439	1,257	267,299	2.64	64.2	12.3	28.9
Phoenix-Mesa-Scottsdale, AZ	11.6	9.1	6.5	50.3	3,251,876	4,193,127	28.9	15.9	485,384	257,590	435,114	1,675,676	2.78	65.1	11.9	27.5
Pine Bluff, AR	13.6	10.2	7.1	48.7	107,341	100,290	-6.6	-10.7	9,274	8,845	-11,360	32,431	2.43	59.8	15.2	33.0
Pittsburgh, PA...............	15.1	11.1	8.9	51.3	2,431,087	2,356,302	-3.1	-1.3	195,598	225,421	169	996,798	2.28	60.5	10.1	33.0
Pittsfield, MA................	16.2	13.1	10.1	51.6	134,953	131,215	-2.7	-3.8	8,866	12,121	-1,606	54,193	2.20	56.2	11.5	35.9
Pocatello, ID................	11.5	8.7	5.5	50.3	75,565	82,842	9.6	5.2	10,543	5,588	-647	31,384	2.65	64.6	8.2	26.6
Portland-South Portland, ME..	15.4	11.5	8.0	51.4	487,568	514,104	5.4	4.1	41,174	39,608	20,096	216,114	2.41	61.4	7.8	29.4
Portland-Vancouver-Hillsboro, OR-WA..	12.3	9.2	5.7	50.5	1,927,881	2,225,996	15.5	11.4	228,316	138,044	162,056	935,722	2.58	63.2	9.4	26.8
Port St. Lucie, FL..............	14.6	13.8	12.6	50.9	319,426	424,107	32.8	13.7	34,908	40,178	62,896	176,539	2.64	65.5	10.4	28.8
Prescott, AZ	17.2	18.8	12.8	51.2	167,517	211,014	26.0	9.9	15,284	23,317	28,757	98,369	2.26	63.3	8.1	28.7
Providence-Warwick, RI-MA...	14.1	9.7	7.4	51.4	1,582,997	1,601,211	1.2	1.3	136,514	123,344	7,768	627,318	2.49	63.6	13.0	30.2
Provo-Orem, UT..............	6.7	4.6	3.2	49.4	376,774	526,885	39.8	20.3	100,502	19,182	25,762	167,853	3.59	81.7	7.6	12.4
Pueblo, CO.................	13.5	10.7	8.0	50.7	141,472	159,063	12.4	5.3	15,428	13,937	7,051	65,098	2.49	64.2	13.0	29.9
Punta Gorda, FL..............	17.2	21.4	18.8	51.2	141,627	159,964	12.9	15.6	8,429	20,351	36,551	76,056	2.35	61.4	6.2	30.4
Racine, WI..................	14.6	9.6	6.9	50.5	188,831	195,428	3.5	0.6	19,758	14,415	-4,136	77,473	2.46	67.8	12.9	27.4
Raleigh, NC.................	11.7	7.6	4.6	51.3	797,071	1,130,488	41.8	20.5	128,634	57,841	159,756	493,879	2.66	69.2	11.5	23.9
Rapid City, SD...............	14.7	11.2	6.9	49.3	120,093	134,618	12.1	10.5	15,617	9,237	7,710	58,171	2.44	65.7	9.9	29.2

1. No spouse present

Table C. Metropolitan Areas — Population, Vital Statistics, Health, and Crime

Area name	Persons in group quarters, 2018	Daytime population, 2017 Number	Employment/ residence ratio	Births, 2018 Total	Rate[1]	Deaths, 2018 Number	Rate[1]	Persons under 65 with no health insurance 2017 Number	Percent	Medicare, 2018 Total Beneficiaries	Enrolled in Original Medicare	Enrolled in Medicare Advantage	Serious crimes known to police[2], 2016 Total Number	Rate[3]
	32	33	34	35	36	37	38	39	40	41	42	43	44	45
Mobile, AL	7,277	425,844	1.07	5,337	12.9	4,500	10.9	40,073	11.7	82,690	37,469	45,221	19,114	4,608
Modesto, CA	6,458	523,281	0.89	7,717	14.0	4,050	7.4	32,797	7.0	85,341	46,900	38,441	21,284	3,946
Monroe, LA	6,014	183,835	1.07	2,336	13.2	1,911	10.8	12,585	8.6	33,146	24,142	9,004	11,010	6,147
Monroe, MI	1,463	127,921	0.69	1,501	10.0	1,454	9.7	6,147	5.0	31,822	19,478	12,344	NA	NA
Montgomery, AL	14,692	382,378	1.05	4,717	12.6	3,678	9.9	30,812	10.1	72,737	39,276	33,461	15,006	4,027
Morgantown, WV	8,874	145,472	1.11	1,385	9.9	1,071	7.6	8,279	7.4	21,364	14,260	7,104	2,611	1,879
Morristown, TN	2,420	115,703	0.95	1,226	10.3	1,422	12.0	12,028	12.9	28,058	15,270	12,788	NA	NA
Mount Vernon-Anacortes, WA	1,625	128,724	1.05	1,499	11.7	1,261	9.8	8,563	8.6	30,255	21,794	8,461	4,654	3,774
Muncie, IN	8,885	112,634	0.95	1,139	9.9	1,187	10.3	7,932	9.0	23,528	17,543	5,985	3,733	3,206
Muskegon, MI	5,490	165,604	0.89	2,072	11.9	1,761	10.1	7,681	5.5	38,207	20,086	18,121	5,965	3,450
Myrtle Beach-Conway-North Myrtle Beach, NC-SC	4,675	456,228	0.96	4,047	8.4	5,329	11.1	56,191	16.4	137,591	107,669	29,922	18,354	4,133
Napa, CA	5,018	147,626	1.09	1,356	9.7	1,336	9.6	9,599	8.5	28,962	18,149	10,813	3,122	2,189
Naples-Immokalee-Marco Island, FL	4,550	387,966	1.10	3,201	8.5	3,772	10.0	57,598	22.8	96,246	72,625	23,621	5,458	1,494
Nashville-Davidson--Murfreesboro--Franklin, TN	42,646	1,942,028	1.04	24,229	12.5	15,183	7.9	178,971	11.0	295,702	175,351	120,351	57,751	3,100
New Bern, NC	6,239	125,724	1.00	1,523	12.2	1,270	10.1	11,358	12.0	29,485	25,280	4,205	3,311	2,626
New Haven-Milford, CT	29,659	829,740	0.93	8,651	10.1	7,918	9.2	39,398	5.7	162,867	101,609	61,258	22,967	2,855
New Orleans-Metairie, LA	19,876	1,301,309	1.04	15,624	12.3	12,057	9.5	107,413	10.1	229,040	102,379	126,661	45,319	3,560
New York-Newark-Jersey City, NY-NJ-PA	417,921	20,466,373	1.01	240,404	12.0	158,886	8.0	1,353,247	8.0	3,361,268	2,290,561	1,070,707	345,363	1,712
Dutchess County-Putnam County, NY Div 20524	22,239	D	D	3,325	8.5	3,489	8.9	16,382	5.2	77,099	60,168	16,931	4,737	1,210
Nassau County-Suffolk County, NY Div 35004	49,720	D	D	29,327	10.3	24,480	8.6	127,639	5.4	548,504	429,182	119,322	37,937	1,332
Newark, NJ-PA Div 35084	49,736	2,518,375	0.99	27,047	10.8	20,023	8.0	188,892	8.9	413,100	314,663	98,437	42,192	1,683
New York-Jersey City-White Plains, NY-NJ Div 35614	296,226	14,910,890	1.05	180,705	12.7	110,894	7.8	1,020,334	8.4	2,322,565	1,486,548	836,017	260,497	1,805
Niles-Benton Harbor, MI	3,488	150,504	0.95	1,659	10.8	1,709	11.1	8,845	7.3	35,236	23,134	12,102	4,301	2,790
North Port-Sarasota-Bradenton, FL	10,752	803,883	1.00	6,285	7.6	10,117	12.3	88,122	16.2	236,156	159,350	76,806	18,548	2,365
Norwich-New London, CT	11,134	271,487	1.02	2,581	9.7	2,572	9.6	10,642	5.0	54,518	37,556	16,962	NA	NA
Ocala, FL	9,018	346,489	0.93	3,449	9.6	5,014	13.9	37,422	15.4	111,618	61,555	50,063	9,097	2,627
Ocean City, NJ	2,601	92,065	0.96	804	8.7	1,298	14.0	5,528	8.1	27,128	23,103	4,025	3,047	3,250
Odessa, TX	2,805	158,962	1.03	2,713	16.7	1,253	7.7	29,371	21.1	19,100	13,946	5,154	7,306	4,459
Ogden-Clearfield, UT	6,124	615,191	0.84	10,514	15.6	3,792	5.6	48,857	8.3	83,582	53,162	30,420	15,525	2,375
Oklahoma City, OK	31,843	1,391,913	1.01	18,405	13.2	11,804	8.5	174,860	15.0	222,326	168,611	53,715	49,420	3,600
Olympia-Tumwater, WA	4,096	264,448	0.88	3,187	11.1	2,273	7.9	14,017	6.1	58,026	36,998	21,028	8,728	3,185
Omaha-Council Bluffs, NE-IA	17,538	937,525	1.01	13,207	14.0	6,834	7.3	67,543	8.5	148,620	112,362	36,258	28,659	3,103
Orlando-Kissimmee-Sanford, FL	45,898	2,565,220	1.05	29,075	11.3	18,909	7.3	309,248	14.7	416,995	221,843	195,152	84,795	3,468
Oshkosh-Neenah, WI	7,617	182,112	1.13	1,845	10.8	1,448	8.5	7,302	5.3	32,105	13,746	18,359	3,138	1,848
Owensboro, KY	2,774	120,718	1.04	1,540	12.9	1,224	10.3	5,424	5.6	25,757	18,809	6,948	3,365	2,854
Oxnard-Thousand Oaks-Ventura, CA	11,371	803,484	0.88	9,370	11.0	6,204	7.3	66,579	9.3	145,310	97,052	48,258	18,607	2,189
Palm Bay-Melbourne-Titusville, FL	6,717	580,877	0.97	5,230	8.8	7,377	12.4	58,273	13.0	150,933	91,414	59,519	17,727	3,087
Panama City, FL	6,824	D	D	2,372	11.8	2,180	10.8	23,554	14.8	41,114	30,831	10,283	7,733	3,857
Parkersburg-Vienna, WV	1,007	92,144	1.05	938	10.4	1,109	12.3	5,164	7.2	23,103	17,126	5,977	2,785	3,038
Pensacola-Ferry Pass-Brent, FL	23,874	474,030	0.94	5,801	11.7	5,022	10.1	45,676	11.8	102,353	69,299	33,054	14,557	3,004
Peoria, IL	8,729	378,627	1.03	4,349	11.8	3,846	10.4	16,612	5.5	75,073	53,597	21,476	9,986	2,656
Philadelphia-Camden-Wilmington, PA-NJ-DE-MD	165,994	6,056,169	0.99	68,267	11.2	57,268	9.4	320,010	6.4	1,112,875	784,375	328,500	158,920	2,619
Camden, NJ Div 15804	23,472	1,147,973	0.83	13,119	10.5	11,548	9.3	66,448	6.4	235,820	181,192	54,628	27,687	2,221
Montgomery County-Bucks County-Chester County, PA	43,190	D	D	19,689	9.9	18,033	9.1	85,571	5.3	384,499	272,929	111,570	30,128	1,534
Philadelphia, PA Div 37964	79,228	2,198,338	1.06	27,415	12.8	21,117	9.8	133,533	7.5	361,589	219,684	141,905	77,228	3,619
Wilmington, DE-MD-NJ Div 48864	20,104	729,562	1.01	8,044	11.1	6,570	9.1	34,458	5.8	130,967	110,570	20,397	23,877	3,298
Phoenix-Mesa-Scottsdale, AZ	90,538	4,726,963	1.00	58,227	12.0	35,251	7.3	471,505	12.0	749,287	434,406	314,881	153,716	3,297
Pine Bluff, AR	9,189	88,536	0.95	1,039	11.6	1,073	12.0	5,077	7.6	19,689	14,942	4,747	4,434	4,799
Pittsburgh, PA	61,190	2,353,424	1.02	22,921	9.9	27,576	11.9	90,949	4.9	535,126	203,070	332,056	47,742	2,036
Pittsfield, MA	5,889	126,398	1.00	985	7.8	1,480	11.7	3,110	3.3	34,045	31,344	2,701	2,941	2,323
Pocatello, ID	1,995	82,230	0.92	1,173	13.5	677	7.8	7,649	10.7	14,707	10,364	4,343	2,459	2,913
Portland-South Portland, ME	13,048	531,552	1.00	5,006	9.3	5,084	9.5	38,071	8.9	121,478	78,561	42,917	9,665	1,825
Portland-Vancouver-Hillsboro, OR-WA	38,640	2,458,415	1.01	27,336	11.0	18,027	7.3	153,589	7.4	410,982	173,018	237,964	74,781	3,070
Port St. Lucie, FL	7,244	442,600	0.84	4,257	8.8	5,438	11.3	58,396	16.9	121,110	76,921	44,189	9,315	2,017
Prescott, AZ	4,199	D	D	1,830	7.9	3,011	13.0	20,081	12.9	78,478	56,162	22,316	4,979	2,213
Providence-Warwick, RI-MA	56,754	1,540,670	0.90	16,207	10.0	15,310	9.4	62,972	4.8	334,973	216,453	118,520	5,079	315
Provo-Orem, UT	14,094	596,398	0.92	12,315	19.4	2,438	3.8	45,605	8.1	55,182	32,559	22,623	11,021	1,839
Pueblo, CO	4,514	166,349	1.00	1,831	10.9	1,825	10.9	11,088	8.4	37,517	23,421	14,096	9,901	6,025
Punta Gorda, FL	3,171	173,740	0.86	1,031	5.6	2,802	15.1	18,489	17.1	66,335	42,548	23,787	3,062	1,738
Racine, WI	4,998	180,787	0.84	2,341	11.9	1,716	8.7	9,908	6.2	39,329	22,589	16,740	4,175	2,144
Raleigh, NC	25,041	1,336,484	1.00	15,843	11.6	8,234	6.0	125,467	10.8	182,670	120,394	62,276	NA	NA
Rapid City, SD	3,614	146,752	1.00	1,769	11.9	1,203	8.1	13,484	11.4	32,776	26,259	6,517	4,527	3,107

1. Per 1,000 estimated resident population.   2. Data for serious crimes have not been adjusted for underreporting; this may affect comparability between geographic areas and over time.   3. Per 100,000 population estimated by the FBI.

Table C. Metropolitan Areas — Crime, Education, Money Income, and Poverty

Area name	Serious crimes known to police[2], 2016 (cont.) Rate — Violent	Property	School enrollment and attainment, 2016 — Enrollment[3] Total	Percent private	Attainment[4] High school graduate or less	Bachelor's degree or more	Local government expenditures,[5] 2014-2015 Total current expenditures (mil dol)	Current expenditures per student[6] (dollars)	Per capita income[6] (dollars)	Mean household income (dollars)	Median household income	Percent of households with income less than $50,000	Percent of households with income of $200,000 or more	Percent below poverty level — All persons	Children under 18 years	Age 65 years and older
	46	47	48	49	50	51	52	53	54	55	56	57	58	59	60	61
Mobile, AL...........................	585	4,023	101,336	15.9	47.9	23	563.8	8,947	25,244	63,728	46,023	53.1	3.4	19.6	32.1	9.5
Modesto, CA..........................	624	3,322	152,819	7.3	50.9	17.5	1,127.1	10,685	24,957	75,818	59,514	42.7	3.9	13.5	17.8	11.9
Monroe, LA...........................	1,187	4,960	42,675	14.7	49.8	22.1	343.9	10,798	23,749	61,417	39,610	57.8	3.3	24.3	38.3	15.3
Monroe, MI...........................	NA	NA	34,600	15.5	46.4	17.5	252.8	10,890	30,336	74,748	59,290	40.5	2.8	13.1	17.8	10.3
Montgomery, AL......................	472	3,555	90,815	18.9	42.7	29.4	468.7	8,353	26,286	66,774	49,123	50.7	3.6	18.8	30.4	9.1
Morgantown, WV......................	263	1,616	41,884	7.7	41.5	34	171.0	11,005	28,885	71,906	49,475	50.4	5.8	18.5	14.9	8.6
Morristown, TN......................	NA	NA	28,656	15.3	54.6	14.9	143.4	8,032	23,087	59,264	44,840	54.2	2.2	14.6	23.5	5.7
Mount Vernon-Anacortes, WA.......	187	3,588	26,840	10.5	35.9	28	231.3	12,066	32,995	82,356	66,066	35.9	5.1	11.0	15.8	6.4
Muncie, IN...........................	261	2,945	34,129	8.6	44.7	24.7	155.8	10,048	26,672	64,890	41,255	57.1	3.8	20.4	18.1	7.8
Muskegon, MI........................	436	3,014	41,649	9.4	43.8	19.4	304.8	10,737	25,241	65,219	49,229	50.7	2.7	15.0	20.8	9.4
Myrtle Beach-Conway-North Myrtle Beach, NC-SC........................	461	3,672	85,420	9.4	42.3	24.9	675.1	9,274	27,274	64,514	48,727	51.3	3.2	15.3	27.5	5.2
Napa, CA.............................	419	1,770	33,990	17.8	32.0	36.2	249.0	11,857	42,133	117,159	86,562	28.1	12.4	5.6	3.2	6.4
Naples-Immokalee-Marco Island, FL..................................	263	1,231	64,930	14.4	38.7	37	466.0	10,304	42,082	103,133	66,048	37.5	11.4	12.1	25.6	5.3
Nashville-Davidson--Murfreesboro- -Franklin, TN	622	2,478	464,942	23.0	36.5	36	2,517.2	8,892	33,875	87,562	63,939	37.6	6.5	10.9	15.1	7.4
New Bern, NC........................	246	2,380	28,570	15.6	38.2	25.6	152.5	8,713	27,309	66,803	50,977	49.0	2.9	18.7	34.1	9.4
New Haven-Milford, CT	323	2,532	216,383	24.0	40.6	34.2	2,193.8	17,877	36,047	90,654	66,863	37.2	8.0	10.7	14.4	6.1
New Orleans-Metairie, LA...........	559	3,001	314,621	27.3	41.7	29.5	2,017.5	12,255	29,166	72,130	50,528	49.5	4.9	18.6	27.4	12.7
New York-Newark-Jersey City, NY-NJ-PA.............................	355	1,357	4,977,857	23.0	38.7	39.6	58,321.2	20,452	40,772	110,849	75,368	35.4	13.2	12.8	17.4	11.8
Dutchess County-Putnam County, NY Div 20524	155	1,055	95,980	23.7	35.2	35.6	1,218.5	21,464	40,715	108,689	83,896	30.0	11.5	8.9	12.0	6.6
Nassau County-Suffolk County, NY Div 35004......................	129	1,203	709,685	19.8	34.4	40.6	10,901.2	24,090	44,882	132,981	100,954	24.3	17.8	6.4	7.8	5.8
Newark, NJ-PA Div 35084	284	1,399	633,681	16.3	35.8	41.8	7,596.5	18,628	44,320	122,010	84,310	31.1	16.0	9.3	12.4	8.5
New York-Jersey City-White Plains, NY-NJ Div 35614......	417	1,388	3,538,511	24.8	40.1	39.1	38,605.1	19,955	39,346	105,089	69,228	38.2	12.0	14.7	20.4	13.8
Niles-Benton Harbor, MI.............	452	2,339	35,021	18.0	41.3	25.6	288.0	11,423	28,128	67,006	48,629	51.2	3.3	17.7	29.6	10.4
North Port-Sarasota-Bradenton, FL	341	2,023	134,907	15.5	38.0	33.2	852.4	9,493	35,680	82,540	56,817	43.8	6.4	9.5	12.8	6.7
Norwich-New London, CT	NA	NA	61,596	20.5	36.6	33.4	650.4	17,695	38,662	94,134	71,987	33.6	7.5	8.2	11.5	6.3
Ocala, FL.............................	339	2,288	68,833	16.6	49.7	21.9	362.3	8,522	25,257	60,694	43,910	56.6	2.8	16.1	25.4	7.9
Ocean City, NJ	232	3,019	17,974	18.9	37.7	33.5	256.4	20,181	37,610	88,474	66,953	35.2	6.8	9.7	12.9	6.1
Odessa, TX	714	3,746	44,033	7.6	54.4	13.9	253.0	7,703	24,264	68,570	55,380	43.3	1.4	11.5	11.3	10.3
Ogden-Clearfield, UT	156	2,219	205,571	9.7	31.2	32.4	920.4	6,361	27,941	85,908	71,629	30.5	4.8	7.4	8.4	5.2
Oklahoma City, OK	491	3,109	373,366	12.5	37.8	31	1,758.3	7,509	29,559	77,056	56,260	44.6	4.8	13.9	19.1	8.2
Olympia-Tumwater, WA..............	244	2,941	64,425	16.2	26.3	35.7	452.3	10,954	34,886	86,453	71,765	33.8	5.0	10.7	12.6	5.3
Omaha-Council Bluffs, NE-IA........	351	2,751	246,606	18.4	31.9	36.3	1,705.5	11,126	33,276	84,781	65,619	37.4	5.6	9.6	12.6	7.0
Orlando-Kissimmee-Sanford, FL....	504	2,964	641,046	17.7	34.7	32.1	3,136.0	8,583	28,512	77,135	55,089	45.5	5.5	14.1	20.6	11.0
Oshkosh-Neenah, WI	166	1,683	41,857	13.0	41.6	29.5	242.0	10,805	30,897	74,758	56,678	44.3	4.1	12.1	16.1	9.2
Owensboro, KY	143	2,711	27,935	11.5	46.5	20.3	186.6	9,284	28,410	69,082	48,550	51.2	3.0	17.2	27.9	10.3
Oxnard-Thousand Oaks-Ventura, CA..................................	258	1,932	225,028	14.7	34.0	33.4	1,402.1	9,881	36,907	110,266	82,857	29.2	12.2	9.3	13.2	7.2
Palm Bay-Melbourne-Titusville, FL.	500	2,588	126,930	17.4	35.8	30	601.8	8,326	30,495	73,082	52,540	46.7	4.3	12.3	18.6	7.7
Panama City, FL.....................	477	3,380	43,565	18.5	40.3	24.4	249.1	8,442	26,993	68,124	51,594	48.6	2.8	15.5	21.0	8.8
Parkersburg-Vienna, WV..............	393	2,645	17,643	12.8	45.5	21.1	151.8	10,619	26,098	61,768	43,648	54.5	3.6	20.1	30.5	14.5
Pensacola-Ferry Pass-Brent, FL....	458	2,546	116,554	17.8	35.7	26.8	568.7	8,480	27,497	68,929	53,378	46.4	3.3	13.7	22.1	7.0
Peoria, IL............................	398	2,258	92,437	19.8	37.6	30	670.9	11,272	32,669	80,337	57,453	42.5	5.9	11.5	13.5	5.5
Philadelphia-Camden-Wilmington, PA-NJ-DE-MD	447	2,172	1,510,495	25.9	38.9	37.7	13,596.5	15,791	37,235	95,595	68,572	38.2	9.8	12.8	16.2	9.1
Camden, NJ Div 15804	272	1,949	309,299	15.4	37.7	34.8	3,554.8	17,699	37,371	98,881	77,648	32.1	9.6	8.4	12.0	6.3
Montgomery County-Bucks County-Chester County, PA .	119	1,415	476,900	28.0	30.4	47.9	4,556.9	16,612	46,360	120,790	89,386	26.9	14.6	6.0	7.1	5.8
Philadelphia, PA Div 37964	827	2,792	540,116	33.2	46.7	31.5	3,957.5	14,067	29,586	72,439	47,326	51.8	6.0	21.5	26.9	14.8
Wilmington, DE-MD-NJ Div 48864	513	2,785	184,180	17.1	42.0	32.6	1,527.2	14,613	34,794	90,128	67,359	38.6	8.0	13.6	16.6	8.7
Phoenix-Mesa-Scottsdale, AZ........	427	2,870	1,200,586	11.7	36.3	31.1	5,658.5	7,284	31,096	83,688	61,506	40.4	6.4	13.3	18.8	8.4
Pine Bluff, AR	909	3,890	23,324	10.5	56.8	16.4	151.0	10,014	19,506	52,250	39,914	60.9	1.2	19.8	31.5	11.3
Pittsburgh, PA.......................	289	1,747	503,044	20.0	38.4	35.1	4,540.5	14,844	34,800	80,012	58,521	43.3	5.8	11.0	14.7	8.4
Pittsfield, MA........................	513	1,811	26,878	19.6	38.3	32.3	288.7	17,481	34,735	78,821	57,054	44.6	6.3	9.0	11.8	4.2
Pocatello, ID.........................	286	2,628	25,234	9.7	34.5	29.5	91.0	6,293	24,598	66,834	51,612	49.4	1.7	13.6	12.8	4.8
Portland-South Portland, ME.........	134	1,691	119,068	19.8	31.3	40.5	973.8	13,736	36,909	87,700	68,570	35.6	6.4	7.8	8.9	6.6
Portland-Vancouver-Hillsboro, OR-WA.............................	276	2,794	579,984	17.5	27.4	40.3	3,633.3	10,543	36,303	92,750	71,931	34.4	7.8	10.9	13.5	9.2
Port St. Lucie, FL....................	259	1,758	95,933	19.4	44.1	25.4	511.4	8,642	30,803	76,888	51,392	48.4	5.4	11.4	15.7	7.9
Prescott, AZ..........................	290	1,922	44,822	14.7	35.1	23.7	186.2	7,720	28,335	64,830	50,041	50.0	2.7	14.1	19.3	9.0
Providence-Warwick, RI-MA..........	315	D	391,093	23.0	42.5	31.9	3,320.4	15,041	34,950	86,816	65,226	39.8	6.9	11.4	17.1	8.5
Provo-Orem, UT	78	1,761	239,114	24.2	21.3	41.3	817.7	5,852	24,273	87,138	70,196	33.3	5.7	10.6	9.7	6.1
Pueblo, CO..........................	680	5,345	40,321	7.7	38.7	22.2	219.6	8,048	23,344	58,202	43,148	55.2	1.7	18.1	24.5	9.9
Punta Gorda, FL.....................	222	1,516	22,513	14.2	42.7	23.6	151.0	9,357	29,786	66,009	52,070	48.1	3.0	10.1	11.1	7.5
Racine, WI...........................	219	1,925	45,241	18.8	39.4	27.8	352.6	11,993	32,014	80,199	60,897	41.2	4.4	10.3	18.2	7.0
Raleigh, NC..........................	NA	NA	356,405	15.4	26.8	46.2	1,713.3	8,172	36,054	95,164	72,576	32.7	8.6	10.5	15.2	7.8
Rapid City, SD	495	2,612	35,439	12.6	35.6	28.6	180.6	8,417	28,450	69,430	56,318	43.6	3.3	11.8	13.1	9.2

1. Data for serious crimes have not been adjusted for underreporting; this may affect comparability between geographic areas and over time.   2. Per 100,000 population estimated by the FBI.   3. All persons 3 years old and over enrolled in nursery school through college.   4. Persons 25 years old and over.   5. Elementary and secondary education expenditures.   6. Based on population estimated by the American Community Survey, 2015.

856 (Mobile, AL)—(Rapid City, SD)

Items 46—61

Table C. Metropolitan Areas — **Personal Income and Earnings**

Area name	Personal income, 2017										Earnings, 2017		
	Total (mil dol)	Percent change, 2016-2017	Per capita[1] Dollars	Per capita[1] Rank	Wages and Salaries (mil dol)	Supplements to wages and salaries, employer contributions (mil dol) Pension and insurance	Supplements to wages and salaries, employer contributions (mil dol) Government social insurance	Proprietors' income	Dividends, interest, and rent (mil dol)	Personal transfer receipts (mil dol)	Total (mil dol)	Contributions for government social insurance (mil dol) From employee and self-employed	Contributions for government social insurance (mil dol) From employer
	62	63	64	65	66	67	68	69	70	71	72	73	74
Mobile, AL.................................	15,353	2.4	37,089	345	8,674	1,425	631	1,028	2,512	3,879	11,757	765	631
Modesto, CA................................	23,446	4.9	42,793	216	9,314	1,866	691	2,361	4,001	4,840	14,232	781	691
Monroe, LA.................................	7,021	2.3	39,347	297	3,265	610	210	545	1,117	1,885	4,629	262	210
Monroe, MI.................................	6,789	4.0	45,363	155	2,097	381	153	376	913	1,371	3,007	207	153
Montgomery, AL...........................	15,724	3.5	42,053	233	7,988	1,546	592	1,043	2,987	3,454	11,168	695	592
Morgantown, WV..........................	5,652	4.4	40,745	268	3,424	616	273	286	986	1,096	4,599	284	273
Morristown, TN.............................	4,164	3.3	35,263	368	1,869	348	132	382	569	1,189	2,732	180	132
Mount Vernon-Anacortes, WA........	6,219	6.0	49,505	94	2,542	473	241	547	1,422	1,284	3,802	227	241
Muncie, IN...................................	4,119	3.4	35,762	364	1,987	380	147	210	674	1,203	2,725	177	147
Muskegon, MI..............................	6,453	3.0	37,149	342	2,814	526	214	332	943	1,781	3,885	261	214
Myrtle Beach-Conway-North Myrtle Beach, NC-SC..........	17,217	5.9	37,092	344	6,341	989	494	1,302	3,635	4,951	9,126	685	494
Napa, CA....................................	10,034	5.0	71,174	8	4,473	836	327	1,734	2,366	1,206	7,370	391	327
Naples-Immokalee-Marco Island, FL.................................	32,750	4.4	87,829	4	7,465	900	500	1,812	18,513	3,516	10,677	732	500
Nashville-Davidson--Murfreesboro-Franklin, TN	106,464	6.3	55,944	38	53,718	7,521	3,670	23,383	14,633	13,496	88,292	4,865	3,670
New Bern, NC..............................	5,235	1.7	41,926	235	2,400	542	194	222	1,178	1,354	3,359	208	194
New Haven-Milford, CT.................	46,931	4.0	54,543	51	21,927	3,607	1,670	4,146	8,216	8,748	31,349	1,754	1,670
New Orleans-Metairie, LA..............	62,683	2.8	49,134	98	30,576	5,187	1,994	6,344	12,379	11,621	44,100	2,439	1,994
New York-Newark-Jersey City, NY-NJ-PA	1,443,163	5.9	71,019	9	740,770	104,724	51,143	160,233	305,423	219,035	1,056,870	58,344	51,143
Dutchess County-Putnam County, NY Div 20524.........	22,292	5.5	56,451	X	7,595	1,543	625	1,242	4,046	3,801	11,005	635	625
Nassau County-Suffolk County, NY Div 35004.........	214,259	5.3	74,851	X	81,378	14,360	6,442	17,613	44,870	29,888	119,794	6,551	6,442
Newark, NJ-PA Div 35084	188,926	5.0	74,682	X	91,063	12,223	6,294	20,737	36,968	21,867	130,317	7,593	6,294
New York-Jersey City-White Plains, NY-NJ Div 35614......	1,017,687	6.2	70,022	X	560,734	76,597	37,781	120,642	219,539	163,479	795,754	43,565	37,781
Niles-Benton Harbor, MI................	7,117	4.9	46,133	141	3,145	636	239	360	1,251	1,610	4,379	279	239
North Port-Sarasota-Bradenton, FL.................................	43,476	4.9	54,028	55	14,172	1,881	960	2,751	16,748	8,769	19,765	1,429	960
Norwich-New London, CT	15,261	3.6	56,725	34	7,416	1,490	545	1,357	2,938	2,545	10,808	574	545
Ocala, FL....................................	12,709	4.5	35,864	363	4,252	673	295	642	2,904	4,379	5,862	480	295
Ocean City, NJ	5,456	4.0	58,324	30	1,756	345	152	589	1,389	1,259	2,842	187	152
Odessa, TX	6,417	7.4	40,851	265	4,223	563	291	439	855	1,054	5,516	301	291
Ogden-Clearfield, UT	27,728	5.3	41,674	239	11,878	2,301	968	1,532	5,171	3,642	16,680	996	968
Oklahoma City, OK	65,170	6.2	47,097	128	31,985	5,335	2,419	8,454	12,218	10,426	48,193	2,655	2,419
Olympia-Tumwater, WA.................	13,705	6.5	48,845	102	5,932	1,123	538	868	2,883	2,537	8,461	504	538
Omaha-Council Bluffs, NE-IA........	50,973	3.6	54,615	47	26,478	4,089	2,011	5,982	10,010	6,711	38,560	2,277	2,011
Orlando-Kissimmee-Sanford, FL....	104,107	5.9	41,480	244	62,666	7,992	4,207	6,563	17,147	19,606	81,427	5,051	4,207
Oshkosh-Neenah, WI....................	7,814	3.4	45,852	148	5,114	897	384	417	1,521	1,270	6,812	419	384
Owensboro, KY	4,663	2.7	39,395	296	2,348	390	179	221	774	1,202	3,138	205	179
Oxnard-Thousand Oaks-Ventura, CA.................................	50,551	4.5	59,178	27	19,343	3,535	1,384	4,916	10,627	6,479	29,178	1,613	1,384
Palm Bay-Melbourne-Titusville, FL.	25,683	5.7	43,592	193	11,294	1,668	785	1,167	5,688	6,337	14,914	1,028	785
Panama City, FL..........................	8,341	3.2	41,763	237	3,810	659	280	433	1,854	1,949	5,182	332	280
Parkersburg-Vienna, WV...............	3,514	1.9	38,654	313	1,583	297	133	168	558	1,035	2,180	155	133
Pensacola-Ferry Pass-Brent, FL....	20,286	4.0	41,589	242	8,738	1,498	640	967	4,224	4,631	11,843	764	640
Peoria, IL....................................	17,495	-0.2	46,977	132	9,435	1,644	661	820	3,417	3,173	12,560	723	661
Philadelphia-Camden-Wilmington, PA-NJ-DE-MD	377,223	4.0	61,879	17	183,780	28,393	13,908	44,721	67,849	61,401	270,802	15,630	13,908
Camden, NJ Div 15804	68,600	4.0	54,813	X	29,950	4,823	2,355	4,980	10,530	12,056	42,107	2,588	2,355
Montgomery County-Bucks County-Chester County, PA .	147,593	4.6	74,780	X	70,602	10,059	5,283	9,154	33,361	16,941	95,098	5,734	5,283
Philadelphia, PA Div 37964	123,342	3.3	57,487	X	61,115	9,862	4,687	28,238	17,252	25,452	103,902	5,549	4,687
Wilmington, DE-MD-NJ Div 48864	37,688	4.2	51,960	X	22,113	3,650	1,582	2,350	6,706	6,953	29,694	1,760	1,582
Phoenix-Mesa-Scottsdale, AZ.......	208,896	5.8	44,096	180	112,366	15,397	7,917	15,534	39,083	35,218	151,215	9,371	7,917
Pine Bluff, AR	2,997	0.7	32,942	378	1,426	266	114	178	407	990	1,984	132	114
Pittsburgh, PA.............................	125,649	3.9	53,849	57	65,612	10,678	5,147	10,387	20,778	24,557	91,823	5,547	5,147
Pittsfield, MA..............................	6,833	2.6	54,095	54	2,995	541	215	527	1,414	1,673	4,277	248	215
Pocatello, ID...............................	3,154	4.8	36,987	346	1,371	270	124	166	529	709	1,931	126	124
Portland-South Portland, ME.........	29,053	4.9	54,603	49	14,581	2,328	1,069	2,284	5,749	4,810	20,261	1,307	1,069
Portland-Vancouver-Hillsboro, OR-WA...............................	131,861	5.5	53,751	59	71,320	10,093	6,075	10,885	26,680	18,704	98,373	6,038	6,075
Port St. Lucie, FL........................	24,826	5.1	52,438	67	6,494	974	448	1,032	8,776	4,991	8,948	660	448
Prescott, AZ...............................	8,533	4.9	37,398	334	2,636	444	194	634	2,255	2,626	3,908	322	194
Providence-Warwick, RI-MA..........	84,737	4.1	52,271	71	38,753	6,431	3,022	5,496	14,360	17,499	53,701	3,459	3,022
Provo-Orem, UT	23,518	5.0	38,075	323	11,198	1,717	869	1,984	4,365	2,788	15,768	928	869
Pueblo, CO.................................	6,198	3.7	37,231	340	2,770	427	213	307	1,096	1,836	3,717	233	213
Punta Gorda, FL..........................	7,383	4.8	40,557	272	1,987	287	138	404	2,227	2,415	2,817	250	138
Racine, WI..................................	9,100	3.6	46,412	138	3,789	747	292	333	1,727	1,748	5,161	334	292
Raleigh, NC................................	70,016	5.3	52,444	66	36,866	4,797	2,606	4,897	12,738	8,116	49,166	2,988	2,606
Rapid City, SD............................	6,914	3.1	47,082	129	3,069	531	233	606	1,775	1,222	4,439	276	233

1. Based on the resident population estimated as of July 1 of the year shown.

Table C. Metropolitan Areas — Earnings, Social Security, and Housing

Area name	Earnings, 2017 (cont.) Percent by selected industries									Social Security beneficiaries, December 2017		Supplemental Security Income Recipients, December 2017	Housing units, 2018	
	Farm	Mining, quarrying, and extracting	Construction	Manufacturing	Information; professional, scientific, and technical serviecs	Retail trade	Finance, insurance, real estate, rental and leasing	Health care and social assistance	Government	Number	Rate[1]		Total	Percent change, 2010-2018
	75	76	77	78	79	80	81	82	83	84	85	86	87	88
Mobile, AL..................	0.3	0.4	6.1	15.5	9.8	6.4	8.0	12.6	15.0	91,400	221	15,112	184,688	3.6
Modesto, CA................	7.7	0.0	6.3	12.1	4.4	7.3	4.3	16.2	18.1	88,290	161	21,375	182,290	1.6
Monroe, LA.................	1.0	0.5	6.1	9.6	D	7.1	7.5	18.6	16.0	35,285	198	7,912	80,922	6.7
Monroe, MI.................	0.1	D	7.5	18.8	8.5	6.3	3.2	8.5	12.5	35,240	235	2,523	64,785	2.9
Montgomery, AL............	0.8	0.1	6.1	11.6	D	6.0	D	D	28.3	80,195	214	14,166	168,538	4.3
Morgantown, WV............	-0.2	1.2	7.1	9.6	7.5	5.1	2.7	D	26.8	22,455	162	2,693	60,249	3.3
Morristown, TN............	0.3	D	D	26.7	D	8.1	3.0	D	13.7	30,915	262	3,598	51,552	2.1
Mount Vernon-Anacortes, WA......	4.8	0.1	10.8	14.1	5.7	8.4	7.4	7.3	23.2	30,455	242	2,435	54,443	5.8
Muncie, IN................	-0.2	D	4.5	10.7	6.3	8.5	6.4	20.2	21.8	25,940	225	3,043	52,727	0.7
Muskegon, MI..............	0.5	0.1	6.6	26.2	4.6	9.8	3.9	17.2	13.9	42,360	244	6,212	74,305	1.0
Myrtle Beach-Conway-North Myrtle Beach, NC-SC.........	0.5	0.1	8.9	3.2	6.8	11.0	9.3	11.1	15.9	142,275	307	8,140	302,962	15.0
Napa, CA..................	3.3	D	7.2	23.7	5.5	4.8	5.9	9.1	14.5	27,050	192	2,198	55,460	1.3
Naples-Immokalee-Marco Island, FL.................	1.0	0.1	10.1	2.9	12.1	8.5	11.6	13.1	9.7	93,940	252	4,169	218,281	10.6
Nashville-Davidson--Murfreesboro- -Franklin, TN	0.0	0.1	7.3	7.6	D	6.1	8.6	20.5	8.8	312,765	164	31,518	799,560	13.8
New Bern, NC..............	0.9	0.1	3.7	8.4	D	5.6	D	9.4	48.0	31,285	251	3,261	60,236	5.0
New Haven-Milford, CT...............	0.1	0.1	6.3	8.7	9.8	6.2	6.7	15.3	14.7	165,185	192	20,625	367,745	1.6
New Orleans-Metairie, LA	0.0	3.0	D	7.7	11.1	D	7.4	11.5	14.6	236,755	186	44,619	560,360	2.5
New York-Newark-Jersey City, NY-NJ-PA	0.0	D	D	D	18.5	4.7	19.2	10.4	12.7	3,311,145	163	587,868	8,021,491	3.1
Dutchess County-Putnam County, NY Div 20524	0.2	0.2	D	D	7.7	6.6	4.0	16.5	22.8	79,160	200	6,072	159,838	1.9
Nassau County-Suffolk County, NY Div 35004	0.1	D	7.4	5.5	11.3	6.9	10.7	15.6	17.9	554,050	194	36,775	1,050,369	1.2
Newark, NJ-PA Div 35084	0.0	0.5	D	9.9	17.5	4.9	10.6	9.2	12.8	414,570	164	50,026	994,856	2.0
New York-Jersey City-White Plains, NY-NJ Div 35614	0.0	0.3	4.2	2.6	19.9	4.3	22.1	9.8	11.7	2,263,365	156	494,995	5,816,428	3.6
Niles-Benton Harbor, MI..............	0.8	0.2	4.5	30.5	3.9	5.3	4.8	11.7	13.8	37,685	244	4,668	77,648	0.9
North Port-Sarasota-Bradenton, FL.................	0.6	D	9.4	6.0	11.4	8.9	8.8	16.0	9.9	237,220	295	10,664	438,533	9.3
Norwich-New London, CT	0.4	0.1	5.4	18.7	8.0	5.5	3.2	11.0	25.8	56,025	208	4,467	123,635	2.2
Ocala, FL.................	1.0	0.2	7.3	8.5	6.6	10.9	5.3	18.8	15.2	116,970	330	9,999	170,504	3.9
Ocean City, NJ	0.2	0.1	10.9	1.7	5.1	9.4	7.3	9.9	27.0	28,715	307	1,724	99,436	1.1
Odessa, TX	-0.1	21.1	12.4	6.8	3.7	6.2	5.3	5.9	13.0	20,425	130	3,419	58,680	10.6
Ogden-Clearfield, UT	0.3	D	8.8	14.7	7.9	6.8	6.1	9.6	24.2	84,635	127	6,653	226,369	10.9
Oklahoma City, OK........	0.1	9.9	6.1	5.2	D	5.7	6.5	D	19.9	234,675	170	27,587	579,374	7.5
Olympia-Tumwater, WA.....	1.2	D	6.1	2.9	D	6.4	4.6	13.2	38.5	59,565	212	5,382	117,872	9.0
Omaha-Council Bluffs, NE-IA........	0.6	0.1	5.6	6.0	D	5.3	10.7	11.3	13.7	150,085	161	14,986	390,430	7.8
Orlando-Kissimmee-Sanford, FL...	0.3	0.0	7.0	4.4	13.2	7.0	8.9	11.1	10.7	442,625	176	61,144	1,050,625	11.5
Oshkosh-Neenah, WI	0.3	D	7.3	27.6	7.5	4.7	5.8	9.1	11.8	34,690	204	2,597	76,028	3.7
Owensboro, KY	2.6	0.6	5.1	21.6	D	7.0	D	17.4	11.8	28,325	239	4,060	51,443	4.0
Oxnard-Thousand Oaks-Ventura, CA	4.6	0.7	5.8	13.8	10.4	7.0	8.5	9.5	17.0	139,710	164	16,410	291,019	3.3
Palm Bay-Melbourne-Titusville, FL	0.2	0.0	5.9	17.8	11.3	7.1	4.7	13.3	15.7	160,285	272	11,898	280,398	3.9
Panama City, FL..........	0.0	0.1	6.8	4.9	8.5	8.8	6.1	D	26.1	45,310	227	5,191	114,009	4.8
Parkersburg-Vienna, WV...........	-0.3	0.5	7.2	D	D	8.8	6.4	15.9	22.9	25,035	275	3,781	43,618	0.4
Pensacola-Ferry Pass-Brent, FL...	0.0	0.1	6.0	4.3	9.1	7.0	8.6	15.8	25.0	108,940	223	12,736	215,538	7.0
Peoria, IL................	0.3	D	6.0	22.4	D	5.2	D	15.1	12.0	79,990	215	7,366	166,879	1.6
Philadelphia-Camden-Wilmington, PA-NJ-DE-MD	0.1	D	5.5	6.6	D	5.0	10.0	12.9	11.8	1,131,830	186	180,745	2,497,485	2.6
Camden, NJ Div 15804	0.2	0.0	6.4	8.1	D	8.1	7.8	15.1	18.1	247,460	198	27,329	499,942	2.0
Montgomery County-Bucks County-Chester County, PA	0.1	0.1	7.7	9.3	20.1	6.0	10.5	11.7	7.9	381,735	193	19,692	789,061	3.3
Philadelphia, PA Div 37964	0.0	0.0	3.1	3.5	31.2	2.8	7.8	13.0	12.4	365,880	171	119,997	913,704	2.3
Wilmington, DE-MD-NJ Div 48864	0.2	D	5.7	6.3	12.9	4.9	18.9	13.1	13.7	136,755	189	13,727	294,778	3.1
Phoenix-Mesa-Scottsdale, AZ......	0.5	0.5	6.5	7.5	11.0	7.0	12.6	12.2	12.3	774,275	163	67,335	1,939,993	7.9
Pine Bluff, AR............	4.5	D	D	17.7	D	5.5	D	D	29.4	21,320	234	5,164	42,436	1.2
Pittsburgh, PA............	0.1	1.5	6.4	7.9	12.8	5.3	9.0	14.2	10.8	561,355	241	64,190	1,130,057	2.5
Pittsfield, MA............	0.0	D	D	8.9	9.2	7.3	5.7	19.1	14.3	34,390	272	4,007	69,400	1.3
Pocatello, ID.............	0.7	D	6.8	8.7	5.3	7.8	7.4	15.3	24.0	15,010	176	1,998	34,450	3.8
Portland-South Portland, ME........	0.1	D	6.9	D	10.6	6.7	9.8	14.5	15.4	120,670	227	9,801	275,711	4.9
Portland-Vancouver-Hillsboro, OR-WA..............	0.6	D	7.0	12.5	D	5.7	7.7	D	13.4	409,425	167	45,303	1,008,433	9.0
Port St. Lucie, FL........	0.7	D	7.6	5.1	8.8	8.6	6.4	17.5	14.8	126,305	267	8,644	223,169	3.7
Prescott, AZ..............	0.3	2.4	8.2	6.1	7.1	9.7	5.3	15.5	19.2	79,400	348	3,689	118,394	7.2
Providence-Warwick, RI-MA.........	0.1	D	D	D	8.9	6.6	8.4	14.2	16.1	344,625	213	52,063	705,431	1.7
Provo-Orem, UT...........	0.4	0.0	11.0	9.2	D	10.0	D	D	10.8	57,760	94	4,334	183,886	21.1
Pueblo, CO...............	0.2	D	8.0	8.5	6.8	8.3	3.7	21.6	21.2	37,140	223	6,319	71,451	2.8
Punta Gorda, FL..........	1.9	0.3	8.4	1.7	8.7	12.1	6.8	21.6	14.1	68,380	376	2,779	105,172	4.5
Racine, WI...............	0.2	0.1	5.4	32.5	4.3	6.1	4.5	12.2	13.7	42,660	218	5,618	82,907	0.9
Raleigh, NC..............	0.3	0.1	7.4	8.3	D	5.8	8.1	9.6	13.8	187,115	140	17,068	548,194	17.6
Rapid City, SD............	0.6	0.1	8.6	3.7	D	7.8	7.7	19.0	23.3	33,495	228	2,368	66,790	10.2

1. Per 1,000 resident population estimated as of July 1 of the year shown.

Table C. Metropolitan Areas — Housing, Labor Force, and Employment

Area name	Housing units, 2017 Occupied units Owner-occupied Total	Percent	Median value[1]	Median owner cost as a percent of income With a mortgage	Without a mortgage[2]	Renter-occupied Median rent[3]	Median rent as a percent of income	Internet access	Civilian labor force, 2018 Total	Percent change 2017-2018	Unemployment Total	Rate[4]	Civilian employment[5], 2017 Total	Percent Management, business, science, and arts	Construction, production, and maintenance occupations
	89	90	91	92	93	94	95	96	97	98	99	100	101	102	103
Mobile, AL.................	154,683	64.3	131,200	19.7	10.1	810	31.2	81.6	187,406	0.3	8,798	4.7	173,485	31.6	24.8
Modesto, CA................	173,573	57.2	288,200	23.4	12.2	1,136	30.0	88.2	243,538	0.4	15,598	6.4	236,867	27.2	30.6
Monroe, LA.................	66,881	62.6	136,600	19.6	10.0	745	33.6	73.0	79,517	-0.3	4,180	5.3	76,346	30.2	22.3
Monroe, MI.................	59,528	79.8	165,600	18.3	12.5	781	31.5	85.5	75,765	-0.1	3,169	4.2	72,235	29.8	29.2
Montgomery, AL..........	141,960	63.6	138,100	19.0	10.0	845	32.8	80.8	172,376	-0.1	6,709	3.9	159,669	36.8	21.0
Morgantown, WV..........	51,043	61.6	189,600	17.0	10.0	784	33.1	87.5	68,646	0.9	2,980	4.3	65,052	42.2	17.7
Morristown, TN...........	43,879	70.5	142,700	18.8	10.6	671	27.2	79.3	51,430	0.6	1,967	3.8	51,526	28.4	28.3
Mount Vernon-Anacortes, WA........	49,262	71.8	303,400	22.9	12.8	1,109	28.8	89.5	60,278	1.7	3,126	5.2	57,452	31.9	29.6
Muncie, IN................	46,588	61.4	92,100	16.1	10.0	691	30.2	83.8	54,159	-0.5	2,173	4.0	54,399	33.6	19.8
Muskegon, MI..............	64,581	75.1	119,900	18.6	11.7	697	29.8	83.9	78,196	0.6	3,557	4.5	76,595	28.9	35.5
Myrtle Beach-Conway-North Myrtle Beach, NC-SC..............	184,898	73.0	184,600	22.8	10.5	919	30.6	86.0	198,665	2.0	8,831	4.4	196,148	27.9	20.8
Napa, CA..................	47,848	66.1	628,500	24.8	10.0	1,777	32.8	92.3	74,547	1.5	2,181	2.9	72,349	39.0	18.9
Naples-Immokalee-Marco Island, FL	144,354	73.3	358,900	25.0	13.0	1,281	33.7	89.7	177,351	2.0	6,096	3.4	158,695	31.2	21.8
Nashville-Davidson--Murfreesboro--Franklin, TN.............	717,370	65.0	242,900	20.1	10.0	1,030	27.9	88.5	1,042,994	3.1	28,447	2.7	1,004,234	39.2	21.0
New Bern, NC..............	49,667	64.5	155,600	20.7	10.8	803	27.4	81.8	51,255	-0.6	2,147	4.2	49,291	29.6	25.6
New Haven-Milford, CT...	324,837	62.0	243,400	23.2	15.0	1,107	29.8	85.7	458,747	0.4	20,171	4.4	427,676	42.3	17.4
New Orleans-Metairie, LA	481,828	62.2	193,100	21.9	10.1	965	34.4	81.5	594,960	0.1	27,513	4.6	587,412	37.2	20.2
New York-Newark-Jersey City, NY-NJ-PA	7,204,800	51.8	440,900	25.1	15.2	1,379	31.7	88.0	9,934,779	-0.2	396,503	4.0	10,041,694	42.5	15.9
Dutchess County-Putnam County, NY Div 20524	140,592	73.5	297,500	24.4	14.8	1,187	33.5	91.5	195,019	0.6	7,191	3.7	199,672	39.8	17.5
Nassau County-Suffolk County, NY Div 35004	929,077	80.5	445,100	26.3	17.8	1,697	33.1	91.0	1,485,659	0.3	54,979	3.7	1,445,324	42.7	16.0
Newark, NJ-PA Div 35084	891,015	62.9	386,200	23.8	15.3	1,241	31.3	89.6	1,219,420	-0.8	50,947	4.2	1,280,542	44.1	16.7
New York-Jersey City-White Plains, NY-NJ Div 35614.......	5,244,116	44.3	462,600	25.2	14.6	1,384	31.6	87.1	7,034,681	-0.2	283,386	4.0	7,116,156	42.2	15.6
Niles-Benton Harbor, MI..................	64,166	69.1	150,400	19.1	11.4	750	32.2	84.3	73,328	-1.0	3,152	4.3	73,251	35.1	24.6
North Port-Sarasota-Bradenton, FL .	328,943	74.4	244,400	22.5	12.0	1,171	33.0	89.1	365,815	1.5	12,356	3.4	331,205	34.1	18.0
Norwich-New London, CT	107,229	67.2	239,400	22.9	14.1	1,048	28.9	89.9	137,463	0.0	5,431	4.0	130,248	42.3	17.0
Ocala, FL.................	140,620	76.9	137,300	22.6	10.2	857	28.6	84.2	135,746	1.2	5,825	4.3	123,022	33.4	18.2
Ocean City, NJ...........	39,526	77.5	297,600	25.5	14.9	1,065	31.9	89.1	45,785	-0.7	3,840	8.4	40,891	34.1	16.0
Odessa, TX...............	51,388	64.7	149,500	21.2	11.2	944	26.3	86.8	85,132	8.2	2,289	2.7	74,637	24.8	31.3
Ogden-Clearfield, UT ...	209,577	75.3	251,800	20.4	10.0	931	26.1	92.2	326,065	1.0	10,305	3.2	317,015	38.1	24.8
Oklahoma City, OK........	511,242	63.5	156,800	20.3	10.0	851	27.9	87.2	681,616	1.4	21,273	3.1	666,609	37.9	20.6
Olympia-Tumwater, WA....	112,075	66.4	283,400	22.9	10.7	1,203	30.0	92.8	137,697	2.7	6,553	4.8	129,447	43.0	17.8
Omaha-Council Bluffs, NE-IA..........	359,372	65.0	170,200	19.7	11.8	891	26.5	88.5	485,858	1.1	13,926	2.9	491,755	39.9	20.2
Orlando-Kissimmee-Sanford, FL......	875,259	60.4	219,000	21.7	10.9	1,151	32.7	89.5	1,337,790	2.6	43,843	3.3	1,227,050	36.9	17.3
Oshkosh-Neenah, WI......	70,008	64.8	157,800	19.6	12.5	738	25.0	90.2	92,956	-0.9	2,524	2.7	88,583	36.3	26.6
Owensboro, KY............	48,691	68.9	132,400	19.6	10.2	778	27.9	82.1	56,392	0.1	2,278	4.0	54,553	29.0	25.9
Oxnard-Thousand Oaks-Ventura, CA	272,085	62.8	592,500	26.4	10.6	1,736	33.9	91.5	425,728	0.2	16,066	3.8	419,323	38.0	21.7
Palm Bay-Melbourne-Titusville, FL...	228,385	73.7	195,400	22.4	11.0	1,013	32.1	89.8	276,558	2.6	9,746	3.5	253,410	39.6	18.7
Panama City, FL..........	76,386	62.5	173,700	22.5	10.0	975	30.2	90.1	95,373	0.9	3,818	4.0	86,341	34.0	18.8
Parkersburg-Vienna, WV..................	36,629	69.9	129,100	17.8	10.0	715	28.6	84.2	38,107	-0.6	2,127	5.6	37,700	34.1	22.5
Pensacola-Ferry Pass-Brent, FL......	184,622	67.0	161,300	21.2	10.0	975	31.0	89.5	225,952	1.9	7,825	3.5	215,818	34.5	18.2
Peoria, IL...............	147,367	72.0	138,000	18.9	11.6	727	27.3	84.0	180,042	1.1	9,267	5.1	167,684	37.6	20.7
Philadelphia-Camden-Wilmington, PA-NJ-DE-MD	2,282,935	66.1	250,900	21.5	13.4	1,082	30.5	86.5	3,082,419	0.1	129,553	4.2	2,971,934	44.4	16.7
Camden, NJ Div 15804	460,100	72.6	221,400	23.0	16.2	1,143	31.2	88.4	624,565	-1.3	26,391	4.2	628,412	42.7	17.6
Montgomery County-Bucks County-Chester County, PA ...	743,933	74.4	329,700	21.0	12.4	1,223	28.9	91.3	1,072,028	0.2	37,136	3.5	1,051,722	48.4	15.1
Philadelphia, PA Div 37964	811,603	54.2	184,100	21.3	13.7	980	31.5	79.2	1,005,484	0.6	51,202	5.1	956,060	41.7	16.5
Wilmington, DE-MD-NJ Div 48864 .	267,299	67.5	246,800	20.6	10.5	1,106	29.7	91.8	380,342	0.7	14,824	3.9	335,740	42.7	20.6
Phoenix-Mesa-Scottsdale, AZ.........	1,675,676	63.7	246,900	21.2	10.0	1,091	28.9	90.2	2,407,742	3.9	101,259	4.2	2,214,774	37.4	18.0
Pine Bluff, AR............	32,431	67.8	82,400	18.5	10.0	680	28.9	64.7	35,409	0.0	1,787	5.0	31,339	27.2	33.2
Pittsburgh, PA...........	996,798	69.9	153,300	18.7	11.5	794	27.3	85.8	1,203,534	-0.2	51,233	4.3	1,160,922	41.5	19.1
Pittsfield, MA............	54,193	69.1	205,900	20.3	14.0	818	31.4	86.8	66,109	1.1	2,669	4.0	63,317	35.7	19.2
Pocatello, ID.............	31,384	67.4	156,900	19.5	10.0	678	33.2	87.5	41,686	0.4	1,139	2.7	38,024	39.6	19.2
Portland-South Portland, ME..........	216,114	73.2	259,200	21.3	12.6	990	28.6	90.7	298,848	0.5	8,418	2.8	292,062	41.4	18.9
Portland-Vancouver-Hillsboro, OR-WA	935,722	63.2	376,000	22.3	12.2	1,238	30.4	92.2	1,313,057	0.8	51,060	3.9	1,270,795	42.7	19.4
Port St. Lucie, FL.......	176,539	73.4	208,300	24.1	13.0	1,157	34.4	88.8	216,794	2.3	8,841	4.1	198,659	30.2	19.9
Prescott, AZ.............	98,369	71.3	260,900	24.8	10.4	943	29.9	85.5	105,618	3.5	4,719	4.5	87,202	31.5	19.5
Providence-Warwick, RI-MA...........	627,318	61.9	277,400	22.6	13.9	916	28.3	87.2	858,725	1.1	35,599	4.1	823,381	38.2	19.8
Provo-Orem, UT...........	167,853	66.6	296,600	20.8	10.0	1,008	29.1	95.7	305,442	3.1	8,643	2.8	283,602	41.6	17.2
Pueblo, CO...............	65,098	62.9	163,300	22.6	11.4	781	29.8	82.1	75,912	1.5	3,726	4.9	68,616	30.9	19.9
Punta Gorda, FL..........	76,056	80.6	193,600	23.9	12.2	952	30.9	86.4	70,953	1.0	2,845	4.0	62,848	28.4	16.8
Racine, WI...............	77,473	67.7	169,500	19.2	12.2	825	28.5	90.0	99,570	-0.3	3,600	3.6	96,221	35.4	25.8
Raleigh, NC..............	493,879	67.0	244,500	18.7	10.0	1,073	27.0	92.7	711,326	1.9	24,261	3.4	692,607	48.2	15.5
Rapid City, SD...........	58,171	68.0	192,700	21.3	12.4	828	27.6	87.1	74,411	1.0	2,347	3.2	71,705	30.4	21.5

1. Specified owner-occupied units. lacking complete plumbing facilities.   2. A value of 10.0 represents 10 percent or less; a value of 50.0 represents 50 percent or more.   3. Specified renter-occupied units.   4. Overcrowded or   5. Percent of civilian labor force.   6. Civilian employed persons 16 years old and over.

Table C. Metropolitan Areas — Nonfarm Employment and Agriculture

Area name	Private nonfarm establishments, employment and payroll, 2016									Agriculture, 2017			
	Number of establishments	Employment						Annual payroll		Farms			Farm producers whose primary occupation is farming (percent)
		Total	Health care and social assistance	Manufacturing	Retail trade	Finance and insurance	Professional, scientific, and technical services	Total (mil dol)	Average per employee (dollars)	Number	Percent with: Fewer than 50 acres	1000 acres or more	
	104	105	106	107	108	109	110	111	112	113	114	115	116
Mobile, AL..................................	8,736	151,652	21,180	16,379	21,503	5,636	9,969	6,435	42,432	653	60.9	3.1	39.3
Modesto, CA..............................	8,866	139,192	24,819	19,633	22,899	3,390	6,209	6,240	44,827	3,621	65.3	3.5	51.3
Monroe, LA................................	4,569	67,657	15,895	6,132	10,585	3,513	2,919	2,468	36,478	914	46	3.4	35.7
Monroe, MI................................	2,285	37,503	4,751	7,359	4,933	810	1,285	1,623	43,270	1,085	57.7	4.1	40.5
Montgomery, AL........................	7,713	131,011	21,150	17,848	18,811	4,976	6,331	5,239	39,989	1,996	35.3	7.6	37.5
Morgantown, WV......................	2,868	52,478	15,689	4,436	7,259	929	2,595	2,251	42,894	1,684	34.7	0.5	38.6
Morristown, TN.........................	1,996	40,364	4,986	11,198	6,217	721	529	1,426	35,332	1,532	54.1	0.5	39.6
Mount Vernon-Anacortes, WA.........	3,457	41,928	7,619	5,809	7,553	1,493	1,833	1,874	44,704	1,041	75.7	1.6	40.8
Muncie, IN................................	2,435	42,283	10,360	4,293	6,276	2,902	1,605	1,465	34,658	546	52.9	8.1	45
Muskegon, MI............................	3,114	52,661	10,271	13,060	7,940	1,075	1,474	2,129	40,422	476	61.1	2.3	44
Myrtle Beach-Conway-North Myrtle Beach, NC-SC.......	11,077	133,230	14,952	4,228	28,503	4,205	4,397	4,138	31,056	998	46.1	5.6	45.9
Napa, CA..................................	4,216	62,535	10,068	11,266	7,000	1,414	1,901	3,189	50,994	1,866	74.9	2.8	32.2
Naples-Immokalee-Marco Island, FL	11,698	124,868	18,374	3,290	21,838	4,000	5,248	5,238	41,949	322	77.3	7.1	36.2
Nashville-Davidson--Murfreesboro--Franklin, TN........	42,739	830,183	135,529	71,328	95,245	50,277	44,631	41,634	50,150	14,207	46.9	1.4	34.3
New Bern, NC...........................	2,491	31,512	7,231	3,540	5,175	863	2,067	1,159	36,787	522	38.9	9.6	47.2
New Haven-Milford, CT.............	19,597	341,265	75,605	31,228	42,569	11,735	15,306	17,169	50,311	686	81.9	0.3	38.3
New Orleans-Metairie, LA.........	30,840	506,317	74,235	24,742	65,009	20,492	32,404	23,333	46,083	1,376	72.6	3.6	34.6
New York-Newark-Jersey City, NY-NJ-PA.......	576,580	8,286,695	1,500,059	330,657	947,789	581,450	761,436	573,358	69,190	7,135	73.3	1	40
Dutchess County-Putnam County, NY Div 20524................	NA	NA	NA	NA	NA	NA	NA	NA	NA	709	54.4	3.1	43.7
Nassau County-Suffolk County, NY Div 35004................	NA	NA	NA	NA	NA	NA	NA	NA	NA	592	74.5	0.3	56.1
Newark, NJ-PA Div 35084	NA	NA	NA	NA	NA	NA	NA	NA	NA	3,566	76.2	0.8	32.8
New York-Jersey City-White Plains, NY-NJ Div 35614........	NA	NA	NA	NA	NA	NA	NA	NA	NA	2,268	74.4	0.9	45.2
Niles-Benton Harbor, MI..................	3,520	54,222	9,392	9,337	7,077	1,396	1,983	2,383	43,951	872	57.8	3.3	48.8
North Port-Sarasota-Bradenton, FL ..	22,400	241,057	44,320	15,512	43,252	7,578	14,689	9,658	40,067	1,045	67.7	6.7	44.6
Norwich-New London, CT	5,865	105,998	17,290	13,522	15,036	2,075	8,216	5,249	49,522	823	63.1	0.6	43.3
Ocala, FL..................................	7,004	79,752	15,888	6,725	16,289	2,094	2,894	2,751	34,496	3,985	81.2	1.2	43.8
Ocean City, NJ..........................	3,841	27,491	4,326	577	7,032	1,104	976	1,073	39,031	164	73.8	NA	48.5
Odessa, TX...............................	3,584	57,465	6,976	3,311	8,324	1,506	1,389	2,780	48,383	275	68.7	14.5	28.2
Ogden-Clearfield, UT................	13,665	183,676	23,278	31,241	28,959	7,743	13,128	7,336	39,938	3,347	71.2	6.8	30.5
Oklahoma City, OK...................	35,526	500,388	80,061	28,607	69,021	25,088	31,114	21,547	43,061	10,023	41.5	5.9	33.9
Olympia-Tumwater, WA.............	6,092	71,359	14,503	2,778	12,566	2,753	4,689	2,856	40,028	1,200	77.8	0.6	35.3
Omaha-Council Bluffs, NE-IA.........	23,504	415,490	63,483	30,346	54,874	40,700	25,198	19,447	46,805	5,843	38.9	13.3	43.7
Orlando-Kissimmee-Sanford, FL......	63,244	1,030,199	121,002	36,459	146,554	39,301	67,100	43,645	42,365	3,120	77	3.2	40.8
Oshkosh-Neenah, WI................	3,564	84,456	12,357	21,609	8,751	3,373	3,021	4,271	50,566	957	49.9	2.2	37.8
Owensboro, KY.........................	2,630	45,917	8,651	7,496	6,485	3,386	995	1,841	40,087	1,679	46.8	6.6	37.2
Oxnard-Thousand Oaks-Ventura, CA	20,909	256,376	38,214	24,647	40,861	11,666	22,432	13,358	52,103	2,135	78.4	2.2	43
Palm Bay-Melbourne-Titusville, FL....	13,927	176,190	29,695	18,301	29,198	4,653	14,471	7,665	43,506	522	81	3.1	43.5
Panama City, FL.......................	4,913	64,284	10,319	4,142	12,130	1,550	7,014	2,211	34,399	236	61.9	4.2	23.9
Parkersburg-Vienna, WV...........	2,079	31,946	7,197	2,163	6,338	1,011	916	1,068	33,430	1,137	36.1	0.4	35.3
Pensacola-Ferry Pass-Brent, FL.......	9,435	129,551	25,245	4,495	21,296	8,632	9,068	5,076	39,181	1,348	67.8	2.5	37.5
Peoria, IL..................................	8,403	158,307	31,578	14,477	20,286	6,045	6,442	8,329	52,614	3,495	33.8	10	43
Philadelphia-Camden-Wilmington, PA-NJ-DE-MD........	147,317	2,592,712	495,451	168,986	310,595	178,631	201,082	146,920	56,667	6,506	67.9	1.8	45.3
Camden, NJ Div 15804	NA	NA	NA	NA	NA	NA	NA	NA	NA	1,692	73.5	1.5	46
Montgomery County-Bucks County-Chester County, PA...............	NA	NA	NA	NA	NA	NA	NA	NA	NA	3,035	66.6	1.2	47.7
Philadelphia, PA Div 37964	NA	NA	NA	NA	NA	NA	NA	NA	NA	104	84.6	D	31.8
Wilmington, DE-MD-NJ Div 48864 ..	NA	NA	NA	NA	NA	NA	NA	NA	NA	1,675	63.5	3.2	41.4
Phoenix-Mesa-Scottsdale, AZ..........	94,758	1,672,158	241,617	104,392	216,507	123,074	115,768	79,781	47,711	2,636	74.3	8	47.6
Pine Bluff, AR...........................	1,566	22,560	4,281	5,598	3,716	845	293	802	35,542	1,010	33.7	13.7	46.8
Pittsburgh, PA..........................	59,850	1,084,046	196,741	81,984	128,786	58,542	78,296	52,947	48,842	6,318	40.3	1.3	40.4
Pittsfield, MA............................	3,896	53,308	11,591	5,141	8,396	1,895	2,520	2,379	44,620	475	50.9	1.3	42.6
Pocatello, ID.............................	2,017	24,676	5,215	1,738	4,517	2,435	1,289	806	32,660	757	51.9	9	35.1
Portland-South Portland, ME..........	17,794	237,839	47,072	22,686	35,036	15,926	13,143	10,930	45,956	1,612	61	0.7	44.3
Portland-Vancouver-Hillsboro, OR-WA........	68,550	1,013,165	147,875	103,125	120,027	45,055	74,847	54,577	53,868	11,755	83.4	0.5	32.5
Port St. Lucie, FL......................	11,002	115,981	22,553	5,355	23,514	3,174	6,050	4,260	36,733	1,009	69.4	8.9	44.3
Prescott, AZ.............................	5,825	60,153	13,238	3,508	10,771	1,234	1,768	2,052	34,110	850	73.2	8.5	46.2
Providence-Warwick, RI-MA..........	41,194	631,644	130,743	66,266	83,296	31,003	28,773	28,909	45,768	1,731	73.8	0.2	43.5
Provo-Orem, UT........................	13,056	206,444	25,301	17,565	27,162	5,656	15,055	8,443	40,897	2,881	76.7	3.2	23.9
Pueblo, CO...............................	3,086	49,911	13,215	4,353	8,263	1,143	2,132	1,901	38,081	839	41.7	14.2	37.6
Punta Gorda, FL........................	3,883	37,640	8,823	499	9,256	1,091	1,401	1,263	33,560	306	66.3	6.2	37.2
Racine, WI................................	4,024	66,437	11,043	15,606	9,313	2,058	1,996	3,058	46,029	611	51.7	3.8	42.6
Raleigh, NC..............................	32,560	504,628	67,038	24,091	69,240	25,710	54,757	25,347	50,229	2,292	53.5	3.3	38.3
Rapid City, SD..........................	4,756	56,331	11,321	3,117	10,083	3,012	2,129	2,162	38,373	1,932	22.4	33.9	48.2

Table C. Metropolitan Areas — Agriculture

Area name	Land in farms — Acreage (1,000) [117]	Percent change, 2012-2017 [118]	Average size of farm [119]	Total irrigated (1,000) [120]	Total cropland (1,000) [121]	Value of land and buildings — Average per farm [122]	Average per acre [123]	Value of machinery and equipment, average per farm (dollars) [124]	Value of products sold: Total (mil dol) [125]	Average per farm (acres) [126]	Percent from: Crops [127]	Percent from: Livestock and poultry products [128]	Organic farms (number) [129]	Farms with internet access (percent) [130]	Government payments Total ($1,000) [131]	Percent of farms [132]
Mobile, AL	95	6.9	145	3.1	37.7	688,890	4,738	83,715	90.6	138,712	88.8	11.2	NA	77	1,537	15.8
Modesto, CA	723	-5.9	200	380.6	404.7	3,116,617	15,619	182,695	2,526.3	697,690	53	47	35	82.2	5,006	7.5
Monroe, LA	168	8.2	184	16.1	68.4	685,214	3,717	87,277	166.4	182,111	15.4	84.6	3	76.5	2,500	13.8
Monroe, MI	210	-2.2	193	4.3	194.1	1,190,516	6,156	150,143	174.5	160,833	96.2	3.8	NA	83.5	4,555	43.7
Montgomery, AL	643	0.5	322	10.3	175.2	769,306	2,388	88,952	176.8	88,562	32.3	67.7	3	70.8	7,305	38.3
Morgantown, WV	205	-6.2	122	0.1	66.8	400,195	3,287	59,253	21.2	12,577	38	62	6	69.3	377	6.2
Morristown, TN	139	-10	91	0.4	61.5	478,775	5,278	63,992	39.9	26,023	22.8	77.2	1	67.8	1,647	25.7
Mount Vernon-Anacortes, WA	98	-8.3	94	23.5	65.7	950,360	10,130	129,653	287.1	275,789	66.6	33.4	61	83	407	7.8
Muncie, IN	168	-4.3	307	0.6	157.6	2,038,397	6,633	188,658	92.2	168,773	92.9	7.1	NA	83.5	4,044	56.4
Muskegon, MI	63	-14.9	133	3.6	45.8	852,880	6,425	112,540	74.7	156,884	58.9	41.1	5	82.8	173	11.1
Myrtle Beach-Conway-North Myrtle Beach, NC-SC	215	-3.5	216	2.8	140.3	946,291	4,388	125,160	133.9	134,187	64.9	35.1	8	73.8	2,625	32.1
Napa, CA	256	1	137	60.9	67.7	6,052,361	44,154	94,303	573.2	307,198	97.7	2.3	117	84.7	924	2.1
Naples-Immokalee-Marco Island, FL	148	20.1	461	37.3	82.7	2,189,705	4,749	121,438	189.7	588,994	96.8	3.2	2	83.5	141	5.3
Nashville-Davidson--Murfreesboro--Franklin, TN	1,831	-2	129	3.9	736.4	614,526	4,769	69,619	488.8	34,408	61.6	38.4	26	75.9	14,361	23.2
New Bern, NC	190	7.6	365	4.8	148.5	1,426,209	3,913	210,902	308.6	591,193	28.9	71.1	4	82.2	3,579	50.2
New Haven-Milford, CT	27	-36.3	39	1.3	11.4	922,401	23,490	67,525	111.6	162,720	95.9	4.1	26	78.4	323	5.2
New Orleans-Metairie, LA	263	14.5	191	0.5	85.0	690,802	3,613	78,734	61.3	44,569	74	26	2	76.3	68	1.2
New York-Newark-Jersey City, NY-NJ-PA	532	-4.2	75	26.5	278.9	965,667	12,945	78,433	677.6	94,972	84	16	146	82.8	2,348	5.2
Dutchess County-Putnam County, NY Div 20524	109	-7.6	154	0.9	42.8	1,363,083	8,832	80,530	47.1	66,364	66.6	33.4	18	89.7	242	7.3
Nassau County-Suffolk County, NY Div 35004	31	-20	52	12.2	23.3	646,571	12,371	146,890	225.6	381,044	90.4	9.6	32	84.5	76	2
Newark, NJ-PA Div 35084	236	0.7	66	4.1	119.2	946,242	14,274	61,802	156.4	43,852	81.6	18.4	64	82.2	1,042	5
New York-Jersey City-White Plains, NY-NJ Div 35614	155	-5.1	69	9.3	93.6	955,264	13,935	86,059	248.6	109,621	83	17	32	81.3	988	5.6
Niles-Benton Harbor, MI	145	-7.6	166	20	123.5	1,068,560	6,445	142,166	171.3	196,501	91.4	8.6	15	76.4	2,594	20.6
North Port-Sarasota-Bradenton, FL	264		252	61.8	82.2	2,060,967	8,164	101,807	383.2	366,712	88.5	11.5	4	76.4	499	4
Norwich-New London, CT	60	-7.7	73	0.6	23.9	837,723	11,467	67,605	135.8	164,989	55.5	44.5	22	88	267	6.1
Ocala, FL	331	2.9	83	13.2	79.3	922,892	11,114	47,624	145.5	36,501	41.1	58.9	5	82.3	813	1.4
Ocean City, NJ	8	10.7	50	1.4	3.8	722,280	14,561	59,085	9.8	59,988	89.2	10.8	NA	81.1	D	1.2
Odessa, TX	558	30.1	2,029	0.9	1.9	2,350,073	1,158	63,273	3.4	12,298	7.6	92.4	NA	75.6	57	1.5
Ogden-Clearfield, UT	1,610	2.4	481	150	360.9	1,125,771	2,341	91,422	224.4	67,057	46.5	53.5	19	78.8	9,132	14.2
Oklahoma City, OK	2,509	1.7	250	23.5	899.4	657,494	2,627	81,754	459.5	45,842	23.8	76.2	8	76.1	13,598	18.3
Olympia-Tumwater, WA	62	-18.8	52	6.4	22.1	616,274	11,880	58,420	176.1	146,742	32	68	34	86.8	107	1.9
Omaha-Council Bluffs, NE-IA	2,363	-0.4	404	245.9	2,123.4	2,524,750	6,243	228,075	1,509.8	258,390	75.9	24.1	37	82.4	39,142	60.7
Orlando-Kissimmee-Sanford, FL	853	0	273	65.4	106.4	1,508,463	5,516	67,498	554.5	177,714	87.4	12.6	31	79.6	2,279	5.7
Oshkosh-Neenah, WI	162	4.2	169	0.5	136.2	1,180,421	6,971	140,933	122.2	127,711	40	60	7	76.6	3,326	53.1
Owensboro, KY	415	0.3	247	10.9	320.3	1,135,275	4,593	152,676	388.3	231,278	47.6	52.4	NA	76.4	7,178	46.9
Oxnard-Thousand Oaks-Ventura, CA	260	-7.5	122	98.1	123.4	3,106,351	25,498	127,982	1,633.3	765,008	99.2	0.8	128	80.6	830	2.5
Palm Bay-Melbourne-Titusville, FL	157	6.9	300	10.5	21.0	1,507,864	5,027	62,406	59	112,977	76.9	23.1	1	78.7	186	3.6
Panama City, FL	74	387.8	312	1.8	6.2	1,822,648	5,846	42,449	2.9	12,297	69.6	30.4	NA	69.9	40	4.2
Parkersburg-Vienna, WV	131	4.4	116	0	34.3	329,622	2,852	45,212	8.6	7,532	40.6	59.4	NA	72.1	307	3.4
Pensacola-Ferry Pass-Brent, FL	144	-16.4	107	3.2	85.9	609,257	5,707	67,962	65.5	48,565	89.9	10.1	4	78.1	6,506	17.7
Peoria, IL	1,215	-5.7	348	46	1,107.3	2,895,959	8,331	217,354	818.3	234,133	86.1	13.9	51	78.6	17,261	69.1
Philadelphia-Camden-Wilmington, PA-NJ-DE-MD	656	0.4	101	50.1	466.6	1,077,298	10,688	111,066	1,358.6	208,822	79	21	91	79.9	9,299	12
Camden, NJ Div 15804	155	5.9	92	23.5	90.4	1,032,028	11,270	96,392	223.9	132,345	93.2	6.8	12	81.1	2,024	8.5
Montgomery County-Bucks County-Chester County, PA	259	-0.2	85	2.8	186.2	1,038,608	12,186	105,618	823.6	271,367	79.2	20.8	63	78.8	2,589	9
Philadelphia, PA Div 37964	3	-46.7	26	0.1	0.9	490,433	19,110	47,933	9.8	94,442	97.2	2.8	2	95.2	D	D
Wilmington, DE-MD-NJ Div 48864	239	-1.3	143	23.8	189.2	1,229,570	8,600	139,681	301.3	179,851	67.3	32.7	14	79.6	4,686	21.8
Phoenix-Mesa-Scottsdale, AZ	1,595	-3.4	605	412.4	551.3	2,837,548	4,689	203,720	2,071.1	785,687	37.8	62.2	22	85.1	9,253	12.7
Pine Bluff, AR	533	2.7	527	348.4	421.5	1,715,145	3,252	258,302	477.5	472,780	49.9	50.1	NA	67.1	21,923	47
Pittsburgh, PA	790	-3.3	125	2.8	448.9	681,802	5,450	94,414	258.8	40,969	60.1	39.9	42	74.7	4,448	14.4
Pittsfield, MA	59	-4.9	123	0.3	19.1	943,836	7,644	72,648	23.5	49,453	42.8	57.2	16	85.5	447	7.8
Pocatello, ID	315	6.8	416	40	181.5	812,963	1,953	97,164	37.8	49,943	56.8	43.2	1	81.6	5,606	33.9
Portland-South Portland, ME	129	-12.6	80	2.6	38.8	451,159	5,649	59,199	54.2	33,620	72.3	27.7	106	86.8	1,496	5.6
Portland-Vancouver-Hillsboro, OR-WA	597	-7.3	51	80.8	327.7	739,269	14,558	65,709	1,020.1	86,784	83.2	16.8	162	87.1	3,852	4.1
Port St. Lucie, FL	380	13.5	376	77	118.3	2,008,239	5,337	96,887	252.2	249,942	90.2	9.8	5	76.3	1,434	8.4
Prescott, AZ	822	-0.3	967	7.5	8.0	1,596,867	1,651	63,906	35.7	42,036	40.1	59.9	4	86.4	115	1.5
Providence-Warwick, RI-MA	89	20.6	51	4.9	30.7	877,440	17,087	65,103	93	53,738	73.7	26.3	40	80.6	1,437	9.2
Provo-Orem, UT	568	-3	197	96.4	174.7	1,042,883	5,286	79,177	256.3	88,948	43.1	56.9	6	81.7	2,612	8.6
Pueblo, CO	896	0	1,067	18.1	72.0	1,097,156	1,028	75,875	52	62,033	41	59	7	77.5	2,117	13.9
Punta Gorda, FL	113	-48.1	368	11.6	18.5	2,644,176	7,176	66,706	43.9	143,402	91.8	8.2	2	73.9	329	5.2
Racine, WI	127	15.9	209	1.6	109.8	1,602,954	7,682	181,939	86.4	141,475	74.8	25.2	1	82.3	2,502	44.5
Raleigh, NC	368	-7	161	5.1	218.9	938,272	5,840	103,395	389.9	170,103	61.2	38.8	21	77.6	3,070	23.5
Rapid City, SD	3,757	0.7	1,945	19.8	651.4	2,117,518	1,089	135,596	186.3	96,405	16.2	83.8	3	80	19,255	45.8

Table C. Metropolitan Areas — Water Use, Wholesale Trade, Retail Trade, and Real Estate

Area name	Water use, 2015		Wholesale Trade[1], 2012				Retail Trade[2], 2012				Real estate and rental and leasing,[2] 2012			
	Public supply water withdrawn (mil gal/day)	Public supply gallons withdrawn per person per day	Number of establishments	Number of employees	Sales (mil dol)	Average payroll (mil dol)	Number of establishments	Number of employees	Sales (mil dol)	Average payroll (mil dol)	Number of establishments	Number of employees	Sales (mil dol)	Average payroll (mil dol)
	133	134	135	136	137	138	139	140	141	142	143	144	145	146
Mobile, AL	66.1	159.1	499	6,116	3,680.0	283.8	1,454	19,204	5,102.6	454.7	410	2,125	419.1	83.2
Modesto, CA	80.48	149.5	405	6,087	5,295.1	313.6	1,374	20,970	5,933.6	527.1	433	2,141	387.9	73.2
Monroe, LA	28.58	159.5	187	2,190	1,793.0	96.6	776	9,812	2,528.4	220.3	190	1,154	229.3	38.1
Monroe, MI	9.27	62	89	D	D	D	377	4,977	1,471.2	110.5	78	306	43.8	7.9
Montgomery, AL	44.78	119.8	360	5,844	4,361.6	272.4	1,322	17,359	4,678.9	421.7	309	2,146	377.1	72.4
Morgantown, WV	13.08	94.7	71	486	374.3	17.4	476	7,179	1,843.1	146.7	152	799	128.8	22.1
Morristown, TN	14.46	124	68	943	1,100.5	45.5	391	5,674	1,619.1	131.9	79	297	62.0	8.9
Mount Vernon-Anacortes, WA	20.31	166.7	104	1,277	793.5	58.2	553	6,801	1,999.2	186.8	158	467	81.8	14.4
Muncie, IN	9.58	82	92	894	805.8	32.1	428	6,189	1,519.9	131.9	95	447	90.7	16.5
Muskegon, MI	16.08	93.1	121	D	D	D	552	7,597	1,919.4	171.2	91	457	71.7	14.8
Myrtle Beach-Conway-North Myrtle Beach, NC-SC	52.93	122.5	307	2,149	971.4	87.0	2,037	25,110	6,365.9	556.0	718	5,052	591.6	151.2
Napa, CA	15.28	107.3	167	D	D	D	524	6,318	1,699.0	184.2	207	1,026	160.4	38.2
Naples-Immokalee-Marco Island, FL	51.82	145	306	2,417	2,306.5	163.1	1,418	18,924	5,304.1	511.0	907	2,610	546.6	109.8
Nashville-Davidson--Murfreesboro--Franklin, TN	245.57	134.2	1,760	32,450	48,065.9	1,851.8	6,018	85,291	23,831.1	2,149.6	1,756	10,598	2,557.2	478.8
New Bern, NC	12.73	100.8	91	803	1,408.6	30.5	461	4,882	1,347.4	115.1	111	376	46.1	10.7
New Haven-Milford, CT	54.49	63.4	922	14,185	11,237.2	821.2	2,901	41,925	11,567.5	1,100.7	673	5,378	2,008.0	220.2
New Orleans-Metairie, LA	261.17	206.8	1,411	19,692	33,417.9	1,064.1	4,480	57,986	16,445.2	1,503.7	1,222	7,682	1,793.8	319.7
New York-Newark-Jersey City, NY-NJ-PA	1,549.3	76.8	33,908	412,171	507,384.4	28,173.7	78,193	896,588	270,758.2	25,968.1	33,390	178,052	65,022.2	9,852.3
Dutchess County-Putnam County, NY Div 20524	21.79	55.2	315	2,814	4,858.3	181.1	1,375	17,192	4,744.9	429.7	414	1,533	280.2	53.6
Nassau County-Suffolk County, NY Div 35004	440.59	153.9	5,694	66,586	60,342.0	4,120.9	12,669	156,986	47,799.0	4,388.8	4,008	16,099	4,922.6	835.9
Newark, NJ-PA Div 35084	394.37	157	3,527	58,817	76,074.4	4,651.1	8,600	112,874	36,178.3	3,107.7	2,541	16,253	5,851.7	899.5
New York-Jersey City-White Plains, NY-NJ Div 35614	692.55	48.1	24,372	283,954	366,109.6	19,220.6	55,549	609,536	182,036.0	18,042.0	26,427	144,167	53,967.8	8,063.3
Niles-Benton Harbor, MI	12.42	80.3	133	D	D	D	587	6,783	1,681.1	147.2	152	614	78.3	19.5
North Port-Sarasota-Bradenton, FL	63	81.9	751	6,092	3,496.9	283.0	2,832	37,299	9,942.8	926.9	1,301	4,688	1,068.6	180.5
Norwich-New London, CT	8.11	29.8	150	D	D	D	1,023	14,372	3,679.3	364.3	204	765	182.6	32.0
Ocala, FL	27.71	80.7	277	3,157	1,719.3	143.3	1,152	14,430	4,263.6	353.9	338	1,382	211.8	41.3
Ocean City, NJ	13.61	143.7	60	D	D	D	669	5,803	1,639.4	166.2	218	681	148.7	26.0
Odessa, TX	0.64	4	298	4,659	3,608.8	330.5	451	7,286	2,711.7	218.7	176	1,482	604.9	101.9
Ogden-Clearfield, UT	91.48	142.3	460	5,797	4,437.8	247.6	1,708	25,217	6,975.2	593.7	726	1,965	359.1	61.2
Oklahoma City, OK	139.34	102.6	1,472	21,416	45,661.6	1,219.0	4,318	61,357	19,131.2	1,578.5	1,713	9,151	2,064.4	407.4
Olympia-Tumwater, WA	22.58	83.8	169	1,824	1,252.0	90.8	769	12,317	3,330.8	324.6	325	994	202.1	31.3
Omaha-Council Bluffs, NE-IA	179.36	196	1,139	16,116	19,466.9	866.4	2,705	51,093	14,650.4	1,227.3	1,015	6,759	1,210.3	292.0
Orlando-Kissimmee-Sanford, FL	370.98	155.4	2,582	28,410	24,271.6	1,413.0	8,166	124,686	37,046.0	3,002.2	3,691	27,653	6,908.9	1,046.4
Oshkosh-Neenah, WI	13.99	82.5	136	D	D	D	473	7,892	2,064.9	174.5	113	576	219.2	19.9
Owensboro, KY	14.58	124.1	108	1,392	1,267.3	60.1	456	6,229	1,547.9	141.1	85	591	102.2	19.5
Oxnard-Thousand Oaks-Ventura, CA	130.02	152.9	985	D	D	D	2,562	37,012	11,194.2	1,011.0	1,008	4,568	983.6	196.5
Palm Bay-Melbourne-Titusville, FL	31.45	55.4	451	3,962	1,846.5	195.7	1,955	24,885	6,527.5	606.1	642	2,056	340.7	66.7
Panama City, FL	49.5	250.6	163	1,472	522.2	63.9	857	10,636	2,805.1	256.9	291	1,460	213.3	40.8
Parkersburg-Vienna, WV	7.97	86.3	77	D	D	D	403	6,095	1,416.4	130.3	85	D	D	D
Pensacola-Ferry Pass-Brent, FL	52.48	109.8	330	2,953	1,719.6	124.7	1,477	19,315	5,356.2	468.5	489	1,781	340.3	56.9
Peoria, IL	48.22	127.6	401	6,169	4,946.2	296.2	1,290	19,211	5,010.7	456.4	312	1,335	266.4	43.7
Philadelphia-Camden-Wilmington, PA-NJ-DE-MD	657.43	108.3	6,714	103,885	112,303.8	6,892.7	19,892	297,081	85,570.3	7,755.5	5,229	36,509	13,076.4	1,908.7
Camden, NJ Div 15804	114.55	91.4	1,360	25,642	36,358.5	1,498.0	4,112	63,959	17,767.4	1,638.0	933	7,228	1,743.9	381.8
Montgomery County-Bucks County-Chester County, PA	204.1	104	3,100	47,014	49,846.9	3,504.5	7,186	122,083	38,696.3	3,449.9	1,977	13,567	3,404.4	703.1
Philadelphia, PA Div 37964	270.33	126.8	1,569	23,901	18,664.2	1,509.3	6,206	74,456	18,710.1	1,767.7	1,488	11,801	2,727.4	613.2
Wilmington, DE-MD-NJ Div 48864	68.45	94.6	685	7,328	7,434.2	380.9	2,388	36,583	10,396.5	899.8	831	3,913	5,200.6	210.6
Phoenix-Mesa-Scottsdale, AZ	839.78	183.6	4,058	59,578	61,626.6	3,549.5	10,899	191,751	59,671.8	5,115.0	5,578	30,399	7,712.9	1,367.6
Pine Bluff, AR	12.89	137.6	65	D	D	D	329	3,719	914.8	82.4	70	229	39.7	6.6
Pittsburgh, PA	324.4	137.9	2,561	37,959	42,687.8	2,075.7	8,271	126,114	34,250.1	2,907.5	2,034	12,564	2,998.5	548.8
Pittsfield, MA	14.33	112.1	105	1,242	455.0	58.0	711	8,482	1,916.5	201.7	108	715	99.5	23.1
Pocatello, ID	16.91	201.9	80	D	D	D	299	4,330	1,155.3	95.7	80	221	31.5	5.2
Portland-South Portland, ME	42.09	80	622	7,227	6,787.0	367.3	2,457	32,974	8,665.6	788.1	768	3,495	647.7	132.3
Portland-Vancouver-Hillsboro, OR-WA	260.27	108.9	3,035	44,671	40,137.7	2,629.7	7,084	105,037	29,004.4	2,832.2	3,353	17,891	3,578.8	700.3
Port St. Lucie, FL	44.98	98.9	352	D	D	D	1,438	21,908	6,262.8	600.4	519	2,333	386.7	80.6
Prescott, AZ	21.14	95.1	163	1,385	880.4	59.1	787	9,854	2,504.3	233.3	341	941	153.0	27.7
Providence-Warwick, RI-MA	124.06	76.9	1,675	26,253	31,686.2	1,626.5	5,987	81,494	20,467.4	2,020.3	1,476	6,997	1,413.5	271.7
Provo-Orem, UT	132.26	225.8	377	5,832	3,148.9	300.7	1,553	22,409	6,153.9	534.7	686	1,871	339.0	53.7
Pueblo, CO	41.29	252.4	85	D	D	D	508	7,551	1,952.8	183.4	143	585	105.1	17.7
Punta Gorda, FL	7.51	43.4	94	D	D	D	558	8,000	2,091.3	185.9	232	680	113.1	19.1
Racine, WI	19.14	98.1	170	2,243	1,702.5	118.6	591	8,542	2,182.0	181.6	100	327	58.9	9.7
Raleigh, NC	73.38	57.6	1,212	19,573	19,650.4	1,474.6	3,838	59,857	16,847.3	1,453.3	1,439	7,825	1,764.6	407.5
Rapid City, SD	12.32	85.5	180	1,944	1,287.9	86.1	683	9,154	2,529.9	219.6	192	645	115.1	18.0

1. Merchant wholesalers, except manufacturers' sales branches and offices. 2. Employer establishments.

Table C. Metropolitan Areas — **Professional Services, Manufacturing, and Accommodation and Food Services**

Area name	Professional, scientific, and technical services, 2012				Manufacturing, 2012				Accommodation and food services, 2012			
	Number of establishments	Number of employees	Sales (mil dol)	Average payroll (mil dol)	Number of establishments	Number of employees	Receipts (mil dol)	Annual payroll (mil dol)	Number of establishments	Number of employees	Receipts (mil dol)	Annual payroll (mil dol)
	147	148	149	150	151	152	153	154	155	156	157	158
Mobile, AL	850	9,039	1,175.1	474.0	343	16,063	10,562.7	886.3	671	13,684	617.9	167.9
Modesto, CA	649	5,111	507.5	196.0	395	19,963	11,703.6	1,007.8	813	13,611	705.7	192.6
Monroe, LA	449	2,737	379.1	125.2	136	6,067	2,438.8	286.3	310	6,524	298.1	81.5
Monroe, MI	147	828	129.9	40.6	128	6,591	2,976.5	351.3	259	4,280	179.9	49.6
Montgomery, AL	756	6,906	1,421.8	433.6	287	17,367	14,627.6	896.5	671	13,503	636.6	174.8
Morgantown, WV	234	2,834	405.3	124.7	78	4,133	2,181.4	273.8	317	6,165	267.1	73.8
Morristown, TN	110	438	48.8	14.1	144	10,205	4,224.1	418.1	178	3,065	152.3	40.6
Mount Vernon-Anacortes, WA	300	D	D	D	174	5,269	11,529.4	295.7	330	4,195	291.5	79.1
Muncie, IN	163	1,522	240.5	63.4	130	4,205	1,591.3	191.2	211	4,417	172.7	49.6
Muskegon, MI	223	1,513	182.5	65.7	259	12,483	3,727.0	608.0	335	5,450	236.1	67.6
Myrtle Beach-Conway-North Myrtle Beach, NC-SC	866	3,696	400.6	143.7	216	4,213	2,742.7	222.8	1,489	29,339	1,897.5	499.8
Napa, CA	395	1,801	280.5	101.5	431	10,837	4,623.5	622.5	375	10,466	774.1	247.7
Naples-Immokalee-Marco Island, FL	1,342	4,810	784.7	270.4	197	2,722	607.5	130.0	763	19,624	1,406.5	404.2
Nashville-Davidson--Murfreesboro--Franklin, TN	3,785	38,289	6,215.8	2,520.0	1,488	61,378	28,947.4	2,916.1	3,530	76,659	4,275.8	1,250.6
New Bern, NC	250	1,884	220.7	97.0	85	3,535	1,308.0	164.3	234	4,207	198.3	54.1
New Haven-Milford, CT	1,907	16,222	2,461.1	1,216.8	1,151	31,792	10,818.1	1,879.2	1,969	26,342	1,487.2	411.3
New Orleans-Metairie, LA	3,884	31,419	5,507.7	2,078.7	742	34,170	104,969.4	2,377.1	3,217	69,067	4,502.4	1,259.1
New York-Newark-Jersey City, NY-NJ-PA	69,819	710,316	163,194.8	61,316.7	16,232	346,950	134,229.9	19,621.2	48,312	634,388	49,193.7	13,558.1
Dutchess County-Putnam County, NY Div 20524	1,086	5,256	833.3	299.0	285	10,022	2,790.6	742.5	979	10,711	599.9	162.2
Nassau County-Suffolk County, NY Div 35004	12,457	87,339	13,447.4	5,200.1	3,110	68,546	21,084.1	3,694.2	7,107	89,642	5,929.2	1,628.8
Newark, NJ-PA Div 35084	9,067	112,684	22,364.6	9,712.9	2,448	70,600	38,127.3	4,797.5	5,475	72,580	4,728.5	1,272.8
New York-Jersey City-White Plains, NY-NJ Div 35614	47,209	505,037	126,549.4	46,104.7	10,389	197,783	72,228.0	10,387.1	34,751	461,455	37,936.1	10,494.2
Niles-Benton Harbor, MI	284	2,149	201.0	108.3	289	8,330	1,962.8	388.9	365	5,323	241.7	69.4
North Port-Sarasota-Bradenton, FL	2,703	20,704	1,945.0	841.3	591	13,680	3,538.1	670.9	1,446	26,437	1,429.1	419.4
Norwich-New London, CT	529	8,100	666.1	862.0	172	12,435	4,693.7	950.2	698	28,347	3,023.8	748.7
Ocala, FL	669	3,676	415.5	157.2	178	4,806	1,471.2	212.9	437	7,369	375.2	102.5
Ocean City, NJ	214	D	D	D	66	615	98.2	21.5	903	5,888	593.0	160.0
Odessa, TX	227	1,832	205.4	80.1	251	4,756	1,706.3	265.7	261	6,150	389.0	94.0
Ogden-Clearfield, UT	1,443	10,848	1,407.6	525.8	596	27,115	14,050.6	1,478.6	855	15,956	671.2	190.6
Oklahoma City, OK	4,132	27,776	4,052.7	1,582.9	1,050	31,032	11,209.0	1,338.6	2,685	57,866	2,741.9	749.8
Olympia-Tumwater, WA	593	D	D	D	168	2,883	910.5	123.8	533	7,785	419.2	120.5
Omaha-Council Bluffs, NE-IA	2,342	59,415	3,755.6	2,966.2	656	30,185	17,651.7	1,361.4	1,901	36,416	1,866.7	512.8
Orlando-Kissimmee-Sanford, FL	7,816	58,862	8,811.8	3,756.9	1,337	32,960	11,209.7	1,917.5	4,484	138,873	10,349.4	2,695.0
Oshkosh-Neenah, WI	247	2,575	514.5	134.8	300	23,892	11,476.5	1,321.6	367	5,963	234.6	65.3
Owensboro, KY	169	1,563	105.3	44.8	125	6,938	5,391.9	357.4	193	4,448	191.8	55.3
Oxnard-Thousand Oaks-Ventura, CA	2,634	22,377	3,185.4	2,063.2	867	23,166	8,334.0	1,295.4	1,598	27,725	1,597.4	442.6
Palm Bay-Melbourne-Titusville, FL	1,669	13,893	2,433.6	981.2	407	19,152	5,441.9	1,311.3	1,042	18,994	902.6	257.7
Panama City, FL	434	3,465	493.8	184.2	110	3,904	1,482.5	197.5	497	10,318	581.6	165.7
Parkersburg-Vienna, WV	165	D	D	D	63	2,882	D	207.9	218	D	D	D
Pensacola-Ferry Pass-Brent, FL	1,063	9,010	1,234.8	486.1	229	4,433	2,552.0	262.3	747	14,767	744.0	203.9
Peoria, IL	676	6,718	865.5	374.9	331	19,563	13,708.7	1,081.5	870	15,632	778.2	212.7
Philadelphia-Camden-Wilmington, PA-NJ-DE-MD	18,064	199,353	37,881.9	16,087.3	5,115	172,790	99,584.5	10,453.8	12,771	198,333	11,474.3	3,164.3
Camden, NJ Div 15804	3,281	D	D	D	967	34,775	D	2,101.0	2,395	36,821	1,967.4	525.4
Montgomery County-Bucks County-Chester County, PA	8,266	83,896	15,163.1	6,634.4	2,565	82,694	30,889.5	4,823.6	4,218	66,585	3,705.4	1,043.4
Philadelphia, PA Div 37964	4,370	59,242	12,848.3	5,152.2	1,132	35,487	27,083.4	2,173.3	4,774	69,816	4,429.8	1,218.4
Wilmington, DE-MD-NJ Div 48864	2,147	D	D	D	451	19,834	D	1,356.0	1,384	25,111	1,371.7	377.1
Phoenix-Mesa-Scottsdale, AZ	11,812	91,918	15,658.8	5,865.3	3,000	94,061	36,827.5	5,560.6	7,121	165,154	9,456.3	2,745.4
Pine Bluff, AR	87	594	66.7	28.3	70	5,532	2,226.6	243.5	134	2,365	93.0	23.1
Pittsburgh, PA	5,871	81,204	15,404.9	5,698.3	2,506	90,107	38,416.1	4,812.4	5,374	92,549	4,548.1	1,266.2
Pittsfield, MA	338	2,688	397.7	162.8	151	5,275	1,288.9	310.7	522	7,006	418.7	124.2
Pocatello, ID	165	1,277	84.2	40.3	44	1,633	916.3	67.7	197	3,199	135.5	37.2
Portland-South Portland, ME	1,923	13,183	2,086.5	801.2	662	21,142	6,501.6	1,099.6	1,823	24,102	1,457.2	436.0
Portland-Vancouver-Hillsboro, OR-WA	8,099	68,556	9,720.6	5,233.3	3,058	D	D	D	5,743	86,242	4,870.0	1,428.9
Port St. Lucie, FL	1,211	5,244	685.0	246.3	296	4,883	1,709.0	237.3	724	12,867	642.0	182.8
Prescott, AZ	522	1,748	190.9	74.3	184	2,765	706.9	130.8	548	8,223	407.5	130.8
Providence-Warwick, RI-MA	4,042	27,215	4,161.4	1,605.4	2,183	66,543	19,277.2	3,628.5	4,214	63,818	3,450.4	982.0
Provo-Orem, UT	1,654	16,956	1,741.7	656.3	525	15,963	6,082.1	807.2	709	13,249	577.3	161.5
Pueblo, CO	238	1,744	435.3	157.3	90	4,221	2,333.3	216.8	356	5,698	236.0	67.8
Punta Gorda, FL	381	1,295	138.5	50.5	69	402	90.4	14.6	261	4,804	219.2	61.7
Racine, WI	310	1,967	234.8	91.7	325	15,444	8,100.1	844.4	382	5,974	251.7	70.5
Raleigh, NC	4,656	41,942	7,437.7	3,117.2	738	21,629	17,865.0	1,146.8	2,415	47,908	2,436.0	675.1
Rapid City, SD	372	2,151	243.7	83.2	164	2,383	570.3	95.4	480	7,455	426.6	117.1

Table C. Metropolitan Areas —

Health Care and Social Assistance, Other Services, Nonemployer Businesses, and Residential Construction

Area name	Health care and social assistance, 2012				Other services, 2012				Nonemployer businesses, 2016		Value of residential construction authorized by building permits, 2018	
	Number of establishments	Number of employees	Receipts (mil dol)	Annual payroll (mil dol)	Number of establishments	Number of employees	Receipts (mil dol)	Annual payroll (mil dol)	Number	Receipts (mil dol)	New construction ($1,000)	Number of housing units
	159	160	161	162	163	164	165	166	167	168	169	170
Mobile, AL	734	21,863	2,397.2	927.8	570	3,577	334.8	96.2	30,532	1,104.7	177,668	783
Modesto, CA	1,075	24,257	3,635.0	1,274.8	604	3,817	371.6	118.9	27,775	1,462.1	155,768	759
Monroe, LA	661	14,936	1,407.9	504.3	243	1,568	144.3	42.1	14,096	585.6	94,632	490
Monroe, MI	282	5,347	457.9	193.6	156	727	67.6	17.0	8,280	362.2	73,573	492
Montgomery, AL	875	20,240	2,062.6	869.8	569	3,906	468.3	130.1	24,396	1,029.8	138,587	654
Morgantown, WV	295	14,178	1,582.2	569.5	177	1,316	190.7	34.3	7,204	309.6	32,743	266
Morristown, TN	230	5,680	491.1	189.8	114	526	42.4	12.9	6,519	302.8	68,192	302
Mount Vernon-Anacortes, WA	330	7,152	700.3	296.6	252	1,128	106.0	31.3	7,844	388.2	132,101	585
Muncie, IN	313	9,158	873.1	318.7	174	1,043	105.9	26.2	5,706	210.0	7,440	52
Muskegon, MI	369	11,494	982.3	483.8	250	1,315	120.8	29.6	9,279	361.7	47,920	233
Myrtle Beach-Conway-North Myrtle Beach, NC-SC	878	14,479	1,600.7	571.0	623	3,183	324.9	77.9	35,781	1,636.2	1,468,633	7,446
Napa, CA	404	10,222	1,360.7	553.3	241	1,359	127.7	40.0	11,857	725.8	78,081	269
Naples-Immokalee-Marco Island, FL	995	16,310	2,089.4	772.0	850	5,209	474.4	138.1	38,119	2,217.0	1,339,352	4,386
Nashville-Davidson--Murfreesboro--Franklin, TN	4,208	109,447	13,584.2	5,158.9	2,507	19,844	2,180.7	640.4	172,840	9,276.1	3,936,729	19,159
New Bern, NC	293	8,064	806.0	330.9	167	832	70.7	18.5	7,564	291.6	66,399	389
New Haven-Milford, CT	2,408	73,162	7,788.2	3,238.4	1,717	9,881	977.8	297.8	61,104	3,171.4	165,282	1,166
New Orleans-Metairie, LA	3,205	67,442	7,698.1	2,899.3	1,850	12,712	1,868.6	426.7	119,932	5,485.3	859,241	3,864
New York-Newark-Jersey City, NY-NJ-PA	60,802	1,438,772	161,273.4	66,480.3	48,848	291,897	42,605.8	10,194.7	1,902,946	107,015.8	8,049,786	49,692
Dutchess County-Putnam County, NY Div 20524	1,162	23,662	2,563.7	1,086.5	824	3,627	397.2	105.5	30,916	1,517.8	NA	NA
Nassau County-Suffolk County, NY Div 35004	10,507	207,080	23,582.4	10,013.4	8,013	40,426	4,189.4	1,107.1	267,868	17,109.5	NA	NA
Newark, NJ-PA Div 35084	7,795	155,717	17,765.9	7,176.8	5,410	35,343	3,614.8	1,051.8	209,418	12,494.2	NA	NA
New York-Jersey City-White Plains, NY-NJ Div 35614	41,338	1,052,313	117,361.3	48,203.6	34,601	212,501	34,404.4	7,930.2	1,394,744	75,894.3	NA	NA
Niles-Benton Harbor, MI	399	9,410	816.5	329.2	251	1,199	116.0	32.2	9,862	392.2	92,060	302
North Port-Sarasota-Bradenton, FL	2,393	40,770	4,488.5	1,669.2	1,448	7,481	648.2	176.8	70,304	3,436.7	2,034,249	10,289
Norwich-New London, CT	734	17,357	1,728.0	751.2	459	2,498	274.7	61.9	16,925	826.8	104,339	666
Ocala, FL	878	15,494	1,874.0	674.9	455	2,315	196.6	54.0	24,317	977.6	433,239	2,817
Ocean City, NJ	278	4,767	443.7	186.8	296	1,237	96.3	32.4	8,248	506.0	214,575	643
Odessa, TX	293	7,384	823.7	297.6	250	2,276	340.1	83.5	11,316	541.5	145,006	740
Ogden-Clearfield, UT	1,431	21,624	2,361.9	801.8	809	4,688	374.1	106.9	41,628	1,785.9	818,262	3,672
Oklahoma City, OK	4,134	76,535	9,611.3	3,270.6	2,067	13,049	1,632.8	381.5	108,020	5,135.1	1,286,622	5,730
Olympia-Tumwater, WA	790	13,079	1,584.8	619.1	483	2,769	331.1	98.1	15,022	652.7	332,518	1,750
Omaha-Council Bluffs, NE-IA	2,439	61,248	6,795.6	2,552.5	1,603	10,653	1,536.4	314.5	59,958	2,737.7	704,883	4,788
Orlando-Kissimmee-Sanford, FL	5,726	108,835	13,809.2	4,884.8	3,592	23,294	2,405.8	635.2	226,474	8,636.4	5,320,024	28,882
Oshkosh-Neenah, WI	439	13,580	1,272.0	555.0	257	2,279	221.0	68.1	8,544	388.9	83,546	378
Owensboro, KY	348	7,891	759.3	301.6	167	1,100	83.1	25.8	6,790	282.2	26,039	258
Oxnard-Thousand Oaks-Ventura, CA	2,557	32,438	3,987.6	1,434.5	1,176	7,150	763.3	188.6	69,019	3,743.8	285,879	1,204
Palm Bay-Melbourne-Titusville, FL	1,522	31,218	3,727.6	1,387.7	958	4,563	372.7	117.7	41,969	1,596.3	860,729	2,958
Panama City, FL	515	10,051	1,078.2	412.5	321	1,936	160.6	43.4	15,070	720.4	370,936	1,668
Parkersburg-Vienna, WV	287	7,169	639.4	248.5	152	D	D	D	4,336	170.8	22,020	125
Pensacola-Ferry Pass-Brent, FL	1,019	24,040	2,905.3	1,091.4	594	3,417	307.7	88.5	32,785	1,378.6	501,133	2,568
Peoria, IL	840	30,651	3,197.1	1,286.0	613	6,256	590.3	251.2	19,847	727.0	71,064	334
Philadelphia-Camden-Wilmington, PA-NJ-DE-MD	17,408	463,943	51,028.6	20,690.6	11,378	74,202	9,462.5	2,309.9	425,972	22,507.8	2,141,320	13,156
Camden, NJ Div 15804	3,439	76,614	8,247.2	3,369.2	2,200	13,271	1,065.6	334.8	75,219	4,003.5	NA	NA
Montgomery County-Bucks County-Chester County, PA	6,477	145,503	15,158.5	6,213.8	4,374	28,315	4,325.0	894.6	167,697	10,056.1	NA	NA
Philadelphia, PA Div 37964	5,528	191,974	21,925.2	8,572.2	3,609	24,712	3,271.7	844.7	137,810	5,645.8	NA	NA
Wilmington, DE-MD-NJ Div 48864	1,964	49,852	5,697.8	2,535.4	1,195	7,904	800.2	235.9	45,246	2,802.4	NA	NA
Phoenix-Mesa-Scottsdale, AZ	11,231	207,257	24,523.2	9,574.2	5,505	43,914	4,609.6	1,279.1	329,315	15,914.4	7,450,142	31,343
Pine Bluff, AR	237	4,827	429.9	173.6	105	530	49.1	15.8	4,466	159.3	2,768	30
Pittsburgh, PA	7,942	190,828	18,711.4	7,858.7	5,155	32,089	3,524.7	897.4	147,613	6,726.0	955,079	4,037
Pittsfield, MA	438	11,415	1,091.4	488.4	278	1,675	144.1	39.5	9,985	442.2	81,411	262
Pocatello, ID	335	3,819	314.1	115.4	120	591	61.6	15.7	5,106	202.1	46,617	404
Portland-South Portland, ME	2,038	44,844	4,350.3	1,882.7	1,164	6,448	701.2	179.9	49,267	2,453.6	561,612	2,624
Portland-Vancouver-Hillsboro, OR-WA	7,272	132,399	16,118.5	6,283.0	4,277	25,065	3,122.2	806.2	180,731	8,906.9	2,906,944	14,180
Port St. Lucie, FL	1,191	18,821	2,288.4	829.9	761	3,811	330.2	96.8	40,178	1,736.4	866,089	3,970
Prescott, AZ	759	11,555	1,245.1	517.8	364	1,717	142.9	41.0	18,667	773.2	489,306	2,079
Providence-Warwick, RI-MA	4,650	123,284	11,708.9	5,129.5	3,361	18,660	1,923.7	529.5	111,009	5,165.1	397,975	1,963
Provo-Orem, UT	1,219	21,246	2,228.3	776.1	634	3,398	272.7	73.9	46,845	2,056.2	1,683,855	6,841
Pueblo, CO	419	11,404	1,063.1	458.0	238	1,222	93.1	28.2	8,357	348.9	74,234	479
Punta Gorda, FL	485	8,927	1,119.6	401.0	297	1,326	113.0	33.0	12,658	553.1	529,176	2,068
Racine, WI	459	10,588	764.4	335.7	317	1,839	140.4	44.5	9,668	401.9	94,503	379
Raleigh, NC	3,069	53,424	5,654.4	2,278.0	1,959	13,792	1,557.4	446.6	104,889	4,816.9	2,865,360	15,950
Rapid City, SD	408	11,766	1,318.5	509.7	334	1,801	220.7	45.4	11,175	502.7	142,675	834

Table C. Metropolitan Areas — Government Employment and Payroll, and Local Government Finances

Area name	Government employment and payroll, 2012									Local government finances, 2012				
	Full-time equivalent employees	March payroll (dollars)	March payroll (percent of total)							General revenue				
			Administration, judicial, and legal	Police and corrections	Fire protection	Highways and transportation	Health and welfare	Natural resources and utilities	Education and libraries	Total (mil dol)	Intergovernmental (mil dol)	Taxes		
												Total (mil dol)	Per capita[1] (dollars)	
													Total	Property
	171	172	173	174	175	176	177	178	179	180	181	182	183	184
Mobile, AL..............................	15,334	47,151,677	5.5	11.5	5.1	4.9	9.2	7.3	53.7	1,405.0	626.1	561.4	1,356	491
Modesto, CA..........................	19,446	94,702,481	5.9	8.3	2.5	1.6	11.8	9.4	58.2	2,696.4	1,547.9	554.1	1,062	825
Monroe, LA............................	8,044	23,625,209	7.1	11.1	3.2	2.1	4.4	5.4	65.9	699.4	335.0	289.5	1,628	585
Monroe, MI............................	3,882	16,268,085	7.1	8.4	1.4	3.3	1.1	4.8	72.4	475.7	225.8	166.5	1,102	1,074
Montgomery, AL......................	12,833	40,413,140	4.7	13.6	5.4	3.2	3.3	7.9	56.9	1,415.6	468.2	359.9	954	325
Morgantown, WV.....................	3,679	10,784,021	6.6	6.4	2.1	3.9	3.1	7.2	67.9	282.4	117.1	109.2	814	659
Morristown, TN.......................	3,406	10,523,184	5.5	8.9	3.2	3.2	3.1	11.3	62.6	288.5	121.7	106.7	928	541
Mount Vernon-Anacortes, WA.....	5,963	27,675,332	5.4	5.4	2.0	4.5	41.5	4.7	33.8	852.8	275.6	199.6	1,688	1,157
Muncie, IN............................	3,335	10,832,587	6.2	9.0	3.6	4.7	3.7	4.2	64.9	345.4	171.1	109.1	930	778
Muskegon, MI.........................	5,428	21,789,876	7.5	7.4	2.5	3.3	9.1	3.1	65.4	721.5	413.6	168.4	989	913
Myrtle Beach-Conway-North Myrtle Beach, NC-SC........	13,720	47,691,925	8.0	11.3	4.0	2.9	7.2	7.6	55.9	1,554.9	373.0	787.2	1,995	1,260
Napa, CA..............................	5,012	27,819,123	11.8	13.2	3.0	2.1	9.4	6.0	49.6	811.6	274.6	367.8	2,645	2,138
Naples-Immokalee-Marco Island, FL............................	9,918	41,162,175	6.9	15.7	6.7	3.5	4.2	9.1	52.0	1,300.6	231.7	737.4	2,218	2,006
Nashville-Davidson--Murfreesboro--Franklin, TN	62,367	213,611,379	6.4	10.6	4.9	2.3	11.3	9.7	53.1	5,944.5	1,864.0	2,495.0	1,445	925
New Bern, NC	6,791	24,592,380	3.3	4.8	1.6	1.2	45.2	4.1	38.0	754.9	290.2	112.7	880	654
New Haven-Milford, CT	28,448	140,929,161	3.5	10.1	6.3	2.6	2.7	5.4	68.7	3,790.8	1,443.5	2,034.2	2,358	2,333
New Orleans-Metairie, LA	43,957	168,084,037	8.4	14.9	3.0	2.9	22.4	8.9	37.2	7,012.5	2,504.9	2,443.4	1,991	986
New York-Newark-Jersey City, NY-NJ-PA	859,136	4,981,795,701	4.0	15.9	3.9	8.2	12.0	4.2	49.2	158,755.3	48,519.4	84,882.7	4,280	2,827
Dutchess County-Putnam County, NY Div 20524.......	15,834	82,439,707	5.8	9.6	2.2	4.0	5.7	1.6	70.0	2,303.5	678.0	1,388.4	3,498	2,873
Nassau County-Suffolk County, NY Div 35004	123,812	732,874,581	4.1	11.7	0.9	2.5	7.4	3.2	68.6	20,978.5	5,325.7	13,527.4	4,749	3,856
Newark, NJ-PA Div 35084	95,852	533,906,989	5.6	13.8	3.9	2.5	4.8	4.3	63.1	13,124.9	3,533.4	8,066.3	3,241	3,160
New York-Jersey City-White Plains, NY-NJ Div 35614...	623,638	3,632,574,424	3.8	17.2	4.5	10.3	14.2	4.4	42.7	122,348.4	38,982.3	61,900.6	4,391	2,559
Niles-Benton Harbor, MI	4,813	18,604,576	9.6	10.9	2.0	2.9	2.9	4.5	64.6	601.1	301.4	200.9	1,288	1,264
North Port-Sarasota-Bradenton, FL..................................	26,901	101,649,100	7.7	11.2	6.0	3.4	20.0	5.4	43.7	3,172.2	626.1	1,212.8	1,684	1,368
Norwich-New London, CT	8,967	42,369,410	4.4	7.7	3.8	3.8	2.3	8.0	68.3	1,101.6	386.5	598.5	2,183	2,159
Ocala, FL..............................	10,760	33,096,942	6.2	11.8	9.0	0.5	2.5	5.9	63.0	875.9	312.2	296.0	883	746
Ocean City, NJ	5,885	27,086,618	8.8	13.8	3.3	3.6	9.4	7.3	49.4	701.1	152.6	449.5	4,667	4,561
Odessa, TX	6,915	26,339,816	4.0	7.3	3.2	1.3	27.3	2.1	53.3	690.5	140.4	269.5	1,867	1,389
Ogden-Clearfield, UT	19,885	69,703,618	6.0	9.0	3.0	1.6	5.2	6.0	67.8	1,758.6	707.7	680.0	1,110	794
Oklahoma City, OK	43,376	150,970,463	5.1	11.2	7.5	3.0	11.2	5.1	56.1	4,132.3	1,264.1	1,725.9	1,331	666
Olympia-Tumwater, WA..............	7,290	36,403,899	10.9	9.6	5.9	9.3	2.0	8.9	51.8	946.4	372.7	391.6	1,516	997
Omaha-Council Bluffs, NE-IA......	36,524	145,002,288	4.4	9.9	3.3	3.6	4.1	18.6	55.0	3,737.9	1,239.7	1,804.1	2,037	1,532
Orlando-Kissimmee-Sanford, FL.	79,591	284,688,968	6.3	14.2	7.2	4.2	4.2	8.8	52.4	8,588.1	2,537.2	3,519.5	1,583	1,131
Oshkosh-Neenah, WI	5,300	21,156,305	4.4	11.7	4.6	5.5	11.2	7.1	54.5	697.9	338.4	249.0	1,475	1,436
Owensboro, KY	5,043	15,494,560	4.3	6.6	2.9	2.8	6.8	13.2	62.0	421.7	154.4	115.6	996	570
Oxnard-Thousand Oaks-Ventura, CA..................................	27,714	159,457,912	10.1	10.8	4.6	3.0	13.0	7.6	49.2	4,630.9	2,005.3	1,379.1	1,650	1,378
Palm Bay-Melbourne-Titusville, FL..................................	19,755	66,076,682	7.5	12.3	7.0	4.4	7.8	7.9	52.0	1,764.4	557.0	634.8	1,160	923
Panama City, FL......................	8,675	32,038,863	3.7	6.7	2.4	3.9	34.3	5.0	42.7	881.5	209.8	288.2	1,536	1,098
Parkersburg-Vienna, WV............	3,144	10,362,577	4.7	5.3	2.0	2.6	2.6	6.3	74.9	235.4	113.7	77.6	838	630
Pensacola-Ferry Pass-Brent, FL.	14,772	47,095,540	7.2	13.2	2.2	2.6	3.7	6.5	62.2	1,288.3	501.5	467.6	1,014	750
Peoria, IL..............................	13,803	52,130,853	6.3	10.3	3.9	4.6	3.2	6.6	63.1	1,517.9	612.5	635.6	1,671	1,435
Philadelphia-Camden-Wilmington, PA-NJ-DE-MD	205,195	1,004,418,815	6.6	13.0	2.3	7.2	5.0	5.0	59.4	31,396.9	12,075.3	14,182.1	2,356	1,683
Camden, NJ Div 15804	50,866	263,407,426	3.8	10.2	2.3	2.9	4.8	3.0	70.8	6,825.7	2,374.5	3,161.2	2,520	2,481
Montgomery County-Bucks County-Chester County, PA.................................	55,254	262,211,582	6.4	11.3	0.4	2.9	4.5	3.7	69.4	8,269.3	2,143.8	4,825.6	2,485	2,076
Philadelphia, PA Div 37964	78,984	387,798,667	9.0	16.8	3.9	13.9	6.0	7.3	42.1	13,846.4	6,463.2	5,279.8	2,504	1,061
Wilmington, DE-MD-NJ Div 48864	20,091	91,001,140	5.5	9.7	1.2	2.8	2.8	4.4	71.6	2,455.5	1,093.8	915.5	1,283	1,049
Phoenix-Mesa-Scottsdale, AZ.....	139,712	587,672,336	8.5	13.3	5.3	2.9	6.2	12.0	50.6	15,082.4	5,190.2	6,265.2	1,447	928
Pine Bluff, AR	3,495	9,830,121	6.5	12.0	3.9	3.6	1.5	2.1	68.3	261.9	169.1	57.9	594	257
Pittsburgh, PA........................	76,232	322,348,429	6.5	11.1	1.8	8.6	5.9	6.4	58.3	10,916.6	4,733.0	4,213.3	1,785	1,286
Pittsfield, MA.........................	4,790	19,230,480	4.3	8.5	3.3	5.5	1.3	4.1	71.5	506.3	218.2	246.7	1,897	1,828
Pocatello, ID..........................	2,618	8,746,568	9.9	14.1	5.7	4.5	6.0	6.6	51.4	238.0	114.9	73.0	871	828
Portland-South Portland, ME.......	19,117	71,307,958	5.3	8.8	5.0	4.0	3.6	6.3	65.4	1,897.9	500.0	1,074.0	2,073	2,046
Portland-Vancouver-Hillsboro, OR-WA..............................	70,641	332,827,613	7.2	11.0	5.2	8.1	4.4	8.5	51.7	10,118.9	3,858.3	4,062.9	1,774	1,375
Port St. Lucie, FL.....................	15,221	57,466,642	7.0	15.0	8.7	2.3	1.8	6.2	55.9	1,562.3	448.2	714.5	1,651	1,400
Prescott, AZ	6,155	23,081,009	10.4	13.4	9.4	4.0	2.1	5.5	45.2	648.3	201.2	335.8	1,579	1,029
Providence-Warwick, RI-MA.......	47,209	226,744,364	3.5	10.7	8.1	2.2	1.2	5.2	67.9	6,092.6	2,097.6	3,232.0	2,018	1,964
Provo-Orem, UT......................	14,474	53,579,798	6.4	8.0	2.5	1.5	4.8	8.4	66.6	1,615.5	670.1	586.2	1,064	722
Pueblo, CO............................	5,698	21,434,409	5.8	12.3	11.0	3.0	6.6	9.0	49.7	552.8	247.0	223.3	1,388	895
Punta Gorda, FL......................	4,654	16,650,878	13.2	15.5	8.9	5.6	2.0	7.8	45.5	559.2	101.1	264.1	1,626	1,290
Racine, WI............................	6,208	25,453,020	4.3	13.6	5.6	3.5	5.9	4.0	61.9	757.1	345.7	302.7	1,554	1,513
Raleigh, NC...........................	40,839	150,997,989	3.4	8.5	3.1	3.1	10.3	5.9	61.8	4,020.3	1,569.5	1,583.3	1,332	1,007
Rapid City, SD........................	5,051	15,769,374	6.1	10.9	1.5	3.1	2.5	4.6	66.3	484.3	139.9	245.9	1,773	1,269

1. Based on the resident population estimated as of July 1 of the year shown.

Table C. Metropolitan Areas — Local Government Finances, Government Employment, and Income Taxes

Area name	Local government finances, 2012 (cont.) Direct general expenditure — Total (mil dol)	Per capita¹ (dollars)	Percent of total for: Education	Health and hospitals	Police protection	Public welfare	Highways	Debt outstanding — Total (mil dol)	Per capita¹ (dollars)	Government employment, 2017 — Federal civilian	Federal military	State and local	Individual income tax returns, 2016 — Number of returns	Mean adjusted gross income	Mean income tax
	185	186	187	188	189	190	191	192	193	194	195	196	197	198	199
Mobile, AL	1,433.8	3,464	41.2	6.0	6.8	0.5	8.3	1,386.2	3,349	2,583	2,571	22,829	172,670	50,832	5,953
Modesto, CA	2,792.3	5,352	50.1	6.9	4.9	10.2	3.4	4,496.8	8,619	870	811	28,940	225,840	53,305	5,666
Monroe, LA	748.1	4,208	53.1	2.8	5.8	0.1	2.9	495.7	2,788	529	657	10,907	73,840	51,886	6,065
Monroe, MI	515.6	3,414	53.6	6.7	3.7	0.2	9.1	557.6	3,691	244	239	5,407	74,070	58,219	6,662
Montgomery, AL	1,403.7	3,722	34.2	33.5	5.6	0.3	2.9	1,403.6	3,722	6,590	4,248	33,619	161,960	54,120	6,328
Morgantown, WV	293.9	2,191	58.5	2.3	5.1	0.3	1.8	267.7	1,996	2,073	632	16,954	55,350	60,004	7,704
Morristown, TN	294.2	2,560	53.3	1.8	5.5	4.4	4.6	336.9	2,932	296	338	6,282	49,260	45,445	4,538
Mount Vernon-Anacortes, WA	797.6	6,747	26.4	43.2	2.9	0.1	3.4	556.4	4,706	411	323	11,093	59,440	63,826	7,819
Muncie, IN	323.3	2,755	48.4	0.8	3.9	0.5	2.7	191.9	1,635	299	331	10,799	48,220	46,412	5,013
Muskegon, MI	746.4	4,386	51.2	13.2	3.2	3.6	4.5	688.6	4,046	360	294	7,361	78,670	48,182	5,138
Myrtle Beach-Conway-North Myrtle Beach, NC-SC	1,496.4	3,793	37.4	11.8	6.6	1.4	4.4	2,146.9	5,441	1,161	1,620	21,141	218,450	52,791	6,253
Napa, CA	821.7	5,909	37.5	5.9	7.5	4.2	4.0	746.0	5,365	228	202	10,768	67,610	87,761	13,621
Naples-Immokalee-Marco Island, FL	1,313.8	3,952	37.5	3.0	12.1	0.6	6.0	2,257.5	6,791	707	673	12,696	177,550	125,451	25,354
Nashville-Davidson--Murfreesboro--Franklin, TN	5,917.9	3,427	40.3	11.8	6.7	0.7	3.2	9,772.4	5,660	13,456	5,857	96,597	891,720	70,013	10,451
New Bern, NC	730.7	5,704	24.7	49.9	4.0	4.0	0.8	197.3	1,540	5,848	7,897	8,498	55,820	51,610	5,503
New Haven-Milford, CT	4,427.8	5,132	58.4	0.6	4.3	0.3	2.5	3,649.0	4,229	5,478	1,918	44,839	413,190	71,243	9,930
New Orleans-Metairie, LA	6,862.8	5,593	28.3	16.1	5.5	1.0	4.4	9,273.5	7,557	12,653	7,695	66,881	557,700	60,457	8,521
New York-Newark-Jersey City, NY-NJ-PA	155,295.2	7,831	37.1	7.8	6.1	10.2	2.3	228,317.6	11,513	113,095	42,730	1,168,725	9,932,440	89,412	15,321
Dutchess County-Putnam County, NY Div 20524	2,273.0	5,726	57.0	3.2	3.6	6.6	4.3	1,817.8	4,580	1,448	583	23,059	NA	NA	NA
Nassau County-Suffolk County, NY Div 35004	22,106.9	7,761	50.8	5.4	7.0	5.6	3.2	19,089.0	6,701	16,501	5,108	168,639	NA	NA	NA
Newark, NJ-PA Div 35084	13,275.6	5,334	50.9	2.5	6.4	2.0	2.6	11,054.8	4,442	18,467	5,189	154,434	NA	NA	NA
New York-Jersey City-White Plains, NY-NJ Div 35614	117,639.8	8,345	32.6	8.9	6.0	12.1	2.1	196,356.0	13,928	76,679	31,850	822,593	NA	NA	NA
Niles-Benton Harbor, MI	618.7	3,965	53.9	7.1	5.5	1.4	5.2	398.2	2,551	332	263	8,984	72,730	55,823	7,065
North Port-Sarasota-Bradenton, FL	3,246.3	4,509	31.7	19.9	6.6	0.3	4.4	3,286.5	4,564	2,044	1,518	25,029	379,960	75,138	12,020
Norwich-New London, CT	1,142.0	4,165	60.1	0.7	5.5	0.6	6.1	911.5	3,324	2,787	6,651	28,095	134,930	69,035	9,124
Ocala, FL	879.1	2,623	48.9	2.0	7.6	0.7	6.3	732.6	2,186	694	624	14,401	157,560	46,622	5,387
Ocean City, NJ	808.9	8,400	33.8	1.5	5.3	4.4	4.9	673.4	6,992	450	1,224	8,600	49,930	61,696	7,904
Odessa, TX	691.3	4,790	36.3	40.0	3.5	0.0	2.4	385.4	2,670	198	312	10,119	65,870	53,440	5,948
Ogden-Clearfield, UT	1,761.7	2,877	51.2	2.7	6.1	1.8	3.1	1,655.4	2,703	19,341	6,445	32,033	279,280	63,683	6,878
Oklahoma City, OK	3,850.3	2,970	45.9	9.2	8.1	0.1	5.6	3,940.9	3,039	28,967	10,715	92,877	587,510	63,089	8,245
Olympia-Tumwater, WA	952.8	3,688	42.4	5.4	4.0	0.0	7.1	917.5	3,552	879	800	37,763	134,630	63,310	7,597
Omaha-Council Bluffs, NE-IA	3,646.7	4,118	52.0	2.7	5.1	0.7	4.4	7,717.4	8,714	9,501	9,296	54,046	440,290	69,014	9,041
Orlando-Kissimmee-Sanford, FL	8,694.5	3,910	39.3	3.5	7.5	0.8	5.5	14,655.7	6,591	14,593	4,703	108,231	1,170,410	54,441	7,084
Oshkosh-Neenah, WI	708.5	4,197	35.6	2.5	5.6	20.8	8.3	688.0	4,076	429	436	11,669	83,510	60,508	7,468
Owensboro, KY	454.5	3,917	36.1	5.3	3.4	0.1	3.3	1,881.3	16,214	314	373	6,278	52,910	52,314	5,507
Oxnard-Thousand Oaks-Ventura, CA	4,471.8	5,349	38.6	13.1	7.5	4.6	3.5	3,011.8	3,603	7,273	4,902	38,837	404,630	78,185	11,168
Palm Bay-Melbourne-Titusville, FL	1,830.9	3,345	36.4	11.6	7.9	0.4	4.3	1,872.2	3,421	6,425	2,863	22,153	279,800	58,338	7,764
Panama City, FL	987.2	5,261	32.4	23.6	6.5	0.0	4.6	937.7	4,998	3,875	4,178	10,452	92,710	51,473	6,342
Parkersburg-Vienna, WV	236.3	2,554	64.2	0.1	5.1	0.0	3.8	191.5	2,070	2,491	430	4,536	40,920	49,753	5,399
Pensacola-Ferry Pass-Brent, FL	1,512.8	3,280	44.3	2.8	7.1	0.2	4.4	3,484.8	7,556	6,701	11,396	21,123	219,100	55,037	6,799
Peoria, IL	1,492.8	3,924	48.0	1.3	5.9	1.7	6.8	1,259.9	3,312	2,243	806	19,272	176,160	65,945	8,603
Philadelphia-Camden-Wilmington, PA-NJ-DE-MD	30,309.1	5,036	49.1	6.0	5.4	5.2	2.6	44,541.2	7,400	51,548	22,874	290,421	2,910,020	77,682	11,751
Camden, NJ Div 15804	6,604.3	5,265	56.5	2.6	4.4	2.8	3.3	7,416.2	5,912	7,786	7,630	73,249	NA	NA	NA
Montgomery County-Bucks County-Chester County, PA	8,574.7	4,415	57.3	2.4	4.9	5.8	3.8	11,320.4	5,829	6,105	5,211	77,495	NA	NA	NA
Philadelphia, PA Div 37964	12,546.9	5,950	37.7	11.3	5.9	7.0	1.3	23,338.7	11,068	32,158	6,546	96,768	NA	NA	NA
Wilmington, DE-MD-NJ Div 48864	2,583.2	3,620	58.6	1.0	6.6	0.5	3.1	2,465.8	3,456	5,499	3,487	42,909	NA	NA	NA
Phoenix-Mesa-Scottsdale, AZ	15,046.5	3,475	42.0	5.1	8.3	1.5	4.0	29,018.4	6,702	22,750	14,700	214,350	1,992,560	64,825	8,849
Pine Bluff, AR	262.8	2,696	61.5	0.1	6.9	0.1	4.7	246.8	2,533	1,462	350	8,312	35,200	42,427	3,808
Pittsburgh, PA	10,894.8	4,615	46.7	6.2	3.8	6.8	3.4	20,628.3	8,738	18,203	6,384	98,909	1,181,570	65,188	8,964
Pittsfield, MA	629.4	4,841	60.3	0.5	3.2	0.3	5.9	274.5	2,111	390	296	7,997	64,680	59,768	7,542
Pocatello, ID	221.0	2,637	41.2	2.7	8.1	1.0	5.5	54.8	654	555	277	7,900	34,650	49,044	4,583
Portland-South Portland, ME	1,867.4	3,604	49.3	0.7	4.6	1.6	5.8	1,662.8	3,209	8,973	4,047	28,532	278,400	67,360	8,778
Portland-Vancouver-Hillsboro, OR-WA	9,964.4	4,352	40.1	4.1	5.7	2.0	5.7	15,721.1	6,866	18,399	6,433	124,969	1,161,660	74,633	10,221
Port St. Lucie, FL	1,660.8	3,838	40.0	3.2	8.5	1.4	5.4	2,747.3	6,349	1,018	914	18,536	217,940	68,849	10,223
Prescott, AZ	653.7	3,074	36.5	2.1	7.2	1.8	9.0	725.7	3,413	1,603	516	9,301	104,930	52,696	6,074
Providence-Warwick, RI-MA	5,907.2	3,689	56.8	0.5	6.6	0.5	2.8	4,257.8	2,659	12,074	8,095	82,458	804,300	63,604	8,280
Provo-Orem, UT	1,466.7	2,663	52.0	4.0	6.1	0.1	5.2	2,448.4	4,445	1,040	2,453	30,124	231,170	65,170	7,614
Pueblo, CO	566.4	3,521	40.3	1.5	6.6	5.3	3.7	456.3	2,837	1,106	423	11,706	70,430	48,976	5,199
Punta Gorda, FL	563.6	3,470	33.1	3.8	11.0	1.5	11.1	628.4	3,868	309	324	5,596	82,800	55,617	6,706
Racine, WI	764.1	3,923	45.5	3.8	9.7	5.3	7.3	710.7	3,648	354	506	8,563	96,420	58,017	6,788
Raleigh, NC	4,137.2	3,481	42.6	8.6	6.0	3.5	1.9	9,884.5	8,316	5,951	3,620	91,605	602,250	77,356	10,789
Rapid City, SD	516.0	3,719	46.0	1.5	5.8	0.4	9.0	476.3	3,433	3,158	4,041	8,315	73,280	58,463	7,303

1. Based on the resident population estimated as of July 1 of the year shown.

Table C. Metropolitan Areas — **Land Area and Population**

CBSA/ DIV Code[1]	Area name	Land area[2] (sq mi)	Total persons	Rank	Per square mile	White	Black	American Indian, Alaska Native	Asian and Pacific Islander	Percent Hispanic or Latino[3]	Under 5 years	5 to 17 years	18 to 24 years	25 to 34 years	35 to 44 years	45 to 54 years
		1	2	3	4	5	6	7	8	9	10	11	12	13	14	15
39740	Reading, PA....................	856.4	420,152	128	490.6	72.2	5.1	0.4	1.8	21.9	5.7	16.6	9.6	12.4	11.5	13.3
39820	Redding, CA...................	3,775.4	180,040	232	47.7	83.0	2.0	4.1	4.6	10.3	5.9	15.5	7.6	12.9	11.1	11.5
39900	Reno, NV.......................	6,565.4	469,764	113	71.6	65.4	3.1	2.0	7.8	24.7	5.9	15.6	8.8	15.1	12.3	12.5
40060	Richmond, VA..................	4,575.6	1,306,172	44	285.5	59.1	30.9	0.9	4.9	6.5	5.8	15.8	8.8	14.6	12.7	13.3
40140	Riverside-San Bernardino-Ontario, CA...................	27,266.5	4,622,361	13	169.5	33.5	8.0	0.9	8.4	51.6	6.8	18.9	10.0	14.6	12.9	12.3
40220	Roanoke, VA...................	1,867.6	314,172	161	168.2	79.8	14.6	0.6	3.0	4.0	5.4	15.1	8.0	12.3	11.3	13.4
40340	Rochester, MN.................	2,477.0	219,802	203	88.7	85.7	5.5	0.6	5.7	4.5	6.7	17.7	7.5	13.5	12.8	11.8
40380	Rochester, NY..................	3,265.9	1,071,082	51	328.0	78.1	12.2	0.7	3.6	7.6	5.3	15.2	9.9	13.3	11.2	12.9
40420	Rockford, IL....................	794.0	337,658	153	425.3	71.2	12.7	0.7	3.2	14.6	6.3	17.4	8.4	12.3	11.8	13.1
40580	Rocky Mount, NC..............	1,045.9	146,021	287	139.6	45.8	47.4	1.0	1.0	6.3	5.6	16.6	8.5	11.8	11.2	12.9
40660	Rome, GA......................	509.8	97,927	360	192.1	72.4	15.4	0.7	1.9	11.3	6.1	17.1	10.0	12.9	12.0	12.6
40900	Sacramento--Roseville--Arden-Arcade, CA.................	5,095.1	2,345,210	26	460.3	55.5	8.6	1.5	17.4	21.8	6.0	16.8	9.3	14.3	13.0	12.5
40980	Saginaw, MI....................	800.5	190,800	227	238.4	71.0	19.8	0.9	1.8	8.5	5.7	15.6	9.4	12.5	10.9	12.5
41060	St. Cloud, MN..................	1,751.1	199,801	222	114.1	87.9	7.2	0.7	2.7	3.3	6.5	17.0	13.4	12.7	11.8	11.5
41100	St. George, UT.................	2,427.4	171,700	244	70.7	85.9	1.1	1.5	2.9	10.6	6.7	19.4	8.8	11.5	11.9	9.3
41140	St. Joseph, MO-KS............	1,655.7	126,490	311	76.4	86.9	6.8	1.1	1.9	5.6	6.0	16.0	9.0	13.8	12.7	12.4
41180	St. Louis, MO-IL...............	7,863.5	2,805,465	20	356.8	75.4	19.4	0.7	3.4	3.1	6.0	16.2	8.3	13.7	12.5	12.7
41420	Salem, OR.....................	1,921.5	432,102	126	224.9	70.1	1.8	2.3	4.3	24.5	6.5	17.7	9.8	13.7	12.6	11.5
41500	Salinas, CA....................	3,281.7	435,594	125	132.7	31.5	3.2	0.8	7.9	59.1	7.1	19.0	9.9	14.3	13.0	11.8
41540	Salisbury, MD-DE..............	2,098.6	409,979	131	195.4	73.0	18.8	0.9	2.2	7.2	5.2	14.0	9.1	10.9	9.9	11.7
41620	Salt Lake City, UT.............	7,684.0	1,222,540	47	159.1	73.4	2.3	1.1	7.3	18.2	7.5	19.9	9.5	16.3	14.7	11.2
41660	San Angelo, TX	2,573.5	119,711	325	46.5	54.3	4.3	0.8	1.9	40.3	6.8	17.1	11.6	15.5	11.6	10.3
41700	San Antonio-New Braunfels, TX......	7,313.1	2,518,036	24	344.3	34.7	7.2	0.6	3.4	55.6	6.9	18.3	9.9	15.1	13.3	12.2
41740	San Diego-Carlsbad, CA.......	4,208.8	3,343,364	17	794.4	48.1	5.7	0.9	14.9	34.0	6.2	15.4	10.3	16.5	13.4	12.4
41860	San Francisco-Oakland-Hayward, CA.................	2,470.3	4,729,484	12	1,914.5	42.6	8.3	0.8	30.7	21.9	5.4	14.3	7.7	16.3	14.5	13.6
41860	Oakland-Hayward-Berkeley, CA Div 36084	1,454.4	2,816,968	X	1,936.9	39.5	11.0	0.9	29.3	23.8	5.7	15.6	8.2	15.1	14.4	13.6
41860	San Francisco-Redwood City-South San Francisco, CA Div 41884	495.5	1,652,850	X	3,335.7	42.7	4.6	0.7	36.4	19.5	5.0	11.7	7.1	19.6	15.1	13.4
41860	San Rafael, CA Div 42034....	520.5	259,666	X	498.9	74.5	3.3	0.8	8.7	16.1	4.6	15.4	6.5	8.7	11.7	15.5
41940	San Jose-Sunnyvale-Santa Clara, CA...................	2,679.7	1,999,107	35	746.0	33.8	2.9	0.7	39.4	26.4	6.0	16.1	8.5	16.2	14.4	13.7
42020	San Luis Obispo-Paso Robles-Arroyo Grande, CA............	3,300.6	284,010	170	86.0	71.0	2.3	1.3	5.3	22.8	4.6	13.0	15.2	11.5	11.1	10.9
42100	Santa Cruz-Watsonville, CA...........	445.1	274,255	176	616.2	59.6	1.7	1.2	6.7	34.1	5.1	14.2	14.9	12.1	11.7	12.2
42140	Santa Fe, NM..................	1,910.1	150,056	279	78.6	44.1	1.1	3.1	1.9	51.1	4.3	13.7	7.3	11.2	11.2	12.4
42200	Santa Maria-Santa Barbara, CA......	2,735.1	446,527	122	163.3	46.2	2.4	1.0	7.1	45.8	6.2	15.9	15.8	13.3	11.3	10.7
42220	Santa Rosa, CA................	1,575.9	499,942	107	317.2	65.8	2.4	1.6	6.3	27.2	5.0	14.7	8.1	12.9	12.5	12.7
42340	Savannah, GA..................	1,349.5	389,494	137	288.6	57.2	34.6	0.8	3.3	6.4	6.5	16.3	10.2	15.8	13.0	11.9
42540	Scranton--Wilkes-Barre--Hazleton, PA...	1,746.4	555,485	100	318.1	83.9	4.3	0.4	2.3	10.5	5.2	14.8	8.7	12.6	11.3	13.2
42660	Seattle-Tacoma-Bellevue, WA........	5,869.6	3,939,363	15	671.1	66.9	7.6	2.0	18.6	10.2	6.1	15.3	8.2	17.0	14.5	13.1
42660	Seattle-Bellevue-Everett, WA Div 42644	4,201.8	3,048,064	X	725.4	65.5	7.1	1.8	20.6	10.0	6.0	14.9	8.0	17.4	14.8	13.3
42660	Tacoma-Lakewood, WA Div 45104	1,667.8	891,299	X	534.4	71.8	9.6	2.6	11.8	11.1	6.7	16.8	8.9	15.7	13.3	12.4
42680	Sebastian-Vero Beach, FL	502.8	157,413	264	313.1	76.4	9.7	0.6	2.0	12.7	4.1	12.0	6.2	9.2	8.8	11.1
42700	Sebring, FL....................	1,017.3	105,424	344	103.6	67.6	10.3	0.9	1.8	20.8	4.6	12.5	6.1	9.7	8.7	9.8
43100	Sheboygan, WI.................	511.5	115,456	332	225.7	85.2	2.8	0.8	6.2	6.5	5.5	16.6	8.3	11.6	12.0	13.2
43300	Sherman-Denison, TX..........	932.8	133,991	301	143.6	77.2	7.0	2.3	2.1	13.8	6.4	17.3	8.4	12.4	11.6	12.3
43340	Shreveport-Bossier City, LA	3,188.7	436,341	124	136.8	54.7	40.3	1.0	1.9	3.9	6.7	17.3	8.4	14.0	12.4	11.7
43420	Sierra Vista-Douglas, AZ.......	6,164.6	126,770	310	20.6	57.0	4.8	1.6	3.6	35.6	5.8	15.7	8.9	12.5	11.0	10.6
43580	Sioux City, IA-NE-SD...........	2,936.8	169,045	251	57.6	76.2	4.2	2.0	3.2	16.6	7.2	18.9	9.2	12.4	12.0	11.9
43620	Sioux Falls, SD................	2,575.4	265,653	184	103.2	86.5	6.0	2.6	2.6	4.3	7.6	18.4	8.3	15.3	13.5	11.5
43780	South Bend-Mishawaka, IN-MI........	948.0	322,424	156	340.1	77.1	13.7	1.1	2.9	8.1	6.2	17.0	10.4	12.8	11.6	12.1
43900	Spartanburg, SC...............	1,321.9	341,298	151	258.2	69.3	22.5	0.7	2.7	6.7	6.0	16.9	9.0	13.6	11.8	13.3
44060	Spokane-Spokane Valley, WA........	5,641.5	573,493	98	101.7	87.8	2.9	3.1	4.3	5.7	6.0	16.0	9.0	14.4	12.1	11.9
44100	Springfield, IL.................	1,182.7	207,636	216	175.6	83.3	13.7	0.6	2.6	2.3	5.6	16.5	8.0	12.5	12.3	12.8
44140	Springfield, MA................	1,144.2	631,761	91	552.1	68.8	7.5	0.6	4.0	20.9	4.9	14.8	13.7	12.7	11.0	12.4
44180	Springfield, MO................	3,007.0	466,978	114	155.3	91.8	3.4	1.5	2.3	3.4	6.3	16.2	11.6	13.4	12.0	11.7
44220	Springfield, OH................	396.9	134,585	299	339.1	86.6	10.7	0.9	1.2	3.5	5.9	16.5	9.1	11.7	10.8	12.7
44300	State College, PA..............	1,109.9	162,805	259	146.7	86.6	4.1	0.4	7.4	3.0	3.9	11.2	23.7	13.9	10.7	11.1
44420	Staunton-Waynesboro, VA......	1,002.0	123,007	320	122.8	87.4	8.6	0.7	1.4	3.9	5.5	14.5	7.6	12.5	11.8	13.1
44700	Stockton-Lodi, CA..............	1,392.4	752,660	77	540.5	33.9	8.2	1.2	18.6	41.9	7.1	20.1	9.6	14.1	13.0	12.2
44940	Sumter, SC....................	665.1	106,512	343	160.1	46.5	48.3	0.9	2.3	4.1	6.7	17.1	10.0	14.2	11.2	11.7
45060	Syracuse, NY..................	2,384.9	650,502	88	272.8	83.7	9.5	1.2	3.7	4.3	5.5	15.4	10.7	12.9	11.1	13.0
45220	Tallahassee, FL................	2,387.6	385,145	139	161.3	57.3	33.5	0.8	3.7	6.7	5.3	13.9	18.1	14.1	11.4	11.0
45300	Tampa-St. Petersburg-Clearwater, FL	2,515.0	3,142,663	18	1,249.6	64.1	12.8	0.7	4.5	20.0	5.3	14.6	7.8	13.3	12.3	13.2
45460	Terre Haute, IN................	1,465.2	169,725	248	115.8	90.7	6.4	0.8	1.8	2.3	5.7	15.1	12.2	12.9	11.8	12.3

1. CBSA = Core Based Statistical Area. DIV = Metropolitan Division. See Appendix A for explanation. See Appendix B for list of metropolitan areas or temporarily covered by water. 2. Dry land or land partially or temporarily covered by water. 3. May be of any race.

Table C. Metropolitan Areas — **Population and Households**

Area name	55 to 64 years	65 to 74 years	75 years and over	Percent female	Total persons 2000	Total persons 2010	Percent change 2000-2010	Percent change 2010-2018	Births	Deaths	Net migration	Number	Persons per house-hold	Family house-holds	Female family house-holder[1]	One person
	16	17	18	19	20	21	22	23	24	25	26	27	28	29	30	31
Reading, PA..............................	13.6	9.7	7.6	50.8	373,638	411,556	10.1	2.1	39,838	31,550	450	155,154	2.61	67.8	12.3	24.9
Redding, CA..............................	14.7	12.2	8.6	50.9	163,256	177,221	8.6	1.6	17,094	17,421	3,343	71,968	2.46	66.1	11.5	27.4
Reno, NV..................................	13.3	10.4	6.0	49.6	342,885	425,439	24.1	10.4	44,605	30,640	30,314	182,846	2.51	60.6	10.4	29.9
Richmond, VA...........................	13.5	9.4	6.1	51.7	1,055,683	1,208,089	14.4	8.1	122,833	85,534	60,899	481,559	2.63	65.9	14.1	27.5
Riverside-San Bernardino-Ontario, CA.	11.4	7.7	5.4	50.2	3,254,821	4,224,966	29.8	9.4	503,697	238,596	133,831	1,344,956	3.33	74.3	14.6	20.8
Roanoke, VA..............................	14.4	11.8	8.4	51.6	288,309	308,669	7.1	1.8	27,579	28,256	6,379	130,863	2.33	61.9	11.9	32.4
Rochester, MN..........................	13.4	9.1	7.5	50.8	184,740	206,882	12.0	6.2	23,897	12,732	1,856	85,994	2.50	68.0	8.4	25.6
Rochester, NY...........................	14.3	10.2	7.6	51.4	1,062,452	1,079,697	1.6	-0.8	94,924	79,855	-23,528	433,400	2.38	62.1	13.7	30.4
Rockford, IL..............................	13.6	9.9	7.4	51.0	320,204	349,431	9.1	-3.4	34,698	26,307	-20,375	132,479	2.52	66.6	13.8	28.4
Rocky Mount, NC	14.6	11.4	7.5	52.7	143,026	152,375	6.5	-4.2	14,037	13,393	-7,021	57,083	2.52	65.2	18.6	30.5
Rome, GA.................................	12.6	9.5	7.2	51.7	90,565	96,314	6.3	1.7	9,880	8,606	398	36,927	2.53	72.0	12.5	24.6
Sacramento--Roseville--Arden-Arcade, CA.	12.6	9.1	6.4	51.1	1,796,857	2,149,151	19.6	9.1	225,512	137,873	109,665	829,772	2.76	67.2	12.4	25.2
Saginaw, MI.............................	14.1	10.9	8.3	51.4	210,039	200,169	-4.7	-4.7	18,492	17,084	-10,863	80,958	2.29	62.8	12.9	30.4
St. Cloud, MN...........................	12.2	8.3	6.6	49.6	167,392	189,093	13.0	5.7	20,962	10,825	621	76,342	2.48	64.1	8.4	26.4
St. George, UT..........................	11.0	11.8	9.6	50.5	90,354	138,115	52.9	24.3	18,481	9,929	24,835	56,139	2.92	71.3	8.8	24.3
St. Joseph, MO-KS....................	13.5	9.3	7.4	48.4	122,336	127,327	4.1	-0.7	12,698	10,735	-2,781	47,135	2.51	64.6	10.1	31.5
St. Louis, MO-IL........................	14.2	9.5	7.0	51.5	2,675,343	2,787,752	4.2	0.6	278,468	213,503	-46,493	1,119,347	2.46	63.8	12.4	30.1
Salem, OR...............................	12.0	9.5	6.6	50.3	347,214	390,750	12.5	10.6	43,987	27,819	25,364	144,978	2.85	66.5	10.6	26.5
Salinas, CA..............................	11.2	8.0	5.6	49.1	401,762	415,061	3.3	4.9	53,287	20,307	-12,323	125,518	3.35	73.5	12.7	20.4
Salisbury, MD-DE......................	15.2	14.6	9.5	51.5	312,572	373,760	19.6	9.7	34,524	34,575	35,981	154,115	2.54	67.0	11.7	26.9
Salt Lake City, UT.....................	10.0	6.6	4.2	49.8	939,122	1,087,808	15.8	12.4	154,505	54,593	35,552	396,869	3.00	70.5	10.0	22.3
San Angelo, TX.........................	11.6	8.7	6.8	50.3	105,781	111,825	5.7	7.1	13,156	8,597	3,305	42,667	2.66	63.2	11.5	30.3
San Antonio-New Braunfels, TX....	11.2	7.8	5.2	50.6	1,711,703	2,142,521	25.2	17.5	268,933	134,786	239,501	810,473	3.00	68.8	14.6	25.8
San Diego-Carlsbad, CA.............	11.8	8.1	5.9	49.7	2,813,833	3,095,349	10.0	8.0	358,797	172,073	64,089	1,126,419	2.88	67.3	12.3	23.6
San Francisco-Oakland-Hayward, CA.	12.6	8.9	6.5	50.5	4,123,740	4,335,587	5.1	9.1	427,815	246,820	213,751	1,694,362	2.74	64.1	10.8	26.2
Oakland-Hayward-Berkeley, CA Div 36084.	12.6	8.6	6.0	50.9	2,392,557	2,559,462	7.0	10.1	260,825	143,380	140,805	965,635	2.87	68.8	12.1	22.9
San Francisco-Redwood City-South San Francisco, CA....	12.2	8.9	7.0	49.7	1,483,894	1,523,702	2.7	8.5	148,050	87,739	68,793	624,508	2.60	56.8	9.3	30.9
San Rafael, CA Div 42034..........	15.2	12.9	9.4	51.1	247,289	252,423	2.1	2.9	18,940	15,701	4,153	104,219	2.43	63.4	8.3	29.1
San Jose-Sunnyvale-Santa Clara, CA ...	11.8	7.5	5.9	49.4	1,735,819	1,836,937	5.8	8.8	199,013	84,481	48,707	651,006	3.01	72.0	10.1	20.1
San Luis Obispo-Paso Robles-Arroyo Grande, CA.	13.7	11.9	8.2	49.3	246,681	269,597	9.3	5.3	21,563	19,077	12,023	104,544	2.55	61.8	8.3	26.4
Santa Cruz-Watsonville, CA.........	13.4	10.5	5.9	50.5	255,602	262,356	2.6	4.5	24,369	14,594	2,228	95,940	2.74	64.1	9.4	27.0
Santa Fe, NM...........................	15.6	15.6	8.8	51.5	129,292	144,227	11.6	4.0	10,938	9,193	4,218	60,904	2.39	57.9	10.9	36.5
Santa Maria-Santa Barbara, CA....	11.3	8.4	6.9	50.0	399,347	423,947	6.2	5.3	46,545	24,980	1,215	147,466	2.90	62.5	10.1	25.1
Santa Rosa, CA.........................	14.4	12.1	7.6	51.2	458,614	483,868	5.5	3.3	41,610	33,485	8,231	188,829	2.63	63.0	9.2	29.1
Savannah, GA...........................	11.9	8.7	5.7	51.5	293,000	347,598	18.6	12.1	42,353	24,636	23,958	142,195	2.64	65.4	15.5	26.4
Scranton--Wilkes-Barre--Hazleton, PA.	14.2	11.0	9.0	50.8	560,625	563,617	0.5	-1.4	46,600	57,375	3,075	223,630	2.39	62.8	12.6	31.5
Seattle-Tacoma-Bellevue, WA......	12.3	8.1	5.3	49.9	3,043,878	3,439,805	13.0	14.5	381,978	198,281	315,825	1,490,337	2.55	63.2	9.1	27.1
Seattle-Bellevue-Everett, WA Div 42644	12.3	8.1	5.2	49.8	2,343,058	2,644,588	12.9	15.3	287,861	146,415	261,801	1,169,069	2.52	62.2	8.5	27.5
Tacoma-Lakewood, WA Div 45104	12.5	8.4	5.4	50.3	700,820	795,217	13.5	12.1	94,117	51,866	54,024	321,268	2.67	66.9	11.3	25.9
Sebastian-Vero Beach, FL	15.6	17.3	15.8	52.1	112,947	138,028	22.2	14.0	10,375	15,786	24,647	58,044	2.63	61.7	5.1	32.9
Sebring, FL...............................	13.4	16.6	18.7	51.1	87,366	98,786	13.1	6.7	7,488	12,394	11,590	42,948	2.35	64.0	8.2	31.9
Sheboygan, WI..........................	14.8	10.4	7.6	49.7	112,646	115,510	2.5	0.0	10,402	8,920	-1,499	48,347	2.32	64.8	9.7	28.5
Sherman-Denison, TX.................	13.9	10.3	7.3	51.2	110,595	120,875	9.3	10.9	12,704	11,389	11,842	49,176	2.61	69.7	10.0	24.3
Shreveport-Bossier City, LA	13.0	9.6	7.0	51.9	417,796	439,811	5.3	-0.8	51,450	37,536	-17,484	172,294	2.50	62.9	16.3	32.7
Sierra Vista-Douglas, AZ.............	13.2	12.7	9.6	49.2	117,755	131,357	11.6	-3.5	13,150	10,460	-7,484	48,939	2.39	64.9	10.5	30.3
Sioux City, IA-NE-SD.................	12.7	9.1	6.7	50.1	167,902	168,563	0.4	0.3	19,928	12,515	-6,978	65,877	2.51	67.0	11.2	27.4
Sioux Falls, SD.........................	12.0	8.2	5.2	49.8	187,093	228,262	22.0	16.4	31,701	14,231	19,823	102,654	2.46	63.7	9.3	29.8
South Bend-Mishawaka, IN-MI.....	13.2	9.7	6.9	51.1	316,663	319,213	0.8	1.0	32,926	25,424	-4,189	119,873	2.58	64.8	12.0	29.7
Spartanburg, SC........................	12.9	9.8	6.7	51.6	283,672	313,289	10.4	8.9	32,346	27,423	23,140	126,242	2.58	68.7	14.0	27.1
Spokane-Spokane Valley, WA.......	13.5	10.4	6.6	50.4	469,737	527,753	12.4	8.7	54,126	40,798	32,661	224,113	2.45	63.7	10.6	28.3
Springfield, IL...........................	14.3	10.5	7.4	52.0	201,437	210,170	4.3	-1.2	19,872	16,984	-5,327	89,434	2.27	62.5	13.4	31.1
Springfield, MA.........................	13.6	9.8	7.1	52.1	608,479	621,681	2.2	1.6	51,797	46,448	4,733	238,781	2.49	63.4	16.3	30.0
Springfield, MO.........................	12.3	9.3	7.2	51.0	368,374	436,709	18.6	6.9	46,911	34,232	17,710	183,438	2.44	62.6	10.0	30.0
Springfield, OH.........................	13.9	11.1	8.3	51.6	144,742	138,341	-4.4	-2.7	13,123	14,039	-2,772	54,026	2.43	64.7	12.5	28.7
State College, PA	11.4	8.1	6.2	47.4	135,758	154,001	13.4	5.7	10,163	7,965	6,621	58,629	2.45	56.3	5.7	30.9
Staunton-Waynesboro, VA	14.5	11.6	8.9	50.8	108,988	118,496	8.7	3.8	10,669	10,803	4,678	50,325	2.32	67.1	11.5	27.3
Stockton-Lodi, CA......................	11.2	7.5	5.2	50.2	563,598	685,306	21.6	9.8	83,754	43,565	27,554	226,624	3.21	73.4	13.8	22.3
Sumter, SC...............................	12.7	9.5	6.9	51.9	104,646	107,490	2.7	-0.9	12,090	8,732	-4,323	41,878	2.49	67.6	18.9	28.0
Syracuse, NY............................	14.4	9.7	7.3	51.3	650,154	662,620	1.9	-1.8	59,744	48,748	-23,156	257,704	2.42	62.7	13.3	29.1
Tallahassee, FL.........................	11.7	9.0	5.5	51.9	320,304	368,770	15.1	4.4	33,414	21,918	4,752	147,734	2.45	58.1	12.4	29.0
Tampa-St. Petersburg-Clearwater, FL.	13.7	11.0	8.7	51.5	2,395,997	2,783,462	16.2	12.9	261,857	248,688	344,163	1,209,519	2.52	61.2	12.2	31.1
Terre Haute, IN.........................	12.9	9.8	7.3	49.2	170,943	172,417	0.9	-1.6	16,342	15,649	-3,321	65,394	2.36	59.4	12.9	33.5

1. No spouse present

Area name	Persons in group quarters, 2018	Daytime population, 2017		Births, 2018		Deaths, 2018		Persons under 65 with no health insurance 2017		Medicare, 2018			Serious crimes known to police[2], 2016 Total	
		Number	Employ-ment/residence ratio	Total	Rate[1]	Number	Rate[1]	Number	Percent	Total Ben-eficiaries	Enrolled in Original Medicare	Enrolled in Medicare Advantage	Number	Rate[3]
	32	33	34	35	36	37	38	39	40	41	42	43	44	45
Reading, PA.................................	11,401	396,147	0.89	4,702	11.2	3,887	9.3	25,410	7.5	83,171	53,970	29,201	7,930	1,912
Redding, CA.................................	2,834	180,318	1.01	1,995	11.1	2,144	11.9	10,045	7.1	47,010	45,919	1,091	6,894	3,857
Reno, NV.....................................	5,313	463,543	0.99	5,411	11.5	3,962	8.4	47,928	12.4	86,656	60,156	26,500	14,220	3,108
Richmond, VA..............................	34,165	1,300,025	1.00	14,786	11.3	11,101	8.5	110,360	10.3	229,903	173,451	56,452	NA	NA
Riverside-San Bernardino-Ontario, CA.....	70,935	4,340,671	0.87	60,720	13.1	32,604	7.1	338,901	8.6	653,409	276,002	377,407	138,186	3,065
Roanoke, VA................................	7,906	319,760	1.05	3,288	10.5	3,572	11.4	25,995	10.6	74,718	56,425	18,293	7,873	2,507
Rochester, MN.............................	3,126	224,037	1.05	2,854	13.0	1,584	7.2	8,507	4.7	39,500	21,367	18,133	3,434	1,597
Rochester, NY..............................	40,042	1,083,355	1.01	10,863	10.1	9,877	9.2	41,004	4.8	228,634	82,778	145,856	24,476	2,277
Rockford, IL.................................	5,053	333,239	0.97	4,121	12.2	3,154	9.3	20,593	7.4	67,275	44,564	22,711	11,695	3,467
Rocky Mount, NC	3,033	144,080	0.96	1,607	11.0	1,673	11.5	14,263	12.2	32,711	25,070	7,641	660	448
Rome, GA....................................	3,759	101,172	1.09	1,177	12.0	1,100	11.2	13,871	17.9	20,256	14,003	6,253	3,074	3,188
Sacramento--Roseville--Arden-Arcade, CA....	37,933	2,316,815	0.99	26,960	11.5	18,348	7.8	116,138	6.0	407,647	218,812	188,835	63,979	2,802
Saginaw, MI.................................	6,728	203,709	1.15	2,119	11.1	2,139	11.2	9,118	6.1	44,823	25,178	19,645	4,514	2,352
St. Cloud, MN..............................	8,342	204,088	1.06	2,573	12.9	1,314	6.6	7,829	4.8	34,014	14,127	19,887	5,026	2,574
St. George, UT.............................	2,237	166,491	1.01	2,282	13.3	1,338	7.8	17,854	13.9	36,615	26,586	10,029	3,027	1,895
St. Joseph, MO-KS.......................	8,427	127,680	1.01	1,467	11.6	1,222	9.7	10,859	11.0	24,527	21,310	3,217	5,673	4,481
St. Louis, MO-IL	54,384	2,816,967	1.01	32,255	11.5	27,368	9.8	184,966	8.0	533,926	319,427	214,499	D	D
Salem, OR...................................	12,595	417,375	0.96	5,507	12.7	3,554	8.2	34,251	9.9	80,742	33,849	46,893	12,899	3,098
Salinas, CA.................................	18,086	434,136	0.98	6,006	13.8	2,688	6.2	41,482	11.5	63,309	58,788	4,521	12,218	2,812
Salisbury, MD-DE	13,754	397,498	0.95	4,166	10.2	4,776	11.6	22,770	7.6	106,463	97,005	9,458	12,364	3,108
Salt Lake City, UT........................	15,164	1,279,902	1.12	18,288	15.0	6,941	5.7	115,227	10.8	145,454	83,631	61,823	59,621	5,010
San Angelo, TX	5,315	119,870	1.01	1,545	12.9	1,106	9.2	17,322	17.9	21,648	15,857	5,791	4,387	4,872
San Antonio-New Braunfels, TX......	49,494	2,459,670	0.99	33,545	13.3	17,984	7.1	350,587	16.6	384,397	219,450	164,947	111,800	4,608
San Diego-Carlsbad, CA...............	108,137	3,373,511	1.02	41,635	12.5	23,022	6.9	235,409	8.4	516,596	271,576	245,020	72,330	2,181
San Francisco-Oakland-Hayward, CA.....	88,300	4,829,838	1.04	51,069	10.8	33,652	7.1	222,759	5.6	759,203	427,843	331,360	179,388	3,826
Oakland-Hayward-Berkeley, CA Div 36084........	47,028	2,664,586	0.89	31,213	11.1	19,697	7.0	139,530	5.8	431,635	237,212	194,423	102,705	3,685
San Francisco-Redwood City-South San Francisco, CA......	33,050	1,904,597	1.27	17,727	10.7	11,951	7.2	72,373	5.2	269,921	156,008	113,913	71,233	4,343
San Rafael, CA Div 42034............	8,222	260,655	1.00	2,129	8.2	2,004	7.7	10,856	5.4	57,647	34,623	23,024	5,450	2,087
San Jose-Sunnyvale-Santa Clara, CA......	31,264	2,116,113	1.12	23,134	11.6	11,800	5.9	89,834	5.2	271,866	157,435	114,431	48,918	2,457
San Luis Obispo-Paso Robles-Arroyo Grande, CA...............	16,232	281,441	0.99	2,518	8.9	2,375	8.4	15,624	7.3	61,960	52,650	9,310	7,802	2,768
Santa Cruz-Watsonville, CA...........	14,048	263,602	0.91	2,709	9.9	1,961	7.2	16,345	7.4	48,719	45,187	3,532	10,586	3,857
Santa Fe, NM	2,632	152,883	1.06	1,243	8.3	1,158	7.7	14,894	13.3	37,993	25,642	12,351	4,822	3,238
Santa Maria-Santa Barbara, CA......	19,626	463,391	1.07	5,353	12.0	3,234	7.2	38,236	10.5	74,641	62,440	12,201	11,306	2,536
Santa Rosa, CA............................	10,921	488,328	0.94	4,789	9.6	4,403	8.8	30,617	7.6	102,970	56,160	46,810	9,662	1,924
Savannah, GA..............................	15,596	401,018	1.07	5,006	12.9	3,287	8.4	49,205	15.4	62,901	38,480	24,421	13,576	3,524
Scranton--Wilkes-Barre--Hazleton, PA......	20,016	562,475	1.03	5,568	10.0	6,867	12.4	27,699	6.4	131,514	94,686	36,828	NA	NA
Seattle-Tacoma-Bellevue, WA........	66,193	3,918,738	1.03	47,957	12.2	26,668	6.8	212,710	6.4	581,147	357,150	223,997	161,587	4,243
Seattle-Bellevue-Everett, WA Div 42644....	48,754	3,099,257	1.07	36,235	11.9	19,487	6.4	161,413	6.2	433,911	258,694	175,217	123,038	4,170
Tacoma-Lakewood, WA Div 45104....	17,439	819,481	0.86	11,722	13.2	7,181	8.1	51,297	6.9	147,236	98,456	48,780	38,549	4,496
Sebastian-Vero Beach, FL	1,327	156,572	1.04	1,243	7.9	2,088	13.3	17,515	16.9	50,669	36,735	13,934	3,121	2,077
Sebring, FL..................................	1,734	101,683	0.96	906	8.6	1,637	15.5	12,158	18.5	32,497	20,743	11,754	2,994	2,998
Sheboygan, WI.............................	2,794	116,070	1.01	1,212	10.5	1,060	9.2	5,654	6.1	24,086	12,870	11,216	1,829	1,585
Sherman-Denison, TX...................	2,300	128,080	0.95	1,595	11.9	1,434	10.7	20,827	19.5	27,371	19,829	7,542	2,851	2,263
Shreveport-Bossier City, LA...........	10,237	445,199	1.02	5,599	12.8	4,699	10.8	31,834	8.8	84,802	63,877	20,925	19,710	4,451
Sierra Vista-Douglas, AZ................	5,699	122,141	0.95	1,395	11.0	1,294	10.2	9,661	10.5	31,351	21,793	9,558	3,334	2,653
Sioux City, IA-NE-SD.....................	3,163	168,417	0.99	2,343	13.9	1,466	8.7	12,159	8.7	30,821	23,885	6,936	4,995	2,958
Sioux Falls, SD............................	7,023	263,345	1.03	3,849	14.5	1,780	6.7	18,105	8.2	45,162	33,923	11,239	7,433	2,902
South Bend-Mishawaka, IN-MI........	11,950	314,228	0.95	3,933	12.2	3,014	9.3	25,230	9.8	61,222	40,485	20,737	11,248	3,518
Spartanburg, SC...........................	8,757	348,578	1.09	4,002	11.7	3,515	10.3	34,989	12.9	70,914	42,641	28,273	NA	NA
Spokane-Spokane Valley, WA........	14,640	570,158	1.02	6,662	11.6	5,330	9.3	28,267	6.2	118,375	78,591	39,784	29,586	5,341
Springfield, IL..............................	4,170	217,213	1.10	2,261	10.9	2,267	10.9	9,295	5.5	42,668	27,473	15,195	7,967	3,789
Springfield, MA............................	37,453	623,535	0.97	5,871	9.3	5,810	9.2	16,884	3.4	133,609	94,649	38,960	17,844	2,828
Springfield, MO............................	14,501	465,904	1.02	5,663	12.1	4,369	9.4	43,806	11.7	92,232	49,755	42,477	22,250	4,840
Springfield, OH............................	3,716	125,239	0.84	1,534	11.4	1,675	12.4	7,575	7.2	30,399	15,700	14,699	5,899	4,359
State College, PA.........................	19,621	170,283	1.10	1,155	7.1	1,090	6.7	8,127	6.7	23,905	12,430	11,475	1,871	1,159
Staunton-Waynesboro, VA..............	4,107	109,873	0.78	1,335	10.9	1,316	10.7	10,408	11.1	29,154	25,279	3,875	1,905	1,588
Stockton-Lodi, CA.........................	15,023	707,481	0.88	10,202	13.6	5,566	7.4	48,411	7.6	109,324	67,264	42,060	28,634	3,927
Sumter, SC..................................	2,521	104,845	0.96	1,321	12.4	1,070	10.0	11,061	12.8	21,482	16,728	4,754	4,175	3,878
Syracuse, NY	26,422	658,727	1.01	6,957	10.7	5,962	9.2	26,609	5.1	131,659	72,383	59,276	14,650	2,235
Tallahassee, FL............................	22,195	390,531	1.03	4,021	10.4	2,847	7.4	36,020	11.6	62,919	31,653	31,266	17,984	4,727
Tampa-St. Petersburg-Clearwater, FL......	50,469	3,076,354	0.99	32,220	10.3	33,109	10.5	355,908	14.5	654,363	322,622	331,741	80,785	2,675
Terre Haute, IN............................	12,365	164,314	0.98	1,892	11.1	1,870	11.0	11,620	8.9	35,573	28,986	6,587	NA	NA

1. Per 1,000 estimated resident population. 2. Data for serious crimes have not been adjusted for underreporting; this may affect comparability between geographic areas and over time. 3. Per 100,000 population estimated by the FBI.

Table C. Metropolitan Areas — Crime, Education, Money Income, and Poverty

Area name	Serious crimes known to police[2], 2016 (cont.) Rate — Violent	Property	Education — School enrollment and attainment, 2016 — Enrollment[3] — Total	Percent private	Attainment[4] — High school graduate or less	Bachelor's degree or more	Local government expenditures,[5] 2014-2015 — Total current expenditures (mil dol)	Current expenditures per student (dollars)	Income and poverty, 2017 — Per capita income[6] (dollars)	Mean household income[6] (dollars)	Median household income	Percent of households with income less than $50,000	Percent of households with income of $200,000 or more	Percent below poverty level — All persons	Children under 18 years	Age 65 years and older
	46	47	48	49	50	51	52	53	54	55	56	57	58	59	60	61
Reading, PA	274	1,638	100,353	16.6	50.5	23.8	943.2	13,897	30,081	78,953	61,058	40.5	4.1	11.8	17.4	8.8
Redding, CA	746	3,111	40,249	12.3	36.8	23	300.5	11,286	29,559	73,496	52,439	47.6	4.5	17.7	23.3	9.7
Reno, NV	515	2,593	112,850	11.5	35.2	31	590.8	8,922	34,104	84,079	61,360	39.0	6.0	10.8	12.9	8.4
Richmond, VA	NA	NA	309,100	14.1	35.6	36.8	1,951.5	9,947	34,720	89,615	67,633	36.7	7.3	11.2	15.4	6.3
Riverside-San Bernardino-Ontario, CA	397	2,667	1,301,605	11.3	45.7	21.4	8,287.6	9,908	25,528	81,378	61,994	40.4	5.7	14.4	19.3	11.4
Roanoke, VA	243	2,264	67,999	19.9	40.2	27.6	473.8	10,552	31,272	72,559	54,233	46.0	4.7	13.5	18.9	7.8
Rochester, MN	138	1,460	55,167	13.2	30.8	39.2	368.7	10,698	36,513	92,058	71,985	31.3	6.6	8.3	10.4	5.5
Rochester, NY	281	1,996	260,922	23.7	36.0	34.1	2,870.3	18,165	31,311	75,771	56,969	44.5	4.8	13.9	21.3	7.8
Rockford, IL	871	2,596	82,062	15.0	45.0	21.8	719.6	12,923	28,732	71,888	55,484	43.5	3.4	13.1	19.5	5.8
Rocky Mount, NC	448	D	33,564	9.5	52.3	19.2	213.5	8,628	23,320	56,313	42,784	57.2	2.2	18.6	26.6	10.7
Rome, GA	321	2,868	23,309	15.2	54.3	18.9	167.0	10,157	24,446	62,691	45,854	53.3	3.1	19.8	30.3	5.1
Sacramento--Roseville--Arden-Arcade, CA	411	2,391	614,488	11.1	32.8	32.7	3,588.6	9,944	33,548	90,806	67,902	36.9	7.9	13.1	15.4	9.3
Saginaw, MI	609	1,743	46,176	12.3	42.3	20.4	303.0	10,773	26,263	62,214	45,331	54.6	2.7	17.4	23.2	6.2
St. Cloud, MN	199	2,376	53,938	17.1	35.8	29	324.1	10,646	30,647	77,934	61,943	41.2	3.9	11.1	13.3	8.4
St. George, UT	169	1,726	44,178	10.4	32.8	26.9	199.9	6,398	27,580	78,203	54,842	43.9	4.1	12.0	15.1	7.4
St. Joseph, MO-KS	420	4,061	29,335	8.5	51.4	18.8	173.2	9,463	24,264	62,943	47,309	51.9	2.3	14.0	19.8	7.2
St. Louis, MO-IL	D	2,490	681,512	24.8	34.2	34.6	4,736.8	11,504	33,987	82,841	61,571	40.7	5.9	11.6	16.0	7.3
Salem, OR	229	2,869	106,256	13.1	42.5	24.5	707.8	10,423	26,268	72,806	56,163	43.9	3.3	16.1	22.2	9.1
Salinas, CA	419	2,393	125,848	11.5	50.0	24.8	822.9	10,838	27,997	92,289	71,274	33.5	7.0	11.4	15.9	7.6
Salisbury, MD-DE	405	2,704	89,003	12.3	43.2	27.8	755.3	13,872	32,184	80,287	59,273	42.6	5.4	12.6	19.8	6.1
Salt Lake City, UT	411	4,599	350,866	12.9	31.3	35.5	1,511.8	6,672	31,039	90,790	71,510	32.4	6.7	8.9	10.6	6.9
San Angelo, TX	334	4,539	29,934	7.4	43.0	23.2	181.2	8,811	27,482	71,577	50,894	49.1	3.8	11.3	15.0	8.6
San Antonio-New Braunfels, TX	526	4,082	665,684	12.0	40.9	28.1	3,936.0	8,878	27,280	77,001	56,774	44.1	5.2	14.5	21.2	10.4
San Diego-Carlsbad, CA	330	1,850	877,730	14.8	31.0	38.8	4,990.5	9,905	36,697	103,215	76,207	32.8	10.9	11.8	15.7	8.6
San Francisco-Oakland-Hayward, CA	478	3,348	1,113,725	19.4	26.5	49.3	6,243.0	10,631	52,261	140,720	101,714	25.7	21.4	8.8	10.2	8.4
Oakland-Hayward-Berkeley, CA Div 36084	503	3,182	714,202	15.8	29.2	44.7	3,932.8	9,838	45,265	127,173	95,902	26.7	17.9	9.2	10.9	8.0
San Francisco-Redwood City-South San Francisco, CA	482	3,861	340,398	26.2	23.8	55.1	1,883.7	12,209	61,517	156,745	112,832	24.6	25.9	8.2	8.8	9.6
San Rafael, CA Div 42034	182	1,905	59,125	23.0	16.3	58.6	426.5	12,843	68,879	170,204	113,908	23.1	26.7	8.2	10.2	6.0
San Jose-Sunnyvale-Santa Clara, CA	280	2,177	522,342	21.5	26.7	50.8	3,058.0	10,643	51,857	153,684	117,474	21.8	25.7	7.3	7.9	7.5
San Luis Obispo-Paso Robles-Arroyo Grande, CA	396	2,373	77,950	8.7	28.6	34.6	359.7	10,343	35,982	92,729	71,880	35.3	8.3	12.1	12.3	5.1
Santa Cruz-Watsonville, CA	401	3,455	84,565	15.9	30.3	40.2	444.5	10,820	39,580	111,228	79,705	31.7	15.6	12.7	12.7	7.9
Santa Fe, NM	373	2,865	29,667	11.2	33.0	40.3	185.9	9,847	35,719	82,225	58,821	42.9	6.5	11.8	18.2	8.3
Santa Maria-Santa Barbara, CA	342	2,193	136,935	8.7	36.2	35.2	726.3	10,591	35,090	101,807	71,106	34.8	10.6	14.5	18.8	8.5
Santa Rosa, CA	372	1,552	117,540	9.8	29.9	35.8	771.7	10,855	40,392	103,489	80,409	30.7	10.3	9.2	10.8	6.3
Savannah, GA	417	3,107	105,453	19.4	38.2	30.4	530.5	9,104	29,463	77,354	56,610	43.9	4.5	14.5	20.8	8.4
Scranton--Wilkes-Barre--Hazleton, PA	NA	NA	120,670	25.6	48.2	25.6	1,006.5	13,232	28,061	67,798	50,891	49.1	3.1	14.0	24.6	7.5
Seattle-Tacoma-Bellevue, WA	353	3,890	891,228	16.9	27.2	41.9	5,631.5	10,808	43,203	109,619	82,133	28.6	12.0	9.0	11.0	8.0
Seattle-Bellevue-Everett, WA Div 42644	313	3,856	685,666	17.5	24.6	46.4	4,251.7	10,874	46,330	116,322	87,187	26.7	13.8	8.7	10.9	8.3
Tacoma-Lakewood, WA Div 45104	490	4,006	205,562	15.0	36.8	26	1,379.8	10,609	32,540	85,228	69,278	35.5	5.5	10.0	11.4	7.0
Sebastian-Vero Beach, FL	230	1,848	29,116	15.5	42.1	30.4	156.1	8,636	34,232	82,567	49,177	50.8	6.6	8.7	8.5	7.8
Sebring, FL	328	2,671	17,513	7.1	53.7	17.8	111.1	9,058	21,795	50,430	35,543	64.1	1.4	20.2	37.6	7.4
Sheboygan, WI	155	1,430	27,193	16.2	41.7	25.2	208.8	10,831	30,536	73,466	58,361	42.5	2.9	7.2	6.6	6.1
Sherman-Denison, TX	273	1,990	32,478	12.9	41.0	19.9	195.3	8,935	27,795	71,992	56,718	45.1	3.5	13.7	20.0	8.9
Shreveport-Bossier City, LA	651	3,801	103,293	12.4	46.4	22.1	828.6	11,064	23,934	58,180	38,627	59.3	3.2	23.9	37.2	10.3
Sierra Vista-Douglas, AZ	341	2,313	27,248	10.5	33.0	24.7	157.7	8,117	27,157	65,303	51,816	48.8	3.2	14.1	19.4	8.5
Sioux City, IA-NE-SD	300	2,658	42,638	15.8	46.1	22.1	355.5	11,461	29,089	74,337	57,207	42.8	3.3	12.2	17.4	7.1
Sioux Falls, SD	388	2,514	62,830	18.7	33.3	32.2	339.8	8,195	32,550	80,800	64,882	38.6	4.8	6.8	6.8	3.1
South Bend-Mishawaka, IN-MI	463	3,055	85,226	32.9	42.3	27.9	453.1	9,903	27,592	70,720	51,880	47.7	3.8	15.0	20.1	8.8
Spartanburg, SC	NA	NA	81,485	14.1	42.6	24.1	515.1	9,966	26,000	66,737	50,074	49.9	3.1	13.7	19.9	10.5
Spokane-Spokane Valley, WA	336	5,006	136,291	19.2	30.6	29.7	880.9	10,684	30,125	74,322	53,321	46.7	4.2	14.0	17.1	6.8
Springfield, IL	740	3,049	49,120	14.1	35.3	32.2	392.6	12,175	34,286	80,267	61,573	40.6	5.7	16.2	25.6	6.3
Springfield, MA	538	2,290	175,542	17.5	41.2	32	1,407.9	15,381	30,442	77,195	55,379	45.5	5.5	15.5	22.6	11.2
Springfield, MO	604	4,236	119,888	17.9	39.6	28.4	582.0	8,562	26,237	64,627	48,151	51.7	3.2	15.1	19.4	7.3
Springfield, OH	348	4,011	31,205	21.7	50.6	20.1	218.4	10,476	26,111	62,706	46,665	52.1	1.9	15.3	20.8	6.7
State College, PA	94	1,065	59,875	7.3	34.4	45.5	197.0	15,018	29,433	75,792	55,895	45.6	5.5	18.3	12.3	5.8
Staunton-Waynesboro, VA	133	1,456	23,794	17.2	50.5	23.9	169.6	10,226	28,938	71,344	54,249	46.9	3.9	11.9	14.2	8.0
Stockton-Lodi, CA	824	3,104	207,721	12.0	48.9	18.9	1,377.5	9,803	26,529	82,227	61,164	41.2	6.2	15.5	22.5	10.1
Sumter, SC	591	3,287	26,616	25.0	48.2	19.6	158.0	9,339	22,963	58,254	45,585	54.1	2.7	18.8	29.7	10.1
Syracuse, NY	276	1,958	164,064	21.8	38.5	31.8	1,813.9	17,718	30,929	75,799	56,780	43.7	4.4	14.0	20.7	8.2
Tallahassee, FL	632	4,095	126,474	15.4	30.9	39.4	404.2	8,327	27,732	71,247	50,825	49.0	4.7	18.2	19.8	4.5
Tampa-St. Petersburg-Clearwater, FL	341	2,334	694,320	17.3	39.9	30	3,617.0	8,983	30,738	74,499	52,212	47.5	5.1	13.9	19.4	10.1
Terre Haute, IN	NA	NA	42,629	12.2	49.4	19.3	240.8	9,543	24,946	60,268	43,843	55.0	2.2	16.1	20.6	6.6

1. Data for serious crimes have not been adjusted for underreporting; this may affect comparability between geographic areas and over time.   2. Per 100,000 population estimated by the FBI.   3. All persons 3 years old and over enrolled in nursery school through college.   4. Persons 25 years old and over.   5. Elementary and secondary education expenditures.   6. Based on population estimated by the American Community Survey, 2015.

Table C. Metropolitan Areas — **Personal Income and Earnings**

	Personal income, 2017										Earnings, 2017		
			Per capita[1]			Supplements to wages and salaries, employer contributions (mil dol)						Contributrions for government social insurance (mil dol)	
Area name	Total (mil dol)	Percent change, 2016-2017	Dollars	Rank	Wages and Salaries (mil dol)	Pension and insurance	Government social insurance	Proprietors' income	Dividends, interest, and rent (mil dol)	Personal transfer receipts (mil dol)	Total (mil dol)	From employee and self-employed	From employer
	62	63	64	65	66	67	68	69	70	71	72	73	74
Reading, PA	19,765	4.2	47,302	123	8,888	1,710	724	1,462	3,185	4,007	12,785	765	724
Redding, CA	8,041	3.8	44,691	171	3,048	669	222	670	1,560	2,348	4,609	295	222
Reno, NV	25,766	8.5	55,460	42	11,566	1,994	856	1,931	7,465	3,608	16,348	925	856
Richmond, VA	70,660	4.9	54,597	50	37,437	5,843	2,666	6,774	13,603	10,390	52,720	3,144	2,666
Riverside-San Bernardino-Ontario, CA	178,883	4.9	39,052	302	72,251	15,126	5,230	13,576	29,021	34,753	106,183	6,142	5,230
Roanoke, VA	14,113	2.6	44,928	163	7,338	1,226	546	879	2,882	3,056	9,990	648	546
Rochester, MN	11,101	3.7	50,856	79	6,796	981	496	568	1,909	1,692	8,840	541	496
Rochester, NY	52,968	4.6	49,138	97	25,948	5,106	2,134	4,047	8,702	11,507	37,235	2,102	2,134
Rockford, IL	14,273	3.2	42,192	230	7,376	1,388	526	588	2,235	2,955	9,879	572	526
Rocky Mount, NC	5,569	3.1	37,949	328	2,383	425	179	244	1,002	1,630	3,231	221	179
Rome, GA	3,632	4.0	37,204	341	1,803	320	126	296	614	966	2,544	158	126
Sacramento--Roseville--Arden-Arcade, CA	125,039	4.2	53,783	58	60,884	13,437	3,995	10,374	23,411	21,054	88,689	4,697	3,995
Saginaw, MI	7,311	3.6	38,090	322	3,939	713	299	348	1,098	2,187	5,299	351	299
St. Cloud, MN	8,681	3.7	43,894	187	4,995	849	387	622	1,462	1,624	6,854	409	387
St. George, UT	5,825	5.8	35,161	369	2,450	418	196	415	1,444	1,293	3,480	237	196
St. Joseph, MO-KS	4,741	3.0	37,350	338	2,629	442	189	269	762	1,137	3,529	219	189
St. Louis, MO-IL	147,100	3.5	52,398	68	76,911	11,281	5,425	10,190	30,924	24,472	103,807	6,250	5,425
Salem, OR	17,369	5.5	40,869	263	8,016	1,711	724	1,538	3,089	4,140	11,989	736	724
Salinas, CA	23,820	4.3	54,395	53	9,972	2,060	779	3,763	5,637	3,271	16,574	796	779
Salisbury, MD-DE	18,692	3.3	46,056	142	6,793	1,284	519	1,977	3,806	4,806	10,572	663	519
Salt Lake City, UT	58,525	4.6	48,645	106	39,236	6,196	2,994	5,345	12,249	6,895	53,771	3,143	2,994
San Angelo, TX	5,122	1.8	42,847	214	2,257	409	165	388	1,190	1,066	3,220	179	165
San Antonio-New Braunfels, TX	110,855	4.4	44,880	166	54,043	8,596	3,868	11,707	20,411	19,383	78,215	4,245	3,868
San Diego-Carlsbad, CA	193,296	3.8	57,913	32	99,206	17,984	7,132	15,797	43,916	26,513	140,119	7,693	7,132
San Francisco-Oakland-Hayward, CA	432,360	6.5	91,459	3	231,154	30,099	13,659	46,916	102,750	37,242	321,828	17,674	13,659
Oakland-Hayward-Berkeley, CA Div 36084	206,365	6.6	73,423	X	88,796	14,023	5,950	18,129	41,364	22,629	126,897	7,024	5,950
San Francisco-Redwood City-South San Francisco, CA	193,493	6.4	116,859	X	133,818	14,752	7,157	24,305	50,551	12,432	180,033	9,835	7,157
San Rafael, CA Div 42034	32,503	5.7	124,552	X	8,540	1,324	552	4,482	10,835	2,181	14,898	815	552
San Jose-Sunnyvale-Santa Clara, CA	193,098	6.7	96,623	2	144,846	13,421	7,300	13,391	40,097	13,466	178,958	10,118	7,300
San Luis Obispo-Paso Robles-Arroyo Grande, CA	15,680	5.2	55,328	43	5,855	1,301	404	2,068	4,082	2,276	9,627	535	404
Santa Cruz-Watsonville, CA	17,665	5.4	64,028	16	5,595	1,109	403	2,284	4,115	2,150	9,391	497	403
Santa Fe, NM	8,264	2.8	55,553	41	2,904	499	214	572	2,764	1,361	4,189	288	214
Santa Maria-Santa Barbara, CA	26,647	4.7	59,460	25	11,404	2,189	817	3,468	8,081	3,290	17,877	942	817
Santa Rosa, CA	30,398	5.4	60,286	19	11,673	2,083	841	3,970	7,288	4,307	18,568	1,054	841
Savannah, GA	17,131	3.5	44,204	176	8,780	1,518	627	963	3,288	3,082	11,889	689	627
Scranton--Wilkes-Barre--Hazleton, PA	24,416	3.1	43,959	184	11,375	2,226	956	1,502	4,129	6,066	16,060	1,012	956
Seattle-Tacoma-Bellevue, WA	267,654	6.7	69,214	12	152,159	18,559	12,133	23,205	61,812	28,148	206,056	11,841	12,133
Seattle-Bellevue-Everett, WA Div 42644	224,505	6.7	75,078	X	134,029	15,377	10,438	19,889	54,173	20,552	179,733	10,327	10,438
Tacoma-Lakewood, WA Div 45104	43,149	6.5	49,214	X	18,130	3,182	1,695	3,316	7,639	7,595	26,323	1,514	1,695
Sebastian-Vero Beach, FL	11,312	5.0	73,274	7	2,414	325	165	578	5,343	1,844	3,481	264	165
Sebring, FL	3,441	3.5	33,446	377	1,070	179	77	140	767	1,325	1,466	124	77
Sheboygan, WI	5,777	4.8	50,081	84	3,096	544	230	570	1,051	910	4,441	273	230
Sherman-Denison, TX	5,410	4.5	41,250	252	2,086	330	149	294	904	1,334	2,860	177	149
Shreveport-Bossier City, LA	18,811	-0.1	42,662	217	8,459	1,656	575	1,251	3,644	4,637	11,940	672	575
Sierra Vista-Douglas, AZ	4,902	3.7	39,294	298	1,883	428	154	291	982	1,564	2,757	177	154
Sioux City, IA-NE-SD	8,087	-1.0	47,962	111	3,923	667	302	897	1,552	1,313	5,789	347	302
Sioux Falls, SD	14,496	1.8	55,947	37	7,503	1,070	540	2,081	3,021	1,669	11,193	655	540
South Bend-Mishawaka, IN-MI	14,701	5.8	45,681	153	6,393	1,067	476	1,376	2,459	2,828	9,311	569	476
Spartanburg, SC	13,676	4.3	40,898	262	7,341	1,167	549	830	2,672	3,065	9,887	643	549
Spokane-Spokane Valley, WA	24,453	5.1	43,338	200	11,901	1,948	1,091	1,587	4,888	5,574	16,527	1,023	1,091
Springfield, IL	9,635	1.9	46,165	140	5,170	1,071	345	471	2,023	1,775	7,057	381	345
Springfield, MA	31,357	2.8	49,643	91	13,929	2,871	956	2,036	4,711	7,845	19,791	1,059	956
Springfield, MO	18,018	4.0	38,968	303	9,045	1,445	647	1,590	3,066	3,935	12,727	805	647
Springfield, OH	5,287	3.2	39,289	299	2,120	392	160	232	816	1,474	2,905	186	160
State College, PA	7,182	4.9	44,152	177	3,888	1,437	295	529	1,423	1,078	6,149	313	295
Staunton-Waynesboro, VA	5,177	4.4	42,436	223	2,130	386	155	331	1,007	1,121	3,002	201	155
Stockton-Lodi, CA	31,920	6.0	42,822	215	12,327	2,598	912	2,594	5,109	6,970	18,431	1,029	912
Sumter, SC	3,941	3.0	36,887	348	1,927	400	159	188	671	1,113	2,674	164	159
Syracuse, NY	30,973	4.1	47,298	124	15,308	3,299	1,253	2,248	4,867	6,833	22,108	1,235	1,253
Tallahassee, FL	15,685	4.6	40,994	259	8,137	1,486	552	875	3,235	2,874	11,050	663	552
Tampa-St. Petersburg-Clearwater, FL	139,319	4.2	45,067	160	70,444	9,737	4,767	6,563	27,786	29,995	91,512	5,957	4,767
Terre Haute, IN	6,250	3.7	36,769	352	2,899	557	217	329	1,035	1,747	4,001	259	217

1. Based on the resident population estimated as of July 1 of the year shown.

Table C. Metropolitan Areas — Earnings, Social Security, and Housing

Area name	Earnings, 2017 (cont.) Percent by selected industries Farm	Mining, quarrying, and extracting	Construc-tion	Manufac-turing	Informa-tion; pro-fessional, scientific, and technical servievs	Retail trade	Finance, insur-ance, real estate, rental and leasing	Health care and social assistance	Govern-ment	Social Security beneficiaries, December 2017 Number	Rate[1]	Supple-mental Security Income Recipi-ents, December 2017	Housing units, 2018 Total	Percent change, 2010-2018
	75	76	77	78	79	80	81	82	83	84	85	86	87	88
Reading, PA...............................	0.5	0.1	6.9	19.1	7.3	5.9	5.2	14.2	13.0	87,295	209	10,821	167,366	1.5
Redding, CA...............................	1.3	0.2	6.9	3.8	6.7	9.5	5.6	19.2	23.0	49,275	274	9,858	79,194	2.4
Reno, NV....................................	0.1	D	11.4	8.0	D	D	D	D	15.7	86,725	187	7,204	203,135	8.7
Richmond, VA............................	0.0	0.1	5.6	5.3	11.6	4.9	D	11.7	18.1	239,935	185	27,888	534,800	5.4
Riverside-San Bernardino-Ontario, CA	0.7	0.2	8.7	7.0	5.1	7.9	4.4	11.7	23.5	671,110	147	133,940	1,574,493	4.9
Roanoke, VA..............................	-0.1	D	D	11.0	D	6.3	7.4	17.0	15.0	76,650	244	8,446	146,755	1.2
Rochester, MN...........................	-0.8	0.1	5.5	10.8	4.0	5.0	3.5	48.3	9.8	40,310	185	2,795	95,296	8.1
Rochester, NY............................	0.5	0.8	5.6	12.7	11.0	5.5	5.9	13.7	16.6	240,765	223	32,415	482,293	2.9
Rockford, IL...............................	0.0	D	5.2	26.8	4.7	5.7	5.7	15.8	13.0	71,720	212	8,164	145,812	-0.1
Rocky Mount, NC.......................	1.2	0.1	6.2	21.1	D	8.0	D	D	18.5	35,810	244	6,409	68,171	1.6
Rome, GA..................................	0.7	D	2.7	18.0	5.5	6.9	4.4	25.3	14.0	22,280	228	3,335	40,636	0.2
Sacramento--Roseville--Arden-Arcade, CA	0.6	0.1	7.2	3.7	10.4	5.6	7.7	11.9	31.3	395,625	170	80,876	911,208	4.5
Saginaw, MI...............................	-0.6	0.1	4.5	19.8	5.8	7.4	6.2	19.4	14.3	49,570	258	8,422	87,817	1.1
St. Cloud, MN............................	1.2	0.2	10.5	14.1	D	7.4	6.7	17.5	14.1	34,785	176	2,818	82,530	5.7
St. George, UT...........................	0.0	0.2	10.7	5.4	7.5	9.8	8.7	17.4	13.6	36,865	223	1,430	71,363	23.6
St. Joseph, MO-KS.....................	0.9	D	6.6	23.9	D	6.3	6.3	14.3	15.4	26,215	207	2,827	54,067	0.8
St. Louis, MO-IL........................	0.1	D	D	10.3	D	5.4	10.1	12.9	12.4	558,800	199	58,432	1,262,828	3.1
Salem, OR.................................	2.7	D	7.7	6.4	4.7	6.3	6.4	14.6	30.6	84,060	198	9,160	159,845	5.7
Salinas, CA...............................	12.6	0.4	4.4	2.5	5.1	5.2	4.8	7.7	23.6	62,705	143	8,493	142,399	2.4
Salisbury, MD-DE.......................	4.2	D	8.8	D	D	8.7	6.6	15.2	16.0	109,510	270	7,802	251,593	8.9
Salt Lake City, UT.......................	0.0	0.3	7.2	8.5	D	7.3	12.4	7.7	14.7	148,090	123	14,455	426,128	11.1
San Angelo, TX..........................	1.0	5.3	D	D	D	D	D	15.1	24.6	22,680	190	2,926	49,482	4.3
San Antonio-New Braunfels, TX......	0.0	D	7.7	4.5	9.3	6.3	11.7	11.0	20.9	398,500	161	60,691	904,717	8.0
San Diego-Carlsbad, CA...............	0.5	0.0	5.4	8.6	17.3	5.0	7.9	8.7	23.6	496,190	149	83,185	1,224,375	5.1
San Francisco-Oakland-Hayward, CA	0.1	D	5.1	6.3	28.6	4.3	11.9	7.8	11.9	687,075	145	131,951	1,825,087	4.8
Oakland-Hayward-Berkeley, CA Div 36084	0.1	0.0	7.3	9.8	18.6	5.2	8.0	11.4	14.5	397,925	142	75,913	1,030,996	4.9
San Francisco-Redwood City-South San Francisco, CA	0.0	0.0	3.5	3.9	36.3	3.6	14.7	5.1	10.0	237,315	143	52,667	680,909	5.1
San Rafael, CA Div 42034	0.3	D	7.1	5.6	20.0	6.2	11.7	10.6	12.0	51,835	199	3,371	113,182	1.8
San Jose-Sunnyvale-Santa Clara, CA	0.2	0.0	3.7	22.2	D	3.3	5.0	6.2	6.2	242,470	121	46,092	697,934	7.4
San Luis Obispo-Paso Robles-Arroyo Grande, CA	4.1	0.1	9.8	5.6	9.5	8.1	5.8	10.4	20.9	59,855	211	4,532	122,979	4.8
Santa Cruz-Watsonville, CA...........	6.0	0.0	7.7	6.7	9.0	7.7	6.3	13.1	18.7	46,545	169	5,719	106,728	2.2
Santa Fe, NM.............................	-0.1	0.8	5.1	1.2	12.5	8.5	6.8	14.2	27.0	37,345	251	2,669	73,456	3.0
Santa Maria-Santa Barbara, CA......	5.4	1.0	4.9	7.4	13.7	5.6	7.4	11.0	19.9	72,830	163	8,807	158,333	3.6
Santa Rosa, CA..........................	2.9	0.1	9.6	12.0	9.6	7.2	7.0	13.3	13.9	99,625	198	9,121	205,225	0.3
Savannah, GA............................	0.1	0.0	4.9	15.8	5.6	6.6	5.8	D	18.5	66,995	173	8,454	163,944	8.5
Scranton--Wilkes-Barre--Hazleton, PA	0.1	0.4	5.7	11.7	D	6.9	6.3	D	14.5	140,295	253	17,517	264,545	2.2
Seattle-Tacoma-Bellevue, WA........	0.1	0.1	6.6	9.6	22.1	9.0	6.5	9.4	14.0	565,835	146	69,241	1,617,435	10.5
Seattle-Bellevue-Everett, WA Div 42644	0.1	0.1	6.3	10.3	24.6	9.3	6.6	8.4	11.6	414,230	139	49,482	1,266,387	11.3
Tacoma-Lakewood, WA Div 45104	0.2	0.1	8.3	5.2	4.7	7.2	5.8	16.1	30.3	151,605	173	19,759	351,048	7.9
Sebastian-Vero Beach, FL..............	0.7	D	7.3	4.1	12.6	9.3	9.4	17.4	10.3	51,485	333	2,548	81,043	6.2
Sebring, FL................................	5.4	0.0	4.4	2.7	3.8	10.7	3.9	23.4	16.9	34,400	334	2,870	55,759	0.7
Sheboygan, WI...........................	1.1	D	5.3	41.8	3.0	5.1	6.7	11.4	8.9	25,865	224	1,768	51,340	1.1
Sherman-Denison, TX..................	0.4	0.8	9.7	14.5	4.3	7.8	8.5	18.2	14.2	28,295	216	3,024	56,731	5.6
Shreveport-Bossier City, LA	0.0	4.2	D	D	D	7.9	5.4	17.8	22.9	89,200	202	20,370	204,121	5.8
Sierra Vista-Douglas, AZ..............	3.5	0.2	3.6	1.2	8.5	6.2	3.4	9.0	47.5	32,540	261	3,122	61,328	3.9
Sioux City, IA-NE-SD...................	3.8	D	7.4	D	D	6.2	6.4	D	12.2	32,595	193	2,572	71,199	3.7
Sioux Falls, SD..........................	1.1	D	6.9	8.7	7.5	7.3	D	D	8.7	45,115	174	3,401	111,732	16.6
South Bend-Mishawaka, IN-MI.......	-0.1	D	5.8	15.8	9.9	6.0	5.3	D	9.8	65,335	203	6,835	143,520	2.0
Spartanburg, SC.........................	0.1	D	6.8	25.5	D	6.1	5.0	D	16.4	76,870	230	8,245	145,546	6.4
Spokane-Spokane Valley, WA........	0.2	D	6.7	7.2	7.2	7.6	8.5	D	20.3	120,960	214	16,293	250,034	8.5
Springfield, IL............................	0.3	D	4.5	2.9	D	5.9	8.5	D	25.1	45,290	217	4,694	97,681	2.2
Springfield, MA..........................	0.0	D	6.1	8.5	5.9	D	7.6	18.9	21.9	133,370	211	33,820	257,927	1.2
Springfield, MO..........................	-0.1	D	D	9.1	9.8	7.4	6.1	17.1	13.8	97,200	210	9,828	205,482	6.8
Springfield, OH..........................	-0.2	0.6	4.3	16.4	3.1	6.5	8.6	15.8	15.7	31,160	232	4,008	61,289	-0.2
State College, PA........................	0.3	0.3	4.6	4.8	7.9	4.4	4.4	10.1	50.3	24,640	151	1,435	67,144	6.1
Staunton-Waynesboro, VA	1.3	D	D	17.9	3.7	6.5	4.3	D	17.6	30,990	254	2,184	54,592	3.7
Stockton-Lodi, CA.......................	4.1	0.1	6.0	7.5	3.8	6.8	4.8	11.9	21.6	111,295	149	28,681	245,541	5.0
Sumter, SC................................	0.4	0.0	7.3	16.4	3.6	5.8	3.0	12.5	33.7	23,890	224	4,197	48,284	4.9
Syracuse, NY	0.2	D	5.1	9.9	D	6.0	7.1	D	20.6	140,530	215	18,837	296,351	3.0
Tallahassee, FL..........................	0.6	D	4.5	2.1	D	5.7	6.2	D	35.3	66,175	173	10,119	172,340	5.7
Tampa-St. Petersburg-Clearwater, FL	0.2	0.0	5.9	5.8	D	7.8	12.0	13.6	12.8	684,490	221	79,291	1,435,316	6.1
Terre Haute, IN...........................	0.4	2.9	7.3	18.6	3.7	7.1	D	15.2	17.9	38,755	228	4,492	75,763	2.2

1. Per 1,000 resident population estimated as of July 1 of the year shown.

Table C. Metropolitan Areas — Housing, Labor Force, and Employment

	Housing units, 2017								Civilian labor force, 2018				Civilian employment[5], 2017		
	Occupied units										Unemployment		Percent		
		Owner-occupied				Renter-occupied									
Area name	Total	Percent	Median value[1]	With a mortgage	Without a mortgage[2]	Median rent[3]	Median rent as a percent of income	Internet access	Total	Percent change 2017-2018	Total	Rate[4]	Total	Management, business, science, and arts	Construction, production, and maintenance occupations
	89	90	91	92	93	94	95	96	97	98	99	100	101	102	103
Reading, PA..........................	155,154	72.3	173,700	21.7	13.7	864	29.7	85.7	212,528	0.0	8,842	4.2	203,508	32.7	27.1
Redding, CA............................	71,968	64.5	248,900	23.4	12.8	984	35.4	86.8	74,215	0.2	3,669	4.9	76,203	32.8	20.7
Reno, NV...............................	182,846	58.4	329,200	22.0	10.0	974	28.1	86.7	252,010	4.8	9,153	3.6	237,150	32.5	22.1
Richmond, VA..........................	481,559	66.2	237,900	20.1	10.0	1,060	29.4	87.5	675,649	0.5	21,329	3.2	651,053	41.5	18.1
Riverside-San Bernardino-Ontario, CA................	1,344,956	63.0	342,300	25.5	12.4	1,268	34.4	90.5	2,053,401	1.8	86,587	4.2	1,942,095	29.8	26.1
Roanoke, VA...........................	130,863	68.8	185,400	20.1	10.0	789	28.7	82.3	156,379	-0.2	4,639	3.0	149,297	37.5	20.0
Rochester, MN.........................	85,994	74.7	212,200	19.1	10.0	902	27.3	90.4	123,420	1.2	3,079	2.5	115,087	46.9	18.1
Rochester, NY.........................	433,400	66.6	144,500	19.8	12.3	870	32.0	86.9	522,110	0.5	22,104	4.2	530,551	40.7	18.7
Rockford, IL...........................	132,479	69.0	121,500	19.4	11.8	775	29.4	87.9	167,669	1.3	9,618	5.7	158,461	30.4	28.2
Rocky Mount, NC	57,083	60.3	115,800	19.6	14.7	742	28.2	73.2	65,029	-0.9	3,661	5.6	64,188	28.4	28.0
Rome, GA..............................	36,927	62.7	135,000	19.6	10.0	750	30.4	82.8	44,274	0.1	1,906	4.3	42,226	28.0	29.9
Sacramento--Roseville--Arden-Arcade, CA..................	829,772	60.2	390,000	23.9	11.8	1,246	32.4	91.2	1,095,762	1.8	40,617	3.7	1,068,785	40.6	17.2
Saginaw, MI............................	80,958	70.8	104,300	19.7	11.6	740	32.0	82.8	86,849	-0.9	4,152	4.8	81,985	29.5	26.2
St. Cloud, MN.........................	76,342	70.1	179,300	19.3	10.9	768	28.5	89.1	111,550	-0.2	3,400	3.0	108,679	33.9	26.3
St. George, UT........................	56,139	68.9	279,800	24.3	10.0	984	30.8	89.7	73,929	4.5	2,517	3.4	69,929	31.4	23.1
St. Joseph, MO-KS....................	47,135	65.2	122,000	18.3	11.0	733	26.4	75.0	63,265	-1.2	1,877	3.0	56,765	29.2	28.9
St. Louis, MO-IL......................	1,119,347	68.9	172,200	19.1	11.1	868	29.4	87.6	1,459,246	-0.1	49,950	3.4	1,399,000	40.2	19.2
Salem, OR.............................	144,978	61.5	241,700	22.4	11.3	967	29.3	90.1	201,371	0.9	8,696	4.3	188,632	30.8	26.1
Salinas, CA............................	125,518	51.3	517,000	26.1	10.2	1,467	32.9	89.3	224,057	1.9	14,047	6.3	191,091	28.5	32.0
Salisbury, MD-DE	154,115	74.8	244,800	22.0	10.7	948	29.4	85.3	191,345	1.3	9,321	4.9	183,030	35.7	21.6
Salt Lake City, UT....................	396,869	68.0	294,800	21.1	10.0	1,068	27.5	93.1	653,521	1.0	19,912	3.0	626,754	40.5	20.5
San Angelo, TX........................	42,667	64.7	138,600	20.8	11.4	822	29.2	82.4	55,730	1.4	1,762	3.2	55,530	33.9	21.3
San Antonio-New Braunfels, TX...	810,473	63.3	170,100	21.1	10.7	959	30.4	85.3	1,189,665	1.7	39,332	3.3	1,134,679	35.7	20.5
San Diego-Carlsbad, CA..............	1,126,419	53.5	563,800	25.4	11.0	1,598	33.4	92.8	1,592,193	1.1	52,663	3.3	1,611,175	41.9	15.9
San Francisco-Oakland-Hayward, CA.............	1,694,362	54.6	849,500	24.3	10.4	1,853	28.6	92.1	2,584,338	1.3	70,153	2.7	2,510,338	49.6	13.5
Oakland-Hayward-Berkeley, CA Div 36084	965,635	59.2	716,500	24.4	10.6	1,752	30.5	92.6	1,412,785	1.0	43,238	3.1	1,429,732	46.6	15.9
San Francisco-Redwood City-South San Francisco, CA...	624,508	46.1	1,095,800	24.1	10.0	2,003	25.8	91.3	1,030,442	2.0	23,552	2.3	952,751	53.4	10.5
San Rafael, CA Div 42034..........	104,219	63.6	1,014,000	24.3	12.0	2,094	33.0	93.5	141,111	0.8	3,363	2.4	127,855	55.4	9.3
San Jose-Sunnyvale-Santa Clara, CA................	651,006	57.2	957,700	24.2	10.2	2,213	28.7	94.3	1,079,673	0.8	28,843	2.7	1,042,417	52.7	14.4
San Luis Obispo-Paso Robles-Arroyo Grande, CA........	104,544	60.4	574,400	26.1	10.5	1,403	31.6	91.2	140,920	0.2	4,151	2.9	131,832	38.9	18.2
Santa Cruz-Watsonville, CA.........	95,940	62.2	775,000	25.9	12.2	1,680	35.6	90.0	142,618	-0.2	6,984	4.9	137,657	43.1	19.4
Santa Fe, NM..........................	60,904	71.0	292,600	22.7	10.0	976	29.7	83.3	73,974	0.9	3,065	4.1	69,080	43.9	11.7
Santa Maria-Santa Barbara, CA...	147,466	51.1	567,600	24.8	10.7	1,587	32.7	91.3	216,698	0.6	8,437	3.9	219,313	35.6	20.6
Santa Rosa, CA........................	188,829	61.3	628,400	25.9	12.0	1,607	33.1	92.1	262,348	0.7	7,187	2.7	259,305	38.4	19.6
Savannah, GA..........................	142,195	59.8	185,000	20.4	10.3	1,031	29.9	89.6	188,764	1.5	6,849	3.6	183,237	36.4	21.7
Scranton--Wilkes-Barre--Hazleton, PA...............	223,630	65.8	140,200	19.5	13.1	764	26.9	82.2	276,860	-0.5	13,975	5.0	264,472	32.5	26.2
Seattle-Tacoma-Bellevue, WA...	1,490,337	60.0	439,800	22.6	11.8	1,443	29.1	93.5	2,113,294	2.0	81,595	3.9	2,020,278	46.0	17.7
Seattle-Bellevue-Everett, WA Div 42664	1,169,069	59.1	494,700	22.5	11.5	1,510	28.9	94.1	1,689,157	2.0	59,648	3.5	1,613,245	48.9	16.1
Tacoma-Lakewood, WA Div 45104	321,268	63.2	300,200	23.0	12.9	1,197	29.9	91.2	424,137	2.1	21,947	5.2	407,033	34.3	24.0
Sebastian-Vero Beach, FL	58,044	77.9	200,000	22.8	11.7	906	36.7	84.4	65,104	1.5	2,786	4.3	60,000	33.7	17.8
Sebring, FL.............................	42,948	71.3	100,200	22.0	10.9	782	31.2	78.9	36,472	-0.1	1,756	4.8	31,032	31.6	22.3
Sheboygan, WI.........................	48,347	69.0	154,900	18.9	12.5	716	24.6	88.6	62,903	0.3	1,571	2.5	60,484	31.2	31.4
Sherman-Denison, TX.................	49,176	67.1	139,500	19.3	11.2	870	27.5	84.2	63,488	2.4	2,061	3.2	60,493	29.8	28.9
Shreveport-Bossier City, LA........	172,294	60.5	149,400	21.4	10.4	789	34.7	77.6	187,820	0.0	9,730	5.2	178,627	33.0	24.4
Sierra Vista-Douglas, AZ............	48,939	69.6	155,600	19.4	10.0	807	24.8	86.9	49,774	0.7	2,789	5.6	47,159	36.8	15.7
Sioux City, IA-NE-SD.................	65,877	69.2	136,000	18.1	10.0	735	24.2	82.9	91,907	1.4	2,376	2.6	84,364	28.7	33.7
Sioux Falls, SD........................	102,654	67.6	194,700	19.6	10.0	783	25.9	89.3	152,131	1.4	3,863	2.5	143,734	38.5	21.4
South Bend-Mishawaka, IN-MI.....	119,873	70.4	127,300	17.8	10.0	770	26.8	83.9	161,106	1.3	5,863	3.6	156,266	34.8	26.0
Spartanburg, SC.......................	126,242	69.0	130,800	18.4	10.0	788	27.3	82.2	159,482	1.0	5,084	3.2	153,606	30.6	29.7
Spokane-Spokane Valley, WA......	224,113	64.4	220,800	21.7	10.7	852	30.3	89.5	267,247	2.0	14,408	5.4	260,250	37.2	20.0
Springfield, IL	89,434	70.7	138,100	18.6	10.5	804	28.0	85.6	111,638	0.2	4,774	4.3	100,347	41.2	17.0
Springfield, MA........................	238,781	60.8	229,100	21.2	14.1	913	32.0	84.8	322,787	2.5	13,427	4.2	297,461	38.4	18.5
Springfield, MO........................	183,438	63.5	148,200	18.3	10.5	732	27.9	85.5	230,332	0.8	6,232	2.7	221,901	35.1	20.2
Springfield, OH........................	54,026	65.9	121,000	19.1	10.0	675	25.5	86.5	62,963	-1.0	2,870	4.6	60,046	29.9	28.4
State College, PA	58,629	62.4	232,300	20.1	10.9	920	35.7	90.1	79,859	1.0	2,585	3.2	76,120	50.7	13.6
Staunton-Waynesboro, VA	50,325	70.5	194,300	21.5	10.1	841	27.2	79.5	59,303	0.6	1,673	2.8	57,497	32.3	24.4
Stockton-Lodi, CA.....................	226,624	57.0	349,200	23.6	11.1	1,148	33.4	86.5	326,387	0.8	19,571	6.0	314,196	28.2	29.9
Sumter, SC.............................	41,878	64.9	123,500	18.7	10.0	770	32.5	79.4	44,120	0.5	1,776	4.0	44,354	28.2	29.9
Syracuse, NY	257,704	66.8	139,400	19.1	11.9	821	28.7	85.9	306,225	0.6	13,282	4.3	308,734	39.3	17.8
Tallahassee, FL	147,734	59.2	182,600	20.5	10.0	977	34.6	88.7	193,504	1.4	6,692	3.5	182,693	43.9	12.8
Tampa-St. Petersburg-Clearwater, FL..................	1,209,519	64.4	191,200	22.0	11.9	1,070	31.7	89.0	1,530,842	1.3	53,140	3.5	1,422,855	37.7	17.4
Terre Haute, IN........................	65,394	66.6	88,800	18.1	10.7	717	29.7	83.8	77,259	0.3	3,432	4.4	75,458	29.3	28.3

1. Specified owner-occupied units.   2. A value of 10.0 represents 10 percent or less; a value of 50.0 represents 50 percent or more.   3. Specified renter-occupied units.   4. Overcrowded or lacking complete plumbing facilities.   5. Percent of civilian labor force.   6. Civilian employed persons 16 years old and over.

Table C. Metropolitan Areas — **Nonfarm Employment and Agriculture**

	Private nonfarm establishments, employment and payroll, 2016									Agriculture, 2017			
		Employment						Annual payroll		Farms			Farm producers whose primary occupation is farming (percent)
											Percent with:		
Area name	Number of establishments	Total	Health care and social assistance	Manufacturing	Retail trade	Finance and insurance	Professional, scientific, and technical services	Total (mil dol)	Average per employee (dollars)	Number	Fewer than 50 acres	1000 acres or more	
	104	105	106	107	108	109	110	111	112	113	114	115	116
Reading, PA	8,406	156,856	25,628	31,471	20,744	5,848	6,585	7,191	45,846	1,809	49	0.9	52.9
Redding, CA	4,148	50,069	10,486	2,291	9,769	2,012	2,778	1,997	39,875	1,337	71.4	4.6	31.5
Reno, NV	12,258	187,281	24,432	15,680	24,213	5,947	10,183	8,191	43,737	355	69.9	7.3	43.5
Richmond, VA	31,416	534,087	82,177	30,247	68,145	43,804	42,344	26,271	49,189	3,037	49.1	5.8	41.8
Riverside-San Bernardino-Ontario, CA	71,807	1,135,984	169,097	95,592	187,129	26,904	38,085	46,053	40,541	3,729	86.4	1.9	41.2
Roanoke, VA	8,060	138,091	26,039	15,900	18,370	7,531	5,613	5,732	41,509	2,011	36	1.5	39.3
Rochester, MN	5,141	110,849	22,112	8,083	13,593	2,205	D	5,910	53,316	3,960	34.6	6.6	45.2
Rochester, NY	24,792	452,595	83,678	53,595	58,873	15,622	28,480	19,866	43,894	4,215	41.9	4.9	53.2
Rockford, IL	7,290	133,721	21,736	32,537	16,357	3,908	5,100	5,665	42,366	1,193	52.1	6.1	42.6
Rocky Mount, NC	2,773	49,114	8,273	10,748	6,586	1,616	1,072	1,754	35,707	674	39.5	10.8	47.6
Rome, GA	1,960	35,518	7,943	6,617	4,435	757	690	1,338	37,679	547	51.7	2	35.2
Sacramento--Roseville--Arden-Arcade, CA	48,044	716,965	116,478	33,879	101,368	43,136	51,354	36,876	51,433	4,737	73	3.9	43.9
Saginaw, MI	4,261	78,672	17,499	11,722	12,759	2,770	2,470	3,159	40,154	1,250	44.2	5.8	42.1
St. Cloud, MN	5,328	98,724	19,345	15,008	13,461	4,337	3,089	4,225	42,793	3,767	26.1	2.7	48
St. George, UT	4,795	49,056	9,298	2,574	9,117	1,436	2,076	1,638	33,389	537	60.5	5.8	26.8
St. Joseph, MO-KS	2,969	49,464	9,545	10,854	6,731	2,013	1,402	2,009	40,620	2,641	32.3	7.6	37.9
St. Louis, MO-IL	77,550	1,237,942	197,634	106,639	149,086	64,894	82,749	61,227	49,459	11,057	40.9	6.3	37.1
Salem, OR	9,459	119,006	22,262	12,416	18,939	3,295	4,104	4,453	37,415	4,004	73.2	2.3	41.5
Salinas, CA	8,632	107,865	15,749	7,660	17,472	2,793	7,115	4,836	44,837	1,104	45.6	20.2	44.3
Salisbury, MD-DE	10,558	125,065	24,164	13,390	24,385	3,698	3,941	4,669	37,333	2,237	51.7	6.6	54.3
Salt Lake City, UT	32,433	591,571	64,642	52,388	67,430	42,743	47,697	29,179	49,324	1,132	75.8	4.7	30.5
San Angelo, TX	2,827	40,249	7,412	3,210	6,878	1,578	1,411	1,522	37,825	1,478	51.8	13.9	30.9
San Antonio-New Braunfels, TX	44,993	859,299	132,641	44,606	113,098	70,533	48,801	37,333	43,446	14,960	48.4	4.8	35.4
San Diego-Carlsbad, CA	83,146	1,248,369	167,831	100,498	155,358	55,355	124,846	69,458	55,639	5,082	90.8	0.8	36.2
San Francisco-Oakland-Hayward, CA	128,309	2,091,071	262,136	121,499	214,057	120,684	247,679	175,468	83,913	1,499	63.4	8.5	42.6
Oakland-Hayward-Berkeley, CA Div 36084	NA	NA	NA	NA	NA	NA	NA	NA	NA	905	69.2	7.1	41.1
San Francisco-Redwood City-South San Francisco, CA	NA	NA	NA	NA	NA	NA	NA	NA	NA	251	67.7	6	47.7
San Rafael, CA Div 42034	NA	NA	NA	NA	NA	NA	NA	NA	NA	343	44.9	14	42.6
San Jose-Sunnyvale-Santa Clara, CA	49,243	1,033,551	112,364	86,058	86,999	22,957	139,437	115,442	111,695	1,500	70.7	7.5	45.2
San Luis Obispo-Paso Robles-Arroyo Grande, CA	8,227	90,392	15,256	6,447	14,452	2,334	4,843	3,796	41,994	2,349	56.4	7.8	40.8
Santa Cruz-Watsonville, CA	7,028	77,903	13,290	5,158	12,527	2,364	4,360	3,561	45,715	625	80.5	2.1	43.2
Santa Fe, NM	4,726	46,628	8,833	820	9,424	1,600	2,423	1,847	39,613	639	67.9	9.7	35.7
Santa Maria-Santa Barbara, CA	11,640	146,896	22,301	14,459	19,614	4,108	9,719	7,310	49,766	1,467	60.7	9.5	44
Santa Rosa, CA	13,887	168,218	25,469	19,805	25,566	6,285	8,973	8,559	50,879	3,594	73.7	3.5	40.6
Savannah, GA	9,070	150,906	21,498	17,840	21,387	3,149	6,014	6,182	40,965	416	59.1	6	36.9
Scranton--Wilkes-Barre--Hazleton, PA	13,233	239,561	47,843	28,036	32,440	10,735	9,574	9,247	38,599	1,124	33	1.4	38.9
Seattle-Tacoma-Bellevue, WA	103,741	1,670,179	227,208	165,444	180,479	60,699	131,521	112,533	67,378	4,961	88.8	0.2	33.9
Seattle-Bellevue-Everett, WA Div 42644	NA	NA	NA	NA	NA	NA	NA	NA	NA	3,354	89.4	0.3	34.9
Tacoma-Lakewood, WA Div 45104	NA	NA	NA	NA	NA	NA	NA	NA	NA	1,607	87.4	0.2	31.8
Sebastian-Vero Beach, FL	4,249	43,224	9,241	1,655	9,199	1,417	1,932	1,623	37,545	450	76.2	5.1	42.6
Sebring, FL	1,913	20,419	5,793	764	4,643	596	690	635	31,108	989	66.4	6.1	45.7
Sheboygan, WI	2,662	54,987	6,591	17,857	5,997	2,083	1,122	2,430	44,197	958	43.6	3.9	49.6
Sherman-Denison, TX	2,526	38,357	8,095	7,031	6,279	1,810	988	1,389	36,220	2,845	61.4	2.4	32.3
Shreveport-Bossier City, LA	9,957	155,073	34,643	9,024	24,526	4,576	6,230	6,020	38,823	2,255	48.4	6	38.3
Sierra Vista-Douglas, AZ	2,150	25,795	4,892	391	5,343	469	3,563	928	35,983	1,083	39.6	17.7	47.4
Sioux City, IA-NE-SD	4,414	77,851	12,251	14,855	10,217	3,248	1,585	3,078	39,534	3,647	28	13.5	48.3
Sioux Falls, SD	7,645	139,797	28,023	14,055	18,676	14,060	5,076	6,127	43,830	3,048	34.5	15.3	44
South Bend-Mishawaka, IN-MI	6,525	127,435	20,573	17,962	16,605	4,035	5,113	5,254	41,230	1,376	53.3	5.5	42.2
Spartanburg, SC	6,639	133,952	17,186	30,783	15,477	2,216	3,819	5,773	43,100	1,674	62.5	0.6	30.7
Spokane-Spokane Valley, WA	13,926	196,629	40,265	16,403	28,218	11,258	9,299	8,555	43,510	3,800	57.2	5.6	35.9
Springfield, IL	5,181	87,354	24,074	2,736	12,791	5,779	4,906	3,523	40,334	1,469	42.7	12.9	45
Springfield, MA	13,303	233,240	62,780	22,068	31,289	11,432	8,472	9,759	41,840	1,215	61.3	0.2	39.4
Springfield, MO	12,003	185,045	34,401	15,614	25,872	8,521	9,046	7,109	38,417	7,601	40.2	1.6	38.9
Springfield, OH	2,287	41,915	8,325	6,070	5,144	2,583	1,167	1,493	35,621	742	56.7	7	36.2
State College, PA	3,347	45,292	8,884	3,906	8,030	1,252	2,974	1,733	38,267	1,023	41.3	1.4	47
Staunton-Waynesboro, VA	2,793	40,530	7,077	7,286	6,316	969	1,027	1,506	37,152	1,665	45.7	2.6	44.6
Stockton-Lodi, CA	11,237	177,161	28,448	17,986	26,507	6,256	5,011	7,604	42,921	3,430	62.1	5.4	55
Sumter, SC	1,773	32,672	5,179	6,207	4,800	808	849	1,123	34,372	524	55.7	7.3	45.7
Syracuse, NY	15,258	260,468	49,780	22,968	36,652	11,787	15,759	11,246	43,175	1,926	37	3.6	49.1
Tallahassee, FL	8,943	112,385	21,118	3,115	19,227	4,734	10,751	4,365	38,841	1,648	62.1	2.7	34.3
Tampa-St. Petersburg-Clearwater, FL	77,204	1,091,950	185,350	55,492	154,097	75,908	96,889	50,068	45,852	4,325	80.3	1.8	39.7
Terre Haute, IN	3,554	57,209	11,796	10,271	8,962	1,658	1,310	2,102	36,738	1,795	44.4	9.4	41.1

Table C. Metropolitan Areas — **Agriculture**

Area name	Land in farms Acreage (1,000)	Percent change, 2012-2017	Acres Average size of farm	Total irrigated (1,000)	Total cropland (1,000)	Value of land and buildings (dollars) Average per farm	Average per acre	Value of machinery and equipment, average per farm (dollars)	Value of products sold: Total (mil dol)	Average per farm (acres)	Percent from: Crops	Live-stock and poultry products	Organic farms (number)	Farms with internet access (percent)	Government payments Total ($1,000)	Percent of farms
	117	118	119	120	121	122	123	124	125	126	127	128	129	130	131	132
Reading, PA	225	-3.9	124	1.5	184.5	1,392,374	11,209	138,139	554.7	306,609	43.8	56.2	72	68.4	3,038	22.1
Redding, CA	410	8.9	307	48.8	38.9	895,229	2,919	51,324	62.2	46,546	35	65	16	81.5	547	2
Reno, NV	501	13.2	1,412	43.6	22.2	1,449,321	1,026	61,699	19.9	56,166	45.8	54.2	14	86.5	174	5.1
Richmond, VA	669	3.1	220	13	356.0	898,183	4,079	105,412	247.8	81,597	55.5	44.5	10	77.1	9,265	21.2
Riverside-San Bernardino-Ontario, CA	332	-21.2	89	148.4	209.0	1,647,577	18,504	95,567	1,305.9	350,203	61.4	38.6	253	79.1	2,268	2.4
Roanoke, VA	315	-5.2	156	0.6	117.9	604,500	3,864	75,565	90.5	44,978	26.1	73.9	10	71	1,000	8.2
Rochester, MN	1,140	-1.5	288	7.5	934.5	1,760,727	6,115	212,289	930.9	235,069	51.7	48.3	76	80	30,766	65.6
Rochester, NY	900	-3	214	7	701.5	836,920	3,920	180,390	956.7	226,983	54.5	45.5	261	70.7	16,376	22.4
Rockford, IL	292	-8	245	2.5	267.0	1,811,732	7,399	155,547	185.6	155,583	77	23	15	82.6	10,252	48.6
Rocky Mount, NC	278	4.2	413	4.7	203.6	1,562,533	3,783	258,892	367.9	545,798	59.4	40.6	17	68	4,904	44.7
Rome, GA	75	6.7	137	0.7	21.7	665,898	4,866	88,750	53.4	97,700	10.2	89.8	NA	77.3	442	13.5
Sacramento--Roseville--Arden-Arcade, CA	929	0.2	196	360.9	468.5	1,852,189	9,440	103,724	1,081.4	228,294	84.7	15.3	178	86.4	5,225	7.3
Saginaw, MI	327	5.6	262	1.7	300.5	1,518,681	5,805	162,378	170.3	136,206	87.9	12.1	12	79.4	6,853	63.1
St. Cloud, MN	846	-10.6	224	68.5	671.7	1,116,661	4,974	184,892	955.2	253,558	25.4	74.6	62	77.4	7,628	53.6
St. George, UT	155	4.8	289	13	22.3	1,078,857	3,737	61,328	16.5	30,648	39.3	60.7	3	76.9	190	3.2
St. Joseph, MO-KS	768	-5.1	291	4.2	583.3	1,061,151	3,648	121,612	287.9	109,001	84.3	15.7	1	75.9	14,004	54.8
St. Louis, MO-IL	2,780	-4.6	251	12.2	2,129.8	1,547,992	6,158	144,778	1,375.5	124,397	74.7	25.3	24	76	44,123	46.8
Salem, OR	438	1.5	109	123	345.0	1,156,225	10,580	127,386	836.3	208,874	84.6	15.4	72	85.2	2,771	6.6
Salinas, CA	1,340	5.7	1,214	294.6	366.7	8,944,364	7,368	805,557	4,116.1	3,728,396	99.1	0.9	191	75.5	1,269	7.4
Salisbury, MD-DE	523	0.4	234	117.5	418.0	1,709,210	7,315	200,515	1,827.9	817,121	17	83	13	77	17,204	43.7
Salt Lake City, UT	411	-3.4	363	29.3	32.6	953,913	2,628	70,367	60.7	53,581	38.8	61.2	11	79.6	594	2.5
San Angelo, TX	1,426	-1.9	965	20.5	129.4	1,276,926	1,324	77,290	109.3	73,955	27.6	72.4	1	76.1	3,282	13.1
San Antonio-New Braunfels, TX	3,657	0.4	244	87.8	613.5	767,866	3,141	56,604	407.3	27,225	37.6	62.4	13	71.5	10,124	6.7
San Diego-Carlsbad, CA	222	0.3	44	42.7	64.1	1,014,281	23,209	43,529	831.4	163,601	93.5	6.5	419	84.2	558	1.1
San Francisco-Oakland-Hayward, CA	525	0.1	350	38.1	79.4	2,439,344	6,965	81,559	304.2	202,908	62.2	37.8	109	85.7	1,416	6.9
Oakland-Hayward-Berkeley, CA Div 36084	339	10.9	374	30.1	58.8	2,629,149	7,022	76,063	129.4	142,977	77.4	22.6	22	84.5	704	6.2
San Francisco-Redwood City-South San Francisco, CA	46	-4.4	184	3	6.9	1,817,211	9,902	73,187	79.4	316,430	98.2	1.8	20	88	0	0.8
San Rafael, CA Div 42034	140	-18	408	5	13.7	2,393,810	5,862	102,187	95.3	277,962	11.6	88.4	67	86.9	712	13.1
San Jose-Sunnyvale-Santa Clara, CA	808	-3.1	539	37.3	69.9	2,800,069	5,197	93,026	473.1	315,395	89.6	10.4	109	84.2	1,093	6.1
San Luis Obispo-Paso Robles-Arroyo Grande, CA	931	-30.4	396	75.8	246.4	2,991,940	7,547	87,783	701.6	298,676	95.2	4.8	132	84.4	4,285	9.4
Santa Cruz-Watsonville, CA	64	-36.1	102	20.1	23.5	2,183,024	21,352	116,842	606.5	970,464	98.7	1.3	130	85.1	37	1.9
Santa Fe, NM	D	-100	D	15.6	23.7	932,061	D	65,568	25.4	39,798	54.5	45.5	14	77	367	5.5
Santa Maria-Santa Barbara, CA	715	2	487	119.9	146.3	5,060,151	10,381	183,019	1,519.9	1,036,090	98	2	163	87.7	854	5.2
Santa Rosa, CA	567	-3.8	158	86.4	129.9	3,501,852	22,186	77,693	919.1	255,719	66.9	33.1	332	87.7	2,410	3.8
Savannah, GA	81	36.2	195	3.5	33.7	642,800	3,300	100,149	31.5	75,671	87.9	12.1	5	81.3	402	15.1
Scranton--Wilkes-Barre--Hazleton, PA	147	-9.5	131	0.5	77.4	663,210	5,073	80,161	47.5	42,264	62.7	37.3	1	73.2	1,259	26.2
Seattle-Tacoma-Bellevue, WA	151	-9.4	31	15.5	64.3	744,589	24,396	47,150	357.9	72,144	54.9	45.1	87	88	1,295	3.1
Seattle-Bellevue-Everett, WA Div 42644	106	-10.1	31	12.5	52.3	808,104	25,655	48,710	293	87,367	57	43	70	88.3	1,224	3.5
Tacoma-Lakewood, WA Div 45104	46	-7.5	28	3	12.1	612,026	21,490	43,894	64.9	40,371	45.4	54.6	17	87.4	71	2.2
Sebastian-Vero Beach, FL	183	12.4	406	52.9	55.5	2,330,718	5,745	90,644	106.5	236,611	89.3	10.7	9	68.2	426	7.1
Sebring, FL	376	-23.3	380	73.3	87.6	1,484,269	3,906	92,897	196.7	198,865	72.5	27.5	2	71.1	2,471	11
Sheboygan, WI	196	-3	205	0.3	164.3	1,348,670	6,594	198,127	213.4	222,785	22.6	77.4	14	84.2	1,215	39.5
Sherman-Denison, TX	430	-0.3	151	2.3	207.0	1,023,105	6,770	68,105	66.2	23,259	60.8	39.2	1	81	4,729	9.9
Shreveport-Bossier City, LA	501	14.4	222	25	158.8	666,795	3,003	90,658	105.4	46,754	49	51	NA	72.5	2,799	8.1
Sierra Vista-Douglas, AZ	973	6.2	899	86	152.9	1,802,553	2,005	99,038	144.7	133,648	56.9	43.1	4	78.9	3,119	10.6
Sioux City, IA-NE-SD	1,690	-2.5	463	105.4	1,487.9	3,176,752	6,855	271,967	1,650.5	452,567	46.4	53.6	9	81.1	36,507	75.7
Sioux Falls, SD	1,429	-6	469	34.3	1,230.4	2,633,238	5,616	236,521	920.2	301,909	60.6	39.4	6	81.8	23,562	68.3
South Bend-Mishawaka, IN-MI	348	2.3	253	99.4	297.5	1,548,314	6,113	178,869	257.3	187,018	71.1	28.9	13	77.3	8,438	43.5
Spartanburg, SC	140	-6.4	83	1.9	41.6	537,310	6,444	47,999	40.8	24,397	55.2	44.8	NA	76.1	907	10.4
Spokane-Spokane Valley, WA	1,125	1.5	296	21.2	474.9	792,706	2,679	71,324	152	39,992	73.5	26.5	51	83.5	8,903	14.9
Springfield, IL	699	4.1	476	4.6	635.8	4,123,080	8,661	259,955	442.3	301,075	92.6	7.4	3	79.2	10,299	65.3
Springfield, MA	87	-6.5	71	1.9	32.3	625,784	8,776	66,789	71.9	59,192	79.2	20.8	35	83	835	7.8
Springfield, MO	1,209	-0.6	159	3.3	360.6	517,580	3,255	58,141	272.7	35,876	13.2	86.8	61	72.1	2,387	6.2
Springfield, OH	171	-1.9	230	1.8	151.4	1,738,039	7,542	165,062	126.5	170,443	79.2	20.8	NA	80.5	6,001	43.3
State College, PA	150	-7.5	146	0.4	88.3	981,430	6,700	92,395	91.5	89,421	35.3	64.7	23	68.5	2,266	24
Staunton-Waynesboro, VA	291	11.8	175	2.5	116.8	1,222,854	6,999	101,481	292.5	175,704	12.8	87.2	5	71.5	1,049	15.7
Stockton-Lodi, CA	773	-1.8	225	487.1	524.4	3,384,002	15,020	189,084	2,176	634,404	74.8	25.2	35	81.7	5,788	6.9
Sumter, SC	168	-4.7	320	19.1	91.4	958,464	2,995	134,000	153.4	292,763	32.6	67.4	5	79.6	1,534	30.7
Syracuse, NY	419	-3.1	217	2.5	258.9	676,931	3,113	142,481	333.3	173,037	26.6	73.4	95	81.9	3,359	20.8
Tallahassee, FL	350	19.5	212	9.3	64.5	811,049	3,823	54,877	134.5	81,627	64.7	35.3	12	76.2	1,600	8.5
Tampa-St. Petersburg-Clearwater, FL	425	-5.6	98	31.5	111.1	958,142	9,761	57,092	534.9	123,682	82.5	17.5	30	76.9	1,773	5.7
Terre Haute, IN	565	-0.7	315	9.5	483.9	1,655,786	5,259	166,884	297.3	165,637	90	10	5	75.6	11,152	61.3

Table C. Metropolitan Areas — Water Use, Wholesale Trade, Retail Trade, and Real Estate

Area name	Water use, 2015		Wholesale Trade[1], 2012				Retail Trade[2], 2012				Real estate and rental and leasing,[2] 2012			
	Public supply water withdrawn (mil gal/day)	Public supply gallons withdrawn per person per day	Number of establishments	Number of employees	Sales (mil dol)	Average payroll (mil dol)	Number of establishments	Number of employees	Sales (mil dol)	Average payroll (mil dol)	Number of establishments	Number of employees	Sales (mil dol)	Average payroll (mil dol)
	133	134	135	136	137	138	139	140	141	142	143	144	145	146
Reading, PA	31.85	76.7	354	6,912	4,277.4	362.2	1,256	20,219	5,719.4	494.3	246	1,249	213.0	41.4
Redding, CA	33.47	186.4	158	1,437	1,023.9	59.8	647	8,980	2,507.1	241.4	207	765	121.4	22.1
Reno, NV	58.21	129.1	584	8,064	6,401.9	414.6	1,411	21,644	6,173.0	580.9	672	3,245	1,049.1	124.3
Richmond, VA	177.19	139.4	1,349	21,390	20,135.9	1,158.4	4,251	64,627	16,923.0	1,530.7	1,288	8,019	1,667.1	345.4
Riverside-San Bernardino-Ontario, CA	778.43	173.4	4,061	55,568	49,713.0	2,646.5	9,744	160,809	49,439.3	4,142.4	3,608	16,254	3,307.2	620.1
Roanoke, VA	41.18	130.9	434	6,455	3,944.5	340.1	1,226	18,356	4,658.8	424.8	361	1,693	283.0	57.0
Rochester, MN	16.91	79.1	171	2,237	1,675.9	108.3	823	12,429	2,948.5	271.3	194	803	149.2	24.0
Rochester, NY	114.43	105.8	1,041	13,319	7,667.8	692.4	3,549	57,373	13,433.0	1,266.8	1,069	7,229	1,212.2	257.3
Rockford, IL	32.79	96.3	364	4,362	2,903.0	219.4	1,094	15,667	4,147.5	358.1	236	1,573	178.9	45.3
Rocky Mount, NC	12.42	83.9	128	2,404	2,899.8	109.2	551	6,475	1,606.6	140.2	126	464	73.5	14.7
Rome, GA	11.8	122.3	74	812	691.5	33.8	386	3,986	1,022.4	89.3	76	252	41.7	8.2
Sacramento--Roseville--Arden-Arcade, CA	340.07	149.5	1,768	24,256	30,299.6	1,354.9	5,715	89,921	25,231.7	2,423.6	2,832	14,883	2,682.4	598.9
Saginaw, MI	0.42	2.2	181	1,975	1,264.9	96.7	870	12,210	2,913.3	262.8	132	602	101.1	16.3
St. Cloud, MN	16.66	85.7	225	4,802	2,975.1	220.1	790	12,674	3,428.2	287.7	196	900	146.3	25.1
St. George, UT	49.38	317.3	149	1,284	1,514.7	47.4	574	7,375	1,900.8	168.4	306	702	95.2	18.7
St. Joseph, MO-KS	18.41	145.1	133	2,102	1,983.2	91.9	440	6,469	1,627.6	140.6	124	D	D	D
St. Louis, MO-IL	459.39	163.4	3,234	52,073	56,278.9	2,936.0	9,170	140,597	44,947.4	3,614.6	2,904	17,590	3,989.1	764.2
Salem, OR	76.88	187.5	293	3,958	3,290.9	187.9	1,228	17,043	4,222.9	413.9	476	2,158	289.1	61.7
Salinas, CA	38.23	88.1	346	4,574	5,775.2	278.9	1,316	16,335	4,457.4	437.2	444	1,873	436.3	69.6
Salisbury, MD-DE	29.56	74.8	321	3,198	3,074.0	154.2	1,959	22,278	5,698.2	523.9	562	2,528	400.9	85.4
Salt Lake City, UT	413.16	353	1,666	27,811	19,766.8	1,643.3	3,499	57,496	17,675.2	1,573.1	1,961	9,056	1,937.9	379.9
San Angelo, TX	1.24	10.4	115	D	D	D	422	5,980	1,823.3	150.0	134	595	92.7	16.5
San Antonio-New Braunfels, TX	255.85	107.3	1,816	D	D	D	5,984	96,472	32,018.0	2,399.0	2,102	15,075	3,359.6	662.5
San Diego-Carlsbad, CA	408.82	123.9	3,883	59,227	35,937.4	4,055.0	9,219	138,929	39,786.1	3,787.5	5,401	28,321	7,895.7	1,308.8
San Francisco-Oakland-Hayward, CA	472.83	101.5	5,594	81,370	73,423.7	5,831.6	13,370	195,011	63,799.7	6,071.0	6,785	40,566	14,041.3	2,383.1
Oakland-Hayward-Berkeley, CA Div 36084	308.71	111.7	3,119	51,504	44,467.8	3,551.0	6,703	102,866	32,748.9	3,008.4	3,226	16,093	4,354.7	794.9
San Francisco-Redwood City-South San Francisco, CA	135.93	83.4	2,116	27,086	27,091.4	2,099.8	5,614	77,447	25,963.3	2,517.8	2,970	22,018	8,228.1	1,419.5
San Rafael, CA Div 42034	28.19	107.9	359	2,780	1,864.6	180.8	1,053	14,698	5,087.5	544.8	589	2,455	1,458.6	168.7
San Jose-Sunnyvale-Santa Clara, CA	199.83	101.1	2,349	84,942	92,134.3	10,863.8	5,032	85,434	40,681.9	3,247.2	2,479	12,943	4,484.6	767.8
San Luis Obispo-Paso Robles-Arroyo Grande, CA	29.1	103.4	289	D	D	D	1,177	13,992	3,624.0	361.5	430	1,552	278.4	52.2
Santa Cruz-Watsonville, CA	18.45	67.3	266	5,614	5,898.2	297.2	887	11,120	4,368.0	294.7	363	1,271	264.1	41.8
Santa Fe, NM	10.57	71.1	111	867	773.2	37.4	813	8,981	2,324.5	250.1	280	933	181.8	36.9
Santa Maria-Santa Barbara, CA	49.94	112.3	406	5,325	3,475.6	397.1	1,509	18,781	4,853.8	501.5	691	3,047	570.7	113.7
Santa Rosa, CA	40.49	80.6	593	8,047	4,443.2	557.8	1,768	23,032	6,016.3	655.8	679	2,824	631.1	103.4
Savannah, GA	66.47	175.3	348	4,265	6,501.3	216.0	1,407	18,108	4,967.3	427.7	445	1,954	404.7	63.4
Scranton--Wilkes-Barre--Hazleton, PA	62.18	111.4	569	9,845	7,916.9	425.6	2,277	32,708	11,676.8	720.0	357	1,640	353.7	57.2
Seattle-Tacoma-Bellevue, WA	373.55	100.1	4,652	65,726	55,450.8	4,041.0	10,862	163,846	80,843.3	5,007.9	5,996	31,037	7,372.8	1,461.3
Seattle-Bellevue-Everett, WA Div 42644	263.14	91.1	3,966	56,555	47,745.2	3,591.1	8,708	130,735	70,728.9	4,063.0	5,049	26,364	6,535.2	1,302.6
Tacoma-Lakewood, WA Div 45104	110.41	130.8	686	9,171	7,705.6	449.9	2,154	33,111	10,114.4	944.9	947	4,673	837.6	158.6
Sebastian-Vero Beach, FL	16.94	114.5	125	D	D	D	659	7,958	1,881.3	189.1	231	1,213	162.3	36.9
Sebring, FL	7.49	75.3	57	D	D	D	316	4,292	1,112.5	100.2	87	264	51.2	7.5
Sheboygan, WI	15.8	136.7	86	1,002	593.9	47.9	395	6,124	1,400.0	133.5	73	298	58.2	10.4
Sherman-Denison, TX	21.61	172.2	100	905	906.6	36.6	417	5,685	1,620.2	137.9	109	327	48.9	8.6
Shreveport-Bossier City, LA	64.6	145.6	487	7,141	6,959.9	343.2	1,641	22,553	6,759.2	557.8	462	3,206	620.0	123.9
Sierra Vista-Douglas, AZ	16.15	127.7	47	269	133.9	10.1	408	5,266	1,267.3	115.2	113	424	57.1	11.4
Sioux City, IA-NE-SD	21.67	128.2	242	3,529	4,024.5	168.6	652	9,729	2,409.8	203.7	143	679	87.2	18.3
Sioux Falls, SD	21.85	79.7	440	6,274	4,859.6	319.5	981	16,468	4,854.0	385.7	293	1,511	299.3	56.7
South Bend-Mishawaka, IN-MI	22.91	71.6	352	4,687	3,447.2	229.0	1,027	15,578	4,032.2	362.8	246	1,281	213.2	42.5
Spartanburg, SC	37.66	115.8	428	5,915	5,383.9	301.5	1,168	14,364	4,162.4	333.6	241	1,133	188.7	40.3
Spokane-Spokane Valley, WA	145.99	266.5	586	D	D	D	1,777	26,212	6,902.3	700.5	644	3,143	531.3	104.3
Springfield, IL	24.02	113.8	206	3,433	3,525.5	155.9	785	12,269	3,205.4	283.0	215	849	154.4	25.7
Springfield, MA	63.47	100.4	470	8,257	7,835.9	436.2	2,119	30,551	7,502.9	727.9	478	2,274	569.0	81.5
Springfield, MO	42.64	93.4	527	8,382	5,528.0	354.2	1,646	24,111	6,492.0	552.8	520	2,647	375.5	75.4
Springfield, OH	16.17	118.9	88	2,274	2,697.8	111.4	403	5,708	1,541.5	128.0	95	468	56.8	12.5
State College, PA	17.87	111.3	90	873	538.9	42.5	481	7,570	1,748.7	155.7	133	1,036	255.5	34.7
Staunton-Waynesboro, VA	8.28	68.9	90	1,190	438.9	52.9	465	5,926	1,528.2	134.3	134	424	45.0	11.2
Stockton-Lodi, CA	93.39	128.6	515	9,279	11,713.5	495.7	1,602	24,097	7,059.5	616.4	572	2,655	464.7	97.2
Sumter, SC	14.6	135.8	69	635	342.0	28.8	398	4,416	1,096.8	85.4	78	258	28.9	6.4
Syracuse, NY	94.13	142.5	685	11,688	17,632.5	597.7	2,257	36,012	8,919.9	802.6	700	4,109	704.0	159.0
Tallahassee, FL	35.54	94	285	D	D	D	1,227	17,445	4,073.0	382.0	438	2,112	295.1	62.2
Tampa-St. Petersburg-Clearwater, FL	299.64	100.7	3,244	40,574	34,352.8	2,027.1	9,767	136,584	39,880.0	3,530.2	3,941	17,281	3,803.9	672.2
Terre Haute, IN	15.14	88.5	135	D	D	D	635	8,698	2,233.2	180.8	116	570	93.5	18.9

1. Merchant wholesalers, except manufacturers' sales branches and offices. 2. Employer establishments.

Table C. Metropolitan Areas — Professional Services, Manufacturing, and Accommodation and Food Services

Area name	Professional, scientific, and technical services, 2012				Manufacturing, 2012				Accommodation and food services, 2012			
	Number of establishments	Number of employees	Sales (mil dol)	Average payroll (mil dol)	Number of establishments	Number of employees	Receipts (mil dol)	Annual payroll (mil dol)	Number of establishments	Number of employees	Receipts (mil dol)	Annual payroll (mil dol)
	147	148	149	150	151	152	153	154	155	156	157	158
Reading, PA	703	D	D	D	498	29,439	10,905.1	1,547.9	754	12,294	548.8	155.6
Redding, CA	358	D	D	D	147	1,990	511.9	93.7	376	5,421	285.5	76.7
Reno, NV	1,625	9,036	1,435.9	540.1	448	14,065	6,444.7	843.5	987	28,209	1,870.1	583.2
Richmond, VA	3,513	32,374	5,370.9	2,052.1	889	29,624	27,862.1	1,722.4	2,516	48,940	2,419.9	696.4
Riverside-San Bernardino-Ontario, CA	5,671	33,151	4,350.9	1,587.8	3,261	88,341	32,728.6	4,043.2	6,476	128,108	8,088.9	2,150.4
Roanoke, VA	773	5,088	632.5	261.7	309	15,342	5,067.6	743.0	665	12,830	592.8	172.4
Rochester, MN	368	11,211	1,098.1	677.9	194	12,474	4,784.7	741.7	493	8,963	441.5	124.4
Rochester, NY	2,481	24,105	3,556.2	1,390.8	1,326	56,345	20,527.1	3,110.6	2,383	36,363	1,740.8	499.6
Rockford, IL	667	4,418	717.0	220.8	678	32,643	14,051.7	1,895.8	635	10,964	531.9	147.7
Rocky Mount, NC	201	1,066	109.1	42.5	119	9,582	4,213.2	455.8	244	4,714	204.8	56.0
Rome, GA	186	809	104.1	35.0	100	5,567	3,615.6	265.3	183	3,593	163.4	46.9
Sacramento--Roseville--Arden-Arcade, CA	5,860	50,049	10,506.0	3,539.0	1,348	32,798	10,949.4	1,820.9	4,221	76,566	4,851.1	1,263.4
Saginaw, MI	318	2,226	299.2	109.3	206	11,249	4,523.3	653.2	368	7,829	373.8	97.6
St. Cloud, MN	359	D	D	D	318	14,205	4,221.1	604.2	419	7,450	311.7	84.8
St. George, UT	433	D	D	D	133	1,838	415.3	76.1	307	5,140	282.3	74.4
St. Joseph, MO-KS	184	1,131	128.8	54.6	110	12,749	7,338.7	492.7	223	D	D	D
St. Louis, MO-IL	7,187	83,135	14,035.8	5,306.9	2,641	99,727	61,153.6	6,113.4	6,026	120,774	6,396.3	1,759.0
Salem, OR	781	4,222	484.6	183.1	412	10,956	2,965.0	415.7	809	12,587	746.7	203.9
Salinas, CA	806	7,448	847.3	338.0	263	6,078	2,258.9	252.3	979	17,786	1,328.8	378.0
Salisbury, MD-DE	742	D	D	D	263	12,888	5,301.6	483.0	1,263	18,991	1,296.5	358.3
Salt Lake City, UT	4,213	40,353	6,437.6	2,413.6	1,394	48,107	22,944.7	2,761.9	2,149	42,602	2,217.2	646.5
San Angelo, TX	213	1,362	159.7	58.6	102	D	1,276.3	D	231	4,761	237.4	64.7
San Antonio-New Braunfels, TX	4,713	44,402	7,158.5	2,719.4	1,207	40,835	18,863.7	1,918.7	4,448	101,868	5,687.6	1,548.8
San Diego-Carlsbad, CA	12,528	134,334	24,111.3	9,099.2	2,891	97,346	33,320.5	6,196.1	6,880	147,457	10,403.8	2,857.4
San Francisco-Oakland-Hayward, CA	19,772	214,269	59,734.6	20,918.1	3,931	110,944	80,170.9	8,312.6	12,156	197,200	14,277.7	4,118.8
Oakland-Hayward-Berkeley, CA Div 36084	8,734	87,351	19,476.4	7,526.8	2,386	78,796	D	5,592.8	5,436	79,002	4,852.4	1,340.7
San Francisco-Redwood City-South San Francisco, CA	9,294	117,823	38,220.9	12,693.3	1,326	30,213	D	2,627.2	5,969	106,620	8,695.6	2,552.5
San Rafael, CA Div 42034	1,744	9,095	2,037.3	698.0	219	1,935	D	92.7	751	11,578	729.7	225.6
San Jose-Sunnyvale-Santa Clara, CA	8,465	125,608	30,165.3	13,558.7	2,447	103,203	42,041.7	9,264.8	4,487	73,416	4,859.1	1,349.7
San Luis Obispo-Paso Robles-Arroyo Grande, CA	868	4,914	673.1	269.5	382	6,107	2,854.0	285.7	865	14,254	824.8	229.5
Santa Cruz-Watsonville, CA	880	4,268	603.0	249.2	293	4,479	1,213.4	219.2	678	10,032	586.0	168.6
Santa Fe, NM	625	2,604	356.9	151.5	138	719	131.0	27.5	421	9,049	592.4	179.9
Santa Maria-Santa Barbara, CA	1,347	9,785	1,751.7	654.0	458	13,896	4,157.6	851.5	1,087	20,623	1,428.9	400.1
Santa Rosa, CA	1,514	9,140	1,244.4	524.0	821	19,324	6,131.7	1,085.2	1,192	17,606	1,058.7	301.8
Savannah, GA	833	6,360	692.4	274.9	208	15,862	10,027.5	1,138.9	1,033	19,741	1,097.8	296.2
Scranton--Wilkes-Barre--Hazleton, PA	1,111	8,480	925.1	352.4	581	27,852	12,229.0	1,255.8	1,390	20,178	960.9	249.9
Seattle-Tacoma-Bellevue, WA	12,651	117,190	21,306.5	9,251.6	3,584	155,814	77,904.1	9,877.4	8,964	135,680	8,755.3	2,557.9
Seattle-Bellevue-Everett, WA Div 42644	11,224	107,726	20,263.1	8,705.3	3,018	139,787	73,443.1	9,080.9	7,411	113,145	7,392.3	2,189.1
Tacoma-Lakewood, WA Div 45104	1,427	9,464	1,043.4	546.3	566	16,027	4,461.0	796.5	1,553	22,535	1,363.0	368.8
Sebastian-Vero Beach, FL	454	1,601	229.1	84.3	84	1,487	D	68.7	250	4,351	225.1	66.2
Sebring, FL	132	602	57.5	18.4	44	570	214.0	22.7	147	2,331	110.6	30.7
Sheboygan, WI	179	1,240	207.9	65.8	230	16,716	7,346.2	825.1	269	4,151	188.8	53.4
Sherman-Denison, TX	227	844	99.0	32.7	112	6,886	2,574.9	288.3	224	4,305	200.2	57.1
Shreveport-Bossier City, LA	894	5,650	756.8	265.3	294	9,906	7,610.9	533.8	821	21,991	1,491.1	349.4
Sierra Vista-Douglas, AZ	217	4,592	586.7	254.7	43	279	141.0	14.2	277	3,875	173.4	48.4
Sioux City, IA-NE-SD	306	1,520	178.5	67.1	183	15,637	10,083.3	584.0	411	6,796	312.3	86.0
Sioux Falls, SD	587	D	D	D	260	13,256	4,720.2	584.5	535	11,487	535.9	159.1
South Bend-Mishawaka, IN-MI	563	5,073	1,374.8	279.6	435	16,080	7,230.4	829.5	624	11,677	516.5	147.6
Spartanburg, SC	474	4,904	698.1	265.2	425	25,455	15,562.6	1,351.9	586	10,544	498.9	134.0
Spokane-Spokane Valley, WA	1,337	D	D	D	566	15,225	D	723.6	1,171	18,692	1,099.7	310.1
Springfield, IL	542	4,460	556.4	227.4	114	2,858	688.9	140.1	544	9,678	444.7	130.5
Springfield, MA	1,214	8,727	1,111.4	446.2	717	23,526	7,355.7	1,240.8	1,312	20,253	978.6	276.9
Springfield, MO	1,042	7,464	1,131.2	410.6	477	14,338	5,202.5	607.4	938	17,836	761.9	224.2
Springfield, OH	166	1,172	141.2	58.3	158	6,116	2,832.4	275.0	235	4,288	197.0	53.2
State College, PA	365	3,204	432.1	191.2	145	3,960	1,053.5	181.9	311	6,352	289.0	79.7
Staunton-Waynesboro, VA	187	1,469	92.3	70.3	124	6,667	2,437.0	320.0	227	3,992	183.9	52.3
Stockton-Lodi, CA	780	4,463	491.1	190.0	517	18,703	9,212.4	879.0	997	15,422	808.6	211.0
Sumter, SC	126	714	75.8	23.2	71	5,524	1,817.5	214.6	158	2,951	127.0	34.9
Syracuse, NY	1,435	14,683	2,187.0	815.3	579	23,640	10,592.6	1,283.4	1,600	24,414	1,158.4	330.5
Tallahassee, FL	1,454	D	D	D	141	2,861	D	138.7	755	D	D	D
Tampa-St. Petersburg-Clearwater, FL	10,447	85,745	12,902.8	5,325.3	2,121	51,778	18,823.8	2,583.0	5,275	100,640	6,300.5	1,646.5
Terre Haute, IN	257	1,453	145.3	54.2	174	12,457	5,125.1	604.5	385	6,822	291.4	82.5

Table C. Metropolitan Areas —

Health Care and Social Assistance, Other Services, Nonemployer Businesses, and Residential Construction

Area name	Health care and social assistance, 2012				Other services, 2012				Nonemployer businesses, 2016		Value of residential construction authorized by building permits, 2018	
	Number of establish-ments	Number of employees	Receipts (mil dol)	Annual payroll (mil dol)	Number of establish-ments	Number of employees	Receipts (mil dol)	Annual payroll (mil dol)	Number	Receipts (mil dol)	New construc-tion ($1,000)	Number of housing units
	159	160	161	162	163	164	165	166	167	168	169	170
Reading, PA..........................	827	25,605	2,588.9	1,067.0	767	4,046	363.5	101.5	24,485	1,137.4	103,485	600
Redding, CA..........................	634	10,525	1,324.6	469.3	296	1,658	162.7	48.2	11,825	539.3	78,562	306
Reno, NV..............................	1,191	23,356	3,028.7	1,167.9	731	4,788	675.8	142.5	32,018	1,855.4	866,623	4,450
Richmond, VA........................	3,086	77,601	9,636.5	3,570.9	2,343	16,581	1,941.2	497.6	87,390	3,776.0	999,979	6,061
Riverside-San Bernardino-Ontario, CA...................	7,983	147,321	19,611.4	7,140.3	4,688	30,021	2,676.3	788.6	308,401	13,635.0	3,538,857	14,809
Roanoke, VA..........................	784	24,402	2,855.7	1,119.8	644	3,814	287.1	88.7	19,230	796.9	109,372	515
Rochester, MN.......................	549	22,061	2,524.6	908.0	368	2,406	208.4	59.1	14,589	657.2	375,614	1,816
Rochester, NY	2,645	78,759	7,020.1	3,004.4	1,691	9,959	979.4	264.8	63,267	2,877.8	339,259	2,206
Rockford, IL...........................	738	20,948	2,479.1	953.1	601	3,558	336.6	91.8	20,915	763.7	33,350	265
Rocky Mount, NC	348	6,552	552.6	216.7	184	D	D	D	8,323	302.2	36,261	235
Rome, GA..............................	281	8,058	1,049.2	412.6	104	831	64.9	19.5	6,742	254.1	33,901	210
Sacramento--Roseville--Arden-Arcade, CA.......	5,224	109,282	17,012.0	6,397.8	3,327	24,372	2,889.2	797.2	167,269	8,301.7	2,093,979	7,873
Saginaw, MI...........................	582	17,262	1,766.5	712.8	328	1,943	161.3	45.2	10,443	403.3	47,805	333
St. Cloud, MN........................	497	18,050	1,736.2	799.1	438	2,932	286.2	73.2	13,265	650.7	164,395	770
St. George, UT.......................	500	7,443	830.8	271.4	188	1,043	87.9	24.3	13,717	649.4	535,219	2,889
St. Joseph, MO-KS.................	380	8,613	902.6	367.8	208	1,294	140.0	39.2	6,408	259.3	18,211	93
St. Louis, MO-IL.....................	8,729	185,365	18,992.4	7,415.9	4,924	33,886	3,497.5	1,037.4	187,228	8,303.7	1,635,614	7,338
Salem, OR.............................	1,162	19,987	1,955.5	833.3	571	2,726	241.4	74.3	21,285	978.1	383,215	1,684
Salinas, CA............................	994	14,898	2,151.0	838.2	560	3,765	457.6	111.7	25,072	1,420.2	225,274	732
Salisbury, MD-DE..................	1,062	22,506	2,375.2	963.4	711	4,120	359.8	107.3	29,115	1,485.7	535,425	3,642
Salt Lake City, UT.................	3,025	61,712	7,734.6	2,715.1	1,930	12,970	1,348.9	402.0	88,227	4,391.4	1,770,443	8,750
San Angelo, TX	270	6,877	701.7	303.3	213	1,158	130.1	31.8	8,772	340.7	56,755	262
San Antonio-New Braunfels, TX...............................	5,165	124,245	13,302.5	4,824.4	3,055	21,342	1,912.9	575.5	179,833	8,370.3	2,001,886	11,497
San Diego-Carlsbad, CA.......	8,522	151,783	21,337.8	7,872.6	5,193	41,437	4,080.6	1,179.4	277,207	13,981.5	2,210,176	9,834
San Francisco-Oakland-Hayward, CA.............	13,665	244,910	38,656.8	14,517.2	8,720	66,357	12,726.2	2,535.8	447,000	26,072.8	4,363,842	17,421
Oakland-Hayward-Berkeley, CA Div 36084	7,150	133,199	21,211.7	7,813.2	4,276	30,323	3,881.3	1,077.8	238,323	12,557.4	NA	NA
San Francisco-Redwood City-South San Francisco, CA..............	5,398	95,851	15,342.8	5,855.6	3,801	31,495	8,261.0	1,298.0	170,821	10,698.2	NA	NA
San Rafael, CA Div 42034....	1,117	15,860	2,102.3	848.3	643	4,539	583.8	160.1	37,856	2,817.1	NA	NA
San Jose-Sunnyvale-Santa Clara, CA..............	5,506	100,436	17,164.2	6,157.0	3,076	21,108	3,516.2	733.7	147,097	8,605.2	2,023,434	8,744
San Luis Obispo-Paso Robles-Arroyo Grande, CA	1,010	14,086	1,580.5	650.0	430	2,668	216.9	60.5	25,329	1,347.8	270,306	1,050
Santa Cruz-Watsonville, CA...	893	12,989	1,689.9	622.3	451	2,973	328.1	98.5	25,079	1,268.8	59,875	426
Santa Fe, NM........................	513	8,697	961.0	384.4	335	1,892	268.6	66.4	16,294	757.5	65,954	273
Santa Maria-Santa Barbara, CA	1,360	20,279	2,637.3	949.2	725	4,544	933.5	142.1	34,480	1,960.7	204,861	928
Santa Rosa, CA.....................	1,462	23,222	3,156.2	1,198.4	853	4,845	494.1	146.9	45,132	2,320.8	1,065,856	3,279
Savannah, GA.......................	830	20,161	2,442.9	911.6	498	3,921	368.3	118.2	27,032	1,149.3	628,544	3,158
Scranton--Wilkes-Barre--Hazleton, PA..............	1,764	43,487	4,120.7	1,722.2	1,012	5,221	498.0	131.3	30,691	1,493.6	119,906	553
Seattle-Tacoma-Bellevue, WA	10,994	207,089	26,020.0	10,446.3	7,088	43,847	10,657.9	1,493.5	263,135	13,822.8	5,514,574	28,186
Seattle-Bellevue-Everett, WA Div 42644	9,079	163,844	20,650.8	8,327.4	5,760	35,714	9,897.2	1,252.5	219,280	11,742.8	NA	NA
Tacoma-Lakewood, WA Div 45104	1,915	43,245	5,369.3	2,118.8	1,328	8,133	760.7	241.0	43,855	2,080.0	NA	NA
Sebastian-Vero Beach, FL	466	7,828	886.2	333.8	280	1,395	124.5	34.6	13,415	678.3	520,258	1,372
Sebring, FL............................	325	5,021	576.5	194.8	134	504	37.4	9.1	5,715	221.0	55,084	271
Sheboygan, WI.......................	299	6,483	597.2	247.8	202	992	67.4	19.5	5,536	245.0	48,926	191
Sherman-Denison, TX............	381	9,105	809.1	337.4	139	834	81.0	27.5	9,935	497.1	123,504	757
Shreveport-Bossier City, LA ...	1,150	35,588	3,413.9	1,334.0	581	3,848	379.2	103.9	33,622	1,363.4	232,444	1,219
Sierra Vista-Douglas, AZ........	273	4,896	408.9	167.4	150	684	53.1	16.1	6,703	203.1	39,907	227
Sioux City, IA-NE-SD..............	487	11,259	1,083.6	409.5	317	2,057	192.8	55.5	10,323	490.6	97,004	468
Sioux Falls, SD......................	636	24,272	2,615.5	1,082.9	478	2,699	293.8	76.5	19,514	1,027.8	391,642	2,388
South Bend-Mishawaka, IN-MI	704	18,666	2,226.8	752.1	517	3,460	318.4	91.6	18,906	753.3	163,658	738
Spartanburg, SC....................	613	11,037	1,165.9	495.2	443	3,072	334.2	82.5	20,788	931.3	445,607	2,685
Spokane-Spokane Valley, WA	1,598	D	D	D	888	D	D	D	33,117	1,493.8	637,724	3,174
Springfield, IL	457	20,585	2,565.9	894.3	490	3,383	422.4	126.1	13,101	502.8	84,409	506
Springfield, MA......................	1,596	55,768	4,697.9	2,118.5	1,110	7,289	661.2	187.6	37,642	1,751.7	152,142	659
Springfield, MO.....................	1,095	33,457	3,330.3	1,366.5	815	5,245	457.3	131.9	34,179	1,576.7	396,800	1,953
Springfield, OH......................	313	10,029	912.0	334.8	212	1,363	134.3	40.5	6,613	250.0	18,048	68
State College, PA..................	363	7,882	767.4	316.6	249	1,471	131.7	37.0	10,130	457.9	83,405	328
Staunton-Waynesboro, VA	244	6,985	733.2	275.4	237	1,272	121.3	36.9	7,286	332.3	54,167	317
Stockton-Lodi, CA..................	1,361	27,052	3,447.7	1,264.8	841	5,038	445.0	135.0	38,315	2,028.6	1,003,804	3,280
Sumter, SC............................	188	5,504	471.1	184.1	130	996	77.4	27.8	6,047	207.7	35,594	279
Syracuse, NY........................	1,666	46,313	5,000.1	1,985.0	1,157	7,013	701.6	199.0	37,562	1,665.4	144,258	738
Tallahassee, FL.....................	851	19,656	2,074.4	853.0	692	4,701	687.4	176.0	26,597	984.0	342,588	3,201
Tampa-St. Petersburg-Clearwater, FL.............	8,585	162,388	21,286.9	7,571.4	4,856	28,790	2,982.5	812.9	246,143	10,436.9	4,619,882	17,452
Terre Haute, IN.....................	458	10,665	1,309.9	409.5	262	1,677	144.4	39.2	7,864	277.3	14,026	130

Table C. Metropolitan Areas — Government Employment and Payroll, and Local Government Finances

Area name	Full-time equivalent employees	March payroll (dollars)	Adminis-tration, judicial, and legal	Police and corrections	Fire protection	Highways and transpor-tation	Health and welfare	Natural resources and utilities	Education and libraries	Total (mil dol)	Inter-govern-mental (mil dol)	Total (mil dol)	Per capita[1] Total	Per capita[1] Property
	171	172	173	174	175	176	177	178	179	180	181	182	183	184
Reading, PA.............	14,566	69,528,665	6.1	16.3	5.1	2.6	4.7	5.3	58.7	2,039.3	792.5	835.6	2,021	1,642
Redding, CA..............	6,528	30,533,939	6.7	8.7	2.8	3.4	15.6	9.0	52.2	922.9	498.8	217.9	1,220	1,000
Reno, NV..................	13,611	57,292,494	10.4	14.1	5.7	4.2	4.2	8.4	50.4	1,736.5	755.1	608.1	1,402	1,025
Richmond, VA............	47,868	168,064,481	7.1	13.2	5.2	1.8	6.2	5.1	57.6	4,453.2	1,860.0	1,873.9	1,521	1,127
Riverside-San Bernardino-Ontario, CA..................	137,986	750,815,862	7.1	10.8	3.0	2.2	12.9	6.4	55.7	22,872.7	12,544.1	5,769.7	1,326	1,022
Roanoke, VA.............	11,938	41,210,661	8.0	9.5	5.8	2.0	5.0	6.0	62.2	1,089.3	447.6	480.6	1,550	1,087
Rochester, MN..........	6,278	37,136,188	6.6	8.4	1.8	3.7	9.6	6.9	60.3	935.5	426.1	273.1	1,303	1,205
Rochester, NY...........	48,625	209,834,432	4.8	9.5	2.6	3.2	6.4	4.2	67.9	6,041.6	2,624.6	2,577.1	2,381	1,781
Rockford, IL..............	11,902	48,299,662	5.1	11.8	5.6	3.5	3.6	7.1	62.7	1,352.3	558.1	615.0	1,777	1,610
Rocky Mount, NC	8,741	30,617,673	3.2	6.0	2.3	1.7	32.7	6.1	46.8	725.6	291.0	136.9	903	699
Rome, GA.................	3,631	12,476,709	5.7	9.3	4.2	4.2	1.7	5.5	67.7	620.3	284.0	151.4	1,574	957
Sacramento--Roseville--Arden-Arcade, CA..................	74,788	405,371,174	6.2	12.5	5.4	3.7	8.2	11.7	48.6	11,604.0	5,395.4	3,303.5	1,504	1,115
Saginaw, MI.............	5,686	21,466,345	8.3	8.5	2.2	2.7	9.8	4.8	61.7	786.5	475.8	154.2	777	684
St. Cloud, MN...........	5,890	30,573,727	7.4	9.3	1.2	4.2	13.3	3.7	58.2	806.5	393.2	236.4	1,241	1,100
St. George, UT..........	4,130	14,492,173	7.3	10.1	1.7	2.6	6.5	13.4	56.5	453.7	154.1	197.8	1,366	972
St. Joseph, MO-KS....	4,475	13,492,001	5.7	7.9	3.9	3.6	2.8	5.1	69.9	408.2	157.7	172.1	1,346	855
St. Louis, MO-IL........	99,216	391,779,336	5.2	10.7	5.1	5.6	2.8	5.2	63.6	10,918.1	3,849.2	5,146.2	1,841	1,249
Salem, OR................	13,276	58,238,836	5.8	9.3	3.5	3.1	4.0	3.9	68.1	1,449.9	756.3	442.2	1,116	1,009
Salinas, CA..............	16,674	95,953,296	5.6	9.2	2.7	3.8	28.8	5.1	41.4	3,062.0	1,376.2	682.3	1,599	1,199
Salisbury, MD-DE	12,705	51,865,541	5.6	9.0	1.0	1.9	3.6	5.9	70.9	1,432.6	624.3	557.2	1,459	1,077
Salt Lake City, UT......	36,279	131,818,213	7.3	10.3	5.1	9.5	5.0	8.7	51.6	3,934.4	1,398.7	1,572.5	1,399	1,008
San Angelo, TX	4,541	12,163,357	8.9	16.3	6.6	1.5	3.5	6.2	55.4	335.7	127.3	150.0	1,306	1,006
San Antonio-New Braunfels, TX........................	94,742	356,044,474	4.4	8.7	3.2	3.7	9.8	10.5	58.5	8,697.5	3,005.2	3,729.5	1,669	1,358
San Diego-Carlsbad, CA.........	97,178	529,647,292	9.3	10.8	3.9	3.4	11.1	7.0	52.0	16,495.7	6,780.5	5,691.2	1,791	1,381
San Francisco-Oakland-Hayward, CA..................	155,343	998,941,828	7.6	12.2	5.4	11.0	17.4	9.2	35.0	32,009.2	10,425.4	11,842.8	2,658	1,820
Oakland-Hayward-Berkeley, CA Div 36084	87,214	540,452,372	5.4	11.4	5.0	8.5	17.1	9.7	40.0	17,465.2	6,071.1	5,674.3	2,154	1,538
San Francisco-Redwood City-South San Francisco, CA	59,585	406,735,774	10.1	13.4	5.7	15.2	18.9	8.4	27.1	13,022.2	4,026.7	5,343.5	3,414	2,179
San Rafael, CA Div 42034......	8,544	51,753,682	10.8	11.2	8.5	4.2	8.9	10.4	44.3	1,521.9	327.6	825.0	3,222	2,533
San Jose-Sunnyvale-Santa Clara, CA..................	61,998	413,816,866	7.6	10.1	4.9	4.9	20.6	6.4	42.8	13,018.5	4,094.2	4,897.7	2,585	1,941
San Luis Obispo-Paso Robles-Arroyo Grande, CA.........	8,194	48,094,004	7.2	11.4	2.8	2.5	6.9	6.4	57.6	1,189.7	435.4	547.8	1,994	1,615
Santa Cruz-Watsonville, CA.....	9,292	50,504,116	8.1	10.1	3.9	7.3	13.5	7.9	47.1	1,432.9	632.4	483.8	1,813	1,441
Santa Fe, NM..........	4,848	18,022,225	9.3	12.0	6.4	3.8	4.1	9.6	48.1	527.4	253.9	199.3	1,361	807
Santa Maria-Santa Barbara, CA	15,712	89,085,924	7.3	11.4	5.3	3.7	14.4	7.2	48.4	2,761.9	960.5	877.6	2,035	1,531
Santa Rosa, CA........	16,072	90,178,192	9.5	12.6	3.9	2.6	12.9	7.2	47.9	2,545.8	918.8	972.6	1,978	1,555
Savannah, GA..........	13,962	46,151,027	10.0	13.9	3.6	3.3	6.0	6.9	53.1	1,947.0	409.1	744.0	2,056	1,229
Scranton--Wilkes-Barre--Hazleton, PA.................	16,712	64,672,766	7.6	11.9	3.2	3.8	5.2	5.6	61.4	1,935.2	804.6	806.0	1,430	1,072
Seattle-Tacoma-Bellevue, WA..	109,144	628,710,550	8.0	10.0	6.7	11.2	9.8	13.4	38.7	18,576.7	5,896.1	7,417.8	2,088	1,239
Seattle-Bellevue-Everett, WA Div 42644......................	85,210	497,008,852	7.8	10.1	6.0	12.0	11.7	13.8	36.5	15,276.4	4,566.4	6,183.2	2,256	1,287
Tacoma-Lakewood, WA Div 45104	23,934	131,701,698	8.7	9.5	9.2	8.4	2.7	12.1	47.1	3,300.2	1,329.7	1,234.7	1,521	1,076
Sebastian-Vero Beach, FL	4,188	14,858,891	4.7	16.3	4.8	5.0	5.1	12.6	48.7	445.1	88.8	266.5	1,896	1,553
Sebring, FL.............	3,358	10,445,615	8.2	12.8	2.4	5.5	3.7	6.4	56.9	264.2	111.3	100.2	1,021	799
Sheboygan, WI.........	4,469	19,622,392	8.8	8.8	2.1	5.2	8.0	3.0	63.5	489.1	213.6	207.1	1,801	1,746
Sherman-Denison, TX..	5,248	18,290,717	5.6	9.2	3.5	2.7	4.2	4.8	69.0	414.8	144.6	188.3	1,544	1,271
Shreveport-Bossier City, LA	18,558	60,559,700	6.4	15.5	6.0	2.9	2.1	5.0	60.8	1,909.4	657.9	985.4	2,204	997
Sierra Vista-Douglas, AZ.........	4,879	16,984,358	11.7	10.2	5.2	2.9	3.0	3.3	61.1	397.9	175.5	144.2	1,092	821
Sioux City, IA-NE-SD....	7,016	27,062,681	5.1	8.4	2.6	4.9	5.3	5.2	67.0	775.3	326.0	295.7	1,751	1,347
Sioux Falls, SD.........	7,176	25,345,869	6.6	9.8	3.7	4.0	2.2	5.5	66.9	751.2	210.8	404.9	1,707	1,166
South Bend-Mishawaka, IN-MI	10,955	36,623,695	5.5	11.4	6.3	4.0	1.2	6.4	63.3	1,211.4	523.3	434.1	1,362	1,022
Spartanburg, SC........	15,589	60,744,767	3.4	5.1	1.5	0.6	46.5	4.0	38.2	1,645.4	411.5	361.9	1,142	1,015
Spokane-Spokane Valley, WA..	15,408	75,996,689	9.2	11.0	6.8	7.0	5.4	7.5	51.4	2,043.9	939.8	680.9	1,279	830
Springfield, IL	9,009	38,285,598	5.0	9.2	3.6	4.6	2.0	19.1	56.1	823.8	336.6	347.9	1,641	1,427
Springfield, MA.........	24,505	106,805,892	3.3	9.5	6.2	2.5	1.8	7.6	67.7	2,499.8	1,290.8	947.8	1,515	1,471
Springfield, MO.........	15,530	53,052,304	4.5	7.1	2.8	3.8	8.8	10.0	56.5	1,328.3	481.9	530.1	1,192	662
Springfield, OH.........	5,386	19,627,638	7.6	10.0	4.2	2.3	8.2	4.4	57.6	501.3	270.1	168.3	1,227	774
State College, PA......	3,965	14,048,206	7.5	8.6	0.0	7.9	9.9	5.8	58.3	455.2	154.4	216.4	1,394	1,018
Staunton-Waynesboro, VA	4,314	12,615,495	6.6	13.2	3.6	1.7	3.9	3.8	64.6	321.2	157.8	126.3	1,064	712
Stockton-Lodi, CA......	23,911	123,453,125	6.5	12.7	3.3	2.6	14.7	5.0	53.3	3,894.2	2,276.8	855.2	1,217	851
Sumter, SC..............	6,341	17,021,292	4.2	6.1	1.7	1.8	1.6	3.3	80.4	271.8	124.5	114.5	1,060	719
Syracuse, NY	30,026	133,886,154	3.8	8.2	2.5	4.2	6.3	4.1	69.2	3,812.8	1,691.2	1,541.0	2,332	1,687
Tallahassee, FL.........	14,377	48,690,908	8.9	11.4	3.1	5.3	3.7	13.3	50.6	1,358.3	476.8	458.3	1,221	865
Tampa-St. Petersburg-Clearwater, FL.................	98,152	350,589,348	7.0	15.7	5.6	4.0	2.8	8.5	53.8	9,943.4	3,586.7	3,926.4	1,381	1,060
Terre Haute, IN..........	5,719	18,131,023	7.8	8.7	4.1	4.4	5.0	5.4	63.3	562.1	284.5	168.7	978	782

1. Based on the resident population estimated as of July 1 of the year shown.

Area name	Direct general expenditure Total (mil dol)	Per capita[1] (dollars)	Percent of total for: Education	Health and hospitals	Police protection	Public welfare	Highways	Debt outstanding Total (mil dol)	Per capita[1] (dollars)	Government employment, 2017 Federal civilian	Federal military	State and local	Individual income tax returns, 2016 Number of returns	Mean adjusted gross income	Mean income tax
	185	186	187	188	189	190	191	192	193	194	195	196	197	198	199
Reading, PA..................................	2,024.3	4,896	54.5	3.4	4.1	7.2	2.8	3,478.7	8,413	944	1,055	21,427	203,120	58,467	7,047
Redding, CA..................................	906.1	5,074	43.3	8.1	5.8	10.6	4.0	544.3	3,048	1,315	302	11,550	76,910	53,589	5,742
Reno, NV..................................	1,700.3	3,919	35.7	1.0	6.7	4.2	3.4	4,528.8	10,439	3,733	1,284	24,652	225,740	73,430	11,447
Richmond, VA..................................	4,393.3	3,566	45.4	3.2	6.9	3.5	2.9	4,997.3	4,056	17,216	14,665	96,089	615,770	68,250	9,130
Riverside-San Bernardino-Ontario, CA..................................	23,480.7	5,398	39.0	11.9	6.3	7.3	4.9	24,738.9	5,687	20,835	23,768	236,980	1,887,660	53,810	5,533
Roanoke, VA..................................	1,134.6	3,659	44.3	2.7	5.5	7.8	1.9	1,358.0	4,379	3,860	1,020	17,404	145,970	58,088	6,937
Rochester, MN..................................	953.0	4,547	35.9	2.2	5.0	7.4	11.0	3,142.1	14,990	970	767	11,614	109,150	68,995	8,852
Rochester, NY..................................	6,147.1	5,680	50.8	4.1	3.8	11.1	4.2	4,984.9	4,606	4,905	1,713	70,012	518,350	60,071	7,387
Rockford, IL..................................	1,291.0	3,731	51.6	1.6	7.8	2.7	5.4	877.0	2,534	900	699	16,091	160,240	53,917	6,177
Rocky Mount, NC..................................	764.0	5,037	34.6	34.0	5.2	5.1	1.5	144.7	954	387	324	9,984	65,210	46,662	4,743
Rome, GA..................................	658.4	6,846	27.4	47.2	2.2	0.1	2.6	238.0	2,474	202	260	5,479	39,590	50,508	5,213
Sacramento--Roseville--Arden-Arcade, CA..................................	11,753.9	5,351	35.4	5.1	5.1	7.8	5.9	20,700.4	9,424	14,323	4,172	233,089	1,041,850	68,582	8,779
Saginaw, MI..................................	801.9	4,043	42.8	14.5	5.8	0.7	5.8	494.0	2,490	1,457	314	9,317	89,760	48,021	5,364
St. Cloud, MN..................................	798.0	4,189	41.0	7.6	5.1	5.3	11.0	1,171.2	6,149	2,393	678	11,128	93,140	61,034	7,763
St. George, UT..................................	401.3	2,771	50.1	0.8	7.7	0.0	6.0	585.2	4,041	584	659	7,842	67,010	57,070	6,228
St. Joseph, MO-KS..................................	361.2	2,824	56.2	2.3	8.0	0.6	5.5	644.5	5,038	637	423	9,066	54,660	50,676	5,527
St. Louis, MO-IL..................................	11,016.7	3,940	50.5	2.4	7.4	0.6	5.2	13,307.4	4,760	28,591	13,454	137,584	1,356,180	68,804	9,632
Salem, OR..................................	1,466.0	3,699	55.7	4.1	5.3	0.2	4.7	2,202.9	5,558	1,371	1,022	44,127	183,470	54,996	5,739
Salinas, CA..................................	2,904.3	6,806	36.5	22.7	4.6	5.4	2.6	1,444.4	3,385	5,201	4,748	28,817	196,270	62,999	7,729
Salisbury, MD-DE..................................	1,397.6	3,660	55.9	1.9	6.1	1.0	2.5	1,055.9	2,765	1,111	1,891	22,410	190,380	57,150	6,888
Salt Lake City, UT..................................	3,773.6	3,358	42.9	1.2	5.6	2.1	5.3	7,423.5	6,606	12,623	5,062	96,411	534,240	66,615	8,504
San Angelo, TX..................................	359.0	3,125	52.5	3.3	5.7	0.2	2.7	590.0	5,137	1,208	3,367	7,894	52,370	54,304	7,037
San Antonio-New Braunfels, TX....	8,877.6	3,974	45.3	13.6	5.3	1.8	3.0	21,467.3	9,609	35,985	37,273	132,779	1,094,440	59,074	7,644
San Diego-Carlsbad, CA..................................	16,846.0	5,302	37.0	9.8	5.3	6.9	2.9	27,732.0	8,729	47,386	100,959	197,739	1,561,790	74,248	10,382
San Francisco-Oakland-Hayward, CA..................................	31,954.0	7,172	25.5	16.6	5.8	5.5	3.3	56,702.8	12,726	32,577	9,073	287,500	2,322,840	120,653	21,775
Oakland-Hayward-Berkeley, CA Div 36084..........................	18,716.4	7,105	26.5	15.3	5.6	5.5	3.2	31,762.2	12,057	14,008	5,626	151,698	NA	NA	NA
San Francisco-Redwood City-South San Francisco, CA....	11,668.6	7,455	22.7	19.9	6.1	5.8	3.5	22,636.4	14,463	17,814	2,949	120,773	NA	NA	NA
San Rafael, CA Div 42034..........	1,569.1	6,127	34.5	6.9	6.2	4.1	3.1	2,304.2	8,998	755	498	15,029	NA	NA	NA
San Jose-Sunnyvale-Santa Clara, CA..................................	12,193.4	6,437	32.5	22.1	5.1	5.2	2.2	18,023.9	9,514	10,310	3,411	86,702	944,090	150,896	27,867
San Luis Obispo-Paso Robles-Arroyo Grande, CA..............	1,206.8	4,391	38.5	5.9	6.2	8.2	3.9	850.7	3,096	562	507	22,345	131,340	69,481	9,013
Santa Cruz-Watsonville, CA..........	1,415.2	5,305	36.6	6.6	6.3	8.5	2.3	1,074.8	4,029	543	390	19,407	130,730	79,736	11,812
Santa Fe, NM..................................	578.2	3,950	45.8	1.3	6.0	2.2	3.5	916.2	6,259	988	387	14,463	75,700	69,520	10,082
Santa Maria-Santa Barbara, CA....	2,786.6	6,462	32.4	18.7	5.7	6.7	3.0	1,346.9	3,123	3,636	3,093	32,176	201,430	72,985	10,610
Santa Rosa, CA..................................	2,601.9	5,290	35.4	10.3	6.3	6.4	5.0	2,547.1	5,179	1,403	1,474	27,667	242,950	74,009	10,122
Savannah, GA..................................	1,874.0	5,178	31.0	28.9	9.3	0.3	2.3	889.2	2,457	2,923	5,403	21,201	167,790	58,311	6,866
Scranton--Wilkes-Barre--Hazleton, PA..................................	2,105.8	3,736	51.8	0.4	3.4	5.0	4.2	2,409.6	4,275	4,304	1,409	25,299	273,140	51,261	5,995
Seattle-Tacoma-Bellevue, WA.......	17,216.0	4,847	33.8	9.8	5.1	1.0	5.3	30,708.3	8,645	34,472	44,943	243,514	1,881,230	94,630	15,327
Seattle-Bellevue-Everett, WA Div 42644..........................	13,942.5	5,088	31.5	11.7	5.0	1.1	5.2	26,143.1	9,540	22,458	13,498	196,446	NA	NA	NA
Tacoma-Lakewood, WA Div 45104..........................	3,273.5	4,033	43.7	2.1	5.8	0.6	5.6	4,565.2	5,624	12,014	31,445	47,068	NA	NA	NA
Sebastian-Vero Beach, FL	470.0	3,343	38.2	4.8	9.4	0.8	8.2	436.2	3,103	365	275	4,729	74,040	87,256	14,924
Sebring, FL..................................	276.6	2,818	46.6	3.7	7.8	0.6	6.0	143.0	1,457	271	183	3,793	42,110	40,133	3,792
Sheboygan, WI..................................	492.9	4,286	55.2	3.6	5.7	6.1	8.2	375.9	3,269	197	318	5,592	58,650	58,998	6,957
Sherman-Denison, TX..................	423.3	3,471	54.8	3.3	5.1	0.0	6.0	717.6	5,885	334	260	6,576	57,330	56,567	6,664
Shreveport-Bossier City, LA	1,871.4	4,185	49.7	1.4	7.4	0.2	3.7	1,823.7	4,078	4,913	6,756	25,571	189,090	52,253	6,214
Sierra Vista-Douglas, AZ..............	407.1	3,082	44.0	3.5	12.3	4.9	7.3	161.6	1,223	4,834	4,071	6,230	51,680	47,084	4,575
Sioux City, IA-NE-SD..................................	799.7	4,734	53.5	7.0	4.5	1.1	5.7	754.0	4,464	929	636	10,123	79,020	58,659	7,397
Sioux Falls, SD..................................	772.0	3,254	47.6	1.5	5.3	0.5	10.0	951.0	4,008	2,757	1,516	11,251	131,530	72,983	10,786
South Bend-Mishawaka, IN-MI......	1,028.2	3,227	51.4	1.7	4.7	1.1	3.4	1,041.8	3,270	972	972	14,851	148,960	57,453	7,313
Spartanburg, SC..................................	1,655.8	5,223	33.7	46.8	3.0	0.4	1.0	1,083.5	3,418	599	1,248	22,244	145,510	52,270	5,713
Spokane-Spokane Valley, WA.......	2,096.5	3,939	45.9	6.2	5.2	0.2	4.3	1,764.2	3,315	5,150	4,366	35,462	255,100	59,121	7,318
Springfield, IL..................................	869.8	4,103	52.8	1.5	7.5	0.9	4.5	2,540.3	11,983	1,830	463	18,839	104,530	64,363	8,384
Springfield, MA..................................	2,618.5	4,185	57.6	0.6	4.8	0.6	3.1	1,821.1	2,910	5,311	1,645	47,946	291,590	59,116	7,224
Springfield, MO..................................	1,305.4	2,936	50.3	8.6	6.8	0.8	6.6	1,931.0	4,343	2,472	1,538	26,192	200,210	54,085	6,504
Springfield, OH..................................	474.6	3,459	49.3	5.8	5.9	6.2	3.3	206.0	1,502	574	339	6,402	62,720	47,399	4,745
State College, PA..................................	453.5	2,923	51.0	2.2	3.5	7.9	6.1	486.7	3,136	477	449	49,688	59,660	67,532	8,800
Staunton-Waynesboro, VA	339.0	2,856	51.3	2.7	4.7	6.7	3.4	294.4	2,480	275	382	8,420	57,510	51,649	5,196
Stockton-Lodi, CA..................................	3,717.2	5,291	40.5	9.2	5.9	8.8	3.5	3,309.2	4,710	3,085	1,145	39,894	309,720	56,746	6,155
Sumter, SC..................................	256.2	2,371	54.5	1.2	7.1	0.3	2.5	245.3	2,270	1,207	5,251	5,342	46,710	42,219	3,876
Syracuse, NY..................................	4,111.0	6,220	49.2	3.2	3.0	9.8	5.1	4,285.9	6,485	4,980	1,143	49,014	305,600	61,318	7,586
Tallahassee, FL..................................	1,372.1	3,655	40.1	1.3	7.9	0.1	7.2	4,333.3	11,544	2,092	701	57,127	163,620	55,675	7,045
Tampa-St. Petersburg-Clearwater, FL..................................	10,477.2	3,685	38.4	3.3	8.7	2.4	4.2	11,252.6	3,958	23,594	12,077	124,925	1,422,350	59,831	8,289
Terre Haute, IN..................................	504.6	2,925	50.6	6.3	3.2	0.5	3.2	559.6	3,244	1,294	498	11,313	73,810	47,043	4,771

1. Based on the resident population estimated as of July 1 of the year shown.

Table C. Metropolitan Areas — Land Area and Population

CBSA/ DIV Code[1]	Area name	Land area[2] (sq mi)	Population, 2018			Population characteristics, 2018										
						Race alone or in combination, not Hispanic or Latino (percent)					Age (percent)					
			Total persons	Rank	Per square mile	White	Black	American Indian, Alaska Native	Asian and Pacific Islander	Percent Hispanic or Latino[3]	Under 5 years	5 to 17 years	18 to 24 years	25 to 34 years	35 to 44 years	45 to 54 years
		1	2	3	4	5	6	7	8	9	10	11	12	13	14	15
45500	Texarkana, TX-AR	2,043.0	150,242	278	73.5	67.3	25.6	1.5	1.5	6.2	6.5	17.1	8.2	13.4	12.6	12.4
45540	The Villages, FL	557.1	128,754	307	231.1	85.8	7.4	0.7	1.2	5.7	2.0	5.1	3.1	5.8	5.9	6.7
45780	Toledo, OH	1,363.4	602,871	93	442.2	76.3	16.2	0.8	2.2	7.0	6.1	16.3	10.6	13.6	11.4	12.2
45820	Topeka, KS	3,232.6	232,594	195	72.0	80.6	7.9	2.5	1.9	10.5	6.1	17.5	8.1	11.9	11.7	12.0
45940	Trenton, NJ	224.4	369,811	145	1,648.0	50.3	20.5	0.5	12.6	18.1	5.7	15.6	11.4	12.5	12.7	13.9
46060	Tucson, AZ	9,187.2	1,039,073	53	113.1	53.2	4.2	3.0	4.2	37.6	5.6	15.2	11.8	12.8	11.4	11.0
46140	Tulsa, OK	6,269.7	993,797	55	158.5	70.3	9.7	13.0	3.3	10.2	6.7	18.0	8.6	13.8	12.6	12.2
46220	Tuscaloosa, AL	2,846.3	243,575	190	85.6	60.4	34.7	0.6	1.8	3.8	6.0	15.0	15.3	14.5	11.9	11.4
46340	Tyler, TX	921.5	230,221	198	249.8	60.7	18.1	0.8	2.2	19.9	6.9	17.7	9.6	13.7	11.8	11.7
46520	Urban Honolulu, HI	600.6	980,080	56	1,631.8	31.8	3.7	1.5	78.6	10.0	6.3	14.9	9.3	15.2	12.8	11.9
46540	Utica-Rome, NY	2,623.8	291,410	167	111.1	85.9	6.2	0.6	3.9	5.2	5.5	15.6	9.2	12.3	11.0	12.9
46660	Valdosta, GA	1,607.2	146,174	286	90.9	56.7	35.3	0.8	2.6	6.6	6.7	17.1	14.9	14.9	11.3	10.9
46700	Vallejo-Fairfield, CA	821.8	446,610	121	543.5	41.9	15.9	1.3	19.9	26.9	6.0	16.1	8.7	14.7	12.6	12.6
47020	Victoria, TX	1,734.1	99,619	354	57.4	46.2	6.2	0.6	1.5	46.6	6.8	18.2	9.1	13.7	12.0	11.1
47220	Vineland-Bridgeton, NJ	483.4	150,972	276	312.3	47.5	20.1	1.4	1.9	31.4	6.3	17.6	8.1	14.3	13.0	13.1
47260	Virginia Beach-Norfolk-Newport News, VA-NC.	2,682.7	1,728,733	37	644.4	57.7	32.2	1.1	5.6	7.0	6.3	15.7	10.6	15.5	12.4	12.0
47300	Visalia-Porterville, CA	4,824.4	465,861	115	96.6	29.4	1.6	1.2	4.2	65.2	7.9	22.7	10.1	14.2	12.7	11.0
47380	Waco, TX	1,802.6	271,942	179	150.9	56.8	15.5	0.7	2.2	26.5	6.9	17.5	14.0	13.3	11.5	10.8
47460	Walla Walla, WA	2,138.6	64,981	380	30.4	74.3	2.5	1.7	3.2	20.6	5.4	15.4	12.5	12.7	11.4	11.2
47580	Warner Robins, GA	775.6	193,835	225	249.9	56.6	34.7	0.8	3.8	6.7	6.3	18.2	9.4	14.2	12.7	12.7
47900	Washington-Arlington-Alexandria, DC-VA-MD-WV	6,246.9	6,249,950	6	1,000.5	47.5	26.5	0.8	12.2	16.1	6.5	16.5	8.7	15.0	14.4	13.8
47900	Silver Spring-Frederick-Rockville, MD Div 43524	1,153.5	1,308,215	X	1,134.1	51.5	18.0	0.6	14.8	18.0	6.2	17.0	8.0	12.7	13.6	14.0
47900	Washington-Arlington-Alexandria, DC-VA-MD-WV Div 47894	5,093.4	4,941,735	X	970.2	46.5	28.7	0.8	11.5	15.6	6.5	16.4	8.9	15.6	14.6	13.7
47940	Waterloo-Cedar Falls, IA	1,503.2	169,659	249	112.9	86.0	8.9	0.5	2.9	3.8	6.2	15.8	13.8	12.5	11.5	10.7
48060	Watertown-Fort Drum, NY	1,268.7	111,755	337	88.1	83.5	7.5	1.0	2.8	7.8	7.8	16.2	12.3	17.1	11.6	10.4
48140	Wausau, WI	1,545.3	135,428	297	87.6	89.9	1.4	0.9	6.6	2.8	5.9	16.9	7.6	12.0	12.3	13.1
48260	Weirton-Steubenville, WV-OH	579.9	117,064	331	201.9	93.9	5.1	0.6	0.8	1.4	4.8	14.1	8.7	10.7	10.7	13.0
48300	Wenatchee, WA	4,740.4	119,943	324	25.3	67.8	0.9	1.6	1.8	29.7	6.4	17.9	8.1	12.5	11.8	11.2
48540	Wheeling, WV-OH	943.4	140,045	293	148.4	94.9	4.3	0.6	0.8	1.1	4.9	14.2	8.1	12.0	11.3	12.6
48620	Wichita, KS	5,011.9	644,888	89	128.7	74.6	8.8	1.9	4.6	13.3	6.7	18.8	9.1	13.7	12.3	11.5
48660	Wichita Falls, TX	2,619.6	151,306	274	57.8	69.8	10.4	1.4	2.8	17.9	6.2	16.1	12.4	14.5	11.5	11.0
48700	Williamsport, PA	1,228.8	113,664	335	92.5	92.5	6.0	0.6	1.0	2.1	5.3	15.1	8.9	13.1	11.1	12.6
48900	Wilmington, NC	1,063.5	294,436	165	276.9	78.5	14.5	1.0	2.0	6.0	5.1	14.1	11.6	12.9	12.4	12.8
49020	Winchester, VA-WV	1,062.8	139,810	294	131.5	83.3	6.3	0.7	2.2	9.7	6.0	16.2	8.2	12.2	12.1	13.7
49180	Winston-Salem, NC	2,008.6	671,456	84	334.3	69.4	18.8	0.8	2.3	10.5	5.6	16.5	8.7	12.3	11.7	13.9
49340	Worcester, MA-CT	2,023.6	947,866	57	468.4	78.5	5.3	0.6	5.5	12.0	5.3	15.6	9.7	13.0	12.1	14.2
49420	Yakima, WA	4,294.5	251,446	188	58.6	44.3	1.3	4.5	2.0	49.9	8.1	21.5	9.5	13.4	11.8	11.0
49620	York-Hanover, PA	904.2	448,273	120	495.8	84.6	6.9	0.5	2.0	7.9	5.7	16.4	8.1	12.4	12.0	13.7
49660	Youngstown-Warren-Boardman, OH-PA	1,702.1	538,952	104	316.6	84.6	11.9	0.7	1.1	3.7	5.2	14.9	8.4	11.5	10.9	12.7
49700	Yuba City, CA	1,234.5	174,848	241	141.6	52.9	4.0	2.6	14.6	30.3	7.4	19.3	9.0	14.9	12.3	11.3
49740	Yuma, AZ	5,514.0	212,128	210	38.5	31.4	2.3	1.3	1.9	64.3	7.2	18.0	11.2	13.9	11.0	10.1

1. CBSA = Core Based Statistical Area. DIV = Metropolitan Division. See Appendix A for explanation. See Appendix B for list of metropolitan areas or temporarily covered by water. 2. Dry land or land partially or temporarily covered by water. 3. May be of any race.

Table C. Metropolitan Areas — **Population and Households**

Area name	Age (percent) (cont.)				Population change and components of change, 2000-2018							Households, 2017				
					Total persons		Percent change		Components of change, 2010-2018						Percent	
	55 to 64 years	65 to 74 years	75 years and over	Percent female	2000	2010	2000-2010	2010-2018	Births	Deaths	Net migration	Number	Persons per house-hold	Family house-holds	Female family house-holder[1]	One person
	16	17	18	19	20	21	22	23	24	25	26	27	28	29	30	31
Texarkana, TX-AR................	12.7	9.8	7.2	50.2	143,377	149,194	4.1	0.7	16,172	13,327	-1,710	55,934	2.60	65.5	13.3	30.6
The Villages, FL....................	13.9	33.1	24.5	50.1	53,345	93,420	75.1	37.8	3,818	12,808	43,639	55,097	2.11	66.3	3.5	29.2
Toledo, OH	13.5	9.5	6.7	51.3	618,203	610,002	-1.3	-1.2	61,528	48,392	-20,390	245,035	2.39	62.4	14.2	30.6
Topeka, KS	14.2	10.6	7.9	51.1	224,551	233,867	4.1	-0.5	24,185	19,414	-5,964	96,822	2.35	63.6	8.1	31.2
Trenton, NJ	13.1	8.5	6.6	51.1	350,761	367,511	4.8	0.6	34,662	23,990	-8,539	128,757	2.79	66.3	12.9	28.4
Tucson, AZ	12.5	11.2	8.5	50.8	843,746	980,263	16.2	6.0	96,599	75,418	38,490	403,574	2.46	61.5	12.4	29.8
Tulsa, OK	12.7	9.1	6.4	50.9	859,532	937,532	9.1	6.0	109,788	76,238	23,197	379,757	2.57	66.0	13.4	28.6
Tuscaloosa, AL.....................	11.9	8.5	5.6	51.7	203,009	230,176	13.4	5.8	23,830	17,489	7,009	84,249	2.73	66.4	16.3	27.9
Tyler, TX	12.2	9.2	7.3	51.7	174,706	209,725	20.0	9.8	25,372	16,735	11,910	77,292	2.88	70.9	10.0	25.2
Urban Honolulu, HI................	11.9	9.6	8.1	49.7	876,156	953,206	8.8	2.8	109,256	62,703	-19,098	312,625	3.04	70.4	13.2	24.4
Utica-Rome, NY	14.4	10.6	8.6	50.3	299,896	299,330	-0.2	-2.6	26,475	26,271	-8,098	113,323	2.47	62.4	11.9	32.6
Valdosta, GA.........................	10.9	7.9	5.3	51.3	119,560	139,660	16.8	4.7	16,649	9,505	-817	53,619	2.64	63.1	14.8	26.9
Vallejo-Fairfield, CA..............	13.5	9.7	6.1	50.3	394,542	413,298	4.8	8.1	42,613	26,078	17,074	151,127	2.88	70.9	14.4	23.2
Victoria, TX...........................	12.6	9.4	7.2	51.0	91,016	94,003	3.3	6.0	11,199	7,184	1,601	35,635	2.77	66.7	11.5	25.9
Vineland-Bridgeton, NJ	12.3	8.7	6.5	49.0	146,438	156,633	7.0	-3.6	16,548	12,164	-10,118	50,696	2.77	70.3	21.2	24.8
Virginia Beach-Norfolk-Newport News, VA-NC.	12.8	8.6	6.0	50.8	1,580,057	1,676,823	6.1	3.1	184,903	112,379	-20,469	641,881	2.58	67.1	14.6	26.8
Visalia-Porterville, CA............	9.9	6.7	4.7	50.0	368,021	442,181	20.2	5.4	62,255	23,912	-14,597	137,576	3.34	77.3	17.4	18.0
Waco, TX...............................	11.4	8.3	6.3	51.2	232,093	252,766	8.9	7.6	30,390	18,663	7,585	97,310	2.63	66.2	15.4	27.7
Walla Walla, WA....................	12.7	10.5	8.2	49.0	59,244	62,859	6.1	3.4	5,814	5,138	1,466	24,256	2.47	67.2	10.7	27.2
Warner Robins, GA	12.7	8.2	5.5	51.9	144,021	179,604	24.7	7.9	19,923	12,037	6,322	70,479	2.65	72.1	16.7	23.9
Washington-Arlington-Alexandria, DC-VA-MD-WV...	12.2	7.8	5.2	51.1	4,837,428	5,636,363	16.5	10.9	665,561	279,389	225,170	2,203,717	2.77	65.9	11.9	27.2
Silver Spring-Frederick-Rockville, MD Div 43524	13.2	8.7	6.6	51.5	1,068,618	1,205,355	12.8	8.5	130,738	62,652	35,107	465,548	2.78	70.4	11.4	24.2
Washington-Arlington-Alexandria, DC-VA-MD-WV Div 4	12.0	7.6	4.8	51.0	3,768,810	4,431,008	17.6	11.5	534,823	216,737	190,063	1,738,169	2.77	64.7	12.0	28.0
Waterloo-Cedar Falls, IA........	12.4	9.6	7.6	50.8	163,706	167,819	2.5	1.1	17,285	12,673	-2,653	67,711	2.41	62.7	8.1	29.8
Watertown-Fort Drum, NY......	10.9	8.0	5.7	47.4	111,738	116,234	4.0	-3.9	17,056	7,329	-14,329	41,548	2.58	64.0	9.8	29.4
Wausau, WI...........................	14.5	10.0	7.7	49.7	125,834	134,061	6.5	1.0	13,201	9,534	-2,234	55,084	2.43	64.5	6.2	27.9
Weirton-Steubenville, WV-OH	15.7	12.8	9.6	51.3	132,008	124,450	-5.7	-5.9	9,210	13,914	-2,573	48,242	2.41	63.5	11.8	30.3
Wenatchee, WA.....................	13.5	10.9	7.7	49.8	99,219	110,887	11.8	8.2	12,064	8,031	5,093	42,468	2.75	70.5	11.0	23.4
Wheeling, WV-OH	15.4	12.3	9.2	50.1	153,172	147,960	-3.4	-5.3	11,883	15,414	-4,276	51,143	2.62	64.0	9.3	32.3
Wichita, KS	12.9	8.7	6.3	50.4	579,839	630,923	8.8	2.2	74,307	46,795	-13,346	246,524	2.58	64.2	12.1	28.9
Wichita Falls, TX	12.8	8.6	7.0	48.5	151,524	151,474	0.0	-0.1	15,694	12,683	-3,176	55,426	2.45	62.0	12.6	33.3
Williamsport, PA	14.6	10.8	8.5	51.0	120,044	116,114	-3.3	-2.1	10,254	10,423	-2,245	46,122	2.33	64.7	9.6	28.4
Wilmington, NC	13.3	10.9	6.9	51.9	201,389	254,881	26.6	15.5	23,650	19,312	34,795	117,982	2.37	57.6	11.0	35.3
Winchester, VA-WV	13.7	10.5	7.3	50.2	102,997	128,475	24.7	8.8	12,908	9,725	8,171	51,174	2.66	70.2	10.6	23.6
Winston-Salem, NC...............	13.8	10.2	7.3	51.9	569,207	640,537	12.5	4.8	61,195	51,497	21,590	263,215	2.48	65.4	12.0	30.2
Worcester, MA-CT	14.4	9.2	6.6	50.7	860,054	916,764	6.6	3.4	80,730	65,331	16,124	352,356	2.58	64.4	12.3	28.0
Yakima, WA...........................	10.8	8.0	5.8	50.0	222,581	243,240	9.3	3.4	33,531	15,851	-9,471	82,107	3.00	72.4	14.8	23.4
York-Hanover, PA	14.2	10.1	7.4	50.6	381,751	435,008	14.0	3.0	40,590	32,619	5,722	171,781	2.54	69.0	10.3	24.0
Youngstown-Warren-Boardman, OH-PA........	15.1	11.9	9.5	51.0	602,964	565,781	-6.2	-4.7	46,312	57,303	-15,617	231,423	2.27	61.1	13.7	33.1
Yuba City, CA	11.7	8.2	6.0	49.8	139,149	166,902	19.9	4.8	20,899	11,154	-1,815	58,173	2.94	67.8	10.6	26.0
Yuma, AZ..............................	9.8	9.2	9.5	48.5	160,026	195,750	22.3	8.4	25,471	11,828	2,437	74,620	2.71	75.0	15.1	20.5

1. No spouse present

882 (Texarkana, TX-AR)—(Yuma, AZ)

Items 16—31

Area name	Persons in group quarters, 2018	Daytime population, 2017		Births, 2018		Deaths, 2018		Persons under 65 with no health insurance 2017		Medicare, 2018			Serious crimes known to police[2], 2016 Total	
		Number	Employment/ residence ratio	Total	Rate[1]	Number	Rate[1]	Number	Percent	Total Beneficiaries	Enrolled in Original Medicare	Enrolled in Medicare Advantage	Number	Rate[3]
	32	33	34	35	36	37	38	39	40	41	42	43	44	45
Texarkana, TX-AR..............	7,800	156,423	1.07	1,911	12.7	1,685	11.2	15,640	13.3	30,852	23,541	7,311	5,622	3,760
The Villages, FL...................	8,197	136,899	1.47	456	3.5	1,920	14.9	5,512	11.9	71,177	41,740	29,437	1,385	1,110
Toledo, OH..........................	17,030	622,382	1.07	7,201	11.9	5,952	9.9	34,770	7.0	116,389	66,184	50,205	21,268	3,519
Topeka, KS..........................	5,044	233,689	1.00	2,724	11.7	2,353	10.1	16,939	9.0	50,236	42,836	7,400	9,894	4,256
Trenton, NJ..........................	20,371	432,022	1.32	4,198	11.4	3,018	8.2	29,244	9.7	64,746	45,186	19,560	8,075	2,181
Tucson, AZ..........................	25,279	1,024,071	1.00	11,251	10.8	9,977	9.6	87,312	10.9	219,585	116,876	102,709	48,485	4,763
Tulsa, OK	15,529	995,999	1.01	13,012	13.1	9,861	9.9	127,899	15.4	179,602	126,196	53,406	41,467	4,212
Tuscaloosa, AL....................	12,554	242,841	1.01	2,888	11.9	2,236	9.2	18,892	9.6	44,604	28,648	15,956	7,614	3,156
Tyler, TX	4,800	233,229	1.06	3,109	13.5	2,152	9.3	36,912	19.8	44,072	30,468	13,604	736	327
Urban Honolulu, HI...............	35,936	991,743	1.01	12,368	12.6	8,600	8.8	32,629	4.1	179,460	93,156	86,304	33,923	3,407
Utica-Rome, NY	14,550	294,795	1.01	3,026	10.4	3,140	10.8	12,551	5.5	66,747	39,899	26,848	6,313	2,155
Valdosta, GA........................	6,303	145,017	0.99	1,908	13.1	1,243	8.5	21,144	17.7	23,420	17,018	6,402	5,178	3,613
Vallejo-Fairfield, CA..............	11,396	394,356	0.75	5,155	11.5	3,624	8.1	20,814	5.7	77,395	44,216	33,179	13,741	3,140
Victoria, TX.........................	1,961	101,205	1.02	1,294	13.0	913	9.2	15,113	18.4	18,761	12,801	5,960	NA	NA
Vineland-Bridgeton, NJ	9,974	153,238	1.01	1,774	11.8	1,447	9.6	14,511	12.1	28,059	21,601	6,458	6,434	4,156
Virginia Beach-Norfolk-Newport News, VA-NC.	71,961	1,734,610	1.01	21,472	12.4	14,795	8.6	135,185	9.6	292,342	232,975	59,367	54,553	3,163
Visalia-Porterville, CA............	5,053	455,590	0.95	6,970	15.0	3,052	6.6	35,272	8.8	61,291	50,428	10,863	13,232	2,876
Waco, TX.............................	10,372	274,202	1.06	3,666	13.5	2,386	8.8	40,045	18.1	46,324	29,550	16,774	8,470	3,210
Walla Walla, WA...................	4,894	66,724	1.07	683	10.5	648	10.0	3,773	7.8	14,113	12,748	1,365	2,212	3,414
Warner Robins, GA	4,103	192,344	1.00	2,332	12.0	1,645	8.5	22,996	14.2	31,888	23,567	8,321	7,568	3,992
Washington-Arlington-Alexandria, DC-VA-MD-WV..............	105,865	6,363,885	1.04	79,710	12.8	38,932	6.2	449,770	8.4	834,286	709,743	124,543	131,916	2,144
Silver Spring-Frederick-Rockville, MD Div 43524	13,361	1,259,184	0.93	15,449	11.8	8,148	6.2	82,918	7.5	200,730	177,398	23,332	21,216	1,640
Washington-Arlington-Alexandria, DC-VA-MD-WV Div 4	92,504	5,104,701	1.08	64,261	13.0	30,784	6.2	366,852	8.6	633,556	532,345	101,211	110,700	2,278
Waterloo-Cedar Falls, IA	6,711	176,358	1.07	2,047	12.1	1,559	9.2	6,704	5.0	33,620	23,329	10,291	4,142	2,424
Watertown-Fort Drum, NY	6,135	117,962	1.07	1,859	16.6	920	8.2	4,315	4.7	19,849	13,447	6,402	2,360	2,016
Wausau, WI..........................	1,561	139,535	1.05	1,534	11.3	1,140	8.4	7,250	6.5	26,915	14,257	12,658	1,967	1,446
Weirton-Steubenville, WV-OH	3,400	113,743	0.88	1,048	9.0	1,670	14.3	6,227	6.9	30,278	19,998	10,280	2,340	1,960
Wenatchee, WA....................	1,121	116,730	0.97	1,432	11.9	982	8.2	9,572	10.0	24,779	19,081	5,698	2,795	2,376
Wheeling, WV-OH	6,754	145,239	1.07	1,254	9.0	1,805	12.9	7,142	6.7	33,963	18,809	15,154	2,723	1,905
Wichita, KS...........................	11,482	646,719	1.00	8,461	13.1	5,818	9.0	58,931	10.9	112,335	88,350	23,985	4,563	709
Wichita Falls, TX	12,683	150,830	0.99	1,782	11.8	1,611	10.6	20,649	17.7	28,292	23,006	5,286	5,120	3,410
Williamsport, PA...................	5,261	114,956	1.02	1,152	10.1	1,313	11.6	5,887	6.7	26,290	17,341	8,949	1,990	1,720
Wilmington, NC	9,602	293,089	1.04	2,892	9.8	2,548	8.7	29,170	12.6	56,992	44,998	11,994	9,376	3,317
Winchester, VA-WV..............	2,697	137,796	0.98	1,581	11.3	1,243	8.9	12,560	11.3	27,257	23,418	3,839	2,163	1,613
Winston-Salem, NC...............	13,530	645,963	0.93	7,307	10.9	6,441	9.6	70,395	13.0	135,695	60,618	75,077	NA	NA
Worcester, MA-CT.................	32,969	884,073	0.87	9,612	10.1	8,344	8.8	26,739	3.5	176,241	115,739	60,502	D	D
Yakima, WA..........................	3,506	249,878	1.00	3,866	15.4	2,052	8.2	27,117	12.9	41,847	33,714	8,133	9,818	3,916
York-Hanover, PA	8,691	408,250	0.83	4,859	10.8	4,081	9.1	23,695	6.5	90,689	57,225	33,464	8,068	1,821
Youngstown-Warren-Boardman, OH-PA.......	18,629	523,863	0.92	5,582	10.4	6,852	12.7	29,320	7.1	134,880	66,241	68,639	NA	NA
Yuba City, CA	1,892	158,152	0.78	2,584	14.8	1,334	7.6	11,864	8.1	29,390	27,762	1,628	5,313	3,115
Yuma, AZ..............................	9,283	204,888	0.97	2,981	14.1	1,621	7.6	22,653	14.2	34,508	26,766	7,742	NA	NA

1. Per 1,000 estimated resident population.   2. Data for serious crimes have not been adjusted for underreporting; this may affect comparability between geographic areas and over time.   3. Per 100,000 population estimated by the FBI.

Area name	Serious crimes known to police[2], 2016 (cont.) Rate		Education						Income and poverty, 2017							
			School enrollment and attainment, 2016				Local government expenditures,[5] 2014-2015							Percent below poverty level		
			Enrollment[3]		Attainment[4]											
	Violent	Property	Total	Percent private	High school graduate or less	Bachelor's degree or more	Total current expenditures (mil dol)	Current expenditures per student (dollars)	Per capita income[6] (dollars)	Mean household income (dollars)	Median household income	Percent of households with income less than $50,000	Percent of households with income of $200,000 or more	All persons	Children under 18 years	Age 65 years and older
	46	47	48	49	50	51	52	53	54	55	56	57	58	59	60	61
Texarkana, TX-AR	447	3,312	36,843	6.5	47.1	20.4	244.3	9,146	25,416	65,937	47,722	52.1	2.5	14.9	20.1	8.3
The Villages, FL	234	876	D	D	36.7	33	77.3	9,303	32,484	68,865	54,057	46.7	3.6	8.1	12.9	4.9
Toledo, OH	617	2,902	157,562	14.2	40.9	27.1	1,134.1	11,264	28,584	69,121	50,389	49.6	3.9	15.9	21.5	7.6
Topeka, KS	392	3,865	53,303	14.3	39.2	31.3	404.9	10,515	28,533	67,963	56,834	44.1	2.1	10.9	13.9	5.1
Trenton, NJ	403	1,779	96,707	24.1	35.1	43.9	1,104.2	18,651	42,268	116,672	79,173	33.6	15.3	11.7	16.5	7.8
Tucson, AZ	496	4,267	263,036	11.3	32.1	33.6	1,090.0	7,581	28,655	71,284	51,425	48.5	4.4	16.7	22.4	8.9
Tulsa, OK	589	3,623	251,216	15.9	39.0	27.6	1,343.6	8,040	28,265	71,534	52,275	47.5	4.1	14.3	20.4	7.3
Tuscaloosa, AL	368	2,788	64,676	10.4	45.4	29.4	314.5	9,336	24,848	66,054	51,164	48.0	2.8	16.3	20.5	8.0
Tyler, TX	327	D	60,952	10.7	34.4	26.8	293.8	8,473	26,039	72,587	54,339	46.5	4.8	16.6	19.7	9.5
Urban Honolulu, HI	335	3,073	235,177	23.0	34.7	34.7	2,344.5	12,855	35,143	103,713	81,284	29.9	10.6	8.4	10.2	8.8
Utica-Rome, NY	266	1,889	66,595	15.4	45.0	22.5	718.2	16,204	26,870	66,335	52,214	47.6	2.5	15.6	24.9	7.3
Valdosta, GA	320	3,293	39,338	9.2	49.2	25.7	213.9	9,139	21,460	54,808	40,391	58.3	2.1	26.0	31.6	23.8
Vallejo-Fairfield, CA	462	2,678	109,641	13.8	36.0	26.6	620.4	9,372	34,216	97,373	77,133	32.2	8.8	9.9	15.1	6.5
Victoria, TX	NA	NA	24,399	14.9	46.9	19.9	155.2	9,166	25,932	69,660	51,923	47.0	3.6	16.6	22.3	8.6
Vineland-Bridgeton, NJ	518	3,638	35,386	7.3	56.3	18.1	480.7	17,340	25,217	70,626	52,627	46.9	3.4	19.2	32.5	7.1
Virginia Beach-Norfolk-Newport News, VA-NC	352	2,811	447,593	16.1	33.1	32.1	2,818.9	10,599	32,493	82,927	64,255	38.4	5.4	12.3	18.7	7.5
Visalia-Porterville, CA	353	2,523	137,455	7.3	57.1	14.3	1,073.9	10,507	19,697	64,624	46,266	52.4	3.5	24.6	33.2	14.1
Waco, TX	424	2,786	77,196	22.6	43.2	24.1	484.7	8,880	24,851	66,419	45,961	53.5	3.9	18.9	24.7	10.2
Walla Walla, WA	250	3,164	17,710	23.8	31.8	27.8	101.8	10,749	30,702	80,581	54,157	45.0	4.4	11.6	15.3	5.6
Warner Robins, GA	452	3,540	50,474	14.6	37.8	27.7	317.1	9,544	27,016	71,392	54,802	43.5	3.2	14.1	23.2	5.3
Washington-Arlington-Alexandria, DC-VA-MD-WV	301	1,843	1,627,437	20.2	27.5	50.8	13,113.2	14,022	47,285	128,402	99,669	23.2	17.2	7.9	10.3	7.0
Silver Spring-Frederick-Rockville, MD Div 43524	189	1,452	344,711	19.7	24.2	54.9	2,866.5	14,684	48,986	135,159	100,856	22.3	18.4	7.0	9.1	7.5
Washington-Arlington-Alexandria, DC-VA-MD-WV Div 4	331	1,947	1,282,726	20.3	28.4	49.7	10,246.7	13,847	46,830	126,593	99,134	23.4	16.9	8.1	10.7	6.9
Waterloo-Cedar Falls, IA	442	1,981	48,768	15.4	37.1	28.8	324.0	11,964	28,875	70,578	52,318	46.9	3.5	14.1	15.6	5.8
Watertown-Fort Drum, NY	240	1,776	24,639	13.1	45.2	21.2	238.1	15,742	23,356	59,281	47,101	53.0	1.9	15.6	23.1	6.5
Wausau, WI	132	1,314	31,763	16.2	42.1	25.8	228.4	11,454	32,126	77,209	58,173	43.7	4.0	10.4	13.4	9.7
Weirton-Steubenville, WV-OH	159	1,801	25,209	20.0	49.8	16.7	176.1	10,896	24,385	59,307	45,971	53.6	2.0	16.0	21.0	11.8
Wenatchee, WA	144	2,232	29,393	8.0	44.7	24.6	238.9	11,204	28,518	74,418	58,990	42.5	4.7	16.4	22.5	13.1
Wheeling, WV-OH	350	1,555	29,757	13.5	49.5	20.7	209.5	11,052	27,304	69,104	49,343	50.6	2.8	11.5	12.7	6.9
Wichita, KS	709	D	175,782	15.7	36.3	31.1	1,098.5	9,557	27,498	70,563	54,432	45.9	3.5	13.4	17.6	8.5
Wichita Falls, TX	362	3,047	38,718	8.2	45.5	22.5	218.1	8,957	23,598	58,933	45,267	54.2	2.0	16.2	19.2	11.8
Williamsport, PA	206	1,515	24,827	17.1	47.2	24.1	228.5	14,275	27,568	66,930	50,909	49.0	3.0	12.2	16.9	7.2
Wilmington, NC	364	2,953	68,786	12.5	30.5	38.3	319.2	8,864	33,940	79,375	52,416	47.1	5.9	15.0	20.4	7.4
Winchester, VA-WV	139	1,474	34,389	20.2	44.7	25.4	247.0	11,769	30,186	79,841	65,334	37.6	4.2	8.5	8.4	8.5
Winston-Salem, NC	NA	NA	159,860	16.2	42.1	26.4	864.5	8,521	28,360	69,547	49,162	50.6	3.9	16.2	25.3	9.4
Worcester, MA-CT	D	1,600	235,328	20.3	38.0	35	2,100.9	14,507	35,468	91,200	69,412	37.3	8.1	10.6	13.0	8.3
Yakima, WA	300	3,616	71,240	9.9	52.9	17.6	561.7	10,469	20,989	61,787	47,402	52.1	2.9	18.1	27.6	10.0
York-Hanover, PA	235	1,587	99,999	18.6	48.9	25.3	841.9	12,615	31,149	79,562	63,519	37.5	4.0	9.5	13.5	5.9
Youngstown-Warren-Boardman, OH-PA	NA	NA	115,468	13.1	52.5	21.5	955.5	12,461	26,691	61,534	45,382	55.2	2.6	15.9	25.7	7.7
Yuba City, CA	398	2,718	46,397	9.2	45.5	17.3	340.8	9,617	24,802	71,091	58,727	43.0	3.0	12.6	15.9	8.9
Yuma, AZ	NA	NA	54,223	5.8	54.3	13.5	254.9	6,851	21,665	60,110	46,798	52.4	1.6	18.3	24.9	14.5

1. Data for serious crimes have not been adjusted for underreporting; this may affect comparability between geographic areas and over time.   2.   Per 100,000 population estimated by the FBI.   3.   All persons 3 years old and over enrolled in nursery school through college.   4.   Persons 25 years old and over.   5.   Elementary and secondary education expenditures.   6.   Based on population estimated by the American Community Survey, 2015.

Table C. Metropolitan Areas — **Personal Income and Earnings**

Area name	Personal income, 2017										Earnings, 2017		
	Total (mil dol)	Percent change, 2016-2017	Per capita[1] Dollars	Rank	Wages and Salaries (mil dol)	Supplements to wages and salaries, employer contributions (mil dol) Pension and insurance	Government social insurance	Proprietors' income	Dividends, interest, and rent (mil dol)	Personal transfer receipts (mil dol)	Total (mil dol)	Contributions for government social insurance (mil dol) From employee and self-employed	From employer
	62	63	64	65	66	67	68	69	70	71	72	73	74
Texarkana, TX-AR	5,508	2.5	36,634	354	2,545	459	188	366	963	1,488	3,557	220	188
The Villages, FL	5,440	5.1	43,464	196	1,272	217	91	192	1,716	2,249	1,772	200	91
Toledo, OH	27,065	2.5	44,834	165	14,783	2,634	1,105	2,179	4,141	5,801	20,701	1,173	1,105
Topeka, KS	10,271	2.5	44,054	183	5,277	897	395	765	1,799	2,186	7,334	465	395
Trenton, NJ	24,861	4.8	66,343	15	16,414	2,352	1,189	1,912	5,227	3,463	21,867	1,282	1,189
Tucson, AZ	42,585	5.4	41,637	241	18,459	3,262	1,352	2,933	9,507	10,033	26,006	1,697	1,352
Tulsa, OK	51,359	7.8	51,841	72	22,216	3,386	1,695	9,959	9,779	8,034	37,255	1,984	1,695
Tuscaloosa, AL	8,949	4.0	36,858	350	4,698	908	336	455	1,641	2,051	6,396	405	336
Tyler, TX	10,749	2.0	47,200	127	4,800	737	339	1,892	1,995	2,103	7,767	419	339
Urban Honolulu, HI	56,084	3.2	56,728	33	28,660	6,001	2,283	3,985	11,920	7,926	40,928	2,357	2,283
Utica-Rome, NY	12,503	5.5	42,588	220	5,347	1,360	446	701	1,987	3,392	7,853	464	446
Valdosta, GA	5,052	3.9	34,739	373	2,421	541	177	221	970	1,199	3,360	191	177
Vallejo-Fairfield, CA	21,879	6.4	49,116	99	8,901	1,811	627	1,113	3,776	3,738	12,453	713	627
Victoria, TX	4,221	0.6	42,363	227	1,890	311	132	267	863	967	2,601	151	132
Vineland-Bridgeton, NJ	5,933	3.0	38,893	305	2,911	563	241	490	874	1,685	4,206	260	241
Virginia Beach-Norfolk-Newport News, VA-NC	83,678	3.4	48,502	107	43,301	8,583	3,394	3,274	18,145	14,261	58,551	3,402	3,394
Visalia-Porterville, CA	18,467	5.1	39,756	288	6,822	1,627	510	2,700	2,974	4,230	11,659	561	510
Waco, TX	10,550	4.3	39,263	300	5,519	901	392	762	1,722	2,336	7,574	430	392
Walla Walla, WA	2,789	3.0	43,157	207	1,280	243	126	265	618	639	1,913	108	126
Warner Robins, GA	7,662	4.2	39,954	282	3,625	929	278	306	1,433	1,614	5,138	291	278
Washington-Arlington-Alexandria, DC-VA-MD-WV	432,558	4.3	69,581	11	256,079	40,911	18,405	40,526	84,347	39,587	355,921	19,840	18,405
Silver Spring-Frederick-Rockville, MD Div 43524	106,137	4.8	80,969	X	43,840	6,924	3,164	17,488	21,987	8,435	71,416	3,913	3,164
Washington-Arlington-Alexandria, DC-VA-MD-WV Div 4	326,422	4.1	66,538	X	212,240	33,987	15,240	23,038	62,361	31,152	284,505	15,927	15,240
Waterloo-Cedar Falls, IA	7,382	3.0	43,452	198	4,110	747	323	432	1,428	1,429	5,611	352	323
Watertown-Fort Drum, NY	5,146	4.2	45,069	159	2,669	749	251	216	924	1,077	3,885	191	251
Wausau, WI	6,463	3.5	47,617	117	3,474	651	260	500	1,090	1,025	4,886	298	260
Weirton-Steubenville, WV-OH	4,507	3.4	38,116	321	1,658	322	133	207	631	1,408	2,319	164	133
Wenatchee, WA	5,574	4.6	47,045	131	2,290	383	237	511	1,324	1,150	3,421	196	237
Wheeling, WV-OH	6,486	9.8	45,918	147	3,118	515	239	664	1,154	1,573	4,535	294	239
Wichita, KS	30,801	2.3	47,708	115	14,354	2,431	1,101	3,846	6,603	4,899	21,732	1,299	1,101
Wichita Falls, TX	6,143	0.7	40,617	271	2,657	528	200	404	1,291	1,463	3,790	212	200
Williamsport, PA	4,707	2.6	41,346	248	2,331	504	192	223	788	1,159	3,250	204	192
Wilmington, NC	12,222	4.8	42,413	225	5,970	894	431	815	2,947	2,521	8,110	528	431
Winchester, VA-WV	6,348	4.8	46,036	143	2,956	496	217	445	1,084	1,054	4,114	259	217
Winston-Salem, NC	28,851	4.8	43,207	204	13,497	1,895	974	1,989	5,217	6,049	18,355	1,212	974
Worcester, MA-CT	50,647	4.6	53,738	60	21,605	3,966	1,510	3,753	7,124	8,829	30,833	1,661	1,510
Yakima, WA	10,341	3.8	41,331	250	4,426	739	476	1,040	1,854	2,613	6,681	352	476
York-Hanover, PA	21,156	4.1	47,427	121	9,056	1,658	744	1,256	3,248	3,989	12,714	783	744
Youngstown-Warren-Boardman, OH-PA	22,029	2.4	40,649	270	9,101	1,722	714	1,669	3,640	6,182	13,206	840	714
Yuba City, CA	7,238	4.2	41,673	240	2,514	616	190	698	1,238	1,753	4,019	218	190
Yuma, AZ	7,212	5.5	34,752	372	2,937	578	255	1,229	1,047	1,631	4,998	261	255

1. Based on the resident population estimated as of July 1 of the year shown.

Table C. Metropolitan Areas — Earnings, Social Security, and Housing

Area name	Earnings, 2017 (cont.) Percent by selected industries									Social Security beneficiaries, December 2017		Supplemental Security Income Recipients, December 2017	Housing units, 2018	
	Farm	Mining, quarrying, and extracting	Construction	Manufacturing	Information; professional, scientific, and technical serviecs	Retail trade	Finance, insurance, real estate, rental and leasing	Health care and social assistance	Government	Number	Rate[1]		Total	Percent change, 2010-2018
	75	76	77	78	79	80	81	82	83	84	85	86	87	88
Texarkana, TX-AR	0.6	D	5.7	11.2	D	7.2	6.4	D	24.2	33,040	220	6,468	66,152	3.0
The Villages, FL	1.2	0.5	10.8	4.4	5.8	8.4	6.9	15.3	20.8	69,110	552	1,664	72,385	36.5
Toledo, OH	0.0	D	7.0	18.1	D	6.3	6.8	D	15.1	118,155	196	19,435	275,110	0.6
Topeka, KS	0.2	0.5	6.3	7.0	D	4.8	D	14.9	22.3	52,100	223	5,684	105,388	1.5
Trenton, NJ	0.0	0.6	3.1	4.9	21.1	3.8	11.6	9.0	17.9	65,520	175	9,683	145,121	1.4
Tucson, AZ	0.3	0.7	5.0	10.0	10.0	6.6	6.4	14.3	24.3	221,130	216	20,644	462,749	5.0
Tulsa, OK	0.1	D	5.3	9.9	D	5.3	5.4	10.8	8.7	191,090	193	22,278	434,419	6.0
Tuscaloosa, AL	0.7	2.0	5.3	20.6	D	5.8	D	D	28.7	49,755	205	8,345	110,472	8.3
Tyler, TX	0.3	12.2	5.8	5.3	7.2	10.1	7.4	19.9	11.8	45,425	199	5,476	91,101	4.3
Urban Honolulu, HI	0.2	0.1	7.8	1.9	7.8	5.3	6.6	10.5	31.8	175,700	178	15,735	352,527	4.6
Utica-Rome, NY	0.5	0.6	4.1	9.6	6.4	6.1	7.1	16.3	30.1	71,655	244	9,594	139,327	1.3
Valdosta, GA	0.6	D	D	D	D	D	D	D	35.0	25,770	177	5,152	62,357	8.6
Vallejo-Fairfield, CA	1.2	0.2	9.8	13.1	4.3	6.6	3.6	15.9	25.1	77,730	174	12,068	158,808	4.0
Victoria, TX	-0.3	8.6	8.3	D	D	8.3	5.4	D	17.0	19,850	199	2,742	40,870	4.5
Vineland-Bridgeton, NJ	1.5	0.4	6.5	15.0	D	7.3	3.0	15.9	25.9	30,885	202	5,919	56,490	1.1
Virginia Beach-Norfolk-Newport News, VA-NC	0.0	D	D	7.3	9.5	5.1	D	10.3	35.8	305,245	177	34,873	724,153	5.2
Visalia-Porterville, CA	15.7	0.0	4.3	7.9	4.7	6.2	3.5	6.8	23.4	65,140	140	18,963	150,210	6.0
Waco, TX	-0.2	D	8.2	17.5	5.5	6.5	D	10.7	16.4	48,345	180	8,003	110,206	7.2
Walla Walla, WA	9.9	D	4.3	14.2	D	4.5	4.3	15.3	25.1	14,180	219	1,528	27,075	5.8
Warner Robins, GA	0.5	D	D	D	D	5.7	D	6.8	51.8	33,615	175	5,237	80,735	8.3
Washington-Arlington-Alexandria, DC-VA-MD-WV	0.0	D	D	D	D	D	D	D	26.8	678,950	123	62,591	2,375,815	6.3
Silver Spring-Frederick-Rockville, MD Div 43524	0.0	D	D	D	21.3	D	D	D	19.6	177,140	135	16,528	489,705	5.1
Washington-Arlington-Alexandria, DC-VA-MD-WV Div 4	0.0	0.0	4.9	1.2	27.1	3.0	5.9	6.0	28.6	501,810	119	46,063	1,886,110	6.6
Waterloo-Cedar Falls, IA	0.9	0.1	5.8	23.6	D	6.6	D	13.0	15.8	35,570	209	3,519	74,423	4.3
Watertown-Fort Drum, NY	1.0	0.4	4.5	3.6	2.6	6.0	2.2	10.6	57.4	22,005	193	2,636	60,049	3.6
Wausau, WI	1.4	0.2	5.2	22.3	4.9	6.0	10.5	15.2	11.2	28,575	211	1,960	59,734	3.5
Weirton-Steubenville, WV-OH	-0.1	D	6.0	18.9	D	7.0	4.0	18.0	13.3	32,865	278	3,937	57,598	-1.3
Wenatchee, WA	8.3	D	5.8	4.4	D	10.5	4.2	15.1	20.9	25,460	215	2,035	55,247	7.3
Wheeling, WV-OH	-0.3	D	D	D	14.8	6.4	4.6	D	11.9	36,375	258	4,234	68,801	-1.1
Wichita, KS	0.7	D	6.3	21.2	D	5.6	8.3	D	12.8	119,700	185	12,783	277,738	4.1
Wichita Falls, TX	0.0	3.9	4.7	9.5	D	7.6	D	D	30.4	30,080	199	4,439	65,437	0.9
Williamsport, PA	0.2	3.4	6.8	16.6	5.4	6.7	4.1	16.7	19.1	28,375	249	3,253	53,540	2.0
Wilmington, NC	0.8	D	7.6	6.0	D	7.8	7.6	10.8	19.7	59,720	207	5,307	142,840	11.5
Winchester, VA-WV	0.1	D	D	13.1	D	8.2	7.5	D	18.5	28,545	207	2,368	60,900	7.0
Winston-Salem, NC	0.4	0.1	5.5	13.2	D	6.7	D	D	10.3	145,515	218	14,226	301,120	4.9
Worcester, MA-CT	0.0	D	D	12.7	9.7	5.9	6.6	15.7	16.3	177,415	188	25,001	386,318	2.8
Yakima, WA	14.5	0.0	5.1	8.3	3.0	7.3	3.2	14.2	18.7	44,215	177	7,355	89,130	4.3
York-Hanover, PA	0.0	0.2	9.4	18.7	6.0	5.7	4.5	13.9	13.3	96,140	216	8,375	184,869	3.5
Youngstown-Warren-Boardman, OH-PA	0.0	0.3	7.1	15.7	4.2	8.0	5.9	16.9	15.3	141,965	262	18,829	259,329	-0.2
Yuba City, CA	6.8	0.5	6.6	4.1	D	6.8	4.0	12.7	33.2	30,930	178	8,052	63,170	2.7
Yuma, AZ	17.3	D	3.4	3.6	5.0	8.2	3.3	9.9	27.1	37,195	179	4,629	93,565	6.5

1. Per 1,000 resident population estimated as of July 1 of the year shown.

Table C. Metropolitan Areas — Housing, Labor Force, and Employment

Area name	Housing units, 2017								Civilian labor force, 2018		Unemployment		Civilian employment[5], 2017		
	Occupied units													Percent	
			Owner-occupied			Renter-occupied									
				Median owner cost as a percent of income			Median rent as a percent of income			Percent change 2017-2018				Management, business, science, and arts	Construction, production, and maintenance occupations
	Total	Percent	Median value[1]	With a mortgage	Without a mortgage[2]	Median rent[3]	of income	Internet access	Total		Total	Rate[4]	Total		
	89	90	91	92	93	94	95	96	97	98	99	100	101	102	103
Texarkana, TX-AR	55,934	60.8	116,500	17.3	10.8	667	26.7	75.6	64,702	0.2	3,192	4.9	61,721	32.3	27.4
The Villages, FL	55,097	91.8	259,000	24.1	10.0	804	29.3	88.0	31,241	2.9	1,592	5.1	NA	NA	NA
Toledo, OH	245,035	61.5	130,700	18.6	11.5	709	26.6	87.0	301,725	-0.5	14,816	4.9	289,519	35.4	24.9
Topeka, KS	96,822	67.6	132,600	18.8	11.0	763	27.8	82.4	120,102	0.0	4,150	3.5	112,101	38.6	23.1
Trenton, NJ	128,757	63.5	293,800	23.6	14.7	1,271	30.7	86.3	196,494	0.5	7,217	3.7	184,030	46.6	16.3
Tucson, AZ	403,574	63.9	182,300	20.8	10.0	887	32.8	89.4	486,261	2.0	21,828	4.5	439,775	37.5	16.9
Tulsa, OK	379,757	64.9	150,700	19.5	10.5	823	28.2	85.4	479,874	0.5	16,669	3.5	461,464	36.8	23.0
Tuscaloosa, AL	84,249	64.9	158,500	20.0	10.0	825	28.6	84.4	115,365	1.6	4,375	3.8	103,971	34.1	24.4
Tyler, TX	77,292	67.1	155,900	19.7	10.4	883	28.8	88.4	107,543	1.3	3,909	3.6	99,294	34.6	23.3
Urban Honolulu, HI	312,625	56.4	680,200	25.5	10.0	1,712	34.3	89.0	465,193	-0.9	10,863	2.3	469,673	35.4	17.3
Utica-Rome, NY	113,323	68.0	118,000	19.0	12.5	712	28.6	83.7	129,719	0.1	5,872	4.5	130,165	34.6	20.4
Valdosta, GA	53,619	54.3	123,600	18.7	10.0	771	28.7	78.4	64,535	0.1	2,613	4.0	59,988	33.3	21.4
Vallejo-Fairfield, CA	151,127	59.2	411,700	24.3	11.3	1,549	32.1	93.0	209,721	0.6	8,168	3.9	206,151	32.6	24.4
Victoria, TX	35,635	65.9	140,800	19.2	10.0	887	27.0	79.9	46,675	0.9	1,779	3.8	46,895	31.8	26.3
Vineland-Bridgeton, NJ	50,696	66.2	162,100	23.4	15.6	1,053	43.6	83.8	64,289	-1.5	4,161	6.5	62,435	26.9	29.7
Virginia Beach-Norfolk-Newport News, VA-NC.	641,881	62.0	245,900	23.0	10.9	1,124	30.8	88.7	849,659	0.2	27,686	3.3	798,977	38.7	19.1
Visalia-Porterville, CA	137,576	54.9	204,300	24.0	10.0	911	34.4	82.5	204,589	-0.1	19,649	9.6	182,722	26.3	34.0
Waco, TX	97,310	59.2	133,700	20.2	11.6	816	31.9	83.1	125,454	0.5	4,499	3.6	121,275	32.4	24.0
Walla Walla, WA	24,256	61.6	226,500	19.5	10.0	954	33.2	89.7	31,059	1.6	1,483	4.8	28,187	34.4	27.9
Warner Robins, GA	70,479	65.1	124,300	18.8	10.0	866	28.8	86.5	86,242	1.4	3,586	4.2	84,820	35.7	23.5
Washington-Arlington-Alexandria, DC-VA-MD-WV	2,203,717	63.6	424,600	21.5	10.0	1,629	28.8	93.0	3,393,091	0.7	112,135	3.3	3,344,339	52.4	12.6
Silver Spring-Frederick-Rockville, MD Div 43524	465,548	67.1	439,800	21.3	10.0	1,658	30.0	94.1	685,820	0.4	22,158	3.2	702,478	53.3	12.2
Washington-Arlington-Alexandria, DC-VA-MD-WV Div 4	1,738,169	62.7	419,800	21.6	10.0	1,621	28.5	92.7	2,707,271	0.7	89,977	3.3	2,641,861	52.2	12.7
Waterloo-Cedar Falls, IA	67,711	68.5	153,900	20.0	10.5	736	26.9	85.5	89,342	0.9	2,352	2.6	88,468	33.8	24.8
Watertown-Fort Drum, NY	41,548	55.9	148,300	21.3	11.7	1,005	32.8	87.6	44,691	-0.5	2,510	5.6	42,042	32.6	23.8
Wausau, WI	55,084	71.6	148,400	18.9	10.8	685	25.7	87.6	74,073	0.0	1,975	2.7	71,385	37.2	26.7
Weirton-Steubenville, WV-OH	48,242	69.0	95,300	17.1	10.0	670	27.1	81.4	50,206	-0.3	3,106	6.2	51,704	28.7	26.7
Wenatchee, WA	42,468	63.1	284,600	22.0	10.8	852	25.0	86.9	67,183	2.9	3,214	4.8	54,026	34.1	29.3
Wheeling, WV-OH	51,143	79.3	113,800	16.2	10.0	613	26.0	77.4	66,156	1.5	3,480	5.3	60,754	30.6	25.6
Wichita, KS	246,524	64.8	138,500	19.4	11.3	789	28.0	86.7	309,600	0.7	11,497	3.7	307,367	36.2	24.5
Wichita Falls, TX	55,426	63.0	103,400	20.7	11.7	760	32.4	79.6	65,868	1.0	2,223	3.4	63,980	30.6	26.2
Williamsport, PA	46,122	68.7	160,800	20.3	11.8	754	28.2	86.0	57,134	-1.2	2,740	4.8	53,649	31.1	25.0
Wilmington, NC	117,982	63.6	230,400	21.3	11.7	911	28.8	86.2	149,245	1.2	5,645	3.8	140,772	39.3	18.1
Winchester, VA-WV	51,174	72.1	224,000	20.8	10.0	952	25.5	84.5	71,900	1.1	2,085	2.9	69,461	33.8	26.8
Winston-Salem, NC	263,215	67.8	148,600	18.8	10.0	730	29.5	84.0	326,280	0.6	12,128	3.7	306,572	34.8	25.8
Worcester, MA-CT	352,356	64.2	269,600	21.2	13.9	974	29.0	88.6	514,096	2.3	18,822	3.7	473,591	40.9	19.5
Yakima, WA	82,107	60.2	177,700	23.9	11.0	771	27.4	86.0	129,176	3.0	8,190	6.3	101,101	27.4	38.5
York-Hanover, PA	171,781	73.7	179,900	21.2	13.4	954	29.1	85.4	234,141	-0.3	9,024	3.9	224,848	34.3	25.2
Youngstown-Warren-Boardman, OH-PA	231,423	69.8	109,800	19.0	11.5	654	28.6	83.7	241,186	-1.4	13,973	5.8	240,573	30.9	27.3
Yuba City, CA	58,173	60.0	266,300	24.3	11.0	1,018	29.7	87.9	74,555	1.0	5,255	7.0	70,839	29.9	29.0
Yuma, AZ	74,620	67.1	132,500	22.3	10.0	863	25.7	84.5	97,636	2.0	16,639	17.0	79,447	25.3	31.5

1. Specified owner-occupied units.   2. A value of 10.0 represents 10 percent or less; a value of 50.0 represents 50 percent or more.   3. Specified renter-occupied units.   4. Overcrowded or lacking complete plumbing facilities.   5. Percent of civilian labor force.   6. Civilian employed persons 16 years old and over.

Table C. Metropolitan Areas — **Nonfarm Employment and Agriculture**

Area name	Private nonfarm establishments, employment and payroll, 2016									Agriculture, 2017			
	Number of establish-ments	Employment						Annual payroll		Farms			Farm producers whose primary occupation is farming (percent)
		Total	Health care and social assistance	Manufactur-ing	Retail trade	Finance and insurance	Professional, scientific, and technical ser-vices	Total (mil dol)	Average per employee (dollars)	Number	Percent with:		
											Fewer than 50 acres	1000 acres or more	
	104	105	106	107	108	109	110	111	112	113	114	115	116
Texarkana, TX-AR.............	3,119	46,989	8,850	5,767	8,440	1,786	1,882	1,702	36,212	2,433	40.1	4.3	36.1
The Villages, FL..............	1,453	20,883	4,277	1,219	3,710	685	679	757	36,272	1,307	75.7	1.9	37
Toledo, OH	13,276	277,280	47,828	42,502	32,804	7,357	12,434	11,767	42,437	2,240	49.2	6.1	38.5
Topeka, KS	5,157	88,164	19,996	8,221	11,325	5,803	4,858	3,688	41,835	4,511	29	9.4	34.9
Trenton, NJ	9,675	190,694	29,108	6,182	23,562	14,882	21,617	12,290	64,448	323	72.1	0.6	35.1
Tucson, AZ	20,180	316,661	61,442	22,850	48,632	12,820	17,161	12,446	39,305	661	79.7	7.9	42.9
Tulsa, OK	24,403	402,661	62,596	52,563	50,789	17,581	22,871	18,262	45,354	9,398	44.7	4.8	33.5
Tuscaloosa, AL................	4,531	83,110	13,137	16,079	11,281	1,857	2,427	3,249	39,092	1,327	35.4	6	35.2
Tyler, TX	5,775	91,444	22,480	6,924	13,229	4,603	4,959	3,780	41,337	2,928	58.8	1.1	31.7
Urban Honolulu, HI.............	21,404	359,766	53,010	10,060	47,049	16,355	18,257	16,369	45,499	927	91.3	1.7	55.4
Utica-Rome, NY	6,014	100,364	21,648	12,725	14,246	6,945	3,851	3,890	38,762	1,563	30.4	2	46.2
Valdosta, GA..................	3,072	44,213	8,319	3,623	7,244	1,184	1,304	1,408	31,847	909	42.2	9.2	37.5
Vallejo-Fairfield, CA...........	6,984	111,150	23,200	9,272	20,042	4,378	3,334	5,541	49,855	849	65.3	8.1	44.6
Victoria, TX...................	2,475	35,081	7,361	2,034	6,395	951	1,168	1,423	40,577	2,541	42	5.9	32.3
Vineland-Bridgeton, NJ	2,815	46,097	9,750	7,815	7,412	1,071	1,005	1,818	39,439	560	63.6	2	48
Virginia Beach-Norfolk-Newport News, VA-NC.	37,474	609,784	92,737	58,447	91,276	25,038	52,233	25,597	41,977	1,502	60	7.7	39.3
Visalia-Porterville, CA..........	6,301	94,534	15,764	13,440	16,450	3,060	2,711	3,706	39,198	4,187	57.6	5.4	52.3
Waco, TX......................	5,391	106,443	18,449	14,117	12,542	5,281	5,178	3,902	36,654	4,469	54.3	4.4	32.7
Walla Walla, WA	1,486	20,611	4,277	3,572	2,410	676	499	783	37,970	1,160	48.3	18.3	42
Warner Robins, GA	3,144	46,006	7,555	6,930	8,823	1,279	4,008	1,613	35,060	694	50.3	4.5	33.3
Washington-Arlington-Alexandria, DC-VA-MD-WV.................	152,428	2,609,262	316,315	49,092	279,618	99,793	534,533	168,930	64,743	8,859	59.9	2.4	38.3
Silver Spring-Frederick-Rockville, MD Div 43524	NA	NA	NA	NA	NA	NA	NA	NA	NA	1,931	58.2	2.5	40.3
Washington-Arlington-Alexandria, DC-VA-MD-WV Div 4	NA	NA	NA	NA	NA	NA	NA	NA	NA	6,928	60.4	2.4	37.7
Waterloo-Cedar Falls, IA	4,095	81,282	18,029	14,388	11,123	3,404	3,772	3,069	37,757	2,691	38.2	8.2	42.6
Watertown-Fort Drum, NY	2,443	30,183	6,395	2,339	6,710	686	931	1,085	35,961	792	26.5	5.6	51.5
Wausau, WI	3,353	64,918	10,357	17,196	7,743	4,457	1,523	2,724	41,954	2,237	33.8	2.9	50.2
Weirton-Steubenville, WV-OH	2,202	34,917	7,612	5,532	5,049	737	824	1,250	35,800	781	32.5	0.1	36.3
Wenatchee, WA..................	3,278	35,775	6,776	2,124	6,361	858	1,417	1,481	41,411	1,564	57.9	12.1	48.4
Wheeling, WV-OH	3,316	56,234	13,632	2,395	8,992	2,269	2,673	2,073	36,868	1,596	29.6	0.8	38
Wichita, KS	14,955	260,343	40,723	48,772	34,807	8,435	11,813	11,160	42,867	5,276	32.8	15.7	37.2
Wichita Falls, TX	3,411	46,764	11,438	4,527	7,753	1,703	1,713	1,653	35,354	1,997	28.8	18.1	36.5
Williamsport, PA	2,745	45,232	8,956	7,543	7,555	1,503	1,419	1,705	37,700	1,043	32.2	1.3	38.6
Wilmington, NC	8,291	104,226	18,822	6,566	17,488	3,252	5,968	4,304	41,291	395	58.2	3.3	47.5
Winchester, VA-WV	3,186	54,164	10,100	6,909	8,546	2,790	2,899	2,112	38,986	1,645	53.2	2.2	34.8
Winston-Salem, NC..............	13,255	235,668	44,844	30,150	29,835	11,399	8,457	10,642	45,159	3,825	52.9	1.2	40
Worcester, MA-CT...............	20,110	331,536	75,741	39,163	44,969	17,129	18,728	15,767	47,559	2,214	66.4	0.3	38.5
Yakima, WA	4,674	68,496	13,849	9,237	10,404	1,497	1,736	2,677	39,080	2,952	74.1	3.8	44.3
York-Hanover, PA	8,646	164,632	25,020	30,464	22,078	3,726	5,947	6,975	42,367	2,067	62	2	39.3
Youngstown-Warren-Boardman, OH-PA........	12,261	198,976	42,525	33,719	30,241	5,487	4,548	7,263	36,504	2,978	48.3	1.4	37.7
Yuba City, CA	2,524	30,787	6,193	1,966	6,026	1,007	1,382	1,276	41,448	1,921	53.5	5.2	53.1
Yuma, AZ......................	2,963	42,536	7,324	3,124	8,262	1,014	1,250	1,379	32,412	456	60.7	13.2	50.4

Table C. Metropolitan Areas — **Agriculture**

	Agriculture, 2017 (cont.)															
	Land in farms					Value of land and buildings (dollars)		Value of machinery and equipmnet, average per farm (dollars)	Value of products sold:				Organic farms (number)	Farms with internet access (percent)	Government payments	
			Acres								Percent from:					
Area name	Acreage (1,000)	Percent change, 2012-2017	Average size of farm	Total irrigated (1,000)	Total cropland (1,000)	Average per farm	Average per acre		Total (mil dol)	Average per farm (acres)	Crops	Livestock and poultry products			Total ($1,000)	Percent of farms
	117	118	119	120	121	122	123	124	125	126	127	128	129	130	131	132
Texarkana, TX-AR	580	-4.6	239	24.8	191.5	655,739	2,749	84,649	180.5	74,199	24.9	75.1	NA	73.4	6,849	17.8
The Villages, FL	177	-3.4	135	2	21.3	816,314	6,025	50,217	54.5	41,666	36.7	63.3	8	74.7	1,099	16.7
Toledo, OH	531	0.8	237	4.4	498.0	1,653,342	6,979	176,446	383	171,002	77.4	22.6	15	78.1	17,507	62.1
Topeka, KS	1,610	0.3	357	29.6	815.2	852,691	2,389	103,730	351.5	77,915	61.6	38.4	7	77.1	10,303	43.2
Trenton, NJ	25	27.8	78	1	15.8	1,414,873	18,114	83,437	25	77,344	80.1	19.9	12	73.4	149	8
Tucson, AZ	2,618	D	3,960	30	40.7	2,088,809	527	79,142	75.5	114,174	84.3	15.7	3	72	1,234	5.4
Tulsa, OK	2,653	-3.7	282	16.9	518.9	615,238	2,179	60,741	314.7	33,485	25	75	3	74.1	9,321	10.3
Tuscaloosa, AL	358	2.4	269	3.9	71.3	709,104	2,631	83,763	190.9	143,833	9.9	90.1	4	71.5	4,211	39.9
Tyler, TX	272	-10.1	93	1.9	64.3	487,136	5,248	52,759	53.6	18,308	68.6	31.4	NA	71.8	94	1.2
Urban Honolulu, HI	72	3.8	77	11.7	23.1	1,920,260	24,794	92,037	151.4	163,305	90.4	9.6	25	71.1	350	10.8
Utica-Rome, NY	311	-10.1	199	0.9	188.7	500,447	2,519	115,581	158.4	101,364	27.4	72.6	43	73.4	1,533	19.1
Valdosta, GA	310	15.6	341	39.8	150.6	1,283,208	3,764	154,355	195.2	214,726	73.2	26.8	3	73.3	5,651	41.6
Vallejo-Fairfield, CA	343	-15.8	404	110.4	152.1	3,691,320	9,148	178,302	296.6	349,337	83.8	16.2	63	85.2	2,554	13.9
Victoria, TX	806	-13.6	317	8.2	119.4	887,059	2,796	65,326	76	29,923	51	49	NA	70.1	3,621	8.9
Vineland-Bridgeton, NJ	66	2.7	118	20	49.6	1,159,638	9,801	150,220	212.6	379,730	97.5	2.5	8	77.5	665	9.6
Virginia Beach-Norfolk-Newport News, VA-NC	363	4.2	242	5.7	264.3	1,148,721	4,756	136,712	272.9	181,706	67.2	32.8	9	84.7	10,901	31.8
Visalia-Porterville, CA	1,250	0.9	299	568.2	721.4	3,501,053	11,726	218,462	4,474.8	1,068,739	49.7	50.3	104	78.2	13,824	10.4
Waco, TX	965	3.1	216	6.2	466.3	683,249	3,164	81,994	337.6	75,544	30.2	69.8	4	72.7	9,061	14.2
Walla Walla, WA	946	0.4	815	104.6	715.3	1,874,169	2,298	196,451	30.7	26,471	86.4	13.6	13	84.1	20,303	44.8
Warner Robins, GA	150	3.2	216	38.1	80.9	912,148	4,224	128,716	133.2	191,960	65.2	34.8	NA	83.6	1,402	28.2
Washington-Arlington-Alexandria, DC-VA-MD-WV	1,147	-3.8	129	7.1	599.9	1,039,181	8,026	82,091	448.5	50,631	59.6	40.4	76	83.5	8,552	11.2
Silver Spring-Frederick-Rockville, MD Div 43524	254	3.7	132	2.3	189.4	1,208,668	9,185	116,267	174.2	90,193	58.2	41.8	35	83.1	5,159	23
Washington-Arlington-Alexandria, DC-VA-MD-WV Div 4	893	-5.7	129	4.8	410.5	991,941	7,696	72,565	274.4	39,604	60.4	39.6	41	83.5	3,393	8
Waterloo-Cedar Falls, IA	862	-2.7	320	0.9	812.7	2,765,372	8,630	252,938	757.9	281,635	64.3	35.7	15	82.2	22,822	76.4
Watertown-Fort Drum, NY	247	-14.9	312	0.4	168.8	836,501	2,677	170,553	165.1	208,404	21.6	78.4	31	74.7	1,986	22.3
Wausau, WI	473	-1.2	212	7	322.9	1,004,890	4,751	161,949	413.6	184,888	24.4	75.6	51	73	1,226	29.2
Weirton-Steubenville, WV-OH	100	8.4	128	0.1	40.7	639,277	5,011	79,855	11	14,059	47.4	52.6	NA	77.8	192	6.9
Wenatchee, WA	883	-0.8	564	40.1	573.5	1,209,012	2,143	104,421	444.4	284,169	97.9	2.1	77	80.9	16,065	24.6
Wheeling, WV-OH	229	-0.2	143	0.1	75.0	486,981	3,396	79,205	31.9	19,969	28.2	71.8	5	71.1	169	3.9
Wichita, KS	2,913	2	552	125.8	1,977.2	1,298,337	2,351	153,110	759.5	143,955	58	42	16	78.5	33,115	54.2
Wichita Falls, TX	1,578	2.4	790	10.7	378.0	1,314,140	1,663	86,950	161.9	81,049	16.3	83.7	NA	77.4	8,463	28.4
Williamsport, PA	186	17.5	178	0.2	79.0	913,566	5,119	69,673	63.7	61,086	48.1	51.9	8	67	2,683	40.6
Wilmington, NC	65	11.4	165	1.9	41.4	948,987	5,735	100,043	201.1	509,147	19.1	80.9	9	79.2	583	17.7
Winchester, VA-WV	242	-0.4	147	0.2	82.1	723,372	4,922	61,643	72.5	44,068	40.9	59.1	6	73.3	322	8.3
Winston-Salem, NC	385	1.3	101	2.1	181.5	551,408	5,485	63,812	267	69,798	29	71	15	73.6	1,509	10.4
Worcester, MA-CT	147	-8	67	1.9	56.8	751,336	11,293	57,343	110.3	49,813	57	43	32	81.4	1,147	7.3
Yakima, WA	1,781	0.1	603	260	344.0	1,662,431	2,755	174,332	1,988	673,451	71.3	28.7	84	79	5,221	6.5
York-Hanover, PA	253	-3.6	122	0.7	199.2	1,002,707	8,201	105,569	260.9	126,235	51.7	48.3	25	74.5	4,781	17.8
Youngstown-Warren-Boardman, OH-PA	355	0.7	119	1	236.8	555,675	4,667	104,689	190.4	63,938	50.5	49.5	39	74	4,148	22
Yuba City, CA	560	-0.4	292	271.2	336.7	2,657,292	9,107	207,693	591.3	307,805	96	4	63	80.4	10,515	10.3
Yuma, AZ	247	15.2	542	181.4	234.3	5,006,515	9,235	462,680	D	D	D	D	34	84.4	3,789	14.9

Table C. Metropolitan Areas — Water Use, Wholesale Trade, Retail Trade, and Real Estate

Area name	Water use, 2015		Wholesale Trade[1], 2012				Retail Trade[2], 2012				Real estate and rental and leasing,[2] 2012			
	Public supply water withdrawn (mil gal/day)	Public supply gallons withdrawn per person per day	Number of establish-ments	Number of employees	Sales (mil dol)	Average payroll (mil dol)	Number of establish-ments	Number of employees	Sales (mil dol)	Average payroll (mil dol)	Number of establish-ments	Number of employees	Sales (mil dol)	Average payroll (mil dol)
	133	134	135	136	137	138	139	140	141	142	143	144	145	146
Texarkana, TX-AR................	19.83	132.4	132	1,974	2,955.7	87.5	577	7,946	2,151.3	185.7	131	589	110.1	20.1
The Villages, FL....................	24.13	203	45	D	D	D	217	2,840	908.8	62.1	79	176	25.6	5.7
Toledo, OH	89.2	147.2	649	9,697	7,499.0	479.7	2,001	31,636	8,224.9	732.7	547	3,285	2,664.1	183.5
Topeka, KS	18.66	79.8	192	2,204	1,496.3	107.9	801	10,823	2,632.3	233.1	218	946	138.5	27.3
Trenton, NJ	37.62	101.3	354	D	D	D	1,305	18,794	5,127.4	477.9	347	1,934	729.3	91.8
Tucson, AZ	175.4	173.7	703	6,172	3,099.3	269.6	2,770	43,642	11,377.2	1,094.8	1,250	6,042	973.5	205.5
Tulsa, OK	133.35	135.9	1,210	16,787	15,854.1	976.9	3,066	44,465	12,865.2	1,081.7	1,097	6,653	1,083.1	261.7
Tuscaloosa, AL.....................	37.53	156.4	160	1,774	1,240.0	86.6	835	10,366	2,796.3	233.7	192	1,511	166.7	45.0
Tyler, TX	42.89	192.4	215	D	D	D	829	11,883	3,388.9	293.6	281	1,477	301.0	61.6
Urban Honolulu, HI................	168.78	169	1,167	13,446	8,052.8	596.9	2,889	46,165	13,036.4	1,233.1	1,219	7,213	2,553.5	340.7
Utica-Rome, NY	61.66	208.6	205	2,626	1,249.6	116.1	1,017	13,905	3,556.1	308.4	204	799	126.9	22.4
Valdosta, GA........................	14.47	101.3	128	1,261	1,438.4	48.5	563	6,439	1,880.1	142.3	142	1,467	107.4	26.5
Vallejo-Fairfield, CA..............	52.18	119.7	249	4,165	2,803.7	215.6	1,060	17,610	5,106.6	469.9	381	1,629	389.2	59.2
Victoria, TX	12.4	124.1	115	1,716	1,251.0	91.8	397	5,629	1,698.7	143.3	129	1,057	604.9	59.8
Vineland-Bridgeton, NJ	15.72	100.9	152	3,223	2,422.4	133.6	512	7,201	2,049.0	175.0	120	471	96.2	15.8
Virginia Beach-Norfolk-Newport News, VA-NC.	167.4	97.1	1,282	18,502	16,160.5	1,040.2	5,848	87,532	21,164.8	1,960.2	2,017	14,556	2,348.7	549.1
Visalia-Porterville, CA............	70.33	152.9	325	4,564	3,890.5	191.8	1,044	14,210	3,903.5	340.6	306	1,421	249.0	40.9
Waco, TX.............................	43.7	166.3	248	D	D	D	898	11,518	3,321.4	258.7	228	1,531	290.6	64.7
Walla Walla, WA...................	13.72	213.4	88	673	602.4	25.8	201	2,433	586.0	59.1	62	187	23.0	5.2
Warner Robins, GA................	27.15	144.3	73	D	D	D	581	7,789	2,146.6	179.0	151	519	81.0	14.4
Washington-Arlington-Alexandria, DC-VA-MD-WV...	568.53	93.2	3,527	49,567	57,941.8	3,388.0	16,124	264,471	74,306.7	7,157.0	6,881	53,448	15,623.8	3,069.8
Silver Spring-Frederick-Rockville, MD Div 43524 ...	368.73	286.9	875	11,325	11,642.7	792.1	3,438	58,054	16,973.9	1,633.0	1,570	13,206	4,741.5	869.1
Washington-Arlington-Alexandria, DC-VA-MD-WV Div 4	199.8	41.5	2,652	38,242	46,299.2	2,595.9	12,686	206,417	57,332.8	5,524.0	5,311	40,242	10,882.3	2,200.7
Waterloo-Cedar Falls, IA........	18.33	107.4	197	3,210	2,774.7	154.0	639	10,445	2,555.7	225.1	164	706	141.0	22.9
Watertown-Fort Drum, NY......	9.29	79	67	870	345.2	34.7	476	6,849	1,937.9	161.4	119	588	103.9	17.8
Wausau, WI	10.98	80.8	180	2,955	1,276.6	126.2	472	9,545	2,572.4	208.5	83	412	79.2	11.9
Weirton-Steubenville, WV-OH	15.44	128.1	71	D	D	D	372	5,013	1,195.3	105.3	67	306	35.9	8.4
Wenatchee, WA.....................	16.74	144.1	127	D	D	D	477	5,701	1,434.5	146.9	145	475	63.0	13.5
Wheeling, WV-OH	19.98	138.6	126	D	D	D	585	8,547	2,283.3	189.1	117	601	84.5	16.8
Wichita, KS	73.91	114.7	727	9,369	9,027.7	524.5	2,115	31,655	8,362.2	740.0	650	4,202	610.9	138.1
Wichita Falls, TX	11.7	77.6	163	1,255	715.2	58.5	544	7,725	2,105.4	174.4	170	822	169.1	30.2
Williamsport, PA	8.78	75.7	108	2,110	1,271.2	82.6	503	7,404	1,878.1	154.7	89	618	120.0	24.4
Wilmington, NC	9.02	32.4	315	2,837	1,368.8	136.0	1,174	14,996	4,258.4	367.1	425	2,314	395.5	86.3
Winchester, VA-WV	5.8	43.3	129	D	D	D	537	8,118	2,358.1	195.3	127	432	90.4	14.8
Winston-Salem, NC...............	68.6	104	608	8,614	5,513.2	389.1	2,151	27,365	7,696.4	651.1	530	2,200	739.1	77.4
Worcester, MA-CT.................	259.35	277.2	827	12,550	7,416.0	685.2	2,928	43,798	12,212.7	1,080.8	643	2,883	651.1	124.6
Yakima, WA	30	120.6	234	4,373	3,335.1	198.3	713	9,575	2,560.2	246.1	249	974	132.0	26.7
York-Hanover, PA	34.82	78.6	359	6,685	4,340.8	301.4	1,297	21,024	5,192.4	463.9	258	1,470	263.7	51.8
Youngstown-Warren-Boardman, OH-PA........	51.89	94.4	538	7,293	4,748.0	345.2	2,094	29,036	7,127.0	610.9	384	3,946	486.5	114.2
Yuba City, CA	22.56	132	96	D	D	D	414	5,557	1,459.7	136.6	134	559	68.5	14.4
Yuma, AZ.............................	36.29	177.7	137	2,433	1,439.8	102.5	449	7,408	1,996.0	171.9	159	639	91.9	18.0

1. Merchant wholesalers, except manufacturers' sales branches and offices. 2. Employer establishments.

Table C. Metropolitan Areas

Professional Services, Manufacturing, and Accommodation and Food Services

Area name	Professional, scientific, and technical services, 2012				Manufacturing, 2012				Accommodation and food services, 2012			
	Number of establish-ments	Number of employees	Sales (mil dol)	Average payroll (mil dol)	Number of establish-ments	Number of employees	Receipts (mil dol)	Annual payroll (mil dol)	Number of establish-ments	Number of employees	Receipts (mil dol)	Annual payroll (mil dol)
	147	148	149	150	151	152	153	154	155	156	157	158
Texarkana, TX-AR.................	208	1,126	118.7	38.6	99	5,410	2,601.2	308.5	270	5,616	260.2	74.3
The Villages, FL....................	128	500	53.9	21.0	36	942	461.9	40.7	106	2,464	117.2	35.9
Toledo, OH	1,127	D	D	D	732	35,417	35,387.1	2,068.8	1,420	26,503	1,122.3	320.8
Topeka, KS	517	D	D	D	131	5,986	2,893.2	270.6	434	D	D	D
Trenton, NJ...........................	1,591	21,394	5,318.1	2,127.7	246	7,070	2,220.3	378.2	812	11,894	731.4	201.0
Tucson, AZ	2,531	16,514	2,241.1	940.0	640	24,297	8,686.6	1,906.7	1,787	42,311	2,154.7	637.4
Tulsa, OK	2,808	D	D	D	1,317	52,150	24,817.4	2,774.6	1,901	37,592	1,899.4	537.9
Tuscaloosa, AL......................	357	2,263	328.8	102.3	172	12,576	14,491.5	745.1	418	9,331	443.6	113.5
Tyler, TX	596	4,265	689.9	244.8	189	6,739	5,066.1	318.0	405	9,236	427.1	124.3
Urban Honolulu, HI................	2,399	18,234	2,895.1	1,105.4	544	9,076	D	370.8	2,355	57,486	5,273.2	1,333.0
Utica-Rome, NY	469	3,829	573.9	215.9	296	12,368	4,147.5	581.4	727	12,339	862.6	219.5
Valdosta, GA.........................	239	1,235	144.3	51.3	103	3,263	2,683.6	142.3	322	5,907	255.2	68.6
Vallejo-Fairfield, CA..............	547	3,258	415.3	150.6	259	9,266	11,412.2	558.9	711	11,129	625.6	163.2
Victoria, TX...........................	173	899	118.4	42.6	77	2,090	2,172.9	136.0	204	3,702	192.7	50.8
Vineland-Bridgeton, NJ	207	D	D	D	162	8,055	2,812.0	351.2	265	3,555	173.7	43.6
Virginia Beach-Norfolk-Newport News, VA-NC.	4,187	51,649	9,454.7	3,521.0	847	54,304	15,652.6	2,873.8	3,805	74,606	3,885.1	1,062.9
Visalia-Porterville, CA............	407	D	D	D	237	11,412	8,362.4	538.0	568	8,540	451.9	118.1
Waco, TX...............................	377	2,607	337.8	140.5	240	14,284	6,478.1	682.2	502	9,682	475.4	130.6
Walla Walla, WA....................	117	459	46.0	17.6	137	3,450	1,773.2	159.6	147	1,998	95.8	28.4
Warner Robins, GA	312	3,445	450.1	174.3	85	5,334	2,785.0	216.8	343	6,719	310.2	80.9
Washington-Arlington-Alexandria, DC-VA-MD-WV.........................	30,747	517,949	125,259.6	49,288.9	2,091	49,219	15,671.4	3,030.8	12,138	247,606	17,932.2	4,868.0
Silver Spring-Frederick-Rockville, MD Div 43524	6,546	80,941	15,488.5	7,179.1	544	14,259	5,408.7	974.0	2,259	39,978	2,529.6	701.8
Washington-Arlington-Alexandria, DC-VA-MD-WV Div 4	24,201	437,008	109,771.1	42,109.9	1,547	34,961	10,262.7	2,056.8	9,879	207,628	15,402.6	4,166.1
Waterloo-Cedar Falls, IA	280	3,998	310.2	210.6	213	15,285	10,703.1	762.0	370	7,330	342.8	91.2
Watertown-Fort Drum, NY	142	1,092	115.9	45.4	66	2,247	770.5	102.6	335	4,117	198.8	57.0
Wausau, WI...........................	225	1,943	284.9	113.9	238	14,472	4,306.0	654.1	305	4,458	180.7	51.8
Weirton-Steubenville, WV-OH	155	D	D	D	77	5,822	3,877.9	314.9	276	4,415	375.3	63.3
Wenatchee, WA......................	217	1,070	116.2	45.4	109	2,005	635.0	99.6	341	4,174	233.2	73.2
Wheeling, WV-OH	268	2,501	287.4	105.6	106	2,887	981.8	117.4	322	6,150	371.3	85.2
Wichita, KS............................	1,350	11,334	1,676.4	603.6	687	46,169	23,736.2	2,589.4	1,320	25,323	1,163.6	321.8
Wichita Falls, TX	250	1,551	212.3	72.3	142	5,114	1,434.9	238.1	286	D	D	D
Williamsport, PA	200	2,151	184.5	74.5	160	8,162	3,186.7	371.5	296	4,696	237.9	62.6
Wilmington, NC	937	5,852	1,090.5	295.5	207	5,268	2,640.9	349.5	746	13,951	673.8	185.5
Winchester, VA-WV	269	1,885	178.2	85.7	119	6,864	3,469.8	346.3	294	5,209	255.3	68.9
Winston-Salem, NC	1,288	8,118	1,077.1	446.8	671	26,926	18,915.9	1,212.5	1,133	20,985	989.5	278.5
Worcester, MA-CT..................	1,945	D	D	D	1,132	40,227	12,621.8	2,273.0	1,956	27,526	1,425.5	400.0
Yakima, WA...........................	319	2,023	193.3	80.5	232	8,152	2,622.2	327.3	416	5,364	281.5	79.8
York-Hanover, PA	705	5,671	635.2	279.4	568	31,890	11,489.4	1,602.6	791	13,391	593.3	165.9
Youngstown-Warren-Boardman, OH-PA........	917	5,807	560.3	218.3	730	31,925	14,956.5	1,845.3	1,140	24,546	1,101.8	309.3
Yuba City, CA........................	204	978	118.4	46.1	100	2,091	650.7	99.0	224	3,374	171.4	44.9
Yuma, AZ...............................	221	1,364	132.3	68.0	68	2,084	884.3	79.8	329	5,736	307.5	76.2

Table C. Metropolitan Areas — Health Care and Social Assistance, Other Services, Nonemployer Businesses, and Residential Construction

Area name	Health care and social assistance, 2012				Other services, 2012				Nonemployer businesses, 2016		Value of residential construction authorized by building permits, 2018	
	Number of establish-ments	Number of employees	Receipts (mil dol)	Annual payroll (mil dol)	Number of establish-ments	Number of employees	Receipts (mil dol)	Annual payroll (mil dol)	Number	Receipts (mil dol)	New construc-tion ($1,000)	Number of housing units
	159	160	161	162	163	164	165	166	167	168	169	170
Texarkana, TX-AR.................	370	8,528	889.6	333.1	212	1,253	110.7	32.9	8,398	365.8	20,526	191
The Villages, FL....................	146	2,956	381.2	123.8	64	304	22.2	6.7	6,367	254.4	552,266	2,076
Toledo, OH	1,611	45,338	4,689.0	1,918.0	1,012	6,823	597.0	174.5	34,728	1,536.3	218,881	1,096
Topeka, KS	609	19,147	1,803.3	791.6	449	3,859	347.5	108.9	13,114	558.7	69,458	356
Trenton, NJ	1,165	28,970	2,981.0	1,326.6	815	6,403	1,245.5	239.1	25,163	1,388.3	54,986	501
Tucson, AZ	2,777	56,539	6,617.5	2,441.8	1,483	10,691	1,008.6	281.2	65,734	2,585.0	1,065,133	4,404
Tulsa, OK	2,640	57,324	6,459.5	2,399.4	1,479	9,217	1,253.9	281.4	73,270	3,391.2	699,056	3,412
Tuscaloosa, AL.....................	479	14,351	1,485.8	644.6	259	1,660	154.9	43.1	14,068	627.0	232,463	1,047
Tyler, TX	640	21,211	2,527.9	969.6	347	2,613	252.8	87.5	18,574	909.1	160,273	660
Urban Honolulu, HI................	2,520	50,049	6,302.6	2,481.0	2,012	14,967	1,522.4	411.8	66,902	3,377.8	645,840	2,410
Utica-Rome, NY	724	21,377	1,820.7	801.3	501	4,229	251.1	82.6	15,305	617.3	53,534	275
Valdosta, GA........................	400	8,078	828.5	305.9	174	1,111	78.5	22.0	8,668	403.6	193,721	1,126
Vallejo-Fairfield, CA..............	861	21,490	3,241.8	1,204.0	552	3,228	326.8	102.6	24,790	1,026.7	241,759	990
Victoria, TX..........................	314	6,698	684.2	276.3	158	1,175	163.1	46.9	6,586	262.6	14,816	70
Vineland-Bridgeton, NJ	417	8,593	872.1	338.7	240	1,253	97.1	27.3	5,987	281.7	7,332	74
Virginia Beach-Norfolk-Newport News, VA-NC.	3,558	88,360	9,916.7	4,051.8	2,792	18,235	2,070.9	534.5	103,185	4,158.7	1,039,235	5,604
Visalia-Porterville, CA............	836	15,488	1,610.2	632.1	383	2,114	219.4	60.0	19,951	967.9	292,423	1,528
Waco, TX..............................	574	17,072	1,527.0	641.3	379	2,408	236.0	65.4	16,514	766.4	169,632	850
Walla Walla, WA....................	171	4,358	455.3	204.5	88	D	D	D	3,410	142.3	57,477	225
Warner Robins, GA	351	7,250	654.0	264.3	181	983	79.5	22.9	12,230	376.4	207,916	1,378
Washington-Arlington-Alexandria, DC-VA-MD-WV..............	15,282	295,912	36,062.8	14,351.2	12,704	147,087	35,947.3	8,469.9	549,377	25,296.4	4,671,847	25,757
Silver Spring-Frederick-Rockville, MD Div 43524	4,197	73,187	8,433.4	3,585.4	2,317	21,946	4,674.0	1,095.5	131,677	6,645.7	NA	NA
Washington-Arlington-Alexandria, DC-VA-MD-WV Div 4	11,085	222,725	27,629.4	10,765.8	10,387	125,141	31,273.3	7,374.5	417,700	18,650.7	NA	NA
Waterloo-Cedar Falls, IA........	446	12,695	1,142.7	482.3	309	1,779	161.8	43.2	9,942	453.4	72,688	335
Watertown-Fort Drum, NY	277	6,183	536.8	247.5	187	912	83.3	21.0	5,280	209.8	14,606	138
Wausau, WI..........................	367	10,123	1,133.0	459.7	221	1,313	138.5	37.7	7,846	389.5	68,221	308
Weirton-Steubenville, WV-OH	295	7,787	682.8	262.3	179	953	64.5	18.5	5,260	187.9	6,477	26
Wenatchee, WA.....................	285	6,275	701.9	314.4	205	720	79.7	19.0	6,395	303.5	160,244	807
Wheeling, WV-OH	521	12,959	1,076.5	427.5	291	1,936	174.3	45.2	6,716	268.0	14,505	116
Wichita, KS...........................	1,710	42,014	4,111.4	1,693.2	983	6,533	748.0	191.4	40,865	1,785.4	321,449	1,958
Wichita Falls, TX	414	11,201	1,080.1	404.4	242	1,300	124.4	32.5	9,557	438.3	45,144	320
Williamsport, PA	287	8,233	825.8	345.7	240	1,546	152.8	35.4	6,249	278.7	30,510	140
Wilmington, NC	845	13,790	1,374.7	550.2	495	2,759	244.2	70.6	25,015	1,158.8	608,104	2,450
Winchester, VA-WV...............	383	8,763	1,051.5	423.6	215	1,204	101.6	30.6	8,976	404.5	180,562	934
Winston-Salem, NC...............	1,155	39,069	3,997.0	1,523.5	848	4,224	485.5	115.3	46,045	1,866.8	634,069	3,499
Worcester, MA-CT.................	2,274	67,479	6,940.7	3,070.9	1,518	8,318	808.2	227.2	59,570	2,890.7	355,745	1,769
Yakima, WA..........................	557	12,903	1,431.4	574.7	281	1,449	130.9	34.3	9,261	447.9	125,061	578
York-Hanover, PA	924	24,161	2,604.4	1,031.9	783	5,242	651.3	139.7	26,109	1,244.4	167,150	916
Youngstown-Warren-Boardman, OH-PA.......	1,755	40,695	3,681.2	1,454.5	946	5,527	442.5	117.9	34,284	1,452.0	82,056	374
Yuba City, CA	329	5,566	789.3	253.2	155	724	67.1	20.7	9,308	514.5	119,613	476
Yuma, AZ..............................	359	7,092	794.1	282.4	194	1,099	77.8	25.0	9,022	350.4	160,551	1,015

Area name	Government employment and payroll, 2012									Local government finances, 2012				
	Full-time equivalent employees	March payroll (dollars)	March payroll (percent of total)							General revenue				
			Adminis-tration, judicial, and legal	Police and corrections	Fire protection	Highways and transpor-tation	Health and welfare	Natural resources and utilities	Education and libraries	Total (mil dol)	Inter-govern-mental (mil dol)	Taxes		
												Total (mil dol)	Per capita[1] (dollars)	
													Total	Property
	171	172	173	174	175	176	177	178	179	180	181	182	183	184
Texarkana, TX-AR................	6,292	19,132,215	5.6	9.2	3.4	2.8	3.9	5.8	68.2	458.1	217.9	156.0	1,042	715
The Villages, FL...................	1,509	4,669,736	4.3	3.1	1.1	6.4	1.4	4.3	72.3	251.5	43.7	105.9	1,042	834
Toledo, OH	20,923	85,663,164	9.0	10.9	7.2	4.7	9.5	5.3	52.3	2,794.2	1,171.7	1,080.1	1,774	1,098
Topeka, KS	10,897	35,463,350	4.3	10.3	3.4	3.2	2.7	5.2	70.1	954.7	354.8	369.2	1,574	1,171
Trenton, NJ...........................	15,352	84,285,619	4.4	12.4	3.3	2.0	4.4	4.9	64.8	2,164.5	711.0	1,168.1	3,172	3,117
Tucson, AZ...........................	31,634	115,785,276	10.5	14.5	6.6	3.5	2.2	7.1	52.9	3,257.1	1,214.5	1,427.3	1,438	1,057
Tulsa, OK	33,451	106,348,173	5.8	9.5	5.7	4.2	2.6	6.1	63.2	2,858.0	992.1	1,256.0	1,319	714
Tuscaloosa, AL......................	11,519	40,376,521	3.7	7.3	3.3	3.6	45.3	3.8	32.1	1,108.1	293.7	229.4	983	397
Tyler, TX	8,764	29,028,100	7.6	10.8	2.8	1.5	6.8	3.6	65.8	648.3	207.0	325.4	1,515	1,170
Urban Honolulu, HI.................	9,304	47,881,176	14.1	35.4	14.0	2.6	6.8	20.8	0.0	2,232.4	331.8	1,316.4	1,348	833
Utica-Rome, NY	13,622	60,609,793	5.4	11.3	5.5	6.7	5.6	4.7	59.5	1,597.5	779.4	603.1	2,024	1,388
Valdosta, GA.........................	7,094	22,829,566	3.5	7.5	1.9	1.7	36.8	2.6	44.7	654.5	164.9	169.0	1,171	661
Vallejo-Fairfield, CA...............	14,386	72,410,858	7.6	13.9	3.4	2.8	9.9	7.1	53.4	1,896.3	937.5	594.6	1,413	1,051
Victoria, TX...........................	5,691	19,191,140	4.0	10.2	2.9	1.9	29.7	3.0	47.2	483.0	112.9	173.9	1,800	1,367
Vineland-Bridgeton, NJ	7,697	36,180,326	5.2	9.1	0.8	1.2	4.3	5.3	72.5	886.9	544.0	234.1	1,483	1,435
Virginia Beach-Norfolk-Newport News, VA-NC.	78,042	285,080,100	5.2	9.8	4.7	2.6	8.9	7.9	57.4	7,361.3	2,849.8	2,945.6	1,733	1,190
Visalia-Porterville, CA............	21,502	97,324,423	4.7	7.2	1.7	1.1	30.4	3.5	50.1	3,132.9	1,499.7	450.9	998	665
Waco, TX...............................	11,156	37,341,296	5.7	11.3	3.0	2.0	4.2	8.5	64.1	1,218.5	462.8	380.3	1,484	1,179
Walla Walla, WA....................	2,119	9,087,256	8.5	10.7	5.3	6.5	9.7	4.4	51.5	269.2	118.5	82.8	1,307	907
Warner Robins, GA	6,945	22,535,113	5.6	9.7	2.9	2.1	4.2	3.2	70.2	591.5	229.4	253.3	1,365	800
Washington-Arlington-Alexandria, DC-VA-MD-WV..........................	238,082	1,225,240,040	6.3	10.4	4.1	8.1	7.2	5.9	54.7	35,371.1	10,257.7	19,074.9	3,255	1,833
Silver Spring-Frederick-Rockville, MD Div 43524	49,143	284,578,074	3.5	7.4	4.0	2.8	6.0	9.5	65.7	6,273.9	1,440.7	3,712.4	2,984	1,415
Washington-Arlington-Alexandria, DC-VA-MD-WV Div 4	188,939	940,661,966	7.1	11.3	4.2	9.7	7.5	4.8	51.4	29,097.2	8,817.0	15,362.6	3,328	1,946
Waterloo-Cedar Falls, IA........	5,986	22,105,854	5.2	9.3	3.5	4.9	8.6	9.6	56.3	779.9	309.2	283.0	1,677	1,331
Watertown-Fort Drum, NY......	5,239	20,682,670	6.0	6.1	2.2	6.7	6.7	3.0	66.9	631.5	312.9	217.3	1,807	1,154
Wausau, WI...........................	5,721	22,517,091	4.6	6.0	1.9	5.6	19.3	2.6	59.4	701.3	346.1	232.0	1,722	1,622
Weirton-Steubenville, WV-OH	4,496	13,800,652	7.0	10.6	2.3	5.5	8.0	7.2	56.9	422.2	201.3	126.9	1,036	755
Wenatchee, WA.....................	4,724	22,972,485	4.8	6.6	2.1	5.8	6.9	31.1	41.1	513.2	239.9	153.9	1,361	918
Wheeling, WV-OH	5,774	18,658,082	6.6	9.0	3.0	7.2	6.7	13.1	53.0	499.7	202.4	181.6	1,241	837
Wichita, KS...........................	24,964	87,029,872	6.0	10.7	4.3	3.5	5.1	4.4	64.0	2,420.1	936.4	884.7	1,391	1,088
Wichita Falls, TX	6,724	21,253,583	6.4	13.3	6.1	3.0	9.1	5.3	54.1	453.8	154.7	207.0	1,372	1,062
Williamsport, PA....................	3,615	14,906,594	7.7	7.9	1.8	4.3	2.7	6.0	68.7	451.3	198.0	155.7	1,329	953
Wilmington, NC	13,583	50,754,541	2.9	7.0	2.4	1.1	45.2	4.5	33.4	1,618.1	350.1	385.0	1,461	1,059
Winchester, VA-WV	5,411	16,715,382	6.8	13.2	4.1	1.2	2.9	3.6	66.6	418.3	170.3	190.4	1,454	1,027
Winston-Salem, NC	1,023,990	75,606,649	4.5	8.8	4.0	1.2	8.6	5.0	65.1	1,918.0	964.0	681.2	1,052	828
Worcester, MA-CT.................	32,279	147,826,569	3.6	7.7	4.7	3.3	1.4	4.3	74.0	3,495.3	1,632.4	1,503.7	1,628	1,589
Yakima, WA...........................	8,019	34,900,911	7.0	10.7	3.2	2.8	3.3	5.9	66.0	970.4	601.4	232.4	941	607
York-Hanover, PA	12,293	50,416,660	6.7	12.2	1.5	2.7	6.3	3.6	64.5	1,771.5	572.5	787.5	1,799	1,467
Youngstown-Warren-Boardman, OH-PA........	20,254	71,750,350	7.4	10.2	3.8	3.6	7.7	6.8	59.4	1,994.8	1,016.8	698.5	1,251	866
Yuba City, CA	6,669	32,864,622	7.3	8.3	2.0	2.2	10.3	3.3	64.0	941.7	532.4	189.6	1,129	918
Yuma, AZ..............................	7,924	25,609,990	12.0	12.1	3.1	2.2	2.4	7.3	59.9	638.9	314.0	221.6	1,108	716

1. Based on the resident population estimated as of July 1 of the year shown.

Table C. Metropolitan Areas — Local Government Finances, Government Employment, and Income Taxes

Area name	Local government finances, 2012 (cont.) Direct general expenditure — Total (mil dol)	Per capita¹ (dollars)	Percent of total for: Education	Health and hospitals	Police protection	Public welfare	Highways	Debt outstanding — Total (mil dol)	Per capita¹ (dollars)	Government employment, 2017 — Federal civilian	Federal military	State and local	Individual income tax returns, 2016 — Number of returns	Mean adjusted gross income	Mean income tax
	185	186	187	188	189	190	191	192	193	194	195	196	197	198	199
Texarkana, TX-AR	437.3	2,921	59.2	2.4	5.9	1.0	4.9	430.1	2,873	3,904	411	9,007	61,980	49,512	5,572
The Villages, FL	263.4	2,592	27.3	1.6	6.0	0.5	7.8	594.1	5,846	1,734	211	3,047	57,090	76,131	10,808
Toledo, OH	2,631.6	4,323	42.5	7.5	6.3	6.1	4.2	2,796.0	4,593	2,164	1,612	42,145	283,390	55,323	6,658
Topeka, KS	921.3	3,928	54.3	2.2	6.2	0.2	4.0	1,441.3	6,144	3,648	956	23,009	108,740	54,227	5,976
Trenton, NJ	2,145.5	5,825	52.3	0.9	5.3	4.3	1.4	1,928.9	5,237	2,347	730	37,533	174,760	92,659	15,431
Tucson, AZ	3,531.8	3,559	37.0	3.1	9.1	2.7	5.3	5,788.9	5,833	12,845	8,121	67,186	441,640	56,276	6,565
Tulsa, OK	2,829.0	2,972	48.0	4.0	5.9	0.6	8.2	3,865.4	4,061	4,767	3,674	49,326	422,380	63,433	8,128
Tuscaloosa, AL	1,116.2	4,783	30.5	41.4	4.7	0.0	5.1	682.1	2,923	1,983	995	25,250	95,470	53,861	6,359
Tyler, TX	645.1	3,003	55.0	5.1	5.6	0.2	3.4	1,145.0	5,330	643	483	13,505	98,700	59,423	7,889
Urban Honolulu, HI	1,596.7	1,635	0.0	1.5	15.2	0.0	7.8	5,300.0	5,428	30,692	52,182	69,038	481,540	65,538	8,105
Utica-Rome, NY	1,653.0	5,546	53.3	2.7	2.8	10.6	6.2	1,633.5	5,480	2,426	493	27,512	132,770	51,190	5,517
Valdosta, GA	724.2	5,017	28.8	47.7	4.1	0.7	2.5	413.2	2,862	1,178	4,691	11,682	56,010	44,623	4,656
Vallejo-Fairfield, CA	1,873.8	4,454	35.1	6.1	9.3	7.8	4.2	1,624.0	3,860	3,716	6,915	22,144	207,680	65,466	7,487
Victoria, TX	470.7	4,872	36.4	29.6	5.8	0.0	7.0	443.6	4,591	208	205	6,900	43,460	57,536	7,173
Vineland-Bridgeton, NJ	880.4	5,580	60.1	2.7	3.8	3.4	2.5	354.4	2,246	621	284	11,921	66,150	47,683	4,692
Virginia Beach-Norfolk-Newport News, VA-NC	7,765.7	4,568	42.7	6.6	4.8	4.0	3.4	9,372.3	5,513	57,522	81,330	104,965	801,810	59,748	6,977
Visalia-Porterville, CA	3,186.6	7,050	39.0	24.4	3.2	8.0	4.7	1,380.8	3,055	1,062	685	31,225	178,610	44,391	4,279
Waco, TX	1,187.0	4,631	42.3	2.5	5.0	0.6	1.8	11,603.4	45,270	3,136	627	15,806	112,730	51,504	5,958
Walla Walla, WA	257.4	4,061	43.0	9.4	5.8	0.0	7.2	267.1	4,213	1,462	161	4,787	27,520	61,057	7,547
Warner Robins, GA	571.7	3,082	54.7	6.0	6.4	0.1	5.0	263.3	1,419	14,996	3,786	12,316	82,820	51,966	5,123
Washington-Arlington-Alexandria, DC-VA-MD-WV	35,473.9	6,053	40.6	3.4	5.3	10.4	3.3	44,210.4	7,544	383,582	65,064	329,641	3,051,850	91,483	14,199
Silver Spring-Frederick-Rockville, MD Div 43524	6,498.3	5,222	51.5	1.7	5.2	3.2	3.5	7,084.9	5,694	52,588	9,623	54,692	NA	NA	NA
Washington-Arlington-Alexandria, DC-VA-MD-WV Div 4	28,975.7	6,277	38.1	3.8	5.3	12.0	3.3	37,125.5	8,043	330,994	55,441	274,949	NA	NA	NA
Waterloo-Cedar Falls, IA	855.9	5,072	49.6	11.0	4.2	0.3	7.5	561.2	3,325	627	622	13,801	75,350	58,874	6,761
Watertown-Fort Drum, NY	631.0	5,247	49.6	3.4	2.6	9.2	6.9	554.7	4,612	3,069	15,058	8,256	50,570	48,723	4,844
Wausau, WI	710.6	5,274	41.9	10.2	3.9	18.8	7.9	440.9	3,273	409	358	7,568	67,740	60,360	7,657
Weirton-Steubenville, WV-OH	426.7	3,482	52.1	4.9	6.0	2.5	5.9	341.9	2,790	261	406	5,325	54,600	46,690	4,707
Wenatchee, WA	488.0	4,317	47.1	12.8	4.5	0.0	5.8	1,944.4	17,202	860	307	8,498	57,380	58,250	7,228
Wheeling, WV-OH	488.4	3,335	43.9	3.2	5.0	2.6	4.4	552.7	3,775	603	500	8,900	64,790	53,447	6,334
Wichita, KS	2,506.2	3,940	49.5	4.3	5.3	0.1	5.5	6,729.7	10,580	4,972	5,259	36,999	291,950	60,446	7,502
Wichita Falls, TX	440.1	2,918	47.9	5.2	7.0	0.7	4.4	688.7	4,566	1,891	6,330	10,347	61,920	51,508	5,730
Williamsport, PA	560.5	4,783	43.8	0.0	2.2	3.1	4.4	997.6	8,514	367	283	8,666	53,770	49,639	5,239
Wilmington, NC	1,610.9	6,115	23.7	45.2	4.9	2.9	1.0	1,660.3	6,303	1,099	868	22,495	129,510	63,521	8,596
Winchester, VA-WV	404.5	3,090	60.9	0.7	5.4	3.3	1.5	564.7	4,314	2,182	489	8,084	64,290	60,494	7,208
Winston-Salem, NC	2,021.7	3,121	49.9	5.3	7.8	4.7	1.7	1,785.1	2,756	2,012	1,521	29,617	297,690	56,799	6,868
Worcester, MA-CT	3,721.4	4,029	62.3	0.4	3.9	0.2	3.5	2,671.4	2,892	3,353	2,151	56,763	457,210	69,534	9,333
Yakima, WA	1,052.2	4,260	60.9	3.2	4.2	0.8	4.9	606.3	2,455	1,250	752	16,832	109,230	49,165	5,516
York-Hanover, PA	1,790.5	4,089	47.4	3.5	3.3	9.2	2.6	2,454.1	5,605	4,274	1,311	15,873	223,680	59,059	6,869
Youngstown-Warren-Boardman, OH-PA	2,023.9	3,626	53.2	5.1	6.2	4.2	4.0	1,224.6	2,194	1,991	1,386	27,768	262,100	48,140	5,345
Yuba City, CA	962.8	5,733	49.2	5.2	4.2	8.2	2.8	640.8	3,816	1,636	4,073	9,767	69,170	49,976	4,778
Yuma, AZ	616.3	3,081	47.8	2.1	6.0	2.5	4.6	668.5	3,342	3,503	4,961	10,743	84,260	41,809	3,859

1. Based on the resident population estimated as of July 1 of the year shown.

Cities of 25,000 or More

(For explanation of symbols, see page viii)

Page

897	City Highlights and Rankings
907	City Column Headings
910	Table D
910	**AL**(Alabaster)—**AR**(Hot Springs)
922	**AR**(Jacksonville)—**CA**(Davis)
934	**CA**(Delano)—**CA**(Menifee)
946	**CA**(Menlo Park)—**CA**(San Dimas)
958	**CA**(San Francisco)—**CO**(Broomfield)
970	**CO**(Castle Rock)—**FL**(Daytona Beach)
982	**FL**(Deerfield Beach)—**FL**(Winter Springs)
994	**GA**(Albany)—**IL**(Buffalo Grove)
1006	**IL**(Burbank)—**IL**(Vernon Hills)
1018	**IL**(Waukegan)—**IA**(West Des Moines)
1030	**KS**(Dodge City)—**MA**(Barnstable Town)
1042	**MA**(Beverly)—**MI**(Novi)
1054	**MI**(Oak Park)—**MS**(Tupelo)
1066	**MO**(Ballwin)—**NJ**(Fort Lee)
1078	**NJ**(Garfield)—**NY**(White Plains)
1090	**NY**(Yonkers)—**OH**(Grove City)
1102	**OH**(Hamilton)—**OR**(Portland)
1114	**OR**(Redmond)—**TN**(Collierville)
1126	**TN**(Columbia)—**TX**(Hurst)
1138	**TX**(Irving)—**UT**(Holladay)
1150	**UT**(Kaysville)—**WA**(Olympia)
1162	**WA**(Pasco)—**WY**(Laramie)

City Highlights and Rankings

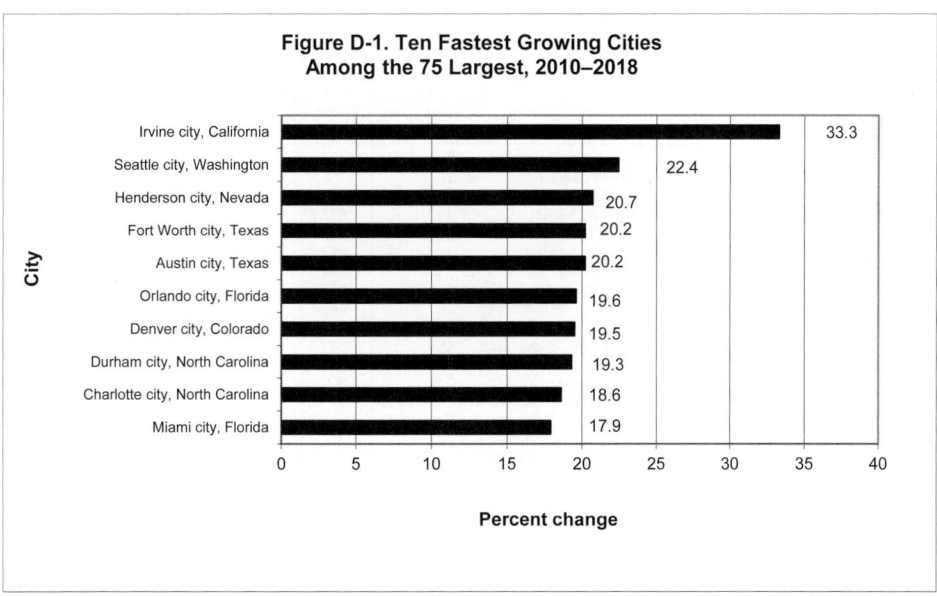

Figure D-1. Ten Fastest Growing Cities Among the 75 Largest, 2010–2018

City	Percent change
Irvine city, California	33.3
Seattle city, Washington	22.4
Henderson city, Nevada	20.7
Fort Worth city, Texas	20.2
Austin city, Texas	20.2
Orlando city, Florida	19.6
Denver city, Colorado	19.5
Durham city, North Carolina	19.3
Charlotte city, North Carolina	18.6
Miami city, Florida	17.9

In 2018, 10 cities had more than 1 million residents, led by New York City with nearly 8.4 million people, Los Angeles with nearly 4.0 million people, and Chicago with 2.7 million people. California had 14 cities among the nation's 75 most populous, as well as 4 among the top 15 (Los Angeles, San Diego, San Jose, and San Francisco). Texas had 9 cities in the top 75, and had 5 among the top 15 (Houston, San Antonio, Dallas, Austin, and Fort Worth).

Among the largest cities, 50 had growth rates equaling 5 percent or higher from 2010 to 2018 and 33 had growth rates at 10 percent or higher. Many of these cities were in the south. Irvine, CA had the highest growth rate at 33.3 percent. Texas had two cities in the top ten (Austin and Fort Worth), as did Florida (Orlando and Miami) and North Carolina (Charlotte and Durham). Forty-seven of the largest cities equaled or exceeded the U.S. growth rate of 6.0 percent.

Among the 75 largest cities, nine lost population between 2010 and 2018. Detroit lost nearly 6 percent of its population while St. Louis, Cleveland, Toledo, and Baltimore each lost 3 percent or more.

New Orleans, with a 13.7 percent increase, was among the top twenty cities for population growth. Though New Orleans lost more than half of its population after Hurricane Katrina in 2005, it has grown by more than two-thirds between 2006 and 2018. It was the nineteenth fastest growing city from 2010 to 2018, but its 2018 population is still about 19 percent below its pre-Katrina total.

Among all cities of 25,000 or more, 10 cities had unemployment rates of 10 percent or more, significantly lower than eight years earlier, when 555 cities had an unemployment rate of 10 percent or more. Ten of the twenty-five cities with the highest unemployment rates were located in California, five were in Michigan, three were in Texas, two each in New Jersey and Illinois, and one in Pennsylvania. Among the largest cities, Detroit, MI had the highest unemployment rate at 9.0 percent followed by Newark, NJ at 7.0 percent. Lincoln, NE and San Francisco, CA had the lowest unemployment rates at 2.5 percent and 2.4 percent respectively. Among all cities, 893 had unemployment rates of 4.0 percent or lower. Six of the ten cities with the lowest unemployment rates were in Iowa, two were in California, and one each were in Idaho and Michigan. No unemployment data are available for Hawaiian cities, but Honolulu county had an unemployment rate of 2.2 percent, lower than any of the 75 largest cities.

While the 2010 census provided updated counts of the population and basic demographic characteristics, updated information on social and economic characteristics is now obtained through the ongoing American Community Survey (ACS). For states, counties, and metropolitan areas, the official intercensal estimates are provided by age, sex, race, and Hispanic origin through the Population Estimates Program. Estimates of these demographic characteristics are not included for cities through the Population Estimates Program, but are available through the ACS. This book includes ACS 1-year estimates for 2017, including data on education, income, housing characteristics, and more.

Among the largest cities, San Francisco, San Jose, and Irvine were the top three for both median income and median housing value. Seattle, Oakland, Washington, DC, and San Diego also ranked in the top ten for both median income and housing value. Plano, TX ranked fourth for median household income, but its median housing value ranked only 20th among the large cities. Los Angeles and New York ranked 7th and 8th for median housing value, but their median household incomes ranked 23rd and 27th among large cities. San Francisco tops the ranking with an estimated median housing value of $1,104,100. Detroit and Cleveland had the lowest median housing values among the large cities in 2017, at $50,200 and $70,200 respectively. They also had the lowest median incomes among the largest cities.

Among the 75 largest cities in 2017, there were six cities where 10 percent or more of residents had moved from another state or county within the previous year. This may result from population growth: Irvine, CA had one of the highest growth rates in recent years as well as one of the highest proportions of people who had moved there in the past year. Irvine has a strong technological economy as well as a large university. Other cities have large shifts because of student or military population groups: East Lansing, MI—site of Michigan State University—lost 1.2 percent of its population from 2010 to 2018 but 29.1 percent of its residents had moved there within the past year, reflecting the 61.6 percent of residents who were between the ages of 18 and 24, well above the 9.5 percent national average.

75 Largest Cities by 2018 Population
Selected rankings

Population, 2018

Population rank	City	Population [col 2]
1	New York city, New York	8,398,748
2	Los Angeles city, California	3,990,456
3	Chicago city, Illinois	2,705,994
4	Houston city, Texas	2,325,502
5	Phoenix city, Arizona	1,660,272
6	Philadelphia city, Pennsylvania	1,584,138
7	San Antonio city, Texas	1,532,233
8	San Diego city, California	1,425,976
9	Dallas city, Texas	1,345,047
10	San Jose city, California	1,030,119
11	Austin city, Texas	964,254
12	Jacksonville city, Florida	903,889
13	Fort Worth city, Texas	895,008
14	Columbus city, Ohio	892,533
15	San Francisco city, California	883,305
16	Charlotte city, North Carolina	872,498
17	Indianapolis city, Indiana	867,125
18	Seattle city, Washington	744,955
19	Denver city, Colorado	716,492
20	Washington city, District of Columbia	702,455
21	Boston city, Massachusetts	694,583
22	El Paso city, Texas	682,669
23	Detroit city, Michigan	672,662
24	Nashville-Davidson, Tennessee	669,053
25	Portland city, Oregon	653,115
26	Memphis city, Tennessee	650,618
27	Oklahoma City city, Oklahoma	649,021
28	Las Vegas city, Nevada	644,644
29	Louisville/Jefferson, Kentucky	620,118
30	Baltimore city, Maryland	602,495
31	Milwaukee city, Wisconsin	592,025
32	Albuquerque city, New Mexico	560,218
33	Tucson city, Arizona	545,975
34	Fresno city, California	530,093
35	Mesa city, Arizona	508,958
36	Sacramento city, California	508,529
37	Atlanta city, Georgia	498,044
38	Kansas City city, Missouri	491,918
39	Colorado Springs city, Colorado	472,688
40	Miami city, Florida	470,914
41	Raleigh city, North Carolina	469,298
42	Omaha city, Nebraska	468,262
43	Long Beach city, California	467,354
44	Virginia Beach city, Virginia	450,189
45	Oakland city, California	429,082
46	Minneapolis city, Minnesota	425,403
47	Tulsa city, Oklahoma	400,669
48	Arlington city, Texas	398,112
49	Tampa city, Florida	392,890
50	New Orleans city, Louisiana	391,006
51	Wichita city, Kansas	389,255
52	Cleveland city, Ohio	383,793
53	Bakersfield city, California	383,579
54	Aurora city, Colorado	374,114
55	Anaheim city, California	352,005
56	Urban Honolulu CDP, Hawaii	347,397
57	Santa Ana city, California	332,725
58	Riverside city, California	330,063
59	Corpus Christi city, Texas	326,554
60	Lexington-Fayette, Kentucky	323,780
61	Stockton city, California	311,178
62	Henderson city, Nevada	310,390
63	St. Paul city, Minnesota	307,695
64	St. Louis city, Missouri	302,838
65	Cincinnati city, Ohio	302,605
66	Pittsburgh city, Pennsylvania	301,048
67	Greensboro city, North Carolina	294,722
68	Anchorage municipality, Alaska	291,538
69	Plano city, Texas	288,061
70	Lincoln city, Nebraska	287,401
71	Orlando city, Florida	285,713
72	Irvine city, California	282,572
73	Newark city, New Jersey	282,090
74	Toledo city, Ohio	274,975
75	Durham city, North Carolina	274,291

Land area, 2018

Population rank	Land area rank	City	Land area (square miles) [col 1]
68	1	Anchorage municipality, Alaska	1706.4
12	2	Jacksonville city, Florida	747.7
4	3	Houston city, Texas	637.0
27	4	Oklahoma City city, Oklahoma	606.4
5	5	Phoenix city, Arizona	517.7
7	6	San Antonio city, Texas	484.6
24	7	Nashville-Davidson, Tennessee	475.6
2	8	Los Angeles city, California	468.7
17	9	Indianapolis city, Indiana	361.6
13	10	Fort Worth city, Texas	344.8
9	11	Dallas city, Texas	339.6
8	12	San Diego city, California	325.6
11	13	Austin city, Texas	320.8
26	14	Memphis city, Tennessee	317.4
38	15	Kansas City city, Missouri	314.9
16	16	Charlotte city, North Carolina	306.6
1	17	New York city, New York	300.4
60	18	Lexington-Fayette, Kentucky	283.6
29	19	Louisville/Jefferson, Kentucky	263.4
22	20	El Paso city, Texas	257.4
44	21	Virginia Beach city, Virginia	244.7
33	22	Tucson city, Arizona	238.0
3	23	Chicago city, Illinois	227.4
14	24	Columbus city, Ohio	218.8
47	25	Tulsa city, Oklahoma	197.5
39	26	Colorado Springs city, Colorado	195.0
32	27	Albuquerque city, New Mexico	187.2
10	28	San Jose city, California	177.1
50	29	New Orleans city, Louisiana	169.4
51	30	Wichita city, Kansas	161.2
59	31	Corpus Christi city, Texas	159.7
54	32	Aurora city, Colorado	153.5
19	33	Denver city, Colorado	153.3
53	34	Bakersfield city, California	149.7
41	35	Raleigh city, North Carolina	145.3
28	36	Las Vegas city, Nevada	141.8
23	37	Detroit city, Michigan	138.7
42	38	Omaha city, Nebraska	138.2
35	39	Mesa city, Arizona	138.0
37	40	Atlanta city, Georgia	135.6
6	41	Philadelphia city, Pennsylvania	134.2
25	42	Portland city, Oregon	133.4
67	43	Greensboro city, North Carolina	128.9
34	44	Fresno city, California	114.3
49	45	Tampa city, Florida	114.0
75	46	Durham city, North Carolina	112.2
71	47	Orlando city, Florida	110.1
62	48	Henderson city, Nevada	104.7
36	49	Sacramento city, California	97.8
31	50	Milwaukee city, Wisconsin	96.2
48	51	Arlington city, Texas	95.8
70	52	Lincoln city, Nebraska	94.8
18	53	Seattle city, Washington	83.9
58	54	Riverside city, California	81.3
30	55	Baltimore city, Maryland	80.9
74	56	Toledo city, Ohio	80.5
65	57	Cincinnati city, Ohio	77.9
52	58	Cleveland city, Ohio	77.7
69	59	Plano city, Texas	71.7
72	60	Irvine city, California	65.6
61	61	Stockton city, California	61.7
64	62	St. Louis city, Missouri	61.7
20	63	Washington city, District of Columbia	61.1
56	64	Urban Honolulu CDP, Hawaii	60.5
45	65	Oakland city, California	55.9
66	66	Pittsburgh city, Pennsylvania	55.4
46	67	Minneapolis city, Minnesota	54.0
63	68	St. Paul city, Minnesota	52.0
43	69	Long Beach city, California	50.7
55	70	Anaheim city, California	50.3
21	71	Boston city, Massachusetts	48.3
15	72	San Francisco city, California	46.9
40	73	Miami city, Florida	36.0
57	74	Santa Ana city, California	27.4
73	75	Newark city, New Jersey	24.1

Population density, 2018

Population rank	Density rank	City	Density (per square kilometer) [col 4]
1	1	New York city, New York	27,958.5
15	2	San Francisco city, California	18,833.8
21	3	Boston city, Massachusetts	14,380.6
40	4	Miami city, Florida	13,080.9
57	5	Santa Ana city, California	12,143.2
3	6	Chicago city, Illinois	11,899.7
6	7	Philadelphia city, Pennsylvania	11,804.3
73	8	Newark city, New Jersey	11,705.0
20	9	Washington city, District of Columbia	11,496.8
43	10	Long Beach city, California	9,218.0
18	11	Seattle city, Washington	8,879.1
2	12	Los Angeles city, California	8,513.9
46	13	Minneapolis city, Minnesota	7,877.8
45	14	Oakland city, California	7,675.9
30	15	Baltimore city, Maryland	7,447.4
55	16	Anaheim city, California	6,998.1
31	17	Milwaukee city, Wisconsin	6,154.1
63	18	St. Paul city, Minnesota	5,917.2
10	19	San Jose city, California	5,816.6
56	20	Urban Honolulu CDP, Hawaii	5,742.1
66	21	Pittsburgh city, Pennsylvania	5,434.1
36	22	Sacramento city, California	5,199.7
61	23	Stockton city, California	5,043.4
52	24	Cleveland city, Ohio	4,939.4
64	25	St. Louis city, Missouri	4,908.2
25	26	Portland city, Oregon	4,895.9
23	27	Detroit city, Michigan	4,849.8
19	28	Denver city, Colorado	4,673.8
34	29	Fresno city, California	4,637.7
28	30	Las Vegas city, Nevada	4,546.1
8	31	San Diego city, California	4,379.5
72	32	Irvine city, California	4,307.5
48	33	Arlington city, Texas	4,155.7
14	34	Columbus city, Ohio	4,079.2
58	35	Riverside city, California	4,059.8
69	36	Plano city, Texas	4,017.6
9	37	Dallas city, Texas	3,960.7
65	38	Cincinnati city, Ohio	3,884.5
35	39	Mesa city, Arizona	3,688.1
37	40	Atlanta city, Georgia	3,672.9
4	41	Houston city, Texas	3,650.7
49	42	Tampa city, Florida	3,446.4
74	43	Toledo city, Ohio	3,415.8
42	44	Omaha city, Nebraska	3,388.3
41	45	Raleigh city, North Carolina	3,229.9
5	46	Phoenix city, Arizona	3,207.0
7	47	San Antonio city, Texas	3,161.9
70	48	Lincoln city, Nebraska	3,031.7
11	49	Austin city, Texas	3,005.8
32	50	Albuquerque city, New Mexico	2,992.6
62	51	Henderson city, Nevada	2,964.6
16	52	Charlotte city, North Carolina	2,845.7
22	53	El Paso city, Texas	2,652.2
13	54	Fort Worth city, Texas	2,595.7
71	55	Orlando city, Florida	2,595.0
53	56	Bakersfield city, California	2,562.3
75	57	Durham city, North Carolina	2,444.7
54	58	Aurora city, Colorado	2,437.2
39	59	Colorado Springs city, Colorado	2,424.0
51	60	Wichita city, Kansas	2,414.7
17	61	Indianapolis city, Indiana	2,398.0
29	62	Louisville/Jefferson, Kentucky	2,354.3
50	63	New Orleans city, Louisiana	2,308.2
33	64	Tucson city, Arizona	2,294.0
67	65	Greensboro city, North Carolina	2,286.4
26	66	Memphis city, Tennessee	2,049.8
59	67	Corpus Christi city, Texas	2,044.8
47	68	Tulsa city, Oklahoma	2,028.7
44	69	Virginia Beach city, Virginia	1,839.8
38	70	Kansas City city, Missouri	1562.1
24	71	Nashville-Davidson, Tennessee	1406.8
12	72	Jacksonville city, Florida	1208.9
60	73	Lexington-Fayette, Kentucky	1141.7
27	74	Oklahoma City city, Oklahoma	1070.3
68	75	Anchorage municipality, Alaska	170.8

75 Largest Cities by 2018 Population
Selected rankings

Percent population change, 2010–2018				Percent White alone, 2017				Percent Black alone, 2017			
Population rank	Percent change rank	City	Percent change [col 26]	Population rank	White rank	City	Percent White [col 5]	Population rank	Black rank	City	Percent Black [col 6]
72	1	Irvine city, California	33.3	59	1	Corpus Christi city, Texas	90.4	23	1	Detroit city, Michigan	79.0
18	2	Seattle city, Washington	22.4	70	2	Lincoln city, Nebraska	84.9	26	2	Memphis city, Tennessee	63.7
62	3	Henderson city, Nevada	20.7	35	3	Mesa city, Arizona	80.1	30	3	Baltimore city, Maryland	62.7
11	4	Austin city, Texas	20.2	7	4	San Antonio city, Texas	79.8	50	4	New Orleans city, Louisiana	59.5
13	4	Fort Worth city, Texas	20.2	39	5	Colorado Springs city, Colorado	78.8	37	5	Atlanta city, Georgia	52.8
71	6	Orlando city, Florida	19.6	42	6	Omaha city, Nebraska	78.3	73	6	Newark city, New Jersey	50.7
19	7	Denver city, Colorado	19.5	25	7	Portland city, Oregon	77.3	52	7	Cleveland city, Ohio	48.7
75	8	Durham city, North Carolina	19.3	32	8	Albuquerque city, New Mexico	76.5	64	8	St. Louis city, Missouri	46.8
16	9	Charlotte city, North Carolina	18.6	22	9	El Paso city, Texas	76.0	20	9	Washington city, District of Columbia	45.9
40	10	Miami city, Florida	17.9	62	10	Henderson city, Nevada	75.6	67	10	Greensboro city, North Carolina	42.9
49	11	Tampa city, Florida	16.9	60	11	Lexington-Fayette, Kentucky	75.5	65	11	Cincinnati city, Ohio	42.5
20	12	Washington city, District of Columbia	16.7	19	12	Denver city, Colorado	75.4	6	12	Philadelphia city, Pennsylvania	42.0
37	12	Atlanta city, Georgia	16.7	40	13	Miami city, Florida	74.2	31	13	Milwaukee city, Wisconsin	39.0
41	14	Raleigh city, North Carolina	16.1	5	14	Phoenix city, Arizona	73.4	75	14	Durham city, North Carolina	38.4
35	15	Mesa city, Arizona	15.7	33	15	Tucson city, Arizona	71.8	16	15	Charlotte city, North Carolina	34.4
7	16	San Antonio city, Texas	15.5	11	16	Austin city, Texas	71.6	12	16	Jacksonville city, Florida	31.6
54	17	Aurora city, Colorado	15.2	51	16	Wichita city, Kansas	71.6	3	17	Chicago city, Illinois	29.8
5	18	Phoenix city, Arizona	14.7	29	18	Louisville/Jefferson, Kentucky	69.3	41	18	Raleigh city, North Carolina	29.2
50	19	New Orleans city, Louisiana	13.7	53	19	Tampa city, Florida	68.6	14	19	Columbus city, Ohio	28.6
39	20	Colorado Springs city, Colorado	13.2	27	20	Oklahoma City city, Oklahoma	67.5	38	20	Kansas City city, Missouri	28.5
14	21	Columbus city, Ohio	13.1	18	21	Seattle city, Washington	67.2	17	21	Indianapolis city, Indiana	27.8
21	22	Boston city, Massachusetts	12.4	66	22	Pittsburgh city, Pennsylvania	67.0	71	22	Orlando city, Florida	27.5
9	23	Dallas city, Texas	12.3	49	23	Tampa city, Florida	66.5	74	22	Toledo city, Ohio	27.5
25	24	Portland city, Oregon	11.9	69	24	Plano city, Texas	65.9	24	24	Nashville-Davidson, Tennessee	27.3
27	24	Oklahoma City city, Oklahoma	11.9	44	25	Virginia Beach city, Virginia	65.5	21	25	Boston city, Massachusetts	25.9
46	26	Minneapolis city, Minnesota	11.2	8	26	San Diego city, California	64.6	48	26	Arlington city, Texas	25.0
4	27	Houston city, Texas	11.1	47	27	Tulsa city, Oklahoma	64.5	9	27	Dallas city, Texas	24.5
70	27	Lincoln city, Nebraska	11.1	24	28	Nashville-Davidson, Tennessee	64.2	1	28	New York city, New York	24.3
24	29	Nashville-Davidson, Tennessee	10.9	13	29	Fort Worth city, Texas	63.5	29	29	Louisville/Jefferson, Kentucky	24.1
69	29	Plano city, Texas	10.9	74	30	Toledo city, Ohio	63.1	49	30	Tampa city, Florida	23.9
28	31	Las Vegas city, Nevada	10.3	9	31	Dallas city, Texas	62.9	45	31	Oakland city, California	23.4
53	32	Bakersfield city, California	10.1	46	32	Minneapolis city, Minnesota	62.8	4	32	Houston city, Texas	22.9
12	33	Jacksonville city, Florida	10.0	17	33	Indianapolis city, Indiana	62.7	66	33	Pittsburgh city, Pennsylvania	22.1
45	34	Oakland city, California	9.8	28	34	Las Vegas city, Nevada	62.1	44	34	Virginia Beach city, Virginia	19.0
15	35	San Francisco city, California	9.7	54	34	Aurora city, Colorado	62.1	40	35	Miami city, Florida	18.0
67	36	Greensboro city, North Carolina	9.6	68	36	Anchorage municipality, Alaska	61.9	46	35	Minneapolis city, Minnesota	18.0
8	37	San Diego city, California	9.5	55	37	Anaheim city, California	61.4	13	37	Fort Worth city, Texas	17.7
60	38	Lexington-Fayette, Kentucky	9.4	34	38	Fresno city, California	60.4	63	38	St. Paul city, Minnesota	17.1
36	39	Sacramento city, California	9.0	38	39	Kansas City city, Missouri	60.0	54	39	Aurora city, Colorado	15.9
48	39	Arlington city, Texas	9.0	48	40	Arlington city, Texas	59.4	27	40	Oklahoma City city, Oklahoma	15.1
58	41	Riverside city, California	8.6	4	41	Houston city, Texas	59.3	47	41	Tulsa city, Oklahoma	14.9
10	42	San Jose city, California	8.2	14	42	Columbus city, Ohio	59.0	60	42	Lexington-Fayette, Kentucky	14.5
63	43	St. Paul city, Minnesota	7.9	12	43	Jacksonville city, Florida	57.9	36	43	Sacramento city, California	14.0
38	44	Kansas City city, Missouri	7.0	41	44	Raleigh city, North Carolina	56.8	43	44	Long Beach city, California	12.7
59	44	Corpus Christi city, Texas	7.0	71	45	Orlando city, Florida	56.5	42	45	Omaha city, Nebraska	12.3
61	46	Stockton city, California	6.7	63	46	St. Paul city, Minnesota	55.8	61	45	Stockton city, California	12.3
34	47	Fresno city, California	6.6	21	47	Boston city, Massachusetts	52.8	51	47	Wichita city, Kansas	11.0
17	48	Indianapolis city, Indiana	5.7	2	48	Los Angeles city, California	50.9	28	48	Las Vegas city, Nevada	10.7
22	49	El Paso city, Texas	5.3	43	48	Long Beach city, California	50.9	2	49	Los Angeles city, California	9.1
2	50	Los Angeles city, California	5.2	65	50	Cincinnati city, Ohio	50.4	19	49	Denver city, Colorado	9.1
55	51	Anaheim city, California	4.6	3	51	Chicago city, Illinois	49.9	69	49	Plano city, Texas	9.1
29	52	Louisville/Jefferson, Kentucky	4.2	75	52	Durham city, North Carolina	49.8	11	52	Austin city, Texas	7.7
42	53	Omaha city, Nebraska	4.0	16	53	Charlotte city, North Carolina	49.2	34	52	Fresno city, California	7.7
6	54	Philadelphia city, Pennsylvania	3.8	67	54	Greensboro city, North Carolina	48.2	53	54	Bakersfield city, California	7.6
33	55	Tucson city, Arizona	3.7	58	55	Riverside city, California	48.1	5	55	Phoenix city, Arizona	7.2
56	56	Urban Honolulu CDP, Hawaii	2.9	72	56	Irvine city, California	46.5	7	56	San Antonio city, Texas	7.0
44	57	Virginia Beach city, Virginia	2.8	64	57	St. Louis city, Missouri	46.3	18	57	Seattle city, Washington	6.9
1	58	New York city, New York	2.7	15	58	San Francisco city, California	45.6	58	58	Riverside city, California	6.7
32	59	Albuquerque city, New Mexico	2.6	31	59	Milwaukee city, Wisconsin	44.0	62	59	Henderson city, Nevada	6.3
57	60	Santa Ana city, California	2.4	1	60	New York city, New York	42.2	8	60	San Diego city, California	6.2
47	61	Tulsa city, Oklahoma	2.2	6	61	Philadelphia city, Pennsylvania	42.1	39	61	Colorado Springs city, Colorado	5.6
65	62	Cincinnati city, Ohio	1.9	36	62	Sacramento city, California	41.4	25	62	Portland city, Oregon	5.5
51	63	Wichita city, Kansas	1.8	20	63	Washington city, District of Columbia	41.0	15	63	San Francisco city, California	5.2
73	63	Newark city, New Jersey	1.8	61	64	Stockton city, California	39.7	68	64	Anchorage municipality, Alaska	5.0
43	65	Long Beach city, California	1.1	37	65	Atlanta city, Georgia	39.2	33	65	Tucson city, Arizona	4.8
3	66	Chicago city, Illinois	0.4	10	66	San Jose city, California	39.1	70	66	Lincoln city, Nebraska	4.1
68	67	Anchorage municipality, Alaska	-0.1	52	66	Cleveland city, Ohio	39.1	59	67	Corpus Christi city, Texas	4.0
26	68	Memphis city, Tennessee	-0.2	57	68	Santa Ana city, California	35.0	35	68	Mesa city, Arizona	3.8
31	69	Milwaukee city, Wisconsin	-0.4	45	69	Oakland city, California	34.2	22	69	El Paso city, Texas	3.7
66	70	Pittsburgh city, Pennsylvania	-1.4	50	70	New Orleans city, Louisiana	33.8	32	70	Albuquerque city, New Mexico	3.1
30	71	Baltimore city, Maryland	-3.0	30	71	Baltimore city, Maryland	30.1	10	71	San Jose city, California	2.9
52	72	Cleveland city, Ohio	-3.2	26	72	Memphis city, Tennessee	29.2	55	72	Anaheim city, California	2.8
74	73	Toledo city, Ohio	-4.3	73	73	Newark city, New Jersey	27.1	56	73	Urban Honolulu CDP, Hawaii	2.0
64	74	St. Louis city, Missouri	-5.1	56	74	Urban Honolulu CDP, Hawaii	16.1	72	74	Irvine city, California	1.8
23	75	Detroit city, Michigan	-5.8	23	75	Detroit city, Michigan	14.5	57	75	Santa Ana city, California	0.9

75 Largest Cities by 2018 Population
Selected rankings

Percent American Indian, Alaska Native alone, 2017				Percent Asian and Pacific Islander alone, 2017				Percent Hispanic or Latino,[1] 2017			
Population rank	American Indian, Alaska Native rank	City	Percent American Indian, Alaska Native [col 7]	Population rank	Asian and Pacific Islander rank	City	Percent Asian and Pacific Islander [col 8]	Population rank	Hispanic or Latino rank	City	Percent Hispanic or Latino [col 12]
68	1	Anchorage municipality, Alaska	7.8	56	1	Urban Honolulu CDP, Hawaii	55.0	22	1	El Paso city, Texas	81.4
32	2	Albuquerque city, New Mexico	4.4	72	2	Irvine city, California	41.5	57	2	Santa Ana city, California	76.5
47	3	Tulsa city, Oklahoma	4.3	10	3	San Jose city, California	35.6	40	3	Miami city, Florida	71.7
33	4	Tucson city, Arizona	4.2	15	4	San Francisco city, California	34.7	7	4	San Antonio city, Texas	64.1
27	5	Oklahoma City city, Oklahoma	2.4	61	5	Stockton city, California	21.0	59	5	Corpus Christi city, Texas	63.1
5	6	Phoenix city, Arizona	2.0	63	6	St. Paul city, Minnesota	19.9	55	6	Anaheim city, California	55.0
35	6	Mesa city, Arizona	2.0	69	7	Plano city, Texas	19.7	58	7	Riverside city, California	54.7
46	8	Minneapolis city, Minnesota	1.7	36	8	Sacramento city, California	18.9	53	8	Bakersfield city, California	50.9
19	9	Denver city, Colorado	1.1	8	9	San Diego city, California	17.2	32	9	Albuquerque city, New Mexico	49.6
34	9	Fresno city, California	1.1	55	10	Anaheim city, California	16.6	34	10	Fresno city, California	49.0
39	9	Colorado Springs city, Colorado	1.1	18	11	Seattle city, Washington	15.8	2	11	Los Angeles city, California	48.9
36	12	Sacramento city, California	1.0	45	12	Oakland city, California	15.5	33	12	Tucson city, Arizona	44.9
25	13	Portland city, Oregon	0.9	1	13	New York city, New York	14.5	4	13	Houston city, Texas	44.6
11	14	Austin city, Texas	0.8	34	14	Fresno city, California	14.1	43	14	Long Beach city, California	43.2
28	14	Las Vegas city, Nevada	0.8	43	15	Long Beach city, California	13.5	61	15	Stockton city, California	43.1
54	14	Aurora city, Colorado	0.8	57	16	Santa Ana city, California	12.0	5	16	Phoenix city, Arizona	42.9
58	14	Riverside city, California	0.8	2	17	Los Angeles city, California	11.5	9	17	Dallas city, Texas	41.9
63	14	St. Paul city, Minnesota	0.8	68	18	Anchorage municipality, Alaska	10.8	73	18	Newark city, New Jersey	36.2
10	19	San Jose city, California	0.7	62	19	Henderson city, Nevada	10.6	13	19	Fort Worth city, Texas	36.1
43	19	Long Beach city, California	0.7	21	20	Boston city, Massachusetts	9.7	11	20	Austin city, Texas	34.2
45	19	Oakland city, California	0.7	58	21	Riverside city, California	8.4	28	20	Las Vegas city, Nevada	34.2
70	19	Lincoln city, Nebraska	0.7	25	22	Portland city, Oregon	8.1	10	22	San Jose city, California	32.1
2	23	Los Angeles city, California	0.6	54	23	Aurora city, Colorado	7.8	71	23	Orlando city, Florida	30.8
8	23	San Diego city, California	0.6	11	24	Austin city, Texas	7.6	8	24	San Diego city, California	30.2
38	23	Kansas City city, Missouri	0.6	6	25	Philadelphia city, Pennsylvania	7.3	19	25	Denver city, Colorado	29.9
53	23	Bakersfield city, California	0.6	53	26	Bakersfield city, California	7.2	48	25	Arlington city, Texas	29.9
16	27	Charlotte city, North Carolina	0.5	28	27	Las Vegas city, Nevada	7.1	1	27	New York city, New York	29.2
22	27	El Paso city, Texas	0.5	44	28	Virginia Beach city, Virginia	6.8	3	28	Chicago city, Illinois	29.0
31	27	Milwaukee city, Wisconsin	0.5	3	29	Chicago city, Illinois	6.7	45	29	Oakland city, California	28.4
40	27	Miami city, Florida	0.5	4	30	Houston city, Texas	6.5	35	30	Mesa city, Arizona	28.3
42	27	Omaha city, Nebraska	0.5	66	30	Pittsburgh city, Pennsylvania	6.5	36	31	Sacramento city, California	28.2
51	27	Wichita city, Kansas	0.5	16	32	Charlotte city, North Carolina	6.4	54	32	Aurora city, Colorado	27.6
52	27	Cleveland city, Ohio	0.5	46	32	Minneapolis city, Minnesota	6.4	49	33	Tampa city, Florida	26.4
61	27	Stockton city, California	0.5	14	34	Columbus city, Ohio	6.0	21	34	Boston city, Massachusetts	20.4
67	27	Greensboro city, North Carolina	0.5	48	35	Arlington city, Texas	5.7	27	35	Oklahoma City city, Oklahoma	20.0
1	36	New York city, New York	0.4	12	36	Jacksonville city, Florida	5.3	31	36	Milwaukee city, Wisconsin	19.1
6	36	Philadelphia city, Pennsylvania	0.4	41	37	Raleigh city, North Carolina	5.1	39	37	Colorado Springs city, Colorado	17.5
7	36	San Antonio city, Texas	0.4	51	38	Wichita city, Kansas	5.0	51	37	Wichita city, Kansas	17.5
18	36	Seattle city, Washington	0.4	70	38	Lincoln city, Nebraska	5.0	47	39	Tulsa city, Oklahoma	16.9
23	36	Detroit city, Michigan	0.4	75	38	Durham city, North Carolina	5.0	15	40	San Francisco city, California	15.2
30	36	Baltimore city, Maryland	0.4	27	41	Oklahoma City city, Oklahoma	4.6	6	41	Philadelphia city, Pennsylvania	14.8
55	36	Anaheim city, California	0.4	67	42	Greensboro city, North Carolina	4.5	62	42	Henderson city, Nevada	14.7
59	36	Corpus Christi city, Texas	0.4	13	43	Fort Worth city, Texas	4.4	69	42	Plano city, Texas	14.7
64	36	St. Louis city, Missouri	0.4	31	44	Milwaukee city, Wisconsin	4.3	16	44	Charlotte city, North Carolina	14.3
69	36	Plano city, Texas	0.4	49	44	Tampa city, Florida	4.3	42	45	Omaha city, Nebraska	14.1
3	46	Chicago city, Illinois	0.3	71	44	Orlando city, Florida	4.3	75	46	Durham city, North Carolina	13.2
4	46	Houston city, Texas	0.3	20	47	Washington city, District of Columbia	4.1	52	47	Cleveland city, Ohio	12.4
9	46	Dallas city, Texas	0.3	47	47	Tulsa city, Oklahoma	4.1	20	48	Washington city, District of Columbia	11.0
13	46	Fort Worth city, Texas	0.3	5	49	Phoenix city, Arizona	4.0	41	48	Raleigh city, North Carolina	11.0
14	46	Columbus city, Ohio	0.3	37	49	Atlanta city, Georgia	4.0	46	48	Minneapolis city, Minnesota	11.0
15	46	San Francisco city, California	0.3	19	51	Denver city, Colorado	3.9	17	51	Indianapolis city, Indiana	10.9
21	46	Boston city, Massachusetts	0.3	9	52	Dallas city, Texas	3.7	72	52	Irvine city, California	10.6
41	46	Raleigh city, North Carolina	0.3	42	52	Omaha city, Nebraska	3.7	24	53	Nashville-Davidson, Tennessee	10.4
48	46	Arlington city, Texas	0.3	24	54	Nashville-Davidson, Tennessee	3.6	25	53	Portland city, Oregon	10.4
57	46	Santa Ana city, California	0.3	60	54	Lexington-Fayette, Kentucky	3.6	12	55	Jacksonville city, Florida	9.9
60	46	Lexington-Fayette, Kentucky	0.3	64	56	St. Louis city, Missouri	3.4	63	56	St. Paul city, Minnesota	9.8
12	57	Jacksonville city, Florida	0.2	38	57	Kansas City city, Missouri	3.2	38	57	Kansas City city, Missouri	9.4
17	57	Indianapolis city, Indiana	0.2	17	58	Indianapolis city, Indiana	3.1	68	58	Anchorage municipality, Alaska	9.2
20	57	Washington city, District of Columbia	0.2	33	58	Tucson city, Arizona	3.1	44	59	Virginia Beach city, Virginia	8.2
24	57	Nashville-Davidson, Tennessee	0.2	29	60	Louisville/Jefferson, Kentucky	2.9	74	59	Toledo city, Ohio	8.2
26	57	Memphis city, Tennessee	0.2	32	60	Albuquerque city, New Mexico	2.9	26	61	Memphis city, Tennessee	7.7
44	57	Virginia Beach city, Virginia	0.2	50	60	New Orleans city, Louisiana	2.9	70	61	Lincoln city, Nebraska	7.7
49	57	Tampa city, Florida	0.2	30	63	Baltimore city, Maryland	2.7	23	63	Detroit city, Michigan	7.2
50	57	New Orleans city, Louisiana	0.2	7	64	San Antonio city, Texas	2.6	60	63	Lexington-Fayette, Kentucky	7.2
56	57	Urban Honolulu CDP, Hawaii	0.2	65	64	Cincinnati city, Ohio	2.6	56	65	Urban Honolulu CDP, Hawaii	6.9
62	57	Henderson city, Nevada	0.2	39	66	Colorado Springs city, Colorado	2.4	67	65	Greensboro city, North Carolina	6.9
66	57	Pittsburgh city, Pennsylvania	0.2	52	66	Cleveland city, Ohio	2.4	18	67	Seattle city, Washington	6.7
72	57	Irvine city, California	0.2	59	66	Corpus Christi city, Texas	2.4	14	68	Columbus city, Ohio	6.3
73	57	Newark city, New Jersey	0.2	35	69	Mesa city, Arizona	2.0	29	69	Louisville/Jefferson, Kentucky	5.8
74	57	Toledo city, Ohio	0.2	23	70	Detroit city, Michigan	1.8	50	70	New Orleans city, Louisiana	5.7
75	57	Durham city, North Carolina	0.2	73	70	Newark city, New Jersey	1.8	30	71	Baltimore city, Maryland	5.3
29	72	Louisville/Jefferson, Kentucky	0.1	26	72	Memphis city, Tennessee	1.7	37	72	Atlanta city, Georgia	4.3
37	72	Atlanta city, Georgia	0.1	22	73	El Paso city, Texas	1.5	64	73	St. Louis city, Missouri	4.0
65	72	Cincinnati city, Ohio	0.1	40	74	Miami city, Florida	1.4	65	74	Cincinnati city, Ohio	3.9
71	72	Orlando city, Florida	0.1	74	75	Toledo city, Ohio	1.3	66	75	Pittsburgh city, Pennsylvania	3.0

75 Largest Cities by 2018 Population
Selected rankings

Percent under 18 years old, 2017

Population rank	Under 18 years old rank	City	Percent under 18 years old [col 14]
53	1	Bakersfield city, California	29.8
34	2	Fresno city, California	28.2
61	3	Stockton city, California	27.1
13	4	Fort Worth city, Texas	27.0
48	4	Arlington city, Texas	27.0
22	6	El Paso city, Texas	26.9
27	7	Oklahoma City city, Oklahoma	26.4
57	7	Santa Ana city, California	26.4
5	9	Phoenix city, Arizona	26.2
31	10	Milwaukee city, Wisconsin	25.8
63	11	St. Paul city, Minnesota	25.7
35	12	Mesa city, Arizona	25.5
4	13	Houston city, Texas	25.4
26	14	Memphis city, Tennessee	25.3
54	15	Aurora city, Colorado	25.2
9	16	Dallas city, Texas	25.1
23	17	Detroit city, Michigan	24.9
7	18	San Antonio city, Texas	24.8
42	18	Omaha city, Nebraska	24.8
59	18	Corpus Christi city, Texas	24.8
17	21	Indianapolis city, Indiana	24.6
51	21	Wichita city, Kansas	24.6
73	21	Newark city, New Jersey	24.6
68	24	Anchorage municipality, Alaska	24.5
47	25	Tulsa city, Oklahoma	24.1
58	26	Riverside city, California	23.9
55	27	Anaheim city, California	23.8
28	28	Las Vegas city, Nevada	23.7
39	28	Colorado Springs city, Colorado	23.7
72	30	Irvine city, California	23.4
36	31	Sacramento city, California	23.3
16	32	Charlotte city, North Carolina	23.1
70	32	Lincoln city, Nebraska	23.1
74	32	Toledo city, Ohio	23.1
12	35	Jacksonville city, Florida	22.9
52	35	Cleveland city, Ohio	22.9
29	37	Louisville/Jefferson, Kentucky	22.8
32	37	Albuquerque city, New Mexico	22.8
38	39	Kansas City city, Missouri	22.7
14	40	Columbus city, Ohio	22.6
44	41	Virginia Beach city, Virginia	22.3
71	42	Orlando city, Florida	22.2
10	43	San Jose city, California	22.1
43	43	Long Beach city, California	22.1
69	45	Plano city, Texas	21.9
6	46	Philadelphia city, Pennsylvania	21.8
75	47	Durham city, North Carolina	21.5
33	48	Tucson city, Arizona	21.3
41	49	Raleigh city, North Carolina	21.1
60	49	Lexington-Fayette, Kentucky	21.1
65	49	Cincinnati city, Ohio	21.1
24	52	Nashville-Davidson, Tennessee	21.0
67	52	Greensboro city, North Carolina	21.0
49	54	Tampa city, Florida	20.9
3	55	Chicago city, Illinois	20.8
1	56	New York city, New York	20.7
2	57	Los Angeles city, California	20.6
30	57	Baltimore city, Maryland	20.6
11	59	Austin city, Texas	20.3
62	59	Henderson city, Nevada	20.3
50	61	New Orleans city, Louisiana	20.1
8	62	San Diego city, California	19.9
19	62	Denver city, Colorado	19.9
46	62	Minneapolis city, Minnesota	19.9
45	65	Oakland city, California	19.7
64	66	St. Louis city, Missouri	19.4
37	67	Atlanta city, Georgia	18.9
25	68	Portland city, Oregon	18.4
20	69	Washington city, District of Columbia	18.0
40	70	Miami city, Florida	17.7
56	71	Urban Honolulu CDP, Hawaii	16.9
18	72	Seattle city, Washington	15.8
21	73	Boston city, Massachusetts	15.5
66	74	Pittsburgh city, Pennsylvania	14.3
15	75	San Francisco city, California	13.4

Percent 65 years old and over, 2017

Population rank	65 years old and over rank	City	Percent 65 years old and over [col 20]
62	1	Henderson city, Nevada	20.7
56	2	Urban Honolulu CDP, Hawaii	19.7
40	3	Miami city, Florida	16.2
35	4	Mesa city, Arizona	15.8
32	5	Albuquerque city, New Mexico	15.5
15	6	San Francisco city, California	15.4
66	6	Pittsburgh city, Pennsylvania	15.4
51	8	Wichita city, Kansas	14.7
33	9	Tucson city, Arizona	14.6
29	10	Louisville/Jefferson, Kentucky	14.4
1	11	New York city, New York	14.3
28	12	Las Vegas city, Nevada	14.2
47	12	Tulsa city, Oklahoma	14.2
50	14	New Orleans city, Louisiana	14.1
74	14	Toledo city, Ohio	14.1
23	16	Detroit city, Michigan	14.0
39	17	Colorado Springs city, Colorado	13.9
59	17	Corpus Christi city, Texas	13.9
67	19	Greensboro city, North Carolina	13.8
44	20	Virginia Beach city, Virginia	13.7
52	20	Cleveland city, Ohio	13.7
12	22	Jacksonville city, Florida	13.5
30	22	Baltimore city, Maryland	13.5
6	24	Philadelphia city, Pennsylvania	13.4
45	25	Oakland city, California	13.2
69	26	Plano city, Texas	13.1
70	26	Lincoln city, Nebraska	13.1
42	28	Omaha city, Nebraska	13.0
65	28	Cincinnati city, Ohio	13.0
60	30	Lexington-Fayette, Kentucky	12.9
64	30	St. Louis city, Missouri	12.9
10	32	San Jose city, California	12.8
49	32	Tampa city, Florida	12.8
22	34	El Paso city, Texas	12.7
36	34	Sacramento city, California	12.7
38	34	Kansas City city, Missouri	12.7
18	37	Seattle city, Washington	12.6
8	38	San Diego city, California	12.5
25	38	Portland city, Oregon	12.5
26	38	Memphis city, Tennessee	12.5
2	41	Los Angeles city, California	12.4
3	42	Chicago city, Illinois	12.2
7	42	San Antonio city, Texas	12.2
17	42	Indianapolis city, Indiana	12.2
20	45	Washington city, District of Columbia	12.1
27	45	Oklahoma City city, Oklahoma	12.1
75	45	Durham city, North Carolina	12.1
21	48	Boston city, Massachusetts	11.7
61	48	Stockton city, California	11.7
19	50	Denver city, Colorado	11.6
24	50	Nashville-Davidson, Tennessee	11.6
43	50	Long Beach city, California	11.6
34	53	Fresno city, California	11.4
37	54	Atlanta city, Georgia	11.2
54	55	Aurora city, Colorado	11.0
53	56	Bakersfield city, California	10.8
5	57	Phoenix city, Arizona	10.7
31	57	Milwaukee city, Wisconsin	10.7
55	57	Anaheim city, California	10.7
4	60	Houston city, Texas	10.6
73	60	Newark city, New Jersey	10.6
9	62	Dallas city, Texas	10.5
68	62	Anchorage municipality, Alaska	10.5
71	62	Orlando city, Florida	10.5
16	65	Charlotte city, North Carolina	10.3
14	66	Columbus city, Ohio	10.2
48	66	Arlington city, Texas	10.2
63	66	St. Paul city, Minnesota	10.2
41	69	Raleigh city, North Carolina	10.1
46	70	Minneapolis city, Minnesota	10.0
13	71	Fort Worth city, Texas	9.9
58	72	Riverside city, California	9.7
11	73	Austin city, Texas	9.4
72	74	Irvine city, California	9.2
57	75	Santa Ana city, California	8.3

Percent high school graduate or less, 2017

Population rank	Percent high school graduate or less rank	City	Percent high school graduate or less [col 40]
57	1	Santa Ana city, California	64.0
73	2	Newark city, New Jersey	60.5
61	3	Stockton city, California	52.2
52	4	Cleveland city, Ohio	51.6
23	5	Detroit city, Michigan	51.5
6	6	Philadelphia city, Pennsylvania	50.4
74	7	Toledo city, Ohio	49.4
40	8	Miami city, Florida	49.1
31	9	Milwaukee city, Wisconsin	48.0
53	10	Bakersfield city, California	46.9
59	11	Corpus Christi city, Texas	46.5
55	12	Anaheim city, California	46.4
26	13	Memphis city, Tennessee	46.1
9	14	Dallas city, Texas	45.2
30	15	Baltimore city, Maryland	45.0
58	16	Riverside city, California	44.8
34	17	Fresno city, California	44.5
4	18	Houston city, Texas	43.8
28	19	Las Vegas city, Nevada	43.3
22	20	El Paso city, Texas	43.2
17	21	Indianapolis city, Indiana	43.0
7	22	San Antonio city, Texas	42.9
1	23	New York city, New York	42.7
13	24	Fort Worth city, Texas	42.5
2	25	Los Angeles city, California	41.6
5	26	Phoenix city, Arizona	41.2
54	27	Aurora city, Colorado	40.1
29	28	Louisville/Jefferson, Kentucky	39.6
12	29	Jacksonville city, Florida	39.1
43	30	Long Beach city, California	38.7
49	30	Tampa city, Florida	38.7
27	32	Oklahoma City city, Oklahoma	38.6
51	33	Wichita city, Kansas	38.3
3	34	Chicago city, Illinois	37.9
48	34	Arlington city, Texas	37.9
65	34	Cincinnati city, Ohio	37.9
50	37	New Orleans city, Louisiana	37.7
47	38	Tulsa city, Oklahoma	37.6
33	39	Tucson city, Arizona	37.5
14	40	Columbus city, Ohio	36.3
38	41	Kansas City city, Missouri	36.2
64	42	St. Louis city, Missouri	35.5
35	43	Mesa city, Arizona	35.4
36	44	Sacramento city, California	35.2
45	45	Oakland city, California	34.8
63	46	St. Paul city, Minnesota	34.6
56	47	Urban Honolulu CDP, Hawaii	34.1
71	48	Orlando city, Florida	33.5
21	49	Boston city, Massachusetts	33.4
42	50	Omaha city, Nebraska	33.1
10	51	San Jose city, California	32.5
66	52	Pittsburgh city, Pennsylvania	32.3
67	52	Greensboro city, North Carolina	32.3
24	54	Nashville-Davidson, Tennessee	32.2
62	55	Henderson city, Nevada	31.2
32	56	Albuquerque city, New Mexico	31.0
68	57	Anchorage municipality, Alaska	30.4
37	58	Atlanta city, Georgia	29.7
19	59	Denver city, Colorado	29.0
70	60	Lincoln city, Nebraska	28.5
75	60	Durham city, North Carolina	28.5
44	62	Virginia Beach city, Virginia	28.1
16	63	Charlotte city, North Carolina	27.8
11	64	Austin city, Texas	27.1
60	64	Lexington-Fayette, Kentucky	27.1
20	66	Washington city, District of Columbia	27.0
8	67	San Diego city, California	26.9
39	68	Colorado Springs city, Colorado	26.2
46	69	Minneapolis city, Minnesota	25.1
41	70	Raleigh city, North Carolina	23.8
25	71	Portland city, Oregon	23.6
15	72	San Francisco city, California	23.3
69	73	Plano city, Texas	18.6
18	74	Seattle city, Washington	15.2
72	75	Irvine city, California	13.4

75 Largest Cities by 2018 Population
Selected rankings

Percent college graduates (bachelor's degree or more), 2017

Population rank	Percent college graduate rank	City	Percent college graduates [col 41]
72	1	Irvine city, California	66.1
18	2	Seattle city, Washington	62.6
15	3	San Francisco city, California	57.8
69	4	Plano city, Texas	57.5
20	5	Washington city, District of Columbia	57.3
11	6	Austin city, Texas	51.0
41	6	Raleigh city, North Carolina	51.0
46	8	Minneapolis city, Minnesota	50.8
75	9	Durham city, North Carolina	50.3
25	10	Portland city, Oregon	49.9
19	11	Denver city, Colorado	49.3
37	12	Atlanta city, Georgia	49.2
21	13	Boston city, Massachusetts	48.2
8	14	San Diego city, California	45.6
16	15	Charlotte city, North Carolina	45.0
66	16	Pittsburgh city, Pennsylvania	44.1
60	17	Lexington-Fayette, Kentucky	43.6
10	18	San Jose city, California	43.4
45	19	Oakland city, California	42.4
24	20	Nashville-Davidson, Tennessee	41.2
63	21	St. Paul city, Minnesota	40.1
39	22	Colorado Springs city, Colorado	39.0
3	23	Chicago city, Illinois	38.8
70	24	Lincoln city, Nebraska	38.5
67	25	Greensboro city, North Carolina	38.1
1	26	New York city, New York	37.3
49	26	Tampa city, Florida	37.3
64	28	St. Louis city, Missouri	37.1
56	29	Urban Honolulu CDP, Hawaii	36.5
32	30	Albuquerque city, New Mexico	36.3
42	30	Omaha city, Nebraska	36.3
65	32	Cincinnati city, Ohio	35.8
44	33	Virginia Beach city, Virginia	35.3
50	33	New Orleans city, Louisiana	35.3
71	35	Orlando city, Florida	35.2
14	36	Columbus city, Ohio	35.1
68	36	Anchorage municipality, Alaska	35.1
2	38	Los Angeles city, California	34.4
38	39	Kansas City city, Missouri	34.3
62	40	Henderson city, Nevada	33.9
36	41	Sacramento city, California	32.8
4	42	Houston city, Texas	32.7
9	43	Dallas city, Texas	32.2
17	44	Indianapolis city, Indiana	32.1
43	45	Long Beach city, California	31.1
27	46	Oklahoma City city, Oklahoma	30.9
30	47	Baltimore city, Maryland	30.6
47	47	Tulsa city, Oklahoma	30.6
51	49	Wichita city, Kansas	30.5
54	50	Aurora city, Colorado	30.3
40	51	Miami city, Florida	30.1
29	52	Louisville/Jefferson, Kentucky	29.9
13	53	Fort Worth city, Texas	29.7
5	54	Phoenix city, Arizona	28.4
6	55	Philadelphia city, Pennsylvania	28.3
35	56	Mesa city, Arizona	28.2
12	57	Jacksonville city, Florida	28.1
48	58	Arlington city, Texas	27.9
33	59	Tucson city, Arizona	27.7
7	60	San Antonio city, Texas	26.5
26	61	Memphis city, Tennessee	25.7
55	61	Anaheim city, California	25.7
28	63	Las Vegas city, Nevada	25.1
22	64	El Paso city, Texas	24.7
58	65	Riverside city, California	23.7
31	66	Milwaukee city, Wisconsin	23.6
53	67	Bakersfield city, California	21.4
34	68	Fresno city, California	21.3
59	68	Corpus Christi city, Texas	21.3
61	70	Stockton city, California	18.5
74	70	Toledo city, Ohio	18.5
52	72	Cleveland city, Ohio	17
73	73	Newark city, New Jersey	15.5
23	74	Detroit city, Michigan	14.6
57	75	Santa Ana city, California	14.3

Percent female-headed family households, 2017

Population rank	Female households rank	City	Percent female households [col 31]
23	1	Detroit city, Michigan	26.3
73	2	Newark city, New Jersey	26.1
26	3	Memphis city, Tennessee	22.6
30	4	Baltimore city, Maryland	21.7
52	4	Cleveland city, Ohio	21.7
31	6	Milwaukee city, Wisconsin	21.0
22	7	El Paso city, Texas	20.1
74	8	Toledo city, Ohio	19.1
34	9	Fresno city, California	18.6
6	10	Philadelphia city, Pennsylvania	17.8
58	10	Riverside city, California	17.8
1	12	New York city, New York	17.6
50	13	New Orleans city, Louisiana	17.4
53	14	Bakersfield city, California	17.0
59	15	Corpus Christi city, Texas	16.7
71	15	Orlando city, Florida	16.7
57	17	Santa Ana city, California	16.4
61	17	Stockton city, California	16.4
64	19	St. Louis city, Missouri	16.3
4	20	Houston city, Texas	16.0
7	20	San Antonio city, Texas	16.0
12	20	Jacksonville city, Florida	16.0
21	23	Boston city, Massachusetts	15.8
40	23	Miami city, Florida	15.8
43	23	Long Beach city, California	15.8
37	26	Atlanta city, Georgia	15.7
65	26	Cincinnati city, Ohio	15.7
55	28	Anaheim city, California	15.6
9	29	Dallas city, Texas	15.4
14	29	Columbus city, Ohio	15.4
48	29	Arlington city, Texas	15.4
75	32	Durham city, North Carolina	15.3
3	33	Chicago city, Illinois	15.2
29	33	Louisville/Jefferson, Kentucky	15.2
28	35	Las Vegas city, Nevada	15.1
47	35	Tulsa city, Oklahoma	15.1
67	37	Greensboro city, North Carolina	14.9
33	38	Tucson city, Arizona	14.6
5	39	Phoenix city, Arizona	14.5
36	39	Sacramento city, California	14.5
45	39	Oakland city, California	14.5
13	42	Fort Worth city, Texas	14.4
17	43	Indianapolis city, Indiana	13.9
54	43	Aurora city, Colorado	13.9
2	45	Los Angeles city, California	13.8
20	45	Washington city, District of Columbia	13.8
49	45	Tampa city, Florida	13.8
41	48	Raleigh city, North Carolina	13.7
24	49	Nashville-Davidson, Tennessee	13.4
38	49	Kansas City city, Missouri	13.4
16	51	Charlotte city, North Carolina	13.3
35	52	Mesa city, Arizona	13.2
56	53	Urban Honolulu CDP, Hawaii	13.1
63	54	St. Paul city, Minnesota	13.0
51	55	Wichita city, Kansas	12.9
32	56	Albuquerque city, New Mexico	12.8
68	56	Anchorage municipality, Alaska	12.8
44	58	Virginia Beach city, Virginia	12.7
27	59	Oklahoma City city, Oklahoma	12.3
42	59	Omaha city, Nebraska	12.3
10	61	San Jose city, California	12.0
66	62	Pittsburgh city, Pennsylvania	11.3
60	63	Lexington-Fayette, Kentucky	11.2
8	64	San Diego city, California	11.0
62	65	Henderson city, Nevada	10.5
39	66	Colorado Springs city, Colorado	10.4
69	67	Plano city, Texas	9.7
70	68	Lincoln city, Nebraska	9.5
25	69	Portland city, Oregon	9.4
11	70	Austin city, Texas	9.3
46	71	Minneapolis city, Minnesota	9.0
19	72	Denver city, Colorado	8.9
15	73	San Francisco city, California	8.4
72	74	Irvine city, California	8.0
18	75	Seattle city, Washington	6.6

Percent of households composed of one person, 2017

Population rank	One-person household rank	City	Percent one-person households [col 33]
65	1	Cincinnati city, Ohio	46.6
50	2	New Orleans city, Louisiana	45.7
20	3	Washington city, District of Columbia	45.2
52	4	Cleveland city, Ohio	44.7
66	5	Pittsburgh city, Pennsylvania	43.4
6	6	Philadelphia city, Pennsylvania	43.2
64	6	St. Louis city, Missouri	43.2
37	8	Atlanta city, Georgia	43.1
46	9	Minneapolis city, Minnesota	41.0
23	10	Detroit city, Michigan	40.4
30	11	Baltimore city, Maryland	40.0
18	12	Seattle city, Washington	37.8
26	13	Memphis city, Tennessee	37.7
49	13	Tampa city, Florida	37.7
74	15	Toledo city, Ohio	37.6
17	16	Indianapolis city, Indiana	37.4
3	17	Chicago city, Illinois	37.3
19	18	Denver city, Colorado	37.2
21	19	Boston city, Massachusetts	37.0
31	20	Milwaukee city, Wisconsin	36.8
38	21	Kansas City city, Missouri	36.5
15	22	San Francisco city, California	36.4
32	23	Albuquerque city, New Mexico	35.6
40	24	Miami city, Florida	35.4
56	25	Urban Honolulu CDP, Hawaii	35.2
9	26	Dallas city, Texas	34.8
47	26	Tulsa city, Oklahoma	34.8
11	28	Austin city, Texas	34.5
14	28	Columbus city, Ohio	34.5
75	30	Durham city, North Carolina	34.3
33	31	Tucson city, Arizona	34.2
73	31	Newark city, New Jersey	34.2
67	33	Greensboro city, North Carolina	34.1
63	34	St. Paul city, Minnesota	33.7
16	35	Charlotte city, North Carolina	33.6
25	36	Portland city, Oregon	33.5
24	37	Nashville-Davidson, Tennessee	32.6
42	37	Omaha city, Nebraska	32.6
41	39	Raleigh city, North Carolina	32.4
45	39	Oakland city, California	32.4
29	41	Louisville/Jefferson, Kentucky	32.3
1	42	New York city, New York	32.2
4	43	Houston city, Texas	32.0
36	44	Sacramento city, California	31.3
2	45	Los Angeles city, California	31.1
51	46	Wichita city, Kansas	31.0
60	47	Lexington-Fayette, Kentucky	30.9
27	48	Oklahoma City city, Oklahoma	30.8
70	48	Lincoln city, Nebraska	30.8
71	48	Orlando city, Florida	30.8
43	51	Long Beach city, California	30.4
12	52	Jacksonville city, Florida	29.9
28	53	Las Vegas city, Nevada	29.3
7	54	San Antonio city, Texas	29.1
5	55	Phoenix city, Arizona	28.3
39	56	Colorado Springs city, Colorado	28.1
35	57	Mesa city, Arizona	27.7
8	58	San Diego city, California	26.9
59	59	Corpus Christi city, Texas	26.6
13	60	Fort Worth city, Texas	26.3
62	60	Henderson city, Nevada	26.3
54	62	Aurora city, Colorado	25.4
68	63	Anchorage municipality, Alaska	25.3
34	64	Fresno city, California	24.2
48	64	Arlington city, Texas	24.2
22	66	El Paso city, Texas	24.1
44	67	Virginia Beach city, Virginia	23.9
61	68	Stockton city, California	23.6
69	69	Plano city, Texas	23.5
72	70	Irvine city, California	20.6
53	71	Bakersfield city, California	20.0
10	72	San Jose city, California	18.9
58	73	Riverside city, California	18.3
55	74	Anaheim city, California	17.7
57	75	Santa Ana city, California	12.7

75 Largest Cities by 2018 Population
Selected rankings

Median household income, 2017				Median value of owner-occupied housing units, 2017				Percent with commutes of 30 minutes or more, 2017			
Population rank	Median income rank	City	Median income (dollars) [col 42]	Population rank	Median value rank	City	Median value (dollars) [col 53]	Population rank	Commutes of 30 minutes or more rank	City	Commutes of 30 minutes or more [col 56]
15	1	San Francisco city, California	110,816	15	1	San Francisco city, California	$1,104,100	1	1	New York city, New York	71.3
10	2	San Jose city, California	104,675	10	2	San Jose city, California	$854,700	3	2	Chicago city, Illinois	62.5
72	3	Irvine city, California	104,185	72	3	Irvine city, California	$822,100	15	3	San Francisco city, California	57.4
69	4	Plano city, Texas	94,306	56	4	Urban Honolulu CDP, Hawaii	$696,800	6	4	Philadelphia city, Pennsylvania	55.3
18	5	Seattle city, Washington	86,822	45	5	Oakland city, California	$686,700	21	5	Boston city, Massachusetts	55.0
20	6	Washington city, District of Columbia	82,372	18	6	Seattle city, Washington	$673,100	2	6	Los Angeles city, California	53.7
68	7	Anchorage municipality, Alaska	79,166	2	7	Los Angeles city, California	$647,000	45	7	Oakland city, California	53.6
8	8	San Diego city, California	76,662	1	8	New York city, New York	$609,500	73	7	Newark city, New Jersey	53.6
44	9	Virginia Beach city, Virginia	72,586	20	9	Washington city, District of Columbia	$607,200	20	9	Washington city, District of Columbia	53.4
45	10	Oakland city, California	70,577	8	10	San Diego city, California	$600,300	10	10	San Jose city, California	51.2
55	11	Anaheim city, California	70,395	55	11	Anaheim city, California	$577,500	40	11	Miami city, Florida	50.6
62	12	Henderson city, Nevada	69,667	43	12	Long Beach city, California	$557,700	43	12	Long Beach city, California	50.2
56	13	Urban Honolulu CDP, Hawaii	69,193	21	13	Boston city, Massachusetts	$540,600	30	13	Baltimore city, Maryland	48.7
11	14	Austin city, Texas	67,755	57	14	Santa Ana city, California	$494,700	54	14	Aurora city, Colorado	47.3
58	15	Riverside city, California	66,928	25	15	Portland city, Oregon	$427,500	18	15	Seattle city, Washington	46.7
21	16	Boston city, Massachusetts	66,758	19	16	Denver city, Colorado	$395,100	55	16	Anaheim city, California	45.8
25	17	Portland city, Oregon	66,187	58	17	Riverside city, California	$368,600	58	17	Riverside city, California	44.6
57	18	Santa Ana city, California	65,655	36	18	Sacramento city, California	$335,900	9	18	Dallas city, Texas	44.1
19	19	Denver city, Colorado	65,224	11	19	Austin city, Texas	$332,700	48	18	Arlington city, Texas	44.1
41	20	Raleigh city, North Carolina	64,660	69	20	Plano city, Texas	$329,500	69	18	Plano city, Texas	44.1
54	21	Aurora city, Colorado	63,055	40	21	Miami city, Florida	$322,100	4	21	Houston city, Texas	44.0
16	22	Charlotte city, North Carolina	61,350	68	22	Anchorage municipality, Alaska	$320,000	13	22	Fort Worth city, Texas	41.1
1	23	New York city, New York	60,879	62	23	Henderson city, Nevada	$311,200	25	23	Portland city, Oregon	40.2
46	24	Minneapolis city, Minnesota	60,789	54	24	Aurora city, Colorado	$299,600	37	24	Atlanta city, Georgia	40.1
43	25	Long Beach city, California	60,557	37	25	Atlanta city, Georgia	$299,400	5	25	Phoenix city, Arizona	39.6
13	26	Fort Worth city, Texas	60,205	44	26	Virginia Beach city, Virginia	$282,300	57	26	Santa Ana city, California	39.3
2	27	Los Angeles city, California	60,197	61	27	Stockton city, California	$282,000	19	27	Denver city, Colorado	38.9
39	28	Colorado Springs city, Colorado	59,514	39	28	Colorado Springs city, Colorado	$265,400	71	27	Orlando city, Florida	38.9
24	29	Nashville-Davidson, Tennessee	57,737	3	29	Chicago city, Illinois	$255,900	28	29	Las Vegas city, Nevada	38.1
37	30	Atlanta city, Georgia	57,597	46	30	Minneapolis city, Minnesota	$250,400	12	30	Jacksonville city, Florida	37.6
53	31	Bakersfield city, California	57,105	24	31	Nashville-Davidson, Tennessee	$246,800	49	31	Tampa city, Florida	35.8
48	32	Arlington city, Texas	57,083	28	32	Las Vegas city, Nevada	$245,500	35	32	Mesa city, Arizona	35.7
36	33	Sacramento city, California	56,943	41	33	Raleigh city, North Carolina	$239,700	36	33	Sacramento city, California	35.3
28	34	Las Vegas city, Nevada	56,699	53	33	Bakersfield city, California	$239,700	16	34	Charlotte city, North Carolina	35.2
5	35	Phoenix city, Arizona	56,696	73	35	Newark city, New Jersey	$235,000	24	35	Nashville-Davidson, Tennessee	35.0
42	36	Omaha city, Nebraska	56,406	34	36	Fresno city, California	$234,500	72	36	Irvine city, California	34.9
75	37	Durham city, North Carolina	56,375	49	37	Tampa city, Florida	$233,800	11	37	Austin city, Texas	34.3
70	38	Lincoln city, Nebraska	56,160	71	38	Orlando city, Florida	$232,600	66	38	Pittsburgh city, Pennsylvania	33.7
60	39	Lexington-Fayette, Kentucky	56,137	5	39	Phoenix city, Arizona	$231,000	41	39	Raleigh city, North Carolina	33.2
3	40	Chicago city, Illinois	55,295	75	40	Durham city, North Carolina	$230,100	8	40	San Diego city, California	33.1
35	41	Mesa city, Arizona	55,014	50	41	New Orleans city, Louisiana	$227,800	61	40	Stockton city, California	33.1
63	42	St. Paul city, Minnesota	54,290	35	42	Mesa city, Arizona	$224,700	7	42	San Antonio city, Texas	33.0
59	43	Corpus Christi city, Texas	53,605	16	43	Charlotte city, North Carolina	$215,500	23	43	Detroit city, Michigan	32.8
27	44	Oklahoma City city, Oklahoma	52,062	63	44	St. Paul city, Minnesota	$211,100	64	44	St. Louis city, Missouri	31.7
29	45	Louisville/Jefferson, Kentucky	51,960	32	45	Albuquerque city, New Mexico	$196,900	63	45	St. Paul city, Minnesota	31.6
14	46	Columbus city, Ohio	51,708	60	46	Lexington-Fayette, Kentucky	$193,100	56	46	Urban Honolulu CDP, Hawaii	31.5
12	47	Jacksonville city, Florida	51,497	9	47	Dallas city, Texas	$190,600	62	47	Henderson city, Nevada	30.7
61	48	Stockton city, California	51,336	12	48	Jacksonville city, Florida	$177,000	46	48	Minneapolis city, Minnesota	30.2
38	49	Kansas City city, Missouri	51,330	4	49	Houston city, Texas	$173,600	17	49	Indianapolis city, Indiana	30.0
4	50	Houston city, Texas	50,896	70	50	Lincoln city, Nebraska	$171,300	44	50	Virginia Beach city, Virginia	29.6
9	51	Dallas city, Texas	50,627	13	51	Fort Worth city, Texas	$169,400	50	51	New Orleans city, Louisiana	29.4
51	52	Wichita city, Kansas	50,504	48	52	Arlington city, Texas	$167,800	33	52	Tucson city, Arizona	28.3
49	53	Tampa city, Florida	50,489	6	53	Philadelphia city, Pennsylvania	$166,200	53	53	Bakersfield city, California	28.2
32	54	Albuquerque city, New Mexico	50,456	29	54	Louisville/Jefferson, Kentucky	$160,500	65	53	Cincinnati city, Ohio	28.2
7	55	San Antonio city, Texas	50,044	27	55	Oklahoma City city, Oklahoma	$158,200	22	55	El Paso city, Texas	28.1
34	56	Fresno city, California	48,600	42	56	Omaha city, Nebraska	$157,100	29	56	Louisville/Jefferson, Kentucky	27.9
71	57	Orlando city, Florida	47,594	67	57	Greensboro city, North Carolina	$157,000	38	57	Kansas City city, Missouri	27.8
17	58	Indianapolis city, Indiana	47,225	30	58	Baltimore city, Maryland	$154,400	31	58	Milwaukee city, Wisconsin	27.7
30	59	Baltimore city, Maryland	47,131	38	59	Kansas City city, Missouri	$152,900	52	58	Cleveland city, Ohio	27.7
67	60	Greensboro city, North Carolina	47,043	14	60	Columbus city, Ohio	$151,400	75	60	Durham city, North Carolina	26.9
47	61	Tulsa city, Oklahoma	45,894	33	61	Tucson city, Arizona	$150,400	32	61	Albuquerque city, New Mexico	26.5
66	62	Pittsburgh city, Pennsylvania	45,851	7	62	San Antonio city, Texas	$148,200	26	62	Memphis city, Tennessee	25.9
22	63	El Paso city, Texas	44,754	65	63	Cincinnati city, Ohio	$143,100	14	63	Columbus city, Ohio	25.3
33	64	Tucson city, Arizona	41,613	64	64	St. Louis city, Missouri	$141,400	39	64	Colorado Springs city, Colorado	25.0
64	65	St. Louis city, Missouri	41,441	59	65	Corpus Christi city, Texas	$141,300	34	65	Fresno city, California	24.1
40	66	Miami city, Florida	40,327	47	66	Tulsa city, Oklahoma	$139,700	27	66	Oklahoma City city, Oklahoma	23.6
6	67	Philadelphia city, Pennsylvania	39,759	17	67	Indianapolis city, Indiana	$137,600	67	67	Greensboro city, North Carolina	23.2
26	68	Memphis city, Tennessee	39,333	51	68	Wichita city, Kansas	$135,100	60	68	Lexington-Fayette, Kentucky	21.0
31	69	Milwaukee city, Wisconsin	39,098	22	69	El Paso city, Texas	$127,700	74	68	Toledo city, Ohio	21.0
65	70	Cincinnati city, Ohio	38,938	66	70	Pittsburgh city, Pennsylvania	$123,600	68	70	Anchorage municipality, Alaska	17.2
74	71	Toledo city, Ohio	37,339	31	71	Milwaukee city, Wisconsin	$122,300	70	71	Lincoln city, Nebraska	16.8
50	72	New Orleans city, Louisiana	36,999	26	72	Memphis city, Tennessee	$98,700	59	72	Corpus Christi city, Texas	16.4
73	73	Newark city, New Jersey	35,167	74	73	Toledo city, Ohio	$78,400	42	73	Omaha city, Nebraska	15.5
23	74	Detroit city, Michigan	30,344	52	74	Cleveland city, Ohio	$70,200	47	74	Tulsa city, Oklahoma	14.9
52	75	Cleveland city, Ohio	28,974	23	75	Detroit city, Michigan	$50,200	51	75	Wichita city, Kansas	13.8

75 Largest Cities by 2018 Population
Selected rankings

Median non-family household Income, 2016

Population rank	Poverty rate rank	City	Poverty rate [col 46]
15	1	San Francisco city, California	89,046
72	2	Irvine city, California	71,866
20	3	Washington city, District of Columbia	68,067
10	4	San Jose city, California	65,579
18	5	Seattle city, Washington	63,990
8	6	San Diego city, California	58,268
45	7	Oakland city, California	58,222
69	8	Plano city, Texas	57,497
21	9	Boston city, Massachusetts	55,011
68	10	Anchorage municipality, Alaska	53,445
11	11	Austin city, Texas	52,363
19	12	Denver city, Colorado	51,754
55	13	Anaheim city, California	50,832
43	14	Long Beach city, California	50,556
57	15	Santa Ana city, California	49,661
44	16	Virginia Beach city, Virginia	48,537
41	17	Raleigh city, North Carolina	47,727
46	18	Minneapolis city, Minnesota	46,974
37	19	Atlanta city, Georgia	46,710
25	20	Portland city, Oregon	45,988
62	21	Henderson city, Nevada	45,860
1	22	New York city, New York	45,326
16	23	Charlotte city, North Carolina	45,114
2	24	Los Angeles city, California	44,981
24	25	Nashville-Davidson, Tennessee	44,802
36	26	Sacramento city, California	44,623
3	27	Chicago city, Illinois	43,203
54	28	Aurora city, Colorado	42,286
71	29	Orlando city, Florida	41,881
56	30	Urban Honolulu CDP, Hawaii	41,475
9	31	Dallas city, Texas	41,042
5	32	Phoenix city, Arizona	40,490
75	33	Durham city, North Carolina	40,386
13	34	Fort Worth city, Texas	40,324
14	35	Columbus city, Ohio	40,191
4	36	Houston city, Texas	40,156
63	37	St. Paul city, Minnesota	39,933
39	38	Colorado Springs city, Colorado	39,767
48	39	Arlington city, Texas	38,251
58	40	Riverside city, California	38,186
42	41	Omaha city, Nebraska	37,778
53	42	Bakersfield city, California	37,225
35	43	Mesa city, Arizona	37,200
38	44	Kansas City city, Missouri	36,654
28	45	Las Vegas city, Nevada	36,294
70	46	Lincoln city, Nebraska	36,029
49	47	Tampa city, Florida	35,576
30	48	Baltimore city, Maryland	35,393
60	49	Lexington-Fayette, Kentucky	35,303
27	50	Oklahoma City city, Oklahoma	34,789
67	51	Greensboro city, North Carolina	34,484
17	52	Indianapolis city, Indiana	33,403
12	53	Jacksonville city, Florida	33,227
7	54	San Antonio city, Texas	32,570
34	55	Fresno city, California	32,499
29	56	Louisville/Jefferson, Kentucky	32,446
66	57	Pittsburgh city, Pennsylvania	32,064
32	58	Albuquerque city, New Mexico	31,646
47	59	Tulsa city, Oklahoma	31,467
59	60	Corpus Christi city, Texas	31,432
40	61	Miami city, Florida	30,928
51	62	Wichita city, Kansas	30,779
64	63	St. Louis city, Missouri	30,273
61	64	Stockton city, California	30,195
65	65	Cincinnati city, Ohio	30,112
33	66	Tucson city, Arizona	29,361
31	67	Milwaukee city, Wisconsin	29,343
26	68	Memphis city, Tennessee	27,670
74	69	Toledo city, Ohio	26,412
50	70	New Orleans city, Louisiana	25,921
22	71	El Paso city, Texas	25,736
6	72	Philadelphia city, Pennsylvania	23,144
73	73	Newark city, New Jersey	22,513
52	74	Cleveland city, Ohio	21,257
23	75	Detroit city, Michigan	20,445

Unemployment rate, 2018

Population rank	Unemployment rate rank	City	Unemployment rate [col 64]
23	1	Detroit city, Michigan	9.0
73	2	Newark city, New Jersey	7.0
61	3	Stockton city, California	6.9
52	4	Cleveland city, Ohio	6.5
34	5	Fresno city, California	5.8
74	5	Toledo city, Ohio	5.8
30	7	Baltimore city, Maryland	5.7
20	8	Washington city, District of Columbia	5.6
6	9	Philadelphia city, Pennsylvania	5.5
53	9	Bakersfield city, California	5.5
68	9	Anchorage municipality, Alaska	5.5
28	12	Las Vegas city, Nevada	5.0
50	12	New Orleans city, Louisiana	5.0
43	14	Long Beach city, California	4.8
2	15	Los Angeles city, California	4.7
33	15	Tucson city, Arizona	4.7
26	17	Memphis city, Tennessee	4.6
59	17	Corpus Christi city, Texas	4.6
32	19	Albuquerque city, New Mexico	4.5
65	19	Cincinnati city, Ohio	4.5
62	21	Henderson city, Nevada	4.4
5	22	Phoenix city, Arizona	4.3
37	22	Atlanta city, Georgia	4.3
67	22	Greensboro city, North Carolina	4.3
3	25	Chicago city, Illinois	4.2
4	25	Houston city, Texas	4.2
66	25	Pittsburgh city, Pennsylvania	4.2
1	28	New York city, New York	4.1
22	28	El Paso city, Texas	4.1
29	28	Louisville/Jefferson, Kentucky	4.1
35	28	Mesa city, Arizona	4.1
31	32	Milwaukee city, Wisconsin	4.0
14	33	Columbus city, Ohio	3.9
36	33	Sacramento city, California	3.9
39	33	Colorado Springs city, Colorado	3.9
51	33	Wichita city, Kansas	3.9
16	37	Charlotte city, North Carolina	3.8
40	37	Miami city, Florida	3.8
58	37	Riverside city, California	3.8
64	37	St. Louis city, Missouri	3.8
9	41	Dallas city, Texas	3.7
12	42	Jacksonville city, Florida	3.6
13	42	Fort Worth city, Texas	3.6
25	42	Portland city, Oregon	3.6
41	42	Raleigh city, North Carolina	3.6
47	42	Tulsa city, Oklahoma	3.6
49	42	Tampa city, Florida	3.6
54	42	Aurora city, Colorado	3.6
17	49	Indianapolis city, Indiana	3.5
38	49	Kansas City city, Missouri	3.5
48	49	Arlington city, Texas	3.5
75	49	Durham city, North Carolina	3.5
45	53	Oakland city, California	3.4
7	54	San Antonio city, Texas	3.3
60	54	Lexington-Fayette, Kentucky	3.3
69	54	Plano city, Texas	3.3
8	57	San Diego city, California	3.2
18	57	Seattle city, Washington	3.2
19	57	Denver city, Colorado	3.2
27	57	Oklahoma City city, Oklahoma	3.2
42	61	Omaha city, Nebraska	3.1
55	61	Anaheim city, California	3.1
71	61	Orlando city, Florida	3.1
21	64	Boston city, Massachusetts	3.0
57	64	Santa Ana city, California	3.0
44	66	Virginia Beach city, Virginia	2.9
63	67	St. Paul city, Minnesota	2.8
72	67	Irvine city, California	2.8
10	69	San Jose city, California	2.7
11	69	Austin city, Texas	2.7
24	71	Nashville-Davidson, Tennessee	2.6
46	72	Minneapolis city, Minnesota	2.5
70	72	Lincoln city, Nebraska	2.5
15	74	San Francisco city, California	2.4
56	75	Urban Honolulu CDP, Hawaii	NA

Percent change in civilian labor force, 2017-2018

Population rank	Percent change rank	City	Percent change [col 62]
35	1	Mesa city, Arizona	4.0
5	2	Phoenix city, Arizona	3.9
19	3	Denver city, Colorado	3.4
21	3	Boston city, Massachusetts	3.4
39	3	Colorado Springs city, Colorado	3.4
54	3	Aurora city, Colorado	3.4
11	7	Austin city, Texas	3.2
24	7	Nashville-Davidson, Tennessee	3.2
62	9	Henderson city, Nevada	2.8
28	10	Las Vegas city, Nevada	2.6
71	10	Orlando city, Florida	2.6
13	12	Fort Worth city, Texas	2.4
48	12	Arlington city, Texas	2.4
9	14	Dallas city, Texas	2.3
69	14	Plano city, Texas	2.3
15	16	San Francisco city, California	2.0
18	16	Seattle city, Washington	2.0
33	16	Tucson city, Arizona	2.0
16	19	Charlotte city, North Carolina	1.8
36	19	Sacramento city, California	1.8
41	19	Raleigh city, North Carolina	1.8
58	19	Riverside city, California	1.8
70	19	Lincoln city, Nebraska	1.8
4	24	Houston city, Texas	1.7
7	24	San Antonio city, Texas	1.7
12	24	Jacksonville city, Florida	1.7
17	27	Indianapolis city, Indiana	1.4
22	27	El Paso city, Texas	1.4
27	27	Oklahoma City city, Oklahoma	1.4
75	27	Durham city, North Carolina	1.4
26	31	Memphis city, Tennessee	1.3
42	32	Omaha city, Nebraska	1.2
49	32	Tampa city, Florida	1.2
8	34	San Diego city, California	1.1
37	34	Atlanta city, Georgia	1.1
29	36	Louisville/Jefferson, Kentucky	1.0
72	36	Irvine city, California	1.0
45	38	Oakland city, California	0.9
57	38	Santa Ana city, California	0.9
53	38	Bakersfield city, California	0.9
55	38	Anaheim city, California	0.9
2	42	Los Angeles city, California	0.8
10	42	San Jose city, California	0.8
20	42	Washington city, District of Columbia	0.8
34	42	Fresno city, California	0.8
43	42	Long Beach city, California	0.8
6	47	Philadelphia city, Pennsylvania	0.7
25	47	Portland city, Oregon	0.7
40	47	Miami city, Florida	0.7
61	47	Stockton city, California	0.7
63	47	St. Paul city, Minnesota	0.7
14	52	Columbus city, Ohio	0.6
46	52	Minneapolis city, Minnesota	0.6
51	52	Wichita city, Kansas	0.6
32	55	Albuquerque city, New Mexico	0.5
47	55	Tulsa city, Oklahoma	0.5
65	55	Cincinnati city, Ohio	0.5
44	58	Virginia Beach city, Virginia	0.4
23	59	Detroit city, Michigan	0.2
50	59	New Orleans city, Louisiana	0.2
59	61	Corpus Christi city, Texas	0.1
38	62	Kansas City city, Missouri	0.0
56	62	Urban Honolulu CDP, Hawaii	0.0
30	64	Baltimore city, Maryland	-0.1
67	64	Greensboro city, North Carolina	-0.1
66	66	Pittsburgh city, Pennsylvania	-0.2
1	67	New York city, New York	-0.3
60	67	Lexington-Fayette, Kentucky	-0.3
52	69	Cleveland city, Ohio	-0.4
64	69	St. Louis city, Missouri	-0.4
74	71	Toledo city, Ohio	-0.7
31	72	Milwaukee city, Wisconsin	-0.8
73	73	Newark city, New Jersey	-0.9
3	74	Chicago city, Illinois	-1.1
68	75	Anchorage municipality, Alaska	-1.2

75 Largest Cities by 2018 Population
Selected rankings

Per capita local government taxes, 2012				Per capita city government debt outstanding, 2012				Violent crime rate, 2016 (violent crimes known to police)			
Population rank	Local taxes rank	City	Local per capita taxes (dollars) [col 121]	Population rank	Debt rank	City	Debt per capita (dollars) [col 138]	Population rank	Violent crime rate rank	City	Violent crimes (per 100,000 population) [col 37]
20	1	Washington city, District of Columbia....	9,344	20	1	Washington city, District of Columbia....	17,761	23	1	Detroit city, Michigan	2,049
1	2	New York city, New York	5,077	37	2	Atlanta city, Georgia	16,770	64	2	St. Louis city, Missouri	1,913
15	3	San Francisco city, California	3,430	15	3	San Francisco city, California	15,759	26	3	Memphis city, Tennessee	1,826
21	4	Boston city, Massachusetts	2,844	1	4	New York city, New York	15,714	30	4	Baltimore city, Maryland	1,780
6	5	Philadelphia city, Pennsylvania	2,089	12	5	Jacksonville city, Florida	12,465	52	5	Cleveland city, Ohio	1,695
30	6	Baltimore city, Maryland	1,989	23	6	Detroit city, Michigan	11,720	38	6	Kansas City city, Missouri	1,657
24	7	Nashville-Davidson, Tennessee	1,952	19	7	Denver city, Colorado	11,106	31	7	Milwaukee city, Wisconsin	1,534
68	8	Anchorage municipality, Alaska	1,830	51	8	Wichita city, Kansas	9,003	45	8	Oakland city, California	1,426
44	9	Virginia Beach city, Virginia	1,817	46	9	Minneapolis city, Minnesota	8,754	61	9	Stockton city, California	1,421
19	10	Denver city, Colorado	1,748	24	10	Nashville-Davidson, Tennessee	7,828	17	10	Indianapolis city, Indiana	1,374
64	11	St. Louis city, Missouri	1,706	3	11	Chicago city, Illinois	7,811	74	11	Toledo city, Ohio	1,192
38	12	Kansas City city, Missouri	1,599	17	12	Indianapolis city, Indiana	7,191	68	12	Anchorage municipality, Alaska	1,144
18	13	Seattle city, Washington	1,438	18	13	Seattle city, Washington	6,556	20	13	Washington city, District of Columbia...	1,132
45	14	Oakland city, California	1,420	52	14	Cleveland city, Ohio	6,465	32	14	Albuquerque city, New Mexico	1,112
65	15	Cincinnati city, Ohio	1,400	4	15	Houston city, Texas	6,459	46	15	Minneapolis city, Minnesota	1,109
50	16	New Orleans city, Louisiana	1,349	11	16	Austin city, Texas	6,438	3	16	Chicago city, Illinois	1,108
37	17	Atlanta city, Georgia	1,173	9	17	Dallas city, Texas	6,389	24	17	Nashville-Davidson, Tennessee	1,107
46	18	Minneapolis city, Minnesota	1,170	7	18	San Antonio city, Texas	6,374	47	18	Tulsa city, Oklahoma	1,095
66	19	Pittsburgh city, Pennsylvania	1,166	38	19	Kansas City city, Missouri	6,347	37	19	Atlanta city, Georgia	1,084
12	20	Jacksonville city, Florida	1,104	39	20	Colorado Springs city, Colorado	6,097	50	20	New Orleans city, Louisiana	1,070
73	21	Newark city, New Jersey	1,099	72	21	Irvine city, California	6,096	51	21	Wichita city, Kansas	1,064
23	22	Detroit city, Michigan	1,078	58	22	Riverside city, California	6,092	4	22	Houston city, Texas	1,026
52	23	Cleveland city, Ohio	1,071	10	23	San Jose city, California	6,013	6	23	Philadelphia city, Pennsylvania	979
17	24	Indianapolis city, Indiana	1,064	68	24	Anchorage municipality, Alaska	5,991	65	24	Cincinnati city, Ohio	938
60	25	Lexington-Fayette, Kentucky	1,045	2	25	Los Angeles city, California	5,983	73	25	Newark city, New Jersey	937
25	26	Portland city, Oregon	1,016	64	26	St. Louis city, Missouri	5,832	40	26	Miami city, Florida	887
27	27	Oklahoma City city, Oklahoma	1,003	48	27	Arlington city, Texas	5,724	28	27	Las Vegas city, Nevada	849
2	28	Los Angeles city, California	997	45	28	Oakland city, California	5,709	71	28	Orlando city, Florida	838
40	29	Miami city, Florida	976	25	29	Portland city, Oregon	5,608	33	29	Tucson city, Arizona	795
14	30	Columbus city, Ohio	958	5	30	Phoenix city, Arizona	5,557	27	30	Oklahoma City city, Oklahoma	783
3	31	Chicago city, Illinois	930	50	31	New Orleans city, Louisiana	5,454	66	31	Pittsburgh city, Pennsylvania	782
69	32	Plano city, Texas	907	55	32	Anaheim city, California	5,304	9	32	Dallas city, Texas	762
42	33	Omaha city, Nebraska	903	43	33	Long Beach city, California	5,095	75	33	Durham city, North Carolina	747
71	34	Orlando city, Florida	895	6	34	Philadelphia city, Pennsylvania	4,985	16	34	Charlotte city, North Carolina	732
4	35	Houston city, Texas	888	70	35	Lincoln city, Nebraska	4,876	2	35	Los Angeles city, California	719
43	36	Long Beach city, California	877	71	36	Orlando city, Florida	4,219	7	36	San Antonio city, Texas	718
10	37	San Jose city, California	876	30	37	Baltimore city, Maryland	4,208	36	37	Sacramento city, California	716
9	38	Dallas city, Texas	872	16	38	Charlotte city, North Carolina	4,165	15	38	San Francisco city, California	711
47	39	Tulsa city, Oklahoma	862	49	39	Tampa city, Florida	3,945	59	39	Corpus Christi city, Texas	710
8	40	San Diego city, California	838	44	40	Virginia Beach city, Virginia	3,811	21	40	Boston city, Massachusetts	707
16	41	Charlotte city, North Carolina	803	26	41	Memphis city, Tennessee	3,791	29	41	Louisville/Jefferson, Kentucky	678
26	42	Memphis city, Tennessee	789	32	42	Albuquerque city, New Mexico	3,769	5	42	Phoenix city, Arizona	674
13	43	Fort Worth city, Texas	783	59	43	Corpus Christi city, Texas	3,689	19	43	Denver city, Colorado	658
55	44	Anaheim city, California	779	54	44	Aurora city, Colorado	3,582	63	44	St. Paul city, Minnesota	648
49	45	Tampa city, Florida	774	35	45	Mesa city, Arizona	3,305	67	45	Greensboro city, North Carolina	643
36	46	Sacramento city, California	771	60	46	Lexington-Fayette, Kentucky	3,277	12	46	Jacksonville city, Florida	625
29	47	Louisville/Jefferson, Kentucky	753	47	47	Tulsa city, Oklahoma	3,179	18	47	Seattle city, Washington	614
75	48	Durham city, North Carolina	717	14	48	Columbus city, Ohio	3,153	34	48	Fresno city, California	611
67	49	Greensboro city, North Carolina	711	65	49	Cincinnati city, Ohio	3,091	43	49	Long Beach city, California	597
11	50	Austin city, Texas	709	13	50	Fort Worth city, Texas	3,084	1	50	New York city, New York	573
41	51	Raleigh city, North Carolina	679	63	51	St. Paul city, Minnesota	2,646	42	51	Omaha city, Nebraska	567
5	52	Phoenix city, Arizona	663	29	52	Louisville/Jefferson, Kentucky	2,633	48	52	Arlington city, Texas	557
32	52	Albuquerque city, New Mexico	663	8	53	San Diego city, California	2,563	14	53	Columbus city, Ohio	544
72	54	Irvine city, California	656	21	54	Boston city, Massachusetts	2,454	54	54	Aurora city, Colorado	532
48	55	Arlington city, Texas	644	42	55	Omaha city, Nebraska	2,411	13	55	Fort Worth city, Texas	530
54	56	Aurora city, Colorado	638	41	56	Raleigh city, North Carolina	2,373	58	56	Riverside city, California	529
58	57	Riverside city, California	631	73	57	Newark city, New Jersey	2,366	49	57	Tampa city, Florida	507
57	58	Santa Ana city, California	621	66	58	Pittsburgh city, Pennsylvania	2,300	25	58	Portland city, Oregon	502
74	59	Toledo city, Ohio	618	36	59	Sacramento city, California	2,286	39	59	Colorado Springs city, Colorado	496
59	60	Corpus Christi city, Texas	614	22	60	El Paso city, Texas	2,270	53	60	Bakersfield city, California	481
63	61	St. Paul city, Minnesota	602	33	61	Tucson city, Arizona	2,236	57	61	Santa Ana city, California	478
22	62	El Paso city, Texas	572	27	62	Oklahoma City city, Oklahoma	2,199	35	62	Mesa city, Arizona	429
61	63	Stockton city, California	544	31	63	Milwaukee city, Wisconsin	2,181	11	63	Austin city, Texas	408
7	64	San Antonio city, Texas	534	34	64	Fresno city, California	2,099	22	64	El Paso city, Texas	390
33	64	Tucson city, Arizona	534	40	65	Miami city, Florida	2,095	8	65	San Diego city, California	377
34	66	Fresno city, California	529	61	66	Stockton city, California	1,926	10	66	San Jose city, California	373
70	67	Lincoln city, Nebraska	516	75	67	Durham city, North Carolina	1,661	70	67	Lincoln city, Nebraska	358
31	68	Milwaukee city, Wisconsin	505	67	68	Greensboro city, North Carolina	1,603	55	68	Anaheim city, California	342
39	69	Colorado Springs city, Colorado	494	69	69	Plano city, Texas	1,293	60	69	Lexington-Fayette, Kentucky	341
62	70	Henderson city, Nevada	487	74	70	Toledo city, Ohio	1,260	62	70	Henderson city, Nevada	212
51	71	Wichita city, Kansas	435	62	71	Henderson city, Nevada	1,165	44	71	Virginia Beach city, Virginia	155
53	72	Bakersfield city, California	417	57	72	Santa Ana city, California	1,080	69	72	Plano city, Texas	139
35	73	Mesa city, Arizona	346	28	73	Las Vegas city, Nevada	1,069	72	73	Irvine city, California	57
28	74	Las Vegas city, Nevada	336	53	74	Bakersfield city, California	966	41	74	Raleigh city, North Carolina	NA
56	75	Urban Honolulu CDP, Hawaii	NA	56	75	Urban Honolulu CDP, Hawaii	NA	56	74	Urban Honolulu CDP, Hawaii	NA

75 Largest Cities by 2018 Population
Selected rankings

Property crime rate, 2016 (property crimes known to police)				Full-time equivalent local government employees, 2012				Local government employee payroll for March 2012			
Population rank	property crime rate rank	City	Property crimes (per 100,000) population) [col 38]	Population rank	Government employees rank	City	Government employees [col 108]	Population rank	Government employee payroll rank	City	Government payroll (thousands of dollars) [col 109]
32	1	Albuquerque city, New Mexico...	6,861	1	1	New York city, New York	404,260	1	1	New York city, New York	2,380,283,176
64	2	St. Louis city, Missouri	5,931	2	2	Los Angeles city, California	47,505	2	2	Los Angeles city, California	361,983,103
47	3	Tulsa city, Oklahoma	5,904	20	3	Washington city, District of Columbia	34,002	15	3	San Francisco city, California	217,722,943
33	4	Tucson city, Arizona	5,859	6	4	Philadelphia city, Pennsylvania	29,409	20	4	Washington city, District of Columbia	194,813,463
26	5	Memphis city, Tennessee	5,640	15	5	San Francisco city, California	28,349	3	5	Chicago city, Illinois	175,627,618
45	6	Oakland city, California	5,636	30	6	Baltimore city, Maryland	26,392	6	6	Philadelphia city, Pennsylvania	148,399,324
18	7	Seattle city, Washington	5,489	3	7	Chicago city, Illinois	25,630	30	7	Baltimore city, Maryland	122,552,640
15	8	San Francisco city, California	5,441	26	8	Memphis city, Tennessee	24,196	21	8	Boston city, Massachusetts	112,444,857
51	9	Wichita city, Kansas	5,388	24	9	Nashville-Davidson, Tennessee	21,697	4	9	Houston city, Texas	99,616,057
52	9	Cleveland city, Ohio	5,388	4	10	Houston city, Texas	21,007	24	10	Nashville-Davidson, Tennessee	83,700,973
37	11	Atlanta city, Georgia	5,249	21	11	Boston city, Massachusetts	19,230	26	11	Memphis city, Tennessee	79,305,378
71	12	Orlando city, Florida	5,220	44	12	Virginia Beach city, Virginia	18,286	18	12	Seattle city, Washington	71,586,796
7	13	San Antonio city, Texas	5,190	7	13	San Antonio city, Texas	15,382	7	13	San Antonio city, Texas	70,371,976
25	14	Portland city, Oregon	5,189	9	14	Dallas city, Texas	14,235	5	14	Phoenix city, Arizona	69,633,897
65	15	Cincinnati city, Ohio	5,162	5	15	Phoenix city, Arizona	13,392	9	15	Dallas city, Texas	67,511,933
68	16	Anchorage municipality, Alaska	4,898	11	16	Austin city, Texas	12,580	11	16	Austin city, Texas	64,599,610
17	17	Indianapolis city, Indiana	4,795	23	17	Detroit city, Michigan	12,364	44	17	Virginia Beach city, Virginia	64,539,702
30	18	Baltimore city, Maryland	4,778	17	18	Indianapolis city, Indiana	12,328	19	18	Denver city, Colorado	62,559,560
23	19	Detroit city, Michigan	4,744	19	19	Denver city, Colorado	11,914	8	19	San Diego city, California	62,476,850
20	20	Washington city, District of Columbia	4,597	18	20	Seattle city, Washington	10,193	23	20	Detroit city, Michigan	57,433,160
53	21	Bakersfield city, California	4,524	12	21	Jacksonville city, Florida	10,137	68	21	Anchorage municipality, Alaska	51,971,256
29	22	Louisville/Jefferson, Kentucky	4,442	68	22	Anchorage municipality, Alaska	9,819	17	22	Indianapolis city, Indiana	49,785,804
38	23	Kansas City city, Missouri	4,374	8	23	San Diego city, California	9,425	12	23	Jacksonville city, Florida	46,960,164
4	24	Houston city, Texas	4,321	29	24	Louisville/Jefferson, Kentucky	8,264	14	24	Columbus city, Ohio	42,573,757
46	25	Minneapolis city, Minnesota	4,222	37	25	Atlanta city, Georgia	8,214	10	25	San Jose city, California	38,715,963
40	26	Miami city, Florida	4,221	14	26	Columbus city, Ohio	8,035	39	26	Colorado Springs city, Colorado	37,084,390
60	27	Lexington-Fayette, Kentucky	4,121	16	27	Charlotte city, North Carolina	7,449	43	27	Long Beach city, California	36,050,392
16	28	Charlotte city, North Carolina	4,098	52	28	Cleveland city, Ohio	7,389	25	28	Portland city, Oregon	35,656,383
14	29	Columbus city, Ohio	4,090	39	29	Colorado Springs city, Colorado	6,835	16	29	Charlotte city, North Carolina	34,348,745
31	30	Milwaukee city, Wisconsin	4,064	50	30	New Orleans city, Louisiana	6,570	32	30	Albuquerque city, New Mexico	33,331,138
74	31	Toledo city, Ohio	4,020	13	31	Fort Worth city, Texas	6,536	52	31	Cleveland city, Ohio	33,318,506
50	32	New Orleans city, Louisiana	3,920	38	32	Kansas City city, Missouri	6,482	29	32	Louisville/Jefferson, Kentucky	32,734,538
34	33	Fresno city, California	3,911	31	33	Milwaukee city, Wisconsin	6,455	31	33	Milwaukee city, Wisconsin	32,385,292
27	34	Oklahoma City city, Oklahoma	3,901	32	34	Albuquerque city, New Mexico	6,438	13	34	Fort Worth city, Texas	32,292,472
61	35	Stockton city, California	3,773	64	35	St. Louis city, Missouri	6,234	37	35	Atlanta city, Georgia	31,551,612
42	36	Omaha city, Nebraska	3,767	22	36	El Paso city, Texas	5,996	45	36	Oakland city, California	30,153,764
59	37	Corpus Christi city, Texas	3,719	43	37	Long Beach city, California	5,861	36	37	Sacramento city, California	29,508,935
24	38	Nashville-Davidson, Tennessee	3,704	25	38	Portland city, Oregon	5,804	65	38	Cincinnati city, Ohio	26,843,252
5	39	Phoenix city, Arizona	3,690	65	39	Cincinnati city, Ohio	5,222	46	39	Minneapolis city, Minnesota	26,103,507
19	40	Denver city, Colorado	3,599	10	40	San Jose city, California	5,214	50	40	New Orleans city, Louisiana	26,033,023
12	41	Jacksonville city, Florida	3,582	46	41	Minneapolis city, Minnesota	5,068	73	41	Newark city, New Jersey	25,580,741
39	42	Colorado Springs city, Colorado	3,559	33	42	Tucson city, Arizona	4,691	64	42	St. Louis city, Missouri	25,364,525
11	43	Austin city, Texas	3,509	36	43	Sacramento city, California	4,483	27	43	Oklahoma City city, Oklahoma	24,268,820
58	44	Riverside city, California	3,457	27	44	Oklahoma City city, Oklahoma	4,418	22	44	El Paso city, Texas	23,812,936
9	45	Dallas city, Texas	3,400	49	45	Tampa city, Florida	4,247	49	45	Tampa city, Florida	22,517,912
13	46	Fort Worth city, Texas	3,315	66	46	Pittsburgh city, Pennsylvania	4,176	33	46	Tucson city, Arizona	21,780,237
75	47	Durham city, North Carolina	3,281	45	47	Oakland city, California	3,940	38	47	Kansas City city, Missouri	21,087,489
66	48	Pittsburgh city, Pennsylvania	3,263	41	48	Raleigh city, North Carolina	3,936	35	48	Mesa city, Arizona	20,622,110
63	49	St. Paul city, Minnesota	3,228	47	49	Tulsa city, Oklahoma	3,932	40	49	Miami city, Florida	18,642,774
67	50	Greensboro city, North Carolina	3,214	60	50	Lexington-Fayette, Kentucky	3,926	34	50	Fresno city, California	18,551,770
3	51	Chicago city, Illinois	3,197	73	51	Newark city, New Jersey	3,857	63	51	St. Paul city, Minnesota	18,028,194
48	52	Arlington city, Texas	3,154	40	52	Miami city, Florida	3,807	28	52	Las Vegas city, Nevada	17,371,881
6	53	Philadelphia city, Pennsylvania	3,141	35	53	Mesa city, Arizona	3,616	47	53	Tulsa city, Oklahoma	16,951,552
70	54	Lincoln city, Nebraska	3,105	34	54	Fresno city, California	3,214	66	54	Pittsburgh city, Pennsylvania	16,527,485
36	55	Sacramento city, California	3,085	67	55	Greensboro city, North Carolina	3,098	60	55	Lexington-Fayette, Kentucky	16,180,537
54	56	Aurora city, Colorado	3,066	63	56	St. Paul city, Minnesota	3,092	41	56	Raleigh city, North Carolina	15,850,858
43	57	Long Beach city, California	2,985	51	57	Wichita city, Kansas	2,864	55	57	Anaheim city, California	15,281,363
28	58	Las Vegas city, Nevada	2,889	42	58	Omaha city, Nebraska	2,835	42	58	Omaha city, Nebraska	15,258,712
55	59	Anaheim city, California	2,720	71	59	Orlando city, Florida	2,773	58	59	Riverside city, California	15,114,251
2	60	Los Angeles city, California	2,474	59	60	Corpus Christi city, Texas	2,747	71	60	Orlando city, Florida	14,180,368
10	61	San Jose city, California	2,375	57	61	Santa Ana city, California	2,711	62	61	Henderson city, Nevada	13,759,509
35	62	Mesa city, Arizona	2,345	70	62	Lincoln city, Nebraska	2,609	54	62	Aurora city, Colorado	13,742,359
73	63	Newark city, New Jersey	2,241	28	63	Las Vegas city, Nevada	2,582	70	63	Lincoln city, Nebraska	13,359,820
44	64	Virginia Beach city, Virginia	2,183	54	64	Aurora city, Colorado	2,579	57	64	Santa Ana city, California	12,719,386
21	65	Boston city, Massachusetts	2,150	48	65	Arlington city, Texas	2,551	61	65	Stockton city, California	12,427,436
49	66	Tampa city, Florida	2,075	58	66	Riverside city, California	2,260	51	66	Wichita city, Kansas	12,396,633
57	67	Santa Ana city, California	2,069	62	67	Henderson city, Nevada	2,239	48	67	Arlington city, Texas	12,130,944
8	68	San Diego city, California	2,025	55	68	Anaheim city, California	2,214	67	68	Greensboro city, North Carolina	11,503,988
69	69	Plano city, Texas	1,904	74	69	Toledo city, Ohio	2,146	59	69	Corpus Christi city, Texas	10,789,288
62	70	Henderson city, Nevada	1881	69	70	Plano city, Texas	2089	69	70	Plano city, Texas	10395648
22	71	El Paso city, Texas	1798	61	71	Stockton city, California	2010	74	71	Toledo city, Ohio	10282276
1	72	New York city, New York	1462	53	72	Bakersfield city, California	1424	53	72	Bakersfield city, California	8316644
72	73	Irvine city, California	1401	75	73	Durham city, North Carolina	1086	72	73	Irvine city, California	6075973
41	74	Raleigh city, North Carolina	NA	72	74	Irvine city, California	977	75	74	Durham city, North Carolina	4030398
56	74	Urban Honolulu CDP, Hawaii	NA	56	75	Urban Honolulu CDP, Hawaii	NA	56	75	Urban Honolulu CDP, Hawaii	NA

Table D. Cities — **Land Area and Population**

STATE Place code	City		Population, 2018			Race 2017						
							Race alone[2] (percent)					
		Land area[1] (sq. mi)	Total persons 2018	Rank	Per square mile	White	Black or African American	American Indian, Alaskan Native	Asian	Hawaiian Pacific Islander	Some other race	Two or more races (percent)
		1	2	3	4	5	6	7	8	9	10	11

1. Dry land or land partially or temporarily covered by water.   2. Hispanic or Latino persons may be of any race.

Table D. Cities — **Population**

City	Percent Hispanic or Latino[1], 2017	Percent foreign born, 2017	Age of population (percent), 2017							Median age, 2017	Percent female, 2017	Population			
												Census counts		Percent change	
			Under 18 years	18 to 24 years	25 to 34 years	35 to 44 years	45 to 54 years	55 to 64 years	65 years and over			2000	2010	2000-2010	2001-2018
	12	13	14	15	16	17	18	19	20	21	22	23	24	25	26

1. May be of any race.

Table D. Cities — **Households, Group Quarters, Crime, and Education**

City	Households, 2017							Persons in group quarters, 2017	Serious crimes known to police[2], 2016				Educational attainment, 2017		
			Percent						Total		Rate[3]			Attainment[4] (percent)	
	Number	Persons per household	Family	Married couple family	Female family	Non-family	One person		Number	Rate	Violent	Property	Population age 25 and over	High school graduate or less	Bachelor's degree or more
	27	28	29	30	31	32	33	34	35	36	37	38	39	40	41

1. No spouse present.   2. Data for serious crimes have not been adjusted for underreporting. This may affect comparability between geographic areas and over time.   3. Per 100,000 population estimated by the FBI.   4. Persons 25 years old and over.

Table D. Cities — **Income and Housing**

City	Money income, 2017					Median earnings, 2017			Housing units, 2017				
	Households			Median family income	Median non-family income	All persons	Men	Women	Total	Occupied	Percent owner occupied	Median value (dollars)	Median gross rent (dollars)
	Median income	Percent with income less than $20,000	Percent with income of $200,000 or more										
	42	43	44	45	46	47	48	49	50	51	52	53	54

Table D. Cities — **Commuting, Computer Access, Migration, Labor Force, and Employment**

City	Commuting[1], 2017		Computer access[2], 2017		Migration, 2017		Civilian labor force, 2018				Civilian employment[4], 2017			
	Percent		Percent						Unemployment		Population age 16 and older		Population age 16 to 64	
	Commuting	With commutes of 30 minutes or more	With a computer in the house	With Internet access	Percent who lived in the same house one year ago	Percent who lived in another state or county one year ago	Total	Percent change 2016 -2017	Total	Rate[3]	Number	Percent in labor force	Number	Percent who worked full-year full-time
	55	56	57	58	59	60	61	62	63	64	65	66	67	68

1. Employed persons.   2. Households.   3. Percent of civilian labor force.   4. Persons 16 years old and over.

Table D. Cities — **Construction, Wholesale Trade, and Retail Trade**

City	Value of residential construction authorized by building permits, 2018			Wholesale trade[1], 2012				Retail trade[2], 2012			
	New construction ($1,000)	Number of housing units	Percent single family	Number of establishments	Number of employees	Sales (mil dol)	Annual payroll (mil dol)	Number of establish- ments	Number of employees	Sales (mil dol)	Annual payroll (mil dol)
	69	70	71	72	73	74	75	76	77	78	79

1. Merchant wholesalers except manufacturers' sales branches and offices.   2. Establishments with payroll.

Table D. Cities — **Real Estate, Professional Services, and Manufacturing**

City	Real estate and rental and leasing, 2012				Professional, scientific, and technical services[1], 2012				Manufacturing, 2012			
	Number of establish- ments	Number of employees	Receipts (mil dol)	Annual payroll (mil dol)	Number of establish- ments	Number of employees	Receipts (mil dol)	Annual payroll (mil dol)	Number of establish- ments	Number of employees	Receipts (mil dol)	Annual payroll (mil dol)
	80	81	82	83	84	85	86	87	88	89	90	91

1. Establishments subject to federal tax.

Table D. Cities — **Accommodation and Food Services, Arts, Entertainment, and Recreation, and Health Care and Social Assistance**

City	Accommodation and food services, 2012				Arts, entertainment, and recreation[1], 2012				Health care and social assistance,[1] 2012			
	Number of establish- ments	Number of employees	Receipts (mil dol)	Annual payroll (mil dol)	Number of establish- ments	Number of employees	Receipts (mil dol)	Annual payroll (mil dol)	Number of establish- ments	Number of employees	Receipts (mil dol)	Annual payroll (mil dol)
	92	93	94	95	96	97	98	99	100	101	102	103

1. Establishments subject to federal tax.

Table D. Cities — **Other Services and Government Employment and Payroll**

City	Other services[1]				Government employment and payroll, 2012									
					Full-time equivalent employees	March payroll								
						Total (dollars)	Perent of total for:							
	Number of establish-ments	Number of employees	Receipts (mil dol)	Annual payroll (mil dol)			Admin-istrative, judicial, and legal	Police and corrections	Fire protection	Highways and trans-portation	Health and welfare	Natural resources and utilities	Education and libraries
	104	105	106	107	108	109	110	111	112	113	114	115	116

1. Establishments subject to federal tax.

Table D. Cities — **City Government Finances**

City	City government finances, 2012										
	General revenue								General expenditure		
		Intergovernmental		Taxes							
						Per capita[1] (dollars)				Per capita[1] (dollars)	
	Total (mil dol)	Total (mil dol)	Percent from state government	Total (mil dol)	Total	Property	Sales and gross receipts	Total (mil dol)	Total	Capital outlays
	117	118	119	120	121	122	123	124	125	126

1. Based on population estimated as of July 1 of the year shown.

Table D. Cities — **City Government Finances**

City	City government finances, 2012 (cont.)									
	General expenditure (cont.)									
	Percent of total for:									
	Public welfare	Highways	Parking facilities	Education	Health and hospitals	Police protection	Sewerage and sanitation	Parks and recreation	Housing and community development	Interest on debt
	127	128	129	130	131	132	133	134	135	136

Table D. Cities — **City Government Finances, City Government Employment, and Climate**

City	City government finances, 2012 (cont.)			Climate[2]							
	Debt outstanding			Average daily temperature							
				Mean		Limits					
	Total (mil dol)	Per capita[1] (dollars)	Debt issued during year	January	July	January[3]	July[4]	Annual precipitation (inches)	Heating degree days	Cooling degree days
	137	138	139	140	141	142	143	144	145	146

1. Based on the population estimated as of July 1 of the year shown.   2. Represents normal values based on the 30-year period, 1971±2000.   3. Average daily minimum.   4. Average daily maximum.

Table D. Cities — **Land Area and Population**

STATE Place code	City	Population, 2018				Race 2017 Race alone² (percent)						Two or more races (percent)
		Land area¹ (sq. mi)	Total persons 2018	Rank	Per square mile	White	Black or African American	American Indian, Alaskan Native	Asian	Hawaiian Pacific Islander	Some other race	
		1	2	3	4	5	6	7	8	9	10	11
00 00000	United States	3,532,614.3	327,167,434	X	92.6	72.3	12.7	0.8	5.6	0.2	5.1	3.3
01 00000	ALABAMA	50,646.6	4,887,871	X	96.5	68.0	26.8	0.5	1.4	0.0	1.4	1.9
01 00820	Alabaster................	25.2	33,340	1,147	1,323.0	69.2	17.8	0.0	0.0	0.0	9.3	3.7
01 03076	Auburn	60.1	65,738	563	1,093.8	72.8	15.5	0.2	9.0	0.0	0.5	2.0
01 05980	Bessemer................	40.5	26,538	1,378	655.3	NA	NA	NA	NA	NA	NA	NA
01 07000	Birmingham.............	146.1	209,880	107	1,436.6	24.6	71.1	0.2	1.2	0.1	1.3	1.5
01 20104	Decatur..................	54.1	54,264	705	1,003.0	72.6	19.4	0.0	0.3	0.0	4.9	2.8
01 21184	Dothan...................	89.7	68,247	529	760.8	64.4	32.2	0.1	1.0	0.0	0.1	2.2
01 24184	Enterprise...............	30.6	28,269	1,310	923.8	75.7	19.4	0.4	3.5	0.0	0.0	1.0
01 26896	Florence.................	26.4	40,428	944	1,531.4	NA	NA	NA	NA	NA	NA	NA
01 28696	Gadsden	37.3	35,157	1,091	942.5	NA	NA	NA	NA	NA	NA	NA
01 35800	Homewood..............	8.3	25,397	1,403	3,059.9	NA	NA	NA	NA	NA	NA	NA
01 35896	Hoover	47.9	85,108	395	1,776.8	75.3	15.2	0.1	6.6	0.0	0.7	2.1
01 37000	Huntsville	214.4	197,318	122	920.3	61.3	31.4	0.2	2.8	0.0	1.5	2.8
01 45784	Madison	30.3	50,440	763	1,664.7	76.5	11.1	0.9	5.9	0.0	2.3	3.3
01 50000	Mobile	139.4	189,572	131	1,359.9	42.9	52.3	0.2	1.6	0.0	1.1	1.9
01 51000	Montgomery.............	159.8	198,218	119	1,240.4	33.8	60.3	0.2	3.0	0.0	1.0	1.7
01 57048	Opelika..................	59.7	30,555	1,231	511.8	NA	NA	NA	NA	NA	NA	NA
01 59472	Phenix City.............	28.0	36,435	1,056	1,301.3	45.0	44.6	0.4	0.2	0.0	7.1	2.7
01 62328	Prattville	33.9	35,662	1,079	1,052.0	72.2	22.6	0.3	2.3	0.0	0.0	2.5
01 77256	Tuscaloosa..............	61.7	101,113	306	1,638.8	49.0	46.4	0.8	1.9	0.1	0.2	1.7
01 78552	Vestavia Hills...........	19.9	34,461	1,105	1,731.7	NA	NA	NA	NA	NA	NA	NA
02 00000	ALASKA	570,983.2	737,438	X	1.3	64.2	3.0	14.9	6.7	1.2	1.5	8.6
02 03000	Anchorage...............	1,706.4	291,538	68	170.8	61.9	5.0	7.8	10.8	2.6	2.4	9.5
02 24230	Fairbanks................	31.8	31,516	1,204	991.1	63.8	7.6	13.5	2.3	0.4	1.4	11.1
02 36400	Juneau...................	2,703.9	32,113	1,185	11.9	67.2	0.2	8.6	6.8	0.5	1.5	15.2
04 00000	ARIZONA	113,590.7	7,171,646	X	63.1	77.6	4.4	4.5	3.3	0.2	6.2	3.8
04 02830	Apache Junction	35.1	41,739	912	1,189.1	NA	NA	NA	NA	NA	NA	NA
04 04720	Avondale.................	45.2	85,835	388	1,899.0	74.2	8.7	2.2	1.8	0.7	8.6	3.9
04 07940	Buckeye.................	393.1	74,370	479	189.2	65.6	4.6	1.8	5.3	0.4	18.6	3.7
04 08220	Bullhead City............	59.4	40,421	945	680.5	86.2	1.6	0.4	1.7	0.2	6.8	3.1
04 10530	Casa Grande............	110.6	57,232	664	517.5	64.0	7.8	10.6	1.2	0.2	6.2	10.0
04 12000	Chandler.................	65.0	257,165	82	3,956.4	77.5	5.9	0.8	9.9	0.2	1.7	4.0
04 22220	El Mirage................	9.9	35,670	1,078	3,603.0	70.0	9.4	1.3	2.4	0.0	12.4	4.5
04 23620	Flagstaff.................	66.0	73,964	485	1,120.7	85.9	1.5	3.8	2.7	0.4	0.9	4.8
04 23760	Florence.................	62.6	26,419	1,383	422.0	84.7	7.5	4.6	0.0	0.2	1.0	2.0
04 27400	Gilbert...................	68.1	248,279	88	3,645.8	84.7	2.6	0.7	5.0	0.0	2.6	4.3
04 27820	Glendale.................	59.5	250,702	87	4,213.5	74.6	7.9	2.1	4.6	0.7	6.0	4.1
04 28380	Goodyear................	191.2	82,835	410	433.2	71.8	8.7	2.6	5.6	0.0	7.8	3.4
04 37620	Kingman.................	37.5	30,314	1,243	808.4	NA	NA	NA	NA	NA	NA	NA
04 39370	Lake Havasu City........	46.3	55,090	691	1,189.8	NA	NA	NA	NA	NA	NA	NA
04 44270	Marana	121.0	47,007	826	388.5	83.0	0.6	0.8	4.3	1.0	4.5	5.8
04 44410	Maricopa................	42.8	50,024	768	1,168.8	77.3	6.4	0.9	5.1	0.1	2.5	7.7
04 46000	Mesa	138.0	508,958	35	3,688.1	80.1	3.8	2.0	2.0	0.4	7.7	3.9
04 51600	Oro Valley...............	35.6	45,395	844	1,275.1	89.5	3.6	0.5	3.9	0.0	0.8	1.7
04 54050	Peoria...................	175.7	172,259	152	980.4	83.6	2.8	0.6	4.5	0.4	4.2	3.9
04 55000	Phoenix..................	517.7	1,660,272	5	3,207.0	73.4	7.2	2.0	4.0	0.2	9.0	4.2
04 57380	Prescott..................	44.9	43,314	881	964.7	91.3	0.3	0.9	1.7	0.0	1.7	4.2
04 57450	Prescott Valley...........	40.9	45,751	843	1,118.6	92.2	1.0	0.3	1.9	0.0	2.6	1.9
04 58150	Queen Creek............	30.1	42,503	896	1,412.1	91.4	1.0	0.6	1.4	0.5	1.9	3.2
04 62140	Sahuarita................	31.5	30,282	1,245	961.3	90.4	4.0	0.0	2.1	0.0	1.4	2.1
04 63470	San Luis.................	34.1	33,490	1,145	982.1	NA	NA	NA	NA	NA	NA	NA
04 65000	Scottsdale...............	184.0	255,310	85	1,387.6	89.0	2.6	0.7	4.8	0.0	0.9	2.1
04 66820	Sierra Vista.............	152.2	44,420	861	291.9	76.3	7.5	2.7	4.6	0.9	1.8	6.2
04 71510	Surprise.................	108.2	138,161	198	1,276.9	87.5	3.5	0.5	2.2	0.0	4.1	2.3
04 73000	Tempe...................	40.0	192,364	129	4,809.1	67.1	6.5	3.0	7.9	0.2	11.3	3.9
04 77000	Tucson...................	238.0	545,975	33	2,294.0	71.8	4.8	4.2	3.1	0.2	10.1	5.9
04 85540	Yuma....................	121.0	97,908	317	809.2	75.8	3.6	2.1	2.6	0.1	10.9	5.0
05 00000	ARKANSAS	52,034.6	3,013,825	X	57.9	76.3	15.3	0.6	1.6	0.3	3.1	2.8
05 04840	Bella Vista..............	45.3	28,661	1,298	632.7	NA	NA	NA	NA	NA	NA	NA
05 05290	Benton...................	22.4	36,403	1,060	1,625.1	NA	NA	NA	NA	NA	NA	NA
05 05320	Bentonville..............	33.2	51,111	753	1,539.5	77.9	1.8	1.5	13.2	0.5	2.1	2.9
05 15190	Conway..................	45.9	66,426	553	1,447.2	74.0	17.5	0.0	2.6	0.0	3.1	2.8
05 23290	Fayetteville..............	54.0	86,751	384	1,606.5	78.0	8.4	0.7	4.5	0.1	4.7	3.6
05 24550	Fort Smith...............	63.3	87,845	377	1,387.8	63.3	8.7	1.0	5.4	0.0	13.6	8.0
05 33400	Hot Springs.............	36.5	37,169	1,034	1,018.3	73.4	15.5	0.3	0.3	0.0	6.8	3.8

1. Dry land or land partially or temporarily covered by water.   2. Hispanic or Latino persons may be of any race.

Table D. Cities — **Population**

City	Percent Hispanic or Latino[1], 2017	Percent foreign born, 2017	Age of population (percent), 2017							Median age, 2017	Percent female, 2017	Population			
			Under 18 years	18 to 24 years	25 to 34 years	35 to 44 years	45 to 54 years	55 to 64 years	65 years and over			Census counts		Percent change	
												2000	2010	2000-2010	2001-2018
	12	13	14	15	16	17	18	19	20	21	22	23	24	25	26
United States	18.1	13.7	22.6	9.5	13.8	12.6	13.0	12.9	15.6	38.1	50.8	281,421,906	308,758,105	9.7	6.0
ALABAMA	4.1	3.5	22.4	9.7	12.9	12.2	12.9	13.4	16.5	38.9	51.6	4,447,100	4,780,138	7.5	2.3
Alabaster..........................	12.1	6.8	28.7	7.6	9.9	19.4	12.7	11.8	10.0	36.8	52.7	22,619	31,091	37.5	7.2
Auburn	3.3	11.5	16.5	33.0	13.4	10.2	9.9	6.4	10.6	25.3	49.1	42,987	53,453	24.3	23.0
Bessemer..........................	8.6	6.4	22.1	11.9	8.9	13.3	10.9	14.6	18.3	39.3	46.4	29,672	27,688	-6.7	-4.2
Birmingham.......................	3.8	3.2	19.4	11.4	18.2	11.1	11.3	13.6	14.9	35.8	52.3	242,820	212,003	-12.7	-1.0
Decatur.............................	12.9	6.0	19.7	9.6	11.5	11.9	15.0	13.7	18.7	41.7	50.5	53,929	55,783	3.4	-2.7
Dothan..............................	4.4	2.1	25.1	7.1	14.9	11.9	11.7	12.9	16.4	37.3	53.0	57,737	65,774	13.9	3.8
Enterprise.........................	10.2	6.6	21.6	5.5	15.7	15.4	13.4	13.6	14.9	39.3	51.2	21,178	26,601	25.6	6.3
Florence...........................	4.9	3.0	18.2	14.5	15.9	9.1	10.7	11.5	20.1	35.5	51.7	36,264	39,516	9.0	2.3
Gadsden...........................	6.8	3.2	22.1	9.1	9.4	12.6	11.3	14.2	21.3	42.8	51.2	38,978	36,902	-5.3	-4.7
Homewood........................	9.1	6.4	23.1	14.4	17.3	13.0	11.6	9.5	11.2	31.8	52.5	25,043	25,183	0.6	0.8
Hoover	3.2	9.8	22.0	6.2	13.3	14.1	12.5	14.2	17.7	41.0	52.5	62,742	80,621	28.5	5.6
Huntsville	5.9	6.7	21.2	10.6	14.8	12.5	11.9	13.1	15.9	37.3	52.6	158,216	180,416	14.0	9.4
Madison	6.8	8.4	23.1	8.8	12.4	13.5	13.8	13.9	14.6	40.3	51.6	29,329	43,190	47.3	16.8
Mobile	3.1	3.4	20.3	10.7	16.3	11.6	12.4	13.3	15.4	37.3	51.9	198,915	194,664	-2.1	-2.6
Montgomery......................	3.7	5.3	24.0	10.4	14.6	12.8	11.9	12.0	14.3	36.0	53.3	201,568	205,501	2.0	-3.5
Opelika.............................	1.9	3.2	19.3	6.7	16.3	9.7	17.2	11.9	19.1	44.2	56.0	23,498	26,425	12.5	15.6
Phenix City.......................	8.9	3.5	30.4	10.2	16.9	10.6	11.8	10.1	10.0	30.0	50.6	28,265	32,861	16.3	10.9
Prattville	0.6	3.1	21.6	8.6	14.7	15.9	12.2	13.8	13.2	37.2	50.9	24,303	34,013	40.0	4.8
Tuscaloosa........................	2.3	4.1	18.0	25.3	16.1	11.0	8.7	10.2	10.7	28.6	52.3	77,906	90,373	16.0	11.9
Vestavia Hills....................	4.5	6.1	26.3	6.3	8.6	16.1	13.7	13.8	15.2	39.9	54.2	24,476	33,878	38.4	1.7
ALASKA...........................	7.0	7.9	25.0	9.9	16.0	13.1	12.0	12.7	11.2	34.5	47.9	626,932	710,249	13.3	3.8
Anchorage........................	9.2	11.8	24.5	10.1	17.0	14.1	11.7	12.1	10.5	34.0	49.2	260,283	291,829	12.1	-0.1
Fairbanks	11.5	4.2	24.8	19.3	19.9	8.0	7.3	9.9	10.8	27.9	44.5	30,224	31,556	4.4	-0.1
Juneau	6.6	7.9	21.6	9.2	14.5	13.9	13.9	15.2	11.8	38.2	47.0	30,711	31,275	1.8	2.7
ARIZONA..........................	31.4	13.2	23.3	9.6	13.6	12.2	12.1	12.1	17.1	37.7	50.3	5,130,632	6,392,288	24.6	12.2
Apache Junction	9.3	7.2	12.1	7.8	6.4	9.4	12.5	17.6	34.3	55.8	52.3	31,814	35,723	12.3	16.8
Avondale...........................	58.9	17.3	28.2	10.3	17.4	15.4	9.9	9.6	9.2	31.4	52.8	35,883	76,132	112.2	12.7
Buckeye............................	42.7	14.4	26.0	10.7	15.2	14.2	14.6	7.8	11.5	33.5	45.4	6,537	50,861	678.0	46.2
Bullhead City.....................	25.9	9.4	18.0	5.0	14.9	6.7	9.9	14.9	30.4	50.7	53.9	33,769	39,541	17.1	2.2
Casa Grande......................	37.9	9.4	23.9	8.5	13.6	12.4	11.4	11.1	19.1	39.0	48.0	25,224	48,555	92.5	17.9
Chandler	17.7	15.4	25.3	7.8	13.2	15.3	14.7	11.8	11.8	37.3	50.3	176,581	236,187	33.8	8.9
El Mirage..........................	49.3	13.4	26.5	5.7	15.7	16.8	14.0	9.6	11.7	36.0	47.5	7,609	31,797	317.9	12.2
Flagstaff	19.6	4.9	19.1	29.1	15.1	9.8	8.5	9.0	9.5	26.5	49.1	52,894	66,023	24.8	12.0
Florence	38.4	14.9	11.0	6.6	21.2	16.7	16.7	9.1	18.7	39.6	24.9	17,054	25,563	49.9	3.3
Gilbert	17.5	7.9	29.3	8.2	13.7	15.8	14.0	9.9	9.1	34.4	50.9	109,697	208,387	90.0	19.1
Glendale...........................	37.4	17.9	26.8	11.1	15.1	11.3	14.0	10.6	11.0	32.4	51.0	218,812	226,099	3.3	10.9
Goodyear..........................	29.6	14.6	23.8	8.4	12.0	15.9	13.4	12.0	14.6	38.5	53.1	18,911	65,254	245.1	26.9
Kingman...........................	18.0	1.5	24.0	6.9	15.7	9.5	8.9	12.6	22.5	37.6	48.3	20,069	28,069	39.9	8.0
Lake Havasu City...............	13.1	5.2	10.6	5.8	7.2	6.1	15.8	18.9	35.7	58.4	51.1	41,938	52,531	25.3	4.9
Marana	25.0	9.1	24.4	11.7	11.8	14.6	9.5	10.7	17.3	36.4	52.7	13,556	34,556	154.9	36.0
Maricopa	27.0	8.8	27.4	7.1	10.3	17.6	12.8	9.7	15.2	38.0	50.0	1,040	43,490	4,081.7	15.0
Mesa	28.3	11.7	25.5	8.7	14.6	12.5	11.9	11.0	15.8	35.6	51.2	396,375	440,084	11.0	15.7
Oro Valley	18.6	9.7	18.3	6.1	6.7	8.9	11.3	16.1	32.6	54.0	51.2	29,700	41,028	38.1	10.6
Peoria..............................	15.1	8.8	21.4	9.1	12.1	12.3	14.0	14.5	16.6	41.0	52.5	108,364	154,090	42.2	11.8
Phoenix............................	42.9	19.3	26.2	9.9	15.7	13.7	12.8	11.0	10.7	33.8	50.1	1,321,045	1,446,914	9.5	14.7
Prescott............................	10.1	6.4	12.6	10.2	6.7	8.9	8.6	17.9	35.0	58.2	49.9	33,938	39,766	17.2	8.9
Prescott Valley	24.4	9.2	22.3	3.3	12.3	9.5	11.8	13.9	26.9	46.4	49.4	23,535	38,880	65.2	17.7
Queen Creek......................	15.0	4.4	32.2	5.9	9.1	21.6	14.6	7.0	9.6	36.6	50.7	4,316	26,323	509.9	61.5
Sahuarita..........................	36.1	14.1	27.1	5.0	12.1	13.3	9.7	11.7	20.9	38.8	53.2	3,242	25,289	680.0	19.7
San Luis	95.5	45.5	29.7	12.2	13.6	14.6	12.3	9.8	7.6	30.0	41.3	15,322	27,909	82.1	20.0
Scottsdale	10.5	11.1	17.6	5.8	15.0	10.1	13.7	15.5	22.4	46.0	49.6	202,705	217,464	7.3	17.4
Sierra Vista	20.0	9.1	23.2	8.2	14.7	12.1	9.7	11.0	21.0	37.7	51.0	37,775	45,263	19.8	-1.9
Surprise............................	19.2	7.4	18.9	7.3	11.3	13.7	13.9	9.7	25.3	44.3	51.5	30,848	117,501	280.9	17.6
Tempe..............................	23.8	15.7	15.6	22.7	21.7	11.3	9.2	9.6	9.9	29.9	46.7	158,625	161,777	2.0	18.9
Tucson	44.9	14.4	21.3	15.0	14.8	11.4	11.5	11.5	14.6	34.1	50.1	486,699	526,635	8.2	3.7
Yuma...............................	60.1	24.3	26.5	12.5	15.0	10.9	10.0	9.6	15.5	32.2	52.1	77,515	90,717	17.0	7.9
ARKANSAS	7.4	4.7	23.6	9.6	12.7	12.3	12.5	12.7	16.5	38.1	50.7	2,673,400	2,916,028	9.1	3.4
Bella Vista	2.9	2.0	16.2	4.1	10.2	9.5	8.3	20.9	30.7	55.6	50.9	16,582	26,512	59.9	8.1
Benton..............................	7.2	5.4	23.8	9.8	11.1	17.7	12.6	10.7	14.3	37.7	51.6	21,906	30,723	40.2	18.5
Bentonville........................	9.5	16.1	27.5	7.6	15.8	16.7	12.2	10.0	10.3	33.9	46.9	19,730	35,325	79.0	44.7
Conway............................	4.0	7.2	21.5	21.7	15.9	10.3	12.4	7.9	10.2	28.5	52.3	43,167	58,871	36.4	12.8
Fayetteville.......................	8.4	4.5	19.6	27.5	16.3	11.6	8.3	7.1	9.5	26.6	50.3	58,047	73,573	26.7	17.9
Fort Smith	19.8	11.5	23.3	10.4	12.6	12.8	13.9	13.2	13.7	37.2	52.0	80,268	86,269	7.5	1.8
Hot Springs	10.0	3.9	20.9	12.1	14.5	8.8	10.3	13.3	20.2	38.6	52.8	35,750	36,416	1.9	2.1

1. May be of any race.

Table D. Cities — Households, Group Quarters, Crime, and Education

City	Households, 2017 Number (27)	Persons per household (28)	Percent Family (29)	Percent Married couple family (30)	Percent Female headed¹ (31)	Percent Non-family (32)	Percent One person (33)	Persons in group quarters, 2017 (34)	Serious crimes Total Number (35)	Serious crimes Total Rate (36)	Rate³ Violent (37)	Rate³ Property (38)	Population age 25 and over (39)	Attainment⁴ High school graduate or less (40)	Attainment⁴ Bachelor's degree or more (41)
United States	120,062,818	2.65	65.5	48.2	12.4	34.5	27.9	8,087,237	9,167,220	2,837	386	2,451	221,250,083	39.1	32.0
ALABAMA	1,841,665	2.58	65.4	46.5	14.6	34.6	29.9	118,973	169,248	3,480	532	2,948	3,309,607	44.6	25.5
Alabaster	10,888	3.02	80.4	63.9	11.6	19.6	17.6	NA	585	1,771	294	1,477	21,145	32.1	34.5
Auburn	23,506	2.50	47.5	38.8	7.4	52.5	37.1	5,212	1,335	2,090	329	1,761	32,310	20.4	51.9
Bessemer	10,068	2.53	57.2	28.7	22.5	42.8	32.9	867	3,166	11,906	2,869	9,037	17,426	58.3	12.7
Birmingham	90,186	2.26	50.1	22.4	22.5	49.9	41.2	9,214	15,890	7,476	1,609	5,867	147,226	41.4	26.7
Decatur	22,205	2.40	62.4	45.1	16.0	37.6	31.8	NA	2,754	4,973	278	4,695	38,432	41.2	24.3
Dothan	25,192	2.65	64.3	43.4	17.3	35.7	31.0	891	3,374	4,885	819	4,065	45,773	39.5	26.2
Enterprise	11,695	2.39	60.8	44.6	15.3	39.2	32.7	NA	881	3,121	347	2,774	20,611	34.2	31.9
Florence	17,277	2.19	58.5	38.8	13.1	41.5	33.5	1,935	1,596	3,974	488	3,486	26,811	40.1	28.2
Gadsden	14,445	2.39	47.9	26.4	18.2	52.1	48.6	946	2,985	8,309	1,292	7,017	24,394	51.5	20.5
Homewood	9,755	2.41	60.7	49.2	9.5	39.3	34.8	1,940	1,058	4,097	325	3,772	15,927	14.9	68.4
Hoover	34,058	2.48	69.4	57.4	8.8	30.6	26.3	372	1,266	1,479	121	1,357	60,924	16.5	57.0
Huntsville	84,750	2.21	58.9	39.0	15.6	41.1	35.5	7,988	11,185	5,808	928	4,880	133,240	28.6	42.0
Madison	20,343	2.47	70.2	57.5	12.3	29.8	25.2	NA	1,220	2,556	438	2,118	34,354	15.8	56.8
Mobile	78,145	2.37	54.6	34.5	17.3	45.4	40.5	5,004	13,478	5,393	684	4,709	131,218	41.1	29.5
Montgomery	78,217	2.47	60.7	34.3	21.2	39.3	34.8	6,343	10,204	5,113	609	4,504	130,862	41.1	32.0
Opelika	12,328	2.39	56.7	34.7	20.4	43.3	31.8	818	1,697	5,623	732	4,891	22,402	38.3	28.0
Phenix City	14,296	2.61	59.7	38.4	17.5	40.3	36.0	NA	2,144	5,566	849	4,717	22,535	43.3	26.1
Prattville	13,638	2.58	73.7	50.2	18.3	26.3	23.6	537	1,445	4,048	235	3,813	24,942	39.8	27.4
Tuscaloosa	36,209	2.52	54.3	33.9	18.3	45.7	35.7	9,214	4,212	4,215	480	3,735	56,876	37.5	39.9
Vestavia Hills	13,054	2.62	71.1	61.0	9.0	28.9	23.9	NA	422	1,234	73	1,161	23,121	9.9	70.8
ALASKA	250,741	2.84	66.8	49.4	11.4	33.2	25.3	27,545	30,842	4,157	804	3,353	481,561	36.0	28.8
Anchorage	107,373	2.68	65.8	47.9	12.8	34.2	25.3	7,128	18,071	6,042	1,144	4,898	192,466	30.4	35.1
Fairbanks	9,901	2.88	69.1	48.8	11.7	30.9	18.7	3,087	1,573	4,847	687	4,159	17,689	32.5	27.3
Juneau	12,429	2.53	61.6	49.1	10.5	38.4	29.1	593	1,877	5,694	855	4,839	22,225	24.6	41.5
ARIZONA	2,552,972	2.69	64.7	47.3	12.1	35.3	27.8	155,143	239,015	3,448	470	2,978	4,711,362	37.0	29.4
Apache Junction	16,761	2.41	53.8	39.0	10.4	46.2	38.1	NA	1,038	2,696	280	2,415	32,519	46.3	13.1
Avondale	26,223	3.20	76.6	48.4	20.3	23.4	20.1	NA	3,495	4,283	286	3,997	51,666	44.8	18.4
Buckeye	18,135	3.38	81.1	64.3	12.0	18.9	14.4	7,202	1,060	1,642	54	1,588	43,311	41.1	19.0
Bullhead City	18,135	2.21	56.0	38.8	11.4	44.0	35.7	NA	1,504	3,815	251	3,564	30,955	55.3	9.6
Casa Grande	17,516	3.15	70.8	47.2	15.8	29.2	23.6	280	2,028	3,900	546	3,354	37,500	52.5	16.5
Chandler	91,671	2.75	66.8	50.7	11.4	33.2	25.3	933	6,710	2,523	210	2,313	169,500	25.5	43.8
El Mirage	12,077	2.92	70.2	42.9	22.3	29.8	27.3	NA	1,126	3,276	215	3,060	23,904	54.2	12.3
Flagstaff	24,493	2.44	49.5	35.8	10.2	50.5	32.8	12,320	3,121	4,385	372	4,012	37,338	18.6	49.6
Florence	4,630	2.70	70.7	49.3	10.1	29.3	27.3	13,581	173	556	71	485	21,495	58.1	11.9
Gilbert	81,415	2.97	71.6	58.6	9.7	28.4	20.2	511	3,603	1,408	81	1,327	151,505	21.0	42.8
Glendale	79,570	3.05	67.0	42.9	16.6	33.0	26.1	3,888	14,009	5,766	496	5,271	153,246	47.7	20.9
Goodyear	25,532	2.98	77.6	63.1	9.4	22.4	17.1	3,801	2,373	2,893	378	2,515	54,186	31.2	34.1
Kingman	11,141	2.53	68.4	44.2	15.1	31.6	26.4	1,268	1,581	5,439	347	5,091	20,375	48.5	17.9
Lake Havasu City	25,132	2.16	64.9	56.3	5.5	35.1	26.6	227	1,359	2,529	262	2,266	45,522	45.5	16.0
Marana	15,612	2.82	75.5	64.9	6.9	24.5	16.8	NA	1,085	2,535	93	2,441	28,601	17.1	44.5
Maricopa	16,342	2.94	66.3	58.1	5.0	33.7	29.0	NA	745	1,501	195	1,306	31,448	39.7	23.3
Mesa	177,276	2.78	65.8	47.7	13.2	34.2	27.7	3,787	13,265	2,773	429	2,345	326,533	35.4	28.2
Oro Valley	19,266	2.30	69.4	60.9	6.3	30.6	24.7	NA	682	1,547	66	1,481	33,549	17.7	57.3
Peoria	62,112	2.68	67.8	53.7	10.2	32.2	27.6	1,409	4,059	2,322	200	2,122	116,927	31.0	33.7
Phoenix	559,155	2.87	63.6	42.1	14.5	36.4	28.3	18,916	69,252	4,365	674	3,690	1,038,987	41.2	28.4
Prescott	18,647	2.16	62.6	54.8	5.2	37.4	27.9	2,435	1,094	2,585	402	2,183	32,979	24.6	35.3
Prescott Valley	18,313	2.42	67.9	53.6	11.0	32.1	27.0	231	1,072	2,499	182	2,317	33,085	44.7	17.7
Queen Creek	12,358	3.17	77.2	71.7	2.9	22.8	19.3	NA	NA	NA	NA	NA	24,323	27.4	34.9
Sahuarita	10,558	2.77	75.4	56.5	8.2	24.6	22.0	NA	398	1,543	89	1,454	19,884	21.2	41.2
San Luis	7,936	3.84	90.6	68.0	13.3	9.4	9.4	1,934	466	1,446	121	1,325	18,839	71.8	4.8
Scottsdale	110,192	2.25	56.7	46.3	6.6	43.3	33.8	1,822	6,067	2,519	153	2,365	191,521	15.9	56.8
Sierra Vista	17,819	2.27	63.0	48.7	12.8	37.0	31.2	2,383	1,363	3,171	198	2,973	29,448	24.0	31.7
Surprise	50,799	2.63	73.5	62.7	8.3	26.5	21.1	371	2,624	2,008	103	1,905	98,930	33.7	27.0
Tempe	70,555	2.49	45.2	29.5	9.0	54.8	36.1	9,607	9,046	5,063	505	4,559	114,154	26.6	42.6
Tucson	211,560	2.40	54.8	33.6	14.6	45.2	34.2	27,016	35,510	6,654	795	5,859	341,440	37.5	27.7
Yuma	35,353	2.63	75.8	48.8	20.4	24.2	20.1	2,687	3,722	2,388	338	2,051	58,286	48.0	18.2
ARKANSAS	1,153,082	2.53	65.5	47.9	12.8	34.5	29.1	84,942	114,134	3,819	551	3,269	2,008,398	47.3	23.4
Bella Vista	12,174	2.33	71.0	66.3	4.7	29.0	23.4	NA	259	916	233	683	22,716	30.2	31.4
Benton	13,447	2.63	63.9	46.0	12.8	36.1	31.2	487	1,728	4,948	507	4,442	23,745	37.5	27.9
Bentonville	18,071	2.68	68.6	61.4	5.6	31.4	23.7	808	755	1,625	187	1,438	32,024	24.3	54.5
Conway	24,623	2.49	63.4	44.0	14.2	36.6	29.6	4,518	3,315	5,015	511	4,504	37,388	30.8	44.6
Fayetteville	34,393	2.27	51.3	33.4	9.7	48.7	33.5	7,207	4,194	4,950	542	4,408	45,087	24.1	49.4
Fort Smith	34,903	2.48	58.4	41.1	11.0	41.6	34.6	1,592	5,943	6,710	806	5,904	58,333	49.2	20.4
Hot Springs	14,008	2.51	50.1	36.6	8.5	49.9	42.9	1,814	3,170	8,876	778	8,097	24,738	47.2	18.4

1. No spouse present.   2. Data for serious crimes have not been adjusted for underreporting. This may affect comparability between geographic areas and over time.   3. Per 100,000 population estimated by the FBI.   4. Persons 25 years old and over.

City	Money income, 2017					Median earnings, 2017			Housing units, 2017				
	Households												
	Median income	Percent with income less than $20,000	Percent with income of $200,000 or more	Median family income	Median non-family income	All persons	Men	Women	Total	Occupied	Percent owner occupied	Median value[1] (dollars)	Median gross rent (dollars)
	42	43	44	45	46	47	48	49	50	51	52	53	54
United States	60,336	15.5	6.9	73,891	35,980	33,646	40,228	28,737	137,407,308	120,062,818	63.9	217,600	1,012
ALABAMA	48,123	21.3	3.6	61,512	26,647	30,528	36,713	24,616	2,258,669	1,841,665	68.0	141,300	750
Alabaster	69,741	5.7	3.8	80,541	58,693	36,991	39,012	32,268	11,320	10,888	85.9	166,600	1,111
Auburn	51,832	22.3	6.2	101,720	25,617	18,979	21,744	11,849	29,299	23,506	46.8	261,000	830
Bessemer	29,482	37.4	0.5	35,643	24,058	20,953	21,175	20,190	14,025	10,068	47.4	81,200	690
Birmingham	33,553	30.7	2.2	43,931	24,261	24,560	27,218	22,404	114,102	90,186	44.7	87,800	790
Decatur	47,811	18.3	3.2	62,172	24,857	24,589	30,017	21,578	25,236	22,205	67.2	141,400	630
Dothan	44,280	21.6	4.3	60,237	28,066	30,831	36,331	24,686	30,274	25,192	59.3	156,800	712
Enterprise	62,248	14.0	3.8	68,152	42,489	38,567	49,206	27,152	12,584	11,695	57.9	198,000	855
Florence	38,486	25.9	3.1	57,502	21,429	23,297	28,460	21,037	19,815	17,277	50.2	137,700	632
Gadsden	24,462	43.3	0.4	44,159	16,289	20,573	22,277	19,251	19,554	14,445	64.0	62,100	553
Homewood	84,390	6.4	13.2	108,023	51,322	41,989	60,966	30,884	11,501	9,755	70.5	331,000	1,065
Hoover	84,054	7.7	13.1	107,358	46,004	44,915	51,598	37,200	37,695	34,058	67.3	283,500	1,075
Huntsville	50,704	21.8	6.3	73,415	31,350	31,058	40,375	24,205	92,769	84,750	55.1	170,900	777
Madison	78,668	8.0	10.8	108,408	49,865	52,694	65,587	36,824	21,592	20,343	71.3	246,900	950
Mobile	40,316	29.3	3.7	57,261	24,671	30,484	34,136	26,429	93,985	78,145	52.8	124,800	797
Montgomery	42,419	24.6	3.4	54,342	30,056	25,504	29,050	22,547	92,631	78,217	54.7	119,500	827
Opelika	47,468	19.5	0.4	58,230	32,714	27,357	32,126	25,315	13,713	12,328	70.0	135,800	691
Phenix City	35,461	35.5	2.0	42,241	17,083	31,525	35,043	25,343	16,111	14,296	52.1	117,300	759
Prattville	52,090	19.4	4.8	64,879	37,353	30,453	38,386	20,911	14,425	13,638	56.7	178,200	968
Tuscaloosa	47,243	24.5	4.1	60,652	28,132	21,638	25,790	20,192	48,587	36,209	47.5	170,500	826
Vestavia Hills	101,233	6.3	19.6	134,257	37,066	51,380	75,006	40,722	14,459	13,054	72.7	381,900	1,327
ALASKA	73,181	10.2	7.3	86,831	48,441	37,326	43,350	31,734	316,968	250,741	63.5	273,100	1,201
Anchorage	79,166	7.3	8.8	91,590	53,445	41,094	45,460	36,456	117,298	107,373	58.5	320,000	1,291
Fairbanks	65,514	6.8	3.7	76,613	46,034	32,085	38,040	27,701	12,704	9,901	44.4	187,500	1,305
Juneau	92,310	8.9	11.4	111,891	56,156	45,647	47,436	42,999	13,732	12,429	64.6	379,400	1,092
ARIZONA	56,581	15.5	5.4	67,886	36,607	31,651	35,887	28,139	2,999,185	2,552,972	64.7	223,400	1,020
Apache Junction	44,110	20.5	0.7	56,454	28,719	22,497	27,143	20,863	22,653	16,761	81.8	83,300	698
Avondale	55,468	14.3	2.5	58,793	35,814	31,351	35,541	27,502	28,072	26,223	60.1	207,300	1,126
Buckeye	74,970	8.4	2.5	79,842	48,971	31,361	32,378	30,259	20,815	18,135	77.9	216,400	1,241
Bullhead City	38,207	20.1	1.3	46,192	25,940	25,089	25,134	25,060	25,725	18,135	57.8	129,100	774
Casa Grande	50,435	19.0	1.9	54,463	28,372	24,784	26,639	22,262	21,133	17,516	59.2	139,200	854
Chandler	76,860	7.5	10.1	96,757	51,482	42,670	50,335	38,212	97,629	91,671	65.4	292,800	1,254
El Mirage	53,275	12.0	0.2	54,850	37,605	31,533	37,012	28,750	13,555	12,077	55.5	153,200	1,198
Flagstaff	56,059	16.4	5.6	82,281	35,193	21,168	26,172	14,739	28,956	24,493	51.6	344,600	1,300
Florence	43,434	15.1	1.8	46,284	28,082	17,037	15,271	25,710	6,772	4,630	77.5	128,200	704
Gilbert	84,699	6.2	9.1	99,024	50,020	43,531	51,645	37,331	87,145	81,415	70.5	320,000	1,384
Glendale	53,753	18.0	3.9	63,779	33,969	29,755	31,775	26,089	86,539	79,570	52.4	220,600	974
Goodyear	87,481	6.8	9.4	95,977	52,739	39,099	48,667	31,281	29,103	25,532	76.9	298,900	1,359
Kingman	45,760	18.8	1.8	53,660	21,485	27,235	26,291	30,202	12,822	11,141	68.8	146,600	789
Lake Havasu City	53,440	19.8	3.4	68,539	28,876	28,065	28,645	27,077	32,130	25,132	72.2	248,100	836
Marana	78,869	6.1	5.7	95,038	50,582	38,165	46,390	31,403	18,223	15,612	85.1	251,100	1,110
Maricopa	58,508	13.8	4.6	72,596	40,947	40,741	45,085	35,494	20,274	16,342	81.0	197,500	1,214
Mesa	55,014	13.7	4.1	67,826	37,200	30,910	35,388	26,873	208,391	177,276	61.6	224,700	1,003
Oro Valley	74,661	8.6	11.2	91,347	47,265	46,140	56,978	35,180	22,227	19,266	73.9	300,500	1,221
Peoria	72,142	11.6	6.4	89,730	40,927	39,324	46,761	32,193	69,003	62,112	76.3	255,800	1,155
Phoenix	56,696	14.0	5.6	65,509	40,490	31,917	34,625	30,162	618,561	559,155	56.1	231,000	1,013
Prescott	61,428	11.0	3.9	82,216	38,562	31,104	34,169	27,069	20,987	18,647	69.2	331,000	892
Prescott Valley	50,245	16.4	0.4	57,218	29,205	26,884	30,838	21,919	20,150	18,313	66.1	244,900	968
Queen Creek	96,802	6.3	8.6	101,904	0	46,926	65,644	33,690	14,322	12,358	87.9	363,200	1,455
Sahuarita	79,534	10.5	3.8	84,554	49,334	37,058	50,264	30,779	11,509	10,558	89.3	207,200	1,093
San Luis	46,783	25.8	1.1	48,774	0	19,308	21,548	14,555	8,604	7,936	65.0	117,000	686
Scottsdale	88,407	10.0	17.3	108,728	62,292	50,851	60,138	42,443	133,883	110,192	66.2	473,300	1,315
Sierra Vista	61,121	12.6	2.6	75,258	43,566	34,378	42,971	23,985	21,080	17,819	56.1	183,800	957
Surprise	65,898	8.0	3.7	75,230	39,439	36,025	41,333	32,183	58,397	50,799	74.2	231,900	1,268
Tempe	51,986	19.7	4.6	70,224	40,868	30,516	32,011	28,261	79,710	70,555	39.1	266,900	1,182
Tucson	41,613	24.4	2.0	51,296	29,361	24,586	26,517	22,261	238,999	211,560	51.1	150,400	817
Yuma	50,195	20.8	2.2	55,610	23,340	29,843	35,073	24,387	40,828	35,353	61.5	143,400	904
ARKANSAS	45,869	20.6	3.0	57,421	25,188	30,050	34,561	25,470	1,370,109	1,153,082	65.3	128,500	711
Bella Vista	65,782	9.2	4.7	79,034	23,836	36,299	42,427	30,016	12,904	12,174	90.8	163,400	961
Benton	52,070	16.0	1.9	70,761	32,432	34,119	42,585	31,314	14,934	13,447	68.1	147,100	773
Bentonville	82,596	8.5	11.1	101,915	49,119	50,227	61,592	38,821	19,060	18,071	48.5	236,100	970
Conway	43,182	19.3	4.2	58,860	27,614	26,920	28,148	26,306	27,328	24,623	47.5	178,800	778
Fayetteville	42,365	23.8	4.9	63,401	24,763	27,273	31,424	23,317	37,431	34,393	38.5	218,300	732
Fort Smith	38,294	19.9	2.4	53,167	25,509	26,758	31,112	22,282	38,998	34,903	50.1	121,900	619
Hot Springs	36,349	29.1	2.3	65,548	21,807	23,949	30,038	20,176	19,064	14,008	53.4	112,100	677

1. Specified owner-occupied units. $2,000,000 represents $2,000,000 or more.

Table D. Cities — Commuting, Computer Access, Migration, Labor Force, and Employment

City	Commuting[1], 2017		Computer access[2], 2017		Migration, 2017		Civilian labor force, 2018				Civilian employment[4], 2017			
	Percent		Percent						Unemployment		Population age 16 and older		Population age 16 to 64	
	Commuting	With commutes of 30 minutes or more	With a computer in the house	With Internet access	Percent who lived in the same house one year ago	Percent who lived in another state or county one year ago	Total	Percent change 2017-2018	Total	Rate[3]	Number	Percent in labor force	Number	Percent who worked full-year full-time
	55	56	57	58	59	60	61	62	63	64	65	66	67	68
United States	76.4	38.5	90.8	83.1	85.7	6.2	161,640,240	0.9	6,296,296	3.9	260,564,248	63.2	209,748,536	50.8
ALABAMA	85.7	34.1	86.1	77.5	86.3	5.7	2,198,837	0.9	86,490	3.9	3,906,384	56.5	3,103,168	47.3
Alabaster	85.4	52.1	98.0	92.6	85.8	8.2	18,007	1.4	499	2.8	24,506	69.5	21,197	56.3
Auburn	79.8	22.7	96.5	89.3	79.3	13.1	29,732	1.5	1,118	3.8	54,805	53.8	48,027	36.6
Bessemer	75.7	42.7	75.1	63.2	NA	NA	9,744	0.9	506	5.2	21,563	50.9	16,738	33.8
Birmingham	78.9	28.1	83.9	72.7	78.5	5.9	92,365	1.1	4,252	4.6	174,925	60.5	143,247	44.6
Decatur	89.8	20.6	87.9	78.1	86.2	7.8	26,491	2.5	972	3.7	44,726	56.5	34,585	47.4
Dothan	87.4	20.2	85.1	80.1	85.7	5.4	29,441	1.0	1,202	4.1	52,515	58.7	41,442	48.9
Enterprise	89.4	24.5	88.4	81.3	72.7	17.0	10,894	-0.1	448	4.1	23,183	61.9	18,979	52.6
Florence	85.4	13.5	86.1	75.8	70.6	11.7	18,125	0.3	767	4.2	33,372	58.0	25,373	43.9
Gadsden	87.2	13.6	76.6	68.9	83.5	4.8	13,465	0.0	663	4.9	28,512	44.1	20,952	34.9
Homewood	83.6	11.2	96.9	95.4	83.2	8.0	14,120	1.4	376	2.7	20,195	70.2	17,349	51.9
Hoover	82.4	35.4	97.2	94.7	80.6	8.6	45,038	1.5	1,273	2.8	68,116	68.6	53,118	56.7
Huntsville	86.1	19.9	91.1	85.7	78.6	7.9	96,290	2.2	3,538	3.7	157,874	63.2	126,760	51.2
Madison	87.4	24.5	96.4	92.3	86.1	6.0	25,278	2.1	750	3.0	40,360	64.1	33,010	58.4
Mobile	85.8	27.4	86.0	75.6	87.1	3.5	85,885	0.5	4,368	5.1	155,930	56.7	126,623	47.3
Montgomery	84.9	18.1	87.7	75.8	78.0	7.8	92,200	-0.2	3,775	4.1	157,881	58.4	129,426	43.2
Opelika	NA	9.8	86.7	80.3	86.3	6.5	14,103	1.8	548	3.9	24,657	61.1	18,884	52.8
Phenix City	84.9	21.7	91.2	76.4	81.9	10.9	15,242	1.7	576	3.8	27,389	56.6	23,584	38.1
Prattville	87.1	28.2	88.9	85.7	86.0	10.0	17,041	0.1	608	3.6	28,954	61.3	24,242	49.5
Tuscaloosa	83.3	13.3	89.1	77.4	73.3	13.2	46,616	1.6	2,008	4.3	84,047	56.7	73,284	41.3
Vestavia Hills	83.5	23.4	93.6	90.1	84.1	5.9	17,783	1.5	450	2.5	26,255	68.4	21,055	55.8
ALASKA	69.3	18.4	94.2	85.9	81.5	7.4	356,886	-1.1	23,511	6.6	573,196	68.0	490,155	48.7
Anchorage	76.7	17.2	95.9	90.2	79.2	7.5	151,950	-1.2	8,348	5.5	228,778	72.6	197,817	55.5
Fairbanks	74.7	8.9	92.4	86.5	73.8	10.5	12,352	-0.7	881	7.1	24,293	68.0	20,860	52.0
Juneau	60.7	9.0	96.1	91.7	81.2	6.5	17,232	-0.3	762	4.4	25,845	68.0	22,072	44.6
ARIZONA	76.5	37.3	92.2	85.2	82.4	6.3	3,439,755	3.4	166,205	4.8	5,571,583	59.9	4,370,733	49.5
Apache Junction	81.3	48.7	89.0	74.5	80.4	12.3	15,281	3.5	916	6.0	36,370	39.4	22,452	35.0
Avondale	77.7	47.0	93.6	84.1	83.3	5.7	44,688	4.1	2,014	4.5	62,741	68.9	55,033	53.4
Buckeye	80.7	51.2	94.9	90.6	80.6	5.3	28,653	4.0	1,475	5.1	52,374	56.5	44,507	47.7
Bullhead City	76.0	18.7	86.8	75.3	83.6	5.8	17,055	3.6	1,012	5.9	33,510	48.8	21,268	43.7
Casa Grande	82.3	32.4	92.9	85.4	80.5	10.6	25,051	3.7	1,320	5.3	43,913	58.1	33,339	44.6
Chandler	79.4	34.6	96.5	92.0	80.6	6.3	149,563	3.9	5,513	3.7	196,777	70.3	166,934	58.3
El Mirage	80.6	43.8	91.5	85.2	81.6	4.1	16,834	4.0	773	4.6	27,474	65.8	23,349	50.8
Flagstaff	72.0	10.0	94.5	82.9	67.0	19.8	43,123	2.0	1,677	3.9	60,069	69.0	53,203	36.9
Florence	NA	41.8	92.9	88.7	77.0	16.1	3,609	3.9	196	5.4	23,474	14.9	18,591	13.0
Gilbert	80.6	45.0	98.3	95.7	80.2	6.8	138,244	3.9	4,788	3.5	181,595	70.8	159,517	55.4
Glendale	77.8	48.0	92.3	81.1	80.9	4.3	125,036	3.8	5,490	4.4	188,399	64.7	161,172	50.7
Goodyear	76.2	45.8	97.7	90.2	84.3	6.9	39,304	3.9	1,663	4.2	63,056	60.9	51,430	55.5
Kingman	NA	13.2	95.8	91.6	62.8	15.4	13,438	3.2	704	5.2	23,235	48.2	16,612	46.4
Lake Havasu City	69.7	11.7	90.0	81.9	83.9	7.6	24,709	3.6	1,337	5.4	49,754	44.2	30,352	47.0
Marana	86.4	61.1	97.6	96.6	85.0	5.9	23,162	1.9	802	3.5	34,725	62.3	26,999	56.0
Maricopa	77.3	66.1	95.1	88.0	81.9	11.6	24,981	3.6	1,157	4.6	36,484	60.4	29,195	54.5
Mesa	75.4	35.7	94.1	87.9	81.0	6.2	252,652	4.0	10,473	4.1	383,655	64.6	305,420	53.1
Oro Valley	82.4	45.8	95.7	90.9	77.0	9.3	19,742	2.0	856	4.3	37,586	49.0	23,114	50.3
Peoria	77.8	48.1	95.0	90.8	84.9	4.6	89,861	4.0	3,584	4.0	136,190	64.5	108,221	54.4
Phoenix	74.1	39.6	91.7	84.1	84.9	3.7	840,443	3.9	35,737	4.3	1,246,705	67.3	1,072,325	53.0
Prescott	76.6	12.8	95.3	90.2	88.5	7.0	18,418	3.4	920	5.0	37,884	42.0	22,939	40.1
Prescott Valley	81.8	17.4	92.5	84.4	80.6	14.8	22,136	3.4	892	4.0	35,909	50.9	23,942	42.6
Queen Creek	72.4	55.0	NA	NA	75.7	9.8	20,185	4.1	710	3.5	28,189	67.5	24,401	52.6
Sahuarita	83.8	60.3	96.0	93.0	85.6	10.1	12,642	1.8	474	3.7	21,959	57.7	15,830	52.2
San Luis	75.5	52.2	86.5	82.6	NA	NA	17,928	2.6	6,777	37.8	23,816	57.0	21,337	40.8
Scottsdale	74.1	31.2	97.0	93.2	80.8	7.2	145,902	4.0	5,144	3.5	212,383	63.1	156,386	55.9
Sierra Vista	72.9	18.8	94.8	90.3	75.6	13.3	18,362	0.8	919	5.0	33,363	60.0	24,357	57.3
Surprise	80.8	43.4	95.0	91.1	89.8	4.2	57,884	4.1	2,701	4.7	111,809	58.6	77,947	56.3
Tempe	72.6	21.6	96.2	87.4	73.4	7.4	114,042	3.9	4,353	3.8	159,413	68.6	141,163	49.1
Tucson	73.6	28.3	92.0	84.2	74.7	7.4	260,618	2.0	12,258	4.7	435,409	61.2	357,241	43.5
Yuma	85.7	13.8	89.0	84.0	82.6	7.0	44,987	2.0	4,981	11.1	73,417	59.9	58,584	52.7
ARKANSAS	83.3	27.1	86.3	72.5	84.5	6.9	1,351,496	0.3	50,037	3.7	2,375,324	58.0	1,878,300	49.6
Bella Vista	83.9	42.4	99.5	77.7	84.2	8.7	12,230	1.6	474	3.9	24,378	53.2	15,619	58.6
Benton	89.5	44.0	90.9	85.4	82.2	7.4	17,182	0.4	541	3.1	28,310	65.4	23,184	62.7
Bentonville	87.6	13.4	95.2	59.5	78.6	9.3	26,102	1.1	682	2.6	36,937	69.9	31,858	66.6
Conway	84.2	26.3	90.0	80.7	86.5	6.9	33,532	0.1	1,076	3.2	53,067	64.1	46,354	47.2
Fayetteville	74.2	20.6	96.4	88.2	69.4	16.0	47,325	1.5	1,277	2.7	69,511	64.5	61,371	44.0
Fort Smith	79.0	8.6	87.3	78.2	80.2	8.1	39,604	-0.2	1,438	3.6	70,878	62.8	58,814	49.4
Hot Springs	70.4	16.4	85.1	74.0	81.4	10.3	14,569	1.3	679	4.7	29,737	51.0	22,283	43.4

1. Employed persons.   2. Households.   3. Percent of civilian labor force.   4. Persons 16 years old and over.

Table D. Cities — Construction, Wholesale Trade, and Retail Trade

City	Value of residential construction authorized by building permits, 2018			Wholesale trade[1], 2012				Retail trade[2], 2012			
	New construction ($1,000)	Number of housing units	Percent single family	Number of establishments	Number of employees	Sales (mil dol)	Annual payroll (mil dol)	Number of establishments	Number of employees	Sales (mil dol)	Annual payroll (mil dol)
	69	70	71	72	73	74	75	76	77	78	79
United States	271,119,545	1,328,827	64.4	355,983	4,880,666	5,208,023.5	287,549.6	1,062,083	14,703,529	4,219,821.9	369,001.4
ALABAMA	3,046,657	14,824	87.5	4,600	60,332	57,746.6	2,894.7	18,211	218,531	58,565.0	5,123.1
Alabaster	19,967	65	100.0	44	579	489.1	26.3	92	1,773	388.8	39.2
Auburn	176,970	678	86.0	34	217	235.5	9.0	206	3,180	779.4	70.4
Bessemer	6,071	37	100.0	58	944	417.9	52.0	194	2,746	732.0	70.4
Birmingham	34,316	250	26.4	500	9,168	7,099.9	481.8	943	12,300	3,305.9	318.1
Decatur	11,530	58	100.0	77	1,316	1,022.6	56.7	332	4,256	1,140.4	99.1
Dothan	54,606	231	76.2	148	D	D	D	501	7,114	1,990.0	173.0
Enterprise	15,748	90	94.4	11	38	13.6	1.4	155	1,802	521.3	47.9
Florence	12,204	150	46.0	49	584	209.3	22.4	302	4,139	967.8	88.7
Gadsden	1,470	16	100.0	39	351	293.5	14.5	229	3,037	731.2	60.6
Homewood	17,644	42	100.0	65	775	499.4	42.2	224	3,152	662.1	76.7
Hoover	142,287	312	100.0	80	1,134	2,347.7	102.5	384	7,578	2,425.7	200.6
Huntsville	84,276	1,312	94.6	225	3,051	3,197.3	168.8	999	14,677	3,945.3	360.9
Madison	139,038	408	100.0	52	728	426.2	39.6	131	2,356	550.6	52.7
Mobile	26,466	126	84.1	353	4,191	2,717.6	205.9	968	14,109	3,661.5	339.7
Montgomery	35,683	241	100.0	274	4,739	3,703.7	214.7	874	11,871	3,163.3	294.6
Opelika	61,939	258	100.0	32	373	261.3	18.4	206	2,732	725.2	58.3
Phenix City	24,762	165	50.3	10	D	D	D	125	1,683	413.4	36.8
Prattville	56,148	185	100.0	19	84	33.2	2.7	152	2,669	621.9	60.7
Tuscaloosa	184,087	822	42.9	77	955	638.5	48.4	475	6,821	1,782.8	149.8
Vestavia Hills	43,087	88	100.0	39	220	213.9	14.5	156	1,659	396.1	43.3
ALASKA	429,020	1,677	73.2	638	7,734	5,216.3	440.9	2,508	33,721	10,474.3	977.4
Anchorage	306,813	1,083	80.2	336	5,228	3,147.7	296.6	860	15,253	4,966.8	462.2
Fairbanks	0	0	0.0	47	531	309.2	29.6	208	3,630	1,300.3	116.3
Juneau	NA	NA	NA	36	265	196.9	12.8	142	1,821	491.4	53.0
ARIZONA	9,727,722	41,664	77.1	5,570	73,496	69,437.3	4,144.3	17,479	286,184	84,716.5	7,367.8
Apache Junction	17,961	163	68.1	11	D	D	D	90	1,591	515.0	41.0
Avondale	55,801	232	100.0	15	161	73.6	8.2	113	3,480	1,360.9	107.5
Buckeye	565,473	2,194	100.0	15	106	71.4	4.9	50	597	260.8	14.1
Bullhead City	37,581	161	100.0	9	64	26.3	2.4	119	2,195	552.0	52.5
Casa Grande	61,795	252	100.0	25	403	196.3	17.9	190	3,440	896.6	75.4
Chandler	303,418	1,331	37.0	228	4,007	5,269.8	257.8	658	13,607	4,225.0	382.5
El Mirage	1,449	4	100.0	4	36	16.5	1.3	26	498	117.5	12.0
Flagstaff	73,331	375	98.9	68	554	377.7	26.2	322	5,224	1,383.9	120.5
Florence	68,362	233	100.0	1	D	D	D	12	142	39.9	3.1
Gilbert	352,256	1,789	81.6	143	1,264	666.2	63.7	470	9,470	2,762.7	251.0
Glendale	49,156	191	100.0	118	1,188	834.2	47.7	674	12,710	3,821.3	320.8
Goodyear	383,875	1,332	93.5	23	D	D	D	141	3,318	788.1	74.7
Kingman	45,881	274	96.7	22	211	115.2	7.7	128	2,586	896.1	59.8
Lake Havasu City	77,586	425	84.9	48	223	86.2	9.0	215	2,843	914.5	71.1
Marana	287,264	1,108	74.7	20	108	41.2	5.1	114	2,868	865.1	73.1
Maricopa	239,692	988	100.0	7	16	4.6	0.6	26	729	213.8	16.1
Mesa	805,825	2,919	91.1	292	3,313	2,705.3	168.9	1,315	22,342	5,819.7	549.5
Oro Valley	92,591	331	94.0	23	57	52.4	3.6	90	2,092	496.7	46.5
Peoria	239,051	1,428	87.2	60	289	266.3	12.7	387	8,515	2,657.7	235.0
Phoenix	1,472,958	7,262	51.4	1,853	30,877	31,193.7	1,638.2	3,712	60,797	18,448.4	1,620.7
Prescott	155,605	692	51.9	62	557	453.8	29.8	279	4,290	1,030.2	102.4
Prescott Valley	141,152	540	91.9	31	430	305.1	15.7	100	1,348	360.2	32.2
Queen Creek	485,293	1,296	100.0	7	14	5.0	0.6	50	973	227.1	20.0
Sahuarita	99,281	366	100.0	3	D	D	D	23	730	192.6	16.4
San Luis	43,584	294	100.0	8	233	36.1	11.0	36	591	136.0	10.2
Scottsdale	389,108	1,179	52.6	505	4,707	4,011.1	311.5	1,218	18,728	5,848.1	574.5
Sierra Vista	12,407	68	100.0	12	86	25.4	2.4	160	2,810	686.5	63.9
Surprise	414,651	1,415	92.9	27	401	159.2	16.0	169	4,396	1,137.0	105.7
Tempe	315,215	1,760	7.0	436	8,635	8,373.2	562.7	755	14,805	7,231.6	431.6
Tucson	301,151	1,540	44.2	446	4,468	2,221.8	192.0	1,883	30,599	7,878.2	774.0
Yuma	85,191	487	99.6	80	1,615	963.8	67.0	302	5,503	1,528.9	132.8
ARKANSAS	1,829,441	10,179	72.2	2,884	34,492	31,256.1	1,630.8	10,923	135,448	36,815.3	3,061.5
Bella Vista	67,927	260	100.0	12	20	21.6	0.9	25	307	60.7	5.8
Benton	32,506	150	98.7	23	138	130.1	5.6	127	1,859	659.5	46.2
Bentonville	299,922	1,805	28.2	86	1,135	1,338.4	79.1	119	2,488	1,024.2	68.7
Conway	53,658	329	64.7	57	618	460.6	27.8	284	4,730	1,246.1	100.9
Fayetteville	179,302	701	100.0	54	550	372.7	25.1	419	7,043	1,766.8	156.5
Fort Smith	49,677	269	72.5	171	2,184	1,605.2	98.1	521	7,161	1,767.6	157.2
Hot Springs	14,887	90	55.6	43	409	151.5	14.7	364	4,655	1,242.1	108.3

1. Merchant wholesalers except manufacturers' sales branches and offices. 2. Establishments with payroll.

Table D. Cities — Real Estate, Professional Services, and Manufacturing

City	Real estate and rental and leasing, 2012				Professional, scientific, and technical services[1], 2012				Manufacturing, 2012			
	Number of establishments	Number of employees	Receipts (mil dol)	Annual payroll (mil dol)	Number of establishments	Number of employees	Receipts (mil dol)	Annual payroll (mil dol)	Number of establishments	Number of employees	Receipts (mil dol)	Annual payroll (mil dol)
	80	81	82	83	84	85	86	87	88	89	90	91
United States	354,106	1,923,770	487,655.2	85,326.0	851,542	7,997,617	1,440,060.5	566,412.5	297,191	11,214,165	5,696,729.6	593,397.0
ALABAMA........................	3,858	22,852	3,919.4	819.6	9,062	88,566	16,043.5	5,633.1	4,283	232,650	124,809.8	11,099.5
Alabaster........................	17	54	11.1	1.8	58	528	119.8	20.0	26	1,145	478.6	63.1
Auburn............................	54	299	45.0	8.5	125	1,074	102.4	44.3	60	3,523	D	141.7
Bessemer........................	27	159	26.3	6.6	72	D	D	D	41	1,549	466.6	70.1
Birmingham.....................	281	3,076	417.2	129.1	834	D	D	D	249	10,654	4,118.4	568.2
Decatur...........................	57	218	43.9	6.7	139	978	110.2	44.0	82	4,735	4,680.9	284.7
Dothan............................	94	D	D	D	192	D	D	D	78	D	1,285.1	D
Enterprise.......................	40	198	19.6	4.1	49	425	74.3	21.0	18	844	D	32.6
Florence..........................	77	309	47.2	9.1	134	D	D	D	53	2,616	631.6	82.3
Gadsden	39	182	34.3	5.0	99	1,065	55.2	29.2	48	3,839	1,058.2	162.3
Homewood.......................	59	362	70.9	17.5	157	1,291	225.2	76.1	24	1,121	564.1	55.4
Hoover	95	675	274.1	36.2	281	D	D	D	25	345	49.7	13.1
Huntsville	311	D	D	D	999	28,634	6,933.7	2,324.3	173	13,598	6,213.8	771.4
Madison	56	266	48.8	8.9	150	D	D	D	32	977	D	48.4
Mobile	310	1,554	312.4	60.4	701	D	D	D	152	8,817	3,274.4	471.1
Montgomery.....................	219	1,890	339.1	64.8	575	5,871	1,258.6	386.5	172	10,902	9,125.1	528.6
Opelika...........................	40	149	17.8	4.0	62	D	D	D	34	2,067	D	93.7
Phenix City.....................	34	95	16.7	2.5	46	170	16.6	4.4	31	D	1,110.6	113.0
Prattville	35	138	20.4	3.9	54	276	28.7	10.8	15	839	651.5	54.1
Tuscaloosa......................	124	1,192	129.1	35.8	232	1,584	260.5	78.4	53	4,454	4,234.8	221.7
Vestavia Hills..................	81	1,191	389.9	73.2	173	D	D	D	15	47	D	1.9
ALASKA	872	4,212	1,022.7	187.6	1,866	17,328	3,140.3	1,163.5	527	12,450	D	514.5
Anchorage.......................	383	2,403	631.3	112.1	1,128	13,444	2,515.7	954.8	182	2,049	479.8	95.7
Fairbanks........................	88	468	116.2	25.1	137	D	D	D	37	239	D	10.7
Juneau	61	249	42.2	7.0	86	D	D	D	26	236	75.4	11.7
ARIZONA.........................	8,089	40,479	9,329.7	1,693.2	16,112	119,843	19,041.9	7,272.6	4,269	131,941	51,243.5	8,193.2
Apache Junction	40	141	22.6	2.6	22	76	7.6	2.2	13	85	D	3.5
Avondale.........................	42	118	15.7	3.1	47	197	14.8	5.4	9	29	12.9	1.5
Buckeye..........................	19	59	9.6	2.0	37	196	32.4	10.6	11	203	D	6.4
Bullhead City...................	52	187	20.0	4.5	45	D	D	D	6	39	D	1.3
Casa Grande...................	52	198	39.6	5.6	59	D	D	D	37	1,753	1,807.3	96.5
Chandler.........................	304	896	252.4	34.7	642	3,678	535.3	203.9	165	7,413	2,535.2	459.9
El Mirage........................	10	D	D	D	7	18	2.4	0.4	13	251	74.4	12.3
Flagstaff.........................	129	450	101.0	16.3	249	D	D	D	58	3,453	2,006.0	287.8
Florence	4	D	D	D	8	23	1.4	0.8	NA	NA	NA	NA
Gilbert	292	787	170.2	33.4	533	D	D	D	118	1,887	338.2	84.8
Glendale.........................	215	820	160.3	26.3	308	D	D	D	134	2,988	829.9	156.5
Goodyear........................	62	136	25.4	4.4	88	480	48.3	24.1	22	1,220	384.0	58.7
Kingman..........................	35	94	14.4	2.6	48	D	D	D	11	133	47.4	5.1
Lake Havasu City.............	80	277	38.8	6.6	96	319	26.2	9.5	65	916	217.3	34.4
Marana...........................	31	81	12.7	2.8	57	D	D	D	30	1,028	344.7	59.1
Maricopa.........................	15	29	4.7	0.7	38	94	6.4	4.0	11	148	D	6.4
Mesa..............................	547	2,280	456.6	72.6	1,021	5,199	668.1	255.6	245	7,319	3,353.0	583.2
Oro Valley	60	D	D	D	123	447	49.3	36.5	10	2,279	803.0	215.5
Peoria.............................	156	621	111.0	20.1	219	D	D	D	49	874	177.8	36.4
Phoenix..........................	1,894	13,507	2,965.5	673.8	4,848	43,895	7,794.4	2,992.6	1,338	38,642	12,978.9	2,175.5
Prescott..........................	127	254	52.5	7.3	218	D	D	D	61	1,457	404.8	76.0
Prescott Valley	36	99	21.8	4.0	42	336	43.9	21.0	31	603	149.6	24.3
Queen Creek....................	24	D	D	D	52	136	13.3	4.6	5	27	D	1.3
Sahuarita........................	10	17	2.7	0.4	14	34	3.1	1.2	3	D	D	D
San Luis	5	D	D	D	6	D	D	D	5	D	D	D
Scottsdale.......................	983	5,713	2,175.5	276.0	1,986	D	D	D	216	7,082	4,532.5	612.3
Sierra Vista	60	317	42.5	9.0	103	D	D	D	11	57	7.8	1.7
Surprise..........................	63	148	31.2	4.2	81	D	D	D	19	281	143.7	8.9
Tempe.............................	407	3,684	1,027.0	165.6	970	12,464	2,302.8	772.1	373	15,660	5,445.1	914.4
Tucson	735	3,966	628.3	129.9	1,563	10,568	1,457.1	581.5	393	6,648	1,551.5	312.7
Yuma..............................	124	513	71.6	14.0	171	D	D	D	42	1,800	785.5	71.2
ARKANSAS	2,802	12,867	1,922.7	409.8	5,655	31,871	4,464.9	1,549.2	2,688	153,706	62,712.9	6,290.8
Bella Vista	24	D	D	D	34	65	9.3	2.6	NA	NA	NA	NA
Benton............................	26	53	14.9	1.3	62	250	26.1	8.8	35	561	133.7	24.4
Bentonville......................	67	286	68.9	14.3	225	D	D	D	21	304	135.3	12.0
Conway...........................	94	402	98.9	17.6	168	D	D	D	54	3,479	1,156.6	168.0
Fayetteville.....................	137	2,012	133.0	52.1	364	1,850	231.9	87.0	57	4,106	1,031.7	156.0
Fort Smith	156	813	124.2	25.5	272	D	D	D	148	13,228	4,983.3	538.8
Hot Springs.....................	73	302	48.2	8.4	147	D	D	D	33	800	147.3	37.0

1. Establishments subject to federal tax.

Table D. Cities — Accommodation and Food Services, Arts, Entertainment, and Recreation, and Health Care and Social Assistance

City	Accommodation and food services, 2012				Arts, entertainment, and recreation[1], 2012				Health care and social assistance,[1] 2012			
	Number of establishments	Number of employees	Receipts (mil dol)	Annual payroll (mil dol)	Number of establishments	Number of employees	Receipts (mil dol)	Annual payroll (mil dol)	Number of establishments	Number of employees	Receipts (mil dol)	Annual payroll (mil dol)
	92	93	94	95	96	97	98	99	100	101	102	103
United States	662,489	12,007,689	708,138.6	196,103.3	99,659	1,486,462	161,690.3	50,328.5	690,525	9,542,138	1,008,744.6	409,811.9
ALABAMA	8,339	157,337	7,576.5	2,071.1	782	10,487	885.0	178.3	8,489	142,386	14,627.8	5,995.0
Alabaster	48	1,162	60.6	17.0	5	D	D	D	85	D	D	D
Auburn	198	3,581	163.3	41.4	13	D	D	D	103	D	D	D
Bessemer	95	1,734	86.8	24.2	7	89	6.5	2.0	85	D	D	D
Birmingham	564	11,239	625.3	185.7	38	570	38.8	10.9	615	12,973	1,675.5	690.7
Decatur	140	2,847	134.6	38.0	10	171	6.8	2.2	217	2,511	271.7	95.3
Dothan	223	4,538	209.2	56.1	18	D	D	D	257	D	D	D
Enterprise	73	1,202	58.3	14.4	9	D	D	D	75	D	D	D
Florence	129	3,445	141.4	42.9	10	D	D	D	183	3,575	406.3	142.1
Gadsden	90	2,203	101.3	27.6	6	D	D	D	182	5,271	564.2	244.0
Homewood	117	2,294	132.3	35.5	6	D	D	D	182	5,513	800.3	271.4
Hoover	187	4,241	244.5	72.4	20	213	19.4	3.1	219	3,211	266.0	124.0
Huntsville	527	11,685	575.1	162.0	53	831	33.1	12.8	596	9,963	1,301.2	536.7
Madison	109	1,795	93.9	24.8	11	105	3.9	1.2	110	D	D	D
Mobile	488	10,868	488.5	134.3	41	1,339	25.6	7.7	469	10,192	1,150.0	515.1
Montgomery	471	9,716	462.3	127.8	28	D	D	D	539	D	D	D
Opelika	98	2,049	94.4	25.6	3	D	D	D	82	D	D	D
Phenix City	67	1,285	60.2	14.6	3	D	D	D	53	D	D	D
Prattville	85	2,148	103.2	28.2	7	D	D	D	73	D	D	D
Tuscaloosa	284	6,941	344.2	86.9	13	157	8.5	3.2	217	D	D	D
Vestavia Hills	77	1,770	83.6	23.4	13	226	19.2	8.0	118	D	D	D
ALASKA	2,126	26,836	2,221.3	626.0	441	4,161	328.4	68.0	1,851	21,389	2,810.2	1,098.5
Anchorage	788	14,957	1,106.2	338.1	108	D	D	D	962	12,792	1,783.5	682.5
Fairbanks	138	2,215	177.4	46.9	31	D	D	D	165	2,316	301.7	136.0
Juneau	119	1,329	81.5	24.1	27	D	D	D	92	644	90.1	33.2
ARIZONA	11,669	251,455	13,996.6	4,030.3	1,424	33,881	3,279.3	1,088.3	15,041	184,186	20,221.1	7,974.6
Apache Junction	45	665	28.9	7.9	4	D	D	D	48	1,078	84.4	37.2
Avondale	86	1,658	82.7	22.2	7	D	D	D	104	1,026	109.9	35.9
Buckeye	46	798	35.8	9.3	4	163	5.7	2.3	16	D	D	D
Bullhead City	85	1,091	54.2	14.5	7	167	4.0	1.5	109	2,009	285.4	97.3
Casa Grande	114	D	D	D	7	D	D	D	144	1,810	164.5	71.2
Chandler	474	10,996	559.8	181.3	63	2,325	434.4	62.7	676	7,874	833.7	289.4
El Mirage	11	128	7.1	1.6	NA	NA	NA	NA	6	D	D	D
Flagstaff	300	6,034	326.5	86.4	29	440	27.4	9.3	286	2,220	273.8	105.4
Florence	24	D	D	D	2	D	D	D	17	D	D	D
Gilbert	287	6,139	297.6	85.7	48	1,045	48.7	14.8	619	5,146	520.0	191.9
Glendale	381	8,050	387.3	108.4	40	D	D	D	574	7,794	931.5	370.5
Goodyear	113	2,899	141.1	39.2	12	D	D	D	129	3,464	369.7	146.7
Kingman	92	1,681	74.6	21.2	5	D	D	D	103	D	D	D
Lake Havasu City	134	2,333	97.3	29.5	12	D	D	D	165	2,272	263.2	93.2
Marana	96	2,178	121.3	36.3	14	454	19.5	9.8	44	D	D	D
Maricopa	30	479	23.2	5.9	3	D	D	D	33	D	D	D
Mesa	733	14,688	685.3	202.1	76	1,920	85.3	29.5	1,135	14,098	1,418.9	568.5
Oro Valley	67	1,998	87.2	30.1	14	D	D	D	117	D	D	D
Peoria	243	5,889	281.9	85.8	31	480	28.5	9.0	368	4,425	462.6	214.7
Phoenix	2,493	57,339	3,479.6	992.4	295	6,038	626.0	312.8	3,435	45,960	5,433.6	2,241.6
Prescott	154	2,390	116.7	34.9	17	163	10.3	3.5	323	3,046	292.3	110.1
Prescott Valley	75	1,112	49.3	14.8	11	241	7.4	2.9	103	1,203	95.9	41.0
Queen Creek	38	698	31.9	9.4	4	109	6.9	1.7	71	D	D	D
Sahuarita	19	438	15.1	4.0	2	D	D	D	19	D	D	D
San Luis	14	206	9.5	2.2	1	D	D	D	14	123	10.6	4.7
Scottsdale	746	22,062	1,370.6	421.5	145	3,996	294.0	97.4	1,422	13,486	1,598.1	648.8
Sierra Vista	100	2,058	91.3	26.4	8	D	D	D	135	1,490	125.8	49.2
Surprise	140	3,145	151.8	42.8	11	210	10.9	4.1	165	1,110	119.2	43.1
Tempe	563	12,672	646.1	183.9	60	1,217	267.5	181.7	507	7,866	855.5	321.6
Tucson	1,214	26,136	1,235.4	350.0	117	1,487	61.4	17.9	1,485	19,878	2,194.4	824.6
Yuma	227	4,641	254.2	64.1	14	D	D	D	273	D	D	D
ARKANSAS	5,473	95,854	4,307.3	1,182.5	563	5,927	499.0	104.3	5,936	86,999	8,540.6	3,495.8
Bella Vista	20	D	D	D	2	D	D	D	26	402	28.6	11.3
Benton	62	1,080	51.2	13.5	9	53	1.6	0.5	80	1,254	91.3	43.5
Bentonville	123	2,365	111.2	30.2	10	119	8.0	2.2	99	1,121	120.3	44.2
Conway	172	4,248	177.6	48.5	11	D	D	D	206	2,682	239.8	96.7
Fayetteville	326	6,288	270.4	77.3	28	309	13.5	4.3	304	4,648	483.1	202.3
Fort Smith	245	5,188	232.1	67.2	16	D	D	D	299	6,889	843.4	335.9
Hot Springs	194	4,178	178.1	52.6	27	D	D	D	199	2,884	369.2	142.9

1. Establishments subject to federal tax.

Table D. Cities — **Other Services and Government Employment and Payroll**

City	Other services[1]				Government employment and payroll, 2012								
					Full-time equivalent employees	March payroll							
						Total (dollars)	Perent of total for:						
	Number of establishments	Number of employees	Receipts (mil dol)	Annual payroll (mil dol)			Administrative, judicial, and legal	Police and corrections	Fire protection	Highways and transportation	Health and welfare	Natural resources and utilities	Education and libraries
	104	105	106	107	108	109	110	111	112	113	114	115	116
United States	422,719	2,543,493	230,974.9	69,948.3	X	X	X	X	X	X	X	X	X
ALABAMA	5,009	31,262	3,191.9	893.0	X	X	X	X	X	X	X	X	X
Alabaster........................	36	177	12.5	3.9	226	902,906	9.2	32.9	29.4	6.0	0.0	14.0	4.0
Auburn...........................	70	342	24.8	7.2	541	1,872,172	15.3	25.8	16.5	9.6	0.9	24.2	4.1
Bessemer........................	45	470	67.5	19.5	570	2,109,401	7.5	25.2	23.3	0.5	0.9	32.7	1.8
Birmingham.....................	308	3,072	292.1	97.3	4,784	19,867,336	9.5	27.6	17.4	3.5	0.9	29.6	4.1
Decatur..........................	77	654	60.7	18.3	695	2,762,157	6.2	20.0	17.7	5.1	1.4	45.8	0.0
Dothan...........................	145	D	D	D	980	3,540,917	11.7	22.1	20.0	3.1	0.8	33.9	0.0
Enterprise.......................	45	236	21.2	6.5	572	1,406,470	3.3	16.3	8.9	3.8	48.7	17.5	0.8
Florence.........................	70	471	30.4	9.5	814	2,966,594	5.4	16.5	13.1	6.3	0.6	51.8	0.0
Gadsden.........................	51	332	33.7	10.1	813	2,569,152	8.3	19.3	20.9	8.8	0.9	30.2	2.8
Homewood.......................	63	1,403	81.3	31.4	357	1,440,394	4.5	33.6	23.3	6.7	0.0	16.2	7.0
Hoover	79	450	43.0	12.5	663	3,382,691	10.6	31.1	26.9	5.3	0.7	8.2	7.7
Huntsville	269	2,553	476.6	101.5	2,636	11,833,638	8.9	19.0	14.5	7.2	2.2	32.4	0.0
Madison	54	366	30.0	9.7	374	1,553,149	16.6	30.8	22.6	2.6	0.0	24.9	0.0
Mobile	311	2,205	183.3	55.0	2,894	9,605,291	10.7	26.2	21.6	4.7	1.5	25.1	3.9
Montgomery	243	1,612	142.5	42.9	2,884	10,068,707	8.1	26.1	17.3	7.2	0.4	29.4	2.1
Opelika..........................	49	232	22.7	6.1	355	1,405,862	10.4	27.1	19.6	3.6	0.5	35.2	2.4
Phenix City.....................	46	253	19.0	6.6	795	2,466,225	53.9	13.6	9.1	2.5	0.4	18.3	0.5
Prattville	44	210	18.2	5.4	328	1,108,761	10.0	29.2	32.0	3.9	0.0	16.8	0.0
Tuscaloosa......................	103	1,037	83.4	26.8	1,302	4,845,351	13.7	29.6	21.7	13.7	0.3	17.3	0.0
Vestavia Hills...................	55	493	33.3	12.2	264	1,136,169	7.5	27.3	44.1	1.9	0.0	6.9	5.2
ALASKA	882	4,807	495.9	152.7	X	X	X	X	X	X	X	X	X
Anchorage.......................	400	2,688	261.8	87.3	9,819	51,971,256	4.5	7.8	6.6	5.5	1.4	9.1	63.8
Fairbanks........................	82	408	40.9	12.3	207	1,185,064	19.9	35.9	23.3	6.8	8.7	5.4	0.0
Juneau...........................	45	202	18.7	5.3	1,960	10,163,476	5.6	5.4	3.1	7.4	27.2	8.1	43.2
ARIZONA	7,025	46,847	4,192.9	1,223.9	X	X	X	X	X	X	X	X	X
Apache Junction	31	165	25.8	8.4	234	1,013,473	20.4	42.8	0.0	10.1	7.9	13.1	5.7
Avondale.........................	58	399	27.3	8.4	512	2,677,540	26.3	33.3	15.4	3.4	3.4	12.3	1.8
Buckeye.........................	12	37	3.0	0.8	391	1,821,664	27.3	19.8	28.2	3.6	1.6	9.5	2.0
Bullhead City....................	36	207	15.3	4.8	298	1,290,523	21.2	44.5	0.0	12.9	1.8	11.0	0.0
Casa Grande....................	61	361	28.4	8.8	385	1,771,597	18.0	31.5	19.5	7.8	0.7	17.0	3.4
Chandler.........................	257	1,995	169.0	53.6	1,623	9,363,010	16.5	33.2	15.8	6.3	4.4	16.4	3.0
El Mirage........................	13	58	3.7	1.3	144	789,368	14.2	35.0	17.6	4.7	0.0	9.4	0.0
Flagstaff.........................	123	695	58.4	17.0	767	3,403,748	18.4	24.3	12.4	4.2	3.2	21.7	4.8
Florence.........................	3	D	D	D	163	645,551	22.7	26.9	19.9	12.8	1.7	13.7	2.3
Gilbert	212	1,299	91.0	27.5	1,117	5,590,864	15.8	33.0	20.5	2.9	0.1	18.9	0.0
Glendale.........................	250	1,436	143.9	40.6	1,775	9,436,681	12.7	32.7	19.8	5.2	1.8	16.0	2.7
Goodyear........................	48	281	17.3	5.6	482	2,715,439	27.9	20.6	25.2	2.4	0.0	14.0	0.0
Kingman.........................	41	257	19.9	6.4	335	1,383,755	16.2	24.7	22.1	11.4	0.0	22.8	0.0
Lake Havasu City...............	117	416	37.7	9.5	484	2,122,419	13.0	26.9	20.4	8.0	0.0	20.7	0.0
Marana..........................	69	387	30.7	10.5	306	1,328,433	22.4	36.4	0.0	14.2	1.2	11.8	0.0
Maricopa........................	23	D	D	D	204	1,087,610	13.2	32.5	35.7	1.6	0.0	5.6	2.4
Mesa	552	3,294	272.4	78.7	3,616	20,622,110	15.1	36.5	16.1	6.6	1.6	17.7	1.6
Oro Valley	49	327	22.6	8.3	311	1,409,218	13.9	47.7	0.0	6.6	0.8	15.0	4.3
Peoria...........................	157	942	72.8	23.1	1,162	6,255,922	23.5	26.8	16.6	7.4	0.0	20.3	2.2
Phoenix..........................	1,631	14,684	1,515.2	403.1	13,392	69,633,897	11.5	35.6	16.7	9.5	5.0	18.7	1.5
Prescott..........................	111	551	45.7	13.9	538	2,411,836	19.0	24.9	16.7	6.7	0.0	14.5	3.4
Prescott Valley	54	199	17.3	4.8	189	851,635	20.9	38.1	0.0	4.8	7.5	7.0	8.5
Queen Creek....................	21	101	6.9	2.3	217	1,060,750	23.5	0.0	16.7	8.1	23.4	23.1	0.0
Sahuarita........................	8	91	4.3	1.9	131	644,309	29.4	41.1	0.0	11.3	0.0	7.5	0.0
San Luis.........................	3	6	0.3	0.1	233	639,318	48.6	5.8	13.3	7.7	0.0	21.5	0.0
Scottsdale.......................	533	3,863	294.6	94.1	2,454	13,029,893	23.6	31.2	13.0	3.8	2.1	18.0	3.7
Sierra Vista	47	253	19.6	6.5	380	1,580,863	16.3	28.2	17.1	6.7	1.2	17.2	2.1
Surprise.........................	87	462	30.5	9.9	738	4,192,160	14.5	25.4	22.6	5.1	6.0	22.1	0.0
Tempe	292	2,006	188.3	62.7	1,762	9,492,774	16.0	31.6	13.1	6.2	9.5	18.8	1.5
Tucson	756	4,997	423.7	128.2	4,691	21,780,237	12.6	30.8	18.8	10.4	3.2	19.2	0.0
Yuma............................	115	709	52.0	16.5	946	3,797,070	16.5	30.3	16.4	7.6	3.3	23.1	0.0
ARKANSAS	3,157	17,091	1,427.6	423.7	X	X	X	X	X	X	X	X	X
Bella Vista	11	D	D	D	93	498,217	10.0	35.9	53.0	1.1	0.0	0.0	0.0
Benton...........................	48	216	21.4	5.5	270	875,166	13.5	25.7	22.5	4.2	2.4	27.6	0.0
Bentonville	62	475	27.9	13.7	435	1,712,143	20.1	20.9	18.7	4.1	0.0	33.1	3.1
Conway..........................	100	535	40.7	11.2	474	1,540,085	12.3	31.7	27.5	7.8	0.0	17.9	0.0
Fayetteville......................	111	661	43.6	14.9	692	2,378,996	14.3	27.3	16.7	11.7	2.3	20.9	0.0
Fort Smith.......................	143	751	62.0	17.6	880	3,505,049	10.2	26.1	17.9	14.1	2.6	29.1	0.0
Hot Springs	82	454	27.2	9.5	597	2,082,915	9.8	24.7	17.9	10.7	1.2	28.2	0.0

1. Establishments subject to federal tax.

Table D. Cities — City Government Finances

City	City government finances, 2012									
	General revenue							General expenditure		
		Intergovernmental		Taxes					Per capita[1] (dollars)	
					Per capita[1] (dollars)					
	Total (mil dol)	Total (mil dol)	Percent from state government	Total (mil dol)	Total	Property	Sales and gross receipts	Total (mil dol)	Total	Capital outlays
	117	118	119	120	121	122	123	124	125	126
United States	X	X	X	X	X	X	X	X	X	X
ALABAMA	X	X	X	X	X	X	X	X	X	X
Alabaster	27.6	0.0	0.0	19.2	619	107	511	23.9	773	0
Auburn	94.7	3.9	77.7	64.8	1,135	368	766	67.3	1,180	135
Bessemer	51.9	5.8	81.8	34.8	1,279	240	1,039	52.4	1,924	4
Birmingham	436.4	42.3	52.9	334.4	1,583	243	985	466.4	2,207	235
Decatur	174.2	68.7	100.0	61.6	1,103	209	877	202.0	3,616	209
Dothan	93.4	4.5	88.0	70.5	1,046	66	980	98.8	1,467	83
Enterprise	30.6	1.8	95.9	23.0	826	157	670	32.1	1,155	209
Florence	64.7	4.1	76.8	43.9	1,107	284	821	58.6	1,477	59
Gadsden	64.3	6.9	28.4	44.2	1,206	66	731	60.4	1,647	45
Homewood	54.6	1.8	36.5	50.5	1,996	632	1,363	51.4	2,034	100
Hoover	104.2	6.8	51.4	83.0	998	121	853	95.0	1,143	78
Huntsville	329.0	28.2	93.3	217.9	1,186	320	866	337.4	1,836	440
Madison	51.4	5.9	79.3	34.9	777	291	451	50.2	1,117	123
Mobile	353.3	20.4	65.4	248.6	1,275	83	1,192	344.5	1,767	296
Montgomery	280.1	36.3	46.1	169.8	830	151	679	218.0	1,065	80
Opelika	54.6	2.4	35.3	39.9	1,425	328	810	51.4	1,834	224
Phenix City	33.7	1.9	100.0	26.0	717	165	552	36.4	1,007	213
Prattville	35.5	1.0	99.2	26.5	765	71	695	28.2	814	6
Tuscaloosa	163.4	34.6	20.3	77.7	834	145	637	163.0	1,750	124
Vestavia Hills	34.2	1.8	33.1	29.1	857	387	470	34.6	1,017	160
ALASKA	X	X	X	X	X	X	X	X	X	X
Anchorage	1,296.8	572.1	91.3	546.6	1,830	1,623	208	1,251.1	4,190	417
Fairbanks	42.7	11.6	100.0	21.4	659	432	227	39.7	1,220	110
Juneau	316.5	94.8	75.9	83.0	2,561	1,130	1,431	302.2	9,325	1,605
ARIZONA	X	X	X	X	X	X	X	X	X	X
Apache Junction	26.7	11.0	100.0	11.6	316	0	316	29.2	793	0
Avondale	84.4	25.7	100.0	40.9	523	67	456	73.8	945	93
Buckeye	61.1	12.9	69.2	27.9	512	172	339	48.2	882	7
Bullhead City	48.4	17.4	91.6	11.3	286	0	285	42.5	1,075	35
Casa Grande	70.3	17.3	83.1	29.4	586	128	458	77.3	1,541	234
Chandler	333.6	72.6	90.2	151.1	617	130	487	266.6	1,089	179
El Mirage	30.1	8.5	100.0	9.5	290	94	196	33.0	1,011	114
Flagstaff	130.0	35.8	90.1	54.3	801	176	624	120.0	1,768	130
Florence	23.1	8.7	80.8	6.8	254	38	210	20.6	772	122
Gilbert	261.7	63.3	83.0	136.2	614	108	503	189.6	854	154
Glendale	324.3	103.3	81.2	145.1	625	87	538	226.0	974	13
Goodyear	108.3	19.5	99.3	60.0	864	237	627	78.8	1,135	56
Kingman	39.6	14.2	100.0	12.5	439	0	439	31.4	1,108	1
Lake Havasu City	80.6	21.3	85.8	26.9	509	186	322	98.9	1,874	405
Marana	50.4	18.1	58.5	27.9	760	14	742	43.7	1,189	179
Maricopa	36.8	14.6	100.0	19.2	428	242	187	33.5	747	45
Mesa	511.1	172.3	70.6	156.6	346	32	309	601.2	1,330	186
Oro Valley	29.7	10.8	100.0	15.4	373	0	373	29.9	723	49
Peoria	190.2	41.3	95.5	90.5	566	140	418	239.6	1,498	187
Phoenix	2,902.9	848.4	63.4	987.1	663	152	507	2,651.7	1,780	445
Prescott	74.7	16.1	77.8	30.5	761	71	684	77.2	1,928	429
Prescott Valley	38.2	14.1	87.4	14.0	357	47	310	41.2	1,051	74
Queen Creek	50.6	8.0	99.8	20.6	739	223	477	52.0	1,861	347
Sahuarita	26.6	12.6	63.4	10.0	379	11	368	22.4	852	221
San Luis	21.1	8.0	87.4	6.9	228	0	228	26.1	861	37
Scottsdale	477.7	126.1	80.7	238.4	1,068	291	776	562.4	2,518	823
Sierra Vista	48.4	13.6	97.0	18.9	407	9	398	48.8	1,052	142
Surprise	112.2	31.8	91.0	40.3	332	56	276	106.8	880	55
Tempe	344.4	69.4	71.3	183.5	1,097	215	883	286.8	1,715	177
Tucson	736.3	277.8	53.0	280.3	534	76	458	608.5	1,159	174
Yuma	125.5	30.9	90.5	51.1	545	108	435	125.6	1,341	167
ARKANSAS	X	X	X	X	X	X	X	X	X	X
Bella Vista	12.2	6.0	28.9	3.3	122	28	94	12.1	440	15
Benton	23.3	4.6	40.9	12.8	398	73	324	22.8	712	138
Bentonville	57.6	8.2	48.3	30.3	790	159	630	57.0	1,486	389
Conway	95.8	7.8	55.2	33.5	532	61	471	88.6	1,408	244
Fayetteville	107.6	24.4	45.2	48.2	626	53	572	96.7	1,256	246
Fort Smith	133.9	29.8	38.6	61.3	700	146	554	126.0	1,439	456
Hot Springs	69.7	12.2	60.6	26.7	752	1	751	69.2	1,951	328

1. Based on population estimated as of July 1 of the year shown.

Table D. Cities — City Government Finances

City	City government finances, 2012 (cont.)									
	General expenditure (cont.)									
	Percent of total for:									
	Public welfare	Highways	Parking facilities	Education	Health and hospitals	Police protection	Sewerage and sanitation	Parks and recreation	Housing and community development	Interest on debt
	127	128	129	130	131	132	133	134	135	136
United States	X	X	X	X	X	X	X	X	X	X
ALABAMA	X	X	X	X	X	X	X	X	X	X
Alabaster................................	0.0	6.5	0.0	0.0	0.0	25.9	23.2	8.6	0.0	0.0
Auburn..................................	0.0	5.6	0.0	0.0	2.5	16.6	14.8	7.9	1.4	12.2
Bessemer...............................	0.0	6.1	0.0	0.0	0.0	21.1	6.2	3.2	0.0	6.0
Birmingham...........................	0.0	12.7	1.3	0.0	0.0	16.8	0.0	4.0	1.4	4.9
Decatur	0.3	5.0	0.0	53.7	2.3	6.1	12.6	3.4	0.9	1.1
Dothan	0.0	10.4	0.0	4.0	2.8	16.8	17.1	8.5	0.5	3.4
Enterprise..............................	0.0	8.4	0.0	16.6	0.7	13.2	23.7	7.3	0.0	8.6
Florence................................	0.0	9.8	0.0	14.4	0.0	15.5	16.1	11.6	0.3	2.8
Gadsden................................	0.0	6.2	0.0	0.0	0.0	16.2	16.8	9.0	2.3	4.3
Homewood.............................	0.1	5.6	0.0	28.6	0.0	16.9	4.9	6.2	0.0	4.2
Hoover..................................	0.0	9.1	0.0	2.1	0.3	21.8	8.8	8.6	0.0	4.5
Huntsville..............................	0.2	6.6	0.5	5.6	1.2	12.4	8.8	9.0	2.3	8.1
Madison................................	0.0	14.5	0.0	0.0	0.0	14.0	12.2	7.0	0.0	6.1
Mobile..................................	0.0	7.7	2.7	0.0	0.4	12.3	20.0	8.1	0.1	4.3
Montgomery...........................	0.0	5.6	1.7	0.0	0.0	20.0	7.3	12.6	1.3	6.6
Opelika.................................	0.0	8.4	0.0	14.7	0.6	16.6	11.9	9.8	0.5	6.3
Phenix City............................	0.0	1.8	0.0	5.6	0.3	16.9	14.0	10.2	0.0	3.9
Prattville...............................	0.0	0.0	0.0	0.0	0.0	22.0	13.5	6.2	0.0	8.8
Tuscaloosa............................	0.1	14.2	0.3	7.9	0.1	17.4	9.0	8.0	1.4	2.3
Vestavia Hills.........................	0.0	4.8	0.0	0.7	0.5	12.9	7.4	16.4	0.0	5.5
ALASKA	X	X	X	X	X	X	X	X	X	X
Anchorage.............................	0.0	5.9	0.4	53.2	2.1	9.9	5.0	1.7	0.0	2.8
Fairbanks	0.0	33.1	0.6	0.0	0.0	15.6	0.0	0.0	0.0	0.5
Juneau	0.0	4.5	0.0	28.1	32.3	5.7	3.6	4.3	1.4	3.0
ARIZONA	X	X	X	X	X	X	X	X	X	X
Apache Junction	0.0	24.4	0.0	0.0	0.0	30.0	0.0	11.6	6.9	0.0
Avondale...............................	3.8	15.7	0.0	0.0	0.0	31.7	20.3	3.4	4.4	6.6
Buckeye................................	0.0	4.5	0.0	0.0	0.0	19.8	24.3	3.3	0.4	17.7
Bullhead City.........................	0.0	20.8	0.0	0.0	4.2	23.1	21.7	7.4	1.4	6.7
Casa Grande..........................	0.0	8.0	0.0	0.0	0.0	17.5	17.4	8.7	0.9	6.8
Chandler...............................	0.0	7.7	0.0	0.0	0.0	21.8	19.2	0.9	13.7	4.7
El Mirage..............................	0.0	8.4	0.0	0.0	1.4	31.0	25.8	3.8	0.3	1.9
Flagstaff...............................	0.0	14.0	0.0	0.0	0.0	13.5	14.1	0.0	12.3	3.7
Florence	0.0	8.9	3.0	0.0	0.0	25.5	11.9	4.9	4.2	6.6
Gilbert	0.0	20.7	0.0	0.0	0.0	19.1	13.1	5.3	0.8	8.4
Glendale...............................	0.0	3.3	0.2	0.0	0.0	22.4	12.4	4.5	6.7	18.5
Goodyear..............................	0.0	2.1	0.0	0.0	0.0	16.8	9.8	9.8	5.8	13.2
Kingman...............................	0.0	5.6	0.0	0.0	0.0	23.3	22.2	11.9	2.1	2.3
Lake Havasu City...................	0.0	6.5	0.0	0.0	0.0	11.7	38.4	6.7	0.4	10.7
Marana.................................	0.0	15.9	0.0	0.0	0.0	23.0	2.8	3.8	0.9	10.8
Maricopa...............................	0.0	3.8	0.0	0.0	0.0	20.8	0.0	6.7	29.9	3.2
Mesa	0.6	10.4	0.0	0.0	0.0	26.2	11.2	7.4	3.3	6.1
Oro Valley	0.0	14.5	0.0	0.0	0.0	40.4	0.0	9.9	0.0	0.0
Peoria..................................	0.0	9.6	0.0	0.2	0.0	12.3	12.7	11.6	0.7	5.5
Phoenix................................	0.0	6.6	0.0	0.9	0.0	17.8	11.1	7.4	7.3	10.4
Prescott................................	0.0	26.8	0.1	0.0	0.0	16.5	17.0	7.8	0.3	3.3
Prescott Valley	0.0	10.3	0.0	0.0	0.0	20.4	14.9	3.7	0.0	11.3
Queen Creek..........................	0.0	6.0	0.0	0.0	0.0	3.2	8.0	12.7	1.3	8.9
Sahuarita..............................	0.0	27.9	0.0	0.0	0.0	23.8	7.8	5.8	0.0	11.5
San Luis...............................	0.5	5.6	0.0	0.0	0.0	14.5	18.2	0.0	0.6	24.2
Scottsdale.............................	0.0	5.4	0.0	0.0	0.0	14.2	16.1	6.3	1.5	9.3
Sierra Vista	0.0	26.3	0.0	0.0	0.0	32.3	13.8	9.6	2.6	2.4
Surprise................................	0.0	14.1	0.0	0.0	0.0	19.0	11.3	12.5	5.8	4.6
Tempe..................................	0.0	10.3	0.0	0.0	0.0	21.8	10.9	1.8	14.8	5.2
Tucson	0.0	5.0	0.0	0.0	0.0	21.9	6.7	8.0	12.2	6.0
Yuma...................................	0.0	11.8	0.0	0.0	0.6	17.9	15.0	9.1	1.2	11.1
ARKANSAS	X	X	X	X	X	X	X	X	X	X
Bella Vista	0.0	26.0	0.0	0.0	0.0	19.9	13.8	0.0	0.0	0.0
Benton..................................	0.0	22.3	0.0	0.0	1.5	20.7	12.3	6.4	0.0	7.0
Bentonville	0.0	16.9	0.0	0.0	0.0	12.6	25.2	11.3	0.2	5.6
Conway................................	0.0	14.7	0.0	0.0	0.4	11.7	15.7	4.1	0.0	15.9
Fayetteville...........................	0.0	11.2	1.0	0.0	1.0	16.4	26.2	5.7	0.5	5.3
Fort Smith	0.0	13.8	0.2	0.0	0.1	12.5	25.6	2.5	1.0	8.9
Hot Springs	0.0	6.7	0.2	0.0	0.9	15.8	27.9	2.4	0.4	2.1

City	City government finances, 2012 (cont.)			Climate[2]						
	Debt outstanding			Average daily temperature						
				Mean		Limits		Annual precipitation (inches)	Heating degree days	Cooling degree days
	Total (mil dol)	Per capita[1] (dollars)	Debt issued during year	January	July	January[3]	July[4]			
	137	138	139	140	141	142	143	144	145	146
United States	X	X	X	X	X	X	X	X	X	X
ALABAMA...........................	X	X	X	X	X	X	X	X	X	X
Alabaster..............................	101.5	3,276	0.0	NA	NA	NA	NA	NA	NA	NA
Auburn.................................	229.8	4,028	11.0	44.7	79.9	34.2	89.7	52.63	2,507	1,932
Bessemer............................	103.0	3,783	12.0	42.9	81.0	30.8	93.6	59.38	2,766	1,943
Birmingham.........................	573.7	2,715	109.7	42.6	80.2	32.3	90.6	53.99	2,823	1,881
Decatur...............................	508.8	9,106	6.5	38.9	79.2	29.1	90.3	55.31	3,469	1,609
Dothan	84.7	1,257	3.4	47.7	81.3	36.2	93.3	56.61	2,058	2,264
Enterprise............................	79.9	2,876	8.3	NA	NA	NA	NA	NA	NA	NA
Florence..............................	116.3	2,932	59.9	39.9	80.2	30.7	90.6	55.80	3,236	1,789
Gadsden	75.3	2,052	5.0	40.3	79.8	29.9	90.5	56.10	3,220	1,716
Homewood...........................	49.2	1,946	0.3	42.6	80.2	32.3	90.6	53.99	2,823	1,881
Hoover	108.5	1,306	58.5	42.9	81.0	30.8	93.6	59.38	2,766	1,943
Huntsville............................	774.8	4,216	13.8	39.8	79.5	30.7	89.4	57.51	3,262	1,671
Madison	75.1	1,672	13.3	46.6	81.8	35.5	92.7	54.77	2,194	2,252
Mobile.................................	547.6	2,809	13.3	50.1	81.5	39.5	91.2	66.29	1,681	2,539
Montgomery.........................	275.9	1,348	38.8	46.6	81.8	35.5	92.7	54.77	2,194	2,252
Opelika................................	162.2	5,790	70.3	NA	NA	NA	NA	NA	NA	NA
Phenix City..........................	139.4	3,853	52.5	46.8	82.0	36.6	91.7	48.57	2,154	2,296
Prattville.............................	61.2	1,766	5.6	NA	NA	NA	NA	NA	NA	NA
Tuscaloosa..........................	198.6	2,132	1.3	42.9	80.4	32.5	90.8	54.99	2,787	1,893
Vestavia Hills......................	41.6	1,224	0.0	NA	NA	NA	NA	NA	NA	NA
ALASKA..............................	X	X	X	X	X	X	X	X	X	X
Anchorage...........................	1,789.0	5,991	62.0	15.8	58.4	9.3	65.3	16.08	10,470	3
Fairbanks	2.3	71	0.0	-9.7	62.4	-19.0	73.0	10.34	13,980	74
Juneau................................	193.0	5,956	14.8	25.7	56.8	20.7	64.3	58.33	8,574	0
ARIZONA	X	X	X	X	X	X	X	X	X	X
Apache Junction	10.8	294	0.0	52.7	89.5	40.0	104.3	12.29	1,542	3,443
Avondale.............................	93.9	1,202	0.0	54.7	93.5	41.3	107.6	9.03	1,173	4,166
Buckeye	160.3	2,937	1.5	NA	NA	NA	NA	NA	NA	NA
Bullhead City.......................	73.4	1,858	0.0	54.4	95.6	43.3	111.7	5.84	1,164	4,508
Casa Grande.......................	119.9	2,388	14.4	52.4	90.4	37.3	105.1	9.22	1,572	3,554
Chandler	579.4	2,367	0.0	54.3	91.3	41.5	105.7	9.23	1,271	3,798
El Mirage.............................	27.3	836	0.0	NA	NA	NA	NA	NA	NA	NA
Flagstaff..............................	118.5	1,746	34.4	29.7	66.1	16.5	82.2	22.91	6,999	126
Florence	18.6	697	0.0	NA	NA	NA	NA	NA	NA	NA
Gilbert	479.5	2,159	37.9	54.3	91.3	41.5	105.7	9.23	1,271	3,798
Glendale..............................	1,053.0	4,536	86.3	52.5	90.6	39.2	104.2	7.78	1,535	3,488
Goodyear	426.4	6,140	38.6	NA	NA	NA	NA	NA	NA	NA
Kingman..............................	55.1	1,944	11.1	NA	NA	NA	NA	NA	NA	NA
Lake Havasu City................	321.9	6,096	8.4	53.9	95.2	42.9	107.5	6.25	1,230	4,523
Marana	94.8	2,584	0.1	NA	NA	NA	NA	NA	NA	NA
Maricopa.............................	19.3	430	0.0	NA	NA	NA	NA	NA	NA	NA
Mesa	1,494.6	3,305	352.1	54.3	91.3	41.5	105.7	9.23	1,271	3,798
Oro Valley	64.1	1,547	21.8	50.6	86.3	34.6	100.7	12.40	1,831	2,810
Peoria.................................	511.6	3,199	51.7	54.7	93.5	41.3	107.6	9.03	1,173	4,166
Phoenix...............................	8,278.0	5,557	760.6	54.2	92.8	43.4	104.2	8.29	1,125	4,189
Prescott..............................	73.2	1,829	3.5	37.1	73.4	23.3	88.3	19.19	4,849	742
Prescott Valley	104.9	2,678	33.8	NA	NA	NA	NA	NA	NA	NA
Queen Creek.......................	165.6	5,930	0.1	NA	NA	NA	NA	NA	NA	NA
Sahuarita............................	56.9	2,161	0.4	NA	NA	NA	NA	NA	NA	NA
San Luis.............................	169.5	5,602	0.0	NA	NA	NA	NA	NA	NA	NA
Scottsdale...........................	1,200.6	5,375	53.3	54.2	92.8	43.4	104.2	8.29	1,125	4,189
Sierra Vista........................	37.2	803	9.3	47.7	79.1	33.7	92.6	14.02	2,369	1,739
Surprise..............................	37.0	305	0.0	54.7	93.5	41.3	107.6	9.03	1,173	4,166
Tempe.................................	740.2	4,427	68.6	54.1	89.9	40.1	103.6	9.36	1,390	3,655
Tucson................................	1,174.4	2,236	152.8	54.0	88.5	41.9	100.5	12.00	1,333	3,501
Yuma..................................	302.8	3,234	0.0	58.1	94.1	46.2	107.3	3.01	782	4,540
ARKANSAS	X	X	X	X	X	X	X	X	X	X
Bella Vista	0.0	0	0.0	NA	NA	NA	NA	NA	NA	NA
Benton................................	44.1	1,373	0.0	NA	NA	NA	NA	NA	NA	NA
Bentonville	97.5	2,541	0.0	NA	NA	NA	NA	NA	NA	NA
Conway...............................	383.2	6,092	0.0	38.3	82.1	28.1	92.4	48.67	3,320	1,961
Fayetteville.........................	139.6	1,813	0.0	34.3	78.9	24.2	89.1	46.02	4,166	1,439
Fort Smith	454.0	5,184	22.1	38.0	82.2	27.8	92.9	43.87	3,437	1,929
Hot Springs	68.3	1,925	1.0	40.2	82.2	29.6	94.3	57.69	3,133	1,993

1. Based on the population estimated as of July 1 of the year shown.   2. Represents normal values based on the 30-year period, 1971±2000.   3. Average daily minimum.   4. Average daily maximum.

Table D. Cities — Land Area and Population

STATE Place code	City	Land area[1] (sq. mi)	Total persons 2018	Rank	Per square mile	White	Black or African American	American Indian, Alaskan Native	Asian	Hawaiian Pacific Islander	Some other race	Two or more races (percent)
		1	2	3	4	5	6	7	8	9	10	11
	ARKANSAS— Cont'd											
05 34750	Jacksonville	28.6	28,287	1,309	989.1	51.2	35.1	0.1	1.0	0.0	10.6	2.0
05 35710	Jonesboro	80.0	76,990	456	962.4	71.5	17.5	0.1	1.7	0.0	3.1	6.0
05 41000	Little Rock	119.2	197,881	121	1,660.1	49.8	41.9	0.3	3.4	0.1	1.6	2.9
05 50450	North Little Rock	52.3	66,127	558	1,264.4	42.9	53.2	0.1	0.9	0.0	1.1	1.8
05 53390	Paragould	31.7	28,912	1,289	912.1	NA	NA	NA	NA	NA	NA	NA
05 55310	Pine Bluff	43.8	42,271	903	965.1	NA	NA	NA	NA	NA	NA	NA
05 60410	Rogers	38.2	67,600	538	1,769.6	87.3	2.6	0.9	3.4	1.0	1.8	3.0
05 61670	Russellville	28.3	29,325	1,277	1,036.2	90.7	2.6	0.0	1.5	0.0	0.9	4.3
05 63800	Sherwood	20.8	31,237	1,210	1,501.8	NA	NA	NA	NA	NA	NA	NA
05 66080	Springdale	46.8	81,029	426	1,731.4	60.1	1.1	0.7	1.5	5.5	26.0	5.1
05 68810	Texarkana	41.9	29,972	1,255	715.3	62.8	32.0	2.1	0.0	0.0	0.9	2.2
05 74540	West Memphis	28.9	24,636	1,422	852.5	NA	NA	NA	NA	NA	NA	NA
06 00000	**CALIFORNIA**	155,793.7	39,557,045	X	253.9	58.6	5.7	0.8	14.6	0.4	15.0	4.9
06 00296	Adelanto	52.9	34,160	1,117	645.7	59.6	22.4	0.0	1.1	1.5	12.1	3.3
06 00562	Alameda	10.4	78,338	442	7,532.5	49.6	8.4	1.0	27.7	0.2	5.2	7.9
06 00884	Alhambra	7.6	84,649	400	11,138.0	20.8	1.0	0.3	57.7	1.3	16.5	2.3
06 00947	Aliso Viejo	6.9	51,783	742	7,504.8	65.1	0.3	0.9	17.0	0.1	9.2	7.4
06 02000	Anaheim	50.3	352,005	55	6,998.1	61.4	2.8	0.4	16.6	0.3	14.7	3.8
06 02252	Antioch	29.3	111,535	267	3,806.7	40.8	19.4	0.4	13.1	0.8	15.3	10.3
06 02364	Apple Valley	74.9	73,508	488	981.4	82.3	8.2	0.6	2.8	0.0	1.3	4.9
06 02462	Arcadia	10.9	58,610	645	5,377.1	22.5	1.6	0.1	66.2	0.0	7.9	1.8
06 03064	Atascadero	26.1	30,330	1,242	1,162.1	86.5	2.4	1.0	2.1	0.0	4.5	3.6
06 03162	Atwater	6.1	29,479	1,275	4,832.6	65.9	5.2	0.0	1.4	0.3	22.1	5.1
06 03386	Azusa	9.7	49,958	769	5,150.3	48.8	3.7	2.2	15.2	0.1	22.1	7.8
06 03526	Bakersfield	149.7	383,579	53	2,562.3	68.6	7.6	0.6	7.2	0.3	12.4	3.4
06 03666	Baldwin Park	6.6	75,813	463	11,486.8	37.3	2.6	2.4	16.7	2.0	36.7	2.3
06 03820	Banning	23.3	31,253	1,209	1,341.3	67.9	7.5	0.0	12.1	0.2	7.3	5.0
06 04758	Beaumont	30.0	49,241	782	1,641.4	70.6	7.2	1.3	5.3	0.7	11.5	3.4
06 04870	Bell	2.5	35,728	1,077	14,291.2	NA	NA	NA	NA	NA	NA	NA
06 04982	Bellflower	6.1	77,131	451	12,644.4	33.2	14.2	0.4	11.6	1.1	35.8	3.8
06 04996	Bell Gardens	2.5	42,331	901	16,932.4	NA	NA	NA	NA	NA	NA	NA
06 05108	Belmont	4.6	27,113	1,353	5,894.1	56.9	0.9	0.3	33.6	1.4	0.9	6.0
06 05290	Benicia	12.9	28,306	1,307	2,194.3	75.1	2.3	0.4	9.6	0.0	4.5	8.2
06 06000	Berkeley	10.5	121,643	232	11,585.0	57.7	9.2	0.6	19.4	0.7	4.8	7.6
06 06308	Beverly Hills	5.7	34,183	1,115	5,997.0	83.8	2.1	0.0	9.2	0.0	1.2	3.6
06 08100	Brea	12.2	43,601	875	3,573.9	64.1	2.3	1.6	24.3	0.6	2.1	5.0
06 08142	Brentwood	14.9	63,800	586	4,281.9	68.2	3.2	1.2	9.8	2.3	6.2	9.0
06 08786	Buena Park	10.5	82,421	412	7,849.6	47.2	4.7	2.2	26.5	0.3	14.6	4.5
06 08954	Burbank	17.3	103,695	297	5,993.9	74.9	4.5	0.4	10.8	0.0	3.6	5.8
06 09066	Burlingame	4.4	30,467	1,235	6,924.3	55.2	2.9	0.8	27.1	0.6	7.0	6.4
06 09710	Calexico	8.6	40,139	956	4,667.3	NA	NA	NA	NA	NA	NA	NA
06 10046	Camarillo	19.7	69,127	519	3,509.0	74.8	1.5	1.1	13.8	0.8	2.9	5.1
06 10345	Campbell	6.1	42,466	898	6,961.6	67.4	4.9	1.0	18.6	0.3	1.3	6.6
06 11194	Carlsbad	37.8	115,877	249	3,065.5	84.3	1.1	0.2	8.5	0.3	1.7	4.0
06 11530	Carson	18.7	91,909	354	4,914.9	33.9	20.5	0.6	25.8	0.4	11.2	7.5
06 12048	Cathedral City	22.5	54,902	697	2,440.1	76.0	4.8	1.7	5.7	0.0	7.6	4.3
06 12524	Ceres	9.4	48,769	791	5,188.2	63.1	6.3	1.1	7.7	0.2	17.8	3.6
06 12552	Cerritos	8.7	50,462	761	5,800.2	21.0	7.3	0.2	54.4	1.8	6.5	8.9
06 13014	Chico	33.5	94,776	335	2,829.1	81.8	2.7	0.7	6.0	0.0	4.7	4.1
06 13210	Chino	29.6	91,583	358	3,094.0	50.1	6.2	0.6	13.2	1.2	23.7	5.0
06 13214	Chino Hills	44.7	83,447	406	1,866.8	51.8	2.7	0.4	34.0	0.0	7.8	3.3
06 13392	Chula Vista	49.6	271,651	76	5,476.8	65.2	6.7	0.8	13.9	0.8	7.5	5.1
06 13588	Citrus Heights	14.2	87,910	376	6,190.8	80.3	4.5	0.5	2.9	0.1	5.7	5.9
06 13756	Claremont	13.4	36,478	1,054	2,722.2	59.8	9.3	1.3	12.5	0.0	8.8	8.2
06 14218	Clovis	24.6	112,022	262	4,553.7	73.6	2.1	0.6	10.1	0.9	8.2	4.5
06 14260	Coachella	30.1	45,839	842	1,522.9	NA	NA	NA	NA	NA	NA	NA
06 14890	Colton	15.5	54,741	701	3,531.7	51.5	10.7	1.9	3.9	0.1	29.0	3.0
06 15044	Compton	10.0	96,617	325	9,661.7	26.9	30.1	0.5	0.2	0.0	40.7	1.5
06 16000	Concord	30.6	129,688	212	4,238.2	62.8	3.2	0.4	14.2	0.0	14.5	4.9
06 16350	Corona	39.4	168,819	154	4,284.7	56.2	8.0	0.3	9.2	0.4	21.1	4.9
06 16532	Costa Mesa	15.8	113,615	255	7,190.8	77.5	1.7	0.2	7.7	1.4	7.8	3.7
06 16742	Covina	7.0	47,963	809	6,851.9	59.2	1.3	1.8	19.7	0.2	14.6	3.3
06 17568	Culver City	5.1	39,214	985	7,689.0	60.6	9.6	0.1	15.9	0.5	6.9	6.3
06 17610	Cupertino	11.3	60,170	620	5,324.8	NA	NA	NA	NA	NA	NA	NA
06 17750	Cypress	6.6	48,958	788	7,417.9	58.1	1.8	0.9	32.4	0.3	1.9	4.6
06 17918	Daly City	7.6	107,008	285	14,080.0	18.2	3.5	0.5	57.6	0.2	12.9	7.1
06 17946	Dana Point	6.5	33,730	1,133	5,189.2	74.8	3.8	0.0	4.2	0.0	11.0	6.1
06 17988	Danville	18.1	44,650	856	2,466.9	NA	NA	NA	NA	NA	NA	NA
06 18100	Davis	9.9	69,289	517	6,998.9	64.7	2.5	0.6	20.2	0.2	3.2	8.7

1. Dry land or land partially or temporarily covered by water.   2. Hispanic or Latino persons may be of any race.

Table D. Cities — **Population**

City	Percent Hispanic or Latino[1], 2017	Percent foreign born, 2017	Age of population (percent), 2017 Under 18 years	18 to 24 years	25 to 34 years	35 to 44 years	45 to 54 years	55 to 64 years	65 years and over	Median age, 2017	Percent female, 2017	Population Census counts 2000	2010	Population Percent change 2000-2010	2001-2018
	12	13	14	15	16	17	18	19	20	21	22	23	24	25	26
ARKANSAS— Cont'd															
Jacksonville....................	14.4	7.6	30.9	6.6	15.8	10.7	6.9	13.6	15.4	32.0	55.5	29,916	28,356	-5.2	-0.2
Jonesboro............................	6.2	5.7	23.9	13.9	13.3	15.2	10.6	9.8	13.3	33.5	50.9	55,515	67,291	21.2	14.4
Little Rock	6.6	7.2	25.1	7.8	15.6	14.2	11.2	12.6	13.5	36.2	51.4	183,133	193,490	5.7	2.3
North Little Rock	4.8	1.8	21.3	12.5	16.9	10.4	10.6	12.1	16.3	34.8	53.0	60,433	62,368	3.2	6.0
Paragould	0.6	1.8	25.8	11.2	12.1	14.3	11.9	11.8	13.0	36.0	50.5	22,017	26,293	19.4	10.0
Pine Bluff............................	2.5	2.5	24.6	11.4	14.5	10.5	12.2	13.4	13.4	34.7	51.3	55,085	49,057	-10.9	-13.8
Rogers	34.2	18.8	28.8	10.0	16.3	13.8	15.1	7.5	8.6	32.2	52.5	38,829	56,021	44.3	20.7
Russellville	13.3	7.1	22.3	20.4	16.0	9.3	9.3	7.3	15.5	30.9	48.9	23,682	28,113	18.7	4.3
Sherwood............................	7.5	6.5	18.5	11.8	10.8	11.9	15.9	13.7	17.4	42.6	52.7	21,511	29,626	37.7	5.4
Springdale...........................	36.7	23.6	31.7	8.5	12.1	15.6	12.2	8.8	11.1	32.6	49.0	45,798	70,808	54.6	14.4
Texarkana	4.3	1.0	21.4	12.5	12.1	9.5	13.5	13.7	17.3	40.6	50.4	26,448	29,905	13.1	0.2
West Memphis	0.7	0.5	27.9	8.0	13.9	12.6	11.0	11.4	15.4	35.2	53.8	27,666	26,245	-5.1	-6.1
CALIFORNIA.....................	39.1	26.9	22.9	9.6	15.2	13.2	13.1	12.0	13.9	36.5	50.3	33,871,648	37,254,523	10.0	6.2
Adelanto..............................	65.4	17.0	37.4	10.1	14.9	15.8	10.3	7.2	4.2	26.8	48.5	18,130	31,760	75.2	7.6
Alameda..............................	13.7	25.2	22.1	5.9	16.0	16.2	11.9	11.2	16.6	38.9	55.0	72,259	73,812	2.1	6.1
Alhambra.............................	32.2	53.4	14.6	7.5	15.9	15.5	13.8	12.2	20.5	42.5	51.9	85,804	83,118	-3.1	1.8
Aliso Viejo...........................	25.9	24.9	25.3	8.8	14.8	14.8	16.7	11.4	8.1	36.3	51.1	40,166	48,098	19.7	7.7
Anaheim...............................	55.0	37.1	23.8	11.6	15.6	13.5	13.6	11.2	10.7	34.3	49.6	328,014	336,443	2.6	4.6
Antioch................................	34.0	23.5	26.1	8.6	13.9	12.4	15.1	12.7	11.1	36.2	50.8	90,532	102,745	13.5	8.6
Apple Valley	37.3	9.1	27.2	8.7	11.8	12.4	11.0	13.2	15.8	37.6	52.3	54,239	69,146	27.5	6.3
Arcadia................................	12.1	54.1	23.1	5.5	12.8	15.1	15.1	12.2	16.3	40.3	50.3	53,054	56,327	6.2	4.1
Atascadero...........................	17.8	9.6	19.6	9.5	16.3	9.2	10.3	16.8	18.3	37.8	49.0	26,411	28,306	7.2	7.2
Atwater................................	51.4	17.5	25.6	14.0	11.7	13.0	15.0	10.5	10.2	33.4	51.8	23,113	28,215	22.1	4.5
Azusa..................................	60.8	32.0	21.6	20.8	13.3	13.1	10.8	9.8	10.6	29.3	53.1	44,712	46,567	4.1	7.3
Bakersfield..........................	50.9	18.2	29.8	9.7	15.4	12.4	11.6	10.2	10.8	31.3	51.3	247,057	348,255	41.0	10.1
Baldwin Park........................	75.7	42.7	22.7	9.9	18.5	13.2	11.8	11.0	12.9	34.1	50.4	75,837	75,397	-0.6	0.6
Banning...............................	47.5	27.1	27.7	5.5	10.2	14.3	8.0	6.7	27.5	40.1	54.0	23,562	29,590	25.6	5.6
Beaumont............................	47.5	16.0	30.3	8.6	13.9	10.6	11.6	12.8	12.2	32.7	52.3	11,384	36,859	223.8	33.6
Bell.....................................	94.2	47.3	26.3	9.9	16.7	12.2	14.7	9.5	10.6	32.2	50.2	36,664	35,473	-3.2	0.7
Bellflower	50.8	29.6	22.9	11.5	14.1	13.3	16.3	10.3	11.5	35.8	50.4	72,878	76,610	5.1	0.7
Bell Gardens	97.2	43.8	30.7	11.6	14.0	14.7	12.9	7.7	8.4	29.4	49.0	44,054	42,053	-4.5	0.7
Belmont...............................	4.9	33.0	23.3	5.5	11.9	15.0	16.1	11.1	17.1	40.5	52.5	25,123	25,840	2.9	4.9
Benicia................................	13.9	13.4	22.4	4.7	7.1	17.9	12.8	16.9	18.3	44.1	50.9	26,865	26,994	0.5	4.9
Berkeley..............................	13.3	20.7	13.9	25.2	18.5	11.4	8.7	9.3	13.0	30.0	50.8	102,743	112,494	9.5	8.1
Beverly Hills........................	6.0	34.0	20.7	5.7	10.6	11.0	15.0	12.2	24.8	45.9	52.2	33,784	33,940	0.5	0.7
Brea....................................	26.2	22.1	21.4	7.1	10.3	16.2	17.8	12.0	15.2	41.9	51.3	35,410	39,189	10.7	11.3
Brentwood...........................	18.7	12.7	24.3	8.8	10.5	10.0	16.0	14.4	15.9	43.0	50.4	23,302	51,624	121.5	23.6
Buena Park..........................	41.4	36.6	22.2	11.1	15.9	12.7	12.6	11.9	13.7	35.5	50.0	78,282	80,619	3.0	2.2
Burbank...............................	19.9	28.7	18.6	8.0	18.0	13.5	14.1	12.8	14.9	38.9	52.3	100,316	103,358	3.0	0.3
Burlingame...........................	13.7	28.0	22.7	4.3	12.7	16.4	14.8	12.2	17.0	40.7	51.7	28,158	28,806	2.3	5.8
Calexico..............................	97.3	46.7	29.5	8.0	12.4	11.4	14.3	11.3	13.0	35.1	54.3	27,109	38,573	42.3	4.1
Camarillo.............................	24.0	14.6	19.7	10.8	8.4	12.9	14.1	14.1	20.1	44.0	49.3	57,077	65,154	14.2	6.1
Campbell..............................	16.5	23.2	20.9	3.9	14.0	15.0	20.1	13.3	12.8	43.3	51.1	38,138	40,572	6.4	4.7
Carlsbad..............................	14.4	13.6	22.7	6.0	7.8	12.8	17.3	14.7	18.7	45.4	50.9	78,247	105,329	34.6	10.0
Carson................................	39.6	35.9	21.2	10.9	11.8	13.0	12.4	12.7	18.0	39.1	51.9	89,730	91,714	2.2	0.2
Cathedral City	53.2	27.7	20.9	9.8	13.2	12.1	13.0	14.8	16.0	41.2	48.4	42,647	51,254	20.2	7.1
Ceres..................................	59.9	24.8	29.9	12.2	16.0	9.9	13.4	9.5	9.1	28.7	47.1	34,609	45,891	32.6	6.3
Cerritos...............................	13.1	41.8	17.0	8.4	12.1	11.2	14.4	15.5	21.5	46.3	51.8	51,488	49,051	-4.7	2.9
Chico..................................	19.5	7.8	18.6	21.6	15.3	10.3	9.8	10.2	14.3	30.8	52.0	59,954	86,807	44.8	9.2
Chino..................................	51.8	23.0	21.6	7.9	16.0	15.8	14.8	11.7	12.1	37.8	41.2	67,168	78,078	16.2	17.3
Chino Hills...........................	27.7	28.8	23.4	8.7	13.2	15.6	15.3	12.5	11.4	37.4	53.5	66,787	74,799	12.0	11.6
Chula Vista..........................	59.7	30.6	25.5	10.3	13.6	14.5	12.2	12.1	11.9	35.5	51.8	173,556	243,923	40.5	11.4
Citrus Heights......................	18.2	14.2	21.3	6.5	19.0	12.0	13.0	11.8	16.4	37.4	50.5	85,071	83,274	-2.1	5.6
Claremont	26.6	12.3	22.9	14.5	8.1	13.1	11.8	8.5	21.1	39.6	53.4	33,998	34,873	2.6	4.6
Clovis..................................	29.1	11.3	27.1	9.5	13.7	11.3	12.7	11.0	14.7	34.8	51.1	68,468	95,835	40.0	16.9
Coachella............................	96.8	38.7	15.5	7.9	17.5	16.8	21.7	13.0	7.6	39.7	53.3	22,724	40,714	79.2	12.6
Colton.................................	70.1	23.0	28.2	9.1	20.7	11.2	12.2	8.6	9.9	30.6	54.4	47,662	52,150	9.4	5.0
Compton..............................	68.6	30.0	29.9	11.2	14.1	13.9	13.6	9.7	7.6	30.7	50.2	93,493	96,411	3.1	0.2
Concord...............................	27.6	26.1	21.7	6.9	14.5	14.0	12.7	13.0	17.2	39.3	50.6	121,780	122,168	0.3	6.2
Corona................................	43.0	21.8	26.6	11.1	14.2	12.9	15.1	10.4	9.8	33.0	49.9	124,966	152,511	22.0	10.7
Costa Mesa.........................	35.2	21.9	20.4	9.4	21.0	13.8	14.7	9.0	11.6	34.6	50.1	108,724	110,078	1.2	3.2
Covina.................................	57.9	30.6	20.9	11.4	13.0	15.0	14.3	12.3	13.1	38.0	54.6	46,837	47,792	2.0	0.4
Culver City	18.5	27.5	19.0	7.6	16.9	15.6	15.2	12.7	13.1	38.1	53.0	38,816	38,917	0.3	0.8
Cupertino.............................	3.2	54.5	24.5	4.4	8.4	14.0	20.1	13.1	15.6	44.1	50.7	50,546	58,572	15.9	2.7
Cypress...............................	20.1	31.5	20.5	8.5	10.5	12.1	16.9	14.3	17.2	43.5	52.1	46,229	47,860	3.5	2.3
Daly City.............................	26.8	51.7	18.4	9.7	18.0	14.1	10.4	13.3	16.1	37.9	51.5	103,621	101,132	-2.4	5.8
Dana Point..........................	22.0	13.2	18.9	6.7	8.5	11.3	17.2	21.6	15.8	48.5	47.4	35,110	33,296	-5.2	1.3
Danville...............................	5.6	16.8	20.9	7.8	3.6	10.3	19.4	16.2	21.8	49.2	52.4	41,715	41,849	0.3	6.7
Davis..................................	14.2	16.6	15.6	34.2	12.3	9.0	9.0	9.2	10.7	25.1	54.6	60,308	65,639	8.8	5.6

1. May be of any race.

Table D. Cities — Households, Group Quarters, Crime, and Education

City	Households, 2017							Persons in group quarters, 2017	Serious crimes known to police[2], 2016				Educational attainment, 2017		
			Percent						Total		Rate[3]			Attainment[4] (percent)	
	Number	Persons per household	Family	Married couple family	Female headed[1]	Non-family	One person		Number	Rate	Violent	Property	Population age 25 and over	High school graduate or less	Bachelor's degree or more
	27	28	29	30	31	32	33	34	35	36	37	38	39	40	41

City	27	28	29	30	31	32	33	34	35	36	37	38	39	40	41
ARKANSAS— Cont'd															
Jacksonville..................	9,867	2.80	71.1	43.7	21.1	28.9	28.0	863	1,559	5,435	861	4,574	17,813	40.0	16.3
Jonesboro......................	29,975	2.41	62.1	44.5	13.2	37.9	27.2	3,703	3,767	5,007	518	4,489	47,148	43.1	30.0
Little Rock....................	79,869	2.44	58.3	38.6	16.6	41.7	34.9	3,726	16,828	8,465	1,534	6,931	133,196	30.1	44.6
North Little Rock	26,595	2.45	55.5	29.3	22.3	44.5	40.2	773	3,433	5,098	753	4,345	43,686	42.1	27.6
Paragould......................	10,592	2.59	65.7	41.4	19.7	34.3	23.6	652	1,541	5,454	570	4,884	17,676	48.4	17.4
Pine Bluff.....................	16,179	2.41	58.5	31.3	23.2	41.5	33.1	3,989	3,491	7,938	1,603	6,335	27,503	51.3	20.6
Rogers	23,710	2.78	75.9	61.6	11.9	24.1	20.0	467	2,580	3,993	520	3,473	40,642	46.7	33.4
Russellville...................	10,392	2.50	59.0	41.5	14.6	41.0	32.6	3,332	1,459	4,968	637	4,332	16,813	38.6	32.7
Sherwood......................	13,385	2.32	62.7	47.2	9.7	37.3	33.9	NA	1,415	4,613	525	4,088	21,642	34.7	29.3
Springdale....................	26,417	3.08	75.2	50.9	13.6	24.8	20.9	1,039	NA	NA	NA	NA	49,248	56.1	17.3
Texarkana.....................	12,953	2.45	66.0	43.4	19.7	34.0	28.1	1,300	1,878	6,172	598	5,574	21,810	51.5	23.5
West Memphis	10,000	2.32	53.4	27.6	22.6	46.6	40.8	535	1,665	6,709	1,866	4,843	15,248	56.3	18.0
CALIFORNIA.....................	13,005,097	2.98	68.5	49.6	13.0	31.5	24.0	817,862	1,176,866	2,998	445	2,553	26,679,273	37.4	33.6
Adelanto.......................	7,154	4.40	92.3	55.6	27.1	7.7	6.5	2,599	836	2,497	824	1,673	17,878	63.6	4.4
Alameda.......................	30,662	2.54	58.8	47.1	8.4	41.2	29.7	1,272	2,171	2,727	190	2,538	56,992	23.4	53.3
Alhambra......................	30,255	2.79	69.3	47.8	14.2	30.7	23.5	844	2,253	2,619	170	2,449	66,570	41.3	34.9
Aliso Viejo	18,519	2.77	69.3	53.6	9.7	30.7	27.1	392	440	869	57	812	34,039	19.2	53.3
Anaheim.......................	98,734	3.52	74.0	51.9	15.6	26.0	17.7	4,877	10,826	3,062	342	2,720	227,623	46.4	25.7
Antioch........................	34,423	3.23	78.2	46.0	24.9	21.8	15.3	587	4,450	3,970	678	3,292	72,879	41.7	21.4
Apple Valley	24,050	3.02	72.8	50.6	17.6	27.2	23.7	513	2,049	2,816	432	2,385	46,910	47.2	16.4
Arcadia........................	18,428	3.16	79.1	59.5	14.2	20.9	15.9	625	1,725	2,933	141	2,792	42,013	23.9	53.3
Atascadero....................	11,482	2.62	64.5	54.9	7.9	35.5	23.9	NA	584	1,940	276	1,664	21,570	26.9	26.5
Atwater........................	8,821	3.32	74.6	50.6	20.6	25.4	20.7	NA	1,209	4,107	690	3,417	17,731	52.5	12.6
Azusa..........................	12,760	3.45	77.7	53.6	16.1	22.3	13.1	5,846	1,314	2,608	347	2,260	28,725	49.2	22.7
Bakersfield	118,508	3.18	73.9	48.1	17.0	26.1	20.0	4,270	18,959	5,005	481	4,524	230,158	46.9	21.4
Baldwin Park	17,725	4.28	86.4	57.8	19.7	13.6	10.3	472	1,805	2,332	376	1,956	51,439	61.4	11.5
Banning.......................	9,443	3.19	64.7	44.5	11.9	35.3	30.9	1,133	824	2,642	474	2,167	20,851	52.7	13.0
Beaumont......................	13,043	3.59	82.2	64.2	11.0	17.8	14.8	NA	1,203	2,659	318	2,340	28,733	40.1	23.6
Bell...........................	9,071	3.87	81.6	44.6	22.7	18.4	16.9	NA	1,015	2,793	641	2,151	22,861	71.9	8.6
Bellflower	24,796	3.11	73.4	44.5	18.2	26.6	21.1	667	2,382	3,023	497	2,525	50,973	50.8	16.1
Bell Gardens	9,729	4.35	88.9	48.3	28.8	11.1	6.8	NA	1,097	2,533	358	2,175	24,638	77.8	4.5
Belmont.......................	10,362	2.56	69.5	62.7	5.3	30.5	27.0	633	408	1,484	113	1,371	19,327	7.7	72.5
Benicia........................	10,585	2.68	78.0	58.7	10.4	22.0	18.2	NA	559	1,968	67	1,901	20,668	21.3	44.8
Berkeley.......................	43,770	2.48	49.0	37.4	7.6	51.0	29.0	13,780	6,022	4,910	491	4,419	74,482	10.7	71.8
Beverly Hills	14,552	2.37	62.4	49.0	8.3	37.6	32.6	NA	1,522	4,346	303	4,044	25,394	18.6	60.0
Brea...........................	15,308	2.78	74.7	59.2	11.2	25.3	19.6	150	1,523	3,586	217	3,370	30,593	20.6	51.8
Brentwood.....................	20,872	2.98	81.1	69.9	7.4	18.9	14.8	NA	1,415	2,338	215	2,124	41,740	24.3	35.8
Buena Park	23,627	3.47	80.0	52.1	21.7	20.0	14.8	988	2,837	3,387	297	3,089	55,369	40.3	32.1
Burbank........................	40,981	2.54	58.2	42.5	10.5	41.8	32.8	544	3,137	2,967	199	2,769	76,947	26.1	40.7
Burlingame....................	11,876	2.54	65.0	54.2	7.1	35.0	24.6	NA	1,112	3,611	201	3,410	22,393	9.7	71.8
Calexico.......................	8,862	4.55	81.4	59.0	16.2	18.6	14.4	NA	1,431	3,548	407	3,141	25,214	58.8	12.2
Camarillo.....................	25,361	2.65	71.0	56.8	10.2	29.0	24.3	635	1,248	1,833	181	1,653	47,171	21.9	44.8
Campbell......................	16,689	2.47	58.9	47.0	5.7	41.1	31.2	347	1,414	3,411	261	3,150	31,223	19.3	51.3
Carlsbad.......................	45,588	2.52	68.6	55.6	11.2	31.4	24.8	573	2,397	2,084	182	1,902	82,252	14.4	62.7
Carson.........................	26,070	3.52	79.7	49.0	23.4	20.3	15.9	882	2,929	3,129	539	2,589	62,961	41.5	26.1
Cathedral City	19,811	2.74	60.3	42.8	10.8	39.7	33.3	385	1,249	2,299	280	2,020	37,821	49.1	18.1
Ceres..........................	13,586	3.53	83.1	57.4	15.3	16.9	13.5	NA	1,464	3,027	385	2,642	28,180	61.1	10.4
Cerritos.......................	15,478	3.29	85.6	69.3	11.9	14.4	11.9	147	2,375	4,735	221	4,514	38,072	19.0	54.1
Chico..........................	37,547	2.39	53.0	36.0	12.0	47.0	30.8	3,740	3,583	3,932	322	3,611	55,827	24.1	36.8
Chino..........................	20,484	3.42	77.0	58.2	16.3	23.0	19.4	19,808	2,358	2,708	238	2,470	63,311	46.9	20.3
Chino Hills....................	23,170	3.46	88.4	70.3	11.8	11.6	9.4	NA	1,072	1,357	75	1,282	54,622	24.3	41.5
Chula Vista....................	80,417	3.34	80.3	57.7	16.5	19.7	15.3	1,953	4,950	1,832	258	1,575	173,547	40.3	28.1
Citrus Heights	33,598	2.59	61.9	44.7	10.3	38.1	28.0	786	3,072	3,498	451	3,047	63,416	36.0	23.1
Claremont	11,159	2.82	74.1	61.5	9.7	25.9	20.9	4,511	1,019	2,788	161	2,626	22,545	14.8	56.4
Clovis	35,855	3.05	74.0	50.7	16.6	26.0	19.3	477	3,228	3,049	241	2,808	69,540	30.1	31.5
Coachella......................	18,551	2.45	44.7	34.7	6.3	55.3	53.4	NA	1,463	3,222	355	2,868	34,790	82.9	4.5
Colton.........................	16,810	3.24	75.2	47.1	22.3	24.8	19.5	320	1,859	3,374	387	2,987	34,350	52.8	17.5
Compton	23,360	4.15	83.6	47.1	27.4	16.4	13.6	721	3,657	3,699	1,142	2,557	57,505	68.5	8.8
Concord........................	45,868	2.80	70.1	54.8	10.2	29.9	23.2	1,353	4,784	3,683	344	3,339	92,591	28.9	37.1
Corona.........................	47,942	3.48	77.4	60.7	11.3	22.6	17.5	779	3,878	2,329	111	2,218	104,579	37.5	26.6
Costa Mesa....................	40,927	2.73	61.6	45.7	9.1	38.4	24.9	1,952	5,022	4,412	362	4,050	79,905	33.2	40.1
Covina.........................	15,243	3.15	72.1	45.8	23.2	27.9	21.5	468	1,453	2,952	333	2,619	32,820	36.4	27.7
Culver City	17,399	2.24	52.9	40.3	9.3	47.1	38.9	332	2,273	5,700	534	5,165	28,828	16.6	58.5
Cupertino......................	21,707	2.78	77.5	69.2	7.0	22.5	19.8	436	1,068	1,752	116	1,636	43,220	10.2	76.1
Cypress........................	16,164	3.03	81.2	62.8	15.0	18.8	16.4	129	844	1,703	125	1,578	34,842	25.0	46.8
Daly City......................	29,162	3.64	74.2	46.7	16.4	25.8	19.9	911	1,875	1,742	227	1,515	76,900	35.3	34.2
Dana Point	14,608	2.31	57.5	48.1	5.7	42.5	34.3	NA	623	1,814	186	1,627	25,276	23.3	51.0
Danville.......................	17,251	2.58	74.8	63.7	8.8	25.2	21.8	200	374	833	20	813	31,914	12.9	66.5
Davis..........................	23,271	2.88	51.1	41.9	5.7	48.9	24.7	1,908	1,773	2,604	159	2,445	34,601	8.4	73.0

1. No spouse present. 2. Data for serious crimes have not been adjusted for underreporting. This may affect comparability between geographic areas and over time. 3. Per 100,000 population estimated by the FBI. 4. Persons 25 years old and over.

City	Money income, 2017 Households			Median family income	Median non-family income	Median earnings, 2017 All persons	Men	Women	Housing units, 2017 Total	Occupied	Percent owner occupied	Median value[1] (dollars)	Median gross rent (dollars)
	Median income	Percent with income less than $20,000	Percent with income of $200,000 or more										
	42	43	44	45	46	47	48	49	50	51	52	53	54
ARKANSAS— Cont'd													
Jacksonville	46,320	19.0	0.4	50,907	29,898	31,103	33,488	26,264	12,518	9,867	47.0	127,800	834
Jonesboro	49,563	18.4	3.9	65,958	25,580	27,551	31,586	25,148	32,470	29,975	51.0	153,000	765
Little Rock	57,534	15.5	6.7	74,390	37,912	35,867	40,602	32,635	93,514	79,869	55.9	169,900	875
North Little Rock	40,579	25.9	1.9	52,344	30,840	26,580	33,771	23,643	33,230	26,595	43.5	137,600	772
Paragould	41,815	18.7	0.4	49,952	24,347	26,009	31,471	22,834	11,393	10,592	57.2	119,700	692
Pine Bluff	33,157	25.9	0.9	41,189	24,630	25,330	23,115	26,411	19,837	16,179	54.4	70,100	693
Rogers	60,527	12.6	7.3	64,589	38,092	31,865	35,762	27,958	24,944	23,710	56.6	171,600	877
Russellville	40,175	22.2	1.8	56,811	22,364	20,366	30,956	16,277	11,881	10,392	54.8	153,700	626
Sherwood	60,226	15.5	8.3	71,403	34,499	36,450	49,572	30,225	14,765	13,385	72.9	146,300	831
Springdale	51,152	6.4	2.1	56,230	35,835	29,876	31,786	23,807	27,877	26,417	53.2	144,400	756
Texarkana	42,475	24.5	0.9	54,028	24,035	22,626	35,066	18,638	14,914	12,953	50.7	128,000	734
West Memphis	28,903	37.3	0.6	32,309	21,085	25,139	30,402	19,535	10,987	10,000	49.6	88,300	660
CALIFORNIA	71,805	13.1	11.1	82,009	46,599	35,544	40,557	30,598	14,177,270	13,005,097	54.8	509,400	1,447
Adelanto	46,954	21.6	0.0	46,351	18,565	25,637	27,753	22,097	7,619	7,154	49.3	198,500	1,180
Alameda	89,979	9.9	13.3	108,648	71,038	51,315	52,022	50,687	33,179	30,662	45.7	891,700	1,790
Alhambra	61,724	17.6	5.2	68,474	45,929	36,288	37,420	35,682	32,017	30,255	38.2	597,200	1,350
Aliso Viejo	101,418	8.1	14.5	117,833	73,050	47,170	60,126	40,593	19,586	18,519	59.0	632,900	2,273
Anaheim	70,395	12.4	7.5	72,477	50,832	30,477	32,252	26,747	102,542	98,734	44.1	577,500	1,578
Antioch	70,696	15.7	7.8	71,484	57,912	34,068	38,309	30,883	35,295	34,423	61.6	408,100	1,708
Apple Valley	55,951	16.3	5.5	58,040	31,881	30,203	47,735	23,334	25,244	24,050	63.1	249,900	1,053
Arcadia	98,242	9.0	16.4	108,815	45,410	49,284	51,847	42,868	20,191	18,428	62.1	1,073,900	1,461
Atascadero	75,934	7.0	7.4	84,658	50,659	35,365	40,581	31,183	11,986	11,482	69.0	483,400	1,409
Atwater	54,128	13.2	0.4	52,923	31,422	23,651	29,884	20,580	9,301	8,821	45.4	224,600	994
Azusa	66,335	11.3	1.8	68,682	52,243	25,232	30,448	22,925	13,865	12,760	53.4	442,000	1,361
Bakersfield	57,105	14.2	4.8	60,183	37,225	31,808	40,270	25,519	126,624	118,508	56.1	239,700	1,082
Baldwin Park	67,472	12.1	3.0	68,230	24,250	26,282	29,510	21,514	18,482	17,725	53.6	416,500	1,457
Banning	39,157	22.6	0.4	42,986	24,914	23,091	22,299	25,197	9,868	9,443	63.6	244,100	1,005
Beaumont	75,689	13.5	7.3	82,172	31,817	31,764	32,344	31,271	13,475	13,043	73.1	322,000	1,065
Bell	38,429	23.2	0.0	44,215	26,696	22,150	27,059	17,101	9,238	9,071	31.9	411,000	1,194
Bellflower	60,233	14.3	2.5	67,046	32,771	30,841	35,852	27,098	26,047	24,796	38.1	471,800	1,371
Bell Gardens	41,257	20.1	0.0	39,658	17,940	20,369	22,320	15,172	9,840	9,729	23.9	405,800	1,149
Belmont	137,104	8.9	34.8	191,446	75,729	90,956	106,566	71,152	11,057	10,362	57.6	1,538,500	2,335
Benicia	117,555	5.0	23.0	119,141	58,274	65,250	76,301	52,071	10,724	10,585	72.4	617,900	1,951
Berkeley	86,497	16.6	18.7	134,089	48,686	31,870	34,818	30,413	47,286	43,770	44.0	993,500	1,627
Beverly Hills	83,874	12.0	24.9	121,782	57,989	52,376	65,423	39,632	17,954	14,552	42.0	2,000,000	2,075
Brea	93,963	4.3	15.7	108,250	75,093	51,269	58,420	39,649	15,777	15,308	66.8	686,800	1,847
Brentwood	105,294	6.6	13.1	116,633	44,265	46,841	67,310	37,120	21,693	20,872	79.3	599,800	2,069
Buena Park	65,139	15.5	4.0	68,606	40,963	29,100	30,723	26,247	25,161	23,627	52.9	570,900	1,567
Burbank	71,558	15.9	10.5	90,181	47,085	40,992	43,368	39,390	42,567	40,981	40.8	723,000	1,635
Burlingame	125,134	3.5	28.7	169,390	80,701	74,065	86,467	60,222	12,714	11,876	50.2	1,987,300	2,229
Calexico	42,155	26.2	3.3	50,912	0	21,535	30,423	14,838	11,557	8,862	59.1	220,700	853
Camarillo	101,310	8.8	17.2	113,138	54,478	50,367	55,597	42,327	26,668	25,361	67.2	622,100	1,962
Campbell	122,107	9.5	24.5	155,625	80,069	65,201	81,822	60,048	17,075	16,689	49.8	1,115,800	2,186
Carlsbad	101,646	7.8	20.3	121,266	62,212	60,638	75,718	45,283	49,194	45,588	66.3	809,700	1,998
Carson	66,784	9.9	5.8	75,104	40,813	30,145	30,595	28,191	26,724	26,070	70.3	467,600	1,314
Cathedral City	53,596	18.3	3.5	59,845	27,811	27,206	27,327	26,892	25,215	19,811	60.7	279,300	1,154
Ceres	57,660	15.4	1.6	58,065	35,632	26,492	33,496	22,862	13,845	13,586	58.5	268,900	1,170
Cerritos	104,247	8.6	17.1	115,841	38,375	46,533	51,057	41,655	16,303	15,478	81.2	686,300	2,129
Chico	50,544	22.7	4.9	66,301	31,905	26,027	27,639	24,322	41,153	37,547	43.4	332,300	983
Chino	72,396	9.2	6.8	80,534	35,353	31,606	36,174	28,569	22,105	20,484	59.7	465,000	1,626
Chino Hills	99,763	6.8	14.5	105,306	47,250	47,052	59,491	35,476	25,173	23,170	78.2	610,900	1,925
Chula Vista	77,273	11.4	6.9	85,490	37,386	37,056	42,068	31,024	87,930	80,417	56.7	497,800	1,604
Citrus Heights	58,774	10.1	3.2	71,582	43,473	35,631	41,335	29,531	35,093	33,598	55.2	302,300	1,211
Claremont	106,568	8.0	18.7	121,008	52,270	47,157	59,616	31,383	11,726	11,159	67.1	650,700	1,612
Clovis	78,146	10.1	8.2	87,941	50,071	39,468	48,088	35,106	37,541	35,855	62.9	319,100	1,164
Coachella	27,233	37.9	2.0	47,909	14,383	22,071	27,794	18,264	19,155	18,551	76.7	228,100	739
Colton	51,535	14.1	3.3	56,889	32,880	31,991	39,236	23,669	19,605	16,810	47.2	273,500	1,135
Compton	50,637	16.8	2.5	52,813	31,867	28,758	30,844	25,441	24,328	23,360	52.3	346,300	1,193
Concord	89,118	9.3	10.4	99,194	52,679	41,782	46,546	36,272	48,559	45,868	61.9	572,800	1,750
Corona	83,345	10.4	9.1	87,277	52,301	35,305	41,068	29,931	50,301	47,942	65.0	470,300	1,540
Costa Mesa	78,904	9.2	9.9	85,564	61,493	36,778	38,997	33,884	42,440	40,927	40.1	744,900	1,798
Covina	71,356	6.8	4.8	77,524	53,955	35,218	37,763	32,314	16,119	15,243	60.7	520,000	1,399
Culver City	100,744	9.2	16.0	126,198	73,019	65,454	71,768	59,438	18,554	17,399	47.7	846,400	1,934
Cupertino	151,051	6.1	34.3	182,064	70,858	89,128	120,183	51,419	24,068	21,707	61.6	1,707,600	2,950
Cypress	101,265	8.0	11.1	111,240	47,997	48,416	52,175	42,073	16,432	16,164	69.9	642,600	1,844
Daly City	90,888	7.0	11.9	98,865	53,762	36,991	40,122	35,264	30,412	29,162	57.6	786,200	2,152
Dana Point	94,133	8.5	20.0	130,729	60,293	51,820	75,922	32,335	16,589	14,608	57.8	890,900	2,105
Danville	137,520	10.0	35.1	172,016	68,665	72,887	106,947	58,588	17,848	17,251	87.1	1,110,400	2,345
Davis	72,800	18.2	16.8	140,396	36,614	21,834	31,123	12,976	24,992	23,271	46.4	649,700	1,515

1. Based on population estimated by the American Community Survey. 2. Includes units rented or sold but not occupied. 3. Specified owner-occupied units; $1,000,000 represents $1,000,000 or more. 4. 50.0 represents 50 percent or more. 5. 10.0 represents 10 percent or less.

Table D. Cities — Commuting, Computer Access, Migration, Labor Force, and Employment

City	Commuting 2017 Percent — Commuting	With commutes of 30 minutes or more	Computer access 2017 Percent — With a computer in the house	With Internet access	Migration 2017 — Percent who lived in the same house one year ago	Percent who lived in another state or county one year ago	Civilian labor force 2018 — Total	Percent change 2017-2018	Unemployment Total	Rate³	Civilian employment 2017 — Population age 16 and older Number	Percent in labor force	Population age 16 to 64 Number	Percent who worked full-year full-time
	55	56	57	58	59	60	61	62	63	64	65	66	67	68
ARKANSAS— Cont'd														
Jacksonville	NA	25.9	93.1	74.9	82.2	10.0	11,718	0.1	495	4.2	20,804	58.1	16,416	53.1
Jonesboro	86.0	19.4	91.7	85.4	72.2	10.0	38,062	0.9	1,180	3.1	60,032	66.5	49,929	49.7
Little Rock	81.9	15.7	90.0	80.9	86.0	5.7	97,434	0.4	3,393	3.5	152,849	67.6	126,073	57.7
North Little Rock	81.4	14.0	85.2	72.0	85.1	2.2	29,766	0.3	1,114	3.7	53,212	62.2	42,471	42.4
Paragould	NA	28.1	90.4	80.4	78.9	6.6	12,399	0.0	459	3.7	21,647	59.2	17,987	44.5
Pine Bluff	89.8	14.8	83.7	57.7	84.1	6.8	16,746	0.4	1,007	6.0	33,303	54.5	27,547	40.6
Rogers	87.9	11.8	93.6	55.2	85.2	7.5	35,205	1.3	919	2.6	49,155	72.3	43,468	63.0
Russellville	79.4	26.0	89.4	77.8	64.4	12.2	13,447	-0.1	537	4.0	23,411	59.5	18,873	39.3
Sherwood	79.6	31.3	90.8	86.2	90.4	2.5	15,923	0.2	484	3.0	25,955	65.5	20,560	62.8
Springdale	83.6	23.1	90.7	74.7	84.8	6.9	38,933	1.5	1,018	2.6	59,092	69.4	49,927	59.8
Texarkana	82.3	12.5	85.4	77.9	84.1	8.4	13,620	-0.2	713	5.2	26,986	56.6	21,285	47.4
West Memphis	84.2	17.0	77.6	72.0	84.1	6.6	10,574	0.1	498	4.7	17,555	56.2	13,905	47.2
CALIFORNIA	73.9	44.1	93.5	87.3	87.0	4.9	19,398,212	1.0	815,410	4.2	31,510,759	63.7	26,005,942	47.9
Adelanto	72.8	60.0	95.0	86.2	87.8	5.8	9,662	1.3	737	7.6	22,898	52.0	21,469	32.1
Alameda	59.1	52.7	94.2	87.5	88.1	5.1	42,116	1.0	1,179	2.8	62,878	67.6	49,741	54.4
Alhambra	76.8	52.0	90.1	85.5	91.7	2.9	46,858	0.8	1,871	4.0	74,492	60.3	56,952	51.6
Aliso Viejo	80.6	37.4	NA	NA	84.1	4.2	30,470	1.0	792	2.6	39,765	75.0	35,569	52.9
Anaheim	76.9	45.8	93.6	88.6	89.6	2.9	172,097	0.9	5,307	3.1	277,723	66.7	240,183	49.7
Antioch	64.6	65.6	93.7	89.1	86.2	5.5	51,295	0.9	2,095	4.1	86,577	64.8	74,125	44.1
Apple Valley	87.3	38.5	95.4	90.8	82.9	2.2	29,075	1.8	1,391	4.8	55,987	52.9	44,462	40.5
Arcadia	77.9	50.8	94.4	90.7	93.2	4.2	29,964	0.8	1,051	3.5	47,703	59.8	38,148	51.8
Atascadero	77.0	30.6	97.3	90.7	90.4	4.3	15,499	0.2	404	2.6	25,059	61.1	19,487	44.8
Atwater	78.5	28.8	92.3	89.0	74.4	2.7	11,985	0.0	923	7.7	22,606	64.3	19,600	41.7
Azusa	75.4	46.5	93.1	85.0	87.2	4.2	25,222	0.5	1,127	4.5	40,248	64.8	34,954	46.0
Bakersfield	81.7	28.2	95.0	86.7	84.8	3.6	176,474	0.9	9,651	5.5	280,124	61.1	238,896	41.7
Baldwin Park	76.4	51.9	94.0	89.0	94.6	1.2	34,916	0.7	1,725	4.9	60,957	66.7	51,126	49.8
Banning	85.0	27.2	85.7	65.9	90.4	4.4	11,230	1.3	563	5.0	23,310	42.2	14,712	38.5
Beaumont	77.1	55.9	97.4	88.2	90.7	5.6	21,928	2.0	729	3.3	34,851	62.8	29,110	48.0
Bell	71.8	62.6	89.4	77.4	NA	NA	15,227	0.6	774	5.1	27,343	63.0	23,539	47.4
Bellflower	81.2	50.3	90.9	78.2	93.9	1.5	36,808	0.7	1,911	5.2	61,926	67.6	52,964	52.8
Bell Gardens	75.1	63.1	83.2	74.5	NA	NA	18,282	0.5	856	4.7	31,425	62.4	27,845	44.8
Belmont	73.4	46.1	NA	NA	85.4	7.7	16,655	1.9	367	2.2	21,391	69.8	16,761	57.1
Benicia	76.1	48.0	NA	NA	88.8	7.7	14,979	0.8	444	3.0	22,493	67.8	17,313	62.3
Berkeley	32.0	44.8	96.7	92.8	71.1	18.5	63,561	0.9	1,791	2.8	107,447	62.2	91,596	37.0
Beverly Hills	76.2	44.5	92.2	91.6	88.2	2.8	18,509	0.7	744	4.0	28,477	60.9	19,920	51.3
Brea	78.8	50.8	97.0	94.0	87.3	4.7	22,813	1.2	664	2.9	34,353	68.2	27,849	53.9
Brentwood	74.3	65.5	95.3	93.0	88.8	5.5	29,101	0.8	984	3.4	49,666	63.3	39,740	47.6
Buena Park	80.5	48.0	94.1	90.7	89.0	4.4	40,651	0.8	1,289	3.2	66,684	65.3	55,340	45.0
Burbank	83.2	43.6	92.5	88.0	89.4	3.5	59,868	0.9	3,151	5.3	86,929	70.9	71,285	52.7
Burlingame	55.0	48.9	97.8	95.9	85.0	6.6	18,411	2.1	399	2.2	24,444	69.6	19,242	55.0
Calexico	67.2	28.5	88.7	82.1	NA	NA	18,054	-1.1	5,375	29.8	29,867	52.3	24,607	32.8
Camarillo	81.8	33.0	95.9	92.1	87.5	3.9	33,623	0.2	974	2.9	55,954	64.7	42,326	51.6
Campbell	79.9	44.4	96.6	92.2	85.5	7.3	26,083	0.9	622	2.4	33,298	71.7	27,971	58.1
Carlsbad	73.2	43.4	97.1	94.1	84.1	6.4	55,322	1.1	1,695	3.1	92,724	63.0	71,149	50.6
Carson	79.4	38.9	92.0	86.0	94.1	1.2	46,518	0.8	2,286	4.9	75,217	61.5	58,559	49.0
Cathedral City	79.0	15.7	87.1	83.2	84.0	4.8	26,230	1.7	1,054	4.0	44,656	57.3	35,895	43.8
Ceres	86.4	34.5	89.4	85.9	87.0	5.5	21,657	0.1	1,633	7.5	35,372	62.5	30,944	41.5
Cerritos	86.3	57.5	97.1	94.1	93.7	3.9	25,710	0.6	1,005	3.9	43,418	61.7	32,456	53.6
Chico	74.5	11.0	95.7	91.2	80.2	10.3	48,744	0.7	1,871	3.8	78,562	63.9	65,241	36.8
Chino	79.8	50.9	96.6	91.0	82.4	13.3	42,664	2.0	1,428	3.3	73,269	48.1	62,365	38.2
Chino Hills	85.5	64.1	98.8	95.4	90.3	8.4	43,956	2.1	1,198	2.7	63,473	62.8	54,335	46.8
Chula Vista	77.8	51.2	95.3	87.7	89.6	2.8	123,401	1.0	4,431	3.6	210,270	65.3	178,154	41.6
Citrus Heights	79.1	43.7	94.0	85.6	81.0	10.0	43,922	1.9	1,630	3.7	72,176	62.2	57,741	45.9
Claremont	64.4	37.7	96.8	92.8	83.8	11.5	17,041	0.8	735	4.3	28,461	60.6	20,842	42.1
Clovis	85.9	17.1	93.9	90.6	82.0	4.9	53,522	1.2	2,091	3.9	82,711	62.1	66,603	49.5
Coachella	NA	25.7	92.1	82.6	NA	NA	20,041	1.0	2,157	10.8	39,675	71.2	36,244	41.4
Colton	79.2	28.0	90.2	84.7	92.4	0.8	24,747	1.5	1,029	4.2	41,112	61.5	35,663	50.5
Compton	81.9	53.8	90.6	67.4	NA	NA	39,641	0.9	2,517	6.3	71,032	61.5	63,607	48.0
Concord	68.5	51.7	94.3	88.0	85.7	5.6	66,480	0.9	1,879	2.8	103,418	65.4	81,105	50.1
Corona	79.1	55.5	95.2	91.5	87.3	6.6	84,274	2.0	2,801	3.3	129,144	68.9	112,696	50.8
Costa Mesa	78.3	29.9	95.6	90.6	88.7	3.3	66,237	1.0	1,730	2.6	92,582	72.0	79,340	54.1
Covina	79.3	62.9	95.4	89.8	90.4	2.5	24,300	0.7	1,201	4.9	39,975	65.6	33,631	45.1
Culver City	80.5	45.0	95.4	89.3	81.3	8.0	23,097	0.7	1,017	4.4	32,393	73.4	27,259	59.4
Cupertino	72.1	49.1	95.9	93.4	87.3	7.5	29,968	0.9	778	2.6	48,156	63.2	38,671	55.9
Cypress	79.0	54.5	94.3	90.7	88.3	8.7	25,227	1.2	791	3.1	41,153	62.0	32,737	48.8
Daly City	59.1	53.4	94.1	87.2	91.3	5.8	64,812	2.0	1,453	2.2	89,227	68.4	72,011	56.8
Dana Point	71.8	42.1	96.2	93.4	84.4	4.1	18,931	1.0	511	2.7	28,312	65.4	22,935	46.0
Danville	73.6	50.0	96.0	94.7	89.2	6.3	21,004	1.0	583	2.8	36,486	60.7	26,727	46.6
Davis	55.7	28.0	98.1	95.4	67.1	16.4	35,722	1.8	953	2.7	59,760	59.8	52,390	31.7

1. Employed persons.   2. Households.   3. Percent of civilian labor force.   4. Persons 16 years old and over.

Table D. Cities — Construction, Wholesale Trade, and Retail Trade

City	Value of residential construction authorized by building permits, 2018			Wholesale trade[1], 2012				Retail trade[2], 2012			
	New construction ($1,000)	Number of housing units	Percent single family	Number of establishments	Number of employees	Sales (mil dol)	Annual payroll (mil dol)	Number of establish-ments	Number of employees	Sales (mil dol)	Annual payroll (mil dol)
	69	70	71	72	73	74	75	76	77	78	79

City	69	70	71	72	73	74	75	76	77	78	79
ARKANSAS— Cont'd											
Jacksonville	5,405	53	66.0	10	84	66.9	3.8	89	1,404	396.8	36.7
Jonesboro	77,042	635	63.5	94	1,133	643.5	50.6	406	6,053	1,556.4	135.5
Little Rock	124,998	470	69.1	358	6,552	3,801.0	340.0	994	14,533	4,025.2	354.2
North Little Rock	20,906	135	64.4	196	3,234	3,898.4	185.7	417	6,092	1,557.4	138.8
Paragould	19,214	158	68.4	26	378	459.2	15.1	130	1,608	395.9	33.7
Pine Bluff	334	7	14.3	40	354	189.0	14.8	248	3,072	744.6	71.2
Rogers	113,770	702	62.8	60	510	619.9	30.8	297	5,130	1,162.2	114.4
Russellville	5,195	61	100.0	47	384	296.7	16.6	216	2,815	782.7	60.7
Sherwood	35,377	205	100.0	30	188	93.2	8.1	94	1,899	763.9	53.7
Springdale	61,692	227	100.0	144	1,569	1,133.8	74.0	247	3,448	1,011.1	86.8
Texarkana	6,242	29	100.0	37	D	D	D	113	1,324	416.4	29.7
West Memphis	1,476	12	100.0	38	717	1,799.2	32.4	102	1,660	617.7	35.6
CALIFORNIA	27,844,627	113,502	51.8	52,664	723,526	666,652.2	48,408.7	106,419	1,540,055	481,800.5	43,361.0
Adelanto	2,051	16	100.0	7	114	42.2	4.5	19	286	80.8	8.0
Alameda	4,092	31	100.0	63	2,252	2,887.1	218.6	155	1,956	492.2	54.1
Alhambra	4,303	34	100.0	234	999	476.8	31.3	233	3,923	1,636.6	116.7
Aliso Viejo	0	0	0.0	74	1,311	1,010.6	133.6	82	1,210	500.3	43.2
Anaheim	42,205	572	21.2	799	9,520	7,153.5	562.0	826	13,333	3,757.9	374.1
Antioch	25,059	121	52.1	23	316	276.1	18.2	216	3,781	939.3	102.9
Apple Valley	12,684	79	100.0	10	32	8.6	1.2	113	2,311	598.1	53.9
Arcadia	48,280	90	87.8	284	1,066	527.0	39.5	295	4,276	860.3	94.2
Atascadero	6,151	29	100.0	30	210	66.5	9.5	116	1,230	298.5	30.7
Atwater	505	3	100.0	8	D	D	D	74	1,314	257.5	27.3
Azusa	40,595	177	22.0	75	1,416	883.0	103.9	94	1,147	470.7	33.6
Bakersfield	308,554	1,108	95.8	274	3,933	3,693.1	216.0	960	18,130	5,263.8	454.7
Baldwin Park	14,119	79	100.0	151	860	373.8	34.0	130	2,106	535.3	52.4
Banning	300	1	100.0	11	347	72.0	10.9	58	616	176.7	16.6
Beaumont	177,383	684	100.0	9	27	3.9	0.8	57	1,297	348.8	32.0
Bell	7,448	54	18.5	71	1,564	1,029.1	83.9	51	458	128.5	10.8
Bellflower	7,424	51	37.3	34	226	98.4	10.3	174	1,970	551.5	53.2
Bell Gardens	7,762	49	18.4	39	474	178.2	18.6	79	1,127	321.2	30.9
Belmont	8,373	12	100.0	19	D	D	D	57	761	292.3	28.8
Benicia	250	1	100.0	66	1,134	733.7	63.0	71	844	266.6	31.0
Berkeley	35,817	195	33.8	94	1,175	565.1	82.4	497	5,449	1,341.0	164.2
Beverly Hills	99,040	51	86.3	158	778	647.5	48.2	429	5,382	2,912.3	275.0
Brea	3,331	9	66.7	263	3,865	3,321.6	215.5	321	6,133	1,260.4	134.2
Brentwood	66,667	324	100.0	14	59	18.3	2.5	142	2,263	557.2	54.7
Buena Park	7,299	34	100.0	204	3,037	2,044.9	165.9	202	3,987	1,731.1	134.4
Burbank	3,320	17	100.0	208	2,987	4,628.6	209.3	399	7,310	2,316.8	191.7
Burlingame	85,362	301	11.0	136	978	870.8	64.3	159	2,011	776.4	79.8
Calexico	1,752	10	100.0	58	403	416.3	11.7	136	1,997	432.4	40.7
Camarillo	93,220	526	49.2	147	2,132	1,157.4	130.2	313	5,248	1,526.8	133.7
Campbell	20,352	69	91.3	74	D	D	D	182	2,925	757.9	83.6
Carlsbad	81,160	261	98.9	292	5,465	3,115.2	354.2	485	7,796	2,649.1	215.9
Carson	9,195	153	2.6	337	6,718	5,893.4	352.1	210	4,267	1,398.5	148.4
Cathedral City	18,456	92	100.0	24	127	37.6	4.6	145	2,002	790.1	65.7
Ceres	7,921	37	100.0	22	335	281.9	16.9	89	1,606	443.7	38.5
Cerritos	0	0	0.0	254	5,230	5,454.5	329.6	233	7,278	2,479.9	213.9
Chico	89,101	449	75.9	84	831	399.3	40.8	419	6,368	1,790.7	165.7
Chino	193,271	891	49.0	457	5,476	3,872.9	265.8	266	4,563	1,188.9	105.8
Chino Hills	63,418	235	98.3	90	248	203.5	8.8	140	2,399	635.6	57.1
Chula Vista	401,377	1,751	29.4	299	1,793	1,406.4	77.9	616	11,228	2,744.4	273.1
Citrus Heights	4,514	20	100.0	16	58	70.0	3.3	263	4,698	1,029.7	103.2
Claremont	12,371	70	54.3	20	86	48.1	4.1	80	1,102	379.7	34.8
Clovis	268,900	1,107	80.6	47	190	189.9	9.0	267	5,059	1,496.3	130.8
Coachella	683	8	0.0	22	460	162.5	29.0	49	671	259.6	15.9
Colton	15,672	82	100.0	44	770	642.1	36.6	103	1,508	480.9	44.2
Compton	1,856	16	37.5	141	2,276	1,584.9	122.5	160	1,571	368.8	31.3
Concord	2,631	20	90.0	116	896	444.6	53.7	423	7,650	2,376.7	225.2
Corona	94,894	465	38.7	288	5,898	7,239.0	355.9	450	8,115	2,616.1	218.4
Costa Mesa	48,728	163	100.0	288	4,160	17,724.3	315.1	748	13,371	3,815.5	386.4
Covina	1,972	7	100.0	67	405	143.3	18.1	154	2,746	671.1	78.3
Culver City	42,413	247	11.7	110	2,279	1,690.9	200.3	287	5,510	1,660.3	154.5
Cupertino	35,455	64	64.1	71	1,507	1,092.5	107.8	121	D	D	D
Cypress	22,899	173	100.0	101	3,164	3,767.2	259.9	103	1,617	614.0	46.7
Daly City	9,101	18	100.0	35	D	D	D	193	3,738	885.4	91.3
Dana Point	86,046	85	100.0	51	232	155.8	12.7	102	1,042	340.4	27.3
Danville	18,018	24	100.0	44	173	167.2	10.3	124	1,610	548.1	45.5
Davis	72,033	324	14.5	16	256	495.9	21.3	124	2,061	466.0	50.5

1. Merchant wholesalers except manufacturers' sales branches and offices. 2. Establishments with payroll.

Real Estate, Professional Services, and Manufacturing

City	Real estate and rental and leasing, 2012				Professional, scientific, and technical services[1], 2012				Manufacturing, 2012			
	Number of establishments	Number of employees	Receipts (mil dol)	Annual payroll (mil dol)	Number of establishments	Number of employees	Receipts (mil dol)	Annual payroll (mil dol)	Number of establishments	Number of employees	Receipts (mil dol)	Annual payroll (mil dol)
	80	81	82	83	84	85	86	87	88	89	90	91
ARKANSAS— Cont'd												
Jacksonville	44	170	24.3	4.4	34	191	14.4	5.0	23	543	D	27.2
Jonesboro	110	469	79.0	12.8	157	D	D	D	80	4,781	1,900.6	203.7
Little Rock	377	2,450	423.0	89.3	1,182	D	D	D	166	8,152	4,227.1	419.7
North Little Rock	89	440	89.0	13.4	175	1,435	172.4	62.8	62	1,978	D	93.1
Paragould	30	D	D	D	47	423	38.2	18.6	37	3,299	D	128.4
Pine Bluff	53	173	26.7	4.4	57	D	D	D	48	4,258	1,859.3	185.2
Rogers	83	322	65.1	13.2	216	1,644	275.6	87.7	53	5,462	1,753.7	217.3
Russellville	59	174	26.2	4.9	105	D	D	D	40	4,067	1,339.7	149.1
Sherwood	28	80	21.3	2.5	43	539	113.1	30.5	17	D	D	D
Springdale	74	254	39.7	7.5	135	D	D	D	101	7,619	2,375.8	265.0
Texarkana	27	D	D	D	41	D	D	D	26	2,303	D	D
West Memphis	30	168	20.0	5.0	37	D	D	D	25	815	469.3	31.6
CALIFORNIA	49,276	273,511	78,740.2	13,467.5	113,553	1,270,902	227,858.9	87,924.6	38,741	1,163,341	512,303.2	69,316.8
Adelanto	9	21	3.3	0.4	7	75	11.0	4.5	42	1,108	263.4	55.3
Alameda	95	382	65.5	13.6	234	2,323	614.3	222.1	50	3,006	1,130.2	274.0
Alhambra	117	396	66.2	15.1	220	D	D	D	76	1,252	307.3	64.9
Aliso Viejo	79	D	D	D	288	3,609	843.5	364.2	30	378	58.0	21.7
Anaheim	381	3,684	508.9	131.9	681	4,384	760.1	251.7	693	19,991	4,824.4	1,071.6
Antioch	60	266	43.1	7.5	92	600	103.3	28.6	22	235	125.9	12.2
Apple Valley	37	179	23.1	4.3	68	339	33.2	12.1	25	319	D	15.4
Arcadia	175	483	98.1	17.1	258	D	D	D	47	905	194.3	46.0
Atascadero	27	D	D	D	74	D	D	D	26	109	15.8	4.6
Atwater	12	32	4.9	0.6	10	27	3.0	1.0	13	368	D	18.9
Azusa	22	46	13.8	1.5	35	309	64.0	22.4	100	4,979	1,505.2	318.8
Bakersfield	343	1,907	335.7	69.5	798	D	D	D	143	2,541	646.2	110.3
Baldwin Park	22	119	17.8	4.2	31	143	12.0	4.6	85	1,533	285.7	63.8
Banning	29	216	38.8	6.0	14	145	9.5	3.7	22	326	72.9	14.2
Beaumont	24	77	10.2	1.7	19	45	4.4	1.7	14	361	102.3	15.9
Bell	12	D	D	D	16	405	45.4	18.2	30	1,711	657.2	85.4
Bellflower	78	249	48.7	10.7	60	317	17.0	6.3	33	254	46.8	11.2
Bell Gardens	10	36	10.0	0.9	10	153	14.6	5.2	50	863	156.7	32.5
Belmont	49	533	67.1	25.6	107	508	62.1	41.7	20	352	D	19.2
Benicia	43	187	47.1	8.7	98	580	92.2	36.8	70	2,579	7,511.9	195.5
Berkeley	198	744	175.2	40.0	605	3,646	692.1	295.7	152	3,744	D	241.1
Beverly Hills	481	2,312	1,293.7	155.3	1,017	5,275	1,681.6	538.7	57	348	33.9	9.2
Brea	97	536	118.4	26.9	288	D	D	D	152	5,251	1,292.7	254.2
Brentwood	55	173	40.2	6.8	84	280	36.7	12.6	17	232	D	12.3
Buena Park	57	218	40.3	6.9	110	960	135.1	50.1	109	3,966	1,990.3	204.1
Burbank	242	2,976	1,052.6	246.5	608	D	D	D	191	5,031	1,269.2	284.4
Burlingame	149	935	213.8	44.8	272	D	D	D	49	1,679	D	98.9
Calexico	24	104	9.3	1.8	42	112	12.2	3.4	12	265	D	20.8
Camarillo	87	608	111.7	28.3	299	2,498	601.1	181.4	134	4,292	1,636.8	230.4
Campbell	85	448	155.2	36.3	312	D	D	D	92	1,840	431.0	113.7
Carlsbad	314	1,571	330.6	74.0	894	D	D	D	160	12,711	4,983.1	1,024.6
Carson	64	625	453.8	62.4	101	970	159.8	40.6	230	9,808	15,329.4	624.3
Cathedral City	38	182	40.7	5.8	40	99	11.0	2.7	13	29	5.5	1.3
Ceres	30	110	24.6	4.0	25	311	34.0	14.1	21	391	90.1	16.8
Cerritos	79	226	56.8	9.6	188	D	D	D	88	2,532	509.8	111.1
Chico	137	769	88.0	18.4	291	D	D	D	71	1,549	568.6	65.1
Chino	78	289	66.4	11.5	148	1,068	130.1	42.1	220	5,480	1,465.1	232.5
Chino Hills	66	116	36.2	4.9	169	428	66.5	18.7	10	72	D	1.4
Chula Vista	241	987	217.4	34.8	357	D	D	D	126	4,237	1,363.4	330.2
Citrus Heights	79	408	46.7	11.6	122	1,252	128.6	50.2	12	31	3.2	1.0
Claremont	58	180	24.5	7.7	133	D	D	D	20	620	114.6	26.2
Clovis	79	276	49.5	7.6	155	894	88.8	35.3	42	2,866	D	131.0
Coachella	17	58	8.7	1.8	6	D	D	D	11	773	433.2	37.5
Colton	34	222	39.8	7.7	49	D	D	D	53	2,758	1,090.7	95.5
Compton	21	61	13.2	2.3	15	D	D	D	129	4,001	1,184.2	178.4
Concord	148	996	215.3	48.3	298	3,084	581.0	226.3	106	1,779	464.2	97.9
Corona	175	641	156.0	25.2	319	1,877	210.8	106.2	341	12,813	4,810.5	586.6
Costa Mesa	298	3,347	666.1	135.9	687	8,743	2,097.9	740.2	232	6,196	1,541.4	321.1
Covina	94	479	63.9	16.8	148	946	131.5	44.7	89	1,490	344.0	69.4
Culver City	107	1,251	229.6	59.8	424	D	D	D	53	1,612	367.4	84.7
Cupertino	104	401	256.0	28.6	444	2,980	1,111.0	417.2	35	927	382.1	90.2
Cypress	65	277	58.0	13.3	118	979	212.8	55.6	35	1,287	588.1	92.4
Daly City	54	273	136.9	13.2	69	291	25.2	8.4	20	283	D	7.2
Dana Point	78	163	34.4	7.8	168	548	113.1	46.1	24	155	37.3	7.0
Danville	103	379	148.2	26.7	223	956	185.9	66.9	11	125	D	5.1
Davis	116	619	75.6	21.2	205	D	D	D	22	627	D	32.0

1. Establishments subject to federal tax.

Table D. Cities — Accommodation and Food Services, Arts, Entertainment, and Recreation, and Health Care and Social Assistance

City	Accommodation and food services, 2012				Arts, entertainment, and recreation[1], 2012				Health care and social assistance,[1] 2012			
	Number of establish-ments	Number of employees	Receipts (mil dol)	Annual payroll (mil dol)	Number of establish-ments	Number of employees	Receipts (mil dol)	Annual payroll (mil dol)	Number of establish-ments	Number of employees	Receipts (mil dol)	Annual payroll (mil dol)
	92	93	94	95	96	97	98	99	100	101	102	103
ARKANSAS— Cont'd												
Jacksonville	61	1,010	44.9	12.3	5	D	D	D	51	D	D	D
Jonesboro	193	4,134	182.9	50.6	14	184	7.4	3.1	284	D	D	D
Little Rock	593	12,849	626.5	185.9	64	677	40.9	13.3	825	10,939	1,405.6	615.5
North Little Rock	227	4,536	213.5	63.3	20	D	D	D	212	2,659	322.4	127.2
Paragould	61	D	D	D	4	D	D	D	73	D	D	D
Pine Bluff	102	D	D	D	3	D	D	D	153	D	D	D
Rogers	145	3,735	169.7	52.0	9	174	11.6	4.9	164	D	D	D
Russellville	103	2,256	101.8	24.9	9	42	2.0	0.4	112	D	D	D
Sherwood	43	673	34.9	8.9	3	D	D	D	68	D	D	D
Springdale	134	2,345	106.4	30.2	12	D	D	D	139	3,900	446.2	171.2
Texarkana	69	D	D	D	5	D	D	D	50	D	D	D
West Memphis	68	1,158	65.6	15.7	5	D	D	D	66	D	D	D
CALIFORNIA	78,560	1,394,984	90,830.4	25,147.8	19,010	245,599	34,302.9	11,726.7	89,999	1,005,201	127,355.7	48,372.7
Adelanto	14	D	D	D	1	D	D	D	4	D	D	D
Alameda	208	2,505	145.4	38.8	28	566	281.4	169.8	182	2,115	251.2	88.4
Alhambra	196	3,107	170.3	46.8	15	D	D	D	265	2,672	292.9	102.2
Aliso Viejo	68	1,335	87.1	24.8	15	D	D	D	119	D	D	D
Anaheim	692	23,526	1,589.1	507.2	75	D	D	D	825	11,330	1,388.6	525.8
Antioch	129	1,981	105.6	29.7	13	D	D	D	210	D	D	D
Apple Valley	85	D	D	D	7	D	D	D	190	D	D	D
Arcadia	212	3,593	220.4	59.1	70	D	D	D	383	D	D	D
Atascadero	70	926	53.1	12.9	9	127	4.6	1.6	85	D	D	D
Atwater	35	532	27.7	6.5	3	69	3.6	1.0	23	D	D	D
Azusa	73	895	48.0	12.8	3	D	D	D	44	523	27.4	11.7
Bakersfield	675	12,835	713.4	189.0	59	2,198	85.8	29.3	973	11,550	1,564.5	498.1
Baldwin Park	85	1,201	74.2	18.5	2	D	D	D	77	D	D	D
Banning	46	751	41.3	10.1	NA	NA	NA	NA	41	653	93.4	23.7
Beaumont	45	629	33.1	10.0	4	D	D	D	41	D	D	D
Bell	54	580	35.7	8.8	1	D	D	D	30	279	20.7	8.9
Bellflower	117	1,294	72.6	18.7	8	170	7.6	2.4	143	D	D	D
Bell Gardens	53	669	50.4	10.7	2	D	D	D	26	526	40.3	15.0
Belmont	62	716	58.0	13.2	5	D	D	D	47	D	D	D
Benicia	60	767	40.2	10.6	6	112	8.9	1.7	51	D	D	D
Berkeley	437	6,068	383.7	114.8	62	836	131.8	27.2	401	3,197	463.0	188.7
Beverly Hills	200	8,518	782.3	248.1	857	3,764	1,868.9	804.7	1,091	5,921	1,249.2	360.7
Brea	160	4,045	232.7	69.9	18	221	20.7	4.9	158	D	D	D
Brentwood	102	1,623	88.8	23.1	10	D	D	D	98	D	D	D
Buena Park	185	2,924	183.6	46.4	13	D	D	D	161	1,619	170.0	58.5
Burbank	325	6,840	532.9	130.3	308	D	D	D	467	D	D	D
Burlingame	145	4,340	387.8	115.5	18	216	19.1	4.6	179	2,136	426.2	133.0
Calexico	53	852	44.7	11.6	2	D	D	D	16	115	12.0	4.3
Camarillo	165	3,099	173.5	47.2	21	379	23.1	7.4	236	2,256	202.5	78.3
Campbell	133	2,474	150.8	42.2	19	D	D	D	193	D	D	D
Carlsbad	251	7,216	468.8	154.5	59	2,435	246.6	49.3	290	3,598	496.5	180.1
Carson	158	2,289	144.2	34.6	17	D	D	D	146	1,327	109.9	42.4
Cathedral City	85	1,365	67.0	19.6	10	D	D	D	53	462	29.2	13.1
Ceres	58	1,188	52.0	13.4	4	54	5.6	0.7	39	345	34.5	12.9
Cerritos	146	D	D	D	10	D	D	D	196	2,163	236.9	89.7
Chico	247	4,730	213.1	60.4	23	556	19.7	6.3	374	3,766	383.8	139.8
Chino	149	2,564	127.7	36.8	26	441	22.0	7.2	190	2,297	255.9	84.2
Chino Hills	116	2,267	114.5	33.9	13	324	19.0	6.0	108	661	71.1	23.0
Chula Vista	385	6,198	357.9	96.7	35	829	66.2	15.1	506	4,450	514.8	213.8
Citrus Heights	126	2,343	113.2	32.5	18	D	D	D	148	1,507	122.3	49.4
Claremont	97	1,667	90.5	24.3	11	D	D	D	141	1,336	118.8	48.2
Clovis	197	3,352	167.2	46.2	16	D	D	D	187	D	D	D
Coachella	46	753	35.2	8.2	1	D	D	D	10	D	D	D
Colton	85	1,150	58.0	15.2	4	D	D	D	79	D	D	D
Compton	94	1,207	77.6	18.5	4	D	D	D	62	527	41.3	17.7
Concord	247	3,850	229.6	61.7	30	714	40.8	12.1	333	3,810	420.7	163.9
Corona	276	4,993	261.4	70.9	29	D	D	D	315	3,204	333.1	119.1
Costa Mesa	422	8,168	530.6	147.9	54	581	50.5	12.4	344	3,573	343.0	121.0
Covina	114	1,803	98.7	26.0	10	D	D	D	199	2,636	265.1	113.9
Culver City	183	3,434	231.9	63.6	129	626	172.6	43.9	181	5,143	367.4	142.9
Cupertino	150	2,728	168.4	45.5	15	203	12.8	3.5	184	D	D	D
Cypress	105	1,460	88.3	23.2	26	393	30.3	10.6	114	1,648	166.5	66.6
Daly City	145	2,549	165.7	42.9	11	D	D	D	241	D	D	D
Dana Point	111	3,674	299.2	94.4	21	D	D	D	97	613	66.3	23.1
Danville	96	1,576	85.1	25.8	18	330	35.2	9.5	132	1,097	114.6	45.2
Davis	182	D	D	D	17	266	9.0	3.2	118	1,483	229.0	63.5

1. Establishments subject to federal tax.

Table D. Cities — Other Services and Government Employment and Payroll

City	Other services[1] Number of establishments	Number of employees	Receipts (mil dol)	Annual payroll (mil dol)	Government employment and payroll, 2012 Full-time equivalent employees	March payroll Total (dollars)	Percent of total for: Administrative, judicial, and legal	Police and corrections	Fire protection	Highways and transportation	Health and welfare	Natural resources and utilities	Education and libraries
	104	105	106	107	108	109	110	111	112	113	114	115	116
ARKANSAS— Cont'd													
Jacksonville	24	124	8.6	2.6	351	1,152,915	9.7	28.8	19.4	4.2	5.3	27.7	0.0
Jonesboro	90	653	67.9	19.3	689	2,345,837	8.5	24.7	13.3	9.8	1.2	42.4	0.0
Little Rock	291	2,215	176.7	54.2	2,851	11,721,278	7.5	27.1	19.0	8.2	12.4	20.1	0.0
North Little Rock	118	1,132	69.5	23.3	971	3,614,112	10.1	25.8	20.1	6.7	0.9	29.4	2.5
Paragould	34	D	D	D	282	995,938	7.4	13.5	10.1	7.0	0.0	34.9	0.0
Pine Bluff	56	D	D	D	430	1,262,555	9.4	40.1	30.3	11.6	2.7	0.0	0.0
Rogers	64	326	28.7	7.6	478	1,723,247	11.6	29.5	25.6	5.5	1.0	18.2	4.6
Russellville	62	350	23.9	8.9	247	826,281	6.7	26.5	27.2	7.8	0.0	20.1	0.0
Sherwood	41	196	17.8	5.0	260	794,982	19.0	40.7	0.0	5.0	4.1	26.7	0.1
Springdale	87	778	60.4	21.5	584	1,997,062	10.3	28.7	23.9	6.6	1.7	21.9	3.3
Texarkana	34	D	D	D	237	974,321	9.2	47.4	27.7	4.9	2.8	2.3	0.0
West Memphis	37	D	D	D	383	1,214,605	9.2	23.7	21.2	5.8	0.8	25.0	1.3
CALIFORNIA	46,852	299,033	29,320.9	8,446.1	X	X	X	X	X	X	X	X	X
Adelanto	5	D	D	D	122	519,045	17.9	63.0	0.0	6.8	0.0	11.6	0.0
Alameda	104	556	42.8	12.8	658	4,669,134	6.4	25.2	22.5	8.7	5.7	19.2	3.1
Alhambra	97	427	40.9	11.2	423	2,729,610	8.0	33.5	27.5	3.8	4.0	18.8	4.5
Aliso Viejo	41	D	D	D	20	114,486	83.1	0.0	0.0	0.0	0.0	16.9	0.0
Anaheim	354	2,718	252.4	74.3	2,214	15,281,363	10.2	31.2	18.4	2.6	1.6	22.9	1.9
Antioch	88	506	37.6	12.3	306	1,931,728	10.7	57.2	0.0	6.0	2.1	20.9	0.0
Apple Valley	38	261	13.8	6.6	115	584,392	38.7	9.0	0.0	3.2	20.4	28.7	0.0
Arcadia	97	448	32.9	10.0	327	2,164,149	7.3	33.8	24.4	10.7	0.9	4.2	5.7
Atascadero	31	126	12.9	3.7	131	738,888	19.1	30.8	22.5	9.0	0.0	14.3	0.0
Atwater	19	88	7.8	1.8	124	673,870	13.1	42.2	13.9	5.5	4.6	18.3	0.0
Azusa	61	287	23.1	6.8	312	2,003,992	16.2	36.1	0.0	4.3	3.4	34.3	3.5
Bakersfield	360	2,420	249.6	70.7	1,424	8,316,644	6.2	38.5	18.9	8.6	0.9	17.6	0.0
Baldwin Park	35	125	13.5	3.8	227	1,307,981	10.1	58.7	0.0	11.0	9.8	10.4	0.0
Banning	24	139	11.8	4.4	195	1,176,594	19.1	35.3	0.3	9.9	1.7	30.2	0.0
Beaumont	41	189	16.1	4.3	168	910,677	6.3	58.6	0.8	7.4	3.3	11.9	0.0
Bell	24	190	12.3	4.4	208	970,721	15.5	65.9	0.0	1.2	2.2	15.3	0.0
Bellflower	120	540	54.4	14.6	135	560,170	32.9	10.6	0.0	29.1	9.0	18.3	0.0
Bell Gardens	35	341	26.4	8.6	195	974,379	15.1	53.7	0.0	4.2	3.0	14.3	0.0
Belmont	51	D	D	D	110	851,441	1.4	33.4	0.0	4.3	7.0	30.3	0.0
Benicia	57	552	58.2	25.0	293	1,695,705	13.1	23.5	18.0	3.4	0.0	29.9	7.0
Berkeley	184	1,327	101.2	57.4	1,669	13,806,771	10.8	38.3	13.0	4.5	13.4	11.2	4.6
Beverly Hills	286	1,965	162.3	48.7	680	6,033,141	8.8	32.8	21.5	1.8	6.2	14.5	3.8
Brea	82	920	94.9	35.4	435	2,822,410	14.6	42.7	17.3	2.4	1.3	14.0	0.0
Brentwood	74	455	37.4	12.5	277	2,032,978	16.0	33.4	0.0	3.6	6.7	27.5	0.0
Buena Park	76	D	D	D	314	1,712,183	10.2	51.5	0.0	9.3	10.0	14.8	0.0
Burbank	249	2,438	233.0	94.4	1,339	10,789,444	10.5	20.6	13.7	5.7	4.5	35.6	3.0
Burlingame	116	720	62.3	18.2	257	2,033,098	7.4	25.4	24.0	8.9	0.0	20.2	9.2
Calexico	14	D	D	D	180	959,584	5.6	39.4	18.0	0.4	3.6	18.6	2.2
Camarillo	100	687	46.9	15.2	150	1,175,192	38.2	4.5	0.0	28.2	1.2	24.7	0.0
Campbell	176	1,133	97.9	32.0	194	1,441,718	19.7	44.4	0.0	5.3	0.4	13.4	0.0
Carlsbad	145	1,476	146.1	43.5	776	4,824,420	15.7	25.6	15.4	11.2	1.9	15.0	9.2
Carson	96	716	83.4	24.7	510	2,517,774	28.5	6.7	0.0	15.0	7.7	26.1	0.0
Cathedral City	80	514	39.8	11.8	175	1,230,278	13.0	52.3	30.1	4.1	0.0	0.6	0.0
Ceres	43	562	63.2	34.2	182	1,207,924	11.0	48.7	18.9	7.5	0.0	8.8	0.0
Cerritos	58	521	37.0	16.0	300	1,151,269	17.9	4.7	0.0	2.1	2.0	12.8	8.8
Chico	143	775	76.5	23.2	388	2,759,409	11.9	39.0	24.3	7.0	1.6	8.0	0.0
Chino	127	1,343	98.7	42.2	425	2,145,199	12.8	49.4	0.0	3.6	12.3	20.9	0.0
Chino Hills	55	285	14.7	4.4	182	1,001,156	45.8	0.0	0.0	13.9	6.0	34.0	0.0
Chula Vista	207	1,602	108.9	37.2	1,114	7,346,424	14.6	37.1	17.1	15.8	1.2	10.8	2.8
Citrus Heights	80	443	53.8	12.3	204	1,278,252	11.3	69.4	0.0	6.6	1.3	2.7	0.0
Claremont	34	142	8.7	2.6	169	958,849	29.8	43.5	0.0	0.0	0.0	26.7	0.0
Clovis	111	729	59.0	17.3	505	2,897,575	9.7	32.5	16.7	12.7	3.2	20.0	0.0
Coachella	13	D	D	D	79	428,436	23.4	3.0	0.0	9.0	11.1	39.1	0.0
Colton	48	489	60.2	13.4	360	2,494,835	14.1	29.0	19.7	3.6	3.4	18.7	1.8
Compton	60	552	35.1	14.2	329	1,870,002	18.8	5.9	37.1	8.5	3.7	15.6	0.0
Concord	206	1,154	132.7	40.1	443	2,858,330	14.9	60.6	0.0	9.1	1.2	10.7	0.0
Corona	219	1,374	108.4	31.0	692	4,620,304	10.2	34.8	23.7	7.6	2.3	16.8	2.3
Costa Mesa	316	1,916	167.0	46.4	499	4,282,210	13.5	43.0	28.9	5.5	1.1	5.7	0.0
Covina	104	497	48.3	13.9	187	1,234,035	14.5	55.3	0.0	3.8	3.1	11.5	0.0
Culver City	130	1,050	82.8	22.7	409	1,848,474	11.4	41.4	12.9	4.7	9.6	15.5	0.0
Cupertino	66	268	25.6	7.0	154	1,132,814	34.4	0.0	0.0	21.5	0.0	26.3	0.0
Cypress	64	663	99.0	34.4	171	1,179,800	19.6	48.1	0.0	5.4	0.7	14.5	0.0
Daly City	83	D	D	D	560	4,065,527	12.0	29.6	20.8	3.3	3.1	19.2	3.3
Dana Point	60	358	91.5	9.6	66	459,856	20.0	0.0	0.0	25.3	33.8	14.3	0.0
Danville	46	239	14.8	4.5	101	575,902	34.0	3.2	0.0	27.3	0.0	27.4	0.0
Davis	65	350	29.0	8.9	423	2,817,726	14.4	26.2	16.3	3.9	5.3	24.3	0.0

1. Establishments subject to federal tax.

Table D. Cities — City Government Finances

Items 117—126

City	General revenue Total (mil dol)	Intergovernmental Total (mil dol)	Percent from state government	Taxes Total (mil dol)	Taxes Per capita (dollars) Total	Property	Sales and gross receipts	General expenditure Total (mil dol)	General expenditure Per capita (dollars) Total	Capital outlays
	117	118	119	120	121	122	123	124	125	126
ARKANSAS— Cont'd										
Jacksonville	66.7	10.5	44.6	9.9	344	27	317	75.1	2,619	339
Jonesboro	78.3	23.6	30.3	30.7	435	65	371	71.4	1,014	147
Little Rock	376.0	98.2	37.1	121.4	617	247	370	369.8	1,881	297
North Little Rock	90.5	26.5	30.0	39.2	606	159	447	97.5	1,506	165
Paragould	29.1	6.0	40.6	7.3	270	31	239	27.7	1,027	152
Pine Bluff	45.8	15.6	31.1	17.4	370	78	293	42.9	915	56
Rogers	66.9	18.0	35.4	33.4	565	89	476	49.1	832	178
Russellville	28.8	7.4	31.7	14.0	492	24	468	23.4	820	49
Sherwood	26.4	11.3	17.7	7.8	261	19	243	26.0	868	128
Springdale	72.7	20.3	30.2	29.9	406	72	333	53.9	732	67
Texarkana	31.4	6.9	34.8	13.5	449	104	344	26.4	879	33
West Memphis	33.0	8.5	26.7	13.1	507	50	458	32.5	1,262	139
CALIFORNIA	X	X	X	X	X	X	X	X	X	X
Adelanto	12.0	0.9	64.5	6.2	197	83	105	18.3	586	65
Alameda	117.1	11.9	69.1	72.8	961	544	346	118.5	1,564	250
Alhambra	94.9	11.0	57.2	48.2	570	309	260	85.5	1,012	77
Aliso Viejo	19.0	1.4	100.0	14.0	283	134	120	22.2	448	112
Anaheim	697.7	119.6	21.0	267.6	779	340	436	658.5	1,917	451
Antioch	69.2	16.1	79.1	35.4	336	194	139	57.9	550	87
Apple Valley	55.7	5.3	91.3	27.5	389	258	118	55.8	790	105
Arcadia	68.8	2.9	73.3	48.5	848	441	400	64.5	1,130	99
Atascadero	31.8	7.6	92.3	15.9	555	349	188	28.1	978	301
Atwater	26.6	3.9	48.1	8.3	291	192	93	49.2	1,714	675
Azusa	58.3	7.2	30.8	36.3	767	353	363	55.0	1,161	37
Bakersfield	360.1	84.2	69.9	149.4	417	223	192	382.6	1,069	301
Baldwin Park	50.2	15.9	46.5	25.1	328	172	153	43.8	572	46
Banning	33.1	4.9	90.4	13.0	427	251	175	30.4	1,003	237
Beaumont	83.3	0.7	100.0	14.4	366	160	203	79.5	2,017	1,172
Bell	29.7	1.8	72.8	16.9	471	317	154	30.0	835	223
Bellflower	32.9	3.7	60.2	25.4	328	163	163	34.3	442	71
Bell Gardens	36.8	3.6	71.1	22.7	531	201	329	31.1	726	78
Belmont	43.6	2.2	83.1	25.6	965	712	247	44.8	1,687	160
Benicia	43.3	1.4	100.0	29.1	1,061	603	453	46.0	1,679	414
Berkeley	293.3	31.1	90.2	147.9	1,281	526	494	300.7	2,605	242
Beverly Hills	261.2	5.5	72.9	142.7	4,124	1,370	2,727	226.1	6,532	1,003
Brea	90.0	3.5	86.5	56.2	1,395	893	497	87.6	2,176	593
Brentwood	78.8	1.8	100.0	33.7	628	397	152	88.6	1,654	238
Buena Park	87.0	7.0	64.8	64.8	788	449	336	105.8	1,285	278
Burbank	265.6	36.3	55.0	147.7	1,412	849	560	282.4	2,701	443
Burlingame	72.1	2.7	100.0	42.6	1,436	445	977	70.0	2,356	686
Calexico	34.0	6.5	59.4	15.9	405	203	194	33.5	852	103
Camarillo	73.4	5.0	40.6	40.7	617	335	278	73.6	1,117	261
Campbell	46.2	3.4	53.9	33.2	823	390	428	49.3	1,222	160
Carlsbad	179.5	13.2	50.3	112.9	1,033	528	496	160.2	1,465	200
Carson	105.5	19.8	56.9	74.0	799	340	456	135.1	1,459	403
Cathedral City	70.1	6.3	64.9	52.7	1,002	695	304	69.7	1,324	144
Ceres	34.3	3.7	83.6	18.9	406	213	188	38.7	834	89
Cerritos	96.9	2.0	89.7	65.5	1,320	774	541	96.8	1,950	141
Chico	99.3	7.9	55.7	69.9	799	467	330	91.9	1,050	275
Chino	102.9	7.3	90.6	54.2	677	425	248	109.3	1,365	144
Chino Hills	60.2	3.8	89.2	21.6	283	154	126	65.7	861	137
Chula Vista	240.2	25.5	80.3	126.8	501	240	258	247.0	976	73
Citrus Heights	52.7	10.0	85.5	32.4	382	164	216	48.9	578	136
Claremont	35.2	1.7	82.5	23.2	653	293	356	34.7	978	122
Clovis	110.7	10.2	67.2	46.4	470	218	249	105.9	1,074	201
Coachella	37.8	11.0	71.9	18.0	421	228	167	49.1	1,150	551
Colton	50.0	6.2	92.7	27.9	524	332	190	44.1	829	84
Compton	98.6	17.9	28.9	54.6	558	319	236	114.4	1,170	108
Concord	120.0	9.6	80.8	70.7	566	241	321	128.3	1,026	86
Corona	225.6	16.4	78.9	106.2	672	397	245	219.2	1,388	272
Costa Mesa	117.6	9.7	76.3	92.1	823	381	439	111.9	1,001	113
Covina	49.3	4.1	69.9	32.6	672	369	300	49.1	1,013	132
Culver City	173.5	27.4	43.4	99.6	2,528	1,144	1,336	143.8	3,651	482
Cupertino	60.4	2.0	89.4	42.9	716	306	399	59.2	989	78
Cypress	43.8	2.7	66.2	33.4	683	409	270	44.8	917	226
Daly City	103.9	12.0	48.5	57.4	551	324	225	112.7	1,082	108
Dana Point	29.3	1.6	100.0	25.1	740	287	445	31.5	929	121
Danville	35.0	6.4	100.0	21.8	508	306	190	34.7	809	181
Davis	96.8	18.9	87.5	47.1	714	397	221	90.4	1,372	150

1. Based on population estimated as of July 1 of the year shown.

City	City government finances, 2012 (cont.)									
	General expenditure (cont.)									
	Percent of total for:									
	Public welfare	Highways	Parking facilities	Education	Health and hospitals	Police protection	Sewerage and sanitation	Parks and recreation	Housing and community development	Interest on debt
	127	128	129	130	131	132	133	134	135	136
ARKANSAS— Cont'd										
Jacksonville	0.0	4.8	0.0	0.0	51.2	10.2	15.6	3.1	0.4	2.2
Jonesboro	0.0	12.4	0.0	0.0	1.1	17.0	17.2	3.4	0.5	15.4
Little Rock	0.0	4.7	0.2	0.0	5.8	15.0	12.9	10.2	2.6	6.0
North Little Rock	0.0	6.2	0.0	0.0	0.4	18.6	16.6	6.3	3.6	5.9
Paragould	0.2	9.6	0.0	0.0	0.5	10.6	23.1	6.0	0.0	2.5
Pine Bluff	0.5	10.5	0.0	0.0	0.1	24.5	18.2	6.0	4.3	1.9
Rogers	0.0	9.9	0.0	0.0	0.8	17.6	15.7	9.0	0.0	5.8
Russellville	0.0	20.6	0.0	0.0	1.1	18.7	18.5	6.1	0.0	0.0
Sherwood	0.0	20.6	0.0	0.0	1.0	23.1	14.0	13.5	0.0	1.2
Springdale	0.0	8.2	0.0	0.0	1.0	20.7	17.2	4.4	1.2	9.5
Texarkana	0.0	5.7	0.0	0.0	1.2	28.6	21.0	1.4	0.8	3.8
West Memphis	0.0	13.7	0.0	0.0	0.5	20.8	16.6	4.2	2.0	3.0
CALIFORNIA	X	X	X	X	X	X	X	X	X	X
Adelanto	0.0	9.8	0.0	0.0	1.4	25.8	0.0	4.3	9.3	0.0
Alameda	0.0	8.5	0.8	0.0	14.8	22.2	8.2	11.0	6.1	3.5
Alhambra	0.0	9.2	2.7	0.0	0.1	28.1	12.5	7.4	4.9	4.2
Aliso Viejo	0.0	15.3	0.0	0.0	1.0	28.2	0.0	7.9	0.5	9.0
Anaheim	0.0	8.5	0.0	0.0	0.1	16.5	8.2	12.1	18.0	10.6
Antioch	0.0	16.1	0.0	0.0	2.4	43.6	4.2	9.6	8.8	3.6
Apple Valley	0.0	8.4	0.0	0.0	2.9	19.9	23.3	8.7	11.7	5.3
Arcadia	0.0	9.9	0.0	0.0	6.9	25.6	2.2	4.2	3.1	1.5
Atascadero	0.0	7.5	0.0	0.0	0.0	21.1	6.6	9.2	20.1	4.0
Atwater	0.0	2.7	0.0	0.0	0.0	14.1	51.3	3.5	5.4	8.0
Azusa	0.0	3.3	0.0	0.0	1.2	30.7	8.1	6.3	8.1	11.6
Bakersfield	0.0	10.0	0.0	0.0	0.0	17.9	17.4	6.8	2.6	3.6
Baldwin Park	0.0	15.9	0.0	0.0	0.0	41.3	0.6	8.7	17.9	3.9
Banning	0.0	11.9	0.0	0.0	0.3	24.5	18.5	2.1	18.5	4.9
Beaumont	0.0	3.8	0.0	0.0	0.6	12.7	7.1	4.6	0.6	0.5
Bell	0.0	6.8	0.0	0.0	0.0	22.5	4.9	3.5	21.8	9.1
Bellflower	0.0	31.2	0.0	0.0	0.0	30.7	0.0	6.3	6.8	6.6
Bell Gardens	0.0	13.1	0.0	0.0	0.0	42.3	7.6	15.9	3.0	3.7
Belmont	0.0	9.5	0.0	0.0	0.0	21.4	17.5	8.4	8.9	2.3
Benicia	0.0	7.0	0.0	0.0	0.0	19.3	14.2	10.6	0.2	3.1
Berkeley	0.0	7.4	2.4	0.0	11.4	18.1	14.2	5.9	6.0	1.9
Beverly Hills	0.0	5.7	21.3	0.0	4.9	17.9	10.5	9.5	0.1	1.7
Brea	0.0	14.6	0.0	0.0	4.1	30.3	6.4	10.8	11.8	1.2
Brentwood	0.0	14.0	0.0	0.0	0.0	18.8	17.9	12.0	9.8	9.7
Buena Park	0.0	12.0	0.0	0.0	0.3	20.3	3.1	4.7	23.0	5.3
Burbank	0.0	7.2	0.3	0.0	4.6	15.9	9.3	5.7	14.2	5.8
Burlingame	0.0	24.2	2.0	0.0	0.0	13.4	14.4	8.0	0.0	2.4
Calexico	0.0	6.0	0.0	0.0	0.9	30.5	16.3	3.8	10.3	0.4
Camarillo	0.0	24.2	0.0	0.0	0.3	20.3	17.6	0.9	6.1	5.0
Campbell	0.0	13.9	0.0	0.0	0.0	26.2	0.0	12.0	10.3	3.4
Carlsbad	0.0	8.7	0.0	0.0	8.2	17.9	8.5	13.4	4.7	1.6
Carson	0.0	13.8	1.0	0.0	0.1	16.4	0.1	13.3	26.3	7.1
Cathedral City	0.0	9.7	0.0	0.0	4.2	22.1	0.6	1.4	22.4	15.6
Ceres	0.0	8.7	0.0	0.0	1.2	28.2	19.7	5.0	9.7	5.6
Cerritos	0.0	10.6	0.0	0.0	0.3	14.0	3.4	14.7	6.5	8.1
Chico	0.0	17.5	1.9	0.0	0.3	23.6	6.6	3.2	11.8	6.1
Chino	0.0	13.4	0.0	0.0	0.0	25.6	18.7	5.2	15.2	6.1
Chino Hills	0.0	20.8	0.0	0.0	0.0	17.3	14.6	6.5	0.4	6.1
Chula Vista	0.0	10.6	0.1	0.0	0.9	20.6	17.6	9.9	2.7	7.6
Citrus Heights	0.0	22.4	0.0	0.0	1.3	38.7	1.2	0.1	14.3	2.1
Claremont	0.0	12.7	0.0	0.0	0.8	28.4	15.5	9.0	4.2	2.9
Clovis	0.0	10.8	0.0	0.0	0.7	21.2	28.1	5.4	3.1	2.4
Coachella	0.0	33.0	0.0	0.0	0.4	12.4	16.2	10.2	4.8	5.7
Colton	0.0	6.2	0.0	0.0	1.3	23.1	11.2	3.9	8.2	9.8
Compton	0.0	8.3	0.0	0.0	0.0	15.0	9.0	2.9	15.0	1.3
Concord	0.0	12.7	0.0	0.0	0.0	33.4	16.2	6.9	3.5	2.3
Corona	0.0	4.4	0.1	0.0	0.5	18.5	23.8	3.9	7.9	9.2
Costa Mesa	0.0	8.7	0.0	0.0	1.0	33.4	0.0	6.1	2.3	2.0
Covina	0.0	5.4	0.2	0.0	0.7	30.8	3.6	5.8	13.9	6.1
Culver City	0.0	5.6	0.2	0.0	3.7	19.6	11.6	4.8	13.5	6.5
Cupertino	0.0	11.9	0.0	0.0	0.3	28.1	2.6	25.6	1.8	3.2
Cypress	0.0	21.7	0.0	0.0	0.5	31.3	3.4	13.1	11.8	1.7
Daly City	0.0	10.1	0.0	0.0	0.5	24.9	20.5	8.8	1.7	0.4
Dana Point	0.0	24.9	0.0	0.0	1.0	30.4	0.0	14.2	0.0	1.4
Danville	0.0	21.8	0.0	0.0	1.0	21.0	0.0	21.4	0.4	1.5
Davis	0.0	8.9	0.0	0.0	0.0	16.4	20.0	26.2	3.7	2.4

Table D. Cities — City Government Finances, City Government Employment, and Climate

City	City government finances, 2012 (cont.) Debt outstanding Total (mil dol)	Per capita[1] (dollars)	Debt issued during year	Climate[2] Average daily temperature Mean January	July	Limits January[3]	July[4]	Annual precipitation (inches)	Heating degree days	Cooling degree days
	137	138	139	140	141	142	143	144	145	146
ARKANSAS— Cont'd										
Jacksonville	28.9	1,008	1.9	38.2	79.9	27.4	91.1	50.56	3,470	1,699
Jonesboro	298.0	4,230	2.9	35.6	81.6	25.8	92.3	46.18	3,737	1,858
Little Rock	511.4	2,601	23.9	40.1	82.4	30.8	92.8	50.93	3,084	2,086
North Little Rock	204.0	3,152	19.6	40.1	82.4	30.8	92.8	50.93	3,084	2,086
Paragould	25.8	953	7.4	NA	NA	NA	NA	NA	NA	NA
Pine Bluff	29.1	619	9.6	40.8	82.4	31.5	92.4	52.48	2,935	2,099
Rogers	160.5	2,718	85.8	32.9	77.5	22.0	88.8	46.92	4,483	1,269
Russellville	0.0	0	0.0	NA	NA	NA	NA	NA	NA	NA
Sherwood	8.3	277	0.0	NA	NA	NA	NA	NA	NA	NA
Springdale	110.5	1,501	0.0	34.3	78.9	24.2	89.1	46.02	4,166	1,439
Texarkana	34.1	1,136	0.0	44.3	82.7	35.6	92.7	47.38	2,421	2,280
West Memphis	31.2	1,214	0.0	37.5	81.5	28.5	90.9	52.80	3,417	1,903
CALIFORNIA	X	X	X	X	X	X	X	X	X	X
Adelanto	0.0	0	0.0	NA	NA	NA	NA	NA	NA	NA
Alameda	152.6	2,014	3.6	50.9	64.9	44.7	72.7	22.94	2,400	377
Alhambra	70.5	834	0.0	56.3	75.6	42.6	89.0	18.56	1,295	1,575
Aliso Viejo	34.0	686	0.0	56.7	72.4	47.2	82.3	14.03	1,465	1,183
Anaheim	1,822.5	5,304	0.0	56.9	73.2	45.2	84.0	11.23	1,286	1,294
Antioch	41.8	397	0.0	45.7	74.4	37.8	90.7	13.33	2,714	1,179
Apple Valley	63.0	893	0.0	45.5	80.0	31.4	99.1	6.20	2,929	1,735
Arcadia	40.4	707	0.0	56.3	75.6	42.6	89.0	18.56	1,295	1,575
Atascadero	27.6	962	0.0	47.3	71.6	33.1	91.3	14.71	2,932	785
Atwater	93.3	3,253	0.0	NA	NA	NA	NA	NA	NA	NA
Azusa	235.4	4,970	0.0	54.6	73.8	41.5	88.7	16.96	1,727	1,191
Bakersfield	345.9	966	49.8	47.8	83.1	39.3	96.9	6.49	2,120	2,286
Baldwin Park	66.8	873	0.0	56.3	75.6	42.6	89.0	18.56	1,295	1,575
Banning	48.2	1,591	0.0	NA	NA	NA	NA	NA	NA	NA
Beaumont	9.6	244	0.4	NA	NA	NA	NA	NA	NA	NA
Bell	55.7	1,550	0.0	58.8	76.6	47.9	88.9	14.44	949	1,837
Bellflower	31.8	410	0.0	57.0	73.8	46.0	82.9	12.94	1,211	1,186
Bell Gardens	36.7	856	0.0	58.8	76.6	47.9	88.9	14.44	949	1,837
Belmont	38.8	1,460	0.0	48.1	69.7	36.4	88.2	28.71	2,769	569
Benicia	55.1	2,008	4.3	46.3	71.2	38.8	87.4	19.58	2,757	786
Berkeley	188.8	1,635	0.0	50.0	62.8	43.6	70.4	25.40	2,857	142
Beverly Hills	142.3	4,111	0.0	57.9	69.5	49.4	76.9	18.68	1,379	893
Brea	39.1	971	0.0	56.9	73.2	45.2	84.0	11.23	1,286	1,294
Brentwood	194.1	3,622	22.4	NA	NA	NA	NA	NA	NA	NA
Buena Park	115.5	1,403	0.0	57.0	73.8	46.0	82.9	12.94	1,211	1,186
Burbank	463.3	4,430	9.8	54.8	75.5	42.0	88.9	17.49	1,575	1,455
Burlingame	33.1	1,114	0.0	50.0	62.7	42.9	70.5	23.35	2,720	184
Calexico	2.8	71	0.0	55.8	91.4	41.3	107.0	2.96	1,080	3,952
Camarillo	90.1	1,367	7.6	55.7	66.0	45.3	74.0	13.61	1,961	389
Campbell	28.0	694	0.1	48.7	70.3	38.8	85.4	22.64	2,641	613
Carlsbad	65.0	594	0.2	54.7	67.6	45.4	72.1	11.13	2,009	505
Carson	217.3	2,347	0.0	56.3	69.4	46.2	77.6	14.79	1,526	742
Cathedral City	271.4	5,160	0.3	57.3	92.1	44.2	108.2	5.23	951	4,224
Ceres	50.3	1,083	0.0	47.2	77.7	40.1	93.6	13.12	2,358	1,570
Cerritos	153.8	3,099	0.0	57.0	73.8	46.0	82.9	12.94	1,211	1,186
Chico	163.2	1,865	0.8	44.5	76.9	35.2	93.0	26.23	2,945	1,334
Chino	211.8	2,645	12.9	54.6	73.8	41.5	88.7	16.96	1,727	1,191
Chino Hills	127.2	1,667	0.0	56.9	73.2	45.2	84.0	11.23	1,286	1,294
Chula Vista	512.8	2,027	4.0	57.3	70.1	46.1	76.1	9.95	1,321	862
Citrus Heights	28.5	337	0.0	46.9	77.7	39.2	94.8	24.61	2,532	1,528
Claremont	26.2	739	0.0	54.6	73.8	41.5	88.7	16.96	1,727	1,191
Clovis	232.4	2,358	0.0	46.0	81.4	38.4	96.6	11.23	2,447	1,963
Coachella	94.7	2,219	2.4	NA	NA	NA	NA	NA	NA	NA
Colton	96.4	1,813	0.0	54.4	79.6	41.8	96.0	16.43	1,599	1,937
Compton	73.6	752	0.0	57.0	73.8	46.0	82.9	12.94	1,211	1,186
Concord	63.7	510	0.0	46.3	71.2	38.8	87.4	19.58	2,757	786
Corona	346.1	2,191	25.3	54.7	75.9	41.5	92.0	12.00	1,599	1,534
Costa Mesa	38.8	347	0.0	55.9	67.3	48.2	71.4	11.65	1,719	543
Covina	86.2	1,779	2.3	54.6	73.8	41.5	88.7	16.96	1,727	1,191
Culver City	206.5	5,244	0.0	56.7	70.8	46.1	80.0	13.32	1,344	959
Cupertino	43.9	734	43.9	48.7	70.3	38.8	85.4	22.64	2,641	613
Cypress	8.8	181	0.0	57.0	73.8	46.0	82.9	12.94	1,211	1,186
Daly City	45.3	435	0.0	50.6	57.3	44.6	61.1	19.77	3,665	17
Dana Point	8.2	241	0.0	55.4	68.7	43.9	77.3	13.56	1,756	666
Danville	12.9	300	0.0	47.5	72.4	39.3	85.2	23.96	3,267	983
Davis	55.0	835	0.0	45.2	74.3	37.1	92.7	19.05	2,853	1,127

1. Based on the population estimated as of July 1 of the year shown.   2. Represents normal values based on the 30-year period, 1971±2000.   3. Average daily minimum.   4. Average daily maximum.

Table D. Cities — **Land Area and Population**

STATE Place code	City	Population, 2018				Race 2017 — Race alone[2] (percent)						Two or more races (percent)
		Land area[1] (sq. mi)	Total persons 2018	Rank	Per square mile	White	Black or African American	American Indian, Alaskan Native	Asian	Hawaiian Pacific Islander	Some other race	
		1	2	3	4	5	6	7	8	9	10	11
	CALIFORNIA— Cont'd											
06 18,394	Delano..................................	14.3	53,014	731	3,707.3	69.3	5.3	0.3	12.5	0.0	10.7	1.9
06 18,996	Desert Hot Springs...............	30.2	28,885	1,290	956.5	77.6	8.2	1.7	3.7	0.0	5.2	3.6
06 19,192	Diamond Bar........................	14.9	56,275	674	3,776.8	26.7	3.9	0.3	59.8	0.2	5.1	4.0
06 19,766	Downey................................	12.4	112,269	261	9,054.0	56.4	3.0	0.2	6.0	0.4	30.5	3.6
06 20,018	Dublin..................................	15.2	63,445	588	4,174.0	38.4	2.9	0.4	50.0	1.0	2.1	5.2
06 20,956	East Palo Alto.....................	2.5	29,519	1,273	11,807.6	34.7	12.5	0.4	6.6	5.2	37.1	3.5
06 21,712	El Cajon..............................	14.5	103,241	300	7,120.1	74.0	6.6	0.3	4.5	0.3	8.2	6.1
06 21,782	El Centro.............................	11.5	44,120	868	3,836.5	36.7	2.3	0.4	1.0	0.4	54.7	4.4
06 22,020	Elk Grove............................	42.0	172,886	149	4,116.3	47.9	10.0	0.4	27.7	2.3	3.7	8.0
06 22,230	El Monte..............................	9.6	115,586	250	12,040.2	28.5	0.4	0.2	29.0	1.2	38.8	1.9
06 22,300	El Paso de Robles (Paso Robles).................................	19.6	32,212	1,181	1,643.5	91.3	0.8	0.0	0.7	0.0	4.8	2.4
06 22,678	Encinitas	19.0	62,904	595	3,310.7	85.3	0.4	0.5	4.6	0.3	3.7	5.2
06 22,804	Escondido............................	37.2	152,213	173	4,091.7	64.8	1.8	0.5	5.0	0.1	22.9	5.0
06 23,042	Eureka.................................	9.4	26,998	1,361	2,872.1	73.9	4.8	1.8	12.8	0.0	3.1	3.7
06 23,182	Fairfield	41.0	116,884	244	2,850.8	44.7	16.4	0.7	18.7	1.7	9.6	8.1
06 24,638	Folsom................................	27.8	79,022	439	2,842.5	68.8	2.7	0.3	18.4	0.4	2.1	7.4
06 24,680	Fontana...............................	43.1	213,739	105	4,959.1	38.2	9.4	0.9	4.7	0.1	41.5	5.2
06 25,338	Foster City..........................	3.8	34,151	1,118	8,987.1	44.9	3.8	0.0	45.3	0.0	1.9	4.1
06 25,380	Fountain Valley	9.1	55,814	679	6,133.4	53.5	0.2	0.2	36.6	0.0	4.0	5.5
06 26,000	Fremont...............................	77.5	237,807	96	3,068.5	22.4	2.0	0.5	61.3	0.4	8.0	5.4
06 27,000	Fresno.................................	114.3	530,093	34	4,637.7	60.4	7.7	1.1	14.1	0.1	12.0	4.6
06 28,000	Fullerton..............................	22.4	139,640	191	6,233.9	54.8	2.7	0.2	24.4	0.4	12.6	5.0
06 28,168	Gardena..............................	5.8	59,721	628	10,296.7	25.8	19.2	0.2	26.8	0.4	23.5	4.1
06 29,000	Garden Grove......................	18.0	172,646	150	9,591.4	39.4	1.0	0.3	44.5	0.1	12.7	2.1
06 29,504	Gilroy..................................	16.5	58,756	639	3,561.0	71.0	1.8	0.3	12.5	0.0	7.9	6.5
06 30,000	Glendale..............................	30.5	201,361	112	6,602.0	77.3	2.3	0.2	13.0	0.1	3.4	3.7
06 30,014	Glendora	19.5	52,002	738	2,666.8	68.3	1.6	1.3	12.1	0.4	4.8	11.6
06 30,378	Goleta.................................	7.9	30,821	1,224	3,901.4	71.2	1.3	0.0	6.7	0.0	14.7	6.1
06 31,960	Hanford...............................	17.1	56,910	668	3,328.1	75.5	2.9	0.9	6.2	0.0	8.2	6.4
06 32,548	Hawthorne...........................	6.1	86,965	382	14,256.6	25.9	26.5	0.3	11.3	0.4	32.1	3.7
06 33,000	Hayward..............................	45.5	159,620	160	3,508.1	30.0	9.2	0.6	26.5	1.8	23.9	7.9
06 33,182	Hemet.................................	29.3	85,275	393	2,910.4	71.3	8.8	1.5	3.2	0.0	10.3	4.9
06 33,434	Hesperia.............................	72.7	95,274	333	1,310.5	84.2	4.1	0.2	2.9	0.0	5.8	2.7
06 33,588	Highland..............................	18.7	55,406	686	2,962.9	56.7	5.9	1.9	7.8	3.7	14.9	9.1
06 34,120	Hollister..............................	7.3	39,749	969	5,445.1	77.6	0.3	0.4	2.3	0.0	15.1	4.3
06 36,000	Huntington Beach	27.0	200,641	113	7,431.1	73.7	1.4	0.6	12.1	0.2	6.9	5.1
06 36,056	Huntington Park...................	3.0	58,173	648	19,391.0	60.8	3.4	1.4	0.4	0.1	33.5	0.4
06 36,294	Imperial Beach....................	4.3	27,447	1,338	6,383.0	67.0	5.5	1.5	7.1	0.2	12.8	5.8
06 36,448	Indio...................................	33.2	91,240	361	2,748.2	63.3	2.1	0.2	2.0	0.0	29.8	2.6
06 36,546	Inglewood............................	9.1	109,419	277	12,024.1	27.1	40.7	1.9	2.0	2.1	23.8	2.4
06 36,770	Irvine..................................	65.6	282,572	72	4,307.5	46.5	1.8	0.2	41.5	0.3	4.4	5.3
06 39,220	Laguna Hills........................	6.6	31,024	1,216	4,700.6	69.7	4.1	0.2	13.3	0.0	5.2	7.6
06 39,248	Laguna Niguel.....................	14.7	66,266	556	4,507.9	72.9	0.6	0.0	13.8	0.2	5.2	7.4
06 39,290	La Habra.............................	7.4	62,183	600	8,403.1	50.3	2.3	0.6	10.5	0.0	29.7	6.6
06 39,486	Lake Elsinore......................	38.3	68,183	531	1,780.2	37.0	6.6	0.3	9.6	0.0	42.9	3.6
06 39,496	Lake Forest.........................	16.6	85,623	389	5,158.0	63.4	1.6	2.9	22.1	0.0	5.7	4.3
06 39,892	Lakewood............................	9.4	80,140	433	8,525.5	50.9	8.9	0.8	18.4	0.3	14.7	6.1
06 40,004	La Mesa..............................	9.1	59,556	629	6,544.6	74.8	4.4	1.5	8.3	0.3	2.4	8.3
06 40,032	La Mirada............................	7.8	48,683	792	6,241.4	45.8	1.9	1.5	22.9	0.1	21.2	6.7
06 40,130	Lancaster............................	94.3	159,053	161	1,686.7	66.2	15.7	0.9	5.5	0.2	7.2	4.3
06 40,340	La Puente............................	3.5	39,908	965	11,402.3	37.4	1.7	0.5	7.9	0.3	50.7	1.5
06 40,354	La Quinta............................	35.3	41,535	918	1,176.6	84.1	2.3	0.3	5.8	0.0	4.4	3.1
06 40,830	La Verne..............................	8.4	32,206	1,182	3,834.0	73.6	2.3	1.1	9.8	0.0	8.7	4.6
06 40,886	Lawndale.............................	2.0	32,754	1,162	16,377.0	32.2	9.8	0.0	10.5	0.3	43.0	4.2
06 41,124	Lemon Grove.......................	3.9	26,969	1,362	6,915.1	64.4	16.2	0.0	6.4	0.6	6.2	6.2
06 41,474	Lincoln................................	23.5	47,978	808	2,041.6	79.0	1.2	0.2	7.4	0.4	6.6	5.3
06 41,992	Livermore............................	27.0	90,269	365	3,343.3	77.6	1.6	0.3	12.9	0.6	2.1	4.8
06 42,202	Lodi....................................	13.7	66,995	544	4,890.1	60.7	3.2	0.9	9.0	0.3	4.1	21.8
06 42,524	Lompoc...............................	11.6	42,760	890	3,686.2	68.8	2.1	1.9	3.5	0.5	19.5	3.6
06 43,000	Long Beach.........................	50.7	467,354	43	9,218.0	50.9	12.7	0.7	13.5	0.7	18.0	3.6
06 43,280	Los Altos............................	6.5	30,531	1,232	4,697.1	63.7	0.8	0.2	29.0	0.0	0.4	5.8
06 44,000	Los Angeles	468.7	3,990,456	2	8,513.9	50.9	9.1	0.6	11.5	0.2	24.3	3.5
06 44,028	Los Banos	10.0	40,074	957	4,007.4	33.3	1.4	0.6	2.4	0.0	55.1	7.2
06 44,112	Los Gatos...........................	11.4	30,680	1,228	2,691.2	NA	NA	NA	NA	NA	NA	NA
06 44,574	Lynwood..............................	4.8	70,504	510	14,688.3	42.2	5.6	0.8	1.4	0.0	49.7	0.3
06 45,022	Madera................................	15.8	65,706	565	4,158.6	56.5	5.8	1.5	1.7	0.0	33.3	1.4
06 45,400	Manhattan Beach.................	3.9	35,532	1,081	9,110.8	NA	NA	NA	NA	NA	NA	NA
06 45,484	Manteca..............................	20.9	81,592	422	3,903.9	68.3	4.0	0.7	11.0	0.3	7.9	7.8
06 46,114	Martinez..............................	12.6	38,402	1,001	3,047.8	72.3	4.9	0.2	10.5	0.0	6.0	6.1
06 46,492	Maywood.............................	1.2	27,298	1,345	22,748.3	NA	NA	NA	NA	NA	NA	NA
06 46,842	Menifee...............................	46.5	92,595	351	1,991.3	60.9	5.7	0.7	6.5	0.4	20.7	5.2

1. Dry land or land partially or temporarily covered by water.   2. Hispanic or Latino persons may be of any race.

Table D. Cities — Population

City	Percent Hispanic or Latino[1], 2017	Percent foreign born, 2017	Age of population (percent), 2017							Median age, 2017	Percent female, 2017	Population			
			Under 18 years	18 to 24 years	25 to 34 years	35 to 44 years	45 to 54 years	55 to 64 years	65 years and over			Census counts		Percent change	
												2000	2010	2000-2010	2001-2018
	12	13	14	15	16	17	18	19	20	21	22	23	24	25	26
CALIFORNIA— Cont'd															
Delano..................	76.8	35.5	26.4	11.2	19.8	14.6	9.9	9.5	8.7	30.7	43.4	38,824	53,040	36.6	0.0
Desert Hot Springs..............	51.6	22.3	26.4	6.5	9.8	14.8	14.8	12.9	14.8	39.8	50.6	16,582	27,052	63.1	6.8
Diamond Bar......................	20.4	44.5	23.9	6.4	12.9	14.9	15.0	12.3	14.4	38.3	50.8	56,287	55,552	-1.3	1.3
Downey......................	77.4	32.1	24.4	8.3	18.0	11.5	12.4	13.3	12.2	34.7	51.2	107,323	111,775	4.1	0.4
Dublin......................	10.1	39.4	27.0	3.6	16.6	18.4	14.4	9.3	10.7	35.8	50.8	29,973	46,036	53.6	37.8
East Palo Alto..................	61.5	43.7	23.8	8.9	16.4	15.3	18.6	8.1	9.1	35.5	51.0	29,506	28,155	-4.6	4.8
El Cajon......................	27.8	28.9	26.2	8.0	19.4	12.0	10.4	11.9	12.1	32.8	51.4	94,869	99,513	4.9	3.7
El Centro......................	87.2	27.2	30.3	10.0	17.4	11.2	8.8	10.7	11.7	30.7	52.4	37,835	42,588	12.6	3.6
Elk Grove......................	20.8	25.9	24.3	9.2	13.6	12.0	14.6	12.7	13.7	37.9	51.5	59,984	153,010	155.1	13.0
El Monte......................	66.0	52.3	23.3	10.9	16.1	12.8	13.5	11.2	12.2	34.8	48.5	115,965	113,507	-2.1	1.8
El Paso de Robles (Paso Robles)......................	33.1	15.4	22.9	9.1	13.1	17.0	11.3	15.0	11.6	39.0	53.5	24,297	29,750	22.4	8.3
Encinitas......................	15.5	12.4	20.2	4.6	9.5	13.6	17.8	17.2	17.2	46.3	48.3	58,014	59,515	2.6	5.7
Escondido......................	53.0	26.3	24.2	10.1	17.5	12.1	13.6	11.2	11.3	34.2	49.7	133,559	143,972	7.8	5.7
Eureka......................	14.8	8.0	18.7	11.6	13.9	11.2	14.4	14.1	16.0	40.3	52.7	26,128	27,196	4.1	-0.7
Fairfield......................	25.0	21.4	26.0	9.3	15.1	14.3	12.1	11.2	12.0	34.7	50.0	96,178	105,425	9.6	10.9
Folsom......................	12.5	16.3	24.5	5.7	11.1	14.9	18.9	10.9	14.0	41.3	49.2	51,884	72,196	39.1	9.5
Fontana......................	68.2	22.2	29.8	13.3	14.9	14.4	13.2	8.4	6.1	29.3	48.8	128,929	196,472	52.4	8.8
Foster City......................	13.3	45.9	22.7	4.4	20.9	13.9	12.7	10.5	14.9	36.6	50.1	28,803	30,567	6.1	11.7
Fountain Valley	17.2	29.6	20.6	8.7	9.9	11.4	15.8	12.0	21.5	44.4	52.6	54,978	55,360	0.7	0.8
Fremont......................	13.2	48.8	23.8	6.1	16.2	16.0	14.7	10.7	12.4	37.4	51.1	203,413	214,072	5.2	11.1
Fresno......................	49.0	19.2	28.2	10.8	16.2	12.8	10.6	10.0	11.4	31.5	51.0	427,652	497,102	16.2	6.6
Fullerton......................	40.0	29.9	22.2	10.7	15.2	12.8	13.0	12.3	13.7	36.4	48.0	126,003	135,237	7.3	3.3
Gardena......................	41.2	35.8	17.7	7.7	16.4	13.5	11.9	15.2	17.6	40.6	51.2	57,746	58,829	1.9	1.5
Garden Grove	33.3	44.4	19.9	10.8	14.3	12.7	14.6	13.4	14.4	39.6	51.2	165,196	170,956	3.5	1.0
Gilroy......................	54.6	23.1	31.4	6.5	10.7	17.5	13.8	9.5	10.6	35.5	50.0	41,464	48,888	17.9	20.2
Glendale......................	16.8	53.6	16.5	7.9	15.7	10.9	16.1	14.9	18.1	43.9	53.5	194,973	191,687	-1.7	5.0
Glendora......................	31.3	21.4	21.5	6.3	12.1	15.2	14.2	15.5	15.2	42.0	52.7	49,415	50,253	1.7	3.5
Goleta......................	39.5	22.9	22.2	10.5	16.8	12.6	11.4	10.5	16.0	35.4	48.1	55,204	29,914	-45.8	3.0
Hanford......................	51.0	19.0	27.6	9.2	16.2	12.6	13.8	10.1	10.6	33.4	48.1	41,686	54,371	30.4	4.7
Hawthorne......................	50.5	35.1	26.0	9.0	18.2	13.8	14.7	9.0	9.2	33.2	49.6	84,112	84,293	0.2	3.2
Hayward......................	40.9	38.2	22.2	10.1	17.7	13.3	14.7	10.9	11.0	34.9	50.8	140,030	144,332	3.1	10.6
Hemet......................	47.7	15.0	25.8	8.0	11.4	9.9	10.3	13.3	21.3	39.7	52.0	58,812	78,627	33.7	8.5
Hesperia......................	56.7	14.7	33.2	9.1	12.6	11.6	12.5	10.9	10.0	31.7	49.7	62,582	90,117	44.0	5.7
Highland......................	57.0	19.1	31.3	9.3	15.3	11.8	13.1	9.0	10.2	31.2	50.1	44,605	53,100	19.0	4.3
Hollister......................	72.0	26.5	28.9	11.8	13.2	14.9	14.0	9.6	7.6	31.6	51.5	34,413	34,757	1.0	14.4
Huntington Beach	18.7	15.8	19.9	6.7	13.6	12.4	14.8	14.1	18.5	42.8	50.4	189,594	191,037	0.8	5.0
Huntington Park......................	96.1	44.4	28.4	12.2	17.6	12.9	10.9	10.4	7.5	29.8	47.8	61,348	58,112	-5.3	0.1
Imperial Beach......................	51.9	25.6	19.1	12.1	19.1	13.3	14.6	10.8	11.1	34.2	48.2	26,992	26,324	-2.5	4.3
Indio......................	66.0	22.9	15.8	8.0	16.3	11.5	14.2	15.5	18.7	43.5	53.5	49,116	79,138	61.1	15.3
Inglewood......................	51.5	25.3	24.1	8.6	15.9	13.9	13.1	10.8	13.8	36.5	51.4	112,580	109,672	-2.6	-0.2
Irvine......................	10.6	40.0	23.4	12.2	15.7	15.5	13.9	10.1	9.2	34.1	51.6	143,072	212,043	48.2	33.3
Laguna Hills......................	23.6	24.1	24.0	6.3	13.6	16.5	9.6	12.2	17.7	37.2	51.7	31,178	30,212	-3.1	2.7
Laguna Niguel......................	9.9	24.3	20.1	5.4	8.8	11.0	14.7	18.6	21.3	48.8	50.2	61,891	62,985	1.8	5.2
La Habra	64.8	27.2	26.8	9.0	16.7	12.8	12.2	11.3	11.3	33.4	48.2	58,974	60,264	2.2	3.2
Lake Elsinore	55.9	23.8	33.4	9.9	17.3	14.0	9.9	9.5	6.0	28.9	52.9	28,928	53,312	84.3	27.9
Lake Forest	22.8	25.4	19.6	7.8	17.3	12.2	16.6	13.1	13.4	38.9	51.5	58,707	77,448	31.9	10.6
Lakewood......................	32.7	21.9	21.7	8.7	15.4	13.1	14.0	12.3	14.8	38.6	53.0	79,345	80,060	0.9	0.1
La Mesa	24.4	16.5	21.0	10.2	18.3	12.8	11.1	12.3	14.2	35.2	54.0	54,749	57,012	4.1	4.5
La Mirada	40.7	26.2	17.7	13.0	13.0	12.7	11.9	15.1	16.6	40.0	50.0	46,783	48,525	3.7	0.3
Lancaster......................	43.9	8.8	28.1	9.5	13.2	14.6	12.7	12.6	9.2	34.1	47.9	118,718	156,642	31.9	1.5
La Puente......................	85.7	40.7	24.2	11.8	16.6	11.2	13.3	12.4	10.4	32.5	49.4	41,063	39,832	-3.0	0.2
La Quinta......................	27.2	15.0	19.1	6.0	7.9	9.2	11.5	17.6	28.6	50.9	50.9	23,694	37,475	58.2	10.8
La Verne......................	38.7	16.9	21.2	10.2	9.6	10.2	16.6	14.0	18.1	44.1	52.1	31,638	31,121	-1.6	3.5
Lawndale......................	62.4	36.8	20.3	6.4	20.9	14.0	14.7	12.7	11.0	37.0	50.7	31,711	32,769	3.3	0.0
Lemon Grove	37.7	16.7	27.2	5.9	21.3	12.0	9.0	13.9	10.7	32.9	50.1	24,918	25,318	1.6	6.5
Lincoln......................	20.5	15.1	24.4	6.9	11.1	12.1	10.0	9.8	25.8	41.5	53.1	11,205	42,926	283.1	11.8
Livermore......................	18.9	19.0	22.9	6.7	14.0	14.1	15.2	13.4	13.7	39.5	49.8	73,345	81,414	11.0	10.9
Lodi......................	34.1	17.5	30.0	8.1	14.5	13.9	10.0	10.4	13.1	32.4	53.1	56,999	62,134	9.0	7.8
Lompoc......................	61.5	23.2	30.0	9.6	14.8	11.4	11.6	11.9	10.7	32.1	45.3	41,103	42,438	3.2	0.8
Long Beach	43.2	25.4	22.1	10.4	17.1	13.6	13.2	12.0	11.6	35.3	51.6	461,522	462,211	0.1	1.1
Los Altos	6.8	29.2	24.3	5.4	8.4	9.9	17.1	14.8	20.1	46.1	51.9	27,693	29,024	4.8	5.2
Los Angeles	48.9	36.9	20.6	10.3	17.9	14.3	13.2	11.4	12.4	35.8	50.4	3,694,820	3,792,820	2.7	5.2
Los Banos	73.9	27.2	37.1	7.5	13.7	12.0	9.3	10.2	10.2	29.2	48.8	25,869	35,971	39.1	11.4
Los Gatos......................	12.4	22.3	26.6	5.1	8.6	11.6	18.7	12.3	17.1	43.3	51.5	28,592	29,718	3.9	3.2
Lynwood......................	90.9	35.8	29.5	12.5	17.5	13.3	10.6	9.7	6.9	30.1	52.9	69,845	69,766	-0.1	1.1
Madera......................	75.6	25.5	34.5	10.9	14.3	14.6	10.2	6.6	8.9	28.0	51.0	43,207	61,416	42.1	7.0
Manhattan Beach..................	8.4	15.0	28.9	4.7	9.0	13.4	20.8	12.4	10.8	41.3	53.5	33,852	35,132	3.8	1.1
Manteca......................	42.7	15.1	25.0	9.7	13.3	12.8	14.2	11.2	13.8	36.5	50.9	49,258	67,286	36.6	21.3
Martinez......................	14.8	11.3	18.0	8.6	12.2	13.8	16.8	13.2	17.4	43.4	51.4	35,866	36,036	0.5	6.6
Maywood......................	97.4	41.9	30.0	10.6	17.1	11.1	16.2	7.7	7.3	30.0	49.3	28,083	27,395	-2.4	-0.4
Menifee......................	36.9	15.4	22.0	9.4	14.0	11.2	11.6	13.9	17.9	39.1	50.6	NA	77,496	**********	19.5

1. May be of any race.

City	Households, 2017								Serious crimes known to police[2], 2016				Educational attainment, 2017		
			Percent						Total		Rate[3]			Attainment[4] (percent)	
	Number	Persons per household	Family	Married couple family	Female headed[1]	Non-family	One person	Persons in group quarters, 2017	Number	Rate	Violent	Property	Population age 25 and over	High school graduate or less	Bachelor's degree or more
	27	28	29	30	31	32	33	34	35	36	37	38	39	40	41
CALIFORNIA— Cont'd															
Delano	11,906	3.69	84.3	61.5	15.7	15.7	11.5	9,255	1,816	3,449	501	2,947	33,198	71.5	6.1
Desert Hot Springs	12,081	2.36	45.9	25.0	14.1	54.1	49.2	NA	1,151	4,028	787	3,241	19,293	65.3	12.2
Diamond Bar	17,250	3.27	81.2	66.5	10.3	18.8	15.3	185	997	1,744	115	1,629	39,449	20.8	58.3
Downey	33,578	3.35	78.2	52.2	18.6	21.8	17.7	670	3,744	3,264	325	2,939	76,120	41.4	25.2
Dublin	20,362	2.93	73.6	65.2	5.5	26.4	19.2	1,261	1,184	1,959	144	1,815	42,263	17.6	65.4
East Palo Alto	8,903	3.33	69.0	46.9	17.5	31.0	21.8	NA	639	2,133	404	1,729	20,043	51.4	24.6
El Cajon	33,587	3.02	69.5	44.2	19.0	30.5	25.1	2,431	2,841	2,719	378	2,341	68,375	41.9	21.0
El Centro	10,591	4.14	82.0	46.1	26.1	18.0	15.8	525	2,519	5,697	464	5,234	26,511	52.6	16.0
Elk Grove	53,661	3.18	77.5	59.3	14.4	22.5	18.5	955	2,889	1,702	322	1,380	114,292	26.9	36.9
El Monte	27,987	4.10	83.1	50.0	23.1	16.9	12.6	1,246	2,949	2,513	382	2,131	76,395	70.2	11.8
El Paso de Robles (Paso Robles)	12,300	2.58	61.9	48.7	9.5	38.1	26.2	NA	1,044	3,269	210	3,059	21,714	34.2	24.2
Encinitas	25,149	2.50	66.1	54.9	4.6	33.9	24.9	347	1,142	1,796	165	1,631	47,539	17.2	58.6
Escondido	46,250	3.23	71.6	48.9	13.6	28.4	20.2	2,363	3,841	2,512	363	2,149	99,880	46.6	22.6
Eureka	11,620	2.24	44.1	31.3	8.8	55.9	46.3	1,150	1,776	6,582	945	5,637	18,957	33.7	30.3
Fairfield	37,324	3.06	76.0	51.6	16.1	24.0	19.3	1,916	3,321	2,900	416	2,484	75,192	34.1	27.7
Folsom	28,094	2.63	74.9	63.8	7.0	25.1	21.6	4,238	1,460	1,890	98	1,792	54,412	19.4	49.2
Fontana	52,767	4.00	87.3	60.7	19.7	12.7	10.6	589	5,266	2,513	415	2,098	120,697	53.0	18.1
Foster City	12,422	2.76	70.4	59.4	8.8	29.6	22.8	NA	375	1,100	94	1,006	25,090	13.5	67.5
Fountain Valley	17,574	3.17	79.1	59.8	12.3	20.9	18.0	537	1,506	2,629	110	2,519	39,781	27.4	42.2
Fremont	72,148	3.23	82.8	70.4	9.3	17.2	13.5	1,588	5,135	2,177	178	1,999	164,649	24.1	55.5
Fresno	169,409	3.06	69.1	40.9	18.6	30.9	24.2	9,474	23,729	4,522	611	3,911	321,638	44.5	21.3
Fullerton	45,632	3.00	70.1	51.8	11.8	29.9	22.4	3,455	3,940	2,775	240	2,535	94,152	30.7	41.0
Gardena	21,189	2.80	65.2	43.9	18.7	34.8	29.4	811	1,820	2,995	556	2,439	44,940	44.5	20.9
Garden Grove	48,036	3.59	79.9	55.4	15.1	20.1	14.4	1,912	4,867	2,762	309	2,452	120,866	50.1	22.5
Gilroy	16,961	3.37	74.8	52.4	16.8	25.2	19.6	450	1,924	3,554	336	3,218	35,809	37.7	29.3
Glendale	74,613	2.70	68.7	51.0	12.3	31.3	25.4	1,719	3,677	1,812	112	1,700	153,511	36.3	38.7
Glendora	17,200	2.99	76.8	61.4	11.0	23.2	16.1	1,011	1,431	2,732	134	2,598	37,864	25.2	43.7
Goleta	10,301	2.99	67.9	57.7	6.7	32.1	20.0	292	521	1,673	119	1,554	20,942	27.4	41.1
Hanford	18,215	3.08	80.5	55.8	19.3	19.5	13.2	473	1,762	3,148	475	2,673	35,695	42.1	16.3
Hawthorne	29,450	2.96	64.5	35.6	18.5	35.5	28.1	659	3,187	3,569	732	2,837	57,076	44.4	24.9
Hayward	46,860	3.35	73.9	51.4	15.8	26.1	18.9	3,457	5,272	3,272	392	2,880	108,534	44.0	27.1
Hemet	29,725	2.84	62.7	44.3	12.5	37.3	29.9	821	4,005	4,721	724	3,997	56,433	46.2	13.4
Hesperia	25,398	3.73	82.6	60.4	15.2	17.4	16.4	NA	2,133	2,272	356	1,916	54,679	56.1	10.5
Highland	15,488	3.56	79.5	56.5	16.0	20.5	15.2	NA	1,373	2,488	433	2,055	32,861	45.5	18.1
Hollister	9,583	3.87	81.4	63.4	11.7	18.6	13.8	NA	512	1,349	306	1,043	22,030	49.6	17.6
Huntington Beach	77,155	2.60	66.1	48.5	11.5	33.9	25.5	1,113	4,889	2,396	177	2,218	148,159	22.9	41.6
Huntington Park	13,649	4.30	88.0	48.4	27.0	12.0	9.6	NA	2,451	4,106	776	3,330	34,905	80.8	5.7
Imperial Beach	9,752	2.72	64.5	33.8	17.5	35.5	27.3	NA	443	1,604	257	1,347	18,869	44.3	23.8
Indio	35,675	2.50	58.8	45.3	7.2	41.2	37.7	737	2,381	2,669	490	2,179	68,460	57.2	14.9
Inglewood	35,788	3.04	66.2	35.2	21.6	33.8	28.8	NA	3,286	2,932	741	2,192	74,499	45.2	20.5
Irvine	97,161	2.78	67.9	56.8	8.0	32.1	20.6	7,515	3,889	1,458	57	1,401	178,607	13.4	66.1
Laguna Hills	10,726	2.87	73.4	57.7	11.0	26.6	19.7	NA	570	1,779	106	1,673	21,798	22.5	50.5
Laguna Niguel	26,133	2.52	70.9	60.1	7.7	29.1	24.2	367	816	1,230	98	1,132	49,446	16.7	55.2
La Habra	17,473	3.55	78.2	57.9	13.1	21.8	16.1	413	1,454	2,327	163	2,164	40,149	42.9	27.0
Lake Elsinore	16,388	4.05	84.5	56.0	18.6	15.5	12.9	NA	2,020	3,161	243	2,918	37,646	48.6	15.1
Lake Forest	29,519	2.84	68.9	50.4	12.2	31.1	23.4	595	851	1,019	126	893	61,218	20.8	48.3
Lakewood	25,186	3.21	74.0	49.4	15.8	26.0	21.3	165	2,744	3,350	272	3,077	56,372	30.3	27.0
La Mesa	22,385	2.64	60.2	41.9	14.2	39.8	30.6	830	1,866	3,075	325	2,750	41,320	26.3	38.3
La Mirada	14,417	3.20	82.3	62.5	15.6	17.7	15.6	2,919	974	1,959	171	1,788	34,009	30.3	35.4
Lancaster	48,327	3.18	75.8	53.9	14.3	24.2	21.3	6,735	4,591	2,835	681	2,154	99,954	43.2	18.0
La Puente	8,713	4.62	87.8	49.3	26.3	12.2	8.4	94	691	1,688	320	1,368	25,821	68.6	11.6
La Quinta	16,406	2.51	70.0	56.5	8.0	30.0	26.7	NA	1,171	2,852	209	2,643	30,931	26.7	34.3
La Verne	11,550	2.75	64.8	51.0	8.7	35.2	30.1	748	602	1,824	124	1,699	22,280	25.6	38.0
Lawndale	11,385	2.89	66.2	37.6	14.3	33.8	29.8	NA	722	2,151	578	1,573	24,250	48.7	20.5
Lemon Grove	9,209	2.92	70.9	44.7	21.5	29.1	22.1	NA	648	2,402	515	1,887	18,128	46.4	17.2
Lincoln	17,784	2.67	74.4	60.0	9.3	25.6	23.7	NA	570	1,207	61	1,146	32,741	31.2	28.9
Livermore	33,085	2.72	68.9	56.3	8.0	31.1	27.2	453	2,458	2,745	194	2,550	63,580	24.2	47.0
Lodi	22,454	2.90	70.3	48.3	15.4	29.7	25.3	683	2,286	3,513	539	2,974	40,789	43.3	21.8
Lompoc	12,942	3.13	70.8	47.9	14.5	29.2	21.7	2,971	1,199	2,692	498	2,193	26,275	50.9	15.6
Long Beach	167,447	2.75	60.6	38.6	15.8	39.4	30.4	8,851	17,070	3,583	597	2,985	316,829	38.7	31.1
Los Altos	9,984	3.05	81.9	73.4	7.5	18.1	14.2	292	356	1,148	42	1,106	21,607	3.7	86.2
Los Angeles	1,384,851	2.83	59.0	38.6	13.8	41.0	31.1	84,045	127,968	3,193	719	2,474	2,767,070	41.6	34.4
Los Banos	11,127	3.51	72.1	52.3	15.3	27.9	23.4	163	1,282	3,397	321	3,076	21,710	61.4	9.9
Los Gatos	10,870	2.79	77.2	63.0	9.7	22.8	20.1	380	637	2,058	68	1,990	20,978	12.1	70.9
Lynwood	15,263	4.46	90.3	55.4	24.0	9.7	8.5	3,010	2,182	3,011	647	2,364	41,291	71.5	8.3
Madera	18,079	3.61	75.4	54.4	14.3	24.6	19.1	NA	2,364	3,651	780	2,871	35,705	63.6	11.9
Manhattan Beach	13,007	2.76	71.4	54.8	12.6	28.6	22.8	NA	1,083	3,012	147	2,865	23,845	9.6	74.5
Manteca	24,573	3.20	74.1	55.0	13.3	25.9	19.2	671	2,944	3,818	316	3,502	51,751	49.5	16.2
Martinez	15,455	2.44	64.2	44.0	17.9	35.8	26.7	647	909	2,359	132	2,226	28,148	21.3	44.2
Maywood	6,532	4.20	85.3	53.2	27.7	14.7	11.5	NA	563	2,012	436	1,576	16,387	81.5	4.8
Menifee	28,891	3.13	71.3	54.3	12.6	28.7	26.0	199	2,254	2,529	151	2,378	62,144	38.3	20.2

1. No spouse present.   2. Data for serious crimes have not been adjusted for underreporting. This may affect comparability between geographic areas and over time.   3. Per 100,000 population estimated by the FBI.   4. Persons 25 years old and over.

City	Money income, 2017					Median earnings, 2017			Housing units, 2017				
	Households												
	Median income	Percent with income less than $20,000	Percent with income of $200,000 or more	Median family income	Median non-family income	All persons	Men	Women	Total	Occupied	Percent owner occupied	Median value[1] (dollars)	Median gross rent (dollars)
	42	43	44	45	46	47	48	49	50	51	52	53	54
CALIFORNIA— Cont'd													
Delano	45,528	15.0	1.2	46,765	25,953	19,681	23,685	16,152	13,251	11,906	65.1	173,500	785
Desert Hot Springs	24,512	36.8	0.4	40,504	22,453	23,802	23,766	23,902	14,841	12,081	37.8	177,900	900
Diamond Bar	97,280	6.4	11.7	111,052	64,347	49,562	54,840	37,235	17,628	17,250	76.4	647,700	2,270
Downey	72,178	9.0	6.5	75,893	51,783	35,325	41,846	31,081	34,635	33,578	52.2	556,600	1,372
Dublin	149,026	3.1	32.2	171,435	62,191	81,859	107,940	60,467	20,686	20,362	62.6	884,200	2,615
East Palo Alto	65,864	14.2	4.8	69,480	49,709	32,707	33,948	32,354	9,699	8,903	44.9	826,800	1,539
El Cajon	50,312	17.3	5.2	60,919	33,570	29,339	29,758	28,971	34,498	33,587	38.5	458,100	1,232
El Centro	44,012	20.6	4.6	49,508	33,380	26,105	27,379	24,474	12,302	10,591	51.1	189,200	812
Elk Grove	89,404	9.1	9.9	98,160	42,060	39,542	47,871	33,442	55,525	53,661	72.8	403,300	1,688
El Monte	51,730	16.9	1.1	51,591	26,220	21,645	25,038	17,170	29,443	27,987	42.3	442,100	1,224
El Paso de Robles (Paso Robles)	64,766	9.8	6.5	92,895	40,166	34,222	50,657	26,506	12,934	12,300	52.8	460,500	1,376
Encinitas	107,329	6.0	24.5	130,957	60,002	51,955	61,799	40,922	27,199	25,149	62.6	908,500	1,849
Escondido	62,210	10.6	4.9	67,595	39,244	31,056	35,642	24,403	48,576	46,250	49.3	442,800	1,438
Eureka	42,209	20.0	1.6	70,167	30,507	27,557	31,148	25,230	13,307	11,620	44.8	270,200	827
Fairfield	81,231	9.1	9.6	90,885	47,867	39,616	41,820	36,776	39,011	37,324	54.9	415,700	1,611
Folsom	116,592	5.5	17.9	136,502	55,787	65,789	81,456	52,149	29,102	28,094	69.8	521,600	1,667
Fontana	67,067	10.4	4.9	70,562	38,769	30,588	35,481	24,427	54,941	52,767	66.9	373,600	1,269
Foster City	144,357	4.0	35.2	180,011	97,719	83,926	100,627	79,559	13,112	12,422	55.4	1,342,200	2,916
Fountain Valley	84,790	11.3	14.0	100,421	30,657	38,595	41,370	37,750	18,178	17,574	74.6	737,400	1,774
Fremont	127,093	6.0	25.9	136,781	61,790	66,686	83,345	50,299	76,172	72,148	63.9	927,500	2,280
Fresno	48,600	21.0	3.8	53,428	32,499	26,591	30,409	23,456	180,495	169,409	47.1	234,500	954
Fullerton	77,385	11.4	10.3	90,254	49,501	31,949	39,821	27,971	48,826	45,632	50.3	672,300	1,609
Gardena	47,272	22.0	2.7	58,577	34,988	28,535	31,186	26,802	21,865	21,189	43.7	491,300	1,193
Garden Grove	66,842	14.3	7.2	70,905	43,224	30,831	35,199	26,243	49,168	48,036	51.6	558,800	1,426
Gilroy	87,039	6.6	17.2	109,692	48,367	39,734	49,716	32,875	16,990	16,961	63.0	663,000	1,896
Glendale	58,861	21.6	8.8	68,676	37,511	36,561	40,220	32,485	79,620	74,613	33.0	790,300	1,549
Glendora	108,615	6.4	14.3	113,618	65,951	50,075	53,841	39,552	17,987	17,200	74.8	603,900	1,603
Goleta	87,771	6.0	8.0	102,660	46,792	37,457	37,162	38,760	10,898	10,301	47.5	801,800	2,022
Hanford	67,487	13.3	3.3	64,884	60,854	30,312	34,505	24,421	19,463	18,215	64.5	222,600	858
Hawthorne	50,063	19.1	3.6	59,563	27,213	30,713	32,507	28,031	31,590	29,450	24.0	601,400	1,183
Hayward	89,925	7.6	8.9	92,356	61,450	41,095	43,760	38,586	50,226	46,860	52.5	595,500	1,795
Hemet	39,801	24.1	1.0	53,262	22,943	25,363	31,293	19,609	32,461	29,725	60.7	194,900	1,074
Hesperia	55,418	17.7	1.5	61,352	17,866	31,179	36,731	25,984	26,335	25,398	67.8	238,600	1,150
Highland	59,400	13.6	6.6	66,700	25,165	28,765	36,264	25,639	16,532	15,488	64.2	328,400	1,156
Hollister	74,614	6.1	7.9	75,860	66,020	33,314	39,452	24,167	10,395	9,583	68.1	472,600	1,362
Huntington Beach	87,120	9.8	14.1	100,871	58,205	43,874	55,474	35,740	82,344	77,155	58.2	738,600	1,823
Huntington Park	45,152	16.6	1.5	45,286	30,927	21,541	23,460	17,918	14,177	13,649	31.3	442,500	998
Imperial Beach	54,770	9.8	2.7	64,855	42,476	30,780	30,890	30,597	11,774	9,752	34.4	575,700	1,283
Indio	45,278	21.6	2.0	61,703	28,537	31,429	41,651	24,519	43,804	35,675	72.7	277,400	1,006
Inglewood	51,456	17.6	4.5	58,342	34,027	29,544	29,555	29,526	38,029	35,788	36.0	528,300	1,260
Irvine	104,185	12.6	18.7	123,501	71,866	57,465	75,067	41,761	103,560	97,161	46.8	822,100	2,262
Laguna Hills	87,011	5.8	17.8	104,819	80,444	38,382	44,198	31,231	11,507	10,726	65.9	762,000	1,995
Laguna Niguel	102,386	8.5	19.2	124,935	80,546	58,800	78,501	43,300	28,033	26,133	75.1	809,500	2,260
La Habra	78,597	9.1	6.6	84,407	41,060	32,152	32,439	31,912	18,279	17,473	60.3	571,400	1,578
Lake Elsinore	67,988	12.3	2.4	68,721	34,081	24,277	38,547	16,727	17,342	16,388	65.1	347,000	1,356
Lake Forest	99,913	6.9	12.5	120,015	65,880	47,475	52,509	38,331	30,230	29,519	69.2	626,900	1,920
Lakewood	83,485	11.5	6.1	92,074	40,778	41,893	46,787	37,423	25,795	25,186	70.3	583,200	1,829
La Mesa	67,086	13.6	5.9	77,344	45,659	39,253	45,906	35,481	23,692	22,385	45.4	559,900	1,448
La Mirada	94,386	8.8	12.2	106,609	47,905	40,510	51,636	33,402	14,586	14,417	80.0	574,500	1,466
Lancaster	52,878	18.4	3.2	56,112	31,232	35,793	39,775	30,969	52,933	48,327	54.7	262,400	1,193
La Puente	66,242	11.3	0.4	69,332	28,672	25,914	27,112	23,690	9,025	8,713	57.4	429,600	1,344
La Quinta	74,903	12.1	15.0	88,605	40,493	38,449	50,735	26,980	28,035	16,406	76.2	402,600	1,164
La Verne	83,592	13.9	15.7	127,771	25,158	42,072	47,651	38,864	12,027	11,550	72.0	601,000	1,316
Lawndale	54,972	17.2	0.9	54,610	38,963	31,478	35,686	22,023	11,800	11,385	27.1	437,800	1,333
Lemon Grove	51,237	11.2	1.0	61,518	46,603	31,559	35,706	26,922	10,208	9,209	48.7	430,400	1,246
Lincoln	75,359	8.8	7.0	102,056	40,469	41,759	51,844	33,909	18,136	17,784	82.5	458,400	1,533
Livermore	118,406	4.0	25.2	153,005	58,058	61,326	77,266	42,148	34,624	33,085	72.0	745,600	1,868
Lodi	51,902	14.3	3.5	63,142	24,375	31,755	39,782	23,965	23,172	22,454	48.0	326,800	1,074
Lompoc	51,649	22.2	2.8	53,623	41,169	27,141	32,917	23,695	13,518	12,942	42.4	357,800	1,175
Long Beach	60,557	14.7	7.3	67,882	50,556	34,788	37,456	31,403	175,632	167,447	40.6	557,700	1,278
Los Altos	223,644	2.2	55.9	249,750	130,969	88,945	101,905	76,852	10,554	9,984	80.8	2,000,000	3,223
Los Angeles	60,197	17.4	9.0	67,685	44,981	31,191	33,807	27,249	1,496,661	1,384,851	36.6	647,000	1,397
Los Banos	47,453	13.7	5.2	46,206	51,560	29,674	32,273	23,881	11,378	11,127	56.6	326,300	1,152
Los Gatos	150,610	5.6	35.6	169,186	87,132	72,143	112,412	53,887	11,435	10,870	67.7	1,658,000	2,673
Lynwood	48,812	16.7	0.9	53,430	19,018	27,763	28,072	27,484	15,515	15,263	43.9	412,500	1,196
Madera	42,144	25.6	1.3	46,292	21,015	19,051	29,144	12,455	18,463	18,079	46.5	210,800	983
Manhattan Beach	155,977	2.4	40.2	203,333	96,905	82,250	153,146	51,736	14,915	13,007	65.9	2,000,000	2,539
Manteca	71,324	14.8	5.3	76,552	39,544	39,072	50,633	28,825	25,772	24,573	62.6	374,800	1,330
Martinez	101,959	8.7	14.3	124,312	70,521	59,930	73,571	42,940	15,953	15,455	68.5	602,800	1,576
Maywood	40,938	18.5	0.7	42,968	30,530	21,432	22,745	18,239	6,709	6,532	22.7	361,600	992
Menifee	65,995	12.0	4.9	77,281	27,094	36,572	45,216	26,576	30,337	28,891	75.9	339,000	1,448

1. Based on population estimated by the American Community Survey.   2. Includes units rented or sold but not occupied.   3. Specified owner-occupied units; $1,000,000 represents $1,000,000 or more.   4. 50.0 represents 50 percent or more.   5. 10.0 represents 10 percent or less.

Table D. Cities — Commuting, Computer Access, Migration, Labor Force, and Employment

City	Commuting[1], 2017		Computer access[2], 2017		Migration, 2017		Civilian labor force, 2018				Civilian employment[4], 2017			
	Percent		Percent						Unemployment		Population age 16 and older		Population age 16 to 64	
	Commuting	With commutes of 30 minutes or more	With a computer in the house	With Internet access	Percent who lived in the same house one year ago	Percent who lived in another state or county one year ago	Total	Percent change 2017-2018	Total	Rate[3]	Number	Percent in labor force	Number	Percent who worked full-year full-time
	55	56	57	58	59	60	61	62	63	64	65	66	67	68
CALIFORNIA— Cont'd														
Delano	72.3	17.4	64.6	57.9	83.1	12.5	21,921	-1.4	4,957	22.6	40,289	54.0	35,672	29.1
Desert Hot Springs	80.6	40.9	77.9	68.0	82.6	9.1	11,584	1.3	651	5.6	21,942	51.5	17,683	38.7
Diamond Bar	77.1	63.0	98.2	96.9	89.6	3.8	30,583	0.8	1,128	3.7	44,957	63.9	36,770	49.8
Downey	82.4	55.1	94.9	85.2	93.8	0.8	57,887	0.9	2,593	4.5	88,430	65.7	74,675	51.7
Dublin	67.6	57.3	98.4	96.3	81.3	10.0	31,492	1.1	838	2.7	46,077	70.9	39,580	62.5
East Palo Alto	70.9	49.8	88.6	77.6	94.6	3.7	15,060	2.0	404	2.7	24,015	70.7	21,319	53.9
El Cajon	74.8	45.5	93.8	88.8	80.2	7.0	45,468	1.1	1,657	3.6	79,732	63.4	67,166	44.8
El Centro	82.5	18.0	88.1	82.3	86.1	4.9	18,463	-1.3	2,566	13.9	32,262	55.7	27,058	33.0
Elk Grove	74.9	50.5	95.7	91.2	88.9	3.8	82,936	2.0	2,673	3.2	135,683	63.8	112,218	47.9
El Monte	77.5	43.9	89.1	75.2	95.8	1.5	52,061	0.8	2,419	4.6	92,463	62.9	78,267	42.6
El Paso de Robles (Paso Robles)	85.0	28.6	97.8	89.2	89.1	5.4	16,236	0.0	465	2.9	25,313	73.7	21,601	55.4
Encinitas	71.7	38.4	96.3	93.4	86.0	6.0	33,555	1.2	892	2.7	52,055	66.6	41,209	51.5
Escondido	79.1	45.2	93.2	85.7	84.1	1.7	69,638	1.1	2,201	3.2	119,456	66.6	102,289	50.0
Eureka	73.5	13.5	97.2	88.6	73.8	14.5	12,842	0.6	447	3.5	22,728	56.2	18,369	41.3
Fairfield	78.1	43.7	95.0	91.8	85.7	6.8	53,536	0.6	1,966	3.7	89,371	65.1	75,410	49.4
Folsom	77.4	40.8	97.0	95.4	85.7	7.3	37,266	1.9	1,033	2.8	60,835	61.2	49,924	52.4
Fontana	76.8	49.0	96.6	87.8	90.6	3.6	98,759	1.8	3,767	3.8	156,447	66.7	143,615	48.5
Foster City	73.5	49.2	98.1	94.7	75.2	12.9	20,082	1.9	411	2.0	27,519	71.0	22,396	62.0
Fountain Valley	87.5	44.8	93.2	88.2	94.5	0.8	28,661	0.9	871	3.0	46,206	57.4	34,102	46.2
Fremont	71.1	59.0	98.5	93.8	88.2	5.6	120,129	1.0	3,183	2.6	184,698	66.7	155,601	58.7
Fresno	80.7	24.1	89.6	81.0	84.2	3.6	233,148	0.8	13,568	5.8	393,230	61.4	333,081	40.5
Fullerton	80.0	48.4	95.6	91.3	86.0	6.0	70,861	1.0	2,128	3.0	112,039	65.1	92,794	47.5
Gardena	75.3	40.3	88.5	77.0	92.9	1.3	30,559	0.7	1,437	4.7	50,584	60.5	39,972	45.4
Garden Grove	80.8	47.7	93.7	88.2	91.6	2.8	82,647	0.9	2,671	3.2	144,107	62.3	119,096	46.5
Gilroy	73.6	59.3	97.0	92.6	NA	NA	29,827	0.8	947	3.2	42,100	68.9	36,005	48.2
Glendale	78.2	43.7	86.2	82.0	90.8	2.5	104,600	0.9	4,614	4.4	173,218	59.5	136,527	45.5
Glendora	82.2	54.7	95.6	92.0	91.2	2.3	26,380	0.8	1,130	4.3	43,092	65.8	35,138	54.1
Goleta	66.9	16.0	95.4	90.5	83.5	5.1	17,149	0.6	416	2.4	25,013	71.9	20,043	50.1
Hanford	77.7	34.1	94.4	83.5	84.2	6.4	25,112	1.1	1,605	6.4	43,024	62.3	37,058	48.6
Hawthorne	77.7	48.1	91.5	84.5	86.2	1.7	45,317	1.0	2,173	4.8	67,204	69.7	59,123	49.3
Hayward	71.5	56.8	96.2	91.5	90.3	5.2	78,891	0.9	2,541	3.2	129,478	69.0	111,845	55.7
Hemet	79.5	46.7	89.7	83.5	84.2	5.8	29,704	1.8	1,762	5.9	66,360	50.3	48,208	38.4
Hesperia	78.8	61.4	94.2	91.1	NA	NA	35,810	1.7	1,874	5.2	68,246	54.9	58,795	38.8
Highland	79.0	33.4	97.1	83.4	96.1	1.4	24,728	1.7	1,003	4.1	39,789	60.7	34,168	43.3
Hollister	76.7	53.8	NA	NA	76.6	14.3	19,475	0.7	1,120	5.8	27,967	68.8	25,157	43.2
Huntington Beach	78.0	47.8	96.4	88.7	88.9	3.6	109,811	1.0	3,143	2.9	166,784	66.2	129,428	51.7
Huntington Park	65.4	56.9	90.4	78.0	92.8	0.9	26,845	0.6	1,237	4.6	44,035	65.3	39,600	47.5
Imperial Beach	77.5	44.9	95.6	86.4	83.4	3.8	12,063	1.0	519	4.3	22,728	68.8	19,698	50.3
Indio	81.0	21.2	89.4	79.6	94.3	2.1	40,551	1.6	2,235	5.5	76,410	57.5	59,578	44.4
Inglewood	77.7	47.1	91.9	82.4	89.3	1.6	53,325	1.0	2,962	5.6	85,974	64.9	70,764	50.3
Irvine	74.2	34.9	98.6	93.3	78.7	10.1	145,653	1.0	4,060	2.8	220,151	63.3	194,584	46.9
Laguna Hills	77.0	31.3	NA	NA	90.1	3.5	17,270	1.0	473	2.7	24,485	69.5	18,943	48.6
Laguna Niguel	79.2	44.8	98.6	95.3	85.1	5.5	35,743	1.1	1,005	2.8	54,473	62.8	40,329	51.3
La Habra	79.0	45.2	94.6	90.4	87.8	6.9	31,214	1.1	965	3.1	48,024	71.0	40,958	50.4
Lake Elsinore	83.7	68.9	96.7	87.7	89.3	6.0	29,979	1.9	1,206	4.0	45,882	66.4	41,916	40.8
Lake Forest	80.3	38.4	97.6	93.8	88.0	4.7	48,575	1.1	1,289	2.7	69,802	69.4	58,538	55.0
Lakewood	83.7	43.8	94.3	90.9	92.5	0.9	43,436	0.8	1,900	4.4	65,052	63.7	53,070	52.4
La Mesa	82.2	35.8	95.0	91.5	80.0	5.5	30,881	1.1	1,002	3.2	47,906	65.5	39,372	51.6
La Mirada	81.1	55.5	98.3	91.5	90.3	2.9	24,509	0.9	1,088	4.4	41,720	64.0	33,563	50.1
Lancaster	83.7	28.5	90.3	80.9	91.4	3.1	65,576	0.8	4,337	6.6	120,708	52.6	105,955	42.8
La Puente	74.8	49.7	93.7	86.2	NA	NA	19,274	0.8	927	4.8	31,707	63.8	27,497	50.1
La Quinta	68.6	19.0	90.7	87.8	89.8	4.2	19,089	1.9	839	4.4	34,320	50.3	22,486	37.8
La Verne	76.8	47.6	91.6	87.6	88.9	3.9	16,212	0.9	718	4.4	26,083	65.7	20,193	44.0
Lawndale	87.2	32.1	91.2	83.1	NA	NA	16,789	0.9	726	4.3	26,775	68.1	23,132	54.8
Lemon Grove	75.5	30.8	91.0	85.0	NA	NA	12,567	0.8	475	3.8	20,202	67.0	17,313	49.7
Lincoln	79.2	44.7	94.7	87.0	92.3	4.3	19,173	1.7	644	3.4	37,531	55.7	25,234	56.9
Livermore	79.7	47.9	94.6	91.5	84.5	5.6	48,826	1.1	1,240	2.5	71,781	69.1	59,424	59.3
Lodi	80.4	36.4	92.2	87.4	82.0	4.8	29,705	1.0	1,733	5.8	48,820	62.5	40,197	44.5
Lompoc	64.4	36.4	89.1	82.7	82.3	2.3	17,444	0.3	886	5.1	31,688	57.6	27,037	40.5
Long Beach	76.8	50.2	92.9	83.4	88.3	4.0	240,159	0.8	11,467	4.8	375,636	65.8	321,097	49.6
Los Altos	81.6	42.5	98.4	92.1	85.5	10.7	14,861	0.9	364	2.4	24,475	62.5	18,297	49.3
Los Angeles	69.7	53.7	92.5	84.4	88.8	3.0	2,080,175	0.8	97,557	4.7	3,271,960	66.9	2,776,855	48.7
Los Banos	83.5	50.6	94.9	81.5	86.5	5.3	16,721	0.0	1,738	10.4	25,865	63.0	21,876	41.6
Los Gatos	76.8	49.2	98.3	95.3	85.9	5.2	16,145	0.9	437	2.7	23,745	64.5	18,490	55.8
Lynwood	81.5	57.2	88.7	64.3	NA	NA	28,801	0.8	1,582	5.5	52,269	57.2	47,386	40.6
Madera	67.3	43.2	84.5	74.4	84.5	5.8	27,639	0.8	2,129	7.7	45,585	57.7	39,776	38.6
Manhattan Beach	77.7	41.2	97.9	96.0	87.5	3.2	20,003	0.8	683	3.4	26,942	65.0	23,081	54.0
Manteca	86.5	41.0	91.6	86.8	85.8	3.8	36,855	0.9	1,652	4.5	61,377	58.1	50,407	47.2
Martinez	75.5	46.7	91.6	90.5	82.2	6.2	20,799	1.0	609	2.9	32,415	67.4	25,757	53.0
Maywood	75.1	67.5	86.4	70.5	NA	NA	12,520	0.7	554	4.4	19,915	63.3	17,903	47.6
Menifee	79.6	59.6	93.1	89.6	86.2	3.7	38,737	1.9	1,640	4.2	73,361	55.9	57,153	44.6

1. Employed persons.　　2. Households.　　3. Percent of civilian labor force.　　4. Persons 16 years old and over.

Table D. Cities — Construction, Wholesale Trade, and Retail Trade

City	Value of residential construction authorized by building permits, 2018			Wholesale trade[1], 2012				Retail trade[2], 2012			
	New construction ($1,000)	Number of housing units	Percent single family	Number of establishments	Number of employees	Sales (mil dol)	Annual payroll (mil dol)	Number of establishments	Number of employees	Sales (mil dol)	Annual payroll (mil dol)
	69	70	71	72	73	74	75	76	77	78	79
CALIFORNIA— Cont'd											
Delano	38,973	253	43.9	20	180	189.0	7.9	80	1,045	277.3	26.3
Desert Hot Springs	8,425	39	100.0	1	D	D	D	40	549	144.4	13.1
Diamond Bar	11,536	31	100.0	249	634	1,359.9	29.2	113	1,062	311.6	23.4
Downey	13,834	56	100.0	97	813	338.5	37.5	275	4,421	1,163.8	107.2
Dublin	300,975	786	78.2	64	323	222.6	20.3	175	3,862	1,329.0	124.1
East Palo Alto	403	2	100.0	5	D	D	D	24	926	270.5	24.8
El Cajon	23,850	101	100.0	134	1,080	556.8	49.7	445	6,280	1,756.0	158.4
El Centro	10,548	100	16.0	53	433	294.8	15.8	200	4,172	925.9	91.7
Elk Grove	145,955	693	100.0	42	347	83.9	18.9	280	5,913	1,823.8	173.9
El Monte	39,647	300	13.0	294	1,887	808.8	71.4	274	3,254	1,676.8	111.8
El Paso de Robles (Paso Robles)	17,516	109	19.3	47	328	129.7	14.1	151	2,429	625.2	61.4
Encinitas	37,291	157	100.0	96	462	212.1	24.3	282	3,927	1,119.7	110.9
Escondido	24,224	218	9.2	132	1,165	545.8	54.2	541	9,202	2,786.0	263.2
Eureka	480	4	100.0	42	388	134.3	15.8	233	3,186	971.3	84.0
Fairfield	88,152	314	100.0	69	1,393	869.7	72.1	311	5,307	1,398.6	133.8
Folsom	174,249	785	54.0	44	374	788.8	36.4	282	5,534	1,639.5	151.0
Fontana	135,966	498	82.9	145	3,620	1,811.5	165.0	321	5,905	2,145.1	171.5
Foster City	0	0	0.0	60	D	D	D	31	876	305.0	25.3
Fountain Valley	2,903	11	100.0	105	1,076	657.1	60.4	221	3,205	1,298.6	88.7
Fremont	475,905	1,967	8.1	458	9,470	13,487.4	720.4	411	7,229	2,617.9	231.1
Fresno	304,354	1,239	66.3	514	7,741	5,459.8	388.1	1,539	22,005	5,960.2	555.9
Fullerton	13,948	80	23.8	236	2,434	2,539.6	141.5	374	5,211	1,516.4	130.8
Gardena	16,776	103	95.1	164	1,540	642.6	63.2	177	2,197	754.0	66.5
Garden Grove	33,357	137	81.0	232	2,465	1,239.7	113.3	402	5,005	1,656.2	134.7
Gilroy	95,130	391	32.5	41	D	D	D	313	5,155	1,191.9	111.9
Glendale	22,252	144	62.5	254	1,911	1,386.6	97.1	731	11,330	3,138.2	300.7
Glendora	17,116	50	100.0	34	362	162.9	25.1	131	2,471	688.2	64.0
Goleta	9,790	44	100.0	52	999	620.2	95.5	127	2,317	727.7	66.4
Hanford	56,487	202	90.1	26	325	191.2	18.5	168	2,905	741.6	67.5
Hawthorne	34,049	49	73.5	67	1,209	480.3	56.2	183	3,443	1,382.2	101.6
Hayward	108,922	287	99.0	457	6,380	4,546.4	386.7	399	5,840	1,765.7	162.5
Hemet	18,179	63	100.0	21	124	69.1	4.0	203	3,658	845.5	93.6
Hesperia	44,171	283	88.0	42	186	231.4	7.7	173	2,101	615.5	45.9
Highland	18,364	65	100.0	14	D	D	D	59	836	234.9	21.1
Hollister	113,182	371	100.0	20	212	72.2	10.3	88	1,192	318.2	32.5
Huntington Beach	29,759	121	43.8	403	4,714	10,353.7	291.2	556	8,069	2,505.6	233.2
Huntington Park	40	1	100.0	55	740	399.3	28.5	182	2,196	622.7	55.4
Imperial Beach	13,999	95	36.8	6	9	3.3	0.3	30	224	45.3	4.4
Indio	50,599	322	100.0	35	373	166.7	15.3	162	2,624	862.9	79.5
Inglewood	3,781	20	5.0	81	2,277	977.4	76.3	257	3,440	1,219.9	85.6
Irvine	782,106	3,410	54.7	986	18,431	30,339.3	1,395.5	593	9,845	4,254.4	363.2
Laguna Hills	1,500	1	100.0	94	623	282.3	41.9	186	2,324	452.6	51.3
Laguna Niguel	72,476	303	1.3	63	264	95.4	11.1	133	2,959	1,254.0	107.5
La Habra	6,273	33	93.9	72	416	247.9	22.0	173	3,158	912.1	78.9
Lake Elsinore	121,193	408	100.0	37	272	79.4	10.4	157	2,732	784.9	69.5
Lake Forest	71,482	237	100.0	187	3,004	1,741.4	213.4	205	3,212	1,068.1	116.0
Lakewood	6,631	27	11.1	32	142	38.9	5.3	228	4,820	1,104.4	106.2
La Mesa	11,076	105	29.5	23	192	66.6	8.5	229	3,846	1,070.3	101.9
La Mirada	1,474	9	100.0	125	3,047	2,257.2	185.6	88	1,375	391.9	40.2
Lancaster	32,556	153	66.7	68	867	887.2	30.5	300	4,983	1,562.3	132.5
La Puente	10,910	45	91.1	24	110	40.7	3.6	92	1,111	243.8	25.7
La Quinta	41,425	201	63.2	17	33	34.7	3.3	93	2,204	637.4	57.4
La Verne	10,442	45	15.6	66	691	527.1	37.9	74	1,298	355.7	27.2
Lawndale	3,072	13	100.0	15	111	39.2	4.8	87	774	208.4	19.2
Lemon Grove	4,121	33	33.3	9	46	16.7	2.8	77	1,227	411.6	35.5
Lincoln	31,345	92	100.0	16	151	55.5	6.3	52	975	268.0	24.8
Livermore	64,496	317	39.1	162	3,292	2,192.9	228.9	281	3,560	1,212.0	126.4
Lodi	66,639	247	100.0	39	265	639.3	14.3	209	3,353	974.6	93.3
Lompoc	400	3	100.0	9	51	12.6	2.2	111	1,395	371.9	35.3
Long Beach	40,109	201	63.7	318	4,469	6,962.3	284.9	957	13,033	3,783.9	334.5
Los Altos	49,507	65	63.1	17	D	D	D	102	D	D	D
Los Angeles	3,872,425	16,299	16.2	8,552	83,938	63,834.9	4,787.1	11,359	133,706	40,156.9	3,735.0
Los Banos	62,295	284	100.0	11	131	122.9	4.9	74	1,197	270.5	26.6
Los Gatos	33,912	31	100.0	28	D	D	D	176	D	D	D
Lynwood	857	6	100.0	39	580	312.5	28.8	118	1,386	322.3	27.6
Madera	27,975	178	100.0	22	250	213.0	14.2	173	2,163	556.1	50.7
Manhattan Beach	80,139	121	100.0	40	D	D	D	178	2,924	772.1	69.1
Manteca	161,174	524	98.5	26	393	225.1	13.9	177	3,440	824.0	85.3
Martinez	1,888	6	100.0	23	D	D	D	57	1,031	309.8	32.5
Maywood	323	2	0.0	20	432	233.0	20.4	54	472	107.1	9.3
Menifee	264,395	976	100.0	14	57	39.8	2.4	87	1,672	417.3	37.9

1. Merchant wholesalers except manufacturers' sales branches and offices.   2. Establishments with payroll.

City	Real estate and rental and leasing, 2012				Professional, scientific, and technical services[1], 2012				Manufacturing, 2012			
	Number of establishments	Number of employees	Receipts (mil dol)	Annual payroll (mil dol)	Number of establishments	Number of employees	Receipts (mil dol)	Annual payroll (mil dol)	Number of establishments	Number of employees	Receipts (mil dol)	Annual payroll (mil dol)
	80	81	82	83	84	85	86	87	88	89	90	91
CALIFORNIA— Cont'd												
Delano.................................	19	69	10.6	1.6	20	D	D	D	11	85	38.3	2.9
Desert Hot Springs...............	10	D	D	D	8	215	4.4	2.9	NA	NA	NA	NA
Diamond Bar........................	98	D	D	D	234	D	D	D	14	231	D	9.9
Downey...............................	153	1,051	130.9	28.1	145	D	D	D	79	1,968	1,037.0	95.1
Dublin.................................	55	214	73.4	10.1	190	1,452	291.3	124.2	18	1,281	509.7	118.6
East Palo Alto.....................	20	92	48.2	4.5	19	D	D	D	6	D	D	D
El Cajon	158	625	90.8	20.7	199	2,323	151.5	60.1	162	4,472	D	242.7
El Centro	46	207	45.5	6.7	90	D	D	D	16	204	D	7.7
Elk Grove	110	427	68.7	12.9	198	D	D	D	30	532	111.0	22.4
El Monte.............................	72	390	52.0	11.1	105	D	D	D	142	2,558	515.5	113.7
El Paso de Robles (Paso Robles)...................	55	178	26.8	5.3	77	273	31.3	12.1	67	2,175	524.6	101.9
Encinitas	181	428	86.5	19.1	525	1,658	350.3	110.8	41	186	48.2	10.7
Escondido	180	937	862.9	53.1	337	1,810	230.1	84.0	165	2,794	D	125.1
Eureka................................	61	263	46.4	8.4	103	D	D	D	29	541	109.6	19.1
Fairfield..............................	99	406	106.4	15.0	156	D	D	D	60	2,638	1,718.9	152.8
Folsom................................	103	489	95.5	17.6	327	D	D	D	26	674	198.9	49.2
Fontana...............................	88	538	131.0	25.1	89	411	34.7	10.0	105	4,084	1,574.6	197.3
Foster City..........................	50	352	119.1	24.9	151	2,145	485.6	210.3	11	817	D	D
Fountain Valley	106	346	80.4	15.6	231	D	D	D	86	2,752	2,318.1	165.1
Fremont..............................	240	1,052	392.8	54.1	1,047	13,204	2,603.7	1,153.9	328	18,254	5,194.0	1,594.2
Fresno................................	506	3,269	512.4	105.4	1,121	D	D	D	335	12,295	4,367.7	522.7
Fullerton.............................	172	684	123.9	23.6	378	3,338	471.3	246.0	195	6,326	2,032.2	315.5
Gardena..............................	54	332	27.1	7.8	69	364	27.2	10.6	224	4,643	891.1	222.1
Garden Grove	138	495	125.3	19.1	244	D	D	D	272	7,436	1,533.1	355.2
Gilroy.................................	40	136	48.6	4.7	73	382	51.8	19.1	54	1,346	498.9	68.7
Glendale.............................	310	2,740	1,391.5	162.4	888	D	D	D	198	4,473	842.3	237.4
Glendora.............................	63	256	46.6	7.8	114	692	77.5	31.3	41	827	363.0	37.9
Goleta	52	278	43.8	9.9	158	D	D	D	109	5,347	1,857.5	408.2
Hanford...............................	50	200	34.3	4.8	52	268	30.2	10.9	29	894	D	35.3
Hawthorne...........................	64	427	74.0	13.7	72	514	87.5	23.5	67	3,043	D	209.5
Hayward.............................	171	1,330	279.1	57.6	262	D	D	D	315	10,345	4,108.1	608.5
Hemet................................	74	345	51.8	8.1	75	333	33.7	11.6	21	748	169.0	36.2
Hesperia.............................	54	187	31.5	5.6	51	450	30.8	8.0	53	392	55.4	16.2
Highland.............................	20	57	10.4	1.4	24	113	16.3	3.4	9	168	D	5.8
Hollister.............................	32	81	20.9	2.8	46	147	15.6	4.6	38	1,274	341.6	D
Huntington Beach	319	1,411	311.7	62.6	769	D	D	D	320	12,880	D	1,221.6
Huntington Park	21	104	13.7	2.4	26	240	16.0	6.1	100	2,565	441.3	99.1
Imperial Beach	20	D	D	D	21	88	9.2	2.5	NA	NA	NA	NA
Indio	45	232	38.4	7.8	73	D	D	D	25	329	48.7	13.1
Inglewood............................	65	939	147.2	31.8	73	D	D	D	68	2,175	D	99.3
Irvine..................................	647	10,154	2,790.0	512.7	2,768	D	D	D	427	27,718	11,089.1	1,999.5
Laguna Hills	93	631	88.9	28.8	335	1,852	279.2	119.9	49	426	74.9	20.6
Laguna Niguel	108	446	112.4	22.8	298	872	138.3	41.2	24	209	D	12.2
La Habra	48	128	33.4	3.9	80	381	47.0	13.4	57	829	168.9	38.3
Lake Elsinore	39	103	20.6	3.6	55	235	35.7	8.0	65	790	113.3	31.5
Lake Forest	115	1,051	165.2	49.8	412	3,461	683.1	298.9	96	5,765	1,446.9	283.3
Lakewood............................	36	147	28.9	4.4	67	367	30.4	11.8	10	238	D	8.7
La Mesa..............................	133	884	104.7	26.8	229	1,068	128.8	51.4	21	115	18.7	4.0
La Mirada............................	56	501	98.5	23.4	67	355	47.1	17.3	58	2,267	590.8	93.1
Lancaster............................	132	545	134.8	19.0	149	D	D	D	57	983	219.7	36.2
La Puente............................	19	62	10.5	2.0	15	239	32.2	16.5	13	105	9.3	2.6
La Quinta	87	190	44.5	7.5	89	339	65.4	25.8	4	6	1.1	0.3
La Verne..............................	34	153	21.1	4.6	72	290	37.7	11.8	55	1,093	204.7	53.5
Lawndale.............................	22	295	59.8	9.2	43	D	D	D	18	239	D	10.5
Lemon Grove	16	71	22.3	1.9	23	119	6.7	2.7	9	81	16.3	3.8
Lincoln................................	38	86	18.0	2.4	44	216	18.0	6.8	10	601	176.9	30.1
Livermore............................	99	525	173.9	24.0	204	D	D	D	132	3,690	1,339.4	234.4
Lodi....................................	77	403	39.7	10.1	104	656	71.3	25.7	80	2,124	561.9	81.6
Lompoc...............................	31	146	18.8	4.1	35	D	D	D	23	573	108.4	25.5
Long Beach..........................	502	3,660	2,647.9	266.4	1,036	7,701	1,489.9	485.4	234	8,027	4,464.4	758.2
Los Altos.............................	98	304	114.2	21.0	275	D	D	D	23	189	30.0	12.6
Los Angeles.........................	5,948	36,498	14,628.8	2,035.5	14,376	134,211	30,105.0	10,658.0	5,034	101,103	43,502.5	4,752.3
Los Banos............................	23	59	8.4	1.2	18	86	7.9	3.3	9	553	D	26.3
Los Gatos............................	105	366	123.7	18.9	277	1,637	303.1	122.9	32	488	169.9	36.6
Lynwood..............................	16	100	10.7	4.5	15	96	7.2	2.2	51	1,057	236.6	42.3
Madera................................	35	148	19.2	4.0	38	D	D	D	35	1,055	445.4	51.3
Manhattan Beach.................	127	430	272.3	23.1	308	1,384	312.1	121.5	19	82	D	2.9
Manteca..............................	56	231	50.5	9.3	54	319	23.7	9.4	22	972	D	57.2
Martinez..............................	41	171	35.4	5.8	78	D	D	D	18	907	D	111.5
Maywood.............................	3	4	0.2	0.0	4	D	D	D	16	228	D	6.9
Menifee...............................	50	242	36.5	6.8	52	174	13.4	3.8	16	266	61.8	11.7

1. Establishments subject to federal tax.

Accommodation and Food Services, Arts, Entertainment, and Recreation, and Health Care and Social Assistance

City	Accommodation and food services, 2012				Arts, entertainment, and recreation[1], 2012				Health care and social assistance,[1] 2012			
	Number of establishments	Number of employees	Receipts (mil dol)	Annual payroll (mil dol)	Number of establishments	Number of employees	Receipts (mil dol)	Annual payroll (mil dol)	Number of establishments	Number of employees	Receipts (mil dol)	Annual payroll (mil dol)
	92	93	94	95	96	97	98	99	100	101	102	103
CALIFORNIA— Cont'd												
Delano	43	432	23.3	5.2	2	D	D	D	66	D	D	D
Desert Hot Springs	36	353	19.2	4.8	2	D	D	D	11	61	4.0	1.5
Diamond Bar	123	1,370	75.1	23.4	6	114	7.9	2.0	165	1,273	115.1	42.3
Downey	213	4,046	247.7	66.5	12	D	D	D	278	5,105	739.3	295.8
Dublin	141	2,588	181.4	45.7	15	D	D	D	117	1,174	151.5	51.5
East Palo Alto	14	660	46.3	16.6	2	D	D	D	12	D	D	D
El Cajon	236	3,169	173.6	44.6	13	189	15.1	2.8	205	3,958	345.4	143.9
El Centro	116	1,870	97.1	25.8	5	D	D	D	121	925	100.5	38.7
Elk Grove	206	3,919	212.5	57.4	16	D	D	D	275	2,744	414.4	112.2
El Monte	164	1,488	91.3	20.8	4	D	D	D	147	1,988	157.8	60.8
El Paso de Robles (Paso Robles)	114	2,080	119.4	31.2	13	D	D	D	71	736	45.7	15.7
Encinitas	214	4,943	277.9	78.7	46	366	24.4	7.6	362	2,859	347.1	124.7
Escondido	263	4,164	233.7	60.5	24	D	D	D	313	3,443	351.6	138.1
Eureka	135	1,649	92.7	25.5	12	186	5.8	2.1	108	1,163	110.5	46.1
Fairfield	211	3,101	190.2	46.8	18	D	D	D	219	2,316	348.6	100.5
Folsom	180	3,470	169.3	49.0	22	490	21.7	6.2	231	D	D	D
Fontana	219	3,451	188.4	48.0	18	D	D	D	159	D	D	D
Foster City	59	1,120	80.5	22.4	3	D	D	D	76	D	D	D
Fountain Valley	146	2,203	128.3	34.6	21	D	D	D	377	D	D	D
Fremont	381	5,412	331.7	87.2	32	722	36.4	11.3	577	6,977	1,074.4	399.9
Fresno	927	16,854	841.3	233.1	77	2,455	94.6	31.0	1,397	17,786	2,161.5	877.0
Fullerton	323	5,151	293.1	76.7	26	399	28.0	7.4	374	D	D	D
Gardena	202	2,258	130.3	33.5	7	D	D	D	137	2,174	270.4	96.6
Garden Grove	396	6,025	389.7	98.0	23	D	D	D	456	4,760	527.1	180.1
Gilroy	127	2,168	124.6	31.7	8	D	D	D	116	D	D	D
Glendale	403	6,449	400.5	111.6	163	755	117.6	36.7	968	8,146	871.9	316.1
Glendora	88	1,402	74.6	20.7	16	D	D	D	192	D	D	D
Goleta	102	1,752	104.7	27.1	4	145	6.5	2.2	112	1,339	152.1	57.9
Hanford	91	1,597	84.0	21.8	5	109	3.3	0.6	147	1,349	140.9	50.6
Hawthorne	124	1,650	108.8	25.2	14	222	16.5	4.3	125	1,950	189.7	72.8
Hayward	297	3,731	225.0	55.7	16	308	15.4	7.9	231	4,468	704.8	308.2
Hemet	144	2,179	112.1	32.1	10	D	D	D	213	2,976	305.8	105.1
Hesperia	104	1,773	88.6	23.7	6	D	D	D	77	700	70.2	24.3
Highland	56	753	43.6	11.0	3	D	D	D	49	D	D	D
Hollister	53	645	35.5	8.8	6	D	D	D	59	D	D	D
Huntington Beach	441	8,517	534.8	151.5	67	754	58.6	12.8	609	4,641	531.3	204.7
Huntington Park	99	1,374	82.7	20.6	2	D	D	D	125	1,294	152.6	47.9
Imperial Beach	33	351	20.6	4.8	3	D	D	D	19	367	27.3	11.4
Indio	106	2,965	229.2	63.3	21	D	D	D	114	1,760	238.1	80.6
Inglewood	168	2,570	145.5	38.5	32	1,156	168.8	33.9	237	3,724	505.3	167.9
Irvine	606	14,173	907.9	244.5	234	8,490	501.7	114.6	954	8,749	1,347.3	422.5
Laguna Hills	94	1,905	103.5	30.4	9	D	D	D	334	D	D	D
Laguna Niguel	119	1,929	110.3	29.0	25	D	D	D	215	1,500	138.1	58.8
La Habra	136	1,866	102.6	28.6	5	D	D	D	99	D	D	D
Lake Elsinore	98	1,432	77.8	21.6	9	D	D	D	57	297	31.1	11.4
Lake Forest	181	2,897	173.1	46.3	27	359	26.9	7.2	189	4,891	328.9	178.3
Lakewood	156	3,191	169.1	46.4	10	205	16.5	3.7	159	2,002	319.3	106.1
La Mesa	167	3,198	172.3	52.7	13	D	D	D	322	D	D	D
La Mirada	98	1,486	85.4	21.3	10	D	D	D	104	1,392	127.6	49.9
Lancaster	205	3,762	184.0	47.1	13	D	D	D	365	5,673	790.7	256.4
La Puente	68	734	41.5	10.1	1	D	D	D	52	352	27.9	9.6
La Quinta	73	3,254	207.1	67.1	17	498	37.2	13.8	71	389	46.6	18.3
La Verne	78	1,240	64.9	18.0	12	195	12.3	3.5	62	427	37.8	13.3
Lawndale	46	610	38.0	9.2	4	11	4.2	0.8	60	294	29.4	10.6
Lemon Grove	48	643	35.3	8.8	3	38	1.3	0.5	31	622	44.5	17.3
Lincoln	50	D	D	D	7	D	D	D	71	D	D	D
Livermore	180	2,541	153.7	42.3	23	D	D	D	150	1,658	225.7	78.3
Lodi	127	1,893	98.6	26.8	9	266	12.6	3.7	176	D	D	D
Lompoc	82	1,055	62.9	16.2	2	D	D	D	57	D	D	D
Long Beach	877	16,971	984.1	276.1	94	1,467	109.3	28.3	1,053	12,915	1,473.7	546.7
Los Altos	85	1,252	84.0	26.0	14	D	D	D	136	1,133	165.0	54.6
Los Angeles	8,009	138,886	9,295.6	2,593.6	7,686	31,974	9,416.1	3,866.7	9,711	109,130	13,605.4	4,917.1
Los Banos	57	804	43.0	11.4	2	D	D	D	41	273	29.1	10.2
Los Gatos	124	2,447	145.9	46.4	16	D	D	D	296	2,222	320.7	125.2
Lynwood	79	1,053	64.6	14.9	NA	NA	NA	NA	110	D	D	D
Madera	79	1,081	57.8	13.4	6	75	3.4	0.9	105	D	D	D
Manhattan Beach	154	3,688	247.0	75.6	73	281	48.9	19.8	187	D	D	D
Manteca	117	1,839	103.7	26.1	10	323	18.4	5.9	103	D	D	D
Martinez	79	753	43.4	10.9	6	D	D	D	41	D	D	D
Maywood	39	425	24.1	6.0	NA	NA	NA	NA	22	D	D	D
Menifee	67	1,348	75.4	21.6	8	D	D	D	87	1,573	128.0	50.8

1. Establishments subject to federal tax.

Table D. Cities — Other Services and Government Employment and Payroll

City	Other services[1]				Government employment and payroll, 2012								
						March payroll							
							Percent of total for:						
	Number of establishments	Number of employees	Receipts (mil dol)	Annual payroll (mil dol)	Full-time equivalent employees	Total (dollars)	Administrative, judicial, and legal	Police and corrections	Fire protection	Highways and transportation	Health and welfare	Natural resources and utilities	Education and libraries
	104	105	106	107	108	109	110	111	112	113	114	115	116
CALIFORNIA— Cont'd													
Delano	21	58	7.4	1.3	220	881,307	8.4	41.4	0.0	13.6	3.9	30.6	0.0
Desert Hot Springs	17	47	3.1	0.8	73	440,127	17.0	60.5	0.0	11.0	10.1	1.4	0.0
Diamond Bar	54	D	D	D	72	380,697	40.0	0.0	0.0	16.5	10.9	32.6	0.0
Downey	126	702	60.2	15.2	505	3,402,608	8.6	42.0	25.6	4.8	1.5	12.4	2.5
Dublin	83	D	D	D	106	716,632	36.7	5.5	0.8	23.0	3.5	24.9	0.0
East Palo Alto	11	D	D	D	112	1,036,706	21.8	57.6	0.0	11.0	9.5	0.0	0.0
El Cajon	171	1,183	130.3	31.8	443	2,609,521	7.2	42.2	14.7	6.2	11.0	13.4	0.0
El Centro	52	239	21.3	6.3	964	4,003,786	4.7	10.9	5.9	2.3	69.2	5.8	0.5
Elk Grove	137	707	57.1	16.3	280	1,987,037	15.1	76.6	0.0	2.4	1.4	1.1	0.0
El Monte	132	434	49.1	10.7	336	2,338,846	6.8	63.2	0.0	15.0	2.5	12.4	0.0
El Paso de Robles (Paso Robles)	43	247	23.8	6.5	164	981,684	11.7	27.8	19.1	3.0	4.3	20.5	2.9
Encinitas	141	825	67.4	21.3	242	1,673,551	30.3	0.0	25.3	14.3	0.8	20.7	0.0
Escondido	225	1,215	123.8	34.8	1,133	10,074,411	16.4	29.3	13.9	7.9	0.9	24.7	3.3
Eureka	73	461	45.5	12.5	282	1,300,511	8.5	31.6	18.8	2.4	4.7	21.0	0.0
Fairfield	121	906	97.2	32.5	645	3,404,101	10.9	36.3	15.3	11.5	3.2	11.0	0.0
Folsom	97	764	50.8	16.0	483	3,244,300	14.2	23.2	21.7	8.2	0.0	28.9	1.6
Fontana	170	945	83.8	23.5	767	4,073,819	10.2	49.0	0.0	8.3	6.6	23.2	0.0
Foster City	20	D	D	D	192	1,556,154	16.6	27.7	24.1	6.3	0.0	25.3	0.0
Fountain Valley	84	562	47.6	14.9	232	1,801,733	11.7	37.6	26.9	4.9	0.9	10.1	0.0
Fremont	276	1,983	276.4	67.3	881	7,171,062	20.6	30.1	20.1	9.2	7.6	8.2	0.0
Fresno	536	3,750	381.1	106.9	3,214	18,551,770	10.2	39.0	13.4	20.0	0.0	15.9	0.0
Fullerton	185	884	110.0	26.1	676	4,122,933	7.6	39.6	18.4	6.3	5.0	12.8	3.4
Gardena	124	780	69.3	20.9	419	2,062,110	7.9	42.6	0.0	28.2	6.3	8.7	0.0
Garden Grove	216	884	78.3	21.3	657	4,420,328	10.0	44.2	22.5	0.7	7.8	7.6	0.0
Gilroy	82	713	68.2	19.1	258	1,936,702	13.1	41.6	20.3	4.9	2.7	13.4	0.0
Glendale	308	2,190	165.1	65.5	1,864	13,741,087	17.0	23.8	18.6	3.2	4.9	27.1	3.1
Glendora	78	D	D	D	321	1,582,591	10.6	43.7	0.0	11.9	6.9	19.8	7.2
Goleta	48	D	D	D	47	334,846	63.8	0.0	0.0	23.1	5.9	7.2	0.0
Hanford	43	192	17.7	4.8	259	1,321,734	9.8	38.2	13.4	8.8	0.0	24.1	0.0
Hawthorne	97	369	35.3	7.5	283	1,907,186	16.2	40.8	0.0	5.5	2.8	5.5	0.0
Hayward	202	1,576	223.3	52.6	761	6,582,512	8.9	39.0	24.1	6.2	3.7	9.7	2.7
Hemet	88	384	31.1	8.2	409	2,543,919	11.5	33.8	20.3	7.4	2.2	11.7	3.6
Hesperia	83	355	37.7	10.1	127	669,050	29.0	0.1	0.0	16.7	15.9	0.0	0.0
Highland	29	147	9.2	2.7	38	273,354	31.6	0.0	0.0	15.6	10.8	4.6	0.0
Hollister	50	D	D	D	131	912,911	12.2	25.2	24.4	4.8	4.9	18.9	0.0
Huntington Beach	309	1,944	159.4	52.3	1,071	7,579,599	14.4	34.3	23.5	5.3	1.3	14.6	2.6
Huntington Park	49	417	37.5	10.0	208	1,200,684	11.4	67.5	0.0	5.5	5.1	6.0	0.0
Imperial Beach	23	100	6.1	1.9	82	452,081	44.4	0.0	17.6	4.4	3.2	9.8	0.0
Indio	59	314	27.8	7.7	253	1,534,809	8.8	49.5	0.0	12.9	5.9	15.1	0.0
Inglewood	122	934	85.6	23.8	724	3,812,741	19.1	49.5	0.0	10.8	5.9	11.8	2.9
Irvine	293	2,511	248.1	68.7	977	6,075,973	20.0	39.1	0.0	10.5	2.9	13.8	0.0
Laguna Hills	68	390	33.7	10.7	40	246,065	39.8	0.0	0.0	13.2	20.3	26.7	0.0
Laguna Niguel	92	520	41.6	11.9	79	590,935	24.7	1.6	0.0	17.2	21.8	28.0	0.0
La Habra	95	531	47.0	10.7	325	1,702,615	11.2	45.6	0.0	0.0	0.0	0.0	0.0
Lake Elsinore	66	351	29.9	8.7	66	784,724	0.4	0.0	0.0	8.2	0.0	11.8	0.0
Lake Forest	111	695	85.9	20.7	79	477,565	58.7	1.2	0.0	5.1	13.9	21.1	0.0
Lakewood	76	D	D	D	255	1,549,892	26.5	6.5	0.0	16.3	2.1	41.0	0.0
La Mesa	106	820	54.6	17.8	283	1,642,547	12.9	41.7	20.9	5.6	2.7	10.2	0.0
La Mirada	33	141	6.3	2.0	142	702,597	25.1	9.5	0.0	0.0	9.3	25.7	0.0
Lancaster	167	864	78.2	22.3	338	1,643,288	21.1	3.3	0.0	28.3	10.6	32.5	0.0
La Puente	35	121	7.6	2.2	44	173,692	49.1	0.0	0.0	14.7	2.7	17.6	0.0
La Quinta	39	168	10.1	2.9	94	580,882	30.3	0.0	0.0	26.7	22.0	0.0	0.0
La Verne	38	215	12.2	3.4	200	1,245,972	16.1	41.5	26.1	2.8	0.0	10.1	0.0
Lawndale	65	299	25.9	6.0	72	370,627	35.6	0.0	0.0	27.9	0.0	17.4	0.0
Lemon Grove	44	150	11.9	3.3	50	320,723	14.9	0.0	50.2	14.0	7.5	6.0	0.0
Lincoln	34	D	D	D	204	1,072,286	18.7	28.4	11.2	10.5	9.3	10.6	1.8
Livermore	109	D	D	D	431	3,325,675	14.6	36.7	0.0	16.4	4.9	18.3	6.5
Lodi	100	559	54.0	15.2	481	2,698,469	10.3	27.2	16.3	7.0	1.8	29.2	2.7
Lompoc	37	D	D	D	391	1,833,592	11.8	26.5	9.3	5.4	0.4	32.9	2.7
Long Beach	514	3,723	492.5	110.7	5,861	36,050,392	7.5	28.9	14.8	19.5	6.1	12.6	1.4
Los Altos	51	D	D	D	127	885,014	8.2	40.0	0.0	11.6	3.4	17.8	0.0
Los Angeles	5,383	33,721	2,988.4	814.2	47,505	361,983,103	11.8	27.5	11.6	12.8	4.2	30.5	1.2
Los Banos	22	100	7.8	2.4	285	749,390	11.4	40.2	15.6	5.1	2.2	19.0	0.0
Los Gatos	88	419	37.6	11.5	148	1,210,153	16.6	44.9	0.0	10.6	7.2	6.5	7.5
Lynwood	52	296	21.9	5.7	230	916,329	42.8	2.5	0.0	20.8	5.6	28.3	0.0
Madera	43	202	19.6	4.9	274	1,196,996	16.2	35.6	0.0	9.9	12.2	22.5	0.0
Manhattan Beach	76	594	37.8	12.1	381	1,720,027	11.4	41.4	12.9	4.7	9.6	15.5	0.0
Manteca	76	307	28.1	6.9	345	2,165,170	13.0	35.1	16.6	6.2	1.2	25.5	0.0
Martinez	41	166	22.5	5.1	52	324,363	4.1	88.0	0.0	0.0	4.6	1.4	0.0
Maywood	27	98	6.0	1.9	18	66,828	51.7	0.0	0.0	0.0	5.9	31.7	0.0
Menifee	43	233	27.6	5.1	23	165,702	68.9	0.0	0.0	10.5	13.6	0.0	0.0

1. Establishments subject to federal tax.

Table D. Cities — City Government Finances

City	City government finances, 2012									
	General revenue							General expenditure		
	Intergovernmental			Taxes						
						Per capita[1] (dollars)				Per capita[1] (dollars)	
	Total (mil dol)	Total (mil dol)	Percent from state government	Total (mil dol)	Total	Property	Sales and gross receipts	Total (mil dol)	Total	Capital outlays
	117	118	119	120	121	122	123	124	125	126
CALIFORNIA— Cont'd										
Delano................................	32.5	6.6	92.1	16.4	313	163	105	31.3	597	53
Desert Hot Springs................	20.2	3.1	33.2	12.4	446	214	213	27.4	988	219
Diamond Bar........................	24.3	2.3	77.9	16.9	300	165	128	31.6	561	189
Downey................................	89.0	11.9	58.4	53.0	468	227	239	98.0	866	54
Dublin..................................	67.1	3.0	97.7	50.4	1,032	529	415	63.3	1,298	122
East Palo Alto.......................	36.0	3.8	90.2	24.9	858	568	285	31.6	1,090	142
El Cajon	103.0	8.1	84.7	70.6	695	308	385	103.4	1,017	157
El Centro	182.9	11.7	52.8	25.2	582	256	318	173.8	4,019	507
Elk Grove	117.6	21.2	77.7	55.8	352	138	210	116.8	737	118
El Monte	92.1	16.0	67.9	64.7	561	290	268	92.7	803	118
El Paso de Robles (Paso Robles)..	46.5	6.6	62.1	30.0	983	513	466	43.1	1,414	272
Encinitas	74.3	4.1	60.5	49.4	809	584	217	77.2	1,265	265
Escondido	143.3	14.3	60.1	78.5	531	315	209	135.9	919	78
Eureka.................................	46.5	7.0	68.0	27.9	1,036	386	648	49.7	1,845	324
Fairfield...............................	135.2	23.7	86.3	87.3	811	437	371	120.8	1,122	219
Folsom................................	106.2	4.7	81.7	61.5	840	482	272	106.9	1,459	214
Fontana...............................	243.1	25.3	66.9	150.7	748	563	182	241.4	1,198	265
Foster City...........................	51.6	1.9	100.0	38.7	1,203	920	277	53.2	1,654	65
Fountain Valley	51.8	4.2	91.1	35.6	630	394	227	53.9	954	197
Fremont...............................	214.4	29.7	64.9	141.4	637	367	230	244.1	1,100	468
Fresno.................................	632.4	127.3	42.9	267.5	529	240	287	528.7	1,045	197
Fullerton..............................	151.4	23.8	80.4	79.9	576	371	202	188.8	1,362	506
Gardena..............................	78.5	10.8	48.9	56.0	938	205	564	63.5	1,065	158
Garden Grove	143.3	12.1	44.0	78.1	448	263	183	176.5	1,012	138
Gilroy..................................	73.7	6.7	42.5	38.7	762	281	360	72.6	1,432	389
Glendale..............................	315.9	29.1	55.9	145.8	748	379	366	334.4	1,717	239
Glendora..............................	41.0	5.3	97.4	28.1	553	361	190	34.8	685	69
Goleta	31.1	4.4	87.8	22.0	727	257	426	33.8	1,118	384
Hanford	41.5	3.7	86.5	19.3	355	224	123	40.0	736	127
Hawthorne............................	103.1	37.8	12.8	48.4	564	260	302	99.8	1,163	96
Hayward..............................	216.5	39.7	29.1	108.3	724	336	353	190.5	1,273	255
Hemet.................................	71.2	3.5	72.5	44.9	552	243	299	68.8	846	126
Hesperia..............................	73.7	15.0	93.8	44.5	483	317	165	101.5	1,103	350
Highland..............................	29.3	5.5	73.6	17.0	315	231	64	34.1	631	199
Hollister...............................	49.1	1.4	100.0	27.1	753	551	186	40.2	1,115	356
Huntington Beach	237.1	14.8	87.5	142.7	732	378	348	245.0	1,257	137
Huntington Park	53.9	9.0	53.2	35.6	605	397	207	47.0	799	63
Imperial Beach......................	31.4	1.9	89.6	17.2	640	488	150	27.2	1,012	70
Indio...................................	79.4	8.3	78.1	47.6	577	315	258	80.9	980	123
Inglewood............................	168.9	42.5	51.9	97.4	874	422	400	161.6	1,451	100
Irvine..................................	221.8	16.6	67.8	150.8	656	245	405	296.0	1,289	255
Laguna Hills	26.8	8.5	93.2	16.2	524	301	209	23.6	764	235
Laguna Niguel......................	38.2	3.2	97.6	31.8	495	300	189	40.3	626	203
La Habra..............................	54.3	8.3	81.6	32.0	521	283	239	52.1	847	84
Lake Elsinore	62.9	4.4	97.8	38.1	682	451	180	70.3	1,261	194
Lake Forest..........................	48.6	4.3	66.7	38.8	491	253	234	69.4	879	338
Lakewood............................	58.5	5.6	92.9	38.4	474	248	223	55.1	680	68
La Mesa	60.0	3.3	82.3	42.5	729	333	392	58.2	999	181
La Mirada	53.4	5.0	48.8	36.5	744	494	247	62.4	1,271	395
Lancaster.............................	155.7	14.4	70.0	98.7	621	395	225	158.8	999	170
La Puente............................	17.0	3.2	83.5	10.1	251	139	110	16.8	417	64
La Quinta.............................	92.3	4.4	99.5	69.5	1,801	1,413	377	79.1	2,049	214
La Verne..............................	36.0	1.3	97.5	23.8	756	457	290	35.3	1,123	55
Lawndale.............................	21.9	4.6	43.6	15.6	470	264	205	22.6	682	195
Lemon Grove	23.6	3.5	40.3	12.9	495	317	176	23.1	888	142
Lincoln.................................	39.4	1.9	82.7	16.0	363	218	137	39.2	887	142
Livermore.............................	144.6	12.8	81.4	70.9	848	452	391	146.1	1,746	314
Lodi....................................	74.4	14.8	61.1	37.4	591	232	358	65.7	1,040	203
Lompoc................................	49.0	7.6	70.8	20.7	479	244	198	57.4	1,329	168
Long Beach..........................	1,850.9	195.5	44.1	411.4	877	543	331	1,760.6	3,753	846
Los Altos	38.7	1.3	98.4	24.5	820	464	333	41.7	1,397	179
Los Angeles	9,274.5	847.5	41.5	3,849.3	997	441	528	8,678.1	2,247	524
Los Banos	30.8	1.2	94.3	16.0	437	268	87	30.9	844	146
Los Gatos............................	39.5	1.7	100.0	30.5	1,010	550	425	44.6	1,477	382
Lynwood..............................	48.4	7.5	65.9	33.0	465	265	191	48.6	685	116
Madera................................	61.9	6.4	52.4	35.7	571	205	290	58.8	939	220
Manhattan Beach..................	64.9	2.0	100.0	40.2	1,132	649	468	68.9	1,939	189
Manteca...............................	96.8	11.6	80.0	40.6	571	382	177	94.8	1,335	419
Martinez..............................	24.4	2.4	100.0	18.2	493	310	179	24.1	653	42
Maywood..............................	11.1	1.5	55.8	8.9	321	203	117	10.0	361	22
Menifee	33.2	8.6	100.0	19.8	243	138	102	27.8	341	43

1. Based on population estimated as of July 1 of the year shown.

Table D. Cities — **City Government Finances**

City		City government finances, 2012 (cont.)								
		General expenditure (cont.)								
		Percent of total for:								
	Public welfare	Highways	Parking facilities	Education	Health and hospitals	Police protection	Sewerage and sanitation	Parks and recreation	Housing and community development	Interest on debt
	127	128	129	130	131	132	133	134	135	136
CALIFORNIA— Cont'd										
Delano...............................	0.0	7.9	0.1	0.0	0.7	35.9	16.1	5.8	6.3	4.8
Desert Hot Springs...............	0.0	19.3	0.0	0.0	1.2	32.8	0.0	2.7	15.7	5.8
Diamond Bar.......................	0.0	11.3	0.0	0.0	0.4	17.3	1.0	17.5	2.2	2.7
Downey..............................	0.0	10.4	0.0	0.0	3.3	29.8	2.0	12.8	8.4	2.2
Dublin................................	0.0	9.9	0.0	0.0	0.9	23.6	5.1	13.7	4.2	0.4
East Palo Alto......................	0.0	15.7	0.0	0.0	0.0	32.7	8.2	3.9	9.5	7.2
El Cajon	0.0	7.2	0.0	0.0	4.9	29.0	15.2	4.3	14.7	2.9
El Centro............................	0.0	3.7	0.0	0.0	71.3	5.1	5.8	1.4	1.4	2.7
Elk Grove...........................	0.0	20.1	0.0	0.0	0.7	26.4	11.1	0.6	15.2	3.0
El Monte.............................	0.0	8.9	0.1	0.0	0.1	24.2	0.0	3.9	14.8	4.7
El Paso de Robles (Paso Robles)...............................	0.0	14.0	0.0	0.0	0.0	18.5	11.1	8.4	4.2	5.6
Encinitas	0.0	11.1	0.0	0.0	1.4	14.8	5.7	11.7	3.2	0.4
Escondido...........................	0.0	9.0	0.0	0.0	1.1	26.8	15.4	5.9	4.7	6.9
Eureka...............................	0.0	7.4	0.3	0.0	0.2	21.6	17.7	5.2	11.4	6.1
Fairfield..............................	0.0	22.4	0.0	0.0	0.9	26.9	0.0	8.9	8.3	6.3
Folsom...............................	0.0	7.4	0.0	0.0	0.6	18.0	10.0	10.4	7.7	6.6
Fontana..............................	0.0	16.0	0.0	0.0	0.0	21.8	4.9	5.1	16.6	14.1
Foster City..........................	0.0	4.8	0.0	0.0	0.0	17.3	12.1	18.0	5.0	0.0
Fountain Valley	0.0	16.9	0.0	0.0	5.8	26.6	8.8	7.4	11.0	1.2
Fremont..............................	0.1	18.2	0.0	0.0	4.6	27.3	2.1	6.1	8.7	3.7
Fresno...............................	0.0	9.2	0.9	0.0	1.8	27.9	21.5	4.8	2.7	8.1
Fullerton.............................	0.0	19.9	0.0	0.0	3.1	19.1	8.1	6.3	16.0	3.9
Gardena.............................	0.0	12.4	0.0	0.0	3.2	33.0	1.6	5.6	7.1	2.4
Garden Grove......................	0.0	9.7	0.0	0.0	3.7	26.6	4.0	4.9	25.2	3.8
Gilroy.................................	0.0	3.9	0.0	0.0	0.1	23.5	11.0	1.2	31.3	2.7
Glendale.............................	0.0	6.5	1.9	0.0	0.2	20.8	9.9	5.1	16.0	1.2
Glendora............................	0.0	7.3	0.0	0.0	0.3	38.7	0.0	9.5	14.0	4.6
Goleta................................	0.0	35.2	0.0	0.0	1.4	19.9	0.0	7.5	6.3	2.1
Hanford..............................	0.0	14.3	0.0	0.0	1.1	20.5	28.6	8.9	2.1	3.4
Hawthorne..........................	0.0	13.4	0.0	0.0	0.0	30.2	0.7	1.5	12.0	4.8
Hayward.............................	0.0	22.7	0.0	0.0	1.1	29.9	8.1	0.9	3.9	2.6
Hemet	0.0	13.6	0.0	0.0	0.3	23.8	21.6	1.1	10.9	0.9
Hesperia............................	0.0	18.2	0.0	0.0	1.8	12.4	0.0	0.0	33.4	8.9
Highland.............................	0.0	33.6	0.0	0.0	3.7	20.5	0.0	3.0	9.1	8.3
Hollister..............................	0.0	9.2	0.0	0.0	1.5	15.8	30.4	3.1	12.4	4.5
Huntington Beach	0.0	12.4	1.3	0.0	1.9	28.9	8.3	6.7	4.8	2.2
Huntington Park	0.0	8.1	1.2	0.0	5.3	33.4	0.8	4.2	12.8	4.9
Imperial Beach.....................	0.0	9.3	0.0	0.0	0.7	26.9	16.9	5.6	13.1	5.9
Indio..................................	0.0	11.9	0.0	0.0	5.2	25.3	0.2	5.0	15.5	8.5
Inglewood...........................	0.0	9.8	0.2	0.0	1.6	19.3	8.5	5.2	14.3	7.4
Irvine.................................	0.0	25.6	0.0	0.0	1.6	18.7	0.0	21.6	1.9	12.6
Laguna Hills	0.0	25.2	0.0	0.0	0.3	27.3	0.0	23.3	0.3	2.6
Laguna Niguel......................	0.0	23.9	0.0	0.0	0.8	23.4	0.0	17.7	0.2	0.0
La Habra	0.0	8.8	0.0	0.0	1.8	30.7	10.8	10.5	12.4	2.9
Lake Elsinore.......................	0.0	5.0	0.0	0.0	0.7	12.7	0.0	16.1	15.7	24.3
Lake Forest.........................	0.0	38.6	0.0	0.0	0.2	18.1	0.0	16.3	6.7	0.7
Lakewood...........................	0.0	18.5	0.0	0.0	0.5	20.7	12.1	21.5	3.7	3.9
La Mesa.............................	0.0	19.6	0.3	0.0	0.9	25.3	16.9	6.5	1.6	2.5
La Mirada...........................	0.0	37.1	0.0	0.0	0.1	12.1	0.0	18.7	14.6	3.8
Lancaster...........................	0.0	12.1	0.0	0.0	0.4	17.3	0.0	6.5	26.8	11.9
La Puente...........................	0.0	11.0	0.0	0.0	1.7	27.8	3.9	17.2	8.0	4.3
La Quinta	0.0	10.7	0.0	0.0	0.5	15.3	0.0	8.3	24.6	17.5
La Verne.............................	0.0	8.7	0.0	0.0	5.5	33.7	3.3	6.8	15.6	2.9
Lawndale............................	0.0	12.3	0.0	0.0	0.6	20.2	0.2	10.8	29.6	4.8
Lemon Grove	0.0	4.3	0.0	0.0	0.7	19.3	17.8	3.7	15.4	4.9
Lincoln...............................	0.0	14.1	0.0	0.0	0.0	13.0	24.9	4.2	2.1	3.8
Livermore............................	0.0	17.3	0.0	0.0	0.4	17.7	12.7	1.7	2.3	2.6
Lodi...................................	0.0	12.3	0.0	0.0	0.6	24.8	16.8	7.4	2.4	0.1
Lompoc..............................	0.0	9.5	0.0	0.0	0.6	34.0	20.4	5.7	8.5	1.8
Long Beach.........................	0.0	3.4	0.0	0.0	3.0	11.4	5.2	7.6	7.6	4.6
Los Altos	0.0	14.1	0.0	0.0	0.8	22.9	12.7	6.1	2.6	0.2
Los Angeles	0.0	8.1	0.4	0.0	2.6	19.6	8.6	4.5	4.2	6.1
Los Banos..........................	0.0	9.9	0.0	0.0	0.3	24.6	26.0	13.3	5.1	2.8
Los Gatos..........................	0.0	12.1	0.0	0.0	0.3	26.6	0.3	7.1	9.0	2.5
Lynwood.............................	0.0	22.5	0.0	0.0	1.0	16.7	1.5	5.8	13.5	1.6
Madera..............................	0.0	25.5	0.1	0.0	1.7	16.8	19.2	6.0	4.6	5.3
Manhattan Beach.................	0.0	10.0	4.3	0.0	4.5	30.5	9.0	13.7	0.0	1.3
Manteca.............................	0.0	16.3	0.0	0.0	0.3	15.0	25.2	6.9	13.6	4.5
Martinez.............................	0.0	10.7	1.3	0.0	0.0	41.2	0.0	13.9	0.1	3.6
Maywood............................	0.0	11.2	0.0	0.0	0.0	39.4	0.0	6.2	4.2	10.1
Menifee..............................	0.0	9.1	0.0	0.0	1.3	31.9	0.0	0.0	6.7	0.3

City	City government finances, 2012 (cont.)			Climate[2]							
	Debt outstanding		Debt issued during year	Average daily temperature				Annual precipitation (inches)	Heating degree days	Cooling degree days
				Mean		Limits				
	Total (mil dol)	Per capita[1] (dollars)		January	July	January[3]	July[4]			
	137	138	139	140	141	142	143	144	145	146
CALIFORNIA— Cont'd										
Delano	62.8	1,196	0.0	46.6	81.1	36.5	99.0	7.34	2,434	1,990
Desert Hot Springs	12.2	440	6.2	NA	NA	NA	NA	NA	NA	NA
Diamond Bar	0.0	0	12.0	54.6	73.8	41.5	88.7	16.96	1,727	1,191
Downey	63.1	558	1.5	57.0	73.8	46.0	82.9	12.94	1,211	1,186
Dublin	6.2	127	0.0	47.2	72.0	37.4	89.1	14.82	2,755	858
East Palo Alto	47.6	1,643	0.0	49.0	68.0	40.4	78.8	15.71	2,584	452
El Cajon	68.2	671	0.1	54.9	74.7	41.6	87.0	11.96	1,560	1,371
El Centro	100.3	2,320	0.0	55.8	91.4	41.3	107.0	2.96	1,080	3,852
Elk Grove	95.6	603	0.0	46.3	75.4	38.8	92.4	17.93	2,666	1,248
El Monte	168.9	1,465	13.3	56.3	75.6	42.6	89.0	18.56	1,295	1,575
El Paso de Robles (Paso Robles)	54.4	1,784	6.4	NA	NA	NA	NA	NA	NA	NA
Encinitas	40.7	667	0.0	55.5	75.1	42.5	88.6	15.10	1,464	1,436
Escondido	191.9	1,298	11.4	55.5	75.1	42.5	88.6	15.10	1,464	1,436
Eureka	109.2	4,052	9.4	47.9	58.1	40.8	63.3	38.10	4,430	7
Fairfield	271.5	2,523	10.5	46.1	72.6	37.5	88.8	23.46	2,649	975
Folsom	237.5	3,241	15.0	46.9	77.7	39.2	94.8	24.61	2,532	1,528
Fontana	677.9	3,364	0.8	56.6	78.3	45.3	95.0	14.77	1,364	1,901
Foster City	0.0	0	0.0	48.4	68.0	39.1	80.8	20.16	2,764	422
Fountain Valley	9.7	171	0.0	58.0	72.9	46.6	87.7	13.84	1,153	1,299
Fremont	313.6	1,414	53.3	49.8	68.0	42.0	78.3	14.85	2,367	530
Fresno	1,062.2	2,099	0.0	46.0	81.4	38.4	96.6	11.23	2,447	1,963
Fullerton	195.2	1,408	0.0	56.9	73.2	45.2	84.0	11.23	1,286	1,294
Gardena	24.8	415	0.0	56.3	69.4	46.2	77.6	14.79	1,526	742
Garden Grove	179.2	1,028	6.7	58.0	72.9	46.6	87.7	13.84	1,153	1,299
Gilroy	54.9	1,083	0.0	49.7	72.0	39.4	88.3	20.60	2,278	913
Glendale	322.6	1,656	38.3	54.8	75.5	42.0	88.9	17.49	1,575	1,455
Glendora	46.8	921	0.0	54.6	73.8	41.5	88.7	16.96	1,727	1,191
Goleta	15.7	518	0.0	53.1	67.0	40.8	76.7	16.93	2,121	482
Hanford	43.0	792	0.0	44.7	79.6	35.7	95.9	8.58	2,749	1,724
Hawthorne	104.9	1,223	0.0	57.1	69.3	48.6	75.3	13.15	1,274	679
Hayward	196.8	1,315	0.0	49.7	64.6	41.7	75.2	26.30	2,810	261
Hemet	13.7	168	0.0	52.4	79.9	38.4	97.8	12.55	1,914	1,903
Hesperia	168.7	1,834	0.0	45.5	80.0	31.4	99.1	6.20	2,929	1,735
Highland	73.8	1,364	0.0	54.4	79.6	41.8	96.0	16.43	1,599	1,937
Hollister	43.7	1,213	0.0	49.5	66.6	37.8	80.9	13.61	2,724	405
Huntington Beach	257.9	1,323	36.3	55.9	67.3	48.2	71.4	11.65	1,719	543
Huntington Park	42.4	720	0.0	58.3	74.2	48.5	83.8	15.14	928	1,506
Imperial Beach	40.1	1,493	0.0	57.3	70.1	46.1	76.1	9.95	1,321	862
Indio	184.2	2,232	0.0	56.8	92.8	42.0	107.1	3.15	903	4,388
Inglewood	277.3	2,489	30.8	57.1	69.3	48.6	75.3	13.15	1,274	679
Irvine	1,400.1	6,096	270.1	54.5	72.1	41.4	83.8	13.87	1,794	1,102
Laguna Hills	15.6	507	0.0	56.7	72.4	47.2	82.3	14.03	1,465	1,183
Laguna Niguel	0.0	0	0.0	55.4	68.7	43.9	77.3	13.56	1,756	666
La Habra	55.8	908	0.0	56.9	73.2	45.2	84.0	11.23	1,286	1,294
Lake Elsinore	410.2	7,355	1.5	52.2	79.6	38.3	98.1	12.09	1,924	1,874
Lake Forest	18.8	238	11.0	56.7	72.4	47.2	82.3	14.03	1,465	1,183
Lakewood	42.5	525	0.0	57.0	73.8	46.0	82.9	12.94	1,211	1,186
La Mesa	46.3	795	0.9	57.1	73.0	45.7	83.6	13.75	1,313	1,261
La Mirada	92.9	1,893	1.9	58.8	76.6	47.9	88.9	14.44	949	1,837
Lancaster	431.7	2,716	0.0	43.9	80.8	31.0	95.5	7.40	3,241	1,733
La Puente	9.5	236	0.0	58.8	76.6	47.9	88.9	14.44	949	1,837
La Quinta	324.4	8,401	0.0	NA	NA	NA	NA	NA	NA	NA
La Verne	19.4	618	0.0	54.6	73.8	41.5	88.7	16.96	1,727	1,191
Lawndale	21.1	635	0.0	57.1	69.3	48.6	75.3	13.15	1,274	679
Lemon Grove	26.5	1,021	0.0	NA	NA	NA	NA	NA	NA	NA
Lincoln	35.5	801	0.0	NA	NA	NA	NA	NA	NA	NA
Livermore	175.1	2,093	0.0	47.2	72.0	37.4	89.1	14.82	2,755	858
Lodi	0.2	4	0.0	46.1	73.8	37.5	91.1	18.22	2,710	1,057
Lompoc	54.1	1,253	0.0	53.7	64.5	41.4	75.4	15.85	2,250	322
Long Beach	2,390.0	5,095	112.4	57.0	73.8	46.0	82.9	12.94	1,211	1,186
Los Altos	1.9	62	0.0	49.0	68.0	40.4	78.8	15.71	2,584	452
Los Angeles	23,104.2	5,983	2,268.6	58.3	74.2	48.5	83.8	15.14	928	1,506
Los Banos	28.4	774	0.0	45.9	78.1	36.8	94.6	9.95	2,570	1,547
Los Gatos	23.8	789	0.0	48.7	70.3	38.8	85.4	22.64	2,641	613
Lynwood	30.0	423	0.0	58.3	74.2	48.5	83.8	15.14	928	1,506
Madera	114.1	1,823	0.0	45.7	79.6	37.2	96.5	11.94	2,670	1,706
Manhattan Beach	37.6	1,058	0.0	57.1	69.3	48.6	75.3	13.15	1,274	679
Manteca	214.3	3,017	1.7	46.0	77.3	38.1	93.8	13.84	2,563	1,456
Martinez	29.2	790	18.7	46.3	71.2	38.8	87.4	19.58	2,757	786
Maywood	0.0	0	0.0	58.3	74.2	48.5	83.8	15.14	928	1,506
Menifee	20.0	246	20.0	NA	NA	NA	NA	NA	NA	NA

1. Based on the population estimated as of July 1 of the year shown. 2. Represents normal values based on the 30-year period, 1971±2000. 3. Average daily minimum. 4. Average daily maximum.

Table D. Cities — **Land Area and Population**

STATE Place code	City	Land area[1] (sq. mi)	Total persons 2018	Rank	Per square mile	Race 2017 — Race alone[2] (percent) White	Black or African American	American Indian, Alaskan Native	Asian	Hawaiian Pacific Islander	Some other race	Two or more races (percent)
		1	2	3	4	5	6	7	8	9	10	11
	CALIFORNIA— Cont'd											
06 46,870	Menlo Park	10.0	34,549	1,103	3,454.9	63.6	1.4	2.8	15.4	6.0	6.2	4.7
06 46,898	Merced	23.2	83,316	408	3,591.2	66.7	4.7	1.2	15.8	0.2	7.6	3.8
06 47,766	Milpitas	13.7	80,430	431	5,870.8	17.0	6.0	0.4	61.9	0.7	7.5	6.6
06 48,256	Mission Viejo	17.7	95,202	334	5,378.6	77.1	1.3	0.9	11.6	0.1	4.4	4.5
06 48,354	Modesto	43.0	215,030	104	5,000.7	76.0	5.0	0.9	6.9	1.6	5.0	4.6
06 48,648	Monrovia	13.6	36,715	1,045	2,699.6	59.8	2.0	2.5	13.3	0.0	19.1	3.3
06 48,788	Montclair	5.5	39,437	980	7,170.4	66.8	2.9	0.2	9.8	0.2	16.9	3.3
06 48,816	Montebello	8.3	62,632	597	7,546.0	61.3	2.8	0.5	12.6	0.3	21.0	1.5
06 48,872	Monterey	8.6	28,289	1,308	3,289.4	80.5	4.6	0.0	6.0	0.0	1.7	7.2
06 48,914	Monterey Park	7.7	60,401	618	7,844.3	11.2	1.0	0.0	65.4	0.8	19.7	2.0
06 49,138	Moorpark	12.6	36,576	1,050	2,902.9	75.0	2.3	1.9	7.3	0.2	5.4	8.0
06 49,270	Moreno Valley	51.3	209,050	110	4,075.0	30.6	16.4	0.8	6.1	0.6	43.3	2.2
06 49,278	Morgan Hill	12.8	45,135	847	3,526.2	78.0	1.6	1.0	12.7	0.0	3.6	3.1
06 49,670	Mountain View	12.0	83,377	407	6,948.1	49.9	0.9	0.1	37.2	0.1	8.0	3.7
06 50,076	Murrieta	33.6	114,985	251	3,422.2	63.1	4.9	0.8	8.8	0.2	11.1	11.0
06 50,258	Napa	18.0	79,263	437	4,403.5	82.9	0.4	0.5	2.8	0.1	10.0	3.3
06 50,398	National City	7.3	61,431	606	8,415.2	64.2	5.6	0.5	16.6	0.9	8.6	3.7
06 50,916	Newark	13.9	48,198	802	3,467.5	30.3	5.2	0.6	33.2	1.4	20.7	8.6
06 51,182	Newport Beach	23.8	85,326	392	3,585.1	89.2	0.9	0.1	6.3	0.2	0.6	2.8
06 51,560	Norco	13.8	26,610	1,373	1,928.3	75.4	5.7	0.6	4.6	0.1	10.4	3.1
06 52,526	Norwalk	9.7	105,120	292	10,837.1	32.2	3.0	0.2	13.8	0.5	48.2	2.2
06 52,582	Novato	27.4	55,655	680	2,031.2	66.2	2.5	0.0	6.8	0.1	19.4	5.0
06 53,000	Oakland	55.9	429,082	45	7,675.9	34.2	23.4	0.7	15.5	0.6	17.9	7.6
06 53,070	Oakley	15.9	42,129	904	2,649.6	57.1	13.8	0.0	8.9	0.3	16.2	3.7
06 53,322	Oceanside	41.2	176,080	147	4,273.8	69.8	5.0	1.4	7.9	0.4	9.5	5.9
06 53,896	Ontario	50.0	181,107	141	3,622.1	49.7	5.1	2.1	7.1	0.1	31.6	4.3
06 53,980	Orange	25.7	139,484	193	5,427.4	72.7	1.2	0.5	11.2	0.1	11.1	3.3
06 54,652	Oxnard	27.0	209,877	108	7,773.2	76.1	2.9	2.0	7.0	0.2	9.3	2.6
06 54,806	Pacifica	12.7	38,759	995	3,051.9	61.2	2.6	0.3	22.5	0.3	5.6	7.5
06 55,156	Palmdale	106.1	156,667	164	1,476.6	40.0	13.2	1.5	4.1	0.6	34.6	5.9
06 55,184	Palm Desert	26.8	53,185	727	1,984.5	85.1	1.8	0.9	6.4	0.0	2.3	3.4
06 55,254	Palm Springs	93.9	48,375	797	515.2	82.2	5.3	1.4	5.0	0.6	3.0	2.6
06 55,282	Palo Alto	23.9	66,666	549	2,789.4	59.3	2.3	0.5	32.9	0.0	1.2	3.9
06 55,520	Paradise	18.3	26,800	1,367	1,464.5	NA	NA	NA	NA	NA	NA	NA
06 55,618	Paramount	4.7	54,387	704	11,571.7	34.6	8.6	0.2	3.2	1.8	49.2	2.6
06 56,000	Pasadena	23.0	141,371	187	6,146.6	51.5	8.3	0.2	17.4	0.1	17.9	4.5
06 56,700	Perris	31.6	79,133	438	2,504.2	29.2	5.6	0.0	2.3	0.1	60.3	2.6
06 56,784	Petaluma	14.4	61,917	603	4,299.8	76.4	1.3	1.1	3.0	0.3	12.1	5.7
06 56,924	Pico Rivera	8.3	62,888	596	7,576.9	46.8	1.4	0.4	5.4	0.4	44.1	1.6
06 57,456	Pittsburg	17.3	72,437	495	4,187.1	31.2	15.9	1.9	15.0	1.3	20.9	13.8
06 57,526	Placentia	6.6	51,671	744	7,828.9	70.7	1.5	2.4	15.5	0.5	6.3	3.1
06 57,764	Pleasant Hill	7.1	34,903	1,093	4,915.9	76.1	2.5	0.0	12.0	0.0	4.6	4.7
06 57,792	Pleasanton	24.1	82,372	414	3,417.9	57.2	2.8	0.5	31.2	0.6	1.7	5.9
06 58,072	Pomona	23.0	152,361	172	6,624.4	42.3	5.9	3.4	12.6	0.0	31.9	3.9
06 58,240	Porterville	18.6	59,988	624	3,225.2	82.2	0.7	1.3	4.2	0.0	8.6	3.0
06 58,520	Poway	39.1	49,704	773	1,271.2	75.8	0.9	0.0	12.0	0.3	6.2	4.8
06 59,444	Rancho Cordova	35.0	74,585	475	2,131.0	61.0	10.0	0.4	9.4	1.0	11.7	6.5
06 59,451	Rancho Cucamonga	40.1	177,751	145	4,432.7	58.1	8.5	0.8	15.8	0.1	9.9	6.9
06 59,514	Rancho Palos Verdes	13.5	41,928	906	3,105.8	59.3	1.4	0.6	29.8	0.0	2.5	6.4
06 59,587	Rancho Santa Margarita	12.9	48,325	798	3,746.1	79.8	2.3	0.0	10.1	0.0	2.1	5.6
06 59,920	Redding	59.6	91,772	356	1,539.8	86.0	1.4	3.2	4.8	0.0	1.2	3.4
06 59,962	Redlands	35.8	71,586	502	1,999.6	63.5	10.5	0.7	11.6	0.0	8.0	5.7
06 60,018	Redondo Beach	6.2	67,412	540	10,872.9	69.0	3.1	0.3	13.0	0.2	7.7	6.7
06 60,102	Redwood City	19.3	86,200	385	4,466.3	59.9	3.1	0.3	14.5	0.4	16.7	5.2
06 60,466	Rialto	23.9	103,440	298	4,328.0	58.2	14.0	1.0	2.8	0.0	20.0	4.0
06 60,620	Richmond	30.1	110,146	275	3,659.3	49.2	18.5	0.6	13.1	0.4	12.1	6.2
06 60,704	Ridgecrest	20.9	28,940	1,287	1,384.7	77.9	5.6	0.2	6.4	0.0	3.1	6.8
06 62,000	Riverside	81.3	330,063	58	4,059.8	48.1	6.7	0.8	8.4	0.1	31.9	4.1
06 62,364	Rocklin	19.8	67,221	541	3,395.0	74.4	2.4	0.5	11.0	0.0	4.9	6.7
06 62,546	Rohnert Park	7.0	43,753	873	6,250.4	71.1	1.7	0.0	9.2	0.0	13.4	4.8
06 62,896	Rosemead	5.2	54,412	703	10,463.8	12.9	0.2	1.6	64.6	0.1	19.6	1.0
06 62,938	Roseville	43.1	139,117	195	3,227.8	78.6	2.3	0.9	10.2	1.1	2.9	4.1
06 64,000	Sacramento	97.8	508,529	36	5,199.7	41.4	14.0	1.0	18.9	2.0	15.0	7.5
06 64,224	Salinas	23.4	156,259	165	6,677.7	31.3	1.3	0.2	5.2	0.1	58.5	3.4
06 65,000	San Bernardino	62.0	215,941	103	3,482.9	59.3	13.0	0.5	3.5	0.1	18.1	5.5
06 65,028	San Bruno	5.5	43,047	882	7,826.7	38.2	1.2	0.3	28.8	4.4	17.2	9.8
06 65,042	San Buenaventura (Ventura)	21.9	111,128	271	5,074.3	86.6	2.5	0.4	2.9	0.0	2.7	5.0
06 65,070	San Carlos	5.5	30,364	1,241	5,520.7	NA	NA	NA	NA	NA	NA	NA
06 65,084	San Clemente	18.4	64,857	574	3,524.8	83.6	0.3	0.2	4.0	0.1	7.1	4.6
06 66,000	San Diego	325.6	1,425,976	8	4,379.5	64.6	6.2	0.6	17.2	0.4	5.8	5.2
06 66,070	San Dimas	15.0	33,982	1,122	2,265.5	70.0	0.8	0.3	19.2	0.0	6.3	3.4

1. Dry land or land partially or temporarily covered by water. 2. Hispanic or Latino persons may be of any race.

Table D. Cities — Population

City	Percent Hispanic or Latino[1], 2017	Percent foreign born, 2017	Age of population (percent), 2017							Median age, 2017	Percent female, 2017	Population Census counts		Percent change	
			Under 18 years	18 to 24 years	25 to 34 years	35 to 44 years	45 to 54 years	55 to 64 years	65 years and over			2000	2010	2000-2010	2001-2018
	12	13	14	15	16	17	18	19	20	21	22	23	24	25	26
CALIFORNIA— Cont'd															
Menlo Park	19.2	29.4	27.3	5.9	11.5	16.9	12.1	13.7	12.7	38.0	48.0	30,785	32,019	4.0	7.9
Merced	56.3	22.7	30.0	12.0	15.2	12.3	10.9	9.7	10.0	30.7	52.4	63,893	78,957	23.6	5.5
Milpitas	15.2	49.5	25.3	7.0	17.9	16.5	13.2	10.0	10.3	34.9	47.2	62,698	66,820	6.6	20.4
Mission Viejo	15.1	19.5	20.4	7.1	10.6	12.2	15.1	17.7	16.8	44.7	50.7	93,102	93,112	0.0	2.2
Modesto	39.4	20.4	24.1	9.6	15.1	11.8	12.1	12.1	15.2	35.8	50.9	188,856	203,119	7.6	5.9
Monrovia	43.7	25.1	19.0	7.0	15.4	16.3	15.2	12.3	14.9	40.8	50.8	36,929	36,600	-0.9	0.3
Montclair	74.6	33.9	27.3	12.2	12.6	11.7	11.7	12.7	11.9	33.6	52.9	33,049	36,649	10.9	7.6
Montebello	77.9	37.3	23.3	8.4	16.3	14.5	10.6	10.8	16.0	36.2	51.2	62,150	62,490	0.5	0.2
Monterey	12.6	14.4	15.9	13.1	15.9	13.1	11.0	11.1	19.9	38.9	50.3	29,674	27,697	-6.7	2.1
Monterey Park	27.6	55.7	15.5	7.4	14.0	14.5	11.7	15.0	22.0	43.0	51.0	60,051	60,226	0.3	0.3
Moorpark	35.6	17.0	22.4	10.3	12.7	13.8	13.1	16.6	11.1	38.1	49.5	31,415	34,517	9.9	6.0
Moreno Valley	62.2	24.5	28.3	12.1	16.6	13.7	11.7	9.0	8.5	30.5	50.6	142,381	193,305	35.8	8.1
Morgan Hill	34.5	18.7	25.0	7.4	11.8	12.2	15.5	16.7	11.3	40.3	52.5	33,556	37,905	13.0	19.1
Mountain View	18.5	48.0	18.2	8.6	24.4	16.3	10.9	10.0	11.5	34.5	47.1	70,708	73,997	4.7	12.7
Murrieta	28.1	13.4	30.2	8.5	11.4	12.3	12.6	11.6	13.4	34.9	52.9	44,282	103,680	134.1	10.9
Napa	38.9	19.6	22.6	8.6	14.2	12.5	14.1	11.6	16.4	38.5	50.8	72,585	77,097	6.2	2.8
National City	66.9	36.1	21.7	15.0	17.3	11.9	11.0	10.1	13.0	32.3	50.1	54,260	58,560	7.9	4.9
Newark	31.0	35.1	18.7	8.5	19.1	13.3	13.7	14.5	12.2	36.7	51.4	42,471	42,573	0.2	13.2
Newport Beach	7.1	12.1	18.0	4.9	10.8	10.9	15.4	16.6	23.4	49.6	51.2	70,032	85,222	21.7	0.1
Norco	29.4	8.9	21.2	11.2	10.8	13.9	17.9	13.1	11.9	40.0	47.8	24,157	27,032	11.9	-1.6
Norwalk	71.6	36.9	22.3	10.8	14.2	14.7	13.5	11.1	13.4	36.5	49.8	103,298	105,549	2.2	-0.4
Novato	23.3	21.4	18.3	10.6	11.9	12.7	12.1	15.8	18.6	43.3	50.2	47,630	51,872	8.9	7.3
Oakland	28.4	28.1	19.7	7.6	19.1	15.9	12.6	12.0	13.2	36.7	50.8	399,484	390,792	-2.2	9.8
Oakley	36.0	21.9	32.2	9.1	12.6	15.1	12.8	10.2	8.0	31.2	51.7	25,619	35,432	38.3	18.9
Oceanside	36.2	21.2	20.5	9.7	15.1	11.4	11.8	14.0	17.4	39.0	49.1	161,029	167,382	3.9	5.2
Ontario	67.9	26.9	25.3	11.0	16.7	13.6	11.8	11.0	10.6	33.2	50.4	158,007	163,925	3.7	10.5
Orange	40.5	23.6	19.0	13.3	17.4	13.4	12.8	11.9	12.1	35.2	50.3	128,821	136,432	5.9	2.2
Oxnard	75.6	34.2	27.1	10.5	15.5	14.0	11.7	11.2	9.9	32.6	50.0	170,358	197,964	16.2	6.0
Pacifica	19.1	19.1	15.8	8.5	11.9	10.7	18.5	15.6	18.9	47.3	51.5	38,390	37,304	-2.8	3.9
Palmdale	58.7	23.7	29.5	10.8	13.9	11.3	14.5	10.8	9.2	31.3	49.9	116,670	152,751	30.9	2.6
Palm Desert	18.0	12.5	13.8	4.0	11.1	8.1	7.8	15.8	39.5	59.2	52.5	41,155	48,450	17.7	9.8
Palm Springs	25.0	20.1	11.3	5.6	6.1	12.0	14.0	17.1	33.9	55.7	41.3	42,807	44,540	4.0	8.6
Palo Alto	5.9	34.0	24.5	6.5	12.9	13.1	13.5	11.2	18.4	39.8	51.0	58,598	64,395	9.9	3.5
Paradise	8.7	3.1	22.1	7.0	15.5	7.5	10.0	14.4	23.5	43.1	54.2	26,408	26,199	-0.8	2.3
Paramount	82.4	32.1	29.4	12.4	16.7	12.7	13.3	8.1	7.5	29.3	49.2	55,266	54,098	-2.1	0.5
Pasadena	35.1	32.0	18.5	8.7	19.2	14.4	15.3	9.9	14.0	37.4	51.4	133,936	137,120	2.4	3.1
Perris	84.3	32.0	33.5	12.8	17.0	12.9	11.3	6.3	6.2	27.4	48.5	36,189	68,565	89.5	15.4
Petaluma	23.9	13.9	24.3	5.4	10.9	16.4	15.5	12.1	15.4	40.6	49.8	54,548	57,938	6.2	6.9
Pico Rivera	86.3	29.1	23.2	11.2	11.7	13.7	14.3	10.4	15.5	38.1	52.3	63,428	62,948	-0.8	-0.1
Pittsburg	42.5	29.8	22.4	9.9	16.0	15.2	10.8	12.1	13.7	35.9	51.0	56,769	63,259	11.4	14.5
Placentia	47.1	22.6	23.3	11.3	16.1	11.7	11.8	12.8	13.0	34.7	51.1	46,488	50,917	9.5	1.5
Pleasant Hill	10.2	24.4	19.1	8.8	19.4	13.8	11.0	15.9	12.0	37.4	51.9	32,837	33,101	0.8	5.4
Pleasanton	7.7	32.0	21.0	7.1	10.1	14.5	18.0	15.3	13.9	43.7	49.3	63,654	70,282	10.4	17.2
Pomona	71.1	37.1	24.8	12.4	14.2	14.3	13.6	9.6	11.1	33.9	49.9	149,473	149,030	-0.3	2.2
Porterville	65.7	21.9	29.5	11.0	14.9	11.9	14.1	6.8	11.8	32.1	48.1	39,615	58,152	46.8	3.2
Poway	13.6	18.3	21.2	9.2	10.2	11.1	16.5	15.5	16.2	43.0	50.7	48,044	47,806	-0.5	4.0
Rancho Cordova	21.8	25.1	23.3	7.5	17.8	16.1	10.8	12.3	12.1	36.1	49.2	55,060	64,805	17.7	15.1
Rancho Cucamonga	38.1	20.5	25.2	10.2	15.2	12.5	13.6	12.5	10.8	34.6	51.4	127,743	165,380	29.5	7.5
Rancho Palos Verdes	11.4	27.6	24.0	5.4	6.9	10.3	14.0	13.9	25.6	47.7	53.9	41,145	41,660	1.3	0.6
Rancho Santa Margarita	24.1	14.2	24.6	7.9	15.0	14.4	14.6	15.0	8.4	36.5	52.8	47,214	47,855	1.4	1.0
Redding	11.9	8.6	21.5	9.0	15.4	10.9	11.8	13.9	17.6	37.9	51.9	80,865	89,861	11.1	2.1
Redlands	30.3	15.8	19.8	9.3	15.8	11.3	11.7	15.2	16.9	39.1	50.2	63,591	68,675	8.0	4.2
Redondo Beach	15.6	18.2	19.6	5.4	17.5	12.8	17.5	14.7	12.6	41.1	48.0	63,261	66,924	5.8	0.7
Redwood City	30.4	35.2	18.5	6.7	19.5	15.8	15.3	12.0	12.1	38.4	47.5	75,402	76,822	1.9	12.2
Rialto	73.9	26.0	27.2	12.0	16.2	13.4	12.0	10.9	8.3	31.7	52.4	91,873	99,112	7.9	4.4
Richmond	47.6	35.0	22.2	11.0	16.6	13.8	13.9	10.3	12.2	35.1	50.6	99,216	103,262	4.1	6.7
Ridgecrest	16.8	8.2	24.6	8.3	12.0	15.1	13.6	12.1	14.4	38.9	47.8	24,927	27,616	10.8	4.8
Riverside	54.7	23.2	23.9	13.9	17.5	12.2	12.8	9.9	9.7	30.9	50.2	255,166	304,033	19.2	8.6
Rocklin	16.2	13.4	26.3	11.6	10.6	14.9	15.0	9.9	11.8	35.8	52.1	36,330	57,131	57.3	17.7
Rohnert Park	25.7	17.9	18.3	14.0	17.2	11.5	12.9	13.4	12.6	35.3	52.9	42,236	40,818	-3.4	7.2
Rosemead	29.3	59.2	18.4	8.9	14.2	9.6	13.2	18.5	17.1	43.5	49.7	53,505	53,771	0.5	1.2
Roseville	15.3	14.1	22.9	7.7	12.2	13.7	14.5	12.3	16.7	39.3	50.8	79,921	119,156	49.1	16.8
Sacramento	28.2	22.3	23.3	8.5	18.0	13.5	11.5	12.5	12.7	35.2	51.1	407,018	466,390	14.6	9.0
Salinas	78.8	38.4	30.6	9.4	16.2	14.7	10.6	9.5	9.1	31.4	48.6	151,060	150,615	-0.3	3.7
San Bernardino	64.7	21.1	27.9	10.9	15.0	14.2	10.4	11.4	10.2	31.7	51.5	185,401	209,662	13.1	3.0
San Bruno	29.2	41.2	19.0	7.4	16.7	13.8	13.8	13.5	15.9	39.5	51.5	40,165	41,067	2.2	4.8
San Buenaventura (Ventura)	36.6	14.9	21.5	7.1	16.1	12.9	12.2	13.1	17.1	38.7	50.2	100,916	107,236	6.3	3.6
San Carlos	6.9	18.7	25.9	5.0	13.7	14.0	18.3	11.7	11.4	38.7	51.2	27,718	28,376	2.4	7.0
San Clemente	17.3	13.4	18.8	6.8	9.9	9.9	16.3	16.8	21.4	48.0	50.8	49,936	63,478	27.1	2.2
San Diego	30.2	25.9	19.9	11.1	19.8	13.9	12.0	10.8	12.5	34.5	49.2	1,223,400	1,301,949	6.4	9.5
San Dimas	30.8	24.2	18.1	9.2	11.1	10.4	16.7	11.6	23.0	46.5	51.9	34,980	33,375	-4.6	1.8

1. May be of any race.

Table D. Cities — Households, Group Quarters, Crime, and Education

City	Households, 2017 Number	Persons per household	Percent Family	Married couple family	Female headed[1]	Non-family	One person	Persons in group quarters, 2017	Serious crimes known to police[2], 2016 Total Number	Rate	Rate[3] Violent	Property	Educational attainment, 2017 Population age 25 and over	Attainment[4] (percent) High school graduate or less	Bachelor's degree or more
	27	28	29	30	31	32	33	34	35	36	37	38	39	40	41
CALIFORNIA— Cont'd															
Menlo Park	11,235	2.96	61.4	53.9	4.8	38.6	28.8	1,063	653	1,936	89	1,847	22,966	20.1	66.9
Merced	26,278	3.12	66.4	36.8	21.4	33.6	25.8	1,049	3,263	3,926	588	3,338	48,219	52.4	15.8
Milpitas	22,128	3.44	84.3	68.1	9.9	15.7	12.1	2,004	1,887	2,359	120	2,239	52,906	27.2	50.1
Mission Viejo	33,936	2.78	76.1	62.8	10.7	23.9	17.3	1,771	1,058	1,080	77	1,004	69,626	17.7	50.4
Modesto	72,621	2.91	70.6	49.8	16.2	29.4	24.6	2,688	11,428	5,368	988	4,380	142,099	45.7	18.9
Monrovia	13,126	2.81	69.2	44.5	16.4	30.8	25.3	NA	892	2,370	159	2,211	27,446	25.6	44.0
Montclair	10,284	3.79	82.4	51.8	20.9	17.6	14.7	272	1,923	4,920	537	4,383	23,779	52.4	11.3
Montebello	18,928	3.31	81.2	45.9	23.5	18.8	16.1	453	2,192	3,414	333	3,081	43,115	52.6	20.1
Monterey	12,005	2.16	47.4	39.1	4.7	52.6	38.4	2,690	1,183	4,150	351	3,799	20,346	21.5	54.0
Monterey Park	19,850	3.06	71.8	45.3	17.2	28.2	20.3	226	1,835	2,974	212	2,761	47,079	47.0	30.2
Moorpark	11,860	3.10	77.8	70.0	6.1	22.2	19.1	NA	333	914	102	813	24,765	24.0	42.1
Moreno Valley	48,908	4.22	83.8	55.9	20.7	16.2	12.0	802	6,981	3,385	418	2,967	123,536	55.0	15.0
Morgan Hill	14,927	3.00	79.8	62.8	12.1	20.2	15.5	291	724	1,645	186	1,459	30,422	28.0	38.3
Mountain View	33,177	2.45	53.6	44.4	5.9	46.4	33.6	317	1,908	2,335	162	2,173	59,559	18.3	67.5
Murrieta	32,407	3.48	78.5	58.7	15.3	21.5	16.5	602	1,652	1,488	44	1,444	69,389	30.2	32.9
Napa	28,790	2.74	65.2	51.6	9.3	34.8	28.9	870	1,875	2,312	365	1,947	54,932	31.2	36.5
National City	15,746	3.50	78.0	45.6	23.6	22.0	18.2	6,225	1,643	2,669	434	2,236	38,818	49.9	13.4
Newark	13,999	3.38	81.9	57.5	17.5	18.1	10.7	NA	1,294	2,820	235	2,584	34,588	44.0	32.8
Newport Beach	37,968	2.26	57.4	51.1	2.8	42.6	35.2	511	2,351	2,687	126	2,562	66,421	9.7	68.3
Norco	7,160	3.34	80.6	61.0	12.8	19.4	17.3	2,828	823	3,149	195	2,954	18,118	39.5	16.7
Norwalk	27,661	3.75	82.7	60.7	16.4	17.3	13.0	2,464	2,382	2,217	390	1,827	70,967	50.5	19.5
Novato	21,219	2.61	68.3	55.3	6.3	31.7	25.4	670	1,118	1,987	142	1,845	39,788	26.9	43.2
Oakland	158,851	2.63	55.0	33.9	14.5	45.0	32.4	6,694	30,011	7,061	1,426	5,636	309,387	34.8	42.4
Oakley	10,461	3.98	86.6	69.8	14.3	13.4	10.2	NA	474	1,165	135	1,030	24,484	39.8	20.5
Oceanside	61,138	2.87	69.2	52.3	12.1	30.8	24.4	789	5,003	2,821	360	2,461	123,019	32.6	35.0
Ontario	50,572	3.46	80.1	52.8	19.4	19.9	15.3	741	5,320	3,082	349	2,733	112,006	50.7	17.4
Orange	42,663	3.13	72.1	50.5	13.6	27.9	17.7	7,142	2,836	1,999	161	1,839	95,053	34.5	36.5
Oxnard	52,717	3.96	80.4	51.6	20.0	19.6	14.1	1,454	7,021	3,359	453	2,905	131,022	52.5	17.8
Pacifica	14,773	2.63	67.8	53.0	9.4	32.2	23.2	216	557	1,405	164	1,241	29,561	21.5	49.3
Palmdale	42,005	3.74	78.5	53.8	18.4	21.5	17.3	255	3,425	2,148	437	1,711	93,979	53.2	12.8
Palm Desert	25,162	2.09	56.7	46.5	5.3	43.3	36.8	323	2,221	4,228	147	4,082	43,515	30.2	37.0
Palm Springs	23,745	2.01	44.8	32.3	9.6	55.2	42.2	505	3,029	6,322	574	5,748	39,990	26.9	42.0
Palo Alto	25,439	2.62	66.4	58.3	5.2	33.6	25.8	509	1,509	2,242	108	2,133	46,368	3.9	86.1
Paradise	10,403	2.52	55.2	41.1	11.3	44.8	38.3	513	547	2,062	170	1,892	18,931	33.3	25.3
Paramount	14,247	3.83	78.8	45.1	22.6	21.2	17.9	330	2,057	3,695	562	3,133	31,956	58.3	12.4
Pasadena	54,177	2.57	58.0	43.3	11.5	42.0	33.5	3,662	3,923	2,738	333	2,405	103,915	26.0	51.6
Perris	15,947	4.86	86.4	64.4	14.4	13.6	8.2	NA	2,383	3,125	295	2,830	41,785	66.3	7.2
Petaluma	21,564	2.79	70.0	58.3	8.9	30.0	25.3	747	1,308	2,147	328	1,818	42,750	28.0	38.1
Pico Rivera	17,195	3.67	78.7	53.1	18.2	21.3	19.8	482	1,841	2,856	341	2,514	41,654	59.1	14.1
Pittsburg	20,784	3.45	78.7	47.1	20.1	21.3	15.1	373	2,253	3,188	393	2,795	48,870	45.9	18.1
Placentia	16,122	3.21	77.5	57.1	12.7	22.5	16.1	418	867	1,642	146	1,496	34,102	27.4	37.2
Pleasant Hill	13,447	2.57	61.9	48.7	9.3	38.1	27.4	405	1,589	4,522	225	4,297	25,222	14.9	54.9
Pleasanton	30,435	2.72	76.1	67.5	5.9	23.9	18.3	333	1,704	2,092	123	1,969	59,614	12.8	65.0
Pomona	38,980	3.80	76.8	50.7	16.6	23.2	17.4	4,701	5,443	3,532	498	3,034	96,060	54.7	17.4
Porterville	16,065	3.60	80.3	51.8	20.8	19.7	14.0	1,397	1,530	2,712	381	2,331	35,204	63.6	11.1
Poway	16,807	2.95	75.0	58.4	12.4	25.0	20.5	538	520	1,028	128	899	34,796	22.2	51.8
Rancho Cordova	25,850	2.82	66.8	41.0	15.6	33.2	21.7	555	1,680	2,325	339	1,986	50,868	41.7	21.9
Rancho Cucamonga	52,731	3.30	79.2	60.0	14.5	20.8	15.1	3,171	4,257	2,404	150	2,254	114,588	28.2	36.7
Rancho Palos Verdes	15,053	2.78	77.8	70.4	5.4	22.2	19.7	530	444	1,034	63	971	29,939	10.2	66.5
Rancho Santa Margarita	17,565	2.78	78.0	62.2	13.4	22.0	18.2	NA	315	635	97	538	32,897	19.5	47.1
Redding	38,036	2.35	60.4	43.8	12.2	39.6	31.7	2,299	4,557	4,958	783	4,174	63,836	34.2	24.7
Redlands	26,264	2.62	61.9	45.4	13.7	38.1	29.5	2,785	3,138	4,390	315	4,075	50,739	28.8	43.4
Redondo Beach	28,081	2.41	61.5	49.1	7.9	38.5	29.9	NA	1,902	2,779	234	2,545	50,963	15.3	60.5
Redwood City	32,344	2.62	64.6	51.8	8.9	35.4	25.3	1,898	1,667	1,915	188	1,727	64,841	25.7	52.2
Rialto	26,699	3.86	82.6	58.2	16.6	17.4	12.9	592	2,338	2,250	434	1,816	62,981	58.7	11.5
Richmond	37,029	2.94	67.6	41.9	20.8	32.4	24.4	1,238	4,804	4,333	919	3,414	73,564	43.5	28.9
Ridgecrest	10,869	2.64	58.5	44.0	10.2	41.5	30.8	NA	714	2,462	514	1,948	19,383	39.9	24.2
Riverside	86,905	3.60	74.6	50.7	17.8	25.4	18.3	14,983	12,990	3,986	529	3,457	203,706	44.8	23.7
Rocklin	22,184	2.88	74.7	59.8	11.6	25.3	20.9	896	1,267	2,043	105	1,939	40,282	19.1	44.6
Rohnert Park	16,369	2.61	59.0	41.8	9.7	41.0	27.7	NA	947	2,217	477	1,739	28,993	32.5	31.9
Rosemead	15,097	3.57	82.3	59.5	15.0	17.7	13.2	673	1,416	2,569	303	2,266	39,645	60.2	20.9
Roseville	50,198	2.68	71.5	56.1	10.5	28.5	23.7	1,002	3,515	2,652	150	2,501	93,940	23.4	40.1
Sacramento	189,193	2.61	59.5	37.7	14.5	40.5	31.3	8,957	18,832	3,801	716	3,085	342,577	35.2	32.8
Salinas	41,218	3.79	80.4	56.3	17.6	19.6	15.0	1,496	5,747	3,621	633	2,987	94,583	64.6	14.8
San Bernardino	60,714	3.38	76.3	41.9	22.8	23.7	18.9	11,761	12,056	5,548	1,324	4,224	132,776	61.3	11.7
San Bruno	14,773	2.90	64.2	48.5	11.1	35.8	27.5	NA	1,215	2,786	250	2,536	31,909	24.4	45.3
San Buenaventura (Ventura)	41,338	2.64	60.7	42.5	12.4	39.3	31.8	1,835	4,118	3,736	334	3,402	79,118	29.5	33.7
San Carlos	11,022	2.76	73.4	64.7	6.9	26.6	19.1	NA	NA	NA	NA	NA	21,090	5.5	74.9
San Clemente	25,366	2.56	72.1	59.4	9.9	27.9	22.0	375	874	1,326	114	1,212	48,503	18.7	49.3
San Diego	504,208	2.74	60.2	44.9	11.0	39.8	26.9	36,547	33,956	2,402	377	2,025	979,135	26.9	45.6
San Dimas	12,266	2.73	62.8	50.9	6.9	37.2	29.3	871	846	2,425	235	2,190	24,973	24.3	37.2

1. No spouse present.   2. Data for serious crimes have not been adjusted for underreporting. This may affect comparability between geographic areas and over time.   3. Per 100,000 population estimated by the FBI.   4. Persons 25 years old and over.

Table D. Cities — Income and Housing

City	Money income, 2017					Median earnings, 2017			Housing units, 2017				
	Households												
	Median income	Percent with income less than $20,000	Percent with income of $200,000 or more	Median family income	Median non-family income	All persons	Men	Women	Total	Occupied	Percent owner occupied	Median value[1] (dollars)	Median gross rent (dollars)
	42	43	44	45	46	47	48	49	50	51	52	53	54
CALIFORNIA— Cont'd													
Menlo Park	127,873	7.8	37.7	200,351	65,369	61,206	75,846	40,812	12,358	11,235	58.5	2,000,000	2,380
Merced	40,573	28.4	3.9	43,197	28,876	25,326	29,872	20,688	27,988	26,278	40.3	222,700	1,032
Milpitas	127,984	7.2	27.3	132,050	73,883	54,058	73,706	41,125	23,929	22,128	64.9	854,100	2,422
Mission Viejo	102,787	6.4	17.5	120,847	60,334	50,433	64,191	40,525	36,252	33,936	78.1	694,600	2,199
Modesto	56,493	14.5	3.1	62,092	40,252	31,083	35,420	26,958	75,600	72,621	53.9	279,600	1,148
Monrovia	82,657	6.2	14.0	98,417	58,411	45,933	50,307	40,791	14,299	13,126	51.8	678,100	1,531
Montclair	55,859	18.5	1.4	56,851	30,274	23,755	27,156	20,411	10,521	10,284	45.7	383,500	1,281
Montebello	53,676	11.7	3.2	55,184	27,053	25,964	29,815	24,258	19,708	18,928	40.7	496,600	1,310
Monterey	72,190	8.2	8.9	93,703	61,576	37,376	37,021	37,672	13,571	12,005	34.7	720,300	1,730
Monterey Park	56,260	13.4	8.5	60,955	45,360	27,466	30,005	25,310	21,687	19,850	52.3	642,600	1,418
Moorpark	97,650	5.5	20.0	113,248	66,639	47,133	51,839	41,242	12,381	11,860	75.2	652,700	1,997
Moreno Valley	62,198	9.4	2.6	62,280	40,024	27,470	31,843	23,769	52,130	48,908	58.8	305,900	1,443
Morgan Hill	131,724	6.0	27.8	141,048	83,205	52,129	61,959	50,652	15,456	14,927	73.4	872,600	1,570
Mountain View	135,115	9.7	30.3	172,276	99,502	80,861	105,983	56,329	36,021	33,177	41.3	1,461,400	2,353
Murrieta	82,249	9.0	8.2	90,241	46,798	32,291	54,399	23,141	34,564	32,407	67.7	417,000	1,725
Napa	82,361	7.4	10.0	100,608	51,523	39,115	45,884	30,633	31,801	28,790	60.5	633,200	1,763
National City	40,967	21.4	2.3	44,709	30,938	24,062	28,551	20,914	17,035	15,746	35.7	426,900	1,119
Newark	102,880	10.2	16.9	102,986	85,615	45,795	49,918	41,936	14,325	13,999	63.9	757,600	2,192
Newport Beach	127,104	6.9	32.5	164,065	81,280	65,049	82,140	47,443	46,237	37,968	58.5	1,902,000	2,103
Norco	100,671	9.3	10.5	105,695	51,044	41,831	62,154	33,336	7,595	7,160	83.7	546,600	1,343
Norwalk	74,730	7.4	2.8	80,661	39,742	35,030	37,341	28,462	28,983	27,661	65.9	441,000	1,527
Novato	106,680	8.1	19.4	126,735	62,200	38,919	41,630	32,334	22,798	21,219	65.4	821,500	2,098
Oakland	70,577	16.1	12.4	77,401	58,222	40,234	40,540	39,612	168,166	158,851	39.3	686,700	1,394
Oakley	101,030	7.1	11.9	111,628	33,619	40,840	50,653	31,071	10,461	10,461	76.5	443,100	1,600
Oceanside	71,609	9.1	8.2	83,035	43,834	32,425	38,953	27,686	66,925	61,138	58.6	514,600	1,755
Ontario	60,086	11.8	3.3	62,194	38,703	30,220	32,476	24,929	53,608	50,572	53.5	369,700	1,449
Orange	91,092	9.3	14.0	98,701	58,274	36,534	37,238	35,586	44,790	42,663	57.2	656,300	1,689
Oxnard	68,994	7.3	4.5	69,071	51,194	29,096	31,133	24,661	55,545	52,717	54.1	458,400	1,530
Pacifica	113,595	9.1	15.6	129,074	82,639	52,883	55,792	51,698	15,300	14,773	68.1	878,300	2,353
Palmdale	60,518	14.7	3.4	63,670	38,750	29,586	35,599	25,191	45,168	42,005	60.4	274,100	1,298
Palm Desert	60,160	15.6	7.0	80,000	37,988	32,488	35,980	27,298	43,891	25,162	61.7	350,900	1,299
Palm Springs	51,055	20.3	11.5	64,641	37,205	32,426	35,688	31,009	37,480	23,745	59.5	393,200	1,088
Palo Alto	153,802	9.8	42.9	204,690	86,533	95,073	138,588	60,575	27,072	25,439	52.6	2,000,000	2,673
Paradise	47,732	18.4	5.7	58,981	25,955	25,600	26,220	25,411	11,541	10,403	70.5	208,000	1,086
Paramount	54,501	13.8	1.4	58,148	25,521	29,733	35,220	25,008	14,999	14,247	35.4	351,200	1,335
Pasadena	76,972	15.2	13.6	92,116	54,846	40,341	43,309	36,373	61,511	54,177	42.4	802,500	1,611
Perris	62,340	10.8	0.8	60,772	37,500	27,289	31,326	22,334	16,685	15,947	65.6	283,300	1,366
Petaluma	89,152	10.0	12.1	103,673	51,137	47,944	58,333	40,165	22,284	21,564	61.9	642,300	1,842
Pico Rivera	73,727	12.6	2.9	76,609	37,810	34,266	37,707	27,587	17,520	17,195	71.3	447,100	1,324
Pittsburg	65,497	7.9	6.3	61,428	55,276	30,863	34,993	25,581	22,642	20,784	55.0	387,700	1,720
Placentia	89,449	7.5	8.9	100,752	51,332	39,014	43,886	32,284	16,382	16,122	62.2	613,000	1,777
Pleasant Hill	106,599	7.3	16.8	131,364	58,655	51,037	60,126	42,483	14,002	13,447	64.4	725,500	2,060
Pleasanton	152,123	5.9	36.9	179,977	90,331	76,317	99,453	51,937	32,950	30,435	69.0	997,500	2,346
Pomona	58,837	15.4	5.3	59,117	40,019	25,215	28,785	20,461	41,592	38,980	55.0	405,000	1,259
Porterville	40,002	23.5	1.9	36,530	25,553	22,966	26,423	21,249	17,835	16,065	48.4	169,500	1,002
Poway	100,555	8.8	17.9	120,567	59,139	49,441	60,269	37,244	17,884	16,807	77.2	676,200	1,450
Rancho Cordova	64,088	10.4	5.4	68,985	51,618	32,449	36,217	30,000	26,715	25,850	52.6	304,400	1,200
Rancho Cucamonga	90,034	6.8	9.0	97,822	61,126	40,547	50,475	31,640	55,895	52,731	63.8	488,000	1,773
Rancho Palos Verdes	144,907	7.7	36.9	159,340	56,790	71,951	94,155	50,960	16,566	15,053	78.5	1,211,700	2,355
Rancho Santa Margarita	105,869	5.9	17.1	117,357	60,965	56,327	71,810	48,653	17,565	17,565	70.8	653,300	2,091
Redding	50,320	20.6	4.2	64,732	26,550	30,840	32,914	29,453	40,133	38,036	53.4	260,000	1,039
Redlands	65,053	15.2	10.6	87,342	44,596	40,379	39,435	40,854	29,115	26,264	59.5	383,800	1,209
Redondo Beach	104,715	7.7	23.9	127,415	69,310	56,767	70,376	45,108	31,072	28,081	51.6	907,400	1,972
Redwood City	116,966	7.3	24.7	122,255	98,850	52,120	61,580	46,080	33,166	32,344	50.5	1,196,500	2,327
Rialto	57,065	13.6	0.7	61,576	31,522	26,865	30,925	22,470	28,261	26,699	61.2	307,900	1,227
Richmond	67,102	14.0	7.1	67,508	42,349	33,981	35,915	31,616	40,489	37,029	50.9	495,400	1,460
Ridgecrest	56,357	21.3	5.8	77,913	26,558	27,894	35,090	23,489	12,621	10,869	57.5	177,900	872
Riverside	66,928	12.7	5.7	73,467	38,186	27,207	31,548	23,557	91,403	86,905	53.1	368,600	1,352
Rocklin	98,247	10.2	10.6	110,306	40,402	42,451	56,040	32,391	22,596	22,184	64.3	478,700	1,697
Rohnert Park	72,630	12.4	4.5	93,171	42,458	36,716	46,276	25,811	17,052	16,369	53.4	485,000	1,785
Rosemead	53,594	19.0	4.0	58,563	27,362	29,196	30,287	28,058	16,066	15,097	47.8	568,800	1,332
Roseville	80,426	12.6	10.8	96,212	46,321	45,997	52,148	38,240	52,739	50,198	65.2	441,100	1,582
Sacramento	56,943	17.4	6.1	64,554	44,623	35,064	36,406	32,052	199,760	189,193	48.6	335,900	1,215
Salinas	60,370	11.3	2.5	62,890	32,860	25,922	27,014	23,944	42,742	41,218	45.8	431,500	1,388
San Bernardino	46,510	20.1	1.2	52,122	29,693	25,198	30,052	21,341	68,414	60,714	49.2	245,900	1,038
San Bruno	102,008	7.4	16.7	120,806	68,301	50,077	60,339	34,557	14,955	14,773	52.3	937,600	2,151
San Buenaventura (Ventura)	72,100	13.9	6.4	82,720	44,744	35,688	40,401	28,010	43,665	41,338	52.4	545,900	1,580
San Carlos	204,436	2.1	51.4	217,465	116,551	101,486	112,144	86,818	11,345	11,022	74.4	1,623,000	2,414
San Clemente	101,743	6.6	19.9	131,109	52,386	48,880	72,003	36,591	29,616	25,366	65.8	894,500	1,830
San Diego	76,662	11.3	11.8	90,695	58,268	38,044	41,788	34,122	543,238	504,208	47.1	600,300	1,642
San Dimas	86,492	16.6	8.9	108,586	50,858	51,308	74,448	29,377	12,949	12,266	72.9	557,900	1,747

1. Based on population estimated by the American Community Survey.   2. Includes units rented or sold but not occupied.   3. Specified owner-occupied units; $1,000,000 represents $1,000,000 or more.   4. 50.0 represents 50 percent or more.   5. 10.0 represents 10 percent or less.

Table D. Cities — Commuting, Computer Access, Migration, Labor Force, and Employment

City	Commuting¹, 2017 Percent — Commuting	With commutes of 30 minutes or more	Computer access², 2017 Percent — With a computer in the house	With Internet access	Migration, 2017 — Percent who lived in the same house one year ago	Percent who lived in another state or county one year ago	Civilian labor force, 2018 — Total	Percent change 2017-2018	Unemployment Total	Rate³	Civilian employment⁴, 2017 — Population age 16 and older Number	Percent in labor force	Population age 16 to 64 Number	Percent who worked full-year full-time
	55	56	57	58	59	60	61	62	63	64	65	66	67	68
CALIFORNIA— Cont'd														
Menlo Park	66.0	38.7	99.1	92.8	86.4	9.3	19,709	2.1	396	2.0	25,807	65.8	21,461	50.7
Merced	82.8	27.3	89.6	86.0	89.0	5.3	34,180	0.2	2,304	6.7	60,865	53.7	52,520	37.9
Milpitas	78.3	47.2	99.1	97.6	89.8	2.9	41,734	0.8	1,159	2.8	60,335	69.7	52,312	58.7
Mission Viejo	78.4	41.6	97.5	94.2	88.0	2.2	50,302	1.0	1,487	3.0	79,044	66.7	62,875	53.3
Modesto	83.8	33.8	92.6	87.3	83.7	5.5	95,118	0.6	5,549	5.8	168,274	59.8	135,774	44.0
Monrovia	74.7	54.8	96.0	87.6	NA	NA	21,139	0.8	836	4.0	31,029	64.6	25,506	55.6
Montclair	71.6	43.4	92.8	84.1	89.8	7.1	19,234	2.0	679	3.5	30,076	61.5	25,395	40.5
Montebello	75.7	58.8	93.1	84.9	91.9	2.8	29,248	0.7	1,474	5.0	50,356	63.9	40,250	48.6
Monterey	60.6	18.0	94.3	92.2	70.2	22.9	15,629	2.2	408	2.6	25,132	65.5	19,419	50.0
Monterey Park	82.6	55.8	89.4	85.3	90.9	3.1	29,759	0.9	1,262	4.2	52,720	55.1	39,285	48.2
Moorpark	87.1	46.0	92.0	91.3	91.4	3.3	19,704	0.4	595	3.0	29,476	72.5	25,399	53.7
Moreno Valley	78.9	53.3	94.9	90.1	88.6	3.7	94,540	1.6	4,223	4.5	155,439	64.2	137,726	44.7
Morgan Hill	79.3	62.1	97.4	90.2	86.7	4.4	24,210	1.0	683	2.8	34,657	71.1	29,568	53.6
Mountain View	66.9	28.8	96.6	92.8	78.8	11.5	51,463	1.0	995	1.9	67,382	74.4	58,039	62.4
Murrieta	79.3	44.2	96.8	93.0	80.6	6.5	55,299	2.0	1,930	3.5	83,285	61.0	68,077	41.1
Napa	79.9	26.9	93.9	89.2	88.4	4.0	42,414	1.5	1,312	3.1	64,314	67.5	51,259	49.3
National City	66.1	42.2	92.3	83.5	89.2	4.2	24,927	0.8	1,109	4.4	49,296	64.5	41,323	47.7
Newark	71.1	46.2	96.7	94.3	93.2	2.8	25,071	0.9	695	2.8	40,128	68.3	34,334	57.9
Newport Beach	81.1	36.9	96.9	94.7	90.2	3.0	45,649	1.1	1,227	2.7	72,764	62.9	52,625	52.1
Norco	82.0	52.4	91.4	88.3	88.8	6.1	11,764	2.0	426	3.6	22,299	52.9	19,113	42.7
Norwalk	80.9	54.3	93.4	83.2	91.9	2.1	50,867	0.6	2,347	4.6	84,997	64.0	70,792	52.9
Novato	63.1	54.5	93.9	91.9	87.9	3.8	29,970	0.8	725	2.4	46,885	64.8	36,486	46.2
Oakland	50.2	53.6	91.4	85.2	85.6	6.3	214,483	0.9	7,387	3.4	349,595	69.1	293,494	50.2
Oakley	73.3	52.5	97.0	91.9	92.6	2.3	19,851	0.9	695	3.5	29,633	70.2	26,316	48.1
Oceanside	79.3	43.4	94.8	90.5	81.8	6.0	82,681	1.1	2,819	3.4	143,878	64.0	113,218	50.0
Ontario	81.8	45.6	95.2	85.5	89.4	3.8	86,199	1.9	3,094	3.6	136,692	65.7	118,108	49.0
Orange	80.6	41.9	94.8	92.6	90.0	3.2	73,060	1.1	2,131	2.9	117,192	65.4	100,162	50.0
Oxnard	80.5	26.3	93.2	84.3	90.6	3.5	101,142	0.1	4,847	4.8	159,066	68.5	138,212	49.2
Pacifica	70.8	54.6	97.7	92.1	87.0	7.3	24,348	2.0	564	2.3	33,791	70.8	26,394	60.6
Palmdale	76.5	53.1	94.7	90.5	91.7	1.9	64,875	0.9	4,142	6.4	116,600	58.2	102,172	41.1
Palm Desert	71.4	12.4	91.9	84.9	87.9	5.3	24,770	1.9	1,068	4.3	46,088	52.8	25,203	51.2
Palm Springs	73.0	19.4	91.4	87.0	78.0	9.9	22,944	2.1	922	4.0	43,561	50.2	27,256	40.3
Palo Alto	58.1	33.5	96.5	93.9	81.3	10.4	35,970	1.0	784	2.2	53,033	62.7	40,705	55.6
Paradise	80.3	21.8	94.8	91.8	85.6	4.9	11,260	0.7	537	4.8	21,132	51.1	14,848	38.7
Paramount	77.4	56.5	90.2	75.4	NA	NA	24,923	0.9	1,272	5.1	40,944	61.2	36,847	46.1
Pasadena	69.6	46.4	93.0	85.2	87.0	4.3	79,762	0.8	3,170	4.0	119,945	67.1	99,908	52.2
Perris	76.1	56.0	96.3	89.1	86.0	3.6	30,576	1.4	1,493	4.9	54,338	68.1	49,532	50.2
Petaluma	71.8	53.9	94.0	89.6	86.3	8.0	33,600	0.8	817	2.4	47,650	65.3	38,246	48.9
Pico Rivera	87.2	49.7	90.3	81.4	96.5	0.4	30,748	0.9	1,597	5.2	51,238	60.2	41,381	55.2
Pittsburg	66.2	62.9	96.4	93.2	87.9	3.2	34,501	0.9	1,278	3.7	57,892	64.8	48,011	45.3
Placentia	81.7	41.9	98.2	93.3	89.2	3.2	26,158	1.0	779	3.0	41,221	71.3	34,441	58.2
Pleasant Hill	63.7	43.9	95.4	93.3	85.9	4.8	18,316	1.0	520	2.8	28,838	68.5	24,639	44.9
Pleasanton	69.4	51.1	97.2	93.4	86.4	6.3	41,765	1.0	1,060	2.5	67,661	70.2	56,114	57.4
Pomona	71.7	43.4	94.9	88.6	89.2	3.1	68,410	0.7	3,467	5.1	119,492	62.3	102,549	46.8
Porterville	79.0	22.2	90.2	84.7	89.4	1.7	25,449	-0.1	3,006	11.8	44,290	58.4	37,317	37.1
Poway	81.6	40.3	96.1	91.1	84.9	2.8	25,925	1.3	703	2.7	41,132	64.4	33,014	49.5
Rancho Cordova	81.7	38.8	94.8	90.7	80.8	7.3	35,002	1.6	1,325	3.8	57,956	68.1	49,054	46.8
Rancho Cucamonga	81.4	43.2	96.5	93.8	84.0	6.9	96,492	2.0	2,978	3.1	137,268	67.6	118,104	46.6
Rancho Palos Verdes	82.7	59.5	93.7	91.2	89.8	4.9	19,865	0.8	752	3.8	33,032	58.0	22,174	49.7
Rancho Santa Margarita	84.3	48.8	97.6	95.4	88.3	1.3	28,104	1.1	758	2.7	38,115	72.6	34,015	56.8
Redding	79.8	11.2	92.5	84.5	86.1	4.0	39,647	0.3	1,739	4.4	73,972	58.2	57,795	41.7
Redlands	83.4	28.6	91.2	84.6	87.3	6.9	35,746	2.1	1,149	3.2	59,428	59.2	47,318	45.0
Redondo Beach	81.6	46.1	97.3	92.2	85.2	5.5	41,721	0.8	1,599	3.8	55,809	69.8	47,268	58.4
Redwood City	71.1	41.0	96.3	92.8	82.9	7.2	51,173	2.0	1,089	2.1	71,969	71.4	61,475	55.4
Rialto	81.0	44.6	93.5	80.3	88.2	2.2	44,861	1.5	2,025	4.5	78,639	65.6	70,038	44.2
Richmond	64.2	60.8	93.4	88.7	88.2	7.0	53,335	0.9	1,919	3.6	88,273	66.5	74,838	49.8
Ridgecrest	76.3	11.3	82.9	77.7	83.4	6.4	13,679	1.3	406	3.0	22,614	59.8	18,453	46.6
Riverside	77.3	44.6	94.0	87.6	86.0	6.0	153,975	1.8	5,878	3.8	260,853	63.6	228,936	44.4
Rocklin	79.2	39.7	93.3	90.5	84.1	10.2	32,415	2.0	983	3.0	49,635	69.0	42,009	53.2
Rohnert Park	73.0	36.5	95.9	90.1	83.2	2.5	23,487	0.7	625	2.7	35,496	69.8	30,092	51.0
Rosemead	78.4	46.4	90.9	80.8	92.9	1.6	25,350	0.4	1,099	4.3	45,706	58.4	36,385	43.5
Roseville	77.3	40.2	93.9	88.9	85.6	7.9	67,687	2.0	2,026	3.0	108,051	63.7	85,489	52.3
Sacramento	72.8	35.3	93.4	89.2	83.8	6.0	235,087	1.8	9,156	3.9	396,307	64.3	332,377	48.4
Salinas	69.6	22.2	91.3	86.1	92.7	2.9	81,832	1.8	6,816	8.3	114,183	64.3	99,910	44.3
San Bernardino	74.0	39.0	91.9	76.3	87.5	3.6	85,182	1.5	4,413	5.2	163,978	56.2	141,804	38.2
San Bruno	68.2	44.4	94.6	91.7	88.8	8.0	26,987	2.0	614	2.3	36,437	70.8	29,566	57.2
San Buenaventura (Ventura)	79.3	32.5	94.5	90.5	84.2	5.9	56,155	0.3	1,821	3.2	89,600	64.5	70,694	49.4
San Carlos	73.9	50.5	98.4	96.7	83.7	8.4	17,789	2.1	397	2.2	23,329	75.1	19,845	59.0
San Clemente	74.6	46.1	97.8	93.7	86.7	4.1	32,161	1.0	910	2.8	54,419	64.4	40,448	50.2
San Diego	75.4	33.1	96.0	91.3	81.5	6.8	719,981	1.1	23,061	3.2	1,166,285	68.3	989,315	51.3
San Dimas	77.9	53.4	91.0	84.3	88.9	3.1	18,124	0.7	762	4.2	29,100	56.0	21,191	47.9

1. Employed persons. 2. Households. 3. Percent of civilian labor force. 4. Persons 16 years old and over.

Table D. Cities — Construction, Wholesale Trade, and Retail Trade

City	Value of residential construction authorized by building permits, 2018			Wholesale trade[1], 2012				Retail trade[2], 2012			
	New construction ($1,000)	Number of housing units	Percent single family	Number of establishments	Number of employees	Sales (mil dol)	Annual payroll (mil dol)	Number of establishments	Number of employees	Sales (mil dol)	Annual payroll (mil dol)
	69	70	71	72	73	74	75	76	77	78	79
CALIFORNIA— Cont'd											
Menlo Park	56,324	203	27.6	33	468	410.3	40.2	122	1,502	438.2	48.9
Merced	19,548	77	100.0	37	742	1,669.5	35.7	227	3,728	945.6	89.5
Milpitas	405,746	1,583	26.2	143	4,902	4,031.6	568.9	307	5,295	1,132.7	119.5
Mission Viejo	4,512	16	100.0	107	576	268.8	39.3	356	6,275	1,726.5	159.4
Modesto	56,954	298	74.8	113	1,977	2,459.5	99.8	683	10,639	2,347.6	237.2
Monrovia	4,976	24	100.0	89	709	545.3	34.5	109	1,951	779.4	62.0
Montclair	39,142	221	4.5	82	593	226.0	23.9	243	4,021	1,003.5	93.6
Montebello	1,911	11	100.0	114	1,826	1,166.8	90.1	203	3,498	817.9	76.0
Monterey	351	2	100.0	36	382	1,264.0	28.0	199	2,265	464.5	59.9
Monterey Park	6,159	20	100.0	207	1,082	878.6	44.2	202	1,671	399.6	34.6
Moorpark	11,576	28	100.0	53	774	411.4	40.9	55	890	227.3	22.6
Moreno Valley	322,159	1,226	69.7	30	663	544.9	23.8	311	5,600	1,696.8	136.7
Morgan Hill	123,796	526	41.1	58	1,873	1,259.4	115.3	105	D	D	D
Mountain View	73,060	351	20.5	106	2,330	2,021.6	246.3	244	4,078	1,222.6	126.3
Murrieta	131,777	536	74.1	97	667	425.6	30.9	218	3,873	1,082.7	97.5
Napa	12,743	49	100.0	69	437	309.9	24.7	315	4,374	1,128.4	125.6
National City	18,595	150	0.7	87	1,198	702.7	55.7	304	5,393	1,395.9	140.2
Newark	131,280	454	61.9	61	1,443	788.0	61.8	168	2,856	684.3	69.8
Newport Beach	122,723	174	74.7	190	1,183	976.1	98.6	441	6,409	2,885.4	252.0
Norco	0	0	0	27	469	175.8	13.5	86	1,093	337.4	28.9
Norwalk	2,159	11	100.0	88	639	469.4	29.8	178	3,078	1,101.5	88.1
Novato	12,289	62	22.6	73	579	450.4	38.8	162	2,538	834.3	80.7
Oakland	786,344	3,639	6.3	376	4,921	3,620.2	263.0	1,014	10,458	3,029.1	311.7
Oakley	58,514	184	100.0	9	D	D	D	38	366	124.8	10.8
Oceanside	58,108	401	30.4	149	1,476	696.8	75.4	389	6,742	1,677.8	166.9
Ontario	255,023	1,326	79.6	681	11,341	14,205.7	557.2	579	13,650	4,833.5	378.2
Orange	7,803	30	80.0	333	3,442	4,940.7	176.7	558	7,821	2,152.9	207.9
Oxnard	34,649	115	33.9	183	3,805	5,873.6	213.8	430	6,729	2,363.1	194.0
Pacifica	6,820	13	100.0	7	D	D	D	61	699	194.3	16.8
Palmdale	16,561	65	100.0	28	128	87.5	4.2	299	6,423	1,557.0	144.8
Palm Desert	40,625	129	47.3	74	389	215.3	17.5	453	6,199	2,309.1	160.9
Palm Springs	40,588	152	82.2	35	535	309.8	27.3	184	2,480	733.1	66.8
Palo Alto	72,564	110	100.0	76	D	D	D	317	5,759	2,461.0	261.4
Paradise	6,685	26	100.0	6	D	D	D	77	791	190.8	19.4
Paramount	8,299	36	69.4	212	1,709	989.1	73.8	110	1,202	326.9	30.2
Pasadena	95,179	524	5.9	163	1,382	2,271.6	79.9	594	9,409	2,700.9	256.4
Perris	23,489	115	100.0	20	265	204.0	12.6	92	2,151	609.3	52.9
Petaluma	13,900	56	69.6	101	2,055	1,396.4	198.1	262	3,233	875.4	96.3
Pico Rivera	2,993	13	100.0	84	1,923	1,419.8	97.3	113	2,571	1,480.3	55.9
Pittsburg	20,780	135	51.9	32	324	185.9	19.2	99	2,084	524.4	53.0
Placentia	0	0	0.0	108	923	329.5	51.3	96	1,099	356.1	33.2
Pleasant Hill	12,560	37	100.0	29	172	112.4	8.8	146	2,490	607.5	56.9
Pleasanton	33,704	96	43.8	135	5,394	2,651.3	430.8	330	6,278	1,662.3	190.3
Pomona	50,514	292	64.7	301	3,224	2,099.4	139.4	293	3,308	845.7	76.5
Porterville	21,216	82	90.2	24	127	42.0	5.9	147	2,231	513.7	52.2
Poway	8,641	14	100.0	96	2,136	1,103.5	131.1	144	2,679	969.9	77.4
Rancho Cordova	63,154	217	100.0	173	2,537	1,593.6	179.2	218	3,332	929.1	91.9
Rancho Cucamonga	62,220	185	68.6	322	3,710	3,866.2	174.8	436	8,160	2,025.3	192.2
Rancho Palos Verdes	11,673	27	100.0	53	163	209.1	8.4	46	388	128.2	10.0
Rancho Santa Margarita	0	0	0	59	550	364.4	30.7	72	1,504	540.6	43.3
Redding	26,226	103	100.0	115	1,223	918.6	51.6	444	7,061	1,974.7	192.8
Redlands	21,277	92	100.0	56	495	190.5	19.2	240	4,676	2,221.1	118.9
Redondo Beach	40,911	117	89.7	64	311	156.2	15.0	274	3,969	869.7	94.8
Redwood City	26,580	136	29.4	65	1,049	1,124.1	110.9	204	4,486	1,656.7	172.2
Rialto	15,107	130	50.0	54	698	739.7	34.3	152	2,173	541.9	52.3
Richmond	68,109	386	24.9	99	1,431	1,476.7	83.3	238	3,600	1,092.5	105.9
Ridgecrest	10,234	94	100.0	4	D	D	D	82	1,246	272.4	28.2
Riverside	99,459	674	25.4	293	4,399	2,747.6	223.9	829	13,943	4,127.4	385.4
Rocklin	207,537	585	100.0	65	1,562	785.8	86.0	149	1,824	616.0	59.6
Rohnert Park	49,068	264	100.0	41	692	299.9	40.5	106	2,088	637.6	57.9
Rosemead	18,332	96	67.7	107	450	245.6	13.5	172	1,583	460.9	34.2
Roseville	220,814	808	100.0	108	1,597	1,587.0	90.0	588	13,555	4,159.6	380.2
Sacramento	466,986	2,324	69.3	488	7,125	9,800.4	381.3	1,200	18,042	4,363.3	447.7
Salinas	39,472	163	35.0	123	1,861	1,717.4	124.3	428	6,955	1,928.3	175.7
San Bernardino	12,704	86	72.1	128	2,392	2,145.2	102.9	526	8,518	2,610.4	216.6
San Bruno	2,599	9	44.4	36	798	1,046.6	96.4	149	2,508	528.7	59.6
San Buenaventura (Ventura)	20,917	110	63.6	167	1,531	762.2	83.3	517	6,814	1,824.7	183.5
San Carlos	6,561	16	62.5	103	885	488.8	52.5	142	1,828	490.1	55.9
San Clemente	54,423	110	88.2	162	1,826	810.7	119.4	204	2,501	670.2	68.7
San Diego	902,488	4,452	17.4	1,823	35,353	24,027.1	2,803.8	4,119	61,044	17,869.3	1,740.7
San Dimas	1,468	2	100.0	75	704	304.0	36.4	112	1,792	538.4	45.5

1. Merchant wholesalers except manufacturers' sales branches and offices.   2. Establishments with payroll.

Table D. Cities — Real Estate, Professional Services, and Manufacturing

City	Real estate and rental and leasing, 2012				Professional, scientific, and technical services¹, 2012				Manufacturing, 2012			
	Number of establishments	Number of employees	Receipts (mil dol)	Annual payroll (mil dol)	Number of establishments	Number of employees	Receipts (mil dol)	Annual payroll (mil dol)	Number of establishments	Number of employees	Receipts (mil dol)	Annual payroll (mil dol)
	80	81	82	83	84	85	86	87	88	89	90	91
CALIFORNIA— Cont'd												
Menlo Park	84	374	119.4	18.4	336	D	D	D	56	2,390	D	199.1
Merced	69	322	48.1	10.2	84	D	D	D	28	1,234	273.9	55.5
Milpitas	72	394	207.8	18.2	265	D	D	D	157	8,969	4,539.3	968.4
Mission Viejo	161	775	177.2	37.0	469	D	D	D	51	440	275.1	26.6
Modesto	207	925	194.6	31.8	390	D	D	D	91	7,104	D	441.5
Monrovia	58	202	32.3	8.1	152	2,436	594.7	198.6	94	2,885	719.6	171.7
Montclair	32	179	97.5	13.0	25	217	12.4	5.8	85	938	121.3	31.4
Montebello	55	309	76.9	14.6	66	375	41.1	12.3	71	2,433	753.8	101.7
Monterey	88	312	64.7	10.7	238	D	D	D	44	717	116.9	37.5
Monterey Park	89	296	53.3	13.6	158	D	D	D	42	593	89.3	24.3
Moorpark	35	137	22.6	4.9	94	313	49.0	17.9	52	1,349	398.3	73.8
Moreno Valley	73	312	60.1	8.9	85	509	32.6	12.4	23	802	233.3	32.3
Morgan Hill	65	232	49.9	8.0	142	2,207	183.8	71.9	79	3,047	933.8	193.4
Mountain View	121	668	151.4	33.2	584	17,005	3,739.2	1,721.2	121	3,230	825.0	231.9
Murrieta	118	326	62.7	12.5	206	873	98.4	34.8	63	609	108.9	27.0
Napa	101	472	90.9	17.1	210	957	151.4	55.6	110	1,899	1,079.0	127.4
National City	50	288	51.0	10.6	46	473	44.5	15.9	70	1,045	D	44.2
Newark	42	132	46.2	5.3	132	1,882	561.3	168.0	67	2,348	806.2	148.0
Newport Beach	698	4,870	1,633.4	354.5	1,244	8,075	1,727.4	632.4	86	3,739	547.2	180.8
Norco	38	108	19.4	3.4	75	1,221	142.0	76.0	33	449	71.6	20.6
Norwalk	44	194	45.2	6.9	66	D	D	D	52	698	174.2	28.2
Novato	105	D	D	D	233	D	D	D	52	557	D	30.2
Oakland	482	2,716	672.7	126.2	1,414	10,188	2,035.0	834.8	333	6,555	1,744.2	314.1
Oakley	18	78	18.0	4.3	25	102	8.8	2.9	7	201	D	7.6
Oceanside	157	562	121.3	19.3	310	2,326	256.5	95.6	164	4,715	1,537.3	221.0
Ontario	182	1,205	368.5	65.3	256	D	D	D	391	11,003	4,490.4	494.1
Orange	259	1,787	400.2	84.1	713	D	D	D	287	6,122	1,980.3	301.4
Oxnard	139	694	144.8	27.4	213	D	D	D	172	6,057	3,144.4	359.9
Pacifica	28	64	12.5	2.5	72	272	30.5	9.7	9	139	D	4.1
Palmdale	102	326	51.4	8.5	95	D	D	D	35	4,686	D	D
Palm Desert	144	713	131.3	32.2	260	862	140.2	41.9	40	196	23.4	6.1
Palm Springs	123	573	120.2	20.7	191	664	110.6	32.3	27	624	242.9	23.3
Palo Alto	197	1,214	562.6	101.1	838	11,477	3,506.9	1,646.9	81	6,683	2,798.4	597.1
Paradise	25	204	30.2	4.3	34	107	9.0	2.7	16	85	D	3.3
Paramount	33	192	28.8	4.7	38	384	35.3	13.8	205	4,348	1,996.3	204.6
Pasadena	322	1,704	320.0	64.2	1,212	D	D	D	89	1,016	172.5	47.9
Perris	32	110	24.5	4.8	29	133	17.0	5.7	39	1,034	166.0	34.9
Petaluma	70	347	64.0	10.8	207	D	D	D	100	3,106	1,069.6	156.8
Pico Rivera	34	214	58.7	11.8	30	229	21.4	8.1	60	1,446	433.3	59.6
Pittsburg	25	231	75.7	11.2	49	310	27.6	12.1	40	2,175	D	149.4
Placentia	61	362	68.3	14.1	112	377	65.9	17.6	108	3,097	757.0	153.9
Pleasant Hill	46	233	67.3	15.2	135	779	143.3	53.2	17	78	D	3.3
Pleasanton	176	748	218.6	40.7	553	7,366	1,220.2	707.5	78	1,560	836.9	109.3
Pomona	76	475	141.3	21.1	112	D	D	D	212	4,462	991.4	202.3
Porterville	33	115	18.6	2.8	45	185	15.3	4.3	16	868	312.0	29.4
Poway	89	353	53.1	11.5	252	1,442	304.0	99.7	117	9,014	3,400.3	652.7
Rancho Cordova	108	532	79.7	20.4	235	D	D	D	115	4,676	1,083.4	329.7
Rancho Cucamonga	177	1,031	236.0	40.9	400	D	D	D	246	8,056	3,331.7	401.0
Rancho Palos Verdes	66	D	D	D	138	585	104.4	49.0	11	63	D	2.8
Rancho Santa Margarita	65	148	49.0	8.1	191	1,525	234.9	55.4	42	2,892	682.8	202.3
Redding	148	550	85.4	16.5	280	D	D	D	83	757	162.0	32.5
Redlands	72	293	56.3	9.5	209	1,046	152.6	48.7	58	1,140	305.6	39.5
Redondo Beach	111	309	43.9	9.7	329	D	D	D	35	183	D	5.2
Redwood City	129	628	222.9	26.3	444	7,705	2,124.6	913.7	75	1,834	660.3	107.8
Rialto	48	204	31.0	6.1	32	208	16.6	7.5	70	1,567	410.5	74.0
Richmond	72	370	107.6	14.4	139	1,720	313.7	150.6	118	3,925	11,604.0	268.8
Ridgecrest	25	141	20.6	3.7	53	1,267	142.5	65.6	4	22	D	0.5
Riverside	341	1,685	308.8	59.2	625	4,385	630.9	250.0	264	9,041	2,802.9	410.9
Rocklin	104	407	79.5	18.3	170	1,185	267.0	79.6	45	916	173.2	47.1
Rohnert Park	49	248	58.1	11.3	67	424	45.2	16.6	38	791	240.4	44.1
Rosemead	28	70	15.0	1.6	78	389	35.5	12.1	53	670	D	19.8
Roseville	238	1,902	349.5	82.7	494	8,360	3,354.9	878.1	69	1,325	296.8	77.5
Sacramento	573	3,255	622.2	160.8	1,775	16,337	3,011.6	1,134.8	322	7,890	3,149.8	404.4
Salinas	116	586	141.3	22.3	226	D	D	D	77	2,255	903.1	105.0
San Bernardino	125	514	93.1	16.8	239	D	D	D	122	2,811	929.3	118.4
San Bruno	44	156	67.8	7.6	82	1,002	379.3	116.3	13	D	D	D
San Buenaventura (Ventura)	190	1,046	207.7	39.3	467	D	D	D	157	2,717	517.2	119.4
San Carlos	55	277	74.1	14.6	205	D	D	D	90	1,460	D	88.4
San Clemente	138	386	87.7	17.1	381	D	D	D	99	1,448	314.0	72.1
San Diego	2,764	17,178	4,869.5	851.4	7,387	100,220	18,660.6	7,260.6	1,137	41,655	14,667.0	2,613.2
San Dimas	55	535	66.7	16.9	135	1,890	352.9	135.7	71	1,267	D	61.9

1. Establishments subject to federal tax.

Table D. Cities — Accommodation and Food Services, Arts, Entertainment, and Recreation, and Health Care and Social Assistance

City	Accommodation and food services, 2012				Arts, entertainment, and recreation[1], 2012				Health care and social assistance,[1] 2012			
	Number of establishments	Number of employees	Receipts (mil dol)	Annual payroll (mil dol)	Number of establishments	Number of employees	Receipts (mil dol)	Annual payroll (mil dol)	Number of establishments	Number of employees	Receipts (mil dol)	Annual payroll (mil dol)
	92	93	94	95	96	97	98	99	100	101	102	103
CALIFORNIA— Cont'd												
Menlo Park	104	1,790	139.2	43.6	17	D	D	D	136	988	157.7	64.5
Merced	131	2,340	107.7	28.6	11	113	7.0	1.8	245	2,514	266.6	96.1
Milpitas	282	4,613	320.4	86.0	21	D	D	D	210	2,097	351.1	107.7
Mission Viejo	193	3,372	184.2	53.7	26	D	D	D	466	D	D	D
Modesto	394	7,262	391.0	107.5	30	469	32.2	6.4	580	10,528	1,492.8	561.7
Monrovia	108	1,787	109.3	29.1	15	D	D	D	83	1,573	150.0	63.4
Montclair	83	1,650	82.2	23.8	7	D	D	D	96	1,960	168.3	59.6
Montebello	130	1,741	101.4	26.2	6	D	D	D	171	D	D	D
Monterey	212	5,518	416.3	131.8	22	D	D	D	280	D	D	D
Monterey Park	177	2,613	149.0	40.7	8	D	D	D	262	3,352	515.5	164.7
Moorpark	41	835	48.9	14.1	11	62	4.5	1.3	40	659	51.7	22.4
Moreno Valley	213	3,468	191.9	49.7	11	137	6.3	1.7	206	D	D	D
Morgan Hill	113	1,457	89.8	23.6	9	D	D	D	96	D	D	D
Mountain View	314	4,218	296.3	90.7	19	487	228.8	14.2	302	D	D	D
Murrieta	148	2,672	135.9	36.2	33	475	27.1	7.9	256	3,678	504.8	176.8
Napa	205	3,698	270.3	79.2	18	330	12.8	4.0	225	2,573	344.6	136.0
National City	169	2,512	145.8	35.9	7	D	D	D	148	2,719	229.2	83.2
Newark	162	2,273	149.0	39.7	7	D	D	D	73	D	D	D
Newport Beach	369	11,543	805.0	251.5	95	954	123.4	41.8	887	D	D	D
Norco	72	1,532	221.1	22.5	7	D	D	D	39	D	D	D
Norwalk	138	1,902	110.9	29.2	7	198	10.0	2.5	135	D	D	D
Novato	122	1,804	98.9	28.4	19	289	14.5	5.1	150	1,781	258.6	94.9
Oakland	967	13,126	833.7	237.5	66	2,500	383.9	195.8	837	10,763	1,560.7	744.1
Oakley	25	D	D	D	3	D	D	D	24	D	D	D
Oceanside	306	5,216	354.8	87.9	32	826	47.6	13.6	290	2,490	295.4	117.0
Ontario	332	6,564	383.2	104.6	19	D	D	D	186	D	D	D
Orange	398	6,959	424.2	114.0	36	358	25.4	5.6	597	8,280	979.2	407.1
Oxnard	282	4,397	264.2	68.2	28	414	25.9	6.5	373	3,719	448.7	170.8
Pacifica	67	633	43.7	11.5	6	D	D	D	47	D	D	D
Palmdale	206	4,388	228.8	62.4	12	D	D	D	176	1,715	185.6	59.5
Palm Desert	194	5,547	365.5	109.1	37	1,326	97.5	32.4	226	2,038	226.0	76.2
Palm Springs	262	6,904	411.2	124.8	27	1,116	216.2	34.6	239	4,434	735.1	243.8
Palo Alto	280	6,048	422.3	131.5	31	530	36.4	12.6	329	D	D	D
Paradise	40	D	D	D	6	D	D	D	87	D	D	D
Paramount	73	683	41.0	9.9	2	D	D	D	78	1,276	153.4	58.7
Pasadena	473	9,619	617.4	184.7	150	954	136.2	50.7	873	10,536	1,619.4	533.6
Perris	68	1,017	55.9	14.7	4	D	D	D	34	498	47.0	17.2
Petaluma	162	2,080	125.4	33.8	29	659	49.4	12.6	165	2,145	253.5	83.3
Pico Rivera	118	1,627	105.0	26.5	4	D	D	D	74	931	85.5	31.9
Pittsburg	84	1,394	73.9	19.6	4	76	3.8	1.0	65	693	54.3	24.0
Placentia	91	1,268	74.5	19.3	7	D	D	D	125	2,113	211.4	91.8
Pleasant Hill	93	1,540	106.1	28.9	14	204	10.2	4.5	114	1,550	164.1	57.1
Pleasanton	240	3,856	247.7	70.1	37	D	D	D	273	3,240	621.3	164.5
Pomona	195	2,940	169.5	48.4	12	D	D	D	272	3,383	335.7	125.5
Porterville	81	1,268	60.0	14.8	4	D	D	D	126	D	D	D
Poway	105	1,280	69.7	20.1	24	D	D	D	148	D	D	D
Rancho Cordova	144	2,383	136.5	37.8	15	D	D	D	98	3,006	767.2	253.0
Rancho Cucamonga	312	7,074	366.2	105.5	31	299	42.0	6.4	386	4,315	417.1	156.3
Rancho Palos Verdes	38	1,388	127.9	38.1	12	D	D	D	120	D	D	D
Rancho Santa Margarita	83	1,423	76.4	22.1	16	D	D	D	83	D	D	D
Redding	254	4,374	228.7	62.0	25	D	D	D	465	6,274	676.0	257.0
Redlands	174	3,257	163.8	44.1	13	194	12.7	4.7	289	3,092	466.2	151.4
Redondo Beach	212	4,099	247.5	78.7	42	D	D	D	204	1,310	193.7	70.3
Redwood City	216	2,841	205.9	55.3	30	799	45.3	13.2	273	D	D	D
Rialto	89	1,287	71.8	18.0	6	98	17.2	3.3	87	733	63.4	25.8
Richmond	123	1,053	72.7	18.7	16	D	D	D	118	2,201	345.6	138.1
Ridgecrest	60	939	45.2	12.0	6	61	1.4	0.4	56	D	D	D
Riverside	535	9,620	516.6	142.1	52	723	46.2	12.7	761	12,615	1,758.6	662.6
Rocklin	80	1,274	65.2	19.0	13	D	D	D	137	D	D	D
Rohnert Park	87	1,698	95.0	27.2	12	D	D	D	69	556	81.6	20.8
Rosemead	157	2,023	112.0	29.5	6	155	9.1	2.8	127	1,343	141.6	46.4
Roseville	365	7,478	394.2	113.6	37	766	43.4	11.9	450	D	D	D
Sacramento	1,093	20,289	1,145.7	327.5	90	2,682	303.0	111.5	1,052	15,968	2,608.6	1,092.1
Salinas	253	3,746	221.3	57.4	11	D	D	D	276	2,941	365.6	148.3
San Bernardino	342	5,741	303.7	82.1	25	D	D	D	364	5,388	522.1	207.2
San Bruno	129	1,868	119.7	33.7	9	D	D	D	104	1,117	171.6	55.4
San Buenaventura (Ventura)	327	5,534	319.0	91.8	47	731	45.3	12.4	440	4,394	516.3	195.0
San Carlos	116	1,498	104.4	27.0	15	86	7.5	1.4	94	646	67.7	25.3
San Clemente	162	2,475	136.2	36.7	34	D	D	D	201	D	D	D
San Diego	3,527	80,688	5,590.8	1,561.3	403	8,652	1,213.2	467.7	3,572	40,873	5,882.8	2,308.0
San Dimas	77	1,183	71.5	19.0	16	D	D	D	101	1,648	157.6	61.0

1. Establishments subject to federal tax.

City	Other services[1]				Government employment and payroll, 2012								
						March payroll							
							Percent of total for:						
	Number of establishments	Number of employees	Receipts (mil dol)	Annual payroll (mil dol)	Full-time equivalent employees	Total (dollars)	Admin-istrative, judicial, and legal	Police and corrections	Fire protection	Highways and trans-portation	Health and welfare	Natural resources and utilities	Education and libraries
	104	105	106	107	108	109	110	111	112	113	114	115	116
CALIFORNIA— Cont'd													
Menlo Park	62	D	D	D	265	1,760,354	14.1	39.6	0.0	11.5	2.4	17.6	6.2
Merced	59	326	26.8	8.3	442	2,547,548	11.6	31.0	16.4	3.0	2.2	22.9	0.0
Milpitas	108	1,035	201.8	34.8	391	3,312,573	25.8	33.3	22.1	4.4	1.1	10.0	0.0
Mission Viejo	169	1,052	91.3	28.5	180	959,036	31.7	0.0	0.0	15.3	6.3	22.8	18.2
Modesto	237	1,355	141.6	35.1	1,217	6,592,366	14.4	32.0	18.1	7.5	1.5	23.8	0.0
Monrovia	67	392	51.0	11.7	256	1,668,764	17.2	33.0	27.7	1.5	3.1	13.2	3.5
Montclair	73	398	35.7	9.4	251	1,296,597	25.0	33.8	17.4	1.8	13.1	5.5	0.0
Montebello	81	611	42.8	10.4	486	2,561,705	6.5	30.7	19.8	32.0	1.1	6.0	0.0
Monterey	57	547	34.6	13.1	506	3,399,804	0.1	18.1	19.6	2.7	1.3	10.8	4.3
Monterey Park	81	333	32.7	7.0	327	1,888,775	11.2	36.1	23.6	5.9	0.0	17.1	5.2
Moorpark	25	126	12.5	3.2	67	465,036	35.0	0.0	0.0	14.4	20.2	30.4	0.0
Moreno Valley	121	474	34.7	10.2	743	3,360,444	15.3	2.0	2.4	17.1	12.4	15.5	1.9
Morgan Hill	68	347	34.4	9.8	182	1,516,788	12.8	39.9	0.0	2.3	1.1	25.1	0.0
Mountain View	137	800	84.5	25.9	600	5,229,873	11.3	28.6	21.6	9.3	5.2	17.2	4.4
Murrieta	142	925	70.6	22.7	339	2,066,931	19.5	46.2	23.2	0.5	0.0	6.5	3.4
Napa	119	638	58.5	17.7	431	3,308,340	12.4	30.1	19.6	7.4	8.5	18.7	0.0
National City	104	512	41.9	13.0	361	2,077,359	8.6	42.0	20.4	3.0	4.5	9.8	7.3
Newark	63	D	D	D	169	764,266	14.7	51.1	0.0	5.4	1.7	15.4	0.0
Newport Beach	205	1,435	107.2	31.2	797	6,997,470	14.3	26.3	21.3	6.9	1.1	16.5	4.6
Norco	62	303	27.3	8.0	81	317,544	33.7	2.4	2.2	9.4	11.1	25.1	0.0
Norwalk	72	363	35.5	10.3	339	1,671,145	18.7	10.3	0.0	35.5	8.6	18.6	0.0
Novato	87	853	75.5	28.5	190	1,241,125	11.4	43.9	0.0	18.8	2.5	18.0	0.0
Oakland	594	3,810	392.7	119.0	3,940	30,153,764	10.1	31.4	20.4	17.1	7.7	5.5	3.1
Oakley	23	58	7.1	1.9	26	121,823	56.5	10.1	0.0	3.7	0.0	20.3	0.0
Oceanside	178	1,117	103.6	31.0	950	5,925,758	16.2	36.9	16.2	3.6	4.4	18.2	2.3
Ontario	177	2,305	216.1	68.5	1,078	8,143,877	8.3	39.1	22.6	0.5	2.8	14.8	2.5
Orange	279	2,345	198.3	65.4	662	5,240,608	10.8	40.5	25.9	5.9	1.0	10.0	3.4
Oxnard	159	939	94.1	25.7	1,267	7,972,661	9.1	36.5	12.3	4.2	8.3	23.4	2.6
Pacifica	29	D	D	D	186	1,351,528	12.4	28.8	17.8	10.7	2.1	16.8	0.0
Palmdale	89	433	30.0	9.6	315	1,381,568	13.7	8.9	0.0	20.8	15.6	20.9	2.9
Palm Desert	117	624	45.2	14.4	122	957,854	30.8	0.0	0.0	28.3	24.5	7.0	0.0
Palm Springs	80	514	32.2	10.3	513	3,307,054	15.7	33.0	17.9	11.3	2.5	5.4	3.1
Palo Alto	104	1,104	97.7	36.6	921	7,610,093	16.4	17.4	16.0	3.9	0.9	38.7	3.0
Paradise	41	123	12.7	3.3	88	528,134	9.9	38.1	34.1	5.6	8.4	2.9	0.0
Paramount	67	609	74.6	24.1	210	830,396	17.7	15.7	0.0	19.4	8.9	20.4	0.0
Pasadena	333	2,438	363.4	87.9	1,821	13,044,662	12.2	21.1	13.6	1.9	4.8	27.1	0.2
Perris	32	156	23.1	4.6	76	396,603	36.6	0.0	0.0	22.9	32.0	8.5	0.0
Petaluma	106	599	49.6	15.6	301	2,362,449	10.3	35.7	22.9	9.0	1.1	20.1	0.0
Pico Rivera	68	535	59.8	17.1	288	1,134,401	19.4	0.0	0.0	28.7	11.6	40.3	0.0
Pittsburg	44	530	53.6	17.1	267	1,784,475	10.5	44.3	0.0	7.0	2.9	12.6	0.0
Placentia	63	401	47.0	11.9	175	1,008,861	10.4	58.5	0.0	7.4	1.7	17.6	0.0
Pleasant Hill	55	410	36.4	10.9	125	907,055	21.9	52.8	0.0	22.8	2.3	0.0	0.0
Pleasanton	135	1,000	105.4	37.9	509	4,073,003	13.7	23.1	30.7	5.5	2.2	14.7	4.4
Pomona	133	729	74.7	22.6	630	2,988,643	8.4	51.9	0.0	5.9	6.3	15.1	2.8
Porterville	35	165	14.0	5.3	323	1,445,053	12.8	29.5	14.5	7.6	0.7	28.3	2.8
Poway	88	592	49.4	15.7	291	1,821,500	20.9	0.0	28.9	10.0	4.0	27.1	0.0
Rancho Cordova	81	482	53.1	16.4	67	438,835	46.2	0.0	0.0	25.2	6.1	0.0	0.0
Rancho Cucamonga	215	1,149	89.7	27.4	639	3,536,504	13.7	0.0	32.8	6.4	4.3	31.3	5.3
Rancho Palos Verdes	20	103	5.8	1.7	69	423,058	29.0	0.0	0.0	13.7	0.0	30.2	0.0
Rancho Santa Margarita	52	288	21.8	5.6	27	142,356	100.0	0.0	0.0	0.0	0.0	0.0	0.0
Redding	185	1,012	97.6	30.5	747	5,047,088	9.6	20.1	14.2	8.9	1.6	42.2	0.0
Redlands	110	567	48.6	15.6	429	2,798,020	10.0	32.4	23.6	5.8	1.1	19.2	3.1
Redondo Beach	123	745	68.2	17.6	980	23,723,684	11.5	36.3	24.3	11.4	4.1	9.3	3.2
Redwood City	122	D	D	D	543	4,492,820	13.2	30.5	20.6	0.0	1.1	19.6	6.0
Rialto	61	322	37.7	10.1	357	2,259,378	9.8	38.9	27.3	6.1	4.1	10.2	0.0
Richmond	88	448	49.5	16.7	843	5,538,248	8.5	38.6	12.2	3.0	6.2	8.4	4.2
Ridgecrest	29	124	10.7	3.1	106	565,833	18.2	47.9	0.0	13.3	4.0	14.5	0.0
Riverside	366	2,248	213.7	58.3	2,260	15,114,251	6.2	28.2	15.6	5.5	4.5	29.8	1.6
Rocklin	72	487	38.0	11.3	287	1,697,873	10.7	35.7	20.8	8.4	6.6	17.7	0.0
Rohnert Park	55	337	34.1	9.8	176	1,106,615	17.8	57.7	0.0	0.0	1.6	22.9	0.0
Rosemead	91	245	22.4	5.1	102	521,909	25.8	14.7	0.0	10.3	10.6	24.2	0.0
Roseville	179	1,842	231.3	58.3	1,160	7,733,037	12.9	18.3	15.7	2.8	2.2	35.9	2.0
Sacramento	612	3,879	358.6	106.5	4,483	29,508,935	6.7	46.8	16.2	10.8	3.9	15.6	0.0
Salinas	164	962	110.0	28.5	553	3,536,035	7.9	43.0	21.0	11.8	4.5	3.6	5.1
San Bernardino	202	974	78.5	24.7	1,527	9,251,817	6.8	36.8	22.6	1.2	6.6	19.6	1.2
San Bruno	96	679	64.5	18.7	262	1,918,097	12.9	28.0	20.2	5.7	0.5	17.9	6.2
San Buenaventura (Ventura)	197	993	93.1	27.9	659	4,241,287	13.8	29.9	21.1	8.7	1.1	23.0	0.0
San Carlos	83	914	67.7	24.1	99	739,930	23.5	0.0	27.1	4.5	4.5	27.8	0.0
San Clemente	88	489	39.8	11.5	220	909,552	22.8	0.0	0.0	23.9	7.3	44.4	0.0
San Diego	1,994	16,826	1,333.9	457.3	9,425	62,476,850	19.9	28.7	13.9	2.4	0.3	25.5	2.3
San Dimas	50	D	D	D	106	558,552	25.6	0.0	0.0	20.9	21.8	31.7	0.0

1. Establishments subject to federal tax.

City Government Finances

City	City government finances, 2012									
	General revenue							General expenditure		
		Intergovernmental		Taxes						
						Per capita[1] (dollars)			Per capita[1] (dollars)	
	Total (mil dol)	Total (mil dol)	Percent from state government	Total (mil dol)	Total	Property	Sales and gross receipts	Total (mil dol)	Total	Capital outlays
	117	118	119	120	121	122	123	124	125	126
CALIFORNIA— Cont'd										
Menlo Park	57.5	3.5	90.3	37.8	1,149	690	444	61.2	1,859	334
Merced	96.3	17.9	51.3	32.3	401	192	205	102.4	1,271	255
Milpitas	117.5	7.2	69.9	80.2	1,162	727	430	122.5	1,776	418
Mission Viejo	74.4	7.3	60.1	55.9	588	365	219	78.4	825	168
Modesto	229.0	48.3	51.3	90.4	440	167	270	226.5	1,101	147
Monrovia	51.2	2.2	84.3	38.6	1,042	714	321	56.5	1,525	198
Montclair	47.1	5.3	94.7	33.5	892	526	363	50.6	1,346	152
Montebello	97.7	20.3	71.7	57.3	904	479	394	66.8	1,053	70
Monterey	96.6	3.5	87.7	44.7	1,575	505	1,065	99.9	3,520	328
Monterey Park	60.2	3.6	69.4	41.1	674	471	200	56.7	929	44
Moorpark	30.0	1.5	80.3	17.5	500	296	187	35.7	1,021	81
Moreno Valley	147.5	17.1	68.1	88.6	446	252	192	166.7	838	157
Morgan Hill	67.3	2.7	96.6	37.9	960	628	229	61.1	1,548	436
Mountain View	174.0	5.3	63.1	102.5	1,337	778	411	183.3	2,392	549
Murrieta	80.7	26.1	46.3	39.0	366	220	142	83.1	780	255
Napa	110.6	18.2	18.2	57.4	732	363	365	117.8	1,502	144
National City	79.9	19.2	23.1	47.7	801	407	387	70.4	1,183	258
Newark	41.0	2.5	91.0	33.4	766	334	424	40.3	924	81
Newport Beach	200.4	9.9	61.5	127.8	1,472	878	579	233.0	2,684	829
Norco	33.0	2.3	44.5	21.6	787	582	187	36.0	1,314	451
Norwalk	85.6	27.5	48.8	49.4	464	166	296	67.8	637	38
Novato	49.0	2.3	100.0	35.6	669	475	189	48.6	913	211
Oakland	1,343.3	204.3	54.6	570.6	1,420	810	448	1,312.4	3,266	765
Oakley	29.3	2.8	84.6	16.7	447	271	122	25.9	696	242
Oceanside	233.9	38.0	49.7	106.3	620	416	200	212.9	1,241	113
Ontario	317.2	21.8	84.9	172.3	1,031	570	459	290.2	1,736	274
Orange	142.3	16.7	75.8	101.3	726	444	279	160.6	1,151	284
Oxnard	312.9	40.3	93.9	115.8	575	339	234	320.7	1,592	328
Pacifica	41.0	2.7	100.0	20.9	544	352	188	44.4	1,157	119
Palmdale	135.7	21.8	54.2	85.7	550	380	156	117.3	753	85
Palm Desert	168.1	3.9	64.2	125.5	2,515	1,931	574	156.3	3,132	538
Palm Springs	141.9	13.2	18.3	76.2	1,662	780	860	157.5	3,436	660
Palo Alto	217.5	3.5	57.6	84.1	1,269	530	666	250.9	3,789	623
Paradise	16.8	4.1	95.7	11.0	420	262	156	14.4	551	19
Paramount	37.4	3.7	65.3	29.9	546	300	244	36.2	660	87
Pasadena	411.2	38.8	79.2	194.6	1,402	638	686	403.1	2,905	429
Perris	49.1	3.7	86.4	26.8	376	223	151	54.9	770	150
Petaluma	90.6	5.2	59.0	46.6	792	514	263	83.8	1,424	233
Pico Rivera	61.1	23.1	28.9	26.9	422	222	200	71.3	1,118	307
Pittsburg	89.1	17.2	34.3	46.4	708	555	146	101.3	1,544	207
Placentia	41.3	4.4	89.2	26.6	512	274	225	39.0	750	113
Pleasant Hill	28.8	3.6	100.0	22.5	664	309	316	29.7	877	199
Pleasanton	134.8	6.1	84.2	81.3	1,125	737	334	130.6	1,807	174
Pomona	196.5	41.6	62.7	104.5	692	386	299	201.6	1,334	134
Porterville	49.1	8.8	73.5	21.3	387	135	246	51.3	933	177
Poway	88.7	1.8	88.7	67.5	1,375	1,096	258	85.0	1,731	191
Rancho Cordova	68.7	14.0	40.7	44.1	660	234	422	65.9	985	308
Rancho Cucamonga	230.6	19.5	59.9	162.0	950	784	163	207.7	1,218	193
Rancho Palos Verdes	29.2	1.6	88.9	24.4	577	282	294	28.5	673	66
Rancho Santa Margarita	16.9	2.4	90.6	13.9	285	143	138	17.3	354	60
Redding	182.1	39.5	29.9	57.9	638	314	302	162.8	1,795	572
Redlands	93.8	3.7	75.1	56.2	805	451	352	85.8	1,228	162
Redondo Beach	117.9	8.1	72.6	58.6	867	423	419	113.6	1,680	108
Redwood City	145.3	7.3	85.5	81.5	1,028	589	431	149.2	1,881	250
Rialto	107.1	8.8	38.5	65.0	639	365	273	111.4	1,095	208
Richmond	254.5	35.4	49.7	151.0	1,416	681	645	274.3	2,573	398
Ridgecrest	21.9	1.1	90.4	15.8	556	343	211	20.8	736	131
Riverside	410.7	63.1	60.7	197.7	631	327	295	486.0	1,551	356
Rocklin	52.5	5.7	74.5	32.4	549	319	184	53.8	911	89
Rohnert Park	59.0	3.3	100.0	32.1	780	488	289	57.7	1,402	280
Rosemead	34.4	2.8	59.2	25.5	469	313	155	32.2	592	173
Roseville	251.3	19.4	55.2	91.7	738	331	402	243.4	1,960	236
Sacramento	884.8	128.8	66.1	366.7	771	418	342	806.3	1,695	296
Salinas	117.7	16.6	57.5	82.1	532	198	333	122.6	794	103
San Bernardino	250.9	21.3	61.3	132.6	621	311	305	230.8	1,081	128
San Bruno	58.6	3.4	100.0	29.7	704	334	342	51.8	1,228	135
San Buenaventura (Ventura)	132.2	9.8	64.9	71.9	662	319	341	135.5	1,247	155
San Carlos	46.8	1.0	100.0	27.3	933	565	359	38.4	1,315	156
San Clemente	74.5	6.4	93.0	44.4	685	501	177	82.7	1,276	289
San Diego	2,616.7	370.0	40.2	1,122.2	838	439	397	2,361.5	1,763	396
San Dimas	30.5	1.5	86.2	23.3	690	367	317	33.2	982	105

1. Based on population estimated as of July 1 of the year shown.

Table D. Cities — **City Government Finances**

956 CA(Menlo Park)—CA(San Dimas)

City	City government finances, 2012 (cont.) General expenditure (cont.) Percent of total for:									
	Public welfare	Highways	Parking facilities	Education	Health and hospitals	Police protection	Sewerage and sanitation	Parks and recreation	Housing and community development	Interest on debt
	127	128	129	130	131	132	133	134	135	136
CALIFORNIA— Cont'd										
Menlo Park	0.0	9.7	2.0	0.0	0.0	23.7	0.7	24.5	5.2	7.1
Merced	0.0	14.7	0.0	0.0	0.2	17.9	21.6	4.9	8.8	3.6
Milpitas	0.0	8.7	0.0	0.0	10.6	17.8	7.2	5.0	24.5	5.9
Mission Viejo	0.0	22.7	0.0	0.0	2.2	20.0	0.0	20.2	7.8	1.5
Modesto	0.0	11.8	0.5	0.3	0.4	20.9	16.0	9.7	4.4	2.0
Monrovia	0.0	4.3	0.0	0.0	3.4	33.5	2.0	4.6	10.1	7.2
Montclair	0.0	8.2	0.0	0.0	8.2	20.5	7.9	8.1	24.7	6.2
Montebello	0.0	6.7	0.0	0.0	0.3	27.9	5.1	15.8	5.7	8.2
Monterey	0.0	11.5	6.8	0.0	0.0	12.8	1.9	15.4	6.0	0.7
Monterey Park	0.0	6.8	0.0	0.0	1.2	26.8	11.0	5.8	9.8	4.7
Moorpark	0.0	11.6	0.0	0.0	1.1	18.2	0.9	12.0	18.3	2.7
Moreno Valley	0.0	19.1	0.0	0.0	1.3	26.1	0.0	9.0	14.2	3.7
Morgan Hill	0.0	10.4	0.0	0.0	0.0	18.6	10.0	10.1	21.8	3.2
Mountain View	0.0	4.2	0.1	0.0	0.0	16.0	15.2	21.1	2.5	1.5
Murrieta	0.0	30.4	0.0	0.0	0.0	29.4	0.0	11.0	5.8	4.3
Napa	0.0	15.7	0.4	0.0	2.6	16.9	17.1	6.9	13.2	1.1
National City	0.0	3.6	0.0	0.0	1.7	30.9	9.9	3.5	23.8	4.2
Newark	0.0	12.0	0.0	0.0	0.6	32.5	0.4	11.1	0.5	1.2
Newport Beach	0.0	13.8	0.0	0.0	2.6	17.7	1.5	10.0	0.0	3.5
Norco	0.0	9.4	0.0	0.0	5.5	12.6	18.0	6.1	16.3	12.3
Norwalk	0.0	12.1	0.7	0.0	7.3	19.7	0.0	10.0	18.0	8.9
Novato	0.0	12.8	0.0	0.0	1.2	25.4	0.0	19.0	6.7	9.6
Oakland	0.0	3.5	0.7	0.0	5.4	14.9	3.4	3.6	9.4	7.2
Oakley	0.0	20.6	0.0	0.0	0.7	28.9	0.0	14.6	12.4	5.7
Oceanside	0.0	7.9	0.8	0.0	0.1	22.7	19.9	6.2	10.5	3.6
Ontario	0.0	7.4	0.0	0.0	0.4	24.6	11.6	5.0	10.1	4.7
Orange	0.0	11.8	0.0	0.0	6.7	23.1	3.8	11.6	10.8	2.7
Oxnard	0.0	12.2	0.3	0.0	0.0	21.3	22.0	10.3	4.4	7.3
Pacifica	0.0	14.4	0.0	0.0	1.7	20.3	20.0	8.3	0.5	4.7
Palmdale	0.0	15.6	0.0	0.0	0.7	16.8	2.5	12.1	20.8	10.5
Palm Desert	0.0	10.2	0.0	0.0	2.6	10.4	0.0	10.7	38.1	11.7
Palm Springs	0.0	15.8	0.3	0.0	0.8	12.8	3.7	14.0	5.4	3.7
Palo Alto	0.0	4.4	0.1	2.9	0.3	13.8	24.8	13.4	0.2	1.9
Paradise	0.0	15.3	0.0	0.0	1.1	27.0	4.7	0.2	1.9	7.0
Paramount	0.0	18.4	0.0	0.0	0.0	29.4	0.0	12.7	10.6	4.9
Pasadena	0.0	6.9	2.7	0.0	4.4	15.8	4.9	10.1	6.4	3.9
Perris	0.0	14.3	0.0	0.0	0.8	20.1	3.8	3.3	23.1	17.7
Petaluma	0.0	9.4	0.0	0.0	1.0	18.2	19.3	5.4	15.3	10.8
Pico Rivera	0.0	35.5	0.0	0.0	0.0	14.1	0.0	10.4	18.0	0.0
Pittsburg	0.0	7.8	0.0	0.0	0.4	18.5	2.0	3.9	33.7	17.9
Placentia	0.0	16.3	0.0	0.0	0.3	28.1	8.9	5.7	6.5	3.6
Pleasant Hill	0.0	29.3	0.0	0.0	0.6	35.4	0.8	0.0	9.2	2.4
Pleasanton	0.0	10.4	0.0	0.0	0.2	18.3	10.1	17.9	1.6	2.7
Pomona	0.0	15.1	0.0	0.0	0.0	20.1	6.5	1.6	23.4	13.4
Porterville	0.0	8.0	0.1	0.0	0.2	15.8	24.2	9.3	3.5	6.2
Poway	0.0	11.2	0.0	0.0	0.4	12.3	9.1	7.3	12.9	15.2
Rancho Cordova	0.0	34.1	0.0	0.0	0.7	24.0	0.0	1.0	7.5	1.7
Rancho Cucamonga	0.0	11.8	0.0	1.1	1.4	12.6	1.6	3.3	19.8	13.7
Rancho Palos Verdes	0.0	21.5	0.0	0.0	0.7	14.0	1.6	11.5	1.2	3.6
Rancho Santa Margarita	0.0	22.7	0.0	0.0	2.1	43.6	0.0	5.7	0.0	3.1
Redding	0.0	8.9	0.0	0.0	0.4	15.2	34.2	5.3	9.1	2.7
Redlands	0.0	5.8	0.0	0.0	5.2	24.9	19.0	6.7	5.8	3.4
Redondo Beach	0.0	6.3	0.0	0.0	4.0	24.5	5.8	5.0	14.1	1.4
Redwood City	0.0	12.8	1.2	0.0	0.5	20.3	14.1	6.2	5.9	3.2
Rialto	0.0	8.0	0.0	0.4	4.0	23.1	8.6	5.0	18.0	8.2
Richmond	0.0	11.3	0.0	0.0	0.5	23.5	3.7	1.7	15.8	7.2
Ridgecrest	0.0	9.8	0.0	0.0	0.0	30.5	5.8	8.8	15.7	7.3
Riverside	0.0	11.4	1.0	0.0	0.1	18.0	8.8	5.0	13.1	6.9
Rocklin	0.0	10.2	0.0	0.0	0.0	21.7	0.0	12.6	9.7	4.8
Rohnert Park	0.0	4.3	0.0	0.0	1.7	17.8	25.1	6.1	17.1	5.0
Rosemead	0.0	5.7	0.0	0.0	0.9	20.7	0.0	7.6	18.2	4.3
Roseville	0.0	11.4	0.0	0.0	0.0	12.0	14.3	9.5	4.3	15.7
Sacramento	0.0	18.4	1.9	0.0	2.2	16.9	15.2	7.8	3.6	5.8
Salinas	0.0	8.9	1.2	0.0	3.6	33.3	3.9	3.8	3.4	1.3
San Bernardino	0.0	5.3	0.0	0.0	1.1	29.7	15.7	3.3	9.8	1.9
San Bruno	0.0	6.9	0.0	0.0	0.0	23.1	16.6	12.8	1.6	0.9
San Buenaventura (Ventura)	0.0	11.6	0.5	0.0	0.2	22.4	15.1	9.0	2.0	3.7
San Carlos	0.0	9.3	0.2	0.0	0.0	18.2	15.9	9.3	3.0	2.2
San Clemente	0.0	8.3	0.0	0.0	3.0	14.5	11.0	25.3	3.1	1.1
San Diego	0.0	9.7	0.1	0.0	0.6	12.7	12.6	9.9	19.7	6.2
San Dimas	0.0	13.5	0.1	0.0	0.4	15.5	0.1	11.6	10.1	3.7

Table D. Cities — City Government Finances, City Government Employment, and Climate

City	City government finances, 2012 (cont.) Debt outstanding Total (mil dol)	Per capita[1] (dollars)	Debt issued during year	Climate[2] Average daily temperature Mean January	July	Limits January[3]	July[4]	Annual precipitation (inches)	Heating degree days	Cooling degree days
	137	138	139	140	141	142	143	144	145	146
CALIFORNIA— Cont'd										
Menlo Park	89.8	2,729	9.8	49.0	68.0	40.4	78.8	15.71	2,584	452
Merced	93.3	1,159	0.0	46.3	78.6	37.5	96.5	12.50	2,602	1,578
Milpitas	171.2	2,482	0.0	50.5	70.9	41.7	84.3	15.08	2,171	811
Mission Viejo	47.5	500	0.0	56.7	72.4	47.2	82.3	14.03	1,465	1,183
Modesto	441.0	2,144	52.8	47.2	77.7	40.1	93.6	13.12	2,358	1,570
Monrovia	103.5	2,796	0.0	56.1	75.3	44.3	89.4	21.09	1,398	1,558
Montclair	77.9	2,073	0.0	54.6	73.8	41.5	88.7	16.96	1,727	1,191
Montebello	88.0	1,388	0.0	58.8	76.6	47.9	88.9	14.44	949	1,837
Monterey	14.8	521	0.0	51.6	60.2	43.4	68.1	20.35	3,092	74
Monterey Park	83.1	1,363	0.0	56.3	75.6	42.6	89.0	18.56	1,295	1,575
Moorpark	27.6	788	0.0	54.7	68.3	41.2	80.7	18.41	1,911	602
Moreno Valley	91.6	461	0.0	54.2	77.4	42.0	93.5	10.67	1,674	1,697
Morgan Hill	124.6	3,156	0.0	43.5	70.7	37.5	78.2	23.73	4,566	747
Mountain View	83.5	1,090	39.4	49.0	68.0	40.4	78.8	15.71	2,584	452
Murrieta	90.8	852	0.0	52.2	79.6	38.3	98.1	12.09	1,924	1,874
Napa	95.7	1,221	0.0	47.9	68.6	39.2	82.6	26.46	2,689	529
National City	84.5	1,419	0.0	57.3	70.1	46.1	76.1	9.95	1,321	862
Newark	11.4	261	9.7	49.8	68.0	42.0	78.3	14.85	2,367	530
Newport Beach	270.0	3,110	2.6	55.9	67.3	48.2	71.4	11.65	1,719	543
Norco	136.8	4,999	0.0	NA	NA	NA	NA	NA	NA	NA
Norwalk	142.9	1,342	2.1	57.0	73.8	46.0	82.9	12.94	1,211	1,186
Novato	141.1	2,647	0.0	48.8	67.7	41.3	80.9	34.29	2,621	451
Oakland	2,294.4	5,709	429.5	50.9	64.9	44.7	72.7	22.94	2,400	377
Oakley	39.5	1,060	0.0	45.7	74.4	37.8	90.7	13.33	2,714	1,179
Oceanside	200.5	1,168	7.7	54.7	67.6	45.4	72.1	11.13	2,009	505
Ontario	212.5	1,271	0.9	54.6	73.8	41.5	88.7	16.96	1,727	1,191
Orange	107.1	768	3.0	58.0	72.9	46.6	82.7	13.84	1,153	1,299
Oxnard	484.3	2,404	9.3	55.6	65.9	45.5	72.7	15.62	1,936	403
Pacifica	52.3	1,363	0.0	49.4	62.8	42.9	71.1	20.11	2,862	142
Palmdale	251.2	1,614	2.2	46.6	81.7	34.3	97.5	7.36	2,704	1,998
Palm Desert	450.5	9,024	1.0	56.8	92.8	42.0	107.1	3.15	903	4,388
Palm Springs	165.5	3,611	68.9	57.3	92.1	44.2	108.2	5.23	951	4,224
Palo Alto	142.0	2,144	17.2	49.0	68.0	40.4	78.8	15.71	2,584	452
Paradise	14.9	568	0.0	45.7	77.8	37.7	91.7	56.20	3,145	1,464
Paramount	69.2	1,262	0.0	57.0	73.8	46.0	82.9	12.94	1,211	1,186
Pasadena	766.2	5,522	88.3	56.1	75.3	44.3	89.4	21.09	1,398	1,558
Perris	262.8	3,686	0.0	51.2	78.3	36.1	97.8	11.40	2,123	1,710
Petaluma	244.3	4,153	12.9	48.4	67.3	38.9	82.7	25.86	2,741	385
Pico Rivera	49.9	784	0.0	58.3	74.2	48.5	83.8	15.14	928	1,506
Pittsburg	474.6	7,230	0.0	45.7	74.4	37.8	90.7	13.33	2,714	1,179
Placentia	28.8	554	0.0	58.0	72.9	46.6	82.7	13.84	1,153	1,299
Pleasant Hill	21.7	641	0.0	46.3	71.2	38.8	87.4	19.58	2,757	786
Pleasanton	82.6	1,143	0.0	47.2	72.0	37.4	89.1	14.82	2,755	858
Pomona	411.1	2,721	0.0	54.6	73.8	41.5	88.7	16.96	1,727	1,191
Porterville	72.6	1,321	0.1	48.7	82.8	39.4	98.1	11.49	2,053	2,246
Poway	246.1	5,010	0.2	55.3	70.9	43.5	80.8	11.97	1,808	979
Rancho Cordova	23.3	349	0.0	48.2	77.4	41.3	93.8	19.87	2,226	1,597
Rancho Cucamonga	503.8	2,954	0.4	56.6	78.3	45.3	95.0	14.77	1,364	1,901
Rancho Palos Verdes	24.4	575	0.3	56.3	69.4	46.2	77.6	14.79	1,526	742
Rancho Santa Margarita	11.4	233	0.0	56.7	72.4	47.2	82.3	14.03	1,465	1,183
Redding	140.7	1,552	25.2	45.5	81.3	35.5	98.5	33.52	2,961	1,741
Redlands	63.1	903	0.0	52.9	78.0	40.4	94.4	13.62	1,904	1,714
Redondo Beach	53.3	789	0.0	57.1	69.3	48.6	75.3	13.15	1,274	679
Redwood City	164.1	2,069	10.0	48.4	68.0	39.1	80.8	20.16	2,764	422
Rialto	226.0	2,222	0.0	54.4	79.6	41.8	96.0	16.43	1,599	1,937
Richmond	657.3	6,165	25.9	50.0	62.7	42.9	70.5	23.35	2,720	184
Ridgecrest	40.5	1,430	0.0	NA	NA	NA	NA	NA	NA	NA
Riverside	1,908.6	6,092	61.7	55.3	78.7	42.7	94.1	10.22	1,475	1,863
Rocklin	85.0	1,439	11.8	46.9	77.7	39.2	94.8	24.61	2,532	1,528
Rohnert Park	71.7	1,743	0.0	48.7	67.6	39.5	82.2	31.01	2,694	526
Rosemead	43.5	799	0.0	56.3	75.6	42.6	89.0	18.56	1,295	1,575
Roseville	1,069.1	8,607	0.0	46.9	77.7	39.2	94.8	24.61	2,532	1,528
Sacramento	1,087.3	2,286	1.8	46.3	75.4	38.8	92.4	17.93	2,666	1,248
Salinas	42.6	276	18.0	51.2	63.2	41.3	71.3	12.91	2,770	210
San Bernardino	121.7	570	0.0	54.4	79.6	41.8	96.0	16.43	1,599	1,937
San Bruno	11.6	274	0.0	49.4	62.8	42.9	71.1	20.11	2,862	142
San Buenaventura (Ventura)	122.9	1,132	23.5	55.6	65.9	45.5	72.7	15.62	1,936	403
San Carlos	24.3	832	0.0	48.4	68.0	39.1	80.8	20.16	2,764	422
San Clemente	18.2	280	5.0	55.4	68.7	43.9	77.3	13.56	1,756	666
San Diego	3,433.7	2,563	465.2	57.8	70.9	49.7	75.8	10.77	1,063	866
San Dimas	19.7	582	0.0	54.6	73.8	41.5	88.7	16.96	1,727	1,191

1. Based on the population estimated as of July 1 of the year shown. 2. Represents normal values based on the 30-year period, 1971±2000. 3. Average daily minimum. 4. Average daily maximum.

Table D. Cities — **Land Area and Population**

STATE Place code	City	Land area[1] (sq. mi)	Total persons 2018	Rank	Per square mile	Race 2017 Race alone[2] (percent) White	Black or African American	American Indian, Alaskan Native	Asian	Hawaiian Pacific Islander	Some other race	Two or more races (percent)
		1	2	3	4	5	6	7	8	9	10	11
	CALIFORNIA— Cont'd											
06 67,000	San Francisco......................	46.9	883,305	15	18,833.8	45.6	5.2	0.3	34.7	0.4	8.1	5.7
06 67,042	San Gabriel.........................	4.1	40,335	951	9,837.8	19.2	0.7	0.8	59.6	0.0	15.7	4.0
06 67,112	San Jacinto	25.7	48,867	789	1,901.4	72.3	7.1	3.2	2.6	0.0	8.6	6.2
06 68,000	San Jose.........................	177.1	1,030,119	10	5,816.6	39.1	2.9	0.7	35.6	0.5	16.0	5.4
06 68,028	San Juan Capistrano	14.4	36,013	1,066	2,500.9	59.5	0.4	0.0	5.0	0.0	27.4	7.7
06 68,084	San Leandro	13.3	89,703	366	6,744.6	37.8	9.1	1.0	36.9	1.4	6.5	7.3
06 68,154	San Luis Obispo..................	13.1	47,446	816	3,621.8	85.5	1.3	0.6	5.5	0.0	3.2	4.0
06 68,196	San Marcos......................	24.4	96,847	324	3,969.1	78.5	1.5	0.9	8.7	0.1	3.9	6.3
06 68,252	San Mateo.......................	12.2	105,025	293	8,608.6	52.7	1.4	0.5	23.6	3.5	12.7	5.5
06 68,294	San Pablo........................	2.6	31,124	1,212	11,970.8	50.5	13.3	0.7	16.3	0.2	15.2	3.7
06 68,364	San Rafael.......................	16.6	58,704	640	3,536.4	69.8	1.2	0.8	4.5	0.0	17.8	6.0
06 68,378	San Ramon.......................	18.7	75,839	461	4,055.6	36.8	3.5	0.5	49.8	0.5	1.7	7.1
06 69,000	Santa Ana	27.4	332,725	57	12,143.2	35.0	0.9	0.3	12.0	0.4	49.9	1.5
06 69,070	Santa Barbara	19.5	91,350	360	4,684.6	76.1	2.2	0.2	3.7	0.0	14.9	2.9
06 69,084	Santa Clara......................	18.4	129,488	214	7,037.4	36.4	4.2	0.1	45.0	0.2	8.2	5.8
06 69,088	Santa Clarita	65.9	210,089	106	3,188.0	69.4	4.1	1.4	12.3	0.1	6.2	6.5
06 69,112	Santa Cruz.......................	12.7	64,725	576	5,096.5	73.7	1.4	0.6	11.0	0.2	7.3	5.7
06 69,196	Santa Maria......................	22.8	107,408	282	4,710.9	81.1	1.1	0.7	5.8	0.0	7.5	3.7
06 70,000	Santa Monica....................	8.4	91,411	359	10,882.3	71.9	4.2	0.0	10.5	0.2	5.5	7.6
06 70,042	Santa Paula	4.5	30,011	1,253	6,669.1	90.8	0.3	0.1	2.3	0.0	4.8	1.7
06 70,098	Santa Rosa.......................	42.5	177,586	146	4,178.5	63.2	3.1	1.7	5.4	1.0	19.5	6.0
06 70,224	Santee...........................	16.5	58,115	649	3,522.1	81.9	1.9	1.1	5.2	0.0	4.8	5.1
06 70,280	Saratoga	12.8	30,599	1,229	2,390.5	NA	NA	NA	NA	NA	NA	NA
06 70,742	Seaside..........................	9.2	33,930	1,125	3,688.0	64.5	8.6	0.5	12.6	2.0	5.0	6.9
06 72,016	Simi Valley	41.5	125,851	221	3,032.6	79.0	1.5	0.2	11.1	0.0	4.0	4.2
06 72,520	Soledad..........................	4.4	26,013	1,394	5,912.0	46.3	6.9	0.5	1.8	0.1	43.0	1.3
06 73,080	South Gate	7.2	94,443	340	13,117.1	58.9	0.7	1.3	0.9	0.0	36.4	1.8
06 73,220	South Pasadena	3.4	25,611	1,400	7,532.6	53.9	2.3	0.9	33.5	0.0	5.3	4.1
06 73,262	South San Francisco.............	9.2	67,733	536	7,362.3	26.0	2.3	0.4	46.0	1.0	19.0	5.2
06 73,962	Stanton..........................	3.1	38,234	1,006	12,333.5	51.9	0.9	0.8	28.4	1.2	12.0	4.9
06 75,000	Stockton.........................	61.7	311,178	61	5,043.4	39.7	12.3	0.5	21.0	0.7	12.9	12.9
06 75,630	Suisun City.......................	4.1	29,713	1,263	7,247.1	43.6	10.6	1.3	34.8	0.0	3.8	5.8
06 77,000	Sunnyvale	22.0	153,185	169	6,963.0	37.9	1.7	0.4	47.4	0.2	7.2	5.2
06 78,120	Temecula.........................	37.3	114,742	252	3,076.2	66.3	4.6	0.5	7.1	0.2	12.5	8.8
06 78,148	Temple City	4.0	36,120	1,063	9,030.0	23.7	0.5	1.2	58.2	0.0	14.0	2.5
06 78,582	Thousand Oaks..................	55.3	127,690	217	2,309.0	81.3	1.3	0.4	10.3	0.1	1.8	5.0
06 80,000	Torrance.........................	20.5	145,182	181	7,082.0	44.7	2.7	0.3	39.0	0.5	6.1	6.6
06 80,238	Tracy............................	22.1	91,812	355	4,154.4	56.2	4.5	0.2	18.3	2.0	10.3	8.6
06 80,644	Tulare...........................	20.4	64,475	578	3,160.5	75.1	4.5	0.9	1.0	0.5	14.1	3.9
06 80,812	Turlock..........................	16.9	73,504	489	4,349.3	72.5	1.4	0.6	7.2	0.1	12.7	5.5
06 80,854	Tustin...........................	11.1	79,795	434	7,188.7	46.8	5.4	0.3	25.7	0.0	16.3	5.4
06 80,994	Twentynine Palms...............	58.8	26,418	1,384	449.3	71.3	14.1	1.4	1.6	1.0	0.2	10.3
06 81,204	Union City	19.4	74,559	476	3,843.2	20.8	5.3	0.8	56.8	1.5	9.7	5.1
06 81,344	Upland...........................	15.6	77,000	454	4,935.9	68.5	3.5	0.6	8.7	0.0	11.7	7.0
06 81,554	Vacaville.........................	29.2	100,154	309	3,429.9	68.3	9.9	0.2	6.5	0.9	7.0	7.2
06 81,666	Vallejo	30.7	121,913	230	3,971.1	33.5	19.5	0.4	23.0	0.9	16.7	6.0
06 82,590	Victorville........................	73.6	122,312	228	1,661.8	64.6	10.3	0.4	4.9	0.2	12.3	7.3
06 82,954	Visalia...........................	37.9	133,800	205	3,530.3	69.9	2.4	0.9	5.1	0.0	15.6	6.1
06 82,996	Vista............................	18.7	101,224	305	5,413.0	86.2	2.9	0.2	3.5	0.1	4.2	2.9
06 83,332	Walnut...........................	9.0	30,006	1,254	3,334.0	23.9	2.2	1.5	63.0	0.0	5.4	3.7
06 83,346	Walnut Creek	19.8	69,825	514	3,526.5	67.5	3.1	0.4	19.3	0.2	2.4	7.1
06 83,542	Wasco...........................	9.4	27,976	1,321	2,976.2	78.7	7.1	0.7	1.6	0.5	9.5	1.7
06 83,668	Watsonville......................	6.7	53,920	714	8,047.8	41.4	1.5	0.0	2.7	0.1	52.5	1.7
06 84,200	West Covina	16.0	106,311	289	6,644.4	31.9	4.4	0.6	33.4	0.2	24.9	4.5
06 84,410	West Hollywood	1.9	36,854	1,040	19,396.8	78.0	5.2	0.0	7.5	0.0	6.7	2.7
06 84,550	Westminster	10.0	90,938	363	9,093.8	37.8	1.0	1.0	50.9	0.3	5.2	3.8
06 84,816	West Sacramento	21.5	53,727	720	2,498.9	65.1	4.7	0.2	13.5	1.9	6.4	8.2
06 85,292	Whittier..........................	14.6	86,064	386	5,894.8	48.1	1.2	0.6	5.0	0.0	40.9	4.3
06 85,446	Wildomar.........................	23.7	37,280	1,030	1,573.0	65.2	0.5	1.0	3.6	3.7	22.4	3.6
06 85,922	Windsor..........................	7.3	27,849	1,325	3,814.9	72.1	1.1	2.0	2.8	0.0	15.9	6.2
06 86,328	Woodland.........................	15.3	60,531	616	3,956.3	74.8	2.5	0.7	6.4	0.1	9.6	5.9
06 86,832	Yorba Linda......................	19.8	67,787	535	3,423.6	74.0	1.1	0.0	20.7	0.2	0.5	3.5
06 86,972	Yuba City........................	14.9	66,992	545	4,496.1	62.6	3.2	1.7	20.8	0.9	4.4	6.4
06 87,042	Yucaipa	28.3	53,682	721	1,896.9	NA	NA	NA	NA	NA	NA	NA
08 00,000	**COLORADO**	103,638.7	5,695,564	X	55.0	84.2	4.1	1.0	3.2	0.1	3.9	3.5
08 03,455	Arvada...........................	38.8	120,492	236	3,105.5	91.8	1.0	0.6	2.4	0.0	1.7	2.7
08 04,000	Aurora	153.5	374,114	54	2,437.2	62.1	15.9	0.8	7.8	0.3	8.2	4.8
08 07,850	Boulder	26.3	107,353	283	4,081.9	87.6	1.3	0.1	5.1	0.0	1.3	4.5
08 08,675	Brighton..........................	21.2	41,254	927	1,945.9	88.5	2.0	1.0	3.2	0.1	2.7	2.5
08 09,280	Broomfield	33.0	69,267	518	2,099.0	85.8	1.5	0.5	6.7	0.0	0.8	4.7

1. Dry land or land partially or temporarily covered by water.   2. Hispanic or Latino persons may be of any race.

Table D. Cities — **Population**

City	Percent Hispanic or Latino[1], 2017	Percent foreign born, 2017	Under 18 years	18 to 24 years	25 to 34 years	35 to 44 years	45 to 54 years	55 to 64 years	65 years and over	Median age, 2017	Percent female, 2017	Census counts 2000	Census counts 2010	Percent change 2000-2010	Percent change 2001-2018
	12	13	14	15	16	17	18	19	20	21	22	23	24	25	26
CALIFORNIA— Cont'd															
San Francisco	15.2	35.6	13.4	7.2	23.5	15.7	13.4	11.5	15.4	38.3	49.1	776,733	805,184	3.7	9.7
San Gabriel	23.8	54.3	15.7	10.1	17.8	12.7	14.0	13.6	16.1	39.6	51.5	39,804	39,644	-0.4	1.7
San Jacinto	54.5	22.8	31.1	11.5	9.7	13.0	13.2	11.2	10.2	33.4	54.7	23,779	44,224	86.0	10.5
San Jose	32.1	40.3	22.1	8.8	16.2	14.6	13.7	11.9	12.8	36.8	49.5	894,943	952,060	6.4	8.2
San Juan Capistrano	37.4	26.2	17.9	7.1	9.9	9.4	19.2	12.0	24.5	48.2	54.4	33,826	34,426	1.8	4.6
San Leandro	21.8	39.9	17.8	6.6	13.7	14.0	11.3	16.7	19.9	43.5	53.7	79,452	84,967	6.9	5.6
San Luis Obispo	20.5	8.3	10.4	34.0	14.4	9.4	10.0	8.6	13.2	28.5	49.3	44,174	45,164	2.2	5.1
San Marcos	45.0	26.4	26.1	8.9	14.8	15.9	12.0	8.9	13.3	35.3	50.5	54,977	83,642	52.1	15.8
San Mateo	25.6	32.7	22.6	7.0	14.6	16.7	13.1	10.0	16.0	38.7	50.5	92,482	97,207	5.1	8.0
San Pablo	59.9	48.6	17.9	12.2	16.6	17.0	13.6	11.5	11.2	37.0	49.8	30,215	29,512	-2.3	5.5
San Rafael	27.0	26.4	23.7	6.5	10.2	13.8	16.2	8.6	20.9	41.8	49.1	56,063	57,696	2.9	1.7
San Ramon	5.6	34.6	29.9	5.9	9.6	18.2	16.4	10.4	9.6	38.8	51.2	44,722	71,423	59.7	6.2
Santa Ana	76.5	43.6	26.4	10.7	17.3	13.7	13.1	10.4	8.3	32.0	49.0	337,977	324,778	-3.9	2.4
Santa Barbara	31.9	18.5	14.1	12.3	18.4	12.1	11.3	13.2	18.7	39.1	48.9	92,325	88,380	-4.3	3.4
Santa Clara	15.8	44.8	19.1	11.4	20.7	15.4	11.8	8.7	12.9	34.3	47.8	102,361	116,497	13.8	11.2
Santa Clarita	31.7	20.8	25.1	9.1	13.7	12.2	14.9	13.1	11.9	37.0	50.8	151,088	204,142	35.1	2.9
Santa Cruz	20.6	19.4	11.4	28.9	13.9	9.9	11.4	12.1	12.4	30.9	51.1	54,593	59,943	9.8	8.0
Santa Maria	75.7	35.1	30.2	13.0	12.5	13.0	12.2	9.5	9.5	30.0	52.5	77,423	99,595	28.6	7.8
Santa Monica	14.7	26.5	15.3	7.8	18.1	15.1	11.6	11.9	20.3	41.1	52.4	84,084	89,742	6.7	1.9
Santa Paula	81.7	28.0	25.4	9.9	14.8	13.6	13.6	10.2	12.4	34.9	48.3	28,598	29,272	2.4	2.5
Santa Rosa	32.5	21.2	21.1	8.2	15.7	12.8	11.6	13.0	17.5	38.5	52.9	147,595	175,082	18.6	1.4
Santee	20.4	10.0	20.3	8.9	13.7	11.2	14.9	16.3	14.8	42.8	54.8	52,975	53,420	0.8	8.8
Saratoga	1.9	41.5	22.2	4.1	7.0	10.5	18.8	18.2	19.3	49.0	49.8	29,843	29,993	0.5	2.0
Seaside	41.5	28.5	19.7	11.8	18.7	11.2	16.3	12.2	10.2	34.5	49.1	31,696	33,025	4.2	2.7
Simi Valley	25.9	19.0	22.6	8.2	13.7	12.1	15.7	12.6	15.0	39.7	50.5	111,351	124,243	11.6	1.3
Soledad	79.0	37.4	24.4	10.1	14.0	18.4	17.4	11.2	4.6	35.8	32.3	11,263	25,738	128.5	1.1
South Gate	95.0	41.6	27.3	11.2	15.7	13.7	12.2	9.5	10.3	31.6	51.3	96,375	94,412	-2.0	0.0
South Pasadena	21.9	26.7	22.4	6.4	16.9	13.3	15.4	13.6	11.9	38.7	49.4	24,292	25,601	5.4	0.0
South San Francisco	31.2	41.5	20.6	7.4	14.3	13.9	13.1	14.2	16.6	40.7	52.2	60,552	63,660	5.1	6.4
Stanton	49.8	44.7	29.4	8.8	16.9	13.5	11.6	8.3	11.4	33.1	51.1	37,403	37,827	1.1	1.1
Stockton	43.1	25.8	27.1	10.9	14.9	12.9	11.6	10.9	11.7	32.9	52.4	243,771	291,731	19.7	6.7
Suisun City	22.6	31.1	21.3	11.1	18.9	10.8	11.3	14.3	12.3	34.1	50.2	26,118	28,057	7.4	5.9
Sunnyvale	15.6	48.6	19.8	6.2	22.5	15.6	13.0	10.9	12.0	36.1	48.1	131,760	140,060	6.3	9.4
Temecula	31.2	14.9	28.2	8.1	13.9	13.4	14.5	10.2	11.7	34.9	50.3	57,716	100,020	73.3	14.7
Temple City	23.8	50.1	23.1	6.8	11.0	12.1	16.4	12.1	18.4	42.0	47.4	33,377	35,550	6.5	1.6
Thousand Oaks	17.2	15.4	22.4	8.4	9.7	11.4	15.4	13.3	19.5	43.6	52.6	117,005	126,481	8.1	1.0
Torrance	18.6	32.9	20.4	5.7	13.9	12.8	14.9	13.9	18.3	42.9	51.4	137,946	145,173	5.2	0.0
Tracy	38.2	27.0	28.4	9.8	12.5	14.4	15.5	10.1	9.2	34.4	48.8	56,929	83,406	46.5	10.1
Tulare	65.3	18.5	35.3	10.1	17.6	9.4	10.2	8.3	9.0	27.8	50.3	43,994	59,296	34.8	8.7
Turlock	39.3	22.7	24.7	11.2	15.1	13.2	12.4	9.7	13.7	34.5	50.9	55,810	68,621	23.0	7.1
Tustin	36.0	32.5	24.9	7.5	16.0	14.4	15.7	10.5	11.0	35.9	52.1	67,504	75,317	11.6	5.9
Twentynine Palms	22.4	8.7	28.7	26.7	18.6	10.3	3.6	6.9	5.1	23.3	42.7	14,764	25,048	69.7	5.5
Union City	18.3	48.2	16.1	7.9	18.3	13.6	15.0	14.5	14.6	40.9	48.6	66,869	69,533	4.0	7.2
Upland	51.8	16.2	21.9	10.6	15.9	8.6	14.4	14.1	14.5	38.1	51.7	68,393	73,718	7.8	4.5
Vacaville	28.9	12.9	19.4	9.4	16.0	11.1	14.3	14.7	15.0	39.7	49.9	88,625	92,422	4.3	8.4
Vallejo	28.0	25.5	22.4	9.3	15.4	12.4	12.1	13.5	14.9	36.5	52.2	116,760	115,897	-0.7	5.2
Victorville	58.6	20.9	28.8	9.7	14.8	13.4	12.6	10.1	10.5	33.3	50.5	64,029	115,899	81.0	5.5
Visalia	53.7	13.5	29.7	10.4	15.1	12.9	10.3	10.8	10.8	31.2	53.4	91,565	124,520	36.0	7.5
Vista	52.4	26.3	25.3	10.2	15.3	15.6	13.4	9.6	10.5	34.4	48.5	89,857	93,349	3.9	8.4
Walnut	19.8	47.6	19.1	7.8	15.2	10.5	13.0	19.7	14.7	42.9	51.4	30,004	29,177	-2.8	2.8
Walnut Creek	10.5	23.0	18.6	4.0	11.7	11.8	12.4	13.5	27.9	48.2	52.9	64,296	64,165	-0.2	8.8
Wasco	79.2	31.8	21.1	13.8	23.2	15.2	6.7	12.8	7.1	30.2	40.1	21,263	25,552	20.2	9.5
Watsonville	83.4	41.4	29.1	12.6	15.8	12.1	11.8	9.1	9.4	30.5	47.9	44,265	51,204	15.7	5.3
West Covina	52.2	38.6	21.2	8.7	17.0	12.7	12.7	12.1	15.5	37.0	50.3	105,080	106,108	1.0	0.2
West Hollywood	15.3	28.7	3.5	4.5	30.1	18.8	15.7	15.0	12.4	40.4	42.2	35,716	34,393	-3.7	7.2
Westminster	24.2	46.1	19.4	7.9	14.3	12.9	17.0	12.0	16.5	42.0	53.1	88,207	89,613	1.6	1.5
West Sacramento	21.8	32.4	23.1	6.8	16.5	15.3	11.2	11.6	15.5	36.6	51.9	31,615	48,744	54.2	10.2
Whittier	66.7	14.8	25.0	9.7	14.2	13.4	13.2	10.5	13.9	35.4	51.8	83,680	85,313	2.0	0.9
Wildomar	45.5	17.2	25.4	12.1	14.0	12.8	11.1	11.0	13.8	34.0	48.2	14,064	32,210	129.0	15.7
Windsor	30.2	13.1	22.3	11.2	7.5	14.4	12.3	17.1	15.2	41.7	51.0	22,744	26,795	17.8	3.9
Woodland	53.7	22.9	26.1	10.0	14.7	14.5	12.6	10.9	11.1	34.6	48.1	49,151	55,553	13.0	9.0
Yorba Linda	14.4	17.8	21.8	8.3	8.7	11.9	13.5	18.0	17.9	44.6	51.2	58,918	64,169	8.9	5.6
Yuba City	30.3	25.2	25.7	8.3	17.5	10.4	12.1	11.6	14.5	34.5	49.1	36,758	65,634	78.6	2.1
Yucaipa	44.4	14.4	24.3	11.1	14.9	9.7	13.0	13.0	14.0	34.5	51.3	41,207	51,347	24.6	4.5
COLORADO	21.5	9.8	22.5	9.3	15.5	13.6	12.7	12.6	13.8	36.8	49.7	4,301,261	5,029,316	16.9	13.2
Arvada	15.7	5.6	21.0	6.6	15.1	13.7	13.0	14.5	16.1	39.8	50.7	102,153	106,722	4.5	12.9
Aurora	27.6	22.9	25.2	8.9	16.9	14.6	12.4	11.0	11.0	34.4	50.5	276,393	324,675	17.5	15.2
Boulder	10.1	10.7	14.2	30.9	16.6	10.7	9.0	8.4	10.2	27.2	48.7	94,673	97,640	3.1	9.9
Brighton	42.4	9.9	25.9	8.1	19.0	14.1	12.0	10.2	10.7	32.4	47.0	20,905	33,845	61.9	21.9
Broomfield	12.4	9.1	23.5	7.5	14.6	14.6	15.1	11.7	12.9	38.4	50.0	38,272	55,856	45.9	24.0

1. May be of any race.

Table D. Cities — Households, Group Quarters, Crime, and Education

City	Households, 2017							Persons in group quarters, 2017	Serious crimes known to police[2], 2016				Educational attainment, 2017		
			Percent						Total		Rate[3]			Attainment[4] (percent)	
	Number	Persons per household	Family	Married couple family	Female headed[1]	Non-family	One person		Number	Rate	Violent	Property	Population age 25 and over	High school graduate or less	Bachelor's degree or more
	27	28	29	30	31	32	33	34	35	36	37	38	39	40	41

City	27	28	29	30	31	32	33	34	35	36	37	38	39	40	41
CALIFORNIA— Cont'd															
San Francisco	360,323	2.40	47.6	36.0	8.4	52.4	36.4	20,312	53,592	6,152	711	5,441	702,525	23.3	57.8
San Gabriel	11,929	3.34	78.2	45.2	17.8	21.8	17.1	720	753	1,856	241	1,614	30,053	51.5	32.7
San Jacinto	12,864	3.73	78.8	51.6	17.8	21.2	16.3	222	1,801	3,794	270	3,524	27,670	59.4	8.7
San Jose	321,913	3.17	73.2	54.7	12.0	26.8	18.9	14,714	28,636	2,749	373	2,375	715,929	32.5	43.4
San Juan Capistrano	14,296	2.51	63.4	53.4	6.1	36.6	32.4	NA	523	1,421	236	1,185	27,049	39.1	34.4
San Leandro	33,458	2.69	63.1	42.0	15.7	36.9	27.5	519	4,017	4,372	530	3,842	68,463	41.0	32.6
San Luis Obispo	18,260	2.53	38.5	28.6	6.2	61.5	31.5	1,404	2,254	4,718	373	4,345	26,456	22.8	48.3
San Marcos	29,611	3.22	73.5	55.7	11.6	26.5	18.6	971	1,342	1,415	208	1,207	62,531	36.7	35.8
San Mateo	39,660	2.60	63.0	50.3	9.1	37.0	29.6	1,517	2,383	2,274	231	2,043	73,762	22.9	55.6
San Pablo	9,633	3.18	72.8	42.0	12.5	27.2	20.9	519	1,427	4,652	694	3,958	21,777	55.7	14.6
San Rafael	24,038	2.37	57.2	42.6	10.8	42.8	33.4	2,087	1,962	3,301	419	2,882	41,216	19.4	54.2
San Ramon	24,317	3.12	81.1	70.4	8.3	18.9	16.0	121	862	1,121	51	1,070	48,746	9.9	73.9
Santa Ana	76,650	4.31	79.5	53.3	16.4	20.5	12.7	3,420	8,592	2,546	478	2,069	210,242	64.0	14.3
Santa Barbara	40,145	2.26	45.2	34.6	7.1	54.8	37.8	1,373	3,457	3,737	429	3,307	67,809	22.1	54.4
Santa Clara	43,159	2.83	69.5	54.8	9.5	30.5	20.0	4,888	2,973	2,319	124	2,195	88,352	22.1	56.5
Santa Clarita	67,564	3.09	73.8	56.6	10.7	26.2	20.8	1,982	3,336	1,519	151	1,368	138,852	25.3	36.6
Santa Cruz	23,585	2.32	47.1	37.0	5.5	52.9	35.1	10,234	4,131	6,358	802	5,556	38,803	21.6	53.6
Santa Maria	27,968	3.79	77.6	51.6	17.7	22.4	16.8	1,092	3,144	2,960	476	2,484	60,749	60.9	10.7
Santa Monica	45,258	2.00	42.4	32.4	7.2	57.6	46.5	1,571	4,514	4,806	506	4,300	70,976	15.1	66.1
Santa Paula	8,696	3.47	82.4	55.0	18.3	17.6	13.0	NA	423	1,374	260	1,114	19,611	61.9	12.2
Santa Rosa	64,155	2.68	61.2	46.0	10.7	38.8	31.7	3,096	3,668	2,080	373	1,707	123,920	29.3	35.2
Santee	19,356	2.91	74.0	50.8	17.0	26.0	19.3	1,824	1,027	1,751	191	1,560	41,138	33.7	28.5
Saratoga	11,497	2.67	77.9	69.2	6.5	22.1	20.4	225	314	1,008	90	918	22,784	9.0	79.9
Seaside	10,081	3.25	71.6	56.8	10.0	28.4	23.7	1,330	735	2,110	368	1,743	23,399	42.4	26.2
Simi Valley	40,822	3.09	72.7	55.7	11.3	27.3	19.8	875	1,740	1,367	137	1,231	87,792	30.0	33.5
Soledad	3,555	4.93	90.9	72.8	15.3	9.1	9.1	8,749	288	1,161	306	855	17,203	69.2	5.2
South Gate	24,019	3.97	83.9	48.1	19.2	16.1	12.5	NA	4,095	4,231	682	3,549	58,687	68.9	9.3
South Pasadena	10,045	2.57	65.6	49.3	9.9	34.4	25.9	NA	694	2,643	103	2,540	18,408	9.9	67.9
South San Francisco	20,939	3.18	75.3	54.8	15.8	24.7	19.7	807	1,565	2,302	219	2,083	48,559	33.1	36.0
Stanton	10,401	3.68	83.3	59.1	18.3	16.7	13.3	265	865	2,214	335	1,879	23,803	50.8	22.9
Stockton	91,392	3.33	72.2	48.1	16.4	27.8	23.6	6,582	16,015	5,194	1,421	3,773	192,375	52.2	18.5
Suisun City	8,888	3.32	82.2	64.4	13.1	17.8	11.7	NA	734	2,466	269	2,197	20,026	39.3	24.3
Sunnyvale	55,024	2.77	69.2	57.8	6.7	30.8	20.2	971	2,298	1,491	103	1,389	113,723	20.9	61.6
Temecula	34,277	3.33	81.1	65.1	13.3	18.9	15.8	58	2,732	2,389	127	2,262	72,785	26.8	34.4
Temple City	11,294	3.18	76.0	56.3	10.7	24.0	19.0	NA	629	1,722	134	1,588	25,470	28.0	40.6
Thousand Oaks	46,017	2.76	68.4	59.8	7.6	31.6	24.3	1,854	1,850	1,425	126	1,298	89,298	17.4	51.6
Torrance	54,327	2.67	70.9	56.2	8.6	29.1	24.2	1,494	3,479	2,334	173	2,161	108,446	22.4	51.1
Tracy	25,830	3.51	79.9	59.1	13.8	20.1	14.2	251	2,050	2,334	172	2,162	56,108	40.5	21.9
Tulare	18,153	3.50	79.9	53.9	19.8	20.1	14.2	391	1,988	3,160	356	2,804	34,842	59.2	9.3
Turlock	25,562	2.85	71.4	52.6	13.4	28.6	21.0	589	2,887	3,953	526	3,427	47,195	43.7	26.1
Tustin	27,780	2.86	67.0	48.5	13.6	33.0	24.1	1,008	1,926	2,359	147	2,212	54,414	29.3	45.5
Twentynine Palms	7,547	3.04	76.0	55.6	9.5	24.0	17.9	3,577	456	1,740	351	1,389	11,826	42.0	18.0
Union City	22,684	3.29	81.4	65.0	12.6	18.6	14.2	807	2,178	2,885	372	2,513	57,268	37.4	33.5
Upland	25,582	2.98	74.9	49.4	16.5	25.1	17.5	638	2,544	3,306	316	2,990	51,984	28.9	34.8
Vacaville	34,017	2.74	68.6	50.8	13.5	31.4	24.0	6,851	2,264	2,318	212	2,106	71,220	35.6	22.2
Vallejo	41,719	2.89	66.6	41.9	17.4	33.4	28.3	1,545	5,863	4,794	861	3,933	83,302	37.2	27.1
Victorville	35,088	3.38	72.2	43.9	21.4	27.8	21.2	3,871	4,276	3,464	606	2,858	75,272	51.1	11.1
Visalia	43,785	3.00	71.2	48.5	15.8	28.8	24.4	1,472	4,676	3,564	366	3,199	79,653	35.5	23.8
Vista	31,618	3.15	74.2	54.4	16.0	25.8	20.3	2,046	1,987	1,942	364	1,579	65,517	48.4	21.9
Walnut	9,094	3.32	85.5	72.2	11.4	14.5	11.8	NA	541	1,777	82	1,695	22,071	22.4	53.3
Walnut Creek	31,648	2.18	55.4	49.6	4.4	44.6	36.7	845	2,198	3,146	112	3,035	53,990	8.9	68.6
Wasco	6,111	3.53	84.9	66.3	14.5	15.1	13.8	5,434	NA	NA	NA	NA	17,589	75.4	3.6
Watsonville	14,374	3.74	77.1	55.6	15.1	22.9	21.1	339	1,976	3,652	440	3,212	31,516	68.0	9.5
West Covina	29,807	3.58	79.8	57.5	14.4	20.2	13.9	976	3,076	2,823	243	2,580	75,381	38.8	31.8
West Hollywood	23,725	1.56	28.3	22.2	3.8	71.7	56.1	NA	1,876	5,127	751	4,375	34,119	18.9	58.8
Westminster	28,876	3.16	74.8	52.0	15.8	25.2	22.4	313	3,029	3,272	334	2,938	66,544	42.3	28.7
West Sacramento	19,351	2.74	64.1	45.4	13.4	35.9	29.0	NA	1,452	2,712	435	2,277	37,523	37.1	25.5
Whittier	26,722	3.19	72.6	50.3	13.1	27.4	20.2	1,668	3,048	3,469	294	3,176	56,753	42.0	25.2
Wildomar	9,562	3.85	84.8	62.3	13.4	15.2	13.8	NA	704	1,939	135	1,804	23,111	46.4	19.0
Windsor	9,153	2.99	72.6	59.6	7.7	27.4	18.8	NA	395	1,431	304	1,127	18,308	35.6	30.0
Woodland	20,960	2.81	68.6	52.2	11.9	31.4	24.5	1,117	1,740	2,940	368	2,571	38,315	43.2	25.4
Yorba Linda	22,410	3.03	85.0	74.4	7.6	15.0	12.2	248	766	1,115	60	1,055	47,711	19.8	53.7
Yuba City	22,172	2.97	64.8	48.8	10.9	35.2	27.4	919	2,302	3,426	405	3,021	44,141	44.9	17.5
Yucaipa	15,993	3.32	74.5	50.8	12.4	25.5	22.3	599	1,275	2,374	210	2,164	34,666	40.8	22.8
COLORADO	2,139,207	2.57	63.9	49.7	9.5	36.1	27.1	119,289	170,833	3,083	343	2,741	3,822,068	29.7	41.2
Arvada	47,083	2.50	67.9	54.2	8.9	32.1	25.5	550	3,108	2,652	173	2,479	85,655	30.8	41.1
Aurora	128,100	2.85	66.5	44.8	13.9	33.5	25.4	2,354	13,186	3,598	532	3,066	241,793	40.1	30.3
Boulder	42,177	2.27	41.6	32.3	5.6	58.4	31.8	11,179	3,436	3,147	238	2,909	58,799	7.6	78.2
Brighton	12,595	3.05	72.8	55.5	14.4	27.2	19.7	1,782	1,481	3,860	375	3,485	26,521	50.8	19.4
Broomfield	27,665	2.46	64.3	52.9	8.1	35.7	25.0	291	1,647	2,460	51	2,409	47,160	19.2	55.1

1. No spouse present. 2. Data for serious crimes have not been adjusted for underreporting. This may affect comparability between geographic areas and over time. 3. Per 100,000 population estimated by the FBI. 4. Persons 25 years old and over.

Table D. Cities — Income and Housing

City	Money income, 2017 — Median income	Households — Percent with income less than $20,000	Percent with income of $200,000 or more	Median family income	Median non-family income	Median earnings, 2017 — All persons	Men	Women	Housing units, 2017 — Total	Occupied	Percent owner occupied	Median value[1] (dollars)	Median gross rent (dollars)
	42	43	44	45	46	47	48	49	50	51	52	53	54
CALIFORNIA— Cont'd													
San Francisco	110,816	12.4	25.6	131,244	89,046	60,093	65,125	52,304	397,566	360,323	36.5	1,104,100	1,836
San Gabriel	56,859	11.8	7.0	57,563	22,368	32,178	36,165	29,176	13,130	11,929	40.0	695,200	1,366
San Jacinto	50,748	20.0	0.0	52,188	0	26,160	36,304	21,197	13,962	12,864	63.5	242,200	1,243
San Jose	104,675	8.9	21.4	119,331	65,579	45,345	52,863	36,446	338,738	321,913	57.4	854,700	2,109
San Juan Capistrano	83,388	9.8	17.5	100,213	51,608	38,954	34,811	40,360	15,490	14,296	70.3	693,900	2,224
San Leandro	64,923	13.7	8.6	85,798	37,494	41,884	46,708	37,375	34,430	33,458	56.5	597,000	1,591
San Luis Obispo	60,239	19.1	7.1	105,203	39,495	26,457	28,670	21,649	20,529	18,260	41.3	628,200	1,456
San Marcos	76,272	8.6	11.6	87,369	32,037	34,583	39,134	30,433	30,321	29,611	64.8	525,200	1,523
San Mateo	108,058	8.4	25.9	130,818	75,920	63,223	73,427	52,001	42,198	39,660	52.4	1,093,900	2,480
San Pablo	56,392	18.2	2.6	60,430	32,797	27,085	31,167	21,542	10,108	9,633	44.7	369,700	1,465
San Rafael	99,278	10.5	25.2	135,239	59,586	53,711	65,246	40,726	24,982	24,038	49.4	947,300	1,986
San Ramon	161,870	5.8	40.4	184,424	106,875	90,195	117,013	70,155	25,334	24,317	73.3	957,800	2,296
Santa Ana	65,655	8.8	4.4	64,156	49,661	26,043	28,295	22,109	79,680	76,650	46.0	494,700	1,496
Santa Barbara	79,740	13.6	15.3	106,272	66,104	41,297	46,538	38,235	42,769	40,145	41.7	1,037,400	1,751
Santa Clara	115,375	7.4	22.6	122,267	79,883	56,049	72,239	35,147	45,265	43,159	42.7	1,001,100	2,298
Santa Clarita	90,961	6.9	12.4	110,916	51,965	42,273	52,302	35,172	68,912	67,564	66.7	536,700	1,825
Santa Cruz	71,442	22.1	16.3	106,214	47,896	28,145	30,785	23,214	25,827	23,585	46.1	860,600	1,780
Santa Maria	60,320	11.1	2.0	60,903	36,068	25,116	29,384	21,862	28,574	27,968	50.3	350,200	1,331
Santa Monica	90,088	14.8	18.9	113,903	65,344	57,705	71,495	45,471	49,919	45,258	29.9	1,237,500	1,743
Santa Paula	62,594	11.1	2.3	64,068	47,584	26,647	32,177	18,301	9,156	8,696	55.5	411,400	1,208
Santa Rosa	75,356	10.8	8.0	94,000	44,339	36,108	40,032	31,247	68,100	64,155	55.0	568,200	1,540
Santee	90,271	6.4	6.2	97,879	51,073	40,521	48,702	31,170	19,967	19,356	69.8	447,500	1,805
Saratoga	186,851	8.6	47.3	228,438	100,568	110,932	136,038	72,454	11,571	11,497	81.7	2,000,000	0
Seaside	81,575	9.5	3.0	94,482	39,651	31,078	36,679	22,017	10,921	10,081	45.7	495,500	1,780
Simi Valley	90,200	7.5	11.5	100,335	60,857	42,782	51,507	33,010	41,959	40,822	69.2	602,800	1,944
Soledad	56,542	5.6	3.6	57,624	29,632	19,582	20,043	18,951	3,982	3,555	64.1	380,400	1,553
South Gate	50,355	16.5	1.8	50,455	32,353	22,806	26,751	18,260	24,605	24,019	42.9	420,800	1,111
South Pasadena	99,895	5.6	24.1	129,605	72,923	61,648	72,373	55,969	11,197	10,045	50.7	1,087,100	1,691
South San Francisco	94,459	9.6	16.4	110,556	52,068	40,670	41,130	40,342	21,953	20,939	56.5	873,000	1,974
Stanton	56,413	13.3	2.6	53,421	61,926	26,957	34,258	21,132	10,613	10,401	40.8	366,800	1,484
Stockton	51,336	18.1	4.5	58,014	30,195	28,693	31,713	23,499	100,823	91,392	50.3	282,000	1,059
Suisun City	76,938	8.6	4.2	83,335	51,438	36,701	41,147	31,791	9,015	8,888	61.7	364,800	1,668
Sunnyvale	134,234	7.1	29.9	143,306	100,672	67,670	83,176	55,370	58,590	55,024	46.6	1,220,900	2,390
Temecula	89,173	7.8	11.9	102,115	56,078	41,052	52,142	33,141	36,409	34,277	63.3	457,300	1,868
Temple City	80,695	11.1	13.4	96,997	48,722	49,990	55,745	42,216	12,645	11,294	60.3	715,900	1,462
Thousand Oaks	100,338	7.9	22.2	125,909	51,835	50,174	62,006	36,574	48,242	46,017	71.4	728,700	2,007
Torrance	88,860	9.6	12.6	103,546	50,923	47,588	53,655	40,204	57,351	54,327	56.6	760,300	1,672
Tracy	89,936	10.1	9.8	99,229	47,292	42,909	51,657	35,214	26,940	25,830	63.2	456,100	1,726
Tulare	51,940	15.1	3.5	53,379	37,086	31,312	35,785	25,424	19,958	18,153	51.4	210,800	1,034
Turlock	59,836	17.0	5.0	66,488	33,811	29,678	32,698	23,612	26,507	25,562	53.4	305,100	1,121
Tustin	81,285	9.7	11.7	94,805	66,215	41,331	50,305	31,869	29,154	27,780	46.9	668,500	1,883
Twentynine Palms	47,355	12.7	0.4	46,091	31,434	25,549	28,412	18,997	8,523	7,547	29.8	116,100	856
Union City	117,526	3.9	18.8	129,914	76,256	49,170	55,782	41,617	23,985	22,684	65.8	805,100	2,050
Upland	70,760	8.8	7.9	78,304	53,740	35,554	42,158	26,854	26,210	25,582	56.2	495,700	1,382
Vacaville	80,425	9.1	7.5	95,070	45,280	38,168	51,426	29,185	35,140	34,017	57.8	426,400	1,586
Vallejo	65,493	13.2	6.9	78,535	38,701	35,628	41,055	27,660	44,225	41,719	55.1	373,100	1,404
Victorville	50,997	14.5	2.2	60,652	40,898	26,805	40,558	18,534	37,487	35,088	55.6	221,500	1,151
Visalia	64,482	13.0	6.1	74,073	36,793	34,574	36,504	31,566	46,059	43,785	60.3	233,900	967
Vista	68,130	9.3	4.9	71,384	46,127	30,692	32,110	26,449	32,796	31,618	52.3	478,000	1,605
Walnut	94,667	8.1	14.0	109,443	27,224	37,196	46,489	30,848	9,409	9,094	83.8	776,000	2,210
Walnut Creek	100,180	9.6	24.1	144,258	57,778	71,874	101,619	47,454	33,990	31,648	65.9	814,600	2,110
Wasco	32,526	19.0	0.0	35,369	0	21,634	25,184	15,991	6,770	6,111	68.5	154,500	673
Watsonville	58,420	13.2	4.5	62,937	26,011	25,123	26,654	22,052	14,730	14,374	48.3	450,100	1,384
West Covina	81,170	10.5	8.6	89,494	33,906	36,833	38,152	36,008	31,146	29,807	62.7	559,200	1,629
West Hollywood	67,956	15.7	12.4	104,051	62,951	52,099	58,381	50,077	26,582	23,725	20.5	897,800	1,634
Westminster	57,938	18.7	6.5	68,369	25,964	30,231	35,302	25,876	29,785	28,876	51.6	600,100	1,601
West Sacramento	60,912	22.7	9.6	80,105	28,080	31,632	38,481	27,209	20,379	19,351	53.2	391,000	915
Whittier	66,525	15.4	7.0	74,883	36,669	38,516	40,633	36,835	27,693	26,722	59.2	581,300	1,329
Wildomar	81,805	7.8	10.5	94,888	39,673	32,172	40,601	24,560	9,752	9,562	76.0	360,200	1,445
Windsor	114,278	8.6	13.4	120,551	63,420	38,031	49,887	26,681	9,662	9,153	73.1	610,200	1,733
Woodland	60,221	11.7	2.4	71,362	50,724	34,162	37,493	30,189	21,838	20,960	49.0	358,200	1,082
Yorba Linda	132,952	2.7	29.6	153,087	51,772	63,699	75,825	53,842	23,237	22,410	82.5	913,700	2,275
Yuba City	51,497	16.0	2.7	61,225	38,719	30,668	35,900	21,232	23,765	22,172	55.7	274,800	1,014
Yucaipa	62,978	11.1	8.9	75,568	29,423	36,308	46,203	25,807	16,903	15,993	68.5	351,700	1,045
COLORADO	69,117	11.8	7.8	84,918	44,139	36,804	42,277	31,268	2,385,495	2,139,207	65.2	348,900	1,240
Arvada	81,787	8.2	8.1	99,434	47,886	42,388	52,906	34,186	48,629	47,083	76.1	382,700	1,243
Aurora	63,055	9.4	4.8	74,160	42,286	33,952	36,944	30,693	134,175	128,100	60.6	299,600	1,321
Boulder	66,524	16.6	12.6	115,513	43,069	25,946	30,310	22,099	45,026	42,177	45.4	694,900	1,542
Brighton	75,306	12.3	6.7	79,902	44,987	39,311	41,495	35,806	13,075	12,595	71.8	327,800	1,144
Broomfield	90,939	8.0	12.5	120,435	53,735	47,996	56,788	41,271	28,534	27,665	67.1	416,600	1,565

1. Based on population estimated by the American Community Survey.   2. Includes units rented or sold but not occupied.   3. Specified owner-occupied units; $1,000,000 represents $1,000,000 or more.   4. 50.0 represents 50 percent or more.   5. 10.0 represents 10 percent or less.

Table D. Cities — Commuting, Computer Access, Migration, Labor Force, and Employment

City	Commuting[1], 2017 Commuting	Commuting[1], 2017 Percent With commutes of 30 minutes or more	Computer access[2], 2017 Percent With a computer in the house	Computer access[2], 2017 Percent With Internet access	Migration, 2017 Percent who lived in the same house one year ago	Migration, 2017 Percent who lived in another state or county one year ago	Civilian labor force, 2018 Total	Civilian labor force, 2018 Percent change 2017-2018	Civilian labor force, 2018 Unemployment Total	Civilian labor force, 2018 Unemployment Rate[3]	Civilian employment[4], 2017 Population age 16 and older Number	Civilian employment[4], 2017 Population age 16 and older Percent in labor force	Civilian employment[4], 2017 Population age 16 to 64 Number	Civilian employment[4], 2017 Population age 16 to 64 Percent who worked full-year full-time
	55	56	57	58	59	60	61	62	63	64	65	66	67	68
CALIFORNIA— Cont'd														
San Francisco	32.4	57.4	93.1	87.6	85.2	7.9	575,567	2.0	13,545	2.4	777,887	71.5	641,662	57.2
San Gabriel	71.3	49.8	91.1	81.1	93.2	3.6	21,592	0.6	801	3.7	35,430	60.8	28,915	51.0
San Jacinto	76.4	54.4	95.9	87.0	82.9	2.2	18,774	1.6	981	5.2	35,381	54.7	30,465	33.2
San Jose	75.4	51.2	95.5	91.2	85.8	4.7	555,419	0.8	15,076	2.7	832,198	68.5	699,886	54.1
San Juan Capistrano	80.7	27.2	94.5	89.3	NA	NA	17,341	1.2	488	2.8	30,601	56.9	21,774	48.8
San Leandro	63.4	58.8	91.6	87.5	90.0	4.7	47,262	1.0	1,478	3.1	76,019	60.0	57,956	49.4
San Luis Obispo	76.2	12.7	97.5	93.4	72.3	12.1	25,544	0.4	637	2.5	43,163	64.1	36,868	36.6
San Marcos	79.3	35.4	95.6	90.8	88.1	2.6	42,490	1.2	1,336	3.1	73,109	67.0	60,281	52.2
San Mateo	68.5	45.6	94.3	90.8	88.2	5.9	64,485	2.0	1,342	2.1	82,775	69.7	66,001	56.1
San Pablo	62.6	57.2	92.8	88.8	92.9	4.5	14,021	1.0	487	3.5	26,675	62.8	23,183	42.0
San Rafael	65.7	43.4	93.2	84.7	80.2	10.1	32,823	0.8	768	2.3	46,104	64.4	33,760	52.7
San Ramon	68.0	57.1	97.3	96.5	86.9	8.2	40,075	1.1	1,065	2.7	55,887	69.1	48,606	56.5
Santa Ana	71.8	39.3	94.2	88.6	89.6	2.3	158,918	0.9	4,690	3.0	255,193	69.9	227,326	50.0
Santa Barbara	71.0	11.6	93.6	86.9	76.9	7.1	50,510	0.8	1,306	2.6	80,962	73.0	63,780	56.8
Santa Clara	72.6	29.7	97.1	94.3	78.4	9.4	70,227	0.9	1,712	2.4	105,841	65.5	89,451	52.0
Santa Clarita	76.3	54.3	95.3	93.7	86.3	2.9	113,566	1.2	4,933	4.3	163,666	67.6	138,511	50.5
Santa Cruz	61.1	29.3	94.8	89.1	72.8	16.6	33,290	0.0	1,096	3.3	58,731	64.3	50,695	35.0
Santa Maria	71.4	23.6	91.1	87.5	88.5	3.3	49,106	0.4	3,099	6.3	77,619	66.1	67,401	53.2
Santa Monica	63.4	43.8	91.8	88.8	82.8	5.6	57,019	0.9	2,534	4.4	79,835	66.6	61,136	50.8
Santa Paula	85.7	36.9	89.4	84.6	NA	NA	14,038	-0.2	1,059	7.5	23,624	60.6	19,853	40.7
Santa Rosa	76.4	28.6	94.1	89.7	84.9	5.1	89,474	0.7	2,526	2.8	143,101	64.1	112,373	49.6
Santee	87.4	35.8	94.3	90.1	83.0	2.2	29,451	1.3	910	3.1	48,430	67.4	39,850	51.2
Saratoga	72.0	49.5	NA	NA	93.0	2.4	14,973	0.8	412	2.8	24,821	53.3	18,863	47.7
Seaside	78.6	25.0	91.4	88.7	85.1	11.5	17,646	2.2	472	2.7	28,210	70.9	24,743	47.9
Simi Valley	79.2	52.9	93.5	92.1	89.7	2.6	68,155	0.3	2,115	3.1	101,811	65.1	82,717	47.4
Soledad	75.7	26.2	NA	NA	83.8	13.6	8,228	1.5	796	9.7	20,441	33.2	19,243	29.2
South Gate	69.4	54.0	90.5	84.4	90.3	0.9	43,134	0.6	2,114	4.9	73,020	66.2	63,147	44.5
South Pasadena	80.0	54.1	98.5	95.6	NA	NA	15,084	1.0	591	3.9	21,210	72.1	18,134	59.6
South San Francisco	55.3	48.2	92.5	88.4	93.2	4.3	39,204	1.9	914	2.3	54,825	70.6	43,644	58.2
Stanton	78.6	42.7	93.5	88.9	89.5	4.3	18,695	0.9	606	3.2	28,274	66.4	23,868	46.8
Stockton	82.0	33.1	90.6	80.2	87.1	4.7	131,246	0.7	9,034	6.9	235,383	59.5	198,977	43.4
Suisun City	81.1	53.4	94.4	89.6	87.3	5.2	14,409	0.2	519	3.6	24,044	68.6	20,410	48.3
Sunnyvale	72.3	34.1	97.3	92.8	79.6	8.8	87,870	0.9	1,913	2.2	126,174	71.0	107,697	59.8
Temecula	76.1	45.8	98.8	94.7	83.9	6.9	55,360	2.1	1,919	3.5	85,486	66.3	72,144	49.1
Temple City	77.6	48.9	95.5	90.8	93.5	1.5	18,437	0.8	707	3.8	28,990	58.6	22,299	54.6
Thousand Oaks	78.0	33.5	95.2	93.7	89.6	4.0	65,497	0.4	1,979	3.0	103,794	64.2	78,598	50.4
Torrance	83.1	41.1	95.3	90.9	87.6	4.5	79,148	0.8	3,018	3.8	120,616	62.2	93,751	51.7
Tracy	78.1	65.1	99.0	95.6	90.0	5.1	43,603	0.9	1,677	3.8	68,483	66.9	60,107	50.5
Tulare	82.3	27.4	89.4	76.3	81.2	4.0	27,848	0.3	1,674	6.0	43,099	62.3	37,323	50.0
Turlock	82.3	33.8	91.9	86.6	84.5	5.6	33,916	0.7	1,614	4.8	57,835	64.4	47,754	43.6
Tustin	84.0	35.4	96.6	91.8	85.2	4.0	43,193	1.0	1,210	2.8	62,718	71.4	53,870	51.9
Twentynine Palms	71.5	5.5	92.6	86.8	60.2	28.1	7,056	2.0	373	5.3	19,006	74.4	17,653	61.2
Union City	72.3	60.6	96.1	90.1	93.3	2.5	37,636	1.0	1,126	3.0	64,233	67.9	53,201	60.7
Upland	78.0	47.3	93.8	87.0	87.3	8.1	39,646	2.0	1,322	3.3	61,698	65.5	50,544	48.5
Vacaville	81.0	37.6	94.4	92.4	84.1	7.4	46,237	0.7	1,565	3.4	82,887	58.1	67,841	44.7
Vallejo	68.8	54.2	93.8	89.5	85.1	9.8	57,149	0.6	2,508	4.4	97,971	63.7	79,766	44.0
Victorville	79.2	53.6	94.4	86.3	79.3	5.3	46,115	1.5	2,615	5.7	91,095	55.4	78,213	38.0
Visalia	78.3	21.4	94.3	85.8	86.8	4.2	61,549	0.3	3,049	5.0	97,761	65.3	83,365	46.0
Vista	82.7	37.7	96.1	89.0	87.9	3.6	45,358	1.0	1,606	3.5	78,087	69.3	67,428	54.5
Walnut	78.2	53.3	99.0	97.5	89.3	4.1	16,139	0.6	579	3.6	25,416	61.6	20,971	53.1
Walnut Creek	62.2	57.7	95.3	92.0	84.0	10.4	34,725	1.1	976	2.8	58,339	57.2	38,843	58.1
Wasco	85.1	24.7	51.1	47.7	83.1	13.8	8,719	-0.6	1,228	14.1	21,959	44.2	20,030	29.2
Watsonville	73.4	37.2	87.6	77.0	NA	NA	26,247	-1.1	2,740	10.4	39,466	67.6	34,380	43.5
West Covina	84.7	57.6	94.9	88.5	88.5	2.7	53,457	0.8	2,450	4.6	87,202	65.3	70,535	51.2
West Hollywood	68.4	49.5	94.0	89.8	87.2	4.4	27,460	0.7	1,444	5.3	35,890	78.9	31,283	63.2
Westminster	78.3	43.7	89.8	87.7	91.4	1.4	42,307	0.9	1,416	3.3	75,940	61.2	60,818	43.0
West Sacramento	67.1	44.1	91.5	83.0	81.1	11.5	25,684	1.8	1,027	4.0	42,446	63.8	34,167	46.4
Whittier	81.4	62.6	90.2	82.1	90.0	1.7	44,237	0.8	2,008	4.5	67,544	60.0	55,446	53.8
Wildomar	84.9	42.9	95.0	91.3	NA	NA	17,576	1.8	684	3.9	28,997	60.5	23,906	42.1
Windsor	78.4	22.5	92.0	88.7	90.4	4.1	14,218	0.7	382	2.7	22,093	72.8	17,899	50.4
Woodland	79.1	27.6	89.5	84.4	90.6	2.5	30,536	1.5	1,624	5.3	45,858	64.5	39,189	49.2
Yorba Linda	82.6	59.9	97.1	96.1	90.8	3.2	35,317	1.0	962	2.7	55,892	63.4	43,677	48.1
Yuba City	80.4	42.9	88.9	81.9	87.6	4.9	31,508	0.9	2,367	7.5	51,494	54.6	41,820	41.0
Yucaipa	88.1	49.3	95.6	88.8	92.3	2.2	25,248	1.7	857	3.4	41,907	64.2	34,377	49.8
COLORADO	74.9	37.4	94.2	88.0	82.0	9.7	3,096,358	3.5	101,606	3.3	4,488,813	68.2	3,715,114	54.1
Arvada	82.0	44.0	94.8	88.4	86.9	5.8	68,419	3.3	2,070	3.0	95,950	70.4	76,916	60.4
Aurora	76.2	47.3	95.0	88.5	81.7	9.7	196,376	3.4	7,015	3.6	284,965	72.1	244,578	56.7
Boulder	51.6	19.1	97.4	93.5	61.7	19.0	65,513	3.7	1,782	2.7	93,957	65.6	83,020	36.8
Brighton	78.0	63.8	92.6	86.5	81.8	7.9	20,453	3.2	699	3.4	30,834	67.2	26,519	59.1
Broomfield	77.2	45.3	96.2	93.5	80.3	16.8	39,816	3.2	1,165	2.9	53,967	73.4	45,140	61.1

1. Employed persons.　2. Households.　3. Percent of civilian labor force.　4. Persons 16 years old and over.

Table D. Cities — Construction, Wholesale Trade, and Retail Trade

City	Value of residential construction authorized by building permits, 2018			Wholesale trade[1], 2012				Retail trade[2], 2012			
	New construction ($1,000)	Number of housing units	Percent single family	Number of establishments	Number of employees	Sales (mil dol)	Annual payroll (mil dol)	Number of establishments	Number of employees	Sales (mil dol)	Annual payroll (mil dol)
	69	70	71	72	73	74	75	76	77	78	79
CALIFORNIA— Cont'd											
San Francisco	1,001,632	5,178	0.5	1,066	12,056	11,121.7	850.7	3,573	43,378	14,632.7	1,455.0
San Gabriel	4,915	24	100.0	128	479	219.8	15.3	211	1,577	473.4	36.5
San Jacinto	23,361	158	100.0	13	59	27.0	2.1	50	861	214.3	22.6
San Jose	378,860	2,836	8.4	1,023	42,254	49,902.3	5,435.8	2,297	40,525	14,982.0	1,850.7
San Juan Capistrano	23,461	73	58.9	62	339	254.3	19.5	128	1,795	714.4	61.3
San Leandro	160	2	100.0	249	3,095	1,784.4	179.0	305	5,619	4,342.8	158.5
San Luis Obispo	45,461	257	47.5	83	1,001	442.4	42.4	365	4,892	1,390.7	134.8
San Marcos	66,176	256	52.3	133	1,494	606.3	65.6	246	4,005	1,194.8	115.7
San Mateo	15,498	83	9.6	87	839	586.3	61.8	378	6,587	1,817.9	200.3
San Pablo	680	4	100.0	8	30	11.4	1.0	77	947	227.9	22.5
San Rafael	7,751	11	100.0	124	1,151	763.5	73.0	344	5,031	1,757.0	185.3
San Ramon	68,008	160	100.0	98	1,095	2,125.6	86.1	117	2,015	671.5	64.0
Santa Ana	115,920	621	19.6	555	6,699	3,284.1	352.4	822	11,680	3,169.4	309.8
Santa Barbara	33,677	300	40.3	110	1,641	832.1	115.2	531	6,881	1,537.8	181.2
Santa Clara	313,858	1,248	13.1	378	12,811	10,163.3	1,455.7	352	5,045	2,126.5	215.2
Santa Clarita	136,538	433	85.9	198	3,225	7,495.9	181.0	535	9,774	2,781.7	257.4
Santa Cruz	2,251	44	100.0	59	1,181	594.5	70.1	255	3,098	773.2	81.7
Santa Maria	29,277	171	92.4	109	1,108	692.5	54.8	367	5,362	1,561.2	144.1
Santa Monica	62,890	88	78.4	159	1,317	675.4	71.4	682	10,986	4,981.6	451.1
Santa Paula	760	3	100.0	16	D	D	D	55	705	193.2	17.9
Santa Rosa	707,322	1,701	95.9	166	1,963	1,002.8	113.8	654	10,479	2,817.5	292.1
Santee	20,744	157	16.6	46	410	152.7	18.9	123	2,861	750.0	73.1
Saratoga	35,770	40	100.0	25	D	D	D	34	D	D	D
Seaside	0	0	0.0	13	D	D	D	98	1,427	526.3	48.7
Simi Valley	66,799	243	37.0	144	1,371	847.5	70.8	413	5,841	1,672.1	145.6
Soledad	23,588	72	100.0	7	70	55.4	4.4	27	259	79.1	6.4
South Gate	1,418	28	100.0	79	1,000	650.4	41.1	165	2,220	686.4	53.4
South Pasadena	3,410	8	50.0	36	130	159.3	7.6	56	720	196.3	19.3
South San Francisco	34,345	198	0.5	330	5,622	4,819.0	441.5	187	3,063	1,133.4	96.8
Stanton	14,477	52	100.0	28	D	D	D	104	1,162	386.5	30.1
Stockton	104,569	324	100.0	239	4,944	5,746.4	249.4	695	10,893	3,295.0	277.1
Suisun City	3,826	18	44.4	5	D	D	D	31	316	79.6	7.7
Sunnyvale	150,711	794	34.5	210	13,280	9,873.2	2,070.1	279	5,005	1,693.0	148.4
Temecula	17,052	90	100.0	150	2,522	2,074.4	101.5	439	8,208	2,541.9	214.3
Temple City	22,151	83	100.0	91	352	104.0	8.8	99	1,152	299.8	27.6
Thousand Oaks	15,927	61	29.5	158	2,474	5,097.7	275.4	545	9,016	2,880.6	267.4
Torrance	10,492	44	100.0	607	5,653	9,142.9	349.4	663	11,780	3,783.7	319.2
Tracy	312,899	940	68.5	62	1,275	2,123.1	88.6	235	3,772	1,041.6	93.5
Tulare	76,938	530	66.0	50	515	233.8	23.8	181	2,794	808.1	63.7
Turlock	10,469	45	100.0	64	696	377.1	35.5	209	3,514	956.6	86.3
Tustin	20,687	89	67.4	192	2,126	1,489.7	157.5	282	6,234	2,205.6	177.2
Twentynine Palms	1,776	28	100.0	4	17	9.3	0.6	31	312	75.0	7.1
Union City	29,701	86	100.0	139	3,705	2,980.9	306.2	107	2,198	621.1	62.9
Upland	43,167	160	100.0	120	664	276.2	25.2	240	3,685	882.0	91.3
Vacaville	50,180	220	89.1	36	332	320.6	15.6	323	5,699	1,586.2	136.8
Vallejo	13,835	51	100.0	28	794	434.0	36.2	233	3,910	1,147.5	114.0
Victorville	76,430	267	100.0	32	241	314.6	8.8	318	6,108	1,710.9	154.4
Visalia	132,680	577	90.3	126	1,321	1,749.7	69.2	396	6,664	1,873.7	166.6
Vista	87,513	485	37.1	201	3,510	1,611.1	184.4	252	4,089	1,219.6	106.9
Walnut	6,032	13	100.0	229	925	557.6	37.6	105	1,008	232.5	20.0
Walnut Creek	22,629	309	8.7	68	595	1,067.3	50.8	308	6,753	1,972.8	221.6
Wasco	24,703	313	39.9	3	D	D	D	41	426	98.5	8.5
Watsonville	9,816	107	51.4	54	1,108	941.3	57.4	146	2,398	2,233.3	65.5
West Covina	3,705	9	100.0	88	433	203.6	17.9	292	5,618	1,476.3	137.6
West Hollywood	34,055	138	13.0	103	527	222.6	29.4	331	3,472	1,179.9	115.1
Westminster	19,706	133	57.9	118	533	307.3	24.1	453	5,841	1,466.4	145.4
West Sacramento	31,861	153	54.9	140	3,579	5,481.1	185.2	124	2,110	547.8	55.1
Whittier	1,530	7	42.9	71	342	114.4	12.0	200	2,993	619.8	66.5
Wildomar	12,042	42	100.0	8	31	5.8	0.7	39	377	110.5	10.6
Windsor	363	4	100.0	23	441	297.5	22.1	52	1,077	263.2	30.4
Woodland	67,737	249	84.3	77	829	565.9	44.8	154	2,515	703.3	66.7
Yorba Linda	45,511	175	81.1	124	1,029	775.1	74.6	114	1,557	565.2	46.0
Yuba City	11,842	28	100.0	44	372	199.2	19.4	247	4,003	1,015.1	97.0
Yucaipa	19,692	144	33.3	15	62	22.7	2.0	89	995	271.5	24.6
COLORADO	10,230,540	42,627	61.3	5,733	75,717	77,035.0	4,762.1	18,474	245,704	67,815.2	6,508.6
Arvada	136,413	507	99.0	83	880	498.7	59.0	259	3,832	1,145.4	99.5
Aurora	513,260	2,615	54.5	230	5,173	6,512.0	258.0	908	15,374	4,095.7	376.0
Boulder	136,967	747	10.7	187	3,538	1,572.6	297.4	574	8,079	2,002.7	229.8
Brighton	107,201	297	100.0	25	462	250.7	24.9	100	2,136	683.4	52.2
Broomfield	199,222	785	74.8	52	D	D	D	261	4,606	1,000.2	101.7

1. Merchant wholesalers except manufacturers' sales branches and offices. 2. Establishments with payroll.

Real Estate, Professional Services, and Manufacturing

City	Real estate and rental and leasing, 2012				Professional, scientific, and technical services[1], 2012				Manufacturing, 2012			
	Number of establish-ments	Number of employees	Receipts (mil dol)	Annual payroll (mil dol)	Number of establish-ments	Number of employees	Receipts (mil dol)	Annual payroll (mil dol)	Number of establish-ments	Number of employees	Receipts (mil dol)	Annual payroll (mil dol)
	80	81	82	83	84	85	86	87	88	89	90	91
CALIFORNIA— Cont'd												
San Francisco	1,828	15,000	6,000.9	1,071.1	6,233	82,644	28,932.6	8,880.3	693	7,506	D	327.6
San Gabriel	81	209	44.7	6.0	144	483	49.4	15.3	43	389	56.0	13.7
San Jacinto	22	63	13.8	1.3	15	126	8.9	4.2	30	354	45.2	12.2
San Jose	1,045	5,858	1,734.1	314.5	2,961	39,395	9,252.2	4,203.2	897	32,421	15,126.0	2,545.5
San Juan Capistrano	74	237	68.9	14.0	219	993	197.0	63.5	28	792	272.1	51.3
San Leandro	129	905	283.7	43.6	123	D	D	D	182	4,777	1,833.5	233.7
San Luis Obispo	137	693	116.7	25.1	338	D	D	D	73	1,170	219.2	52.4
San Marcos	103	377	79.4	15.8	233	D	D	D	157	4,276	D	204.5
San Mateo	182	789	420.2	55.7	532	D	D	D	46	601	D	36.6
San Pablo	17	59	11.9	1.6	12	95	8.0	3.1	10	50	D	2.1
San Rafael	161	794	806.7	46.0	493	D	D	D	76	632	157.8	32.1
San Ramon	131	D	D	D	523	7,408	2,010.9	642.3	27	302	D	18.1
Santa Ana	316	2,685	564.8	123.4	1,013	D	D	D	771	19,771	5,177.3	938.8
Santa Barbara	287	1,101	228.5	47.7	647	D	D	D	96	998	197.0	51.4
Santa Clara	177	1,396	691.0	107.1	920	D	D	D	508	15,935	4,524.8	1,286.2
Santa Clarita	233	1,129	228.7	48.7	511	D	D	D	231	8,930	2,137.1	549.9
Santa Cruz	87	286	75.5	8.3	283	D	D	D	90	1,324	346.2	64.2
Santa Maria	100	522	89.8	17.0	147	D	D	D	89	2,996	790.2	118.9
Santa Monica	418	3,011	1,488.6	234.2	1,162	8,835	2,052.7	791.5	88	807	172.9	38.0
Santa Paula	22	111	32.5	6.0	21	146	17.4	6.0	23	433	81.8	19.2
Santa Rosa	254	1,131	247.9	41.8	608	4,438	446.1	232.5	153	4,862	1,036.0	344.0
Santee	58	270	38.3	8.6	72	D	D	D	84	1,353	D	65.9
Saratoga	85	219	79.9	14.2	167	D	D	D	14	252	D	24.7
Seaside	12	66	11.0	2.0	18	D	D	D	10	85	3.7	1.5
Simi Valley	118	557	168.5	25.9	369	2,804	537.5	176.7	130	3,504	833.5	189.1
Soledad	12	45	5.3	1.0	4	32	1.6	0.7	4	73	D	2.8
South Gate	41	202	45.9	8.1	28	402	45.0	18.4	121	4,380	1,778.1	206.4
South Pasadena	58	D	D	D	141	D	D	D	13	86	D	3.0
South San Francisco	76	666	132.1	27.1	187	D	D	D	111	10,909	D	1,501.6
Stanton	19	84	24.1	3.2	31	D	D	D	63	702	101.6	31.4
Stockton	253	1,338	218.7	48.2	370	D	D	D	166	5,937	2,921.8	277.1
Suisun City	10	23	4.0	0.9	18	89	8.0	3.0	7	22	3.1	0.6
Sunnyvale	153	960	227.4	45.3	804	18,744	5,191.0	1,991.2	225	25,088	10,930.7	2,976.8
Temecula	184	706	142.9	26.4	368	D	D	D	125	5,024	3,482.1	298.6
Temple City	41	D	D	D	76	235	26.3	7.7	24	149	14.3	4.1
Thousand Oaks	279	971	217.6	50.5	807	D	D	D	124	3,346	1,238.8	239.2
Torrance	343	1,992	374.5	76.2	879	D	D	D	248	12,560	11,915.2	799.0
Tracy	76	181	51.3	7.4	106	D	D	D	52	2,358	1,110.0	110.2
Tulare	46	149	26.3	3.7	47	322	46.6	16.0	27	1,940	2,387.4	99.7
Turlock	58	280	33.7	7.1	74	D	D	D	71	2,986	1,675.0	122.7
Tustin	172	853	210.1	42.1	549	D	D	D	98	3,270	679.2	193.1
Twentynine Palms	11	77	17.9	2.8	15	D	D	D	NA	NA	NA	NA
Union City	40	162	39.3	7.5	109	D	D	D	81	3,879	1,033.7	226.9
Upland	102	876	99.4	49.3	209	1,306	185.3	64.5	95	981	198.4	46.1
Vacaville	106	542	123.2	18.1	114	632	67.7	26.4	44	2,425	D	138.6
Vallejo	73	300	80.3	10.0	95	D	D	D	32	356	D	16.1
Victorville	88	465	57.7	12.2	103	D	D	D	18	1,222	665.7	49.7
Visalia	131	834	120.0	25.9	245	D	D	D	67	2,417	1,355.8	121.5
Vista	138	738	172.1	27.4	230	1,448	254.4	77.5	178	7,380	2,754.2	405.5
Walnut	56	D	D	D	107	340	55.3	13.1	30	318	84.6	17.4
Walnut Creek	224	1,209	285.4	68.5	691	6,364	1,516.1	549.4	32	591	D	33.9
Wasco	14	37	6.6	1.1	4	20	2.4	0.5	6	104	D	5.8
Watsonville	60	256	46.9	8.8	72	D	D	D	57	1,381	353.8	59.3
West Covina	82	421	55.4	14.7	144	D	D	D	16	632	104.1	35.0
West Hollywood	146	820	248.1	40.6	398	2,286	623.2	201.7	36	225	31.0	8.4
Westminster	93	300	81.0	12.0	145	635	68.8	25.2	93	775	106.4	30.0
West Sacramento	77	604	123.5	25.4	83	D	D	D	64	3,118	D	165.9
Whittier	102	338	57.2	9.6	166	755	83.9	25.8	47	732	223.4	31.7
Wildomar	15	123	9.5	2.7	23	D	D	D	8	75	D	4.6
Windsor	23	160	41.9	4.6	57	335	82.2	13.8	26	570	122.3	31.5
Woodland	60	300	55.2	10.6	81	D	D	D	57	2,002	D	92.5
Yorba Linda	102	293	60.3	12.2	246	D	D	D	54	1,386	714.1	106.8
Yuba City	78	420	47.8	10.8	103	484	48.6	18.0	43	1,144	457.9	62.2
Yucaipa	45	152	21.2	4.8	59	175	19.2	5.3	20	326	39.2	12.4
COLORADO	9,295	38,706	8,482.5	1,569.6	23,761	175,448	32,686.8	12,537.0	4,898	114,632	50,447.1	6,230.1
Arvada	125	276	48.7	9.2	382	1,535	215.1	79.5	110	2,139	615.1	128.0
Aurora	298	1,233	267.5	46.2	635	D	D	D	122	2,400	644.1	118.3
Boulder	316	1,091	258.0	42.8	1,346	D	D	D	216	7,153	2,744.6	521.0
Brighton	34	114	13.8	3.3	50	D	D	D	22	697	222.2	38.9
Broomfield	96	313	77.1	11.4	323	D	D	D	82	3,087	3,918.4	188.5

1. Establishments subject to federal tax.

Table D. Cities — Accommodation and Food Services, Arts, Entertainment, and Recreation, and Health Care and Social Assistance

City	Accommodation and food services, 2012				Arts, entertainment, and recreation[1], 2012				Health care and social assistance,[1] 2012			
	Number of establishments	Number of employees	Receipts (mil dol)	Annual payroll (mil dol)	Number of establishments	Number of employees	Receipts (mil dol)	Annual payroll (mil dol)	Number of establishments	Number of employees	Receipts (mil dol)	Annual payroll (mil dol)
	92	93	94	95	96	97	98	99	100	101	102	103
CALIFORNIA— Cont'd												
San Francisco	4,059	73,417	6,142.7	1,841.6	320	6,226	1,006.9	402.9	2,413	18,874	2,647.7	1,112.5
San Gabriel	176	1,866	105.8	26.5	3	D	D	D	209	D	D	D
San Jacinto	40	628	27.2	6.9	NA	NA	NA	NA	31	234	22.6	8.2
San Jose	1,916	31,023	1,919.1	523.7	141	4,615	413.7	177.4	2,175	24,468	3,274.0	1,300.7
San Juan Capistrano	73	1,257	72.0	21.1	15	325	32.8	6.9	115	1,172	106.9	43.2
San Leandro	191	2,329	146.2	37.7	12	D	D	D	240	3,538	346.0	150.9
San Luis Obispo	218	4,125	220.9	62.5	12	164	6.9	2.3	302	3,655	493.7	183.6
San Marcos	169	2,973	180.6	46.5	17	D	D	D	135	1,504	166.4	68.7
San Mateo	313	4,808	325.1	89.5	29	D	D	D	417	4,045	533.1	182.6
San Pablo	60	739	38.6	9.7	1	D	D	D	29	D	D	D
San Rafael	224	2,841	163.4	47.3	63	352	83.8	17.7	235	3,214	429.2	221.2
San Ramon	148	2,324	159.8	41.1	19	520	27.8	8.6	273	2,624	416.2	140.8
Santa Ana	542	7,493	462.8	121.3	25	226	31.1	6.2	708	9,016	1,138.6	464.2
Santa Barbara	421	8,143	494.4	143.1	62	721	53.2	16.6	469	3,762	656.2	216.6
Santa Clara	400	7,151	581.1	157.9	31	2,308	382.4	216.1	211	D	D	D
Santa Clarita	327	6,766	351.4	98.9	117	1,303	86.4	30.6	468	4,669	577.5	213.6
Santa Cruz	256	4,446	253.9	74.7	24	906	59.8	21.6	173	1,586	166.8	71.0
Santa Maria	178	2,596	144.9	39.6	14	249	11.8	3.8	274	2,403	258.2	98.4
Santa Monica	454	12,289	947.7	276.5	677	1,752	660.2	254.2	841	5,314	753.0	267.1
Santa Paula	42	D	D	D	5	29	1.6	0.4	36	257	29.5	11.9
Santa Rosa	389	5,764	355.0	95.6	52	826	50.3	22.4	579	8,031	1,158.3	525.6
Santee	108	1,620	85.1	24.6	12	D	D	D	70	450	42.3	16.6
Saratoga	64	883	58.5	15.6	6	78	7.1	2.7	102	D	D	D
Seaside	71	1,005	65.6	17.6	2	D	D	D	15	D	D	D
Simi Valley	251	3,984	230.6	59.4	45	D	D	D	324	2,835	295.7	109.2
Soledad	21	D	D	D	NA	NA	NA	NA	7	42	9.1	2.3
South Gate	108	1,192	74.4	17.5	6	D	D	D	75	841	82.5	28.5
South Pasadena	61	882	45.7	13.4	39	D	D	D	106	717	73.8	27.1
South San Francisco	204	3,673	316.2	82.3	17	D	D	D	162	2,570	353.5	192.7
Stanton	82	924	52.9	13.0	6	D	D	D	31	D	D	D
Stockton	424	6,912	366.5	95.4	34	716	47.6	17.9	587	9,180	993.6	391.5
Suisun City	31	426	23.3	5.9	4	D	D	D	17	54	5.3	2.1
Sunnyvale	346	4,781	349.1	86.3	34	D	D	D	390	3,554	486.8	163.1
Temecula	281	9,653	965.6	240.6	28	697	33.3	9.3	311	2,408	227.9	86.7
Temple City	64	836	47.4	11.5	4	8	1.6	0.3	95	D	D	D
Thousand Oaks	317	6,760	378.5	109.1	96	684	71.5	26.4	636	6,430	1,012.7	325.7
Torrance	419	8,055	498.1	139.8	55	D	D	D	1,030	9,696	1,168.6	428.5
Tracy	137	2,191	111.1	28.9	16	D	D	D	158	D	D	D
Tulare	80	1,403	74.5	19.3	7	D	D	D	100	D	D	D
Turlock	146	2,528	128.2	35.1	14	D	D	D	154	1,477	166.6	56.7
Tustin	232	4,167	224.8	65.2	20	D	D	D	346	3,588	605.0	147.8
Twentynine Palms	49	661	48.0	9.9	3	D	D	D	12	D	D	D
Union City	113	1,771	95.5	26.3	7	D	D	D	116	1,019	90.2	38.7
Upland	145	D	D	D	23	D	D	D	346	D	D	D
Vacaville	168	3,293	173.1	48.6	16	411	22.5	5.3	167	2,305	379.6	145.5
Vallejo	167	2,623	147.9	38.4	17	1,257	78.4	21.8	214	4,353	620.0	337.9
Victorville	175	3,245	167.9	46.5	12	D	D	D	199	3,415	365.9	130.7
Visalia	234	4,245	216.8	60.7	11	293	17.9	3.9	349	3,648	417.3	160.1
Vista	171	2,150	114.0	29.2	10	288	22.6	6.6	207	2,342	240.7	88.8
Walnut	48	539	29.1	7.5	6	D	D	D	87	702	41.8	19.2
Walnut Creek	202	4,358	259.1	78.0	28	363	25.0	7.5	442	D	D	D
Wasco	28	D	D	D	1	D	D	D	13	D	D	D
Watsonville	90	1,218	72.9	17.9	6	D	D	D	139	2,047	245.2	88.9
West Covina	196	3,421	184.5	48.2	11	D	D	D	314	D	D	D
West Hollywood	229	7,741	543.1	166.4	482	D	D	D	248	1,104	177.3	57.1
Westminster	245	2,672	144.5	39.6	14	D	D	D	281	2,520	273.5	96.0
West Sacramento	91	D	D	D	9	D	D	D	67	D	D	D
Whittier	177	2,662	149.2	42.8	10	D	D	D	295	D	D	D
Wildomar	31	402	22.3	5.8	7	D	D	D	53	1,307	161.0	68.4
Windsor	52	D	D	D	5	89	4.1	1.4	37	230	17.3	6.3
Woodland	104	D	D	D	9	124	3.6	1.1	85	1,376	153.3	86.4
Yorba Linda	92	1,710	83.5	24.6	25	D	D	D	167	D	D	D
Yuba City	124	2,121	110.6	28.1	14	D	D	D	196	D	D	D
Yucaipa	55	764	39.2	10.6	11	D	D	D	83	D	D	D
COLORADO	12,744	240,484	13,617.7	3,994.6	1,950	41,585	3,048.6	1,082.5	12,701	140,738	14,693.2	6,167.1
Arvada	186	3,172	160.0	45.6	24	225	9.3	2.8	216	2,393	194.0	72.0
Aurora	577	10,728	567.1	162.5	44	760	41.5	13.5	575	7,897	607.0	279.9
Boulder	429	8,834	501.9	149.9	102	970	50.4	16.4	579	4,074	429.0	172.7
Brighton	83	1,338	72.1	19.3	7	D	D	D	76	D	D	D
Broomfield	143	2,944	169.6	54.7	20	D	D	D	135	1,542	167.0	62.6

1. Establishments subject to federal tax.

Items 92—103

Table D. Cities — Other Services and Government Employment and Payroll

City	Other services[1] Number of establish-ments	Number of employees	Receipts (mil dol)	Annual payroll (mil dol)	Full-time equivalent employees	March payroll Total (dollars)	Admin-istrative, judicial, and legal	Police and corrections	Fire protection	Highways and trans-portation	Health and welfare	Natural resources and utilities	Education and libraries
	104	105	106	107	108	109	110	111	112	113	114	115	116
CALIFORNIA— Cont'd													
San Francisco	1,603	10,876	1,109.6	320.2	28,349	217,722,943	13.9	17.4	7.3	22.7	24.7	11.1	2.1
San Gabriel	96	408	39.5	11.3	191	1,327,334	11.3	38.5	24.6	6.9	3.8	11.2	0.0
San Jacinto	34	D	D	D	65	267,518	30.0	0.0	0.0	10.8	18.2	28.6	0.0
San Jose	1,175	6,748	929.6	202.4	5,214	38,715,963	8.8	33.1	18.0	9.9	1.0	14.9	3.3
San Juan Capistrano	48	217	27.5	7.0	115	698,016	51.1	0.6	0.0	8.3	1.4	33.4	0.0
San Leandro	163	1,027	148.8	32.8	375	2,465,492	13.1	40.7	0.0	11.7	4.5	15.4	7.2
San Luis Obispo	106	523	45.2	13.0	406	3,104,703	10.0	27.1	17.3	3.8	5.5	22.1	0.0
San Marcos	120	713	60.9	18.7	279	1,870,622	14.4	0.0	37.4	21.7	5.6	15.9	0.0
San Mateo	203	D	D	D	610	5,077,524	8.5	28.2	20.6	5.7	5.0	23.9	4.0
San Pablo	34	189	13.0	3.7	74	394,492	49.3	1.6	0.0	13.4	12.2	22.1	0.0
San Rafael	194	1,244	151.0	45.2	864	2,915,776	12.5	26.3	32.7	4.3	0.0	17.6	4.1
San Ramon	112	897	75.3	23.7	279	2,017,589	12.1	37.5	0.0	31.3	1.9	13.4	0.0
Santa Ana	390	2,175	232.8	64.4	2,711	12,719,386	0.7	3.5	1.9	0.5	0.5	0.5	0.1
Santa Barbara	186	1,179	94.1	27.8	1,156	7,284,111	11.3	26.7	14.2	12.8	3.2	19.5	2.7
Santa Clara	235	1,567	145.2	45.6	961	8,545,138	10.4	22.6	18.9	6.8	0.6	30.5	3.6
Santa Clarita	255	1,689	176.5	43.8	434	2,697,699	16.1	0.0	0.0	6.2	6.5	35.1	0.0
Santa Cruz	86	701	70.7	23.5	774	4,763,881	12.0	20.2	14.4	4.6	2.0	33.9	8.6
Santa Maria	115	781	97.3	22.6	497	2,980,086	10.3	35.8	13.6	5.8	5.2	22.7	3.8
Santa Monica	353	2,604	175.5	57.6	2,163	15,220,984	14.3	23.8	11.2	20.8	3.2	14.6	3.3
Santa Paula	27	65	7.4	1.7	110	646,323	13.8	38.3	18.1	4.2	7.2	16.1	0.0
Santa Rosa	252	1,669	155.6	51.2	1,213	8,220,156	11.3	23.5	16.6	10.0	2.3	23.5	0.0
Santee	91	554	55.8	16.7	148	1,012,079	28.3	0.6	51.2	9.9	1.2	8.9	0.0
Saratoga	30	141	14.2	3.4	58	435,826	25.2	0.0	0.0	22.5	22.1	14.1	0.0
Seaside	49	196	21.9	5.6	158	994,460	9.5	41.0	20.0	8.9	0.9	6.0	0.0
Simi Valley	155	1,140	145.1	27.9	592	3,356,138	14.7	32.1	0.0	21.1	15.4	16.6	0.0
Soledad	4	16	1.4	0.3	45	264,288	21.2	60.5	0.0	1.9	0.0	16.4	0.0
South Gate	76	242	20.4	4.9	318	1,634,468	11.2	44.3	0.0	17.0	9.3	18.2	0.0
South Pasadena	40	185	13.1	3.6	168	950,670	11.5	35.7	20.9	5.1	8.3	7.4	9.4
South San Francisco	114	1,365	141.2	47.8	497	3,574,682	9.0	29.5	25.0	5.7	0.7	17.9	6.9
Stanton	52	290	23.7	6.8	38	219,326	37.8	0.0	0.0	18.7	21.0	22.5	0.0
Stockton	289	1,996	163.5	53.9	2,010	12,427,436	7.5	55.8	14.5	0.7	2.3	9.7	2.3
Suisun City	26	82	7.1	2.2	85	454,879	15.9	38.0	4.6	17.0	8.7	8.9	0.0
Sunnyvale	167	956	108.4	37.1	870	7,456,793	9.7	27.3	18.0	7.5	4.3	20.3	3.7
Temecula	183	1,029	84.1	22.4	200	1,117,348	29.5	0.5	0.7	25.3	14.8	29.0	0.0
Temple City	57	216	18.4	4.3	75	319,507	42.5	0.0	0.0	0.0	0.0	25.4	0.0
Thousand Oaks	209	1,193	114.8	31.6	440	2,648,993	26.5	1.5	0.0	28.8	2.2	20.8	12.0
Torrance	244	1,814	167.6	51.1	1,361	10,031,057	10.8	31.2	18.3	15.1	4.3	10.6	3.4
Tracy	100	467	54.4	18.3	420	2,906,444	11.9	31.9	22.5	6.6	1.4	20.4	0.0
Tulare	53	314	42.3	11.1	347	1,781,358	7.7	33.8	16.3	2.3	3.5	23.6	2.6
Turlock	89	557	53.2	15.3	394	2,010,112	13.5	34.3	14.7	8.6	2.6	22.0	0.0
Tustin	115	974	97.2	28.4	338	2,566,292	15.4	48.7	0.0	14.6	2.0	11.4	0.0
Twentynine Palms	17	95	7.7	2.4	26	143,616	18.5	18.8	0.0	23.3	0.0	39.5	0.0
Union City	68	618	95.8	22.4	252	1,774,885	14.0	49.2	0.0	3.0	5.2	19.0	0.0
Upland	130	575	53.8	14.8	892	4,437,479	3.7	19.6	11.3	3.4	2.6	5.7	1.6
Vacaville	115	578	46.5	13.3	584	4,121,808	12.2	30.0	19.8	13.3	4.5	20.2	0.0
Vallejo	105	454	43.4	12.4	573	3,266,338	8.6	32.1	16.0	8.2	5.4	28.1	0.0
Victorville	89	506	48.5	13.3	340	1,783,174	43.6	0.0	0.0	23.9	2.4	30.1	0.0
Visalia	159	989	95.7	27.0	612	3,335,649	7.1	37.8	15.7	9.2	6.0	23.1	0.0
Vista	114	744	73.7	22.1	290	1,741,746	25.7	0.0	39.6	9.1	5.0	16.8	0.0
Walnut	49	269	24.4	7.7	52	276,966	49.6	0.0	0.0	21.7	8.9	19.8	0.0
Walnut Creek	154	2,209	191.8	80.2	389	2,700,536	16.3	37.1	0.0	5.7	0.7	23.8	0.0
Wasco	12	D	D	D	60	270,885	30.6	0.0	0.0	10.8	0.0	46.4	0.0
Watsonville	64	225	22.2	6.1	373	2,335,983	9.1	27.3	13.3	4.5	1.8	31.8	5.7
West Covina	85	472	27.2	8.0	445	2,840,481	9.7	46.0	25.6	12.3	2.3	4.1	0.0
West Hollywood	167	1,186	102.6	24.5	216	1,683,338	37.7	0.0	0.0	20.8	29.7	11.7	0.0
Westminster	142	768	59.5	22.1	290	1,903,418	13.5	58.3	0.0	6.1	4.4	8.3	0.0
West Sacramento	87	674	95.2	28.0	402	3,250,336	14.1	25.4	25.1	1.9	6.5	14.5	0.0
Whittier	107	517	43.8	12.2	478	2,572,894	10.2	44.2	0.0	4.8	6.2	21.3	5.7
Wildomar	17	D	D	D	12	48,677	78.0	0.0	0.0	0.0	0.0	0.0	0.0
Windsor	24	D	D	D	98	584,900	39.6	0.0	0.0	13.3	0.0	47.2	0.0
Woodland	72	394	32.9	9.0	304	1,839,421	7.6	32.0	20.0	4.8	13.1	16.1	2.4
Yorba Linda	77	517	47.3	14.9	130	661,872	25.1	0.0	0.0	10.0	1.5	30.7	18.9
Yuba City	80	502	45.5	14.6	299	1,719,010	11.1	33.5	26.1	7.0	0.0	20.2	0.0
Yucaipa	42	177	13.9	3.4	44	165,657	7.8	0.0	0.0	38.1	0.0	54.1	0.0
COLORADO	7,918	46,005	3,942.1	1,242.3	X	X	X	X	X	X	X	X	X
Arvada	164	824	65.2	20.3	661	3,647,076	20.5	35.5	0.0	9.8	4.4	22.2	0.0
Aurora	396	2,655	208.3	66.3	2,579	13,742,359	13.6	38.9	14.9	4.2	2.6	20.7	1.4
Boulder	215	1,177	93.8	31.3	1,108	6,200,124	15.9	23.9	11.2	6.6	1.6	26.0	4.7
Brighton	47	213	22.1	5.8	297	2,531,155	9.4	15.0	0.0	3.0	57.8	11.9	0.0
Broomfield	92	520	39.4	13.2	687	3,465,198	16.4	35.0	0.0	2.4	18.0	19.6	3.9

1. Establishments subject to federal tax.

Table D. Cities — City Government Finances

City	General revenue Total (mil dol)	Intergovernmental Total (mil dol)	Intergovernmental Percent from state government	Taxes Total (mil dol)	Taxes Per capita (dollars) Total	Taxes Per capita (dollars) Property	Taxes Per capita (dollars) Sales and gross receipts	General expenditure Total (mil dol)	General expenditure Per capita (dollars) Total	General expenditure Per capita (dollars) Capital outlays
	117	118	119	120	121	122	123	124	125	126
CALIFORNIA— Cont'd										
San Francisco	7,274.1	2,355.9	68.6	2,846.2	3,430	1,747	885	5,704.0	6,875	846
San Gabriel	37.1	3.0	81.2	25.2	626	356	258	40.2	999	177
San Jacinto	28.1	1.5	100.0	14.5	318	213	92	31.0	681	34
San Jose	1,721.1	116.7	56.0	863.4	876	456	363	1,428.0	1,449	178
San Juan Capistrano	47.2	4.4	76.8	30.4	856	577	270	40.6	1,144	265
San Leandro	123.0	8.3	72.0	88.5	1,016	465	517	121.7	1,398	127
San Luis Obispo	81.4	6.3	56.0	48.1	1,049	330	716	76.5	1,668	350
San Marcos	121.3	7.6	84.2	76.6	879	491	384	132.6	1,523	283
San Mateo	145.7	11.0	62.3	86.7	867	454	370	148.4	1,483	264
San Pablo	44.1	1.8	97.0	39.1	1,326	549	776	38.0	1,291	386
San Rafael	85.9	4.1	86.9	52.8	903	369	506	87.5	1,496	47
San Ramon	74.2	3.7	100.0	41.1	557	343	208	75.1	1,017	190
Santa Ana	440.5	127.5	23.8	205.9	621	334	285	391.8	1,181	145
Santa Barbara	246.8	36.0	63.6	102.8	1,149	512	631	228.4	2,550	530
Santa Clara	280.5	11.7	71.5	124.3	1,039	577	456	212.3	1,776	110
Santa Clarita	152.4	24.6	54.9	80.2	448	205	233	145.6	814	191
Santa Cruz	132.1	4.8	59.8	60.6	977	437	528	145.4	2,345	279
Santa Maria	117.0	16.8	78.0	58.2	574	182	391	112.6	1,111	201
Santa Monica	560.2	57.7	51.4	332.1	3,618	1,337	2,095	538.6	5,867	1,727
Santa Paula	29.3	4.2	87.4	12.9	428	275	94	23.2	771	142
Santa Rosa	262.1	24.5	59.6	119.5	702	255	435	250.3	1,470	305
Santee	44.7	2.6	60.7	34.2	616	379	155	49.1	885	180
Saratoga	20.9	1.1	97.2	15.0	490	306	160	22.6	736	169
Seaside	27.0	2.8	39.4	22.4	662	372	288	30.5	899	206
Simi Valley	96.1	10.2	52.4	62.4	497	300	194	92.5	736	103
Soledad	15.7	1.0	97.1	6.1	229	125	103	14.9	563	43
South Gate	80.6	17.7	38.8	36.7	383	216	166	67.6	707	121
South Pasadena	28.7	3.5	84.1	19.0	731	429	296	28.2	1,089	148
South San Francisco	128.4	5.4	89.0	77.6	1,179	732	371	122.6	1,863	259
Stanton	32.9	2.6	78.3	26.3	682	496	169	38.1	989	253
Stockton	381.7	98.9	79.6	161.7	544	215	325	384.7	1,293	244
Suisun City	27.1	4.4	39.6	13.1	458	385	71	30.3	1,061	113
Sunnyvale	274.8	32.4	34.0	112.9	770	377	386	274.4	1,871	145
Temecula	113.3	14.0	33.6	69.7	665	351	310	129.7	1,238	371
Temple City	15.4	1.3	81.7	11.0	305	164	133	14.2	393	12
Thousand Oaks	143.2	11.9	64.9	84.5	660	350	305	145.4	1,135	190
Torrance	261.0	41.4	39.9	155.5	1,056	365	677	234.0	1,589	118
Tracy	114.6	11.3	53.2	47.1	556	256	297	128.6	1,519	332
Tulare	97.1	4.2	71.5	38.5	632	245	375	90.8	1,492	464
Turlock	69.6	5.8	56.0	34.6	496	222	216	83.2	1,193	431
Tustin	77.0	3.6	66.8	51.5	661	437	220	77.9	1,001	98
Twentynine Palms	11.2	1.2	85.8	9.5	370	226	143	12.3	477	86
Union City	85.1	5.7	83.5	61.0	850	562	282	92.0	1,283	294
Upland	71.1	4.5	65.1	37.7	502	337	159	74.2	987	59
Vacaville	153.8	33.0	26.6	79.6	848	575	270	156.0	1,662	571
Vallejo	195.2	49.6	22.5	64.7	549	229	308	152.7	1,295	112
Victorville	115.4	9.5	68.3	53.9	448	251	195	130.1	1,082	123
Visalia	157.6	23.1	61.9	68.5	540	218	320	143.8	1,134	282
Vista	132.0	9.1	80.1	57.8	601	345	252	117.1	1,217	321
Walnut	21.5	1.3	82.0	13.1	436	322	106	20.0	668	25
Walnut Creek	70.1	2.6	97.1	45.9	699	317	354	80.4	1,224	103
Wasco	13.5	2.6	29.2	5.5	217	145	72	13.2	517	75
Watsonville	67.3	6.4	30.2	31.1	599	394	194	72.0	1,387	113
West Covina	102.2	8.7	74.3	63.9	594	395	196	91.9	854	133
West Hollywood	88.9	5.0	44.0	55.8	1,601	602	980	93.6	2,685	485
Westminster	91.7	10.4	70.7	68.6	750	538	210	114.0	1,245	487
West Sacramento	140.9	23.6	64.6	66.7	1,344	812	401	129.2	2,601	822
Whittier	79.8	8.9	72.4	41.7	483	250	231	82.4	954	94
Wildomar	9.4	3.2	100.0	5.9	177	97	62	9.3	280	7
Windsor	23.5	2.8	29.7	16.3	603	373	188	23.2	859	257
Woodland	72.5	12.3	93.9	44.7	793	310	482	78.0	1,385	376
Yorba Linda	62.1	4.6	47.2	35.0	526	382	138	79.9	1,201	263
Yuba City	54.9	5.2	89.4	33.0	508	270	193	59.0	910	163
Yucaipa	28.1	0.9	94.5	20.9	398	293	82	29.1	554	111
COLORADO	X	X	X	X	X	X	X	X	X	X
Arvada	132.6	21.2	32.5	67.8	619	84	534	119.2	1,086	160
Aurora	380.8	48.7	50.2	216.5	638	102	536	400.3	1,180	162
Boulder	219.5	16.4	84.1	150.1	1,471	286	1,185	210.4	2,063	39
Brighton	32.9	3.4	84.3	21.9	624	53	567	24.3	691	69
Broomfield	149.9	15.4	40.7	113.5	1,924	654	1,161	109.7	1,860	53

1. Based on population estimated as of July 1 of the year shown.

City	City government finances, 2012 (cont.)									
	General expenditure (cont.)									
	Percent of total for:									
	Public welfare	Highways	Parking facilities	Education	Health and hospitals	Police protection	Sewerage and sanitation	Parks and recreation	Housing and community development	Interest on debt
	127	128	129	130	131	132	133	134	135	136
CALIFORNIA— Cont'd										
San Francisco	8.5	4.4	2.4	0.0	30.2	6.6	4.7	4.3	4.2	7.1
San Gabriel	0.0	12.3	0.0	0.0	0.0	30.1	0.2	11.5	3.0	0.2
San Jacinto	0.0	13.6	0.0	0.0	0.0	28.1	10.6	3.1	13.0	4.6
San Jose	0.0	6.0	0.5	0.0	0.1	17.6	18.1	6.3	3.6	18.3
San Juan Capistrano	0.0	12.0	0.0	0.0	1.3	17.5	6.8	9.2	9.6	7.7
San Leandro	0.0	9.1	0.2	0.0	1.1	22.2	6.5	5.1	9.9	2.9
San Luis Obispo	0.0	16.3	3.7	0.0	0.0	20.2	13.2	9.3	2.1	2.5
San Marcos	0.0	12.9	0.0	0.0	3.2	11.1	0.0	7.4	24.5	11.5
San Mateo	0.0	10.7	1.3	0.0	1.3	19.6	17.8	9.7	2.9	4.2
San Pablo	0.0	22.7	0.0	0.0	0.4	36.6	0.0	6.8	8.3	9.8
San Rafael	0.0	8.4	3.3	0.0	6.9	21.6	0.0	11.4	2.3	2.2
San Ramon	0.0	11.3	0.0	0.0	0.0	21.4	0.0	20.7	7.9	7.1
Santa Ana	0.0	9.8	1.0	0.0	2.9	30.3	5.4	5.0	15.2	5.2
Santa Barbara	0.0	12.0	2.9	0.0	0.2	15.2	15.9	8.4	3.7	1.3
Santa Clara	0.0	9.0	0.6	0.0	2.0	19.7	16.4	8.4	2.4	4.7
Santa Clarita	0.0	30.6	0.0	0.0	0.1	13.0	0.3	12.7	3.7	3.5
Santa Cruz	0.0	6.8	2.2	0.0	1.0	27.5	18.8	8.9	8.5	2.8
Santa Maria	0.0	11.1	0.0	0.0	0.0	18.5	25.1	6.9	0.4	3.7
Santa Monica	0.0	6.8	0.2	0.0	3.3	13.7	7.2	9.9	25.8	2.8
Santa Paula	0.0	10.9	0.0	0.0	0.8	23.3	14.7	14.4	4.7	6.1
Santa Rosa	0.0	11.5	1.9	0.0	0.9	17.4	23.0	7.1	3.3	7.1
Santee	0.0	15.5	0.0	0.0	6.2	21.7	0.0	3.5	17.3	4.1
Saratoga	0.0	23.5	0.0	0.0	3.2	18.0	0.0	18.8	0.4	2.4
Seaside	0.0	9.8	0.0	0.0	0.6	36.9	0.0	8.6	10.5	5.0
Simi Valley	0.0	9.2	0.0	0.0	1.4	30.9	17.3	1.0	10.4	3.5
Soledad	0.0	13.2	0.0	0.0	1.3	25.1	31.6	3.9	2.2	2.7
South Gate	0.0	24.1	0.0	0.0	0.1	28.3	7.2	6.6	3.6	9.8
South Pasadena	0.0	13.6	0.1	0.0	1.0	25.7	4.3	10.7	1.7	0.0
South San Francisco	0.0	19.1	0.7	0.0	6.2	17.3	14.3	8.2	4.4	5.1
Stanton	0.0	6.3	0.0	0.0	0.2	22.4	1.8	5.3	35.3	8.9
Stockton	0.0	9.4	0.6	0.0	0.6	24.6	11.6	5.1	6.1	5.1
Suisun City	0.0	7.8	0.0	0.0	0.0	16.2	0.0	6.2	22.0	8.1
Sunnyvale	0.0	8.6	0.5	0.3	0.5	11.3	28.1	8.2	2.4	1.5
Temecula	0.0	19.9	0.0	0.0	0.2	17.4	4.7	15.3	10.4	3.5
Temple City	0.0	9.2	1.0	0.0	1.7	23.9	0.2	13.7	6.8	1.8
Thousand Oaks	0.0	22.4	0.0	0.0	0.5	17.9	13.0	6.9	8.4	2.8
Torrance	0.0	12.5	0.0	0.0	4.5	28.2	6.5	8.3	2.8	3.0
Tracy	0.0	6.2	0.0	0.0	0.4	16.6	24.2	12.4	3.8	5.1
Tulare	0.0	20.9	0.0	0.0	1.3	13.0	23.7	3.4	6.2	11.6
Turlock	0.0	9.9	0.0	0.0	0.5	33.2	16.6	4.4	11.0	1.6
Tustin	0.0	13.4	0.0	0.0	0.0	29.4	0.0	4.0	8.8	9.1
Twentynine Palms	0.0	17.8	0.0	0.0	5.0	25.2	0.0	13.8	5.5	4.2
Union City	0.0	8.6	0.0	0.0	0.6	22.1	0.8	13.1	17.7	7.7
Upland	0.0	9.8	0.0	0.0	1.4	22.4	19.7	2.8	10.4	2.3
Vacaville	0.0	6.6	0.0	0.0	4.4	17.0	29.3	4.9	18.9	3.8
Vallejo	0.0	10.3	0.0	0.0	0.4	22.0	15.1	0.9	18.2	3.0
Victorville	0.0	6.3	0.0	0.0	0.4	13.7	19.3	5.0	2.1	11.3
Visalia	0.0	12.5	0.0	0.0	0.0	19.7	23.2	7.4	2.8	1.1
Vista	0.0	9.8	0.0	0.0	3.8	15.0	17.2	7.4	9.0	7.5
Walnut	0.0	20.0	0.0	0.0	0.6	30.8	0.0	17.0	5.4	5.1
Walnut Creek	0.0	11.1	4.4	0.0	0.0	23.7	0.0	30.1	1.5	0.3
Wasco	0.0	17.2	0.0	0.0	1.0	28.0	26.1	0.0	8.4	1.4
Watsonville	0.0	7.2	0.0	0.0	1.0	19.7	25.5	4.2	6.2	0.5
West Covina	0.0	14.3	0.4	0.0	2.6	31.7	0.0	5.3	5.0	7.9
West Hollywood	0.0	10.7	3.8	0.0	7.0	16.4	2.5	5.8	5.8	3.5
Westminster	0.0	7.6	0.0	0.0	0.9	22.8	0.0	3.0	44.5	5.1
West Sacramento	0.0	18.1	0.0	0.0	0.3	13.0	10.0	6.8	11.0	8.6
Whittier	0.0	9.9	0.0	0.0	0.0	33.8	13.2	11.2	4.0	4.8
Wildomar	0.0	21.2	0.0	0.0	2.4	22.8	0.0	0.9	0.0	0.0
Windsor	0.0	20.4	0.0	0.0	1.0	24.7	0.0	3.9	13.1	4.1
Woodland	0.0	17.7	0.0	0.0	0.0	19.0	12.1	6.1	4.4	3.6
Yorba Linda	0.0	25.6	0.0	0.0	0.0	14.8	6.4	14.1	10.6	6.2
Yuba City	0.0	6.1	0.0	0.0	0.8	23.5	22.2	5.7	6.5	1.7
Yucaipa	0.0	24.1	0.0	0.0	4.3	22.0	0.0	13.1	11.5	2.4
COLORADO	X	X	X	X	X	X	X	X	X	X
Arvada	0.0	15.3	0.0	0.0	0.0	19.8	10.3	18.6	8.4	1.3
Aurora	0.0	13.0	0.0	0.0	0.0	21.5	14.3	11.3	2.9	2.2
Boulder	0.0	17.2	3.0	0.0	0.0	21.6	5.5	19.0	9.4	2.5
Brighton	0.0	11.9	0.0	0.0	0.0	22.3	16.7	14.5	0.0	7.4
Broomfield	10.4	8.0	0.0	0.0	1.6	14.4	5.1	12.8	0.0	12.6

City Government Finances, City Government Employment, and Climate

City	City government finances, 2012 (cont.)			Climate[2]						
	Debt outstanding		Debt issued during year	Average daily temperature				Annual precipitation (inches)	Heating degree days	Cooling degree days
				Mean		Limits				
	Total (mil dol)	Per capita[1] (dollars)		January	July	January[3]	July[4]			
	137	138	139	140	141	142	143	144	145	146
CALIFORNIA— Cont'd										
San Francisco	13,075.2	15,759	3,426.5	52.3	61.3	46.4	68.2	22.28	2,597	163
San Gabriel	3.0	74	3.3	56.3	75.6	42.6	89.0	18.56	1,295	1,575
San Jacinto	24.5	538	0.0	NA	NA	NA	NA	NA	NA	NA
San Jose	5,924.6	6,013	690.9	50.5	70.9	41.7	84.3	15.08	2,171	811
San Juan Capistrano	68.5	1,928	0.0	55.4	68.7	43.9	77.3	13.56	1,756	666
San Leandro	78.3	899	0.0	50.0	62.8	43.6	70.4	25.40	2,857	142
San Luis Obispo	65.5	1,429	0.0	53.3	66.5	41.9	80.3	24.36	2,138	476
San Marcos	501.2	5,755	0.0	56.4	71.6	45.1	82.2	13.69	1,514	1,047
San Mateo	159.9	1,599	0.0	48.4	68.0	39.1	80.8	20.16	2,764	422
San Pablo	81.2	2,754	0.2	48.8	67.7	41.3	80.9	34.29	2,621	451
San Rafael	46.5	794	0.1	48.8	67.7	41.3	80.9	34.29	2,621	451
San Ramon	108.0	1,464	11.6	47.2	72.0	37.4	89.1	14.82	2,755	858
Santa Ana	358.1	1,080	0.0	58.0	72.9	46.6	87.7	13.84	1,153	1,299
Santa Barbara	112.5	1,257	1.5	53.1	67.0	40.8	76.7	16.93	2,121	482
Santa Clara	388.8	3,251	0.0	50.5	70.9	41.7	84.3	15.08	2,171	811
Santa Clarita	94.2	526	0.0	50.3	74.1	36.1	94.2	13.96	2,502	1,139
Santa Cruz	79.2	1,278	0.0	50.6	63.7	40.2	74.8	30.67	2,836	162
Santa Maria	66.7	658	51.7	51.6	63.5	39.3	73.5	14.01	2,783	121
Santa Monica	353.1	3,846	20.3	57.0	65.5	50.2	68.8	13.27	1,810	429
Santa Paula	69.0	2,299	0.0	54.7	68.3	41.2	80.7	18.41	1,911	602
Santa Rosa	483.1	2,836	59.1	48.7	67.6	39.5	82.2	31.01	2,694	526
Santee	52.7	950	3.0	57.1	73.0	45.7	83.6	13.75	1,313	1,261
Saratoga	12.0	391	12.0	50.5	70.9	41.7	84.3	15.08	2,171	811
Seaside	39.4	1,164	0.0	51.6	60.2	43.4	68.1	20.35	3,092	74
Simi Valley	147.8	1,177	0.0	53.7	76.0	39.5	95.0	17.79	1,822	1,485
Soledad	45.3	1,710	0.0	NA	NA	NA	NA	NA	NA	NA
South Gate	167.3	1,750	0.0	58.3	74.2	48.5	83.8	15.14	928	1,506
South Pasadena	7.3	280	0.0	NA	NA	NA	NA	NA	NA	NA
South San Francisco	146.4	2,225	0.0	49.4	62.8	42.9	71.1	20.11	2,862	142
Stanton	76.1	1,975	0.0	58.0	72.9	46.6	87.7	13.84	1,153	1,299
Stockton	572.9	1,926	0.1	46.0	77.3	38.1	93.8	13.84	2,563	1,456
Suisun City	69.5	2,431	0.5	46.1	72.6	37.5	88.8	23.46	2,649	975
Sunnyvale	125.4	855	0.0	50.5	70.9	41.7	84.3	15.08	2,171	811
Temecula	96.6	922	0.0	51.2	78.3	36.1	97.8	11.40	2,123	1,710
Temple City	6.3	174	0.0	56.3	75.6	42.6	89.0	18.56	1,295	1,575
Thousand Oaks	133.2	1,040	0.0	53.7	76.0	39.5	95.0	17.79	1,822	1,485
Torrance	148.8	1,010	0.0	56.3	69.4	46.2	77.6	14.79	1,526	742
Tracy	222.9	2,633	0.0	47.1	76.4	38.5	92.5	12.51	2,421	1,470
Tulare	200.3	3,290	0.0	45.8	79.3	37.4	93.8	11.03	2,588	1,685
Turlock	69.6	997	0.0	46.4	77.6	39.0	93.3	12.43	2,519	1,506
Tustin	193.5	2,486	8.9	54.5	72.1	41.4	83.8	13.87	1,794	1,102
Twentynine Palms	11.0	429	0.0	50.0	88.4	36.1	105.8	4.57	1,910	3,064
Union City	178.1	2,483	0.0	49.8	68.0	42.0	78.3	14.85	2,367	530
Upland	41.7	555	0.0	54.6	73.8	41.5	88.7	16.96	1,727	1,191
Vacaville	190.4	2,028	31.2	47.2	77.3	38.8	95.8	24.55	2,410	1,498
Vallejo	192.2	1,630	0.0	46.3	71.2	38.8	87.4	19.58	2,757	786
Victorville	370.9	3,084	0.0	45.5	80.0	31.4	99.1	6.20	2,929	1,735
Visalia	31.2	246	0.0	45.8	79.3	37.4	93.8	11.03	2,588	1,685
Vista	245.6	2,552	0.0	56.4	71.6	45.1	82.2	13.69	1,514	1,047
Walnut	28.7	956	0.0	54.6	73.8	41.5	88.7	16.96	1,727	1,191
Walnut Creek	4.9	74	0.2	47.5	72.4	39.3	85.2	23.96	3,267	983
Wasco	4.4	173	0.0	NA	NA	NA	NA	NA	NA	NA
Watsonville	36.2	698	0.0	49.7	62.4	38.7	72.0	23.25	3,080	123
West Covina	181.9	1,691	8.9	56.3	75.6	42.6	89.0	18.56	1,295	1,575
West Hollywood	100.2	2,875	0.0	58.3	74.2	48.5	83.8	15.14	928	1,506
Westminster	142.2	1,553	0.0	58.0	72.9	46.6	82.7	13.84	1,153	1,299
West Sacramento	368.8	7,425	94.7	46.3	75.4	38.8	92.4	17.93	2,666	1,248
Whittier	98.6	1,142	7.7	56.3	75.6	42.6	89.0	18.56	1,295	1,575
Wildomar	0.0	0	0.0	NA	NA	NA	NA	NA	NA	NA
Windsor	27.1	1,000	12.5	NA	NA	NA	NA	NA	NA	NA
Woodland	111.4	1,977	5.9	45.7	76.4	37.6	94.0	20.78	2,683	1,417
Yorba Linda	117.7	1,769	2.7	56.9	73.2	45.2	84.0	11.23	1,286	1,294
Yuba City	63.6	980	0.0	46.3	78.9	37.8	96.3	22.07	2,488	1,687
Yucaipa	35.9	684	0.0	52.9	78.0	40.4	94.4	13.62	1,904	1,714
COLORADO	X	X	X	X	X	X	X	X	X	X
Arvada	120.5	1,098	0.0	31.2	71.5	15.6	88.3	18.17	5,988	496
Aurora	1,215.3	3,582	2.6	29.2	73.4	15.2	88.0	15.81	6,128	696
Boulder	155.7	1,527	18.5	32.5	71.6	19.2	87.2	19.93	5,687	552
Brighton	76.1	2,167	0.0	NA	NA	NA	NA	NA	NA	NA
Broomfield	293.0	4,968	0.0	32.5	71.6	19.2	87.2	19.93	5,687	552

1. Based on the population estimated as of July 1 of the year shown.　　2. Represents normal values based on the 30-year period, 1971±2000.　　3. Average daily minimum.　　4. Average daily maximum.

Table D. Cities — Land Area and Population

STATE Place code	City	Land area[1] (sq. mi)	Total persons 2018	Rank	Per square mile	White	Black or African American	American Indian, Alaskan Native	Asian	Hawaiian Pacific Islander	Some other race	Two or more races (percent)
								Race 2017 — Race alone[2] (percent)				
		1	2	3	4	5	6	7	8	9	10	11
	COLORADO— Cont'd											
08 12,415	Castle Rock	34.3	64,827	575	1,890.0	89.8	0.6	0.3	2.1	0.1	4.4	2.7
08 12,815	Centennial	29.6	110,831	272	3,744.3	87.6	3.5	0.0	3.6	0.0	2.7	2.5
08 16,000	Colorado Springs	195.0	472,688	39	2,424.0	78.8	5.6	1.1	2.4	0.5	5.2	6.3
08 16,495	Commerce City	35.7	58,449	646	1,637.2	80.5	8.3	0.9	2.3	0.0	5.7	2.3
08 20,000	Denver	153.3	716,492	19	4,673.8	75.4	9.1	1.1	3.9	0.2	7.0	3.4
08 24,785	Englewood	6.6	34,690	1,100	5,256.1	90.9	0.8	0.4	1.0	0.0	4.9	2.0
08 27,425	Fort Collins	56.7	167,830	157	2,960.0	89.5	1.9	1.1	3.2	0.1	1.0	3.2
08 27,865	Fountain	22.5	30,454	1,236	1,353.5	69.1	11.6	0.6	8.2	0.0	2.7	7.9
08 31,660	Grand Junction	39.4	63,374	589	1,608.5	89.6	1.5	0.9	2.9	1.0	2.6	1.4
08 32,155	Greeley	48.8	107,348	284	2,199.8	87.6	2.0	0.8	1.2	0.0	6.4	2.1
08 43,000	Lakewood	43.0	156,798	162	3,646.5	88.2	1.0	1.5	3.4	0.0	2.4	3.4
08 45,255	Littleton	12.6	48,007	806	3,810.1	88.0	3.8	0.6	2.3	0.0	2.6	2.7
08 45,970	Longmont	27.6	96,577	326	3,499.2	87.1	0.9	0.8	3.4	0.0	3.8	3.9
08 46,465	Loveland	34.2	77,446	446	2,264.5	95.2	0.2	0.9	1.1	0.0	1.3	1.4
08 54,330	Northglenn	7.4	39,010	990	5,271.6	84.3	1.3	0.6	5.4	0.0	3.5	4.9
08 57,630	Parker	21.8	55,636	681	2,552.1	85.7	3.1	0.3	6.0	0.0	1.5	3.4
08 62,000	Pueblo	55.8	111,750	264	2,002.7	74.7	2.4	5.0	1.1	0.1	12.1	4.5
08 77,290	Thornton	35.3	139,436	194	3,950.0	87.1	2.4	0.6	4.8	0.0	2.5	2.6
08 83,835	Westminster	31.6	113,479	256	3,591.1	84.9	1.2	0.9	6.3	0.1	2.9	3.6
08 84,440	Wheat Ridge	9.3	31,400	1,206	3,376.3	88.1	1.8	0.7	0.4	0.0	3.8	5.2
09 00,000	**CONNECTICUT**	4,842.7	3,572,665	X	737.7	75.9	10.6	0.3	4.6	0.0	5.3	3.3
09 08,000	Bridgeport	16.1	144,900	182	9,000.0	41.4	35.6	0.6	3.6	0.0	14.5	4.2
09 08,420	Bristol	26.4	60,032	623	2,273.9	83.7	7.0	0.8	0.7	0.0	3.5	4.4
09 18,430	Danbury	41.9	84,730	399	2,022.2	57.4	11.3	0.1	6.3	0.0	22.7	2.2
09 37,000	Hartford	17.4	122,587	227	7,045.2	27.7	36.2	0.1	3.8	0.0	25.4	6.8
09 46,450	Meriden	23.8	59,540	630	2,501.7	76.2	14.3	0.3	1.9	0.0	5.2	2.0
09 47,290	Middletown	41.0	46,146	836	1,125.5	72.3	17.6	1.1	5.9	0.0	0.7	2.4
09 47,500	Milford	21.9	53,120	729	2,425.6	86.2	5.9	0.2	5.0	0.0	0.8	1.9
09 49,880	Naugatuck	16.3	31,288	1,208	1,919.5	NA	NA	NA	NA	NA	NA	NA
09 50,370	New Britain	13.4	72,453	494	5,406.9	74.2	13.1	0.0	3.3	0.0	6.5	2.9
09 52,000	New Haven	18.7	130,418	210	6,974.2	43.3	35.2	0.1	4.9	0.0	13.0	3.6
09 52,280	New London	5.6	26,939	1,363	4,810.5	57.8	8.0	0.0	3.6	0.0	17.9	12.7
09 55,990	Norwalk	22.9	89,047	371	3,888.5	73.3	14.0	0.5	4.1	0.1	5.3	2.7
09 56,200	Norwich	28.1	39,136	988	1,392.7	70.2	11.5	0.3	10.6	0.0	0.6	6.8
09 68,100	Shelton	30.6	41,097	931	1,343.0	88.8	3.8	0.0	5.2	0.0	0.5	1.7
09 73,000	Stamford	37.6	129,775	211	3,451.5	67.3	8.1	0.8	8.8	0.1	12.4	2.4
09 76,500	Torrington	39.8	34,228	1,113	860.0	87.4	5.8	0.2	4.5	0.0	0.5	1.7
09 80,000	Waterbury	28.5	108,093	281	3,792.7	61.1	18.5	0.2	2.3	0.0	11.9	6.0
09 82,800	West Haven	10.8	54,879	698	5,081.4	62.3	19.8	0.5	5.0	0.0	7.7	4.8
10 00,000	**DELAWARE**	1,948.2	967,171	X	496.4	68.8	21.9	0.3	4.0	0.0	1.9	3.0
10 21,200	Dover	23.7	38,079	1,012	1,606.7	44.3	42.4	0.4	4.2	0.0	0.6	8.1
10 50,670	Newark	9.2	33,673	1,135	3,660.1	75.9	8.2	1.0	10.0	0.3	1.2	3.4
10 77,580	Wilmington	10.9	70,635	509	6,480.3	37.0	60.3	0.1	0.8	0.0	0.6	1.1
11 00,000	**DISTRICT OF COLUMBIA**	61.1	702,455	X	11,496.8	41.0	45.9	0.2	4.1	0.0	5.8	3.0
11 50,000	Washington	61.1	702,455	20	11,496.8	41.0	45.9	0.2	4.1	0.0	5.8	3.0
12 00,000	**FLORIDA**	53,648.6	21,299,325	X	397.0	75.1	16.2	0.3	2.8	0.1	2.9	2.6
12 00,950	Altamonte Springs	9.1	44,241	866	4,861.6	71.9	18.1	0.2	4.4	0.0	1.6	3.9
12 01,700	Apopka	33.5	53,489	724	1,596.7	NA	NA	NA	NA	NA	NA	NA
12 02,681	Aventura	2.7	37,988	1,014	14,069.6	NA	NA	NA	NA	NA	NA	NA
12 07,300	Boca Raton	28.9	99,244	312	3,434.0	87.3	4.9	0.0	3.1	0.0	3.0	1.6
12 07,525	Bonita Springs	38.7	57,370	659	1,482.4	NA	NA	NA	NA	NA	NA	NA
12 07,875	Boynton Beach	16.2	78,050	443	4,817.9	57.9	37.8	0.1	2.4	0.0	1.0	0.9
12 07,950	Bradenton	14.4	57,644	656	4,003.1	76.7	15.7	0.0	0.7	0.0	4.7	2.2
12 10,275	Cape Coral	105.8	189,343	132	1,789.6	91.5	3.6	0.4	2.0	0.0	0.8	1.6
12 11,050	Casselberry	6.9	28,876	1,291	4,184.9	72.6	11.9	1.4	5.1	0.5	2.6	6.0
12 12,875	Clearwater	26.0	116,478	246	4,479.9	76.0	12.8	1.3	2.1	0.0	5.5	2.3
12 12,925	Clermont	14.3	36,693	1,046	2,565.9	NA	NA	NA	NA	NA	NA	NA
12 13,275	Coconut Creek	11.2	61,361	607	5,478.7	80.0	14.4	0.0	2.0	0.0	1.0	2.6
12 14,125	Cooper City	8.0	35,853	1,073	4,481.6	82.5	5.2	0.4	2.9	0.0	2.6	6.3
12 14,250	Coral Gables	12.9	50,999	754	3,953.4	91.4	3.6	0.0	2.7	0.0	0.4	2.0
12 14,400	Coral Springs	22.9	133,507	206	5,830.0	65.3	20.6	0.2	7.0	0.0	2.0	4.8
12 15,968	Cutler Bay	9.9	44,867	851	4,532.0	86.4	10.1	0.0	0.4	0.0	2.6	0.5
12 16,335	Dania Beach	7.8	32,271	1,176	4,137.3	73.3	20.0	0.0	3.2	0.0	1.3	2.3
12 16,475	Davie	35.0	106,558	288	3,044.5	69.9	14.6	0.0	4.3	0.4	6.1	4.6
12 16,525	Daytona Beach	65.6	68,866	520	1,049.8	57.8	34.0	0.5	3.1	0.1	1.6	2.8

1. Dry land or land partially or temporarily covered by water.   2. Hispanic or Latino persons may be of any race.

Table D. Cities — Population

City	Percent Hispanic or Latino[1], 2017	Percent foreign born, 2017	Age of population (percent), 2017							Median age, 2017	Percent female, 2017	Population			
			Under 18 years	18 to 24 years	25 to 34 years	35 to 44 years	45 to 54 years	55 to 64 years	65 years and over			Census counts		Percent change	
												2000	2010	2000-2010	2001-2018
	12	13	14	15	16	17	18	19	20	21	22	23	24	25	26
COLORADO— Cont'd															
Castle Rock............	12.0	5.8	29.1	7.8	12.1	16.5	15.7	9.6	9.2	35.6	49.7	20,224	48,254	138.6	34.3
Centennial...............	8.9	8.8	23.5	7.2	11.3	14.0	13.5	15.4	15.1	41.0	49.6	NA	100,635	**********	10.1
Colorado Springs.........	17.5	7.0	23.7	10.4	16.5	12.4	11.6	11.5	13.9	34.7	49.6	360,890	417,433	15.7	13.2
Commerce City............	47.1	11.5	33.7	8.0	15.5	16.6	11.4	7.1	7.7	31.2	50.5	20,991	45,905	118.7	27.3
Denver......................	29.9	15.0	19.9	8.1	22.9	15.9	11.6	10.0	11.6	34.5	49.9	554,636	599,815	8.1	19.5
Englewood................	19.0	4.8	14.5	7.6	20.5	13.1	11.2	15.8	17.2	39.2	47.4	31,727	30,259	-4.6	14.6
Fort Collins..............	14.6	7.8	20.8	22.7	16.9	11.0	10.0	8.7	9.8	28.4	49.7	118,652	144,855	22.1	15.9
Fountain..................	25.7	11.4	35.0	3.7	22.7	17.8	13.5	5.4	1.9	30.0	53.2	15,197	25,932	70.6	17.4
Grand Junction...........	15.3	8.5	21.5	12.8	14.1	12.6	10.7	11.7	16.6	36.3	51.2	41,986	59,034	40.6	7.4
Greeley...................	37.8	12.8	23.0	15.0	14.8	11.7	12.4	10.7	12.4	32.4	50.5	76,930	92,945	20.8	15.5
Lakewood..................	25.4	8.8	19.8	9.9	15.8	13.0	12.2	13.3	15.9	37.9	50.8	144,126	142,626	-1.0	9.9
Littleton.................	14.0	5.8	19.7	7.5	14.2	13.1	12.4	14.5	18.7	42.2	51.6	40,340	41,633	3.2	15.3
Longmont..................	24.2	11.9	25.3	7.3	12.5	16.3	13.8	12.2	12.6	37.8	51.1	71,093	86,310	21.4	11.9
Loveland..................	9.9	3.6	16.3	8.5	14.6	13.3	11.6	15.3	20.4	43.0	52.2	50,608	66,890	32.2	15.8
Northglenn...............	36.4	11.0	27.9	12.8	17.3	14.9	9.4	9.3	8.3	30.0	49.4	31,575	35,762	13.3	9.1
Parker....................	10.1	8.5	30.0	8.4	11.3	18.0	14.3	11.1	6.7	35.3	51.0	23,558	45,337	92.4	22.7
Pueblo....................	50.3	4.0	21.7	10.4	13.4	11.4	13.2	12.7	17.0	38.1	51.5	102,121	106,544	4.3	4.9
Thornton..................	35.4	12.6	27.8	5.9	15.2	14.4	15.5	11.0	10.2	35.6	48.9	82,384	118,784	44.2	17.4
Westminster..............	21.2	8.4	20.9	9.2	17.2	14.4	12.2	11.6	14.4	36.6	50.4	100,940	106,144	5.2	6.9
Wheat Ridge..............	16.2	3.1	17.6	7.1	20.3	13.2	13.6	9.3	18.9	38.6	51.4	32,913	30,180	-8.3	4.0
CONNECTICUT...............	16.1	14.8	20.7	9.8	12.4	11.7	14.4	14.3	16.8	40.9	51.2	3,405,565	3,574,147	5.0	0.0
Bridgeport...............	40.0	32.4	22.8	12.4	15.1	13.4	12.6	12.3	11.3	34.8	50.2	139,529	144,239	3.4	0.5
Bristol...................	16.1	7.3	18.2	8.6	13.4	12.5	11.4	16.6	19.3	42.8	50.4	60,062	60,474	0.7	-0.7
Danbury...................	28.3	33.0	19.0	10.2	15.3	14.5	13.0	12.6	15.3	38.2	49.3	74,848	80,907	8.1	4.7
Hartford..................	45.1	23.6	25.2	15.2	16.7	11.1	11.5	9.7	10.6	30.7	52.5	121,578	124,770	2.6	-1.7
Meriden...................	27.0	11.1	15.8	6.8	12.5	16.5	13.5	16.5	18.4	44.0	52.6	58,244	60,841	4.5	-2.1
Middletown................	9.6	10.9	16.4	14.2	16.1	12.2	10.7	15.1	15.4	38.7	49.7	43,167	47,648	10.4	-3.2
Milford...................	8.5	12.8	18.7	7.1	10.0	11.0	18.0	16.0	19.2	46.8	47.7		51,271	NA	3.6
Naugatuck.................	10.6	11.1	20.4	8.9	13.3	13.0	13.4	15.8	15.1	38.9	50.1	30,989	31,885	2.9	-1.9
New Britain...............	42.2	17.4	21.6	9.2	18.8	12.0	11.4	12.4	14.6	35.6	54.3	71,538	73,202	2.3	-1.0
New Haven.................	29.3	14.7	22.3	16.7	18.2	13.2	10.8	9.1	9.8	30.4	49.6	123,626	129,884	5.1	0.4
New London................	34.1	16.9	16.8	16.0	14.4	9.1	18.4	13.3	12.0	38.0	48.7	25,671	27,620	7.6	-2.5
Norwalk...................	34.8	29.7	20.9	8.1	17.0	11.4	16.4	12.9	13.3	38.5	52.8	82,951	85,623	3.2	4.0
Norwich...................	10.4	15.9	19.6	8.2	13.6	8.9	14.7	15.5	19.6	44.6	51.8	36,117	40,495	12.1	-3.4
Shelton...................	6.2	13.6	17.6	12.4	9.3	11.4	14.6	16.3	18.4	43.9	54.0	38,101	39,562	3.8	3.9
Stamford..................	27.7	35.3	19.6	9.2	16.0	15.5	12.8	11.4	15.7	38.0	51.4	117,083	122,633	4.7	5.8
Torrington................	9.2	12.6	17.3	6.0	11.7	11.7	18.4	14.8	20.2	46.6	48.8	35,202	36,386	3.4	-5.9
Waterbury.................	41.0	18.9	25.9	9.0	15.5	9.9	13.6	11.1	14.9	34.7	53.2	107,271	110,329	2.9	-2.0
West Haven................	29.3	14.6	20.6	12.7	19.8	11.4	12.0	12.5	11.0	33.5	49.5	52,360	55,564	6.1	-1.2
DELAWARE......................	9.3	10.2	21.2	8.7	13.6	11.5	12.9	13.9	18.0	40.1	51.6	783,600	897,934	14.6	7.7
Dover.....................	4.8	10.8	18.2	16.7	15.6	11.0	12.5	9.5	16.5	34.0	53.8	32,135	35,804	11.4	6.4
Newark....................	7.7	12.7	9.8	44.1	11.9	6.7	6.4	8.6	12.4	22.9	55.0	28,547	31,491	10.3	6.9
Wilmington................	8.4	7.6	23.0	9.3	16.2	13.2	12.2	11.8	14.4	36.4	51.7	72,664	70,835	-2.5	-0.3
DISTRICT OF COLUMBIA....	11.0	14.7	18.0	10.8	23.4	14.7	11.0	10.1	12.1	34.0	52.6	572,059	601,766	5.2	16.7
Washington................	11.0	14.7	18.0	10.8	23.4	14.7	11.0	10.1	12.1	34.0	52.6	572,059	601,766	5.2	16.7
FLORIDA........................	25.6	20.9	20.0	8.4	12.9	12.1	13.2	13.3	20.1	42.0	51.1	15,982,378	18,804,580	17.7	13.3
Altamonte Springs..............	25.3	16.9	14.3	10.4	19.5	14.7	11.7	13.3	16.0	38.9	53.9	41,200	41,614	1.0	6.3
Apopka....................	27.3	14.1	23.2	10.3	15.2	12.8	12.2	9.2	17.1	35.5	48.9	26,642	42,140	58.2	26.9
Aventura..................	42.3	52.3	14.1	3.3	7.5	13.0	16.2	17.6	28.4	53.0	51.0	25,267	35,762	41.5	6.2
Boca Raton................	14.5	19.9	17.9	8.0	11.8	8.6	13.2	15.6	24.9	47.9	52.4	74,764	84,409	12.9	17.6
Bonita Springs............	34.1	30.0	14.2	3.7	10.8	8.3	9.2	14.4	39.3	56.4	52.2	32,797	43,928	33.9	30.6
Boynton Beach.............	13.9	24.7	18.6	7.0	18.0	11.7	13.1	12.3	19.2	39.6	50.3	60,389	68,213	13.0	14.4
Bradenton.................	18.1	14.2	17.7	8.2	13.9	9.8	10.2	15.1	25.1	45.4	53.4	49,504	49,270	-0.5	17.0
Cape Coral................	21.7	16.7	17.7	6.8	10.0	11.4	13.0	16.5	24.6	47.9	50.3	102,286	154,314	50.9	22.7
Casselberry..............	24.2	9.4	19.9	7.2	17.1	12.4	12.6	15.7	15.1	39.2	46.1	22,629	26,120	15.4	10.6
Clearwater................	24.0	19.0	20.9	6.3	11.6	14.0	13.4	14.4	19.4	42.3	55.5	108,787	109,019	0.2	6.8
Clermont	10.7	12.8	22.4	8.6	7.8	12.4	13.2	15.0	20.7	44.5	54.1	9,333	28,791	208.5	27.4
Coconut Creek.............	21.7	30.1	20.5	8.6	9.6	14.1	15.5	11.7	20.0	42.9	53.0	43,566	53,037	21.7	15.7
Cooper City...............	32.8	25.5	24.9	9.7	7.9	14.7	17.5	11.1	14.2	40.3	52.0	27,939	28,537	2.1	25.6
Coral Gables..............	57.7	36.1	21.2	14.1	9.9	11.9	11.1	12.4	19.4	38.5	52.6	42,249	46,747	10.6	9.1
Coral Springs.............	27.0	33.0	25.8	8.4	12.9	14.9	13.7	12.8	11.6	37.3	53.6	117,549	122,091	3.9	9.4
Cutler Bay................	70.4	45.3	22.9	7.6	13.8	12.9	15.8	12.8	14.2	37.7	54.0	NA	40,286	**********	11.4
Dania Beach	36.1	32.0	23.2	5.7	14.2	13.8	14.8	15.1	13.2	39.9	52.9	20,061	29,737	48.2	8.5
Davie.....................	36.2	29.9	23.5	10.3	12.8	12.9	13.0	14.0	13.6	37.6	53.6	75,720	91,950	21.4	15.9
Daytona Beach	8.0	8.6	19.5	11.3	16.1	9.6	11.1	13.6	18.9	38.1	48.7	64,112	61,575	-4.0	11.8

1. May be of any race.

Table D. Cities — Households, Group Quarters, Crime, and Education

City	Households, 2017							Persons in group quarters, 2017	Serious crimes known to police[2], 2016				Educational attainment, 2017		
			Percent						Total		Rate[3]			Attainment[4] (percent)	
	Number	Persons per household	Family	Married couple family	Female headed[1]	Non-family	One person		Number	Rate	Violent	Property	Population age 25 and over	High school graduate or less	Bachelor's degree or more
	27	28	29	30	31	32	33	34	35	36	37	38	39	40	41
COLORADO— Cont'd															
Castle Rock	21,037	2.93	79.9	68.7	7.1	20.1	14.9	NA	932	1,632	88	1,544	39,309	18.3	47.3
Centennial	40,480	2.67	73.8	60.5	9.7	26.2	20.5	2,137	1,568	1,407	148	1,259	76,453	15.8	61.1
Colorado Springs	181,677	2.52	63.3	47.0	10.4	36.7	28.1	6,641	18,822	4,055	496	3,559	306,529	26.2	39.0
Commerce City	15,237	3.65	80.3	60.3	13.9	19.7	14.8	329	2,013	3,637	437	3,200	32,617	47.0	22.8
Denver	296,938	2.32	48.3	34.7	8.9	51.7	37.2	14,839	29,766	4,257	658	3,599	507,664	29.0	49.3
Englewood	15,833	2.14	52.1	39.6	6.7	47.9	38.0	525	1,763	5,238	229	5,009	26,813	32.2	39.0
Fort Collins	60,376	2.59	52.8	41.2	7.6	47.2	27.1	8,536	4,391	2,667	209	2,458	93,240	21.1	53.0
Fountain	10,055	2.96	81.7	63.1	13.0	18.3	12.6	NA	827	2,941	349	2,593	18,269	24.6	32.6
Grand Junction	26,006	2.30	54.9	43.0	8.1	45.1	37.6	2,654	3,374	5,565	518	5,047	41,040	36.0	31.8
Greeley	36,963	2.68	69.5	53.2	13.1	30.5	22.2	6,560	3,745	3,654	458	3,196	65,437	43.1	26.4
Lakewood	64,260	2.37	58.2	40.6	13.0	41.8	31.2	2,464	9,329	6,036	566	5,470	108,873	31.7	40.6
Littleton	20,138	2.32	61.7	45.5	10.6	38.3	29.2	528	1,345	2,844	102	2,743	34,435	24.7	50.6
Longmont	37,073	2.52	68.6	48.6	13.2	31.4	25.0	589	2,598	2,786	316	2,469	63,423	28.4	44.2
Loveland	33,384	2.28	59.6	47.5	7.5	40.4	31.9	505	2,195	2,853	247	2,606	57,713	29.4	40.6
Northglenn	12,229	3.17	73.5	52.2	15.3	26.5	20.3	NA	1,496	3,750	353	3,397	23,070	40.7	17.1
Parker	18,796	2.88	76.9	62.6	8.5	23.1	16.2	NA	638	1,266	91	1,174	33,368	14.5	51.6
Pueblo	44,459	2.42	60.7	39.1	16.2	39.3	33.4	3,698	8,572	7,798	987	6,811	75,366	42.1	19.0
Thornton	45,908	2.97	69.9	54.1	11.5	30.1	22.8	NA	4,786	3,507	350	3,158	90,899	40.3	26.8
Westminster	45,750	2.46	61.1	45.3	12.4	38.9	28.5	419	4,300	3,755	238	3,517	78,821	31.2	36.5
Wheat Ridge	13,923	2.20	54.1	38.8	13.1	45.9	35.5	617	1,600	5,097	350	4,747	23,548	31.8	38.3
CONNECTICUT	1,356,762	2.56	64.7	47.9	12.3	35.3	29.0	114,538	72,787	2,035	227	1,808	2,493,854	36.7	38.7
Bridgeport	48,023	2.96	65.5	32.6	24.2	34.5	27.5	4,464	4,373	2,951	752	2,199	94,978	59.0	16.4
Bristol	26,090	2.28	59.0	41.5	12.0	41.0	34.8	728	1,012	1,674	94	1,580	44,045	45.6	23.6
Danbury	30,963	2.65	60.4	42.7	12.4	39.6	29.3	3,344	1,524	1,786	189	1,597	60,301	45.0	33.0
Hartford	42,395	2.74	58.2	22.8	27.6	41.8	33.3	7,362	6,550	5,294	1,093	4,200	73,624	62.0	16.6
Meriden	27,864	2.11	51.2	36.1	9.9	48.8	45.8	1,052	1,594	2,665	380	2,285	46,383	55.0	22.3
Middletown	19,458	2.17	54.6	35.0	14.2	45.4	38.0	4,304	997	2,140	150	1,990	32,262	41.8	34.0
Milford	20,753	2.51	64.6	51.4	10.0	35.4	28.8	435	1,249	2,324	63	2,260	38,928	31.1	40.5
Naugatuck	11,713	2.66	69.0	50.3	13.5	31.0	26.8	306	582	1,849	118	1,732	22,223	36.1	24.6
New Britain	28,305	2.48	58.8	35.3	18.8	41.2	36.2	2,583	2,337	3,214	297	2,917	50,332	59.5	18.6
New Haven	47,579	2.56	47.9	22.7	19.9	52.1	41.5	9,241	6,717	5,150	938	4,212	79,829	44.5	34.4
New London	12,176	1.97	37.8	25.0	9.8	62.2	47.7	3,028	939	3,466	720	2,746	18,174	48.4	29.7
Norwalk	33,535	2.63	65.4	49.0	11.9	34.6	29.3	667	1,723	1,936	332	1,605	63,230	38.3	40.2
Norwich	16,798	2.32	59.4	43.0	13.0	40.6	34.3	428	742	1,866	304	1,561	28,521	50.2	18.3
Shelton	15,694	2.61	67.3	57.4	6.4	32.7	27.6	508	465	1,117	70	1,047	28,983	34.8	37.4
Stamford	51,254	2.53	58.8	42.8	12.2	41.2	30.7	1,115	2,441	1,876	272	1,604	93,226	32.0	49.8
Torrington	14,547	2.32	58.9	45.0	8.5	41.1	33.5	801	643	1,857	176	1,681	26,509	45.4	24.6
Waterbury	39,869	2.67	60.7	29.0	25.7	39.3	34.1	2,019	4,759	4,387	510	3,877	70,684	57.1	17.0
West Haven	18,854	2.74	59.8	38.9	15.8	40.2	30.3	3,189	1,186	2,164	248	1,916	36,571	49.2	23.5
DELAWARE	357,937	2.62	65.9	49.4	11.8	34.1	27.7	25,034	31,178	3,275	509	2,766	673,686	41.8	31.5
Dover	14,328	2.31	53.7	33.8	18.0	46.3	36.6	4,514	2,188	5,785	814	4,970	24,423	38.5	29.6
Newark	10,375	2.59	48.2	35.5	6.4	51.8	32.0	6,969	879	2,563	332	2,231	15,580	25.0	47.2
Wilmington	30,272	2.23	45.6	21.0	19.1	54.4	47.9	3,456	4,846	6,713	1,790	4,924	48,130	54.2	25.9
DISTRICT OF COLUMBIA	281,475	2.32	42.4	25.1	13.8	57.6	45.2	39,935	40,930	6,009	1,206	4,803	494,614	27.0	57.3
Washington	281,475	2.32	42.4	25.1	13.8	57.6	45.2	39,935	39,023	5,729	1,132	4,597	494,614	27.0	57.3
FLORIDA	7,689,964	2.67	64.3	46.7	12.7	35.7	28.8	428,146	642,512	3,117	430	2,687	15,020,177	40.5	29.7
Altamonte Springs	20,508	2.14	53.1	39.6	10.6	46.9	36.5	NA	1,687	3,878	349	3,529	33,326	19.1	42.5
Apopka	17,496	2.94	72.2	49.0	17.2	27.8	21.8	NA	2,232	4,482	450	4,032	34,272	45.0	27.8
Aventura	18,646	2.04	48.5	41.3	4.1	51.5	45.1	NA	1,993	5,243	168	5,075	31,552	16.3	48.7
Boca Raton	40,455	2.34	53.5	46.1	4.3	46.5	39.5	3,659	2,734	2,880	252	2,628	72,745	20.3	56.3
Bonita Springs	21,592	2.59	71.2	60.1	5.8	28.8	25.7	NA	NA	NA	NA	NA	46,046	41.1	34.0
Boynton Beach	27,522	2.80	57.3	38.9	14.5	42.7	33.6	746	4,067	5,412	659	4,754	57,762	40.8	28.7
Bradenton	21,531	2.55	55.2	42.6	10.6	44.8	38.1	1,503	2,041	3,676	591	3,085	41,853	43.8	24.1
Cape Coral	66,046	2.76	69.3	56.4	9.9	30.7	27.1	763	3,305	1,840	125	1,715	138,316	44.5	23.1
Casselberry	11,951	2.37	50.0	32.8	13.1	50.0	36.5	NA	1,220	4,482	562	3,920	20,681	29.0	26.1
Clearwater	45,734	2.48	58.5	39.0	15.8	41.5	35.6	1,929	4,391	3,855	558	3,297	84,055	43.5	29.1
Clermont	13,549	2.58	69.2	59.9	8.2	30.8	22.9	NA	773	2,331	160	2,171	24,318	42.2	32.8
Coconut Creek	23,976	2.53	60.2	44.7	11.5	39.8	33.3	NA	1,322	2,180	120	2,060	43,265	35.1	34.9
Cooper City	11,206	3.19	81.0	61.4	17.9	19.0	14.5	NA	473	1,282	95	1,187	23,370	32.6	38.7
Coral Gables	17,787	2.60	66.3	55.1	7.6	33.7	27.5	4,862	1,627	3,130	148	2,982	33,055	13.1	71.7
Coral Springs	41,195	3.22	74.8	50.3	18.2	25.2	21.8	NA	2,620	1,998	159	1,838	87,582	28.8	41.4
Cutler Bay	12,680	3.52	75.2	43.2	25.5	24.8	21.1	416	1,683	3,675	332	3,343	31,327	38.2	33.3
Dania Beach	11,039	2.89	72.4	46.4	22.9	27.6	25.3	NA	1,292	4,062	591	3,471	22,788	35.8	31.2
Davie	34,885	2.96	68.6	46.6	15.7	31.4	21.3	1,737	3,199	3,115	222	2,893	69,664	31.7	42.0
Daytona Beach	27,042	2.41	49.6	26.5	16.6	50.4	40.4	2,904	5,011	7,651	1,243	6,408	47,125	42.2	21.3

1. No spouse present. 2. Data for serious crimes have not been adjusted for underreporting. This may affect comparability between geographic areas and over time. 3. Per 100,000 population estimated by the FBI. 4. Persons 25 years old and over.

Table D. Cities — Income and Housing

City	Money income, 2017 Households					Median earnings, 2017			Housing units, 2017				
	Median income	Percent with income less than $20,000	Percent with income of $200,000 or more	Median family income	Median non-family income	All persons	Men	Women	Total	Occupied	Percent owner occupied	Median value[1] (dollars)	Median gross rent (dollars)
	42	43	44	45	46	47	48	49	50	51	52	53	54
COLORADO— Cont'd													
Castle Rock	105,008	5.9	13.0	118,280	50,486	46,769	65,516	32,888	21,525	21,037	74.3	424,800	1,492
Centennial	106,012	4.4	15.4	124,645	60,689	51,055	61,859	41,309	41,157	40,480	79.7	446,000	1,747
Colorado Springs	59,514	13.5	5.2	71,772	39,767	32,433	36,574	27,777	190,025	181,677	57.8	265,400	1,093
Commerce City	70,271	6.3	2.5	71,994	58,082	35,840	37,771	31,563	15,683	15,237	70.3	330,100	1,307
Denver	65,224	13.1	9.6	85,166	51,754	41,316	46,999	36,964	320,551	296,938	50.0	395,100	1,286
Englewood	65,123	10.6	3.4	81,777	45,303	40,554	46,143	34,336	16,972	15,833	48.8	359,300	1,273
Fort Collins	60,731	14.3	5.7	86,319	37,962	26,413	31,502	20,992	63,244	60,376	53.4	366,500	1,316
Fountain	72,754	6.3	3.1	72,623	61,363	37,417	51,964	22,032	10,675	10,055	65.7	235,900	1,566
Grand Junction	50,071	22.2	3.3	66,566	31,521	26,736	36,029	16,578	27,347	26,006	56.5	246,600	846
Greeley	53,379	17.8	2.6	66,358	34,911	30,755	35,917	23,113	39,027	36,963	60.2	248,000	935
Lakewood	67,255	11.4	5.9	82,575	47,866	36,986	41,087	31,675	67,415	64,260	58.8	385,200	1,354
Littleton	72,449	11.8	9.8	93,521	48,820	42,032	47,666	40,121	21,229	20,138	57.7	418,900	1,286
Longmont	73,832	10.8	7.5	89,395	44,390	37,314	44,677	31,746	38,431	37,073	59.5	366,900	1,300
Loveland	60,933	15.5	2.8	80,594	39,036	37,380	44,603	30,812	36,179	33,384	66.7	316,700	1,197
Northglenn	78,598	4.1	6.2	80,396	50,246	36,016	39,306	31,429	12,927	12,229	55.0	315,500	1,367
Parker	107,761	4.1	10.1	116,531	71,964	55,571	70,165	34,384	19,857	18,796	72.8	433,700	1,523
Pueblo	36,124	27.5	1.6	48,867	22,769	24,074	26,240	21,562	48,864	44,459	55.6	139,500	756
Thornton	77,092	9.4	3.7	82,425	51,286	37,470	47,390	30,890	48,251	45,908	74.0	324,800	1,424
Westminster	64,214	8.9	4.4	81,354	48,006	36,292	43,697	30,042	47,792	45,750	63.5	341,200	1,370
Wheat Ridge	61,761	19.7	5.7	75,032	31,289	32,057	32,532	30,774	14,055	13,923	47.8	397,800	1,180
CONNECTICUT	74,168	11.9	11.3	93,870	44,532	41,053	49,253	33,975	1,517,495	1,356,762	66.2	273,100	1,125
Bridgeport	45,048	24.1	3.3	52,768	24,022	25,813	28,108	22,587	56,057	48,023	45.5	177,600	1,091
Bristol	61,184	12.4	5.2	76,535	42,679	40,204	44,007	37,889	28,892	26,090	59.7	201,600	1,021
Danbury	65,596	13.0	6.1	73,512	58,930	32,471	35,542	29,071	34,314	30,963	57.9	314,300	1,428
Hartford	33,677	31.4	1.6	37,198	22,402	25,003	27,423	22,949	51,141	42,395	24.1	168,000	926
Meriden	55,721	8.9	2.6	72,761	47,128	43,965	47,899	42,012	30,987	27,864	57.9	169,100	920
Middletown	57,128	19.4	3.6	83,571	41,860	40,899	45,451	36,539	21,354	19,458	50.8	241,500	1,111
Milford	86,683	6.5	11.6	111,622	46,672	58,643	61,775	52,047	23,433	20,753	78.6	286,400	1,541
Naugatuck	70,839	7.9	3.9	95,192	40,050	36,581	39,063	31,615	12,549	11,713	64.1	208,100	1,068
New Britain	43,574	19.2	1.4	47,809	35,981	33,670	39,208	31,332	31,284	28,305	41.4	157,900	942
New Haven	44,445	25.3	3.7	54,618	30,889	26,890	28,910	25,706	54,906	47,579	28.8	194,200	1,127
New London	65,489	16.8	4.0	74,226	37,402	34,635	55,077	24,545	12,861	12,176	41.8	165,400	942
Norwalk	70,236	13.0	12.8	78,750	59,671	37,710	42,908	33,154	35,825	33,535	51.6	423,500	1,575
Norwich	49,780	24.5	5.4	74,081	19,940	28,541	35,401	25,779	20,363	16,798	57.0	174,200	834
Shelton	88,850	11.6	8.5	113,927	35,972	45,617	55,460	42,163	16,958	15,694	77.5	345,600	1,407
Stamford	87,316	9.4	18.6	106,011	62,257	45,189	51,053	36,593	56,952	51,254	53.3	517,700	1,705
Torrington	62,438	13.7	2.8	78,987	42,168	37,402	42,335	32,991	16,862	14,547	67.5	157,900	928
Waterbury	42,969	28.5	1.9	54,209	27,337	30,076	30,949	27,442	47,682	39,869	44.3	134,000	922
West Haven	64,243	12.6	3.1	72,100	48,456	30,523	36,713	23,350	21,867	18,854	54.3	189,800	1,165
DELAWARE	62,852	14.9	6.8	77,082	37,458	36,315	40,854	31,966	432,853	357,937	70.9	252,800	1,086
Dover	51,205	22.4	5.0	56,247	34,007	26,775	30,785	23,402	15,847	14,328	51.3	184,700	928
Newark	51,356	27.5	6.0	100,649	25,348	7,566	14,000	6,398	11,091	10,375	45.0	283,100	1,140
Wilmington	35,963	29.6	5.7	42,518	31,695	35,376	36,077	32,326	35,522	30,272	43.8	176,800	963
DISTRICT OF COLUMBIA	82,372	17.1	16.7	106,528	68,067	54,604	60,167	51,904	314,843	281,475	42.2	607,200	1,499
Washington	82,372	17.1	16.7	106,528	68,067	54,604	60,167	51,904	314,843	281,475	42.2	607,200	1,499
FLORIDA	52,594	16.7	5.4	64,003	33,962	30,471	33,572	26,412	9,441,585	7,689,964	65.2	214,000	1,128
Altamonte Springs	49,948	11.8	3.7	61,245	40,616	33,949	35,326	32,677	23,967	20,508	40.7	183,000	1,146
Apopka	49,472	9.3	5.2	61,079	31,672	29,229	35,105	23,650	18,613	17,496	69.0	228,400	1,133
Aventura	57,399	19.3	14.5	104,598	41,067	37,559	37,884	36,135	32,054	18,646	65.0	366,400	1,782
Boca Raton	80,815	12.4	18.5	109,408	50,591	45,960	70,367	31,134	54,380	40,455	75.9	459,200	1,483
Bonita Springs	67,654	8.5	8.8	71,850	50,214	31,719	35,761	26,184	37,065	21,592	75.1	332,500	1,203
Boynton Beach	51,372	15.3	3.7	54,088	46,380	30,751	31,652	27,393	35,142	27,522	59.5	200,200	1,495
Bradenton	43,603	18.7	1.7	54,588	32,486	26,995	31,154	23,851	28,267	21,531	55.8	187,200	1,086
Cape Coral	54,358	14.2	3.9	67,194	34,469	30,825	31,513	29,462	86,155	66,046	74.2	225,800	1,216
Casselberry	48,859	20.7	0.9	57,328	29,297	31,586	36,073	26,656	13,202	11,951	56.6	123,900	1,022
Clearwater	44,062	19.6	3.1	56,071	30,329	29,887	31,155	27,126	57,763	45,734	55.4	207,200	984
Clermont	68,383	15.4	4.7	80,016	35,608	34,593	41,142	32,073	16,178	13,549	74.1	237,200	1,543
Coconut Creek	60,363	13.0	3.5	66,892	38,665	35,312	37,484	29,594	27,320	23,976	68.0	181,500	1,649
Cooper City	101,011	4.8	10.8	102,440	56,522	43,019	51,340	40,959	11,452	11,206	85.5	373,300	2,200
Coral Gables	105,516	8.4	25.7	148,850	56,739	51,686	69,867	40,257	21,586	17,787	67.2	860,600	1,658
Coral Springs	72,557	9.2	10.1	79,181	50,361	36,149	42,853	30,789	44,453	41,195	62.1	347,400	1,468
Cutler Bay	71,529	11.1	4.2	73,563	41,027	34,457	37,122	30,879	13,718	12,680	70.3	281,700	1,424
Dania Beach	48,827	16.5	2.1	49,236	32,368	25,852	27,364	21,250	14,045	11,039	56.0	194,300	1,238
Davie	63,243	16.5	11.1	76,238	37,753	34,801	40,073	30,420	39,459	34,885	70.3	281,200	1,449
Daytona Beach	33,228	28.7	1.0	41,756	25,459	25,189	26,056	23,873	32,727	27,042	44.5	147,700	925

1. Based on population estimated by the American Community Survey. 2. Includes units rented or sold but not occupied. 3. Specified owner-occupied units; $1,000,000 represents $1,000,000 or more. 4. 50.0 represents 50 percent or more. 5. 10.0 represents 10 percent or less.

Table D. Cities — Commuting, Computer Access, Migration, Labor Force, and Employment

City	Commuting¹, 2017		Computer access², 2017		Migration, 2017		Civilian labor force, 2018				Civilian employment⁴, 2017			
	Percent		Percent						Unemployment		Population age 16 and older		Population age 16 to 64	
	Commuting	With commutes of 30 minutes or more	With a computer in the house	With Internet access	Percent who lived in the same house one year ago	Percent who lived in another state or county one year ago	Total	Percent change 2017-2018	Total	Rate³	Number	Percent in labor force	Number	Percent who worked full-year full-time
	55	56	57	58	59	60	61	62	63	64	65	66	67	68
COLORADO— Cont'd														
Castle Rock	76.6	46.7	97.9	96.4	82.4	8.2	34,332	3.4	989	2.9	46,375	72.9	40,651	56.6
Centennial	78.4	37.8	96.9	94.3	85.8	8.3	64,256	3.4	1,830	2.8	86,591	70.8	69,958	57.2
Colorado Springs	77.5	25.0	94.7	89.8	76.3	9.3	234,693	3.4	9,090	3.9	366,117	66.4	301,458	52.1
Commerce City	74.3	55.3	95.1	86.1	87.4	7.6	28,865	3.4	1,013	3.5	38,901	72.7	34,580	55.3
Denver	67.9	38.9	93.5	87.3	79.3	12.0	412,817	3.4	13,146	3.2	577,520	72.0	495,645	59.9
Englewood	75.2	43.6	92.8	85.1	75.0	17.7	21,192	3.4	683	3.2	30,209	73.0	24,275	64.2
Fort Collins	69.3	21.5	96.8	90.1	75.0	12.4	100,795	3.6	2,708	2.7	134,838	69.0	118,640	44.5
Fountain	73.1	40.0	NA	NA	77.4	16.4	12,883	4.0	610	4.7	20,896	72.0	20,329	51.4
Grand Junction	78.4	6.4	87.5	82.3	74.1	5.7	30,970	3.2	1,254	4.0	50,867	62.8	40,499	39.9
Greeley	77.9	32.6	92.4	80.1	82.8	9.1	53,844	4.8	1,761	3.3	83,750	63.5	70,637	47.8
Lakewood	76.3	41.8	94.5	89.6	82.3	8.6	87,144	3.4	2,823	3.2	128,877	68.6	104,236	57.3
Littleton	73.0	42.6	96.0	93.2	82.5	14.2	26,466	3.4	806	3.0	38,923	65.8	30,089	57.6
Longmont	75.0	36.4	94.8	88.4	82.0	11.3	53,292	3.7	1,700	3.2	73,480	73.4	61,604	55.5
Loveland	86.3	35.5	96.6	90.2	83.5	9.4	43,215	3.7	1,341	3.1	65,295	62.2	49,662	53.9
Northglenn	77.8	54.2	96.3	83.4	79.4	8.9	21,539	3.2	763	3.5	28,860	74.9	25,613	60.3
Parker	83.1	45.8	99.3	96.4	85.5	9.7	31,902	3.4	936	2.9	39,599	79.3	35,944	60.0
Pueblo	85.2	17.0	86.1	75.1	85.1	5.9	48,665	1.4	2,594	5.3	90,001	56.9	71,057	44.5
Thornton	81.2	54.6	95.6	88.4	84.8	6.1	76,913	3.4	2,515	3.3	103,186	73.1	89,217	56.4
Westminster	80.7	43.3	93.5	87.8	82.1	13.9	66,033	3.4	2,164	3.3	91,457	70.2	75,212	60.1
Wheat Ridge	73.3	40.7	92.4	84.4	75.7	14.6	17,158	3.3	622	3.6	26,610	70.1	20,698	55.7
CONNECTICUT	78.3	35.2	90.9	85.1	88.2	5.0	1,905,312	0.4	78,242	4.1	2,937,891	65.7	2,336,797	50.7
Bridgeport	70.7	43.8	85.1	77.1	87.0	3.4	69,676	0.1	4,204	6.0	116,382	64.9	99,760	39.0
Bristol	79.9	41.9	89.3	80.4	86.1	5.1	33,221	0.5	1,519	4.6	50,293	66.3	38,696	56.9
Danbury	77.9	39.5	91.9	85.3	87.2	6.1	47,230	0.0	1,609	3.4	70,162	70.6	57,103	47.9
Hartford	61.2	27.0	81.0	67.2	79.5	5.5	53,353	-0.1	3,734	7.0	96,674	58.3	83,564	36.3
Meriden	75.8	29.4	79.4	63.3	87.0	5.1	32,135	0.1	1,536	4.8	52,021	63.0	40,971	56.9
Middletown	77.3	33.7	86.5	73.9	89.7	6.8	26,265	0.6	1,047	4.0	39,545	64.0	32,399	50.1
Milford	84.4	30.2	93.0	88.6	87.9	4.0	30,459	0.5	1,145	3.8	NA	NA	NA	NA
Naugatuck	72.3	48.2	94.8	88.4	NA	NA	17,447	0.7	815	4.7	25,367	70.8	20,621	55.3
New Britain	79.1	22.7	82.6	68.3	86.9	4.1	36,815	0.4	2,059	5.6	58,483	58.6	47,866	45.4
New Haven	59.7	24.9	87.6	81.2	77.9	9.4	64,773	0.0	3,281	5.1	105,483	63.4	92,706	36.4
New London	72.5	16.7	89.8	81.7	84.6	8.6	12,101	-0.3	665	5.5	22,586	66.6	19,346	50.1
Norwalk	73.1	37.0	93.3	87.8	90.8	4.0	50,799	0.4	1,873	3.7	72,582	74.0	60,748	50.0
Norwich	85.7	30.3	79.7	78.4	89.0	0.9	20,328	0.0	913	4.5	32,808	62.2	25,082	46.8
Shelton	85.6	38.6	87.6	82.1	88.1	7.2	22,194	0.4	919	4.1	34,701	71.4	27,099	58.3
Stamford	66.8	35.3	93.9	88.3	85.4	6.3	70,883	0.5	2,609	3.7	108,126	70.5	87,619	53.1
Torrington	85.7	34.5	87.1	83.6	87.8	4.0	19,174	0.4	901	4.7	29,326	66.2	22,348	54.3
Waterbury	79.6	29.2	81.4	71.0	88.9	4.1	50,973	0.6	3,350	6.6	83,474	59.3	67,334	41.6
West Haven	79.8	25.3	89.7	85.7	81.2	8.5	30,195	0.3	1,433	4.7	44,557	75.4	38,540	53.6
DELAWARE	82.0	35.9	92.9	85.9	87.2	5.6	482,465	1.2	18,128	3.8	781,963	59.3	608,746	50.1
Dover	80.0	23.1	89.8	84.3	78.0	9.3	15,564	0.4	812	5.2	31,362	59.9	25,164	43.4
Newark	63.1	25.6	96.7	82.3	64.6	18.7	16,527	0.9	590	3.6	31,254	55.9	27,045	26.1
Wilmington	68.2	24.9	90.7	72.5	83.2	5.7	33,922	0.7	1,812	5.3	56,315	52.3	46,069	44.6
DISTRICT OF COLUMBIA	34.4	53.4	91.9	82.1	80.9	9.7	404,610	0.8	22,470	5.6	579,654	70.5	495,662	56.2
Washington	34.4	53.4	91.9	82.1	80.9	9.7	404,610	0.8	22,470	5.6	579,654	70.5	495,662	56.2
FLORIDA	79.4	42.7	91.9	82.7	84.5	7.1	10,234,770	1.4	365,097	3.6	17,280,632	58.4	13,065,400	50.0
Altamonte Springs	84.2	39.9	96.4	90.9	88.4	5.4	26,282	2.6	857	3.3	38,865	64.6	31,787	52.3
Apopka	74.5	56.9	92.5	83.9	92.9	3.4	27,781	2.6	816	2.9	41,524	66.0	32,729	56.7
Aventura	79.7	53.4	89.3	77.0	87.3	7.6	17,366	0.6	625	3.6	33,677	56.8	22,838	54.0
Boca Raton	78.7	27.3	97.3	91.3	81.0	10.3	52,928	1.1	1,627	3.1	82,163	57.0	57,738	45.8
Bonita Springs	78.1	44.2	94.6	89.7	89.9	5.9	25,088	1.9	820	3.3	49,214	45.6	27,151	51.2
Boynton Beach	83.6	36.6	94.9	83.6	78.9	9.4	39,270	0.9	1,446	3.7	64,687	62.1	49,762	54.7
Bradenton	82.4	41.2	91.0	82.2	86.1	6.8	26,196	1.3	906	3.5	47,624	53.5	33,454	47.8
Cape Coral	83.5	43.1	95.2	90.4	85.0	4.8	89,176	1.9	3,022	3.4	156,332	59.5	111,266	54.5
Casselberry	70.4	28.7	97.1	86.0	89.5	8.0	15,754	2.6	512	3.2	23,407	61.6	19,114	56.5
Clearwater	71.1	35.4	89.3	78.6	80.5	8.2	58,372	1.4	1,903	3.3	94,707	60.3	72,260	50.4
Clermont	85.3	63.1	97.2	94.0	86.9	11.1	16,498	2.6	544	3.3	28,465	64.5	21,176	55.8
Coconut Creek	83.7	47.6	94.0	86.8	79.7	7.7	33,256	1.1	1,038	3.1	49,957	64.4	37,776	54.1
Cooper City	84.8	60.1	97.9	93.8	90.2	4.2	20,453	1.1	569	2.8	27,863	66.4	22,771	52.2
Coral Gables	75.8	35.6	97.7	93.8	80.5	10.7	26,881	0.8	928	3.5	41,196	59.6	31,269	48.5
Coral Springs	82.0	53.1	98.4	93.5	83.2	7.6	74,475	1.2	2,460	3.3	102,980	72.5	87,588	52.1
Cutler Bay	81.0	74.4	93.2	85.5	NA	NA	23,831	0.6	858	3.6	35,929	68.9	29,544	59.6
Dania Beach	67.6	40.4	90.2	78.8	86.1	6.6	16,725	1.1	603	3.6	26,222	60.8	21,988	40.0
Davie	87.4	49.4	95.0	88.7	83.0	7.1	59,311	1.2	1,766	3.0	83,409	62.8	69,060	45.6
Daytona Beach	77.0	18.9	87.5	68.7	82.1	7.3	31,382	1.0	1,425	4.5	56,110	53.5	43,234	43.4

1. Employed persons.   2. Households.   3. Percent of civilian labor force.   4. Persons 16 years old and over.

City	Value of residential construction authorized by building permits, 2018			Wholesale trade[1], 2012				Retail trade[2], 2012			
	New construction ($1,000)	Number of housing units	Percent single family	Number of establishments	Number of employees	Sales (mil dol)	Annual payroll (mil dol)	Number of establishments	Number of employees	Sales (mil dol)	Annual payroll (mil dol)
	69	70	71	72	73	74	75	76	77	78	79
COLORADO— Cont'd											
Castle Rock	344,550	1,499	70.5	30	D	D	D	189	2,800	698.3	61.0
Centennial	61,502	273	96.3	189	3,340	12,326.3	261.0	264	4,771	1,842.4	159.3
Colorado Springs	NA	NA	NA	325	3,638	2,062.8	210.3	1,621	24,923	6,966.7	660.4
Commerce City	193,427	759	94.7	140	2,530	1,915.3	128.8	105	1,333	468.0	39.3
Denver	1,452,879	7,878	30.8	1,175	17,997	14,625.8	1,090.1	2,282	26,469	7,111.4	725.7
Englewood	42,172	204	45.1	100	1,489	754.3	84.5	203	2,525	876.6	72.2
Fort Collins	208,562	1,071	37.2	108	D	D	D	617	9,667	2,309.8	229.5
Fountain	NA	NA	NA	3	D	D	D	37	1,021	283.6	25.7
Grand Junction	NA	NA	NA	167	1,556	706.3	70.9	477	6,718	1,749.6	171.6
Greeley	112,986	538	64.7	77	1,110	790.0	51.2	291	4,986	1,379.5	132.7
Lakewood	119,805	792	13.3	129	930	1,069.2	68.6	669	10,547	2,528.7	263.6
Littleton	28,137	135	51.9	60	901	833.2	60.7	244	4,098	1,390.7	138.9
Longmont	270,926	1,067	46.8	69	775	427.5	52.2	270	3,932	1,137.4	105.0
Loveland	115,006	592	40.9	79	1,202	484.9	57.9	320	5,233	1,401.1	123.9
Northglenn	2,109	10	0.0	18	201	47.2	6.8	105	1,817	584.0	62.9
Parker	203,849	863	47.3	30	228	190.4	17.6	153	2,728	837.5	71.6
Pueblo	NA	NA	NA	58	704	341.3	29.7	406	6,473	1,653.1	157.5
Thornton	301,740	993	83.0	29	213	116.7	16.9	189	4,625	1,326.7	126.4
Westminster	49,393	182	100.0	72	1,572	1,733.1	183.3	322	6,329	1,552.3	145.2
Wheat Ridge	6,429	20	100.0	68	680	274.3	35.3	163	2,222	659.2	63.2
CONNECTICUT	1,112,212	4,815	53.0	3,675	58,814	161,962.2	3,934.4	12,597	182,528	51,632.5	4,974.5
Bridgeport	5,889	54	46.3	138	D	D	D	266	3,050	900.7	93.0
Bristol	6,134	39	79.5	38	342	180.9	16.3	170	2,867	824.5	75.6
Danbury	27,877	126	63.5	109	1,316	1,349.4	85.0	454	8,144	2,283.3	221.8
Hartford	673	5	100.0	112	2,244	1,317.7	107.6	357	3,053	1,813.7	100.6
Meriden	8,589	76	0.0	38	306	165.0	15.1	228	3,081	750.7	68.0
Middletown	3,023	16	100.0	44	1,087	800.9	65.3	120	1,690	457.4	45.7
Milford	13,578	167	19.2	98	1,476	792.5	87.7	323	5,819	1,667.1	149.2
Naugatuck	0	0	0.0	21	480	331.4	29.1	66	1,031	320.9	28.6
New Britain	7,323	84	4.8	39	402	179.8	21.3	146	1,691	553.7	45.6
New Haven	54,090	460	0.9	74	D	D	D	322	3,135	835.6	84.8
New London	6,124	37	100.0	13	D	D	D	101	1,343	463.7	42.2
Norwalk	12,563	29	62.1	129	2,445	1,940.3	142.7	343	5,913	1,719.0	217.9
Norwich	3,010	27	100.0	20	571	381.6	38.9	125	2,053	477.6	45.9
Shelton	12,615	62	96.8	56	D	D	D	90	1,821	831.5	65.7
Stamford	56,635	124	87.1	213	5,498	109,632.9	713.5	482	6,199	1,626.0	178.9
Torrington	721	3	100.0	32	D	D	D	159	2,832	931.4	75.3
Waterbury	1,504	27	55.6	80	803	519.7	46.1	425	6,035	1,620.9	152.8
West Haven	1,446	11	81.8	60	1,248	626.2	70.0	110	1,361	351.0	35.7
DELAWARE	788,602	6,003	91.2	835	7,653	5,628.9	385.9	3,616	51,711	14,456.0	1,270.1
Dover	42,654	206	76.2	38	296	114.7	13.2	205	3,883	1,005.0	85.7
Newark	2,091	21	100.0	41	195	117.5	9.5	176	2,877	921.4	81.8
Wilmington	8,665	35	100.0	114	878	767.7	50.7	303	2,882	862.8	84.2
DISTRICT OF COLUMBIA	518,239	4,615	2.4	335	3,415	2,591.9	260.6	1,710	19,780	4,439.9	525.2
Washington	518,239	4,615	2.4	335	3,415	2,591.9	260.6	1,710	19,780	4,439.9	525.2
FLORIDA	31,543,714	144,427	67.2	27,109	252,418	252,626.6	12,867.6	71,189	947,877	273,867.1	24,033.5
Altamonte Springs	4,969	29	100.0	77	1,929	423.7	42.2	342	5,824	1,363.3	127.9
Apopka	71,525	266	98.1	67	724	226.1	26.4	155	2,058	625.8	49.2
Aventura	7,000	6	0.0	142	476	1,807.9	35.5	375	9,146	2,197.9	206.7
Boca Raton	80,031	136	82.4	379	4,030	4,550.7	313.9	652	9,944	2,534.2	293.6
Bonita Springs	310,507	1,541	40.0	43	525	373.7	28.1	187	2,067	484.2	48.9
Boynton Beach	32,280	281	5.3	105	828	627.9	48.3	377	5,602	1,279.4	120.7
Bradenton	108,069	1,024	17.4	43	288	161.6	13.6	265	3,701	1,102.0	95.9
Cape Coral	500,597	2,601	86.3	100	294	140.4	12.3	404	6,381	1,692.8	150.1
Casselberry	646	4	100.0	26	111	53.1	4.2	128	2,264	478.2	52.0
Clearwater	62,493	537	8.0	143	1,373	633.3	75.8	647	9,790	2,790.5	261.7
Clermont	110,445	707	53.3	21	82	58.2	2.4	147	2,818	733.0	63.3
Coconut Creek	2,196	16	100.0	58	237	221.5	12.6	153	3,213	1,345.4	118.9
Cooper City	4,043	15	100.0	39	D	D	D	81	1,450	346.6	38.9
Coral Gables	26,978	35	100.0	180	1,576	9,268.1	128.7	297	4,154	1,556.6	152.6
Coral Springs	7,343	33	100.0	239	1,345	632.7	62.3	455	7,810	2,066.6	197.0
Cutler Bay	1,658	10	100.0	28	116	26.7	3.2	165	2,223	546.1	50.3
Dania Beach	7,863	37	100.0	129	857	529.1	39.0	183	1,613	510.5	45.7
Davie	12,944	41	100.0	262	1,782	688.4	76.7	405	5,802	2,050.3	170.3
Daytona Beach	37,536	141	100.0	79	627	253.7	26.3	461	6,387	1,687.6	152.6

1. Merchant wholesalers except manufacturers' sales branches and offices. 2. Establishments with payroll.

City	Real estate and rental and leasing, 2012				Professional, scientific, and technical services[1], 2012				Manufacturing, 2012			
	Number of establish-ments	Number of employees	Receipts (mil dol)	Annual payroll (mil dol)	Number of establish-ments	Number of employees	Receipts (mil dol)	Annual payroll (mil dol)	Number of establish-ments	Number of employees	Receipts (mil dol)	Annual payroll (mil dol)
	80	81	82	83	84	85	86	87	88	89	90	91
COLORADO— Cont'd												
Castle Rock	78	202	39.4	6.8	195	D	D	D	16	221	D	9.5
Centennial	250	998	354.1	53.2	695	3,802	1,019.8	274.6	69	1,750	667.5	112.4
Colorado Springs	845	2,875	545.3	102.9	1,907	D	D	D	351	8,351	2,236.8	473.5
Commerce City	48	531	114.8	20.7	43	293	229.5	19.6	87	2,851	5,446.3	164.6
Denver	1,451	9,373	2,723.8	488.3	4,273	D	D	D	759	17,032	5,343.9	761.4
Englewood	87	377	113.3	18.9	161	D	D	D	128	2,688	522.0	118.8
Fort Collins	298	1,258	173.5	40.5	877	6,219	736.6	343.1	109	5,760	3,156.6	361.8
Fountain	9	47	2.8	0.9	20	97	3.4	1.2	7	145	D	7.6
Grand Junction	195	663	143.5	26.7	365	D	D	D	93	1,938	382.8	78.8
Greeley	119	518	73.6	16.7	181	D	D	D	53	4,235	3,090.6	145.1
Lakewood	251	791	145.6	27.9	823	D	D	D	99	1,112	270.5	51.5
Littleton	89	410	52.1	12.4	346	4,994	1,110.9	517.6	32	4,492	1,698.0	414.4
Longmont	121	362	80.1	12.2	379	4,846	752.7	392.9	118	2,180	599.1	141.3
Loveland	110	577	74.2	19.1	260	1,265	144.6	54.4	99	2,619	756.9	199.0
Northglenn	31	107	18.8	3.5	59	256	22.9	8.6	26	425	100.2	19.9
Parker	71	118	30.1	4.5	220	687	102.7	36.3	27	399	D	15.2
Pueblo	108	523	83.1	15.4	185	D	D	D	54	1,733	821.0	72.1
Thornton	81	487	118.9	13.9	171	1,048	124.5	45.4	16	250	D	12.9
Westminster	157	568	114.5	20.7	378	D	D	D	53	747	270.3	42.9
Wheat Ridge	53	272	40.7	9.7	189	D	D	D	42	1,007	293.8	54.2
CONNECTICUT	3,219	19,778	5,349.5	958.4	9,176	96,768	17,863.9	8,316.7	4,350	163,847	55,160.1	10,546.2
Bridgeport	94	406	79.7	15.6	208	D	D	D	139	3,274	1,063.3	168.4
Bristol	40	151	31.1	5.5	67	302	40.4	15.8	130	2,827	663.8	148.5
Danbury	84	1,711	327.0	105.0	226	2,662	597.8	264.5	93	5,623	2,084.0	376.1
Hartford	164	1,337	270.0	66.6	392	5,588	1,361.1	488.4	68	1,013	207.6	44.6
Meriden	44	505	47.4	17.8	76	760	108.3	45.2	66	2,433	940.2	173.9
Middletown	39	248	37.7	10.2	108	D	D	D	52	3,583	2,078.3	231.1
Milford	51	D	D	D	178	2,832	268.5	104.6	151	3,305	1,532.1	214.8
Naugatuck	14	D	D	D	32	213	24.5	9.7	47	1,168	386.1	61.1
New Britain	40	184	44.2	6.2	84	D	D	D	94	2,959	758.3	165.2
New Haven	128	751	151.1	31.4	365	2,957	599.6	267.5	70	2,250	510.5	114.6
New London	24	147	24.3	5.7	96	D	D	D	15	212	D	9.0
Norwalk	95	327	81.0	15.6	340	3,538	837.7	299.1	100	1,733	404.2	120.5
Norwich	35	D	D	D	63	894	118.3	54.5	25	699	132.4	35.9
Shelton	38	605	89.0	23.4	140	1,681	394.2	141.0	64	2,951	1,302.9	191.0
Stamford	217	1,369	456.5	114.3	641	D	D	D	104	1,959	495.4	106.4
Torrington	25	102	14.1	3.6	61	463	74.5	35.4	65	1,870	422.2	92.3
Waterbury	72	293	70.0	10.1	146	D	D	D	153	3,206	956.8	157.0
West Haven	43	132	39.5	5.1	61	D	D	D	49	1,411	382.6	73.7
DELAWARE	1,111	5,402	5,471.2	264.9	2,536	D	D	D	573	26,355	22,597.4	1,393.2
Dover	75	286	50.3	10.6	159	D	D	D	19	1,518	940.3	91.7
Newark	49	192	409.9	5.4	115	D	D	D	25	932	276.4	66.4
Wilmington	204	805	1,802.6	35.2	585	D	D	D	66	999	D	53.8
DISTRICT OF COLUMBIA	1,112	10,103	3,213.9	673.7	4,831	89,224	29,796.2	10,549.2	113	1,361	309.8	61.5
Washington	1,112	10,103	3,213.9	673.7	4,831	89,224	29,796.2	10,549.2	113	1,361	309.8	61.5
FLORIDA	29,845	139,955	30,560.1	5,337.4	70,617	436,764	69,653.4	26,855.4	12,890	277,089	96,924.1	14,270.0
Altamonte Springs	109	1,328	141.9	42.8	293	1,495	158.6	57.3	40	307	45.4	11.9
Apopka	34	90	19.6	2.6	96	354	38.7	13.1	27	360	88.0	15.1
Aventura	206	737	136.8	26.3	362	944	181.4	59.5	13	149	D	4.4
Boca Raton	432	3,486	519.2	170.9	1,457	D	D	D	153	2,052	451.1	113.8
Bonita Springs	119	399	75.8	18.8	198	962	183.2	56.3	24	146	19.5	4.6
Boynton Beach	116	610	108.0	20.3	353	1,510	207.6	76.2	64	735	153.3	33.8
Bradenton	79	390	70.6	10.9	220	D	D	D	30	1,819	995.3	132.5
Cape Coral	292	534	104.5	17.6	348	D	D	D	85	548	84.2	25.4
Casselberry	46	329	40.6	10.9	89	414	34.4	11.9	26	298	39.2	12.5
Clearwater	280	1,132	166.8	39.4	694	D	D	D	97	1,674	319.2	64.9
Clermont	83	205	38.0	6.0	105	340	36.5	12.6	9	65	7.3	1.0
Coconut Creek	46	1,730	603.7	81.4	166	725	108.1	29.6	14	216	67.0	7.5
Cooper City	42	91	15.9	2.6	180	404	60.8	17.0	7	21	2.2	0.7
Coral Gables	359	1,144	331.7	54.6	1,505	D	D	D	28	447	D	25.9
Coral Springs	217	765	177.5	30.6	752	2,530	355.4	106.9	59	775	197.7	40.5
Cutler Bay	28	68	8.8	1.8	72	344	18.6	6.2	4	9	D	0.3
Dania Beach	58	301	83.0	16.7	137	D	D	D	44	696	136.0	31.9
Davie	196	604	147.1	24.9	538	D	D	D	88	1,879	924.1	130.4
Daytona Beach	143	667	137.5	25.6	312	D	D	D	63	1,532	376.6	82.0

1. Establishments subject to federal tax.

Accommodation and Food Services, Arts, Entertainment, and Recreation, and Health Care and Social Assistance

City	Accommodation and food services, 2012				Arts, entertainment, and recreation[1], 2012				Health care and social assistance,[1] 2012			
	Number of establish-ments	Number of employees	Receipts (mil dol)	Annual payroll (mil dol)	Number of establish-ments	Number of employees	Receipts (mil dol)	Annual payroll (mil dol)	Number of establish-ments	Number of employees	Receipts (mil dol)	Annual payroll (mil dol)
	92	93	94	95	96	97	98	99	100	101	102	103
COLORADO— Cont'd												
Castle Rock	103	1,843	88.7	26.4	16	D	D	D	107	D	D	D
Centennial	207	3,322	186.9	57.4	34	D	D	D	365	2,886	309.3	118.6
Colorado Springs	1,040	23,240	1,274.8	344.7	133	1,678	92.3	27.7	1,477	15,806	1,630.5	678.0
Commerce City	58	926	47.2	11.4	2	D	D	D	26	D	D	D
Denver	1,982	42,906	2,884.9	823.2	235	5,851	687.1	309.6	1,695	25,982	3,209.7	1,299.9
Englewood	95	1,448	75.2	21.7	8	D	D	D	206	D	D	D
Fort Collins	427	8,329	374.5	113.7	66	910	47.5	15.0	546	6,422	677.3	306.6
Fountain	45	967	37.6	9.6	1	D	D	D	22	155	15.1	5.9
Grand Junction	211	4,578	218.7	67.6	20	321	12.9	3.7	309	D	D	D
Greeley	184	3,501	157.6	47.0	23	216	6.4	2.1	222	2,645	241.0	98.5
Lakewood	378	7,456	385.9	117.3	44	641	29.8	9.3	487	7,651	747.3	321.9
Littleton	135	D	D	D	20	D	D	D	215	2,503	244.6	108.5
Longmont	187	3,623	177.6	53.6	26	167	8.5	2.1	250	2,606	228.9	107.6
Loveland	194	4,019	189.3	53.5	30	159	8.5	2.6	224	2,558	257.2	104.5
Northglenn	45	922	46.2	14.4	8	239	10.1	2.7	53	D	D	D
Parker	106	2,252	101.4	32.7	16	287	16.5	5.5	160	1,259	131.5	51.3
Pueblo	286	4,992	205.1	60.2	20	D	D	D	319	D	D	D
Thornton	164	3,197	178.1	48.7	23	D	D	D	155	2,057	211.7	89.3
Westminster	231	5,395	292.5	86.3	29	610	30.4	9.2	246	2,827	313.2	146.7
Wheat Ridge	91	1,347	68.7	20.1	16	83	5.2	1.5	168	D	D	D
CONNECTICUT	8,263	134,546	9,542.1	2,590.8	1,160	14,862	1,538.5	418.5	7,876	131,732	13,333.4	6,058.8
Bridgeport	227	2,202	148.4	36.4	23	366	29.6	6.3	217	4,554	524.5	261.5
Bristol	108	1,222	70.9	19.2	13	381	32.1	8.0	101	1,854	157.9	72.5
Danbury	211	3,531	226.6	63.2	19	226	14.3	4.5	216	D	D	D
Hartford	326	4,429	297.2	82.4	13	201	38.9	6.7	237	5,215	831.5	439.4
Meriden	116	1,292	67.8	17.0	4	D	D	D	98	1,770	163.6	80.8
Middletown	110	1,311	86.4	24.9	8	58	5.2	1.2	116	2,661	282.4	126.8
Milford	172	2,632	141.5	39.4	20	296	17.6	7.4	139	2,189	248.7	116.0
Naugatuck	51	474	23.7	5.8	3	D	D	D	36	728	49.5	25.3
New Britain	91	1,195	66.5	18.1	8	66	9.3	1.4	104	1,728	213.0	93.8
New Haven	337	4,119	284.4	75.6	24	D	D	D	269	4,257	438.6	190.6
New London	89	1,217	68.1	20.3	11	32	2.6	0.9	84	D	D	D
Norwalk	251	2,845	219.3	61.1	54	916	118.8	42.0	192	2,678	308.7	141.5
Norwich	93	D	D	D	7	D	D	D	114	2,071	199.2	89.0
Shelton	112	1,915	117.2	36.3	10	118	9.5	2.6	105	2,312	243.7	118.4
Stamford	389	5,995	451.2	133.7	52	1,193	404.4	75.7	351	4,135	495.2	221.6
Torrington	79	959	55.1	14.4	13	91	5.9	1.4	112	1,801	182.1	71.6
Waterbury	231	3,063	158.2	43.5	11	99	6.2	1.4	230	4,952	513.4	234.8
West Haven	110	1,471	86.4	22.4	4	D	D	D	59	D	D	D
DELAWARE	1,987	35,609	2,148.4	566.7	302	5,087	490.5	148.6	1,964	30,400	3,173.7	1,434.8
Dover	151	4,280	387.3	78.2	17	D	D	D	188	3,325	290.5	129.7
Newark	133	3,183	177.0	45.9	10	143	6.6	1.8	133	D	D	D
Wilmington	197	2,964	169.2	48.2	28	243	17.8	5.4	258	3,681	330.2	137.8
DISTRICT OF COLUMBIA	2,371	60,370	5,101.6	1,504.8	210	5,103	778.3	327.3	1,353	24,356	2,870.9	1,203.4
Washington	2,371	60,370	5,101.6	1,504.8	210	5,103	778.3	327.3	1,353	24,356	2,870.9	1,203.4
FLORIDA	37,118	786,082	49,817.9	13,598.2	6,594	136,273	14,212.0	4,120.2	51,567	614,004	76,785.9	27,914.4
Altamonte Springs	140	3,730	196.0	61.3	21	D	D	D	244	D	D	D
Apopka	67	D	D	D	8	131	6.8	2.5	69	658	84.0	38.9
Aventura	109	3,319	244.7	73.0	23	168	12.3	3.3	291	D	D	D
Boca Raton	362	10,342	697.3	208.7	89	728	54.8	14.7	726	6,025	893.3	349.7
Bonita Springs	116	D	D	D	31	876	58.0	19.2	115	975	135.0	47.5
Boynton Beach	197	4,235	220.6	63.8	26	D	D	D	340	D	D	D
Bradenton	134	2,396	122.9	35.8	25	191	14.9	6.3	291	7,453	892.2	318.4
Cape Coral	212	3,797	181.0	52.6	35	238	17.4	3.5	270	2,503	346.7	110.5
Casselberry	70	873	46.2	11.5	10	85	4.3	1.5	63	D	D	D
Clearwater	346	7,252	482.0	130.8	54	917	45.3	10.5	468	5,606	706.4	279.5
Clermont	91	1,932	93.6	26.1	16	D	D	D	151	D	D	D
Coconut Creek	80	1,383	69.2	18.3	21	D	D	D	101	D	D	D
Cooper City	49	687	33.2	9.0	13	D	D	D	132	D	D	D
Coral Gables	246	5,972	363.6	117.6	51	321	44.2	14.9	528	D	D	D
Coral Springs	275	4,612	264.7	71.0	75	551	40.1	9.7	469	D	D	D
Cutler Bay	66	D	D	D	8	63	3.5	0.8	64	D	D	D
Dania Beach	83	1,723	129.3	31.1	24	D	D	D	45	D	D	D
Davie	195	D	D	D	48	D	D	D	252	D	D	D
Daytona Beach	256	5,862	321.0	91.6	38	D	D	D	237	4,513	412.7	178.0

1. Establishments subject to federal tax.

— **Other Services and Government Employment and Payroll**

City	Other services[1]				Government employment and payroll, 2012								
					Full-time equivalent employees	March payroll							
						Total (dollars)	Percent of total for:						
	Number of establishments	Number of employees	Receipts (mil dol)	Annual payroll (mil dol)			Administrative, judicial, and legal	Police and corrections	Fire protection	Highways and transportation	Health and welfare	Natural resources and utilities	Education and libraries
	104	105	106	107	108	109	110	111	112	113	114	115	116
COLORADO— Cont'd													
Castle Rock	98	511	34.5	11.9	454	2,257,316	12.3	18.0	21.0	7.0	3.2	27.7	0.0
Centennial	167	809	75.5	22.6	56	312,389	97.1	0.0	0.0	0.0	0.0	0.0	0.0
Colorado Springs	703	4,195	357.7	115.6	6,835	37,084,390	4.0	14.0	7.5	3.0	35.7	34.0	0.0
Commerce City	90	712	87.2	22.8	331	1,840,907	22.9	42.5	0.0	11.7	8.4	14.5	0.0
Denver	1,071	8,716	708.5	244.9	11,914	62,559,560	13.5	28.4	10.9	11.0	11.2	19.1	2.3
Englewood	118	799	76.5	27.1	496	2,612,051	12.2	19.8	16.5	5.4	2.5	32.9	2.4
Fort Collins	247	1,400	92.3	31.1	1,475	7,276,841	19.4	25.1	0.0	10.9	0.5	39.9	0.0
Fountain	15	61	5.4	1.2	195	852,760	16.1	9.5	14.2	2.6	3.5	38.5	0.0
Grand Junction	187	1,438	129.5	36.6	684	3,402,863	13.8	30.4	21.4	6.4	0.5	21.7	0.0
Greeley	117	634	55.5	16.1	980	4,950,974	9.9	28.6	15.1	7.5	1.4	32.8	0.0
Lakewood	250	1,404	103.2	35.4	1,014	5,146,071	18.0	47.7	0.0	3.7	1.4	18.8	0.0
Littleton	105	756	64.3	24.2	427	2,523,624	11.4	21.4	46.3	4.8	4.3	5.3	4.2
Longmont	150	783	56.9	19.1	895	4,775,325	12.8	26.4	13.8	4.3	4.2	29.7	3.4
Loveland	134	851	75.9	24.6	677	3,104,613	23.9	23.9	13.3	6.0	0.0	25.8	3.5
Northglenn	48	237	18.5	5.9	323	4,495,142	20.4	39.8	0.0	2.3	0.0	30.8	0.0
Parker	122	772	57.9	17.7	295	1,383,773	22.2	35.4	0.0	13.3	0.0	22.5	0.0
Pueblo	142	832	57.8	18.7	859	4,316,626	8.8	33.4	18.2	8.7	0.5	28.3	0.0
Thornton	101	778	51.3	20.7	842	4,836,932	20.0	27.9	10.2	10.4	4.4	24.7	0.0
Westminster	135	894	56.6	20.4	992	5,125,430	12.9	29.5	16.6	4.2	3.5	24.3	3.3
Wheat Ridge	109	562	56.1	16.5	198	835,164	27.5	56.8	0.0	15.6	0.0	0.0	0.0
CONNECTICUT	5,816	34,073	3,031.0	960.6	X	X	X	X	X	X	X	X	X
Bridgeport	153	654	68.5	19.9	4,248	23,926,290	4.5	12.4	5.7	0.9	3.3	1.9	70.6
Bristol	76	373	31.9	9.4	1,756	9,163,919	3.3	10.9	5.8	2.6	1.2	5.4	69.3
Danbury	159	986	86.8	26.3	1,817	10,016,152	3.5	11.0	8.0	3.2	1.8	2.8	68.2
Hartford	214	1,242	113.2	33.1	5,207	24,306,797	2.8	9.1	6.3	1.0	3.8	0.9	76.1
Meriden	67	388	30.1	9.1	1,673	9,260,984	3.4	12.3	8.7	1.1	3.7	5.2	65.5
Middletown	77	441	48.9	14.4	1,621	8,623,913	3.5	13.7	9.7	2.6	6.4	5.0	55.8
Milford	126	752	61.9	20.0	2,207	11,763,788	2.2	6.1	6.4	1.6	1.9	2.6	77.1
Naugatuck	36	134	12.9	3.6	976	4,533,881	3.1	10.0	5.6	1.8	1.8	2.7	73.9
New Britain	74	358	28.8	9.3	2,064	11,112,239	2.6	10.0	9.5	2.3	1.6	6.1	66.2
New Haven	170	901	83.8	27.2	4,808	23,846,140	3.9	13.4	10.0	1.1	2.8	3.0	65.4
New London	53	336	24.9	8.5	789	3,869,245	5.6	17.4	11.4	1.4	2.1	4.5	54.9
Norwalk	178	1,009	93.6	30.5	2,837	13,813,488	4.1	12.3	8.1	3.0	1.2	1.8	68.2
Norwich	59	459	28.3	10.5	984	5,092,687	3.2	11.7	7.1	3.7	4.1	20.9	47.0
Shelton	69	379	25.9	8.9	952	5,269,099	4.2	8.4	0.5	4.0	2.3	3.1	77.5
Stamford	251	1,622	134.5	42.7	3,375	22,400,736	3.9	13.4	9.4	1.1	5.3	3.3	60.5
Torrington	69	433	30.9	10.6	923	4,776,132	2.9	12.2	7.3	3.8	3.3	2.6	66.3
Waterbury	144	916	93.7	26.2	3,875	18,570,027	3.9	12.3	7.5	1.2	2.6	5.2	67.1
West Haven	74	338	35.7	10.1	1,404	6,641,617	4.9	17.7	4.6	4.7	2.6	0.6	64.8
DELAWARE	1,190	7,668	617.2	207.1	X	X	X	X	X	X	X	X	X
Dover	59	509	30.1	11.0	348	1,666,145	16.3	43.4	1.4	2.0	1.1	25.4	3.3
Newark	53	290	15.9	6.3	258	1,304,591	12.9	41.6	0.4	3.6	4.4	29.6	0.0
Wilmington	116	825	80.0	23.8	1,254	5,779,211	16.3	41.1	15.0	4.0	5.1	11.7	0.0
DISTRICT OF COLUMBIA	940	7,719	633.3	194.1	X	X	X	X	X	X	X	X	X
Washington	940	7,719	633.3	194.1	34,002	194,813,463	15.0	19.3	5.8	2.2	15.5	8.1	25.7
FLORIDA	27,843	145,010	12,202.5	3,616.4	X	X	X	X	X	X	X	X	X
Altamonte Springs	107	D	D	D	387	1,562,231	12.2	35.2	0.0	2.6	0.0	35.5	1.2
Apopka	58	268	18.9	5.7	391	1,780,824	13.9	31.5	26.1	2.1	0.0	17.9	0.0
Aventura	79	867	43.0	16.3	366	1,349,401	17.9	28.7	27.3	9.0	0.5	15.5	0.0
Boca Raton	314	1,584	114.4	35.2	1,418	6,984,386	9.9	26.8	24.4	3.6	0.1	27.8	2.2
Bonita Springs	86	306	19.6	6.8	55	213,459	44.7	0.0	0.0	0.0	0.0	11.7	0.0
Boynton Beach	159	1,102	75.5	26.0	747	4,117,701	10.9	32.9	22.3	0.2	0.5	25.1	2.4
Bradenton	83	288	22.5	6.3	434	1,525,511	8.1	37.6	20.9	3.9	0.5	24.1	0.0
Cape Coral	227	1,016	67.2	21.0	1,360	5,329,766	17.8	25.1	19.0	5.1	0.4	27.7	0.0
Casselberry	63	237	16.4	4.8	217	833,769	18.9	28.6	21.7	6.1	0.0	23.7	0.0
Clearwater	197	921	75.6	21.2	1,653	6,760,407	11.2	29.1	14.6	5.7	0.6	28.3	3.3
Clermont	64	393	27.0	9.0	262	960,550	4.5	26.8	25.5	20.2	0.0	23.0	0.0
Coconut Creek	70	365	23.8	7.0	330	1,913,611	28.0	41.4	1.7	4.0	0.0	17.4	0.0
Cooper City	48	326	25.4	9.0	138	525,375	17.6	0.0	0.0	0.0	0.0	48.0	0.0
Coral Gables	131	897	65.6	19.8	793	4,845,710	17.3	32.6	27.2	4.5	0.5	12.9	0.0
Coral Springs	235	860	68.5	19.5	845	4,451,797	13.6	41.1	25.3	2.0	0.0	11.7	0.0
Cutler Bay	37	155	13.9	4.3	47	173,292	50.2	1.3	0.0	11.8	0.0	32.6	0.0
Dania Beach	93	1,143	60.0	18.5	113	516,841	46.4	0.0	0.0	4.7	3.0	37.2	0.0
Davie	230	1,116	121.6	32.4	617	4,513,053	8.3	40.2	31.1	7.0	1.3	8.4	0.0
Daytona Beach	122	572	38.3	13.6	1,046	4,375,710	11.9	39.3	11.4	5.1	1.4	26.4	0.0

1. Establishments subject to federal tax.

City	City government finances, 2012									
	General revenue							General expenditure		
		Intergovernmental			Taxes					
						Per capita[1] (dollars)			Per capita[1] (dollars)	
	Total (mil dol)	Total (mil dol)	Percent from state government	Total (mil dol)	Total	Property	Sales and gross receipts	Total (mil dol)	Total	Capital outlays
	117	118	119	120	121	122	123	124	125	126
COLORADO— Cont'd										
Castle Rock..........................	72.3	4.3	100.0	39.3	764	86	677	61.6	1,198	135
Centennial..........................	67.4	9.9	66.5	52.6	505	129	376	66.6	640	152
Colorado Springs	1,020.1	65.7	31.6	214.4	494	52	442	968.4	2,233	239
Commerce City	59.2	2.8	60.8	47.8	984	138	846	61.0	1,256	0
Denver	2,940.6	477.1	60.5	1,107.9	1,748	610	1,138	2,623.4	4,139	261
Englewood	60.4	3.3	42.3	31.3	1,002	139	864	53.0	1,698	1
Fort Collins........................	238.1	30.8	16.5	125.6	843	119	724	233.7	1,569	354
Fountain	12.7	1.1	60.7	10.1	374	74	300	26.4	981	22
Grand Junction....................	114.1	18.2	45.4	60.4	1,009	214	795	130.2	2,176	564
Greeley	114.2	13.2	62.0	60.1	630	105	514	99.4	1,042	109
Lakewood...........................	155.5	22.9	36.1	96.4	663	105	514	144.6	994	114
Littleton	70.6	17.6	14.5	32.8	749	95	655	75.6	1,725	102
Longmont	98.1	6.6	75.4	57.7	650	161	388	98.8	1,114	42
Loveland	115.2	11.2	96.5	59.5	847	268	579	109.1	1,554	315
Northglenn	32.1	4.4	67.4	19.9	539	82	457	33.8	914	210
Parker	53.8	8.3	22.1	33.0	699	35	636	55.5	1,175	321
Pueblo	152.7	29.0	69.9	79.2	734	146	589	141.8	1,315	332
Thornton............................	147.1	14.0	41.5	89.2	717	95	617	134.0	1,078	204
Westminster.......................	153.4	13.5	40.6	99.8	914	126	788	145.3	1,330	246
Wheat Ridge	30.8	2.8	58.9	23.1	752	27	726	32.0	1,043	219
CONNECTICUT................	X	X	X	X	X	X	X	X	X	X
Bridgeport	693.1	370.2	98.3	277.5	1,888	1,865	23	743.6	5,058	849
Bristol...............................	263.8	119.3	95.5	120.4	1,987	1,939	38	318.7	5,258	1,671
Danbury	280.7	82.5	95.8	171.7	2,074	2,030	44	248.5	3,001	199
Hartford.............................	809.1	477.2	84.9	283.3	2,262	2,204	49	793.7	6,336	712
Meriden	212.7	85.0	99.7	110.3	1,819	1,801	2	226.8	3,739	412
Middletown.........................	189.7	68.5	99.3	101.5	2,142	2,129	12	158.3	3,339	308
Milford	203.4	27.7	97.5	162.8	3,160	3,130	13	206.1	4,000	448
Naugatuck..........................	113.1	38.6	96.7	67.3	2,115	2,091	21	123.1	3,870	120
New Britain.........................	264.0	124.4	97.4	111.2	1,521	1,505	16	274.7	3,758	394
New Haven	723.5	431.0	93.9	232.5	1,776	1,722	46	1,130.4	8,633	3,741
New London........................	123.5	69.0	97.3	39.7	1,438	1,415	23	112.6	4,081	298
Norwalk.............................	353.8	52.6	97.8	263.8	3,023	2,994	29	360.1	4,125	476
Norwich.............................	159.1	79.8	97.7	64.1	1,584	1,562	13	163.0	4,029	489
Shelton..............................	121.4	15.0	88.2	99.0	2,457	2,415	42	115.7	2,872	166
Stamford............................	535.4	50.2	94.1	426.4	3,408	3,340	47	551.6	4,408	402
Torrington..........................	128.3	39.4	97.2	77.2	2,158	2,136	0	121.9	3,409	87
Waterbury	498.5	253.0	94.0	220.5	2,006	1,989	11	626.2	5,696	845
West Haven	172.1	67.7	99.0	89.3	1,617	1,606	11	169.2	3,062	287
DELAWARE	X	X	X	X	X	X	X	X	X	X
Dover	42.7	9.6	91.3	15.8	426	298	91	55.8	1,506	400
Newark..............................	23.4	3.3	100.0	8.4	258	155	72	32.7	1,010	108
Wilmington	193.4	38.2	53.3	110.5	1,550	547	108	166.5	2,334	116
DISTRICT OF COLUMBIA....	X	X	X	X	X	X	X	X	X	X
Washington	10,710.4	3,077.7	0.0	5,933.8	9,344	2,957	2,601	11,199.3	17,636	2,228
FLORIDA..........................	X	X	X	X	X	X	X	X	X	X
Altamonte Springs................	42.8	3.7	94.1	21.6	515	214	300	30.6	731	144
Apopka..............................	48.2	9.5	80.2	19.4	437	163	273	45.1	1,012	64
Aventura............................	42.7	11.2	85.4	25.0	671	315	355	38.3	1,028	79
Boca Raton	195.4	30.0	30.6	109.3	1,242	718	524	210.8	2,397	278
Bonita Springs.....................	18.8	4.9	87.3	11.2	243	125	118	17.6	382	76
Boynton Beach....................	116.4	15.6	61.0	50.6	721	474	247	120.3	1,714	146
Bradenton	58.2	10.3	29.0	24.6	488	329	158	58.4	1,157	9
Cape Coral.........................	245.7	47.7	80.3	92.3	572	430	143	240.6	1,492	184
Casselberry........................	34.0	7.5	31.2	12.8	484	228	256	41.1	1,552	195
Clearwater..........................	200.9	27.4	47.6	81.7	751	363	387	194.0	1,782	189
Clermont	32.1	6.1	87.7	12.5	423	203	221	30.7	1,043	125
Coconut Creek.....................	61.2	5.4	70.6	29.6	537	289	249	52.9	959	77
Cooper City	35.4	2.6	92.2	17.7	547	292	255	32.2	994	12
Coral Gables.......................	158.0	11.2	62.7	97.1	1,954	1,350	604	127.4	2,564	171
Coral Springs......................	123.2	15.5	67.5	65.4	521	261	253	133.1	1,060	84
Cutler Bay	23.2	9.8	41.7	11.1	260	99	161	26.0	611	269
Dania Beach	52.7	10.5	66.3	24.3	793	518	275	52.7	1,718	156
Davie................................	104.7	13.7	53.9	70.6	738	407	331	98.2	1,027	73
Daytona Beach	124.9	15.8	46.5	44.7	724	392	332	118.4	1,915	146

1. Based on population estimated as of July 1 of the year shown.

City	City government finances, 2012 (cont.)									
	General expenditure (cont.)									
	Percent of total for:									
	Public welfare	Highways	Parking facilities	Education	Health and hospitals	Police protection	Sewerage and sanitation	Parks and recreation	Housing and community development	Interest on debt
	127	128	129	130	131	132	133	134	135	136
COLORADO— Cont'd										
Castle Rock	0.0	16.9	0.0	0.0	0.0	12.1	16.6	16.7	0.0	4.0
Centennial	0.0	26.3	0.0	0.0	0.0	29.9	0.0	9.5	5.1	0.2
Colorado Springs	0.0	8.7	0.2	0.0	53.3	9.2	3.9	2.2	0.5	2.8
Commerce City	0.0	7.9	0.0	0.0	0.0	23.6	3.0	10.5	3.7	7.1
Denver	6.4	5.9	0.0	0.0	2.0	8.6	3.3	7.4	4.4	11.0
Englewood	0.0	6.9	0.0	0.0	0.0	19.6	18.4	14.4	2.6	5.1
Fort Collins	0.0	22.5	0.0	0.0	0.0	13.6	7.0	20.8	0.0	1.9
Fountain	0.0	4.7	0.0	0.0	0.8	19.5	0.0	3.1	0.3	0.0
Grand Junction	0.0	12.8	0.3	0.0	0.0	27.0	12.8	14.2	1.8	5.2
Greeley	0.0	6.4	0.3	0.0	0.0	27.1	11.9	13.9	4.4	3.0
Lakewood	0.0	10.8	0.0	0.0	0.9	27.9	2.2	12.3	1.2	1.7
Littleton	0.4	8.2	0.0	0.0	0.0	14.2	10.6	3.0	0.1	2.6
Longmont	0.0	1.0	0.2	0.0	0.0	22.5	18.0	19.4	5.9	2.3
Loveland	0.0	11.3	0.0	0.0	0.0	15.0	10.4	11.8	13.3	0.5
Northglenn	1.3	36.3	0.0	0.0	0.0	21.1	7.6	18.5	0.7	0.0
Parker	0.0	15.6	0.0	0.0	0.0	16.9	2.2	37.3	2.0	5.8
Pueblo	0.0	5.5	0.8	0.0	0.0	18.6	20.0	6.8	11.0	1.6
Thornton	0.0	19.8	0.0	0.0	0.0	19.1	12.4	16.7	1.5	2.1
Westminster	0.0	5.0	0.0	0.0	0.0	13.9	6.9	14.9	9.1	4.9
Wheat Ridge	0.0	14.0	0.0	0.0	0.0	32.8	6.3	20.9	0.0	0.3
CONNECTICUT	X	X	X	X	X	X	X	X	X	X
Bridgeport	0.4	1.9	0.3	44.8	0.5	12.4	5.2	0.8	1.2	5.5
Bristol	0.0	5.0	0.0	63.2	2.8	4.2	3.8	1.2	0.3	0.8
Danbury	0.2	4.2	0.5	53.7	1.2	6.5	3.4	2.5	0.2	2.4
Hartford	1.6	3.6	0.1	58.0	1.8	8.2	0.4	0.2	8.4	1.9
Meriden	0.6	1.9	0.1	57.5	1.4	5.2	4.0	0.9	0.4	1.6
Middletown	0.1	2.3	0.3	50.9	0.6	8.1	3.9	1.7	0.3	1.8
Milford	0.5	1.5	0.0	54.6	1.2	4.9	13.6	0.5	0.4	1.1
Naugatuck	0.2	2.0	0.0	56.2	0.8	4.8	6.3	1.1	0.0	3.5
New Britain	0.1	4.1	0.0	51.5	0.6	12.7	4.6	3.5	1.1	5.1
New Haven	0.0	1.2	1.6	66.9	0.3	3.3	1.0	0.5	1.0	1.6
New London	0.0	9.3	0.5	48.4	0.2	11.0	4.0	8.9	1.6	1.9
Norwalk	0.0	4.6	1.3	50.9	0.6	5.2	5.7	3.8	0.4	3.4
Norwich	1.6	10.4	0.2	52.7	0.0	7.4	10.4	1.5	1.0	0.7
Shelton	0.0	2.6	0.0	60.5	2.6	4.5	4.5	1.7	0.1	2.3
Stamford	2.7	1.6	0.6	47.9	4.0	10.2	4.2	0.6	0.6	3.4
Torrington	0.0	4.5	0.0	56.8	5.0	6.7	4.0	1.2	0.2	1.8
Waterbury	0.6	1.7	0.0	58.3	0.5	4.8	4.0	0.7	1.1	4.5
West Haven	0.2	3.3	0.0	53.9	0.9	7.6	10.9	1.1	0.5	4.1
DELAWARE	X	X	X	X	X	X	X	X	X	X
Dover	0.0	4.4	0.0	0.0	0.1	25.4	18.7	1.5	0.7	0.2
Newark	0.0	8.2	2.2	0.0	0.0	30.5	22.1	7.9	1.1	0.3
Wilmington	0.0	5.8	4.3	0.0	0.0	30.6	10.4	4.8	6.2	3.2
DISTRICT OF COLUMBIA	X	X	X	X	X	X	X	X	X	X
Washington	25.6	4.7	0.2	21.2	6.0	5.0	5.3	1.8	4.9	4.5
FLORIDA	X	X	X	X	X	X	X	X	X	X
Altamonte Springs	0.0	19.8	0.0	0.0	0.0	30.9	9.3	11.4	0.0	0.1
Apopka	0.0	5.4	0.0	0.0	8.7	26.1	18.4	5.7	0.0	1.3
Aventura	0.0	8.4	0.0	17.8	0.0	41.5	0.0	7.7	0.0	3.2
Boca Raton	0.0	5.0	0.0	0.0	0.0	17.6	14.0	17.3	0.2	1.6
Bonita Springs	0.0	31.5	0.0	0.0	1.0	9.5	0.0	12.6	1.6	7.3
Boynton Beach	0.0	1.9	0.0	0.0	0.0	21.9	20.0	8.6	0.3	2.3
Bradenton	0.0	3.5	1.4	0.0	0.0	22.9	24.5	5.3	9.3	1.9
Cape Coral	0.0	10.9	0.0	10.4	0.0	15.1	5.4	7.0	3.0	4.8
Casselberry	0.0	6.3	0.0	0.0	0.1	13.0	22.3	3.0	0.0	1.2
Clearwater	0.1	6.4	2.0	0.0	3.0	19.9	21.2	14.6	0.6	1.4
Clermont	0.0	3.8	0.0	0.0	0.0	20.7	33.3	12.1	0.0	0.5
Coconut Creek	0.0	3.4	0.0	0.0	0.0	29.3	2.2	9.1	1.0	1.9
Cooper City	0.0	2.4	0.1	0.0	0.0	31.4	17.8	9.4	0.0	0.4
Coral Gables	0.0	4.8	3.5	0.0	0.0	29.1	12.4	6.3	0.5	1.9
Coral Springs	0.0	4.5	0.0	0.0	6.2	37.8	6.6	11.4	0.0	1.5
Cutler Bay	0.0	2.3	0.0	0.0	0.0	30.8	0.0	32.3	0.0	3.8
Dania Beach	0.0	4.0	2.3	0.0	0.0	19.8	10.2	6.8	0.0	1.4
Davie	0.0	8.0	0.0	0.0	0.0	36.2	0.0	7.4	2.6	3.2
Daytona Beach	0.0	11.2	0.0	0.0	0.0	29.4	13.1	11.5	1.8	3.5

Table D. Cities — City Government Finances, City Government Employment, and Climate

City	City government finances, 2012 (cont.) Debt outstanding — Total (mil dol)	Per capita[1] (dollars)	Debt issued during year	Climate[2] Average daily temperature Mean — January	Mean — July	Limits — January[3]	Limits — July[4]	Annual precipitation (inches)	Heating degree days	Cooling degree days
	137	138	139	140	141	142	143	144	145	146
COLORADO— Cont'd										
Castle Rock	110.8	2,154	0.0	NA	NA	NA	NA	NA	NA	NA
Centennial	2.8	27	0.0	NA	NA	NA	NA	NA	NA	NA
Colorado Springs	2,643.8	6,097	167.5	28.1	69.6	14.5	84.4	17.40	6,480	404
Commerce City	182.6	3,760	0.1	NA	NA	NA	NA	NA	NA	NA
Denver	7,039.4	11,106	660.3	31.2	71.5	15.6	88.3	18.17	5,988	496
Englewood	89.9	2,879	0.3	28.2	70.2	12.7	85.8	17.06	6,773	435
Fort Collins	216.4	1,453	11.2	28.2	71.5	14.5	86.2	13.98	6,256	524
Fountain	29.0	1,078	9.0	NA	NA	NA	NA	NA	NA	NA
Grand Junction	74.2	1,241	0.0	27.4	77.5	16.8	91.9	9.06	5,489	1,098
Greeley	155.4	1,629	0.0	27.8	74.0	15.6	88.7	14.22	5,980	759
Lakewood	74.1	509	0.0	28.2	70.2	12.7	85.8	17.06	6,773	435
Littleton	52.5	1,198	2.4	28.2	70.2	12.7	85.8	17.06	6,773	435
Longmont	86.1	971	2.5	27.1	72.2	12.0	88.9	14.15	6,415	587
Loveland	5.0	71	0.0	28.2	71.5	14.5	86.2	13.98	6,256	524
Northglenn	9.0	244	0.0	30.0	72.0	16.2	87.9	13.25	6,074	590
Parker	55.9	1,184	0.0	NA	NA	NA	NA	NA	NA	NA
Pueblo	144.1	1,337	15.5	30.8	77.0	14.7	93.8	12.60	5,346	997
Thornton	191.4	1,539	0.0	30.0	72.0	16.2	87.9	13.25	6,074	590
Westminster	297.6	2,724	5.2	29.2	73.4	15.2	88.0	15.81	6,128	696
Wheat Ridge	2.7	86	0.0	31.2	71.5	15.6	88.3	18.17	5,988	496
CONNECTICUT	X	X	X	X	X	X	X	X	X	X
Bridgeport	742.4	5,050	77.6	29.9	74.0	22.9	81.9	44.15	5,466	789
Bristol	95.9	1,582	23.9	23.4	70.5	12.6	83.3	51.03	6,825	395
Danbury	169.5	2,047	37.8	26.5	72.5	17.6	83.9	51.77	6,159	597
Hartford	413.5	3,301	78.1	25.9	73.6	16.3	83.8	44.29	6,121	654
Meriden	121.0	1,994	1.8	28.3	73.4	20.3	84.2	52.35	5,791	669
Middletown	145.6	3,071	0.0	29.9	74.0	22.9	81.9	44.15	5,466	789
Milford	167.9	3,259	24.1	29.9	74.0	22.9	81.9	44.15	5,466	789
Naugatuck	75.9	2,387	0.0	29.9	74.0	22.9	81.9	44.15	5,466	789
New Britain	280.1	3,831	34.0	28.3	73.4	20.3	84.2	52.35	5,791	669
New Haven	585.6	4,473	50.6	25.9	72.5	16.9	82.8	52.73	6,271	558
New London	63.6	2,305	6.8	28.9	71.8	20.0	80.7	48.72	5,799	511
Norwalk	269.9	3,093	45.1	27.8	73.4	18.8	84.2	48.38	5,854	652
Norwich	48.2	1,190	17.7	27.6	73.2	17.3	83.8	52.78	5,916	627
Shelton	84.7	2,103	22.7	29.9	74.0	22.9	81.9	44.15	5,466	789
Stamford	448.3	3,582	64.9	28.7	73.5	19.2	85.4	52.79	5,582	692
Torrington	36.3	1,015	0.0	23.6	69.5	13.9	80.7	54.59	6,839	323
Waterbury	472.8	4,301	67.1	25.9	72.5	16.9	82.8	52.73	6,271	558
West Haven	122.2	2,213	51.1	25.9	72.5	16.9	82.8	52.73	6,271	558
DELAWARE	X	X	X	X	X	X	X	X	X	X
Dover	41.3	1,115	4.1	35.3	77.8	26.9	87.4	46.28	4,212	1,262
Newark	13.6	418	12.7	32.5	76.4	23.5	87.6	45.35	4,746	1,047
Wilmington	353.0	4,950	53.2	31.5	76.6	23.7	86.0	42.81	4,888	1,125
DISTRICT OF COLUMBIA	X	X	X	X	X	X	X	X	X	X
Washington	11,278.8	17,761	1,642.8	34.9	79.2	27.3	88.3	39.35	4,055	1,531
FLORIDA	X	X	X	X	X	X	X	X	X	X
Altamonte Springs	0.0	0	0.0	58.7	81.5	47.0	91.9	51.31	799	3,017
Apopka	33.4	751	0.0	58.7	81.5	47.0	91.9	51.31	799	3,017
Aventura	32.5	872	6.8	67.9	82.7	62.6	87.0	46.60	141	4,090
Boca Raton	139.0	1,580	0.0	67.2	83.3	57.8	91.8	57.27	219	4,241
Bonita Springs	24.3	526	0.0	64.3	82.0	53.4	91.2	51.90	316	3,646
Boynton Beach	126.0	1,795	0.0	66.2	82.5	57.3	90.1	61.39	246	3,999
Bradenton	34.5	683	0.0	61.6	81.9	50.9	91.3	54.12	538	3,327
Cape Coral	907.6	5,629	196.0	62.7	81.3	50.3	91.3	50.07	427	3,287
Casselberry	20.3	766	9.1	NA	NA	NA	NA	NA	NA	NA
Clearwater	247.9	2,276	47.0	61.3	82.5	52.4	89.7	44.77	591	3,482
Clermont	19.7	668	0.0	NA	NA	NA	NA	NA	NA	NA
Coconut Creek	22.8	413	0.0	67.2	83.3	57.8	91.8	57.27	219	4,241
Cooper City	6.1	189	1.5	67.5	82.6	59.2	89.8	64.19	167	4,120
Coral Gables	79.3	1,596	50.7	67.9	82.7	62.6	87.0	46.60	141	4,090
Coral Springs	71.6	570	8.8	67.2	83.3	57.8	91.8	57.27	219	4,241
Cutler Bay	18.6	437	3.6	NA	NA	NA	NA	NA	NA	NA
Dania Beach	30.3	988	3.6	NA	NA	NA	NA	NA	NA	NA
Davie	144.9	1,515	20.0	66.2	82.5	57.3	90.1	61.39	246	3,999
Daytona Beach	154.8	2,505	36.2	57.1	81.2	44.5	91.2	57.03	954	2,819

1. Based on the population estimated as of July 1 of the year shown. 2. Represents normal values based on the 30-year period, 1971±2000. 3. Average daily minimum. 4. Average daily maximum.

Table D. Cities — **Land Area and Population**

STATE Place code	City	Land area[1] (sq. mi)	Total persons 2018	Rank	Per square mile	White	Black or African American	American Indian, Alaskan Native	Asian	Hawaiian Pacific Islander	Some other race	Two or more races (percent)
			Population, 2018			**Race 2017 — Race alone[2] (percent)**						
		1	2	3	4	5	6	7	8	9	10	11
	FLORIDA— Cont'd											
12 16,725	Deerfield Beach	14.9	80,863	428	5,427.0	62.4	29.8	0.1	3.7	0.0	1.0	3.1
12 16,875	DeLand	18.8	33,532	1,143	1,783.6	75.9	15.9	0.5	3.4	0.0	3.0	1.3
12 17,100	Delray Beach	15.9	69,358	516	4,362.1	62.6	32.5	0.0	2.8	0.0	1.2	0.9
12 17,200	Deltona..................	37.3	91,951	353	2,465.2	73.9	11.6	0.4	1.3	0.0	11.2	1.7
12 17,935	Doral	13.8	61,824	604	4,480.0	93.7	1.5	0.0	2.8	0.0	1.3	0.6
12 18,575	Dunedin..................	10.4	36,580	1,049	3,517.3	NA	NA	NA	NA	NA	NA	NA
12 24,000	Fort Lauderdale..................	34.6	182,595	139	5,277.3	60.4	33.3	0.0	1.0	0.0	3.5	1.8
12 24,125	Fort Myers	39.8	82,254	416	2,066.7	62.4	21.5	0.1	4.9	0.1	9.0	2.0
12 24,300	Fort Pierce	23.7	46,071	837	1,943.9	58.4	34.3	1.0	0.7	0.0	3.8	0.4	1.4
12 25,175	Gainesville	63.0	133,857	204	2,124.7	66.4	20.6	0.2	6.4	0.1	1.6	4.7
12 27,322	Greenacres	5.8	41,084	932	7,083.4	63.3	25.5	0.1	2.8	0.0	5.0	3.2
12 28,452	Hallandale Beach..................	4.2	39,940	963	9,509.5	68.1	24.0	0.0	2.0	0.0	3.1	2.8
12 30,000	Hialeah	21.4	238,942	95	11,165.5	93.4	2.1	0.0	0.9	0.0	3.1	0.5
12 32,000	Hollywood	27.3	154,823	167	5,671.2	67.5	18.3	0.4	3.1	0.0	8.1	2.7
12 32,275	Homestead..................	15.1	70,477	511	4,667.4	76.8	16.2	1.2	1.1	0.0	2.3	2.4
12 35,000	Jacksonville	747.7	903,889	12	1,208.9	57.9	31.6	0.2	5.3	0.0	2.0	3.0
12 35,875	Jupiter	21.6	65,524	567	3,033.5	88.1	1.0	0.3	3.9	0.0	2.8	3.9
12 36,950	Kissimmee	20.8	73,597	486	3,538.3	64.2	10.4	0.4	5.1	0.1	11.6	8.2
12 38,250	Lakeland	66.1	110,516	273	1,672.0	73.0	20.8	0.3	2.7	0.2	1.5	1.5
12 39,075	Lake Worth..................	5.9	38,267	1,005	6,485.9	71.3	11.7	2.4	2.2	0.0	7.7	4.7
12 39,425	Largo	18.4	84,996	396	4,619.3	86.4	6.8	0.2	2.6	0.2	1.6	2.2
12 39,525	Lauderdale Lakes	3.7	36,324	1,061	9,817.3	NA	NA	NA	NA	NA	NA	NA
12 39,550	Lauderhill..................	8.5	72,094	498	8,481.6	13.4	81.8	0.6	0.6	0.0	2.1	1.6
12 43,125	Margate	8.8	58,656	643	6,665.5	65.5	26.3	0.0	2.4	0.0	2.5	3.3
12 43,975	Melbourne..................	44.0	82,826	411	1,882.4	77.0	9.7	0.3	6.8	0.0	2.5	3.8
12 45,000	Miami	36.0	470,914	40	13,080.9	74.2	18.0	0.5	1.4	0.0	3.8	2.1
12 45,025	Miami Beach	7.7	91,718	357	11,911.4	74.1	4.7	0.5	0.6	0.0	17.3	2.8
12 45,060	Miami Gardens..................	18.2	113,069	258	6,212.6	26.2	68.5	0.1	1.5	0.0	2.3	1.3
12 45,100	Miami Lakes..................	5.7	31,628	1,199	5,548.8	NA	NA	NA	NA	NA	NA	NA
12 45,975	Miramar	28.8	140,823	189	4,889.7	45.7	44.3	0.3	3.2	0.0	2.2	4.3
12 49,425	North Lauderdale	4.6	44,391	863	9,650.2	38.7	48.8	0.2	2.1	0.0	3.6	6.6
12 49,450	North Miami..................	8.4	62,996	592	7,499.5	34.6	59.4	0.1	0.9	0.0	4.0	1.0
12 49,475	North Miami Beach	4.8	45,887	841	9,559.8	49.4	42.1	0.0	3.6	0.0	3.7	1.1
12 49,675	North Port..................	99.5	68,628	522	689.7	86.9	7.4	0.0	3.9	0.0	0.3	1.6
12 50,575	Oakland Park..................	7.5	45,339	845	6,045.2	58.0	31.0	0.4	3.3	0.0	3.4	3.8
12 50,750	Ocala..................	47.3	60,429	617	1,277.6	77.2	18.3	0.1	1.6	0.5	0.0	2.3
12 51,075	Ocoee	15.2	47,720	811	3,139.5	62.9	22.0	0.6	6.1	0.0	5.6	2.7
12 53,000	Orlando	110.1	285,713	71	2,595.0	56.5	27.5	0.1	4.3	0.0	7.5	4.0
12 53,150	Ormond Beach..................	33.1	43,475	877	1,313.4	90.2	3.5	0.0	3.8	0.0	0.3	2.2
12 53,575	Oviedo	15.5	41,557	917	2,681.1	83.3	6.5	0.0	5.8	0.0	1.9	2.5
12 54,000	Palm Bay..................	97.8	114,194	254	1,167.6	76.0	15.4	1.0	1.8	0.0	3.7	2.1
12 54,075	Palm Beach Gardens...........	56.3	56,284	673	999.7	89.1	2.1	0.2	4.2	0.0	0.9	3.5
12 54,200	Palm Coast	95.1	87,607	379	921.2	79.4	13.2	0.3	3.5	0.0	2.4	1.3
12 54,700	Panama City	35.0	36,908	1,038	1,054.5	67.8	26.0	0.0	0.9	0.0	2.2	3.1
12 55,775	Pembroke Pines..................	32.8	172,374	151	5,255.3	61.5	23.4	0.5	6.3	0.1	3.8	4.3
12 55,925	Pensacola	22.6	52,713	733	2,332.4	62.9	29.5	0.0	0.6	0.0	1.9	5.1
12 56,975	Pinellas Park	16.0	53,098	730	3,318.6	74.6	6.3	0.0	8.5	0.0	3.6	7.0
12 57,425	Plantation	21.7	94,288	342	4,345.1	70.1	17.1	0.2	4.2	0.0	3.2	5.2
12 57,550	Plant City..................	27.6	39,156	987	1,418.7	72.5	17.5	0.4	2.1	0.0	4.1	3.4
12 58,050	Pompano Beach	24.0	111,954	263	4,664.8	60.9	34.1	0.1	0.6	0.0	1.5	2.8
12 58,575	Port Orange	26.7	64,252	582	2,406.4	86.3	6.5	0.6	2.5	0.0	1.7	2.4
12 58,715	Port St. Lucie	119.2	195,248	124	1,638.0	75.2	18.4	0.2	2.6	0.0	1.6	2.0
12 60,975	Riviera Beach..................	8.3	34,834	1,097	4,196.9	NA	NA	NA	NA	NA	NA	NA
12 62,100	Royal Palm Beach	11.5	40,018	960	3,479.8	75.2	16.7	0.5	4.5	0.0	2.4	0.7
12 62,625	St. Cloud	20.3	54,115	709	2,665.8	73.3	7.3	1.1	0.2	0.0	15.1	2.8
12 63,000	St. Petersburg	61.8	265,098	79	4,289.6	70.1	21.6	0.2	3.8	0.0	1.0	3.4
12 63,650	Sanford	23.2	60,035	622	2,587.7	55.3	28.3	0.2	3.5	0.0	7.2	5.5
12 64,175	Sarasota..................	14.7	57,738	654	3,927.8	80.5	15.8	0.4	1.6	0.0	0.3	1.4
12 69,700	Sunrise	16.2	95,458	331	5,892.5	55.2	33.4	0.5	4.9	0.0	3.5	2.4
12 70,600	Tallahassee	100.4	193,551	127	1,927.8	57.6	33.8	0.1	4.1	0.0	1.8	2.6
12 70,675	Tamarac	11.6	66,054	559	5,694.3	58.3	32.9	0.1	5.3	0.0	2.4	1.0
12 71,000	Tampa	114.0	392,890	49	3,446.4	66.5	23.9	0.2	4.3	0.0	1.3	3.8
12 71,900	Titusville	29.2	46,497	835	1,592.4	81.0	8.1	1.0	3.4	1.8	1.6	3.1
12 75,812	Wellington	45.3	65,200	571	1,439.3	81.8	11.5	0.3	3.0	0.0	0.5	2.9
12 76,582	Weston	24.6	71,210	505	2,894.7	78.9	7.1	0.0	6.1	0.2	2.2	5.6
12 76,600	West Palm Beach	54.8	111,398	268	2,032.8	58.4	34.6	0.0	2.3	0.0	3.5	1.2
12 78,250	Winter Garden..................	16.3	45,266	846	2,777.1	66.4	16.0	0.0	4.1	0.0	10.5	3.0
12 78,275	Winter Haven	32.0	43,020	884	1,344.4	72.5	21.5	0.0	1.4	0.3	1.2	3.1
12 78,300	Winter Park	8.7	31,059	1,214	3,570.0	84.4	6.2	0.0	4.5	0.0	1.9	3.0
12 78,325	Winter Springs	14.9	37,321	1,027	2,504.8	85.5	2.5	0.0	4.1	0.0	1.5	6.4

1. Dry land or land partially or temporarily covered by water. 2. Hispanic or Latino persons may be of any race.

Table D. Cities — **Population**

City	Percent Hispanic or Latino[1], 2017	Percent foreign born, 2017	Age of population (percent), 2017							Median age, 2017	Percent female, 2017	Population			
			Under 18 years	18 to 24 years	25 to 34 years	35 to 44 years	45 to 54 years	55 to 64 years	65 years and over			Census counts		Percent change	
												2000	2010	2000-2010	2001-2018
	12	13	14	15	16	17	18	19	20	21	22	23	24	25	26
FLORIDA— Cont'd															
Deerfield Beach	21.2	41.1	19.1	10.0	13.9	14.0	8.3	13.7	20.9	40.4	51.6	64,583	75,021	16.2	7.8
DeLand	11.6	8.3	11.9	12.6	6.7	11.2	13.6	15.1	28.8	51.1	54.0	20,904	26,894	28.7	24.7
Delray Beach	8.9	23.5	18.0	5.0	13.3	11.6	13.4	13.8	24.8	46.4	52.9	60,020	60,623	1.0	14.4
Deltona	36.8	9.6	25.2	8.1	11.6	14.6	13.3	12.2	15.1	38.5	50.2	69,543	85,117	22.4	8.0
Doral	83.0	62.2	25.3	7.7	15.9	15.3	15.9	11.1	8.9	35.6	50.8	20,438	45,709	123.6	35.3
Dunedin	4.2	9.7	7.7	6.9	7.8	7.0	15.4	18.5	36.6	56.9	52.7	35,691	35,338	-1.0	3.5
Fort Lauderdale	21.6	24.5	18.4	6.7	17.1	11.5	14.7	15.0	16.6	42.1	48.7	152,397	165,763	8.8	10.2
Fort Myers	23.7	21.4	19.6	7.9	14.4	13.1	13.2	11.5	20.2	40.2	50.9	48,208	62,316	29.3	32.0
Fort Pierce	27.6	18.3	22.3	9.7	13.1	9.3	12.6	17.3	15.8	40.7	50.5	37,516	41,941	11.8	9.8
Gainesville	12.1	11.1	12.9	33.8	17.6	8.2	8.1	8.8	10.5	26.7	53.4	95,447	124,266	30.2	7.7
Greenacres	40.8	39.9	26.2	9.3	12.0	13.7	14.5	8.8	15.6	37.3	49.1	27,569	37,632	36.5	9.2
Hallandale Beach	37.5	51.7	14.9	7.6	16.9	11.6	10.2	15.7	23.1	44.2	52.0	34,282	37,113	8.3	7.6
Hialeah	96.2	75.2	16.4	7.2	11.4	12.2	17.7	13.8	21.2	46.5	51.8	226,419	224,687	-0.8	6.3
Hollywood	40.6	37.3	21.8	7.9	14.0	13.5	14.5	11.8	16.4	39.6	50.0	139,357	140,711	1.0	10.0
Homestead	68.1	38.7	27.8	11.3	16.6	15.3	11.1	7.9	10.1	32.1	49.0	31,909	60,752	90.4	16.0
Jacksonville	9.9	12.1	22.9	9.1	16.6	12.7	12.7	12.5	13.5	35.8	51.6	735,617	821,764	11.7	10.0
Jupiter	14.6	10.2	22.5	5.2	10.8	11.7	14.8	12.3	22.7	44.7	51.4	39,328	55,310	40.6	18.5
Kissimmee	68.7	28.1	24.7	11.5	16.9	15.3	14.9	7.1	9.5	33.0	45.5	47,814	59,600	24.6	23.5
Lakeland	15.6	10.9	18.8	11.3	12.9	12.0	13.7	11.5	19.8	41.0	53.5	78,452	97,309	24.0	13.6
Lake Worth	53.1	44.9	20.4	8.9	16.9	14.4	12.6	11.7	15.2	36.7	46.8	35,133	34,889	-0.7	9.7
Largo	12.5	14.2	15.2	8.2	13.0	10.8	12.4	14.4	26.0	47.3	50.9	69,371	79,358	14.4	7.1
Lauderdale Lakes	2.0	50.3	21.5	8.0	14.4	14.3	13.6	10.1	18.0	38.1	51.5	31,705	32,784	3.4	10.8
Lauderhill	8.4	31.4	29.4	10.3	10.9	13.4	13.3	11.6	11.1	34.3	53.2	57,585	66,939	16.2	7.7
Margate	23.4	36.7	13.6	6.1	14.2	12.6	12.0	15.8	25.8	48.3	52.9	53,909	53,120	-1.5	10.4
Melbourne	9.0	11.3	19.7	7.6	11.1	10.4	12.5	14.5	24.3	46.6	51.4	71,382	76,247	6.8	8.6
Miami	71.7	58.4	17.7	8.2	16.7	14.8	14.9	11.6	16.2	39.8	50.7	362,470	399,530	10.2	17.9
Miami Beach	54.7	50.0	17.2	7.3	14.4	15.8	15.1	12.6	17.6	42.8	48.5	87,933	87,739	-0.2	4.5
Miami Gardens	27.7	33.4	24.9	9.7	15.8	14.0	11.7	11.2	12.8	34.6	52.9	NA	107,162	**********	5.5
Miami Lakes	85.0	51.6	19.9	10.5	12.3	12.6	15.9	11.0	17.8	41.4	53.8	22,676	29,377	29.6	7.7
Miramar	39.6	35.2	24.5	8.5	14.2	16.9	15.0	10.3	10.5	35.9	50.7	72,739	121,958	67.7	15.5
North Lauderdale	31.8	44.3	24.8	7.9	18.2	15.5	18.0	9.1	6.5	34.0	50.3	32,264	41,092	27.4	8.0
North Miami	32.3	56.3	24.5	6.4	13.4	17.6	14.5	11.6	12.0	38.7	49.0	59,880	58,598	-2.1	7.5
North Miami Beach	32.4	57.7	22.0	9.8	14.5	10.2	15.3	15.6	12.7	39.8	49.4	40,786	42,517	4.2	7.9
North Port	14.6	14.2	18.4	10.4	11.1	10.7	12.8	13.1	23.5	44.2	54.2	22,797	57,333	151.5	19.7
Oakland Park	27.0	32.5	15.4	6.9	12.7	13.0	20.1	19.5	12.4	47.0	43.7	30,966	41,299	33.4	9.8
Ocala	17.6	7.6	22.5	8.2	12.5	14.7	14.1	10.7	17.3	39.3	50.9	45,943	56,566	23.1	6.8
Ocoee	20.2	24.2	24.8	6.2	16.8	12.3	19.9	10.3	9.8	37.1	49.5	24,391	35,711	46.4	33.6
Orlando	30.8	24.6	22.2	9.5	21.8	15.3	11.3	9.3	10.5	33.0	51.3	185,951	238,813	28.4	19.6
Ormond Beach	7.8	8.4	16.2	5.6	8.6	11.7	11.5	14.7	31.8	52.3	51.8	36,301	39,477	8.7	10.1
Oviedo	19.5	10.3	26.7	9.9	11.1	11.9	16.9	13.5	10.1	36.4	49.3	26,316	33,473	27.2	24.2
Palm Bay	16.7	10.5	21.0	9.6	14.4	11.9	12.7	16.1	14.2	38.5	47.6	79,413	104,008	31.0	9.8
Palm Beach Gardens	10.9	14.2	15.2	4.7	10.3	11.3	12.3	17.0	29.1	52.5	54.7	35,058	49,100	40.1	14.6
Palm Coast	11.4	12.0	18.2	8.4	9.1	10.2	10.6	15.4	28.1	48.2	53.0	32,732	75,205	129.8	16.5
Panama City	10.9	11.3	17.1	9.0	12.7	12.7	13.4	13.3	21.8	42.8	52.9	36,417	34,608	-5.0	6.6
Pembroke Pines	42.0	33.8	20.8	9.0	13.9	13.0	15.5	12.5	15.4	39.7	52.3	137,427	154,898	12.7	11.3
Pensacola	9.0	3.4	23.8	9.1	15.8	10.9	10.9	12.9	16.5	36.0	53.1	56,255	52,009	-7.5	1.4
Pinellas Park	13.9	17.2	21.7	3.9	16.2	10.8	13.7	13.4	20.3	42.6	51.9	45,658	49,348	8.1	7.6
Plantation	29.5	33.4	20.1	7.5	15.9	11.0	14.1	12.9	18.6	40.9	52.7	82,934	84,880	2.3	11.1
Plant City	28.1	9.5	25.8	8.1	15.3	15.0	13.6	8.8	13.4	35.4	54.8	29,915	34,779	16.3	12.6
Pompano Beach	18.8	27.0	16.3	7.9	14.1	11.1	15.3	16.7	18.6	45.5	47.1	78,191	99,844	27.7	12.1
Port Orange	9.0	7.7	17.3	8.7	12.0	10.7	12.7	14.4	24.2	45.5	52.8	45,823	56,620	23.6	13.5
Port St. Lucie	18.3	17.7	20.8	8.4	11.1	11.6	13.9	12.8	21.4	43.3	50.7	88,769	164,194	85.0	18.9
Riviera Beach	5.9	16.6	23.6	10.2	13.1	11.9	11.5	11.3	18.4	36.5	50.6	29,884	32,504	8.8	7.2
Royal Palm Beach	30.1	29.9	21.0	6.3	10.1	16.3	12.5	15.0	18.8	42.7	52.5	21,523	34,196	58.9	17.0
St. Cloud	48.4	11.3	26.3	11.9	12.9	14.4	10.8	11.3	12.4	32.1	51.7	20,074	37,816	88.4	43.1
St. Petersburg	6.1	12.0	16.2	6.9	16.1	11.2	14.3	15.1	20.3	44.8	51.8	248,232	245,176	-1.2	8.1
Sanford	28.0	9.6	27.5	5.6	20.7	13.8	11.0	9.2	12.1	32.6	51.5	38,291	53,910	40.8	11.4
Sarasota	13.8	18.3	14.5	8.0	14.3	9.6	15.3	12.9	29.3	48.2	50.9	52,715	52,102	-1.2	10.8
Sunrise	31.3	40.1	21.9	5.4	16.1	16.1	12.0	11.6	16.9	38.1	54.4	85,779	84,305	-1.7	13.2
Tallahassee	7.1	7.4	15.8	29.1	16.8	10.0	8.9	9.3	10.1	27.0	53.1	150,624	181,211	20.3	6.8
Tamarac	25.5	35.7	17.2	7.4	9.3	12.1	12.3	12.6	29.0	48.9	53.9	55,588	60,245	8.4	9.6
Tampa	26.4	17.7	20.9	10.7	16.3	13.5	13.8	12.0	12.8	36.6	50.7	303,447	336,154	10.8	16.9
Titusville	8.0	3.0	17.8	8.6	14.4	7.5	11.5	15.7	24.5	45.7	54.7	40,670	43,626	7.3	6.6
Wellington	26.7	26.0	24.0	5.5	11.5	13.5	15.7	13.6	16.2	41.2	53.7	38,216	56,697	48.4	15.0
Weston	48.1	42.2	27.4	7.5	7.7	11.0	19.9	13.7	12.7	42.4	51.1	49,286	65,419	32.7	8.9
West Palm Beach	27.2	29.6	20.4	10.4	13.9	12.6	11.2	12.1	19.4	39.7	52.0	82,103	100,666	22.6	10.7
Winter Garden	18.1	21.3	25.6	6.0	8.8	11.5	19.0	15.5	13.6	42.4	51.5	14,351	34,767	142.3	30.2
Winter Haven	16.8	6.5	25.1	6.7	12.5	10.8	10.9	8.7	25.4	39.3	53.7	26,487	34,548	30.4	24.5
Winter Park	8.1	12.3	17.6	8.1	9.9	9.0	12.1	18.2	25.1	50.0	51.3	24,090	27,713	15.0	12.1
Winter Springs	18.9	8.6	17.0	7.5	13.0	12.5	17.8	13.2	19.0	45.0	51.6	31,666	33,327	5.2	12.0

1. May be of any race.

City	Number (27)	Persons per household (28)	Family (29)	Married couple family (30)	Female headed[1] (31)	Non-family (32)	One person (33)	Persons in group quarters, 2017 (34)	Number (35)	Rate (36)	Violent (37)	Property (38)	Population age 25 and over (39)	High school graduate or less (40)	Bachelor's degree or more (41)
				Percent					Total		Rate[3]			Attainment[4] (percent)	
FLORIDA— Cont'd															
Deerfield Beach	30,853	2.58	50.8	34.7	11.6	49.2	40.2	1,091	2,470	3,060	343	2,717	57,074	47.5	24.6
DeLand	14,440	2.08	53.5	40.4	9.1	46.5	42.8	2,434	1,625	5,262	576	4,686	24,542	35.9	32.5
Delray Beach	27,750	2.44	53.3	39.4	9.2	46.7	38.3	1,155	3,229	4,791	574	4,217	52,942	32.5	43.9
Deltona	30,261	2.99	77.7	51.0	14.8	22.3	16.1	NA	NA	NA	NA	NA	60,500	47.5	15.2
Doral	17,604	3.47	81.5	56.3	15.3	18.5	12.3	NA	1,794	3,077	137	2,940	40,961	25.0	43.5
Dunedin	19,473	1.84	45.5	34.5	8.4	54.5	49.3	637	749	2,061	149	1,913	31,183	27.0	38.5
Fort Lauderdale	69,899	2.53	47.2	32.4	11.4	52.8	42.5	3,466	11,774	6,497	631	5,866	134,908	36.9	35.1
Fort Myers	29,430	2.62	57.1	41.1	12.0	42.9	34.4	2,917	3,110	4,061	1,237	2,825	57,990	44.5	29.9
Fort Pierce	16,476	2.72	58.0	29.1	17.6	42.0	36.8	703	1,859	4,132	705	3,428	31,005	58.7	14.6
Gainesville	51,104	2.33	33.7	23.6	7.8	66.3	50.2	13,372	5,778	4,403	663	3,740	70,548	29.1	44.0
Greenacres	13,117	3.09	70.9	44.6	20.1	29.1	26.3	NA	1,091	2,722	362	2,360	26,259	49.5	19.7
Hallandale Beach	16,711	2.38	47.8	33.5	9.7	52.2	41.6	NA	1,803	4,512	606	3,906	30,844	44.1	28.2
Hialeah	77,399	3.07	71.1	44.8	18.5	28.9	24.4	2,086	6,177	2,580	242	2,337	183,146	66.0	14.4
Hollywood	54,454	2.79	58.6	36.3	15.1	41.4	36.2	1,496	5,564	3,672	379	3,294	107,966	42.8	25.8
Homestead	18,279	3.80	81.4	42.9	25.8	18.6	15.5	451	3,529	5,213	1,183	4,030	42,569	48.6	26.3
Jacksonville	338,564	2.58	63.4	42.1	16.0	36.6	29.9	19,723	37,042	4,207	625	3,582	606,913	39.1	28.1
Jupiter	25,431	2.53	62.0	51.0	7.2	38.0	31.2	NA	1,408	2,191	229	1,962	46,923	21.4	49.4
Kissimmee	22,086	3.20	70.0	45.5	17.4	30.0	21.6	427	3,178	4,464	714	3,750	45,331	39.9	19.4
Lakeland	41,134	2.51	59.9	42.9	12.7	40.1	32.9	4,878	5,448	5,151	319	4,832	75,556	46.1	24.8
Lake Worth	12,641	2.97	61.2	30.0	16.9	38.8	27.8	591	2,388	6,281	1,341	4,939	26,942	59.4	19.2
Largo	36,735	2.29	51.8	38.0	9.8	48.2	37.0	827	3,379	4,151	479	3,672	64,864	44.9	23.6
Lauderdale Lakes	13,096	2.73	59.0	31.4	18.3	41.0	35.8	360	1,951	5,539	752	4,787	25,432	58.4	18.3
Lauderhill	22,167	3.22	66.2	31.4	25.3	33.8	28.8	616	2,986	4,118	902	3,216	43,363	54.8	15.6
Margate	24,643	2.36	57.5	38.4	14.8	42.5	38.0	NA	1,096	1,889	231	1,658	46,965	51.4	19.4
Melbourne	32,258	2.47	53.3	38.5	12.3	46.7	40.7	2,465	3,975	4,913	824	4,089	59,620	40.0	26.2
Miami	170,005	2.67	57.3	34.6	15.8	42.7	35.4	9,672	22,963	5,109	887	4,221	343,318	49.1	30.1
Miami Beach	43,959	2.08	44.9	31.6	9.3	55.1	44.0	1,069	9,359	10,046	1,009	9,037	69,651	29.9	47.3
Miami Gardens	27,517	4.08	77.6	36.3	35.0	22.4	19.5	1,343	4,414	3,860	650	3,210	74,377	59.8	13.8
Miami Lakes	9,735	3.19	73.5	47.3	18.9	26.5	22.4	NA	622	1,989	99	1,889	21,659	33.4	32.4
Miramar	41,430	3.38	74.5	51.4	18.9	25.5	17.0	141	3,186	2,271	318	1,953	94,008	34.3	28.3
North Lauderdale	15,322	2.88	57.4	29.9	19.0	42.6	39.2	NA	1,150	2,600	473	2,128	29,712	62.5	14.3
North Miami	17,740	3.43	70.2	39.6	18.9	29.8	25.7	1,328	3,052	4,846	721	4,126	43,027	52.7	23.6
North Miami Beach	12,418	3.53	71.6	47.2	17.4	28.4	24.3	NA	1,988	4,473	677	3,796	30,111	42.9	22.4
North Port	23,269	2.84	70.3	49.2	15.4	29.7	23.7	NA	950	1,499	140	1,358	47,201	51.3	17.5
Oakland Park	17,332	2.59	53.6	33.3	12.2	46.4	32.1	NA	2,277	5,071	483	4,588	34,977	42.2	28.9
Ocala	22,487	2.50	57.4	36.6	16.6	42.6	33.4	2,790	3,637	6,207	790	5,417	40,956	51.8	25.2
Ocoee	14,511	3.18	78.4	65.8	8.5	21.6	17.2	NA	1,705	3,761	296	3,466	32,015	26.1	42.2
Orlando	107,590	2.59	55.9	35.1	16.7	44.1	30.8	1,945	16,826	6,059	838	5,220	191,250	33.5	35.2
Ormond Beach	19,564	2.15	57.1	47.1	6.7	42.9	37.5	677	1,804	4,365	489	3,877	33,492	33.6	29.4
Oviedo	13,634	2.98	74.7	61.6	8.5	25.3	20.4	91	439	1,108	197	911	25,862	19.2	50.6
Palm Bay	38,707	2.87	66.2	45.0	13.6	33.8	26.7	567	2,357	2,166	474	1,692	77,468	44.9	20.3
Palm Beach Gardens	24,256	2.25	58.0	48.7	7.4	42.0	35.7	386	1,496	2,780	139	2,641	44,062	20.7	52.2
Palm Coast	32,334	2.73	69.8	50.8	14.1	30.2	21.2	179	NA	NA	NA	NA	64,912	43.5	22.2
Panama City	16,811	2.16	49.9	30.5	14.2	50.1	43.7	620	2,374	6,111	710	5,401	27,340	42.4	26.3
Pembroke Pines	56,680	3.00	70.8	53.5	12.9	29.2	22.4	836	4,092	2,419	202	2,217	119,729	31.2	34.1
Pensacola	22,826	2.28	59.0	40.9	15.1	41.0	33.1	507	2,532	4,739	651	4,088	35,245	27.2	39.2
Pinellas Park	20,282	2.56	58.0	40.8	9.3	42.0	34.1	880	2,861	5,490	405	5,085	39,341	45.7	24.7
Plantation	33,537	2.79	69.0	47.9	12.4	31.0	23.8	381	3,298	3,506	231	3,275	68,050	26.5	45.6
Plant City	14,599	2.64	65.1	40.0	16.8	34.9	23.6	NA	1,408	3,710	414	3,297	25,582	45.2	21.9
Pompano Beach	42,621	2.49	51.9	33.5	13.6	48.1	37.0	4,164	6,136	5,611	851	4,759	83,809	48.3	25.6
Port Orange	25,943	2.43	64.6	47.3	15.0	35.4	28.3	NA	1,538	2,540	101	2,439	46,763	44.0	23.3
Port St. Lucie	65,514	2.88	71.5	53.3	11.5	28.5	21.2	701	2,689	1,475	148	1,326	134,092	47.6	21.3
Riviera Beach	12,190	2.82	60.2	28.9	19.9	39.8	33.4	NA	1,816	5,294	1,385	3,909	22,942	43.7	25.7
Royal Palm Beach	12,563	3.05	76.2	62.4	12.7	23.8	21.7	NA	915	2,386	329	2,057	28,064	40.0	28.0
St. Cloud	15,091	3.37	69.3	51.5	14.1	30.7	26.3	425	881	1,863	283	1,580	31,677	42.3	17.8
St. Petersburg	109,834	2.34	51.8	37.0	10.2	48.2	38.5	5,752	14,531	5,599	665	4,934	202,625	36.0	34.0
Sanford	19,306	3.01	69.5	47.7	14.8	30.5	23.3	1,298	3,354	5,682	918	4,764	39,687	38.6	26.6
Sarasota	24,894	2.15	50.6	35.6	11.6	49.4	41.9	3,538	2,490	4,468	522	3,946	44,153	36.8	36.7
Sunrise	30,548	3.06	67.7	46.1	16.8	32.3	28.1	785	3,328	3,525	267	3,258	68,565	37.1	30.7
Tallahassee	77,176	2.30	45.8	30.9	11.4	54.2	33.5	13,461	12,759	6,660	880	5,780	105,318	21.1	50.0
Tamarac	27,783	2.35	57.1	35.1	17.0	42.9	38.7	NA	1,520	2,320	203	2,117	49,499	39.7	27.9
Tampa	154,040	2.42	53.8	34.7	13.8	46.2	37.7	12,297	9,706	2,582	507	2,075	263,730	38.7	37.3
Titusville	19,133	2.40	54.1	40.9	10.8	45.9	40.3	432	2,223	4,862	776	4,085	34,036	38.4	23.9
Wellington	20,145	3.22	79.3	67.8	8.4	20.7	17.3	NA	1,132	1,775	176	1,600	45,721	29.7	41.9
Weston	22,246	3.19	84.1	68.5	12.2	15.9	12.8	NA	379	535	51	484	46,134	15.2	68.0
West Palm Beach	39,657	2.71	55.3	36.7	14.3	44.7	34.3	2,937	6,553	6,063	883	5,181	76,298	35.7	37.0
Winter Garden	16,319	2.64	67.4	54.8	8.7	32.6	27.0	504	1,561	3,756	322	3,434	29,777	24.7	47.2
Winter Haven	15,443	2.63	61.5	41.6	12.9	38.5	34.2	629	1,535	3,988	509	3,479	28,187	43.9	18.9
Winter Park	13,582	2.14	52.7	41.3	7.7	47.3	41.3	1,772	1,135	3,739	329	3,409	22,951	12.4	64.1
Winter Springs	14,645	2.50	68.2	56.6	9.0	31.8	28.6	NA	494	1,407	154	1,254	27,675	22.3	50.6

1. No spouse present. 2. Data for serious crimes have not been adjusted for underreporting. This may affect comparability between geographic areas and over time. 3. Per 100,000 population estimated by the FBI. 4. Persons 25 years old and over.

City	Money income, 2017					Median earnings, 2017			Housing units, 2017				
	Households			Median family income	Median non-family income	All persons	Men	Women	Total	Occupied	Percent owner occupied	Median value[1] (dollars)	Median gross rent (dollars)
	Median income	Percent with income less than $20,000	Percent with income of $200,000 or more										
	42	43	44	45	46	47	48	49	50	51	52	53	54
FLORIDA— Cont'd													
Deerfield Beach	46,238	21.9	2.5	55,273	30,849	26,672	29,637	23,655	38,810	30,853	56.4	165,100	1,286
DeLand	43,131	23.4	2.8	58,040	21,920	32,643	36,091	30,946	16,248	14,440	62.6	197,100	878
Delray Beach	63,357	12.9	9.2	77,394	42,937	34,502	40,597	29,392	34,753	27,750	59.5	317,400	1,416
Deltona	53,171	17.5	0.7	57,472	30,981	31,756	40,327	26,000	33,181	30,261	68.8	148,500	1,115
Doral	71,150	8.0	7.1	71,444	54,788	31,879	36,251	27,588	24,394	17,604	50.0	376,200	1,812
Dunedin	46,154	21.4	4.4	68,340	31,270	34,410	42,201	29,134	22,840	19,473	67.2	175,400	952
Fort Lauderdale	56,309	17.5	10.4	76,325	40,853	31,082	36,358	25,666	93,917	69,899	51.8	329,500	1,217
Fort Myers	45,511	19.2	4.7	55,082	28,316	27,191	28,685	26,258	39,355	29,430	47.3	230,800	982
Fort Pierce	32,073	25.1	0.3	37,350	25,461	22,283	24,843	18,430	20,696	16,476	52.8	91,500	952
Gainesville	34,226	31.6	3.3	58,731	22,214	19,985	19,428	20,309	63,440	51,104	40.1	156,900	947
Greenacres	45,566	17.3	2.6	50,921	25,309	25,976	25,148	26,979	15,899	13,117	67.0	169,700	1,355
Hallandale Beach	41,171	23.2	1.2	50,326	33,413	25,657	26,698	23,221	27,668	16,711	48.1	237,600	1,248
Hialeah	34,512	30.8	1.2	41,542	15,226	22,756	25,912	20,844	80,649	77,399	45.1	232,600	1,085
Hollywood	50,775	14.5	4.6	60,282	39,424	30,887	32,308	26,405	68,321	54,454	56.4	261,700	1,179
Homestead	47,426	16.9	4.7	44,568	48,641	22,084	22,441	21,116	19,450	18,279	43.7	223,200	1,303
Jacksonville	51,497	16.9	3.7	64,742	33,227	31,470	35,377	28,610	382,572	338,564	54.7	177,000	988
Jupiter	80,481	9.0	14.1	101,168	56,517	46,817	54,254	40,293	32,740	25,431	76.0	382,200	1,638
Kissimmee	39,871	16.4	1.3	41,649	31,921	23,251	27,448	20,668	28,190	22,086	37.5	166,800	1,141
Lakeland	46,466	21.7	3.6	57,419	32,037	31,338	35,205	26,638	50,917	41,134	54.4	150,800	981
Lake Worth	35,987	18.4	3.7	43,107	28,795	22,095	25,869	19,586	14,869	12,641	44.5	206,900	1,107
Largo	43,363	18.8	2.2	61,433	29,042	30,752	31,602	27,247	45,788	36,735	58.6	129,500	1,047
Lauderdale Lakes	36,544	28.8	0.3	47,856	20,199	24,143	26,237	22,108	16,186	13,096	50.4	100,400	988
Lauderhill	38,471	24.1	1.1	45,130	30,069	25,144	29,174	22,184	28,070	22,167	50.0	174,600	1,171
Margate	44,114	23.5	1.7	54,994	23,698	28,137	30,506	25,987	29,603	24,643	67.8	204,500	1,330
Melbourne	43,979	21.6	2.7	63,095	29,483	29,419	35,085	24,584	36,654	32,258	62.0	162,100	979
Miami	40,327	26.8	5.6	41,874	30,928	26,794	30,245	24,540	201,784	170,005	28.9	322,100	1,165
Miami Beach	50,152	23.7	8.3	69,764	36,769	35,067	40,338	27,737	70,349	43,959	35.6	458,800	1,306
Miami Gardens	46,450	21.2	1.3	49,734	19,857	26,299	25,538	26,909	30,983	27,517	65.0	192,700	1,243
Miami Lakes	63,683	13.0	6.1	91,068	44,733	37,492	55,805	31,916	10,283	9,735	53.4	387,100	1,604
Miramar	70,381	9.3	7.1	76,193	50,584	37,561	39,337	35,148	44,287	41,430	66.8	314,600	1,236
North Lauderdale	36,210	25.3	1.7	52,584	30,217	26,746	30,882	22,461	16,193	15,322	54.6	162,900	1,414
North Miami	44,567	20.9	2.7	47,833	26,254	25,555	26,009	24,604	20,107	17,740	44.7	214,500	1,133
North Miami Beach	46,574	20.2	2.2	55,367	26,771	27,532	30,073	24,175	14,737	12,418	56.6	188,600	1,138
North Port	53,662	5.7	1.6	65,294	29,655	26,582	35,640	25,586	27,457	23,269	73.0	175,300	1,186
Oakland Park	51,317	13.3	4.7	65,427	39,491	30,165	30,170	30,157	19,904	17,332	60.0	205,600	1,182
Ocala	41,951	24.4	2.8	44,374	31,690	30,270	30,430	30,019	26,251	22,487	48.5	137,100	849
Ocoee	80,502	13.0	8.7	86,417	36,796	40,511	41,309	38,208	15,736	14,511	73.7	273,700	1,204
Orlando	47,594	18.0	5.2	49,076	41,881	27,568	31,067	24,742	128,403	107,590	33.4	232,600	1,152
Ormond Beach	57,860	14.8	7.1	77,174	30,733	36,478	39,984	35,033	21,347	19,564	75.3	209,700	1,070
Oviedo	92,635	10.2	10.0	111,492	28,486	45,253	63,303	28,975	13,897	13,634	80.0	273,300	1,458
Palm Bay	46,301	13.0	1.7	49,466	35,261	26,263	30,733	23,722	42,975	38,707	68.5	153,200	1,039
Palm Beach Gardens	82,623	9.8	16.2	107,045	52,223	48,135	51,846	38,882	30,204	24,256	73.4	363,600	1,673
Palm Coast	49,578	13.6	1.7	55,213	36,463	24,955	28,400	23,544	36,950	32,334	75.0	215,300	1,241
Panama City	43,249	20.5	4.7	67,927	30,635	27,712	26,917	30,162	19,746	16,811	51.2	157,900	891
Pembroke Pines	72,056	13.7	6.7	87,743	40,539	40,596	42,448	36,025	63,099	56,680	68.8	300,600	1,378
Pensacola	44,220	21.2	3.7	61,713	30,809	31,178	36,556	26,209	25,365	22,826	59.2	193,200	923
Pinellas Park	42,868	20.8	1.7	51,082	26,150	30,252	34,899	27,895	23,448	20,282	61.5	162,500	1,006
Plantation	73,817	12.7	8.7	77,556	52,269	40,084	42,084	33,672	37,752	33,537	63.1	317,700	1,551
Plant City	52,319	16.3	3.4	63,393	39,754	33,062	35,992	31,769	16,270	14,599	57.4	160,600	910
Pompano Beach	49,419	19.5	4.1	66,087	34,985	27,575	30,654	22,909	57,675	42,621	53.4	197,400	1,249
Port Orange	50,130	16.6	3.6	69,008	28,773	28,457	33,509	26,535	27,586	25,943	68.8	170,600	1,148
Port St. Lucie	57,045	12.2	2.2	60,542	35,791	29,254	36,083	22,453	73,060	65,514	73.8	205,000	1,361
Riviera Beach	41,276	23.7	5.6	49,363	28,225	25,578	26,512	21,922	16,252	12,190	46.9	198,700	1,124
Royal Palm Beach	70,428	5.4	3.6	77,529	41,031	35,994	37,160	32,172	14,094	12,563	89.5	254,000	1,478
St. Cloud	55,011	12.1	3.4	71,020	31,825	27,360	29,489	22,302	18,369	15,091	77.0	209,300	978
St. Petersburg	55,134	17.4	6.2	75,582	37,353	32,490	36,048	31,360	137,350	109,834	61.0	198,400	1,083
Sanford	50,841	18.7	2.5	52,161	41,578	29,097	32,069	23,188	20,176	19,306	50.5	146,900	1,077
Sarasota	51,422	15.7	7.2	67,429	37,521	29,979	35,418	26,858	32,215	24,894	58.5	283,600	1,076
Sunrise	61,887	14.9	3.4	74,915	33,194	36,965	38,771	36,013	33,935	30,548	70.6	200,500	1,674
Tallahassee	45,153	20.9	4.9	69,400	30,647	23,215	24,214	22,815	88,957	77,176	43.0	202,400	1,014
Tamarac	41,737	15.3	1.7	54,551	28,920	30,320	30,367	30,261	31,327	27,783	74.7	170,300	1,316
Tampa	50,489	21.2	7.8	64,692	35,576	31,003	35,729	26,445	175,475	154,040	46.7	233,800	1,082
Titusville	40,940	19.1	1.3	54,517	29,387	23,974	28,431	21,198	24,680	19,133	70.3	148,900	875
Wellington	89,227	5.3	15.4	100,733	62,007	41,530	47,376	35,674	25,188	20,145	77.6	397,600	1,837
Weston	97,908	6.1	18.8	105,929	75,525	44,647	57,419	31,956	25,494	22,246	75.8	504,800	1,962
West Palm Beach	51,871	16.4	5.0	60,712	41,967	27,536	31,475	24,098	51,684	39,657	51.3	256,600	1,248
Winter Garden	60,006	18.9	12.5	89,342	31,733	35,019	41,627	29,658	19,230	16,319	66.3	328,700	922
Winter Haven	46,264	24.6	6.1	52,559	27,664	29,921	40,324	25,896	18,535	15,443	51.1	169,700	875
Winter Park	87,088	11.5	18.5	115,401	50,983	55,516	67,074	38,347	15,695	13,582	69.2	428,400	1,341
Winter Springs	75,105	17.0	8.6	94,029	42,791	42,355	52,334	36,699	16,038	14,645	82.6	255,200	1,284

1. Based on population estimated by the American Community Survey.   2. Includes units rented or sold but not occupied.   3. Specified owner-occupied units; $1,000,000 represents $1,000,000 or more.   4. 50.0 represents 50 percent or more.   5. 10.0 represents 10 percent or less.

Table D. Cities — Commuting, Computer Access, Migration, Labor Force, and Employment

City	Commuting[1], 2017 — Percent Commuting	With commutes of 30 minutes or more	Computer access[2], 2017 — With a computer in the house	With Internet access	Migration, 2017 — Percent who lived in the same house one year ago	Percent who lived in another state or county one year ago	Civilian labor force, 2018 — Total	Percent change 2017-2018	Unemployment Total	Rate[3]	Civilian employment[4], 2017 — Population age 16 and older Number	Percent in labor force	Population age 16 to 64 Number	Percent who worked full-year full-time
	55	56	57	58	59	60	61	62	63	64	65	66	67	68
FLORIDA— Cont'd														
Deerfield Beach	82.6	45.7	90.2	82.6	74.5	9.7	40,967	1.2	1,421	3.5	66,307	65.1	49,465	51.1
DeLand	70.5	32.6	90.4	73.6	86.8	8.0	14,112	1.2	573	4.1	29,152	45.0	19,787	44.8
Delray Beach	80.6	33.6	93.2	86.2	84.2	6.3	36,259	0.9	1,234	3.4	57,782	63.3	40,708	52.9
Deltona	86.9	58.8	94.4	81.5	87.0	8.6	44,280	1.1	1,710	3.9	70,636	55.3	56,947	46.7
Doral	77.4	39.3	93.3	88.7	85.6	7.7	31,726	0.8	1,053	3.3	47,088	70.9	41,677	60.1
Dunedin	86.4	30.0	88.5	78.9	83.1	9.4	18,319	1.5	610	3.3	34,567	52.0	21,192	51.5
Fort Lauderdale	77.8	38.0	93.2	84.7	81.1	6.7	97,245	1.0	3,430	3.5	150,951	64.4	121,002	50.1
Fort Myers	78.8	38.0	87.7	78.8	84.2	6.8	34,767	1.8	1,294	3.7	65,870	58.1	49,714	51.9
Fort Pierce	80.3	38.8	81.1	69.1	87.9	3.1	18,952	1.8	1,219	6.4	36,752	58.3	29,570	44.4
Gainesville	66.7	17.3	93.9	86.5	70.5	15.2	67,761	1.1	2,478	3.7	117,282	60.0	103,336	38.2
Greenacres	76.5	44.8	90.3	82.3	86.7	5.0	21,924	1.1	714	3.3	31,216	61.9	24,871	50.7
Hallandale Beach	78.6	51.4	89.7	78.3	81.2	10.8	18,511	0.8	688	3.7	34,267	60.5	25,065	48.4
Hialeah	74.1	50.5	83.1	67.0	91.9	2.6	114,846	0.4	4,554	4.0	204,263	58.7	153,394	54.0
Hollywood	78.1	47.8	92.2	85.0	87.4	6.4	81,503	1.1	2,763	3.4	124,728	63.8	99,496	51.0
Homestead	67.7	68.3	93.8	83.9	88.0	4.6	32,023	-0.2	1,351	4.2	52,816	68.5	45,778	45.2
Jacksonville	79.8	37.6	90.0	81.4	80.5	6.2	460,539	1.7	16,693	3.6	709,981	65.8	589,809	53.6
Jupiter	80.0	27.5	96.9	88.7	88.8	4.0	34,736	1.0	994	2.9	52,362	62.9	37,647	55.6
Kissimmee	79.6	60.2	88.9	74.3	82.8	11.6	37,745	2.4	1,374	3.6	55,509	67.1	48,727	46.0
Lakeland	82.6	25.8	87.5	64.9	78.3	12.5	46,543	1.4	1,932	4.2	90,100	57.2	68,707	49.0
Lake Worth	60.8	48.7	91.1	65.6	85.7	5.2	19,592	0.7	682	3.5	30,953	60.6	25,161	53.6
Largo	76.9	28.3	86.8	77.1	81.7	5.8	41,860	1.5	1,457	3.5	73,335	56.7	51,307	58.1
Lauderdale Lakes	77.7	42.3	91.8	63.5	77.0	4.4	17,699	0.9	684	3.9	29,232	58.2	22,744	45.9
Lauderhill	80.4	44.0	89.0	59.5	85.7	2.9	36,142	1.0	1,460	4.0	53,205	61.8	45,217	44.7
Margate	82.9	42.9	92.7	83.3	88.3	5.5	30,837	1.3	1,155	3.7	51,132	66.1	36,054	54.6
Melbourne	78.7	24.3	86.2	81.5	87.3	5.9	39,276	2.5	1,415	3.6	67,392	51.1	47,465	47.1
Miami	68.1	50.6	88.2	65.2	85.6	4.4	230,536	0.7	8,774	3.8	390,223	62.1	315,270	55.3
Miami Beach	50.1	44.5	91.1	77.4	77.6	8.2	56,884	0.7	1,695	3.0	77,836	68.2	61,584	55.6
Miami Gardens	86.5	53.8	89.7	71.0	90.9	1.7	53,345	0.4	2,627	4.9	88,846	58.6	74,315	49.2
Miami Lakes	85.7	45.7	96.3	90.5	93.2	3.2	16,284	0.8	557	3.4	25,606	62.5	20,082	48.5
Miramar	87.4	53.2	96.9	86.5	92.9	4.0	77,397	1.1	2,523	3.3	109,326	72.1	94,618	57.6
North Lauderdale	83.0	49.1	95.9	86.5	78.8	2.7	23,900	1.1	895	3.7	34,950	75.0	32,087	50.8
North Miami	76.0	53.6	91.6	74.0	84.3	5.4	30,866	0.3	1,348	4.4	48,613	63.7	41,141	50.5
North Miami Beach	82.0	53.2	91.2	81.0	91.8	3.7	22,810	0.5	876	3.8	34,984	65.8	29,388	45.5
North Port	89.2	49.9	90.4	83.2	89.6	7.2	29,251	1.6	1,059	3.6	55,419	60.7	39,844	58.7
Oakland Park	79.0	40.6	95.4	88.2	86.3	5.0	26,474	1.2	889	3.4	39,118	71.8	33,528	46.1
Ocala	83.2	23.9	85.4	76.8	81.5	9.0	25,066	1.1	1,024	4.1	46,951	54.7	36,718	48.1
Ocoee	76.5	64.9	97.4	91.5	NA	NA	26,704	2.7	755	2.8	35,854	69.6	31,289	54.3
Orlando	76.0	38.9	95.7	83.4	78.5	11.0	167,009	2.6	5,103	3.1	223,697	71.9	194,185	53.6
Ormond Beach	80.3	19.0	86.6	79.8	84.8	5.0	19,903	1.3	721	3.6	36,696	52.1	23,076	54.0
Oviedo	83.0	47.5	93.9	91.6	84.8	7.9	22,534	2.6	635	2.8	31,627	68.6	27,507	47.3
Palm Bay	79.8	35.4	93.3	88.1	86.1	4.1	53,038	2.4	1,934	3.6	91,807	60.5	75,910	49.0
Palm Beach Gardens	77.9	24.5	95.0	92.0	84.0	6.6	28,950	1.1	870	3.0	47,382	58.0	31,342	56.2
Palm Coast	89.5	38.1	92.3	74.6	87.0	10.0	37,239	1.7	1,502	4.0	74,306	46.6	49,455	42.3
Panama City	77.1	18.5	89.0	83.6	77.9	7.0	16,872	1.0	780	4.6	31,591	58.0	23,542	41.2
Pembroke Pines	88.9	54.8	95.2	87.8	89.4	6.3	92,077	1.1	2,897	3.1	139,658	64.3	113,453	58.2
Pensacola	82.0	15.5	92.1	82.2	80.3	8.0	27,742	2.0	818	2.9	41,809	63.6	33,133	50.6
Pinellas Park	82.8	25.5	88.9	81.1	86.0	4.8	26,513	1.5	870	3.3	42,585	59.3	31,851	55.6
Plantation	82.2	42.6	95.4	87.3	80.9	7.4	54,550	1.2	1,613	3.0	77,462	64.8	60,017	51.1
Plant City	87.6	32.7	94.9	84.3	78.9	9.7	19,766	1.3	652	3.3	30,041	66.7	24,866	56.8
Pompano Beach	73.3	34.1	86.2	78.0	81.4	6.6	52,949	0.9	2,056	3.9	94,526	58.6	73,962	47.1
Port Orange	77.8	25.7	94.9	84.1	88.0	3.4	31,774	1.3	1,041	3.3	53,248	57.7	37,979	47.4
Port St. Lucie	80.6	43.1	95.9	92.3	86.2	9.1	91,937	2.3	3,507	3.8	154,862	56.7	114,299	50.7
Riviera Beach	80.5	22.4	87.0	77.4	84.0	6.6	16,398	0.6	716	4.4	27,262	60.9	20,876	47.1
Royal Palm Beach	82.6	48.6	96.8	92.3	NA	NA	21,093	0.9	677	3.2	31,085	63.3	23,828	55.1
St. Cloud	75.8	58.6	95.3	88.9	91.2	2.4	25,380	2.5	867	3.4	38,857	65.7	32,477	52.2
St. Petersburg	77.8	32.0	91.3	81.9	87.1	5.5	141,103	1.4	4,529	3.2	224,458	62.7	170,893	54.6
Sanford	86.4	47.8	91.6	80.8	78.2	14.1	28,456	2.5	1,190	4.2	44,212	63.0	37,032	53.0
Sarasota	75.6	24.5	90.2	81.6	81.6	9.3	28,368	1.6	907	3.2	49,652	49.1	32,982	45.3
Sunrise	82.3	39.2	93.6	65.1	89.4	3.8	52,568	1.0	1,752	3.3	76,362	64.7	60,455	54.3
Tallahassee	80.2	16.3	95.9	88.6	69.7	13.3	101,016	1.3	3,627	3.6	164,814	66.9	145,550	42.5
Tamarac	86.1	50.3	94.2	86.6	82.9	6.7	34,617	1.1	1,260	3.6	55,308	59.6	36,238	52.6
Tampa	77.2	35.8	92.5	85.5	77.3	8.9	200,112	1.2	7,143	3.6	313,418	66.0	263,904	51.6
Titusville	80.8	42.5	90.7	88.0	78.5	5.2	21,057	2.5	785	3.7	38,319	51.7	26,994	44.5
Wellington	72.9	57.4	97.9	95.6	89.8	4.6	34,703	1.1	1,055	3.0	51,229	64.4	40,701	50.1
Weston	75.8	54.6	NA	NA	85.2	7.4	36,885	1.1	1,092	3.0	54,447	64.5	45,409	51.4
West Palm Beach	76.8	28.2	91.6	82.5	79.7	10.7	59,264	1.0	2,068	3.5	90,408	64.8	69,080	54.0
Winter Garden	75.4	51.0	90.7	82.0	81.9	7.2	23,095	2.7	719	3.1	34,621	69.6	28,701	62.5
Winter Haven	83.4	35.1	82.9	57.8	77.7	12.5	17,360	2.0	833	4.8	32,064	46.5	21,573	45.0
Winter Park	79.3	29.1	96.3	91.1	87.9	6.2	15,206	2.5	467	3.1	26,267	56.0	18,505	48.7
Winter Springs	82.3	51.2	97.5	94.5	86.6	6.9	20,275	2.5	629	3.1	31,377	59.4	24,407	54.9

1. Employed persons.　2. Households.　3. Percent of civilian labor force.　4. Persons 16 years old and over.

Table D. Cities — Construction, Wholesale Trade, and Retail Trade

City	Value of residential construction authorized by building permits, 2018			Wholesale trade[1], 2012				Retail trade[2], 2012			
	New construction ($1,000)	Number of housing units	Percent single family	Number of establishments	Number of employees	Sales (mil dol)	Annual payroll (mil dol)	Number of establishments	Number of employees	Sales (mil dol)	Annual payroll (mil dol)
	69	70	71	72	73	74	75	76	77	78	79
FLORIDA— Cont'd											
Deerfield Beach	24,807	243	7.0	218	2,314	10,619.2	148.1	298	3,593	1,084.7	99.1
DeLand	155,039	649	71.0	45	209	116.2	10.7	175	2,527	752.9	66.0
Delray Beach	29,168	74	73.0	112	564	548.9	32.4	380	4,553	1,576.5	139.0
Deltona	63,894	242	99.2	10	D	D	D	97	1,566	368.2	35.7
Doral	317,508	2,112	22.5	1,540	13,960	31,206.3	805.1	445	6,595	2,137.1	195.8
Dunedin	20,153	74	97.3	29	265	114.0	8.9	123	1,010	233.2	25.7
Fort Lauderdale	156,610	339	32.2	571	5,787	4,332.2	299.5	1,161	12,021	4,045.3	367.8
Fort Myers	517,954	2,777	30.6	167	2,206	1,030.4	96.2	688	9,914	2,678.6	251.3
Fort Pierce	24,687	149	40.9	35	360	225.0	16.8	220	2,803	919.2	77.6
Gainesville	45,255	942	13.6	135	1,457	1,010.0	67.6	547	8,426	2,169.4	189.1
Greenacres	5,174	32	53.1	27	108	35.5	5.1	94	1,481	469.2	42.6
Hallandale Beach	7,989	43	23.3	80	429	248.2	20.4	137	1,858	437.1	44.0
Hialeah	40,809	278	27.0	515	3,886	1,380.5	132.7	1,060	10,595	2,456.0	240.2
Hollywood	80,096	334	62.3	285	2,279	1,521.9	131.5	573	6,316	1,916.1	159.0
Homestead	75,409	343	97.1	41	288	179.1	11.0	182	2,386	656.3	51.3
Jacksonville	1,241,460	7,003	54.0	1,075	18,668	18,797.6	1,056.4	3,011	43,471	12,498.4	1,114.5
Jupiter	67,774	118	96.6	100	669	352.8	36.1	257	2,886	673.8	77.3
Kissimmee	124,105	749	48.9	49	D	D	D	366	4,823	1,248.2	107.1
Lakeland	93,021	435	100.0	156	2,930	7,572.0	187.5	559	8,370	2,282.0	200.0
Lake Worth	22,418	135	28.1	43	331	126.8	21.2	120	888	256.9	24.5
Largo	18,662	79	100.0	102	D	D	D	330	4,311	1,033.1	112.4
Lauderdale Lakes	0	0	0.0	20	102	33.4	2.8	73	1,072	253.1	26.1
Lauderhill	940	12	41.7	41	D	D	D	198	1,478	364.1	37.0
Margate	15,801	145	61.4	62	411	354.4	17.4	171	2,476	889.2	78.1
Melbourne	69,244	215	97.7	102	1,461	820.5	80.6	464	6,067	1,626.6	155.3
Miami	831,911	4,625	1.7	1,440	8,474	7,906.8	371.9	2,398	21,175	6,476.3	551.4
Miami Beach	30,977	31	100.0	151	415	275.6	19.3	561	5,912	1,556.8	145.4
Miami Gardens	1,845	16	100.0	180	3,106	2,120.4	149.9	302	4,416	1,685.6	138.4
Miami Lakes	46,273	209	100.0	113	1,305	835.1	68.0	72	1,372	559.3	49.3
Miramar	12,493	183	3.3	198	2,748	2,686.5	197.4	198	3,297	1,659.5	96.3
North Lauderdale	0	0	0.0	7	D	D	D	70	961	241.1	24.2
North Miami	3,735	17	100.0	76	364	210.0	18.5	188	1,749	462.3	46.5
North Miami Beach	3,208	13	69.2	57	156	76.7	6.6	191	2,470	1,125.3	69.9
North Port	376,776	1,274	100.0	23	133	41.1	3.9	80	1,454	375.3	35.2
Oakland Park	3,561	25	92.0	114	811	360.5	49.2	252	2,047	654.6	55.5
Ocala	65,189	226	100.0	166	2,285	1,310.3	109.1	631	9,325	2,756.9	228.6
Ocoee	140,662	428	100.0	32	632	675.2	40.5	160	2,639	564.9	54.3
Orlando	440,491	3,079	25.7	634	8,653	5,585.7	443.6	1,580	27,103	8,359.0	641.1
Ormond Beach	36,111	109	60.6	44	767	287.7	31.1	195	2,299	579.6	55.4
Oviedo	51,086	129	98.4	31	D	D	D	148	2,331	405.9	44.8
Palm Bay	159,030	689	100.0	32	202	71.9	8.4	170	2,500	736.5	63.0
Palm Beach Gardens	108,968	285	76.8	68	341	138.0	14.8	348	6,747	1,555.8	167.7
Palm Coast	226,055	909	83.1	36	100	27.0	3.2	140	2,406	588.2	58.2
Panama City	36,420	111	100.0	68	765	247.4	31.0	338	4,441	1,199.2	113.9
Pembroke Pines	93,034	602	36.7	202	702	334.8	32.1	577	10,690	3,250.8	264.3
Pensacola	24,906	112	100.0	67	641	246.2	27.8	418	6,109	1,366.9	130.7
Pinellas Park	24,923	289	5.2	166	2,065	728.0	83.2	284	3,773	1,371.7	103.5
Plantation	33,025	263	12.9	120	490	277.2	31.8	348	5,590	1,724.9	134.2
Plant City	17,552	132	100.0	79	1,769	1,236.6	70.7	157	2,140	698.8	53.4
Pompano Beach	42,138	334	16.5	454	6,291	4,882.2	310.0	624	8,020	4,203.6	258.0
Port Orange	58,516	203	100.0	34	D	D	D	164	2,608	585.4	58.6
Port St. Lucie	485,251	2,943	71.4	81	489	148.1	19.5	334	8,054	2,257.6	240.5
Riviera Beach	43,293	309	24.3	102	2,211	1,640.8	133.5	106	878	354.3	29.7
Royal Palm Beach	40,213	125	93.6	32	184	124.2	7.4	154	3,525	975.5	88.3
St. Cloud	292,592	960	100.0	12	D	D	D	127	1,765	490.8	41.8
St. Petersburg	156,405	1,003	33.4	187	2,580	1,218.2	128.5	905	13,444	4,893.4	361.6
Sanford	140,455	653	57.1	88	1,374	538.6	64.0	358	5,781	1,758.4	148.0
Sarasota	111,503	549	16.9	88	651	303.2	32.0	505	5,274	1,363.5	141.3
Sunrise	0	0	0.0	262	2,458	1,729.8	140.2	544	10,882	2,776.1	241.5
Tallahassee	210,916	1,524	26.0	176	1,987	1,622.5	155.3	854	13,278	3,039.5	290.5
Tamarac	18,349	162	100.0	60	1,056	609.3	50.8	131	2,294	530.4	78.0
Tampa	453,158	1,788	62.0	646	9,863	9,457.0	490.2	1,878	24,934	7,449.8	673.5
Titusville	16,870	103	98.1	21	236	100.8	11.2	168	2,468	612.6	59.0
Wellington	33,699	52	92.3	78	239	386.9	12.4	243	3,279	570.2	69.5
Weston	8,653	37	100.0	279	1,712	2,552.4	102.4	134	2,210	864.1	70.8
West Palm Beach	49,500	363	11.0	146	1,663	1,282.1	90.9	535	8,040	2,939.5	248.0
Winter Garden	278,185	569	100.0	41	446	359.2	15.9	158	2,483	603.2	53.6
Winter Haven	176,638	774	100.0	45	1,427	534.7	34.0	201	2,939	801.8	72.5
Winter Park	57,412	114	100.0	52	335	233.1	16.8	232	2,936	816.0	80.3
Winter Springs	15,796	33	100.0	28	125	30.6	5.5	43	453	182.0	13.4

1. Merchant wholesalers except manufacturers' sales branches and offices.   2. Establishments with payroll.

City	Real estate and rental and leasing, 2012				Professional, scientific, and technical services[1], 2012				Manufacturing, 2012			
	Number of establish-ments	Number of employees	Receipts (mil dol)	Annual payroll (mil dol)	Number of establish-ments	Number of employees	Receipts (mil dol)	Annual payroll (mil dol)	Number of establish-ments	Number of employees	Receipts (mil dol)	Annual payroll (mil dol)
	80	81	82	83	84	85	86	87	88	89	90	91
FLORIDA— Cont'd												
Deerfield Beach	122	846	131.8	33.0	338	2,736	400.9	136.7	107	2,166	751.5	109.1
DeLand	56	207	30.3	5.3	131	573	65.2	21.3	57	1,798	358.7	76.5
Delray Beach	152	673	85.9	19.7	467	1,971	299.1	98.3	73	585	136.6	21.5
Deltona	18	24	3.5	0.6	67	193	17.8	5.4	3	D	D	D
Doral	212	1,180	264.7	49.9	560	D	D	D	127	2,765	533.1	112.8
Dunedin	42	87	23.3	4.0	154	544	91.0	26.6	18	234	D	11.1
Fort Lauderdale	708	3,644	1,279.5	186.4	2,319	14,924	2,716.3	1,134.6	282	3,899	975.0	177.2
Fort Myers	212	1,133	239.2	40.0	486	6,661	1,451.1	576.0	93	1,720	396.6	75.2
Fort Pierce	61	221	41.6	7.7	137	D	D	D	26	495	108.8	21.3
Gainesville	201	1,076	156.0	32.4	472	2,740	317.7	130.2	86	1,558	587.6	82.4
Greenacres	22	55	23.2	2.4	96	629	52.3	17.5	4	56	D	1.4
Hallandale Beach	92	188	43.0	7.3	183	663	109.6	34.7	34	334	52.9	11.4
Hialeah	250	682	126.3	20.8	348	1,631	208.5	68.1	436	4,833	837.4	174.1
Hollywood	297	3,294	231.6	94.1	905	3,385	541.2	200.0	96	1,125	249.1	44.8
Homestead	43	141	17.7	3.4	80	344	33.6	13.4	19	221	D	8.6
Jacksonville	1,093	6,806	1,758.4	308.0	2,865	28,566	5,420.9	2,114.3	579	21,616	10,146.3	1,252.8
Jupiter	160	862	98.9	30.5	452	D	D	D	57	777	D	68.0
Kissimmee	147	584	102.0	15.8	177	811	73.7	22.8	28	125	D	4.2
Lakeland	194	1,027	197.6	34.5	357	D	D	D	82	3,922	1,614.7	155.8
Lake Worth	43	88	31.0	3.3	120	D	D	D	45	244	36.8	9.1
Largo	115	569	108.6	20.9	220	2,075	310.6	103.4	107	2,541	531.7	128.3
Lauderdale Lakes	20	282	50.3	10.1	28	D	D	D	8	32	2.3	0.6
Lauderhill	56	635	134.3	22.4	98	342	46.2	12.8	19	158	D	5.5
Margate	51	171	34.4	4.5	133	648	71.1	23.4	30	154	14.8	5.1
Melbourne	170	628	103.9	19.7	399	3,608	775.2	251.9	96	5,615	2,026.1	392.0
Miami	1,169	4,273	1,121.7	207.2	3,517	D	D	D	343	3,948	887.3	142.4
Miami Beach	457	1,556	402.9	70.2	661	D	D	D	29	99	13.4	2.9
Miami Gardens	69	266	70.9	9.7	78	335	30.7	18.5	68	1,871	338.3	79.1
Miami Lakes	85	607	137.0	28.8	270	1,165	271.1	70.2	24	2,155	578.1	148.6
Miramar	72	466	80.6	15.6	270	D	D	D	33	825	209.5	37.4
North Lauderdale	18	70	25.2	2.4	40	D	D	D	11	44	D	1.5
North Miami	90	276	54.4	9.5	158	521	84.3	25.4	27	468	51.4	17.4
North Miami Beach	72	239	34.3	9.2	213	734	97.9	31.4	23	247	D	12.8
North Port	29	50	6.0	2.0	62	137	13.0	4.1	12	247	D	9.7
Oakland Park	96	430	59.5	12.9	220	D	D	D	103	724	157.5	34.1
Ocala	171	897	130.2	27.8	383	1,854	216.2	81.0	105	3,819	1,196.5	169.6
Ocoee	30	241	37.3	8.6	92	412	38.8	12.8	13	192	D	4.7
Orlando	762	7,122	2,384.5	297.4	2,017	D	D	D	253	11,032	4,157.9	783.3
Ormond Beach	74	338	53.8	11.0	172	654	98.2	30.8	40	820	116.8	32.7
Oviedo	66	186	41.7	5.7	140	D	D	D	13	44	D	1.7
Palm Bay	54	143	24.5	4.2	99	D	D	D	39	8,936	2,317.2	672.1
Palm Beach Gardens	138	730	253.4	36.1	499	D	D	D	24	489	D	39.2
Palm Coast	98	D	D	D	128	288	42.8	12.6	21	428	D	20.4
Panama City	98	488	90.8	15.9	199	D	D	D	39	1,448	739.4	92.9
Pembroke Pines	159	506	135.3	19.8	563	1,725	276.4	78.8	46	249	44.4	9.8
Pensacola	122	590	114.5	18.9	450	D	D	D	49	766	361.0	41.0
Pinellas Park	67	263	56.7	11.4	167	D	D	D	238	7,383	2,189.6	333.8
Plantation	198	1,034	102.6	38.4	723	D	D	D	41	268	29.7	10.0
Plant City	46	146	41.2	4.9	91	D	D	D	49	1,795	748.9	76.0
Pompano Beach	228	930	191.6	35.6	471	1,768	287.0	89.9	250	5,908	1,497.3	326.0
Port Orange	94	362	53.1	10.2	120	901	112.2	36.9	18	210	28.5	7.4
Port St. Lucie	139	353	59.0	10.1	277	D	D	D	48	840	332.3	38.3
Riviera Beach	44	312	36.6	10.6	49	464	52.6	14.6	69	1,424	463.1	63.0
Royal Palm Beach	23	38	10.3	1.6	117	547	59.2	26.1	5	15	D	0.6
St. Cloud	43	132	15.4	2.8	53	163	14.0	4.5	15	163	D	7.1
St. Petersburg	347	1,614	298.8	58.1	1,158	11,396	1,508.6	594.7	148	4,906	1,377.7	262.0
Sanford	70	417	107.4	13.6	128	D	D	D	59	1,596	652.5	69.0
Sarasota	242	768	190.2	30.9	622	D	D	D	57	552	D	30.1
Sunrise	122	492	115.4	20.6	364	2,464	366.1	135.5	71	495	165.2	25.8
Tallahassee	331	1,808	256.7	54.4	1,158	D	D	D	77	1,297	382.7	66.0
Tamarac	63	250	47.5	7.7	166	553	71.6	28.5	20	370	52.6	15.1
Tampa	856	5,003	1,353.4	236.3	2,675	31,236	6,007.1	2,573.3	303	5,894	2,751.2	266.4
Titusville	35	121	19.4	3.1	95	565	76.9	27.8	37	433	43.6	15.4
Wellington	117	203	54.6	8.9	319	776	116.3	37.7	22	191	D	5.8
Weston	165	346	86.0	13.6	485	1,320	1,009.4	95.4	20	153	D	5.0
West Palm Beach	260	1,144	229.8	51.3	1,119	D	D	D	103	1,822	343.3	103.7
Winter Garden	63	199	43.3	7.2	110	377	39.9	14.1	26	470	186.1	17.1
Winter Haven	59	305	69.0	10.4	120	497	56.7	24.6	28	513	293.4	26.9
Winter Park	134	416	89.2	15.7	476	2,577	409.0	162.9	32	185	D	7.5
Winter Springs	42	D	D	D	101	230	27.4	10.9	13	82	12.8	3.0

1. Establishments subject to federal tax.

Table D. Cities — Accommodation and Food Services, Arts, Entertainment, and Recreation, and Health Care and Social Assistance

City	Accommodation and food services, 2012				Arts, entertainment, and recreation[1], 2012				Health care and social assistance,[1] 2012			
	Number of establish-ments	Number of employees	Receipts (mil dol)	Annual payroll (mil dol)	Number of establish-ments	Number of employees	Receipts (mil dol)	Annual payroll (mil dol)	Number of establish-ments	Number of employees	Receipts (mil dol)	Annual payroll (mil dol)
	92	93	94	95	96	97	98	99	100	101	102	103
FLORIDA— Cont'd												
Deerfield Beach	155	2,717	163.2	44.0	38	241	25.1	6.5	168	D	D	D
DeLand	94	1,414	61.1	17.5	13	123	6.2	2.2	120	1,769	166.1	69.1
Delray Beach	211	4,061	273.6	79.2	49	255	28.5	6.0	383	4,546	761.1	220.0
Deltona	40	500	25.4	5.7	7	D	D	D	84	805	65.8	24.4
Doral	228	3,851	320.6	83.4	41	D	D	D	211	1,991	219.2	60.8
Dunedin	100	1,271	62.0	16.6	10	34	2.2	0.6	116	D	D	D
Fort Lauderdale	710	20,279	1,934.4	464.8	144	962	172.8	31.6	863	12,461	1,320.6	599.4
Fort Myers	282	5,994	305.0	89.8	33	1,294	66.5	24.3	374	5,692	734.2	298.9
Fort Pierce	126	2,222	105.7	30.7	11	241	26.7	8.7	161	3,140	489.6	153.0
Gainesville	380	8,375	391.2	105.3	43	854	29.3	8.4	379	6,465	967.8	305.0
Greenacres	58	939	46.3	12.2	11	56	2.6	0.7	84	622	60.8	18.0
Hallandale Beach	85	2,230	121.5	35.0	31	D	D	D	148	D	D	D
Hialeah	347	3,876	238.1	61.1	35	180	14.7	3.0	784	9,203	1,171.2	341.0
Hollywood	330	5,683	427.6	115.8	88	1,142	170.7	30.4	544	D	D	D
Homestead	93	1,813	102.5	26.2	8	D	D	D	148	1,687	165.8	54.6
Jacksonville	1,765	33,931	1,820.0	501.7	204	4,730	435.0	228.5	2,029	D	D	D
Jupiter	151	3,307	179.7	61.8	45	1,168	82.3	31.5	326	D	D	D
Kissimmee	209	5,035	345.2	88.3	19	D	D	D	284	4,309	608.9	218.7
Lakeland	246	5,649	294.2	83.3	19	348	16.8	6.2	352	7,330	896.2	289.6
Lake Worth	63	683	38.8	11.2	15	D	D	D	73	1,043	105.6	40.2
Largo	183	2,788	146.3	39.2	30	D	D	D	242	7,076	803.8	308.4
Lauderdale Lakes	35	391	24.5	6.3	NA	NA	NA	NA	86	1,412	256.4	72.5
Lauderhill	82	944	61.7	14.2	15	D	D	D	127	D	D	D
Margate	98	D	D	D	13	168	7.8	2.5	159	2,272	365.7	109.6
Melbourne	213	4,009	194.2	58.9	27	D	D	D	408	7,860	928.5	375.3
Miami	1,267	26,462	1,914.9	527.4	207	3,993	846.1	359.3	1,679	17,673	2,388.6	733.1
Miami Beach	626	23,117	2,085.9	568.7	114	639	135.8	30.7	404	2,235	306.7	113.0
Miami Gardens	100	1,628	91.0	22.0	22	D	D	D	144	1,173	127.5	45.6
Miami Lakes	54	1,634	101.3	26.2	16	D	D	D	197	D	D	D
Miramar	118	1,660	95.1	23.5	25	D	D	D	223	1,967	419.1	91.0
North Lauderdale	28	364	20.1	5.1	6	23	15.7	1.3	44	D	D	D
North Miami	104	1,478	83.9	21.4	18	113	14.5	2.4	129	2,233	175.9	88.9
North Miami Beach	124	1,833	98.1	26.6	16	280	9.5	1.9	212	D	D	D
North Port	38	682	30.9	9.3	5	D	D	D	44	529	51.6	15.8
Oakland Park	100	1,691	90.7	26.4	14	D	D	D	149	D	D	D
Ocala	251	5,431	277.0	76.1	17	D	D	D	535	8,831	1,199.2	423.3
Ocoee	77	904	48.0	13.4	17	D	D	D	104	D	D	D
Orlando	999	26,376	1,938.1	473.7	144	16,398	2,187.0	457.1	879	11,319	1,616.4	697.7
Ormond Beach	118	2,321	112.8	33.4	28	339	19.2	6.3	226	D	D	D
Oviedo	62	1,202	54.4	15.1	14	115	5.7	1.5	123	D	D	D
Palm Bay	108	1,820	81.1	22.2	15	D	D	D	131	1,612	113.2	50.2
Palm Beach Gardens	143	4,820	235.6	85.0	40	D	D	D	319	3,706	535.7	163.4
Palm Coast	91	D	D	D	17	D	D	D	148	D	D	D
Panama City	167	3,198	158.1	45.4	18	D	D	D	294	6,840	827.5	314.0
Pembroke Pines	285	5,958	330.2	92.6	57	500	31.2	6.7	576	D	D	D
Pensacola	212	5,204	250.7	75.2	15	709	16.7	5.1	343	6,294	856.9	350.2
Pinellas Park	106	1,876	134.8	38.0	13	122	8.7	2.1	136	1,898	203.6	78.2
Plantation	188	3,356	218.5	56.0	51	405	26.1	7.4	586	6,332	923.7	328.2
Plant City	76	D	D	D	6	D	D	D	122	D	D	D
Pompano Beach	249	3,807	258.2	69.0	50	1,455	129.3	42.4	295	3,416	395.6	135.1
Port Orange	103	2,310	99.2	30.7	20	D	D	D	133	D	D	D
Port St. Lucie	204	3,628	180.6	48.3	36	D	D	D	370	5,191	645.7	223.1
Riviera Beach	39	836	62.1	13.2	10	289	18.8	5.1	41	D	D	D
Royal Palm Beach	95	1,883	101.7	28.4	14	140	6.0	2.1	121	1,020	115.9	46.0
St. Cloud	61	1,042	46.1	13.8	5	D	D	D	72	D	D	D
St. Petersburg	525	9,116	540.4	147.3	72	1,850	212.6	143.0	799	8,081	1,079.9	424.7
Sanford	119	2,238	104.8	30.3	15	D	D	D	118	1,977	292.3	101.4
Sarasota	286	6,049	377.5	110.2	41	843	33.5	11.3	449	4,964	632.8	228.5
Sunrise	187	4,135	217.4	61.9	38	D	D	D	260	3,931	557.9	269.7
Tallahassee	588	13,051	593.0	160.9	56	691	72.6	14.7	576	D	D	D
Tamarac	63	926	55.1	12.4	20	187	11.5	3.3	216	3,052	340.0	122.6
Tampa	1,087	25,033	1,655.4	420.6	152	5,489	847.6	350.2	1,345	16,190	2,907.9	955.1
Titusville	95	1,730	81.8	23.1	6	120	6.0	2.0	141	D	D	D
Wellington	105	2,479	107.4	33.3	64	D	D	D	245	D	D	D
Weston	97	2,066	122.1	35.9	26	D	D	D	258	D	D	D
West Palm Beach	356	6,424	390.8	105.9	52	1,061	115.7	33.7	543	8,828	1,360.8	428.4
Winter Garden	62	D	D	D	23	D	D	D	82	938	79.0	29.9
Winter Haven	119	1,878	90.7	26.6	12	D	D	D	163	D	D	D
Winter Park	153	3,518	183.9	59.3	38	D	D	D	307	3,291	428.3	170.9
Winter Springs	36	497	19.9	7.0	19	D	D	D	40	D	D	D

1. Establishments subject to federal tax.

Table D. Cities — Other Services and Government Employment and Payroll

City	Other services[1] Number of establish-ments	Number of employees	Receipts (mil dol)	Annual payroll (mil dol)	Government employment and payroll, 2012 Full-time equivalent employees	March payroll Total (dollars)	Percent of total for: Admin-istrative, judicial, and legal	Police and corrections	Fire protection	Highways and trans-portation	Health and welfare	Natural resources and utilities	Education and libraries
	104	105	106	107	108	109	110	111	112	113	114	115	116
FLORIDA— Cont'd													
Deerfield Beach	154	534	48.1	11.9	608	3,242,063	11.8	0.0	36.3	1.9	4.4	33.5	0.0
DeLand	75	321	23.6	7.6	339	1,192,527	21.8	28.4	14.3	9.1	0.0	23.5	0.0
Delray Beach	180	854	61.4	17.8	762	3,820,363	10.4	30.3	26.8	3.3	0.8	22.2	0.0
Deltona.............................	34	111	6.8	1.9	304	1,105,426	18.7	0.0	34.0	5.8	0.9	31.1	0.0
Doral.................................	141	1,116	195.1	39.7	269	1,347,474	13.6	55.1	0.0	6.7	0.0	8.2	0.0
Dunedin.............................	62	216	14.1	5.4	343	1,392,549	13.9	0.0	21.1	7.5	1.6	43.2	5.9
Fort Lauderdale.................	617	3,575	397.5	120.8	2,346	13,506,065	10.3	32.6	25.0	0.5	4.6	19.2	0.0
Fort Myers........................	248	1,391	112.7	34.8	902	3,718,361	15.0	32.5	18.3	2.3	1.3	27.1	0.0
Fort Pierce........................	78	337	24.3	8.8	620	2,494,232	7.9	24.2	0.0	3.9	1.4	41.0	0.0
Gainesville........................	188	1,011	72.3	24.6	2,090	9,866,610	13.9	18.0	9.1	12.0	1.5	36.0	0.0
Greenacres........................	45	127	9.8	3.0	180	934,096	15.0	34.9	33.1	2.2	0.0	2.1	0.0
Hallandale Beach..............	98	469	33.8	11.8	437	2,597,020	14.5	36.5	23.5	4.3	3.1	15.3	0.0
Hialeah.............................	410	1,449	138.7	34.8	1,644	7,468,317	8.8	33.3	26.1	4.7	2.0	17.7	4.4
Hollywood	256	1,597	140.4	43.2	1,340	7,260,474	10.2	35.7	23.9	4.1	2.7	17.3	0.0
Homestead........................	51	169	12.9	3.3	375	2,068,115	10.3	44.1	0.0	4.5	0.9	33.5	0.0
Jacksonville......................	1,274	7,216	656.4	208.6	10,137	46,960,164	11.8	32.9	13.5	4.4	2.3	13.0	2.0
Jupiter..............................	154	899	68.0	26.5	368	1,870,904	18.7	37.5	0.0	8.8	0.2	23.5	0.0
Kissimmee........................	109	409	27.9	7.1	912	3,901,999	9.5	20.8	12.3	5.7	0.0	51.1	0.0
Lakeland...........................	135	802	69.7	22.6	2,156	10,065,334	11.3	18.9	7.3	4.3	2.7	48.5	1.5
Lake Worth........................	66	303	22.4	6.9	267	1,224,227	13.4	0.0	0.0	3.3	7.0	68.8	1.3
Largo...............................	167	822	61.4	18.5	823	3,637,673	0.0	25.8	22.2	6.2	1.2	25.5	3.2
Lauderdale Lakes	26	93	10.1	2.1	79	272,557	39.0	0.0	0.0	5.4	19.3	16.1	0.0
Lauderhill.........................	91	328	27.4	7.0	410	2,557,908	13.6	36.5	29.7	0.9	1.2	14.4	0.0
Margate............................	101	343	34.4	7.5	486	2,719,607	9.8	35.2	29.2	0.0	0.8	18.8	0.0
Melbourne........................	173	963	67.9	26.7	870	3,653,445	13.0	26.1	21.7	11.7	0.9	24.0	0.0
Miami...............................	815	4,921	337.4	100.8	3,807	18,642,774	9.5	38.6	27.3	0.0	1.0	10.5	0.0
Miami Beach	201	1,617	138.3	31.8	1,861	12,515,293	9.7	37.2	16.1	3.6	1.8	12.8	0.0
Miami Gardens..................	70	347	28.4	7.8	499	2,715,980	13.8	61.9	0.0	4.0	1.2	10.9	0.0
Miami Lakes......................	42	596	33.0	12.2	31	181,241	72.9	0.0	0.0	4.7	0.0	22.4	0.0
Miramar............................	102	488	48.4	15.7	758	4,183,683	11.9	34.2	25.2	4.0	4.9	19.8	0.0
North Lauderdale	29	148	16.0	4.7	153	612,914	14.4	0.0	35.9	6.8	9.5	24.3	0.0
North Miami......................	96	627	34.0	10.9	424	1,773,052	15.3	47.6	0.0	2.6	1.4	24.9	1.4
North Miami Beach	78	383	28.4	8.4	481	2,472,451	13.4	37.7	0.0	7.0	0.3	17.7	1.3
North Port.........................	38	124	11.1	3.5	511	2,449,083	12.2	24.5	20.8	13.4	0.8	17.6	0.0
Oakland Park.....................	163	497	61.2	13.6	238	1,116,830	16.6	0.0	36.2	5.5	0.7	31.5	2.1
Ocala................................	186	1,226	89.7	29.7	961	3,935,258	12.7	25.3	17.5	2.8	1.6	37.3	0.0
Ocoee..............................	56	321	19.2	6.5	332	1,430,323	11.3	31.2	19.8	7.4	8.7	21.6	0.0
Orlando	540	4,699	341.4	120.0	2,773	14,180,368	10.1	36.7	27.1	2.9	0.6	17.8	0.0
Ormond Beach...................	72	368	21.4	7.0	333	1,242,053	17.4	24.9	18.0	7.1	0.0	25.6	0.0
Oviedo..............................	54	224	14.5	4.1	281	1,140,501	10.0	30.2	24.7	5.4	5.6	24.1	0.0
Palm Bay..........................	89	348	28.7	9.3	738	2,860,974	8.8	34.4	22.7	12.9	2.8	18.3	0.0
Palm Beach Gardens...........	103	689	49.4	17.3	497	2,744,921	6.6	31.5	34.9	3.9	0.0	13.0	0.0
Palm Coast.......................	58	222	15.1	4.1	367	1,477,520	33.5	0.4	16.8	0.0	0.0	49.3	0.0
Panama City	85	526	40.6	11.7	560	1,720,128	8.5	23.2	16.5	21.6	2.5	23.8	0.0
Pembroke Pines.................	180	882	72.7	21.1	811	4,498,652	8.1	38.2	36.8	0.0	0.5	11.6	0.0
Pensacola.........................	116	886	68.1	20.8	835	3,072,149	10.7	26.9	15.4	10.9	2.2	25.7	4.6
Pinellas Park.....................	135	807	86.2	25.7	495	2,118,077	13.5	29.2	22.2	4.8	5.1	17.7	4.0
Plantation	174	912	96.6	27.0	805	3,820,829	9.6	44.3	2.6	5.4	9.5	17.4	1.1
Plant City..........................	52	319	26.0	8.6	501	1,604,248	10.1	22.3	11.9	11.1	2.3	30.0	3.2
Pompano Beach	268	1,609	151.4	45.6	750	3,541,060	16.9	0.0	31.9	13.8	1.8	23.5	0.0
Port Orange	84	382	25.9	7.6	401	1,524,545	16.2	27.0	16.3	4.0	8.0	26.5	0.0
Port St. Lucie	151	676	48.4	14.7	947	4,712,445	20.9	40.2	0.0	10.1	2.4	19.5	0.0
Riviera Beach	67	390	47.2	14.7	471	2,072,288	16.7	31.0	21.2	5.6	2.0	15.3	1.1
Royal Palm Beach	60	401	25.2	7.5	102	467,299	20.4	0.0	0.0	30.5	0.0	29.3	0.0
St. Cloud	42	183	11.5	3.7	437	1,502,512	12.4	20.0	15.5	4.7	0.0	25.9	0.0
St. Petersburg...................	399	1,874	149.2	46.8	3,700	17,064,309	4.8	45.6	11.2	0.8	1.0	27.0	1.2
Sanford............................	99	498	30.5	11.1	571	2,356,239	8.5	26.8	18.3	14.9	0.6	25.6	0.0
Sarasota...........................	176	1,055	66.7	21.9	650	3,097,398	13.3	41.0	0.0	3.7	1.8	26.4	0.0
Sunrise.............................	125	556	39.2	11.0	946	5,498,554	12.5	33.9	21.2	2.4	0.9	25.6	0.0
Tallahassee.......................	317	2,012	143.4	46.5	3,027	13,645,644	13.9	19.4	10.3	12.4	2.1	36.5	0.0
Tamarac...........................	58	193	15.6	4.2	364	1,617,407	25.5	0.0	24.3	8.4	1.2	29.4	0.0
Tampa..............................	787	5,615	363.3	119.3	4,247	22,517,912	11.0	35.8	17.2	4.0	2.4	25.2	0.0
Titusville...........................	72	353	28.7	9.0	452	1,810,027	17.0	25.5	15.5	4.3	0.7	33.4	0.0
Wellington	83	454	38.0	12.5	322	1,314,469	22.1	0.0	0.0	3.5	0.0	40.8	0.0
Weston.............................	88	469	30.5	8.7	10	117,886	74.7	0.0	0.0	0.0	0.0	25.3	0.0
West Palm Beach	237	1,177	88.5	27.3	1,355	7,409,659	10.2	30.9	19.4	4.7	1.3	25.2	2.2
Winter Garden...................	45	318	31.2	9.7	272	1,145,114	16.2	35.8	18.5	3.2	0.0	17.7	0.0
Winter Haven	60	247	20.2	5.6	460	1,697,693	17.7	25.5	18.1	2.2	0.0	25.4	2.8
Winter Park	115	579	36.5	12.4	506	2,395,109	10.5	24.5	19.9	4.4	0.8	35.0	0.0
Winter Springs	26	98	6.0	1.7	207	765,305	16.8	45.2	0.0	0.0	0.0	34.3	0.0

1. Establishments subject to federal tax.

Table D. Cities — City Government Finances

City	General revenue Total (mil dol)	Intergovernmental Total (mil dol)	Intergovernmental Percent from state government	Taxes Total (mil dol)	Taxes Per capita¹ (dollars) Total	Taxes Per capita¹ (dollars) Property	Taxes Per capita¹ (dollars) Sales and gross receipts	General expenditure Total (mil dol)	General expenditure Per capita¹ (dollars) Total	General expenditure Per capita¹ (dollars) Capital outlays
	117	118	119	120	121	122	123	124	125	126
FLORIDA— Cont'd										
Deerfield Beach	110.6	11.2	65.6	51.7	667	441	223	119.1	1,535	67
DeLand	35.7	3.0	61.4	17.0	614	289	325	31.5	1,139	109
Delray Beach	122.1	11.8	68.8	77.5	1,240	937	301	117.6	1,882	71
Deltona	54.5	13.8	48.2	29.8	348	137	212	53.3	623	113
Doral	55.0	5.7	60.4	41.1	848	410	438	61.9	1,277	597
Dunedin	36.4	4.4	84.4	17.5	493	184	309	42.1	1,185	73
Fort Lauderdale	351.8	52.9	32.9	172.6	1,007	601	406	357.5	2,086	178
Fort Myers	148.2	15.3	59.3	61.9	943	526	416	154.4	2,352	195
Fort Pierce	68.9	10.3	85.1	26.0	609	360	249	79.2	1,855	305
Gainesville	206.3	24.2	47.3	64.4	510	212	298	208.2	1,648	273
Greenacres	21.6	4.0	80.4	13.4	347	173	174	20.5	533	30
Hallandale Beach	73.9	8.7	37.1	31.8	827	546	281	76.5	1,992	86
Hialeah	219.5	58.6	43.0	103.2	442	208	234	207.3	887	63
Hollywood	276.4	29.3	52.2	122.9	843	565	278	276.3	1,896	231
Homestead	81.0	20.4	49.7	25.1	395	226	168	68.8	1,081	164
Jacksonville	1,946.9	245.5	61.0	924.4	1,104	595	506	1,888.1	2,255	340
Jupiter	55.9	5.9	86.7	35.6	621	347	274	60.5	1,056	189
Kissimmee	69.7	20.4	62.5	27.9	438	199	239	82.5	1,296	259
Lakeland	186.5	38.4	30.2	50.0	502	262	240	203.7	2,048	303
Lake Worth	47.4	10.9	39.7	14.0	389	189	201	55.1	1,538	116
Largo	106.7	10.7	72.0	39.5	505	186	318	110.7	1,416	238
Lauderdale Lakes	26.2	4.3	77.6	11.9	352	170	182	26.8	792	44
Lauderhill	67.1	12.7	52.9	27.3	394	187	208	71.1	1,026	65
Margate	70.3	9.0	65.1	33.0	598	364	233	69.8	1,266	200
Melbourne	117.4	17.7	39.8	45.0	584	287	297	113.2	1,469	76
Miami	722.3	172.2	31.3	406.9	976	638	338	740.7	1,777	262
Miami Beach	529.5	21.7	43.5	328.2	3,597	1,276	2,320	497.2	5,448	572
Miami Gardens	83.2	27.7	43.3	41.1	368	176	192	85.3	765	86
Miami Lakes	18.1	3.9	79.9	12.9	422	185	237	19.4	635	118
Miramar	143.9	25.7	45.7	72.6	562	324	239	135.3	1,048	75
North Lauderdale	36.7	5.7	71.1	13.9	327	169	158	33.0	775	30
North Miami	74.3	14.3	45.8	30.1	493	287	206	78.4	1,282	99
North Miami Beach	69.4	10.5	84.8	22.9	528	290	238	79.6	1,838	147
North Port	74.1	8.3	65.2	22.7	389	138	251	78.1	1,339	244
Oakland Park	60.8	8.4	54.6	23.5	546	294	252	60.3	1,403	122
Ocala	118.1	16.3	79.4	40.2	707	380	327	106.1	1,865	168
Ocoee	39.5	8.6	94.4	16.4	428	253	175	40.9	1,066	54
Orlando	675.7	172.7	30.5	223.8	895	417	478	644.8	2,578	124
Ormond Beach	49.2	7.5	40.8	21.3	554	253	301	51.7	1,346	298
Oviedo	37.7	4.2	64.8	18.8	531	271	260	40.7	1,151	91
Palm Bay	95.5	22.5	37.8	43.8	421	236	184	96.4	925	142
Palm Beach Gardens	72.5	6.7	77.4	55.9	1,116	914	202	73.8	1,475	130
Palm Coast	61.9	7.9	63.6	23.7	306	196	111	75.5	974	151
Panama City	60.3	8.8	82.6	27.9	771	279	492	64.4	1,779	119
Pembroke Pines	252.5	67.1	81.6	92.9	581	321	260	310.7	1,942	78
Pensacola	126.4	46.1	16.9	42.4	804	266	538	157.0	2,977	968
Pinellas Park	65.8	7.8	64.1	31.4	631	274	357	68.5	1,377	108
Plantation	103.5	13.9	50.3	55.4	628	333	295	108.1	1,225	75
Plant City	47.9	7.5	73.4	20.0	554	231	323	40.6	1,128	97
Pompano Beach	157.1	12.7	50.4	84.6	819	496	323	202.4	1,959	236
Port Orange	65.3	6.6	74.6	25.0	440	215	225	62.8	1,105	37
Port St. Lucie	168.3	26.2	39.2	71.3	422	209	214	184.5	1,092	286
Riviera Beach	85.9	14.2	26.9	47.7	1,438	1,016	422	92.1	2,775	315
Royal Palm Beach	21.1	5.0	54.1	11.9	338	100	237	26.3	747	203
St. Cloud	51.0	4.2	78.7	15.3	386	160	226	64.8	1,632	228
St. Petersburg	377.4	80.5	33.2	139.7	565	303	262	403.2	1,630	142
Sanford	92.0	18.1	67.1	32.7	597	311	286	78.2	1,427	372
Sarasota	157.9	32.8	32.3	54.1	1,023	523	501	163.4	3,091	774
Sunrise	184.3	17.8	52.4	62.2	698	352	347	170.9	1,920	274
Tallahassee	339.4	52.0	38.9	105.7	565	184	381	370.9	1,983	425
Tamarac	73.4	11.5	50.2	31.8	507	261	245	68.8	1,097	20
Tampa	643.2	135.9	37.9	270.1	774	350	424	634.2	1,817	201
Titusville	55.0	7.1	79.7	25.9	589	263	326	44.4	1,010	129
Wellington	61.9	10.3	59.9	28.2	481	219	261	61.6	1,048	256
Weston	90.1	5.2	88.6	38.6	569	177	392	83.3	1,228	132
West Palm Beach	226.7	39.5	30.6	109.6	1,069	714	355	255.4	2,491	117
Winter Garden	39.8	5.5	93.8	20.7	560	226	334	40.6	1,096	279
Winter Haven	52.2	3.8	56.0	20.8	594	282	312	58.7	1,677	299
Winter Park	63.4	8.3	60.7	29.5	1,019	622	397	65.0	2,246	474
Winter Springs	27.7	4.0	89.0	13.1	389	125	264	26.4	786	144

1. Based on population estimated as of July 1 of the year shown.

Table D. Cities — **City Government Finances**

City	City government finances, 2012 (cont.) General expenditure (cont.) Percent of total for:									
	Public welfare	Highways	Parking facilities	Education	Health and hospitals	Police protection	Sewerage and sanitation	Parks and recreation	Housing and community development	Interest on debt
	127	128	129	130	131	132	133	134	135	136
FLORIDA— Cont'd										
Deerfield Beach	2.1	2.3	1.5	0.0	0.0	18.0	25.4	5.7	0.3	1.7
DeLand	0.0	8.4	0.0	0.0	0.0	21.9	18.8	9.0	1.4	1.9
Delray Beach	0.0	3.6	0.7	0.0	0.0	25.3	3.7	15.4	1.8	2.5
Deltona...........................	0.0	8.7	0.0	0.0	0.0	17.3	17.9	5.0	6.3	2.0
Doral..............................	0.0	13.4	0.0	0.0	0.0	19.6	0.0	27.0	0.0	2.4
Dunedin..........................	0.0	7.2	0.0	0.0	0.0	9.4	14.6	15.8	0.0	0.9
Fort Lauderdale..................	0.0	3.4	3.0	0.0	0.0	27.5	5.4	11.4	4.4	0.7
Fort Myers.......................	0.0	10.3	0.7	0.0	0.0	19.9	24.4	9.3	1.3	3.9
Fort Pierce	0.0	4.7	0.0	0.0	0.0	14.8	34.2	10.9	6.0	5.4
Gainesville	0.7	8.6	0.2	0.0	0.1	18.0	17.1	7.9	3.6	7.8
Greenacres	0.0	8.7	0.0	0.0	0.0	35.2	5.1	6.4	0.0	0.9
Hallandale Beach................	1.2	1.0	0.0	0.0	0.0	25.2	20.9	3.0	3.1	1.7
Hialeah...........................	0.0	4.5	0.0	0.0	0.0	23.0	17.8	7.3	2.2	2.2
Hollywood........................	0.0	2.8	2.4	0.0	0.0	25.1	19.0	7.2	1.2	3.5
Homestead.......................	1.6	5.0	0.0	0.0	0.0	28.2	30.0	12.4	6.6	0.8
Jacksonville......................	2.5	7.5	0.2	0.0	3.3	15.9	10.3	4.6	0.7	8.6
Jupiter............................	0.0	10.0	0.0	0.0	0.0	32.3	4.8	3.6	0.0	2.5
Kissimmee	0.0	15.8	0.0	0.0	0.0	21.3	9.0	13.5	1.1	1.6
Lakeland	0.0	11.1	0.4	0.0	0.0	17.3	14.6	14.0	3.0	1.7
Lake Worth.......................	0.0	2.8	0.2	0.0	0.0	27.6	23.1	9.1	0.0	0.7
Largo..............................	0.0	3.0	0.0	0.0	0.0	17.3	27.9	13.2	2.4	0.4
Lauderdale Lakes	0.0	1.7	0.0	0.0	9.4	27.5	7.2	4.2	0.0	4.7
Lauderhill........................	0.0	1.7	0.0	0.0	6.5	22.9	6.6	4.3	3.2	4.5
Margate...........................	0.0	3.6	0.0	0.0	0.0	27.0	14.4	4.2	3.5	3.0
Melbourne........................	0.0	12.5	0.2	0.0	0.0	16.1	13.2	8.2	2.2	0.5
Miami.............................	0.2	9.5	3.7	0.0	0.0	18.5	3.2	14.9	5.4	5.4
Miami Beach.....................	0.4	3.6	6.2	0.0	3.2	17.9	10.5	14.6	4.3	2.3
Miami Gardens..................	0.0	6.2	0.0	0.0	0.0	36.6	0.0	14.2	6.2	5.6
Miami Lakes......................	0.0	8.4	0.0	0.0	0.0	33.7	0.0	12.1	0.0	1.3
Miramar...........................	0.0	5.5	0.0	0.0	0.0	29.7	6.2	8.7	0.9	3.6
North Lauderdale	0.0	3.0	0.0	0.0	0.0	26.0	17.3	11.7	2.6	1.3
North Miami......................	0.0	9.0	0.0	0.0	0.0	28.7	22.0	7.0	7.1	2.4
North Miami Beach	0.0	1.7	0.0	0.0	0.0	31.6	17.5	6.7	2.7	2.4
North Port........................	0.6	22.2	0.0	0.0	0.0	16.2	17.0	6.4	0.0	0.6
Oakland Park	0.0	6.0	0.0	0.0	0.0	20.6	19.4	7.9	0.0	1.9
Ocala..............................	0.3	12.3	0.0	0.0	0.0	20.5	21.8	6.8	1.2	1.9
Ocoee.............................	0.0	8.8	0.0	0.0	0.0	20.3	13.9	5.3	0.0	3.7
Orlando...........................	0.0	6.8	2.6	0.0	1.0	19.2	13.7	12.9	1.7	7.0
Ormond Beach...................	0.0	9.6	0.0	0.0	0.0	14.8	20.0	21.6	0.0	0.6
Oviedo............................	0.0	31.0	0.0	0.0	0.0	16.7	17.4	8.4	0.0	3.0
Palm Bay.........................	0.0	10.3	0.0	0.0	0.0	21.3	19.2	3.6	3.9	4.7
Palm Beach Gardens...........	0.0	1.7	0.0	0.0	0.0	30.2	0.0	12.4	0.0	1.4
Palm Coast	0.0	16.0	0.0	0.0	0.0	3.5	36.5	6.2	0.0	1.3
Panama City	0.0	8.9	0.0	0.0	0.0	14.5	8.1	9.2	1.3	0.7
Pembroke Pines.................	0.5	1.7	0.0	0.0	0.0	15.3	12.6	5.8	3.4	5.5
Pensacola........................	0.0	3.8	0.3	0.0	0.0	13.4	4.1	25.3	10.0	4.8
Pinellas Park	0.0	6.9	0.0	0.0	4.5	20.1	24.8	8.4	0.0	0.7
Plantation........................	0.0	2.8	0.0	0.0	7.5	32.2	15.5	12.9	1.7	1.6
Plant City.........................	0.0	8.8	0.0	0.0	0.0	19.8	27.0	8.6	1.2	1.3
Pompano Beach	0.0	2.1	0.0	0.0	7.0	18.5	11.1	7.3	1.9	0.6
Port Orange	0.0	8.8	0.0	0.0	0.0	18.5	37.4	7.4	0.7	2.5
Port St. Lucie	0.0	24.4	0.0	0.0	0.7	19.0	7.9	6.5	2.6	16.5
Riviera Beach....................	0.2	7.4	0.0	0.0	0.0	18.1	17.9	6.3	0.2	1.0
Royal Palm Beach	0.0	11.4	0.0	0.0	0.0	27.6	0.0	26.9	0.0	0.6
St. Cloud..........................	0.0	25.8	0.0	0.0	3.0	12.6	26.0	4.3	0.2	6.7
St. Petersburg...................	0.0	9.3	1.1	0.0	3.1	22.0	21.3	14.7	2.3	1.5
Sanford...........................	0.7	8.9	0.0	0.0	0.0	15.9	18.1	5.9	1.9	2.5
Sarasota..........................	0.0	7.1	0.7	0.0	0.0	17.6	23.5	19.7	10.7	3.1
Sunrise...........................	0.0	3.6	0.0	0.0	0.0	29.4	25.2	8.3	0.6	0.8
Tallahassee	0.0	15.1	0.0	0.0	0.0	13.2	31.4	5.6	1.8	2.3
Tamarac	0.0	6.9	0.0	0.0	0.0	17.5	11.9	5.4	1.8	1.9
Tampa............................	0.0	8.7	2.2	0.0	0.0	23.8	21.2	8.9	5.4	4.1
Titusville	0.0	4.6	0.0	0.0	0.0	24.8	18.5	2.8	7.4	1.2
Wellington	0.0	15.3	0.0	0.0	0.0	12.1	9.3	6.6	0.0	1.2
Weston............................	0.0	0.8	0.0	0.0	0.0	12.7	18.5	6.4	1.7	0.6
West Palm Beach	0.0	4.1	1.6	0.0	0.7	18.7	24.9	7.1	2.6	4.0
Winter Garden...................	0.1	13.7	0.2	0.0	0.0	17.5	15.8	18.6	0.0	2.5
Winter Haven	1.2	4.2	2.4	0.0	0.0	17.1	25.7	14.3	0.4	3.8
Winter Park	0.0	2.8	0.0	0.0	0.0	17.7	13.9	8.8	0.0	2.4
Winter Springs	0.0	10.9	0.0	0.0	0.0	28.7	22.0	7.4	0.0	2.2

Table D. Cities — City Government Finances, City Government Employment, and Climate

City	City government finances, 2012 (cont.)			Climate[2]						
	Debt outstanding		Debt issued during year	Average daily temperature				Annual precipitation (inches)	Heating degree days	Cooling degree days
				Mean		Limits				
	Total (mil dol)	Per capita[1] (dollars)		January	July	January[3]	July[4]			
	137	138	139	140	141	142	143	144	145	146

FLORIDA— Cont'd

City	137	138	139	140	141	142	143	144	145	146
Deerfield Beach	72.1	929	0.0	67.2	83.3	57.8	91.8	57.27	219	4,241
DeLand	33.4	1,206	9.3	NA	NA	NA	NA	NA	NA	NA
Delray Beach	86.4	1,383	5.4	66.2	82.5	57.3	90.1	61.39	246	3,999
Deltona	97.2	1,137	0.3	57.1	81.2	44.5	91.2	57.03	954	2,819
Doral	26.4	544	0.0	NA	NA	NA	NA	NA	NA	NA
Dunedin	35.3	995	0.0	60.9	82.5	50.2	91.3	52.42	623	3,414
Fort Lauderdale	587.6	3,429	67.9	67.5	82.6	59.2	89.8	64.19	167	4,120
Fort Myers	377.2	5,747	15.1	64.9	83.0	54.5	91.7	54.19	302	3,957
Fort Pierce	216.8	5,076	1.1	62.6	81.7	50.7	91.5	53.50	477	3,430
Gainesville	1,189.9	9,418	161.7	54.4	81.1	41.8	92.4	49.56	1,249	2,608
Greenacres	4.0	105	0.0	66.2	82.5	57.3	90.1	61.39	246	3,999
Hallandale Beach	31.5	819	0.0	68.1	83.7	59.6	90.9	58.53	149	4,361
Hialeah	169.3	725	81.6	67.9	82.7	62.6	87.0	46.60	141	4,090
Hollywood	379.0	2,602	4.3	67.5	82.6	59.2	89.8	64.19	167	4,120
Homestead	18.5	291	0.0	67.0	81.8	56.2	90.6	55.55	238	3,923
Jacksonville	10,439.0	12,465	630.5	54.5	82.5	42.6	92.7	51.88	1,222	2,810
Jupiter	66.9	1,167	0.0	66.2	82.5	57.3	90.1	61.39	246	3,999
Kissimmee	457.1	7,175	151.7	59.7	81.8	47.7	91.6	48.01	694	3,111
Lakeland	951.3	9,565	203.4	62.5	84.0	51.1	94.6	49.13	487	3,886
Lake Worth	74.3	2,072	6.8	65.1	81.1	52.5	91.3	58.44	273	3,438
Largo	31.5	403	14.0	61.3	82.5	52.4	89.7	44.77	591	3,482
Lauderdale Lakes	28.4	838	0.0	67.2	83.3	57.8	91.8	57.27	219	4,241
Lauderhill	118.7	1,711	18.3	67.5	82.6	59.2	89.8	64.19	167	4,120
Margate	53.5	971	0.0	67.2	83.3	57.8	91.8	57.27	219	4,241
Melbourne	132.5	1,720	1.5	60.9	81.2	50.0	90.5	48.29	595	3,186
Miami	873.2	2,095	120.6	68.1	83.7	59.6	90.9	58.53	149	4,361
Miami Beach	465.1	5,097	56.6	68.1	83.7	59.6	90.9	58.53	149	4,361
Miami Gardens	111.4	999	55.0	NA	NA	NA	NA	NA	NA	NA
Miami Lakes	7.5	246	7.3	NA	NA	NA	NA	NA	NA	NA
Miramar	182.5	1,414	0.0	68.1	83.7	59.6	90.9	58.53	149	4,361
North Lauderdale	8.6	203	0.0	67.5	82.6	59.2	89.8	64.19	167	4,120
North Miami	21.9	359	0.0	68.1	83.7	59.6	90.9	58.53	149	4,361
North Miami Beach	111.2	2,568	18.3	68.1	83.7	59.6	90.9	58.53	149	4,361
North Port	54.0	925	17.5	NA	NA	NA	NA	NA	NA	NA
Oakland Park	38.9	904	18.2	67.5	82.6	59.2	89.8	64.19	167	4,120
Ocala	201.6	3,544	13.9	58.1	81.7	45.7	92.2	49.68	902	2,971
Ocoee	54.8	1,428	2.1	NA	NA	NA	NA	NA	NA	NA
Orlando	1,055.4	4,219	67.0	60.9	82.4	49.9	92.2	48.35	580	3,428
Ormond Beach	54.1	1,408	5.6	60.9	82.4	49.9	92.2	48.35	580	3,428
Oviedo	79.7	2,256	1.3	58.7	81.5	47.0	91.9	51.31	799	3,017
Palm Bay	157.8	1,514	5.5	60.9	81.2	50.0	90.5	48.29	595	3,186
Palm Beach Gardens	25.8	515	4.4	66.2	82.5	57.3	90.1	61.39	246	3,999
Palm Coast	176.4	2,276	2.2	57.4	82.8	46.4	92.0	49.79	909	3,193
Panama City	35.5	980	0.0	50.3	80.0	38.7	89.0	64.76	1,810	2,174
Pembroke Pines	388.8	2,430	12.3	67.5	82.6	59.2	89.8	64.19	167	4,120
Pensacola	213.6	4,050	0.0	52.0	82.6	42.7	90.7	64.28	1,498	2,650
Pinellas Park	31.8	640	0.0	61.7	83.4	54.0	90.2	49.58	548	3,718
Plantation	39.9	452	2.8	67.5	82.6	59.2	89.8	64.19	167	4,120
Plant City	68.0	1,886	0.0	61.1	81.5	49.8	90.8	51.17	625	3,261
Pompano Beach	88.3	855	28.1	67.2	83.3	57.8	91.8	57.27	219	4,241
Port Orange	156.3	2,751	13.3	57.1	81.2	44.5	91.2	57.03	954	2,819
Port St. Lucie	1,015.1	6,008	42.9	64.5	81.8	54.7	89.5	59.53	315	3,600
Riviera Beach	67.2	2,025	26.5	66.2	82.5	57.3	90.1	61.39	246	3,999
Royal Palm Beach	20.5	582	20.5	NA	NA	NA	NA	NA	NA	NA
St. Cloud	123.7	3,114	57.6	NA	NA	NA	NA	NA	NA	NA
St. Petersburg	562.7	2,275	53.9	61.7	83.4	54.0	90.2	49.58	548	3,718
Sanford	79.7	1,455	6.1	58.7	81.5	47.0	91.9	51.31	799	3,017
Sarasota	156.6	2,962	30.9	61.7	83.4	54.0	90.2	49.58	548	3,718
Sunrise	298.7	3,356	9.6	67.5	82.6	59.2	89.8	64.19	167	4,120
Tallahassee	1,263.4	6,754	173.5	51.8	82.4	39.7	92.0	63.21	1,604	2,551
Tamarac	60.4	963	23.3	67.2	83.3	57.8	91.8	57.27	219	4,241
Tampa	1,377.0	3,945	202.8	61.3	82.5	52.4	89.7	44.77	591	3,482
Titusville	56.5	1,285	3.6	59.9	82.4	49.5	91.4	52.79	677	3,300
Wellington	22.8	388	0.0	66.2	82.5	57.3	90.1	61.39	246	3,999
Weston	12.6	186	0.0	67.5	82.6	59.2	89.8	64.19	167	4,120
West Palm Beach	437.5	4,267	0.0	66.2	82.5	57.3	90.1	61.39	246	3,999
Winter Garden	22.0	596	0.0	NA	NA	NA	NA	NA	NA	NA
Winter Haven	89.2	2,549	27.3	62.3	82.3	51.0	92.5	50.22	538	3,551
Winter Park	187.9	6,488	28.7	NA	NA	NA	NA	NA	NA	NA
Winter Springs	34.5	1,028	14.4	60.9	82.4	49.9	92.2	48.35	580	3,428

1. Based on the population estimated as of July 1 of the year shown.   2. Represents normal values based on the 30-year period, 1971±2000.   3. Average daily minimum.   4. Average daily maximum.

Table D. Cities — Land Area and Population

STATE Place code	City	Land area[1] (sq. mi)	Total persons 2018	Rank	Per square mile	White	Black or African American	American Indian, Alaskan Native	Asian	Hawaiian Pacific Islander	Some other race	Two or more races (percent)
		1	2	3	4	5	6	7	8	9	10	11
13 00,000	GEORGIA	57,715.3	10,519,475	X	182.3	58.7	31.6	0.4	3.9	0.1	2.6	2.7
13 01,052	Albany	55.1	75,249	469	1,365.7	23.0	72.6	0.2	0.6	0.0	1.0	2.6
13 01,696	Alpharetta	26.9	66,255	557	2,463.0	58.7	11.9	0.0	20.5	0.0	1.5	7.5
13 03,436	Athens-Clarke County	116.4	125,964	219	1,082.2	62.6	27.5	0.0	4.0	0.0	2.6	3.3
13 04,000	Atlanta	135.6	498,044	37	3,672.9	39.2	52.8	0.1	4.0	0.0	1.3	2.5
13 04,200	Augusta-Richmond County ..	302.3	196,939	123	651.5	35.8	57.6	0.2	2.0	0.1	1.0	3.4
13 19,000	Columbus	216.4	194,160	126	897.2	43.5	46.5	0.1	2.5	0.1	3.2	4.1
13 21,380	Dalton	20.5	33,500	1,144	1,634.1	86.6	5.1	0.0	1.4	0.0	5.0	1.9
13 23,900	Douglasville	22.6	34,190	1,114	1,512.8	NA	NA	NA	NA	NA	NA	NA
13 24,600	Duluth	10.2	29,527	1,272	2,894.8	43.2	15.3	0.0	27.5	0.0	10.2	3.9
13 24,768	Dunwoody	13.0	49,459	776	3,804.5	62.3	13.0	1.9	15.8	0.0	1.4	5.6
13 25,720	East Point	14.7	34,849	1,096	2,370.7	23.3	71.6	0.0	1.2	0.1	0.5	3.3
13 31,908	Gainesville	32.8	41,464	921	1,264.1	73.2	18.6	1.3	1.5	0.0	3.6	1.8
13 38,964	Hinesville	18.2	32,872	1,158	1,806.2	39.2	49.0	0.3	2.4	0.8	1.9	6.4
13 42,425	Johns Creek	30.8	84,310	403	2,737.3	60.4	13.9	0.1	24.1	0.0	0.5	1.1
13 43,192	Kennesaw	9.6	34,172	1,116	3,559.6	NA	NA	NA	NA	NA	NA	NA
13 44,340	LaGrange	42.1	30,291	1,244	719.5	36.7	53.2	0.3	3.3	0.0	5.3	1.2
13 45,488	Lawrenceville	13.5	29,795	1,261	2,207.0	52.8	33.0	0.0	4.6	0.6	7.9	1.2
13 49,008	Macon-Bibb County	249.4	153,095	170	613.9	40.4	55.0	0.3	2.1	0.0	0.3	1.9
13 49,756	Marietta	23.3	60,806	613	2,609.7	55.2	32.1	0.0	3.5	0.0	6.0	3.3
13 51,670	Milton	38.5	39,217	984	1,018.6	67.7	12.2	0.0	17.7	0.0	0.5	2.0
13 55,020	Newnan	19.2	39,784	968	2,072.1	65.3	26.0	0.4	4.5	0.0	0.8	3.1
13 59,724	Peachtree City	24.6	35,766	1,075	1,453.9	81.6	3.1	0.0	4.9	0.0	3.2	7.2
13 66,668	Rome	31.5	36,634	1,047	1,163.0	71.4	22.7	0.1	3.1	0.0	1.4	1.3
13 67,284	Roswell	40.7	94,650	337	2,325.6	73.9	15.3	0.2	3.0	0.0	3.2	4.4
13 68,516	Sandy Springs	37.7	108,797	279	2,885.9	73.7	14.7	0.7	8.2	0.0	0.8	1.9
13 69,000	Savannah	103.9	145,862	179	1,403.9	36.6	55.8	0.1	1.7	0.9	1.1	3.7
13 71,492	Smyrna	15.6	56,706	670	3,635.0	50.2	31.7	0.1	9.0	0.0	5.1	3.9
13 73,256	Statesboro	14.9	31,667	1,198	2,125.3	51.8	37.4	0.6	2.3	0.0	2.7	5.2
13 73,704	Stockbridge	13.7	29,638	1,267	2,163.4	NA	NA	NA	NA	NA	NA	NA
13 78,800	Valdosta	36.0	56,426	672	1,567.4	35.7	56.2	0.0	2.2	0.1	5.0	0.8
13 80,508	Warner Robins	36.5	75,797	464	2,076.6	51.2	37.8	0.1	3.4	0.0	0.7	6.7
15 00,000	HAWAII	6,422.4	1,420,491	X	221.2	25.0	1.6	0.2	38.2	10.2	1.5	23.3
15 06,290	East Honolulu CDP	23.0	NA	0	NA	28.3	1.8	0.1	50.7	2.7	0.3	16.1
15 14,650	Hilo CDP	53.4	NA	0	NA	22.4	0.4	0.2	29.0	8.9	0.9	38.3
15 22,700	Kahului CDP	14.4	NA	0	NA	8.5	0.6	0.1	60.7	9.0	0.0	21.1
15 23,150	Kailua CDP (Honolulu County)	7.8	NA	0	NA	45.8	1.1	0.2	20.1	7.2	0.6	24.9
15 28,250	Kaneohe CDP	6.5	NA	0	NA	22.5	0.4	0.0	36.4	7.3	0.5	32.8
15 51,050	Mililani Town CDP	4.0	NA	0	NA	20.8	1.7	0.0	43.2	7.5	1.2	25.5
15 62,600	Pearl City CDP	9.1	NA	0	NA	17.0	0.6	0.0	50.5	7.2	0.5	24.3
15 71,550	Urban Honolulu CDP	60.5	347,397	56	5,742.1	16.1	2.0	0.2	55.0	6.5	1.4	18.8
15 79,700	Waipahu CDP	2.7	NA	0	NA	2.7	0.5	0.0	72.9	10.0	0.2	13.6
16 00,000	IDAHO	82,645.1	1,754,208	X	21.2	90.0	0.7	1.3	1.3	0.2	3.4	3.1
16 08,830	Boise City	83.7	228,790	97	2,733.5	88.7	2.1	0.3	2.8	0.1	1.7	4.4
16 12,250	Caldwell	22.2	56,541	671	2,546.9	75.6	0.2	0.5	0.8	0.7	16.4	5.7
16 16,750	Coeur d'Alene	15.9	51,303	749	3,226.6	NA	NA	NA	NA	NA	NA	NA
16 39,700	Idaho Falls	23.3	61,535	605	2,641.0	84.8	1.0	0.4	1.7	0.5	7.7	3.8
16 46,540	Lewiston	17.3	32,817	1,160	1,896.9	95.0	0.0	1.2	2.3	0.0	0.7	0.8
16 52,120	Meridian	33.6	106,804	286	3,178.7	92.7	0.1	0.1	2.1	0.0	0.9	4.1
16 56,260	Nampa	32.2	96,252	328	2,989.2	82.9	1.3	0.9	0.6	0.1	10.6	3.6
16 64,090	Pocatello	32.7	56,266	675	1,720.7	88.5	0.5	3.7	2.2	0.0	2.2	2.9
16 64,810	Post Falls	14.6	34,691	1,099	2,376.1	NA	NA	NA	NA	NA	NA	NA
16 67,420	Rexburg	9.8	28,687	1,297	2,927.2	NA	NA	NA	NA	NA	NA	NA
16 82,810	Twin Falls	19.3	49,764	771	2,578.4	89.7	1.6	0.5	4.0	0.0	2.7	1.5
17 00,000	ILLINOIS	55,514.0	12,741,080	X	229.5	71.2	14.2	0.2	5.4	0.0	6.2	2.6
17 00,243	Addison	9.8	36,724	1,043	3,747.3	66.2	6.9	0.4	5.2	0.0	16.6	4.7
17 00,685	Algonquin	12.2	30,910	1,220	2,533.6	NA	NA	NA	NA	NA	NA	NA
17 01,114	Alton	15.5	26,528	1,379	1,711.5	66.2	25.9	0.2	1.6	0.0	1.0	5.1
17 02,154	Arlington Heights	16.6	75,249	469	4,533.1	83.2	3.2	0.0	8.1	0.0	3.6	1.8
17 03,012	Aurora	45.0	199,602	118	4,435.6	57.9	10.0	0.5	10.2	0.5	17.4	3.4
17 04,013	Bartlett	15.7	40,931	936	2,607.1	73.3	0.6	0.0	23.1	0.0	1.4	1.5
17 04,078	Batavia	10.5	26,316	1,386	2,506.3	NA	NA	NA	NA	NA	NA	NA
17 04,845	Belleville	23.2	41,290	926	1,779.7	NA	NA	NA	NA	NA	NA	NA
17 05,092	Belvidere	12.1	25,194	1,409	2,082.1	NA	NA	NA	NA	NA	NA	NA
17 05,573	Berwyn	3.9	54,917	696	14,081.3	54.4	7.0	0.0	2.4	0.0	31.6	4.6
17 06,613	Bloomington	27.1	77,962	445	2,876.8	77.8	10.2	0.6	9.3	0.0	0.3	1.8
17 07,133	Bolingbrook	24.6	75,178	471	3,056.0	46.5	21.4	0.0	13.7	0.0	15.9	2.5
17 09,447	Buffalo Grove	9.5	40,853	939	4,300.3	67.5	2.0	0.5	25.2	0.0	2.1	2.7

1. Dry land or land partially or temporarily covered by water.   2. Hispanic or Latino persons may be of any race.

Table D. Cities — **Population**

City	Percent Hispanic or Latino[1], 2017	Percent foreign born, 2017	Age of population (percent), 2017							Median age, 2017	Percent female, 2017	Population Census counts		Population Percent change	
			Under 18 years	18 to 24 years	25 to 34 years	35 to 44 years	45 to 54 years	55 to 64 years	65 years and over			2000	2010	2000-2010	2001-2018
	12	13	14	15	16	17	18	19	20	21	22	23	24	25	26
GEORGIA	9.6	10.2	24.1	9.8	13.6	13.3	13.6	12.2	13.4	36.8	51.4	8,186,453	9,688,709	18.4	8.6
Albany	2.3	1.7	23.2	10.8	15.2	13.5	9.7	12.4	15.1	35.6	53.6	76,939	77,431	0.6	-2.8
Alpharetta	10.0	27.7	25.2	6.9	10.4	16.4	16.9	14.2	10.0	38.6	52.1	34,854	57,383	64.6	15.5
Athens-Clarke County	11.0	9.7	17.3	27.8	15.0	11.6	9.3	8.6	10.5	28.1	52.2	NA	115,441	NA	9.1
Atlanta	4.3	7.5	18.9	13.4	20.7	13.7	12.3	9.8	11.2	33.3	51.0	416,474	426,821	2.5	16.7
Augusta-Richmond County	5.2	3.9	23.2	11.7	15.9	11.5	11.6	12.6	13.5	34.2	52.0		195,847	NA	0.6
Columbus	7.6	5.1	24.9	10.3	15.7	12.7	11.6	11.9	12.9	34.4	51.3	186,291	190,573	2.3	1.9
Dalton	57.5	34.5	26.8	14.0	14.1	16.4	10.3	9.4	8.9	29.4	51.7	27,912	33,091	18.6	1.2
Douglasville	10.0	6.0	23.1	7.2	19.3	13.6	16.7	13.0	7.2	35.7	57.1	20,065	30,960	54.3	10.4
Duluth	22.4	38.5	21.7	8.1	12.9	18.7	13.6	13.4	11.7	38.5	49.4	22,122	26,672	20.6	10.7
Dunwoody	9.9	24.3	22.7	6.5	15.4	14.4	16.3	12.2	12.5	38.1	54.6	32,808	46,253	41.0	6.9
East Point	12.3	8.0	28.3	7.8	15.6	17.8	9.7	10.0	10.8	33.3	52.4	39,595	33,453	-15.5	4.2
Gainesville	40.7	22.5	25.6	11.2	17.0	12.7	10.2	9.3	13.8	32.6	53.8	25,578	34,041	33.1	21.8
Hinesville	16.1	6.4	26.8	13.7	22.7	11.8	9.6	9.4	6.0	28.9	50.5	30,392	33,333	9.7	-1.4
Johns Creek	6.2	31.3	27.5	6.5	8.3	14.9	18.8	15.2	8.8	40.4	50.7	NA	76,640	NA	10.0
Kennesaw	29.0	14.1	23.4	12.4	17.7	14.7	16.2	9.7	6.0	32.1	54.0	21,675	30,592	41.1	11.7
LaGrange	6.9	4.7	27.3	14.3	9.6	12.9	12.6	10.8	12.6	33.8	52.2	25,998	29,374	13.0	3.1
Lawrenceville	39.6	27.8	23.5	9.1	15.1	13.8	11.1	13.3	14.0	36.0	48.7	22,397	27,238	21.6	9.4
Macon-Bibb County	3.3	2.9	24.7	10.4	13.0	11.3	12.4	13.2	15.0	36.0	53.2	NA	155,795	NA	-1.7
Marietta	19.2	24.7	22.6	12.1	20.1	12.0	10.1	11.6	11.6	32.3	48.8	58,748	56,594	-3.7	7.4
Milton	2.6	20.2	25.9	8.6	11.8	12.3	24.7	10.8	5.8	36.8	48.9	NA	32,835	NA	19.4
Newnan	14.6	12.6	24.5	13.5	9.8	8.5	21.8	11.7	10.3	36.1	52.0	16,242	32,898	102.5	20.9
Peachtree City	9.3	13.0	25.5	4.4	9.7	10.7	13.5	17.2	18.9	44.8	52.3	31,580	34,366	8.8	4.1
Rome	21.3	13.7	23.0	10.5	13.3	15.5	13.8	7.5	16.5	37.2	55.9	34,980	36,392	4.0	0.7
Roswell	16.1	18.4	25.6	7.1	12.6	14.7	14.2	11.6	14.3	38.5	52.2	79,334	88,332	11.3	7.2
Sandy Springs	14.9	21.7	19.0	7.8	20.1	13.5	13.1	12.6	13.8	36.6	53.1	85,781	93,820	9.4	16.0
Savannah	4.3	6.0	19.5	14.2	17.6	11.6	11.7	12.5	12.9	34.3	53.5	131,510	137,002	4.2	6.5
Smyrna	14.5	16.1	23.6	4.7	22.1	18.9	12.0	9.0	9.7	34.8	53.8	40,999	51,188	24.9	10.8
Statesboro	5.5	4.6	12.5	46.4	12.2	7.6	4.8	6.7	9.9	22.5	50.9	22,698	28,375	25.0	11.6
Stockbridge	5.6	14.3	23.9	13.6	13.9	15.2	15.7	9.1	8.5	33.6	58.8	9,853	26,436	168.3	12.1
Valdosta	6.3	3.9	25.1	20.6	14.3	11.8	8.6	9.6	9.9	26.6	50.7	43,724	54,764	25.2	3.0
Warner Robins	10.4	7.7	26.3	7.3	16.4	15.2	10.6	11.4	12.9	35.0	54.0	48,804	69,066	41.5	9.7
HAWAII	10.5	18.6	21.4	8.7	14.4	12.7	12.2	12.8	17.8	39.2	49.8	1,211,537	1,360,307	12.3	4.4
East Honolulu CDP	4.0	18.7	19.3	6.8	7.8	11.7	12.5	14.4	27.5	48.0	48.6	NA	NA	NA	NA
Hilo CDP	13.8	5.4	21.1	9.9	13.7	8.7	13.0	13.1	20.4	40.2	53.3	40,759	NA	NA	NA
Kahului CDP	8.3	28.3	22.3	9.6	13.7	11.9	7.9	13.6	21.0	38.0	47.0	20,146	NA	NA	NA
Kailua CDP (Honolulu County)	8.8	10.4	21.1	7.1	13.2	11.6	14.2	12.7	19.9	42.0	49.9	36,513	NA	NA	NA
Kaneohe CDP	5.4	11.5	20.2	7.0	13.6	13.5	11.4	12.0	22.3	41.5	51.5	34,970	NA	NA	NA
Mililani Town CDP	7.8	11.0	19.7	7.8	12.1	12.4	9.8	13.7	24.4	43.8	51.5	28,608	NA	NA	NA
Pearl City CDP	4.2	12.5	17.1	11.2	13.1	8.8	11.5	12.6	25.6	44.8	49.8	30,976	NA	NA	NA
Urban Honolulu CDP	6.9	27.5	16.9	7.7	16.4	12.6	13.3	13.4	19.7	41.9	50.8	NA	337,721	NA	2.9
Waipahu CDP	6.8	43.0	21.6	10.4	15.0	12.5	13.8	9.0	17.7	37.7	51.7	33,108	NA	NA	NA
IDAHO	12.4	5.9	25.8	9.4	12.9	12.6	11.6	12.4	15.3	36.3	49.8	1,293,953	1,567,657	21.2	11.9
Boise City	9.2	6.9	21.8	10.6	16.0	13.3	12.8	11.8	13.8	36.1	49.2	185,787	209,389	12.7	9.3
Caldwell	34.5	7.9	35.8	10.5	17.0	11.2	10.1	8.9	6.5	26.6	54.2	25,967	46,319	78.4	22.1
Coeur d'Alene	3.4	2.7	20.5	10.0	15.7	10.0	11.6	14.7	17.4	38.4	49.3	34,514	44,159	27.9	16.2
Idaho Falls	16.0	7.4	29.4	9.5	16.0	10.3	11.1	11.2	12.6	30.8	51.9	50,730	57,130	12.6	7.7
Lewiston	4.5	1.5	22.0	9.3	12.5	12.6	12.2	11.3	20.1	40.8	50.2	30,904	31,894	3.2	2.9
Meridian	7.7	4.3	29.3	8.0	12.0	14.2	13.8	10.1	12.6	35.8	50.4	34,919	76,959	120.4	38.8
Nampa	25.6	7.5	26.5	12.7	14.1	15.3	8.4	9.6	13.4	33.3	48.0	51,867	81,843	57.8	17.6
Pocatello	9.6	3.4	22.9	15.7	16.6	11.5	9.2	11.2	12.9	31.5	52.3	51,466	54,233	5.4	3.7
Post Falls	7.2	2.3	35.1	6.8	14.2	15.7	8.1	9.5	10.7	32.4	52.4	17,247	27,758	60.9	25.0
Rexburg	11.1	9.9	25.7	38.6	17.3	8.1	3.8	2.0	4.5	22.8	49.9	17,257	25,485	47.7	12.6
Twin Falls	16.0	10.7	26.2	8.8	15.4	14.5	11.2	11.0	13.0	33.9	49.5	34,469	44,313	28.6	12.3
ILLINOIS	17.2	14.3	22.6	9.4	13.8	12.9	13.1	13.0	15.2	38.0	50.8	12,419,293	12,831,572	3.3	-0.7
Addison	46.0	33.2	28.1	6.6	16.9	10.2	13.5	10.3	14.5	33.4	53.0	35,914	37,062	3.2	-0.9
Algonquin	5.1	12.0	22.5	6.9	11.3	11.1	19.5	17.2	11.4	44.0	52.8	23,276	30,061	29.2	2.8
Alton	1.4	2.5	23.5	8.0	14.4	14.0	12.8	13.8	13.4	36.9	46.4	30,496	27,948	-8.4	-5.1
Arlington Heights	8.2	19.8	21.3	4.5	11.5	12.8	14.6	15.0	20.4	45.0	52.3	76,031	75,187	-1.1	0.1
Aurora	43.7	28.8	28.6	8.3	11.7	17.3	13.9	9.6	10.5	35.6	49.6	142,990	197,914	38.4	0.9
Bartlett	9.4	21.9	19.9	10.5	12.2	15.4	15.6	14.7	11.7	39.6	46.6	36,706	41,152	12.1	-0.5
Batavia	9.6	5.6	24.4	5.1	8.8	13.8	15.0	15.5	17.3	43.3	54.7	23,866	26,180	9.7	0.5
Belleville	0.3	0.9	25.1	7.9	15.0	10.3	15.2	11.9	14.7	36.7	52.4	41,410	44,296	7.0	-6.8
Belvidere	31.8	11.1	23.7	10.4	12.1	13.6	11.7	11.3	17.3	37.2	54.3	20,820	25,644	23.2	-1.8
Berwyn	58.1	25.4	27.5	8.8	13.5	13.3	15.8	11.6	9.5	35.2	50.0	54,016	56,653	4.9	-3.1
Bloomington	4.9	10.1	20.6	13.9	15.4	12.9	12.0	12.1	13.2	35.1	52.5	64,808	76,701	18.4	1.6
Bolingbrook	23.7	25.1	25.7	8.5	15.2	13.3	16.9	10.9	9.6	35.7	50.6	56,321	73,365	30.3	2.5
Buffalo Grove	7.2	32.0	21.2	6.7	11.9	13.9	15.8	15.4	15.2	43.2	52.7	42,909	41,505	-3.3	-1.6

1. May be of any race.

Table D. Cities — **Households, Group Quarters, Crime, and Education**

City	Households, 2017 Number	Persons per household	Family	Married couple family	Female headed[1]	Non-family	One person	Persons in group quarters, 2017	Serious crimes — Total Number	Total Rate	Violent Rate[3]	Property Rate[3]	Population age 25 and over	High school graduate or less	Bachelor's degree or more
	27	28	29	30	31	32	33	34	35	36	37	38	39	40	41
GEORGIA............................	3,745,074	2.72	67.4	47.8	14.9	32.6	26.7	258,793	350,760	3,402	398	3,004	6,896,026	41.0	30.9
Albany	28,147	2.40	57.4	26.3	26.9	42.6	37.8	3,911	4,493	6,045	1,174	4,870	47,261	45.3	23.2
Alpharetta............................	23,696	2.76	73.3	61.2	8.9	26.7	23.4	NA	1,343	2,068	54	2,014	44,671	12.3	69.7
Athens-Clarke County	47,821	2.41	53.3	35.8	12.4	46.7	28.9	10,626	4,633	3,738	430	3,308	69,187	33.2	44.2
Atlanta	199,717	2.27	45.5	26.1	15.7	54.5	43.1	32,310	29,925	6,332	1,084	5,249	329,115	29.7	49.2
Augusta-Richmond County ..	69,283	2.69	58.9	33.7	20.3	41.1	34.1	9,521	9,498	4,817	429	4,388	127,457	47.4	21.5
Columbus	70,306	2.64	59.4	37.2	18.8	40.6	35.6	8,334	10,803	5,339	598	4,741	125,754	41.7	25.7
Dalton..................................	10,492	3.13	69.5	47.7	15.7	30.5	22.6	874	1,216	3,578	332	3,245	20,000	64.5	17.8
Douglasville........................	14,185	2.29	55.3	34.3	18.7	44.7	37.1	1,171	1,943	5,837	586	5,251	23,483	32.8	33.7
Duluth	10,550	2.78	78.5	58.1	14.3	21.5	16.7	NA	803	2,702	538	2,164	20,696	22.8	53.2
Dunwoody............................	20,792	2.39	63.3	49.5	10.1	36.7	32.0	NA	2,145	4,357	158	4,198	35,104	11.6	71.2
East Point...........................	13,889	2.52	48.7	20.4	21.5	51.3	44.6	323	4,115	11,497	1,179	10,318	22,537	40.0	32.3
Gainesville..........................	13,471	2.91	67.4	42.4	17.1	32.6	26.8	1,118	1,567	3,975	411	3,564	25,488	53.2	25.8
Hinesville............................	12,792	2.55	66.3	46.8	17.6	33.7	24.7	483	1,577	4,711	681	4,030	19,739	31.3	22.2
Johns Creek	29,623	2.84	80.1	70.1	5.9	19.9	18.2	NA	714	844	32	812	55,700	9.8	69.7
Kennesaw............................	12,762	2.68	63.6	46.8	16.1	36.4	25.0	NA	673	1,968	193	1,775	22,057	31.5	37.6
LaGrange	10,475	2.83	61.6	34.7	21.7	38.4	35.2	815	1,790	5,787	508	5,279	17,797	54.5	20.3
Lawrenceville.......................	10,714	2.76	56.6	34.7	17.9	43.4	38.0	NA	1,069	3,458	291	3,167	20,119	51.1	27.7
Macon-Bibb County.............	56,151	2.61	58.9	34.7	20.2	41.1	36.6	6,262	NA	NA	NA	NA	99,200	45.0	24.8
Marietta	23,711	2.46	56.2	35.3	17.3	43.8	34.2	2,594	2,515	4,226	391	3,834	39,873	35.8	38.1
Milton	13,266	2.93	75.5	67.5	6.5	24.5	20.9	NA	348	903	26	877	25,489	9.7	68.6
Newnan	14,402	2.67	66.1	44.8	18.2	33.9	27.6	NA	1,221	3,202	564	2,638	24,141	36.2	29.4
Peachtree City.....................	13,754	2.56	68.2	56.5	10.6	31.8	25.0	NA	564	1,594	54	1,540	24,723	17.8	55.7
Rome...................................	15,185	2.30	63.1	45.8	14.3	36.9	34.0	1,421	1,665	4,590	593	3,997	24,187	51.6	25.7
Roswell................................	34,784	2.71	64.2	52.3	9.8	35.8	27.6	1,845	1,928	149	1,779	63,843	23.9	55.7
Sandy Springs......................	47,371	2.24	52.6	39.8	8.2	47.4	36.5	462	2,954	2,743	109	2,635	78,111	17.3	66.4
Savannah	53,703	2.53	57.7	33.4	19.3	42.3	31.5	10,566	9,936	4,118	487	3,631	97,045	40.0	27.5
Smyrna................................	24,536	2.30	62.7	44.2	14.6	37.3	30.6	NA	1,745	3,053	343	2,710	40,631	20.6	53.7
Statesboro	10,682	2.14	42.6	29.3	8.8	57.4	31.7	8,540	1,284	4,119	318	3,801	12,906	40.4	28.8
Stockbridge.........................	10,915	2.67	71.2	28.8	33.0	28.8	26.0	NA	NA	NA	NA	NA	18,192	27.6	46.3
Valdosta..............................	21,166	2.55	51.4	28.7	18.6	48.6	34.4	2,037	3,263	5,839	369	5,471	30,408	51.4	30.2
Warner Robins	29,658	2.54	69.8	44.6	18.9	30.2	23.9	316	4,605	6,188	664	5,524	50,283	34.2	31.4
HAWAII.................................	458,078	3.02	69.9	50.9	12.8	30.1	24.4	44,435	47,170	3,302	309	2,993	997,744	35.8	32.9
East Honolulu CDP	15,723	2.96	78.1	60.1	12.0	21.9	17.8	268	NA	NA	NA	NA	34,605	21.1	55.0
Hilo CDP...............................	16,394	2.66	66.1	39.3	20.0	33.9	26.7	1,350	NA	NA	NA	NA	31,022	41.6	30.1
Kahului CDP.........................	7,959	3.69	71.0	49.7	12.1	29.0	19.6	1,327	NA	NA	NA	NA	20,903	50.2	20.6
Kailua CDP (Honolulu County)................	12,132	2.98	72.2	57.5	10.7	27.8	21.7	202	NA	NA	NA	NA	26,067	28.8	45.6
Kaneohe CDP	10,252	2.99	74.1	59.2	12.7	25.9	20.9	734	NA	NA	NA	NA	22,889	33.3	38.0
Mililani Town CDP	8,783	3.07	79.7	66.2	9.3	20.3	17.5	NA	NA	NA	NA	NA	19,556	31.4	38.0
Pearl City CDP	13,465	3.09	77.6	53.5	15.3	22.4	20.0	1,677	NA	NA	NA	NA	31,064	36.8	33.9
Urban Honolulu CDP............	129,548	2.60	58.4	39.8	13.1	41.6	35.2	13,397	NA	NA	NA	NA	264,120	34.1	36.5
Waipahu CDP.......................	8,083	4.91	80.1	55.5	18.6	19.9	16.6	1,493	NA	NA	NA	NA	27,970	50.9	16.4
IDAHO	625,135	2.70	67.1	54.1	8.7	32.9	27.5	29,946	33,233	1,974	230	1,744	1,111,788	37.3	26.8
Boise City	89,803	2.49	55.4	43.4	8.2	44.6	37.0	3,164	5,791	2,623	298	2,326	153,175	29.8	39.3
Caldwell...............................	15,586	3.42	74.1	54.4	13.0	25.9	19.9	1,337	1,159	2,195	248	1,947	29,361	47.3	17.6
Coeur d'Alene......................	21,212	2.33	59.9	40.7	14.1	40.1	34.1	1,228	1,591	3,172	345	2,827	35,158	28.9	32.2
Idaho Falls...........................	23,429	2.56	64.4	49.4	10.7	35.6	32.0	1,120	1,620	2,717	424	2,293	37,323	33.9	32.2
Lewiston	12,347	2.49	72.1	56.7	10.8	27.9	24.2	960	1,376	4,212	141	4,072	21,799	36.9	23.3
Meridian...............................	35,323	2.82	63.7	54.1	5.1	36.3	33.1	NA	1,562	1,660	112	1,548	62,675	28.4	32.3
Nampa.................................	33,258	2.76	63.2	46.7	12.8	36.8	29.3	1,914	2,975	3,251	363	2,888	56,924	45.7	18.1
Pocatello.............................	20,688	2.58	60.9	44.1	9.6	39.1	26.5	1,785	1,837	3,373	380	2,993	33,884	34.2	31.9
Post Falls............................	10,873	3.03	73.6	59.6	8.8	26.4	24.6	299	830	2,675	229	2,446	19,371	30.4	17.0
Rexburg	7,440	3.17	81.5	76.8	3.9	18.5	16.0	371	198	704	32	672	8,546	13.1	38.1
Twin Falls	19,037	2.53	67.5	44.8	13.6	32.5	24.7	1,117	1,227	2,552	327	2,225	32,017	40.2	19.7
ILLINOIS...............................	4,808,672	2.60	64.1	47.4	12.1	35.9	29.7	300,775	318,160	2,485	436	2,049	8,707,057	37.0	34.4
Addison	13,118	2.94	70.9	47.9	16.3	29.1	23.8	NA	703	1,887	134	1,753	25,318	54.9	20.6
Algonquin............................	9,343	2.70	81.7	72.2	5.8	18.3	15.9	NA	393	1,281	39	1,242	17,781	20.3	47.9
Alton....................................	10,829	2.41	55.4	30.7	19.6	44.6	39.0	628	1,358	5,062	682	4,380	18,289	43.4	19.6
Arlington Heights	30,984	2.39	66.2	57.1	5.8	33.8	29.3	NA	780	1,025	76	949	55,759	19.3	62.1
Aurora..................................	67,111	2.99	71.1	54.3	13.6	28.9	23.3	1,834	3,498	1,739	314	1,425	127,645	44.6	29.6
Bartlett................................	13,818	3.29	79.7	65.3	6.7	20.3	15.9	NA	282	678	77	601	31,703	27.5	42.0
Batavia	10,217	2.52	75.3	65.2	9.3	24.7	23.1	NA	440	1,657	98	1,559	18,217	18.9	53.7
Belleville..............................	18,499	2.18	49.7	29.7	14.4	50.3	47.4	1,251	1,930	4,635	610	4,025	27,911	37.0	23.8
Belvidere	9,732	2.81	72.2	45.7	18.4	27.8	21.3	NA	345	1,377	259	1,118	18,197	51.9	21.9
Berwyn.................................	18,363	3.01	62.9	44.0	11.9	37.1	29.5	NA	1,405	2,495	302	2,193	35,375	44.3	22.8
Bloomington	32,145	2.36	58.3	46.9	8.2	41.7	33.9	2,212	1,654	2,104	391	1,714	51,074	26.6	49.7
Bolingbrook	21,994	3.27	80.6	60.6	14.8	19.4	14.3	NA	1,102	1,480	212	1,268	47,511	33.6	38.2
Buffalo Grove	15,746	2.61	74.2	62.9	8.4	25.8	24.5	NA	222	535	31	503	29,733	13.5	64.3

1. No spouse present. 2. Data for serious crimes have not been adjusted for underreporting. This may affect comparability between geographic areas and over time. 3. Per 100,000 population estimated by the FBI. 4. Persons 25 years old and over.

City	Median income	Percent with income less than $20,000	Percent with income of $200,000 or more	Median family income	Median non-family income	All persons	Men	Women	Total	Occupied	Percent owner occupied	Median value[1] (dollars)	Median gross rent (dollars)
	Money income, 2017 — Households					Median earnings, 2017			Housing units, 2017				
	42	43	44	45	46	47	48	49	50	51	52	53	54
GEORGIA	56,183	16.5	5.8	67,983	34,224	32,010	37,222	27,421	4,282,254	3,745,074	62.9	173,700	958
Albany	33,434	29.3	1.8	41,019	26,036	24,417	26,202	22,152	33,510	28,147	38.2	97,400	671
Alpharetta	108,188	6.6	27.5	142,444	63,179	63,466	76,824	46,846	26,000	23,696	70.0	416,500	1,457
Athens-Clarke County	39,714	26.2	3.1	54,162	24,178	21,310	24,364	17,495	52,395	47,821	39.7	167,400	843
Atlanta	57,597	19.7	11.9	78,645	46,710	37,612	42,268	32,906	245,063	199,717	43.8	299,400	1,104
Augusta-Richmond County	37,073	25.5	1.9	49,054	25,554	23,165	24,606	20,848	86,354	69,283	51.9	101,600	840
Columbus	42,107	25.1	3.4	59,942	28,417	26,703	31,700	22,838	84,742	70,306	47.5	139,000	840
Dalton	42,284	24.6	4.3	52,445	21,842	28,091	30,693	19,336	12,015	10,492	39.6	149,300	710
Douglasville	52,567	10.3	1.9	60,610	41,203	38,123	31,958	39,507	15,267	14,185	41.0	171,200	986
Duluth	62,460	10.2	7.1	68,371	46,183	36,434	49,472	31,201	11,431	10,550	66.0	252,100	1,336
Dunwoody	95,062	8.5	16.7	111,588	64,564	53,990	71,398	42,048	23,385	20,792	55.0	434,000	1,443
East Point	40,329	25.6	0.8	48,769	35,295	30,445	35,385	27,071	17,163	13,889	39.6	134,600	1,051
Gainesville	44,798	13.3	4.8	51,074	36,973	26,403	30,093	21,478	16,144	13,471	43.2	189,800	952
Hinesville	46,517	17.8	0.0	49,521	45,247	26,163	32,465	21,361	15,415	12,792	43.5	111,900	925
Johns Creek	110,482	4.4	22.7	125,565	46,033	52,381	71,776	40,317	30,790	29,623	73.8	414,200	1,721
Kennesaw	67,965	9.5	6.6	74,578	45,586	34,961	41,480	31,491	13,204	12,762	69.1	194,200	1,478
LaGrange	31,120	36.6	1.0	36,297	24,034	22,359	30,439	13,945	11,831	10,475	35.7	143,100	726
Lawrenceville	49,093	16.8	5.4	61,366	35,464	32,283	36,790	24,106	10,834	10,714	52.8	174,000	1,043
Macon-Bibb County	37,477	25.9	4.2	52,993	30,449	26,766	30,410	25,584	69,954	56,151	53.7	117,400	808
Marietta	53,821	9.8	6.3	60,672	42,036	31,331	35,544	28,126	25,828	23,711	39.4	271,700	1,068
Milton	138,152	7.0	33.5	177,994	45,156	71,404	83,665	52,139	13,266	13,266	78.2	549,700	1,331
Newnan	57,643	17.0	6.1	74,418	40,152	31,247	41,654	24,554	14,998	14,402	49.6	191,100	1,098
Peachtree City	96,239	8.6	12.2	114,645	51,074	51,551	76,862	31,574	14,223	13,754	69.5	327,300	1,384
Rome	33,093	30.2	2.0	46,077	23,418	24,511	24,609	24,279	16,639	15,185	43.0	159,800	744
Roswell	82,743	9.2	16.5	117,080	51,203	43,755	50,854	40,846	36,556	34,784	63.6	367,900	1,271
Sandy Springs	74,223	6.8	15.9	110,538	51,899	46,505	52,196	40,813	51,522	47,371	44.6	499,200	1,294
Savannah	42,869	23.4	2.8	55,284	27,175	25,793	27,371	23,622	63,833	53,703	43.7	148,800	975
Smyrna	83,622	9.6	9.2	91,057	60,000	41,382	57,432	45,285	27,583	24,536	54.3	296,100	1,277
Statesboro	29,448	37.2	2.1	45,532	17,050	10,616	11,780	8,601	12,353	10,682	32.6	127,800	750
Stockbridge	57,825	17.9	3.9	66,738	36,986	35,534	25,950	40,514	11,132	10,915	55.5	189,500	1,185
Valdosta	26,516	38.8	2.6	40,874	16,702	24,019	28,857	20,967	24,368	21,166	32.5	122,000	764
Warner Robins	51,435	17.9	2.3	52,514	40,111	30,663	37,383	26,713	33,517	29,658	55.7	100,100	899
HAWAII	77,765	12.1	9.1	91,460	41,972	37,247	42,189	32,265	542,955	458,078	58.5	617,400	1,573
East Honolulu CDP	113,201	4.6	20.8	128,519	75,750	52,508	60,302	47,344	18,221	15,723	83.9	960,100	2,603
Hilo CDP	56,902	22.2	2.3	63,581	32,069	27,481	33,362	24,240	19,429	16,394	59.3	329,600	893
Kahului CDP	77,955	15.5	8.8	83,989	40,427	33,633	34,818	32,270	9,070	7,959	60.2	610,700	1,115
Kailua CDP (Honolulu County)	120,453	6.9	23.4	128,119	62,242	48,722	61,869	37,358	13,251	12,132	72.5	1,000,500	2,299
Kaneohe CDP	105,119	4.2	12.6	118,180	49,871	42,350	50,109	36,445	11,177	10,252	71.9	789,200	2,030
Mililani Town CDP	80,282	8.9	5.9	90,812	56,029	40,447	43,627	31,236	8,783	8,783	74.9	623,700	1,725
Pearl City CDP	97,521	8.4	10.7	105,292	61,382	40,703	45,507	35,602	14,291	13,465	72.1	669,300	1,890
Urban Honolulu CDP	69,193	13.7	9.2	87,905	41,475	38,070	42,138	33,121	151,619	129,548	45.1	696,800	1,470
Waipahu CDP	78,094	13.6	13.6	84,191	36,719	26,802	31,799	24,660	8,623	8,083	55.0	624,900	1,211
IDAHO	52,225	15.0	3.3	64,178	30,706	27,589	34,165	20,894	721,818	625,135	69.7	207,100	822
Boise City	55,943	16.3	4.9	79,519	35,039	30,367	35,940	23,413	95,527	89,803	60.3	242,000	909
Caldwell	51,086	13.0	3.1	53,518	35,830	25,015	25,454	23,496	16,636	15,586	59.5	153,100	889
Coeur d'Alene	51,566	13.6	2.8	61,912	38,242	26,454	32,387	21,944	22,752	21,212	54.8	251,100	959
Idaho Falls	47,125	20.2	2.3	58,923	25,887	26,405	31,655	18,855	24,472	23,429	63.3	148,500	689
Lewiston	56,503	12.8	3.1	69,866	30,779	30,456	38,345	22,039	13,490	12,347	75.8	198,700	663
Meridian	64,273	13.1	5.9	82,128	41,380	38,534	45,490	30,482	37,848	35,323	76.0	271,800	976
Nampa	42,302	18.7	2.1	48,465	25,790	21,934	26,203	20,129	34,751	33,258	56.0	171,100	915
Pocatello	45,839	17.1	1.4	57,126	27,976	22,262	30,472	15,506	22,897	20,688	61.7	143,000	655
Post Falls	55,931	7.8	1.3	63,714	32,292	31,390	41,339	22,139	11,857	10,873	75.2	224,600	1,097
Rexburg	25,878	40.5	0.6	27,084	19,040	9,615	12,841	6,541	10,544	7,440	29.4	189,500	660
Twin Falls	46,201	14.9	0.7	54,079	32,820	26,405	32,280	17,264	19,946	19,037	68.5	158,000	757
ILLINOIS	62,992	15.1	7.5	79,168	38,105	35,868	42,238	30,039	5,359,416	4,808,672	66.2	195,300	974
Addison	46,425	18.0	4.4	60,669	31,173	30,640	35,045	25,563	13,831	13,118	57.8	254,500	980
Algonquin	107,244	4.2	12.0	125,498	36,576	50,580	64,289	32,295	10,151	9,343	86.4	273,200	1,686
Alton	36,198	27.5	1.1	45,213	25,680	22,303	29,909	20,003	12,877	10,829	63.6	83,900	681
Arlington Heights	101,634	6.4	15.6	124,379	64,365	52,404	71,614	42,352	32,263	30,984	73.0	377,500	1,245
Aurora	70,367	10.1	5.1	76,747	48,930	35,576	42,227	26,985	69,722	67,111	67.2	177,700	1,223
Bartlett	95,966	7.5	15.1	115,328	43,156	47,533	53,529	36,352	14,507	13,818	84.5	271,900	1,682
Batavia	102,158	8.3	17.3	121,354	52,881	56,005	76,463	35,625	10,466	10,217	78.2	315,200	1,105
Belleville	45,001	20.7	1.6	62,722	30,942	30,942	33,741	28,929	21,575	18,499	60.4	93,800	802
Belvidere	55,074	12.0	0.8	58,956	31,972	22,210	29,317	15,487	10,504	9,732	74.8	101,700	847
Berwyn	55,606	19.7	4.1	62,632	31,040	31,381	30,826	32,772	20,689	18,363	50.9	212,400	942
Bloomington	67,471	22.6	8.2	95,231	34,092	41,782	51,816	33,461	35,411	32,145	62.8	165,800	829
Bolingbrook	92,769	7.7	9.3	98,735	51,776	44,266	51,697	35,441	22,835	21,994	80.1	227,300	1,474
Buffalo Grove	117,318	8.4	21.8	140,546	76,218	61,325	71,872	51,634	16,546	15,746	76.0	339,900	1,498

1. Based on population estimated by the American Community Survey.   2. Includes units rented or sold but not occupied.   3. Specified owner-occupied units; $1,000,000 represents $1,000,000 or more.   4. 50.0 represents 50 percent or more.   5. 10.0 represents 10 percent or less.

Table D. Cities — Commuting, Computer Access, Migration, Labor Force, and Employment

City	Commuting[1], 2017 Percent — Commuting	With commutes of 30 minutes or more	Computer access[2], 2017 Percent — With a computer in the house	With Internet access	Migration, 2017 — Percent who lived in the same house one year ago	Percent who lived in another state or county one year ago	Civilian labor force, 2018 — Total	Percent change 2017-2018	Unemployment — Total	Rate[3]	Civilian employment[4], 2017 — Population age 16 and older — Number	Percent in labor force	Population age 16 to 64 — Number	Percent who worked full-year full-time
	55	56	57	58	59	60	61	62	63	64	65	66	67	68
GEORGIA	78.7	42.8	90.9	82.0	85.1	7.9	5,107,656	1.0	201,245	3.9	8,196,727	63.3	6,794,877	51.3
Albany	74.3	17.5	87.1	73.4	76.1	5.4	31,016	-1.4	1,636	5.3	56,528	56.3	45,700	40.4
Alpharetta	70.1	43.2	NA	NA	86.7	7.1	36,558	1.3	1,128	3.1	50,964	69.7	44,361	60.5
Athens-Clarke County	72.3	14.9	95.4	88.1	69.5	17.9	61,475	0.9	2,430	4.0	NA	NA	NA	NA
Atlanta	66.5	40.1	89.9	83.9	76.8	12.1	256,630	1.1	10,970	4.3	403,495	67.5	348,825	52.5
Augusta-Richmond County	77.5	19.9	86.7	76.4	80.6	8.5	86,626	0.8	4,460	5.1	NA	NA	NA	NA
Columbus	79.5	16.1	87.5	75.7	76.0	11.9	79,354	0.4	4,029	5.1	150,917	59.4	125,842	44.3
Dalton	81.2	21.6	88.8	80.5	91.6	3.0	14,286	0.7	710	5.0	26,100	68.6	23,095	52.1
Douglasville	83.8	57.5	92.5	73.8	70.3	21.4	17,153	1.1	735	4.3	26,424	71.7	23,999	60.6
Duluth	81.1	62.9	NA	NA	83.4	8.7	16,120	1.1	536	3.3	23,419	64.1	19,961	51.0
Dunwoody	82.1	37.9	98.1	95.9	82.4	12.0	27,699	1.3	838	3.0	40,052	69.5	33,864	60.2
East Point	68.5	46.3	90.0	83.0	85.4	5.4	17,014	0.8	926	5.4	25,667	66.7	21,861	53.9
Gainesville	70.2	27.9	92.2	83.8	81.3	11.3	19,487	1.7	663	3.4	31,120	68.2	25,534	57.1
Hinesville	88.1	26.4	96.6	93.0	58.7	23.0	15,126	1.0	609	4.0	25,054	74.1	23,074	52.8
Johns Creek	78.2	52.6	98.7	96.1	88.7	7.9	45,185	1.2	1,441	3.2	64,003	71.9	56,554	58.1
Kennesaw	71.7	56.0	NA	NA	86.9	1.7	20,237	1.2	651	3.2	27,725	73.0	25,666	51.7
LaGrange	81.9	19.9	78.2	57.7	86.4	5.6	15,101	-2.0	634	4.2	22,697	55.1	18,868	41.9
Lawrenceville	79.9	52.0	97.2	87.3	88.3	6.6	14,533	1.0	584	4.0	23,251	71.6	19,067	54.2
Macon-Bibb County	83.7	22.2	89.1	75.4	84.6	7.7	69,212	-0.5	3,129	4.5	119,644	56.0	96,735	44.6
Marietta	75.7	49.0	96.6	84.9	77.6	12.7	35,850	1.2	1,199	3.3	48,387	69.6	41,288	53.6
Milton	75.9	46.5	NA	NA	90.0	4.4	20,105	1.3	640	3.2	30,978	71.7	28,723	59.6
Newnan	73.8	41.3	94.6	82.7	77.4	8.9	18,111	1.0	697	3.8	31,103	65.6	27,112	53.3
Peachtree City	72.2	34.6	94.4	90.5	84.0	13.4	18,373	1.4	564	3.1	27,722	59.8	21,041	54.0
Rome	68.2	23.2	87.6	76.5	83.2	6.7	15,426	0.1	715	4.6	28,593	56.3	22,604	48.7
Roswell	74.9	55.8	96.8	88.5	89.4	5.2	54,073	1.3	1,641	3.0	72,704	69.6	59,122	60.2
Sandy Springs	73.9	42.0	97.3	92.8	81.5	13.2	64,667	1.4	1,985	3.1	89,090	74.0	74,314	66.5
Savannah	74.3	23.4	90.4	79.3	73.9	10.3	67,962	1.4	2,806	4.1	119,770	63.2	100,900	48.4
Smyrna	83.7	49.8	98.3	96.4	80.5	7.9	35,342	1.4	1,182	3.3	43,756	76.2	38,245	64.6
Statesboro	70.2	19.4	89.7	79.3	48.4	27.0	14,212	2.1	792	5.6	27,842	55.2	24,748	23.8
Stockbridge	79.9	55.2	87.5	85.6	89.4	7.2	14,307	1.1	684	4.8	23,020	74.1	20,541	54.7
Valdosta	86.5	10.1	81.8	44.5	84.2	9.0	25,383	0.1	1,146	4.5	42,939	58.2	37,398	42.1
Warner Robins	83.3	28.6	92.6	85.5	79.4	8.3	33,203	1.4	1,372	4.1	56,826	68.0	47,095	49.9
HAWAII	67.6	40.8	91.3	84.3	87.3	5.0	678,734	-0.7	16,606	2.4	1,153,457	65.3	899,707	56.2
East Honolulu CDP	77.5	60.6	92.9	90.3	91.8	2.4	NA	NA	NA	NA	38,892	57.3	26,019	59.1
Hilo CDP	76.1	9.1	84.3	65.3	94.1	2.2	NA	NA	NA	NA	37,146	58.0	27,940	44.7
Kahului CDP	68.0	25.9	82.9	78.9	88.6	5.9	NA	NA	NA	NA	24,313	64.0	17,862	61.9
Kailua CDP (Honolulu County)	70.8	57.6	91.7	85.9	83.4	7.8	NA	NA	NA	NA	29,472	67.4	22,229	59.4
Kaneohe CDP	73.0	55.4	92.4	89.5	87.9	5.1	NA	NA	NA	NA	25,787	64.5	18,772	55.9
Mililani Town CDP	82.8	55.5	93.8	87.8	85.3	3.7	NA	NA	NA	NA	22,248	60.9	15,661	55.3
Pearl City CDP	74.0	42.0	92.1	90.5	91.5	2.1	NA	NA	NA	NA	36,574	61.9	25,458	60.8
Urban Honolulu CDP	58.9	31.5	89.9	83.4	85.1	5.1	NA	NA	NA	NA	297,902	65.4	228,983	57.1
Waipahu CDP	57.9	58.6	88.8	70.8	NA	NA	NA	NA	NA	NA	33,498	64.2	26,221	54.5
IDAHO	79.1	24.5	91.3	82.7	83.0	7.8	857,049	2.7	24,317	2.8	1,328,549	62.1	1,065,955	47.8
Boise City	82.6	15.9	88.3	80.2	83.6	5.8	129,671	4.2	3,094	2.4	184,338	68.7	153,161	53.4
Caldwell	74.8	41.7	94.8	88.5	75.3	9.7	25,688	3.9	850	3.3	36,422	63.4	32,886	46.1
Coeur d'Alene	86.2	14.5	93.5	84.3	85.2	5.8	25,640	2.6	876	3.4	41,930	58.7	33,093	45.2
Idaho Falls	81.6	12.6	91.8	84.1	73.9	7.7	30,071	3.4	747	2.5	44,907	64.7	37,237	47.7
Lewiston	81.6	13.1	85.5	79.1	84.4	8.3	17,785	-0.5	471	2.6	25,638	64.5	19,265	51.0
Meridian	86.1	23.3	91.5	84.9	82.7	11.4	50,782	4.3	1,283	2.5	74,753	64.2	62,191	50.0
Nampa	78.9	38.5	86.3	75.6	75.0	10.8	42,579	3.7	1,306	3.1	71,975	62.8	59,442	46.2
Pocatello	73.0	11.6	96.1	85.1	76.8	10.0	28,178	0.4	767	2.7	44,214	60.3	37,120	41.1
Post Falls	83.2	19.2	94.1	89.1	86.4	2.8	17,521	2.8	569	3.2	22,467	67.1	18,899	50.1
Rexburg	58.5	9.9	98.0	68.8	67.2	14.9	15,570	2.3	266	1.7	18,508	65.6	17,436	22.1
Twin Falls	84.4	11.9	93.9	80.3	83.9	5.6	23,736	1.5	656	2.8	37,607	69.2	31,216	56.0
ILLINOIS	73.0	45.0	90.3	83.2	87.1	4.7	6,469,668	-0.3	278,349	4.3	10,249,521	65.0	8,301,926	51.3
Addison	82.3	35.7	84.9	77.3	86.7	5.1	19,159	-0.9	714	3.7	28,888	67.9	23,265	55.0
Algonquin	81.1	54.8	97.8	94.6	94.2	3.2	17,322	-0.1	620	3.6	20,787	74.9	17,908	56.6
Alton	82.6	36.8	84.8	78.2	84.5	6.5	11,583	0.2	715	6.2	21,430	62.7	17,846	39.4
Arlington Heights	76.6	46.7	95.6	91.9	89.2	3.2	40,813	-0.7	1,216	3.0	62,208	67.4	46,901	59.2
Aurora	78.0	40.3	93.0	85.4	86.2	5.5	102,699	0.7	4,563	4.4	152,370	71.1	131,022	55.7
Bartlett	82.7	56.8	93.9	89.7	90.4	7.9	23,054	-0.9	731	3.2	37,510	67.9	32,197	56.5
Batavia	80.6	42.4	94.8	93.7	87.2	7.3	14,051	1.8	598	4.3	20,286	68.8	15,805	55.8
Belleville	89.2	37.5	85.0	77.0	84.1	3.2	22,284	0.4	1,106	5.0	32,666	70.9	26,561	56.4
Belvidere	NA	32.4	90.3	88.0	86.9	10.6	11,820	0.4	816	6.9	21,969	67.9	17,190	37.4
Berwyn	61.6	57.0	89.6	79.0	NA	NA	27,041	-0.9	1,129	4.2	41,664	68.3	36,399	53.2
Bloomington	83.9	12.2	94.5	86.4	88.9	4.6	39,801	-1.0	1,711	4.3	63,833	66.5	53,544	50.7
Bolingbrook	88.7	55.0	95.5	90.6	88.5	9.4	40,410	-1.0	1,487	3.7	56,096	73.8	49,155	59.9
Buffalo Grove	76.9	46.1	93.8	90.8	86.5	6.7	24,726	0.6	835	3.4	33,508	70.0	27,238	58.8

1. Employed persons.   2. Households.   3. Percent of civilian labor force.   4. Persons 16 years old and over.

Table D. Cities — Construction, Wholesale Trade, and Retail Trade

City	Value of residential construction authorized by building permits, 2018			Wholesale trade[1], 2012				Retail trade[2], 2012			
	New construction ($1,000)	Number of housing units	Percent single family	Number of establishments	Number of employees	Sales (mil dol)	Annual payroll (mil dol)	Number of establishments	Number of employees	Sales (mil dol)	Annual payroll (mil dol)
	69	70	71	72	73	74	75	76	77	78	79
GEORGIA	11,146,199	59,315	71.3	10,637	150,168	143,645.3	8,476.3	33,426	433,840	119,801.5	10,290.1
Albany	5,785	48	62.5	111	1,406	824.7	63.5	458	6,179	1,449.6	129.6
Alpharetta	177,324	475	100.0	161	3,714	5,088.0	345.2	372	7,362	1,931.3	170.7
Athens-Clarke County	79,858	606	56.9	99	1,801	1,947.0	85.0	516	6,963	1,684.2	145.6
Atlanta	1,080,870	6,496	18.2	698	11,556	9,224.9	748.9	1,875	24,977	6,088.3	633.1
Augusta-Richmond County	65,317	503	67.8	182	1,856	864.7	81.5	812	10,830	2,627.3	229.5
Columbus	91,855	501	65.1	157	1,843	1,550.1	80.6	796	11,371	2,847.8	250.2
Dalton	NA	NA	NA	108	1,489	756.2	57.6	259	2,644	678.8	59.3
Douglasville	54,761	172	100.0	20	146	65.8	7.0	253	4,228	922.8	82.2
Duluth	17,625	63	100.0	127	3,067	2,088.3	243.7	199	2,792	1,032.1	82.9
Dunwoody	21,418	63	100.0	60	978	713.5	98.7	250	5,168	916.8	106.9
East Point	10,002	106	100.0	30	640	501.8	29.6	90	1,196	267.7	23.2
Gainesville	97,875	893	33.9	92	D	D	D	299	3,927	1,007.8	95.0
Hinesville	42,602	181	100.0	6	D	D	D	127	1,682	402.9	35.9
Johns Creek	67,645	211	100.0	67	231	116.5	17.8	149	1,831	395.3	40.8
Kennesaw	6,642	40	45.0	80	1,153	832.4	62.3	189	3,621	840.4	78.5
LaGrange	14,798	70	100.0	32	609	287.4	18.2	184	2,600	738.7	64.3
Lawrenceville	57,844	476	9.7	115	1,926	1,257.1	109.0	309	3,550	882.0	81.9
Macon-Bibb County	24,851	145	100.0	122	D	D	D	629	7,527	1,820.1	166.1
Marietta	52,076	203	100.0	275	3,494	2,618.4	199.5	447	6,196	1,976.9	173.8
Milton	44,875	191	100.0	20	147	118.9	9.7	56	916	187.9	18.3
Newnan	157,331	793	42.2	33	D	D	D	200	3,261	798.6	73.3
Peachtree City	63,673	230	100.0	75	1,037	874.5	65.6	145	2,641	617.7	55.5
Rome	NA	NA	NA	54	693	605.1	29.3	283	3,352	840.9	76.5
Roswell	71,032	209	100.0	177	1,786	1,397.9	140.4	324	5,202	1,762.9	163.1
Sandy Springs	186,263	550	87.5	147	3,515	7,647.4	330.3	252	3,933	1,342.8	131.9
Savannah	79,543	399	100.0	180	1,884	3,630.1	102.2	869	11,121	2,862.9	260.4
Smyrna	46,587	198	100.0	73	2,229	2,185.5	138.4	189	2,894	1,028.8	79.6
Statesboro	8,027	100	85.0	23	141	152.5	6.2	202	2,828	655.9	59.1
Stockbridge	41,774	135	100.0	11	38	9.7	0.9	95	1,819	443.8	43.5
Valdosta	84,752	417	100.0	85	822	1,113.3	32.0	370	4,978	1,314.1	109.7
Warner Robins	75,732	703	32.6	22	221	71.1	7.5	291	4,392	1,107.7	98.9
HAWAII	1,359,881	4,659	55.6	1,561	16,686	9,608.0	724.5	4,643	68,360	18,901.7	1,835.0
East Honolulu CDP	NA	NA	NA	33	65	22.5	2.4	55	962	343.3	27.9
Hilo CDP	NA	NA	NA	71	839	328.1	31.4	228	3,849	969.6	101.6
Kahului CDP	NA	NA	NA	52	637	513.5	31.8	194	4,127	1,252.3	124.8
Kailua CDP (Honolulu County)	NA	NA	NA	17	62	21.4	2.8	96	1,388	322.1	32.7
Kaneohe CDP	NA	NA	NA	12	19	11.5	1.0	119	1,597	481.5	46.5
Mililani Town CDP	NA	NA	NA	9	16	2.9	0.5	34	974	253.0	25.5
Pearl City CDP	NA	NA	NA	38	463	261.9	19.3	65	2,081	672.5	49.9
Urban Honolulu CDP	NA	NA	NA	782	9,002	5,712.8	399.8	1,851	26,485	7,684.2	748.6
Waipahu CDP	NA	NA	NA	56	790	292.5	35.1	106	2,248	866.1	76.8
IDAHO	3,099,095	15,824	76.9	1,739	21,470	17,906.0	960.8	5,815	72,980	20,444.3	1,794.0
Boise City	273,650	1,140	74.0	376	5,188	5,866.3	287.1	916	13,392	3,485.8	335.1
Caldwell	84,045	680	84.1	29	299	130.4	10.6	121	1,512	430.0	38.0
Coeur d'Alene	97,624	644	41.0	50	612	398.5	26.2	309	4,575	1,433.8	118.5
Idaho Falls	38,713	279	100.0	114	1,210	2,531.3	62.0	362	5,209	1,529.1	119.4
Lewiston	14,515	58	86.2	37	472	314.2	18.8	191	2,163	670.5	54.6
Meridian	581,464	3,141	58.6	93	2,282	1,086.7	100.6	246	4,537	1,648.6	139.2
Nampa	150,209	1,089	78.7	78	939	707.4	44.7	300	5,210	1,634.4	136.4
Pocatello	26,181	247	99.2	69	656	473.3	25.4	219	2,935	848.4	69.2
Post Falls	122,987	697	76.5	27	143	72.8	7.4	99	1,762	600.9	48.3
Rexburg	89,894	723	9.3	20	285	157.5	8.4	105	1,542	358.6	32.7
Twin Falls	57,302	298	86.6	75	810	336.8	31.3	314	4,308	1,122.4	102.5
ILLINOIS	4,036,281	21,510	46.7	16,036	255,531	295,457.0	15,973.3	39,947	592,942	166,634.5	14,576.1
Addison	7,175	30	100.0	198	3,798	2,418.5	282.6	96	1,807	709.5	72.4
Algonquin	12,274	86	100.0	23	95	69.6	7.5	158	3,492	706.1	66.4
Alton	140	1	100.0	27	284	219.5	14.5	150	2,233	500.2	51.8
Arlington Heights	24,936	89	69.7	151	3,104	2,632.1	263.1	203	3,354	749.7	97.9
Aurora	33,656	121	100.0	150	2,943	26,798.1	179.4	566	9,344	2,025.4	191.3
Bartlett	2,411	13	100.0	57	751	578.0	41.7	41	615	138.7	13.2
Batavia	31,466	153	7.2	78	799	539.8	49.0	90	1,634	394.1	34.5
Belleville	8,017	35	100.0	42	549	330.1	27.1	188	2,333	577.7	60.5
Belvidere	695	7	100.0	12	91	101.2	4.5	86	1,140	354.8	27.0
Berwyn	2,188	12	100.0	12	37	10.8	1.4	112	836	226.5	21.8
Bloomington	6,392	70	31.4	73	D	D	D	360	5,463	1,396.1	120.9
Bolingbrook	2,772	22	100.0	103	3,334	3,837.2	212.6	214	5,088	1,377.5	135.6
Buffalo Grove	0	0	0.0	122	2,672	2,796.2	181.6	128	1,340	381.3	40.2

1. Merchant wholesalers except manufacturers' sales branches and offices.   2. Establishments with payroll.

Table D. Cities — Real Estate, Professional Services, and Manufacturing

City	Real estate and rental and leasing, 2012				Professional, scientific, and technical services[1], 2012				Manufacturing, 2012			
	Number of establish-ments	Number of employees	Receipts (mil dol)	Annual payroll (mil dol)	Number of establish-ments	Number of employees	Receipts (mil dol)	Annual payroll (mil dol)	Number of establish-ments	Number of employees	Receipts (mil dol)	Annual payroll (mil dol)
	80	81	82	83	84	85	86	87	88	89	90	91
GEORGIA......................	10,484	55,551	14,232.4	2,703.7	28,018	239,289	41,359.0	15,587.7	7,456	333,837	155,836.8	15,316.6
Albany................................	130	493	87.1	15.3	197	D	D	D	60	2,943	D	172.1
Alpharetta.........................	203	1,412	723.0	90.7	847	13,182	2,303.2	1,072.3	21	412	D	27.7
Athens-Clarke County	190	926	140.6	27.0	300	D	D	D	78	5,115	2,004.8	229.5
Atlanta..............................	1,121	9,940	2,333.2	660.6	3,501	52,799	12,632.0	4,945.1	295	7,404	3,609.7	356.0
Augusta-Richmond County ..	201	1,069	248.9	37.9	473	D	D	D	111	7,884	5,452.2	451.0
Columbus	237	1,461	258.1	55.7	346	D	D	D	122	6,977	1,937.2	297.0
Dalton	41	158	35.4	5.2	123	D	D	D	147	10,548	4,437.1	403.8
Douglasville......................	50	204	53.1	5.6	113	604	56.4	22.1	20	D	69.0	D
Duluth	98	459	112.5	23.3	279	2,539	420.2	172.3	39	1,549	553.4	127.0
Dunwoody	123	1,450	871.4	84.1	572	6,017	1,408.3	415.3	14	54	9.2	1.8
East Point.........................	33	301	93.9	11.3	51	D	D	D	24	648	348.8	32.4
Gainesville........................	71	254	69.6	10.5	178	D	D	D	86	8,909	4,539.2	335.2
Hinesville	41	159	23.1	4.8	41	D	D	D	4	D	D	D
Johns Creek	99	D	D	D	580	D	D	D	14	D	D	D
Kennesaw	43	220	61.9	8.7	145	980	130.0	42.9	51	1,225	550.7	60.0
LaGrange	42	193	28.8	5.2	65	746	40.9	19.9	57	5,180	2,151.0	258.5
Lawrenceville.....................	71	367	85.4	15.0	231	D	D	D	67	2,258	1,017.4	99.4
Macon-Bibb County.............	126	575	116.3	18.0	284	D	D	D	71	D	929.5	D
Marietta............................	186	884	174.8	41.4	557	D	D	D	109	3,408	1,129.4	161.1
Milton...............................	24	D	D	D	205	4,498	264.7	132.2	6	16	D	0.6
Newnan	68	185	39.4	6.8	92	514	49.6	22.3	31	1,019	330.9	40.1
Peachtree City....................	74	158	32.4	7.0	172	D	D	D	39	1,864	789.3	97.9
Rome................................	61	202	33.1	6.2	146	700	85.0	31.2	61	3,069	2,196.8	142.6
Roswell.............................	179	787	172.4	34.4	750	D	D	D	57	636	113.0	30.6
Sandy Springs....................	334	2,561	796.8	127.6	970	15,638	2,999.5	1,194.6	30	529	156.7	22.9
Savannah..........................	246	1,266	247.7	38.9	496	D	D	D	104	3,234	1,475.3	166.2
Smyrna.............................	87	297	62.2	12.4	280	8,545	575.5	275.5	40	1,132	208.7	40.4
Statesboro.........................	56	266	44.6	6.7	87	D	D	D	26	1,163	359.6	43.1
Stockbridge........................	38	151	35.8	4.6	73	454	64.7	16.6	12	D	21.3	D
Valdosta............................	100	1,363	89.3	24.2	172	D	D	D	65	2,208	2,117.3	89.1
Warner Robins	79	303	50.0	7.6	158	D	D	D	25	519	D	28.4
HAWAII.............................	1,919	11,369	3,411.2	483.9	3,188	20,998	3,229.4	1,225.0	796	11,440	D	465.0
East Honolulu CDP	49	105	18.6	4.2	110	282	33.8	12.2	3	9	1.6	0.4
Hilo CDP............................	80	358	59.7	9.4	98	D	D	D	46	425	D	16.8
Kahului CDP.......................	52	535	142.3	21.3	43	258	27.7	9.5	18	95	17.3	3.1
Kailua CDP (Honolulu County).............................	54	176	31.5	7.2	95	D	D	D	13	47	5.7	1.5
Kaneohe CDP	26	89	11.6	3.0	50	D	D	D	15	120	16.9	4.1
Mililani Town CDP	6	28	3.2	0.7	17	D	D	D	NA	NA	NA	NA
Pearl City CDP	21	101	22.5	4.4	36	224	27.6	10.3	12	171	D	6.6
Urban Honolulu CDP...........	825	5,335	1,834.2	255.2	1,694	14,113	2,397.4	907.6	351	5,599	1,152.7	200.0
Waipahu CDP......................	34	182	27.7	5.7	20	226	15.2	5.4	20	359	128.8	13.0
IDAHO..............................	2,033	6,268	1,039.9	184.2	4,177	D	D	D	1,759	52,084	20,201.4	2,445.5
Boise City	452	1,905	341.1	61.6	1,150	9,739	1,465.6	588.0	216	12,584	D	855.5
Caldwell............................	36	183	17.7	4.2	49	D	D	D	53	D	579.1	63.7
Coeur d'Alene....................	103	404	92.6	13.1	244	2,077	149.0	74.7	63	1,116	D	47.4
Idaho Falls........................	101	366	67.8	11.7	282	D	D	D	80	1,528	472.1	54.6
Lewiston............................	35	D	D	D	77	D	D	D	27	D	D	D
Meridian............................	101	236	40.4	10.5	197	1,595	242.0	88.2	55	1,143	D	46.4
Nampa..............................	77	186	21.2	4.6	141	798	73.2	31.0	78	3,627	1,102.2	140.3
Pocatello...........................	69	D	D	D	138	D	D	D	33	1,499	D	61.6
Post Falls..........................	33	91	10.5	2.3	57	275	44.3	11.2	49	1,109	320.4	44.4
Rexburg............................	46	149	22.5	2.6	58	D	D	D	18	415	55.6	13.7
Twin Falls..........................	87	259	45.4	7.1	174	D	D	D	59	1,669	683.0	64.1
ILLINOIS...........................	12,035	76,794	23,649.1	3,816.1	38,540	355,434	68,675.2	27,645.3	13,868	542,004	281,037.8	28,413.7
Addison.............................	42	347	75.6	16.6	94	455	89.2	21.9	310	5,793	1,395.5	279.1
Algonquin	23	D	D	D	111	340	48.7	17.3	23	391	84.6	20.1
Alton	34	109	15.7	3.5	63	D	D	D	22	1,105	442.7	50.3
Arlington Heights................	96	633	105.7	32.7	488	D	D	D	71	1,902	980.2	109.7
Aurora..............................	130	676	147.4	22.5	450	2,399	351.6	125.4	138	8,689	4,775.2	512.4
Bartlett.............................	22	61	10.8	1.9	148	319	58.9	19.0	29	999	273.5	53.2
Batavia.............................	26	100	13.6	3.2	138	D	D	D	88	3,758	1,380.5	182.1
Belleville...........................	55	169	31.9	5.4	153	D	D	D	38	1,347	380.4	61.5
Belvidere...........................	15	45	6.4	1.1	31	D	D	D	39	6,985	5,764.7	374.7
Berwyn..............................	27	68	14.4	1.6	71	1,276	49.3	27.9	15	486	D	28.0
Bloomington	95	439	107.7	14.1	238	D	D	D	49	1,525	554.8	71.0
Bolingbrook.......................	39	190	34.0	6.3	154	1,517	178.4	76.7	54	3,763	1,169.0	181.2
Buffalo Grove.....................	47	261	56.0	11.4	313	3,419	392.2	178.1	53	3,097	1,205.8	154.6

1. Establishments subject to federal tax.

Accommodation and Food Services, Arts, Entertainment, and Recreation, and Health Care and Social Assistance

City	Accommodation and food services, 2012				Arts, entertainment, and recreation[1], 2012				Health care and social assistance,[1] 2012			
	Number of establishments	Number of employees	Receipts (mil dol)	Annual payroll (mil dol)	Number of establishments	Number of employees	Receipts (mil dol)	Annual payroll (mil dol)	Number of establishments	Number of employees	Receipts (mil dol)	Annual payroll (mil dol)
	92	93	94	95	96	97	98	99	100	101	102	103
GEORGIA	18,815	353,638	18,976.6	5,173.4	2,232	28,800	2,877.8	953.0	20,166	256,945	28,196.2	11,171.4
Albany	211	D	D	D	15	D	D	D	238	D	D	D
Alpharetta	286	6,486	342.2	98.9	33	D	D	D	389	3,667	556.5	236.2
Athens-Clarke County	342	6,927	307.6	83.9	27	354	20.5	5.5	394	D	D	D
Atlanta	1,618	42,124	3,023.4	844.6	272	3,724	871.2	309.6	1,336	17,100	2,332.0	908.9
Augusta-Richmond County	424	9,448	447.0	125.6	28	D	D	D	577	9,118	1,230.5	456.4
Columbus	442	10,453	519.3	149.2	30	427	26.0	6.5	520	6,215	649.7	261.6
Dalton	120	D	D	D	7	D	D	D	122	D	D	D
Douglasville	129	2,867	130.6	36.6	4	D	D	D	115	1,033	118.2	46.4
Duluth	144	1,624	82.0	22.3	19	D	D	D	166	D	D	D
Dunwoody	141	3,952	244.2	73.0	17	D	D	D	202	3,057	258.8	98.0
East Point	72	1,504	97.0	26.8	14	D	D	D	83	1,789	177.9	59.5
Gainesville	151	2,837	163.0	43.3	15	D	D	D	271	D	D	D
Hinesville	80	1,307	68.7	14.9	3	D	D	D	49	525	40.8	18.1
Johns Creek	137	2,100	98.6	30.2	20	557	47.0	15.0	158	D	D	D
Kennesaw	111	2,319	109.7	31.5	15	D	D	D	85	D	D	D
LaGrange	86	1,738	76.2	21.7	7	D	D	D	79	D	D	D
Lawrenceville	128	2,022	107.6	29.9	15	D	D	D	262	D	D	D
Macon-Bibb County	266	4,795	207.3	58.8	11	D	D	D	365	D	D	D
Marietta	289	4,708	264.5	74.0	24	174	19.7	3.8	392	D	D	D
Milton	44	635	34.6	9.8	17	171	13.5	3.2	28	D	D	D
Newnan	112	2,784	129.1	37.1	7	189	9.1	2.2	93	D	D	D
Peachtree City	100	2,410	112.6	35.3	20	D	D	D	119	D	D	D
Rome	138	3,070	136.6	40.0	11	D	D	D	215	D	D	D
Roswell	237	4,531	234.3	68.0	51	D	D	D	352	5,025	553.5	202.6
Sandy Springs	266	4,373	280.1	75.7	33	577	39.2	11.4	640	8,319	1,459.9	597.1
Savannah	571	12,766	759.1	203.0	40	D	D	D	486	8,390	1,182.6	453.3
Smyrna	161	2,788	152.3	41.7	19	291	13.0	4.8	208	1,508	188.3	61.4
Statesboro	124	D	D	D	4	D	D	D	148	D	D	D
Stockbridge	83	1,205	57.8	14.1	8	D	D	D	143	D	D	D
Valdosta	214	4,519	199.0	53.2	13	D	D	D	275	D	D	D
Warner Robins	157	3,608	168.4	44.7	11	234	7.1	2.4	179	D	D	D
HAWAII	3,518	98,364	9,536.7	2,536.0	398	7,327	571.1	168.2	2,794	26,788	3,180.4	1,347.2
East Honolulu CDP	65	D	D	D	12	D	D	D	64	548	56.6	19.3
Hilo CDP	146	2,239	133.8	33.2	6	D	D	D	176	2,291	225.8	99.0
Kahului CDP	84	1,703	123.3	31.2	10	D	D	D	75	704	99.2	42.4
Kailua CDP (Honolulu County)	86	1,446	81.3	20.9	9	D	D	D	113	D	D	D
Kaneohe CDP	74	1,140	76.8	17.5	12	D	D	D	81	725	78.1	31.0
Mililani Town CDP	41	1,055	60.1	15.0	3	119	8.8	1.8	19	180	19.9	10.1
Pearl City CDP	74	1,346	79.7	19.3	3	146	11.9	2.5	76	785	82.2	31.8
Urban Honolulu CDP	1,471	38,426	3,944.0	955.4	103	1,558	117.6	31.5	1,262	11,394	1,445.9	615.3
Waipahu CDP	77	1,007	64.5	15.0	3	5	0.7	0.1	86	749	74.2	28.6
IDAHO	3,564	54,257	2,680.2	726.1	573	6,755	355.9	102.6	4,271	49,613	4,281.1	1,636.4
Boise City	617	11,334	523.9	154.0	56	1,166	44.4	12.3	793	D	D	D
Caldwell	65	1,007	46.6	12.2	5	D	D	D	93	1,484	160.5	55.9
Coeur d'Alene	184	3,531	181.2	51.4	28	244	18.5	5.6	274	D	D	D
Idaho Falls	191	3,578	159.1	46.2	13	D	D	D	416	D	D	D
Lewiston	95	D	D	D	13	D	D	D	119	1,820	167.6	56.4
Meridian	178	3,513	161.9	44.2	25	439	19.6	5.9	279	D	D	D
Nampa	159	2,965	122.8	34.2	16	D	D	D	197	3,419	215.1	99.1
Pocatello	151	2,633	111.4	30.7	17	D	D	D	245	D	D	D
Post Falls	57	735	34.0	9.7	8	65	4.8	1.2	83	1,406	124.7	47.3
Rexburg	48	840	30.4	8.5	7	60	1.8	0.5	84	D	D	D
Twin Falls	140	2,486	123.3	32.4	23	D	D	D	235	D	D	D
ILLINOIS	27,117	469,870	27,937.4	7,707.1	3,564	49,286	5,591.9	1,678.3	27,624	383,980	39,270.3	16,150.8
Addison	73	D	D	D	8	D	D	D	50	969	81.3	41.9
Algonquin	82	1,821	81.9	26.2	16	D	D	D	89	733	76.2	36.1
Alton	92	1,842	85.5	26.3	11	D	D	D	92	D	D	D
Arlington Heights	148	2,732	161.0	45.4	29	274	16.7	5.1	351	D	D	D
Aurora	257	4,005	227.2	56.8	34	973	161.4	29.9	304	4,552	575.3	222.8
Bartlett	36	460	24.8	6.5	7	D	D	D	49	D	D	D
Batavia	63	1,094	50.3	15.2	5	D	D	D	57	D	D	D
Belleville	142	D	D	D	14	D	D	D	159	4,006	362.8	191.6
Belvidere	49	D	D	D	5	D	D	D	45	D	D	D
Berwyn	86	D	D	D	6	42	2.7	0.7	130	3,811	433.8	197.0
Bloomington	223	4,927	234.3	67.4	33	601	18.3	6.0	204	2,790	335.9	142.6
Bolingbrook	154	3,230	173.5	49.0	19	569	17.7	8.6	138	D	D	D
Buffalo Grove	101	1,514	92.8	28.1	14	D	D	D	172	1,506	181.5	64.6

1. Establishments subject to federal tax.

Table D. Cities — Other Services and Government Employment and Payroll

City	Other services[1] Number of establishments	Number of employees	Receipts (mil dol)	Annual payroll (mil dol)	Full-time equivalent employees	Total (dollars)	Admin-istrative, judicial, and legal	Police and corrections	Fire protection	Highways and trans-portation	Health and welfare	Natural resources and utilities	Education and libraries
	104	105	106	107	108	109	110	111	112	113	114	115	116
GEORGIA	11,682	71,989	6,311.9	1,949.9	X	X	X	X	X	X	X	X	X
Albany	113	D	D	D	1,213	4,293,454	11.1	19.0	17.2	7.2	2.0	31.0	0.0
Alpharetta	138	D	D	D	443	2,007,691	5.5	32.0	22.6	9.9	0.0	9.9	0.0
Athens-Clarke County	153	929	66.0	21.6	1,759	6,225,567	17.5	31.3	12.0	9.2	0.6	19.8	3.4
Atlanta	879	8,945	574.9	212.4	8,214	31,551,612	15.9	34.2	13.9	16.0	0.2	18.5	0.0
Augusta-Richmond County	220	1,531	148.4	44.6	2,708	8,108,733	23.7	31.7	13.0	8.3	1.7	16.6	2.0
Columbus	259	1,902	157.2	51.1	3,147	10,081,655	11.8	34.7	14.0	7.5	4.7	18.9	2.8
Dalton	57	D	D	D	692	2,865,431	2.7	12.6	11.3	8.7	0.3	61.7	0.0
Douglasville	80	369	35.4	10.7	232	792,422	15.8	53.4	0.0	14.1	0.0	8.0	0.0
Duluth	133	785	73.7	21.0	140	565,431	33.5	44.9	0.0	10.3	0.0	10.1	0.0
Dunwoody	73	435	28.6	8.8	67	294,800	23.0	77.0	0.0	0.0	0.0	0.0	0.0
East Point	38	747	41.5	13.4	535	1,898,606	17.4	33.8	15.0	2.6	0.0	22.3	0.0
Gainesville	86	398	34.2	9.9	670	2,183,927	9.3	16.9	16.0	8.4	2.2	43.8	0.0
Hinesville	39	208	14.9	4.4	201	695,457	7.4	56.2	19.8	0.0	3.5	2.5	0.0
Johns Creek	78	D	D	D	8	41,438	87.5	12.5	0.0	0.0	0.0	0.0	0.0
Kennesaw	99	963	111.3	41.3	205	735,014	16.6	34.2	0.0	9.0	2.2	24.9	0.0
LaGrange	45	D	D	D	408	1,594,338	6.9	28.0	14.4	4.1	0.7	29.6	0.0
Lawrenceville	135	767	85.7	27.2	246	987,618	20.7	41.4	0.0	4.4	0.0	30.9	0.0
Macon-Bibb County	145	839	91.3	25.4	1,169	3,501,960	8.9	33.1	34.1	4.1	1.9	14.4	0.0
Marietta	220	1,340	152.1	45.4	734	3,368,637	23.6	11.1	12.3	4.3	11.8	24.4	0.0
Milton	30	D	D	D	121	520,911	22.5	27.5	44.2	3.3	0.0	2.5	0.0
Newnan	69	308	24.4	6.4	267	989,419	6.4	31.3	19.7	8.0	0.0	19.0	0.6
Peachtree City	86	758	53.4	17.9	270	1,079,307	11.4	29.0	29.7	14.7	0.0	5.3	3.6
Rome	62	429	39.4	10.8	589	1,937,155	8.3	18.6	26.8	11.5	0.6	25.2	0.0
Roswell	200	1,408	111.7	41.6	741	2,812,794	17.5	29.3	11.9	8.4	0.0	29.5	0.0
Sandy Springs	170	D	D	D	295	1,455,396	3.8	60.7	34.3	0.0	0.0	0.0	0.0
Savannah	221	1,473	144.6	43.6	2,548	9,836,488	9.9	34.9	11.9	8.9	2.7	25.8	0.0
Smyrna	102	452	41.9	12.4	391	1,523,989	10.9	37.3	23.1	6.6	3.6	14.0	2.3
Statesboro	55	288	21.2	5.4	279	845,101	12.3	28.4	12.3	12.1	0.0	32.0	0.0
Stockbridge	38	175	12.6	3.1	68	227,107	32.1	0.0	0.0	21.8	0.0	33.5	0.0
Valdosta	92	512	31.4	8.5	574	1,813,002	8.4	32.3	17.3	9.7	3.4	24.8	0.0
Warner Robins	81	473	34.5	10.5	536	1,642,600	10.8	31.9	21.3	10.1	3.3	20.5	0.0
HAWAII	1,519	11,014	877.5	279.0	X	X	X	X	X	X	X	X	X
East Honolulu CDP	24	101	4.3	1.6	NA	NA	NA	NA	NA	NA	NA	NA	NA
Hilo CDP	68	351	30.2	8.4	NA	NA	NA	NA	NA	NA	NA	NA	NA
Kahului CDP	53	471	34.8	11.6	NA	NA	NA	NA	NA	NA	NA	NA	NA
Kailua CDP (Honolulu County)	47	196	15.1	4.7	NA	NA	NA	NA	NA	NA	NA	NA	NA
Kaneohe CDP	38	268	20.0	7.2	NA	NA	NA	NA	NA	NA	NA	NA	NA
Mililani Town CDP	15	93	5.1	2.0	NA	NA	NA	NA	NA	NA	NA	NA	NA
Pearl City CDP	43	187	21.3	6.1	NA	NA	NA	NA	NA	NA	NA	NA	NA
Urban Honolulu CDP	721	6,242	481.7	157.1	NA	NA	NA	NA	NA	NA	NA	NA	NA
Waipahu CDP	53	276	23.2	6.9	NA	NA	NA	NA	NA	NA	NA	NA	NA
IDAHO	2,055	9,826	849.8	240.9	X	X	X	X	X	X	X	X	X
Boise City	371	2,083	162.4	51.1	1,617	7,522,788	17.0	29.2	23.6	4.2	0.9	17.7	4.2
Caldwell	46	290	30.2	8.4	228	861,823	8.7	36.4	24.0	12.2	0.0	13.3	3.2
Coeur d'Alene	82	447	32.5	10.0	318	1,619,497	16.8	30.1	21.9	7.8	0.2	19.0	3.2
Idaho Falls	92	448	42.2	11.5	659	2,848,455	10.4	20.7	20.0	4.4	0.0	33.4	2.9
Lewiston	65	381	28.8	8.9	314	1,377,725	8.6	24.1	24.4	12.2	3.9	16.1	2.7
Meridian	90	556	37.4	13.7	343	1,643,338	14.3	34.7	25.5	8.1	0.0	15.4	0.0
Nampa	100	578	47.8	14.8	565	2,435,649	5.6	35.1	21.4	3.5	2.1	14.7	2.4
Pocatello	76	416	39.1	9.5	561	2,333,293	10.6	25.9	18.5	10.3	1.9	26.0	2.6
Post Falls	48	236	18.4	5.5	169	673,051	14.6	40.3	0.0	12.1	1.2	22.8	0.0
Rexburg	25	D	D	D	115	440,960	21.3	29.6	8.0	11.5	0.8	17.1	0.0
Twin Falls	87	614	50.1	14.4	284	1,088,260	9.5	36.0	16.2	11.3	4.2	14.9	5.2
ILLINOIS	18,681	117,388	10,571.7	3,334.1	X	X	X	X	X	X	X	X	X
Addison	113	775	89.8	27.4	245	1,559,535	9.6	44.1	0.0	4.2	9.2	20.0	8.6
Algonquin	66	364	22.1	7.5	143	751,901	11.3	26.1	0.0	11.5	0.3	33.9	0.0
Alton	46	251	16.2	5.6	230	1,141,005	7.5	40.6	24.3	8.2	1.8	13.2	0.0
Arlington Heights	138	912	99.9	29.3	594	3,727,355	11.4	27.0	22.6	8.1	2.6	6.6	15.0
Aurora	159	1,044	120.6	29.7	1,402	8,465,715	9.4	32.8	18.5	7.5	8.1	14.5	5.4
Bartlett	33	142	18.3	4.9	166	992,280	14.8	48.1	0.0	13.2	11.3	12.4	0.0
Batavia	55	509	52.3	18.0	160	528,428	11.6	29.4	18.9	8.0	7.5	24.3	0.0
Belleville	96	635	49.6	15.9	345	1,469,633	6.3	35.6	25.0	5.2	0.0	14.8	4.1
Belvidere	30	231	17.9	6.1	125	645,335	6.9	38.7	26.4	8.1	0.0	13.1	4.0
Berwyn	53	214	19.6	4.7	402	2,004,230	7.2	46.5	25.8	5.7	1.5	5.4	6.1
Bloomington	127	1,022	74.9	28.0	723	3,168,188	7.2	25.0	19.2	14.3	0.0	27.5	5.8
Bolingbrook	79	424	31.8	10.7	391	2,517,306	8.3	44.4	26.4	8.1	0.0	9.5	0.0
Buffalo Grove	77	463	37.9	11.1	255	1,764,688	6.4	35.2	28.3	6.6	3.6	14.2	0.0

1. Establishments subject to federal tax.

City	City government finances, 2012									
	General revenue							General expenditure		
		Intergovernmental		Taxes					Per capita[1] (dollars)	
					Per capita[1] (dollars)					
	Total (mil dol)	Total (mil dol)	Percent from state government	Total (mil dol)	Total	Property	Sales and gross receipts	Total (mil dol)	Total	Capital outlays
	117	118	119	120	121	122	123	124	125	126
GEORGIA..........................	X	X	X	X	X	X	X	X	X	X
Albany	124.2	55.1	36.8	24.1	312	164	148	134.7	1,739	76
Alpharetta...........................	73.1	15.6	8.8	42.0	678	393	285	72.3	1,166	291
Athens-Clarke County	206.5	69.1	26.0	71.2	598	405	191	249.4	2,095	484
Atlanta................................	1,789.4	282.2	8.0	521.0	1,173	704	465	1,567.5	3,530	1,093
Augusta-Richmond County ..	364.7	133.0	12.9	103.4	524	291	230	341.5	1,731	350
Columbus	354.1	116.0	29.3	135.0	675	498	175	364.1	1,820	349
Dalton	69.4	16.5	0.3	14.2	427	283	144	82.6	2,478	515
Douglasville........................	27.0	7.1	10.3	13.8	441	190	246	34.0	1,088	313
Duluth	24.7	9.0	7.9	11.7	419	226	192	21.2	761	234
Dunwoody	20.5	0.6	15.1	17.6	372	123	247	26.5	560	185
East Point	49.3	11.3	1.5	20.7	582	366	216	55.0	1,547	287
Gainesville.........................	78.3	19.3	20.5	21.8	626	363	263	70.8	2,035	502
Hinesville...........................	30.4	10.9	1.3	9.9	287	163	124	30.3	873	89
Johns Creek	48.5	16.3	1.2	29.0	352	203	148	41.5	504	64
Kennesaw	26.5	5.0	1.3	14.0	449	296	154	24.9	796	112
LaGrange	35.7	9.6	8.9	4.7	155	1	153	44.0	1,454	186
Lawrenceville......................	22.3	5.6	4.6	5.4	185	59	120	28.0	952	219
Macon-Bibb County.............	105.9	49.5	9.0	37.3	239	126	113	116.6	748	73
Marietta	82.2	22.8	7.9	30.6	524	231	293	98.4	1,683	284
Milton	21.7	4.6	14.9	15.2	433	294	139	20.2	577	192
Newnan	30.9	10.4	1.6	10.9	320	137	184	29.9	875	209
Peachtree City....................	37.7	9.3	2.0	19.4	559	360	199	41.6	1,200	340
Rome..................................	65.6	22.8	6.9	19.0	526	247	230	61.5	1,706	503
Roswell...............................	94.1	26.7	5.7	44.7	478	286	192	94.3	1,006	196
Sandy Springs	95.9	28.3	2.8	60.0	604	296	307	75.2	757	151
Savannah............................	345.6	126.6	7.8	105.1	739	418	308	307.5	2,161	358
Smyrna...............................	56.3	11.1	0.4	27.0	513	327	184	52.4	994	224
Statesboro..........................	31.5	5.9	3.1	9.5	316	131	185	31.3	1,045	125
Stockbridge	16.8	7.3	22.1	4.0	149	1	148	12.9	481	83
Valdosta.............................	56.4	22.7	6.1	17.4	302	105	197	59.7	1,036	254
Warner Robins	55.2	4.5	3.8	28.0	390	229	159	54.2	755	88
HAWAII..............................	X	X	X	X	X	X	X	X	X	X
East Honolulu CDP	NA	NA	NA	NA	NA	NA	NA	NA	NA	NA
Hilo CDP.............................	NA	NA	NA	NA	NA	NA	NA	NA	NA	NA
Kahului CDP.......................	NA	NA	NA	NA	NA	NA	NA	NA	NA	NA
Kailua CDP (Honolulu County).............................	NA	NA	NA	NA	NA	NA	NA	NA	NA	NA
Kaneohe CDP	NA	NA	NA	NA	NA	NA	NA	NA	NA	NA
Mililani Town CDP	NA	NA	NA	NA	NA	NA	NA	NA	NA	NA
Pearl City CDP	NA	NA	NA	NA	NA	NA	NA	NA	NA	NA
Urban Honolulu CDP...........	NA	NA	NA	NA	NA	NA	NA	NA	NA	NA
Waipahu CDP......................	NA	NA	NA	NA	NA	NA	NA	NA	NA	NA
IDAHO	X	X	X	X	X	X	X	X	X	X
Boise City	272.0	25.8	66.8	117.7	555	507	48	267.8	1,262	173
Caldwell..............................	38.9	8.0	82.7	14.3	300	279	21	36.7	769	225
Coeur d'Alene.....................	48.9	9.7	58.0	22.9	502	399	102	55.8	1,224	307
Idaho Falls.........................	69.3	13.2	98.9	29.0	500	478	22	71.2	1,228	104
Lewiston	41.1	7.7	98.7	16.4	511	463	48	40.2	1,252	159
Meridian..............................	53.9	9.9	100.0	23.3	290	242	48	42.4	528	89
Nampa................................	96.5	19.8	60.9	39.9	476	446	30	87.0	1,036	141
Pocatello.............................	63.5	14.4	48.1	27.0	493	456	37	67.9	1,239	121
Post Falls...........................	27.0	5.7	100.0	8.8	307	307	0	21.0	732	124
Rexburg..............................	28.6	9.7	87.9	4.9	188	131	58	28.9	1,102	434
Twin Falls	39.5	5.6	70.4	19.5	433	398	35	33.6	747	116
ILLINOIS............................	X	X	X	X	X	X	X	X	X	X
Addison	44.5	12.7	100.0	22.1	594	338	250	39.8	1,067	5
Algonquin	27.6	11.4	100.0	12.4	415	200	215	21.1	704	36
Alton	40.8	15.1	100.0	14.7	535	282	253	34.8	1,267	124
Arlington Heights	98.7	20.5	94.8	68.0	897	574	324	81.7	1,078	28
Aurora................................	238.0	71.0	89.2	134.1	671	453	211	225.1	1,127	121
Bartlett...............................	31.0	7.0	96.0	17.3	415	315	93	29.2	703	48
Batavia	30.0	8.1	95.0	13.2	500	278	223	38.7	1,468	511
Belleville.............................	58.9	17.0	97.2	27.8	641	477	164	95.3	2,198	622
Belvidere	21.8	7.4	92.3	8.4	331	227	105	17.2	679	20
Berwyn...............................	69.4	14.0	73.5	38.6	679	499	163	80.9	1,425	107
Bloomington	114.7	26.3	94.5	54.8	704	308	396	104.9	1,349	122
Bolingbrook	85.6	23.0	91.1	43.5	588	210	348	83.2	1,124	65
Buffalo Grove	47.2	12.4	82.1	22.3	535	338	184	50.5	1,215	102

1. Based on population estimated as of July 1 of the year shown.

City	City government finances, 2012 (cont.)									
	General expenditure (cont.)									
	Percent of total for:									
	Public welfare	Highways	Parking facilities	Education	Health and hospitals	Police protection	Sewerage and sanitation	Parks and recreation	Housing and community development	Interest on debt
	127	128	129	130	131	132	133	134	135	136
GEORGIA........................	X	X	X	X	X	X	X	X	X	X
Albany	0.0	4.9	0.0	0.0	0.0	11.4	15.9	5.6	5.6	1.4
Alpharetta	0.0	23.5	0.0	0.0	0.0	19.9	4.3	8.5	0.0	1.8
Athens-Clarke County	0.2	4.4	1.6	0.0	5.2	11.0	11.5	5.5	1.8	0.4
Atlanta	1.2	2.2	0.0	1.3	0.1	11.0	13.8	4.1	1.0	10.4
Augusta-Richmond County ..	0.2	6.6	0.1	0.0	6.2	11.7	18.1	4.9	6.5	1.3
Columbus	0.0	10.1	0.0	0.0	8.2	13.4	10.9	3.8	2.8	2.7
Dalton	0.8	5.6	0.0	0.0	0.0	10.7	27.0	11.8	0.1	2.3
Douglasville	0.0	4.7	0.0	0.0	0.0	25.3	15.3	31.6	0.8	3.5
Duluth	0.0	21.9	0.5	0.0	0.0	31.7	0.0	12.3	0.9	2.1
Dunwoody	0.0	22.3	0.0	0.0	0.0	22.3	2.5	23.3	8.6	0.3
East Point	0.0	6.9	0.0	0.0	0.0	25.4	20.7	2.7	3.3	3.1
Gainesville	4.3	4.3	0.0	0.0	0.0	12.4	22.0	12.2	0.9	2.6
Hinesville	0.0	11.7	0.0	0.0	0.0	23.7	19.6	1.5	4.0	1.6
Johns Creek	0.0	20.6	0.0	0.0	0.0	21.0	0.0	3.6	6.9	0.5
Kennesaw	0.0	17.6	0.0	0.0	0.0	21.1	7.9	9.3	2.7	4.0
LaGrange	0.0	12.7	0.0	0.0	0.5	20.4	32.2	2.5	1.6	0.5
Lawrenceville.....................	0.0	16.5	0.0	0.0	0.0	37.1	18.1	0.0	1.5	0.0
Macon-Bibb County.............	0.0	2.6	0.1	0.0	0.4	20.4	8.6	5.0	5.9	1.3
Marietta	5.6	11.8	0.0	0.0	0.0	14.3	14.3	5.3	3.3	4.2
Milton..............................	0.0	25.7	0.0	0.0	0.7	15.0	0.0	2.8	3.7	0.3
Newnan	0.0	11.4	0.0	0.0	0.2	21.1	23.1	3.7	1.2	0.0
Peachtree City...................	0.3	7.9	0.0	0.0	0.7	16.0	2.6	8.7	0.1	1.9
Rome	0.0	8.7	0.8	0.1	0.0	12.5	22.9	2.5	2.4	0.5
Roswell	0.0	12.1	0.0	0.0	0.0	17.7	10.8	11.8	2.1	1.2
Sandy Springs...................	0.0	27.3	0.0	0.0	0.0	23.0	1.9	6.3	1.1	0.3
Savannah	0.3	4.5	2.1	0.0	0.0	20.3	17.7	6.9	10.8	1.5
Smyrna............................	0.0	22.7	0.0	0.0	0.0	14.8	15.7	4.7	0.3	3.6
Statesboro	0.0	8.4	0.0	0.0	0.3	19.2	31.7	2.2	2.0	0.1
Stockbridge	0.0	17.1	0.0	0.0	0.0	8.4	17.0	3.3	1.1	5.7
Valdosta...........................	0.0	12.1	0.0	0.0	0.0	21.5	25.4	2.4	1.0	0.2
Warner Robins	0.2	11.8	0.0	0.0	0.8	25.1	22.9	3.7	3.1	0.0
HAWAII............................	X	X	X	X	X	X	X	X	X	X
East Honolulu CDP	NA	NA	NA	NA	NA	NA	NA	NA	NA	NA
Hilo CDP...........................	NA	NA	NA	NA	NA	NA	NA	NA	NA	NA
Kahului CDP......................	NA	NA	NA	NA	NA	NA	NA	NA	NA	NA
Kailua CDP (Honolulu County)...........................	NA	NA	NA	NA	NA	NA	NA	NA	NA	NA
Kaneohe CDP	NA	NA	NA	NA	NA	NA	NA	NA	NA	NA
Mililani Town CDP	NA	NA	NA	NA	NA	NA	NA	NA	NA	NA
Pearl City CDP	NA	NA	NA	NA	NA	NA	NA	NA	NA	NA
Urban Honolulu CDP...........	NA	NA	NA	NA	NA	NA	NA	NA	NA	NA
Waipahu CDP.....................	NA	NA	NA	NA	NA	NA	NA	NA	NA	NA
IDAHO.............................	X	X	X	X	X	X	X	X	X	X
Boise City	0.0	0.9	0.0	0.0	0.0	16.9	19.6	7.6	2.4	0.6
Caldwell...........................	0.0	10.3	0.0	0.0	0.0	19.7	16.9	5.7	0.0	1.3
Coeur d'Alene....................	0.0	10.0	0.3	0.0	0.0	18.0	32.7	5.5	0.2	1.6
Idaho Falls	0.0	6.6	0.0	0.0	4.4	14.1	16.6	12.8	0.0	0.1
Lewiston	0.0	13.4	0.0	0.0	0.0	15.9	27.8	7.7	3.2	0.7
Meridian...........................	0.0	0.0	0.0	0.0	0.0	26.6	23.6	9.0	0.4	0.3
Nampa.............................	0.0	7.3	0.1	0.0	0.6	21.3	17.3	14.0	0.9	3.1
Pocatello..........................	0.0	9.8	0.0	0.0	4.3	16.7	12.7	5.2	1.4	1.8
Post Falls.........................	0.0	12.2	0.0	0.0	0.0	22.6	27.3	8.3	0.0	3.4
Rexburg...........................	0.0	9.2	0.0	0.0	0.7	6.6	16.2	20.9	2.6	1.0
Twin Falls	0.0	14.4	0.2	0.0	1.0	21.5	19.5	6.3	1.9	0.8
ILLINOIS..........................	X	X	X	X	X	X	X	X	X	X
Addison	0.0	16.5	0.0	0.0	0.0	38.7	13.7	0.0	0.0	6.6
Algonquin	0.0	19.0	0.0	0.0	0.0	39.5	10.4	8.0	0.0	0.9
Alton	0.0	13.1	0.0	0.0	0.5	25.5	14.9	8.3	0.0	2.0
Arlington Heights................	0.0	12.4	1.5	0.0	1.8	26.6	1.9	0.9	0.4	2.9
Aurora.............................	0.0	10.8	0.6	0.0	0.4	28.0	2.2	3.8	2.0	11.6
Bartlett............................	0.0	16.3	0.7	0.0	0.0	37.2	10.5	8.1	0.0	7.2
Batavia	0.0	37.4	0.0	0.0	0.0	19.8	6.2	0.0	0.0	1.8
Belleville	0.0	8.5	0.0	0.0	0.0	9.1	31.1	1.7	0.0	4.9
Belvidere	0.0	14.5	0.0	0.0	0.1	33.8	11.9	1.0	0.0	2.3
Berwyn	0.3	11.0	0.1	0.0	0.0	26.6	8.8	2.9	4.0	5.8
Bloomington	0.0	5.5	0.9	0.0	0.0	14.8	15.4	16.9	0.6	2.8
Bolingbrook	0.0	14.2	0.0	0.0	0.0	22.2	9.2	11.1	0.3	10.3
Buffalo Grove	0.0	6.9	0.3	0.0	0.0	24.6	16.7	6.1	0.0	0.4

City	City government finances, 2012 (cont.) Debt outstanding — Total (mil dol)	Per capita[1] (dollars)	Debt issued during year	Climate[2] — Average daily temperature — Mean — January	July	Limits — January[3]	July[4]	Annual precipitation (inches)	Heating degree days	Cooling degree days
	137	138	139	140	141	142	143	144	145	146
GEORGIA...............	X	X	X	X	X	X	X	X	X	X
Albany....................	71.8	926	16.6	47.5	81.4	35.1	92.5	53.40	2,106	2,264
Alpharetta...............	54.6	880	29.0	39.5	77.2	29.1	87.5	51.82	3,490	1,327
Athens-Clarke County..........	263.4	2,214	18.1	42.2	79.8	32.9	90.2	47.83	2,861	1,785
Atlanta....................	7,446.5	16,770	997.4	41.7	79.5	31.3	90.6	49.10	3,004	1,679
Augusta-Richmond County ..	619.6	3,141	0.0	44.8	80.8	33.1	92.0	44.58	2,525	1,986
Columbus...............	514.9	2,574	66.6	46.8	82.0	36.6	91.7	48.57	2,154	2,296
Dalton....................	51.3	1,540	0.5	39.4	78.0	28.8	89.8	53.64	3,534	1,393
Douglasville..........	43.7	1,399	13.4	NA	NA	NA	NA	NA	NA	NA
Duluth....................	10.1	363	0.0	NA	NA	NA	NA	NA	NA	NA
Dunwoody..............	7.3	154	5.2	NA	NA	NA	NA	NA	NA	NA
East Point..............	99.0	2,784	0.0	42.7	80.0	33.5	89.4	50.20	2,827	1,810
Gainesville.............	711.3	20,464	0.0	36.0	72.9	24.7	84.0	58.19	4,421	752
Hinesville..............	24.5	706	1.8	51.6	82.6	40.7	93.3	48.32	1,551	2,539
Johns Creek..........	3.2	39	0.2	NA	NA	NA	NA	NA	NA	NA
Kennesaw..............	25.6	819	0.0	NA	NA	NA	NA	NA	NA	NA
LaGrange...............	38.1	1,257	0.0	42.2	78.7	31.3	89.3	53.38	3,078	1,551
Lawrenceville..........	0.0	0	0.0	NA	NA	NA	NA	NA	NA	NA
Macon-Bibb County.............	46.4	298	19.4	45.5	81.1	34.5	91.8	45.00	2,364	2,115
Marietta.................	100.1	1,712	0.0	39.4	77.9	28.5	89.3	54.43	3,505	1,403
Milton....................	1.1	32	0.0	NA	NA	NA	NA	NA	NA	NA
Newnan..................	38.2	1,119	0.0	NA	NA	NA	NA	NA	NA	NA
Peachtree City..........	15.8	457	0.0	42.6	79.4	31.8	90.5	50.10	2,958	1,679
Rome.....................	63.5	1,764	0.0	39.4	77.5	29.1	87.7	56.16	3,510	1,360
Roswell..................	12.2	130	1.7	39.5	77.2	29.1	87.5	51.82	3,490	1,327
Sandy Springs.........	2.8	29	0.0	NA	NA	NA	NA	NA	NA	NA
Savannah...............	184.3	1,296	0.0	49.2	82.1	38.0	92.3	49.58	1,799	2,454
Smyrna..................	50.4	956	0.0	42.7	80.0	33.5	89.4	50.20	2,827	1,810
Statesboro..............	18.7	623	0.1	NA	NA	NA	NA	NA	NA	NA
Stockbridge	17.6	656	0.4	NA	NA	NA	NA	NA	NA	NA
Valdosta................	48.0	832	12.1	50.0	80.9	38.0	92.0	53.06	1,782	2,319
Warner Robins	39.6	552	31.7	45.5	81.1	34.5	91.8	45.00	2,364	2,115
HAWAII.................	X	X	X	X	X	X	X	X	X	X
East Honolulu CDP	NA	NA	NA	NA	NA	NA	NA	NA	NA	NA
Hilo CDP................	NA	NA	NA	NA	NA	NA	NA	NA	NA	NA
Kahului CDP............	NA	NA	NA	NA	NA	NA	NA	NA	NA	NA
Kailua CDP (Honolulu County)...........	NA	NA	NA	NA	NA	NA	NA	NA	NA	NA
Kaneohe CDP	NA	NA	NA	NA	NA	NA	NA	NA	NA	NA
Mililani Town CDP	NA	NA	NA	NA	NA	NA	NA	NA	NA	NA
Pearl City CDP	NA	NA	NA	NA	NA	NA	NA	NA	NA	NA
Urban Honolulu CDP...........	NA	NA	NA	NA	NA	NA	NA	NA	NA	NA
Waipahu CDP............	NA	NA	NA	NA	NA	NA	NA	NA	NA	NA
IDAHO.................	X	X	X	X	X	X	X	X	X	X
Boise City..............	79.7	375	36.5	30.2	74.7	23.6	89.2	12.19	5,727	807
Caldwell................	12.5	263	0.0	29.3	68.8	19.6	85.7	10.90	6,749	410
Coeur d'Alene..........	31.6	692	7.6	28.4	68.7	22.1	82.6	26.07	6,540	426
Idaho Falls.............	21.5	370	1.6	19.3	68.4	11.1	85.9	11.02	7,917	322
Lewiston	6.6	205	0.0	33.7	73.5	28.0	87.6	12.74	5,220	792
Meridian................	1.3	17	1.3	29.4	71.8	22.1	89.2	9.94	5,752	579
Nampa...................	58.7	700	6.7	28.9	73.3	20.8	90.5	11.37	5,873	692
Pocatello...............	24.5	448	0.0	24.4	69.2	16.3	87.5	12.58	7,109	387
Post Falls..............	11.1	387	0.0	NA	NA	NA	NA	NA	NA	NA
Rexburg................	14.4	549	10.0	NA	NA	NA	NA	NA	NA	NA
Twin Falls	43.5	967	0.0	28.2	72.2	19.7	87.9	9.42	6,300	587
ILLINOIS.............	X	X	X	X	X	X	X	X	X	X
Addison	59.7	1,602	6.8	22.0	73.3	14.3	83.5	36.27	6,498	830
Algonquin	13.6	453	0.1	NA	NA	NA	NA	NA	NA	NA
Alton....................	20.7	752	0.0	27.7	78.4	19.4	88.1	38.54	5,149	1,354
Arlington Heights.................	53.7	709	19.6	22.0	73.3	14.3	83.5	36.27	6,498	830
Aurora..................	553.2	2,769	9.1	20.0	72.4	10.5	84.2	38.39	6,859	661
Bartlett.................	54.9	1,320	13.6	19.3	72.6	10.9	83.0	37.22	6,975	679
Batavia	54.8	2,077	1.0	NA	NA	NA	NA	NA	NA	NA
Belleville	71.6	1,652	32.1	30.9	78.1	22.1	89.6	39.37	4,612	1,339
Belvidere	5.1	199	0.0	NA	NA	NA	NA	NA	NA	NA
Berwyn	97.3	1,712	7.4	25.8	75.3	17.3	86.2	40.96	5,555	1,027
Bloomington	96.3	1,238	12.7	22.4	75.2	13.7	85.6	37.45	6,190	998
Bolingbrook	272.1	3,679	5.0	23.1	74.8	14.2	86.8	37.94	6,053	942
Buffalo Grove..........	2.2	52	0.0	18.4	72.1	9.6	82.3	36.56	7,149	624

1. Based on the population estimated as of July 1 of the year shown.   2. Represents normal values based on the 30-year period, 1971±2000.   3. Average daily minimum.   4. Average daily maximum.

Table D. Cities — **Land Area and Population**

STATE Place code	City	Land area[1] (sq. mi)	Population, 2018 Total persons 2018	Rank	Per square mile	Race 2017 Race alone[2] (percent) White	Black or African American	American Indian, Alaskan Native	Asian	Hawaiian Pacific Islander	Some other race	Two or more races (percent)
		1	2	3	4	5	6	7	8	9	10	11
	ILLINOIS— Cont'd											
17 09,642	Burbank....................	4.2	28,534	1,302	6,793.8	75.0	5.2	0.0	1.3	0.0	13.8	4.7
17 10,487	Calumet City	7.2	36,240	1,062	5,033.3	NA	NA	NA	NA	NA	NA	NA
17 11,163	Carbondale..................	17.3	25,376	1,405	1,466.8	60.0	28.4	0.0	4.2	0.0	2.8	4.6
17 11,332	Carol Stream................	9.1	39,601	976	4,351.8	64.5	5.7	0.7	20.3	0.0	5.9	2.8
17 11,358	Carpentersville.............	7.9	37,744	1,018	4,777.7	41.2	13.6	1.2	9.1	0.0	31.8	3.0
17 12,385	Champaign..................	22.8	88,029	375	3,860.9	64.1	19.8	0.2	11.9	0.0	1.0	3.0
17 14,000	Chicago.....................	227.4	2,705,994	3	11,899.7	49.9	29.8	0.3	6.7	0.0	10.6	2.8
17 14,026	Chicago Heights..........	10.2	29,571	1,271	2,899.1	26.2	40.4	0.0	0.0	0.0	30.1	3.4
17 14,351	Cicero.......................	5.9	81,597	421	13,830.0	34.3	1.6	0.0	0.6	0.0	61.8	1.7
17 15,599	Collinsville.................	14.7	24,621	1,423	1,674.9	NA	NA	NA	NA	NA	NA	NA
17 17,887	Crystal Lake...............	18.8	40,036	959	2,129.6	NA	NA	NA	NA	NA	NA	NA
17 18,563	Danville.....................	18.0	30,898	1,222	1,716.6	62.2	32.1	0.1	1.5	0.0	0.5	3.6
17 18,823	Decatur	42.3	71,290	504	1,685.3	70.0	22.3	0.5	0.8	0.0	0.4	5.9
17 19,161	DeKalb	16.1	42,611	892	2,646.6	71.9	14.6	0.0	2.4	0.0	5.0	6.1
17 19,642	Des Plaines................	14.3	58,959	637	4,123.0	76.5	2.7	0.0	10.8	0.4	6.3	3.3
17 20,591	Downers Grove............	14.5	49,387	777	3,406.0	85.7	5.8	0.1	5.5	0.0	1.2	1.8
17 22,255	East St. Louis.............	13.9	26,346	1,385	1,895.4	NA	NA	NA	NA	NA	NA	NA
17 23,074	Elgin........................	37.5	111,683	265	2,978.2	64.1	4.3	2.2	4.0	0.0	22.4	3.0
17 23,256	Elk Grove Village	11.5	32,458	1,171	2,822.4	NA	NA	NA	NA	NA	NA	NA
17 23,620	Elmhurst....................	10.3	46,558	834	4,520.2	89.9	0.5	0.2	7.3	0.0	0.6	1.5
17 24,582	Evanston....................	7.8	74,106	483	9,500.8	65.2	18.4	0.0	8.7	0.0	2.6	5.0
17 27,884	Freeport	11.6	23,920	1,429	2,062.1	75.8	18.3	0.4	1.0	0.0	0.0	4.5
17 28,326	Galesburg	17.7	30,432	1,237	1,719.3	79.0	13.5	0.3	1.6	0.0	2.5	3.1
17 29,730	Glendale Heights	5.4	33,928	1,126	6,283.0	53.9	6.8	0.7	23.5	0.0	10.2	4.9
17 29,756	Glen Ellyn	6.8	27,928	1,323	4,107.1	NA	NA	NA	NA	NA	NA	NA
17 29,938	Glenview	14.0	47,258	824	3,375.6	NA	NA	NA	NA	NA	NA	NA
17 30,926	Granite City................	19.3	28,476	1,304	1,475.4	NA	NA	NA	NA	NA	NA	NA
17 32,018	Gurnee	13.5	30,576	1,230	2,264.9	67.8	6.6	0.6	15.8	0.0	6.2	3.1
17 32,746	Hanover Park	6.3	37,747	1,017	5,991.6	62.4	8.1	0.3	9.1	0.4	14.2	5.5
17 33,383	Harvey.......................	6.2	24,641	1,421	3,974.4	20.8	70.1	0.0	3.3	0.0	4.1	1.7
17 34,722	Highland Park.............	12.2	29,622	1,269	2,428.0	NA	NA	NA	NA	NA	NA	NA
17 35,411	Hoffman Estates	21.1	51,197	752	2,426.4	51.1	3.6	0.0	30.0	0.0	9.2	6.2
17 38,570	Joliet........................	64.1	148,099	176	2,310.4	62.6	17.0	0.2	1.8	0.1	14.7	3.7
17 38,934	Kankakee	15.0	26,052	1,393	1,736.8	57.7	36.2	0.3	0.3	0.0	3.2	2.4
17 41,183	Lake in the Hills..........	10.4	28,835	1,294	2,772.6	90.5	1.1	0.0	4.0	0.0	0.6	3.7
17 42,028	Lansing	7.5	27,657	1,332	3,687.6	43.7	43.8	1.6	2.1	0.0	5.7	3.1
17 44,407	Lombard.....................	10.2	44,523	858	4,365.0	78.3	4.1	0.0	13.5	0.0	1.5	2.5
17 45,694	McHenry.....................	14.6	27,022	1,358	1,850.8	NA	NA	NA	NA	NA	NA	NA
17 48,242	Melrose Park...............	4.2	24,925	1,415	5,934.5	48.3	5.7	0.9	0.4	0.0	43.7	1.1
17 49,867	Moline	16.8	41,902	907	2,494.2	84.0	7.4	0.7	3.3	0.0	1.6	3.1
17 51,089	Mount Prospect...........	10.7	54,198	707	5,065.2	77.2	2.8	0.2	16.5	0.0	1.3	1.9
17 51,349	Mundelein	9.5	31,234	1,211	3,287.8	81.2	0.2	0.7	9.5	0.4	5.0	3.0
17 51,622	Naperville	38.8	148,304	175	3,822.3	73.7	4.3	0.0	18.9	0.0	0.4	2.7
17 53,000	Niles	5.8	29,184	1,282	5,031.7	72.8	3.0	0.5	18.5	0.0	1.2	4.0
17 53,234	Normal	18.7	54,742	700	2,927.4	85.3	9.4	0.0	3.8	0.0	0.1	1.3
17 53,481	Northbrook	13.2	33,167	1,150	2,512.7	82.9	1.9	0.0	14.5	0.0	0.1	0.6
17 53,559	North Chicago	8.0	29,770	1,262	3,721.3	50.0	24.5	0.0	5.3	0.2	16.3	3.8
17 54,638	Oak Forest.................	6.0	27,406	1,339	4,567.7	78.0	7.4	0.0	7.2	0.0	6.3	1.1
17 54,820	Oak Lawn...................	8.6	55,511	684	6,454.8	81.4	4.0	0.0	5.4	0.0	5.3	3.9
17 54,885	Oak Park....................	4.7	52,265	737	11,120.2	74.7	15.7	0.0	4.0	0.0	1.4	4.2
17 55,249	O'Fallon.....................	15.3	29,584	1,270	1,933.6	68.3	20.3	0.0	3.5	0.0	2.9	5.0
17 56,640	Orland Park................	22.0	58,312	647	2,650.5	NA	NA	NA	NA	NA	NA	NA
17 56,887	Oswego......................	14.9	35,237	1,090	2,364.9	NA	NA	NA	NA	NA	NA	NA
17 57,225	Palatine	13.6	68,053	532	5,003.9	66.9	1.9	0.1	10.0	0.0	17.1	4.1
17 57,875	Park Ridge	7.1	37,240	1,032	5,245.1	NA	NA	NA	NA	NA	NA	NA
17 58,447	Pekin........................	14.6	32,255	1,179	2,209.2	NA	NA	NA	NA	NA	NA	NA
17 59,000	Peoria.......................	48.2	111,388	269	2,311.0	63.1	26.5	0.1	5.6	0.0	1.5	3.1
17 60,287	Plainfield	24.5	44,138	867	1,801.6	79.7	6.4	0.0	8.5	0.5	1.8	3.1
17 62,367	Quincy.......................	15.7	40,042	958	2,550.4	90.0	6.0	0.4	0.8	0.0	0.0	2.8
17 65,000	Rockford....................	64.4	146,526	178	2,275.2	69.2	22.0	0.3	2.7	0.0	2.3	3.5
17 65,078	Rock Island................	16.9	37,678	1,019	2,229.5	67.3	19.9	0.8	6.1	0.5	1.2	4.2
17 65,442	Romeoville.................	19.0	39,624	974	2,085.5	61.5	11.1	0.0	6.2	0.0	14.7	6.4
17 66,040	Round Lake Beach	5.0	27,325	1,342	5,465.0	73.3	7.8	0.0	1.8	0.0	14.3	2.8
17 66,703	St. Charles.................	14.4	33,032	1,155	2,293.9	88.2	2.5	0.4	5.1	0.0	1.4	2.4
17 68,003	Schaumburg................	19.3	73,509	487	3,808.8	62.8	4.5	0.2	26.3	0.0	2.9	3.4
17 70,122	Skokie.......................	10.1	63,280	590	6,265.3	64.5	6.6	0.1	23.5	0.4	1.1	3.8
17 72,000	Springfield.................	61.0	114,694	253	1,880.2	73.0	20.0	0.0	3.4	0.1	0.2	3.3
17 73,157	Streamwood................	7.8	39,570	977	5,073.1	65.2	9.2	0.6	10.8	0.0	12.4	1.8
17 75,484	Tinley Park	16.1	56,204	676	3,490.9	89.9	3.2	0.0	4.2	0.0	1.8	0.8
17 77,005	Urbana	11.8	42,046	905	3,563.2	56.7	19.6	0.1	19.4	0.1	0.4	3.7
17 77,694	Vernon Hills................	7.7	26,641	1,371	3,459.9	NA	NA	NA	NA	NA	NA	NA

1. Dry land or land partially or temporarily covered by water.   2. Hispanic or Latino persons may be of any race.

Table D. Cities — **Population**

City	Percent Hispanic or Latino[1], 2017	Percent foreign born, 2017	Age of population (percent), 2017							Median age, 2017	Percent female, 2017	Population			
			Under 18 years	18 to 24 years	25 to 34 years	35 to 44 years	45 to 54 years	55 to 64 years	65 years and over			Census counts		Percent change	
												2000	2010	2000-2010	2001-2018
	12	13	14	15	16	17	18	19	20	21	22	23	24	25	26
ILLINOIS— Cont'd															
Burbank	35.9	29.4	25.2	9.7	11.7	17.0	7.7	13.4	15.5	38.2	49.3	27,902	28,925	3.7	-1.4
Calumet City	15.7	7.9	26.9	15.9	11.7	13.6	9.3	12.3	10.3	30.4	55.4	39,071	37,116	-5.0	-2.4
Carbondale	8.6	9.9	11.7	44.3	14.1	8.1	6.2	7.2	8.3	22.8	47.0	20,681	26,411	27.7	-3.9
Carol Stream	20.7	26.3	22.4	9.7	14.5	13.1	12.7	14.8	12.8	36.7	50.3	40,438	39,576	-2.1	0.1
Carpentersville	53.2	30.5	34.3	10.9	13.1	14.9	12.7	8.6	5.5	28.6	48.1	30,586	37,678	23.2	0.2
Champaign	7.1	14.3	17.8	30.0	12.3	12.9	9.6	8.4	8.9	26.6	51.3	67,518	81,272	20.4	8.3
Chicago	29.0	20.8	20.8	10.1	20.0	13.7	12.0	11.2	12.2	34.6	51.5	2,896,016	2,695,624	-6.9	0.4
Chicago Heights	43.1	15.8	28.9	9.2	16.9	13.1	10.4	6.9	14.6	31.3	49.7	32,776	30,365	-7.4	-2.6
Cicero	90.5	40.5	28.4	10.2	15.7	15.7	12.9	8.8	8.2	32.7	49.5	85,616	84,241	-1.6	-3.1
Collinsville	4.3	1.9	21.7	7.7	14.3	11.9	7.9	17.6	19.0	38.8	58.7	24,707	25,665	3.9	-4.1
Crystal Lake	13.4	9.1	30.1	6.0	11.2	13.8	14.1	11.1	13.6	36.6	48.9	38,000	40,766	7.3	-1.8
Danville	5.7	3.0	26.4	9.3	12.9	10.8	11.9	12.1	16.6	36.3	49.0	33,904	33,029	-2.6	-6.5
Decatur	3.3	2.7	22.0	10.5	12.8	11.6	9.9	12.9	20.4	38.9	53.7	81,860	76,131	-7.0	-6.4
DeKalb	16.8	12.9	19.7	29.0	15.9	9.0	7.5	10.0	8.9	25.9	53.4	39,018	44,123	13.1	-3.4
Des Plaines	18.8	34.7	18.7	5.3	13.3	12.8	13.0	16.8	20.2	45.0	51.6	58,720	58,385	-0.6	1.0
Downers Grove	5.8	10.7	22.4	6.5	12.1	12.8	13.0	15.7	17.4	42.6	52.7	48,724	48,874	0.3	1.0
East St. Louis	0.2	0.3	23.8	11.6	10.9	14.5	10.5	13.7	15.0	39.6	53.7	31,542	26,933	-14.6	-2.2
Elgin	46.6	23.8	27.1	9.5	12.2	14.2	14.1	11.7	11.2	35.9	50.1	94,487	108,147	14.5	3.3
Elk Grove Village	11.0	24.3	16.5	8.0	13.8	14.6	11.5	14.9	20.7	41.7	48.6	34,727	33,143	-4.6	-2.1
Elmhurst	8.9	11.4	22.1	12.1	6.4	9.9	16.6	15.0	17.9	44.4	51.4	42,762	44,135	3.2	5.5
Evanston	12.0	21.0	18.6	16.8	11.5	11.5	13.6	11.3	16.6	37.7	51.2	74,239	74,483	0.3	-0.5
Freeport	4.7	2.5	19.8	8.6	12.1	8.1	13.3	17.2	20.9	46.7	52.5	26,443	25,641	-3.0	-6.7
Galesburg	8.6	4.6	18.9	12.6	11.9	12.5	10.7	14.6	18.8	39.7	48.6	33,706	32,195	-4.5	-5.5
Glendale Heights	30.8	35.0	21.1	9.4	16.7	14.0	15.2	12.2	11.5	36.4	48.7	31,765	34,291	8.0	-1.1
Glen Ellyn	3.4	9.3	26.1	7.4	10.1	12.1	15.9	13.2	15.3	40.7	51.3	26,999	27,783	2.9	0.5
Glenview	7.6	22.5	24.3	5.4	6.3	11.0	14.0	16.0	22.9	46.9	50.2	41,847	44,722	6.9	5.7
Granite City	9.0	2.2	19.0	8.7	14.6	11.7	12.8	16.7	16.4	40.8	50.5	31,301	29,807	-4.8	-4.5
Gurnee	15.3	18.3	22.2	12.1	9.9	12.1	16.2	17.0	10.5	40.7	56.4	28,834	31,226	8.3	-2.1
Hanover Park	37.7	26.3	28.2	11.7	11.8	17.3	10.5	10.1	10.4	33.4	51.8	38,278	38,103	-0.5	-0.9
Harvey	21.3	14.6	25.1	11.0	10.8	12.2	15.0	10.2	15.8	37.1	55.7	30,000	25,264	-15.8	-2.5
Highland Park	4.5	10.5	24.4	2.9	5.9	8.2	15.7	19.6	23.3	50.4	50.9	31,365	29,745	-5.2	-0.4
Hoffman Estates	15.0	33.6	23.1	5.8	15.7	12.2	12.5	13.9	16.8	39.1	49.9	49,495	51,891	4.8	-1.3
Joliet	33.3	16.3	26.9	10.3	15.3	13.9	13.3	10.1	10.3	33.7	49.8	106,221	147,435	38.8	0.5
Kankakee	24.5	10.4	25.6	9.4	14.4	14.2	10.5	10.9	15.0	35.3	51.3	27,491	27,562	0.3	-5.5
Lake in the Hills	15.5	13.6	25.6	12.5	12.2	17.5	13.3	11.8	7.1	34.6	50.8	23,152	29,013	25.3	-0.6
Lansing	15.5	7.2	25.4	10.0	6.9	13.6	15.1	12.1	17.0	39.7	58.6	28,332	28,351	0.1	-2.4
Lombard	6.5	15.1	19.5	9.3	15.8	14.0	12.5	15.1	13.8	38.9	51.9	42,322	43,304	2.3	2.8
McHenry	20.5	9.3	19.5	11.1	12.1	12.8	17.7	15.0	11.7	40.9	51.2	21,501	27,019	25.7	0.0
Melrose Park	74.3	35.4	26.1	8.6	16.6	16.0	13.5	11.2	8.1	34.1	44.4	23,171	25,414	9.7	-1.9
Moline	16.1	10.3	21.3	8.6	11.8	12.1	14.0	11.9	20.3	41.6	51.6	43,768	43,519	-0.6	-3.7
Mount Prospect	11.7	34.3	24.2	5.5	12.7	15.3	16.3	10.6	15.4	39.0	47.8	56,265	55,037	-2.2	-1.5
Mundelein	35.8	30.8	27.6	6.8	15.8	15.1	11.3	10.9	12.5	34.8	49.7	30,935	30,979	0.1	0.8
Naperville	5.1	20.2	25.4	8.7	10.2	15.1	15.3	12.8	12.6	38.7	51.2	128,358	142,154	10.7	4.3
Niles	11.6	41.5	13.6	7.0	15.1	10.3	12.4	16.8	24.7	48.5	55.1	30,068	29,815	-0.8	-2.1
Normal	7.6	6.8	18.3	30.0	11.5	9.8	10.2	8.6	11.6	26.1	51.0	45,386	52,543	15.8	4.2
Northbrook	2.0	22.4	24.2	5.7	7.6	9.4	15.9	16.4	20.9	46.7	53.0	33,435	33,202	-0.7	-0.1
North Chicago	31.7	14.7	17.2	31.6	25.6	8.7	5.6	5.8	5.6	25.2	39.5	35,918	32,574	-9.3	-8.6
Oak Forest	16.2	15.2	19.5	9.5	8.1	12.6	18.2	16.5	15.6	45.2	47.1	28,051	27,954	-0.3	-2.0
Oak Lawn	20.2	20.4	21.9	7.7	15.1	12.3	12.1	13.5	17.5	38.1	50.5	55,245	56,690	2.6	-2.1
Oak Park	7.0	8.6	24.6	4.9	13.4	15.3	15.5	9.7	16.5	39.5	50.9	52,524	51,878	-1.2	0.7
O'Fallon	2.6	6.8	26.5	7.6	17.5	12.5	15.5	9.0	11.4	34.5	54.6	21,910	28,750	31.2	2.9
Orland Park	5.7	15.4	20.0	5.5	12.0	11.8	11.3	15.2	24.3	45.7	50.6	51,077	56,638	10.9	3.0
Oswego	12.6	8.7	29.8	10.4	11.7	16.1	11.2	11.0	9.8	31.8	49.9	13,326	30,452	128.5	15.7
Palatine	24.4	27.0	25.3	5.7	17.9	12.5	12.3	13.5	13.0	35.8	50.8	65,479	68,551	4.7	-0.7
Park Ridge	4.3	14.6	26.9	5.9	5.5	15.5	12.8	13.9	19.6	42.3	52.0	37,775	37,479	-0.8	-0.6
Pekin	3.1	1.1	20.6	7.1	14.7	10.5	13.1	14.8	19.2	41.8	52.0	33,857	34,095	0.7	-5.4
Peoria	6.2	9.1	23.8	10.0	13.9	11.7	12.1	11.9	16.8	36.5	52.2	112,936	115,108	1.9	-3.2
Plainfield	15.9	13.9	31.6	9.1	8.9	16.8	15.9	9.0	8.6	35.2	50.9	13,038	39,854	205.7	10.7
Quincy	1.4	1.7	24.6	9.5	12.5	12.4	10.7	10.7	19.7	36.7	51.3	40,366	40,705	0.8	-1.6
Rockford	18.9	13.8	24.7	8.7	13.7	11.3	11.8	13.2	16.5	37.2	51.3	150,115	153,283	2.1	-4.4
Rock Island	14.9	14.5	21.3	15.0	11.7	15.1	8.2	12.2	16.5	36.0	51.3	39,684	39,003	-1.7	-3.4
Romeoville	28.1	25.1	26.6	10.9	9.4	14.3	16.9	10.4	11.6	37.8	55.7	21,153	39,634	87.4	0.0
Round Lake Beach	50.1	25.7	27.2	12.1	16.0	13.1	10.0	12.7	9.0	32.0	46.5	25,859	28,100	8.7	-2.8
St. Charles	6.3	8.0	23.4	6.8	9.6	14.7	16.9	12.3	16.4	43.5	50.2	27,896	32,321	15.9	2.2
Schaumburg	7.4	31.8	20.4	5.0	14.6	16.9	14.2	13.0	15.9	39.9	51.6	75,386	74,229	-1.5	-1.0
Skokie	15.3	38.5	22.5	7.1	9.6	13.1	13.6	14.7	19.3	43.4	54.8	63,348	64,845	2.4	-2.4
Springfield	3.0	5.0	22.3	8.8	14.0	11.2	12.7	13.9	17.2	39.4	53.1	111,454	116,998	5.0	-2.0
Streamwood	40.0	29.5	23.0	8.9	16.1	12.6	15.5	12.1	11.9	36.1	52.3	36,407	39,839	9.4	-0.7
Tinley Park	12.0	9.0	19.7	8.1	12.8	10.8	14.3	19.7	14.7	44.2	51.7	48,401	56,836	17.4	-1.1
Urbana	6.8	24.2	11.2	39.5	16.5	7.9	4.8	7.6	12.5	24.8	45.1	36,395	41,675	14.5	0.9
Vernon Hills	10.9	28.2	25.6	5.2	11.3	14.7	14.2	15.1	13.8	41.5	52.6	20,120	25,030	24.4	6.4

1. May be of any race.

Table D. Cities — Households, Group Quarters, Crime, and Education

City	Households, 2017							Persons in group quarters, 2017	Serious crimes known to police[2], 2016				Educational attainment, 2017		
				Percent					Total		Rate[3]			Attainment[4] (percent)	
	Number	Persons per household	Family	Married couple family	Female headed[1]	Non-family	One person		Number	Rate	Violent	Property	Population age 25 and over	High school graduate or less	Bachelor's degree or more
	27	28	29	30	31	32	33	34	35	36	37	38	39	40	41

ILLINOIS— Cont'd

City	27	28	29	30	31	32	33	34	35	36	37	38	39	40	41
Burbank	8,705	3.21	73.6	53.8	13.3	26.4	25.1	232	474	1,625	240	1,385	18,347	56.2	15.3
Calumet City	11,800	3.10	69.3	25.5	33.4	30.7	27.9	NA	1,569	4,238	570	3,668	20,957	42.2	15.4
Carbondale	9,764	2.13	38.0	18.3	18.4	62.0	38.7	4,710	984	3,731	523	3,208	11,224	21.1	44.8
Carol Stream	13,978	2.83	71.2	55.0	13.7	28.8	20.7	NA	342	845	89	756	27,090	35.7	41.2
Carpentersville	11,242	3.39	68.6	50.4	13.0	31.4	27.7	NA	699	1,808	80	1,728	20,905	60.1	17.2
Champaign	35,590	2.23	42.3	31.7	8.0	57.7	42.6	7,933	3,655	4,198	773	3,425	45,610	19.8	48.9
Chicago	1,047,695	2.54	52.7	32.5	15.2	47.3	37.3	58,015	117,329	4,305	1,108	3,197	1,879,622	37.9	38.8
Chicago Heights	9,261	3.15	64.3	35.1	23.1	35.7	33.5	719	980	3,237	578	2,659	18,485	54.4	16.5
Cicero	22,600	3.62	76.9	49.4	16.5	23.1	18.5	780	1,975	2,357	314	2,043	50,616	70.6	10.7
Collinsville	11,439	2.26	58.7	38.4	12.7	41.3	31.2	NA	789	3,207	215	2,992	18,340	32.1	29.8
Crystal Lake	16,093	2.91	76.8	60.2	10.3	23.2	17.6	292	668	1,655	109	1,546	30,082	27.4	41.1
Danville	11,796	2.58	59.6	35.8	20.7	40.4	30.9	2,498	2,391	7,488	1,556	5,932	21,153	51.3	16.5
Decatur	28,341	2.30	54.3	36.0	14.5	45.7	40.9	3,599	3,049	4,194	539	3,655	46,382	44.8	20.2
DeKalb	15,315	2.54	51.8	35.4	15.5	48.2	33.4	3,705	1,661	3,860	518	3,342	21,901	33.9	27.7
Des Plaines	21,382	2.68	71.9	57.3	9.5	28.1	25.0	933	617	1,051	87	964	44,330	34.7	38.0
Downers Grove	19,734	2.43	64.4	54.0	8.5	35.6	30.2	712	684	1,371	66	1,305	34,572	15.9	57.8
East St. Louis	10,655	2.49	51.2	17.9	26.5	48.8	44.3	NA	1,361	5,084	2,828	2,256	17,228	52.6	12.5
Elgin	37,195	3.03	71.8	53.5	12.6	28.2	23.3	1,661	1,801	1,595	209	1,386	72,556	47.7	23.1
Elk Grove Village	11,648	2.48	65.8	53.1	7.1	34.2	29.5	NA	535	1,609	75	1,534	22,050	29.0	33.1
Elmhurst	17,367	2.69	70.9	61.8	6.8	29.1	26.5	1,252	562	1,213	56	1,157	31,562	17.7	57.5
Evanston	27,760	2.44	52.6	41.7	7.4	47.4	34.4	6,994	1,801	2,379	172	2,207	48,251	21.5	63.8
Freeport	10,720	2.21	64.3	42.5	15.5	35.7	30.2	715	700	2,886	198	2,688	17,449	44.3	24.3
Galesburg	12,579	2.22	51.0	32.9	10.8	49.0	41.9	4,172	1,111	3,573	399	3,174	21,970	49.3	16.8
Glendale Heights	11,097	2.97	69.8	45.7	16.8	30.2	21.9	NA	590	1,712	78	1,633	22,934	37.8	29.2
Glen Ellyn	10,615	2.63	72.2	60.7	9.6	27.8	23.8	NA	270	955	92	863	18,572	13.5	69.0
Glenview	17,249	2.64	70.8	62.3	6.3	29.2	28.2	806	652	1,358	85	1,273	32,505	19.6	63.3
Granite City	11,887	2.46	64.5	48.4	12.0	35.5	30.0	250	791	2,737	661	2,076	21,285	51.9	11.6
Gurnee	11,415	2.69	70.3	53.2	14.5	29.7	24.7	NA	1,293	4,169	74	4,095	20,207	20.8	55.1
Hanover Park	11,049	3.20	77.3	55.4	17.8	22.7	17.4	NA	295	768	102	667	21,279	41.1	30.1
Harvey	7,008	2.97	67.0	31.0	30.7	33.0	30.3	NA	734	2,915	743	2,172	13,459	52.5	11.9
Highland Park	12,506	2.47	74.4	67.3	5.1	25.6	21.9	269	286	962	71	891	22,629	10.2	77.6
Hoffman Estates	18,143	2.74	73.8	60.7	7.6	26.2	23.0	NA	484	928	105	822	35,581	26.1	50.2
Joliet	46,721	3.09	68.9	51.0	12.5	31.1	26.7	2,947	3,289	2,224	330	1,894	92,380	50.7	20.6
Kankakee	9,435	2.58	55.8	31.7	18.7	44.2	37.7	1,681	1,233	4,651	698	3,953	16,944	54.8	15.0
Lake in the Hills	10,094	2.97	75.0	64.2	5.2	25.0	19.5	NA	171	589	83	507	18,572	36.5	28.4
Lansing	11,805	2.62	65.4	39.5	22.4	34.6	30.9	NA	1,999	7,052	399	6,653	20,022	45.9	21.5
Lombard	17,066	2.46	64.6	49.3	10.0	35.4	30.1	545	994	2,266	109	2,157	30,337	25.9	46.7
McHenry	9,474	2.80	78.5	58.8	9.9	21.5	17.3	NA	443	1,667	150	1,516	18,619	38.6	27.2
Melrose Park	7,507	3.31	66.5	44.8	12.4	33.5	25.1	117	372	1,466	201	1,265	16,299	64.3	13.5
Moline	17,305	2.29	62.1	43.7	12.2	37.9	33.2	NA	1,655	3,893	461	3,432	27,944	38.2	26.4
Mount Prospect	19,777	2.66	72.9	64.4	5.8	27.1	22.1	NA	590	1,076	47	1,028	37,002	31.8	45.8
Mundelein	11,729	3.09	82.9	69.0	10.0	17.1	11.5	NA	322	1,016	85	931	23,972	36.5	38.9
Naperville	50,008	2.92	77.7	69.2	5.8	22.3	16.3	2,798	1,687	1,139	63	1,077	97,975	12.6	69.6
Niles	12,726	2.44	62.9	48.4	10.7	37.1	32.6	1,288	731	2,446	97	2,349	25,670	38.9	36.3
Normal	19,180	2.62	55.9	42.6	10.8	44.1	27.6	4,694	1,224	2,237	263	1,973	28,441	22.5	48.3
Northbrook	13,023	2.68	78.0	71.3	6.7	22.0	22.0	721	393	1,165	33	1,132	25,008	9.8	75.5
North Chicago	7,074	2.43	54.9	34.2	14.2	45.1	38.6	10,265	NA	NA	NA	NA	14,076	44.2	27.8
Oak Forest	11,169	2.47	60.8	44.4	10.9	39.2	32.0	NA	342	1,218	150	1,068	19,658	38.2	28.7
Oak Lawn	20,930	2.66	64.9	52.7	8.7	35.1	32.5	514	1,016	1,789	139	1,650	39,510	31.5	36.8
Oak Park	21,589	2.40	60.2	47.5	9.2	39.8	31.7	535	1,603	3,061	206	2,855	36,835	11.6	73.1
O'Fallon	11,292	2.68	69.6	52.6	12.2	30.4	27.1	NA	563	1,937	155	1,782	19,952	16.4	52.4
Orland Park	21,928	2.67	74.2	60.9	7.9	25.8	22.9	625	1,359	2,303	42	2,261	44,130	30.2	46.6
Oswego	11,419	3.25	77.1	69.7	4.4	22.9	15.5	NA	431	1,243	92	1,150	22,215	28.0	43.7
Palatine	27,190	2.52	64.1	45.8	13.0	35.9	30.6	201	637	917	53	864	47,351	25.9	51.4
Park Ridge	13,908	2.67	70.2	59.3	9.3	29.8	27.1	575	387	1,024	32	992	25,303	18.3	60.7
Pekin	14,503	2.25	58.6	43.0	10.7	41.4	34.2	1,638	803	2,430	421	2,009	24,799	47.2	18.6
Peoria	45,862	2.43	56.3	40.1	11.9	43.7	38.9	4,062	5,304	4,608	760	3,848	76,632	37.0	35.7
Plainfield	12,870	3.50	90.1	77.4	8.7	9.9	7.7	NA	367	852	86	766	26,765	23.8	49.0
Quincy	15,987	2.44	61.0	48.3	11.7	39.0	31.2	1,250	1,532	3,755	512	3,243	26,581	42.7	23.5
Rockford	59,068	2.44	58.9	35.7	17.0	41.1	36.8	3,987	8,036	5,453	1,664	3,789	98,649	50.3	19.2
Rock Island	15,961	2.23	55.6	36.7	15.7	44.4	39.0	2,978	1,200	3,113	410	2,703	24,577	42.1	25.2
Romeoville	12,372	3.19	73.3	60.9	9.3	26.7	21.3	1,282	668	1,681	113	1,568	25,503	42.5	26.5
Round Lake Beach	8,236	3.31	82.0	61.7	15.5	18.0	16.3	NA	619	2,227	137	2,090	16,643	52.0	17.8
St. Charles	11,817	2.67	72.9	58.6	11.9	27.1	23.2	482	553	1,648	128	1,520	22,341	22.9	51.5
Schaumburg	29,898	2.43	63.0	52.0	7.9	37.0	32.3	NA	1,760	2,354	99	2,255	54,522	23.7	52.9
Skokie	22,323	2.83	67.2	56.5	7.3	32.8	29.7	820	1,715	2,646	244	2,402	45,041	28.0	48.1
Springfield	51,116	2.17	57.0	36.2	15.9	43.0	35.9	3,722	6,459	5,541	1,116	4,425	78,970	35.5	34.1
Streamwood	12,935	3.16	77.8	60.3	12.4	22.2	17.2	NA	614	1,509	118	1,391	28,022	44.9	26.1
Tinley Park	22,000	2.53	67.8	57.7	8.2	32.2	30.4	NA	814	1,423	84	1,339	40,180	35.1	35.5
Urbana	17,182	2.03	39.2	25.0	9.4	60.8	44.7	7,127	1,705	4,015	382	3,634	20,706	20.8	59.6
Vernon Hills	8,997	2.43	61.0	52.1	5.9	39.0	33.7	397	1,494	71	1,422	15,169	16.4	58.7

1. No spouse present.   2. Data for serious crimes have not been adjusted for underreporting. This may affect comparability between geographic areas and over time.   3. Per 100,000 population estimated by the FBI.   4. Persons 25 years old and over.

Table D. Cities — Income and Housing

City	Money income, 2017					Median earnings, 2017			Housing units, 2017				
	Households												
	Median income	Percent with income less than $20,000	Percent with income of $200,000 or more	Median family income	Median non-family income	All persons	Men	Women	Total	Occupied	Percent owner occupied	Median value[1] (dollars)	Median gross rent (dollars)
	42	43	44	45	46	47	48	49	50	51	52	53	54

ILLINOIS— Cont'd

City	42	43	44	45	46	47	48	49	50	51	52	53	54
Burbank	54,804	9.8	5.4	69,259	38,980	36,646	46,140	27,860	9,089	8,705	74.5	181,000	956
Calumet City	43,763	19.7	0.0	47,045	27,963	24,784	26,321	22,742	14,241	11,800	49.1	96,100	948
Carbondale	20,230	49.8	2.8	24,989	15,175	12,109	12,734	12,010	13,378	9,764	33.1	124,700	687
Carol Stream	78,268	6.7	6.1	89,563	56,970	40,146	43,644	35,077	14,581	13,978	65.8	238,200	1,156
Carpentersville	59,247	12.0	3.6	65,581	47,939	30,114	37,483	22,907	11,550	11,242	73.4	167,400	1,040
Champaign	43,785	27.4	8.0	75,150	23,646	22,932	24,953	20,983	40,496	35,590	39.8	173,400	870
Chicago	55,295	20.5	7.7	64,441	43,203	36,069	40,577	31,777	1,212,932	1,047,695	44.9	255,900	1,067
Chicago Heights	52,734	23.5	0.3	67,685	26,698	34,655	38,050	31,280	10,330	9,261	69.1	96,600	900
Cicero	51,186	12.8	0.9	53,437	27,647	27,528	31,526	24,959	25,265	22,600	50.7	158,300	885
Collinsville	50,909	24.8	1.7	60,588	30,980	30,604	44,230	21,115	12,542	11,439	79.0	119,600	817
Crystal Lake	86,986	8.0	9.9	102,543	41,334	45,228	52,617	33,981	16,502	16,093	74.7	235,400	1,321
Danville	37,407	30.4	2.7	43,697	25,880	27,360	30,496	25,465	14,496	11,796	58.8	62,300	686
Decatur	43,225	23.9	2.0	60,899	26,900	26,032	36,942	21,007	34,633	28,341	67.2	80,100	662
DeKalb	43,270	26.0	1.5	58,602	28,272	15,627	22,214	11,607	16,722	15,315	33.4	151,100	801
Des Plaines	69,525	15.1	6.8	81,229	36,625	40,528	46,065	32,129	22,922	21,382	78.7	253,300	1,108
Downers Grove	85,888	14.1	13.4	110,790	37,919	50,576	67,230	36,387	21,040	19,734	77.2	360,100	1,346
East St. Louis	19,867	50.2	1.2	40,625	11,794	21,527	26,127	14,369	13,429	10,655	43.4	62,100	588
Elgin	67,646	12.1	3.5	75,227	41,091	32,158	34,522	31,231	39,192	37,195	70.5	189,000	976
Elk Grove Village	79,887	6.6	6.3	94,503	46,540	42,078	48,854	38,750	12,554	11,648	68.9	270,600	1,185
Elmhurst	102,693	7.8	21.7	143,872	48,499	51,789	69,966	35,867	18,196	17,367	85.8	410,500	1,507
Evanston	77,821	15.0	14.2	115,940	41,040	38,100	44,257	31,277	31,593	27,760	55.5	374,300	1,393
Freeport	36,771	27.6	2.4	51,066	25,132	22,733	33,466	18,955	12,575	10,720	62.3	68,200	655
Galesburg	39,483	27.8	0.6	60,382	19,858	21,609	27,031	19,159	14,885	12,579	57.9	77,200	581
Glendale Heights	75,580	6.9	1.8	80,015	48,413	32,808	40,483	26,998	11,872	11,097	66.9	190,000	1,246
Glen Ellyn	120,573	10.9	27.5	141,422	43,809	51,306	78,549	30,197	11,234	10,615	77.0	445,900	993
Glenview	102,255	6.5	24.2	135,777	56,643	51,779	67,887	35,236	19,271	17,249	83.4	511,400	1,856
Granite City	50,075	26.4	0.0	63,995	19,203	27,758	32,002	26,076	14,153	11,887	61.9	82,700	709
Gurnee	87,932	9.8	14.4	109,913	57,699	42,847	60,674	30,333	11,846	11,415	70.4	271,400	1,138
Hanover Park	68,050	9.0	0.7	71,482	46,681	32,102	42,079	27,141	11,164	11,049	75.7	193,500	1,456
Harvey	28,966	32.1	2.5	32,736	25,935	26,239	30,771	23,611	10,404	7,008	57.9	72,300	848
Highland Park	152,374	8.5	37.7	171,823	58,764	70,331	83,858	32,322	13,254	12,506	83.0	605,900	1,843
Hoffman Estates	83,077	7.0	10.4	94,517	50,507	41,485	50,308	39,944	18,758	18,143	71.2	277,200	1,371
Joliet	65,725	12.1	4.2	78,929	34,244	31,992	41,794	25,516	50,687	46,721	71.1	179,700	988
Kankakee	32,906	32.1	1.1	48,466	20,854	30,387	31,869	21,735	11,981	9,435	56.0	88,700	686
Lake in the Hills	90,974	2.7	8.2	100,111	52,049	41,863	51,397	37,350	10,094	10,094	82.2	213,100	1,486
Lansing	49,799	10.2	2.4	54,986	44,208	34,727	47,485	27,246	13,125	11,805	58.6	123,500	962
Lombard	81,718	7.1	6.7	93,520	55,811	51,044	55,796	41,718	18,029	17,066	74.0	247,900	1,365
McHenry	69,824	15.3	5.7	80,777	31,245	35,601	42,414	28,807	9,892	9,474	74.7	203,600	1,155
Melrose Park	50,429	17.2	1.8	54,725	45,620	25,229	26,886	21,085	8,192	7,507	41.7	185,700	1,053
Moline	51,643	14.7	3.7	70,059	32,905	29,189	33,865	24,708	19,436	17,305	64.6	116,100	798
Mount Prospect	77,369	10.6	8.5	90,676	35,660	46,567	52,209	36,268	21,545	19,777	68.2	331,000	1,110
Mundelein	92,642	5.0	5.1	98,764	58,203	40,000	46,218	30,512	12,396	11,729	74.8	231,900	1,445
Naperville	126,217	4.0	19.4	141,634	65,538	56,457	80,806	34,898	52,763	50,008	78.2	410,000	1,454
Niles	58,129	18.8	2.7	78,892	26,692	40,376	46,883	32,541	13,296	12,726	75.8	291,800	985
Normal	60,577	24.6	5.2	94,128	30,095	27,190	34,033	19,932	21,543	19,180	56.8	173,900	764
Northbrook	142,920	8.0	30.3	162,148	38,003	70,330	104,117	43,625	14,901	13,023	85.3	516,600	2,055
North Chicago	32,882	24.4	0.6	47,603	22,576	21,145	21,365	20,000	8,209	7,074	32.8	118,300	1,075
Oak Forest	63,067	14.4	1.8	72,364	46,244	37,615	40,498	36,479	11,211	11,169	75.9	187,500	1,097
Oak Lawn	66,912	13.6	5.1	91,706	33,687	42,402	51,684	33,413	23,375	20,930	77.8	211,000	1,049
Oak Park	92,713	13.8	18.3	128,034	56,494	58,275	66,008	50,118	23,198	21,589	58.8	388,600	1,176
O'Fallon	71,201	11.1	10.3	90,275	57,379	42,462	46,662	38,310	12,404	11,292	60.7	208,900	1,017
Orland Park	82,112	4.7	9.8	95,173	41,928	42,206	46,761	39,538	22,528	21,928	83.7	273,000	1,223
Oswego	125,084	2.2	19.2	137,342	66,102	45,059	47,347	32,124	11,920	11,419	82.6	268,900	796
Palatine	71,794	11.2	11.2	99,413	56,260	45,668	54,266	35,904	29,254	27,190	67.2	285,300	1,233
Park Ridge	105,773	6.9	21.3	136,159	51,032	61,548	72,295	52,123	15,089	13,908	84.7	427,200	1,456
Pekin	52,112	15.8	2.3	64,930	31,609	29,256	37,313	21,969	15,406	14,503	72.5	103,600	669
Peoria	48,146	23.2	4.8	65,917	30,232	30,885	36,336	26,812	55,675	45,862	59.7	131,100	738
Plainfield	123,242	3.6	18.4	130,527	80,477	56,090	65,855	36,766	13,104	12,870	91.5	328,400	1,750
Quincy	41,635	22.7	3.9	62,479	25,234	30,740	38,845	20,991	17,820	15,987	66.0	119,900	660
Rockford	44,765	23.1	2.8	53,536	26,795	27,005	31,621	24,256	67,220	59,068	56.2	88,800	742
Rock Island	47,043	26.0	1.1	58,990	34,313	24,290	30,718	17,160	17,791	15,961	60.9	106,200	668
Romeoville	75,067	7.6	0.8	78,637	41,104	35,291	41,474	26,565	14,163	12,372	85.4	176,100	1,634
Round Lake Beach	81,752	8.4	4.8	87,634	41,250	35,813	38,704	31,945	8,728	8,236	75.1	142,500	1,330
St. Charles	94,292	6.0	18.3	125,993	57,158	47,252	68,118	35,453	12,088	11,817	71.6	287,400	1,378
Schaumburg	80,227	9.5	11.2	94,203	52,138	49,438	55,721	42,440	32,017	29,898	66.1	285,700	1,394
Skokie	65,792	13.5	10.6	86,919	29,747	38,514	44,349	34,934	24,472	22,323	65.8	327,600	1,184
Springfield	51,313	21.6	4.6	69,995	33,150	32,652	42,007	30,101	56,522	51,116	63.5	124,400	749
Streamwood	79,202	8.3	6.6	87,977	51,005	36,600	42,115	30,314	13,643	12,935	85.3	204,400	1,511
Tinley Park	76,172	7.0	3.2	95,965	46,461	42,499	57,573	31,948	23,406	22,000	84.6	234,400	1,235
Urbana	32,071	30.3	2.8	57,023	22,692	20,100	20,559	16,367	18,902	17,182	37.3	143,200	752
Vernon Hills	86,351	12.6	16.5	121,500	60,785	61,773	69,615	51,323	9,329	8,997	64.3	346,800	1,663

1. Based on population estimated by the American Community Survey.   2. Includes units rented or sold but not occupied.   3. Specified owner-occupied units; $1,000,000 represents $1,000,000 or more.   4. 50.0 represents 50 percent or more.   5. 10.0 represents 10 percent or less.

Table D. Cities — Commuting, Computer Access, Migration, Labor Force, and Employment

City	Commuting[1], 2017 Percent Commuting	With commutes of 30 minutes or more	Computer access[2], 2017 Percent With a computer in the house	With Internet access	Migration, 2017 Percent who lived in the same house one year ago	Percent who lived in another state or county one year ago	Civilian labor force, 2018 Total	Percent change 2017-2018	Unemployment Total	Rate[3]	Civilian employment[4], 2017 Population age 16 and older Number	Percent in labor force	Population age 16 to 64 Number	Percent who worked full-year full-time
	55	56	57	58	59	60	61	62	63	64	65	66	67	68
ILLINOIS— Cont'd														
Burbank	75.7	54.4	89.2	80.8	NA	NA	13,991	-1.0	566	4.0	21,789	61.8	17,439	45.1
Calumet City	69.2	60.0	84.1	77.9	85.4	0.8	15,989	-1.8	994	6.2	27,672	69.1	23,915	39.1
Carbondale	69.0	13.1	93.7	85.2	56.0	30.0	11,670	0.3	550	4.7	22,881	46.6	20,760	20.7
Carol Stream	80.6	45.0	95.1	91.7	84.2	9.1	23,608	-0.9	704	3.0	32,110	72.1	26,983	59.1
Carpentersville	77.0	41.5	97.0	92.7	88.8	4.5	19,361	1.9	1,245	6.4	26,411	75.4	24,322	48.3
Champaign	69.9	6.9	95.6	84.4	76.1	11.5	44,168	0.3	1,910	4.3	73,011	60.4	65,195	41.7
Chicago	48.6	62.5	88.7	79.1	85.4	3.6	1,345,740	-1.1	56,985	4.2	2,212,557	66.7	1,880,019	50.3
Chicago Heights	76.0	44.2	78.8	72.7	NA	NA	12,647	-1.8	750	5.9	21,762	64.3	17,411	54.9
Cicero	69.7	58.7	88.8	71.1	91.0	2.3	35,959	-1.1	1,535	4.3	61,831	66.6	55,080	53.1
Collinsville	89.0	34.0	85.0	82.1	86.1	10.4	12,986	0.3	598	4.6	20,933	63.2	16,009	45.7
Crystal Lake	82.5	40.6	95.3	93.1	88.5	4.8	22,438	-0.9	694	3.1	35,324	71.0	28,920	54.1
Danville	79.4	17.1	77.8	70.6	86.2	3.4	12,365	-2.1	843	6.8	24,872	51.2	19,412	39.5
Decatur	82.4	13.1	88.0	79.3	81.1	4.2	32,609	1.0	2,027	6.2	55,032	59.4	41,031	43.5
DeKalb	80.2	24.6	91.8	83.2	75.9	9.8	22,562	1.3	1,017	4.5	35,203	62.4	31,399	33.1
Des Plaines	74.5	42.8	93.1	87.8	91.3	1.8	32,179	-0.8	1,092	3.4	49,357	64.6	37,582	58.3
Downers Grove	74.2	47.4	92.5	90.6	85.6	5.3	27,170	-0.8	767	2.8	38,541	64.4	30,066	54.6
East St. Louis	70.5	35.7	73.0	57.7	95.7	1.6	9,027	0.8	750	8.3	21,487	52.0	17,490	29.1
Elgin	80.2	41.2	92.9	88.3	90.6	4.5	57,901	1.1	3,106	5.4	86,622	70.5	73,761	53.9
Elk Grove Village	83.5	33.2	93.1	88.0	89.8	3.2	18,852	-0.8	603	3.2	25,131	65.7	19,073	60.5
Elmhurst	68.3	49.0	94.3	92.2	91.2	5.0	23,536	-0.8	689	2.9	38,494	67.0	29,923	51.5
Evanston	46.8	51.8	94.2	88.6	80.9	7.8	38,931	-0.7	1,260	3.2	62,669	57.8	50,243	41.8
Freeport	NA	16.2	87.4	77.4	86.6	4.5	10,744	1.3	609	5.7	20,020	57.6	14,933	42.4
Galesburg	79.0	11.8	79.4	71.2	89.7	5.0	12,411	-1.2	704	5.7	27,016	53.4	20,998	35.8
Glendale Heights	79.7	43.7	95.4	91.9	83.9	3.9	18,976	-0.9	651	3.4	26,938	75.3	23,136	61.4
Glen Ellyn	75.3	45.2	97.1	94.7	85.7	7.9	14,109	-0.7	411	2.9	22,019	64.3	17,739	49.7
Glenview	68.3	50.7	91.5	87.9	94.0	2.2	23,089	-0.7	663	2.9	37,226	56.8	26,633	46.5
Granite City	85.4	29.1	89.2	79.0	NA	NA	13,205	0.2	679	5.1	24,318	57.1	19,482	39.4
Gurnee	85.4	43.7	96.7	92.9	81.2	9.2	17,578	1.4	722	4.1	25,424	76.1	22,208	59.1
Hanover Park	80.5	46.3	95.7	85.1	87.0	5.5	20,437	-1.0	843	4.1	26,616	73.2	22,934	54.7
Harvey	75.0	56.1	89.5	75.7	NA	NA	8,055	-1.7	639	7.9	16,921	49.9	13,598	27.3
Highland Park	70.0	41.6	NA	NA	90.0	4.1	15,524	1.4	543	3.5	24,918	60.6	17,671	46.7
Hoffman Estates	77.4	54.1	97.2	93.6	87.3	4.9	29,659	-0.8	907	3.1	40,566	68.0	32,145	54.1
Joliet	86.9	48.3	91.4	85.0	87.3	7.4	74,167	-1.2	3,665	4.9	111,639	69.9	96,522	55.8
Kankakee	78.1	20.6	79.0	65.9	90.5	1.5	11,257	1.0	842	7.5	20,378	59.1	16,467	45.4
Lake in the Hills	88.7	50.0	NA	NA	86.9	5.5	16,045	-0.9	556	3.5	23,214	83.1	21,075	59.0
Lansing	82.4	55.4	91.2	86.8	NA	NA	14,119	-1.0	680	4.8	23,963	60.2	18,703	44.8
Lombard	80.8	51.7	94.2	91.7	82.6	4.5	24,959	-0.7	763	3.1	35,012	70.9	29,146	58.7
McHenry	89.1	42.8	94.4	92.9	93.5	2.8	14,102	-0.7	496	3.5	22,236	67.4	19,094	45.9
Melrose Park	65.3	39.9	86.5	71.3	NA	NA	11,783	-0.9	487	4.1	19,130	66.4	17,118	47.9
Moline	83.1	17.0	89.0	81.4	82.3	3.8	21,870	1.0	1,100	5.0	32,196	67.5	24,102	51.2
Mount Prospect	76.9	51.7	92.5	83.8	87.2	3.8	29,005	-0.7	849	2.9	41,339	67.9	33,230	56.5
Mundelein	82.6	43.7	96.2	92.5	90.2	6.5	18,567	1.4	794	4.3	27,747	71.0	23,161	62.4
Naperville	74.1	49.8	98.2	96.3	87.3	8.4	78,025	-0.8	2,325	3.0	115,742	69.6	97,029	55.0
Niles	77.2	58.3	81.2	75.6	NA	NA	13,630	-0.8	467	3.4	28,158	58.5	20,179	51.6
Normal	79.3	14.8	92.8	77.2	79.0	10.4	28,083	-1.0	1,146	4.1	45,616	63.9	39,254	42.6
Northbrook	67.6	52.8	94.0	92.4	NA	NA	16,110	-0.7	476	3.0	28,261	61.0	20,822	54.2
North Chicago	43.5	20.1	93.1	82.7	69.5	25.4	9,205	1.4	554	6.0	23,081	79.0	21,552	59.1
Oak Forest	80.6	57.4	94.5	85.0	NA	NA	14,878	-1.1	563	3.8	23,279	67.1	18,948	54.4
Oak Lawn	76.9	63.6	85.7	75.9	NA	NA	28,161	-1.0	1,070	3.8	44,518	60.4	34,719	49.1
Oak Park	56.1	69.0	93.3	86.2	89.4	4.0	29,452	-0.8	924	3.1	41,620	71.3	32,985	56.4
O'Fallon	88.0	35.7	98.0	94.9	83.6	9.8	14,052	0.7	608	4.3	22,734	69.3	19,283	54.8
Orland Park	83.0	56.4	93.2	87.6	89.5	3.9	30,122	-0.8	954	3.2	49,495	60.7	35,116	55.6
Oswego	80.5	41.1	NA	NA	NA	NA	18,926	-0.7	618	3.3	27,237	73.6	23,596	59.9
Palatine	75.7	49.0	94.9	89.0	83.7	4.8	38,913	-0.8	1,232	3.2	53,236	71.9	44,349	57.4
Park Ridge	68.3	50.4	93.3	88.5	89.9	0.9	19,348	-0.8	580	3.0	28,550	61.3	21,184	55.7
Pekin	93.1	25.7	89.3	82.3	87.1	4.8	15,237	0.8	857	5.6	28,107	55.6	21,528	48.0
Peoria	79.7	15.5	86.5	74.1	84.4	3.5	52,609	1.2	2,995	5.7	90,635	58.5	71,241	43.9
Plainfield	85.2	54.5	98.1	95.9	89.6	5.3	22,692	-0.8	700	3.1	32,849	73.8	28,966	54.2
Quincy	75.8	12.0	88.2	79.0	82.7	5.6	19,528	1.5	786	4.0	31,410	61.6	23,489	52.6
Rockford	75.2	24.7	89.2	80.2	82.7	5.6	67,017	1.2	4,548	6.8	115,847	62.7	91,386	42.6
Rock Island	75.9	20.6	87.5	80.6	80.9	5.6	18,240	1.1	1,009	5.5	31,775	60.8	25,418	40.0
Romeoville	81.6	44.9	95.8	91.6	93.3	2.5	19,710	-1.0	868	4.4	31,182	67.5	26,460	53.9
Round Lake Beach	83.5	57.8	89.5	85.4	NA	NA	15,241	1.6	1,015	6.7	20,914	76.1	18,450	62.4
St. Charles	72.2	51.1	95.2	92.2	84.1	6.5	18,628	1.7	704	3.8	25,395	73.0	20,145	61.9
Schaumburg	79.8	49.0	95.0	92.7	88.7	5.2	43,629	-0.7	1,331	3.1	59,762	71.6	48,166	63.0
Skokie	67.3	46.8	87.9	81.8	89.9	2.4	32,341	-0.8	1,048	3.2	50,665	59.5	38,319	51.1
Springfield	83.6	13.6	87.5	78.4	80.5	5.8	59,338	0.1	2,673	4.5	91,787	60.0	72,089	48.2
Streamwood	84.9	50.4	94.8	89.7	NA	NA	23,209	-0.9	882	3.8	32,964	70.4	28,075	56.6
Tinley Park	80.3	44.9	92.5	87.1	92.8	3.4	31,677	-0.9	1,000	3.2	46,219	68.1	38,056	47.7
Urbana	51.8	11.0	94.8	77.1	68.1	21.5	21,090	0.2	931	4.4	37,869	54.3	32,612	34.2
Vernon Hills	77.0	44.9	91.6	87.1	87.8	5.6	15,370	1.5	569	3.7	16,880	71.2	13,857	61.1

1. Employed persons.　2. Households.　3. Percent of civilian labor force.　4. Persons 16 years old and over.

Table D. Cities — Construction, Wholesale Trade, and Retail Trade

City	Value of residential construction authorized by building permits, 2018			Wholesale trade[1], 2012				Retail trade[2], 2012			
	New construction ($1,000)	Number of housing units	Percent single family	Number of establishments	Number of employees	Sales (mil dol)	Annual payroll (mil dol)	Number of establishments	Number of employees	Sales (mil dol)	Annual payroll (mil dol)
	69	70	71	72	73	74	75	76	77	78	79
ILLINOIS— Cont'd											
Burbank	1,329	8	100.0	6	25	6.3	0.6	90	1,363	370.6	25.7
Calumet City	0	0	0.0	12	D	D	D	173	2,769	550.6	57.6
Carbondale	1,021	7	100.0	10	108	32.8	4.7	157	2,760	760.2	56.4
Carol Stream	150	2	100.0	109	2,642	3,245.6	162.4	91	1,508	606.1	43.9
Carpentersville	0	0	0.0	14	D	D	D	52	882	251.1	19.5
Champaign	158,854	1,107	11.9	66	1,267	670.3	52.9	394	6,538	1,496.1	132.6
Chicago	811,168	6,449	6.8	2,310	37,189	33,135.0	2,291.0	7,285	85,388	22,627.3	2,221.8
Chicago Heights	0	0	0.0	37	1,028	850.8	52.8	68	758	172.0	15.8
Cicero	0	0	0.0	37	638	460.5	29.8	134	2,028	638.7	46.1
Collinsville	4,166	31	35.5	27	201	135.3	10.1	89	1,754	465.6	39.7
Crystal Lake	6,190	20	100.0	68	662	565.9	35.7	210	3,601	940.5	83.8
Danville	819	5	100.0	42	D	D	D	150	2,342	537.7	50.3
Decatur	400	1	100.0	83	1,104	2,699.4	56.1	296	4,330	1,204.4	106.5
DeKalb	3,142	23	100.0	15	D	D	D	133	2,587	508.9	50.7
Des Plaines	41,323	209	45.9	138	2,522	3,236.9	181.8	171	3,047	972.2	96.9
Downers Grove	28,994	63	100.0	113	2,190	3,356.2	202.4	227	4,336	1,393.7	112.5
East St. Louis	0	0	0.0	20	201	462.1	8.2	61	378	91.2	9.3
Elgin	31,402	146	100.0	193	3,654	3,558.4	242.5	240	3,813	1,223.6	105.5
Elk Grove Village	0	0	0.0	447	7,000	5,203.5	432.9	116	2,416	692.4	70.3
Elmhurst	88,325	259	36.7	130	3,294	1,738.7	321.0	158	2,107	726.8	65.1
Evanston	6,439	12	33.3	53	529	468.7	33.7	213	3,480	940.1	95.6
Freeport	200	1	100.0	22	161	104.1	5.8	111	1,665	380.4	36.5
Galesburg	921	10	40.0	23	362	188.5	15.0	153	3,184	717.4	70.5
Glendale Heights	0	0	0.0	66	1,605	1,089.3	101.3	68	1,459	410.3	38.7
Glen Ellyn	18,442	29	100.0	32	340	188.3	19.0	95	1,154	271.5	25.2
Glenview	51,149	209	19.6	100	1,478	1,320.7	86.2	159	3,471	1,344.4	153.0
Granite City	920	6	100.0	27	311	290.1	14.0	88	1,361	376.4	36.8
Gurnee	3,522	22	100.0	64	869	752.5	45.7	255	4,991	1,080.4	98.3
Hanover Park	302	1	100.0	29	1,122	1,993.0	59.8	68	872	216.5	19.1
Harvey	0	0	0.0	22	320	102.2	15.7	64	362	108.6	8.2
Highland Park	29,206	77	29.9	48	172	715.5	14.9	166	2,543	1,008.3	82.9
Hoffman Estates	14,350	71	100.0	80	1,536	1,900.4	178.6	116	2,421	792.2	78.3
Joliet	57,277	285	86.7	93	1,662	1,981.6	93.5	408	6,796	1,819.2	161.5
Kankakee	7,600	56	0.0	31	591	442.4	22.2	84	1,152	292.6	26.5
Lake in the Hills	2,700	11	100.0	21	D	D	D	43	708	221.3	19.9
Lansing	0	0	0.0	31	310	117.6	20.6	103	1,840	430.2	44.8
Lombard	8,648	27	100.0	106	1,333	3,230.1	72.3	239	4,273	911.9	91.9
McHenry	10,390	84	100.0	50	2,143	975.7	109.9	130	1,633	406.3	38.1
Melrose Park	400	4	0.0	59	1,157	832.9	67.1	100	2,887	931.5	73.3
Moline	3,637	46	32.6	34	D	D	D	259	4,706	1,022.6	104.8
Mount Prospect	1,582	4	100.0	81	1,167	1,546.9	87.3	162	3,666	4,621.7	110.6
Mundelein	4,921	35	94.3	69	698	552.8	45.2	110	1,413	332.5	32.4
Naperville	149,994	572	47.7	224	2,764	3,346.8	193.6	518	9,553	4,083.3	277.8
Niles	1,100	2	100.0	100	2,067	1,060.5	148.9	273	6,549	1,744.6	155.6
Normal	5,037	95	38.9	24	D	D	D	131	2,949	701.4	59.6
Northbrook	22,398	37	100.0	188	3,410	5,037.6	390.6	259	4,718	1,282.0	139.8
North Chicago	0	0	0.0	11	415	352.7	29.2	35	124	69.5	3.0
Oak Forest	750	4	100.0	21	89	40.6	3.4	59	630	184.5	14.8
Oak Lawn	790	3	100.0	28	89	34.9	3.0	162	3,509	1,151.6	95.4
Oak Park	27,663	313	2.9	22	46	58.3	2.3	154	1,491	311.4	31.7
O'Fallon	45,886	166	100.0	15	68	64.4	3.1	84	2,087	860.4	62.7
Orland Park	9,287	29	100.0	51	350	129.1	17.4	371	8,020	1,924.8	186.5
Oswego	48,021	438	25.6	25	117	64.1	6.6	94	2,158	463.8	44.6
Palatine	5,126	11	100.0	69	446	414.6	20.3	186	3,623	853.2	84.9
Park Ridge	15,115	27	100.0	52	191	275.6	12.6	93	1,009	340.9	32.3
Pekin	602	4	100.0	15	D	D	D	125	2,127	574.9	51.7
Peoria	11,285	32	100.0	150	2,501	1,151.3	116.8	502	7,845	1,927.7	188.2
Plainfield	40,778	180	100.0	28	361	318.9	29.1	97	1,781	459.8	37.4
Quincy	9,824	45	95.6	71	1,290	693.4	52.9	256	4,452	985.0	94.2
Rockford	8,492	62	25.8	187	2,468	1,826.9	122.4	551	8,326	2,140.2	193.8
Rock Island	962	3	100.0	64	1,280	853.6	61.3	79	969	240.6	25.4
Romeoville	27,214	157	28.7	67	1,833	5,959.8	104.7	59	1,194	330.6	23.6
Round Lake Beach	164	1	100.0	6	18	5.0	0.8	54	1,518	323.6	32.1
St. Charles	15,667	124	22.6	102	1,005	1,648.1	55.9	160	3,016	906.6	82.0
Schaumburg	1,438	4	100.0	270	4,850	6,838.8	373.8	483	11,457	2,790.9	301.5
Skokie	6,564	14	100.0	122	D	D	D	334	5,566	1,148.2	125.8
Springfield	45,312	293	25.3	130	2,845	2,386.0	122.5	586	10,451	2,625.3	242.6
Streamwood	0	0	0.0	21	83	41.8	3.7	88	1,637	374.7	37.3
Tinley Park	6,854	27	100.0	64	739	394.4	38.2	157	3,495	1,195.9	93.4
Urbana	29,422	185	21.6	27	D	D	D	83	1,532	423.9	38.8
Vernon Hills	29,511	54	100.0	68	2,464	2,447.8	174.3	214	5,361	2,085.3	149.8

1. Merchant wholesalers except manufacturers' sales branches and offices. 2. Establishments with payroll.

Table D. Cities — **Real Estate, Professional Services, and Manufacturing**

City	Real estate and rental and leasing, 2012				Professional, scientific, and technical services[1], 2012				Manufacturing, 2012			
	Number of establish-ments	Number of employees	Receipts (mil dol)	Annual payroll (mil dol)	Number of establish-ments	Number of employees	Receipts (mil dol)	Annual payroll (mil dol)	Number of establish-ments	Number of employees	Receipts (mil dol)	Annual payroll (mil dol)
	80	81	82	83	84	85	86	87	88	89	90	91
ILLINOIS— Cont'd												
Burbank..........................	7	19	2.6	0.4	28	92	6.9	2.3	6	47	D	2.4
Calumet City	17	95	27.8	2.4	30	D	D	D	10	485	231.5	25.8
Carbondale........................	51	287	40.7	5.9	59	D	D	D	13	276	D	12.3
Carol Stream......................	36	267	56.9	10.0	90	494	86.9	25.8	95	4,421	1,452.3	237.5
Carpentersville....................	22	91	13.0	3.4	36	D	D	D	24	1,720	538.9	114.1
Champaign........................	108	1,117	307.5	45.4	245	D	D	D	55	1,692	656.3	86.6
Chicago............................	3,076	23,960	7,312.7	1,464.7	10,102	147,767	36,711.4	14,148.1	1,870	58,435	26,503.4	2,891.9
Chicago Heights..................	15	164	58.8	9.0	26	149	10.4	4.9	52	2,462	1,775.4	143.8
Cicero..............................	14	70	16.4	2.7	36	206	15.0	4.4	70	2,847	818.5	144.4
Collinsville........................	26	158	27.4	6.2	83	621	69.6	28.3	11	98	D	3.6
Crystal Lake......................	44	197	33.9	7.5	204	763	190.2	44.2	76	2,902	770.8	138.0
Danville............................	31	114	16.2	2.8	59	349	40.9	15.0	48	3,425	1,654.4	180.8
Decatur............................	73	432	89.0	11.4	126	1,036	119.8	45.4	81	7,384	13,124.3	380.7
DeKalb.............................	41	340	84.7	10.6	48	146	18.8	4.1	27	987	D	42.6
Des Plaines.......................	82	1,134	1,241.2	67.9	273	D	D	D	127	5,811	1,498.2	300.7
Downers Grove...................	104	504	124.9	26.5	343	3,641	798.1	288.8	62	3,257	808.2	202.8
East St. Louis.....................	14	45	15.3	1.8	13	D	D	D	11	169	61.6	8.2
Elgin...............................	78	298	75.2	13.2	275	1,441	213.8	73.2	182	7,541	2,914.3	396.1
Elk Grove Village	59	695	109.0	32.2	179	1,872	339.1	146.4	406	13,764	3,678.1	712.1
Elmhurst..........................	65	367	99.6	17.0	244	1,290	193.2	85.6	75	1,574	427.8	95.0
Evanston..........................	106	443	91.9	18.5	412	D	D	D	48	1,051	255.0	51.9
Freeport...........................	20	68	8.6	1.8	59	345	38.1	14.7	36	1,727	402.7	89.4
Galesburg	27	107	14.9	2.4	56	285	26.1	10.1	30	732	D	29.5
Glendale Heights	15	151	97.0	5.6	43	142	16.6	5.9	47	3,195	845.5	177.9
Glen Ellyn.........................	44	278	247.0	19.2	180	484	128.6	26.7	9	D	2.3	D
Glenview...........................	85	475	446.8	31.4	280	2,042	250.5	161.9	47	635	165.2	37.8
Granite City.......................	30	150	19.6	4.9	32	214	26.6	10.4	30	4,619	2,895.2	320.6
Gurnee............................	37	175	52.1	8.6	126	488	59.5	21.2	67	2,485	890.5	140.1
Hanover Park......................	13	D	D	D	38	151	26.7	5.4	11	645	217.1	31.4
Harvey.............................	9	63	19.7	3.2	8	48	2.3	1.0	22	1,384	771.4	75.1
Highland Park	61	186	88.8	10.9	232	D	D	D	24	115	12.3	3.4
Hoffman Estates	32	123	49.8	6.7	223	1,756	291.5	133.3	25	824	290.7	67.3
Joliet...............................	83	400	66.1	14.4	235	12	D	D	73	3,592	2,050.1	225.9
Kankakee	26	75	13.1	2.6	53	D	D	D	29	1,347	1,122.5	83.6
Lake in the Hills..................	10	22	3.6	0.4	53	236	48.9	14.7	18	133	D	6.1
Lansing............................	25	95	15.1	3.8	46	169	21.1	7.6	29	1,427	348.7	60.1
Lombard...........................	76	2,385	474.0	96.8	222	2,198	376.2	172.9	58	895	170.8	44.5
McHenry...........................	31	D	D	D	77	D	D	D	58	1,296	242.2	60.0
Melrose Park......................	20	106	26.8	4.9	23	83	8.2	2.1	97	4,615	1,763.8	222.9
Moline	56	286	74.2	8.4	112	D	D	D	39	2,353	1,518.8	140.6
Mount Prospect...................	45	235	50.8	15.4	176	2,613	107.1	270.5	39	1,541	536.1	97.6
Mundelein.........................	23	66	11.9	2.4	107	590	108.0	47.9	59	1,625	451.6	80.5
Naperville..........................	207	731	212.6	33.0	1,076	D	D	D	82	1,751	570.1	88.3
Niles...............................	46	319	45.9	11.5	89	472	65.9	22.7	55	1,914	667.9	113.0
Normal.............................	34	256	37.5	7.9	68	D	D	D	16	1,881	D	110.0
Northbrook........................	152	2,172	237.2	61.1	578	D	D	D	79	2,299	514.6	113.0
North Chicago.....................	4	29	4.8	0.8	16	D	D	D	15	6,797	2,649.0	D
Oak Forest........................	14	64	7.2	2.9	48	131	20.5	5.8	14	366	D	16.0
Oak Lawn..........................	38	162	27.7	5.8	95	D	D	D	27	436	128.7	21.9
Oak Park...........................	83	352	86.0	14.7	288	D	D	D	18	158	21.7	5.4
O'Fallon...........................	37	143	25.6	6.3	85	1,347	224.8	91.9	11	276	143.6	10.8
Orland Park.......................	74	201	68.1	8.1	237	1,155	156.2	64.1	33	414	146.6	18.0
Oswego............................	25	D	D	D	71	D	D	D	23	477	D	21.9
Palatine............................	72	198	39.9	7.0	349	1,385	221.4	84.5	43	1,882	566.4	85.8
Park Ridge........................	68	D	D	D	252	874	133.5	45.1	10	358	80.9	10.7
Pekin..............................	20	57	9.2	1.3	41	251	21.0	9.2	30	1,003	960.8	60.6
Peoria.............................	152	778	137.6	26.5	356	D	D	D	84	3,270	3,634.4	162.3
Plainfield..........................	29	128	38.7	7.4	134	801	113.1	58.2	21	620	D	39.0
Quincy.............................	50	201	30.4	5.6	116	693	66.3	25.0	45	1,744	651.1	85.8
Rockford...........................	144	1,187	133.5	34.0	418	2,844	539.9	150.2	340	15,649	5,385.6	961.7
Rock Island	22	66	12.2	2.0	112	D	D	D	39	1,390	455.3	64.7
Romeoville........................	22	435	71.1	23.9	38	346	43.1	12.5	50	1,642	564.9	85.4
Round Lake Beach	9	25	5.3	0.6	20	74	5.0	2.4	7	67	D	1.9
St. Charles........................	79	456	262.5	22.0	213	D	D	D	93	5,614	1,569.4	280.4
Schaumburg.......................	148	1,064	356.5	64.7	713	10,430	2,509.6	777.0	151	3,929	1,699.7	201.9
Skokie.............................	103	670	179.7	36.8	383	D	D	D	134	5,070	1,263.7	258.2
Springfield.........................	152	676	136.6	22.0	414	3,918	504.4	206.6	66	2,116	497.3	107.6
Streamwood.......................	21	247	67.4	13.8	81	236	22.9	7.3	34	764	188.1	37.3
Tinley Park........................	35	135	46.3	4.5	140	990	136.0	48.8	38	1,063	253.5	56.4
Urbana.............................	31	1,483	202.8	62.7	72	D	D	D	21	D	320.6	50.9
Vernon Hills.......................	24	D	D	D	160	1,632	384.7	139.2	24	1,696	622.7	133.0

1. Establishments subject to federal tax.

Table D. Cities — Accommodation and Food Services, Arts, Entertainment, and Recreation, and Health Care and Social Assistance

City	Accommodation and food services, 2012				Arts, entertainment, and recreation[1], 2012				Health care and social assistance,[1] 2012			
	Number of establish-ments	Number of employees	Receipts (mil dol)	Annual payroll (mil dol)	Number of establish-ments	Number of employees	Receipts (mil dol)	Annual payroll (mil dol)	Number of establish-ments	Number of employees	Receipts (mil dol)	Annual payroll (mil dol)
	92	93	94	95	96	97	98	99	100	101	102	103
ILLINOIS— Cont'd												
Burbank	50	742	37.9	10.4	3	D	D	D	36	D	D	D
Calumet City	79	1,238	63.8	16.5	3	37	2.1	0.6	58	798	48.1	23.9
Carbondale	95	D	D	D	4	D	D	D	90	D	D	D
Carol Stream	76	991	58.0	13.5	9	62	3.5	0.8	56	456	43.3	17.0
Carpentersville	37	859	34.9	10.1	4	D	D	D	20	D	D	D
Champaign	301	6,636	298.9	82.6	23	D	D	D	155	D	D	D
Chicago	6,022	115,965	8,996.4	2,481.8	716	11,186	2,159.3	742.9	5,253	73,916	6,786.9	2,549.9
Chicago Heights	46	576	26.8	8.0	1	D	D	D	52	713	57.4	23.5
Cicero	86	1,040	64.0	16.5	5	34	3.0	0.5	60	505	41.7	14.5
Collinsville	67	1,471	64.6	18.7	9	D	D	D	50	D	D	D
Crystal Lake	120	2,615	143.7	41.2	18	106	6.5	1.3	185	2,021	186.4	82.5
Danville	87	1,544	65.9	18.9	7	55	2.8	0.8	77	1,103	96.0	44.9
Decatur	179	3,415	152.1	43.8	13	279	8.2	4.1	206	D	D	D
DeKalb	99	1,677	69.6	19.5	3	D	D	D	53	D	D	D
Des Plaines	163	2,001	135.4	30.3	14	D	D	D	211	2,857	244.0	99.0
Downers Grove	154	3,004	175.7	52.0	16	208	8.5	2.6	215	D	D	D
East St. Louis	35	D	D	D	1	D	D	D	29	D	D	D
Elgin	185	3,061	147.6	41.1	19	D	D	D	246	2,757	302.9	148.7
Elk Grove Village	114	1,739	121.7	33.6	14	D	D	D	130	D	D	D
Elmhurst	108	1,721	92.5	25.7	17	117	7.6	1.9	219	D	D	D
Evanston	238	3,779	274.7	77.2	42	393	24.7	8.6	259	4,212	630.9	389.4
Freeport	64	889	41.2	10.4	8	D	D	D	62	D	D	D
Galesburg	92	1,464	65.9	18.5	3	24	0.8	0.2	67	1,761	183.4	64.6
Glendale Heights	45	706	42.6	10.1	9	D	D	D	33	D	D	D
Glen Ellyn	61	959	51.4	13.8	9	D	D	D	92	1,095	190.8	87.2
Glenview	158	2,761	163.8	52.1	34	328	45.9	20.6	254	3,243	317.0	133.0
Granite City	67	1,011	46.0	12.7	6	D	D	D	67	D	D	D
Gurnee	136	3,217	166.2	47.8	15	D	D	D	166	1,442	196.1	77.9
Hanover Park	36	446	26.2	5.9	3	73	3.6	0.8	32	286	24.4	8.9
Harvey	40	744	41.1	12.3	NA	NA	NA	NA	42	D	D	D
Highland Park	90	1,506	91.0	28.9	30	393	19.9	9.5	155	D	D	D
Hoffman Estates	117	1,993	130.7	36.7	15	D	D	D	226	D	D	D
Joliet	235	5,812	555.9	117.0	16	277	67.5	9.0	337	4,717	581.8	230.6
Kankakee	53	D	D	D	5	D	D	D	71	D	D	D
Lake in the Hills	29	524	25.4	7.8	8	D	D	D	51	583	38.8	16.8
Lansing	62	1,206	57.9	15.9	6	D	D	D	57	504	38.4	15.2
Lombard	148	3,359	210.1	62.0	14	320	14.7	4.6	147	2,367	232.5	95.6
McHenry	83	1,267	53.3	15.2	7	55	4.6	1.2	91	D	D	D
Melrose Park	72	D	D	D	6	D	D	D	106	D	D	D
Moline	156	2,771	128.6	36.9	11	D	D	D	163	2,283	237.6	107.0
Mount Prospect	112	1,568	86.8	23.9	8	D	D	D	118	2,071	159.2	61.2
Mundelein	75	1,082	53.2	13.5	12	D	D	D	48	296	26.4	10.5
Naperville	361	7,975	472.3	129.5	58	730	82.7	29.4	589	D	D	D
Niles	135	D	D	D	9	D	D	D	147	2,732	262.6	89.7
Normal	106	2,742	132.3	36.2	10	D	D	D	74	1,254	119.4	45.5
Northbrook	96	2,082	140.2	46.3	33	D	D	D	269	3,224	294.6	125.2
North Chicago	31	390	19.8	4.9	NA	NA	NA	NA	8	D	D	D
Oak Forest	37	593	28.3	7.6	4	D	D	D	45	869	44.4	23.5
Oak Lawn	108	2,406	172.7	39.1	12	144	7.9	1.8	239	D	D	D
Oak Park	101	1,703	86.0	26.0	25	275	23.2	5.9	262	4,148	374.6	171.8
O'Fallon	69	D	D	D	8	D	D	D	69	D	D	D
Orland Park	170	4,254	207.9	61.7	20	D	D	D	293	4,528	413.6	185.3
Oswego	60	1,375	66.7	19.5	10	108	5.4	1.2	70	D	D	D
Palatine	111	1,558	80.0	22.1	18	D	D	D	134	1,711	101.3	39.2
Park Ridge	66	887	51.4	13.9	11	D	D	D	242	D	D	D
Pekin	86	1,460	62.7	17.3	9	D	D	D	68	926	65.6	30.9
Peoria	326	6,429	294.4	84.8	27	955	36.5	13.6	334	6,614	826.5	352.7
Plainfield	85	1,610	75.6	19.6	7	D	D	D	115	D	D	D
Quincy	126	2,186	98.8	28.2	11	D	D	D	97	2,168	334.1	112.8
Rockford	336	7,122	344.0	97.8	28	317	17.3	4.8	365	5,805	856.7	340.5
Rock Island	62	1,356	157.5	22.1	7	D	D	D	75	D	D	D
Romeoville	61	1,259	58.0	17.6	10	420	22.6	6.8	31	D	D	D
Round Lake Beach	31	484	31.5	8.2	7	87	5.3	1.3	26	D	D	D
St. Charles	114	2,960	140.1	44.4	17	D	D	D	149	1,471	169.2	71.4
Schaumburg	265	7,508	488.2	150.8	31	777	47.5	11.9	261	3,141	316.3	118.4
Skokie	155	3,453	232.9	63.6	22	D	D	D	346	3,873	352.6	149.3
Springfield	402	8,032	383.4	114.2	43	D	D	D	286	9,744	1,233.0	436.3
Streamwood	64	991	53.1	13.9	3	15	0.9	0.3	52	1,247	126.7	50.0
Tinley Park	130	2,621	147.9	38.4	18	216	30.4	5.9	162	2,257	259.1	86.1
Urbana	108	1,781	84.3	23.4	11	D	D	D	45	D	D	D
Vernon Hills	95	1,717	103.9	30.6	16	D	D	D	106	1,089	161.7	55.2

1. Establishments subject to federal tax.

Table D. Cities — Other Services and Government Employment and Payroll

City	Other services[1] Number of establishments	Number of employees	Receipts (mil dol)	Annual payroll (mil dol)	Government employment and payroll, 2012 — Full-time equivalent employees	March payroll Total (dollars)	Percent of total for: Administrative, judicial, and legal	Police and corrections	Fire protection	Highways and transportation	Health and welfare	Natural resources and utilities	Education and libraries
	104	105	106	107	108	109	110	111	112	113	114	115	116
ILLINOIS— Cont'd													
Burbank	39	134	11.1	3.7	134	786,445	7.6	47.7	28.5	12.5	0.0	0.0	0.0
Calumet City	34	108	11.2	3.2	270	1,459,484	9.0	47.4	26.2	6.4	3.6	3.2	4.2
Carbondale	42	152	13.2	3.2	243	1,024,650	20.3	36.8	14.6	7.4	0.7	17.5	0.0
Carol Stream	59	257	23.2	7.0	178	1,066,716	18.8	48.5	0.0	9.7	2.2	4.7	13.5
Carpentersville	30	124	8.9	2.6	197	1,212,358	9.8	38.1	25.5	7.4	4.7	10.2	0.0
Champaign	103	766	51.3	17.7	613	3,303,325	9.3	26.5	21.3	13.7	2.4	1.6	17.9
Chicago	3,455	21,793	1,817.1	565.1	25,630	175,627,618	2.8	74.4	7.6	3.4	2.3	5.3	1.0
Chicago Heights	40	189	15.1	5.0	294	1,453,188	3.9	43.8	28.2	5.0	0.3	9.0	5.7
Cicero	71	248	23.0	5.9	584	2,867,400	8.1	39.8	18.0	10.1	11.3	7.3	1.8
Collinsville	38	200	17.5	5.2	169	956,282	5.4	39.2	23.4	8.4	4.4	16.9	0.0
Crystal Lake	109	730	55.8	17.6	309	1,877,299	13.5	27.5	25.3	5.8	2.7	10.3	9.1
Danville	49	270	24.0	6.7	294	1,321,594	8.4	29.2	21.7	13.2	2.3	14.1	5.3
Decatur	102	865	126.6	28.1	554	2,990,379	8.4	39.2	24.9	9.4	4.8	6.5	5.6
DeKalb	43	312	15.5	5.5	198	1,271,653	11.8	36.9	32.8	11.6	1.9	5.0	0.0
Des Plaines	142	940	130.6	36.5	446	2,438,468	5.2	30.6	34.3	7.1	3.0	5.9	10.5
Downers Grove	115	1,076	103.5	31.9	390	2,164,897	16.2	30.8	26.2	1.6	2.8	10.9	8.4
East St. Louis	16	108	5.7	1.8	189	693,926	9.2	35.2	34.7	6.6	4.3	0.0	2.0
Elgin	143	1,294	139.9	49.7	718	4,472,423	10.3	39.1	24.6	3.4	0.0	18.7	0.0
Elk Grove Village	106	964	120.0	35.0	298	2,048,828	10.7	36.3	32.2	8.8	6.0	5.0	0.0
Elmhurst	94	781	68.0	22.5	587	3,047,235	10.6	25.1	12.8	8.0	0.0	13.7	21.9
Evanston	113	739	46.4	16.6	756	4,935,582	8.8	31.1	21.1	2.8	8.4	20.2	3.5
Freeport	46	195	13.7	3.9	191	868,424	5.9	37.1	28.7	6.7	0.0	12.7	3.3
Galesburg	53	D	D	D	284	1,182,039	9.7	30.8	19.6	8.9	4.7	17.2	4.2
Glendale Heights	39	299	36.2	11.3	240	1,253,066	11.8	42.0	0.0	9.8	5.4	20.6	0.0
Glen Ellyn	48	261	20.7	6.6	170	812,456	21.3	30.1	0.0	7.6	0.0	23.8	11.9
Glenview	126	726	57.9	19.6	368	2,419,770	8.4	26.3	34.2	5.3	3.0	8.4	10.8
Granite City	48	394	45.7	14.2	233	1,173,888	7.7	32.1	27.6	12.2	4.4	14.0	0.0
Gurnee	64	491	47.5	14.0	198	1,570,289	5.9	45.6	29.7	8.4	0.0	3.7	0.0
Hanover Park	34	330	19.3	6.6	207	1,331,356	9.4	44.7	23.0	7.5	3.0	8.6	0.0
Harvey	19	77	6.6	1.6	195	871,135	8.5	48.6	27.8	8.3	0.3	6.5	0.0
Highland Park	101	582	48.4	15.2	227	1,445,604	8.6	30.8	26.4	9.8	1.3	11.6	0.0
Hoffman Estates	59	416	19.3	8.7	347	2,420,731	11.8	35.1	29.9	4.6	1.4	10.1	0.0
Joliet	151	1,366	144.2	44.6	941	6,790,745	6.4	38.7	25.4	6.8	1.3	12.5	3.8
Kankakee	41	246	22.9	6.8	264	1,273,939	5.5	35.8	24.1	7.9	6.7	10.1	4.5
Lake in the Hills	43	168	14.6	4.0	131	726,848	15.2	43.1	0.0	11.6	4.1	15.1	0.0
Lansing	48	561	57.3	16.4	200	1,054,688	6.3	47.0	25.7	7.3	0.0	5.9	5.3
Lombard	107	701	75.0	22.0	289	1,794,844	9.3	33.8	26.1	6.4	0.8	8.5	8.0
McHenry	72	377	28.3	8.4	136	766,529	11.7	38.7	0.0	16.4	0.0	26.3	0.0
Melrose Park	42	D	D	D	274	1,377,728	3.3	43.1	26.6	6.0	1.7	8.5	5.6
Moline	84	478	32.8	10.5	392	2,247,548	10.9	28.1	19.6	8.6	0.7	17.4	6.2
Mount Prospect	81	458	39.5	12.0	445	2,620,859	6.5	27.8	21.6	6.5	3.5	10.4	15.1
Mundelein	71	374	31.2	9.8	167	523,415	11.5	34.6	14.6	10.6	0.0	10.8	0.0
Naperville	249	1,950	138.1	45.2	1,141	6,999,358	11.3	27.3	20.8	10.0	0.0	21.1	9.4
Niles	74	463	36.0	10.0	277	1,803,453	9.8	28.4	25.4	11.8	9.9	11.0	0.0
Normal	49	391	26.9	9.3	426	2,272,555	9.0	24.8	18.8	7.7	0.7	25.9	7.3
Northbrook	87	584	39.7	14.6	275	2,019,890	9.3	35.9	30.6	13.5	2.9	7.8	0.0
North Chicago	10	D	D	D	176	982,302	7.8	51.2	16.6	5.2	4.6	10.0	4.6
Oak Forest	38	172	15.2	3.9	137	814,381	8.2	43.6	26.4	10.5	0.1	10.0	0.0
Oak Lawn	91	709	57.2	17.9	421	2,260,980	6.9	39.4	25.9	7.3	0.7	8.8	7.3
Oak Park	100	582	47.7	14.0	450	2,566,842	9.0	37.0	19.6	5.0	4.3	3.8	10.5
O'Fallon	47	304	27.7	8.3	177	876,752	17.3	46.2	0.5	7.4	7.7	15.6	4.9
Orland Park	121	1,053	78.1	27.9	409	2,080,080	14.2	43.9	0.0	6.5	0.0	22.3	8.2
Oswego	58	331	28.0	9.2	107	609,946	20.4	64.0	0.0	0.0	0.0	15.5	0.0
Palatine	135	781	61.8	19.8	348	2,424,446	10.2	40.9	30.9	4.8	1.1	3.4	0.0
Park Ridge	61	352	31.7	10.3	255	1,549,882	7.5	29.7	26.8	7.3	4.0	6.5	14.1
Pekin	58	255	15.5	5.3	259	1,110,590	5.2	29.2	27.7	6.0	1.0	5.6	4.2
Peoria	158	3,995	358.2	183.6	831	4,963,632	9.9	36.9	26.3	5.9	1.3	5.1	5.3
Plainfield	61	426	29.8	9.2	131	858,893	12.3	62.1	0.0	9.7	0.0	13.1	0.0
Quincy	88	476	38.8	11.9	391	1,653,065	8.8	30.0	19.6	12.1	0.3	15.1	5.2
Rockford	242	1,586	154.2	43.7	1,085	6,113,597	5.6	33.3	36.5	5.3	7.4	4.8	4.2
Rock Island	50	370	31.5	9.6	372	1,377,794	14.6	16.8	10.5	8.7	9.2	29.1	7.6
Romeoville	40	474	48.6	14.5	297	1,580,154	8.8	38.4	18.0	2.8	3.6	17.7	0.0
Round Lake Beach	26	118	7.7	2.5	90	514,049	11.2	62.5	0.0	8.6	4.5	13.1	0.0
St. Charles	85	647	44.9	15.4	264	1,823,844	18.8	26.0	21.1	7.0	0.0	19.6	0.0
Schaumburg	197	1,612	162.4	51.5	536	3,458,405	11.4	32.6	25.6	5.7	7.4	8.7	0.0
Skokie	157	1,128	107.7	36.5	593	3,361,285	7.8	29.7	23.3	2.7	5.7	10.6	14.6
Springfield	184	1,494	123.1	38.3	1,621	10,142,573	6.4	16.0	12.6	5.8	1.5	56.2	1.6
Streamwood	55	288	22.7	6.3	179	1,160,444	8.6	42.2	27.2	3.9	3.6	10.8	0.0
Tinley Park	57	343	25.6	8.5	346	1,824,694	11.4	45.9	13.6	6.6	0.8	8.0	9.0
Urbana	33	193	14.3	4.6	302	1,464,071	11.1	26.0	23.5	13.2	5.3	4.2	11.9
Vernon Hills	34	373	21.8	8.8	101	697,505	10.9	66.3	0.0	16.7	0.0	0.0	0.0

1. Establishments subject to federal tax.

Table D. Cities — City Government Finances

City	City government finances, 2012									
	General revenue							General expenditure		
		Intergovernmental		Taxes						
						Per capita[1] (dollars)			Per capita[1] (dollars)	
	Total (mil dol)	Total (mil dol)	Percent from state government	Total (mil dol)	Total	Property	Sales and gross receipts	Total (mil dol)	Total	Capital outlays
	117	118	119	120	121	122	123	124	125	126

ILLINOIS— Cont'd										
Burbank...........................	19.3	6.5	97.7	12.0	410	185	219	17.0	584	9
Calumet City	50.9	11.6	90.1	34.2	919	681	229	45.9	1,232	103
Carbondale.......................	32.4	10.9	88.9	14.1	533	69	464	31.8	1,202	47
Carol Stream.....................	28.1	11.1	91.6	10.1	252	15	219	25.3	631	60
Carpentersville..................	32.2	12.8	86.2	12.7	332	234	98	36.5	955	239
Champaign........................	100.8	38.9	81.8	49.4	597	285	312	101.7	1,229	343
Chicago...........................	6,690.6	1,758.6	65.4	2,526.4	930	327	547	7,439.1	2,740	425
Chicago Heights.................	44.6	13.6	76.8	22.9	750	593	155	45.7	1,500	202
Cicero.............................	111.4	23.7	88.5	72.9	863	556	300	108.6	1,285	185
Collinsville.......................	30.2	11.1	94.1	12.0	478	200	278	29.1	1,154	106
Crystal Lake......................	53.2	19.4	99.7	23.3	576	375	201	54.2	1,341	305
Danville	42.4	15.6	82.1	19.3	590	227	363	42.8	1,309	210
Decatur...........................	75.9	32.1	85.6	34.5	458	179	279	89.1	1,182	206
DeKalb............................	53.3	19.6	68.3	26.9	614	331	283	45.2	1,031	260
Des Plaines......................	103.1	31.2	96.3	57.8	982	617	358	92.0	1,563	249
Downers Grove..................	65.8	18.9	98.8	39.1	793	447	346	58.7	1,190	157
East St. Louis....................	38.6	19.9	85.1	15.8	592	444	148	38.3	1,439	101
Elgin..............................	136.9	44.5	93.0	66.3	605	479	126	125.2	1,141	155
Elk Grove Village	60.1	13.5	93.1	37.1	1,113	630	466	64.9	1,946	411
Elmhurst..........................	70.4	17.9	99.2	36.4	806	479	320	65.4	1,450	192
Evanston..........................	123.4	24.9	70.5	64.7	858	533	298	116.5	1,544	176
Freeport..........................	29.6	13.3	99.7	8.0	317	186	130	28.8	1,144	64
Galesburg	39.9	19.3	93.4	14.5	455	218	236	38.4	1,207	64
Glendale Heights	35.6	10.2	99.2	15.9	460	241	210	43.0	1,246	422
Glen Ellyn........................	37.6	7.6	88.9	16.6	602	374	215	32.5	1,176	174
Glenview..........................	101.0	27.2	76.5	62.0	1,377	1,042	336	95.5	2,120	282
Granite City......................	40.9	13.0	100.0	18.6	629	472	157	45.0	1,521	211
Gurnee............................	38.2	22.9	85.8	9.6	307	0	307	34.9	1,121	11
Hanover Park	38.2	10.2	89.4	21.6	563	376	180	53.4	1,392	426
Harvey............................	23.0	6.4	100.0	13.8	543	424	119	25.1	990	34
Highland Park	56.2	12.1	93.3	29.2	978	521	419	47.5	1,591	94
Hoffman Estates	82.1	13.5	91.6	51.3	982	736	239	64.6	1,237	110
Joliet..............................	202.1	70.4	93.0	72.3	488	283	198	177.8	1,199	22
Kankakee.........................	60.8	25.8	88.2	20.1	735	562	173	66.7	2,438	258
Lake in the Hills.................	20.2	7.5	78.9	9.1	314	217	97	18.0	620	82
Lansing...........................	33.0	8.0	94.6	18.5	649	445	203	35.4	1,241	283
Lombard..........................	90.1	27.3	90.2	20.3	464	194	270	97.6	2,231	83
McHenry..........................	24.8	12.3	96.4	6.7	249	217	33	23.4	873	150
Melrose Park.....................	43.6	13.9	98.6	23.4	918	732	185	48.9	1,914	285
Moline............................	72.2	20.2	84.2	35.3	819	413	405	74.2	1,720	148
Mount Prospect..................	70.6	19.0	93.5	43.9	805	533	265	70.0	1,283	142
Mundelein	36.2	9.6	91.1	18.0	577	372	205	32.6	1,046	94
Naperville.........................	169.6	55.1	89.1	79.8	555	355	183	143.7	999	101
Niles..............................	48.5	18.9	99.5	23.3	776	251	518	41.3	1,378	19
Normal	80.5	31.2	99.5	31.3	581	208	372	77.3	1,435	387
Northbrook.......................	51.6	18.4	98.1	23.9	715	481	233	52.8	1,578	131
North Chicago....................	26.1	8.5	79.5	13.3	441	299	138	26.6	885	25
Oak Forest........................	21.4	5.3	98.7	12.5	444	315	129	20.9	744	55
Oak Lawn.........................	62.1	19.1	99.2	28.3	496	394	96	68.1	1,194	211
Oak Park..........................	89.0	14.1	80.8	58.0	1,115	815	268	90.4	1,737	226
O'Fallon..........................	33.2	13.4	98.6	10.8	370	237	133	31.4	1,072	258
Orland Park	85.4	30.2	96.4	33.9	592	346	245	81.3	1,420	303
Oswego...........................	21.0	9.6	98.5	6.3	198	46	152	17.5	553	6
Palatine...........................	81.2	22.0	76.2	45.6	660	486	175	87.2	1,262	293
Park Ridge	46.1	10.0	100.0	30.9	818	523	283	47.4	1,255	36
Pekin.............................	40.2	14.5	81.3	13.8	404	189	215	48.4	1,417	388
Peoria.............................	185.6	76.4	95.2	81.2	702	306	396	173.5	1,500	288
Plainfield	34.8	10.0	90.4	14.1	348	155	193	27.5	680	54
Quincy............................	46.5	24.3	86.8	13.5	330	59	271	36.7	898	111
Rockford..........................	205.7	107.8	79.0	75.0	497	396	100	178.2	1,180	127
Rock Island	69.8	23.7	74.6	23.3	601	427	175	75.1	1,934	393
Romeoville	58.3	11.7	84.0	28.8	726	381	336	58.2	1,465	267
Round Lake Beach	17.9	8.1	98.7	8.5	305	231	74	22.5	802	338
St. Charles	51.7	14.2	98.9	26.8	807	424	383	54.5	1,637	225
Schaumburg......................	155.0	40.4	92.8	70.0	937	341	596	138.1	1,847	106
Skokie............................	104.2	37.0	66.4	60.5	929	512	413	82.4	1,265	140
Springfield........................	137.9	49.3	90.7	68.8	587	235	353	135.8	1,159	63
Streamwood......................	29.9	8.7	93.2	15.7	390	250	135	26.2	650	57
Tinley Park	70.3	22.1	99.9	36.1	632	519	114	61.1	1,069	254
Urbana............................	47.8	17.7	62.5	22.2	531	252	279	48.4	1,159	285
Vernon Hills......................	21.2	13.2	99.1	5.7	222	0	222	18.9	740	29

1. Based on population estimated as of July 1 of the year shown.

City	City government finances, 2012 (cont.)								
	General expenditure (cont.)								
	Percent of total for:								
	Public welfare	Highways	Parking facilities	Education	Health and hospitals	Police protection	Sewerage and sanitation	Parks and recreation	Housing and community development	Interest on debt
	127	128	129	130	131	132	133	134	135	136

City	127	128	129	130	131	132	133	134	135	136
ILLINOIS— Cont'd										
Burbank........................	0.0	11.1	0.0	0.0	0.0	42.1	0.0	0.0	0.0	2.8
Calumet City	0.0	11.2	0.0	0.0	1.3	21.0	3.8	0.0	0.3	4.9
Carbondale	0.0	7.9	0.6	0.0	0.0	26.7	11.0	1.0	10.1	4.7
Carol Stream.................	0.0	12.8	0.0	0.0	0.0	46.9	11.5	0.0	0.0	1.4
Carpentersville..............	0.0	38.6	0.0	0.0	0.0	24.1	5.9	0.7	0.0	5.8
Champaign....................	0.3	8.8	2.1	0.0	0.0	19.0	14.5	0.0	0.8	3.1
Chicago........................	4.6	9.7	0.1	0.0	2.5	18.0	5.3	0.5	4.4	12.5
Chicago Heights.............	0.0	5.4	0.0	0.0	0.0	23.2	9.3	0.0	6.0	4.9
Cicero..........................	0.3	10.4	0.0	0.0	1.4	22.1	4.8	0.3	1.6	5.0
Collinsville	0.0	8.9	0.0	0.0	0.6	27.3	16.9	0.0	0.0	5.9
Crystal Lake..................	0.0	25.3	0.0	0.0	0.2	19.8	6.0	1.9	0.0	2.7
Danville	0.0	17.2	0.0	0.0	0.0	16.9	12.9	5.0	1.7	1.3
Decatur........................	0.0	29.1	0.0	0.0	0.0	25.2	3.2	0.1	2.3	5.8
DeKalb.........................	0.0	13.3	0.0	0.0	0.0	23.6	3.7	0.0	0.6	2.7
Des Plaines	0.0	20.8	0.2	0.0	0.0	21.7	6.9	0.0	0.3	2.6
Downers Grove	0.0	18.1	1.8	0.0	0.0	24.0	7.0	0.0	0.0	5.8
East St. Louis................	0.0	6.6	0.0	0.0	0.0	18.9	0.4	0.0	6.8	5.2
Elgin............................	0.0	11.0	0.0	0.0	0.0	27.7	8.5	13.6	1.2	2.1
Elk Grove Village	0.0	19.6	0.0	0.0	0.0	23.4	3.9	0.0	0.0	5.1
Elmhurst.......................	0.0	18.1	1.0	0.0	0.4	21.5	11.4	1.7	0.0	4.4
Evanston.......................	1.7	7.6	6.0	0.0	2.3	18.5	5.9	10.8	6.7	7.0
Freeport	0.0	13.2	0.0	0.0	0.3	14.5	17.8	0.4	0.0	4.6
Galesburg.....................	0.0	25.9	0.0	0.0	0.0	14.5	5.0	7.5	0.0	3.6
Glendale Heights	0.0	11.3	0.0	0.0	0.0	37.4	2.1	17.7	0.0	7.1
Glen Ellyn.....................	0.0	21.1	0.6	0.0	0.0	22.1	17.3	8.7	0.0	1.6
Glenview.......................	0.0	8.2	0.3	0.0	0.0	12.5	5.1	0.0	0.0	5.3
Granite City..................	0.0	20.6	0.0	0.0	0.0	20.0	15.5	0.0	0.0	3.9
Gurnee	0.0	13.7	0.0	0.0	0.0	33.2	3.7	0.6	0.0	1.0
Hanover Park.................	0.0	10.2	0.9	0.0	0.0	43.0	3.1	0.0	0.0	2.1
Harvey..........................	0.0	17.0	0.7	0.0	0.0	22.3	4.4	0.3	0.0	8.0
Highland Park	0.0	10.3	2.4	0.0	0.0	27.0	7.1	5.1	0.0	3.1
Hoffman Estates	0.0	14.7	0.0	0.0	0.9	25.3	5.6	4.4	0.0	8.8
Joliet...........................	0.0	9.3	0.7	0.0	0.0	20.1	10.8	4.0	1.9	1.3
Kankakee......................	0.0	10.0	0.0	0.0	0.0	14.5	21.2	0.0	1.5	5.0
Lake in the Hills............	0.0	10.4	0.0	0.0	0.0	38.8	0.0	8.9	0.0	1.8
Lansing	0.0	15.2	0.0	0.0	0.0	25.7	5.9	0.0	0.0	2.9
Lombard........................	0.0	4.1	0.1	0.0	0.0	13.3	3.6	0.0	0.0	8.5
McHenry.......................	0.0	14.9	0.0	0.0	0.0	39.0	22.4	8.5	0.0	2.9
Melrose Park.................	0.0	8.0	0.0	0.0	0.0	22.1	4.8	2.9	0.0	7.5
Moline	0.0	12.6	0.3	0.0	0.0	17.7	10.4	7.3	0.0	5.5
Mount Prospect..............	1.4	12.6	0.5	0.0	0.2	19.8	8.5	0.5	1.3	1.5
Mundelein.....................	0.0	20.8	0.1	0.0	0.0	30.0	6.2	0.0	0.0	3.3
Naperville.....................	0.0	19.4	0.7	0.0	0.0	24.1	7.8	5.9	0.0	3.5
Niles............................	0.0	16.1	0.0	0.0	0.0	31.3	5.8	3.8	0.0	1.7
Normal.........................	0.0	7.7	0.0	0.0	0.0	14.0	6.7	12.9	0.2	5.5
Northbrook....................	0.0	16.7	0.3	0.0	0.0	24.8	2.5	0.0	0.0	5.0
North Chicago................	0.0	8.1	0.0	0.0	0.0	30.4	1.8	0.0	1.3	5.2
Oak Forest....................	0.0	17.8	1.0	0.0	0.0	37.1	4.8	0.0	0.0	2.4
Oak Lawn......................	0.3	14.0	0.1	0.0	0.0	20.6	8.3	0.6	0.3	5.5
Oak Park.......................	0.0	7.1	4.0	0.0	1.3	20.3	6.0	0.0	4.7	3.1
O'Fallon........................	0.1	13.1	0.0	0.0	0.0	15.5	10.4	15.1	0.0	9.0
Orland Park...................	0.0	27.8	0.4	0.0	0.0	21.1	12.3	10.6	0.0	3.0
Oswego.........................	0.0	11.6	0.0	0.0	0.0	45.1	16.3	0.0	0.0	9.0
Palatine........................	0.0	7.7	0.6	0.0	0.0	41.7	6.7	0.0	0.2	6.5
Park Ridge	0.0	7.0	0.8	0.0	0.0	19.5	10.4	0.0	0.0	3.3
Pekin...........................	0.0	9.3	0.0	0.0	0.0	17.4	28.2	0.0	1.1	3.9
Peoria..........................	0.0	15.7	1.7	0.0	0.0	20.6	1.4	1.5	2.0	5.8
Plainfield	0.0	20.5	0.0	0.0	0.0	39.3	16.5	0.0	0.0	10.9
Quincy..........................	0.0	11.6	0.0	0.0	0.3	22.6	10.1	1.7	2.9	2.4
Rockford.......................	9.5	16.5	0.7	0.0	0.0	25.1	3.9	0.0	5.8	2.4
Rock Island	0.0	8.4	0.2	0.0	0.0	15.4	24.0	9.0	0.4	0.8
Romeoville....................	0.0	11.3	0.0	0.0	0.0	20.1	10.5	6.5	0.0	8.6
Round Lake Beach	0.0	7.7	0.0	0.0	0.0	28.5	0.0	0.6	0.0	4.2
St. Charles....................	0.0	20.9	0.0	0.0	1.2	19.4	13.9	0.0	0.0	9.3
Schaumburg...................	0.8	12.2	0.1	0.0	0.5	18.6	4.6	1.6	0.3	10.1
Skokie..........................	0.0	10.7	0.1	0.0	1.7	19.6	5.0	2.4	1.0	3.2
Springfield....................	0.0	12.3	1.1	0.0	0.0	27.2	4.0	0.0	3.0	2.0
Streamwood...................	0.0	17.6	0.0	0.0	0.0	33.2	9.7	1.3	0.0	1.6
Tinley Park	0.0	17.1	0.9	0.0	0.0	26.6	4.6	0.0	0.0	3.6
Urbana.........................	0.3	29.3	1.4	0.0	0.0	17.9	3.0	0.3	7.3	1.1
Vernon Hills..................	0.0	21.7	0.0	0.0	0.0	46.0	0.0	4.1	0.0	7.1

City	City government finances, 2012 (cont.)			Climate[2]						
	Debt outstanding		Debt issued during year	Average daily temperature				Annual precipitation (inches)	Heating degree days	Cooling degree days
				Mean		Limits				
	Total (mil dol)	Per capita[1] (dollars)		January	July	January[3]	July[4]			
	137	138	139	140	141	142	143	144	145	146

ILLINOIS— Cont'd

City	137	138	139	140	141	142	143	144	145	146
Burbank	10.1	346	0.0	23.5	75.5	16.2	84.7	38.35	6,083	1,001
Calumet City	52.6	1,413	0.0	22.0	74.2	14.8	83.7	38.65	6,355	866
Carbondale	33.7	1,276	6.6	NA	NA	NA	NA	NA	NA	NA
Carol Stream	7.2	180	0.0	23.1	74.8	14.2	86.8	37.94	6,053	942
Carpentersville	49.4	1,295	0.0	19.3	72.6	10.9	83.0	37.22	6,975	679
Champaign	74.8	904	0.0	33.7	79.0	25.0	89.5	47.93	4,183	1,501
Chicago	21,209.6	7,811	2,295.0	25.3	75.4	18.3	84.4	38.01	5,787	994
Chicago Heights	67.7	2,223	46.7	22.0	74.2	14.8	83.7	38.65	6,355	866
Cicero	108.3	1,282	0.0	22.0	73.3	14.3	83.5	36.27	6,498	830
Collinsville	47.8	1,894	0.0	NA	NA	NA	NA	NA	NA	NA
Crystal Lake	42.4	1,049	0.0	28.6	76.3	19.0	87.2	46.96	5,168	1,112
Danville	12.0	367	4.4	25.8	75.3	17.3	86.2	40.96	5,555	1,027
Decatur	96.9	1,286	1.9	25.8	76.2	17.1	87.8	39.74	5,458	1,142
DeKalb	29.2	667	1.0	18.5	73.1	10.3	83.6	37.38	6,979	736
Des Plaines	71.7	1,218	4.0	22.0	73.3	14.3	83.5	36.27	6,498	830
Downers Grove	80.1	1,623	0.0	23.1	74.8	14.2	86.8	37.94	6,053	942
East St. Louis	25.4	954	0.0	29.1	78.6	20.0	88.7	40.33	4,826	1,378
Elgin	106.3	969	10.2	19.3	72.6	10.9	83.0	37.22	6,975	679
Elk Grove Village	52.6	1,579	0.3	22.0	73.3	14.3	83.5	36.27	6,498	830
Elmhurst	61.9	1,371	0.0	23.1	74.8	14.2	86.8	37.94	6,053	942
Evanston	237.9	3,154	19.4	22.0	72.9	13.7	83.2	36.80	6,630	702
Freeport	32.6	1,295	0.0	17.2	71.9	9.0	82.0	34.79	7,317	611
Galesburg	27.4	863	7.9	21.3	74.9	13.5	84.5	37.22	6,347	941
Glendale Heights	49.6	1,437	0.0	22.0	73.3	14.3	83.5	36.27	6,498	830
Glen Ellyn	13.3	482	0.0	21.7	74.4	12.2	85.7	38.58	6,359	888
Glenview	137.4	3,052	11.0	22.0	73.3	14.3	83.5	36.27	6,498	830
Granite City	30.0	1,015	2.2	27.7	78.4	19.4	88.1	38.54	5,149	1,354
Gurnee	16.1	518	10.0	19.9	72.2	12.1	82.2	35.50	6,955	634
Hanover Park	24.0	625	7.0	18.4	72.1	9.6	82.3	36.56	7,149	624
Harvey	50.8	2,004	0.0	22.0	74.2	14.8	83.7	38.65	6,355	866
Highland Park	44.8	1,503	4.6	22.0	72.9	13.7	83.2	36.80	6,630	702
Hoffman Estates	193.6	3,703	2.5	18.4	72.1	9.6	82.3	36.56	7,149	624
Joliet	61.9	417	12.6	21.7	73.7	13.5	84.6	36.96	6,464	809
Kankakee	78.1	2,856	8.7	21.7	74.4	12.2	85.7	38.58	6,359	888
Lake in the Hills	7.6	261	0.0	NA	NA	NA	NA	NA	NA	NA
Lansing	20.8	728	1.5	21.7	74.4	12.2	85.7	38.58	6,359	888
Lombard	219.0	5,007	0.0	23.1	74.8	14.2	86.8	37.94	6,053	942
McHenry	17.9	668	0.0	NA	NA	NA	NA	NA	NA	NA
Melrose Park	80.3	3,147	11.7	NA	NA	NA	NA	NA	NA	NA
Moline	79.9	1,853	18.2	21.8	76.4	13.3	85.1	35.10	6,179	1,100
Mount Prospect	40.7	745	9.3	22.0	73.3	14.3	83.5	36.27	6,498	830
Mundelein	21.6	693	0.0	18.4	72.1	9.6	82.3	36.56	7,149	624
Naperville	178.8	1,244	25.1	23.1	74.8	14.2	86.8	37.94	6,053	942
Niles	18.8	626	4.4	22.0	73.3	14.3	83.5	36.27	6,498	830
Normal	87.9	1,632	0.0	25.8	76.2	17.1	87.8	39.74	5,458	1,142
Northbrook	72.5	2,166	3.0	22.0	72.9	13.7	83.2	36.80	6,630	702
North Chicago	31.9	1,060	2.1	20.3	71.5	12.0	81.7	34.09	7,031	613
Oak Forest	30.0	1,067	0.0	22.0	74.2	14.8	83.7	38.65	6,355	866
Oak Lawn	87.5	1,535	9.2	23.5	75.5	16.2	84.7	38.35	6,083	1,001
Oak Park	104.7	2,013	11.4	22.0	73.3	14.3	83.5	36.27	6,498	830
O'Fallon	47.3	1,618	0.0	NA	NA	NA	NA	NA	NA	NA
Orland Park	81.7	1,427	10.0	23.5	75.5	16.2	84.7	38.35	6,083	1,001
Oswego	34.4	1,087	4.1	NA	NA	NA	NA	NA	NA	NA
Palatine	119.0	1,722	8.2	18.4	72.1	9.6	82.3	36.56	7,149	624
Park Ridge	45.7	1,210	7.5	22.0	73.3	14.3	83.5	36.27	6,498	830
Pekin	49.3	1,445	2.2	24.4	75.8	15.7	87.4	35.71	5,695	1,088
Peoria	222.0	1,920	9.4	22.5	75.1	14.3	85.7	36.03	6,097	998
Plainfield	63.7	1,575	8.4	NA	NA	NA	NA	NA	NA	NA
Quincy	20.2	494	0.0	24.9	76.8	16.0	88.0	35.63	5,707	1,117
Rockford	164.6	1,090	17.5	19.0	72.9	10.8	83.1	36.63	6,933	768
Rock Island	36.5	939	12.7	21.8	76.4	13.3	85.1	35.10	6,179	1,100
Romeoville	169.7	4,271	2.3	NA	NA	NA	NA	NA	NA	NA
Round Lake Beach	25.1	897	4.0	19.9	72.2	12.1	82.2	35.50	6,955	634
St. Charles	142.6	4,289	12.8	19.3	72.6	10.9	83.0	37.22	6,975	679
Schaumburg	302.1	4,043	23.0	18.4	72.1	9.6	82.3	36.56	7,149	624
Skokie	66.5	1,022	0.0	22.0	73.3	14.3	83.5	36.27	6,498	830
Springfield	703.4	6,000	0.3	25.1	76.3	17.1	86.5	35.56	5,596	1,165
Streamwood	10.0	249	0.0	19.3	72.6	10.9	83.0	37.22	6,975	679
Tinley Park	45.9	803	5.2	21.8	76.4	13.3	85.1	35.10	6,179	1,100
Urbana	11.4	273	0.0	20.7	73.2	12.4	83.7	34.47	6,606	774
Vernon Hills	24.7	969	9.5	NA	NA	NA	NA	NA	NA	NA

1. Based on the population estimated as of July 1 of the year shown.   2. Represents normal values based on the 30-year period, 1971±2000.   3. Average daily minimum.   4. Average daily maximum.

Table D. Cities — Land Area and Population

STATE Place code	City	Land area¹ (sq. mi)	Total persons 2018	Rank	Per square mile	White	Black or African American	American Indian, Alaskan Native	Asian	Hawaiian Pacific Islander	Some other race	Two or more races (percent)
		1	2	3	4	5	6	7	8	9	10	11
	ILLINOIS— Cont'd											
17 79,293	Waukegan	24.3	86,792	383	3,571.7	37.0	22.5	1.1	4.9	0.1	31.1	3.2
17 80,060	West Chicago	15.4	27,045	1,357	1,756.2	60.2	3.7	0.1	8.7	0.0	25.7	1.6
17 81,048	Wheaton	11.3	53,150	728	4,703.5	82.6	6.5	0.0	6.0	0.0	0.9	3.9
17 81,087	Wheeling	8.7	38,878	992	4,468.7	62.6	5.8	0.7	17.3	0.6	10.3	2.8
17 82,075	Wilmette	5.4	27,265	1,346	5,049.1	NA	NA	NA	NA	NA	NA	NA
17 83,245	Woodridge	9.7	33,566	1,139	3,460.4	73.8	7.2	0.0	11.8	0.0	1.1	6.1
18 00,000	**INDIANA**	35,826.2	6,691,878	X	186.8	83.7	9.4	0.2	2.2	0.0	1.9	2.7
18 01,468	Anderson	42.7	55,037	692	1,288.9	78.7	13.1	0.6	1.4	0.0	2.0	4.1
18 05,860	Bloomington	23.3	84,981	397	3,647.3	81.8	3.8	0.2	9.5	0.1	0.5	4.1
18 10,342	Carmel	47.5	93,510	346	1,968.6	81.5	2.8	0.9	11.4	0.1	0.3	3.0
18 14,734	Columbus	28.0	47,543	814	1,698.0	83.6	2.5	0.0	11.6	0.0	1.2	1.1
18 16,138	Crown Point	17.8	30,059	1,251	1,688.7	83.0	5.5	0.0	2.1	0.0	2.8	6.6
18 19,486	East Chicago	14.1	27,930	1,322	1,980.9	25.2	34.6	0.1	0.0	0.0	39.2	0.9
18 20,728	Elkhart	27.1	52,367	736	1,932.4	74.9	18.2	0.0	0.5	0.1	3.9	2.4
18 22,000	Evansville	47.3	117,963	241	2,493.9	82.0	12.6	0.2	0.5	0.0	1.4	3.2
18 23,278	Fishers	35.3	93,362	347	2,644.8	83.6	7.2	0.0	6.4	0.0	1.1	1.8
18 25,000	Fort Wayne	110.6	267,633	77	2,419.8	72.6	15.0	0.3	5.5	0.0	1.7	4.9
18 27,000	Gary	49.7	75,282	468	1,514.7	15.7	79.1	0.1	0.2	0.0	3.0	1.9
18 28,386	Goshen	16.7	33,566	1,139	2,009.9	92.0	1.2	0.1	1.9	0.0	2.5	2.3
18 29,898	Greenwood	27.9	58,778	638	2,106.7	NA	NA	NA	NA	NA	NA	NA
18 31,000	Hammond	22.8	75,795	465	3,324.3	49.0	20.2	0.4	1.9	0.0	24.8	3.7
18 34,114	Hobart	26.2	28,040	1,317	1,070.2	79.9	7.7	1.3	0.9	0.4	2.9	7.0
18 36,000	Indianapolis	361.6	867,125	17	2,398.0	62.7	27.8	0.2	3.1	0.0	2.3	3.8
18 38,358	Jeffersonville	34.1	47,432	817	1,391.0	81.3	13.0	0.1	0.9	0.0	0.1	4.6
18 40,392	Kokomo	36.6	57,869	652	1,581.1	NA	NA	NA	NA	NA	NA	NA
18 40,788	Lafayette	29.4	72,168	496	2,454.7	87.5	6.9	0.1	0.9	0.0	2.9	1.8
18 42,426	Lawrence	20.1	49,046	786	2,440.1	54.1	34.9	0.3	3.5	0.0	2.2	5.1
18 46,908	Marion	15.6	28,047	1,316	1,797.9	NA	NA	NA	NA	NA	NA	NA
18 48,528	Merrillville	33.2	34,750	1,098	1,046.7	44.5	40.9	0.3	1.2	0.0	8.3	4.9
18 48,798	Michigan City	19.7	31,118	1,213	1,579.6	64.0	27.4	0.0	1.7	0.0	1.3	5.5
18 49,932	Mishawaka	17.6	49,931	770	2,837.0	80.0	11.0	0.6	1.6	0.2	0.1	6.6
18 51,876	Muncie	27.4	68,529	524	2,501.1	82.0	11.1	0.0	1.3	0.0	0.6	5.1
18 52,326	New Albany	14.9	36,604	1,048	2,456.6	84.7	11.1	0.0	1.2	0.0	0.9	2.1
18 54,180	Noblesville	33.2	63,133	591	1,901.6	90.5	4.0	0.1	1.8	0.0	0.5	3.1
18 60,246	Plainfield	25.2	34,386	1,108	1,364.5	NA	NA	NA	NA	NA	NA	NA
18 61,092	Portage	25.5	36,806	1,042	1,443.4	NA	NA	NA	NA	NA	NA	NA
18 64,260	Richmond	24.0	35,353	1,087	1,473.0	86.3	9.6	0.3	1.2	0.0	0.3	2.3
18 68,220	Schererville	14.8	28,501	1,303	1,925.7	80.9	6.2	0.0	1.1	0.0	3.4	8.4
18 71,000	South Bend	41.5	101,860	304	2,454.5	64.5	25.7	0.3	1.0	0.0	4.1	4.4
18 75,428	Terre Haute	34.5	60,753	614	1,761.0	83.0	9.2	0.4	1.0	0.2	0.9	5.2
18 78,326	Valparaiso	16.3	33,729	1,134	2,069.3	94.0	2.7	0.0	1.5	0.0	0.9	0.9
18 82,700	Westfield	30.4	41,528	919	1,366.1	NA	NA	NA	NA	NA	NA	NA
18 82,862	West Lafayette	13.6	48,308	801	3,552.1	66.2	6.4	0.8	22.6	0.2	0.0	3.8
19 00,000	**IOWA**	55,854.0	3,156,145	X	56.5	90.0	3.4	0.3	2.6	0.2	1.3	2.2
19 01,855	Ames	27.4	67,154	542	2,450.9	82.5	3.9	0.1	11.4	0.0	0.3	1.9
19 02,305	Ankeny	29.9	65,284	569	2,183.4	94.9	2.4	0.1	1.5	0.0	0.0	1.2
19 06,355	Bettendorf	21.3	36,543	1,052	1,715.6	89.2	1.9	0.0	6.2	0.0	0.1	2.5
19 09,550	Burlington	14.4	24,838	1,418	1,724.9	NA	NA	NA	NA	NA	NA	NA
19 11,755	Cedar Falls	28.9	41,048	934	1,420.3	91.2	2.9	0.0	4.4	0.0	0.0	1.6
19 12,000	Cedar Rapids	70.8	133,174	208	1,881.0	83.2	8.4	0.2	2.9	0.3	2.4	2.5
19 14,430	Clinton	35.2	25,184	1,410	715.5	90.0	3.6	0.1	1.1	0.0	0.0	5.2
19 16,860	Council Bluffs	42.9	62,421	599	1,455.0	89.1	1.5	0.7	0.1	0.0	4.6	4.0
19 19,000	Davenport	63.5	102,085	303	1,607.6	82.8	10.5	0.3	2.6	0.0	0.3	3.4
19 21,000	Des Moines	88.2	216,853	101	2,458.7	72.9	10.5	0.4	8.1	0.1	3.3	4.7
19 22,395	Dubuque	30.6	57,941	651	1,893.5	89.7	4.1	0.1	1.4	3.0	0.7	1.2
19 28,515	Fort Dodge	16.0	24,098	1,427	1,506.1	87.0	6.5	0.1	2.3	0.0	1.9	2.2
19 38,595	Iowa City	25.6	76,290	458	2,980.1	80.2	6.7	0.1	8.7	0.0	0.9	3.4
19 49,485	Marion	17.6	39,979	961	2,271.5	NA	NA	NA	NA	NA	NA	NA
19 49,755	Marshalltown	19.3	27,068	1,356	1,402.5	84.9	1.1	0.0	3.6	0.0	6.2	4.2
19 50,160	Mason City	27.8	27,093	1,354	974.6	NA	NA	NA	NA	NA	NA	NA
19 60,465	Ottumwa	15.9	24,550	1,424	1,544.0	80.2	4.0	0.0	0.9	2.4	10.1	2.4
19 73,335	Sioux City	58.4	82,396	413	1,410.9	82.8	3.9	2.9	3.4	0.7	2.6	3.8
19 79,950	Urbandale	22.5	43,949	872	1,953.3	92.1	3.3	0.1	2.5	0.0	0.6	1.4
19 82,425	Waterloo	61.5	67,798	534	1,102.4	75.7	15.9	0.3	2.3	0.3	1.6	3.9
19 83,910	West Des Moines	47.1	66,641	551	1,414.9	85.8	3.5	0.0	8.0	0.0	0.1	2.5

1. Dry land or land partially or temporarily covered by water. 2. Hispanic or Latino persons may be of any race.

Table D. Cities — Population

City	Percent Hispanic or Latino[1], 2017	Percent foreign born, 2017	Age of population (percent), 2017							Median age, 2017	Percent female, 2017	Population			
			Under 18 years	18 to 24 years	25 to 34 years	35 to 44 years	45 to 54 years	55 to 64 years	65 years and over			Census counts		Percent change	
												2000	2010	2000-2010	2001-2018
	12	13	14	15	16	17	18	19	20	21	22	23	24	25	26
ILLINOIS— Cont'd															
Waukegan	53.6	31.0	27.6	11.6	14.8	14.0	11.6	10.3	10.0	32.0	50.0	87,901	89,072	1.3	-2.6
West Chicago	50.0	30.9	29.6	9.8	14.2	11.4	15.9	11.6	7.5	32.5	47.5	23,469	27,221	16.0	-0.6
Wheaton	5.8	13.5	22.8	10.6	14.3	7.7	14.4	12.8	17.4	37.9	51.8	55,416	53,014	-4.3	0.3
Wheeling	24.8	41.2	20.4	7.9	18.1	11.6	11.4	14.1	16.4	37.1	50.7	34,496	37,642	9.1	3.3
Wilmette	1.7	15.8	31.5	5.1	3.1	12.5	13.9	15.3	18.6	43.5	49.2	27,651	27,057	-2.1	0.8
Woodridge	19.5	26.8	23.2	9.4	14.0	14.6	13.3	13.3	12.2	36.5	50.9	30,934	32,980	6.6	1.8
INDIANA	6.9	5.3	23.6	9.9	13.0	12.3	12.8	13.0	15.4	37.7	50.7	6,080,485	6,484,061	6.6	3.2
Anderson	7.4	3.7	21.4	9.4	14.5	12.1	11.5	12.4	18.6	39.2	52.1	59,734	56,169	-6.0	-2.0
Bloomington	4.9	12.5	11.0	40.9	15.0	9.8	5.9	7.8	9.5	24.3	49.2	69,291	80,314	15.9	5.8
Carmel	2.5	11.4	26.4	7.1	9.4	15.8	14.6	12.4	14.2	39.5	50.3	37,733	79,189	109.9	18.1
Columbus	5.5	12.3	22.3	8.2	16.3	12.7	12.3	10.7	17.6	37.4	50.5	39,059	44,088	12.9	7.8
Crown Point	12.4	4.9	21.1	6.9	13.4	14.4	14.5	9.8	19.9	42.5	50.8	19,806	27,868	40.7	7.9
East Chicago	58.4	16.7	30.1	8.2	11.1	13.4	9.2	15.1	12.8	35.4	54.9	32,414	29,698	-8.4	-6.0
Elkhart	23.5	11.3	24.4	9.9	15.0	11.4	13.2	11.4	14.7	35.4	53.3	51,874	51,932	0.1	0.8
Evansville	2.9	2.6	20.3	10.8	15.5	11.6	12.8	12.2	17.0	37.2	52.2	121,582	120,075	-1.2	-1.8
Fishers	4.6	11.1	29.4	6.3	14.1	14.2	16.2	11.0	9.0	35.3	52.1	37,835	77,325	104.4	20.7
Fort Wayne	9.7	8.7	24.9	9.8	14.7	11.8	12.1	12.6	14.1	35.6	51.7	205,727	253,739	23.3	5.5
Gary	5.7	1.9	23.5	9.0	10.6	13.5	11.4	13.9	18.1	39.5	53.5	102,746	80,315	-21.8	-6.3
Goshen	24.6	13.1	28.0	8.5	12.5	13.2	7.9	12.2	17.6	35.6	51.9	29,383	32,107	9.3	4.5
Greenwood	7.7	7.7	22.9	9.5	18.0	15.4	11.8	9.0	13.5	34.8	50.6	36,037	51,183	42.0	14.8
Hammond	40.0	12.8	28.4	11.0	14.3	12.3	11.3	11.3	11.4	32.8	50.7	83,048	80,824	-2.7	-6.2
Hobart	10.1	3.8	26.3	8.7	11.5	11.1	9.3	15.9	17.3	38.5	53.6	25,363	29,382	15.8	-4.6
Indianapolis	10.9	10.4	24.6	9.3	17.2	12.9	11.8	12.0	12.2	34.2	51.7	NA	820,436	NA	5.7
Jeffersonville	6.5	3.8	22.8	6.7	14.6	14.2	12.2	14.7	14.8	38.7	54.1	27,362	45,031	64.6	5.3
Kokomo	3.8	1.7	21.6	9.2	12.5	9.8	12.4	15.3	19.3	41.7	53.1	46,113	58,061	25.9	-0.3
Lafayette	16.5	8.9	23.7	10.9	18.3	11.1	11.3	10.8	13.9	33.2	48.5	56,397	68,862	22.1	4.8
Lawrence	9.5	8.9	28.5	8.9	13.2	14.4	12.6	12.2	10.2	34.4	52.1	38,915	46,003	18.2	6.6
Marion	6.3	0.7	21.4	15.3	10.8	7.1	10.8	12.4	22.3	37.5	55.1	31,320	29,926	-4.5	-6.3
Merrillville	12.9	6.8	20.6	6.1	16.0	13.1	14.7	12.8	16.7	40.8	54.8	30,560	34,973	14.4	-0.6
Michigan City	3.6	3.5	22.9	8.5	18.6	11.3	11.2	15.5	11.9	35.0	49.0	32,900	31,454	-4.4	-1.1
Mishawaka	6.0	7.4	25.0	10.0	18.3	11.8	9.7	10.9	14.3	33.3	54.4	46,557	48,309	3.8	3.4
Muncie	3.7	2.6	16.7	28.5	12.4	10.2	8.3	10.6	13.2	28.0	51.8	67,430	70,210	4.1	-2.4
New Albany	6.8	3.3	22.1	9.7	13.0	14.0	14.0	13.2	14.0	39.0	49.0	37,603	36,349	-3.3	0.7
Noblesville	4.6	2.7	29.2	7.0	15.0	16.1	11.5	9.0	12.3	34.3	50.4	28,590	52,217	82.6	20.9
Plainfield	2.9	4.5	23.3	9.9	10.2	12.6	15.9	12.3	15.8	39.4	50.7	18,396	27,694	50.5	24.2
Portage	23.0	3.3	23.0	11.3	12.6	15.4	13.1	12.2	12.3	36.2	52.3	33,496	36,830	10.0	-0.1
Richmond	5.0	2.2	19.5	9.8	14.5	9.7	13.6	14.4	18.6	40.5	52.4	39,124	36,779	-6.0	-3.9
Schererville	19.8	7.9	15.6	10.1	8.8	11.4	17.3	15.4	21.3	47.1	52.4	24,851	29,247	17.7	-2.6
South Bend	15.1	7.9	24.8	11.3	15.1	12.3	12.5	10.7	13.3	34.3	50.1	107,789	101,241	-6.1	0.6
Terre Haute	3.5	2.3	20.0	20.2	14.6	10.3	11.1	10.2	13.7	31.4	49.2	59,614	60,785	2.0	-0.1
Valparaiso	7.3	4.8	20.7	14.9	14.9	12.2	10.5	8.9	17.9	34.7	51.5	27,428	31,738	15.7	6.3
Westfield	2.4	5.1	29.7	7.9	12.8	15.7	16.5	8.4	9.1	34.6	52.7	9,293	30,134	224.3	37.8
West Lafayette	4.7	24.9	9.1	60.5	10.0	6.1	3.8	4.0	6.5	21.9	46.8	28,778	42,008	46.0	15.0
IOWA	5.9	5.3	23.2	10.2	12.5	11.9	12.2	13.3	16.7	38.3	50.3	2,926,324	3,046,872	4.1	3.6
Ames	3.5	13.2	11.8	40.6	14.4	8.6	6.0	8.4	10.3	23.8	45.9	50,731	59,037	16.4	13.7
Ankeny	2.2	3.2	26.1	10.5	16.8	14.3	12.1	8.9	11.4	32.8	49.7	27,117	45,612	68.2	43.1
Bettendorf	4.6	7.1	27.7	5.9	13.0	12.6	13.4	12.7	14.7	38.1	51.1	31,275	33,213	6.2	10.0
Burlington	4.2	1.9	23.2	8.9	10.6	11.0	12.1	13.1	21.1	41.8	52.6	26,839	25,606	-4.6	-3.0
Cedar Falls	1.6	5.3	15.5	29.1	12.3	8.3	8.9	10.1	15.8	29.2	52.2	36,145	39,259	8.6	4.6
Cedar Rapids	4.7	6.3	23.8	9.9	15.3	12.6	11.3	11.1	16.0	35.9	51.4	120,758	126,430	4.7	5.3
Clinton	4.0	3.0	20.6	8.3	13.3	9.3	13.1	16.7	18.6	43.2	50.7	27,772	26,880	-3.2	-6.3
Council Bluffs	10.0	5.5	23.0	11.0	10.9	12.8	13.0	13.7	15.5	38.9	51.6	58,268	62,227	6.8	0.3
Davenport	8.8	4.4	22.3	10.4	14.0	12.5	12.5	13.7	14.7	38.0	50.7	98,359	99,693	1.4	2.4
Des Moines	14.4	13.7	24.3	11.0	16.4	13.0	11.6	11.4	12.3	33.6	51.2	198,682	204,183	2.8	6.2
Dubuque	2.1	4.8	20.5	12.8	14.5	10.3	11.9	13.1	16.9	37.2	51.8	57,686	57,605	-0.1	0.6
Fort Dodge	6.7	5.2	20.1	15.1	13.6	10.2	11.6	13.3	16.2	36.0	47.8	25,136	25,206	0.3	-4.4
Iowa City	7.2	14.6	13.7	36.0	14.3	9.4	7.9	8.2	10.5	25.2	49.7	62,220	67,946	9.2	12.3
Marion	0.0	1.3	21.6	10.1	9.9	13.8	16.4	14.2	14.2	40.9	51.9	26,294	35,160	33.7	13.7
Marshalltown	30.1	15.5	26.1	8.4	13.0	14.1	8.6	11.9	17.9	37.0	49.7	26,009	27,557	6.0	-1.8
Mason City	5.6	0.8	20.7	8.8	13.8	10.8	10.9	14.3	20.7	42.3	53.6	29,172	28,079	-3.7	-3.5
Ottumwa	14.9	5.5	23.3	10.9	11.5	14.1	13.1	13.0	14.0	37.8	49.6	24,998	25,021	0.1	-1.9
Sioux City	19.8	11.0	27.3	10.5	13.5	12.2	11.4	11.6	13.5	34.2	51.0	85,013	82,693	-2.7	-0.4
Urbandale	3.2	4.7	30.9	4.6	13.1	12.3	14.0	13.2	11.9	35.8	53.0	29,072	39,459	35.7	11.4
Waterloo	7.4	6.7	23.0	9.8	14.5	10.8	12.3	13.7	15.8	37.1	51.6	68,747	68,408	-0.5	-0.9
West Des Moines	4.9	10.6	24.3	6.2	17.6	13.3	14.0	10.4	14.2	36.5	50.0	46,403	56,706	22.2	17.5

1. May be of any race.

Table D. Cities — Households, Group Quarters, Crime, and Education

City	Households, 2017							Persons in group quarters, 2017	Serious crimes known to police[2], 2016				Educational attainment, 2017		
			Percent						Total		Rate[3]			Attainment[4] (percent)	
	Number	Persons per household	Family	Married couple family	Female headed[1]	Non-family	One person		Number	Rate	Violent	Property	Population age 25 and over	High school graduate or less	Bachelor's degree or more
	27	28	29	30	31	32	33	34	35	36	37	38	39	40	41

City	27	28	29	30	31	32	33	34	35	36	37	38	39	40	41
ILLINOIS— Cont'd															
Waukegan	29,913	2.90	69.4	42.2	18.7	30.6	25.5	2,143	2,736	3,097	508	2,589	53,987	58.4	14.1
West Chicago	6,794	3.42	74.7	52.2	14.8	25.3	20.8	NA	327	1,190	124	1,066	14,284	48.9	32.9
Wheaton	19,445	2.59	69.3	60.1	6.9	30.7	25.1	3,052	364	676	59	617	35,509	14.7	63.9
Wheeling	14,280	2.67	65.7	43.7	18.2	34.3	29.5	501	464	1,216	123	1,093	27,641	29.6	44.5
Wilmette	9,326	2.91	79.7	73.2	5.1	20.3	18.4	NA	319	1,161	40	1,121	17,289	5.8	85.7
Woodridge	12,576	2.64	69.5	56.1	9.9	30.5	24.3	NA	483	1,444	111	1,334	22,462	21.1	53.7
INDIANA	2,557,299	2.53	64.9	48.2	11.8	35.1	28.9	187,264	198,604	2,994	405	2,589	4,435,317	44.1	26.8
Anderson	23,532	2.22	54.7	33.3	17.2	45.3	39.7	2,340	2,534	4,596	435	4,161	37,683	52.3	16.1
Bloomington	32,643	2.17	42.3	28.9	10.9	57.7	36.1	14,693	3,081	3,634	446	3,189	41,161	21.8	56.8
Carmel	34,928	2.65	74.3	64.2	6.2	25.7	21.0	557	828	914	28	886	61,988	10.5	72.4
Columbus	19,336	2.49	63.7	46.8	12.5	36.3	29.5	882	1,977	4,187	72	4,115	34,118	35.6	40.3
Crown Point	11,846	2.40	65.9	52.2	12.7	34.1	33.6	1,486	371	1,276	31	1,245	21,542	32.2	33.4
East Chicago	10,727	2.62	64.0	34.5	25.3	36.0	34.8	NA	1,271	4,459	674	3,786	17,405	62.6	7.8
Elkhart	20,425	2.39	61.2	31.8	22.1	38.8	33.9	937	3,055	5,818	1,507	4,312	32,763	58.4	13.2
Evansville	52,799	2.16	51.3	31.9	14.1	48.7	38.9	4,115	6,643	5,540	635	4,905	81,350	42.8	22.6
Fishers	32,159	2.83	75.2	58.7	11.0	24.8	20.7	NA	965	1,059	27	1,032	58,540	10.4	68.6
Fort Wayne	101,062	2.48	60.2	40.4	13.4	39.8	32.3	4,595	9,964	3,808	397	3,411	166,488	41.5	25.0
Gary	29,978	2.52	61.9	23.1	31.7	38.1	33.5	788	4,077	5,326	601	4,725	51,571	54.3	13.5
Goshen	11,808	2.72	73.6	53.0	14.5	26.4	22.9	1,320	1,322	3,986	151	3,835	21,208	51.8	25.7
Greenwood	25,112	2.45	65.2	48.6	13.0	34.8	27.0	480	2,184	3,865	462	3,403	41,869	35.3	38.3
Hammond	26,914	2.81	61.9	37.6	18.5	38.1	32.2	966	3,296	4,280	701	3,579	46,423	57.5	13.8
Hobart	10,153	2.82	71.8	54.9	12.0	28.2	23.4	NA	1,374	4,868	291	4,578	18,785	40.3	24.4
Indianapolis	334,101	2.52	58.6	35.4	13.9	45.2	37.4	15,924	53,447	6,169	1,374	4,795	566,821	43.0	32.1
Jeffersonville	18,830	2.45	62.5	45.0	11.6	37.5	29.8	NA	1,435	3,032	137	2,895	33,239	44.2	16.8
Kokomo	25,178	2.16	55.8	38.0	15.2	44.2	40.4	1,003	2,201	3,796	761	3,035	38,358	55.8	16.2
Lafayette	30,593	2.28	54.2	34.3	13.5	45.8	36.2	1,366	3,376	4,718	503	4,215	46,587	42.2	26.9
Lawrence	17,651	2.75	62.6	48.0	10.6	37.4	35.1	158	6	12	2	10	30,482	38.7	35.2
Marion	11,009	2.25	63.2	35.7	24.3	36.8	34.1	4,031	1,271	4,394	398	3,996	18,250	47.5	20.4
Merrillville	15,018	2.36	60.2	41.7	14.6	39.8	30.9	413	1,370	3,884	139	3,745	26,287	49.1	23.9
Michigan City	12,686	2.28	51.6	30.2	15.9	48.4	40.9	2,824	1,630	5,181	591	4,590	21,739	51.5	14.5
Mishawaka	20,208	2.35	53.6	32.7	14.4	46.4	39.5	1,080	2,688	5,569	342	5,227	31,508	41.1	24.2
Muncie	27,760	2.21	48.7	29.7	14.3	51.3	36.6	7,143	3,007	4,292	360	3,932	37,487	46.1	24.1
New Albany	14,059	2.46	55.4	34.5	15.3	44.6	36.1	1,138	1,192	3,239	120	3,119	24,314	47.2	23.5
Noblesville	23,113	2.67	68.3	53.7	11.3	31.7	24.6	795	NA	NA	NA	NA	39,841	23.6	49.1
Plainfield	11,786	2.50	67.9	49.8	10.9	32.1	29.5	1,826	1,006	3,225	285	2,939	20,891	37.5	25.6
Portage	13,988	2.69	68.4	36.9	26.0	31.6	25.6	NA	160	436	33	403	24,841	50.4	17.8
Richmond	15,107	2.20	58.2	38.9	18.5	41.8	34.8	2,393	NA	NA	NA	NA	25,216	44.0	22.8
Schererville	12,647	2.25	64.1	50.5	8.0	35.9	30.8	NA	NA	NA	NA	NA	21,244	29.4	37.0
South Bend	36,161	2.57	57.1	35.6	16.2	42.9	35.9	3,096	6,203	6,104	1,020	5,084	61,440	46.6	24.2
Terre Haute	23,293	2.26	51.3	29.7	18.0	48.7	39.4	7,784	3,307	5,436	258	5,178	36,132	44.3	23.7
Valparaiso	13,480	2.18	54.6	39.8	11.9	45.4	36.5	3,479	409	1,247	85	1,162	21,203	34.9	38.5
Westfield	14,119	2.82	74.5	61.3	13.2	25.5	20.7	NA	435	1,139	63	1,076	24,910	12.8	59.9
West Lafayette	14,148	2.38	37.9	28.6	7.3	62.1	33.4	14,459	509	1,100	123	977	14,638	12.6	76.3
IOWA	1,257,505	2.42	63.2	50.5	8.6	36.8	29.2	100,003	74,501	2,377	291	2,086	2,093,909	38.4	28.9
Ames	25,877	2.13	40.6	36.4	2.6	59.4	31.7	11,362	1,184	1,785	161	1,624	31,672	16.1	63.3
Ankeny	23,793	2.59	61.5	50.1	6.8	38.5	24.6	805	891	1,504	218	1,286	39,610	20.5	44.9
Bettendorf	13,719	2.60	65.2	52.2	10.8	34.8	29.8	NA	633	1,761	164	1,597	23,780	22.5	51.2
Burlington	10,908	2.19	58.9	44.8	11.3	41.1	35.3	454	1,238	4,879	816	4,063	16,531	37.8	21.7
Cedar Falls	14,687	2.32	55.4	47.9	5.9	44.6	31.5	4,074	775	1,861	158	1,702	21,125	21.5	50.3
Cedar Rapids	54,284	2.38	58.0	43.3	10.7	42.0	34.5	3,152	5,491	4,186	297	3,889	87,695	32.3	33.2
Clinton	10,875	2.32	55.3	37.0	16.4	44.7	32.8	635	1,392	5,373	896	4,478	18,398	55.9	15.5
Council Bluffs	23,967	2.51	58.6	43.9	11.0	41.4	34.0	2,110	4,016	6,411	239	6,172	41,089	47.7	19.6
Davenport	38,402	2.58	54.7	38.8	10.3	45.3	36.3	3,368	5,751	5,577	727	4,850	68,868	43.7	24.3
Des Moines	84,654	2.51	57.5	37.1	14.5	42.5	33.0	4,878	10,377	4,906	710	4,197	140,856	46.7	26.2
Dubuque	23,773	2.29	56.3	40.6	9.9	43.7	35.5	3,897	2,073	3,512	356	3,156	38,840	35.8	33.4
Fort Dodge	9,592	2.23	56.0	35.1	12.5	44.0	35.9	2,750	1,144	4,659	586	4,072	15,639	47.3	13.4
Iowa City	30,418	2.27	41.4	34.9	5.4	58.6	32.8	6,636	1,755	2,324	265	2,059	38,152	17.2	62.9
Marion	15,553	2.51	69.1	52.7	10.9	30.9	24.2	307	683	1,805	196	1,609	26,937	30.4	33.3
Marshalltown	11,203	2.43	63.7	43.5	14.2	36.3	30.8	1,077	987	3,572	583	2,990	18,548	52.6	18.4
Mason City	12,467	2.11	59.5	43.9	12.8	40.5	34.0	945	1,163	4,271	140	4,131	19,235	39.6	18.2
Ottumwa	10,896	2.26	62.2	44.1	12.2	37.8	29.7	801	1,207	4,918	440	4,478	16,772	44.0	19.5
Sioux City	31,176	2.61	62.5	40.5	14.5	37.5	29.2	2,778	3,658	4,417	442	3,975	52,304	47.6	23.0
Urbandale	15,551	2.69	68.8	60.1	5.8	31.2	23.1	352	776	1,724	153	1,571	27,222	19.1	46.3
Waterloo	28,449	2.34	58.6	40.8	10.8	41.4	35.4	941	2,633	3,845	740	3,105	45,407	45.1	20.8
West Des Moines	27,041	2.32	58.8	47.1	7.9	41.2	30.6	378	1,662	2,532	227	2,305	43,907	17.3	54.3

1. No spouse present. 2. Data for serious crimes have not been adjusted for underreporting. This may affect comparability between geographic areas and over time. 3. Per 100,000 population estimated by the FBI. 4. Persons 25 years old and over.

City	Money income, 2017					Median earnings, 2017			Housing units, 2017				
	Households			Median family income	Median non-family income	All persons	Men	Women	Total	Occupied	Percent owner occupied	Median value[1] (dollars)	Median gross rent (dollars)
	Median income	Percent with income less than $20,000	Percent with income of $200,000 or more										
	42	43	44	45	46	47	48	49	50	51	52	53	54
ILLINOIS— Cont'd													
Waukegan	48,029	14.5	3.2	52,999	37,698	25,944	28,081	22,134	32,005	29,913	48.1	138,800	920
West Chicago	73,677	13.6	11.0	90,526	31,801	30,591	38,701	26,454	7,053	6,794	69.2	243,600	945
Wheaton	95,538	8.2	18.6	121,016	51,258	44,201	59,060	34,173	20,733	19,445	73.8	336,800	1,358
Wheeling	62,429	9.5	4.2	70,442	51,206	30,743	30,677	30,947	14,671	14,280	57.4	190,900	1,182
Wilmette	154,664	8.8	41.2	199,664	40,710	70,046	106,899	42,455	10,556	9,326	88.5	731,700	1,388
Woodridge	83,235	6.9	8.9	91,858	42,126	42,495	50,315	36,073	13,387	12,576	64.9	280,700	1,440
INDIANA	54,181	16.1	3.9	68,085	31,574	32,069	40,283	26,129	2,885,342	2,557,299	69.0	141,100	793
Anderson	31,911	31.0	0.9	37,196	26,015	21,274	29,834	17,091	29,349	23,532	53.8	69,500	686
Bloomington	38,897	32.1	2.8	65,684	21,941	14,954	16,322	13,505	35,102	32,643	34.2	196,900	837
Carmel	109,858	3.2	21.8	135,827	57,850	61,179	79,469	47,689	37,900	34,928	74.8	345,900	1,150
Columbus	60,143	13.5	4.5	78,636	35,102	35,723	45,861	30,015	21,636	19,336	64.4	163,300	890
Crown Point	67,671	14.6	4.2	84,125	0	42,092	57,418	34,727	12,057	11,846	80.7	190,800	993
East Chicago	34,358	25.8	0.5	40,663	27,239	29,427	32,709	26,772	14,793	10,727	42.8	71,100	666
Elkhart	41,786	23.1	0.9	49,457	28,917	28,077	32,186	25,250	23,625	20,425	50.5	95,500	675
Evansville	36,690	27.4	1.9	50,483	25,423	26,540	31,995	21,998	58,698	52,799	57.1	92,700	712
Fishers	113,560	1.8	16.6	128,048	59,274	60,937	75,005	46,401	33,466	32,159	82.0	274,000	1,226
Fort Wayne	46,599	18.2	3.2	57,432	30,225	29,513	35,744	24,147	113,739	101,062	60.5	117,900	721
Gary	26,669	36.8	1.4	31,133	19,032	22,253	26,741	19,872	43,234	29,978	54.9	66,900	733
Goshen	53,196	15.5	2.8	61,271	32,920	31,026	38,474	22,136	12,747	11,808	56.5	117,400	813
Greenwood	65,547	8.7	2.6	86,058	47,810	40,312	48,694	31,484	26,137	25,112	61.4	148,400	984
Hammond	45,999	22.3	1.1	52,144	31,743	27,272	34,384	21,609	30,129	26,914	54.9	89,200	823
Hobart	53,123	9.7	0.6	58,316	35,568	33,601	42,895	27,886	10,768	10,153	73.8	127,000	881
Indianapolis	47,225	20.0	4.2	59,275	33,403	31,282	34,781	28,139	384,967	334,101	53.5	137,600	870
Jeffersonville	54,415	13.9	0.4	60,734	41,758	32,678	34,792	31,876	21,505	18,830	67.5	134,000	785
Kokomo	41,233	24.4	0.9	55,470	27,739	26,924	30,692	25,914	29,399	25,178	64.9	80,900	683
Lafayette	45,315	17.0	1.3	57,936	32,749	27,795	36,323	22,425	33,724	30,593	52.4	105,300	798
Lawrence	50,606	18.4	3.2	78,398	28,078	37,392	39,045	35,406	19,401	17,651	64.3	152,200	901
Marion	32,913	30.0	0.0	34,466	27,529	14,177	22,106	12,258	13,769	11,009	57.2	73,200	682
Merrillville	65,675	11.8	1.5	74,209	48,934	41,449	51,702	32,190	16,658	15,018	71.2	137,000	1,056
Michigan City	35,445	25.3	0.6	51,604	25,984	24,436	30,933	21,136	14,615	12,686	48.3	84,800	703
Mishawaka	41,081	21.9	1.1	48,710	27,785	25,597	34,813	20,654	24,796	20,208	50.0	101,500	804
Muncie	30,555	34.2	0.5	49,505	20,297	15,533	17,035	13,453	32,779	27,760	44.4	72,100	692
New Albany	47,247	22.8	2.2	60,782	31,979	34,112	36,498	31,667	17,171	14,059	56.5	119,200	757
Noblesville	78,605	6.9	7.7	89,903	45,443	43,607	52,282	34,006	24,265	23,113	72.8	196,900	963
Plainfield	53,301	8.0	2.8	71,225	41,935	34,459	36,212	31,981	12,393	11,786	56.7	182,800	987
Portage	50,821	22.3	1.0	54,034	34,670	31,970	41,814	22,775	14,346	13,988	58.0	151,700	855
Richmond	35,725	21.7	3.4	51,727	25,865	25,532	25,904	24,107	18,369	15,107	56.9	91,000	708
Schererville	66,883	11.4	5.2	83,847	34,001	40,549	45,788	33,412	13,161	12,647	78.9	210,100	919
South Bend	42,007	22.4	2.4	51,559	29,726	26,676	31,165	21,801	45,688	36,161	56.5	87,600	758
Terre Haute	34,575	29.2	1.5	42,890	26,050	19,852	24,046	16,690	26,311	23,293	55.3	79,400	739
Valparaiso	57,386	16.8	5.9	79,272	40,622	35,978	56,375	26,913	14,097	13,480	48.6	201,900	895
Westfield	88,036	7.1	11.1	102,787	55,195	42,531	60,340	34,612	15,594	14,119	84.5	261,900	1,027
West Lafayette	30,880	37.9	6.5	88,519	17,888	7,016	7,402	6,589	15,622	14,148	31.9	195,800	802
IOWA	58,570	14.3	4.0	75,076	34,335	33,349	40,624	27,348	1,397,739	1,257,505	71.6	149,100	760
Ames	51,860	22.0	5.5	102,971	29,301	14,357	15,777	12,603	27,913	25,877	41.7	216,000	916
Ankeny	83,416	3.7	7.5	106,549	58,109	40,562	57,520	32,031	24,815	23,793	76.8	235,500	1,058
Bettendorf	75,052	9.2	9.8	91,974	41,034	41,481	53,733	33,572	15,708	13,719	75.1	199,300	895
Burlington	43,342	21.0	3.8	64,334	30,472	30,964	41,229	21,550	12,091	10,908	63.0	97,000	860
Cedar Falls	51,458	13.4	4.3	84,314	28,932	20,878	28,036	13,747	15,302	14,687	62.9	187,100	780
Cedar Rapids	56,096	11.2	2.6	69,660	38,567	33,529	37,334	30,576	60,024	54,284	70.7	143,600	767
Clinton	40,770	23.7	1.9	55,115	24,661	26,260	33,960	21,515	12,523	10,875	63.7	94,600	640
Council Bluffs	52,544	17.3	2.5	69,986	31,722	32,648	35,475	29,416	26,074	23,967	62.9	124,800	769
Davenport	50,081	16.8	2.3	65,051	36,789	31,144	40,578	25,790	44,913	38,402	65.3	130,900	766
Des Moines	51,355	17.1	2.4	59,109	37,216	31,111	35,903	26,568	93,513	84,654	61.0	134,300	818
Dubuque	53,709	16.8	3.7	75,188	33,185	32,056	38,999	27,423	26,746	23,773	66.7	144,200	764
Fort Dodge	34,294	32.4	2.5	48,557	17,000	22,919	29,508	21,110	10,832	9,592	54.4	105,600	624
Iowa City	50,320	23.2	4.9	85,132	30,676	20,834	21,393	19,901	33,178	30,418	49.6	219,100	970
Marion	76,337	9.7	4.8	91,711	32,819	35,201	46,321	31,457	16,329	15,553	78.5	162,200	599
Marshalltown	47,851	20.3	1.4	51,367	29,933	31,697	41,160	24,462	11,723	11,203	63.4	96,800	733
Mason City	52,266	16.5	2.9	69,655	31,133	33,189	40,097	30,047	13,890	12,467	63.3	125,800	725
Ottumwa	44,691	20.0	0.7	54,055	27,705	29,837	40,164	20,577	11,935	10,896	67.3	77,700	726
Sioux City	53,332	17.9	2.5	65,711	32,984	31,128	37,174	24,087	34,054	31,176	62.1	115,700	753
Urbandale	81,199	7.2	13.2	110,780	44,898	45,896	52,372	37,330	16,077	15,551	79.0	225,500	870
Waterloo	42,346	20.5	2.9	52,339	28,903	26,736	31,463	21,725	32,228	28,449	59.3	125,200	715
West Des Moines	76,431	8.4	8.9	100,327	56,580	47,559	53,273	40,056	29,063	27,041	64.4	225,200	999

1. Based on population estimated by the American Community Survey.   2. Includes units rented or sold but not occupied.   3. Specified owner-occupied units; $1,000,000 represents $1,000,000 or more.   4. 50.0 represents 50 percent or more.   5. 10.0 represents 10 percent or less.

Table D. Cities — Commuting, Computer Access, Migration, Labor Force, and Employment

City	Commuting¹, 2017		Computer access², 2017		Migration, 2017		Civilian labor force, 2018		Unemployment		Civilian employment⁴, 2017			
	Percent		Percent								Population age 16 and older		Population age 16 to 64	
	Commuting	With commutes of 30 minutes or more	With a computer in the house	With Internet access	Percent who lived in the same house one year ago	Percent who lived in another state or county one year ago	Total	Percent change 2017 -2018	Total	Rate³	Number	Percent in labor force	Number	Percent who worked full-year full-time
	55	56	57	58	59	60	61	62	63	64	65	66	67	68
ILLINOIS— Cont'd														
Waukegan	72.8	37.5	92.9	83.5	82.6	4.7	45,527	1.4	2,678	5.9	67,201	71.2	58,293	50.8
West Chicago	80.9	30.2	94.3	83.9	NA	NA	14,128	-0.8	542	3.8	16,947	72.1	15,184	53.0
Wheaton	73.4	34.5	92.7	90.4	84.6	9.4	28,696	-0.8	825	2.9	42,458	65.1	33,198	50.2
Wheeling	76.3	38.0	92.1	82.5	85.2	7.3	22,631	-0.6	715	3.2	31,630	73.6	25,291	62.5
Wilmette	71.7	53.9	95.2	92.7	91.2	4.0	12,820	-0.6	358	2.8	19,894	61.6	14,826	46.1
Woodridge	68.5	50.9	94.7	93.3	80.4	10.6	20,159	-0.8	599	3.0	26,851	74.8	22,777	58.0
INDIANA	82.4	31.1	88.8	80.8	85.5	6.3	3,381,713	1.4	116,133	3.4	5,275,305	63.4	4,251,419	51.4
Anderson	79.4	32.6	82.0	71.1	84.0	3.9	23,550	1.3	1,007	4.3	43,882	54.9	33,743	39.5
Bloomington	64.4	14.0	93.0	86.4	56.4	22.6	38,241	1.7	1,508	3.9	77,380	57.7	69,268	30.3
Carmel	81.7	34.6	97.6	96.6	83.2	8.0	50,641	1.5	1,334	2.6	70,720	70.5	57,509	59.5
Columbus	81.1	19.8	90.0	80.6	81.0	6.8	25,930	1.7	667	2.6	39,078	63.9	30,458	51.4
Crown Point	83.0	40.2	88.6	87.5	90.8	2.1	15,457	1.1	659	4.3	24,134	61.3	18,172	50.3
East Chicago	75.3	36.3	76.9	56.7	86.2	10.0	10,051	0.5	665	6.6	20,467	53.4	16,860	43.6
Elkhart	74.2	24.5	84.5	75.3	79.7	8.6	27,246	3.6	857	3.1	38,804	63.9	31,468	49.1
Evansville	84.2	17.7	85.7	77.0	78.1	6.6	60,147	1.5	2,041	3.4	96,201	60.6	76,206	48.3
Fishers	78.1	42.3	99.1	97.2	88.1	7.6	51,827	1.4	1,350	2.6	66,190	74.5	58,041	65.1
Fort Wayne	82.6	21.5	91.3	84.9	84.2	4.9	128,440	1.9	4,243	3.3	198,548	66.0	162,626	51.4
Gary	78.8	37.8	79.7	65.5	86.8	3.6	27,131	0.7	1,949	7.2	61,751	47.8	47,944	34.8
Goshen	65.7	15.0	83.1	79.5	83.0	6.3	18,048	3.4	457	2.5	24,789	62.2	18,896	54.3
Greenwood	89.5	38.5	95.9	92.7	82.7	12.3	30,397	1.4	915	3.0	49,772	69.9	41,432	62.2
Hammond	85.3	34.1	84.5	69.9	83.4	5.4	34,827	0.8	1,815	5.2	57,174	60.4	48,430	41.5
Hobart	79.8	32.9	95.3	89.0	85.2	3.1	14,979	0.7	731	4.9	22,275	59.7	17,280	47.7
Indianapolis	81.6	30.0	86.5	79.7	84.9	5.0	449,411	1.4	15,747	3.5	NA	NA	NA	NA
Jeffersonville	83.7	24.3	92.8	77.7	89.3	4.8	25,243	0.8	761	3.0	38,013	65.8	31,047	52.8
Kokomo	80.6	19.2	85.5	74.1	83.6	5.5	25,865	-0.9	1,121	4.3	44,683	57.5	33,995	46.5
Lafayette	78.1	13.2	92.5	88.3	70.9	8.8	38,896	1.9	1,133	2.9	55,208	69.3	45,310	56.8
Lawrence	87.6	44.0	82.6	78.8	89.5	3.5	26,777	1.2	849	3.2	36,063	68.2	31,104	50.9
Marion	76.7	17.7	84.3	64.0	80.5	4.2	12,697	1.1	549	4.3	23,063	51.2	16,643	33.4
Merrillville	83.7	40.3	90.5	86.4	NA	NA	17,175	1.3	942	5.5	29,249	67.3	23,256	56.1
Michigan City	83.5	18.2	83.9	70.1	82.1	9.4	12,695	0.2	598	4.7	25,366	56.7	21,604	36.7
Mishawaka	86.5	20.9	89.3	82.8	84.3	6.2	26,259	1.4	853	3.2	37,204	70.3	30,263	52.1
Muncie	71.3	20.0	88.4	77.1	72.8	11.1	31,213	-0.4	1,354	4.3	58,396	58.2	49,341	33.5
New Albany	88.8	22.4	88.7	75.2	82.9	10.0	18,638	1.0	657	3.5	28,914	64.3	23,910	53.4
Noblesville	82.3	34.0	95.0	93.8	85.3	8.0	35,064	1.4	958	2.7	46,087	74.9	38,420	59.4
Plainfield	81.0	29.5	94.4	87.7	74.3	12.0	16,242	1.6	513	3.2	24,527	66.1	19,601	56.7
Portage	85.2	46.1	87.7	75.0	85.5	8.8	18,047	0.7	794	4.4	30,374	61.1	25,728	47.5
Richmond	72.8	11.6	85.8	68.4	84.3	5.4	15,255	1.3	586	3.8	29,515	56.8	22,877	45.5
Schererville	85.5	42.3	90.4	87.1	89.7	5.0	16,245	1.0	595	3.7	24,929	63.7	18,827	52.1
South Bend	78.6	16.8	78.3	70.3	86.6	5.9	48,467	1.6	1,950	4.0	75,121	62.8	62,363	45.1
Terre Haute	78.9	12.6	89.5	85.3	74.9	11.1	25,694	0.3	1,191	4.6	49,686	59.0	41,438	38.8
Valparaiso	76.5	30.2	90.0	82.9	79.5	13.0	16,718	0.8	596	3.6	26,544	62.5	20,662	51.7
Westfield	85.9	34.8	NA	NA	87.3	7.7	22,135	1.6	585	2.6	29,189	73.5	25,559	57.0
West Lafayette	47.0	12.9	99.5	88.3	51.3	29.3	21,684	2.2	635	2.9	44,294	55.6	41,151	20.6
IOWA	81.4	20.7	89.5	81.7	85.4	6.5	1,686,840	0.5	42,560	2.5	2,498,697	67.3	1,974,073	56.8
Ames	67.7	19.4	94.1	68.8	60.1	19.0	39,888	0.9	583	1.5	59,774	60.0	52,925	34.4
Ankeny	83.4	27.3	95.4	90.3	83.0	5.8	35,793	2.1	700	2.0	47,711	79.6	40,587	74.1
Bettendorf	87.9	11.1	91.9	88.7	81.1	7.4	18,005	0.8	417	2.3	26,788	68.8	21,525	57.3
Burlington	81.4	9.7	86.5	78.5	76.9	9.3	12,049	-0.9	417	3.5	19,286	66.0	14,152	56.2
Cedar Falls	81.7	6.4	91.8	80.6	72.8	13.6	22,659	1.4	424	1.9	32,872	70.8	26,851	40.5
Cedar Rapids	85.6	15.1	92.4	86.0	84.1	6.3	71,084	0.7	2,115	3.0	103,941	68.8	82,754	57.1
Clinton	78.3	14.5	84.3	78.8	76.6	3.6	11,688	-2.4	402	3.4	21,236	60.5	16,425	47.4
Council Bluffs	81.4	20.1	89.0	79.8	86.6	5.6	31,310	0.8	785	2.5	49,541	68.3	39,902	55.7
Davenport	87.2	12.3	86.2	80.0	89.9	2.8	50,325	0.8	1,693	3.4	82,902	62.5	67,832	50.5
Des Moines	80.7	16.3	90.5	80.9	82.4	6.6	113,478	1.6	3,434	3.0	169,827	70.1	143,088	57.3
Dubuque	84.1	6.2	90.8	82.6	82.8	7.2	32,714	1.4	801	2.4	47,436	65.3	37,617	51.4
Fort Dodge	79.2	12.7	86.3	73.3	82.6	7.8	12,163	-1.1	423	3.5	19,837	55.7	15,938	46.4
Iowa City	58.7	18.8	97.0	90.3	67.9	13.4	42,773	-0.1	805	1.9	66,256	67.0	58,295	37.2
Marion	91.0	12.5	92.6	86.3	87.9	6.6	20,622	0.9	508	2.5	32,596	78.7	27,008	60.3
Marshalltown	80.3	10.3	82.2	69.5	82.9	5.3	11,705	-0.9	611	5.2	21,499	62.7	16,436	58.2
Mason City	90.2	8.5	88.5	81.8	88.9	3.7	14,792	0.5	403	2.7	22,374	66.7	16,714	59.1
Ottumwa	89.9	9.3	88.4	78.0	84.4	4.7	12,032	0.1	445	3.7	20,221	61.8	16,650	50.2
Sioux City	84.5	11.8	90.0	77.6	89.2	3.0	44,194	1.6	1,154	2.6	63,200	66.8	51,881	56.1
Urbandale	89.6	15.1	96.6	88.6	89.2	5.0	25,058	1.9	489	2.0	30,310	74.8	25,277	66.3
Waterloo	77.4	7.6	86.6	79.0	82.9	5.7	33,577	0.7	1,142	3.4	53,893	65.9	43,185	52.7
West Des Moines	84.5	13.4	95.6	87.9	83.0	11.8	39,029	1.9	759	1.9	49,307	71.4	40,362	64.5

1. Employed persons.   2. Households.   3. Percent of civilian labor force.   4. Persons 16 years old and over.

Table D. Cities — Construction, Wholesale Trade, and Retail Trade

City	Value of residential construction authorized by building permits, 2018			Wholesale trade[1], 2012				Retail trade[2], 2012			
	New construction ($1,000)	Number of housing units	Percent single family	Number of establishments	Number of employees	Sales (mil dol)	Annual payroll (mil dol)	Number of establishments	Number of employees	Sales (mil dol)	Annual payroll (mil dol)
	69	70	71	72	73	74	75	76	77	78	79
ILLINOIS— Cont'd											
Waukegan	2,827	17	100.0	65	1,228	1,089.5	83.7	209	3,534	1,105.5	133.6
West Chicago	381	2	100.0	61	1,725	746.3	91.4	77	1,098	360.6	32.2
Wheaton	8,567	22	100.0	50	D	D	D	176	2,564	508.7	50.3
Wheeling	6,321	39	100.0	143	2,705	1,386.7	156.5	90	1,437	387.8	41.5
Wilmette	32,409	35	100.0	33	69	103.7	4.1	98	1,255	245.6	33.2
Woodridge	20,293	78	100.0	64	2,715	1,589.2	157.6	98	2,039	526.8	51.5
INDIANA	4,879,857	21,480	76.4	6,460	91,474	81,173.4	4,650.5	21,601	309,552	85,858.0	7,078.7
Anderson	2,309	11	100.0	36	D	D	D	234	3,713	1,008.3	83.7
Bloomington	NA	NA	NA	40	444	172.5	22.8	386	6,729	1,480.9	132.7
Carmel	259,078	757	61.6	135	1,253	1,277.1	106.2	289	5,860	1,749.0	168.1
Columbus	NA	NA	NA	53	895	681.4	49.3	193	3,316	829.1	75.4
Crown Point	74,764	253	100.0	38	D	D	D	75	895	236.8	22.0
East Chicago	801	7	0	35	D	D	D	47	356	120.1	7.8
Elkhart	4,864	26	100.0	144	2,148	1,552.6	109.2	258	3,871	1,039.2	93.7
Evansville	9,683	71	100.0	219	4,224	2,315.7	264.0	730	11,717	2,871.9	268.3
Fishers	226,501	698	97.1	83	1,279	847.7	83.2	185	3,340	974.1	83.5
Fort Wayne	NA	NA	NA	412	5,926	6,481.8	278.0	1,096	18,193	4,689.3	426.8
Gary	1,127	6	100.0	44	928	661.1	43.3	173	1,321	596.3	26.9
Goshen	10,195	47	100.0	30	825	530.5	32.8	162	2,853	779.2	65.8
Greenwood	77,647	318	100.0	45	1,444	883.1	87.1	327	6,283	1,488.0	138.5
Hammond	662	3	100.0	81	D	D	D	196	3,401	1,185.3	79.1
Hobart	5,655	23	100.0	26	D	D	D	224	4,767	1,210.7	105.5
Indianapolis	407,467	2,286	47.7	1,210	22,417	17,495.9	1,279.5	2,725	42,887	13,502.0	1,070.3
Jeffersonville	62,928	446	34.3	49	686	899.7	38.8	120	1,524	415.4	38.2
Kokomo	27,016	212	71.7	50	498	469.3	28.2	297	4,441	1,060.7	94.2
Lafayette	17,380	141	42.6	81	1,088	600.2	46.6	416	7,125	1,844.9	158.1
Lawrence	22,895	112	100.0	45	780	664.6	40.1	120	1,957	467.6	43.6
Marion	5,963	33	100.0	21	206	95.7	7.4	176	2,595	668.9	55.6
Merrillville	11,838	83	59.0	37	D	D	D	204	3,524	1,049.1	88.4
Michigan City	5,009	22	100.0	36	448	266.0	19.3	250	3,669	736.3	67.8
Mishawaka	42,685	329	17.6	61	679	706.9	35.2	371	6,956	1,843.0	151.6
Muncie	4,273	28	100.0	53	551	381.5	19.7	355	5,605	1,266.9	117.5
New Albany	8,608	45	100.0	48	509	301.0	21.0	144	2,129	508.3	50.0
Noblesville	172,870	597	100.0	68	634	325.3	35.9	231	4,179	1,028.1	93.8
Plainfield	70,453	304	100.0	32	2,638	2,509.8	127.5	135	2,794	782.2	64.2
Portage	17,940	103	100.0	24	481	501.3	27.5	91	1,828	490.5	39.4
Richmond	8,999	88	10.2	38	352	241.7	16.5	208	3,244	850.5	72.5
Schererville	20,715	65	84.6	19	130	51.7	6.1	105	2,289	598.8	55.5
South Bend	NA	NA	NA	154	2,577	1,673.0	124.2	315	5,010	1,310.0	127.9
Terre Haute	8,575	74	52.7	77	971	395.4	37.9	330	4,709	998.1	92.0
Valparaiso	36,541	134	79.1	42	550	236.6	28.3	193	3,356	854.6	76.4
Westfield	295,942	910	100.0	30	722	804.8	55.3	85	1,872	467.8	42.5
West Lafayette	180,706	1,124	2.1	5	15	2.2	0.3	61	1,350	300.6	25.6
IOWA	2,249,100	11,518	63.5	4,302	58,872	62,318.3	2,841.8	12,046	174,556	44,905.6	3,865.3
Ames	69,642	439	21.9	35	204	102.0	9.8	212	4,054	937.4	86.2
Ankeny	179,235	890	66.5	40	1,385	1,852.5	76.7	142	3,622	1,175.9	94.1
Bettendorf	43,516	164	81.7	42	466	570.2	23.8	95	1,525	358.6	39.9
Burlington	3,150	29	58.6	24	377	939.4	17.8	114	1,524	307.2	32.6
Cedar Falls	28,289	111	95.5	48	961	646.7	49.7	154	2,884	678.7	60.5
Cedar Rapids	44,679	472	31.1	219	3,999	2,352.7	219.9	489	11,220	3,525.8	272.5
Clinton	4,750	40	32.5	22	155	188.1	5.7	127	2,161	509.2	45.4
Council Bluffs	31,224	118	88.1	67	1,010	1,416.1	50.6	236	5,340	1,462.8	116.1
Davenport	13,088	68	100.0	180	2,928	1,425.4	139.1	478	8,922	2,337.4	209.0
Des Moines	91,767	571	31.5	270	4,570	3,586.5	243.0	647	9,121	2,190.1	215.3
Dubuque	26,512	68	100.0	81	883	870.3	39.7	336	6,175	1,355.8	127.8
Fort Dodge	8,877	52	100.0	36	544	228.3	29.6	151	2,488	569.8	52.6
Iowa City	62,492	321	41.1	34	676	502.3	27.6	247	4,188	927.7	101.9
Marion	26,415	246	65.0	29	257	106.8	10.9	120	1,894	456.6	41.3
Marshalltown	11,373	89	55.1	23	346	225.9	19.4	125	1,923	405.0	41.2
Mason City	5,177	21	61.9	45	584	587.7	27.6	179	3,317	753.3	71.5
Ottumwa	345	3	100.0	24	177	281.4	7.1	119	2,164	488.7	46.0
Sioux City	13,094	55	96.4	129	2,034	1,640.3	91.5	388	6,950	1,675.3	148.6
Urbandale	58,036	213	83.1	96	1,331	1,041.5	81.9	148	2,686	1,017.6	92.9
Waterloo	11,455	63	85.7	80	1,370	961.3	60.8	300	5,413	1,274.6	120.3
West Des Moines	158,170	645	45.4	63	723	1,145.8	42.9	389	8,652	1,620.3	164.8

1. Merchant wholesalers except manufacturers' sales branches and offices.   2. Establishments with payroll.

Table D. Cities — Real Estate, Professional Services, and Manufacturing

City	Real estate and rental and leasing, 2012				Professional, scientific, and technical services[1], 2012				Manufacturing, 2012			
	Number of establishments	Number of employees	Receipts (mil dol)	Annual payroll (mil dol)	Number of establishments	Number of employees	Receipts (mil dol)	Annual payroll (mil dol)	Number of establishments	Number of employees	Receipts (mil dol)	Annual payroll (mil dol)
	80	81	82	83	84	85	86	87	88	89	90	91
ILLINOIS— Cont'd												
Waukegan	52	239	61.7	8.2	162	D	D	D	81	4,911	1,775.3	314.4
West Chicago	19	129	44.2	8.8	78	800	255.7	58.8	94	4,848	2,358.0	245.6
Wheaton	66	209	51.0	8.1	413	D	D	D	21	440	D	11.9
Wheeling	30	116	28.1	4.2	124	976	245.8	57.2	141	7,219	2,463.4	346.7
Wilmette	38	D	D	D	174	390	77.3	26.0	11	95	13.4	3.1
Woodridge	31	303	62.1	11.4	115	924	133.2	66.7	40	1,714	481.7	77.3
INDIANA	5,729	31,715	6,547.9	1,171.7	12,780	99,322	14,627.5	5,453.3	8,141	452,513	242,763.8	23,041.3
Anderson	58	276	42.1	7.7	107	513	42.1	13.9	48	982	383.8	48.4
Bloomington	134	709	132.7	22.7	219	D	D	D	40	1,182	241.2	D
Carmel	200	1,684	1,226.0	116.1	575	3,523	604.7	250.0	61	827	D	40.4
Columbus	60	218	38.5	7.2	137	D	D	D	100	10,319	5,398.3	500.9
Crown Point	32	105	15.4	2.8	102	724	104.2	33.1	36	838	D	35.7
East Chicago	12	173	50.5	9.5	16	193	24.4	13.4	42	7,628	5,950.8	662.5
Elkhart	76	452	90.7	16.9	136	D	D	D	314	16,342	4,442.2	707.8
Evansville	178	1,359	201.9	40.1	355	D	D	D	173	7,490	2,730.9	322.8
Fishers	86	267	80.1	12.2	340	D	D	D	37	685	185.6	42.0
Fort Wayne	307	1,715	327.5	60.5	719	D	D	D	352	14,791	4,689.3	736.2
Gary	40	347	61.9	9.3	44	D	D	D	42	6,100	4,920.5	465.3
Goshen	36	126	18.2	3.3	67	397	35.4	12.0	103	14,551	4,138.7	617.4
Greenwood	67	247	68.4	7.6	121	819	94.6	30.4	41	1,175	496.5	70.8
Hammond	38	284	60.7	13.8	92	D	D	D	59	3,013	2,166.5	170.1
Hobart	22	79	14.1	2.3	44	D	D	D	19	816	D	31.4
Indianapolis	1,177	11,003	2,038.4	451.9	2,572	31,210	5,676.0	2,251.5	813	41,099	27,082.4	2,493.8
Jeffersonville	41	313	57.6	11.4	100	642	81.8	24.1	77	5,491	1,891.2	249.7
Kokomo	64	300	49.5	8.7	100	600	57.6	21.5	62	D	D	D
Lafayette	103	496	99.6	16.6	177	D	D	D	81	11,970	11,260.2	713.8
Lawrence	40	217	36.3	8.8	100	1,046	175.5	60.2	25	363	D	14.9
Marion	29	121	14.4	2.9	54	292	26.1	8.6	38	3,034	1,474.2	200.8
Merrillville	66	525	67.7	18.5	179	1,403	137.5	58.3	25	452	D	16.8
Michigan City	29	131	30.0	3.4	61	333	37.9	11.7	59	2,978	1,323.9	145.8
Mishawaka	56	374	68.2	12.6	109	D	D	D	85	2,618	1,071.2	119.6
Muncie	71	314	54.3	9.6	124	D	D	D	64	1,955	638.9	86.2
New Albany	35	133	17.1	3.6	117	D	D	D	83	4,966	1,660.8	246.4
Noblesville	57	170	50.0	6.5	182	708	90.1	32.6	46	2,056	753.2	95.0
Plainfield	30	252	25.8	8.5	51	387	47.2	16.3	21	582	205.4	24.2
Portage	30	140	24.9	5.4	40	239	24.9	10.8	20	2,252	2,221.9	151.4
Richmond	38	158	31.0	5.0	62	323	23.8	8.9	70	4,238	1,843.2	185.9
Schererville	34	201	46.0	7.4	88	D	D	D	12	374	D	19.1
South Bend	107	659	100.9	22.8	269	D	D	D	164	7,099	2,747.8	370.2
Terre Haute	72	414	69.8	14.9	163	1,035	102.5	38.7	74	6,131	1,922.0	300.0
Valparaiso	62	346	53.3	9.7	150	850	100.6	37.4	46	1,909	959.1	107.0
Westfield	24	131	15.0	4.0	72	234	25.1	9.7	19	1,092	234.3	44.2
West Lafayette	36	182	25.6	5.1	59	D	D	D	15	488	116.3	27.2
IOWA	2,742	12,031	2,268.3	425.9	6,169	48,261	6,396.9	2,454.9	3,598	203,722	116,668.8	10,021.2
Ames	72	364	55.3	11.2	135	D	D	D	43	3,163	2,048.5	180.0
Ankeny	58	148	31.5	4.9	91	463	55.4	23.8	27	3,429	3,100.7	185.8
Bettendorf	45	D	D	D	103	431	48.8	16.2	27	3,277	1,415.5	207.7
Burlington	25	623	110.3	24.4	45	238	25.6	8.8	26	2,687	913.6	110.1
Cedar Falls	49	224	50.1	6.5	98	2,726	150.9	151.5	43	1,523	393.3	69.6
Cedar Rapids	159	744	172.7	28.1	360	3,991	504.1	239.3	120	15,535	8,635.1	1,164.2
Clinton	26	89	14.9	2.9	47	221	17.0	6.7	30	2,803	4,090.3	156.2
Council Bluffs	70	329	51.2	8.3	103	D	D	D	39	3,878	D	167.8
Davenport	121	566	155.1	21.9	271	1,963	252.4	86.8	98	6,751	4,872.0	387.3
Des Moines	212	1,470	302.4	56.6	550	6,032	895.0	375.5	155	6,111	4,837.8	293.4
Dubuque	80	318	61.8	10.7	130	D	D	D	87	3,472	1,283.3	159.6
Fort Dodge	35	D	D	D	64	1,039	34.0	52.4	33	1,006	D	53.5
Iowa City	75	326	63.0	11.7	148	D	D	D	42	2,852	2,889.9	132.3
Marion	24	D	D	D	55	357	46.9	21.3	39	633	123.6	28.6
Marshalltown	27	D	D	D	37	306	46.3	11.9	30	4,891	D	241.9
Mason City	44	116	21.6	3.1	60	D	D	D	37	2,333	1,240.8	109.0
Ottumwa	20	86	12.2	2.9	41	D	D	D	17	D	D	D
Sioux City	83	496	61.9	12.7	176	D	D	D	77	4,428	2,997.7	172.8
Urbandale	43	245	52.4	7.0	178	1,832	517.5	150.7	35	1,403	548.8	83.4
Waterloo	83	387	67.2	10.9	114	D	D	D	98	11,343	9,231.0	577.4
West Des Moines	120	906	193.1	50.2	359	4,625	709.2	247.2	32	1,031	238.7	49.4

1. Establishments subject to federal tax.

Accommodation and Food Services, Arts, Entertainment, and Recreation, and Health Care and Social Assistance

City	Accommodation and food services, 2012				Arts, entertainment, and recreation[1], 2012				Health care and social assistance,[1] 2012			
	Number of establish-ments	Number of employees	Receipts (mil dol)	Annual payroll (mil dol)	Number of establish-ments	Number of employees	Receipts (mil dol)	Annual payroll (mil dol)	Number of establish-ments	Number of employees	Receipts (mil dol)	Annual payroll (mil dol)
	92	93	94	95	96	97	98	99	100	101	102	103
ILLINOIS— Cont'd												
Waukegan	133	1,955	117.5	30.2	13	228	14.6	3.3	102	2,622	313.1	118.7
West Chicago	46	567	27.5	7.3	8	104	6.4	1.7	39	463	43.9	15.0
Wheaton	111	1,954	95.4	29.0	19	D	D	D	173	2,236	205.0	92.6
Wheeling	57	D	D	D	3	31	1.9	0.6	69	897	57.7	26.2
Wilmette	50	D	D	D	17	D	D	D	117	1,034	80.0	32.5
Woodridge	55	965	50.5	14.1	12	231	12.5	4.0	78	443	46.8	18.2
INDIANA	13,057	255,223	13,076.6	3,432.7	1,559	23,917	3,152.7	761.2	12,360	206,531	21,191.4	8,625.9
Anderson	148	2,940	123.6	36.2	19	D	D	D	137	2,075	182.3	76.1
Bloomington	340	7,466	320.5	87.5	15	D	D	D	237	4,035	430.7	181.7
Carmel	185	3,477	180.6	55.8	53	590	40.5	11.1	391	D	D	D
Columbus	167	3,488	160.7	43.7	13	148	5.0	1.5	157	D	D	D
Crown Point	69	1,271	51.6	14.7	10	D	D	D	90	1,145	161.3	56.8
East Chicago	39	D	D	D	1	D	D	D	25	D	D	D
Elkhart	161	3,011	128.0	35.9	9	102	4.4	1.9	129	2,634	317.3	126.3
Evansville	403	9,956	511.6	133.5	39	847	67.1	10.5	405	6,878	732.3	335.7
Fishers	175	3,719	185.5	48.2	34	D	D	D	208	D	D	D
Fort Wayne	614	14,022	590.8	175.7	69	D	D	D	691	18,728	1,992.0	878.5
Gary	87	1,078	119.7	22.5	6	D	D	D	88	1,360	86.0	35.2
Goshen	88	1,742	78.3	20.9	5	D	D	D	82	1,106	106.4	53.7
Greenwood	152	4,007	177.8	52.2	13	D	D	D	159	D	D	D
Hammond	145	D	D	D	9	D	D	D	86	D	D	D
Hobart	73	1,440	66.3	18.9	12	D	D	D	58	D	D	D
Indianapolis	1,988	45,071	2,532.3	704.9	221	D	D	D	1,867	36,083	4,152.6	1,810.4
Jeffersonville	90	D	D	D	10	D	D	D	113	D	D	D
Kokomo	175	3,811	157.7	45.4	17	D	D	D	180	D	D	D
Lafayette	222	4,819	220.1	61.7	19	300	7.8	2.4	237	4,108	437.4	191.0
Lawrence	81	D	D	D	12	D	D	D	54	D	D	D
Marion	84	1,540	67.8	18.3	4	D	D	D	117	D	D	D
Merrillville	132	3,016	167.2	45.4	10	213	9.5	3.1	238	D	D	D
Michigan City	100	3,199	274.3	57.2	3	40	1.7	0.4	82	D	D	D
Mishawaka	200	4,928	221.2	62.2	17	D	D	D	153	D	D	D
Muncie	171	3,804	149.0	42.5	17	163	5.6	1.7	213	D	D	D
New Albany	85	D	D	D	8	D	D	D	146	D	D	D
Noblesville	107	2,503	119.1	34.3	21	D	D	D	128	D	D	D
Plainfield	89	1,947	96.7	26.6	7	D	D	D	46	D	D	D
Portage	81	1,687	81.6	20.3	10	D	D	D	69	976	86.3	32.1
Richmond	119	2,480	107.7	31.2	8	49	1.8	0.6	105	D	D	D
Schererville	96	2,116	88.9	27.7	6	D	D	D	81	670	59.9	25.5
South Bend	234	4,026	180.5	52.6	14	D	D	D	238	5,356	735.7	255.2
Terre Haute	231	4,616	201.8	58.6	14	D	D	D	210	3,875	484.6	171.0
Valparaiso	117	2,468	107.6	31.2	10	D	D	D	152	2,234	223.6	93.3
Westfield	63	1,494	64.3	18.4	14	D	D	D	52	D	D	D
West Lafayette	129	2,599	113.0	30.0	6	D	D	D	46	D	D	D
IOWA	7,047	115,134	5,468.7	1,466.6	993	13,165	1,305.5	255.5	5,582	78,961	7,151.2	3,356.8
Ames	195	3,976	160.9	45.2	15	308	12.5	4.4	96	1,702	217.7	103.8
Ankeny	100	2,414	109.4	31.1	13	150	6.4	2.3	88	925	74.7	32.2
Bettendorf	70	1,919	134.2	30.7	10	D	D	D	108	2,123	185.4	93.7
Burlington	80	1,689	71.7	21.2	9	D	D	D	56	D	D	D
Cedar Falls	110	2,719	94.9	30.9	15	D	D	D	70	D	D	D
Cedar Rapids	372	7,177	316.2	94.2	36	915	31.4	8.9	302	4,513	532.9	246.0
Clinton	76	1,377	93.3	20.1	7	D	D	D	65	987	85.4	33.0
Council Bluffs	159	4,908	393.2	86.2	13	D	D	D	143	D	D	D
Davenport	285	6,066	266.6	78.3	27	D	D	D	241	3,098	348.5	158.8
Des Moines	537	9,062	464.2	133.8	57	601	36.0	10.3	366	7,237	912.1	461.0
Dubuque	181	3,760	145.4	43.6	30	1,253	135.0	29.9	154	2,900	320.2	179.6
Fort Dodge	79	1,347	60.6	16.5	10	31	2.3	0.5	70	D	D	D
Iowa City	214	D	D	D	19	D	D	D	145	1,949	198.8	81.8
Marion	53	880	36.2	10.1	8	D	D	D	50	721	47.7	20.7
Marshalltown	79	1,049	43.7	11.9	4	D	D	D	36	D	D	D
Mason City	83	1,464	60.4	16.8	10	D	D	D	67	D	D	D
Ottumwa	71	1,188	46.2	13.1	9	D	D	D	63	D	D	D
Sioux City	232	D	D	D	26	D	D	D	190	2,778	287.8	121.9
Urbandale	81	1,762	88.7	23.4	19	D	D	D	73	1,189	68.9	30.2
Waterloo	169	3,684	214.3	51.0	21	179	11.7	3.4	154	2,109	227.0	109.8
West Des Moines	214	4,793	244.9	74.5	26	D	D	D	257	3,685	465.1	241.5

1. Establishments subject to federal tax.

Table D. Cities — Other Services and Government Employment and Payroll

City	Other services[1] Number of establish-ments	Number of employees	Receipts (mil dol)	Annual payroll (mil dol)	Full-time equivalent employees	Government employment and payroll, 2012 — March payroll Total (dollars)	Percent of total for: Admin-istrative, judicial, and legal	Police and corrections	Fire protection	Highways and trans-portation	Health and welfare	Natural resources and utilities	Education and libraries
	104	105	106	107	108	109	110	111	112	113	114	115	116
ILLINOIS— Cont'd													
Waukegan	90	374	30.5	9.1	502	3,187,722	12.7	40.5	27.8	4.1	1.1	8.7	5.1
West Chicago	41	238	37.0	10.5	117	799,988	15.4	54.5	0.0	9.6	0.7	18.2	0.0
Wheaton	86	578	31.9	12.0	437	2,488,726	8.6	34.0	12.7	8.3	0.0	11.5	18.2
Wheeling	63	347	44.9	9.4	232	1,575,381	12.4	38.6	25.9	1.8	8.3	8.9	0.0
Wilmette	59	364	33.8	10.9	220	1,531,248	12.5	32.9	25.0	14.4	0.9	11.8	0.0
Woodridge	42	429	12.7	12.4	165	972,329	16.5	46.7	0.0	5.4	0.0	13.1	14.2
INDIANA	8,429	54,735	5,020.8	1,548.5	X	X	X	X	X	X	X	X	X
Anderson	85	519	38.8	12.0	638	2,851,826	7.5	21.3	15.8	10.2	3.5	35.9	0.0
Bloomington	117	1,148	86.0	27.5	814	3,124,701	11.6	21.8	16.1	13.9	5.2	29.9	0.0
Carmel	145	861	63.7	22.3	467	2,600,210	3.5	30.7	43.9	10.0	0.0	10.1	0.0
Columbus	72	502	46.4	13.8	432	1,650,956	6.5	22.9	26.7	7.3	1.6	34.1	0.0
Crown Point	73	560	52.3	16.4	201	804,519	8.2	32.5	18.8	9.5	0.4	23.3	0.0
East Chicago	23	128	12.0	3.5	698	2,567,542	8.3	26.6	16.1	7.5	4.7	36.8	0.0
Elkhart	102	757	71.7	22.9	536	2,197,116	9.6	30.1	28.2	10.0	0.6	18.8	0.0
Evansville	234	2,033	185.2	56.8	1,278	5,214,822	2.6	31.8	24.3	11.2	3.0	24.8	0.0
Fishers	97	503	32.5	10.3	389	1,761,025	11.8	31.1	35.0	5.2	0.0	6.0	0.0
Fort Wayne	462	3,446	282.9	96.5	2,016	8,885,678	3.7	33.2	19.0	14.2	5.3	20.6	0.0
Gary	67	396	46.9	12.4	1,123	2,786,750	11.6	16.2	20.1	6.3	10.1	27.4	0.0
Goshen	54	D	D	D	227	709,892	8.9	38.2	24.5	7.4	0.8	13.4	0.0
Greenwood	101	880	101.2	32.1	279	1,071,961	16.9	33.3	24.5	11.2	0.0	12.1	0.0
Hammond	107	762	80.9	23.2	849	3,866,970	4.7	34.3	24.6	4.0	3.3	25.4	0.0
Hobart	62	410	42.4	12.6	245	963,819	14.4	31.6	27.9	6.1	0.0	15.8	0.0
Indianapolis	1,040	10,121	1,009.7	343.3	12,328	49,785,804	10.1	20.7	10.8	4.3	40.3	12.3	0.0
Jeffersonville	66	556	87.2	16.9	348	1,320,589	10.0	25.0	25.4	9.1	2.7	26.2	0.0
Kokomo	100	D	D	D	458	1,913,705	2.4	27.7	28.3	8.2	3.0	16.6	0.0
Lafayette	147	919	77.8	25.0	727	2,921,411	4.8	26.6	23.4	22.4	1.3	19.2	0.0
Lawrence	58	217	23.6	6.3	310	1,228,922	6.9	27.5	42.0	4.8	1.5	16.4	0.0
Marion	48	255	24.2	7.2	258	851,770	12.9	39.0	29.5	14.0	1.8	2.1	0.0
Merrillville	65	497	47.3	14.9	123	450,414	14.0	61.3	1.8	18.1	0.0	2.7	0.0
Michigan City	51	258	17.2	5.5	429	1,619,412	5.6	25.8	23.0	10.4	1.1	32.5	0.0
Mishawaka	92	578	41.4	14.5	503	2,151,708	6.9	27.5	24.4	4.6	0.7	31.4	0.0
Muncie	100	658	53.2	16.5	505	1,776,621	4.8	23.6	21.0	18.0	2.0	19.4	0.0
New Albany	66	330	28.2	7.9	265	917,338	5.7	32.4	36.7	5.6	3.3	8.7	0.0
Noblesville	75	484	34.1	10.6	368	1,696,635	8.6	26.2	41.3	9.3	0.0	13.7	0.0
Plainfield	49	570	37.3	14.9	268	950,626	7.8	22.5	43.0	4.3	0.0	21.5	0.0
Portage	48	374	27.4	9.2	254	948,853	7.5	31.0	27.5	15.8	0.6	16.7	0.0
Richmond	44	180	12.4	3.9	513	1,860,795	5.6	18.1	16.9	7.3	0.0	51.7	0.0
Schererville	62	588	52.8	16.0	180	726,293	13.7	41.3	15.8	13.1	0.0	16.0	0.0
South Bend	167	1,443	141.4	42.6	1,318	5,351,987	3.8	29.1	24.4	12.9	2.3	21.5	0.0
Terre Haute	91	666	55.3	17.5	615	2,301,273	8.2	27.5	28.9	17.6	1.5	14.9	0.0
Valparaiso	87	594	43.2	16.2	288	1,148,922	5.9	21.1	26.3	6.8	0.0	39.9	0.0
Westfield	43	296	23.5	7.3	176	867,739	19.6	28.0	32.8	8.5	1.6	9.5	0.0
West Lafayette	24	197	10.2	3.7	229	856,416	6.6	32.8	21.3	4.1	5.3	24.8	0.0
IOWA	4,687	23,537	2,103.6	598.9	X	X	X	X	X	X	X	X	X
Ames	69	451	33.2	10.8	616	2,954,800	12.2	13.1	10.5	21.5	2.3	30.9	5.6
Ankeny	64	D	D	D	283	1,240,311	16.5	23.8	24.3	9.4	0.0	18.9	4.5
Bettendorf	53	297	15.9	5.6	243	1,226,060	11.1	23.4	12.3	14.0	5.9	13.4	10.5
Burlington	47	248	20.8	6.4	239	935,691	5.6	25.4	21.5	13.3	0.5	20.2	7.2
Cedar Falls	51	454	36.1	12.0	478	2,270,443	8.5	9.9	7.7	7.0	0.6	57.2	2.9
Cedar Rapids	209	1,602	138.5	47.7	1,296	6,423,374	10.4	21.6	12.8	16.4	1.8	24.1	3.3
Clinton	47	172	15.3	4.4	210	897,240	6.0	29.8	22.4	15.6	2.5	17.4	5.3
Council Bluffs	102	553	47.5	14.5	471	2,609,951	9.1	27.0	20.1	6.8	10.1	21.8	5.0
Davenport	162	1,345	100.9	34.1	906	4,276,351	9.9	26.0	20.2	14.2	1.5	17.2	5.2
Des Moines	289	2,035	156.6	53.2	1,956	10,193,831	8.0	24.9	16.0	11.6	5.0	26.6	3.2
Dubuque	124	804	67.4	20.0	645	3,046,153	13.2	22.4	16.1	21.5	5.8	14.0	4.4
Fort Dodge	36	286	34.2	9.2	118	524,670	9.2	38.3	26.4	3.8	0.0	16.1	6.2
Iowa City	90	577	45.4	14.4	20	1,762,642	14.5	13.9	9.2	13.9	4.6	17.2	6.5
Marion	47	242	23.0	6.9	184	916,685	6.3	31.1	21.9	10.4	6.4	17.3	6.7
Marshalltown	41	238	19.3	4.7	231	825,058	5.3	30.0	16.7	12.6	5.2	25.4	4.7
Mason City	58	375	29.2	9.1	326	1,435,146	5.2	16.5	11.1	10.8	8.2	18.1	25.1
Ottumwa	32	185	14.3	5.3	247	856,818	6.4	16.0	15.1	23.1	5.3	28.1	3.8
Sioux City	120	879	56.6	19.4	794	3,661,919	9.1	25.7	18.3	17.6	2.2	19.7	3.4
Urbandale	61	470	34.2	12.7	223	998,550	11.0	20.8	15.3	12.5	1.1	26.9	9.6
Waterloo	97	708	57.5	17.4	603	2,720,527	5.5	26.6	21.7	9.9	2.6	18.8	4.1
West Des Moines	89	585	36.6	14.7	435	2,294,576	8.6	23.7	13.4	9.2	16.6	19.7	4.4

1. Establishments subject to federal tax.

Table D. Cities — City Government Finances

City	General revenue Total (mil dol) [117]	Intergovernmental Total (mil dol) [118]	Intergovernmental Percent from state government [119]	Taxes Total (mil dol) [120]	Taxes Per capita Total [121]	Taxes Per capita Property [122]	Taxes Per capita Sales and gross receipts [123]	General expenditure Total (mil dol) [124]	General expenditure Per capita Total [125]	General expenditure Per capita Capital outlays [126]
ILLINOIS— Cont'd										
Waukegan	87.3	16.1	90.5	46.7	525	307	218	72.7	819	47
West Chicago	29.0	8.4	99.1	8.9	324	172	153	28.0	1,022	227
Wheaton	56.0	12.7	96.7	32.9	616	438	167	46.6	872	33
Wheeling	45.9	10.7	93.0	29.0	765	553	212	45.1	1,188	197
Wilmette	38.5	7.6	85.0	22.4	821	509	287	38.9	1,425	199
Woodridge	30.1	9.8	82.4	14.4	434	225	199	26.2	789	18
INDIANA	X	X	X	X	X	X	X	X	X	X
Anderson	84.2	19.0	48.2	36.3	652	443	39	65.2	1,172	281
Bloomington	85.2	17.5	64.4	44.3	539	434	15	72.9	886	129
Carmel	111.9	17.9	66.3	72.8	871	597	53	93.8	1,122	60
Columbus	72.5	21.0	50.2	29.8	657	647	11	59.6	1,314	244
Crown Point	35.9	4.6	85.5	17.3	616	580	36	21.8	773	94
East Chicago	103.6	44.0	82.6	50.0	1,697	1,676	21	63.2	2,147	65
Elkhart	70.5	21.2	34.3	30.9	606	596	10	59.6	1,167	88
Evansville	183.6	54.1	55.1	68.3	568	460	15	192.0	1,598	442
Fishers	58.2	7.3	74.3	35.2	430	286	25	55.3	676	109
Fort Wayne	289.9	59.4	54.7	141.1	554	423	16	257.6	1,011	147
Gary	181.4	65.4	74.4	81.4	1,028	1,008	20	145.6	1,839	385
Goshen	35.1	9.7	53.7	14.5	454	447	7	47.8	1,498	416
Greenwood	47.0	10.2	33.2	19.8	376	365	12	34.0	645	24
Hammond	192.8	73.8	83.1	63.5	797	775	22	155.5	1,953	159
Hobart	40.0	5.7	88.9	23.0	794	772	22	36.0	1,242	112
Indianapolis	2,604.6	712.4	81.1	887.7	1,064	601	112	3,151.6	3,777	1,038
Jeffersonville	55.6	10.3	33.9	27.6	605	592	13	57.7	1,264	472
Kokomo	76.1	16.8	67.8	44.3	777	655	2	63.7	1,118	63
Lafayette	99.8	25.3	67.7	44.5	637	508	7	75.9	1,086	2
Lawrence	36.4	5.3	60.9	19.2	411	308	19	34.5	739	4
Marion	32.5	6.6	85.0	19.7	665	514	11	37.1	1,252	46
Merrillville	30.3	3.8	91.0	20.7	587	559	28	18.3	518	137
Michigan City	59.4	25.0	70.4	17.2	553	532	21	50.5	1,621	213
Mishawaka	83.6	10.9	75.5	54.8	1,142	914	13	78.3	1,630	554
Muncie	72.4	20.0	73.9	29.0	414	346	11	72.9	1,040	117
New Albany	59.3	15.9	55.8	20.6	564	548	16	50.5	1,385	371
Noblesville	84.0	18.9	89.5	45.5	823	556	66	67.7	1,226	347
Plainfield	48.8	11.2	29.1	24.9	854	718	136	35.1	1,203	268
Portage	42.2	5.4	93.6	22.3	604	531	19	46.8	1,270	181
Richmond	48.2	15.7	58.1	13.4	368	357	11	46.4	1,269	343
Schererville	33.2	3.7	90.7	21.3	734	702	32	19.4	667	73
South Bend	201.3	37.3	61.0	106.9	1,060	823	30	141.5	1,404	147
Terre Haute	82.6	28.3	35.8	31.8	519	512	8	64.3	1,051	189
Valparaiso	44.4	6.4	59.9	22.8	713	632	30	35.7	1,116	232
Westfield	33.7	3.8	75.3	18.3	572	359	56	25.9	808	40
West Lafayette	32.5	8.8	47.0	12.7	416	322	9	24.7	808	153
IOWA	X	X	X	X	X	X	X	X	X	X
Ames	250.4	24.1	59.9	29.1	475	382	93	219.0	3,578	476
Ankeny	57.6	6.0	79.4	32.3	658	584	74	69.7	1,421	618
Bettendorf	52.9	7.7	67.3	30.2	883	675	208	55.4	1,617	483
Burlington	34.5	5.6	56.2	17.9	700	447	253	35.7	1,395	364
Cedar Falls	77.7	19.4	43.0	31.2	783	598	185	81.6	2,049	977
Cedar Rapids	405.0	168.3	22.7	115.9	905	655	249	457.5	3,573	2,065
Clinton	48.5	10.4	28.4	20.3	761	562	198	67.1	2,521	1,417
Council Bluffs	118.7	29.8	38.3	61.1	983	702	281	111.9	1,801	467
Davenport	165.6	37.9	52.7	84.9	837	610	227	177.4	1,749	508
Des Moines	404.2	93.7	24.5	156.5	757	643	114	460.9	2,228	484
Dubuque	135.5	48.8	22.7	45.3	780	520	260	160.4	2,763	1,348
Fort Dodge	36.9	6.2	50.6	17.7	717	531	186	39.3	1,589	605
Iowa City	138.3	36.0	53.0	63.8	906	715	191	128.1	1,819	366
Marion	36.5	5.5	81.7	22.6	630	474	156	37.9	1,056	306
Marshalltown	34.2	10.2	31.7	16.6	595	411	184	35.1	1,262	431
Mason City	52.9	17.0	23.3	20.8	748	531	218	45.1	1,625	357
Ottumwa	40.4	7.9	63.1	16.8	679	503	177	37.3	1,505	459
Sioux City	139.6	32.9	58.3	63.3	766	553	213	143.7	1,737	477
Urbandale	41.8	4.8	80.6	29.6	721	645	76	40.8	995	315
Waterloo	115.1	25.8	46.6	59.1	865	644	221	119.5	1,749	524
West Des Moines	100.9	15.8	70.7	63.9	1,076	976	100	85.4	1,439	353

1. Based on population estimated as of July 1 of the year shown.

City	City government finances, 2012 (cont.) General expenditure (cont.) Percent of total for:									
	Public welfare	Highways	Parking facilities	Education	Health and hospitals	Police protection	Sewerage and sanitation	Parks and recreation	Housing and community development	Interest on debt
	127	128	129	130	131	132	133	134	135	136
ILLINOIS— Cont'd										
Waukegan	0.0	11.3	0.5	0.0	0.0	30.6	9.2	0.0	1.6	5.9
West Chicago	0.0	15.8	0.4	0.0	0.0	30.2	28.0	0.7	0.0	2.8
Wheaton	0.0	14.4	1.4	0.0	0.0	27.1	7.8	1.1	0.0	4.7
Wheeling	0.0	15.8	0.1	0.0	0.0	27.4	4.3	0.0	0.0	7.2
Wilmette	0.0	14.4	0.8	0.0	0.6	24.7	15.4	0.0	0.0	5.9
Woodridge	0.0	11.2	0.0	0.0	0.0	36.6	9.9	0.1	0.0	4.4
INDIANA	X	X	X	X	X	X	X	X	X	X
Anderson	0.0	5.6	0.1	0.0	0.3	14.5	38.2	1.7	3.5	2.5
Bloomington	0.0	7.2	2.0	0.0	1.5	13.2	15.3	10.4	1.4	3.6
Carmel	0.0	9.2	0.0	0.0	0.0	16.1	5.8	3.9	6.8	11.8
Columbus	0.0	3.5	0.0	0.0	0.5	9.2	28.6	6.4	0.8	4.1
Crown Point	0.0	12.6	0.0	0.0	0.3	15.8	28.1	3.3	0.0	1.9
East Chicago	0.0	1.5	0.0	0.0	4.1	14.6	18.5	4.4	3.2	0.9
Elkhart	0.0	9.1	0.0	0.0	0.0	15.2	19.4	5.4	1.3	2.0
Evansville	0.0	4.5	0.1	0.0	0.4	13.7	25.8	6.1	1.4	1.4
Fishers	0.0	15.5	0.0	0.0	0.0	12.7	15.0	1.2	0.0	7.5
Fort Wayne	0.0	6.4	0.2	0.0	0.9	19.3	29.0	5.5	5.1	2.8
Gary	0.0	2.5	0.0	0.0	2.6	8.6	23.7	5.0	3.3	1.1
Goshen	0.0	13.7	1.0	0.0	0.0	8.2	27.0	2.5	1.1	7.9
Greenwood	0.0	14.9	0.0	0.0	0.0	16.9	24.3	2.9	0.0	3.6
Hammond	0.0	2.9	0.0	0.0	0.0	16.8	11.7	12.4	3.7	2.7
Hobart	0.0	12.7	0.0	0.0	0.1	10.5	26.5	4.8	0.0	0.9
Indianapolis	0.0	1.2	0.4	0.0	35.8	6.6	8.7	11.7	4.3	10.4
Jeffersonville	0.0	1.9	0.0	0.0	0.6	13.1	50.7	3.9	2.0	4.1
Kokomo	0.0	6.8	0.0	0.0	0.0	19.6	18.4	4.5	3.7	1.9
Lafayette	0.0	6.9	0.0	0.0	0.0	16.5	15.5	7.3	3.9	5.6
Lawrence	0.0	3.7	0.0	0.0	2.8	16.4	18.9	3.1	0.0	1.4
Marion	0.0	5.7	0.0	0.0	0.0	20.7	14.4	2.8	0.0	1.5
Merrillville	0.0	6.0	0.0	0.0	0.0	21.1	8.9	0.9	0.0	4.6
Michigan City	0.0	3.1	0.0	0.0	0.5	13.7	18.8	10.2	2.7	3.3
Mishawaka	0.0	3.8	0.0	0.0	1.4	11.5	26.4	3.8	0.9	3.5
Muncie	0.0	3.7	0.1	0.0	0.3	11.3	46.5	1.9	1.2	2.0
New Albany	0.0	2.5	0.9	0.0	0.8	9.6	21.0	4.4	6.5	5.0
Noblesville	0.0	5.0	0.2	0.0	0.2	11.2	32.6	4.6	0.0	13.9
Plainfield	0.0	3.4	0.0	0.0	0.0	12.1	14.0	10.2	0.0	3.2
Portage	0.0	7.4	0.0	0.0	0.2	9.3	26.6	6.0	0.0	5.4
Richmond	0.0	3.5	0.1	0.0	1.1	13.2	43.5	6.3	0.0	2.2
Schererville	0.0	8.6	0.0	0.0	0.3	23.5	39.5	5.2	0.0	2.5
South Bend	0.0	5.8	0.5	0.0	0.3	16.8	22.7	12.5	1.8	5.0
Terre Haute	0.0	7.4	0.0	0.0	0.4	14.5	16.6	4.9	14.2	3.8
Valparaiso	0.0	12.1	0.1	0.0	0.0	9.7	21.3	7.1	0.0	3.4
Westfield	0.0	6.4	0.0	0.0	0.0	16.6	19.5	1.9	0.0	6.9
West Lafayette	0.0	12.3	0.0	0.0	0.0	16.7	38.4	6.0	2.0	4.7
IOWA	X	X	X	X	X	X	X	X	X	X
Ames	0.5	2.1	0.3	0.0	72.3	3.5	4.7	2.0	0.3	2.0
Ankeny	0.4	27.0	0.0	0.0	3.9	9.7	21.2	8.8	0.0	7.2
Bettendorf	0.0	12.9	0.0	0.0	0.0	11.1	12.3	17.3	0.9	8.1
Burlington	0.0	6.6	0.2	0.0	2.2	14.7	12.6	9.1	0.0	6.4
Cedar Falls	0.0	13.0	0.2	0.0	0.3	5.2	6.7	5.8	2.0	1.5
Cedar Rapids	0.0	7.6	0.9	0.0	0.2	7.2	13.4	2.0	1.6	3.1
Clinton	0.0	10.7	0.1	0.0	2.5	7.2	48.1	3.5	1.1	3.6
Council Bluffs	0.0	3.7	0.1	0.0	2.9	13.5	11.9	3.6	1.1	1.9
Davenport	0.0	4.9	0.6	0.0	0.0	13.1	17.7	6.8	6.3	6.4
Des Moines	2.3	11.4	1.8	0.0	0.0	12.6	19.8	4.9	6.4	5.1
Dubuque	0.3	10.6	1.2	0.0	1.4	7.8	26.9	4.5	3.9	3.8
Fort Dodge	0.8	9.9	0.4	0.0	0.1	9.5	14.8	11.3	1.5	5.7
Iowa City	0.0	8.1	3.7	0.0	0.5	8.4	16.3	4.9	8.7	4.8
Marion	0.0	7.5	0.0	0.0	0.1	13.8	13.7	4.6	1.9	5.3
Marshalltown	0.1	16.2	0.1	0.0	4.0	15.0	32.3	6.4	5.1	2.3
Mason City	1.7	6.4	0.2	0.0	4.0	12.0	17.3	4.5	0.0	4.0
Ottumwa	0.3	19.9	0.0	0.0	1.4	12.0	30.9	4.9	0.0	2.4
Sioux City	0.0	5.9	1.1	0.0	0.4	12.2	17.1	8.9	5.9	5.4
Urbandale	0.0	28.4	0.0	0.0	0.1	15.2	5.4	9.9	1.4	4.5
Waterloo	0.2	14.3	0.3	0.0	1.7	13.5	9.5	5.5	7.5	3.5
West Des Moines	1.3	14.3	0.0	0.0	5.2	10.7	16.9	5.3	0.9	4.8

City	City government finances, 2012 (cont.)			Climate[2]						
	Debt outstanding		Debt issued during year	Average daily temperature				Annual precipitation (inches)	Heating degree days	Cooling degree days
				Mean		Limits				
	Total (mil dol)	Per capita[1] (dollars)		January	July	January[3]	July[4]			
	137	138	139	140	141	142	143	144	145	146

City	137	138	139	140	141	142	143	144	145	146
ILLINOIS— Cont'd										
Waukegan	133.5	1,504	26.6	20.3	71.5	12.0	81.7	34.09	7,031	613
West Chicago	20.8	757	0.0	NA	NA	NA	NA	NA	NA	NA
Wheaton	45.4	849	0.0	23.1	74.8	14.2	86.8	37.94	6,053	942
Wheeling	84.5	2,228	8.5	18.4	72.1	9.6	82.3	36.56	7,149	624
Wilmette	76.2	2,790	14.3	22.0	73.3	14.3	83.5	36.27	6,498	830
Woodridge	24.8	746	3.3	23.1	74.8	14.2	86.8	37.94	6,053	942
INDIANA	X	X	X	X	X	X	X	X	X	X
Anderson	127.1	2,286	25.5	25.7	74.0	18.4	83.8	39.82	5,807	872
Bloomington	159.2	1,937	55.7	27.9	75.4	19.3	86.0	44.91	5,348	1,017
Carmel	367.8	4,400	0.0	25.3	74.2	17.0	84.5	42.85	5,901	873
Columbus	109.4	2,413	0.0	27.9	75.9	19.1	86.4	41.94	5,367	1,059
Crown Point	22.4	795	1.9	NA	NA	NA	NA	NA	NA	NA
East Chicago	42.0	1,427	0.0	23.7	74.0	15.3	84.8	38.13	6,055	887
Elkhart	28.7	562	0.0	22.8	72.1	14.3	83.3	38.56	6,487	663
Evansville	274.1	2,281	67.7	33.2	79.6	24.8	90.5	45.76	4,140	1,616
Fishers	131.1	1,603	33.0	25.3	74.2	17.0	84.5	42.85	5,901	873
Fort Wayne	435.4	1,708	0.0	23.6	73.4	16.1	84.3	36.55	6,205	830
Gary	85.2	1,076	21.7	22.2	73.5	13.9	83.9	38.02	6,497	776
Goshen	101.3	3,178	9.3	24.3	73.7	17.0	84.5	36.59	6,075	826
Greenwood	30.0	570	0.0	25.7	74.7	18.0	84.0	40.24	5,783	942
Hammond	112.1	1,407	0.0	22.2	73.5	13.9	83.9	38.02	6,497	776
Hobart	25.7	886	0.0	22.2	73.5	13.9	83.9	38.02	6,497	776
Indianapolis	6,001.3	7,191	2,503.6	26.5	75.4	18.5	85.6	40.95	5,521	1,042
Jeffersonville	54.0	1,182	0.0	31.3	75.8	21.4	88.5	45.47	4,829	1,079
Kokomo	32.5	570	0.0	22.8	73.0	15.0	84.1	41.54	6,368	771
Lafayette	133.7	1,913	0.0	23.0	73.5	14.3	84.5	36.90	6,206	842
Lawrence	27.5	589	0.0	25.7	74.7	18.0	84.0	40.24	5,783	942
Marion	11.4	385	0.0	24.2	73.8	16.3	84.5	39.01	6,143	819
Merrillville	22.7	644	0.2	21.1	72.7	12.1	83.6	40.04	6,642	734
Michigan City	54.0	1,733	7.8	23.4	73.0	15.7	83.1	39.70	6,294	812
Mishawaka	117.0	2,436	0.0	24.3	73.7	17.0	84.5	36.59	6,075	826
Muncie	33.5	478	0.0	24.4	72.5	15.9	83.9	41.23	6,215	717
New Albany	61.3	1,681	0.0	31.3	75.8	21.4	88.5	45.47	4,829	1,079
Noblesville	240.4	4,350	12.0	25.3	74.2	17.0	84.5	42.85	5,901	873
Plainfield	56.2	1,924	0.0	NA	NA	NA	NA	NA	NA	NA
Portage	59.2	1,607	0.0	22.9	73.0	15.5	83.1	40.06	6,270	745
Richmond	34.6	947	0.0	25.7	73.1	17.2	84.6	39.55	5,942	769
Schererville	18.2	626	0.0	NA	NA	NA	NA	NA	NA	NA
South Bend	230.5	2,286	60.5	23.4	73.0	15.7	83.1	39.70	6,294	812
Terre Haute	52.7	860	0.0	26.5	76.2	17.7	87.3	42.47	5,433	1,107
Valparaiso	56.6	1,769	9.8	22.9	73.0	15.5	83.1	40.06	6,270	745
Westfield	55.7	1,737	0.0	NA	NA	NA	NA	NA	NA	NA
West Lafayette	40.9	1,338	2.5	25.2	75.5	17.2	86.3	36.32	5,732	1,024
IOWA	X	X	X	X	X	X	X	X	X	X
Ames	127.9	2,091	71.7	18.5	73.8	9.6	84.3	34.07	6,791	830
Ankeny	178.3	3,634	21.3	18.2	74.8	8.7	85.8	33.38	6,961	881
Bettendorf	119.0	3,478	20.8	21.1	76.2	13.2	85.4	34.11	6,246	1,072
Burlington	62.6	2,447	19.5	22.8	76.3	15.1	85.4	37.94	5,948	1,095
Cedar Falls	86.6	2,177	4.4	16.1	73.6	6.3	85.0	33.15	7,348	758
Cedar Rapids	538.7	4,206	127.7	19.9	74.8	11.5	85.3	36.62	6,488	910
Clinton	83.3	3,130	29.0	20.4	74.7	12.5	85.0	35.68	6,416	915
Council Bluffs	125.8	2,024	15.1	21.1	76.2	10.4	87.7	33.25	6,323	1,057
Davenport	324.8	3,202	66.5	21.1	76.2	13.2	85.4	34.11	6,246	1,072
Des Moines	556.3	2,689	43.7	20.4	76.1	11.7	86.0	34.72	6,436	1,052
Dubuque	185.8	3,199	67.9	17.8	75.1	8.7	85.4	33.96	6,891	908
Fort Dodge	80.9	3,272	8.5	15.4	73.1	5.8	84.3	34.39	7,513	746
Iowa City	187.9	2,668	19.6	21.7	76.9	13.4	87.5	37.27	6,052	1,134
Marion	67.4	1,881	13.8	16.8	73.9	7.1	84.4	36.40	7,191	787
Marshalltown	31.2	1,121	12.4	16.8	73.9	7.1	84.4	36.40	7,191	787
Mason City	60.3	2,170	1.5	13.9	72.4	5.1	83.3	34.48	7,765	655
Ottumwa	37.1	1,498	13.2	NA	NA	NA	NA	NA	NA	NA
Sioux City	249.2	3,013	42.4	18.6	74.6	8.5	86.2	25.99	6,900	914
Urbandale	55.3	1,347	9.4	20.4	76.1	11.7	86.0	34.72	6,436	1,052
Waterloo	115.2	1,686	21.4	16.1	73.6	6.3	85.0	33.15	7,348	758
West Des Moines	136.6	2,302	44.3	20.4	76.1	11.7	86.0	34.72	6,436	1,052

1. Based on the population estimated as of July 1 of the year shown. 2. Represents normal values based on the 30-year period, 1971±2000. 3. Average daily minimum. 4. Average daily maximum.

Table D. Cities — **Land Area and Population**

STATE Place code	City	Land area[1] (sq. mi)	Total persons 2018	Rank	Per square mile	White	Black or African American	American Indian, Alaskan Native	Asian	Hawaiian Pacific Islander	Some other race	Two or more races (percent)
			Population, 2018			Race 2017						
						Race alone[2] (percent)						
		1	2	3	4	5	6	7	8	9	10	11
20 00,000	KANSAS	81,759.2	2,911,505	X	35.6	84.5	5.7	0.7	2.9	0.1	2.5	3.5
20 18,250	Dodge City	14.6	27,329	1,341	1,871.8	NA	NA	NA	NA	NA	NA	NA
20 25,325	Garden City	10.8	26,546	1,376	2,458.0	90.4	3.7	0.0	3.2	0.0	0.5	2.3
20 33,625	Hutchinson	24.6	40,623	942	1,651.3	89.1	4.6	1.0	0.2	0.0	1.5	3.5
20 36,000	Kansas City	124.8	152,958	171	1,225.6	58.0	22.7	0.4	4.4	0.0	9.1	5.4
20 38,900	Lawrence	34.1	97,286	320	2,853.0	80.1	4.7	3.1	6.7	0.0	0.5	4.9
20 39,000	Leavenworth	24.5	36,062	1,065	1,471.9	76.1	15.7	1.4	0.7	0.0	0.9	5.2
20 39,075	Leawood	15.1	34,689	1,101	2,297.3	NA	NA	NA	NA	NA	NA	NA
20 39,350	Lenexa	34.1	55,294	687	1,621.5	81.7	7.5	0.0	8.2	0.0	0.1	2.5
20 44,250	Manhattan	19.8	54,959	694	2,775.7	82.5	3.9	0.8	6.2	0.5	1.1	4.9
20 52,575	Olathe	61.6	139,605	192	2,266.3	84.1	6.5	0.3	4.8	0.1	1.1	3.2
20 53,775	Overland Park	75.2	192,536	128	2,560.3	82.4	4.8	0.9	8.5	0.1	1.4	1.8
20 62,700	Salina	25.7	46,716	831	1,817.7	87.4	3.5	0.1	2.5	0.0	2.1	4.4
20 64,500	Shawnee	42.0	65,845	562	1,567.7	NA	NA	NA	NA	NA	NA	NA
20 71,000	Topeka	61.4	125,904	220	2,050.6	78.5	11.8	0.6	1.8	0.0	3.0	4.4
20 79,000	Wichita	161.2	389,255	51	2,414.7	71.6	11.0	0.5	5.0	0.2	6.8	4.9
21 00,000	KENTUCKY	39,490.3	4,468,402	X	113.2	86.9	8.1	0.2	1.5	0.1	0.9	2.3
21 08,902	Bowling Green	38.7	68,401	526	1,767.5	74.1	11.4	0.0	4.7	2.3	2.8	4.8
21 17,848	Covington	13.2	40,366	949	3,058.0	81.4	10.1	0.3	0.7	0.0	3.3	4.3
21 24,274	Elizabethtown	26.7	30,157	1,249	1,129.5	78.9	13.3	0.2	4.2	0.0	1.1	2.2
21 27,982	Florence	10.7	32,479	1,169	3,035.4	83.4	8.3	0.0	2.4	0.0	2.7	3.2
21 28,900	Frankfort	14.8	27,679	1,331	1,870.2	72.4	19.3	0.4	1.0	0.0	3.2	3.7
21 30,700	Georgetown	16.5	34,395	1,107	2,084.5	86.1	4.7	0.2	0.7	0.0	1.9	6.4
21 35,866	Henderson	16.1	28,432	1,305	1,766.0	NA	NA	NA	NA	NA	NA	NA
21 37,918	Hopkinsville	31.7	31,026	1,215	978.7	66.1	30.8	0.3	1.8	0.0	0.1	0.9
21 40,222	Jeffersontown	10.3	27,997	1,320	2,718.2	76.3	9.0	0.0	7.5	0.2	3.2	3.9
21 46,027	Lexington-Fayette	283.6	323,780	60	1,141.7	75.5	14.5	0.3	3.6	0.0	2.3	3.7
21 48,003	Louisville/Jefferson County	263.4	620,118	29	2,354.3	69.3	24.1	0.1	2.9	0.0	1.2	2.3
21 56,136	Nicholasville	14.0	30,829	1,223	2,202.1	NA	NA	NA	NA	NA	NA	NA
21 58,620	Owensboro	20.5	59,809	626	2,917.5	88.0	6.7	0.3	0.6	0.0	0.2	4.2
21 58,836	Paducah	20.2	24,850	1,416	1,230.2	NA	NA	NA	NA	NA	NA	NA
21 65,226	Richmond	20.3	35,894	1,071	1,768.2	NA	NA	NA	NA	NA	NA	NA
22 00,000	LOUISIANA	43,203.9	4,659,978	X	107.9	61.7	32.5	0.5	1.8	0.0	1.6	1.8
22 00,975	Alexandria	28.5	46,776	830	1,641.3	36.6	56.2	0.4	4.3	0.0	1.2	1.4
22 05,000	Baton Rouge	86.4	221,599	99	2,564.8	39.5	53.9	0.5	3.5	0.1	1.1	1.4
22 08,920	Bossier City	43.5	68,235	530	1,568.6	64.8	29.3	0.4	1.2	0.2	1.2	2.8
22 13,960	Central	62.2	28,864	1,292	464.1	NA	NA	NA	NA	NA	NA	NA
22 36,255	Houma	14.4	32,864	1,159	2,282.2	57.4	31.4	2.0	0.6	0.0	4.8	3.9
22 39,475	Kenner	14.9	66,657	550	4,473.6	61.0	26.7	0.0	3.6	0.0	5.6	3.2
22 40,735	Lafayette	55.5	126,143	218	2,272.8	60.2	33.4	0.2	3.2	0.0	1.1	2.0
22 41,155	Lake Charles	43.2	78,001	444	1,805.6	48.6	47.3	0.1	2.5	0.0	0.5	1.0
22 51,410	Monroe	29.3	47,877	810	1,634.0	37.2	60.9	0.0	0.9	0.0	0.5	0.5
22 54,035	New Iberia	11.1	29,099	1,284	2,621.5	NA	NA	NA	NA	NA	NA	NA
22 55,000	New Orleans	169.4	391,006	50	2,308.2	33.8	59.5	0.2	2.9	0.0	1.4	2.1
22 70,000	Shreveport	107.1	188,987	133	1,764.6	35.1	59.1	0.5	1.7	0.0	0.6	2.9
22 70,805	Slidell	15.3	27,711	1,329	1,811.2	NA	NA	NA	NA	NA	NA	NA
23 00,000	MAINE	30,844.7	1,338,404	X	43.4	94.4	1.2	0.7	1.1	0.0	0.2	2.3
23 02,795	Bangor	34.3	31,997	1,188	932.9	88.7	2.6	3.0	1.9	0.0	0.5	3.2
23 38,740	Lewiston	34.1	35,944	1,070	1,054.1	89.8	3.7	0.7	0.9	0.0	0.0	4.9
23 60,545	Portland	21.6	66,417	554	3,074.9	83.5	10.5	0.2	3.4	0.0	0.6	1.7
23 71,990	South Portland	12.1	25,606	1,401	2,116.2	NA	NA	NA	NA	NA	NA	NA
24 00,000	MARYLAND	9,710.9	6,042,718	X	622.3	54.9	29.9	0.3	6.5	0.0	5.0	3.4
24 01,600	Annapolis	7.2	39,174	986	5,440.8	59.6	20.3	0.6	4.7	0.0	13.8	1.0
24 04,000	Baltimore	80.9	602,495	30	7,447.4	30.1	62.7	0.4	2.7	0.0	1.7	2.4
24 08,775	Bowie	19.2	58,682	642	3,056.4	34.1	54.5	0.0	5.4	0.0	3.3	2.6
24 18,750	College Park	5.6	32,196	1,184	5,749.3	60.7	20.4	0.0	11.5	0.0	5.6	1.8
24 30,325	Frederick	23.2	72,146	497	3,109.7	67.9	14.2	0.2	7.5	0.0	3.4	6.7
24 31,175	Gaithersburg	10.3	68,289	527	6,630.0	43.1	17.1	0.5	16.0	0.0	19.7	3.7
24 36,075	Hagerstown	12.2	40,205	953	3,295.5	72.0	13.5	0.1	1.4	0.0	5.6	7.5
24 45,900	Laurel	4.8	25,723	1,399	5,359.0	24.8	50.3	0.8	7.8	0.0	11.8	4.5
24 67,675	Rockville	13.6	68,268	528	5,019.7	53.6	10.0	0.7	21.7	0.0	9.3	4.7
24 69,925	Salisbury	13.7	32,809	1,161	2,394.8	51.0	42.0	0.0	2.1	0.0	1.1	3.7
25 00,000	MASSACHUSETTS	7,801.2	6,902,149	X	884.8	78.5	7.8	0.2	6.6	0.0	3.8	3.1
25 00,840	Agawam Town	23.3	28,854	1,293	1,238.4	NA	NA	NA	NA	NA	NA	NA
25 02,690	Attleboro	26.8	45,117	848	1,683.5	85.5	3.8	0.0	3.1	0.0	4.2	3.4
25 03,690	Barnstable Town	59.9	44,460	860	742.2	90.0	5.9	0.0	0.6	0.0	0.8	2.7

1. Dry land or land partially or temporarily covered by water.   2. Hispanic or Latino persons may be of any race.

Table D. Cities — **Population**

City	Percent Hispanic or Latino[1], 2017	Percent foreign born, 2017	Age of population (percent), 2017							Median age, 2017	Percent female, 2017	Population			
												Census counts		Percent change	
			Under 18 years	18 to 24 years	25 to 34 years	35 to 44 years	45 to 54 years	55 to 64 years	65 years and over			2000	2010	2000-2010	2001-2018
	12	13	14	15	16	17	18	19	20	21	22	23	24	25	26
KANSAS	11.9	6.9	24.5	10.2	13.2	12.2	11.8	12.9	15.4	36.7	50.1	2,688,418	2,853,126	6.1	2.0
Dodge City	65.1	35.4	31.5	11.7	13.5	13.2	9.9	9.7	10.5	29.4	46.5	25,176	27,326	8.5	0.0
Garden City	54.3	22.3	30.3	10.8	15.0	11.8	10.9	9.7	11.6	30.3	48.2	28,451	26,727	-6.1	-0.7
Hutchinson	13.1	1.8	21.7	10.4	11.2	13.2	13.0	11.7	18.8	39.8	50.3	40,787	42,179	3.4	-3.7
Kansas City	30.3	15.3	28.1	9.0	15.0	12.5	11.8	12.0	11.5	33.7	50.5	146,866	145,785	-0.7	4.9
Lawrence	6.7	7.9	16.7	26.6	17.0	10.9	8.3	8.8	11.7	27.9	51.7	80,098	87,757	9.6	10.9
Leavenworth	10.8	2.7	26.2	6.0	13.4	15.4	14.2	12.2	12.5	37.6	43.3	35,420	35,247	-0.5	2.3
Leawood	1.5	6.5	25.4	5.0	8.2	12.3	13.8	16.8	18.4	44.3	55.9	27,656	31,888	15.3	8.8
Lenexa	7.1	12.0	25.5	6.4	13.5	16.2	13.1	11.3	14.0	37.2	51.3	40,238	48,212	19.8	14.7
Manhattan	7.4	7.9	15.9	35.3	17.8	8.9	6.0	7.7	8.4	24.6	50.5	44,831	52,158	16.3	5.4
Olathe	10.0	11.2	29.3	8.2	12.2	17.0	12.2	10.6	10.5	35.2	50.9	92,962	125,900	35.4	10.9
Overland Park	7.4	11.5	21.7	9.1	15.1	12.1	14.0	12.6	15.5	38.5	49.8	149,080	173,329	16.3	11.1
Salina	12.5	4.6	23.5	8.9	14.4	12.7	11.5	12.8	16.2	37.3	52.3	45,679	47,778	4.6	-2.2
Shawnee	6.9	4.0	24.8	7.8	13.1	12.2	14.9	13.8	13.5	38.7	51.4	47,996	62,207	29.6	5.8
Topeka	14.4	4.6	23.3	9.3	14.9	11.8	11.2	12.0	17.5	36.6	50.8	122,377	127,631	4.3	-1.4
Wichita	17.5	10.4	24.6	9.7	14.6	11.9	11.6	12.9	14.7	35.9	50.7	344,284	382,423	11.1	1.8
KENTUCKY	3.5	3.8	22.8	9.4	12.9	12.5	13.1	13.4	15.9	38.9	50.7	4,041,769	4,339,333	7.4	3.0
Bowling Green	7.0	12.0	21.4	24.9	16.7	7.5	10.3	8.7	10.4	26.7	53.2	49,296	59,031	19.7	15.9
Covington	7.1	4.8	19.7	6.4	19.0	13.9	12.3	14.4	14.4	37.3	50.8	43,370	40,506	-6.6	-0.3
Elizabethtown	4.2	4.6	25.6	8.5	12.8	17.4	12.4	12.0	11.3	36.7	51.7	22,542	28,049	24.4	7.5
Florence	4.7	11.9	22.0	7.5	15.4	12.1	13.7	10.1	19.2	39.6	53.1	23,551	29,537	25.4	10.0
Frankfort	5.0	5.0	19.3	7.3	13.3	11.6	19.6	14.1	14.8	44.2	50.7	27,741	27,269	-1.7	1.5
Georgetown	5.2	4.6	27.1	10.6	15.7	15.3	11.4	9.5	10.4	33.4	51.0	18,080	29,138	61.2	18.0
Henderson	1.3	1.8	22.2	6.4	11.3	12.1	13.6	14.1	20.3	43.6	54.4	27,373	28,925	5.7	-1.7
Hopkinsville	0.9	2.0	27.7	6.3	11.8	12.6	13.4	13.4	14.8	39.1	53.0	30,089	32,034	6.5	-3.1
Jeffersontown	5.6	10.1	18.0	6.3	13.9	11.6	14.8	15.2	20.2	45.3	52.2	26,633	27,813	4.4	0.7
Lexington-Fayette	7.2	8.6	21.1	13.9	15.7	13.2	11.7	11.5	12.9	34.3	50.8	260,512	295,867	13.6	9.4
Louisville/Jefferson County ...	5.8	8.4	22.8	9.3	15.2	12.2	12.6	13.5	14.4	36.9	51.3	NA	595,386	NA	4.2
Nicholasville	2.0	5.3	23.1	8.5	14.4	14.8	13.1	10.2	15.9	36.9	52.4	19,680	28,040	42.5	9.9
Owensboro	4.5	2.9	25.6	10.0	13.2	10.8	12.1	10.5	17.8	36.6	52.9	54,067	57,454	6.3	4.1
Paducah	3.3	2.3	18.9	9.0	13.1	11.8	14.3	14.2	18.8	42.6	50.8	26,307	25,027	-4.9	-0.7
Richmond	2.3	3.6	17.6	28.3	14.9	10.8	8.1	7.8	12.6	26.3	55.5	27,152	31,319	15.3	14.6
LOUISIANA	5.2	4.1	23.7	9.7	14.0	12.6	12.3	12.9	14.9	36.8	51.1	4,468,976	4,533,485	1.4	2.8
Alexandria	2.2	3.9	23.0	11.0	12.9	11.6	11.5	14.1	15.9	37.8	51.9	46,342	47,917	3.4	-2.4
Baton Rouge	3.4	5.1	22.6	17.1	15.9	10.2	10.2	10.4	13.5	30.8	53.3	227,818	229,422	0.7	-3.4
Bossier City	10.4	4.2	25.2	11.4	15.4	14.0	9.8	10.4	13.9	34.1	52.6	56,461	61,769	9.4	10.5
Central	1.2	1.8	22.0	9.9	8.1	12.6	13.2	20.0	14.2	42.4	46.3	NA	26,869	NA	7.4
Houma	6.1	2.8	23.7	8.6	12.5	13.1	12.9	13.7	15.4	38.2	51.4	32,393	33,661	3.9	-2.4
Kenner	27.3	21.1	22.8	8.4	16.5	10.6	11.1	14.6	16.0	36.9	52.6	70,517	66,685	-5.4	0.0
Lafayette	3.3	4.9	22.6	11.4	14.5	12.8	12.4	13.0	13.3	35.6	51.6	110,257	121,667	10.3	3.7
Lake Charles	3.4	2.7	19.7	10.8	15.0	10.1	12.7	14.5	17.2	38.7	51.8	71,757	72,264	0.7	7.9
Monroe	1.1	1.3	26.6	12.4	14.3	11.0	10.1	12.1	13.5	32.3	53.7	53,107	48,914	-7.9	-2.1
New Iberia	4.9	3.1	23.6	10.0	15.9	8.8	14.6	12.0	15.1	35.8	55.2	32,623	30,617	-6.1	-5.0
New Orleans	5.7	5.3	20.1	9.0	18.1	13.4	12.1	13.2	14.1	36.7	52.5	484,674	343,828	-29.1	13.7
Shreveport	2.6	2.6	24.7	9.1	15.5	11.9	11.2	12.1	15.5	35.4	52.8	200,145	200,405	0.1	-5.7
Slidell	5.6	4.8	23.1	9.3	8.7	15.6	10.8	14.1	18.4	41.5	54.9	25,695	27,216	5.9	1.8
MAINE	1.6	3.4	19.0	8.2	11.9	11.3	13.8	15.7	20.0	44.6	51.0	1,274,923	1,328,369	4.2	0.8
Bangor	3.2	4.7	15.3	12.0	15.9	7.8	15.9	16.2	17.0	44.4	51.7	31,473	33,024	4.9	-3.1
Lewiston	0.9	4.8	15.0	13.8	9.9	8.6	15.3	17.4	20.1	46.6	49.3	35,690	36,592	2.5	-1.8
Portland	3.7	12.5	15.1	10.4	23.3	14.1	9.8	12.1	15.2	35.6	50.9	64,249	66,193	3.0	0.3
South Portland	3.5	3.3	16.2	10.4	12.2	14.3	9.7	13.5	23.7	41.7	48.5	23,324	25,004	7.2	2.4
MARYLAND	10.1	15.3	22.3	8.9	13.8	12.8	14.0	13.4	14.9	38.7	51.5	5,296,486	5,773,798	9.0	4.7
Annapolis	24.6	21.3	20.8	5.7	19.5	11.6	13.6	14.1	14.7	38.2	49.1	35,838	38,289	6.8	2.3
Baltimore	5.3	8.7	20.6	9.6	19.2	12.4	12.0	12.7	13.5	35.3	53.1	651,154	620,862	-4.7	-3.0
Bowie	7.6	18.2	22.2	8.2	12.0	10.4	17.7	14.7	14.8	43.1	51.4	50,269	55,335	10.1	6.0
College Park	19.6	22.1	10.8	50.6	15.9	5.7	5.8	5.1	6.1	21.5	49.5	24,657	30,397	23.3	5.9
Frederick	15.0	18.8	21.3	8.9	15.5	14.4	13.3	13.0	13.7	38.5	50.8	52,767	65,287	23.7	10.5
Gaithersburg	27.8	33.7	26.4	6.4	16.3	14.5	12.2	11.5	12.7	35.6	49.6	52,613	59,903	13.9	14.0
Hagerstown	8.8	6.2	22.7	8.4	16.3	11.4	17.2	11.3	12.8	37.2	54.1	36,687	39,757	8.4	1.1
Laurel	16.8	31.8	19.6	5.9	24.6	14.1	15.1	12.5	8.0	34.9	52.0	19,960	24,925	24.9	3.2
Rockville	15.9	33.5	23.1	5.1	15.2	17.2	11.6	11.5	16.4	39.1	52.9	47,388	61,255	29.3	11.4
Salisbury	4.0	10.1	22.0	20.4	12.1	9.8	9.8	14.2	11.6	30.8	58.9	23,743	30,230	27.3	8.5
MASSACHUSETTS	11.8	16.9	20.0	10.2	14.2	12.2	13.7	13.6	16.1	39.5	51.4	6,349,097	6,547,790	3.1	5.4
Agawam Town	7.0	10.2	20.8	3.2	12.9	12.8	17.8	11.5	21.0	45.7	50.0	28,144	28,438	1.0	1.5
Attleboro	9.5	8.1	20.2	8.1	17.1	10.8	15.7	10.7	17.3	39.6	51.5	42,068	43,586	3.6	3.5
Barnstable Town	6.8	17.9	18.0	6.5	11.8	7.5	15.7	16.8	23.6	48.9	50.4	47,821	45,187	-5.5	-1.6

1. May be of any race.

City	Households, 2017								Serious crimes known to police[2], 2016				Educational attainment, 2017		
			Percent						Total		Rate[3]			Attainment[4] (percent)	
	Number	Persons per household	Family	Married couple family	Female headed[1]	Non-family	One person	Persons in group quarters, 2017	Number	Rate	Violent	Property	Population age 25 and over	High school graduate or less	Bachelor's degree or more
	27	28	29	30	31	32	33	34	35	36	37	38	39	40	41
KANSAS	1,128,983	2.51	65.0	50.7	9.9	35.0	29.0	80,160	89,427	3,076	380	2,696	1,904,528	34.8	33.7
Dodge City	9,025	2.97	67.7	47.6	14.7	32.3	19.8	620	973	3,475	361	3,115	15,570	59.2	19.7
Garden City	9,206	2.95	69.0	43.1	15.1	31.0	24.5	605	1,002	3,706	518	3,188	16,383	55.7	14.8
Hutchinson	16,115	2.39	60.0	44.7	12.7	40.0	30.1	2,595	2,117	5,109	451	4,657	27,915	34.2	19.7
Kansas City	56,677	2.72	64.3	38.3	18.8	35.7	30.3	1,138	NA	NA	NA	NA	97,572	53.3	15.6
Lawrence	38,591	2.27	49.1	37.2	8.5	50.9	33.4	7,492	NA	NA	NA	NA	53,825	20.4	49.5
Leavenworth	12,844	2.55	63.6	42.8	14.4	36.4	34.2	3,470	1,514	4,194	657	3,537	24,561	39.7	30.2
Leawood	13,231	2.61	74.0	70.1	3.0	26.0	22.4	NA	427	1,215	85	1,130	24,104	5.6	80.8
Lenexa	20,868	2.55	66.7	54.8	9.6	33.3	26.3	NA	998	1,870	133	1,737	36,480	18.7	55.9
Manhattan	21,521	2.35	46.9	36.4	9.1	53.1	33.2	6,082	NA	NA	NA	NA	27,626	18.1	56.4
Olathe	48,080	2.83	72.9	60.3	8.6	27.1	22.6	1,532	2,349	1,727	163	1,564	85,917	22.0	49.3
Overland Park	78,536	2.42	62.9	51.6	8.5	37.1	30.5	1,151	3,179	1,681	199	1,482	132,444	15.4	61.4
Salina	18,389	2.48	57.1	45.0	9.0	42.9	36.9	1,389	2,044	4,276	429	3,847	31,775	39.7	28.6
Shawnee	25,238	2.58	70.5	57.8	8.0	29.5	24.5	361	1,320	2,012	209	1,803	44,174	18.1	50.2
Topeka	54,707	2.23	55.2	42.9	9.1	44.8	38.8	4,531	7,859	6,180	559	5,621	85,353	39.1	33.3
Wichita	152,691	2.52	62.7	44.1	12.9	37.3	31.0	5,179	25,252	6,452	1,064	5,388	256,658	38.3	30.5
KENTUCKY	1,725,034	2.51	65.5	48.6	12.2	34.5	28.6	131,983	107,466	2,422	232	2,190	3,018,953	46.7	24.0
Bowling Green	24,927	2.39	55.3	35.0	14.7	44.7	31.5	7,581	2,992	4,634	324	4,311	35,957	39.5	29.0
Covington	18,152	2.17	46.8	27.5	13.0	53.2	43.3	1,117	1,548	3,767	499	3,268	29,916	47.9	24.2
Elizabethtown	12,361	2.35	59.5	45.0	9.3	40.5	36.2	1,033	547	1,834	228	1,606	19,808	28.8	26.9
Florence	12,502	2.56	69.9	54.4	9.8	30.1	21.5	NA	1,471	4,502	245	4,258	22,800	37.8	23.2
Frankfort	12,186	2.19	58.4	32.4	17.8	41.6	37.2	1,335	1,209	4,329	405	3,925	20,597	43.4	28.6
Georgetown	14,004	2.44	64.4	44.7	13.9	35.6	31.3	1,376	979	2,966	173	2,793	22,100	44.4	23.2
Henderson	12,423	2.21	58.2	32.7	19.7	41.8	38.8	1,646	826	2,858	197	2,661	20,778	56.9	14.5
Hopkinsville	12,688	2.30	53.2	31.6	18.7	46.8	40.3	1,665	1,021	3,169	292	2,877	20,333	47.7	17.4
Jeffersontown	12,036	2.26	63.6	47.7	9.8	36.4	31.3	NA	674	2,496	122	2,374	20,739	34.6	37.3
Lexington-Fayette	129,140	2.40	57.4	41.6	11.2	42.6	30.9	12,491	14,182	4,462	341	4,121	209,203	27.1	43.6
Louisville/Jefferson County	246,707	2.46	60.3	40.2	15.2	39.7	32.3	15,537	35,015	5,120	678	4,442	421,939	39.6	29.9
Nicholasville	10,940	2.65	65.3	40.0	20.9	34.7	23.3	NA	1,111	3,692	176	3,516	19,988	53.2	15.5
Owensboro	25,247	2.27	63.4	40.1	18.0	36.6	33.3	2,171	2,806	4,727	234	4,493	38,274	42.6	22.0
Paducah	11,064	2.15	48.8	33.8	13.8	51.2	44.8	1,155	1,309	5,271	362	4,908	18,007	41.8	26.8
Richmond	13,071	2.37	52.4	30.7	19.4	47.6	30.3	4,451	1,455	4,284	227	4,057	19,163	37.8	29.2
LOUISIANA	1,737,123	2.62	63.7	42.8	15.9	36.3	30.7	129,589	180,888	3,864	566	3,298	3,120,277	48.9	23.8
Alexandria	17,024	2.65	61.0	29.6	25.7	39.0	36.3	2,245	4,974	10,376	1,842	8,534	31,242	52.4	23.6
Baton Rouge	82,571	2.63	55.9	30.0	20.8	44.1	34.8	8,035	12,077	5,288	938	4,350	135,845	40.6	32.2
Bossier City	27,511	2.39	66.3	42.1	17.3	33.7	28.8	2,902	3,791	5,464	843	4,621	43,487	43.3	21.8
Central	9,627	3.00	76.2	60.0	11.3	23.8	18.1	54	NA	NA	NA	NA	19,747	49.9	20.9
Houma	13,019	2.54	57.2	29.9	17.2	42.8	34.6	NA	1,578	4,586	485	4,101	22,539	60.5	16.8
Kenner	23,906	2.80	65.2	43.2	19.0	34.8	28.4	488	2,429	3,617	289	3,328	46,401	50.0	21.6
Lafayette	48,712	2.51	56.3	36.5	14.4	43.7	34.6	4,481	7,058	5,475	497	4,977	83,767	41.8	37.4
Lake Charles	34,153	2.17	51.0	32.8	15.6	49.0	41.0	2,863	3,807	4,953	851	4,102	53,544	38.6	29.7
Monroe	17,812	2.52	58.4	30.5	24.8	41.6	34.7	3,529	6,139	12,358	3,005	9,352	29,510	49.1	25.9
New Iberia	11,276	2.59	59.5	43.1	10.9	40.5	36.8	388	NA	NA	NA	NA	19,649	59.6	14.9
New Orleans	154,560	2.45	46.8	26.4	17.4	53.2	45.7	14,181	19,820	4,990	1,070	3,920	278,629	37.7	35.3
Shreveport	74,614	2.50	57.1	30.8	20.7	42.9	38.3	4,957	12,586	6,406	949	5,457	126,972	45.6	23.8
Slidell	9,440	2.90	67.0	40.4	18.0	33.0	26.2	473	1,329	4,728	374	4,355	18,858	40.9	25.1
MAINE	540,959	2.40	61.0	48.8	8.3	39.0	30.5	36,280	23,560	1,769	124	1,646	971,740	38.6	32.1
Bangor	13,301	2.18	52.4	39.6	10.8	47.6	36.4	2,871	1,415	4,386	232	4,153	23,204	34.7	37.5
Lewiston	16,570	2.05	47.8	36.1	7.2	52.2	38.4	2,253	786	2,176	180	1,996	25,820	51.9	19.2
Portland	29,722	2.19	41.3	31.6	6.9	58.7	41.0	1,835	1,991	2,970	292	2,677	49,813	25.4	49.6
South Portland	10,673	2.33	54.5	36.6	10.8	45.5	36.6	646	643	2,504	171	2,333	18,700	29.8	38.3
MARYLAND	2,207,343	2.68	66.6	47.7	14.2	33.4	27.4	140,661	165,845	2,757	472	2,284	4,167,604	34.6	39.7
Annapolis	16,027	2.42	55.8	40.4	8.9	44.2	35.4	557	1,188	2,992	630	2,363	28,928	34.5	45.4
Baltimore	240,280	2.44	50.3	23.9	21.7	49.7	40.0	24,671	40,557	6,559	1,780	4,778	426,682	45.0	30.6
Bowie	20,073	2.91	72.3	54.1	15.4	27.7	23.0	375	811	1,383	94	1,289	40,978	26.7	43.9
College Park	7,233	3.02	43.7	35.5	5.8	56.3	35.6	10,450	NA	NA	NA	NA	12,468	28.4	48.1
Frederick	28,966	2.40	58.9	46.2	9.9	41.1	32.4	1,980	1,754	2,494	488	2,007	49,848	28.4	44.3
Gaithersburg	24,459	2.79	67.4	46.1	16.4	32.6	27.1	NA	NA	NA	NA	NA	46,200	33.2	49.0
Hagerstown	16,438	2.39	56.1	34.4	17.5	43.9	35.5	967	1,493	3,680	569	3,111	27,789	55.4	14.7
Laurel	9,665	2.66	52.2	36.5	12.2	47.8	34.8	NA	1,120	4,239	413	3,826	19,291	24.4	48.0
Rockville	25,621	2.64	65.6	49.1	12.5	34.4	27.2	731	NA	NA	NA	NA	49,164	20.1	59.7
Salisbury	13,239	2.38	44.9	19.7	21.3	55.1	40.4	1,288	1,992	5,961	889	5,072	18,888	39.9	31.9
MASSACHUSETTS	2,604,954	2.54	63.4	47.0	12.2	36.6	28.6	250,594	132,016	1,938	377	1,561	4,788,573	33.5	43.4
Agawam Town	11,752	2.41	63.3	51.5	8.2	36.7	30.0	583	570	1,976	281	1,695	21,939	37.7	35.8
Attleboro	17,419	2.53	68.7	45.1	15.5	31.3	25.4	529	872	1,972	210	1,761	31,989	35.8	35.0
Barnstable Town	17,528	2.49	66.7	47.7	13.3	33.3	26.1	510	911	2,072	453	1,619	33,322	34.9	37.2

1. No spouse present. 2. Data for serious crimes have not been adjusted for underreporting. This may affect comparability between geographic areas and over time. 3. Per 100,000 population estimated by the FBI. 4. Persons 25 years old and over.

Table D. Cities — Income and Housing

City	Money income, 2017 Households: Median income	Percent with income less than $20,000	Percent with income of $200,000 or more	Median family income	Median non-family income	Median earnings, 2017: All persons	Men	Women	Housing units, 2017: Total	Occupied	Percent owner occupied	Median value¹ (dollars)	Median gross rent (dollars)
	42	43	44	45	46	47	48	49	50	51	52	53	54
KANSAS	56,422	14.9	4.6	72,057	32,327	31,839	38,674	26,113	1,273,776	1,128,983	65.9	150,600	815
Dodge City	46,842	11.2	2.5	56,098	38,646	30,021	31,170	25,025	9,159	9,025	52.4	103,800	684
Garden City	52,317	10.0	0.8	52,204	49,220	28,959	36,422	19,904	10,092	9,206	59.2	151,600	792
Hutchinson	47,577	17.1	3.5	54,239	24,381	24,311	26,257	22,849	18,839	16,115	67.4	95,900	729
Kansas City	45,118	20.8	1.5	54,898	26,830	29,191	34,812	23,255	63,583	56,677	54.7	103,800	830
Lawrence	48,827	21.4	3.7	76,977	31,246	22,446	25,039	20,938	41,343	38,591	44.5	203,800	872
Leavenworth	52,875	15.4	1.7	66,551	36,146	34,515	39,295	28,314	14,142	12,844	55.5	118,300	905
Leawood	149,502	5.2	36.9	189,577	51,336	68,120	121,862	38,728	13,988	13,231	89.0	464,600	1,636
Lenexa	81,082	6.3	12.8	100,581	60,898	48,783	60,873	38,705	22,419	20,868	59.1	263,300	1,129
Manhattan	48,813	18.5	3.9	67,417	39,527	17,847	22,816	13,673	24,617	21,521	43.1	210,200	888
Olathe	87,052	6.0	7.3	103,310	47,712	42,391	49,543	37,627	50,390	48,080	73.2	239,100	949
Overland Park	79,070	7.2	11.6	105,848	45,673	42,104	53,526	34,443	81,985	78,536	62.0	270,800	1,101
Salina	46,182	15.7	2.7	69,715	29,567	29,090	29,354	28,276	21,151	18,389	63.7	122,700	724
Shawnee	89,190	9.6	10.4	100,340	46,206	45,078	54,490	36,715	26,233	25,238	74.6	240,000	933
Topeka	48,847	17.6	1.2	65,630	32,144	32,958	38,588	27,231	59,890	54,707	55.9	97,300	775
Wichita	50,504	18.8	3.1	63,834	30,779	29,978	35,535	23,518	172,824	152,691	58.6	135,100	786
KENTUCKY	48,375	20.7	3.6	61,593	27,249	30,663	36,142	25,455	1,984,235	1,725,034	66.5	141,000	724
Bowling Green	40,814	21.3	2.9	50,350	29,669	20,208	22,125	16,768	27,787	24,927	37.3	153,500	771
Covington	36,539	28.6	1.5	48,689	26,953	29,622	32,662	27,085	21,018	18,152	45.4	109,800	666
Elizabethtown	55,173	18.3	4.4	72,223	32,753	36,167	41,952	30,098	13,037	12,361	45.6	179,400	761
Florence	63,584	9.0	2.7	85,402	35,768	31,833	32,487	30,147	13,439	12,502	45.6	164,300	860
Frankfort	48,991	12.4	1.8	54,434	35,157	29,010	26,598	31,130	13,402	12,186	61.0	132,700	779
Georgetown	56,676	13.7	3.0	71,180	36,205	30,882	38,400	25,665	14,833	14,004	48.0	168,000	786
Henderson	34,791	22.4	1.6	48,123	24,660	26,085	29,700	22,094	14,184	12,423	59.1	109,800	639
Hopkinsville	40,204	32.9	1.4	53,682	23,668	25,788	36,348	21,362	14,839	12,688	52.3	121,100	666
Jeffersontown	65,964	5.0	5.9	86,512	45,332	36,525	46,555	26,122	12,180	12,036	50.8	184,600	885
Lexington-Fayette	56,137	16.9	6.2	75,756	35,303	30,005	32,862	25,783	141,630	129,140	70.2	193,100	854
Louisville/Jefferson County	51,960	18.6	4.2	67,965	32,446	31,988	37,319	28,167	275,166	246,707	55.3	160,500	810
Nicholasville	50,568	23.5	2.7	54,611	30,781	28,125	32,475	22,269	11,724	10,940	59.7	137,400	732
Owensboro	41,986	23.6	2.7	49,956	26,502	26,718	36,169	22,955	26,875	25,247	52.2	120,900	805
Paducah	43,933	15.9	4.2	54,486	29,666	31,164	36,465	25,478	12,793	11,064	53.4	128,500	588
Richmond	36,318	30.4	2.4	50,746	25,402	15,341	16,921	12,366	15,015	13,071	55.0	159,300	656
LOUISIANA	46,145	23.1	4.0	60,510	26,106	30,544	38,263	24,454	2,061,582	1,737,123	29.9	162,500	836
Alexandria	40,782	24.9	4.8	46,237	31,166	27,797	30,452	25,349	20,992	17,024	65.2	140,000	845
Baton Rouge	40,796	28.9	4.5	58,785	24,857	23,174	28,849	20,718	100,585	82,571	51.0	178,300	855
Bossier City	46,911	23.8	2.0	57,257	35,875	33,136	37,052	30,771	30,921	27,511	49.0	159,900	958
Central	86,556	8.9	2.5	89,513	57,393	41,747	46,635	31,338	10,738	9,627	55.0	220,500	1,014
Houma	35,254	34.7	5.2	50,262	20,768	24,938	36,050	23,299	14,328	13,019	90.2	143,700	756
Kenner	57,009	18.3	4.8	67,338	36,250	31,845	36,771	27,439	26,867	23,906	60.1	179,600	926
Lafayette	41,964	23.7	6.4	57,703	29,826	29,227	37,146	22,287	55,533	48,712	57.9	193,000	856
Lake Charles	43,939	19.1	4.0	59,612	31,966	29,586	36,726	22,549	39,196	34,153	56.1	167,100	846
Monroe	28,957	38.4	3.6	37,712	21,116	25,029	31,147	18,314	21,871	17,812	56.9	157,500	660
New Iberia	32,219	30.3	1.5	41,961	25,983	26,970	30,046	21,855	14,403	11,276	45.3	110,700	628
New Orleans	36,999	31.0	5.1	55,138	25,921	29,751	35,465	25,875	191,688	154,560	48.5	227,800	962
Shreveport	32,983	32.1	4.1	45,579	20,700	24,303	28,341	22,137	87,890	74,614	47.2	155,300	760
Slidell	54,835	15.2	1.3	63,041	23,582	34,019	37,038	30,850	10,534	9,440	48.9	168,600	1,112
MAINE	56,277	16.9	4.1	72,177	31,688	31,552	36,359	27,724	742,644	540,959	72.4	191,200	806
Bangor	45,506	23.4	3.6	60,317	30,054	26,642	30,191	21,483	15,561	13,301	73.2	146,900	859
Lewiston	38,992	29.3	1.4	66,652	22,760	30,365	25,265	21,442	17,087	16,570	50.4	135,000	715
Portland	56,326	20.0	4.0	91,333	42,351	35,931	38,943	32,085	35,010	29,722	56.3	291,200	1,067
South Portland	61,282	12.0	3.9	79,923	44,230	31,660	31,433	31,847	11,967	10,673	47.1	249,500	1,246
MARYLAND	80,776	10.7	11.3	98,393	50,457	42,149	49,045	37,218	2,449,123	2,207,343	67.7	312,500	1,337
Annapolis	93,194	12.9	13.6	108,330	65,899	39,496	40,435	39,041	17,529	16,027	66.7	425,600	1,462
Baltimore	47,131	23.7	5.0	58,613	35,393	35,251	37,111	32,471	294,534	240,280	50.9	154,400	1,035
Bowie	105,481	4.1	17.6	123,825	61,418	51,972	47,493	57,179	20,923	20,073	47.4	339,000	1,835
College Park	61,518	22.8	11.6	98,338	42,704	10,766	16,690	9,007	7,870	7,233	81.7	316,900	1,467
Frederick	73,457	8.6	6.4	94,921	52,155	42,127	50,909	36,328	31,002	28,966	47.6	275,900	1,352
Gaithersburg	82,077	9.6	10.6	92,656	61,918	43,849	50,979	36,763	25,713	24,459	58.2	427,700	1,581
Hagerstown	37,179	30.8	0.7	50,382	23,615	30,898	38,908	21,637	18,468	16,438	49.4	143,900	778
Laurel	78,924	9.6	8.2	94,074	61,021	42,976	44,206	41,360	9,935	9,665	39.1	240,000	1,470
Rockville	100,388	6.1	16.4	118,742	78,712	52,178	62,681	45,507	27,094	25,621	49.1	484,000	1,875
Salisbury	37,066	28.2	1.3	37,354	33,067	23,778	31,731	20,685	15,337	13,239	54.7	141,200	945
MASSACHUSETTS	77,385	14.0	12.2	98,758	43,824	41,700	50,224	35,704	2,894,590	2,604,954	28.2	385,400	1,208
Agawam Town	71,374	9.2	6.6	98,941	41,998	50,865	51,531	48,951	12,288	11,752	62.3	252,300	1,087
Attleboro	63,388	13.8	6.6	85,297	27,158	41,803	41,806	41,750	19,600	17,419	75.7	284,600	1,059
Barnstable Town	69,271	10.6	7.6	83,176	50,009	36,020	41,878	30,149	25,050	17,528	68.4	399,000	1,367

1. Based on population estimated by the American Community Survey.   2. Includes units rented or sold but not occupied.   3. Specified owner-occupied units; $1,000,000 represents $1,000,000 or more.   4. 50.0 represents 50 percent or more.   5. 10.0 represents 10 percent or less.

Table D. Cities — Commuting, Computer Access, Migration, Labor Force, and Employment

City	Commuting[1], 2017		Computer access[2], 2017		Migration, 2017		Civilian labor force, 2018		Unemployment		Civilian employment[4], 2017			
											Population age 16 and older		Population age 16 to 64	
	Percent		Percent											
	Commuting	With commutes of 30 minutes or more	With a computer in the house	With Internet access	Percent who lived in the same house one year ago	Percent who lived in another state or county one year ago	Total	Percent change 2017-2018	Total	Rate[3]	Number	Percent in labor force	Number	Percent who worked full-year full-time
	55	56	57	58	59	60	61	62	63	64	65	66	67	68
KANSAS	82.4	21.0	90.7	82.6	83.9	7.1	1,482,220	0.2	49,833	3.4	2,279,858	66.5	1,832,407	55.2
Dodge City	NA	6.9	86.0	73.3	81.4	6.5	13,670	-3.3	361	2.6	19,584	75.8	16,695	58.3
Garden City	93.2	4.1	87.6	80.1	86.3	5.1	14,857	1.7	381	2.6	20,439	76.9	17,227	56.7
Hutchinson	83.5	12.7	88.5	81.0	77.4	11.0	19,004	-0.1	734	3.9	33,629	63.3	25,904	53.0
Kansas City	82.6	25.3	87.1	74.4	89.1	5.3	71,216	0.8	3,436	4.8	115,847	65.6	97,962	52.0
Lawrence	75.3	22.3	96.7	89.3	69.6	12.1	52,564	0.0	1,579	3.0	80,992	69.5	69,837	46.0
Leavenworth	75.8	19.4	90.4	75.2	73.9	17.6	14,041	0.9	583	4.2	27,603	61.9	23,071	56.4
Leawood	81.0	31.9	98.8	96.9	92.5	3.8	17,592	1.0	475	2.7	27,112	61.1	20,724	51.8
Lenexa	84.9	21.5	98.6	94.5	81.5	9.6	31,452	1.0	920	2.9	40,982	71.1	33,502	65.0
Manhattan	66.7	11.3	95.1	90.4	69.5	15.1	29,130	1.0	766	2.6	48,414	68.2	43,639	39.1
Olathe	84.5	24.4	95.7	93.3	87.2	4.6	78,749	1.1	2,191	2.8	101,771	77.3	87,363	61.7
Overland Park	82.1	22.0	94.7	91.7	82.6	6.8	109,600	1.0	3,158	2.9	155,055	71.0	125,409	58.9
Salina	85.5	8.2	87.5	84.2	83.5	6.4	25,570	-1.5	811	3.2	37,042	65.9	29,435	55.7
Shawnee	86.5	26.7	97.0	94.7	86.2	5.2	36,553	1.1	1,133	3.1	50,899	72.9	42,070	58.7
Topeka	82.0	10.6	85.7	68.5	83.1	6.9	63,187	0.0	2,359	3.7	99,945	63.2	77,819	54.1
Wichita	84.1	13.8	91.0	82.5	79.7	7.1	186,675	0.6	7,298	3.9	304,057	65.6	246,724	52.8
KENTUCKY	82.0	29.9	86.3	78.1	84.5	6.6	2,061,622	0.4	89,310	4.3	3,553,101	59.3	2,844,053	48.5
Bowling Green	79.5	16.1	89.2	82.6	70.3	15.6	32,793	0.5	1,281	3.9	54,073	65.8	47,110	39.5
Covington	73.6	20.4	88.6	76.9	76.3	13.8	19,119	1.2	761	4.0	32,665	61.1	26,842	45.7
Elizabethtown	88.8	31.7	90.0	69.6	77.4	8.3	14,275	1.0	564	4.0	23,390	64.4	19,995	53.0
Florence	77.2	30.9	91.5	87.7	82.1	9.6	16,745	1.1	596	3.6	25,842	67.4	19,628	61.2
Frankfort	79.1	15.9	83.6	76.4	79.4	11.4	14,214	1.1	551	3.9	23,611	66.7	19,453	53.3
Georgetown	82.0	25.8	89.5	81.9	80.4	9.0	17,606	-0.6	593	3.4	26,659	70.6	22,977	56.4
Henderson	89.0	24.9	72.4	60.1	88.8	6.3	13,322	0.7	546	4.1	23,594	49.7	17,682	50.0
Hopkinsville	85.8	8.7	81.3	74.8	76.9	5.1	12,179	1.5	706	5.8	23,255	53.4	18,698	41.6
Jeffersontown	76.9	30.5	93.8	91.0	89.3	2.6	16,005	1.0	541	3.4	23,388	70.3	17,843	65.2
Lexington-Fayette	78.6	21.0	94.0	88.7	75.2	7.7	174,849	-0.3	5,801	3.3	260,333	68.7	218,950	50.4
Louisville/Jefferson County	77.8	27.9	90.0	84.3	84.1	4.3	400,587	1.0	16,269	4.1	NA	NA	NA	NA
Nicholasville	87.7	34.4	85.9	80.5	80.0	9.6	15,220	-0.1	570	3.7	23,476	61.4	18,834	52.4
Owensboro	88.0	12.2	83.6	76.9	81.4	4.5	27,239	0.1	1,130	4.1	45,588	61.9	34,993	52.6
Paducah	89.4	19.0	87.1	81.4	92.8	2.8	10,458	-1.0	632	6.0	20,819	57.8	16,135	49.4
Richmond	78.1	24.3	91.2	77.4	65.4	12.8	18,407	1.5	758	4.1	30,086	62.0	25,642	35.5
LOUISIANA	82.7	33.9	86.0	74.9	87.1	5.4	2,103,495	0.0	102,704	4.9	3,699,819	58.9	3,003,708	47.6
Alexandria	76.5	11.7	85.2	78.9	86.8	4.5	18,830	-1.6	1,053	5.6	38,201	57.8	30,660	43.9
Baton Rouge	81.6	21.7	86.0	76.8	82.4	5.3	113,676	0.4	5,404	4.8	179,962	64.0	149,445	43.5
Bossier City	82.0	12.9	90.8	51.6	86.3	8.7	30,188	0.0	1,319	4.4	53,000	60.3	43,461	54.0
Central	85.5	49.8	NA	NA	82.5	7.6	15,630	0.5	579	3.7	22,850	65.2	18,740	57.0
Houma	84.2	26.8	83.3	74.3	83.9	5.5	13,958	-0.8	719	5.2	26,736	53.7	21,593	40.1
Kenner	77.9	34.6	85.7	74.6	87.7	2.8	33,273	0.1	1,419	4.3	52,834	63.7	42,037	56.1
Lafayette	82.5	22.9	88.0	80.5	82.4	8.8	59,839	0.4	2,791	4.7	101,654	62.6	84,730	49.8
Lake Charles	84.3	6.0	84.5	73.4	81.9	5.2	42,063	1.4	1,669	4.0	63,659	64.9	50,426	50.2
Monroe	83.5	10.3	76.0	68.0	82.4	2.3	19,861	-0.4	1,241	6.2	37,502	56.6	30,949	43.5
New Iberia	83.3	29.5	82.5	80.2	84.4	2.7	10,869	-1.4	717	6.6	23,361	54.9	18,880	39.2
New Orleans	66.9	29.4	84.9	74.0	86.1	5.5	178,845	0.2	8,954	5.0	321,901	60.1	266,679	45.5
Shreveport	85.1	13.6	84.1	67.5	86.0	3.7	82,116	-0.1	4,555	5.5	148,519	58.4	118,778	46.2
Slidell	83.4	45.9	91.5	86.1	81.2	7.7	12,407	0.0	608	4.9	21,807	59.4	16,685	50.1
MAINE	78.6	32.7	89.7	82.2	86.2	6.3	698,745	0.0	23,524	3.4	1,114,189	63.0	847,448	51.1
Bangor	71.1	16.7	90.5	81.1	82.8	8.9	16,780	0.4	574	3.4	28,187	56.9	22,753	44.9
Lewiston	76.3	24.5	84.3	78.1	80.7	10.8	17,199	-0.3	606	3.5	31,847	58.8	24,561	45.2
Portland	64.0	16.5	89.6	84.2	76.6	12.0	39,043	0.6	1,020	2.6	57,459	70.5	47,324	50.4
South Portland	74.7	18.9	93.6	91.2	87.4	7.0	14,803	0.5	391	2.6	21,834	66.9	15,804	53.5
MARYLAND	73.7	52.8	93.0	87.3	86.3	6.3	3,197,137	0.1	125,485	3.9	4,855,374	67.9	3,952,788	55.6
Annapolis	75.3	36.2	94.0	87.0	81.5	7.4	22,274	0.2	691	3.1	32,076	72.5	26,282	58.5
Baltimore	59.7	48.7	86.5	75.5	85.0	6.0	289,758	-0.1	16,454	5.7	498,844	61.7	416,292	47.8
Bowie	74.6	56.4	98.8	96.4	91.5	4.4	34,360	-0.4	1,130	3.3	48,219	70.8	39,477	59.1
College Park	52.1	49.0	96.4	84.7	67.9	28.3	14,882	-0.6	746	5.0	29,137	56.1	27,163	28.2
Frederick	77.6	46.5	96.8	93.7	77.0	11.0	37,524	0.2	1,377	3.7	57,976	72.4	48,230	58.1
Gaithersburg	72.6	54.0	95.6	84.7	80.6	6.5	36,334	0.7	1,185	3.3	52,217	69.7	43,479	57.2
Hagerstown	72.2	34.9	83.6	71.0	77.1	3.4	19,026	-0.5	1,010	5.3	31,902	58.4	26,725	42.6
Laurel	76.7	60.9	95.4	87.1	80.4	9.0	15,659	-0.2	621	4.0	21,512	77.8	19,435	64.5
Rockville	67.1	54.9	96.5	92.6	77.9	11.6	37,337	0.5	1,098	2.9	53,744	70.4	42,558	59.6
Salisbury	78.6	24.4	87.2	77.1	74.3	6.5	15,261	0.4	896	5.9	26,021	65.2	22,204	35.8
MASSACHUSETTS	70.0	46.2	91.2	86.2	86.7	6.2	3,805,450	3.0	127,048	3.3	5,660,731	66.7	4,552,907	51.5
Agawam Town	NA	26.7	91.1	87.2	91.5	1.2	16,607	2.6	586	3.5	23,193	67.5	17,125	63.0
Attleboro	84.4	46.4	92.9	89.0	87.8	5.0	25,394	2.6	888	3.5	36,540	64.8	28,807	55.7
Barnstable Town	71.8	27.7	95.3	89.7	87.6	7.6	24,644	2.5	984	4.0	37,310	66.0	26,882	50.8

1. Employed persons.　2. Households.　3. Percent of civilian labor force.　4. Persons 16 years old and over.

City	Value of residential construction authorized by building permits, 2018			Wholesale trade[1], 2012				Retail trade[2], 2012			
	New construction ($1,000)	Number of housing units	Percent single family	Number of establishments	Number of employees	Sales (mil dol)	Annual payroll (mil dol)	Number of establishments	Number of employees	Sales (mil dol)	Annual payroll (mil dol)
	69	70	71	72	73	74	75	76	77	78	79
KANSAS	1,888,570	9,478	56.7	3,790	52,168	60,226.3	3,055.4	10,548	145,480	38,276.5	3,325.0
Dodge City	4,479	30	86.7	44	535	470.1	27.0	108	1,697	469.2	38.7
Garden City	8,087	48	100.0	27	199	227.0	9.5	149	2,259	538.9	49.9
Hutchinson	6,157	41	29.3	50	630	742.0	25.0	202	2,967	705.3	66.8
Kansas City	33,340	178	89.9	197	4,909	4,507.3	256.9	405	6,193	1,594.1	155.6
Lawrence	99,316	714	45.1	53	413	168.8	16.7	333	5,800	1,253.6	118.2
Leavenworth	5,735	29	100.0	9	D	D	D	110	1,589	405.0	34.5
Leawood	53,374	137	40.9	34	407	217.0	33.5	137	2,931	520.8	74.5
Lenexa	124,028	360	79.7	289	4,625	2,981.9	267.5	200	3,850	2,504.9	122.2
Manhattan	22,863	72	88.9	31	480	144.0	19.7	260	5,438	1,031.9	111.4
Olathe	206,253	813	52.3	154	3,054	3,163.4	177.9	336	6,935	2,223.4	179.6
Overland Park	375,755	2,107	19.0	248	7,767	18,445.8	776.3	739	13,517	3,011.8	310.8
Salina	5,494	27	85.2	72	898	704.3	43.4	243	3,949	1,112.7	86.1
Shawnee	56,261	215	68.4	58	805	700.8	45.9	175	3,243	761.8	72.7
Topeka	19,191	82	100.0	120	1,342	845.1	62.1	574	8,921	2,185.9	197.4
Wichita	130,999	858	62.0	515	7,443	7,544.6	436.2	1,477	24,136	6,284.9	572.7
KENTUCKY	2,267,765	13,826	56.2	3,690	57,630	71,745.9	3,090.3	15,224	202,615	54,870.0	4,619.2
Bowling Green	142,747	1,447	19.3	108	1,303	2,669.4	65.2	449	6,831	1,634.5	150.6
Covington	0	0	0.0	26	D	D	D	121	1,297	396.0	33.7
Elizabethtown	16,933	108	64.8	36	319	194.9	14.2	264	4,076	1,089.3	97.1
Florence	NA	NA	NA	40	D	D	D	295	6,297	1,571.5	138.6
Frankfort	3,128	39	23.1	22	D	D	D	137	1,965	476.8	42.0
Georgetown	NA	NA	NA	18	D	D	D	107	1,687	510.4	35.6
Henderson	1,719	18	66.7	34	D	D	D	152	2,089	665.2	51.4
Hopkinsville	5,747	39	84.6	50	739	958.0	28.8	169	2,369	717.7	61.0
Jeffersontown	10,259	55	78.2	163	2,822	1,782.0	150.6	145	2,960	1,005.9	85.4
Lexington-Fayette	183,119	1,789	41.0	352	7,283	4,517.8	527.7	1,192	19,820	4,994.8	466.9
Louisville/Jefferson County	657,818	3,263	36.3	1,006	15,867	13,048.4	836.7	2,659	41,294	10,964.4	1,004.0
Nicholasville	14,467	91	93.4	27	D	D	D	117	1,996	741.7	56.1
Owensboro	24,115	247	89.9	67	943	527.4	41.0	336	4,944	1,209.2	111.0
Paducah	9,613	41	70.7	72	D	D	D	320	5,310	1,415.2	120.6
Richmond	15,527	224	61.6	18	99	134.9	3.7	199	2,976	712.7	59.7
LOUISIANA	3,108,408	15,835	86.7	4,823	64,259	68,012.8	3,260.2	16,743	220,257	61,396.4	5,334.6
Alexandria	19,414	74	100.0	73	914	443.7	37.0	385	5,698	1,633.6	142.8
Baton Rouge	91,135	340	82.9	306	3,894	2,296.2	192.8	1,146	16,570	4,262.5	409.4
Bossier City	53,681	322	100.0	77	1,165	822.5	55.7	379	5,660	1,621.7	137.8
Central	22,077	162	100.0	9	33	250.0	3.7	40	867	203.6	18.8
Houma	NA	NA	NA	68	686	325.7	42.9	167	2,292	639.3	51.6
Kenner	19,987	63	96.8	113	883	385.7	48.5	266	4,356	1,554.2	130.9
Lafayette	NA	NA	NA	276	3,728	1,815.8	182.4	808	12,699	3,434.7	316.5
Lake Charles	85,982	651	52.4	72	847	764.6	33.7	442	6,000	1,812.8	143.5
Monroe	23,305	140	53.6	81	1,211	1,198.0	53.9	400	5,914	1,452.5	131.1
New Iberia	4,545	29	51.7	54	695	330.9	34.5	208	2,791	743.1	68.9
New Orleans	264,117	1,303	40.2	256	3,794	2,687.0	191.5	1,275	12,371	3,245.1	337.8
Shreveport	74,762	290	100.0	294	D	D	D	875	12,231	3,645.9	311.7
Slidell	1,739	10	100.0	27	158	337.9	7.3	282	4,263	1,096.7	96.6
MAINE	959,299	4,697	77.9	1,344	14,753	12,961.3	691.5	6,351	80,155	21,521.7	1,884.6
Bangor	8,526	49	75.5	63	849	463.0	41.9	310	6,147	1,819.4	136.7
Lewiston	12,759	89	22.5	37	657	300.1	30.0	157	1,935	710.1	46.6
Portland	15,598	78	33.3	174	2,511	1,899.3	129.6	395	4,893	1,551.1	135.3
South Portland	3,733	22	100.0	50	811	2,204.9	43.1	244	4,606	1,131.5	98.7
MARYLAND	3,701,849	18,647	69.6	4,768	73,369	60,734.2	4,378.5	18,179	281,678	76,379.7	7,168.5
Annapolis	9,798	56	89.3	62	404	423.4	22.4	488	7,230	1,508.1	172.2
Baltimore	235,027	1,547	6.4	544	8,592	7,954.3	495.2	1,839	15,747	3,647.7	379.0
Bowie	NA	NA	NA	14	168	62.8	11.9	149	3,864	884.7	82.7
College Park	NA	NA	NA	11	55	15.5	4.5	69	1,686	494.9	46.8
Frederick	39,828	196	89.3	78	844	448.2	45.2	320	5,293	1,594.9	145.0
Gaithersburg	3,134	20	50.0	76	1,339	619.5	79.4	337	6,863	2,146.6	197.4
Hagerstown	6,014	40	100.0	51	463	287.1	20.7	207	4,043	1,212.7	101.4
Laurel	10,547	53	66.0	11	195	101.4	9.1	138	2,078	542.5	48.4
Rockville	20,570	92	23.9	74	1,661	4,078.6	182.6	321	5,420	1,877.2	162.5
Salisbury	5,871	41	61.0	58	707	461.6	31.3	234	4,178	987.1	91.9
MASSACHUSETTS	4,157,964	17,044	42.1	6,619	114,195	123,904.4	8,035.1	24,311	351,598	92,915.4	9,161.7
Agawam Town	4,569	23	82.6	49	729	819.9	46.1	75	922	262.8	26.5
Attleboro	13,855	61	90.2	32	496	227.5	26.1	134	2,277	638.5	51.3
Barnstable Town	53,490	440	9.5	47	444	185.9	22.3	384	4,724	1,267.9	127.6

1. Merchant wholesalers except manufacturers' sales branches and offices. 2. Establishments with payroll.

Table D. Cities — Real Estate, Professional Services, and Manufacturing

City	Real estate and rental and leasing, 2012				Professional, scientific, and technical services[1], 2012				Manufacturing, 2012			
	Number of establish-ments	Number of employees	Receipts (mil dol)	Annual payroll (mil dol)	Number of establish-ments	Number of employees	Receipts (mil dol)	Annual payroll (mil dol)	Number of establish-ments	Number of employees	Receipts (mil dol)	Annual payroll (mil dol)
	80	81	82	83	84	85	86	87	88	89	90	91
KANSAS	2,999	14,256	2,743.1	507.6	7,071	60,615	8,562.6	3,577.1	2,875	152,423	86,076.3	7,578.3
Dodge City	21	D	D	D	42	D	D	D	17	D	D	D
Garden City	26	69	13.5	2.3	54	D	D	D	12	D	D	7.6
Hutchinson	52	145	22.9	3.9	82	D	D	D	41	1,579	441.5	70.9
Kansas City	128	519	107.4	18.4	173	D	D	D	161	10,043	10,883.2	640.0
Lawrence	141	D	D	D	249	D	D	D	45	2,467	957.6	103.4
Leavenworth	25	130	39.4	3.8	73	D	D	D	17	685	178.8	28.4
Leawood	102	D	D	D	236	D	D	D	14	189	26.4	9.8
Lenexa	105	588	133.8	31.5	319	D	D	D	135	6,020	2,108.2	298.4
Manhattan	102	D	D	D	117	D	D	D	34	673	137.0	28.9
Olathe	131	585	134.3	24.4	342	1,676	199.2	77.5	100	5,995	1,402.8	337.4
Overland Park	362	2,042	672.6	98.2	1,219	D	D	D	84	2,007	667.9	95.7
Salina	59	199	48.3	6.0	101	D	D	D	55	3,944	1,128.0	159.4
Shawnee	77	306	61.9	10.1	168	929	127.9	46.9	46	1,586	D	105.0
Topeka	173	803	124.1	24.6	382	D	D	D	84	4,722	2,456.0	220.0
Wichita	478	3,607	493.4	121.0	1,002	8,827	1,463.6	506.0	442	25,801	10,181.7	1,336.6
KENTUCKY	3,534	18,250	4,845.5	637.3	8,064	62,431	7,746.8	2,799.3	3,782	213,545	129,284.4	10,140.1
Bowling Green	102	363	73.7	10.4	181	D	D	D	95	7,873	5,079.8	402.6
Covington	32	203	62.0	10.6	124	D	D	D	28	746	215.7	33.6
Elizabethtown	61	304	42.3	7.6	110	D	D	D	51	4,727	2,009.7	220.6
Florence	49	260	71.8	7.9	102	1,559	106.1	43.1	38	3,293	1,633.6	176.6
Frankfort	27	154	13.2	3.5	102	714	77.5	30.0	15	550	104.0	23.3
Georgetown	32	D	D	D	53	261	31.3	12.5	22	7,150	D	502.3
Henderson	36	D	D	D	62	364	31.7	11.1	54	2,214	1,110.0	98.3
Hopkinsville	44	124	19.1	3.1	58	D	D	D	49	4,305	D	191.7
Jeffersontown	85	586	185.4	19.1	180	3,598	284.8	154.5	93	3,786	999.1	163.6
Lexington-Fayette	431	2,128	442.3	76.6	1,067	10,048	1,438.1	560.1	224	8,005	2,922.0	351.1
Louisville/Jefferson County	926	7,168	2,895.1	289.1	2,191	21,986	3,257.7	1,129.8	718	40,666	28,642.1	2,159.3
Nicholasville	21	87	10.8	2.2	52	286	63.6	15.3	51	2,245	588.9	79.9
Owensboro	63	427	57.1	11.7	128	D	D	D	64	3,644	2,865.5	159.3
Paducah	58	252	47.8	8.1	140	D	D	D	36	D	D	D
Richmond	42	150	29.2	4.2	77	D	D	D	32	1,896	D	83.4
LOUISIANA	4,500	31,298	7,486.4	1,461.4	11,669	87,367	13,417.4	4,986.5	3,308	136,327	271,191.1	8,489.3
Alexandria	98	472	76.2	15.2	202	1,325	163.5	55.0	37	1,826	753.8	99.6
Baton Rouge	339	1,827	382.5	71.7	1,144	D	D	D	185	4,968	D	343.8
Bossier City	79	508	104.5	16.1	116	D	D	D	47	1,018	D	47.8
Central	15	42	5.7	0.8	25	75	9.7	3.2	21	155	D	5.6
Houma	61	589	138.9	37.8	145	925	121.6	47.4	32	1,045	228.4	59.8
Kenner	86	622	156.8	20.9	159	1,862	349.7	122.5	54	1,074	182.8	43.0
Lafayette	334	2,352	623.9	122.8	1,009	7,293	1,312.5	444.7	129	3,831	1,042.7	171.7
Lake Charles	117	480	85.9	16.5	275	1,775	214.0	77.5	39	1,224	1,251.5	76.1
Monroe	119	811	137.7	26.1	292	D	D	D	41	1,356	455.0	66.4
New Iberia	56	311	60.9	12.3	100	400	51.5	15.9	49	1,703	566.7	100.5
New Orleans	379	2,156	411.6	79.1	1,421	D	D	D	144	6,049	4,352.7	335.6
Shreveport	285	2,266	439.8	90.1	574	D	D	D	145	4,796	3,670.1	251.9
Slidell	37	365	116.2	26.1	139	583	62.2	21.6	26	1,895	D	115.8
MAINE	1,580	6,242	1,100.4	220.6	3,457	21,188	3,061.0	1,134.1	1,650	49,238	16,044.5	2,424.3
Bangor	90	404	80.3	14.5	157	D	D	D	37	775	167.2	34.7
Lewiston	48	222	31.1	6.6	83	D	D	D	65	1,507	430.2	65.7
Portland	226	1,453	291.5	56.6	586	5,193	1,044.1	380.9	101	2,425	747.5	112.2
South Portland	48	459	93.8	16.4	101	686	96.6	37.9	33	1,452	247.9	86.6
MARYLAND	6,001	42,838	13,410.1	2,253.2	19,529	D	D	D	3,096	100,079	39,533.0	5,908.9
Annapolis	98	449	115.3	25.7	371	D	D	D	37	324	65.5	14.9
Baltimore	596	4,055	883.7	187.6	1,524	20,740	4,544.9	1,808.5	409	11,748	5,043.3	574.0
Bowie	28	170	59.1	7.0	167	D	D	D	6	19	2.6	0.7
College Park	19	77	10.8	2.5	75	D	D	D	6	101	D	4.3
Frederick	99	462	123.1	23.3	369	D	D	D	59	2,045	D	129.9
Gaithersburg	95	514	181.9	30.3	415	D	D	D	35	1,039	397.5	72.6
Hagerstown	65	251	58.6	8.6	113	1,009	111.0	43.9	61	3,335	1,870.3	199.2
Laurel	42	655	104.1	25.6	74	930	154.4	60.6	12	115	D	8.2
Rockville	131	1,785	1,087.7	198.4	861	18,500	3,927.4	1,747.3	61	1,516	348.0	107.9
Salisbury	77	478	55.7	16.0	156	D	D	D	46	2,713	882.7	109.7
MASSACHUSETTS	6,485	42,788	13,628.4	2,357.9	21,203	243,993	57,979.0	22,938.7	6,806	234,168	81,927.8	14,395.3
Agawam Town	20	77	20.6	3.4	65	707	80.2	36.0	54	2,280	779.8	112.5
Attleboro	26	115	23.8	5.4	59	342	38.7	16.0	88	3,518	926.6	223.9
Barnstable Town	70	227	72.0	9.2	201	D	D	D	46	897	215.2	51.6

1. Establishments subject to federal tax.

Accommodation and Food Services, Arts, Entertainment, and Recreation, and Health Care and Social Assistance

City	Accommodation and food services, 2012				Arts, entertainment, and recreation[1], 2012				Health care and social assistance,[1] 2012			
	Number of establish-ments	Number of employees	Receipts (mil dol)	Annual payroll (mil dol)	Number of establish-ments	Number of employees	Receipts (mil dol)	Annual payroll (mil dol)	Number of establish-ments	Number of employees	Receipts (mil dol)	Annual payroll (mil dol)
	92	93	94	95	96	97	98	99	100	101	102	103
KANSAS	5,943	106,850	4,873.4	1,342.9	668	9,807	615.7	170.2	5,977	93,121	9,677.8	3,955.4
Dodge City	71	D	D	D	5	D	D	D	53	D	D	D
Garden City..................	66	1,333	67.5	17.5	4	37	0.8	0.3	68	981	66.9	26.7
Hutchinson..................	99	1,867	82.0	23.3	1	D	D	D	103	1,783	206.1	89.5
Kansas City..................	227	4,773	254.8	69.8	24	D	D	D	224	D	D	D
Lawrence	270	6,211	249.2	69.3	22	327	36.2	3.7	203	2,798	242.1	93.0
Leavenworth	59	974	43.6	11.6	6	39	1.0	0.2	65	D	D	D
Leawood	73	2,185	96.2	31.7	14	D	D	D	158	1,906	259.5	108.9
Lenexa	106	1,884	94.5	28.0	18	D	D	D	144	4,505	700.3	214.6
Manhattan..................	168	3,912	150.0	41.4	8	D	D	D	132	1,402	163.2	57.6
Olathe	234	5,437	245.6	70.9	32	D	D	D	244	D	D	D
Overland Park..................	456	10,355	538.6	162.8	71	1,583	78.0	25.7	664	12,623	1,736.3	705.9
Salina..................	132	2,986	115.8	31.0	10	D	D	D	137	2,391	231.7	93.3
Shawnee	109	2,166	95.9	27.2	12	D	D	D	121	1,609	123.8	58.3
Topeka	330	6,636	291.1	80.0	32	D	D	D	358	5,825	699.8	308.8
Wichita	962	19,526	918.8	255.2	78	1,300	48.4	18.5	977	18,132	2,250.5	883.1
KENTUCKY	7,678	156,965	7,500.1	2,083.5	931	11,322	862.3	237.6	9,449	127,446	11,985.2	5,178.2
Bowling Green	243	5,498	255.4	68.2	15	425	12.3	4.3	289	D	D	D
Covington..................	125	1,793	117.0	29.4	9	D	D	D	39	D	D	D
Elizabethtown..................	112	2,798	132.4	37.0	9	115	5.2	1.4	204	D	D	D
Florence	161	3,755	201.4	55.7	21	500	20.0	5.8	136	2,375	210.7	92.3
Frankfort..................	88	1,698	83.5	22.2	6	D	D	D	109	1,198	100.9	45.0
Georgetown..................	80	D	D	D	5	D	D	D	93	D	D	D
Henderson	81	1,388	64.2	16.5	9	D	D	D	105	D	D	D
Hopkinsville..................	77	1,524	67.6	19.2	5	39	1.9	0.6	120	1,151	111.2	36.4
Jeffersontown..................	108	2,931	141.4	41.9	18	397	13.0	4.8	101	2,692	165.9	77.6
Lexington-Fayette	772	17,490	939.4	270.7	91	1,469	110.6	37.9	895	12,181	1,255.7	587.7
Louisville/Jefferson County ...	1,651	39,711	2,006.3	572.1	220	3,486	288.7	88.2	2,072	32,822	3,186.5	1,478.1
Nicholasville..................	53	D	D	D	9	D	D	D	67	551	35.4	17.4
Owensboro..................	134	3,481	150.9	44.1	13	D	D	D	235	D	D	D
Paducah..................	174	3,615	161.2	46.8	10	D	D	D	187	D	D	D
Richmond..................	113	2,762	121.8	33.3	11	D	D	D	134	1,421	115.1	50.1
LOUISIANA..................	9,019	193,928	11,697.9	3,110.7	1,085	18,036	2,224.7	606.4	10,240	167,792	15,869.9	6,156.9
Alexandria..................	165	3,114	158.9	43.1	11	D	D	D	277	5,734	754.5	262.4
Baton Rouge	699	15,983	881.3	244.6	65	1,706	232.9	31.8	746	12,755	1,183.1	497.2
Bossier City..................	202	7,287	643.8	129.8	23	935	126.5	17.7	153	2,187	184.1	66.4
Central	15	363	12.6	3.5	4	D	D	D	36	473	33.6	14.0
Houma	90	1,690	114.5	33.7	9	78	3.3	1.2	145	D	D	D
Kenner	184	3,718	210.3	58.3	20	D	D	D	149	1,864	186.3	74.9
Lafayette	542	12,372	689.9	202.6	50	D	D	D	756	14,701	1,619.6	624.3
Lake Charles	197	6,132	579.2	125.3	24	D	D	D	314	5,528	599.3	241.0
Monroe	167	3,761	170.7	46.2	17	310	15.7	2.3	346	5,454	463.4	179.3
New Iberia	81	D	D	D	10	D	D	D	157	D	D	D
New Orleans	1,300	35,510	2,765.4	764.7	129	3,024	367.8	140.6	628	8,481	1,013.6	371.5
Shreveport	460	12,644	750.2	196.0	43	D	D	D	687	D	D	D
Slidell	180	3,220	150.4	41.0	4	D	D	D	196	D	D	D
MAINE..................	3,958	49,672	2,901.3	850.8	585	4,484	368.2	96.3	3,071	41,700	3,486.8	1,613.4
Bangor	139	3,366	222.7	58.4	8	D	D	D	211	4,175	353.1	166.6
Lewiston..................	74	1,015	51.8	14.3	11	D	D	D	98	1,182	131.6	53.6
Portland..................	330	5,887	312.7	99.7	39	404	34.3	8.7	278	4,363	470.5	216.3
South Portland	124	2,729	137.4	41.5	11	D	D	D	106	1,379	150.4	64.4
MARYLAND	11,344	204,222	12,516.8	3,410.5	1,561	24,878	2,726.9	806.3	13,217	168,241	18,823.4	7,784.6
Annapolis	194	4,975	299.5	91.6	NA	NA	NA	NA	143	1,523	189.2	69.3
Baltimore..................	1,541	21,832	1,607.8	435.6	NA	NA	NA	NA	1,069	16,427	1,991.0	827.4
Bowie..................	72	1,969	110.3	30.4	NA	NA	NA	NA	188	1,744	157.8	67.7
College Park	111	1,966	116.5	30.5	NA	NA	NA	NA	29	175	16.3	7.5
Frederick..................	218	4,153	220.7	64.6	NA	NA	NA	NA	318	4,441	550.3	212.9
Gaithersburg..................	204	3,774	267.0	71.0	NA	NA	NA	NA	170	1,725	182.4	60.5
Hagerstown..................	127	2,416	121.7	34.9	NA	NA	NA	NA	132	1,703	199.8	82.6
Laurel	79	1,725	94.2	26.6	NA	NA	NA	NA	94	1,192	123.7	48.6
Rockville..................	252	4,133	278.5	76.7	NA	NA	NA	NA	278	4,285	845.6	434.3
Salisbury	143	2,552	128.3	31.6	NA	NA	NA	NA	161	2,553	311.6	133.3
MASSACHUSETTS.............	16,898	273,185	17,509.0	5,019.8	2,277	35,108	3,412.3	1,261.8	13,136	237,631	26,639.0	12,209.0
Agawam Town..................	58	618	30.0	7.9	9	D	D	D	53	1,341	109.3	47.0
Attleboro..................	83	D	D	D	9	102	3.7	1.9	90	2,274	169.0	83.7
Barnstable Town	196	2,834	192.1	58.4	21	136	11.2	2.6	157	2,523	267.3	130.6

1. Establishments subject to federal tax.

Table D. Cities — Other Services and Government Employment and Payroll

City	Other services[1]				Government employment and payroll, 2012								
					Full-time equivalent employees	March payroll							
							Percent of total for:						
	Number of establishments	Number of employees	Receipts (mil dol)	Annual payroll (mil dol)		Total (dollars)	Administrative, judicial, and legal	Police and corrections	Fire protection	Highways and transportation	Health and welfare	Natural resources and utilities	Education and libraries
	104	105	106	107	108	109	110	111	112	113	114	115	116
KANSAS	3,957	21,148	1,920.4	560.0	X	X	X	X	X	X	X	X	X
Dodge City	37	229	22.9	5.6	249	803,190	14.8	27.3	12.1	6.2	2.3	27.5	6.6
Garden City..................	35	D	D	D	310	1,086,046	12.7	30.4	12.2	6.7	0.7	30.7	0.0
Hutchinson	66	343	20.9	7.2	392	1,720,937	8.7	26.7	25.6	7.2	2.1	25.6	0.0
Kansas City..................	157	827	89.5	25.3	2,707	14,492,572	12.6	24.6	15.1	5.6	5.3	29.9	0.0
Lawrence	117	713	43.2	14.4	1,978	10,089,159	4.2	10.8	8.9	2.8	58.2	13.8	0.0
Leavenworth	44	255	17.7	5.7	268	973,969	12.2	33.1	20.9	8.2	4.8	17.2	0.0
Leawood	48	451	48.8	18.0	262	1,218,472	17.8	32.5	22.4	11.6	1.7	11.1	0.0
Lenexa	68	538	49.5	18.3	414	1,898,039	18.6	33.0	22.5	12.1	0.0	11.7	0.0
Manhattan	72	D	D	D	362	1,385,412	18.7	0.0	25.9	14.5	5.9	32.8	0.0
Olathe	158	1,168	93.9	28.8	826	3,674,590	18.5	24.2	20.1	16.9	2.0	17.6	0.0
Overland Park	304	1,696	122.8	39.0	899	4,414,214	19.0	34.6	19.7	13.5	0.9	8.8	0.0
Salina..........................	87	D	D	D	484	1,858,261	10.4	24.5	22.0	12.0	3.3	23.9	0.0
Shawnee......................	76	534	37.2	13.3	287	1,666,597	13.6	38.1	23.7	12.5	0.8	9.1	0.0
Topeka	190	1,382	108.7	34.1	1,062	3,978,506	7.7	32.8	28.1	11.7	1.6	15.4	0.0
Wichita	560	4,092	364.5	115.2	2,864	12,396,633	10.7	30.7	18.5	13.7	3.8	15.4	2.9
KENTUCKY	4,793	31,452	2,830.7	850.2	X	X	X	X	X	X	X	X	X
Bowling Green	137	784	69.1	19.1	699	2,772,912	7.1	20.2	19.5	5.5	2.9	30.0	0.0
Covington....................	74	318	25.9	8.4	421	1,788,490	6.5	36.3	30.5	3.6	11.9	5.7	0.0
Elizabethtown..............	66	436	37.9	11.0	289	996,440	11.3	24.1	21.7	8.8	0.0	27.7	0.0
Florence	67	538	35.4	12.7	198	919,937	6.2	36.7	28.5	4.6	0.0	11.5	0.0
Frankfort......................	38	233	14.8	4.7	530	2,153,521	5.6	15.6	18.6	4.9	2.2	22.3	0.0
Georgetown.................	38	166	11.3	3.2	179	621,131	11.9	34.9	35.4	6.1	0.0	6.7	0.0
Henderson...................	41	D	D	D	454	1,639,406	10.9	14.7	13.1	5.8	6.0	45.6	0.0
Hopkinsville.................	39	229	21.7	5.9	398	1,517,254	6.4	20.1	21.3	2.1	5.3	33.5	0.0
Jeffersontown..............	78	735	118.2	28.7	108	518,932	9.2	65.9	0.0	12.9	5.5	1.6	1.2
Lexington-Fayette	393	3,062	238.3	81.6	3,926	16,180,537	10.0	31.5	18.1	5.0	11.0	15.2	3.0
Louisville/Jefferson County ...	1,023	8,809	890.5	254.0	8,264	32,734,538	10.3	29.9	8.6	12.9	15.7	14.6	2.2
Nicholasville................	46	174	21.5	4.3	214	748,387	13.4	32.1	20.0	4.1	0.0	17.4	0.0
Owensboro..................	90	706	49.6	17.4	840	3,418,017	7.9	17.9	10.1	5.1	3.1	53.8	0.0
Paducah.......................	76	584	48.2	13.4	537	2,054,380	7.5	18.4	12.7	12.4	7.8	37.6	0.0
Richmond.....................	48	242	17.3	4.8	264	708,015	11.1	30.0	21.4	6.8	9.1	12.4	0.0
LOUISIANA..................	5,092	36,098	3,916.0	1,216.5	X	X	X	X	X	X	X	X	X
Alexandria....................	89	539	45.5	13.2	858	3,139,622	13.3	29.0	18.9	9.8	0.4	22.4	0.0
Baton Rouge................	392	4,825	381.6	214.7	7,745	28,842,476	18.7	20.3	13.5	8.8	15.7	11.6	4.2
Bossier City.................	98	634	55.2	15.9	738	2,695,669	13.1	32.2	30.2	2.8	1.1	15.5	0.0
Central	24	115	12.9	4.0	11	24,511	92.3	7.7	0.0	0.0	0.0	0.0	0.0
Houma	57	527	77.3	29.1	2,552	9,484,779	6.9	16.5	2.3	2.5	60.4	8.0	3.4
Kenner	107	759	114.6	27.1	633	2,227,138	15.0	42.0	19.4	6.5	3.2	7.8	0.0
Lafayette	232	2,047	253.7	62.1	3,047	10,656,600	18.8	30.9	10.4	8.4	1.8	24.1	2.4
Lake Charles................	98	793	74.7	23.3	1,030	3,427,311	10.3	24.5	19.4	6.9	0.4	29.2	0.0
Monroe	65	549	40.9	12.8	1,137	2,092,527	21.1	3.5	2.5	12.5	15.1	42.2	0.0
New Iberia...................	69	388	35.3	10.7	222	646,974	12.2	1.2	36.3	13.5	4.6	27.2	0.0
New Orleans	364	2,537	210.4	62.9	6,570	26,033,023	13.9	33.2	9.9	2.7	8.0	23.7	1.6
Shreveport...................	252	2,069	184.1	54.8	2,841	10,287,795	8.1	28.1	26.4	6.9	2.4	18.7	7.2
Slidell	83	392	28.4	8.2	294	1,068,129	19.4	46.5	0.0	11.4	0.0	18.5	0.0
MAINE.........................	2,041	9,424	881.5	242.9	X	X	X	X	X	X	X	X	X
Bangor	71	499	47.6	12.4	1,172	4,803,542	4.3	9.1	8.0	17.8	2.9	5.2	50.9
Lewiston......................	60	355	30.1	8.5	1,063	4,275,573	4.7	10.1	8.1	4.7	0.9	4.1	64.8
Portland.......................	167	1,005	87.6	26.5	2,667	11,280,661	5.1	9.2	9.4	4.1	13.4	3.5	50.8
South Portland	63	561	29.1	10.6	774	2,806,318	7.4	11.7	11.2	5.1	0.2	9.9	54.4
MARYLAND..................	7,877	57,077	5,195.8	1,677.9	X	X	X	X	X	X	X	X	X
Annapolis.....................	153	1,410	122.6	50.1	620	3,140,557	12.6	28.5	24.6	16.2	0.0	13.6	0.0
Baltimore.....................	682	6,054	643.0	173.9	26,392	122,552,640	6.0	16.4	7.7	3.4	7.5	8.8	48.9
Bowie..........................	43	274	19.4	6.5	332	1,491,481	15.5	19.2	0.0	6.4	9.8	36.4	0.0
College Park	45	300	26.5	9.3	308	540,180	25.6	19.0	0.0	6.4	12.3	21.9	0.0
Frederick.....................	147	996	81.8	25.1	560	2,537,922	10.7	39.5	0.0	8.4	5.7	23.2	0.0
Gaithersburg................	133	875	110.8	28.8	303	1,564,931	28.1	25.0	0.0	16.4	6.3	21.9	0.0
Hagerstown..................	81	428	34.6	11.4	445	2,038,054	10.3	26.5	16.9	6.9	0.7	32.9	0.0
Laurel..........................	51	465	33.5	12.3	197	975,036	19.1	49.9	0.0	7.4	0.0	18.1	0.0
Rockville......................	185	1,289	135.0	38.5	652	3,046,807	18.3	18.4	0.0	9.1	8.6	45.6	0.0
Salisbury.....................	83	757	60.2	19.3	375	1,345,111	6.4	35.5	18.2	7.5	4.4	26.4	0.0
MASSACHUSETTS.............	11,154	67,531	5,985.4	1,892.2	X	X	X	X	X	X	X	X	X
Agawam Town..............	46	197	22.9	5.6	958	3,825,533	4.3	9.2	8.3	3.0	2.5	2.9	64.5
Attleboro......................	67	272	24.0	6.7	1,376	5,707,365	4.1	9.4	7.8	1.4	1.4	7.2	68.0
Barnstable Town	119	629	54.1	17.3	1,040	5,101,618	12.3	17.0	0.0	7.1	2.3	6.5	50.4

1. Establishments subject to federal tax.

Table D. Cities — City Government Finances

City	City government finances, 2012									
	General revenue							General expenditure		
		Intergovernmental		Taxes						
					Per capita[1] (dollars)				Per capita[1] (dollars)	
	Total (mil dol)	Total (mil dol)	Percent from state government	Total (mil dol)	Total	Property	Sales and gross receipts	Total (mil dol)	Total	Capital outlays
	117	118	119	120	121	122	123	124	125	126
KANSAS	X	X	X	X	X	X	X	X	X	X
Dodge City	42.1	4.4	73.2	19.0	676	272	403	61.8	2,199	497
Garden City	32.6	5.3	13.6	13.7	508	224	285	32.2	1,196	137
Hutchinson	47.8	10.1	16.6	24.0	572	287	285	36.3	867	15
Kansas City	345.7	20.8	59.0	197.9	1,342	609	724	304.9	2,068	35
Lawrence	300.0	35.4	66.1	51.1	569	251	318	265.3	2,952	315
Leavenworth	35.9	6.9	24.9	18.7	523	329	194	39.7	1,108	180
Leawood	52.4	9.2	26.4	36.5	1,121	518	604	38.2	1,173	233
Lenexa	84.1	15.1	53.5	48.4	979	537	442	101.5	2,056	664
Manhattan	75.3	14.5	19.2	38.3	675	346	329	70.4	1,243	66
Olathe	165.1	23.5	34.3	90.7	697	288	410	149.2	1,147	163
Overland Park	224.8	42.2	25.4	90.5	506	129	377	208.7	1,166	223
Salina	68.5	10.3	26.4	25.7	535	240	295	75.4	1,572	264
Shawnee	54.4	10.0	26.2	38.6	607	330	277	48.9	769	62
Topeka	206.4	27.9	31.8	106.8	835	320	515	153.6	1,201	139
Wichita	562.5	102.8	20.6	167.5	435	306	129	543.6	1,410	223
KENTUCKY	X	X	X	X	X	X	X	X	X	X
Bowling Green	98.4	10.3	24.6	55.7	916	177	90	76.0	1,251	71
Covington	71.2	13.5	27.4	40.2	989	171	183	54.8	1,350	183
Elizabethtown	45.8	8.2	36.9	25.3	863	132	268	37.6	1,280	347
Florence	43.3	5.6	79.1	28.8	928	238	141	28.8	926	346
Frankfort	67.6	2.6	55.3	25.5	937	148	150	57.0	2,091	104
Georgetown	46.6	3.3	36.0	15.8	523	64	100	38.6	1,277	68
Henderson	46.8	13.7	10.5	17.3	597	254	172	40.9	1,415	213
Hopkinsville	42.0	7.0	7.7	23.2	702	139	127	37.4	1,128	88
Jeffersontown	25.4	1.1	76.1	17.1	637	144	99	23.6	876	92
Lexington-Fayette	544.8	60.2	29.6	318.9	1,045	282	143	440.5	1,443	142
Louisville/Jefferson County	935.3	222.4	25.0	456.1	753	225	93	992.9	1,640	335
Nicholasville	20.8	2.5	72.9	13.4	473	139	110	18.1	638	35
Owensboro	98.3	27.0	14.9	35.0	602	166	123	105.2	1,812	630
Paducah	63.2	11.9	37.1	32.6	1,297	237	164	49.1	1,954	263
Richmond	34.6	1.4	35.9	20.5	631	93	132	25.5	785	137
LOUISIANA	X	X	X	X	X	X	X	X	X	X
Alexandria	82.5	13.7	28.9	53.7	1,121	153	967	92.8	1,936	198
Baton Rouge	959.1	199.4	55.2	458.1	1,992	692	1,300	1,203.6	5,233	1,750
Bossier City	108.4	8.2	55.5	71.3	1,090	181	909	129.1	1,975	823
Central	9.1	0.3	100.0	8.6	313	0	313	4.7	169	2
Houma	411.9	103.8	73.9	117.3	3,483	1,624	1,859	430.0	12,764	2,321
Kenner	77.5	40.2	21.3	22.2	332	125	207	70.3	1,050	164
Lafayette	402.4	70.2	47.1	201.1	1,631	828	803	443.4	3,597	882
Lake Charles	116.9	27.3	9.2	70.1	952	108	845	117.0	1,590	348
Monroe	129.3	28.8	34.5	77.5	1,564	218	1,346	140.8	2,843	755
New Iberia	32.2	4.6	29.3	21.4	693	131	562	42.4	1,376	297
New Orleans	1,505.1	535.6	44.1	499.4	1,349	692	647	1,604.4	4,334	1,371
Shreveport	369.6	59.6	35.0	209.5	1,037	312	725	315.2	1,560	169
Slidell	55.2	15.5	65.5	27.4	1,001	202	798	55.1	2,012	612
MAINE	X	X	X	X	X	X	X	X	X	X
Bangor	131.1	38.3	93.4	54.2	1,653	1,624	29	165.2	5,035	1,527
Lewiston	117.7	52.6	84.0	49.4	1,355	1,342	13	112.8	3,095	292
Portland	318.6	71.3	78.7	144.3	2,178	2,129	49	329.4	4,972	746
South Portland	82.8	11.7	92.5	61.0	2,430	2,411	20	82.1	3,270	347
MARYLAND	X	X	X	X	X	X	X	X	X	X
Annapolis	82.8	14.6	35.6	43.3	1,125	985	140	65.6	1,703	14
Baltimore	3,407.6	1,720.1	81.7	1,238.8	1,989	1,226	267	3,659.5	5,874	527
Bowie	46.8	10.8	16.7	27.6	491	444	47	42.1	748	0
College Park	15.3	2.1	19.1	9.8	315	239	76	14.1	451	4
Frederick	90.8	14.2	14.9	46.5	700	655	45	84.6	1,273	9
Gaithersburg	54.0	13.4	7.5	31.2	495	390	104	49.4	783	40
Hagerstown	57.3	7.1	21.8	26.1	645	527	114	50.2	1,239	16
Laurel	29.2	4.0	20.5	20.5	800	757	43	25.4	992	3
Rockville	92.8	17.8	12.0	40.8	644	553	86	94.1	1,486	5
Salisbury	51.7	5.3	32.3	22.5	725	675	49	39.7	1,279	49
MASSACHUSETTS	NA	NA	NA	NA	NA	NA	NA	NA	NA	NA
Agawam Town	84.8	27.5	99.5	50.0	1,745	1,720	26	102.8	3,589	65
Attleboro	126.9	47.0	97.8	61.9	1,412	1,380	32	113.5	2,593	116
Barnstable Town	177.7	41.0	87.9	109.9	2,458	2,319	139	175.2	3,917	633

1. Based on population estimated as of July 1 of the year shown.

City	City government finances, 2012 (cont.)									
	General expenditure (cont.)									
	Percent of total for:									
	Public welfare	Highways	Parking facilities	Education	Health and hospitals	Police protection	Sewerage and sanitation	Parks and recreation	Housing and community development	Interest on debt
	127	128	129	130	131	132	133	134	135	136
KANSAS	X	X	X	X	X	X	X	X	X	X
Dodge City	0.0	1.2	0.0	0.0	0.8	7.8	35.2	17.9	0.0	16.3
Garden City......................	0.0	11.0	0.0	0.0	0.0	19.9	11.8	14.6	0.0	1.0
Hutchinson.......................	0.0	4.4	0.0	0.0	1.3	22.1	23.3	12.7	0.0	3.8
Kansas City......................	0.0	2.6	0.2	0.0	3.4	15.9	7.5	2.3	1.5	23.3
Lawrence.........................	0.0	2.7	0.5	0.0	59.4	5.5	8.3	3.1	1.3	2.8
Leavenworth	0.0	10.0	0.0	0.0	0.0	17.1	12.8	5.5	9.0	2.9
Leawood	0.0	22.0	0.0	0.0	0.0	21.4	0.0	17.6	0.0	6.5
Lenexa.............................	0.0	20.0	0.0	0.0	0.0	12.2	3.8	8.5	0.0	16.9
Manhattan........................	0.0	6.3	0.0	0.0	1.1	17.5	8.4	8.0	1.8	12.6
Olathe.............................	0.0	15.8	0.0	0.0	0.2	13.0	15.5	3.6	0.0	9.4
Overland Park...................	0.0	21.1	0.0	0.0	0.0	14.4	2.5	5.2	0.0	25.8
Salina..............................	0.0	9.2	0.0	0.0	1.6	11.2	10.5	9.0	5.0	11.5
Shawnee..........................	0.0	12.9	0.0	0.0	0.0	24.3	6.3	9.2	0.0	18.0
Topeka.............................	1.1	9.1	1.4	0.0	0.0	20.4	12.2	10.5	1.5	7.1
Wichita............................	0.0	13.4	0.0	0.0	0.7	13.7	8.7	4.9	0.0	31.2
KENTUCKY	X	X	X	X	X	X	X	X	X	X
Bowling Green	0.0	9.4	0.0	0.0	0.0	12.0	10.5	10.4	6.4	20.5
Covington.........................	0.0	7.9	3.6	0.0	0.0	19.6	4.0	2.4	21.8	12.5
Elizabethtown...................	0.0	9.8	0.1	0.0	0.0	10.7	9.3	8.0	0.0	3.4
Florence..........................	0.0	44.2	0.0	0.0	0.0	16.0	5.1	0.0	0.0	10.7
Frankfort..........................	0.0	3.8	0.0	0.0	5.8	7.9	12.9	5.0	0.0	2.6
Georgetown......................	0.2	3.1	0.0	0.0	0.0	7.8	10.8	2.3	1.1	49.3
Henderson	0.0	5.4	0.0	0.0	0.0	9.2	27.0	2.5	13.3	1.8
Hopkinsville......................	0.7	5.7	0.0	0.0	0.0	20.8	13.6	1.2	13.7	14.5
Jeffersontown...................	0.0	9.1	0.0	0.0	0.0	23.5	4.4	2.6	2.8	37.7
Lexington-Fayette	2.0	2.5	0.3	0.0	3.6	10.8	15.8	4.0	1.1	4.1
Louisville/Jefferson County ...	1.2	6.8	7.9	5.7	3.3	10.2	1.5	5.7	6.5	9.9
Nicholasville.....................	0.0	18.8	0.0	0.0	0.0	22.5	18.6	0.0	0.0	5.0
Owensboro.......................	0.0	5.3	0.2	0.0	0.0	7.1	17.8	7.1	27.9	10.8
Paducah...........................	0.0	8.5	0.0	3.6	0.0	12.3	6.2	4.9	18.9	2.5
Richmond.........................	0.0	3.7	0.0	0.0	0.0	13.5	29.4	8.7	7.4	15.3
LOUISIANA......................	X	X	X	X	X	X	X	X	X	X
Alexandria........................	0.0	13.7	0.0	0.0	0.0	18.0	11.3	3.8	8.9	3.0
Baton Rouge.....................	0.2	8.7	0.1	1.3	8.7	10.5	28.4	2.0	5.2	5.2
Bossier City......................	0.0	1.7	0.0	0.0	0.4	15.1	16.6	5.5	6.7	5.7
Central	0.0	4.9	0.0	0.0	2.1	3.8	0.0	0.0	0.0	0.0
Houma.............................	0.4	4.2	0.0	0.0	41.2	6.3	5.5	2.3	1.7	1.6
Kenner.............................	0.0	19.8	0.0	0.0	0.2	23.7	14.3	6.4	1.0	2.8
Lafayette..........................	0.2	7.6	0.2	0.0	1.4	12.7	9.1	6.0	5.0	8.8
Lake Charles.....................	0.7	13.5	0.0	0.0	0.5	14.4	17.5	8.9	13.5	3.4
Monroe............................	0.1	4.4	0.0	0.0	0.0	13.1	9.8	5.7	17.4	5.8
New Iberia	0.4	16.2	0.0	0.0	0.0	14.0	25.5	5.1	10.0	4.0
New Orleans	0.2	7.6	0.1	0.0	0.8	8.9	13.7	5.5	15.5	5.9
Shreveport	0.0	4.5	0.2	0.0	0.0	18.2	14.6	9.9	7.6	4.3
Slidell	0.0	11.7	0.0	0.0	0.7	14.9	13.3	2.9	10.4	1.7
MAINE.............................	X	X	X	X	X	X	X	X	X	X
Bangor	0.0	0.0	0.4	26.4	2.3	4.8	3.0	22.8	0.9	2.0
Lewiston...........................	0.9	3.4	0.0	49.5	0.0	5.9	6.7	0.6	1.5	5.2
Portland...........................	7.7	5.4	0.6	30.3	1.3	4.1	8.1	2.0	1.0	5.2
South Portland	0.3	4.6	0.0	52.3	0.0	5.4	11.2	4.3	0.0	1.6
MARYLAND	X	X	X	X	X	X	X	X	X	X
Annapolis.........................	0.0	7.2	2.3	0.0	0.0	25.6	12.0	5.3	0.0	5.0
Baltimore..........................	0.0	5.7	0.8	38.4	3.3	10.2	6.6	1.6	2.1	1.4
Bowie..............................	0.0	11.4	0.0	0.0	0.5	17.6	23.4	16.4	0.1	1.5
College Park	0.0	22.3	1.0	0.0	0.6	7.3	18.8	9.4	1.5	2.1
Frederick..........................	0.0	10.8	3.8	0.0	0.0	30.2	13.3	9.7	0.6	5.8
Gaithersburg	0.0	8.4	0.0	0.0	1.2	15.6	4.7	20.3	1.6	11.6
Hagerstown.......................	0.0	5.9	1.4	0.0	0.0	23.0	29.3	6.2	1.0	2.0
Laurel..............................	0.0	4.9	0.0	0.0	0.0	34.6	4.6	9.1	0.2	1.9
Rockville..........................	0.0	12.9	2.9	0.0	0.4	17.1	13.5	19.7	4.1	4.0
Salisbury..........................	0.0	9.1	1.5	0.0	0.5	25.3	23.5	5.2	2.1	3.6
MASSACHUSETTS............	X	X	X	X	X	X	X	X	X	X
Agawam Town...................	0.1	2.9	0.0	52.9	1.8	4.2	4.3	0.8	0.0	0.8
Attleboro..........................	0.6	3.1	0.0	63.9	0.2	5.5	8.6	1.4	0.5	2.3
Barnstable Town	0.2	2.3	0.0	45.7	0.6	6.2	4.5	2.8	0.2	2.5

City	Debt outstanding Total (mil dol)	Per capita[1] (dollars)	Debt issued during year	Mean January	Mean July	Limits January[3]	Limits July[4]	Annual precipitation (inches)	Heating degree days	Cooling degree days
	137	138	139	140	141	142	143	144	145	146
KANSAS	X	X	X	X	X	X	X	X	X	X
Dodge City	220.7	7,857	12.2	30.1	79.8	18.7	92.8	22.35	5,037	1,481
Garden City	42.2	1,564	3.5	28.6	77.8	14.7	92.1	18.77	5,423	1,191
Hutchinson	54.3	1,294	5.6	28.5	79.9	17.0	92.7	30.32	5,146	1,454
Kansas City	1,786.2	12,115	126.8	29.1	79.0	19.9	89.4	40.17	4,847	1,406
Lawrence	287.4	3,197	46.3	29.9	80.2	20.5	90.6	39.78	4,685	1,582
Leavenworth	32.8	917	10.5	26.6	79.1	16.4	89.8	40.94	5,331	1,356
Leawood	60.6	1,863	5.3	29.1	79.0	19.9	89.4	40.17	4,847	1,406
Lenexa	280.1	5,672	46.2	29.1	79.0	19.9	89.4	40.17	4,847	1,406
Manhattan	344.8	6,084	41.3	27.8	79.9	16.1	92.5	34.80	5,120	1,465
Olathe	1,141.4	8,779	55.5	29.1	79.0	19.9	89.4	40.17	4,847	1,406
Overland Park	1,428.3	7,983	15.2	29.1	79.0	19.9	89.4	40.17	4,847	1,406
Salina	168.5	3,513	22.8	29.0	81.3	18.8	93.3	32.19	4,952	1,600
Shawnee	215.7	3,390	22.2	29.1	79.0	19.9	89.4	40.17	4,847	1,406
Topeka	364.4	2,850	72.6	27.2	78.4	17.2	89.1	35.64	5,225	1,357
Wichita	3,471.3	9,003	335.8	30.2	81.0	20.3	92.9	30.38	4,765	1,658
KENTUCKY	X	X	X	X	X	X	X	X	X	X
Bowling Green	283.6	4,667	7.1	34.2	78.5	25.4	89.2	51.63	4,243	1,413
Covington	162.2	3,993	3.6	32.0	76.1	24.1	85.9	45.91	4,713	1,154
Elizabethtown	55.2	1,880	18.5	NA	NA	NA	NA	NA	NA	NA
Florence	69.3	2,230	3.1	NA	NA	NA	NA	NA	NA	NA
Frankfort	46.6	1,711	0.0	30.3	75.2	20.8	86.9	43.56	5,129	994
Georgetown	473.4	15,642	0.0	NA	NA	NA	NA	NA	NA	NA
Henderson	50.4	1,744	15.8	32.6	77.6	23.6	88.4	44.77	4,374	1,344
Hopkinsville	170.2	5,136	12.2	33.2	78.2	24.4	88.5	50.92	4,298	1,433
Jeffersontown	160.3	5,960	0.0	33.0	78.4	24.9	87.0	44.54	4,352	1,443
Lexington-Fayette	1,000.4	3,277	37.3	31.6	75.9	22.5	86.3	46.39	4,769	1,094
Louisville/Jefferson County	1,594.3	2,633	310.5	NA	NA	NA	NA	NA	NA	NA
Nicholasville	32.1	1,130	3.5	NA	NA	NA	NA	NA	NA	NA
Owensboro	399.8	6,888	55.2	33.5	79.2	24.4	90.7	46.53	4,159	1,565
Paducah	39.7	1,583	6.6	35.2	79.9	27.2	90.8	46.04	3,893	1,635
Richmond	104.2	3,208	2.7	34.7	75.8	25.6	87.0	47.33	4,231	1,150
LOUISIANA	X	X	X	X	X	X	X	X	X	X
Alexandria	94.9	1,980	2.6	48.1	83.3	38.0	92.8	61.44	1,908	2,602
Baton Rouge	1,639.8	7,130	219.4	50.1	81.7	40.2	90.7	63.08	1,689	2,628
Bossier City	360.5	5,513	5.7	48.3	81.0	37.4	91.0	61.06	1,981	2,220
Central	0.0	0	0.0	NA	NA	NA	NA	NA	NA	NA
Houma	213.1	6,326	64.3	53.1	82.5	43.4	90.7	63.67	1,346	2,804
Kenner	61.5	919	19.6	52.6	82.7	43.4	91.1	64.16	1,417	2,773
Lafayette	1,132.6	9,186	183.7	51.3	82.2	41.6	91.2	60.54	1,531	2,671
Lake Charles	92.3	1,253	3.7	50.9	82.6	41.2	91.0	57.19	1,546	2,705
Monroe	177.3	3,581	34.9	44.6	83.0	33.5	94.1	58.04	2,399	2,311
New Iberia	38.7	1,257	24.3	51.3	82.3	41.4	91.1	60.89	1,544	2,680
New Orleans	2,018.9	5,454	51.5	52.7	82.2	43.3	90.9	65.15	1,416	2,686
Shreveport	540.8	2,676	85.6	46.4	83.4	36.5	93.3	51.30	2,251	2,405
Slidell	25.1	916	0.0	50.7	82.1	40.2	91.1	62.66	1,652	2,548
MAINE	X	X	X	X	X	X	X	X	X	X
Bangor	109.4	3,335	32.1	18.0	69.2	8.3	79.6	39.57	7,676	313
Lewiston	152.4	4,182	7.6	20.5	71.4	11.5	81.5	45.79	7,107	465
Portland	423.0	6,384	38.7	21.7	68.7	12.5	78.8	45.83	7,318	347
South Portland	50.1	1,994	30.0	NA	NA	NA	NA	NA	NA	NA
MARYLAND	X	X	X	X	X	X	X	X	X	X
Annapolis	96.8	2,513	0.0	32.8	77.5	23.8	87.7	44.78	4,695	1,162
Baltimore	2,621.6	4,208	13.3	36.8	81.7	29.4	90.6	43.59	4,720	1,147
Bowie	18.0	320	0.1	31.8	75.2	21.2	87.1	44.66	4,970	917
College Park	8.4	269	0.0	NA	NA	NA	NA	NA	NA	NA
Frederick	224.2	3,375	31.4	33.3	77.9	25.1	88.9	40.64	4,430	1,272
Gaithersburg	142.6	2,261	0.0	31.8	75.3	23.8	85.4	43.08	4,990	983
Hagerstown	66.0	1,630	7.9	29.3	75.2	20.8	86.1	39.45	5,249	902
Laurel	10.1	396	0.1	NA	NA	NA	NA	NA	NA	NA
Rockville	135.9	2,144	40.7	31.8	75.3	23.8	85.4	43.08	4,990	983
Salisbury	70.9	2,286	15.2	NA	NA	NA	NA	NA	NA	NA
MASSACHUSETTS	X	X	X	X	X	X	X	X	X	X
Agawam Town	25.0	871	6.2	NA	NA	NA	NA	NA	NA	NA
Attleboro	72.7	1,660	1.5	27.4	72.2	17.8	83.0	48.34	6,012	558
Barnstable Town	131.5	2,941	18.5	29.2	70.5	21.2	77.8	43.03	6,026	413

1. Based on the population estimated as of July 1 of the year shown.   2. Represents normal values based on the 30-year period, 1971±2000.   3. Average daily minimum.   4. Average daily maximum.

Table D. Cities — **Land Area and Population**

STATE Place code	City	Land area[1] (sq. mi)	Population, 2018 Total persons 2018	Rank	Per square mile	White	Black or African American	American Indian, Alaskan Native	Asian	Hawaiian Pacific Islander	Some other race	Two or more races (percent)
		1	2	3	4	5	6	7	8	9	10	11
	MASSACHUSETTS— Cont'd											
25 05,595	Beverly	15.1	42,312	902	2,802.1	92.0	3.2	0.6	2.3	0.0	0.3	1.6
25 07,000	Boston	48.3	694,583	21	14,380.6	52.8	25.9	0.3	9.7	0.0	7.2	4.1
25 07,740	Braintree Town	13.8	37,250	1,031	2,699.3	79.2	2.4	0.6	15.9	0.0	0.6	1.3
25 09,000	Brockton	21.3	95,777	330	4,496.6	34.2	41.3	0.5	2.3	0.0	18.4	3.4
25 11,000	Cambridge	6.4	118,977	237	18,590.2	67.5	10.4	0.1	16.7	0.1	1.6	3.6
25 13,205	Chelsea	2.2	40,160	955	18,254.5	56.6	6.9	0.0	6.6	0.0	7.8	22.1
25 13,660	Chicopee	22.9	55,582	683	2,427.2	83.0	7.1	0.1	0.9	0.0	7.5	1.4
25 21,990	Everett	3.4	46,880	828	13,788.2	58.4	17.5	0.0	3.1	0.0	14.6	6.4
25 23,000	Fall River	33.1	89,661	367	2,708.8	75.9	10.9	0.0	2.3	0.0	7.0	3.9
25 23,875	Fitchburg	27.8	40,882	938	1,470.6	83.0	4.6	0.1	1.4	0.0	7.7	3.3
25 25,172	Franklin Town	26.6	33,230	1,149	1,249.2	NA	NA	NA	NA	NA	NA	NA
25 26,150	Gloucester	26.2	30,401	1,239	1,160.3	NA	NA	NA	NA	NA	NA	NA
25 29,405	Haverhill	33.0	64,041	583	1,940.6	84.1	5.0	0.0	1.2	0.0	3.0	6.7
25 30,840	Holyoke	21.2	40,358	950	1,903.7	90.4	1.9	0.3	1.0	0.0	2.3	4.0
25 34,550	Lawrence	6.9	80,376	432	11,648.7	78.7	3.9	0.3	0.5	0.0	13.2	3.3
25 35,075	Leominster	28.8	41,823	909	1,452.2	78.4	10.0	0.0	6.1	0.0	2.2	3.3
25 37,000	Lowell	13.6	111,670	266	8,211.0	62.5	6.8	0.7	25.4	0.1	3.2	1.3
25 37,490	Lynn	10.7	94,654	336	8,846.2	51.8	14.2	0.5	7.0	0.0	21.1	5.4
25 37,875	Malden	5.0	61,036	610	12,207.2	46.9	19.3	0.0	27.0	0.0	3.3	3.5
25 38,715	Marlborough	20.9	39,825	967	1,905.5	77.1	2.4	0.0	4.0	0.0	13.6	2.9
25 39,835	Medford	8.1	57,765	653	7,131.5	78.6	7.6	0.0	11.3	0.0	0.4	2.1
25 40,115	Melrose	4.7	28,193	1,312	5,998.5	85.7	4.0	0.0	8.5	0.0	0.5	1.2
25 40,710	Methuen Town	22.2	50,698	757	2,283.7	71.1	6.9	0.4	5.6	0.0	8.1	7.9
25 45,000	New Bedford	20.0	95,315	332	4,765.8	65.0	5.9	0.0	2.1	0.0	21.4	5.6
25 45,560	Newton	17.8	88,904	372	4,994.6	76.2	3.7	0.0	15.0	0.0	1.1	4.0
25 46,330	Northampton	34.2	28,726	1,296	839.9	89.4	2.1	0.0	3.3	0.0	1.9	3.4
25 52,490	Peabody	16.2	53,278	726	3,288.8	89.2	3.2	0.0	2.0	0.0	2.3	3.3
25 53,960	Pittsfield	40.5	42,533	895	1,050.2	86.7	3.5	0.6	1.0	0.0	3.1	5.0
25 55,745	Quincy	16.6	94,580	339	5,697.6	55.7	4.9	0.1	34.9	0.4	1.9	2.2
25 56,585	Revere	5.7	53,821	718	9,442.3	78.4	7.1	0.0	3.8	0.0	7.4	3.3
25 59,105	Salem	8.3	43,559	876	5,248.1	81.3	6.4	0.3	2.2	0.0	6.8	3.0
25 62,535	Somerville	4.1	81,562	423	19,893.2	77.4	7.6	0.0	9.3	0.0	2.1	3.6
25 67,000	Springfield	31.9	155,032	166	4,859.9	66.7	21.5	0.7	1.8	0.0	5.5	3.8
25 69,170	Taunton	46.7	57,296	663	1,226.9	78.4	6.1	0.0	0.8	0.0	6.7	7.9
25 72,600	Waltham	12.7	62,962	594	4,957.6	76.7	5.6	0.3	10.1	0.0	4.4	2.8
25 73,440	Watertown Town	4.0	35,954	1,068	8,988.5	83.3	1.9	1.2	10.4	0.0	1.1	2.0
25 76,030	Westfield	46.3	41,680	913	900.2	NA	NA	NA	NA	NA	NA	NA
25 77,890	West Springfield Town	16.7	28,747	1,295	1,721.4	NA	NA	NA	NA	NA	NA	NA
25 78,972	Weymouth Town	16.8	57,719	655	3,435.7	84.9	4.9	0.3	6.9	0.0	1.5	1.6
25 81,035	Woburn	12.6	40,397	947	3,206.1	79.5	8.5	0.0	8.6	0.0	1.0	2.3
25 82,000	Worcester	37.4	185,877	136	4,970.0	69.6	12.9	1.0	6.8	0.0	4.3	5.4
26 00,000	**MICHIGAN**	56,602.9	9,995,915	X	176.6	78.4	13.8	0.5	3.1	0.0	1.1	3.0
26 01,380	Allen Park	7.0	27,076	1,355	3,868.0	NA	NA	NA	NA	NA	NA	NA
26 03,000	Ann Arbor	27.9	121,890	231	4,368.8	70.1	7.1	0.3	18.4	0.0	0.2	3.9
26 05,920	Battle Creek	42.6	51,247	751	1,203.0	72.4	18.2	0.5	2.8	0.1	0.5	5.4
26 06,020	Bay City	10.2	33,019	1,156	3,237.2	94.0	1.6	0.0	0.2	0.0	0.9	3.3
26 12,060	Burton	23.4	28,652	1,299	1,224.4	88.0	5.7	0.2	3.0	0.5	0.0	2.6
26 21,000	Dearborn	24.2	94,333	341	3,898.1	89.9	3.7	0.0	2.1	0.0	0.2	4.1
26 21,020	Dearborn Heights	11.7	55,616	682	4,753.5	83.1	10.2	0.1	2.1	0.0	2.3	2.3
26 22,000	Detroit	138.7	672,662	23	4,849.8	14.5	79.0	0.4	1.8	0.0	2.6	1.7
26 24,120	East Lansing	13.4	47,988	807	3,581.2	79.2	5.7	0.1	10.6	0.1	0.8	3.5
26 24,290	Eastpointe	5.2	32,347	1,174	6,220.6	39.7	56.8	0.6	0.1	0.0	0.6	2.3
26 27,440	Farmington Hills	33.3	81,093	425	2,435.2	62.8	17.5	0.2	16.6	0.0	0.4	2.5
26 29,000	Flint	33.4	95,943	329	2,872.5	38.2	53.4	0.8	1.3	0.0	1.1	5.2
26 31,420	Garden City	5.9	26,545	1,377	4,499.2	87.2	4.3	0.2	1.6	0.0	0.2	6.5
26 34,000	Grand Rapids	44.4	200,217	115	4,509.4	65.9	19.7	0.3	3.5	0.0	5.8	4.7
26 38,640	Holland	16.7	33,327	1,148	1,995.6	79.5	3.8	0.0	0.7	0.0	10.6	5.4
26 40,680	Inkster	6.3	24,381	1,426	3,870.0	NA	NA	NA	NA	NA	NA	NA
26 41,420	Jackson	10.9	32,605	1,166	2,991.3	74.2	18.4	0.4	0.9	0.0	0.9	5.3
26 42,160	Kalamazoo	24.7	76,545	457	3,099.0	69.3	22.2	0.1	2.4	0.0	0.3	5.8
26 42,820	Kentwood	20.9	51,868	741	2,481.7	63.1	21.2	0.1	9.8	0.0	1.0	4.8
26 46,000	Lansing	39.2	118,427	240	3,021.1	60.7	23.1	0.6	5.6	0.0	2.3	7.7
26 47,800	Lincoln Park	5.8	36,517	1,053	6,296.0	77.5	6.2	0.3	0.5	0.0	11.6	4.1
26 49,000	Livonia	35.7	93,971	344	2,632.2	90.3	5.2	0.1	2.7	0.0	0.2	1.6
26 50,560	Madison Heights	7.1	30,039	1,252	4,230.8	74.5	9.3	0.1	9.8	0.0	0.3	6.1
26 53,780	Midland	34.4	41,800	911	1,215.1	89.9	1.5	1.1	4.6	0.0	0.6	2.2
26 56,020	Mount Pleasant	7.7	25,388	1,404	3,297.1	85.1	4.0	0.9	4.4	0.0	0.5	5.2
26 56,320	Muskegon	14.1	37,287	1,029	2,644.5	57.4	32.7	0.4	0.4	0.0	0.8	8.3
26 59,440	Novi	30.2	60,951	612	2,018.2	64.3	7.9	0.4	25.0	0.0	0.2	2.2

1. Dry land or land partially or temporarily covered by water.   2. Hispanic or Latino persons may be of any race.

Table D. Cities — **Population**

City	Percent Hispanic or Latino[1] 2017	Percent foreign born, 2017	Age of population (percent), 2017							Median age, 2017	Percent female, 2017	Population			
			Under 18 years	18 to 24 years	25 to 34 years	35 to 44 years	45 to 54 years	55 to 64 years	65 years and over			Census counts		Percent change	
												2000	2010	2000-2010	2001-2018
	12	13	14	15	16	17	18	19	20	21	22	23	24	25	26
MASSACHUSETTS— Cont'd															
Beverly	4.3	6.7	16.3	14.2	12.3	9.6	12.8	15.5	19.2	42.1	55.1	39,862	39,504	-0.9	7.1
Boston	20.4	29.3	15.5	15.0	24.3	12.4	11.1	10.0	11.7	32.3	51.7	589,141	617,786	4.9	12.4
Braintree Town	1.5	16.0	22.4	4.4	12.5	16.5	13.8	12.5	18.0	41.0	54.0	33,698	35,726	6.0	4.3
Brockton	9.3	29.9	24.9	10.8	12.9	12.9	12.7	12.5	13.3	36.1	54.1	94,304	93,767	-0.6	2.1
Cambridge	8.4	27.7	11.7	19.5	30.0	11.4	7.1	8.0	12.2	30.5	49.9	101,355	105,176	3.8	13.1
Chelsea	58.9	47.3	27.6	8.3	20.2	16.3	8.8	10.2	8.7	32.1	49.8	35,080	35,170	0.3	14.2
Chicopee	21.5	6.6	23.9	11.3	12.3	12.4	13.0	12.3	14.8	37.1	50.9	54,653	55,305	1.2	0.5
Everett	27.2	40.4	22.0	6.3	18.1	15.5	12.3	11.3	14.5	37.6	49.9	38,037	41,650	9.5	12.6
Fall River	10.2	22.4	22.3	8.8	11.9	12.7	14.1	14.2	15.9	40.4	53.0	91,938	88,857	-3.4	0.9
Fitchburg	25.9	8.3	18.5	13.9	12.3	8.8	15.9	14.7	15.7	40.8	48.8	39,102	40,325	3.1	1.4
Franklin Town	1.1	8.3	24.2	10.4	12.5	12.3	13.6	13.5	13.6	37.1	47.8	29,560	31,633	7.0	5.0
Gloucester	3.5	12.0	19.5	5.7	11.9	9.9	14.0	17.9	21.1	47.7	50.5	30,273	28,789	-4.9	5.6
Haverhill	20.5	8.5	24.4	7.7	14.1	12.3	14.9	14.8	11.8	37.5	51.9	58,969	60,878	3.2	5.2
Holyoke	53.9	4.8	23.9	5.8	17.3	12.6	14.0	12.4	14.0	37.1	53.5	39,838	39,881	0.1	1.2
Lawrence	84.7	37.9	27.2	12.2	16.4	12.0	11.5	9.9	10.8	31.4	50.9	72,043	76,348	6.0	5.3
Leominster	15.6	19.7	24.6	8.8	12.5	13.9	13.4	14.0	12.8	38.4	49.9	41,303	40,760	-1.3	2.6
Lowell	19.9	33.2	20.3	13.7	14.3	14.9	12.4	12.4	12.1	35.8	49.3	105,167	106,528	1.3	4.8
Lynn	37.7	37.9	20.3	10.6	16.5	13.6	13.3	12.2	13.6	36.4	48.2	89,050	90,333	1.4	4.8
Malden	6.8	45.2	17.9	11.9	24.5	12.8	10.3	9.8	12.8	32.2	56.6	56,340	59,416	5.5	2.7
Marlborough	11.3	24.2	20.3	8.5	14.9	15.6	12.6	14.5	13.6	38.7	54.1	36,255	38,497	6.2	3.4
Medford	2.6	19.2	12.2	13.9	22.6	14.2	9.7	13.6	13.9	36.1	50.9	55,765	56,304	1.0	2.6
Melrose	3.8	15.9	19.4	6.7	13.5	18.0	16.2	7.9	18.3	39.2	53.4	27,134	26,966	-0.6	4.6
Methuen Town	31.9	22.8	20.2	9.4	13.2	13.7	16.1	11.9	15.3	38.9	51.4	43,789	47,320	8.1	7.1
New Bedford	19.7	20.2	20.9	9.9	16.5	12.1	14.0	11.6	15.0	37.2	51.5	93,768	95,068	1.4	0.3
Newton	6.2	22.9	20.1	14.0	9.9	11.2	15.6	11.8	17.4	40.4	54.7	83,829	85,114	1.5	4.5
Northampton	8.6	7.2	17.6	14.8	13.7	10.6	11.8	12.6	18.9	39.0	56.4	28,978	28,552	-1.5	0.6
Peabody	9.1	15.8	16.6	7.2	14.1	10.3	11.8	17.8	22.3	46.2	52.2	48,129	51,266	6.5	3.9
Pittsfield	6.4	6.1	18.6	7.9	9.8	11.7	14.6	17.4	20.0	46.8	54.7	45,793	44,741	-2.3	-4.9
Quincy	2.9	33.6	14.8	7.1	20.1	15.9	11.4	14.7	15.9	39.6	51.0	88,025	92,262	4.8	2.5
Revere	33.9	38.1	24.1	5.2	15.6	17.5	13.7	11.1	12.7	36.3	51.4	47,283	51,737	9.4	4.0
Salem	21.1	14.6	18.6	12.4	18.5	11.2	12.1	11.1	16.0	35.2	57.1	40,407	41,314	2.2	5.4
Somerville	13.2	23.3	12.7	13.0	34.8	11.9	8.7	9.7	9.2	31.2	49.1	77,478	75,651	-2.4	7.8
Springfield	44.9	10.6	23.8	14.0	13.8	12.0	11.7	12.5	12.3	34.0	53.0	152,082	153,173	0.7	1.2
Taunton	10.5	12.5	26.6	7.0	10.3	15.8	11.5	14.9	13.9	38.9	50.8	55,976	55,874	-0.2	2.5
Waltham	14.5	28.4	16.2	15.4	17.5	15.0	11.7	13.3	10.8	35.4	51.4	59,226	60,621	2.4	3.9
Watertown Town	9.6	25.5	12.3	6.6	21.9	15.7	13.2	12.6	17.7	40.0	53.7	32,986	31,977	-3.1	12.4
Westfield	7.3	12.5	18.2	17.6	13.2	15.2	8.6	15.4	11.9	35.4	52.3	40,072	41,092	2.5	1.4
West Springfield Town	12.7	7.3	18.1	8.9	13.9	7.9	19.4	10.2	21.7	46.5	49.9	27,899	28,391	1.8	1.3
Weymouth Town	5.3	12.1	17.3	9.1	15.3	10.1	15.0	15.1	18.1	42.3	51.5	53,988	53,762	-0.4	7.4
Woburn	5.1	17.0	19.1	5.4	16.9	11.4	14.1	14.5	18.7	42.6	48.8	37,258	38,882	4.4	3.9
Worcester	22.8	18.8	19.5	16.2	15.7	11.4	11.2	12.4	13.6	34.2	52.7	172,648	181,009	4.8	2.7
MICHIGAN	5.1	7.1	21.8	9.7	12.7	11.6	13.3	14.1	16.7	39.8	50.7	9,938,444	9,884,117	-0.5	1.1
Allen Park	13.2	2.6	21.7	4.8	12.9	15.2	16.6	14.0	14.7	41.2	49.8	29,376	28,212	-4.0	-4.0
Ann Arbor	4.4	20.8	12.9	31.2	18.4	9.8	8.3	7.4	12.1	27.7	50.9	114,024	113,973	0.0	6.9
Battle Creek	7.3	5.7	25.8	7.4	14.3	11.9	11.6	12.0	17.1	37.5	51.3	53,364	52,400	-1.8	-2.2
Bay City	8.0	0.8	19.2	10.4	14.5	14.8	13.9	15.7	11.5	39.1	51.4	36,817	34,931	-5.1	-5.5
Burton	2.1	4.2	24.3	5.9	10.2	15.3	12.9	16.3	15.0	41.7	52.9	30,308	29,999	-1.0	-4.5
Dearborn	3.4	29.7	30.4	11.6	12.6	12.8	11.7	9.1	11.9	30.8	51.1	97,775	98,148	0.4	-3.9
Dearborn Heights	6.6	23.5	26.5	10.4	13.6	12.6	12.5	11.3	13.1	34.5	51.2	58,264	57,774	-0.8	-3.7
Detroit	7.2	6.1	24.9	10.2	15.3	11.4	12.0	12.2	14.0	34.6	52.6	951,270	713,885	-25.0	-5.8
East Lansing	4.7	13.0	7.0	61.6	8.7	4.6	2.8	7.7	7.6	21.4	52.0	46,525	48,585	4.4	-1.2
Eastpointe	1.8	2.3	22.0	13.1	13.6	13.1	17.1	11.7	9.3	36.8	53.6	34,077	32,403	-4.9	-0.2
Farmington Hills	2.1	23.5	16.6	7.5	14.6	13.0	14.2	14.4	19.7	43.4	50.6	82,111	79,722	-2.9	1.7
Flint	4.7	3.3	21.4	14.0	13.5	10.2	14.0	13.2	13.8	37.4	49.8	124,943	102,230	-18.2	-6.1
Garden City	4.7	4.7	19.2	9.8	12.8	10.3	16.6	17.1	14.2	43.3	51.4	30,047	27,636	-8.0	-3.9
Grand Rapids	16.1	13.1	22.2	13.9	20.2	11.6	9.6	11.2	11.4	31.1	49.9	197,800	188,031	-4.9	6.5
Holland	31.0	8.7	23.9	20.8	10.7	11.7	9.8	7.8	15.2	28.8	54.3	35,048	33,093	-5.6	0.7
Inkster	5.6	3.2	24.3	11.8	15.3	9.6	10.6	13.9	14.7	33.2	57.6	30,115	25,366	-15.8	-3.9
Jackson	7.2	2.0	24.6	8.0	14.2	14.2	16.5	9.8	12.7	36.5	49.6	36,316	33,479	-7.8	-2.6
Kalamazoo	6.7	5.5	17.7	28.8	16.3	9.2	8.3	8.3	11.3	26.8	49.7	77,145	74,261	-3.7	3.1
Kentwood	7.2	15.3	24.2	6.3	16.8	13.4	13.3	10.8	15.2	36.8	55.3	45,255	48,701	7.6	6.5
Lansing	12.7	15.4	22.8	12.4	17.5	12.9	12.5	10.4	11.5	33.3	52.5	119,128	114,253	-4.1	3.7
Lincoln Park	27.0	8.4	26.8	8.2	12.3	12.2	14.1	12.4	14.0	36.8	50.9	40,008	38,085	-4.8	-4.1
Livonia	2.5	8.4	18.3	7.1	12.8	11.7	12.3	17.0	20.7	45.1	51.6	100,545	96,857	-3.7	-3.0
Madison Heights	3.5	12.4	13.8	11.5	13.0	12.7	17.5	16.7	14.8	44.3	48.5	31,101	29,694	-4.5	1.2
Midland	4.5	8.8	22.4	10.5	15.5	12.4	11.2	11.0	16.9	36.0	52.2	41,685	41,869	0.4	-0.2
Mount Pleasant	5.1	5.7	10.9	49.3	14.0	5.5	5.8	6.6	7.9	22.4	50.9	25,946	26,016	0.3	-2.4
Muskegon	10.6	2.2	19.3	14.3	15.3	12.6	12.4	11.9	14.2	35.5	47.7	40,105	38,399	-4.3	-2.9
Novi	2.5	24.8	22.2	9.9	12.1	12.3	16.8	14.8	11.9	39.6	49.7	47,386	55,232	16.6	10.4

1. May be of any race.

City	Households, 2017							Persons in group quarters, 2017	Serious crimes known to police[2], 2016				Educational attainment, 2017		
			Percent						Total		Rate[3]			Attainment[4] (percent)	
	Number	Persons per household	Family	Married couple family	Female headed[1]	Non-family	One person		Number	Rate	Violent	Property	Population age 25 and over	High school graduate or less	Bachelor's degree or more
	27	28	29	30	31	32	33	34	35	36	37	38	39	40	41
MASSACHUSETTS— Cont'd															
Beverly	16,369	2.33	57.1	45.3	8.7	42.9	36.1	3,607	395	956	157	799	29,034	31.8	47.4
Boston	268,304	2.37	47.8	28.0	15.8	52.2	37.0	46,196	19,256	2,857	707	2,150	474,814	33.4	48.2
Braintree Town	14,495	2.53	61.7	51.8	7.4	38.3	28.9	552	754	2,001	239	1,763	27,198	32.5	45.4
Brockton	33,258	2.83	68.2	39.3	22.4	31.8	28.2	1,584	3,324	3,492	1,081	2,411	61,534	50.9	19.7
Cambridge	45,177	2.14	41.5	32.4	6.4	58.5	38.8	17,137	2,665	2,400	265	2,135	78,158	11.4	80.4
Chelsea	13,436	2.94	59.7	34.1	18.1	40.3	31.2	734	1,285	3,205	923	2,282	25,800	62.4	17.1
Chicopee	22,041	2.46	58.8	39.0	14.5	41.2	33.4	NA	1,581	2,779	466	2,313	35,963	45.1	19.0
Everett	16,983	2.72	64.5	44.1	13.5	35.5	28.9	NA	819	1,752	334	1,418	33,223	55.8	26.1
Fall River	38,261	2.30	61.0	34.9	19.6	39.0	32.4	1,470	2,633	2,979	1,094	1,885	61,538	59.7	16.3
Fitchburg	15,421	2.53	57.7	34.8	14.8	42.3	31.2	1,771	1,159	2,869	775	2,095	27,566	48.0	21.0
Franklin Town	12,152	2.62	69.1	61.3	6.3	30.9	26.1	1,108	99	298	3	295	21,611	17.7	62.1
Gloucester	12,867	2.32	64.3	50.6	9.0	35.7	28.5	299	302	1,012	245	768	22,569	35.3	40.4
Haverhill	23,812	2.63	67.3	41.9	17.4	32.7	26.0	956	1,355	2,156	593	1,562	43,182	39.0	33.5
Holyoke	15,861	2.48	57.4	27.9	23.3	42.6	36.5	1,025	2,448	6,009	1,070	4,939	28,381	53.3	18.4
Lawrence	25,836	3.05	73.7	31.8	32.1	26.3	20.9	1,272	2,106	2,612	740	1,872	48,573	61.5	10.5
Leominster	15,497	2.66	63.2	47.0	10.6	36.8	26.8	392	1,211	2,915	650	2,265	27,742	42.3	27.9
Lowell	39,016	2.73	60.6	34.2	18.8	39.4	30.6	4,733	2,587	2,330	342	1,988	73,431	56.1	22.9
Lynn	33,654	2.77	59.8	36.1	17.7	40.2	34.0	798	2,636	2,851	772	2,079	65,054	55.5	19.2
Malden	22,610	2.70	63.0	43.8	15.3	37.0	26.8	NA	886	1,450	277	1,173	42,972	37.2	39.5
Marlborough	15,871	2.48	64.5	44.7	13.7	35.5	28.3	549	722	1,810	401	1,409	28,407	37.5	37.3
Medford	23,517	2.35	52.3	40.8	8.2	47.7	32.8	2,445	759	1,323	155	1,168	42,740	25.8	56.7
Melrose	12,067	2.33	60.1	53.6	3.4	39.9	31.5	274	233	830	68	762	20,947	15.9	62.2
Methuen Town	17,339	2.87	72.3	50.1	15.7	27.7	19.3	438	900	1,803	158	1,645	35,346	46.4	26.4
New Bedford	39,377	2.37	61.4	34.5	19.9	38.6	30.7	1,935	3,735	3,951	855	3,097	65,812	56.4	18.4
Newton	31,504	2.57	74.7	61.1	11.8	25.3	20.7	8,035	688	772	52	720	58,668	10.3	77.7
Northampton	10,616	2.34	59.3	44.1	11.9	40.7	32.2	3,758	727	2,549	438	2,111	19,336	21.5	56.8
Peabody	23,029	2.27	60.9	44.0	10.6	39.1	36.2	611	896	1,707	392	1,314	40,396	42.5	31.1
Pittsfield	19,299	2.15	50.5	35.0	12.0	49.5	41.6	1,188	1,359	3,158	792	2,366	31,278	37.7	31.3
Quincy	38,420	2.42	55.5	43.4	8.4	44.5	34.6	1,163	1,914	2,048	437	1,612	73,520	35.6	43.7
Revere	18,939	2.84	62.9	42.8	12.5	37.1	31.4	279	1,405	2,625	490	2,136	38,150	57.1	21.8
Salem	18,157	2.29	54.1	34.2	15.5	45.9	36.6	1,918	1,164	2,714	305	2,409	29,965	30.2	47.7
Somerville	34,271	2.29	42.9	32.3	7.3	57.1	33.2	3,049	1,413	1,747	255	1,492	60,445	23.0	66.2
Springfield	57,158	2.61	64.5	28.4	29.4	35.5	31.5	5,789	6,664	4,324	1,032	3,293	96,288	53.4	19.4
Taunton	20,964	2.69	62.3	40.7	16.9	37.7	29.9	739	952	1,678	358	1,321	37,907	48.6	20.6
Waltham	23,655	2.32	54.7	46.2	5.2	45.3	34.0	7,633	787	1,237	156	1,082	42,685	29.3	53.2
Watertown Town	15,824	2.23	52.2	39.0	6.8	47.8	32.5	404	438	1,264	110	1,154	28,999	20.6	63.7
Westfield	15,658	2.44	60.5	39.2	12.4	39.5	28.4	3,549	643	1,542	223	1,319	26,769	41.4	30.9
West Springfield Town	12,792	2.23	51.8	34.2	7.4	48.2	41.2	NA	1,394	4,859	655	4,204	20,967	41.1	35.3
Weymouth Town	23,675	2.37	59.8	44.4	10.6	40.2	30.0	457	688	1,225	287	939	41,678	33.2	39.1
Woburn	15,811	2.49	63.1	45.6	9.4	36.9	27.3	303	528	1,332	207	1,125	29,966	34.4	41.7
Worcester	72,067	2.38	51.0	28.8	18.4	49.0	39.9	14,484	7,010	3,798	892	2,906	119,405	44.4	30.0
MICHIGAN	3,930,017	2.48	64.1	47.2	12.0	35.9	29.6	229,856	235,192	2,369	459	1,910	6,819,310	38.0	29.1
Allen Park	11,065	2.44	68.9	56.0	7.9	31.1	26.3	NA	553	2,027	194	1,833	19,942	32.1	26.4
Ann Arbor	46,946	2.32	44.3	36.3	5.5	55.7	33.0	12,621	2,268	1,927	179	1,748	67,897	11.8	74.6
Battle Creek	21,086	2.37	60.2	36.8	19.0	39.8	34.7	1,371	2,929	4,809	979	3,831	34,261	45.1	25.4
Bay City	14,842	2.20	53.3	35.0	12.9	46.7	40.5	475	1,133	3,360	614	2,746	23,370	40.6	19.7
Burton	11,386	2.50	65.3	48.8	14.6	34.7	25.8	NA	871	3,049	382	2,668	19,977	45.8	15.6
Dearborn	29,913	3.15	69.6	51.6	13.0	30.4	26.9	369	3,145	3,323	367	2,956	54,823	46.3	28.3
Dearborn Heights	19,939	2.77	66.1	44.2	14.4	33.9	26.9	505	1,292	2,313	371	1,943	35,158	45.1	22.4
Detroit	264,360	2.49	53.4	19.9	26.3	46.6	40.4	13,684	45,492	6,793	2,049	4,744	436,996	51.5	14.6
East Lansing	13,582	2.36	31.8	23.1	5.8	68.2	39.9	16,568	837	1,728	239	1,488	15,300	16.9	63.6
Eastpointe	13,087	2.47	62.1	25.2	28.0	37.9	31.5	177	1,328	4,061	816	3,245	21,103	45.3	14.3
Farmington Hills	34,069	2.36	66.0	53.4	10.0	34.0	29.5	697	1,134	1,389	98	1,291	61,547	19.7	54.9
Flint	41,302	2.26	55.3	20.7	27.3	44.7	39.8	3,105	4,888	5,011	1,587	3,424	62,363	47.9	12.8
Garden City	10,423	2.55	69.6	51.2	11.2	30.4	25.2	65	562	2,099	265	1,833	18,924	47.0	12.3
Grand Rapids	74,169	2.58	56.2	36.7	13.5	43.8	31.5	7,705	5,661	2,880	675	2,205	127,052	35.7	37.0
Holland	11,375	2.58	61.9	47.1	9.8	38.1	32.3	3,705	966	2,852	348	2,504	18,274	35.0	36.6
Inkster	9,566	2.52	57.9	24.5	28.7	42.1	36.6	365	1,048	4,269	1,316	2,953	15,632	53.8	9.2
Jackson	13,733	2.32	54.2	24.9	19.3	45.8	40.9	822	1,912	5,783	1,234	4,549	22,050	47.3	15.6
Kalamazoo	29,325	2.35	45.4	27.5	12.2	54.6	39.3	6,975	4,152	5,435	1,212	4,223	40,533	28.7	37.1
Kentwood	21,913	2.34	59.2	38.5	17.5	40.8	35.2	448	1,633	3,147	312	2,834	35,939	39.2	35.7
Lansing	48,190	2.37	49.5	28.2	16.8	50.5	39.3	1,041	4,700	4,080	1,180	2,900	74,870	38.3	27.1
Lincoln Park	14,804	2.47	58.3	37.0	14.8	41.7	37.9	62	1,379	3,746	728	3,018	23,836	58.7	7.1
Livonia	36,593	2.53	72.2	59.9	7.5	27.8	24.4	1,557	1,839	1,952	153	1,799	70,177	26.5	36.4
Madison Heights	13,826	2.16	53.8	36.1	11.7	46.2	36.6	NA	723	2,386	267	2,119	22,461	43.0	23.5
Midland	17,365	2.36	63.2	48.2	12.1	36.8	28.4	1,258	559	1,323	114	1,209	28,329	25.8	48.1
Mount Pleasant	7,760	2.49	43.4	35.6	7.2	56.6	34.0	6,532	422	1,619	257	1,362	10,288	21.8	49.8
Muskegon	14,085	2.29	49.9	23.0	19.6	50.1	45.1	5,946	1,746	4,542	713	3,829	25,324	52.3	13.5
Novi	23,542	2.52	67.6	55.0	8.2	32.4	28.0	347	693	1,166	57	1,109	40,501	18.3	60.0

1. No spouse present. 2. Data for serious crimes have not been adjusted for underreporting. This may affect comparability between geographic areas and over time. 3. Per 100,000 population estimated by the FBI. 4. Persons 25 years old and over.

Table D. Cities — Income and Housing

City	Median income	Percent with income less than $20,000	Percent with income of $200,000 or more	Median family income	Median non-family income	All persons	Men	Women	Total	Occupied	Percent owner occupied	Median value[1] (dollars)	Median gross rent (dollars)
	42	43	44	45	46	47	48	49	50	51	52	53	54
MASSACHUSETTS— Cont'd													
Beverly	80,910	16.3	9.4	98,963	41,464	41,585	51,838	31,252	16,532	16,369	57.9	436,600	1,174
Boston	66,758	21.4	10.9	76,603	55,011	38,884	41,776	35,067	293,538	268,304	35.2	540,600	1,541
Braintree Town	99,026	6.0	13.8	130,231	73,500	54,651	61,073	52,412	15,840	14,495	76.1	453,600	1,305
Brockton	58,357	16.9	1.7	68,922	28,014	34,261	37,183	32,732	35,787	33,258	54.8	264,200	1,125
Cambridge	97,316	13.7	21.0	140,994	77,115	45,924	52,207	40,443	48,913	45,177	35.7	773,200	2,102
Chelsea	53,595	20.5	3.6	58,724	30,399	31,163	35,588	27,300	13,857	13,436	25.9	322,700	1,392
Chicopee	49,975	20.6	1.7	58,975	34,901	30,839	36,685	27,560	23,803	22,041	52.2	188,900	959
Everett	65,320	14.7	3.8	73,760	39,838	39,545	42,340	36,359	18,256	16,983	40.1	407,300	1,391
Fall River	43,235	25.5	2.3	50,160	29,642	32,207	40,453	25,013	43,134	38,261	35.7	249,300	758
Fitchburg	54,525	17.0	3.9	59,318	48,194	35,341	40,848	30,991	16,661	15,421	55.9	196,900	958
Franklin Town	113,397	9.4	17.9	150,903	38,883	61,585	71,053	51,134	12,283	12,152	79.8	436,700	1,306
Gloucester	67,384	12.6	8.2	85,976	43,487	40,581	50,629	31,453	14,929	12,867	62.8	435,700	1,149
Haverhill	76,028	11.6	5.2	83,731	44,125	39,653	51,553	31,559	24,986	23,812	60.0	310,700	1,178
Holyoke	34,990	31.4	4.4	49,273	24,259	31,201	37,011	29,819	17,578	15,861	40.2	173,300	836
Lawrence	41,499	20.1	3.1	45,000	26,667	24,487	28,912	21,018	27,561	25,836	26.1	282,300	1,128
Leominster	68,327	15.1	5.1	78,322	40,122	35,994	39,610	31,635	16,241	15,497	56.4	235,000	944
Lowell	50,391	26.6	4.2	56,483	30,273	32,224	35,635	28,781	42,531	39,016	42.0	270,100	1,103
Lynn	48,900	24.4	3.4	66,036	23,185	31,557	35,886	26,882	34,486	33,654	45.6	336,100	1,071
Malden	62,770	18.9	3.4	71,033	39,311	35,059	37,794	31,665	23,823	22,610	35.5	427,900	1,574
Marlborough	76,348	9.3	10.0	93,934	51,861	41,953	53,604	31,227	17,836	15,871	59.1	367,000	1,431
Medford	102,094	9.8	14.0	128,723	67,161	52,415	60,828	50,541	25,045	23,517	58.2	501,400	1,635
Melrose	117,806	10.0	21.3	161,912	42,910	62,382	71,727	54,230	12,466	12,067	66.1	581,600	1,401
Methuen Town	71,730	12.9	5.2	83,538	41,413	39,969	32,410	31,691	18,512	17,339	71.7	326,000	1,147
New Bedford	45,784	24.7	2.8	56,711	26,243	31,259	35,623	27,835	42,804	39,377	38.7	236,200	812
Newton	144,403	5.0	34.8	167,375	72,636	59,679	82,293	43,810	33,331	31,504	72.8	930,400	1,754
Northampton	66,497	13.8	9.0	94,214	38,224	32,254	45,612	25,625	11,625	10,616	56.8	308,500	1,149
Peabody	67,313	13.2	5.0	90,894	41,631	42,309	51,076	32,079	24,155	23,029	63.3	377,200	1,190
Pittsfield	45,731	24.0	5.4	73,131	26,803	32,027	42,038	26,115	22,282	19,299	64.6	172,000	755
Quincy	77,765	16.1	10.8	98,833	54,390	46,582	50,880	41,666	41,582	38,420	49.6	426,200	1,395
Revere	61,085	20.8	3.6	78,056	24,865	37,448	46,702	30,811	20,466	18,939	49.0	356,600	1,509
Salem	67,389	20.8	10.1	77,934	43,001	37,487	47,326	32,212	19,093	18,157	52.7	361,200	1,163
Somerville	89,478	14.4	14.6	107,967	76,668	50,231	53,423	48,035	36,788	34,271	34.4	666,500	1,671
Springfield	36,234	31.2	2.2	42,204	22,803	26,587	29,156	25,334	61,632	57,158	44.0	152,200	835
Taunton	59,143	15.6	5.7	72,285	41,058	36,438	45,932	27,965	22,421	20,964	68.2	274,700	983
Waltham	87,598	14.0	13.0	120,050	56,694	41,767	41,790	41,748	26,016	23,655	55.6	566,000	1,460
Watertown Town	89,250	8.3	13.5	100,667	70,476	53,568	67,372	49,058	16,733	15,824	48.4	484,800	1,892
Westfield	61,575	13.0	5.1	72,098	50,625	35,682	41,717	26,927	16,030	15,658	61.8	223,900	958
West Springfield Town	51,696	25.4	5.9	66,885	27,074	36,863	50,579	27,338	13,037	12,792	61.6	242,000	809
Weymouth Town	81,648	7.9	8.2	107,348	53,505	42,214	46,454	40,502	24,302	23,675	70.7	371,200	1,472
Woburn	75,590	9.5	12.8	86,938	39,778	42,147	51,674	38,661	16,961	15,811	66.6	466,700	1,574
Worcester	41,561	27.7	2.9	55,245	31,712	32,460	38,015	30,660	79,626	72,067	38.9	221,600	1,019
MICHIGAN	54,909	16.1	4.8	69,664	32,401	31,713	39,822	26,156	4,595,274	3,930,017	71.3	155,700	835
Allen Park	71,160	10.5	4.8	77,252	48,553	41,728	49,679	36,973	11,591	11,065	84.6	130,000	1,055
Ann Arbor	70,499	15.4	10.2	102,428	51,045	25,748	28,191	22,272	49,094	46,946	47.5	323,400	1,214
Battle Creek	37,561	26.5	2.2	49,049	26,049	23,257	30,292	21,155	23,560	21,086	58.7	84,500	699
Bay City	41,567	24.6	0.8	52,214	25,332	26,189	31,667	21,063	16,562	14,842	68.9	65,900	564
Burton	47,048	17.6	0.4	51,047	36,762	25,547	26,456	23,970	12,216	11,386	76.4	91,200	714
Dearborn	46,662	21.9	4.5	53,248	35,030	25,719	30,146	20,800	33,431	29,913	65.9	144,900	942
Dearborn Heights	47,204	15.6	3.5	52,786	32,507	31,265	39,186	24,593	21,352	19,939	68.0	114,000	1,013
Detroit	30,344	36.3	1.0	36,939	20,445	24,677	25,599	23,169	363,525	264,360	46.9	50,200	782
East Lansing	40,438	25.1	5.1	89,595	26,731	6,568	7,009	6,107	15,691	13,582	33.2	192,100	939
Eastpointe	47,517	21.0	0.4	48,743	40,800	30,916	37,497	26,768	14,027	13,087	59.3	77,700	1,063
Farmington Hills	82,592	9.3	9.7	97,466	51,692	50,902	63,187	40,099	36,312	34,069	62.2	257,000	1,223
Flint	26,901	36.6	0.4	32,704	20,041	17,141	19,498	16,050	56,993	41,302	59.4	27,400	683
Garden City	59,225	9.8	1.4	70,438	34,708	32,083	39,527	28,830	10,649	10,423	81.9	112,000	1,093
Grand Rapids	48,521	17.0	2.6	56,974	36,637	27,050	29,350	25,078	79,837	74,169	56.8	144,200	910
Holland	57,517	13.5	4.0	74,859	24,446	25,809	31,381	20,663	11,923	11,375	63.4	145,800	880
Inkster	28,815	33.8	0.0	40,742	20,576	22,180	25,836	20,154	11,450	9,566	41.1	40,600	870
Jackson	31,388	31.4	1.1	41,364	19,974	24,946	28,248	21,890	16,440	13,733	52.2	66,200	626
Kalamazoo	42,271	20.8	4.6	58,750	33,851	19,187	21,302	17,276	31,945	29,325	46.9	100,500	776
Kentwood	51,415	12.0	4.9	63,500	30,309	32,226	45,025	27,321	22,112	21,913	54.2	154,500	849
Lansing	39,957	23.3	0.6	47,527	33,370	25,272	26,552	24,304	55,054	48,190	49.7	85,700	787
Lincoln Park	42,330	21.2	0.6	51,405	24,903	32,040	41,010	23,148	16,224	14,804	71.4	78,100	810
Livonia	82,410	6.2	4.7	92,537	42,178	39,643	48,688	31,954	38,128	36,593	87.4	190,000	1,026
Madison Heights	49,727	23.2	3.5	60,845	38,068	37,198	42,491	25,125	14,550	13,826	58.4	126,200	918
Midland	65,756	14.3	7.9	80,717	31,528	33,270	50,080	23,877	18,943	17,365	64.6	153,500	723
Mount Pleasant	39,220	27.8	2.9	62,824	25,170	8,551	9,449	7,296	9,031	7,760	40.6	138,700	738
Muskegon	29,529	38.8	0.8	37,812	17,924	20,484	20,924	20,070	15,923	14,085	43.2	80,100	670
Novi	89,447	7.8	15.6	104,553	45,726	50,161	62,349	35,690	25,213	23,542	64.0	332,700	1,426

1. Based on population estimated by the American Community Survey.   2. Includes units rented or sold but not occupied.   3. Specified owner-occupied units; $1,000,000 represents $1,000,000 or more.   4. 50.0 represents 50 percent or more.   5. 10.0 represents 10 percent or less.

Table D. Cities — Commuting, Computer Access, Migration, Labor Force, and Employment

City	Commuting[1], 2017 Commuting	With commutes of 30 minutes or more	Computer access[2], 2017 With a computer in the house	With Internet access	Migration, 2017 Percent who lived in the same house one year ago	Percent who lived in another state or county one year ago	Civilian labor force, 2018 Total	Percent change 2017-2018	Unemployment Total	Rate[3]	Civilian employment[4], 2017 Population age 16 and older Number	Percent in labor force	Population age 16 to 64 Number	Percent who worked full-year full-time
	55	56	57	58	59	60	61	62	63	64	65	66	67	68
MASSACHUSETTS— Cont'd														
Beverly	69.6	38.9	88.3	84.6	84.4	5.0	24,024	2.6	715	3.0	35,436	63.1	27,403	49.1
Boston	37.6	55.0	91.5	84.8	80.3	10.7	394,317	3.4	11,724	3.0	589,324	69.6	509,340	51.5
Braintree Town	71.2	57.9	92.2	86.1	90.9	6.2	21,226	3.6	668	3.1	30,063	70.2	23,388	61.0
Brockton	73.2	46.2	88.7	80.5	87.8	5.7	49,201	2.9	2,201	4.5	75,986	67.1	63,249	50.2
Cambridge	28.3	42.2	91.8	86.3	72.0	17.2	70,081	3.5	1,477	2.1	102,191	67.2	88,368	49.0
Chelsea	50.3	51.6	89.0	80.9	79.9	7.5	21,068	3.5	673	3.2	29,983	72.5	26,502	50.9
Chicopee	85.1	18.2	88.9	83.9	85.3	5.9	28,399	2.5	1,275	4.5	43,534	60.6	35,292	45.8
Everett	58.0	57.7	82.6	76.3	NA	NA	27,060	3.4	753	2.8	37,053	69.4	30,356	53.5
Fall River	79.6	34.7	81.0	68.4	82.9	6.4	41,085	2.4	2,383	5.8	71,180	59.3	57,003	45.5
Fitchburg	79.6	35.2	86.2	81.2	87.4	4.9	20,535	3.6	924	4.5	34,426	62.6	28,013	49.6
Franklin Town	75.5	53.3	97.9	94.3	85.8	5.5	18,570	3.6	564	3.0	25,942	70.4	21,469	58.9
Gloucester	75.0	33.5	90.1	88.2	87.4	3.8	16,402	3.5	689	4.2	25,436	63.5	19,069	49.9
Haverhill	75.8	47.7	93.1	85.3	89.1	2.3	35,923	2.6	1,231	3.4	49,244	71.1	41,760	52.5
Holyoke	82.5	21.5	81.0	72.0	87.8	5.2	16,790	2.6	920	5.5	32,206	55.5	26,575	36.3
Lawrence	64.7	19.4	88.2	75.4	89.4	3.7	36,894	2.1	2,304	6.2	62,061	70.4	53,403	46.0
Leominster	82.6	39.9	94.2	88.0	88.6	4.8	23,333	3.5	873	3.7	32,637	69.0	27,317	54.1
Lowell	73.9	35.7	78.6	71.4	83.2	6.1	57,506	3.0	2,191	3.8	91,318	62.8	77,891	44.4
Lynn	70.0	51.4	85.9	79.4	85.9	8.4	48,636	2.5	1,755	3.6	77,196	64.8	64,388	49.7
Malden	51.3	65.0	90.7	84.9	83.9	8.1	35,047	3.4	1,036	3.0	51,451	64.7	43,629	50.8
Marlborough	80.4	45.0	97.5	95.0	82.0	7.5	24,192	2.7	683	2.8	32,928	76.1	27,495	55.7
Medford	59.6	52.8	91.3	89.8	84.2	7.1	35,268	3.4	952	2.7	51,538	72.6	43,516	59.2
Melrose	52.6	68.9	90.2	87.2	NA	NA	17,099	3.6	450	2.6	23,483	74.3	18,305	66.6
Methuen Town	83.3	38.0	90.5	88.8	89.3	2.9	27,972	2.3	1,055	3.8	41,498	70.7	33,788	49.4
New Bedford	73.1	34.8	82.5	75.1	87.2	4.1	47,939	1.2	2,903	6.1	78,317	61.3	64,006	44.9
Newton	63.0	49.8	96.1	94.1	85.5	9.5	49,135	3.5	1,205	2.5	73,640	68.9	58,122	52.2
Northampton	70.0	33.1	93.2	88.2	81.7	7.6	16,793	2.5	417	2.5	24,281	63.4	18,890	47.5
Peabody	84.4	37.9	90.3	85.5	83.2	6.7	30,063	2.4	918	3.1	45,142	64.8	33,323	56.6
Pittsfield	81.8	10.3	87.1	80.4	88.2	2.8	21,803	0.6	942	4.3	35,723	59.7	27,210	40.6
Quincy	57.0	61.1	89.1	83.9	84.4	7.9	55,763	3.5	1,719	3.1	81,748	70.7	66,736	55.8
Revere	51.8	63.5	89.7	80.2	89.4	5.8	29,843	3.5	985	3.3	41,577	68.1	34,720	56.8
Salem	65.9	44.3	87.0	80.8	86.3	5.8	24,910	2.4	863	3.5	36,263	66.1	29,305	48.7
Somerville	34.8	59.6	90.4	87.0	79.9	10.8	53,909	3.5	1,178	2.2	71,913	77.6	64,437	57.7
Springfield	77.4	22.1	80.2	69.9	83.0	5.8	65,609	2.3	4,073	6.2	122,973	56.0	103,884	36.3
Taunton	83.9	44.1	89.8	84.4	91.8	5.1	31,038	3.1	1,228	4.0	43,339	66.6	35,412	51.1
Waltham	71.9	41.8	95.2	86.4	81.7	11.3	38,571	3.6	1,048	2.7	53,610	70.9	46,840	48.6
Watertown Town	65.2	57.0	90.6	89.8	84.9	7.9	23,455	3.5	533	2.3	31,529	72.8	25,204	63.5
Westfield	87.0	29.2	93.0	87.8	75.9	11.1	21,974	2.5	850	3.9	34,792	67.2	29,850	47.5
West Springfield Town	86.0	27.0	82.1	78.1	NA	NA	15,186	2.5	574	3.8	24,158	61.3	17,937	45.9
Weymouth Town	79.5	51.1	96.0	89.8	81.8	8.7	32,254	3.3	1,073	3.3	47,710	75.7	37,436	54.2
Woburn	74.6	39.2	90.9	88.3	88.5	3.9	23,847	3.5	679	2.8	34,055	67.4	26,640	61.6
Worcester	72.7	29.9	85.2	80.0	85.9	6.3	94,705	2.4	3,666	3.9	153,494	56.3	128,188	41.9
MICHIGAN	82.5	32.9	90.0	82.3	85.8	5.9	4,902,069	0.3	203,224	4.1	8,052,502	61.5	6,387,389	48.4
Allen Park	88.8	26.2	92.6	83.7	94.9	2.9	14,240	0.6	482	3.4	21,636	65.2	17,658	58.4
Ann Arbor	52.4	25.1	94.9	86.9	69.0	16.9	65,149	0.7	1,630	2.5	107,475	64.3	92,811	39.3
Battle Creek	83.8	16.7	88.2	78.5	80.1	6.5	22,868	-1.7	1,135	5.0	39,503	58.7	30,731	40.6
Bay City	81.8	15.6	89.2	82.4	87.1	6.9	15,634	-1.1	967	6.2	27,307	67.5	23,503	46.8
Burton	82.9	26.4	90.3	86.5	NA	NA	13,357	0.0	658	4.9	22,888	63.3	18,586	44.8
Dearborn	83.2	27.2	91.8	85.8	86.4	5.2	39,020	0.6	1,326	3.4	68,930	55.0	57,725	35.2
Dearborn Heights	82.1	30.2	91.2	84.0	88.4	4.6	25,306	0.5	969	3.8	42,318	58.4	35,025	42.2
Detroit	71.0	32.8	83.1	66.0	84.5	4.3	248,927	0.2	22,454	9.0	525,680	53.0	431,224	35.4
East Lansing	53.7	12.3	95.5	85.3	44.5	29.1	23,975	0.0	619	2.6	45,947	54.2	42,240	17.1
Eastpointe	86.1	40.7	90.3	87.5	84.9	7.8	15,508	0.6	920	5.9	26,223	67.8	23,189	48.4
Farmington Hills	89.5	41.4	94.2	91.3	83.1	10.5	44,911	1.0	959	2.1	69,080	64.3	53,117	55.8
Flint	79.7	24.9	75.3	58.9	83.0	5.4	33,646	-0.6	2,971	8.8	78,114	54.6	64,801	30.3
Garden City	86.8	33.6	89.1	84.7	90.1	2.4	14,884	0.6	525	3.5	22,093	64.0	18,320	54.9
Grand Rapids	74.9	15.6	90.6	84.3	77.3	8.0	104,863	1.0	4,147	4.0	160,293	69.9	137,545	50.5
Holland	80.7	16.7	86.6	82.3	79.2	12.1	17,374	1.1	565	3.3	26,292	67.1	21,266	45.3
Inkster	80.4	35.4	87.6	66.1	NA	NA	8,949	0.3	694	7.8	18,860	54.0	15,277	34.7
Jackson	79.4	21.5	88.6	80.9	80.5	5.0	13,953	-0.2	917	6.6	25,921	54.9	21,775	39.0
Kalamazoo	75.5	17.0	92.6	82.8	67.9	11.0	37,096	0.1	1,583	4.3	64,341	62.9	55,775	35.5
Kentwood	78.3	15.9	90.8	84.0	86.6	4.5	30,379	1.2	851	2.8	40,248	66.6	32,368	59.6
Lansing	76.3	15.6	90.5	77.4	75.9	10.8	59,278	-0.5	3,078	5.2	92,263	67.5	79,036	46.7
Lincoln Park	87.9	33.3	82.2	63.0	NA	NA	17,408	0.5	695	4.0	27,624	57.5	22,486	47.2
Livonia	87.9	33.4	92.4	89.9	90.7	3.2	52,651	0.6	1,211	2.3	79,838	63.0	60,323	52.9
Madison Heights	86.0	34.3	90.9	86.0	86.2	6.0	15,729	0.8	752	4.8	26,346	66.9	21,892	53.2
Midland	85.3	18.4	93.2	87.9	77.6	7.3	20,796	0.6	667	3.2	33,570	61.0	26,430	50.5
Mount Pleasant	70.5	11.3	94.2	83.0	51.0	31.2	12,642	-1.1	502	4.0	23,400	56.9	21,369	24.1
Muskegon	76.9	22.2	83.5	67.3	70.5	8.3	14,108	0.1	1,083	7.7	31,688	49.9	26,274	30.8
Novi	87.3	45.5	95.5	90.4	83.4	10.5	33,459	1.0	749	2.2	47,768	70.4	40,661	58.3

1. Employed persons.   2. Households.   3. Percent of civilian labor force.   4. Persons 16 years old and over.

Table D. Cities — Construction, Wholesale Trade, and Retail Trade

City	Value of residential construction authorized by building permits, 2018			Wholesale trade[1], 2012				Retail trade[2], 2012			
	New construction ($1,000)	Number of housing units	Percent single family	Number of establishments	Number of employees	Sales (mil dol)	Annual payroll (mil dol)	Number of establishments	Number of employees	Sales (mil dol)	Annual payroll (mil dol)
	69	70	71	72	73	74	75	76	77	78	79
MASSACHUSETTS— Cont'd											
Beverly	7,817	20	85.0	41	274	134.9	14.2	139	2,099	690.4	75.2
Boston	855,137	3,602	1.4	517	9,559	7,074.8	716.3	2,161	28,148	7,885.6	807.6
Braintree Town	4,279	15	86.7	62	1,246	1,014.3	92.0	283	5,695	1,394.2	140.3
Brockton	8,055	63	61.9	60	1,117	2,195.0	66.9	331	4,816	1,305.4	128.6
Cambridge	120,324	674	5.0	75	2,383	1,696.9	498.0	455	6,195	1,366.5	153.5
Chelsea	7,854	40	2.5	83	D	D	D	95	1,884	485.7	43.8
Chicopee	4,034	19	100.0	36	1,193	1,014.4	57.3	158	2,538	728.7	63.1
Everett	1,661	13	15.4	46	1,375	1,194.3	76.1	118	1,880	451.8	43.4
Fall River	4,919	42	100.0	67	1,218	454.9	57.8	284	3,310	811.3	83.8
Fitchburg	2,341	14	100.0	34	292	146.2	13.0	114	1,234	318.6	30.9
Franklin Town	52,605	354	26.0	45	1,609	1,499.3	91.0	106	1,651	413.7	42.4
Gloucester	15,509	47	44.7	47	385	675.1	24.3	129	1,514	344.3	37.0
Haverhill	14,631	83	68.7	48	626	261.0	36.0	146	2,420	677.7	59.5
Holyoke	2,202	15	33.3	25	483	149.6	23.2	229	4,017	717.2	79.8
Lawrence	1,991	18	44.4	57	1,311	899.2	103.3	196	1,593	486.4	47.3
Leominster	6,825	50	28.0	45	541	290.1	30.7	234	4,584	1,004.1	91.2
Lowell	5,798	50	46.0	58	945	501.5	51.4	225	2,474	725.6	63.0
Lynn	5,667	48	29.2	38	381	402.6	21.4	221	2,345	668.2	65.5
Malden	680	5	100.0	36	398	295.8	23.5	133	1,280	330.2	30.2
Marlborough	3,666	26	100.0	79	1,587	1,340.6	120.7	221	3,452	800.8	76.1
Medford	2,645	19	5.3	44	789	301.8	41.7	163	2,317	692.4	61.9
Melrose	5,135	19	100.0	4	D	D	D	57	664	178.2	19.3
Methuen Town	28,302	87	100.0	33	D	D	D	110	2,240	530.3	52.5
New Bedford	6,046	54	74.1	98	1,933	1,299.7	92.6	287	3,185	792.3	71.4
Newton	17,662	47	61.7	102	1,642	1,542.7	136.1	322	4,523	1,111.1	136.8
Northampton	7,203	29	72.4	26	D	D	D	176	2,277	548.9	59.6
Peabody	7,962	29	72.4	59	1,497	5,754.2	116.6	298	5,204	1,256.0	134.2
Pittsfield	990	5	100.0	54	655	284.0	28.6	186	2,985	789.5	73.5
Quincy	13,458	116	12.9	65	1,188	592.7	97.2	234	4,022	1,113.6	107.2
Revere	4,633	31	29.0	25	D	D	D	117	1,717	422.0	35.8
Salem	1,381	11	27.3	36	274	147.9	14.3	164	2,242	469.6	51.4
Somerville	28,712	170	18.8	39	489	246.5	25.9	183	3,203	759.4	74.0
Springfield	16,089	63	100.0	105	1,487	1,386.7	90.4	468	5,777	1,384.6	134.6
Taunton	14,897	81	75.3	59	2,147	1,566.7	127.8	220	3,261	718.4	76.7
Waltham	33,116	89	64.0	94	D	D	D	232	3,100	1,041.0	97.7
Watertown Town	29,094	127	24.4	31	391	146.2	20.1	144	2,660	889.9	84.5
Westfield	8,861	45	100.0	43	1,006	1,897.0	45.0	123	1,944	450.2	43.8
West Springfield Town	4,320	19	73.7	58	830	295.0	44.8	194	3,483	1,249.9	105.2
Weymouth Town	36,954	153	25.5	51	343	386.3	19.0	198	2,472	757.5	74.1
Woburn	14,883	55	92.7	201	4,360	2,476.5	299.1	185	3,843	1,053.8	112.2
Worcester	29,292	167	60.5	178	2,454	1,098.5	118.1	564	7,853	1,991.5	198.9
MICHIGAN	4,569,368	19,580	79.8	9,392	132,490	115,704.9	7,474.6	34,858	441,190	119,302.0	10,527.3
Allen Park	0	0	0.0	15	145	113.7	7.8	110	1,877	387.3	37.8
Ann Arbor	32,012	126	100.0	77	452	227.3	27.9	507	8,042	1,758.5	184.5
Battle Creek	2,779	9	100.0	31	440	468.0	21.3	247	3,200	796.6	70.2
Bay City	8,699	24	100.0	36	614	222.7	22.1	145	1,187	251.0	27.4
Burton	5,224	46	100.0	24	723	162.7	44.1	153	2,299	505.4	52.4
Dearborn	8,596	29	100.0	140	1,314	1,896.2	82.7	539	6,554	1,568.3	147.9
Dearborn Heights	2,445	9	100.0	44	157	69.3	7.1	181	1,602	400.2	33.3
Detroit	40,341	170	30.6	409	7,378	7,269.3	430.5	2,092	11,850	3,196.3	251.5
East Lansing	722	6	100.0	8	45	29.6	3.1	85	1,293	303.8	24.7
Eastpointe	157	1	100.0	14	47	9.6	1.2	126	1,120	304.3	35.7
Farmington Hills	8,810	26	100.0	182	2,605	2,587.7	175.7	298	4,091	1,269.7	118.6
Flint	9,507	161	0.0	62	885	587.8	37.2	377	3,419	740.2	73.0
Garden City	0	0	0.0	12	D	D	D	103	906	326.1	27.0
Grand Rapids	116,534	814	15.2	218	5,550	4,778.9	303.7	545	6,140	1,672.6	164.4
Holland	2,866	11	81.8	36	373	403.2	25.1	158	2,040	571.4	47.2
Inkster	0	0	0.0	5	D	D	D	53	278	74.9	5.5
Jackson	0	0	0.0	58	1,008	615.9	47.2	173	1,735	398.3	41.7
Kalamazoo	12,318	47	95.7	86	1,218	600.9	63.3	271	2,495	586.6	64.1
Kentwood	16,876	100	70.0	128	2,727	1,345.8	152.5	284	4,399	894.9	89.8
Lansing	35,831	261	10.0	107	1,728	2,126.3	82.5	430	6,033	1,623.4	150.3
Lincoln Park	0	0	0.0	10	D	D	D	123	1,315	320.8	29.8
Livonia	14,661	58	100.0	244	3,484	4,012.5	211.0	467	7,544	1,929.3	190.0
Madison Heights	1,357	12	100.0	107	1,638	1,062.7	88.5	178	3,280	1,059.3	85.0
Midland	5,141	39	89.7	29	219	674.5	13.8	241	3,558	887.7	77.5
Mount Pleasant	0	0	0.0	24	292	227.4	10.2	114	2,381	556.0	52.0
Muskegon	3,554	16	100.0	34	808	291.0	37.8	126	1,911	518.1	48.5
Novi	28,666	147	100.0	147	2,514	4,754.7	173.2	355	6,929	1,800.8	168.0

1. Merchant wholesalers except manufacturers' sales branches and offices. 2. Establishments with payroll.

City	Real estate and rental and leasing, 2012				Professional, scientific, and technical services[1], 2012				Manufacturing, 2012			
	Number of establish-ments	Number of employees	Receipts (mil dol)	Annual payroll (mil dol)	Number of establish-ments	Number of employees	Receipts (mil dol)	Annual payroll (mil dol)	Number of establish-ments	Number of employees	Receipts (mil dol)	Annual payroll (mil dol)
	80	81	82	83	84	85	86	87	88	89	90	91
MASSACHUSETTS—Cont'd												
Beverly	40	226	65.8	9.7	175	1,223	238.9	90.9	56	2,099	594.9	156.1
Boston	1,030	10,940	3,760.4	812.7	3,017	57,617	17,290.7	6,428.1	284	6,965	3,334.5	386.6
Braintree Town	73	1,395	247.5	74.4	206	D	D	D	27	1,842	450.2	140.9
Brockton	51	183	48.0	7.8	133	D	D	D	68	2,022	421.8	87.6
Cambridge	159	983	360.7	52.3	892	24,581	7,324.8	3,022.0	68	1,810	464.6	113.9
Chelsea	33	184	26.2	6.5	33	1,405	47.5	25.6	37	1,604	391.5	69.8
Chicopee	43	164	29.6	4.8	47	544	46.8	19.2	70	3,014	938.8	169.4
Everett	23	85	13.8	3.5	31	D	D	D	45	705	151.2	33.6
Fall River	75	292	51.5	11.1	149	D	D	D	133	4,419	894.1	182.1
Fitchburg	29	98	16.1	3.2	46	227	27.2	11.3	58	1,701	509.9	90.9
Franklin Town	29	123	55.0	8.3	106	944	96.4	50.7	55	3,313	4,723.8	197.9
Gloucester	28	D	D	D	83	D	D	D	47	2,248	D	171.1
Haverhill	46	263	51.1	11.6	91	621	81.2	29.0	82	2,653	719.3	132.3
Holyoke	39	316	32.4	11.8	67	D	D	D	63	1,672	353.9	82.6
Lawrence	42	220	43.9	8.8	69	D	D	D	91	4,080	813.6	189.4
Leominster	43	298	52.5	14.5	96	554	77.1	29.0	88	2,714	1,094.8	142.2
Lowell	68	315	64.8	11.6	132	D	D	D	76	3,530	1,396.0	263.6
Lynn	47	222	58.0	8.5	82	D	D	D	36	3,277	D	241.3
Malden	46	174	44.4	8.5	64	300	35.7	15.4	40	1,439	436.5	64.4
Marlborough	51	206	63.9	9.2	198	D	D	D	66	3,867	1,795.8	295.1
Medford	34	148	53.8	11.0	119	497	67.5	32.1	39	450	77.5	23.5
Melrose	20	72	25.3	3.3	75	253	35.9	14.8	9	84	D	4.4
Methuen Town	38	D	D	D	85	374	54.6	17.4	42	1,448	635.2	85.2
New Bedford	81	296	63.8	12.1	160	D	D	D	109	4,990	1,543.5	202.6
Newton	155	2,297	2,336.2	131.9	607	D	D	D	51	685	D	47.9
Northampton	36	108	218.4	3.4	125	D	D	D	27	1,072	527.1	52.0
Peabody	41	393	75.7	16.1	101	1,263	182.3	85.7	58	2,187	1,063.9	159.0
Pittsfield	40	244	27.7	7.7	133	D	D	D	51	2,555	506.3	168.8
Quincy	84	455	91.4	25.9	266	D	D	D	42	593	D	33.0
Revere	18	219	29.4	6.9	46	146	14.2	4.9	12	D	D	D
Salem	42	206	55.0	8.4	167	D	D	D	33	734	133.0	33.9
Somerville	63	267	60.7	12.9	174	D	D	D	53	1,142	375.5	80.2
Springfield	109	658	100.7	25.0	325	D	D	D	98	4,029	1,528.2	237.0
Taunton	36	109	22.0	4.0	101	1,018	163.9	62.1	49	4,336	1,714.7	436.9
Waltham	106	894	257.3	51.8	385	11,201	2,336.7	1,198.6	95	4,122	1,130.4	244.5
Watertown Town	31	183	55.0	11.5	135	D	D	D	46	1,161	363.5	89.8
Westfield	32	144	31.4	5.0	59	640	85.4	34.6	92	3,103	858.0	169.0
West Springfield Town	34	90	18.2	3.4	78	498	75.3	27.3	59	1,657	439.0	81.8
Weymouth Town	46	182	44.7	10.3	120	1,165	207.3	88.8	33	495	177.0	25.2
Woburn	84	859	163.1	50.3	302	D	D	D	131	4,341	2,050.1	347.5
Worcester	152	707	200.3	28.7	419	D	D	D	163	7,061	2,300.6	426.2
MICHIGAN	7,826	48,706	11,974.5	1,806.9	21,532	238,884	34,273.5	15,936.8	12,444	514,058	238,892.4	27,611.4
Allen Park	21	399	37.1	12.9	55	593	77.8	25.3	19	158	17.2	5.1
Ann Arbor	146	1,591	367.8	76.4	634	5,588	925.1	397.5	66	1,132	201.1	53.4
Battle Creek	42	247	38.5	7.5	93	D	D	D	57	7,973	4,180.7	449.3
Bay City	24	113	12.3	2.3	91	650	61.7	29.7	50	1,974	589.5	118.2
Burton	21	98	15.2	3.2	42	240	33.2	7.1	32	334	106.0	15.6
Dearborn	95	D	D	D	267	11,832	664.8	1,048.8	79	9,205	D	660.1
Dearborn Heights	46	D	D	D	75	257	20.1	8.3	24	172	34.3	8.4
Detroit	266	1,293	212.4	45.8	682	15,164	3,821.7	1,259.7	382	17,613	19,668.1	1,008.9
East Lansing	54	D	D	D	129	D	D	D	5	D	D	0.7
Eastpointe	13	49	6.9	1.7	31	D	D	D	14	137	17.6	4.3
Farmington Hills	168	3,544	490.9	133.8	734	D	D	D	88	1,849	495.7	106.3
Flint	67	440	64.4	15.1	134	D	D	D	70	6,444	D	486.1
Garden City	11	D	D	D	20	103	8.8	3.7	18	204	31.2	9.5
Grand Rapids	194	1,027	162.3	43.8	569	D	D	D	293	17,974	7,029.5	968.4
Holland	46	225	51.8	7.0	82	D	D	D	96	7,866	2,614.0	331.6
Inkster	13	D	D	D	11	D	D	D	14	185	37.6	9.1
Jackson	31	150	23.1	4.0	91	D	D	D	92	2,477	709.6	122.5
Kalamazoo	82	669	66.4	17.7	200	D	D	D	107	3,950	1,417.5	215.2
Kentwood	48	254	101.3	10.2	124	1,622	303.9	103.1	122	9,987	2,414.6	441.7
Lansing	94	511	84.1	20.5	240	D	D	D	90	4,856	3,904.7	289.1
Lincoln Park	11	D	D	D	26	237	17.0	6.5	15	178	D	6.3
Livonia	105	607	124.1	21.4	376	D	D	D	251	9,447	3,667.7	504.5
Madison Heights	41	489	100.2	28.3	109	2,800	341.5	147.8	156	3,674	881.6	195.9
Midland	52	242	34.2	8.1	112	D	D	D	47	5,897	3,495.9	454.0
Mount Pleasant	32	980	57.2	24.5	67	D	D	D	24	434	D	18.6
Muskegon	18	121	14.3	2.7	79	D	D	D	63	3,241	931.9	148.9
Novi	81	388	98.6	16.0	314	4,877	715.8	271.8	73	1,726	450.0	99.4

1. Establishments subject to federal tax.

Table D. Cities — Accommodation and Food Services, Arts, Entertainment, and Recreation, and Health Care and Social Assistance

City	Accommodation and food services, 2012				Arts, entertainment, and recreation,[1] 2012				Health care and social assistance,[1] 2012			
	Number of establishments	Number of employees	Receipts (mil dol)	Annual payroll (mil dol)	Number of establishments	Number of employees	Receipts (mil dol)	Annual payroll (mil dol)	Number of establishments	Number of employees	Receipts (mil dol)	Annual payroll (mil dol)
	92	93	94	95	96	97	98	99	100	101	102	103
MASSACHUSETTS— Cont'd												
Beverly	115	D	D	D	20	D	D	D	128	D	D	D
Boston	2,276	52,474	4,409.2	1,271.2	215	D	D	D	935	18,605	3,118.9	1,413.4
Braintree Town	124	2,474	142.7	42.4	18	D	D	D	86	2,494	250.8	104.6
Brockton	153	2,206	123.9	36.4	10	166	6.5	1.8	193	5,657	650.7	302.7
Cambridge	466	9,912	784.2	227.4	46	771	164.9	19.5	226	3,649	628.1	254.3
Chelsea	71	746	46.9	11.9	2	D	D	D	35	629	48.9	22.2
Chicopee	115	1,553	79.4	22.2	5	55	4.4	1.1	45	1,055	113.9	43.4
Everett	91	D	D	D	5	109	5.6	1.7	38	D	D	D
Fall River	182	D	D	D	12	120	7.1	1.8	196	5,222	598.4	259.4
Fitchburg	83	1,145	56.0	14.9	3	D	D	D	68	1,217	113.4	45.8
Franklin Town	68	1,532	90.2	24.5	14	D	D	D	54	779	75.9	31.3
Gloucester	117	1,078	72.4	21.0	13	93	12.1	4.1	60	687	65.7	29.6
Haverhill	131	1,829	100.6	28.9	23	551	30.4	10.5	103	2,729	284.2	119.1
Holyoke	92	1,516	77.7	21.2	11	154	5.0	2.0	77	1,518	115.5	58.1
Lawrence	119	D	D	D	4	83	1.9	0.7	82	1,243	149.0	68.2
Leominster	107	2,048	93.9	28.3	16	D	D	D	91	1,667	171.2	69.6
Lowell	218	D	D	D	14	128	8.9	2.5	133	3,122	284.3	143.1
Lynn	140	D	D	D	16	74	3.8	1.2	99	2,137	142.9	73.1
Malden	95	1,129	65.6	19.1	5	D	D	D	81	3,105	759.8	393.0
Marlborough	133	2,397	139.9	39.1	17	374	22.9	6.0	77	1,549	133.4	57.5
Medford	102	1,323	95.0	24.2	12	D	D	D	94	1,788	210.8	94.1
Melrose	40	467	25.4	6.4	6	34	2.2	0.8	74	D	D	D
Methuen Town	104	1,800	96.9	27.4	11	234	10.6	3.6	92	2,434	285.6	124.6
New Bedford	216	D	D	D	17	196	10.9	3.1	137	2,981	245.8	115.8
Newton	191	4,920	381.6	109.6	47	703	86.8	41.7	354	5,904	636.5	291.6
Northampton	105	1,982	92.3	30.0	18	244	11.3	3.2	116	1,464	160.8	76.5
Peabody	141	2,605	154.7	46.5	7	20	2.1	0.4	107	2,241	326.5	148.1
Pittsfield	141	1,849	90.2	26.8	19	236	14.2	3.4	143	1,881	179.7	82.1
Quincy	241	3,168	205.7	55.1	25	252	23.6	6.8	216	5,889	618.3	243.1
Revere	96	1,142	79.0	17.9	8	D	D	D	45	D	D	D
Salem	132	1,707	116.4	31.4	18	D	D	D	101	D	D	D
Somerville	195	2,436	167.1	49.0	16	122	9.6	2.4	83	1,859	219.9	94.5
Springfield	268	4,663	236.2	65.1	15	126	10.0	2.6	301	7,082	910.0	482.5
Taunton	111	D	D	D	6	D	D	D	93	1,312	137.9	60.8
Waltham	304	3,249	244.9	68.9	23	496	33.8	7.2	135	1,854	207.3	102.0
Watertown Town	84	996	61.7	16.6	17	D	D	D	69	764	93.8	34.9
Westfield	78	1,356	61.7	18.4	9	95	3.6	1.1	67	758	74.6	33.8
West Springfield Town	105	2,119	109.8	31.3	9	D	D	D	68	1,694	109.4	58.5
Weymouth Town	102	1,520	73.7	19.1	12	D	D	D	135	D	D	D
Woburn	102	2,048	148.1	39.2	24	346	15.8	4.5	119	3,488	393.7	153.8
Worcester	441	6,201	342.0	95.4	26	420	21.3	7.0	395	12,907	1,671.6	839.6
MICHIGAN	19,491	347,337	17,962.4	4,871.7	2,706	32,268	2,881.5	1,119.9	21,447	270,655	27,434.6	11,943.9
Allen Park	68	1,258	61.4	18.3	8	D	D	D	72	752	78.4	32.4
Ann Arbor	381	8,311	467.1	131.5	37	156	10.6	3.3	307	D	D	D
Battle Creek	140	D	D	D	12	128	4.6	1.3	147	1,939	187.9	82.0
Bay City	102	1,744	59.5	19.7	15	D	D	D	104	1,410	154.2	66.0
Burton	56	1,191	53.5	14.3	8	D	D	D	83	D	D	D
Dearborn	257	4,444	236.5	67.6	18	D	D	D	368	3,186	479.1	179.2
Dearborn Heights	97	1,408	65.6	17.2	5	79	5.2	1.6	94	D	D	D
Detroit	933	20,452	2,237.3	495.8	49	2,577	500.3	295.9	668	21,711	2,848.7	1,101.4
East Lansing	121	2,411	100.0	26.3	5	28	0.9	0.3	109	2,481	410.1	139.5
Eastpointe	47	704	33.1	9.1	5	D	D	D	81	D	D	D
Farmington Hills	175	2,826	137.7	40.1	25	480	16.2	6.2	395	5,861	509.0	236.8
Flint	179	2,260	102.2	25.3	5	D	D	D	148	2,244	254.3	97.4
Garden City	46	740	28.2	7.6	2	D	D	D	73	D	D	D
Grand Rapids	408	8,881	448.6	130.1	56	1,134	38.9	11.2	393	7,651	938.5	470.8
Holland	79	1,893	78.4	24.5	5	178	5.2	1.8	106	1,892	160.2	79.9
Inkster	22	187	13.4	3.1	NA	NA	NA	NA	16	63	4.7	1.5
Jackson	96	1,480	65.6	17.9	9	D	D	D	134	1,613	206.7	111.5
Kalamazoo	210	4,849	194.0	61.6	27	397	17.4	6.2	168	2,775	310.1	160.3
Kentwood	106	2,408	117.2	32.5	16	D	D	D	99	2,708	326.4	158.6
Lansing	233	4,028	181.5	50.1	24	449	82.3	10.9	213	2,226	253.4	123.9
Lincoln Park	67	895	45.1	10.9	4	16	0.8	0.2	45	D	D	D
Livonia	259	5,903	276.8	81.4	23	D	D	D	448	4,931	510.1	217.3
Madison Heights	101	1,743	87.2	23.8	13	116	6.0	1.8	93	1,696	141.7	72.2
Midland	111	2,562	122.9	37.3	14	305	14.1	4.9	166	D	D	D
Mount Pleasant	73	D	D	D	4	D	D	D	103	D	D	D
Muskegon	72	1,276	57.1	16.1	9	201	10.7	3.5	91	D	D	D
Novi	161	3,802	205.2	60.5	20	D	D	D	227	2,509	311.6	114.5

1. Establishments subject to federal tax.

Table D. Cities — Other Services and Government Employment and Payroll

City	Other services[1]				Government employment and payroll, 2012								
					Full-time		March payroll						
							Percent of total for:						
	Number of establish-ments	Number of employees	Receipts (mil dol)	Annual payroll (mil dol)	Full-time equivalent employees	Total (dollars)	Admin-istrative, judicial, and legal	Police and corrections	Fire protection	Highways and trans-portation	Health and welfare	Natural resources and utilities	Education and libraries
	104	105	106	107	108	109	110	111	112	113	114	115	116

City	104	105	106	107	108	109	110	111	112	113	114	115	116
MASSACHUSETTS— Cont'd													
Beverly	63	329	28.7	8.5	996	4,817,626	4.0	11.2	9.0	4.5	1.8	2.6	66.3
Boston	1,253	9,009	772.9	242.2	19,230	112,444,857	3.5	18.3	12.2	2.2	8.9	3.5	49.1
Braintree Town	91	1,006	75.5	22.8	1,198	6,476,545	2.5	10.2	9.4	2.2	1.8	15.8	58.0
Brockton	146	1,021	74.7	25.7	3,168	15,359,504	2.3	8.6	7.5	1.3	0.8	2.7	75.2
Cambridge	153	1,154	107.3	39.0	5,751	29,806,492	5.4	9.0	6.6	1.8	37.9	3.3	26.6
Chelsea	36	251	36.9	7.1	1,195	6,010,338	2.8	12.8	10.5	1.7	2.0	0.7	68.2
Chicopee	72	406	28.9	9.7	1,968	9,607,115	2.4	8.9	8.8	2.2	1.0	8.2	68.6
Everett	74	439	37.2	11.3	1,148	6,059,197	2.8	14.5	12.3	1.2	2.1	1.4	63.1
Fall River	150	728	56.9	17.6	2,306	10,353,050	2.4	15.4	12.8	3.5	0.6	2.2	61.8
Fitchburg	50	241	23.4	6.3	1,151	5,547,200	3.4	9.4	7.3	2.6	1.4	5.1	70.3
Franklin Town	58	546	44.2	13.5	966	4,884,796	3.9	7.4	6.9	0.9	1.2	3.4	75.4
Gloucester	53	223	18.9	5.7	1,097	5,414,614	3.5	6.3	6.5	1.4	2.1	2.0	78.1
Haverhill	84	417	36.6	12.5	1,832	8,913,896	3.7	7.9	7.8	2.3	3.5	5.7	67.6
Holyoke	46	229	15.1	4.7	1,884	8,334,885	2.7	13.7	8.2	1.9	1.5	16.1	55.4
Lawrence	88	567	48.9	15.2	537	3,239,260	9.3	38.4	19.3	2.8	4.3	18.5	2.0
Leominster	67	278	23.7	6.4	1,158	5,702,455	3.5	8.2	8.6	2.7	4.5	1.1	71.5
Lowell	142	671	60.4	19.1	2,860	17,379,993	21.6	7.8	6.2	1.2	1.9	2.6	57.2
Lynn	98	492	40.5	12.2	3,200	15,232,790	2.0	9.3	9.0	0.6	2.4	2.0	71.9
Malden	96	609	50.6	17.0	1,385	7,796,658	4.0	11.7	8.4	1.5	2.2	1.1	67.0
Marlborough	68	703	100.0	29.9	1,155	5,341,768	2.6	10.8	7.8	2.2	2.8	3.2	68.1
Medford	110	657	57.4	19.1	1,214	5,909,654	4.2	14.6	12.9	2.3	1.5	3.3	61.4
Melrose	42	212	18.3	6.1	763	3,328,642	4.7	9.6	9.5	2.3	3.8	3.1	64.8
Methuen Town	57	326	24.1	8.9	1,087	7,336,774	2.5	10.2	7.0	2.2	1.2	5.3	71.1
New Bedford	137	787	79.6	21.8	2,769	11,838,508	3.4	15.9	8.7	0.5	2.2	2.3	64.5
Newton	178	1,202	106.0	36.3	2,832	16,441,085	4.0	8.3	7.3	3.8	2.0	4.3	68.5
Northampton	60	325	25.5	8.5	1,315	6,640,659	6.9	16.3	15.0	3.3	4.8	8.4	45.1
Peabody	116	626	68.0	15.6	1,445	6,993,068	3.9	10.1	8.5	2.0	3.4	9.6	59.9
Pittsfield	73	363	30.8	10.9	1,418	6,191,800	2.1	11.1	7.7	3.1	2.0	2.3	70.3
Quincy	182	1,019	102.2	29.6	2,107	11,341,562	3.7	14.1	12.3	2.7	1.9	3.4	58.4
Revere	76	312	30.3	7.5	1,148	6,190,389	2.9	10.4	9.9	1.4	2.2	0.9	70.9
Salem	92	548	44.5	13.3	1,293	5,566,047	3.8	10.4	7.7	2.3	1.1	2.1	70.6
Somerville	109	1,376	119.9	44.1	1,637	10,044,072	4.6	10.5	15.6	1.3	3.6	1.4	56.7
Springfield	183	1,829	123.1	43.5	6,400	28,244,315	2.7	10.9	5.2	0.8	1.6	1.8	75.7
Taunton	80	381	28.6	8.7	1,574	7,371,663	2.8	12.1	9.6	1.1	6.5	4.4	62.0
Waltham	135	747	59.8	21.5	1,543	7,799,064	4.9	13.2	11.2	3.6	1.6	2.7	59.4
Watertown Town	77	1,305	112.4	47.4	718	3,483,060	6.4	20.3	14.0	1.6	1.6	4.8	50.1
Westfield	57	288	29.1	10.3	1,493	7,020,504	2.4	7.7	7.1	1.5	0.9	11.5	68.2
West Springfield Town	63	469	44.3	12.1	976	3,909,287	3.2	12.1	9.7	5.8	0.8	0.5	65.8
Weymouth Town	110	532	44.7	13.4	1,151	5,346,322	0.0	0.0	0.0	0.0	0.0	0.0	100.0
Woburn	102	D	D	D	1,052	4,899,436	3.8	10.6	8.5	4.3	1.8	2.5	67.9
Worcester	254	1,668	157.3	46.3	5,736	34,255,682	3.1	10.9	7.3	1.4	1.6	2.9	72.6
MICHIGAN	13,062	75,714	6,509.2	1,982.4	X	X	X	X	X	X	X	X	X
Allen Park	43	278	19.6	4.6	145	695,062	17.1	36.5	23.7	3.5	2.1	12.0	1.1
Ann Arbor	148	945	71.1	25.5	1,014	4,848,561	15.1	39.8	10.1	6.4	0.3	20.8	0.0
Battle Creek	75	D	D	D	520	2,297,856	15.9	27.9	16.4	20.0	2.1	17.3	0.0
Bay City	61	390	30.3	10.7	307	1,423,139	12.6	19.6	15.4	7.2	3.8	41.4	0.0
Burton	55	260	23.3	7.6	88	380,820	19.8	42.5	6.3	13.2	3.7	10.2	0.0
Dearborn	192	864	64.3	17.4	923	3,654,827	12.9	29.4	13.1	4.0	5.7	11.8	4.5
Dearborn Heights	83	282	25.1	6.7	306	1,426,569	13.6	40.6	19.1	3.5	0.6	11.8	3.5
Detroit	609	3,355	261.9	82.4	12,364	57,433,160	8.6	36.8	19.2	8.8	3.7	16.3	1.7
East Lansing	25	167	11.3	3.3	396	1,817,436	16.7	32.0	14.5	2.5	2.2	20.9	4.6
Eastpointe	54	259	22.1	6.3	180	830,736	14.8	39.6	19.5	6.0	0.0	11.0	3.5
Farmington Hills	155	1,573	97.8	33.6	445	2,178,404	16.2	39.5	19.9	10.2	0.0	13.4	0.0
Flint	105	665	52.6	13.9	3,484	16,192,746	3.4	5.1	4.1	1.1	80.7	4.6	0.0
Garden City	51	249	19.2	5.3	125	1,093,459	18.2	37.0	20.6	11.9	0.0	10.8	1.6
Grand Rapids	229	1,640	123.7	40.7	1,502	7,515,829	14.9	31.3	17.1	6.5	4.9	18.7	5.4
Holland	60	528	48.1	16.3	501	2,186,069	19.7	18.0	6.4	11.0	2.5	31.8	8.0
Inkster	15	74	2.7	1.8	210	862,765	16.2	39.6	11.9	3.5	10.7	10.1	0.0
Jackson	55	448	37.4	11.5	317	1,468,468	14.1	26.2	16.9	10.7	9.1	20.9	0.0
Kalamazoo	135	1,028	100.7	33.6	737	3,816,582	9.9	48.7	0.0	14.8	4.0	21.7	0.0
Kentwood	68	759	66.8	26.7	223	1,105,109	17.7	43.8	20.2	4.1	0.4	7.1	0.0
Lansing	145	D	D	D	1,615	8,042,053	9.4	18.0	12.0	4.6	2.5	31.5	0.0
Lincoln Park	60	339	32.7	10.6	136	745,448	11.3	45.2	24.4	3.7	3.5	7.7	0.1
Livonia	212	1,646	201.4	50.7	675	3,250,072	15.0	29.9	18.3	6.5	2.1	12.7	4.9
Madison Heights	86	577	55.1	18.3	168	954,270	18.4	39.5	19.8	4.4	6.9	6.2	3.1
Midland	83	593	47.7	13.7	384	1,817,246	18.5	13.7	13.1	13.3	3.3	24.4	7.5
Mount Pleasant	43	302	15.7	4.7	138	584,882	17.9	28.1	11.5	10.7	3.3	20.6	0.0
Muskegon	43	230	20.5	5.8	249	1,066,412	10.8	37.4	17.3	11.3	4.4	11.2	0.0
Novi	95	941	74.1	26.9	303	1,465,600	14.7	34.8	16.3	10.0	0.9	6.5	8.2

1. Establishments subject to federal tax.

Table D. Cities — City Government Finances

City	City government finances, 2012									
	General revenue							General expenditure		
		Intergovernmental		Taxes					Per capita[1] (dollars)	
					Per capita[1] (dollars)					
	Total (mil dol)	Total (mil dol)	Percent from state government	Total (mil dol)	Total	Property	Sales and gross receipts	Total (mil dol)	Total	Capital outlays
	117	118	119	120	121	122	123	124	125	126
MASSACHUSETTS— Cont'd										
Beverly	134.3	32.2	93.2	84.0	2,083	2,032	50	122.1	3,027	262
Boston	3,134.7	946.2	90.8	1,822.2	2,844	2,612	231	3,160.4	4,932	468
Braintree Town	122.1	30.7	98.2	76.9	2,110	2,032	78	126.4	3,467	261
Brockton	341.1	188.9	94.9	118.0	1,255	1,218	36	341.2	3,628	290
Cambridge	1,412.6	295.2	74.5	338.8	3,195	2,843	352	1,310.4	12,357	887
Chelsea	149.1	80.2	94.0	48.9	1,320	1,254	66	146.8	3,958	166
Chicopee	183.1	93.0	88.2	72.3	1,298	1,255	43	183.1	3,289	279
Everett	159.8	65.9	97.2	88.8	2,084	2,072	12	163.2	3,832	25
Fall River	291.2	173.4	87.5	84.8	956	911	46	273.3	3,082	273
Fitchburg	133.3	69.5	95.2	44.8	1,108	1,068	40	123.9	3,067	250
Franklin Town	113.1	39.1	99.7	62.6	1,932	1,864	68	108.1	3,337	214
Gloucester	108.7	22.2	85.3	70.1	2,398	2,265	133	118.1	4,041	621
Haverhill	179.2	72.3	95.2	91.2	1,477	1,436	41	178.9	2,897	125
Holyoke	180.1	108.6	96.0	51.5	1,283	1,249	34	193.1	4,810	387
Lawrence	293.4	219.3	93.9	57.3	741	711	30	270.5	3,497	39
Leominster	137.6	72.2	98.2	57.3	1,401	1,379	22	130.9	3,200	778
Lowell	379.7	222.6	91.4	119.6	1,102	1,055	47	358.5	3,303	268
Lynn	304.3	187.6	95.4	107.6	1,179	1,155	24	313.0	3,429	13
Malden	196.5	94.6	92.6	74.5	1,234	1,215	19	199.3	3,301	386
Marlborough	132.1	30.2	96.1	91.0	2,319	2,265	54	126.8	3,229	96
Medford	142.6	31.8	91.0	94.1	1,650	1,604	46	142.2	2,492	58
Melrose	82.1	18.2	97.0	52.8	1,924	1,914	10	86.2	3,141	285
Methuen Town	133.7	50.8	97.6	70.6	1,469	1,434	35	135.9	2,829	221
New Bedford	342.6	197.7	87.3	103.4	1,091	1,041	50	319.6	3,371	394
Newton	352.9	45.9	82.2	268.4	3,076	2,977	99	348.0	3,989	200
Northampton	93.2	21.7	85.3	47.2	1,647	1,575	72	100.6	3,506	673
Peabody	155.1	38.9	89.5	98.2	1,894	1,799	95	155.3	2,995	158
Pittsfield	156.1	75.8	92.6	70.5	1,592	1,549	43	180.6	4,076	509
Quincy	303.7	68.6	83.6	184.2	1,983	1,919	64	317.7	3,420	279
Revere	167.2	86.7	75.9	74.7	1,396	1,343	53	159.6	2,981	128
Salem	150.4	51.6	89.1	76.8	1,818	1,779	39	149.1	3,528	208
Somerville	214.8	65.2	90.3	115.7	1,489	1,387	102	222.7	2,865	243
Springfield	710.6	501.8	92.6	183.4	1,192	1,136	56	702.0	4,562	459
Taunton	200.1	101.1	96.2	78.0	1,394	1,336	58	198.2	3,540	473
Waltham	215.4	26.2	94.8	161.6	2,606	2,487	119	206.3	3,326	185
Watertown Town	111.0	16.6	95.8	77.8	2,365	2,342	23	108.0	3,282	224
Westfield	141.0	61.2	91.3	63.5	1,541	1,514	27	132.3	3,207	439
West Springfield Town	111.8	41.7	97.5	63.7	2,226	2,135	90	122.2	4,273	802
Weymouth Town	149.6	43.6	97.1	86.4	1,571	1,532	40	133.5	2,426	127
Woburn	134.2	22.5	96.5	94.7	2,436	2,328	108	140.9	3,624	251
Worcester	673.9	351.9	90.1	250.3	1,373	1,328	45	681.7	3,738	461
MICHIGAN	X	X	X	X	X	X	X	X	X	X
Allen Park	38.0	4.5	94.9	19.7	707	622	85	43.2	1,545	192
Ann Arbor	205.6	39.3	54.4	89.8	775	705	70	199.0	1,717	426
Battle Creek	117.1	35.5	38.6	47.3	913	607	16	105.6	2,035	231
Bay City	52.3	16.3	64.9	12.8	371	359	12	52.6	1,522	200
Burton	18.2	5.5	93.6	4.3	148	132	16	18.3	623	116
Dearborn	175.2	29.5	56.1	86.0	888	866	22	163.2	1,685	219
Dearborn Heights	74.1	29.6	29.1	28.0	490	465	25	61.3	1,071	5
Detroit	2,146.1	681.0	63.6	750.8	1,078	381	362	2,248.4	3,227	289
East Lansing	62.4	13.1	74.3	22.1	455	428	27	63.0	1,296	67
Eastpointe	33.6	7.4	68.2	15.1	466	436	30	35.4	1,090	71
Farmington Hills	79.0	13.9	86.1	37.4	463	453	10	81.3	1,007	37
Flint	502.1	117.5	72.0	32.2	321	147	26	538.2	5,357	401
Garden City	29.5	6.1	87.6	10.9	398	370	28	24.0	874	14
Grand Rapids	321.9	89.0	37.4	121.3	637	264	15	325.6	1,709	174
Holland	45.8	12.0	77.2	16.8	504	489	15	51.4	1,542	413
Inkster	43.4	14.9	32.0	13.5	537	526	11	41.5	1,654	64
Jackson	52.5	18.8	34.8	18.5	555	325	11	61.6	1,847	294
Kalamazoo	130.6	43.5	46.0	43.7	580	555	25	121.7	1,617	207
Kentwood	37.6	7.9	86.2	20.9	420	392	28	37.4	753	60
Lansing	199.5	45.8	54.5	68.7	601	343	13	191.2	1,673	175
Lincoln Park	33.8	9.0	78.1	15.8	418	401	17	38.4	1,019	22
Livonia	124.8	25.5	60.0	56.3	586	566	21	115.2	1,199	38
Madison Heights	38.4	6.7	70.4	20.2	674	650	24	43.5	1,448	121
Midland	69.8	10.8	85.7	36.7	874	857	17	61.2	1,460	164
Mount Pleasant	19.8	5.1	79.3	8.1	309	295	14	19.6	748	41
Muskegon	40.9	9.9	74.7	17.3	468	235	33	46.3	1,248	68
Novi	64.1	7.6	98.2	31.7	557	530	26	58.8	1,034	128

1. Based on population estimated as of July 1 of the year shown.

City	Public welfare	Highways	Parking facilities	Education	Health and hospitals	Police protection	Sewerage and sanitation	Parks and recreation	Housing and community development	Interest on debt
	127	128	129	130	131	132	133	134	135	136
MASSACHUSETTS— Cont'd										
Beverly	0.3	3.4	0.0	51.9	0.4	5.3	7.8	1.4	0.2	2.4
Boston	1.5	1.6	0.1	34.9	9.0	10.0	7.1	2.1	3.3	1.8
Braintree Town	0.2	4.6	0.0	56.1	0.2	6.0	1.8	2.0	0.0	0.6
Brockton	0.3	2.4	0.1	69.7	0.2	5.1	4.9	0.4	0.7	2.6
Cambridge	0.1	0.8	0.1	15.3	59.9	2.3	2.5	1.4	0.1	0.8
Chelsea	0.4	1.5	0.0	55.8	0.0	5.6	1.8	0.1	1.3	0.9
Chicopee	0.5	2.5	0.0	55.4	0.2	5.1	10.9	1.4	1.6	1.4
Everett	0.3	4.8	0.3	53.5	0.9	5.4	1.6	0.1	0.5	1.6
Fall River	1.1	2.7	0.1	60.7	1.7	6.0	7.2	0.5	2.1	2.7
Fitchburg	0.4	3.8	0.1	55.3	0.5	5.0	7.7	0.4	1.1	1.6
Franklin Town	0.2	3.8	0.0	62.7	0.2	4.0	5.2	0.4	0.0	1.5
Gloucester	0.3	1.0	0.0	46.4	0.3	4.3	12.1	0.2	0.8	2.6
Haverhill	0.4	2.6	0.0	57.9	0.5	4.9	6.4	0.2	0.8	1.7
Holyoke	3.6	2.3	0.1	57.6	0.3	6.1	4.9	0.6	1.3	0.8
Lawrence	0.2	1.0	0.1	69.2	0.0	4.2	3.9	0.2	0.5	1.9
Leominster	0.3	5.4	0.0	62.2	0.3	4.8	12.4	0.5	0.4	0.5
Lowell	0.3	1.5	0.8	55.4	0.5	6.0	5.9	0.7	2.2	2.0
Lynn	0.3	2.2	0.3	60.6	0.0	5.4	1.5	0.1	1.5	1.0
Malden	0.1	1.8	0.0	51.9	0.3	4.9	1.7	0.4	2.1	1.9
Marlborough	0.1	6.3	0.0	59.3	0.3	5.4	5.3	0.2	0.3	0.9
Medford	0.2	2.1	0.0	42.8	0.3	7.6	4.1	0.4	1.6	0.9
Melrose	0.5	2.1	0.0	46.0	1.6	4.2	1.7	2.4	0.1	2.2
Methuen Town	0.4	4.2	0.0	68.1	0.5	6.5	5.7	0.1	0.7	1.2
New Bedford	1.1	1.1	0.2	57.4	1.0	6.6	5.2	0.4	1.7	2.7
Newton	0.1	2.9	0.0	59.6	0.6	4.5	3.4	1.2	1.0	2.4
Northampton	0.8	3.6	0.4	37.7	1.9	16.0	5.4	0.3	2.0	2.3
Peabody	0.1	2.7	0.0	56.3	0.7	5.9	2.5	1.9	2.2	0.9
Pittsfield	0.3	5.5	0.6	46.8	0.5	4.6	5.2	1.1	1.2	1.6
Quincy	0.5	2.3	0.0	39.4	0.6	6.9	3.3	0.7	2.0	1.2
Revere	0.7	1.0	0.1	51.2	0.2	5.2	7.3	0.3	0.7	1.4
Salem	0.2	3.0	0.5	53.2	0.3	5.4	2.7	1.9	0.9	1.3
Somerville	0.2	2.5	0.0	35.0	0.5	6.5	3.8	0.4	2.1	1.0
Springfield	0.4	1.8	0.0	65.3	0.2	5.5	1.3	1.2	0.9	1.9
Taunton	4.3	2.3	0.0	50.4	0.4	5.5	8.7	0.5	0.9	1.4
Waltham	0.2	3.7	0.1	36.6	0.4	6.4	4.4	0.7	0.6	1.4
Watertown Town	0.1	3.1	0.0	42.6	0.5	6.9	4.0	0.5	0.0	1.3
Westfield	0.5	3.3	0.0	62.6	1.6	4.9	3.8	1.5	0.2	1.7
West Springfield Town	0.5	8.0	0.0	57.3	1.3	5.5	3.0	0.4	0.7	0.9
Weymouth Town	0.4	2.0	0.0	50.6	0.4	6.9	5.0	0.4	0.7	1.5
Woburn	0.3	2.9	0.0	54.1	0.4	6.0	2.5	0.5	0.0	1.5
Worcester	0.0	3.3	0.2	50.4	0.0	6.0	6.2	0.7	1.5	4.3
MICHIGAN	X	X	X	X	X	X	X	X	X	X
Allen Park	0.0	6.4	0.0	0.0	0.0	14.5	38.3	2.2	0.9	7.5
Ann Arbor	0.0	12.0	16.4	0.0	0.0	13.0	19.6	7.4	7.6	4.1
Battle Creek	0.0	15.2	1.0	0.0	0.0	14.4	15.7	5.1	11.4	2.5
Bay City	0.0	12.0	0.0	0.0	0.0	11.7	20.5	1.6	9.1	4.9
Burton	0.0	14.3	0.0	0.0	2.0	21.7	30.0	0.2	0.0	1.5
Dearborn	0.0	11.9	0.7	0.0	0.0	20.4	25.1	8.8	1.7	3.2
Dearborn Heights	0.0	9.4	0.0	0.0	0.0	18.9	29.2	1.7	1.5	3.4
Detroit	0.3	4.1	0.2	2.6	3.2	16.5	19.9	1.5	2.3	14.4
East Lansing	0.0	8.7	6.6	0.0	0.1	13.6	17.4	9.9	5.3	4.2
Eastpointe	0.0	7.5	0.0	0.0	0.0	24.2	26.9	3.0	5.4	0.5
Farmington Hills	0.0	12.0	0.0	0.0	0.0	23.0	18.5	10.0	0.4	1.0
Flint	0.0	2.0	0.0	0.0	71.4	4.3	4.8	0.9	4.2	1.0
Garden City	0.0	11.4	0.0	0.0	0.2	16.2	27.1	1.4	0.6	2.6
Grand Rapids	0.0	8.3	1.9	0.0	0.0	14.7	16.6	1.9	16.1	6.7
Holland	0.2	23.5	0.0	0.0	0.6	14.8	25.5	11.0	1.1	2.2
Inkster	0.0	5.5	0.0	0.0	0.0	15.9	18.5	2.0	23.8	3.0
Jackson	0.0	33.1	0.4	0.0	0.0	12.4	10.4	5.3	12.6	2.4
Kalamazoo	0.0	11.0	0.0	0.0	0.0	27.5	24.5	3.5	2.8	2.5
Kentwood	0.0	17.7	0.0	0.0	0.0	26.5	9.2	5.2	0.1	2.3
Lansing	0.0	9.1	3.2	0.0	0.0	16.0	13.6	7.6	1.0	5.1
Lincoln Park	0.0	8.0	0.0	0.0	0.0	21.1	23.4	1.1	2.1	1.9
Livonia	0.0	11.9	0.0	0.0	0.0	19.1	24.0	8.3	8.3	1.5
Madison Heights	0.0	12.4	0.0	0.0	0.0	20.1	32.9	1.9	4.4	0.4
Midland	0.0	14.5	0.2	0.0	0.0	11.9	18.0	11.9	1.8	1.5
Mount Pleasant	0.0	13.1	1.1	0.0	0.0	24.5	10.3	7.8	4.3	1.3
Muskegon	0.0	13.1	0.0	0.0	0.0	19.8	27.3	2.8	7.1	1.1
Novi	0.0	18.7	0.0	0.0	0.0	19.2	17.0	6.8	0.0	4.0

City Government Finances, City Government Employment, and Climate

City	City government finances, 2012 (cont.)			Climate[2]						
	Debt outstanding		Debt issued during year	Average daily temperature				Annual precipitation (inches)	Heating degree days	Cooling degree days
				Mean		Limits				
	Total (mil dol)	Per capita[1] (dollars)		January	July	January[3]	July[4]			
	137	138	139	140	141	142	143	144	145	146
MASSACHUSETTS— Cont'd										
Beverly	89.1	2,208	0.0	28.8	72.6	20.4	82.1	45.51	5,704	582
Boston	1,572.5	2,454	245.5	29.3	73.9	22.1	82.2	42.53	5,630	777
Braintree Town	145.9	4,001	8.7	NA	NA	NA	NA	NA	NA	NA
Brockton	242.9	2,583	12.5	27.9	72.1	17.8	83.2	48.25	6,008	529
Cambridge	340.3	3,209	55.5	29.3	73.9	22.1	82.2	42.53	5,630	777
Chelsea	35.1	947	2.0	29.3	73.9	22.1	82.2	42.53	5,630	777
Chicopee	51.4	924	11.0	21.5	68.9	10.4	81.7	48.07	7,312	287
Everett	61.8	1,452	1.4	29.3	73.9	22.1	82.2	42.53	5,630	777
Fall River	271.7	3,064	39.8	28.5	74.2	20.0	83.1	50.77	5,734	740
Fitchburg	74.6	1,846	20.7	24.2	71.9	15.2	81.0	49.13	6,576	548
Franklin Town	55.4	1,710	16.4	NA	NA	NA	NA	NA	NA	NA
Gloucester	137.0	4,689	26.4	28.8	72.6	20.4	82.1	45.51	5,704	582
Haverhill	94.2	1,525	3.0	25.3	72.2	15.6	83.5	46.88	6,435	550
Holyoke	104.5	2,604	16.8	21.5	68.9	10.4	81.7	48.07	7,312	287
Lawrence	148.3	1,917	0.0	24.5	71.8	14.5	82.9	44.09	6,539	510
Leominster	58.1	1,421	13.9	24.2	71.9	15.2	81.0	49.13	6,576	548
Lowell	256.6	2,363	32.8	23.6	72.4	14.1	84.5	43.14	6,575	532
Lynn	67.5	740	0.0	29.3	73.9	22.1	82.2	42.53	5,630	777
Malden	106.3	1,761	5.1	29.3	73.9	22.1	82.2	42.53	5,630	777
Marlborough	60.4	1,537	31.1	25.9	73.4	16.2	84.0	45.87	6,060	651
Medford	45.4	795	34.5	29.3	73.9	22.1	82.2	42.53	5,630	777
Melrose	63.4	2,311	5.5	29.3	73.9	22.1	82.2	42.53	5,630	777
Methuen Town	66.0	1,374	0.5	24.5	71.8	14.5	82.9	44.09	6,539	510
New Bedford	257.5	2,716	19.6	28.5	74.2	20.0	83.1	50.77	5,734	740
Newton	217.6	2,495	9.9	25.9	73.4	16.2	84.0	45.87	6,060	651
Northampton	81.7	2,847	20.6	22.3	71.2	11.2	83.2	44.57	6,856	452
Peabody	45.3	874	10.0	28.8	72.6	20.4	82.1	45.51	5,704	582
Pittsfield	87.1	1,966	7.2	19.9	67.6	11.2	77.5	48.71	7,689	222
Quincy	211.7	2,279	14.8	26.0	71.6	18.1	81.2	51.19	6,371	558
Revere	59.8	1,117	0.2	29.3	73.9	22.1	82.2	42.53	5,630	777
Salem	62.2	1,472	6.0	28.8	72.6	20.4	82.1	45.51	5,704	582
Somerville	99.6	1,281	18.7	29.3	73.9	22.1	82.2	42.53	5,630	777
Springfield	260.5	1,693	0.0	25.7	73.7	17.2	84.9	46.16	6,104	759
Taunton	120.6	2,154	0.7	27.4	72.2	17.8	83.0	48.34	6,012	558
Waltham	106.4	1,717	23.1	25.4	71.5	15.7	82.7	46.95	6,370	485
Watertown Town	44.3	1,348	4.0	29.3	73.9	22.1	82.2	42.53	5,630	777
Westfield	98.9	2,398	0.0	21.5	68.9	10.4	81.7	48.07	7,312	287
West Springfield Town	43.5	1,522	0.0	NA	NA	NA	NA	NA	NA	NA
Weymouth Town	91.2	1,657	25.5	NA	NA	NA	NA	NA	NA	NA
Woburn	86.3	2,221	30.5	25.5	71.5	15.7	82.5	48.31	6,401	472
Worcester	657.7	3,607	57.8	23.6	70.1	15.8	79.3	49.05	6,831	371
MICHIGAN	X	X	X	X	X	X	X	X	X	X
Allen Park	85.9	3,076	3.7	24.5	73.5	17.8	83.4	32.89	6,422	736
Ann Arbor	244.9	2,113	25.9	23.4	72.6	16.6	83.0	35.35	6,503	691
Battle Creek	87.6	1,690	0.0	23.1	71.0	15.3	82.5	35.15	6,742	559
Bay City	72.6	2,101	3.7	21.0	71.5	13.8	81.5	31.25	7,106	545
Burton	12.1	411	3.5	21.3	70.6	13.3	82.0	31.61	7,005	555
Dearborn	274.1	2,831	7.6	24.7	73.7	16.1	85.7	33.58	6,224	788
Dearborn Heights	58.1	1,016	3.6	24.7	73.7	16.1	85.7	33.58	6,224	788
Detroit	8,166.1	11,720	1,166.2	24.7	73.7	16.1	85.7	33.58	6,224	788
East Lansing	60.8	1,250	0.0	21.6	70.3	13.9	82.1	31.53	7,098	558
Eastpointe	15.3	472	0.4	25.3	73.6	18.8	83.3	33.97	6,160	757
Farmington Hills	17.7	219	0.0	24.7	73.7	16.1	85.7	33.58	6,224	788
Flint	170.4	1,696	13.5	21.3	70.6	13.3	82.0	31.61	7,005	555
Garden City	50.5	1,842	12.9	24.7	73.7	16.1	85.7	33.58	6,224	788
Grand Rapids	552.9	2,902	23.4	22.4	71.4	15.6	82.3	37.13	6,896	613
Holland	47.8	1,433	12.8	24.4	71.4	17.6	82.5	36.25	6,589	611
Inkster	48.3	1,924	9.7	24.5	73.5	17.8	83.4	32.89	6,422	736
Jackson	42.3	1,268	13.0	22.2	71.3	14.7	82.7	30.67	6,873	570
Kalamazoo	453.2	6,023	117.6	24.3	73.2	17.0	84.2	37.41	6,235	773
Kentwood	20.1	405	0.0	22.4	71.4	15.6	82.3	37.13	6,896	613
Lansing	693.1	6,066	30.4	21.6	70.3	13.9	82.1	31.53	7,098	558
Lincoln Park	16.7	443	0.0	24.5	73.5	17.8	83.4	32.89	6,422	736
Livonia	52.7	549	0.0	24.7	73.7	16.1	85.7	33.58	6,224	788
Madison Heights	14.5	483	0.0	24.7	73.7	16.1	85.7	33.58	6,224	788
Midland	35.9	855	4.6	22.9	72.7	16.2	83.8	30.69	6,645	679
Mount Pleasant	13.0	496	1.5	20.7	70.6	13.5	82.2	31.57	7,329	492
Muskegon	30.6	826	6.5	23.5	69.9	17.1	80.0	32.88	6,943	487
Novi	48.0	844	0.0	22.1	71.0	14.3	81.7	29.28	6,989	550

1. Based on the population estimated as of July 1 of the year shown.   2. Represents normal values based on the 30-year period, 1971±2000.   3. Average daily minimum.   4. Average daily maximum.

Table D. Cities — **Land Area and Population**

STATE Place code	City	Land area[1] (sq. mi)	Total persons 2018	Rank	Per square mile	White	Black or African American	American Indian, Alaskan Native	Asian	Hawaiian Pacific Islander	Some other race	Two or more races (percent)
								Race 2017				
			Population, 2018					Race alone[2] (percent)				
		1	2	3	4	5	6	7	8	9	10	11
	MICHIGAN— Cont'd											
26 59,920	Oak Park	5.2	29,628	1,268	5,697.7	32.3	62.6	0.0	1.0	0.0	0.1	4.0
26 65,440	Pontiac	19.9	59,772	627	3,003.6	45.0	44.3	0.3	0.4	0.0	2.9	7.0
26 65,560	Portage	32.3	49,216	784	1,523.7	85.4	4.9	0.2	6.4	0.0	0.3	2.8
26 65,820	Port Huron	8.1	28,927	1,288	3,571.2	84.6	6.5	0.0	0.9	0.2	1.9	5.8
26 69,035	Rochester Hills	32.8	74,696	474	2,277.3	81.8	3.3	0.2	10.8	0.0	0.6	3.3
26 69,800	Roseville	9.8	47,377	819	4,834.4	71.1	21.6	0.4	2.1	0.1	1.2	3.4
26 70,040	Royal Oak	11.8	59,461	632	5,039.1	91.5	3.0	0.2	2.9	0.0	0.6	1.8
26 70,520	Saginaw	17.1	48,323	799	2,825.9	43.1	47.7	0.7	0.1	0.0	2.2	6.2
26 70,760	St. Clair Shores	11.7	59,409	634	5,077.7	91.4	5.5	0.1	1.4	0.0	0.3	1.4
26 74,900	Southfield	26.3	73,158	490	2,781.7	20.5	71.0	0.0	2.1	0.0	1.3	5.0
26 74,960	Southgate	6.9	29,088	1,285	4,215.7	NA	NA	NA	NA	NA	NA	NA
26 76,460	Sterling Heights	36.4	132,964	209	3,652.9	82.2	6.1	0.3	7.0	0.0	3.0	1.4
26 79,000	Taylor	23.6	61,148	609	2,591.0	74.6	17.4	0.6	1.7	0.0	1.6	3.9
26 80,700	Troy	33.5	84,272	404	2,515.6	68.2	3.7	0.5	25.3	0.0	0.4	1.9
26 84,000	Warren	34.4	134,587	202	3,912.4	67.9	20.7	0.0	9.3	0.1	0.4	1.6
26 86,000	Westland	20.4	81,720	419	4,005.9	72.4	17.7	0.8	4.1	0.0	1.0	4.0
26 88,900	Wyandotte	5.3	24,935	1,414	4,704.7	NA	NA	NA	NA	NA	NA	NA
26 88,940	Wyoming	24.6	75,820	462	3,082.1	74.0	6.0	0.9	2.0	0.2	9.4	7.5
27 00,000	MINNESOTA	79,625.4	5,611,179	X	70.5	82.7	6.5	1.1	4.9	0.0	2.0	2.8
27 01,486	Andover	33.9	33,072	1,153	975.6	89.9	5.3	0.0	2.4	0.0	0.0	2.4
27 01,900	Apple Valley	17.0	54,121	708	3,183.6	74.8	9.5	0.4	9.6	0.0	0.9	5.0
27 06,382	Blaine	32.9	65,212	570	1,982.1	79.5	6.0	1.3	6.4	0.0	4.1	2.7
27 06,616	Bloomington	34.7	85,578	390	2,466.2	75.2	13.2	0.1	4.3	0.0	2.8	4.5
27 07,948	Brooklyn Center	8.0	30,910	1,220	3,863.8	36.7	28.8	0.0	22.8	0.0	8.6	3.0
27 07,966	Brooklyn Park	26.1	80,610	430	3,088.5	46.0	27.7	0.8	19.7	0.0	1.6	4.2
27 08,794	Burnsville	24.8	61,203	608	2,467.9	77.6	10.4	0.2	4.1	0.2	3.2	4.3
27 13,114	Coon Rapids	22.6	62,527	598	2,766.7	85.1	7.2	0.1	4.0	0.0	0.5	3.1
27 13,456	Cottage Grove	33.6	37,208	1,033	1,107.4	82.1	4.4	0.0	11.5	0.0	0.6	1.5
27 17,000	Duluth	71.7	85,884	387	1,197.8	90.2	2.2	1.9	1.3	0.1	0.5	3.9
27 17,288	Eagan	31.2	66,527	552	2,132.3	74.6	11.5	0.0	9.5	0.4	1.4	2.6
27 18,116	Eden Prairie	32.5	64,334	581	1,979.5	82.9	3.5	0.0	9.0	0.0	2.2	2.5
27 18,188	Edina	15.5	52,490	735	3,386.5	89.4	1.8	0.4	5.9	0.0	0.5	2.0
27 22,814	Fridley	10.2	27,742	1,328	2,719.8	58.7	10.8	0.5	11.7	0.4	10.7	7.3
27 31,076	Inver Grove Heights	27.9	35,481	1,085	1,271.7	83.2	5.8	0.2	3.7	0.0	3.9	3.2
27 35,180	Lakeville	36.1	65,877	561	1,824.8	90.1	3.2	0.1	3.0	0.1	1.1	2.3
27 39,878	Mankato	19.1	42,610	893	2,230.9	87.4	5.2	0.0	4.1	0.0	0.3	2.9
27 40,166	Maple Grove	32.6	71,807	501	2,202.7	78.8	10.2	0.3	6.3	0.0	0.9	3.5
27 40,382	Maplewood	17.0	41,004	935	2,412.0	71.8	9.4	1.5	13.7	0.0	0.4	3.1
27 43,000	Minneapolis	54.0	425,403	46	7,877.8	62.8	18.0	1.7	6.4	0.0	6.7	4.3
27 43,252	Minnetonka	26.9	53,953	713	2,005.7	82.1	8.5	0.4	7.0	0.1	0.1	1.8
27 43,864	Moorhead	22.3	43,349	880	1,943.9	89.1	5.6	0.8	1.5	0.0	1.7	1.2
27 47,680	Oakdale	11.0	28,022	1,318	2,547.5	78.5	10.9	0.2	7.2	0.0	0.5	2.8
27 49,300	Owatonna	14.5	25,766	1,398	1,777.0	NA	NA	NA	NA	NA	NA	NA
27 51,730	Plymouth	32.7	79,450	436	2,429.7	81.9	5.2	0.9	9.1	0.0	0.1	2.9
27 54,214	Richfield	6.7	35,990	1,067	5,371.6	61.0	14.8	1.1	6.6	0.0	12.3	4.2
27 54,880	Rochester	55.2	116,961	242	2,118.9	80.1	8.2	0.3	6.5	0.0	0.8	4.2
27 55,852	Roseville	13.0	36,433	1,057	2,802.5	80.9	5.4	0.0	8.5	0.0	0.7	4.5
27 56,896	St. Cloud	40.0	68,043	533	1,701.1	78.5	14.1	0.6	3.0	0.0	0.4	3.3
27 57,220	St. Louis Park	10.6	49,039	787	4,626.3	87.1	6.7	0.2	2.3	0.2	0.5	3.0
27 58,000	St. Paul	52.0	307,695	63	5,917.2	55.8	17.1	0.8	19.9	0.0	2.5	3.9
27 58,738	Savage	15.6	31,694	1,197	2,031.7	70.7	14.5	0.0	11.3	0.0	0.0	3.5
27 59,350	Shakopee	28.1	41,362	924	1,472.0	84.5	4.5	0.6	6.3	0.1	2.2	1.7
27 59,998	Shoreview	10.8	27,210	1,348	2,519.4	NA	NA	NA	NA	NA	NA	NA
27 71,032	Winona	18.9	26,813	1,366	1,418.7	93.0	1.5	0.4	2.4	0.0	0.0	2.8
27 71,428	Woodbury	34.9	71,306	503	2,043.2	80.1	6.3	0.3	10.2	0.0	0.4	2.6
28 00,000	MISSISSIPPI	46,924.4	2,986,530	X	63.6	58.2	38.0	0.5	0.9	0.0	1.0	1.4
28 06,220	Biloxi	43.0	45,968	839	1,069.0	69.2	18.5	0.8	7.3	0.4	0.7	3.2
28 14,420	Clinton	41.8	25,179	1,411	602.4	NA	NA	NA	NA	NA	NA	NA
28 29,180	Greenville	26.9	29,898	1,258	1,111.4	NA	NA	NA	NA	NA	NA	NA
28 29,700	Gulfport	55.6	71,870	499	1,292.6	56.2	40.1	0.8	0.4	0.0	0.8	1.6
28 31,020	Hattiesburg	53.4	45,951	840	860.5	42.7	53.1	0.1	1.2	0.0	0.2	2.8
28 33,700	Horn Lake	16.0	27,127	1,352	1,695.4	41.3	51.3	0.1	0.3	0.0	5.3	1.7
28 36,000	Jackson	111.1	164,422	158	1,479.9	14.3	84.5	0.0	0.5	0.0	0.1	0.6
28 46,640	Meridian	53.7	37,325	1,026	695.1	NA	NA	NA	NA	NA	NA	NA
28 54,040	Olive Branch	37.2	38,149	1,010	1,025.5	NA	NA	NA	NA	NA	NA	NA
28 55,760	Pearl	25.5	26,471	1,381	1,038.1	NA	NA	NA	NA	NA	NA	NA
28 69,280	Southaven	41.3	54,944	695	1,330.4	70.9	21.4	0.0	2.9	0.0	2.2	2.6
28 74,840	Tupelo	64.4	38,206	1,007	593.3	60.2	36.9	0.0	2.0	0.0	0.2	0.8

1. Dry land or land partially or temporarily covered by water.   2. Hispanic or Latino persons may be of any race.

Table D. Cities — **Population**

City	Percent Hispanic or Latino[1], 2017	Percent foreign born, 2017	Under 18 years	18 to 24 years	25 to 34 years	35 to 44 years	45 to 54 years	55 to 64 years	65 years and over	Median age, 2017	Percent female, 2017	Census counts 2000	Census counts 2010	Percent change 2000-2010	Percent change 2001-2018
	12	13	14	15	16	17	18	19	20	21	22	23	24	25	26
MICHIGAN— Cont'd															
Oak Park	1.1	7.2	25.8	11.0	14.0	15.3	10.2	10.1	13.6	34.4	55.0	29,793	29,408	-1.3	0.7
Pontiac	22.6	11.3	26.6	12.3	14.3	12.6	12.7	11.9	9.5	32.3	52.0	66,337	59,631	-10.1	0.2
Portage	3.4	9.9	22.9	10.8	9.9	15.7	11.1	13.0	16.8	39.7	51.2	44,897	46,307	3.1	6.3
Port Huron	9.1	3.3	22.2	13.0	14.5	9.9	12.8	13.2	14.4	35.6	51.2	32,338	30,199	-6.6	-4.2
Rochester Hills	3.2	17.9	22.4	5.7	12.4	12.8	13.5	15.0	18.3	42.8	51.6	68,825	70,985	3.1	5.2
Roseville	2.2	3.2	22.8	8.8	14.9	11.2	14.2	14.1	14.0	37.8	50.8	48,129	47,338	-1.6	0.1
Royal Oak	3.9	7.5	18.1	5.7	22.7	14.4	10.6	12.3	16.2	36.8	49.9	60,062	57,231	-4.7	3.9
Saginaw	14.7	0.8	26.0	9.8	16.6	11.2	11.9	12.1	12.4	33.3	48.6	61,799	51,483	-16.7	-6.1
St. Clair Shores	3.1	4.6	18.1	7.0	12.4	11.4	11.7	16.9	22.5	45.8	52.2	63,096	59,765	-5.3	-0.6
Southfield	2.7	8.0	18.7	9.4	14.4	10.4	13.1	14.6	19.4	42.9	54.4	78,296	71,717	-8.4	2.0
Southgate	9.9	7.6	17.6	8.6	17.2	7.6	12.6	17.8	18.5	44.5	51.9	30,136	30,047	-0.3	-3.2
Sterling Heights	5.7	30.0	20.0	9.6	15.0	12.2	14.5	11.8	16.9	39.6	50.9	124,471	129,675	4.2	2.5
Taylor	6.0	4.5	24.5	9.1	14.4	10.3	14.3	13.6	13.9	37.3	52.4	65,868	63,131	-4.2	-3.1
Troy	2.4	31.0	21.5	8.3	12.5	13.5	15.4	12.9	15.9	40.7	50.6	80,959	80,972	0.0	4.1
Warren	2.0	15.1	21.5	8.1	15.6	10.6	14.0	14.1	16.1	39.6	50.2	138,247	134,056	-3.0	0.4
Westland	4.5	9.7	19.0	7.0	15.4	11.9	14.0	15.0	17.7	41.7	53.4	86,602	84,153	-2.8	-2.9
Wyandotte	4.1	2.2	18.5	5.2	16.7	14.5	10.7	16.5	17.8	41.7	48.8	28,006	25,883	-7.6	-3.7
Wyoming	21.1	10.8	24.5	6.3	17.2	12.5	13.1	13.9	12.6	36.4	50.7	69,368	72,117	4.0	5.1
MINNESOTA	5.3	8.7	23.3	9.0	13.6	12.6	12.7	13.5	15.4	37.9	50.1	4,919,479	5,303,925	7.8	5.8
Andover	2.7	3.5	25.7	10.3	8.7	12.2	21.3	11.7	10.3	40.4	51.8	26,588	30,588	15.0	8.1
Apple Valley	4.0	14.4	24.6	8.7	11.2	13.1	14.8	12.2	15.4	38.6	49.7	45,527	49,092	7.8	10.2
Blaine	5.2	9.5	24.3	7.1	12.3	16.7	12.7	14.7	12.3	38.8	49.5	44,942	57,179	27.2	14.0
Bloomington	7.4	13.5	18.4	6.9	14.1	10.0	13.6	15.8	21.1	45.6	51.4	85,172	82,893	-2.7	3.2
Brooklyn Center	12.9	26.4	30.7	8.8	17.5	14.3	9.0	9.5	10.3	31.2	48.8	29,172	30,169	3.4	2.5
Brooklyn Park	4.4	24.8	27.3	5.7	14.3	15.0	11.5	13.2	13.0	37.0	51.6	67,388	75,776	12.4	6.4
Burnsville	10.9	15.6	22.7	9.2	12.2	16.2	12.1	11.9	15.5	38.0	52.7	60,220	60,286	0.1	1.5
Coon Rapids	2.5	10.0	22.5	7.5	16.2	12.8	11.2	14.7	15.0	38.1	51.3	61,607	61,485	-0.2	1.7
Cottage Grove	5.7	8.4	30.4	6.7	12.9	17.1	14.6	10.0	8.4	35.0	48.6	30,582	34,591	13.1	7.6
Duluth	2.7	4.4	18.2	20.6	12.5	10.4	10.6	12.5	15.3	34.0	51.7	86,918	86,266	-0.8	-0.4
Eagan	3.9	15.3	23.8	6.1	17.1	13.8	12.8	14.3	12.2	37.2	52.1	63,557	64,150	0.9	3.7
Eden Prairie	3.2	13.1	22.2	5.5	11.4	15.3	15.2	16.8	13.6	42.0	51.0	54,901	60,797	10.7	5.8
Edina	2.2	9.4	24.5	4.7	8.2	11.7	16.9	11.7	22.2	45.4	51.1	47,425	47,980	1.2	9.4
Fridley	15.5	24.3	21.4	12.2	14.3	13.8	11.9	13.0	13.4	36.4	48.5	27,449	27,222	-0.8	1.9
Inver Grove Heights	10.7	8.4	19.4	8.1	14.7	11.8	14.7	14.5	16.8	40.9	50.1	29,751	33,986	14.2	4.4
Lakeville	4.9	8.3	31.2	5.5	12.3	13.5	14.5	14.4	8.7	35.8	50.0	43,128	55,999	29.8	17.6
Mankato	3.7	7.3	17.3	32.1	14.1	8.9	7.5	9.1	11.0	25.3	49.1	32,427	39,856	22.9	6.9
Maple Grove	1.5	10.8	27.8	4.5	12.3	15.8	15.1	12.2	12.2	37.9	51.4	50,365	61,548	22.2	16.7
Maplewood	7.4	14.7	22.1	7.8	16.3	14.1	10.2	13.5	16.1	37.4	50.7	34,947	38,013	8.8	7.9
Minneapolis	11.0	16.5	19.9	13.1	22.1	13.7	11.1	10.0	10.0	32.4	49.9	382,618	382,603	0.0	11.2
Minnetonka	2.2	12.9	20.1	5.1	18.3	10.6	11.0	16.3	18.7	41.3	51.7	51,301	49,737	-3.0	8.5
Moorhead	5.1	7.3	23.7	16.0	15.8	13.7	8.9	8.8	13.3	30.7	48.8	32,177	39,439	22.6	9.9
Oakdale	5.2	8.1	17.1	8.5	17.4	8.2	11.7	18.6	18.5	43.6	54.8	26,653	27,364	2.7	2.4
Owatonna	8.3	5.4	24.3	7.9	10.6	10.9	14.6	14.0	17.7	41.7	50.5	22,434	25,619	14.2	0.6
Plymouth	5.3	12.1	23.8	6.6	11.6	14.5	13.0	16.1	14.4	40.0	53.9	65,894	70,589	7.1	12.6
Richfield	18.5	17.6	19.4	6.8	22.3	12.5	12.7	12.4	13.9	35.6	46.8	34,439	35,094	1.9	2.6
Rochester	5.6	14.5	24.1	8.3	15.9	13.9	11.5	11.6	14.8	35.9	52.2	85,806	106,801	24.5	9.5
Roseville	2.7	10.9	17.1	10.4	13.3	12.3	10.1	14.0	22.9	41.7	53.2	33,690	33,661	-0.1	8.2
St. Cloud	3.0	13.2	21.0	19.7	14.7	10.6	9.3	12.3	12.4	30.7	49.7	59,107	65,926	11.5	3.2
St. Louis Park	2.5	7.5	16.6	7.5	24.0	13.0	12.5	12.9	13.5	36.4	47.9	44,126	45,206	2.4	8.5
St. Paul	9.8	20.9	25.7	11.9	18.1	13.3	10.4	10.3	10.2	31.4	50.7	287,151	285,067	-0.7	7.9
Savage	1.1	16.9	29.5	7.7	10.7	14.4	15.3	14.4	8.0	36.9	48.8	21,115	26,912	27.5	17.8
Shakopee	6.5	12.2	25.9	10.2	15.2	17.9	14.3	8.9	7.7	34.1	48.4	20,568	37,063	80.2	11.6
Shoreview	2.4	11.3	20.0	4.5	10.2	12.7	18.0	16.9	17.7	45.9	51.0	25,924	25,043	-3.4	8.7
Winona	2.4	3.2	12.7	28.4	12.8	8.7	8.1	12.6	16.6	29.9	48.8	27,069	27,601	2.0	-2.9
Woodbury	4.1	12.2	29.0	7.9	10.0	15.4	14.8	10.9	12.1	37.9	51.8	46,463	61,965	33.4	15.1
MISSISSIPPI	2.9	2.2	23.9	10.4	12.2	12.7	12.4	12.8	15.6	37.5	51.5	2,844,658	2,968,118	4.3	0.6
Biloxi	7.5	9.5	21.7	13.8	15.5	12.4	10.2	13.5	12.9	34.4	45.7	50,644	44,249	-12.6	3.9
Clinton	5.5	3.3	26.2	8.8	14.9	9.3	10.0	12.6	18.1	35.0	58.9	23,347	25,215	8.0	-0.1
Greenville	1.2	1.1	25.9	7.2	13.2	10.9	11.4	14.7	16.7	38.3	54.5	41,633	34,403	-17.4	-13.1
Gulfport	5.0	3.7	24.6	9.1	18.5	9.7	13.1	10.4	14.5	33.8	54.1	71,127	67,786	-4.7	6.0
Hattiesburg	3.7	2.7	18.2	22.7	18.3	11.7	8.8	8.4	12.0	28.0	54.3	44,779	45,748	2.2	0.4
Horn Lake	6.3	5.5	30.8	13.7	13.6	16.4	11.3	6.5	7.7	30.1	53.4	14,099	26,068	84.9	4.1
Jackson	1.2	1.2	25.2	11.8	16.1	11.5	11.3	11.8	12.4	33.0	52.9	184,256	173,590	-5.8	-5.3
Meridian	3.7	2.2	22.9	7.2	14.3	12.3	13.8	12.8	16.6	38.3	52.6	39,968	41,137	2.9	-9.3
Olive Branch	4.9	3.1	23.6	7.9	15.4	11.9	14.0	12.1	15.1	37.4	49.7	21,054	33,487	59.1	13.9
Pearl	4.6	2.9	26.9	9.5	15.7	14.2	9.3	10.2	14.2	32.5	52.2	21,961	25,700	17.0	3.0
Southaven	3.7	3.8	24.6	8.2	12.7	17.1	11.7	11.2	14.6	37.7	53.0	28,977	48,979	69.0	12.2
Tupelo	1.6	2.6	27.4	7.5	11.9	13.1	14.5	9.8	15.7	37.4	52.9	34,211	37,680	10.1	1.4

1. May be of any race.

City	Households, 2017							Persons in group quarters, 2017	Serious crimes known to police[2], 2016				Educational attainment, 2017		
			Percent						Total		Rate[3]			Attainment[4] (percent)	
	Number	Persons per household	Family	Married couple family	Female headed[1]	Non-family	One person		Number	Rate	Violent	Property	Population age 25 and over	High school graduate or less	Bachelor's degree or more
	27	28	29	30	31	32	33	34	35	36	37	38	39	40	41
MICHIGAN— Cont'd															
Oak Park	11,233	2.63	57.4	32.3	19.5	42.6	36.8	67	672	2,252	352	1,900	18,721	34.9	31.5
Pontiac	22,367	2.58	53.4	19.5	21.9	46.6	40.9	2,055	NA	NA	NA	NA	36,523	59.7	9.2
Portage	20,758	2.34	60.8	48.9	9.5	39.2	33.7	NA	1,395	2,873	206	2,667	32,410	21.9	45.8
Port Huron	12,228	2.34	55.8	37.0	15.8	44.2	32.4	NA	1,030	3,530	963	2,567	18,830	47.2	17.1
Rochester Hills	29,118	2.50	73.4	63.0	6.6	26.6	22.2	1,292	NA	NA	NA	NA	53,377	18.8	57.5
Roseville	19,878	2.37	62.3	31.8	22.4	37.7	32.6	NA	2,078	4,356	518	3,838	32,482	50.4	11.0
Royal Oak	28,879	2.04	47.1	39.4	5.3	52.9	42.1	265	679	1,144	109	1,034	45,034	22.8	55.9
Saginaw	21,228	2.23	55.0	26.9	20.1	45.0	37.7	1,360	1,645	3,361	1,467	1,894	31,285	57.2	10.6
St. Clair Shores	26,481	2.24	58.7	40.1	12.0	41.3	36.0	374	930	1,552	199	1,353	44,618	36.5	25.2
Southfield	30,093	2.38	54.4	33.9	18.3	45.6	37.9	1,498	2,364	3,219	266	2,954	52,617	27.1	40.8
Southgate	12,723	2.28	59.9	40.5	15.4	40.1	33.4	NA	946	3,244	271	2,973	21,464	44.2	21.2
Sterling Heights	49,939	2.64	71.3	55.4	11.0	28.7	25.5	975	1,744	1,316	174	1,142	93,359	40.9	29.3
Taylor	23,158	2.61	64.6	37.1	20.5	35.4	25.3	718	1,869	3,049	607	2,442	40,730	51.1	14.8
Troy	31,954	2.61	74.0	64.3	5.8	26.0	22.4	338	1,416	1,691	93	1,598	58,792	16.2	64.0
Warren	54,699	2.44	63.5	39.2	17.5	36.5	31.6	1,293	4,227	3,117	516	2,601	94,999	45.8	19.6
Westland	35,914	2.25	56.3	38.7	12.8	43.7	39.7	877	2,015	2,469	370	2,099	60,476	42.7	21.2
Wyandotte	11,589	2.15	55.3	39.6	13.3	44.7	35.5	81	434	1,734	196	1,538	19,052	36.6	22.4
Wyoming	28,330	2.66	66.9	46.9	14.2	33.1	26.1	444	2,111	2,781	464	2,317	52,592	46.3	22.8
MINNESOTA	2,162,211	2.52	64.2	51.2	8.9	35.8	28.4	132,035	131,150	2,376	243	2,133	3,778,416	31.8	36.1
Andover	10,734	3.06	82.0	67.9	8.9	18.0	15.0	NA	NA	NA	NA	NA	21,081	22.6	38.6
Apple Valley	19,481	2.68	72.0	61.5	7.8	28.0	23.9	NA	1,213	2,349	124	2,225	34,933	28.0	41.1
Blaine	23,708	2.72	73.7	61.1	9.7	26.3	22.4	102	1,791	2,838	124	2,714	44,289	35.3	32.0
Bloomington	36,455	2.33	57.6	44.2	10.2	42.4	35.7	1,038	2,987	3,428	203	3,225	64,120	25.4	40.6
Brooklyn Center	9,676	3.18	64.8	36.1	20.1	35.2	28.4	211	1,196	3,871	363	3,509	18,774	44.4	20.6
Brooklyn Park	27,849	2.88	70.5	52.2	13.6	29.5	24.4	274	2,738	3,431	388	3,043	53,998	31.0	33.9
Burnsville	25,055	2.44	65.0	43.4	16.3	35.0	28.4	399	1,778	2,882	203	2,679	41,822	33.1	35.7
Coon Rapids	22,987	2.71	63.4	48.1	11.8	36.6	30.2	408	1,889	3,028	167	2,861	43,869	41.1	25.5
Cottage Grove	11,211	3.27	83.6	72.3	8.0	16.4	14.2	82	585	1,618	47	1,571	23,168	24.1	41.1
Duluth	34,939	2.29	50.1	37.7	8.9	49.9	38.1	6,131	4,139	4,808	362	4,445	52,672	27.7	38.8
Eagan	26,342	2.52	68.6	53.1	12.1	31.4	24.5	324	1,184	1,775	60	1,715	46,675	19.1	52.1
Eden Prairie	26,270	2.44	71.8	58.6	8.8	28.2	23.0	190	765	1,195	56	1,138	46,574	12.0	65.5
Edina	21,689	2.38	65.1	57.9	4.3	34.9	32.7	264	961	1,900	51	1,849	36,768	10.5	70.5
Fridley	10,286	2.69	65.1	46.3	7.5	34.9	29.8	136	1,048	3,768	280	3,488	18,500	53.0	22.8
Inver Grove Heights	15,024	2.34	65.1	49.0	14.3	34.9	30.0	180	879	2,508	240	2,268	25,655	27.1	38.5
Lakeville	20,990	3.03	81.9	68.9	10.9	18.1	14.6	NA	656	1,065	68	997	40,379	20.5	50.0
Mankato	16,468	2.35	49.0	32.6	8.2	51.0	26.2	3,596	1,441	3,489	271	3,218	21,384	25.0	43.0
Maple Grove	26,289	2.70	77.0	67.1	6.8	23.0	17.7	62	1,231	1,764	63	1,701	48,115	17.2	55.2
Maplewood	16,219	2.46	62.2	44.0	12.4	37.8	28.3	1,043	1,854	4,514	248	4,266	28,700	36.6	32.4
Minneapolis	176,416	2.30	43.3	30.8	9.0	56.7	41.0	17,338	22,216	5,331	1,109	4,222	282,898	25.1	50.8
Minnetonka	23,405	2.25	59.2	46.8	9.7	40.8	33.5	441	798	1,533	56	1,477	39,745	17.3	57.5
Moorhead	16,450	2.37	54.8	40.9	11.2	45.2	35.3	3,584	1,040	2,447	160	2,287	25,695	26.5	36.9
Oakdale	11,201	2.49	70.2	48.7	17.7	29.8	23.1	203	896	3,176	160	3,017	20,881	31.7	31.4
Owatonna	10,411	2.39	63.7	54.8	5.1	36.3	31.7	470	650	2,523	148	2,376	17,222	40.9	26.1
Plymouth	31,135	2.49	67.9	55.3	8.5	32.1	26.2	966	1,057	1,373	62	1,310	54,535	16.9	58.5
Richfield	15,784	2.27	55.2	38.0	9.8	44.8	32.8	295	996	2,736	214	2,521	26,669	30.1	43.1
Rochester	46,645	2.43	64.2	50.7	10.1	35.8	27.6	2,255	2,721	2,401	214	2,188	78,270	25.0	47.5
Roseville	16,145	2.16	57.9	46.3	8.4	42.1	35.3	1,474	1,884	5,240	197	5,043	26,341	17.5	57.3
St. Cloud	26,416	2.29	51.3	39.2	9.9	48.7	34.0	5,025	3,073	4,563	435	4,128	38,816	31.6	33.5
St. Louis Park	23,582	2.05	44.6	35.7	5.0	55.4	40.5	694	1,251	2,565	135	2,430	37,201	14.4	60.9
St. Paul	112,467	2.65	56.1	38.6	13.0	43.9	33.7	8,759	11,781	3,876	648	3,228	191,150	34.6	40.1
Savage	10,165	3.08	79.2	65.3	9.7	20.8	14.4	NA	458	1,472	119	1,353	19,690	22.1	48.9
Shakopee	14,196	2.80	67.3	58.7	4.8	32.7	24.3	1,110	861	2,125	165	1,959	26,141	31.5	38.0
Shoreview	11,438	2.32	65.6	55.8	7.2	34.4	28.7	236	NA	NA	NA	NA	20,224	15.4	55.4
Winona	10,497	2.22	44.9	36.8	5.3	55.1	37.1	3,541	850	3,148	170	2,978	15,827	25.4	33.0
Woodbury	24,363	2.85	77.1	64.0	7.3	22.9	18.0	NA	1,385	2,006	67	1,940	44,024	17.5	53.9
MISSISSIPPI	1,091,980	2.65	65.6	44.2	16.4	34.4	30.0	92,944	91,115	3,049	280	2,768	1,959,341	46.0	21.9
Biloxi	16,614	2.58	58.5	43.2	9.7	41.5	31.4	2,967	2,875	6,257	396	5,860	29,608	37.1	24.8
Clinton	9,555	2.58	61.6	41.8	17.7	38.4	34.8	448	NA	NA	NA	NA	16,319	22.9	44.6
Greenville	11,959	2.38	58.6	31.1	20.8	41.4	38.9	462	2,057	6,482	277	6,205	19,336	46.5	21.8
Gulfport	28,157	2.50	66.1	35.5	22.2	33.9	29.9	1,560	4,057	5,583	314	5,269	47,616	41.8	21.1
Hattiesburg	17,622	2.37	47.5	26.5	15.9	52.5	37.8	3,613	2,899	6,167	313	5,855	26,840	31.1	39.5
Horn Lake	8,299	3.26	68.1	34.3	24.1	31.9	25.7	NA	721	2,663	74	2,589	15,058	45.5	14.0
Jackson	61,957	2.57	61.1	28.8	25.2	38.9	33.4	7,865	9,335	5,489	853	4,636	105,376	43.8	25.2
Meridian	16,027	2.28	58.1	36.5	19.4	41.9	37.4	1,333	2,047	5,200	594	4,606	26,512	41.1	24.1
Olive Branch	13,708	2.73	68.3	52.4	10.9	31.7	26.3	NA	999	2,736	183	2,553	25,664	41.0	22.3
Pearl	10,128	2.61	61.2	41.3	13.5	38.8	32.5	NA	NA	NA	NA	NA	16,878	50.5	16.5
Southaven	19,774	2.72	70.2	53.2	10.4	29.8	24.6	NA	1,539	2,887	111	2,776	36,325	37.3	25.0
Tupelo	15,084	2.48	62.1	38.3	19.9	37.9	32.2	712	NA	NA	NA	NA	24,800	32.5	34.5

1. No spouse present. 2. Data for serious crimes have not been adjusted for underreporting. This may affect comparability between geographic areas and over time. 3. Per 100,000 population estimated by the FBI. 4. Persons 25 years old and over.

Table D. Cities — Income and Housing

City	Money income, 2017					Median earnings, 2017			Housing units, 2017				
	Households			Median family income	Median non-family income	All persons	Men	Women	Total	Occupied	Percent owner occupied	Median value[1] (dollars)	Median gross rent (dollars)
	Median income	Percent with income less than $20,000	Percent with income of $200,000 or more										
	42	43	44	45	46	47	48	49	50	51	52	53	54

MICHIGAN— Cont'd													
Oak Park	51,337	14.0	4.1	58,386	40,152	36,074	40,921	35,242	12,215	11,233	61.1	125,700	1,078
Pontiac	34,091	31.4	1.2	41,049	22,005	22,852	26,039	20,331	26,049	22,367	42.3	62,000	773
Portage	60,864	9.8	6.0	90,439	37,648	36,326	46,287	29,624	21,817	20,758	69.4	166,800	793
Port Huron	41,377	23.5	0.8	52,795	26,914	24,797	28,113	20,487	13,188	12,228	52.8	92,400	751
Rochester Hills	93,573	8.3	13.9	110,853	51,485	56,816	73,163	47,846	30,556	29,118	80.8	285,300	1,268
Roseville	45,283	17.8	1.4	53,280	33,418	31,451	36,212	26,948	21,093	19,878	64.1	85,900	996
Royal Oak	79,343	8.8	8.4	102,042	65,850	53,244	69,708	49,228	30,757	28,879	68.1	224,000	1,020
Saginaw	25,796	40.1	0.5	33,916	16,922	21,604	24,510	18,287	23,863	21,228	53.0	37,500	707
St. Clair Shores	59,246	10.5	3.3	69,945	42,128	36,766	49,014	28,483	28,110	26,481	79.8	135,900	931
Southfield	58,813	11.7	4.6	73,662	41,531	37,964	40,693	35,003	33,020	30,093	47.7	157,400	1,060
Southgate	54,649	18.6	3.4	77,488	34,536	36,291	46,698	30,921	14,124	12,723	68.3	115,900	803
Sterling Heights	64,668	11.5	4.5	71,193	42,503	36,203	42,412	26,175	51,902	49,939	70.7	187,800	951
Taylor	46,681	15.9	1.3	50,425	35,683	30,832	35,230	26,299	25,546	23,158	58.7	100,000	799
Troy	95,825	7.9	13.1	112,487	50,949	56,828	76,558	40,321	33,765	31,954	72.1	297,600	1,194
Warren	46,347	17.2	1.9	53,292	32,871	31,150	36,051	27,290	58,813	54,699	68.3	124,700	910
Westland	47,943	14.1	1.4	64,459	35,674	31,720	37,448	28,476	38,220	35,914	61.2	121,000	855
Wyandotte	47,586	18.7	3.4	66,745	30,549	37,680	50,552	31,610	12,577	11,589	67.0	111,200	678
Wyoming	56,774	17.0	2.3	65,847	31,179	30,863	39,117	24,699	30,860	28,330	69.1	127,500	852
MINNESOTA	68,388	11.7	7.2	86,416	40,222	37,397	43,323	31,706	2,437,726	2,162,211	71.6	224,000	939
Andover	112,109	2.6	11.1	122,917	52,855	53,561	62,190	44,569	10,861	10,734	90.2	293,600	1,696
Apple Valley	82,100	6.2	8.1	101,001	50,915	46,651	49,875	42,245	19,919	19,481	75.8	264,300	1,406
Blaine	77,135	4.9	6.9	86,407	46,590	41,228	42,392	37,020	24,833	23,708	90.0	231,200	1,057
Bloomington	69,642	9.4	6.8	92,116	46,777	40,923	42,721	39,352	38,670	36,455	68.2	243,500	1,160
Brooklyn Center	54,465	18.3	2.7	60,659	40,633	29,737	34,157	24,481	9,676	9,676	60.6	171,000	1,024
Brooklyn Park	71,213	9.3	5.4	78,310	47,973	40,788	45,230	37,673	28,512	27,849	71.8	227,800	971
Burnsville	66,783	10.8	4.4	80,376	42,921	36,066	43,886	30,571	25,915	25,055	60.9	241,200	1,269
Coon Rapids	72,114	5.5	2.8	87,003	42,933	36,725	41,271	33,522	23,678	22,987	79.7	193,500	1,092
Cottage Grove	94,715	3.0	8.7	101,871	50,300	47,106	51,440	42,279	11,914	11,211	91.3	242,700	1,673
Duluth	49,078	18.6	3.9	73,560	27,701	24,537	30,242	21,241	37,100	34,939	59.2	165,200	788
Eagan	86,611	10.2	13.2	107,884	52,380	47,279	55,786	40,729	27,037	26,342	68.4	288,500	1,113
Eden Prairie	105,918	5.4	20.5	123,511	61,681	55,847	73,090	41,180	27,086	26,270	75.8	355,800	1,356
Edina	101,850	11.9	27.6	143,946	39,563	62,100	81,549	45,658	23,577	21,689	72.3	471,400	1,211
Fridley	53,241	9.0	1.4	62,325	38,078	27,698	32,260	21,687	10,478	10,286	58.1	207,600	889
Inver Grove Heights	77,959	7.7	10.5	93,122	46,466	42,490	52,203	35,724	16,298	15,024	73.6	251,900	994
Lakeville	111,813	3.7	14.0	127,726	50,393	52,422	69,710	42,007	21,319	20,990	85.2	307,700	1,645
Mankato	45,820	16.5	3.0	73,614	27,946	21,026	24,070	16,474	18,066	16,468	53.6	180,400	917
Maple Grove	110,288	3.8	14.1	124,534	61,295	60,702	67,767	50,692	27,385	26,289	84.3	294,200	1,444
Maplewood	59,795	11.4	5.3	81,265	36,947	34,048	36,627	30,514	16,615	16,219	67.1	214,600	1,116
Minneapolis	60,789	17.2	7.9	82,994	46,974	34,941	37,375	31,040	188,084	176,416	47.5	250,400	989
Minnetonka	82,663	9.7	14.9	113,627	49,148	52,064	65,149	44,770	24,178	23,405	65.3	342,100	1,295
Moorhead	53,517	16.8	2.3	72,821	36,975	32,901	40,207	23,808	17,848	16,450	59.2	190,600	804
Oakdale	76,949	8.4	5.4	90,851	52,483	39,099	47,556	33,898	11,747	11,201	80.8	218,000	1,119
Owatonna	53,871	13.3	3.8	67,291	28,378	32,272	38,133	24,988	10,967	10,411	71.8	166,600	832
Plymouth	97,770	6.5	20.7	128,542	48,559	57,084	70,373	46,355	32,288	31,135	73.0	361,900	1,371
Richfield	67,562	13.0	3.7	78,521	54,222	36,453	39,395	32,698	16,276	15,784	59.9	225,700	1,106
Rochester	75,464	10.9	7.3	96,241	50,161	43,153	49,082	38,927	49,829	46,645	67.8	211,900	982
Roseville	76,156	8.9	6.3	103,470	56,465	44,736	51,793	36,032	16,612	16,145	65.9	265,900	991
St. Cloud	46,048	22.6	2.0	70,290	27,925	24,137	25,920	22,469	27,823	26,416	54.5	154,600	720
St. Louis Park	81,293	9.6	10.7	109,899	60,543	51,898	61,507	46,502	24,866	23,582	57.0	255,000	1,220
St. Paul	54,290	16.7	5.1	67,552	39,933	30,910	32,233	29,349	118,045	112,467	48.8	211,100	948
Savage	108,516	3.6	18.1	114,657	60,000	41,627	55,839	35,776	10,165	10,165	83.3	316,200	1,306
Shakopee	91,413	5.0	8.2	116,556	51,830	47,834	54,218	40,927	14,439	14,196	75.5	260,100	1,144
Shoreview	84,316	9.9	10.4	126,111	45,131	53,674	61,942	45,474	12,204	11,438	79.4	284,200	1,339
Winona	47,194	18.8	2.1	67,951	35,039	18,600	21,768	16,095	11,318	10,497	60.0	148,900	642
Woodbury	101,069	3.5	15.1	115,383	57,871	51,021	61,928	39,390	25,229	24,363	81.3	328,000	1,457
MISSISSIPPI	43,529	23.9	2.6	55,937	23,654	29,818	34,616	24,441	1,323,754	1,091,980	68.5	120,200	742
Biloxi	50,074	15.8	3.8	64,249	32,359	26,221	30,580	20,753	20,155	16,614	40.1	157,600	883
Clinton	55,449	10.7	3.0	68,631	39,975	32,698	39,632	30,550	10,962	9,555	67.0	175,900	1,006
Greenville	29,269	36.7	2.2	40,045	20,754	26,230	28,983	21,643	13,734	11,959	50.9	73,300	680
Gulfport	35,758	29.2	1.9	46,543	23,595	22,361	31,578	19,691	34,063	28,157	50.8	124,600	823
Hattiesburg	31,087	30.9	0.9	47,919	21,624	18,605	23,404	14,069	21,897	17,622	37.1	108,600	812
Horn Lake	52,305	5.9	1.2	55,311	43,630	30,302	30,645	30,067	9,357	8,299	49.6	101,900	991
Jackson	39,004	24.4	2.3	52,599	27,788	25,822	26,462	25,106	72,430	61,957	49.3	93,400	819
Meridian	36,857	26.4	4.0	49,162	25,689	30,958	34,826	26,175	19,431	16,027	51.7	82,200	694
Olive Branch	62,961	8.8	2.7	73,846	40,085	36,447	41,959	30,888	14,972	13,708	78.3	176,300	1,077
Pearl	56,371	13.2	0.0	63,702	38,212	33,245	35,323	30,668	11,196	10,128	63.5	120,300	920
Southaven	61,987	8.9	4.2	81,392	37,557	36,029	46,274	31,017	21,967	19,774	74.4	149,400	955
Tupelo	50,263	23.6	4.7	62,464	26,612	31,137	38,715	25,521	17,694	15,084	60.2	138,700	714

1. Based on population estimated by the American Community Survey.   2. Includes units rented or sold but not occupied.   3. Specified owner-occupied units; $1,000,000 represents $1,000,000 or more.   4. 50.0 represents 50 percent or more.   5. 10.0 represents 10 percent or less.

Table D. Cities — Commuting, Computer Access, Migration, Labor Force, and Employment

City	Commuting[1], 2017 Percent		Computer access[2], 2017 Percent		Migration, 2017		Civilian labor force, 2018		Civilian employment[4], 2017					
									Unemployment		Population age 16 and older		Population age 16 to 64	
	Commuting	With commutes of 30 minutes or more	With a computer in the house	With Internet access	Percent who lived in the same house one year ago	Percent who lived in another state or county one year ago	Total	Percent change 2017-2018	Total	Rate[3]	Number	Percent in labor force	Number	Percent who worked full-year full-time
	55	56	57	58	59	60	61	62	63	64	65	66	67	68
MICHIGAN— Cont'd														
Oak Park	79.1	32.9	93.9	89.5	88.2	6.8	14,518	0.8	815	5.6	22,464	68.2	18,441	53.9
Pontiac	66.5	28.4	88.4	78.9	84.6	5.3	25,384	0.7	2,006	7.9	45,603	63.7	39,901	38.2
Portage	88.0	17.8	92.1	90.2	87.3	4.8	25,295	0.3	790	3.1	39,169	67.5	30,981	55.9
Port Huron	74.4	19.6	87.3	79.8	81.3	3.8	12,885	0.5	832	6.5	23,464	61.4	19,274	42.0
Rochester Hills	85.2	36.4	96.1	92.3	91.4	3.7	40,109	1.0	1,108	2.8	59,320	63.6	45,752	57.3
Roseville	85.4	40.1	88.0	81.6	84.9	6.4	23,489	0.6	1,224	5.2	37,699	67.6	31,059	55.8
Royal Oak	87.1	36.0	94.0	90.3	84.9	7.0	38,907	1.0	795	2.0	49,630	71.9	40,061	68.2
Saginaw	77.3	13.7	78.4	67.3	80.1	4.9	18,867	-1.3	1,587	8.4	36,994	56.8	30,940	36.6
St. Clair Shores	90.5	37.5	90.0	83.7	89.8	5.5	31,653	0.7	1,235	3.9	50,055	61.9	36,630	52.6
Southfield	86.5	35.2	90.8	86.2	87.0	7.1	35,377	0.8	1,700	4.8	61,232	61.7	47,010	50.0
Southgate	88.6	39.8	87.2	82.4	87.4	8.2	15,797	0.6	486	3.1	24,775	64.0	19,389	48.4
Sterling Heights	84.8	43.7	91.6	86.7	87.9	6.0	68,039	0.8	2,616	3.8	109,750	62.1	87,328	49.4
Taylor	84.7	26.3	90.2	73.6	82.8	3.2	29,056	0.4	1,510	5.2	47,774	62.2	39,254	49.2
Troy	88.3	38.0	96.9	94.7	89.0	5.9	44,131	1.0	1,212	2.7	67,911	64.8	54,593	54.7
Warren	87.6	33.5	87.3	82.5	86.1	6.2	64,298	0.7	3,136	4.9	109,140	60.1	87,427	48.9
Westland	85.0	39.4	89.9	80.6	84.2	3.4	44,022	0.5	1,607	3.7	67,452	65.0	52,974	53.5
Wyandotte	88.9	35.5	87.3	75.6	91.9	2.1	13,479	0.6	480	3.6	20,783	62.5	16,338	60.0
Wyoming	79.1	23.5	86.6	78.9	84.2	4.7	44,722	1.1	1,452	3.2	58,760	69.8	49,202	51.9
MINNESOTA	78.0	32.1	92.1	85.8	85.8	6.9	3,070,224	0.4	89,339	2.9	4,422,835	69.5	3,563,931	55.1
Andover	82.6	49.5	98.3	93.7	88.8	3.4	18,905	0.8	456	2.4	25,877	76.4	22,501	60.2
Apple Valley	82.3	37.6	93.7	88.6	85.6	7.7	30,347	0.8	745	2.5	40,740	72.8	32,665	64.3
Blaine	83.1	40.2	92.7	89.8	94.4	3.9	36,878	0.7	929	2.5	50,524	72.3	42,588	59.4
Bloomington	78.7	26.6	94.3	90.2	86.2	6.1	46,582	0.7	1,229	2.6	72,012	67.9	53,897	57.1
Brooklyn Center	76.9	32.2	88.1	75.2	86.6	4.1	15,428	0.5	503	3.3	22,064	69.5	18,870	52.5
Brooklyn Park	75.5	39.6	95.5	88.7	91.3	3.4	42,720	0.6	1,234	2.9	60,935	70.5	50,477	57.9
Burnsville	78.1	37.9	94.1	88.2	82.5	8.1	35,734	0.6	893	2.5	49,625	72.3	40,103	53.5
Coon Rapids	83.9	38.3	93.5	88.6	85.5	8.0	35,588	0.6	973	2.7	50,615	71.7	41,193	56.7
Cottage Grove	84.3	35.5	NA	NA	90.9	5.3	20,585	0.6	516	2.5	27,091	77.1	24,014	58.7
Duluth	75.9	12.5	91.3	85.1	75.4	11.1	45,799	-0.2	1,337	2.9	72,172	66.2	59,026	40.8
Eagan	80.6	32.7	96.3	89.8	86.5	7.1	40,055	0.8	921	2.3	52,925	74.0	44,821	62.1
Eden Prairie	77.3	30.4	95.5	92.2	90.4	3.0	36,696	0.8	820	2.2	52,392	71.9	43,603	59.8
Edina	77.1	28.9	93.3	89.8	86.0	6.6	26,001	0.8	585	2.2	41,014	62.4	29,487	55.2
Fridley	78.9	25.7	93.6	89.5	89.1	6.9	14,931	0.6	467	3.1	22,319	67.2	18,593	43.2
Inver Grove Heights	84.9	36.5	95.9	93.5	84.9	6.2	19,912	0.6	519	2.6	29,168	68.2	23,233	53.2
Lakeville	79.2	48.1	97.1	94.4	88.8	5.5	36,174	0.9	850	2.3	46,129	77.5	40,602	59.2
Mankato	84.6	13.5	94.3	84.6	77.4	13.2	26,005	0.6	623	2.4	36,016	70.5	31,365	39.7
Maple Grove	82.3	36.4	98.6	94.2	90.6	3.4	41,514	0.7	910	2.2	53,018	74.1	44,322	63.7
Maplewood	74.0	34.3	90.4	85.2	83.3	6.9	20,919	0.6	610	2.9	32,756	67.3	26,182	56.9
Minneapolis	61.4	30.2	92.9	84.0	76.6	9.6	241,344	0.6	6,071	2.5	345,840	74.6	303,511	51.9
Minnetonka	75.4	30.5	95.5	93.0	84.8	6.6	30,383	0.7	689	2.3	43,747	70.8	33,840	61.3
Moorhead	78.8	10.0	92.3	83.1	80.8	11.5	24,411	0.4	603	2.5	33,490	68.2	27,821	50.2
Oakdale	83.4	35.8	96.2	92.6	86.9	8.3	16,176	0.6	439	2.7	23,844	71.6	18,663	58.2
Owatonna	84.7	22.3	92.8	90.2	89.3	8.1	14,293	0.1	408	2.9	20,170	64.4	15,676	49.8
Plymouth	82.9	29.7	95.2	92.3	84.2	5.1	44,532	0.8	1,032	2.3	61,881	73.7	50,585	62.5
Richfield	69.4	25.7	90.6	84.9	82.0	8.1	20,169	0.7	501	2.5	30,017	75.4	24,996	59.5
Rochester	72.1	11.6	94.3	87.9	85.7	6.9	64,888	1.2	1,448	2.2	90,674	71.1	73,530	58.4
Roseville	74.5	31.6	88.2	84.1	83.6	7.7	19,545	0.7	473	2.4	30,628	69.1	22,309	59.3
St. Cloud	79.4	14.3	93.1	84.9	73.1	16.8	36,966	-0.2	1,172	3.2	52,576	70.4	44,471	42.5
St. Louis Park	79.0	27.5	95.4	92.7	79.1	6.4	30,786	0.8	669	2.2	41,550	76.1	34,943	66.5
St. Paul	66.1	31.6	93.6	86.5	78.2	9.2	158,501	0.7	4,379	2.8	235,661	70.8	204,537	48.4
Savage	83.0	38.5	97.1	92.9	85.9	10.2	18,524	0.9	442	2.4	23,465	79.0	20,946	60.0
Shakopee	85.7	32.4	94.1	86.9	87.6	10.1	23,262	0.7	547	2.4	31,240	77.2	28,106	63.0
Shoreview	76.9	37.6	92.7	88.5	87.3	9.3	15,037	0.7	351	2.3	22,082	69.8	17,350	62.3
Winona	80.5	16.6	91.6	88.3	69.4	15.7	15,424	-0.6	418	2.7	23,862	70.6	19,394	43.0
Woodbury	80.1	34.6	97.7	95.4	87.8	5.6	39,477	0.9	856	2.2	52,187	74.2	43,760	61.4
MISSISSIPPI	85.5	33.3	84.6	72.7	86.6	6.5	1,275,721	-0.4	60,729	4.8	2,351,836	56.5	1,886,117	46.4
Biloxi	76.3	17.6	90.9	83.9	78.2	14.1	19,596	-0.1	874	4.5	37,229	62.9	31,309	47.6
Clinton	82.8	35.9	85.0	84.0	82.1	8.8	13,184	-0.5	465	3.5	18,822	64.5	14,273	61.4
Greenville	88.5	10.3	82.2	63.3	90.4	4.1	11,186	-2.7	741	6.6	22,027	58.8	17,202	42.9
Gulfport	87.6	21.2	83.8	76.5	77.2	11.7	28,925	-0.1	1,343	4.6	55,838	63.8	45,394	45.3
Hattiesburg	77.6	17.4	90.7	76.3	69.8	18.6	21,940	0.2	950	4.3	38,013	66.2	32,565	39.9
Horn Lake	NA	35.7	95.1	94.2	72.6	15.3	12,938	0.8	504	3.9	19,541	68.2	17,451	51.0
Jackson	83.1	24.4	86.7	80.8	78.9	8.0	73,854	-0.7	3,536	4.8	129,211	63.7	108,435	46.9
Meridian	83.6	18.5	81.5	69.2	81.0	7.4	14,703	-2.9	783	5.3	29,807	54.9	23,506	51.0
Olive Branch	91.3	42.5	89.9	82.1	77.5	10.9	19,951	0.9	642	3.2	29,978	65.7	24,333	54.7
Pearl	82.9	21.5	93.8	90.5	83.3	6.9	12,914	-0.6	465	3.6	20,517	72.0	16,743	69.4
Southaven	84.2	33.8	96.7	91.5	83.5	8.3	27,796	0.8	932	3.4	42,323	69.7	34,431	62.4
Tupelo	86.8	16.9	86.5	69.8	86.4	5.2	17,362	-0.9	704	4.1	29,062	59.4	23,062	53.1

1. Employed persons.　2. Households.　3. Percent of civilian labor force.　4. Persons 16 years old and over.

Table D. Cities — Construction, Wholesale Trade, and Retail Trade

City	Value of residential construction authorized by building permits, 2018			Wholesale trade[1], 2012				Retail trade[2], 2012			
	New construction ($1,000)	Number of housing units	Percent single family	Number of establishments	Number of employees	Sales (mil dol)	Annual payroll (mil dol)	Number of establishments	Number of employees	Sales (mil dol)	Annual payroll (mil dol)
	69	70	71	72	73	74	75	76	77	78	79
MICHIGAN— Cont'd											
Oak Park	1,832	14	100.0	63	600	307.9	37.6	121	980	220.7	22.4
Pontiac	429	3	100.0	43	D	D	D	190	1,572	414.7	39.7
Portage	25,372	159	35.8	46	903	352.9	70.5	302	5,471	1,137.7	105.7
Port Huron	166	2	100.0	20	194	120.3	10.2	115	1,145	299.2	29.2
Rochester Hills	52,214	118	100.0	89	959	865.6	77.0	247	5,126	1,393.8	127.7
Roseville	230	1	100.0	45	593	670.2	34.0	250	4,380	1,170.5	99.1
Royal Oak	41,241	142	100.0	55	590	1,218.9	36.5	224	2,496	634.0	65.1
Saginaw	6,906	55	9.1	35	544	276.8	28.0	146	874	188.6	18.5
St. Clair Shores	4,427	25	100.0	38	187	95.9	9.2	174	2,098	565.5	55.8
Southfield	5,685	15	100.0	149	2,717	3,983.5	188.2	421	5,634	2,009.7	163.2
Southgate	270	1	100.0	7	7	D	D	130	2,593	740.5	64.9
Sterling Heights	18,669	107	36.4	151	1,914	845.2	111.2	449	7,490	1,976.7	186.4
Taylor	5,585	20	100.0	66	1,096	783.5	53.2	326	5,342	1,360.1	125.1
Troy	37,878	156	89.7	331	6,106	4,293.4	363.9	550	10,978	3,608.5	299.7
Warren	6,090	92	26.1	165	3,181	1,893.9	188.7	460	5,305	1,498.3	137.6
Westland	8,076	65	100.0	51	477	258.8	24.8	305	4,569	1,094.1	99.9
Wyandotte	4,742	21	100.0	14	D	D	D	86	467	127.7	11.2
Wyoming	3,789	30	80.0	166	3,842	3,083.0	206.9	257	4,053	1,114.2	115.0
MINNESOTA	5,720,813	25,673	52.9	6,569	108,467	104,485.1	7,170.1	19,109	288,888	78,898.2	6,857.5
Andover	19,704	60	100.0	11	36	15.8	1.4	37	601	140.2	11.3
Apple Valley	82,576	498	13.5	22	83	37.5	3.8	119	3,499	924.7	85.0
Blaine	84,623	259	100.0	72	1,059	555.4	53.8	222	4,265	966.4	92.8
Bloomington	1,678	7	100.0	193	5,005	5,106.6	355.4	522	12,250	3,007.9	330.6
Brooklyn Center	1,040	5	100.0	25	508	285.1	24.1	72	1,863	658.2	55.7
Brooklyn Park	32,059	124	100.0	80	1,488	1,018.1	85.7	155	3,311	979.3	87.7
Burnsville	21,063	156	14.1	159	D	D	D	333	5,998	1,506.7	163.7
Coon Rapids	49,463	277	7.9	24	331	107.0	15.7	180	4,610	1,314.0	113.7
Cottage Grove	49,964	184	97.8	11	D	D	D	48	956	236.4	21.0
Duluth	27,677	206	23.3	93	1,063	531.9	52.7	427	6,141	1,384.7	130.1
Eagan	15,638	43	100.0	143	2,815	1,679.9	184.4	163	3,258	1,040.7	81.2
Eden Prairie	72,140	409	12.0	177	2,957	5,430.6	223.2	242	5,876	2,684.5	201.2
Edina	130,699	359	20.3	129	1,086	1,118.7	75.6	299	6,044	1,173.2	135.4
Fridley	12,254	83	18.1	70	9,569	5,882.7	1,457.6	86	2,040	591.5	53.8
Inver Grove Heights	32,737	130	100.0	20	D	D	D	69	1,520	766.8	54.1
Lakeville	170,822	604	83.9	45	D	D	D	120	2,125	664.4	53.6
Mankato	51,303	335	40.3	55	980	715.9	48.6	271	5,743	1,334.6	122.3
Maple Grove	106,642	500	55.0	86	935	601.4	53.7	183	4,073	1,016.9	91.2
Maplewood	2,055	7	100.0	38	425	219.9	23.7	229	4,308	1,218.2	110.9
Minneapolis	757,061	3,625	4.5	483	7,802	6,079.5	477.3	1,123	14,533	4,070.0	397.3
Minnetonka	51,514	240	26.3	131	3,457	2,016.4	204.4	294	5,982	1,771.5	167.8
Moorhead	47,852	329	40.7	31	433	356.1	22.1	113	1,992	471.4	42.2
Oakdale	379	2	100.0	40	480	579.2	33.5	64	1,514	365.5	31.7
Owatonna	22,691	131	29.0	22	323	216.3	18.5	103	2,096	469.4	45.5
Plymouth	133,770	374	100.0	203	5,086	4,243.4	356.7	183	3,279	1,175.4	96.4
Richfield	41,906	291	2.7	15	285	69.5	19.1	116	2,488	3,045.5	74.6
Rochester	281,920	1,415	24.5	71	905	471.2	44.1	507	9,720	2,224.4	213.7
Roseville	12,553	77	23.4	68	1,075	796.5	59.0	304	6,393	1,200.6	130.6
St. Cloud	25,135	109	100.0	75	2,002	970.1	92.7	326	6,280	1,548.2	141.3
St. Louis Park	358	1	100.0	108	1,486	781.5	92.4	205	4,325	1,292.0	127.0
St. Paul	119,172	706	3.5	270	4,879	3,332.8	295.3	739	9,230	1,959.9	208.7
Savage	77,852	284	81.0	33	594	1,002.6	30.7	83	1,069	286.1	23.5
Shakopee	50,307	179	65.4	54	1,186	939.9	83.8	116	2,294	688.9	52.2
Shoreview	2,068	8	100.0	23	D	D	D	38	696	153.6	16.7
Winona	13,725	88	10.2	33	354	200.2	15.4	113	2,298	532.8	46.8
Woodbury	152,549	682	60.6	38	D	D	D	232	4,979	1,005.9	93.7
MISSISSIPPI	1,193,505	6,883	89.1	2,484	30,351	28,303.0	1,373.6	11,594	136,032	37,053.2	2,968.4
Biloxi	33,727	184	100.0	37	417	188.9	14.3	209	2,470	542.5	51.4
Clinton	8,560	35	100.0	13	96	44.1	3.6	84	960	240.7	21.9
Greenville	1,283	5	100.0	40	333	825.3	15.5	168	1,891	405.4	36.0
Gulfport	21,671	137	100.0	84	869	392.0	41.4	385	5,435	1,432.3	123.6
Hattiesburg	10,938	52	100.0	85	866	532.1	33.8	453	7,195	4,103.8	149.6
Horn Lake	6,222	63	100.0	17	D	D	D	70	1,069	266.2	24.0
Jackson	4,606	21	100.0	244	3,355	2,146.6	162.5	700	9,327	2,606.3	236.8
Meridian	1,819	14	85.7	58	1,362	1,511.3	61.2	344	4,598	1,193.9	104.4
Olive Branch	46,581	321	100.0	51	1,000	862.2	45.5	122	1,896	646.7	50.2
Pearl	12,371	61	73.8	68	1,095	777.5	59.8	115	1,947	483.3	48.5
Southaven	49,907	368	100.0	38	1,464	2,194.9	63.9	214	3,945	1,123.1	94.4
Tupelo	19,934	107	100.0	113	1,169	819.3	48.5	374	6,061	1,350.0	127.5

1. Merchant wholesalers except manufacturers' sales branches and offices.   2. Establishments with payroll.

Table D. Cities — Real Estate, Professional Services, and Manufacturing

City	Real estate and rental and leasing, 2012				Professional, scientific, and technical services[1], 2012				Manufacturing, 2012			
	Number of establishments	Number of employees	Receipts (mil dol)	Annual payroll (mil dol)	Number of establishments	Number of employees	Receipts (mil dol)	Annual payroll (mil dol)	Number of establishments	Number of employees	Receipts (mil dol)	Annual payroll (mil dol)
	80	81	82	83	84	85	86	87	88	89	90	91
MICHIGAN— Cont'd												
Oak Park	30	D	D	D	39	317	71.7	23.1	45	812	154.8	42.8
Pontiac	45	221	36.5	8.3	41	370	46.4	19.0	43	984	615.6	61.1
Portage	52	1,240	93.4	41.2	139	1,131	176.4	60.9	56	6,306	D	415.8
Port Huron	23	71	10.2	1.7	66	D	D	D	45	2,633	1,562.4	130.0
Rochester Hills	48	199	31.4	6.2	250	2,652	439.3	181.0	97	4,059	1,368.3	215.9
Roseville	46	301	54.9	12.4	52	288	18.1	9.4	128	3,854	761.8	216.3
Royal Oak	65	284	39.1	11.7	289	D	D	D	66	1,118	412.6	54.1
Saginaw	20	61	10.5	1.9	81	D	D	D	57	2,770	948.9	155.1
St. Clair Shores	41	130	23.1	3.4	161	781	90.7	36.7	39	1,191	382.1	60.6
Southfield	219	3,050	707.3	151.1	731	13,009	2,655.0	1,221.5	72	3,434	D	207.9
Southgate	21	D	D	D	32	230	21.4	8.4	7	D	D	D
Sterling Heights	93	549	121.6	19.3	265	D	D	D	254	15,436	10,090.2	1,077.1
Taylor	45	312	76.9	9.5	93	D	D	D	80	2,506	817.5	133.8
Troy	152	1,427	287.5	58.2	869	16,374	2,482.5	1,139.0	251	5,912	2,053.0	308.7
Warren	99	605	130.0	25.9	192	13,153	410.5	1,111.3	320	13,623	9,322.0	847.9
Westland	52	D	D	D	64	308	35.0	11.0	67	1,690	441.3	78.6
Wyandotte	9	D	D	D	43	138	19.8	7.1	31	1,430	716.3	142.2
Wyoming	73	669	147.0	27.6	108	D	D	D	155	6,340	1,682.6	298.2
MINNESOTA	6,300	34,499	7,827.9	1,396.0	16,260	D	D	D	7,313	297,884	123,076.3	15,822.6
Andover	45	162	19.1	3.6	64	129	16.1	5.4	12	165	D	6.4
Apple Valley	53	201	46.9	5.4	162	D	D	D	13	506	D	32.0
Blaine	61	190	57.9	6.1	112	D	D	D	160	2,730	1,018.4	138.7
Bloomington	199	4,195	904.5	204.9	564	D	D	D	120	4,999	1,673.6	314.9
Brooklyn Center	32	131	30.4	5.6	60	438	76.7	30.4	26	1,719	335.2	99.3
Brooklyn Park	55	299	48.8	11.3	129	1,205	373.8	58.3	113	5,330	1,491.8	294.6
Burnsville	118	503	114.9	18.3	289	1,438	260.1	94.4	94	3,051	850.4	163.6
Coon Rapids	62	199	43.3	8.6	113	842	138.1	49.1	50	2,992	990.6	184.4
Cottage Grove	21	D	D	D	33	94	8.7	3.3	11	1,173	D	82.1
Duluth	120	657	103.9	19.7	229	D	D	D	89	2,381	D	124.9
Eagan	106	799	163.5	35.3	337	D	D	D	86	3,073	1,166.7	165.1
Eden Prairie	124	916	692.7	60.9	430	4,020	819.8	326.0	110	7,861	2,647.8	545.5
Edina	195	1,617	290.7	80.5	492	D	D	D	62	3,155	866.6	221.5
Fridley	36	D	D	D	77	302	72.0	17.1	113	5,972	1,933.4	340.2
Inver Grove Heights	27	168	19.7	4.2	84	398	60.9	24.1	27	832	321.3	40.5
Lakeville	64	122	33.5	4.6	167	523	86.0	25.8	55	2,932	760.7	133.7
Mankato	70	539	63.0	12.9	117	D	D	D	49	2,644	3,469.1	126.6
Maple Grove	86	191	43.4	7.3	275	1,183	202.1	76.0	95	6,410	1,689.4	404.0
Maplewood	43	176	29.9	4.4	93	374	47.5	14.0	24	541	183.8	26.2
Minneapolis	684	4,056	764.1	195.6	2,338	31,241	6,957.8	2,808.4	427	12,837	3,944.2	689.5
Minnetonka	140	1,091	307.6	73.9	438	D	D	D	81	4,523	2,144.7	354.0
Moorhead	30	145	16.3	3.2	48	D	D	D	21	699	D	29.4
Oakdale	27	D	D	D	87	877	157.0	64.4	28	673	151.6	31.2
Owatonna	20	235	15.2	4.4	46	158	15.3	5.1	36	4,139	D	188.5
Plymouth	137	710	405.0	39.0	500	6,498	990.9	362.5	167	10,038	3,905.4	684.6
Richfield	27	384	36.7	8.3	100	450	58.9	26.5	15	46	D	1.2
Rochester	149	676	134.6	21.4	226	D	D	D	56	7,887	2,962.0	543.3
Roseville	53	352	106.4	17.5	213	2,187	545.6	150.0	56	1,644	616.8	91.4
St. Cloud	104	478	87.5	16.4	149	D	D	D	59	4,810	1,515.6	204.2
St. Louis Park	131	2,014	235.5	66.1	370	D	D	D	64	1,517	330.8	77.5
St. Paul	349	2,485	1,113.1	125.8	868	6,532	1,088.9	446.2	225	6,867	2,018.1	380.6
Savage	41	81	24.2	3.4	109	D	D	D	42	1,165	349.1	59.2
Shakopee	44	110	30.7	3.8	120	D	D	D	43	2,790	1,493.2	194.6
Shoreview	25	D	D	D	112	340	52.2	19.4	34	1,368	400.8	92.0
Winona	33	100	15.4	1.9	61	D	D	D	65	3,317	1,069.7	162.6
Woodbury	74	D	D	D	266	1,287	179.2	68.3	22	686	279.7	42.6
MISSISSIPPI	2,374	10,235	1,709.3	334.1	4,727	30,071	4,009.1	1,443.3	2,252	132,789	66,441.6	5,919.1
Biloxi	69	279	64.1	9.7	135	D	D	D	20	265	D	8.5
Clinton	33	D	D	D	58	353	36.9	13.5	8	D	D	6.4
Greenville	35	127	17.5	4.3	57	D	D	D	23	740	526.6	35.6
Gulfport	121	598	110.4	18.6	185	D	D	D	57	1,788	D	82.3
Hattiesburg	99	424	91.7	15.3	187	D	D	D	57	2,861	825.1	105.4
Horn Lake	22	106	22.8	3.1	14	102	6.4	2.4	14	683	D	35.3
Jackson	232	1,458	313.1	65.5	552	D	D	D	103	2,717	855.6	132.7
Meridian	69	242	54.7	7.4	118	D	D	D	46	1,331	448.3	47.5
Olive Branch	19	56	13.8	2.3	40	176	15.0	5.0	54	1,854	742.3	86.4
Pearl	43	218	25.5	6.6	30	169	31.9	6.3	25	628	156.7	25.9
Southaven	40	135	42.9	5.3	75	538	57.3	14.6	15	D	142.1	D
Tupelo	77	343	64.5	11.0	162	1,025	104.0	44.4	72	3,811	1,605.0	172.4

1. Establishments subject to federal tax.

Table D. Cities — Accommodation and Food Services, Arts, Entertainment, and Recreation, and Health Care and Social Assistance

City	Accommodation and food services, 2012				Arts, entertainment, and recreation[1], 2012				Health care and social assistance,[1] 2012			
	Number of establish-ments	Number of employees	Receipts (mil dol)	Annual payroll (mil dol)	Number of establish-ments	Number of employees	Receipts (mil dol)	Annual payroll (mil dol)	Number of establish-ments	Number of employees	Receipts (mil dol)	Annual payroll (mil dol)
	92	93	94	95	96	97	98	99	100	101	102	103
MICHIGAN— Cont'd												
Oak Park	43	D	D	D	1	D	D	D	80	555	41.2	16.1
Pontiac	102	1,226	76.3	18.3	9	96	8.4	1.6	114	1,294	156.3	59.4
Portage	142	D	D	D	14	76	4.1	0.9	160	1,924	167.2	75.6
Port Huron	64	1,016	39.8	11.6	11	132	5.3	1.5	127	1,263	153.2	78.4
Rochester Hills	105	2,490	109.1	33.8	20	D	D	D	290	3,201	358.3	139.4
Roseville	109	2,763	116.3	33.6	9	133	4.3	1.4	102	D	D	D
Royal Oak	157	3,304	170.7	49.2	15	D	D	D	175	D	D	D
Saginaw	76	948	44.7	12.0	2	D	D	D	111	1,788	193.9	83.0
St. Clair Shores	116	D	D	D	22	D	D	D	203	D	D	D
Southfield	240	4,113	234.8	65.0	21	256	17.6	7.1	692	8,755	934.5	419.4
Southgate	92	2,179	99.8	29.7	4	D	D	D	75	835	90.1	34.6
Sterling Heights	226	4,510	191.9	55.7	27	D	D	D	349	3,546	324.1	132.3
Taylor	143	2,257	103.7	28.0	15	D	D	D	121	1,790	160.6	65.4
Troy	269	6,231	342.7	102.3	34	D	D	D	477	D	D	D
Warren	296	5,058	236.0	66.5	23	D	D	D	338	D	D	D
Westland	151	2,695	119.6	32.6	16	D	D	D	120	1,569	132.3	54.9
Wyandotte	60	604	28.1	7.7	4	D	D	D	46	D	D	D
Wyoming	128	2,271	99.7	27.0	11	D	D	D	102	D	D	D
MINNESOTA	11,345	221,859	11,722.6	3,238.0	1,927	27,308	2,355.8	917.7	11,233	189,308	15,774.4	7,258.9
Andover	19	339	15.5	4.0	6	50	2.1	0.7	43	559	40.0	16.5
Apple Valley	72	1,751	80.2	22.9	10	D	D	D	113	1,128	115.6	47.6
Blaine	109	2,569	117.6	34.4	23	D	D	D	100	1,342	135.0	48.8
Bloomington	266	8,597	540.8	163.0	25	D	D	D	221	3,751	287.0	122.0
Brooklyn Center	48	1,089	53.9	12.7	5	D	D	D	75	963	59.8	29.6
Brooklyn Park	84	1,407	61.5	17.2	17	D	D	D	102	2,753	156.1	60.5
Burnsville	129	2,756	129.5	38.5	30	560	19.8	5.8	209	D	D	D
Coon Rapids	110	2,581	128.3	36.6	15	314	17.3	4.4	127	D	D	D
Cottage Grove	32	652	27.9	8.1	5	59	2.2	0.8	44	D	D	D
Duluth	227	5,656	250.0	71.8	28	286	10.4	3.7	263	5,585	485.0	214.0
Eagan	153	3,503	216.5	51.8	16	D	D	D	164	2,756	242.0	94.3
Eden Prairie	149	3,143	165.8	49.4	31	D	D	D	147	2,642	494.2	125.1
Edina	104	2,811	161.3	46.9	26	D	D	D	365	D	D	D
Fridley	48	D	D	D	8	D	D	D	77	D	D	D
Inver Grove Heights	52	971	43.3	13.0	6	60	3.4	1.0	59	944	58.2	28.1
Lakeville	65	1,687	69.7	20.5	13	D	D	D	102	D	D	D
Mankato	140	3,421	138.6	37.9	9	171	6.6	1.5	123	2,577	231.0	109.7
Maple Grove	113	3,337	169.1	48.5	14	D	D	D	150	2,340	223.3	94.4
Maplewood	108	2,244	104.6	30.3	16	D	D	D	155	2,048	258.9	103.9
Minneapolis	1,141	27,424	1,646.9	469.0	169	2,816	501.8	258.8	818	16,746	1,296.2	670.3
Minnetonka	112	2,594	147.1	44.7	29	D	D	D	167	2,597	499.3	141.1
Moorhead	57	1,584	59.7	18.0	7	D	D	D	79	1,420	94.8	40.5
Oakdale	40	963	68.0	16.0	12	D	D	D	42	522	41.1	13.4
Owatonna	66	1,448	54.8	15.6	8	D	D	D	72	D	D	D
Plymouth	131	2,863	137.0	41.4	21	384	25.4	6.2	198	2,705	421.0	189.0
Richfield	62	1,172	66.6	20.0	6	23	1.8	0.6	76	1,832	107.1	50.3
Rochester	292	7,130	374.5	106.7	28	613	20.9	6.9	260	6,019	558.8	248.2
Roseville	118	3,330	164.7	51.5	14	D	D	D	142	3,636	299.1	147.0
St. Cloud	163	3,714	163.6	44.9	28	359	23.8	5.7	166	5,141	424.5	257.6
St. Louis Park	96	2,413	135.1	40.2	28	D	D	D	198	D	D	D
St. Paul	599	11,383	589.0	173.3	84	1,613	203.0	98.9	685	15,640	1,017.7	535.3
Savage	43	D	D	D	9	203	14.3	3.9	47	428	34.8	14.0
Shakopee	78	D	D	D	17	D	D	D	72	695	58.6	29.0
Shoreview	30	629	27.3	7.8	9	42	4.1	1.1	68	703	56.7	26.4
Winona	88	1,902	68.3	18.3	12	154	6.9	2.7	43	D	D	D
Woodbury	114	2,800	133.5	38.7	22	D	D	D	188	2,604	312.7	125.7
MISSISSIPPI	5,177	116,238	6,999.2	1,765.0	467	6,178	453.1	115.8	5,149	84,441	8,730.7	3,450.8
Biloxi	127	10,835	1,089.8	266.2	21	1,448	114.4	27.6	128	D	D	D
Clinton	56	1,270	60.0	14.3	9	D	D	D	48	834	57.9	22.5
Greenville	71	1,709	115.4	27.9	5	D	D	D	110	D	D	D
Gulfport	197	5,065	345.8	81.8	12	D	D	D	209	D	D	D
Hattiesburg	232	5,570	248.9	68.4	16	D	D	D	199	5,424	709.3	332.0
Horn Lake	52	1,260	59.3	15.3	5	D	D	D	17	D	D	D
Jackson	370	7,443	378.2	103.7	22	449	42.9	10.6	515	10,396	1,297.0	513.0
Meridian	154	3,512	168.4	44.0	8	48	2.5	0.6	169	D	D	D
Olive Branch	70	1,581	77.6	19.9	10	D	D	D	54	D	D	D
Pearl	73	1,563	86.6	21.6	5	D	D	D	31	333	42.0	12.4
Southaven	125	3,105	149.8	39.2	8	D	D	D	137	D	D	D
Tupelo	165	4,002	173.2	47.7	11	D	D	D	188	D	D	D

1. Establishments subject to federal tax.

Table D. Cities — Other Services and Government Employment and Payroll

City	Other services[1] Number of establishments	Number of employees	Receipts (mil dol)	Annual payroll (mil dol)	Government employment and payroll, 2012 — March payroll — Full-time equivalent employees	Total (dollars)	Percent of total for: Administrative, judicial, and legal	Police and corrections	Fire protection	Highways and transportation	Health and welfare	Natural resources and utilities	Education and libraries
	104	105	106	107	108	109	110	111	112	113	114	115	116
MICHIGAN— Cont'd													
Oak Park	34	197	21.9	6.4	185	937,924	18.6	60.3	0.0	10.5	1.9	3.7	3.3
Pontiac	58	439	46.2	13.5	430	1,925,926	17.1	26.9	21.9	5.4	1.8	16.6	1.4
Portage	89	659	53.5	16.1	226	1,051,828	15.4	37.7	18.1	12.3	4.6	4.9	0.0
Port Huron	34	193	10.0	3.1	265	1,254,174	10.2	26.7	19.4	6.8	0.5	25.3	0.0
Rochester Hills	83	472	31.1	9.7	212	1,126,747	28.0	1.5	20.1	6.3	0.0	29.2	0.0
Roseville	76	425	36.9	10.6	272	1,442,763	17.1	38.9	18.8	5.1	2.8	6.5	2.7
Royal Oak	118	650	59.8	17.3	321	1,931,268	16.4	25.4	37.1	2.0	1.2	5.2	3.3
Saginaw	45	245	21.6	5.7	613	1,804,633	11.1	28.9	17.4	6.3	2.1	29.3	0.0
St. Clair Shores	98	577	33.0	10.4	289	1,541,860	15.0	42.8	21.6	1.7	0.7	11.6	5.1
Southfield	115	631	59.1	16.2	690	3,446,012	19.1	28.8	18.1	5.7	1.0	8.4	6.3
Southgate	53	532	55.1	15.3	177	773,845	14.0	43.0	18.7	6.4	1.2	9.7	2.6
Sterling Heights	175	950	85.3	27.6	579	3,290,094	12.5	40.0	22.0	5.0	1.9	8.5	3.7
Taylor	103	974	88.6	37.0	369	1,754,345	13.6	40.4	19.0	6.4	4.2	14.1	0.3
Troy	178	1,647	169.1	58.1	515	2,464,478	14.8	42.0	3.2	8.2	0.0	17.1	6.8
Warren	214	1,570	191.9	60.4	409	1,654,082	24.5	41.8	6.8	11.2	1.1	10.9	0.0
Westland	110	720	74.4	21.5	341	1,711,074	17.2	33.4	26.3	2.7	4.2	10.7	4.8
Wyandotte	35	171	15.2	4.9	264	1,258,764	6.9	21.7	11.9	10.2	0.2	39.9	0.0
Wyoming	110	771	68.1	21.3	303	1,910,038	15.8	32.7	7.9	12.1	3.7	22.2	0.0
MINNESOTA	8,286	51,746	4,542.3	1,382.9	X	X	X	X	X	X	X	X	X
Andover	33	253	11.5	4.8	57	306,532	24.8	0.0	6.4	37.0	5.8	20.9	0.0
Apple Valley	57	492	35.1	12.2	229	1,179,963	20.1	31.5	5.2	9.3	0.0	23.8	0.0
Blaine	116	899	89.2	27.5	193	1,113,430	14.4	41.7	4.5	11.3	3.0	15.1	0.0
Bloomington	150	1,477	137.0	42.8	580	3,330,394	17.4	31.1	1.2	8.0	13.9	19.4	0.0
Brooklyn Center	20	99	4.8	1.7	190	907,979	13.2	39.3	1.8	9.0	0.9	16.1	0.0
Brooklyn Park	80	457	34.6	12.1	439	1,758,756	8.0	36.5	10.9	10.9	10.0	15.7	0.0
Burnsville	117	802	66.9	22.7	283	1,681,229	9.1	34.0	19.2	3.9	1.0	16.7	0.0
Coon Rapids	75	502	44.9	12.5	274	1,545,147	17.1	30.9	13.2	6.2	5.6	15.0	0.0
Cottage Grove	38	203	11.3	4.1	144	711,248	12.8	41.8	9.7	7.9	5.8	15.7	0.0
Duluth	124	909	75.2	20.9	1,045	5,036,775	9.3	20.6	16.0	20.5	3.8	18.3	4.0
Eagan	111	1,396	130.4	45.7	268	1,561,646	13.0	28.8	3.4	11.0	7.1	30.5	0.0
Eden Prairie	117	971	89.6	26.0	328	1,743,608	14.5	34.2	4.6	8.2	2.3	23.7	0.0
Edina	90	1,073	83.2	30.7	352	1,123,601	13.6	25.8	14.8	13.3	1.1	27.2	0.0
Fridley	46	383	32.9	12.9	159	814,545	21.9	36.8	8.3	11.3	0.0	18.0	0.0
Inver Grove Heights	43	276	24.6	8.0	165	851,190	11.3	30.5	5.7	13.8	7.8	30.9	0.0
Lakeville	77	546	41.2	13.2	211	1,082,740	14.0	36.0	3.4	11.5	2.5	18.7	0.0
Mankato	71	547	40.6	13.8	247	1,231,381	15.7	27.7	8.8	14.5	6.7	19.1	0.0
Maple Grove	104	862	68.6	24.4	296	1,469,495	14.2	34.1	4.5	6.8	2.2	24.2	0.0
Maplewood	70	359	31.7	10.1	213	1,114,986	14.1	35.4	13.8	12.7	0.3	17.3	0.0
Minneapolis	680	5,266	422.1	142.9	5,068	26,103,507	17.5	27.4	10.3	12.5	9.5	21.9	0.0
Minnetonka	96	717	40.5	15.2	278	1,451,759	17.2	30.1	6.4	12.6	6.1	22.6	0.0
Moorhead	62	311	23.5	7.3	325	1,425,672	7.7	22.3	13.7	9.6	0.7	41.4	0.0
Oakdale	34	D	D	D	111	601,791	15.3	41.9	9.3	5.0	3.9	15.6	0.0
Owatonna	52	278	35.4	7.6	211	1,033,223	2.7	19.8	4.9	11.0	1.6	48.8	5.9
Plymouth	94	765	62.7	24.2	284	1,540,683	14.5	33.6	5.5	10.0	5.3	23.7	0.0
Richfield	51	337	26.5	10.6	152	758,629	14.7	33.6	0.0	13.7	5.8	23.9	0.0
Rochester	145	1,329	90.8	32.3	902	4,970,436	6.7	22.3	13.1	9.3	0.0	38.4	6.2
Roseville	88	825	60.5	20.8	191	1,032,673	11.9	37.1	9.1	3.6	4.1	15.9	0.0
St. Cloud	98	941	91.9	28.1	476	2,084,342	8.3	31.7	16.1	9.7	5.9	21.3	0.0
St. Louis Park	109	545	35.9	12.0	270	1,697,664	10.1	28.0	11.9	8.0	13.9	19.8	0.0
St. Paul	371	2,885	226.3	78.2	3,092	18,028,194	10.8	29.1	17.9	10.0	8.1	20.1	4.0
Savage	53	500	26.3	9.9	118	627,032	15.4	38.4	2.4	14.5	0.0	16.4	0.0
Shakopee	59	314	34.7	9.9	200	1,024,903	11.0	30.0	5.6	7.6	0.0	27.1	0.0
Shoreview	19	D	D	D	99	459,573	15.0	0.0	37.1	15.7	12.0	15.7	0.0
Winona	41	230	21.4	6.2	178	771,072	9.5	27.9	14.3	9.5	3.1	24.9	4.4
Woodbury	84	800	48.3	18.2	208	1,116,340	7.1	20.7	13.8	10.0	0.0	38.6	5.6
MISSISSIPPI	2,801	15,027	1,359.2	402.3	X	X	X	X	X	X	X	X	X
Biloxi	44	285	23.6	7.4	618	2,485,229	7.2	33.9	31.9	11.2	2.3	9.3	0.0
Clinton	28	135	13.3	3.9	200	583,437	12.6	31.2	23.8	11.1	0.0	20.4	0.0
Greenville	45	366	32.0	9.5	418	1,079,087	14.6	25.9	20.6	12.0	0.0	22.1	0.0
					2,468	12,266,312	2.9	7.1	4.8	1.2	81.1	1.5	0.0
Gulfport	102	537	46.0	14.7	695	1,732,465	13.4	28.5	23.1	10.4	3.7	17.8	0.0
Hattiesburg	84	551	43.3	12.9	207	963,937	6.8	40.4	27.4	12.4	0.0	9.9	0.0
Horn Lake	20	107	13.7	3.6	1,879	5,259,822	12.8	36.0	22.9	4.9	6.7	16.7	0.0
Jackson	192	1,476	118.0	40.1	506	1,342,577	12.8	26.9	25.1	9.4	2.6	19.3	0.0
Meridian	85	D	D	D	339	1,161,405	13.8	24.1	23.4	3.7	6.6	20.3	0.0
Olive Branch	48	280	22.9	6.8	218	812,891	8.6	31.3	29.5	10.4	2.5	17.7	0.0
Pearl	42	214	24.6	7.2									
Southaven	52	328	24.4	8.1	376	1,251,638	8.3	38.8	36.0	1.8	0.0	15.2	0.0
Tupelo	83	809	70.2	31.0	513	1,717,455	12.7	24.9	21.1	9.8	0.0	29.0	0.0

1. Establishments subject to federal tax.

Table D. Cities — City Government Finances

City	General revenue — Intergovernmental — Total (mil dol) [117]	Intergovernmental Total (mil dol) [118]	Percent from state government [119]	Taxes Total (mil dol) [120]	Taxes Per capita (dollars) Total [121]	Property [122]	Sales and gross receipts [123]	General expenditure Total (mil dol) [124]	Per capita (dollars) Total [125]	Capital outlays [126]
MICHIGAN— Cont'd										
Oak Park	34.3	6.1	77.1	15.3	515	501	14	32.4	1,094	25
Pontiac	80.8	29.4	48.1	29.2	491	278	50	91.7	1,541	157
Portage	42.4	7.6	94.6	24.0	508	481	26	39.8	842	89
Port Huron	56.4	17.9	36.7	21.0	712	492	23	60.3	2,048	427
Rochester Hills	71.4	14.4	64.9	31.6	437	403	34	59.2	819	60
Roseville	60.4	8.9	82.4	25.0	527	511	16	53.3	1,126	43
Royal Oak	80.5	15.1	59.4	31.4	537	481	56	82.6	1,412	97
Saginaw	92.8	33.0	36.6	21.3	420	150	24	92.8	1,827	78
St. Clair Shores	68.3	10.3	86.2	32.7	546	515	32	62.0	1,037	61
Southfield	103.2	22.5	49.8	64.7	892	863	29	95.5	1,316	49
Southgate	30.9	6.3	84.0	16.4	550	533	17	30.8	1,034	2
Sterling Heights	116.0	21.5	85.9	55.5	426	408	17	126.6	970	137
Taylor	98.5	28.2	37.2	43.0	688	652	36	96.7	1,549	17
Troy	91.2	12.7	89.5	49.2	600	579	21	79.5	969	131
Warren	142.5	27.4	77.3	78.9	588	570	18	136.7	1,019	40
Westland	82.4	25.5	58.5	27.2	327	312	14	78.6	943	2
Wyandotte	44.6	7.8	56.0	16.7	656	640	16	53.7	2,107	160
Wyoming	74.0	21.7	50.6	26.8	365	333	32	64.1	874	19
MINNESOTA	X	X	X	X	X	X	X	X	X	X
Andover	22.9	1.9	92.9	12.6	406	393	12	18.3	588	147
Apple Valley	46.2	2.4	99.7	25.9	518	476	43	38.3	766	170
Blaine	45.6	3.0	81.8	23.5	396	359	37	44.2	746	172
Bloomington	120.6	11.3	85.5	69.9	812	609	203	137.2	1,595	316
Brooklyn Center	39.3	5.0	72.8	18.2	595	514	59	39.3	1,280	319
Brooklyn Park	79.5	9.0	54.3	44.0	566	543	23	69.8	898	50
Burnsville	55.1	4.0	78.6	33.5	547	501	46	54.1	885	185
Coon Rapids	50.6	4.4	75.2	28.1	453	367	86	69.6	1,124	385
Cottage Grove	32.6	4.1	86.1	13.7	391	358	32	30.2	858	186
Duluth	206.7	90.6	73.8	42.1	488	216	272	223.1	2,586	972
Eagan	55.0	3.8	90.8	28.6	442	413	29	57.4	885	201
Eden Prairie	70.0	5.2	80.2	37.9	610	555	54	67.1	1,079	147
Edina	63.6	3.2	88.7	32.5	663	592	70	63.8	1,301	290
Fridley	25.2	2.5	85.3	13.4	485	445	39	22.0	798	53
Inver Grove Heights	31.7	4.0	89.5	15.9	466	442	24	53.2	1,557	670
Lakeville	38.7	2.8	74.0	25.0	436	404	32	42.0	732	180
Mankato	77.8	20.6	42.2	21.6	539	345	195	74.6	1,863	805
Maple Grove	94.0	6.8	98.0	34.4	534	494	40	87.7	1,362	607
Maplewood	49.5	5.8	59.6	18.9	481	447	34	51.2	1,300	407
Minneapolis	1,017.5	148.8	51.2	459.8	1,170	858	312	1,439.6	3,663	222
Minnetonka	66.8	15.6	62.1	35.1	686	601	85	65.7	1,286	502
Moorhead	71.8	30.0	77.2	8.2	210	171	39	91.5	2,342	1,042
Oakdale	20.9	1.3	73.5	10.5	379	346	33	27.2	981	403
Owatonna	26.3	7.8	88.0	10.8	426	355	71	25.3	995	237
Plymouth	77.8	8.1	86.5	32.3	443	399	45	66.3	909	162
Richfield	43.3	7.0	35.4	22.3	617	560	57	42.6	1,180	117
Rochester	216.6	36.4	96.7	62.4	572	415	158	238.9	2,190	743
Roseville	33.7	3.3	86.1	17.5	506	445	61	34.0	981	217
St. Cloud	89.0	22.7	89.2	36.3	550	348	201	105.0	1,592	659
St. Louis Park	76.4	3.2	86.2	35.3	760	659	101	77.7	1,676	320
St. Paul	510.2	119.9	59.1	175.4	602	412	190	504.8	1,733	219
Savage	32.0	3.4	94.3	16.3	584	537	46	22.4	802	183
Shakopee	36.9	5.1	99.9	15.9	410	373	37	36.0	928	217
Shoreview	25.3	1.3	99.9	11.3	441	424	17	23.1	899	137
Winona	24.8	11.9	97.0	7.9	284	213	71	23.2	837	90
Woodbury	61.1	3.7	75.8	30.7	475	432	44	55.7	863	229
MISSISSIPPI	X	X	X	X	X	X	X	X	X	X
Biloxi	102.9	58.6	70.6	23.1	518	393	125	110.6	2,484	715
Clinton	22.4	8.4	97.4	8.5	332	293	39	20.7	810	145
Greenville	30.6	10.5	67.0	12.3	368	293	75	32.5	970	190
	510.2	92.4	40.6	32.6	466	348	117	508.4	7,267	1,373
Gulfport	68.9	33.4	74.6	25.2	537	368	168	64.6	1,378	307
Hattiesburg	18.5	4.3	95.2	7.0	264	233	31	15.9	598	35
Horn Lake	222.7	65.9	65.5	79.3	452	389	63	212.1	1,210	208
Jackson	43.9	15.5	100.0	18.6	456	387	69	39.7	973	158
Meridian	42.4	15.2	100.0	15.0	434	379	55	33.8	978	185
Olive Branch	24.5	10.5	91.4	6.9	263	226	37	32.5	1,241	187
Pearl										
Southaven	49.4	12.7	100.0	25.8	512	457	55	48.7	966	118
Tupelo	65.5	32.8	96.4	15.7	442	418	24	62.2	1,751	529

1. Based on population estimated as of July 1 of the year shown.

City	Public welfare	Highways	Parking facilities	Education	Health and hospitals	Police protection	Sewerage and sanitation	Parks and recreation	Housing and community development	Interest on debt
	City government finances, 2012 (cont.)									
	General expenditure (cont.)									
	Percent of total for:									
	127	128	129	130	131	132	133	134	135	136
MICHIGAN— Cont'd										
Oak Park	0.0	4.6	0.0	0.0	0.0	26.1	25.4	3.4	1.7	4.4
Pontiac	0.0	7.1	0.9	0.0	0.0	12.5	18.4	0.4	15.4	3.8
Portage	0.3	15.3	0.0	0.0	0.0	16.1	25.8	5.4	0.7	6.0
Port Huron	0.0	9.9	0.2	0.0	0.0	12.5	24.6	6.6	19.9	4.4
Rochester Hills	0.0	16.6	0.0	0.0	0.0	14.1	16.0	17.9	0.0	1.7
Roseville	0.0	9.7	0.0	0.0	0.9	22.0	20.2	4.1	2.4	0.9
Royal Oak	0.0	8.3	2.6	0.0	0.9	15.6	28.0	4.9	2.8	4.3
Saginaw	0.0	6.8	0.3	0.0	0.0	19.4	19.6	0.4	17.3	1.0
St. Clair Shores	0.0	8.8	0.0	0.0	0.0	18.5	24.7	7.1	0.1	3.1
Southfield	0.0	8.3	0.0	0.0	0.0	25.8	3.3	9.2	0.8	2.2
Southgate	0.0	10.8	0.0	0.0	0.0	19.5	14.2	3.9	0.7	2.6
Sterling Heights	0.0	9.6	0.0	0.0	0.0	23.7	27.1	2.0	0.7	0.9
Taylor	0.0	6.6	0.0	0.0	0.0	13.8	11.6	3.9	20.5	5.2
Troy	0.0	17.7	0.0	0.0	0.0	27.5	18.5	11.2	0.2	3.2
Warren	0.0	10.2	0.0	0.0	0.0	25.5	15.8	5.4	3.9	3.3
Westland	0.0	7.6	0.0	0.0	0.0	18.9	22.4	3.3	2.0	0.4
Wyandotte	0.0	10.3	0.0	0.0	0.0	12.1	10.3	3.8	0.0	1.2
Wyoming	0.0	10.0	0.0	0.0	0.0	23.8	19.2	7.1	14.4	1.7
MINNESOTA	X	X	X	X	X	X	X	X	X	X
Andover	0.0	21.8	0.0	0.0	0.1	14.3	10.5	11.4	13.2	10.2
Apple Valley	0.0	23.5	0.0	0.0	0.0	20.0	12.9	18.3	1.6	4.4
Blaine	0.0	19.5	0.0	0.0	0.0	20.6	22.6	3.2	4.5	4.2
Bloomington	0.0	15.1	0.0	0.0	4.6	18.4	9.8	10.4	0.3	2.3
Brooklyn Center	0.0	19.6	0.0	0.0	0.0	18.2	16.1	7.6	5.8	2.3
Brooklyn Park	0.0	12.2	0.0	0.0	0.0	24.2	11.5	13.9	1.1	5.9
Burnsville	0.0	20.0	0.0	0.0	0.0	22.5	13.2	12.7	0.0	4.0
Coon Rapids	0.0	11.5	0.9	0.0	0.1	12.5	11.3	29.9	4.5	4.1
Cottage Grove	0.0	33.1	0.0	0.0	3.9	16.5	6.7	11.5	4.3	12.1
Duluth	0.0	10.1	0.4	0.0	0.0	13.3	14.3	13.0	4.6	4.5
Eagan	0.0	20.7	0.0	0.0	0.0	19.5	13.7	14.3	0.0	5.8
Eden Prairie	1.2	12.6	0.0	0.0	0.2	17.7	14.4	15.9	4.9	12.0
Edina	0.0	27.8	0.0	0.0	0.8	13.8	14.5	20.4	1.1	3.7
Fridley	0.0	16.8	0.0	0.0	0.0	23.9	27.0	6.0	5.6	0.1
Inver Grove Heights	0.0	24.4	0.0	0.0	0.0	10.4	20.8	20.6	1.3	4.3
Lakeville	0.0	25.3	0.0	0.0	0.0	21.3	9.7	9.7	1.2	8.8
Mankato	0.0	18.4	5.3	0.0	0.0	11.5	15.6	4.6	16.8	3.8
Maple Grove	0.0	38.8	0.0	0.0	0.0	10.9	8.6	15.2	1.5	5.0
Maplewood	0.0	30.5	0.0	0.0	0.3	15.2	9.0	8.7	0.7	17.9
Minneapolis	0.0	6.6	3.3	0.0	1.1	10.1	41.6	7.3	9.6	8.6
Minnetonka	0.0	31.5	0.0	0.0	0.5	16.6	9.2	10.9	8.2	3.8
Moorhead	0.0	11.8	0.0	0.0	0.4	8.0	8.7	5.0	1.2	11.2
Oakdale	0.0	28.1	0.0	0.0	0.0	15.5	10.8	5.0	0.0	3.0
Owatonna	0.0	25.9	0.0	0.0	0.0	16.3	14.0	13.5	3.4	3.0
Plymouth	0.0	16.9	0.0	0.0	0.0	14.7	11.2	18.8	2.0	8.3
Richfield	0.0	7.8	0.0	0.0	0.3	17.0	11.9	11.5	23.0	12.9
Rochester	0.0	14.1	1.4	0.0	0.1	8.6	5.1	7.5	0.2	27.8
Roseville	0.0	14.4	0.0	0.0	0.0	18.2	17.2	12.1	4.2	1.3
St. Cloud	0.0	11.6	1.2	0.0	0.9	15.3	22.1	22.3	1.4	4.9
St. Louis Park	0.0	9.2	0.0	0.0	0.0	9.0	10.3	10.9	1.1	25.9
St. Paul	0.0	12.4	1.3	0.0	0.7	17.5	8.3	15.6	9.7	6.3
Savage	0.0	30.8	0.0	0.0	0.0	19.3	12.0	7.6	0.9	11.4
Shakopee	0.0	22.2	0.0	0.0	0.0	18.6	16.8	12.4	0.0	13.3
Shoreview	0.0	15.7	0.0	0.0	0.0	7.9	23.0	26.0	3.7	6.4
Winona	0.0	12.5	0.0	0.0	0.5	18.9	18.0	13.8	3.7	0.8
Woodbury	0.0	22.0	2.9	0.0	3.0	20.7	11.9	11.7	3.2	3.7
MISSISSIPPI	X	X	X	X	X	X	X	X	X	X
Biloxi	1.0	7.1	0.0	0.0	0.2	13.5	15.9	12.3	0.7	2.1
Clinton	0.0	13.3	0.0	0.0	0.0	19.0	28.7	7.7	0.0	3.8
Greenville	0.4	16.8	0.0	0.0	0.9	22.4	13.5	2.6	0.0	1.1
	0.0	5.6	0.0	0.0	72.1	4.7	4.9	3.1	2.1	1.8
Gulfport	0.0	16.5	0.3	0.0	1.6	16.2	16.4	6.6	2.8	2.3
Hattiesburg	0.0	6.3	0.0	0.0	0.7	27.6	15.3	6.7	0.7	6.2
Horn Lake	0.5	9.5	0.0	0.0	0.5	15.4	16.2	6.3	0.9	4.0
Jackson	0.0	13.7	0.4	0.0	0.0	18.3	14.0	5.1	2.6	5.1
Meridian	0.0	10.9	0.0	0.0	2.5	22.3	22.4	4.0	0.0	5.9
Olive Branch	0.0	22.1	0.0	0.0	1.4	19.0	18.3	4.3	0.0	6.3
Pearl										
Southaven	0.0	2.9	0.0	0.0	0.6	21.9	9.2	9.5	0.0	8.5
Tupelo	0.0	24.5	0.0	0.0	0.0	16.4	11.5	9.2	0.1	4.2

Table D. Cities — City Government Finances, City Government Employment, and Climate

City	City government finances, 2012 (cont.) Debt outstanding Total (mil dol)	Per capita[1] (dollars)	Debt issued during year	Climate[2] Average daily temperature Mean January	July	Limits January[3]	July[4]	Annual precipitation (inches)	Heating degree days	Cooling degree days
	137	138	139	140	141	142	143	144	145	146
MICHIGAN— Cont'd										
Oak Park	45.1	1,521	0.0	24.7	73.7	16.1	85.7	33.58	6,224	788
Pontiac	80.8	1,357	5.6	22.9	71.9	15.9	82.3	30.03	6,680	626
Portage	90.1	1,908	15.0	24.3	73.2	17.0	84.2	37.41	6,235	773
Port Huron	122.4	4,160	21.5	22.8	72.2	15.1	81.9	31.39	6,845	626
Rochester Hills	31.9	441	5.0	22.0	70.6	13.7	82.7	35.74	7,046	523
Roseville	13.3	282	0.3	25.3	73.6	18.8	83.3	33.97	6,160	757
Royal Oak	117.8	2,013	0.0	24.7	73.7	16.1	85.7	33.58	6,224	788
Saginaw	81.9	1,612	13.5	21.4	71.2	14.9	81.9	31.61	7,099	548
St. Clair Shores	53.2	890	9.1	25.3	73.6	18.8	83.3	33.97	6,160	757
Southfield	64.8	893	0.0	24.7	73.7	16.1	85.7	33.58	6,224	788
Southgate	22.5	757	0.3	24.5	73.5	17.8	83.4	32.89	6,422	736
Sterling Heights	63.9	490	13.6	24.4	71.9	18.0	81.8	32.24	6,620	597
Taylor	147.4	2,362	1.4	24.5	73.5	17.8	83.4	32.89	6,422	736
Troy	55.0	669	0.0	22.9	71.9	15.9	82.3	30.03	6,680	626
Warren	159.2	1,186	8.8	24.7	73.7	16.1	85.7	33.58	6,224	788
Westland	12.4	149	0.8	24.6	73.9	17.6	84.7	32.80	6,167	828
Wyandotte	63.3	2,483	0.8	24.5	73.5	17.8	83.4	32.89	6,422	736
Wyoming	117.0	1,595	7.3	22.4	71.4	15.6	82.3	37.13	6,896	613
MINNESOTA	X	X	X	X	X	X	X	X	X	X
Andover	55.4	1,776	0.3	10.9	70.4	1.8	80.5	31.36	8,367	500
Apple Valley	71.3	1,426	9.2	9.2	69.4	-1.1	80.5	29.19	8,805	416
Blaine	51.9	874	1.6	10.9	70.4	1.8	80.5	31.36	8,367	500
Bloomington	158.7	1,844	27.0	13.1	73.2	4.3	83.3	29.41	7,876	699
Brooklyn Center	47.5	1,549	0.0	13.0	71.4	2.8	82.8	30.50	7,983	587
Brooklyn Park	95.6	1,229	16.1	13.0	71.4	2.8	82.8	30.50	7,983	587
Burnsville	62.7	1,026	8.4	13.8	74.0	3.4	85.8	30.44	7,549	803
Coon Rapids	87.0	1,407	9.1	13.0	71.4	2.8	82.8	30.50	7,983	587
Cottage Grove	57.0	1,618	0.0	12.0	72.1	2.5	82.6	29.95	8,032	617
Duluth	251.3	2,914	21.9	8.4	65.5	-1.2	76.3	31.00	9,724	189
Eagan	61.1	943	0.0	13.1	73.2	4.3	83.3	29.41	7,876	699
Eden Prairie	202.7	3,258	11.3	10.2	71.4	-0.3	82.2	28.82	8,429	567
Edina	119.7	2,440	15.0	13.8	74.0	3.4	85.8	30.44	7,549	803
Fridley	14.9	541	0.0	10.9	70.4	1.8	80.5	31.36	8,367	500
Inver Grove Heights	55.6	1,626	4.6	10.1	71.0	0.0	81.3	34.60	8,345	533
Lakeville	90.0	1,570	4.3	13.1	72.2	3.8	83.6	31.43	7,773	658
Mankato	117.0	2,921	4.6	12.5	72.1	2.4	83.4	33.42	8,029	650
Maple Grove	207.8	3,225	5.4	13.0	71.4	2.8	82.8	30.50	7,983	587
Maplewood	157.8	4,004	10.0	14.5	73.0	6.2	83.2	32.59	7,606	715
Minneapolis	3,439.9	8,754	233.0	13.1	73.2	4.3	83.3	29.41	7,876	699
Minnetonka	91.2	1,784	0.0	13.1	73.2	4.3	83.3	29.41	7,876	699
Moorhead	252.1	6,451	10.0	3.8	69.8	-7.1	81.5	21.56	9,628	478
Oakdale	31.2	1,124	10.6	14.5	73.0	6.2	83.2	32.59	7,606	715
Owatonna	49.7	1,954	8.3	NA	NA	NA	NA	NA	NA	NA
Plymouth	108.6	1,490	0.0	13.0	71.4	2.8	82.8	30.50	7,983	587
Richfield	105.3	2,917	11.9	13.1	73.2	4.3	83.3	29.41	7,876	699
Rochester	2,086.4	19,128	285.0	9.8	70.0	0.0	80.9	29.10	8,703	474
Roseville	20.1	581	10.0	14.5	73.0	6.2	83.2	32.59	7,606	715
St. Cloud	413.3	6,266	35.1	8.8	69.8	-1.2	81.7	27.13	8,815	443
St. Louis Park	499.7	10,778	0.0	13.0	71.4	2.8	82.8	30.50	7,983	587
St. Paul	770.7	2,646	98.7	14.5	73.0	6.2	83.2	32.59	7,606	715
Savage	84.5	3,021	10.7	NA	NA	NA	NA	NA	NA	NA
Shakopee	92.8	2,394	0.0	NA	NA	NA	NA	NA	NA	NA
Shoreview	51.1	1,990	8.6	14.5	73.0	6.2	83.2	32.59	7,606	715
Winona	7.0	254	0.0	17.6	75.8	9.2	85.3	34.20	6,839	990
Woodbury	92.0	1,427	1.5	11.5	72.1	1.9	81.9	29.92	8,104	621
MISSISSIPPI	X	X	X	X	X	X	X	X	X	X
Biloxi	68.0	1,528	0.5	50.7	81.7	43.5	88.5	64.84	1,645	2,517
Clinton	36.4	1,422	1.7	NA	NA	NA	NA	NA	NA	NA
Greenville	22.8	681	10.5	42.3	82.6	33.0	92.6	54.20	2,715	2,216
	212.6	3,038	5.0	51.6	82.6	42.6	91.3	65.20	1,514	2,679
Gulfport	89.3	1,904	5.4	47.9	81.7	36.0	92.1	62.47	2,024	2,327
Hattiesburg	35.8	1,350	0.0	NA	NA	NA	NA	NA	NA	NA
Horn Lake	322.3	1,839	62.9	45.0	81.4	35.0	91.4	55.95	2,401	2,264
Jackson	61.0	1,493	9.3	46.1	81.7	34.7	92.9	58.65	2,352	2,173
Meridian	57.9	1,676	15.0	NA	NA	NA	NA	NA	NA	NA
Olive Branch	99.8	3,814	6.4	NA	NA	NA	NA	NA	NA	NA
Pearl										
Southaven	96.2	1,909	8.0	37.9	80.4	27.8	90.3	55.06	3,442	1,749
Tupelo	82.1	2,311	14.6	40.4	80.6	30.5	91.4	55.86	3,086	1,884

1. Based on the population estimated as of July 1 of the year shown. 2. Represents normal values based on the 30-year period, 1971±2000. 3. Average daily minimum. 4. Average daily maximum.

Table D. Cities — **Land Area and Population**

STATE Place code	City	Land area¹ (sq. mi)	Total persons 2018	Rank	Per square mile	White	Black or African American	American Indian, Alaskan Native	Asian	Hawaiian Pacific Islander	Some other race	Two or more races (percent)
		1	2	3	4	5	6	7	8	9	10	11
29 00,000	MISSOURI	68,745.8	6,126,452	X	89.1	82.0	11.4	0.4	2.0	0.1	1.3	2.6
29 03,160	Ballwin	9.0	30,188	1,247	3,354.2	93.9	2.2	0.0	2.3	0.0	0.0	1.6
29 06,652	Blue Springs	22.4	55,104	689	2,460.0	81.8	9.8	0.2	2.5	0.0	2.2	3.4
29 11,242	Cape Girardeau	29.0	39,853	966	1,374.2	80.0	14.4	0.0	2.4	0.1	0.5	2.6
29 13,600	Chesterfield	31.9	47,644	812	1,493.5	83.2	5.0	0.2	10.5	0.0	0.1	1.0
29 15,670	Columbia	65.6	123,180	224	1,877.7	76.2	10.8	0.4	5.8	1.5	0.7	4.7
29 24,778	Florissant	12.6	51,272	750	4,069.2	56.4	34.2	0.5	1.4	0.1	2.1	5.4
29 27,190	Gladstone	8.1	27,317	1,343	3,372.5	NA	NA	NA	NA	NA	NA	NA
29 31,276	Hazelwood	16.1	25,204	1,408	1,565.5	51.0	41.7	0.0	3.6	0.0	1.2	2.5
29 35,000	Independence	77.8	116,925	243	1,502.9	76.2	5.7	0.8	1.2	1.3	11.9	2.9
29 37,000	Jefferson City	36.1	42,838	888	1,186.6	72.0	21.5	0.3	2.7	0.0	0.0	3.5
29 37,592	Joplin	37.7	50,657	759	1,343.7	83.6	3.4	2.8	1.9	0.0	2.2	6.1
29 38,000	Kansas City	314.9	491,918	38	1,562.1	60.0	28.5	0.6	3.2	0.1	4.2	3.4
29 39,044	Kirkwood	9.1	27,758	1,327	3,050.3	NA	NA	NA	NA	NA	NA	NA
29 41,348	Lee's Summit	63.8	98,461	315	1,543.3	88.3	5.9	0.2	2.3	0.1	1.1	2.2
29 42,032	Liberty	28.8	31,779	1,194	1,103.4	NA	NA	NA	NA	NA	NA	NA
29 46,586	Maryland Heights	21.9	27,016	1,359	1,233.6	66.0	15.0	0.0	14.2	0.0	1.2	3.6
29 54,074	O'Fallon	29.7	88,472	374	2,978.9	90.3	2.7	0.0	3.4	0.0	0.0	3.7
29 60,788	Raytown	9.9	28,993	1,286	2,928.6	55.9	36.8	0.0	0.9	0.0	1.9	4.5
29 64,082	St. Charles	24.7	70,764	508	2,864.9	85.7	6.5	0.1	2.6	0.0	0.3	4.8
29 64,550	St. Joseph	44.0	75,959	460	1,726.3	85.4	4.7	0.4	1.3	1.6	3.3	3.5
29 65,000	St. Louis	61.7	302,838	64	4,908.2	46.3	46.8	0.4	3.4	0.0	1.1	1.9
29 65,126	St. Peters	22.5	57,127	665	2,539.0	85.8	5.8	0.0	3.8	0.0	0.5	4.1
29 70,000	Springfield	82.3	168,122	156	2,042.8	89.0	3.6	0.6	2.3	0.2	0.6	3.7
29 75,220	University City	5.9	34,322	1,110	5,817.3	56.9	32.5	0.2	8.0	0.2	0.0	2.2
29 78,442	Wentzville	20.2	41,164	930	2,037.8	NA	NA	NA	NA	NA	NA	NA
29 79,820	Wildwood	66.6	35,517	1,083	533.3	88.9	2.3	0.0	5.1	0.0	0.7	3.0
30 00,000	MONTANA	145,546.1	1,062,305	X	7.3	88.6	0.4	6.2	0.7	0.1	0.7	3.3
30 06,550	Billings	44.0	109,550	276	2,489.8	88.4	1.1	3.9	0.8	0.5	1.0	4.3
30 08,950	Bozeman	20.1	48,532	794	2,414.5	NA	NA	NA	NA	NA	NA	NA
30 11,390	Butte-Silver Bow	715.8	34,284	1,111	47.9	NA	NA	NA	NA	NA	NA	NA
30 32,800	Great Falls	23.0	58,701	641	2,552.2	87.4	0.9	5.0	0.6	0.1	1.2	4.8
30 35,600	Helena	16.7	32,315	1,175	1,935.0	NA	NA	NA	NA	NA	NA	NA
30 50,200	Missoula	29.3	74,428	478	2,540.2	92.9	0.1	1.4	1.9	0.0	0.4	3.3
31 00,000	NEBRASKA	76,817.6	1,929,268	X	25.1	87.3	4.6	0.8	2.5	0.1	2.0	2.7
31 03,950	Bellevue	16.6	53,627	722	3,230.5	80.5	5.4	0.6	2.3	0.5	7.1	3.6
31 17,670	Fremont	10.4	26,509	1,380	2,548.9	NA	NA	NA	NA	NA	NA	NA
31 19,595	Grand Island	29.7	51,478	748	1,733.3	83.2	2.0	0.8	1.6	0.3	9.9	2.3
31 25,055	Kearney	14.1	33,761	1,131	2,394.4	92.8	0.5	0.1	1.8	0.0	2.3	2.5
31 28,000	Lincoln	94.8	287,401	70	3,031.7	84.9	4.1	0.7	5.0	0.1	1.4	3.9
31 37,000	Omaha	138.2	468,262	42	3,388.3	78.3	12.3	0.5	3.7	0.1	1.7	3.3
32 00,000	NEVADA	109,780.2	3,034,392	X	27.6	64.6	9.2	1.3	8.5	0.7	11.1	4.6
32 09,700	Carson City	144.7	55,414	685	383.0	80.6	1.6	3.1	3.1	0.3	8.8	2.5
32 31,900	Henderson	104.7	310,390	62	2,964.6	75.6	6.3	0.2	10.6	0.2	3.0	4.0
32 40,000	Las Vegas	141.8	644,644	28	4,546.1	62.1	10.7	0.8	7.1	0.9	13.8	4.7
32 51,800	North Las Vegas	98.0	245,949	90	2,509.7	51.1	21.3	0.8	7.6	0.3	13.4	5.5
32 60,600	Reno	108.7	250,998	86	2,309.1	74.3	3.1	1.2	6.8	0.9	8.6	5.0
32 68,400	Sparks	35.8	104,246	296	2,911.9	77.3	1.3	1.9	6.2	0.0	6.4	6.8
33 00,000	NEW HAMPSHIRE	8,953.5	1,356,458	X	151.5	93.1	1.7	0.1	2.7	0.0	0.3	2.1
33 14,200	Concord	64.0	43,412	878	678.3	91.2	3.9	0.7	2.3	0.0	0.4	1.4
33 18,820	Dover	26.7	31,771	1,195	1,189.9	NA	NA	NA	NA	NA	NA	NA
33 45,140	Manchester	33.1	112,525	259	3,399.5	87.9	5.1	0.1	3.7	0.1	1.0	2.1
33 50,260	Nashua	30.8	89,246	370	2,897.6	78.6	5.7	0.1	10.1	0.0	0.9	4.6
33 65,140	Rochester	45.1	31,366	1,207	695.5	NA	NA	NA	NA	NA	NA	NA
34 00,000	NEW JERSEY	7,354.4	8,908,520	X	1,211.3	67.9	13.5	0.2	9.8	0.0	6.0	2.5
34 02,080	Atlantic City	10.8	37,804	1,016	3,500.4	25.6	32.9	0.0	15.5	0.0	22.0	3.9
34 03,580	Bayonne	5.8	65,083	572	11,221.2	67.8	7.0	0.3	6.5	0.0	13.6	4.9
34 05,170	Bergenfield	2.9	27,479	1,337	9,475.5	58.9	9.3	0.0	25.8	0.0	4.1	1.9
34 07,600	Bridgeton	6.2	24,442	1,425	3,942.3	NA	NA	NA	NA	NA	NA	NA
34 10,000	Camden	8.9	73,973	484	8,311.6	31.1	43.0	0.6	3.1	0.2	17.6	4.5
34 13,690	Clifton	11.3	85,273	394	7,546.3	62.9	5.5	0.1	11.7	0.0	17.5	2.3
34 19,390	East Orange	3.9	64,457	579	16,527.4	3.5	85.1	0.0	2.0	0.0	9.0	0.4
34 21,000	Elizabeth	12.3	128,885	215	10,478.5	40.6	18.4	0.6	1.3	0.0	36.1	3.0
34 21,480	Englewood	4.9	28,624	1,300	5,841.6	54.8	30.5	0.0	10.2	0.0	1.2	3.3
34 22,470	Fair Lawn	5.1	33,128	1,151	6,495.7	NA	NA	NA	NA	NA	NA	NA
34 24,420	Fort Lee	2.5	37,921	1,015	15,168.4	55.1	2.2	0.6	35.9	0.0	1.9	4.2

1. Dry land or land partially or temporarily covered by water.   2. Hispanic or Latino persons may be of any race.

1066   MO(Ballwin)—NJ(Fort Lee)   Items 1—11

Table D. Cities — Population

City	Percent Hispanic or Latino[1], 2017	Percent foreign born, 2017	Age of population (percent), 2017 Under 18 years	18 to 24 years	25 to 34 years	35 to 44 years	45 to 54 years	55 to 64 years	65 years and over	Median age, 2017	Percent female, 2017	Census counts 2000	Census counts 2010	Percent change 2000-2010	Percent change 2001-2018
	12	13	14	15	16	17	18	19	20	21	22	23	24	25	26
MISSOURI	4.2	4.2	22.7	9.4	13.3	11.9	12.7	13.5	16.5	38.5	50.9	5,595,211	5,988,952	7.0	2.3
Ballwin	1.2	5.0	23.5	6.0	10.9	14.1	16.4	12.0	17.2	42.4	50.5	31,283	30,420	-2.8	-0.8
Blue Springs	7.8	3.4	27.2	6.8	12.7	12.8	13.5	11.7	15.2	38.1	50.9	48,080	52,620	9.4	4.7
Cape Girardeau	2.0	5.4	19.8	22.2	11.7	9.0	10.4	9.8	17.2	32.1	53.7	35,349	38,001	7.5	4.9
Chesterfield	1.0	13.3	21.1	7.4	9.1	11.4	12.9	14.1	23.9	45.8	51.1	46,802	47,484	1.5	0.3
Columbia	3.5	6.8	17.9	25.8	16.0	11.8	8.9	8.9	10.8	28.0	51.5	84,531	109,044	29.0	13.0
Florissant	1.9	4.6	24.7	8.1	11.4	12.7	13.1	14.1	15.8	38.4	55.6	50,497	52,299	3.6	-2.0
Gladstone	7.2	3.2	21.8	4.0	16.1	12.2	12.3	15.0	18.5	40.7	50.7	26,365	25,442	-3.5	7.4
Hazelwood	9.5	10.0	30.1	9.9	12.0	18.8	8.2	11.3	9.7	31.3	52.1	26,206	25,680	-2.0	-1.9
Independence	14.6	7.9	25.4	8.2	12.3	12.7	10.6	14.1	16.7	37.8	51.8	113,288	116,800	3.1	0.1
Jefferson City	5.3	5.3	20.8	10.8	13.8	12.4	12.9	12.3	17.1	38.1	46.7	39,636	43,121	8.8	-0.7
Joplin	3.9	4.3	22.1	9.1	16.3	12.8	11.2	11.7	16.7	37.4	49.3	45,504	50,793	11.6	-0.3
Kansas City	9.4	7.7	22.7	9.2	17.9	12.9	12.8	11.8	12.7	35.1	51.4	441,545	459,937	4.2	7.0
Kirkwood	3.2	6.0	21.9	4.9	11.5	10.4	12.3	14.5	24.5	46.8	53.0	27,324	27,546	0.8	0.8
Lee's Summit	4.9	4.2	27.3	6.5	11.9	13.6	12.2	13.2	15.3	38.2	51.9	70,700	91,366	29.2	7.8
Liberty	3.1	0.5	21.9	13.0	9.9	12.7	12.0	17.3	13.2	39.7	52.3	26,232	29,190	11.3	8.9
Maryland Heights	4.4	20.7	14.9	12.8	19.3	10.3	11.3	13.4	17.9	37.6	50.5	25,756	27,449	6.6	-1.6
O'Fallon	4.2	3.9	29.7	6.8	13.4	15.1	13.0	10.5	11.6	35.1	48.1	46,169	79,493	72.2	11.3
Raytown	5.3	4.0	17.1	9.7	12.7	11.1	15.3	16.7	17.3	44.7	54.0	30,388	29,475	-3.0	-1.6
St. Charles	4.0	5.5	15.8	15.2	16.6	12.3	11.0	12.4	16.8	36.9	53.6	60,321	66,140	9.6	7.0
St. Joseph	7.7	5.6	23.0	10.6	15.6	10.9	12.1	11.7	16.1	35.7	50.8	73,990	76,786	3.8	-1.1
St. Louis	4.0	7.7	19.4	9.4	20.1	13.1	11.9	13.3	12.9	35.6	51.5	348,189	319,275	-8.3	-5.1
St. Peters	1.9	4.2	24.9	6.9	15.7	13.1	12.8	15.1	11.5	36.7	50.1	51,381	52,578	2.3	8.7
Springfield	5.1	3.1	18.2	19.3	15.4	9.9	10.8	10.4	16.1	32.7	51.6	151,580	159,453	5.2	5.4
University City	2.6	7.6	13.6	16.5	14.8	10.3	7.9	14.7	22.1	39.9	56.1	37,428	35,253	-5.8	-2.6
Wentzville	1.5	1.0	32.1	4.8	13.8	19.0	11.4	8.2	10.7	34.4	53.6	6,896	29,366	325.8	40.2
Wildwood	4.8	7.4	27.5	7.5	5.5	13.5	18.7	13.9	13.5	42.2	52.3	32,884	35,320	7.4	0.6
MONTANA	3.7	2.2	21.9	9.2	12.6	11.9	11.7	14.5	18.1	40.0	49.9	902,195	989,409	9.7	7.4
Billings	6.3	3.0	22.6	7.2	15.6	12.5	11.3	12.9	17.9	38.8	51.3	89,847	104,294	16.1	5.0
Bozeman	3.3	3.3	16.5	28.2	17.5	11.3	9.0	9.6	7.9	27.0	48.7	27,509	37,290	35.6	30.1
Butte-Silver Bow	4.6	1.1	20.4	11.8	11.0	12.1	10.5	15.5	18.7	39.4	50.4	NA	33,505	NA	2.3
Great Falls	5.3	3.3	19.6	9.2	14.8	11.0	12.0	14.6	18.8	41.9	50.3	56,690	59,100	4.3	-0.7
Helena	5.5	0.9	18.9	7.9	11.5	14.0	12.9	15.2	19.7	43.3	51.0	25,780	28,545	10.7	13.2
Missoula	2.4	3.4	18.7	17.6	18.9	12.8	9.2	10.1	12.6	31.9	49.9	57,053	66,828	17.1	11.4
NEBRASKA	10.9	7.5	24.7	9.7	13.5	12.3	11.7	12.7	15.4	36.5	50.0	1,711,263	1,826,305	6.7	5.6
Bellevue	16.3	9.0	22.9	12.2	17.1	10.7	12.1	11.1	13.9	33.5	50.3	44,382	51,531	16.1	4.1
Fremont	15.9	8.6	25.3	10.2	15.0	10.0	10.6	12.6	16.3	34.8	52.8	25,174	26,413	4.9	0.4
Grand Island	30.5	12.7	28.5	7.3	14.2	12.5	11.0	12.2	14.3	35.0	49.3	42,940	48,651	13.3	5.8
Kearney	9.7	4.3	21.8	18.2	13.6	11.6	11.3	10.6	13.0	32.5	51.6	27,431	30,939	12.8	9.1
Lincoln	7.7	9.0	23.1	15.7	14.3	12.4	10.5	10.8	13.1	32.9	49.7	225,581	258,602	14.6	11.1
Omaha	14.1	10.9	24.8	9.8	16.1	12.3	11.8	12.1	13.0	34.5	50.7	390,007	450,238	15.4	4.0
NEVADA	28.8	19.9	22.8	8.4	14.5	13.3	13.2	12.4	15.3	38.0	49.8	1,998,257	2,700,679	35.2	12.4
Carson City	24.2	11.0	19.9	7.4	14.1	12.0	11.9	16.0	18.8	41.9	47.7	52,457	55,274	5.4	0.3
Henderson	14.7	13.4	20.3	7.1	12.1	13.3	13.3	13.1	20.7	43.1	51.0	175,381	257,073	46.6	20.7
Las Vegas	34.2	21.8	23.7	7.4	14.9	13.6	14.0	12.2	14.2	37.8	50.0	478,434	584,509	22.2	10.3
North Las Vegas	43.0	25.5	28.7	9.7	13.9	14.2	13.1	10.0	10.4	32.9	50.2	115,488	216,670	87.6	13.5
Reno	26.1	16.0	22.4	11.3	16.7	11.4	12.1	11.7	14.5	34.8	50.3	180,480	225,411	24.9	11.4
Sparks	27.7	12.5	21.3	7.2	14.1	14.3	13.5	12.9	16.7	40.3	49.5	66,346	91,066	37.3	14.5
NEW HAMPSHIRE	3.8	6.2	19.2	9.4	12.2	11.3	14.6	15.6	17.6	43.2	50.4	1,235,786	1,316,464	6.5	3.0
Concord	3.0	8.6	15.4	8.2	16.0	11.0	18.2	15.0	16.3	44.5	49.8	40,687	42,683	4.9	1.7
Dover	2.3	9.1	12.2	12.1	19.4	9.6	12.5	16.5	17.7	41.7	53.9	26,884	29,994	11.6	5.9
Manchester	10.0	12.5	21.0	9.2	19.5	13.2	13.7	10.9	12.4	35.2	48.2	107,006	109,549	2.4	2.7
Nashua	12.7	17.0	19.8	10.4	14.6	11.3	13.0	15.3	15.6	38.3	52.0	86,605	86,478	-0.1	3.2
Rochester	1.4	5.7	21.0	6.8	14.0	10.2	15.4	12.6	20.1	44.3	47.6	28,461	29,776	4.6	5.3
NEW JERSEY	20.4	22.8	22.0	8.8	12.9	12.9	14.2	13.5	15.7	39.8	51.2	8,414,350	8,791,962	4.5	1.3
Atlantic City	34.2	30.6	24.6	10.0	13.2	12.6	13.9	12.5	13.2	36.5	50.8	40,517	39,558	-2.4	-4.4
Bayonne	37.3	29.7	21.5	8.0	13.4	15.0	14.0	13.4	14.6	39.0	51.9	61,842	63,015	1.9	3.3
Bergenfield	26.9	34.3	23.9	10.0	14.4	15.2	11.1	11.1	14.4	36.4	54.1	26,247	26,821	2.2	2.5
Bridgeton	49.9	23.8	33.8	11.3	14.3	16.7	7.9	10.6	5.4	28.6	45.1	22,771	25,414	11.6	-3.8
Camden	46.6	16.4	30.2	9.7	13.2	15.8	10.8	9.9	10.4	32.1	55.2	79,904	77,043	-3.6	-4.0
Clifton	40.3	38.5	19.0	11.6	12.0	14.6	14.8	12.4	15.5	39.7	52.0	78,672	84,117	6.9	1.4
East Orange	12.3	31.6	21.3	10.4	16.4	14.5	13.6	10.5	13.3	37.1	54.8	69,824	64,169	-8.1	0.4
Elizabeth	67.8	44.5	28.1	9.1	14.0	14.9	13.1	10.7	10.1	34.4	50.3	120,568	124,972	3.7	3.1
Englewood	25.5	35.6	21.1	8.4	9.9	12.3	18.6	13.2	16.4	44.0	56.2	26,203	27,111	3.5	5.6
Fair Lawn	16.3	31.4	22.7	11.7	7.1	10.9	15.5	14.4	17.7	41.8	51.2	31,637	32,388	2.4	2.3
Fort Lee	15.8	45.9	16.1	6.2	13.9	12.7	12.2	12.7	26.2	46.0	52.0	35,461	35,402	-0.2	7.1

1. May be of any race.

Table D. Cities — Households, Group Quarters, Crime, and Education

City	Households, 2017							Persons in group quarters, 2017	Serious crimes known to police[2], 2016				Educational attainment, 2017		
			Percent						Total		Rate[3]			Attainment[4] (percent)	
	Number	Persons per household	Family	Married couple family	Female headed[1]	Non-family	One person		Number	Rate	Violent	Property	Population age 25 and over	High school graduate or less	Bachelor's degree or more
	27	28	29	30	31	32	33	34	35	36	37	38	39	40	41
MISSOURI	2,385,135	2.49	64.0	47.7	11.7	36.0	29.5	174,867	202,193	3,318	519	2,799	4,150,275	41.1	29.1
Ballwin	11,704	2.58	69.7	59.5	6.2	30.3	24.6	NA	247	807	36	771	21,292	20.4	56.3
Blue Springs	19,311	2.83	74.9	57.7	8.5	25.1	21.3	NA	1,581	2,904	149	2,755	36,257	33.6	29.5
Cape Girardeau	14,178	2.56	55.5	34.2	14.3	44.5	28.9	2,909	1,864	4,691	594	4,097	22,716	35.9	38.3
Chesterfield	20,161	2.31	62.1	53.4	5.9	37.9	34.1	937	925	1,930	119	1,811	34,018	12.4	67.9
Columbia	47,678	2.38	50.9	35.0	10.3	49.1	36.8	8,450	3,762	3,105	427	2,679	68,551	24.7	49.8
Florissant	20,275	2.50	64.5	37.5	22.6	35.5	31.6	843	1,270	2,430	188	2,242	34,543	38.3	24.7
Gladstone	11,817	2.30	55.3	42.3	10.1	44.7	40.2	NA	777	2,863	313	2,550	20,130	36.5	30.0
Hazelwood	9,089	2.76	63.8	43.2	17.1	36.2	27.6	NA	1,013	3,949	557	3,391	15,171	38.8	29.5
Independence	45,560	2.55	62.6	41.0	16.3	37.4	32.3	1,252	6,990	5,957	512	5,445	77,919	48.3	19.3
Jefferson City	16,448	2.32	57.9	38.3	13.6	42.1	34.5	4,699	1,492	3,456	403	3,053	29,304	39.8	29.5
Joplin	21,487	2.31	56.6	45.0	7.2	43.4	35.3	1,779	4,123	7,929	635	7,294	35,290	38.1	25.7
Kansas City	204,678	2.34	53.2	34.7	13.4	46.8	36.5	8,900	28,847	6,030	1,657	4,374	332,935	36.2	34.3
Kirkwood	12,189	2.24	61.2	51.9	8.6	38.8	34.8	295	530	1,907	104	1,803	20,218	13.6	67.2
Lee's Summit	36,237	2.66	72.1	59.0	9.0	27.9	24.5	NA	1,730	1,805	109	1,697	64,304	24.0	47.2
Liberty	11,266	2.68	71.9	50.6	18.4	28.1	23.1	1,332	543	1,769	270	1,498	20,523	28.9	36.6
Maryland Heights	11,894	2.22	57.3	41.1	14.4	42.7	31.6	630	525	1,918	201	1,717	19,507	22.5	49.0
O'Fallon	30,224	2.88	78.6	61.0	11.4	21.4	18.4	NA	1,082	1,257	82	1,174	55,604	26.2	43.0
Raytown	13,292	2.16	54.1	36.9	15.0	45.9	38.9	518	1,584	5,392	613	4,779	21,377	45.5	21.4
St. Charles	28,324	2.21	57.8	47.6	7.2	42.2	31.9	7,682	1,901	2,741	199	2,542	48,509	30.7	34.7
St. Joseph	28,999	2.49	62.0	43.7	12.4	38.0	34.2	4,414	4,974	6,495	559	5,937	50,866	51.6	17.5
St. Louis	138,513	2.16	47.8	28.2	16.3	52.2	43.2	10,043	24,670	7,844	1,913	5,931	219,910	35.5	37.1
St. Peters	20,595	2.76	70.9	55.5	10.0	29.1	25.1	NA	1,307	2,260	166	2,094	38,977	28.8	42.9
Springfield	73,568	2.13	49.5	33.5	12.7	50.5	39.9	10,746	16,502	9,805	1,337	8,467	104,755	37.6	29.2
University City	16,603	2.06	44.5	31.9	10.3	55.5	44.5	301	1,640	4,685	726	3,960	24,128	27.6	53.3
Wentzville	14,047	2.80	74.4	61.4	9.2	25.6	21.9	NA	551	1,492	165	1,327	24,862	29.5	33.9
Wildwood	12,084	2.93	88.4	76.9	8.9	11.6	9.6	NA	NA	NA	NA	NA	23,076	10.3	67.8
MONTANA	423,091	2.41	62.1	50.4	7.7	37.9	30.4	28,803	31,816	3,052	368	2,683	723,666	35.1	32.3
Billings	46,642	2.28	60.9	46.3	9.8	39.1	30.9	3,151	5,741	5,151	462	4,689	77,012	32.0	35.1
Bozeman	19,411	2.21	46.6	36.2	6.8	53.4	30.0	3,760	1,413	3,158	342	2,816	25,754	15.6	61.3
Butte-Silver Bow	15,470	2.08	56.2	42.0	10.2	43.8	39.0	1,493	1,857	5,348	282	5,066	22,881	39.7	22.4
Great Falls	24,161	2.21	56.2	43.8	8.4	43.8	38.0	1,776	3,116	5,218	278	4,940	39,208	43.6	26.4
Helena	14,418	2.06	51.2	38.5	9.1	48.8	42.5	1,683	1,419	4,570	676	3,893	23,006	23.5	48.0
Missoula	31,756	2.21	46.4	37.4	6.5	53.6	36.4	3,119	4,148	5,772	527	5,245	46,680	19.1	51.7
NEBRASKA	754,490	2.48	64.3	50.9	8.9	35.7	29.2	52,015	48,713	2,554	291	2,263	1,259,254	35.0	31.7
Bellevue	20,592	2.59	69.6	51.5	10.5	30.4	24.2	121	1,068	1,897	131	1,766	34,673	31.4	33.7
Fremont	11,349	2.32	66.9	51.3	9.2	33.1	20.7	874	655	2,473	215	2,257	17,528	44.2	18.2
Grand Island	19,270	2.64	66.7	50.9	12.0	33.3	25.2	898	1,793	3,449	333	3,117	33,244	48.8	22.3
Kearney	13,066	2.39	56.8	43.8	8.2	43.2	36.2	2,040	819	2,447	227	2,220	19,979	34.7	33.0
Lincoln	111,610	2.43	58.9	44.4	9.5	41.1	30.8	13,286	9,736	3,463	358	3,105	174,241	28.5	38.5
Omaha	184,938	2.46	60.4	43.0	12.3	39.6	32.6	11,889	19,338	4,334	567	3,767	305,440	33.1	36.3
NEVADA	1,094,613	2.70	64.0	44.9	13.0	36.0	28.1	38,240	95,983	3,265	678	2,587	2,063,180	42.0	24.9
Carson City	22,773	2.31	62.3	44.4	10.4	37.7	31.6	2,203	1,125	2,060	282	1,778	39,773	41.0	23.7
Henderson	116,407	2.59	66.5	52.1	10.5	33.5	26.3	1,439	6,101	2,092	212	1,881	219,459	31.2	33.9
Las Vegas	233,581	2.71	63.8	42.3	15.1	36.2	29.3	8,221	59,520	3,738	849	2,889	441,667	43.3	25.1
North Las Vegas	72,620	3.32	74.7	48.8	16.7	25.3	19.8	1,972	7,553	3,166	954	2,212	149,647	51.3	16.9
Reno	100,794	2.42	54.0	38.2	11.3	46.0	34.5	5,403	9,650	3,946	702	3,244	165,105	32.8	35.2
Sparks	39,746	2.53	64.7	49.2	10.6	35.3	27.1	255	2,885	2,966	447	2,519	72,105	40.7	22.4
NEW HAMPSHIRE	528,700	2.46	65.5	52.1	8.5	34.5	26.2	42,483	22,831	1,710	198	1,513	958,005	35.0	36.9
Concord	17,729	2.25	60.3	46.1	12.2	39.7	28.2	3,132	1,011	2,373	253	2,119	32,870	36.1	35.3
Dover	14,841	2.05	47.6	36.7	4.6	52.4	35.4	NA	464	1,494	151	1,343	23,769	34.4	40.0
Manchester	46,172	2.35	54.6	34.1	14.1	45.4	31.0	2,864	3,755	3,403	674	2,729	77,526	42.8	28.3
Nashua	36,257	2.39	61.6	43.4	12.2	38.4	30.7	1,730	1,393	1,578	182	1,396	61,698	33.8	38.3
Rochester	13,340	2.29	56.9	43.7	6.2	43.1	34.5	NA	1,117	3,711	356	3,356	22,247	50.4	19.1
NEW JERSEY	3,218,798	2.74	69.4	51.4	13.0	30.6	25.4	183,073	160,066	1,790	245	1,545	6,234,538	37.3	39.7
Atlantic City	15,491	2.44	50.6	21.8	23.3	49.4	42.9	679	2,287	5,834	1,224	4,609	25,128	61.3	16.5
Bayonne	26,487	2.52	60.6	40.3	16.6	39.4	36.1	NA	890	1,336	221	1,115	47,388	40.3	38.6
Bergenfield	8,277	3.37	75.4	56.9	13.7	24.6	19.4	71	107	387	29	358	18,467	34.7	46.5
Bridgeton	6,058	3.47	71.8	23.6	40.4	28.2	21.2	3,470	1,177	4,711	901	3,811	13,458	75.3	6.6
Camden	26,292	2.75	62.6	19.7	37.4	37.4	31.9	2,145	4,218	5,587	2,085	3,502	44,743	64.9	9.4
Clifton	29,740	2.89	71.5	46.5	19.4	28.5	25.3	776	1,510	1,749	234	1,515	60,094	43.2	35.6
East Orange	22,871	2.81	60.2	26.3	22.9	39.8	31.6	1,060	1,335	2,061	675	1,386	44,677	52.7	20.3
Elizabeth	40,273	3.18	69.8	36.6	24.4	30.2	24.6	2,102	5,188	4,019	816	3,202	81,815	64.1	13.7
Englewood	10,796	2.68	66.0	46.5	12.8	34.0	30.0	187	386	1,346	213	1,133	20,525	34.2	43.3
Fair Lawn	10,307	3.25	82.3	67.6	9.5	17.7	15.8	NA	462	1,373	74	1,299	22,123	26.2	51.4
Fort Lee	16,937	2.24	59.4	44.0	10.9	40.6	36.9	NA	296	806	101	705	29,456	28.1	58.6

1. No spouse present. 2. Data for serious crimes have not been adjusted for underreporting. This may affect comparability between geographic areas and over time. 3. Per 100,000 population estimated by the FBI. 4. Persons 25 years old and over.

City	Money income, 2017					Median earnings, 2017			Housing units, 2017				
	Households												
	Median income	Percent with income less than $20,000	Percent with income of $200,000 or more	Median family income	Median non-family income	All persons	Men	Women	Total	Occupied	Percent owner occupied	Median value[1] (dollars)	Median gross rent (dollars)
	42	43	44	45	46	47	48	49	50	51	52	53	54
MISSOURI	53,578	16.2	4.2	67,317	31,917	31,514	36,751	27,009	2,792,445	2,385,135	67.0	156,700	800
Ballwin..................................	85,000	3.9	12.5	105,837	51,806	50,917	56,415	41,894	12,903	11,704	83.3	266,100	1,198
Blue Springs.........................	82,870	5.6	4.0	90,061	44,045	43,071	45,452	37,319	20,668	19,311	75.6	159,200	978
Cape Girardeau.....................	42,735	24.9	0.5	63,636	29,821	21,027	26,515	17,172	16,849	14,178	56.5	157,000	829
Chesterfield..........................	96,871	6.9	18.0	134,308	49,221	59,455	74,702	41,804	20,655	20,161	75.3	372,400	1,244
Columbia...............................	47,043	18.0	5.5	63,873	33,098	21,425	24,013	18,398	53,237	47,678	46.2	187,100	871
Florissant..............................	51,830	10.8	0.8	63,668	31,783	33,965	35,826	32,995	22,060	20,275	67.8	99,100	971
Gladstone.............................	60,472	14.9	3.8	67,471	40,611	33,668	41,651	29,545	12,915	11,817	61.0	142,800	788
Hazelwood............................	63,004	8.7	3.0	76,417	40,860	32,317	41,120	26,309	10,120	9,089	53.3	128,400	879
Independence	49,855	15.1	1.7	56,982	35,439	31,315	36,487	26,586	49,981	45,560	59.4	112,700	837
Jefferson City	45,353	20.0	2.2	58,505	27,748	26,966	26,775	27,087	18,846	16,448	54.5	150,300	631
Joplin....................................	45,830	21.4	0.9	59,298	24,992	30,345	36,765	23,566	23,960	21,487	55.9	124,100	820
Kansas City...........................	51,330	17.6	5.0	68,780	36,654	33,575	37,024	31,328	236,135	204,678	53.8	152,900	919
Kirkwood...............................	86,118	6.1	12.3	115,505	51,385	50,475	60,131	45,023	13,410	12,189	77.7	295,900	1,063
Lee's Summit.........................	86,695	8.2	8.5	99,544	47,690	48,917	57,553	39,656	38,431	36,237	74.9	211,300	1,105
Liberty...................................	69,717	10.4	3.6	81,573	36,179	36,377	50,482	28,179	11,725	11,266	73.5	186,200	849
Maryland Heights.................	67,038	6.3	3.3	74,858	60,866	32,069	49,003	29,806	12,450	11,894	56.1	159,600	1,004
O'Fallon................................	85,831	4.5	6.8	97,249	47,047	47,369	59,665	35,878	31,949	30,224	84.8	228,200	1,069
Raytown................................	50,844	14.3	1.4	68,644	35,074	36,358	40,050	31,656	14,324	13,292	57.6	103,700	1,024
St. Charles............................	63,574	11.3	6.0	86,468	39,452	41,624	39,329	24,586	30,904	28,324	63.4	185,000	983
St. Joseph.............................	43,585	19.3	2.5	53,422	25,786	27,368	33,148	22,651	33,761	28,999	58.9	108,700	727
St. Louis................................	41,441	25.0	3.2	56,652	30,273	31,207	35,316	28,547	176,850	138,513	43.7	141,400	779
St. Peters..............................	76,311	5.6	5.4	92,210	41,091	40,684	46,438	35,703	21,975	20,595	81.8	182,600	1,042
Springfield............................	36,421	24.6	1.6	47,550	25,558	23,704	26,763	21,311	83,791	73,568	43.7	121,100	735
University City.......................	60,654	21.4	13.0	81,022	44,656	32,050	31,832	32,357	17,976	16,603	58.5	211,200	979
Wentzville..............................	83,695	5.7	6.4	96,677	50,235	50,420	58,849	41,485	14,417	14,047	83.2	233,600	888
Wildwood...............................	131,676	3.3	22.9	142,324	52,159	65,084	86,267	49,577	12,341	12,084	91.8	382,900	1,136
MONTANA............................	53,386	16.1	3.5	68,994	31,186	28,925	33,221	24,322	510,408	423,091	69.2	231,300	759
Billings.................................	57,527	13.0	4.1	70,560	35,305	31,913	38,750	26,846	50,676	46,642	63.4	226,100	840
Bozeman...............................	50,143	17.5	3.7	77,885	35,353	21,672	24,588	20,211	20,229	19,411	43.0	368,800	1,016
Butte-Silver Bow	40,326	27.6	1.5	53,638	24,947	27,424	32,127	21,871	16,836	15,470	68.6	143,000	580
Great Falls	43,384	19.7	3.8	60,799	30,715	28,829	31,959	25,804	27,262	24,161	66.5	172,000	660
Helena...................................	54,488	9.2	4.8	80,729	41,549	31,122	38,909	25,846	15,546	14,418	56.8	253,100	763
Missoula................................	44,241	24.7	3.5	83,207	24,249	21,162	20,600	21,880	33,936	31,756	44.2	279,800	772
NEBRASKA..........................	59,970	13.3	4.4	75,112	35,607	33,314	40,448	27,439	837,540	754,490	66.3	155,800	801
Bellevue................................	66,473	10.5	3.3	80,127	40,254	34,713	40,203	29,513	22,219	20,592	62.2	147,100	944
Fremont................................	51,022	17.1	1.8	57,413	32,030	27,030	38,428	22,915	12,035	11,349	55.8	134,600	700
Grand Island	55,735	12.0	4.3	68,396	40,170	35,277	39,768	30,163	20,729	19,270	60.2	144,500	615
Kearney................................	51,321	23.4	4.0	86,415	27,167	28,397	36,212	24,128	13,780	13,066	57.8	187,000	748
Lincoln..................................	56,160	13.4	4.4	75,146	36,029	31,268	36,112	26,660	119,639	111,610	58.8	171,300	818
Omaha...................................	56,406	14.3	4.8	72,055	37,778	33,114	38,051	30,046	199,510	184,938	56.8	157,100	892
NEVADA................................	58,003	14.1	4.8	68,276	38,579	32,322	36,726	29,422	1,249,733	1,094,613	56.6	258,200	1,051
Carson City	55,700	13.3	3.7	70,968	39,796	32,170	34,707	27,530	23,893	22,773	52.4	256,100	1,027
Henderson............................	69,667	10.0	8.9	85,567	45,860	40,362	48,731	34,207	132,788	116,407	64.3	311,200	1,228
Las Vegas.............................	56,699	16.3	4.7	67,201	36,294	32,753	36,899	30,297	259,374	233,581	51.8	245,500	1,071
North Las Vegas	56,059	12.3	1.3	57,490	42,248	31,030	35,290	26,509	77,359	72,620	59.5	226,600	1,136
Reno......................................	57,125	13.9	4.7	70,220	41,140	32,191	36,290	29,196	108,877	100,794	48.6	328,700	946
Sparks...................................	58,961	11.0	3.5	65,938	41,755	33,493	41,369	26,373	41,471	39,746	54.7	305,800	1,028
NEW HAMPSHIRE	73,381	10.7	8.3	91,029	41,469	37,858	46,197	31,360	634,689	528,700	69.8	263,600	1,072
Concord	63,489	10.2	5.1	82,022	37,405	35,016	39,147	29,562	18,820	17,729	49.8	215,700	1,036
Dover	73,478	13.3	4.3	77,159	64,055	42,192	52,989	32,606	15,503	14,841	50.3	251,700	1,199
Manchester...........................	56,819	15.0	3.1	64,632	46,167	34,924	40,373	30,170	49,506	46,172	40.5	226,900	1,065
Nashua..................................	70,261	12.0	8.9	87,393	40,178	37,240	50,265	29,947	37,414	36,257	54.0	273,900	1,207
Rochester..............................	60,572	16.3	1.5	80,995	30,363	34,857	37,810	31,272	14,570	13,340	61.4	200,700	992
NEW JERSEY.......................	80,088	12.1	13.0	97,300	44,186	41,556	50,432	34,602	3,615,891	3,218,798	63.8	334,900	1,284
Atlantic City..........................	26,182	40.8	1.6	32,990	17,160	21,608	22,451	20,887	20,531	15,491	23.0	158,400	849
Bayonne................................	60,529	20.2	6.3	75,471	37,625	40,434	43,802	36,543	29,664	26,487	36.5	313,200	1,238
Bergenfield...........................	91,533	14.1	14.0	109,753	37,143	40,103	45,960	33,069	8,441	8,277	63.6	376,100	1,277
Bridgeton.............................	31,065	25.4	2.8	31,981	24,906	17,775	16,662	20,626	6,814	6,058	27.7	77,900	1,202
Camden................................	24,540	41.0	0.0	29,822	16,512	18,053	21,531	16,925	31,217	26,292	39.6	84,700	887
Clifton...................................	70,387	14.0	7.1	84,249	31,163	33,516	41,450	25,534	30,932	29,740	55.6	337,300	1,335
East Orange..........................	52,165	18.7	2.0	58,790	37,482	30,979	31,200	30,875	27,693	22,871	24.3	187,500	1,103
Elizabeth...............................	46,754	15.5	2.0	48,105	30,722	27,228	32,912	22,025	43,325	40,273	21.7	272,700	1,162
Englewood............................	80,294	6.7	12.8	90,045	54,590	41,707	50,027	40,607	11,721	10,796	55.6	373,300	1,471
Fair Lawn..............................	125,430	2.4	16.8	137,670	56,409	55,880	56,402	54,734	10,618	10,307	78.0	438,800	1,857
Fort Lee.................................	81,081	18.8	11.1	102,095	44,595	51,797	65,935	44,679	18,391	16,937	58.4	367,000	1,720

1. Based on population estimated by the American Community Survey.   2. Includes units rented or sold but not occupied.   3. Specified owner-occupied units; $1,000,000 represents $1,000,000 or more.   4. 50.0 represents 50 percent or more.   5. 10.0 represents 10 percent or less.

Table D. Cities — Commuting, Computer Access, Migration, Labor Force, and Employment

City	Commuting[1], 2017 Percent — Commuting	With commutes of 30 minutes or more	Computer access[2], 2017 Percent — With a computer in the house	With Internet access	Migration, 2017 — Percent who lived in the same house one year ago	Percent who lived in another state or county one year ago	Civilian labor force, 2018 — Total	Percent change 2017-2018	Unemployment — Total	Rate[3]	Population age 16 and older — Number	Percent in labor force	Population age 16 to 64 — Number	Percent who worked full-year full-time
	55	56	57	58	59	60	61	62	63	64	65	66	67	68
MISSOURI	82.2	32.5	89.7	80.8	84.6	7.3	3,052,386	-0.3	97,578	3.2	4,885,700	63.0	3,875,431	52.5
Ballwin	87.8	41.4	94.0	93.3	91.6	5.0	16,812	-0.1	390	2.3	24,084	71.3	18,902	60.3
Blue Springs	89.0	46.7	95.0	90.1	88.8	2.2	30,751	0.5	1,028	3.3	41,335	69.4	32,989	61.5
Cape Girardeau	78.9	15.5	90.6	84.7	77.6	9.0	19,620	0.2	567	2.9	32,245	55.0	25,524	38.5
Chesterfield	80.4	35.1	92.3	91.9	82.4	8.0	24,727	-0.1	567	2.3	39,156	62.2	27,760	54.1
Columbia	71.6	14.3	91.3	80.7	71.4	12.2	66,331	-0.4	1,498	2.3	102,784	67.6	89,692	43.4
Florissant	82.9	36.9	89.7	84.4	83.0	6.0	27,800	-0.3	961	3.5	39,930	65.7	31,784	53.0
Gladstone	83.4	28.3	90.5	86.7	84.6	9.5	14,652	-0.1	464	3.2	21,700	71.8	16,668	56.0
Hazelwood	NA	43.7	95.8	83.8	NA	NA	13,635	-0.1	479	3.5	17,995	71.0	15,533	58.4
Independence	87.5	39.4	90.7	83.4	92.1	2.9	57,804	0.1	2,374	4.1	91,332	61.4	71,689	52.8
Jefferson City	82.2	9.0	85.6	58.6	85.0	6.3	20,291	-1.6	553	2.7	34,462	60.0	27,140	54.5
Joplin	85.1	11.4	87.9	76.9	85.7	7.6	25,391	-0.5	699	2.8	40,848	64.6	32,255	59.2
Kansas City	82.6	27.8	90.4	81.0	80.6	7.7	259,254	0.0	9,158	3.5	388,400	69.1	326,097	57.4
Kirkwood	86.5	21.7	94.7	88.1	90.1	4.6	15,757	-0.1	356	2.3	22,192	64.1	15,419	58.3
Lee's Summit	84.9	40.2	93.8	89.8	85.7	4.2	54,994	0.4	1,439	2.6	72,911	69.4	58,050	62.6
Liberty	84.2	36.7	93.0	90.9	82.0	9.2	16,493	-0.1	477	2.9	25,876	68.1	21,719	52.7
Maryland Heights	85.3	20.8	96.1	93.8	81.2	9.8	15,965	-0.1	415	2.6	23,366	67.2	18,528	62.0
O'Fallon	89.1	40.5	97.2	91.9	91.6	2.9	49,045	-0.1	1,204	2.5	64,306	72.9	54,173	61.5
Raytown	92.1	31.5	93.9	81.0	86.2	7.9	15,226	-0.1	681	4.5	24,942	65.7	19,888	59.5
St. Charles	83.9	27.4	94.7	85.9	86.2	9.2	38,827	-0.2	1,065	2.7	60,290	69.3	48,500	52.7
St. Joseph	82.7	10.4	78.0	71.2	82.9	8.3	37,500	-1.3	1,142	3.0	60,700	59.3	48,392	48.5
St. Louis	72.0	31.7	87.6	77.7	82.4	9.8	153,678	-0.4	5,878	3.8	255,283	66.1	215,460	51.5
St. Peters	87.9	36.4	94.9	92.2	91.8	4.0	33,928	-0.2	846	2.5	44,130	71.4	37,562	59.9
Springfield	77.8	14.5	90.2	75.2	73.3	10.1	85,724	0.8	2,293	2.7	139,604	62.0	112,645	46.4
University City	79.5	13.0	88.3	82.9	78.2	12.2	18,548	-0.2	562	3.0	30,271	54.4	22,620	45.6
Wentzville	91.9	51.4	96.7	92.2	NA	NA	21,222	0.1	530	2.5	28,728	69.1	24,511	59.0
Wildwood	76.7	53.1	98.7	94.7	86.8	4.1	18,846	-0.3	424	2.2	26,932	68.4	22,148	53.0
MONTANA	76.5	17.6	88.7	81.3	85.0	6.9	528,244	0.6	19,656	3.7	846,678	63.8	656,462	49.8
Billings	83.5	9.5	91.3	85.7	82.9	6.8	56,114	0.0	1,866	3.3	87,458	68.1	67,818	57.9
Bozeman	72.6	6.6	98.1	92.2	68.0	15.1	29,712	2.9	704	2.4	40,099	74.0	36,439	45.2
Butte-Silver Bow	77.4	7.9	83.0	70.5	85.5	7.4	17,238	0.6	692	4.0	NA	NA	NA	NA
Great Falls	80.3	6.3	84.0	79.6	83.7	7.7	27,990	0.2	1,007	3.6	45,581	61.5	35,228	51.6
Helena	79.3	6.5	88.9	77.6	80.8	8.0	17,114	0.7	537	3.1	26,471	67.1	20,287	59.1
Missoula	75.2	7.2	91.0	87.6	75.8	8.8	40,339	1.2	1,274	3.2	61,225	71.0	51,982	43.1
NEBRASKA	81.7	19.0	90.8	84.3	83.8	7.0	1,020,197	0.8	28,509	2.8	1,496,751	70.1	1,201,846	58.5
Bellevue	80.8	20.1	94.0	91.3	76.3	12.5	26,788	1.1	809	3.0	42,596	72.7	35,150	57.1
Fremont	81.6	17.7	92.4	84.4	77.9	9.4	13,848	1.3	377	2.7	20,749	69.6	16,326	57.6
Grand Island	80.3	14.3	92.4	85.3	86.9	3.1	26,265	0.3	837	3.2	38,109	72.2	30,701	61.6
Kearney	83.6	14.2	95.4	86.7	69.6	12.0	19,291	1.8	450	2.3	26,404	71.5	22,078	56.5
Lincoln	82.5	16.8	94.0	87.9	78.0	8.6	156,391	1.8	3,981	2.5	225,377	71.7	187,988	56.6
Omaha	81.5	15.5	90.2	84.3	82.8	6.3	240,861	1.2	7,521	3.1	364,316	70.8	303,431	55.5
NEVADA	78.5	33.5	93.3	83.0	82.0	5.9	1,500,377	2.9	68,418	4.6	2,390,188	63.7	1,931,509	51.8
Carson City	81.3	28.7	91.2	82.5	82.5	9.6	25,718	1.4	1,216	4.7	45,270	61.3	34,978	56.9
Henderson	83.3	30.7	94.0	89.8	83.2	6.2	156,325	2.8	6,956	4.4	248,901	60.6	186,206	53.6
Las Vegas	79.1	38.1	93.1	78.9	82.3	5.3	308,428	2.6	15,367	5.0	505,498	64.0	414,400	51.9
North Las Vegas	83.3	45.9	95.2	84.4	82.8	5.3	111,937	2.7	5,975	5.3	180,630	63.9	155,322	51.7
Reno	75.8	20.1	92.6	81.1	79.3	7.8	135,130	4.8	4,851	3.6	197,733	69.0	161,699	54.2
Sparks	80.6	27.0	94.9	86.8	84.1	4.1	54,881	4.8	1,962	3.6	82,683	68.1	65,818	56.0
NEW HAMPSHIRE	80.9	38.3	93.7	88.3	85.2	7.1	761,752	1.0	19,240	2.5	1,118,608	67.9	882,287	54.2
Concord	83.5	26.4	90.9	87.7	82.1	7.7	22,770	0.8	499	2.2	37,695	65.9	30,691	53.2
Dover	86.2	31.2	95.7	89.3	75.6	11.9	18,416	1.1	400	2.2	28,207	72.2	22,641	61.5
Manchester	80.6	26.2	92.5	87.8	75.1	11.7	64,187	1.1	1,656	2.6	90,055	72.0	76,275	54.7
Nashua	79.6	36.5	93.2	91.6	81.2	9.6	50,296	1.3	1,469	2.9	73,476	68.9	59,683	55.1
Rochester	78.8	38.3	92.5	86.6	86.1	4.8	17,556	1.2	413	2.4	24,934	65.7	18,748	61.8
NEW JERSEY	71.0	47.3	92.6	86.3	89.4	5.1	4,422,942	-0.7	183,375	4.1	7,265,350	65.4	5,848,878	52.4
Atlantic City	47.9	25.3	81.9	68.6	85.3	3.5	14,406	-1.0	1,111	7.7	29,777	57.0	24,700	38.8
Bayonne	50.2	59.0	91.6	79.2	84.1	5.2	32,544	-0.9	1,421	4.4	54,425	62.1	44,593	47.4
Bergenfield	70.5	50.5	NA	NA	NA	NA	14,503	-0.8	449	3.1	22,106	71.5	18,097	53.6
Bridgeton	NA	30.2	90.3	68.4	79.1	5.4	7,975	-1.2	646	8.1	17,137	48.5	15,803	36.9
Camden	54.1	36.4	81.3	57.1	86.4	6.8	25,349	-1.8	2,253	8.9	54,363	57.5	46,382	36.9
Clifton	72.3	37.1	88.7	85.5	91.7	3.2	43,894	-0.8	1,831	4.2	71,888	68.3	58,454	53.2
East Orange	50.5	45.5	88.8	85.2	85.1	7.5	28,984	-1.0	1,918	6.6	52,740	66.5	44,070	48.1
Elizabeth	62.5	30.2	86.9	77.3	86.8	6.4	61,355	-1.0	3,127	5.1	97,630	70.1	84,456	56.8
Englewood	55.3	54.4	95.2	87.5	87.2	2.8	14,876	-0.8	549	3.7	23,624	70.6	18,837	60.6
Fair Lawn	63.6	50.0	95.0	88.9	NA	NA	17,797	-0.7	580	3.3	26,797	64.3	20,834	49.5
Fort Lee	56.7	53.8	90.1	85.7	91.5	3.3	18,973	-0.8	490	2.6	32,448	62.1	22,504	57.3

1. Employed persons. 2. Households. 3. Percent of civilian labor force. 4. Persons 16 years old and over.

Construction, Wholesale Trade, and Retail Trade

City	Value of residential construction authorized by building permits, 2018			Wholesale trade[1], 2012				Retail trade[2], 2012			
	New construction ($1,000)	Number of housing units	Percent single family	Number of establishments	Number of employees	Sales (mil dol)	Annual payroll (mil dol)	Number of establishments	Number of employees	Sales (mil dol)	Annual payroll (mil dol)
	69	70	71	72	73	74	75	76	77	78	79
MISSOURI	3,167,067	16,875	67.4	6,557	96,683	91,916.4	4,978.9	21,456	302,568	90,546.6	7,278.2
Ballwin	4,925	17	100.0	16	49	57.5	2.5	88	1,585	644.5	47.4
Blue Springs	39,727	399	57.9	42	304	280.9	17.1	160	3,296	929.4	76.1
Cape Girardeau	19,543	751	13.3	88	1,141	655.7	47.6	299	4,617	1,240.7	101.1
Chesterfield	NA	NA	NA	146	2,241	1,231.8	161.8	315	5,198	1,093.6	112.9
Columbia	61,087	263	99.2	98	1,158	461.5	55.6	537	10,468	3,251.6	254.7
Florissant	0	0	0.0	18	55	27.7	2.0	176	3,083	789.0	73.0
Gladstone	2,611	17	100.0	16	43	19.5	1.9	82	1,845	489.2	45.3
Hazelwood	0	0	0.0	53	1,573	1,366.0	87.1	142	3,422	2,338.6	137.3
Independence	22,825	151	51.0	71	473	165.7	20.6	456	8,382	2,068.8	196.1
Jefferson City	9,619	48	91.7	60	2,030	915.7	58.0	258	4,881	1,191.7	110.5
Joplin	31,560	241	65.1	99	1,568	691.6	60.1	378	6,152	1,819.7	135.3
Kansas City	278,664	2,154	37.7	614	10,628	14,577.6	675.7	1,458	24,531	7,537.3	620.8
Kirkwood	35,296	93	100.0	35	228	105.1	13.6	128	2,693	738.1	66.5
Lee's Summit	129,784	548	61.9	98	1,351	799.3	72.6	290	5,326	1,337.8	126.7
Liberty	11,479	39	100.0	23	235	216.3	13.1	86	1,299	300.9	31.6
Maryland Heights	6,801	25	100.0	235	5,339	4,493.9	360.0	117	2,674	4,687.1	107.1
O'Fallon	62,970	317	95.0	72	D	D	D	199	3,400	962.6	85.0
Raytown	659	5	100.0	22	162	69.0	9.5	92	1,528	364.0	35.7
St. Charles	77,036	312	92.3	82	1,620	1,102.6	100.2	257	4,047	1,085.4	92.7
St. Joseph	8,826	50	84.0	92	1,627	1,421.4	72.0	321	5,412	1,353.4	119.5
St. Louis	62,601	661	24.4	452	7,692	5,916.4	423.3	923	9,422	2,471.9	231.1
St. Peters	77,472	618	7.8	74	D	D	D	325	6,097	1,695.3	149.1
Springfield	66,837	429	24.7	328	6,097	4,390.8	269.4	967	16,828	4,329.5	388.8
University City	2,267	6	100.0	23	298	226.8	20.4	86	781	156.9	18.2
Wentzville	125,398	418	95.0	26	D	D	D	100	2,179	583.1	58.2
Wildwood	NA	NA	NA	30	82	30.8	4.5	35	452	97.4	10.8
MONTANA	869,896	5,099	63.0	1,288	13,034	12,645.8	577.1	4,831	55,418	15,623.6	1,346.5
Billings	123,467	718	78.8	236	3,832	2,734.4	190.2	618	9,047	2,761.8	240.4
Bozeman	152,504	838	31.1	60	549	286.0	20.8	357	5,153	1,192.1	120.8
Butte-Silver Bow	19,667	185	29.7	37	348	189.3	14.3	172	2,203	610.1	51.7
Great Falls	12,290	65	81.5	92	1,011	847.3	45.7	314	4,496	1,268.2	109.5
Helena	32,586	186	29.6	49	425	295.9	17.8	220	3,292	803.0	77.6
Missoula	89,258	462	59.5	104	1,372	1,023.3	63.8	476	6,831	1,677.6	153.7
NEBRASKA	1,309,845	7,866	62.3	2,720	34,409	42,619.0	1,675.4	7,279	105,953	30,470.7	2,440.4
Bellevue	40,948	151	100.0	15	68	28.8	4.3	110	2,318	661.9	55.4
Fremont	12,449	45	95.6	30	395	566.6	20.6	131	2,220	1,026.6	56.2
Grand Island	14,001	94	66.0	75	1,089	707.6	56.0	273	4,710	1,198.9	107.1
Kearney	37,966	148	94.6	46	698	816.6	34.0	190	3,245	756.9	69.9
Lincoln	278,819	1,532	56.1	242	3,927	2,924.6	159.2	946	16,644	4,184.1	375.6
Omaha	281,353	2,887	42.8	667	10,205	12,272.0	565.0	1,634	33,150	8,083.1	793.0
NEVADA	3,400,610	17,645	73.7	2,501	27,649	19,841.7	1,516.2	8,135	129,977	38,234.2	3,454.1
Carson City	59,901	310	58.1	89	519	276.4	25.2	212	3,139	918.2	92.6
Henderson	413,802	3,883	61.1	196	1,314	776.5	92.8	721	13,600	5,601.8	398.5
Las Vegas	493,766	1,973	90.9	431	3,801	2,620.7	222.9	1,705	29,614	8,550.0	770.5
North Las Vegas	235,089	1,840	85.2	160	2,944	2,079.2	157.1	291	6,155	1,725.4	147.9
Reno	570,375	3,234	41.8	302	4,234	3,320.6	229.2	975	15,952	4,519.4	438.6
Sparks	132,805	664	54.1	227	3,506	2,699.0	172.5	304	4,346	1,158.3	106.8
NEW HAMPSHIRE	875,243	4,445	61.0	1,543	21,140	18,029.2	1,307.9	6,127	95,660	26,018.2	2,403.6
Concord	14,323	100	30.0	53	934	600.2	49.4	279	5,383	1,391.2	125.3
Dover	37,585	268	33.6	34	445	170.6	26.2	96	1,391	339.4	38.6
Manchester	31,288	210	71.9	192	3,297	2,037.3	253.4	464	7,470	2,173.8	198.4
Nashua	38,634	309	27.8	127	1,591	1,231.6	105.3	455	9,973	2,735.4	244.2
Rochester	13,562	116	53.4	14	D	D	D	123	2,506	621.8	67.2
NEW JERSEY	4,220,431	27,942	37.0	12,760	208,830	288,467.8	14,976.8	31,722	436,299	133,665.7	12,676.0
Atlantic City	37,941	279	3.2	12	388	95.8	12.0	330	3,060	641.0	61.1
Bayonne	67,495	757	2.0	48	1,157	1,944.2	72.5	190	1,864	467.1	43.6
Bergenfield	4,032	27	92.6	32	202	122.1	10.5	88	702	178.8	19.5
Bridgeton	922	9	100.0	18	249	68.3	7.1	92	842	337.1	24.3
Camden	6,491	72	100.0	53	1,070	711.4	56.4	211	1,129	305.5	28.3
Clifton	9,878	53	35.8	181	2,492	1,275.3	140.4	281	4,593	1,260.5	121.2
East Orange	27,914	286	4.9	16	169	350.2	9.0	133	1,073	310.1	25.7
Elizabeth	15,419	275	1.5	118	3,077	2,824.0	198.0	540	6,663	1,489.2	132.4
Englewood	4,018	29	10.3	88	1,119	577.9	65.1	163	1,915	1,037.0	93.1
Fair Lawn	6,492	34	100.0	51	376	180.0	18.7	94	1,142	482.4	42.5
Fort Lee	18,534	78	11.5	147	950	13,212.0	91.3	127	917	350.4	26.8

1. Merchant wholesalers except manufacturers' sales branches and offices. 2. Establishments with payroll.

Table D. Cities — **Real Estate, Professional Services, and Manufacturing**

City	Real estate and rental and leasing, 2012				Professional, scientific, and technical services[1], 2012				Manufacturing, 2012			
	Number of establishments	Number of employees	Receipts (mil dol)	Annual payroll (mil dol)	Number of establishments	Number of employees	Receipts (mil dol)	Annual payroll (mil dol)	Number of establishments	Number of employees	Receipts (mil dol)	Annual payroll (mil dol)
	80	81	82	83	84	85	86	87	88	89	90	91
MISSOURI	6,165	33,447	6,730.0	1,297.9	13,221	136,446	24,006.6	8,518.4	6,097	243,208	111,535.4	11,920.8
Ballwin	22	57	11.2	2.1	66	132	15.3	6.0	7	50	D	D
Blue Springs	69	199	31.6	5.7	110	564	65.7	25.8	35	905	196.0	41.5
Cape Girardeau	89	263	49.1	7.5	108	D	D	D	40	1,959	2,326.0	110.1
Chesterfield	129	673	162.9	27.9	394	13,252	2,523.7	849.6	57	1,345	376.0	76.5
Columbia	192	852	153.7	27.5	346	3,314	396.5	148.0	72	2,930	1,280.6	123.0
Florissant	28	170	23.7	4.5	56	318	20.4	9.0	10	49	3.1	D
Gladstone	48	345	35.2	11.9	75	D	D	D	7	D	D	D
Hazelwood	29	193	34.5	5.5	46	D	D	D	35	3,589	1,384.6	228.3
Independence	105	593	138.5	20.2	225	1,035	89.4	34.3	72	4,011	1,235.8	227.1
Jefferson City	54	207	42.2	6.3	203	D	D	D	35	2,574	2,091.7	122.0
Joplin	77	407	68.1	11.4	146	D	D	D	83	5,204	2,217.7	227.6
Kansas City	578	4,517	1,142.9	221.8	1,507	D	D	D	374	17,035	8,635.1	935.0
Kirkwood	43	D	D	D	133	613	98.8	33.0	28	643	173.8	32.9
Lee's Summit	120	370	82.9	14.6	305	D	D	D	71	D	482.1	101.9
Liberty	35	160	25.8	3.9	114	D	D	D	22	927	D	40.6
Maryland Heights	57	371	130.2	19.0	157	3,597	566.4	254.7	107	3,658	1,408.7	207.4
O'Fallon	80	339	58.9	11.6	124	791	323.9	65.9	56	4,204	985.7	204.9
Raytown	23	108	16.0	2.8	58	318	30.4	13.6	26	302	38.8	13.6
St. Charles	104	519	285.3	25.8	245	3,406	195.4	81.6	66	1,654	463.4	84.7
St. Joseph	92	323	58.8	9.8	145	D	D	D	88	D	D	474.4
St. Louis	411	2,432	1,003.0	102.5	1,003	D	D	D	484	17,422	10,737.0	975.2
St. Peters	64	235	46.8	7.4	140	755	82.9	31.0	49	1,365	1,527.5	64.4
Springfield	342	2,232	308.2	65.4	665	D	D	D	239	10,927	4,323.9	478.9
University City	39	404	55.6	13.4	86	241	28.4	10.3	13	112	D	6.0
Wentzville	12	44	8.4	1.3	40	159	15.9	6.2	21	2,315	D	183.2
Wildwood	29	D	D	D	112	364	57.0	18.1	4	12	D	D
MONTANA	1,726	5,207	835.4	162.3	3,501	16,363	2,160.8	784.0	1,237	15,729	11,535.2	714.5
Billings	231	828	152.5	28.0	518	3,166	554.9	178.6	128	2,078	D	127.4
Bozeman	162	420	78.0	14.0	409	1,609	218.3	81.0	79	932	223.2	38.3
Butte-Silver Bow	47	137	15.1	3.2	107	654	73.9	30.8	35	492	D	31.5
Great Falls	104	296	49.0	8.2	171	D	D	D	43	832	D	40.7
Helena	79	265	60.0	10.0	197	1,490	191.1	76.7	38	380	D	17.1
Missoula	158	818	113.4	27.1	415	2,625	305.0	129.2	64	573	160.4	D
NEBRASKA	2,001	10,068	1,732.0	388.5	4,426	74,339	5,705.2	3,628.5	1,844	92,409	57,499.2	4,002.8
Bellevue	50	167	37.5	5.0	85	D	D	D	13	578	126.4	22.9
Fremont	33	167	22.7	4.1	38	152	15.7	5.8	35	1,126	990.8	45.2
Grand Island	73	293	54.1	9.0	99	D	D	D	58	6,981	5,695.9	270.6
Kearney	50	146	37.2	4.2	80	536	65.9	24.4	29	710	130.2	28.7
Lincoln	323	1,561	243.8	53.6	783	8,731	1,254.8	444.0	210	11,045	5,711.5	557.2
Omaha	605	5,464	926.8	248.9	1,472	54,641	3,129.5	2,713.5	381	16,879	9,325.5	718.3
NEVADA	3,866	22,412	4,981.2	814.7	8,076	47,386	7,722.2	2,813.8	1,706	38,123	14,719.1	1,979.3
Carson City	111	304	51.7	9.5	292	D	D	D	122	2,798	634.0	162.7
Henderson	395	1,468	332.9	63.9	929	3,835	633.2	229.3	122	3,591	1,459.3	170.9
Las Vegas	904	5,221	900.9	202.0	2,331	13,142	2,330.1	827.8	197	2,631	896.8	127.8
North Las Vegas	103	630	126.9	24.9	136	D	D	D	107	3,260	856.0	139.6
Reno	454	2,345	523.8	86.2	1,172	7,000	1,131.1	437.9	231	7,327	3,300.4	385.2
Sparks	108	561	102.9	20.7	146	D	D	D	171	5,510	2,459.4	391.3
NEW HAMPSHIRE	1,338	7,044	1,593.1	309.7	3,794	29,853	3,910.7	1,678.8	1,851	66,636	18,895.6	3,923.8
Concord	66	330	74.2	13.3	224	D	D	D	63	1,332	330.9	62.2
Dover	35	358	42.1	10.5	103	D	D	D	44	919	141.4	44.7
Manchester	132	1,348	276.1	69.3	438	D	D	D	116	5,175	1,189.9	263.6
Nashua	109	414	94.6	17.1	324	D	D	D	117	8,970	D	801.7
Rochester	22	75	12.0	2.2	39	389	32.2	14.6	34	1,135	248.3	59.6
NEW JERSEY	8,749	53,751	17,327.6	2,813.1	29,289	305,648	58,415.3	23,862.4	7,758	230,697	108,855.0	14,094.8
Atlantic City	47	475	111.2	15.8	68	D	D	D	6	54	D	1.0
Bayonne	40	203	36.6	7.8	83	685	72.3	36.4	32	931	528.6	53.4
Bergenfield	15	24	5.6	1.2	46	154	20.4	6.1	17	158	D	7.5
Bridgeton	13	109	15.1	2.4	31	142	13.2	5.0	11	627	D	33.3
Camden	37	D	D	D	49	D	D	D	47	1,487	488.4	119.5
Clifton	95	586	117.1	25.7	253	1,866	281.3	114.1	144	5,418	1,781.7	339.4
East Orange	59	323	55.6	8.7	40	D	D	D	12	112	D	4.1
Elizabeth	98	447	216.1	19.7	116	D	D	D	69	2,138	935.4	106.5
Englewood	67	538	192.2	31.5	117	650	136.9	44.5	54	1,240	667.7	61.3
Fair Lawn	35	D	D	D	197	1,219	374.1	71.3	35	1,421	529.1	93.8
Fort Lee	118	499	133.9	21.1	269	1,142	480.9	92.0	14	203	D	8.2

1. Establishments subject to federal tax.

Table D. Cities — Accommodation and Food Services, Arts, Entertainment, and Recreation, and Health Care and Social Assistance

City	Accommodation and food services, 2012				Arts, entertainment, and recreation[1], 2012				Health care and social assistance,[1] 2012			
	Number of establishments	Number of employees	Receipts (mil dol)	Annual payroll (mil dol)	Number of establishments	Number of employees	Receipts (mil dol)	Annual payroll (mil dol)	Number of establishments	Number of employees	Receipts (mil dol)	Annual payroll (mil dol)
	92	93	94	95	96	97	98	99	100	101	102	103
MISSOURI	12,459	239,264	12,430.3	3,409.2	1,626	26,954	3,047.3	1,099.3	14,644	184,918	17,917.0	7,524.7
Ballwin	42	774	31.8	8.9	11	D	D	D	41	D	D	D
Blue Springs	114	2,209	103.1	28.4	24	D	D	D	129	D	D	D
Cape Girardeau	123	3,435	142.1	40.4	14	134	31.8	7.6	227	3,601	404.0	160.5
Chesterfield	175	4,601	217.4	66.7	31	303	18.5	5.2	260	D	D	D
Columbia	367	8,566	354.6	99.6	38	D	D	D	436	5,081	598.8	232.3
Florissant	108	2,211	103.2	28.2	9	179	6.5	1.8	178	2,003	180.9	83.4
Gladstone	41	756	33.9	10.5	5	D	D	D	69	508	44.4	18.4
Hazelwood	69	1,138	60.5	14.5	7	D	D	D	69	616	49.4	20.5
Independence	223	5,275	236.3	71.0	18	D	D	D	243	5,483	603.8	221.8
Jefferson City	152	3,034	126.0	37.8	16	D	D	D	175	3,035	336.4	152.1
Joplin	194	4,298	199.8	56.2	10	82	5.0	1.4	235	D	D	D
Kansas City	1,098	25,669	1,630.0	452.9	129	3,506	747.5	292.7	1,153	15,415	1,821.9	778.3
Kirkwood	65	1,509	68.4	21.0	13	84	5.9	1.9	100	700	105.4	39.1
Lee's Summit	183	3,599	156.7	47.1	25	371	19.3	3.6	270	D	D	D
Liberty	63	1,380	57.8	18.0	9	89	2.7	0.8	110	D	D	D
Maryland Heights	94	3,434	445.0	76.8	11	D	D	D	65	2,502	451.7	108.7
O'Fallon	155	D	D	D	24	D	D	D	179	D	D	D
Raytown	47	658	29.3	8.7	4	D	D	D	47	837	44.3	18.0
St. Charles	209	5,808	481.2	101.0	27	D	D	D	194	2,341	235.7	101.5
St. Joseph	177	3,925	175.6	47.4	12	D	D	D	242	D	D	D
St. Louis	1,036	22,069	1,255.7	371.4	81	4,971	819.6	293.0	927	11,437	1,124.3	388.0
St. Peters	181	3,751	163.4	47.8	27	514	18.2	6.3	231	2,273	249.7	105.0
Springfield	646	13,397	578.7	172.8	58	D	D	D	577	9,875	1,108.5	556.9
University City	82	1,295	66.4	19.4	6	D	D	D	163	1,216	57.8	24.6
Wentzville	73	D	D	D	4	D	D	D	75	824	63.4	28.0
Wildwood	28	D	D	D	6	288	4.9	1.0	58	652	56.1	25.0
MONTANA	3,458	46,251	2,420.5	649.5	899	8,346	676.6	130.3	2,545	24,420	2,508.0	1,040.9
Billings	346	7,362	421.5	113.8	89	847	119.0	13.9	412	5,194	686.5	303.8
Bozeman	190	3,550	160.6	45.5	46	715	36.9	10.1	220	1,633	174.1	72.1
Butte-Silver Bow	147	2,244	102.4	28.7	29	214	19.0	2.8	111	1,672	143.0	71.5
Great Falls	210	3,656	182.1	48.7	61	D	D	D	187	2,481	314.9	109.4
Helena	149	2,758	126.5	35.9	38	D	D	D	183	1,477	147.6	60.3
Missoula	275	5,444	282.1	75.2	60	656	56.0	9.2	341	4,181	428.3	166.2
NEBRASKA	4,326	70,128	3,094.5	855.4	557	7,147	471.2	110.6	4,282	57,239	5,706.7	2,397.7
Bellevue	104	1,961	88.7	25.9	10	D	D	D	94	D	D	D
Fremont	75	1,208	50.1	14.0	5	D	D	D	81	D	D	D
Grand Island	139	2,398	107.7	31.3	21	356	24.2	5.8	147	2,176	206.4	88.1
Kearney	123	2,815	107.4	30.4	12	D	D	D	123	D	D	D
Lincoln	635	12,813	573.3	149.5	78	D	D	D	761	10,250	1,055.7	489.8
Omaha	1,164	23,447	1,115.1	325.7	123	2,255	138.6	36.4	1,308	D	D	D
NEVADA	5,815	296,762	27,481.5	8,555.6	1,179	25,232	3,507.5	732.8	5,766	77,665	9,936.7	3,598.2
Carson City	159	2,740	133.4	41.2	43	1,064	94.0	27.2	198	2,390	334.4	123.6
Henderson	478	14,087	1,083.9	313.2	132	2,709	246.3	66.1	715	D	D	D
Las Vegas	1,140	40,393	2,979.2	962.3	260	4,052	877.0	165.9	1,677	23,573	3,082.1	1,070.0
North Las Vegas	224	7,028	515.5	157.2	27	D	D	D	195	D	D	D
Reno	697	21,617	1,436.8	452.8	105	1,995	139.2	39.9	815	10,429	1,415.2	595.9
Sparks	193	4,855	313.9	92.6	30	926	49.7	15.0	166	2,231	218.6	76.3
NEW HAMPSHIRE	3,606	54,047	2,942.3	890.9	536	10,803	681.9	192.0	2,775	35,400	4,001.6	1,769.7
Concord	120	2,629	122.9	41.6	15	227	11.6	3.5	158	2,713	340.2	176.7
Dover	88	1,552	78.5	23.4	7	29	2.3	0.3	111	D	D	D
Manchester	304	5,518	290.4	87.8	34	879	85.2	38.3	274	3,595	423.1	222.6
Nashua	232	4,426	224.1	68.4	28	534	27.4	7.4	270	3,480	458.1	196.6
Rochester	80	969	51.8	13.8	2	D	D	D	61	627	83.9	34.7
NEW JERSEY	20,127	291,933	19,673.6	5,386.8	2,821	39,560	3,690.4	1,238.1	23,088	297,847	32,634.9	13,027.7
Atlantic City	228	38,593	3,539.1	1,154.8	13	D	D	D	45	D	D	D
Bayonne	125	1,247	72.0	18.6	9	D	D	D	153	1,338	140.8	57.1
Bergenfield	42	284	18.5	4.4	2	D	D	D	64	527	47.5	16.0
Bridgeton	41	364	17.4	4.4	NA	NA	NA	NA	28	230	20.9	9.3
Camden	87	723	46.7	11.5	5	D	D	D	70	2,037	176.9	98.4
Clifton	159	2,027	125.1	31.3	18	D	D	D	367	3,382	338.6	131.9
East Orange	44	593	35.2	8.0	3	D	D	D	103	1,643	123.2	52.2
Elizabeth	249	2,725	206.5	52.3	10	D	D	D	201	2,087	165.7	69.3
Englewood	63	787	54.2	14.2	17	D	D	D	209	D	D	D
Fair Lawn	65	673	49.4	10.9	13	191	9.2	2.6	174	1,903	217.8	88.3
Fort Lee	116	1,113	88.2	18.7	14	37	4.5	1.2	190	D	D	D

1. Establishments subject to federal tax.

Table D. Cities — Other Services and Government Employment and Payroll

Other services[1] — columns 104–107. Government employment and payroll, 2012 (March payroll; columns 108–116 show percent of total for the indicated function).

City	Number of establishments [104]	Number of employees [105]	Receipts (mil dol) [106]	Annual payroll (mil dol) [107]	Full-time equivalent employees [108]	Total (dollars) [109]	Administrative, judicial, and legal [110]	Police and corrections [111]	Fire protection [112]	Highways and transportation [113]	Health and welfare [114]	Natural resources and utilities [115]	Education and libraries [116]
MISSOURI	8,441	49,408	4,235.2	1,361.6	X	X	X	X	X	X	X	X	X
Ballwin	42	351	20.0	7.0	0	0	0.0	0.0	0.0	0.0	0.0	0.0	0.0
Blue Springs	80	447	37.2	11.3	262	1,043,733	19.7	47.3	0.0	9.7	0.9	18.0	0.0
Cape Girardeau	86	502	37.7	12.2	634	1,734,259	10.2	18.8	19.9	13.6	0.0	29.9	5.9
Chesterfield	104	824	48.3	20.3	272	943,362	17.5	48.7	0.0	16.3	0.0	12.9	0.0
Columbia	211	1,418	87.7	32.1	1,462	5,497,108	19.3	10.6	11.4	6.9	6.7	33.2	0.0
Florissant	81	495	46.3	15.9	357	1,267,576	12.1	34.2	0.4	11.1	12.2	29.7	0.0
Gladstone	46	241	19.1	6.4	214	773,534	15.6	32.5	18.4	8.2	3.9	21.3	0.0
Hazelwood	38	323	41.2	10.4	195	925,216	9.7	45.0	25.1	8.3	0.5	6.9	0.0
Independence	153	825	65.0	20.0	1,064	6,218,560	8.1	26.4	15.4	4.9	2.8	41.9	0.0
Jefferson City	87	566	39.6	12.1	415	1,606,150	17.3	28.1	18.7	13.4	4.3	18.2	0.0
Joplin	111	749	48.9	16.7	548	1,718,395	9.6	29.9	20.7	11.8	6.0	12.5	4.3
Kansas City	634	4,554	358.7	119.1	6,482	21,087,489	9.4	47.9	29.2	7.6	1.6	0.9	0.0
Kirkwood	48	369	30.9	11.0	247	1,279,082	4.4	28.6	22.0	4.0	0.0	32.0	0.0
Lee's Summit	135	732	56.2	16.9	662	3,026,236	14.1	26.0	24.8	12.2	1.2	15.7	0.0
Liberty	46	301	25.2	7.0	236	903,212	17.2	26.6	21.9	6.0	2.2	21.9	0.0
Maryland Heights	44	455	39.8	16.5	213	1,068,259	19.4	51.3	0.0	8.8	0.8	12.2	0.0
O'Fallon	118	905	70.2	23.2	411	1,761,725	11.2	39.0	0.0	8.3	0.2	28.0	0.0
Raytown	48	344	41.1	11.9	163	693,572	15.3	25.3	23.0	16.1	0.7	19.6	0.0
St. Charles	132	941	76.1	24.6	509	2,509,796	9.9	33.7	23.0	9.7	0.0	13.6	0.0
St. Joseph	125	D	D	D	663	2,327,632	8.6	25.3	21.9	12.5	6.9	20.6	0.0
St. Louis	462	2,903	291.4	85.6	6,234	25,364,525	13.6	42.1	13.8	12.2	1.8	10.5	0.0
St. Peters	137	949	82.4	23.7	494	2,194,343	14.2	29.0	0.0	11.7	1.0	34.9	0.0
Springfield	408	2,992	241.6	75.3	2,692	13,095,113	4.7	15.6	8.4	9.6	2.7	34.5	0.0
University City	50	496	44.1	17.7	298	1,365,064	15.3	34.6	18.6	11.0	0.0	13.0	5.7
Wentzville	54	351	32.5	10.2	193	721,735	12.9	42.6	0.0	13.1	0.0	18.1	0.0
Wildwood	25	124	5.2	1.8	22	125,285	42.6	1.4	0.0	18.0	0.0	3.7	X
MONTANA	1,583	7,375	732.0	192.6	X	X	X	X	X	X	X	X	X
Billings	235	1,446	135.1	38.4	872	4,012,052	9.7	22.7	20.9	15.3	1.0	18.6	2.7
Bozeman	89	485	35.9	11.5	338	1,647,964	17.1	21.0	15.4	5.9	2.9	25.5	4.6
Butte-Silver Bow	57	228	22.8	6.3	430	1,750,790	15.7	24.3	18.9	14.2	2.0	21.6	0.0
Great Falls	87	593	44.9	14.1	488	2,209,954	12.9	30.2	16.9	10.2	6.8	19.7	3.2
Helena	67	355	29.9	8.9	301	1,298,064	13.5	27.1	14.7	7.9	4.9	23.7	0.0
Missoula	155	1,073	81.3	28.1	447	1,919,831	13.5	30.6	24.9	10.1	1.2	12.0	0.0
NEBRASKA	3,155	16,918	1,516.3	447.6	X	X	X	X	X	X	X	X	X
Bellevue	71	407	32.4	10.8	265	938,368	6.4	36.6	4.0	16.6	2.5	17.7	7.0
Fremont	51	D	D	D	278	1,259,723	10.6	16.8	8.8	6.2	0.0	47.0	2.3
Grand Island	102	D	D	D	596	2,645,689	9.6	16.2	16.0	8.3	0.3	43.9	3.6
Kearney	62	354	32.6	9.7	270	1,071,385	12.0	30.1	5.2	9.0	0.0	29.1	4.9
Lincoln	426	2,442	167.1	57.2	2,609	13,359,820	7.8	16.2	13.7	9.9	9.9	36.2	2.7
Omaha	770	6,202	489.2	176.4	2,835	15,258,712	6.3	39.2	26.1	8.5	2.6	11.0	3.8
NEVADA	2,935	20,584	1,790.5	543.2	X	X	X	X	X	X	X	X	X
Carson City	95	552	42.3	14.2	599	3,175,867	20.0	28.1	15.2	8.9	6.6	14.1	2.2
Henderson	315	2,190	175.4	53.3	2,239	13,759,509	18.4	29.3	14.7	1.2	2.0	25.6	0.0
Las Vegas	661	5,005	401.8	125.7	2,582	17,371,881	20.0	12.6	31.6	6.1	2.8	17.6	0.0
North Las Vegas	126	1,726	146.2	47.7	1,363	9,456,660	14.1	46.1	18.2	3.1	4.2	11.5	1.3
Reno	357	2,581	191.6	64.3	1,190	7,727,021	13.9	33.3	27.4	3.9	0.0	11.5	0.0
Sparks	153	958	119.1	35.2	500	2,883,097	19.7	31.5	22.6	3.6	0.0	21.4	0.0
NEW HAMPSHIRE	2,267	12,435	1,111.0	350.4	X	X	X	X	X	X	X	X	X
Concord	114	604	51.3	16.7	511	2,745,870	14.5	22.9	23.9	13.9	5.1	10.5	4.7
Dover	57	336	22.4	7.3	877	3,404,621	4.9	9.4	7.4	1.9	0.4	5.5	67.4
Manchester	216	1,767	144.0	51.4	3,353	14,363,066	3.8	12.5	9.5	7.7	2.7	7.3	55.0
Nashua	150	1,349	117.8	41.6	2,841	11,458,659	3.6	11.3	8.2	3.9	1.1	3.4	67.9
Rochester	44	232	20.0	6.0	998	3,938,623	4.0	9.1	4.3	1.9	0.5	3.1	75.7
NEW JERSEY	15,754	89,543	7,479.9	2,333.1	X	X	X	X	X	X	X	X	X
Atlantic City	50	743	49.3	16.0	1,521	8,728,573	8.1	41.3	24.3	1.3	7.3	9.0	1.9
Bayonne	110	457	28.1	8.9	2,167	12,420,526	2.7	16.8	11.4	3.3	4.4	2.0	58.3
Bergenfield	51	132	11.9	2.8	255	1,134,735	8.1	48.9	3.6	7.5	2.5	16.0	6.5
Bridgeton	22	89	9.0	2.2	17	61,842	0.0	0.0	0.0	0.0	100.0	0.0	0.0
Camden	54	388	28.9	9.9	98	380,956	0.0	0.0	0.0	0.0	100.0	0.0	4.0
Clifton	158	743	68.1	21.7	557	3,601,939	8.2	40.5	27.4	6.6	4.9	6.5	67.4
East Orange	57	D	D	D	2,832	17,819,602	3.5	12.8	6.9	1.2	5.1	2.4	1.8
Elizabeth	189	1,214	102.9	54.0	1,367	7,810,360	7.8	38.8	26.4	7.8	8.7	0.5	56.7
Englewood	86	425	36.5	11.9	885	5,644,368	2.5	19.1	9.9	1.8	4.0	3.8	7.1
Fair Lawn	82	345	40.2	12.5	256	1,498,256	15.9	40.2	1.4	5.4	2.1	22.3	4.2
Fort Lee	89	263	26.0	7.0	326	1,959,502	8.0	51.4	17.5	5.4	6.0	4.7	

1. Establishments subject to federal tax.

Table D. Cities — City Government Finances

City	General revenue Total (mil dol)	Intergovernmental Total (mil dol)	Intergovernmental Percent from state government	Taxes Total (mil dol)	Taxes Per capita[1] (dollars) Total	Property	Sales and gross receipts	General expenditure Total (mil dol)	Per capita[1] (dollars) Total	Capital outlays
	117	118	119	120	121	122	123	124	125	126
MISSOURI	X	X	X	X	X	X	X	X	X	X
Ballwin	18.7	9.4	1.9	5.3	173	15	159	18.7	613	106
Blue Springs	53.1	13.3	54.5	24.5	462	193	260	57.4	1,082	459
Cape Girardeau	57.8	5.4	100.0	35.6	921	61	860	52.2	1,349	435
Chesterfield	34.7	22.0	9.0	9.6	202	20	182	34.5	723	209
Columbia	138.4	19.3	25.9	63.8	563	95	468	212.6	1,877	640
Florissant	33.1	18.3	15.6	8.4	161	11	147	32.8	626	96
Gladstone	29.7	4.2	55.7	15.5	597	132	465	27.7	1,069	194
Hazelwood	38.3	16.6	5.6	17.5	683	419	264	41.8	1,627	196
Independence	188.3	31.9	65.8	87.8	748	125	624	191.9	1,636	278
Jefferson City	59.3	4.3	100.0	36.2	838	120	718	57.9	1,340	163
Joplin	79.1	7.5	60.0	45.9	914	50	864	75.9	1,511	421
Kansas City	1,256.7	117.6	15.8	742.9	1,599	266	877	1,156.0	2,489	448
Kirkwood	31.5	7.3	39.6	15.7	568	296	272	30.7	1,115	279
Lee's Summit	126.6	6.4	34.2	72.9	788	290	499	116.7	1,263	277
Liberty	33.0	1.0	69.8	19.8	663	218	445	32.0	1,073	157
Maryland Heights	47.8	14.1	52.2	24.5	891	113	778	36.8	1,340	394
O'Fallon	65.0	5.7	97.0	39.2	478	97	381	58.2	710	117
Raytown	24.5	1.7	100.0	13.8	468	60	405	23.7	802	108
St. Charles	85.0	6.1	40.0	58.8	884	225	659	87.4	1,314	334
St. Joseph	112.7	24.2	75.0	53.0	685	173	513	85.5	1,107	153
St. Louis	986.4	175.2	99.4	544.6	1,706	233	878	1,082.7	3,391	490
St. Peters	69.7	8.7	23.6	38.5	712	244	469	72.3	1,337	393
Springfield	302.8	56.5	34.5	151.6	934	123	811	276.2	1,702	333
University City	39.5	14.2	32.7	14.1	401	174	227	40.5	1,149	172
Wentzville	32.7	2.6	11.6	20.8	663	174	488	39.1	1,245	374
Wildwood	13.3	6.4	6.0	5.9	164	64	100	11.4	318	100
MONTANA	X	X	X	X	X	X	X	X	X	X
Billings	139.3	26.8	53.7	38.1	356	286	52	121.4	1,134	258
Bozeman	47.2	7.7	100.0	17.3	446	415	31	47.1	1,218	295
Butte-Silver Bow	75.8	25.6	85.0	27.7	820	793	27	64.6	1,913	455
Great Falls	59.8	11.2	86.2	17.7	300	264	36	59.2	1,004	125
Helena	39.8	8.5	54.5	9.3	320	301	19	38.1	1,306	175
Missoula	74.2	24.8	96.6	28.9	422	381	42	74.8	1,093	151
NEBRASKA	X	X	X	X	X	X	X	X	X	X
Bellevue	47.3	5.6	93.3	31.0	589	275	302	46.0	874	117
Fremont	32.4	11.1	42.3	11.6	439	202	237	26.6	1,007	230
Grand Island	57.1	7.8	100.0	23.4	468	139	329	52.8	1,053	87
Kearney	41.2	6.7	95.0	15.3	478	83	395	40.5	1,270	296
Lincoln	295.4	84.6	29.9	137.0	516	178	338	277.5	1,045	307
Omaha	610.0	80.9	60.1	392.9	903	317	586	580.3	1,333	325
NEVADA	X	X	X	X	X	X	X	X	X	X
Carson City	111.3	36.0	61.3	38.3	701	418	283	103.8	1,902	301
Henderson	402.5	181.2	47.5	129.1	487	256	231	422.6	1,594	454
Las Vegas	801.6	407.6	63.4	200.6	336	186	150	876.8	1,470	462
North Las Vegas	281.9	110.2	80.4	84.1	377	246	131	281.1	1,260	340
Reno	315.2	72.0	57.4	121.3	526	255	271	287.2	1,245	153
Sparks	93.5	28.6	69.1	34.8	378	260	118	85.8	933	92
NEW HAMPSHIRE	X	X	X	X	X	X	X	X	X	X
Concord	62.7	3.7	75.0	39.6	931	895	36	59.6	1,402	31
Dover	105.4	21.2	95.8	64.9	2,139	2,120	18	90.6	2,982	200
Manchester	391.9	151.9	74.0	152.0	1,379	1,330	50	436.7	3,964	479
Nashua	282.0	81.9	99.2	176.1	2,033	2,010	23	264.6	3,055	177
Rochester	102.0	39.7	96.1	54.8	1,835	1,692	143	100.7	3,371	643
NEW JERSEY	X	X	X	X	X	X	X	X	X	X
Atlantic City	265.6	40.5	25.2	197.6	4,993	4,875	117	225.7	5,703	269
Bayonne	247.8	88.4	85.4	137.0	2,113	2,095	18	277.8	4,287	148
Bergenfield	32.3	2.9	94.6	28.1	1,033	1,005	28	28.7	1,057	46
Bridgeton	34.1	9.2	55.7	12.4	491	454	37	34.9	1,382	155
Camden	232.9	174.8	71.9	30.2	391	338	53	160.2	2,073	195
Clifton	115.4	15.5	73.5	84.3	990	936	54	103.5	1,216	37
East Orange	399.7	273.1	95.8	111.4	1,730	1,712	17	362.6	5,630	108
Elizabeth	263.2	59.9	65.7	151.2	1,191	1,058	134	254.8	2,007	251
Englewood	130.4	25.5	71.3	98.9	3,607	3,555	52	132.8	4,840	411
Fair Lawn	44.1	4.4	97.6	38.3	1,166	1,116	50	39.3	1,195	65
Fort Lee	75.6	8.8	24.0	61.9	1,726	1,666	61	78.8	2,198	328

1. Based on population estimated as of July 1 of the year shown.

Table D. Cities — **City Government Finances**

City	City government finances, 2012 (cont.)									
	General expenditure (cont.)									
	Percent of total for:									
	Public welfare	Highways	Parking facilities	Education	Health and hospitals	Police protection	Sewerage and sanitation	Parks and recreation	Housing and community development	Interest on debt
	127	128	129	130	131	132	133	134	135	136
MISSOURI	X	X	X	X	X	X	X	X	X	X
Ballwin...........................	0.0	26.8	0.0	0.0	0.0	25.3	1.6	20.8	0.0	6.3
Blue Springs.....................	0.0	4.3	0.0	0.0	0.0	16.3	33.2	7.3	0.0	6.1
Cape Girardeau	0.0	23.1	0.0	0.0	0.6	13.1	19.5	15.6	0.7	2.2
Chesterfield......................	0.0	20.9	0.0	0.0	0.0	22.6	0.8	28.1	0.0	8.7
Columbia.........................	0.3	9.2	2.5	0.0	2.7	7.7	25.4	7.7	0.9	2.5
Florissant	0.0	13.2	0.0	0.0	1.9	30.6	0.5	18.0	2.8	1.4
Gladstone........................	0.0	11.8	0.0	0.0	0.8	18.2	17.1	13.9	1.8	5.2
Hazelwood.......................	0.0	0.9	0.0	0.0	0.0	19.1	0.3	8.1	0.0	2.2
Independence	1.9	13.2	0.0	0.0	1.6	15.3	15.0	3.9	0.4	8.1
Jefferson City	0.0	20.0	1.2	0.0	1.0	18.7	8.8	13.4	0.7	3.2
Joplin.............................	0.3	11.6	0.1	0.0	3.2	12.8	22.9	7.3	2.2	0.8
Kansas City......................	0.5	13.1	0.4	0.0	4.6	17.1	7.8	4.6	3.5	8.1
Kirkwood.........................	0.0	5.0	0.0	0.0	0.0	21.3	10.0	12.4	0.0	1.8
Lee's Summit	0.0	15.2	0.0	0.0	0.0	15.6	11.5	6.5	1.2	3.3
Liberty	0.0	13.8	0.0	0.0	0.0	14.6	20.9	11.7	4.7	6.1
Maryland Heights	0.9	36.0	0.0	0.0	0.0	26.9	8.2	10.0	3.4	3.1
O'Fallon..........................	0.0	16.9	0.0	0.0	0.0	20.3	13.7	13.5	0.3	7.4
Raytown..........................	0.0	5.9	0.0	0.0	0.0	28.8	18.1	6.2	2.8	11.3
St. Charles	0.0	22.9	0.1	0.0	0.0	21.1	5.4	10.0	0.6	8.9
St. Joseph	2.1	11.2	0.4	0.0	5.5	11.2	14.3	7.0	1.5	5.9
St. Louis..........................	0.0	2.3	0.9	0.0	3.6	23.2	1.7	2.2	2.7	8.4
St. Peters........................	0.0	24.8	0.0	0.0	0.7	19.4	20.1	17.9	0.2	4.6
Springfield.......................	0.4	10.7	0.1	0.0	2.9	23.9	12.1	10.6	0.9	5.3
University City...................	0.0	18.3	0.5	0.0	0.0	18.1	6.7	8.2	3.5	2.0
Wentzville........................	0.0	14.6	0.0	0.0	0.0	18.0	37.0	7.4	0.0	5.5
Wildwood	0.0	34.1	0.0	0.0	0.0	26.6	0.1	4.4	0.0	1.4
MONTANA	X	X	X	X	X	X	X	X	X	X
Billings...........................	0.0	16.9	1.9	0.0	0.6	16.1	21.3	3.4	2.8	1.8
Bozeman.........................	11.0	10.4	0.8	0.0	0.0	20.0	29.4	0.9	0.2	3.2
Butte-Silver Bow	0.2	7.2	0.2	0.0	7.7	10.3	23.9	4.7	0.4	2.6
Great Falls	0.0	12.3	1.1	0.0	0.0	20.7	22.3	10.6	4.0	2.1
Helena............................	0.0	10.7	5.1	0.0	0.4	18.4	19.1	15.1	0.1	3.1
Missoula..........................	0.2	13.6	1.8	0.0	1.9	17.8	14.7	6.3	1.4	3.5
NEBRASKA.......................	X	X	X	X	X	X	X	X	X	X
Bellevue..........................	0.0	10.3	0.0	0.0	0.0	34.9	13.4	5.1	0.4	3.6
Fremont...........................	0.0	16.1	0.0	0.0	0.0	16.9	17.3	8.7	9.2	1.3
Grand Island	0.0	12.5	0.1	0.0	0.0	16.4	18.8	8.4	1.9	2.1
Kearney..........................	0.0	21.9	0.1	0.0	0.0	16.5	18.4	15.8	3.0	0.7
Lincoln...........................	2.3	19.2	1.4	0.0	4.4	12.9	12.2	4.2	3.8	1.5
Omaha............................	0.3	10.5	0.8	0.0	0.0	16.3	19.0	13.1	0.3	7.2
NEVADA..........................	X	X	X	X	X	X	X	X	X	X
Carson City	2.3	10.5	0.0	0.0	4.2	15.9	10.8	10.1	1.5	9.1
Henderson	0.0	1.7	0.0	0.0	0.0	17.2	10.2	28.6	2.7	2.3
Las Vegas........................	0.1	6.9	0.4	0.0	0.4	14.6	13.4	11.0	2.7	3.5
North Las Vegas	0.0	13.1	0.0	0.0	0.0	26.3	10.0	10.6	2.4	3.8
Reno..............................	0.0	9.4	0.0	0.0	0.0	18.6	14.1	3.8	6.8	15.2
Sparks............................	0.0	7.6	0.0	0.0	0.0	23.2	17.6	6.4	0.6	13.5
NEW HAMPSHIRE	X	X	X	X	X	X	X	X	X	X
Concord	1.8	11.5	1.5	0.0	0.3	16.9	15.6	4.2	0.0	4.5
Dover.............................	0.9	5.5	0.4	50.9	0.0	7.9	7.8	2.6	0.3	5.1
Manchester	0.3	5.2	0.6	39.2	1.3	7.0	4.3	1.3	0.9	5.3
Nashua...........................	0.3	2.6	0.0	55.6	0.3	6.6	7.7	1.0	0.5	4.0
Rochester........................	0.6	7.4	0.0	57.0	0.0	6.1	4.6	0.7	0.3	2.9
NEW JERSEY.....................	X	X	X	X	X	X	X	X	X	X
Atlantic City	0.6	1.1	0.0	0.0	1.7	16.6	1.7	3.0	11.8	1.9
Bayonne..........................	0.0	0.6	0.5	41.0	0.5	9.0	4.6	1.2	21.6	4.2
Bergenfield.......................	0.0	7.1	0.0	0.0	1.5	23.3	16.4	2.7	0.0	1.9
Bridgeton.........................	0.0	3.9	0.0	0.0	0.4	15.8	23.3	1.5	13.4	0.5
Camden...........................	0.0	2.8	0.0	0.0	1.1	17.8	5.7	1.0	24.6	2.6
Clifton............................	0.1	2.8	0.0	0.0	1.0	20.0	12.8	1.5	3.1	2.4
East Orange......................	0.0	0.5	0.1	63.0	1.4	7.5	2.7	0.7	4.4	0.7
Elizabeth.........................	0.0	2.3	0.8	0.0	2.2	17.0	12.9	4.9	15.8	1.7
Englewood	0.0	2.1	0.0	52.5	0.6	9.2	4.3	0.7	5.2	1.0
Fair Lawn.........................	0.2	2.9	0.0	0.0	1.8	20.0	13.4	4.5	0.0	3.4
Fort Lee...........................	0.3	3.2	1.7	0.0	1.8	18.2	8.2	2.4	8.3	3.6

City Government Finances, City Government Employment, and Climate

City	City government finances, 2012 (cont.)			Climate[2]						
	Debt outstanding			Average daily temperature						
				Mean		Limits				
	Total (mil dol)	Per capita[1] (dollars)	Debt issued during year	January	July	January[3]	July[4]	Annual precipitation (inches)	Heating degree days	Cooling degree days
	137	138	139	140	141	142	143	144	145	146
MISSOURI	X	X	X	X	X	X	X	X	X	X
Ballwin	17.1	563	0.0	27.5	78.1	17.3	89.2	38.00	5,199	1,293
Blue Springs	129.0	2,432	12.5	24.6	76.6	14.9	87.2	41.18	5,623	1,137
Cape Girardeau	56.2	1,453	14.5	32.4	79.5	24.0	90.1	46.54	4,344	1,515
Chesterfield	69.9	1,467	0.0	27.5	78.1	17.3	89.2	38.00	5,199	1,293
Columbia	354.5	3,130	121.7	27.8	77.4	18.2	88.6	40.28	5,177	1,246
Florissant	22.1	421	7.2	29.6	80.2	21.2	89.8	38.75	4,758	1,561
Gladstone	41.1	1,585	0.0	29.3	81.3	20.7	90.5	35.51	4,734	1,676
Hazelwood	43.7	1,703	7.9	29.6	80.2	21.2	89.8	38.75	4,758	1,561
Independence	427.5	3,645	74.2	26.6	77.1	17.1	87.5	43.14	5,373	1,176
Jefferson City	62.3	1,443	0.0	28.2	77.9	17.7	89.4	39.59	5,158	1,261
Joplin	15.0	299	1.4	33.1	79.9	23.7	90.4	46.07	4,253	1,555
Kansas City	2,948.0	6,347	651.3	29.3	81.3	20.7	90.5	35.51	4,734	1,676
Kirkwood	23.0	833	0.0	29.6	80.2	21.2	89.8	38.75	4,758	1,561
Lee's Summit	98.3	1,064	7.9	24.6	76.6	14.9	87.2	41.18	5,623	1,137
Liberty	47.2	1,585	5.9	26.6	77.1	17.1	87.5	43.14	5,373	1,176
Maryland Heights	17.8	647	0.0	29.5	80.7	21.2	90.5	38.84	4,650	1,633
O'Fallon	231.0	2,818	8.6	28.3	79.0	19.0	90.2	38.28	5,020	1,399
Raytown	54.1	1,832	0.0	24.6	76.6	14.9	87.2	41.18	5,623	1,137
St. Charles	217.8	3,273	9.9	27.5	78.1	17.3	89.2	38.00	5,199	1,293
St. Joseph	532.1	6,888	30.2	26.4	78.7	15.9	89.9	35.24	5,345	1,339
St. Louis	1,862.1	5,832	143.8	29.5	80.7	21.2	90.5	38.84	4,650	1,633
St. Peters	126.3	2,335	11.7	28.3	79.0	19.0	90.2	38.28	5,020	1,399
Springfield	1,021.0	6,292	42.8	31.7	78.5	21.8	89.9	44.97	4,602	1,366
University City	13.5	382	6.6	29.5	80.7	21.2	90.5	38.84	4,650	1,633
Wentzville	64.6	2,058	31.8	NA	NA	NA	NA	NA	NA	NA
Wildwood	5.1	142	0.0	27.5	78.1	17.3	89.2	38.00	5,199	1,293
MONTANA	X	X	X	X	X	X	X	X	X	X
Billings	108.2	1,011	7.4	24.0	72.0	15.1	85.8	14.77	7,006	583
Bozeman	35.1	906	4.1	22.6	65.3	12.0	81.8	16.45	7,984	216
Butte-Silver Bow	42.1	1,246	15.8	17.6	62.7	5.4	79.8	12.78	9,399	127
Great Falls	39.4	668	0.9	21.7	66.2	11.3	82.0	14.89	7,828	288
Helena	45.1	1,546	0.5	20.2	67.8	9.9	83.4	11.32	7,975	277
Missoula	84.9	1,240	6.4	23.5	66.9	16.2	83.6	13.82	7,622	256
NEBRASKA	X	X	X	X	X	X	X	X	X	X
Bellevue	65.0	1,234	8.2	21.7	76.7	11.6	87.4	30.22	6,311	1,095
Fremont	38.9	1,473	4.0	21.1	76.2	10.4	87.7	29.80	6,444	1,004
Grand Island	50.6	1,010	9.3	22.4	75.8	12.2	87.1	25.89	6,385	1,027
Kearney	40.8	1,277	10.8	22.4	74.7	11.0	85.7	25.20	6,652	852
Lincoln	1,294.9	4,876	354.0	22.4	77.8	11.5	89.6	28.37	6,242	1,154
Omaha	1,049.9	2,411	111.5	21.7	76.7	11.6	87.4	30.22	6,311	1,095
NEVADA	X	X	X	X	X	X	X	X	X	X
Carson City	282.0	5,168	35.1	33.7	70.0	21.7	89.2	10.36	5,661	419
Henderson	308.8	1,165	35.1	47.0	91.2	36.8	104.1	4.49	2,239	3,214
Las Vegas	637.5	1,069	51.5	47.0	91.2	36.8	104.1	4.49	2,239	3,214
North Las Vegas	473.2	2,122	27.1	47.0	91.2	36.8	104.1	4.49	2,239	3,214
Reno	1,243.0	5,389	55.4	33.6	71.3	21.8	91.2	7.48	5,600	493
Sparks	243.8	2,649	0.0	33.6	71.3	21.8	91.2	7.48	5,600	493
NEW HAMPSHIRE	X	X	X	X	X	X	X	X	X	X
Concord	67.0	1,577	8.1	20.1	70.0	9.7	82.9	37.60	7,478	442
Dover	72.6	2,392	9.7	23.3	70.7	13.1	83.2	42.80	6,748	427
Manchester	566.8	5,145	160.3	18.8	68.4	5.2	82.1	39.82	7,742	263
Nashua	156.2	1,803	14.8	22.8	70.8	12.1	82.5	45.43	6,834	445
Rochester	80.7	2,701	11.6	23.3	70.7	13.1	83.2	42.80	6,748	427
NEW JERSEY	X	X	X	X	X	X	X	X	X	X
Atlantic City	164.0	4,143	51.6	35.2	75.2	29.0	80.6	38.37	4,480	951
Bayonne	460.2	7,102	0.0	31.3	77.2	24.4	85.2	46.25	4,843	1,220
Bergenfield	14.8	544	0.0	28.6	75.0	19.5	85.5	51.50	5,522	824
Bridgeton	15.0	593	0.0	NA	NA	NA	NA	NA	NA	NA
Camden	77.8	1,007	0.0	32.3	76.3	23.2	87.8	48.25	4,801	1,054
Clifton	71.7	842	15.7	28.6	75.0	19.5	85.5	51.50	5,522	824
East Orange	100.2	1,556	0.0	31.3	77.2	24.4	85.2	46.25	4,843	1,220
Elizabeth	124.1	978	19.1	29.6	74.5	19.8	85.7	50.94	5,450	787
Englewood	44.8	1,633	0.0	29.6	75.3	22.7	82.5	46.33	5,367	882
Fair Lawn	38.7	1,176	0.0	28.6	75.0	19.5	85.5	51.50	5,522	824
Fort Lee	62.2	1,736	14.1	29.6	75.3	22.7	82.5	46.33	5,367	882

1. Based on the population estimated as of July 1 of the year shown.   2. Represents normal values based on the 30-year period, 1971±2000.   3. Average daily minimum.   4. Average daily maximum.

Table D. Cities — Land Area and Population

STATE Place code	City	Land area[1] (sq. mi)	Total persons 2018	Rank	Per square mile	White	Black or African American	American Indian, Alaskan Native	Asian	Hawaiian Pacific Islander	Some other race	Two or more races (percent)
		1	2	3	4	5	6	7	8	9	10	11
	NEW JERSEY— Cont'd											
34 25,770	Garfield	2.1	31,866	1,191	15,174.3	85.1	3.4	0.0	1.5	0.0	5.6	4.4
34 28,680	Hackensack	4.2	44,522	859	10,600.5	50.6	27.8	0.2	13.7	0.0	4.3	3.4
34 32,250	Hoboken	1.3	53,455	725	41,119.2	79.4	2.3	0.0	9.0	0.0	1.8	7.5
34 36,000	Jersey City	14.7	265,549	78	18,064.6	34.3	23.5	0.7	26.5	0.0	11.6	3.4
34 36,510	Kearny	8.8	41,422	923	4,707.0	61.5	5.4	0.2	7.9	0.0	21.2	3.7
34 40,350	Linden	10.7	42,538	894	3,975.5	53.3	28.4	0.3	5.1	0.5	10.1	2.3
34 41,310	Long Branch	5.1	30,406	1,238	5,962.0	68.0	15.4	0.0	0.6	0.0	13.7	2.3
34 46,680	Millville	42.0	27,633	1,333	657.9	NA	NA	NA	NA	NA	NA	NA
34 51,000	Newark	24.1	282,090	73	11,705.0	27.1	50.7	0.2	1.8	0.1	17.9	2.3
34 51,210	New Brunswick	5.2	56,100	678	10,788.5	67.1	13.2	0.0	13.1	0.1	5.8	0.7
34 55,950	Paramus	10.4	26,558	1,375	2,553.7	NA	NA	NA	NA	NA	NA	NA
34 56,550	Passaic	3.1	69,948	513	22,563.9	80.3	6.4	0.0	2.0	0.0	10.8	0.5
34 57,000	Paterson	8.4	145,627	180	17,336.5	32.3	24.9	0.0	4.5	0.0	34.6	3.7
34 58,200	Perth Amboy	4.7	51,928	739	11,048.5	71.0	14.8	0.0	1.0	0.0	10.9	2.3
34 59,190	Plainfield	6.0	50,693	758	8,448.8	30.5	45.0	0.2	1.4	0.3	20.7	2.0
34 61,530	Rahway	3.9	29,880	1,260	7,661.5	51.2	30.9	0.3	4.2	0.0	11.5	1.8
34 65,790	Sayreville	15.8	44,556	857	2,820.0	67.2	15.7	0.0	12.7	0.0	2.8	1.6
34 74,000	Trenton	7.6	83,974	405	11,049.2	40.6	53.8	0.1	0.5	0.0	3.6	1.4
34 74,630	Union City	1.3	68,520	525	52,707.7	77.4	4.3	0.2	2.8	0.0	12.1	3.2
34 76,070	Vineland	68.4	59,966	625	876.7	74.2	16.1	0.1	1.5	0.3	4.7	3.1
34 79,040	Westfield	6.7	29,881	1,259	4,459.9	86.4	2.4	0.0	7.3	0.0	1.5	2.4
34 79,610	West New York	1.0	52,990	732	52,990.0	56.2	2.0	0.0	6.3	0.0	31.4	4.0
35 00,000	**NEW MEXICO**	121,311.9	2,095,428	X	17.3	75.8	2.1	9.6	1.4	0.1	7.7	3.3
35 01,780	Alamogordo	21.4	31,701	1,196	1,481.4	84.3	3.0	1.1	1.1	0.0	3.7	6.7
35 02,000	Albuquerque	187.2	560,218	32	2,992.6	76.5	3.1	4.4	2.9	0.1	9.1	4.0
35 12,150	Carlsbad	31.1	29,331	1,276	943.1	NA	NA	NA	NA	NA	NA	NA
35 16,420	Clovis	23.6	38,680	996	1,639.0	59.4	5.9	0.3	1.0	0.0	25.2	8.1
35 25,800	Farmington	34.4	44,788	853	1,302.0	62.5	1.8	24.1	1.1	0.2	4.1	6.2
35 32,520	Hobbs	26.4	38,277	1,004	1,449.9	82.7	6.8	1.4	0.0	0.0	6.5	2.6
35 39,380	Las Cruces	76.9	102,926	301	1,338.4	83.4	3.3	1.2	1.4	0.0	7.3	3.3
35 63,460	Rio Rancho	103.4	98,023	316	948.0	86.1	2.1	1.6	1.6	0.1	4.0	4.4
35 64,930	Roswell	29.7	47,635	813	1,603.9	86.8	1.8	0.7	0.0	0.0	6.8	3.9
35 70,500	Santa Fe	52.2	84,612	401	1,620.9	86.8	1.8	1.4	1.9	0.3	5.6	2.4
36 00,000	**NEW YORK**	47,123.4	19,542,209	X	414.7	63.1	15.8	0.4	8.7	0.0	8.9	3.0
36 01,000	Albany	21.4	97,279	321	4,545.7	53.3	28.4	0.3	8.8	0.0	3.2	6.0
36 03,078	Auburn	8.3	26,454	1,382	3,187.2	85.6	6.2	0.0	1.2	0.0	1.3	5.7
36 06,607	Binghamton	10.5	44,785	854	4,265.2	71.5	13.9	0.2	7.0	0.0	1.0	6.5
36 11,000	Buffalo	40.4	256,304	83	6,344.2	46.7	35.8	0.3	6.7	0.0	6.2	4.2
36 24,229	Elmira	7.3	27,204	1,349	3,726.6	74.9	17.4	0.1	1.6	0.0	1.1	4.8
36 27,485	Freeport	4.6	43,044	883	9,357.4	38.8	24.9	0.3	0.7	0.0	18.9	16.4
36 29,113	Glen Cove	6.7	27,201	1,350	4,059.9	55.7	13.6	0.0	3.7	0.0	22.0	4.9
36 32,402	Harrison	16.8	27,896	1,324	1,660.5	76.5	6.3	0.3	7.8	0.0	7.1	1.9
36 33,139	Hempstead	3.7	55,255	688	14,933.8	13.9	44.3	0.9	3.1	0.0	32.2	5.7
36 38,077	Ithaca	5.4	30,999	1,217	5,740.6	69.0	4.2	0.1	21.3	0.0	1.8	3.7
36 38,264	Jamestown	8.9	29,315	1,278	3,293.8	87.6	4.7	0.0	0.3	0.0	3.1	4.3
36 42,554	Lindenhurst	3.8	26,902	1,364	7,079.5	NA	NA	NA	NA	NA	NA	NA
36 43,335	Long Beach	2.2	33,534	1,142	15,242.7	83.1	4.6	0.1	4.3	0.0	6.8	1.0
36 47,042	Middletown	5.1	27,815	1,326	5,453.9	54.2	23.9	1.0	4.4	0.0	11.2	5.2
36 49,121	Mount Vernon	4.4	67,593	539	15,362.0	18.0	69.5	0.5	3.4	0.0	6.0	2.6
36 50,034	Newburgh	3.8	28,164	1,313	7,411.6	39.0	22.5	0.0	1.7	0.0	32.0	4.8
36 50,617	New Rochelle	10.4	78,742	441	7,571.3	56.2	20.2	0.0	5.0	0.2	14.6	3.8
36 51,000	New York	300.4	8,398,748	1	27,958.5	42.2	24.3	0.4	14.5	0.1	15.2	3.4
36 51,055	Niagara Falls	14.1	48,144	804	3,414.5	67.0	26.2	1.7	2.3	0.0	0.3	2.4
36 53,682	North Tonawanda	10.1	30,372	1,240	3,007.1	NA	NA	NA	NA	NA	NA	NA
36 55,530	Ossining	3.2	24,998	1,413	7,811.9	41.2	13.9	0.4	6.1	0.0	34.0	4.4
36 59,223	Port Chester	2.3	29,282	1,279	12,731.3	NA	NA	NA	NA	NA	NA	NA
36 59,641	Poughkeepsie	5.1	30,469	1,234	5,974.3	51.1	35.8	2.2	0.3	0.0	3.1	7.5
36 63,000	Rochester	35.8	206,284	111	5,762.1	45.5	40.7	0.9	3.8	0.0	4.3	4.8
36 63,418	Rome	74.9	32,204	1,183	430.0	84.7	7.5	0.3	1.8	0.0	1.4	4.3
36 65,255	Saratoga Springs	28.1	28,005	1,319	996.6	91.8	2.2	0.3	3.2	0.0	1.0	1.5
36 65,508	Schenectady	10.8	65,575	566	6,071.8	60.8	21.8	0.3	7.6	0.0	4.3	5.1
36 70,420	Spring Valley	2.0	32,261	1,178	16,130.5	45.2	33.3	0.1	2.7	0.0	16.7	1.9
36 73,000	Syracuse	25.0	142,749	185	5,710.0	52.7	31.0	1.0	8.7	0.0	1.9	4.7
36 75,484	Troy	10.4	49,374	778	4,747.5	65.4	17.7	0.0	5.3	0.0	3.1	8.4
36 76,540	Utica	16.8	60,100	621	3,577.4	61.9	16.2	0.4	13.3	0.0	5.8	2.5
36 76,705	Valley Stream	3.5	37,523	1,023	10,720.9	35.2	35.9	0.0	9.8	0.0	12.0	7.2
36 78,608	Watertown	9.0	25,290	1,407	2,810.0	79.4	13.5	1.1	1.2	0.0	0.2	4.6
36 81,677	White Plains	9.8	58,111	650	5,929.7	56.8	13.3	0.2	7.9	0.0	19.3	2.5

1. Dry land or land partially or temporarily covered by water.   2. Hispanic or Latino persons may be of any race.

Table D. Cities — **Population**

City	Percent Hispanic or Latino[1], 2017	Percent foreign born, 2017	Age of population (percent), 2017							Median age, 2017	Percent female, 2017	Census counts		Percent change	
			Under 18 years	18 to 24 years	25 to 34 years	35 to 44 years	45 to 54 years	55 to 64 years	65 years and over			2000	2010	2000-2010	2001-2018
	12	13	14	15	16	17	18	19	20	21	22	23	24	25	26
NEW JERSEY— Cont'd															
Garfield	34.2	42.0	21.0	10.1	17.0	13.8	13.1	13.0	12.1	36.0	53.1	29,786	30,494	2.4	4.5
Hackensack	41.6	38.1	19.2	9.1	16.6	15.3	14.4	12.0	13.4	39.0	53.4	42,677	43,014	0.8	3.5
Hoboken	19.3	16.0	15.4	10.4	35.3	16.2	10.0	6.6	6.2	31.3	47.9	38,577	50,015	29.6	6.9
Jersey City	29.5	42.0	21.2	7.7	23.9	15.1	11.3	9.4	11.4	33.8	50.6	240,055	247,639	3.2	7.2
Kearny	48.1	47.6	18.7	7.9	17.1	12.5	16.3	13.2	14.2	38.7	47.2	40,513	40,714	0.5	1.7
Linden	30.7	36.0	20.4	4.3	16.8	14.7	13.9	14.6	15.3	40.5	53.0	39,394	40,525	2.9	5.0
Long Branch	31.2	28.5	21.0	9.1	13.6	14.0	13.3	14.0	15.0	38.6	46.4	31,340	30,717	-2.0	-1.0
Millville	12.8	2.7	19.4	8.0	9.7	10.2	21.7	13.9	17.1	46.3	49.8	26,847	28,417	5.8	-2.8
Newark	36.2	33.2	24.6	10.0	16.3	14.4	13.0	11.1	10.6	34.4	51.6	273,546	277,107	1.3	1.8
New Brunswick	44.5	35.3	24.7	31.3	14.4	11.8	6.7	4.9	6.1	22.6	52.3	48,573	54,500	12.2	2.9
Paramus	8.0	32.3	18.9	6.2	9.4	12.3	15.1	15.4	22.7	48.0	55.2	25,737	26,342	2.4	0.8
Passaic	74.2	41.8	34.5	9.8	15.7	12.7	10.2	9.5	7.5	29.0	48.4	67,861	69,811	2.9	0.2
Paterson	60.6	42.5	27.2	10.9	15.9	12.4	12.9	10.1	10.6	32.0	52.4	149,222	146,181	-2.0	-0.4
Perth Amboy	76.5	47.5	28.4	10.2	13.0	14.5	12.7	9.8	11.3	33.6	51.5	47,303	50,827	7.4	2.2
Plainfield	51.2	33.1	24.5	9.1	17.9	16.9	12.1	8.1	11.3	33.3	47.7	47,829	49,694	3.9	2.0
Rahway	31.2	21.4	17.8	7.5	14.2	18.1	12.3	15.9	14.1	39.7	50.9	26,500	27,324	3.1	9.4
Sayreville	19.0	26.0	20.7	5.1	18.9	12.1	13.1	17.8	12.4	40.2	53.7	40,377	42,753	5.9	4.2
Trenton	36.6	25.0	26.3	11.6	13.8	14.3	13.3	10.6	10.1	33.8	49.9	85,403	84,964	-0.5	-1.2
Union City	74.3	58.5	22.0	10.1	15.6	18.3	14.4	9.7	9.9	36.8	52.1	67,088	66,439	-1.0	3.1
Vineland	42.4	12.9	23.3	9.9	13.8	12.6	11.7	12.8	15.8	37.3	53.5	56,271	60,737	7.9	-1.3
Westfield	7.6	11.2	29.9	7.0	5.1	13.0	18.3	13.8	12.9	41.8	51.5	29,644	30,296	2.2	-1.4
West New York	77.5	62.2	21.8	7.5	22.0	17.0	11.3	9.6	10.8	34.3	48.0	45,768	49,700	8.6	6.6
NEW MEXICO	48.8	9.4	23.5	9.9	13.1	12.0	11.5	13.3	16.8	37.7	50.5	1,819,046	2,059,180	13.2	1.8
Alamogordo	27.3	5.4	21.1	9.8	14.3	13.9	9.0	16.7	15.1	39.3	47.5	35,582	30,417	-14.5	4.2
Albuquerque	49.6	9.3	22.8	9.0	15.6	12.9	11.8	12.4	15.5	37.0	51.2	448,607	546,191	21.8	2.6
Carlsbad	44.8	3.5	21.8	12.3	15.6	10.1	11.1	15.2	13.9	35.2	48.4	25,625	26,236	2.4	11.8
Clovis	49.0	12.4	28.7	11.2	16.5	13.5	9.4	10.5	10.2	30.7	48.8	32,667	37,794	15.7	2.3
Farmington	32.8	7.1	27.7	12.5	14.2	13.9	7.5	10.6	13.5	33.0	50.4	37,844	45,965	21.5	-2.6
Hobbs	54.9	16.5	28.4	9.9	14.4	12.0	11.7	11.3	12.3	32.9	47.4	28,657	34,201	19.3	11.9
Las Cruces	61.1	12.5	23.6	15.0	13.1	11.9	10.3	11.7	14.3	33.8	49.8	74,267	97,728	31.6	5.3
Rio Rancho	43.2	6.4	24.0	7.9	13.5	13.6	12.3	13.5	15.2	38.4	51.6	51,765	87,375	68.8	12.2
Roswell	57.5	14.7	25.9	11.3	14.6	12.0	8.4	12.1	15.7	34.0	51.4	45,293	48,416	6.9	-1.6
Santa Fe	57.2	14.5	19.2	8.2	13.4	11.7	11.7	14.2	21.7	42.4	52.8	62,203	80,878	30.0	4.6
NEW YORK	19.2	22.9	20.9	9.4	14.7	12.5	13.4	13.1	15.9	38.7	51.4	18,976,457	19,378,124	2.1	0.8
Albany	10.6	15.3	19.1	20.5	15.2	11.7	10.4	9.6	13.5	31.2	52.8	95,658	97,841	2.3	-0.6
Auburn	5.6	3.9	21.9	6.3	12.4	13.7	14.5	13.7	17.5	40.9	49.1	28,574	27,688	-3.1	-4.5
Binghamton	5.8	10.7	18.8	16.2	10.8	10.5	13.2	14.1	16.4	38.8	52.0	47,380	47,406	0.1	-5.5
Buffalo	12.1	10.1	22.3	11.9	19.0	10.9	11.5	12.4	12.0	32.9	52.2	292,648	261,372	-10.7	-1.9
Elmira	4.7	2.7	23.2	11.9	18.3	9.9	14.0	10.9	11.7	33.0	48.5	30,940	29,242	-5.5	-7.0
Freeport	50.2	30.5	21.3	10.0	11.1	15.0	13.3	11.9	17.3	40.7	54.0	43,783	42,843	-2.1	0.5
Glen Cove	24.4	29.8	29.2	5.4	12.6	13.2	12.1	12.3	15.2	36.8	53.7	26,622	26,952	1.2	0.9
Harrison	11.0	23.9	20.2	18.2	9.3	11.3	14.6	13.1	13.3	37.8	50.2	24,154	27,465	13.7	1.6
Hempstead	46.2	40.4	28.8	9.4	12.4	12.8	13.4	10.8	12.3	34.5	53.2	56,554	54,018	-4.5	2.3
Ithaca	7.2	19.2	13.2	49.1	12.4	9.2	7.1	3.6	5.4	21.9	50.9	29,287	30,013	2.5	3.3
Jamestown	8.1	3.1	20.3	11.9	13.4	11.3	12.9	13.9	16.4	39.5	47.6	31,730	31,160	-1.8	-5.9
Lindenhurst	26.7	13.8	21.9	12.9	14.8	9.7	17.5	14.6	8.5	35.1	51.0	27,819	27,262	-2.0	-1.3
Long Beach	13.4	13.0	13.3	10.6	12.8	7.8	14.9	20.2	20.5	48.7	52.9	35,462	33,331	-6.0	0.6
Middletown	40.8	15.6	30.2	6.5	18.9	10.9	9.3	9.2	14.9	32.7	50.6	25,388	27,902	9.9	-0.3
Mount Vernon	13.0	29.2	16.6	7.8	17.8	12.7	13.1	12.8	19.1	40.6	56.2	68,381	67,303	-1.6	0.4
Newburgh	53.7	24.3	26.8	12.0	14.9	15.0	9.9	9.5	12.0	32.0	46.5	28,259	28,903	2.3	-2.6
New Rochelle	28.7	33.6	18.1	13.1	11.0	12.5	14.2	14.8	16.4	40.6	51.8	72,182	77,098	6.8	2.1
New York	29.2	37.1	20.7	8.8	18.0	13.7	12.8	11.7	14.3	36.6	52.3	8,008,278	8,174,988	2.1	2.7
Niagara Falls	4.0	4.6	23.0	9.8	12.7	11.2	13.2	14.0	16.1	38.5	51.8	55,593	50,173	-9.7	-4.0
North Tonawanda	0.5	2.0	13.7	6.5	14.8	10.7	14.5	19.1	20.7	48.8	50.5	33,262	31,574	-5.1	-3.8
Ossining	46.3	39.8	21.0	8.5	15.1	17.2	16.6	11.8	9.8	36.8	46.4	24,010	25,054	4.3	-0.2
Port Chester	69.3	51.7	27.5	5.7	13.5	21.1	7.6	10.7	14.0	38.1	48.8	27,867	28,975	4.0	1.1
Poughkeepsie	16.0	16.7	17.2	7.9	17.4	12.5	17.8	10.7	16.4	40.7	45.4	29,871	30,828	3.2	-1.2
Rochester	17.5	10.1	21.2	11.4	20.3	11.4	12.5	11.4	11.8	33.3	51.7	219,773	210,684	-4.1	-2.1
Rome	9.5	3.5	20.2	6.5	18.0	11.1	12.6	12.5	19.1	37.6	51.1	34,950	33,718	-3.5	-4.5
Saratoga Springs	2.1	11.1	12.8	10.0	18.1	11.0	14.7	13.5	19.9	43.9	49.6	26,186	26,565	1.4	5.4
Schenectady	10.0	16.1	20.7	12.2	13.2	11.8	15.0	14.4	12.7	38.1	53.9	61,821	66,157	7.0	-0.9
Spring Valley	29.1	42.5	33.7	10.6	8.6	18.9	11.3	7.7	9.3	32.8	47.2	25,464	31,306	22.9	3.1
Syracuse	10.0	14.0	22.9	18.8	13.6	10.3	11.5	11.0	11.9	30.7	52.8	147,306	145,206	-1.4	-1.7
Troy	10.4	8.0	19.3	21.7	16.1	12.7	11.3	9.9	9.0	30.2	49.9	49,170	50,162	2.0	-1.6
Utica	12.0	19.9	23.4	13.6	13.1	9.8	13.8	10.9	15.4	34.9	52.6	60,651	62,239	2.6	-3.4
Valley Stream	21.6	31.8	22.4	10.7	11.2	10.1	20.7	14.4	10.4	40.5	52.6	36,368	37,366	2.7	0.4
Watertown	4.3	3.1	20.2	10.8	21.3	6.9	14.4	10.3	16.1	34.0	51.8	26,705	26,816	0.4	-5.7
White Plains	36.4	28.1	18.7	9.9	15.3	11.6	14.5	13.9	15.9	39.8	50.4	53,077	56,859	7.1	2.2

1. May be of any race.

Table D. Cities — Households, Group Quarters, Crime, and Education

City	Households, 2017								Serious crimes known to police[2], 2016				Educational attainment, 2017		
			Percent						Total		Rate[3]			Attainment[4] (percent)	
	Number	Persons per household	Family	Married couple family	Female headed[1]	Non-family	One person	Persons in group quarters, 2017	Number	Rate	Violent	Property	Population age 25 and over	High school graduate or less	Bachelor's degree or more
	27	28	29	30	31	32	33	34	35	36	37	38	39	40	41
NEW JERSEY— Cont'd															
Garfield	11,673	2.77	69.8	40.0	21.7	30.2	24.4	44	669	2,098	279	1,818	22,349	56.5	20.0
Hackensack	19,000	2.31	56.0	33.6	17.2	44.0	37.6	1,402	781	1,737	196	1,541	32,455	35.0	37.5
Hoboken	23,410	2.30	44.1	35.5	7.1	55.9	33.2	1,346	1,064	1,967	224	1,743	40,908	12.5	79.1
Jersey City	99,363	2.70	60.3	39.1	14.5	39.7	30.0	2,546	5,759	2,164	479	1,684	192,390	34.6	47.2
Kearny	13,640	2.96	74.3	51.2	16.6	25.7	19.8	NA	858	2,033	201	1,831	31,347	53.1	28.5
Linden	15,223	2.81	71.5	47.5	18.7	28.5	24.9	NA	1,118	2,656	323	2,333	32,420	46.2	23.1
Long Branch	12,498	2.45	53.4	32.0	12.0	46.6	36.6	NA	859	2,775	346	2,429	21,485	42.5	35.0
Millville	12,204	2.27	59.8	37.3	16.6	40.2	36.4	NA	1,937	6,874	791	6,083	20,280	54.9	18.0
Newark	98,678	2.76	61.9	29.1	26.1	38.1	34.2	12,567	8,945	3,178	937	2,241	186,458	60.5	15.5
New Brunswick	15,383	3.11	59.1	27.4	23.3	40.9	26.8	9,198	1,644	2,876	686	2,190	25,080	58.2	25.6
Paramus	8,424	3.01	80.9	70.8	6.1	19.1	17.2	1,689	1,180	4,377	122	4,255	20,234	31.3	47.0
Passaic	19,890	3.56	75.8	34.4	31.9	24.2	21.8	NA	1,504	2,119	561	1,558	39,679	68.7	16.0
Paterson	44,010	3.33	75.7	36.9	29.5	24.3	19.7	2,166	4,280	2,906	765	2,142	91,997	68.1	11.1
Perth Amboy	16,290	3.21	74.0	36.1	26.6	26.0	23.2	610	1,016	1,925	398	1,527	32,420	64.6	11.4
Plainfield	15,930	3.15	71.2	32.0	28.8	28.8	25.3	1,084	1,304	2,546	676	1,870	34,059	61.3	15.6
Rahway	12,205	2.46	63.0	41.4	13.1	37.0	32.5	NA	385	1,292	124	1,168	22,484	39.0	32.4
Sayreville	17,175	2.64	66.9	51.8	10.4	33.1	29.8	NA	403	893	66	826	33,636	42.5	34.8
Trenton	27,324	3.01	56.4	22.8	25.8	43.6	37.3	2,781	3,313	3,961	1,347	2,613	52,760	63.6	11.2
Union City	22,927	3.05	71.0	38.6	20.5	29.0	20.6	512	1,345	1,940	304	1,635	47,822	61.4	21.6
Vineland	20,463	2.84	75.0	45.0	23.5	25.0	19.5	2,177	2,709	4,454	488	3,966	40,315	50.1	21.8
Westfield	10,156	2.96	78.8	69.0	7.5	21.2	20.0	NA	260	855	16	838	19,223	12.7	73.5
West New York	18,494	2.93	72.6	44.1	16.2	27.4	21.0	NA	680	1,264	243	1,020	38,317	50.3	33.2
NEW MEXICO	767,705	2.66	62.4	42.9	13.4	37.6	32.0	42,965	96,550	4,640	702	3,937	1,391,475	40.5	27.1
Alamogordo	13,341	2.30	55.2	41.6	10.9	44.8	40.3	554	1,125	3,656	374	3,283	21,595	39.4	18.6
Albuquerque	221,418	2.50	58.1	38.9	12.8	41.9	35.6	5,841	44,773	7,973	1,112	6,861	381,067	31.0	36.3
Carlsbad	11,243	2.51	62.4	44.1	8.1	37.6	31.5	NA	1,290	4,367	450	3,917	18,952	50.0	18.2
Clovis	14,748	2.67	67.7	38.1	21.1	32.3	29.3	485	2,608	6,565	561	6,004	23,938	39.5	23.5
Farmington	14,794	2.98	69.8	44.6	16.0	30.2	23.0	1,384	2,150	5,086	693	4,393	27,167	41.8	22.6
Hobbs	12,705	2.82	75.5	50.9	14.7	24.5	22.4	1,896	2,116	5,378	562	4,816	23,306	54.5	15.1
Las Cruces	39,176	2.53	58.8	37.5	15.4	41.2	32.2	2,432	5,039	4,923	245	4,678	62,453	34.2	28.6
Rio Rancho	34,189	2.80	71.6	52.0	13.7	28.4	24.1	NA	2,465	2,582	225	2,357	65,442	34.9	27.7
Roswell	17,590	2.74	64.8	40.9	15.6	35.2	28.9	1,676	2,443	5,031	640	4,391	31,343	51.3	17.6
Santa Fe	33,767	2.44	52.6	34.8	12.5	47.4	41.7	1,416	3,558	4,203	383	3,820	60,850	36.2	40.4
NEW YORK	7,304,332	2.64	63.3	44.0	14.2	36.7	29.7	576,151	379,466	1,922	376	1,546	13,821,132	39.7	36.0
Albany	39,646	2.21	42.4	23.0	14.7	57.6	41.5	10,651	4,323	4,384	864	3,520	59,307	34.8	41.0
Auburn	11,523	2.11	52.0	28.9	17.3	48.0	41.1	2,347	933	3,474	477	2,998	19,168	42.0	23.0
Binghamton	19,775	2.20	43.4	22.7	16.9	56.6	45.9	1,660	2,194	4,792	771	4,021	29,386	45.1	21.4
Buffalo	110,678	2.26	50.9	25.0	19.6	49.1	40.4	8,980	13,456	5,227	1,110	4,117	170,150	42.0	27.7
Elmira	8,769	2.75	62.7	32.2	22.5	37.3	32.0	3,617	1,171	4,183	346	3,836	18,017	57.0	14.6
Freeport	14,728	2.92	67.5	38.9	22.2	32.5	29.0	460	803	1,849	244	1,605	29,865	49.8	26.8
Glen Cove	9,216	2.90	70.8	45.8	16.4	29.2	25.5	765	125	455	62	393	17,981	46.3	37.3
Harrison	8,588	2.88	71.6	61.0	6.8	28.4	21.6	3,849	127	445	4	442	17,601	26.3	57.3
Hempstead	16,750	3.28	71.7	35.5	28.3	28.3	25.5	902	1,125	2,014	716	1,298	34,463	56.7	18.9
Ithaca	10,619	2.21	29.2	17.3	8.6	70.8	40.9	7,532	966	3,122	233	2,890	11,675	20.7	66.7
Jamestown	12,436	2.32	56.7	29.9	14.7	43.3	34.8	744	1,288	4,311	753	3,558	20,084	51.3	17.2
Lindenhurst	7,514	3.61	85.9	64.2	17.1	14.1	10.5	43	NA	NA	NA	NA	17,695	32.6	30.2
Long Beach	14,953	2.19	51.6	38.1	10.4	48.4	40.3	984	305	908	68	840	25,701	28.4	47.6
Middletown	8,428	3.26	66.8	44.6	21.3	33.2	23.8	421	814	2,933	537	2,396	17,642	58.9	17.8
Mount Vernon	28,111	2.41	57.6	30.1	20.1	42.4	37.7	961	1,691	2,455	666	1,789	51,894	47.1	24.8
Newburgh	10,484	2.62	56.9	29.8	18.8	43.1	35.5	919	1,288	4,572	1,431	3,142	17,364	57.8	20.0
New Rochelle	28,514	2.69	69.0	51.5	11.5	31.0	26.6	3,294	1,350	1,679	218	1,462	55,033	34.9	47.5
New York	3,159,674	2.67	59.8	36.6	17.6	40.2	32.2	175,311	174,402	2,036	573	1,462	6,076,781	42.7	37.3
Niagara Falls	21,326	2.26	57.5	30.9	19.6	42.5	35.8	356	2,968	6,098	1,161	4,937	32,581	46.9	17.3
North Tonawanda	14,611	2.07	54.3	39.2	11.8	45.7	36.3	175	609	1,988	180	1,808	24,322	44.3	24.7
Ossining	10,025	2.62	68.6	54.9	6.4	31.4	26.8	1,877	172	674	67	607	19,813	50.2	29.0
Port Chester	9,123	3.35	72.9	52.2	14.1	27.1	24.4	NA	550	1,849	148	1,701	20,624	51.7	25.9
Poughkeepsie	13,285	2.23	47.2	28.5	15.9	52.8	45.1	933	833	2,753	773	1,979	22,920	39.7	24.2
Rochester	90,303	2.19	47.6	19.7	23.5	52.4	41.6	9,842	9,658	4,607	880	3,727	140,179	46.7	25.7
Rome	12,299	2.45	60.8	37.6	18.3	39.2	32.0	2,291	671	2,075	161	1,914	23,804	51.3	19.7
Saratoga Springs	13,144	1.93	54.0	49.0	3.1	46.0	38.6	2,677	591	2,110	229	1,882	21,635	20.7	55.3
Schenectady	21,353	2.91	50.0	30.1	14.7	50.0	42.8	3,566	2,706	4,154	921	3,233	44,031	46.9	22.7
Spring Valley	9,595	3.35	73.4	50.3	15.3	26.6	24.1	96	511	1,556	381	1,175	17,961	60.1	16.4
Syracuse	54,062	2.36	50.3	25.2	19.7	49.7	38.7	16,022	5,714	3,970	739	3,232	83,688	47.5	27.7
Troy	20,637	2.17	44.3	21.8	17.1	55.7	41.4	4,856	2,154	4,319	726	3,593	29,270	39.4	25.3
Utica	23,480	2.46	53.2	29.1	15.7	46.8	43.3	2,956	2,651	4,355	634	3,720	38,223	50.1	19.3
Valley Stream	12,041	3.15	83.8	59.4	17.1	16.2	15.7	NA	NA	NA	NA	NA	25,408	31.5	40.1
Watertown	10,845	2.30	50.4	33.0	12.9	49.6	44.3	705	1,352	5,051	676	4,375	17,714	52.8	18.7
White Plains	21,986	2.62	62.7	46.7	9.7	37.3	29.5	1,363	1,052	1,790	206	1,584	42,127	30.2	50.5

1. No spouse present.   2. Data for serious crimes have not been adjusted for underreporting. This may affect comparability between geographic areas and over time.   3. Per 100,000 population estimated by the FBI.   4. Persons 25 years old and over.

Table D. Cities — Income and Housing

City	Money income, 2017					Median earnings, 2017			Housing units, 2017				
	Households												
	Median income	Percent with income less than $20,000	Percent with income of $200,000 or more	Median family income	Median non-family income	All persons	Men	Women	Total	Occupied	Percent owner occupied	Median value[1] (dollars)	Median gross rent (dollars)
	42	43	44	45	46	47	48	49	50	51	52	53	54
NEW JERSEY— Cont'd													
Garfield	59,971	15.7	6.5	65,415	36,610	36,021	46,044	26,415	12,666	11,673	35.5	320,900	1,305
Hackensack	70,663	17.0	4.1	80,023	49,151	41,189	48,242	36,188	20,593	19,000	35.9	297,800	1,307
Hoboken	155,317	8.1	36.3	170,544	130,439	80,322	86,486	73,045	26,155	23,410	34.6	698,100	2,182
Jersey City	66,264	16.7	13.0	77,643	49,698	41,965	49,769	35,911	114,196	99,363	31.2	379,900	1,338
Kearny	65,553	11.9	3.1	68,295	41,048	32,449	35,514	30,283	14,635	13,640	46.0	338,200	1,199
Linden	66,212	12.5	3.0	79,316	42,403	39,643	41,340	34,775	16,461	15,223	61.2	281,100	1,180
Long Branch	62,418	18.4	6.6	66,862	53,010	26,180	29,909	22,268	14,451	12,498	42.7	376,400	1,227
Millville	55,563	27.8	0.8	72,766	20,924	36,754	37,816	36,359	13,944	12,204	63.7	148,800	786
Newark	35,167	32.9	2.1	39,624	22,513	27,435	31,373	24,551	113,025	98,678	25.2	235,000	1,063
New Brunswick	30,049	35.2	2.2	42,783	19,641	21,558	23,801	19,591	16,230	15,383	21.1	276,000	1,414
Paramus	106,653	8.0	22.5	129,139	32,467	49,833	62,260	37,078	9,215	8,424	84.7	604,700	1,579
Passaic	36,723	26.6	1.6	31,733	25,641	21,725	22,398	20,499	20,611	19,890	20.4	346,100	1,144
Paterson	41,367	27.5	1.0	43,247	23,953	26,269	30,578	21,945	47,927	44,010	26.6	241,800	1,179
Perth Amboy	47,351	23.2	0.2	45,629	35,565	26,401	31,494	22,152	17,908	16,290	23.9	232,200	1,283
Plainfield	53,806	18.5	3.6	54,855	32,245	31,876	35,067	27,760	17,407	15,930	40.6	262,900	1,123
Rahway	81,374	14.0	8.6	105,422	48,831	51,672	61,056	37,412	13,199	12,205	54.8	247,300	1,226
Sayreville	81,746	7.7	6.5	96,490	53,396	45,886	52,126	40,168	17,494	17,175	63.2	296,400	1,240
Trenton	31,882	35.9	1.9	42,367	16,610	24,982	26,458	22,326	34,673	27,324	37.4	98,100	1,086
Union City	40,468	22.1	3.2	43,542	25,919	24,131	26,588	20,823	25,623	22,927	18.0	335,600	1,215
Vineland	60,493	15.5	4.6	68,174	30,683	31,094	38,922	23,259	21,690	20,463	70.8	171,900	1,079
Westfield	194,089	7.9	48.8	250	34,944	76,076	101,613	43,057	11,249	10,156	84.0	822,700	1,755
West New York	56,414	14.0	5.9	51,670	58,555	29,367	31,512	22,214	20,428	18,494	19.5	288,900	1,244
NEW MEXICO	46,744	21.2	3.4	58,308	29,887	28,062	31,663	24,171	937,976	767,705	67.9	171,300	813
Alamogordo	42,208	18.9	0.8	55,764	33,097	23,081	27,828	18,564	15,375	13,341	55.7	121,700	720
Albuquerque	50,456	18.1	3.8	67,301	31,646	31,177	33,529	28,641	244,656	221,418	60.6	196,900	837
Carlsbad	56,763	15.2	1.4	59,013	46,907	35,051	47,939	22,876	12,794	11,243	69.7	134,900	1,029
Clovis	42,657	19.6	2.1	48,820	30,790	28,273	31,315	21,856	16,669	14,748	52.2	161,400	853
Farmington	55,357	14.3	3.8	59,927	40,013	27,134	35,110	21,539	17,425	14,794	71.6	189,000	866
Hobbs	50,783	21.0	3.4	62,175	22,772	30,123	44,371	20,743	15,090	12,705	59.8	149,200	797
Las Cruces	36,364	27.0	2.5	55,794	23,042	23,338	25,463	21,727	46,372	39,176	56.2	144,100	743
Rio Rancho	57,349	17.7	1.9	68,922	28,773	32,216	37,456	29,912	36,632	34,189	74.5	187,900	1,104
Roswell	43,989	23.0	1.3	49,959	25,657	25,779	30,963	21,778	20,469	17,590	65.4	107,300	814
Santa Fe	57,022	14.5	4.6	71,350	40,677	30,986	31,666	30,178	40,130	33,767	61.3	283,000	998
NEW YORK	64,894	16.5	9.8	80,114	40,350	37,329	42,037	32,231	8,327,621	7,304,332	53.8	314,500	1,226
Albany	49,307	22.8	4.1	65,122	39,720	29,071	31,236	27,197	48,019	39,646	37.2	177,100	988
Auburn	39,820	25.2	1.8	59,266	27,228	30,810	42,415	23,530	13,284	11,523	48.6	99,800	736
Binghamton	31,461	36.7	1.1	45,276	20,338	22,903	21,605	25,550	22,515	19,775	41.1	84,000	757
Buffalo	34,814	30.2	2.3	45,332	26,012	25,127	27,166	23,136	133,239	110,678	41.0	92,700	725
Elmira	41,013	22.5	0.5	44,993	26,923	22,973	23,657	22,580	11,845	8,769	47.8	77,300	732
Freeport	73,067	13.6	8.2	95,057	50,776	40,379	41,002	37,003	15,076	14,728	63.5	349,300	1,365
Glen Cove	71,337	13.4	11.8	86,639	37,770	36,643	42,235	31,589	10,370	9,216	47.0	490,900	1,589
Harrison	147,024	7.2	40.1	222,577	47,917	50,334	61,376	40,893	9,098	8,588	61.5	882,000	2,332
Hempstead	61,073	19.9	4.9	68,726	28,317	30,996	32,126	27,434	18,586	16,750	44.9	318,000	1,317
Ithaca	30,448	39.1	5.6	85,399	20,821	10,997	15,189	8,165	11,339	10,619	25.4	240,300	1,156
Jamestown	34,014	31.0	0.4	42,796	21,200	22,163	24,944	20,378	14,632	12,436	52.1	58,400	599
Lindenhurst	105,410	5.7	10.9	112,971	60,047	40,674	45,978	31,594	8,223	7,514	89.1	353,800	1,586
Long Beach	96,310	11.1	13.7	106,465	78,645	53,965	62,683	47,722	17,085	14,953	58.3	521,400	2,064
Middletown	59,098	18.1	2.9	68,444	30,798	25,024	26,003	23,343	10,362	8,428	61.1	207,800	1,351
Mount Vernon	55,564	14.5	5.7	70,840	31,221	35,422	37,191	34,038	29,594	28,111	37.2	341,400	1,375
Newburgh	53,564	20.7	1.1	75,231	35,746	33,159	35,994	28,891	12,760	10,484	38.0	164,600	1,075
New Rochelle	84,516	9.5	22.8	112,143	57,216	37,697	46,381	33,978	29,478	28,514	58.8	595,000	1,432
New York	60,879	20.0	10.3	68,353	45,326	38,430	41,604	35,210	3,497,344	3,159,674	32.7	609,500	1,379
Niagara Falls	38,555	26.4	1.2	46,949	25,456	27,725	35,780	25,560	26,134	21,326	60.4	78,100	656
North Tonawanda	54,031	10.9	0.4	69,673	38,572	35,395	43,821	27,306	16,324	14,611	68.1	116,200	645
Ossining	63,856	15.3	14.5	66,370	53,649	33,990	36,060	27,117	10,853	10,025	49.2	361,800	1,617
Port Chester	67,276	12.7	7.8	65,251	46,125	30,811	31,194	29,920	10,215	9,123	37.9	425,900	1,576
Poughkeepsie	41,802	24.1	2.9	63,545	30,960	31,661	35,368	26,451	14,877	13,285	35.6	192,200	1,093
Rochester	33,588	33.1	2.6	41,591	26,924	27,261	30,640	24,701	104,723	90,303	38.0	82,400	833
Rome	39,448	25.4	3.2	59,503	23,596	30,369	31,518	28,987	14,588	12,299	54.8	89,700	727
Saratoga Springs	80,827	13.3	9.2	111,346	41,357	50,874	52,012	47,040	14,293	13,144	52.1	338,000	1,037
Schenectady	42,565	25.4	1.3	58,739	30,772	27,165	26,762	27,764	33,651	21,353	52.4	105,900	864
Spring Valley	46,053	19.3	3.4	56,451	25,065	25,779	30,543	21,412	10,201	9,595	25.3	320,200	1,239
Syracuse	35,568	31.4	1.8	42,224	27,643	24,940	26,898	23,378	66,998	54,062	36.9	90,100	791
Troy	44,367	30.9	2.4	62,336	31,574	26,754	27,306	26,368	24,288	20,637	34.6	157,600	917
Utica	36,364	30.8	3.1	47,926	21,403	24,711	22,066	26,029	28,510	23,480	48.9	95,000	696
Valley Stream	102,690	5.2	12.5	111,619	51,024	46,467	51,882	41,510	12,778	12,041	83.4	431,900	1,738
Watertown	37,736	29.0	2.5	46,239	21,430	28,755	32,264	21,997	13,025	10,845	42.1	117,000	761
White Plains	100,577	12.6	19.2	112,640	69,395	41,335	44,749	31,619	24,188	21,986	55.3	575,100	1,686

1. Based on population estimated by the American Community Survey.   2. Includes units rented or sold but not occupied.   3. Specified owner-occupied units; $1,000,000 represents $1,000,000 or more.   4. 50.0 represents 50 percent or more.   5. 10.0 represents 10 percent or less.

Table D. Cities — Commuting, Computer Access, Migration, Labor Force, and Employment

City	Commuting¹, 2017 Percent — Commuting	With commutes of 30 minutes or more	Computer access², 2017 Percent — With a computer in the house	With Internet access	Migration, 2017 — Percent who lived in the same house one year ago	Percent who lived in another state or county one year ago	Civilian labor force, 2018 — Total	Percent change 2017-2018	Unemployment Total	Rate³	Civilian employment⁴, 2017 — Population age 16 and older Number	Percent in labor force	Population age 16 to 64 Number	Percent who worked full-year full-time
	55	56	57	58	59	60	61	62	63	64	65	66	67	68
NEW JERSEY— Cont'd														
Garfield	67.9	48.4	93.2	86.8	90.9	4.3	15,704	-0.9	869	5.5	26,523	66.5	22,588	49.5
Hackensack	57.0	48.0	92.3	88.4	78.6	11.7	23,756	-0.8	1,010	4.3	37,985	68.9	31,902	56.5
Hoboken	22.1	80.0	96.7	95.7	77.7	10.8	36,348	-0.4	773	2.1	46,839	80.0	43,426	70.0
Jersey City	29.6	66.4	92.8	87.0	84.5	7.9	138,953	-0.8	5,713	4.1	218,574	67.8	187,805	56.5
Kearny	61.0	53.1	88.0	86.0	88.7	5.0	20,322	-0.3	950	4.7	35,831	62.0	29,766	52.8
Linden	69.4	43.3	87.1	79.0	91.1	4.5	21,595	-0.7	1,032	4.8	34,932	64.8	28,350	52.6
Long Branch	70.7	43.8	92.5	85.7	84.6	4.1	15,936	-0.4	651	4.1	25,018	66.1	20,414	45.9
Millville	NA	24.7	88.7	77.5	NA	NA	12,791	-1.5	816	6.4	23,148	61.3	18,375	47.4
Newark	56.1	53.6	88.4	68.1	90.6	4.1	114,544	-0.9	8,014	7.0	222,814	60.1	192,679	42.2
New Brunswick	64.0	35.0	83.7	64.3	84.5	6.8	26,663	-0.4	949	3.6	43,949	50.2	40,454	33.1
Paramus	72.1	38.0	NA	NA	NA	NA	12,471	-0.9	419	3.4	22,464	58.0	16,318	49.9
Passaic	50.9	41.3	89.5	84.3	93.9	2.7	28,660	-1.3	1,658	5.8	48,968	62.8	43,634	41.2
Paterson	63.3	29.1	87.6	73.6	90.3	2.3	59,849	-1.0	4,588	7.7	113,658	59.8	97,894	48.5
Perth Amboy	64.3	39.1	91.8	58.8	94.3	2.1	24,634	-0.7	1,582	6.4	40,021	60.5	34,039	47.0
Plainfield	68.9	52.8	79.4	50.2	90.3	3.1	26,354	-0.8	1,530	5.8	39,703	65.3	33,917	57.8
Rahway	67.4	53.8	92.8	87.2	80.2	5.6	14,635	-1.1	658	4.5	25,181	66.0	20,920	58.2
Sayreville	76.1	53.0	94.2	90.4	90.4	6.2	23,871	-0.5	890	3.7	36,691	72.1	31,072	57.2
Trenton	57.6	29.9	82.3	54.3	80.0	3.6	38,413	0.2	2,405	6.3	64,433	56.1	55,888	39.4
Union City	27.4	63.9	91.9	84.9	95.4	1.9	34,144	-0.9	1,544	4.5	57,698	64.8	50,696	49.6
Vineland	80.1	29.7	91.0	85.5	86.7	4.8	27,379	-1.7	1,693	6.2	47,663	66.9	38,113	46.5
Westfield	57.5	61.3	94.0	88.6	91.3	1.2	13,814	-0.6	384	2.8	22,511	62.4	18,576	50.5
West New York	34.8	70.2	91.7	83.2	88.1	5.8	27,915	-0.6	1,097	3.9	43,268	71.9	37,431	55.0
NEW MEXICO	79.4	28.0	86.6	76.1	87.3	5.6	940,359	0.4	46,536	4.9	1,654,690	56.8	1,304,761	45.2
Alamogordo	80.7	9.8	87.9	79.6	81.5	6.4	12,850	-1.2	567	4.4	25,539	63.6	20,826	52.2
Albuquerque	79.0	26.5	92.1	84.2	86.7	4.5	277,151	0.5	12,376	4.5	445,845	62.7	359,220	49.1
Carlsbad	NA	33.7	92.6	85.1	80.1	10.7	15,632	7.4	528	3.4	22,789	62.5	18,790	52.6
Clovis	NA	9.6	91.7	76.4	75.5	8.4	17,081	-2.8	699	4.1	29,643	67.3	25,587	58.3
Farmington	78.0	14.5	87.7	80.5	87.6	3.6	20,297	-2.3	1,001	4.9	33,669	61.0	27,526	50.8
Hobbs	NA	15.8	86.5	75.2	84.4	4.1	16,027	7.7	698	4.4	28,600	57.2	23,974	44.8
Las Cruces	68.9	22.2	92.5	76.1	84.1	6.1	46,710	1.3	2,283	4.9	80,110	57.5	65,604	41.4
Rio Rancho	82.7	42.3	95.2	90.4	90.9	6.4	45,247	0.4	2,185	4.8	75,138	57.0	60,541	48.6
Roswell	84.4	14.3	80.2	68.8	75.6	7.3	20,089	-1.0	1,019	5.1	38,597	57.0	30,785	46.3
Santa Fe	82.6	14.6	87.6	81.4	90.6	4.4	42,731	0.9	1,737	4.1	70,151	60.2	51,970	50.8
NEW YORK	53.1	51.7	90.1	82.8	89.4	4.7	9,574,706	0.1	393,648	4.1	16,178,211	63.2	13,017,162	50.2
Albany	62.2	15.1	88.9	80.4	77.4	12.0	46,996	0.4	2,046	4.4	81,449	64.8	68,223	45.7
Auburn	80.0	15.2	81.5	71.2	80.4	6.6	11,565	0.3	587	5.1	21,590	56.4	16,914	41.6
Binghamton	73.4	11.9	79.9	71.4	73.5	11.6	17,984	0.3	944	5.2	37,705	51.7	30,303	32.5
Buffalo	67.3	23.7	87.8	79.0	78.5	4.8	109,125	-0.3	6,176	5.7	208,115	62.9	177,151	42.8
Elmira	69.1	19.8	90.5	80.1	83.8	3.4	9,645	-0.7	587	6.1	21,786	53.6	18,535	35.2
Freeport	67.0	51.9	90.8	88.7	NA	NA	22,883	0.1	1,015	4.4	34,964	66.0	27,419	59.7
Glen Cove	76.9	35.1	87.4	78.8	95.3	3.0	14,214	0.5	529	3.7	20,349	63.9	16,169	53.8
Harrison	57.6	42.4	NA	NA	88.3	9.4	13,520	0.9	543	4.0	23,623	62.3	19,827	44.3
Hempstead	60.9	47.1	88.5	78.3	87.8	3.7	27,778	0.2	1,297	4.7	41,463	61.4	34,594	52.1
Ithaca	26.0	13.7	94.0	81.7	60.8	22.8	13,151	0.3	540	4.1	27,917	47.2	26,228	18.7
Jamestown	81.8	13.2	87.8	79.1	84.8	4.1	11,704	-0.7	654	5.6	24,326	56.3	19,474	36.4
Lindenhurst	78.4	54.1	95.9	94.3	91.4	3.4	15,286	-0.1	546	3.6	22,306	74.7	19,995	54.0
Long Beach	66.4	63.2	92.9	87.6	85.9	1.6	19,799	0.4	649	3.3	29,693	63.7	22,773	50.6
Middletown	75.1	35.5	90.9	74.3	80.5	2.3	13,748	1.0	601	4.4	20,167	64.3	16,006	47.3
Mount Vernon	45.3	55.8	90.5	51.7	90.4	3.7	33,361	0.7	1,754	5.3	59,192	63.3	46,089	60.9
Newburgh	58.3	29.1	83.2	69.9	89.1	3.5	12,308	1.0	642	5.2	21,857	62.6	18,452	49.0
New Rochelle	50.1	50.5	93.6	83.8	89.0	4.2	39,188	0.8	1,700	4.3	67,471	66.1	54,369	45.7
New York	22.3	71.3	90.0	81.6	90.2	4.5	4,119,533	-0.3	170,167	4.1	7,020,073	63.8	5,784,444	50.4
Niagara Falls	83.8	27.9	83.4	71.5	92.3	2.6	21,006	-0.5	1,408	6.7	37,835	59.6	30,008	45.6
North Tonawanda	85.6	25.0	84.3	79.5	89.3	3.0	15,388	-0.2	683	4.4	26,951	62.6	20,645	56.4
Ossining	53.8	52.1	86.7	77.3	90.9	4.5	13,274	0.9	473	3.6	23,151	68.9	20,400	50.2
Port Chester	58.0	36.1	89.5	81.8	NA	NA	16,787	1.1	544	3.2	23,083	70.3	18,773	50.0
Poughkeepsie	70.6	37.3	87.1	79.5	86.8	6.8	13,472	0.5	632	4.7	26,289	61.6	21,266	49.4
Rochester	70.1	21.0	83.8	74.6	78.0	6.9	89,964	0.2	5,411	6.0	168,720	61.2	144,075	42.2
Rome	82.5	20.0	83.8	79.0	90.0	2.6	13,425	0.3	630	4.7	26,321	49.4	20,131	44.3
Saratoga Springs	76.3	38.4	94.0	90.9	80.9	12.5	13,993	0.7	506	3.6	25,289	65.9	19,702	59.2
Schenectady	76.9	31.9	93.0	86.1	89.5	5.3	30,060	0.5	1,424	4.7	54,035	60.7	45,716	46.0
Spring Valley	54.7	36.1	86.2	72.3	NA	NA	14,941	0.9	514	3.4	22,165	71.4	19,162	42.6
Syracuse	62.6	14.0	78.3	68.0	77.4	9.6	57,995	0.4	3,053	5.3	115,200	53.0	98,204	33.7
Troy	67.2	23.0	87.9	81.4	68.0	18.6	23,016	0.4	1,121	4.9	41,141	63.1	36,694	40.7
Utica	73.5	14.0	81.9	73.6	82.8	6.4	23,425	-0.2	1,222	5.2	47,750	55.6	38,395	40.7
Valley Stream	67.0	64.8	96.4	91.4	NA	NA	19,737	0.2	732	3.7	30,528	73.7	26,566	55.5
Watertown	73.0	13.9	85.7	75.2	78.5	11.1	10,502	-0.4	544	5.2	20,804	53.7	16,667	44.7
White Plains	59.1	34.8	94.0	92.6	86.7	7.0	32,374	1.0	1,082	3.3	49,093	70.9	39,690	55.2

1. Employed persons. 2. Households. 3. Percent of civilian labor force. 4. Persons 16 years old and over.

Table D. Cities — Construction, Wholesale Trade, and Retail Trade

City	Value of residential construction authorized by building permits, 2018			Wholesale trade[1], 2012				Retail trade[2], 2012			
	New construction ($1,000)	Number of housing units	Percent single family	Number of establishments	Number of employees	Sales (mil dol)	Annual payroll (mil dol)	Number of establishments	Number of employees	Sales (mil dol)	Annual payroll (mil dol)
	69	70	71	72	73	74	75	76	77	78	79

City	69	70	71	72	73	74	75	76	77	78	79
NEW JERSEY— Cont'd											
Garfield	1,668	11	45.5	42	407	223.0	18.5	81	825	213.1	20.6
Hackensack	2,550	84	2.4	182	1,678	1,878.3	95.9	259	3,895	1,208.7	112.4
Hoboken	484,669	221	3.6	48	269	396.8	14.6	164	1,297	314.1	30.6
Jersey City	142,865	2,493	41.2	191	4,740	12,481.7	338.8	807	9,038	2,568.1	241.5
Kearny	142	4	50.0	75	1,611	2,672.4	112.5	104	1,643	402.9	43.2
Linden	47,028	282	1.8	119	1,875	2,144.0	104.5	183	2,770	843.2	66.8
Long Branch	25,477	366	10.1	20	113	73.3	3.7	89	1,000	268.7	28.6
Millville	1,165	14	100.0	27	468	282.8	28.1	88	1,798	460.5	41.2
Newark	46,549	504	1.0	335	5,162	5,373.5	322.4	913	5,918	2,173.9	173.8
New Brunswick	128,677	619	0.5	60	839	751.1	41.8	121	736	179.5	15.9
Paramus	16,594	37	100.0	112	2,436	2,254.0	277.8	618	15,076	3,833.9	364.1
Passaic	4,055	50	12.0	80	768	311.9	30.2	260	2,083	541.7	49.8
Paterson	16,326	302	3.6	194	2,269	1,075.2	105.3	541	3,169	849.8	74.6
Perth Amboy	11,883	129	20.2	34	1,109	1,079.3	85.1	208	1,281	324.3	30.8
Plainfield	8,070	92	2.2	25	D	D	D	125	633	210.9	17.7
Rahway	28,648	446	1.6	67	808	1,282.7	55.6	70	651	321.8	21.9
Sayreville	1,643	31	25.8	57	511	562.7	31.4	104	1,185	406.6	29.1
Trenton	2	15	0.0	49	733	745.6	37.2	242	1,208	341.6	27.9
Union City	13,474	95	2.1	48	203	107.7	8.7	270	1,209	340.8	27.0
Vineland	2,989	26	84.6	78	1,429	1,467.9	65.5	271	3,918	1,066.4	95.1
Westfield	19,245	68	89.7	23	D	D	D	131	1,394	262.4	28.2
West New York	64,476	311	0.0	33	D	D	D	213	1,141	288.9	27.1
NEW MEXICO	1,037,554	4,813	91.3	1,646	17,448	10,720.4	814.6	6,590	90,792	25,179.3	2,214.5
Alamogordo	NA	NA	NA	11	D	D	D	136	1,966	525.3	46.6
Albuquerque	222,659	1,115	100.0	700	8,712	4,784.9	429.6	1,885	31,702	9,067.4	817.5
Carlsbad	34,930	244	56.6	21	148	74.1	6.9	118	1,753	476.4	44.9
Clovis	19,182	110	50.9	30	297	117.0	9.6	176	2,391	596.7	54.0
Farmington	8,395	45	91.1	103	921	466.2	48.5	319	4,848	1,378.0	123.9
Hobbs	35,130	166	100.0	69	877	465.5	45.0	146	2,271	749.8	57.5
Las Cruces	124,123	649	81.2	66	473	224.5	22.7	398	6,973	1,719.0	150.3
Rio Rancho	122,618	580	95.5	24	D	D	D	115	2,593	732.5	62.1
Roswell	7,150	41	100.0	33	336	163.5	12.4	211	2,992	863.1	69.9
Santa Fe	65,954	273	89.0	81	683	606.3	29.8	714	7,979	2,063.4	225.7
NEW YORK	6,692,382	37,778	26.6	28,853	325,663	341,735.0	19,833.3	77,463	905,325	251,167.7	23,641.2
Albany	16,647	102	5.9	115	1,234	2,016.9	65.1	477	7,460	1,710.7	170.1
Auburn	0	0	0.0	20	209	353.0	9.3	130	2,095	501.8	45.0
Binghamton	8,994	48	0.0	61	658	687.6	26.4	183	2,279	563.7	48.1
Buffalo	55,289	256	11.3	253	3,776	2,011.9	178.1	939	10,760	1,972.0	200.0
Elmira	23,460	151	0.0	38	448	194.6	19.4	86	1,051	308.2	27.3
Freeport	1,127	3	100.0	75	737	348.1	31.7	192	1,963	803.0	63.3
Glen Cove	1,675	4	50.0	36	140	173.8	6.6	115	1,192	534.5	42.8
Harrison	83,672	455	6.6	58	1,192	4,816.8	148.3	53	423	82.1	12.0
Hempstead	0	0	0.0	31	297	136.8	16.5	198	1,830	893.6	56.3
Ithaca	46,212	340	4.4	13	98	23.2	3.5	177	3,072	729.8	71.0
Jamestown	0	0	0.0	39	221	130.7	8.2	126	1,462	391.5	36.0
Lindenhurst	2,086	13	100.0	39	D	D	D	118	804	306.8	27.2
Long Beach	3,800	19	100.0	30	443	225.2	23.6	85	629	171.5	17.1
Middletown	15,934	66	100.0	25	247	257.0	9.5	133	2,251	591.3	51.0
Mount Vernon	529	6	33.3	91	1,605	896.2	71.5	227	2,427	597.7	59.4
Newburgh	1,255	10	100.0	47	378	849.8	15.9	114	2,067	558.2	48.1
New Rochelle	8,272	40	25.0	85	821	611.8	64.9	252	2,869	1,150.2	95.9
New York	484,404	3,698	0.2	15,124	148,956	173,797.8	9,474.6	34,215	318,004	92,265.0	9,163.8
Niagara Falls	0	0	0.0	30	D	D	D	261	3,751	843.2	67.1
North Tonawanda	2,540	15	66.7	27	640	159.4	27.3	80	804	210.8	21.0
Ossining	555	2	100.0	14	70	102.9	4.5	78	542	156.6	16.1
Port Chester	0	0	0.0	44	428	189.0	22.5	140	1,997	624.4	58.8
Poughkeepsie	14,000	78	0.0	23	D	D	D	158	2,246	497.8	50.0
Rochester	28,683	437	4.8	279	3,486	1,528.7	175.7	783	7,561	1,414.1	161.5
Rome	19,986	88	9.1	20	148	56.4	6.1	134	2,050	539.5	47.8
Saratoga Springs	58,845	279	27.2	28	278	260.8	18.0	154	2,059	575.3	48.7
Schenectady	479	2	100.0	34	354	306.2	15.9	203	1,642	460.5	43.9
Spring Valley	4,049	22	36.4	52	259	388.1	14.1	102	1,146	265.5	24.8
Syracuse	15,962	126	10.3	145	2,316	1,344.5	108.7	573	7,928	1,726.2	168.5
Troy	8,742	61	4.9	30	D	D	D	148	1,648	487.5	44.5
Utica	0	0	0.0	63	877	636.7	41.8	180	2,547	686.9	58.7
Valley Stream	460	2	100.0	68	432	395.6	27.0	203	2,570	654.1	55.4
Watertown	0	0	0.0	21	290	143.2	11.7	185	3,253	858.3	71.7
White Plains	14,492	107	29.0	100	1,551	4,084.6	159.5	422	7,482	1,956.9	204.0

1. Merchant wholesalers except manufacturers' sales branches and offices.   2. Establishments with payroll.

City	Real estate and rental and leasing, 2012				Professional, scientific, and technical services[1], 2012				Manufacturing, 2012			
	Number of establish-ments	Number of employees	Receipts (mil dol)	Annual payroll (mil dol)	Number of establish-ments	Number of employees	Receipts (mil dol)	Annual payroll (mil dol)	Number of establish-ments	Number of employees	Receipts (mil dol)	Annual payroll (mil dol)
	80	81	82	83	84	85	86	87	88	89	90	91
NEW JERSEY— Cont'd												
Garfield	12	110	9.9	3.2	35	183	14.2	5.1	56	576	146.0	27.2
Hackensack	126	573	206.3	27.3	425	D	D	D	83	1,190	233.2	55.4
Hoboken	81	472	108.6	17.5	209	1,148	266.1	80.8	22	184	33.9	9.7
Jersey City	233	1,129	301.2	53.8	587	D	D	D	99	2,493	857.6	101.8
Kearny	34	227	68.4	12.1	47	227	34.4	11.0	47	1,272	617.1	73.7
Linden	34	187	51.6	9.4	53	1,152	166.5	92.7	105	3,184	14,465.7	223.0
Long Branch	29	76	32.3	3.2	46	183	19.2	10.7	17	250	D	12.2
Millville	12	51	10.6	1.7	44	213	24.5	6.3	43	2,425	450.4	104.5
Newark	214	2,108	518.5	77.8	407	6,545	1,896.8	727.0	251	6,686	3,139.4	358.9
New Brunswick	46	263	166.0	12.3	130	D	D	D	52	842	381.4	46.7
Paramus	73	692	725.3	60.1	216	D	D	D	17	265	78.2	15.9
Passaic	44	124	26.7	4.2	60	360	31.9	10.3	101	1,388	226.0	55.4
Paterson	70	382	54.5	12.6	75	D	D	D	225	4,649	1,167.9	222.8
Perth Amboy	30	135	33.1	4.9	47	D	D	D	37	1,099	579.3	52.3
Plainfield	18	60	12.9	2.2	38	192	21.7	9.4	23	390	D	12.7
Rahway	20	257	35.9	14.9	29	264	29.6	15.4	40	3,169	425.3	361.1
Sayreville	20	95	22.3	3.6	103	857	120.9	64.8	32	1,262	1,031.9	87.6
Trenton	52	352	273.6	16.9	112	D	D	D	53	1,273	D	65.2
Union City	50	147	27.0	3.5	87	314	48.3	10.8	42	339	58.8	10.0
Vineland	76	276	62.5	10.6	119	D	D	D	86	3,864	1,553.6	169.0
Westfield	29	119	56.6	5.4	153	830	170.9	56.6	7	85	11.1	2.2
West New York	57	405	135.5	19.3	70	167	22.7	6.2	40	188	23.2	6.3
NEW MEXICO	2,369	9,754	1,960.4	368.7	4,634	42,423	7,376.4	2,677.8	1,389	26,731	29,102.4	1,349.2
Alamogordo	43	136	17.5	3.3	48	219	17.0	7.1	10	118	D	3.1
Albuquerque	851	4,012	782.3	141.7	2,015	D	D	D	482	10,810	D	522.8
Carlsbad	28	142	33.8	7.5	46	D	D	D	16	252	D	13.8
Clovis	57	204	30.2	5.5	68	439	36.7	14.2	17	120	D	D
Farmington	82	592	167.0	28.6	174	D	D	D	46	519	124.8	27.3
Hobbs	59	459	169.8	36.5	56	403	52.4	23.0	29	479	D	D
Las Cruces	160	563	89.5	15.5	257	D	D	D	55	948	D	30.1
Rio Rancho	58	157	35.2	6.9	100	D	D	D	29	3,562	D	235.3
Roswell	71	201	30.5	5.7	94	954	166.4	62.9	25	95	D	4.0
Santa Fe	229	847	162.7	33.7	477	D	D	D	87	456	D	18.4
NEW YORK	32,033	166,315	56,409.8	8,654.4	58,867	557,669	127,952.2	47,330.7	16,475	426,621	148,879.9	22,073.3
Albany	146	951	161.4	32.4	418	5,267	1,121.9	408.4	63	1,500	684.8	67.5
Auburn	40	121	21.6	3.1	54	D	D	D	49	2,185	858.0	115.1
Binghamton	61	245	29.4	5.9	121	D	D	D	49	1,261	603.4	55.5
Buffalo	257	2,117	240.0	61.9	662	D	D	D	321	11,225	5,260.6	600.2
Elmira	34	137	30.1	7.5	50	D	D	D	29	1,823	385.6	86.9
Freeport	38	176	24.9	6.9	119	447	66.6	20.2	77	1,736	324.3	69.5
Glen Cove	24	93	20.6	4.5	87	335	57.3	20.8	22	254	D	9.6
Harrison	80	718	256.3	48.2	186	D	D	D	7	54	6.5	1.8
Hempstead	51	275	67.0	9.0	96	D	D	D	19	221	D	11.0
Ithaca	53	372	54.2	11.4	123	D	D	D	32	397	63.9	19.9
Jamestown	26	D	D	D	64	D	D	D	62	1,733	251.3	68.4
Lindenhurst	13	54	7.2	2.0	67	221	25.6	8.5	37	368	96.7	17.4
Long Beach	49	129	42.9	5.6	102	203	31.3	9.6	6	15	2.6	0.6
Middletown	26	76	15.8	1.9	50	209	24.6	11.2	29	685	166.3	30.5
Mount Vernon	133	468	86.2	18.4	101	D	D	D	99	2,363	676.9	99.6
Newburgh	27	127	17.9	3.9	60	D	D	D	47	696	109.9	26.9
New Rochelle	202	770	265.6	32.8	228	D	D	D	46	744	159.1	41.2
New York	19,341	107,333	42,465.9	6,213.2	26,420	321,736	92,285.6	32,985.0	5,572	68,953	14,816.3	2,898.8
Niagara Falls	44	223	38.4	7.2	84	D	D	D	43	1,662	1,071.8	116.3
North Tonawanda	12	48	4.6	1.3	35	429	45.3	12.2	62	1,440	437.1	66.3
Ossining	21	60	21.5	2.4	56	228	31.7	12.4	5	D	D	D
Port Chester	40	119	33.4	5.7	61	187	27.4	9.5	33	874	130.1	36.0
Poughkeepsie	61	263	48.3	7.7	131	D	D	D	27	2,474	D	238.8
Rochester	261	2,499	291.6	92.4	639	7,429	1,143.0	421.6	417	19,217	7,492.3	1,164.8
Rome	41	152	24.5	4.6	75	D	D	D	37	1,439	957.7	75.1
Saratoga Springs	51	209	51.4	7.5	153	D	D	D	22	1,441	561.2	73.4
Schenectady	55	225	49.9	7.2	148	D	D	D	53	2,742	1,093.1	193.2
Spring Valley	65	212	37.0	5.2	71	167	74.5	32.1	20	159	29.9	6.4
Syracuse	258	2,011	311.6	91.5	473	D	D	D	111	3,772	1,656.4	181.3
Troy	45	214	42.4	6.9	110	D	D	D	32	620	88.8	24.3
Utica	52	213	27.6	4.7	135	D	D	D	68	1,708	322.2	73.4
Valley Stream	48	218	54.2	10.0	146	1,088	128.2	54.0	25	92	15.2	3.6
Watertown	43	232	46.9	6.4	57	D	D	D	15	818	D	47.7
White Plains	187	892	374.9	59.3	632	5,332	1,359.2	492.6	33	338	56.4	14.5

1. Establishments subject to federal tax.

Accommodation and Food Services, Arts, Entertainment, and Recreation, and Health Care and Social Assistance

City	Accommodation and food services, 2012				Arts, entertainment, and recreation[1], 2012				Health care and social assistance[1], 2012			
	Number of establish-ments	Number of employees	Receipts (mil dol)	Annual payroll (mil dol)	Number of establish-ments	Number of employees	Receipts (mil dol)	Annual payroll (mil dol)	Number of establish-ments	Number of employees	Receipts (mil dol)	Annual payroll (mil dol)
	92	93	94	95	96	97	98	99	100	101	102	103
NEW JERSEY— Cont'd												
Garfield	43	343	28.9	7.8	1	D	D	D	29	313	13.6	6.1
Hackensack	120	D	D	D	12	D	D	D	342	D	D	D
Hoboken	219	D	D	D	24	D	D	D	125	2,091	237.4	98.6
Jersey City	471	4,941	422.5	97.5	47	484	52.6	13.9	439	6,026	521.3	210.3
Kearny	56	532	33.2	8.7	3	D	D	D	68	D	D	D
Linden	95	986	62.1	14.7	6	74	3.8	1.1	63	1,413	115.3	44.9
Long Branch	93	1,567	88.5	25.3	6	137	4.3	1.2	84	D	D	D
Millville	56	673	42.5	8.7	3	D	D	D	59	939	73.2	33.9
Newark	536	7,920	582.4	146.1	15	D	D	D	310	4,836	383.4	162.7
New Brunswick	161	2,009	127.1	35.8	4	D	D	D	80	D	D	D
Paramus	156	3,372	221.9	58.6	22	D	D	D	199	2,320	258.7	100.4
Passaic	115	674	46.1	9.7	12	100	4.7	1.4	103	D	D	D
Paterson	232	D	D	D	12	D	D	D	156	1,927	192.0	71.6
Perth Amboy	102	614	41.5	8.7	3	D	D	D	66	1,254	70.5	30.2
Plainfield	75	613	33.5	7.8	1	D	D	D	71	947	78.0	32.2
Rahway	53	524	34.2	8.4	3	D	D	D	39	D	D	D
Sayreville	82	677	37.9	9.2	10	203	15.2	5.0	50	D	D	D
Trenton	140	D	D	D	6	D	D	D	94	1,646	147.3	64.5
Union City	126	831	53.8	12.9	5	D	D	D	156	1,745	91.7	40.7
Vineland	128	2,165	98.9	26.5	7	D	D	D	164	2,173	268.1	95.2
Westfield	74	D	D	D	11	218	10.1	4.2	150	1,979	178.7	81.2
West New York	87	669	42.8	11.0	9	D	D	D	95	D	D	D
NEW MEXICO	4,177	82,601	4,349.7	1,250.4	488	10,536	1,207.2	219.7	3,970	67,477	6,071.0	2,449.7
Alamogordo	75	D	D	D	7	D	D	D	67	801	75.0	26.8
Albuquerque	1,281	29,238	1,579.0	454.3	138	D	D	D	1,468	25,832	2,659.8	1,045.2
Carlsbad	69	1,320	78.4	20.0	4	D	D	D	52	1,124	152.2	54.9
Clovis	78	1,927	77.4	21.9	7	42	1.6	0.5	94	D	D	D
Farmington	129	3,091	150.4	41.9	11	D	D	D	193	D	D	D
Hobbs	98	1,703	110.1	24.6	7	D	D	D	68	D	D	D
Las Cruces	276	6,189	262.7	72.6	18	383	9.9	2.9	379	8,409	840.8	336.9
Rio Rancho	91	2,066	90.2	26.7	15	D	D	D	122	1,646	119.9	51.6
Roswell	119	2,281	106.2	28.0	5	D	D	D	134	3,029	289.8	111.6
Santa Fe	349	7,896	532.7	158.5	58	186	28.8	8.2	362	3,454	397.5	170.6
NEW YORK	49,731	679,146	49,285.5	13,734.3	9,600	103,072	16,431.7	4,940.4	43,548	540,067	55,599.5	22,400.9
Albany	453	5,990	373.4	98.6	21	730	12.9	4.8	216	3,700	522.7	199.4
Auburn	94	1,291	54.4	15.1	11	61	3.8	1.2	101	1,097	105.3	48.2
Binghamton	171	3,078	154.7	38.0	12	D	D	D	103	1,390	167.0	74.4
Buffalo	660	11,300	510.5	158.3	44	820	185.7	95.7	363	7,108	684.7	361.8
Elmira	63	995	42.7	10.7	7	137	7.2	1.5	70	794	85.7	36.4
Freeport	95	638	48.3	12.2	20	92	18.8	2.7	109	1,395	96.8	41.3
Glen Cove	82	D	D	D	10	135	15.3	3.2	118	D	D	D
Harrison	67	D	D	D	25	197	12.4	4.6	87	D	D	D
Hempstead	121	983	63.5	14.5	5	D	D	D	115	1,342	148.1	53.1
Ithaca	203	2,774	153.0	43.5	10	67	6.9	1.8	68	669	57.7	22.6
Jamestown	72	733	37.0	8.9	10	D	D	D	55	543	54.4	18.6
Lindenhurst	80	893	52.0	12.7	8	D	D	D	52	555	46.4	18.9
Long Beach	91	1,052	61.6	17.7	11	97	8.0	1.8	94	D	D	D
Middletown	67	616	30.1	8.4	5	D	D	D	71	2,591	332.5	147.7
Mount Vernon	104	692	49.5	11.4	15	159	13.2	5.3	111	927	75.2	29.0
Newburgh	87	1,121	79.9	18.1	5	D	D	D	76	887	81.0	32.2
New Rochelle	208	1,949	139.6	37.0	35	D	D	D	234	3,089	327.0	117.8
New York	21,506	304,855	27,452.9	7,757.8	4,956	50,582	11,117.6	3,322.1	18,267	234,221	22,637.1	8,976.3
Niagara Falls	171	5,873	883.7	134.7	13	D	D	D	68	1,178	67.5	32.2
North Tonawanda	55	642	27.4	8.3	7	50	2.7	0.7	53	301	22.2	9.5
Ossining	44	417	28.0	10.4	6	31	4.9	1.4	33	337	27.3	11.1
Port Chester	98	948	70.4	20.3	8	D	D	D	39	469	77.9	30.2
Poughkeepsie	126	D	D	D	5	7	0.7	0.2	103	2,052	299.4	131.4
Rochester	570	7,114	366.7	105.5	64	1,228	62.6	20.8	264	5,172	420.6	192.5
Rome	81	D	D	D	15	66	3.3	1.0	85	1,234	94.7	41.1
Saratoga Springs	170	3,198	196.3	57.3	39	949	162.4	34.0	109	1,410	158.0	74.2
Schenectady	182	1,857	93.1	25.5	8	402	80.7	11.6	138	1,958	182.0	82.2
Spring Valley	46	D	D	D	4	D	D	D	40	509	41.2	14.9
Syracuse	386	6,146	311.3	92.3	29	162	13.8	4.3	316	4,768	625.4	249.8
Troy	146	1,747	95.0	28.2	7	D	D	D	107	1,509	139.2	62.8
Utica	158	D	D	D	8	52	2.6	0.7	143	2,547	301.7	130.7
Valley Stream	82	1,147	66.7	17.9	14	62	7.4	1.9	134	954	157.5	46.6
Watertown	105	2,206	96.5	28.7	10	50	2.6	0.7	96	1,331	140.6	63.4
White Plains	203	3,100	235.8	75.9	31	233	28.3	5.7	348	5,680	639.1	303.9

1. Establishments subject to federal tax.

Table D. Cities — Other Services and Government Employment and Payroll

City	Other services[1] Number of establishments	Number of employees	Receipts (mil dol)	Annual payroll (mil dol)	Government employment and payroll, 2012 Full-time equivalent employees	March payroll Total (dollars)	Percent of total for: Administrative, judicial, and legal	Police and corrections	Fire protection	Highways and transportation	Health and welfare	Natural resources and utilities	Education and libraries
	104	105	106	107	108	109	110	111	112	113	114	115	116
NEW JERSEY— Cont'd													
Garfield	65	268	29.8	8.1	172	1,065,564	10.9	55.4	1.4	9.0	14.1	5.5	3.1
Hackensack	117	757	63.8	20.3	540	2,983,931	6.1	38.2	33.3	3.4	8.9	5.9	3.9
Hoboken	118	D	D	D	712	4,180,854	7.4	42.5	22.9	2.8	7.1	10.6	3.1
Jersey City	318	1,625	144.0	44.1	2,936	18,762,329	8.1	43.6	27.3	3.2	7.6	6.7	2.0
Kearny	58	241	26.5	6.9	326	2,506,387	6.0	43.9	30.5	0.2	2.6	7.9	1.8
Linden	101	647	63.6	20.9	585	3,237,694	11.7	49.9	25.1	3.6	5.9	2.5	0.8
Long Branch	52	195	11.3	3.2	338	2,021,115	9.6	41.0	10.8	0.7	12.9	21.3	3.7
Millville	32	147	9.8	3.3	210	1,102,759	14.1	44.9	6.7	4.0	8.6	14.2	0.0
Newark	425	4,834	339.5	123.8	3,857	25,580,741	14.8	36.1	19.3	0.6	13.6	10.8	2.2
New Brunswick	74	535	49.5	15.3	1,983	11,480,514	2.4	14.2	6.5	0.7	1.8	3.7	67.3
Paramus	63	494	49.3	22.3	293	1,879,108	9.0	31.6	18.6	10.8	1.2	13.4	8.4
Passaic	90	251	20.0	5.3	563	3,095,395	9.0	45.4	25.9	6.9	9.0	1.7	2.3
Paterson	183	1,164	94.0	28.2	1,472	8,450,610	6.5	42.6	30.2	1.1	8.2	5.3	1.6
Perth Amboy	89	736	67.5	23.4	401	2,317,835	10.2	44.0	15.6	5.1	10.9	6.6	1.8
Plainfield	75	266	22.3	6.6	551	3,548,125	11.6	36.0	23.0	0.9	9.8	7.5	2.9
Rahway	42	162	19.7	5.2	277	1,741,702	7.4	40.4	21.7	9.0	8.1	6.9	4.4
Sayreville	87	372	38.5	11.7	240	1,549,628	10.5	59.2	0.8	2.5	2.2	9.8	4.9
Trenton	83	359	27.6	7.6	2,747	16,968,078	3.1	14.5	9.4	0.5	3.5	5.2	60.7
Union City	105	233	17.4	4.5	2,174	11,223,072	2.5	14.9	0.8	0.1	2.4	3.3	73.7
Vineland	108	538	44.6	12.1	718	3,828,158	13.3	30.7	5.0	1.6	10.8	34.6	2.3
Westfield	83	465	40.5	11.7	238	1,357,302	9.1	33.5	21.3	15.6	9.8	5.2	5.0
West New York	75	228	17.6	4.0	1,416	9,134,998	2.4	10.3	4.4	1.4	1.5	0.3	79.2
NEW MEXICO	2,182	12,810	1,115.9	349.7	X	X	X	X	X	X	X	X	X
Alamogordo	38	202	14.8	4.1	280	741,098	18.0	39.9	1.3	4.0	10.8	22.4	3.5
Albuquerque	718	4,969	379.7	125.0	6,438	33,331,138	10.6	29.5	14.1	15.4	8.8	17.0	1.5
Carlsbad	39	195	24.0	6.2	381	1,625,310	11.0	22.8	19.6	11.1	0.7	23.8	1.9
Clovis	55	332	26.5	7.3	383	1,169,467	11.4	25.1	25.2	9.8	5.3	18.8	2.8
Farmington	116	973	105.0	36.0	882	3,555,193	11.2	22.9	12.7	4.9	2.4	35.0	4.8
Hobbs	62	571	72.3	23.8	403	1,643,293	10.3	27.3	18.4	9.1	3.7	22.7	2.5
Las Cruces	138	753	51.6	16.6	1,337	4,708,150	16.1	21.4	12.0	10.4	4.2	18.4	1.9
Rio Rancho	67	437	31.6	12.0	606	2,382,289	13.5	29.4	20.0	10.8	8.8	12.6	4.3
Roswell	46	222	19.0	5.4	548	1,751,942	8.5	26.4	20.7	10.4	1.6	25.5	3.2
Santa Fe	162	866	71.7	23.4	1,540	6,258,370	13.8	15.1	12.9	7.7	6.4	28.1	2.3
NEW YORK	34,948	168,002	14,493.2	4,209.4	X	X	X	X	X	X	X	X	X
Albany	146	825	81.6	24.9	1,455	6,784,879	6.9	38.4	23.1	4.0	10.7	16.1	0.0
Auburn	53	242	19.2	5.0	306	1,503,241	6.8	27.5	30.2	4.3	6.2	19.5	0.0
Binghamton	81	439	34.3	10.7	581	2,791,570	8.2	32.5	25.6	1.7	4.0	21.6	0.0
Buffalo	301	1,577	149.1	47.0	8,627	45,770,501	2.5	13.0	9.3	1.2	2.8	5.8	63.6
Elmira	29	155	12.6	3.8	297	1,470,047	6.0	34.4	27.9	5.6	6.2	16.6	0.0
Freeport	95	491	40.6	11.1	414	2,410,577	14.5	41.4	0.5	2.6	0.9	35.0	0.0
Glen Cove	71	259	21.8	5.5	313	2,051,266	16.9	46.0	2.4	7.0	7.0	17.7	0.0
Harrison	44	D	D	D	272	1,502,544	14.2	43.3	8.0	7.9	2.8	13.9	7.7
Hempstead	97	562	59.8	16.0	437	2,884,577	9.4	54.8	2.8	5.5	2.5	17.0	3.8
Ithaca	42	274	21.6	6.5	454	2,158,827	9.3	24.0	19.7	8.1	0.9	28.6	0.0
Jamestown	44	211	19.7	5.0	658	3,048,026	3.6	13.9	18.8	8.5	1.7	2.6	51.0
Lindenhurst	102	289	31.4	6.7	72	206,485	20.7	0.0	5.1	24.6	6.2	32.4	0.0
Long Beach	54	178	8.6	2.4	484	2,657,473	9.3	32.7	12.4	11.0	4.5	25.8	0.0
Middletown	54	376	29.6	8.9	283	1,449,586	12.4	41.3	15.8	7.3	3.0	20.2	0.0
Mount Vernon	128	768	87.4	28.0	873	4,489,959	6.4	36.3	23.8	1.9	2.2	13.5	2.9
Newburgh	62	479	52.2	12.3	258	1,411,393	6.5	44.1	27.5	10.5	1.6	9.6	0.0
New Rochelle	157	669	59.3	15.7	652	4,204,505	7.5	35.0	29.4	4.5	9.0	14.1	0.0
New York	15,271	69,456	5,597.1	1,634.2	404,260	2,380,283,106	3.2	19.0	5.4	13.7	18.1	4.4	34.0
Niagara Falls	62	323	23.2	6.3	687	3,126,887	0.0	30.2	23.2	0.0	6.6	0.0	0.0
North Tonawanda	56	153	11.3	3.0	281	1,334,637	8.0	28.4	16.0	17.6	0.8	25.8	0.0
Ossining	38	109	10.2	2.8	186	1,201,283	12.6	41.7	0.4	13.3	0.9	24.9	0.0
Port Chester	73	282	34.4	9.6	227	2,070,548	10.9	52.5	7.8	6.0	2.3	13.1	0.0
Poughkeepsie	71	288	25.8	7.1	365	2,055,377	6.9	43.5	19.1	6.3	5.4	15.8	0.0
Rochester	274	1,741	176.4	53.9	9,049	47,150,145	2.7	13.0	6.6	0.8	3.9	4.3	67.0
Rome	56	208	21.1	5.3	373	1,669,365	8.0	27.2	30.1	12.6	4.5	16.3	0.0
Saratoga Springs	49	232	18.3	5.5	349	1,565,062	9.5	32.3	19.4	23.7	4.3	7.4	0.0
Schenectady	90	526	61.4	17.3	637	3,109,293	5.4	38.3	21.7	5.1	10.0	14.6	0.0
Spring Valley	36	94	11.3	1.8	298	901,316	12.0	64.5	0.6	10.1	7.0	0.4	0.0
Syracuse	198	1,576	131.3	43.9	5,644	31,187,441	1.4	12.0	7.9	4.1	2.4	3.2	68.9
Troy	55	398	31.1	12.3	598	3,268,327	9.0	41.8	17.7	4.1	9.7	13.5	0.0
Utica	75	516	35.6	12.4	614	2,894,903	5.7	39.6	26.6	3.3	11.4	9.1	0.0
Valley Stream	116	1,253	73.5	22.6	225	1,128,453	12.8	3.8	0.6	18.2	0.6	37.3	6.6
Watertown	47	259	24.6	6.6	370	1,573,042	9.1	22.3	27.5	9.6	5.8	20.8	2.5
White Plains	141	958	83.4	26.2	1,041	6,536,682	8.4	25.5	18.2	8.2	6.7	11.5	3.6

1. Establishments subject to federal tax.

City	City government finances, 2012									
	General revenue							General expenditure		
	Intergovernmental			Taxes						
					Per capita[1] (dollars)				Per capita[1] (dollars)	
	Total (mil dol)	Total (mil dol)	Percent from state government	Total (mil dol)	Total	Property	Sales and gross receipts	Total (mil dol)	Total	Capital outlays
	117	118	119	120	121	122	123	124	125	126
NEW JERSEY— Cont'd										
Garfield	35.0	4.4	66.3	24.7	798	774	23	30.5	985	29
Hackensack	89.8	9.7	58.1	74.7	1,693	1,640	53	81.7	1,851	0
Hoboken	112.1	26.1	53.1	59.5	1,137	1,071	66	110.1	2,106	65
Jersey City	597.9	170.1	64.9	235.7	918	842	76	580.2	2,260	102
Kearny	76.1	28.2	95.1	41.5	994	966	27	71.6	1,713	127
Linden	93.5	30.9	71.2	55.1	1,345	1,310	36	93.7	2,288	123
Long Branch	71.9	21.4	25.7	37.9	1,241	1,202	40	74.6	2,445	343
Millville	50.7	12.0	68.9	21.9	765	691	74	49.8	1,738	61
Newark	845.2	438.4	36.2	305.9	1,099	784	156	860.7	3,093	368
New Brunswick	273.2	161.6	90.4	60.6	1,087	1,034	52	308.3	5,532	930
Paramus	60.6	4.7	91.3	49.5	1,859	1,738	120	49.8	1,869	77
Passaic	116.8	43.8	42.5	59.3	840	818	22	115.2	1,634	39
Paterson	273.4	94.3	64.3	140.1	959	943	17	265.5	1,818	72
Perth Amboy	99.9	23.5	45.3	58.9	1,136	1,119	17	92.3	1,780	148
Plainfield	100.9	20.9	40.2	54.9	1,089	1,063	26	102.8	2,039	6
Rahway	52.2	8.2	52.9	35.2	1,263	1,210	53	40.3	1,445	119
Sayreville	48.5	12.4	79.2	29.1	663	632	31	48.1	1,097	44
Trenton	505.3	395.0	94.6	79.2	938	887	51	482.0	5,714	70
Union City	355.1	263.5	96.4	81.0	1,184	1,161	23	313.3	4,583	154
Vineland	73.4	16.1	56.5	36.7	602	549	53	67.7	1,110	67
Westfield	37.4	4.0	79.9	29.6	967	909	57	39.3	1,283	88
West New York	209.6	134.4	93.8	51.2	986	966	20	216.0	4,160	249
NEW MEXICO	X	X	X	X	X	X	X	X	X	X
Alamogordo	41.0	11.2	83.4	17.7	560	107	454	39.0	1,236	363
Albuquerque	951.2	282.5	80.4	367.8	663	244	419	827.4	1,491	292
Carlsbad	58.1	6.7	35.3	37.8	1,412	97	1,316	48.5	1,811	487
Clovis	56.3	14.0	34.5	27.9	706	44	662	57.5	1,457	483
Farmington	92.1	35.8	11.0	27.5	600	38	562	99.0	2,161	207
Hobbs	89.8	35.4	93.8	38.4	1,098	56	1,042	69.8	1,994	1,088
Las Cruces	182.5	39.2	26.8	96.3	953	139	815	144.3	1,429	190
Rio Rancho	95.2	13.7	34.9	54.3	599	175	424	87.0	959	166
Roswell	55.1	34.8	96.0	9.3	192	110	82	56.9	1,173	255
Santa Fe	162.5	78.1	73.2	35.9	518	123	395	178.9	2,584	479
NEW YORK	X	X	X	X	X	X	X	X	X	X
Albany	252.8	90.3	28.3	61.5	625	548	77	277.7	2,820	454
Auburn	42.1	14.9	40.5	12.2	447	408	39	47.1	1,722	251
Binghamton	80.6	30.7	45.7	35.7	765	729	37	75.4	1,615	190
Buffalo	1,438.1	1,151.5	83.0	149.0	573	504	69	1,532.1	5,896	790
Elmira	41.8	23.4	53.0	11.6	398	367	31	41.7	1,427	358
Freeport	62.3	3.3	46.3	42.5	985	940	44	67.6	1,566	34
Glen Cove	53.4	17.4	54.0	30.6	1,125	1,054	71	56.1	2,063	478
Harrison	13.5	1.5	60.8	10.7	385	338	47	12.1	434	112
Hempstead	71.2	3.7	54.3	55.6	1,013	971	42	80.4	1,463	51
Ithaca	58.8	12.2	65.1	33.1	1,088	633	455	57.2	1,881	235
Jamestown	70.2	29.9	76.1	15.0	487	459	28	77.7	2,528	164
Lindenhurst	11.6	1.7	75.6	7.0	257	207	50	11.3	413	55
Long Beach	66.7	9.4	52.8	33.6	1,002	859	144	74.0	2,210	91
Middletown	41.5	13.3	24.7	19.0	681	633	47	38.9	1,397	51
Mount Vernon	96.7	15.2	70.5	70.8	1,042	724	319	104.4	1,537	169
Newburgh	57.5	23.9	52.4	21.2	742	667	74	56.9	1,989	235
New Rochelle	134.5	29.2	42.3	80.1	1,022	628	394	133.3	1,700	146
New York	85,078.0	30,398.8	83.5	42,476.1	5,077	2,176	970	81,160.8	9,701	1,196
Niagara Falls	98.1	50.3	53.9	40.9	824	581	243	127.6	2,570	657
North Tonawanda	43.9	17.1	37.3	18.6	596	510	86	41.6	1,330	104
Ossining	33.4	8.9	10.1	20.3	805	760	45	37.3	1,479	39
Port Chester	36.3	5.3	14.4	23.6	808	753	54	37.3	1,275	86
Poughkeepsie	58.3	29.4	22.7	19.2	624	566	58	54.6	1,777	206
Rochester	1,215.0	931.5	73.2	180.9	859	798	61	1,222.9	5,805	517
Rome	49.4	15.0	77.6	25.0	760	462	298	50.7	1,538	140
Saratoga Springs	48.9	5.5	67.4	32.2	1,193	719	474	43.3	1,605	81
Schenectady	89.2	31.5	44.8	29.9	453	405	48	98.0	1,484	180
Spring Valley	34.8	11.4	13.6	21.9	684	651	33	34.7	1,083	29
Syracuse	822.4	598.0	72.4	96.4	668	613	55	858.4	5,950	640
Troy	90.3	48.5	30.6	21.6	433	387	47	91.3	1,830	238
Utica	93.1	41.6	48.0	37.0	597	363	234	94.1	1,521	162
Valley Stream	33.6	2.5	57.9	27.0	716	656	60	37.3	987	118
Watertown	42.6	26.8	23.3	8.9	316	265	50	49.0	1,746	140
White Plains	165.8	12.3	50.2	108.8	1,897	862	1,035	178.6	3,112	124

1. Based on population estimated as of July 1 of the year shown.

City	Public welfare	Highways	Parking facilities	Education	Health and hospitals	Police protection	Sewerage and sanitation	Parks and recreation	Housing and community development	Interest on debt
	127	128	129	130	131	132	133	134	135	136
NEW JERSEY— Cont'd										
Garfield	0.0	4.9	0.0	0.0	1.2	28.2	11.9	2.8	13.2	2.5
Hackensack	0.3	1.3	0.4	0.0	1.2	17.9	12.8	1.5	6.5	1.4
Hoboken	0.0	2.5	7.0	0.0	0.5	13.9	4.0	1.6	15.2	3.1
Jersey City	0.0	2.1	1.3	0.0	2.2	16.2	14.1	1.4	13.6	4.6
Kearny	0.0	7.5	0.1	0.0	1.0	20.6	13.2	0.8	0.0	3.6
Linden	0.8	2.4	0.6	0.0	0.9	15.3	6.7	2.6	6.2	1.7
Long Branch	0.0	2.4	0.0	0.0	1.1	15.9	20.9	1.9	20.8	3.0
Millville	0.0	2.0	0.0	0.0	0.0	13.2	16.0	1.1	16.4	2.3
Newark	0.3	0.7	0.4	0.2	4.3	15.3	9.7	2.5	24.4	3.2
New Brunswick	0.0	1.0	16.5	54.0	0.2	6.3	3.2	1.5	2.1	2.1
Paramus	0.1	3.7	0.0	0.0	3.0	23.8	11.3	5.3	0.0	2.7
Passaic	0.0	2.5	0.6	0.0	2.3	17.6	7.6	3.5	20.1	0.7
Paterson	0.0	3.0	1.9	0.0	4.0	17.4	9.1	2.0	10.5	1.2
Perth Amboy	0.1	2.3	0.6	0.0	0.6	15.2	8.7	1.9	19.0	3.0
Plainfield	0.0	6.3	0.0	0.0	0.6	15.9	18.4	1.4	13.0	1.7
Rahway	0.0	12.8	2.0	0.0	0.8	23.3	11.5	1.3	12.1	2.9
Sayreville	0.0	4.9	0.0	0.0	0.6	24.7	13.2	3.4	5.0	3.8
Trenton	0.0	0.8	0.8	58.2	0.5	6.3	3.8	0.3	4.5	2.6
Union City	0.0	2.3	0.7	64.8	0.6	6.4	1.9	0.7	4.1	0.9
Vineland	0.0	5.5	0.0	0.0	6.5	25.3	10.8	1.0	11.4	1.3
Westfield	0.0	5.2	0.5	0.0	2.2	16.1	8.8	2.6	0.0	1.6
West New York	0.0	1.4	0.6	65.2	0.6	5.6	1.5	0.6	5.1	1.0
NEW MEXICO	X	X	X	X	X	X	X	X	X	X
Alamogordo	3.1	26.7	0.0	0.0	0.0	16.5	10.5	11.1	3.1	3.2
Albuquerque	3.0	8.8	0.6	0.0	3.4	19.6	11.0	13.3	4.4	3.2
Carlsbad	0.0	11.5	0.0	0.0	1.6	17.0	21.2	11.8	0.0	0.8
Clovis	0.0	8.5	0.0	0.0	0.2	12.6	18.1	12.9	5.5	1.0
Farmington	0.0	12.8	0.0	0.0	1.2	15.7	9.6	13.8	1.3	0.6
Hobbs	0.0	29.3	0.0	0.0	1.5	6.2	12.9	10.4	0.0	0.0
Las Cruces	0.0	12.7	0.0	0.0	0.2	17.7	14.3	7.1	8.6	3.4
Rio Rancho	0.5	17.8	0.0	1.7	0.0	19.1	15.5	6.6	0.4	4.5
Roswell	0.0	8.7	0.0	0.0	0.0	19.1	9.7	11.3	0.0	1.5
Santa Fe	2.8	5.9	2.5	0.0	1.6	12.5	12.4	13.0	6.7	6.9
NEW YORK	X	X	X	X	X	X	X	X	X	X
Albany	0.0	5.6	0.0	0.0	0.2	17.8	5.3	1.6	23.5	17.5
Auburn	0.0	13.1	0.7	0.0	0.1	17.6	14.0	3.7	9.5	4.2
Binghamton	0.0	7.1	1.1	0.0	0.2	14.2	12.9	3.0	6.5	4.6
Buffalo	0.0	2.4	0.1	58.2	0.1	5.2	5.6	0.8	7.1	2.0
Elmira	0.0	21.6	0.6	0.0	0.5	16.9	2.2	3.1	4.9	2.6
Freeport	0.0	3.4	0.1	0.0	0.0	22.9	5.8	6.0	1.8	4.8
Glen Cove	0.0	9.1	0.0	0.0	0.6	22.5	4.1	13.1	9.0	6.4
Harrison	0.0	7.9	0.0	0.0	0.0	4.4	33.2	0.4	0.0	15.8
Hempstead	0.0	2.8	0.3	0.0	0.0	25.2	3.6	3.9	1.3	2.5
Ithaca	0.0	9.6	2.5	0.0	0.1	13.5	10.9	10.1	0.0	4.4
Jamestown	0.0	6.4	0.1	44.5	0.1	7.1	9.8	2.5	0.0	1.1
Lindenhurst	0.0	23.9	0.2	0.0	0.0	0.7	5.7	10.7	1.3	4.1
Long Beach	0.0	0.4	0.0	0.0	0.0	16.1	15.3	10.1	0.0	2.7
Middletown	0.0	5.3	0.0	0.0	0.0	19.0	11.9	6.4	5.3	3.9
Mount Vernon	0.0	2.6	0.1	0.0	0.4	19.2	7.2	5.0	2.7	3.0
Newburgh	0.0	3.7	0.2	0.0	0.1	24.8	13.6	2.8	1.7	4.8
New Rochelle	0.0	5.4	1.6	0.0	0.3	22.3	5.0	4.2	10.9	6.0
New York	15.7	1.8	0.1	27.7	10.4	6.2	5.6	1.3	5.8	5.3
Niagara Falls	0.0	16.1	0.0	0.0	0.1	14.7	2.8	4.1	5.6	2.1
North Tonawanda	0.0	12.9	0.0	0.0	0.1	13.1	15.2	4.4	0.0	1.2
Ossining	0.0	7.2	0.1	0.0	0.3	20.5	6.4	6.1	8.8	5.0
Port Chester	0.0	4.5	0.2	0.0	0.7	20.4	7.3	4.6	1.8	9.9
Poughkeepsie	0.0	9.9	0.9	0.0	0.2	23.5	8.9	1.2	1.5	3.8
Rochester	0.0	1.8	0.6	55.2	0.1	6.7	2.7	1.4	7.0	0.4
Rome	0.0	13.1	0.6	0.0	0.1	12.0	8.8	4.1	5.0	4.1
Saratoga Springs	0.0	10.1	0.2	0.0	0.1	23.1	9.2	8.2	0.6	3.2
Schenectady	0.0	7.4	0.7	0.0	0.1	16.3	15.5	2.0	4.8	6.5
Spring Valley	0.0	3.7	0.1	0.0	0.1	24.6	0.3	1.4	24.9	4.1
Syracuse	0.0	4.0	0.0	53.9	0.1	5.2	1.8	0.9	7.1	6.5
Troy	0.0	7.6	0.0	0.0	0.2	18.6	6.2	3.0	21.6	5.7
Utica	0.0	8.1	0.5	0.0	0.8	16.1	5.0	3.3	19.4	5.5
Valley Stream	0.0	15.7	0.7	0.0	0.4	0.6	12.9	12.6	0.0	5.6
Watertown	0.0	10.7	0.1	0.0	0.0	15.9	10.4	3.1	0.9	3.8
White Plains	0.0	8.2	7.1	0.0	0.0	18.6	5.2	4.4	3.7	1.8

City	City government finances, 2012 (cont.)			Climate[2]						
	Debt outstanding		Debt issued during year	Average daily temperature				Annual precipitation (inches)	Heating degree days	Cooling degree days
				Mean		Limits				
	Total (mil dol)	Per capita[1] (dollars)		January	July	January[3]	July[4]			
	137	138	139	140	141	142	143	144	145	146
NEW JERSEY— Cont'd										
Garfield	21.5	693	2.6	28.6	75.0	19.5	85.5	51.50	5,522	824
Hackensack	36.0	817	0.0	28.6	75.0	19.5	85.5	51.50	5,522	824
Hoboken	101.0	1,932	0.0	29.6	75.3	22.7	82.5	46.33	5,367	882
Jersey City	847.1	3,300	36.1	29.6	75.3	22.7	82.5	46.33	5,367	882
Kearny	83.3	1,995	9.1	31.3	77.2	24.4	85.2	46.25	4,843	1,220
Linden	46.6	1,137	15.0	28.5	74.0	18.2	85.8	51.61	5,595	757
Long Branch	70.9	2,322	0.0	31.7	74.1	22.8	82.6	48.63	5,168	750
Millville	39.9	1,390	9.2	32.7	76.3	24.1	85.9	43.20	4,835	1,009
Newark	658.6	2,366	2.2	31.3	77.2	24.4	85.2	46.25	4,843	1,220
New Brunswick	406.3	7,289	53.2	29.7	74.8	21.1	85.4	48.78	5,346	816
Paramus	39.3	1,477	0.0	28.6	75.0	19.5	85.5	51.50	5,522	824
Passaic	18.9	269	0.0	28.6	75.0	19.5	85.5	51.50	5,522	824
Paterson	119.6	819	5.1	28.6	75.0	19.5	85.5	51.50	5,522	824
Perth Amboy	91.3	1,761	13.7	29.7	74.8	21.1	85.4	48.78	5,346	816
Plainfield	48.0	952	0.1	30.0	74.9	21.5	86.6	49.63	5,266	854
Rahway	64.7	2,321	0.0	29.6	74.5	19.8	85.7	50.94	5,450	787
Sayreville	53.0	1,208	6.3	29.7	74.8	21.1	85.4	48.78	5,346	816
Trenton	390.2	4,626	34.2	30.4	75.2	21.3	86.9	48.83	5,262	903
Union City	82.9	1,213	0.0	29.6	75.3	22.7	82.5	46.33	5,367	882
Vineland	133.2	2,183	0.0	26.7	70.4	16.8	81.7	53.28	6,281	438
Westfield	20.7	675	0.0	30.0	74.9	21.5	86.6	49.63	5,266	854
West New York	52.4	1,010	0.0	29.6	75.3	22.7	82.5	46.33	5,367	882
NEW MEXICO	X	X	X	X	X	X	X	X	X	X
Alamogordo	58.7	1,859	25.6	42.2	79.7	28.9	93.0	13.20	31	1,715
Albuquerque	2,091.8	3,769	165.1	35.7	78.5	23.8	92.3	9.47	4,281	1,290
Carlsbad	40.7	1,520	8.7	42.7	81.7	27.5	95.8	14.15	2,823	2,029
Clovis	25.6	649	13.2	37.9	77.5	25.0	91.0	18.50	3,955	1,305
Farmington	1,802.6	39,348	11.1	29.8	74.9	17.9	90.7	8.39	5,508	805
Hobbs	58.7	1,677	0.0	42.9	80.1	29.1	93.5	18.15	2,849	1,842
Las Cruces	152.7	1,512	18.5	39.0	78.7	21.1	94.9	11.44	3,818	1,364
Rio Rancho	236.5	2,609	12.4	33.8	73.9	19.7	90.0	9.28	4,981	773
Roswell	18.0	371	0.0	40.0	80.8	24.4	94.8	13.34	3,332	1,814
Santa Fe	381.4	5,509	62.7	29.3	69.8	15.5	85.6	14.22	6,073	414
NEW YORK	X	X	X	X	X	X	X	X	X	X
Albany	773.1	7,851	27.8	22.2	71.1	13.3	82.2	38.60	6,860	544
Auburn	52.9	1,933	0.0	23.7	71.2	16.0	81.5	36.98	6,694	528
Binghamton	115.0	2,462	10.4	21.7	68.7	15.0	78.1	38.65	7,237	396
Buffalo	609.4	2,345	116.7	24.5	70.8	17.8	79.6	40.54	6,692	548
Elmira	36.3	1,243	8.5	23.9	70.3	15.0	82.3	34.95	6,806	446
Freeport	138.4	3,205	19.4	30.7	73.8	24.2	81.0	42.97	5,504	779
Glen Cove	81.8	3,010	11.6	31.9	74.2	25.4	82.8	46.36	5,231	839
Harrison	65.6	2,358	21.0	NA	NA	NA	NA	NA	NA	NA
Hempstead	47.9	872	0.0	31.9	74.2	25.4	82.8	46.36	5,231	839
Ithaca	76.9	2,530	0.0	22.6	68.7	13.9	80.1	36.71	7,182	312
Jamestown	36.2	1,179	4.0	22.3	69.2	14.1	80.1	45.68	7,048	389
Lindenhurst	5.9	218	0.0	30.7	73.8	24.2	81.0	42.97	5,504	779
Long Beach	54.6	1,631	2.5	31.8	74.8	24.7	82.9	42.46	4,947	949
Middletown	84.2	3,024	23.7	26.5	73.0	17.5	84.0	44.00	5,820	674
Mount Vernon	56.4	831	0.0	29.7	74.2	20.1	86.0	46.46	5,400	770
Newburgh	100.8	3,527	0.0	26.6	74.3	17.1	84.9	45.79	5,813	790
New Rochelle	141.5	1,805	20.0	29.7	74.2	20.1	86.0	46.46	5,400	770
New York	131,462.0	15,714	16,736.2	32.1	76.5	26.2	84.2	49.69	4,754	1,151
Niagara Falls	72.6	1,461	7.4	24.2	71.4	16.8	81.8	33.93	6,752	508
North Tonawanda	13.9	445	3.3	24.2	71.4	16.8	81.8	33.93	6,752	508
Ossining	25.9	1,027	2.3	NA	NA	NA	NA	NA	NA	NA
Port Chester	50.5	1,727	13.4	28.4	73.8	21.0	82.5	50.45	5,660	716
Poughkeepsie	86.8	2,825	12.4	24.5	71.9	14.7	83.6	44.12	6,438	550
Rochester	496.9	2,359	124.1	23.9	70.7	16.6	81.4	33.98	6,728	576
Rome	46.6	1,415	0.8	20.8	70.2	11.9	81.3	46.27	7,146	416
Saratoga Springs	36.7	1,362	3.4	20.9	71.2	11.6	83.0	43.31	6,904	477
Schenectady	159.7	2,417	13.3	22.2	71.1	13.3	82.2	38.60	6,860	544
Spring Valley	16.9	528	0.2	27.3	73.1	18.2	83.8	51.01	5,809	642
Syracuse	1,117.3	7,744	121.3	22.7	70.9	14.0	81.7	40.05	6,803	551
Troy	99.0	1,985	0.0	22.2	71.1	13.3	82.2	38.60	6,860	544
Utica	95.0	1,535	6.0	22.2	70.5	12.6	83.2	41.90	6,855	441
Valley Stream	28.5	756	3.5	22.2	70.5	12.6	83.2	41.90	6,855	441
Watertown	24.2	862	0.0	18.6	70.2	9.1	79.4	42.57	7,517	421
White Plains	106.6	1,858	45.7	29.7	74.2	20.1	86.0	46.46	5,400	770

1. Based on the population estimated as of July 1 of the year shown.   2. Represents normal values based on the 30-year period, 1971±2000.   3. Average daily minimum.   4. Average daily maximum.

Table D. Cities — **Land Area and Population**

STATE Place code	City	Land area[1] (sq. mi)	Population, 2018			Race 2017 — Race alone[2] (percent)						
			Total persons 2018	Rank	Per square mile	White	Black or African American	American Indian, Alaskan Native	Asian	Hawaiian Pacific Islander	Some other race	Two or more races (percent)
		1	2	3	4	5	6	7	8	9	10	11
	NEW YORK— Cont'd											
36 84,000	Yonkers	18.0	199,663	117	11,092.4	53.2	18.2	1.2	7.5	0.1	16.7	3.1
37 00,000	NORTH CAROLINA	48,619.4	10,383,620	X	213.6	68.8	21.5	1.2	2.9	0.1	3.0	2.6
37 01,520	Apex	19.1	53,852	717	2,819.5	79.6	8.6	0.3	8.2	0.0	0.1	3.2
37 02,080	Asheboro	18.8	25,844	1,396	1,374.7	73.5	11.4	0.4	0.0	0.0	10.0	4.8
37 02,140	Asheville	45.6	92,452	352	2,027.5	83.8	12.7	0.2	1.1	0.0	0.6	1.6
37 09,060	Burlington	29.4	53,748	719	1,828.2	62.4	26.0	0.0	3.0	0.3	7.4	0.9
37 10,740	Cary	57.3	168,160	155	2,934.7	68.4	6.1	0.3	20.1	0.0	2.3	2.6
37 11,800	Chapel Hill	21.5	60,988	611	2,836.7	72.1	10.8	0.0	11.9	0.0	1.2	4.0
37 12,000	Charlotte	306.6	872,498	16	2,845.7	49.2	34.4	0.5	6.4	0.0	6.3	3.1
37 14,100	Concord	63.0	94,130	343	1,494.1	66.3	21.1	0.8	4.7	0.0	5.1	2.0
37 19,000	Durham	112.2	274,291	75	2,444.7	49.8	38.4	0.2	5.0	0.0	3.2	3.3
37 22,920	Fayetteville	147.9	209,468	109	1,416.3	44.6	41.7	1.1	3.2	0.7	2.8	5.8
37 25,480	Garner	15.6	30,502	1,233	1,955.3	NA	NA	NA	NA	NA	NA	NA
37 25,580	Gastonia	51.6	77,024	452	1,492.7	65.4	28.1	0.3	1.7	0.0	2.2	2.3
37 26,880	Goldsboro	28.5	34,234	1,112	1,201.2	42.2	47.3	0.2	2.7	0.2	0.7	6.7
37 28,000	Greensboro	128.9	294,722	67	2,286.4	48.2	42.9	0.5	4.5	0.1	1.6	2.3
37 28,080	Greenville	35.6	93,137	348	2,616.2	57.7	35.7	0.0	1.3	0.2	3.3	1.9
37 31,060	Hickory	29.6	40,925	937	1,382.6	70.2	12.1	0.0	5.5	0.0	7.8	4.3
37 31,400	High Point	55.8	112,316	260	2,012.8	52.4	36.0	0.7	7.0	0.0	1.2	2.7
37 33,120	Huntersville	40.5	57,098	666	1,409.8	76.4	16.6	0.3	1.7	0.0	2.2	2.9
37 33,560	Indian Trail	22.1	39,619	975	1,792.7	83.1	9.5	0.0	1.7	0.2	1.3	4.2
37 34,200	Jacksonville	48.6	72,896	492	1,499.9	67.6	21.2	0.5	3.9	0.0	0.1	6.6
37 35,200	Kannapolis	32.6	49,761	772	1,526.4	62.5	21.0	0.0	4.7	0.3	9.5	2.0
37 41,960	Matthews	17.1	32,635	1,164	1,908.5	84.7	7.4	0.4	1.4	0.0	1.9	4.2
37 43,920	Monroe	29.8	35,311	1,088	1,184.9	60.8	26.1	0.0	1.0	0.4	9.5	2.3
37 44,220	Mooresville	24.4	38,431	999	1,575.0	81.9	11.3	0.1	2.4	0.0	1.0	3.4
37 46,340	New Bern	28.3	30,113	1,250	1,064.1	50.8	34.5	0.0	8.4	0.0	6.1	0.2
37 55,000	Raleigh	145.3	469,298	41	3,229.9	56.8	29.2	0.3	5.1	0.1	6.1	2.4
37 57,500	Rocky Mount	44.2	54,242	706	1,227.2	NA	NA	NA	NA	NA	NA	NA
37 58,860	Salisbury	22.2	33,834	1,130	1,524.1	56.6	40.1	0.0	0.3	0.1	0.9	2.0
37 59,280	Sanford	29.1	29,917	1,257	1,028.1	NA	NA	NA	NA	NA	NA	NA
37 67,420	Thomasville	16.8	26,635	1,372	1,585.4	77.5	12.8	1.5	0.0	0.0	2.9	5.3
37 70,540	Wake Forest	16.4	44,046	871	2,685.7	76.0	20.0	0.0	1.9	0.0	0.1	2.0
37 74,440	Wilmington	51.7	122,607	226	2,371.5	77.2	17.3	0.4	1.0	0.9	0.7	2.5
37 74,540	Wilson	31.1	49,329	779	1,586.1	45.2	47.0	0.7	1.3	0.0	4.3	1.5
37 75,000	Winston-Salem	132.6	246,328	89	1,857.7	58.0	33.8	0.5	3.0	0.1	2.0	2.6
38 00,000	NORTH DAKOTA	68,999.4	760,077	X	11.0	86.6	3.1	5.5	1.7	0.1	1.1	2.0
38 07,200	Bismarck	33.7	73,112	491	2,169.5	90.7	2.5	3.9	1.0	0.0	0.2	1.8
38 25,700	Fargo	49.7	124,844	222	2,512.0	83.9	7.9	1.3	3.9	0.1	0.4	2.7
38 32,060	Grand Forks	27.2	56,948	667	2,093.7	85.0	5.8	3.4	3.6	0.0	1.0	1.2
38 53,380	Minot	27.2	47,370	820	1,741.5	84.8	5.5	2.9	2.2	0.7	0.7	3.1
38 84,780	West Fargo	16.0	36,566	1,051	2,285.4	NA	NA	NA	NA	NA	NA	NA
39 00,000	OHIO	40,860.8	11,689,442	X	286.1	81.3	12.4	0.2	2.2	0.0	0.9	2.9
39 01,000	Akron	61.9	198,006	120	3,198.8	59.7	31.1	0.3	4.0	0.1	0.2	4.5
39 03,828	Barberton	9.0	26,072	1,390	2,896.9	NA	NA	NA	NA	NA	NA	NA
39 04,720	Beavercreek	26.6	47,391	818	1,781.6	NA	NA	NA	NA	NA	NA	NA
39 07,200	Bowling Green	12.7	31,578	1,202	2,486.5	87.3	7.3	0.1	0.8	0.0	0.9	3.5
39 09,680	Brunswick	12.9	34,897	1,094	2,705.2	90.9	4.0	0.0	2.3	0.0	0.0	2.9
39 12,000	Canton	25.8	70,458	512	2,730.9	73.3	19.4	0.2	0.5	0.1	0.1	6.3
39 15,000	Cincinnati	77.9	302,605	65	3,884.5	50.4	42.5	0.1	2.6	0.2	0.9	3.3
39 16,000	Cleveland	77.7	383,793	52	4,939.4	39.1	48.7	0.5	2.4	0.0	4.0	5.3
39 16,014	Cleveland Heights	8.1	44,373	864	5,478.1	48.3	41.0	0.2	7.7	0.0	0.5	2.2
39 18,000	Columbus	218.8	892,533	14	4,079.2	59.0	28.6	0.3	6.0	0.0	2.2	3.8
39 19,778	Cuyahoga Falls	25.8	49,272	781	1,909.8	NA	NA	NA	NA	NA	NA	NA
39 21,000	Dayton	55.4	140,640	190	2,538.6	53.5	40.9	0.3	0.6	0.0	1.0	3.7
39 21,434	Delaware	19.3	39,930	964	2,068.9	NA	NA	NA	NA	NA	NA	NA
39 22,694	Dublin	24.6	48,647	793	1,977.5	NA	NA	NA	NA	NA	NA	NA
39 25,256	Elyria	20.6	53,881	716	2,615.6	74.9	17.3	0.1	0.2	0.0	0.4	7.1
39 25,704	Euclid	10.7	46,946	827	4,387.5	NA	NA	NA	NA	NA	NA	NA
39 25,914	Fairborn	14.6	33,658	1,136	2,305.3	83.6	8.4	0.0	3.9	0.0	0.0	4.2
39 25,970	Fairfield	20.9	42,613	891	2,038.9	79.3	13.5	0.0	4.7	0.0	1.6	0.9
39 27,048	Findlay	19.6	41,324	925	2,108.4	89.5	3.1	0.3	0.6	0.0	1.6	5.0
39 29,106	Gahanna	12.4	35,551	1,080	2,867.0	NA	NA	NA	NA	NA	NA	NA
39 29,428	Garfield Heights	7.2	27,687	1,330	3,845.4	NA	NA	NA	NA	NA	NA	NA
39 31,860	Green	32.1	25,783	1,397	803.2	NA	NA	NA	NA	NA	NA	NA
39 32,592	Grove City	17.0	41,625	915	2,448.5	92.2	1.7	0.8	1.9	0.0	0.0	3.3

1. Dry land or land partially or temporarily covered by water.   2. Hispanic or Latino persons may be of any race.

Table D. Cities — **Population**

Items 12—26

City	Percent Hispanic or Latino[1], 2017	Percent foreign born, 2017	Age of population (percent), 2017							Median age, 2017	Percent female, 2017	Population			
												Census counts		Percent change	
			Under 18 years	18 to 24 years	25 to 34 years	35 to 44 years	45 to 54 years	55 to 64 years	65 years and over			2000	2010	2000-2010	2001-2018
	12	13	14	15	16	17	18	19	20	21	22	23	24	25	26
NEW YORK— Cont'd															
Yonkers	38.6	29.9	22.1	9.0	13.8	13.9	13.3	10.8	17.1	38.7	51.3	196,086	196,018	0.0	1.9
NORTH CAROLINA	9.4	8.1	22.4	9.5	13.2	12.7	13.5	12.8	15.9	38.8	51.3	8,049,313	9,535,736	18.5	8.9
Apex	5.6	11.3	28.9	4.5	10.3	20.6	18.9	8.9	7.9	38.1	50.5	20,212	37,621	86.1	43.1
Asheboro	19.3	11.2	24.8	8.3	14.7	14.8	10.5	10.6	16.4	36.6	52.1	21,672	25,390	17.2	1.8
Asheville	6.3	6.8	16.9	6.6	16.4	16.2	12.0	12.0	19.9	40.7	52.3	68,889	83,433	21.1	10.8
Burlington	20.2	13.3	20.7	9.2	13.9	11.2	13.7	12.6	18.7	39.8	51.7	44,917	50,862	13.2	5.7
Cary	8.4	23.5	24.9	6.2	11.8	14.5	16.0	13.7	12.8	39.9	50.2	94,536	135,777	43.6	23.9
Chapel Hill	5.8	11.1	17.1	33.0	13.3	10.1	8.4	6.7	11.4	24.9	52.3	48,715	57,220	17.5	6.6
Charlotte	14.3	17.1	23.1	9.8	18.1	14.6	13.4	10.8	10.3	34.4	51.8	540,828	735,692	36.0	18.6
Concord	15.1	10.9	26.5	7.2	13.1	16.1	14.2	10.8	12.0	37.5	49.2	55,977	79,317	41.7	18.7
Durham	13.2	15.1	21.5	10.6	19.4	13.8	12.0	10.7	12.1	34.2	53.4	187,035	229,878	22.9	19.3
Fayetteville	12.5	7.0	22.6	15.6	18.2	11.0	10.1	10.3	12.2	30.4	49.2	121,015	200,565	65.7	4.4
Garner	6.5	5.3	24.3	7.2	19.3	7.1	17.7	13.6	10.9	34.0	49.0	17,757	25,776	45.2	18.3
Gastonia	10.8	5.7	22.8	8.3	12.6	13.6	13.0	13.0	16.7	39.7	52.9	66,277	71,722	8.2	7.4
Goldsboro	5.3	4.0	21.6	13.2	13.8	9.8	12.7	11.7	17.1	36.7	51.0	39,043	35,454	-9.2	-3.4
Greensboro	6.9	10.8	21.0	12.7	14.5	12.6	13.3	12.1	13.8	36.4	52.9	223,891	268,924	20.1	9.6
Greenville	5.5	4.0	19.9	24.3	16.7	10.4	9.9	8.1	10.7	27.7	55.1	60,476	84,722	40.1	9.9
Hickory	11.5	9.3	21.6	9.9	13.9	12.6	13.4	11.3	17.3	38.7	54.1	37,222	40,015	7.5	2.3
High Point	9.1	13.0	24.0	9.1	14.4	13.2	11.7	11.8	15.8	36.9	54.2	85,839	104,514	21.8	7.5
Huntersville	7.0	7.0	30.3	2.0	10.8	18.9	16.1	12.0	9.9	38.7	50.8	24,960	46,763	87.4	22.1
Indian Trail	7.5	11.8	31.5	7.7	14.5	14.1	14.1	8.7	9.5	30.9	52.3	11,905	33,573	182.0	18.0
Jacksonville	16.1	5.2	23.1	37.0	17.2	6.7	5.2	4.4	6.3	22.4	38.6	66,715	70,169	5.2	3.9
Kannapolis	17.4	10.5	26.6	7.7	14.1	12.5	13.4	9.5	16.1	36.5	52.6	36,910	42,607	15.4	16.8
Matthews	13.6	9.6	27.6	7.4	11.9	13.9	11.0	11.9	16.3	38.0	48.0	22,127	27,189	22.9	20.0
Monroe	32.8	18.9	27.4	10.5	12.3	12.7	15.2	10.3	11.6	34.9	51.8	26,228	32,784	25.0	7.7
Mooresville	7.4	7.4	29.1	6.9	12.9	14.5	14.4	7.7	14.5	35.7	53.0	18,823	34,331	82.4	11.9
New Bern	13.0	11.1	23.5	9.7	14.7	9.8	10.0	13.6	18.7	37.8	52.1	23,128	29,343	26.9	2.6
Raleigh	11.0	14.0	21.1	12.8	18.9	14.9	12.6	9.5	10.1	33.4	51.5	276,093	404,073	46.4	16.1
Rocky Mount	3.8	3.4	18.5	7.7	12.8	16.0	12.9	14.9	17.2	42.1	55.5	55,893	57,700	3.2	-6.0
Salisbury	3.8	1.8	23.0	11.3	12.7	11.5	8.9	12.4	20.2	37.4	51.3	26,462	33,533	26.7	0.9
Sanford	26.0	12.2	25.2	9.2	14.2	13.0	14.3	14.6	9.5	36.4	49.7	23,220	28,218	21.5	6.0
Thomasville	18.9	9.4	25.9	8.3	13.4	13.4	12.1	12.5	14.5	37.3	51.3	19,788	26,776	35.3	-0.5
Wake Forest	2.5	6.4	32.3	5.3	11.0	14.3	15.8	9.3	12.0	36.4	51.8	12,588	30,099	139.1	46.3
Wilmington	6.2	5.1	17.3	16.0	14.9	11.1	12.9	11.6	16.2	36.7	53.9	75,838	106,454	40.4	15.2
Wilson	12.2	8.3	25.1	9.1	11.9	11.2	12.5	14.2	16.0	37.8	57.2	44,405	49,160	10.7	0.3
Winston-Salem	14.1	10.2	22.5	11.1	14.8	12.4	12.3	12.8	14.2	36.1	52.6	185,776	229,634	23.6	7.3
NORTH DAKOTA	3.5	4.1	22.9	11.4	15.1	11.8	10.9	12.9	14.9	35.4	48.6	642,200	672,576	4.7	13.0
Bismarck	2.2	2.9	21.8	8.9	15.8	12.7	11.5	13.4	16.0	37.3	50.0	55,532	61,301	10.4	19.3
Fargo	2.9	8.6	21.0	17.1	19.6	11.9	9.6	9.9	10.9	30.7	48.7	90,599	105,610	16.6	18.2
Grand Forks	4.0	7.1	19.6	22.2	16.8	10.2	9.0	10.6	11.7	28.9	47.4	49,321	52,921	7.3	7.6
Minot	4.8	5.3	22.5	13.8	17.2	11.7	10.9	10.9	12.9	32.1	48.7	36,567	41,097	12.4	15.3
West Fargo	2.7	2.2	23.7	8.7	15.3	16.4	14.0	13.4	8.6	36.9	47.7	14,940	25,854	73.1	41.4
OHIO	3.7	4.5	22.3	9.2	13.1	11.9	13.0	13.8	16.6	39.3	51.0	11,353,140	11,536,757	1.6	1.3
Akron	2.8	6.8	20.9	11.8	15.7	10.6	12.6	13.6	14.8	36.4	52.8	217,074	199,135	-8.3	-0.6
Barberton	2.4	1.5	22.7	5.3	15.7	9.5	13.5	15.0	18.2	41.3	57.5	27,899	26,552	-4.8	-1.8
Beavercreek	2.2	8.9	24.2	7.1	13.3	13.9	12.7	15.7	13.1	38.6	48.9	37,984	45,177	18.9	4.9
Bowling Green	6.1	2.9	10.3	46.1	13.5	6.8	5.6	7.8	9.9	23.6	47.8	29,636	30,055	1.4	5.1
Brunswick	6.9	7.2	23.3	8.4	12.4	14.4	13.5	12.6	15.4	38.1	52.6	33,388	34,279	2.7	1.8
Canton	3.3	2.1	23.5	10.3	14.7	13.2	12.2	13.0	13.1	36.2	52.2	80,806	73,043	-9.6	-3.5
Cincinnati	3.9	6.3	21.1	13.1	19.2	11.8	10.9	10.9	13.0	32.7	51.5	331,285	296,893	-10.4	1.9
Cleveland	12.4	5.7	22.9	9.9	15.5	11.8	12.4	13.8	13.7	36.2	52.6	478,403	396,629	-17.1	-3.2
Cleveland Heights	2.3	11.3	19.7	13.1	19.5	9.4	10.2	11.2	17.0	33.6	55.7	49,958	46,268	-7.4	-4.1
Columbus	6.3	12.0	22.6	11.4	20.7	12.8	11.8	10.5	10.2	32.2	51.0	711,470	789,011	10.9	13.1
Cuyahoga Falls	0.8	3.3	19.3	8.3	18.1	12.1	12.0	13.2	16.9	38.6	51.5	49,374	49,580	0.4	-0.6
Dayton	4.1	4.8	20.5	15.1	16.9	9.6	12.4	13.5	12.0	33.4	49.4	166,179	141,995	-14.6	-1.0
Delaware	2.3	2.5	25.5	11.6	14.0	16.3	11.6	8.2	12.8	34.5	52.6	25,243	34,758	37.7	14.9
Dublin	0.6	20.1	29.5	6.8	9.3	15.4	16.1	12.7	10.2	38.2	48.4	31,392	41,364	31.8	17.6
Elyria	6.0	3.0	18.1	10.6	13.5	10.3	14.1	15.6	17.9	43.5	54.2	55,953	54,528	-2.5	-1.2
Euclid	1.5	3.0	17.9	8.6	14.1	11.6	11.1	19.7	17.0	42.3	54.6	52,717	48,901	-7.2	-4.0
Fairborn	1.7	4.4	18.5	18.2	17.9	10.7	9.8	10.8	14.0	31.5	54.0	32,052	32,932	2.7	2.2
Fairfield	8.7	12.8	21.1	7.6	11.9	14.2	12.2	14.3	18.7	41.8	51.9	42,097	42,505	1.0	0.3
Findlay	8.0	4.5	20.8	10.5	17.7	13.0	13.2	10.5	14.4	35.5	52.3	38,967	41,185	5.7	0.3
Gahanna	4.8	5.3	25.0	4.5	12.0	15.0	13.5	13.1	16.9	39.5	50.4	32,636	33,230	1.8	7.0
Garfield Heights	3.0	4.7	22.8	6.6	18.4	9.8	10.1	13.2	19.2	36.8	55.9	30,734	28,849	-6.1	-4.0
Green	0.3	4.2	17.4	7.7	10.0	10.6	16.2	18.6	19.6	49.3	50.3	22,817	25,735	12.8	0.2
Grove City	1.6	1.7	26.0	5.4	13.9	12.3	12.9	15.5	14.1	39.0	54.1	27,075	35,609	31.5	16.9

1. May be of any race.

Table D. Cities — Households, Group Quarters, Crime, and Education

City	Households, 2017 Number	Persons per household	Percent Family	Married couple family	Female headed[1]	Non-family	One person	Persons in group quarters, 2017	Serious crimes known to police[2], 2016 Total Number	Rate	Violent	Property	Population age 25 and over	High school graduate or less	Bachelor's degree or more
	27	28	29	30	31	32	33	34	35	36	37	38	39	40	41
NEW YORK— Cont'd															
Yonkers	75,981	2.62	62.5	40.0	16.1	37.5	33.0	2,926	3,130	1,549	467	1,082	139,232	44.5	32.1
NORTH CAROLINA	3,955,069	2.53	65.5	48.2	12.7	34.5	28.6	266,771	315,534	3,110	372	2,737	6,991,185	38.0	31.3
Apex	18,089	2.78	73.6	60.7	9.8	26.4	19.4	210	641	1,354	85	1,270	33,616	12.5	64.4
Asheboro	11,486	2.18	58.2	32.0	17.0	41.8	40.0	837	1,605	6,119	396	5,722	17,301	52.0	15.3
Asheville	42,045	2.11	45.5	35.0	7.9	54.5	41.6	3,233	4,894	5,465	600	4,866	70,348	24.4	50.9
Burlington	22,507	2.36	63.6	39.4	18.5	36.4	32.7	992	2,225	4,217	743	3,474	37,950	50.4	21.3
Cary	62,831	2.64	72.3	62.5	7.5	27.7	22.8	360	1,807	1,096	92	1,005	114,350	14.4	68.2
Chapel Hill	19,303	2.53	48.7	43.4	4.4	51.3	28.5	9,667	1,476	2,460	188	2,272	29,161	9.4	77.0
Charlotte	331,822	2.55	58.5	41.0	13.3	41.5	33.6	12,224	43,292	4,830	732	4,098	575,876	27.8	45.0
Concord	33,305	2.73	72.5	55.9	11.3	27.5	23.5	1,212	2,329	2,604	139	2,465	60,968	37.1	37.1
Durham	110,017	2.34	56.6	37.4	15.3	43.4	34.3	10,598	10,623	4,028	747	3,281	182,055	28.5	50.3
Fayetteville	83,558	2.35	57.1	38.7	14.1	42.9	37.8	13,809	10,732	5,308	757	4,550	129,733	34.4	26.3
Garner	10,323	2.77	74.1	56.9	12.4	25.9	16.5	NA	1,079	3,785	302	3,483	19,770	33.9	36.4
Gastonia	30,097	2.50	60.2	38.9	15.3	39.8	29.6	1,437	4,016	5,346	767	4,579	52,787	44.6	21.3
Goldsboro	14,329	2.30	59.3	36.9	20.2	40.7	34.3	2,197	2,388	6,657	1,084	5,573	22,948	44.8	23.6
Greensboro	115,802	2.38	57.5	38.0	14.9	42.5	34.1	14,322	11,132	3,857	643	3,214	192,538	32.3	38.1
Greenville	36,029	2.39	50.9	33.1	15.4	49.1	35.4	5,908	3,834	4,178	508	3,670	51,468	24.7	42.3
Hickory	16,527	2.39	59.4	47.3	10.2	40.6	34.0	1,270	2,118	5,238	408	4,830	27,865	37.8	32.2
High Point	40,437	2.65	66.7	43.5	18.7	33.3	27.8	3,965	4,704	4,221	647	3,574	74,347	36.4	30.8
Huntersville	20,073	2.78	72.9	64.2	5.6	27.1	23.2	NA	1,220	2,262	117	2,145	38,050	17.1	57.5
Indian Trail	11,667	3.34	83.7	65.3	11.5	16.3	12.3	NA	NA	NA	NA	NA	23,697	33.0	35.7
Jacksonville	19,630	2.75	71.8	53.3	14.6	28.2	25.2	18,510	1,246	1,868	162	1,707	28,843	30.1	26.3
Kannapolis	18,838	2.74	70.8	46.2	18.1	29.2	25.0	336	1,054	2,249	252	1,997	34,169	41.1	21.5
Matthews	10,700	2.97	72.7	60.6	8.5	27.3	22.0	NA	1,121	3,570	146	3,423	20,868	17.9	58.8
Monroe	11,487	3.00	72.6	48.5	14.6	27.4	22.2	607	2,191	6,264	649	5,615	21,778	54.5	14.1
Mooresville	13,833	2.72	71.8	54.6	9.6	28.2	23.2	NA	1,543	4,229	274	3,955	24,202	29.9	40.6
New Bern	12,906	2.26	54.3	38.2	11.5	45.7	37.8	413	1,170	3,882	411	3,471	19,783	38.5	28.3
Raleigh	183,672	2.43	56.6	38.7	13.7	43.4	32.4	18,105	NA	NA	NA	NA	306,942	23.8	51.0
Rocky Mount	22,650	2.36	61.6	34.3	23.3	38.4	32.1	1,154	2,542	4,586	785	3,801	40,269	52.2	21.1
Salisbury	12,577	2.42	56.5	31.4	18.9	43.5	40.1	3,414	1,994	5,844	973	4,871	22,239	39.6	25.6
Sanford	10,467	2.73	71.5	43.3	15.5	28.5	23.7	744	12	41	3	37	19,239	46.9	25.7
Thomasville	11,056	2.36	59.1	42.2	13.4	40.9	35.6	447	1,188	4,381	321	4,060	17,507	53.3	10.0
Wake Forest	14,617	2.85	75.7	62.4	11.5	24.3	17.4	NA	1,008	2,520	135	2,385	26,256	17.5	53.4
Wilmington	51,862	2.20	49.7	35.2	12.2	50.3	40.8	5,133	5,530	4,692	644	4,048	79,336	27.8	43.4
Wilson	20,191	2.38	63.1	39.1	20.7	36.9	33.1	1,385	2,091	4,204	521	3,684	32,457	48.5	24.9
Winston-Salem	94,344	2.48	58.6	39.3	14.9	41.4	36.0	10,549	13,461	5,528	749	4,779	162,433	36.1	34.6
NORTH DAKOTA	316,306	2.31	60.1	48.3	7.4	39.9	31.7	26,143	19,305	2,547	251	2,296	495,904	33.5	30.7
Bismarck	31,597	2.19	57.9	44.3	9.4	42.1	34.6	2,243	2,698	3,683	292	3,391	49,615	29.9	35.5
Fargo	54,351	2.18	51.5	39.6	7.7	48.5	32.9	5,069	4,329	3,571	388	3,184	76,506	22.9	42.2
Grand Forks	25,130	2.07	43.5	32.7	7.4	56.5	43.4	3,892	1,972	3,409	308	3,101	32,560	25.3	36.3
Minot	19,319	2.40	54.7	42.7	7.7	45.3	39.2	1,347	1,517	2,959	273	2,686	30,395	39.9	32.6
West Fargo	14,493	2.46	71.6	57.7	8.3	28.4	19.7	82	560	1,582	186	1,396	24,154	18.3	45.1
OHIO	4,667,192	2.43	63.2	45.8	12.5	36.8	30.3	317,470	334,234	2,878	300	2,577	7,981,885	43.1	28.0
Akron	84,331	2.28	53.4	27.9	19.7	46.6	37.8	5,339	9,934	5,036	654	4,382	133,076	46.3	21.3
Barberton	11,015	2.34	62.8	41.0	16.6	37.2	32.4	370	874	3,339	287	3,053	18,811	63.5	12.1
Beavercreek	18,791	2.47	69.6	55.9	8.2	30.4	26.6	385	1,101	2,368	71	2,297	32,127	18.8	56.2
Bowling Green	11,858	2.17	48.2	30.6	10.7	51.8	31.3	6,100	602	1,917	134	1,783	13,859	22.5	44.5
Brunswick	13,026	2.66	73.6	58.1	8.5	26.4	22.3	NA	249	716	72	644	23,828	39.6	25.8
Canton	30,708	2.22	59.0	23.8	26.9	41.0	34.7	2,621	4,368	6,096	987	5,109	46,909	54.5	11.9
Cincinnati	140,911	2.04	41.8	22.0	15.7	58.2	46.6	13,675	18,231	6,100	938	5,162	198,191	37.9	35.8
Cleveland	171,717	2.17	46.9	19.8	21.7	53.1	44.7	12,747	27,354	7,082	1,695	5,388	259,124	51.6	17.0
Cleveland Heights	19,090	2.29	51.2	36.6	11.8	48.8	37.5	872	1,142	2,555	324	2,231	29,950	18.1	56.6
Columbus	355,414	2.41	54.2	33.3	15.4	45.8	34.5	24,225	39,967	4,634	544	4,090	581,506	36.3	35.1
Cuyahoga Falls	22,879	2.13	55.0	39.5	11.3	45.0	38.7	520	1,210	2,466	137	2,330	35,635	33.0	32.2
Dayton	57,649	2.19	50.5	24.4	22.1	49.5	41.4	14,261	8,702	6,204	1,041	5,163	90,350	46.8	17.7
Delaware	14,076	2.64	62.8	49.8	11.1	37.2	35.2	2,250	963	2,491	189	2,302	24,774	31.0	33.2
Dublin	15,146	3.05	82.2	75.6	3.9	17.8	15.7	NA	547	1,193	50	1,143	29,585	11.9	72.4
Elyria	24,481	2.17	56.4	33.9	18.5	43.6	37.8	NA	1,645	3,067	300	2,767	38,444	43.8	17.7
Euclid	23,555	1.98	48.4	25.5	18.8	51.6	46.5	644	1,604	3,383	580	2,803	34,710	43.5	19.7
Fairborn	13,264	2.48	57.2	36.9	15.9	42.8	30.2	739	1,002	2,983	253	2,730	21,247	33.7	26.1
Fairfield	17,707	2.37	61.6	45.8	9.8	38.4	32.0	636	1,155	2,698	257	2,441	30,334	43.8	28.6
Findlay	17,966	2.21	55.8	36.8	10.2	44.2	36.2	1,701	1,415	3,438	284	3,154	28,392	43.0	27.2
Gahanna	13,425	2.52	71.7	56.5	10.6	28.3	24.3	NA	809	2,321	57	2,263	23,972	26.1	46.8
Garfield Heights	11,433	2.39	59.2	24.7	27.7	40.8	32.5	471	419	1,500	236	1,264	19,648	51.1	14.3
Green	10,562	2.42	69.4	61.6	6.3	30.6	23.7	NA	NA	NA	NA	NA	19,276	34.5	32.4
Grove City	16,362	2.53	71.2	54.6	11.0	28.8	23.3	NA	1,731	4,310	110	4,201	28,623	34.9	35.8

1. No spouse present.   2. Data for serious crimes have not been adjusted for underreporting. This may affect comparability between geographic areas and over time.   3. Per 100,000 population estimated by the FBI.   4. Persons 25 years old and over.

Table D. Cities — Income and Housing

City	Money income, 2017 Median income	Households Percent with income less than $20,000	Percent with income of $200,000 or more	Median family income	Median non-family income	Median earnings, 2017 All persons	Men	Women	Housing units, 2017 Total	Occupied	Percent owner occupied	Median value[1] (dollars)	Median gross rent (dollars)
	42	43	44	45	46	47	48	49	50	51	52	53	54
NEW YORK— Cont'd													
Yonkers........................	59,846	16.4	7.9	69,909	41,303	36,078	41,874	30,013	80,434	75,981	44.1	429,300	1,384
NORTH CAROLINA............	52,752	17.3	4.9	65,964	31,627	31,347	36,026	27,127	4,622,656	3,955,069	65.4	171,200	861
Apex............................	112,676	6.4	15.3	133,033	66,935	56,727	77,174	40,481	18,913	18,089	75.7	331,200	1,204
Asheboro......................	32,466	32.6	0.3	40,854	20,774	21,813	26,006	18,838	12,034	11,486	38.5	130,800	668
Asheville......................	50,184	16.6	6.1	80,505	35,943	31,284	32,418	29,917	47,697	42,045	51.8	267,000	1,088
Burlington....................	40,050	21.1	2.9	53,101	22,846	26,984	28,373	25,873	25,223	22,507	48.4	135,900	783
Cary............................	99,209	4.5	14.9	120,216	58,730	54,170	71,170	41,748	65,006	62,831	69.9	356,800	1,204
Chapel Hill...................	64,759	13.1	15.7	137,724	37,921	22,706	26,184	14,866	20,755	19,303	44.9	412,800	1,183
Charlotte.....................	61,350	12.9	8.2	75,564	45,114	36,267	40,768	32,136	359,326	331,822	53.2	215,500	1,088
Concord.......................	67,844	9.2	7.0	83,718	36,905	37,283	40,045	36,215	34,824	33,305	69.5	212,300	903
Durham........................	56,375	13.9	6.4	80,254	40,386	36,968	40,659	34,870	118,995	110,017	47.8	230,100	1,014
Fayetteville..................	42,629	22.6	1.5	52,478	29,411	24,873	26,433	21,982	96,784	83,558	44.2	132,400	883
Garner.........................	62,274	7.8	2.8	72,500	42,153	34,924	37,464	30,473	10,960	10,323	72.5	184,100	1,087
Gastonia......................	46,688	25.7	2.3	65,289	24,946	28,018	31,968	26,075	33,143	30,097	52.3	149,600	831
Goldsboro.....................	35,679	29.8	3.5	45,569	29,253	17,626	24,711	13,766	16,559	14,329	41.9	129,500	728
Greensboro...................	47,043	19.1	4.1	60,993	34,484	29,366	32,332	26,340	130,620	115,802	50.3	157,000	826
Greenville....................	39,423	29.6	3.5	61,924	27,637	22,473	30,332	18,512	41,920	36,029	35.2	156,700	818
Hickory.......................	49,301	20.1	5.3	67,546	22,045	25,934	27,494	21,535	18,863	16,527	57.3	164,400	654
High Point	49,860	16.9	2.8	61,030	29,817	29,748	31,329	26,007	45,823	40,437	57.0	144,600	840
Huntersville..................	101,188	4.6	15.4	114,170	60,404	60,979	75,270	45,135	21,006	20,073	76.2	307,800	1,395
Indian Trail	83,395	5.9	8.7	90,256	41,819	40,264	45,618	30,446	11,858	11,667	88.3	218,900	1,665
Jacksonville..................	43,839	16.3	2.7	46,662	36,267	23,289	23,684	21,292	22,461	19,630	30.2	149,000	1,011
Kannapolis....................	49,710	15.2	2.7	56,210	26,511	26,444	31,757	24,018	20,435	18,838	60.3	135,800	746
Matthews.....................	81,009	9.4	8.2	93,838	46,812	38,430	44,126	32,330	11,132	10,700	68.8	255,900	1,305
Monroe........................	56,562	15.7	0.8	67,032	36,702	27,015	36,391	21,966	12,595	11,487	60.1	146,200	981
Mooresville...................	66,176	12.0	4.2	71,569	35,083	36,594	44,189	31,765	14,755	13,833	65.2	232,700	1,049
New Bern	38,739	22.1	1.5	53,264	21,459	25,513	30,872	20,629	15,297	12,906	48.9	152,300	766
Raleigh........................	64,660	9.7	6.6	82,597	47,727	37,442	41,606	34,855	203,936	183,672	53.4	239,700	1,082
Rocky Mount.................	42,643	29.0	2.6	51,941	20,319	30,108	27,112	31,103	28,170	22,650	48.0	108,300	879
Salisbury......................	37,034	29.6	2.3	50,228	21,126	25,933	28,518	19,994	14,575	12,577	50.4	138,700	750
Sanford.......................	52,143	14.5	1.7	57,833	36,266	29,233	31,468	26,103	11,483	10,467	55.4	156,500	745
Thomasville..................	41,346	19.6	0.3	49,565	24,585	27,095	30,163	25,484	12,401	11,056	54.0	117,500	658
Wake Forest.................	88,159	3.3	7.5	104,687	54,313	47,454	65,956	36,563	15,233	14,617	71.1	293,100	1,122
Wilmington...................	46,079	24.8	6.6	70,450	31,637	30,746	35,250	22,491	59,338	51,862	46.7	249,400	902
Wilson.........................	47,440	18.5	0.7	61,098	29,030	28,936	30,875	27,090	22,506	20,191	53.2	141,200	768
Winston-Salem..............	44,146	22.9	4.7	57,733	29,254	29,269	33,384	25,885	108,432	94,344	53.3	146,300	774
NORTH DAKOTA.................	61,843	14.3	5.2	81,869	35,233	35,999	41,686	30,726	374,591	316,306	63.4	194,700	785
Bismarck......................	62,755	14.7	2.9	81,075	31,395	38,675	44,463	32,222	34,542	31,597	63.0	247,400	852
Fargo..........................	59,542	16.2	4.9	76,132	36,313	31,331	32,258	30,760	59,891	54,351	46.6	213,300	785
Grand Forks..................	40,982	26.6	3.4	82,834	30,807	28,932	32,464	24,154	26,901	25,130	40.8	201,900	739
Minot..........................	61,823	10.0	3.5	85,570	36,092	32,319	36,754	25,351	23,741	19,319	58.7	202,400	794
West Fargo	90,753	4.7	16.7	104,269	51,771	45,416	50,869	39,933	14,726	14,493	74.7	244,900	870
OHIO............................	54,021	16.9	4.3	69,632	32,007	31,982	39,819	26,728	5,201,701	4,667,192	65.8	144,200	772
Akron..........................	36,816	27.7	1.9	45,541	25,906	23,812	28,684	20,276	94,758	84,331	51.4	81,600	731
Barberton	39,711	21.3	0.8	60,366	21,803	30,333	37,604	24,620	11,891	11,015	60.0	83,700	701
Beavercreek..................	96,200	5.7	7.6	103,093	52,108	51,466	61,780	41,810	19,485	18,791	73.7	189,300	1,193
Bowling Green	36,214	26.2	1.4	56,733	21,420	10,809	13,192	8,445	12,763	11,858	34.3	168,100	708
Brunswick.....................	67,352	8.8	2.3	79,275	31,646	32,462	40,708	30,199	14,266	13,026	75.0	171,600	833
Canton	30,046	34.9	0.7	37,394	21,538	20,206	25,778	16,785	34,954	30,708	44.5	74,200	676
Cincinnati	38,938	27.7	3.8	55,434	30,112	28,547	31,401	25,511	164,944	140,911	37.0	143,100	697
Cleveland	28,974	37.4	1.2	35,053	21,257	25,057	27,862	22,328	212,726	171,717	40.4	70,200	704
Cleveland Heights..............	53,587	22.0	6.4	75,844	31,953	32,186	32,178	32,189	21,890	19,090	52.4	131,600	931
Columbus.....................	51,708	17.6	2.4	61,094	40,191	31,401	34,334	29,253	391,716	355,414	44.7	151,400	917
Cuyahoga Falls	53,972	13.6	1.6	72,481	36,870	36,990	44,649	29,317	24,506	22,879	61.4	122,800	798
Dayton........................	30,643	34.3	0.7	39,599	20,860	19,329	20,518	17,771	74,369	57,649	43.8	63,900	679
Delaware......................	70,641	12.9	4.3	95,894	38,299	36,923	50,307	29,791	15,949	14,076	66.4	178,000	865
Dublin.........................	128,034	3.6	24.3	146,586	68,625	65,586	90,656	45,921	15,820	15,146	79.3	367,100	1,320
Elyria..........................	38,538	25.0	1.9	52,292	26,536	27,083	31,769	23,412	27,081	24,481	61.6	99,200	695
Euclid..........................	36,950	29.3	1.0	47,073	22,307	27,264	29,053	26,953	26,400	23,555	45.0	83,300	766
Fairborn.......................	56,716	17.0	0.3	61,271	34,827	23,234	29,992	21,784	14,994	13,264	43.5	115,500	778
Fairfield.......................	57,237	11.7	3.2	74,444	40,696	37,123	44,426	30,132	18,843	17,707	65.4	152,700	868
Findlay........................	45,405	15.6	3.8	57,783	30,377	30,985	36,095	25,382	19,576	17,966	60.9	118,600	708
Gahanna	81,661	9.1	6.2	95,553	47,303	40,836	53,056	32,189	13,425	13,425	72.0	206,200	1,056
Garfield Heights.............	40,056	19.3	0.5	46,250	31,007	29,017	31,774	24,805	12,960	11,433	63.3	67,400	936
Green..........................	76,903	12.7	4.3	89,236	28,630	37,739	46,128	31,094	10,989	10,562	77.2	195,400	754
Grove City....................	82,195	6.3	5.8	87,620	53,164	47,255	51,058	42,076	17,368	16,362	75.6	189,400	1,010

1. Based on population estimated by the American Community Survey.   2. Includes units rented or sold but not occupied.   3. Specified owner-occupied units; $1,000,000 represents $1,000,000 or more.   4. 50.0 represents 50 percent or more.   5. 10.0 represents 10 percent or less.

City	Commuting[1], 2017		Computer access[2], 2017		Migration, 2017		Civilian labor force, 2018				Civilian employment[4], 2017			
	Percent		Percent						Unemployment		Population age 16 and older		Population age 16 to 64	
	Commuting	With commutes of 30 minutes or more	With a computer in the house	With Internet access	Percent who lived in the same house one year ago	Percent who lived in another state or county one year ago	Total	Percent change 2017 -2018	Total	Rate[3]	Number	Percent in labor force	Number	Percent who worked full-year full-time
	55	56	57	58	59	60	61	62	63	64	65	66	67	68
NEW YORK— Cont'd														
Yonkers	52.1	50.5	89.3	80.4	89.2	4.7	95,784	0.8	4,388	4.6	162,327	64.0	127,800	50.9
NORTH CAROLINA	81.1	33.6	89.4	81.2	85.1	7.2	4,981,834	0.9	194,514	3.9	8,248,651	62.4	6,618,653	51.2
Apex	83.7	37.6	97.8	92.8	83.6	7.2	27,523	2.0	819	3.0	37,797	75.3	33,796	64.8
Asheboro	NA	31.1	89.7	77.1	84.1	3.5	10,991	-0.3	444	4.0	20,157	57.9	15,926	47.1
Asheville	73.7	14.0	89.0	83.0	83.4	7.3	51,224	2.0	1,541	3.0	77,600	67.1	59,315	54.8
Burlington	88.1	18.7	87.3	74.5	82.4	7.7	25,883	0.8	1,002	3.9	43,838	60.7	33,732	50.6
Cary	78.9	26.9	98.3	95.1	84.2	9.4	93,021	1.9	2,830	3.0	129,314	69.8	107,988	58.3
Chapel Hill	57.8	21.0	97.0	86.1	59.8	25.6	30,230	1.2	1,150	3.8	49,464	58.9	42,800	35.8
Charlotte	76.3	35.2	94.0	87.4	82.3	6.5	486,874	1.8	18,330	3.8	681,901	71.5	593,843	56.7
Concord	78.4	44.9	91.4	85.8	81.6	6.0	47,825	1.8	1,743	3.6	70,092	70.6	59,038	56.4
Durham	78.7	26.9	91.7	85.4	78.4	10.5	145,646	1.4	5,102	3.5	216,119	68.1	183,771	55.9
Fayetteville	76.6	19.1	90.5	85.4	75.9	13.5	76,964	0.1	4,274	5.6	166,952	66.4	141,309	52.9
Garner	85.7	40.4	97.2	92.7	82.0	13.0	16,350	2.1	555	3.4	22,248	65.2	19,091	47.7
Gastonia	82.4	39.9	85.0	76.9	83.3	7.5	36,922	1.7	1,567	4.2	61,223	63.7	48,424	50.4
Goldsboro	77.4	24.7	83.7	79.6	77.1	8.5	12,009	-1.5	699	5.8	28,622	57.7	22,590	39.7
Greensboro	81.4	23.2	85.4	69.3	82.3	7.3	144,679	-0.1	6,178	4.3	237,710	64.6	197,613	47.4
Greenville	83.1	26.1	92.8	85.0	66.9	16.6	47,927	0.6	2,135	4.5	75,595	63.1	65,721	40.1
Hickory	81.8	19.4	89.0	83.0	85.6	8.2	20,388	0.1	740	3.6	32,679	67.4	25,642	56.7
High Point	81.2	26.2	92.6	86.5	80.6	8.0	53,776	-0.3	2,331	4.3	87,961	64.5	70,418	48.3
Huntersville	77.4	47.8	97.5	95.0	87.8	8.5	33,476	1.9	1,032	3.1	41,089	68.4	35,500	60.0
Indian Trail	84.6	60.1	97.8	93.6	80.8	14.1	20,897	1.7	686	3.3	28,187	70.6	24,495	59.7
Jacksonville	58.1	12.8	94.1	88.3	61.6	28.5	19,713	-0.6	1,129	5.7	56,902	79.3	52,335	65.4
Kannapolis	82.5	38.7	93.4	84.7	86.7	7.4	23,327	1.8	932	4.0	39,713	68.6	31,362	53.3
Matthews	87.2	39.8	95.4	92.7	85.0	9.7	17,923	1.8	585	3.3	23,912	65.1	18,691	54.7
Monroe	84.0	39.6	93.4	89.2	82.8	6.3	17,263	1.6	673	3.9	27,031	66.1	22,961	51.6
Mooresville	83.1	30.5	96.6	89.1	81.2	10.2	20,480	1.8	779	3.8	28,411	66.7	22,932	54.0
New Bern	82.0	24.2	88.4	74.3	85.9	7.4	12,408	-0.6	533	4.3	23,404	64.0	17,884	51.9
Raleigh	78.7	33.2	96.0	92.2	80.7	7.2	256,041	1.8	9,099	3.6	376,170	71.5	329,039	56.9
Rocky Mount	82.3	23.3	85.4	71.9	78.6	10.7	23,115	-1.2	1,566	6.8	46,171	58.2	36,782	49.5
Salisbury	73.3	27.7	84.6	73.0	84.1	7.9	13,820	1.3	649	4.7	26,707	54.1	19,872	42.8
Sanford	77.2	38.1	85.9	76.7	90.8	5.9	12,428	-0.5	584	4.7	22,521	69.6	19,735	54.1
Thomasville	NA	28.8	84.7	75.1	79.5	10.9	12,103	0.3	503	4.2	20,853	66.7	16,990	49.7
Wake Forest	80.9	51.9	NA	NA	83.4	8.3	22,060	2.0	728	3.3	30,753	68.0	25,687	53.3
Wilmington	80.1	13.5	92.9	78.2	79.6	10.3	62,993	1.3	2,474	3.9	100,255	64.3	80,995	49.9
Wilson	90.6	27.7	85.9	76.2	82.6	4.3	20,687	-2.1	1,455	7.0	38,387	61.2	30,486	49.9
Winston-Salem	84.0	23.7	90.1	81.0	86.1	6.0	117,808	0.7	4,824	4.1	196,588	59.5	161,885	47.8
NORTH DAKOTA	81.6	13.1	90.5	80.5	81.8	9.7	404,299	-1.5	10,544	2.6	599,020	71.2	486,351	58.1
Bismarck	88.6	6.9	89.9	82.1	80.4	7.2	37,618	-2.3	1,002	2.7	57,762	68.7	46,332	60.8
Fargo	82.2	5.6	93.8	85.4	74.3	10.7	69,238	-0.9	1,603	2.3	100,390	79.0	86,918	56.9
Grand Forks	77.6	9.3	89.6	75.5	70.6	17.7	31,620	-2.6	684	2.2	45,890	72.6	39,364	47.6
Minot	80.3	10.8	93.1	86.7	79.0	9.1	23,321	-1.5	642	2.8	38,048	74.2	31,883	55.2
West Fargo	84.1	6.9	95.3	91.5	84.0	5.5	21,041	-0.9	449	2.1	27,713	83.7	24,641	68.1
OHIO	83.3	30.8	89.6	82.7	85.3	5.6	5,754,931	-0.3	263,346	4.6	9,366,669	62.9	7,427,053	50.8
Akron	79.7	24.0	85.9	79.0	84.2	5.0	90,513	-0.9	4,809	5.3	160,761	62.4	131,401	44.5
Barberton	75.7	19.2	79.8	74.1	86.2	2.7	12,522	-1.1	650	5.2	20,588	64.8	15,825	55.0
Beavercreek	87.0	11.8	94.2	91.5	85.8	10.4	23,439	-0.3	833	3.6	37,088	63.9	30,968	55.4
Bowling Green	69.1	17.5	93.9	86.2	49.8	20.5	16,931	-0.3	716	4.2	28,966	73.5	25,821	29.0
Brunswick	87.9	39.4	92.5	87.2	90.8	4.0	20,074	-0.2	830	4.1	27,727	68.1	22,373	57.1
Canton	77.0	24.8	86.9	79.5	76.4	3.2	31,448	-0.5	1,834	5.8	56,534	60.8	47,275	40.7
Cincinnati	71.4	28.2	88.6	80.0	75.2	8.1	145,761	0.5	6,569	4.5	242,324	67.3	203,031	49.3
Cleveland	70.8	27.7	81.8	68.9	80.0	4.5	159,277	-0.4	10,412	6.5	307,229	59.2	254,296	40.6
Cleveland Heights	76.9	29.7	92.0	81.3	86.5	4.4	22,835	-0.2	1,043	4.6	36,909	61.1	29,334	46.6
Columbus	80.1	25.3	93.2	87.2	78.1	6.8	467,144	0.6	18,070	3.9	701,068	69.8	611,234	52.0
Cuyahoga Falls	91.6	24.5	91.2	84.6	87.9	5.5	26,430	-0.7	1,165	4.4	40,629	71.3	32,305	57.7
Dayton	74.5	21.3	84.8	76.9	71.5	9.4	58,333	-0.4	3,147	5.4	114,501	56.3	97,637	32.4
Delaware	83.8	43.0	94.7	88.3	85.3	5.7	21,133	0.6	762	3.6	29,910	72.2	24,862	62.0
Dublin	83.6	29.6	NA	NA	88.0	6.7	25,876	0.7	857	3.3	34,383	69.0	29,660	52.7
Elyria	86.2	28.1	87.5	75.0	83.4	2.9	27,178	-0.4	1,541	5.7	45,203	60.5	35,577	49.2
Euclid	81.1	34.6	81.6	71.1	86.4	3.2	22,637	-0.5	1,389	6.1	39,910	59.5	31,882	46.0
Fairborn	76.4	25.6	93.1	87.2	77.4	14.8	16,940	-0.1	725	4.3	27,985	68.7	23,277	43.1
Fairfield	91.2	32.1	93.4	88.0	86.5	5.7	24,214	0.3	881	3.6	34,764	67.7	26,805	62.3
Findlay	84.1	14.5	93.1	90.7	79.8	7.6	21,705	-0.6	781	3.6	33,330	67.7	27,398	53.8
Gahanna	91.1	26.5	95.9	91.5	88.8	4.8	20,262	0.5	701	3.5	26,648	70.0	20,903	62.6
Garfield Heights	80.1	27.2	85.2	77.4	NA	NA	13,703	-0.1	848	6.2	22,401	61.5	17,069	49.2
Green	87.5	22.7	93.2	91.4	94.8	0.9	13,779	-0.8	580	4.2	21,917	65.5	16,874	54.7
Grove City	89.6	34.1	96.2	94.8	81.7	5.7	22,203	0.6	808	3.6	31,685	68.8	25,816	59.1

1. Employed persons.   2. Households.   3. Percent of civilian labor force.   4. Persons 16 years old and over.

Table D. Cities — Construction, Wholesale Trade, and Retail Trade

City	Value of residential construction authorized by building permits, 2018			Wholesale trade[1], 2012				Retail trade[2], 2012			
	New construction ($1,000)	Number of housing units	Percent single family	Number of establishments	Number of employees	Sales (mil dol)	Annual payroll (mil dol)	Number of establishments	Number of employees	Sales (mil dol)	Annual payroll (mil dol)
	69	70	71	72	73	74	75	76	77	78	79
NEW YORK— Cont'd											
Yonkers	61,971	609	1.6	161	1,348	852.6	72.2	657	9,473	2,708.5	250.0
NORTH CAROLINA	13,581,958	71,691	71.5	9,713	136,174	105,275.6	7,853.7	34,288	446,373	120,691.0	10,421.2
Apex	370,722	2,241	74.7	44	753	621.3	39.8	131	2,427	657.6	56.1
Asheboro	8,008	102	78.4	33	313	180.7	11.8	196	2,375	556.5	48.5
Asheville	86,211	404	82.7	155	1,477	883.6	71.4	776	11,310	2,822.0	265.2
Burlington	39,336	352	93.2	81	1,025	423.2	40.9	367	5,655	1,236.2	120.3
Cary	282,273	1,562	69.4	144	1,776	2,938.5	134.8	495	9,194	2,877.2	229.4
Chapel Hill	108,705	718	8.9	27	141	176.5	7.7	199	2,833	684.1	72.3
Charlotte	NA	NA	NA	1,540	25,446	19,884.6	1,617.4	2,600	39,240	10,901.0	960.8
Concord	NA	NA	NA	113	1,941	1,285.3	92.3	489	9,070	2,228.3	189.2
Durham	463,290	3,230	58.6	173	5,168	4,131.5	426.0	871	13,896	3,313.6	317.4
Fayetteville	56,001	241	100.0	104	2,032	663.0	79.3	825	12,882	3,625.9	311.0
Garner	65,813	542	46.1	57	1,381	1,135.3	57.4	112	1,911	490.5	42.2
Gastonia	87,300	339	82.9	86	848	328.4	34.2	378	5,774	1,341.6	125.3
Goldsboro	11,439	59	89.8	56	1,306	1,019.9	54.9	311	4,058	1,143.7	90.6
Greensboro	142,866	846	70.6	541	7,993	9,675.9	453.6	1,232	19,426	4,950.9	488.9
Greenville	102,495	714	43.3	70	700	350.5	35.0	421	6,355	1,589.1	141.5
Hickory	NA	NA	NA	129	4,126	3,196.1	196.6	454	6,897	1,934.2	165.6
High Point	42,614	267	100.0	298	4,852	3,737.6	268.8	410	4,792	1,347.0	114.9
Huntersville	NA	NA	NA	66	621	341.0	41.8	161	2,686	782.3	65.0
Indian Trail	NA	NA	NA	84	838	379.9	44.2	91	1,494	468.6	42.2
Jacksonville	3,212	23	82.6	26	109	73.0	4.5	340	5,936	1,691.7	141.4
Kannapolis	NA	NA	NA	25	178	118.1	8.3	158	1,596	398.1	36.6
Matthews	NA	NA	NA	53	549	204.2	31.8	170	3,135	1,099.4	85.6
Monroe	13,968	88	100.0	76	1,328	647.5	58.3	230	3,076	861.7	68.7
Mooresville	NA	NA	NA	81	690	499.8	38.7	226	3,734	1,130.1	84.1
New Bern	28,818	145	100.0	33	D	D	D	248	3,073	834.7	72.9
Raleigh	736,510	4,211	31.0	570	8,627	5,399.8	577.4	1,698	27,148	7,268.5	688.9
Rocky Mount	1,150	10	100.0	74	1,406	1,071.4	63.1	331	4,143	1,014.0	89.4
Salisbury	NA	NA	NA	47	945	612.8	38.8	203	2,948	832.5	70.1
Sanford	13,716	74	100.0	22	D	D	D	192	2,658	706.4	58.3
Thomasville	4,783	32	100.0	30	453	211.9	22.1	128	1,458	354.7	31.5
Wake Forest	151,130	764	99.7	26	139	96.6	7.8	87	1,725	489.2	43.6
Wilmington	NA	NA	NA	139	1,191	570.6	58.3	764	10,389	3,009.5	261.3
Wilson	14,636	128	100.0	76	742	444.0	30.7	263	3,268	899.3	76.9
Winston-Salem	191,648	1,335	93.7	239	3,943	2,266.4	189.6	1,008	15,129	4,067.8	365.3
NORTH DAKOTA	607,898	3,211	59.3	1,430	18,880	28,150.8	1,078.2	3,185	47,186	15,519.8	1,204.4
Bismarck	55,585	292	67.1	115	1,967	1,346.8	106.9	357	6,779	1,948.7	175.8
Fargo	171,790	1,210	25.9	251	5,114	4,124.9	288.3	518	11,065	3,299.9	266.9
Grand Forks	41,679	227	59.9	59	965	697.8	50.3	279	5,654	1,501.8	126.4
Minot	12,283	55	100.0	68	1,285	2,418.1	80.1	250	5,160	1,686.7	149.6
West Fargo	115,430	541	74.3	41	477	194.6	23.5	91	1,133	373.8	27.1
OHIO	5,189,339	24,221	67.4	11,744	182,791	155,426.0	9,627.2	36,531	549,152	153,554.0	13,099.3
Akron	NA	NA	NA	217	2,998	1,695.8	153.6	612	7,731	1,906.6	185.0
Barberton	945	7	100.0	22	523	113.2	17.8	71	780	171.4	15.5
Beavercreek	NA	NA	NA	23	167	327.3	9.5	216	4,600	941.1	87.2
Bowling Green	NA	NA	NA	15	116	109.0	6.5	99	1,599	368.3	34.6
Brunswick	9,218	61	100.0	48	532	238.0	27.5	93	1,759	727.5	48.8
Canton	2,406	22	36.4	89	1,263	770.9	58.2	249	3,432	823.7	73.9
Cincinnati	92,265	730	13.4	358	5,890	6,371.5	337.1	941	13,549	3,977.7	350.4
Cleveland	15,323	148	77.0	577	9,142	5,475.0	465.9	1,206	10,637	2,764.9	244.1
Cleveland Heights	0	0	0.0	8	43	11.8	1.6	97	1,340	294.9	32.8
Columbus	564,422	4,297	12.9	807	17,060	14,346.8	1,005.3	2,566	46,211	13,114.2	1,178.1
Cuyahoga Falls	NA	NA	NA	39	573	243.9	26.5	171	3,313	1,015.8	79.1
Dayton	17,142	174	4.0	158	3,063	12,234.4	182.6	375	3,791	870.1	88.8
Delaware	113,811	623	58.4	14	120	40.6	6.4	118	1,738	539.0	44.8
Dublin	72,455	199	97.0	88	1,426	1,730.1	115.1	118	2,215	997.6	79.5
Elyria	13,364	115	83.5	56	309	150.4	12.6	219	3,567	887.5	79.0
Euclid	0	0	0.0	34	533	206.2	25.9	84	993	235.3	22.0
Fairborn	24,654	96	100.0	11	330	338.2	17.0	78	1,061	300.0	22.6
Fairfield	3,247	17	100.0	72	1,793	1,060.2	92.0	175	3,937	1,355.5	133.3
Findlay	10,726	53	69.8	40	638	483.4	29.8	205	3,287	823.7	72.0
Gahanna	4,535	13	100.0	38	619	358.8	28.4	87	1,378	475.2	39.6
Garfield Heights	0	0	0.0	27	404	152.7	15.1	78	960	211.5	18.5
Green	NA	NA	NA	31	457	465.3	45.9	55	1,490	706.3	46.3
Grove City	39,163	136	100.0	32	869	592.4	38.9	121	3,256	1,130.1	76.0

1. Merchant wholesalers except manufacturers' sales branches and offices. 2. Establishments with payroll.

Table D. Cities — Real Estate, Professional Services, and Manufacturing

City	Real estate and rental and leasing, 2012				Professional, scientific, and technical services[1], 2012				Manufacturing, 2012			
	Number of establishments	Number of employees	Receipts (mil dol)	Annual payroll (mil dol)	Number of establishments	Number of employees	Receipts (mil dol)	Annual payroll (mil dol)	Number of establishments	Number of employees	Receipts (mil dol)	Annual payroll (mil dol)
	80	81	82	83	84	85	86	87	88	89	90	91
NEW YORK— Cont'd												
Yonkers	363	1,099	341.3	42.1	254	D	D	D	88	2,755	984.9	141.4
NORTH CAROLINA	10,140	47,155	9,301.7	1,942.6	22,730	190,441	30,520.8	12,461.5	8,953	403,593	202,344.6	18,191.2
Apex	27	74	12.0	2.8	158	611	83.3	27.8	34	1,042	1,399.5	63.7
Asheboro	38	152	34.8	4.5	76	358	28.0	10.0	63	6,915	3,002.3	245.9
Asheville	244	785	163.3	26.3	575	D	D	D	130	4,595	983.8	224.4
Burlington	66	419	106.4	18.7	107	828	75.6	33.9	92	3,671	855.4	141.8
Cary	218	681	151.2	29.9	903	D	D	D	68	1,693	696.0	79.4
Chapel Hill	88	381	67.0	13.7	293	D	D	D	17	D	7.4	D
Charlotte	1,372	8,759	2,045.6	494.7	3,202	D	D	D	643	21,152	9,376.1	1,164.0
Concord	103	464	88.7	13.4	207	D	D	D	87	4,261	1,352.5	190.7
Durham	275	1,601	337.0	66.8	973	D	D	D	144	7,368	4,773.1	499.7
Fayetteville	264	1,622	314.8	54.9	443	D	D	D	63	2,169	616.0	109.6
Garner	33	128	39.8	4.6	76	558	63.6	21.5	22	684	611.1	39.6
Gastonia	90	546	125.8	21.3	170	D	D	D	104	5,248	1,597.3	223.9
Goldsboro	44	216	23.0	6.0	104	614	61.0	22.9	49	3,089	808.7	137.0
Greensboro	455	3,181	525.0	135.4	936	D	D	D	308	16,855	22,411.9	1,025.3
Greenville	125	546	86.3	17.7	228	D	D	D	35	424	84.9	15.1
Hickory	100	324	88.9	9.9	199	1,198	602.5	54.9	161	5,444	1,261.8	195.0
High Point	115	754	127.8	25.4	273	D	D	D	241	12,901	3,676.7	541.1
Huntersville	62	160	42.1	8.0	183	856	120.2	52.3	25	706	209.7	35.8
Indian Trail	21	55	11.9	2.1	59	174	17.3	6.4	53	830	197.3	35.3
Jacksonville	100	390	73.2	12.0	152	D	D	D	12	D	D	D
Kannapolis	33	142	18.6	4.1	56	D	D	D	28	468	101.5	22.4
Matthews	50	236	32.3	7.5	144	690	89.7	35.9	34	713	296.9	38.6
Monroe	43	135	28.6	5.4	90	422	47.5	18.4	89	6,657	2,763.7	321.8
Mooresville	64	191	45.4	7.3	147	1,618	202.9	72.6	73	2,277	825.9	109.7
New Bern	51	223	29.9	7.0	111	D	D	D	34	2,008	683.6	100.2
Raleigh	735	5,229	1,173.6	305.0	2,185	22,893	4,304.5	1,706.4	267	5,229	1,842.0	270.5
Rocky Mount	77	357	54.8	12.0	125	803	83.1	33.8	43	4,002	940.1	217.5
Salisbury	44	205	18.3	4.3	97	529	64.3	20.7	66	1,904	585.2	84.1
Sanford	38	144	26.2	5.2	66	D	D	D	44	4,754	1,224.1	195.9
Thomasville	24	D	D	D	44	141	15.6	3.5	86	2,096	642.1	79.0
Wake Forest	33	76	17.9	3.2	116	D	D	D	14	111	18.0	6.2
Wilmington	249	1,574	260.9	58.6	652	D	D	D	91	3,247	1,623.2	250.0
Wilson	65	229	41.2	5.8	97	D	D	D	59	6,692	12,784.2	334.9
Winston-Salem	293	1,575	276.0	58.3	672	D	D	D	200	8,322	4,017.0	410.7
NORTH DAKOTA	912	5,157	1,445.1	247.5	1,706	13,633	1,836.9	732.4	745	23,541	14,427.4	1,042.8
Bismarck	122	389	101.5	13.2	274	D	D	D	57	824	D	35.8
Fargo	238	1,613	286.7	62.0	411	D	D	D	126	6,087	2,601.4	278.6
Grand Forks	73	481	83.5	14.3	117	D	D	D	42	2,015	564.1	73.6
Minot	68	D	D	D	119	D	D	D	26	346	110.3	13.9
West Fargo	21	D	D	D	38	D	D	D	42	2,294	791.0	109.1
OHIO	9,932	60,966	16,132.7	2,441.8	23,851	228,728	35,259.4	13,870.3	14,482	627,124	313,630.0	33,135.4
Akron	167	1,062	182.7	40.1	449	D	D	D	269	8,672	3,477.8	461.5
Barberton	6	19	1.9	0.4	27	D	D	D	50	1,938	530.0	97.4
Beavercreek	46	176	56.2	4.8	188	D	D	D	28	D	76.3	D
Bowling Green	38	159	21.8	4.3	49	D	D	D	35	1,906	729.3	87.6
Brunswick	22	92	17.7	2.3	56	390	35.0	12.3	49	969	204.1	45.2
Canton	71	248	39.3	8.2	155	D	D	D	136	8,020	6,885.8	429.7
Cincinnati	405	2,489	609.1	120.1	1,118	19,286	3,946.0	1,410.5	363	12,881	7,058.1	760.4
Cleveland	349	3,895	816.6	177.7	1,159	17,004	3,382.2	1,318.3	805	22,075	7,794.7	1,192.0
Cleveland Heights	50	166	27.9	4.4	104	D	D	D	8	46	6.3	1.5
Columbus	904	6,933	1,893.8	317.8	2,055	D	D	D	518	19,881	9,829.7	1,036.6
Cuyahoga Falls	42	197	26.6	5.6	108	867	73.7	33.2	76	2,565	857.7	128.3
Dayton	136	713	118.0	24.4	306	D	D	D	266	9,794	2,940.7	467.6
Delaware	36	117	25.0	5.8	54	355	48.7	14.7	38	2,755	2,055.5	169.2
Dublin	75	673	434.5	29.4	369	3,381	496.2	250.6	33	1,051	404.2	58.3
Elyria	48	223	34.8	7.1	79	D	D	D	100	4,869	1,604.5	260.5
Euclid	49	355	51.3	9.7	42	361	39.4	16.1	75	5,059	1,704.4	368.8
Fairborn	35	161	23.0	4.0	76	D	D	D	12	443	85.9	22.3
Fairfield	50	299	94.5	11.8	82	D	D	D	82	3,088	880.8	140.4
Findlay	50	382	46.4	12.4	108	649	87.7	34.2	56	5,654	2,137.3	287.6
Gahanna	40	159	35.3	6.3	143	973	120.1	46.4	27	754	235.0	32.9
Garfield Heights	20	69	10.8	2.8	48	360	46.8	20.8	18	838	186.7	40.7
Green	22	176	38.5	6.0	77	958	102.9	39.9	37	1,479	458.4	66.2
Grove City	34	164	36.7	6.5	46	389	52.7	14.4	29	1,545	393.2	70.7

1. Establishments subject to federal tax.

City	Accommodation and food services, 2012				Arts, entertainment, and recreation[1], 2012				Health care and social assistance,[1] 2012			
	Number of establish-ments	Number of employees	Receipts (mil dol)	Annual payroll (mil dol)	Number of establish-ments	Number of employees	Receipts (mil dol)	Annual payroll (mil dol)	Number of establish-ments	Number of employees	Receipts (mil dol)	Annual payroll (mil dol)
	92	93	94	95	96	97	98	99	100	101	102	103
NEW YORK— Cont'd												
Yonkers.................	351	3,484	259.8	65.3	46	1,168	286.4	45.1	403	4,301	453.0	184.7
NORTH CAROLINA.............	19,496	358,602	18,622.3	5,040.6	2,696	37,335	3,805.3	1,167.0	19,152	292,709	27,305.8	11,432.3
Apex....................	90	1,635	79.2	21.5	10	D	D	D	104	D	D	D
Asheboro................	102	1,875	87.1	22.8	8	D	D	D	121	D	D	D
Asheville...............	541	11,795	698.6	201.3	64	1,459	103.0	35.1	530	7,203	898.5	383.9
Burlington..............	188	4,010	175.6	50.4	16	D	D	D	208	3,755	374.2	204.6
Cary....................	372	7,249	386.6	114.4	56	956	57.7	17.6	471	4,842	566.0	221.9
Chapel Hill.............	220	4,078	221.9	63.0	29	97	12.9	4.1	209	D	D	D
Charlotte...............	1,888	40,752	2,413.6	659.0	231	5,691	619.8	322.6	1,739	25,574	3,149.2	1,263.4
Concord.................	233	6,309	337.1	89.4	46	2,034	599.3	132.0	197	3,012	361.3	155.4
Durham..................	645	12,968	767.1	209.7	64	731	58.8	11.4	604	8,801	935.0	342.0
Fayetteville............	480	10,965	516.5	143.3	42	D	D	D	597	9,245	705.4	309.7
Garner..................	66	1,528	68.1	18.8	4	D	D	D	83	934	84.4	31.8
Gastonia................	191	3,998	199.4	51.2	20	224	11.9	2.6	270	D	D	D
Goldsboro...............	144	2,625	129.6	33.4	13	128	5.8	1.4	156	2,442	232.0	104.5
Greensboro..............	789	16,835	856.6	237.3	72	1,183	77.5	21.7	723	12,951	1,352.5	583.9
Greenville..............	288	6,910	313.5	85.4	23	D	D	D	332	D	D	D
Hickory.................	219	4,748	210.4	59.9	12	130	7.0	2.3	237	D	D	D
High Point..............	229	D	D	D	20	234	18.3	2.9	235	4,742	580.3	213.0
Huntersville............	99	2,246	118.5	33.8	28	703	130.4	49.4	145	D	D	D
Indian Trail............	55	887	41.7	10.8	11	114	7.9	1.7	43	337	33.1	11.5
Jacksonville............	219	4,593	257.1	60.9	15	203	9.4	2.8	179	D	D	D
Kannapolis..............	74	D	D	D	10	D	D	D	48	934	81.5	36.3
Matthews................	104	2,147	103.8	28.4	22	250	19.1	4.6	129	D	D	D
Monroe..................	105	1,927	91.2	24.5	8	D	D	D	116	D	D	D
Mooresville.............	159	2,948	149.8	40.0	44	D	D	D	147	2,454	339.9	123.9
New Bern................	123	2,528	108.2	30.7	15	213	8.3	2.6	147	D	D	D
Raleigh.................	1,145	24,150	1,237.1	348.9	135	4,102	350.3	97.6	1,291	18,328	1,959.5	866.1
Rocky Mount.............	146	3,442	150.4	41.8	20	D	D	D	192	3,250	310.3	125.0
Salisbury...............	138	2,714	123.3	34.0	13	85	5.4	1.7	157	D	D	D
Sanford.................	92	1,665	77.3	20.9	6	D	D	D	123	2,042	213.9	78.1
Thomasville.............	72	D	D	D	7	D	D	D	35	745	46.6	21.9
Wake Forest.............	57	1,050	47.5	14.0	17	195	9.0	2.3	93	1,027	78.7	31.8
Wilmington..............	440	9,326	440.1	124.0	48	544	29.8	8.0	547	8,125	895.9	369.0
Wilson..................	124	2,521	133.0	32.7	11	D	D	D	151	D	D	D
Winston-Salem...........	539	11,157	564.9	159.4	56	548	32.9	8.9	510	9,646	868.9	430.6
NORTH DAKOTA.............	1,935	35,698	2,045.1	521.3	259	2,153	145.3	34.2	1,235	15,038	1,809.1	775.9
Bismarck................	162	4,873	236.6	69.4	23	D	D	D	196	D	D	D
Fargo...................	316	8,386	389.1	114.6	52	662	51.3	10.4	284	5,329	931.1	386.1
Grand Forks.............	174	4,076	173.4	51.4	24	D	D	D	97	D	D	D
Minot...................	150	3,741	203.9	56.9	19	D	D	D	102	D	D	D
West Fargo..............	38	D	D	D	6	D	D	D	39	D	D	D
OHIO....................	23,432	437,293	20,652.8	5,742.7	2,869	36,390	3,903.5	1,464.8	22,945	393,909	34,637.9	15,470.9
Akron...................	407	5,634	257.4	69.3	31	310	42.4	9.4	351	7,424	853.5	418.3
Barberton...............	46	D	D	D	3	D	D	D	75	2,196	237.1	87.3
Beavercreek.............	105	2,738	140.8	37.8	4	D	D	D	121	D	D	D
Bowling Green...........	117	2,586	89.2	23.7	10	D	D	D	75	D	D	D
Brunswick...............	63	1,072	50.8	13.5	9	D	D	D	51	762	51.6	27.8
Canton..................	170	2,652	119.8	31.6	14	123	7.4	1.6	154	3,277	373.8	185.5
Cincinnati..............	738	15,321	858.6	247.4	82	1,803	462.6	323.2	652	15,018	2,070.9	917.9
Cleveland...............	980	16,885	950.9	254.3	63	2,425	509.8	290.4	402	7,946	537.2	237.2
Cleveland Heights.......	80	1,005	55.6	16.3	9	51	2.1	0.6	85	1,247	77.8	38.2
Columbus................	1,959	42,063	2,259.0	637.6	152	3,969	354.9	122.1	1,620	31,398	3,077.4	1,331.6
Cuyahoga Falls..........	119	2,339	111.2	32.1	9	D	D	D	130	2,582	252.4	100.3
Dayton..................	276	4,570	206.8	57.9	17	210	23.6	5.6	285	5,572	659.7	342.5
Delaware................	87	1,313	62.5	17.1	8	D	D	D	92	1,626	86.5	40.9
Dublin..................	123	3,294	167.6	52.9	27	D	D	D	195	D	D	D
Elyria..................	118	2,230	96.8	26.9	8	74	2.5	1.0	115	D	D	D
Euclid..................	71	D	D	D	7	D	D	D	98	2,556	121.2	62.9
Fairborn................	74	1,535	71.9	20.2	7	D	D	D	39	D	D	D
Fairfield...............	104	1,990	100.4	25.7	9	D	D	D	136	D	D	D
Findlay.................	147	3,530	146.5	42.1	8	51	1.6	0.4	125	D	D	D
Gahanna.................	104	1,861	89.4	24.3	12	D	D	D	140	2,473	261.4	110.1
Garfield Heights........	46	654	29.6	7.2	4	10	0.8	0.2	62	614	63.7	33.4
Green...................	54	949	45.3	12.2	10	106	6.9	2.1	67	D	D	D
Grove City..............	110	2,387	130.7	34.8	14	D	D	D	94	1,147	128.8	47.1

1. Establishments subject to federal tax.

Table D. Cities — Other Services and Government Employment and Payroll

City	Other services[1]				Government employment and payroll, 2012								
					Full-time equivalent employees	Total (dollars)	March payroll — Percent of total for:						
	Number of establishments	Number of employees	Receipts (mil dol)	Annual payroll (mil dol)			Administrative, judicial, and legal	Police and corrections	Fire protection	Highways and transportation	Health and welfare	Natural resources and utilities	Education and libraries
	104	105	106	107	108	109	110	111	112	113	114	115	116
NEW YORK— Cont'd													
Yonkers	305	1,248	129.1	34.1	5,538	39,341,604	3.2	17.5	10.4	1.0	2.7	6.0	58.2
NORTH CAROLINA	11,506	64,643	5,548.4	1,664.9	X	X	X	X	X	X	X	X	X
Apex	64	436	30.8	10.3	344	1,509,120	15.4	23.1	14.9	7.4	4.6	28.3	0.0
Asheboro	43	265	27.2	7.5	349	1,396,592	5.9	23.8	15.1	5.8	2.2	22.5	0.0
Asheville	214	1,148	87.1	27.3	1,057	3,889,185	9.1	23.7	24.5	5.3	3.3	19.0	0.0
Burlington	86	514	39.3	11.9	628	2,130,883	10.7	32.6	15.8	5.7	0.1	29.4	0.0
Cary	196	1,880	141.3	54.1	1,135	5,112,012	14.8	23.3	19.4	15.6	0.0	21.6	0.0
Chapel Hill	59	545	34.2	13.1	840	3,017,788	12.7	26.8	15.1	19.0	2.7	8.1	3.9
Charlotte	1,161	9,188	865.2	265.7	7,449	34,348,745	9.7	36.0	16.2	12.9	2.2	17.0	0.0
Concord	134	672	60.1	15.6	923	3,576,064	7.2	20.8	21.3	7.1	4.4	23.7	0.0
Durham	306	2,624	221.3	72.2	1,086	4,030,398	25.2	0.0	0.0	16.5	6.6	47.8	0.0
Fayetteville	256	1,445	107.3	33.2	1,960	7,748,728	4.9	24.8	14.8	6.6	0.8	30.0	0.0
Garner	52	338	30.0	8.8	177	821,893	16.4	47.7	0.0	3.4	1.0	15.0	0.0
Gastonia	122	742	51.1	16.1	935	3,494,489	15.2	23.5	14.9	10.2	1.1	28.7	0.0
Goldsboro	73	484	38.1	11.4	449	1,502,437	12.1	25.9	19.1	3.7	0.8	27.4	0.0
Greensboro	413	2,580	239.4	71.4	3,098	11,503,988	8.8	28.2	17.9	6.9	2.9	20.8	2.5
Greenville	103	692	52.0	14.4	1,347	5,208,426	6.5	18.6	12.5	6.2	2.4	34.6	0.0
Hickory	105	824	63.2	18.2	636	2,107,555	11.1	23.4	23.3	9.5	0.2	23.5	3.6
High Point	150	1,094	111.3	31.0	1,446	5,797,223	10.4	32.4	13.1	5.0	2.2	31.9	3.2
Huntersville	71	360	27.5	8.2	161	688,375	25.1	57.8	0.0	7.5	0.0	9.6	0.0
Indian Trail	60	283	24.5	6.8	48	144,392	56.2	0.0	0.0	9.0	0.0	9.0	0.0
Jacksonville	109	795	48.3	16.8	542	2,172,480	13.1	25.3	14.1	6.1	0.2	19.4	0.0
Kannapolis	48	D	D	D	289	1,109,005	13.6	30.3	23.4	4.8	0.0	27.8	0.0
Matthews	66	310	21.4	6.9	163	577,637	14.5	49.3	6.0	9.7	1.3	6.1	0.0
Monroe	82	392	37.1	11.2	511	1,971,029	15.1	20.8	15.3	6.0	0.0	37.8	0.0
Mooresville	81	506	50.3	12.2	760	1,406,044	10.4	25.8	21.5	3.5	0.0	23.4	4.8
New Bern	54	280	22.6	6.9	449	1,701,922	12.5	25.9	16.3	4.6	1.3	33.6	0.0
Raleigh	712	5,192	401.9	131.8	3,936	15,850,858	10.6	25.2	16.4	6.4	0.7	28.5	0.0
Rocky Mount	89	D	D	D	1,002	3,610,762	13.3	21.6	15.9	8.8	1.5	39.0	0.0
Salisbury	41	338	22.5	8.0	458	1,569,483	17.2	19.6	16.0	10.0	0.7	25.8	0.0
Sanford	52	284	18.9	6.3	345	1,295,948	13.5	31.2	15.8	6.0	2.5	21.9	0.0
Thomasville	45	207	22.4	5.7	377	1,184,674	5.8	27.3	23.1	5.5	0.0	20.8	0.0
Wake Forest	46	310	31.0	9.2	200	792,417	16.8	36.0	0.0	10.9	6.1	19.0	0.0
Wilmington	240	1,326	102.4	32.2	949	3,706,301	13.1	34.8	22.0	7.7	2.3	17.8	0.0
Wilson	74	D	D	D	776	2,938,961	12.7	19.6	12.6	8.5	5.3	36.1	0.0
Winston-Salem	276	1,682	131.3	43.3	2,489	8,460,457	12.1	31.4	15.9	7.1	5.7	23.1	0.0
NORTH DAKOTA	1,296	6,652	721.6	189.3	X	X	X	X	X	X	X	X	X
Bismarck	138	D	D	D	605	2,280,206	9.2	23.4	16.3	8.9	10.4	15.3	4.2
Fargo	226	1,642	138.6	44.9	836	3,889,052	10.7	22.5	14.1	18.2	12.7	15.1	3.8
Grand Forks	99	642	52.1	15.8	549	2,249,631	11.5	21.4	13.7	14.6	8.9	22.9	0.0
Minot	84	521	48.4	14.6	348	1,359,688	12.5	26.4	15.9	13.9	0.0	20.0	3.8
West Fargo	52	313	35.3	9.8	120	521,710	16.1	47.5	0.0	0.0	0.0	30.4	6.0
OHIO	15,038	99,624	8,638.0	2,607.8	X	X	X	X	X	X	X	X	X
Akron	272	1,576	104.3	34.7	1,872	8,159,087	15.0	31.5	21.9	4.1	0.5	18.7	0.0
Barberton	36	195	19.1	6.4	256	1,078,359	17.1	23.7	20.5	6.9	9.7	22.1	0.0
Beavercreek	54	443	31.1	9.3	144	794,411	6.5	49.4	0.0	17.6	4.9	14.0	0.0
Bowling Green	40	190	9.6	3.5	302	1,389,538	15.6	20.6	19.6	2.1	0.6	31.6	0.0
Brunswick	59	422	39.6	12.5	156	716,777	14.6	38.7	22.6	9.5	2.3	6.8	0.0
Canton	115	597	54.1	15.3	914	3,932,055	14.5	23.0	20.1	7.9	7.6	22.3	0.0
Cincinnati	415	3,189	264.2	77.6	5,222	26,843,252	9.4	25.7	17.7	5.4	8.4	28.9	0.0
Cleveland	546	3,780	261.7	90.6	7,389	33,318,506	12.7	29.1	13.0	9.9	7.8	25.3	0.0
Cleveland Heights	52	306	27.0	8.7	461	2,098,391	11.2	30.1	23.8	3.9	3.6	16.1	0.0
Columbus	916	8,412	668.6	217.0	8,035	42,573,757	14.7	32.2	23.9	4.3	5.7	16.8	0.0
Cuyahoga Falls	92	522	39.1	12.7	489	2,562,538	13.6	24.8	17.8	10.3	2.3	25.4	0.0
Dayton	176	1,277	133.1	38.3	1,940	9,617,585	13.2	22.8	17.4	11.8	4.6	25.3	0.0
Delaware	33	D	D	D	269	1,371,645	23.1	26.5	19.6	10.0	0.0	17.2	0.0
Dublin	34	D	D	D	836	2,882,615	15.9	35.7	0.0	4.5	15.6	11.3	0.0
Elyria	56	340	58.0	8.9	532	2,415,086	14.1	27.3	15.3	5.3	6.2	26.7	0.0
Euclid	50	149	11.5	3.3	454	1,882,329	12.3	36.1	22.3	4.1	5.6	15.3	0.0
Fairborn	38	187	15.5	4.8	222	557,607	20.8	22.1	26.3	4.5	1.3	11.4	0.0
Fairfield	82	590	60.6	17.0	340	1,631,218	20.0	30.2	17.2	8.1	0.0	22.3	0.0
Findlay	81	587	46.9	15.2	325	1,499,497	13.1	24.6	25.6	9.6	3.8	22.6	0.0
Gahanna	58	676	49.3	18.0	274	1,378,735	13.1	50.2	0.0	7.2	1.6	18.8	0.0
Garfield Heights	32	205	11.2	3.5	204	993,260	15.9	40.2	25.6	1.0	4.0	2.4	0.0
Green	41	531	92.4	27.9	131	615,958	19.2	0.0	49.5	27.4	0.0	2.9	0.0
Grove City	57	1,019	73.6	25.3	169	893,462	12.9	61.0	0.0	6.2	0.0	15.6	0.0

1. Establishments subject to federal tax.

City	General revenue							General expenditure		
		Intergovernmental		Taxes					Per capita[1] (dollars)	
					Per capita[1] (dollars)					
	Total (mil dol)	Total (mil dol)	Percent from state government	Total (mil dol)	Total	Property	Sales and gross receipts	Total (mil dol)	Total	Capital outlays
	117	118	119	120	121	122	123	124	125	126
NEW YORK— Cont'd										
Yonkers........................	973.8	463.3	98.2	426.2	2,146	1,487	460	967.5	4,872	267
NORTH CAROLINA.............	X	X	X	X	X	X	X	X	X	X
Apex........................	41.1	5.4	89.2	23.2	575	413	161	41.1	1,016	152
Asheboro........................	28.8	4.7	94.5	15.9	623	480	143	29.2	1,140	28
Asheville........................	115.3	28.1	51.3	66.5	775	542	233	121.5	1,415	244
Burlington........................	64.2	9.0	59.4	35.6	695	482	213	62.8	1,224	7
Cary	187.2	16.9	75.1	100.1	687	482	205	218.0	1,496	577
Chapel Hill........................	80.0	23.1	43.6	48.5	826	614	212	68.9	1,174	154
Charlotte	1,401.8	250.6	43.7	622.1	803	489	314	1,294.8	1,671	438
Concord........................	109.3	19.4	51.2	56.1	682	525	158	107.7	1,311	79
Durham........................	303.7	47.0	61.0	171.9	717	538	179	302.6	1,262	129
Fayetteville........................	208.3	50.9	51.4	95.2	472	298	174	235.1	1,166	340
Garner........................	26.6	2.9	28.3	20.3	760	553	207	24.8	926	110
Gastonia........................	81.0	9.5	71.1	46.3	636	418	218	85.6	1,176	76
Goldsboro........................	41.9	6.6	92.5	22.8	633	417	216	47.0	1,303	68
Greensboro........................	371.9	60.4	63.7	196.6	711	528	183	412.3	1,492	244
Greenville........................	116.0	31.1	70.0	46.0	525	360	165	107.6	1,228	125
Hickory........................	61.0	10.1	62.0	33.9	844	579	265	60.2	1,500	170
High Point	158.5	22.3	59.1	81.9	768	572	196	167.5	1,571	282
Huntersville........................	34.2	5.5	74.2	22.2	450	329	122	35.6	722	217
Indian Trail	10.0	2.4	32.5	6.4	182	142	41	7.7	220	16
Jacksonville........................	66.3	10.7	56.8	31.8	458	272	186	75.1	1,079	221
Kannapolis........................	41.5	5.6	64.3	25.1	572	425	147	48.1	1,099	338
Matthews........................	20.9	3.5	73.5	14.5	506	361	145	19.8	691	109
Monroe........................	55.3	6.6	75.2	24.8	738	578	160	69.9	2,080	827
Mooresville........................	65.3	6.7	75.3	35.6	1,034	845	189	71.2	2,068	563
New Bern........................	44.8	7.8	87.0	19.3	636	440	196	43.0	1,416	135
Raleigh........................	555.4	92.1	53.9	287.3	679	448	231	527.4	1,245	199
Rocky Mount........................	82.1	24.8	46.4	31.3	549	385	164	81.9	1,437	161
Salisbury........................	55.5	5.3	90.5	21.9	656	510	146	64.5	1,931	175
Sanford	35.2	4.6	61.9	18.2	628	419	210	34.4	1,189	24
Thomasville........................	26.0	4.5	82.6	14.1	525	395	129	26.2	973	39
Wake Forest........................	31.1	3.1	92.3	26.4	802	585	216	34.4	1,042	231
Wilmington	128.8	25.2	52.9	76.2	693	481	212	132.5	1,206	224
Wilson	71.8	10.0	67.7	27.6	557	410	147	70.7	1,427	69
Winston-Salem........................	293.3	50.8	63.3	139.2	594	431	163	303.3	1,294	272
NORTH DAKOTA.................	X	X	X	X	X	X	X	X	X	X
Bismarck........................	128.3	46.0	40.5	37.1	571	261	310	118.8	1,827	623
Fargo........................	237.9	83.4	99.5	72.5	658	188	465	229.3	2,080	749
Grand Forks........................	100.1	20.7	28.9	38.0	709	279	430	59.4	1,106	129
Minot	75.0	19.3	56.5	37.3	849	247	603	44.2	1,005	135
West Fargo	34.8	5.1	100.0	10.6	384	237	147	41.1	1,488	814
OHIO	X	X	X	X	X	X	X	X	X	X
Akron........................	350.3	65.6	64.3	174.5	879	131	9	337.8	1,701	101
Barberton........................	31.7	6.9	86.9	14.0	533	53	31	30.8	1,170	202
Beavercreek........................	25.7	8.8	100.0	12.8	279	249	24	26.8	583	125
Bowling Green	36.0	6.4	100.0	21.2	667	71	53	36.9	1,161	103
Brunswick........................	26.4	4.7	51.4	15.9	463	47	13	22.8	662	108
Canton........................	118.3	36.4	85.3	46.7	642	37	21	113.3	1,558	208
Cincinnati	947.1	392.8	17.6	415.4	1,400	180	74	783.9	2,641	864
Cleveland........................	897.0	231.8	58.8	419.1	1,071	143	124	897.7	2,294	222
Cleveland Heights.................	55.8	10.6	84.0	31.9	699	210	54	57.2	1,254	119
Columbus........................	1,434.3	260.4	47.1	776.6	958	53	57	1,353.3	1,670	431
Cuyahoga Falls.................	65.4	9.3	91.5	31.4	637	219	19	59.4	1,207	245
Dayton........................	304.4	74.9	66.0	118.0	832	117	10	297.8	2,099	314
Delaware........................	45.0	6.0	28.6	20.7	578	47	21	56.6	1,578	458
Dublin........................	103.4	5.5	100.0	74.6	1,739	85	61	90.8	2,117	497
Elyria........................	65.0	18.3	87.1	27.5	508	62	44	62.4	1,153	112
Euclid........................	62.8	10.1	90.8	28.1	581	104	4	73.1	1,514	131
Fairborn........................	38.1	6.6	99.9	16.6	498	73	74	37.4	1,124	168
Fairfield........................	52.2	6.6	100.0	29.3	686	121	80	61.3	1,438	11
Findlay........................	47.4	7.7	100.0	24.9	599	67	8	43.6	1,050	149
Gahanna........................	35.0	5.1	65.6	19.0	562	61	37	38.9	1,150	171
Garfield Heights.................	34.7	4.5	59.7	21.3	748	365	31	32.2	1,130	3
Green........................	27.4	4.6	79.0	20.6	800	59	29	25.0	969	123
Grove City	38.4	8.3	45.2	24.0	651	84	43	33.8	917	213

1. Based on population estimated as of July 1 of the year shown.

City	Public welfare	Highways	Parking facilities	Education	Health and hospitals	Police protection	Sewerage and sanitation	Parks and recreation	Housing and community development	Interest on debt
				City government finances, 2012 (cont.)						
				General expenditure (cont.)						
				Percent of total for:						
	127	128	129	130	131	132	133	134	135	136
NEW YORK— Cont'd										
Yonkers	0.0	0.9	0.5	52.5	0.1	8.5	2.4	1.0	0.9	3.4
NORTH CAROLINA	X	X	X	X	X	X	X	X	X	X
Apex	0.0	9.5	0.0	0.0	2.8	16.4	27.0	10.3	2.5	2.0
Asheboro	0.0	8.3	0.0	0.0	0.1	21.9	25.3	5.2	4.4	0.7
Asheville	0.0	11.4	6.4	0.0	0.1	18.3	8.4	17.4	4.6	1.0
Burlington	0.0	3.6	0.0	0.0	0.0	23.7	18.2	9.5	2.5	2.6
Cary	0.0	5.6	0.0	0.0	0.0	10.3	37.2	10.3	1.6	2.8
Chapel Hill	0.0	7.2	2.8	0.0	0.0	17.7	7.9	9.7	8.4	3.6
Charlotte	0.0	9.3	0.1	0.0	0.0	19.2	21.6	2.2	6.0	10.5
Concord	0.0	5.4	0.0	0.0	0.0	16.5	22.1	5.5	14.1	2.4
Durham	0.0	10.6	0.6	0.0	0.0	20.7	18.7	6.5	7.1	5.9
Fayetteville	0.0	4.9	1.7	0.0	0.0	18.9	35.9	6.3	3.1	2.1
Garner	0.0	19.6	0.0	0.0	0.0	27.7	7.0	11.0	3.5	2.1
Gastonia	0.0	10.5	1.2	0.0	0.0	19.9	26.7	5.9	5.3	3.9
Goldsboro	0.0	9.3	0.0	0.0	0.0	21.0	16.1	5.8	8.1	2.6
Greensboro	0.0	9.9	0.4	0.0	0.1	17.5	24.6	17.5	4.9	2.7
Greenville	0.0	8.9	0.1	0.0	0.0	22.4	22.7	8.4	5.4	2.9
Hickory	0.0	10.0	0.0	0.0	0.1	18.2	21.0	5.9	0.9	0.8
High Point	0.0	8.3	0.2	0.0	0.1	15.8	29.1	8.4	4.3	4.7
Huntersville	0.0	24.6	0.0	0.0	1.1	36.8	1.5	16.6	4.1	3.6
Indian Trail	0.0	12.0	0.0	0.0	0.2	17.8	38.0	0.6	12.1	1.2
Jacksonville	0.0	5.6	0.0	0.0	0.0	20.5	39.6	8.4	2.4	3.8
Kannapolis	0.0	7.6	0.0	0.0	0.0	14.6	9.5	9.7	2.7	4.1
Matthews	0.0	12.0	0.0	0.0	0.0	32.5	9.0	16.0	2.3	1.5
Monroe	0.0	3.6	0.0	0.0	0.1	13.8	9.2	5.7	1.3	0.9
Mooresville	0.0	5.1	0.0	0.0	0.0	9.5	29.1	9.2	9.4	12.4
New Bern	0.0	7.7	0.0	0.0	0.0	30.7	26.9	5.0	4.4	3.1
Raleigh	0.2	6.1	1.7	0.0	0.0	19.1	14.8	23.5	4.8	5.4
Rocky Mount	0.0	9.3	0.0	0.0	0.0	18.5	26.3	9.8	4.8	1.0
Salisbury	0.0	7.1	0.0	0.0	0.0	10.8	24.8	3.7	1.0	4.6
Sanford	0.0	6.4	0.0	0.0	0.2	24.4	26.0	2.5	7.0	4.5
Thomasville	0.0	7.7	0.0	0.0	0.1	20.4	26.1	8.1	3.0	3.4
Wake Forest	0.0	17.8	0.0	0.0	0.0	19.6	7.2	10.3	0.0	2.7
Wilmington	0.0	10.5	2.9	0.0	0.0	20.7	15.0	8.1	1.1	7.7
Wilson	0.6	5.3	0.2	0.0	0.0	18.4	20.5	7.6	5.6	3.2
Winston-Salem	0.0	6.9	0.9	0.0	0.0	21.2	27.1	7.5	5.2	7.0
NORTH DAKOTA	X	X	X	X	X	X	X	X	X	X
Bismarck	0.0	24.2	0.9	0.0	2.1	9.9	17.2	6.8	0.7	2.1
Fargo	4.1	24.0	0.3	0.0	0.0	12.3	6.2	5.9	0.9	7.6
Grand Forks	0.0	6.9	0.6	0.0	2.9	14.2	20.7	2.9	5.6	13.8
Minot	0.0	12.9	0.3	0.0	0.0	16.1	18.8	4.7	0.0	1.5
West Fargo	0.0	39.8	0.0	0.0	0.0	11.7	25.6	0.8	0.0	9.2
OHIO	X	X	X	X	X	X	X	X	X	X
Akron	0.0	2.5	1.8	0.0	1.6	10.0	12.3	1.6	3.3	7.7
Barberton	0.0	7.0	0.0	0.0	0.0	16.3	30.7	3.3	3.5	1.0
Beavercreek	0.0	39.4	0.0	0.0	0.6	27.4	0.0	12.8	2.3	3.6
Bowling Green	0.0	18.5	0.0	0.0	0.2	14.7	20.9	5.0	0.0	3.1
Brunswick	0.0	16.1	0.0	0.0	0.4	28.0	10.3	6.3	1.3	1.4
Canton	0.0	11.9	0.3	0.0	5.6	18.0	15.3	1.7	0.0	0.9
Cincinnati	0.0	7.1	1.4	0.0	3.5	14.5	34.1	4.3	5.1	2.9
Cleveland	1.2	3.1	0.7	0.0	4.6	19.2	6.3	4.4	9.1	9.8
Cleveland Heights	0.0	12.2	1.9	0.0	2.4	15.6	7.3	6.2	7.6	1.5
Columbus	0.0	9.9	0.2	0.0	2.8	18.9	20.2	10.2	2.3	6.4
Cuyahoga Falls	0.0	8.0	0.0	0.0	0.0	15.5	16.0	12.1	2.4	2.6
Dayton	0.8	8.7	0.0	0.0	0.0	14.5	12.3	2.9	7.3	0.8
Delaware	0.0	8.1	0.1	0.0	0.0	10.0	11.3	20.5	0.8	7.8
Dublin	0.0	5.5	0.0	0.0	0.3	11.4	6.9	18.8	0.0	2.5
Elyria	0.0	9.1	0.0	0.0	5.9	20.7	28.4	3.7	2.1	2.2
Euclid	0.0	2.8	0.0	0.0	0.5	15.6	17.9	2.5	1.4	1.9
Fairborn	0.0	14.7	0.0	0.0	0.0	15.7	20.6	0.7	1.8	2.3
Fairfield	0.0	27.4	0.0	0.0	0.0	16.3	11.4	7.3	0.0	2.2
Findlay	0.0	12.0	0.2	0.0	4.9	14.8	17.2	3.5	0.0	3.6
Gahanna	0.0	13.2	0.2	2.8	1.0	22.0	20.7	10.3	0.0	2.6
Garfield Heights	0.8	3.9	0.0	1.6	0.6	19.0	5.9	2.2	0.4	4.5
Green	0.0	27.0	0.0	0.0	3.3	7.4	0.7	5.3	0.0	7.8
Grove City	0.0	24.3	0.0	0.0	0.0	28.2	2.0	7.8	0.0	4.8

Table D. Cities — City Government Finances, City Government Employment, and Climate

City	City government finances, 2012 (cont.) Debt outstanding Total (mil dol)	Per capita[1] (dollars)	Debt issued during year	Climate[2] Average daily temperature Mean January	July	Limits January[3]	July[4]	Annual precipitation (inches)	Heating degree days	Cooling degree days
	137	138	139	140	141	142	143	144	145	146
NEW YORK— Cont'd										
Yonkers	757.7	3,815	113.7	29.7	74.2	20.1	86.0	46.46	5,400	770
NORTH CAROLINA	X	X	X	X	X	X	X	X	X	X
Apex	63.3	1,566	35.0	NA	NA	NA	NA	NA	NA	NA
Asheboro	9.3	363	0.0	NA	NA	NA	NA	NA	NA	NA
Asheville	110.4	1,286	39.2	36.4	73.9	26.6	84.3	37.32	4,237	877
Burlington	62.0	1,208	18.4	38.7	79.3	27.6	90.6	45.08	3,588	1,489
Cary	243.8	1,672	11.3	39.5	78.7	30.1	87.9	46.49	3,431	1,456
Chapel Hill	60.5	1,030	33.5	38.5	79.4	27.8	88.6	48.04	3,650	1,491
Charlotte	3,227.6	4,165	470.5	41.7	80.3	32.1	90.1	43.51	3,162	1,681
Concord	100.3	1,221	19.4	39.4	79.2	27.9	90.3	47.30	3,463	1,540
Durham	398.4	1,661	15.6	39.7	78.8	29.6	89.1	43.05	3,465	1,521
Fayetteville	204.6	1,014	10.6	41.7	80.4	31.1	90.4	46.78	3,097	1,721
Garner	13.9	520	0.0	NA	NA	NA	NA	NA	NA	NA
Gastonia	94.3	1,295	6.0	42.0	79.9	31.7	89.9	49.19	3,009	1,701
Goldsboro	50.9	1,411	14.3	43.4	81.2	33.0	91.4	49.84	2,771	1,922
Greensboro	443.1	1,603	48.7	39.7	78.6	29.0	88.9	42.89	3,443	1,438
Greenville	143.1	1,633	4.3	42.0	78.8	31.9	88.4	49.30	3,113	1,516
Hickory	38.0	947	3.4	39.0	77.7	29.2	87.8	48.98	3,608	1,333
High Point	267.0	2,504	53.4	39.7	78.2	29.6	89.0	46.19	3,399	1,424
Huntersville	41.4	839	24.3	NA	NA	NA	NA	NA	NA	NA
Indian Trail	2.4	69	0.0	NA	NA	NA	NA	NA	NA	NA
Jacksonville	103.2	1,484	51.6	44.7	80.2	33.9	89.5	54.07	2,656	1,832
Kannapolis	67.9	1,550	17.0	39.4	79.2	27.9	90.3	47.30	3,463	1,540
Matthews	6.0	211	0.0	NA	NA	NA	NA	NA	NA	NA
Monroe	59.6	1,773	2.8	41.5	79.0	31.0	89.7	48.73	3,125	1,538
Mooresville	220.0	6,392	65.4	NA	NA	NA	NA	NA	NA	NA
New Bern	76.1	2,504	3.5	NA	NA	NA	NA	NA	NA	NA
Raleigh	1,004.7	2,373	218.5	39.1	79.4	28.1	89.9	45.70	3,514	1,550
Rocky Mount	10.0	175	2.4	41.1	79.2	30.8	89.7	46.51	3,215	1,518
Salisbury	81.1	2,426	8.3	40.2	78.7	29.5	89.5	42.86	3,356	1,466
Sanford	51.3	1,774	0.0	NA	NA	NA	NA	NA	NA	NA
Thomasville	42.9	1,594	11.3	NA	NA	NA	NA	NA	NA	NA
Wake Forest	32.8	993	6.3	NA	NA	NA	NA	NA	NA	NA
Wilmington	205.6	1,872	30.7	44.8	80.1	33.3	90.0	58.44	2,606	1,791
Wilson	113.0	2,279	12.2	40.4	79.2	29.5	90.2	47.18	3,328	1,575
Winston-Salem	727.7	3,105	38.5	39.7	78.2	29.6	89.0	46.19	3,399	1,424
NORTH DAKOTA	X	X	X	X	X	X	X	X	X	X
Bismarck	97.9	1,506	12.3	10.2	70.4	-0.6	84.5	16.84	8,802	471
Fargo	566.3	5,136	79.8	6.8	70.6	-2.3	82.2	21.19	9,092	533
Grand Forks	382.8	7,136	24.1	5.3	69.4	-4.3	81.9	19.60	9,489	420
Minot	41.8	952	7.0	7.5	68.4	-1.8	80.4	18.65	9,479	422
West Fargo	120.7	4,372	17.9	NA	NA	NA	NA	NA	NA	NA
OHIO	X	X	X	X	X	X	X	X	X	X
Akron	794.0	3,998	96.9	27.2	74.1	20.1	83.9	36.07	5,752	856
Barberton	16.6	631	0.0	29.1	73.6	20.3	85.0	39.16	5,348	813
Beavercreek	12.0	260	4.2	27.6	73.1	19.5	83.5	40.06	5,531	768
Bowling Green	24.2	761	3.4	23.1	72.9	15.2	84.2	33.18	6,492	690
Brunswick	11.1	322	0.4	25.7	71.9	18.8	81.4	38.71	6,121	702
Canton	20.1	276	0.0	25.2	71.8	17.4	82.3	38.47	6,154	678
Cincinnati	917.4	3,091	175.8	30.6	76.8	22.7	86.8	39.57	4,841	1,210
Cleveland	2,530.4	6,465	194.4	25.7	71.9	18.8	81.4	38.71	6,121	702
Cleveland Heights	18.6	407	0.0	25.7	71.9	18.8	81.4	38.71	6,121	702
Columbus	2,555.4	3,153	190.4	28.3	74.7	20.2	85.6	40.03	5,349	935
Cuyahoga Falls	55.8	1,133	3.3	29.1	73.6	20.3	85.0	39.16	5,348	813
Dayton	131.3	926	0.2	26.3	74.3	19.0	84.2	39.58	5,690	935
Delaware	89.4	2,492	2.2	25.1	73.0	16.6	84.6	37.58	6,178	739
Dublin	57.2	1,334	0.0	28.3	74.7	20.2	85.6	40.03	5,349	935
Elyria	50.5	934	13.2	27.1	73.8	19.3	85.0	38.02	5,731	818
Euclid	40.5	839	19.4	23.0	68.8	14.3	80.0	47.33	6,956	372
Fairborn	21.9	657	0.0	27.9	77.0	20.6	87.2	39.41	5,343	1,214
Fairfield	32.0	750	0.0	28.7	76.6	19.9	88.1	43.36	5,261	1,135
Findlay	18.2	439	2.7	24.5	73.6	17.4	83.5	36.91	6,194	809
Gahanna	26.3	777	5.8	28.3	75.1	20.3	85.3	38.52	5,492	951
Garfield Heights	27.3	959	0.0	25.7	71.9	18.8	81.4	38.71	6,121	702
Green	58.3	2,261	7.2	NA	NA	NA	NA	NA	NA	NA
Grove City	35.9	973	0.0	28.3	74.7	20.2	85.6	40.03	5,349	935

1. Based on the population estimated as of July 1 of the year shown.   2. Represents normal values based on the 30-year period, 1971±2000.   3. Average daily minimum.   4. Average daily maximum.

Table D. Cities — Land Area and Population

STATE Place code	City	Land area[1] (sq. mi)	Total persons 2018	Rank	Per square mile	White	Black or African American	American Indian, Alaskan Native	Asian	Hawaiian Pacific Islander	Some other race	Two or more races (percent)
		1	2	3	4	5	6	7	8	9	10	11
	OHIO— Cont'd											
39 33,012	Hamilton	21.5	62,174	601	2,891.8	86.7	6.7	0.4	0.7	0.0	1.4	4.1
39 35,476	Hilliard	14.3	36,414	1,059	2,546.4	NA	NA	NA	NA	NA	NA	NA
39 36,610	Huber Heights	22.2	38,174	1,009	1,719.5	74.0	17.7	0.4	2.1	0.0	0.1	5.7
39 39,872	Kent	9.2	29,662	1,266	3,224.1	77.2	6.0	0.6	8.1	0.0	1.8	6.3
39 40,040	Kettering	18.7	55,103	690	2,946.7	91.8	3.1	0.2	2.8	0.0	0.9	1.2
39 41,664	Lakewood	5.5	50,100	766	9,109.1	87.5	4.7	0.3	2.1	0.0	0.6	4.7
39 41,720	Lancaster	18.9	40,414	946	2,138.3	NA	NA	NA	NA	NA	NA	NA
39 43,554	Lima	13.5	36,862	1,039	2,730.5	62.1	27.2	0.0	0.4	0.0	1.0	9.2
39 44,856	Lorain	23.7	64,028	584	2,701.6	71.5	16.6	1.2	1.6	0.0	2.9	6.1
39 47,138	Mansfield	30.8	46,560	833	1,511.7	70.3	22.1	0.4	0.2	0.0	1.1	5.9
39 47,754	Marion	11.8	36,087	1,064	3,058.2	87.6	6.8	0.4	0.0	0.0	0.3	4.8
39 48,188	Mason	19.2	33,586	1,138	1,749.3	NA	NA	NA	NA	NA	NA	NA
39 48,244	Massillon	19.0	32,410	1,172	1,705.8	82.4	9.9	1.6	0.0	0.0	0.6	5.4
39 48,790	Medina	11.6	26,072	1,390	2,247.6	NA	NA	NA	NA	NA	NA	NA
39 49,056	Mentor	27.8	47,273	823	1,700.5	NA	NA	NA	NA	NA	NA	NA
39 49,840	Middletown	26.1	48,861	790	1,872.1	76.7	13.0	0.4	1.1	0.0	3.2	5.6
39 54,040	Newark	20.8	50,029	767	2,405.2	NA	NA	NA	NA	NA	NA	NA
39 56,882	North Olmsted	11.7	31,591	1,200	2,700.1	90.8	1.8	0.0	2.4	0.0	0.5	4.5
39 56,966	North Ridgeville	23.4	33,889	1,129	1,448.2	NA	NA	NA	NA	NA	NA	NA
39 57,008	North Royalton	21.3	30,239	1,246	1,419.7	89.4	2.5	0.5	4.0	0.0	0.0	3.6
39 61,000	Parma	20.0	78,751	440	3,937.6	89.9	3.8	0.6	1.5	0.0	1.1	3.1
39 66,390	Reynoldsburg	11.1	38,278	1,003	3,448.5	NA	NA	NA	NA	NA	NA	NA
39 67,468	Riverside	9.7	25,151	1,412	2,592.9	83.0	7.5	0.0	1.0	0.0	5.8	2.6
39 70,380	Sandusky	9.7	24,714	1,419	2,547.8	73.3	23.1	0.5	0.1	0.0	1.1	1.9
39 71,682	Shaker Heights	6.3	27,302	1,344	4,333.7	51.9	40.1	0.3	4.0	0.0	0.0	3.8
39 74,118	Springfield	25.7	59,282	636	2,306.7	76.4	16.2	0.6	1.0	0.0	0.4	5.4
39 74,944	Stow	17.1	34,857	1,095	2,038.4	89.6	4.3	0.9	3.5	0.0	0.3	1.4
39 75,098	Strongsville	24.6	44,853	852	1,823.3	90.9	1.7	0.0	4.4	0.0	0.4	2.6
39 77,000	Toledo	80.5	274,975	74	3,415.8	63.1	27.5	0.2	1.3	0.0	3.1	4.6
39 77,588	Troy	12.0	26,132	1,388	2,177.7	89.7	3.5	0.4	4.1	0.0	0.0	2.3
39 79,002	Upper Arlington	9.8	35,522	1,082	3,624.7	NA	NA	NA	NA	NA	NA	NA
39 80,892	Warren	16.0	38,382	1,002	2,398.9	70.5	21.4	0.0	0.5	0.0	0.5	7.1
39 83,342	Westerville	12.6	40,387	948	3,205.3	86.9	8.3	0.0	1.9	0.0	0.0	3.0
39 83,622	Westlake	15.9	32,233	1,180	2,027.2	88.2	4.0	0.0	4.3	0.0	0.1	3.4
39 86,548	Wooster	16.8	26,560	1,374	1,581.0	92.0	1.4	0.0	4.6	0.0	0.0	2.0
39 86,772	Xenia	13.0	26,783	1,368	2,060.2	NA	NA	NA	NA	NA	NA	NA
39 88,000	Youngstown	33.9	64,958	573	1,916.2	46.5	41.2	0.6	0.9	0.1	2.7	8.0
39 88,084	Zanesville	11.8	25,364	1,406	2,149.5	NA	NA	NA	NA	NA	NA	NA
40 00,000	**OKLAHOMA**	68,596.0	3,943,079	X	57.5	72.2	7.3	7.7	2.2	0.2	2.7	7.7
40 04,450	Bartlesville	22.8	36,423	1,058	1,597.5	77.5	3.6	10.6	0.6	0.0	0.5	7.3
40 09,050	Broken Arrow	61.8	109,171	278	1,766.5	77.7	4.2	4.7	4.1	0.1	1.5	7.7
40 23,200	Edmond	84.7	93,127	349	1,099.5	79.5	6.0	1.8	3.9	0.0	1.5	7.3
40 23,950	Enid	74.0	49,585	774	670.1	81.5	4.2	3.3	0.0	4.2	2.2	4.6
40 41,850	Lawton	81.4	92,859	350	1,140.8	58.0	17.7	5.4	3.3	0.7	3.4	11.4
40 48,350	Midwest City	24.4	57,325	661	2,349.4	67.5	20.6	5.0	0.5	0.0	0.6	5.7
40 49,200	Moore	21.8	62,103	602	2,848.8	79.7	4.5	3.1	2.1	0.0	1.1	9.4
40 50,050	Muskogee	43.2	37,402	1,024	865.8	52.5	14.0	17.1	1.2	0.0	5.8	9.5
40 52,500	Norman	178.8	123,471	223	690.6	75.6	5.4	3.3	4.2	0.0	2.4	9.1
40 55,000	Oklahoma City	606.4	649,021	27	1,070.3	67.5	15.1	2.4	4.6	0.1	3.9	6.5
40 56,650	Owasso	17.6	36,722	1,044	2,086.5	75.6	5.3	7.6	2.5	0.6	1.2	7.2
40 59,850	Ponca City	18.4	24,033	1,428	1,306.1	70.8	4.4	10.8	0.1	0.0	7.5	6.4
40 66,800	Shawnee	44.1	31,434	1,205	712.8	70.6	4.9	18.5	0.2	0.4	0.4	4.9
40 70,300	Stillwater	29.5	50,391	764	1,708.2	80.8	4.3	3.2	5.4	0.1	1.1	5.2
40 75,000	Tulsa	197.5	400,669	47	2,028.7	64.5	14.9	4.3	4.1	0.1	4.9	7.1
41 00,000	**OREGON**	95,987.7	4,190,713	X	43.7	84.4	1.9	1.2	4.4	0.4	3.0	4.8
41 01,000	Albany	17.5	54,453	702	3,111.6	90.2	0.3	0.7	2.2	0.0	1.9	4.7
41 05,350	Beaverton	19.6	98,962	313	5,049.1	72.6	2.0	1.2	15.1	0.0	3.7	5.4
41 05,800	Bend	33.1	97,590	318	2,948.3	93.7	1.0	0.6	2.1	0.0	0.8	1.8
41 15,800	Corvallis	14.2	58,641	644	4,129.6	84.0	0.7	0.4	9.1	0.4	1.2	4.3
41 23,850	Eugene	44.2	171,245	153	3,874.3	84.4	1.2	0.3	4.4	0.1	3.7	6.0
41 30,550	Grants Pass	11.5	38,191	1,008	3,321.0	NA	NA	NA	NA	NA	NA	NA
41 31,250	Gresham	23.4	110,158	274	4,707.6	76.4	6.7	1.6	5.3	0.0	4.9	5.1
41 34,100	Hillsboro	25.7	108,389	280	4,217.5	71.5	2.5	0.1	12.0	0.4	5.9	7.6
41 38,500	Keizer	7.2	39,692	971	5,512.8	NA	NA	NA	NA	NA	NA	NA
41 40,550	Lake Oswego	10.8	39,532	978	3,660.4	81.8	1.3	0.1	6.9	0.5	2.4	7.0
41 45,000	McMinnville	10.6	34,617	1,102	3,265.8	85.7	2.0	0.4	2.2	0.6	3.1	6.0
41 47,000	Medford	25.8	82,347	415	3,191.7	89.7	0.5	3.2	1.5	0.0	2.4	2.7
41 55,200	Oregon City	9.9	37,129	1,036	3,750.4	NA	NA	NA	NA	NA	NA	NA
41 59,000	Portland	133.4	653,115	25	4,895.9	77.3	5.5	0.9	8.1	0.8	2.1	5.4

1. Dry land or land partially or temporarily covered by water.   2. Hispanic or Latino persons may be of any race.

Table D. Cities — **Population**

City	Percent Hispanic or Latino[1], 2017	Percent foreign born, 2017	Age of population (percent), 2017							Median age, 2017	Percent female, 2017	Population			
			Under 18 years	18 to 24 years	25 to 34 years	35 to 44 years	45 to 54 years	55 to 64 years	65 years and over			Census counts		Percent change	
												2000	2010	2000-2010	2001-2018
	12	13	14	15	16	17	18	19	20	21	22	23	24	25	26
OHIO— Cont'd															
Hamilton	5.7	3.7	22.8	10.2	13.1	12.2	13.4	13.0	15.2	37.0	49.8	60,690	62,272	2.6	-0.2
Hilliard	4.5	4.5	26.0	7.2	10.7	15.1	16.7	14.6	9.8	39.8	51.6	24,230	28,233	16.5	29.0
Huber Heights	0.8	3.4	23.0	12.0	10.2	11.5	16.2	12.8	14.5	38.6	54.4	38,212	38,102	-0.3	0.2
Kent	3.0	9.1	11.2	41.7	13.6	6.3	7.7	7.7	11.8	24.1	52.0	27,906	28,906	3.6	2.6
Kettering	1.5	4.6	21.3	6.9	15.5	13.3	12.4	13.6	16.9	39.8	51.8	57,502	56,143	-2.4	-1.9
Lakewood	5.6	9.7	17.4	8.1	23.5	15.3	10.9	11.8	12.9	35.5	50.2	56,646	52,131	-8.0	-3.9
Lancaster	1.4	0.8	23.4	9.2	15.2	11.1	12.3	13.2	15.5	36.8	50.9	35,335	38,762	9.7	4.3
Lima	3.5	1.5	24.9	12.4	16.5	10.9	13.3	9.1	12.9	32.6	47.7	40,081	38,627	-3.6	-4.6
Lorain	29.8	2.3	23.9	9.2	12.2	12.5	11.5	12.9	17.8	40.0	51.9	68,652	64,099	-6.6	-0.1
Mansfield	3.9	1.6	22.1	9.8	14.1	15.3	12.0	11.0	15.6	38.2	48.7	49,346	47,830	-3.1	-2.7
Marion	2.4	3.7	20.8	9.1	17.5	13.5	12.0	12.0	15.3	37.3	45.1	35,318	36,828	4.3	-2.0
Mason	3.6	13.3	27.7	5.1	10.9	12.6	18.7	12.7	12.3	40.6	47.9	22,016	30,850	40.1	8.9
Massillon	1.8	0.8	20.1	8.4	9.8	9.8	13.8	15.0	23.1	46.1	51.2	31,325	32,257	3.0	0.5
Medina	1.9	1.5	26.8	9.9	15.1	12.6	11.8	10.0	13.7	33.6	48.0	25,139	26,663	6.1	-2.2
Mentor	2.7	4.1	18.7	6.5	9.2	10.9	15.5	16.6	22.5	47.3	53.2	50,278	47,161	-6.2	0.2
Middletown	7.4	3.6	25.9	9.5	11.8	10.5	10.6	15.6	16.0	36.2	53.6	51,605	48,678	-5.7	0.4
Newark	0.5	2.3	23.0	8.6	13.7	12.0	12.4	13.3	17.0	38.4	53.1	46,279	47,558	2.8	5.2
North Olmsted	2.1	9.3	21.5	6.2	10.7	12.4	9.8	18.0	21.5	44.1	48.4	34,113	32,713	-4.1	-3.4
North Ridgeville	0.3	1.9	25.4	3.1	12.0	13.7	13.3	13.0	19.5	43.2	52.8	22,338	29,466	31.9	15.0
North Royalton	0.5	10.0	19.4	7.0	14.0	9.9	16.9	11.6	21.2	44.6	53.2	28,648	30,452	6.3	-0.7
Parma	4.5	8.3	16.5	9.4	13.8	10.5	13.7	18.2	17.9	44.7	51.0	85,655	81,589	-4.7	-3.5
Reynoldsburg	4.4	7.5	24.2	9.0	15.6	13.8	13.0	13.5	10.7	36.3	52.5	32,069	35,920	12.0	6.6
Riverside	9.8	7.7	21.7	8.5	19.3	9.9	15.7	7.4	17.4	35.5	47.4	23,545	25,175	6.9	-0.1
Sandusky	9.4	2.5	22.8	8.4	13.9	10.6	10.9	15.3	18.0	38.5	47.4	27,844	25,919	-6.9	-4.6
Shaker Heights	2.1	9.7	26.7	4.7	12.2	12.0	12.7	11.7	19.9	40.1	55.7	29,405	28,509	-3.0	-4.2
Springfield	4.1	2.8	24.9	11.5	11.7	10.5	12.1	11.9	17.4	36.3	53.4	65,358	60,565	-7.3	-2.1
Stow	0.8	2.8	22.5	7.5	12.7	15.0	13.0	12.9	16.5	39.0	49.8	32,139	34,837	8.4	0.1
Strongsville	3.0	7.4	22.8	6.3	9.4	12.0	14.0	14.1	21.5	44.7	50.1	43,858	44,750	2.0	0.2
Toledo	8.2	4.1	23.1	10.8	15.4	11.0	12.7	12.9	14.1	35.4	52.0	313,619	287,319	-8.4	-4.3
Troy	4.1	4.8	28.6	7.6	14.0	14.7	12.7	10.5	11.9	34.9	47.6	21,999	25,209	14.6	3.7
Upper Arlington	2.4	9.0	25.5	4.2	13.4	14.8	14.0	13.0	15.2	39.2	52.0	33,686	33,691	0.0	5.4
Warren	4.2	2.1	23.1	11.4	12.0	10.9	12.7	13.3	16.6	39.2	50.3	46,832	41,583	-11.2	-7.7
Westerville	2.2	5.6	21.5	9.1	11.6	12.5	10.1	14.9	20.3	40.5	50.6	35,318	36,273	2.7	11.3
Westlake	1.4	10.2	22.8	5.7	9.2	9.3	13.5	15.5	23.8	47.2	51.7	31,719	32,729	3.2	-1.5
Wooster	2.5	7.2	13.4	19.4	10.3	10.3	11.4	11.5	23.7	40.9	51.9	24,811	26,175	5.5	1.5
Xenia	1.0	0.8	19.9	5.0	12.2	11.7	14.5	11.2	25.5	46.7	53.5	24,164	25,658	6.2	4.4
Youngstown	12.5	2.2	22.1	10.6	11.9	13.2	12.2	13.8	16.2	38.7	49.9	82,026	66,952	-18.4	-3.0
Zanesville	0.3	0.0	24.9	6.7	17.2	12.4	10.3	12.7	15.8	36.2	48.8	25,586	25,473	-0.4	-0.4
OKLAHOMA	10.6	5.7	24.5	9.7	13.7	12.4	11.9	12.5	15.3	36.6	50.4	3,450,654	3,751,583	8.7	5.1
Bartlesville	8.3	3.6	24.7	8.1	14.0	10.7	11.4	12.5	18.6	38.0	52.2	34,748	35,736	2.8	1.9
Broken Arrow	7.4	6.5	26.5	7.1	13.8	12.7	14.4	11.9	13.6	36.8	50.8	74,859	98,838	32.0	10.5
Edmond	5.8	6.3	25.5	9.8	14.0	13.2	9.5	12.3	15.7	35.6	52.5	68,315	81,149	18.8	14.8
Enid	13.9	7.5	27.1	10.0	14.1	11.3	11.3	12.3	13.9	34.2	51.2	47,045	49,379	5.0	0.4
Lawton	14.0	5.9	23.9	15.3	15.8	12.0	11.1	9.9	11.9	31.2	48.6	92,757	96,867	4.4	-4.1
Midwest City	4.9	2.0	24.2	6.8	15.0	11.7	12.5	13.1	16.6	38.0	53.4	54,088	54,371	0.5	5.4
Moore	12.3	4.7	25.7	11.2	15.0	16.1	11.7	10.1	10.1	34.3	53.1	41,138	55,083	33.9	12.7
Muskogee	8.3	4.9	25.0	11.0	11.8	12.2	12.6	12.6	14.7	36.3	51.9	38,310	39,223	2.4	-4.6
Norman	7.8	7.1	18.4	21.1	17.5	11.4	9.9	9.4	12.2	30.2	49.4	95,694	110,925	15.9	11.3
Oklahoma City	20.0	11.0	26.4	8.8	15.9	13.1	11.9	11.7	12.1	34.2	50.4	506,132	580,247	14.6	11.9
Owasso	2.5	4.1	25.6	8.6	14.8	17.1	8.7	12.3	12.9	36.1	49.8	18,502	29,871	61.4	22.9
Ponca City	12.0	2.8	24.3	8.1	10.2	12.8	10.3	14.1	20.3	40.2	50.1	25,919	25,401	-2.0	-5.4
Shawnee	6.6	2.8	21.1	12.9	14.9	12.3	10.4	12.5	15.9	35.7	51.7	28,692	29,855	4.1	5.3
Stillwater	4.9	10.5	15.0	40.0	12.3	10.3	6.1	6.8	9.5	23.0	49.6	39,065	45,691	17.0	10.3
Tulsa	16.9	11.1	24.1	9.7	15.6	12.2	12.0	12.3	14.2	35.5	52.0	393,049	392,010	-0.3	2.2
OREGON	13.1	9.9	21.1	8.9	14.0	13.3	12.5	13.2	17.1	39.3	50.4	3,421,399	3,831,075	12.0	9.4
Albany	10.8	4.8	24.2	9.3	12.5	13.2	13.7	10.6	16.6	38.0	51.5	40,852	50,142	22.7	8.6
Beaverton	13.2	21.9	19.3	9.1	18.6	13.9	13.6	11.5	13.9	36.4	52.4	76,129	89,732	17.9	10.3
Bend	11.6	7.2	24.0	5.5	14.0	13.6	13.0	11.5	18.4	40.4	53.7	52,029	76,651	47.3	27.3
Corvallis	6.5	11.9	13.3	30.8	17.3	9.5	6.7	9.8	12.7	27.5	49.0	49,322	54,494	10.5	7.6
Eugene	8.6	7.3	17.1	17.7	15.0	11.7	10.6	11.2	16.6	35.2	50.9	137,893	156,428	13.4	9.5
Grants Pass	11.8	3.8	25.9	8.4	11.1	13.0	10.3	15.0	16.3	37.0	49.8	23,003	35,923	56.2	6.3
Gresham	17.4	17.2	23.8	9.0	14.3	14.5	12.0	13.2	13.1	37.2	50.2	90,205	105,639	17.1	4.3
Hillsboro	24.4	18.7	24.1	8.7	19.9	16.0	12.0	10.3	9.0	33.5	49.8	70,186	92,274	31.5	17.5
Keizer	19.5	8.3	24.3	7.7	13.2	11.2	13.6	15.9	14.1	38.0	50.8	32,203	36,434	13.1	8.9
Lake Oswego	8.0	12.7	23.2	3.7	6.4	11.4	17.6	16.8	20.9	47.8	50.9	35,278	36,759	4.2	7.5
McMinnville	21.6	9.5	22.9	12.5	12.8	11.4	8.2	13.0	19.2	36.4	46.5	26,499	32,182	21.4	7.6
Medford	15.1	7.5	23.9	9.7	13.1	11.6	10.8	11.9	19.0	37.7	52.0	63,154	74,943	18.7	9.9
Oregon City	7.4	3.6	22.0	9.5	11.8	14.4	14.1	12.7	15.5	39.1	48.8	25,754	32,623	26.7	13.8
Portland	10.4	13.7	18.4	8.0	19.9	16.9	13.2	11.0	12.5	36.8	50.4	529,121	583,792	10.3	11.9

1. May be of any race.

Table D. Cities — **Households, Group Quarters, Crime, and Education**

City	Households, 2017							Persons in group quarters, 2017	Serious crimes known to police[2], 2016				Educational attainment, 2017		
			Percent						Total		Rate[3]			Attainment[4] (percent)	
	Number	Persons per household	Family	Married couple family	Female headed[1]	Non-family	One person		Number	Rate	Violent	Property	Population age 25 and over	High school graduate or less	Bachelor's degree or more
	27	28	29	30	31	32	33	34	35	36	37	38	39	40	41

City	27	28	29	30	31	32	33	34	35	36	37	38	39	40	41
OHIO— Cont'd															
Hamilton	23,957	2.52	58.7	35.4	17.9	41.3	31.4	1,742	3,723	5,964	525	5,439	41,594	53.9	17.7
Hilliard	13,310	2.68	80.2	68.9	6.8	19.8	17.2	NA	407	1,168	106	1,062	23,973	22.2	55.9
Huber Heights	15,680	2.45	72.0	46.6	18.3	28.0	23.7	NA	1,365	3,575	225	3,350	25,127	39.5	22.9
Kent	11,268	2.16	42.3	29.1	5.9	57.7	41.5	5,536	563	1,877	223	1,654	14,088	25.7	47.5
Kettering	25,375	2.17	55.9	43.5	8.9	44.1	37.9	515	1,081	1,952	132	1,820	39,914	28.3	35.7
Lakewood	25,633	1.95	41.7	30.4	8.9	58.3	45.7	313	944	1,875	125	1,750	37,437	25.9	49.1
Lancaster	15,693	2.50	63.9	42.5	17.5	36.1	28.7	1,007	1,979	4,953	358	4,595	27,156	50.2	19.1
Lima	14,774	2.35	60.3	29.1	23.0	39.7	34.9	2,408	2,615	6,934	944	5,990	23,316	52.3	12.0
Lorain	26,351	2.40	61.6	35.8	19.5	38.4	33.4	657	918	1,444	200	1,244	42,668	53.3	11.1
Mansfield	18,549	2.12	51.7	28.7	17.9	48.3	41.7	6,780	2,825	6,055	461	5,594	31,405	53.8	18.3
Marion	13,706	2.33	60.3	43.2	12.3	39.7	35.1	5,551	1,427	3,934	295	3,639	26,262	53.2	13.7
Mason	12,752	2.58	67.3	56.6	8.1	32.7	26.8	NA	337	1,020	18	1,002	22,330	26.7	55.4
Massillon	14,050	2.25	61.7	42.0	12.8	38.3	29.9	795	784	2,430	310	2,120	23,127	57.0	14.7
Medina	9,975	2.58	63.6	46.6	13.1	36.4	34.1	NA	108	227	4	223	16,552	33.3	39.1
Mentor	20,136	2.32	61.7	49.3	7.2	38.3	30.3	NA	1,094	2,335	109	2,226	35,262	33.5	34.4
Middletown	19,883	2.38	54.1	36.4	14.5	45.9	39.0	698	3,551	7,281	523	6,759	31,052	53.3	17.2
Newark	19,291	2.50	63.0	40.4	16.3	37.0	31.1	1,202	484	1,007	25	982	33,810	48.7	19.0
North Olmsted	13,118	2.38	64.1	52.6	5.8	35.9	33.5	450	645	2,025	82	1,943	22,970	33.8	33.3
North Ridgeville	13,292	2.50	73.1	57.6	10.0	26.9	22.4	NA	205	619	36	583	23,899	35.0	29.5
North Royalton	12,874	2.33	61.8	56.5	4.7	38.2	34.9	307	NA	NA	NA	NA	22,310	26.8	43.1
Parma	33,748	2.32	61.7	42.7	12.8	38.3	31.3	1,000	1,210	1,521	136	1,385	58,637	48.1	21.2
Reynoldsburg	13,983	2.47	64.9	40.4	19.6	35.1	29.8	40	1,436	3,839	233	3,606	23,065	33.8	33.8
Riverside	10,573	2.37	68.7	46.1	13.2	31.3	26.2	NA	673	2,701	205	2,496	17,509	43.2	21.1
Sandusky	11,040	2.20	49.8	28.4	15.9	50.2	41.3	513	956	3,812	179	3,633	17,076	52.0	18.4
Shaker Heights	11,109	2.45	64.7	44.4	17.1	35.3	31.1	NA	NA	NA	NA	NA	18,816	14.0	65.3
Springfield	23,550	2.39	58.5	34.5	17.2	41.5	33.1	2,831	4,451	7,480	691	6,790	37,656	58.3	16.1
Stow	14,581	2.36	62.9	49.5	7.6	37.1	27.2	337	672	1,931	86	1,845	24,323	21.6	52.1
Strongsville	17,846	2.49	71.0	61.5	7.5	29.0	26.3	NA	901	2,019	43	1,976	31,746	23.7	47.8
Toledo	117,449	2.29	54.9	28.8	19.1	45.1	37.6	7,407	14,510	5,213	1,192	4,020	182,635	49.4	18.5
Troy	9,065	2.81	63.1	46.8	8.2	36.9	29.0	NA	761	2,956	117	2,839	16,495	42.8	31.1
Upper Arlington	13,789	2.55	69.0	57.9	8.2	31.0	25.3	NA	558	1,587	46	1,542	24,867	7.6	79.0
Warren	17,224	2.16	53.3	22.6	25.7	46.7	39.1	2,384	1,744	4,359	577	3,782	25,926	59.6	15.7
Westerville	15,348	2.58	69.8	59.5	8.1	30.2	25.1	2,128	962	2,479	54	2,425	28,974	24.0	51.8
Westlake	13,341	2.36	61.5	52.8	5.6	38.5	31.5	765	475	1,468	43	1,425	23,072	19.8	53.6
Wooster	12,254	1.91	45.8	32.0	10.0	54.2	49.4	3,216	849	3,158	272	2,887	17,875	45.2	31.0
Xenia	11,643	2.19	61.2	42.0	15.1	38.8	34.9	1,055	882	3,387	204	3,184	19,958	53.2	16.6
Youngstown	26,746	2.25	52.5	21.9	26.7	47.5	42.4	4,437	2,862	4,459	662	3,797	43,450	62.1	11.3
Zanesville	10,296	2.42	61.9	36.1	19.9	38.1	35.8	436	1,425	5,590	373	5,217	17,356	58.3	12.4
OKLAHOMA	1,470,364	2.60	65.6	48.0	12.5	34.4	28.5	109,498	134,685	3,433	450	2,983	2,586,414	43.0	25.5
Bartlesville	14,610	2.48	63.7	46.3	12.3	36.3	31.7	659	1,241	3,377	297	3,080	24,754	43.8	29.8
Broken Arrow	39,869	2.76	75.1	58.7	11.7	24.9	21.0	448	2,462	2,278	154	2,124	73,311	27.1	34.5
Edmond	34,670	2.61	66.7	50.2	13.5	33.3	26.1	1,398	1,529	1,664	145	1,520	59,420	18.6	52.7
Enid	18,047	2.69	63.0	44.8	10.7	37.0	32.1	1,683	2,255	4,317	410	3,907	31,596	46.3	22.6
Lawton	33,863	2.50	59.3	39.4	15.1	40.7	32.3	8,903	4,472	4,638	810	3,828	56,958	38.5	22.0
Midwest City	23,063	2.47	61.0	35.8	18.7	39.0	34.0	NA	2,351	4,068	218	3,850	39,531	44.9	19.6
Moore	22,822	2.68	71.7	50.9	16.5	28.3	20.6	439	1,518	2,468	133	2,335	38,776	38.1	28.3
Muskogee	14,864	2.46	64.8	43.9	14.8	35.2	32.8	1,331	1,913	4,996	1,060	3,935	24,223	52.6	20.4
Norman	48,236	2.36	57.5	41.4	10.5	42.5	29.9	8,904	4,326	3,542	277	3,265	74,255	27.3	42.8
Oklahoma City	237,932	2.65	61.6	44.2	12.3	38.4	30.8	12,418	30,059	4,684	783	3,901	416,688	38.6	30.9
Owasso	13,741	2.58	65.5	46.7	13.1	34.5	27.1	NA	868	2,442	217	2,225	23,456	34.7	30.4
Ponca City	10,291	2.33	61.5	44.2	12.9	38.5	32.9	680	1,181	4,792	872	3,919	16,703	45.7	19.7
Shawnee	11,981	2.47	58.2	38.8	14.1	41.8	37.1	1,633	1,684	5,336	840	4,496	20,592	51.5	17.6
Stillwater	18,189	2.36	45.0	31.4	8.7	55.0	33.0	6,966	1,729	3,483	290	3,193	22,446	29.9	47.2
Tulsa	162,640	2.43	57.7	38.3	15.1	42.3	34.8	6,845	28,400	6,999	1,095	5,904	266,312	37.6	30.6
OREGON	1,603,635	2.53	63.0	48.7	9.9	37.0	27.7	89,553	132,175	3,229	265	2,964	2,901,195	32.3	33.7
Albany	20,274	2.61	69.7	49.5	15.5	30.3	24.9	897	1,555	2,959	82	2,878	35,781	33.9	22.6
Beaverton	39,301	2.46	60.5	47.2	8.2	39.5	28.6	1,012	1,614	1,649	147	1,501	69,837	23.3	47.9
Bend	37,831	2.48	72.9	56.9	9.9	27.1	20.2	602	2,124	2,380	112	2,268	66,695	21.9	44.4
Corvallis	23,686	2.20	49.8	38.9	8.2	50.2	27.6	5,937	1,636	2,918	136	2,783	32,446	12.0	60.0
Eugene	70,253	2.31	52.0	40.4	7.9	48.0	32.7	6,445	6,938	4,208	368	3,840	110,156	19.8	44.1
Grants Pass	16,007	2.29	56.7	39.0	13.5	43.3	33.2	977	2,112	5,660	257	5,402	24,681	43.5	18.2
Gresham	40,669	2.68	65.8	46.0	14.6	34.2	27.7	1,958	3,506	3,145	385	2,760	74,572	38.7	22.6
Hillsboro	38,749	2.72	66.6	51.3	11.8	33.4	24.0	1,509	2,371	2,270	299	1,971	71,853	24.7	44.3
Keizer	13,515	2.88	65.3	45.8	13.2	34.7	24.2	366	840	2,201	173	2,028	26,737	41.1	26.1
Lake Oswego	15,346	2.54	74.1	64.7	6.7	25.9	21.8	218	481	1,238	82	1,155	28,682	6.7	73.7
McMinnville	13,097	2.48	56.0	45.0	8.6	44.0	36.8	1,803	887	2,590	175	2,415	22,188	28.8	28.8
Medford	32,615	2.45	60.4	42.9	12.7	39.6	31.8	1,745	6,114	7,567	505	7,062	54,309	38.5	22.9
Oregon City	12,445	2.86	72.9	54.8	12.1	27.1	20.2	NA	814	2,231	206	2,025	24,903	31.8	27.5
Portland	265,700	2.38	52.0	39.0	9.4	48.0	33.5	16,645	36,544	5,691	502	5,189	476,631	23.6	49.9

1. No spouse present.   2. Data for serious crimes have not been adjusted for underreporting. This may affect comparability between geographic areas and over time.   3. Per 100,000 population estimated by the FBI.   4. Persons 25 years old and over.

City	Money income, 2017					Median earnings, 2017			Housing units, 2017				
	Households			Median family income	Median non-family income	All persons	Men	Women	Total	Occupied	Percent owner occupied	Median value[1] (dollars)	Median gross rent (dollars)
	Median income	Percent with income less than $20,000	Percent with income of $200,000 or more										
	42	43	44	45	46	47	48	49	50	51	52	53	54
OHIO— Cont'd													
Hamilton	50,830	20.8	1.2	56,875	32,208	31,170	36,372	27,373	26,302	23,957	58.0	105,400	763
Hilliard	98,912	4.7	10.3	111,239	40,833	56,865	68,793	46,534	13,377	13,310	75.0	268,400	1,014
Huber Heights	52,720	12.2	3.5	57,183	40,390	30,394	40,991	24,089	16,409	15,680	71.7	104,400	840
Kent	53,414	25.3	3.2	65,419	25,728	15,215	19,220	11,562	14,067	11,268	38.7	139,700	872
Kettering	54,375	14.3	4.3	78,000	32,732	35,691	41,425	31,538	26,805	25,375	62.0	133,100	748
Lakewood	50,363	16.5	5.0	77,488	38,155	39,030	45,058	35,183	27,689	25,633	41.7	156,800	778
Lancaster	45,065	19.3	1.2	53,862	27,315	23,907	30,124	20,636	18,064	15,693	53.6	117,400	829
Lima	36,257	29.7	0.0	37,131	25,157	26,292	33,711	18,230	17,242	14,774	43.9	66,600	614
Lorain	32,379	33.5	0.7	42,730	19,880	24,322	30,557	21,025	30,710	26,351	52.7	85,800	675
Mansfield	33,331	25.8	1.5	40,586	27,454	22,538	25,267	21,993	21,589	18,549	53.9	79,500	558
Marion	35,625	26.0	0.9	43,430	25,147	28,940	30,934	25,337	15,947	13,706	57.4	72,600	714
Mason	92,822	4.9	13.2	109,031	52,050	47,140	60,283	38,244	13,012	12,752	78.1	259,600	1,114
Massillon	44,244	19.4	0.6	49,928	29,744	31,148	36,648	25,499	16,037	14,050	62.4	94,800	643
Medina	59,888	17.9	2.1	85,009	24,432	29,214	33,340	24,398	10,268	9,975	61.2	179,000	889
Mentor	70,171	8.2	5.9	88,052	40,693	41,323	53,484	35,303	21,721	20,136	86.6	184,400	874
Middletown	41,720	27.5	0.7	59,862	30,376	30,713	33,225	25,956	22,743	19,883	52.1	105,700	756
Newark	42,201	16.6	2.4	48,963	29,480	26,489	29,304	24,835	22,674	19,291	60.6	126,200	765
North Olmsted	62,855	12.1	3.9	81,830	37,838	40,862	46,656	33,488	13,928	13,118	77.7	154,300	871
North Ridgeville	67,107	12.0	2.1	75,200	41,665	38,169	45,803	32,136	13,917	13,292	84.1	182,600	841
North Royalton	67,970	7.6	9.6	100,504	36,910	42,283	46,168	39,727	13,677	12,874	75.7	210,400	857
Parma	54,588	11.4	1.0	67,952	39,244	32,553	40,631	27,649	36,243	33,748	70.1	116,400	819
Reynoldsburg	60,892	13.7	3.8	83,856	31,381	32,094	31,742	32,458	15,299	13,983	59.0	158,700	978
Riverside	51,282	14.3	0.5	52,365	43,146	30,455	36,926	23,674	11,766	10,573	52.3	85,700	804
Sandusky	37,592	29.5	1.1	52,999	25,042	27,608	33,847	23,162	13,110	11,040	47.9	76,800	632
Shaker Heights	77,083	15.7	19.4	109,676	34,563	44,612	70,123	31,767	12,157	11,109	61.1	241,000	1,049
Springfield	37,474	21.6	1.3	43,382	30,606	21,415	22,051	20,888	28,584	23,550	52.3	78,900	666
Stow	77,139	10.6	5.0	86,875	51,866	41,725	52,127	35,712	15,701	14,581	64.2	185,400	1,037
Strongsville	84,373	6.6	7.8	106,966	44,320	46,645	50,821	41,505	18,861	17,846	81.2	200,000	1,039
Toledo	37,339	27.8	1.1	47,686	26,412	26,159	29,455	23,716	137,831	117,449	51.0	78,400	675
Troy	63,198	13.0	2.8	77,449	34,012	37,216	46,440	29,154	10,211	9,065	59.2	133,200	807
Upper Arlington	119,075	5.1	23.5	144,172	70,081	64,981	78,189	52,251	14,402	13,789	81.7	416,400	1,255
Warren	28,483	35.5	0.3	41,738	20,956	20,384	21,150	19,134	20,083	17,224	48.3	65,900	637
Westerville	87,971	10.2	8.1	99,033	45,661	42,301	51,521	33,306	16,263	15,348	79.8	228,900	1,080
Westlake	84,285	7.0	14.1	106,496	52,250	50,837	63,497	38,739	13,704	13,341	71.4	265,600	1,161
Wooster	44,266	22.5	3.7	52,769	30,211	21,455	30,376	20,121	13,663	12,254	59.8	136,200	649
Xenia	46,750	25.9	1.3	57,291	25,057	29,936	35,264	25,370	13,118	11,643	63.3	100,900	730
Youngstown	28,843	37.1	1.1	34,304	21,326	20,665	21,685	18,424	32,648	26,746	53.3	41,400	594
Zanesville	33,541	32.6	0.5	38,942	19,908	17,278	18,241	16,778	11,728	10,296	49.0	68,300	685
OKLAHOMA	50,051	18.4	3.6	61,471	28,870	30,479	35,769	25,036	1,734,074	1,470,364	65.5	137,400	780
Bartlesville	50,187	21.6	4.0	59,218	25,587	27,645	34,024	24,113	17,201	14,610	65.7	119,300	625
Broken Arrow	68,811	7.8	5.4	80,375	41,582	37,309	47,026	31,505	42,652	39,869	74.0	168,200	1,028
Edmond	69,570	11.8	11.1	86,541	40,844	37,049	49,595	31,667	38,049	34,670	65.3	232,900	972
Enid	47,235	15.9	1.4	59,658	26,524	27,318	35,609	21,983	21,453	18,047	60.5	114,400	847
Lawton	47,591	20.0	0.7	54,977	29,799	23,740	31,651	20,186	40,172	33,863	45.9	120,500	778
Midwest City	43,384	19.8	0.6	52,095	28,554	27,596	31,987	24,008	25,363	23,063	57.3	112,500	805
Moore	64,715	12.7	2.0	71,441	34,027	33,055	39,208	30,087	24,626	22,822	66.3	142,800	957
Muskogee	32,922	35.0	1.1	46,176	16,457	27,335	29,671	24,519	17,704	14,864	53.6	97,600	632
Norman	54,065	15.6	5.5	68,624	32,310	26,564	30,216	22,119	53,475	48,236	49.1	174,900	879
Oklahoma City	52,062	15.9	4.3	67,201	34,789	31,589	38,370	27,446	268,953	237,932	59.5	158,200	841
Owasso	61,068	6.8	0.6	71,240	48,681	32,024	39,194	29,920	14,571	13,741	68.0	175,100	901
Ponca City	42,452	19.5	1.0	56,162	26,097	26,973	29,874	25,187	12,224	10,291	68.3	95,300	627
Shawnee	37,178	27.3	2.6	52,645	22,918	23,162	29,629	19,493	13,475	11,981	52.7	112,300	642
Stillwater	29,756	30.7	1.8	66,046	21,567	12,031	15,518	10,472	21,931	18,189	36.3	177,500	787
Tulsa	45,894	21.1	5.0	56,706	31,467	29,511	33,285	25,059	187,612	162,640	51.2	139,700	811
OREGON	60,212	15.1	5.7	73,202	36,665	32,137	37,715	27,107	1,768,582	1,603,635	62.8	319,200	1,079
Albany	54,449	16.1	3.1	64,479	35,090	31,126	40,217	23,489	21,876	20,274	57.8	233,200	958
Beaverton	71,979	11.1	6.4	86,572	46,544	36,849	47,413	30,260	41,084	39,301	49.9	389,500	1,327
Bend	66,455	8.5	4.7	75,571	40,686	31,498	41,565	23,907	41,772	37,831	59.4	400,700	1,222
Corvallis	51,132	23.3	4.2	69,381	32,423	19,267	18,945	19,569	25,871	23,686	39.7	372,100	1,044
Eugene	50,592	21.0	4.9	74,736	26,218	23,891	26,416	20,914	74,725	70,253	48.7	279,000	937
Grants Pass	40,963	29.0	2.3	51,329	26,278	27,933	32,407	25,170	16,685	16,007	46.7	228,000	869
Gresham	51,130	15.7	2.1	63,144	35,465	32,407	37,915	26,083	43,333	40,669	58.0	296,300	1,112
Hillsboro	83,992	5.1	5.6	91,019	61,684	40,179	50,178	27,999	41,602	38,749	55.1	350,000	1,445
Keizer	63,253	14.1	4.7	74,639	50,342	31,969	36,374	30,102	14,521	13,515	57.6	249,100	1,065
Lake Oswego	108,807	5.0	23.7	135,163	60,130	60,737	86,918	33,034	16,756	15,346	77.8	662,300	1,614
McMinnville	53,837	19.5	2.9	71,627	39,076	29,564	34,920	22,223	13,707	13,097	63.8	261,500	948
Medford	48,825	20.3	3.1	54,596	32,231	28,746	32,872	25,030	35,284	32,615	55.0	270,400	948
Oregon City	77,338	3.0	7.1	94,247	50,313	41,470	48,838	35,656	13,007	12,445	74.0	357,800	1,165
Portland	66,187	16.2	8.3	85,262	45,988	36,382	40,216	32,037	284,258	265,700	53.6	427,500	1,216

1. Based on population estimated by the American Community Survey.   2. Includes units rented or sold but not occupied.   3. Specified owner-occupied units; $1,000,000 represents $1,000,000 or more.   4. 50.0 represents 50 percent or more.   5. 10.0 represents 10 percent or less.

Table D. Cities — Commuting, Computer Access, Migration, Labor Force, and Employment

City	Commuting[1], 2017 Percent Commuting	With commutes of 30 minutes or more	Computer access[2], 2017 Percent With a computer in the house	With Internet access	Migration, 2017 Percent who lived in the same house one year ago	Percent who lived in another state or county one year ago	Civilian labor force, 2018 Total	Percent change 2017-2018	Unemployment Total	Rate[3]	Population age 16 and older Number	Percent in labor force	Population age 16 to 64 Number	Percent who worked full-year full-time
	55	56	57	58	59	60	61	62	63	64	65	66	67	68
OHIO— Cont'd														
Hamilton	79.3	40.4	88.0	82.4	82.7	5.1	27,981	0.4	1,272	4.5	49,341	62.0	39,875	51.2
Hilliard	88.1	31.6	97.3	91.5	83.9	5.2	19,562	0.7	632	3.2	28,511	71.8	24,986	59.3
Huber Heights	93.6	28.9	93.4	90.5	86.7	4.5	18,081	-0.5	798	4.4	30,911	67.8	25,304	55.8
Kent	76.9	29.0	96.1	74.9	64.6	23.9	16,657	-1.0	702	4.2	26,932	68.1	23,413	30.2
Kettering	85.0	16.3	93.3	88.6	80.8	7.2	28,973	-0.2	1,140	3.9	45,599	64.7	36,193	54.1
Lakewood	81.6	31.3	92.7	85.0	81.3	6.2	29,891	-0.2	1,196	4.0	42,398	74.1	35,912	63.4
Lancaster	79.7	39.7	86.7	76.4	84.9	3.9	18,143	0.3	832	4.6	31,777	60.5	25,523	46.6
Lima	80.7	16.0	85.5	75.4	76.7	5.2	14,537	-1.6	804	5.5	28,653	62.4	23,856	44.7
Lorain	78.6	33.1	85.4	70.0	NA	NA	27,463	-0.8	1,924	7.0	50,713	52.7	39,365	35.3
Mansfield	83.7	18.2	85.5	69.4	79.0	10.6	17,439	-0.8	965	5.5	37,261	47.8	30,073	38.2
Marion	80.1	22.8	86.7	82.1	78.9	7.1	13,871	1.2	687	5.0	30,393	45.8	24,655	34.8
Mason	85.0	25.0	NA	NA	87.8	7.8	17,119	0.4	629	3.7	25,669	69.8	21,567	63.2
Massillon	88.4	19.6	88.6	83.9	83.5	4.0	15,369	-0.2	819	5.3	26,933	55.5	19,455	48.9
Medina	86.0	42.7	94.9	89.3	86.4	10.5	13,235	-0.5	588	4.4	20,336	69.0	16,743	48.3
Mentor	87.2	25.9	93.6	92.1	92.1	4.5	26,576	-0.2	1,117	4.2	39,503	64.6	28,880	57.7
Middletown	NA	33.5	88.6	78.9	83.1	6.4	21,039	0.6	1,118	5.3	36,296	60.8	28,604	51.6
Newark	80.9	33.3	91.6	82.8	85.7	2.0	23,883	0.3	987	4.1	38,852	58.8	30,459	49.8
North Olmsted	83.2	39.4	88.9	82.8	NA	NA	17,410	0.0	764	4.4	25,981	61.7	19,148	52.8
North Ridgeville	86.8	38.7	95.9	90.2	87.1	7.2	17,903	-0.4	800	4.5	26,195	65.5	19,673	56.5
North Royalton	88.7	49.6	92.3	89.1	NA	NA	17,526	0.0	762	4.3	24,746	67.1	18,319	60.0
Parma	84.1	35.0	90.6	84.5	82.0	3.1	42,141	-0.2	2,094	5.0	67,942	63.8	53,807	53.5
Reynoldsburg	83.9	43.2	92.5	87.8	89.1	4.7	20,906	0.5	803	3.8	27,639	73.8	23,936	58.3
Riverside	88.3	10.5	88.1	83.8	86.4	5.6	10,792	-0.3	520	4.8	20,425	65.2	16,059	57.4
Sandusky	80.8	19.2	83.9	64.9	83.8	2.8	11,847	-1.0	738	6.2	19,540	62.8	15,067	50.3
Shaker Heights	78.5	30.3	95.5	90.1	79.0	7.5	14,156	-0.1	580	4.1	21,071	66.7	15,610	52.9
Springfield	79.2	24.9	87.1	78.7	80.4	6.3	25,192	-1.0	1,253	5.0	46,047	59.2	35,768	39.9
Stow	90.7	32.2	91.5	89.1	80.2	7.0	18,572	-0.8	747	4.0	27,510	64.9	21,777	61.0
Strongsville	84.8	47.8	93.8	91.5	NA	NA	24,503	0.0	1,040	4.2	35,693	70.0	26,090	60.3
Toledo	81.1	21.0	88.5	80.0	84.1	4.5	127,901	-0.7	7,451	5.8	219,296	60.5	180,442	42.8
Troy	78.8	35.2	89.6	86.9	89.1	6.2	13,663	-0.3	519	3.8	18,959	72.1	15,874	60.8
Upper Arlington	84.9	18.5	96.4	93.6	85.1	4.3	18,466	0.6	581	3.1	27,179	71.1	21,815	60.6
Warren	91.8	24.9	78.9	66.4	90.7	4.0	13,994	-1.9	1,028	7.3	31,941	47.8	25,365	37.8
Westerville	84.3	28.9	98.1	95.5	88.3	5.3	22,242	0.5	760	3.4	33,605	66.8	25,146	56.3
Westlake	85.5	36.1	91.5	88.4	87.9	4.7	17,085	0.0	692	4.1	25,762	63.0	18,059	55.7
Wooster	79.2	16.7	82.6	75.3	69.4	16.5	13,838	-1.4	513	3.7	23,618	56.7	17,320	41.5
Xenia	83.8	29.5	85.7	83.1	86.7	6.0	11,427	-0.4	561	4.9	22,157	56.9	15,379	48.9
Youngstown	75.2	18.8	81.6	71.4	82.6	9.6	22,459	-1.7	1,638	7.3	51,616	51.7	41,143	34.1
Zanesville	74.9	15.1	81.5	71.9	81.5	2.6	9,766	-1.2	576	5.9	19,577	56.4	15,567	40.0
OKLAHOMA	82.3	26.8	89.2	79.4	83.0	7.3	1,841,872	0.3	62,502	3.4	3,075,002	61.0	2,473,870	49.6
Bartlesville	84.4	15.0	87.0	78.7	82.7	6.9	16,291	-1.1	628	3.9	28,610	56.3	21,746	51.7
Broken Arrow	86.2	22.5	97.1	94.0	85.2	6.2	57,262	0.6	1,717	3.0	84,756	70.1	69,720	56.8
Edmond	81.7	30.8	95.2	91.2	78.3	8.6	48,039	1.5	1,243	2.6	70,311	66.3	55,917	52.8
Enid	83.5	8.9	84.2	70.9	83.9	9.5	21,640	-1.9	684	3.2	37,847	63.2	30,845	52.3
Lawton	71.1	7.1	91.7	85.9	66.2	18.6	36,251	-0.9	1,504	4.1	73,344	65.9	62,194	44.4
Midwest City	86.5	28.8	88.0	77.9	85.2	4.1	26,806	1.4	1,033	3.9	44,889	59.9	35,372	50.3
Moore	83.6	31.1	97.5	89.5	85.2	7.0	31,414	1.5	911	2.9	47,485	74.6	41,258	58.1
Muskogee	82.5	17.5	81.8	63.5	86.3	6.6	16,308	-1.2	649	4.0	29,509	51.9	23,941	42.6
Norman	79.0	31.3	96.7	91.3	69.4	13.9	62,880	1.5	1,784	2.8	102,290	65.0	87,321	46.8
Oklahoma City	83.1	23.6	91.2	84.2	82.0	6.5	319,520	1.4	10,225	3.2	491,576	66.4	413,529	53.0
Owasso	86.8	21.5	92.2	90.3	87.8	5.5	19,026	0.7	560	2.9	27,094	68.9	22,492	58.0
Ponca City	88.2	17.2	91.5	70.6	81.6	5.5	10,395	-1.3	510	4.9	19,158	58.0	14,153	54.2
Shawnee	84.3	23.8	86.7	77.7	82.9	7.5	14,442	-1.5	559	3.9	25,699	57.7	20,734	41.4
Stillwater	72.7	17.4	94.9	83.7	63.9	21.6	24,442	-0.6	692	2.8	43,169	57.8	38,414	28.1
Tulsa	80.9	14.9	89.8	80.2	79.2	6.7	196,950	0.5	7,022	3.6	314,717	65.5	257,777	50.0
OREGON	71.7	32.8	93.2	86.7	83.0	7.7	2,104,516	0.7	87,361	4.2	3,370,795	62.4	2,661,927	47.8
Albany	77.7	26.0	93.0	82.8	88.2	5.8	25,588	1.0	1,153	4.5	42,113	64.5	33,209	52.4
Beaverton	69.1	35.1	96.4	91.3	80.4	8.3	55,666	0.6	1,974	3.5	80,299	71.6	66,731	55.0
Bend	72.2	11.4	94.8	89.9	79.6	9.3	52,592	2.3	1,953	3.7	73,821	64.8	56,407	48.5
Corvallis	60.6	11.6	97.7	89.9	69.8	16.7	31,023	0.1	1,012	3.3	51,384	60.8	44,039	30.2
Eugene	67.2	12.5	95.1	86.1	72.7	10.5	84,561	0.1	3,543	4.2	143,653	63.0	115,550	38.0
Grants Pass	81.3	19.3	90.4	80.7	77.4	2.2	16,147	2.1	896	5.5	28,756	53.7	22,648	39.9
Gresham	71.6	46.5	90.8	83.3	88.3	5.5	55,744	0.7	2,237	4.0	88,052	63.7	73,487	46.3
Hillsboro	71.1	32.5	97.1	93.9	80.4	6.9	58,434	0.6	1,970	3.4	83,694	74.5	74,067	53.7
Keizer	84.0	26.8	96.7	90.5	89.2	7.2	19,665	0.8	787	4.0	31,193	63.6	25,650	49.5
Lake Oswego	76.1	38.6	97.2	95.3	85.1	9.8	21,132	0.7	731	3.5	31,183	63.9	22,988	50.6
McMinnville	81.5	31.7	91.7	81.7	78.0	4.7	16,883	0.9	659	3.9	27,132	57.6	20,547	41.7
Medford	79.6	11.1	90.0	84.5	78.8	5.6	40,377	1.4	1,922	4.8	64,454	58.7	48,898	43.8
Oregon City	76.4	50.0	95.8	90.4	83.4	8.2	19,005	0.6	791	4.2	29,312	70.9	23,686	59.0
Portland	56.7	40.2	94.7	89.6	80.6	9.0	376,355	0.7	13,689	3.6	541,319	70.8	460,077	51.7

1. Employed persons.　2. Households.　3. Percent of civilian labor force.　4. Persons 16 years old and over.

Table D. Cities — **Construction, Wholesale Trade, and Retail Trade**

City	Value of residential construction authorized by building permits, 2018			Wholesale trade[1], 2012				Retail trade[2], 2012			
	New construction ($1,000)	Number of housing units	Percent single family	Number of establishments	Number of employees	Sales (mil dol)	Annual payroll (mil dol)	Number of establish-ments	Number of employees	Sales (mil dol)	Annual payroll (mil dol)
	69	70	71	72	73	74	75	76	77	78	79
OHIO— Cont'd											
Hamilton	10,607	68	100.0	43	800	635.4	43.1	213	3,262	733.6	69.0
Hilliard	26,953	89	100.0	51	700	448.5	36.9	85	1,405	382.8	40.2
Huber Heights	NA	NA	NA	20	394	270.8	20.8	98	2,020	476.1	41.0
Kent	28,078	140	7.1	13	D	D	D	78	1,344	404.7	34.2
Kettering	3,778	17	100.0	26	D	D	D	158	3,328	803.7	80.7
Lakewood	1,202	8	50.0	22	D	D	D	110	1,149	255.6	26.5
Lancaster	12,541	65	87.7	27	368	75.2	14.9	235	3,240	641.9	66.5
Lima	623	4	50.0	49	663	431.3	30.2	125	1,634	463.2	39.7
Lorain	14,125	108	100.0	27	786	333.4	26.3	121	1,836	361.1	39.0
Mansfield	1,345	5	100.0	56	1,001	369.2	44.1	185	2,073	465.0	50.1
Marion	65	5	100.0	18	286	403.2	12.9	112	1,762	446.2	42.3
Mason	52,288	180	94.4	51	1,783	1,023.7	132.9	105	1,864	428.8	46.5
Massillon	11,048	125	38.4	29	419	241.8	21.5	119	2,488	617.7	55.3
Medina	180	4	0.0	50	526	371.0	23.6	111	1,813	384.7	33.8
Mentor	22,256	104	100.0	97	944	439.1	43.2	303	5,884	1,498.9	130.9
Middletown	9,587	54	100.0	33	D	D	D	153	3,372	1,461.3	86.1
Newark	NA	NA	NA	34	514	459.8	22.8	145	1,825	498.5	41.2
North Olmsted	516	2	100.0	22	166	188.0	13.3	250	4,827	1,176.4	114.5
North Ridgeville	58,405	318	96.9	30	442	254.5	18.4	58	647	169.3	14.5
North Royalton	6,996	27	100.0	52	478	357.7	33.4	63	484	112.9	13.8
Parma	1,022	5	100.0	44	851	314.7	32.4	270	3,793	913.3	76.8
Reynoldsburg	6,036	51	2.0	8	D	D	D	119	2,127	1,053.8	79.5
Riverside	NA	NA	NA	9	D	D	D	57	516	144.4	11.9
Sandusky	1,613	6	100.0	31	380	220.9	16.7	101	1,277	330.6	28.8
Shaker Heights	950	2	100.0	10	20	7.1	0.9	47	494	109.2	11.9
Springfield	1,293	5	100.0	50	1,628	2,331.3	82.1	221	3,643	1,118.8	88.4
Stow	6,267	33	100.0	47	590	462.9	34.7	102	2,184	514.7	44.8
Strongsville	21,805	62	100.0	70	1,636	877.5	91.3	240	4,775	1,004.1	95.1
Toledo	2,653	25	80.0	249	3,832	2,592.8	188.6	935	13,004	2,837.1	282.7
Troy	NA	NA	NA	18	253	388.6	11.2	79	1,695	411.5	39.9
Upper Arlington	14,979	12	100.0	14	D	D	D	85	891	192.1	19.3
Warren	0	0	0.0	28	712	772.8	36.5	155	1,907	605.4	48.8
Westerville	38,429	341	14.4	52	494	190.6	21.8	108	1,683	454.8	41.0
Westlake	13,390	23	100.0	82	1,308	830.6	74.6	161	2,377	540.9	50.0
Wooster	5,291	24	66.7	36	476	552.5	19.5	165	2,606	597.9	55.4
Xenia	NA	NA	NA	14	263	285.6	12.0	79	1,259	331.7	32.5
Youngstown	NA	NA	NA	89	1,488	734.0	70.3	219	2,454	473.8	48.8
Zanesville	945	7	42.9	24	251	96.6	8.8	210	3,093	751.9	64.3
OKLAHOMA	2,181,297	10,502	89.1	3,909	50,660	71,892.9	2,718.6	13,051	168,839	50,256.2	4,055.1
Bartlesville	3,004	18	100.0	21	D	D	D	161	D	D	D
Broken Arrow	107,039	455	100.0	125	1,347	691.5	71.5	253	4,115	1,357.3	103.9
Edmond	163,130	487	93.4	96	D	D	D	327	4,505	1,154.8	107.5
Enid	8,124	43	100.0	58	690	1,312.1	33.5	251	3,289	894.8	81.6
Lawton	8,592	40	100.0	49	378	119.1	12.1	352	4,956	1,340.6	112.7
Midwest City	22,757	144	100.0	19	D	D	D	176	4,097	1,280.7	111.1
Moore	41,073	203	100.0	33	D	D	D	147	2,442	638.3	53.5
Muskogee	3,659	17	100.0	45	806	353.8	38.1	215	2,855	806.8	68.8
Norman	115,185	407	97.5	59	746	476.1	39.7	419	7,006	2,124.7	174.3
Oklahoma City	624,429	3,097	95.4	1,025	17,349	43,266.0	1,022.8	2,186	31,326	10,272.1	844.2
Owasso	28,532	130	90.0	15	D	D	D	115	2,434	618.1	50.9
Ponca City	755	3	100.0	23	157	74.9	5.5	126	1,576	431.5	37.3
Shawnee	9,030	63	69.8	29	D	D	D	191	2,675	676.9	59.0
Stillwater	22,783	125	59.2	22	158	163.5	7.5	202	3,157	739.2	66.5
Tulsa	151,853	814	57.9	770	11,810	11,596.9	716.4	1,708	26,411	7,542.2	665.1
OREGON	4,180,894	20,132	55.7	4,393	59,523	48,325.3	3,233.0	13,879	187,402	49,481.1	4,831.5
Albany	48,125	224	69.2	39	369	307.0	16.1	187	2,812	741.1	70.0
Beaverton	37,854	125	100.0	185	2,640	2,230.6	185.4	391	7,600	2,759.6	241.8
Bend	225,999	918	94.2	136	908	621.5	43.0	503	6,406	1,741.9	171.3
Corvallis	39,247	217	20.7	26	D	D	D	212	3,138	676.7	75.6
Eugene	150,550	834	45.8	241	3,013	1,585.8	151.3	726	10,971	2,487.2	271.9
Grants Pass	27,384	126	81.7	25	307	270.2	13.0	241	3,637	872.6	94.9
Gresham	72,386	348	54.6	55	1,615	854.4	73.4	270	3,677	1,087.3	95.5
Hillsboro	77,879	370	59.5	99	1,315	1,047.6	79.5	303	5,624	1,666.9	151.8
Keizer	7,674	42	50.0	11	25	18.9	1.4	83	1,213	255.2	24.0
Lake Oswego	74,671	222	50.5	94	1,457	781.5	136.0	126	D	D	D
McMinnville	37,707	204	46.1	20	111	68.0	5.4	144	2,005	510.0	49.7
Medford	90,506	450	70.2	112	1,139	543.6	46.9	479	7,401	1,965.9	194.4
Oregon City	39,224	146	68.5	14	163	69.3	8.4	98	1,607	448.7	39.4
Portland	860,503	5,648	13.7	1,139	20,024	20,321.0	1,195.1	2,527	32,426	8,508.3	886.3

1. Merchant wholesalers except manufacturers' sales branches and offices.   2. Establishments with payroll.

Table D. Cities — **Real Estate, Professional Services, and Manufacturing**

City	Real estate and rental and leasing, 2012				Professional, scientific, and technical services[1], 2012				Manufacturing, 2012			
	Number of establishments	Number of employees	Receipts (mil dol)	Annual payroll (mil dol)	Number of establishments	Number of employees	Receipts (mil dol)	Annual payroll (mil dol)	Number of establishments	Number of employees	Receipts (mil dol)	Annual payroll (mil dol)
	80	81	82	83	84	85	86	87	88	89	90	91
OHIO— Cont'd												
Hamilton	31	165	34.3	5.3	96	D	D	D	69	1,827	509.6	115.7
Hilliard	39	256	40.3	9.1	85	778	123.9	56.4	28	1,506	436.3	73.5
Huber Heights	25	124	26.4	4.4	32	495	53.8	19.5	31	2,494	1,089.2	237.9
Kent	22	93	11.3	2.9	44	D	D	D	59	1,435	369.6	65.5
Kettering	57	197	60.6	6.9	110	D	D	D	45	1,601	D	73.3
Lakewood	58	322	63.1	12.5	116	388	49.3	20.4	33	587	204.9	30.5
Lancaster	54	215	27.1	4.3	70	D	D	D	45	2,844	864.5	145.2
Lima	29	186	18.9	5.7	73	D	D	D	37	1,724	D	123.5
Lorain	36	118	18.8	3.4	51	D	D	D	40	2,533	D	169.7
Mansfield	58	295	31.0	5.8	117	668	73.7	27.1	96	5,359	2,170.7	257.6
Marion	25	93	14.2	2.1	41	D	D	D	31	2,001	1,291.7	90.7
Mason	30	86	21.6	2.7	110	587	89.7	32.2	32	3,399	1,492.0	197.9
Massillon	24	88	19.8	3.6	44	236	21.2	8.8	60	5,519	1,962.7	218.7
Medina	30	110	24.7	4.1	109	531	55.5	23.3	61	3,036	1,320.6	144.5
Mentor	49	163	47.0	5.1	169	899	118.2	45.6	213	8,675	2,501.6	449.4
Middletown	53	219	40.4	5.9	63	579	51.3	23.3	53	4,040	D	250.4
Newark	42	158	22.9	4.0	82	D	D	D	41	2,302	688.0	103.5
North Olmsted	36	156	28.8	6.1	68	2,306	60.4	33.2	16	208	44.8	8.0
North Ridgeville	12	46	5.2	0.8	43	240	22.5	9.7	42	1,305	318.8	57.3
North Royalton	26	141	38.7	10.6	93	308	44.0	14.6	73	779	113.7	37.3
Parma	57	314	47.8	9.6	91	638	78.4	22.3	32	1,923	692.1	132.2
Reynoldsburg	39	185	42.9	6.5	74	464	40.2	15.9	15	243	D	12.1
Riverside	16	82	23.1	2.5	37	D	D	D	5	90	D	3.1
Sandusky	35	135	19.9	4.1	56	D	D	D	41	1,644	424.9	85.1
Shaker Heights	36	D	D	D	94	D	D	D	NA	NA	NA	NA
Springfield	58	324	35.3	9.3	101	D	D	D	79	2,767	793.4	127.3
Stow	38	169	31.6	4.4	100	864	96.2	42.2	47	1,336	230.6	74.1
Strongsville	53	439	89.0	16.3	121	402	51.7	17.6	72	2,434	685.3	137.3
Toledo	237	1,823	2,219.2	127.8	448	D	D	D	295	11,821	11,102.3	734.4
Troy	21	105	18.5	3.6	59	411	50.8	19.5	49	5,461	2,360.9	285.1
Upper Arlington	42	D	D	D	117	D	D	D	11	61	D	1.5
Warren	32	175	18.6	3.6	97	D	D	D	45	5,428	1,836.3	422.8
Westerville	54	D	D	D	206	2,231	328.1	141.2	34	1,218	354.1	56.2
Westlake	64	258	70.7	11.4	230	1,534	375.8	109.8	49	1,200	295.1	58.0
Wooster	31	107	22.8	3.7	76	746	91.7	33.1	36	3,603	1,406.3	188.9
Xenia	16	43	6.4	1.7	29	118	8.2	2.6	27	493	100.1	27.1
Youngstown	54	357	37.7	7.2	115	D	D	D	90	3,310	719.4	182.1
Zanesville	29	170	24.2	5.0	68	D	D	D	28	D	430.8	46.6
OKLAHOMA	4,000	21,261	4,269.6	898.0	9,428	71,303	10,915.0	4,080.1	3,610	133,064	74,295.4	6,416.0
Bartlesville	39	D	D	D	79	D	D	D	25	D	200.7	D
Broken Arrow	92	227	34.8	7.2	228	1,457	241.0	105.0	132	5,570	1,953.3	332.2
Edmond	181	642	256.3	35.0	430	2,414	312.1	106.9	38	410	78.6	15.7
Enid	72	312	50.1	10.7	107	563	78.8	27.9	50	2,172	D	78.6
Lawton	118	D	D	D	128	D	D	D	39	3,367	D	178.3
Midwest City	74	374	80.1	10.3	93	D	D	D	12	280	83.8	12.8
Moore	47	172	39.0	8.1	64	412	28.4	12.7	25	808	191.2	25.9
Muskogee	48	196	26.7	5.5	75	D	D	D	46	3,200	1,371.0	157.9
Norman	210	975	134.7	35.4	451	D	D	D	69	2,255	1,077.8	101.1
Oklahoma City	893	5,794	1,255.5	266.3	2,357	D	D	D	645	21,675	8,249.8	979.6
Owasso	40	125	20.4	4.6	83	452	38.5	13.8	23	633	D	26.1
Ponca City	27	97	18.0	3.1	67	377	43.2	17.4	34	1,373	488.9	60.8
Shawnee	33	139	21.6	3.8	83	D	D	D	30	2,564	1,032.2	118.3
Stillwater	66	263	46.1	7.3	101	D	D	D	28	946	343.2	37.1
Tulsa	715	5,522	899.2	224.1	1,871	16,400	3,016.5	1,025.7	629	22,012	11,517.9	1,180.7
OREGON	5,644	26,016	4,649.6	902.8	11,564	82,456	11,167.3	5,723.4	5,289	D	D	D
Albany	58	203	31.8	6.6	99	D	D	D	61	D	528.4	D
Beaverton	208	904	162.5	30.0	450	D	D	D	115	6,475	2,817.0	442.4
Bend	257	701	116.7	24.4	500	D	D	D	162	2,444	524.2	117.1
Corvallis	86	D	D	D	208	D	D	D	47	974	235.3	43.4
Eugene	286	1,256	197.0	36.9	673	D	D	D	263	5,512	1,384.9	254.1
Grants Pass	72	248	35.1	6.7	89	D	D	D	68	1,632	318.2	66.0
Gresham	119	445	65.2	11.1	128	D	D	D	73	4,848	1,275.2	291.1
Hillsboro	116	914	467.6	34.3	216	D	D	D	149	D	D	D
Keizer	36	218	22.4	4.3	43	207	22.7	7.9	7	46	6.2	1.5
Lake Oswego	127	627	148.0	38.3	372	3,174	583.8	237.4	36	674	D	54.2
McMinnville	35	120	15.8	2.6	86	D	D	D	63	1,915	776.4	85.2
Medford	145	642	102.9	17.5	242	D	D	D	91	1,599	380.2	66.1
Oregon City	37	109	23.2	4.1	93	D	D	D	47	586	113.8	28.0
Portland	1,221	8,268	1,479.3	357.0	3,434	29,338	5,410.0	2,066.2	978	26,432	8,768.5	1,300.8

1. Establishments subject to federal tax.

Table D. Cities — Accommodation and Food Services, Arts, Entertainment, and Recreation, and Health Care and Social Assistance

City	Accommodation and food services, 2012				Arts, entertainment, and recreation,[1] 2012				Health care and social assistance,[1] 2012			
	Number of establish-ments	Number of employees	Receipts (mil dol)	Annual payroll (mil dol)	Number of establish-ments	Number of employees	Receipts (mil dol)	Annual payroll (mil dol)	Number of establish-ments	Number of employees	Receipts (mil dol)	Annual payroll (mil dol)
	92	93	94	95	96	97	98	99	100	101	102	103
OHIO— Cont'd												
Hamilton	129	2,433	124.0	31.5	6	40	3.8	0.7	111	1,417	122.6	51.6
Hilliard	70	1,572	72.2	20.5	14	224	14.1	4.6	92	D	D	D
Huber Heights	78	1,638	79.2	22.6	6	D	D	D	67	D	D	D
Kent	89	1,426	84.5	18.3	5	D	D	D	38	518	32.6	15.1
Kettering	107	D	D	D	12	413	16.7	6.3	170	D	D	D
Lakewood	115	1,820	86.4	27.6	11	79	4.3	1.0	104	1,259	97.6	40.3
Lancaster	108	2,393	99.5	29.4	10	66	4.6	0.9	146	D	D	D
Lima	77	1,196	63.9	15.8	2	D	D	D	129	2,405	308.3	168.9
Lorain	71	1,107	50.0	12.8	14	104	5.7	1.7	100	1,278	150.0	64.6
Mansfield	111	2,022	86.2	23.9	8	60	2.2	0.5	178	D	D	D
Marion	66	1,259	56.5	14.2	4	D	D	D	108	D	D	D
Mason	98	2,588	129.5	35.3	18	1,038	130.5	32.4	117	1,503	122.9	51.1
Massillon	79	1,175	54.7	14.4	2	D	D	D	70	2,249	205.4	75.4
Medina	59	1,182	50.2	14.5	6	D	D	D	75	D	D	D
Mentor	174	3,813	162.3	46.2	10	D	D	D	155	2,340	211.0	89.2
Middletown	91	2,064	96.7	26.8	6	68	2.6	0.9	117	D	D	D
Newark	97	1,672	72.0	20.0	10	D	D	D	126	3,126	271.2	124.2
North Olmsted	119	2,387	112.3	30.9	7	58	3.3	0.9	72	1,135	77.4	31.0
North Ridgeville	43	611	25.9	6.9	6	64	3.4	1.1	39	521	35.4	13.3
North Royalton	39	398	13.7	3.6	8	D	D	D	59	691	49.7	19.7
Parma	163	2,484	110.1	28.3	11	D	D	D	184	3,232	293.7	139.9
Reynoldsburg	74	D	D	D	7	47	1.9	0.6	104	D	D	D
Riverside	51	D	D	D	3	D	D	D	28	D	D	D
Sandusky	72	865	81.7	13.6	16	D	D	D	58	607	81.9	37.3
Shaker Heights	33	362	19.8	5.2	10	105	6.0	2.1	51	938	50.8	25.1
Springfield	154	3,174	149.7	40.3	12	82	3.9	1.3	188	3,381	255.6	114.1
Stow	86	1,724	78.0	21.0	19	D	D	D	63	1,145	88.2	37.7
Strongsville	122	2,951	127.8	36.6	14	192	30.1	6.8	98	1,391	125.2	54.7
Toledo	632	11,286	485.9	141.1	61	786	167.8	28.9	528	8,914	904.1	446.6
Troy	75	1,906	81.6	23.6	8	D	D	D	74	D	D	D
Upper Arlington	66	1,333	60.8	18.2	6	10	1.0	0.2	70	1,120	86.0	44.6
Warren	89	6,193	301.0	97.1	8	D	D	D	154	D	D	D
Westerville	102	D	D	D	7	D	D	D	222	3,299	342.2	164.6
Westlake	99	2,797	127.0	39.5	10	368	8.6	3.3	236	4,021	374.4	172.0
Wooster	85	1,683	75.0	21.6	5	D	D	D	91	1,529	140.0	69.5
Xenia	50	1,003	42.7	11.1	5	D	D	D	55	485	48.0	17.6
Youngstown	117	D	D	D	9	D	D	D	124	4,127	396.0	180.4
Zanesville	100	2,215	103.0	29.1	7	83	2.8	0.8	117	D	D	D
OKLAHOMA	7,403	143,561	7,121.2	1,908.3	816	22,012	2,526.6	578.2	8,868	128,437	13,382.5	4,996.4
Bartlesville	100	D	D	D	8	D	D	D	119	D	D	D
Broken Arrow	169	D	D	D	25	D	D	D	191	2,529	176.7	71.3
Edmond	202	4,394	197.9	54.0	33	D	D	D	403	3,669	450.9	150.6
Enid	120	2,183	111.9	26.6	11	69	5.8	1.0	172	2,734	250.9	88.2
Lawton	195	4,445	207.1	62.1	17	D	D	D	210	D	D	D
Midwest City	121	2,544	125.1	34.9	11	60	4.2	0.9	188	3,214	418.2	136.1
Moore	105	2,398	117.7	30.2	5	D	D	D	95	D	D	D
Muskogee	106	2,011	88.5	23.5	8	D	D	D	177	D	D	D
Norman	312	7,292	325.2	93.0	41	D	D	D	393	3,976	397.6	155.8
Oklahoma City	1,361	30,537	1,510.0	413.0	141	2,398	459.8	136.5	1,969	31,146	4,098.3	1,466.1
Owasso	76	1,812	82.7	24.2	12	D	D	D	85	D	D	D
Ponca City	54	932	45.7	11.3	3	21	0.7	0.2	81	1,264	109.1	40.3
Shawnee	98	2,180	95.0	25.3	7	D	D	D	99	1,508	120.2	55.9
Stillwater	146	3,143	134.8	36.7	8	D	D	D	98	1,494	114.9	44.2
Tulsa	1,099	D	D	D	114	D	D	D	1,387	22,659	3,105.8	1,205.0
OREGON	10,610	150,482	8,466.8	2,438.5	1,190	16,916	1,176.8	415.8	9,829	105,341	11,016.4	4,533.8
Albany	119	1,905	87.6	24.4	12	D	D	D	98	D	D	D
Beaverton	317	5,077	279.4	81.1	45	564	69.0	13.4	360	3,703	381.2	140.5
Bend	303	4,684	255.1	74.6	44	1,231	47.0	13.8	384	D	D	D
Corvallis	179	2,837	131.5	37.8	14	D	D	D	175	D	D	D
Eugene	526	8,479	417.8	124.4	44	574	25.5	6.4	586	D	D	D
Grants Pass	145	2,089	100.1	29.4	15	D	D	D	178	2,519	235.5	81.6
Gresham	221	3,294	181.5	49.0	21	374	19.7	6.3	284	3,040	247.1	100.5
Hillsboro	237	3,789	222.3	61.7	20	265	13.3	3.5	248	D	D	D
Keizer	56	D	D	D	10	117	5.6	1.9	60	D	D	D
Lake Oswego	113	1,928	111.3	33.3	19	156	10.0	3.4	186	1,643	156.1	60.1
McMinnville	86	1,138	56.6	16.1	6	D	D	D	111	D	D	D
Medford	262	4,049	204.4	59.8	26	355	23.4	5.9	303	D	D	D
Oregon City	79	1,044	55.6	15.6	7	D	D	D	105	D	D	D
Portland	2,522	38,496	2,261.7	671.0	274	3,542	436.5	185.9	1,963	D	D	D

1. Establishments subject to federal tax.

Table D. Cities — Other Services and Government Employment and Payroll

City	Other services[1] — Number of establishments	Number of employees	Receipts (mil dol)	Annual payroll (mil dol)	Government employment and payroll, 2012 — Full-time equivalent employees	March payroll — Total (dollars)	Percent of total for: Administrative, judicial, and legal	Police and corrections	Fire protection	Highways and transportation	Health and welfare	Natural resources and utilities	Education and libraries
	104	105	106	107	108	109	110	111	112	113	114	115	116
OHIO— Cont'd													
Hamilton	73	417	41.3	11.8	648	3,715,041	12.3	21.8	20.8	4.6	2.2	31.0	0.0
Hilliard	43	287	30.7	9.1	138	630,071	19.0	53.4	0.0	3.8	0.0	18.6	0.0
Huber Heights	50	279	20.4	6.7	178	969,065	15.5	36.2	31.4	11.5	0.0	0.2	0.0
Kent	43	273	18.6	6.8	203	1,021,262	8.2	30.7	21.0	16.4	6.0	15.0	0.0
Kettering	72	623	28.5	9.9	489	2,337,531	21.1	27.0	15.6	13.9	0.8	14.6	0.0
Lakewood	55	417	19.5	6.9	462	2,388,158	12.9	31.2	24.7	3.8	7.9	16.6	0.0
Lancaster	61	400	36.0	11.3	414	1,841,272	17.3	24.9	20.9	5.2	0.7	29.3	0.9
Lima	52	297	19.1	5.3	375	1,604,715	20.6	25.2	20.8	9.0	2.6	21.4	0.0
Lorain	58	401	30.2	8.5	466	2,344,000	9.9	33.0	23.6	4.0	5.6	19.7	4.2
Mansfield	87	577	42.8	13.0	423	1,865,914	20.0	26.6	23.0	4.6	1.3	17.6	0.0
Marion	40	285	18.1	5.7	241	1,067,754	11.2	34.1	23.1	9.9	0.0	17.7	0.0
Mason	38	237	13.8	5.4	266	1,194,447	18.2	24.2	20.0	7.6	0.0	21.7	0.0
Massillon	54	340	31.7	10.7	321	1,362,818	15.6	16.2	16.6	5.0	6.2	34.1	0.0
Medina	63	487	36.1	11.8	221	904,261	23.8	27.5	4.7	5.0	3.8	26.8	0.0
Mentor	120	838	57.7	21.3	500	2,127,362	11.3	29.5	28.5	14.3	5.5	10.9	0.0
Middletown	62	465	41.4	13.1	404	1,752,509	12.7	30.0	25.2	6.7	4.9	15.7	0.0
Newark	56	410	27.1	10.1	384	1,681,225	15.2	30.1	24.2	8.0	3.0	18.9	0.0
North Olmsted	100	676	54.7	16.5	255	1,250,704	8.6	28.1	19.4	3.8	2.7	29.3	0.0
North Ridgeville	46	193	19.3	5.1	199	885,287	13.3	28.1	21.5	10.7	2.1	18.6	0.0
North Royalton	58	292	26.0	8.6	185	949,689	9.7	32.8	24.0	9.0	2.8	17.2	0.0
Parma	129	828	74.7	22.5	468	1,957,354	15.6	32.5	28.4	11.6	3.1	4.2	0.0
Reynoldsburg	41	229	17.2	6.2	136	685,686	14.7	61.7	0.0	5.3	1.2	11.6	0.0
Riverside	18	74	5.3	1.7	85	380,891	12.2	46.1	28.8	12.4	0.0	0.0	0.0
Sandusky	33	122	10.0	3.0	231	1,023,311	17.4	23.9	23.6	4.8	2.8	23.4	0.0
Shaker Heights	18	81	5.9	1.7	356	1,867,638	14.5	30.2	20.9	14.6	4.9	6.2	0.0
Springfield	93	634	55.9	15.3	591	2,580,272	18.3	27.7	26.1	4.8	3.8	16.2	0.0
Stow	59	406	27.2	9.1	268	1,324,714	23.7	25.9	29.3	6.1	0.7	9.3	0.0
Strongsville	74	755	53.2	18.6	365	1,769,488	7.3	33.1	24.7	16.5	5.3	11.6	0.0
Toledo	356	2,384	178.0	57.2	2,146	10,282,276	15.9	23.9	36.8	7.3	1.5	13.8	0.0
Troy	48	279	18.0	5.7	184	972,285	13.3	25.7	22.4	11.8	1.3	24.4	0.0
Upper Arlington	29	239	15.7	5.7	239	1,342,741	13.2	27.2	31.7	10.1	4.0	11.5	0.0
Warren	60	319	22.3	6.7	445	1,785,083	16.7	23.0	19.1	3.3	3.9	30.7	0.0
Westerville	63	D	D	D	484	2,542,559	12.4	27.1	26.3	4.3	0.0	26.7	0.0
Westlake	71	678	39.2	14.8	288	1,367,977	13.6	30.0	24.5	2.8	3.2	21.7	0.0
Wooster	44	291	21.3	6.8	879	3,824,028	2.0	5.4	6.8	4.2	78.8	2.8	0.0
Xenia	33	164	12.2	3.6	219	1,060,316	20.5	35.1	21.7	3.3	0.9	13.1	0.0
Youngstown	78	358	25.6	9.2	757	3,252,504	14.0	28.1	18.4	6.3	4.9	27.3	0.0
Zanesville	65	633	43.5	13.4	297	1,096,683	10.0	29.7	21.1	6.3	2.8	25.1	0.0
OKLAHOMA	4,369	26,154	2,610.1	707.1	X	X	X	X	X	X	X	X	X
Bartlesville	51	373	28.3	9.4	344	1,284,794	8.5	23.4	23.5	6.4	0.4	26.0	5.4
Broken Arrow	136	834	88.2	22.0	618	2,786,415	13.1	30.6	27.6	5.5	0.0	17.1	0.0
Edmond	157	902	68.3	20.1	688	3,323,448	15.6	22.5	27.9	6.2	1.5	21.4	0.0
Enid	91	468	48.5	11.7	477	1,757,022	12.4	27.9	23.3	7.6	2.5	18.8	2.4
Lawton	98	659	52.1	17.1	892	3,414,778	14.9	29.7	19.3	9.4	2.0	20.6	1.8
Midwest City	52	415	26.1	8.2	494	2,315,063	15.2	28.4	24.6	3.8	4.3	18.9	0.0
Moore	60	D	D	D	275	1,722,367	12.5	35.2	32.5	2.3	5.4	6.1	0.0
Muskogee	55	470	44.3	11.5	497	1,548,570	8.5	26.0	24.8	12.1	0.0	24.8	0.0
Norman	132	769	56.0	16.9	3,161	15,136,504	3.2	7.5	5.5	2.7	74.3	5.6	0.0
Oklahoma City	835	6,134	660.7	173.6	4,418	24,268,820	9.9	32.6	28.7	9.3	4.5	15.0	0.0
Owasso	44	155	13.3	3.2	219	910,478	15.5	28.5	31.9	5.8	0.7	11.3	0.0
Ponca City	34	192	19.0	4.9	400	1,441,141	9.1	18.8	20.4	7.8	0.7	35.3	2.6
Shawnee	45	248	17.3	5.3	279	1,055,211	16.1	30.3	23.8	5.8	1.6	22.2	0.0
Stillwater	58	D	D	D	1,308	5,630,416	4.6	9.5	6.8	1.6	62.0	12.2	1.1
Tulsa	686	4,968	482.3	149.2	3,932	16,951,552	11.3	27.1	20.9	14.4	1.8	12.8	0.0
OREGON	5,258	28,203	2,519.4	794.3	X	X	X	X	X	X	X	X	X
Albany	63	412	25.0	9.0	389	2,123,666	12.9	24.2	24.6	13.2	0.1	18.7	3.7
Beaverton	180	1,217	116.1	37.3	488	2,217,436	38.8	23.9	0.0	5.4	0.0	10.8	12.0
Bend	159	822	64.7	20.0	432	2,556,081	14.4	29.2	23.0	5.2	3.3	12.8	0.0
Corvallis	75	389	24.1	8.5	430	2,437,922	9.9	21.5	18.9	5.8	8.1	18.9	8.1
Eugene	251	1,832	146.3	47.3	1,983	11,796,504	9.0	18.2	12.2	8.0	1.2	26.1	3.1
Grants Pass	59	285	22.5	6.6	214	1,160,951	18.8	44.3	16.7	2.1	0.0	13.1	0.0
Gresham	117	495	40.4	13.3	515	3,198,886	13.0	29.6	21.1	3.3	0.6	22.0	0.0
Hillsboro	119	947	121.9	49.5	759	4,281,252	14.6	24.9	17.5	3.5	0.0	24.7	6.8
Keizer	34	166	11.3	3.7	89	489,891	18.6	57.2	0.0	2.5	0.0	16.6	0.0
Lake Oswego	74	318	23.2	7.1	325	1,928,696	17.6	21.1	21.4	8.6	1.3	17.6	6.5
McMinnville	40	165	12.8	4.0	252	1,307,113	16.9	18.4	16.1	4.8	2.3	34.2	4.5
Medford	125	860	71.7	26.4	452	2,575,154	14.2	34.5	21.7	15.1	0.1	9.8	0.0
Oregon City	49	254	20.5	7.5	159	835,368	19.0	32.4	0.0	14.2	0.0	19.2	5.8
Portland	1,246	8,014	781.3	237.5	5,804	35,656,383	18.1	25.5	15.0	10.2	0.9	27.3	0.0

1. Establishments subject to federal tax.

City Government Finances

City	General revenue Total (mil dol) 117	Intergovernmental Total (mil dol) 118	Percent from state government 119	Taxes Total (mil dol) 120	Taxes Per capita¹ (dollars) Total 121	Property 122	Sales and gross receipts 123	General expenditure Total (mil dol) 124	Per capita¹ (dollars) Total 125	Capital outlays 126
OHIO— Cont'd										
Hamilton	89.3	12.8	82.9	38.5	618	143	14	83.9	1,348	178
Hilliard	35.0	7.3	60.4	23.3	762	41	50	31.8	1,040	211
Huber Heights	30.3	5.3	52.2	16.8	442	90	32	34.7	911	258
Kent	26.7	4.8	93.2	14.4	488	94	24	31.0	1,046	271
Kettering	81.4	18.4	94.3	48.4	863	160	8	83.8	1,495	462
Lakewood	61.0	11.1	71.9	35.2	685	265	25	53.0	1,032	61
Lancaster	74.4	14.1	95.8	19.9	511	72	1	62.8	1,614	139
Lima	73.9	31.0	93.2	18.5	482	32	28	56.9	1,483	345
Lorain	67.9	22.6	96.7	25.7	402	58	34	56.8	890	61
Mansfield	55.9	12.3	51.1	27.7	588	43	15	51.8	1,101	78
Marion	39.4	10.3	100.0	13.8	375	33	10	36.5	989	43
Mason	54.1	7.0	87.3	29.3	937	192	66	56.2	1,798	343
Massillon	35.7	5.9	26.8	17.4	540	50	45	33.4	1,036	44
Medina	27.0	2.3	92.3	16.9	636	121	21	24.7	931	114
Mentor	61.5	10.0	90.4	40.5	862	94	40	59.9	1,274	0
Middletown	84.2	23.4	47.0	24.4	501	100	5	78.5	1,612	138
Newark	52.3	16.1	92.8	22.0	462	55	6	52.1	1,091	140
North Olmsted	41.3	6.2	95.2	23.4	724	285	44	35.0	1,082	136
North Ridgeville	32.6	5.0	88.6	15.8	516	189	54	29.7	972	100
North Royalton	28.1	4.2	100.0	16.8	554	150	19	25.8	852	47
Parma	80.5	21.4	100.0	48.3	599	109	29	75.6	937	31
Reynoldsburg	27.3	3.4	100.0	14.8	406	60	10	25.5	702	31
Riverside	11.8	3.1	96.7	6.6	263	93	1	11.2	447	11
Sandusky	39.2	10.7	84.2	17.6	686	79	317	32.3	1,262	169
Shaker Heights	52.5	8.5	41.5	33.5	1,195	272	23	57.7	2,057	258
Springfield	86.7	27.8	35.7	38.2	635	49	32	79.9	1,328	177
Stow	35.8	7.4	100.0	21.6	623	215	21	32.9	950	128
Strongsville	63.9	10.5	39.1	39.3	881	209	21	66.8	1,498	383
Toledo	451.3	105.2	62.6	175.0	618	42	23	399.2	1,408	377
Troy	33.3	3.4	70.1	17.1	674	74	29	30.1	1,187	140
Upper Arlington	43.7	6.5	59.0	27.9	815	255	41	52.7	1,538	476
Warren	62.9	13.4	36.4	19.8	486	36	24	56.8	1,394	127
Westerville	85.6	17.7	81.5	50.6	1,359	332	29	96.9	2,605	855
Westlake	58.8	5.1	53.1	39.7	1,222	403	54	49.3	1,518	310
Wooster	134.0	6.0	94.8	14.0	532	83	27	128.8	4,877	371
Xenia	28.5	5.5	95.4	13.4	514	62	40	28.4	1,089	214
Youngstown	104.6	20.7	41.1	54.6	826	37	116	89.8	1,358	37
Zanesville	44.9	17.1	96.5	17.8	701	46	54	34.3	1,347	67
OKLAHOMA	X	X	X	X	X	X	X	X	X	X
Bartlesville	40.2	4.0	79.0	22.5	619	96	523	44.1	1,213	354
Broken Arrow	90.6	4.1	24.8	53.9	528	119	409	91.4	896	239
Edmond	93.1	6.8	73.5	55.3	651	0	651	115.9	1,364	281
Enid	67.3	6.0	81.8	38.4	769	57	712	80.2	1,606	728
Lawton	96.6	12.3	38.3	56.7	575	41	534	92.9	943	108
Midwest City	69.8	4.9	68.6	36.3	646	46	600	62.1	1,107	89
Moore	45.7	1.5	65.9	32.5	561	58	503	41.5	717	95
Muskogee	130.4	3.3	45.2	28.4	729	5	724	134.9	3,462	322
Norman	443.4	6.4	56.7	79.6	687	68	619	422.1	3,646	294
Oklahoma City	1,107.5	90.6	50.5	601.9	1,003	139	865	835.1	1,392	272
Owasso	32.7	0.8	93.6	20.7	658	0	658	29.0	924	98
Ponca City	41.3	2.3	61.5	16.3	655	21	635	56.7	2,278	730
Shawnee	34.1	5.6	40.8	20.1	656	2	653	30.7	1,003	220
Stillwater	49.0	2.9	45.6	29.0	622	29	593	48.2	1,033	155
Tulsa	741.9	77.4	11.3	340.0	862	161	701	712.6	1,806	561
OREGON	X	X	X	X	X	X	X	X	X	X
Albany	59.2	9.0	56.9	32.7	638	505	133	56.1	1,094	127
Beaverton	79.4	16.3	57.8	44.0	475	344	131	78.1	842	126
Bend	88.7	15.0	54.7	44.0	558	331	227	81.1	1,029	162
Corvallis	71.4	12.8	43.7	35.6	647	446	202	62.4	1,135	94
Eugene	265.1	45.3	46.0	119.6	757	620	138	254.5	1,612	275
Grants Pass	36.2	6.8	64.2	20.5	589	453	136	35.8	1,028	164
Gresham	102.2	33.7	52.1	39.5	363	243	120	106.4	979	155
Hillsboro	134.5	12.8	83.8	79.4	832	541	291	124.8	1,309	91
Keizer	21.2	3.3	99.7	10.7	290	216	74	18.1	490	50
Lake Oswego	80.7	14.9	44.5	43.4	1,164	919	245	69.2	1,857	263
McMinnville	37.5	4.1	96.1	15.2	459	360	99	30.1	909	86
Medford	102.4	14.5	49.3	58.0	758	455	303	104.2	1,361	306
Oregon City	52.1	16.8	99.0	19.9	594	337	257	43.8	1,308	472
Portland	1298.8	266.5	44.2	612.5	1,016	708	308	1,280.8	2,124	548

1. Based on population estimated as of July 1 of the year shown.

Table D. Cities — City Government Finances

General expenditure (cont.)

Percent of total for:

City	Public welfare	Highways	Parking facilities	Education	Health and hospitals	Police protection	Sewerage and sanitation	Parks and recreation	Housing and community development	Interest on debt
	127	128	129	130	131	132	133	134	135	136
OHIO— Cont'd										
Hamilton	0.0	6.1	0.5	0.0	1.5	24.9	20.3	0.9	3.4	4.7
Hilliard	0.0	24.2	0.0	0.0	0.5	19.2	1.2	7.4	0.0	8.3
Huber Heights	0.0	13.8	0.0	0.0	3.0	17.2	7.9	12.9	4.7	5.3
Kent	0.4	5.1	0.0	0.0	3.0	20.7	13.4	5.7	2.8	0.8
Kettering	0.0	11.2	0.0	0.0	0.8	17.2	0.0	14.9	1.4	0.8
Lakewood	3.1	12.4	0.5	0.0	0.8	19.5	15.5	4.3	5.6	4.7
Lancaster	0.0	5.4	0.0	0.0	0.4	12.7	21.9	2.9	0.9	23.9
Lima	0.0	16.0	0.0	0.0	0.0	15.9	21.7	1.8	6.7	2.8
Lorain	1.5	5.3	0.0	0.0	2.1	22.9	25.4	0.6	7.9	2.8
Mansfield	0.0	13.1	0.0	1.8	0.0	16.3	8.4	0.5	3.4	0.6
Marion	0.0	8.9	0.0	0.0	1.3	18.4	33.3	2.5	0.0	2.0
Mason	0.0	17.2	0.0	0.0	0.0	10.0	9.1	17.8	0.0	7.0
Massillon	0.0	11.0	0.1	0.0	1.8	14.9	25.5	10.7	0.9	5.3
Medina	0.0	17.5	8.9	0.0	0.0	17.4	12.9	13.7	0.0	1.6
Mentor	0.0	24.6	0.0	0.0	0.0	19.1	0.0	11.9	0.8	2.7
Middletown	0.0	12.5	0.0	0.0	1.0	10.4	16.2	3.7	18.8	2.3
Newark	0.0	9.2	0.0	0.0	0.0	16.1	17.8	0.0	0.0	2.0
North Olmsted	0.9	13.9	0.0	0.0	0.0	15.9	22.0	12.1	0.5	5.6
North Ridgeville	0.0	12.1	0.0	0.0	8.5	17.4	25.4	1.3	4.6	3.6
North Royalton	0.0	20.6	0.0	0.0	0.7	23.5	21.0	1.5	2.7	1.6
Parma	0.0	5.8	0.0	0.0	0.4	40.5	0.5	5.1	11.3	1.6
Reynoldsburg	0.0	5.9	0.0	0.0	0.8	30.8	31.8	3.9	0.0	1.4
Riverside	0.0	14.6	0.0	0.0	0.0	41.2	0.0	0.4	0.0	0.8
Sandusky	0.0	8.5	0.0	0.0	0.0	15.5	25.9	1.2	2.8	6.9
Shaker Heights	0.0	7.5	0.0	0.0	1.0	20.4	8.3	8.9	8.8	1.6
Springfield	0.0	3.0	0.0	0.0	0.0	15.5	8.1	0.0	5.0	1.9
Stow	0.0	10.2	0.0	0.0	0.9	18.9	2.2	7.6	0.0	3.2
Strongsville	0.0	30.1	0.0	0.0	0.5	17.2	11.8	7.8	0.0	4.3
Toledo	0.4	8.8	0.2	0.0	3.7	23.7	22.4	1.8	3.2	5.8
Troy	0.0	7.4	0.4	0.0	1.1	12.4	14.3	12.0	6.3	2.2
Upper Arlington	0.0	34.9	0.0	0.0	0.4	13.2	6.2	6.9	2.2	3.4
Warren	0.0	8.6	0.2	0.0	1.6	12.9	18.9	4.3	7.2	1.3
Westerville	0.0	2.3	0.0	0.0	0.0	14.8	10.3	17.5	0.0	1.5
Westlake	0.0	17.5	0.0	0.0	0.0	13.8	11.8	6.6	0.0	1.6
Wooster	0.0	1.4	0.0	0.0	76.3	4.9	6.2	1.1	0.2	0.4
Xenia	0.0	1.1	0.3	0.0	0.0	19.2	20.9	0.6	1.7	1.4
Youngstown	0.0	6.3	0.1	0.0	1.5	22.0	27.0	2.7	6.8	1.8
Zanesville	0.0	10.9	0.0	0.0	1.2	22.8	24.7	2.4	0.0	3.0
OKLAHOMA	X	X	X	X	X	X	X	X	X	X
Bartlesville	0.0	15.9	0.0	0.0	0.0	12.6	20.7	12.2	2.0	1.5
Broken Arrow	0.0	7.8	0.0	0.0	0.8	18.6	18.5	7.7	0.8	5.5
Edmond	1.6	24.4	0.0	0.0	1.5	11.6	15.1	8.3	0.6	0.3
Enid	0.3	12.1	0.0	0.0	5.1	10.6	19.3	6.6	17.6	0.7
Lawton	0.0	9.4	0.0	5.7	0.9	21.2	15.2	1.3	1.1	1.4
Midwest City	0.0	8.1	0.0	0.0	0.0	23.9	12.5	4.6	7.6	6.6
Moore	0.0	14.8	0.0	0.0	0.0	23.2	14.3	3.7	3.2	1.9
Muskogee	0.0	3.1	0.0	0.0	65.8	5.4	5.9	4.1	0.6	0.1
Norman	0.0	6.6	0.0	0.0	68.5	5.5	5.8	1.8	0.4	3.1
Oklahoma City	0.0	8.8	0.7	2.5	0.9	18.5	8.3	17.3	3.5	5.8
Owasso	0.0	4.3	0.0	0.0	4.7	22.5	13.0	6.5	1.6	5.2
Ponca City	0.0	7.2	0.0	0.0	1.8	11.7	12.2	6.8	1.4	3.7
Shawnee	0.0	12.2	0.0	0.0	0.0	22.5	9.6	3.8	2.4	0.3
Stillwater	0.4	18.2	0.0	0.0	0.2	21.6	13.9	8.0	0.0	2.1
Tulsa	2.1	19.7	1.1	0.0	8.8	12.2	19.9	4.8	0.0	6.0
OREGON	X	X	X	X	X	X	X	X	X	X
Albany	0.0	7.1	0.0	0.0	3.9	21.6	16.2	10.8	0.1	1.7
Beaverton	0.0	7.6	0.0	0.0	0.0	31.5	10.8	0.2	1.1	0.8
Bend	0.0	12.0	0.8	0.0	0.0	21.4	12.9	0.0	4.1	3.6
Corvallis	0.0	5.9	0.2	0.0	0.0	20.1	18.1	9.1	2.8	3.7
Eugene	0.0	2.5	1.5	0.0	0.0	18.2	14.0	9.7	2.9	0.9
Grants Pass	0.0	8.4	0.0	0.0	0.0	30.5	11.8	5.8	3.1	1.3
Gresham	0.0	10.0	0.0	0.0	0.0	20.1	23.2	3.0	1.4	3.3
Hillsboro	0.0	8.1	0.1	0.0	0.0	20.0	22.0	13.5	1.2	2.5
Keizer	0.0	10.4	0.0	0.0	0.0	28.9	33.1	2.7	4.7	7.4
Lake Oswego	0.0	4.0	0.0	0.0	0.0	13.3	14.8	11.9	0.0	6.6
McMinnville	0.0	5.9	0.0	0.0	10.6	19.5	16.7	11.4	0.0	3.2
Medford	0.0	12.8	0.4	0.0	0.0	19.0	14.3	5.7	5.9	15.0
Oregon City	0.0	35.9	0.8	0.0	0.0	15.8	13.8	8.7	1.1	3.8
Portland	0.0	13.9	0.6	0.0	0.0	13.5	20.3	7.8	7.5	7.6

City	City government finances, 2012 (cont.)			Climate[2]						
	Debt outstanding			Average daily temperature						
				Mean		Limits				
	Total (mil dol)	Per capita[1] (dollars)	Debt issued during year	January	July	January[3]	July[4]	Annual precipitation (inches)	Heating degree days	Cooling degree days
	137	138	139	140	141	142	143	144	145	146

OHIO— Cont'd										
Hamilton....................	315.7	5,070	50.5	28.7	76.6	19.9	88.1	43.36	5,261	1,135
Hilliard.......................	62.6	2,046	8.0	NA	NA	NA	NA	NA	NA	NA
Huber Heights............	57.3	1,501	0.6	27.9	77.0	20.6	87.2	39.41	5,343	1,214
Kent...........................	19.1	645	0.0	27.2	74.1	20.1	83.9	36.07	5,752	856
Kettering....................	18.1	324	0.0	27.9	77.0	20.6	87.2	39.41	5,343	1,214
Lakewood...................	92.2	1,795	12.3	25.7	71.9	18.8	81.4	38.71	6,121	702
Lancaster...................	375.7	9,659	0.2	26.5	73.1	17.8	84.4	36.55	5,887	764
Lima..........................	36.5	953	1.1	25.5	73.6	18.1	84.0	37.20	5,932	835
Lorain........................	48.2	755	6.9	27.1	73.8	19.3	85.0	38.02	5,731	818
Mansfield...................	9.9	210	0.4	24.3	71.0	16.2	81.8	43.24	6,364	653
Marion.......................	44.8	1,215	0.0	24.5	72.7	16.0	83.7	38.35	6,300	703
Mason........................	120.3	3,846	16.6	NA	NA	NA	NA	NA	NA	NA
Massillon...................	22.4	697	0.1	25.2	71.8	17.4	82.3	38.47	6,154	678
Medina.......................	45.6	1,720	0.0	23.7	71.3	16.2	82.0	38.34	6,525	558
Mentor.......................	34.9	742	4.4	23.0	68.8	14.3	80.0	47.33	6,956	372
Middletown.................	241.5	4,959	0.3	27.5	74.2	18.3	86.3	39.54	5,609	879
Newark.......................	24.5	514	2.9	25.8	72.7	17.3	83.8	41.62	6,084	687
North Olmsted............	38.8	1,199	1.4	25.7	71.9	18.8	81.4	38.71	6,121	702
North Ridgeville..........	34.1	1,115	4.1	NA	NA	NA	NA	NA	NA	NA
North Royalton...........	40.3	1,328	15.0	25.7	71.9	18.8	81.4	38.71	6,121	702
Parma........................	37.5	465	0.0	25.7	71.9	18.8	81.4	38.71	6,121	702
Reynoldsburg.............	22.9	631	0.0	28.3	75.1	20.3	85.3	38.52	5,492	951
Riverside....................	2.0	79	0.0	NA	NA	NA	NA	NA	NA	NA
Sandusky...................	27.6	1,078	4.1	25.6	73.8	18.9	81.8	34.46	6,065	785
Shaker Heights	27.3	972	0.3	25.7	71.9	18.8	81.4	38.71	6,121	702
Springfield.................	42.8	711	0.0	26.1	73.5	18.2	83.8	37.70	5,921	796
Stow..........................	28.9	832	0.0	27.2	74.1	20.1	83.9	36.07	5,752	856
Strongsville	60.3	1,353	10.7	25.7	71.9	18.8	81.4	38.71	6,121	702
Toledo.......................	357.2	1,260	8.3	27.5	77.6	21.7	87.1	33.52	5,464	1,257
Troy...........................	19.5	768	0.0	NA	NA	NA	NA	NA	NA	NA
Upper Arlington	51.9	1,515	6.0	28.3	75.1	20.3	85.3	38.52	5,492	951
Warren.......................	33.9	832	0.0	24.0	70.2	15.3	82.4	37.80	6,678	458
Westerville.................	75.5	2,027	10.0	27.7	74.4	19.7	85.4	39.35	5,434	924
Westlake....................	43.8	1,350	7.4	27.1	73.8	19.3	85.0	38.02	5,731	818
Wooster.....................	10.1	381	0.0	NA	NA	NA	NA	NA	NA	NA
Xenia.........................	7.4	286	1.1	NA	NA	NA	NA	NA	NA	NA
Youngstown	32.0	483	0.0	24.9	69.9	17.4	81.0	38.02	6,451	552
Zanesville..................	6.6	261	0.0	24.3	68.4	16.3	78.7	36.91	6,639	373
OKLAHOMA................	X	X	X	X	X	X	X	X	X	X
Bartlesville................	60.7	1,673	0.0	35.4	82.2	23.7	94.5	38.99	3,743	1,894
Broken Arrow	183.9	1,802	48.4	34.8	81.3	23.5	92.9	40.46	3,917	1,746
Edmond.....................	136.7	1,609	0.0	36.7	82.0	26.2	93.1	35.85	3,663	1,907
Enid...........................	78.5	1,572	17.0	33.1	82.6	21.9	94.4	34.25	4,269	1,852
Lawton.......................	141.0	1,431	38.0	38.2	84.2	26.4	95.7	31.64	3,326	2,199
Midwest City..............	106.7	1,901	73.2	36.7	82.0	26.2	93.1	35.85	3,663	1,907
Moore........................	71.4	1,232	25.2	36.7	82.0	26.2	93.1	35.85	3,663	1,907
Muskogee	44.3	1,136	5.0	36.1	82.1	25.2	93.1	43.77	3,667	1,858
Norman......................	372.5	3,217	23.4	35.8	82.1	23.2	93.9	41.65	3,713	1,906
Oklahoma City	1,318.9	2,199	185.3	36.7	82.0	26.2	93.1	35.85	3,663	1,907
Owasso......................	39.4	1,254	0.0	NA	NA	NA	NA	NA	NA	NA
Ponca City.................	59.4	2,385	24.9	33.8	82.9	23.8	94.1	36.41	4,053	1,964
Shawnee....................	23.5	767	3.5	37.3	83.0	25.5	94.5	40.87	3,460	2,024
Stillwater...................	38.1	817	4.6	34.5	82.3	21.9	93.6	36.71	3,899	1,881
Tulsa.........................	1,254.1	3,179	126.1	37.4	81.9	27.1	92.2	45.10	3,413	1,905
OREGON....................	X	X	X	X	X	X	X	X	X	X
Albany.......................	122.1	2,381	0.0	40.3	66.5	33.6	81.2	43.66	4,715	247
Beaverton..................	26.4	285	0.0	40.0	66.8	33.8	79.2	39.95	4,723	287
Bend..........................	92.3	1,171	10.9	31.2	63.5	22.6	80.7	11.73	7,042	147
Corvallis....................	59.4	1,080	0.0	38.1	63.8	31.6	77.4	67.76	5,501	139
Eugene......................	418.2	2,649	112.5	39.8	66.2	33.0	81.5	50.90	4,786	242
Grants Pass	12.2	350	0.0	NA	NA	NA	NA	NA	NA	NA
Gresham....................	82.4	758	3.0	40.0	68.3	33.5	81.5	45.70	4,491	450
Hillsboro....................	62.2	652	0.0	40.5	67.6	35.1	80.4	38.19	4,532	323
Keizer.......................	28.7	779	0.0	40.3	66.8	33.5	81.5	40.00	4,784	257
Lake Oswego	156.3	4,196	37.7	41.8	69.3	35.7	82.6	46.05	4,132	475
McMinnville................	22.1	668	5.6	39.6	66.6	33.0	81.9	41.66	4,815	288
Medford......................	380.1	4,966	26.6	39.1	72.7	30.9	90.2	18.37	4,539	711
Oregon City................	33.8	1,009	0.0	41.8	69.3	35.7	82.6	46.05	4,132	475
Portland.....................	3381.1	5,608	353.6	41.8	69.3	35.7	82.6	46.05	4,132	475

1. Based on the population estimated as of July 1 of the year shown.   2. Represents normal values based on the 30-year period, 1971±2000.   3. Average daily minimum.   4. Average daily maximum.

Table D. Cities — **Land Area and Population**

STATE Place code	City	Land area[1] (sq. mi)	Population, 2018 Total persons 2018	Rank	Per square mile	Race 2017 Race alone[2] (percent) White	Black or African American	American Indian, Alaskan Native	Asian	Hawaiian Pacific Islander	Some other race	Two or more races (percent)
		1	2	3	4	5	6	7	8	9	10	11
	OREGON— Cont'd											
41 61,200	Redmond	16.8	30,914	1,219	1,840.1	NA	NA	NA	NA	NA	NA	NA
41 64,900	Salem	48.6	173,442	148	3,568.8	80.2	1.4	0.9	2.7	2.3	5.6	7.0
41 69,600	Springfield	15.8	62,979	593	3,986.0	84.9	0.4	0.9	1.1	0.2	3.6	8.9
41 73,650	Tigard	12.8	54,758	699	4,278.0	84.2	1.0	0.2	7.2	0.0	2.4	4.9
41 74,950	Tualatin	8.2	27,602	1,334	3,366.1	83.7	2.8	1.9	3.0	0.6	1.4	6.6
41 80,150	West Linn	7.4	26,756	1,370	3,615.7	88.2	2.6	0.0	3.7	0.0	3.2	2.3
42 00,000	**PENNSYLVANIA**	44,743.2	12,807,060	X	286.2	80.7	11.2	0.2	3.5	0.0	1.9	2.5
42 02,000	Allentown	17.5	121,433	233	6,939.0	63.9	13.2	1.2	2.3	0.0	14.3	5.1
42 02,184	Altoona	9.8	43,702	874	4,459.4	91.0	3.3	0.0	0.5	0.0	1.0	4.1
42 06,064	Bethel Park	11.7	32,501	1,168	2,777.9	88.6	1.9	0.0	1.8	0.0	0.1	7.5
42 06,088	Bethlehem	19.1	75,790	466	3,968.1	75.5	11.9	0.1	2.5	0.0	4.7	5.2
42 13,208	Chester	4.8	33,909	1,127	7,064.4	18.6	66.6	0.0	1.1	0.0	8.3	5.5
42 21,648	Easton	4.3	27,216	1,347	6,329.3	69.4	18.1	0.0	2.3	0.0	2.1	8.0
42 24,000	Erie	19.1	96,471	327	5,050.8	73.6	14.9	0.1	3.3	0.0	3.6	4.4
42 32,800	Harrisburg	8.1	49,229	783	6,077.7	35.0	56.0	0.4	2.7	0.0	2.1	3.8
42 33,408	Hazleton	6.0	24,703	1,420	4,117.2	79.6	5.0	0.0	1.0	0.0	13.2	1.3
42 41,216	Lancaster	7.2	59,420	633	8,252.8	59.0	19.6	0.1	4.1	0.0	11.7	5.4
42 42,168	Lebanon	4.2	25,902	1,395	6,167.1	68.6	3.1	0.0	1.7	0.0	22.3	4.3
42 50,528	Monroeville	19.7	27,529	1,336	1,397.4	62.9	22.9	0.0	4.4	0.0	0.2	9.6
42 54,656	Norristown	3.5	34,422	1,106	9,834.9	46.6	36.0	0.0	4.8	0.0	9.3	3.2
42 60,000	Philadelphia	134.2	1,584,138	6	11,804.3	42.1	42.0	0.4	7.3	0.0	5.5	2.7
42 61,000	Pittsburgh	55.4	301,048	66	5,434.1	67.0	22.1	0.2	6.5	0.0	0.6	3.6
42 61,536	Plum	28.6	27,135	1,351	948.8	NA	NA	NA	NA	NA	NA	NA
42 63,624	Reading	9.8	88,495	373	9,030.1	49.4	18.2	2.0	0.5	0.0	9.8	20.2
42 69,000	Scranton	25.3	77,182	450	3,050.7	85.6	3.6	0.0	6.2	0.1	0.7	3.7
42 73,808	State College	4.6	42,352	900	9,207.0	84.2	3.8	0.0	10.1	0.0	0.1	1.8
42 85,152	Wilkes-Barre	7.0	40,806	940	5,829.4	68.1	13.1	0.0	1.8	0.2	11.8	4.9
42 85,312	Williamsport	8.7	28,348	1,306	3,258.4	76.4	17.1	0.1	1.4	0.0	1.1	3.9
42 87,048	York	5.3	44,118	869	8,324.2	64.3	26.2	0.0	0.8	0.1	1.1	7.5
44 00,000	**RHODE ISLAND**	1,033.9	1,057,315	X	1,022.6	81.8	6.3	0.5	3.6	0.1	4.5	3.3
44 19,180	Cranston	28.3	81,274	424	2,871.9	78.5	6.0	0.7	8.3	0.1	3.0	3.4
44 22,960	East Providence	13.3	47,476	815	3,569.6	87.6	3.3	0.0	3.4	0.0	3.5	2.2
44 54,640	Pawtucket	8.7	71,847	500	8,258.3	61.1	15.7	0.5	2.3	0.1	13.1	7.2
44 59,000	Providence	18.4	179,335	143	9,746.5	60.9	17.2	0.9	5.2	0.4	11.2	4.3
44 74,300	Warwick	35.0	80,847	429	2,309.9	90.8	1.8	0.0	3.6	0.0	1.1	2.7
44 80,780	Woonsocket	7.7	41,603	916	5,403.0	67.2	10.0	2.6	7.0	0.0	3.5	9.7
45 00,000	**SOUTH CAROLINA**	30,063.8	5,084,127	X	169.1	67.3	27.0	0.3	1.5	0.1	1.6	2.1
45 00,550	Aiken	20.9	30,778	1,225	1,472.6	NA	NA	NA	NA	NA	NA	NA
45 01,360	Anderson	14.5	27,380	1,340	1,888.3	NA	NA	NA	NA	NA	NA	NA
45 13,330	Charleston	110.6	136,208	201	1,231.5	75.6	21.3	0.2	1.0	0.0	0.3	1.7
45 16,000	Columbia	136.0	133,451	207	981.3	50.5	42.6	0.2	3.2	0.0	1.0	2.5
45 25,810	Florence	22.3	37,625	1,022	1,687.2	48.2	45.7	0.0	3.8	0.1	0.1	2.2
45 29,815	Goose Creek	41.4	42,841	887	1,034.8	71.7	14.3	0.3	1.3	0.0	5.2	7.3
45 30,850	Greenville	29.2	68,563	523	2,348.0	69.0	23.9	0.5	2.3	0.4	1.9	2.0
45 30,985	Greer	22.5	32,102	1,186	1,426.8	NA	NA	NA	NA	NA	NA	NA
45 34,045	Hilton Head Island	41.4	39,639	973	957.5	89.8	4.3	0.0	1.2	0.5	3.3	0.9
45 48,535	Mount Pleasant	45.1	89,338	369	1,980.9	88.8	4.2	0.3	2.2	0.0	0.2	4.3
45 49,075	Myrtle Beach	23.6	33,908	1,128	1,436.8	NA	NA	NA	NA	NA	NA	NA
45 50,875	North Charleston	77.5	113,237	257	1,461.1	51.9	43.5	0.3	1.2	0.0	0.4	2.7
45 61,405	Rock Hill	38.0	74,309	480	1,955.5	56.1	38.5	0.2	2.3	0.0	1.6	1.3
45 68,290	Spartanburg	19.8	37,644	1,021	1,901.2	46.1	47.8	0.2	3.0	0.0	0.9	1.9
45 70,270	Summerville	19.5	51,692	743	2,650.9	76.0	15.9	0.0	4.0	0.0	2.3	1.8
45 70,405	Sumter	32.6	39,656	972	1,216.4	41.8	51.6	0.6	1.9	0.1	2.0	2.0
46 00,000	**SOUTH DAKOTA**	75,810.0	882,235	X	11.6	84.7	2.0	8.7	1.2	0.1	0.6	2.6
46 00,100	Aberdeen	16.0	28,562	1,301	1,785.1	NA	NA	NA	NA	NA	NA	NA
46 52,980	Rapid City	54.5	75,443	467	1,384.3	80.1	1.3	11.3	1.7	0.3	1.3	4.0
46 59,020	Sioux Falls	77.5	181,883	140	2,346.9	85.3	6.4	1.6	2.1	0.0	0.8	3.7
47 00,000	**TENNESSEE**	41,236.8	6,770,010	X	164.2	77.7	16.7	0.2	1.8	0.1	1.3	2.1
47 03,440	Bartlett	32.3	59,315	635	1,836.4	73.0	19.9	0.0	3.6	0.0	0.6	2.9
47 08,280	Brentwood	41.1	42,502	897	1,034.1	87.7	3.0	0.0	7.7	0.0	0.2	1.4
47 08,540	Bristol	32.7	26,881	1,365	822.0	NA	NA	NA	NA	NA	NA	NA
47 14,000	Chattanooga	142.9	180,557	142	1,263.5	61.1	32.4	0.1	3.6	0.0	1.2	1.6
47 15,160	Clarksville	98.0	156,794	163	1,599.9	66.7	23.1	0.4	2.2	0.6	1.9	5.1
47 15,400	Cleveland	27.1	44,974	850	1,659.6	80.8	8.1	0.0	3.0	0.0	7.4	0.8
47 16,420	Collierville	36.2	50,616	760	1,398.2	79.1	10.7	0.1	6.1	0.0	0.8	3.1

1. Dry land or land partially or temporarily covered by water.   2. Hispanic or Latino persons may be of any race.

Table D. Cities — **Population**

City	Percent Hispanic or Latino[1], 2017	Percent foreign born, 2017	Age of population (percent), 2017							Median age, 2017	Percent female, 2017	Population			
			Under 18 years	18 to 24 years	25 to 34 years	35 to 44 years	45 to 54 years	55 to 64 years	65 years and over			Census counts		Percent change	
												2000	2010	2000-2010	2001-2018
	12	13	14	15	16	17	18	19	20	21	22	23	24	25	26
OREGON— Cont'd															
Redmond	5.9	4.0	20.0	8.9	14.1	18.7	11.4	14.0	12.9	38.3	51.9	13,481	26,213	94.4	17.9
Salem	24.6	12.9	24.4	9.6	13.6	14.9	12.6	10.1	14.9	37.1	48.0	136,924	154,909	13.1	12.0
Springfield	11.8	4.8	19.7	13.0	14.3	13.7	10.9	12.9	15.6	36.8	49.6	52,864	59,398	12.4	6.0
Tigard	9.5	12.1	24.6	5.7	11.0	20.6	12.3	11.5	14.3	38.7	50.3	41,223	48,205	16.9	13.6
Tualatin	12.7	8.9	21.1	10.7	11.4	16.3	13.4	14.3	12.8	38.9	53.4	22,791	26,114	14.6	5.7
West Linn	5.8	9.1	27.3	5.5	7.9	12.0	17.5	13.0	16.8	42.5	50.7	22,261	25,118	12.8	6.5
PENNSYLVANIA	7.3	7.0	20.8	9.2	13.1	11.6	13.3	14.2	17.8	40.8	51.0	12,281,054	12,702,873	3.4	0.8
Allentown	52.9	22.4	25.9	13.2	17.0	12.1	10.3	10.2	11.3	31.3	51.7	106,632	118,097	10.8	2.8
Altoona	2.8	1.0	22.6	9.4	15.3	13.4	11.3	13.3	14.7	37.1	52.1	49,523	45,997	-7.1	-5.0
Bethel Park	2.7	5.0	20.6	5.1	11.7	9.7	13.9	16.1	23.0	46.6	50.4	33,556	32,323	-3.7	0.6
Bethlehem	28.2	7.8	19.8	16.4	16.2	10.4	10.8	12.6	13.8	32.6	53.1	71,329	74,951	5.1	1.1
Chester	13.1	3.5	25.3	14.2	17.1	10.3	11.4	9.1	12.6	30.8	48.8	36,854	33,906	-8.0	0.0
Easton	15.8	9.3	23.0	15.1	11.9	11.9	11.8	11.0	15.3	35.0	49.1	26,263	26,810	2.1	1.5
Erie	7.5	7.1	22.5	12.7	14.8	11.0	11.4	12.8	14.7	35.0	50.2	103,717	101,747	-1.9	-5.2
Harrisburg	25.4	7.4	29.9	11.0	16.9	11.2	12.3	10.5	8.3	29.8	52.0	48,950	49,522	1.2	-0.6
Hazleton	59.8	35.0	28.2	9.0	18.6	12.2	10.2	8.5	13.3	31.1	55.6	23,329	25,349	8.7	-2.5
Lancaster	35.8	9.8	24.0	14.2	20.1	13.1	9.2	9.1	10.4	30.4	51.5	56,348	59,333	5.3	0.1
Lebanon	39.2	10.6	25.7	11.0	16.8	10.8	12.1	11.0	12.6	33.8	52.8	24,461	25,477	4.2	1.7
Monroeville	0.9	6.6	19.3	6.9	13.1	12.4	12.1	15.6	20.6	43.7	60.1	29,349	28,341	-3.4	-2.9
Norristown	35.6	22.9	24.4	9.4	17.6	18.3	13.8	10.0	6.5	33.8	52.7	31,282	34,339	9.8	0.2
Philadelphia	14.8	13.8	21.8	10.2	19.0	12.3	11.7	11.6	13.4	34.4	52.7	1,517,550	1,526,009	0.6	3.8
Pittsburgh	3.0	8.8	14.3	16.3	22.3	10.2	9.9	11.6	15.4	33.3	50.5	334,563	305,376	-8.7	-1.4
Plum	1.2	1.5	16.2	5.8	10.2	16.0	8.4	16.9	26.5	47.5	51.8	26,940	27,122	0.7	0.0
Reading	66.4	22.2	30.4	12.1	15.0	12.3	11.1	8.9	10.2	29.6	52.0	81,207	88,016	8.4	0.5
Scranton	14.4	12.4	21.6	12.5	13.2	13.0	10.8	11.9	16.9	36.8	50.7	76,415	76,087	-0.4	1.4
State College	3.7	14.7	7.5	61.3	8.7	6.3	5.6	4.3	6.3	21.3	48.1	38,420	41,980	9.3	0.9
Wilkes-Barre	25.9	12.3	22.2	13.4	14.8	10.5	8.8	12.5	17.8	34.8	49.9	43,123	41,498	-3.8	-1.7
Williamsport	2.8	5.8	20.7	16.8	18.6	12.5	10.1	10.3	11.1	30.5	46.4	30,706	29,378	-4.3	-3.5
York	35.7	6.6	28.0	13.2	13.2	13.9	12.5	9.8	9.5	31.0	52.4	40,862	43,807	7.2	0.7
RHODE ISLAND	15.4	13.9	19.5	10.9	13.8	11.6	13.5	14.0	16.7	39.5	51.6	1,048,319	1,052,957	0.4	0.4
Cranston	16.7	15.3	21.9	8.8	13.2	14.6	10.7	13.1	17.7	38.6	48.7	79,269	80,559	1.6	0.9
East Providence	5.5	14.6	15.3	5.6	16.8	11.5	13.6	16.8	20.3	45.7	51.4	48,688	47,010	-3.3	0.9
Pawtucket	24.9	24.0	20.9	9.1	20.0	12.4	11.9	12.1	13.7	35.1	49.0	72,958	71,139	-2.5	1.0
Providence	43.2	30.2	22.4	15.5	16.1	12.3	11.5	10.4	11.8	32.0	51.5	173,618	177,844	2.4	0.8
Warwick	6.2	8.1	17.8	9.1	13.5	11.8	12.1	16.6	19.2	43.2	52.5	85,808	82,674	-3.7	-2.2
Woonsocket	17.1	8.7	21.0	14.6	14.7	11.9	12.7	12.0	13.1	34.8	53.9	43,224	41,199	-4.7	1.0
SOUTH CAROLINA	5.7	4.9	21.9	9.5	12.9	12.3	12.8	13.2	17.2	39.4	51.5	4,012,012	4,625,381	15.3	9.9
Aiken	0.9	2.3	19.5	12.4	7.5	8.3	8.8	14.8	28.7	48.3	55.6	25,337	29,588	16.8	4.0
Anderson	5.9	4.0	18.2	10.7	15.9	13.0	10.3	9.6	22.2	40.4	52.1	25,514	26,433	3.6	3.6
Charleston	3.2	2.9	17.7	12.8	20.1	12.3	10.9	12.7	13.5	34.7	50.8	96,650	120,574	24.8	13.0
Columbia	5.7	5.9	15.5	27.7	17.1	9.8	11.2	9.5	9.3	28.1	49.2	116,278	130,432	12.2	2.3
Florence	2.5	4.3	24.7	5.4	17.2	10.2	13.4	13.0	16.0	37.7	54.2	30,248	37,464	23.9	0.4
Goose Creek	11.7	7.6	26.1	13.5	15.6	10.9	12.0	11.1	10.8	31.4	51.5	29,208	36,432	24.7	17.6
Greenville	6.1	5.9	15.2	12.4	20.7	12.5	11.8	14.2	13.2	35.9	51.2	56,002	59,149	5.6	15.9
Greer	15.4	14.9	16.5	8.3	17.9	13.5	13.4	12.2	18.2	39.6	53.0	16,843	25,827	53.3	24.3
Hilton Head Island	11.9	8.8	13.8	6.5	7.6	6.2	9.7	18.3	37.9	58.4	52.1	33,862	37,094	9.5	6.9
Mount Pleasant	1.7	6.4	21.7	5.0	12.7	12.9	13.3	15.8	18.6	43.5	52.7	47,609	67,812	42.4	31.7
Myrtle Beach	14.4	11.1	18.8	5.4	10.5	12.3	13.0	14.7	25.4	47.0	55.2	22,759	27,094	19.0	25.1
North Charleston	11.1	9.4	23.5	8.3	19.4	13.6	12.3	11.5	11.4	34.5	51.1	79,641	97,559	22.5	16.1
Rock Hill	4.5	5.6	22.8	15.7	13.3	13.1	12.7	11.3	11.0	33.9	52.8	49,765	66,547	33.7	11.7
Spartanburg	3.8	4.5	22.7	14.0	14.6	9.1	12.7	11.7	15.1	34.3	52.0	39,673	36,753	-7.4	2.4
Summerville	10.0	5.1	27.4	9.1	15.1	16.5	10.0	9.4	12.5	33.6	50.7	27,752	42,868	54.5	20.6
Sumter	7.1	4.9	26.5	12.1	15.2	11.7	9.8	9.4	15.2	30.3	54.2	39,643	40,518	2.2	-2.1
SOUTH DAKOTA	3.6	3.4	24.5	9.4	13.3	11.5	11.4	13.5	16.3	36.9	49.6	754,844	814,198	7.9	8.4
Aberdeen	3.6	2.6	21.3	13.5	14.9	10.6	9.9	12.2	17.7	35.4	51.2	24,658	26,108	5.9	9.4
Rapid City	5.1	2.7	23.1	9.1	15.5	10.8	10.9	12.4	18.2	36.4	50.3	59,607	68,461	14.9	10.2
Sioux Falls	5.1	7.6	24.3	9.2	16.8	11.9	12.8	12.3	12.8	34.8	50.5	123,975	153,972	24.2	18.1
TENNESSEE	5.4	5.2	22.5	9.2	13.5	12.5	13.3	13.1	15.9	38.6	51.3	5,689,283	6,346,286	11.5	6.7
Bartlett	3.5	4.7	21.7	6.2	9.4	14.1	14.6	15.1	18.8	43.7	51.0	40,543	56,925	40.4	4.2
Brentwood	2.2	8.4	30.9	8.8	5.1	13.6	19.6	10.6	11.4	39.6	51.7	23,445	37,062	58.1	14.7
Bristol	4.2	2.8	19.8	9.1	12.2	10.2	12.8	16.3	19.5	43.8	51.4	24,821	26,740	7.7	0.5
Chattanooga	6.7	7.1	18.8	10.5	16.6	12.2	11.5	12.7	17.7	38.2	54.2	155,554	170,309	9.5	6.0
Clarksville	11.9	5.1	27.7	11.6	21.5	13.5	9.9	7.7	8.1	29.8	50.3	103,455	132,897	28.5	18.0
Cleveland	12.8	13.1	21.5	16.2	16.3	11.6	14.1	9.3	11.0	32.5	51.8	37,192	41,263	10.9	9.0
Collierville	3.2	7.5	25.6	6.0	12.3	10.7	15.9	15.7	13.8	40.2	53.1	31,872	45,603	43.1	11.0

1. May be of any race.

Table D. Cities — Households, Group Quarters, Crime, and Education

City	Households, 2017								Serious crimes known to police[2], 2016				Educational attainment, 2017		
			Percent						Total		Rate[3]			Attainment[4] (percent)	
	Number	Persons per household	Family	Married couple family	Female headed[1]	Non-family	One person	Persons in group quarters, 2017	Number	Rate	Violent	Property	Population age 25 and over	High school graduate or less	Bachelor's degree or more
	27	28	29	30	31	32	33	34	35	36	37	38	39	40	41
OREGON— Cont'd															
Redmond	12,657	2.35	62.5	43.2	10.6	37.5	32.8	235	1,057	3,624	278	3,347	21,343	44.1	17.0
Salem	58,511	2.76	63.6	46.2	11.2	36.4	29.9	8,268	7,202	4,325	321	4,005	112,140	38.5	28.4
Springfield	24,939	2.47	57.5	41.0	11.1	42.5	32.8	693	3,146	5,144	301	4,843	41,980	41.3	13.3
Tigard	20,673	2.55	64.9	52.7	8.5	35.1	23.4	447	1,679	3,236	256	2,980	37,045	23.4	45.6
Tualatin	10,753	2.53	71.5	57.0	9.7	28.5	19.9	NA	781	2,853	190	2,664	18,652	20.3	46.4
West Linn	9,353	2.83	79.6	68.6	8.6	20.4	18.3	NA	256	952	48	904	17,917	11.1	61.7
PENNSYLVANIA	5,008,751	2.47	63.4	47.5	11.4	36.6	30.4	423,488	263,242	2,059	316	1,743	8,960,842	44.4	31.4
Allentown	43,480	2.67	62.3	33.3	20.6	37.7	27.3	5,142	3,889	3,224	458	2,767	73,873	58.9	14.1
Altoona	18,976	2.27	60.4	34.5	19.7	39.6	33.8	1,022	978	2,166	348	1,818	29,976	56.4	16.7
Bethel Park	13,436	2.39	68.2	53.4	10.3	31.8	27.2	NA	330	1,029	69	960	24,094	26.8	45.0
Bethlehem	27,995	2.51	56.2	39.8	10.0	43.8	34.0	6,237	2,051	2,739	753	1,986	48,792	50.5	26.2
Chester	10,907	2.77	65.5	17.4	37.6	34.5	29.8	3,869	1,585	4,647	1,571	3,075	20,645	63.6	13.8
Easton	9,545	2.47	67.1	39.5	23.5	32.9	28.1	3,559	519	1,927	275	1,652	16,784	58.8	18.0
Erie	38,522	2.39	53.2	33.0	14.8	46.8	37.0	5,487	2,631	2,657	356	2,301	63,063	54.3	20.9
Harrisburg	18,782	2.50	55.4	20.9	27.3	44.6	35.3	2,229	1,868	3,813	1,074	2,739	29,103	52.8	19.4
Hazleton	8,311	2.94	71.8	40.9	22.9	28.2	23.3	290	454	1,836	380	1,456	15,533	60.6	18.5
Lancaster	22,771	2.48	56.6	32.2	19.3	43.4	32.8	3,150	2,651	4,467	821	3,647	36,910	50.9	24.1
Lebanon	9,437	2.69	59.0	31.7	17.8	41.0	31.5	344	679	2,658	235	2,423	16,300	65.7	13.1
Monroeville	11,633	2.33	69.6	55.5	10.3	30.4	26.5	553	599	2,128	267	1,862	20,453	29.0	40.7
Norristown	13,966	2.41	65.1	36.4	19.9	34.9	30.8	836	766	2,225	430	1,795	22,822	51.0	26.6
Philadelphia	606,142	2.53	49.3	25.7	17.8	50.7	43.2	47,625	64,719	4,120	979	3,141	1,075,853	50.4	28.3
Pittsburgh	137,442	2.03	43.0	28.3	11.3	57.0	43.4	24,036	12,234	4,045	782	3,263	210,044	32.3	44.1
Plum	12,589	2.16	65.0	56.9	4.7	35.0	30.9	NA	176	638	109	529	21,250	35.9	30.9
Reading	28,765	2.98	63.5	31.1	24.4	36.5	28.8	2,781	2,888	3,288	680	2,608	50,831	64.9	8.5
Scranton	31,486	2.29	52.7	31.7	13.9	47.3	40.2	5,447	1,912	2,472	279	2,193	51,132	53.9	23.9
State College	12,751	2.34	28.7	26.3	1.7	71.3	43.8	12,612	530	912	67	845	13,231	9.4	76.4
Wilkes-Barre	15,032	2.50	59.3	32.7	21.2	40.7	36.8	3,250	1,316	3,238	531	2,707	26,288	55.7	16.5
Williamsport	11,878	2.11	51.2	30.4	15.6	48.8	40.7	3,422	896	3,072	357	2,716	17,790	40.6	26.7
York	16,298	2.61	58.9	24.6	27.9	41.1	30.9	1,589	1,824	4,144	945	3,199	25,976	71.4	11.4
RHODE ISLAND	408,748	2.49	61.6	45.5	12.1	38.4	32.3	41,924	22,582	2,138	239	1,899	736,969	41.6	33.5
Cranston	28,764	2.69	65.9	50.5	11.1	34.1	27.7	3,760	1,634	2,013	153	1,860	56,227	37.8	35.5
East Providence	21,258	2.20	49.0	36.3	7.6	51.0	45.0	829	619	1,304	145	1,159	37,636	48.2	29.6
Pawtucket	27,548	2.60	61.8	34.1	20.0	38.2	31.1	486	2,375	3,315	426	2,889	50,447	52.4	21.0
Providence	64,156	2.59	55.1	33.4	16.9	44.9	35.6	14,016	6,432	3,586	577	3,009	112,076	54.2	28.3
Warwick	33,749	2.38	63.4	50.9	8.2	36.6	31.2	613	1,686	2,069	75	1,994	59,164	36.2	34.9
Woonsocket	15,652	2.61	61.2	31.9	19.6	38.8	31.8	843	1,184	2,852	511	2,342	26,889	55.3	15.7
SOUTH CAROLINA	1,905,100	2.57	65.8	47.3	14.3	34.2	28.9	136,487	185,824	3,746	502	3,244	3,443,851	42.1	28.0
Aiken	13,137	2.22	63.9	40.8	19.2	36.1	34.1	1,605	2,063	6,698	844	5,854	20,939	36.0	39.1
Anderson	11,653	2.19	55.5	29.1	22.2	44.5	41.0	1,713	2,491	9,051	1,079	7,972	19,387	51.9	24.8
Charleston	56,780	2.36	52.7	39.4	10.9	47.3	37.1	5,825	3,768	2,788	302	2,486	97,246	25.2	52.2
Columbia	48,202	2.17	47.5	29.7	13.5	52.5	42.0	29,044	8,501	6,321	831	5,490	75,965	30.8	44.2
Florence	15,240	2.44	61.1	37.6	23.5	38.9	32.9	613	2,981	7,767	1,068	6,698	26,386	47.4	30.1
Goose Creek	12,972	3.07	76.5	58.3	14.6	23.5	18.3	2,722	1,075	2,588	380	2,208	25,739	35.1	27.2
Greenville	31,367	2.04	47.8	32.4	11.6	52.2	41.8	4,387	3,219	4,901	606	4,295	49,416	29.3	46.3
Greer	10,079	2.31	62.5	49.7	10.9	37.5	33.2	NA	837	2,893	335	2,558	17,695	34.7	38.7
Hilton Head Island	16,563	2.41	64.6	54.9	8.7	35.4	30.5	185	NA	NA	NA	NA	31,925	22.2	53.8
Mount Pleasant	34,298	2.52	70.8	60.4	7.8	29.2	24.5	NA	1,572	1,865	153	1,712	63,519	15.8	62.7
Myrtle Beach	14,866	2.20	52.2	41.2	8.2	47.8	42.1	NA	4,940	15,503	1,692	13,812	24,866	38.8	28.2
North Charleston	45,072	2.38	49.5	32.2	15.3	50.5	43.9	5,345	7,229	6,543	901	5,642	76,917	47.8	25.0
Rock Hill	28,673	2.44	63.0	39.0	17.2	37.0	28.5	3,055	2,993	4,123	616	3,507	44,929	31.2	37.4
Spartanburg	15,080	2.34	57.8	33.4	17.6	42.2	39.3	2,217	2,793	7,334	1,103	6,231	23,713	41.6	29.1
Summerville	17,049	2.88	66.4	49.5	12.8	33.6	27.8	298	2,034	4,056	375	3,681	31,383	34.9	27.5
Sumter	16,337	2.35	63.0	33.8	22.8	37.0	33.5	1,545	1,947	4,765	690	4,074	24,550	39.0	24.8
SOUTH DAKOTA	344,260	2.43	62.0	48.7	8.8	38.0	31.5	33,984	20,762	2,399	418	1,981	574,559	39.0	28.1
Aberdeen	12,228	2.18	52.3	33.1	12.7	47.7	42.7	1,356	756	2,653	470	2,183	18,300	37.6	29.2
Rapid City	29,814	2.37	56.4	41.1	13.6	43.6	38.4	3,716	3,513	4,711	728	3,983	50,504	32.5	30.3
Sioux Falls	72,873	2.34	58.6	44.4	9.6	41.4	33.8	6,077	6,478	3,699	512	3,186	117,660	31.9	33.7
TENNESSEE	2,588,655	2.53	66.0	48.5	12.8	34.0	28.3	154,724	231,932	3,487	633	2,854	4,588,453	44.6	27.3
Bartlett	21,096	2.75	72.2	58.9	9.4	27.8	24.1	1,116	1,161	1,971	321	1,650	42,595	28.7	36.1
Brentwood	13,086	3.25	85.7	80.0	5.0	14.3	12.4	NA	425	994	58	936	25,735	8.2	77.3
Bristol	11,744	2.24	60.0	42.1	16.6	40.0	32.3	574	1,056	3,962	593	3,369	19,080	50.7	24.3
Chattanooga	75,985	2.23	47.7	33.3	11.4	52.3	46.5	9,530	11,622	6,537	1,023	5,513	126,559	40.0	30.5
Clarksville	56,014	2.68	71.1	54.5	12.5	28.9	22.0	3,293	4,824	3,163	615	2,548	93,007	34.0	26.8
Cleveland	16,368	2.52	64.9	48.3	12.9	35.1	27.2	3,176	3,090	6,956	864	6,091	27,719	45.9	21.8
Collierville	18,246	2.75	77.6	70.9	5.1	22.4	18.8	NA	822	1,660	162	1,498	34,403	20.7	55.2

1. No spouse present. 2. Data for serious crimes have not been adjusted for underreporting. This may affect comparability between geographic areas and over time. 3. Per 100,000 population estimated by the FBI. 4. Persons 25 years old and over.

City	Money income, 2017 Households Median income	Percent with income less than $20,000	Percent with income of $200,000 or more	Median family income	Median non-family income	Median earnings, 2017 All persons	Men	Women	Housing units, 2017 Total	Occupied	Percent owner occupied	Median value[1] (dollars)	Median gross rent (dollars)
	42	43	44	45	46	47	48	49	50	51	52	53	54
OREGON— Cont'd													
Redmond	66,910	12.8	2.3	70,166	31,530	35,919	40,591	30,708	13,315	12,657	59.3	275,600	987
Salem	56,186	16.0	2.8	67,914	30,997	30,576	32,098	27,224	64,414	58,511	55.2	234,900	947
Springfield	48,404	18.7	0.7	60,597	29,463	25,325	26,929	22,356	25,546	24,939	51.8	209,800	925
Tigard	81,358	8.7	7.7	93,341	47,364	41,665	51,381	34,706	21,436	20,673	65.3	414,100	1,215
Tualatin	78,044	8.3	11.7	86,094	54,388	38,318	44,481	32,827	11,171	10,753	54.5	427,400	1,318
West Linn	127,411	4.4	22.9	136,354	63,814	59,949	82,302	41,246	9,482	9,353	86.5	484,900	1,633
PENNSYLVANIA	59,195	16.4	6.1	75,949	32,044	35,000	41,182	29,255	5,694,402	5,008,751	68.3	181,200	893
Allentown	39,687	26.3	1.7	45,426	29,322	23,154	26,799	19,073	46,329	43,480	39.8	123,700	933
Altoona	40,509	31.3	1.1	45,485	24,980	23,434	30,235	16,706	20,608	18,976	55.6	84,200	669
Bethel Park	74,322	9.1	4.7	87,426	34,168	45,680	54,221	27,485	13,889	13,436	81.6	180,500	945
Bethlehem	53,504	21.3	5.5	68,291	32,225	31,613	36,462	27,844	30,232	27,995	51.3	169,700	970
Chester	35,426	27.0	1.6	34,735	21,690	22,222	21,390	24,191	13,325	10,907	39.5	67,800	792
Easton	45,256	23.0	3.4	54,275	26,310	25,451	31,271	20,300	10,697	9,545	51.1	119,500	892
Erie	37,721	27.4	0.6	51,046	23,815	22,097	25,088	20,304	44,638	38,522	50.7	88,000	682
Harrisburg	43,801	28.6	1.4	48,116	33,796	25,655	26,464	24,681	24,583	18,782	36.8	79,900	869
Hazleton	46,939	14.7	2.7	48,759	41,098	27,139	28,286	26,617	10,146	8,311	51.1	97,200	799
Lancaster	41,796	20.5	1.5	43,303	38,929	23,518	27,976	20,865	25,632	22,771	41.5	113,400	836
Lebanon	38,091	31.0	0.0	45,080	32,468	27,273	33,100	22,881	10,848	9,437	41.3	87,700	745
Monroeville	63,916	8.6	2.4	77,948	34,097	37,312	46,442	31,547	13,150	11,633	70.9	149,000	1,166
Norristown	43,373	20.4	4.6	48,188	27,459	31,907	39,286	25,993	16,745	13,966	40.3	149,800	1,025
Philadelphia	39,759	31.7	4.3	54,431	23,144	32,011	35,245	30,689	685,988	606,142	49.0	166,200	969
Pittsburgh	45,851	24.5	5.2	66,263	32,064	30,239	33,682	25,641	158,277	137,442	48.9	123,600	925
Plum	69,595	12.5	4.3	85,438	28,771	42,781	46,636	38,875	12,992	12,589	86.3	140,700	810
Reading	31,160	31.7	1.6	38,470	19,716	20,521	23,373	16,367	33,026	28,765	39.9	70,000	758
Scranton	35,904	27.3	1.7	55,653	24,541	26,238	30,797	21,044	36,553	31,486	45.1	108,100	751
State College	40,032	30.8	7.0	102,115	28,419	6,526	9,180	5,217	14,423	12,751	31.4	313,100	955
Wilkes-Barre	33,293	29.3	2.3	42,349	19,862	20,165	22,897	16,153	19,191	15,032	51.1	72,800	672
Williamsport	31,758	30.9	3.2	43,551	21,725	21,120	18,359	22,008	13,658	11,878	40.5	116,500	737
York	30,695	32.4	1.4	31,676	23,867	20,981	21,875	20,360	18,357	16,298	35.0	73,700	803
RHODE ISLAND	63,870	16.6	6.7	84,557	34,234	36,278	42,084	30,413	468,266	408,748	60.8	257,800	941
Cranston	71,263	12.1	6.1	87,561	37,891	41,060	50,045	31,824	30,376	28,764	70.0	245,600	1,039
East Providence	53,969	24.1	4.2	91,913	25,752	41,899	46,865	36,448	22,176	21,258	59.8	221,300	860
Pawtucket	45,380	19.7	2.6	55,949	29,274	29,073	32,239	23,833	30,773	27,548	43.6	189,300	877
Providence	44,517	26.7	5.6	60,213	26,764	25,877	30,985	21,397	76,660	64,156	39.0	203,300	938
Warwick	73,966	13.3	5.6	90,072	37,085	42,185	47,008	37,083	36,526	33,749	73.8	218,400	1,066
Woonsocket	41,390	23.2	1.7	49,202	26,172	26,568	31,109	22,182	18,395	15,652	35.2	173,800	848
SOUTH CAROLINA	50,570	18.5	4.2	62,432	29,644	30,021	34,621	25,125	2,284,820	1,905,100	68.7	161,800	848
Aiken	45,786	14.2	3.3	53,426	32,363	26,815	31,240	25,462	14,021	13,137	62.6	182,400	869
Anderson	30,697	30.4	1.6	37,434	22,244	25,851	31,053	18,204	13,178	11,653	48.7	127,900	742
Charleston	63,364	14.6	10.5	91,099	42,875	38,285	43,890	35,309	65,680	56,780	56.6	344,600	1,236
Columbia	42,646	24.0	6.3	72,797	28,756	21,223	22,436	20,104	55,980	48,202	44.1	192,500	878
Florence	45,104	17.9	2.9	51,418	31,479	25,923	37,064	22,111	16,603	15,240	54.4	148,600	734
Goose Creek	65,406	7.2	4.2	71,476	53,356	29,066	36,582	22,810	14,052	12,972	69.7	195,900	1,280
Greenville	52,900	16.5	9.1	80,106	36,646	33,236	41,460	30,548	35,457	31,367	43.3	282,900	904
Greer	56,027	15.2	1.4	71,430	42,816	32,277	33,887	31,354	10,810	10,079	68.9	165,500	906
Hilton Head Island	73,221	14.5	15.7	101,194	34,995	30,372	31,274	25,714	35,226	16,563	76.4	493,600	1,128
Mount Pleasant	91,259	4.9	18.5	116,630	64,649	50,965	74,516	36,429	38,090	34,298	73.3	449,000	1,660
Myrtle Beach	40,275	26.4	5.6	52,071	30,023	25,888	27,043	24,688	26,511	14,866	52.7	206,800	881
North Charleston	39,265	25.2	2.8	61,213	26,321	24,929	30,349	21,906	50,820	45,072	42.7	179,600	983
Rock Hill	52,663	14.4	4.9	62,434	32,320	30,474	33,715	26,891	30,969	28,673	57.2	159,300	913
Spartanburg	40,156	23.6	4.2	53,304	27,058	24,901	31,954	21,090	17,617	15,080	46.3	118,700	808
Summerville	54,234	10.6	3.4	74,727	40,921	36,090	42,075	31,377	19,018	17,049	58.6	212,600	1,071
Sumter	37,070	27.2	4.5	47,874	22,710	27,700	32,047	22,397	18,068	16,337	45.3	140,200	768
SOUTH DAKOTA	56,521	15.3	3.8	73,236	32,347	31,333	37,012	26,397	392,650	344,260	67.7	167,600	722
Aberdeen	51,739	13.0	2.2	70,569	30,834	32,414	39,367	29,047	12,942	12,228	54.5	153,600	744
Rapid City	49,602	20.0	4.6	70,157	28,249	27,667	29,909	24,665	32,999	29,814	55.3	184,200	826
Sioux Falls	61,915	12.6	4.3	79,479	35,961	32,992	38,773	29,793	77,439	72,873	62.7	193,900	781
TENNESSEE	51,340	18.2	4.4	62,926	30,490	30,994	35,552	26,596	2,958,799	2,588,655	65.4	167,500	833
Bartlett	73,083	4.1	5.2	86,817	50,292	43,391	48,597	40,546	22,575	21,096	87.5	172,100	1,428
Brentwood	157,143	3.6	38.3	179,063	59,824	55,805	91,551	28,599	13,527	13,086	90.5	662,500	2,065
Bristol	37,258	25.3	2.4	57,504	21,723	21,265	26,521	18,154	12,903	11,744	67.9	116,500	736
Chattanooga	41,859	24.4	5.0	67,434	29,423	29,532	33,206	25,887	85,406	75,985	49.5	163,000	818
Clarksville	55,021	16.6	2.5	65,388	31,437	31,372	34,921	26,029	61,873	56,014	52.0	153,800	981
Cleveland	41,016	23.6	2.6	48,883	28,590	23,563	29,073	20,182	18,169	16,368	38.1	185,500	743
Collierville	102,149	7.3	14.6	115,862	61,498	60,801	72,075	45,338	18,384	18,246	77.2	314,700	1,236

1. Based on population estimated by the American Community Survey.   2. Includes units rented or sold but not occupied.   3. Specified owner-occupied units; $1,000,000 represents $1,000,000 or more.   4. 50.0 represents 50 percent or more.   5. 10.0 represents 10 percent or less.

Table D. Cities — Commuting, Computer Access, Migration, Labor Force, and Employment

	Commuting[1], 2017		Computer access[2], 2017		Migration, 2017		Civilian labor force, 2018				Civilian employment[4], 2017			
	Percent		Percent						Unemployment		Population age 16 and older		Population age 16 to 64	
City	Commuting	With commutes of 30 minutes or more	With a computer in the house	With Internet access	Percent who lived in the same house one year ago	Percent who lived in another state or county one year ago	Total	Percent change 2017 -2018	Total	Rate[3]	Number	Percent in labor force	Number	Percent who worked full-year full-time
	55	56	57	58	59	60	61	62	63	64	65	66	67	68
OREGON— Cont'd														
Redmond	75.3	27.3	96.0	92.5	84.0	4.3	12,887	2.1	667	5.2	24,831	70.5	20,960	53.6
Salem	78.3	25.3	92.5	87.4	83.7	8.2	80,670	0.9	3,584	4.4	132,071	60.0	106,767	49.2
Springfield	73.7	19.2	92.4	85.2	84.2	5.9	31,183	0.2	1,515	4.9	51,788	64.7	42,088	43.7
Tigard	76.5	44.9	96.7	92.1	88.9	6.5	30,825	0.7	1,069	3.5	41,292	71.6	33,684	60.0
Tualatin	75.3	29.9	NA	NA	82.2	11.1	15,346	0.8	554	3.6	22,539	76.5	19,034	54.4
West Linn	75.3	46.1	97.6	93.5	93.7	3.7	14,756	0.5	479	3.2	20,102	64.7	15,626	51.1
PENNSYLVANIA	76.2	38.7	88.0	81.2	87.4	5.2	6,424,421	0.0	275,786	4.3	10,459,220	62.4	8,182,677	51.5
Allentown	67.4	24.3	88.9	79.3	80.3	7.8	55,189	0.3	3,744	6.8	92,670	62.2	79,017	45.7
Altoona	78.5	22.8	87.0	80.8	82.8	6.7	19,923	-1.2	939	4.7	35,175	57.1	28,689	45.0
Bethel Park	76.7	52.7	88.8	85.2	90.8	3.8	17,403	0.0	600	3.4	26,371	65.5	18,911	59.2
Bethlehem	80.8	27.8	85.7	79.1	81.8	7.1	37,592	0.4	1,966	5.2	62,969	59.7	52,435	44.9
Chester	69.7	30.0	81.9	76.2	79.0	9.5	13,335	0.0	1,026	7.7	25,819	55.9	21,518	39.3
Easton	72.3	33.8	83.8	72.2	75.5	10.4	12,030	0.4	729	6.1	21,894	57.1	17,734	44.7
Erie	69.7	14.7	85.0	77.3	76.4	4.5	43,378	-1.2	2,290	5.3	77,325	58.0	63,003	41.6
Harrisburg	65.1	16.8	86.5	76.7	73.3	11.5	21,463	-0.2	1,326	6.2	36,056	66.7	31,975	45.9
Hazleton	77.2	18.4	84.1	75.7	81.4	13.1	11,526	-1.0	993	8.6	18,378	65.5	15,096	54.8
Lancaster	65.8	24.5	87.6	72.0	80.7	6.5	26,995	0.7	1,369	5.1	47,008	70.0	40,817	48.0
Lebanon	68.2	23.9	82.8	71.5	71.0	17.2	11,661	1.2	704	6.0	19,476	59.7	16,240	48.6
Monroeville	71.3	49.2	89.6	86.2	91.9	2.8	14,508	0.1	595	4.1	23,920	66.2	18,211	58.1
Norristown	66.4	43.9	87.2	77.0	84.0	5.6	18,130	0.2	801	4.4	27,687	75.2	25,451	55.1
Philadelphia	51.1	55.3	84.1	71.0	86.0	5.0	709,586	0.7	39,322	5.5	1,271,430	58.4	1,059,714	44.1
Pittsburgh	56.6	33.7	89.4	82.1	78.0	8.9	156,476	-0.2	6,527	4.2	263,830	63.2	217,150	48.0
Plum	77.9	48.1	91.6	86.7	NA	NA	14,924	0.0	577	3.9	23,300	69.0	16,076	57.9
Reading	57.7	36.1	86.2	80.0	79.0	7.0	34,004	-0.1	2,267	6.7	64,144	62.8	55,109	39.1
Scranton	77.4	19.0	86.0	77.5	82.4	8.0	36,686	-0.6	1,757	4.8	63,056	54.7	49,913	45.0
State College	34.8	10.2	97.1	87.9	50.6	30.8	16,690	0.9	677	4.1	39,952	46.9	36,920	19.6
Wilkes-Barre	63.5	16.8	82.9	74.6	82.1	7.6	18,520	-0.3	1,190	6.4	33,365	58.1	26,102	37.8
Williamsport	69.6	10.6	89.5	79.6	73.7	9.2	13,306	-1.4	718	5.4	22,917	59.3	19,766	38.7
York	74.0	23.5	81.9	72.6	79.8	6.6	17,760	-0.7	1,353	7.6	33,233	61.8	29,025	38.5
RHODE ISLAND	79.4	34.4	89.7	85.1	88.0	5.7	555,807	0.4	22,636	4.1	877,959	65.4	701,387	50.2
Cranston	79.0	28.4	90.8	85.0	88.1	4.3	41,418	0.5	1,654	4.0	64,753	62.1	50,421	48.2
East Providence	82.8	27.7	81.1	72.5	87.5	3.7	24,379	0.3	1,060	4.3	40,668	63.8	31,006	56.3
Pawtucket	76.8	34.1	87.8	82.3	88.7	2.7	36,504	0.3	1,682	4.6	58,362	69.5	48,482	51.4
Providence	60.5	26.6	86.0	81.7	85.1	6.7	87,007	0.5	4,412	5.1	145,412	62.1	124,126	43.8
Warwick	87.7	33.9	91.2	86.9	90.4	5.0	45,614	0.4	1,589	3.5	68,242	67.9	52,738	57.2
Woonsocket	71.5	34.8	86.1	78.8	80.9	6.5	19,128	0.2	1,030	5.4	33,702	65.2	28,213	38.1
SOUTH CAROLINA	81.8	34.1	88.8	78.7	85.5	7.0	2,323,209	0.7	79,553	3.4	4,049,809	60.4	3,183,992	49.7
Aiken	80.9	28.5	89.1	83.7	80.5	6.0	13,176	0.0	489	3.7	25,960	50.5	17,149	43.2
Anderson	75.9	15.3	83.3	69.1	77.9	5.9	11,442	0.2	412	3.6	22,557	58.5	16,500	50.0
Charleston	79.0	32.8	92.8	79.8	84.6	7.5	73,097	1.4	1,957	2.7	116,672	67.3	97,786	55.5
Columbia	63.5	13.7	91.6	81.1	63.8	24.7	58,554	-0.9	2,261	3.9	115,407	65.6	102,989	41.7
Florence	80.0	18.9	85.9	81.6	82.4	5.1	18,872	0.8	639	3.4	29,454	65.9	23,399	53.5
Goose Creek	71.5	45.9	95.8	89.3	76.7	17.0	19,691	1.5	626	3.2	32,435	70.0	27,815	55.3
Greenville	80.1	22.7	89.2	81.5	74.9	13.4	35,325	0.3	1,022	2.9	59,007	70.2	49,987	57.8
Greer	85.3	28.1	92.5	85.3	84.6	7.9	16,143	0.5	427	2.6	19,910	70.5	15,629	63.3
Hilton Head Island	70.7	17.1	96.4	91.0	86.3	7.5	17,914	2.1	508	2.8	34,973	49.8	19,790	44.8
Mount Pleasant	81.7	33.4	95.3	92.1	85.6	4.1	47,303	1.5	1,092	2.3	70,585	67.5	54,442	60.7
Myrtle Beach	78.5	17.4	89.5	76.3	84.6	6.3	15,410	1.6	743	4.8	27,049	56.3	18,735	45.0
North Charleston	76.3	34.9	88.1	68.5	81.4	7.7	52,945	1.4	1,668	3.2	89,422	67.0	76,535	52.4
Rock Hill	82.2	38.1	93.8	89.0	78.2	10.2	37,901	0.5	1,394	3.7	59,004	68.6	50,959	50.3
Spartanburg	81.4	21.1	82.9	71.2	77.8	7.4	16,859	0.6	608	3.6	29,895	62.5	24,224	48.2
Summerville	85.9	48.9	97.1	90.5	79.8	14.7	24,126	1.2	713	3.0	37,684	64.9	31,490	55.7
Sumter	83.0	20.0	85.2	78.3	76.7	7.7	15,878	0.5	663	4.2	30,556	62.9	24,462	49.2
SOUTH DAKOTA	81.2	16.1	88.4	80.1	84.5	8.3	459,459	0.7	13,860	3.0	679,688	67.9	537,802	56.5
Aberdeen	87.0	3.5	83.9	74.8	77.1	4.0	15,086	-0.2	446	3.0	22,701	71.4	17,733	59.0
Rapid City	83.4	10.0	89.4	80.8	82.1	9.5	36,860	1.0	1,134	3.1	58,692	63.9	45,163	50.7
Sioux Falls	83.9	9.3	93.9	87.1	80.0	12.0	103,848	1.5	2,719	2.6	138,541	74.3	115,887	60.3
TENNESSEE	83.2	34.9	87.4	78.7	85.5	6.4	3,244,921	1.7	113,261	3.5	5,385,691	61.5	4,315,291	51.0
Bartlett	89.0	35.7	92.7	89.3	89.4	3.4	31,174	1.2	937	3.0	47,640	67.0	36,549	56.6
Brentwood	84.7	38.5	98.9	97.6	90.7	7.9	22,004	3.0	547	2.5	31,901	69.0	27,018	47.5
Bristol	91.9	28.1	81.5	78.2	83.3	8.7	11,724	0.4	439	3.7	22,211	56.5	16,971	46.4
Chattanooga	82.5	12.2	86.1	73.7	87.3	5.3	84,952	1.9	3,169	3.7	148,375	59.8	116,718	49.5
Clarksville	87.3	30.7	93.6	88.1	72.3	16.0	61,969	2.4	2,494	4.0	114,427	68.8	102,091	53.8
Cleveland	78.1	20.2	91.9	82.7	78.2	8.7	20,600	-1.0	766	3.7	35,755	65.2	30,850	45.7
Collierville	86.0	43.7	96.1	95.0	90.0	4.9	25,905	1.2	709	2.7	38,954	63.3	32,023	49.7

1. Employed persons.   2. Households.   3. Percent of civilian labor force.   4. Persons 16 years old and over.

Table D. Cities — Construction, Wholesale Trade, and Retail Trade

City	Value of residential construction authorized by building permits, 2018			Wholesale trade[1], 2012				Retail trade[2], 2012			
	New construction ($1,000)	Number of housing units	Percent single family	Number of establishments	Number of employees	Sales (mil dol)	Annual payroll (mil dol)	Number of establishments	Number of employees	Sales (mil dol)	Annual payroll (mil dol)
	69	70	71	72	73	74	75	76	77	78	79
OREGON— Cont'd											
Redmond	107,899	512	82.4	33	206	78.9	8.4	113	1,962	532.5	50.2
Salem	179,228	861	56.8	141	1,652	1,862.8	77.8	604	9,646	2,535.4	252.4
Springfield	22,455	147	34.7	39	873	433.4	35.3	209	3,545	812.2	79.1
Tigard	85,037	368	51.9	148	2,255	2,065.8	150.7	327	7,093	1,827.1	198.3
Tualatin	31,330	99	100.0	107	1,685	785.6	90.2	109	1,837	478.3	43.0
West Linn	12,935	31	100.0	29	93	66.9	5.2	54	473	129.1	12.1
PENNSYLVANIA	4,684,321	23,325	65.7	12,568	195,004	191,170.1	11,203.8	43,952	643,903	178,794.9	15,330.6
Allentown	0	0	0.0	144	2,072	1,088.9	87.3	366	5,377	1,387.1	125.7
Altoona	1,005	9	100.0	47	803	355.3	36.0	248	4,693	1,095.5	94.3
Bethel Park	6,694	26	50.0	32	257	115.6	12.3	109	2,824	628.3	62.0
Bethlehem	8,325	91	18.7	59	D	D	D	214	3,511	919.0	79.5
Chester	0	0	0.0	18	163	78.1	8.3	61	340	119.5	10.6
Easton	0	0	0.0	28	D	D	D	143	1,730	423.5	39.8
Erie	7,702	43	100.0	110	1,629	679.5	74.2	374	5,516	1,018.6	108.5
Harrisburg	5,440	46	6.5	58	1,349	1,837.2	89.7	233	2,682	613.8	56.3
Hazleton	1,170	39	2.6	33	499	151.6	22.7	112	1,124	275.4	22.1
Lancaster	91	1	100.0	60	719	491.1	29.5	364	5,382	1,100.3	117.8
Lebanon	261	2	100.0	18	D	D	D	107	1,260	296.1	31.2
Monroeville	1,258	4	100.0	46	520	195.8	25.6	276	5,452	1,635.0	131.3
Norristown	2,926	11	100.0	43	732	456.5	38.6	92	614	134.5	16.5
Philadelphia	521,128	3,239	21.1	1,047	16,940	13,181.9	973.0	4,506	50,185	12,241.3	1,165.5
Pittsburgh	80,530	643	14.0	399	6,843	7,437.6	393.2	1,202	17,411	4,107.1	410.7
Plum	9,968	52	100.0	29	227	104.4	9.9	51	658	149.3	15.9
Reading	0	0	0.0	47	973	490.8	50.7	227	3,321	1,085.9	88.0
Scranton	749	3	100.0	96	1,385	963.1	62.1	340	4,493	1,127.2	102.9
State College	349	1	100.0	9	51	16.6	2.5	138	1,883	299.4	33.7
Wilkes-Barre	0	0	0.0	46	546	167.9	19.5	260	5,744	4,517.9	139.9
Williamsport	0	0	0.0	40	1,077	638.3	38.4	109	1,683	386.8	38.3
York	212	2	100.0	60	1,005	845.5	38.2	138	2,077	555.9	53.9
RHODE ISLAND	260,274	1,294	72.3	1,158	15,697	22,310.4	1,000.2	3,795	47,688	12,063.9	1,206.6
Cranston	8,131	64	76.6	129	D	D	D	288	4,488	1,135.5	124.6
East Providence	0	0	0.0	81	D	D	D	150	1,954	561.3	50.6
Pawtucket	1,809	15	73.3	64	D	D	D	176	1,604	456.3	41.9
Providence	235	1	100.0	184	1,942	1,475.2	102.4	646	6,835	1,448.7	156.4
Warwick	9,313	63	74.6	140	1,919	909.2	104.8	429	7,656	1,960.7	188.2
Woonsocket	725	6	100.0	33	D	D	D	129	1,366	328.2	35.2
SOUTH CAROLINA	8,143,578	35,487	86.2	4,337	54,949	45,520.9	2,806.2	17,586	220,438	58,093.8	4,954.6
Aiken	21,626	108	100.0	19	92	158.2	4.2	233	3,420	774.1	68.4
Anderson	14,911	154	100.0	35	253	105.4	9.3	279	4,031	819.8	84.6
Charleston	146,388	1,164	69.6	137	1,331	1,032.0	80.8	733	10,061	2,642.6	246.2
Columbia	85,248	477	94.1	206	3,094	2,469.9	181.7	657	10,186	2,631.1	231.5
Florence	25,182	199	83.4	59	973	545.1	45.0	382	5,058	1,162.9	107.6
Goose Creek	50,869	287	100.0	9	D	D	D	74	1,511	387.6	34.0
Greenville	162,009	1,064	22.7	173	2,302	2,438.0	117.4	777	12,402	3,109.2	298.0
Greer	126,807	577	91.3	42	309	134.3	13.1	138	2,345	786.4	63.9
Hilton Head Island	106,643	227	100.0	54	188	132.4	9.7	259	2,750	645.8	67.0
Mount Pleasant	365,095	1,061	73.6	69	388	149.9	24.7	360	5,269	1,145.8	115.5
Myrtle Beach	192,256	550	100.0	82	616	281.5	26.0	683	9,822	2,163.0	206.7
North Charleston	116,347	1,270	35.3	219	3,399	1,876.0	177.0	580	8,363	2,269.3	203.1
Rock Hill	65,917	250	95.2	68	1,091	556.9	57.5	322	4,914	1,279.3	106.0
Spartanburg	6,620	28	100.0	63	508	352.6	26.2	355	5,853	1,418.3	130.5
Summerville	80,000	294	100.0	39	339	279.2	12.0	196	3,764	909.6	82.7
Sumter	NA	NA	NA	31	278	96.0	11.7	289	3,599	754.7	69.1
SOUTH DAKOTA	854,338	4,963	60.1	1,317	15,827	20,411.1	756.9	3,843	49,867	13,791.8	1,127.3
Aberdeen	4,726	63	74.6	42	698	1,225.2	35.3	176	2,778	751.1	70.2
Rapid City	74,001	468	43.6	139	1,600	1,109.9	69.4	475	7,691	2,110.4	183.0
Sioux Falls	314,089	1,981	54.7	324	5,257	3,108.2	267.7	751	14,515	4,340.9	342.0
TENNESSEE	7,048,088	37,169	75.4	5,828	92,537	111,718.4	4,863.3	22,615	306,078	91,641.6	7,420.3
Bartlett	18,788	81	100.0	64	1,097	755.5	62.6	124	2,019	889.8	54.7
Brentwood	69,263	139	100.0	59	785	1,413.2	49.0	175	3,254	1,076.3	102.5
Bristol	8,649	73	52.1	40	394	123.1	12.5	118	1,872	597.2	51.0
Chattanooga	127,270	655	67.3	374	4,859	2,711.5	249.6	1,123	16,813	4,359.1	419.3
Clarksville	96,718	938	71.3	68	952	553.2	43.2	489	7,756	1,983.0	188.4
Cleveland	29,462	218	69.7	41	D	D	D	297	4,319	1,150.0	103.0
Collierville	70,311	183	100.0	50	671	518.5	41.7	213	3,540	852.9	76.9

1. Merchant wholesalers except manufacturers' sales branches and offices.   2. Establishments with payroll.

Real Estate, Professional Services, and Manufacturing

City	Real estate and rental and leasing, 2012				Professional, scientific, and technical services[1], 2012				Manufacturing, 2012			
	Number of establishments	Number of employees	Receipts (mil dol)	Annual payroll (mil dol)	Number of establishments	Number of employees	Receipts (mil dol)	Annual payroll (mil dol)	Number of establishments	Number of employees	Receipts (mil dol)	Annual payroll (mil dol)
	80	81	82	83	84	85	86	87	88	89	90	91
OREGON— Cont'd												
Redmond	42	164	23.8	5.5	43	D	D	D	59	951	221.6	36.9
Salem	271	1,130	173.7	40.0	494	3,110	381.0	145.7	182	5,324	1,708.8	217.6
Springfield	64	274	54.2	8.4	87	572	49.3	20.0	85	2,380	1,240.8	126.6
Tigard	121	615	219.5	27.6	362	D	D	D	93	1,716	D	D
Tualatin	59	595	125.1	23.3	107	D	D	D	121	6,893	2,103.6	410.6
West Linn	41	172	16.9	4.9	122	290	44.4	15.5	10	264	D	D
PENNSYLVANIA	9,438	58,585	13,364.0	2,617.5	29,113	310,692	54,014.0	22,242.0	13,988	543,641	231,396.2	28,057.8
Allentown	95	498	93.0	16.6	214	D	D	D	140	2,442	687.5	115.1
Altoona	41	193	30.0	6.0	87	D	D	D	45	1,006	293.8	39.6
Bethel Park	30	104	32.6	5.2	92	391	69.9	25.5	30	441	82.1	18.1
Bethlehem	62	306	167.0	13.3	176	1,009	152.0	61.7	53	3,306	1,017.5	188.3
Chester	15	D	D	D	14	D	D	D	26	1,401	929.4	99.3
Easton	21	D	D	D	87	369	59.0	15.1	26	505	233.3	22.1
Erie	66	427	61.9	15.9	196	D	D	D	148	5,832	1,842.9	298.2
Harrisburg	44	381	206.6	40.2	256	D	D	D	32	1,432	666.1	84.0
Hazleton	19	51	9.6	1.5	54	472	70.1	11.7	47	2,606	1,393.1	105.5
Lancaster	48	394	65.3	13.7	222	D	D	D	74	3,363	1,357.6	168.3
Lebanon	27	128	17.6	3.8	53	D	D	D	55	1,140	342.7	44.0
Monroeville	58	546	99.3	21.3	100	1,194	155.2	84.5	17	549	D	30.5
Norristown	29	108	36.4	3.7	94	D	D	D	16	470	D	19.6
Philadelphia	1,079	8,856	1,951.0	443.5	2,793	44,342	10,124.7	4,075.8	765	22,558	19,718.6	1,198.5
Pittsburgh	473	3,628	816.9	179.9	1,505	D	D	D	295	7,303	2,054.6	372.7
Plum	17	57	12.4	1.9	37	539	145.0	54.7	26	320	145.4	14.0
Reading	60	436	61.7	14.1	129	D	D	D	94	7,270	3,814.0	457.0
Scranton	54	333	56.8	10.3	205	D	D	D	77	2,100	660.4	91.6
State College	56	401	91.1	15.9	90	D	D	D	5	169	D	10.4
Wilkes-Barre	34	237	58.7	10.4	119	D	D	D	26	1,099	279.5	48.4
Williamsport	28	204	38.7	8.0	75	1,194	86.8	37.2	51	3,612	1,461.4	168.1
York	36	297	39.9	11.4	137	D	D	D	76	3,422	1,334.4	192.6
RHODE ISLAND	1,058	5,615	1,119.8	218.5	2,980	20,991	3,316.8	1,300.2	1,509	39,608	11,262.2	2,076.5
Cranston	66	366	67.9	14.3	222	1,893	287.4	103.5	156	4,275	1,845.9	211.8
East Providence	57	376	165.0	17.0	129	1,318	191.7	68.9	89	2,304	654.6	112.1
Pawtucket	55	311	38.2	12.4	106	D	D	D	132	3,327	733.0	169.5
Providence	208	1,126	227.9	50.4	790	D	D	D	217	3,165	628.4	135.4
Warwick	111	1,102	223.1	42.2	344	D	D	D	130	3,281	1,227.7	199.0
Woonsocket	40	131	18.0	4.5	44	262	40.2	12.7	43	853	178.8	39.5
SOUTH CAROLINA	4,692	23,189	4,334.4	825.9	9,688	79,433	12,645.3	4,789.2	3,854	207,396	99,160.8	10,082.1
Aiken	42	168	27.9	5.6	125	D	D	D	22	1,506	518.0	70.2
Anderson	47	178	34.4	4.7	133	D	D	D	50	1,956	626.4	79.9
Charleston	278	1,716	249.2	57.6	660	D	D	D	77	1,335	521.0	64.7
Columbia	227	1,594	529.1	96.6	838	D	D	D	69	1,172	D	60.3
Florence	79	398	74.6	14.9	132	D	D	D	20	1,773	1,034.8	117.6
Goose Creek	22	90	33.1	3.4	60	1,152	218.9	65.3	13	755	845.2	47.1
Greenville	243	1,308	310.1	54.5	809	D	D	D	104	3,863	1,260.2	160.8
Greer	35	146	25.9	4.9	66	334	57.7	16.7	39	849	372.9	42.0
Hilton Head Island	223	1,158	179.3	45.4	245	1,028	167.3	70.0	28	186	19.7	6.3
Mount Pleasant	183	384	93.3	15.5	415	D	D	D	35	D	D	D
Myrtle Beach	211	2,259	251.5	66.6	218	1,141	152.1	54.1	27	758	D	35.5
North Charleston	148	1,039	209.0	39.9	345	D	D	D	122	11,200	3,422.0	655.8
Rock Hill	77	319	47.2	10.9	160	D	D	D	60	2,691	1,154.2	153.3
Spartanburg	82	404	69.7	18.0	192	D	D	D	32	1,002	296.2	47.6
Summerville	67	248	43.1	8.3	116	D	D	D	27	1,055	374.8	46.2
Sumter	57	208	22.0	5.3	99	517	44.6	11.9	29	D	214.6	D
SOUTH DAKOTA	962	3,526	582.8	105.7	1,806	11,083	1,310.0	479.5	1,025	41,931	16,882.6	1,764.7
Aberdeen	55	D	D	D	67	378	47.4	16.1	31	2,351	873.4	93.8
Rapid City	141	528	92.4	15.1	270	D	D	D	93	1,766	D	74.6
Sioux Falls	236	1,231	268.4	47.6	473	4,266	497.7	210.2	147	9,836	3,126.3	436.3
TENNESSEE	5,470	30,593	6,178.4	1,220.0	10,815	D	D	D	5,823	293,646	139,960.5	14,180.5
Bartlett	35	145	109.4	4.8	104	921	103.5	41.7	34	920	260.5	44.4
Brentwood	94	D	D	D	306	D	D	D	18	173	D	6.9
Bristol	34	93	17.4	2.7	64	569	80.2	34.0	47	2,255	1,512.1	212.0
Chattanooga	290	1,898	384.3	91.1	621	6,999	979.3	362.0	323	18,889	10,598.1	1,048.6
Clarksville	137	605	100.4	18.4	157	D	D	D	45	3,378	1,142.0	159.0
Cleveland	55	254	33.6	7.2	125	786	71.4	30.7	80	5,481	4,457.4	229.6
Collierville	41	149	32.4	5.0	105	416	54.5	25.9	38	2,236	1,536.9	100.0

1. Establishments subject to federal tax.

Accommodation and Food Services, Arts, Entertainment, and Recreation, and Health Care and Social Assistance

City	Accommodation and food services, 2012				Arts, entertainment, and recreation,[1] 2012				Health care and social assistance,[1] 2012			
	Number of establish-ments	Number of employees	Receipts (mil dol)	Annual payroll (mil dol)	Number of establish-ments	Number of employees	Receipts (mil dol)	Annual payroll (mil dol)	Number of establish-ments	Number of employees	Receipts (mil dol)	Annual payroll (mil dol)
	92	93	94	95	96	97	98	99	100	101	102	103
OREGON— Cont'd												
Redmond	93	1,231	64.1	18.9	5	D	D	D	80	D	D	D
Salem	405	6,360	318.8	92.9	30	515	29.4	8.7	502	6,639	715.7	304.0
Springfield	168	2,503	136.0	36.9	20	D	D	D	147	D	D	D
Tigard	167	2,707	155.8	44.5	15	D	D	D	200	2,120	229.1	90.6
Tualatin	80	1,542	78.3	23.3	11	D	D	D	126	1,520	216.2	83.7
West Linn	45	645	34.3	10.2	11	69	2.9	0.7	92	D	D	D
PENNSYLVANIA	27,646	439,159	23,504.2	6,377.4	3,117	67,396	6,763.8	2,052.6	27,983	433,818	43,779.7	19,364.3
Allentown	255	3,394	173.8	50.0	18	184	25.4	5.1	283	4,491	471.4	222.0
Altoona	137	2,176	97.5	27.2	9	D	D	D	157	2,596	276.1	123.2
Bethel Park	65	1,589	63.9	19.8	10	D	D	D	110	1,593	127.4	59.1
Bethlehem	217	4,921	636.2	121.2	9	D	D	D	186	2,369	251.4	124.0
Chester	40	D	D	D	3	D	D	D	44	1,671	222.3	122.8
Easton	110	1,447	71.7	19.1	4	D	D	D	58	653	46.2	22.0
Erie	222	3,551	151.0	40.4	29	D	D	D	285	5,043	619.6	320.3
Harrisburg	183	2,537	136.0	35.5	12	D	D	D	97	1,657	184.2	81.9
Hazleton	60	553	25.4	6.4	4	D	D	D	84	1,485	122.1	50.1
Lancaster	162	2,948	174.5	51.3	12	D	D	D	138	D	D	D
Lebanon	58	609	28.1	6.9	4	43	3.1	0.8	66	D	D	D
Monroeville	128	2,852	150.0	40.8	11	190	5.1	2.3	193	3,252	412.6	162.2
Norristown	59	D	D	D	5	1	0.5	0.1	71	787	84.8	43.2
Philadelphia	3,669	53,533	3,551.7	982.4	208	13,373	1,333.2	697.1	2,647	47,119	5,255.8	2,270.4
Pittsburgh	1,234	22,377	1,306.2	375.3	92	D	D	D	963	19,796	2,162.6	1,330.0
Plum	36	527	24.5	6.9	8	D	D	D	20	112	6.8	3.0
Reading	149	1,822	98.4	24.9	7	236	13.1	5.0	99	2,195	189.6	82.5
Scranton	217	2,965	136.3	35.6	17	367	18.8	4.6	227	5,785	719.2	314.6
State College	135	3,042	126.0	34.8	7	70	5.4	1.5	90	D	D	D
Wilkes-Barre	126	2,784	133.9	37.5	7	D	D	D	111	3,579	442.0	167.6
Williamsport	101	1,570	90.5	24.1	6	44	4.7	1.0	83	1,902	166.3	109.0
York	113	1,581	76.0	22.3	6	D	D	D	57	D	D	D
RHODE ISLAND	2,973	44,063	2,481.3	705.9	406	6,108	593.5	150.4	2,470	35,597	3,467.0	1,535.8
Cranston	182	D	D	D	28	D	D	D	231	2,679	227.2	111.4
East Providence	114	1,746	82.6	21.8	20	D	D	D	141	2,850	305.9	155.3
Pawtucket	139	1,384	74.6	20.0	16	129	16.1	5.1	136	2,049	180.2	81.1
Providence	566	9,893	584.0	169.8	35	1,396	85.4	23.1	415	5,910	770.3	358.2
Warwick	248	4,910	262.4	74.2	31	357	24.5	6.8	303	4,416	385.9	170.1
Woonsocket	93	1,218	57.8	15.7	4	52	2.2	0.6	75	2,245	236.0	95.3
SOUTH CAROLINA	9,828	185,282	9,763.8	2,650.5	1,226	17,936	1,471.4	318.4	8,346	132,360	13,822.7	5,385.0
Aiken	134	3,030	118.0	34.6	19	311	17.8	6.3	153	3,760	381.8	139.0
Anderson	165	3,355	147.6	42.8	10	31	1.2	0.4	162	D	D	D
Charleston	517	11,876	786.3	216.0	67	722	63.0	13.2	423	4,151	582.4	230.9
Columbia	505	11,042	560.3	153.4	30	D	D	D	447	7,578	925.6	362.0
Florence	192	3,845	192.1	51.2	11	264	6.4	3.5	230	D	D	D
Goose Creek	69	1,254	57.0	15.1	6	121	4.0	1.3	44	D	D	D
Greenville	448	10,151	539.9	148.8	50	743	34.0	10.5	436	6,515	671.2	316.3
Greer	74	1,172	55.8	15.5	8	D	D	D	79	949	79.1	32.7
Hilton Head Island	226	5,252	388.2	111.7	53	1,045	73.5	20.5	149	1,681	275.2	72.5
Mount Pleasant	220	4,417	229.8	62.5	39	516	25.3	7.8	316	4,075	548.0	169.8
Myrtle Beach	546	13,643	869.7	232.6	78	1,575	151.3	34.2	219	2,882	566.6	167.6
North Charleston	322	6,364	364.7	92.2	14	1,218	19.2	6.3	282	6,172	858.2	285.2
Rock Hill	196	4,123	200.9	52.8	9	52	4.6	1.0	231	5,653	666.2	221.2
Spartanburg	200	4,453	213.9	61.2	13	D	D	D	168	3,712	492.0	227.8
Summerville	146	2,968	134.8	39.0	11	D	D	D	133	D	D	D
Sumter	128	2,635	112.9	31.4	4	68	3.1	1.3	144	2,705	239.6	100.7
SOUTH DAKOTA	2,363	37,974	1,873.7	514.2	526	4,636	352.8	73.0	1,544	20,514	2,023.2	829.8
Aberdeen	90	1,833	77.5	22.9	22	121	14.3	1.8	81	D	D	D
Rapid City	247	5,808	296.8	84.8	66	D	D	D	265	3,417	424.3	155.5
Sioux Falls	409	10,412	491.0	147.6	118	D	D	D	358	6,363	680.4	300.1
TENNESSEE	12,004	241,348	12,499.0	3,546.5	1,931	20,971	2,793.2	934.8	12,286	220,313	24,541.3	9,564.0
Bartlett	84	1,282	62.5	15.3	10	D	D	D	115	2,716	316.5	97.5
Brentwood	92	1,834	107.5	27.5	55	500	59.6	22.7	220	3,698	460.8	224.1
Bristol	83	1,431	58.5	16.3	11	D	D	D	114	D	D	D
Chattanooga	651	14,791	763.5	220.8	63	1,040	59.8	17.2	661	11,426	1,520.4	604.5
Clarksville	319	5,879	285.5	77.3	14	D	D	D	281	4,771	469.8	173.3
Cleveland	163	D	D	D	8	167	5.9	2.3	169	D	D	D
Collierville	97	2,332	105.5	30.6	12	D	D	D	103	D	D	D

1. Establishments subject to federal tax.

Table D. Cities — Other Services and Government Employment and Payroll

City	Other services[1]				Government employment and payroll, 2012								
							March payroll						
							Percent of total for:						
	Number of establishments	Number of employees	Receipts (mil dol)	Annual payroll (mil dol)	Full-time equivalent employees	Total (dollars)	Administrative, judicial, and legal	Police and corrections	Fire protection	Highways and transportation	Health and welfare	Natural resources and utilities	Education and libraries
	104	105	106	107	108	109	110	111	112	113	114	115	116
OREGON— Cont'd													
Redmond	41	161	19.9	5.4	145	696,980	14.3	31.9	0.0	20.4	5.5	20.4	0.0
Salem	221	1,161	86.8	28.8	1,201	6,557,144	12.3	26.5	18.4	2.9	8.3	17.5	2.8
Springfield	79	375	36.9	11.1	535	3,245,769	12.3	22.4	20.4	10.8	4.0	18.1	2.0
Tigard	107	696	75.5	25.0	286	1,551,160	26.2	36.8	0.0	7.7	0.0	11.2	12.8
Tualatin	79	509	42.7	13.8	147	818,379	22.2	35.7	0.0	9.0	1.8	13.6	10.1
West Linn	37	171	8.2	3.3	104	541,464	20.2	40.2	0.0	4.2	0.0	22.8	12.6
PENNSYLVANIA	20,247	114,850	10,517.4	3,078.9	X	X	X	X	X	X	X	X	X
Allentown	196	1,384	115.2	37.0	870	4,561,766	8.4	33.3	19.8	5.0	8.9	19.7	0.0
Altoona	104	579	37.6	12.7	242	1,031,472	8.7	39.4	29.9	15.7	4.9	1.4	0.0
Bethel Park	80	610	37.9	13.3	127	577,790	11.9	56.2	0.0	16.0	0.0	15.3	0.0
Bethlehem	103	892	72.1	26.8	680	3,090,583	7.7	30.1	17.3	3.5	8.2	18.8	0.0
Chester	33	214	16.3	4.7	305	1,818,516	31.3	36.7	17.7	3.5	2.3	3.4	0.0
Easton	51	249	21.3	6.6	246	1,153,107	13.0	32.8	24.1	5.8	1.5	12.2	0.0
Erie	158	727	55.7	16.7	656	3,187,505	6.2	34.9	25.5	9.0	2.8	15.7	0.0
Harrisburg	73	320	28.9	9.4	534	2,458,452	13.1	41.4	17.4	3.7	6.0	16.7	0.0
Hazleton	40	119	9.2	2.8	93	424,630	10.3	46.4	20.8	13.6	6.5	0.6	0.0
Lancaster	94	499	32.6	11.6	519	2,372,327	5.8	43.9	17.4	3.9	3.7	21.3	0.0
Lebanon	51	208	18.1	5.2	153	662,861	5.0	39.2	17.2	5.8	2.6	30.3	0.0
Monroeville	82	503	30.5	10.6	148	872,947	9.5	53.2	0.0	15.7	2.8	6.5	6.5
Norristown	43	188	24.6	7.4	170	899,425	10.6	61.2	15.6	6.4	0.0	0.7	0.0
Philadelphia	1,947	10,726	869.3	257.8	29,409	148,399,324	18.0	39.0	9.6	3.4	11.1	15.4	1.7
Pittsburgh	589	4,360	396.7	123.0	4,176	16,527,485	9.4	38.3	25.1	11.2	8.9	5.4	0.0
Plum	40	182	17.4	4.7	67	358,089	66.3	0.0	0.0	0.0	0.0	0.0	0.0
Reading	80	473	47.4	14.7	730	12,558,088	5.8	44.6	24.9	0.6	5.6	13.5	1.3
Scranton	123	595	42.9	12.5	484	2,233,185	4.0	40.2	30.7	5.1	1.7	7.2	6.5
State College	41	285	15.2	6.1	165	866,140	14.2	48.6	0.0	13.8	4.0	4.8	0.0
Wilkes-Barre	70	349	30.5	8.2	284	1,342,714	13.0	34.7	27.3	0.0	8.1	12.4	0.0
Williamsport	51	390	28.4	8.2	201	913,971	5.1	32.7	21.3	35.2	1.9	3.5	0.0
York	54	510	48.9	14.2	379	1,772,634	9.4	43.1	18.8	1.0	6.2	13.8	0.0
RHODE ISLAND	1,838	9,862	884.8	273.4	X	X	X	X	X	X	X	X	X
Cranston	157	971	86.9	28.6	2,144	11,389,033	1.9	8.5	6.8	1.5	0.6	0.6	78.6
East Providence	91	431	50.1	14.8	1,234	5,386,925	3.6	8.7	7.8	3.2	0.6	4.6	71.2
Pawtucket	106	623	61.0	18.7	1,817	9,164,839	2.7	8.8	7.2	0.8	1.4	4.4	72.6
Providence	290	1,961	165.9	50.3	5,219	27,174,708	5.3	17.6	13.9	1.5	0.0	6.7	54.9
Warwick	173	1,135	94.7	30.2	2,400	12,798,555	2.8	10.0	12.2	1.9	0.5	3.3	67.2
Woonsocket	60	274	30.1	8.6	1,167	6,516,930	2.3	7.1	7.8	1.5	0.3	1.7	77.9
SOUTH CAROLINA	5,482	34,926	3,006.7	1,000.9	X	X	X	X	X	X	X	X	X
Aiken	48	279	21.0	6.0	346	1,255,386	18.9	27.9	10.5	14.5	0.0	24.7	0.0
Anderson	67	428	30.2	9.8	420	924,851	13.0	31.8	14.8	8.6	2.0	25.1	0.0
Charleston	187	1,286	81.0	28.8	2,045	7,787,974	9.2	27.1	16.5	1.2	1.0	37.8	0.0
Columbia	179	1,789	129.9	41.8	2,261	7,098,669	11.6	20.9	23.5	2.0	2.7	24.7	0.0
Florence	64	571	35.9	10.4	510	1,554,745	9.4	29.2	16.4	5.2	3.3	35.0	0.0
Goose Creek	42	220	15.4	4.7	271	928,636	14.9	34.9	20.4	3.8	0.0	23.9	0.0
Greenville	208	1,367	89.8	31.4	1,049	3,701,819	9.4	20.4	14.8	5.7	1.5	42.0	0.0
Greer	41	195	15.1	4.9	189	659,763	25.5	37.5	20.6	2.5	0.0	13.8	0.0
Hilton Head Island	97	396	33.3	11.0	242	1,283,504	30.6	0.0	57.1	4.6	0.0	0.5	0.0
Mount Pleasant	120	838	59.9	22.1	569	1,912,550	16.4	33.5	20.8	2.0	0.8	24.2	0.0
Myrtle Beach	122	653	47.9	15.1	889	3,176,078	16.3	31.5	18.5	3.8	0.5	25.7	1.3
North Charleston	192	1,544	152.2	49.9	1,049	3,596,992	11.5	39.1	21.3	5.5	0.4	16.7	0.0
Rock Hill	89	787	71.8	22.4	836	2,857,047	21.2	21.2	14.2	3.9	6.3	29.3	0.0
Spartanburg	90	737	58.3	15.4	616	2,210,757	10.5	25.6	11.1	4.0	2.5	41.1	0.0
Summerville	91	560	40.0	14.3	357	1,158,866	7.9	29.3	23.7	1.9	0.0	33.0	0.0
Sumter	73	D	D	D	550	1,497,205	11.8	29.7	18.8	1.8	1.1	29.5	0.0
SOUTH DAKOTA	1,363	6,155	578.2	152.9	X	X	X	X	X	X	X	X	X
Aberdeen	43	198	16.7	4.5	287	1,030,395	10.5	20.7	18.3	13.5	0.0	31.3	4.3
Rapid City	176	1,034	84.9	26.0	868	1,798,797	7.6	17.7	12.4	6.9	0.0	24.6	3.9
Sioux Falls	265	1,851	149.3	47.4	1,148	5,118,747	9.5	24.6	18.4	10.7	7.0	21.1	5.6
TENNESSEE	6,521	44,354	3,896.0	1,201.1	X	X	X	X	X	X	X	X	X
Bartlett	62	614	45.6	14.5	511	2,039,502	14.7	30.7	21.1	6.5	0.0	20.1	0.0
Brentwood	58	427	38.4	11.5	256	1,094,815	19.4	23.6	26.3	6.2	0.0	13.8	5.5
Bristol	47	307	29.4	9.1	919	3,282,369	4.6	12.4	6.6	3.8	0.6	7.7	61.5
Chattanooga	346	2,676	264.2	76.0	3,133	11,941,830	7.9	16.8	12.6	11.2	5.0	42.3	2.0
Clarksville	164	931	71.3	19.9	1,114	3,666,316	6.5	29.4	19.3	13.3	0.6	26.7	0.0
Cleveland	64	748	59.6	18.9	1,030	3,567,674	2.1	10.1	17.6	4.9	1.2	2.8	59.7
Collierville	58	525	30.7	11.5	435	1,694,955	11.6	31.7	20.1	7.3	1.0	19.2	0.0

1. Establishments subject to federal tax.

Table D. Cities — **City Government Finances**

City	General revenue Total (mil dol)	Intergovernmental Total (mil dol)	Intergovernmental Percent from state government	Taxes Total (mil dol)	Taxes Per capita[1] (dollars) Total	Taxes Per capita[1] (dollars) Property	Taxes Per capita[1] (dollars) Sales and gross receipts	General expenditure Total (mil dol)	General expenditure Per capita[1] (dollars) Total	General expenditure Per capita[1] (dollars) Capital outlays
	117	118	119	120	121	122	123	124	125	126
OREGON— Cont'd										
Redmond	35.3	5.9	60.8	13.4	502	328	174	32.9	1,229	258
Salem	251.3	76.0	63.8	101.3	642	489	153	240.9	1,527	209
Springfield	103.6	9.1	99.1	32.9	549	452	97	90.7	1,514	262
Tigard	45.1	9.8	49.5	26.0	522	305	217	43.3	870	90
Tualatin	29.9	5.6	64.3	13.3	498	310	188	27.4	1,025	191
West Linn	24.0	5.0	70.0	11.3	439	271	168	22.2	865	100
PENNSYLVANIA	X	X	X	X	X	X	X	X	X	X
Allentown	129.2	30.4	47.0	56.8	477	247	115	175.0	1,471	88
Altoona	29.3	7.5	47.2	17.6	381	194	73	27.1	587	40
Bethel Park	24.5	2.7	71.8	13.8	427	131	46	25.6	790	60
Bethlehem	101.1	27.5	100.0	47.5	632	280	117	89.6	1,193	0
Chester	47.9	12.2	79.6	19.2	563	252	84	45.6	1,340	83
Easton	52.4	14.3	75.3	14.8	546	331	69	53.4	1,967	129
Erie	113.3	23.8	46.1	46.9	464	337	53	105.0	1,039	74
Harrisburg	93.9	6.2	90.0	30.4	616	345	171	78.7	1,595	121
Hazleton	18.6	7.2	55.0	8.3	329	113	39	13.3	528	65
Lancaster	69.1	11.7	71.8	31.0	522	384	54	87.4	1,472	261
Lebanon	21.7	10.2	34.6	8.3	325	116	37	26.5	1,036	259
Monroeville	23.1	1.7	95.3	19.7	695	159	284	30.1	1,058	116
Norristown	28.2	3.4	47.9	21.6	627	320	95	30.2	875	85
Philadelphia	6,411.8	2,254.7	74.3	3,239.1	2,089	323	474	5,483.2	3,537	209
Pittsburgh	607.0	163.6	87.2	357.2	1,166	443	419	548.9	1,791	25
Plum	13.3	1.8	85.5	9.6	352	192	32	13.6	498	25
Reading	139.8	30.8	89.3	42.9	488	220	111	135.9	1,543	96
Scranton	67.6	10.7	95.5	45.2	593	179	69	70.2	923	3
State College	36.3	5.5	55.6	11.4	272	114	42	35.4	843	78
Wilkes-Barre	52.9	20.4	46.2	24.1	583	208	78	57.3	1,386	201
Williamsport	41.3	20.3	45.8	15.5	526	329	123	30.5	1,035	151
York	68.7	9.7	51.4	24.7	566	395	110	63.2	1,448	39
RHODE ISLAND	X	X	X	X	X	X	X	X	X	X
Cranston	282.2	60.2	92.5	187.4	2,322	2,290	32	256.9	3,184	42
East Providence	148.4	43.6	95.5	91.6	1,942	1,918	24	155.3	3,292	150
Pawtucket	197.7	91.3	77.8	95.5	1,339	1,328	10	192.3	2,697	24
Providence	747.8	292.1	91.6	325.5	1,822	1,765	57	715.3	4,004	160
Warwick	318.8	59.3	98.4	219.5	2,682	2,607	74	303.4	3,707	110
Woonsocket	147.2	67.5	95.5	57.6	1,401	1,352	50	147.3	3,584	80
SOUTH CAROLINA	X	X	X	X	X	X	X	X	X	X
Aiken	42.7	5.6	22.9	23.7	790	330	460	40.3	1,341	206
Anderson	40.2	4.0	38.2	19.7	735	460	275	43.2	1,613	63
Charleston	207.6	27.8	72.1	132.3	1,053	446	607	178.8	1,424	222
Columbia	222.0	28.7	56.5	95.1	721	383	339	189.3	1,435	255
Florence	47.5	3.6	40.8	22.6	603	96	506	40.8	1,086	63
Goose Creek	19.6	0.7	100.0	11.6	298	47	251	20.5	528	67
Greenville	95.3	5.9	100.0	64.6	1,066	598	468	99.6	1,643	290
Greer	28.9	2.8	31.9	15.7	593	370	223	45.5	1,711	36
Hilton Head Island	89.1	35.5	16.2	48.4	1,261	625	586	94.8	2,471	1,299
Mount Pleasant	114.5	34.1	60.2	59.9	833	385	448	106.8	1,486	667
Myrtle Beach	161.3	12.2	83.8	82.5	2,918	878	2,040	123.3	4,360	375
North Charleston	122.2	14.2	23.7	93.4	915	471	408	119.1	1,168	208
Rock Hill	88.3	12.8	15.4	35.8	525	351	174	102.2	1,502	271
Spartanburg	53.3	13.1	6.6	33.4	895	449	446	42.1	1,130	160
Summerville	29.5	3.1	88.8	21.9	494	238	255	26.9	608	53
Sumter	43.8	6.9	24.7	24.0	587	218	369	40.1	980	178
SOUTH DAKOTA	X	X	X	X	X	X	X	X	X	X
Aberdeen	39.6	5.1	70.4	24.2	900	292	609	38.1	1,414	18
Rapid City	138.0	19.9	85.8	75.4	1,077	309	768	126.9	1,813	706
Sioux Falls	226.3	20.3	62.2	149.5	933	282	651	225.7	1,408	474
TENNESSEE	X	X	X	X	X	X	X	X	X	X
Bartlett	55.6	18.3	51.6	21.0	361	305	56	47.7	820	25
Brentwood	49.5	19.7	38.7	18.1	463	278	185	45.0	1,153	330
Bristol	75.0	35.6	60.9	26.6	999	899	101	74.6	2,797	336
Chattanooga	485.4	165.9	19.7	139.3	809	668	141	396.3	2,300	197
Clarksville	137.4	38.8	51.1	37.5	262	197	65	103.9	725	103
Cleveland	109.5	65.6	56.3	19.7	464	400	64	96.6	2,278	237
Collierville	56.6	15.9	37.4	25.4	547	460	87	51.4	1,107	164

1. Based on population estimated as of July 1 of the year shown.

Table D. Cities — **City Government Finances**

City	City government finances, 2012 (cont.)									
	General expenditure (cont.)									
	Percent of total for:									
	Public welfare	Highways	Parking facilities	Education	Health and hospitals	Police protection	Sewerage and sanitation	Parks and recreation	Housing and community development	Interest on debt
	127	128	129	130	131	132	133	134	135	136
OREGON— Cont'd										
Redmond	0.0	21.1	0.0	0.0	0.0	15.5	10.0	8.1	3.5	10.2
Salem	0.0	14.5	0.7	0.0	0.5	13.9	12.1	3.7	13.0	8.7
Springfield	0.0	5.4	0.0	0.0	5.6	16.9	38.3	0.0	1.1	4.0
Tigard	0.3	7.7	0.0	0.0	0.0	32.1	6.0	8.9	0.0	3.8
Tualatin	0.0	6.8	0.1	0.0	0.0	16.5	24.6	7.3	13.2	1.4
West Linn	0.0	8.3	0.0	0.0	0.0	26.6	11.1	13.8	0.0	1.9
PENNSYLVANIA	X	X	X	X	X	X	X	X	X	X
Allentown	0.0	8.9	0.0	0.0	3.5	18.4	23.6	4.4	6.1	2.8
Altoona	0.0	14.2	0.0	0.0	0.0	19.2	3.2	1.2	0.4	4.1
Bethel Park	0.0	22.7	0.0	0.0	0.0	23.6	35.2	3.1	0.5	0.9
Bethlehem	0.0	9.0	0.0	0.0	4.0	14.3	14.7	6.1	3.7	7.6
Chester	0.0	7.2	0.0	0.0	1.1	32.8	3.0	11.5	2.2	2.3
Easton	0.0	6.5	0.4	0.0	0.1	15.5	18.0	5.8	18.7	5.4
Erie	0.0	11.3	0.0	0.0	0.0	14.0	14.2	2.1	11.8	7.3
Harrisburg	0.0	7.4	0.0	0.0	0.2	24.9	23.4	3.9	8.6	3.8
Hazleton	0.0	13.4	0.0	0.0	1.1	27.9	2.4	0.8	7.7	3.1
Lancaster	0.0	5.5	0.0	0.0	0.0	20.9	23.8	6.2	5.6	9.3
Lebanon	0.0	53.3	0.1	0.0	0.7	15.7	0.8	1.4	6.1	0.1
Monroeville	0.0	20.1	0.0	0.0	0.3	34.5	4.7	6.1	1.2	3.1
Norristown	0.0	15.4	0.0	0.0	1.6	24.2	5.2	2.1	0.0	4.5
Philadelphia	10.4	2.1	0.0	1.4	24.8	11.1	7.0	1.5	3.5	3.9
Pittsburgh	0.0	0.6	0.0	0.0	2.5	14.1	2.8	3.0	16.9	6.6
Plum	0.0	28.0	0.0	0.0	0.0	29.8	11.8	0.2	0.0	4.0
Reading	0.0	8.0	0.0	0.0	2.7	20.8	21.1	2.8	14.3	8.1
Scranton	0.0	4.2	3.7	0.0	2.3	23.1	4.8	1.1	0.2	11.1
State College	0.0	15.4	4.9	0.0	0.9	24.5	27.4	3.1	3.2	2.6
Wilkes-Barre	0.0	23.8	0.5	0.0	4.6	16.0	7.5	7.7	7.2	7.7
Williamsport	0.0	28.5	0.0	0.0	0.0	21.9	14.1	2.4	3.5	1.1
York	0.0	6.2	0.9	0.0	3.2	15.4	23.5	4.9	6.1	8.0
RHODE ISLAND	X	X	X	X	X	X	X	X	X	X
Cranston	0.0	6.7	0.0	55.8	1.1	9.1	6.7	0.9	0.6	2.1
East Providence	0.0	3.8	0.0	57.0	0.3	7.9	7.4	1.5	0.8	1.9
Pawtucket	0.0	1.0	0.0	62.2	0.0	8.3	1.9	0.8	1.8	1.1
Providence	0.0	1.4	0.0	53.6	0.0	11.5	1.4	1.2	2.1	5.7
Warwick	0.4	2.3	0.0	56.7	0.1	6.4	4.3	0.7	0.4	1.6
Woonsocket	0.2	1.6	0.0	53.4	0.1	6.0	10.2	0.1	1.1	8.0
SOUTH CAROLINA	X	X	X	X	X	X	X	X	X	X
Aiken	0.0	7.0	0.0	0.0	0.0	22.5	13.8	12.3	1.7	0.1
Anderson	0.0	8.9	1.2	0.0	0.0	14.1	22.7	7.2	3.6	9.8
Charleston	0.4	3.1	5.1	0.0	0.0	22.4	4.6	13.3	3.8	1.7
Columbia	0.0	4.0	1.7	0.0	0.7	13.1	43.5	7.0	3.2	2.4
Florence	0.0	6.9	0.0	0.0	0.1	23.0	19.5	15.0	6.8	1.0
Goose Creek	0.0	12.8	0.0	0.0	0.0	27.9	5.4	24.9	0.0	0.3
Greenville	0.0	7.1	3.2	0.0	0.5	18.3	13.4	14.0	4.6	2.4
Greer	0.0	2.8	0.0	0.0	0.0	10.2	60.8	3.3	1.8	7.7
Hilton Head Island	0.0	1.9	0.0	0.0	0.0	6.5	2.0	0.0	30.1	4.5
Mount Pleasant	0.0	41.5	0.0	0.0	0.0	10.2	14.4	4.9	1.7	4.1
Myrtle Beach	0.0	3.8	1.5	0.0	0.0	16.0	11.8	19.5	3.8	7.6
North Charleston	0.0	4.5	0.5	0.0	0.0	25.1	8.9	5.1	1.0	5.2
Rock Hill	0.0	2.7	0.0	0.0	0.0	13.2	22.9	12.5	2.9	3.6
Spartanburg	0.0	6.2	2.3	0.0	0.0	22.3	4.7	7.7	4.1	5.1
Summerville	0.0	11.9	0.0	0.0	0.0	23.8	8.6	7.7	0.1	1.8
Sumter	0.0	1.7	0.0	0.0	0.0	23.3	16.2	12.9	8.3	0.8
SOUTH DAKOTA	X	X	X	X	X	X	X	X	X	X
Aberdeen	0.0	29.4	0.0	0.0	3.2	9.7	7.1	15.7	0.0	2.8
Rapid City	0.6	19.1	0.5	0.0	2.8	10.2	14.4	12.7	1.8	3.0
Sioux Falls	0.0	19.1	0.9	0.0	4.2	12.3	22.3	14.2	2.2	3.2
TENNESSEE	X	X	X	X	X	X	X	X	X	X
Bartlett	0.7	8.5	0.0	0.0	5.6	26.6	15.0	11.0	0.0	2.2
Brentwood	0.0	19.3	0.0	0.5	0.2	13.3	16.6	5.6	0.0	3.8
Bristol	0.0	4.9	0.0	54.1	0.0	9.0	9.0	5.1	0.9	1.0
Chattanooga	3.7	5.6	0.4	0.0	0.6	13.8	18.8	6.1	2.6	4.4
Clarksville	0.0	10.6	0.3	0.0	0.0	22.6	26.1	6.1	1.6	6.6
Cleveland	0.0	6.0	0.0	47.1	0.6	9.4	11.6	2.5	1.3	2.9
Collierville	0.7	12.6	0.0	0.0	1.6	20.1	14.9	7.5	0.0	2.6

	City government finances, 2012 (cont.)			Climate[2]						
	Debt outstanding			Average daily temperature				Annual precipitation (inches)	Heating degree days	Cooling degree days
City			Debt issued during year	Mean		Limits				
	Total (mil dol)	Per capita[1] (dollars)		January	July	January[3]	July[4]			
	137	138	139	140	141	142	143	144	145	146
OREGON— Cont'd										
Redmond	73.6	2,750	12.3	NA	NA	NA	NA	NA	NA	NA
Salem	711.5	4,509	94.7	40.3	66.8	33.5	81.5	40.00	4,784	257
Springfield	151.8	2,534	3.8	39.8	66.2	33.0	81.5	50.90	4,786	242
Tigard	131.8	2,649	100.1	40.0	66.8	33.8	79.2	39.95	4,723	287
Tualatin	14.5	544	0.0	NA	NA	NA	NA	NA	NA	NA
West Linn	21.7	847	8.5	NA	NA	NA	NA	NA	NA	NA
PENNSYLVANIA	X	X	X	X	X	X	X	X	X	X
Allentown	119.4	1,003	11.6	27.1	73.3	19.1	83.9	45.17	5,830	787
Altoona	38.9	844	1.0	26.5	71.1	18.2	81.9	42.69	6,055	546
Bethel Park	4.8	147	0.0	28.6	73.1	19.8	84.5	37.78	5,727	709
Bethlehem	228.4	3,041	27.6	27.1	73.3	19.1	83.9	45.17	5,830	787
Chester	8.1	239	0.0	33.7	78.7	27.9	87.5	40.66	4,469	1,333
Easton	33.9	1,250	7.7	27.1	73.3	19.1	83.9	45.17	5,830	787
Erie	189.6	1,876	47.4	26.9	72.1	20.3	80.4	42.77	6,243	620
Harrisburg	110.0	2,230	0.0	30.3	75.9	23.1	85.7	41.45	5,201	955
Hazleton	11.6	460	5.6	NA	NA	NA	NA	NA	NA	NA
Lancaster	221.6	3,732	38.9	29.1	74.4	20.7	84.7	43.47	5,448	809
Lebanon	0.3	12	0.0	NA	NA	NA	NA	NA	NA	NA
Monroeville	30.2	1,064	7.5	28.6	73.1	19.8	84.5	37.78	5,727	709
Norristown	23.9	694	0.0	30.2	75.1	20.4	86.6	43.87	5,174	884
Philadelphia	7,729.2	4,985	667.1	32.3	77.6	25.5	85.5	42.05	4,759	1,235
Pittsburgh	704.7	2,300	0.0	27.5	72.6	19.9	82.7	37.85	5,829	726
Plum	50.0	1,825	11.3	28.6	73.1	19.8	84.5	37.78	5,727	709
Reading	256.9	2,918	24.4	27.1	73.6	19.1	83.8	45.28	5,876	723
Scranton	61.9	814	0.0	26.3	72.1	18.5	82.6	37.56	6,234	611
State College	28.2	673	0.0	25.4	71.2	18.3	80.7	39.76	6,345	538
Wilkes-Barre	73.4	1,775	9.2	21.5	67.7	13.2	77.4	47.89	7,466	234
Williamsport	5.4	183	2.3	25.5	72.4	17.9	83.2	41.59	6,063	709
York	128.7	2,949	22.1	30.0	74.6	20.9	86.5	43.00	5,233	862
RHODE ISLAND	X	X	X	X	X	X	X	X	X	X
Cranston	88.4	1,096	19.4	28.7	73.3	20.3	82.6	46.45	5,754	714
East Providence	75.2	1,595	23.3	28.7	73.3	20.3	82.6	46.45	5,754	714
Pawtucket	159.7	2,239	9.4	28.7	73.3	20.3	82.6	46.45	5,754	714
Providence	735.9	4,120	5.4	28.7	73.3	20.3	82.6	46.45	5,754	714
Warwick	170.1	2,078	2.4	28.7	73.3	20.3	82.6	46.45	5,754	714
Woonsocket	202.3	4,921	1.0	25.4	72.3	13.3	84.3	48.75	6,302	534
SOUTH CAROLINA	X	X	X	X	X	X	X	X	X	X
Aiken	2.8	92	0.0	45.6	81.7	33.4	93.7	52.43	2,413	2,081
Anderson	125.4	4,687	53.2	41.7	79.7	31.3	90.5	46.67	3,087	1,700
Charleston	74.3	592	0.0	49.8	82.8	42.4	88.5	46.39	1,755	2,473
Columbia	505.3	3,832	205.7	47.3	83.6	36.5	95.2	47.14	2,044	2,475
Florence	139.9	3,725	7.4	45.0	81.2	35.2	90.7	44.76	2,523	2,029
Goose Creek	1.4	36	0.0	47.9	81.7	36.9	90.9	51.53	2,005	2,306
Greenville	94.3	1,556	17.3	40.8	78.8	31.4	88.8	50.24	3,272	1,526
Greer	93.7	3,527	1.7	NA	NA	NA	NA	NA	NA	NA
Hilton Head Island	127.7	3,326	46.9	47.9	80.5	37.3	88.2	52.52	2,128	2,012
Mount Pleasant	99.4	1,383	0.0	47.1	81.1	37.5	88.5	49.38	2,260	2,124
Myrtle Beach	216.4	7,653	27.5	NA	NA	NA	NA	NA	NA	NA
North Charleston	186.0	1,823	52.5	47.9	81.7	36.9	90.9	51.53	2,005	2,306
Rock Hill	186.9	2,745	54.5	42.2	80.1	32.5	90.1	48.32	2,934	1,721
Spartanburg	205.6	5,518	0.0	42.1	79.3	30.1	91.1	49.95	3,080	1,591
Summerville	7.9	179	0.0	49.1	81.8	38.0	91.8	48.24	1,907	2,251
Sumter	45.0	1,100	4.2	44.9	80.7	33.6	91.8	48.65	2,577	1,913
SOUTH DAKOTA	X	X	X	X	X	X	X	X	X	X
Aberdeen	63.9	2,375	5.3	NA	NA	NA	NA	NA	NA	NA
Rapid City	113.7	1,624	24.2	22.3	70.2	10.3	82.7	18.45	7,623	480
Sioux Falls	307.2	1,916	24.4	14.0	73.0	2.9	85.6	24.69	7,812	747
TENNESSEE	X	X	X	X	X	X	X	X	X	X
Bartlett	40.8	701	9.5	37.3	79.6	27.3	89.9	55.09	3,665	1,635
Brentwood	29.8	765	16.6	NA	NA	NA	NA	NA	NA	NA
Bristol	50.2	1,884	3.1	NA	NA	NA	NA	NA	NA	NA
Chattanooga	733.3	4,256	51.6	39.4	79.6	29.9	89.8	54.52	3,427	1,608
Clarksville	870.1	6,075	29.2	35.2	79.0	25.0	90.4	51.78	4,058	1,512
Cleveland	130.0	3,067	3.1	38.0	77.5	27.7	88.5	55.42	3,782	1,333
Collierville	60.9	1,313	5.0	37.9	81.1	28.2	91.1	53.63	3,491	1,838

1. Based on the population estimated as of July 1 of the year shown. 2. Represents normal values based on the 30-year period, 1971±2000. 3. Average daily minimum. 4. Average daily maximum.

Table D. Cities — **Land Area and Population**

STATE Place code	City	Land area[1] (sq. mi)	Total persons 2018	Rank	Per square mile	White	Black or African American	American Indian, Alaskan Native	Asian	Hawaiian Pacific Islander	Some other race	Two or more races (percent)
			Population, 2018			Race 2017 — Race alone[2] (percent)						
		1	2	3	4	5	6	7	8	9	10	11
	TENNESSEE—Cont'd											
47 16,540	Columbia	32.9	39,376	982	1,196.8	NA	NA	NA	NA	NA	NA	NA
47 16,920	Cookeville	35.4	34,005	1,121	960.6	90.7	4.1	0.1	3.1	0.0	0.5	1.5
47 27,740	Franklin	41.6	80,914	427	1,945.0	82.0	7.9	0.0	7.0	0.0	0.8	2.3
47 28,540	Gallatin	31.8	40,457	943	1,272.2	76.6	13.3	0.0	4.4	0.0	1.3	4.4
47 28,960	Germantown	20.0	39,099	989	1,955.0	87.4	2.8	0.0	7.8	0.0	0.7	1.1
47 33,280	Hendersonville	31.4	57,576	657	1,833.6	87.3	9.5	0.4	0.3	0.2	1.1	1.2
47 37,640	Jackson	58.3	66,903	546	1,147.6	NA	NA	NA	NA	NA	NA	NA
47 38,320	Johnson City	43.1	66,778	547	1,549.4	84.3	7.9	0.3	3.6	0.0	1.2	2.7
47 39,560	Kingsport	52.4	54,076	710	1,032.0	90.2	5.2	0.0	0.9	0.0	0.4	3.3
47 40,000	Knoxville	98.7	187,500	135	1,899.7	76.3	17.4	0.2	2.1	0.0	1.5	2.5
47 41,200	La Vergne	24.6	35,819	1,074	1,456.1	77.0	13.3	0.6	2.8	0.0	1.1	5.2
47 41,520	Lebanon	39.1	35,050	1,092	896.4	NA	NA	NA	NA	NA	NA	NA
47 46,380	Maryville	17.1	29,192	1,281	1,707.1	NA	NA	NA	NA	NA	NA	NA
47 48,000	Memphis	317.4	650,618	26	2,049.8	29.2	63.7	0.2	1.7	0.1	3.7	1.5
47 50,280	Morristown	27.3	29,926	1,256	1,096.2	NA	NA	NA	NA	NA	NA	NA
47 51,560	Murfreesboro	60.9	141,344	188	2,320.9	71.6	21.3	0.2	2.8	0.0	0.7	3.4
47 52,004	Nashville-Davidson	475.6	669,053	24	1,406.8	64.2	27.3	0.2	3.6	0.1	1.5	3.1
47 55,120	Oak Ridge	85.3	29,109	1,283	341.3	79.3	4.4	0.2	3.8	0.0	3.5	8.7
47 69,420	Smyrna	30.3	50,775	755	1,675.7	73.9	18.9	0.2	2.9	0.0	0.8	3.3
47 70,580	Spring Hill	26.8	41,464	921	1,547.2	90.2	2.7	0.0	1.9	0.0	1.7	3.6
48 00,000	**TEXAS**	261,257.3	28,701,845	X	109.9	73.9	12.1	0.5	4.8	0.1	5.9	2.6
48 01,000	Abilene	106.7	122,999	225	1,152.8	67.7	10.6	0.9	2.4	0.0	15.6	2.8
48 01,924	Allen	26.4	103,383	299	3,916.0	70.1	6.5	0.2	17.8	0.0	1.2	4.1
48 03,000	Amarillo	101.6	199,924	116	1,967.8	82.0	6.5	0.4	3.6	0.1	3.3	4.2
48 04,000	Arlington	95.8	398,112	48	4,155.7	59.4	25.0	0.3	5.7	0.1	6.5	2.9
48 05,000	Austin	320.8	964,254	11	3,005.8	71.6	7.7	0.8	7.6	0.0	8.5	3.8
48 06,128	Baytown	36.9	77,024	452	2,087.4	78.2	15.4	0.3	0.7	0.2	3.1	2.2
48 07,000	Beaumont	82.3	118,428	239	1,439.0	45.8	46.8	0.0	2.7	0.1	2.2	2.3
48 07,132	Bedford	10.0	49,464	775	4,946.4	69.4	14.6	1.1	6.5	2.4	1.9	4.0
48 08,236	Big Spring	19.1	28,162	1,314	1,474.5	76.8	6.2	1.4	0.2	0.1	11.9	3.4
48 10,768	Brownsville	132.3	183,392	137	1,386.2	97.1	0.2	0.2	0.2	0.0	2.1	0.2
48 10,912	Bryan	45.7	85,445	391	1,869.7	73.5	16.9	0.1	1.9	0.0	4.9	2.7
48 11,428	Burleson	28.2	47,282	822	1,676.7	89.8	6.8	0.5	1.0	0.0	0.8	1.0
48 13,024	Carrollton	36.6	136,879	199	3,739.9	71.8	10.1	1.0	13.3	0.0	2.2	1.7
48 13,492	Cedar Hill	35.9	48,463	795	1,349.9	32.8	48.6	0.0	8.1	0.0	6.9	3.6
48 13,552	Cedar Park	25.3	76,999	455	3,043.4	78.5	2.7	0.3	8.7	0.1	3.9	5.9
48 15,364	Cleburne	34.9	30,720	1,226	880.2	NA	NA	NA	NA	NA	NA	NA
48 15,976	College Station	51.1	116,218	247	2,274.3	77.5	7.5	0.4	9.9	0.0	1.1	3.5
48 16,432	Conroe	70.2	87,654	378	1,248.6	83.4	10.4	0.2	1.9	0.1	2.5	1.7
48 16,612	Coppell	14.5	41,818	910	2,884.0	67.3	3.8	0.6	22.6	0.0	0.5	5.1
48 16,624	Copperas Cove	18.0	32,658	1,163	1,814.3	66.3	17.1	0.9	3.4	1.1	1.7	9.6
48 17,000	Corpus Christi	159.7	326,554	59	2,044.8	90.4	4.0	0.4	2.4	0.0	1.3	1.4
48 19,000	Dallas	339.6	1,345,047	9	3,960.7	62.9	24.5	0.3	3.7	0.1	6.2	2.4
48 19,624	Deer Park	10.5	33,931	1,124	3,231.5	NA	NA	NA	NA	NA	NA	NA
48 19,792	Del Rio	20.4	35,954	1,068	1,762.5	NA	NA	NA	NA	NA	NA	NA
48 19,972	Denton	96.1	138,541	196	1,441.6	76.8	9.8	0.3	4.7	0.2	4.2	4.0
48 20,092	DeSoto	21.6	53,523	723	2,477.9	25.0	67.7	0.2	0.3	0.0	2.7	4.1
48 21,628	Duncanville	11.2	39,364	983	3,514.6	51.9	34.2	0.0	0.9	0.3	11.7	0.9
48 21,892	Eagle Pass	9.4	29,487	1,274	3,136.9	NA	NA	NA	NA	NA	NA	NA
48 22,660	Edinburg	44.7	98,665	314	2,207.3	89.4	2.4	0.4	3.1	0.0	4.5	0.2
48 24,000	El Paso	257.4	682,669	22	2,652.2	76.0	3.7	0.5	1.5	0.1	15.6	2.6
48 24,768	Euless	16.1	57,346	660	3,561.9	62.3	13.0	0.2	14.4	1.8	2.0	6.3
48 25,452	Farmers Branch	11.8	40,209	952	3,407.5	71.8	8.0	0.1	9.1	0.0	8.3	2.7
48 26,232	Flower Mound	41.9	77,329	448	1,845.6	77.0	6.7	0.3	11.2	0.1	1.2	3.5
48 27,000	Fort Worth	344.8	895,008	13	2,595.7	63.5	17.7	0.3	4.4	0.0	11.2	2.9
48 27,648	Friendswood	20.6	40,181	954	1,950.5	87.3	3.6	0.7	6.5	0.0	0.8	1.0
48 27,684	Frisco	68.0	188,170	134	2,767.2	65.9	6.4	0.5	20.7	0.0	1.6	4.8
48 28,068	Galveston	41.2	50,457	762	1,224.7	74.8	16.7	0.7	3.2	0.0	1.5	3.2
48 29,000	Garland	57.1	242,507	93	4,247.1	66.1	14.6	0.4	10.7	0.0	4.6	3.7
48 29,336	Georgetown	54.8	74,180	481	1,353.6	84.9	5.4	0.2	0.5	0.1	1.0	8.0
48 30,464	Grand Prairie	72.3	194,614	125	2,691.8	60.3	22.2	0.5	7.9	0.1	5.7	3.3
48 30,644	Grapevine	32.0	53,976	712	1,686.8	80.3	3.1	1.2	8.3	0.0	4.7	2.5
48 30,920	Greenville	32.3	28,263	1,311	875.0	71.5	10.4	0.0	0.5	0.2	10.1	7.4
48 31,928	Haltom City	12.4	44,339	865	3,575.7	60.6	6.5	0.0	8.5	0.0	22.3	2.1
48 32,312	Harker Heights	15.6	31,857	1,192	2,042.1	57.5	29.9	0.8	4.7	1.5	1.5	4.0
48 32,372	Harlingen	40.1	65,436	568	1,631.8	90.4	0.8	0.6	2.5	0.0	4.7	0.9
48 35,000	Houston	637.0	2,325,502	4	3,650.7	59.3	22.9	0.3	6.5	0.0	8.8	2.1
48 35,528	Huntsville	35.9	41,521	920	1,156.6	NA	NA	NA	NA	NA	NA	NA
48 35,576	Hurst	10.0	38,992	991	3,899.2	76.8	8.6	0.8	2.7	0.0	8.2	2.9

1. Dry land or land partially or temporarily covered by water.   2. Hispanic or Latino persons may be of any race.

Table D. Cities — Population

City	Percent Hispanic or Latino[1], 2017	Percent foreign born, 2017	Under 18 years	18 to 24 years	25 to 34 years	35 to 44 years	45 to 54 years	55 to 64 years	65 years and over	Median age, 2017	Percent female, 2017	Census counts 2000	Census counts 2010	Percent change 2000-2010	Percent change 2001-2018
	12	13	14	15	16	17	18	19	20	21	22	23	24	25	26
TENNESSEE—Cont'd															
Columbia	11.7	7.1	25.3	10.7	15.4	10.6	10.9	13.8	13.4	34.4	49.8	33,055	34,649	4.8	13.6
Cookeville	4.3	6.7	17.8	25.3	14.9	10.0	11.5	6.6	13.9	28.5	49.6	23,923	31,124	30.1	9.3
Franklin	6.6	11.7	22.2	7.6	13.5	13.9	15.3	12.4	15.0	38.8	52.9	41,842	62,569	49.5	29.3
Gallatin	8.4	8.0	22.4	6.4	15.5	15.5	11.1	12.6	16.5	37.6	50.2	23,230	30,345	30.6	33.3
Germantown	4.4	10.1	19.5	6.0	6.2	12.8	14.2	17.2	24.0	49.6	50.9	37,348	38,838	4.0	0.7
Hendersonville	3.5	6.3	25.3	4.8	13.3	14.5	14.8	12.6	14.6	40.1	54.6	40,620	51,333	26.4	12.2
Jackson	5.5	3.1	23.7	14.9	10.3	11.3	13.1	12.1	14.6	35.8	54.0	59,643	66,847	12.1	0.1
Johnson City	6.2	6.2	20.2	15.0	13.3	14.0	10.3	12.9	14.2	36.9	52.6	55,469	63,380	14.3	5.4
Kingsport	1.6	2.4	22.1	7.5	10.6	11.4	14.2	11.6	22.5	43.3	53.2	44,905	53,007	18.0	2.0
Knoxville	6.4	6.7	20.0	17.6	16.2	11.8	11.8	10.0	12.6	31.9	51.5	173,890	178,310	2.5	5.2
La Vergne	23.5	17.4	24.7	13.2	13.5	15.9	15.9	10.5	6.2	33.9	48.6	18,687	32,597	74.4	9.9
Lebanon	10.9	7.9	27.7	11.5	15.8	11.9	13.4	8.2	11.6	32.0	54.4	20,235	26,172	29.3	33.9
Maryville	1.1	2.6	24.5	14.9	8.6	12.6	13.0	11.4	15.0	37.4	50.5	23,120	27,453	18.7	6.3
Memphis	7.7	6.7	25.3	10.6	16.0	12.2	11.8	11.6	12.5	33.6	52.9	650,100	651,885	0.3	-0.2
Morristown	18.0	9.6	28.6	6.5	12.2	16.1	10.9	9.5	16.3	35.6	48.5	24,965	29,019	16.2	3.1
Murfreesboro	7.6	7.7	26.0	15.7	18.1	13.3	9.3	8.8	8.7	29.1	51.1	68,816	109,073	58.5	29.6
Nashville-Davidson	10.4	13.0	21.0	10.1	20.2	13.8	11.8	11.5	11.6	34.3	51.7	NA	603,427	NA	10.9
Oak Ridge	5.3	8.4	20.7	9.0	14.1	13.9	11.4	12.4	18.5	40.3	50.5	27,387	29,328	7.1	-0.7
Smyrna	7.4	6.7	24.6	9.8	15.3	14.8	14.3	11.1	10.2	35.2	52.9	25,569	40,384	57.9	25.7
Spring Hill	8.0	2.3	38.1	4.2	12.4	17.7	12.1	6.9	8.6	31.5	49.2	7,715	29,110	277.3	42.4
TEXAS	39.4	17.1	26.0	9.9	14.6	13.5	12.5	11.3	12.2	34.7	50.3	20,851,820	25,146,114	20.6	14.1
Abilene	27.0	8.1	23.8	15.4	16.7	11.7	9.3	9.9	13.1	31.1	47.8	115,930	117,512	1.4	4.7
Allen	10.6	19.4	29.8	7.2	8.4	15.8	17.7	12.3	8.7	38.4	52.0	43,554	84,275	93.5	22.7
Amarillo	34.0	12.6	27.2	8.7	15.3	13.2	11.6	11.3	12.7	34.3	49.9	173,627	190,666	9.8	4.9
Arlington	29.9	22.7	27.0	10.7	14.8	14.0	13.2	10.1	10.2	33.1	51.5	332,969	365,337	9.7	9.0
Austin	34.2	18.7	20.3	10.3	22.5	16.0	11.8	9.6	9.4	33.4	49.3	656,562	802,078	22.2	20.2
Baytown	45.7	17.2	26.4	10.5	15.6	13.1	11.8	10.3	12.4	33.4	51.3	66,430	71,635	7.8	7.5
Beaumont	18.0	11.7	26.7	12.3	13.3	12.7	9.6	12.5	13.0	33.2	50.8	113,866	117,278	3.0	1.0
Bedford	12.5	11.6	23.7	6.1	16.2	15.6	11.5	12.5	14.4	37.1	52.8	47,152	46,994	-0.3	5.3
Big Spring	46.5	13.8	21.1	13.9	15.7	15.3	11.2	11.2	11.6	34.7	42.4	25,233	27,282	8.1	3.2
Brownsville	94.0	28.6	29.6	13.8	11.3	12.0	11.4	9.2	12.7	30.3	50.8	139,722	174,748	25.1	4.9
Bryan	40.2	15.3	23.6	15.7	16.3	13.1	10.2	9.7	11.5	31.6	50.4	65,660	76,226	16.1	12.1
Burleson	9.4	4.3	25.9	6.5	11.4	15.9	13.8	13.5	13.0	38.5	53.6	20,976	36,898	75.9	28.1
Carrollton	37.4	30.1	24.4	7.9	13.7	16.8	15.1	12.5	9.6	37.4	51.1	109,576	119,176	8.8	14.9
Cedar Hill	22.9	11.8	26.8	8.6	13.2	12.2	14.9	13.8	10.4	36.0	52.0	32,093	44,992	40.2	7.7
Cedar Park	23.6	15.0	31.0	7.1	15.8	17.4	13.6	7.7	7.2	33.1	47.9	26,049	55,117	111.6	39.7
Cleburne	33.7	2.3	26.9	12.3	11.1	11.8	11.9	8.9	17.1	34.7	47.0	26,005	29,637	14.0	3.7
College Station	15.5	13.3	17.4	38.6	16.0	9.5	6.7	5.9	6.0	22.9	48.5	67,890	94,221	38.8	23.3
Conroe	35.2	15.1	27.6	9.6	16.8	11.1	12.8	9.2	12.9	31.7	51.8	36,811	65,259	77.3	34.3
Coppell	13.6	24.9	23.7	4.6	12.9	12.7	19.0	17.8	9.4	42.6	53.7	35,958	38,666	7.5	8.2
Copperas Cove	19.8	7.2	26.9	9.1	19.9	13.7	12.9	8.6	8.7	33.3	55.1	29,592	32,247	9.0	1.3
Corpus Christi	63.1	8.8	24.8	10.0	14.9	12.4	12.2	11.9	13.9	35.3	50.8	277,454	305,226	10.0	7.0
Dallas	41.9	24.9	25.1	10.1	19.2	13.7	11.1	10.4	10.5	32.4	50.6	1,188,580	1,197,653	0.8	12.3
Deer Park	20.3	5.4	22.7	9.6	13.6	9.8	15.6	16.7	12.0	37.5	47.8	28,520	32,010	12.2	6.0
Del Rio	83.3	24.9	27.2	9.4	13.5	15.3	8.8	9.1	16.7	34.9	47.7	33,867	35,938	6.1	0.0
Denton	25.9	13.2	18.6	21.2	17.2	9.9	10.3	11.4	11.5	29.9	51.3	80,537	116,371	44.5	19.1
DeSoto	14.1	6.7	24.1	6.7	12.2	12.1	18.8	11.6	14.4	42.2	58.9	37,646	49,043	30.3	9.1
Duncanville	44.2	15.5	29.8	10.6	11.6	11.5	13.2	12.5	10.8	33.4	51.1	36,081	38,533	6.8	2.2
Eagle Pass	98.5	29.4	31.0	14.6	8.5	13.5	11.7	8.8	11.9	31.2	50.9	22,413	26,604	18.7	10.8
Edinburg	87.5	18.3	33.6	10.5	16.0	14.1	10.0	7.8	8.0	28.0	53.6	48,465	82,020	69.2	20.3
El Paso	81.4	24.6	26.9	10.7	14.5	12.7	11.5	11.0	12.7	33.4	51.1	563,662	648,254	15.0	5.3
Euless	15.7	22.7	20.7	7.4	16.8	14.5	16.9	13.8	9.9	37.9	50.3	46,005	51,272	11.4	11.8
Farmers Branch	45.4	23.4	23.6	8.3	16.6	13.5	15.1	10.1	12.7	35.7	47.0	27,508	28,616	4.0	40.5
Flower Mound	8.8	13.3	27.1	8.2	7.1	13.2	20.8	12.7	11.0	41.6	51.7	50,702	64,675	27.6	19.6
Fort Worth	36.1	18.0	27.0	9.9	16.7	13.9	12.4	10.2	9.9	32.9	51.2	534,694	744,852	39.3	20.2
Friendswood	16.1	9.9	25.7	8.4	8.0	9.8	15.5	16.3	16.2	43.5	53.3	29,037	35,898	23.6	11.9
Frisco	14.1	23.1	31.5	6.0	10.0	18.8	17.6	8.2	7.9	36.6	49.9	33,714	117,170	247.5	60.6
Galveston	31.8	14.4	15.6	11.8	13.9	14.1	11.3	16.0	17.4	40.5	47.6	57,247	47,743	-16.6	5.7
Garland	39.9	26.9	25.3	9.9	14.5	11.5	13.7	12.8	12.2	35.3	49.6	215,768	226,910	5.2	6.9
Georgetown	18.2	5.1	18.3	10.6	7.5	12.0	12.1	11.2	28.2	45.9	54.5	28,339	47,483	67.6	56.2
Grand Prairie	46.8	21.1	28.6	9.3	14.1	14.1	14.9	10.5	8.6	33.6	51.2	127,427	175,468	37.7	10.9
Grapevine	17.4	16.2	24.4	10.1	13.7	12.0	14.9	15.1	9.8	37.2	48.9	42,059	46,336	10.2	16.5
Greenville	23.6	5.5	26.8	5.6	17.6	13.5	7.8	15.1	13.6	35.0	50.9	23,960	25,528	6.5	10.7
Haltom City	56.5	29.7	33.4	10.1	14.3	15.1	10.9	8.7	7.5	30.1	46.3	39,018	42,373	8.6	4.6
Harker Heights	19.2	13.6	24.1	9.3	14.5	15.5	13.1	13.0	10.5	36.2	48.3	17,308	26,727	54.4	19.2
Harlingen	79.7	14.2	34.5	6.3	14.1	11.2	8.8	10.4	14.8	31.2	48.8	57,564	64,912	12.8	0.8
Houston	44.6	29.1	25.4	9.5	18.5	13.8	11.9	10.4	10.6	33.1	50.0	1,953,631	2,093,615	7.2	11.1
Huntsville	18.7	8.5	10.4	27.5	16.0	10.5	10.2	14.4	11.1	32.3	40.8	35,078	38,550	9.9	7.7
Hurst	23.5	15.7	26.4	9.1	13.5	11.5	14.0	9.0	16.4	36.2	47.5	36,273	37,335	2.9	4.4

1. May be of any race.

Table D. Cities — Households, Group Quarters, Crime, and Education

City	Households, 2017							Persons in group quarters, 2017	Serious crimes known to police[2], 2016				Educational attainment, 2017		
			Percent						Total		Rate[3]			Attainment[4] (percent)	
	Number	Persons per household	Family	Married couple family	Female headed[1]	Non-family	One person		Number	Rate	Violent	Property	Population age 25 and over	High school graduate or less	Bachelor's degree or more
	27	28	29	30	31	32	33	34	35	36	37	38	39	40	41

City	27	28	29	30	31	32	33	34	35	36	37	38	39	40	41
TENNESSEE—Cont'd															
Columbia	13,550	2.74	67.7	45.1	17.6	32.3	29.0	1,145	1,337	3,592	682	2,910	24,510	54.4	17.5
Cookeville	13,332	2.28	48.3	30.4	14.3	51.7	39.6	3,008	1,579	4,890	517	4,373	19,059	44.8	34.1
Franklin	30,018	2.60	70.6	58.7	9.9	29.4	22.0	NA	1,236	1,653	202	1,451	54,983	20.5	61.7
Gallatin	13,680	2.66	73.6	52.2	17.3	26.4	21.4	982	592	1,684	395	1,289	26,582	41.5	27.4
Germantown	15,097	2.59	84.1	76.3	5.1	15.9	14.3	NA	550	1,399	117	1,282	29,142	8.4	64.9
Hendersonville	21,633	2.65	70.3	52.1	12.3	29.7	26.9	NA	952	1,671	133	1,538	40,181	28.6	37.0
Jackson	24,077	2.62	58.2	35.7	16.0	41.8	35.8	3,834	3,579	5,343	946	4,396	41,078	47.0	27.3
Johnson City	27,768	2.23	50.6	34.8	12.0	49.4	38.4	3,986	2,759	4,148	400	3,748	42,670	34.4	39.8
Kingsport	23,534	2.21	62.9	43.3	15.7	37.1	34.0	1,007	2,871	5,411	699	4,712	37,285	45.6	24.9
Knoxville	79,066	2.27	50.7	31.0	14.8	49.3	36.9	7,757	12,013	6,438	897	5,541	116,889	37.9	34.1
La Vergne	12,181	2.93	76.7	55.6	11.0	23.3	20.7	NA	1,728	4,905	1,343	3,563	22,158	44.2	23.8
Lebanon	11,111	2.76	72.8	46.5	20.1	27.2	24.6	1,521	1,150	3,695	649	3,046	19,596	46.2	21.3
Maryville	10,133	2.66	63.6	47.1	11.7	36.4	30.4	1,792	737	2,571	195	2,376	17,414	29.8	39.0
Memphis	246,518	2.58	56.2	28.5	22.6	43.8	37.7	15,066	49,012	7,466	1,826	5,640	417,951	46.1	25.7
Morristown	10,525	2.74	67.1	52.0	13.0	32.9	28.3	888	1,557	5,264	642	4,622	19,317	57.0	14.3
Murfreesboro	48,694	2.71	66.3	47.6	13.0	33.7	21.3	4,182	4,668	3,598	610	2,988	79,406	29.2	42.0
Nashville-Davidson	273,111	2.36	56.6	39.1	13.4	43.4	32.6	22,063	32,172	4,811	1,107	3,704	458,810	32.2	41.2
Oak Ridge	12,093	2.43	65.0	45.7	16.3	35.0	32.0	315	1,083	3,697	676	3,021	20,842	32.1	38.9
Smyrna	18,386	2.70	65.7	46.0	17.3	34.3	25.7	NA	1,521	3,168	529	2,639	32,786	43.0	24.8
Spring Hill	13,682	3.09	86.5	72.9	10.0	13.5	11.9	NA	390	1,037	194	843	24,400	14.2	52.3
TEXAS	9,623,874	2.88	69.6	50.7	13.7	30.4	25.0	606,511	889,989	3,194	434	2,760	18,149,346	41.4	29.6
Abilene	42,828	2.56	66.2	44.5	15.9	33.8	25.7	13,821	4,815	3,930	446	3,484	74,924	45.2	23.3
Allen	33,446	3.00	78.4	66.8	9.2	21.6	18.5	NA	1,223	1,211	79	1,131	63,356	13.9	58.3
Amarillo	76,092	2.61	65.9	48.8	11.6	34.1	28.6	2,019	10,948	5,470	712	4,758	128,534	44.7	23.4
Arlington	131,845	2.98	70.3	49.3	15.4	29.7	24.2	5,098	14,571	3,711	557	3,154	246,767	37.9	27.9
Austin	376,509	2.47	51.8	38.7	9.3	48.2	34.5	20,809	37,478	3,917	408	3,509	659,652	27.1	51.0
Baytown	27,188	2.84	67.8	43.7	17.0	32.2	27.3	723	3,160	4,092	391	3,701	49,180	49.7	13.3
Beaumont	44,960	2.54	65.5	38.0	20.2	34.5	29.2	4,924	6,381	5,395	1,113	4,282	72,755	40.1	24.5
Bedford	20,287	2.42	63.4	43.5	16.1	36.6	30.0	405	1,219	2,448	261	2,187	34,745	24.8	38.2
Big Spring	8,189	2.90	67.7	44.1	15.8	32.3	28.7	5,132	1,580	5,413	596	4,817	18,803	59.7	10.3
Brownsville	52,138	3.49	77.5	51.4	20.0	22.5	21.2	1,508	6,476	3,490	241	3,248	103,812	59.3	21.1
Bryan	30,998	2.57	63.8	34.9	21.4	36.2	30.1	4,221	2,972	3,568	504	3,064	50,975	45.5	26.5
Burleson	16,186	2.76	80.1	55.8	18.4	19.9	16.0	NA	927	2,055	186	1,869	30,305	39.1	25.7
Carrollton	47,064	2.87	70.7	56.1	10.6	29.3	24.2	737	2,879	2,115	162	1,954	91,767	34.0	39.8
Cedar Hill	16,607	2.90	69.6	48.3	16.4	30.4	27.2	594	1,657	3,367	236	3,131	31,511	34.6	32.5
Cedar Park	22,376	3.35	74.3	60.5	9.8	25.7	19.5	NA	1,080	1,564	168	1,396	46,518	22.1	46.6
Cleburne	10,848	2.70	68.3	44.9	17.3	31.7	26.3	903	869	2,890	289	2,601	18,392	57.1	16.5
College Station	38,829	2.61	49.6	37.3	8.9	50.4	28.4	12,284	2,535	2,288	221	2,067	49,966	18.6	58.4
Conroe	29,297	2.83	71.2	53.2	13.0	28.8	22.6	1,564	2,498	3,513	360	3,153	52,936	42.3	25.3
Coppell	16,319	2.56	79.0	68.3	8.9	21.0	21.0	NA	543	1,304	65	1,239	29,963	10.0	68.8
Copperas Cove	10,462	3.10	78.3	58.0	16.5	21.7	20.1	327	1,120	3,370	536	2,834	20,907	35.0	23.3
Corpus Christi	115,797	2.74	67.9	45.8	16.7	32.1	26.6	8,778	14,526	4,429	710	3,719	212,371	46.5	21.3
Dallas	513,084	2.58	57.3	35.7	15.4	42.7	34.8	17,437	54,981	4,162	762	3,400	868,969	45.2	32.2
Deer Park	12,458	2.71	72.9	53.7	14.7	27.1	26.1	NA	657	1,924	190	1,733	22,943	40.2	13.8
Del Rio	12,431	2.67	81.4	51.4	22.0	18.6	17.6	1,005	902	2,493	160	2,333	21,650	56.0	18.8
Denton	49,287	2.56	58.8	44.8	10.9	41.2	29.5	10,185	3,383	2,524	259	2,265	82,062	29.1	39.2
DeSoto	20,307	2.60	69.4	49.5	17.5	30.6	27.4	711	1,849	3,479	327	3,152	37,031	34.5	27.2
Duncanville	12,295	3.19	76.3	54.3	17.7	23.7	20.0	263	1,452	3,623	507	3,117	23,546	43.4	23.9
Eagle Pass	8,369	3.44	81.4	41.1	18.3	18.6	15.9	NA	732	2,502	147	2,355	15,747	61.0	18.9
Edinburg	26,185	3.39	77.5	53.1	19.5	22.5	16.8	1,560	4,537	5,243	409	4,834	50,430	52.1	25.1
El Paso	229,156	2.95	72.5	46.0	20.1	27.5	24.1	7,319	15,039	2,188	390	1,798	426,729	43.2	24.7
Euless	21,465	2.56	64.2	40.7	16.8	35.8	28.9	NA	1,327	2,422	204	2,218	39,664	38.5	30.7
Farmers Branch	13,692	2.70	69.0	54.2	11.7	31.0	23.7	NA	930	2,770	164	2,606	25,245	32.5	41.3
Flower Mound	25,597	2.98	87.3	74.3	8.8	12.7	11.1	NA	698	961	55	906	49,597	14.2	61.7
Fort Worth	299,593	2.87	67.7	46.8	14.4	32.3	26.3	15,855	32,754	3,845	530	3,315	553,149	42.5	29.7
Friendswood	13,393	2.81	72.7	60.7	8.2	27.3	22.3	NA	329	835	69	766	24,949	20.4	52.3
Frisco	58,409	3.03	78.6	66.4	8.5	21.4	17.5	NA	2,546	1,563	80	1,483	110,887	14.7	61.5
Galveston	22,077	2.12	49.8	37.1	10.2	50.2	40.9	3,755	2,015	3,977	482	3,495	36,682	40.6	29.1
Garland	77,072	3.07	72.7	51.0	14.8	27.3	22.8	705	8,430	3,529	321	3,208	153,985	45.7	22.4
Georgetown	26,361	2.60	68.6	54.3	9.0	31.4	29.4	2,063	800	1,186	129	1,057	50,284	30.0	40.5
Grand Prairie	60,843	3.18	77.9	52.5	18.9	22.1	19.1	476	5,114	2,688	309	2,379	120,429	48.1	22.3
Grapevine	19,557	2.75	68.2	53.1	10.7	31.8	22.1	NA	1,343	2,562	166	2,396	35,382	27.2	44.4
Greenville	10,027	2.65	60.2	41.3	14.4	39.8	34.9	854	932	3,492	480	3,012	18,549	45.8	24.3
Haltom City	13,169	3.36	75.9	49.9	17.9	24.1	17.7	NA	1,176	2,639	263	2,377	25,095	65.1	8.3
Harker Heights	10,452	2.95	72.6	53.4	17.9	27.4	20.9	NA	1,016	3,432	243	3,189	20,698	31.9	36.8
Harlingen	19,945	3.20	73.5	48.2	18.6	26.5	23.1	1,697	2,871	4,356	428	3,929	38,809	56.9	18.9
Houston	837,686	2.72	61.3	39.5	16.0	38.7	32.0	33,899	124,816	5,347	1,026	4,321	1,505,869	43.8	32.7
Huntsville	13,556	2.09	44.1	31.4	12.4	55.9	39.8	12,919	932	2,252	416	1,836	25,617	49.8	25.9
Hurst	13,288	2.92	72.0	58.5	12.7	28.0	23.2	NA	1,723	4,379	244	4,135	25,198	43.7	28.7

1. No spouse present.   2. Data for serious crimes have not been adjusted for underreporting. This may affect comparability between geographic areas and over time.   3. Per 100,000 population estimated by the FBI.   4. Persons 25 years old and over.

City	Money income, 2017					Median earnings, 2017			Housing units, 2017				
	Households			Median family income	Median non-family income	All persons	Men	Women	Total	Occupied	Percent owner occupied	Median value[1] (dollars)	Median gross rent (dollars)
	Median income	Percent with income less than $20,000	Percent with income of $200,000 or more										
	42	43	44	45	46	47	48	49	50	51	52	53	54
TENNESSEE—Cont'd													
Columbia	46,536	18.5	1.5	54,399	31,538	30,246	32,274	26,948	14,942	13,550	53.6	148,600	921
Cookeville	36,638	32.2	1.9	54,045	23,071	21,587	25,417	20,181	14,444	13,332	39.1	174,300	665
Franklin	96,199	6.2	13.9	106,733	61,274	41,641	61,040	29,301	30,824	30,018	71.1	412,900	1,422
Gallatin	60,011	14.1	3.8	64,646	30,859	31,783	39,738	27,977	15,228	13,680	61.9	224,100	913
Germantown	124,115	4.4	24.3	133,206	49,202	61,051	76,558	46,631	15,292	15,097	87.3	330,200	1,125
Hendersonville	67,762	6.2	8.8	82,206	46,866	38,069	45,407	33,862	22,901	21,633	70.8	262,900	1,148
Jackson	41,956	25.9	3.3	53,920	27,027	28,784	31,545	24,484	29,054	24,077	50.2	138,400	860
Johnson City	35,700	26.9	5.3	55,951	24,666	22,229	26,791	20,917	31,934	27,768	50.1	166,900	733
Kingsport	35,994	25.1	3.4	51,332	24,577	25,476	31,298	20,599	25,657	23,534	59.8	143,900	628
Knoxville	38,714	27.9	3.5	50,681	26,553	25,517	30,083	21,486	89,070	79,066	45.6	133,900	834
La Vergne	60,634	7.8	6.4	66,253	41,156	31,862	36,998	27,795	12,598	12,181	74.2	169,500	1,115
Lebanon	51,906	15.2	1.8	60,114	29,124	25,543	29,872	22,312	11,972	11,111	48.6	240,700	913
Maryville	58,585	10.2	6.7	82,723	31,863	31,124	35,471	22,478	11,387	10,133	64.2	190,500	695
Memphis	39,333	26.0	3.4	46,985	27,670	27,076	30,625	25,391	298,121	246,518	46.0	98,700	863
Morristown	38,080	23.1	0.8	42,007	18,624	22,189	23,970	21,458	13,022	10,525	55.6	123,000	677
Murfreesboro	64,953	13.4	3.5	76,994	36,963	30,124	31,801	27,013	51,489	48,694	52.3	243,800	970
Nashville-Davidson	57,737	14.0	5.2	67,088	44,802	33,369	35,998	31,498	302,389	273,111	52.6	246,800	1,079
Oak Ridge	52,321	12.3	5.6	66,435	33,282	31,198	31,766	27,286	15,359	12,093	57.3	154,000	768
Smyrna	66,117	9.3	1.9	75,552	34,792	31,854	35,883	30,096	19,241	18,386	46.7	191,800	1,001
Spring Hill	95,537	5.1	5.2	97,088	43,394	41,865	52,464	26,555	15,062	13,682	80.6	279,200	1,392
TEXAS	59,206	15.3	6.6	70,136	36,529	32,264	38,129	27,150	10,933,375	9,623,874	62.0	172,200	987
Abilene	49,365	17.3	3.5	58,064	33,814	24,993	33,666	19,053	48,809	42,828	58.0	114,900	822
Allen	106,475	5.1	20.1	126,234	61,991	54,293	71,514	41,235	35,629	33,446	76.9	322,400	1,618
Amarillo	51,263	16.5	3.9	59,970	31,443	30,527	32,788	25,867	85,201	76,092	60.1	131,400	828
Arlington	57,083	13.2	4.0	66,985	38,251	32,291	36,487	30,262	145,857	131,485	55.6	167,800	990
Austin	67,755	11.6	9.4	87,200	52,363	39,883	42,311	35,796	417,939	376,509	45.0	332,700	1,244
Baytown	56,042	19.2	1.6	63,249	31,151	35,256	42,177	23,126	30,256	27,188	59.5	126,600	924
Beaumont	48,043	21.4	3.8	56,120	26,321	28,144	34,320	24,480	51,998	44,960	57.6	105,000	842
Bedford	64,889	5.0	5.8	87,457	45,015	40,891	49,164	35,494	20,914	20,287	50.4	218,500	1,121
Big Spring	44,079	16.5	1.2	49,969	26,515	22,266	28,009	20,986	10,026	8,189	58.0	96,000	744
Brownsville	36,176	31.3	1.0	44,441	15,356	21,850	24,266	20,009	58,048	52,138	59.5	93,300	690
Bryan	43,283	26.0	1.1	48,529	26,884	25,962	30,924	18,866	34,480	30,998	50.3	129,600	880
Burleson	76,208	3.9	4.7	80,340	44,192	46,188	51,369	39,512	16,783	16,186	73.6	185,600	1,220
Carrollton	77,998	7.4	8.4	89,436	53,061	40,596	43,634	35,548	48,957	47,064	59.5	240,700	1,179
Cedar Hill	75,697	7.7	7.9	85,669	52,044	43,067	50,173	39,255	17,504	16,607	74.4	162,100	1,363
Cedar Park	99,461	6.3	12.1	110,296	56,977	50,687	61,809	35,466	24,026	22,376	68.8	307,200	1,296
Cleburne	48,662	17.2	1.8	55,823	30,280	25,483	33,125	19,284	11,000	10,848	64.3	123,100	902
College Station	44,124	30.8	5.3	76,630	21,038	19,059	23,560	15,257	43,850	38,829	37.8	244,000	945
Conroe	60,931	11.9	4.5	72,880	35,465	35,802	40,722	29,742	32,250	29,297	56.1	196,800	1,011
Coppell	119,872	5.7	22.9	136,284	41,919	60,187	80,053	47,595	16,802	16,319	75.2	397,300	1,307
Copperas Cove	52,896	9.3	1.4	56,488	27,235	26,236	30,166	23,341	12,542	10,462	64.7	112,600	899
Corpus Christi	53,605	17.4	5.2	64,649	31,432	30,697	34,214	26,988	131,980	115,797	56.7	141,300	970
Dallas	50,627	17.8	7.0	55,540	41,042	31,587	33,693	28,702	573,667	513,084	39.4	190,600	992
Deer Park	67,304	7.2	6.3	78,424	32,851	37,766	52,390	27,658	12,976	12,458	73.1	162,600	1,183
Del Rio	37,912	27.9	2.3	40,626	23,188	22,858	26,882	18,913	13,816	12,431	64.0	88,300	658
Denton	51,004	17.2	5.7	76,653	28,633	25,379	30,544	20,579	52,329	49,287	48.2	223,900	1,005
DeSoto	72,049	10.9	4.1	80,900	30,667	41,102	41,770	37,175	21,043	20,307	63.0	168,900	1,023
Duncanville	61,407	12.5	5.1	70,127	40,628	35,322	37,205	30,988	12,755	12,295	67.1	151,500	1,149
Eagle Pass	29,830	33.9	0.4	32,217	0	24,940	27,570	20,257	9,459	8,369	56.7	96,800	630
Edinburg	55,392	24.2	1.9	62,560	36,121	25,938	30,597	20,480	28,063	26,185	53.1	115,200	760
El Paso	44,754	22.1	3.1	50,933	25,736	26,045	30,603	21,983	252,969	229,156	58.9	127,700	832
Euless	61,353	8.3	2.1	81,098	47,477	40,190	47,456	35,910	22,889	21,465	47.5	183,100	1,119
Farmers Branch	67,308	6.3	5.3	68,979	61,872	41,027	40,311	41,355	14,333	13,692	58.0	183,000	1,377
Flower Mound	133,521	2.4	24.6	146,036	72,108	62,180	85,586	51,081	26,616	25,597	88.9	366,600	1,750
Fort Worth	60,205	13.6	4.9	69,973	40,324	35,100	38,152	30,115	329,779	299,593	56.7	169,400	994
Friendswood	101,334	5.7	21.6	130,974	45,732	46,811	71,361	37,240	14,614	13,393	78.4	308,200	1,160
Frisco	122,302	5.8	21.0	141,218	51,869	60,738	90,542	43,073	62,911	58,409	72.4	404,100	1,449
Galveston	46,639	25.4	4.7	60,133	29,961	26,969	30,571	24,451	32,835	22,077	42.7	189,100	896
Garland	57,483	10.1	3.6	65,087	39,179	30,503	32,002	27,198	80,940	77,072	63.1	161,700	1,002
Georgetown	71,829	11.3	9.5	89,107	39,860	31,945	42,138	21,058	27,525	26,361	70.1	280,300	1,130
Grand Prairie	67,099	9.6	2.8	74,485	39,284	35,715	37,429	32,475	66,054	60,843	63.5	164,000	1,056
Grapevine	90,897	11.7	15.2	111,285	61,928	46,414	47,402	44,333	20,321	19,557	52.7	337,100	1,344
Greenville	48,972	21.8	0.9	51,736	0	32,405	40,627	21,135	10,464	10,027	54.5	126,100	985
Haltom City	47,042	14.0	1.5	48,052	39,592	26,472	32,458	21,033	14,016	13,169	53.8	109,900	985
Harker Heights	79,700	14.4	4.1	80,311	75,782	44,370	43,714	45,647	11,509	10,452	64.4	181,800	999
Harlingen	38,250	31.4	1.8	41,415	19,298	22,654	26,154	20,248	22,839	19,945	54.4	95,100	669
Houston	50,896	19.1	7.8	56,751	40,156	31,533	35,482	27,311	958,421	837,686	42.8	173,600	986
Huntsville	35,478	31.8	0.0	43,024	27,870	23,246	26,030	17,232	14,794	13,556	25.1	178,900	831
Hurst	54,952	9.4	5.6	64,247	44,358	27,499	31,927	25,255	14,176	13,288	63.6	187,700	1,112

1. Based on population estimated by the American Community Survey.   2. Includes units rented or sold but not occupied.   3. Specified owner-occupied units; $1,000,000 represents $1,000,000 or more.   4. 50.0 represents 50 percent or more.   5. 10.0 represents 10 percent or less.

Table D. Cities — Commuting, Computer Access, Migration, Labor Force, and Employment

City	Commuting[1], 2017 Commuting	With commutes of 30 minutes or more	Computer access[2], 2017 With a computer in the house	With Internet access	Migration, 2017 Percent who lived in the same house one year ago	Percent who lived in another state or county one year ago	Civilian labor force, 2018 Total	Percent change 2017-2018	Unemployment Total	Rate[3]	Civilian employment[4], 2017 Population age 16 and older Number	Percent in labor force	Population age 16 to 64 Number	Percent who worked full-year full-time
	55	56	57	58	59	60	61	62	63	64	65	66	67	68
TENNESSEE—Cont'd														
Columbia	75.7	41.3	92.3	84.3	87.6	7.2	18,160	3.5	682	3.8	30,075	64.8	24,947	55.0
Cookeville	85.7	17.0	86.1	79.9	72.3	12.5	13,975	1.1	537	3.8	28,116	58.6	23,462	38.9
Franklin	77.8	35.2	96.3	91.1	81.7	12.9	45,105	3.2	1,072	2.4	62,358	70.4	50,594	57.4
Gallatin	74.1	33.9	88.6	81.6	87.1	6.3	19,558	3.2	599	3.1	29,366	63.1	23,218	55.9
Germantown	88.9	27.6	98.1	94.2	86.3	5.7	19,943	1.3	536	2.7	32,419	63.4	23,024	59.5
Hendersonville	85.9	44.8	96.1	89.0	80.0	13.7	32,477	3.2	866	2.7	45,070	72.0	36,656	61.8
Jackson	83.7	16.3	84.2	74.5	85.8	5.3	32,033	1.4	1,302	4.1	52,347	55.8	42,588	46.1
Johnson City	83.8	18.7	85.4	80.7	77.6	11.1	31,436	0.7	1,085	3.5	54,135	60.7	44,759	43.7
Kingsport	77.9	20.4	87.2	78.8	81.6	8.9	22,821	0.2	871	3.8	42,496	54.2	30,565	43.3
Knoxville	79.2	19.7	88.4	77.4	77.6	9.5	96,140	1.2	3,024	3.1	153,077	63.6	129,493	46.2
La Vergne	87.2	51.1	97.5	87.5	91.7	6.9	19,321	3.0	542	2.8	27,973	72.6	25,755	57.3
Lebanon	82.5	32.8	91.7	79.6	86.9	7.7	15,357	3.1	498	3.2	24,333	64.3	20,610	48.1
Maryville	90.0	33.5	93.5	85.9	85.5	3.5	13,623	1.1	408	3.0	23,371	57.8	19,068	44.9
Memphis	83.2	25.9	81.6	70.9	83.8	3.7	294,016	1.3	13,609	4.6	505,207	62.4	423,590	47.6
Morristown	NA	22.6	83.7	74.8	86.6	5.3	11,469	0.5	464	4.0	21,996	54.2	17,158	44.4
Murfreesboro	82.7	36.6	94.5	82.6	79.3	12.7	77,366	3.1	2,118	2.7	104,245	73.1	92,406	55.0
Nashville-Davidson	78.4	35.0	92.9	85.3	81.0	7.6	396,574	3.2	10,438	2.6	NA	NA	NA	NA
Oak Ridge	85.2	38.6	91.5	85.5	79.5	12.0	14,099	1.3	495	3.5	24,141	60.1	18,657	50.1
Smyrna	84.9	47.4	94.9	79.0	90.5	5.4	27,699	3.1	722	2.6	39,125	74.2	34,023	60.8
Spring Hill	80.2	57.5	NA	NA	77.5	18.8	21,832	3.4	595	2.7	28,544	74.7	24,891	50.4
TEXAS	80.6	38.8	91.8	82.9	84.3	6.6	13,848,080	1.9	533,877	3.9	21,761,733	64.3	18,296,241	51.7
Abilene	80.3	9.3	89.2	75.0	75.0	12.0	55,710	1.6	1,842	3.3	97,019	63.3	80,817	48.4
Allen	82.7	48.4	98.7	96.9	84.6	8.9	56,406	2.3	1,823	3.2	74,308	73.4	65,598	55.2
Amarillo	83.3	15.5	93.0	80.8	81.4	7.1	100,947	0.6	2,750	2.7	152,084	66.5	126,594	56.4
Arlington	82.0	44.1	96.3	85.0	87.4	4.8	212,277	2.4	7,504	3.5	302,086	68.2	261,609	52.5
Austin	74.0	34.3	95.7	89.0	78.9	9.6	579,048	3.2	15,894	2.7	775,804	73.7	686,406	58.5
Baytown	83.5	36.9	93.1	84.9	85.2	5.8	34,202	0.8	3,046	8.9	58,753	62.8	49,117	50.7
Beaumont	85.6	21.8	93.0	73.2	88.0	5.7	52,108	0.6	2,917	5.6	89,869	60.5	74,396	52.7
Bedford	80.2	41.1	95.8	91.1	81.3	6.2	29,387	2.4	991	3.4	39,472	72.0	32,342	62.0
Big Spring	74.5	17.4	85.3	66.7	83.3	10.5	9,912	3.1	357	3.6	22,949	50.4	19,604	36.5
Brownsville	84.4	18.4	79.5	35.2	93.3	1.6	74,764	-0.4	4,723	6.3	135,755	55.8	112,477	39.9
Bryan	80.1	11.9	89.2	77.4	76.3	9.5	43,138	3.2	1,234	2.9	66,789	59.3	57,153	48.8
Burleson	84.4	56.2	93.9	91.7	89.0	5.1	24,400	2.4	787	3.2	34,723	68.5	28,899	60.2
Carrollton	81.4	40.6	97.7	90.8	86.8	5.8	81,776	2.3	2,627	3.2	107,472	75.0	94,511	60.7
Cedar Hill	86.3	57.1	97.1	92.6	90.0	2.9	27,218	2.6	1,285	4.7	37,562	68.3	32,488	57.1
Cedar Park	78.2	39.4	97.8	94.3	84.2	8.9	41,741	3.2	1,246	3.0	55,040	70.8	49,594	58.7
Cleburne	NA	39.8	84.5	78.1	90.7	4.4	13,460	2.1	485	3.6	23,065	58.0	17,903	49.0
College Station	79.5	9.8	97.1	86.6	65.2	18.6	60,033	3.3	1,715	2.9	95,268	58.8	88,468	33.2
Conroe	82.0	44.5	92.8	86.9	78.2	7.6	40,386	1.8	1,491	3.7	62,897	66.2	52,050	57.3
Coppell	87.0	37.4	99.1	97.0	87.5	8.1	24,288	2.4	796	3.3	33,367	77.1	29,452	62.0
Copperas Cove	81.9	27.7	93.8	91.8	69.4	24.7	12,803	-0.1	527	4.1	24,766	63.4	21,913	48.6
Corpus Christi	84.2	16.4	90.8	84.0	84.8	4.9	152,754	0.1	7,032	4.6	254,195	63.1	208,968	52.1
Dallas	75.9	44.1	88.9	80.0	81.9	6.9	692,285	2.3	25,664	3.7	1,037,244	69.3	896,549	56.1
Deer Park	84.3	39.6	NA	NA	NA	NA	16,938	0.9	798	4.7	27,608	68.4	23,543	52.0
Del Rio	79.2	7.2	79.5	68.2	92.4	5.4	15,040	1.5	668	4.4	25,784	57.0	20,092	40.9
Denton	77.2	34.6	95.7	91.1	76.3	11.8	74,984	2.4	2,345	3.1	114,783	64.2	99,117	43.9
DeSoto	85.5	52.0	94.8	80.5	85.2	5.6	29,024	2.4	1,491	5.1	41,978	70.2	34,252	59.8
Duncanville	88.6	52.5	92.8	81.3	95.3	1.6	20,513	2.3	863	4.2	29,168	62.2	24,911	52.1
Eagle Pass	NA	21.5	70.6	39.2	NA	NA	12,588	-1.1	1,197	9.5	20,557	42.9	17,105	32.6
Edinburg	80.5	17.9	90.0	74.3	86.6	2.9	41,792	1.8	1,953	4.7	62,666	66.9	55,477	52.5
El Paso	80.0	28.1	87.2	79.7	84.0	4.8	300,501	1.4	12,373	4.1	521,515	62.2	434,900	48.5
Euless	84.2	37.1	98.8	92.0	84.5	7.4	31,637	2.6	1,124	3.6	45,481	71.9	40,030	55.7
Farmers Branch	84.4	34.1	96.9	89.9	84.1	7.3	20,132	2.2	669	3.3	29,225	67.9	24,520	59.2
Flower Mound	84.5	46.3	98.9	97.7	88.4	7.6	43,240	2.3	1,263	2.9	58,408	70.2	49,976	55.2
Fort Worth	82.1	41.1	92.9	85.7	82.4	6.3	427,892	2.4	15,562	3.6	667,185	68.1	580,028	54.2
Friendswood	85.5	49.7	NA	NA	84.3	10.5	19,974	1.8	739	3.7	29,869	63.4	23,730	52.9
Frisco	77.4	48.3	99.1	95.2	83.2	10.7	99,240	2.4	3,099	3.1	126,999	72.7	112,934	60.5
Galveston	79.1	17.2	89.3	81.6	76.0	11.5	24,012	1.8	1,101	4.6	43,582	59.0	34,811	42.8
Garland	80.6	47.5	95.2	89.2	88.7	3.9	125,188	2.4	4,455	3.6	185,030	67.4	155,986	53.6
Georgetown	74.0	41.5	96.6	90.4	88.2	4.7	29,873	3.2	1,075	3.6	58,694	47.9	38,788	47.6
Grand Prairie	84.7	49.2	94.4	86.6	86.7	5.5	100,962	2.4	3,752	3.7	145,147	70.6	128,535	58.2
Grapevine	76.8	35.8	98.0	95.9	74.9	10.0	32,722	2.4	987	3.0	42,813	75.0	37,537	57.2
Greenville	NA	32.4	88.4	76.2	85.0	5.7	11,528	2.1	473	4.1	20,631	57.4	16,912	48.3
Haltom City	78.5	38.1	95.6	90.0	76.9	9.7	22,489	2.3	742	3.3	31,249	67.8	27,905	52.6
Harker Heights	86.3	20.2	98.1	92.1	80.9	11.6	12,641	-0.2	489	3.9	24,791	61.4	21,514	45.4
Harlingen	82.0	18.2	80.5	67.1	89.8	4.9	24,521	-0.1	1,420	5.8	45,473	57.1	35,810	43.2
Houston	77.0	44.0	91.2	82.8	80.9	5.2	1,156,707	1.7	49,068	4.2	1,783,503	66.2	1,537,391	51.4
Huntsville	69.0	23.2	93.3	85.8	72.7	14.5	11,818	1.1	579	4.9	36,982	40.3	32,416	27.6
Hurst	78.7	33.5	92.2	85.8	80.5	3.9	20,472	2.2	705	3.4	29,548	66.5	23,141	50.7

1. Employed persons.   2. Households.   3. Percent of civilian labor force.   4. Persons 16 years old and over.

Construction, Wholesale Trade, and Retail Trade

City	Value of residential construction authorized by building permits, 2018			Wholesale trade[1], 2012				Retail trade[2], 2012			
	New construction ($1,000)	Number of housing units	Percent single family	Number of establishments	Number of employees	Sales (mil dol)	Annual payroll (mil dol)	Number of establishments	Number of employees	Sales (mil dol)	Annual payroll (mil dol)
	69	70	71	72	73	74	75	76	77	78	79
TENNESSEE—Cont'd											
Columbia	11,391	484	95.0	39	496	223.7	30.5	221	2,817	845.7	69.4
Cookeville	36,927	274	54.7	50	887	260.9	35.3	274	4,064	1,040.3	88.8
Franklin	256,166	976	58.5	134	1,764	8,777.6	126.9	477	8,372	2,529.1	225.5
Gallatin	152,030	1,003	53.5	37	530	497.6	26.2	144	2,057	620.6	54.0
Germantown	NA	NA	NA	33	D	D	D	140	1,977	349.6	39.7
Hendersonville	52,769	282	100.0	50	D	D	D	198	2,898	686.8	66.5
Jackson	32,019	153	100.0	117	1,383	688.7	61.0	426	6,689	1,806.3	155.1
Johnson City	43,161	273	36.6	93	1,048	664.6	41.7	436	7,306	1,780.5	155.2
Kingsport	19,999	93	93.5	75	904	642.3	38.8	337	5,487	1,293.3	119.1
Knoxville	83,733	609	55.0	411	5,879	3,451.0	312.1	1,326	22,849	6,049.5	553.2
La Vergne	13,111	74	100.0	74	4,419	12,983.0	187.8	61	667	261.9	18.8
Lebanon	95,110	490	85.3	42	1,219	891.1	66.2	213	2,781	782.1	67.1
Maryville	34,020	172	100.0	29	271	793.8	13.6	174	2,749	605.8	57.1
Memphis	NA	NA	NA	980	20,551	28,725.9	1,109.3	2,365	35,878	18,848.9	999.6
Morristown	15,144	102	100.0	42	D	D	D	248	3,728	961.9	90.9
Murfreesboro	465,249	2,750	54.5	88	925	706.0	48.5	554	8,860	2,448.0	197.9
Nashville-Davidson	1,074,414	6,828	52.1	923	17,595	17,607.0	1,115.0	2,575	37,506	10,138.3	989.0
Oak Ridge	6,795	57	100.0	21	D	D	D	107	1,720	397.7	37.9
Smyrna	64,842	443	70.0	31	831	1,062.2	40.8	149	2,386	592.6	54.0
Spring Hill	206,064	877	100.0	11	423	184.9	14.1	64	1,105	256.0	23.6
TEXAS	34,689,871	192,878	65.4	27,752	408,692	691,242.6	24,826.1	78,281	1,150,148	356,116.4	28,835.5
Abilene	70,693	327	93.3	131	1,619	1,861.9	79.7	533	7,619	2,087.4	181.6
Allen	162,953	1,054	43.4	58	D	D	D	281	5,344	1,113.8	105.1
Amarillo	149,628	656	82.8	216	3,356	2,985.1	174.7	841	12,920	4,067.9	311.0
Arlington	221,832	1,571	39.7	333	5,752	4,034.0	317.8	1,147	17,817	5,419.7	452.1
Austin	1,750,073	13,283	33.4	942	19,901	55,702.0	1,417.1	3,091	49,905	14,738.2	1,363.0
Baytown	76,861	612	44.8	41	460	164.0	19.0	276	4,460	1,572.2	105.0
Beaumont	41,458	283	49.1	180	2,151	1,889.9	117.4	611	9,166	2,511.7	234.4
Bedford	1,257	5	100.0	33	211	113.2	15.0	119	1,747	556.4	46.5
Big Spring	4,829	28	100.0	21	D	D	D	99	1,309	383.9	30.9
Brownsville	67,495	665	100.0	175	1,681	891.1	53.2	563	8,869	2,169.6	181.8
Bryan	103,307	735	64.5	83	1,126	864.9	58.7	299	3,842	1,271.3	93.6
Burleson	66,304	250	100.0	22	138	52.2	5.2	154	3,015	885.6	73.7
Carrollton	266,175	1,209	47.2	394	6,422	5,487.6	365.5	406	4,850	2,173.2	156.5
Cedar Hill	16,956	67	91.0	12	94	65.0	4.7	146	3,056	602.7	57.9
Cedar Park	111,443	811	39.1	44	D	D	D	232	3,735	835.7	75.7
Cleburne	17,772	93	100.0	35	498	315.7	25.1	155	2,084	584.0	51.3
College Station	152,784	1,031	44.5	34	344	235.6	15.6	309	5,876	1,375.4	111.6
Conroe	283,771	1,561	80.0	111	1,352	5,498.0	69.0	382	6,345	2,214.1	171.2
Coppell	20,212	49	100.0	70	2,125	1,442.5	167.5	75	1,605	713.9	59.3
Copperas Cove	26,999	199	93.0	1	D	D	D	70	1,004	278.4	21.5
Corpus Christi	177,983	1,016	100.0	326	4,376	4,143.7	229.2	1,043	16,278	4,939.2	401.2
Dallas	1,094,324	8,047	25.0	1,934	28,244	22,578.0	1,572.1	4,022	57,240	16,889.0	1,603.9
Deer Park	2,135	8	100.0	40	898	466.1	61.6	57	1,014	283.4	22.7
Del Rio	8,393	43	100.0	21	D	D	D	142	1,984	573.3	43.6
Denton	325,373	1,552	64.8	93	1,231	1,208.9	51.8	399	6,463	1,802.7	149.9
DeSoto	50,992	140	100.0	25	368	220.3	22.3	80	1,395	410.9	34.7
Duncanville	2,756	11	100.0	16	D	D	D	130	1,521	558.9	44.0
Eagle Pass	18,124	72	94.4	38	D	D	D	150	2,425	565.9	47.7
Edinburg	153,787	1,443	33.4	73	1,425	688.7	46.3	216	3,856	1,371.8	91.3
El Paso	469,431	2,209	71.9	884	9,548	6,348.6	404.9	2,064	32,405	8,445.4	706.3
Euless	46,336	196	100.0	48	418	306.6	25.7	135	1,595	641.0	46.0
Farmers Branch	461,293	3,355	4.3	207	5,093	3,422.1	356.4	150	2,360	772.0	79.2
Flower Mound	242,357	575	100.0	58	698	790.8	40.4	153	2,668	625.3	60.6
Fort Worth	1,436,250	9,310	58.8	696	16,814	17,624.0	1,062.3	2,047	31,491	10,333.5	866.2
Friendswood	61,841	142	100.0	15	D	D	D	96	1,743	480.3	37.4
Frisco	990,211	4,818	45.8	96	D	D	D	437	9,421	2,468.7	229.1
Galveston	46,257	183	100.0	36	D	D	D	208	2,523	615.4	55.4
Garland	67,835	456	20.2	184	2,917	1,771.9	143.2	608	9,210	2,725.4	226.9
Georgetown	308,927	2,053	59.0	33	D	D	D	190	3,460	1,234.9	95.6
Grand Prairie	114,845	921	12.1	267	5,982	5,073.0	337.2	343	5,605	2,050.9	146.2
Grapevine	79,734	790	2.5	93	1,933	1,902.9	109.6	315	4,979	1,563.4	128.1
Greenville	17,934	141	100.0	23	249	275.3	9.1	139	2,206	636.5	65.5
Haltom City	985	10	80.0	96	1,072	473.3	51.8	144	1,370	509.3	40.0
Harker Heights	47,850	190	83.2	4	24	7.6	0.8	58	1,136	296.4	23.4
Harlingen	27,391	239	74.9	75	738	585.5	27.3	298	4,835	1,183.7	111.2
Houston	2,313,660	13,237	40.9	4,501	77,057	322,772.6	5,461.8	8,592	130,540	41,589.4	3,488.6
Huntsville	61,462	414	12.8	22	D	D	D	138	2,258	696.9	48.1
Hurst	3,571	19	100.0	37	234	154.5	11.8	282	5,108	1,292.0	117.4

1. Merchant wholesalers except manufacturers' sales branches and offices.   2. Establishments with payroll.

Table D. Cities — Real Estate, Professional Services, and Manufacturing

City	Real estate and rental and leasing, 2012				Professional, scientific, and technical services[1], 2012				Manufacturing, 2012			
	Number of establishments	Number of employees	Receipts (mil dol)	Annual payroll (mil dol)	Number of establishments	Number of employees	Receipts (mil dol)	Annual payroll (mil dol)	Number of establishments	Number of employees	Receipts (mil dol)	Annual payroll (mil dol)
	80	81	82	83	84	85	86	87	88	89	90	91
TENNESSEE—Cont'd												
Columbia	50	175	29.4	4.6	70	D	D	D	40	856	187.7	38.2
Cookeville	54	156	31.0	4.2	114	D	D	D	76	2,976	912.5	119.6
Franklin	120	753	357.2	45.0	373	3,940	700.5	271.3	68	1,770	474.7	74.7
Gallatin	38	456	83.3	30.3	53	D	D	D	61	2,257	985.0	92.1
Germantown	42	D	D	D	115	418	67.3	24.9	9	D	3.6	D
Hendersonville	68	251	51.2	8.8	120	D	D	D	48	810	147.5	37.5
Jackson	90	431	68.9	14.1	157	D	D	D	77	7,033	3,426.0	317.7
Johnson City	99	494	80.6	15.0	170	D	D	D	74	3,902	1,278.7	149.8
Kingsport	59	264	46.2	8.5	143	966	104.2	41.9	38	10,628	D	D
Knoxville	396	2,635	470.7	97.2	719	D	D	D	208	D	2,070.7	D
La Vergne	17	136	33.7	6.9	18	233	15.2	15.6	46	3,289	D	167.8
Lebanon	58	228	57.3	9.1	86	D	D	D	47	2,115	1,015.7	111.6
Maryville	32	88	19.0	2.5	97	D	D	D	31	3,037	2,235.1	173.7
Memphis	745	5,964	1,152.7	263.4	1,305	D	D	D	450	18,847	18,372.5	1,096.2
Morristown	49	162	32.5	4.5	60	D	D	D	84	8,441	3,203.3	350.6
Murfreesboro	134	715	238.3	31.7	226	D	D	D	99	5,030	2,935.5	226.9
Nashville-Davidson	897	6,348	1,410.7	284.0	1,922	24,110	4,015.2	1,637.4	552	18,154	7,319.4	851.8
Oak Ridge	42	152	31.4	5.8	143	D	D	D	44	5,527	1,166.0	445.1
Smyrna	26	111	31.0	4.5	53	650	88.2	43.0	31	6,099	7,170.4	405.2
Spring Hill	18	64	16.5	2.9	27	89	12.5	3.4	9	D	D	D
TEXAS	26,639	169,941	38,757.4	7,751.8	62,085	632,486	120,954.5	46,783.6	19,782	767,024	702,603.1	42,529.8
Abilene	162	881	149.9	27.0	255	D	D	D	83	1,991	898.3	84.5
Allen	77	413	84.0	17.6	280	1,169	204.3	83.0	27	987	334.1	64.8
Amarillo	272	1,247	244.3	42.2	463	D	D	D	159	12,263	D	755.5
Arlington	379	1,915	398.2	74.6	736	D	D	D	224	9,679	15,060.3	518.9
Austin	1,548	10,167	2,332.9	520.7	4,826	56,872	11,692.9	4,737.1	616	20,866	11,413.4	1,356.9
Baytown	79	444	84.3	17.5	97	2,249	182.6	303.9	55	5,545	D	545.5
Beaumont	176	1,179	231.5	49.4	370	4,918	871.7	338.4	103	4,671	D	349.7
Bedford	55	209	46.8	9.2	162	805	100.1	37.5	13	111	11.2	4.0
Big Spring	37	146	29.4	4.3	34	169	16.5	6.3	16	495	D	33.4
Brownsville	142	537	63.8	13.2	263	D	D	D	103	2,705	1,215.2	123.5
Bryan	92	558	75.5	16.4	189	D	D	D	69	3,967	928.5	149.1
Burleson	32	106	21.7	3.5	77	321	37.4	9.5	32	920	178.9	38.8
Carrollton	143	1,629	302.6	85.9	407	3,355	571.1	209.8	187	11,424	3,739.1	564.1
Cedar Hill	23	69	14.7	1.6	55	D	D	D	27	782	151.6	27.9
Cedar Park	65	185	68.5	6.1	155	912	142.0	51.6	39	1,200	384.8	75.0
Cleburne	37	120	21.7	3.8	72	434	40.1	18.2	32	1,433	599.9	75.8
College Station	120	638	132.9	20.1	165	D	D	D	13	241	D	13.6
Conroe	83	578	111.4	26.6	203	D	D	D	104	3,733	1,763.5	194.3
Coppell	47	482	113.4	25.0	208	2,604	562.9	231.0	35	1,485	297.0	66.8
Copperas Cove	29	D	D	D	31	138	10.6	3.8	4	7	D	D
Corpus Christi	370	2,602	623.1	121.9	786	5,700	840.3	306.1	168	5,412	D	357.1
Dallas	2,162	20,336	4,905.7	1,160.5	5,407	67,331	14,598.6	5,688.9	1,125	42,824	17,731.3	2,126.8
Deer Park	32	421	104.1	22.0	51	1,007	175.6	55.4	41	4,605	28,034.8	485.4
Del Rio	32	114	16.5	2.7	37	D	D	D	15	176	D	5.0
Denton	149	585	125.7	19.9	260	D	D	D	93	5,210	4,794.0	277.2
DeSoto	39	162	31.9	5.6	48	199	16.9	6.8	27	733	120.5	39.8
Duncanville	38	173	19.2	5.5	54	196	21.3	8.4	22	1,137	223.0	39.0
Eagle Pass	26	71	12.5	1.9	36	D	D	D	14	339	49.0	9.0
Edinburg	60	205	41.5	6.1	148	D	D	D	29	625	215.0	22.9
El Paso	671	2,969	548.7	101.9	1,119	D	D	D	432	11,607	13,170.8	487.1
Euless	40	267	50.6	8.9	86	D	D	D	37	832	197.2	39.3
Farmers Branch	70	929	144.0	47.3	308	4,575	1,077.9	470.0	80	2,707	910.5	117.6
Flower Mound	66	400	66.6	17.0	271	D	D	D	20	636	212.3	36.7
Fort Worth	704	4,977	1,106.6	228.7	1,652	D	D	D	645	39,747	D	2,369.4
Friendswood	44	314	23.4	8.1	128	447	58.6	21.0	16	175	D	7.2
Frisco	135	672	165.1	27.0	552	4,343	778.7	263.7	36	533	233.7	29.2
Galveston	75	403	76.2	15.5	106	D	D	D	29	948	D	48.9
Garland	173	1,113	183.7	33.5	280	3,620	463.2	299.6	264	9,585	5,396.6	427.2
Georgetown	63	228	62.7	13.0	161	616	86.9	30.9	48	1,541	344.6	63.4
Grand Prairie	126	1,945	355.9	83.2	169	1,299	174.6	65.1	181	12,084	4,512.7	758.4
Grapevine	77	785	328.6	40.5	219	1,265	198.4	76.2	43	1,942	D	95.9
Greenville	38	115	20.4	3.3	47	281	49.8	10.4	39	6,681	2,783.6	523.9
Haltom City	38	350	82.6	19.8	56	687	53.9	22.5	90	2,612	684.3	107.5
Harker Heights	32	127	18.7	4.0	28	138	9.6	3.5	4	23	2.6	D
Harlingen	97	443	80.5	9.8	146	D	D	D	49	903	D	40.8
Houston	3,435	28,791	7,005.4	1,456.0	9,252	158,979	38,304.1	14,658.9	2,436	86,899	53,787.1	4,791.2
Huntsville	48	175	42.9	6.1	68	393	27.6	9.8	17	347	D	21.3
Hurst	52	240	72.6	8.6	167	1,037	134.3	59.3	31	467	127.0	22.8

1. Establishments subject to federal tax.

Table D. Cities — Accommodation and Food Services, Arts, Entertainment, and Recreation, and Health Care and Social Assistance

City	Accommodation and food services, 2012				Arts, entertainment, and recreation[1], 2012				Health care and social assistance,[1] 2012			
	Number of establish-ments	Number of employees	Receipts (mil dol)	Annual payroll (mil dol)	Number of establish-ments	Number of employees	Receipts (mil dol)	Annual payroll (mil dol)	Number of establish-ments	Number of employees	Receipts (mil dol)	Annual payroll (mil dol)
	92	93	94	95	96	97	98	99	100	101	102	103
TENNESSEE—Cont'd												
Columbia	101	1,771	81.2	22.3	7	D	D	D	136	D	D	D
Cookeville	137	D	D	D	10	D	D	D	173	D	D	D
Franklin	281	6,519	337.0	97.6	95	D	D	D	285	4,901	744.3	269.8
Gallatin	58	905	44.3	12.2	6	D	D	D	84	D	D	D
Germantown	70	1,454	82.7	22.4	13	130	5.8	1.9	191	D	D	D
Hendersonville	112	2,638	113.7	34.6	26	D	D	D	142	2,039	249.7	85.2
Jackson	210	4,703	220.3	62.4	17	D	D	D	261	D	D	D
Johnson City	239	5,668	249.2	72.7	16	D	D	D	252	D	D	D
Kingsport	193	4,387	199.6	58.9	19	D	D	D	228	3,761	503.7	220.1
Knoxville	714	17,958	865.1	267.4	47	548	34.6	9.6	755	16,303	2,046.1	772.1
La Vergne	29	412	20.6	5.3	NA	NA	NA	NA	15	143	7.3	3.6
Lebanon	108	2,239	98.8	28.6	8	D	D	D	136	2,476	294.2	114.8
Maryville	94	1,644	75.5	22.0	13	D	D	D	140	1,629	171.3	82.1
Memphis	1,243	28,822	1,503.9	425.7	82	1,976	210.8	102.7	1,415	26,987	2,964.4	1,216.1
Morristown	106	D	D	D	9	D	D	D	123	2,306	227.8	96.0
Murfreesboro	314	7,922	356.0	105.3	21	D	D	D	327	6,004	576.4	262.1
Nashville-Davidson	1,714	40,106	2,573.8	759.3	665	4,720	1,476.9	524.5	1,467	30,924	4,176.2	1,568.7
Oak Ridge	74	1,604	76.3	21.4	6	101	4.6	1.6	101	D	D	D
Smyrna	109	2,367	112.1	32.0	6	D	D	D	117	D	D	D
Spring Hill	57	1,188	45.9	14.2	9	19	3.6	0.5	35	D	D	D
TEXAS	48,721	976,390	54,480.8	14,743.8	4,966	83,587	7,770.7	2,523.6	55,176	945,659	93,988.1	36,493.1
Abilene	284	D	D	D	34	258	21.1	4.0	316	7,710	657.8	271.4
Allen	170	3,771	194.3	56.4	24	462	25.4	8.1	259	D	D	D
Amarillo	500	10,147	514.1	139.7	52	687	38.7	11.3	567	10,579	1,228.0	437.8
Arlington	684	15,492	910.8	233.2	67	3,881	616.2	255.2	865	15,821	1,542.7	638.3
Austin	2,517	55,702	3,474.7	962.5	317	4,559	468.8	144.0	2,329	37,842	4,746.7	1,859.6
Baytown	174	3,836	193.7	52.2	12	D	D	D	213	D	D	D
Beaumont	283	6,727	320.7	88.3	35	D	D	D	501	D	D	D
Bedford	93	1,993	98.5	27.8	9	D	D	D	191	D	D	D
Big Spring	71	1,057	61.0	13.8	3	D	D	D	57	D	D	D
Brownsville	299	5,246	244.3	65.5	26	D	D	D	418	13,860	789.1	346.9
Bryan	139	2,436	115.0	32.5	13	D	D	D	186	2,546	275.6	118.1
Burleson	105	2,511	112.7	31.4	8	D	D	D	95	1,020	82.2	34.5
Carrollton	244	3,204	187.6	49.4	27	D	D	D	328	3,721	410.7	148.7
Cedar Hill	86	2,068	97.8	25.6	6	D	D	D	79	1,220	84.9	30.5
Cedar Park	137	2,517	119.2	31.5	20	D	D	D	163	D	D	D
Cleburne	81	1,365	63.3	18.1	7	68	3.7	0.6	99	D	D	D
College Station	287	6,966	327.7	88.0	21	330	14.7	5.0	136	D	D	D
Conroe	164	3,450	175.2	48.5	10	125	11.6	1.4	200	D	D	D
Coppell	73	1,538	93.3	22.2	9	159	6.8	2.3	106	D	D	D
Copperas Cove	50	934	42.1	10.8	3	D	D	D	27	426	22.3	10.3
Corpus Christi	749	15,806	825.4	223.7	57	D	D	D	907	17,743	1,577.5	620.5
Dallas	2,687	59,649	3,851.5	1,087.3	283	4,840	477.0	208.1	3,535	56,873	8,201.1	3,427.0
Deer Park	44	769	46.6	11.2	2	D	D	D	45	D	D	D
Del Rio	87	1,613	76.2	19.5	7	41	1.1	0.5	84	D	D	D
Denton	283	5,961	277.1	75.9	20	291	15.1	4.0	390	6,232	770.2	285.0
DeSoto	60	1,240	63.9	17.8	5	89	5.7	2.1	165	3,622	236.3	105.8
Duncanville	60	1,406	69.0	19.1	5	101	5.7	1.5	101	2,187	105.2	47.1
Eagle Pass	65	D	D	D	7	D	D	D	81	D	D	D
Edinburg	120	1,970	102.3	25.9	12	D	D	D	331	9,143	433.5	212.2
El Paso	1,362	27,187	1,310.8	354.0	89	D	D	D	1,300	26,860	2,875.1	1,005.3
Euless	89	1,538	76.0	20.2	5	D	D	D	77	D	D	D
Farmers Branch	99	1,493	83.9	25.9	6	D	D	D	136	2,292	285.2	112.7
Flower Mound	118	2,866	157.4	42.2	23	411	26.0	7.3	178	1,971	257.9	91.6
Fort Worth	1,288	28,324	1,609.5	440.5	134	2,108	225.1	46.6	1,602	24,161	2,738.6	1,078.8
Friendswood	70	1,121	55.0	14.1	11	D	D	D	111	D	D	D
Frisco	254	6,182	360.8	100.4	41	1,555	148.3	83.1	394	D	D	D
Galveston	212	6,605	391.2	110.0	22	480	35.2	7.9	85	D	D	D
Garland	309	5,540	286.8	79.7	31	504	40.5	9.4	414	7,134	439.2	187.8
Georgetown	103	2,188	109.6	30.5	14	D	D	D	152	2,278	225.8	90.9
Grand Prairie	216	3,855	221.9	54.6	21	D	D	D	234	2,519	181.0	66.5
Grapevine	175	7,278	628.9	152.0	17	379	26.3	5.7	186	D	D	D
Greenville	68	1,304	65.2	17.1	4	D	D	D	110	D	D	D
Haltom City	72	735	37.6	9.0	7	49	4.1	0.5	35	D	D	D
Harker Heights	63	951	37.1	10.2	5	D	D	D	34	D	D	D
Harlingen	170	3,749	203.8	57.5	16	D	D	D	334	11,017	834.5	354.0
Houston	5,645	122,643	7,746.6	2,082.8	442	10,362	1,681.5	523.7	6,526	105,192	11,479.2	4,372.6
Huntsville	94	D	D	D	3	D	D	D	78	D	D	D
Hurst	103	2,129	126.6	32.5	14	182	9.7	2.5	130	D	D	D

1. Establishments subject to federal tax.

Table D. Cities — Other Services and Government Employment and Payroll

City	Other services[1]				Government employment and payroll, 2012								
					Full-time equivalent employees	March payroll							
						Total (dollars)	Percent of total for:						
	Number of establishments	Number of employees	Receipts (mil dol)	Annual payroll (mil dol)			Administrative, judicial, and legal	Police and corrections	Fire protection	Highways and transportation	Health and welfare	Natural resources and utilities	Education and libraries
	104	105	106	107	108	109	110	111	112	113	114	115	116
TENNESSEE—Cont'd													
Columbia	57	381	30.1	9.6	492	1,828,149	7.0	18.8	18.5	8.4	0.0	42.6	0.0
Cookeville	80	413	34.4	9.2	2,260	9,757,664	1.2	3.6	1.9	1.3	85.3	5.8	0.0
Franklin	133	1,096	75.2	26.9	635	2,507,514	14.1	24.5	24.1	7.9	2.9	21.9	0.0
Gallatin	46	230	20.9	6.9	429	1,515,188	8.8	22.7	17.5	5.7	0.0	40.3	0.0
Germantown	51	506	24.7	9.6	286	1,166,262	0.4	46.4	32.0	8.9	0.0	6.3	0.0
Hendersonville	78	421	27.5	8.9	317	1,225,951	9.7	37.8	33.9	3.9	0.4	5.6	0.0
Jackson	91	D	D	D	732	2,706,306	10.3	39.0	26.4	6.9	0.2	15.5	0.0
Johnson City	104	D	D	D	2,069	7,207,080	4.3	9.1	5.7	7.6	0.0	24.2	46.3
Kingsport	83	531	48.6	15.0	2,088	7,112,728	4.6	8.2	5.7	3.4	0.1	9.0	66.2
Knoxville	392	3,196	242.1	83.5	2,544	10,707,196	7.3	20.0	11.8	5.2	1.3	49.6	0.0
La Vergne	24	794	124.4	25.1	165	495,446	15.9	42.8	0.0	4.2	0.0	26.3	4.3
Lebanon	56	657	63.8	20.5	337	1,064,568	9.9	34.9	13.8	8.3	1.8	27.1	0.0
Maryville	50	266	19.8	6.8	929	3,586,065	5.2	6.5	5.0	4.0	0.0	15.5	63.0
Memphis	712	5,678	522.2	172.5	24,196	79,305,378	2.0	15.7	10.1	4.9	0.8	25.5	40.2
Morristown	49	245	21.5	6.7	417	1,625,386	6.0	20.1	18.2	6.1	0.3	38.5	0.0
Murfreesboro	167	1,164	91.2	29.6	2,265	7,333,077	3.8	13.4	9.7	3.3	0.2	20.3	45.7
Nashville-Davidson	868	8,126	726.0	233.6	21,697	83,700,973	6.4	13.3	7.5	1.1	9.0	11.1	49.9
Oak Ridge	44	D	D	D	1,132	4,632,934	5.5	7.1	8.2	4.8	1.0	10.3	62.3
Smyrna	46	442	34.2	16.1	426	1,763,154	14.1	27.9	24.5	2.1	0.0	27.9	0.0
Spring Hill	26	136	10.8	3.2	153	514,319	5.2	29.3	24.9	4.9	0.0	23.4	4.4
TEXAS	28,255	216,219	21,861.4	6,765.6	X	X	X	X	X	X	X	X	X
Abilene	162	1,407	104.9	34.0	1,115	4,154,689	10.5	32.0	23.1	4.8	5.7	16.9	2.3
Allen	81	693	53.5	17.3	662	2,925,255	11.5	28.9	20.0	3.9	2.3	27.3	4.5
Amarillo	296	2,035	192.1	55.1	2,117	7,521,677	9.3	27.1	24.7	8.3	4.8	19.1	2.1
Arlington	374	2,410	207.6	61.6	2,551	12,130,944	13.1	38.1	20.5	5.1	4.7	13.8	2.7
Austin	1,319	11,317	1,060.8	331.5	12,580	64,599,610	10.4	24.1	13.4	7.1	8.1	30.6	1.9
Baytown	87	779	71.7	24.8	748	3,193,832	12.8	28.9	19.0	2.5	7.2	18.6	3.5
Beaumont	178	1,744	180.5	55.1	1,387	7,544,738	11.5	29.5	22.1	6.9	9.1	14.8	1.6
Bedford	55	334	28.4	8.5	396	1,910,062	12.2	44.6	25.8	2.3	0.9	11.0	3.3
Big Spring	28	D	D	D	255	860,648	10.2	23.3	19.7	6.6	10.8	21.6	0.0
Brownsville	98	498	35.4	11.2	1,660	6,576,268	6.3	28.3	16.9	10.1	3.1	22.4	2.2
Bryan	120	727	64.4	18.2	926	4,516,110	3.1	19.6	11.5	1.8	0.7	38.5	3.0
Burleson	66	364	26.8	8.7	314	1,837,857	11.3	27.1	16.3	3.9	5.4	20.8	2.6
Carrollton	168	1,866	164.0	66.9	750	3,791,660	11.3	30.8	28.1	4.7	3.6	12.4	3.2
Cedar Hill	35	227	19.1	5.7	345	1,415,937	9.4	29.5	24.7	6.8	4.1	17.5	2.3
Cedar Park	105	720	53.2	19.3	366	1,608,634	12.6	30.9	18.4	2.3	0.5	20.7	3.2
Cleburne	51	317	28.3	8.6	331	1,384,254	10.9	25.9	23.1	7.1	3.7	23.7	1.6
College Station	75	549	34.1	11.0	818	3,487,614	20.0	22.9	18.5	6.9	0.0	27.4	0.0
Conroe	104	679	59.5	17.1	506	2,148,894	13.0	28.8	20.3	9.4	1.3	18.9	0.0
Coppell	48	964	119.8	36.7	374	2,007,729	18.0	24.0	25.7	6.8	0.9	15.3	4.2
Copperas Cove	42	228	21.2	5.7	265	875,963	7.7	30.2	19.1	1.6	1.2	17.4	2.0
Corpus Christi	358	3,496	346.7	116.1	2,747	10,789,288	5.1	28.6	19.2	4.2	3.3	21.1	1.6
Dallas	1,450	12,565	1,440.8	409.3	14,235	67,511,933	7.3	31.8	17.3	19.3	4.4	14.9	1.2
Deer Park	58	906	130.9	49.5	328	1,382,968	18.7	32.7	5.3	2.7	0.0	31.9	2.9
Del Rio	32	D	D	D	479	1,348,047	13.5	25.7	21.8	5.8	8.4	17.9	0.0
Denton	150	972	89.5	27.1	1,265	6,238,827	15.5	19.1	17.6	2.9	1.6	38.3	2.8
DeSoto	39	154	15.1	4.3	317	1,509,174	9.4	33.2	25.8	4.2	5.1	12.0	3.0
Duncanville	63	321	32.4	8.9	262	1,180,545	13.5	32.0	24.0	4.8	0.9	15.2	3.2
Eagle Pass	29	126	7.5	2.1	351	916,457	7.8	31.5	17.9	15.9	3.9	20.4	1.6
Edinburg	69	313	21.9	6.5	687	2,190,991	12.2	35.3	5.2	5.7	1.0	33.1	3.3
El Paso	714	4,354	334.6	101.8	5,996	23,812,936	7.0	28.9	21.6	16.9	1.4	12.9	2.2
Euless	59	D	D	D	434	2,144,456	12.6	34.2	21.4	3.9	1.0	17.4	4.5
Farmers Branch	53	615	61.6	17.3	372	1,986,448	11.5	30.7	24.2	3.4	5.2	21.2	0.0
Flower Mound	88	931	73.4	25.9	440	1,883,026	25.4	26.1	22.5	3.5	4.1	11.7	3.5
Fort Worth	700	6,296	605.7	172.5	6,536	32,292,472	9.5	36.9	20.2	4.1	1.8	17.7	2.4
Friendswood	57	303	22.4	7.9	194	961,732	21.4	48.5	0.4	6.3	7.0	10.9	5.4
Frisco	142	1,037	80.7	26.6	594	2,715,180	9.9	30.4	23.9	5.3	1.2	19.8	3.8
Galveston	64	301	25.2	8.2	808	3,423,101	7.9	29.1	17.6	21.5	3.7	16.9	0.0
Garland	230	1,159	100.6	32.4	1,920	9,882,194	9.5	22.2	17.3	5.1	4.8	30.5	2.2
Georgetown	75	446	37.7	12.4	540	2,310,226	14.5	21.6	17.8	5.7	3.2	24.6	2.8
Grand Prairie	143	1,111	98.2	32.3	1,169	5,599,824	10.7	29.3	27.8	5.1	5.9	13.3	1.6
Grapevine	69	662	56.1	18.8	572	2,942,808	10.6	24.3	22.7	7.0	1.2	13.7	2.9
Greenville	36	211	16.2	5.5	403	1,671,286	7.6	21.2	16.8	3.9	1.7	41.0	1.8
Haltom City	65	D	D	D	281	1,111,357	13.5	36.6	17.0	6.0	1.5	13.9	4.9
Harker Heights	32	151	9.1	2.7	218	830,939	17.0	29.4	23.6	4.0	1.0	16.2	3.2
Harlingen	91	501	34.2	10.3	751	2,448,262	8.2	27.6	19.8	7.2	2.5	27.1	1.8
Houston	3,244	31,771	3,283.0	1,045.9	21,007	99,616,057	8.7	36.5	20.9	7.6	4.6	8.9	1.5
Huntsville	41	244	21.2	5.3	308	1,115,825	24.2	27.0	5.3	6.6	0.0	23.7	2.4
Hurst	71	450	31.1	10.3	371	1,783,347	13.7	36.1	21.5	5.6	0.0	15.6	6.0

1. Establishments subject to federal tax.

City	City government finances, 2012									
	General revenue							General expenditure		
		Intergovernmental		Taxes						
					Per capita[1] (dollars)				Per capita[1] (dollars)	
	Total (mil dol)	Total (mil dol)	Percent from state government	Total (mil dol)	Total	Property	Sales and gross receipts	Total (mil dol)	Total	Capital outlays
	117	118	119	120	121	122	123	124	125	126

City	117	118	119	120	121	122	123	124	125	126
TENNESSEE—Cont'd										
Columbia	41.4	15.4	53.0	12.6	360	269	88	40.7	1,166	252
Cookeville	277.1	19.0	22.5	9.4	303	201	101	277.4	8,954	919
Franklin	87.6	39.1	37.2	24.4	368	176	192	85.2	1,285	230
Gallatin	34.4	11.7	42.9	11.9	376	302	74	33.1	1,045	154
Germantown	61.8	21.1	73.1	24.7	627	570	58	65.4	1,661	429
Hendersonville	35.8	16.0	45.5	13.8	260	194	66	34.8	655	51
Jackson	87.7	28.3	31.7	40.9	609	491	118	83.5	1,243	137
Johnson City	163.0	78.4	55.6	47.4	732	608	124	167.9	2,594	204
Kingsport	166.0	83.1	48.9	57.0	1,080	915	166	164.5	3,118	644
Knoxville	351.6	81.3	38.7	163.6	898	585	313	318.2	1,747	425
La Vergne	25.4	7.8	50.3	10.3	306	225	80	18.7	553	55
Lebanon	28.1	13.4	31.2	6.1	218	112	106	31.0	1,113	106
Maryville	74.6	37.7	68.6	28.4	1,027	932	95	71.2	2,571	85
Memphis	2,270.7	1,329.3	61.2	520.3	789	551	237	2,276.9	3,451	425
Morristown	51.1	16.0	22.3	12.8	440	314	127	46.1	1,582	230
Murfreesboro	157.1	75.8	58.2	48.0	422	310	112	168.1	1,476	135
Nashville-Davidson	2,398.7	624.4	98.0	1,220.6	1,952	1,260	691	2,431.3	3,888	403
Oak Ridge	134.1	83.4	33.6	34.7	1,182	710	463	107.5	3,666	210
Smyrna	53.2	16.9	24.7	11.2	269	186	83	50.3	1,205	109
Spring Hill	19.8	7.0	49.1	5.7	182	127	55	26.7	857	343
TEXAS	X	X	X	X	X	X	X	X	X	X
Abilene	137.0	15.0	30.9	83.5	697	279	418	116.5	972	130
Allen	117.2	4.4	12.3	78.6	873	457	416	125.1	1,390	272
Amarillo	243.2	33.1	39.3	120.2	614	172	442	262.0	1,339	339
Arlington	460.5	35.2	25.8	242.5	644	301	343	480.0	1,275	145
Austin	1,410.8	92.8	27.1	613.6	709	410	298	1,511.5	1,746	382
Baytown	105.9	8.6	14.0	43.5	589	251	339	126.1	1,710	339
Beaumont	168.9	28.1	23.8	91.4	782	377	405	178.4	1,526	395
Bedford	41.1	0.8	100.0	27.1	562	290	272	42.9	889	121
Big Spring	26.6	1.5	86.7	14.4	521	200	321	29.9	1,081	134
Brownsville	224.1	50.4	11.0	74.7	415	197	218	175.9	976	181
Bryan	85.5	6.5	55.6	40.7	522	297	225	96.3	1,235	236
Burleson	54.3	0.2	84.0	35.0	897	409	488	43.5	1,115	101
Carrollton	128.2	6.2	86.1	88.8	708	435	273	119.3	951	184
Cedar Hill	54.5	2.8	12.5	34.8	748	403	345	54.1	1,163	158
Cedar Park	71.9	5.6	100.0	42.4	732	349	383	67.0	1,156	349
Cleburne	51.2	3.4	11.5	26.3	884	463	421	43.9	1,472	106
College Station	94.1	3.3	25.7	53.8	549	255	294	101.4	1,036	172
Conroe	70.6	1.0	16.8	50.6	824	235	589	74.4	1,211	375
Coppell	72.0	0.3	100.0	58.2	1,451	828	624	65.6	1,638	306
Copperas Cove	25.8	0.6	100.0	14.2	425	258	167	73.0	2,187	1,475
Corpus Christi	357.9	29.6	42.3	191.7	614	280	333	389.3	1,246	290
Dallas	2,544.8	172.7	56.8	1,084.4	872	545	327	2,543.0	2,045	435
Deer Park	42.3	0.3	34.3	19.4	585	370	215	36.3	1,097	77
Del Rio	34.7	4.3	47.7	15.1	418	189	229	37.0	1,026	201
Denton	169.7	11.5	79.7	94.5	765	357	408	149.1	1,207	175
DeSoto	50.0	1.3	100.0	32.7	640	413	227	48.8	954	113
Duncanville	37.1	1.0	60.3	22.7	573	320	253	42.9	1,085	220
Eagle Pass	32.1	2.3	62.3	10.6	387	159	228	32.6	1,184	237
Edinburg	72.5	6.4	81.8	40.8	518	269	249	71.1	903	197
El Paso	743.5	92.0	24.8	386.6	572	287	285	621.6	920	181
Euless	66.2	1.7	13.5	42.6	806	223	583	61.4	1,162	109
Farmers Branch	55.4	0.8	73.5	41.0	1,395	732	663	53.3	1,813	185
Flower Mound	74.2	2.2	6.5	54.3	800	457	343	76.4	1,125	247
Fort Worth	1,108.5	81.2	53.9	609.6	783	466	317	1,116.7	1,434	341
Friendswood	32.1	3.1	8.8	20.8	562	394	168	35.6	963	285
Frisco	214.9	32.8	2.5	125.6	977	507	469	202.2	1,572	466
Galveston	180.4	62.3	54.6	58.9	1,217	502	716	182.3	3,769	1,529
Garland	228.5	19.9	12.3	106.8	457	312	145	234.9	1,004	127
Georgetown	65.1	3.9	87.5	35.5	675	289	386	70.7	1,345	298
Grand Prairie	252.2	40.5	30.9	131.5	723	393	330	217.4	1,195	147
Grapevine	125.9	3.7	100.0	94.8	1,953	609	1,344	92.9	1,916	312
Greenville	39.6	2.4	41.3	19.8	762	371	392	43.8	1,690	468
Haltom City	42.3	2.2	23.7	24.5	565	230	336	38.1	878	131
Harker Heights	24.0	0.5	27.3	15.5	558	324	234	26.5	951	239
Harlingen	87.2	13.1	29.3	40.5	615	250	365	112.2	1,703	650
Houston	3,667.9	315.0	27.9	1,921.4	888	474	414	3,697.9	1,708	274
Huntsville	32.1	1.0	50.9	14.9	376	122	253	30.5	766	52
Hurst	51.1	2.4	26.0	34.8	911	328	583	49.1	1,285	225

1. Based on population estimated as of July 1 of the year shown.

Table D. Cities — **City Government Finances**

City	City government finances, 2012 (cont.)									
	General expenditure (cont.)									
	Percent of total for:									
	Public welfare	Highways	Parking facilities	Education	Health and hospitals	Police protection	Sewerage and sanitation	Parks and recreation	Housing and community development	Interest on debt
	127	128	129	130	131	132	133	134	135	136
TENNESSEE—Cont'd										
Columbia	0.0	10.7	0.0	0.0	0.0	16.5	23.4	4.1	0.0	2.9
Cookeville	0.0	1.2	0.0	0.0	84.6	2.6	1.6	1.0	0.0	1.2
Franklin	0.0	10.0	0.0	0.0	0.0	16.6	17.5	4.0	0.2	6.0
Gallatin	0.0	5.6	0.0	0.0	0.4	19.4	17.8	11.9	0.0	1.4
Germantown	0.0	27.4	0.0	0.0	0.5	17.1	10.4	14.4	2.9	1.4
Hendersonville	0.0	12.3	0.0	0.0	0.0	27.4	13.2	7.3	0.0	1.2
Jackson	0.0	14.0	0.0	0.0	0.2	25.1	12.3	11.3	3.2	3.2
Johnson City	0.5	5.3	0.0	40.8	0.0	8.8	12.9	8.4	0.3	4.0
Kingsport	0.0	3.2	0.0	40.7	0.0	7.2	9.4	4.1	0.3	3.0
Knoxville	0.0	3.1	0.3	0.0	0.0	15.7	31.2	5.9	3.8	8.0
La Vergne	0.7	9.0	0.0	0.0	0.1	30.0	21.7	6.8	0.0	2.9
Lebanon	0.0	8.4	0.0	0.0	0.0	25.7	25.8	7.6	0.0	1.0
Maryville	0.0	3.8	0.0	66.8	0.3	6.3	5.5	2.0	0.0	3.6
Memphis	0.0	1.2	0.0	52.3	0.0	9.9	4.8	1.6	6.4	4.4
Morristown	0.6	10.0	0.0	0.0	0.0	15.5	27.8	3.8	1.6	1.5
Murfreesboro	0.1	11.1	0.1	38.8	0.0	13.6	8.2	6.7	0.8	2.6
Nashville-Davidson	1.3	1.6	0.0	34.8	9.5	8.0	6.5	3.3	0.0	7.0
Oak Ridge	0.0	2.3	0.0	52.8	0.0	6.5	10.1	3.7	0.6	3.4
Smyrna	0.5	5.1	0.0	0.0	0.0	18.7	11.2	12.4	0.3	2.6
Spring Hill	0.0	9.8	0.0	0.0	0.0	14.6	51.6	2.8	0.0	0.9
TEXAS	X	X	X	X	X	X	X	X	X	X
Abilene	0.0	7.3	0.0	0.0	3.8	18.8	16.3	6.3	1.0	2.9
Allen	0.0	4.2	0.0	0.0	0.2	15.6	11.7	22.6	1.0	5.9
Amarillo	0.0	6.1	0.0	0.0	6.0	13.9	17.9	6.7	4.4	2.1
Arlington	0.1	9.3	0.0	0.0	0.9	17.6	13.8	7.7	1.1	26.6
Austin	0.0	7.5	0.0	0.0	6.9	17.8	18.1	8.2	3.3	5.9
Baytown	0.0	9.2	0.0	0.0	3.4	15.7	9.1	9.2	2.3	5.4
Beaumont	0.0	21.9	0.0	0.0	5.1	21.4	8.4	9.5	1.2	4.0
Bedford	0.0	4.8	0.0	0.0	0.8	24.7	12.9	6.3	0.0	5.0
Big Spring	0.0	5.1	0.0	0.0	7.7	15.7	16.2	15.7	0.0	2.1
Brownsville	1.3	7.1	0.3	0.0	1.0	18.2	22.3	5.7	1.0	5.9
Bryan	0.0	9.9	0.0	0.0	0.0	16.0	19.2	3.8	1.3	6.5
Burleson	0.0	9.7	0.0	0.0	1.7	16.8	16.6	12.8	0.0	9.0
Carrollton	0.0	12.5	0.0	0.0	2.0	17.5	10.3	7.8	2.6	6.3
Cedar Hill	0.1	6.3	0.0	0.0	0.3	19.0	15.2	8.6	0.0	7.0
Cedar Park	0.0	19.4	0.0	0.0	0.4	11.4	13.6	7.0	0.0	10.8
Cleburne	0.0	5.5	0.0	0.0	1.7	16.6	19.7	9.4	3.6	4.0
College Station	0.0	15.6	1.2	0.0	0.0	13.7	18.3	9.5	1.4	5.1
Conroe	0.0	11.1	0.0	0.0	0.0	18.9	12.0	15.3	0.4	6.4
Coppell	0.0	7.8	0.0	0.0	0.5	14.6	6.7	17.0	0.0	5.6
Copperas Cove	0.0	63.3	0.0	0.0	0.5	6.3	7.5	2.6	0.0	4.4
Corpus Christi	0.0	10.6	0.1	0.0	1.8	18.9	23.2	9.8	3.9	3.6
Dallas	0.7	5.5	0.0	0.0	1.0	14.0	11.3	7.1	1.9	16.7
Deer Park	0.0	3.7	0.0	0.0	0.6	17.6	14.8	15.5	0.0	4.5
Del Rio	3.2	16.9	0.0	0.0	1.4	17.0	15.7	4.1	0.0	4.6
Denton	0.0	8.4	0.0	0.0	0.6	14.7	25.1	9.1	1.2	4.9
DeSoto	0.0	7.2	0.0	0.0	1.1	16.2	19.1	6.8	0.0	10.7
Duncanville	0.0	7.7	0.0	0.0	0.7	17.1	17.5	22.4	0.0	2.2
Eagle Pass	0.0	20.2	0.0	0.0	0.2	16.0	19.6	9.2	0.0	4.5
Edinburg	0.0	4.6	0.0	0.0	2.0	17.8	26.4	14.6	1.5	3.2
El Paso	0.4	3.1	0.0	0.0	3.3	18.8	16.2	4.6	2.2	8.5
Euless	0.0	6.2	0.0	0.0	0.5	16.4	4.4	12.4	0.1	3.2
Farmers Branch	0.0	11.0	0.0	0.0	1.5	20.8	10.8	13.5	0.0	2.3
Flower Mound	0.2	27.9	0.0	0.0	1.1	16.1	10.1	9.8	0.1	4.3
Fort Worth	0.0	9.2	0.3	0.0	1.3	21.0	19.0	7.6	3.1	5.7
Friendswood	0.0	4.5	0.0	0.0	3.2	21.8	12.3	5.4	1.7	2.4
Frisco	0.0	14.8	0.0	4.9	0.6	9.4	9.2	9.5	0.2	12.3
Galveston	0.0	12.7	0.0	0.0	0.3	9.8	11.8	9.1	14.0	5.5
Garland	0.0	6.6	0.0	0.0	1.3	19.5	18.2	8.0	6.9	6.4
Georgetown	0.0	19.8	0.0	0.0	0.9	12.7	17.5	8.6	0.0	5.3
Grand Prairie	0.0	8.1	0.0	0.0	0.7	16.1	13.9	10.7	14.8	6.4
Grapevine	0.0	8.5	0.0	0.0	0.0	14.9	6.7	16.5	0.0	4.9
Greenville	0.0	8.7	0.0	0.0	0.0	15.0	24.1	3.8	3.9	3.5
Haltom City	0.0	7.6	0.0	0.0	0.9	19.6	15.2	2.7	0.0	5.1
Harker Heights	0.0	3.6	0.0	0.0	0.0	18.2	17.1	6.8	0.0	4.4
Harlingen	0.0	5.5	0.0	0.0	0.6	11.9	13.7	4.7	0.7	3.1
Houston	0.0	10.0	0.2	0.0	3.0	16.1	6.5	2.7	2.5	13.3
Huntsville	0.0	8.0	0.0	0.0	1.5	17.2	34.7	4.6	0.0	4.1
Hurst	0.0	11.9	0.0	0.0	2.5	22.9	10.3	15.1	0.0	3.7

City Government Finances, City Government Employment, and Climate

City	Debt outstanding Total (mil dol)	Debt outstanding Per capita[1] (dollars)	Debt issued during year	Mean January	Mean July	Limits January[3]	Limits July[4]	Annual precipitation (inches)	Heating degree days	Cooling degree days
	137	138	139	140	141	142	143	144	145	146
TENNESSEE—Cont'd										
Columbia	73.5	2,105	17.0	35.6	77.2	25.0	88.5	56.13	4,183	1,267
Cookeville	143.9	4,643	5.1	NA	NA	NA	NA	NA	NA	NA
Franklin	172.8	2,606	19.4	35.1	77.4	25.2	88.9	54.33	4,199	1,294
Gallatin	47.2	1,492	8.7	NA	NA	NA	NA	NA	NA	NA
Germantown	32.1	815	6.0	37.9	81.1	28.2	91.1	53.63	3,491	1,838
Hendersonville	11.8	222	0.3	36.8	79.1	27.9	88.7	48.11	3,677	1,652
Jackson	119.1	1,772	10.0	37.1	79.6	28.2	89.4	54.86	3,649	1,648
Johnson City	422.8	6,531	15.0	34.2	74.2	24.3	84.8	41.33	4,445	956
Kingsport	225.1	4,268	41.5	35.6	76.2	26.2	86.9	44.44	4,178	1,139
Knoxville	920.7	5,055	198.0	38.5	78.7	30.3	88.2	48.22	3,531	1,527
La Vergne	25.9	769	1.0	NA	NA	NA	NA	NA	NA	NA
Lebanon	61.0	2,191	5.9	NA	NA	NA	NA	NA	NA	NA
Maryville	130.5	4,709	0.0	NA	NA	NA	NA	NA	NA	NA
Memphis	2,500.9	3,791	107.2	39.9	82.5	31.3	92.1	54.65	3,041	2,187
Morristown	126.8	4,355	37.3	NA	NA	NA	NA	NA	NA	NA
Murfreesboro	318.3	2,795	1.6	35.4	78.1	25.3	89.1	54.98	4,107	1,388
Nashville-Davidson	4,895.0	7,828	800.3	36.8	79.1	27.9	88.7	48.11	3,677	1,652
Oak Ridge	170.4	5,812	11.1	36.6	77.3	27.2	88.1	55.05	3,993	1,301
Smyrna	71.6	1,717	2.4	36.8	79.1	27.9	88.7	48.11	3,677	1,652
Spring Hill	21.6	692	10.8	NA	NA	NA	NA	NA	NA	NA
TEXAS	X	X	X	X	X	X	X	X	X	X
Abilene	132.7	1,106	22.6	43.5	83.5	31.8	94.8	23.78	2,659	2,386
Allen	179.7	1,997	8.8	41.8	82.4	31.1	92.7	41.01	2,843	2,060
Amarillo	366.9	1,876	40.4	35.8	78.2	22.6	91.0	19.71	4,318	1,344
Arlington	2,154.5	5,724	564.5	44.1	85.0	34.0	95.4	34.73	2,370	2,568
Austin	5,572.8	6,438	681.1	50.2	84.2	40.0	95.0	33.65	1,648	2,974
Baytown	189.8	2,575	22.4	51.6	83.6	41.9	91.6	53.75	1,471	2,841
Beaumont	353.3	3,022	53.2	51.1	83.1	41.1	92.7	57.38	1,548	2,734
Bedford	61.2	1,268	14.8	44.1	85.0	34.0	95.4	34.73	2,370	2,568
Big Spring	23.3	843	0.0	42.7	82.7	29.6	94.3	20.12	2,724	2,243
Brownsville	528.4	2,931	23.6	59.6	83.9	50.5	92.4	27.55	644	3,874
Bryan	362.9	4,655	34.6	50.2	84.6	39.8	95.6	39.67	1,616	2,938
Burleson	130.3	3,340	17.8	NA	NA	NA	NA	NA	NA	NA
Carrollton	168.5	1,343	0.0	44.1	85.0	34.0	95.4	34.73	2,370	2,568
Cedar Hill	156.9	3,375	18.0	43.7	84.3	33.2	94.9	34.54	2,437	2,508
Cedar Park	214.5	3,700	8.4	47.2	83.8	35.1	95.7	36.42	1,998	2,584
Cleburne	132.4	4,443	26.5	45.9	84.5	34.0	97.0	36.25	2,158	2,604
College Station	242.2	2,475	47.0	50.2	84.6	39.8	95.6	39.67	1,616	2,938
Conroe	196.2	3,194	37.9	50.3	83.7	40.0	94.3	49.32	1,647	2,793
Coppell	93.5	2,332	21.3	44.1	85.0	34.0	95.4	34.73	2,370	2,568
Copperas Cove	98.1	2,937	52.5	46.0	83.5	34.0	95.3	32.88	2,190	2,477
Corpus Christi	1,152.6	3,689	80.5	56.1	83.8	46.2	93.2	32.26	950	3,497
Dallas	7,943.6	6,389	1,246.4	45.9	86.5	36.4	96.1	37.05	2,219	2,878
Deer Park	44.9	1,359	0.0	54.3	84.5	45.2	93.6	53.96	1,174	3,179
Del Rio	64.8	1,795	0.1	51.3	85.3	39.7	96.2	18.80	1,417	3,226
Denton	501.7	4,062	45.1	42.7	83.6	32.0	94.1	37.79	2,650	2,269
DeSoto	130.8	2,556	20.2	46.0	84.6	35.0	96.0	38.81	2,130	2,608
Duncanville	19.1	483	6.9	45.9	86.5	36.4	96.1	37.05	2,219	2,878
Eagle Pass	61.2	2,224	14.7	NA	NA	NA	NA	NA	NA	NA
Edinburg	98.1	1,246	24.2	58.7	85.1	48.2	95.5	22.61	719	3,898
El Paso	1,534.1	2,270	166.5	45.1	83.3	32.9	94.5	9.43	2,543	2,254
Euless	51.8	980	9.6	44.1	85.0	34.0	95.4	34.73	2,370	2,568
Farmers Branch	24.3	827	0.0	45.9	86.5	36.4	96.1	37.05	2,219	2,878
Flower Mound	129.5	1,908	3.6	44.1	85.0	34.0	95.4	34.73	2,370	2,568
Fort Worth	2,401.8	3,084	394.8	43.3	84.5	31.4	96.6	34.01	2,509	2,466
Friendswood	66.6	1,804	17.5	54.3	84.5	45.2	93.6	53.96	1,174	3,179
Frisco	640.8	4,982	148.2	41.8	82.4	31.1	92.7	41.01	2,843	2,060
Galveston	316.3	6,539	9.9	55.8	84.3	49.7	88.7	43.84	1,008	3,268
Garland	905.7	3,873	152.4	45.9	86.5	36.4	96.1	37.05	2,219	2,878
Georgetown	168.4	3,205	21.7	47.2	83.8	35.1	95.7	36.42	1,998	2,584
Grand Prairie	447.1	2,458	34.9	44.1	85.0	34.0	95.4	34.73	2,370	2,568
Grapevine	142.7	2,942	0.0	42.4	84.0	30.8	95.5	34.66	2,649	2,340
Greenville	148.3	5,723	11.5	NA	NA	NA	NA	NA	NA	NA
Haltom City	60.4	1,392	15.4	43.0	84.1	31.4	95.7	34.12	2,608	2,358
Harker Heights	50.6	1,819	8.0	NA	NA	NA	NA	NA	NA	NA
Harlingen	118.7	1,803	50.3	58.6	84.4	48.4	94.5	28.13	737	3,736
Houston	13,983.7	6,459	2,478.6	54.3	84.5	45.2	93.6	53.96	1,174	3,179
Huntsville	38.9	977	5.0	48.5	83.2	39.0	93.8	48.51	1,835	2,600
Hurst	57.6	1,508	9.1	44.1	85.0	34.0	95.4	34.73	2,370	2,568

1. Based on the population estimated as of July 1 of the year shown.   2. Represents normal values based on the 30-year period, 1971±2000.   3. Average daily minimum.   4. Average daily maximum.

Table D. Cities — **Land Area and Population**

STATE Place code	City	Land area[1] (sq. mi)	Total persons 2018	Rank	Per square mile	White	Black or African American	American Indian, Alaskan Native	Asian	Hawaiian Pacific Islander	Some other race	Two or more races (percent)
			Population, 2018			**Race 2017** — Race alone[2] (percent)						
		1	2	3	4	5	6	7	8	9	10	11
	TEXAS— Cont'd											
48 37,000	Irving	67.1	242,242	94	3,610.2	47.4	14.9	0.7	18.8	0.0	15.6	2.6
48 38,632	Keller	18.5	47,350	821	2,559.5	NA	NA	NA	NA	NA	NA	NA
48 39,148	Killeen	54.5	149,103	174	2,735.8	43.7	37.5	1.0	5.4	1.4	4.0	6.9
48 39,352	Kingsville	13.8	25,487	1,402	1,846.9	89.2	2.5	0.0	4.2	0.0	2.5	1.6
48 39,952	Kyle	30.2	46,874	829	1,552.1	82.7	8.0	0.9	1.3	0.0	4.4	2.7
48 40,588	Lake Jackson	19.7	27,533	1,335	1,397.6	NA	NA	NA	NA	NA	NA	NA
48 41,212	Lancaster	33.2	39,477	979	1,189.1	NA	NA	NA	NA	NA	NA	NA
48 41,440	La Porte	18.6	35,423	1,086	1,904.5	75.6	13.8	0.2	0.8	0.0	5.6	4.1
48 41,464	Laredo	104.2	261,639	80	2,510.9	95.9	0.2	0.2	0.6	0.0	2.7	0.3
48 41,980	League City	51.3	106,244	290	2,071.0	81.6	8.6	0.2	7.3	0.0	0.6	1.7
48 42,016	Leander	36.6	56,111	677	1,533.1	85.2	4.8	0.0	3.0	0.0	3.5	3.5
48 42,508	Lewisville	36.7	106,586	287	2,904.3	62.7	17.1	0.7	12.1	0.1	3.7	3.6
48 43,012	Little Elm	17.9	50,314	765	2,810.8	68.9	14.7	0.5	7.7	0.0	2.1	6.2
48 43,888	Longview	55.7	81,647	420	1,465.8	71.6	23.1	0.0	1.6	0.5	1.7	1.6
48 45,000	Lubbock	127.8	255,885	84	2,002.2	81.8	8.5	0.8	2.8	0.1	3.8	2.3
48 45,072	Lufkin	34.2	35,510	1,084	1,038.3	68.3	24.7	0.5	2.9	0.0	3.0	0.5
48 45,384	McAllen	65.7	143,433	183	2,183.2	76.1	0.7	0.5	2.4	0.3	19.3	0.7
48 45,744	McKinney	66.9	191,645	130	2,864.6	74.6	12.4	0.5	8.8	0.0	1.5	2.2
48 46,452	Mansfield	36.6	70,981	506	1,939.4	72.3	18.3	0.1	2.8	0.0	2.6	4.0
48 47,892	Mesquite	47.3	142,816	184	3,019.4	67.2	22.7	0.3	2.9	0.0	3.2	3.7
48 48,072	Midland	74.4	142,344	186	1,913.2	82.6	8.3	0.3	2.5	0.0	5.4	0.9
48 48,768	Mission	35.5	84,827	398	2,389.5	86.9	0.1	0.0	1.7	0.0	10.2	1.1
48 48,804	Missouri City	29.0	74,705	473	2,576.0	30.3	37.0	0.0	26.7	0.0	4.2	1.8
48 50,256	Nacogdoches	27.6	33,542	1,141	1,215.3	69.9	25.2	0.9	1.8	0.0	0.6	1.6
48 50,820	New Braunfels	45.0	84,612	401	1,880.3	92.5	1.3	0.5	1.3	0.0	2.1	2.3
48 52,356	North Richland Hills	18.1	70,836	507	3,913.6	82.4	5.1	2.0	4.8	0.1	4.1	1.5
48 53,388	Odessa	45.2	120,568	235	2,667.4	73.0	5.6	0.4	1.8	0.2	14.9	4.1
48 55,080	Paris	35.2	24,839	1,417	705.7	NA	NA	NA	NA	NA	NA	NA
48 56,000	Pasadena	43.6	153,219	168	3,514.2	88.8	3.6	0.2	1.8	0.0	2.8	2.7
48 56,348	Pearland	48.2	122,149	229	2,534.2	63.6	19.0	0.8	11.3	0.0	2.5	2.8
48 57,176	Pflugerville	24.5	64,431	580	2,629.8	66.2	12.7	0.2	4.8	0.0	13.4	2.7
48 57,200	Pharr	23.6	79,707	435	3,377.4	NA	NA	NA	NA	NA	NA	NA
48 58,016	Plano	71.7	288,061	69	4,017.6	65.9	9.1	0.4	19.7	0.1	1.5	3.2
48 58,820	Port Arthur	76.9	55,018	693	715.4	45.1	39.2	1.0	10.3	0.1	2.8	1.4
48 61,796	Richardson	28.6	120,981	234	4,230.1	67.9	10.8	0.2	14.7	0.2	3.3	2.9
48 62,828	Rockwall	29.4	45,112	849	1,534.4	83.4	9.7	0.2	1.9	0.0	0.9	3.8
48 63,284	Rosenberg	36.9	38,061	1,013	1,031.5	71.6	17.4	0.0	2.9	0.0	7.3	0.8
48 63,500	Round Rock	36.1	128,739	216	3,566.2	71.2	12.3	0.1	8.0	0.0	4.5	3.8
48 63,572	Rowlett	20.9	66,285	555	3,171.5	70.3	18.3	0.6	5.7	0.0	1.0	4.1
48 64,472	San Angelo	60.0	100,215	307	1,670.3	77.2	5.5	0.4	1.4	0.1	13.4	2.1
48 65,000	San Antonio	484.6	1,532,233	7	3,161.9	79.8	7.0	0.4	2.6	0.1	7.0	3.1
48 65,516	San Juan	11.6	37,154	1,035	3,202.9	NA	NA	NA	NA	NA	NA	NA
48 65,600	San Marcos	34.0	63,509	587	1,867.9	85.2	5.6	0.1	2.7	0.2	3.0	3.3
48 66,128	Schertz	32.0	41,057	933	1,283.0	62.8	17.6	0.0	4.3	0.6	11.2	3.5
48 66,644	Seguin	37.0	29,700	1,264	802.7	55.1	10.7	0.3	1.6	0.0	30.7	1.7
48 67,496	Sherman	44.0	42,462	899	965.0	84.4	6.4	1.2	3.3	0.0	1.1	3.6
48 68,636	Socorro	21.9	34,533	1,104	1,576.8	49.5	0.0	2.1	0.8	0.0	46.2	1.4
48 69,032	Southlake	21.8	32,269	1,177	1,480.2	NA	NA	NA	NA	NA	NA	NA
48 70,808	Sugar Land	40.5	118,600	238	2,928.4	50.4	3.1	0.2	43.2	0.0	1.4	1.6
48 72,176	Temple	70.3	76,256	459	1,084.7	80.7	14.1	0.3	1.0	0.0	2.8	1.2
48 72,368	Texarkana	29.1	37,295	1,028	1,281.6	59.6	35.5	1.8	1.4	0.0	0.4	1.2
48 72,392	Texas City	64.3	49,153	785	764.4	27.4	0.1	0.6	0.5	1.1	6.3	
48 72,530	The Colony	14.0	43,402	879	3,100.1	75.0	9.2	0.0	9.7	0.1	2.3	3.6
48 74,144	Tyler	56.6	105,729	291	1,868.0	68.4	25.8	0.2	2.0	0.0	1.9	1.7
48 75,428	Victoria	37.2	67,015	543	1,801.5	85.6	8.1	0.8	0.6	0.0	2.7	2.2
48 76,000	Waco	89.0	138,183	197	1,552.6	68.6	20.9	1.0	2.6	0.0	4.8	2.2
48 76,816	Waxahachie	48.8	36,807	1,041	754.2	79.5	11.8	0.5	0.6	0.0	2.4	5.2
48 76,864	Weatherford	27.1	31,836	1,193	1,174.8	NA	NA	NA	NA	NA	NA	NA
48 77,272	Weslaco	17.6	41,171	929	2,339.3	NA	NA	NA	NA	NA	NA	NA
48 79,000	Wichita Falls	72.0	104,576	295	1,452.4	71.3	12.5	1.2	2.0	0.1	8.9	3.9
48 80,356	Wylie	22.1	51,585	746	2,334.2	70.0	10.9	0.7	8.5	0.0	6.4	3.5
49 00,000	**UTAH**	82,195.8	3,161,105	X	38.5	85.7	1.2	1.1	2.4	0.9	5.8	3.0
49 01,310	American Fork	10.7	32,519	1,167	3,039.2	NA	NA	NA	NA	NA	NA	NA
49 07,690	Bountiful	13.2	44,098	870	3,340.8	92.8	0.2	0.9	0.9	0.0	2.9	2.2
49 11,320	Cedar City	35.9	33,055	1,154	920.8	87.9	0.4	4.2	0.4	0.0	3.6	3.5
49 13,850	Clearfield	7.7	31,967	1,189	4,151.6	86.3	1.8	0.1	2.1	0.4	2.8	6.5
49 16,270	Cottonwood Heights	9.2	34,117	1,119	3,708.4	94.3	0.0	0.1	1.7	0.0	0.8	3.1
49 20,120	Draper	30.1	48,319	800	1,605.3	91.9	1.0	0.6	3.3	0.8	0.6	1.9
49 36,070	Holladay	8.5	30,697	1,227	3,611.4	NA	NA	NA	NA	NA	NA	NA

1. Dry land or land partially or temporarily covered by water.   2. Hispanic or Latino persons may be of any race.

Table D. Cities — **Population**

City	Percent Hispanic or Latino[1], 2017	Percent foreign born, 2017	Age of population (percent), 2017							Median age, 2017	Percent female, 2017	Population			
			Under 18 years	18 to 24 years	25 to 34 years	35 to 44 years	45 to 54 years	55 to 64 years	65 years and over			Census counts		Percent change	
												2000	2010	2000-2010	2001-2018
	12	13	14	15	16	17	18	19	20	21	22	23	24	25	26
TEXAS— Cont'd															
Irving	43.6	36.0	28.2	8.2	18.2	17.2	12.1	8.9	7.1	32.1	49.2	191,615	216,285	12.9	12.0
Keller	9.7	9.7	28.4	7.5	9.0	11.9	16.9	14.1	12.3	39.4	52.1	27,345	39,632	44.9	19.5
Killeen	27.8	9.1	29.4	12.3	19.8	14.4	9.2	8.1	6.8	28.7	51.7	86,911	127,696	46.9	16.8
Kingsville	78.4	8.1	24.3	20.0	10.3	14.6	8.1	9.1	13.7	28.2	51.1	25,575	26,213	2.5	-2.8
Kyle	41.1	5.2	30.2	4.7	15.7	19.9	10.8	11.0	7.6	34.8	49.1	5,314	28,256	431.7	65.9
Lake Jackson	27.8	6.7	28.8	7.5	14.2	12.6	9.7	11.3	15.9	34.8	49.4	26,386	26,832	1.7	2.6
Lancaster	20.2	8.5	30.3	6.2	14.5	14.0	8.7	14.4	11.8	34.5	51.3	25,894	36,664	41.6	7.7
La Porte	34.5	7.8	20.2	8.5	15.0	12.1	15.1	14.6	14.5	41.4	52.9	31,880	33,806	6.0	4.8
Laredo	95.3	27.5	33.3	11.2	13.4	13.0	11.5	8.4	9.3	28.8	51.2	176,576	235,809	33.5	11.0
League City	15.2	8.9	32.0	6.3	13.9	16.7	13.3	8.5	9.3	33.6	51.7	45,444	83,563	83.9	27.1
Leander	24.2	9.7	29.1	7.1	15.6	16.6	13.5	9.8	8.3	33.8	52.1	7,596	27,271	259.0	105.8
Lewisville	31.3	24.8	23.0	8.4	24.2	14.7	12.8	8.8	8.1	32.7	50.7	77,737	95,458	22.8	11.7
Little Elm	22.1	20.9	30.3	9.5	9.5	28.4	11.5	5.7	5.0	35.7	48.9	3,646	25,906	610.5	94.2
Longview	20.1	9.7	26.2	10.4	14.5	12.7	11.8	9.9	14.6	34.4	50.7	73,344	80,423	9.7	1.5
Lubbock	36.0	6.7	22.8	18.5	15.5	11.0	9.6	10.6	12.1	30.0	51.4	199,564	229,632	15.1	11.4
Lufkin	29.9	11.6	23.8	13.0	13.2	9.7	10.3	11.5	18.5	35.0	53.3	32,709	35,115	7.4	1.1
McAllen	85.3	29.4	26.6	8.8	12.7	14.6	12.3	11.3	13.8	35.9	48.3	106,414	131,559	23.6	9.0
McKinney	17.3	17.6	30.7	8.1	9.6	18.3	14.8	8.6	9.9	35.9	52.4	54,369	131,160	141.2	46.1
Mansfield	19.0	8.6	28.1	10.5	9.0	14.8	14.8	12.6	10.1	36.9	50.9	28,031	56,415	101.3	25.8
Mesquite	43.6	20.5	31.3	10.1	12.3	12.7	14.9	8.8	9.9	32.5	51.1	124,523	139,593	12.1	2.3
Midland	43.7	15.4	27.3	9.1	17.1	13.5	10.6	11.1	11.3	32.5	48.6	94,996	111,190	17.0	28.0
Mission	88.3	31.3	29.1	13.0	10.3	10.4	10.6	11.1	15.4	31.7	52.9	45,408	77,690	71.1	9.2
Missouri City	17.6	29.2	25.6	6.1	12.5	13.3	11.9	14.9	15.6	39.3	51.7	52,913	66,531	25.7	12.3
Nacogdoches	16.8	7.6	17.1	28.9	12.9	8.7	7.9	9.2	15.3	26.6	53.8	29,914	32,910	10.0	1.9
New Braunfels	32.5	5.5	28.1	6.0	16.0	14.5	9.1	11.3	14.9	34.9	50.7	36,494	57,677	58.0	46.7
North Richland Hills	17.9	10.1	21.8	8.3	12.4	11.5	16.1	12.9	17.0	41.7	51.1	55,635	63,338	13.8	11.8
Odessa	56.8	13.3	28.8	11.3	18.0	11.9	11.1	9.1	9.9	30.2	51.6	90,943	99,876	9.8	20.7
Paris	9.7	0.7	20.9	10.7	13.0	10.1	12.3	11.8	21.1	39.2	56.5	25,898	25,255	-2.5	-1.6
Pasadena	71.3	26.7	31.3	9.8	14.2	13.1	12.2	10.3	9.1	30.7	47.9	141,674	149,307	5.4	2.6
Pearland	24.3	16.7	28.1	7.3	15.2	15.7	12.5	10.9	10.4	34.7	51.0	37,640	93,128	147.4	31.2
Pflugerville	28.7	17.2	23.4	3.9	16.9	14.1	19.1	11.2	11.2	39.3	53.8	16,335	48,366	196.1	33.2
Pharr	95.0	28.7	32.9	11.8	11.1	13.2	10.8	7.7	12.5	29.7	48.5	46,660	70,467	51.0	13.1
Plano	14.7	25.8	21.9	7.6	14.6	14.9	13.6	14.4	13.1	38.9	50.3	222,030	259,857	17.0	10.9
Port Arthur	29.3	22.4	24.2	8.0	14.4	12.1	12.4	14.5	14.5	37.3	51.9	57,755	54,376	-5.9	1.2
Richardson	18.6	25.7	23.6	10.7	13.3	14.1	11.6	10.2	16.4	36.5	51.3	91,802	99,251	8.1	21.9
Rockwall	15.8	11.0	23.5	12.1	10.3	13.7	14.4	11.3	14.8	37.4	49.7	17,976	37,566	109.0	20.1
Rosenberg	63.4	16.4	31.1	9.0	15.6	12.5	11.7	10.0	10.0	31.0	50.3	24,043	31,577	31.3	20.5
Round Rock	29.0	16.2	26.8	11.5	13.7	16.1	14.3	9.4	8.2	33.7	50.1	61,136	100,010	63.6	28.7
Rowlett	14.2	13.4	23.8	4.9	10.6	12.1	21.2	15.7	11.7	43.8	50.7	44,503	56,224	26.4	17.9
San Angelo	44.4	5.6	22.2	11.5	17.7	11.5	9.5	11.7	15.8	34.0	51.6	88,439	93,221	5.4	7.5
San Antonio	64.1	14.0	24.8	10.7	16.3	13.1	12.1	10.7	12.2	33.6	50.7	1,144,646	1,326,768	15.9	15.5
San Juan	98.4	22.9	34.5	11.4	12.5	14.9	11.3	7.3	8.1	27.5	53.5	26,229	33,979	29.5	9.3
San Marcos	43.5	6.7	12.6	41.7	19.1	7.4	6.9	4.4	7.9	23.0	50.0	34,733	45,143	30.0	40.7
Schertz	27.8	6.8	24.2	6.8	11.3	14.2	16.9	13.1	13.4	40.6	49.8	18,694	31,797	70.1	29.1
Seguin	53.4	8.5	23.6	11.4	17.6	11.2	9.6	10.0	16.7	33.6	50.9	22,011	25,601	16.3	16.0
Sherman	26.2	15.3	27.9	11.6	13.5	16.1	11.6	9.3	9.9	32.2	50.0	35,082	38,349	9.3	10.7
Socorro	95.1	34.6	29.2	13.2	18.0	9.0	13.0	9.5	8.0	28.8	52.3	27,152	32,052	18.0	7.7
Southlake	3.0	13.7	35.2	3.3	5.4	15.6	18.1	15.4	7.1	40.9	48.7	21,519	26,573	23.5	21.4
Sugar Land	12.8	36.7	21.1	7.2	13.5	14.2	14.2	16.1	13.8	41.3	50.8	63,328	107,850	70.3	10.0
Temple	26.5	5.2	26.5	9.5	17.2	10.3	11.0	10.5	15.0	32.2	53.4	54,514	66,078	21.2	15.4
Texarkana	6.1	2.7	24.8	9.9	11.4	10.5	11.2	15.1	17.1	39.0	52.7	34,782	36,408	4.7	2.4
Texas City	35.6	11.9	19.3	9.6	14.3	11.8	13.4	15.1	16.4	40.1	53.7	41,521	45,089	8.6	9.0
The Colony	22.3	11.8	25.9	6.2	23.6	15.2	12.1	11.6	5.3	32.0	51.9	26,531	36,308	36.9	19.5
Tyler	21.9	11.4	24.4	13.2	12.8	11.6	10.9	10.6	16.6	34.8	53.1	83,650	96,887	15.8	9.1
Victoria	53.2	7.2	25.5	10.8	14.5	11.7	9.8	12.0	15.6	34.0	52.1	60,603	62,624	3.3	7.0
Waco	33.2	11.2	24.7	19.3	14.4	10.7	8.8	9.8	12.1	28.8	52.2	113,726	124,831	9.8	10.7
Waxahachie	22.7	7.2	22.6	10.5	17.4	8.3	14.6	12.3	14.2	34.7	50.3	21,426	29,538	37.9	24.6
Weatherford	11.2	4.4	21.0	9.3	14.0	11.6	12.5	11.2	20.3	40.8	53.5	19,000	25,788	35.7	23.5
Weslaco	91.0	17.5	33.2	13.6	14.0	10.5	11.1	7.0	10.6	26.5	50.0	26,935	36,774	36.5	12.0
Wichita Falls	21.9	7.9	21.9	16.5	15.0	11.5	10.0	11.2	14.0	32.8	48.3	104,197	104,682	0.5	-0.1
Wylie	16.5	14.4	31.3	8.4	13.0	15.2	17.0	9.0	6.2	32.6	53.2	15,132	41,677	175.4	23.8
UTAH	14.0	8.7	29.8	11.3	14.6	13.7	10.2	9.6	10.8	31.0	49.6	2,233,169	2,763,891	23.8	14.4
American Fork	14.3	8.2	37.1	8.4	13.9	13.0	8.8	7.8	11.1	29.0	51.0	21,941	26,543	21.0	22.5
Bountiful	6.6	7.3	30.2	6.1	15.8	12.2	8.5	10.1	16.9	33.4	50.4	41,301	42,574	3.1	3.6
Cedar City	9.6	3.2	30.4	18.5	13.9	13.2	6.5	8.4	9.0	25.7	49.7	20,527	28,867	40.6	14.5
Clearfield	22.3	9.5	34.2	8.4	20.7	13.6	7.6	7.4	8.2	28.5	51.0	25,974	29,927	15.2	6.8
Cottonwood Heights	3.7	4.6	19.7	6.8	18.5	13.2	13.2	12.1	16.4	38.3	51.9	27,569	33,585	21.8	1.6
Draper	4.9	5.9	32.5	6.5	13.5	15.0	16.3	9.4	6.8	33.8	49.8	25,220	42,272	67.6	14.3
Holladay	3.7	3.8	24.2	8.5	9.0	13.1	11.1	13.3	20.8	41.0	50.3	14,561	30,127	106.9	1.9

1. May be of any race.

Table D. Cities — Households, Group Quarters, Crime, and Education

City	Households, 2017							Persons in group quarters, 2017	Serious crimes known to police[2], 2016				Educational attainment, 2017		
				Percent					Total		Rate[3]			Attainment[4] (percent)	
	Number	Persons per household	Family	Married couple family	Female headed[1]	Non-family	One person		Number	Rate	Violent	Property	Population age 25 and over	High school graduate or less	Bachelor's degree or more
	27	28	29	30	31	32	33	34	35	36	37	38	39	40	41

TEXAS— Cont'd

City	Number	Persons per household	Family	Married couple family	Female headed	Non-family	One person	Group quarters	Number	Rate	Violent	Property	Pop 25+	HS or less	Bachelor's+
Irving	84,371	2.83	68.8	48.6	14.1	31.2	24.2	1,347	7,011	2,912	216	2,696	152,963	40.7	37.7
Keller	15,053	3.12	86.0	71.5	10.3	14.0	10.0	NA	295	627	64	563	30,303	18.2	55.4
Killeen	53,350	2.72	69.4	48.3	19.5	30.6	27.3	NA	4,942	3,450	695	2,755	84,829	32.6	20.7
Kingsville	9,385	2.66	64.3	43.4	8.2	35.7	29.4	1,719	984	3,752	248	3,504	14,881	59.8	14.2
Kyle	15,320	2.82	68.3	56.0	10.1	31.7	22.5	NA	689	1,842	206	1,636	28,307	26.5	38.7
Lake Jackson	9,958	2.75	66.9	55.5	6.3	33.1	28.8	NA	497	1,796	195	1,601	17,499	26.8	35.4
Lancaster	14,092	2.76	63.6	36.5	17.6	36.4	33.8	427	1,501	3,827	574	3,254	25,002	47.8	14.5
La Porte	12,017	2.94	73.8	57.6	9.8	26.2	21.0	NA	675	1,906	206	1,700	25,248	41.2	18.5
Laredo	70,522	3.67	80.1	50.5	22.7	19.9	17.8	3,169	8,830	3,405	362	3,043	145,480	59.6	17.5
League City	35,854	2.92	72.0	57.5	12.2	28.0	22.1	487	2,019	1,990	81	1,910	64,866	23.4	49.4
Leander	14,703	3.45	83.8	68.0	10.2	16.2	13.8	NA	501	1,232	113	1,119	32,344	29.8	33.5
Lewisville	39,357	2.70	63.2	42.6	16.1	36.8	25.8	472	2,811	2,658	208	2,450	73,154	32.1	36.6
Little Elm	13,782	3.38	85.0	71.7	7.2	15.0	12.7	NA	438	1,057	99	958	27,999	17.4	50.1
Longview	29,620	2.67	64.1	41.3	16.7	35.9	31.1	4,137	3,956	4,787	551	4,237	52,682	42.3	20.7
Lubbock	94,480	2.57	59.9	40.8	13.5	40.1	28.9	11,084	15,402	6,090	1,084	5,006	149,014	39.1	31.0
Lufkin	13,752	2.52	61.8	41.2	13.2	38.2	33.0	1,253	1,681	4,595	380	4,215	22,650	40.8	27.5
McAllen	46,598	3.04	74.7	52.5	16.5	25.3	20.3	1,222	4,685	3,294	151	3,143	92,287	44.7	31.5
McKinney	61,833	2.92	78.6	61.3	13.4	21.4	18.2	1,028	2,500	1,473	141	1,332	111,041	23.0	47.2
Mansfield	22,679	3.02	80.8	65.0	9.9	19.2	17.0	NA	844	1,281	102	1,179	42,330	25.7	38.7
Mesquite	44,948	3.18	74.3	48.5	17.3	25.7	22.3	693	6,137	4,210	414	3,796	84,322	51.9	17.2
Midland	48,729	2.76	69.9	55.2	11.8	30.1	26.3	1,779	3,764	2,732	299	2,433	86,474	42.4	29.7
Mission	25,857	3.26	84.4	55.9	22.1	15.6	14.4	NA	2,299	2,725	142	2,582	48,865	53.6	23.1
Missouri City	23,948	3.02	79.4	61.3	15.4	20.6	18.5	NA	1,407	1,861	190	1,670	49,495	27.0	47.6
Nacogdoches	12,013	2.34	51.0	33.1	11.6	49.0	39.1	5,489	988	2,899	349	2,550	18,151	40.3	27.4
New Braunfels	29,931	2.71	67.8	51.3	11.2	32.2	27.1	1,072	1,928	2,629	282	2,347	54,252	35.9	34.3
North Richland Hills	27,650	2.54	64.1	48.5	11.7	35.9	31.4	343	1,499	2,129	183	1,946	49,205	30.2	33.5
Odessa	39,400	2.94	66.6	39.9	18.2	33.4	29.0	1,180	5,114	4,151	808	3,342	70,206	48.6	17.4
Paris	9,699	2.48	51.0	36.4	11.8	49.0	42.5	761	1,159	4,691	684	4,007	16,940	44.9	13.2
Pasadena	47,532	3.21	71.2	48.4	15.3	28.8	25.1	1,131	4,699	3,039	447	2,592	90,416	60.8	12.5
Pearland	42,672	2.92	76.8	66.4	8.8	23.2	17.9	656	2,257	2,001	176	1,824	80,865	17.4	52.3
Pflugerville	20,376	3.09	76.9	68.3	5.3	23.1	16.7	NA	1,092	1,852	244	1,607	45,905	34.9	35.9
Pharr	22,897	3.47	82.4	51.3	24.6	17.6	16.2	NA	2,035	2,618	293	2,324	43,934	57.3	16.3
Plano	106,078	2.68	71.6	58.3	9.7	28.4	23.5	912	5,890	2,043	139	1,904	201,260	18.6	57.5
Port Arthur	21,843	2.51	58.7	38.8	16.0	41.3	35.5	639	2,191	3,947	652	3,295	37,637	60.5	11.2
Richardson	43,017	2.68	63.9	49.2	9.7	36.1	28.4	1,321	2,629	2,322	138	2,184	76,763	23.0	48.7
Rockwall	14,742	2.98	78.1	62.4	10.8	21.9	19.3	NA	849	1,950	92	1,858	28,485	23.4	43.3
Rosenberg	12,898	2.91	71.7	46.2	19.0	28.3	27.9	NA	725	1,994	294	1,700	22,547	43.7	25.6
Round Rock	38,368	3.21	76.8	62.2	10.3	23.2	19.0	550	2,826	2,369	145	2,224	76,273	27.1	44.9
Rowlett	21,703	2.81	84.0	72.3	9.4	16.0	13.6	292	1,023	1,676	151	1,525	43,623	25.9	34.1
San Angelo	35,383	2.53	61.2	45.1	12.5	38.8	32.3	5,463	5,405	5,306	364	4,942	62,975	42.1	22.8
San Antonio	501,645	2.97	64.7	43.0	16.0	35.3	29.1	22,442	88,540	5,908	718	5,190	975,145	42.9	26.5
San Juan	9,181	4.01	89.2	54.4	27.4	10.8	9.9	NA	972	2,622	396	2,225	20,002	56.3	17.8
San Marcos	22,480	2.51	39.6	24.2	8.2	60.4	30.4	6,634	2,231	3,465	353	3,113	28,885	33.4	38.0
Schertz	14,840	2.65	71.6	55.0	13.3	28.4	24.1	293	814	2,075	217	1,859	27,356	29.0	38.5
Seguin	9,954	2.76	74.2	48.6	19.2	25.8	21.6	1,527	1,187	4,192	392	3,800	18,858	61.5	13.8
Sherman	14,828	2.71	65.1	49.0	11.6	34.9	28.1	1,709	1,378	3,350	309	3,041	25,337	41.7	21.1
Socorro	8,873	3.84	90.3	44.6	32.9	9.7	9.3	NA	347	1,037	132	906	19,608	62.6	6.4
Southlake	9,032	3.52	88.7	84.6	3.4	11.3	9.8	NA	415	1,354	62	1,292	19,590	7.6	72.1
Sugar Land	29,065	3.03	77.3	65.4	10.6	22.7	21.5	386	1,537	1,706	85	1,621	63,472	18.8	60.7
Temple	27,395	2.66	61.6	43.0	14.1	38.4	31.9	1,537	2,549	3,472	305	3,167	47,655	33.6	29.7
Texarkana	14,415	2.49	57.7	36.0	14.7	42.3	37.1	1,485	2,189	5,846	839	5,008	24,376	44.8	29.1
Texas City	17,502	2.68	73.6	43.6	21.7	26.4	23.5	1,656	2,008	4,175	518	3,657	34,514	56.0	12.0
The Colony	16,361	2.61	59.5	40.4	16.9	40.5	33.6	NA	555	1,293	154	1,139	29,005	28.1	34.9
Tyler	36,030	2.79	66.2	47.0	12.7	33.8	27.7	4,554	4,177	3,976	409	3,567	65,606	33.6	27.2
Victoria	23,876	2.76	64.6	44.1	12.8	35.4	27.2	1,259	2,584	3,767	392	3,374	42,692	47.4	20.7
Waco	49,706	2.57	61.4	35.7	19.6	38.6	30.6	8,463	5,577	4,168	519	3,649	76,342	44.2	24.8
Waxahachie	12,067	2.82	75.0	59.4	9.3	25.0	22.0	1,348	926	2,711	152	2,559	23,627	49.3	19.6
Weatherford	11,297	2.59	61.2	47.7	9.3	38.8	32.1	1,441	667	2,267	177	2,090	21,374	42.3	21.4
Weslaco	11,278	3.53	80.8	47.0	27.6	19.2	17.6	505	2,109	5,274	430	4,844	21,473	47.8	19.8
Wichita Falls	37,535	2.38	59.6	39.1	14.9	40.4	34.7	15,297	4,179	3,992	425	3,567	64,538	47.9	22.2
Wylie	15,095	3.33	81.4	60.2	17.4	18.6	14.7	NA	467	978	107	871	30,468	28.7	35.5
UTAH	975,448	3.13	74.1	60.7	9.0	25.9	19.6	47,561	97,465	3,194	243	2,952	1,827,035	30.2	34.6
American Fork	7,934	3.68	86.6	70.1	9.9	13.4	11.4	300	882	2,260	61	2,198	16,105	20.2	42.8
Bountiful	14,501	3.01	75.6	66.9	6.1	24.4	22.0	450	793	1,802	107	1,695	28,064	19.1	47.1
Cedar City	9,999	2.95	74.8	55.2	13.2	25.2	15.2	NA	702	2,306	220	2,086	15,252	32.6	35.4
Clearfield	9,288	3.35	80.3	58.6	15.7	19.7	15.9	NA	693	2,251	94	2,157	18,036	34.6	23.0
Cottonwood Heights	12,842	2.64	68.7	57.8	8.3	31.3	23.2	NA	958	2,777	116	2,661	24,966	17.5	54.2
Draper	13,756	3.28	82.6	68.5	5.0	17.4	9.3	2,421	1,490	3,124	155	2,969	29,024	21.1	46.3
Holladay	11,496	2.65	72.0	59.3	9.2	28.0	22.5	NA	NA	NA	NA	NA	20,650	11.9	60.6

1. No spouse present.   2. Data for serious crimes have not been adjusted for underreporting. This may affect comparability between geographic areas and over time.   3. Per 100,000 population estimated by the FBI.   4. Persons 25 years old and over.

Table D. Cities — Income and Housing

City	Money income, 2017					Median earnings, 2017			Housing units, 2017				
	Households												
	Median income	Percent with income less than $20,000	Percent with income of $200,000 or more	Median family income	Median non-family income	All persons	Men	Women	Total	Occupied	Percent owner occupied	Median value[1] (dollars)	Median gross rent (dollars)
	42	43	44	45	46	47	48	49	50	51	52	53	54

City	42	43	44	45	46	47	48	49	50	51	52	53	54
TEXAS— Cont'd													
Irving	62,837	9.1	5.2	69,394	51,457	35,623	41,334	29,750	89,292	84,371	37.9	187,700	1,103
Keller	136,015	4.8	29.1	142,251	67,406	56,288	84,475	39,341	15,604	15,053	80.9	404,100	1,569
Killeen	45,404	14.8	1.0	49,942	34,235	27,123	31,853	21,725	61,000	53,350	43.9	128,300	889
Kingsville	36,348	30.8	4.7	50,515	12,473	25,297	34,053	16,588	10,479	9,385	48.3	74,600	836
Kyle	78,676	4.8	9.6	88,351	52,467	48,047	50,700	46,267	15,649	15,320	71.1	187,300	1,299
Lake Jackson	69,920	5.2	9.4	97,036	39,565	42,386	52,215	35,821	10,675	9,958	64.8	187,100	1,165
Lancaster	42,076	24.2	0.6	49,982	23,582	30,661	32,430	27,965	14,733	14,092	54.6	130,600	968
La Porte	81,987	14.2	6.9	90,087	21,288	37,951	46,952	30,251	13,121	12,017	75.3	141,400	968
Laredo	44,494	23.5	2.4	48,157	26,619	25,433	30,444	18,702	78,073	70,522	60.5	136,400	809
League City	98,593	3.6	12.4	105,648	71,730	56,213	73,632	48,215	37,654	35,854	75.1	253,400	1,286
Leander	99,337	1.9	10.4	107,191	50,217	45,321	51,426	36,233	15,889	14,703	76.1	272,100	1,250
Lewisville	65,578	7.6	3.6	72,647	52,137	38,439	40,566	36,118	43,056	39,357	39.9	222,200	1,222
Little Elm	113,506	2.8	3.7	117,496	43,347	48,361	56,250	40,231	13,782	13,782	83.5	261,900	1,661
Longview	46,081	18.9	3.8	56,116	30,113	24,747	26,397	23,367	34,417	29,620	55.4	145,100	815
Lubbock	45,764	21.7	3.9	63,625	24,149	24,477	27,051	22,004	107,222	94,480	49.7	138,000	900
Lufkin	37,277	27.2	3.0	51,630	20,745	21,454	22,595	20,721	14,287	13,752	48.5	115,000	793
McAllen	44,108	28.1	3.5	54,844	30,517	22,742	29,587	19,305	54,480	46,598	59.2	131,000	746
McKinney	93,546	7.7	12.7	105,186	44,643	46,308	60,450	37,972	64,403	61,833	64.1	317,200	1,377
Mansfield	88,736	6.6	9.8	98,918	54,325	46,941	60,265	31,518	24,279	22,679	76.5	247,600	1,361
Mesquite	54,775	13.9	2.0	62,609	37,143	31,363	35,249	28,988	48,419	44,948	60.7	142,000	1,052
Midland	75,886	10.9	8.5	85,543	50,925	46,041	60,127	30,495	52,141	48,729	66.7	204,100	1,101
Mission	45,285	23.6	4.4	50,207	22,904	21,484	31,614	15,545	30,123	25,857	68.5	104,400	670
Missouri City	76,572	4.7	11.6	79,993	50,890	41,557	45,400	37,924	24,970	23,948	81.6	195,500	1,489
Nacogdoches	41,383	25.1	6.3	56,626	23,683	19,795	21,329	18,663	14,716	12,013	40.9	177,300	761
New Braunfels	58,814	12.3	5.2	73,288	39,604	36,086	41,770	31,222	32,886	29,931	63.0	219,100	1,126
North Richland Hills	67,307	11.0	6.5	86,936	41,073	38,616	42,037	31,967	28,799	27,650	65.0	199,600	1,176
Odessa	58,919	12.9	1.8	63,362	35,257	34,504	41,690	25,933	44,340	39,400	59.2	157,800	948
Paris	33,354	26.5	1.0	43,642	20,412	21,127	20,468	21,625	11,788	9,699	48.3	84,800	678
Pasadena	50,210	21.0	2.6	58,616	27,387	27,180	35,629	18,465	52,211	47,532	53.7	122,900	864
Pearland	105,806	6.8	11.3	120,614	56,653	54,439	56,638	51,357	45,356	42,672	74.6	251,400	1,353
Pflugerville	95,561	3.7	3.6	106,736	58,445	49,240	57,054	41,796	21,562	20,376	78.0	234,300	1,486
Pharr	41,286	29.1	1.3	45,363	19,974	24,503	29,004	17,939	25,785	22,897	60.1	83,100	721
Plano	94,306	6.3	13.1	105,512	57,497	50,628	62,417	40,284	113,234	106,078	59.3	329,500	1,371
Port Arthur	34,309	29.7	1.4	41,609	21,086	24,328	30,619	20,933	26,591	21,843	57.8	64,300	798
Richardson	72,635	9.8	9.2	86,302	45,220	40,847	46,192	32,254	47,306	43,017	57.0	269,900	1,297
Rockwall	89,582	7.3	8.0	104,848	33,759	49,208	52,275	42,130	15,754	14,742	76.5	269,900	1,139
Rosenberg	47,846	16.4	2.0	49,271	36,369	28,091	31,182	25,516	14,853	12,898	51.9	187,400	1,008
Round Rock	79,444	5.2	9.0	84,988	49,572	36,943	40,315	34,150	41,337	38,368	62.2	267,500	1,210
Rowlett	92,877	4.0	8.7	98,968	66,163	51,954	61,313	41,107	22,263	21,703	89.0	227,100	1,579
San Angelo	46,100	16.3	2.5	64,833	31,860	28,254	29,820	26,520	40,865	35,383	60.4	134,600	815
San Antonio	50,044	19.1	3.6	59,810	32,570	29,668	31,624	25,801	552,520	501,645	54.8	148,200	926
San Juan	37,541	27.5	0.8	38,736	11,511	25,285	29,269	20,412	10,117	9,181	76.9	88,000	722
San Marcos	37,634	19.7	0.5	55,469	28,423	16,076	22,258	11,389	24,447	22,480	21.5	154,500	961
Schertz	77,148	10.9	6.5	87,885	48,982	48,064	51,859	37,495	15,165	14,840	75.5	199,200	1,216
Seguin	45,407	24.0	1.1	49,090	19,609	22,244	30,127	17,572	10,713	9,954	60.6	121,200	829
Sherman	45,300	22.4	2.7	57,994	25,885	27,930	31,186	21,650	17,271	14,828	55.3	116,200	860
Socorro	38,961	24.1	1.3	39,671	22,571	20,900	27,341	13,611	9,428	8,873	73.4	103,900	690
Southlake	231,651	2.5	58.8	250	0	81,343	100,402	60,436	9,381	9,032	92.3	714,700	1,294
Sugar Land	110,798	8.0	26.3	132,808	54,626	54,042	66,946	37,095	31,472	29,065	76.9	332,900	1,667
Temple	52,416	15.5	3.1	62,449	38,081	30,932	35,646	29,041	30,721	27,395	53.3	139,000	900
Texarkana	40,597	31.1	3.0	56,934	21,843	30,682	42,971	25,181	17,966	14,415	46.3	142,800	660
Texas City	46,180	16.8	1.7	54,151	32,565	22,170	24,091	20,990	19,720	17,502	54.4	122,900	963
The Colony	76,695	4.0	5.5	90,168	52,574	42,036	50,324	35,887	17,170	16,361	53.9	223,800	1,357
Tyler	51,956	18.2	4.4	59,319	31,705	26,763	35,205	22,871	42,659	36,030	56.4	153,400	888
Victoria	49,525	16.7	3.7	56,864	34,758	29,965	35,457	21,817	27,173	23,876	58.3	144,200	898
Waco	39,063	25.4	2.6	47,217	25,535	22,257	24,245	20,121	55,598	49,706	44.4	117,100	836
Waxahachie	63,456	9.8	5.5	70,245	39,554	31,842	39,935	22,411	12,964	12,067	56.1	161,700	957
Weatherford	62,708	8.9	6.0	74,487	41,250	31,180	37,641	29,784	12,073	11,297	67.2	174,400	1,118
Weslaco	42,002	22.2	0.4	45,116	23,880	21,055	25,988	16,624	14,753	11,278	59.5	82,100	699
Wichita Falls	42,959	23.9	1.5	57,970	26,411	26,512	30,979	22,375	43,939	37,535	54.8	101,900	758
Wylie	93,687	2.0	2.6	95,719	55,674	49,682	53,240	40,960	16,392	15,095	76.6	228,500	1,492
UTAH	68,358	10.4	5.7	77,940	38,344	31,046	40,450	22,448	1,084,685	975,448	69.9	275,100	986
American Fork	75,310	5.6	3.6	80,077	34,545	32,976	42,122	19,265	7,934	7,934	75.7	287,600	1,167
Bountiful	71,808	13.4	9.5	90,875	30,217	36,552	45,690	26,444	14,971	14,501	71.3	323,900	998
Cedar City	45,668	18.1	1.5	60,210	21,922	20,244	30,248	13,567	11,488	9,999	49.9	217,700	722
Clearfield	52,619	10.1	0.3	60,748	27,243	29,026	31,839	25,155	10,234	9,288	61.1	186,800	980
Cottonwood Heights	83,326	5.5	13.3	103,163	60,173	40,143	51,149	31,741	13,627	12,842	71.6	370,600	1,249
Draper	108,016	4.0	15.3	114,867	60,539	38,962	51,188	28,396	14,592	13,756	78.1	462,200	1,371
Holladay	92,676	11.9	15.8	109,092	36,597	38,313	60,327	27,116	12,759	11,496	81.5	457,100	1,109

1. Based on population estimated by the American Community Survey. 2. Includes units rented or sold but not occupied. 3. Specified owner-occupied units; $1,000,000 represents $1,000,000 or more. 4. 50.0 represents 50 percent or more. 5. 10.0 represents 10 percent or less.

Table D. Cities — Commuting, Computer Access, Migration, Labor Force, and Employment

City	Commuting, 2017 Percent — Commuting	With commutes of 30 minutes or more	Computer access, 2017 Percent — With a computer in the house	With Internet access	Migration, 2017 Percent who lived in the same house one year ago	Percent who lived in another state or county one year ago	Civilian labor force, 2018 — Total	Percent change 2017-2018	Unemployment — Total	Rate	Civilian employment, 2017 — Population age 16 and older — Number	Percent in labor force	Population age 16 to 64 — Number	Percent who worked full-year full-time
	55	56	57	58	59	60	61	62	63	64	65	66	67	68
TEXAS— Cont'd														
Irving	83.7	33.2	95.5	84.9	79.8	8.8	132,991	2.3	4,529	3.4	179,710	74.9	162,565	59.7
Keller	82.5	50.7	99.1	97.0	79.6	9.0	24,518	2.4	750	3.1	36,148	66.6	30,322	54.6
Killeen	78.5	25.8	93.9	86.0	74.1	12.1	56,063	0.1	2,716	4.8	107,526	67.2	97,660	48.8
Kingsville	80.5	17.7	92.9	71.9	86.1	7.1	10,839	-0.6	551	5.1	20,934	55.4	17,289	43.5
Kyle	88.0	59.4	98.6	91.6	90.6	2.3	23,392	3.3	675	2.9	31,204	74.2	27,909	58.4
Lake Jackson	81.1	23.3	96.2	93.0	78.4	12.1	13,769	0.9	664	4.8	19,828	64.5	15,461	54.9
Lancaster	NA	57.8	87.9	73.4	89.3	2.4	19,164	2.4	1,100	5.7	28,673	68.3	24,011	53.3
La Porte	80.5	38.8	92.5	86.9	88.8	6.2	18,581	1.1	934	5.0	29,148	65.5	24,012	51.0
Laredo	82.5	21.6	79.7	64.0	88.0	3.1	111,689	1.2	4,162	3.7	184,525	59.4	160,219	47.5
League City	85.1	48.5	98.5	93.3	86.2	6.4	57,330	1.9	2,073	3.6	75,074	69.0	65,309	57.4
Leander	84.0	56.8	NA	NA	81.9	8.8	26,156	3.2	784	3.0	37,179	74.1	32,974	61.9
Lewisville	84.2	40.3	98.7	92.4	77.8	11.6	65,628	2.3	2,103	3.2	83,998	77.8	75,356	61.3
Little Elm	75.5	63.0	NA	NA	82.8	14.6	24,517	2.4	876	3.6	34,657	77.7	32,314	59.9
Longview	80.4	19.5	87.3	81.6	78.1	9.4	37,867	0.6	1,605	4.2	64,203	61.9	52,108	46.8
Lubbock	81.7	10.1	91.9	80.0	74.7	11.3	132,990	0.7	4,040	3.1	201,929	66.2	171,253	47.7
Lufkin	78.8	11.4	87.4	81.1	77.4	11.0	15,046	-1.0	643	4.3	28,427	56.2	21,783	46.2
McAllen	77.0	15.6	87.3	79.9	88.4	5.1	66,260	2.0	3,099	4.7	110,403	61.6	90,706	46.4
McKinney	79.6	44.4	96.8	90.4	83.5	8.5	97,349	2.4	3,411	3.5	131,648	70.7	113,692	58.8
Mansfield	83.5	50.3	98.7	95.9	85.1	6.4	36,957	2.6	1,199	3.2	53,240	68.7	46,254	51.6
Mesquite	77.9	59.2	94.4	91.1	83.5	3.5	76,872	2.2	2,892	3.8	103,561	67.2	89,295	51.1
Midland	85.4	19.1	91.0	84.3	84.0	7.1	84,221	12.6	1,772	2.1	101,786	67.3	86,415	55.8
Mission	83.9	25.0	88.8	73.8	88.0	4.4	34,546	1.5	2,029	5.9	63,030	55.7	50,000	40.2
Missouri City	84.5	47.0	96.8	93.1	92.1	5.7	39,509	1.6	1,823	4.6	55,395	66.6	44,117	57.4
Nacogdoches	74.8	14.7	90.3	75.6	63.5	13.5	14,713	0.7	610	4.1	28,231	56.6	23,083	36.6
New Braunfels	82.3	30.6	90.6	86.2	79.0	11.0	40,759	1.8	1,267	3.1	60,690	67.7	48,399	60.7
North Richland Hills	82.3	43.8	95.3	89.1	84.9	6.8	39,726	2.4	1,236	3.1	56,732	67.3	44,724	56.2
Odessa	78.9	17.6	91.1	85.8	77.8	6.6	65,313	8.4	1,681	2.6	87,869	71.4	76,312	55.2
Paris	78.9	13.6	84.4	63.4	81.3	3.5	11,540	0.7	481	4.2	20,508	57.5	15,264	49.9
Pasadena	79.3	36.1	89.6	85.6	82.1	2.5	67,825	1.1	3,838	5.7	111,273	66.1	97,348	46.3
Pearland	83.7	64.9	96.7	94.2	85.8	8.3	64,776	2.0	2,193	3.4	93,550	72.1	80,528	63.3
Pflugerville	80.8	54.4	98.3	92.3	83.0	11.0	36,446	3.2	1,157	3.2	49,975	70.6	42,887	64.1
Pharr	82.1	10.6	89.6	60.6	92.0	2.0	31,311	1.5	2,230	7.1	55,924	58.8	46,000	46.8
Plano	83.1	44.1	97.8	93.9	88.8	6.4	163,394	2.3	5,398	3.3	231,103	70.2	193,709	60.9
Port Arthur	85.7	23.4	86.3	61.5	86.9	2.2	22,352	-0.4	2,057	9.2	43,405	52.1	35,385	42.4
Richardson	82.0	43.2	97.1	92.8	81.3	10.2	64,719	2.3	2,079	3.2	92,871	62.9	73,728	50.8
Rockwall	76.2	58.2	94.4	90.4	83.6	13.1	23,078	2.3	761	3.3	35,695	61.6	29,172	51.9
Rosenberg	90.0	47.3	95.9	89.3	76.9	4.1	17,925	1.7	722	4.0	27,735	65.3	23,953	48.5
Round Rock	80.5	34.7	97.9	95.1	82.8	9.4	68,559	3.1	2,016	2.9	94,811	71.6	84,721	54.6
Rowlett	84.0	65.4	97.7	96.2	89.1	1.9	35,710	2.5	1,261	3.5	48,190	69.1	41,013	59.4
San Angelo	80.4	8.0	88.5	75.7	77.2	9.0	46,039	1.3	1,480	3.2	75,572	67.2	60,540	56.3
San Antonio	79.3	33.0	89.4	79.2	85.6	4.8	726,266	1.7	23,961	3.3	1,180,076	63.6	995,898	50.5
San Juan	76.9	11.7	93.3	55.6	NA	NA	15,353	1.5	1,204	7.8	25,241	62.5	22,230	49.0
San Marcos	77.7	19.6	95.8	72.9	59.6	17.6	33,107	3.2	1,079	3.3	56,373	64.9	51,361	35.3
Schertz	88.8	42.0	96.0	92.8	83.2	13.5	19,230	1.6	612	3.2	31,001	62.2	25,666	58.3
Seguin	82.3	26.9	85.5	74.3	83.7	6.9	13,378	1.5	450	3.4	22,468	54.7	17,627	50.7
Sherman	79.9	20.4	91.5	85.0	80.9	8.5	19,928	2.4	655	3.3	30,943	62.2	26,806	50.1
Socorro	74.6	32.5	91.2	83.3	NA	NA	14,175	0.9	609	4.3	25,460	63.2	22,743	43.9
Southlake	75.3	47.6	NA	NA	82.3	6.9	15,064	2.5	490	3.3	22,407	68.1	20,140	54.1
Sugar Land	78.7	51.7	97.8	96.0	90.0	6.4	45,606	1.5	1,613	3.5	72,047	64.6	59,855	53.1
Temple	83.6	18.4	90.1	83.4	79.2	5.7	34,910	-0.1	1,198	3.4	55,766	61.7	44,568	55.5
Texarkana	92.5	8.5	76.4	64.1	92.4	3.5	15,447	0.1	751	4.9	29,143	53.0	22,767	46.8
Texas City	79.1	29.8	85.4	76.6	78.4	10.5	21,615	1.3	1,326	6.1	39,888	55.6	31,918	42.1
The Colony	81.8	43.7	98.0	92.0	86.8	10.0	27,731	2.3	985	3.6	32,467	76.6	30,184	63.6
Tyler	83.1	19.6	94.3	87.3	87.2	6.7	51,061	1.3	1,838	3.6	82,353	59.7	64,888	50.6
Victoria	78.5	19.6	87.4	73.2	84.0	4.9	31,346	0.9	1,211	3.9	51,907	64.0	41,431	50.5
Waco	83.3	14.7	85.2	76.0	74.0	11.2	60,961	0.4	2,327	3.8	106,218	61.1	89,693	43.2
Waxahachie	80.8	35.3	97.4	92.4	87.6	5.5	18,175	2.4	608	3.3	28,439	60.5	23,410	47.9
Weatherford	NA	36.3	93.5	88.2	77.2	11.6	13,854	2.2	460	3.3	25,249	59.8	19,029	55.9
Weslaco	77.5	28.4	93.3	85.0	NA	NA	15,844	1.7	1,158	7.3	28,226	56.8	23,939	44.8
Wichita Falls	73.7	8.6	88.6	75.4	77.6	11.1	43,935	1.1	1,544	3.5	84,442	62.7	69,727	48.7
Wylie	80.6	53.6	NA	NA	86.7	7.9	27,698	2.5	881	3.2	37,278	73.5	34,151	61.0
UTAH	76.1	27.3	95.5	87.8	82.9	7.5	1,572,136	1.5	48,978	3.1	2,278,695	68.7	1,943,500	49.8
American Fork	76.6	29.1	98.3	90.4	90.0	5.7	13,885	3.1	444	3.2	19,825	64.0	16,541	51.0
Bountiful	78.0	31.5	95.2	88.4	78.4	15.1	20,857	1.1	672	3.2	31,987	60.0	24,540	48.5
Cedar City	77.2	14.9	96.3	87.6	71.7	15.8	14,616	2.6	542	3.7	22,321	64.9	19,636	34.9
Clearfield	78.6	23.3	94.6	88.9	81.6	7.4	14,519	1.0	519	3.6	21,447	69.7	18,877	51.7
Cottonwood Heights	77.5	26.5	94.1	86.7	81.8	9.9	19,710	1.0	595	3.0	27,770	74.0	22,185	56.7
Draper	81.1	35.3	98.8	92.0	79.8	10.0	22,734	1.1	728	3.2	33,794	68.7	30,579	52.6
Holladay	78.8	19.3	95.0	89.0	NA	NA	15,844	1.1	504	3.2	23,903	65.7	17,514	51.4

1. Employed persons.　2. Households.　3. Percent of civilian labor force.　4. Persons 16 years old and over.

Table D. Cities — Construction, Wholesale Trade, and Retail Trade

City	Value of residential construction authorized by building permits, 2018			Wholesale trade[1], 2012				Retail trade[2], 2012			
	New construction ($1,000)	Number of housing units	Percent single family	Number of establishments	Number of employees	Sales (mil dol)	Annual payroll (mil dol)	Number of establishments	Number of employees	Sales (mil dol)	Annual payroll (mil dol)
	69	70	71	72	73	74	75	76	77	78	79
TEXAS— Cont'd											
Irving	213,534	550	94.0	356	11,506	13,262.4	880.3	606	11,927	4,776.3	357.3
Keller	57,782	109	100.0	26	93	84.4	4.7	104	1,435	420.6	32.8
Killeen	124,074	875	72.1	22	D	D	D	402	6,119	1,679.6	138.6
Kingsville	605	6	100.0	4	D	D	D	100	1,397	494.1	32.1
Kyle	110,224	599	100.0	8	D	D	D	47	997	290.2	22.3
Lake Jackson	12,880	49	100.0	12	63	27.8	5.8	111	2,489	604.1	54.6
Lancaster	30,512	145	100.0	18	D	D	D	63	995	235.8	21.5
La Porte	8,463	64	100.0	50	833	392.3	45.3	70	508	217.3	14.1
Laredo	167,410	1,375	78.4	356	D	D	D	782	D	D	D
League City	175,476	679	100.0	47	D	D	D	181	3,492	1,319.5	103.4
Leander	609,217	2,006	76.8	9	D	D	D	36	807	246.9	18.7
Lewisville	186,477	1,040	33.8	105	2,322	1,992.2	147.4	411	7,286	2,343.5	193.5
Little Elm	389,292	1,162	100.0	8	D	D	D	31	585	177.9	12.9
Longview	28,268	204	63.7	170	2,233	1,211.0	114.1	508	7,547	2,082.8	192.5
Lubbock	296,640	1,330	98.0	317	4,844	4,623.3	239.3	946	15,727	4,583.3	388.0
Lufkin	8,145	71	100.0	47	684	310.6	30.4	271	4,094	1,148.9	100.2
McAllen	105,548	826	65.4	348	3,131	2,539.6	124.1	870	14,085	3,716.8	301.9
McKinney	887,020	3,463	65.9	93	771	705.9	43.3	330	6,634	2,507.3	187.9
Mansfield	200,770	693	80.5	65	1,523	681.2	70.7	141	2,807	785.5	61.8
Mesquite	16,681	70	100.0	63	674	656.6	34.7	431	7,326	2,015.8	180.2
Midland	307,846	1,222	100.0	164	2,436	2,268.9	136.4	453	7,059	2,661.1	201.3
Mission	48,193	411	74.7	68	410	205.9	12.7	231	3,721	1,110.8	85.5
Missouri City	98,070	386	100.0	52	316	225.2	16.6	147	2,936	757.1	60.7
Nacogdoches	357	4	0.0	34	D	D	D	210	2,763	824.0	66.9
New Braunfels	340,201	1,931	70.7	58	D	D	D	276	4,435	1,585.3	125.1
North Richland Hills	80,580	234	100.0	29	188	82.9	9.7	150	3,641	1,423.3	108.1
Odessa	145,006	740	96.8	184	2,717	1,951.1	189.8	401	6,849	2,658.0	208.0
Paris	5,701	37	62.2	34	D	D	D	178	2,252	628.8	53.7
Pasadena	12,471	129	100.0	137	1,665	979.4	92.2	440	6,288	1,733.4	146.8
Pearland	165,613	818	100.0	59	481	302.0	23.9	262	5,120	1,244.6	111.1
Pflugerville	178,968	716	100.0	41	511	243.6	29.2	86	1,515	416.4	35.3
Pharr	55,330	273	80.6	142	1,208	876.6	51.4	179	2,374	622.6	62.7
Plano	151,929	712	34.3	420	7,367	4,626.3	589.3	1,064	20,770	7,683.0	624.0
Port Arthur	9,759	49	100.0	24	D	D	D	187	3,169	865.8	71.9
Richardson	152,344	1,187	7.2	220	8,348	31,123.6	713.3	353	4,650	1,846.0	154.0
Rockwall	76,258	319	100.0	41	D	D	D	202	3,754	1,268.6	97.4
Rosenberg	51,244	244	100.0	23	498	260.2	26.9	161	2,925	954.5	75.2
Round Rock	251,254	1,370	67.3	104	D	D	D	398	8,410	4,317.2	253.1
Rowlett	84,447	646	25.1	33	123	63.4	5.9	92	1,508	409.1	36.6
San Angelo	56,755	262	100.0	94	853	407.1	45.4	398	5,806	1,771.6	145.5
San Antonio	873,970	5,929	55.1	1,287	D	D	D	4,211	72,437	23,870.2	1,785.6
San Juan	12,661	137	100.0	15	D	D	D	60	887	311.7	23.2
San Marcos	86,468	557	100.0	26	D	D	D	405	7,099	1,501.9	128.8
Schertz	97,780	388	100.0	56	D	D	D	50	1,220	362.5	24.4
Seguin	36,075	175	93.1	25	D	D	D	139	1,826	516.0	45.2
Sherman	45,783	390	49.7	47	425	653.6	17.9	207	3,645	1,048.3	86.8
Socorro	15,142	156	71.8	14	140	148.7	6.1	58	695	219.3	13.8
Southlake	122,664	153	76.5	59	591	528.1	40.5	229	5,140	1,760.0	142.1
Sugar Land	73,477	141	100.0	164	1,983	3,499.2	101.2	475	8,226	2,057.7	173.9
Temple	138,078	829	95.2	59	1,974	3,323.9	110.3	286	4,130	1,179.3	95.8
Texarkana	8,208	36	100.0	57	742	2,243.1	30.4	309	5,047	1,276.2	120.7
Texas City	78,509	510	100.0	28	211	113.5	12.0	186	1,575	517.8	49.6
The Colony	149,456	366	100.0	17	D	D	D	69	987	282.7	23.2
Tyler	124,932	437	77.1	114	1,433	533.3	66.2	632	9,824	2,734.3	243.4
Victoria	14,816	70	100.0	82	1,085	557.4	58.6	353	5,240	1,563.4	134.0
Waco	124,828	575	92.9	130	2,062	1,025.9	88.1	589	7,888	2,154.0	176.1
Waxahachie	128,487	652	85.1	31	D	D	D	138	2,364	623.9	53.6
Weatherford	67,514	497	42.1	25	274	362.1	10.5	198	3,255	1,372.8	96.3
Weslaco	24,564	319	58.6	37	417	228.7	13.5	160	2,807	818.9	63.1
Wichita Falls	31,832	223	33.6	116	981	508.4	46.0	434	6,851	1,830.0	154.1
Wylie	164,702	840	65.5	14	D	D	D	62	1,258	340.1	30.4
UTAH	5,610,557	25,574	72.5	3,015	43,523	30,927.9	2,364.4	9,095	133,535	38,024.5	3,334.9
American Fork	87,989	339	71.1	28	439	166.3	17.1	137	2,331	737.3	56.8
Bountiful	25,582	103	41.7	42	263	209.0	14.9	146	1,951	614.2	49.5
Cedar City	57,691	290	66.9	24	183	140.2	7.3	140	1,698	505.3	39.8
Clearfield	13,422	136	1.5	21	302	360.7	12.2	58	549	136.4	11.3
Cottonwood Heights	35,562	92	100.0	41	914	513.9	135.6	70	1,589	1,291.6	68.7
Draper	111,656	377	63.1	51	772	303.2	47.8	186	3,580	1,289.4	117.5
Holladay	11,905	28	85.7	25	189	47.0	6.5	75	784	122.9	15.3

1. Merchant wholesalers except manufacturers' sales branches and offices.   2. Establishments with payroll.

Items 69—79

Table D. Cities — **Real Estate, Professional Services, and Manufacturing**

City	Real estate and rental and leasing, 2012				Professional, scientific, and technical services[1], 2012				Manufacturing, 2012			
	Number of establishments	Number of employees	Receipts (mil dol)	Annual payroll (mil dol)	Number of establishments	Number of employees	Receipts (mil dol)	Annual payroll (mil dol)	Number of establishments	Number of employees	Receipts (mil dol)	Annual payroll (mil dol)
	80	81	82	83	84	85	86	87	88	89	90	91
TEXAS— Cont'd												
Irving	339	4,857	1,213.8	191.9	1,008	D	D	D	160	6,926	3,150.8	425.8
Keller	35	219	78.0	9.7	152	562	116.2	28.5	17	87	16.4	3.7
Killeen	144	580	88.7	19.5	105	1,036	114.2	42.8	15	94	16.0	3.5
Kingsville	26	D	D	D	29	160	13.9	3.5	13	D	D	D
Kyle	13	16	5.9	0.6	12	34	3.2	0.8	7	353	D	20.9
Lake Jackson	21	113	28.2	4.2	46	D	D	D	3	10	D	0.7
Lancaster	20	75	17.6	3.2	17	D	D	D	24	949	341.2	37.1
La Porte	38	469	146.7	27.1	55	1,954	348.4	145.0	39	2,483	4,902.1	214.8
Laredo	199	692	132.4	22.0	316	D	D	D	68	D	D	D
League City	60	182	34.9	6.6	175	1,646	189.3	79.6	26	113	D	5.8
Leander	14	36	6.3	1.0	36	D	D	D	17	174	D	8.6
Lewisville	112	551	139.1	19.7	215	D	D	D	99	2,046	462.9	93.5
Little Elm	7	23	3.1	0.7	26	64	6.6	2.4	7	188	D	D
Longview	149	792	175.3	33.3	313	2,706	390.9	157.3	120	8,520	4,525.5	450.7
Lubbock	367	1,524	263.7	48.2	573	3,620	441.8	164.5	197	4,181	1,348.7	177.3
Lufkin	67	299	48.1	9.5	121	642	77.4	29.0	43	3,980	1,126.2	144.2
McAllen	206	810	213.5	27.2	455	D	D	D	96	2,207	729.1	100.2
McKinney	121	1,027	144.3	33.5	348	D	D	D	70	5,938	4,106.2	469.4
Mansfield	39	140	33.6	6.6	116	545	64.2	24.1	82	2,745	1,053.8	132.4
Mesquite	97	413	84.6	12.7	106	764	62.1	23.1	66	2,300	1,044.8	109.1
Midland	225	1,243	347.7	62.0	445	D	D	D	77	D	393.9	D
Mission	55	219	36.2	6.1	75	438	47.6	17.6	26	312	65.3	8.6
Missouri City	41	93	17.5	3.7	131	D	D	D	26	550	134.5	26.6
Nacogdoches	49	154	27.8	4.1	78	D	D	D	43	3,753	1,244.6	109.5
New Braunfels	101	423	63.9	11.7	153	670	74.9	25.1	60	2,039	587.1	86.6
North Richland Hills	66	280	42.8	9.3	141	D	D	D	20	1,003	409.0	44.1
Odessa	136	815	318.2	40.4	180	D	D	D	122	2,282	780.5	128.0
Paris	43	152	20.0	3.5	46	D	D	D	35	2,757	1,905.5	148.0
Pasadena	128	762	165.0	28.1	157	D	D	D	102	4,633	10,180.0	344.0
Pearland	86	418	104.1	16.1	189	D	D	D	62	1,502	D	81.1
Pflugerville	17	59	14.4	2.2	59	185	16.0	6.4	19	389	78.4	26.2
Pharr	41	264	37.9	6.8	60	770	34.2	14.3	25	333	95.0	12.4
Plano	398	3,742	744.5	192.9	1,492	D	D	D	150	4,601	1,698.4	277.0
Port Arthur	35	282	49.1	10.7	48	471	42.4	19.7	40	4,687	D	447.9
Richardson	172	756	194.7	32.3	682	9,109	2,070.8	693.6	138	7,059	2,336.5	546.5
Rockwall	52	D	D	D	155	D	D	D	41	936	241.2	48.1
Rosenberg	36	123	34.0	4.5	38	D	D	D	22	823	583.8	42.7
Round Rock	119	402	100.1	14.8	311	1,693	252.5	100.6	77	2,828	923.9	159.5
Rowlett	25	52	9.9	1.6	76	502	41.5	11.9	42	592	D	22.5
San Angelo	127	D	D	D	192	D	D	D	88	3,166	1,205.4	123.9
San Antonio	1,500	10,878	2,522.4	478.0	3,338	33,837	5,854.7	2,108.0	742	27,947	14,068.1	1,370.3
San Juan	10	38	3.4	1.4	12	46	4.4	0.9	9	99	D	2.1
San Marcos	75	338	87.0	9.8	96	823	54.9	19.6	40	D	687.6	D
Schertz	27	D	D	D	31	275	29.9	8.7	25	773	165.8	25.2
Seguin	34	192	36.9	7.6	49	198	16.6	6.5	48	3,995	2,029.9	180.9
Sherman	50	178	29.5	4.9	114	395	50.0	17.5	46	4,317	D	191.4
Socorro	8	33	10.2	1.2	7	41	1.7	0.5	14	79	16.7	2.2
Southlake	92	599	98.4	25.3	229	1,624	250.9	81.1	28	295	81.4	14.1
Sugar Land	167	483	155.5	20.7	521	4,603	724.3	604.4	57	3,099	1,374.8	159.4
Temple	80	409	65.1	12.8	117	D	D	D	59	4,222	1,611.1	180.0
Texarkana	78	385	79.6	15.3	123	D	D	D	26	814	276.8	36.9
Texas City	34	281	66.9	11.7	43	D	D	D	25	4,126	40,766.1	498.9
The Colony	17	177	41.1	4.0	51	276	36.3	10.4	NA	NA	NA	NA
Tyler	208	953	217.8	39.9	458	D	D	D	88	4,002	4,317.4	201.7
Victoria	110	714	492.3	39.4	142	D	D	D	55	1,062	D	D
Waco	162	1,293	245.6	55.7	272	D	D	D	134	12,060	5,828.2	576.4
Waxahachie	46	149	31.1	4.7	63	D	D	D	54	3,534	1,293.8	154.3
Weatherford	37	174	24.8	5.4	86	D	D	D	31	825	177.4	40.7
Weslaco	49	201	35.0	4.1	59	D	D	D	12	92	11.7	4.3
Wichita Falls	153	759	153.6	28.2	208	D	D	D	97	3,045	724.1	148.2
Wylie	17	54	11.1	1.6	49	153	14.8	6.1	32	1,788	653.8	75.9
UTAH	4,446	16,197	3,226.1	604.8	8,961	75,648	10,415.5	3,860.6	3,163	108,264	50,046.4	5,762.6
American Fork	60	167	27.7	5.1	118	1,593	235.8	76.3	27	591	D	31.7
Bountiful	81	170	19.1	6.0	192	D	D	D	42	797	1,594.5	52.5
Cedar City	57	140	26.1	4.5	83	385	54.8	14.5	57	1,212	639.8	51.5
Clearfield	25	102	31.3	3.3	59	1,259	142.0	70.8	47	5,724	1,740.4	267.2
Cottonwood Heights	232	745	127.3	30.7	210	1,225	192.1	76.0	23	250	D	14.9
Draper	104	334	55.2	12.8	245	1,348	180.2	73.3	41	1,216	362.4	69.8
Holladay	80	D	D	D	159	D	D	D	11	445	D	22.1

1. Establishments subject to federal tax.

Accommodation and Food Services, Arts, Entertainment, and Recreation, and Health Care and Social Assistance

City	Accommodation and food services, 2012				Arts, entertainment, and recreation[1], 2012				Health care and social assistance,[1] 2012			
	Number of establishments	Number of employees	Receipts (mil dol)	Annual payroll (mil dol)	Number of establishments	Number of employees	Receipts (mil dol)	Annual payroll (mil dol)	Number of establishments	Number of employees	Receipts (mil dol)	Annual payroll (mil dol)
	92	93	94	95	96	97	98	99	100	101	102	103
TEXAS— Cont'd												
Irving	545	11,557	795.8	219.0	41	882	308.9	194.8	524	9,189	1,018.6	422.2
Keller	81	1,232	64.1	17.2	10	D	D	D	116	D	D	D
Killeen	248	5,406	275.3	73.2	20	D	D	D	162	D	D	D
Kingsville	70	D	D	D	4	27	1.9	0.7	49	D	D	D
Kyle	39	461	26.7	7.0	5	D	D	D	42	D	D	D
Lake Jackson	58	1,421	67.1	18.7	6	180	4.8	2.3	127	D	D	D
Lancaster	32	646	34.6	10.3	2	D	D	D	42	882	44.4	19.0
La Porte	68	1,241	60.2	17.1	4	4	0.1	0.1	39	D	D	D
Laredo	388	D	D	D	29	D	D	D	495	D	D	D
League City	121	2,047	101.4	28.6	19	D	D	D	147	D	D	D
Leander	27	405	20.0	5.0	4	D	D	D	37	D	D	D
Lewisville	232	4,707	268.4	69.0	29	D	D	D	235	4,569	466.8	185.6
Little Elm	23	D	D	D	4	85	4.4	1.3	18	160	9.8	3.7
Longview	239	5,463	255.8	71.5	18	233	14.7	4.0	330	D	D	D
Lubbock	597	13,817	697.7	186.1	56	966	44.5	14.4	681	12,591	1,244.5	475.9
Lufkin	122	2,852	129.3	36.8	11	84	4.1	1.0	206	4,992	368.7	159.6
McAllen	402	8,909	434.2	116.1	27	298	31.6	5.0	737	15,849	1,434.3	538.1
McKinney	229	4,652	233.6	66.7	28	756	34.3	12.7	340	5,253	601.0	220.2
Mansfield	118	D	D	D	16	D	D	D	177	1,699	177.1	68.4
Mesquite	217	5,218	270.6	75.1	22	324	22.3	4.3	309	D	D	D
Midland	279	6,352	431.1	102.8	24	D	D	D	319	D	D	D
Mission	135	2,294	119.2	28.9	11	239	10.1	3.2	262	D	D	D
Missouri City	101	1,540	82.2	20.4	10	D	D	D	163	1,529	104.2	40.9
Nacogdoches	105	2,457	96.1	27.0	9	D	D	D	172	2,233	248.4	76.5
New Braunfels	228	4,685	247.9	66.5	27	D	D	D	214	D	D	D
North Richland Hills	127	2,539	118.8	33.0	20	D	D	D	129	2,717	342.9	117.9
Odessa	230	5,893	377.8	90.6	23	239	15.9	2.6	273	5,379	633.2	215.6
Paris	93	1,462	67.5	18.9	8	D	D	D	153	3,443	310.7	115.6
Pasadena	202	3,882	206.4	54.8	10	D	D	D	307	6,675	807.2	289.9
Pearland	180	4,226	212.0	58.5	15	D	D	D	242	2,374	209.8	83.3
Pflugerville	61	1,266	61.4	17.6	7	100	6.1	1.7	59	D	D	D
Pharr	92	1,721	102.4	22.5	10	95	5.8	1.3	141	3,312	128.5	68.5
Plano	681	14,581	846.9	241.8	63	1,334	112.0	25.0	1,326	16,372	2,368.0	869.3
Port Arthur	102	1,890	86.4	24.4	8	D	D	D	111	D	D	D
Richardson	322	5,202	307.9	82.9	31	427	31.0	10.6	479	5,290	475.4	182.8
Rockwall	124	3,006	154.6	46.0	16	D	D	D	168	2,085	270.0	90.3
Rosenberg	92	1,713	89.5	25.8	2	D	D	D	52	D	D	D
Round Rock	278	6,112	340.4	92.7	29	D	D	D	288	D	D	D
Rowlett	70	990	49.9	14.0	9	D	D	D	100	1,983	246.4	72.1
San Angelo	210	4,220	211.7	57.1	22	264	15.8	3.7	225	3,970	425.1	200.0
San Antonio	3,209	79,964	4,616.3	1,242.7	255	D	D	D	3,448	74,255	8,556.3	3,003.7
San Juan	28	363	19.3	4.6	3	D	D	D	52	942	37.0	17.6
San Marcos	212	4,456	215.6	59.6	6	D	D	D	119	D	D	D
Schertz	58	1,287	62.4	17.5	4	D	D	D	44	681	61.7	24.3
Seguin	81	1,368	73.6	17.3	5	D	D	D	89	D	D	D
Sherman	102	2,593	124.4	35.3	13	171	6.6	1.6	208	4,944	426.2	184.1
Socorro	24	263	12.7	3.0	1	D	D	D	12	303	7.1	3.8
Southlake	111	D	D	D	21	D	D	D	193	2,328	300.7	102.7
Sugar Land	328	7,038	377.8	109.4	27	772	63.8	17.7	563	D	D	D
Temple	170	3,451	159.8	44.4	17	136	8.5	2.0	157	D	D	D
Texarkana	134	3,369	158.4	46.2	18	169	6.4	2.4	215	4,013	462.8	181.8
Texas City	74	1,229	55.7	15.6	3	D	D	D	92	2,400	223.0	86.3
The Colony	47	1,083	50.1	14.3	10	136	11.6	2.8	47	D	D	D
Tyler	310	7,298	339.0	97.3	33	D	D	D	465	11,350	1,145.8	482.2
Victoria	176	3,538	182.8	48.4	27	D	D	D	254	D	D	D
Waco	350	7,672	380.5	106.7	29	338	20.8	5.4	317	6,697	512.1	245.1
Waxahachie	80	1,902	85.0	25.3	3	D	D	D	86	D	D	D
Weatherford	116	2,114	98.8	28.6	6	D	D	D	128	1,988	207.2	79.7
Weslaco	84	1,781	86.0	21.4	10	D	D	D	174	D	D	D
Wichita Falls	236	5,370	249.6	76.2	20	D	D	D	305	5,113	540.1	185.9
Wylie	42	D	D	D	5	42	3.6	0.8	50	D	D	D
UTAH	5,108	95,933	4,789.3	1,362.9	790	17,988	982.5	330.3	6,601	77,036	8,253.6	3,016.8
American Fork	82	1,558	69.8	18.5	7	D	D	D	129	D	D	D
Bountiful	69	D	D	D	10	D	D	D	209	D	D	D
Cedar City	82	1,224	57.5	14.8	9	D	D	D	117	D	D	D
Clearfield	32	611	23.0	6.5	5	D	D	D	44	D	D	D
Cottonwood Heights	54	799	43.5	11.6	13	D	D	D	120	D	D	D
Draper	94	1,494	72.3	21.8	15	D	D	D	132	997	104.1	37.5
Holladay	51	578	30.2	8.2	11	D	D	D	96	972	85.2	33.2

1. Establishments subject to federal tax.

City	Other services[1]				Government employment and payroll, 2012								
						March payroll							
							Percent of total for:						
	Number of establishments	Number of employees	Receipts (mil dol)	Annual payroll (mil dol)	Full-time equivalent employees	Total (dollars)	Administrative, judicial, and legal	Police and corrections	Fire protection	Highways and transportation	Health and welfare	Natural resources and utilities	Education and libraries
	104	105	106	107	108	109	110	111	112	113	114	115	116
TEXAS— Cont'd													
Irving	239	2,926	307.3	114.7	1,743	8,046,007	11.8	31.8	18.7	7.1	2.9	19.2	3.6
Keller	55	377	31.5	9.8	322	1,442,647	19.7	27.3	24.3	2.1	4.2	18.4	3.8
Killeen	150	974	79.5	24.9	1,394	4,447,306	9.5	31.5	19.2	10.2	0.6	25.4	2.0
Kingsville	31	D	D	D	241	740,345	13.5	34.2	17.7	5.2	3.4	18.4	2.6
Kyle	18	91	7.2	2.0	143	570,004	14.8	39.7	0.0	1.7	5.7	18.1	3.7
Lake Jackson	28	191	12.6	4.6	223	1,137,302	14.0	31.7	0.5	2.3	1.6	37.2	0.0
Lancaster	24	150	17.5	5.4	197	872,132	6.8	31.3	33.7	2.6	3.3	16.0	2.4
La Porte	42	5,934	655.6	342.7	386	1,606,505	14.9	33.6	6.2	5.1	7.8	22.0	0.0
Laredo	175	975	90.0	24.7	2,366	9,931,436	6.8	30.9	24.7	11.9	8.6	14.4	1.1
League City	93	670	50.8	15.5	495	2,096,779	14.9	38.2	2.0	7.5	5.2	20.9	5.0
Leander	26	146	11.5	3.6	176	773,154	15.8	34.3	18.9	9.2	0.8	16.9	0.0
Lewisville	150	1,053	116.4	32.6	702	3,410,758	13.2	32.7	24.8	4.3	1.7	15.0	2.1
Little Elm	12	44	4.1	1.4	174	691,106	17.2	23.6	29.0	9.8	0.8	13.6	2.1
Longview	155	1,278	152.8	44.8	813	3,225,874	7.0	26.2	26.9	3.4	3.3	21.3	2.7
Lubbock	338	2,485	217.7	69.3	2,120	8,958,861	10.0	27.2	23.3	4.5	2.1	29.5	1.5
Lufkin	75	615	135.8	27.5	429	1,543,350	10.3	27.6	23.6	6.7	2.2	23.4	1.9
McAllen	145	1,046	142.4	30.6	1,664	5,174,843	11.6	30.2	15.6	10.8	1.0	24.6	3.0
McKinney	132	1,023	89.8	27.9	813	4,047,327	14.6	26.8	24.0	4.8	0.1	11.7	2.8
Mansfield	67	D	D	D	451	2,111,359	10.1	41.1	18.9	1.8	1.4	11.7	1.5
Mesquite	122	946	102.3	28.3	1,105	5,253,222	10.9	34.0	25.7	3.7	4.0	15.6	2.0
Midland	157	D	D	D	894	4,038,726	12.2	27.1	26.9	7.2	3.1	13.6	0.0
Mission	72	434	36.4	9.7	597	1,943,490	10.4	37.6	17.4	3.6	1.5	22.5	3.1
Missouri City	68	415	28.1	9.5	283	1,318,714	9.4	42.4	22.9	9.3	0.0	4.5	0.0
Nacogdoches	49	298	23.9	7.2	302	1,195,157	10.1	30.1	23.9	1.7	1.3	26.6	1.9
New Braunfels	105	1,334	54.3	37.3	732	3,498,442	7.2	20.5	22.3	4.6	3.6	21.9	2.5
North Richland Hills	73	459	48.3	13.6	574	2,442,427	13.2	35.1	19.1	9.2	9.3	9.3	4.0
Odessa	149	1,399	178.1	47.0	873	3,249,214	13.9	28.3	26.0	7.1	3.0	16.3	0.0
Paris	58	301	28.1	7.8	203	911,303	16.1	38.4	1.6	2.6	5.8	17.2	7.9
Pasadena	135	1,402	179.6	68.1	960	4,082,891	10.8	48.1	2.1	4.7	5.5	18.7	2.8
Pearland	129	906	77.4	25.7	598	2,337,139	14.4	37.4	8.4	4.4	15.8	16.8	0.0
Pflugerville	51	308	28.6	10.5	253	1,010,931	16.1	44.8	0.0	8.0	1.3	21.6	3.5
Pharr	52	340	29.9	8.1	558	1,780,708	10.5	35.0	15.9	8.1	1.9	18.2	3.4
Plano	419	3,683	759.6	161.0	2,089	10,395,648	9.8	32.0	22.2	2.2	0.0	14.1	5.2
Port Arthur	36	162	11.7	3.2	668	2,985,904	7.8	28.2	20.4	6.1	9.3	23.9	1.7
Richardson	146	1,302	141.4	44.2	1,085	4,745,385	14.8	25.0	17.8	5.0	3.3	20.5	3.5
Rockwall	55	559	27.7	10.4	286	1,221,546	32.3	33.7	9.6	3.1	0.0	16.3	0.0
Rosenberg	53	230	30.8	8.3	213	967,179	15.7	34.7	16.7	5.1	5.0	18.2	0.0
Round Rock	147	1,405	151.8	46.8	471	2,565,694	21.2	46.9	28.7	0.0	0.0	0.7	2.5
Rowlett	74	396	34.4	11.4	332	1,590,040	18.8	30.9	25.7	4.7	2.6	10.7	1.9
San Angelo	161	867	85.1	23.1	915	3,145,374	16.7	27.8	25.3	3.8	3.2	19.2	0.0
San Antonio	1,694	12,508	1,000.7	326.7	15,382	70,371,976	6.9	20.9	12.5	5.3	3.5	46.3	2.1
San Juan	14	D	D	D	204	595,583	10.6	35.0	12.1	4.4	4.5	31.9	0.4
San Marcos	73	D	D	D	528	2,976,832	13.7	28.7	14.8	4.1	4.9	21.3	2.7
Schertz	36	342	28.5	9.8	292	1,152,930	17.4	24.7	12.8	2.8	16.4	9.2	3.8
Seguin	47	323	25.3	7.7	907	3,729,350	5.2	8.3	6.1	1.8	68.5	7.0	0.7
Sherman	43	375	37.8	16.0	387	1,528,362	13.7	25.7	23.1	4.3	3.0	22.7	2.2
Socorro	24	112	8.0	1.6	92	274,728	24.8	59.5	0.0	13.4	2.2	0.0	0.0
Southlake	68	D	D	D	274	1,309,065	24.1	24.8	21.4	7.0	0.0	20.0	2.7
Sugar Land	128	947	72.3	23.2	631	3,018,681	23.4	31.1	19.1	10.0	1.3	10.4	0.0
Temple	104	933	55.9	26.2	731	2,585,537	12.4	26.7	22.3	6.4	2.4	25.4	2.6
Texarkana	91	661	56.2	17.8	562	2,018,866	13.1	24.0	17.3	8.1	4.9	29.4	1.7
Texas City	38	241	27.2	9.5	481	1,954,986	8.1	29.3	20.9	5.9	1.6	25.9	2.0
The Colony	32	157	11.7	3.1	311	1,270,659	11.9	29.0	21.2	3.8	7.3	20.1	4.5
Tyler	170	1,478	125.2	57.0	778	3,106,473	9.1	34.9	25.5	3.1	3.1	18.2	1.7
Victoria	103	D	D	D	566	2,159,618	10.1	31.7	22.5	6.4	0.0	22.4	3.2
Waco	177	1,205	90.1	28.9	1,507	5,739,695	9.4	29.8	17.3	5.4	5.9	25.5	2.4
Waxahachie	42	262	29.4	6.8	264	1,145,356	12.3	28.0	25.5	3.4	3.0	21.1	0.0
Weatherford	63	579	42.4	15.3	345	1,550,071	17.4	23.4	20.0	5.7	2.6	21.9	3.2
Weslaco	45	347	28.5	7.3	368	1,252,682	6.2	31.0	27.7	5.1	2.2	17.8	3.2
Wichita Falls	142	835	70.0	20.7	1,213	4,712,736	7.8	25.5	27.3	8.3	5.3	16.8	1.2
Wylie	33	172	13.3	4.5	191	622,464	4.4	29.0	33.5	4.3	0.0	22.4	6.3
UTAH	3,631	21,705	1,875.3	549.2	X	X	X	X	X	X	X	X	X
American Fork	55	448	23.4	5.8	215	711,482	13.8	21.8	14.3	3.1	1.3	25.9	5.2
Bountiful	72	572	38.0	11.3	195	922,673	14.7	32.2	0.0	14.9	0.0	37.8	0.0
Cedar City	43	174	14.8	3.9	172	568,537	11.0	28.7	7.6	11.9	1.2	27.7	2.2
Clearfield	34	194	11.7	4.6	150	543,342	19.4	32.7	17.0	4.0	0.9	22.9	0.0
Cottonwood Heights	25	150	5.7	1.9	68	323,642	24.8	70.5	0.0	4.6	0.0	0.0	0.0
Draper	78	494	43.8	10.8	152	605,204	26.7	28.9	0.0	17.1	3.4	14.1	0.0
Holladay	40	158	11.1	3.1	18	69,533	64.5	0.0	0.0	0.0	22.6	12.9	0.0

1. Establishments subject to federal tax.

Table D. Cities — City Government Finances

City	General revenue							General expenditure		
	Intergovernmental			Taxes					Per capita[1] (dollars)	
					Per capita[1] (dollars)					
	Total (mil dol)	Total (mil dol)	Percent from state government	Total (mil dol)	Total	Property	Sales and gross receipts	Total (mil dol)	Total	Capital outlays
	117	118	119	120	121	122	123	124	125	126

City	117	118	119	120	121	122	123	124	125	126
TEXAS— Cont'd										
Irving	281.4	21.9	71.5	189.3	839	427	411	289.2	1,281	200
Keller	52.3	5.6	60.6	32.1	765	471	294	46.9	1,117	201
Killeen	120.2	5.4	5.6	62.9	466	248	219	125.1	928	204
Kingsville	22.9	0.6	12.6	12.2	464	228	236	21.7	825	89
Kyle	18.5	1.7	25.7	10.7	346	201	145	21.9	709	200
Lake Jackson	29.0	0.4	54.4	14.7	543	207	335	25.6	942	152
Lancaster	48.5	11.5	23.8	24.6	649	359	290	46.9	1,238	111
La Porte	56.7	0.9	100.0	26.5	769	497	272	48.6	1,407	246
Laredo	394.6	81.6	35.0	126.6	516	281	235	350.9	1,429	400
League City	86.5	3.8	100.0	58.1	658	411	247	73.3	829	130
Leander	26.5	2.2	9.7	17.9	606	377	229	29.0	981	234
Lewisville	95.9	2.2	49.8	62.5	628	286	342	100.9	1,013	207
Little Elm	30.5	4.2	98.1	18.2	629	354	275	39.3	1,357	641
Longview	103.8	12.8	28.3	64.9	798	306	492	94.8	1,166	149
Lubbock	270.7	38.4	30.0	127.0	538	245	293	310.3	1,313	386
Lufkin	50.9	0.7	59.9	25.8	716	272	443	52.9	1,468	203
McAllen	185.3	20.0	21.5	98.4	727	242	485	201.4	1,488	430
McKinney	171.7	14.0	23.8	109.6	764	437	327	184.3	1,284	234
Mansfield	76.9	0.3	100.0	53.1	894	514	381	67.5	1,136	167
Mesquite	149.0	15.9	19.4	81.9	571	255	316	164.5	1,147	212
Midland	147.3	7.4	38.3	94.6	790	273	516	126.0	1,052	145
Mission	73.0	7.2	12.2	38.7	478	266	212	68.7	850	112
Missouri City	57.5	9.1	36.1	36.0	524	363	161	66.1	963	354
Nacogdoches	37.5	1.3	98.2	17.4	514	223	291	34.0	1,005	86
New Braunfels	75.8	2.4	48.3	46.1	754	263	491	79.1	1,294	279
North Richland Hills	83.8	11.2	100.0	46.1	705	344	361	93.1	1,424	490
Odessa	103.9	3.9	38.2	61.7	580	196	384	93.2	877	116
Paris	30.9	2.2	100.0	18.1	722	303	419	29.3	1,166	79
Pasadena	146.5	20.4	12.6	75.9	497	217	280	138.9	910	167
Pearland	113.9	0.6	58.8	76.6	794	500	295	118.6	1,230	308
Pflugerville	42.9	1.9	93.4	26.5	509	326	184	44.6	858	248
Pharr	63.4	5.8	5.1	30.9	422	211	211	59.7	815	150
Plano	386.2	19.2	55.2	247.7	907	528	380	338.6	1,240	181
Port Arthur	104.3	23.2	53.0	35.6	652	306	346	92.8	1,701	263
Richardson	156.9	3.8	94.5	105.8	1,020	591	428	174.7	1,684	269
Rockwall	44.0	0.7	30.2	36.4	910	434	476	49.9	1,249	367
Rosenberg	36.1	5.0	24.6	21.6	665	231	434	29.5	906	207
Round Rock	146.3	3.6	66.0	112.0	1,050	315	735	119.5	1,120	243
Rowlett	58.1	2.1	65.8	33.9	587	420	167	55.7	965	142
San Angelo	93.6	7.0	10.4	55.3	575	299	276	98.6	1,026	216
San Antonio	1,748.6	300.5	51.3	740.3	534	275	253	1,743.3	1,258	188
San Juan	18.0	1.1	32.3	9.7	275	168	107	18.5	524	97
San Marcos	67.7	3.7	100.0	38.5	769	285	485	82.3	1,643	440
Schertz	37.4	1.3	65.0	21.3	611	306	305	31.5	902	81
Seguin	116.5	6.1	85.0	13.9	529	240	289	116.4	4,428	511
Sherman	47.8	2.7	3.7	27.5	704	182	522	48.9	1,254	120
Socorro	7.7	0.5	0.0	6.1	185	124	61	9.8	298	92
Southlake	68.2	0.6	38.4	54.7	1,972	1,139	834	66.5	2,398	864
Sugar Land	160.2	31.2	93.8	77.6	948	347	601	161.5	1,972	729
Temple	85.5	3.7	93.7	46.0	666	317	349	91.2	1,319	299
Texarkana	47.9	0.8	78.3	31.7	853	368	485	49.1	1,322	277
Texas City	68.4	8.3	43.2	43.1	944	451	493	58.5	1,280	147
The Colony	38.4	2.1	73.4	25.5	652	384	268	46.1	1,181	397
Tyler	128.9	15.0	13.7	61.9	623	142	481	120.1	1,209	168
Victoria	78.7	5.7	39.9	49.8	773	320	453	89.3	1,386	576
Waco	359.0	127.8	9.2	97.3	762	414	348	344.8	2,700	343
Waxahachie	40.4	0.2	100.0	28.8	928	477	451	33.9	1,090	82
Weatherford	34.6	3.2	80.9	20.7	782	306	475	43.0	1,627	441
Weslaco	37.6	0.7	25.3	22.1	599	267	332	35.9	972	114
Wichita Falls	120.3	13.6	34.0	66.3	633	276	357	114.0	1,088	129
Wylie	43.1	1.6	92.9	30.5	688	467	221	53.2	1,199	374
UTAH	X	X	X	X	X	X	X	X	X	X
American Fork	30.4	2.8	100.0	13.6	497	205	291	29.8	1,092	170
Bountiful	25.9	3.0	48.4	13.7	320	93	227	21.6	504	27
Cedar City	26.1	3.3	64.2	13.5	465	185	280	21.4	736	103
Clearfield	27.3	4.4	91.5	11.8	387	164	223	21.4	704	59
Cottonwood Heights	14.9	1.2	96.8	12.7	374	206	168	16.8	494	109
Draper	36.2	2.5	98.9	24.0	544	247	297	32.8	742	114
Holladay	17.7	2.0	70.1	11.7	434	197	236	15.0	555	0

1. Based on population estimated as of July 1 of the year shown.

Table D. Cities — City Government Finances

	City government finances, 2012 (cont.)									
	General expenditure (cont.)									
City	Percent of total for:									
	Public welfare	Highways	Parking facilities	Education	Health and hospitals	Police protection	Sewerage and sanitation	Parks and recreation	Housing and community development	Interest on debt
	127	128	129	130	131	132	133	134	135	136
TEXAS— Cont'd										
Irving	0.0	6.3	0.0	0.0	0.3	18.5	10.7	16.0	1.7	6.2
Keller	0.0	17.7	0.0	0.0	0.0	17.1	7.0	11.8	0.0	10.1
Killeen	0.2	9.1	0.0	0.0	0.4	19.5	23.3	5.7	0.3	4.1
Kingsville	0.0	9.8	0.0	0.0	1.5	31.1	19.6	0.9	0.0	1.3
Kyle	0.0	2.5	0.0	0.0	0.7	17.1	24.0	10.5	0.0	11.7
Lake Jackson	0.0	11.4	0.0	0.0	3.4	18.2	19.4	20.7	0.0	5.0
Lancaster	0.0	1.7	0.0	0.0	0.3	12.2	16.8	4.5	18.4	8.3
La Porte	0.0	8.4	0.0	0.0	0.0	21.8	10.5	11.3	0.0	3.9
Laredo	0.2	2.1	0.4	0.0	4.1	15.0	11.2	3.3	3.8	5.2
League City	0.0	10.6	0.0	0.0	3.9	20.7	11.4	6.2	0.2	5.1
Leander	0.0	21.6	0.0	0.0	0.6	14.8	12.0	7.8	0.0	17.7
Lewisville	0.0	16.6	0.0	0.0	1.2	21.6	6.1	10.4	2.2	6.4
Little Elm	0.0	4.0	0.0	0.0	0.3	8.7	13.3	2.7	0.0	4.5
Longview	0.0	10.3	0.0	0.0	1.5	21.3	12.6	8.8	7.2	2.4
Lubbock	0.0	7.3	0.0	0.0	1.8	16.3	18.4	5.2	1.4	10.2
Lufkin	0.0	14.7	0.0	0.0	1.2	15.2	18.1	7.6	0.3	13.8
McAllen	0.6	11.5	0.4	0.0	0.8	16.5	22.1	10.4	1.7	2.6
McKinney	0.0	8.4	0.0	0.0	0.8	10.9	11.9	6.8	0.3	6.0
Mansfield	0.0	9.9	0.0	0.0	0.6	14.5	12.1	8.2	0.0	8.1
Mesquite	0.0	6.4	0.0	0.0	0.8	18.5	13.6	7.0	8.4	4.2
Midland	0.0	5.4	0.0	0.0	3.3	17.0	15.9	13.4	0.6	2.3
Mission	0.0	8.3	0.0	0.0	0.5	20.0	10.6	12.1	1.7	18.9
Missouri City	0.0	12.6	0.0	0.0	0.3	16.3	9.7	12.1	0.5	7.8
Nacogdoches	0.0	4.3	0.0	0.0	0.0	20.6	28.3	4.4	0.0	1.2
New Braunfels	0.0	16.3	0.0	0.0	0.9	17.7	16.5	7.8	0.3	6.0
North Richland Hills	0.0	7.5	0.0	0.0	0.9	17.6	8.3	14.6	0.0	2.6
Odessa	0.1	14.4	0.0	0.0	0.7	18.6	16.0	6.7	2.6	1.6
Paris	0.0	12.8	0.0	0.0	10.9	19.7	12.9	3.9	4.1	2.1
Pasadena	0.3	19.6	0.0	0.0	2.5	30.9	13.9	6.5	7.8	3.5
Pearland	0.0	21.9	0.0	0.0	3.6	13.1	14.4	6.1	0.0	12.2
Pflugerville	0.0	14.9	0.0	0.0	0.0	22.4	18.1	6.3	0.0	7.6
Pharr	0.0	17.9	0.0	0.0	3.4	23.5	9.1	9.1	2.3	3.4
Plano	0.0	5.1	0.0	0.0	1.0	16.3	18.5	12.9	0.8	4.2
Port Arthur	2.1	10.7	0.0	0.0	3.3	19.4	20.8	2.7	3.2	3.5
Richardson	0.0	11.9	0.0	0.0	1.1	13.7	17.6	8.7	0.0	6.6
Rockwall	0.0	20.4	0.0	0.0	1.1	16.8	11.8	16.8	0.0	11.1
Rosenberg	0.0	19.1	0.0	0.0	0.8	23.4	17.4	3.5	0.0	6.0
Round Rock	0.0	13.0	0.0	0.0	0.7	19.5	9.2	7.3	0.4	5.1
Rowlett	0.0	13.1	0.0	0.0	1.6	18.1	14.7	6.6	0.0	6.4
San Angelo	0.0	7.5	0.0	0.0	3.5	15.8	10.8	5.9	3.1	4.7
San Antonio	7.8	6.4	0.3	0.0	1.9	17.7	19.6	7.8	2.9	1.6
San Juan	0.0	7.7	0.0	0.0	0.0	18.3	23.7	7.5	0.0	4.2
San Marcos	0.0	3.2	0.0	0.0	2.0	17.4	16.7	3.5	0.8	8.8
Schertz	0.0	7.2	0.0	0.0	12.4	14.7	16.9	4.0	0.0	6.6
Seguin	0.0	2.2	0.0	0.0	64.9	4.6	5.0	2.7	0.0	6.7
Sherman	0.1	14.6	0.0	0.0	1.2	15.7	18.0	4.8	0.6	2.0
Socorro	0.0	16.3	0.0	0.0	4.1	19.1	0.0	1.1	2.7	3.8
Southlake	0.0	16.1	0.0	0.0	0.0	12.5	7.7	19.6	0.0	8.2
Sugar Land	0.0	21.1	0.0	0.0	0.4	10.2	11.7	4.0	0.2	5.9
Temple	0.0	5.4	0.0	0.0	0.9	17.8	21.2	9.8	0.0	5.0
Texarkana	0.0	16.5	0.0	0.0	1.7	19.3	24.5	4.0	0.9	4.9
Texas City	0.0	17.5	0.0	0.0	0.7	18.1	12.1	12.9	0.8	4.6
The Colony	0.0	20.7	0.0	0.0	0.0	26.6	8.9	7.9	0.0	5.3
Tyler	0.0	11.3	0.0	0.0	0.0	18.5	17.1	3.5	6.7	14.7
Victoria	0.0	29.4	0.0	0.0	0.0	15.1	11.6	3.8	1.2	5.0
Waco	0.0	2.2	0.0	0.0	2.2	10.3	12.3	7.5	1.0	48.3
Waxahachie	0.0	7.3	0.0	0.0	2.2	18.4	13.9	8.1	0.0	10.0
Weatherford	0.0	29.0	0.0	0.0	0.1	15.8	13.4	5.2	0.0	6.7
Weslaco	0.0	3.7	0.0	0.0	1.2	15.5	23.6	1.3	0.0	10.1
Wichita Falls	0.0	8.9	0.0	0.0	4.1	17.6	17.4	5.8	5.2	1.7
Wylie	0.0	21.8	0.0	0.0	0.5	9.5	11.2	16.0	0.0	9.1
UTAH	X	X	X	X	X	X	X	X	X	X
American Fork	0.0	15.1	0.0	0.0	4.9	14.4	17.4	12.8	0.9	3.0
Bountiful	0.0	19.3	0.0	0.0	0.0	26.9	15.0	11.0	3.2	0.7
Cedar City	0.0	17.1	0.0	0.0	0.0	18.7	14.8	18.3	3.1	4.1
Clearfield	0.0	8.5	0.0	0.0	0.0	19.0	14.3	16.1	2.4	4.6
Cottonwood Heights	0.0	31.0	0.0	0.0	0.0	0.9	1.2	1.1	0.0	0.0
Draper	0.0	22.1	0.0	0.0	0.6	12.1	7.5	9.8	9.4	3.2
Holladay	0.0	9.9	0.0	0.0	0.0	21.1	1.5	5.1	20.2	6.0

Table D. Cities — City Government Finances, City Government Employment, and Climate

City	City government finances, 2012 (cont.)			Climate[2]						
	Debt outstanding		Debt issued during year	Average daily temperature				Annual precipitation (inches)	Heating degree days	Cooling degree days
	Total (mil dol)	Per capita[1] (dollars)		Mean		Limits				
				January	July	January[3]	July[4]			
	137	138	139	140	141	142	143	144	145	146
TEXAS— Cont'd										
Irving	567.8	2,515	137.2	45.9	86.5	36.4	96.1	37.05	2,219	2,878
Keller	128.2	3,054	0.0	43.0	84.1	31.4	95.7	34.12	2,608	2,358
Killeen	238.9	1,773	75.1	46.0	83.5	34.0	95.3	32.88	2,190	2,477
Kingsville	28.3	1,072	10.0	55.9	84.3	43.4	95.5	29.03	1,001	3,404
Kyle	69.4	2,246	7.7	NA	NA	NA	NA	NA	NA	NA
Lake Jackson	42.1	1,549	0.0	54.0	83.7	45.4	90.2	50.66	1,234	3,003
Lancaster	96.3	2,540	0.0	44.4	84.0	33.3	95.7	38.69	2,380	2,452
La Porte	45.1	1,307	0.0	51.6	83.6	41.9	91.6	53.75	1,471	2,841
Laredo	576.1	2,347	109.7	55.6	88.5	43.7	101.6	21.53	931	4,213
League City	210.1	2,379	39.8	52.7	82.7	43.1	91.2	51.73	1,365	2,815
Leander	176.0	5,952	0.0	NA	NA	NA	NA	NA	NA	NA
Lewisville	244.1	2,452	15.1	42.7	83.6	32.0	94.1	37.79	2,650	2,269
Little Elm	74.2	2,564	0.0	NA	NA	NA	NA	NA	NA	NA
Longview	160.6	1,975	39.2	45.4	83.4	33.7	94.5	49.06	2,319	2,355
Lubbock	1,342.1	5,681	257.0	38.1	79.8	24.4	91.9	18.69	3,508	1,769
Lufkin	179.5	4,983	21.3	48.6	82.6	37.9	93.5	46.62	1,900	2,480
McAllen	182.6	1,349	18.6	58.7	85.1	48.2	95.5	22.61	719	3,898
McKinney	313.4	2,184	16.9	41.8	82.4	31.1	92.7	41.01	2,843	2,060
Mansfield	183.2	3,084	26.8	43.7	84.3	33.2	94.9	34.54	2,437	2,508
Mesquite	242.0	1,687	42.9	45.9	86.5	36.4	96.1	37.05	2,219	2,878
Midland	125.3	1,046	6.0	44.5	81.8	29.5	95.6	14.84	2,479	2,241
Mission	387.2	4,787	51.7	58.8	86.3	47.5	97.7	22.13	740	4,128
Missouri City	174.1	2,535	5.1	51.8	84.1	41.6	93.7	49.34	1,475	2,950
Nacogdoches	62.8	1,856	1.7	46.5	83.9	36.4	93.5	48.36	2,150	2,555
New Braunfels	122.5	2,004	19.1	48.6	82.7	35.5	94.7	35.74	1,840	2,545
North Richland Hills	95.6	1,463	9.4	44.1	85.0	34.0	95.4	34.73	2,370	2,568
Odessa	124.0	1,168	0.0	43.2	81.7	29.6	94.3	14.80	2,716	2,139
Paris	25.2	1,004	0.0	40.6	83.1	29.9	94.3	47.82	2,972	2,197
Pasadena	223.9	1,467	34.6	54.3	84.5	45.2	93.6	53.96	1,174	3,179
Pearland	497.5	5,162	21.5	54.3	84.5	45.2	93.6	53.96	1,174	3,179
Pflugerville	167.6	3,224	21.9	NA	NA	NA	NA	NA	NA	NA
Pharr	103.3	1,410	2.2	60.1	85.9	50.3	96.1	22.96	624	4,181
Plano	352.8	1,293	21.4	44.1	85.0	34.0	95.4	34.73	2,370	2,568
Port Arthur	88.1	1,615	9.5	52.2	82.7	42.9	91.6	59.89	1,447	2,823
Richardson	311.9	3,007	21.2	45.9	86.5	36.4	96.1	37.05	2,219	2,878
Rockwall	163.4	4,091	17.3	NA	NA	NA	NA	NA	NA	NA
Rosenberg	52.3	1,608	15.4	NA	NA	NA	NA	NA	NA	NA
Round Rock	260.2	2,439	16.1	47.2	83.8	35.1	95.7	36.42	1,998	2,584
Rowlett	119.6	2,070	9.2	42.1	82.8	30.8	94.2	40.06	2,710	2,212
San Angelo	234.6	2,440	163.8	44.9	82.4	31.8	94.4	20.91	2,396	2,383
San Antonio	8,830.9	6,374	589.4	50.3	84.3	38.6	94.6	32.92	1,573	3,038
San Juan	24.6	697	5.9	60.1	85.9	50.3	96.1	22.96	624	4,181
San Marcos	264.7	5,283	17.2	49.9	84.4	38.6	95.1	37.19	1,629	2,913
Schertz	73.9	2,118	13.8	NA	NA	NA	NA	NA	NA	NA
Seguin	172.6	6,568	18.6	NA	NA	NA	NA	NA	NA	NA
Sherman	23.5	602	0.0	41.5	82.8	32.2	92.7	42.04	2,850	2,137
Socorro	12.3	374	8.1	44.9	83.6	29.2	98.7	9.71	2,557	2,372
Southlake	179.6	6,478	11.1	NA	NA	NA	NA	NA	NA	NA
Sugar Land	363.3	4,437	130.2	51.8	84.1	41.6	93.7	49.34	1,475	2,950
Temple	177.8	2,572	24.1	46.1	83.7	34.9	95.0	35.81	2,191	2,551
Texarkana	69.8	1,880	0.0	41.6	82.6	30.7	93.1	51.24	2,893	2,138
Texas City	91.3	1,997	31.9	55.8	84.3	49.7	88.7	43.84	1,008	3,268
The Colony	97.6	2,499	7.6	42.7	83.6	32.0	94.1	37.79	2,650	2,269
Tyler	428.2	4,307	9.4	47.5	83.4	37.7	93.6	45.27	1,958	2,521
Victoria	179.1	2,780	9.7	53.2	84.2	43.6	93.4	40.10	1,248	3,203
Waco	8,413.1	65,880	7.3	46.1	85.4	35.1	96.7	33.34	2,164	2,840
Waxahachie	170.0	5,475	0.0	NA	NA	NA	NA	NA	NA	NA
Weatherford	117.6	4,447	33.5	NA	NA	NA	NA	NA	NA	NA
Weslaco	115.6	3,134	11.5	58.6	84.5	47.7	95.4	25.37	755	3,791
Wichita Falls	168.4	1,607	0.0	40.5	84.8	28.9	97.2	28.83	3,024	2,396
Wylie	119.8	2,699	5.4	NA	NA	NA	NA	NA	NA	NA
UTAH	X	X	X	X	X	X	X	X	X	X
American Fork	62.3	2,284	1.7	NA	NA	NA	NA	NA	NA	NA
Bountiful	18.1	421	0.0	29.1	75.8	21.6	88.4	22.40	5,937	861
Cedar City	21.1	725	0.0	NA	NA	NA	NA	NA	NA	NA
Clearfield	24.6	809	0.0	27.6	74.2	18.6	89.9	20.75	6,142	746
Cottonwood Heights	0.0	0	0.0	NA	NA	NA	NA	NA	NA	NA
Draper	33.1	749	0.0	31.6	78.0	22.0	95.3	15.76	5,251	1,172
Holladay	20.8	770	9.2	NA	NA	NA	NA	NA	NA	NA

1. Based on the population estimated as of July 1 of the year shown.   2. Represents normal values based on the 30-year period, 1971±2000.   3. Average daily minimum.   4. Average daily maximum.

Table D. Cities — Land Area and Population

STATE Place code	City	Land area[1] (sq. mi)	Total persons 2018	Rank	Per square mile	Race 2017 Race alone[2] (percent) White	Black or African American	American Indian, Alaskan Native	Asian	Hawaiian Pacific Islander	Some other race	Two or more races (percent)
		1	2	3	4	5	6	7	8	9	10	11
	UTAH— Cont'd											
49 40,360	Kaysville	10.5	32,095	1,187	3,056.7	NA	NA	NA	NA	NA	NA	NA
49 43,660	Layton	22.3	77,303	449	3,466.5	88.6	1.2	0.8	2.7	1.1	0.8	4.8
49 44,320	Lehi	27.9	66,037	560	2,366.9	89.1	0.7	1.3	3.0	1.1	1.8	3.0
49 45,860	Logan	17.7	51,619	745	2,916.3	88.2	1.2	0.9	2.1	0.3	3.9	3.4
49 49,710	Midvale	5.9	33,636	1,137	5,701.0	80.1	2.8	0.0	6.7	1.7	5.7	3.0
49 53,230	Murray	12.3	49,308	780	4,008.8	86.2	3.2	0.0	1.0	1.0	5.4	3.2
49 55,980	Ogden	27.3	87,325	380	3,198.7	79.9	2.6	1.4	0.6	0.2	10.6	4.7
49 57,300	Orem	18.5	97,521	319	5,271.4	89.7	0.5	0.8	3.0	1.9	2.0	2.0
49 60,930	Pleasant Grove	9.1	38,428	1,000	4,222.9	90.8	0.4	0.7	1.3	1.0	4.6	1.2
49 62,470	Provo	41.7	116,702	245	2,798.6	88.4	1.1	0.3	3.0	0.5	3.4	3.4
49 64,340	Riverton	12.6	44,419	862	3,525.3	NA	NA	NA	NA	NA	NA	NA
49 65,110	Roy	7.9	38,773	993	4,908.0	86.9	0.4	0.0	2.2	0.3	6.7	3.5
49 65,330	St. George	76.9	87,178	381	1,133.7	89.0	1.1	0.1	3.1	1.5	3.3	1.9
49 67,000	Salt Lake City	111.2	200,591	114	1,803.9	73.0	1.7	1.7	5.4	1.9	12.9	3.3
49 67,440	Sandy	23.8	96,901	323	4,071.5	91.7	0.5	0.3	2.6	0.3	2.9	1.5
49 70,850	South Jordan	22.2	74,149	482	3,340.0	88.5	0.5	0.3	4.5	1.6	2.0	2.6
49 71,290	Spanish Fork	16.0	39,961	962	2,497.6	95.0	0.1	0.1	0.3	1.0	1.2	2.3
49 72,280	Springville	14.3	33,104	1,152	2,315.0	85.3	1.1	0.2	1.1	0.0	8.8	3.4
49 75,360	Taylorsville	10.9	60,192	619	5,522.2	70.3	1.2	2.2	5.4	0.4	15.9	4.7
49 76,680	Tooele	24.1	35,251	1,089	1,462.7	88.0	0.5	0.7	0.0	0.8	6.3	3.6
49 82,950	West Jordan	32.3	116,046	248	3,592.8	73.2	1.3	0.7	3.3	0.4	17.9	3.3
49 83,470	West Valley City	35.5	136,401	200	3,842.3	55.6	3.0	0.7	5.1	2.7	26.4	6.4
50 00,000	VERMONT	9,217.9	626,299	X	67.9	94.2	1.3	0.4	1.8	0.0	0.2	2.1
50 10,675	Burlington	10.3	42,899	886	4,165.0	80.8	6.4	0.1	10.3	0.0	0.3	2.1
51 00,000	VIRGINIA	39,481.9	8,517,685	X	215.7	67.5	19.2	0.3	6.4	0.0	2.6	3.9
51 01,000	Alexandria	14.9	160,530	159	10,773.8	61.6	23.4	0.4	5.8	0.0	4.9	3.9
51 07,784	Blacksburg	19.7	44,678	855	2,267.9	79.6	3.9	0.1	14.1	0.1	1.1	1.0
51 14,968	Charlottesville	10.2	48,117	805	4,717.4	70.3	18.9	0.4	8.2	0.1	0.3	1.8
51 16,000	Chesapeake	338.5	242,634	92	716.8	60.8	30.6	0.2	3.2	0.0	0.9	4.2
51 21,344	Danville	42.8	40,693	941	950.8	46.1	43.8	0.1	0.8	0.4	0.2	8.7
51 35,000	Hampton	51.4	134,313	203	2,613.1	40.5	49.5	0.3	2.5	0.1	2.5	4.6
51 35,624	Harrisonburg	17.3	54,033	711	3,123.3	78.6	7.9	0.0	3.6	0.0	1.1	8.7
51 44,984	Leesburg	12.4	53,917	715	4,348.1	79.9	6.1	0.3	4.8	0.0	3.8	5.0
51 47,672	Lynchburg	49.0	82,126	417	1,676.0	64.4	27.6	0.7	2.7	0.1	1.1	3.5
51 48,952	Manassas	9.9	41,641	914	4,206.2	62.1	11.4	0.1	7.2	0.0	11.1	8.1
51 56,000	Newport News	69.1	178,626	144	2,585.0	48.9	40.6	0.5	3.2	0.1	1.5	5.2
51 57,000	Norfolk	53.3	244,076	91	4,579.3	46.3	41.4	0.4	3.5	0.1	3.3	4.8
51 61,832	Petersburg	22.7	31,567	1,203	1,390.6	15.6	75.9	0.0	0.8	0.1	5.7	1.9
51 64,000	Portsmouth	33.3	94,632	338	2,841.8	39.5	53.3	0.5	1.4	0.1	1.2	4.0
51 67,000	Richmond	59.9	228,783	98	3,819.4	45.6	47.1	0.0	2.0	0.0	1.5	3.6
51 68,000	Roanoke	42.5	99,920	310	2,351.1	61.3	28.2	0.3	3.1	0.0	2.2	4.8
51 76,432	Suffolk	399.2	91,185	362	228.4	51.7	41.6	0.4	2.2	0.0	0.3	3.8
51 82,000	Virginia Beach	244.7	450,189	44	1,839.8	65.5	19.0	0.2	6.8	0.1	2.6	5.9
51 86,720	Winchester	9.2	28,108	1,315	3,055.2	76.0	12.5	0.0	1.5	0.3	4.5	5.2
53 00,000	WASHINGTON	66,453.0	7,535,591	X	113.4	75.4	3.7	1.3	8.5	0.7	4.6	5.9
53 03,180	Auburn	29.5	81,905	418	2,776.4	69.2	3.9	1.1	11.2	3.7	5.8	5.1
53 05,210	Bellevue	33.5	147,599	177	4,405.9	56.2	2.7	0.3	34.4	0.8	2.0	3.8
53 05,280	Bellingham	27.7	90,665	364	3,273.1	84.2	1.4	1.4	5.4	0.0	1.3	6.2
53 07,380	Bothell	13.7	46,657	832	3,405.6	64.3	1.3	0.7	23.0	0.4	6.6	3.6
53 07,695	Bremerton	28.5	41,235	928	1,446.8	77.7	5.6	0.9	7.8	0.5	1.8	5.8
53 08,850	Burien	10.1	51,908	740	5,139.4	52.0	10.7	0.5	19.0	1.5	11.7	4.6
53 17,635	Des Moines	6.4	32,364	1,173	5,056.9	51.2	7.2	0.3	12.1	6.5	13.5	9.2
53 20,750	Edmonds	8.9	42,767	889	4,805.3	NA	NA	NA	NA	NA	NA	NA
53 22,640	Everett	33.2	111,262	270	3,351.3	73.3	6.0	0.3	8.3	0.3	5.2	6.8
53 23,515	Federal Way	22.2	97,044	322	4,371.4	51.6	12.5	0.7	14.2	1.1	10.7	9.2
53 33,805	Issaquah	12.1	39,378	981	3,254.4	65.8	1.6	0.1	24.9	0.0	6.1	1.5
53 35,275	Kennewick	27.4	82,943	409	3,027.1	79.3	2.1	2.0	3.1	0.0	10.6	2.9
53 35,415	Kent	33.7	129,618	213	3,846.2	51.1	9.4	0.7	21.5	0.6	9.7	7.0
53 35,940	Kirkland	17.8	89,557	368	5,031.3	74.5	1.9	0.1	14.3	0.0	1.6	7.6
53 36,745	Lacey	17.0	50,718	756	2,983.4	70.4	5.2	0.2	9.1	1.9	3.0	10.1
53 37,900	Lake Stevens	8.9	33,378	1,146	3,750.3	87.7	2.3	0.4	5.0	0.0	0.5	4.2
53 38,038	Lakewood	17.1	60,538	615	3,540.2	59.5	11.1	2.1	9.6	5.2	1.6	10.9
53 40,245	Longview	14.9	38,112	1,011	2,557.9	79.7	3.8	1.7	2.0	0.9	1.5	10.4
53 40,840	Lynnwood	7.8	38,511	998	4,937.3	61.5	6.8	0.6	14.3	0.1	7.2	9.4
53 43,955	Marysville	20.6	69,779	515	3,387.3	80.7	1.3	1.1	6.9	0.9	2.7	6.4
53 47,560	Mount Vernon	12.3	35,741	1,076	2,905.8	69.1	1.2	3.1	2.7	0.3	20.6	3.0
53 51,300	Olympia	18.2	52,555	734	2,887.6	81.9	4.3	2.1	7.1	0.2	0.0	4.4

1. Dry land or land partially or temporarily covered by water.   2. Hispanic or Latino persons may be of any race.

City	Percent Hispanic or Latino[1], 2017	Percent foreign born, 2017	Age of population (percent), 2017							Median age, 2017	Percent female, 2017	Population			
			Under 18 years	18 to 24 years	25 to 34 years	35 to 44 years	45 to 54 years	55 to 64 years	65 years and over			Census counts		Percent change	
												2000	2010	2000-2010	2001-2018
	12	13	14	15	16	17	18	19	20	21	22	23	24	25	26
UTAH— Cont'd															
Kaysville	5.5	1.5	29.3	11.5	9.5	10.8	14.9	11.9	12.1	34.6	46.9	20,351	27,578	35.5	16.4
Layton	11.5	5.5	30.0	10.2	14.3	14.1	10.0	10.7	10.6	31.8	49.5	58,474	67,500	15.4	14.5
Lehi	9.1	6.2	44.4	7.8	13.5	18.3	5.2	6.1	4.7	22.7	50.1	19,028	47,776	151.1	38.2
Logan	11.7	7.0	20.8	32.5	17.4	9.1	5.7	6.3	8.2	24.1	47.1	42,670	48,218	13.0	7.1
Midvale	23.8	16.8	23.8	6.8	24.7	16.4	9.0	11.2	8.1	32.8	51.1	27,029	27,999	3.6	20.1
Murray	11.4	9.1	19.4	9.4	17.4	11.3	9.3	15.9	17.2	38.7	54.8	34,024	46,685	37.2	5.6
Ogden	33.0	11.7	27.5	11.6	16.5	13.0	9.8	10.9	10.9	32.0	48.9	77,226	82,838	7.3	5.4
Orem	13.1	10.0	31.2	18.7	15.3	10.2	8.3	7.1	9.1	25.0	48.6	84,324	88,328	4.7	10.4
Pleasant Grove	14.0	8.6	27.9	16.5	15.4	10.3	10.7	7.6	11.6	28.5	47.0	23,468	33,547	42.9	14.5
Provo	17.3	11.7	21.1	34.0	17.6	9.2	6.4	5.4	6.2	24.0	51.3	105,166	112,487	7.0	3.7
Riverton	3.2	4.3	36.6	7.2	10.3	19.4	11.7	7.4	7.4	32.2	51.1	25,011	38,832	55.3	14.4
Roy	16.0	4.5	28.4	8.7	16.9	11.2	11.1	11.4	12.2	32.4	49.8	32,885	36,891	12.2	5.1
St. George	11.2	7.1	24.2	11.1	11.9	10.1	9.2	10.0	23.6	38.1	49.6	49,663	72,759	46.5	19.8
Salt Lake City	20.8	16.3	21.9	13.0	21.5	14.4	9.4	9.2	10.5	31.2	50.5	181,743	186,443	2.6	7.6
Sandy	12.1	9.4	26.0	9.6	12.5	12.6	11.6	13.5	14.1	36.4	50.0	88,418	89,977	1.8	7.7
South Jordan	6.8	6.2	32.0	6.1	12.8	15.4	13.0	9.1	11.6	34.0	52.2	29,437	50,473	71.5	46.9
Spanish Fork	13.8	8.5	36.8	12.6	13.8	15.4	10.8	4.4	6.2	25.2	48.3	20,246	34,748	71.6	15.0
Springville	19.2	10.7	37.7	11.4	15.8	11.7	8.6	6.2	8.6	25.4	45.8	20,424	29,584	44.8	11.9
Taylorsville	25.4	16.4	22.4	8.4	15.1	13.3	14.5	13.5	12.8	37.6	47.8	57,439	58,691	2.2	2.6
Tooele	16.5	2.1	29.3	10.8	13.3	14.1	12.8	10.7	9.0	32.7	51.7	22,502	31,603	40.4	11.5
West Jordan	24.6	12.7	30.9	9.2	17.2	15.5	11.9	8.3	6.9	31.2	50.1	68,336	103,601	51.6	12.0
West Valley City	36.5	22.0	30.5	10.1	16.1	14.8	11.0	7.8	9.6	31.0	46.9	108,896	129,491	18.9	5.3
VERMONT	1.9	4.5	18.9	10.7	11.8	11.1	13.3	15.4	18.8	42.6	50.6	608,827	625,744	2.8	0.1
Burlington	5.1	14.6	13.1	34.6	16.8	7.5	10.1	6.3	11.5	26.1	49.3	38,889	42,417	9.1	1.1
VIRGINIA	9.3	12.5	22.1	9.7	13.8	13.1	13.5	12.9	15.0	38.2	50.8	7,078,515	8,001,055	13.0	6.5
Alexandria	16.6	31.0	18.0	5.9	21.9	19.6	12.6	10.7	11.2	37.0	52.0	128,283	140,008	9.1	14.7
Blacksburg	6.2	10.7	12.7	55.7	10.9	6.7	3.4	3.4	7.2	21.8	42.6	39,573	42,528	7.5	5.1
Charlottesville	5.6	20.1	15.9	21.8	18.5	12.6	10.1	9.0	12.1	31.2	54.3	45,049	43,425	-3.6	10.8
Chesapeake	6.2	6.4	24.3	8.8	13.5	13.5	14.0	13.1	12.8	36.7	51.1	199,184	222,306	11.6	9.1
Danville	4.4	2.7	22.3	8.0	12.0	12.2	11.1	14.1	20.3	40.6	54.7	48,411	43,077	-11.0	-5.5
Hampton	5.7	4.5	20.9	11.7	15.5	11.9	11.4	13.6	15.0	36.6	51.5	146,437	137,384	-6.2	-2.2
Harrisonburg	19.8	18.8	17.1	33.9	13.9	10.5	8.1	8.0	8.4	24.3	52.8	40,468	48,900	20.8	10.5
Leesburg	19.1	19.1	27.3	10.6	12.4	15.0	16.6	10.2	8.0	34.6	48.7	28,311	42,614	50.5	26.5
Lynchburg	4.0	4.7	19.4	25.7	13.5	9.6	7.9	9.7	14.3	27.8	54.2	65,269	75,533	15.7	8.7
Manassas	36.1	27.2	31.6	7.1	16.3	12.7	13.0	12.3	7.2	31.8	48.1	35,135	37,819	7.6	10.1
Newport News	9.1	7.1	23.2	12.0	17.0	11.6	11.6	11.9	12.7	33.4	51.6	180,150	180,994	0.5	-1.3
Norfolk	8.0	6.9	19.8	18.1	19.2	11.1	10.1	10.7	10.9	30.5	47.7	234,403	242,827	3.6	0.5
Petersburg	5.2	3.6	20.5	8.1	18.0	9.8	13.6	12.6	17.4	38.6	54.5	33,740	32,435	-3.9	-2.7
Portsmouth	4.4	3.3	23.0	9.9	15.5	12.6	11.7	12.6	14.6	36.0	52.3	100,565	95,527	-5.0	-0.9
Richmond	6.7	6.1	17.8	13.0	21.5	11.8	11.2	12.1	12.7	34.0	52.8	197,790	204,327	3.3	12.0
Roanoke	6.4	7.4	21.7	6.8	15.4	13.0	13.0	13.3	16.9	40.0	52.1	94,911	96,912	2.1	3.1
Suffolk	4.4	3.7	24.4	7.1	14.5	12.4	14.5	13.0	14.2	37.3	51.6	63,677	84,572	32.8	7.8
Virginia Beach	8.2	9.4	22.3	9.5	16.7	13.0	12.7	12.3	13.7	36.2	50.8	425,257	437,903	3.0	2.8
Winchester	18.1	13.2	21.9	13.3	15.3	9.4	11.6	12.1	16.3	34.7	50.4	23,585	26,223	11.2	7.2
WASHINGTON	12.7	14.3	22.2	8.9	14.9	13.2	12.8	12.9	15.1	37.7	50.1	5,894,121	6,724,540	14.1	12.1
Auburn	11.7	24.0	25.0	8.2	16.3	14.3	12.3	14.9	8.9	35.3	49.5	40,314	70,164	74.0	16.7
Bellevue	7.4	39.1	19.7	5.3	20.3	13.6	15.8	11.3	14.1	37.4	48.0	109,569	127,885	16.7	15.4
Bellingham	8.0	9.3	13.0	24.3	13.3	12.4	8.5	11.2	17.3	34.5	50.2	67,171	81,252	21.0	11.6
Bothell	14.0	24.9	21.5	6.5	18.5	16.3	13.1	7.3	16.9	36.7	51.2	30,150	39,868	32.2	17.0
Bremerton	6.9	8.4	15.8	15.6	19.6	9.2	11.7	11.0	17.3	34.4	49.7	37,259	37,876	1.7	8.9
Burien	22.8	26.9	21.8	7.9	13.0	13.8	13.9	13.2	16.4	40.4	49.5	31,881	48,081	50.8	8.0
Des Moines	16.8	17.1	18.9	11.2	15.7	11.8	12.8	13.8	15.7	39.7	50.2	29,267	29,654	1.3	9.1
Edmonds	3.6	11.2	14.0	10.0	11.8	9.3	13.1	16.4	25.4	49.0	52.2	39,515	39,747	0.6	7.6
Everett	15.5	18.8	19.7	13.0	17.2	12.8	13.0	13.3	11.1	35.2	48.0	91,488	103,070	12.7	7.9
Federal Way	20.7	25.9	21.9	11.6	14.3	13.9	13.8	10.5	14.2	36.9	50.2	83,259	89,300	7.3	8.7
Issaquah	12.8	31.1	23.0	3.4	16.6	18.9	12.7	10.7	14.8	37.1	52.0	11,212	30,440	171.5	29.4
Kennewick	32.2	13.9	27.4	9.3	15.1	12.1	9.6	10.5	16.0	34.3	49.6	54,693	73,995	35.3	12.1
Kent	15.0	33.7	23.7	10.2	16.3	13.9	12.1	11.9	11.8	34.8	48.4	79,524	118,614	49.2	9.3
Kirkland	5.5	24.9	21.2	6.5	18.4	16.6	12.4	13.5	11.4	36.8	51.2	45,054	80,585	78.9	11.1
Lacey	10.1	11.6	22.0	12.7	14.4	13.2	10.3	11.2	16.1	35.9	51.4	31,226	42,586	36.4	19.1
Lake Stevens	19.7	9.7	32.7	7.1	17.1	13.1	11.9	11.9	6.1	32.2	51.0	6,361	28,061	341.1	18.9
Lakewood	16.3	12.9	23.3	10.4	17.7	11.6	9.9	12.5	14.6	33.7	51.1	58,211	57,532	-1.2	5.2
Longview	15.6	4.5	24.7	7.2	13.0	10.7	12.5	13.5	18.5	38.2	51.5	34,660	36,831	6.3	3.5
Lynnwood	15.3	30.9	23.7	9.2	12.5	14.8	12.9	13.6	13.4	39.0	49.0	33,847	35,873	6.0	7.4
Marysville	9.4	8.9	25.9	7.4	11.6	13.8	15.7	12.0	13.6	39.0	49.4	25,315	60,007	137.0	16.3
Mount Vernon	31.8	17.4	21.7	11.7	15.3	11.6	12.2	9.9	17.7	36.3	49.6	26,232	31,720	20.9	12.7
Olympia	6.6	8.9	15.1	10.0	16.5	15.0	13.1	11.6	18.7	40.2	52.8	42,514	46,881	10.3	12.1

1. May be of any race.

City	Households, 2017							Serious crimes known to police[2], 2016					Educational attainment, 2017		
			Percent						Total		Rate[3]			Attainment[4] (percent)	
	Number	Persons per household	Family	Married couple family	Female headed[1]	Non-family	One person	Persons in group quarters, 2017	Number	Rate	Violent	Property	Population age 25 and over	High school graduate or less	Bachelor's degree or more
	27	28	29	30	31	32	33	34	35	36	37	38	39	40	41
UTAH— Cont'd															
Kaysville	9,578	3.32	81.3	72.6	7.7	18.7	18.2	NA	289	931	58	873	18,808	14.7	44.9
Layton	23,579	3.25	79.3	67.7	7.5	20.7	14.8	141	1,825	2,418	172	2,246	45,842	31.0	34.9
Lehi	15,897	3.94	85.2	77.3	5.5	14.8	13.0	NA	846	1,391	127	1,265	29,962	16.0	47.7
Logan	18,161	2.66	54.1	41.4	9.2	45.9	24.6	2,717	906	1,785	102	1,682	23,906	23.1	39.4
Midvale	13,840	2.39	55.3	42.2	10.4	44.7	37.3	NA	NA	NA	NA	NA	23,043	28.7	34.6
Murray	18,488	2.65	67.1	51.3	10.9	32.9	23.8	NA	3,811	7,659	553	7,106	35,103	31.6	35.6
Ogden	30,058	2.81	65.2	45.8	13.7	34.8	28.6	2,616	4,509	5,247	514	4,733	53,086	48.0	22.2
Orem	28,262	3.41	79.4	65.6	10.1	20.6	12.9	1,537	2,512	2,627	68	2,559	48,946	20.3	42.3
Pleasant Grove	12,277	3.16	77.4	63.7	6.1	22.6	13.7	NA	268	687	31	657	21,600	17.2	44.9
Provo	34,962	3.01	70.0	57.8	7.3	30.0	17.7	12,134	2,866	2,476	129	2,348	52,660	21.6	42.3
Riverton	11,399	3.79	95.5	85.4	6.2	4.5	2.7	NA	NA	NA	NA	NA	24,339	15.1	43.1
Roy	12,558	3.06	73.8	56.5	8.6	26.2	23.3	NA	744	1,949	113	1,837	24,255	40.2	19.0
St. George	29,352	2.84	66.1	54.1	10.0	33.9	29.8	983	1,626	1,989	196	1,793	54,642	28.8	27.4
Salt Lake City	78,086	2.49	51.7	39.3	8.6	48.3	35.3	6,228	18,287	9,430	920	8,510	130,440	27.7	46.8
Sandy	31,784	3.01	79.2	65.2	8.6	20.8	17.2	414	3,312	3,501	170	3,331	61,888	23.1	41.2
South Jordan	21,745	3.26	81.7	76.5	4.0	18.3	15.7	NA	1,620	2,307	77	2,230	43,903	15.3	43.6
Spanish Fork	10,385	3.71	87.0	77.4	6.7	13.0	11.8	940	552	1,433	26	1,407	19,967	28.8	31.3
Springville	8,394	3.95	83.5	76.0	6.3	16.5	10.8	NA	695	2,117	85	2,032	16,946	28.3	32.9
Taylorsville	21,791	2.75	72.1	48.3	14.9	27.9	21.3	NA	NA	NA	NA	NA	41,484	39.5	25.5
Tooele	10,812	3.18	81.3	60.8	11.8	18.7	17.7	NA	1,515	4,529	436	4,093	20,755	41.6	21.0
West Jordan	32,635	3.47	79.1	63.8	11.1	20.9	14.9	533	3,963	3,489	275	3,214	68,168	42.0	21.0
West Valley City	40,010	3.40	75.1	51.4	16.2	24.9	17.4	310	7,256	5,275	596	4,679	80,936	52.3	13.4
VERMONT	256,629	2.33	59.9	46.7	9.2	40.1	31.0	25,053	11,591	1,856	158	1,697	439,267	36.4	38.3
Burlington	15,571	2.26	37.6	26.2	9.0	62.4	38.3	7,007	1,505	3,545	344	3,201	22,059	33.6	48.4
VIRGINIA	3,120,880	2.64	67.0	50.9	11.8	33.0	26.6	242,294	174,714	2,077	218	1,859	5,779,221	34.4	38.7
Alexandria	69,667	2.28	50.9	37.9	9.5	49.1	39.9	1,456	3,128	2,014	185	1,828	121,705	19.7	62.5
Blacksburg	12,166	2.91	38.2	30.2	6.5	61.8	31.4	9,127	456	1,024	97	928	14,094	13.4	76.2
Charlottesville	19,100	2.35	39.1	25.8	9.3	60.9	37.9	3,101	1,477	3,144	526	2,618	29,925	23.9	56.3
Chesapeake	83,402	2.83	76.6	56.4	15.0	23.4	20.5	4,206	7,008	2,962	412	2,550	160,787	30.1	35.1
Danville	18,149	2.18	54.6	31.5	19.2	45.4	38.2	1,593	1,872	4,491	804	3,687	28,665	47.8	18.0
Hampton	53,267	2.44	62.9	40.8	18.0	37.1	30.9	4,589	5,099	3,763	323	3,440	90,781	35.0	28.2
Harrisonburg	16,885	2.77	58.3	39.2	13.0	41.7	25.4	7,410	1,217	2,297	219	2,078	26,530	44.6	37.9
Leesburg	18,823	2.87	70.0	57.6	9.9	30.0	24.3	NA	932	1,758	209	1,549	33,701	24.5	54.5
Lynchburg	27,814	2.52	56.6	37.1	16.0	43.4	34.2	10,874	2,114	2,635	375	2,260	44,468	35.2	33.3
Manassas	12,807	3.23	76.8	56.2	14.7	23.2	18.6	NA	938	2,219	291	1,928	25,461	41.0	30.1
Newport News	69,249	2.46	63.4	37.5	19.6	36.6	30.8	9,330	6,454	3,552	472	3,080	116,240	38.9	25.3
Norfolk	87,857	2.48	57.4	36.2	16.9	42.6	33.5	26,579	11,261	4,583	659	3,923	151,907	37.3	29.2
Petersburg	13,230	2.35	60.3	21.8	30.1	39.7	34.8	630	1,312	4,063	740	3,323	22,684	53.6	18.4
Portsmouth	36,246	2.51	56.0	36.6	16.3	44.0	38.2	3,702	6,226	6,498	796	5,702	63,441	40.5	22.5
Richmond	87,401	2.48	46.1	26.5	14.9	53.9	41.6	10,487	9,343	4,200	569	3,632	157,287	37.3	38.6
Roanoke	42,133	2.33	48.9	30.2	13.5	51.1	43.0	1,732	4,615	4,616	412	4,204	71,363	45.7	23.2
Suffolk	33,077	2.71	71.7	54.9	13.8	28.3	26.0	450	2,398	2,714	281	2,434	61,850	40.4	26.1
Virginia Beach	168,818	2.61	68.7	50.2	12.7	31.3	23.9	9,338	10,590	2,338	155	2,183	307,404	28.1	35.3
Winchester	10,222	2.63	56.5	39.2	10.1	43.5	33.5	1,043	842	3,077	223	2,854	18,111	44.4	32.5
WASHINGTON	2,840,377	2.56	64.6	49.9	9.8	35.4	26.5	142,990	276,676	3,796	302	3,494	5,101,968	30.8	35.5
Auburn	29,701	2.66	64.4	44.9	15.8	35.6	24.9	557	3,958	5,048	423	4,625	53,137	42.1	23.4
Bellevue	59,588	2.40	67.0	58.3	6.1	33.0	24.7	1,337	4,787	3,365	98	3,268	108,363	15.2	68.2
Bellingham	39,465	2.13	44.4	36.2	5.9	55.6	34.9	4,883	4,974	5,783	262	5,522	55,820	25.3	44.8
Bothell	17,365	2.48	64.4	51.4	6.1	35.6	26.2	589	1,265	2,886	114	2,772	31,434	23.2	54.0
Bremerton	17,628	2.16	54.0	37.7	14.6	46.0	35.2	3,008	1,778	4,460	502	3,959	28,163	31.6	23.7
Burien	18,792	2.72	71.0	49.9	10.2	29.0	25.2	477	2,830	5,556	489	5,067	36,286	40.4	30.8
Des Moines	11,523	2.66	60.2	47.7	6.1	39.8	32.2	642	1,413	4,482	374	4,108	21,832	36.3	29.8
Edmonds	19,172	2.18	56.6	43.0	8.8	43.4	31.4	372	1,229	2,947	177	2,769	32,065	16.9	48.2
Everett	42,895	2.47	53.9	35.6	10.6	46.1	33.0	4,175	6,099	5,596	450	5,146	74,169	36.6	24.7
Federal Way	35,162	2.72	65.1	43.8	15.4	34.9	25.2	969	6,479	6,725	474	6,251	64,378	37.8	26.3
Issaquah	15,575	2.39	64.2	56.7	5.3	35.8	30.1	NA	1,186	3,179	99	3,080	27,593	11.7	68.3
Kennewick	29,353	2.74	64.3	47.5	11.0	35.7	29.0	1,209	2,442	3,059	232	2,827	51,703	46.1	23.7
Kent	43,906	2.88	69.1	52.3	12.8	30.9	22.3	2,227	7,906	6,148	292	5,856	84,915	44.5	23.2
Kirkland	36,175	2.41	64.0	55.0	6.1	36.0	27.7	1,375	2,098	2,367	93	2,275	64,055	12.6	62.0
Lacey	19,010	2.57	69.9	55.0	13.0	30.1	22.6	947	1,833	3,882	231	3,651	32,498	29.3	31.6
Lake Stevens	10,500	3.12	74.7	54.6	12.6	25.3	20.5	NA	565	1,797	213	1,584	19,733	32.5	26.7
Lakewood	23,192	2.55	66.1	45.8	15.8	33.9	27.6	1,080	3,398	5,649	751	4,898	39,974	40.2	25.1
Longview	15,027	2.44	56.5	34.0	16.3	43.5	36.5	1,002	2,075	5,630	388	5,242	25,627	39.9	14.9
Lynnwood	13,708	2.73	68.0	52.0	11.5	32.0	24.8	791	2,769	7,440	387	7,053	25,697	28.4	28.5
Marysville	25,410	2.69	68.3	49.7	12.0	31.7	26.7	458	2,075	3,044	232	2,812	45,947	43.3	17.9
Mount Vernon	13,592	2.52	62.4	40.0	16.5	37.6	30.7	821	1,412	4,090	255	3,835	23,352	43.8	23.0
Olympia	23,648	2.12	49.5	37.7	9.1	50.5	36.5	1,357	2,699	5,295	394	4,901	38,635	21.3	44.0

1. No spouse present.   2. Data for serious crimes have not been adjusted for underreporting. This may affect comparability between geographic areas and over time.   3. Per 100,000 population estimated by the FBI.   4. Persons 25 years old and over.

Table D. Cities — Income and Housing

City	Money income, 2017 Households			Median family income	Median non-family income	Median earnings, 2017 All persons	Men	Women	Housing units, 2017 Total	Occupied	Percent owner occupied	Median value[1] (dollars)	Median gross rent (dollars)
	Median income	Percent with income less than $20,000	Percent with income of $200,000 or more										
	42	43	44	45	46	47	48	49	50	51	52	53	54

City	42	43	44	45	46	47	48	49	50	51	52	53	54
UTAH— Cont'd													
Kaysville	93,663	5.1	4.6	113,258	51,602	40,097	62,129	20,152	9,661	9,578	87.3	324,100	910
Layton	76,371	4.8	3.6	82,929	48,450	32,120	50,189	22,230	24,865	23,579	77.4	252,300	976
Lehi	90,888	5.6	6.6	100,075	43,637	40,696	61,759	18,945	16,600	15,897	76.7	346,200	1,371
Logan	38,858	19.2	0.9	48,319	29,701	17,633	20,742	15,002	19,687	18,161	37.7	183,000	754
Midvale	55,076	17.1	3.2	66,714	36,151	32,281	31,829	33,034	15,102	13,840	44.0	248,200	1,006
Murray	62,058	10.1	5.7	71,485	41,386	32,628	39,516	26,466	19,717	18,488	68.2	294,700	1,085
Ogden	44,965	19.1	2.6	54,721	31,531	26,532	28,342	24,513	32,642	30,058	55.2	182,600	794
Orem	61,729	11.6	4.6	64,183	39,206	23,866	33,744	16,270	30,331	28,262	55.3	266,600	1,006
Pleasant Grove	67,269	7.5	3.2	69,131	44,304	28,123	39,238	19,202	12,435	12,277	69.4	287,400	1,123
Provo	43,126	19.4	3.6	47,833	32,225	15,429	20,702	11,754	36,817	34,962	39.2	256,900	830
Riverton	103,911	2.0	10.1	105,381	45,984	44,197	70,120	27,686	11,447	11,399	91.0	354,500	1,764
Roy	65,673	5.1	2.4	75,224	41,474	31,927	42,698	23,184	13,316	12,558	81.6	189,100	1,071
St. George	54,210	15.3	3.6	66,751	31,990	26,231	29,416	21,049	35,834	29,352	64.2	289,500	943
Salt Lake City	58,688	18.7	6.8	75,015	40,649	31,105	32,833	27,401	85,135	78,086	48.9	307,900	946
Sandy	88,481	8.5	8.3	98,861	35,854	37,320	50,045	27,551	33,338	31,784	77.6	347,300	1,168
South Jordan	103,534	5.5	13.5	115,899	48,350	50,295	70,198	29,499	22,244	21,745	83.4	385,600	1,391
Spanish Fork	75,236	7.1	4.6	78,092	31,753	30,269	39,064	22,085	10,773	10,385	72.9	256,600	997
Springville	70,217	8.6	2.7	71,701	47,142	34,403	42,905	21,340	8,593	8,394	71.5	258,300	1,058
Taylorsville	62,044	11.7	1.3	71,961	39,935	30,561	31,906	28,569	22,989	21,791	69.3	244,100	1,011
Tooele	60,590	2.3	2.2	61,455	38,719	28,058	36,987	20,552	11,338	10,812	85.6	203,700	1,074
West Jordan	74,400	4.1	3.9	77,105	56,041	32,266	41,313	26,395	33,066	32,635	73.2	283,700	1,308
West Valley City	65,143	8.0	2.6	69,219	43,406	30,624	34,799	26,514	41,138	40,010	69.5	219,800	1,041
VERMONT	57,513	15.3	5.2	74,426	34,754	31,457	35,578	27,410	335,248	256,629	69.5	226,300	950
Burlington	47,117	24.6	8.3	71,366	32,477	16,766	19,522	15,157	16,123	15,571	36.7	271,400	1,217
VIRGINIA	71,535	12.6	9.9	86,279	43,210	37,483	45,226	31,126	3,512,917	3,120,880	66.6	273,400	1,179
Alexandria	100,530	6.8	15.9	118,757	81,512	54,026	60,847	50,409	76,588	69,667	42.5	573,200	1,693
Blacksburg	46,897	30.6	6.8	96,040	26,346	8,459	8,409	8,501	14,749	12,166	35.3	296,300	1,098
Charlottesville	55,601	16.3	11.4	90,099	45,305	35,159	36,785	32,445	20,638	19,100	43.9	284,800	1,106
Chesapeake	76,629	10.2	6.7	86,675	47,400	40,292	50,319	31,686	90,870	83,402	73.2	270,200	1,218
Danville	33,375	26.9	2.5	47,514	22,378	23,237	26,760	20,006	22,078	18,149	49.7	89,700	686
Hampton	54,062	16.6	2.7	68,705	37,266	29,576	34,066	25,783	60,116	53,267	54.9	184,100	1,072
Harrisonburg	47,633	19.5	1.4	66,094	29,199	15,840	27,301	11,728	18,295	16,885	42.5	202,600	881
Leesburg	93,791	6.9	14.9	120,673	58,530	42,591	54,021	31,764	18,925	18,823	70.8	429,900	1,598
Lynchburg	45,239	19.4	2.6	56,955	29,870	19,765	25,291	13,574	32,466	27,814	49.0	160,400	837
Manassas	78,397	6.7	11.0	82,071	58,845	36,871	44,232	31,544	13,841	12,807	65.4	319,800	1,443
Newport News	49,716	20.1	1.9	57,991	31,190	31,163	37,324	25,284	77,767	69,249	49.9	192,500	995
Norfolk	49,445	21.4	4.2	58,740	35,439	26,247	29,266	23,534	97,931	87,857	43.5	204,400	989
Petersburg	40,585	19.3	2.2	45,738	29,746	28,461	35,669	24,211	16,359	13,230	38.7	110,500	898
Portsmouth	50,242	18.1	1.7	61,227	36,781	29,922	37,583	24,394	40,891	36,246	54.1	175,200	976
Richmond	46,261	24.5	5.9	61,338	36,033	28,264	29,765	26,811	100,120	87,401	43.4	233,200	946
Roanoke	43,799	24.5	3.6	55,650	25,656	28,662	31,360	26,067	47,006	42,133	51.4	136,300	790
Suffolk	70,277	18.0	5.9	87,072	28,716	37,271	46,195	30,374	36,845	33,077	66.9	252,000	1,051
Virginia Beach	72,586	8.6	6.8	86,305	48,537	36,753	44,411	30,046	184,999	168,818	64.5	282,300	1,321
Winchester	50,579	11.3	3.3	66,875	38,940	28,224	31,982	21,236	11,520	10,222	50.1	236,100	876
WASHINGTON	70,979	12.1	8.5	84,594	44,213	38,437	46,620	31,202	3,103,263	2,840,377	62.8	339,000	1,216
Auburn	69,243	11.6	3.5	81,522	45,965	36,916	41,006	31,606	31,794	29,701	54.4	323,100	1,233
Bellevue	121,168	8.8	27.2	142,665	83,037	73,092	90,460	50,391	64,692	59,588	54.9	806,800	1,837
Bellingham	53,369	22.8	4.0	75,048	29,938	29,717	31,706	21,337	40,793	39,465	49.1	372,600	1,061
Bothell	92,034	8.8	10.8	114,973	60,205	54,714	70,210	41,426	17,547	17,365	65.2	540,800	1,663
Bremerton	47,581	18.9	3.2	59,380	35,712	30,018	32,298	22,770	19,567	17,628	47.6	237,500	956
Burien	71,089	12.4	8.4	85,888	35,525	35,140	36,069	32,182	20,234	18,792	52.9	393,500	1,353
Des Moines	62,020	5.9	3.2	82,164	46,098	38,026	40,451	36,245	12,243	11,523	58.5	360,800	1,310
Edmonds	84,222	6.0	15.7	102,804	59,585	44,421	49,659	39,329	20,442	19,172	69.7	564,200	1,323
Everett	61,248	14.4	2.6	78,872	46,896	33,500	37,485	27,462	45,413	42,895	45.9	325,900	1,220
Federal Way	61,804	12.4	7.1	70,588	42,704	35,160	36,830	30,085	36,546	35,162	53.1	340,500	1,274
Issaquah	118,620	5.7	18.5	160,445	64,954	77,225	115,336	45,018	16,538	15,575	61.1	590,400	2,072
Kennewick	51,061	17.6	4.3	61,959	27,273	28,934	33,678	23,840	31,127	29,353	60.0	200,500	897
Kent	67,497	11.2	4.4	71,193	48,304	35,437	36,561	32,270	45,588	43,906	52.4	343,700	1,369
Kirkland	106,722	7.6	21.8	141,379	59,525	62,493	81,092	46,992	38,611	36,175	63.8	682,300	1,768
Lacey	72,967	9.0	4.6	80,304	56,774	36,988	45,518	29,154	19,683	19,010	57.4	263,400	1,481
Lake Stevens	81,838	6.9	4.3	93,262	56,609	41,547	50,549	34,740	10,569	10,500	71.6	363,400	1,571
Lakewood	55,211	15.2	2.8	61,892	40,368	30,075	33,171	24,141	24,641	23,192	45.6	276,900	1,083
Longview	39,304	25.7	1.6	49,236	24,981	27,149	31,022	21,832	15,783	15,027	51.2	184,600	827
Lynnwood	71,421	13.9	4.3	91,456	43,393	39,449	47,629	32,157	14,923	13,708	59.8	411,100	1,185
Marysville	80,981	8.6	4.8	92,008	49,571	41,718	60,854	31,457	26,144	25,410	69.1	337,000	1,314
Mount Vernon	60,082	15.1	3.9	70,402	30,383	30,459	37,011	25,942	13,887	13,592	65.4	269,300	1,072
Olympia	58,657	15.6	5.2	83,255	44,693	32,288	40,639	30,377	24,307	23,648	49.7	314,100	1,125

1. Based on population estimated by the American Community Survey.   2. Includes units rented or sold but not occupied.   3. Specified owner-occupied units; $1,000,000 represents $1,000,000 or more.   4. 50.0 represents 50 percent or more.   5. 10.0 represents 10 percent or less.

Table D. Cities — Commuting, Computer Access, Migration, Labor Force, and Employment

City	Commuting[1], 2017		Computer access[2], 2017		Migration, 2017		Civilian labor force, 2018				Civilian employment[4], 2017				
	Percent		Percent						Unemployment		Population age 16 and older		Population age 16 to 64		
	Commuting	With commutes of 30 minutes or more	With a computer in the house	With Internet access	Percent who lived in the same house one year ago	Percent who lived in another state or county one year ago	Total	Percent change 2017-2018	Total	Rate[3]	Number	Percent in labor force	Number	Percent who worked full-year full-time
	55	56	57	58	59	60	61	62	63	64	65	66	67	68
UTAH— Cont'd														
Kaysville	76.7	31.8	96.9	93.8	81.6	12.3	14,669	1.1	384	2.6	23,221	63.5	19,375	51.7
Layton	79.9	35.9	95.4	90.7	82.5	7.0	38,871	1.2	1,183	3.0	56,982	70.9	48,833	53.2
Lehi	72.2	36.5	96.6	92.8	85.2	6.5	27,632	3.2	835	3.0	36,851	72.7	33,921	50.7
Logan	71.2	12.8	94.8	78.6	69.1	15.6	27,945	1.0	743	2.7	41,180	69.5	36,974	36.2
Midvale	77.9	23.0	97.9	87.1	84.0	8.2	20,204	1.1	644	3.2	26,308	75.8	23,633	55.4
Murray	79.4	17.1	90.9	85.9	84.8	4.5	29,229	1.0	889	3.0	40,823	66.0	32,364	50.3
Ogden	77.9	19.7	91.1	80.7	76.3	8.1	41,439	1.0	1,621	3.9	65,830	63.9	56,379	51.5
Orem	78.0	18.6	98.3	90.7	78.1	5.6	51,262	3.0	1,455	2.8	69,949	72.3	61,062	44.4
Pleasant Grove	75.5	26.9	98.3	87.9	79.1	9.0	19,296	3.0	552	2.9	29,677	69.4	25,155	49.3
Provo	63.0	15.7	97.6	67.9	65.3	14.9	67,248	3.0	1,797	2.7	94,299	69.9	87,020	32.0
Riverton	80.2	41.5	NA	NA	87.7	3.5	23,785	1.2	666	2.8	29,335	71.3	26,122	52.2
Roy	83.2	20.1	97.6	90.6	89.0	4.7	19,095	0.9	704	3.7	28,825	71.2	24,115	60.0
St. George	79.9	6.2	89.6	82.9	82.1	10.5	37,854	4.5	1,279	3.4	66,484	57.3	46,545	43.7
Salt Lake City	66.9	18.9	94.5	86.2	79.7	9.3	115,105	0.9	3,378	2.9	160,223	72.9	139,120	52.8
Sandy	76.6	29.5	96.0	90.1	86.7	4.8	53,732	1.0	1,599	3.0	74,416	66.5	60,834	52.5
South Jordan	77.5	42.1	99.1	89.5	83.5	7.1	36,147	1.0	1,043	2.9	50,440	71.1	42,220	58.6
Spanish Fork	76.3	26.5	97.8	92.4	86.5	4.5	18,006	3.2	531	2.9	26,347	70.8	23,905	51.4
Springville	78.1	19.6	98.5	90.6	83.7	4.3	16,660	3.1	472	2.8	21,534	63.4	18,655	48.1
Taylorsville	73.5	21.3	94.6	88.6	85.0	6.3	33,794	0.9	1,067	3.2	47,536	72.3	39,872	54.9
Tooele	71.0	48.3	97.4	92.4	83.5	10.5	16,774	0.8	611	3.6	25,764	71.4	22,642	53.0
West Jordan	77.3	35.8	97.5	94.2	85.8	3.5	62,467	1.0	1,820	2.9	83,937	76.7	76,102	54.7
West Valley City	76.9	30.9	96.0	88.2	83.2	5.3	70,702	0.9	2,263	3.2	99,911	74.6	86,802	58.2
VERMONT	74.9	31.3	89.5	81.0	86.6	6.4	346,061	0.0	9,223	2.7	519,579	65.4	402,429	50.8
Burlington	50.3	19.5	90.9	82.6	63.4	18.1	24,223	-0.1	551	2.3	36,981	66.8	32,127	36.9
VIRGINIA	77.4	42.5	91.8	84.5	84.7	8.8	4,331,380	0.5	128,579	3.0	6,813,344	65.7	5,541,740	54.1
Alexandria	59.0	54.8	97.2	92.4	82.4	12.1	100,409	1.1	2,255	2.2	133,653	78.0	115,763	64.3
Blacksburg	60.4	11.4	98.1	95.9	68.0	14.1	20,316	-0.1	736	3.6	39,177	47.6	35,950	20.8
Charlottesville	59.0	14.5	96.4	85.7	70.5	16.3	26,014	1.0	662	2.5	40,900	61.0	35,088	46.2
Chesapeake	85.0	42.0	95.6	91.0	86.1	8.2	121,125	0.3	3,685	3.0	187,990	65.9	157,122	54.9
Danville	78.3	16.3	82.3	74.8	86.9	6.4	19,579	-1.7	989	5.1	32,556	54.8	24,224	41.5
Hampton	83.1	30.8	91.7	82.4	81.1	10.8	64,378	0.0	2,596	4.0	108,943	64.9	88,691	51.1
Harrisonburg	70.1	10.7	91.3	81.6	73.2	19.3	24,736	-0.1	857	3.5	46,199	58.0	41,671	36.4
Leesburg	74.5	45.1	93.5	90.7	84.7	7.2	29,527	1.2	701	2.4	41,363	80.7	37,037	60.7
Lynchburg	74.6	14.0	90.4	78.7	76.4	11.3	35,927	-0.3	1,437	4.0	67,388	59.1	55,841	36.4
Manassas	76.2	61.2	93.0	89.0	82.2	13.3	21,856	1.1	585	2.7	29,523	79.5	26,548	55.9
Newport News	78.0	30.0	88.2	67.5	83.0	10.1	88,872	0.0	3,207	3.6	142,093	66.7	119,384	53.2
Norfolk	71.9	24.5	92.0	86.0	71.9	17.2	111,524	0.0	4,028	3.6	200,866	70.3	174,089	53.9
Petersburg	82.8	23.0	85.8	77.6	72.5	17.0	13,120	-0.2	798	6.1	25,893	59.7	20,383	46.2
Portsmouth	82.8	34.0	91.2	81.7	83.7	8.5	44,095	-0.3	1,792	4.1	75,036	64.2	61,183	52.8
Richmond	69.9	21.7	90.0	74.5	78.9	11.7	117,259	0.4	4,134	3.5	190,929	64.1	162,117	45.1
Roanoke	78.1	32.3	87.1	74.9	79.8	8.9	48,774	-0.3	1,575	3.2	80,239	63.3	63,372	53.2
Suffolk	84.5	50.8	91.7	79.6	79.1	12.7	44,014	0.1	1,419	3.2	69,965	65.8	57,179	54.7
Virginia Beach	82.6	29.6	95.9	90.4	82.2	8.9	232,342	0.4	6,647	2.9	360,489	69.9	298,954	58.2
Winchester	63.1	33.0	87.0	76.7	87.6	9.1	14,588	0.9	427	2.9	23,011	66.9	18,450	50.5
WASHINGTON	71.7	40.8	94.2	89.0	82.2	7.8	3,793,095	2.0	170,796	4.5	5,939,508	64.6	4,821,749	50.5
Auburn	73.0	50.4	93.9	92.0	80.1	9.0	41,888	2.0	1,714	4.1	62,665	68.4	55,588	52.0
Bellevue	64.4	34.5	97.4	93.2	80.6	8.9	81,003	2.0	2,561	3.2	119,549	65.2	99,252	54.2
Bellingham	71.2	15.2	94.5	88.1	72.3	10.0	46,859	1.7	2,117	4.5	78,299	62.8	62,858	38.3
Bothell	62.3	61.1	94.6	89.7	81.2	11.8	25,865	1.9	941	3.6	35,170	67.4	27,808	54.4
Bremerton	58.3	30.7	93.9	87.9	75.8	14.0	17,393	2.4	988	5.7	35,012	62.8	27,930	51.8
Burien	67.2	49.5	91.1	89.1	84.6	5.7	27,677	2.1	1,131	4.1	41,525	67.8	33,070	47.1
Des Moines	75.6	43.0	96.7	94.2	81.3	4.9	16,588	2.0	681	4.1	26,271	66.1	21,379	53.4
Edmonds	74.7	54.0	96.3	93.7	83.9	9.8	23,327	2.1	837	3.6	37,028	61.3	26,306	54.5
Everett	71.4	44.2	94.1	87.9	79.7	6.8	56,864	1.8	2,329	4.1	90,883	67.4	78,671	50.1
Federal Way	70.9	56.2	95.3	87.8	77.0	6.4	50,464	2.0	2,073	4.1	77,640	68.4	63,943	52.2
Issaquah	58.5	56.8	96.3	95.2	79.8	13.5	21,209	2.0	666	3.1	29,366	69.7	23,818	58.2
Kennewick	84.5	20.2	88.1	77.0	83.5	6.2	40,814	2.4	2,091	5.1	61,874	59.5	48,784	47.0
Kent	68.0	47.8	96.0	92.8	78.3	10.4	66,027	2.0	2,693	4.1	100,814	69.1	85,671	51.6
Kirkland	66.2	44.0	97.9	93.9	77.9	8.3	53,243	1.8	1,774	3.3	71,891	71.0	61,804	55.1
Lacey	80.6	37.1	94.6	93.1	82.1	8.3	21,647	2.8	1,126	5.2	39,823	63.4	31,803	56.2
Lake Stevens	81.6	62.1	95.6	90.0	NA	NA	17,379	1.9	681	3.9	22,746	71.0	20,745	55.6
Lakewood	78.7	33.5	95.4	88.5	83.7	8.1	26,195	2.2	1,507	5.8	47,884	58.7	39,052	47.6
Longview	76.7	22.2	87.1	78.8	69.5	11.6	15,360	0.7	935	6.1	29,226	53.0	22,288	36.6
Lynnwood	67.2	57.7	96.1	91.6	86.8	6.7	20,513	2.0	820	4.0	30,197	67.4	25,087	48.3
Marysville	81.1	47.2	93.4	89.2	83.2	5.1	35,527	1.9	1,411	4.0	53,513	66.5	44,123	52.7
Mount Vernon	75.2	23.5	90.6	82.0	80.0	3.8	15,656	1.8	840	5.4	28,469	64.3	22,255	45.7
Olympia	77.2	24.2	92.9	85.2	72.7	14.5	27,530	2.6	1,237	4.5	44,618	61.4	34,969	43.2

1. Employed persons.   2. Households.   3. Percent of civilian labor force.   4. Persons 16 years old and over.

Table D. Cities — **Construction, Wholesale Trade, and Retail Trade**

City	Value of residential construction authorized by building permits, 2018			Wholesale trade[1], 2012				Retail trade[2], 2012			
	New construction ($1,000)	Number of housing units	Percent single family	Number of establishments	Number of employees	Sales (mil dol)	Annual payroll (mil dol)	Number of establishments	Number of employees	Sales (mil dol)	Annual payroll (mil dol)
	69	70	71	72	73	74	75	76	77	78	79

City	69	70	71	72	73	74	75	76	77	78	79
UTAH— Cont'd											
Kaysville	56,119	170	100.0	22	269	117.4	11.7	62	707	169.1	17.7
Layton	92,145	468	91.2	47	321	117.8	10.7	295	4,761	1,123.0	106.0
Lehi	337,038	1,341	100.0	22	303	180.4	15.0	144	2,159	637.8	63.4
Logan	30,872	203	74.9	67	606	435.2	23.7	248	3,710	725.7	71.2
Midvale	52,442	488	16.4	48	604	354.9	25.5	149	2,153	554.8	53.1
Murray	46,764	132	100.0	109	1,032	520.2	54.1	353	5,656	1,921.1	161.3
Ogden	10,478	63	57.1	100	1,412	949.3	67.5	344	3,839	1,121.8	93.9
Orem	106,894	545	53.2	102	1,421	658.4	62.1	451	7,296	1,843.7	165.6
Pleasant Grove	44,860	112	92.9	19	75	28.7	2.6	65	675	219.9	21.0
Provo	88,669	457	37.4	55	1,506	1,153.2	99.6	317	4,334	1,205.9	98.9
Riverton	56,575	189	78.3	21	76	42.2	2.7	68	1,184	261.9	25.9
Roy	6,784	56	62.5	7	D	D	D	72	906	236.3	19.3
St. George	189,233	1,309	75.4	106	D	D	D	425	5,477	1,468.9	126.9
Salt Lake City	143,326	902	12.1	603	12,541	10,292.8	748.3	918	14,096	4,071.1	374.7
Sandy	38,634	235	23.0	130	1,173	847.6	59.8	382	6,580	2,199.2	187.0
South Jordan	256,386	1,092	87.5	38	1,231	900.5	73.8	112	2,249	662.1	55.5
Spanish Fork	108,081	427	98.8	19	186	106.2	7.3	88	1,077	204.4	19.6
Springville	48,958	219	50.7	25	639	228.5	25.2	74	1,095	301.6	23.9
Taylorsville	25,717	158	31.6	18	76	41.8	2.9	101	1,695	375.1	36.2
Tooele	30,124	234	62.4	7	D	D	D	75	1,334	361.7	31.4
West Jordan	136,045	658	64.4	76	1,201	1,118.5	66.9	207	3,971	945.0	84.5
West Valley City	54,253	209	95.2	143	2,669	1,906.8	143.3	280	5,549	1,457.0	157.9
VERMONT	365,383	2,080	54.4	696	9,464	6,450.1	464.4	3,509	38,910	9,933.8	967.1
Burlington	26,974	188	3.7	48	539	327.8	37.4	224	3,271	610.2	75.9
VIRGINIA	5,830,512	31,977	67.0	6,232	88,353	86,613.6	4,983.1	27,415	410,918	110,002.4	10,007.9
Alexandria	21,577	112	100.0	82	1,139	502.8	61.6	480	7,180	2,416.0	222.6
Blacksburg	14,850	58	100.0	14	D	D	D	97	1,363	284.4	22.3
Charlottesville	45,773	180	34.4	48	513	183.3	23.7	331	3,925	747.9	82.8
Chesapeake	291,400	1,031	89.3	239	3,447	2,225.2	169.7	789	15,088	4,114.9	336.7
Danville	692	3	100.0	50	545	285.2	24.5	306	4,165	965.0	87.2
Hampton	11,156	179	100.0	71	886	344.7	39.3	436	6,791	1,512.5	148.3
Harrisonburg	12,514	88	62.5	57	1,006	405.9	43.2	334	5,664	1,519.8	144.6
Leesburg	24,799	117	100.0	27	366	172.4	19.0	266	5,403	1,388.7	124.5
Lynchburg	19,225	138	42.0	69	877	509.0	39.0	385	7,371	1,995.2	178.2
Manassas	19,044	87	86.2	41	D	D	D	194	2,778	895.3	86.1
Newport News	22,907	124	100.0	110	1,438	851.3	72.7	686	9,879	2,480.8	229.7
Norfolk	74,834	594	53.4	209	3,287	3,195.3	161.6	867	12,440	2,683.2	281.6
Petersburg	1,204	13	100.0	21	570	560.1	16.2	145	1,426	334.5	33.0
Portsmouth	17,058	137	100.0	48	688	249.5	32.0	273	3,081	699.5	71.1
Richmond	80,046	563	48.5	269	3,767	3,288.5	201.3	808	8,666	1,955.2	206.1
Roanoke	13,719	115	27.8	180	2,727	1,398.0	130.3	535	9,912	2,461.0	230.1
Suffolk	101,412	717	69.9	54	961	666.0	49.8	226	3,536	958.9	79.1
Virginia Beach	119,041	779	68.5	391	6,893	8,187.6	477.1	1,500	22,723	5,671.5	521.6
Winchester	22,122	158	12.7	39	677	286.8	26.1	283	4,126	888.5	94.4
WASHINGTON	9,807,980	47,746	49.6	7,733	103,307	83,313.4	5,789.8	21,588	307,089	118,924.0	8,722.5
Auburn	18,521	50	100.0	174	3,739	4,631.5	198.0	281	4,676	1,475.0	140.8
Bellevue	261,184	924	23.5	324	4,333	5,128.3	368.3	673	12,225	4,113.9	412.6
Bellingham	104,534	718	26.9	147	D	D	D	532	8,805	2,243.5	206.9
Bothell	151,731	482	58.5	63	1,357	1,465.7	112.4	100	1,451	363.3	41.6
Bremerton	35,730	190	67.4	27	191	83.1	9.6	134	1,704	572.5	55.8
Burien	9,287	41	68.3	23	138	33.0	4.7	163	2,013	573.1	58.3
Des Moines	41,892	120	60.8	15	116	91.7	10.1	38	360	93.3	10.2
Edmonds	22,402	65	87.7	39	201	177.8	12.4	133	1,449	448.2	43.9
Everett	37,224	245	47.8	134	2,108	1,355.6	129.1	449	6,782	2,023.4	194.6
Federal Way	24,863	65	100.0	54	450	250.1	22.5	257	4,441	1,184.1	118.0
Issaquah	85,940	243	81.9	44	272	372.7	17.3	136	3,108	2,801.7	110.1
Kennewick	134,475	679	54.6	67	659	927.9	31.5	378	6,113	1,620.4	148.4
Kent	118,978	400	76.3	430	8,772	6,803.7	509.9	340	4,711	1,447.2	137.9
Kirkland	325,098	2,644	10.9	104	1,023	656.4	81.0	216	4,128	1,776.8	148.9
Lacey	127,914	844	23.8	23	493	421.0	24.6	148	3,567	869.8	92.1
Lake Stevens	79,638	253	93.7	6	40	15.9	1.2	45	848	219.2	20.3
Lakewood	46,998	311	20.9	67	834	1,407.2	41.8	227	2,725	701.2	69.7
Longview	3,647	18	100.0	39	637	712.5	30.9	175	3,043	796.3	78.7
Lynnwood	62,526	364	19.0	95	794	407.1	44.8	425	7,823	2,042.0	210.1
Marysville	79,456	345	70.7	34	236	117.4	12.5	172	3,450	933.4	88.4
Mount Vernon	28,258	172	100.0	32	385	219.6	18.1	135	2,017	491.7	53.0
Olympia	22,633	145	23.4	39	390	461.9	24.3	367	5,515	1,396.7	142.3

1. Merchant wholesalers except manufacturers' sales branches and offices.   2. Establishments with payroll.

Table D. Cities — Real Estate, Professional Services, and Manufacturing

City	Real estate and rental and leasing, 2012				Professional, scientific, and technical services[1], 2012				Manufacturing, 2012			
	Number of establishments	Number of employees	Receipts (mil dol)	Annual payroll (mil dol)	Number of establishments	Number of employees	Receipts (mil dol)	Annual payroll (mil dol)	Number of establishments	Number of employees	Receipts (mil dol)	Annual payroll (mil dol)
	80	81	82	83	84	85	86	87	88	89	90	91
UTAH— Cont'd												
Kaysville	36	77	11.5	2.4	90	647	74.6	35.3	15	180	37.4	7.1
Layton	111	313	69.3	9.9	177	D	D	D	43	870	372.5	39.8
Lehi	58	70	17.2	3.3	173	D	D	D	32	518	198.1	27.0
Logan	108	396	57.3	14.3	179	D	D	D	112	7,049	2,431.3	301.9
Midvale	69	468	105.0	25.5	92	D	D	D	34	435	D	18.9
Murray	134	1,271	154.0	51.4	300	2,624	380.0	136.7	118	1,590	320.6	65.0
Ogden	100	413	51.5	10.6	245	D	D	D	134	7,939	3,135.1	383.0
Orem	185	566	108.3	15.8	358	7,806	401.3	195.9	122	2,729	780.8	124.9
Pleasant Grove	48	98	13.9	3.4	99	670	83.9	32.6	30	238	D	9.1
Provo	120	569	85.7	13.1	346	D	D	D	81	1,908	376.7	96.3
Riverton	41	95	15.9	2.7	89	191	14.6	4.9	8	D	D	0.7
Roy	19	54	5.6	1.0	29	249	16.2	8.5	17	65	8.1	D
St. George	218	541	77.1	14.8	324	D	D	D	87	1,376	322.3	55.1
Salt Lake City	528	3,093	878.2	142.4	1,434	16,666	3,114.5	1,238.7	457	24,316	11,969.2	1,556.7
Sandy	202	654	157.6	28.0	443	2,500	324.0	131.8	103	2,619	891.9	137.8
South Jordan	93	253	42.3	10.3	230	1,478	223.0	60.7	23	D	D	D
Spanish Fork	29	60	12.7	2.1	80	381	36.1	9.2	39	1,771	671.8	94.5
Springville	19	21	2.9	0.6	66	320	29.0	10.5	46	3,092	1,538.7	143.1
Taylorsville	48	157	20.9	4.6	85	D	D	D	17	601	85.8	26.6
Tooele	19	61	8.5	1.3	32	165	13.4	6.1	19	729	343.7	D
West Jordan	82	181	30.4	5.2	153	D	D	D	106	2,439	895.2	116.7
West Valley City	73	525	111.5	24.5	118	D	D	D	156	4,762	2,397.5	240.5
VERMONT	741	3,092	509.9	103.6	2,093	15,781	1,762.8	730.9	1,013	31,487	9,315.5	1,594.3
Burlington	61	347	91.9	15.5	267	D	D	D	24	613	192.2	30.9
VIRGINIA	8,862	54,246	11,758.9	2,378.3	29,176	416,651	90,042.2	35,093.6	5,101	228,197	96,389.9	11,586.1
Alexandria	240	1,475	524.1	76.6	1,228	16,537	3,436.0	1,497.8	72	1,332	273.0	57.9
Blacksburg	50	393	73.4	14.9	153	D	D	D	20	1,473	514.6	99.8
Charlottesville	99	502	107.6	19.7	316	D	D	D	46	455	98.7	21.6
Chesapeake	273	1,227	291.6	52.9	509	7,649	1,029.3	412.6	130	3,965	1,504.2	211.6
Danville	64	339	48.7	9.1	72	D	D	D	46	4,635	1,703.0	223.7
Hampton	114	750	117.3	23.7	273	D	D	D	68	2,189	508.3	114.9
Harrisonburg	72	351	75.9	10.9	137	D	D	D	46	2,556	832.6	99.4
Leesburg	64	288	136.2	14.5	302	D	D	D	11	347	D	D
Lynchburg	109	447	79.9	14.5	199	D	D	D	83	8,339	2,749.6	504.3
Manassas	52	229	64.0	11.4	212	D	D	D	32	4,012	1,365.7	366.4
Newport News	254	1,672	276.5	60.3	361	D	D	D	91	26,503	5,578.9	1,558.5
Norfolk	291	2,496	430.8	127.7	700	D	D	D	130	6,866	1,812.5	328.2
Petersburg	32	223	27.2	5.8	34	D	D	D	28	1,646	D	91.0
Portsmouth	71	332	52.6	9.7	144	D	D	D	56	2,196	447.1	97.6
Richmond	258	1,539	304.3	67.1	844	10,249	2,511.6	888.8	187	5,882	16,885.9	386.3
Roanoke	155	950	141.8	31.0	326	D	D	D	100	3,869	1,629.7	174.8
Suffolk	67	243	37.5	8.1	121	D	D	D	46	1,996	1,521.0	103.6
Virginia Beach	649	6,165	902.5	210.7	1,391	17,195	3,883.4	1,188.8	207	5,616	1,954.2	255.1
Winchester	59	260	56.4	8.0	130	D	D	D	23	2,197	866.2	117.6
WASHINGTON	9,913	45,209	9,695.5	1,895.1	19,882	D	D	D	6,992	248,192	131,530.6	14,461.8
Auburn	86	344	96.7	13.9	120	D	D	D	159	9,859	1,243.4	582.4
Bellevue	517	3,594	974.9	195.2	1,260	14,873	2,735.3	1,204.9	115	1,733	621.1	87.9
Bellingham	199	847	193.4	27.6	432	D	D	D	126	3,061	D	129.2
Bothell	75	269	75.9	9.9	201	D	D	D	38	3,273	1,724.1	260.6
Bremerton	67	218	38.4	6.6	83	D	D	D	21	578	D	27.2
Burien	72	226	38.4	6.5	95	477	40.2	15.8	28	82	D	2.8
Des Moines	16	36	6.0	1.1	32	106	9.0	3.5	6	18	3.2	0.8
Edmonds	76	205	46.1	10.6	174	755	109.3	45.1	19	214	D	9.2
Everett	168	1,056	172.8	36.9	312	D	D	D	134	43,136	D	3,324.1
Federal Way	101	442	92.4	15.2	167	1,491	176.7	97.4	25	347	D	12.5
Issaquah	77	311	89.4	14.5	189	1,046	145.5	96.2	27	1,407	505.4	96.3
Kennewick	117	683	123.7	19.6	202	D	D	D	45	714	293.9	37.4
Kent	155	866	200.1	36.9	217	1,766	282.1	127.2	247	14,012	7,642.4	924.1
Kirkland	182	867	643.3	64.0	457	D	D	D	50	668	146.4	34.4
Lacey	54	210	45.1	6.0	74	2,388	319.2	147.8	17	415	D	19.8
Lake Stevens	30	D	D	D	20	69	7.1	2.5	12	D	5.4	D
Lakewood	102	445	85.3	12.9	111	544	55.3	21.0	36	585	D	24.6
Longview	55	208	34.2	5.8	83	D	D	D	37	2,469	1,391.6	203.7
Lynnwood	90	307	99.0	13.1	155	D	D	D	48	675	213.4	31.0
Marysville	63	218	67.8	9.8	60	336	31.8	8.4	55	1,672	340.2	68.8
Mount Vernon	56	143	24.1	4.4	117	512	64.3	22.6	32	673	328.2	26.9
Olympia	114	428	88.3	14.2	280	1,524	210.6	88.8	32	514	205.9	24.6

1. Establishments subject to federal tax.

Accommodation and Food Services, Arts, Entertainment, and Recreation, and Health Care and Social Assistance

City	Accommodation and food services, 2012				Arts, entertainment, and recreation,[1] 2012				Health care and social assistance,[1] 2012			
	Number of establish-ments	Number of employees	Receipts (mil dol)	Annual payroll (mil dol)	Number of establish-ments	Number of employees	Receipts (mil dol)	Annual payroll (mil dol)	Number of establish-ments	Number of employees	Receipts (mil dol)	Annual payroll (mil dol)
	92	93	94	95	96	97	98	99	100	101	102	103
UTAH— Cont'd												
Kaysville	16	354	11.4	3.4	6	239	14.9	3.3	52	D	D	D
Layton	149	3,414	138.2	40.9	19	D	D	D	156	2,734	304.0	116.0
Lehi	50	1,117	48.2	12.4	17	D	D	D	62	D	D	D
Logan	120	2,287	98.7	26.6	19	244	10.7	1.9	175	D	D	D
Midvale	94	1,572	73.1	21.6	6	D	D	D	53	D	D	D
Murray	113	2,538	120.0	40.6	13	D	D	D	298	D	D	D
Ogden	184	3,206	124.0	36.2	14	D	D	D	270	D	D	D
Orem	152	3,262	148.0	43.6	43	D	D	D	238	4,058	391.5	134.5
Pleasant Grove	29	280	12.9	3.1	11	35	4.6	0.8	60	D	D	D
Provo	186	3,335	143.9	40.6	32	387	25.6	7.2	285	D	D	D
Riverton	48	758	32.8	9.6	5	10	0.8	0.2	79	D	D	D
Roy	40	661	29.6	7.4	5	55	1.5	0.6	53	D	D	D
St. George	216	3,957	197.1	55.1	30	393	13.9	4.6	383	D	D	D
Salt Lake City	735	16,057	961.6	277.0	77	1,617	227.7	90.4	587	5,979	775.9	270.9
Sandy	188	3,696	173.1	49.7	28	D	D	D	272	D	D	D
South Jordan	68	1,569	65.6	20.3	13	D	D	D	123	D	D	D
Spanish Fork	40	664	28.4	7.4	7	D	D	D	59	644	44.7	15.2
Springville	39	D	D	D	7	26	1.6	0.3	63	D	D	D
Taylorsville	83	1,618	80.8	21.1	11	D	D	D	100	1,045	93.1	34.5
Tooele	45	755	33.8	8.9	6	60	3.3	1.1	58	D	D	D
West Jordan	116	2,362	125.2	32.2	13	D	D	D	170	2,883	365.1	92.4
West Valley City	179	2,987	161.6	43.4	18	D	D	D	101	D	D	D
VERMONT	1,920	31,365	1,564.3	494.0	286	5,468	233.6	73.7	1,370	14,976	1,297.2	578.2
Burlington	151	2,846	172.1	51.6	12	107	7.2	2.0	96	1,655	135.2	70.7
VIRGINIA	16,832	320,514	17,795.9	4,908.6	1,970	35,718	2,993.0	875.7	16,070	236,459	25,556.4	10,868.1
Alexandria	387	8,051	647.5	180.7	41	606	45.8	15.2	343	3,739	466.5	194.6
Blacksburg	100	2,054	91.4	25.1	7	D	D	D	93	1,512	197.5	73.2
Charlottesville	293	5,199	293.3	75.9	25	D	D	D	121	D	D	D
Chesapeake	466	10,267	447.6	121.1	42	D	D	D	456	6,275	637.4	290.0
Danville	139	2,850	120.4	33.6	11	D	D	D	175	3,730	374.9	152.4
Hampton	250	5,380	249.0	72.2	23	D	D	D	217	3,137	322.2	134.7
Harrisonburg	186	4,468	216.0	58.8	11	D	D	D	128	2,006	163.9	75.6
Leesburg	118	2,305	135.4	37.9	11	D	D	D	166	1,736	209.9	92.8
Lynchburg	215	5,071	216.4	61.0	21	243	10.2	3.1	205	D	D	D
Manassas	109	1,587	91.4	24.7	10	116	4.8	1.4	157	D	D	D
Newport News	386	6,621	323.8	87.6	28	D	D	D	327	6,977	693.3	380.1
Norfolk	593	11,264	547.1	148.4	41	504	37.2	10.7	422	6,733	776.7	359.3
Petersburg	79	885	39.1	10.2	6	D	D	D	103	3,619	364.2	135.7
Portsmouth	172	2,624	107.1	29.3	17	119	10.7	2.2	166	3,362	274.4	117.8
Richmond	618	11,470	576.5	184.1	53	896	52.7	10.8	441	11,147	1,922.8	628.0
Roanoke	320	6,509	308.1	94.4	17	188	7.9	2.6	228	4,017	462.5	191.5
Suffolk	147	2,477	122.9	30.6	12	D	D	D	155	2,625	273.4	125.1
Virginia Beach	1,153	21,910	1,202.7	324.3	153	1,714	129.4	31.6	919	12,464	1,177.1	571.3
Winchester	130	2,518	119.1	33.1	12	D	D	D	226	D	D	D
WASHINGTON	16,333	234,145	14,297.3	4,159.7	2,029	41,184	4,079.6	1,177.3	16,888	194,136	20,414.0	8,703.2
Auburn	145	1,859	107.0	30.9	28	D	D	D	163	2,421	232.0	100.8
Bellevue	432	8,993	618.4	184.7	63	1,856	151.9	47.0	887	8,423	958.7	398.7
Bellingham	325	5,589	277.4	84.5	50	434	20.2	6.1	423	4,236	422.2	171.3
Bothell	140	1,982	120.6	32.9	7	D	D	D	152	1,457	128.3	50.7
Bremerton	108	1,440	88.2	22.7	6	76	2.2	0.9	110	2,072	208.8	76.9
Burien	103	1,221	61.3	17.6	11	D	D	D	182	1,404	166.8	67.1
Des Moines	55	744	42.8	12.0	2	D	D	D	55	475	34.1	14.8
Edmonds	113	1,426	83.1	23.3	11	346	20.8	6.3	210	D	D	D
Everett	343	4,457	265.2	72.9	27	364	18.6	6.4	362	5,867	622.3	298.1
Federal Way	221	3,085	182.5	51.8	16	325	14.1	6.6	320	4,356	425.8	144.9
Issaquah	109	1,729	107.2	31.5	8	260	12.5	4.3	200	2,294	388.2	126.9
Kennewick	195	3,554	183.4	51.8	17	575	22.9	8.5	246	3,243	314.4	114.6
Kent	272	3,198	179.9	50.2	21	308	22.3	8.6	283	2,592	199.0	79.1
Kirkland	191	2,958	187.3	57.6	44	801	33.4	12.5	324	D	D	D
Lacey	122	1,852	101.8	28.7	11	D	D	D	114	D	D	D
Lake Stevens	42	621	39.4	9.0	4	145	3.7	1.0	39	276	28.1	10.4
Lakewood	179	2,433	132.6	35.9	16	599	28.9	13.6	192	2,524	199.3	92.3
Longview	104	1,490	63.4	19.3	12	D	D	D	131	1,795	161.7	68.4
Lynnwood	204	3,092	189.1	53.0	9	D	D	D	193	2,322	158.2	62.4
Marysville	104	1,365	81.6	21.4	8	D	D	D	118	1,282	114.0	49.3
Mount Vernon	83	915	52.0	14.4	6	167	6.6	2.4	114	D	D	D
Olympia	215	3,316	166.4	52.7	12	152	7.7	2.3	400	4,538	594.5	232.9

1. Establishments subject to federal tax.

Table D. Cities — Other Services and Government Employment and Payroll

City	Other services[1] Number of establishments (104)	Number of employees (105)	Receipts (mil dol) (106)	Annual payroll (mil dol) (107)	Government employment and payroll, 2012 Full-time equivalent employees (108)	March payroll Total (dollars) (109)	Percent of total for: Administrative, judicial, and legal (110)	Police and corrections (111)	Fire protection (112)	Highways and transportation (113)	Health and welfare (114)	Natural resources and utilities (115)	Education and libraries (116)
UTAH— Cont'd													
Kaysville	27	134	9.5	2.7	134	462,338	10.8	22.9	9.0	7.6	0.0	39.1	0.0
Layton	108	729	48.9	13.9	349	1,449,599	18.3	33.6	21.9	4.9	0.0	21.4	0.0
Lehi	36	203	13.8	4.1	336	1,214,483	12.5	20.4	13.7	4.2	0.0	36.3	4.1
Logan	86	509	36.2	11.4	471	1,727,277	13.4	20.5	14.4	3.6	0.0	36.1	3.5
Midvale	60	338	31.1	8.2	75	305,262	65.6	0.0	0.0	6.5	2.9	20.3	0.0
Murray	138	886	86.2	27.3	431	1,925,114	16.4	23.1	16.8	2.6	0.0	30.9	3.1
Ogden	134	957	76.3	22.7	634	2,507,571	18.7	28.7	20.1	7.0	5.2	16.9	0.0
Orem	137	740	53.8	15.5	516	2,194,808	19.2	27.2	17.2	4.8	2.4	19.7	7.3
Pleasant Grove	38	138	13.3	3.4	245	686,046	17.4	27.3	9.0	3.6	2.6	26.1	8.0
Provo	118	749	59.2	17.7	702	2,815,201	17.2	23.0	14.4	5.6	1.8	29.5	4.4
Riverton	36	173	15.0	3.8	91	415,613	39.8	2.6	0.0	25.0	0.6	22.8	0.0
Roy	38	172	11.7	3.2	176	633,604	20.3	31.4	22.5	4.2	0.0	16.1	0.0
St. George	118	695	59.3	16.2	700	2,450,568	9.2	24.3	5.4	10.7	2.4	44.2	0.0
Salt Lake City	459	4,071	340.1	115.3	2,853	13,446,478	15.0	21.7	15.0	20.9	2.4	14.9	4.1
Sandy	118	785	56.3	19.2	496	2,122,916	21.0	24.1	15.6	9.8	7.5	20.1	0.0
South Jordan	52	295	22.6	6.9	333	1,224,842	20.3	19.7	17.6	6.1	2.9	18.3	0.0
Spanish Fork	38	236	17.2	5.4	215	776,827	12.0	18.4	0.0	6.4	4.3	34.7	2.8
Springville	33	124	10.2	2.2	213	858,647	17.7	20.4	1.6	8.5	0.6	42.5	4.7
Taylorsville	37	220	19.4	5.4	122	499,977	35.5	62.2	0.0	0.0	0.4	0.3	0.0
Tooele	33	D	D	D	184	603,981	20.7	27.5	3.3	5.6	6.8	29.9	3.6
West Jordan	93	670	67.8	22.8	409	1,901,684	7.2	32.4	23.5	4.1	0.0	8.0	0.0
West Valley City	123	642	71.8	20.9	699	2,859,122	17.7	37.1	17.3	7.1	8.8	9.1	0.0
VERMONT	1,057	4,255	398.4	109.0	X	X	X	X	X	X	X	X	X
Burlington	65	361	25.2	9.7	741	3,858,642	9.5	18.3	12.6	11.2	3.0	32.5	2.0
VIRGINIA	11,654	76,041	6,881.1	2,289.3	X	X	X	X	X	X	X	X	X
Alexandria	241	2,374	213.3	75.6	5,221	27,072,935	10.0	12.5	7.7	2.6	12.6	6.5	44.7
Blacksburg	45	D	D	D	360	1,254,541	15.3	27.9	0.6	24.0	1.6	12.0	0.0
Charlottesville	100	817	69.3	23.2	2,140	8,097,522	10.3	6.1	3.5	6.3	5.6	8.0	55.6
Chesapeake	361	2,768	291.0	89.0	9,069	32,784,817	5.1	11.5	6.3	2.1	5.7	4.5	62.1
Danville	84	466	34.2	8.7	2,451	7,816,325	9.2	11.3	5.7	3.0	5.2	9.6	51.6
Hampton	153	854	66.1	21.4	6,070	20,036,058	6.9	11.2	6.1	1.0	5.7	6.3	61.8
Harrisonburg	101	595	47.0	15.8	1,474	5,157,943	4.1	7.6	6.7	5.8	0.3	15.0	53.6
Leesburg	78	478	39.0	13.4	378	1,973,445	18.8	28.6	0.0	10.5	0.0	34.5	1.1
Lynchburg	130	929	73.3	24.1	3,057	9,313,489	8.7	9.6	8.0	2.9	8.1	7.5	52.5
Manassas	121	713	75.6	20.4	1,551	7,149,920	5.0	8.7	4.1	2.5	3.1	8.0	67.1
Newport News	251	1,757	157.4	53.0	8,390	34,469,339	6.2	10.2	4.6	1.3	4.5	9.2	63.2
Norfolk	287	2,254	192.7	73.6	11,723	42,393,144	6.3	13.5	5.5	3.7	10.1	7.2	51.8
Petersburg	63	508	33.1	13.2	1,422	4,584,024	6.0	20.2	8.9	4.5	6.2	4.0	47.4
Portsmouth	128	1,019	117.8	35.7	4,082	15,197,404	6.6	10.7	7.0	0.8	8.6	5.3	58.8
Richmond	370	2,708	213.2	75.5	8,746	33,243,527	9.0	18.5	6.0	1.8	8.7	7.9	42.5
Roanoke	207	1,415	111.5	37.8	3,839	13,972,707	8.1	12.9	8.3	1.7	8.0	2.4	56.6
Suffolk	84	551	35.7	12.1	3,545	11,901,204	10.3	7.7	9.6	2.9	3.6	6.8	58.2
Virginia Beach	724	4,164	320.0	99.7	18,286	64,539,702	3.7	9.5	3.6	0.3	6.6	7.3	60.5
Winchester	69	422	29.0	9.2	1,441	5,056,458	6.8	23.0	6.6	2.0	4.0	7.0	48.8
WASHINGTON	9,852	54,069	4,710.4	1,503.1	X	X	X	X	X	X	X	X	X
Auburn	143	808	83.2	28.8	428	2,532,346	24.2	34.3	0.0	15.0	4.6	18.9	0.0
Bellevue	332	2,177	173.9	64.4	1,278	8,997,838	17.4	19.2	22.6	7.6	8.6	23.3	0.0
Bellingham	201	1,185	106.1	34.2	813	4,462,504	14.2	23.4	26.3	8.6	0.9	16.4	3.3
Bothell	64	407	39.1	10.4	290	2,203,744	15.3	29.0	30.7	8.0	5.8	5.8	0.0
Bremerton	60	300	27.1	8.7	363	2,283,752	11.7	25.1	21.9	5.4	0.6	29.5	0.0
Burien	98	471	39.1	11.3	70	380,590	32.7	0.0	0.0	22.6	20.3	22.5	0.0
Des Moines	23	D	D	D	130	840,420	26.3	37.5	0.0	7.8	4.0	18.8	0.0
Edmonds	59	325	27.2	9.0	206	1,296,656	16.1	35.4	0.0	8.9	4.8	28.4	0.0
Everett	192	1,194	118.6	38.2	1,193	7,513,828	9.0	22.1	21.2	14.6	2.1	22.6	3.2
Federal Way	136	668	49.6	16.5	338	1,899,108	20.8	52.5	0.0	7.2	0.0	15.6	0.0
Issaquah	76	D	D	D	241	1,458,971	48.2	24.1	0.0	5.7	0.0	22.0	0.0
Kennewick	114	736	52.9	17.4	365	2,339,914	19.2	32.4	27.2	7.2	0.0	14.0	0.0
Kent	221	1,354	135.1	42.8	659	3,957,128	25.4	33.2	0.0	11.4	1.3	24.6	0.0
Kirkland	151	703	57.2	18.9	575	3,364,380	21.8	25.2	24.8	2.6	0.0	12.1	0.0
Lacey	71	423	34.4	11.2	244	1,204,776	6.5	40.8	0.0	5.7	7.4	37.2	0.0
Lake Stevens	27	111	6.8	2.1	60	371,914	10.4	53.2	0.0	21.3	10.4	0.0	0.0
Lakewood	130	607	54.2	18.0	252	1,631,866	29.1	53.0	0.0	11.9	1.0	3.8	0.0
Longview	72	459	34.1	10.9	291	1,531,626	13.5	28.3	20.6	13.2	0.0	18.9	5.5
Lynnwood	134	974	87.8	27.1	514	3,172,400	18.5	30.1	20.2	2.4	0.0	17.3	0.0
Marysville	103	496	52.8	13.3	244	1,573,886	23.0	37.9	0.0	9.3	0.0	24.8	0.0
Mount Vernon	55	271	22.6	7.3	209	1,138,810	14.6	30.5	21.7	3.5	0.0	18.1	5.0
Olympia	130	638	50.1	16.9	524	3,201,082	31.0	21.7	21.0	4.7	0.3	21.2	0.0

1. Establishments subject to federal tax.

Table D. Cities — City Government Finances

City	City government finances, 2012									
	General revenue							General expenditure		
		Intergovernmental		Taxes						
						Per capita[1] (dollars)			Per capita[1] (dollars)	
	Total (mil dol)	Total (mil dol)	Percent from state government	Total (mil dol)	Total	Property	Sales and gross receipts	Total (mil dol)	Total	Capital outlays
	117	118	119	120	121	122	123	124	125	126
UTAH— Cont'd										
Kaysville	15.6	1.7	75.8	6.7	236	50	186	10.3	364	62
Layton	45.3	3.8	61.6	25.7	375	112	263	40.3	587	14
Lehi	47.8	1.8	100.0	28.4	552	308	244	36.9	718	82
Logan	58.6	7.2	21.6	20.1	408	111	297	49.7	1,011	194
Midvale	17.3	1.8	50.9	11.1	368	138	230	17.2	568	9
Murray	52.5	4.5	36.2	29.2	604	209	395	48.5	1,005	89
Ogden	102.4	13.2	30.0	48.5	578	280	298	114.7	1,367	205
Orem	78.3	6.3	49.6	38.7	427	131	296	65.7	725	49
Pleasant Grove	23.6	2.0	81.2	9.0	261	99	162	21.4	621	39
Provo	87.3	11.8	35.6	39.2	339	125	214	98.1	850	250
Riverton	19.6	1.5	82.4	10.7	264	47	217	34.9	864	199
Roy	21.0	1.5	77.3	10.5	279	86	193	16.4	436	23
St. George	76.3	3.8	65.5	38.0	504	165	340	76.8	1,020	221
Salt Lake City	529.4	30.7	31.4	201.1	1,062	642	419	382.9	2,021	145
Sandy	79.3	5.3	56.3	44.9	502	168	334	64.8	724	74
South Jordan	55.2	2.4	79.1	34.3	614	349	265	50.1	895	75
Spanish Fork	37.6	1.4	82.8	10.0	277	75	202	31.9	880	170
Springville	25.9	1.1	90.9	10.0	325	103	223	30.3	989	165
Taylorsville	24.7	2.8	76.1	17.3	287	79	208	28.5	473	69
Tooele	20.4	1.8	85.9	11.5	358	130	227	20.7	645	92
West Jordan	65.0	6.3	62.5	35.7	329	119	210	59.0	544	60
West Valley City	134.8	12.6	33.4	67.2	507	262	245	154.8	1,168	359
VERMONT	X	X	X	X	X	X	X	X	X	X
Burlington	110.0	17.7	38.0	38.4	908	674	234	92.8	2,192	417
VIRGINIA	X	X	X	X	X	X	X	X	X	X
Alexandria	694.5	112.0	62.0	498.6	3,394	2,493	843	697.3	4,746	514
Blacksburg	40.4	14.5	48.6	16.4	382	130	252	36.6	855	218
Charlottesville	233.9	98.5	67.6	93.0	2,089	1,298	743	229.9	5,163	617
Chesapeake	886.7	369.8	97.8	422.6	1,852	1,303	538	865.4	3,792	475
Danville	173.3	85.4	95.4	50.7	1,186	638	544	179.2	4,189	318
Hampton	525.3	220.7	90.2	218.7	1,599	1,068	519	516.8	3,777	217
Harrisonburg	165.0	51.6	74.2	63.4	1,238	628	603	166.3	3,246	275
Leesburg	59.3	13.1	95.3	31.9	693	279	414	58.7	1,273	249
Lynchburg	266.8	110.8	87.0	117.5	1,510	897	597	268.3	3,449	589
Manassas	181.8	62.5	84.3	83.5	2,049	1,559	467	169.8	4,168	200
Newport News	774.9	330.7	85.5	322.2	1,785	1,271	515	806.2	4,467	333
Norfolk	1,105.0	447.5	74.8	416.3	1,691	1,027	664	1,153.5	4,686	548
Petersburg	125.4	70.3	87.3	45.2	1,406	1,038	357	129.9	4,039	140
Portsmouth	430.0	216.4	85.2	161.2	1,669	1,218	439	514.7	5,331	1,170
Richmond	1,063.0	471.0	79.9	412.6	1,951	1,242	709	1,029.3	4,866	638
Roanoke	385.6	172.3	96.1	172.9	1,766	1,081	685	378.3	3,865	222
Suffolk	304.8	145.8	82.7	134.3	1,577	1,160	411	324.3	3,808	436
Virginia Beach	1,602.6	600.6	84.2	810.1	1,817	1,221	583	1,799.1	4,036	628
Winchester	116.1	39.1	89.9	61.6	2,267	1,283	983	112.7	4,147	231
WASHINGTON	X	X	X	X	X	X	X	X	X	X
Auburn	109.0	17.7	41.8	43.9	598	200	378	107.6	1,464	393
Bellevue	284.5	33.1	23.5	153.0	1,157	275	833	257.3	1,947	276
Bellingham	120.9	15.0	39.1	67.7	825	212	593	118.7	1,446	280
Bothell	54.5	14.0	63.8	29.4	848	273	531	61.1	1,763	521
Bremerton	57.7	6.4	49.1	25.4	646	218	419	58.3	1,484	236
Burien	28.1	4.7	75.2	18.7	378	142	222	34.9	705	215
Des Moines	29.2	4.6	73.5	12.6	412	142	257	26.8	881	214
Edmonds	45.6	4.4	75.7	28.0	693	332	334	42.6	1,054	137
Everett	182.2	16.6	67.5	108.1	1,033	367	650	170.4	1,629	324
Federal Way	65.3	12.0	93.7	40.0	435	107	311	59.1	643	167
Issaquah	59.7	10.5	71.1	31.0	949	250	650	53.3	1,633	344
Kennewick	68.6	6.5	69.3	41.7	550	142	391	69.4	914	179
Kent	137.7	20.6	82.9	62.9	511	157	335	140.6	1,143	354
Kirkland	106.7	9.7	53.2	61.0	731	262	428	105.7	1,267	159
Lacey	56.2	9.1	68.1	26.8	611	136	454	60.0	1,365	347
Lake Stevens	14.7	2.9	47.3	9.7	333	139	178	9.2	318	2
Lakewood	45.5	9.7	66.3	28.3	480	104	367	49.0	831	168
Longview	58.1	10.3	61.4	25.0	685	222	460	58.2	1,593	375
Lynnwood	66.8	5.6	76.9	38.6	1,065	319	731	58.4	1,610	230
Marysville	60.6	3.7	74.9	30.1	483	246	222	58.8	943	114
Mount Vernon	38.0	3.3	70.9	17.8	552	222	318	33.3	1,033	107
Olympia	99.6	9.9	54.8	50.0	1,045	267	761	116.3	2,434	673

1. Based on population estimated as of July 1 of the year shown.

Table D. Cities — **City Government Finances**

City	City government finances, 2012 (cont.)									
	General expenditure (cont.)									
	Percent of total for:									
	Public welfare	Highways	Parking facilities	Education	Health and hospitals	Police protection	Sewerage and sanitation	Parks and recreation	Housing and community development	Interest on debt
	127	128	129	130	131	132	133	134	135	136
UTAH— Cont'd										
Kaysville..........................	0.0	10.3	0.0	0.0	0.0	7.6	51.5	11.5	0.0	0.4
Layton..............................	0.0	16.8	0.0	0.0	0.0	26.0	19.4	9.8	1.1	0.5
Lehi..................................	0.0	39.4	0.0	0.0	0.0	13.0	21.2	1.1	0.0	4.8
Logan...............................	0.0	14.4	0.0	0.0	0.0	16.5	26.1	11.6	5.4	0.7
Midvale............................	0.0	9.4	0.0	0.0	0.0	30.1	15.3	2.0	3.5	7.1
Murray..............................	0.0	15.6	0.0	0.0	0.0	19.8	13.0	13.4	2.1	1.2
Ogden..............................	0.0	4.7	0.0	0.0	0.0	14.8	16.3	5.7	17.8	2.5
Orem................................	0.0	11.1	0.0	0.0	0.0	20.7	17.2	10.0	3.7	2.9
Pleasant Grove..................	0.0	3.1	0.0	0.0	0.0	20.0	22.6	14.2	0.0	8.8
Provo...............................	0.0	10.5	0.0	0.0	0.0	15.5	9.1	27.2	5.6	4.5
Riverton...........................	0.0	25.5	0.0	0.0	0.0	7.2	8.5	5.8	2.0	36.7
Roy..................................	0.0	7.7	0.0	0.0	0.0	26.4	11.6	13.2	2.1	0.2
St. George........................	0.0	18.8	0.0	0.0	0.0	16.5	19.8	18.3	1.4	6.6
Salt Lake City....................	0.0	10.9	0.0	0.0	0.0	14.9	5.8	5.6	9.0	3.8
Sandy...............................	0.0	7.4	0.0	0.0	0.0	18.4	13.6	11.7	1.0	5.4
South Jordan.....................	0.0	14.1	0.0	0.0	0.0	10.9	6.1	12.5	9.7	3.6
Spanish Fork.....................	0.0	10.9	0.0	0.0	0.0	11.9	16.0	20.8	0.0	2.7
Springville........................	0.0	7.8	0.0	0.0	0.9	12.7	15.8	12.5	0.0	5.5
Taylorsville.......................	0.0	10.3	0.0	0.0	0.0	27.4	1.8	1.8	4.8	1.3
Tooele..............................	0.0	12.0	0.0	0.0	0.0	16.2	9.4	17.6	12.8	5.1
West Jordan......................	0.0	17.8	0.0	0.0	0.0	22.3	18.1	4.0	3.7	2.0
West Valley City.................	0.0	7.4	0.0	0.0	1.1	13.1	5.3	16.7	25.5	4.1
VERMONT.......................	X	X	X	X	X	X	X	X	X	X
Burlington.........................	0.0	9.2	5.2	0.0	0.0	11.3	8.3	8.8	5.6	3.9
VIRGINIA.........................	X	X	X	X	X	X	X	X	X	X
Alexandria........................	6.3	3.7	0.0	34.5	6.0	9.6	6.1	3.7	2.0	2.8
Blacksburg........................	0.0	22.9	0.0	0.0	1.6	19.2	16.1	5.9	6.9	2.2
Charlottesville...................	11.0	6.3	0.1	31.0	8.0	7.1	5.8	5.3	2.3	1.6
Chesapeake.......................	3.3	5.6	0.0	54.2	3.3	4.6	3.4	2.3	0.4	2.3
Danville............................	4.2	5.7	0.0	41.3	2.3	5.5	6.6	2.2	2.3	1.7
Hampton...........................	5.7	1.3	0.1	45.5	0.8	5.2	4.9	6.8	8.5	3.2
Harrisonburg......................	1.8	11.3	0.1	38.9	0.7	4.7	9.4	3.1	0.3	18.0
Leesburg...........................	0.0	9.2	0.0	0.0	0.0	19.2	10.4	11.6	0.0	4.3
Lynchburg.........................	7.1	2.8	0.1	35.8	0.7	6.4	15.5	2.2	2.9	2.8
Manassas..........................	0.7	6.2	0.1	54.0	2.2	7.8	7.8	0.2	2.3	3.2
Newport News....................	5.1	3.9	0.0	42.3	8.5	5.7	4.8	3.1	5.8	3.6
Norfolk.............................	6.6	4.6	1.0	36.0	3.2	5.9	5.3	4.1	9.5	3.1
Petersburg........................	11.4	4.7	0.0	40.0	1.0	9.0	4.0	1.3	1.0	1.0
Portsmouth........................	5.0	1.3	0.2	33.2	2.1	6.8	5.2	2.1	6.8	2.7
Richmond..........................	1.6	2.7	0.0	31.6	4.5	8.9	10.5	2.5	9.1	0.8
Roanoke...........................	15.3	3.5	0.4	39.4	0.9	6.1	2.2	2.5	6.6	3.1
Suffolk..............................	4.4	6.8	0.0	45.2	0.2	6.3	2.0	1.6	1.2	2.8
Virginia Beach....................	3.8	4.8	0.1	46.8	3.0	5.0	7.1	5.9	1.4	3.0
Winchester........................	6.4	5.0	0.8	43.4	1.0	6.4	10.1	2.6	1.9	4.9
WASHINGTON..................	X	X	X	X	X	X	X	X	X	X
Auburn..............................	0.0	19.6	0.0	0.0	0.5	15.0	33.6	9.0	0.2	2.2
Bellevue...........................	0.0	15.0	0.0	0.0	6.3	11.9	18.4	15.2	5.3	2.8
Bellingham........................	0.0	10.0	1.2	0.0	7.0	13.4	14.1	16.3	1.8	1.6
Bothell.............................	0.0	30.3	0.0	0.0	0.2	16.3	12.8	2.0	1.6	0.9
Bremerton.........................	0.0	5.7	0.8	0.0	4.2	18.7	14.8	21.3	1.8	3.3
Burien..............................	0.0	31.7	0.0	0.0	3.0	27.1	2.7	8.9	2.0	2.6
Des Moines.......................	0.1	19.9	0.0	0.0	0.8	24.9	4.7	24.1	0.0	1.4
Edmonds...........................	0.0	7.5	0.0	0.0	0.1	18.8	16.6	11.8	0.0	2.5
Everett.............................	0.2	7.5	0.1	0.0	4.4	15.4	24.4	7.7	1.3	4.0
Federal Way......................	0.2	28.9	0.0	0.0	1.1	27.6	4.7	10.0	2.0	1.0
Issaquah...........................	0.0	14.9	0.0	0.0	0.0	8.3	20.1	9.3	2.9	3.0
Kennewick.........................	0.0	11.4	0.0	0.0	5.3	18.7	4.5	20.4	0.8	2.9
Kent.................................	0.2	5.1	0.0	0.0	1.2	15.6	40.1	11.7	2.0	3.1
Kirkland............................	0.0	10.8	0.1	0.0	0.7	17.1	22.2	8.0	0.0	2.1
Lacey...............................	0.0	19.2	0.0	0.0	2.9	14.1	25.7	13.0	0.0	1.6
Lake Stevens.....................	0.2	13.5	0.0	0.0	0.4	40.6	12.7	1.9	2.0	3.5
Lakewood..........................	1.0	17.8	0.0	0.0	0.6	40.2	7.5	3.3	4.9	0.3
Longview...........................	0.2	8.3	0.0	0.0	0.0	15.9	40.1	5.9	2.7	1.2
Lynnwood..........................	0.0	8.5	0.0	0.0	7.2	19.4	9.5	17.2	1.2	1.4
Marysville.........................	0.0	17.7	0.0	0.0	4.9	14.4	17.3	5.1	0.0	5.8
Mount Vernon....................	0.0	9.6	0.0	0.0	0.5	19.0	29.6	4.4	0.0	2.1
Olympia............................	0.0	6.3	0.0	0.0	1.9	9.4	24.8	12.3	0.4	3.4

City	City government finances, 2012 (cont.)			Climate[2]						
	Debt outstanding		Debt issued during year	Average daily temperature				Annual precipitation (inches)	Heating degree days	Cooling degree days
				Mean		Limits				
	Total (mil dol)	Per capita[1] (dollars)		January	July	January[3]	July[4]			
	137	138	139	140	141	142	143	144	145	146

City	137	138	139	140	141	142	143	144	145	146
UTAH— Cont'd										
Kaysville	2.6	91	0.0	NA	NA	NA	NA	NA	NA	NA
Layton	4.9	71	0.0	27.6	74.2	18.6	89.9	20.75	6,142	746
Lehi	97.2	1,889	0.7	NA	NA	NA	NA	NA	NA	NA
Logan	43.8	891	0.0	21.8	71.6	12.7	88.3	17.86	7,174	522
Midvale	50.8	1,678	1.5	30.4	78.5	22.1	90.9	26.19	5,441	1,197
Murray	36.9	765	6.1	29.2	77.0	21.3	90.6	16.50	5,631	1,066
Ogden	115.6	1,378	7.1	28.1	76.6	20.1	90.0	23.67	5,868	980
Orem	67.1	740	4.3	28.6	76.5	20.3	92.3	12.84	5,564	1,016
Pleasant Grove	62.2	1,801	22.8	NA	NA	NA	NA	NA	NA	NA
Provo	115.1	997	34.5	30.9	76.9	22.5	93.4	20.13	5,264	1,028
Riverton	482.2	11,921	4.6	31.6	78.0	22.0	95.3	15.76	5,251	1,172
Roy	7.2	193	0.6	27.6	74.2	18.6	89.9	20.75	6,142	746
St. George	157.4	2,090	6.1	41.8	86.3	28.9	102.8	8.77	3,103	2,471
Salt Lake City	393.2	2,075	81.7	32.0	78.1	25.4	89.0	17.75	5,095	1,190
Sandy	93.6	1,045	8.3	30.4	78.5	22.1	90.9	26.19	5,441	1,197
South Jordan	71.6	1,279	6.9	31.6	78.0	22.0	95.3	15.76	5,251	1,172
Spanish Fork	24.7	681	0.0	NA	NA	NA	NA	NA	NA	NA
Springville	37.6	1,229	0.0	NA	NA	NA	NA	NA	NA	NA
Taylorsville	10.9	182	0.7	29.2	77.0	21.3	90.6	16.50	5,631	1,066
Tooele	36.8	1,147	15.2	NA	NA	NA	NA	NA	NA	NA
West Jordan	23.2	214	3.3	30.4	78.5	22.1	90.9	26.19	5,441	1,197
West Valley City	149.0	1,125	33.1	29.2	77.0	21.3	90.6	16.50	5,631	1,066
VERMONT	X	X	X	X	X	X	X	X	X	X
Burlington	192.6	4,550	24.3	18.0	70.6	9.3	81.4	36.05	7,665	489
VIRGINIA	X	X	X	X	X	X	X	X	X	X
Alexandria	580.7	3,952	133.6	34.9	79.2	27.3	88.3	39.35	4,055	1,531
Blacksburg	23.1	541	9.5	30.9	71.1	20.6	82.5	42.63	5,559	533
Charlottesville	117.7	2,645	34.1	35.5	76.9	26.2	88.0	48.87	4,103	1,212
Chesapeake	635.5	2,785	137.5	40.1	79.1	32.3	86.8	45.74	3,368	1,612
Danville	152.0	3,554	3.9	36.6	78.8	25.8	90.0	44.98	3,970	1,418
Hampton	359.9	2,630	78.5	39.4	78.5	32.0	85.2	47.90	3,535	1,432
Harrisonburg	500.6	9,773	28.6	30.5	73.5	20.4	85.3	36.12	5,333	758
Leesburg	126.9	2,753	33.9	31.5	75.2	20.8	87.1	43.21	5,031	911
Lynchburg	330.4	4,247	7.0	34.5	75.1	24.5	86.4	43.31	4,354	1,075
Manassas	130.5	3,202	0.0	31.7	75.7	21.9	87.4	41.80	4,925	1,075
Newport News	797.6	4,419	228.9	41.2	80.3	33.8	87.9	43.53	3,179	1,682
Norfolk	1,752.2	7,119	414.1	40.1	79.1	32.3	86.8	45.74	3,368	1,612
Petersburg	34.6	1,076	1.5	39.7	79.6	29.2	91.0	45.26	3,334	1,619
Portsmouth	519.2	5,378	88.9	40.1	79.1	32.3	86.8	45.74	3,368	1,612
Richmond	1,340.2	6,336	260.0	36.4	77.9	27.6	87.5	43.91	3,919	1,435
Roanoke	544.5	5,563	52.3	35.8	76.2	26.6	87.5	42.49	4,284	1,134
Suffolk	538.4	6,320	114.6	39.6	78.5	30.3	88.1	48.71	3,467	1,427
Virginia Beach	1,698.8	3,811	173.0	40.7	78.8	32.2	86.9	44.50	3,336	1,482
Winchester	201.0	7,395	51.9	NA	NA	NA	NA	NA	NA	NA
WASHINGTON	X	X	X	X	X	X	X	X	X	X
Auburn	68.3	929	0.0	40.8	66.4	34.6	77.4	39.59	4,624	219
Bellevue	176.9	1,338	0.0	41.5	65.5	36.0	74.5	38.25	4,615	192
Bellingham	92.2	1,124	49.1	40.5	63.3	34.8	72.5	34.84	4,980	68
Bothell	43.3	1,251	30.0	40.8	65.2	35.2	75.0	35.96	4,756	174
Bremerton	75.6	1,923	12.7	40.1	64.6	34.7	75.2	53.96	4,994	158
Burien	33.0	667	8.6	40.9	65.3	35.9	75.3	37.07	4,797	173
Des Moines	14.4	471	2.0	40.9	65.3	35.9	75.3	37.07	4,797	173
Edmonds	37.6	929	13.8	40.8	65.2	35.2	75.0	35.96	4,756	174
Everett	252.3	2,410	52.2	39.7	63.6	33.6	73.0	37.54	5,199	121
Federal Way	13.7	149	0.0	41.0	65.6	35.1	76.1	38.95	4,650	167
Issaquah	38.5	1,180	5.4	NA	NA	NA	NA	NA	NA	NA
Kennewick	63.3	834	5.4	34.2	75.2	28.0	89.3	8.01	4,731	909
Kent	164.6	1,338	0.0	40.8	66.4	34.6	77.4	39.59	4,624	219
Kirkland	53.5	641	8.3	40.8	65.2	35.2	75.0	35.96	4,756	174
Lacey	24.6	561	1.6	38.1	62.8	31.8	76.1	50.79	5,531	97
Lake Stevens	22.3	768	0.0	NA	NA	NA	NA	NA	NA	NA
Lakewood	12.0	203	1.3	41.0	65.6	35.1	76.1	38.95	4,650	167
Longview	34.6	948	15.4	39.9	64.5	33.8	76.5	48.02	4,900	148
Lynnwood	46.2	1,274	6.4	40.8	65.2	35.2	75.0	35.96	4,756	174
Marysville	92.8	1,487	4.8	39.7	63.6	33.6	73.0	37.54	5,199	121
Mount Vernon	37.4	1,161	0.0	39.9	62.3	34.1	73.0	32.70	5,197	47
Olympia	95.1	1,989	3.4	38.1	62.8	31.8	76.1	50.79	5,531	97

1. Based on the population estimated as of July 1 of the year shown.   2. Represents normal values based on the 30-year period, 1971±2000.   3. Average daily minimum.   4. Average daily maximum.

Table D. Cities — Land Area and Population

STATE Place code	City	Land area[1] (sq. mi)	Population, 2018 Total persons 2018	Rank	Per square mile	Race 2017 — Race alone[2] (percent) White	Black or African American	American Indian, Alaskan Native	Asian	Hawaiian Pacific Islander	Some other race	Two or more races (percent)
		1	2	3	4	5	6	7	8	9	10	11
	WASHINGTON—Cont'd											
53 53,545	Pasco	33.9	74,778	472	2,205.8	67.1	1.4	3.3	3.3	1.0	19.0	5.0
53 56,625	Pullman	10.7	34,019	1,120	3,179.3	75.8	3.6	0.2	11.1	0.5	1.7	7.2
53 56,695	Puyallup	14.1	41,886	908	2,970.6	75.2	5.1	0.1	6.9	0.3	2.2	10.4
53 57,535	Redmond	16.6	67,678	537	4,077.0	54.6	1.9	0.0	35.7	0.0	1.0	6.8
53 57,745	Renton	23.4	102,153	302	4,365.5	53.5	8.4	0.3	18.9	0.9	10.6	7.3
53 58,235	Richland	39.1	57,303	662	1,465.5	83.3	1.5	0.5	5.6	0.0	4.2	4.9
53 61,115	Sammamish	20.4	65,733	564	3,222.2	63.1	1.1	0.6	30.7	0.4	0.7	3.4
53 62,288	SeaTac	10.0	29,239	1,280	2,923.9	39.7	24.9	0.6	15.1	5.2	7.0	7.5
53 63,000	Seattle	83.9	744,955	18	8,879.1	67.2	6.9	0.4	15.8	0.3	2.6	6.8
53 63,960	Shoreline	11.6	56,752	669	4,892.4	67.2	8.3	0.1	13.6	0.0	3.3	7.5
53 67,000	Spokane	68.8	219,190	100	3,185.9	84.9	2.2	1.6	2.8	1.2	1.0	6.4
53 67,167	Spokane Valley	37.7	99,703	311	2,644.6	89.6	1.2	1.7	1.4	0.4	1.4	4.3
53 70,000	Tacoma	49.7	216,279	102	4,351.7	65.9	10.6	1.6	8.1	1.3	3.8	8.7
53 73,465	University Place	8.3	33,740	1,132	4,065.1	66.5	11.4	0.7	11.1	0.0	1.6	8.7
53 74,060	Vancouver	48.9	183,012	138	3,742.6	80.7	2.2	0.4	5.9	1.6	3.2	6.0
53 75,775	Walla Walla	13.5	32,986	1,157	2,443.4	78.9	2.0	0.5	1.2	0.0	9.3	8.0
53 77,105	Wenatchee	10.0	34,329	1,109	3,432.9	NA	NA	NA	NA	NA	NA	NA
53 80,010	Yakima	27.8	93,884	345	3,377.1	74.1	1.0	0.7	1.0	0.0	18.9	4.3
54 00,000	**WEST VIRGINIA**	24,041.2	1,805,832	X	75.1	92.8	4.0	0.1	0.8	0.0	0.7	1.7
54 14,600	Charleston	31.5	47,215	825	1,498.9	77.4	14.7	0.2	2.9	0.0	0.2	4.6
54 39,460	Huntington	16.2	46,048	838	2,842.5	84.9	8.9	0.3	1.8	0.1	2.8	1.3
54 55,756	Morgantown	10.0	30,955	1,218	3,095.5	82.0	7.0	0.5	3.2	0.0	2.8	4.4
54 62,140	Parkersburg	11.8	29,675	1,265	2,514.8	NA	NA	NA	NA	NA	NA	NA
54 86,452	Wheeling	13.8	26,771	1,369	1,939.9	NA	NA	NA	NA	NA	NA	NA
55 00,000	**WISCONSIN**	54,166.3	5,813,568	X	107.3	85.3	6.4	0.8	2.8	0.1	2.2	2.5
55 02,375	Appleton	24.5	74,526	477	3,041.9	83.3	3.4	1.1	8.9	0.1	1.5	1.8
55 06,500	Beloit	17.3	37,018	1,037	2,139.8	63.6	13.0	0.8	2.8	0.0	9.8	10.0
55 10,025	Brookfield	27.3	38,770	994	1,420.1	82.8	1.3	0.0	14.3	0.2	0.2	1.2
55 22,300	Eau Claire	32.6	68,866	520	2,112.5	89.7	1.1	0.7	3.7	3.0	0.1	1.8
55 25,950	Fitchburg	34.9	30,170	1,248	864.5	76.8	15.3	0.0	1.3	0.0	3.6	2.9
55 26,275	Fond du Lac	19.1	42,959	885	2,249.2	86.4	4.1	0.7	1.6	0.0	4.6	2.6
55 27,300	Franklin	34.6	35,872	1,072	1,036.8	82.8	3.9	0.9	7.1	0.0	7.0	4.7
55 31,000	Green Bay	45.5	104,879	294	2,305.0	76.7	4.9	3.4	3.3	0.0	5.2	2.5
55 31,175	Greenfield	11.5	37,358	1,025	3,248.5	82.0	2.8	0.3	7.1	0.0	1.9	1.6
55 37,825	Janesville	34.0	64,565	577	1,899.0	93.4	1.8	0.1	1.0	0.1	4.4	4.7
55 39,225	Kenosha	27.9	100,164	308	3,590.1	77.1	11.6	0.6	1.7	0.0	0.7	2.4
55 40,775	La Crosse	21.7	51,567	747	2,376.4	91.6	2.6	0.4	2.4	0.0	1.7	3.2
55 48,000	Madison	78.8	258,054	81	3,274.8	79.3	5.6	0.4	9.6	0.1	NA	NA
55 48,500	Manitowoc	17.8	32,627	1,165	1,833.0	NA	NA	NA	NA	NA	1.3	1.2
55 51,000	Menomonee Falls	32.9	37,671	1,020	1,145.0	87.4	5.9	0.2	4.1	0.0	7.9	4.2
55 53,000	Milwaukee	96.2	592,025	31	6,154.1	44.0	39.0	0.5	4.3	0.0	1.2	3.4
55 54,875	Mount Pleasant	33.9	27,014	1,360	796.9	84.0	7.7	0.0	3.6	0.0	NA	NA
55 55,750	Neenah	9.3	26,062	1,392	2,802.4	NA	NA	NA	NA	NA	0.2	1.3
55 56,375	New Berlin	36.5	39,733	970	1,088.6	94.1	1.1	0.0	3.3	0.0	5.3	4.3
55 58,800	Oak Creek	28.4	36,470	1,055	1,284.2	76.0	6.9	0.2	6.9	0.3	0.1	2.0
55 60,500	Oshkosh	26.8	66,729	548	2,489.9	91.2	3.9	0.3	2.4	0.0	4.9	6.1
55 66,000	Racine	15.5	77,432	447	4,995.6	65.8	21.8	0.4	1.0	0.0	2.5	4.2
55 72,975	Sheboygan	15.6	48,180	803	3,088.5	79.6	2.8	0.3	10.6	0.0	0.9	3.8
55 77,200	Stevens Point	17.2	26,161	1,387	1,521.0	86.6	0.8	0.0	8.2	0.0	0.0	4.1
55 78,600	Sun Prairie	12.3	33,974	1,123	2,762.1	80.4	10.4	0.1	4.3	0.0	2.2	1.8
55 78,650	Superior	36.6	26,101	1,389	713.1	91.5	0.9	2.2	1.3	0.0	2.6	1.7
55 84,250	Waukesha	25.5	72,549	493	2,845.1	82.8	1.0	0.7	11.2	0.0	0.6	3.3
55 84,475	Wausau	19.3	38,580	997	1,999.0	87.9	3.4	0.1	4.7	0.0	3.5	5.0
55 84,675	Wauwatosa	13.2	48,376	796	3,664.8	79.4	8.9	0.8	2.3	0.0	NA	NA
55 85,300	West Allis	11.4	59,492	631	5,218.6	NA	NA	NA	NA	NA	1.7	2.8
55 85,350	West Bend	15.1	31,590	1,201	2,092.1	NA	NA	NA	NA	NA	NA	NA
56 00,000	**WYOMING**	97,088.7	577,737	X	6.0	91.2	1.0	2.4	0.8	0.0	2.8	4.7
56 13,150	Casper	26.5	57,461	658	2,168.3	NA	NA	NA	NA	NA	NA	NA
56 13,900	Cheyenne	28.5	63,957	585	2,244.1	89.9	1.2	0.4	0.9	0.0	NA	NA
56 31,855	Gillette	23.0	31,903	1,190	1,387.1	NA	NA	NA	NA	NA	0.9	4.7
56 45,050	Laramie	18.3	32,473	1,170	1,774.5	88.0	0.1	2.2	4.2	0.0		

1. Dry land or land partially or temporarily covered by water.   2. Hispanic or Latino persons may be of any race.

Table D. Cities — **Population**

City	Percent Hispanic or Latino[1], 2017	Percent foreign born, 2017	Age of population (percent), 2017							Median age, 2017	Percent female, 2017	Population Census counts		Percent change	
			Under 18 years	18 to 24 years	25 to 34 years	35 to 44 years	45 to 54 years	55 to 64 years	65 years and over			2000	2010	2000-2010	2001-2018
	12	13	14	15	16	17	18	19	20	21	22	23	24	25	26
WASHINGTON—Cont'd															
Pasco	54.4	23.6	31.9	9.9	15.0	14.1	10.0	8.8	10.3	30.3	49.8	32,066	62,160	93.9	20.3
Pullman	8.2	17.1	11.5	50.7	14.2	7.5	4.0	5.9	6.3	22.0	50.6	24,675	29,822	20.9	14.1
Puyallup	5.8	10.0	21.5	7.4	12.9	15.3	13.9	14.0	15.1	40.4	47.7	33,011	37,241	12.8	12.5
Redmond	5.3	43.6	21.2	5.5	21.4	21.7	10.2	7.4	12.6	35.9	50.9	45,256	54,511	20.5	24.2
Renton	17.5	29.5	21.3	8.4	17.7	16.2	13.2	12.1	11.1	36.7	51.7	50,052	91,903	83.6	11.2
Richland	11.3	8.7	22.7	9.9	15.0	13.0	13.9	13.3	12.2	37.4	49.9	38,708	48,105	24.3	19.1
Sammamish	4.0	28.9	28.6	5.2	9.4	19.2	16.6	13.1	8.0	38.2	52.2	34,104	57,445	68.4	14.4
SeaTac	10.1	41.7	23.9	7.0	14.5	19.6	11.9	15.0	8.3	37.5	47.1	25,496	26,901	5.5	8.7
Seattle	6.7	18.3	15.8	9.9	23.1	14.9	12.8	10.9	12.6	35.6	50.3	563,374	608,666	8.0	22.4
Shoreline	11.2	23.8	20.9	7.2	13.8	15.9	14.0	13.4	14.8	39.5	53.5	53,025	53,031	0.0	7.0
Spokane	6.1	5.6	21.5	9.9	17.4	11.6	11.3	12.9	15.4	35.7	50.5	195,629	209,455	7.1	4.6
Spokane Valley	6.6	5.9	20.8	7.1	16.0	12.7	14.1	12.1	17.1	39.5	49.9	NA	89,743	NA	11.1
Tacoma	11.9	12.4	21.4	9.6	17.5	13.9	13.3	11.4	12.9	35.9	49.4	193,556	198,243	2.4	9.1
University Place	9.1	11.3	23.1	9.1	16.8	6.7	13.4	14.0	16.8	36.0	53.4	29,933	31,133	4.0	8.4
Vancouver	14.2	13.4	23.1	8.0	16.2	12.4	12.8	11.8	15.6	37.1	50.4	143,560	167,185	16.5	9.5
Walla Walla	25.0	7.0	19.8	16.4	14.6	15.3	8.0	9.5	16.5	33.9	48.3	29,686	32,439	9.3	1.7
Wenatchee	36.7	15.8	25.1	10.8	15.9	10.5	10.3	12.6	14.9	33.1	50.9	27,856	32,765	17.6	4.8
Yakima	46.5	16.3	27.4	11.0	15.2	12.1	10.0	9.9	14.4	32.5	50.1	71,845	91,276	27.0	2.9
WEST VIRGINIA	1.3	1.6	20.6	9.0	11.5	12.2	13.1	14.4	19.3	42.4	50.6	1,808,344	1,853,001	2.5	-2.5
Charleston	0.9	5.2	23.3	5.8	11.5	12.5	12.5	15.9	18.5	41.3	52.0	53,421	51,338	-3.9	-8.0
Huntington	2.3	2.3	19.3	16.1	11.9	11.0	11.0	13.1	18.5	36.8	51.0	51,475	49,182	-4.5	-6.4
Morgantown	4.3	8.6	10.7	45.1	13.8	8.9	5.2	6.8	9.6	23.1	45.3	26,809	28,343	5.7	9.2
Parkersburg	1.3	0.2	20.0	8.4	11.0	12.6	13.5	14.0	20.6	42.8	51.9	33,099	31,289	-5.5	-5.2
Wheeling	0.8	1.0	20.1	11.5	9.8	11.8	9.5	14.0	23.2	41.6	51.5	31,419	28,485	-9.3	-6.0
WISCONSIN	6.9	5.0	22.1	9.6	12.5	12.1	13.1	14.1	16.5	39.5	50.3	5,363,675	5,687,282	6.0	2.2
Appleton	5.2	6.2	23.2	9.5	14.2	13.1	13.5	13.6	13.0	37.4	52.1	70,087	72,673	3.7	2.5
Beloit	22.8	10.8	30.0	10.3	13.5	12.8	10.8	10.7	12.0	31.2	53.3	35,775	37,007	3.4	0.0
Brookfield	3.2	12.8	23.0	6.1	7.7	13.0	12.9	15.7	21.5	45.2	49.9	38,649	37,919	-1.9	2.2
Eau Claire	2.7	5.9	19.9	20.8	14.5	11.8	9.0	11.5	12.4	31.5	50.6	61,704	66,230	7.3	4.0
Fitchburg	12.4	7.1	22.5	7.3	16.6	8.6	11.3	14.1	19.6	37.2	46.1	20,501	25,161	22.7	19.9
Fond du Lac	8.3	5.7	20.4	10.9	13.9	10.7	11.8	15.5	16.9	39.8	49.7	42,203	43,016	1.9	-0.1
Franklin	7.7	9.0	22.1	5.3	12.5	15.7	14.6	14.6	15.1	40.8	47.8	29,494	35,460	20.2	1.2
Green Bay	14.7	8.5	22.3	11.5	13.6	13.5	12.1	12.6	14.5	37.1	51.0	102,313	103,911	1.6	0.9
Greenfield	11.6	7.5	18.7	4.6	16.2	12.0	11.6	15.3	21.7	43.4	49.7	35,476	36,740	3.6	1.7
Janesville	4.0	2.8	20.8	7.5	12.5	12.2	12.8	14.9	19.3	43.4	52.0	59,498	63,635	7.0	1.5
Kenosha	18.2	10.6	25.0	11.3	14.8	12.0	12.0	11.6	13.2	34.1	51.8	90,352	99,323	9.9	0.8
La Crosse	1.9	1.6	14.3	28.9	14.8	9.9	8.6	8.4	15.1	28.7	49.4	51,818	51,348	-0.9	0.4
Madison	8.1	12.6	16.0	21.8	18.2	13.0	9.5	9.0	12.5	31.3	50.1	208,054	233,163	12.1	10.7
Manitowoc	5.9	3.6	22.7	9.2	9.2	12.2	12.7	14.9	19.0	42.0	52.4	34,053	33,741	-0.9	-3.3
Menomonee Falls	3.6	6.4	23.2	6.0	8.9	14.6	12.8	15.1	19.3	42.8	51.4	32,647	35,625	9.1	5.7
Milwaukee	19.1	10.0	25.8	12.0	16.8	12.5	11.3	10.8	10.7	31.9	52.1	596,974	594,511	-0.4	-0.4
Mount Pleasant	9.0	6.8	15.4	8.7	10.4	11.2	11.2	18.7	24.5	49.3	53.1	NA	26,576	NA	1.6
Neenah	3.3	3.4	26.3	6.8	13.4	11.3	10.2	15.8	16.2	38.9	52.0	24,507	25,501	4.1	2.2
New Berlin	1.4	7.1	19.9	8.0	9.9	8.3	17.1	16.1	20.6	48.2	52.5	38,220	39,583	3.6	0.4
Oak Creek	9.6	14.1	23.8	3.9	15.1	11.8	13.6	16.7	15.1	40.2	51.8	28,456	34,449	21.1	5.9
Oshkosh	2.9	1.9	15.6	19.3	16.9	10.3	14.0	9.9	14.0	34.0	50.4	62,916	66,205	5.2	0.8
Racine	23.4	4.7	27.7	11.1	13.6	12.3	11.4	10.8	13.0	32.8	51.0	81,855	78,848	-3.7	-1.8
Sheboygan	9.9	6.6	23.7	9.6	12.7	13.8	10.5	11.6	18.2	37.4	49.7	50,792	49,390	-2.8	-2.4
Stevens Point	4.3	6.6	12.9	35.1	14.1	5.6	7.5	10.7	14.0	25.9	50.1	24,551	26,702	8.8	-2.0
Sun Prairie	2.9	6.8	25.2	8.0	12.8	14.6	15.3	9.7	14.4	37.7	54.9	20,369	29,538	45.0	15.0
Superior	2.2	2.7	19.8	11.7	15.5	10.9	14.7	12.9	14.4	36.7	52.1	27,368	27,236	-0.5	-4.2
Waukesha	11.4	6.5	17.6	9.9	17.1	13.5	11.3	13.0	17.6	39.0	52.2	64,825	71,222	9.9	1.9
Wausau	5.4	8.0	17.3	9.0	17.0	10.7	13.7	14.3	18.1	40.1	50.4	38,426	39,187	2.0	-1.5
Wauwatosa	4.9	3.3	22.2	4.9	15.4	14.9	13.0	11.3	18.3	38.8	51.2	47,271	46,425	-1.8	4.2
West Allis	9.6	5.9	17.2	6.3	22.6	13.7	12.8	12.5	14.9	37.3	50.9	61,254	60,410	-1.4	-1.5
West Bend	3.7	2.3	19.7	8.0	12.6	14.8	12.1	13.4	19.3	40.3	49.5	28,152	31,187	10.8	1.3
WYOMING	10.0	3.5	23.8	9.2	13.8	12.2	11.2	14.1	15.6	37.5	48.9	493,782	563,773	14.2	2.5
Casper	10.5	3.6	26.4	6.6	13.4	13.4	12.4	11.8	15.9	37.2	50.8	49,644	55,313	11.4	3.9
Cheyenne	13.9	2.8	23.1	8.9	16.0	12.7	11.9	13.3	14.1	36.3	47.2	53,011	59,547	12.3	7.4
Gillette	12.2	3.6	35.3	8.8	16.8	11.0	9.9	12.7	5.5	29.4	48.4	19,646	31,393	59.8	1.6
Laramie	11.1	9.4	16.7	30.8	19.5	10.1	6.6	7.5	8.9	25.9	47.8	27,204	30,816	13.3	5.4

1. May be of any race.

Table D. Cities — Households, Group Quarters, Crime, and Education

City	Households, 2017 — Number	Persons per household	Percent — Family	Married couple family	Female headed[1]	Non-family	One person	Persons in group quarters, 2017	Serious crimes known to police[2], 2016 — Total Number	Total Rate	Rate[3] Violent	Rate[3] Property	Population age 25 and over	Attainment[4] High school graduate or less	Bachelor's degree or more
	27	28	29	30	31	32	33	34	35	36	37	38	39	40	41
WASHINGTON—Cont'd															
Pasco	20,628	3.23	71.5	53.9	12.5	28.5	22.5	NA	1,799	2,531	208	2,323	39,142	47.7	18.3
Pullman	12,446	2.10	31.9	27.2	3.3	68.1	46.0	7,616	726	2,170	149	2,021	12,765	13.5	54.5
Puyallup	16,843	2.39	58.9	41.8	8.9	41.1	31.8	766	2,909	7,242	321	6,921	29,180	40.6	21.4
Redmond	27,101	2.36	64.6	53.2	9.1	35.4	27.7	372	2,022	3,267	136	3,131	47,090	11.7	68.9
Renton	38,103	2.64	67.8	44.8	14.2	32.2	22.8	889	6,110	5,996	335	5,661	71,218	35.4	34.6
Richland	21,822	2.56	65.7	47.9	11.3	34.3	26.0	283	1,446	2,607	180	2,426	37,917	26.3	37.3
Sammamish	21,548	2.99	84.8	77.7	4.8	15.2	13.0	124	462	865	36	830	42,779	9.8	72.7
SeaTac	10,146	2.77	68.0	46.0	14.8	32.0	26.1	1,059	1,749	6,144	530	5,614	20,150	38.0	22.4
Seattle	329,671	2.13	45.9	35.7	6.6	54.1	37.8	21,317	42,743	6,103	614	5,489	538,813	15.2	62.6
Shoreline	20,962	2.59	64.1	47.0	11.7	35.9	27.4	1,875	1,466	2,622	165	2,458	40,394	22.4	48.7
Spokane	90,699	2.31	57.3	38.8	13.0	42.7	33.7	7,344	17,739	8,288	598	7,690	148,792	30.2	30.6
Spokane Valley	41,372	2.35	59.4	44.1	9.4	40.6	31.4	789	5,567	5,804	283	5,521	70,566	31.6	25.2
Tacoma	83,034	2.48	58.8	39.5	12.2	41.2	33.4	7,345	15,784	7,519	954	6,565	147,294	37.8	28.0
University Place	13,438	2.47	61.7	45.5	13.2	38.3	33.0	NA	925	2,786	223	2,564	22,623	22.9	46.5
Vancouver	68,395	2.53	60.0	44.5	10.6	40.0	30.0	2,615	6,208	3,549	385	3,164	120,884	34.7	28.2
Walla Walla	11,603	2.48	60.4	42.0	15.3	39.6	30.9	4,106	1,497	4,631	377	4,254	20,957	32.8	22.4
Wenatchee	11,581	2.87	65.2	41.5	13.8	34.8	24.3	750	1,218	3,591	259	3,331	21,783	43.5	23.4
Yakima	33,768	2.70	63.8	38.3	15.8	36.2	31.3	2,604	5,448	5,789	530	5,259	57,725	50.2	19.0
WEST VIRGINIA	715,308	2.47	64.5	48.4	10.9	35.5	29.9	47,432	44,044	2,405	358	2,047	1,279,350	54.1	20.2
Charleston	20,661	2.22	53.5	34.7	14.6	46.5	39.3	1,977	4,712	9,533	1,556	7,977	33,989	37.9	39.7
Huntington	21,055	2.12	48.4	30.2	13.1	51.6	41.2	3,290	2,771	5,709	785	4,924	30,997	47.3	23.9
Morgantown	10,440	2.46	39.6	28.3	3.2	60.4	37.4	4,829	767	2,466	286	2,179	13,527	23.1	55.0
Parkersburg	13,194	2.25	56.4	35.0	14.8	43.6	38.1	433	1,582	5,118	670	4,448	21,575	53.2	16.3
Wheeling	10,769	2.30	44.0	30.9	9.6	56.0	50.9	1,314	936	3,405	968	2,438	17,786	45.0	32.9
WISCONSIN	2,350,293	2.40	62.9	48.5	9.9	37.1	29.5	145,899	129,399	2,239	306	1,933	3,958,231	38.3	30.4
Appleton	29,323	2.44	66.4	50.9	12.1	33.6	28.5	2,492	1,518	2,039	289	1,750	49,832	34.1	34.5
Beloit	13,459	2.61	63.4	31.6	21.9	36.6	30.7	1,660	1,299	3,522	475	3,048	21,983	51.9	14.9
Brookfield	13,697	2.75	82.5	74.3	6.0	17.5	14.8	449	895	2,353	66	2,287	26,970	16.7	63.7
Eau Claire	27,785	2.37	55.9	40.6	10.9	44.1	32.0	4,028	1,959	2,877	207	2,670	41,406	30.5	33.4
Fitchburg	12,967	2.20	65.5	44.5	13.0	34.5	28.5	890	498	1,742	252	1,490	20,695	17.1	50.0
Fond du Lac	17,837	2.26	59.8	47.1	7.1	40.2	31.6	2,440	1,095	2,552	322	2,230	29,397	41.3	26.3
Franklin	13,922	2.43	64.7	55.4	5.9	35.3	29.8	2,308	704	1,939	58	1,881	26,237	33.4	38.8
Green Bay	43,546	2.33	58.2	39.6	11.7	41.8	34.4	3,563	2,818	2,672	482	2,191	69,571	43.8	26.0
Greenfield	16,003	2.28	55.2	41.1	11.1	44.8	37.5	402	1,131	3,024	230	2,794	28,262	38.6	31.6
Janesville	27,871	2.28	61.6	44.7	12.0	38.4	33.8	841	1,908	2,970	226	2,745	46,190	44.0	22.4
Kenosha	37,867	2.55	59.0	36.8	16.1	41.0	31.8	3,489	2,546	2,547	357	2,190	63,619	41.1	25.3
La Crosse	21,665	2.18	42.0	26.8	8.6	58.0	38.7	4,659	2,424	4,617	251	4,366	29,455	38.1	31.4
Madison	111,035	2.20	46.1	34.8	7.3	53.9	35.7	11,476	7,771	3,082	331	2,751	158,803	18.3	57.0
Manitowoc	13,964	2.29	59.9	42.3	10.5	40.1	32.1	785	1,033	3,142	322	2,820	22,268	42.8	17.9
Menomonee Falls	15,307	2.43	69.1	59.9	6.7	30.9	26.2	NA	452	1,248	44	1,204	26,488	28.4	44.2
Milwaukee	228,054	2.54	53.2	26.7	21.0	46.8	36.8	16,893	33,597	5,598	1,534	4,064	370,407	48.0	23.6
Mount Pleasant	11,395	2.30	63.1	49.8	8.5	36.9	29.5	NA	721	2,743	61	2,682	20,140	27.5	40.1
Neenah	10,595	2.43	63.2	45.7	12.4	36.8	28.0	NA	543	2,101	201	1,899	17,368	41.6	29.5
New Berlin	17,189	2.30	63.9	55.8	5.4	36.1	31.4	NA	433	1,086	30	1,056	28,621	30.2	43.9
Oak Creek	14,559	2.49	65.2	50.0	13.5	34.8	28.3	NA	939	2,657	91	2,567	26,266	38.4	33.8
Oshkosh	27,122	2.18	52.9	37.6	10.2	47.1	32.3	7,550	1,612	2,418	212	2,207	43,389	41.5	29.3
Racine	30,633	2.47	63.1	36.0	21.9	36.9	31.8	1,818	2,654	3,423	473	2,950	47,413	47.1	17.1
Sheboygan	20,719	2.29	58.2	38.9	12.6	41.8	33.3	853	1,194	2,451	269	2,182	32,244	44.4	18.2
Stevens Point	10,709	2.16	41.0	29.7	7.7	59.0	41.6	3,151	478	1,798	192	1,606	13,655	32.6	41.7
Sun Prairie	13,220	2.48	65.4	50.9	10.3	34.6	30.3	151	621	1,885	106	1,779	21,955	21.8	46.8
Superior	11,992	2.13	53.5	31.0	13.3	46.5	35.9	1,039	1,315	4,971	227	4,745	18,224	30.1	26.7
Waukesha	32,294	2.16	56.9	43.9	11.2	43.1	35.1	2,658	1,209	1,674	127	1,547	52,548	30.5	40.0
Wausau	18,292	2.06	51.3	38.9	8.5	48.7	38.4	993	1,073	2,745	292	2,453	28,528	38.7	28.2
Wauwatosa	19,639	2.42	59.9	52.3	4.3	40.1	32.4	717	1,933	4,046	161	3,885	35,176	18.5	59.9
West Allis	26,149	2.26	49.0	33.7	11.6	51.0	41.0	879	2,467	4,074	332	3,742	45,868	43.4	26.1
West Bend	13,830	2.26	60.4	49.0	6.8	39.6	34.0	375	741	2,331	182	2,148	22,846	36.8	25.3
WYOMING	225,796	2.50	64.5	51.6	8.5	35.5	28.5	14,133	12,890	2,202	244	1,957	387,700	36.6	27.6
Casper	23,743	2.34	60.0	45.1	9.8	40.0	33.4	1,138	1,739	2,835	114	2,721	38,012	33.8	26.9
Cheyenne	25,967	2.41	60.7	47.0	8.6	39.3	32.0	946	2,599	4,058	269	3,789	43,262	31.8	32.0
Gillette	10,768	2.87	70.3	51.6	12.2	29.7	22.5	527	770	2,318	187	2,131	17,587	41.1	20.8
Laramie	13,459	2.18	38.5	29.1	7.4	61.5	37.9	2,375	448	1,382	117	1,265	16,652	21.6	55.5

1. No spouse present. 2. Data for serious crimes have not been adjusted for underreporting. This may affect comparability between geographic areas and over time. 3. Per 100,000 population estimated by the FBI. 4. Persons 25 years old and over.

Table D. Cities — Income and Housing

City	Money income, 2017 — Households: Median income (42)	Percent with income less than $20,000 (43)	Percent with income of $200,000 or more (44)	Median family income (45)	Median non-family income (46)	Median earnings, 2017 — All persons (47)	Men (48)	Women (49)	Housing units, 2017 — Total (50)	Occupied (51)	Percent owner occupied (52)	Median value¹ (dollars) (53)	Median gross rent (dollars) (54)
WASHINGTON—Cont'd													
Pasco	59,200	11.9	4.5	69,810	41,550	30,544	36,980	23,080	21,442	20,628	73.4	209,000	798
Pullman	29,593	37.1	4.9	84,464	19,901	10,990	15,793	8,864	13,225	12,446	30.4	277,900	787
Puyallup	63,606	12.0	4.1	80,156	43,789	38,471	44,866	36,347	17,339	16,843	50.2	332,200	1,152
Redmond	122,449	6.9	23.2	145,975	79,308	72,373	101,977	49,574	29,103	27,101	50.1	708,000	1,935
Renton	78,703	8.1	7.5	84,607	52,240	40,733	46,041	35,108	40,116	38,103	51.0	401,600	1,532
Richland	74,447	10.9	6.9	98,525	50,699	46,245	57,165	34,585	23,160	21,822	61.6	247,700	1,080
Sammamish	157,493	1.5	39.6	173,761	100,691	90,967	131,129	42,413	22,081	21,548	87.4	840,200	2,513
SeaTac	60,167	9.1	2.6	73,068	50,313	28,487	31,376	25,526	10,787	10,146	50.1	304,700	1,276
Seattle	86,822	12.2	15.8	121,256	63,990	51,851	60,317	45,307	355,293	329,671	47.1	673,100	1,555
Shoreline	82,069	11.2	12.0	100,833	55,043	42,649	55,169	33,865	21,466	20,962	62.3	555,700	1,593
Spokane	46,543	19.0	2.9	63,239	30,796	30,417	31,231	29,183	97,944	90,699	54.5	190,200	830
Spokane Valley	49,888	16.4	2.8	75,389	30,308	30,968	36,263	28,578	44,237	41,372	59.3	198,600	866
Tacoma	57,164	17.6	4.1	77,092	37,456	35,783	41,146	30,256	90,476	83,034	53.3	269,800	1,071
University Place	62,118	12.7	10.4	84,554	37,850	37,990	50,363	33,224	14,182	13,438	57.3	379,300	1,095
Vancouver	61,079	12.9	4.7	68,051	41,700	34,927	40,050	30,014	72,379	68,395	52.0	290,500	1,183
Walla Walla	49,619	17.8	2.3	58,214	37,837	27,337	29,585	25,964	12,854	11,603	54.6	193,700	1,014
Wenatchee	61,142	19.6	6.0	65,833	29,688	27,587	29,824	23,301	13,116	11,581	56.3	247,100	885
Yakima	41,121	16.9	3.7	46,927	31,774	25,435	30,103	22,898	35,663	33,768	51.7	168,700	761
WEST VIRGINIA	43,469	23.4	2.7	56,086	24,084	28,937	35,166	24,036	892,240	715,308	72.5	119,800	690
Charleston	41,844	26.6	6.4	58,444	28,288	31,872	36,952	23,773	25,477	20,661	62.0	140,800	650
Huntington	26,289	42.5	1.8	42,389	15,801	20,662	22,861	16,980	24,866	21,055	46.5	96,200	643
Morgantown	38,175	34.5	4.8	70,013	19,741	11,201	15,784	8,363	13,030	10,440	37.2	222,500	816
Parkersburg	35,697	28.0	2.2	41,222	24,219	29,422	34,543	21,416	15,248	13,194	63.2	96,400	681
Wheeling	44,143	22.8	2.3	64,242	32,742	26,543	30,073	25,610	14,093	10,769	66.2	115,000	728
WISCONSIN	59,305	14.2	4.4	75,413	35,115	34,841	41,180	28,623	2,695,303	2,350,293	66.6	178,900	819
Appleton	58,374	14.0	6.2	70,241	37,939	32,316	39,876	27,351	31,033	29,323	68.5	148,600	779
Beloit	42,250	23.8	1.4	49,192	21,748	24,836	32,229	20,230	14,509	13,459	57.9	89,000	773
Brookfield	107,511	5.7	16.7	112,215	58,682	51,877	64,691	41,645	14,093	13,697	84.9	323,300	1,635
Eau Claire	52,355	19.8	3.8	72,559	32,078	27,679	34,883	20,073	28,707	27,785	57.2	149,100	781
Fitchburg	69,840	5.7	7.8	89,156	47,847	35,366	38,546	31,629	13,690	12,967	51.7	302,300	979
Fond du Lac	52,590	14.7	2.9	69,519	32,727	30,024	40,363	21,636	18,700	17,837	58.4	126,700	751
Franklin	75,403	8.2	8.0	102,324	38,632	40,573	45,288	37,919	14,331	13,922	73.8	227,300	985
Green Bay	47,794	17.6	2.8	59,256	30,747	29,731	33,634	25,578	46,042	43,546	54.7	138,600	692
Greenfield	62,026	14.6	4.0	82,172	39,769	39,169	42,163	35,404	16,951	16,003	58.4	165,200	987
Janesville	52,191	15.0	1.6	66,231	31,405	30,622	39,650	25,224	29,111	27,871	64.3	133,600	794
Kenosha	52,848	14.3	4.8	62,228	35,706	29,704	36,627	23,030	40,434	37,867	55.0	145,500	883
La Crosse	42,728	22.7	2.2	52,826	33,143	23,169	30,157	13,212	22,809	21,665	40.4	138,100	780
Madison	65,072	16.7	5.9	85,466	42,727	32,303	38,664	27,408	116,145	111,035	48.0	240,700	1,095
Manitowoc	50,736	15.7	1.8	72,596	31,730	36,689	40,994	28,449	15,560	13,964	68.1	101,300	651
Menomonee Falls	80,003	5.9	12.0	99,367	40,024	47,595	55,879	34,828	15,777	15,307	74.5	255,700	1,044
Milwaukee	39,098	25.3	1.8	46,302	29,343	27,798	30,599	25,754	260,581	228,054	40.4	122,300	820
Mount Pleasant	77,915	17.1	6.6	91,856	31,229	44,810	54,550	36,166	11,861	11,395	77.5	190,600	913
Neenah	53,523	14.7	5.4	70,805	34,747	34,787	41,286	27,110	10,888	10,595	64.3	141,000	713
New Berlin	70,758	10.1	5.7	90,810	42,593	49,665	53,330	41,724	17,438	17,189	70.3	263,200	1,102
Oak Creek	71,028	10.9	5.5	78,543	42,162	47,175	49,962	46,265	15,410	14,559	62.3	232,100	979
Oshkosh	49,972	15.5	0.6	63,249	32,436	28,201	35,606	22,271	29,597	27,122	56.6	128,500	734
Racine	43,169	19.4	1.8	47,431	30,096	28,813	31,950	25,846	33,260	30,633	48.0	106,700	760
Sheboygan	45,102	16.9	0.7	58,629	29,567	27,854	32,423	24,148	21,804	20,719	60.2	107,000	667
Stevens Point	40,757	22.8	3.0	69,519	27,792	14,502	18,607	11,869	11,634	10,709	48.8	134,400	711
Sun Prairie	76,887	9.3	4.9	94,486	49,050	43,206	50,133	37,182	13,854	13,220	62.2	236,500	1,031
Superior	53,798	18.5	2.0	66,151	35,817	31,171	35,343	25,923	12,537	11,992	53.8	123,200	769
Waukesha	60,923	12.5	1.8	85,936	40,809	37,579	41,071	34,454	34,247	32,294	58.8	209,800	891
Wausau	36,357	24.1	2.6	53,918	26,146	26,450	25,474	27,412	19,293	18,292	55.2	108,300	633
Wauwatosa	87,128	13.6	8.6	106,816	48,895	50,517	61,336	40,331	21,151	19,639	66.1	246,600	1,052
West Allis	49,377	15.3	0.9	67,277	36,667	35,088	40,522	29,000	28,291	26,149	55.0	144,900	789
West Bend	54,949	13.5	2.4	75,456	30,938	36,336	40,815	29,083	14,317	13,830	65.1	173,400	848
WYOMING	60,434	14.4	3.5	74,868	33,472	32,885	40,838	27,108	276,733	225,796	70.8	214,300	832
Casper	60,385	13.7	4.4	79,066	35,943	39,296	47,496	32,163	26,540	23,743	67.4	207,600	915
Cheyenne	62,049	12.9	1.1	74,854	41,208	35,094	40,802	28,192	29,180	25,967	67.2	206,900	918
Gillette	71,583	13.9	2.0	79,116	57,374	40,137	55,446	30,164	13,372	10,768	72.8	194,100	801
Laramie	33,632	25.5	0.7	63,527	28,463	16,104	19,626	12,302	14,902	13,459	43.1	201,500	731

1. Based on population estimated by the American Community Survey.   2. Includes units rented or sold but not occupied.   3. Specified owner-occupied units; $1,000,000 represents $1,000,000 or more.   4. 50.0 represents 50 percent or more.   5. 10.0 represents 10 percent or less.

Table D. Cities — Commuting, Computer Access, Migration, Labor Force, and Employment

City	Commuting [55]	With commutes of 30 minutes or more [56]	With a computer in the house [57]	With Internet access [58]	Percent who lived in the same house one year ago [59]	Percent who lived in another state or county one year ago [60]	Total [61]	Percent change 2017-2018 [62]	Unemployment Total [63]	Rate [64]	Population age 16 and older Number [65]	Percent in labor force [66]	Population age 16 to 64 Number [67]	Percent who worked full-year full-time [68]
WASHINGTON—Cont'd														
Pasco	79.5	18.5	94.1	84.7	91.6	5.9	33,483	2.1	2,061	6.2	47,716	68.5	40,806	45.4
Pullman	52.9	7.4	98.4	88.0	54.4	29.6	16,187	1.6	710	4.4	30,301	60.9	28,168	23.7
Puyallup	81.4	45.8	93.7	84.8	78.9	10.0	21,861	2.1	1,040	4.8	33,160	67.4	26,961	50.9
Redmond	65.4	36.3	97.9	94.8	77.9	10.1	37,813	1.9	1,167	3.1	51,830	71.8	43,734	58.5
Renton	74.1	56.8	95.4	92.4	77.4	6.6	58,456	2.0	2,147	3.7	82,067	72.7	70,794	56.1
Richland	76.4	17.6	95.3	90.6	80.7	9.6	28,702	2.4	1,392	4.8	44,996	66.3	38,162	52.9
Sammamish	67.6	61.3	NA	NA	86.7	6.1	33,370	2.0	1,060	3.2	48,337	68.9	43,186	49.6
SeaTac	76.5	35.5	94.5	91.3	81.9	11.4	14,989	1.9	644	4.3	22,909	70.3	20,503	47.8
Seattle	47.2	46.7	95.4	91.0	77.8	9.0	460,990	2.0	14,536	3.2	621,509	73.2	530,316	55.7
Shoreline	68.0	54.5	96.4	89.8	78.3	9.0	30,778	2.1	1,100	3.6	45,827	68.5	37,495	54.0
Spokane	76.5	22.1	91.9	87.0	78.7	7.4	104,960	2.0	5,698	5.4	175,089	60.8	141,617	47.9
Spokane Valley	84.0	19.7	91.8	85.1	81.4	6.3	48,943	2.2	2,625	5.4	80,211	66.4	63,443	54.3
Tacoma	74.3	42.3	92.0	82.8	81.4	9.3	104,660	2.1	5,754	5.5	171,992	63.7	144,413	47.1
University Place	80.4	36.4	90.5	85.8	92.1	2.3	17,012	2.1	770	4.5	26,746	64.6	21,130	48.5
Vancouver	76.1	35.2	94.0	89.0	78.4	11.0	86,502	1.2	4,281	4.9	140,044	63.8	112,616	47.8
Walla Walla	71.6	20.4	94.5	85.2	73.2	18.6	14,819	1.5	762	5.1	26,604	53.6	21,190	38.8
Wenatchee	76.7	12.7	95.0	85.9	80.1	7.8	19,735	3.1	968	4.9	25,997	64.8	20,941	51.4
Yakima	78.3	12.9	88.6	81.0	78.1	7.3	47,921	3.2	2,667	5.6	70,310	59.7	56,828	44.8
WEST VIRGINIA	82.8	34.0	84.6	75.3	88.4	5.0	783,344	0.5	41,165	5.3	1,485,052	52.4	1,134,480	43.4
Charleston	79.9	13.0	83.8	75.0	87.2	6.0	22,252	-1.1	1,094	4.9	38,578	55.2	29,714	45.9
Huntington	75.6	15.6	85.9	55.7	82.4	7.7	19,764	-0.5	989	5.0	39,785	46.3	30,905	35.0
Morgantown	61.6	11.0	91.2	81.4	54.4	18.5	14,708	1.1	679	4.6	27,591	58.5	24,664	30.4
Parkersburg	83.0	6.8	80.8	76.1	91.4	2.4	11,987	-0.6	716	6.0	24,488	50.7	18,293	43.9
Wheeling	81.0	17.6	79.8	66.7	88.1	8.1	13,129	1.9	643	4.9	21,469	57.2	15,433	47.8
WISCONSIN	81.1	27.5	89.5	83.2	85.6	5.8	3,133,294	-0.2	93,999	3.0	4,662,901	66.3	3,706,717	54.7
Appleton	82.6	14.5	91.4	86.3	87.1	8.2	40,264	-0.6	1,173	2.9	59,040	70.4	49,446	55.7
Beloit	86.7	28.0	87.3	80.7	80.4	9.0	17,273	-0.4	694	4.0	26,318	62.3	21,900	42.5
Brookfield	86.0	25.0	96.4	92.7	89.9	6.5	19,404	-0.5	535	2.8	30,517	62.0	22,332	55.0
Eau Claire	79.1	10.2	93.0	87.6	75.3	12.9	40,164	-0.3	1,017	2.5	57,220	71.2	48,567	47.2
Fitchburg	73.0	22.0	96.8	91.5	86.7	5.3	16,786	-0.3	355	2.1	23,585	67.8	17,820	60.1
Fond du Lac	87.2	17.9	88.4	80.3	77.9	7.6	23,008	0.8	653	2.8	34,729	65.2	27,501	49.8
Franklin	87.1	37.3	87.3	83.9	84.9	3.7	18,402	-0.6	539	2.9	28,996	60.6	23,522	52.7
Green Bay	81.1	10.5	86.9	82.5	83.8	5.6	55,224	0.4	1,660	3.0	84,360	68.0	69,106	51.9
Greenfield	85.9	33.7	88.1	80.2	82.7	4.1	19,748	-0.6	631	3.2	30,682	65.7	22,703	61.6
Janesville	87.3	21.5	88.7	82.8	85.3	3.8	33,847	0.0	1,077	3.2	52,549	62.7	40,116	52.2
Kenosha	85.4	30.2	87.8	80.1	83.3	7.0	50,748	-0.1	1,951	3.8	77,806	68.1	64,585	50.5
La Crosse	78.7	13.5	89.2	78.5	73.9	12.2	29,643	-0.9	823	2.8	44,664	64.4	36,845	42.3
Madison	61.0	22.1	95.8	87.7	75.5	10.5	156,435	-0.2	3,434	2.2	219,474	70.0	187,452	48.7
Manitowoc	80.7	18.3	85.8	81.5	94.7	1.7	16,116	-1.0	540	3.4	26,243	62.4	20,042	58.5
Menomonee Falls	85.5	25.6	94.2	92.2	88.6	6.7	20,692	-0.7	513	2.5	29,607	68.9	22,366	60.7
Milwaukee	73.4	27.7	82.2	72.2	82.4	4.5	277,608	-0.8	11,208	4.0	456,973	63.5	393,027	47.7
Mount Pleasant	85.2	29.7	91.8	86.9	88.9	3.4	14,290	-0.2	464	3.2	22,777	58.6	16,290	59.6
Neenah	86.5	12.2	92.2	88.3	83.8	6.2	14,172	-1.0	394	2.8	19,668	64.9	15,476	57.4
New Berlin	92.6	24.2	95.1	88.6	90.5	4.7	21,963	-0.5	603	2.7	32,617	65.8	24,432	59.2
Oak Creek	84.9	43.3	92.1	90.5	82.0	5.0	21,096	-0.6	576	2.7	28,652	66.5	23,165	53.5
Oshkosh	78.4	14.9	92.5	87.9	73.8	11.2	35,144	-0.9	985	2.8	57,579	63.3	48,270	46.3
Racine	83.0	25.0	90.6	84.2	82.1	2.6	35,551	-0.4	1,598	4.5	57,864	64.1	47,788	52.3
Sheboygan	77.1	14.5	91.3	82.9	85.4	2.8	25,537	0.3	700	2.7	38,146	64.8	29,352	58.8
Stevens Point	73.3	12.8	87.7	82.4	64.2	17.8	14,762	-1.1	443	3.0	23,207	65.7	19,526	35.8
Sun Prairie	81.7	30.3	93.4	89.9	94.7	2.7	19,591	-0.2	446	2.3	26,122	72.2	21,401	61.1
Superior	76.1	13.0	92.2	84.3	81.9	7.6	14,562	-1.2	513	3.5	21,730	69.3	17,906	52.1
Waukesha	85.1	32.0	92.8	87.2	83.4	6.5	42,207	-0.6	1,166	2.8	61,266	68.8	48,533	58.2
Wausau	85.3	6.3	88.9	83.5	83.1	6.2	19,768	0.0	578	2.9	32,833	65.8	25,835	51.1
Wauwatosa	83.1	27.0	92.2	85.8	85.8	3.9	27,720	-0.5	751	2.7	38,435	68.2	29,589	63.0
West Allis	81.8	24.6	83.9	76.6	86.7	5.2	33,382	-0.7	1,147	3.4	51,378	69.1	42,456	56.6
West Bend	88.1	37.2	87.9	83.1	82.2	6.7	17,123	-0.4	475	2.8	25,912	67.9	19,823	62.6
WYOMING	77.9	16.8	91.7	83.2	83.9	6.1	289,574	-1.1	11,754	4.1	456,056	66.0	365,619	52.1
Casper	86.6	8.3	93.3	83.8	88.0	2.3	28,647	-1.2	1,291	4.5	43,982	68.7	34,959	55.8
Cheyenne	81.2	4.3	92.2	83.5	81.8	5.3	30,939	-1.1	1,250	4.0	50,744	67.4	41,770	56.2
Gillette	80.4	14.4	NA	NA	86.2	3.5	14,788	-1.1	662	4.5	21,132	73.7	19,398	57.6
Laramie	79.1	5.6	92.7	85.0	62.4	16.4	16,943	-0.8	529	3.1	26,864	66.1	24,050	39.6

1. Employed persons. 2. Households. 3. Percent of civilian labor force. 4. Persons 16 years old and over.

Table D. Cities — Construction, Wholesale Trade, and Retail Trade

City	Value of residential construction authorized by building permits, 2018			Wholesale trade[1], 2012				Retail trade[2], 2012			
	New construction ($1,000)	Number of housing units	Percent single family	Number of establishments	Number of employees	Sales (mil dol)	Annual payroll (mil dol)	Number of establishments	Number of employees	Sales (mil dol)	Annual payroll (mil dol)
	69	70	71	72	73	74	75	76	77	78	79
WASHINGTON—Cont'd											
Pasco	128,159	485	100.0	77	939	595.5	46.6	157	2,051	722.8	67.7
Pullman	38,547	234	41.0	11	177	182.1	9.0	51	1,027	222.7	20.4
Puyallup	53,701	277	33.9	39	652	343.0	27.6	239	5,078	1,686.5	152.9
Redmond	292,782	2,193	7.6	173	3,101	4,143.8	257.7	251	3,923	947.4	105.4
Renton	72,029	259	71.0	110	3,308	2,769.4	197.3	264	5,284	1,831.9	165.6
Richland	102,792	331	97.6	19	186	192.6	7.6	143	2,531	680.0	60.7
Sammamish	120,321	282	94.3	31	52	46.8	2.9	47	413	129.3	12.6
SeaTac	11,263	39	89.7	19	177	146.3	10.2	71	943	213.9	18.1
Seattle	1,034,253	7,918	6.6	1,093	16,045	12,790.5	1,049.7	2,530	34,652	40,037.9	1,230.2
Shoreline	65,962	364	24.5	33	135	57.2	5.6	121	2,364	835.7	75.9
Spokane	154,988	855	44.4	249	3,330	1,686.8	158.8	862	13,166	3,132.8	341.2
Spokane Valley	89,746	542	25.1	202	2,963	1,772.5	140.6	476	7,626	1,987.3	207.5
Tacoma	164,154	1,033	12.0	210	2,967	2,750.1	151.2	744	11,177	3,036.6	314.9
University Place	27,156	166	24.7	12	75	49.4	4.1	51	728	154.9	19.8
Vancouver	98,345	1,114	28.5	185	2,441	2,580.9	139.4	555	10,131	2,863.9	278.6
Walla Walla	30,235	117	100.0	54	483	437.5	18.3	150	1,667	386.1	40.7
Wenatchee	23,134	192	21.9	52	587	710.1	27.7	185	2,635	615.3	68.3
Yakima	51,746	251	75.7	108	2,196	1,875.8	100.9	346	5,078	1,334.7	134.8
WEST VIRGINIA	500,078	2,887	81.1	1,334	16,906	14,295.4	761.9	6,393	85,305	22,637.9	1,908.5
Charleston	5,612	23	100.0	121	1,588	1,059.8	78.1	358	5,805	1,495.4	134.6
Huntington	2,161	23	30.4	73	1,250	511.6	62.2	211	2,788	670.4	66.6
Morgantown	3,982	10	100.0	26	142	47.8	5.3	260	4,385	1,081.4	86.6
Parkersburg	291	4	100.0	40	338	134.5	12.1	203	3,074	791.4	68.8
Wheeling	0	0	0.0	62	D	D	D	142	1,690	380.3	37.4
WISCONSIN	4,008,219	19,113	63.0	5,990	97,040	77,066.9	5,253.6	19,272	296,956	78,201.8	6,835.0
Appleton	18,136	62	87.1	98	1,432	5,759.6	66.1	291	4,865	1,306.6	111.5
Beloit	3,136	20	100.0	19	456	292.8	25.0	115	1,756	481.9	40.3
Brookfield	49,662	258	14.3	108	1,733	686.6	105.7	301	5,576	1,022.7	117.4
Eau Claire	39,015	250	32.8	79	1,509	961.9	64.8	340	6,565	1,419.6	131.8
Fitchburg	40,378	338	12.4	25	967	1,149.6	59.0	58	614	173.3	16.1
Fond du Lac	11,510	159	20.8	41	812	610.4	46.3	211	3,688	959.5	81.9
Franklin	13,358	42	100.0	35	402	292.7	23.6	75	2,107	614.6	52.0
Green Bay	23,791	101	100.0	106	2,190	1,714.9	122.4	340	5,909	1,595.9	134.6
Greenfield	5,196	25	36.0	14	192	128.7	7.3	149	3,100	932.8	80.5
Janesville	19,748	88	81.8	75	1,941	1,843.2	96.1	276	5,678	1,422.0	144.0
Kenosha	8,098	33	87.9	56	763	769.3	42.7	295	5,162	1,369.5	114.4
La Crosse	18,525	176	14.8	61	1,690	2,434.7	78.4	251	4,879	976.7	97.7
Madison	306,284	1,443	23.1	270	4,849	2,859.6	252.1	972	17,918	4,804.9	409.1
Manitowoc	6,784	63	17.5	27	461	211.0	23.9	146	2,436	555.8	53.0
Menomonee Falls	52,399	262	46.9	89	1,425	651.3	89.4	126	2,741	700.4	63.1
Milwaukee	20,775	756	5.2	485	11,513	8,694.3	908.5	1,368	15,652	3,894.9	360.3
Mount Pleasant	21,907	84	83.3	21	346	145.5	14.4	64	1,331	441.7	31.9
Neenah	13,910	119	23.5	24	278	252.6	13.1	82	1,520	436.6	34.5
New Berlin	32,204	86	86.0	119	2,332	1,178.0	137.1	96	2,375	579.0	64.6
Oak Creek	5,689	19	100.0	32	1,429	891.0	89.5	80	2,059	718.9	43.7
Oshkosh	7,882	37	78.4	50	1,198	517.4	48.5	250	4,856	1,205.0	107.7
Racine	845	5	100.0	42	448	225.6	22.3	281	3,410	622.1	61.4
Sheboygan	3,003	14	100.0	41	451	304.5	18.9	197	3,362	758.9	74.1
Stevens Point	NA	NA	NA	32	332	270.7	14.4	120	2,003	470.3	39.3
Sun Prairie	NA	NA	NA	33	822	362.4	38.0	70	1,155	305.8	25.6
Superior	NA	NA	NA	39	669	817.8	31.9	113	1,835	541.2	45.8
Waukesha	NA	NA	NA	115	2,148	1,126.3	119.0	213	4,314	1,601.4	120.4
Wausau	NA	NA	NA	44	817	375.7	36.8	187	4,576	1,239.9	101.2
Wauwatosa	NA	NA	NA	56	1,033	652.0	55.5	293	5,436	1,107.9	113.4
West Allis	NA	NA	NA	107	1,830	975.2	99.4	243	4,249	1,154.4	102.4
West Bend	NA	NA	NA	25	201	93.9	8.1	120	2,163	553.4	46.4
WYOMING	593,197	1,812	84.6	709	7,003	5,597.9	398.7	2,681	30,088	9,446.0	796.0
Casper	21,401	94	63.8	80	841	1,414.8	51.5	299	4,299	1,244.2	116.3
Cheyenne	53,877	361	59.0	93	782	336.4	52.5	321	4,632	1,561.0	112.7
Gillette	10,050	37	100.0	49	813	462.8	41.3	160	2,202	757.5	62.0
Laramie	15,589	98	52.0	19	95	127.6	4.0	131	1,671	470.8	35.7

1. Merchant wholesalers except manufacturers' sales branches and offices.   2. Establishments with payroll.

Table D. Cities — Real Estate, Professional Services, and Manufacturing

City	Real estate and rental and leasing, 2012				Professional, scientific, and technical services[1], 2012				Manufacturing, 2012			
	Number of establishments	Number of employees	Receipts (mil dol)	Annual payroll (mil dol)	Number of establishments	Number of employees	Receipts (mil dol)	Annual payroll (mil dol)	Number of establishments	Number of employees	Receipts (mil dol)	Annual payroll (mil dol)
	80	81	82	83	84	85	86	87	88	89	90	91
WASHINGTON—Cont'd												
Pasco	46	224	39.2	6.8	61	369	37.2	16.4	37	D	D	59.8
Pullman	40	180	19.4	4.4	36	304	40.0	17.3	12	D	D	D
Puyallup	86	417	83.6	13.0	119	627	65.7	26.1	43	954	240.9	43.2
Redmond	128	1,207	288.5	71.4	385	D	D	D	127	6,634	3,469.5	443.1
Renton	115	610	212.1	29.7	208	2,109	213.2	103.7	71	13,466	D	994.5
Richland	89	268	46.3	9.2	181	D	D	D	39	1,839	D	119.8
Sammamish	41	D	D	D	197	405	85.7	26.5	6	14	2.5	0.6
SeaTac	40	312	71.5	11.6	17	243	32.8	13.3	15	130	D	6.0
Seattle	1,966	11,652	2,431.3	587.9	4,631	50,113	10,321.5	4,432.8	859	20,323	5,200.2	1,054.2
Shoreline	70	282	64.4	11.6	113	D	D	D	17	147	29.9	5.9
Spokane	281	1,580	283.9	57.9	741	D	D	D	200	4,292	1,101.4	202.5
Spokane Valley	147	814	146.0	26.8	189	1,245	123.8	51.5	189	6,500	2,048.1	324.3
Tacoma	297	1,748	304.2	64.2	504	D	D	D	194	6,347	1,923.4	338.4
University Place	55	D	D	D	66	251	29.2	11.6	17	87	D	2.9
Vancouver	273	1,384	225.1	51.1	570	D	D	D	182	6,379	2,585.4	336.6
Walla Walla	42	128	17.4	4.0	79	356	36.7	14.4	83	1,043	221.4	46.9
Wenatchee	61	211	32.7	5.9	101	D	D	D	23	401	71.9	14.9
Yakima	146	587	81.6	16.1	211	D	D	D	99	2,981	838.8	122.6
WEST VIRGINIA	1,405	6,011	1,255.8	203.8	2,918	23,115	2,804.7	1,053.4	1,245	48,686	24,553.1	2,603.9
Charleston	135	663	154.9	22.9	385	D	D	D	39	528	148.4	22.8
Huntington	74	259	50.9	9.4	135	D	D	D	52	3,170	1,697.1	206.5
Morgantown	79	435	64.2	10.7	126	D	D	D	22	446	D	23.3
Parkersburg	53	239	52.6	7.4	89	D	D	D	25	657	134.7	26.1
Wheeling	49	D	D	D	136	D	D	D	37	D	D	D
WISCONSIN	4,509	23,762	4,358.9	801.1	11,253	98,507	15,028.9	5,701.2	8,995	436,777	177,728.9	21,879.3
Appleton	60	D	D	D	193	1,791	315.2	106.8	104	7,600	D	409.2
Beloit	17	88	66.4	4.6	38	212	20.4	9.2	52	2,599	1,801.2	132.8
Brookfield	94	1,075	88.2	31.8	306	3,589	744.8	278.8	56	1,544	368.5	79.4
Eau Claire	94	462	72.5	14.0	145	1,527	188.2	78.6	79	3,823	1,148.1	170.4
Fitchburg	42	247	46.1	7.9	85	556	90.6	34.8	30	3,154	1,287.1	205.2
Fond du Lac	31	144	25.7	3.7	91	1,050	125.8	63.4	72	4,252	1,894.6	202.1
Franklin	25	127	25.8	3.3	58	424	80.7	23.0	52	3,383	1,221.8	176.4
Green Bay	94	610	93.9	21.6	226	D	D	D	130	10,215	6,399.1	513.4
Greenfield	38	182	31.6	6.8	80	589	63.7	26.0	17	106	D	4.8
Janesville	53	260	74.1	12.6	107	624	70.8	24.5	82	3,985	1,600.9	187.1
Kenosha	67	289	44.5	7.3	125	816	73.3	33.0	99	2,044	738.6	95.7
La Crosse	74	475	70.7	12.9	171	D	D	D	93	4,666	1,527.4	195.8
Madison	369	2,871	759.2	115.5	1,019	13,787	2,399.8	978.8	182	8,788	2,798.2	467.9
Manitowoc	19	D	D	D	58	453	68.2	16.7	75	6,299	1,804.1	295.0
Menomonee Falls	20	260	33.5	14.7	91	1,294	253.1	76.0	176	8,361	3,503.9	464.3
Milwaukee	460	3,036	618.5	127.5	1,091	D	D	D	540	22,779	8,678.9	1,199.8
Mount Pleasant	20	80	9.6	2.8	50	387	38.9	19.2	35	2,073	3,299.8	155.3
Neenah	17	142	151.8	6.5	51	476	60.8	31.5	60	5,008	2,079.0	262.2
New Berlin	27	263	44.5	7.7	109	2,193	348.9	102.6	130	6,222	2,305.6	359.7
Oak Creek	38	405	92.1	16.3	35	414	32.6	12.5	55	3,412	1,390.3	196.4
Oshkosh	53	306	43.0	8.3	100	D	D	D	115	11,025	6,369.1	607.7
Racine	37	121	31.0	3.8	118	D	D	D	143	4,602	1,264.5	245.5
Sheboygan	31	181	41.8	8.1	94	D	D	D	89	6,676	2,068.9	311.6
Stevens Point	19	D	D	D	57	635	57.0	23.5	30	1,791	570.9	73.8
Sun Prairie	25	70	13.3	2.1	60	404	50.5	20.4	29	1,020	283.2	48.2
Superior	34	106	14.5	2.4	55	323	35.1	14.3	40	1,200	D	77.6
Waukesha	56	321	69.7	10.8	188	1,794	285.7	100.4	142	9,474	4,144.2	668.2
Wausau	39	D	D	D	130	D	D	D	64	4,486	1,177.6	184.4
Wauwatosa	45	268	89.0	13.0	236	D	D	D	51	3,718	1,267.0	356.5
West Allis	43	293	77.6	14.4	86	925	100.6	52.4	92	3,448	743.0	196.1
West Bend	18	D	D	D	49	D	D	D	52	1,779	409.9	79.6
WYOMING	1,076	4,546	1,259.1	215.6	2,132	D	D	D	553	10,094	10,783.8	630.6
Casper	124	649	182.3	31.4	216	1,146	166.8	64.1	27	471	91.8	25.8
Cheyenne	112	390	89.7	14.4	414	D	D	D	51	1,132	2,542.4	75.4
Gillette	61	265	72.1	9.9	94	D	D	D	27	482	D	30.7
Laramie	50	132	20.2	3.0	95	D	D	D	21	141	D	5.5

1. Establishments subject to federal tax.

Accommodation and Food Services, Arts, Entertainment, and Recreation, and Health Care and Social Assistance

City	Accommodation and food services, 2012				Arts, entertainment, and recreation[1], 2012				Health care and social assistance,[1] 2012			
	Number of establishments	Number of employees	Receipts (mil dol)	Annual payroll (mil dol)	Number of establishments	Number of employees	Receipts (mil dol)	Annual payroll (mil dol)	Number of establishments	Number of employees	Receipts (mil dol)	Annual payroll (mil dol)
	92	93	94	95	96	97	98	99	100	101	102	103
WASHINGTON—Cont'd												
Pasco	88	1,288	71.1	19.4	10	D	D	D	82	712	67.0	23.5
Pullman	103	1,302	55.6	15.4	4	93	5.0	1.8	58	D	D	D
Puyallup	151	2,421	134.5	41.0	11	149	7.2	2.1	186	D	D	D
Redmond	244	4,597	340.1	100.7	32	D	D	D	210	2,496	242.3	95.7
Renton	241	3,787	253.7	71.3	19	D	D	D	293	3,016	379.9	154.7
Richland	127	2,055	108.4	31.6	13	460	16.3	6.3	213	2,156	238.8	113.7
Sammamish	30	488	26.5	7.7	17	D	D	D	67	452	49.3	20.3
SeaTac	96	2,996	251.0	72.1	2	D	D	D	29	860	20.9	11.6
Seattle	2,823	45,976	3,164.1	970.4	323	4,218	540.3	224.9	2,101	24,068	3,408.6	1,564.3
Shoreline	100	1,054	55.9	15.9	21	698	31.6	10.1	181	1,928	148.4	64.8
Spokane	601	10,256	549.0	165.9	58	883	47.7	12.4	722	13,373	1,618.3	684.5
Spokane Valley	216	3,468	180.3	51.5	23	D	D	D	305	5,354	479.1	203.9
Tacoma	501	7,220	387.9	118.9	45	1,749	231.4	53.3	561	8,906	951.2	503.6
University Place	41	459	25.8	7.3	7	89	4.9	1.1	87	D	D	D
Vancouver	428	6,939	364.3	111.0	38	578	31.7	9.0	514	7,399	755.8	370.4
Walla Walla	114	1,746	83.9	25.4	12	77	4.2	1.7	96	D	D	D
Wenatchee	112	1,622	84.5	25.0	9	74	4.4	1.2	120	D	D	D
Yakima	239	3,527	183.5	53.1	20	491	18.5	7.1	291	4,885	631.0	234.6
WEST VIRGINIA	3,629	66,302	4,036.3	975.9	631	6,055	550.1	98.9	3,734	57,400	5,125.5	2,107.5
Charleston	225	4,651	253.2	69.2	20	267	22.8	5.6	318	4,136	555.2	230.6
Huntington	172	2,964	141.0	38.8	18	D	D	D	176	3,266	356.7	167.6
Morgantown	207	4,596	190.5	52.1	23	182	10.0	2.7	89	D	D	D
Parkersburg	130	2,121	97.5	29.0	21	D	D	D	158	1,922	235.2	94.9
Wheeling	103	2,033	181.0	33.4	27	D	D	D	152	D	D	D
WISCONSIN	14,137	221,567	10,303.3	2,764.3	1,966	28,433	2,548.1	826.1	11,460	175,153	16,357.2	7,784.6
Appleton	211	4,363	168.4	47.9	12	262	8.6	2.9	209	3,503	485.0	217.5
Beloit	90	1,338	63.4	17.0	5	D	D	D	43	D	D	D
Brookfield	124	3,114	159.0	44.7	22	358	14.6	5.7	306	D	D	D
Eau Claire	229	D	D	D	26	411	25.7	5.0	217	5,434	656.6	349.8
Fitchburg	43	930	42.0	12.0	15	D	D	D	35	D	D	D
Fond du Lac	125	2,424	86.8	25.7	18	200	21.7	3.5	139	D	D	D
Franklin	60	768	43.4	10.9	11	D	D	D	91	D	D	D
Green Bay	272	5,414	234.0	68.2	23	D	D	D	204	4,567	663.1	285.6
Greenfield	72	D	D	D	17	D	D	D	134	3,258	279.4	127.6
Janesville	162	3,046	132.5	37.4	15	197	9.0	2.7	104	D	D	D
Kenosha	235	3,801	160.5	45.2	22	D	D	D	282	3,366	297.5	140.4
La Crosse	222	3,923	155.1	45.9	24	D	D	D	100	1,197	86.8	36.7
Madison	743	15,474	718.3	209.5	73	1,144	96.4	19.6	443	10,016	1,248.6	619.4
Manitowoc	86	1,544	57.0	16.8	10	94	9.3	1.6	90	D	D	D
Menomonee Falls	66	1,248	56.4	15.1	11	D	D	D	68	D	D	D
Milwaukee	1,106	D	D	D	87	D	D	D	1,135	18,188	1,518.5	812.0
Mount Pleasant	56	1,290	57.7	16.9	6	D	D	D	82	886	83.4	37.3
Neenah	70	1,153	48.7	13.4	10	D	D	D	85	1,134	170.1	69.1
New Berlin	65	1,345	56.6	15.0	16	D	D	D	84	1,074	99.6	47.1
Oak Creek	68	1,366	75.1	18.9	13	D	D	D	53	580	45.6	19.9
Oshkosh	187	3,495	136.7	39.0	16	147	7.1	2.1	142	2,244	240.8	121.8
Racine	161	D	D	D	29	190	13.5	3.2	139	1,401	91.3	43.1
Sheboygan	132	1,976	79.9	21.5	9	110	5.6	1.5	155	3,073	286.6	143.0
Stevens Point	112	1,748	69.1	18.9	10	D	D	D	81	D	D	D
Sun Prairie	50	844	36.4	9.5	7	D	D	D	52	761	65.7	30.0
Superior	107	1,625	60.4	16.8	13	D	D	D	46	963	50.5	22.5
Waukesha	153	3,185	142.4	42.7	22	321	11.9	3.3	193	2,607	288.5	147.1
Wausau	111	1,690	73.6	21.1	14	137	5.1	1.9	164	D	D	D
Wauwatosa	142	3,107	158.9	47.0	13	D	D	D	329	5,474	602.4	307.0
West Allis	159	D	D	D	13	250	10.5	3.2	159	3,183	277.0	141.5
West Bend	66	1,326	52.2	14.2	11	D	D	D	98	1,085	79.5	33.4
WYOMING	1,799	27,580	1,644.8	468.7	317	2,922	168.9	57.1	1,457	13,706	1,486.2	607.7
Casper	158	3,224	170.2	49.2	17	D	D	D	239	D	D	D
Cheyenne	176	3,518	200.9	53.0	11	D	D	D	237	2,779	258.7	113.1
Gillette	94	1,529	86.2	24.3	8	81	2.7	1.1	80	D	D	D
Laramie	103	1,976	73.8	22.0	9	62	1.7	0.5	99	D	D	D

1. Establishments subject to federal tax.

City	Other services[1] Number of establishments 104	Number of employees 105	Receipts (mil dol) 106	Annual payroll (mil dol) 107	Government employment and payroll, 2012 — March payroll Full-time equivalent employees 108	Total (dollars) 109	Percent of total for: Administrative, judicial, and legal 110	Police and corrections 111	Fire protection 112	Highways and transportation 113	Health and welfare 114	Natural resources and utilities 115	Education and libraries 116
WASHINGTON—Cont'd													
Pasco	63	308	34.5	8.6	285	1,601,010	14.1	30.2	22.2	7.6	4.6	21.0	0.0
Pullman	25	D	D	D	232	989,864	6.3	23.6	22.8	32.0	0.0	11.6	3.7
Puyallup	85	763	64.8	21.2	469	3,001,181	14.9	30.0	21.9	6.7	0.0	16.4	3.2
Redmond	130	892	98.9	30.0	679	4,387,058	20.9	18.6	29.5	4.1	1.4	18.8	0.0
Renton	148	854	76.7	27.0	825	5,336,014	10.3	32.9	23.1	6.5	6.4	17.5	0.0
Richland	68	522	42.4	14.8	499	3,031,486	16.6	16.7	14.9	6.2	1.1	33.3	2.9
Sammamish	31	180	11.4	4.1	85	514,186	26.6	1.0	0.0	28.1	16.1	22.8	0.0
SeaTac	48	687	63.2	17.1	162	1,068,652	30.3	0.6	37.3	13.7	1.2	5.9	0.0
Seattle	1,302	8,892	755.8	250.0	10,193	71,586,796	7.4	21.3	13.4	5.8	3.3	38.0	3.4
Shoreline	63	326	25.3	7.4	222	1,123,950	28.0	39.9	0.0	5.5	0.6	22.6	0.0
Spokane	349	2,163	171.0	52.9	2,161	12,463,086	15.6	21.9	20.6	8.3	0.4	26.4	3.2
Spokane Valley	177	1,222	110.3	35.5	92	466,469	31.8	0.0	0.0	24.5	34.4	9.2	2.1
Tacoma	330	2,444	223.1	75.5	3,458	23,314,293	11.1	13.2	14.4	8.2	0.5	43.6	0.0
University Place	46	293	20.0	7.5	48	264,084	30.6	4.5	0.0	30.0	14.8	9.6	0.0
Vancouver	300	1,562	120.8	37.4	1,018	5,857,054	12.9	26.3	24.0	6.1	0.0	21.4	0.0
Walla Walla	42	240	16.7	6.0	251	1,313,753	15.6	33.8	26.5	0.9	0.3	16.4	3.3
Wenatchee	65	228	21.7	6.0	185	996,105	13.5	30.6	19.2	10.0	2.0	19.4	0.0
Yakima	140	736	62.9	17.7	615	3,330,932	12.9	39.5	16.4	10.4	0.9	18.9	0.0
WEST VIRGINIA	2,003	12,728	1,246.8	343.2	X	X	X	X	X	X	X	X	X
Charleston	110	979	56.3	17.8	826	2,940,542	13.0	28.6	24.9	0.8	1.4	16.3	0.0
Huntington	67	434	39.9	11.4	338	1,166,129	8.3	42.3	27.9	4.5	2.5	8.5	0.0
Morgantown	56	D	D	D	442	1,584,824	7.6	19.5	12.7	10.7	0.3	38.5	4.0
Parkersburg	64	446	33.0	10.3	347	1,079,226	8.0	24.0	18.5	10.1	1.5	34.7	0.0
Wheeling	66	715	76.6	19.2	828	2,250,153	5.6	14.0	15.9	7.2	0.0	55.8	0.0
WISCONSIN	8,338	47,662	4,015.9	1,242.4	X	X	X	X	X	X	X	X	X
Appleton	127	972	89.6	27.8	663	3,090,024	10.6	24.2	16.9	8.2	4.8	15.8	6.5
Beloit	48	195	14.1	4.2	368	1,795,646	10.7	25.3	19.5	14.3	3.6	17.7	4.9
Brookfield	101	1,064	92.4	31.2	333	1,844,609	12.7	28.6	21.1	12.3	0.0	14.9	6.1
Eau Claire	125	901	62.1	19.6	608	2,643,962	9.0	24.0	17.4	10.5	10.6	15.3	5.6
Fitchburg	30	289	28.3	9.4	168	745,550	17.6	38.6	15.3	7.5	2.7	10.2	0.8
Fond du Lac	89	610	40.0	14.2	344	1,652,329	8.9	25.7	21.9	14.0	1.9	15.0	6.8
Franklin	47	329	29.9	10.1	218	1,131,749	9.5	36.1	24.9	12.6	2.8	4.7	5.0
Green Bay	146	913	67.4	21.0	860	4,043,340	7.5	30.8	25.6	11.5	1.1	19.5	0.0
Greenfield	65	456	26.6	10.5	217	1,158,811	11.1	38.6	26.7	12.0	3.2	3.7	3.2
Janesville	99	626	36.7	12.8	482	2,513,217	10.6	24.7	21.6	15.6	3.3	16.1	7.3
Kenosha	147	915	66.9	20.6	811	3,859,872	5.8	28.1	22.1	10.6	2.7	18.1	7.7
La Crosse	93	681	44.6	17.3	567	2,357,551	9.7	24.1	19.2	17.7	2.0	14.4	9.6
Madison	349	2,839	212.6	76.1	3,036	14,945,308	10.6	21.2	12.9	22.9	2.3	18.7	5.5
Manitowoc	55	273	19.5	5.7	355	1,875,536	6.3	20.8	18.2	15.1	0.0	32.1	5.9
Menomonee Falls	63	563	52.2	15.9	252	1,124,295	9.0	39.6	11.5	12.7	2.5	9.8	5.9
Milwaukee	623	4,127	367.3	126.6	6,455	32,385,292	9.5	39.7	17.4	3.2	7.3	12.0	3.2
Mount Pleasant	34	232	17.6	5.4	206	856,388	12.7	34.6	41.4	6.6	0.0	4.6	0.0
Neenah	49	366	27.3	10.1	272	1,262,394	8.6	24.1	29.0	10.9	5.7	15.3	6.4
New Berlin	69	664	69.6	27.6	254	1,283,876	12.9	39.3	15.4	12.5	0.0	11.2	4.4
Oak Creek	42	439	49.7	12.3	266	1,412,700	9.6	31.2	21.6	13.5	2.3	15.7	2.7
Oshkosh	80	687	53.0	18.2	576	2,558,304	7.2	22.6	21.9	15.9	6.5	17.9	5.9
Racine	110	731	40.6	14.4	815	4,196,517	6.8	33.8	20.0	8.7	5.3	19.5	3.6
Sheboygan	83	518	26.7	9.1	431	1,929,836	9.1	27.3	17.8	18.6	2.9	13.8	7.8
Stevens Point	54	298	29.0	8.2	194	851,692	9.1	29.9	22.2	24.4	3.2	11.3	0.0
Sun Prairie	35	202	18.0	4.1	223	1,003,694	14.5	33.1	0.0	9.8	7.1	24.8	7.1
Superior	53	351	28.1	9.0	255	1,159,999	11.2	29.7	15.8	11.8	0.7	18.3	5.6
Waukesha	117	872	73.3	23.8	566	2,950,957	10.7	28.4	19.7	16.3	0.3	16.6	5.6
Wausau	55	328	31.9	9.2	306	1,383,873	11.0	27.3	21.3	24.5	3.8	8.0	0.0
Wauwatosa	68	639	52.4	18.0	414	2,166,975	10.9	28.6	27.5	10.0	3.1	9.0	5.3
West Allis	114	604	68.2	17.0	541	2,746,980	10.4	30.7	21.8	7.9	7.6	15.5	3.5
West Bend	76	464	30.9	10.2	261	1,244,682	11.9	33.2	19.5	9.0	0.0	16.8	5.0
WYOMING	998	5,095	660.2	169.6	X	X	X	X	X	X	X	X	X
Casper	106	687	82.8	22.0	563	2,490,135	12.1	24.0	15.7	5.9	2.6	30.8	0.0
Cheyenne	102	561	47.1	14.6	655	2,479,867	12.4	24.6	20.1	11.9	5.3	17.8	0.0
Gillette	77	512	63.1	17.6	278	1,359,171	21.1	29.1	0.0	9.2	3.7	24.3	0.0
Laramie	56	D	D	D	282	1,207,422	11.8	25.1	22.5	5.3	8.5	26.7	0.0

1. Establishments subject to federal tax.

City	General revenue Total (mil dol)	Intergovernmental Total (mil dol)	Intergovernmental Percent from state government	Taxes Total (mil dol)	Taxes Per capita[1] (dollars) Total	Taxes Per capita[1] (dollars) Property	Taxes Per capita[1] (dollars) Sales and gross receipts	General expenditure Total (mil dol)	General expenditure Per capita[1] (dollars) Total	General expenditure Per capita[1] (dollars) Capital outlays
	117	118	119	120	121	122	123	124	125	126
WASHINGTON—Cont'd										
Pasco	56.3	7.4	83.9	27.7	414	100	307	43.0	644	84
Pullman	28.8	6.2	79.9	14.1	450	166	280	23.2	740	102
Puyallup	56.2	6.0	83.5	28.9	756	220	514	45.2	1,184	149
Redmond	132.9	19.1	27.4	73.4	1,298	388	860	135.8	2,399	780
Renton	182.1	40.0	23.2	80.9	844	338	484	161.6	1,687	421
Richland	85.1	16.9	69.5	35.1	682	273	382	81.3	1,579	382
Sammamish	38.6	2.0	89.9	31.3	638	438	144	30.6	623	115
SeaTac	44.1	5.0	93.3	33.9	1,224	437	770	38.5	1,392	195
Seattle	1,849.1	193.2	68.5	913.5	1,438	626	809	1,658.2	2,611	430
Shoreline	64.6	27.8	75.5	28.7	527	212	300	61.5	1,129	532
Spokane	360.6	46.8	62.8	134.2	641	291	339	346.3	1,653	310
Spokane Valley	47.6	9.5	74.7	34.3	379	118	250	44.6	492	104
Tacoma	497.4	82.6	61.5	160.2	792	300	477	525.2	2,597	668
University Place	20.3	3.7	81.0	12.2	386	120	255	19.2	607	164
Vancouver	216.2	36.9	48.3	102.8	622	244	361	188.0	1,138	228
Walla Walla	47.0	7.8	77.4	16.3	512	186	320	48.0	1,505	391
Wenatchee	35.6	3.6	70.5	20.4	627	183	433	31.6	972	109
Yakima	108.8	28.2	59.7	50.2	539	163	367	101.0	1,085	250
WEST VIRGINIA	NA	NA	NA	NA	NA	NA	NA	NA	NA	NA
Charleston	119.9	8.4	43.3	74.5	1,461	237	1,224	118.2	2,318	327
Huntington	66.4	5.5	20.3	27.6	561	105	408	69.9	1,422	172
Morgantown	47.5	3.6	18.6	18.2	602	114	488	57.9	1,916	338
Parkersburg	38.3	2.2	14.9	16.0	512	159	345	37.9	1,214	142
Wheeling	68.9	4.3	9.3	21.9	776	214	556	77.9	2,759	267
WISCONSIN	NA	NA	NA	NA	NA	NA	NA	NA	NA	NA
Appleton	105.8	35.3	66.9	40.0	547	511	29	95.4	1,306	185
Beloit	62.8	26.8	88.2	19.9	542	506	31	62.9	1,709	281
Brookfield	58.1	9.5	75.4	37.1	977	878	98	58.2	1,531	164
Eau Claire	86.2	27.3	65.5	36.1	536	481	48	88.9	1,320	274
Fitchburg	30.2	5.5	88.9	18.6	718	696	22	39.3	1,517	661
Fond du Lac	60.5	20.6	71.8	21.1	490	445	41	63.0	1,465	223
Franklin	41.4	6.9	92.4	26.8	747	678	68	36.9	1,030	91
Green Bay	138.7	46.3	79.3	53.7	512	485	22	133.7	1,276	218
Greenfield	36.7	6.5	88.9	20.6	556	518	38	41.0	1,106	190
Janesville	81.1	21.4	60.8	31.0	488	455	30	86.4	1,359	476
Kenosha	136.7	40.5	74.7	66.5	666	635	29	121.2	1,213	141
La Crosse	96.0	32.3	81.3	41.7	801	727	63	83.2	1,597	241
Madison	476.1	163.1	64.2	192.4	802	725	69	469.3	1,956	262
Manitowoc	48.5	17.0	90.1	15.7	469	434	32	54.5	1,630	246
Menomonee Falls	46.2	6.0	94.8	25.0	698	656	42	54.6	1,523	188
Milwaukee	1,070.1	483.1	64.8	302.6	505	483	22	1,000.4	1,671	211
Mount Pleasant	34.1	6.0	62.3	15.7	601	545	49	36.3	1,387	0
Neenah	34.2	7.5	78.2	17.5	681	647	32	35.3	1,374	110
New Berlin	42.8	4.9	98.3	23.5	591	549	41	43.8	1,103	116
Oak Creek	39.6	9.3	95.7	20.6	591	532	53	40.8	1,169	139
Oshkosh	88.9	26.0	83.5	36.9	554	503	47	92.9	1,393	336
Racine	138.3	56.9	78.9	49.1	627	593	33	139.8	1,787	186
Sheboygan	64.8	24.2	81.4	26.8	549	494	49	58.7	1,204	114
Stevens Point	34.5	13.5	80.1	14.0	519	471	42	34.2	1,272	140
Sun Prairie	36.3	6.6	89.6	21.4	700	647	49	33.4	1,092	159
Superior	47.8	19.7	86.8	13.1	488	414	69	43.1	1,604	221
Waukesha	94.8	23.2	75.8	53.6	753	709	40	92.3	1,297	257
Wausau	59.2	21.8	72.8	26.1	667	628	35	52.5	1,340	306
Wauwatosa	76.5	14.7	62.5	41.9	891	830	51	68.2	1,451	107
West Allis	89.6	27.7	67.2	39.6	652	626	24	88.3	1,455	97
West Bend	37.8	8.6	79.5	22.6	714	667	45	36.4	1,152	223
WYOMING	NA	NA	NA	NA	NA	NA	NA	NA	NA	NA
Casper	90.9	48.4	57.4	10.7	185	79	91	91.8	1,586	372
Cheyenne	102.2	45.4	60.0	14.2	231	86	144	84.7	1,372	240
Gillette	102.0	79.8	46.5	4.1	129	81	48	73.4	2,334	563
Laramie	40.4	21.5	68.2	5.1	162	66	95	47.7	1,503	636

1. Based on population estimated as of July 1 of the year shown.

City	City government finances, 2012 (cont.)									
	General expenditure (cont.)									
	Percent of total for:									
	Public welfare	Highways	Parking facilities	Education	Health and hospitals	Police protection	Sewerage and sanitation	Parks and recreation	Housing and community development	Interest on debt
	127	128	129	130	131	132	133	134	135	136
WASHINGTON—Cont'd										
Pasco	0.0	12.0	0.0	0.0	5.4	17.4	11.1	11.5	2.3	5.8
Pullman	0.0	11.6	0.0	0.0	6.2	18.7	14.9	9.3	0.0	0.8
Puyallup	0.0	14.1	0.0	0.0	0.3	25.3	23.3	8.8	1.9	6.7
Redmond	0.1	20.2	0.0	0.0	3.2	9.2	16.1	13.1	0.8	2.8
Renton	0.0	13.1	0.0	0.0	0.2	11.9	18.6	6.2	1.5	5.1
Richland	0.0	12.0	0.0	0.0	3.2	11.2	16.4	9.6	5.1	3.3
Sammamish	0.0	22.0	0.0	0.0	0.5	13.9	5.2	17.5	3.3	0.4
SeaTac	0.0	17.5	0.0	0.0	0.0	22.5	3.5	7.6	3.2	0.3
Seattle	6.2	11.8	0.5	0.3	1.1	10.5	29.3	9.1	1.8	4.1
Shoreline	0.0	46.6	0.0	0.0	0.0	16.3	3.4	7.7	2.4	3.0
Spokane	1.1	10.6	0.1	0.0	0.1	12.3	34.0	5.6	2.9	2.6
Spokane Valley	0.0	29.1	0.0	0.0	0.7	37.4	3.1	8.3	3.7	0.9
Tacoma	1.2	12.1	1.0	0.0	2.6	11.0	24.3	5.6	2.6	4.8
University Place	0.0	26.2	0.0	0.0	0.9	17.4	7.1	4.1	4.1	14.1
Vancouver	0.0	18.7	0.7	0.0	0.1	13.2	12.4	8.6	1.9	4.8
Walla Walla	0.0	9.6	0.0	0.0	5.4	12.5	19.2	5.1	0.0	3.1
Wenatchee	0.0	8.3	0.0	0.0	0.6	18.3	19.6	9.2	4.5	4.1
Yakima	0.0	18.3	0.0	0.0	0.4	19.6	13.4	5.3	3.1	2.2
WEST VIRGINIA	NA	NA	NA	NA	NA	NA	NA	NA	NA	NA
Charleston	0.0	12.8	2.4	0.0	0.0	18.6	20.7	8.7	3.5	3.1
Huntington	1.1	3.4	1.2	0.0	0.5	17.3	19.7	5.0	6.2	1.0
Morgantown	0.0	7.3	3.3	0.0	0.1	10.7	27.2	11.8	9.3	1.9
Parkersburg	0.1	17.9	0.6	0.0	0.0	14.6	24.6	1.3	3.6	0.4
Wheeling	0.3	8.2	0.9	0.0	0.0	10.7	13.4	47.9	2.8	1.1
WISCONSIN	NA	NA	NA	NA	NA	NA	NA	NA	NA	NA
Appleton	0.5	20.7	1.8	0.0	1.3	17.2	14.6	5.8	1.5	8.6
Beloit	0.0	15.7	0.0	0.0	2.0	18.6	18.7	5.0	1.7	7.4
Brookfield	0.0	16.4	0.0	0.0	5.1	16.4	24.7	6.6	0.0	4.2
Eau Claire	0.0	26.3	0.5	0.0	7.7	17.5	7.2	8.4	1.3	5.0
Fitchburg	0.0	15.1	0.0	0.0	1.4	15.9	6.7	4.4	0.0	3.0
Fond du Lac	0.0	15.2	1.0	0.0	7.9	15.6	15.7	3.3	5.5	12.5
Franklin	0.0	12.4	0.0	0.0	6.0	25.2	13.8	0.9	1.9	3.9
Green Bay	0.0	15.6	1.6	0.0	0.1	19.6	17.1	7.5	0.1	7.7
Greenfield	0.0	24.5	0.0	0.0	6.1	25.0	12.3	4.7	0.0	3.4
Janesville	1.0	12.8	0.1	0.0	3.5	15.3	28.2	6.8	4.9	2.7
Kenosha	0.0	15.3	0.0	0.0	8.7	23.0	12.6	7.0	3.3	5.4
La Crosse	0.1	15.0	1.9	0.1	0.2	14.5	10.0	13.5	2.4	5.6
Madison	0.0	12.8	1.8	0.0	2.2	14.5	7.9	12.6	8.8	4.6
Manitowoc	0.0	15.2	0.1	0.0	0.4	14.2	10.4	6.0	0.2	12.4
Menomonee Falls	0.0	15.5	0.0	0.0	0.2	16.2	20.2	2.6	0.0	7.8
Milwaukee	0.0	12.7	2.5	0.0	2.4	25.6	14.5	0.3	4.2	5.0
Mount Pleasant	0.0	17.1	0.0	0.0	4.2	20.6	21.1	0.8	0.0	5.8
Neenah	0.0	16.2	0.6	0.0	1.9	17.0	13.8	6.1	0.8	10.8
New Berlin	0.0	19.7	0.0	0.0	2.8	23.9	21.2	4.8	0.0	3.7
Oak Creek	0.0	19.5	0.0	0.0	14.6	24.8	12.2	3.6	0.0	2.2
Oshkosh	0.0	23.8	0.5	0.0	2.4	13.2	11.8	12.9	0.2	8.2
Racine	0.0	14.3	1.2	0.0	5.6	23.4	15.4	8.0	2.0	7.2
Sheboygan	0.0	14.8	0.7	0.0	0.9	20.3	13.9	5.4	6.3	5.0
Stevens Point	0.0	23.7	0.0	0.0	4.9	16.2	9.8	7.6	0.0	4.2
Sun Prairie	0.0	21.7	0.0	0.0	4.2	20.7	12.6	6.0	0.0	10.6
Superior	0.0	18.0	0.0	0.0	0.4	17.5	22.0	4.7	2.4	3.9
Waukesha	0.0	16.2	0.8	0.0	2.6	18.4	16.2	9.4	0.3	5.9
Wausau	0.0	21.0	3.6	0.0	5.0	16.8	11.2	7.1	1.6	3.1
Wauwatosa	0.0	13.3	0.0	0.0	8.5	23.5	12.9	2.4	2.5	4.8
West Allis	0.0	15.5	0.1	0.0	4.5	22.8	11.5	0.5	5.7	4.1
West Bend	0.0	15.4	0.3	0.0	1.8	22.0	12.1	9.0	0.5	10.6
WYOMING	NA	NA	NA	NA	NA	NA	NA	NA	NA	NA
Casper	2.2	10.7	0.0	0.0	1.5	13.9	20.6	12.8	0.5	0.4
Cheyenne	1.4	15.7	0.8	0.0	2.2	15.2	14.6	13.7	0.4	1.9
Gillette	0.0	29.3	0.0	0.0	0.8	10.9	11.6	5.5	1.5	0.5
Laramie	0.0	22.8	0.0	0.0	3.0	15.4	15.8	9.0	1.0	1.4

Table D. Cities — City Government Finances, City Government Employment, and Climate

City	Debt outstanding Total (mil dol)	Per capita[1] (dollars)	Debt issued during year	Average daily temperature Mean January	July	Limits January[3]	July[4]	Annual precipitation (inches)	Heating degree days	Cooling degree days
	137	138	139	140	141	142	143	144	145	146
WASHINGTON—Cont'd										
Pasco	48.6	727	4.2	34.2	75.2	28.0	89.3	8.01	4,731	909
Pullman	7.0	224	0.3	NA	NA	NA	NA	NA	NA	NA
Puyallup	75.3	1,972	2.6	39.9	64.9	32.9	77.8	40.51	4,991	153
Redmond	82.8	1,463	8.0	25.1	55.0	20.0	65.0	82.86	9,630	12
Renton	184.1	1,921	26.1	40.9	65.3	35.9	75.3	37.07	4,797	173
Richland	147.2	2,861	0.3	33.0	73.2	26.0	87.9	7.55	5,133	739
Sammamish	7.7	157	0.0	40.8	65.2	35.2	75.0	35.96	4,756	174
SeaTac	5.8	208	0.0	40.9	65.3	35.9	75.3	37.07	4,797	173
Seattle	4,163.6	6,556	431.3	41.5	65.5	36.0	74.5	38.25	4,615	192
Shoreline	38.3	704	0.0	40.8	65.2	35.2	75.0	35.96	4,756	174
Spokane	189.9	906	0.0	27.3	68.6	21.7	82.5	16.67	6,820	394
Spokane Valley	7.9	88	0.0	NA	NA	NA	NA	NA	NA	NA
Tacoma	1,587.6	7,849	58.5	41.0	65.6	35.1	76.1	38.95	4,650	167
University Place	55.9	1,770	5.9	41.0	65.6	35.1	76.1	38.95	4,650	167
Vancouver	263.9	1,597	10.6	39.0	65.4	32.4	77.3	41.92	4,990	197
Walla Walla	62.5	1,959	0.0	34.7	75.3	28.8	89.9	20.88	4,882	957
Wenatchee	42.9	1,318	18.9	29.2	74.4	23.2	87.8	9.12	5,533	832
Yakima	60.7	653	2.8	29.1	69.1	20.5	87.2	8.26	6,104	431
WEST VIRGINIA	X	X	X	X	X	X	X	X	X	X
Charleston	118.0	2,315	9.2	33.4	73.9	24.2	84.9	44.05	4,644	978
Huntington	44.1	897	2.3	32.1	76.3	23.5	87.1	41.74	4,737	1,128
Morgantown	120.1	3,972	3.8	30.8	73.5	22.3	83.4	43.30	5,174	815
Parkersburg	67.9	2,176	4.9	30.7	75.4	22.3	85.8	40.69	5,091	1,038
Wheeling	49.6	1,759	8.3	29.6	74.8	21.4	85.2	40.34	5,313	926
WISCONSIN	X	X	X	X	X	X	X	X	X	X
Appleton	159.0	2,176	6.9	16.0	71.6	7.8	81.4	30.16	7,721	572
Beloit	93.8	2,547	28.1	19.1	72.4	11.6	82.5	35.25	6,969	664
Brookfield	66.3	1,745	9.1	20.0	74.3	11.5	85.1	32.09	6,886	791
Eau Claire	99.4	1,476	8.5	11.9	71.4	2.5	82.6	32.12	8,196	554
Fitchburg	29.6	1,143	6.6	NA	NA	NA	NA	NA	NA	NA
Fond du Lac	203.2	4,724	19.8	16.6	71.8	9.1	81.1	30.15	7,534	586
Franklin	32.5	906	0.0	20.7	72.0	13.4	81.1	34.81	7,087	616
Green Bay	209.5	1,998	5.7	15.6	69.9	7.1	81.2	29.19	7,963	463
Greenfield	32.8	886	7.3	19.9	73.8	12.7	81.9	33.86	6,847	764
Janesville	106.9	1,682	22.1	17.7	72.1	8.6	83.8	32.78	7,238	629
Kenosha	179.5	1,797	26.2	20.8	71.3	13.2	78.7	34.74	6,999	549
La Crosse	98.7	1,894	17.8	15.9	74.0	6.3	85.2	32.36	7,340	775
Madison	526.8	2,195	99.4	17.3	71.6	9.3	82.1	32.95	7,493	582
Manitowoc	154.4	4,618	11.6	18.7	69.9	10.8	79.6	30.49	7,563	425
Menomonee Falls	94.1	2,625	18.0	16.5	69.3	8.1	80.2	33.45	7,832	407
Milwaukee	1,306.0	2,181	454.0	20.0	74.3	11.5	85.1	32.09	6,886	791
Mount Pleasant	47.2	1,806	5.6	NA	NA	NA	NA	NA	NA	NA
Neenah	75.6	2,939	5.0	NA	NA	NA	NA	NA	NA	NA
New Berlin	45.0	1,133	6.4	19.9	73.8	12.7	81.9	33.86	6,847	764
Oak Creek	112.6	3,230	18.5	20.7	72.0	13.4	81.1	34.81	7,087	616
Oshkosh	221.7	3,326	42.5	16.1	72.0	7.8	81.8	31.57	7,639	591
Racine	233.6	2,986	30.0	20.7	71.3	13.3	78.6	35.35	7,032	567
Sheboygan	62.5	1,281	1.4	20.9	71.4	13.2	81.4	31.90	7,056	559
Stevens Point	44.4	1,651	18.4	NA	NA	NA	NA	NA	NA	NA
Sun Prairie	70.0	2,289	0.0	NA	NA	NA	NA	NA	NA	NA
Superior	54.2	2,019	18.4	12.1	66.6	3.4	76.2	30.78	9,006	241
Waukesha	127.7	1,793	19.3	19.5	73.8	11.4	84.2	34.64	6,893	784
Wausau	50.1	1,279	7.7	13.0	70.1	3.6	80.8	33.36	8,237	464
Wauwatosa	100.8	2,142	19.5	20.0	74.3	11.5	85.1	32.09	6,886	791
West Allis	78.5	1,294	5.9	19.9	73.8	12.7	81.9	33.86	6,847	764
West Bend	79.7	2,525	6.8	18.4	70.6	10.7	81.3	32.85	7,371	502
WYOMING	X	X	X	X	X	X	X	X	X	X
Casper	19.5	338	0.1	22.3	70.0	12.2	86.8	13.03	7,571	428
Cheyenne	86.1	1,395	14.1	25.9	67.7	14.8	81.9	15.45	7,388	273
Gillette	91.7	2,916	2.2	NA	NA	NA	NA	NA	NA	NA
Laramie	44.3	1,394	0.5	20.3	62.9	7.8	79.4	11.19	9,233	75

1. Based on the population estimated as of July 1 of the year shown. 2. Represents normal values based on the 30-year period, 1971±2000. 3. Average daily minimum. 4. Average daily maximum.

Congressional Districts of the 116th Congress

(For explanation of symbols, see page viii)

Page

1177	Congressional District Highlights and Rankings
1184	Congressional District Column Headings
1186	Table E
1186	**AL**(District 1)—**CA**(District 53)
1193	**CO**(District 1)—**IL**(District 2)
1200	**IL**(District 3)—**MA**(District 9)
1207	**MI**(District 1)—**NM**(District 2)
1214	**NM**(District 3)—**OR**(District 2)
1221	**OR**(District 3)—**TX**(District 25)
1228	**TX**(District 26)—**WY**(At Large)

Congressional District Highlights and Rankings

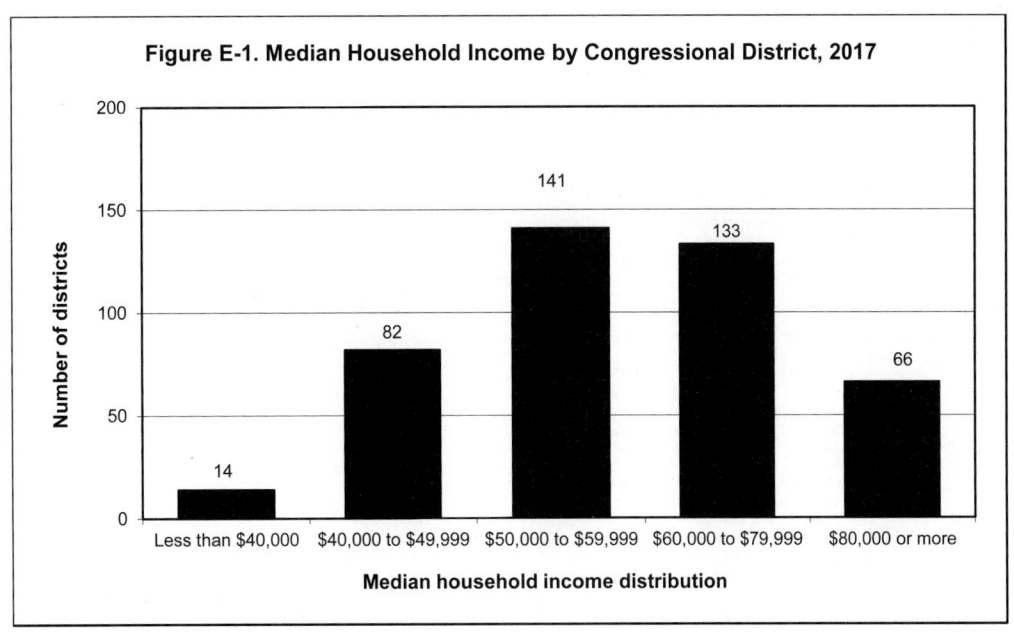

Figure E-1. Median Household Income by Congressional District, 2017

Number of districts

- Less than $40,000: 14
- $40,000 to $49,999: 82
- $50,000 to $59,999: 141
- $60,000 to $79,999: 133
- $80,000 or more: 66

Median household income distribution

Every 10 years, the Census Bureau conducts a count to reapportion the seats in the U.S. House of Representatives. The House's 435 seats are divided among the 50 states. (The District of Columbia has no representative in Congress, although it has a nonvoting delegate.) The seats are reapportioned according to the population measured on April 1 of the census year in order to account for population changes among the states over the previous decade. The number of districts within a state may change after each decennial census, and the districts' boundaries may change more than once during a decade. The 116th Congress which convened in 2019 was the third to reflect the new boundaries based on the 2010 census. The Representatives of the 116th Congress are listed. Most of the data in Table E have been collected or updated for the 116th congress, but some sources were collected for the 115th congress or earlier. Boundary changes between the 114th and 115th congresses occurred in Florida, Minnesota, North Carolina, and Virginia.

As the state with the largest population, California had the most representatives with 53. Texas (36) and New York (27) were second and third largest, respectively. There were 7 states with just 1 representative: Alaska, Delaware, Montana, North Dakota, South Dakota, Vermont, and Wyoming. These states' representatives were considered 'At Large,' as they represented an entire state instead of a specific congressional district within the state.

Because the number of representatives is limited to 435, states with larger population growth add seats, while states with little or no growth lose seats. When the 113th Congress convened in January 2013, eight states had more representatives in congress and 10 states had fewer. Based on the 2010 census, Texas gained 4 seats, Florida gained 2, while Washington, Nevada, Utah, Arizona, Georgia, and South Carolina each gained one seat. New York and Ohio each lost two seats, while Massachusetts, New Jersey, Pennsylvania, Michigan, Illinois, Iowa, Missouri, and Louisiana each lost a seat.

As each decade progresses, population shifts alter the size of districts, leading up to the reapportionment of the next census. After the 2010

census, the population of each congressional district was about 710,000. Based on the 2018 population estimates, the congressional districts average over 750,000 people. Montana's at-large congressional district had over a million people, while Delaware and South Dakota also had at-large seats with above average populations. Texas' 22nd district is the largest apportioned congressional district in the United States with a population over 897,000 in 2017. Rhode Island's two congressional districts have the smallest populations at 539,250 and 520,389. Congressional districts in Nebraska and West Virginia also have smaller populations. For years, Louisiana's 2nd district was the least populous congressional district in the nation due to outmigration after Hurricane Katrina.

While most of the congressional districts had about the same population size, they varied widely in other characteristics. In Colorado's 2nd district, 96.3 percent of the residents were high school graduates, compared with just 57.3 percent in California's 40th district and 59.0 percent in Texas' 33rd district. California's 21st district and Texas' 33rd district had the lowest proportions of college graduates, with only 8.3 and 9.9 percent of their residents holding a bachelor's degree respectively, followed by California's 40th district at 10.6 percent, Texas's 29th district at 10.8 percent, and California's 16th district at 12.1 percent. In New York's 12th district, 74.1 percent of residents were college graduates.

The highest unemployment rates were found in New York's 15th district and Illinois' 1st and 2nd districts, all over 13 percent. Three districts from California, two districts each from Illinois and Michigan along with one district each from Georgia, Ohio, and New York. ranked among the 10 highest unemployment rates. Forty-one congressional districts had 20 percent or more of their populations living in poverty. New York's 15th district had the highest poverty rate in the nation at 36.2 percent and the lowest median household income at $28,042 in 2017. In California's 18th district, the median household income was $134,077, the highest in the nation. Eighty-three congressional districts had median household incomes exceeding $75,000 per year, while fourteen districts had median household incomes below $40,000. The U.S. median household income in 2017 was $60,336

Congressional Districts of the 116th Congress of the United States
Selected Rankings

Population rank	Population, 2017 State congressional district Representative	Population [col 2]	Land area rank	Land area, 2018 State congressional district Representative	Land area (square kilometers) [col 1]	Density rank	Population density, 2017 State congressional district Representative	Population density (per square kilometer) [col 3]
1	MT At large: Greg Gianforte (R)	1,050,493	1	AK At-Large: Don Young (R)	570,886	1	NY 13th: Adriano Espaillat (D)	79,008
2	DE: At-Large: Lisa Blunt Rochester (D)	961,939	2	MT At large: Greg Gianforte (R)	145,545	2	NY 15th: José E. Serrano (D)	53,809
3	TX 22nd: Pete Olson (R)	897,080	3	WY: At-Large Liz Cheney (R)	97,091	3	NY 10th: Jerrold Nadler (D)	52,202
4	ID 1st: Russ Fulcher (R)	890,052	4	SD At-Large: Dusty Johnson (R)	75,809	4	NY 12th: Carolyn B. Maloney (D)	48,288
5	TX 26th: Michael C. Burgess (R)	879,237	5	NM 2nd: Xochitl Torres Small (D)	71,745	5	NY 9th: Yvette D. Clarke (D)	48,252
6	TX 3rd: Van Taylor (R)	870,763	6	OR 2nd: Greg Walden (R)	69,444	6	NY 7th: Nydia M. Velázquez (D)	46,820
7	SD At-Large: Dusty Johnson (R)	869,666	7	ND At-Large: Kelly Armstrong (R)	69,000	7	NY 8th: Hakeem S. Jeffries (D)	27,923
8	FL 9th: Darren Soto (D)	868,945	8	NE 3rd: Adrian Smith (R)	67,429	8	NY 6th: Grace Meng (D)	25,569
9	TX 8th: Kevin Brady (R)	863,498	9	TX 23rd: Will Hurd (R)	58,058	9	NY 14th: Alexandria Ocasio Cortez (D)	24,303
10	NC 12th: Alma S. Adams (D)	860,866	10	NV 2nd: Mark E. Amodei (R)	55,829	10	CA 12th: Nancy Pelosi (D)	19,868
11	NC 4th: David E. Price (D)	856,104	11	AZ 1st: Tom O'Halleran (D)	55,037	11	CA 34th: Jimmy Gomez (D)	16,012
12	TX 31st: John R. Carter (R)	853,799	12	KS 1st: Roger W. Marshall (R)	52,542	12	NY 5th: Gregory W. Meeks (D)	15,376
13	VA 10th: Jennifer Wexton (D)	850,118	13	NV 4th: Steven Horsford (D)	50,997	13	NJ 8th: Albio Sires (D)	14,218
14	TX 10th: Michael T. McCaul (R)	846,261	14	NM 3rd: Ben Ray Luján (D)	44,964	14	IL 4th: Jesus G. "Chuy" Garcia (D)	13,365
15	OR 1st: Suzanne Bonamici (D)	844,175	15	ID 2nd: Michael K. Simpson (R)	43,225	15	CA 37th: Karen Bass (D)	12,912
16	OR 3rd: Earl Blumenauer (D)	842,158	16	UT 2nd: Chris Stewart (R)	40,015	16	MA 7th: Ayanna Presley (D)	12,864
17	NC 2nd: George Holding (R)	835,806	17	ID 1st: Russ Fulcher (R)	39,420	17	CA 40th: Lucille Roybal-Allard (D)	12,804
18	IA 3rd: Cynthia Axne (D)	835,190	18	TX 13th: Mac Thornberry (R)	38,350	18	NY 11th: Max Rose (D)	11,632
19	AZ 7th: Ruben Gallego (D)	833,654	19	OK 3rd: Frank D. Lucas (R)	34,117	19	DC: At-Large: Eleanor Holmes Norton (D)	11,351
20	OR 5th: Kurt Schrader (D)	831,703	20	MN 7th: Collin C. Peterson (D)	33,429	20	IL 7th: Danny K. Davis (D)	11,185
21	TX 35th: Lloyd Doggett (D)	830,041	21	AZ 4th: Paul A. Gosar (R)	33,200	21	CA 43rd: Maxine Waters (D)	10,351
22	FL 10th: Val Butler Demings (D)	830,014	22	CA 8th: Paul Cook (R)	32,868	22	NJ 10th: Donald M. Payne, Jr. (D)	10,311
23	CO 1st: Diana DeGette (D)	826,995	23	CA 1st: Doug LaMalfa (R)	28,088	23	CA 46th: J. Luis Correa (D)	10,256
24	CA 42nd: Ken Calvert (R)	826,899	24	MN 8th: Pete Stauber (R)	27,907	24	PA 2nd: Brendan F. Boyle (D)	9,801
25	ID 2nd: Michael K. Simpson (R)	826,891	25	TX 11th: K. Michael Conaway (R)	27,833	25	NY 16th: Eliot L. Engel (D)	9,474
26	AZ 5th: Andy Biggs (R)	822,497	26	ME 2nd: Jared F. Golden (D)	27,558	26	PA 1st: Brian K. Fitzpatrick (R)	9,338
27	OR 2nd: Greg Walden (R)	821,129	27	TX 19th: Jodey C. Arrington (R)	25,836	27	CA 44th: Nanette Diaz Barragan (D)	9,039
28	OK 5th: Kendra S. Horn (D)	818,162	28	MI 1st: Jack Bergman (R)	25,028	28	NJ 9th: Bill Pascrell, Jr. (D)	8,074
29	CO 4th: Ken Buck (R)	817,251	29	WI 7th: Sean P. Duffy (R)	23,039	29	CA 13th: Barbara Lee (D)	7,921
30	CO 6th: Jason Crow (D)	814,636	30	IA 4th: Steve King (R)	22,756	30	CA 29th: Tony Cárdenas (D)	7,756
31	FL 16th: Vern Buchanan (R)	814,209	31	AR 4th: Bruce Westerman (R)	22,338	31	IL 5th: Michael Quigley (D)	7,626
32	Fl 19th: Francis Rooney (R)	814,074	32	OK 2nd: Markwayne Mullin (R)	20,997	32	FL 24th: Frederica S. Wilson (D)	7,524
33	TX 21st: Chip Roy (R)	809,322	33	UT 3rd: John R. Curtis (R)	20,074	33	CA 38th: Linda T. Sánchez (D)	7,084
34	LA 1st: Steve Scalise (R)	808,968	34	MO 1st: Jason T. Smith (R)	19,901	34	IL 9th: Janice D. Schakowsky (D)	6,952
35	GA 7th: Robert Woodall (R)	807,492	35	UT 1st: Rob Bishop (R)	19,557	35	NV 1st: Dina Titus (D)	6,898
36	AR 3rd: Steve Womack (R)	807,421	36	AR 1st: Eric A. "Rick" Crawford (R)	19,319	36	FL 27th: Donna E. Shalala (D)	6,674
37	MA 7th: Ayanna Presley (D)	806,820	37	WA 5th: Cathy McMorris Rodgers (R)	19,246	37	NY 4th: Kathleen M. Rice (D)	6,583
38	TX 12th: Kay Granger (R)	806,551	38	MO 6th: Sam Graves (R)	18,198	38	CA 32nd: Grace F. Napolitano (D)	5,838
39	TX 20th: Joaquin Castro (D)	806,372	39	OR 4th: Peter A. DeFazio (D)	17,272	39	CA 53rd: Susan A. Davis (D)	5,705
40	UT 4th: Ben McAdams (D)	805,400	40	AZ 3rd: Raul M. Grijalva (D)	15,688	40	Ca 30th: Brad Sherman (D)	5,673
41	VA 1st: Robert J. Wittman (R)	805,159	41	MS 2nd: Bennie G. Thompson (D)	15,551	41	WI 4th: Gwen Moore (D)	5,521
42	FL 15th: Ross Spano (R)	804,652	42	WA 4th: Dan Newsome (R)	15,473	42	VA 8th: Donald S. Beyer, Jr. (D)	5,371
43	OK 1st: Kevin Hern (R)	803,883	43	NY 21st: Elise M. Stefanik (R)	15,114	43	WA 7th: Pramila Jayapal (D)	5,338
44	OR 4th: Peter A. DeFazio (D)	803,611	44	IL 15th: John Shimkus (R)	14,696	44	MN 5th: Ilhan Omar (D)	5,315
45	NV 3rd: Susie Lee (D)	803,545	45	LA 5th: Ralph Lee Abraham (R)	14,453	45	CA 48th: Harley Rouda (D)	4,959
46	NY 13th: Adriano Espaillat (D)	802,800	46	MO 4th: Vicky Hartzler (R)	14,406	46	TX 7th: Lizzie Fletcher (D)	4,937
47	VA 8th: Donald S. Beyer, Jr. (D)	801,609	47	KS 4th: Ron Estes (R)	14,315	47	TX 9th: Al Green (D)	4,766
48	FL 4th: John H. Rutherford (R)	800,494	48	KS 2nd: Steve Watkins (R)	14,144	48	PA 13th: John Joyce (R)	4,695
49	TX 18th: Sheila Jackson-Lee (D)	800,402	49	CA 2nd: Jared Huffman (D)	12,952	49	AZ 9th: Greg Stanton (D)	4,673
50	TX 24th: Kenny Marchant (R)	800,103	50	CA 4th: Tom McClintock (R)	12,837	50	FL 22nd: Theodore E. Deutch (D)	4,593
51	NC 7th: David Rouzer (R)	800,096	51	MS 3rd: Michael Guest (R)	12,754	51	CA 35th: Norma J. Torres (D)	4,413
52	TX 7th: Lizzie Fletcher (D)	800,081	52	LA 4th: Mike Johnson (R)	12,436	52	CA 6th: Doris O. Matsui (D)	4,371
53	CO 2nd: Joe Neguse (D)	799,734	53	IA 2nd: Doug Loebsack (D)	12,262	53	CO 1st: Diana DeGette (D)	4,354
54	CO 5th: Doug Lamborn (R)	799,622	54	KY 1st: James Comer (R)	12,082	54	VA 11th: Gerald E. Connolly (D)	4,203
55	CO 7th: Ed Perlmutter (D)	799,438	55	IA 1st: Abby Finkenauer (D)	12,049	55	WA 9th: Adam Smith (D)	4,172
56	NY 5th: Gregory W. Meeks (D)	798,555	56	MN 1st: Jim Hagedorn (R)	11,974	56	CA 17th: Ro Khanna (D)	4,159
57	LA 2nd: Cedric Richmond (D)	797,298	57	KY 5th: Harold Rogers (R)	11,234	57	TX 32nd: Colin Z. Allred (D)	4,102
58	FL 26th: Debbie Murcasel-Powell (D)	797,160	58	WI 3rd: Ron Kind (D)	11,112	58	TX 29th: Sylvia R. Garcia (D)	4,072
59	LA 6th: Garret Graves (R)	796,589	59	FL 2nd: Neal P. Dunn (R)	11,004	59	AZ 7th: Ruben Gallego (D)	4,069
60	NY 8th: Hakeem S. Jeffries (D)	793,532	60	PA 5th: Mary Gay Scanlon (D)	10,711	60	TX 20th: Joaquin Castro (D)	4,038
61	MO 3rd: Blaine Luetkemeyer (R)	792,954	61	MS 1st: Trent Kelly (R)	10,573	61	FL 13th: Charlie Crist (D)	4,019
62	TX 6th: Ron Wright (R)	792,043	62	IL 18th: Darin LaHood (R)	10,516	62	FL 23rd: Debbie Wasserman Schultz (D)	4,014
63	TX 15th: Vicente Gonzalez (D)	790,730	63	AL 7th: Terri A. Sewell (D)	10,155	63	NY 2nd: Peter T. King (R)	3,973
64	VA 7th: Abigail Davis Spanberger (D)	790,084	64	AL 2nd:Martha Roby (R)	10,143	64	MI 9th: Sander M. Levin (D)	3,924
65	OK 4th: Tom Cole (R)	789,947	65	TX 4th: John Ratcliffe (R)	10,130	65	MI 14th: Brenda L. Lawrence (D)	3,752
66	TX 25th: Roger Williams (R)	789,825	66	VA 5th: Denver Riggleman (R)	10,031	66	MI 13th: Rashida Tlaib (D)	3,647
67	TX 9th: Al Green (D)	789,535	67	CA 23rd: Kevin McCarthy (R)	9,898	67	CA 39th: Gilbert Ray Cisneros, Jr. (D)	3,603
68	NC 8th: Richard Hudson (R)	789,484	68	OK 4th: Tom Cole (R)	9,777	68	TX 33rd: Marc A. Veasey (D)	3,554
69	FL 21st: Lois Frankel (D)	788,240	69	WV 3rd: Carol D. Miller (R)	9,746	69	CA 31st: Pete Aguilar (D)	3,492
70	LA 3rd: Clay Higgins (R)	788,118	70	GA 2nd: Sanford D. Bishop Jr. (D)	9,626	70	IL 8th: Raja Krishnamoorthi (D)	3,468
71	NC 9th: Vacant	788,020	71	TX 28th: Henry Cuellar (D)	9,379	71	NJ 6th: Frank Pallone Jr. (D)	3,450
72	CA 15th: Eric Swalwell (D)	785,387	72	VT 1st: Peter Welch (D)	9,218	72	OH 3rd: Joyce Beatty (D)	3,433
73	GA 5th: John Lewis (D)	784,370	73	TN 7th: Mark E. Green (R)	9,160	73	HI 1st: Ed Case (D)	3,417
74	AZ 6th: David Schweikert (R)	783,087	74	TX 27th: Michael Cloud (R)	9,121	74	TX 18th: Sheila Jackson-Lee (D)	3,402
75	OH 3rd: Joyce Beatty (D)	782,878	75	WA 3rd: Jaime Herrera Beutler (R)	9,116	75	CA 47th: Alan S. Lowenthal (D)	3,346

Congressional Districts of the 116th Congress of the United States
Selected Rankings

Percent Non-Hispanic White alone, 2017			Percent Black alone, 2017			Percent American Indian, Alaska Native alone, 2017		
Non-Hispanic White alone rank	State congressional district Representative	Percent white [col 11]	Black rank	State congressional district Representative	Percent black [col 5]	American Indian Alaska Native rank	State congressional district Representative	Percent American Indian Alaska Native [col 6]
1	KY 5th: Harold Rogers (R)	96.1	1	MS 2nd: Bennie G. Thompson (D)	67.4	1	AZ 1st: Tom O'Halleran (D)	22.7
2	OH 6th: Bill Johnson (R)	94.3	2	TN 9th: Steve Cohen (D)	66.6	2	NM 3rd: Ben Ray Luján (D)	19.1
3	ME 2nd: Jared F. Golden (D)	94.0	3	AL 7th: Terri A. Sewell (D)	63.1	3	OK 2nd: Markwayne Mullin (R)	17.3
4	WV 1st: David McKinley (R)	93.2	4	LA 2nd: Cedric Richmond (D)	62.4	4	AK At-Large: Don Young (R)	14.9
5	VT 1st: Peter Welch (D)	92.8	5	GA 13th: David Scott (D)	60.6	5	SD At-Large: Dusty Johnson (R)	8.7
6	ME 1st: Chellie Pingree (D)	92.7	6	GA 4th: Henry C. "Hank" Johnson Jr. (D)	60.2	6	NC 9th: Vacant	7.6
6	WV 3rd: Carol D. Miller (R)	92.7	7	GA 5th: John Lewis (D)	58.3	7	OK 1st: Kevin Hern (R)	6.3
8	PA 9th: Daniel Meuser (R)	92.5	8	IL 2nd: Robin L. Kelly (D)	57.8	8	MT At large: Greg Gianforte (R)	6.2
9	PA 5th: Mary Gay Scanlon (D)	91.9	9	SC 6th: James E. Clyburn (D)	56.7	9	OK 3rd: Frank D. Lucas (R)	6.1
10	NY 27th: Chris Collins (R)	91.7	10	PA 2nd: Brendan F. Boyle (D)	56.6	10	ND At-Large: Kelly Armstrong (R)	5.5
10	WI 3rd: Ron Kind (D)	91.7	11	MI 14th: Brenda L. Lawrence (D)	56.5	11	AZ 3rd: Raul M. Grijalva (D)	5.4
12	MN 8th: Pete Stauber (R)	91.6	12	MI 13th: Rashida Tlaib (D)	53.8	11	OK 4th: Tom Cole (R)	5.4
13	PA 18th: Michael F. Doyle (D)	91.5	13	FL 20th: Alcee L. Hastings (D)	53.7	13	NM 2nd: Xochitl Torres Small (D)	5.2
13	WI 7th: Sean P. Duffy (R)	91.5	14	OH 11th: Marcia L. Fudge (D)	53.4	14	NM 1st: Debra A. Haaland (D)	4.4
15	IN 6th: Greg Pence (R)	91.4	15	MD 7th: Elijah E. Cummings (D)	52.7	15	OK 5th: Kendra S. Horn (D)	4.1
15	MI 4th: John L. Moolenar (R)	91.4	16	NY 8th: Hakeem S. Jeffries (D)	52.5	16	WA 4th: Dan Newsome (R)	3.2
17	OH 16th: Anthony Gonzalez (R)	91.2	17	GA 2nd: Sanford D. Bishop Jr. (D)	52.1	17	MN 7th: Collin C. Peterson (D)	3.1
17	PA 12th: Fred Keller (R)	91.2	18	NJ 10th: Donald M. Payne, Jr. (D)	51.7	18	AZ 7th: Ruben Gallego (D)	3.0
17	TN 1st: Phil Roe (R)	91.2	19	MD 4th: Anthony G. Brown (D)	51.4	19	AZ 9th: Greg Stanton (D)	2.6
20	OH 7th: Bob Gibbs (R)	91.1	20	IL 1st: Bobby L. Rush (D)	50.3	19	MN 8th: Pete Stauber (R)	2.6
21	MI 1st: Jack Bergman (R)	90.9	21	MO 1st: William Lacy Clay (D)	49.4	19	NV 2nd: Mark E. Amodei (R)	2.6
21	MO 3rd: Blaine Luetkemeyer (R)	90.9	22	FL 24th: Frederica S. Wilson (D)	48.9	22	CO 3rd: Scott R. Tipton (R)	2.4
21	NH 1st: Chris Pappas (D)	90.9	23	NY 5th: Gregory W. Meeks (D)	48.1	22	WI 8th: Mike Gallagher (R)	2.4
24	MO 8th: Jason T. Smith (R)	90.6	24	FL 5th: Al Lawson (D)	47.6	22	WY: At-Large Liz Cheney (R)	2.4
25	IL 15th: John Shimkus (R)	90.5	25	NY 9th: Yvette D. Clarke (D)	46.9	25	MI 1st: Jack Bergman (R)	2.3
26	IN 8th: Larry Bucshon (R)	90.4	26	VA 3rd: Robert C. "Bobby" Scott (D)	46.3	26	OR 2nd: Greg Walden (R)	2.2
27	MI 10th: Paul Mitchell (R)	90.1	27	DC: At-Large: Eleanor Holmes Norton (D)	45.9	27	CA 1st: Doug LaMalfa (R)	2.1
27	WV 2nd: Alexander X. Mooney (R)	90.1	28	IL 7th: Danny K. Davis (D)	45.7	27	CA 2nd: Jared Huffman (D)	2.1
29	PA 3rd: Dwight Evans (D)	90.0	29	NC 1st: G. K. Butterfield (D)	43.7	29	WI 6th: Derek Kilmer (D)	2.0
30	NY 21st: Elise M. Stefanik (R)	89.9	30	TX 30th: Eddie Bernice Johnson (D)	43.1	29	WI 7th: Sean P. Duffy (R)	2.0
31	NH 2nd: Ann M. Kuster (D)	89.8	31	VA 4th: A. Donald McEachin (D)	41.0	31	AZ 6th: David Schweikert (R)	1.9
32	KY 4th: Thomas Massie (R)	89.6	32	MD 5th: Steny H. Hoyer (D)	38.6	32	AZ 4th: Paul A. Gosar (R)	1.8
33	PA 10th: Scott Perry (R)	89.5	33	NC 12th: Alma S. Adams (D)	37.7	32	WA 5th: Cathy McMorris Rodgers (R)	1.8
34	OH 15th: Steve Stivers (R)	89.2	34	PA 1st: Brian K. Fitzpatrick (R)	36.7	34	CA 35th: Norma J. Torres (D)	1.7
34	VA 9th: Morgan Griffith (R)	89.2	34	TX 9th: Al Green (D)	36.7	35	AZ 2nd: Ann Kirkpatrick (D)	1.6
36	WI 6th: Glenn Grothman (R)	89.1	36	NY 15th: José E. Serrano (D)	36.1	35	NC 11th: Mark Meadows (R)	1.6
37	IN 9th: Trey Hollingsworth (R)	88.8	37	LA 5th: Ralph Lee Abraham (R)	36.0	37	CA 8th: Paul Cook (R)	1.4
38	MN 7th: Collin C. Peterson (D)	88.4	38	MS 3rd: Michael Guest (R)	35.6	37	CA 36th: Raul Ruiz (D)	1.4
39	IL 18th: Darin LaHood (R)	88.3	39	MD 2nd: C. A. Dutch Ruppersberger (D)	35.4	37	GA 6th: Lucy McBath (D)	1.4
39	OH 5th: Robert E. Latta (R)	88.3	40	GA 12th: Rick W. Allen (R)	35.2	37	NV 1st: Dina Titus (D)	1.4
41	OH 14th: David P. Joyce (R)	88.2	41	OH 3rd: Joyce Beatty (D)	34.7	41	CA 23rd: Kevin McCarthy (R)	1.3
42	TN 6th: John W. Rose (R)	88.1	42	NY 8th: Sheila Jackson-Lee (D)	34.6	41	ID 1st: Russ Fulcher (R)	1.3
43	IA 1st: Abby Finkenauer (D)	88.0	43	LA 4th: Mike Johnson (R)	34.2	41	KS 2nd: Steve Watkins (R)	1.3
43	MN 6th: Tom Emmer (R)	88.0	44	NY 16th: Eliot L. Engel (D)	33.8	41	UT 3rd: John R. Curtis (R)	1.3
45	MO 7th: Bill Long (R)	87.8	45	WI 4th: Gwen Moore (D)	33.7	41	WA 1st: Suzan K. DelBene (D)	1.3
45	NY 23rd: Tom Reed (R)	87.8	46	GA 8th: Austin Scott (R)	31.3	46	AZ 8th: Debbie Lesko (R)	1.2
47	MI 7th: Tim Walberg (R)	87.5	47	AL 2nd: Martha Roby (R)	30.7	46	CA 4th: Tom McClintock (R)	1.2
48	IA 4th: Steve King (R)	87.4	48	GA 1st: Earl L. "Buddy" Carter (R)	29.3	46	CA 16th: Jim Costa (D)	1.2
48	OH 4th: Jim Jordan (R)	87.4	49	IN 7th: André Carson (D)	29.2	46	CA 25th: Katie Hill (D)	1.2
50	KY 1st: James Comer (R)	87.3	50	FL 10th: Val Butler Demings (D)	28.9	46	CA 32nd: Grace F. Napolitano (D)	1.2
50	NY 22nd: Anthony Brindisi (D)	87.3	51	SC 7th: Tom Rice (R)	28.6	46	CA 50th: Duncan Hunter (R)	1.2
52	MO 6th: Sam Graves (R)	86.9	52	NY 13th: Adriano Espaillat (D)	28.4	46	ID 2nd: Michael K. Simpson (R)	1.2
53	KY 2nd: Brett Guthrie (R)	86.7	53	AL 1st: Bradley Byrne (R)	27.9	46	MN 5th: Ilhan Omar (D)	1.2
53	WI 5th: F. James Sensenbrenner Jr. (R)	86.7	54	MS 1st: Trent Kelly (R)	27.4	54	AR 3rd: Steve Womack (R)	1.1
53	WI 8th: Mike Gallagher (R)	86.7	55	AL 3rd: Mike Rogers (R)	26.3	54	CA 34th: Jimmy Gomez (D)	1.1
56	MO 4th: Vicky Hartzler (R)	86.6	55	SC 5th: Ralph Norman (R)	26.3	54	ME 2nd: Jared F. Golden (D)	1.1
57	NC 11th: Mark Meadows (R)	86.4	57	MA 7th: Ayanna Presley (D)	25.7	54	MS 3rd: Michael Guest (R)	1.1
58	MT At large: Greg Gianforte (R)	86.3	58	LA 3rd: Clay Higgins (R)	24.8	54	NE 1st: Jeff Fortenberry (R)	1.1
59	MO 2nd: Ann Wagner (R)	86.2	59	GA 10th: Jody B. Hice (R)	24.6	54	NC 8th: Richard Hudson (R)	1.1
60	MA 9th: William R. Keating (D)	86.1	60	GA 3rd: A. Drew Ferguson IV (R)	24.4	54	OR 3rd: Earl Blumenauer (D)	1.1
61	MN 1st: Jim Hagedorn (R)	85.8	61	MS 4th: Steven Palazzo (R)	24.1	54	WA 10th: Denny Heck (D)	1.1
62	TN 2nd: Tim Burchett (R)	85.7	61	TN 5th: Jim Cooper (D)	24.1	62	AL 4th: Robert B. Aderholt (R)	1.0
63	OH 8th: Warren Davidson (R)	85.6	63	NC 8th: Richard Hudson (R)	23.8	62	AZ 5th: Andy Biggs (R)	1.0
64	IA 2nd: David Loebsack (D)	85.3	63	SC 2nd: Joe Wilson (R)	23.8	62	CA 3rd: John Garamendi (D)	1.0
65	OH 12th: Troy Balderson (R)	85.1	65	CA 37th: Karen Bass (D)	23.5	62	CA 19th: Zoe Lofgren (D)	1.0
66	OH 2nd: Brad R. Wenstrup (R)	84.8	65	MD 3rd: John P. Sarbanes (D)	23.5	62	CA 24th: Salud O. Carbajal (D)	1.0
67	IN 4th: James R. Baird (R)	84.7	67	CA 43rd: Maxine Waters (D)	23.1	62	CA 26th: Julia Brownley (D)	1.0
68	ND At-Large: Kelly Armstrong (R)	84.4	67	LA 6th: Garret Graves (R)	23.1	62	CO 1st: Diana DeGette (D)	1.0
69	PA 11th: LLloyd Smucker (R)	84.1	69	AR 2nd: J. French Hill (R)	22.9	62	CO 5th: Doug Lamborn (R)	1.0
70	WY: At-Large Liz Cheney (R)	84.0	70	KY 3rd: John A. Yarmuth (D)	22.2	62	LA 1st: Steve Scalise (R)	1.0
71	NE 3rd: Adrian Smith (R)	83.8	70	NC 4th: David E. Price (D)	22.2	62	NV 4th: Steven Horsford (D)	1.0
71	NY 19th: Antonio Delgado (D)	83.8	70	NC 9th: Ted Budd (R)	22.2	62	OR 5th: Kurt Schrader (D)	1.0
73	ID 1st: Russ Fulcher (R)	83.6	73	DE: At-Large: Lisa Blunt Rochester (D)	21.9	62	UT 1st: Rob Bishop (R)	1.0
73	OR 4th: Peter A. DeFazio (D)	83.6	74	TX 6th: Ron Wright (R)	21.7	62	UT 2nd: Chris Stewart (R)	1.0
73	PA 7th: Susan Wild (D)	83.6	75	MO 5th: Emanuel Cleaver (D)	21.5	62	WA 2nd: Rick Larsen (D)	1.0

Congressional Districts of the 116th Congress of the United States
Selected Rankings

Percent Asian or Pacific Islander alone, 2017

Asian or Pacific Islander rank	State congressional district Representative	Percent Asian or Pacific Islander [col 7]
1	HI 1st: Ed Case (D)	58.2
2	CA 17th: Ro Khanna (D)	55.7
3	NY 6th: Grace Meng (D)	40.7
4	CA 27th: Judy Chu (D)	40.6
5	HI 2nd: Tulsi Gabbard (D)	38.6
6	CA 14th: Jackie Speier (D)	36.0
7	CA 15th: Eric Swalwell (D)	35.8
8	CA 12th: Nancy Pelosi (D)	33.2
9	CA 39th: Gilbert Ray Cisneros, Jr. (D)	31.7
10	CA 19th: Zoe Lofgren (D)	29.5
11	CA 45th: Katie Porter (D)	25.8
12	CA 47th: Alan S. Lowenthal (D)	24.3
13	CA 18th: Anna G. Eshoo (D)	24.2
13	WA 9th: Adam Smith (D)	24.2
15	CA 13th: Barbara Lee (D)	21.3
16	CA 52nd: Scott H. Peters (D)	21.2
17	CA 32nd: Grace F. Napolitano (D)	20.3
18	NJ 6th: Frank Pallone Jr. (D)	20.1
19	CA 34th: Jimmy Gomez (D)	19.5
20	NY 7th: Nydia M. Velázquez (D)	19.4
21	TX 22nd: Pete Olson (R)	19.2
22	NY 10th: Jerrold Nadler (D)	18.8
23	CA 48th: Harley Rouda (D)	18.7
24	VA 11th: Gerald E. Connolly (D)	18.5
25	NY 14th: Alexandria Ocasio Cortez (D)	18.1
26	CA 6th: Doris O. Matsui (D)	17.6
27	NJ 12th: Bonnie Watson Coleman (D)	16.8
28	NY 3rd: Thomas R. Souzzi (D)	16.5
29	CA 7th: Ami Bera (D)	16.4
30	CA 38th: Linda T. Sánchez (D)	16.0
31	VA 10th: Jennifer Wexton (D)	15.9
32	TX 3rd: Van Taylor (R)	15.7
33	NV 3rd: Susie Lee (D)	15.5
34	NY 5th: Gregory W. Meeks (D)	15.3
34	NY 11th: Max Rose (D)	15.3
36	CA 9th: Jerry McNerney (D)	15.2
37	CA 33rd: Ted Lieu (D)	15.1
38	CA 53rd: Susan A. Davis (D)	15.0
39	CA 11th: Mark Desaulnier (D)	14.7
40	TX 24th: Kenny Marchant (R)	14.5
41	GA 7th: Robert Woodall (R)	14.2
41	NY 12th: Carolyn B. Maloney (D)	14.2
43	CA 43rd: Maxine Waters (D)	14.0
44	Ca 30th: Brad Sherman (D)	13.4
44	CA 46th: J. Luis Correa (D)	13.4
46	NJ 9th: Bill Pascrell, Jr. (D)	13.3
47	MN 4th: Betty McCollum (D)	13.1
47	WA 7th: Pramila Jayapal (D)	13.1
49	IL 8th: Raja Krishnamoorthi (D)	13.0
50	IL 9th: Janice D. Schakowsky (D)	12.5
51	CA 28th: Adam B. Schiff (D)	12.4
51	MA 5th: Katherine Clark (D)	12.4
53	CA 3rd: John Garamendi (D)	12.3
54	MD 6th: David J. Trone (D)	11.9
54	WA 1st: Suzan K. DelBene (D)	11.9
56	NJ 5th: Josh Gottheimer (D)	11.8
57	CA 5th: Mike Thompson (D)	11.7
57	TX 9th: Al Green (D)	11.7
59	GA 6th: Lucy McBath (D)	11.3
60	IL 10th: Bradley Scott Schneider (D)	11.1
60	TX 7th: Lizzie Fletcher (D)	11.1
62	VA 8th: Donald S. Beyer, Jr. (D)	11.0
63	NJ 7th: Tom Malinowski (D)	10.8
63	NJ 11th: Mikie Sherill (D)	10.8
65	MA 7th: Ayanna Presley (D)	10.4
65	MI 11th: Haley M. Stevens (D)	10.4
65	WA 8th: Kim Schrier (D)	10.4
68	IL 6th: Sean Casten (D)	10.3
69	CA 37th: Karen Bass (D)	10.0
69	CA 42nd: Ken Calvert (R)	10.0
69	PA 13th: John Joyce (R)	10.0
72	CA 16th: Jim Costa (D)	9.9
73	CA 25th: Katie Hill (D)	9.3
73	NV 1st: Dina Titus (D)	9.3
73	NC 4th: David E. Price (D)	9.3

Percent Hispanic or Latino,[1] 2017

Hispanic rank	State congressional district Representative	Percent Hispanic [col 10]
1	CA 40th: Lucille Roybal-Allard (D)	88.1
2	TX 34th: Filemon Vela (D)	85.0
3	TX 15th: Vicente Gonzalez (D)	82.3
4	TX 16th: Veronica Escobar (D)	81.0
5	TX 29th: Sylvia R. Garcia (D)	77.5
6	TX 28th: Henry Cuellar (D)	77.3
7	CA 21st: TJ Cox (D)	75.4
8	FL 25th: Mario Diaz-Balart (R)	75.3
9	FL 27th: Donna E. Shalala (D)	73.2
10	FL 26th: Debbie Murcasel-Powell (D)	72.3
11	CA 44th: Nanette Diaz Barragan (D)	71.6
12	CA 51st: Juan Vargas (D)	70.9
13	TX 23rd: Will Hurd (R)	70.3
14	CA 35th: Norma J. Torres (D)	69.7
14	TX 20th: Joaquin Castro (D)	69.7
16	TX 33rd: Marc A. Veasey (D)	69.3
17	IL 4th: Jesus G. "Chuy" Garcia (D)	68.4
18	CA 29th: Tony Cárdenas (D)	68.1
19	CA 46th: J. Luis Correa (D)	66.6
19	NY 15th: José E. Serrano (D)	66.6
21	AZ 7th: Ruben Gallego (D)	64.3
22	CA 34th: Jimmy Gomez (D)	63.6
23	AZ 3rd: Raul M. Grijalva (D)	63.0
24	CA 41st: Mark Takano (D)	62.8
25	CA 32nd: Grace F. Napolitano (D)	61.9
26	CA 16th: Jim Costa (D)	61.7
27	CA 38th: Linda T. Sánchez (D)	60.3
28	TX 35th: Lloyd Doggett (D)	60.1
29	NM 2nd: Xochitl Torres Small (D)	55.3
30	NY 13th: Adriano Espaillat (D)	54.8
31	NJ 8th: Albio Sires (D)	54.5
32	CA 31st: Pete Aguilar (D)	53.5
33	CA 20th: Jimmy Panetta (D)	53.3
34	TX 27th: Michael Cloud (R)	53.0
35	NM 1st: Debra A. Haaland (D)	49.9
36	CA 22nd: Devin Nunes (R)	48.8
37	CA 36th: Raul Ruiz (D)	48.0
38	NY 14th: Alexandria Ocasio Cortez (D)	47.7
39	CA 43rd: Maxine Waters (D)	47.4
40	NV 1st: Dina Titus (D)	46.3
41	CA 26th: Julia Brownley (D)	45.8
42	CA 10th: Josh Harder (D)	44.3
43	TX 18th: Sheila Jackson-Lee (D)	44.1
44	CA 8th: Paul Cook (R)	43.0
45	FL 9th: Darren Soto (D)	42.0
46	NM 3rd: Ben Ray Luján (D)	41.1
47	TX 9th: Al Green (D)	40.8
48	NY 7th: Nydia M. Velázquez (D)	40.5
49	CA 25th: Katie Hill (D)	39.7
50	CA 19th: Zoe Lofgren (D)	39.6
51	CA 37th: Karen Bass (D)	39.3
51	CA 42nd: Ken Calvert (R)	39.3
53	WA 4th: Dan Newsome (R)	39.2
54	CA 23rd: Kevin McCarthy (R)	39.1
54	TX 11th: K. Michael Conaway (R)	39.1
56	FL 24th: Frederica S. Wilson (D)	39.0
57	TX 30th: Eddie Bernice Johnson (D)	38.2
58	CA 9th: Jerry McNerney (D)	38.1
59	FL 23rd: Debbie Wasserman Schultz (D)	37.9
59	NJ 9th: Bill Pascrell, Jr. (D)	37.9
61	TX 19th: Jodey C. Arrington (R)	36.9
62	CA 24th: Salud O. Carbajal (D)	36.6
63	CA 39th: Gilbert Ray Cisneros, Jr. (D)	35.4
64	CA 47th: Alan S. Lowenthal (D)	34.9
65	CA 50th: Duncan Hunter (R)	33.6
66	IL 3rd: Daniel Lipinski (D)	32.1
66	TX 2nd: Dan Crenshaw (R)	32.1
68	CA 53rd: Susan A. Davis (D)	32.0
69	FL 14th: Kathy Castor (D)	30.5
70	NV 4th: Steven Horsford (D)	30.5
71	TX 7th: Lizzie Fletcher (D)	30.4
72	CA 3rd: John Garamendi (D)	30.3
72	TX 21st: Chip Roy (R)	30.3
74	IL 8th: Raja Krishnamoorthi (D)	29.7
75	CO 7th: Ed Perlmutter (D)	29.4

Percent foreign born, 2017

Foreign-born rank	State congressional district Representative	Percent foreign born [col 13]
1	FL 25th: Mario Diaz-Balart (R)	56.3
2	FL 27th: Donna E. Shalala (D)	53.8
3	NY 6th: Grace Meng (D)	51.6
4	FL 26th: Debbie Murcasel-Powell (D)	50.0
5	CA 17th: Ro Khanna (D)	48.9
6	NY 14th: Alexandria Ocasio Cortez (D)	47.0
7	CA 34th: Jimmy Gomez (D)	46.1
8	NJ 8th: Albio Sires (D)	44.3
9	FL 24th: Frederica S. Wilson (D)	43.9
10	CA 29th: Tony Cárdenas (D)	42.6
11	NY 5th: Gregory W. Meeks (D)	42.2
12	CA 27th: Judy Chu (D)	40.1
13	CA 28th: Adam B. Schiff (D)	39.3
13	NY 9th: Yvette D. Clarke (D)	39.3
15	CA 40th: Lucille Roybal-Allard (D)	39.2
16	CA 46th: J. Luis Correa (D)	38.9
17	NJ 9th: Bill Pascrell, Jr. (D)	38.6
18	CA 14th: Jackie Speier (D)	38.3
19	CA 32nd: Grace F. Napolitano (D)	37.7
20	NY 15th: José E. Serrano (D)	37.4
21	CA 19th: Zoe Lofgren (D)	36.2
22	FL 23rd: Debbie Wasserman Schultz (D)	36.0
23	NY 7th: Nydia M. Velázquez (D)	35.5
24	CA 15th: Eric Swalwell (D)	35.2
25	NY 13th: Adriano Espaillat (D)	35.1
26	TX 9th: Al Green (D)	34.8
27	IL 4th: Jesus G. "Chuy" Garcia (D)	34.2
28	CA 12th: Nancy Pelosi (D)	34.1
29	CA 44th: Nanette Diaz Barragan (D)	33.6
30	Ca 30th: Brad Sherman (D)	33.5
31	TX 33rd: Marc A. Veasey (D)	33.3
32	FL 20th: Alcee L. Hastings (D)	33.1
33	CA 39th: Gilbert Ray Cisneros, Jr. (D)	32.7
34	CA 51st: Juan Vargas (D)	32.6
35	MA 7th: Ayanna Presley (D)	32.5
36	NV 1st: Dina Titus (D)	32.1
36	TX 29th: Sylvia R. Garcia (D)	32.1
38	NY 8th: Hakeem S. Jeffries (D)	31.9
38	VA 11th: Gerald E. Connolly (D)	31.9
40	CA 43rd: Maxine Waters (D)	31.3
41	NY 11th: Max Rose (D)	31.2
42	CA 18th: Anna G. Eshoo (D)	31.0
43	CA 37th: Karen Bass (D)	30.9
43	NY 16th: Eliot L. Engel (D)	30.9
43	WA 9th: Adam Smith (D)	30.9
46	NY 10th: Jerrold Nadler (D)	30.7
47	CA 47th: Alan S. Lowenthal (D)	30.4
48	VA 8th: Donald S. Beyer, Jr. (D)	30.1
49	CA 38th: Linda T. Sánchez (D)	30.0
50	NJ 10th: Donald M. Payne, Jr. (D)	29.9
50	TX 7th: Lizzie Fletcher (D)	29.9
52	NJ 6th: Frank Pallone Jr. (D)	29.6
53	FL 22nd: Theodore E. Deutch (D)	29.5
54	IL 8th: Raja Krishnamoorthi (D)	29.3
55	CA 21st: TJ Cox (D)	29.2
55	CA 45th: Katie Porter (D)	29.2
57	FL 21st: Lois Frankel (D)	28.4
58	CA 35th: Norma J. Torres (D)	28.3
59	CA 13th: Barbara Lee (D)	28.1
59	NJ 12th: Bonnie Watson Coleman (D)	28.1
61	IL 9th: Janice D. Schakowsky (D)	27.1
62	CA 20th: Jimmy Panetta (D)	27.0
63	CA 11th: Mark Desaulnier (D)	26.3
64	NY 12th: Carolyn B. Maloney (D)	25.9
65	GA 7th: Robert Woodall (R)	25.8
66	FL 10th: Val Butler Demings (D)	25.6
66	TX 22nd: Pete Olson (R)	25.6
68	AZ 7th: Ruben Gallego (D)	25.1
69	CA 41st: Mark Takano (D)	24.9
70	MA 5th: Katherine Clark (D)	24.8
71	IL 10th: Bradley Scott Schneider (D)	24.7
72	TX 24th: Kenny Marchant (R)	24.6
73	TX 16th: Veronica Escobar (D)	24.3
74	CA 6th: Doris O. Matsui (D)	24.0
75	CA 16th: Jim Costa (D)	23.9

Congressional Districts of the 116th Congress of the United States
Selected Rankings

Percent under 18 years old, 2017

Under 18 years old rank	State congressional district Representative	Percent under 18 years old [col 15 and 16]
1	TX 15th: Vicente Gonzalez (D)	31.1
1	UT 4th: Ben McAdams (D)	31.1
3	TX 29th: Sylvia R. Garcia (D)	31.0
4	TX 28th: Henry Cuellar (D)	30.7
5	UT 1st: Rob Bishop (R)	30.6
6	TX 33rd: Marc A. Veasey (D)	30.5
7	CA 21st: TJ Cox (D)	30.2
8	TX 34th: Filemon Vela (D)	29.8
8	UT 3rd: John R. Curtis (R)	29.8
10	AZ 7th: Ruben Gallego (D)	29.5
11	CA 22nd: Devin Nunes (R)	29.4
12	CA 16th: Jim Costa (D)	29.2
13	CA 40th: Lucille Roybal-Allard (D)	29.1
14	WA 4th: Dan Newsome (R)	28.7
15	TX 23rd: Will Hurd (R)	28.5
16	CA 42nd: Ken Calvert (R)	28.2
17	UT 2nd: Chris Stewart (R)	27.7
18	CA 44th: Nanette Diaz Barragan (D)	27.6
18	TX 22nd: Pete Olson (R)	27.6
20	TX 30th: Eddie Bernice Johnson (D)	27.5
21	CA 8th: Paul Cook (R)	27.3
21	TX 16th: Veronica Escobar (D)	27.3
23	CA 9th: Jerry McNerney (D)	27.2
23	NY 15th: José E. Serrano (D)	27.2
25	CA 23rd: Kevin McCarthy (R)	27.0
25	GA 7th: Robert Woodall (R)	27.0
27	CA 5th: Lance Gooden (R)	26.8
27	TX 7th: Lizzie Fletcher (D)	26.8
29	ID 2nd: Michael K. Simpson (R)	26.7
30	AZ 3rd: Raul M. Grijalva (D)	26.6
30	CA 10th: Josh Harder (D)	26.6
30	CA 41st: Mark Takano (D)	26.6
30	GA 13th: David Scott (D)	26.6
30	VA 10th: Jennifer Wexton (D)	26.6
35	TX 18th: Sheila Jackson-Lee (D)	26.4
36	AZ 5th: Andy Biggs (R)	26.3
37	CA 25th: Katie Hill (D)	26.2
37	CA 35th: Norma J. Torres (D)	26.2
37	NE 2nd: Don Bacon (R)	26.2
37	TX 6th: Ron Wright (R)	26.2
37	TX 9th: Al Green (D)	26.2
37	TX 31st: John R. Carter (R)	26.2
43	CA 31st: Pete Aguilar (D)	26.1
43	TX 26th: Michael C. Burgess (R)	26.1
45	TX 3rd: Van Taylor (R)	26.0
46	TX 10th: Michael T. McCaul (R)	25.9
47	NV 4th: Steven Horsford (D)	25.8
47	TX 35th: Lloyd Doggett (D)	25.8
49	KS 4th: Ron Estes (R)	25.7
50	CA 51st: Juan Vargas (D)	25.6
50	IN 7th: André Carson (D)	25.6
50	NC 2nd: George Holding (R)	25.6
50	OK 5th: Kendra S. Horn (D)	25.6
54	CO 4th: Ken Buck (R)	25.5
54	GA 4th: Henry C. "Hank" Johnson Jr. (D)	25.5
54	IN 3rd: Jim Banks (R)	25.5
54	KS 3rd: Sharice Davids (D)	25.5
58	IL 11th: Bill Foster (D)	25.4
58	MN 6th: Tom Emmer (R)	25.4
58	TX 11th: K. Michael Conaway (R)	25.4
61	OK 1st: Kevin Hern (R)	25.2
61	TN 9th: Steve Cohen (D)	25.2
61	TX 8th: Kevin Brady (R)	25.2
64	IL 14th: Lauren Underwood (D)	25.1
64	MN 2nd: Angie Craig (D)	25.1
64	NM 2nd: Xochitl Torres Small (D)	25.1
64	TX 19th: Jodey C. Arrington (R)	25.1
64	WA 8th: Kim Schrier (D)	25.1
69	AK At-Large: Don Young (R)	25.0
69	ID 1st: Russ Fulcher (R)	25.0
69	LA 3rd: Clay Higgins (R)	25.0
69	MS 2nd: Bennie G. Thompson (D)	25.0
69	TX 12th: Kay Granger (R)	25.0
69	TX 27th: Michael Cloud (R)	25.0
75	AR 3rd: Steve Womack (R)	24.9

Percent 65 years old and over, 2017

65 years old and over rank	State congressional district Representative	Percent 65 years old and over [col 22 and 23]
1	FL 11th: Daniel Webster (R)	36.3
2	Fl 19th: Francis Rooney (R)	31.6
3	FL 17th: W. Gregory Steube (R)	31.3
4	AZ 4th: Paul A. Gosar (R)	27.6
5	FL 16th: Vern Buchanan (R)	26.7
6	FL 6th: Michael Waltz (R)	25.4
7	FL 18th: Brian J. Mast (R)	25.3
8	FL 21st: Lois Frankel (D)	25.2
9	FL 8th: Bill Posey (R)	24.8
10	FL 12th: Gus M. Bilirakis (R)	24.3
11	FL 13th: Charlie Crist (D)	22.8
12	MI 1st: Jack Bergman (R)	22.7
13	NC 11th: Mark Meadows (R)	22.3
14	AZ 8th: Debbie Lesko (R)	22.0
15	CA 36th: Raul Ruiz (D)	21.9
16	AZ 2nd: Ann Kirkpatrick (D)	21.8
16	MA 9th: William R. Keating (D)	21.8
18	PA 12th: Fred Keller (R)	21.4
19	CA 1st: Doug LaMalfa (R)	20.9
20	CA 4th: Tom McClintock (R)	20.8
21	FL 22nd: Theodore E. Deutch (D)	20.7
22	CA 2nd: Jared Huffman (D)	20.6
22	SC 7th: Tom Rice (R)	20.6
24	NY 3rd: Thomas R. Souzzi (D)	20.4
25	OR 2nd: Greg Walden (R)	20.3
25	OR 4th: Peter A. DeFazio (D)	20.3
25	WV 3rd: Carol D. Miller (R)	20.3
28	ME 2nd: Jared F. Golden (D)	20.2
28	PA 10th: Scott Perry (R)	20.2
30	PA 9th: Daniel Meuser (R)	20.0
30	TN 1st: Phil Roe (R)	20.0
30	VA 9th: Morgan Griffith (R)	20.0
30	WI 7th: Sean P. Duffy (R)	20.0
34	VA 5th: Denver Riggleman (R)	19.9
35	MN 8th: Pete Stauber (R)	19.8
35	OH 16th: Anthony Gonzalez (R)	19.8
35	WA 6th: Derek Kilmer (D)	19.8
38	ME 1st: Chellie Pingree (D)	19.7
38	NY 19th: Antonio Delgado (D)	19.7
38	OH 6th: Bill Johnson (R)	19.7
38	PA 18th: Michael F. Doyle (D)	19.7
42	FL 2nd: Neal P. Dunn (R)	19.5
43	MN 7th: Collin C. Peterson (D)	19.4
43	OH 14th: David P. Joyce (R)	19.4
45	MO 2nd: Ann Wagner (R)	19.2
45	NJ 3rd: Andy Kim (D)	19.2
45	PA 3rd: Dwight Evans (D)	19.2
45	PA 11th: LLloyd Smucker (R)	19.2
49	AR 4th: Bruce Westerman (R)	19.1
49	NE 3rd: Adrian Smith (R)	19.1
51	NC 7th: David Rouzer (R)	18.9
51	WV 1st: David McKinley (R)	18.9
53	FL 25th: Mario Diaz-Balart (R)	18.8
53	NY 27th: Chris Collins (R)	18.8
53	VT 1st: Peter Welch (D)	18.8
53	WV 2nd: Alexander X. Mooney (R)	18.8
57	MI 4th: John L. Moolenar (R)	18.7
57	MO 8th: Jason T. Smith (R)	18.7
57	PA 17th: Conor Lamb (D)	18.7
60	PA 5th: Mary Gay Scanlon (D)	18.6
60	TN 3rd: Chuck Fleischmann (R)	18.6
62	NH 2nd: Ann M. Kuster (D)	18.5
62	NY 22nd: Anthony Brindisi (D)	18.5
62	OK 2nd: Markwayne Mullin (R)	18.5
65	AZ 6th: David Schweikert (R)	18.4
65	CA 48th: Harley Rouda (D)	18.4
65	HI 1st: Ed Case (D)	18.4
65	IL 15th: John Shimkus (R)	18.4
65	IL 17th: Cheri Bustos (D)	18.4
65	MD 1st: Andrew Harris (R)	18.4
65	OH 7th: Bob Gibbs (R)	18.4
72	FL 27th: Donna E. Shalala (D)	18.3
72	IL 18th: Darin LaHood (R)	18.3
72	IA 4th: Steve King (R)	18.3
72	MI 5th: Daniel T. Kildee (D)	18.3

Percent college graduates (bachelor's degree or more), 2017

College graduates rank	State congressional district Representative	Percent college graduates [col 27]
1	NY 12th: Carolyn B. Maloney (D)	74.1
2	CA 18th: Anna G. Eshoo (D)	64.5
3	CA 33rd: Ted Lieu (D)	63.9
4	VA 8th: Donald S. Beyer, Jr. (D)	62.2
5	GA 6th: Lucy McBath (D)	62.0
6	NY 10th: Jerrold Nadler (D)	61.5
7	WA 7th: Pramila Jayapal (D)	60.5
8	CA 12th: Nancy Pelosi (D)	59.6
9	CA 52nd: Scott H. Peters (D)	59.2
10	MA 5th: Katherine Clark (D)	57.6
11	DC At-Large: Eleanor Holmes Norton (D)	57.3
12	VA 11th: Gerald E. Connolly (D)	56.8
13	CA 17th: Ro Khanna (D)	56.4
13	CO 2nd: Joe Neguse (D)	56.4
15	VA 10th: Jennifer Wexton (D)	56.1
16	MD 8th: Jamie Raskin (D)	55.1
17	CA 45th: Katie Porter (D)	55.0
17	IL 5th: Michael Quigley (D)	55.0
19	NC 4th: David E. Price (D)	54.7
20	IL 9th: Janice D. Schakowsky (D)	54.4
21	NJ 11th: Mikie Sherill (R)	54.2
22	TX 3rd: Van Taylor (R)	54.0
23	IL 6th: Sean Casten (D)	53.9
24	NY 3rd: Thomas R. Souzzi (D)	52.6
25	NJ 7th: Tom Malinowski (D)	52.4
26	MA 4th: Joseph P. Kennedy III (D)	52.1
27	MN 3rd: Dean Philips (D)	49.8
28	MO 2nd: Ann Wagner (R)	49.5
29	CT 4th: James A. Himes (D)	49.2
30	CA 14th: Jackie Speier (D)	48.9
30	TX 7th: Lizzie Fletcher (D)	48.9
32	CO 1st: Diana DeGette (D)	48.8
33	MI 11th: Haley M. Stevens (D)	48.4
34	MD 3rd: John P. Sarbanes (D)	48.3
35	CA 13th: Barbara Lee (D)	48.2
35	NJ 5th: Josh Gottheimer (D)	48.2
37	IN 5th: Susan W. Brooks (R)	48.0
38	KS 3rd: Sharice Davids (D)	47.5
39	MA 8th: Stephen F. Lynch (D)	47.2
40	TX 22nd: Pete Olson (R)	47.1
41	MN 5th: Ilhan Omar (D)	47.0
42	TX 21st: Chip Roy (R)	46.6
43	TX 24th: Kenny Marchant (R)	46.3
44	CA 15th: Eric Swalwell (D)	45.9
44	CA 49th: Mike Levin (D)	45.9
44	NY 17th: Nita M. Lowey (D)	45.9
47	PA 7th: Susan Wild (D)	45.5
48	TX 26th: Michael C. Burgess (R)	45.4
49	IL 10th: Bradley Scott Schneider (D)	45.3
50	CA 28th: Adam B. Schiff (D)	45.2
51	Ca 30th: Brad Sherman (D)	45.1
51	CA 48th: Harley Rouda (D)	45.1
51	MA 6th: Seth Moulton (D)	45.1
54	MA 7th: Ayanna Presley (D)	44.9
55	NJ 12th: Bonnie Watson Coleman (D)	44.7
56	AZ 6th: David Schweikert (R)	44.4
57	CA 11th: Mark Desaulnier (D)	44.1
57	PA 6th: Chrissy Houlahan (D)	44.1
59	MN 4th: Betty McCollum (D)	43.5
60	IL 7th: Danny K. Davis (D)	43.3
61	CA 27th: Judy Chu (D)	43.2
61	TX 32nd: Colin Z. Allred (D)	43.2
61	WA 1st: Suzan K. DelBene (D)	43.2
64	CO 6th: Jason Crow (D)	43.1
65	WA 9th: Adam Smith (D)	43.0
66	GA 7th: Robert Woodall (R)	42.6
67	OR 1st: Suzanne Bonamici (D)	42.4
68	CA 2nd: Jared Huffman (D)	42.3
68	WI 2nd: Mark Pocan (D)	42.3
70	UT 3rd: John R. Curtis (R)	42.2
71	MD 6th: David J. Trone (D)	42.1
72	NJ 4th: Christopher H. Smith (R)	41.9
73	NY 4th: Kathleen M. Rice (D)	41.8
74	CA 39th: Gilbert Ray Cisneros, Jr. (D)	41.7
74	NJ 6th: Frank Pallone Jr. (D)	41.7

Congressional Districts of the 116th Congress of the United States
Selected Rankings

Median value of owner-occupied housing units, 2017			Percent female-headed family households, 2017			Percent of households with one person, 2017		
Median value rank	State congressional district Representative	Median value (dollars) [col 43]	Female householder rank	State congressional district Representative	Percent with female householder [col 32]	One-person household rank	State congressional district Representative	Percent one-person households [col 33]
1	CA 18th: Anna G. Eshoo (D)	1,337,300	1	NY 15th: José E. Serrano (D)	35.2	1	PA 2nd: Brendan F. Boyle (D)	47.8
2	CA 33rd: Ted Lieu (D)	1,191,600	2	NY 13th: Adriano Espaillat (D)	25.9	2	NY 12th: Carolyn B. Maloney (D)	47.2
3	CA 12th: Nancy Pelosi (D)	1,120,600	3	CA 44th: Nanette Diaz Barragan (D)	23.9	3	DC: At-Large: Eleanor Holmes Norton (D)	45.2
4	NY 12th: Carolyn B. Maloney (D)	1,004,600	4	IL 2nd: Robin L. Kelly (D)	23.7	4	IL 7th: Danny K. Davis (D)	42.4
5	NY 10th: Jerrold Nadler (D)	1,003,300	5	CA 40th: Lucille Roybal-Allard (D)	23.3	5	PA 14th: Guy Reschenthaler (R)	41.7
6	CA 14th: Jackie Speier (D)	996,800	6	MS 2nd: Bennie G. Thompson (D)	23.1	6	OH 11th: Marcia L. Fudge (D)	41.5
7	CA 17th: Ro Khanna (D)	964,500	7	NY 5th: Gregory W. Meeks (D)	22.8	7	NY 10th: Jerrold Nadler (D)	40.2
8	CA 28th: Adam B. Schiff (D)	827,900	8	NY 8th: Hakeem S. Jeffries (D)	22.7	8	GA 5th: John Lewis (D)	40.1
9	CA 15th: Eric Swalwell (D)	797,600	8	TN 9th: Steve Cohen (D)	22.7	9	MN 5th: Ilhan Omar (D)	38.1
10	CA 19th: Zoe Lofgren (D)	792,000	10	FL 24th: Frederica S. Wilson (D)	22.6	10	CA 37th: Karen Bass (D)	37.9
11	CA 48th: Harley Rouda (D)	759,800	11	LA 2nd: Cedric Richmond (D)	22.3	10	MI 13th: Rashida Tlaib (D)	37.9
12	CA 13th: Barbara Lee (D)	747,900	12	AL 7th: Terri A. Sewell (D)	22.1	10	PA 1st: Brian K. Fitzpatrick (R)	37.9
13	NY 7th: Nydia M. Velázquez (D)	733,200	13	GA 13th: David Scott (D)	22.0	13	CA 12th: Nancy Pelosi (D)	37.8
14	CA 37th: Karen Bass (D)	730,800	14	MI 13th: Rashida Tlaib (D)	21.9	14	MO 1st: William Lacy Clay (D)	37.6
15	CA 52nd: Scott H. Peters (D)	719,900	15	CA 52nd: Sanford D. Bishop Jr. (D)	21.4	15	WA 7th: Pramila Jayapal (D)	37.4
16	CA 45th: Katie Porter (D)	719,700	16	AZ 7th: Ruben Gallego (D)	21.3	16	TN 9th: Steve Cohen (D)	37.3
17	CA 49th: Mike Levin (D)	701,500	17	NJ 10th: Donald M. Payne, Jr. (D)	21.0	17	LA 2nd: Cedric Richmond (D)	37.2
18	CA 27th: Judy Chu (D)	699,800	18	IL 1st: Bobby L. Rush (D)	20.6	18	IN 7th: André Carson (D)	36.9
19	CA 11th: Mark Desaulnier (D)	692,200	19	CA 51st: Juan Vargas (D)	20.5	19	FL 13th: Charlie Crist (D)	36.5
20	Ca 30th: Brad Sherman (D)	691,400	20	OH 11th: Marcia L. Fudge (D)	20.4	19	WI 4th: Gwen Moore (D)	36.5
21	HI 1st: Ed Case (D)	668,900	21	GA 4th: Henry C. "Hank" Johnson Jr. (D)	20.3	21	CA 28th: Adam B. Schiff (D)	36.3
22	CA 39th: Gilbert Ray Cisneros, Jr. (D)	659,100	21	TX 29th: Sylvia R. Garcia (D)	20.3	21	MO 5th: Emanuel Cleaver (D)	36.3
23	NY 9th: Yvette D. Clarke (D)	652,200	21	TX 30th: Eddie Bernice Johnson (D)	20.3	23	FL 22nd: Theodore E. Deutch (D)	36.1
24	CA 2nd: Jared Huffman (D)	649,500	24	TX 9th: Al Green (D)	20.0	24	IL 9th: Janice D. Schakowsky (D)	35.9
25	WA 7th: Pramila Jayapal (D)	644,100	25	FL 5th: Al Lawson (D)	19.9	24	NY 26th: Brian Higgins (D)	35.9
26	NY 3rd: Thomas R. Souzzi (D)	619,200	25	TX 28th: Henry Cuellar (D)	19.9	26	AL 7th: Terri A. Sewell (D)	35.8
27	CA 34th: Jimmy Gomez (D)	612,600	27	FL 20th: Alcee L. Hastings (D)	19.7	27	CO 1st: Diana DeGette (D)	35.6
28	CA 20th: Jimmy Panetta (D)	608,700	27	TX 18th: Sheila Jackson-Lee (D)	19.7	28	SC 6th: James E. Clyburn (D)	35.5
29	NY 6th: Grace Meng (D)	608,400	29	SC 6th: James E. Clyburn (D)	19.6	29	AZ 9th: Greg Stanton (D)	35.4
30	DC: At-Large: Eleanor Holmes Norton (D)	607,200	29	TX 16th: Veronica Escobar (D)	19.6	30	MI 14th: Brenda L. Lawrence (D)	35.2
31	NY 8th: Hakeem S. Jeffries (D)	599,700	31	CA 16th: Jim Costa (D)	19.5	31	NM 1st: Debra A. Haaland (D)	35.1
32	CA 47th: Alan S. Lowenthal (D)	596,600	32	MI 14th: Brenda L. Lawrence (D)	19.4	32	IL 1st: Bobby L. Rush (D)	35.0
33	CA 26th: Julia Brownley (D)	591,700	32	TX 33rd: Marc A. Veasey (D)	19.4	32	OH 9th: Marcy Kaptur (D)	35.0
34	CA 24th: Salud O. Carbajal (D)	572,300	34	MO 1st: William Lacy Clay (D)	19.2	34	IL 5th: Michael Quigley (D)	34.6
35	VA 8th: Donald S. Beyer, Jr. (D)	572,200	34	TX 34th: Filemon Vela (D)	19.2	34	NY 13th: Adriano Espaillat (D)	34.6
36	HI 2nd: Tulsi Gabbard (D)	566,800	36	CA 21st: TJ Cox (D)	19.1	36	OH 13th: Tim Ryan (D)	34.5
37	MA 5th: Katherine Clark (D)	564,400	37	FL 26th: Debbie Murcasel-Powell (D)	18.9	37	CA 33rd: Ted Lieu (D)	34.4
38	CA 43rd: Maxine Waters (D)	562,300	37	TX 15th: Vicente Gonzalez (D)	18.9	38	CA 36th: Raul Ruiz (D)	34.3
39	NY 11th: Max Rose (D)	551,100	37	WI 4th: Gwen Moore (D)	18.9	39	MA 7th: Ayanna Presley (D)	34.2
40	NY 13th: Adriano Espaillat (D)	543,000	40	VA 3rd: Robert C. "Bobby" Scott (D)	18.8	40	IL 13th: Rodney Davis (R)	34.1
41	CA 46th: J. Luis Correa (D)	528,700	41	CA 35th: Norma J. Torres (D)	18.7	41	OH 3rd: Joyce Beatty (D)	34.0
42	CA 5th: Mike Thompson (D)	528,600	41	CA 43rd: Maxine Waters (D)	18.7	42	IL 2nd: Robin L. Kelly (D)	33.7
43	CA 53rd: Susan A. Davis (D)	523,300	41	MD 7th: Elijah E. Cummings (D)	18.7	42	MD 7th: Elijah E. Cummings (D)	33.7
44	NY 14th: Alexandria Ocasio Cortez (D)	512,100	44	PA 1st: Brian K. Fitzpatrick (R)	18.6	42	VA 8th: Donald S. Beyer, Jr. (D)	33.7
45	CT 4th: James A. Himes (D)	507,700	45	GA 5th: John Lewis (D)	18.5	45	NC 12th: Alma S. Adams (D)	33.6
46	CA 38th: Linda T. Sánchez (D)	503,800	46	NY 9th: Yvette D. Clarke (D)	18.4	46	NY 20th: Paul Tonko (D)	33.5
47	MA 7th: Ayanna Presley (D)	496,300	47	MD 4th: Anthony G. Brown (D)	18.3	46	RI 1st: David Cicilline (D)	33.5
48	VA 10th: Jennifer Wexton (D)	493,100	48	CA 31st: Pete Aguilar (D)	18.2	48	KY 3rd: John A. Yarmuth (D)	33.2
49	CA 29th: Tony Cárdenas (D)	489,000	48	OH 3rd: Joyce Beatty (D)	18.2	48	MI 9th: Sander M. Levin (D)	33.2
50	CA 50th: Duncan Hunter (R)	486,600	50	AZ 3rd: Raul M. Grijalva (D)	18.1	48	MS 2nd: Bennie G. Thompson (D)	33.2
51	WA 1st: Suzan K. DelBene (D)	478,900	51	CA 41st: Mark Takano (D)	18.0	51	IL 17th: Cheri Bustos (D)	33.1
52	CA 32nd: Grace F. Napolitano (D)	478,700	51	LA 5th: Ralph Lee Abraham (R)	18.0	52	NV 1st: Dina Titus (D)	33.0
53	VA 11th: Gerald E. Connolly (D)	474,300	51	NY 16th: Eliot L. Engel (D)	18.0	53	AZ 2nd: Ann Kirkpatrick (D)	32.9
54	NY 17th: Nita M. Lowey (D)	473,700	54	NC 1st: G. K. Butterfield (D)	17.6	53	FL 14th: Kathy Castor (D)	32.9
55	NY 4th: Kathleen M. Rice (D)	472,100	55	PA 2nd: Brendan F. Boyle (D)	17.5	55	LA 4th: Mike Johnson (R)	32.6
56	NY 16th: Eliot L. Engel (D)	463,900	56	CA 32nd: Grace F. Napolitano (D)	17.2	55	NY 9th: Yvette D. Clarke (D)	32.6
57	CA 25th: Katie Hill (D)	461,800	57	MD 2nd: C. A. Dutch Ruppersberger (D)	17.0	57	GA 2nd: Sanford D. Bishop Jr. (D)	32.4
58	NY 5th: Gregory W. Meeks (D)	460,300	57	NV 1st: Dina Titus (D)	17.0	57	OH 10th: Michael R. Turner (R)	32.4
59	WA 9th: Adam Smith (D)	458,200	59	FL 10th: Val Butler Demings (D)	16.9	59	NY 8th: Hakeem S. Jeffries (D)	32.2
60	NJ 7th: Tom Malinowski (D)	449,600	59	IL 7th: Danny K. Davis (D)	16.9	60	MI 5th: Daniel T. Kildee (D)	32.0
61	NJ 11th: Mikie Sherill (R)	448,300	59	NJ 8th: Albio Sires (D)	16.9	60	NY 25th: Joseph D. Morelle (D)	32.0
62	MA 6th: Seth Moulton (D)	446,700	62	CA 38th: Linda T. Sánchez (D)	16.8	60	TN 3rd: Chuck Fleischmann (R)	32.0
63	MD 8th: Jamie Raskin (D)	444,000	62	TX 20th: Joaquin Castro (D)	16.8	60	TN 5th: Jim Cooper (D)	32.0
64	CA 40th: Lucille Roybal-Allard (D)	438,800	64	CA 46th: J. Luis Correa (D)	16.6	64	NY 22nd: Anthony Brindisi (D)	31.9
65	MA 8th: Stephen F. Lynch (D)	437,400	64	NJ 9th: Bill Pascrell, Jr. (D)	16.6	65	FL 21st: Lois Frankel (D)	31.8
66	CO 2nd: Joe Neguse (D)	436,300	66	NY 7th: Nydia M. Velázquez (D)	16.5	66	IL 12th: Mike Bost (R)	31.7
67	MA 4th: Joseph P. Kennedy III (D)	431,500	67	FL 25th: Mario Diaz-Balart (D)	16.4	66	ND At-Large: Kelly Armstrong (R)	31.7
68	CA 42nd: Ken Calvert (R)	430,800	67	NY 14th: Alexandria Ocasio Cortez (D)	16.4	66	OH 1st: Steve Chabot (R)	31.7
69	NJ 5th: Josh Gottheimer (D)	429,100	69	OH 9th: Marcy Kaptur (D)	16.3	69	CT 1st: John B. Larson (D)	31.6
70	CA 4th: Tom McClintock (R)	424,900	69	TX 35th: Lloyd Doggett (D)	16.3	69	TX 21st: Chip Roy (R)	31.6
71	CA 44th: Nanette Diaz Barragan (D)	410,200	71	MA 7th: Ayanna Presley (D)	16.1	71	SD At-Large: Dusty Johnson (R)	31.5
72	FL 27th: Donna E. Shalala (D)	395,000	71	TX 23rd: Will Hurd (D)	16.1	72	FL 8th: Bill Posey (R)	31.4
73	CO 1st: Diana DeGette (D)	394,400	71	VA 4th: A. Donald McEachin (D)	16.1	72	NM 3rd: Ben Ray Luján (D)	31.4
74	GA 6th: Lucy McBath (D)	386,800	74	SC 7th: Tom Rice (R)	15.9	74	NC 1st: G. K. Butterfield (D)	31.3
75	OR 3rd: Earl Blumenauer (D)	386,600	75	IN 7th: André Carson (D)	15.8	74	PA 13th: John Joyce (R)	31.3

Congressional Districts of the 116th Congress of the United States
Selected Rankings

Median household income, 2017

Median income rank	State congressional district Representative	Median income (dollars) [col 47]
1	CA 18th: Anna G. Eshoo (D)	134,077
2	CA 17th: Ro Khanna (D)	124,131
3	VA 10th: Jennifer Wexton (D)	122,092
4	CA 15th: Eric Swalwell (D)	116,710
5	NJ 7th: Tom Malinowski (D)	113,993
6	NJ 11th: Mikie Sherill (R)	112,348
7	CA 12th: Nancy Pelosi (D)	111,717
8	CA 14th: Jackie Speier (D)	110,507
9	NY 3rd: Thomas R. Souzzi (D)	107,412
10	NY 12th: Carolyn B. Maloney (D)	107,010
11	VA 11th: Gerald E. Connolly (D)	106,527
12	CA 33rd: Ted Lieu (D)	105,200
13	VA 8th: Donald S. Beyer, Jr. (D)	104,149
14	NY 4th: Kathleen M. Rice (D)	102,205
15	CA 45th: Katie Porter (D)	102,040
16	CA 19th: Zoe Lofgren (D)	101,427
17	MD 8th: Jamie Raskin (D)	100,953
18	MA 4th: Joseph P. Kennedy III (D)	100,742
19	NJ 5th: Josh Gottheimer (D)	100,607
20	IL 6th: Sean Casten (D)	98,889
21	MA 5th: Katherine Clark (D)	98,775
22	NY 2nd: Peter T. King (R)	97,387
23	MD 5th: Steny H. Hoyer (D)	96,325
24	NY 17th: Nita M. Lowey (D)	96,125
25	CA 52nd: Scott H. Peters (D)	95,770
26	TX 3rd: Van Taylor (R)	95,235
27	WA 1st: Suzan K. DelBene (D)	94,638
28	CT 4th: James A. Himes (D)	94,547
29	TX 22nd: Pete Olson (R)	94,048
30	NY 10th: Jerrold Nadler (D)	93,629
31	IL 14th: Lauren Underwood (D)	92,461
32	GA 6th: Lucy McBath (D)	92,317
33	NY 1st: Lee M. Zeldin (R)	92,284
34	TX 26th: Michael C. Burgess (R)	91,650
35	PA 7th: Susan Wild (D)	90,546
36	MA 8th: Stephen F. Lynch (D)	90,323
37	CA 11th: Mark Desaulnier (D)	90,155
38	CA 48th: Harley Rouda (D)	89,807
39	MN 3rd: Dean Philips (D)	89,442
40	CA 39th: Gilbert Ray Cisneros, Jr. (D)	89,300
41	CA 49th: Mike Levin (D)	88,314
42	VA 1st: Robert J. Wittman (R)	88,044
43	MD 3rd: John P. Sarbanes (D)	87,732
44	WA 7th: Pramila Jayapal (D)	86,452
45	NJ 4th: Christopher H. Smith (R)	86,365
46	NY 18th: Sean Patrick Maloney (D)	86,211
47	MA 6th: Seth Moulton (D)	85,951
48	NJ 12th: Bonnie Watson Coleman (D)	85,595
49	PA 8th: Matt Cartwright (D)	84,772
50	CA 42nd: Ken Calvert (R)	83,837
51	WA 8th: Kim Schrier (D)	83,495
52	MI 11th: Haley M. Stevens (D)	82,545
53	NJ 6th: Frank Pallone Jr. (D)	82,451
54	DC: At-Large: Eleanor Holmes Norton (D)	82,372
55	NJ 3rd: Andy Kim (D)	82,301
56	IL 5th: Michael Quigley (D)	82,210
57	PA 6th: Chrissy Houlahan (D)	82,203
58	CA 26th: Julia Brownley (D)	82,029
59	MN 2nd: Angie Craig (D)	81,885
60	Ca 30th: Brad Sherman (D)	81,276
61	MD 4th: Anthony G. Brown (D)	81,151
62	CO 6th: Jason Crow (D)	80,606
63	WA 9th: Adam Smith (D)	80,283
64	IL 10th: Bradley Scott Schneider (D)	80,229
65	HI 1st: Ed Case (D)	80,083
66	CO 2nd: Joe Neguse (D)	80,019
67	MN 6th: Tom Emmer (R)	79,826
68	MO 2nd: Ann Wagner (R)	79,497
69	MD 6th: David J. Trone (D)	79,247
70	CA 5th: Mike Thompson (D)	78,152
71	CA 27th: Judy Chu (D)	77,629
72	VA 7th: Abigail Davis Spanberger (D)	77,533
73	TX 2nd: Dan Crenshaw (D)	77,519
74	CA 50th: Duncan Hunter (R)	77,155
75	CA 13th: Barbara Lee (D)	76,915

Percent of persons below 65 years with no health insurance, 2017

No health insurance rank	State congressional district Representative	Percent with no health insurance [col 59]
1	TX 33rd: Marc A. Veasey (D)	33.5
2	TX 29th: Sylvia R. Garcia (D)	32.6
3	TX 34th: Filemon Vela (D)	29.6
4	TX 15th: Vicente Gonzalez (D)	28.4
5	TX 28th: Henry Cuellar (D)	27.9
6	TX 9th: Al Green (D)	25.8
6	TX 18th: Sheila Jackson-Lee (D)	25.8
8	FL 24th: Frederica S. Wilson (D)	24.6
9	FL 25th: Mario Diaz-Balart (R)	22.9
10	OK 2nd: Markwayne Mullin (R)	22.7
11	TX 5th: Lance Gooden (R)	22.6
12	TX 30th: Eddie Bernice Johnson (D)	21.6
13	TX 11th: K. Michael Conaway (R)	21.4
13	TX 23rd: Will Hurd (R)	21.4
15	TX 16th: Veronica Escobar (D)	21.1
15	TX 36th: Brian Babin (R)	21.1
17	TX 1st: Louie Gohmert (R)	20.9
18	TX 27th: Michael Cloud (R)	20.8
19	NV 1st: Dina Titus (D)	20.5
20	TX 13th: Mac Thornberry (R)	20.2
21	FL 26th: Debbie Murcasel-Powell (D)	20.1
22	FL 21st: Lois Frankel (D)	19.3
22	TX 35th: Lloyd Doggett (D)	19.3
24	TX 32nd: Colin Z. Allred (D)	19.1
25	AZ 7th: Ruben Gallego (D)	19.0
26	FL 20th: Alcee L. Hastings (D)	18.8
27	TX 20th: Joaquin Castro (D)	18.5
28	GA 7th: Robert Woodall (R)	18.5
29	TX 19th: Jodey C. Arrington (R)	18.4
30	GA 9th: Doug Collins (R)	18.3
31	CA 34th: Jimmy Gomez (D)	18.1
32	FI 19th: Francis Rooney (R)	18.0
33	IL 4th: Jesus G. "Chuy" Garcia (D)	17.8
34	TX 4th: John Ratcliffe (R)	17.7
35	FL 10th: Val Butler Demings (D)	17.6
36	TX 14th: Randy K. Weber Sr. (R)	17.4
37	GA 14th: Tom Graves (R)	17.2
38	TX 6th: Ron Wright (R)	17.1
39	GA 4th: Henry C. "Hank" Johnson Jr. (D)	17.0
40	TX 12th: Kay Granger (R)	16.9
41	FL 17th: W. Gregory Steube (R)	16.8
42	FL 22nd: Theodore E. Deutch (D)	16.7
42	TX 7th: Lizzie Fletcher (D)	16.7
42	TX 8th: Kevin Brady (R)	16.7
45	GA 2nd: Sanford D. Bishop Jr. (D)	16.6
45	TX 2nd: Dan Crenshaw (R)	16.6
47	GA 1st: Earl L. "Buddy" Carter (R)	16.5
47	GA 8th: Austin Scott (R)	16.5
49	MS 2nd: Bennie G. Thompson (D)	16.3
49	NJ 8th: Albio Sires (D)	16.3
51	FL 9th: Darren Soto (D)	16.2
52	OK 5th: Kendra S. Horn (D)	16.1
52	SC 6th: James E. Clyburn (D)	16.1
54	GA 12th: Rick W. Allen (R)	15.8
55	SC 7th: Tom Rice (R)	15.7
56	FL 27th: Donna E. Shalala (D)	15.6
56	OK 3rd: Frank D. Lucas (R)	15.6
58	NC 11th: Mark Meadows (R)	15.5
58	TX 24th: Kenny Marchant (R)	15.5
60	CA 46th: J. Luis Correa (D)	15.4
60	FL 13th: Charlie Crist (D)	15.4
62	AK At-Large: Don Young (R)	15.3
62	FL 11th: Daniel Webster (R)	15.3
62	MS 4th: Steven Palazzo (R)	15.3
65	OK 1st: Kevin Hern (R)	15.2
66	FL 16th: Vern Buchanan (R)	15.1
67	FL 6th: Michael Waltz (R)	15.0
67	NC 7th: David Rouzer (R)	15.0
69	GA 13th: David Scott (D)	14.9
69	NJ 9th: Bill Pascrell, Jr. (D)	14.9
69	TX 10th: Michael T. McCaul (R)	14.9
72	FL 14th: Kathy Castor (D)	14.8
72	TX 17th: Bill Flores (R)	14.8
74	FL 18th: Brian J. Mast (R)	14.6
74	GA 5th: John Lewis (D)	14.6

Percent of persons below the poverty level, 2017

Poverty rate rank	State congressional district Representative	Poverty rate [col 49]
1	NY 15th: José E. Serrano (D)	36.2
2	MI 13th: Rashida Tlaib (D)	29.6
3	KY 5th: Harold Rogers (R)	29.1
4	TX 34th: Filemon Vela (D)	27.8
5	LA 2nd: Cedric Richmond (D)	27.1
6	CA 16th: Jim Costa (D)	26.7
7	MS 2nd: Bennie G. Thompson (D)	26.2
8	PA 2nd: Brendan F. Boyle (D)	26.0
9	TX 15th: Vicente Gonzalez (D)	25.7
10	OH 11th: Marcia L. Fudge (D)	25.6
11	NY 13th: Adriano Espaillat (D)	25.4
12	LA 5th: Ralph Lee Abraham (R)	25.1
13	GA 2nd: Sanford D. Bishop Jr. (D)	25.0
14	CA 21st: TJ Cox (D)	24.7
15	AL 7th: Terri A. Sewell (D)	24.6
16	AZ 7th: Ruben Gallego (D)	24.2
17	TX 29th: Sylvia R. Garcia (D)	24.1
18	TN 9th: Steve Cohen (D)	24.0
19	PA 1st: Brian K. Fitzpatrick (R)	23.9
20	SC 6th: James E. Clyburn (D)	23.8
21	TX 28th: Henry Cuellar (D)	23.6
22	WV 3rd: Carol D. Miller (R)	23.3
23	LA 4th: Mike Johnson (R)	23.2
24	NY 7th: Nydia M. Velázquez (D)	23.0
25	CA 40th: Lucille Roybal-Allard (D)	22.6
26	WI 4th: Gwen Moore (D)	22.5
27	TX 18th: Sheila Jackson-Lee (D)	22.4
28	CA 34th: Jimmy Gomez (D)	22.1
29	FL 5th: Al Lawson (D)	22.0
30	OH 3rd: Joyce Beatty (D)	21.9
31	NM 3rd: Ben Ray Luján (D)	21.8
32	NM 2nd: Xochitl Torres Small (D)	21.6
33	IL 7th: Danny K. Davis (D)	21.2
33	TX 33rd: Marc A. Veasey (D)	21.2
35	NY 8th: Hakeem S. Jeffries (D)	21.1
35	NC 1st: G. K. Butterfield (D)	21.1
37	MI 14th: Brenda L. Lawrence (D)	20.9
38	FL 24th: Frederica S. Wilson (D)	20.5
39	TX 16th: Veronica Escobar (D)	20.3
40	MO 8th: Jason T. Smith (R)	20.1
41	AZ 3rd: Raul M. Grijalva (D)	20.0
42	CA 51st: Juan Vargas (D)	19.9
42	OH 9th: Marcy Kaptur (D)	19.9
44	GA 8th: Austin Scott (R)	19.7
44	GA 12th: Rick W. Allen (R)	19.7
44	IN 7th: André Carson (D)	19.7
47	MS 3rd: Michael Guest (R)	19.6
47	OK 2nd: Markwayne Mullin (R)	19.6
49	AR 4th: Bruce Westerman (R)	19.5
49	TX 35th: Lloyd Doggett (D)	19.5
51	TX 30th: Eddie Bernice Johnson (D)	19.3
52	AZ 1st: Tom O'Halleran (D)	19.2
52	GA 5th: John Lewis (D)	19.2
52	SC 7th: Tom Rice (R)	19.2
55	IL 13th: Rodney Davis (R)	18.9
56	NV 1st: Dina Titus (D)	18.8
57	IL 2nd: Robin L. Kelly (D)	18.7
57	MA 7th: Ayanna Presley (D)	18.7
57	NY 26th: Brian Higgins (D)	18.7
57	VA 9th: Morgan Griffith (R)	18.7
61	AR 1st: Eric A. "Rick" Crawford (R)	18.6
61	CA 44th: Nanette Diaz Barragan (D)	18.6
61	MI 5th: Daniel T. Kildee (D)	18.6
64	CA 37th: Karen Bass (D)	18.5
65	TX 1st: Louie Gohmert (R)	18.3
65	TX 17th: Bill Flores (R)	18.3
67	CA 8th: Paul Cook (R)	18.2
67	FL 3rd: Ted S. Yoho (R)	18.2
67	IL 12th: Mike Bost (R)	18.2
70	AL 2nd: Martha Roby (R)	18.0
70	KY 1st: James Comer (R)	18.0
70	MS 4th: Steven Palazzo (R)	18.0
73	CA 6th: Doris O. Matsui (D)	17.9
73	CA 36th: Raul Ruiz (D)	17.9
75	AL 3rd: Mike Rogers (R)	17.8

Table E. Congressional Districts 116th Congress — **Land Area and Population Characteristics**

STATE District	Representative, 116th Congress	Land area,1 2018 (sq mi)	Total persons	Per square mile	Race alone (percent)							Hispanic or Latino[2] (percent)	Non-Hispanic White alone (percent)	Percent female	Percent foreign-born	Percent born in state of residence
					White	Black	Ameri-can Indian, Alaska Native	Asian and Pacific Islander	Some other race (percent)	Two or more races (percent)						
		1	2	3	4	5	6	7	8	9	10	11	12	13	14

1. Dry land or land partially or temporarily covered by water.   2. May be of any race.

Table E. Congressional Districts 116th Congress — **Age and Education**

STATE District	Population and population characteristics, 2017 (cont.)										Education, 2017		
	Age (percent)										Total Enrollment[1]	Attainment[2] (percent)	
	Under 5 years	5 to 17 years	18 to 24 years	25 to 34 years	35 to 44 years	45 to 54 years	55 to 64 years	65 to 74 years	75 years and over	Median age		High school graduate or more	Bachelor's degree or more
	15	16	17	18	19	20	21	22	23	24	25	26	27

1. All persons 3 years old and over enrolled in nursery school through college and graduate or professional school.   2. Persons 25 years old and over.

Table E. Congressional Districts 116th Congress — **Households and Group Quarters**

STATE District	Households, 2017						Total in group quarters, 2017	Group Quarters, 2010				
	Number	Average household size	Family households (percent)	Married couple family (percent)	Female family house-holder[1]	One person households (percent)		Percent 65 years and over	Persons in correctional institutions	Persons in nursing facilities	Persons in college dormitories	Persons in military quarters
	28	29	30	31	32	33	34	35	36	37	38	39

1. No spouse present.

Table E. Congressional Districts 116th Congress — **Housing and Money Income**

STATE District	Housing units, 2017						Money income, 2017		
	Total	Occupied units					Per capita income (dollars)	Households	
		Occupied units as a percent of all units	Owner-occupied			Renter-occupied		Median income (dollars)	Percent with income of $100,000 or more
			Owner-occupied units as a percent of occupied units	Median value[1] (dollars)	Percent valued at $500,000 or more	Median rent[2]			
	40	41	42	43	44	45	46	47	48

1. Specified owner-occupied units.   2. Specified renter-occupied units.

Table E. Congressional Districts 116th Congress — **Poverty, Labor Force, Employment, and Social Security**

STATE District	Poverty, 2017			Civilian labor force, 2016			Civilian employment,[2] 2017				Persons under 65 years of age with no health insur- ance, 2017 (percent)	Social Security beneficiaries, December 2018		Supple- mental Security Income recipients, December 2018
					Unemployment			Percent						
	Persons below poverty level (percent)	Families below poverty level (percent)	Percent of households receiv- ing food stamps in past 12 months	Total	Total	Rate[1]	Total	Manage- ment, business, science, and arts occupa- tions	Service, sales, and office	Construc- tion and production		Number	Rate[3]	
	49	50	51	52	53	54	55	56	57	58	59	60	61	62

1. Percent of civilian labor force. 2. Persons 16 years old and over. 3. Per 1,000 resident population estimated in the 2017 American Community Survey.

Table E. Congressional Districts 116th Congress — **Agriculture**

STATE District	Agriculture 2017									
		Land in farms			Value of products sold				Government payments	
	Number of farms	Acres	Average size of farm (acres)	Harvested cropland (acres)	Total ($1,000)	Average per farm (dollars)	Percent from crops	Percent from livestock and poultry products	Total ($1,000)	Average per farm receiving payments (dollars)
	63	64	65	66	67	68	69	70	71	72

Table E. Congressional Districts 116th Congress — **Nonfarm Employment and Payroll**

STATE District	Private nonfarm employment and payroll, 2016												Annual payroll	
		Employment												
			Percent by selected industries											
	Number of establishments	Total	Manufac- turing	Construc- tion	Wholesale trade	Retail trade	Health care and social assistance	Finance and Insurance	Real estate and rental and leasing	Profes- sional, sci- entific, and technical services	Information		Total (mil dol)	Average per employee (dollars)
	73	74	75	76	77	78	79	80	81	82	83		84	85

Table E. Congressional Districts 116th Congress — **Land Area and Population Characteristics**

STATE District	Representative, 116th Congress	Land area,1 2018 (sq mi)	Population and population characteristics, 2017: Total persons	Per square mile	Race alone (percent): White	Black	American Indian, Alaska Native	Asian and Pacific Islander	Some other race (percent)	Two or more races (percent)	Hispanic or Latino[2] (percent)	Non-Hispanic White alone (percent)	Percent female	Percent foreign-born	Percent born in state of residence
		1	2	3	4	5	6	7	8	9	10	11	12	13	14
UNITED STATES....		3,532,614.3	325,719,178	92.2	72.3	12.7	0.8	5.8	5.1	3.3	18.1	60.6	50.8	13.7	58.2
ALABAMA..............		50,646.7	4,874,747	96.2	68.0	26.8	0.5	1.4	1.4	1.9	4.1	65.5	51.6	3.5	69.9
District 1.................	Bradley Byrne (R).................	6,066.9	713,410	117.6	67.3	27.9	0.9	1.5	1.0	1.4	3.1	65.0	51.8	3.5	68.7
District 2.................	Martha Roby (R)...................	10,142.7	673,776	66.4	64.6	30.7	0.4	1.2	0.8	2.4	3.6	62.0	51.2	2.6	70.4
District 3.................	Mike Rogers (R)....................	7,544.0	710,488	94.2	68.7	26.3	0.2	1.7	1.2	2.0	2.9	67.2	51.2	2.9	65.2
District 4.................	Robert B. Aderholt (R)...........	8,889.0	685,553	77.1	86.7	7.2	1.0	0.6	2.5	2.1	6.7	83.0	51.4	3.9	74.0
District 5.................	Mo Brooks (R).......................	3,678.1	718,713	195.4	75.8	18.0	0.7	1.9	1.5	2.2	5.2	72.2	50.8	4.3	61.9
District 6.................	Gary J. Palmer (R)................	4,171.0	700,401	167.9	78.3	15.9	0.2	1.9	1.7	2.0	4.5	75.9	52.3	4.4	69.9
District 7.................	Terri A. Sewell (D)................	10,155.1	672,406	66.2	33.1	63.1	0.2	1.0	1.1	1.4	3.0	31.7	52.3	2.7	80.1
ALASKA..................		570,886.1	739,795	1.3	64.2	3.0	14.9	7.9	1.5	8.6	7.0	60.6	47.9	7.9	42.5
At Large..................	Don Young (R)......................	570,886.1	739,795	1.3	64.2	3.0	14.9	7.9	1.5	8.6	7.0	60.6	47.9	7.9	42.5
ARIZONA...............		113,590.7	7,016,270	61.8	77.6	4.4	4.5	3.5	6.2	3.8	31.4	54.7	50.3	13.2	39.7
District 1.................	Tom O'Halleran (D)...............	55,037.3	765,810	13.9	66.5	2.3	22.7	2.1	2.6	3.8	23.6	47.9	49.5	6.2	51.9
District 2.................	Ann Kirkpatrick (D)................	7,837.3	720,429	91.9	81.6	4.0	1.6	3.5	5.1	4.1	28.9	60.5	50.5	10.3	37.0
District 3.................	Raul M. Grijalva (D)..............	15,688.4	773,297	49.3	70.0	4.3	5.4	2.2	13.5	4.7	63.0	25.7	50.0	20.6	48.5
District 4.................	Paul A. Gosar (R)..................	33,200.0	771,214	23.2	88.6	1.7	1.8	1.6	3.3	3.1	19.2	74.0	49.6	8.4	28.7
District 5.................	Andy Biggs (R)......................	293.4	822,497	2,802.9	84.5	3.1	1.0	4.6	3.2	3.7	18.3	70.6	51.2	9.3	36.6
District 6.................	David Schweikert (R)............	625.0	783,087	1,252.9	85.0	2.6	1.9	5.4	2.0	3.1	16.6	71.7	51.0	13.8	32.0
District 7.................	Ruben Gallego (D)................	204.9	833,654	4,069.3	66.4	10.4	3.0	2.8	12.6	4.7	64.3	18.4	49.9	25.1	49.8
District 8.................	Debbie Lesko (R)..................	539.8	777,208	1,439.8	82.6	4.2	1.2	4.3	4.4	3.2	19.4	69.3	52.0	9.9	33.6
District 9.................	Greg Stanton (D)....................	164.6	769,074	4,673.2	73.4	6.4	2.6	5.3	8.4	3.7	27.4	56.0	48.8	14.2	38.4
ARKANSAS		52,034.3	3,004,279	57.7	76.3	15.3	0.6	1.9	3.1	2.8	7.4	72.3	50.7	4.7	60.6
District 1.................	Eric A. "Rick" Crawford (R).....	19,318.8	722,287	37.4	77.3	17.1	0.4	0.7	1.1	3.4	3.2	75.5	50.2	1.8	66.3
District 2.................	J. French Hill (R)....................	4,979.0	765,193	153.7	70.6	22.9	0.2	1.7	1.9	2.6	5.3	67.6	51.4	4.3	64.8
District 3.................	Steve Womack (R).................	5,398.6	807,421	149.6	82.9	2.9	1.1	3.9	5.8	3.4	14.6	74.7	50.3	9.1	47.8
District 4.................	Bruce Westerman (R)...........	22,337.8	709,378	31.8	74.1	19.1	0.8	0.9	3.2	1.9	5.9	71.6	51.1	2.9	65.0
CALIFORNIA..........		155,785.7	39,536,653	253.8	58.6	5.7	0.8	15.0	15.0	4.9	39.1	37.0	50.3	26.9	55.6
District 1.................	Doug LaMalfa (R)...................	28,087.7	718,214	25.6	86.0	1.8	2.1	3.1	3.0	4.0	14.0	76.3	49.6	6.6	69.0
District 2.................	Jared Huffman (D)................	12,952.4	717,999	55.4	79.1	1.3	2.1	4.3	7.7	5.6	17.7	70.4	50.5	13.2	59.9
District 3.................	John Garamendi (D).............	6,184.1	750,271	121.3	67.7	6.2	1.0	12.3	6.7	6.1	30.3	46.6	49.7	18.5	61.3
District 4.................	Tom McClintock (R)...............	12,836.8	748,410	58.3	84.8	1.3	1.2	5.7	2.7	4.3	13.8	75.1	50.3	9.5	66.8
District 5.................	Mike Thompson (D)...............	1,730.7	732,438	423.2	61.7	6.0	0.8	11.7	14.1	5.6	29.2	48.5	51.4	21.2	60.5
District 6.................	Doris O. Matsui (D)...............	174.9	764,344	4,371.4	48.4	13.0	0.8	17.6	12.7	7.5	27.6	36.5	51.2	24.0	59.1
District 7.................	Ami Bera (D).........................	548.8	750,860	1,368.3	62.7	6.7	0.5	16.4	5.6	8.2	18.3	52.3	51.1	19.9	60.4
District 8.................	Paul Cook (R).......................	32,867.7	721,449	22.0	76.6	6.9	1.4	3.9	6.1	5.1	43.0	42.9	50.1	13.7	66.1
District 9.................	Jerry McNerney (D)...............	1,250.9	774,266	619.0	52.5	8.9	0.5	15.2	10.6	12.4	38.1	33.9	50.7	22.3	64.7
District 10...............	Josh Harder (D).....................	1,820.3	758,005	416.4	74.1	3.4	0.7	8.3	8.3	5.1	44.3	41.0	50.0	21.3	66.3
District 11...............	Mark Desaulnier (D)..............	489.7	764,135	1,560.3	59.5	7.9	0.5	14.7	10.1	7.2	27.7	44.9	51.3	26.3	53.3
District 12...............	Nancy Pelosi (D)....................	39.0	774,736	19,868.1	47.7	5.3	0.3	33.2	7.9	5.4	14.8	42.2	48.9	34.1	38.7
District 13...............	Barbara Lee (D).....................	96.8	766,731	7,921.0	41.4	16.7	0.7	21.3	12.4	7.4	22.3	34.3	51.6	28.1	48.6
District 14...............	Jackie Speier (D)..................	259.7	756,389	2,913.1	42.4	2.9	0.4	36.0	12.2	6.2	24.0	33.5	50.9	38.3	46.4
District 15...............	Eric Swalwell (D)...................	598.1	785,387	1,313.0	42.2	5.7	0.6	35.8	9.7	6.0	22.5	31.7	50.1	35.2	51.3
District 16...............	Jim Costa (D)........................	2,839.3	729,788	257.0	58.1	5.1	1.2	9.9	22.1	3.6	61.7	21.6	50.2	23.9	65.7
District 17...............	Ro Khanna (D)......................	185.4	771,078	4,159.3	27.6	3.0	0.3	55.7	8.2	5.2	15.0	22.2	49.1	48.9	38.6
District 18...............	Anna G. Eshoo (D)................	696.1	742,728	1,067.0	62.6	1.7	0.6	24.2	5.4	5.4	16.6	52.6	49.5	31.0	46.6
District 19...............	Zoe Lofgren (D)......................	915.9	770,105	840.8	42.8	2.5	1.0	29.5	18.7	5.5	39.6	25.5	49.9	36.2	50.8
District 20...............	Jimmy Panetta (D)................	4,874.1	744,295	152.7	57.9	2.0	0.4	5.5	30.0	4.2	53.3	36.4	49.7	27.0	57.4
District 21...............	TJ Cox (D)............................	6,729.8	723,549	107.5	71.6	3.6	0.8	3.8	17.4	2.8	75.4	15.7	47.1	29.2	62.4
District 22...............	Devin Nunes (R)....................	1,164.9	760,328	652.7	71.1	3.7	0.9	7.8	12.0	4.4	48.8	37.3	50.9	17.4	69.4
District 23...............	Kevin McCarthy (R)................	9,898.4	745,328	75.3	75.2	5.9	1.3	5.6	7.9	4.0	39.1	46.1	48.8	13.2	70.1
District 24...............	Salud O. Carbajal (D)............	6,885.3	740,039	107.5	80.6	1.8	1.0	4.9	7.5	4.2	36.6	53.7	49.8	17.6	60.5
District 25...............	Katie Hill (D)..........................	1,690.7	721,740	426.9	63.3	7.2	1.2	9.3	13.6	5.4	39.7	40.4	49.6	19.0	64.0
District 26...............	Julia Brownley (D).................	939.1	732,091	779.6	80.4	2.1	1.0	7.2	5.1	4.2	45.8	42.6	50.6	22.2	58.7
District 27...............	Judy Chu (D).........................	699.9	717,980	1,025.9	37.0	4.2	0.5	40.6	13.8	3.9	27.8	24.8	51.2	40.1	46.2
District 28...............	Adam B. Schiff (D)................	218.5	719,156	3,292.1	68.2	3.4	0.4	12.4	11.4	4.3	24.2	56.8	49.9	39.3	38.6
District 29...............	Tony Cárdenas (D)................	92.0	713,745	7,755.7	56.7	3.9	0.4	7.3	29.2	2.5	68.1	19.7	50.2	42.6	47.2
District 30...............	Brad Sherman (D).................	135.9	771,201	5,672.7	63.1	4.7	0.5	13.4	13.4	4.8	28.0	50.0	50.6	33.5	46.0
District 31...............	Pete Aguilar (D).....................	218.3	762,208	3,492.2	59.4	11.1	0.7	8.2	15.2	5.4	53.5	25.0	51.1	19.7	65.5
District 32...............	Grace F. Napolitano (D).........	124.2	725,317	5,837.7	43.4	2.2	1.2	20.3	29.1	3.8	61.9	14.3	50.9	37.7	54.2
District 33...............	Ted Lieu (D)..........................	288.6	705,588	2,444.9	72.2	3.2	0.2	15.1	4.1	5.3	13.3	63.8	52.1	22.8	46.2
District 34...............	Jimmy Gomez (D)..................	47.7	763,303	16,012.2	37.0	4.5	1.1	19.5	35.1	2.8	63.6	11.1	48.8	46.1	43.5
District 35...............	Norma J. Torres (D)..............	168.9	745,237	4,412.6	45.8	6.4	1.7	8.1	33.6	4.3	69.7	14.0	49.0	28.3	61.8
District 36...............	Raul Ruiz (D)........................	5,912.5	737,403	124.7	70.8	4.7	1.4	4.0	15.4	3.8	48.0	41.3	50.4	20.6	57.1
District 37...............	Karen Bass (D)......................	55.3	713,530	12,911.5	40.7	23.5	0.4	10.0	22.0	3.5	39.3	24.5	51.9	30.9	48.2
District 38...............	Linda T. Sánchez (D).............	101.4	718,428	7,084.3	41.5	4.2	0.7	16.0	33.7	4.0	60.3	17.3	51.1	30.0	61.1
District 39...............	Gilbert Ray Cisneros, Jr. (D)..	204.4	736,480	3,603.2	50.2	2.3	0.7	31.7	11.1	4.0	35.4	28.4	49.9	32.7	55.3
District 40...............	Lucille Roybal-Allard (D)........	57.7	738,618	12,803.9	53.5	5.3	0.7	2.6	36.0	2.0	88.1	3.8	49.9	39.2	56.2
District 41...............	Mark Takano (D)...................	316.7	765,770	2,418.2	40.5	9.1	0.7	6.2	40.2	3.4	62.8	20.2	49.9	24.9	63.0
District 42...............	Ken Calvert (R).....................	935.9	826,899	883.5	58.0	6.3	0.5	10.0	19.5	5.8	39.3	41.5	50.5	18.9	62.2
District 43...............	Maxine Waters (D)................	72.0	745,656	10,350.6	35.0	23.1	0.8	14.0	23.6	3.6	47.4	13.4	51.9	31.3	54.6
District 44...............	Nanette Diaz Barragan (D)....	79.3	717,097	9,039.4	40.9	14.3	0.7	6.4	34.5	3.1	71.6	6.5	51.5	33.6	58.3
District 45...............	Katie Porter (D)....................	330.5	777,871	2,353.8	60.8	2.0	0.6	25.8	5.8	5.0	18.2	50.1	51.7	29.2	49.5
District 46...............	J. Luis Correa (D)..................	71.6	734,649	10,255.7	51.6	1.9	0.4	13.4	30.2	2.6	66.6	17.2	49.5	38.9	52.2
District 47...............	Alan S. Lowenthal (D)...........	216.3	723,526	3,345.5	53.6	7.1	0.7	24.3	10.3	3.9	34.9	31.4	51.3	30.4	54.1
District 48...............	Harley Rouda (D)..................	145.5	721,632	4,959.2	67.7	1.1	0.4	18.7	7.6	4.6	20.7	55.8	51.1	23.6	53.7
District 49...............	Mike Levin (D).......................	553.4	747,350	1,350.4	76.2	2.5	0.5	8.3	7.2	5.3	28.2	57.9	48.9	18.5	50.7
District 50...............	Duncan Hunter (R)................	2,788.5	754,388	270.5	76.5	2.4	1.2	5.2	9.1	5.5	33.6	55.0	50.5	19.0	56.1
District 51...............	Juan Vargas (D)....................	4,791.6	746,496	155.8	65.3	7.3	0.9	7.8	14.8	3.8	70.9	12.8	48.7	32.6	53.4
District 52...............	Scott H. Peters (D)...............	267.0	768,240	2,877.3	66.4	2.7	0.4	21.2	3.8	5.5	14.6	57.3	49.7	23.5	42.7
District 53...............	Susan A. Davis (D)................	135.7	774,182	5,704.8	62.4	8.2	0.6	15.0	7.0	6.8	32.0	40.5	50.9	22.3	52.1

1. Dry land or land partially or temporarily covered by water. 2. May be of any race.

Table E. Congressional Districts 116th Congress — **Age and Education**

STATE District	Population and population characteristics, 2017 (cont.)										Education, 2017		
	Age (percent)										Total Enrollment[1]	Attainment[2] (percent)	
	Under 5 years	5 to 17 years	18 to 24 years	25 to 34 years	35 to 44 years	45 to 54 years	55 to 64 years	65 to 74 years	75 years and over	Median age		High school graduate or more	Bachelor's degree or more
	15	16	17	18	19	20	21	22	23	24	25	26	27
UNITED STATES	6.1	16.5	9.5	13.8	12.6	13.0	12.9	9.1	6.5	38.1	81,273,337	88.0	32.0
ALABAMA	5.9	16.5	9.7	12.9	12.2	12.9	13.4	9.9	6.6	38.9	1,188,014	86.5	25.5
District 1	6.0	16.7	8.2	12.9	11.9	12.9	13.9	10.7	6.7	40.0	165,205	87.8	25.0
District 2	6.0	16.6	9.7	13.0	12.7	12.8	13.1	9.4	6.7	38.5	156,895	84.7	23.1
District 3	5.7	16.3	10.7	13.0	12.0	12.9	13.0	10.1	6.4	38.1	181,354	85.6	21.7
District 4	6.1	16.8	8.8	11.7	12.1	12.9	13.6	10.8	7.2	40.7	154,735	82.2	17.9
District 5	5.7	16.1	9.3	13.2	12.3	13.6	13.6	9.6	6.6	39.5	181,799	89.0	31.9
District 6	6.0	17.5	8.6	12.3	13.3	13.4	13.1	9.2	6.5	39.1	174,127	91.5	37.6
District 7	5.9	15.6	12.5	14.2	11.4	12.0	13.1	9.3	6.0	36.3	173,899	84.3	20.7
ALASKA	7.2	17.9	9.9	16.0	13.1	12.0	12.7	7.7	3.5	34.5	186,461	91.7	28.8
At Large	7.2	17.9	9.9	16.0	13.1	12.0	12.7	7.7	3.5	34.5	186,461	91.7	28.8
ARIZONA	6.2	17.1	9.6	13.6	12.2	12.1	12.1	10.0	7.1	37.7	1,757,544	87.2	29.4
District 1	5.8	18.1	10.7	12.2	11.6	10.7	12.8	10.7	7.3	37.6	201,965	86.3	25.3
District 2	5.8	14.4	9.5	12.8	10.8	11.6	13.2	12.2	9.6	41.4	162,816	92.1	35.4
District 3	7.0	19.6	13.1	14.1	13.2	11.1	10.5	7.1	4.4	31.8	228,652	76.9	16.8
District 4	4.9	14.2	7.0	10.5	9.9	11.5	14.4	16.2	11.4	48.1	154,343	87.6	19.3
District 5	6.3	20.0	7.0	12.1	13.8	13.3	10.9	9.4	7.2	38.0	223,390	94.0	36.0
District 6	5.7	14.9	6.9	13.9	12.1	13.4	14.8	10.6	7.8	42.3	169,214	93.5	44.4
District 7	8.5	21.0	11.9	16.5	13.2	11.9	9.3	4.8	2.9	29.7	235,936	68.8	13.8
District 8	5.3	15.6	7.7	11.9	12.1	13.4	12.1	12.2	9.7	43.1	177,094	91.7	30.7
District 9	6.3	15.2	12.5	18.2	13.3	12.0	11.0	7.3	4.2	33.5	204,134	90.1	39.7
ARKANSAS	6.2	17.4	9.6	12.7	12.3	12.5	12.7	9.7	6.8	38.1	743,696	86.7	23.4
District 1	6.1	17.1	8.6	12.0	12.3	12.7	13.1	10.5	7.6	39.7	168,237	84.8	16.4
District 2	6.3	16.9	9.7	13.8	12.6	12.6	12.6	9.3	6.0	37.4	194,069	90.4	30.5
District 3	6.6	18.3	10.5	13.8	13.1	12.1	11.5	8.4	5.7	35.5	209,835	86.0	28.8
District 4	5.7	17.1	9.3	11.1	11.3	12.7	13.7	10.9	8.2	40.8	171,555	85.4	17.2
CALIFORNIA	6.2	16.7	9.6	15.2	13.2	13.1	12.0	8.1	5.8	36.5	10,455,915	83.3	33.6
District 1	5.2	14.8	9.4	12.3	10.9	11.7	14.8	12.5	8.4	42.3	167,392	90.0	24.8
District 2	4.8	15.1	7.9	10.3	12.7	13.6	15.0	12.5	8.1	44.3	163,313	91.6	42.3
District 3	6.2	17.2	12.1	14.3	12.0	11.8	12.4	8.4	5.6	35.2	214,542	83.8	25.1
District 4	4.7	16.0	7.4	10.5	11.7	13.3	15.5	12.2	8.6	44.6	174,109	93.5	32.9
District 5	5.2	15.2	8.7	14.1	12.4	12.8	14.2	10.5	6.9	40.2	175,444	87.9	32.4
District 6	7.3	17.1	9.0	17.5	13.6	11.3	11.8	7.0	5.3	34.4	199,336	85.3	28.4
District 7	5.8	17.2	8.2	14.1	12.8	14.2	12.5	9.2	6.1	38.7	192,164	89.8	33.4
District 8	7.7	19.6	10.1	13.5	11.9	12.0	11.7	8.0	5.5	34.2	193,661	83.1	15.9
District 9	6.9	20.3	9.2	13.5	12.8	12.6	12.2	7.5	5.0	35.0	221,852	82.3	21.3
District 10	6.8	19.8	9.7	14.2	12.6	12.8	11.2	7.6	5.3	34.6	209,472	81.0	17.9
District 11	6.0	16.1	8.3	13.2	13.4	13.8	12.8	9.6	6.8	39.7	193,158	87.5	44.1
District 12	4.6	8.6	6.6	24.3	16.1	13.5	11.3	8.4	6.8	38.2	128,834	88.8	59.6
District 13	5.9	13.1	10.0	17.8	14.9	12.0	12.0	9.1	5.3	36.8	192,365	84.9	48.2
District 14	5.4	14.5	8.0	15.6	14.3	13.5	12.7	9.1	7.0	39.4	181,684	89.2	48.9
District 15	5.8	17.3	7.0	14.7	15.2	14.9	12.3	7.4	5.4	38.5	199,959	90.4	45.9
District 16	8.6	20.6	11.1	15.8	12.5	11.2	9.7	6.3	4.2	30.8	223,091	67.2	12.1
District 17	6.2	14.6	7.4	18.8	15.1	14.3	11.0	6.8	5.8	36.8	181,299	91.8	56.4
District 18	5.6	15.9	7.9	14.2	13.2	15.0	13.1	8.3	6.9	39.8	193,662	93.7	64.5
District 19	6.2	17.2	9.3	14.5	14.8	13.3	12.1	7.4	5.1	36.7	210,276	82.3	36.5
District 20	6.3	18.0	11.9	13.9	12.8	12.1	11.6	8.1	5.3	34.9	222,066	75.9	28.0
District 21	8.0	22.2	11.0	16.5	13.3	11.3	9.3	5.2	3.3	30.0	217,910	61.3	8.3
District 22	7.8	21.6	9.8	14.3	12.4	11.1	10.6	7.1	5.3	32.2	231,289	81.8	25.2
District 23	7.2	19.8	9.1	14.6	12.6	12.3	11.7	7.8	4.9	34.5	207,194	81.6	20.7
District 24	5.6	14.9	15.6	12.6	11.0	11.2	12.5	9.6	7.0	36.0	217,528	85.5	34.9
District 25	7.5	18.7	9.5	13.5	11.9	14.7	12.6	6.8	4.8	35.8	207,860	86.0	27.6
District 26	6.2	17.4	9.6	13.2	12.7	13.0	13.0	8.8	6.3	38.0	192,811	84.1	33.6
District 27	5.3	13.6	8.1	14.4	13.2	14.6	13.2	9.1	8.4	41.2	175,113	85.8	43.2
District 28	4.1	10.7	7.5	19.3	14.1	15.2	13.5	8.5	7.1	40.3	143,405	88.4	45.2
District 29	6.2	16.6	10.0	16.7	14.7	12.9	11.6	6.8	4.4	35.3	189,781	71.2	19.8
District 30	5.2	14.2	8.2	15.9	14.1	14.3	13.3	8.0	6.8	39.3	189,938	89.5	45.1
District 31	7.3	18.8	10.5	16.5	12.6	12.4	11.5	6.2	4.1	33.0	226,902	81.0	25.1
District 32	5.4	16.3	10.5	15.0	13.6	13.2	12.1	8.5	5.4	37.1	191,989	76.6	22.7
District 33	4.8	13.7	9.0	13.9	14.1	14.1	13.6	9.9	7.9	41.2	174,408	95.5	63.9
District 34	6.0	14.5	10.8	19.1	14.8	13.4	10.2	6.1	5.1	34.8	189,224	68.0	27.7
District 35	6.7	19.5	11.6	15.6	14.1	12.7	10.1	6.0	3.7	32.6	226,083	71.9	15.9
District 36	5.4	15.3	7.5	11.6	11.9	12.1	14.3	11.9	10.0	43.7	158,470	81.5	20.6
District 37	4.9	13.5	11.2	19.5	14.0	12.8	11.5	7.3	5.3	35.5	180,185	81.3	38.9
District 38	6.0	16.2	10.1	14.7	13.3	13.3	11.7	8.1	6.7	37.0	177,770	82.1	24.6
District 39	6.2	16.1	9.1	13.6	13.2	13.5	13.4	8.9	5.8	38.4	203,607	88.5	41.7
District 40	7.8	21.3	10.8	16.6	12.9	12.6	9.5	5.0	3.4	30.6	230,582	57.3	10.6
District 41	7.0	19.6	12.9	17.0	12.7	12.6	9.0	5.6	3.6	30.7	233,395	75.8	17.4
District 42	7.2	21.0	9.3	13.1	13.5	12.9	11.1	6.8	4.9	34.6	250,801	87.7	26.6
District 43	7.5	16.3	8.7	16.2	13.7	13.3	11.0	7.7	5.5	36.1	192,609	77.9	27.6
District 44	7.4	20.2	10.7	15.3	13.3	12.1	10.6	6.0	4.2	32.3	208,018	65.0	13.3
District 45	5.5	16.2	9.0	14.0	13.6	14.4	13.1	8.0	6.2	38.8	217,867	93.7	55.0
District 46	6.6	17.7	12.1	17.5	13.7	12.8	10.1	5.5	3.9	32.4	211,262	67.4	19.1
District 47	5.7	15.5	10.1	15.3	13.4	14.1	12.5	7.9	5.5	37.5	194,624	81.7	33.1
District 48	5.6	14.5	7.3	13.5	11.8	15.4	13.4	10.3	8.1	42.9	170,817	89.9	45.1
District 49	6.1	16.4	10.0	11.8	12.4	14.5	12.8	9.2	6.8	39.5	185,196	89.8	45.9
District 50	7.0	17.1	8.6	14.1	12.8	13.4	12.4	8.6	6.1	37.3	198,640	87.6	29.4
District 51	7.1	18.5	11.6	16.6	12.8	11.5	10.3	6.7	4.9	32.5	210,158	71.5	14.8
District 52	5.4	13.9	10.2	18.6	13.5	12.9	11.7	8.1	5.6	36.2	204,586	95.5	59.2
District 53	6.4	13.9	10.4	18.8	14.4	11.3	12.0	7.3	5.4	35.2	208,214	89.5	38.6

1. All persons 3 years old and over enrolled in nursery school through college and graduate or professional school. 2. Persons 25 years old and over.

Table E. Congressional Districts 116th Congress — Households and Group Quarters

STATE District	Households, 2017 Number	Average household size	Family households (percent)	Married couple family (percent)	Female family householder[1]	One person households (percent)	Total in group quarters, 2017	Percent 65 years and over	Persons in correctional institutions	Persons in nursing facilities	Persons in college dormitories	Persons in military quarters
	28	29	30	31	32	33	34	35	36	37	38	39
UNITED STATES	120,062,818	2.65	65.5	48.2	12.4	27.9	8,087,237	18.3	2,263,602	1,502,264	2,521,090	338,191
ALABAMA..........................	1,841,665	2.58	65.4	46.5	14.6	29.9	118,973	18.7	41,177	22,995	36,341	2,152
District 1.............................	262,679	2.66	65.3	46.4	15.4	30.5	13,767	19.1	5,651	2,671	2,579	0
District 2.............................	245,124	2.67	66.4	46.1	15.6	29.5	20,304	15.4	13,081	3,727	3,107	1,274
District 3.............................	274,860	2.51	64.4	45.8	14.3	29.6	21,163	15.9	7,014	3,016	6,949	0
District 4.............................	254,061	2.67	67.4	51.2	11.4	29.2	7,793	39.0	2,922	3,652	791	0
District 5.............................	284,883	2.46	66.3	49.8	12.9	28.7	16,687	17.5	5,087	2,879	5,347	823
District 6.............................	262,296	2.63	69.4	54.6	10.9	26.4	11,569	23.8	4,884	2,733	2,830	0
District 7.............................	257,762	2.50	58.4	31.4	22.1	35.8	27,690	15.1	2,538	4,317	14,738	55
ALASKA..............................	250,741	2.84	66.8	49.4	11.4	25.3	27,545	5.9	4,206	1,626	1,872	5,055
At Large	250,741	2.84	66.8	49.4	11.4	25.3	27,545	5.9	4,206	1,626	1,872	5,055
ARIZONA.............................	2,552,972	2.69	64.7	47.3	12.1	27.8	155,143	12.2	67,767	13,819	27,987	5,172
District 1.............................	255,285	2.86	66.8	47.8	13.5	26.8	35,065	4.2	15,071	816	7,630	0
District 2.............................	303,440	2.30	59.3	44.0	10.5	32.9	21,663	19.9	7,538	2,914	118	3,352
District 3.............................	242,271	3.08	73.5	47.3	18.1	19.8	26,922	5.3	11,711	863	6,913	0
District 4.............................	307,261	2.43	64.6	52.1	8.7	28.8	25,001	6.9	19,869	1,431	1,213	1,164
District 5.............................	291,062	2.81	69.9	56.4	9.8	24.1	3,602	55.3	11	859	346	0
District 6.............................	315,622	2.47	62.2	48.5	8.7	30.0	4,932	53.4	10	1,594	274	0
District 7.............................	243,861	3.37	68.8	38.2	21.3	23.4	11,592	5.2	8,915	840	1,162	0
District 8.............................	290,198	2.64	68.5	54.9	9.6	26.4	12,098	30.5	4,624	2,809	861	656
District 9.............................	303,972	2.48	52.3	35.1	11.6	35.4	14,268	12.2	18	1,693	9,470	0
ARKANSAS.........................	1,153,082	2.53	65.5	47.9	12.8	29.1	84,942	21.7	25,844	18,532	24,144	619
District 1.............................	283,126	2.45	65.1	46.6	13.5	29.4	28,322	20.6	15,495	5,770	2,669	0
District 2.............................	293,697	2.55	64.4	46.0	14.3	30.8	16,980	20.1	3,461	3,521	6,184	616
District 3.............................	301,844	2.62	67.9	52.3	10.4	25.8	17,823	21.3	1,599	3,663	9,499	0
District 4.............................	274,415	2.51	64.2	46.6	13.3	30.9	21,817	24.7	5,289	5,578	5,792	3
CALIFORNIA.......................	13,005,097	2.98	68.5	49.6	13.0	24.0	817,862	15.4	256,807	111,884	172,843	57,628
District 1.............................	282,678	2.45	63.4	47.4	11.4	29.1	24,741	14.1	11,908	2,834	2,728	5
District 2.............................	278,942	2.50	61.8	48.1	9.3	30.0	19,470	13.5	9,975	2,246	2,645	393
District 3.............................	251,430	2.90	68.8	51.2	12.0	22.7	22,174	9.1	12,154	1,728	4,981	1,321
District 4.............................	280,226	2.62	71.0	58.5	8.5	24.1	13,469	15.3	8,633	1,677	458	0
District 5.............................	265,405	2.71	64.9	47.6	12.0	28.2	11,947	22.6	1,940	3,657	3,581	0
District 6.............................	277,502	2.72	61.8	39.1	15.6	29.5	10,576	19.4	2,254	1,789	1,493	0
District 7.............................	263,770	2.80	69.9	51.0	12.8	23.3	11,253	23.1	6,682	1,704	22	0
District 8.............................	227,852	3.10	70.2	48.7	15.2	24.4	15,719	10.8	6,717	1,325	117	4,748
District 9.............................	236,131	3.22	75.0	54.6	13.9	20.3	15,082	21.5	1,358	2,403	2,194	0
District 10...........................	237,723	3.15	75.2	54.9	14.0	20.3	8,480	24.1	4,848	2,580	584	0
District 11...........................	267,976	2.82	70.5	53.1	12.5	22.6	8,244	35.3	865	3,004	1,568	0
District 12...........................	328,247	2.31	45.7	34.6	8.0	37.8	16,774	18.3	1,573	2,810	5,993	0
District 13...........................	286,121	2.60	56.0	37.9	12.7	30.6	22,337	13.2	1,044	2,600	11,927	661
District 14...........................	252,322	2.95	69.1	53.1	11.1	23.2	11,447	29.2	1,090	1,939	2,487	0
District 15...........................	253,687	3.06	75.6	60.7	10.5	18.8	9,520	23.6	5,669	2,136	1,076	0
District 16...........................	213,382	3.33	74.0	45.5	19.5	20.2	19,866	11.0	12,113	2,113	1,443	0
District 17...........................	253,748	3.00	74.9	61.1	9.1	17.2	10,679	20.8	2,564	1,666	2,592	0
District 18...........................	269,056	2.70	68.4	56.4	8.2	23.8	16,926	24.9	4	2,889	6,712	5
District 19...........................	228,985	3.31	73.8	54.1	12.8	19.1	12,351	11.7	1,448	916	3,356	0
District 20...........................	224,309	3.18	70.4	53.0	11.7	22.2	30,064	8.9	11,516	2,072	8,411	2,504
District 21...........................	191,271	3.58	81.2	54.2	19.1	15.0	38,082	4.1	44,549	1,252	239	2,038
District 22...........................	244,440	3.08	73.1	50.0	15.4	21.7	7,777	28.5	1,349	1,709	1,566	0
District 23...........................	241,420	3.01	71.1	49.6	13.8	22.7	17,696	9.1	17,160	2,293	560	329
District 24...........................	255,648	2.75	62.1	48.3	9.4	25.8	36,867	7.2	11,387	1,805	15,714	475
District 25...........................	217,168	3.27	76.0	56.5	12.4	19.0	10,717	5.7	7,129	251	1,775	0
District 26...........................	232,050	3.10	71.7	54.6	12.2	22.4	11,872	18.2	1,535	1,644	2,316	1,349
District 27...........................	240,261	2.93	71.2	52.6	12.5	22.5	13,987	25.4	331	3,659	5,809	0
District 28...........................	298,448	2.38	52.7	38.9	9.7	36.3	9,858	32.8	183	3,356	647	0
District 29...........................	212,129	3.34	68.4	45.1	14.9	24.1	5,989	35.7	307	2,842	151	0
District 30...........................	280,607	2.71	63.5	46.4	11.0	27.5	10,245	41.0	20	2,996	2,746	0
District 31...........................	224,483	3.29	75.9	50.1	18.2	18.7	23,585	15.4	5,464	2,391	2,739	0
District 32...........................	194,974	3.66	78.5	53.6	17.2	15.9	12,555	29.1	74	2,895	3,298	0
District 33...........................	290,376	2.35	56.9	45.9	7.5	34.4	22,563	11.2	98	1,851	14,107	0
District 34...........................	254,775	2.91	58.3	34.3	15.4	30.8	21,719	11.7	8,722	3,270	2,438	0
District 35...........................	192,450	3.73	81.1	54.0	18.7	14.9	26,736	11.5	6,996	2,041	1,948	0
District 36...........................	276,677	2.62	60.1	45.1	9.4	34.3	12,479	16.9	9,107	1,504	70	0
District 37...........................	274,250	2.54	51.4	32.6	13.5	37.9	16,259	14.0	155	2,263	7,976	0
District 38...........................	206,255	3.44	78.6	53.8	16.8	16.9	9,916	26.5	156	2,794	3,305	0
District 39...........................	226,049	3.22	79.6	61.9	12.5	15.6	7,728	26.5	2	1,230	2,630	0
District 40...........................	184,167	3.99	82.1	47.0	23.3	14.1	3,218	37.5	7	1,571	5	0
District 41...........................	186,332	4.02	79.3	54.6	18.0	14.7	17,410	11.9	1,171	1,826	7,379	0
District 42...........................	228,811	3.59	80.3	62.8	12.0	16.0	6,455	10.4	5,652	440	161	0
District 43...........................	242,994	3.03	66.8	39.8	18.7	26.9	10,178	27.0	120	2,478	3,293	0
District 44...........................	187,699	3.77	78.2	45.4	23.9	17.8	8,767	16.1	2,843	1,687	587	20
District 45...........................	275,654	2.78	70.7	57.2	9.7	21.3	12,754	22.2	534	789	5,705	0
District 46...........................	188,471	3.82	75.2	49.9	16.6	15.9	15,486	19.0	4,906	2,887	1,967	0
District 47...........................	246,627	2.89	66.2	45.2	14.7	26.4	10,324	31.5	235	2,931	2,040	2
District 48...........................	266,038	2.69	66.2	51.2	9.7	26.1	5,635	30.5	13	1,555	1,249	14
District 49...........................	261,728	2.78	70.5	56.3	10.1	23.1	20,620	6.5	782	1,612	7,910	16,563
District 50...........................	241,359	3.09	74.5	55.6	12.7	19.7	9,014	26.3	889	1,975	757	0
District 51...........................	203,666	3.49	74.7	46.3	20.5	19.4	34,812	4.0	17,756	1,059	0	11,846
District 52...........................	286,069	2.61	61.6	49.9	8.1	25.9	22,337	8.6	2,774	1,881	4,151	15,213
District 53...........................	272,259	2.80	61.9	45.1	12.5	26.7	13,103	28.3	46	3,059	3,237	142

1. No spouse present.

Table E. Congressional Districts 116th Congress — **Housing and Money Income**

STATE District	Housing units, 2017						Money income, 2017		
		Occupied units						Households	
			Owner-occupied			Renter-occupied			
	Total	Occupied units as a percent of all units	Owner-occupied units as a percent of occupied units	Median value[1] (dollars)	Percent valued at $500,000 or more	Median rent[2]	Per capita income (dollars)	Median income (dollars)	Percent with income of $100,000 or more
	40	41	42	43	44	45	46	47	48
UNITED STATES	137,407,308	87.4	63.9	217,600	14.8	1,012	32,397	60,336	27.8
ALABAMA	2,258,669	81.5	68.0	141,300	4.2	750	26,498	48,123	19.7
District 1	339,357	77.4	68.5	147,100	4.5	821	26,195	47,984	19.3
District 2	313,057	78.3	65.2	131,400	3.3	762	24,502	46,579	17.9
District 3	333,318	82.5	69.3	127,600	3.7	703	24,959	46,484	17.3
District 4	316,637	80.2	72.7	117,700	3.5	613	23,326	43,218	15.5
District 5	320,117	89.0	68.9	160,400	3.6	729	30,012	54,707	24.8
District 6	299,457	87.6	74.2	193,400	8.3	971	34,784	65,170	30.9
District 7	336,726	76.5	57.3	96,500	1.9	735	21,293	35,988	11.7
ALASKA	316,968	79.1	63.5	273,100	9.2	1,201	34,222	73,181	35.4
At Large	316,968	79.1	63.5	273,100	9.2	1,201	34,222	73,181	35.4
ARIZONA	2,999,185	85.1	64.7	223,400	9.8	1,020	29,420	56,581	24.4
District 1	338,585	75.4	69.5	180,500	7.3	895	23,909	50,303	19.9
District 2	350,528	86.6	63.6	185,900	7.0	873	31,436	53,516	21.4
District 3	273,572	88.6	63.4	156,800	2.5	926	19,874	47,670	16.4
District 4	400,938	76.6	74.6	194,600	6.5	921	26,199	49,387	17.5
District 5	335,679	86.7	73.2	282,600	10.2	1,223	34,364	71,675	34.9
District 6	363,447	86.8	66.0	346,000	27.9	1,155	44,583	73,425	35.6
District 7	268,990	90.7	47.7	167,900	3.1	914	18,225	43,969	13.7
District 8	326,812	88.8	73.9	242,900	6.4	1,206	33,737	67,699	30.6
District 9	340,634	89.2	48.4	270,100	12.8	1,062	32,889	56,598	25.7
ARKANSAS	1,370,109	84.2	65.3	128,500	3.0	711	25,316	45,869	17.2
District 1	343,260	82.5	64.7	101,300	1.9	651	22,704	41,143	13.4
District 2	342,372	85.8	64.2	149,400	4.4	803	28,698	51,287	21.1
District 3	336,959	89.6	63.0	159,600	3.9	729	27,230	51,335	20.2
District 4	347,518	79.0	69.5	98,500	2.0	623	22,148	40,903	13.5
CALIFORNIA	14,177,270	91.7	54.8	509,400	50.9	1,447	35,046	71,805	35.9
District 1	330,193	85.6	64.7	280,200	15.0	977	29,249	51,478	21.9
District 2	322,256	86.6	63.4	649,500	62.0	1,481	47,178	76,114	39.1
District 3	272,320	92.3	58.4	346,400	22.6	1,273	30,060	65,934	31.3
District 4	361,353	77.5	75.6	424,900	34.7	1,345	38,077	75,841	37.4
District 5	287,187	92.4	62.0	528,600	53.8	1,586	37,781	78,152	37.0
District 6	292,317	94.9	47.4	316,700	15.3	1,172	28,503	54,243	23.9
District 7	275,316	95.8	64.1	379,800	24.4	1,306	34,971	74,608	36.0
District 8	300,582	75.8	60.8	237,200	7.3	1,035	22,726	52,428	21.7
District 9	252,568	93.5	61.5	375,600	26.7	1,147	28,128	65,392	33.4
District 10	248,676	95.6	58.8	323,700	14.0	1,194	26,486	63,223	28.3
District 11	285,066	94.0	64.9	692,200	69.1	1,734	47,527	90,155	45.3
District 12	363,178	90.4	34.2	1,120,600	X	1,820	67,737	111,717	54.2
District 13	303,161	94.4	43.5	747,900	76.5	1,538	42,559	76,915	40.0
District 14	265,781	94.9	58.1	996,800	93.7	2,245	52,107	110,507	54.3
District 15	267,251	94.9	64.3	797,600	85.3	1,972	47,990	116,710	57.3
District 16	226,110	94.4	48.7	215,700	7.1	924	18,866	43,839	15.5
District 17	270,458	93.8	54.5	964,500	89.4	2,418	51,577	124,131	60.6
District 18	286,266	94.0	60.2	1,337,300	94.1	2,210	70,075	134,077	61.8
District 19	239,821	95.5	60.8	792,000	83.9	1,957	40,269	101,427	51.0
District 20	250,973	89.4	55.0	608,700	61.7	1,521	31,124	73,076	35.3
District 21	207,010	92.4	51.5	181,800	3.8	858	16,563	42,621	15.1
District 22	258,846	94.4	57.6	262,500	10.0	1,035	26,507	57,667	26.4
District 23	269,961	89.4	60.5	238,600	5.1	1,014	24,903	55,680	25.0
District 24	283,456	90.2	54.6	572,300	56.9	1,492	35,431	71,356	35.5
District 25	229,818	94.5	67.1	461,800	44.3	1,546	30,875	76,866	37.6
District 26	247,105	93.9	62.3	591,700	63.2	1,721	37,205	82,029	39.8
District 27	262,156	91.6	53.9	699,800	82.6	1,483	38,230	77,629	39.8
District 28	329,410	90.6	33.7	827,900	X	1,504	42,844	65,849	33.4
District 29	223,806	94.8	41.6	489,000	46.7	1,324	22,670	53,347	23.0
District 30	294,339	95.3	51.6	691,400	78.9	1,705	44,527	81,276	41.6
District 31	243,979	92.0	55.4	359,900	20.0	1,271	24,813	61,631	27.0
District 32	204,861	95.2	60.8	478,700	43.6	1,416	26,072	70,390	32.8
District 33	326,448	89.0	50.1	1,191,600	91.5	2,032	70,899	105,200	52.7
District 34	275,827	92.4	20.7	612,600	66.8	1,191	24,145	46,883	20.5
District 35	204,443	94.1	56.9	367,900	13.3	1,340	20,797	60,741	24.6
District 36	373,348	74.1	66.8	270,400	14.3	1,060	28,056	46,494	21.6
District 37	298,878	91.8	35.9	730,800	74.3	1,469	35,481	59,069	28.9
District 38	212,868	96.9	62.1	503,800	50.6	1,447	27,010	72,463	34.6
District 39	237,021	95.4	66.6	659,100	75.9	1,701	35,672	89,300	44.3
District 40	190,279	96.8	34.6	438,800	32.0	1,155	16,495	47,190	15.3
District 41	197,450	94.4	58.3	340,300	11.2	1,356	22,033	64,658	28.5
District 42	240,655	95.1	72.6	430,800	29.7	1,588	30,504	83,837	41.8
District 43	258,334	94.1	40.5	562,300	59.7	1,291	27,435	56,655	26.5
District 44	194,863	96.3	46.1	410,200	25.0	1,193	18,738	50,346	19.0
District 45	289,849	95.1	63.1	719,700	79.8	2,130	46,133	102,040	51.6
District 46	196,441	95.9	41.0	528,700	55.6	1,521	22,734	65,334	27.5
District 47	258,080	95.6	47.1	596,600	67.9	1,367	32,566	68,300	32.6
District 48	290,706	91.5	59.7	759,800	79.9	1,870	49,257	89,807	45.0
District 49	285,539	91.7	60.9	701,500	73.7	1,862	46,013	88,314	45.0
District 50	257,924	93.6	63.3	486,600	47.1	1,488	32,810	77,155	37.9
District 51	230,777	88.3	44.8	347,300	16.2	1,180	19,775	48,043	18.7
District 52	309,435	92.4	54.2	719,900	78.3	1,932	50,066	95,770	48.3
District 53	292,525	93.1	48.7	523,300	53.8	1,541	34,252	72,479	34.9

1. Specified owner-occupied units.   2. Specified renter-occupied units.

Table E. Congressional Districts 116th Congress — Poverty, Labor Force, Employment, and Social Security

STATE District	Poverty, 2017 Persons below poverty level (percent)	Families below poverty level (percent)	Percent of households receiving food stamps in past 12 months	Civilian labor force, 2016 Total	Unemployment Total	Rate[1]	Civilian employment,[2] 2017 Total	Percent Management, business, science, and arts occupations	Number Service, sales, and office	Rate[3] Construction and production	Persons under 65 years of age with no health insurance, 2017 (percent)	Social Security beneficiaries, December 2018		Supplemental Security Income recipients, December 2018
	49	50	51	52	53	54	55	56	57	58	59	60	61	62
UNITED STATES	13.4	9.5	11.7	163,703,561	8,645,230	5.3	155,058,331	38.2	40.8	21.0	10.2	61,362,783	188.4	8,127,634
ALABAMA	16.9	12.8	14.0	2,194,187	128,302	5.8	2,065,885	34.8	40.0	25.2	11.1	1,143,125	234.5	161,635
District 1	17.0	13.1	13.5	313,708	18,343	5.8	295,365	33.2	43.0	23.8	12.5	171,745	240.7	22,015
District 2	18.0	14.2	15.8	296,337	18,475	6.2	277,862	32.0	41.5	26.4	11.0	162,702	241.5	26,605
District 3	17.8	12.7	14.0	315,091	16,827	5.3	298,264	32.4	39.8	27.8	10.6	167,154	235.3	22,169
District 4	17.6	13.9	14.0	289,123	17,228	6.0	271,895	29.3	36.8	34.0	12.8	181,823	265.2	23,691
District 5	13.8	10.3	12.4	343,330	16,132	4.7	327,198	41.1	37.7	21.2	10.7	155,012	215.7	16,256
District 6	9.9	7.3	6.9	341,838	14,898	4.4	326,940	43.6	38.0	18.4	8.2	147,164	210.1	11,487
District 7	24.6	19.8	21.9	294,760	26,399	9.0	268,361	29.4	44.0	26.6	12.1	157,525	234.3	39,412
ALASKA	11.1	7.4	10.8	373,249	28,267	7.6	344,982	37.4	40.6	22.0	15.3	101,402	137.1	12,537
At Large	11.1	7.4	10.8	373,249	28,267	7.6	344,982	37.4	40.6	22.0	15.3	101,402	137.1	12,537
ARIZONA	14.9	10.7	10.8	3,318,675	192,721	5.8	3,125,954	36.1	45.3	18.6	12.0	1,349,458	192.3	118,707
District 1	19.2	13.5	13.7	316,103	25,215	8.0	290,888	32.2	47.9	19.9	12.2	161,026	210.3	17,684
District 2	13.9	9.8	11.9	326,967	22,586	6.9	304,381	40.9	44.7	14.4	8.5	177,632	246.6	14,237
District 3	20.0	16.4	20.2	360,253	28,622	7.9	331,631	25.6	48.0	26.4	14.3	119,308	154.3	18,941
District 4	13.4	9.0	10.2	294,640	18,131	6.2	276,509	29.5	49.0	21.4	12.3	228,335	296.1	12,204
District 5	8.0	6.0	4.9	403,052	15,030	3.7	388,022	44.2	41.9	13.9	9.0	140,565	170.9	6,767
District 6	10.6	7.3	5.2	408,514	18,077	4.4	390,437	45.5	41.2	13.3	9.5	146,473	187.0	7,948
District 7	24.2	20.7	22.1	400,188	27,945	7.0	372,243	22.0	49.0	29.0	19.0	90,219	108.2	22,493
District 8	8.2	5.2	5.4	372,456	16,450	4.4	356,006	39.7	44.6	15.7	8.6	182,278	234.5	8,493
District 9	16.3	10.5	8.0	436,502	20,665	4.7	415,837	41.5	43.7	14.8	12.4	103,622	134.7	9,940
ARKANSAS	16.4	11.6	11.8	1,373,376	76,495	5.6	1,296,881	34.0	39.8	26.2	9.3	696,936	232.0	105,213
District 1	18.6	13.4	15.1	311,052	18,748	6.0	292,304	29.3	40.5	30.2	8.4	186,026	257.6	32,680
District 2	13.5	9.7	8.9	372,307	18,441	5.0	353,866	39.0	41.6	19.5	8.2	163,732	214.0	26,085
District 3	14.5	10.2	9.0	394,374	19,586	5.0	374,788	36.3	38.4	25.3	11.2	159,417	197.4	17,436
District 4	19.5	13.6	14.8	295,643	19,720	6.7	275,923	29.4	38.7	31.9	9.3	187,761	264.7	29,012
CALIFORNIA	13.3	9.6	8.9	19,936,052	1,178,551	5.9	18,757,501	38.7	41.1	20.1	8.1	5,962,804	150.8	1,238,456
District 1	17.1	10.8	10.9	318,885	18,510	5.8	300,375	34.8	44.2	21.0	7.4	184,328	256.6	30,198
District 2	12.3	6.2	7.3	358,015	17,933	5.0	340,082	44.6	39.7	15.7	6.9	155,644	216.8	17,576
District 3	13.6	9.0	11.4	349,737	19,849	5.7	329,888	33.2	40.6	26.2	6.0	129,821	173.0	22,404
District 4	9.3	6.4	5.5	347,108	15,311	4.4	331,797	42.8	42.1	15.1	5.2	174,618	233.3	12,962
District 5	9.8	5.9	7.2	385,750	18,649	4.8	367,101	36.4	43.1	20.5	7.2	142,058	194.0	16,805
District 6	17.9	14.1	13.8	376,638	29,007	7.7	347,631	35.8	44.4	19.7	7.2	112,752	147.5	43,204
District 7	10.3	7.6	8.6	372,142	20,841	5.6	351,301	42.0	42.8	15.2	5.5	131,559	175.2	22,923
District 8	18.2	14.8	17.0	297,411	28,735	9.7	268,676	28.9	44.7	26.4	8.0	128,766	178.5	27,926
District 9	14.8	10.8	12.7	360,035	25,328	7.0	334,707	29.8	42.4	27.8	6.9	120,681	155.9	28,436
District 10	12.9	10.8	11.6	356,227	24,935	7.0	331,292	27.9	42.2	29.9	5.8	120,224	158.6	25,147
District 11	9.8	6.9	7.0	390,410	20,427	5.2	369,983	43.3	40.8	16.0	6.9	127,526	166.9	18,688
District 12	10.2	5.3	4.7	491,224	17,871	3.6	473,353	57.7	33.5	8.8	4.1	107,181	138.3	36,399
District 13	14.2	9.4	7.6	423,047	24,963	5.9	398,084	49.2	35.4	15.4	8.0	107,202	139.8	31,412
District 14	6.4	3.9	2.9	429,375	16,391	3.8	412,984	47.8	39.8	12.4	4.7	114,764	151.7	13,728
District 15	5.1	3.6	4.5	426,758	14,281	3.3	412,477	48.7	36.0	15.3	3.5	98,206	125.0	15,239
District 16	26.7	22.1	24.4	312,623	35,282	11.3	277,341	21.3	43.6	35.2	9.6	97,167	133.1	38,175
District 17	6.4	3.9	3.8	425,966	16,113	3.8	409,853	59.1	28.5	12.4	2.8	87,419	113.4	13,489
District 18	5.8	3.1	2.4	402,600	14,960	3.7	387,640	61.8	29.2	9.0	4.4	102,189	137.6	10,275
District 19	9.1	6.4	7.5	416,491	19,612	4.7	396,879	40.6	40.0	19.4	5.8	91,958	119.4	24,973
District 20	11.5	7.7	8.0	364,811	22,151	6.1	342,660	33.2	38.8	28.0	9.2	113,622	152.7	14,182
District 21	24.7	20.5	21.5	305,024	27,930	9.2	277,094	17.8	36.1	46.1	10.8	83,311	115.1	25,909
District 22	17.7	14.6	17.6	348,946	25,263	7.2	323,683	34.0	41.9	24.1	7.1	115,916	152.5	26,759
District 23	17.8	14.1	12.7	320,373	28,918	9.0	291,455	33.2	41.5	25.4	6.4	118,548	159.1	27,241
District 24	13.6	6.8	6.3	374,391	18,693	5.0	355,698	36.9	43.6	19.6	9.5	136,569	184.5	13,010
District 25	13.2	10.1	7.4	340,928	19,874	5.8	321,054	39.1	40.4	20.5	6.6	102,753	142.4	22,578
District 26	9.3	6.8	7.7	376,605	19,400	5.2	357,205	36.9	40.4	22.7	10.7	122,158	166.9	14,129
District 27	10.3	6.8	3.2	369,575	15,711	4.3	353,864	47.1	40.6	12.3	6.9	116,246	161.9	28,180
District 28	13.8	9.9	6.0	422,589	25,823	6.1	396,766	48.0	39.4	12.6	9.1	93,307	129.7	42,272
District 29	16.4	12.8	11.1	374,906	20,439	5.5	354,467	25.5	46.9	27.6	11.9	80,721	113.1	31,968
District 30	9.4	6.2	4.2	443,021	26,432	6.0	416,589	48.5	38.2	13.3	7.1	112,712	146.2	21,172
District 31	15.7	11.5	14.8	366,151	29,560	8.1	336,591	32.5	42.9	24.6	7.9	97,976	128.5	27,027
District 32	11.8	8.7	7.5	373,856	22,312	6.0	351,544	28.3	46.5	25.2	9.3	106,775	147.2	25,561
District 33	7.9	4.5	1.8	382,756	19,125	5.0	363,631	60.6	32.5	7.0	4.2	115,916	164.3	11,000
District 34	22.1	18.5	12.5	420,269	28,762	6.8	391,507	29.8	46.6	23.6	18.1	80,065	104.9	41,170
District 35	16.3	13.5	14.2	353,998	24,070	6.8	329,928	22.7	43.0	34.3	11.3	84,112	112.9	22,468
District 36	17.9	12.8	9.1	321,163	29,976	9.3	291,187	26.8	50.1	23.2	10.1	164,724	223.4	24,435
District 37	18.5	13.1	8.4	391,822	25,035	6.4	366,787	44.3	41.3	14.4	9.6	95,677	134.1	27,776
District 38	10.2	7.4	6.5	361,234	18,177	5.0	343,057	33.5	42.9	23.6	7.9	112,233	156.2	25,644
District 39	9.9	6.7	6.0	385,772	20,055	5.2	365,717	42.8	41.4	15.7	6.7	109,736	149.0	15,714
District 40	22.6	20.3	18.0	348,339	23,578	6.8	324,761	17.3	47.3	35.4	14.5	73,763	99.9	25,058
District 41	13.8	10.7	12.0	375,789	31,045	8.3	344,744	25.4	42.9	31.7	10.6	95,498	124.7	24,230
District 42	8.4	6.4	6.8	386,358	23,644	6.1	362,714	36.5	42.2	21.3	7.4	112,917	136.6	12,607
District 43	16.6	13.3	10.5	375,884	23,212	6.2	352,672	32.5	46.7	20.8	10.6	97,440	130.7	31,026
District 44	18.6	17.0	16.3	334,697	27,096	8.1	307,601	20.0	47.0	33.0	13.7	90,465	126.2	34,255
District 45	9.1	5.7	3.1	409,768	16,237	4.0	393,531	54.3	36.0	9.7	5.1	113,329	145.7	9,829
District 46	17.0	14.7	12.7	387,372	18,056	4.7	369,316	24.3	47.0	28.7	15.4	77,814	105.9	26,805
District 47	15.5	11.6	9.1	379,738	18,322	4.8	361,416	38.4	42.7	18.9	7.9	99,223	137.1	31,659
District 48	9.6	6.5	5.4	383,958	14,660	3.8	369,298	46.2	40.7	13.1	7.2	124,801	172.9	10,145
District 49	7.6	4.9	4.3	367,474	16,730	4.6	350,744	44.9	40.1	15.0	7.6	118,783	158.9	8,273
District 50	10.2	7.2	7.0	381,059	18,116	4.8	362,943	34.2	45.4	20.5	8.9	124,327	164.8	15,521
District 51	19.9	17.6	18.6	333,930	34,655	10.4	299,275	23.2	52.0	24.9	12.8	117,512	157.4	37,386
District 52	8.2	3.9	3.1	414,643	21,214	5.1	393,429	57.9	33.1	9.0	4.8	111,220	144.8	14,238
District 53	13.2	8.9	7.7	418,411	25,282	6.0	393,129	43.5	43.2	13.3	7.9	108,572	140.2	19,270

1. Percent of civilian labor force.   2. Persons 16 years old and over.   3. Per 1,000 resident population estimated in the 2017 American Community Survey.

Table E. Congressional Districts 116th Congress — Agriculture

STATE District	Agriculture 2017									
	Land in farms				Value of products sold				Government payments	
	Number of farms	Acres	Average size of farm (acres)	Harvested cropland (acres)	Total ($1,000)	Average per farm (dollars)	Percent from crops	Percent from livestock and poultry products	Total ($1,000)	Average per farm receiving payments (dollars)
	63	64	65	66	67	68	69	70	71	72
UNITED STATES	2,042,220	900,217,576	441	320,041,858	388,522,695	190,245	49.8	50.2	8,943,574	13,906
ALABAMA	40,592	8,580,940	211	2,205,766	5,980,595	147,334	20.3	79.7	134,654	8,892
District 1	2,928	652,956	223	227,241	310,410	106,014	76.8	23.2	15,572	16,762
District 2	8,100	2,095,530	259	504,145	1,514,029	186,917	18.4	81.6	43,478	11,103
District 3	5,232	1,104,479	211	215,369	813,111	155,411	20.1	79.9	13,810	7,955
District 4	11,374	1,639,238	144	473,554	2,172,299	190,988	8.7	91.3	24,234	6,379
District 5	5,927	965,903	163	459,776	519,220	87,602	43.1	56.9	14,741	7,456
District 6	2,580	399,443	155	81,843	217,477	84,293	16.4	83.6	4,185	6,707
District 7	4,451	1,723,391	387	243,838	434,050	97,517	19.2	80.8	18,634	8,615
ALASKA	990	849,753	858	31,877	70,459	71,171	42.1	57.9	2,091	9,293
At Large	990	849,753	858	31,877	70,459	71,171	42.1	57.9	2,091	9,293
ARIZONA	19,086	26,125,819	1,369	915,647	3,852,008	201,824	54.4	45.6	22,331	29,735
District 1	13,560	20,195,286	1,489	289,469	1,031,964	76,104	34.3	65.7	6,836	24,768
District 2	1,323	1,040,464	786	88,140	161,280	121,905	59.9	40.1	3,212	25,291
District 3	1,257	3,078,961	2,449	219,807	1,195,275	950,895	54.7	45.3	5,920	39,467
District 4	1,717	1,598,936	931	239,342	1,017,973	592,879	67.6	32.4	4,311	35,628
District 5	435	60,281	139	22,775	126,184	290,078	D	D	1,053	32,906
District 6	297	D	D	21,075	113,635	382,609	92.1	7.9	239	21,727
District 7	106	20,624	195	16,332	102,007	962,330	84.2	15.8	383	42,556
District 8	343	D	D	18,354	86,807	253,082	71.7	28.3	193	9,190
District 9	48	2,095	44	353	16,884	351,750	D	D	184	46,000
ARKANSAS	42,625	13,888,929	326	7,098,672	9,651,160	226,420	37.6	62.4	321,742	38,624
District 1	13,399	7,758,029	579	5,424,425	4,087,818	305,084	77.5	22.5	272,375	48,500
District 2	5,351	1,039,161	194	315,834	422,992	79,049	21.3	78.7	13,321	19,195
District 3	9,329	1,669,233	179	314,685	1,928,511	206,722	2.3	97.7	4,899	10,080
District 4	14,546	3,422,506	235	1,043,728	3,211,839	220,806	10.0	90.0	31,147	20,304
CALIFORNIA	70,521	24,522,801	348	7,857,512	45,154,359	640,297	73.9	26.1	127,938	24,112
District 1	7,949	3,690,258	464	650,694	1,471,521	185,120	81.2	18.8	17,554	27,300
District 2	4,847	1,983,379	409	121,953	1,206,957	249,011	56.6	43.4	2,866	14,697
District 3	5,761	2,222,919	386	1,075,534	2,524,704	438,241	92.6	7.4	27,813	31,356
District 4	5,025	1,537,953	306	149,086	783,366	155,894	70.6	29.4	5,706	16,444
District 5	3,616	502,424	139	106,858	889,982	246,123	89.6	10.4	2,234	17,591
District 6	95	7,171	81	7,171	14,672	154,442	99.6	0.4	232	38,667
District 7	714	134,035	188	30,374	186,365	261,015	63.7	36.3	860	18,696
District 8	830	405,833	489	25,014	160,823	193,763	31.2	68.8	1,370	42,813
District 9	3,034	682,651	225	417,973	1,881,357	620,091	74.8	25.2	5,136	24,226
District 10	4,282	881,704	206	463,869	2,915,414	680,853	56.4	43.6	5,996	18,855
District 11	230	105,382	458	19,726	36,383	158,187	77.0	23.0	332	15,091
District 12	9	89	10	5	452	50,222	D	D	D	D
District 13	35	D	D	34	2,608	74,514	12.6	87.4	D	D
District 14	121	24,065	199	2,329	48,318	399,322	98.3	1.7	D	D
District 15	409	138,780	339	6,969	34,387	84,076	76.5	23.5	194	7,462
District 16	3,710	1,394,781	376	800,605	4,460,128	1,202,191	54.7	45.3	10,377	27,094
District 17	60	D	D	541	11,233	187,217	97.5	2.5	D	D
District 18	492	63,346	129	10,962	195,998	398,370	99.3	0.7	18	3,600
District 19	612	268,704	439	14,521	197,717	323,067	92.1	7.9	490	16,897
District 20	2,210	1,901,631	860	338,292	4,831,405	2,186,156	98.4	1.6	1,925	12,419
District 21	4,578	2,751,011	601	1,718,981	9,790,565	2,138,612	62.0	38.0	18,580	24,609
District 22	3,428	771,371	225	483,801	3,124,957	911,598	60.9	39.1	8,611	28,703
District 23	2,800	1,981,120	708	419,024	2,438,036	870,727	87.9	12.1	4,921	24,605
District 24	4,091	1,708,370	418	237,661	2,708,747	662,123	97.4	2.6	5,168	17,227
District 25	403	36,030	89	7,779	53,369	132,404	D	D	64	6,400
District 26	1,814	193,157	106	69,560	1,128,887	622,319	99.5	0.5	743	16,152
District 27	124	3,062	25	989	24,781	199,847	99.3	0.7	43	14,333
District 28	93	1,488	16	67	965	10,376	72.2	27.8	D	D
District 29	75	1,341	18	686	12,735	169,800	98.7	1.3	D	D
District 30	47	1,864	40	1,529	15,037	319,936	99.7	0.3	D	D
District 31	177	6,904	39	2,458	19,407	109,644	99.5	0.5	124	24,800
District 32	49	804	16	211	15,520	316,735	99.7	0.3	D	D
District 33	101	5,819	58	1,248	9,241	91,495	98.7	1.3	D	D
District 34	12	151	13	13	54	4,500	100.0	0.0	D	D
District 35	168	10,073	60	3,962	207,967	1,237,899	13.0	87.0	310	34,444
District 36	961	185,512	193	106,983	649,142	675,486	86.7	13.3	1,502	34,930
District 37	13	D	D	31	169	13,000	D	D	D	D
District 38	37	179	5	98	5,583	150,892	D	D	D	D
District 39	81	5,324	66	649	10,590	130,741	95.7	4.3	300	50,000
District 40	5	D	D	21	617	123,400	100.0	0.0	D	D
District 41	413	29,236	71	9,848	57,385	138,947	86.6	13.4	16	1,778
District 42	1,178	45,409	39	24,697	212,078	180,032	38.4	61.6	101	11,222
District 43	27	1,709	63	330	8,044	297,926	D	D	139	46,333
District 44	36	188	5	118	21,704	602,889	D	D	D	D
District 45	82	26,333	321	3,066	41,076	500,927	99.9	0.1	3	1,000
District 46	17	D	D	91	4,874	286,706	D	D	D	D
District 47	28	9,985	357	214	5,939	212,107	99.3	0.7	D	D
District 48	28	2,641	94	704	20,354	726,929	99.2	0.8	3	1,000
District 49	813	21,797	27	7,962	174,311	214,405	90.9	9.1	13	2,167
District 50	3,783	153,781	41	37,897	597,859	158,038	94.4	5.6	542	12,044
District 51	697	563,066	808	470,449	1,908,532	2,738,209	66.5	33.5	3,641	32,509
District 52	214	7,688	36	2,821	19,376	90,542	93.3	6.7	D	D
District 53	107	3,830	36	1,054	12,679	118,495	98.8	1.2	D	D

Table E. Congressional Districts 116th Congress — Nonfarm Employment and Payroll

STATE District		Private nonfarm employment and payroll, 2016											Annual payroll	
		Employment												
			Percent by selected industries											
	Number of establishments	Total	Manufac-turing	Construc-tion	Wholesale trade	Retail trade	Health care and social assistance	Finance and Insur-ance	Real estate and rental and leas-ing	Profes-sional, sci-entific, and technical services	Information	Total (mil dol)	Average per employee (dollars)
	73	74	75	76	77	78	79	80	81	82	83	84	85
UNITED STATES	7,757,807	126,752,238	9.1	5.0	4.8	12.6	15.6	5.0	1.7	6.9	2.7	6,435,142	50,769
ALABAMA	99,584	1,673,249	15.0	4.9	4.3	14.2	14.7	4.2	1.4	6.0	2.0	68,971	41,220
District 1	15,611	236,720	11.9	6.8	4.1	16.4	13.3	3.4	2.0	5.2	1.7	9,449	39,918
District 2	14,252	215,224	12.9	4.3	4.8	15.7	17.0	3.7	1.3	4.4	1.5	8,267	38,409
District 3	11,510	179,100	21.7	3.9	3.4	16.6	14.6	2.5	1.1	2.9	1.1	6,150	34,339
District 4	12,538	188,796	27.5	3.8	3.4	15.4	15.9	3.1	0.9	2.0	1.1	6,498	34,418
District 5	15,137	255,797	15.4	4.5	3.8	14.2	15.6	2.7	1.1	15.7	2.1	11,466	44,823
District 6	16,197	251,622	6.8	6.1	5.0	16.3	12.3	8.2	1.5	5.2	4.4	11,807	46,922
District 7	13,840	287,267	16.4	5.4	5.8	9.8	17.6	5.2	1.9	3.9	1.8	13,461	46,857
ALASKA	21,077	266,072	4.8	6.4	3.5	13.2	18.7	2.9	1.7	7.3	2.5	15,239	57,275
At Large	21,077	266,072	4.8	6.4	3.5	13.2	18.7	2.9	1.7	7.3	2.5	15,239	57,275
ARIZONA	139,134	2,379,409	6.1	6.0	3.9	13.5	15.1	6.2	2.0	6.2	2.0	106,431	44,730
District 1	11,927	166,416	9.4	4.2	2.0	17.8	17.2	1.7	1.4	2.7	1.6	6,415	38,550
District 2	15,397	217,943	2.7	4.8	1.4	17.6	22.3	5.1	2.2	7.2	1.8	7,972	36,577
District 3	9,888	165,199	9.9	6.8	4.9	15.0	16.3	1.9	1.3	3.7	2.0	6,621	40,078
District 4	12,645	141,929	6.7	7.0	3.1	20.4	19.1	2.1	1.7	2.5	1.3	4,690	33,041
District 5	14,439	187,758	7.4	8.4	2.3	19.4	15.9	5.2	1.9	5.6	1.7	7,590	40,427
District 6	24,973	379,927	3.5	6.8	2.7	12.2	12.6	10.1	2.4	7.4	2.4	19,556	51,472
District 7	14,033	387,001	9.9	6.9	8.9	7.6	13.1	6.6	1.6	4.8	1.3	19,479	50,334
District 8	11,511	152,527	3.0	6.3	1.7	23.4	23.4	3.0	2.0	3.3	1.0	5,319	34,873
District 9	23,646	475,935	5.7	5.3	4.5	10.6	13.3	9.1	2.8	10.9	3.6	24,710	51,918
ARKANSAS	65,611	1,023,854	15.0	4.5	4.6	14.4	16.7	3.6	1.2	3.7	2.5	40,969	40,015
District 1	13,855	192,289	19.1	3.8	5.3	16.9	19.8	3.1	1.1	2.0	3.3	6,526	33,941
District 2	18,848	294,396	7.0	5.3	5.3	14.5	19.6	5.2	1.5	4.8	4.2	12,285	41,728
District 3	18,788	328,502	15.9	4.2	4.8	13.1	13.2	2.8	1.2	4.5	1.4	15,048	45,809
District 4	13,748	186,615	23.7	4.8	2.5	15.6	16.9	3.2	1.1	2.3	1.0	6,504	34,853
CALIFORNIA	922,477	14,600,349	7.9	5.0	5.8	11.7	13.2	4.2	2.0	8.2	4.9	886,644	60,728
District 1	15,365	171,410	6.9	5.4	3.1	17.9	22.1	3.8	1.7	4.6	1.4	6,766	39,471
District 2	21,721	226,752	8.5	6.1	4.2	15.9	15.9	3.9	2.2	6.1	2.9	11,976	52,816
District 3	11,822	165,851	8.9	6.5	5.1	18.1	17.6	3.3	1.6	3.9	1.7	7,446	44,898
District 4	18,682	222,875	4.0	8.4	2.4	15.8	14.8	6.0	2.6	5.5	2.1	10,422	46,761
District 5	17,266	234,849	11.8	7.4	4.1	14.7	17.6	3.1	1.6	4.4	1.2	12,434	52,945
District 6	15,582	263,366	4.3	6.3	6.0	11.8	18.5	3.1	2.2	7.7	2.7	13,492	51,231
District 7	13,795	213,587	4.9	6.2	5.2	15.4	15.4	9.9	1.8	8.0	2.9	11,861	55,532
District 8	9,402	116,450	4.7	5.7	1.2	19.6	18.5	2.1	2.3	3.2	1.4	4,036	34,655
District 9	10,777	159,812	8.0	7.1	5.9	15.0	17.6	3.9	1.6	2.9	1.2	7,215	45,149
District 10	12,185	190,329	13.6	5.4	5.9	16.7	16.0	2.2	1.5	4.0	1.0	8,414	44,209
District 11	16,983	230,676	4.2	6.9	3.3	15.2	18.4	7.7	2.2	7.5	2.2	13,861	60,090
District 12	32,718	613,587	1.3	3.1	2.5	7.0	10.2	8.7	2.5	17.5	9.9	59,999	97,785
District 13	19,174	300,945	6.4	5.7	4.8	10.1	17.1	3.2	1.8	8.4	3.8	19,734	65,573
District 14	19,454	351,648	6.5	4.9	5.4	10.4	9.1	4.3	2.2	9.5	12.2	37,629	107,006
District 15	16,997	289,706	8.1	7.1	9.4	11.2	11.3	4.2	1.7	11.4	5.8	21,236	73,303
District 16	9,102	149,720	16.1	5.0	6.9	13.7	18.9	1.9	1.5	2.6	1.8	6,272	41,890
District 17	21,411	562,421	15.3	4.3	13.4	5.9	6.2	2.0	1.0	14.2	8.1	68,100	121,084
District 18	22,079	404,129	3.1	2.9	2.9	9.6	17.0	3.2	1.5	14.4	15.8	46,637	115,401
District 19	13,930	202,572	7.0	8.2	5.0	11.4	11.2	2.8	1.8	11.4	5.5	13,440	66,346
District 20	16,384	200,289	7.7	5.5	5.5	17.4	15.5	2.4	1.7	5.6	1.3	8,920	44,537
District 21	6,911	105,964	17.3	4.4	9.0	19.6	11.5	1.2	1.4	1.7	0.7	4,211	39,744
District 22	14,384	208,974	7.6	5.9	3.8	18.2	18.1	4.7	1.9	4.4	1.1	8,408	40,232
District 23	12,055	186,208	4.3	6.2	3.9	14.3	19.1	3.4	1.9	5.8	1.6	7,943	42,659
District 24	20,372	242,652	8.6	5.8	3.7	14.3	15.6	2.7	2.1	6.2	3.4	11,375	46,879
District 25	12,375	161,652	9.9	6.4	4.3	17.6	13.0	2.8	1.9	7.5	1.7	6,773	41,897
District 26	18,932	242,372	9.6	5.1	6.1	15.5	14.2	5.1	1.8	9.2	2.5	13,300	54,874
District 27	21,984	254,910	2.4	2.1	3.1	12.2	18.8	7.4	1.9	9.7	1.9	12,958	50,833
District 28	25,077	337,666	5.5	2.5	2.3	10.5	17.3	2.7	2.7	7.1	14.2	18,737	55,489
District 29	12,253	171,756	15.1	7.5	7.8	13.2	19.6	1.6	2.5	3.4	2.0	8,012	46,645
District 30	30,390	391,843	4.9	3.3	2.9	10.2	13.3	6.5	2.3	6.5	21.4	19,320	49,306
District 31	13,186	240,722	8.0	5.1	5.2	14.2	21.0	3.4	1.4	3.8	2.0	10,292	42,753
District 32	15,315	246,743	16.8	4.5	10.4	14.0	14.2	3.3	1.4	4.1	1.3	11,326	45,901
District 33	40,750	508,491	5.9	1.8	2.6	10.3	11.8	4.5	3.4	13.5	10.6	38,147	75,019
District 34	23,945	349,223	5.6	1.4	9.8	7.1	13.9	7.5	2.2	10.6	4.5	22,693	64,982
District 35	13,495	260,410	12.2	6.4	12.1	13.6	11.2	1.7	1.3	2.0	1.3	11,765	45,177
District 36	12,438	169,377	3.1	6.5	1.8	20.4	16.5	1.8	2.5	2.6	1.5	5,989	35,362
District 37	21,475	295,656	3.0	2.0	3.1	8.8	10.7	3.8	3.0	10.3	18.9	19,212	64,979
District 38	14,810	243,609	13.4	5.8	14.5	13.9	13.7	2.6	1.5	3.2	1.4	10,758	44,160
District 39	19,665	257,648	10.5	8.0	11.5	12.7	9.1	5.7	1.7	5.8	1.3	11,941	46,345
District 40	11,400	211,391	21.6	2.4	16.3	11.4	11.5	1.4	1.2	1.9	0.8	9,117	43,128
District 41	10,126	184,914	8.4	9.0	5.3	16.1	15.2	2.3	1.5	3.3	1.2	7,571	40,945
District 42	11,740	155,850	11.7	15.2	6.4	15.2	11.1	1.8	1.6	4.9	1.1	6,340	40,677
District 43	15,217	291,799	10.9	2.9	6.3	10.3	11.5	2.2	2.5	6.4	2.3	15,274	52,344
District 44	8,735	163,841	20.6	6.1	11.6	10.6	8.6	1.1	1.3	1.8	1.2	7,775	47,455
District 45	26,021	413,301	10.1	5.0	8.1	8.3	8.7	8.4	4.0	14.5	4.7	29,008	70,185
District 46	18,049	392,810	10.6	7.0	5.8	7.7	13.3	4.9	2.0	5.0	1.4	18,892	48,095
District 47	15,770	243,080	7.3	5.3	5.3	12.1	15.1	5.3	1.9	5.6	1.9	12,345	50,786
District 48	25,408	327,565	7.6	4.3	5.0	14.3	12.3	6.7	4.1	10.6	1.5	19,508	59,554
District 49	21,754	276,231	11.8	5.5	6.3	12.8	12.4	2.6	2.0	12.1	2.5	15,097	54,655
District 50	16,313	200,829	7.5	12.7	3.2	17.6	11.5	2.0	1.8	3.9	1.0	7,877	39,223
District 51	10,343	141,209	11.7	3.9	6.7	23.7	14.5	2.4	1.7	3.0	1.6	5,175	36,646
District 52	29,498	525,065	7.6	4.8	6.8	8.8	7.7	6.4	2.6	13.4	4.5	36,033	68,626
District 53	16,279	234,195	3.0	4.8	2.0	13.1	28.2	4.6	2.4	6.7	1.0	10,679	45,598

Table E. Congressional Districts 116th Congress — **Land Area and Population Characteristics**

STATE District	Representative, 116th Congress	Land area[1] 2018 (sq mi)	Population and population characteristics, 2017												
			Total persons	Per square mile	Race alone (percent)				Some other race (percent)	Two or more races (percent)	Hispanic or Latino[2] (percent)	Non-Hispanic White alone (percent)	Percent female	Percent foreign-born	Percent born in state of residence
					White	Black	American Indian, Alaska Native	Asian and Pacific Islander							
		1	2	3	4	5	6	7	8	9	10	11	12	13	14
COLORADO		103,639.8	5,607,154	54.1	84.2	4.1	1.0	3.3	3.9	3.5	21.5	68.2	49.7	9.8	42.1
District 1	Diana DeGette (D)	189.9	826,995	4,354.3	77.9	7.9	1.0	3.7	6.3	3.2	27.5	58.5	49.8	13.6	40.3
District 2	Joe Neguse (D)	7,535.4	799,734	106.1	91.2	1.1	0.7	3.3	1.1	2.7	10.7	82.5	49.5	7.3	35.1
District 3	Scott R. Tipton (R)	49,730.5	749,478	15.1	88.5	0.9	2.4	1.0	4.6	2.6	24.4	70.9	49.9	6.3	48.9
District 4	Ken Buck (R)	38,102.1	817,251	21.4	89.8	1.4	0.6	2.4	3.1	2.9	22.1	71.7	49.4	8.4	47.9
District 5	Doug Lamborn (R)	7,265.8	799,622	110.1	81.0	5.7	1.0	2.7	4.1	5.5	16.4	70.7	48.9	6.2	32.3
District 6	Jason Crow (D)	474.0	814,636	1,718.7	73.8	9.5	0.6	6.7	5.4	4.1	20.2	60.4	50.2	15.9	41.1
District 7	Ed Perlmutter (D)	342.2	799,438	2,336.4	87.8	1.9	0.9	3.5	2.8	3.2	29.4	62.9	50.1	10.6	49.5
CONNECTICUT		4,842.7	3,588,184	740.9	75.9	10.6	0.3	4.6	5.3	3.3	16.1	66.7	51.2	14.8	54.2
District 1	John B. Larson (D)	675.4	710,509	1,052.0	68.4	15.5	0.3	5.4	6.7	3.7	17.1	60.4	51.5	16.0	58.0
District 2	Joe Courtney (D)	1,988.1	705,217	354.7	85.8	3.9	0.5	3.3	2.5	4.0	8.5	81.5	50.2	7.2	54.9
District 3	Rosa L. DeLauro (D)	470.3	716,547	1,523.5	72.9	14.4	0.2	4.2	4.7	3.7	15.2	64.6	51.7	11.5	62.9
District 4	James A. Himes (D)	460.8	737,616	1,600.6	73.5	11.3	0.4	5.7	6.3	2.9	20.8	60.2	51.4	23.8	41.2
District 5	Jahana Haynes (D)	1,248.1	718,295	575.5	79.0	8.0	0.3	4.2	6.3	2.2	18.9	67.1	51.2	15.0	54.4
DELAWARE		1,948.8	961,939	493.6	68.8	21.9	0.3	4.1	1.9	3.0	9.3	62.2	51.6	10.2	43.2
At Large	Lisa Blunt Rochester (D)	1,948.8	961,939	493.6	68.8	21.9	0.3	4.1	1.9	3.0	9.3	62.2	51.6	10.2	43.2
DISTRICT OF COLUMBIA		61.1	693,972	11,350.5	41.0	45.9	0.2	4.2	5.8	3.0	11.0	36.5	52.6	14.7	37.4
Delegate District (At Large)	Eleanor Holmes Norton (D)	61.1	693,972	11,350.5	41.0	45.9	0.2	4.2	5.8	3.0	11.0	36.5	52.6	14.7	37.4
FLORIDA		53,634.0	20,984,400	391.3	75.1	16.2	0.3	2.9	2.9	2.6	25.6	53.8	51.1	20.9	36.0
District 1	Matt Gaetz (R)	4,017.4	770,361	191.8	76.4	13.2	0.4	2.8	2.4	4.8	6.6	72.9	49.6	5.3	38.0
District 2	Neal P. Dunn (R)	11,003.7	731,845	66.5	80.8	13.6	0.3	1.8	0.7	2.7	6.8	75.5	48.9	4.9	51.8
District 3	Ted S. Yoho (R)	3,564.9	739,130	207.3	75.6	15.7	0.4	3.3	1.5	3.6	10.3	67.8	50.6	6.9	49.8
District 4	John H. Rutherford (R)	1,569.8	800,494	509.9	81.2	9.5	0.2	4.7	1.5	2.9	8.8	74.4	50.9	10.6	40.6
District 5	Al Lawson (D)	3,817.6	729,175	191.0	44.5	47.6	0.3	3.3	1.7	2.5	7.9	39.3	51.4	7.6	61.1
District 6	Michael Waltz (R)	2,171.4	764,500	352.1	82.8	10.3	0.5	1.9	2.8	1.7	12.8	73.5	51.2	7.6	34.5
District 7	Stephanie N. Murphy (D)	392.9	772,969	1,967.2	76.6	10.4	0.3	4.5	5.0	3.2	25.9	57.5	51.3	13.5	42.1
District 8	Bill Posey (R)	1,751.5	756,993	432.2	83.2	9.4	0.4	2.4	1.8	2.8	10.8	74.5	51.5	8.6	32.3
District 9	Darren Soto (D)	2,311.9	868,945	375.8	72.8	13.6	0.4	2.9	6.1	4.2	42.0	40.6	50.9	17.4	31.4
District 10	Val Butler Demings (D)	436.5	830,014	1,901.4	54.0	28.9	0.2	5.5	8.1	3.3	27.9	35.6	51.0	25.6	37.3
District 11	Daniel Webster (R)	2,390.1	770,114	322.2	87.6	7.2	0.5	1.5	1.4	1.7	10.2	78.9	52.1	6.7	29.5
District 12	Gus M. Bilirakis (R)	859.4	779,151	906.7	87.9	4.9	0.3	2.9	1.4	2.6	13.0	77.1	51.5	11.1	31.3
District 13	Charlie Crist (D)	181.8	730,650	4,018.8	78.1	12.8	0.4	3.5	1.9	3.3	10.2	70.7	52.0	13.2	34.5
District 14	Kathy Castor (D)	275.9	776,940	2,816.1	71.5	18.0	0.4	4.8	1.7	3.6	30.6	45.5	51.0	20.2	39.2
District 15	Ross Spano (R)	1,087.4	804,652	740.0	73.5	16.6	0.4	3.3	3.5	2.8	22.9	55.7	51.5	13.1	42.1
District 16	Vern Buchanan (R)	1,293.4	814,209	629.5	84.1	8.9	0.2	2.3	2.5	1.9	17.6	70.0	51.4	13.1	30.8
District 17	W. Gregory Steube (R)	5,573.0	778,091	139.6	86.7	7.6	0.3	1.6	2.0	1.9	14.9	74.2	50.7	10.9	32.4
District 18	Brian J. Mast (R)	1,511.3	772,184	510.9	80.3	13.0	0.5	2.5	1.4	2.2	17.2	66.0	51.5	16.0	32.1
District 19	Francis Rooney (R)	750.0	814,074	1,085.5	85.5	7.3	0.1	1.9	3.5	1.7	20.6	68.8	51.5	18.4	23.1
District 20	Alcee L. Hastings (D)	2,159.4	776,092	359.4	38.6	53.7	0.3	2.5	2.5	2.5	24.9	18.3	51.1	33.1	43.5
District 21	Lois Frankel (D)	256.1	788,240	3,077.6	75.9	16.8	0.3	2.7	2.4	1.9	24.1	55.1	51.4	28.4	27.1
District 22	Theodore E. Deutch (D)	164.9	757,352	4,593.0	76.6	15.1	0.1	3.4	2.0	2.8	22.0	57.6	50.4	29.5	27.0
District 23	Debbie Wasserman Schultz (D)	187.8	753,950	4,014.2	72.1	15.6	0.3	4.5	3.6	3.9	37.9	39.6	52.2	36.0	32.1
District 24	Frederica S. Wilson (D)	102.4	770,480	7,523.6	43.7	48.9	0.2	1.2	4.6	1.5	39.0	11.7	51.3	43.9	42.0
District 25	Mario Diaz-Balart (R)	3,505.5	780,826	222.7	90.4	4.5	0.2	1.5	2.1	1.2	75.3	19.0	51.0	56.3	25.9
District 26	Debbie Murcasel-Powell (D)	2,184.5	797,160	364.9	81.8	9.7	0.2	2.7	3.9	1.8	72.3	15.8	50.8	50.0	33.5
District 27	Donna E. Shalala (D)	113.2	755,809	6,674.3	86.0	5.5	0.3	1.5	4.6	2.1	73.2	20.1	51.7	53.8	29.7
GEORGIA		57,597.8	10,429,379	181.1	58.7	31.6	0.4	4.0	2.6	2.7	9.6	52.6	51.4	10.2	55.1
District 1	Earl L. "Buddy" Carter (R)	8,062.0	747,334	92.7	63.4	29.3	0.6	2.3	1.7	2.8	6.9	59.0	50.9	4.9	55.0
District 2	Sanford D. Bishop Jr. (D)	9,626.3	674,100	70.0	42.3	52.1	0.1	1.2	1.8	2.4	5.4	39.4	51.5	3.3	73.8
District 3	A. Drew Ferguson IV (R)	3,836.2	738,066	192.4	69.3	24.4	0.3	2.1	1.5	2.3	6.1	65.1	51.1	5.8	61.0
District 4	Henry C. "Hank" Johnson Jr. (D)	497.0	765,854	1,540.9	26.5	60.2	0.5	5.1	4.0	3.6	9.4	22.2	53.0	16.8	48.9
District 5	John Lewis (D)	264.9	784,370	2,960.8	32.0	58.3	0.2	4.5	2.2	2.9	6.6	28.3	51.8	8.8	54.0
District 6	Lucy McBath (D)	298.9	756,389	2,530.4	67.7	13.4	1.4	11.3	2.4	3.8	13.4	59.1	51.2	22.2	33.0
District 7	Robert Woodall (R)	392.6	807,492	2,056.6	54.4	20.5	0.5	14.2	7.2	3.3	20.0	43.3	50.7	25.8	35.7
District 8	Austin Scott (R)	8,716.9	702,262	80.6	62.4	31.3	0.3	1.5	2.4	2.2	6.3	59.0	50.6	4.4	68.8
District 9	Doug Collins (R)	5,211.6	755,181	144.9	87.8	6.9	0.2	1.5	1.9	1.8	13.1	76.8	50.7	8.2	60.8
District 10	Jody B. Hice (R)	7,096.9	736,838	103.8	68.8	24.6	0.1	2.3	1.4	2.9	5.4	65.3	51.2	5.3	64.8
District 11	Barry Loudermilk (R)	1,070.7	768,968	718.2	74.6	16.4	0.1	3.3	2.5	3.1	11.2	66.6	50.9	12.3	45.3
District 12	Rick W. Allen (R)	8,186.2	722,937	88.3	57.8	35.2	0.3	1.6	2.1	2.9	6.4	54.2	50.8	4.6	67.5
District 13	David Scott (D)	714.2	752,631	1,053.8	31.2	60.6	0.1	2.8	3.2	2.2	10.9	24.6	53.0	11.1	50.0
District 14	Tom Graves (R)	3,623.2	716,957	197.9	85.4	9.3	0.2	1.0	1.8	2.3	11.8	76.1	51.8	6.7	59.3
HAWAII		6,422.5	1,427,538	222.3	25.0	1.6	0.2	48.4	1.5	23.3	10.5	21.8	49.8	18.6	53.0
District 1	Ed Case (D)	209.0	714,328	3,417.0	17.7	1.8	0.1	58.2	1.3	20.8	8.3	15.7	50.2	23.7	52.1
District 2	Tulsi Gabbard (D)	6,213.4	713,210	114.8	32.4	1.4	0.2	38.6	1.7	25.7	12.7	27.9	49.4	13.5	54.0
IDAHO		82,644.5	1,716,943	20.8	90.0	0.7	1.3	1.5	3.4	3.1	12.4	82.0	49.8	5.9	47.6
District 1	Russ Fulcher (R)	39,419.8	890,052	22.6	89.8	0.6	1.3	1.4	3.6	3.3	10.6	83.6	50.0	4.7	42.7
District 2	Michael K. Simpson (R)	43,224.6	826,891	19.1	90.3	0.7	1.2	1.7	3.3	2.8	14.4	80.2	49.5	7.1	53.0
ILLINOIS		55,515.4	12,802,023	230.6	71.2	14.2	0.2	5.5	6.2	2.6	17.2	61.2	50.8	14.3	66.9
District 1	Bobby L. Rush (D)	258.4	720,977	2,790.2	41.8	50.3	0.2	2.0	3.5	2.2	10.9	35.3	53.6	7.3	78.1
District 2	Robin L. Kelly (D)	1,080.7	702,756	650.3	36.3	57.8	0.1	0.6	3.4	1.7	14.9	25.8	53.3	6.2	76.7

1. Dry land or land partially or temporarily covered by water. 2. May be of any race.

Table E. Congressional Districts 116th Congress — **Age and Education**

STATE District	Age (percent) Under 5 years	5 to 17 years	18 to 24 years	25 to 34 years	35 to 44 years	45 to 54 years	55 to 64 years	65 to 74 years	75 years and over	Median age	Education, 2017 Total Enrollment[1]	Attainment[2] (percent) High school graduate or more	Bachelor's degree or more
	15	16	17	18	19	20	21	22	23	24	25	26	27
COLORADO	5.9	16.6	9.3	15.5	13.6	12.7	12.6	8.6	5.2	36.8	1,394,563	91.6	41.2
District 1	6.2	13.8	7.9	21.7	15.6	11.9	10.9	7.3	4.7	35.2	184,074	89.5	48.8
District 2	4.6	14.3	13.3	14.0	11.8	12.9	13.9	9.8	5.4	38.1	217,012	96.3	56.4
District 3	5.5	16.2	8.7	12.8	12.4	12.2	14.5	11.0	6.8	40.3	173,899	90.8	31.0
District 4	6.4	19.0	8.4	13.2	13.7	13.7	12.4	8.2	4.9	37.1	210,672	90.7	36.0
District 5	6.3	17.1	10.2	15.4	12.9	12.2	12.4	8.4	5.1	35.6	204,261	93.5	37.2
District 6	6.1	18.8	8.2	14.7	14.6	13.7	12.0	7.7	4.3	36.5	212,929	91.6	43.1
District 7	6.3	16.7	8.7	16.3	14.1	12.6	12.0	7.9	5.4	36.1	191,716	89.3	34.6
CONNECTICUT	5.1	15.6	9.8	12.4	11.7	14.4	14.3	9.4	7.3	40.9	898,609	90.4	38.7
District 1	5.1	16.0	9.4	12.6	11.9	13.5	14.1	9.8	7.6	40.6	176,181	89.4	37.2
District 2	4.3	14.3	11.6	11.7	10.7	15.0	14.7	10.1	7.6	42.6	173,142	92.6	35.0
District 3	5.2	14.7	11.1	13.6	11.3	13.9	13.7	9.4	7.1	39.4	184,793	92.3	35.5
District 4	5.5	18.0	8.8	11.4	12.6	15.1	13.6	8.1	6.9	40.0	203,441	89.3	49.2
District 5	5.2	14.9	8.2	12.7	12.2	14.3	15.2	9.9	7.4	42.4	161,052	88.6	36.5
DELAWARE	5.7	15.5	8.7	13.6	11.5	12.9	13.9	10.8	7.2	40.1	233,046	90.6	31.5
At Large	5.7	15.5	8.7	13.6	11.5	12.9	13.9	10.8	7.2	40.1	233,046	90.6	31.5
DISTRICT OF COLUMBIA	6.5	11.5	10.8	23.4	14.7	11.0	10.1	6.9	5.2	34.0	167,649	90.2	57.3
Delegate District (At Large)	6.5	11.5	10.8	23.4	14.7	11.0	10.1	6.9	5.2	34.0	167,649	90.2	57.3
FLORIDA	5.4	14.6	8.4	12.9	12.1	13.2	13.3	11.2	8.9	42.0	4,770,596	88.4	29.7
District 1	5.9	15.5	9.8	14.2	11.7	12.7	13.9	9.8	6.6	38.5	178,158	90.9	27.8
District 2	5.1	14.9	9.6	11.8	12.2	12.5	14.4	11.4	8.1	41.9	167,097	88.1	24.6
District 3	5.5	14.9	12.5	13.5	11.9	12.5	12.6	10.1	6.6	37.6	198,865	87.6	26.1
District 4	5.8	14.9	8.4	14.6	12.4	13.8	13.8	10.2	6.0	39.6	179,172	92.6	40.0
District 5	6.2	16.8	12.5	15.9	12.6	11.6	11.6	7.9	5.0	34.0	204,685	86.9	21.3
District 6	4.4	13.1	7.6	10.9	10.5	12.4	15.7	14.3	11.1	47.9	150,553	89.9	23.7
District 7	5.1	14.7	11.3	16.1	13.4	13.2	12.4	8.0	5.8	36.5	209,414	94.6	41.5
District 8	4.6	13.4	7.5	10.4	9.9	13.0	16.4	13.4	11.3	48.5	158,804	91.5	30.0
District 9	6.1	17.3	8.9	13.5	13.7	12.9	11.2	9.5	6.9	38.3	211,294	85.9	23.4
District 10	6.7	17.1	9.3	16.9	13.9	13.5	11.3	7.2	4.1	35.0	215,802	88.1	30.2
District 11	4.0	11.7	6.0	8.1	8.6	11.0	14.4	20.1	16.1	55.5	122,207	89.2	22.0
District 12	4.9	14.2	6.9	10.3	11.5	13.4	14.5	13.2	11.0	46.5	161,299	90.8	27.2
District 13	4.5	12.1	6.7	13.2	11.1	14.0	15.7	12.5	10.3	46.9	138,407	90.4	30.5
District 14	5.9	14.9	10.5	15.8	13.2	14.1	12.3	8.0	5.3	37.1	200,273	89.4	36.4
District 15	6.4	17.5	8.4	13.9	13.7	12.7	11.9	9.2	6.3	37.7	204,210	88.0	25.2
District 16	5.1	14.7	6.1	10.7	11.0	11.9	13.8	14.3	12.4	47.3	161,583	91.1	33.6
District 17	4.5	12.9	6.2	9.6	9.5	11.5	14.4	16.4	14.9	51.5	131,987	87.0	21.7
District 18	4.5	14.2	7.4	10.0	10.8	12.8	14.9	13.4	12.0	47.7	161,671	89.9	32.0
District 19	4.2	12.3	6.6	9.9	10.2	11.4	13.9	16.9	14.7	51.3	150,485	90.6	32.4
District 20	7.2	16.3	9.2	14.7	14.0	13.5	11.3	7.8	6.0	36.6	203,091	83.1	21.1
District 21	5.2	13.7	6.7	12.0	11.3	13.2	12.6	12.0	13.2	46.1	169,514	88.6	35.2
District 22	4.5	13.4	7.2	12.6	12.1	14.1	15.3	11.2	9.5	45.1	167,270	91.6	39.6
District 23	5.6	16.0	7.9	12.3	13.0	15.1	13.1	9.0	8.0	41.0	192,953	92.4	40.6
District 24	6.8	16.2	8.4	15.5	14.3	13.3	12.1	8.0	5.5	37.0	193,597	79.2	20.4
District 25	5.3	13.9	8.3	13.3	12.1	15.3	13.1	10.0	8.8	42.7	166,907	79.4	24.1
District 26	5.4	15.5	9.8	14.0	13.9	15.0	11.8	8.3	6.4	38.7	202,568	81.5	27.5
District 27	5.6	12.7	7.4	14.7	13.7	14.9	12.7	9.4	8.8	42.1	168,730	86.6	40.8
GEORGIA	6.3	17.8	9.8	13.6	13.3	13.6	12.2	8.3	5.1	36.8	2,748,599	87.0	30.9
District 1	6.8	16.9	10.4	15.1	12.1	12.5	12.0	8.8	5.4	35.6	190,237	87.6	25.2
District 2	6.6	17.6	10.4	13.8	11.8	11.8	13.1	8.9	6.0	36.0	182,335	84.0	17.2
District 3	5.8	17.9	9.3	11.9	13.0	14.4	13.0	9.0	5.7	38.6	185,242	87.8	27.6
District 4	6.7	18.8	8.9	13.6	13.9	13.7	13.0	7.4	4.1	36.4	213,485	87.9	30.7
District 5	6.3	14.7	12.9	19.2	13.2	12.6	10.0	6.9	4.2	33.0	208,072	88.6	40.9
District 6	6.1	17.9	6.9	14.3	14.3	15.1	12.9	7.9	4.6	37.8	193,319	94.2	62.0
District 7	6.8	20.2	8.6	12.6	15.8	15.3	10.5	6.4	3.8	36.1	228,521	89.3	42.6
District 8	6.4	17.6	9.9	12.9	12.9	12.7	12.4	9.1	6.2	37.5	178,144	84.9	23.0
District 9	5.7	16.9	8.9	10.8	12.1	13.9	13.4	11.1	7.2	41.4	173,399	82.4	23.6
District 10	5.5	18.2	12.1	12.3	11.9	13.3	12.1	9.3	5.3	36.4	212,306	87.2	26.2
District 11	5.6	17.7	9.5	14.6	14.0	14.7	12.0	7.6	4.3	36.9	209,202	91.3	41.4
District 12	6.3	17.3	11.9	13.3	12.1	12.4	12.5	8.6	5.6	35.9	197,679	83.4	21.5
District 13	7.1	19.5	8.2	13.5	14.9	13.7	11.7	7.5	3.8	36.1	208,587	88.2	27.6
District 14	6.3	18.4	9.1	12.4	13.3	13.7	12.4	8.8	5.6	37.8	168,071	80.3	17.1
HAWAII	6.3	15.2	8.7	14.4	12.7	12.2	12.8	10.1	7.6	39.2	324,608	92.3	32.9
District 1	6.0	13.7	8.5	15.3	12.8	12.8	12.4	10.0	8.4	39.7	164,301	91.4	35.6
District 2	6.6	16.6	8.9	13.6	12.6	11.5	13.1	10.3	6.8	38.6	160,307	93.2	30.1
IDAHO	6.8	19.0	9.4	12.9	12.6	11.6	12.4	9.3	6.0	36.3	454,019	90.8	26.8
District 1	6.3	18.6	8.6	12.1	12.5	12.2	13.2	10.2	6.2	38.2	223,224	91.1	25.4
District 2	7.2	19.5	10.3	13.8	12.6	10.9	11.6	8.4	5.6	34.2	230,795	90.6	28.4
ILLINOIS	6.0	16.6	9.4	13.8	12.9	13.1	13.0	8.8	6.4	38.0	3,216,701	89.1	34.4
District 1	5.8	17.0	9.6	13.2	11.4	12.9	14.6	9.2	6.5	38.7	189,565	88.9	27.6
District 2	5.8	18.4	9.9	11.9	12.2	13.7	13.1	8.8	6.2	37.9	186,376	88.7	21.8

1. All persons 3 years old and over enrolled in nursery school through college and graduate or professional school. 2. Persons 25 years old and over.

Table E. Congressional Districts 116th Congress — **Households and Group Quarters**

STATE District	Households, 2017 — Number	Average household size	Family households (percent)	Married couple family (percent)	Female family house-holder[1] (percent)	One person households (percent)	Total in group quarters, 2017	Percent 65 years and over	Persons in correctional institutions	Persons in nursing facilities	Persons in college dormitories	Persons in military quarters
	28	29	30	31	32	33	34	35	36	37	38	39
COLORADO	2,139,207	2.57	63.9	49.7	9.5	27.1	119,289	14.3	40,568	18,079	29,952	10,945
District 1	347,044	2.34	50.7	37.3	8.9	35.6	15,645	12.3	3,960	2,592	4,940	0
District 2	315,832	2.46	60.2	49.8	6.5	26.9	22,608	11.6	1,634	2,213	11,841	0
District 3	292,491	2.51	64.4	50.3	9.0	29.2	16,479	20.4	3,982	3,460	5,041	0
District 4	295,268	2.71	72.3	58.5	9.6	21.3	17,320	12.8	13,075	2,577	3,993	0
District 5	297,598	2.59	68.5	53.5	9.8	24.5	29,662	6.9	12,094	2,245	2,580	10,678
District 6	291,946	2.77	69.5	52.5	11.2	23.7	7,179	32.7	3,009	2,128	0	267
District 7	299,028	2.64	64.2	47.8	12.1	26.7	10,396	28.1	2,814	2,864	1,557	0
CONNECTICUT	1,356,762	2.56	64.7	47.9	12.3	29.0	114,538	20.9	20,059	26,371	48,537	3,977
District 1	279,014	2.49	61.7	43.6	13.0	31.6	16,433	33.0	1,335	6,778	5,649	0
District 2	273,508	2.43	64.9	49.7	10.9	27.8	40,383	10.7	12,975	4,306	16,779	3,977
District 3	268,206	2.57	62.8	44.6	13.9	30.8	26,914	17.9	902	5,257	16,566	0
District 4	261,440	2.77	69.0	53.0	11.8	25.2	13,567	31.6	1,159	4,719	5,030	0
District 5	274,594	2.55	65.2	48.8	11.8	29.4	17,241	28.1	3,688	5,311	4,513	0
DELAWARE	357,937	2.62	65.9	49.4	11.8	27.7	25,034	16.8	6,457	4,591	10,184	283
At Large	357,937	2.62	65.9	49.4	11.8	27.7	25,034	16.8	6,457	4,591	10,184	283
DISTRICT OF COLUMBIA	281,475	2.32	42.4	25.1	13.8	45.2	39,935	7.8	3,598	3,064	24,087	1,504
Delegate District (At Large)	281,475	2.32	42.4	25.1	13.8	45.2	39,935	7.8	3,598	3,064	24,087	1,504
FLORIDA	7,689,964	2.67	64.3	46.7	12.7	28.8	428,146	17.5	167,453	73,372	85,243	14,612
District 1	297,700	2.48	65.4	47.6	12.7	28.0	31,196	8.8	10,881	2,652	4,832	8,580
District 2	269,813	2.55	65.0	49.9	10.8	28.2	43,895	6.9	32,671	3,280	10,370	513
District 3	266,829	2.64	61.4	45.0	12.1	30.9	34,981	9.3	21,156	3,439	9,235	0
District 4	304,912	2.57	67.1	52.8	10.2	26.1	15,648	18.0	2,597	2,852	2,776	4,662
District 5	269,908	2.58	60.3	34.5	19.9	31.0	32,574	10.6	10,195	2,281	1,357	0
District 6	308,131	2.44	63.3	47.1	11.1	29.9	12,061	20.3	4,351	3,572	5,748	4
District 7	289,203	2.59	62.5	46.7	11.1	27.8	24,143	15.3	757	3,056	13,306	0
District 8	291,341	2.57	62.4	49.4	9.1	31.4	7,553	27.2	3,105	2,612	1,259	182
District 9	273,983	3.14	72.0	50.9	15.0	22.0	8,408	24.1	3,819	1,838	245	0
District 10	278,232	2.95	68.3	46.3	16.9	24.1	8,227	16.2	3,929	2,605	315	0
District 11	321,140	2.34	64.7	51.6	9.5	29.4	17,068	15.3	16,221	2,953	312	0
District 12	314,204	2.45	64.4	48.5	11.5	29.4	10,016	40.5	1,981	2,902	1,050	0
District 13	304,154	2.35	54.4	39.4	10.7	36.5	15,571	35.3	3,506	5,478	1,751	0
District 14	301,090	2.53	58.4	39.6	13.8	32.9	14,931	18.8	3,483	3,007	3,375	324
District 15	278,634	2.84	69.0	50.6	13.4	24.5	13,010	15.6	854	2,303	7,847	0
District 16	315,102	2.55	63.1	50.9	8.7	30.1	9,927	38.1	2,011	3,857	1,569	0
District 17	299,235	2.54	65.6	52.5	9.2	28.1	18,677	15.9	12,761	3,312	606	2
District 18	293,652	2.60	64.7	49.9	10.4	29.6	8,037	25.5	3,930	1,838	339	9
District 19	313,159	2.56	64.7	52.4	8.5	29.5	12,170	26.8	2,727	2,860	2,688	0
District 20	247,808	3.06	63.5	37.5	19.7	29.3	16,936	18.4	10,719	3,611	214	0
District 21	295,802	2.64	62.0	46.4	11.4	31.8	6,889	52.8	619	1,396	19	0
District 22	303,636	2.46	56.0	41.9	10.0	36.1	8,892	29.7	1,291	3,658	3,672	0
District 23	267,627	2.80	66.4	48.3	13.1	27.3	4,137	23.7	938	1,239	1,463	59
District 24	239,380	3.15	64.4	34.5	22.6	30.1	15,258	21.9	3,004	2,733	3,132	0
District 25	246,558	3.12	73.6	49.9	16.4	21.3	12,575	12.7	5,752	717	596	0
District 26	227,080	3.45	77.2	50.8	18.9	17.4	14,592	17.9	4,186	1,100	2,657	277
District 27	271,651	2.74	61.4	41.0	13.7	30.9	10,774	24.6	9	2,221	4,510	0
GEORGIA	3,745,074	2.72	67.4	47.8	14.9	26.7	258,793	12.5	104,012	34,738	72,288	16,072
District 1	276,109	2.62	65.9	46.5	15.1	27.9	25,149	10.4	10,733	3,028	5,798	5,069
District 2	245,599	2.59	63.5	37.2	21.4	32.4	37,419	8.4	17,145	3,559	7,343	5,167
District 3	272,918	2.66	69.8	52.4	13.7	24.6	11,233	20.6	4,777	2,837	4,020	64
District 4	262,056	2.90	68.4	42.8	20.3	26.1	6,345	17.9	4,367	1,472	653	0
District 5	303,273	2.45	49.7	26.6	18.5	40.1	41,837	5.3	6,731	2,500	22,635	78
District 6	284,919	2.64	67.1	54.2	8.8	26.3	3,096	49.0	89	1,109	620	0
District 7	263,436	3.04	77.1	60.8	11.5	18.6	5,596	18.9	4,093	1,167	0	0
District 8	257,564	2.63	67.5	46.8	15.6	26.9	23,698	13.4	13,355	4,044	5,390	401
District 9	263,353	2.82	73.3	56.5	11.7	22.4	11,355	17.7	4,824	2,514	4,115	44
District 10	259,444	2.73	70.5	52.3	13.4	23.6	27,691	12.0	10,678	2,840	9,699	74
District 11	286,732	2.64	67.0	51.9	10.7	26.0	11,387	14.1	3,520	1,539	4,296	36
District 12	246,483	2.79	64.7	45.6	14.6	29.7	35,469	10.7	15,029	3,980	5,294	5,139
District 13	267,301	2.79	69.0	41.7	22.0	26.5	5,945	21.4	3,437	1,322	0	0
District 14	255,887	2.75	73.3	54.9	12.4	21.5	12,573	21.5	5,234	2,827	2,425	0
HAWAII	458,078	3.02	69.9	50.9	12.8	24.4	44,435	12.2	5,673	5,198	7,540	12,551
District 1	234,250	2.95	67.7	48.5	13.3	26.9	22,658	13.3	3,581	2,672	4,641	5,332
District 2	223,828	3.09	72.3	53.5	12.2	21.7	21,777	10.9	2,092	2,526	2,899	7,219
IDAHO	625,135	2.70	67.1	54.1	8.7	27.5	29,946	16.9	11,275	4,820	7,223	466
District 1	323,306	2.70	67.9	55.3	8.3	26.9	18,566	15.4	7,951	2,375	4,359	0
District 2	301,829	2.70	66.3	52.9	9.1	28.1	11,380	19.2	3,324	2,445	2,864	466
ILLINOIS	4,808,672	2.60	64.1	47.4	12.1	29.7	300,775	22.6	70,828	81,516	92,960	12,483
District 1	270,378	2.62	61.0	34.8	20.6	35.0	11,337	21.7	0	4,063	5,957	0
District 2	253,451	2.73	62.5	34.1	23.7	33.7	11,885	31.1	685	5,037	2,054	0

1. No spouse present.

Table E. Congressional Districts 116th Congress — **Housing and Money Income**

STATE District	Housing units, 2017						Money income, 2017		
	Occupied units						Households		
			Owner-occupied			Renter-occupied			
	Total	Occupied units as a percent of all units	Owner-occupied units as a percent of occupied units	Median value[1] (dollars)	Percent valued at $500,000 or more	Median rent[2]	Per capita income (dollars)	Median income (dollars)	Percent with income of $100,000 or more
	40	41	42	43	44	45	46	47	48
COLORADO	2,385,495	89.7	65.2	348,900	23.2	1,240	36,345	69,117	32.7
District 1	373,376	92.9	52.9	394,400	31.9	1,291	42,466	67,441	32.9
District 2	381,482	82.8	67.6	436,300	39.1	1,398	43,235	80,019	39.8
District 3	371,093	78.8	68.1	237,500	17.9	890	29,302	52,765	21.1
District 4	318,045	92.8	71.5	341,400	21.2	1,096	35,195	73,735	34.7
District 5	326,449	91.2	65.2	271,900	11.0	1,120	31,323	64,179	28.8
District 6	303,826	96.1	67.0	383,700	24.2	1,397	38,714	80,606	39.2
District 7	311,224	96.1	66.1	351,600	16.7	1,343	33,508	70,574	31.8
CONNECTICUT	1,517,495	89.4	66.2	273,100	16.8	1,125	42,029	74,168	37.0
District 1	307,367	90.8	64.8	238,400	6.7	1,057	37,148	69,766	33.2
District 2	308,487	88.7	71.5	244,400	8.8	1,030	38,641	73,805	34.9
District 3	299,755	89.5	62.4	252,200	8.3	1,160	36,123	69,178	33.8
District 4	289,675	90.3	65.2	507,700	50.6	1,451	58,307	94,547	48.3
District 5	312,211	88.0	67.0	270,100	11.7	1,045	39,357	71,995	35.2
DELAWARE	432,853	82.7	70.9	252,800	9.2	1,086	33,887	62,852	28.7
At Large	432,853	82.7	70.9	252,800	9.2	1,086	33,887	62,852	28.7
DISTRICT OF COLUMBIA....	314,843	89.4	42.2	607,200	60.3	1,499	52,500	82,372	42.6
Delegate District (At Large)...	314,843	89.4	42.2	607,200	60.3	1,499	52,500	82,372	42.6
FLORIDA............	9,441,585	81.4	65.2	214,000	10.4	1,128	29,838	52,594	22.4
District 1	367,932	80.9	66.8	175,700	6.8	992	29,183	55,229	21.8
District 2	352,875	76.5	72.5	160,200	4.1	896	26,100	48,838	19.0
District 3	316,412	84.3	65.8	154,000	3.4	926	25,983	47,611	18.0
District 4	349,054	87.4	67.8	256,100	12.3	1,161	37,769	68,964	32.7
District 5	317,297	85.1	51.2	125,900	1.7	894	21,033	40,920	11.1
District 6	370,136	83.2	71.2	187,100	5.5	1,044	27,478	48,197	18.0
District 7	322,729	89.6	59.8	238,700	10.0	1,176	33,095	61,423	28.2
District 8	364,154	80.0	74.9	197,100	7.4	989	31,436	52,180	22.6
District 9	362,699	75.5	64.9	187,700	3.0	1,120	23,786	50,964	19.2
District 10	323,758	85.9	53.0	227,100	9.8	1,128	27,306	50,963	22.0
District 11	391,939	81.9	81.3	159,200	3.9	892	26,382	46,001	13.7
District 12	367,384	85.5	71.9	180,200	4.3	1,055	30,360	52,573	22.0
District 13	390,247	77.9	64.8	191,600	11.3	1,040	32,806	50,724	20.4
District 14	337,919	89.1	51.6	232,600	13.8	1,080	33,061	51,774	24.5
District 15	320,680	86.9	63.7	177,000	3.2	1,073	25,785	53,367	21.1
District 16	404,189	78.0	73.9	242,200	14.0	1,191	34,548	59,437	26.0
District 17	391,018	76.5	77.1	170,300	6.1	918	27,152	49,449	18.3
District 18	369,460	79.5	73.8	253,000	14.2	1,282	36,310	58,754	26.4
District 19	478,335	65.5	71.4	265,500	20.4	1,166	37,099	56,828	25.1
District 20	285,595	86.8	55.5	188,100	4.6	1,155	22,021	44,436	16.0
District 21	365,548	80.9	71.5	267,200	15.0	1,374	35,935	58,410	27.2
District 22	391,241	77.6	64.5	312,900	22.7	1,408	41,131	62,353	30.5
District 23	346,151	77.3	66.0	316,400	20.3	1,484	36,096	66,872	30.9
District 24	270,224	88.6	45.2	203,900	8.9	1,128	20,222	41,172	14.6
District 25	285,247	86.4	56.9	267,100	10.3	1,265	23,521	50,120	19.4
District 26	261,655	86.8	61.4	295,800	11.3	1,411	23,880	56,496	24.2
District 27	337,651	80.5	47.7	395,000	38.9	1,349	36,271	56,183	28.8
GEORGIA	4,282,254	87.5	62.9	173,700	8.0	958	29,668	56,183	24.8
District 1	325,443	84.8	60.9	152,800	6.7	933	27,437	51,223	20.8
District 2	302,635	81.2	54.9	99,000	2.0	717	20,794	37,569	13.0
District 3	297,642	91.7	67.4	169,900	5.0	904	29,182	58,949	24.7
District 4	285,964	91.6	59.9	162,900	3.4	1,055	26,415	57,349	22.7
District 5	363,768	83.4	43.9	209,800	18.3	1,065	35,019	51,810	25.0
District 6	306,443	93.0	64.1	386,800	28.2	1,335	50,358	92,317	46.3
District 7	276,835	95.2	70.2	259,100	10.8	1,244	33,275	74,868	36.2
District 8	303,091	85.0	63.2	120,000	2.2	760	23,929	45,279	17.7
District 9	334,242	78.8	75.0	178,500	7.4	772	28,497	56,754	23.6
District 10	299,899	86.5	67.4	172,100	5.1	834	26,433	53,479	22.9
District 11	307,580	93.2	65.3	246,300	13.4	1,173	38,902	72,445	33.8
District 12	303,768	81.1	63.0	119,600	2.2	749	22,161	43,177	16.4
District 13	289,807	92.2	60.8	156,500	2.5	1,011	26,141	55,682	21.5
District 14	285,137	89.7	66.3	142,900	2.9	757	24,113	50,132	18.2
HAWAII	542,955	84.4	58.5	617,400	64.4	1,573	33,882	77,765	37.0
District 1	264,347	88.6	55.2	668,900	71.3	1,631	36,095	80,083	38.7
District 2	278,608	80.3	62.0	566,800	58.0	1,491	31,666	75,289	35.3
IDAHO............	721,818	86.6	69.7	207,100	6.3	822	26,386	52,225	19.9
District 1	374,309	86.4	72.1	225,800	6.9	864	27,677	53,561	21.1
District 2	347,509	86.9	67.0	186,500	5.5	793	24,997	51,307	18.5
ILLINOIS	5,359,416	89.7	66.2	195,300	9.1	974	34,196	62,992	29.8
District 1	310,506	87.1	58.5	184,100	4.2	957	26,993	50,744	21.8
District 2	297,195	85.3	60.7	133,900	1.7	931	24,831	50,391	19.0

1. Specified owner-occupied units.   2. Specified renter-occupied units.

Table E. Congressional Districts 116th Congress — Poverty, Labor Force, Employment, and Social Security

STATE District	Poverty, 2017			Civilian labor force, 2016	Unemployment		Civilian employment,[2] 2017	Percent			Persons under 65 years of age with no health insurance, 2017 (percent)	Social Security beneficiaries, December 2018		Supplemental Security Income recipients, December 2018
	Persons below poverty level (percent)	Families below poverty level (percent)	Percent of households receiving food stamps in past 12 months	Total	Total	Rate[1]	Total	Management, business, science, and arts occupations	Service, sales, and office	Construction and production		Number	Rate[3]	
	49	50	51	52	53	54	55	56	57	58	59	60	61	62
COLORADO	10.3	6.7	7.6	3,027,185	127,259	4.2	2,899,926	41.9	39.4	18.7	8.6	874,819	156.0	73,012
District 1	11.3	7.9	7.5	487,098	14,945	3.1	472,153	47.0	37.2	15.7	9.9	106,298	128.5	15,341
District 2	10.7	4.3	4.7	455,085	18,628	4.1	436,457	49.6	35.3	15.1	6.7	124,152	155.2	4,748
District 3	13.7	9.8	11.6	375,873	22,817	6.1	353,056	34.7	42.0	23.3	11.5	157,423	210.0	14,242
District 4	8.8	5.9	7.8	430,314	16,959	3.9	413,355	40.0	38.6	21.4	7.4	127,215	155.7	9,052
District 5	10.8	8.1	9.4	381,843	21,479	5.6	360,364	40.3	40.9	18.8	8.3	135,472	169.4	10,899
District 6	7.5	5.0	6.1	451,813	17,627	3.9	434,186	42.0	41.1	17.0	7.8	105,909	130.0	9,214
District 7	9.5	6.4	6.4	445,159	14,804	3.3	430,355	37.8	41.4	20.8	8.7	118,350	148.0	9,516
CONNECTICUT	9.6	6.4	12.0	1,922,383	117,360	6.1	1,805,023	43.6	39.9	16.5	6.4	681,765	190.0	66,442
District 1	10.9	6.8	14.4	381,420	23,806	6.2	357,614	43.7	40.5	15.8	5.2	143,259	201.6	17,160
District 2	7.7	4.6	8.9	371,537	17,032	4.6	354,505	42.7	38.6	18.7	4.2	145,039	205.7	9,009
District 3	10.4	6.9	12.8	389,101	26,738	6.9	362,363	42.3	41.7	16.1	4.8	137,509	191.9	15,010
District 4	9.1	6.3	8.6	392,800	26,901	6.8	365,899	46.8	40.0	13.1	10.5	116,920	158.5	10,668
District 5	9.9	7.2	15.4	387,525	22,883	5.9	364,642	42.6	38.7	18.7	7.0	139,038	193.6	14,595
DELAWARE	13.6	9.2	10.4	460,676	24,300	5.3	436,376	40.7	39.3	20.0	6.4	213,246	221.7	17,047
At Large	13.6	9.2	10.4	460,676	24,300	5.3	436,376	40.7	39.3	20.0	6.4	213,246	221.7	17,047
DISTRICT OF COLUMBIA....	16.6	13.3	13.2	405,506	26,726	6.6	378,780	63.3	30.3	6.4	4.2	83,059	119.7	25,755
Delegate District (At Large)...	16.6	13.3	13.2	405,506	26,726	6.6	378,780	63.3	30.3	6.4	4.2	83,059	119.7	25,755
FLORIDA	14.0	10.1	13.6	10,040,987	552,245	5.5	9,488,742	35.2	46.0	18.8	15.9	4,626,156	220.5	576,375
District 1	13.6	9.6	11.9	358,862	19,001	5.3	339,861	35.5	46.4	18.1	13.4	174,155	226.1	17,482
District 2	15.8	10.6	13.4	310,533	19,820	6.4	290,713	35.9	44.0	20.1	14.1	182,443	249.3	20,278
District 3	18.2	12.4	12.9	340,385	19,231	5.6	321,154	38.8	44.4	16.8	12.9	159,023	215.1	19,243
District 4	9.5	6.4	7.2	415,847	18,919	4.5	396,928	44.7	39.9	15.4	11.8	157,232	196.4	12,040
District 5	22.0	16.3	21.9	346,156	27,791	8.0	318,365	30.0	50.3	19.8	14.1	134,822	184.9	27,716
District 6	14.5	10.1	12.6	333,652	16,188	4.9	317,464	32.6	47.0	20.4	15.0	228,782	299.3	17,242
District 7	13.2	8.9	9.5	407,928	16,942	4.2	390,986	45.6	40.6	13.7	9.8	127,722	165.2	13,917
District 8	11.5	6.8	9.6	335,405	15,209	4.5	320,196	38.5	42.8	18.6	13.0	218,839	289.1	15,049
District 9	14.5	11.3	18.0	410,315	19,846	4.8	390,469	31.0	48.7	20.4	16.2	176,092	202.7	26,701
District 10	16.0	13.5	17.0	444,351	24,284	5.5	420,067	33.2	47.6	19.1	17.6	120,710	145.4	23,497
District 11	12.4	8.3	10.9	274,220	20,147	7.3	254,073	29.0	50.4	20.6	15.3	312,187	405.4	16,696
District 12	11.5	8.5	11.2	353,232	18,954	5.4	334,278	37.3	45.3	17.3	13.6	207,510	266.3	15,400
District 13	13.0	7.9	11.0	365,525	19,970	5.5	345,555	36.5	45.9	17.6	15.4	184,083	251.9	18,760
District 14	17.6	12.9	15.0	412,239	23,382	5.7	388,857	41.5	43.1	15.4	14.8	124,783	160.6	26,363
District 15	15.0	11.4	13.3	387,376	17,991	4.6	369,385	34.2	45.7	20.2	14.3	159,235	197.9	21,880
District 16	10.1	6.7	8.8	360,190	16,523	4.6	343,667	35.7	44.8	19.4	15.1	217,334	266.9	11,838
District 17	14.2	9.6	10.8	304,128	16,445	5.4	287,683	27.9	48.6	23.4	16.8	243,762	313.3	14,376
District 18	10.1	6.7	8.6	359,890	17,472	4.9	342,418	36.4	46.2	17.4	14.6	197,810	256.2	12,061
District 19	10.5	7.0	7.7	358,993	17,375	4.8	341,618	31.1	48.4	20.5	18.0	224,493	275.8	12,433
District 20	17.6	12.8	21.6	396,261	26,797	6.8	369,464	28.4	49.7	21.9	18.8	120,118	154.8	25,626
District 21	12.0	7.7	9.6	383,991	22,459	5.8	361,532	34.4	48.8	16.8	19.3	183,164	232.4	10,615
District 22	11.3	7.8	7.2	409,374	23,656	5.8	385,718	39.9	43.9	16.2	16.7	148,708	196.4	13,316
District 23	10.2	8.1	8.7	384,962	21,154	5.5	363,808	43.4	41.3	15.3	13.7	127,781	169.5	13,118
District 24	20.5	16.7	28.6	380,497	35,791	9.4	344,706	25.8	54.2	20.0	24.6	121,217	157.3	49,341
District 25	16.2	13.4	25.2	397,330	16,118	4.1	381,212	26.9	46.6	26.5	22.9	132,650	169.9	43,826
District 26	14.4	12.4	23.1	409,666	22,506	5.5	387,160	30.6	46.9	22.5	20.1	120,095	150.7	40,428
District 27	15.0	12.2	21.8	399,679	18,274	4.6	381,405	41.7	42.5	15.8	15.6	121,406	160.6	37,133
GEORGIA	14.9	11.1	12.6	5,137,885	296,040	5.8	4,841,845	37.2	40.2	22.6	15.4	1,830,266	175.5	259,434
District 1	16.6	12.5	14.0	345,083	23,622	6.8	321,461	33.7	42.5	23.8	16.5	138,633	185.5	17,955
District 2	25.0	20.1	23.2	282,961	27,855	9.8	255,106	27.1	46.2	26.7	16.6	143,183	212.4	31,558
District 3	14.1	10.9	11.5	362,943	21,548	5.9	341,395	33.7	39.3	27.0	12.9	149,387	202.4	19,069
District 4	14.2	11.1	14.8	401,185	25,018	6.2	376,167	35.1	41.9	23.0	17.0	116,271	151.8	21,886
District 5	19.2	14.7	17.3	427,018	29,381	6.9	397,637	45.7	38.7	15.6	14.6	104,003	132.6	26,221
District 6	7.2	4.4	3.9	421,090	16,175	3.8	404,915	55.8	34.8	9.4	11.9	96,325	127.3	5,732
District 7	10.0	7.5	6.3	420,713	18,329	4.4	402,384	42.4	40.1	17.5	18.5	95,134	117.8	9,741
District 8	19.7	14.6	15.3	314,621	20,423	6.5	294,198	33.2	42.1	24.7	16.5	144,750	206.1	24,001
District 9	13.4	10.0	11.5	355,186	13,932	3.9	341,254	30.7	39.8	29.5	18.3	175,757	232.7	15,502
District 10	15.7	10.5	12.2	338,863	15,711	4.6	323,152	34.9	39.2	25.9	11.8	146,498	198.8	18,362
District 11	9.8	6.5	5.6	420,864	16,801	4.0	404,063	44.2	39.0	16.8	13.0	115,594	150.3	9,873
District 12	19.7	14.3	17.0	317,592	22,642	7.1	294,950	32.1	41.5	26.4	15.8	141,728	196.0	23,952
District 13	12.8	10.4	13.5	386,589	26,681	6.9	359,908	33.6	41.8	24.6	14.9	116,507	154.8	18,094
District 14	14.7	11.1	11.8	343,177	17,922	5.2	325,255	28.2	38.3	33.5	17.2	146,496	204.3	17,488
HAWAII	9.5	7.4	10.7	710,267	29,762	4.2	680,505	34.1	48.5	17.4	4.6	271,236	190.0	23,155
District 1	7.9	6.1	8.8	366,453	11,990	3.3	354,463	35.8	47.7	16.5	3.8	133,523	186.9	11,359
District 2	11.2	8.6	12.7	343,814	17,772	5.2	326,042	32.1	49.4	18.5	5.3	137,713	193.1	11,796
IDAHO	12.8	8.6	9.7	820,913	34,000	4.1	786,913	34.6	39.5	25.9	11.9	346,243	201.7	30,870
District 1	12.5	7.9	9.7	418,421	18,102	4.3	400,319	33.4	40.6	26.1	12.5	194,516	218.5	15,325
District 2	13.1	9.4	9.8	402,492	15,898	3.9	386,594	35.8	38.5	25.8	11.3	151,727	183.5	15,545
ILLINOIS	12.6	9.0	12.9	6,642,821	407,967	6.1	6,234,854	37.8	40.8	21.4	7.8	2,243,286	175.2	267,026
District 1	17.8	13.8	20.9	358,033	46,401	13.0	311,632	33.1	46.3	20.6	8.1	125,542	174.1	24,588
District 2	18.7	14.0	22.5	341,297	45,101	13.2	296,196	29.1	45.5	25.5	8.4	132,374	188.4	28,555

1. Percent of civilian labor force.   2. Persons 16 years old and over.   3. Per 1,000 resident population estimated in the 2017 American Community Survey.

Table E. Congressional Districts 116th Congress — **Agriculture**

STATE District		Agriculture 2017								
		Land in farms			Value of products sold				Government payments	
	Number of farms	Acres	Average size of farm (acres)	Harvested cropland (acres)	Total ($1,000)	Average per farm (dollars)	Percent from crops	Percent from livestock and poultry products	Total ($1,000)	Average per farm receiving payments (dollars)
	63	64	65	66	67	68	69	70	71	72
COLORADO	38,893	31,820,957	818	5,916,737	7,491,702	192,623	29.9	70.1	198,697	22,206
District 1	71	6,390	90	523	D	D	D	D	D	D
District 2	3,627	953,177	263	126,497	206,343	56,891	51.3	48.7	1,035	6,273
District 3	14,808	8,719,448	589	1,025,088	967,155	65,313	53.4	46.6	16,655	10,711
District 4	16,578	20,777,185	1,253	4,667,347	6,156,045	371,338	24.5	75.5	178,446	25,540
District 5	3,044	1,225,026	402	47,661	71,820	23,594	32.5	67.5	1,626	11,698
District 6	395	96,913	245	38,832	D	D	D	D	644	9,200
District 7	370	42,818	116	10,789	47,821	129,246	90.4	9.6	D	D
CONNECTICUT	5,521	381,539	69	122,074	580,114	105,074	72.4	27.6	1,850	7,551
District 1	720	41,976	58	17,349	88,995	123,604	97.0	3.0	202	7,481
District 2	2,501	171,834	69	60,637	290,026	115,964	61.6	38.4	869	7,364
District 3	560	22,760	41	8,099	30,317	54,138	D	D	322	11,500
District 4	336	49,386	147	2,989	32,355	96,295	41.5	58.5	10	1,667
District 5	1,404	95,583	68	33,000	138,421	98,590	D	D	446	6,758
DELAWARE	2,302	525,324	228	435,085	1,465,973	636,826	22.2	77.8	15,162	18,604
At Large	2,302	525,324	228	435,085	1,465,973	636,826	22.2	77.8	15,162	18,604
DISTRICT OF COLUMBIA	X	X	X	X	X	X	X	X	X	X
Delegate District (At Large)	X	X	X	X	X	X	X	X	X	X
FLORIDA	47,590	9,731,731	204	2,093,330	7,357,343	154,599	77.5	22.5	59,120	14,795
District 1	2,929	349,886	119	112,935	125,902	42,985	61.0	39.0	9,336	16,322
District 2	7,980	1,696,547	213	398,462	809,576	101,451	39.1	60.9	19,453	20,872
District 3	5,415	531,791	98	87,596	239,941	44,310	61.9	38.1	1,881	9,746
District 4	809	103,274	128	14,834	43,075	53,245	62.4	37.6	301	5,017
District 5	2,815	597,271	212	90,114	290,125	103,064	53.2	46.8	4,332	13,929
District 6	2,353	274,585	117	37,953	354,142	150,507	92.4	7.6	1,507	11,773
District 7	456	41,487	91	3,212	26,224	57,509	91.2	8.8	180	10,000
District 8	1,106	367,011	332	61,950	182,637	165,133	85.7	14.3	703	11,339
District 9	1,290	816,015	633	71,832	238,917	185,207	75.6	24.4	1,739	14,372
District 10	361	18,909	52	5,215	196,875	545,360	99.6	0.4	69	6,900
District 11	4,389	445,594	102	48,445	165,219	37,644	64.8	35.2	1,994	6,391
District 12	1,318	198,908	151	16,710	68,035	51,620	25.8	74.2	944	6,695
District 13	78	198	3	58	877	11,244	D	D	D	D
District 14	249	23,507	94	3,592	34,590	138,916	84.3	15.7	D	D
District 15	2,439	271,445	111	53,811	357,975	146,771	82.2	17.8	1,530	9,000
District 16	1,625	281,092	173	77,338	557,864	343,301	90.4	9.6	540	9,000
District 17	5,060	2,148,236	425	295,998	1,085,016	214,430	60.4	39.6	9,989	14,799
District 18	1,327	545,846	411	199,100	462,117	348,242	93.9	6.1	1,462	16,805
District 19	461	60,374	131	21,045	104,295	226,236	95.8	4.2	36	3,000
District 20	645	295,454	458	235,636	507,802	787,290	98.9	1.1	93	7,154
District 21	403	28,185	70	18,733	187,957	466,395	96.6	3.4	D	D
District 22	95	1,077	11	264	4,866	51,221	95.7	4.3	D	D
District 23	479	3,809	8	910	16,598	34,651	94.2	5.8	D	D
District 24	40	772	19	311	2,007	50,175	D	D	D	D
District 25	831	556,369	670	189,265	474,762	571,314	93.0	7.0	1,511	23,246
District 26	2,298	70,917	31	45,578	800,022	348,138	98.6	1.4	1,500	32,609
District 27	339	3,172	9	2,433	19,925	58,776	97.4	2.6	D	D
GEORGIA	42,439	9,953,730	235	3,628,707	9,573,252	225,577	34.2	65.8	247,428	18,310
District 1	2,271	444,632	196	144,495	285,752	125,827	63.5	36.5	5,441	11,985
District 2	5,565	2,604,471	468	1,196,536	1,835,745	329,873	61.5	38.5	96,196	31,406
District 3	3,547	473,893	134	73,710	386,470	108,957	12.2	87.8	2,164	5,116
District 4	236	19,841	84	3,114	2,128	9,017	54.6	45.4	60	4,615
District 5	37	3,697	100	101	216	5,838	49.1	50.9	97	8,083
District 6	96	3,153	33	323	1,399	14,573	43.5	56.5	D	D
District 7	191	11,824	62	2,645	15,251	79,848	81.1	18.9	20	2,000
District 8	6,410	2,070,355	323	924,328	1,416,022	220,908	64.0	36.0	68,008	22,692
District 9	6,825	670,548	98	151,029	2,238,033	327,917	3.3	96.7	8,570	5,343
District 10	5,529	1,116,120	202	235,447	921,978	166,753	19.6	80.4	12,584	9,717
District 11	969	103,747	107	20,615	97,670	100,795	18.5	81.5	1,105	7,367
District 12	6,001	1,866,526	311	733,828	1,293,651	215,573	51.9	48.1	47,457	19,522
District 13	313	17,735	57	2,715	2,894	9,246	58.9	41.1	26	1,733
District 14	4,449	547,188	123	139,821	1,076,043	241,862	4.5	95.5	5,700	5,449
HAWAII	7,328	1,135,352	155	84,767	563,802	76,938	74.0	26.0	8,362	12,631
District 1	252	12,158	48	3,152	32,162	127,627	91.2	8.8	53	2,524
District 2	7,076	1,123,194	159	81,615	531,641	75,133	72.9	27.1	8,309	12,963
IDAHO	24,996	11,691,912	468	4,576,077	7,567,440	302,746	42.4	57.6	129,605	21,306
District 1	12,254	4,107,446	335	1,325,074	1,577,768	128,755	48.8	51.2	34,226	16,969
District 2	12,742	7,584,466	595	3,251,003	5,989,671	470,073	40.7	59.3	95,379	23,458
ILLINOIS	72,651	27,006,288	372	22,701,382	17,009,972	234,133	81.4	18.6	521,229	10,727
District 1	186	61,309	330	58,228	38,288	205,849	92.4	7.6	198	3,536
District 2	1,119	419,020	374	395,183	295,161	263,772	91.3	8.7	2,900	6,416

Table E. Congressional Districts 116th Congress — **Nonfarm Employment and Payroll**

STATE District	Private nonfarm employment and payroll, 2016											Annual payroll	
	Number of establishments	Employment										Total (mil dol)	Average per employee (dollars)
		Total	Manufac-turing	Construc-tion	Wholesale trade	Retail trade	Health care and social assistance	Finance and Insur-ance	Real estate and rental and leas-ing	Profes-sional, sci-entific, and technical services	Information		
	73	74	75	76	77	78	79	80	81	82	83	84	85
COLORADO	165,264	2,318,190	5.2	6.6	4.4	12.1	13.3	4.6	2.0	8.4	3.7	120,399	51,937
District 1	29,618	496,227	4.1	4.9	5.1	8.5	13.2	5.3	2.4	9.5	3.2	28,878	58,195
District 2	30,011	356,951	7.2	5.3	5.1	13.2	12.3	3.0	2.1	11.2	3.6	18,241	51,103
District 3	25,551	252,456	4.5	9.2	2.9	15.8	17.3	2.8	2.8	4.3	1.7	9,777	38,729
District 4	19,686	241,416	11.4	9.1	3.8	15.1	13.1	4.6	1.3	6.1	4.2	12,339	51,110
District 5	19,829	255,960	4.5	5.6	2.6	14.2	15.8	4.4	1.9	9.1	3.7	11,176	43,665
District 6	20,336	326,513	2.5	5.7	5.9	12.2	14.5	8.2	1.8	7.9	8.1	19,112	58,533
District 7	19,500	269,887	6.2	11.1	5.3	14.7	13.0	3.7	1.7	8.2	2.3	12,821	47,504
CONNECTICUT	89,416	1,533,879	10.1	3.8	4.8	12.2	18.6	8.2	1.3	6.9	2.5	94,659	61,712
District 1	18,540	377,872	11.7	4.2	4.7	10.7	18.0	11.9	1.1	6.6	3.0	22,700	60,073
District 2	14,386	215,723	12.9	3.8	4.0	16.4	17.8	3.2	0.9	5.6	1.7	9,872	45,760
District 3	16,503	308,835	12.2	4.0	4.9	11.1	20.9	3.2	1.4	4.6	1.8	16,067	52,023
District 4	21,896	336,223	4.3	2.7	6.0	10.9	15.7	12.9	1.5	9.9	3.6	30,204	89,834
District 5	17,551	267,494	11.7	4.7	3.7	15.1	22.8	5.1	1.7	5.4	1.8	14,078	52,628
DELAWARE	25,366	400,069	6.8	5.0	4.2	14.0	16.9	10.6	1.6	7.4	1.7	21,196	52,982
At Large	25,366	400,069	6.8	5.0	4.2	14.0	16.9	10.6	1.6	7.4	1.7	21,196	52,982
DISTRICT OF COLUMBIA	23,177	526,879	0.2	1.9	0.9	4.2	13.0	3.4	2.3	19.5	4.3	39,834	75,603
Delegate District (At Large)	23,177	526,879	0.2	1.9	0.9	4.2	13.0	3.4	2.3	19.5	4.3	39,834	75,603
FLORIDA	546,218	8,169,642	3.8	4.9	3.9	13.3	13.3	4.4	2.0	6.1	2.1	363,336	44,474
District 1	16,955	208,689	3.1	6.5	2.8	18.2	17.2	5.4	2.3	7.7	1.3	8,022	38,442
District 2	14,940	173,017	6.6	5.3	3.2	17.7	18.2	3.4	1.8	8.6	2.0	6,191	35,784
District 3	16,478	216,562	6.0	5.3	3.1	17.9	24.3	3.4	1.9	5.3	2.0	8,033	37,093
District 4	23,983	355,941	4.3	5.2	4.7	12.8	14.6	10.1	1.9	6.8	1.8	16,503	46,364
District 5	14,651	231,147	5.7	7.1	4.5	16.2	14.7	5.7	1.7	5.4	3.0	9,979	43,174
District 6	16,927	181,257	6.0	6.4	2.7	19.1	18.9	3.3	2.0	4.3	2.1	6,178	34,083
District 7	24,259	341,794	2.6	6.3	2.6	13.6	15.3	7.4	2.1	9.9	4.0	16,650	48,712
District 8	18,379	219,142	9.1	5.9	2.4	17.6	17.6	2.8	1.8	7.1	1.8	9,227	42,104
District 9	13,478	193,190	5.4	5.9	2.7	17.5	13.9	3.6	3.7	2.9	1.7	7,103	36,769
District 10	22,907	479,029	4.1	4.3	4.7	12.8	7.1	2.0	3.5	5.8	1.8	19,619	40,955
District 11	12,340	140,927	4.0	7.3	2.0	20.6	25.8	2.4	2.0	3.5	1.9	4,728	33,552
District 12	16,550	168,479	4.3	6.8	2.5	20.8	20.5	4.5	1.9	7.3	1.3	6,087	36,131
District 13	21,271	301,078	8.3	4.4	4.4	13.0	19.6	6.5	2.2	7.2	3.2	13,730	45,601
District 14	24,612	424,550	2.9	4.6	4.8	10.2	14.8	8.6	2.0	11.8	3.5	22,164	52,206
District 15	16,463	256,097	6.5	7.6	6.6	15.6	13.2	6.8	2.0	5.7	2.2	10,639	41,542
District 16	21,196	229,239	5.8	6.9	3.7	17.6	18.6	3.2	2.6	6.3	1.5	9,283	40,493
District 17	13,760	137,652	6.5	8.2	2.5	21.8	20.7	3.0	1.9	3.6	1.1	4,846	35,208
District 18	21,571	223,989	3.4	6.2	2.9	18.0	16.9	3.3	2.3	7.2	1.7	9,675	43,194
District 19	25,537	300,371	2.5	9.6	3.0	18.7	16.7	2.9	2.7	5.5	1.8	12,246	40,769
District 20	17,351	255,643	5.6	6.7	8.7	14.0	13.8	3.4	1.8	6.7	5.3	12,014	46,997
District 21	21,658	201,112	1.9	5.7	2.6	17.7	20.0	3.4	2.3	6.5	1.6	8,272	41,133
District 22	33,420	351,980	3.0	5.4	5.4	13.9	12.3	6.5	2.7	10.2	2.5	17,617	50,050
District 23	26,148	295,718	1.9	3.6	4.2	20.6	13.2	4.4	3.9	6.6	2.6	13,511	45,690
District 24	16,401	213,698	5.8	3.5	7.8	13.5	22.7	2.9	1.8	4.4	2.2	9,344	43,727
District 25	26,169	333,224	6.0	5.8	12.6	12.9	8.9	3.9	2.5	4.2	3.4	15,038	45,129
District 26	15,223	131,696	2.5	6.3	5.8	21.0	13.9	4.3	2.6	4.5	1.3	4,538	34,461
District 27	32,348	354,819	0.8	2.6	2.4	13.8	15.1	7.6	2.6	12.1	1.7	19,425	54,745
GEORGIA	228,330	3,804,433	9.7	4.5	5.6	12.8	13.1	4.7	1.6	6.9	3.2	182,911	48,078
District 1	15,774	230,310	11.4	4.3	3.6	15.8	14.9	2.3	1.5	3.8	1.2	8,922	38,738
District 2	12,942	202,809	13.4	3.7	4.8	13.8	18.5	9.6	1.3	4.2	1.3	8,093	39,903
District 3	15,035	226,611	16.4	5.0	4.0	17.3	15.2	3.6	1.1	2.9	1.7	8,445	37,265
District 4	11,245	150,249	11.1	8.0	5.2	17.5	15.0	2.1	1.7	4.4	2.0	5,811	38,673
District 5	22,133	529,484	3.5	2.7	4.3	6.8	12.4	4.2	2.2	9.1	4.9	32,892	62,121
District 6	28,524	478,508	1.7	2.8	6.1	9.4	11.0	9.3	2.1	14.3	8.5	32,963	68,887
District 7	24,763	359,243	8.1	7.2	11.3	13.7	9.1	4.4	1.4	8.6	3.9	18,218	50,711
District 8	13,248	185,537	12.9	3.9	3.6	17.3	17.8	3.7	1.2	4.1	1.1	6,283	33,862
District 9	14,712	201,396	24.2	4.8	4.7	15.8	13.7	2.6	0.9	2.6	1.1	7,617	37,819
District 10	13,100	159,169	12.3	5.4	3.7	17.7	16.1	2.7	1.7	3.3	1.3	5,488	34,480
District 11	21,091	362,353	7.1	6.6	7.9	11.8	9.5	5.8	2.6	9.0	3.5	20,588	56,816
District 12	13,169	210,926	12.5	4.4	3.6	15.8	21.2	2.7	1.2	5.4	1.6	8,130	38,542
District 13	11,107	171,442	6.3	6.6	7.5	18.1	16.5	2.3	2.9	2.5	1.3	6,936	40,455
District 14	10,652	175,666	28.5	3.9	5.0	14.7	12.9	1.9	0.8	2.2	1.1	6,472	36,844
HAWAII	32,350	528,415	2.5	6.3	3.7	13.4	13.4	3.6	2.3	4.3	1.6	22,892	43,323
District 1	18,230	320,441	3.0	7.1	4.6	12.7	14.1	4.9	2.1	5.1	1.9	14,997	46,800
District 2	13,913	185,382	1.9	5.7	2.4	16.2	14.0	1.6	2.8	3.2	1.0	6,974	37,620
IDAHO	45,826	562,282	10.7	6.8	5.6	15.0	16.2	4.0	1.3	5.8	2.3	22,243	39,559
District 1	21,696	242,730	11.8	9.1	4.9	16.1	15.1	4.1	1.4	4.4	2.5	9,003	37,089
District 2	23,825	309,751	10.2	5.2	6.1	14.5	17.6	3.9	1.3	7.1	2.2	12,870	41,550
ILLINOIS	319,605	5,513,071	9.7	3.8	5.8	11.5	14.6	6.3	1.4	7.1	2.2	295,308	53,565
District 1	11,931	191,669	6.0	4.8	3.7	16.6	20.4	2.5	1.4	2.5	1.1	7,874	41,084
District 2	10,151	165,045	18.3	4.3	5.2	13.9	20.1	2.1	1.3	2.4	1.8	6,889	41,740

Table E. Congressional Districts 116th Congress — **Land Area and Population Characteristics**

STATE District	Representative, 116th Congress	Land area,[1] 2018 (sq mi)	Total persons	Per square mile	Race alone (percent) White	Black	American Indian, Alaska Native	Asian and Pacific Islander	Some other race (percent)	Two or more races (percent)	Hispanic or Latino[2] (percent)	Non-Hispanic White alone (percent)	Percent female	Percent foreign-born	Percent born in state of residence
		1	2	3	4	5	6	7	8	9	10	11	12	13	14
ILLINOIS — Cont'd															
District 3	Daniel Lipinski (D)	237.0	725,538	3,061.6	75.3	4.8	0.2	5.2	12.4	2.1	32.1	57.0	49.8	20.8	70.0
District 4	Jesus G. "Chuy" Garcia (D)	52.4	700,585	13,364.8	56.4	4.4	0.4	4.1	31.5	3.2	68.4	22.4	49.8	34.2	51.8
District 5	Michael Quigley (D)	95.6	729,300	7,626.1	80.0	3.1	0.2	7.7	6.0	3.2	19.4	67.5	50.3	21.5	55.7
District 6	Sean Casten (D)	378.9	720,542	1,901.8	80.5	3.1	0.2	10.3	3.0	2.9	10.7	73.7	50.8	15.7	65.1
District 7	Danny K. Davis (D)	62.3	697,263	11,185.4	38.6	45.7	0.2	6.3	6.8	2.4	15.4	30.7	52.1	13.7	62.3
District 8	Raja Krishnamoorthi (D)	205.6	713,012	3,467.7	65.6	5.1	0.5	13.0	12.7	3.1	29.7	50.3	50.0	29.3	58.8
District 9	Janice D. Schakowsky (D)	105.4	732,614	6,951.9	71.9	9.0	0.3	12.5	2.8	3.5	12.7	62.8	51.0	27.1	52.2
District 10	Bradley Scott Schneider (D)	300.1	714,681	2,381.3	69.3	6.9	0.4	11.1	9.6	2.7	23.1	56.7	50.2	24.7	56.2
District 11	Bill Foster (D)	280.6	721,823	2,572.9	65.6	11.2	0.3	8.2	11.1	3.7	27.7	51.0	50.3	21.1	63.7
District 12	Mike Bost (R)	5,008.3	695,178	138.8	77.5	17.0	0.1	1.0	1.3	3.1	3.7	75.3	50.3	2.6	68.7
District 13	Rodney Davis (R)	5,793.4	698,295	120.5	81.1	11.8	0.2	3.8	0.3	2.8	3.3	78.4	50.4	5.5	74.9
District 14	Lauren Underwood (D)	1,597.5	746,748	467.4	86.6	3.1	0.1	4.9	3.4	2.0	12.5	78.0	50.7	9.8	70.0
District 15	John Shimkus (R)	14,695.9	701,482	47.7	92.6	4.1	0.2	0.9	0.4	1.9	2.8	90.5	50.0	1.6	76.2
District 16	Adam Kinzinger (R)	7,917.3	690,420	87.2	90.0	3.9	0.1	1.4	2.2	2.3	9.9	82.9	50.5	5.3	76.3
District 17	Cheri Bustos (D)	6,930.2	689,744	99.5	82.4	12.1	0.2	1.5	1.2	2.5	9.3	75.3	50.7	5.6	71.0
District 18	Darin LaHood (R)	10,515.7	701,065	66.7	90.6	3.9	0.3	3.1	0.4	1.8	2.9	88.3	51.0	4.1	78.3
INDIANA		35,825.6	6,666,818	186.1	83.7	9.4	0.2	2.2	1.9	2.7	6.9	79.2	50.7	5.3	68.0
District 1	Peter J. Visclosky (D)	1,156.8	714,257	617.4	69.7	18.4	0.3	1.4	6.8	3.4	15.8	62.5	50.9	5.9	58.4
District 2	Jackie Walorski (R)	3,958.7	722,928	182.6	86.4	7.2	0.1	1.2	1.9	3.0	9.7	79.4	50.9	5.5	68.5
District 3	Jim Banks (R)	4,180.2	744,914	178.2	87.5	6.0	0.2	2.4	1.1	2.9	6.2	82.9	50.4	4.6	72.9
District 4	James R. Baird (R)	6,351.6	758,815	119.5	88.7	4.1	0.2	3.0	1.9	2.1	6.3	84.7	49.9	5.5	69.2
District 5	Susan W. Brooks (R)	1,924.8	781,441	406.0	83.7	9.1	0.2	3.6	0.8	2.6	4.1	80.8	51.2	6.2	65.2
District 6	Greg Pence (R)	6,206.9	720,147	116.0	93.1	3.0	0.2	1.4	0.5	1.8	2.7	91.4	50.5	2.4	70.5
District 7	André Carson (D)	303.9	755,875	2,487.2	61.2	29.2	0.2	3.3	2.4	3.7	12.0	52.0	51.9	10.8	65.9
District 8	Larry Bucshon (R)	7,255.8	714,623	98.5	91.6	4.0	0.2	1.2	0.8	2.1	2.3	90.4	50.3	2.3	75.8
District 9	Trey Hollingsworth (R)	4,486.8	753,818	168.0	91.3	3.0	0.2	2.4	0.8	2.4	3.4	88.8	50.4	4.0	65.6
IOWA		55,855.1	3,145,711	56.3	90.0	3.4	0.3	2.8	1.3	2.2	5.9	85.9	50.3	5.3	70.2
District 1	Abby Finkenauer (D)	12,048.7	774,043	64.2	91.0	3.9	0.3	2.0	0.9	1.8	4.0	88.0	50.6	4.0	75.1
District 2	David Loebsack (D)	12,261.9	780,802	63.7	89.5	3.9	0.2	2.9	0.9	2.5	5.5	85.3	50.3	5.0	67.3
District 3	Cynthia Axne (D)	8,788.4	835,190	95.0	87.7	4.1	0.3	3.7	1.7	2.6	7.0	83.0	50.6	6.7	67.0
District 4	Steve King (R)	22,756.1	755,676	33.2	91.9	1.6	0.6	2.5	1.8	1.6	7.1	87.4	49.9	5.4	71.8
KANSAS		81,758.4	2,913,123	35.6	84.5	5.7	0.7	3.1	2.5	3.5	11.9	75.9	50.1	6.9	59.6
District 1	Roger W. Marshall (R)	52,541.8	702,327	13.4	89.7	2.7	0.6	1.8	2.1	3.0	16.0	76.6	49.3	7.2	63.8
District 2	Steve Watkins (R)	14,143.9	715,120	50.6	87.3	4.6	1.3	1.8	1.0	4.0	6.7	82.3	49.9	3.3	63.9
District 3	Sharice Davids (D)	757.3	770,493	1,017.4	80.5	8.6	0.4	4.9	2.7	2.8	12.1	71.8	50.9	10.1	45.3
District 4	Ron Estes (R)	14,315.3	725,183	50.7	81.0	6.7	0.6	3.6	4.0	4.1	12.6	73.2	50.4	6.6	66.3
KENTUCKY		39,485.2	4,454,189	112.8	86.9	8.1	0.2	1.5	0.9	2.3	3.5	84.6	50.7	3.8	69.2
District 1	James Comer (R)	12,082.3	716,177	59.3	88.9	7.2	0.2	0.8	0.8	2.1	2.8	87.3	50.2	1.6	69.8
District 2	Brett Guthrie (R)	7,177.7	760,681	106.0	89.2	5.4	0.2	1.6	0.8	2.8	3.6	86.7	50.8	3.5	71.0
District 3	John A. Yarmuth (D)	319.6	746,559	2,336.0	71.0	22.2	0.2	3.1	1.2	2.3	5.5	67.0	51.6	8.2	66.8
District 4	Thomas Massie (R)	4,376.3	760,043	173.7	91.6	3.5	0.1	1.2	1.1	2.4	3.3	89.6	50.4	3.3	62.1
District 5	Harold Rogers (R)	11,233.9	696,337	62.0	96.5	1.4	0.3	0.4	0.3	1.1	0.8	96.1	50.2	0.7	78.2
District 6	Garland "Andy" Barr (R)	4,295.4	774,392	180.3	85.1	8.5	0.2	2.0	1.3	3.0	4.6	82.0	51.0	5.1	68.2
LOUISIANA		43,204.7	4,684,333	108.4	61.7	32.5	0.5	1.8	1.6	1.8	5.2	58.5	51.1	4.1	78.3
District 1	Steve Scalise (R)	4,030.8	808,968	200.7	76.9	14.8	1.0	2.4	2.5	2.3	9.3	70.8	51.4	7.3	73.3
District 2	Cedric Richmond (D)	1,268.4	797,298	628.6	30.8	62.4	0.2	2.5	2.7	1.4	6.7	27.5	52.0	5.3	79.0
District 3	Clay Higgins (R)	6,984.2	788,118	112.8	70.0	24.8	0.2	1.6	1.2	2.1	4.0	67.2	51.3	3.0	84.8
District 4	Mike Johnson (R)	12,436.2	753,143	60.6	60.6	34.2	0.8	1.0	1.1	2.3	4.0	58.1	50.7	2.3	74.1
District 5	Ralph Lee Abraham (R)	14,453.3	740,217	51.2	60.9	36.0	0.3	1.0	0.6	1.3	2.4	59.4	50.1	1.8	81.6
District 6	Garret Graves (R)	4,033.9	796,589	197.5	70.8	23.1	0.6	2.4	1.5	1.6	4.5	67.9	51.0	4.5	77.3
MAINE		30,844.1	1,335,907	43.3	94.4	1.2	0.7	1.2	0.2	2.3	1.6	93.4	51.0	3.4	63.5
District 1	Chellie Pingree (D)	3,286.4	683,279	207.9	94.2	1.7	0.4	1.6	0.2	1.9	1.9	92.7	51.4	4.2	57.3
District 2	Jared F. Golden (D)	27,557.7	652,628	23.7	94.7	0.7	1.1	0.6	0.2	2.7	1.4	94.0	50.5	2.5	70.0
MARYLAND		9,710.7	6,052,177	623.2	54.9	29.9	0.3	6.5	5.0	3.4	10.1	50.7	51.5	15.3	47.2
District 1	Andrew Harris (R)	3,977.1	734,002	184.6	82.1	12.0	0.2	1.8	1.1	2.7	4.1	79.5	50.5	5.4	63.5
District 2	C. A. Dutch Ruppersberger (D)	348.7	765,155	2,194.6	52.4	35.4	0.2	5.9	2.2	3.8	8.0	48.1	52.4	12.5	62.1
District 3	John P. Sarbanes (D)	304.5	763,763	2,508.5	60.3	23.5	0.3	8.8	3.6	3.4	8.6	55.7	52.4	17.6	46.9
District 4	Anthony G. Brown (D)	297.9	761,353	2,556.2	29.5	51.4	0.4	3.3	12.5	2.9	16.6	26.3	51.5	18.3	31.2
District 5	Steny H. Hoyer (D)	1,482.6	768,507	518.3	48.3	38.6	0.3	4.1	4.7	3.9	9.7	44.5	51.1	13.0	38.4
District 6	David J. Trone (D)	1,952.2	779,616	399.3	64.6	12.7	0.3	11.9	6.4	4.1	15.1	57.1	49.8	20.2	43.6
District 7	Elijah E. Cummings (D)	488.2	718,158	1,470.8	35.9	52.7	0.5	7.4	0.8	2.7	3.5	33.9	52.2	11.8	60.3
District 8	Jamie Raskin (D)	859.5	761,623	886.1	65.7	13.5	0.3	8.4	8.6	3.4	14.6	60.1	52.2	23.1	32.8
MASSACHUSETTS		7,800.9	6,859,819	879.4	78.5	7.8	0.2	6.6	3.8	3.1	11.8	71.5	51.4	16.9	60.1
District 1	Richard E. Neal (D)	2,350.2	736,460	313.4	84.7	6.5	0.3	2.5	3.4	2.7	18.2	71.7	52.0	7.9	65.6
District 2	James P. McGovern (D)	1,628.0	744,124	457.1	82.8	5.5	0.4	5.8	1.8	3.7	9.9	76.5	51.2	12.6	64.5
District 3	Lori Trahan (D)	757.6	769,115	1,015.2	80.6	3.4	0.2	8.4	4.3	3.0	20.1	66.4	50.0	18.1	60.0
District 4	Joseph P. Kennedy III (D)	668.2	752,077	1,125.4	85.4	3.5	0.0	6.0	2.0	3.0	5.4	82.2	52.0	13.1	59.5
District 5	Katherine Clark (D)	265.1	766,210	2,890.5	75.7	6.1	0.2	12.4	2.9	2.8	9.2	69.9	51.7	24.8	49.6
District 6	Seth Moulton (D)	526.7	774,450	1,470.4	86.0	4.0	0.2	3.8	3.7	2.4	9.4	81.6	51.5	13.2	68.8
District 7	Ayanna Presley (D)	62.7	806,820	12,864.2	50.9	25.7	0.3	10.4	7.4	5.3	22.5	40.4	51.3	32.5	40.8
District 8	Stephen F. Lynch (D)	326.4	762,640	2,336.8	74.5	10.6	0.2	8.6	3.9	2.2	5.5	71.3	51.9	18.2	63.8
District 9	William R. Keating (D)	1,216.1	747,923	615.0	88.3	3.3	0.2	1.2	4.7	2.3	5.6	86.1	51.1	9.8	70.3

1. Dry land or land partially or temporarily covered by water.   2. May be of any race.

Table E. Congressional Districts 116th Congress — Age and Education

STATE District	Population and population characteristics, 2017 (cont.)										Education, 2017		
	Age (percent)										Total Enrollment[1]	Attainment[2] (percent)	
	Under 5 years	5 to 17 years	18 to 24 years	25 to 34 years	35 to 44 years	45 to 54 years	55 to 64 years	65 to 74 years	75 years and over	Median age		High school graduate or more	Bachelor's degree or more
	15	16	17	18	19	20	21	22	23	24	25	26	27
ILLINOIS — Cont'd													
District 3	7.1	17.7	7.8	13.0	13.7	12.8	13.4	8.2	6.2	37.7	182,716	86.3	30.0
District 4	6.6	17.8	9.6	18.4	15.4	12.5	10.4	5.7	3.6	33.7	178,612	72.3	24.9
District 5	5.5	12.4	9.4	21.7	14.7	12.1	10.9	7.4	5.9	35.6	158,070	92.4	55.0
District 6	5.8	17.9	7.7	11.9	12.3	15.2	14.3	9.0	6.0	40.4	194,311	94.9	53.9
District 7	6.2	13.5	10.6	20.4	13.3	11.9	10.6	7.9	5.5	34.6	165,405	87.1	43.3
District 8	6.4	16.6	8.5	14.6	13.9	13.3	12.6	8.4	5.7	37.3	171,334	86.2	33.3
District 9	6.1	14.4	8.7	13.9	12.9	13.9	12.9	9.3	7.9	40.2	179,400	92.4	54.4
District 10	6.1	18.1	9.5	12.1	12.2	13.6	13.5	8.3	6.6	38.2	185,331	89.3	45.3
District 11	6.2	19.2	8.9	13.0	14.6	13.8	11.8	7.8	4.7	36.9	195,696	85.6	35.3
District 12	6.0	15.9	9.2	13.1	12.2	12.9	14.0	9.7	7.0	39.5	163,999	90.0	23.3
District 13	5.3	14.7	15.5	12.3	11.7	11.5	12.7	9.2	7.1	36.6	206,746	92.7	31.4
District 14	5.6	19.4	8.7	10.7	13.4	15.0	13.6	8.3	5.2	39.2	202,897	93.6	40.4
District 15	6.0	16.6	8.4	12.1	11.9	12.5	14.2	10.2	8.2	40.6	158,109	89.2	19.5
District 16	5.6	16.3	9.5	12.2	11.9	13.1	13.9	10.0	7.6	40.3	167,109	91.2	21.4
District 17	6.1	16.4	8.7	12.1	11.6	12.5	14.1	10.4	8.1	40.7	160,848	87.8	19.8
District 18	5.8	16.5	8.6	11.9	12.3	12.5	14.0	10.2	8.2	40.5	170,177	94.0	33.6
INDIANA	6.3	17.3	9.9	13.0	12.3	12.8	13.0	9.0	6.4	37.7	1,661,841	88.6	26.8
District 1	5.9	17.2	8.8	12.5	12.7	13.0	14.1	9.3	6.7	39.2	170,839	89.5	23.8
District 2	6.6	18.1	9.6	12.3	12.0	12.3	13.0	9.4	6.8	37.9	182,195	85.6	22.6
District 3	6.9	18.7	8.9	13.0	11.6	12.8	12.9	8.9	6.2	37.2	181,798	87.9	22.4
District 4	6.1	16.9	12.5	12.3	11.9	12.7	12.7	8.9	6.4	36.8	209,549	90.6	26.3
District 5	6.0	18.2	7.8	13.2	13.6	13.9	12.7	8.6	6.0	38.5	194,211	94.7	48.0
District 6	5.7	16.3	10.3	11.6	11.7	13.6	13.7	9.8	7.2	40.3	165,653	89.2	22.7
District 7	7.7	17.9	9.9	16.7	12.7	11.9	11.5	7.0	4.7	33.5	191,023	82.1	24.5
District 8	6.0	16.5	9.8	12.4	11.7	12.8	14.0	9.7	7.1	39.1	169,395	88.3	22.3
District 9	5.7	16.0	11.3	13.0	12.5	12.7	13.0	9.4	6.3	38.0	197,178	88.9	26.7
IOWA	6.3	16.9	10.2	12.5	11.9	12.2	13.3	9.3	7.4	38.3	802,489	92.1	28.9
District 1	6.1	16.9	10.1	12.2	11.4	12.4	13.5	9.5	7.9	39.1	196,948	92.9	27.6
District 2	6.1	16.6	11.2	12.2	11.8	12.2	13.2	9.6	7.2	38.2	204,114	92.3	29.8
District 3	6.9	17.9	8.5	13.8	13.4	12.7	12.5	8.4	6.0	37.1	208,856	91.6	32.9
District 4	6.1	16.2	11.3	11.7	10.9	11.3	14.2	9.7	8.7	39.2	192,571	91.6	25.1
KANSAS	6.6	17.8	10.2	13.2	12.2	11.8	12.9	8.8	6.6	36.7	777,271	91.0	33.7
District 1	6.9	17.0	12.5	13.0	11.3	10.4	12.6	8.7	7.5	35.4	191,803	88.2	25.7
District 2	5.9	16.8	11.3	12.4	11.5	12.0	13.3	9.7	7.1	37.9	186,119	92.7	29.9
District 3	6.8	18.7	8.0	13.9	13.8	12.9	12.5	8.1	5.3	36.7	204,510	92.5	47.5
District 4	6.9	18.8	9.0	13.4	11.9	11.7	13.1	8.7	6.5	36.7	194,839	90.4	30.2
KENTUCKY	6.2	16.6	9.4	12.9	12.5	13.1	13.4	9.5	6.4	38.9	1,051,294	86.3	24.0
District 1	6.4	16.6	9.5	11.5	11.8	12.5	13.6	10.5	7.6	40.3	160,558	84.7	16.3
District 2	6.3	17.0	10.0	12.3	12.2	13.4	13.4	9.2	6.2	38.4	185,242	87.1	19.8
District 3	6.4	15.8	8.7	14.9	12.6	12.4	13.4	9.2	6.5	37.9	170,218	90.8	32.5
District 4	6.1	17.9	8.0	12.9	13.0	13.9	13.5	9.0	5.6	39.0	185,706	89.6	29.1
District 5	5.7	16.2	8.7	12.0	12.3	13.7	14.2	10.4	6.6	40.9	152,312	76.3	13.2
District 6	6.3	15.9	11.6	13.5	12.9	12.7	12.4	9.0	5.8	37.1	197,258	88.8	31.7
LOUISIANA	6.5	17.1	9.7	14.0	12.6	12.3	12.9	9.0	5.9	36.8	1,176,248	85.1	23.8
District 1	6.4	16.7	8.4	14.0	12.9	12.6	13.2	9.8	6.0	38.3	202,647	87.7	31.1
District 2	6.5	16.1	9.8	15.0	13.0	12.2	13.4	8.7	5.4	36.6	200,709	82.1	22.3
District 3	7.0	17.9	9.2	14.2	12.3	12.2	13.1	8.3	5.7	36.1	198,810	85.5	22.0
District 4	6.7	17.2	9.8	13.2	12.4	12.0	12.5	9.5	6.6	37.1	180,664	85.7	19.5
District 5	6.3	17.8	10.0	12.7	12.7	12.0	12.8	9.4	6.4	37.5	183,629	81.3	18.2
District 6	6.4	17.1	11.1	14.7	12.1	12.9	12.3	8.3	5.2	35.6	209,789	88.2	28.8
MAINE	4.8	14.2	8.2	11.9	11.3	13.8	15.7	11.9	8.1	44.6	289,898	92.3	32.1
District 1	4.7	14.0	8.2	12.4	11.7	13.9	15.4	11.7	8.0	44.0	148,625	93.4	38.2
District 2	5.0	14.5	8.2	11.3	10.9	13.8	16.1	12.2	8.1	45.1	141,273	91.2	25.6
MARYLAND	6.0	16.3	8.9	13.8	12.8	14.0	13.4	8.8	6.1	38.7	1,536,509	89.9	39.7
District 1	5.0	16.3	8.9	11.5	10.9	14.2	14.8	10.7	7.7	42.6	179,145	90.1	31.5
District 2	6.7	16.6	8.8	16.0	13.5	12.5	13.0	8.0	5.0	36.3	187,316	88.7	32.6
District 3	6.0	14.9	9.3	16.2	13.1	12.4	13.3	8.0	6.7	37.3	193,649	91.2	48.3
District 4	6.7	16.3	8.4	14.3	13.4	14.4	12.8	8.4	5.3	38.1	184,952	87.6	33.0
District 5	5.7	17.1	9.9	13.1	12.7	14.9	13.3	8.4	5.0	38.2	213,533	91.3	35.8
District 6	6.3	16.6	8.6	12.8	13.4	14.9	13.2	8.4	5.9	38.9	198,953	89.6	42.1
District 7	5.7	15.7	9.4	14.1	11.8	14.4	13.3	9.4	6.2	38.9	188,629	88.8	38.0
District 8	6.0	16.4	7.8	12.6	13.2	14.0	13.5	9.4	7.1	40.4	190,332	92.0	55.1
MASSACHUSETTS	5.3	14.7	10.2	14.2	12.2	13.7	13.6	9.3	6.9	39.5	1,714,245	90.8	43.4
District 1	5.2	15.1	10.2	12.6	11.5	13.2	14.4	10.1	7.5	40.8	176,808	87.7	29.5
District 2	4.6	14.9	13.0	12.4	11.5	13.8	13.8	9.5	6.5	39.6	204,984	91.7	39.7
District 3	6.0	16.4	9.6	12.2	12.9	14.8	13.8	8.4	5.8	39.1	194,010	88.7	38.0
District 4	5.1	16.7	9.4	11.6	12.2	15.6	13.7	9.0	6.6	41.1	195,941	93.6	52.1
District 5	5.7	14.8	9.1	15.7	13.4	13.5	12.7	8.3	6.9	38.1	198,120	94.0	57.6
District 6	5.1	15.2	8.7	11.7	11.7	14.8	14.9	10.2	7.7	42.9	176,350	93.0	45.1
District 7	5.0	11.5	15.5	23.9	12.4	10.3	10.1	6.7	4.6	31.7	234,367	86.3	44.9
District 8	5.7	13.9	8.1	15.8	13.3	13.6	13.5	9.1	7.1	39.8	173,643	91.6	47.2
District 9	4.7	14.2	8.2	10.9	10.6	14.2	15.3	12.4	9.4	46.1	160,022	90.5	35.6

1. All persons 3 years old and over enrolled in nursery school through college and graduate or professional school.   2. Persons 25 years old and over.

Table E. Congressional Districts 116th Congress — Households and Group Quarters

STATE District	Households, 2017						Group Quarters, 2010					
	Number	Average household size	Family households (percent)	Married couple family (percent)	Female family house-holder[1]	One person households (percent)	Total in group quarters, 2017	Percent 65 years and over	Persons in correctional institutions	Persons in nursing facilities	Persons in college dormitories	Persons in military quarters
	28	29	30	31	32	33	34	35	36	37	38	39
ILLINOIS — Cont'd												
District 3	245,766	2.91	70.9	53.8	11.0	24.8	10,740	30.2	3,160	3,740	1,890	0
District 4	221,320	3.15	66.6	44.7	14.3	22.7	3,565	34.4	1	1,268	285	0
District 5	297,914	2.41	53.3	42.0	7.5	34.6	10,802	32.7	0	3,882	4,823	0
District 6	262,101	2.71	72.6	60.4	8.3	23.0	9,249	36.8	786	4,034	3,517	16
District 7	287,358	2.33	49.2	27.5	16.9	42.4	27,584	6.3	11,612	3,240	7,992	0
District 8	253,560	2.79	68.8	52.5	11.2	25.6	5,144	45.7	0	2,564	744	0
District 9	289,228	2.46	56.6	46.3	6.9	35.9	22,281	27.4	31	8,543	8,803	0
District 10	252,695	2.75	72.2	57.2	11.2	23.6	20,596	19.5	704	5,665	2,088	12,155
District 11	248,393	2.88	70.4	54.7	11.5	24.4	7,223	33.9	1,085	2,891	1,495	0
District 12	275,493	2.44	62.8	43.4	14.0	31.7	22,721	22.6	10,700	5,209	3,332	307
District 13	282,769	2.32	57.0	42.1	10.7	34.1	41,836	12.5	5,125	5,481	27,454	0
District 14	260,871	2.84	76.5	63.4	9.3	18.8	4,969	33.0	1,364	1,562	158	0
District 15	277,450	2.43	65.6	50.8	10.1	29.2	27,130	23.2	12,642	6,376	3,900	0
District 16	269,928	2.49	67.1	51.2	10.8	27.3	17,744	26.0	6,821	5,619	6,178	0
District 17	281,393	2.36	61.8	43.4	13.3	33.1	24,282	21.2	8,864	5,921	5,835	0
District 18	278,604	2.44	65.4	54.0	8.3	29.0	21,687	27.7	7,248	6,421	6,455	5
INDIANA	2,557,299	2.53	64.9	48.2	11.8	28.9	187,264	20.5	48,694	41,158	75,434	228
District 1	271,891	2.56	65.6	46.1	14.8	29.3	17,193	19.0	7,380	3,116	3,194	0
District 2	269,085	2.60	68.2	51.0	12.2	26.7	22,082	20.0	5,936	4,482	8,659	0
District 3	285,787	2.56	67.0	50.3	11.0	26.8	12,943	33.2	2,229	4,852	3,948	0
District 4	285,845	2.55	66.5	50.4	11.0	26.8	30,884	15.3	7,233	4,934	15,651	0
District 5	303,507	2.52	65.9	52.4	9.8	28.1	15,376	25.1	4,416	4,444	5,257	178
District 6	280,968	2.48	66.9	51.0	10.8	27.0	21,996	23.8	5,096	5,532	8,541	0
District 7	287,062	2.58	55.9	33.9	15.8	36.9	14,594	18.3	3,216	3,152	5,162	50
District 8	284,613	2.41	63.5	48.5	10.8	30.0	27,808	19.4	10,561	5,980	10,509	0
District 9	288,541	2.53	65.0	50.2	10.1	28.2	24,388	17.9	2,627	4,666	14,513	3
IOWA	1,257,505	2.42	63.2	50.5	8.6	29.2	100,003	26.1	13,309	26,871	44,574	3
District 1	309,743	2.42	64.3	50.9	8.6	29.3	25,547	26.1	2,415	7,519	13,934	0
District 2	308,314	2.45	61.8	49.8	8.5	29.7	24,970	21.8	5,185	5,702	11,804	0
District 3	327,485	2.50	63.5	50.1	9.2	28.1	16,856	27.7	3,690	5,218	5,248	0
District 4	311,963	2.32	63.0	51.1	8.0	29.6	32,630	29.1	2,019	8,432	13,588	3
KANSAS	1,128,983	2.51	65.0	50.7	9.9	29.0	80,160	24.4	18,009	20,672	27,754	3,943
District 1	272,763	2.46	63.5	51.0	8.8	29.5	30,560	23.2	5,306	7,084	10,873	3,425
District 2	284,408	2.41	62.8	50.0	8.5	30.8	28,980	17.4	7,436	5,478	12,652	192
District 3	294,229	2.60	67.2	52.7	10.3	27.0	6,088	49.6	1,355	3,598	544	0
District 4	277,583	2.56	66.3	49.1	11.8	28.9	14,532	29.4	3,912	4,512	3,685	326
KENTUCKY	1,725,034	2.51	65.5	48.6	12.2	28.6	131,983	19.2	41,122	26,044	36,340	5,856
District 1	277,330	2.49	64.9	49.6	11.1	30.2	26,743	20.4	7,869	5,548	4,101	3,843
District 2	291,730	2.53	69.3	51.6	12.6	25.7	23,182	21.3	4,501	4,378	7,527	2,013
District 3	303,844	2.40	59.6	40.5	14.3	33.2	16,485	30.7	2,662	4,723	3,307	0
District 4	279,161	2.66	70.1	54.3	11.2	24.6	16,633	21.9	9,255	3,657	1,768	0
District 5	266,693	2.52	66.1	49.1	11.8	29.8	23,934	15.1	12,451	4,570	5,039	0
District 6	306,276	2.45	63.5	47.0	12.1	27.8	25,006	12.1	4,384	3,168	14,598	0
LOUISIANA	1,737,123	2.62	63.7	42.8	15.9	30.7	129,589	16.7	60,804	24,524	24,891	2,861
District 1	303,983	2.61	66.0	48.2	13.2	28.3	14,068	24.4	1,182	2,957	5,469	57
District 2	293,971	2.64	57.4	30.3	22.3	37.2	20,654	12.0	11,687	3,058	4,007	138
District 3	290,886	2.67	63.8	45.1	13.9	30.3	12,552	26.9	4,329	4,273	2,935	0
District 4	287,975	2.54	62.9	41.8	15.1	32.6	22,218	18.4	13,410	5,425	2,390	2,524
District 5	266,365	2.59	65.5	42.8	18.0	29.2	49,345	11.6	28,559	5,925	6,333	142
District 6	293,943	2.67	66.8	48.5	12.9	26.5	10,752	23.4	1,637	2,886	3,757	0
MAINE	540,959	2.40	61.0	48.8	8.3	30.5	36,280	22.5	3,679	7,878	17,251	131
District 1	278,915	2.39	60.2	48.7	7.9	31.1	17,367	24.5	2,708	4,128	7,433	119
District 2	262,044	2.42	61.9	48.9	8.7	29.8	18,913	20.4	971	3,750	9,818	12
MARYLAND	2,207,343	2.68	66.6	47.7	14.2	27.4	140,661	19.4	35,832	28,001	48,141	7,534
District 1	270,843	2.65	70.6	54.7	11.7	23.9	17,035	20.6	5,648	3,465	5,803	7
District 2	284,025	2.61	63.8	41.7	17.0	29.8	23,155	17.1	7,411	3,533	3,971	2,113
District 3	291,605	2.57	61.6	46.4	11.2	30.4	14,170	19.9	583	3,399	6,910	4,515
District 4	268,178	2.82	66.8	41.6	18.3	27.8	6,107	42.2	1,149	2,597	410	115
District 5	261,352	2.86	71.5	52.8	14.2	23.5	20,872	11.8	1,111	2,598	14,602	387
District 6	278,293	2.72	70.6	53.6	12.1	24.1	22,416	17.6	12,569	3,716	2,766	93
District 7	271,895	2.55	59.8	36.3	18.7	33.7	25,132	14.8	6,305	4,677	10,895	0
District 8	281,152	2.67	68.6	54.3	10.5	26.0	11,774	37.8	1,056	4,016	2,784	304
MASSACHUSETTS	2,604,954	2.54	63.4	47.0	12.2	28.6	250,594	17.7	24,683	43,833	135,773	498
District 1	288,980	2.46	62.1	41.3	15.4	31.1	26,186	20.9	1,897	5,855	13,226	0
District 2	278,430	2.52	63.1	47.0	12.3	28.5	42,997	13.9	1,576	5,572	26,184	0
District 3	274,965	2.73	69.2	49.7	13.8	24.5	18,574	19.7	6,829	3,823	4,944	0
District 4	279,277	2.59	70.2	56.7	10.0	24.0	28,044	19.7	2,520	4,914	15,480	25
District 5	289,174	2.55	63.6	51.0	8.8	28.0	28,584	16.5	771	4,440	18,907	113
District 6	294,151	2.57	66.6	51.7	11.0	28.3	19,237	28.9	2,014	4,919	5,965	73
District 7	303,513	2.48	50.4	29.9	16.1	34.2	54,442	4.7	1,895	2,728	42,309	261
District 8	298,060	2.50	61.2	46.8	10.7	30.0	17,126	35.8	3,879	6,322	3,522	261
District 9	298,404	2.45	65.4	49.9	11.5	28.3	15,404	30.2	3,302	5,260	5,236	26

1. No spouse present.

Table E. Congressional Districts 116th Congress — Housing and Money Income

STATE District	Housing units, 2017						Money income, 2017		
	Total	Occupied units	Occupied units — Owner-occupied			Occupied units — Renter-occupied	Households		
		Occupied units as a percent of all units	Owner-occupied units as a percent of occupied units	Median value[1] (dollars)	Percent valued at $500,000 or more	Median rent[2]	Per capita income (dollars)	Median income (dollars)	Percent with income of $100,000 or more
	40	41	42	43	44	45	46	47	48
ILLINOIS — Cont'd									
District 3	263,645	93.2	73.4	231,300	7.1	996	30,790	65,230	31.6
District 4	248,904	88.9	48.1	247,400	8.8	999	23,882	53,955	21.6
District 5	324,705	91.7	55.4	351,100	26.8	1,313	49,928	82,210	41.5
District 6	275,469	95.1	79.6	327,000	20.4	1,294	47,564	98,889	49.5
District 7	344,634	83.4	41.8	273,500	21.8	1,126	41,132	58,444	30.8
District 8	268,273	94.5	67.4	228,900	5.1	1,172	32,072	69,386	30.2
District 9	317,373	91.1	60.5	347,500	24.4	1,118	43,455	70,552	36.1
District 10	271,550	93.1	69.9	270,600	23.5	1,155	44,655	80,229	41.3
District 11	262,646	94.6	72.3	216,200	6.2	1,216	33,836	75,446	35.8
District 12	323,763	85.1	67.1	112,100	1.4	732	26,688	48,570	18.9
District 13	322,259	87.7	64.9	123,000	2.4	767	29,098	51,129	21.9
District 14	272,946	95.6	82.1	264,800	8.1	1,190	40,518	92,461	45.4
District 15	318,026	87.2	75.3	102,600	1.5	657	27,212	52,527	20.0
District 16	300,697	89.8	71.9	139,000	2.3	814	30,293	60,326	24.6
District 17	323,384	87.0	67.9	101,300	1.7	677	25,973	48,036	16.0
District 18	313,441	88.9	75.8	150,200	2.7	764	34,715	65,048	30.0
INDIANA	2,885,342	88.6	69.0	141,100	3.4	793	28,323	54,181	21.7
District 1	308,425	88.2	70.2	155,600	2.9	838	27,967	56,293	23.1
District 2	309,036	87.1	71.0	130,200	2.6	748	26,015	53,440	19.3
District 3	321,764	88.8	72.3	134,400	3.6	720	26,382	53,197	18.4
District 4	317,235	90.1	71.1	141,600	2.3	789	27,852	56,721	22.3
District 5	332,548	91.3	71.4	196,400	8.4	915	39,643	71,573	34.7
District 6	316,397	88.8	72.3	125,800	2.7	730	27,362	52,636	20.3
District 7	335,704	85.5	51.9	119,300	2.3	852	23,345	42,630	14.5
District 8	321,216	88.6	71.2	123,300	2.6	717	27,576	50,666	19.4
District 9	323,017	89.3	70.0	149,600	2.8	793	28,154	54,504	22.5
IOWA	1,397,739	90.0	71.6	149,100	3.2	760	30,865	58,570	24.0
District 1	343,521	90.2	74.3	149,700	2.5	712	30,189	57,295	23.0
District 2	346,355	89.0	70.2	143,300	3.6	779	29,306	54,758	21.8
District 3	356,679	91.8	71.0	170,900	4.6	834	34,187	65,023	28.8
District 4	351,184	88.8	70.8	126,500	2.1	701	29,494	55,496	22.2
KANSAS	1,273,776	88.6	65.9	150,600	3.9	815	30,146	56,422	23.6
District 1	321,959	84.7	65.6	113,300	1.9	720	26,017	49,380	16.6
District 2	321,147	88.6	66.3	133,600	2.3	763	27,389	53,483	19.8
District 3	314,040	93.7	66.3	230,100	9.1	987	39,158	74,120	36.0
District 4	316,630	87.7	65.3	132,400	2.0	775	27,290	53,657	21.1
KENTUCKY	1,984,235	86.9	66.5	141,000	3.7	724	26,779	48,375	19.5
District 1	336,118	82.5	69.6	111,400	2.4	638	22,988	41,930	14.7
District 2	328,832	88.7	68.0	143,600	3.4	738	27,125	50,289	18.6
District 3	335,868	90.5	60.5	169,700	5.4	831	31,101	53,677	23.0
District 4	312,514	89.3	71.1	172,500	5.3	744	31,673	62,095	29.6
District 5	332,437	80.2	69.3	81,500	1.3	572	18,301	31,731	8.5
District 6	338,466	90.5	61.3	160,500	4.5	755	28,599	52,156	21.6
LOUISIANA	2,061,582	84.3	65.2	162,500	4.8	836	25,885	46,145	20.2
District 1	340,790	89.2	69.1	202,500	8.3	958	31,648	58,199	27.4
District 2	354,048	83.0	54.7	158,100	5.7	904	22,863	37,340	14.6
District 3	343,095	84.8	68.5	158,700	3.3	761	25,597	47,741	20.2
District 4	351,759	81.9	62.0	130,000	3.2	738	22,496	37,102	14.2
District 5	331,753	80.3	65.2	115,400	2.6	691	21,060	37,415	14.8
District 6	340,137	86.4	71.4	189,000	5.0	920	31,032	62,374	29.1
MAINE	742,644	72.8	73.2	191,200	6.4	806	31,088	56,277	22.5
District 1	359,829	77.5	72.6	243,400	9.9	910	35,345	64,599	27.6
District 2	382,815	68.5	73.8	146,400	2.7	702	26,632	48,603	17.1
MARYLAND	2,449,123	90.1	66.7	312,500	19.9	1,337	39,960	80,776	40.2
District 1	341,183	79.4	76.1	272,200	13.4	1,030	36,969	73,206	36.1
District 2	308,007	92.2	60.5	238,500	5.2	1,216	32,688	68,204	31.8
District 3	313,684	93.0	65.4	331,600	22.7	1,467	44,698	87,732	44.0
District 4	286,735	93.5	62.9	316,700	17.1	1,412	37,424	81,151	39.7
District 5	282,683	92.5	76.4	330,200	14.0	1,569	40,786	96,325	48.1
District 6	302,546	92.0	67.7	317,500	24.4	1,323	38,735	79,247	39.8
District 7	318,853	85.3	58.0	261,300	22.0	1,118	35,708	60,929	31.1
District 8	295,432	95.2	67.4	444,000	40.2	1,658	52,361	100,953	50.7
MASSACHUSETTS	2,894,590	90.0	62.3	385,400	31.7	1,208	41,821	77,385	39.4
District 1	322,646	89.6	62.8	221,000	5.5	870	31,300	55,465	26.6
District 2	303,616	91.7	62.7	280,500	12.3	1,028	35,820	67,531	33.4
District 3	294,473	93.4	63.8	348,600	23.4	1,151	37,914	75,654	38.8
District 4	294,111	95.0	73.7	431,500	40.7	1,225	52,026	100,742	50.6
District 5	305,997	94.5	60.0	564,400	58.3	1,624	51,768	98,775	49.6
District 6	311,296	94.5	71.1	446,700	38.2	1,232	43,560	85,951	42.8
District 7	326,446	93.0	33.5	496,300	49.3	1,513	37,872	64,310	33.3
District 8	323,528	92.1	63.2	437,400	38.1	1,471	46,791	90,323	45.3
District 9	412,477	72.3	71.6	369,200	25.6	953	39,109	71,685	35.0

1. Specified owner-occupied units.   2. Specified renter-occupied units.

Table E. Congressional Districts 116th Congress — Poverty, Labor Force, Employment, and Social Security

STATE District	Poverty, 2017			Civilian labor force, 2016			Civilian employment[2] 2017				Persons under 65 years of age with no health insurance, 2017 (percent)	Social Security beneficiaries, December 2018		Supplemental Security Income recipients, December 2018
	Persons below poverty level (percent)	Families below poverty level (percent)	Percent of households receiving food stamps in past 12 months	Total	Unemployment Total	Unemployment Rate[1]	Total	Percent Management, business, science, and arts occupations	Service, sales, and office	Construction and production		Number	Rate[3]	
	49	50	51	52	53	54	55	56	57	58	59	60	61	62
ILLINOIS — Cont'd														
District 3	10.0	7.5	11.1	365,642	20,279	5.5	345,363	34.3	40.4	25.3	9.3	118,479	163.3	12,269
District 4	15.8	12.5	18.5	376,011	20,116	5.3	355,895	26.7	43.3	29.9	17.8	77,301	110.3	17,646
District 5	7.9	4.9	6.5	440,301	16,038	3.6	424,263	50.8	36.5	12.7	7.6	97,758	134.0	11,496
District 6	5.2	3.8	4.3	392,066	15,384	3.9	376,682	50.6	36.6	12.7	4.2	118,353	164.3	5,220
District 7	21.2	17.3	20.8	375,785	34,693	9.2	341,092	48.4	38.3	13.3	8.4	100,838	144.6	32,844
District 8	9.0	6.4	9.5	400,618	18,249	4.6	382,369	34.7	41.6	23.6	11.2	107,347	150.6	8,038
District 9	12.2	7.7	8.7	378,395	11,898	3.1	366,497	49.4	38.3	12.3	8.0	124,221	169.6	18,184
District 10	8.6	6.8	9.4	372,978	18,004	4.8	354,974	41.2	39.8	19.0	7.7	112,885	158.0	9,717
District 11	8.3	6.3	11.1	391,198	20,566	5.3	370,632	35.1	41.2	23.7	8.6	102,763	142.4	8,508
District 12	18.2	13.4	16.5	328,624	19,936	6.1	308,688	29.7	43.7	26.6	7.1	148,630	213.8	19,760
District 13	18.9	12.0	13.3	346,160	21,752	6.3	324,408	38.1	41.4	20.5	4.7	138,829	198.8	15,396
District 14	5.3	3.9	6.0	403,397	17,074	4.2	386,323	40.2	41.3	18.5	4.7	119,396	159.9	4,709
District 15	13.6	9.9	14.6	335,663	18,097	5.4	317,566	30.7	39.8	29.6	6.8	158,854	226.5	14,181
District 16	11.0	7.4	11.4	354,069	22,721	6.4	331,348	30.5	41.9	27.7	5.4	149,702	216.8	8,931
District 17	16.6	12.6	17.9	332,438	26,112	7.9	306,326	27.6	42.5	29.8	7.2	157,665	228.6	18,504
District 18	9.3	6.2	9.1	350,146	15,546	4.4	334,600	40.6	39.0	20.4	4.7	152,349	217.3	8,480
INDIANA	13.5	9.2	9.3	3,342,800	158,556	4.7	3,184,244	34.4	38.5	27.1	9.5	1,350,417	202.6	127,408
District 1	14.8	11.6	11.1	342,686	22,398	6.5	320,288	31.8	41.0	27.2	8.9	149,770	209.7	16,017
District 2	13.7	9.6	8.7	356,521	15,609	4.4	340,912	29.5	37.7	32.8	11.5	148,681	205.6	12,882
District 3	12.0	8.4	9.1	375,700	15,590	4.1	360,110	30.2	37.0	32.8	11.7	150,800	202.4	12,936
District 4	12.5	7.7	7.0	389,374	14,624	3.8	374,750	34.5	36.4	29.2	8.2	148,023	195.1	10,333
District 5	8.2	5.8	6.1	411,423	15,414	3.7	396,009	48.0	37.2	14.8	6.3	141,810	181.5	10,015
District 6	13.1	8.0	9.7	361,150	15,348	4.2	345,802	32.8	38.4	28.8	8.8	167,763	233.0	14,498
District 7	19.7	14.5	14.4	378,874	26,579	7.0	352,295	31.1	43.6	25.3	13.8	123,806	163.8	23,639
District 8	14.4	10.5	9.9	352,283	15,834	4.5	336,449	32.6	38.0	29.4	9.0	162,715	227.7	14,828
District 9	13.1	8.3	7.9	374,789	17,160	4.6	357,629	36.7	37.9	25.5	7.4	157,101	208.4	12,260
IOWA	10.7	6.7	9.6	1,679,790	60,190	3.6	1,619,600	35.5	38.9	25.6	5.5	647,462	205.8	51,142
District 1	10.5	6.7	9.3	418,540	15,635	3.7	402,905	34.4	39.5	26.2	5.1	167,407	216.3	13,007
District 2	12.3	7.3	10.0	406,228	16,371	4.0	389,857	35.2	38.6	26.1	5.7	162,658	208.3	15,056
District 3	8.9	6.0	10.0	457,989	15,623	3.4	442,366	38.4	40.6	21.0	5.3	150,010	179.6	13,176
District 4	11.4	6.9	9.0	397,033	12,561	3.2	384,472	33.8	36.5	29.8	6.1	167,387	221.5	9,903
KANSAS	11.9	7.9	7.7	1,499,885	63,084	4.2	1,436,801	38.9	38.5	22.6	10.2	552,973	189.8	47,735
District 1	13.9	7.9	6.5	354,558	12,472	3.5	342,086	34.3	38.6	27.2	10.4	138,355	197.0	9,720
District 2	12.8	7.8	8.6	362,431	15,367	4.2	347,064	36.7	40.8	22.5	9.4	151,038	211.2	14,682
District 3	7.9	6.2	5.0	420,972	15,609	3.7	405,363	47.4	36.1	16.5	10.0	121,842	158.1	9,004
District 4	13.5	9.9	10.6	361,924	19,636	5.4	342,288	35.7	39.1	25.2	11.1	141,738	195.5	14,329
KENTUCKY	17.2	12.9	14.1	2,091,959	115,271	5.5	1,976,688	33.5	40.2	26.3	6.3	989,575	222.2	174,213
District 1	18.0	12.8	13.7	303,536	15,706	5.2	287,830	27.7	40.0	32.3	7.0	180,220	251.6	27,206
District 2	14.9	11.3	11.0	364,982	18,917	5.2	346,065	30.8	39.6	29.6	5.8	167,822	220.6	22,987
District 3	14.0	10.3	12.5	397,957	22,512	5.7	375,445	35.1	41.7	23.2	6.2	147,723	197.9	24,778
District 4	11.9	8.7	10.6	380,078	17,436	4.6	362,642	37.5	40.0	22.4	5.3	148,391	195.2	18,000
District 5	29.1	24.0	24.7	249,108	21,019	8.4	228,089	29.4	41.5	29.1	7.1	193,630	278.1	58,091
District 6	16.6	11.4	12.9	396,298	19,681	5.0	376,617	37.5	39.0	23.5	6.7	151,789	196.0	23,151
LOUISIANA	19.7	14.7	16.4	2,164,374	141,608	6.5	2,022,766	33.4	42.8	23.8	9.7	907,733	193.8	175,204
District 1	14.2	10.7	10.9	399,950	17,332	4.3	382,618	37.4	41.0	21.6	10.4	158,459	195.9	18,381
District 2	27.1	20.8	22.9	366,583	32,471	8.9	334,112	31.2	47.0	21.8	11.1	144,671	181.5	40,660
District 3	17.7	13.5	15.7	374,926	24,533	6.5	350,393	31.4	43.0	25.6	10.5	151,446	192.2	25,285
District 4	23.2	17.5	17.7	314,788	25,413	8.1	289,375	31.4	42.3	26.3	8.9	156,044	207.2	33,008
District 5	25.1	19.2	19.1	301,103	20,610	6.8	280,493	31.0	44.1	24.9	9.6	160,058	216.2	38,687
District 6	12.3	8.4	12.9	407,024	21,249	5.2	385,775	36.4	40.3	23.3	7.8	137,055	172.1	19,183
MAINE	11.1	6.3	12.8	700,979	29,493	4.2	671,486	36.7	41.1	22.1	10.0	344,482	257.9	36,860
District 1	8.7	4.7	9.8	379,834	14,977	3.9	364,857	40.1	40.2	19.7	8.5	169,304	247.8	14,636
District 2	13.6	8.0	16.1	321,145	14,516	4.5	306,629	32.8	42.2	25.0	11.7	175,178	268.4	22,224
MARYLAND	9.3	6.2	10.3	3,268,601	170,419	5.2	3,098,182	45.9	38.0	16.1	7.0	1,001,230	165.4	121,059
District 1	8.6	5.7	10.3	387,398	23,345	6.0	364,053	40.5	39.1	20.4	5.8	161,595	220.2	11,688
District 2	10.5	7.2	13.2	403,074	23,802	5.9	379,272	40.9	40.2	19.0	6.6	127,182	166.2	18,069
District 3	7.8	4.9	7.9	426,653	18,493	4.3	408,160	52.9	34.4	12.7	6.7	119,365	156.3	15,198
District 4	8.0	5.9	8.4	434,089	25,782	5.9	408,307	40.2	41.0	18.8	10.2	105,959	139.2	11,097
District 5	7.1	4.0	7.0	413,696	17,034	4.1	396,662	45.4	38.3	16.4	7.2	113,967	148.3	9,712
District 6	9.9	7.3	10.5	417,494	21,317	5.1	396,177	46.2	37.4	16.4	7.3	124,146	159.2	14,121
District 7	16.6	11.5	19.2	363,304	22,385	6.2	340,919	46.0	40.5	13.5	5.3	129,376	180.1	33,395
District 8	6.3	4.1	5.7	422,893	18,261	4.3	404,632	54.3	34.1	11.6	6.9	119,640	157.1	7,779
MASSACHUSETTS	10.5	7.2	11.7	3,771,625	172,091	4.6	3,599,534	46.1	38.4	15.5	3.3	1,273,360	185.6	184,020
District 1	14.2	10.7	20.4	369,718	20,605	5.6	349,113	36.5	43.4	20.0	3.1	168,512	228.8	37,175
District 2	10.9	7.0	10.8	391,548	17,309	4.4	374,239	42.7	39.8	17.4	3.1	138,993	186.8	20,095
District 3	11.1	8.8	13.8	421,432	19,434	4.6	401,998	41.3	38.4	20.4	4.1	133,480	173.6	23,625
District 4	7.0	4.9	6.9	421,748	16,888	4.0	404,860	53.8	33.5	12.7	1.7	136,395	181.4	10,964
District 5	7.7	5.0	6.4	431,966	16,403	3.8	415,563	56.6	33.1	10.2	3.2	121,421	158.5	11,472
District 6	7.6	4.9	8.8	424,814	14,785	3.5	410,029	46.3	38.6	15.1	2.9	151,599	195.8	13,730
District 7	18.7	13.6	18.2	478,920	30,602	6.4	448,318	47.8	40.4	11.8	4.3	92,085	114.1	30,904
District 8	7.8	5.1	9.7	444,343	21,469	4.8	422,874	48.5	38.7	12.8	2.8	137,767	180.6	17,613
District 9	8.9	6.6	10.2	387,136	14,596	3.8	372,540	38.2	40.4	21.3	4.0	193,108	258.2	18,442

1. Percent of civilian labor force.   2. Persons 16 years old and over.   3. Per 1,000 resident population estimated in the 2017 American Community Survey.

Table E. Congressional Districts 116th Congress — Agriculture

STATE District	Number of farms	Land in farms			Value of products sold				Government payments	
		Acres	Average size of farm (acres)	Harvested cropland (acres)	Total ($1,000)	Average per farm (dollars)	Percent from crops	Percent from livestock and poultry products	Total ($1,000)	Average per farm receiving payments (dollars)
	63	64	65	66	67	68	69	70	71	72
ILLINOIS — Cont'd										
District 3	97	7,643	79	6,731	5,512	56,825	91.1	8.9	45	2,368
District 4	7	D	D	5	149	21,286	D	D	D	D
District 5	10	D	D	21	53	5,300	D	D	D	D
District 6	197	15,572	79	9,818	38,691	196,401	93.6	6.4	417	15,444
District 7	16	668	42	D	1,072	67,000	97.6	2.4	D	D
District 8	32	2,974	93	D	4,267	133,344	78.2	21.8	D	D
District 9	20	286	14	93	245	12,250	90.6	9.4	D	D
District 10	118	10,377	88	7,981	21,179	179,483	96.9	3.1	110	10,000
District 11	121	18,409	152	16,488	13,715	113,347	98.9	1.1	148	3,524
District 12	6,820	1,946,182	285	1,466,610	805,718	118,140	84.2	15.8	41,813	10,414
District 13	7,766	3,135,635	404	2,669,082	1,883,640	242,550	89.4	10.6	52,897	9,823
District 14	2,036	618,099	304	563,973	509,435	250,214	80.5	19.5	11,944	13,792
District 15	21,078	7,426,442	352	6,212,563	4,259,863	202,100	79.8	20.2	170,063	11,271
District 16	9,983	4,128,064	414	3,788,243	2,978,591	298,366	83.3	16.7	80,693	12,544
District 17	9,578	3,577,140	373	2,881,538	2,562,993	267,592	72.6	27.4	79,988	11,942
District 18	13,467	5,638,365	419	4,621,479	3,591,400	266,682	82.0	18.0	79,989	8,430
INDIANA	56,649	14,969,996	264	12,345,774	11,107,336	196,073	64.1	35.9	342,914	12,628
District 1	1,148	340,509	297	308,926	214,590	186,925	89.2	10.8	8,942	15,259
District 2	7,227	1,837,512	254	1,567,768	1,626,207	225,018	55.4	44.6	51,386	14,720
District 3	10,574	2,108,580	199	1,764,657	1,976,214	186,894	47.3	52.7	40,561	8,858
District 4	8,273	3,194,762	386	2,852,760	2,418,273	292,309	71.6	28.4	65,287	13,445
District 5	2,607	846,826	325	787,740	567,515	217,689	87.7	12.3	14,688	10,424
District 6	10,193	2,588,026	254	2,073,367	1,682,472	165,062	68.4	31.6	62,303	12,376
District 7	163	15,719	96	13,871	11,513	70,632	92.3	7.7	419	13,516
District 8	9,750	2,730,610	280	2,135,119	1,896,295	194,492	67.0	33.0	70,322	14,544
District 9	6,714	1,307,452	195	841,566	714,256	106,383	60.3	39.7	29,007	12,423
IOWA	86,104	30,563,878	355	24,347,862	28,956,455	336,296	47.8	52.2	682,995	11,146
District 1	21,735	6,684,219	308	5,250,747	6,067,485	279,157	50.2	49.8	156,577	9,697
District 2	19,439	5,982,719	308	4,032,959	4,288,086	220,592	50.2	49.8	144,109	11,010
District 3	11,923	4,582,245	384	3,312,351	2,634,857	220,989	65.9	34.1	95,406	12,633
District 4	33,007	13,314,695	403	11,751,805	15,966,026	483,716	43.2	56.8	286,904	11,716
KANSAS	58,569	45,759,319	781	21,837,465	18,782,726	320,694	34.4	65.6	509,205	14,089
District 1	27,977	29,850,908	1,067	13,748,148	14,276,677	510,300	28.6	71.4	368,435	17,621
District 2	19,374	7,619,877	393	4,210,470	2,184,002	112,729	63.1	36.9	59,861	6,569
District 3	1,128	202,593	180	127,288	73,657	65,299	81.5	18.5	971	3,996
District 4	10,090	8,085,941	801	3,751,559	2,248,390	222,833	41.9	58.1	79,947	13,596
KENTUCKY	75,966	12,961,784	171	5,474,346	5,737,920	75,533	44.3	55.7	126,697	7,502
District 1	21,346	4,852,908	227	2,696,597	3,093,230	144,909	47.9	52.1	76,262	9,436
District 2	19,839	3,134,196	158	1,336,434	1,157,083	58,324	51.3	48.7	36,761	7,633
District 3	190	10,644	56	2,639	5,100	26,842	85.6	14.4	56	7,000
District 4	11,807	1,645,348	139	555,968	316,984	26,847	62.5	37.5	4,898	4,230
District 5	11,110	1,472,160	133	350,486	244,748	22,030	34.5	65.5	3,322	2,579
District 6	11,674	1,846,528	158	532,222	920,776	78,874	19.5	80.5	5,398	3,512
LOUISIANA	27,386	7,997,511	292	3,314,955	3,172,978	115,861	65.0	35.0	177,399	22,822
District 1	1,724	380,822	221	57,206	71,150	41,270	55.9	44.1	251	12,550
District 2	412	269,457	654	103,019	70,301	170,633	94.4	5.6	330	10,313
District 3	5,682	1,812,789	319	565,038	505,329	88,935	77.2	22.8	50,916	24,562
District 4	7,211	1,572,422	218	430,884	728,780	101,065	25.0	75.0	23,611	17,860
District 5	9,960	3,395,715	341	1,894,297	1,548,447	155,467	77.7	22.3	96,718	24,149
District 6	2,397	566,306	236	264,511	248,972	103,868	71.9	28.1	5,574	17,364
MAINE	7,600	1,307,613	172	360,295	666,962	87,758	61.3	38.7	8,947	10,806
District 1	2,501	204,079	82	53,902	94,149	37,645	66.4	33.6	1,829	12,113
District 2	5,099	1,103,534	216	306,393	572,813	112,338	60.5	39.5	7,118	10,514
MARYLAND	12,429	1,990,122	160	1,290,212	2,472,806	198,955	38.3	61.7	44,410	12,471
District 1	5,298	1,147,145	217	812,238	1,915,054	361,467	33.5	66.5	32,857	14,181
District 2	143	7,808	55	2,261	7,223	50,510	71.1	28.9	111	11,100
District 3	183	14,350	78	7,991	11,926	65,169	83.0	17.0	249	20,750
District 4	129	5,728	44	2,148	8,721	67,605	96.6	3.4	10	2,500
District 5	1,878	182,049	97	89,237	73,022	38,883	79.5	20.5	2,353	8,715
District 6	2,462	330,277	134	179,485	237,611	96,511	38.3	61.7	2,972	7,375
District 7	653	79,254	121	45,853	55,821	85,484	85.6	14.4	1,092	11,258
District 8	1,683	223,511	133	150,999	163,428	97,105	52.8	47.2	4,767	10,641
MASSACHUSETTS	7,241	491,653	68	140,922	475,185	65,624	76.5	23.5	4,004	7,583
District 1	1,955	190,928	98	45,678	73,907	37,804	61.8	38.2	1,502	8,632
District 2	1,721	123,085	72	41,818	143,703	83,500	76.0	24.0	1,146	8,128
District 3	842	36,665	44	12,632	40,465	48,058	74.0	26.0	285	6,477
District 4	656	28,229	43	9,054	32,585	49,672	87.1	12.9	272	4,772
District 5	170	6,214	37	2,032	36,345	213,794	98.2	1.8	20	3,333
District 6	417	19,362	46	7,705	29,882	71,659	86.5	13.5	45	5,625
District 7	27	60	2	30	268	9,926	90.7	9.3	D	D
District 8	175	5,678	32	1,976	9,289	53,080	90.8	9.2	53	5,300
District 9	1,278	81,432	64	19,997	108,740	85,086	73.7	26.3	680	7,727

Table E. Congressional Districts 116th Congress — Nonfarm Employment and Payroll

Private nonfarm employment and payroll, 2016

STATE District	Number of establishments	Employment — Total	Manufacturing	Construction	Wholesale trade	Retail trade	Health care and social assistance	Finance and Insurance	Real estate and rental and leasing	Professional, scientific, and technical services	Information	Annual payroll — Total (mil dol)	Average per employee (dollars)
	73	74	75	76	77	78	79	80	81	82	83	84	85
ILLINOIS — Cont'd													
District 3	15,644	227,989	11.9	6.1	4.9	13.9	14.2	2.5	1.3	4.6	0.8	10,218	44,820
District 4	11,019	140,177	15.5	3.7	7.6	17.5	17.0	2.7	1.1	2.4	1.0	5,593	39,897
District 5	23,375	383,537	7.6	3.4	5.0	10.4	13.2	3.7	2.8	5.7	2.4	20,306	52,945
District 6	25,612	390,897	9.3	4.3	6.2	12.4	12.6	7.3	1.1	7.2	2.7	21,477	54,942
District 7	30,036	817,997	2.6	1.5	2.8	4.7	12.9	16.0	2.1	17.9	5.3	67,193	82,143
District 8	23,551	418,644	12.8	6.1	12.0	9.9	8.3	5.0	1.8	6.9	3.2	24,366	58,202
District 9	20,623	299,523	6.8	2.9	4.5	12.0	23.5	2.9	1.8	5.8	2.1	15,337	51,204
District 10	21,561	368,852	10.4	3.2	12.8	10.8	12.1	7.4	1.1	11.0	1.3	27,883	75,595
District 11	16,098	274,618	9.8	4.0	8.6	16.1	14.1	3.1	1.2	4.8	1.4	12,675	46,154
District 12	14,685	217,707	12.0	4.4	3.5	16.2	19.6	3.2	1.1	4.3	1.1	8,363	38,414
District 13	15,495	246,755	7.4	4.8	4.1	13.9	22.4	4.4	1.7	4.5	2.4	9,796	39,701
District 14	17,645	192,487	13.7	7.7	6.0	15.8	11.9	3.0	1.1	5.8	1.0	8,547	44,402
District 15	15,367	202,608	19.3	4.5	5.7	13.2	18.4	3.6	1.0	2.4	1.3	7,472	36,880
District 16	15,063	223,584	19.9	3.5	4.7	14.9	15.3	3.5	1.1	3.4	1.2	9,297	41,581
District 17	14,851	267,932	15.1	3.4	3.9	11.6	19.4	3.5	0.8	3.8	1.4	13,233	49,388
District 18	16,029	253,201	9.8	4.4	6.4	16.5	14.1	12.3	0.9	3.4	1.3	10,842	42,821
INDIANA	146,078	2,720,277	18.4	4.5	4.3	12.0	15.6	3.7	1.3	4.7	1.6	117,009	43,014
District 1	14,793	237,701	15.0	5.6	3.2	15.5	19.3	2.5	1.2	3.4	1.0	10,201	42,916
District 2	15,621	316,002	33.7	3.1	4.8	10.7	13.2	2.5	0.9	2.6	1.3	13,236	41,886
District 3	17,467	320,650	27.0	4.0	5.1	11.8	15.6	3.6	1.1	2.6	1.5	13,236	41,280
District 4	15,058	255,057	22.9	4.8	4.1	14.7	14.7	2.2	1.1	2.5	1.0	9,902	38,823
District 5	21,571	384,196	6.6	4.3	4.7	11.9	16.1	7.5	1.9	8.2	2.6	18,357	47,781
District 6	14,280	239,973	22.1	4.0	2.8	12.5	17.0	3.1	0.8	3.8	1.0	9,481	39,507
District 7	15,162	350,471	9.5	5.6	5.6	8.8	15.8	4.1	2.2	7.2	3.0	17,748	50,639
District 8	16,244	278,663	20.0	5.6	4.7	13.0	17.8	3.3	1.0	3.2	1.4	11,411	40,949
District 9	15,232	239,013	19.1	5.4	3.6	15.3	16.6	3.0	1.2	3.2	1.2	8,904	37,253
IOWA	81,563	1,354,487	15.4	4.9	5.1	13.8	16.5	7.3	1.0	4.1	2.2	56,930	42,031
District 1	19,583	349,963	18.1	4.5	4.6	13.7	16.4	6.3	0.9	4.0	2.2	14,387	41,110
District 2	18,874	314,996	19.6	5.2	3.8	14.5	18.5	3.3	0.9	3.7	2.0	12,471	39,590
District 3	20,647	375,053	8.2	5.0	5.3	13.7	14.4	13.8	1.4	5.1	2.5	17,821	47,517
District 4	22,066	288,970	18.4	5.4	6.9	14.6	18.5	3.6	0.9	3.2	2.0	10,935	37,840
KANSAS	74,884	1,184,710	13.5	5.5	5.3	13.0	16.2	5.1	1.3	5.5	2.6	51,016	43,062
District 1	20,010	241,515	16.6	4.9	5.8	15.4	18.2	4.0	1.1	3.1	1.9	8,403	34,794
District 2	15,898	235,451	14.1	6.2	3.1	13.7	20.2	4.4	1.1	5.4	1.5	8,825	37,480
District 3	21,283	392,420	8.4	5.4	7.1	11.8	13.6	7.5	1.5	8.1	4.3	20,771	52,930
District 4	17,199	282,513	19.0	6.1	4.3	13.5	16.0	3.3	1.4	4.4	1.9	11,914	42,173
KENTUCKY	92,000	1,603,173	14.7	4.4	4.5	13.4	15.9	4.7	1.1	4.7	2.0	65,243	40,696
District 1	14,355	216,646	22.8	4.4	3.6	15.1	16.1	3.0	1.0	2.6	1.2	7,715	35,611
District 2	14,608	233,403	19.7	4.7	3.0	14.5	16.5	3.7	1.1	2.7	2.8	8,515	36,482
District 3	19,425	415,566	11.0	4.3	4.8	10.6	15.3	7.4	1.3	5.4	2.1	20,441	49,188
District 4	14,364	246,768	13.9	4.4	5.7	13.7	14.0	5.4	1.2	3.2	1.2	10,395	42,123
District 5	11,560	161,572	10.4	2.9	3.3	18.6	22.4	3.4	1.0	5.6	2.6	5,242	32,442
District 6	17,215	286,388	15.2	5.4	4.6	13.9	16.5	2.9	1.3	6.3	2.5	11,846	41,365
LOUISIANA	105,732	1,709,226	6.9	7.9	4.4	14.0	17.2	3.8	1.8	5.7	1.8	75,125	43,953
District 1	21,106	322,609	4.9	5.3	5.3	14.8	17.6	4.6	2.1	5.3	3.3	14,633	45,357
District 2	16,070	296,096	8.4	5.1	3.7	11.0	12.7	3.7	1.8	6.9	1.2	14,281	48,232
District 3	19,703	287,295	8.8	6.1	5.3	14.9	17.8	2.9	2.6	5.4	1.3	12,334	42,931
District 4	15,002	216,636	8.6	6.2	4.3	15.9	21.9	3.3	1.5	3.7	1.4	8,162	37,676
District 5	15,112	210,895	8.0	5.3	3.9	16.7	26.3	4.1	1.4	4.2	2.0	7,468	35,409
District 6	18,207	329,060	5.1	17.8	4.1	14.3	14.0	4.1	1.5	7.2	1.5	15,561	47,290
MAINE	41,178	511,936	9.7	5.0	3.6	16.4	21.8	5.5	1.3	4.5	2.3	21,349	41,703
District 1	23,366	300,426	9.0	4.9	3.5	15.6	21.3	6.0	1.4	5.1	2.1	13,280	44,205
District 2	17,522	207,750	10.9	5.1	3.5	17.8	22.8	4.5	1.2	3.5	2.6	7,845	37,760
MARYLAND	138,480	2,282,725	4.3	6.6	4.0	12.9	16.2	4.4	2.0	12.1	2.3	121,952	53,424
District 1	17,649	196,831	8.7	7.4	3.8	17.6	18.1	2.7	1.4	4.4	1.1	7,615	38,690
District 2	16,457	341,450	8.4	6.9	7.1	13.4	11.4	4.5	1.9	12.2	1.9	18,882	55,301
District 3	21,075	382,835	2.8	5.2	4.3	11.6	16.0	4.0	2.0	12.9	3.4	21,094	55,099
District 4	12,929	198,099	2.3	8.6	4.3	16.4	14.0	2.6	2.7	10.1	2.0	8,801	44,428
District 5	14,122	208,343	2.2	12.5	3.2	15.7	12.9	2.0	2.3	15.7	1.6	9,840	47,232
District 6	18,921	290,187	6.4	6.4	3.7	15.5	14.6	5.4	1.5	12.1	2.9	14,573	50,219
District 7	15,662	300,115	2.2	2.8	2.2	8.9	26.7	6.8	2.1	11.1	1.8	18,207	60,668
District 8	21,085	320,828	2.1	6.8	2.3	10.0	17.5	5.1	2.4	14.9	2.9	20,160	62,837
MASSACHUSETTS	177,631	3,254,781	6.8	4.0	4.4	11.5	19.8	5.8	1.4	8.7	3.5	204,747	62,907
District 1	16,248	253,580	11.2	4.2	3.5	14.2	23.0	4.9	1.2	3.9	1.3	11,130	43,892
District 2	16,760	295,089	9.0	3.5	4.2	13.2	26.1	5.4	1.0	5.5	1.4	13,255	44,920
District 3	16,467	279,026	14.5	4.3	6.3	10.8	19.1	3.6	1.0	9.4	3.7	18,174	65,132
District 4	20,832	340,133	8.4	4.0	7.0	13.7	16.6	3.8	1.7	6.3	3.0	19,735	58,020
District 5	21,006	388,851	4.1	4.3	4.1	10.0	13.9	4.2	1.5	11.8	5.3	26,718	68,711
District 6	21,277	354,981	10.2	5.2	4.7	13.8	19.0	3.3	1.1	8.4	5.4	21,354	60,154
District 7	17,095	504,144	2.1	1.8	2.7	6.9	21.3	6.3	1.7	11.0	4.1	40,035	79,411
District 8	24,588	536,974	3.3	4.3	3.7	9.6	21.4	12.6	1.9	11.7	3.8	39,550	73,654
District 9	22,707	248,225	6.8	7.1	3.9	18.8	21.0	3.0	1.3	5.0	1.4	11,241	45,286

Table E. Congressional Districts 116th Congress — Land Area and Population Characteristics

STATE District	Representative, 116th Congress	Land area,1 2018 (sq mi)	Total persons	Per square mile	White	Black	American Indian, Alaska Native	Asian and Pacific Islander	Some other race (percent)	Two or more races (percent)	Hispanic or Latino[2] (percent)	Non-Hispanic White alone (percent)	Percent female	Percent foreign-born	Percent born in state of residence
		1	2	3	4	5	6	7	8	9	10	11	12	13	14
MICHIGAN		56,559.4	9,962,311	176.1	78.4	13.8	0.5	3.1	1.1	3.0	5.1	75.0	50.7	7.1	76.1
District 1	Jack Bergman (R)	25,028.3	698,974	27.9	92.0	1.5	2.3	0.7	0.4	3.1	1.9	90.9	49.3	1.9	79.0
District 2	Bill Huizenga (R)	3,297.3	737,365	223.6	84.6	6.6	0.6	2.2	2.5	3.6	9.3	78.8	51.0	5.4	78.9
District 3	Justin Amash (R)	2,629.5	743,830	282.9	83.9	8.3	0.3	2.2	2.0	3.3	8.0	78.7	49.6	6.2	78.2
District 4	John L. Moolenar (R)	8,458.0	702,994	83.1	93.9	1.9	0.7	1.0	0.3	2.2	3.2	91.4	49.9	2.3	85.0
District 5	Daniel T. Kildee (D)	2,348.9	677,788	288.6	77.1	17.3	0.5	0.9	0.7	3.5	4.9	73.9	51.4	2.7	83.7
District 6	Fred Upton (R)	3,547.7	718,436	202.5	84.7	8.0	0.5	1.7	1.3	3.8	6.3	80.4	50.6	4.5	69.5
District 7	Tim Walberg (R)	4,227.9	701,645	166.0	91.2	4.2	0.5	1.0	0.6	2.5	4.7	87.5	49.9	2.4	74.9
District 8	Elissa Slotkin (D)	1,503.1	736,333	489.9	85.2	5.8	0.3	4.4	1.0	3.4	5.2	81.5	50.7	8.6	73.9
District 9	Sander M. Levin (D)	183.7	720,890	3,924.2	77.7	14.2	0.4	4.8	0.8	2.1	2.5	75.9	50.7	12.4	74.8
District 10	Paul Mitchell (R)	4,142.2	717,703	173.3	92.4	2.8	0.3	1.8	0.7	2.1	3.3	90.1	50.9	5.7	83.7
District 11	Haley M. Stevens (D)	419.1	727,901	1,736.8	81.0	5.5	0.3	10.4	0.3	2.4	3.0	78.7	50.9	14.4	70.0
District 12	Debbie Dingell (D)	403.2	708,060	1,756.2	78.7	10.5	0.2	5.5	1.5	3.6	6.2	74.4	51.0	12.6	68.0
District 13	Rashida Tlaib (D)	184.9	674,157	3,646.6	38.5	53.8	0.5	1.6	3.0	2.6	8.4	33.8	52.3	8.9	74.9
District 14	Brenda L. Lawrence (D)	185.6	696,235	3,752.1	34.0	56.5	0.3	5.1	0.9	3.2	4.0	31.3	52.2	10.5	71.5
MINNESOTA		79,625.5	5,576,606	70.0	82.7	6.5	1.1	4.9	2.0	2.8	5.3	79.9	50.1	8.7	67.4
District 1	Jim Hagedorn (R)	11,974.1	675,755	56.4	90.0	3.2	0.3	2.8	1.7	2.1	6.3	85.8	50.1	6.9	68.2
District 2	Angie Craig (D)	2,437.9	705,074	289.2	83.9	5.1	0.4	5.0	2.5	3.2	6.3	80.6	50.2	9.0	66.8
District 3	Dean Philips (D)	527.0	714,299	1,355.4	80.2	8.3	0.4	7.1	1.1	3.0	3.7	77.9	51.3	11.7	62.4
District 4	Betty McCollum (D)	332.6	714,075	2,147.0	70.6	10.6	0.6	13.1	1.8	3.3	6.8	66.4	51.3	14.8	61.2
District 5	Ilhan Omar (D)	135.7	721,389	5,315.3	65.3	16.8	1.2	6.8	1.8	4.1	9.9	62.3	49.8	16.2	54.0
District 6	Tom Emmer (R)	2,881.6	716,009	248.5	89.6	4.0	0.4	2.3	1.2	2.5	3.1	88.0	49.6	5.1	77.5
District 7	Collin C. Peterson (D)	33,429.2	662,695	19.8	90.9	1.7	3.1	0.9	1.4	2.0	4.3	88.4	49.5	3.3	71.4
District 8	Pete Stauber (R)	27,907.4	667,310	23.9	92.7	1.1	2.6	0.9	0.3	2.5	1.8	91.6	49.2	1.9	78.9
MISSISSIPPI		46,923.1	2,984,100	63.6	58.2	38.0	0.5	1.0	1.0	1.4	2.9	56.6	51.5	2.2	72.0
District 1	Trent Kelly (R)	10,572.9	764,896	72.3	68.2	27.4	0.1	0.7	1.7	1.8	3.2	66.7	51.4	2.2	65.0
District 2	Bennie G. Thompson (D)	15,551.4	701,238	45.1	30.5	67.4	0.3	0.5	0.6	0.8	1.7	29.8	52.1	1.3	84.9
District 3	Michael Guest (R)	12,754.2	749,247	58.7	60.3	35.6	1.1	1.1	1.0	1.0	2.2	59.1	51.5	2.3	77.0
District 4	Steven Palazzo (R)	8,044.5	768,719	95.6	71.4	24.1	0.3	1.6	0.8	1.9	4.2	68.4	51.1	3.0	62.3
MISSOURI		68,746.3	6,113,532	88.9	82.0	11.4	0.4	2.2	1.3	2.6	4.2	79.4	50.9	4.2	66.0
District 1	William Lacy Clay (D)	225.2	729,026	3,237.0	42.8	49.4	0.3	3.5	1.2	2.7	3.6	40.5	52.9	7.0	68.3
District 2	Ann Wagner (R)	465.8	764,043	1,640.3	88.3	4.0	0.1	4.4	0.8	2.4	3.0	86.2	51.3	7.6	65.4
District 3	Blaine Luetkemeyer (R)	6,851.5	792,954	115.7	92.5	3.4	0.2	1.2	0.3	2.4	2.1	90.9	50.0	2.2	75.0
District 4	Vicky Hartzler (R)	14,406.0	769,533	53.4	89.2	4.5	0.6	1.8	1.0	2.9	3.9	86.6	50.0	2.7	63.0
District 5	Emanuel Cleaver (D)	2,425.2	770,628	317.8	68.2	21.5	0.3	2.2	4.7	3.1	9.2	63.8	51.1	6.3	59.8
District 6	Sam Graves (R)	18,195.5	773,740	42.5	89.2	4.2	0.5	2.0	1.0	3.0	4.1	86.9	51.1	3.1	64.8
District 7	Bill Long (R)	6,272.8	777,380	123.9	91.6	1.9	0.9	1.5	1.1	3.0	5.3	87.8	51.0	3.2	59.2
District 8	Jason T. Smith (R)	19,901.1	736,228	37.0	92.3	4.5	0.3	0.8	0.5	1.5	2.2	90.6	49.6	1.7	73.1
MONTANA		145,545.4	1,050,493	7.2	88.6	0.4	6.2	0.8	0.7	3.2	3.7	86.3	49.9	2.2	53.1
At Large	Greg Gianforte (R)	145,545.4	1,050,493	7.2	88.6	0.4	6.2	0.8	0.7	3.2	3.7	86.3	49.9	2.2	53.1
NEBRASKA		76,818.1	1,920,076	25.0	87.3	4.6	0.8	2.5	2.0	2.7	10.9	79.0	50.0	7.5	64.5
District 1	Jeff Fortenberry (R)	8,879.0	648,060	73.0	88.4	2.8	1.1	2.9	2.0	2.7	9.3	81.8	49.8	7.4	65.7
District 2	Don Bacon (R)	509.7	668,800	1,312.1	81.5	9.5	0.4	3.8	1.5	3.2	11.6	72.1	50.5	9.3	59.4
District 3	Adrian Smith (R)	67,429.4	603,216	8.9	92.6	1.2	0.9	0.7	2.6	2.0	12.0	83.8	49.9	5.4	68.9
NEVADA		109,780.2	2,998,039	27.3	64.6	9.2	1.3	9.2	11.1	4.6	28.8	48.8	49.8	19.9	25.9
District 1	Dina Titus (D)	104.5	720,730	6,897.7	48.2	11.9	1.4	9.3	24.5	4.7	46.3	28.7	49.2	32.1	23.1
District 2	Mark E. Amodei (R)	55,829.3	720,704	12.9	80.5	1.9	2.6	4.5	6.3	4.1	23.0	65.8	49.1	11.3	31.4
District 3	Susie Lee (D)	2,848.9	803,545	282.1	66.7	7.8	0.2	15.5	4.7	5.1	16.8	56.2	51.1	18.3	21.7
District 4	Steven Horsford (D)	50,997.4	753,060	14.8	62.8	14.9	1.0	6.8	9.8	4.6	30.5	43.9	49.6	18.1	27.9
NEW HAMPSHIRE		8,952.7	1,342,795	150.0	93.1	1.7	0.1	2.7	0.3	2.1	3.8	90.3	50.4	6.2	41.8
District 1	Chris Pappas (D)	2,464.5	673,194	273.2	93.5	1.6	0.1	2.5	0.3	2.0	3.5	90.9	50.4	5.8	42.3
District 2	Ann M. Kuster (D)	6,488.2	669,601	103.2	92.6	1.7	0.2	2.9	0.4	2.2	4.1	89.8	50.5	6.6	41.2
NEW JERSEY		7,355.1	9,005,644	1,224.4	67.9	13.5	0.2	9.9	6.0	2.5	20.4	54.8	51.2	22.8	51.9
District 1	Donald Norcross (D)	350.2	729,675	2,083.5	68.7	16.9	0.2	5.6	5.5	3.1	14.1	61.8	51.5	9.8	54.6
District 2	Jefferson Van Drew (D)	2,095.0	713,380	340.5	75.3	12.7	0.6	4.1	4.6	2.7	16.5	64.9	51.1	10.4	59.8
District 3	Andy Kim (D)	898.2	746,035	830.6	80.1	11.7	0.1	3.6	1.8	2.8	8.4	74.6	51.2	8.9	60.9
District 4	Christopher H. Smith (R)	691.2	756,825	1,095.0	83.9	6.6	0.1	4.7	2.6	2.1	10.8	76.4	51.9	12.2	59.7
District 5	Josh Gottheimer (D)	991.6	746,385	752.7	79.1	5.2	0.1	11.8	1.9	1.9	15.2	66.9	51.7	20.6	51.9
District 6	Frank Pallone Jr. (D)	215.2	742,483	3,449.5	62.2	10.3	0.2	20.1	4.5	2.6	22.5	46.1	50.8	29.6	48.6
District 7	Tom Malinowski (D)	969.9	754,222	777.6	79.2	5.0	0.1	10.8	2.7	2.3	12.0	70.5	50.8	19.1	56.1
District 8	Albio Sires (D)	54.7	777,484	14,218.0	57.3	9.4	0.3	9.1	20.2	3.8	54.5	25.8	50.2	44.3	36.1
District 9	Bill Pascrell Jr. (D)	95.3	769,504	8,073.9	62.6	9.6	0.1	13.3	11.7	2.7	37.9	38.1	51.1	38.6	43.0
District 10	Donald M. Payne, Jr. (D)	75.8	781,893	10,310.7	27.8	51.7	0.3	7.7	10.1	2.4	21.1	18.1	52.2	29.9	48.7
District 11	Mikie Sherill (R)	505.8	729,569	1,442.3	81.8	3.7	0.2	10.8	1.5	2.0	11.4	72.6	51.1	19.9	57.4
District 12	Bonnie Watson Coleman (D)	412.1	758,189	1,839.8	59.3	17.9	0.1	16.8	3.6	2.3	18.5	46.3	50.5	28.1	47.7
NEW MEXICO		121,310.0	2,088,070	17.2	75.8	2.1	9.6	1.5	7.7	3.3	48.8	37.4	50.5	9.4	54.3
District 1	Debra A. Haaland (D)	4,600.8	696,688	151.4	78.4	2.7	4.4	2.3	8.6	3.6	49.9	39.9	51.2	9.7	53.6
District 2	Xochitl Torres Small (D)	71,745.4	694,692	9.7	83.7	2.1	5.2	0.8	5.5	2.7	55.3	36.1	49.2	11.7	51.0

1. Dry land or land partially or temporarily covered by water.   2. May be of any race.

Table E. Congressional Districts 116th Congress — **Age and Education**

STATE District	Population and population characteristics, 2017 (cont.)										Education, 2017		
	Age (percent)											Attainment[2] (percent)	
	Under 5 years	5 to 17 years	18 to 24 years	25 to 34 years	35 to 44 years	45 to 54 years	55 to 64 years	65 to 74 years	75 years and over	Median age	Total Enrollment[1]	High school graduate or more	Bachelor's degree or more
	15	16	17	18	19	20	21	22	23	24	25	26	27
MICHIGAN	5.7	16.1	9.7	12.7	11.6	13.3	14.1	9.8	6.9	39.8	2,452,202	90.9	29.1
District 1	4.7	13.9	8.7	10.4	10.4	12.7	16.6	13.2	9.4	46.6	143,176	92.6	26.3
District 2	6.3	17.1	10.2	13.1	11.6	12.5	13.2	9.2	6.8	37.6	184,956	90.5	27.2
District 3	6.4	17.6	9.6	13.8	12.6	12.8	12.9	8.4	5.8	37.1	189,805	91.9	32.6
District 4	5.1	15.5	10.9	11.2	10.9	13.0	14.7	10.9	7.8	41.6	174,651	91.3	22.4
District 5	5.7	16.1	8.3	12.3	11.3	13.3	14.7	10.5	7.8	41.8	156,344	89.8	19.8
District 6	6.1	16.6	10.7	12.1	11.5	12.6	13.9	9.9	6.7	38.7	182,263	90.8	28.1
District 7	5.4	16.1	8.4	11.8	11.4	13.9	15.1	10.5	7.3	42.3	165,805	92.5	24.1
District 8	5.4	16.4	12.4	11.9	11.7	13.8	13.4	9.4	5.6	38.4	208,968	94.5	41.5
District 9	5.5	14.4	8.3	15.0	12.1	14.0	13.9	9.5	7.2	40.3	153,772	90.3	30.4
District 10	5.1	16.4	7.7	11.2	11.7	14.6	15.2	10.7	7.3	43.0	165,293	91.1	23.6
District 11	5.2	16.3	8.0	11.8	12.5	14.9	15.0	9.5	6.7	42.0	177,702	95.0	48.4
District 12	5.6	15.5	13.6	14.0	11.8	13.3	12.4	8.6	5.2	35.9	214,792	90.7	34.7
District 13	7.1	16.5	10.1	14.7	11.5	12.8	12.5	8.7	6.2	36.4	166,164	83.2	16.1
District 14	6.8	16.8	8.9	14.4	11.6	12.3	13.7	8.7	6.8	37.4	168,511	87.4	30.7
MINNESOTA	6.3	16.9	9.0	13.6	12.6	12.7	13.5	8.8	6.6	37.9	1,404,105	93.1	36.1
District 1	6.1	17.0	10.1	12.3	11.9	12.0	13.5	9.2	7.9	38.3	173,409	92.6	29.4
District 2	6.3	18.8	8.1	12.8	13.4	14.2	13.2	7.9	5.3	37.5	188,954	94.4	39.2
District 3	6.7	17.0	6.1	12.7	13.3	13.8	14.9	9.2	6.3	40.4	169,382	96.3	49.8
District 4	6.8	16.7	9.5	15.5	12.5	12.1	12.7	8.4	5.9	36.0	190,809	91.2	43.5
District 5	6.3	14.3	10.9	20.9	13.7	11.3	10.7	6.9	5.0	33.8	185,899	91.0	47.0
District 6	6.5	18.9	9.7	12.1	13.3	13.9	12.8	7.7	5.0	37.0	189,148	94.5	31.0
District 7	6.3	17.1	8.7	11.2	11.1	11.8	14.5	10.3	9.1	40.8	156,435	91.6	22.1
District 8	5.6	15.7	8.8	10.9	11.3	12.5	15.5	11.5	8.3	42.8	150,069	92.9	23.7
MISSISSIPPI	6.1	17.8	10.4	12.2	12.7	12.4	12.8	9.4	6.2	37.5	779,151	84.4	21.9
District 1	5.9	17.7	10.5	11.9	13.0	12.6	12.5	9.5	6.3	38.1	196,735	83.6	20.4
District 2	6.2	18.8	10.7	11.8	12.7	12.2	12.7	9.0	5.8	36.7	193,661	81.4	19.1
District 3	5.8	17.7	10.4	11.9	12.9	12.3	13.1	9.5	6.5	37.5	198,089	85.8	25.8
District 4	6.5	17.2	10.0	12.9	12.1	12.7	12.9	9.4	6.4	37.4	190,666	86.4	22.0
MISSOURI	6.1	16.6	9.4	13.3	11.9	12.7	13.5	9.5	7.0	38.5	1,484,234	89.7	29.1
District 1	6.5	15.4	10.1	16.5	12.5	12.0	13.6	7.7	5.8	36.0	181,147	89.4	31.9
District 2	5.4	15.9	7.2	12.3	11.7	13.6	14.8	11.0	8.2	42.8	177,635	95.4	49.5
District 3	6.1	17.7	8.5	12.6	12.6	13.3	13.7	9.4	6.3	38.9	193,654	90.4	27.0
District 4	6.2	16.4	12.3	12.7	11.1	12.0	12.7	9.7	6.9	36.9	195,929	89.2	26.0
District 5	6.7	16.6	8.5	15.4	12.4	12.3	13.0	8.7	6.3	36.9	180,274	89.0	27.7
District 6	6.0	17.5	9.5	12.2	12.4	13.0	13.0	9.3	7.1	38.6	193,836	91.3	27.6
District 7	6.3	16.6	10.6	12.9	11.4	12.3	12.7	9.9	7.3	37.9	195,371	88.9	25.0
District 8	5.8	16.6	8.7	12.0	11.3	12.6	14.3	10.7	8.1	40.9	166,388	83.5	16.3
MONTANA	5.8	16.0	9.2	12.6	11.9	11.7	14.5	10.9	7.2	40.0	236,016	93.0	32.3
At Large	5.8	16.0	9.2	12.6	11.9	11.7	14.5	10.9	7.2	40.0	236,016	93.0	32.3
NEBRASKA	6.9	17.9	9.7	13.5	12.3	11.7	12.7	8.7	6.6	36.5	507,288	91.3	31.7
District 1	6.8	17.1	12.1	13.3	12.0	11.4	12.4	8.7	6.3	35.6	179,078	92.5	31.9
District 2	7.5	18.8	8.6	15.3	13.6	12.2	11.7	7.6	4.8	34.9	180,521	91.3	40.0
District 3	6.3	17.6	8.4	11.7	11.2	11.5	14.2	10.1	8.9	39.9	147,689	90.1	22.5
NEVADA	6.1	16.7	8.4	14.5	13.3	13.2	12.4	9.6	5.7	38.0	697,092	86.8	24.9
District 1	5.8	16.1	9.5	16.5	13.1	14.3	11.7	7.9	5.1	36.5	158,656	78.1	15.7
District 2	5.8	15.8	8.5	13.9	12.1	12.9	13.9	10.7	6.2	39.7	167,319	88.8	27.6
District 3	5.7	16.2	7.3	14.3	14.4	13.2	12.2	10.3	6.4	39.3	187,738	93.2	32.8
District 4	7.2	18.6	8.3	13.6	13.5	12.5	11.9	9.3	5.1	36.7	183,379	86.0	22.2
NEW HAMPSHIRE	4.7	14.5	9.4	12.2	11.3	14.6	15.6	10.7	6.9	43.2	300,223	93.1	36.9
District 1	4.8	14.4	9.6	13.2	11.4	14.7	15.2	10.3	6.4	42.0	149,690	93.0	37.8
District 2	4.6	14.5	9.3	11.2	11.2	14.5	16.1	11.0	7.5	44.3	150,533	93.1	36.1
NEW JERSEY	5.8	16.2	8.8	12.9	12.9	14.2	13.5	8.9	6.8	39.8	2,226,989	89.9	39.7
District 1	5.7	16.7	8.7	13.2	12.8	13.8	13.4	9.0	6.7	39.4	181,784	90.2	32.8
District 2	5.4	15.9	8.6	11.7	11.8	13.6	14.8	10.6	7.7	42.2	166,328	88.4	28.0
District 3	4.9	15.6	8.2	11.5	11.5	14.4	14.7	10.7	8.5	43.5	172,671	93.4	33.8
District 4	6.9	16.9	8.3	11.5	10.7	13.8	14.1	9.5	8.4	40.7	193,855	92.4	41.9
District 5	5.2	17.1	8.3	9.8	12.7	15.7	14.5	9.2	7.5	42.6	189,560	93.7	48.2
District 6	5.7	15.8	10.4	14.0	13.3	13.3	13.7	8.5	5.4	37.7	197,472	89.2	41.7
District 7	5.0	17.5	7.9	9.8	12.3	16.0	15.4	9.1	7.0	43.1	187,055	94.1	52.4
District 8	7.0	14.4	8.7	19.8	16.1	12.5	10.8	6.1	4.4	35.0	170,288	80.4	34.4
District 9	6.4	15.6	9.0	14.7	13.2	13.6	12.8	8.3	6.4	37.8	188,819	85.5	33.9
District 10	6.5	16.9	9.6	15.7	13.7	13.4	11.6	7.3	5.2	35.9	208,752	86.3	30.6
District 11	5.1	15.5	8.4	10.4	12.7	15.5	14.5	9.8	8.1	43.3	177,677	94.8	54.2
District 12	5.5	16.4	9.4	12.3	13.6	14.8	12.3	9.0	6.8	39.5	192,728	90.9	44.7
NEW MEXICO	6.1	17.4	9.9	13.1	12.0	11.5	13.3	10.2	6.6	37.7	536,849	86.1	27.1
District 1	5.6	15.9	8.9	14.2	12.9	12.4	13.8	10.0	6.2	38.6	172,218	89.6	34.0
District 2	6.5	18.6	11.4	12.8	11.2	10.5	12.5	9.5	7.0	35.6	188,593	81.7	19.5

1. All persons 3 years old and over enrolled in nursery school through college and graduate or professional school.   2. Persons 25 years old and over.

Table E. Congressional Districts 116th Congress — Households and Group Quarters

STATE District	Households, 2017						Total in group quarters, 2017	Group Quarters, 2010			
	Number	Average household size	Family households (percent)	Married couple family (percent)	Female family householder[1]	One person households (percent)		Percent 65 years and over	Persons in correctional institutions	Persons in nursing facilities	Persons in college dormitories	Persons in military quarters
	28	29	30	31	32	33	34	35	36	37	38	39
MICHIGAN	3,930,017	2.48	64.1	47.2	12.0	29.6	229,856	19.8	62,083	42,473	78,033	214
District 1	284,799	2.37	63.3	50.5	8.2	30.3	24,096	20.2	12,990	4,884	5,714	129
District 2	279,944	2.56	67.2	51.5	10.9	27.2	21,029	17.4	5,021	2,948	6,414	0
District 3	278,077	2.61	67.7	51.9	10.7	25.5	18,583	18.1	7,012	3,695	5,151	82
District 4	273,635	2.47	65.3	51.7	9.2	27.9	27,895	13.6	9,024	3,606	13,524	0
District 5	283,633	2.35	62.3	41.8	14.9	32.0	9,891	33.6	1,630	3,103	1,303	3
District 6	286,594	2.45	64.5	49.0	10.8	28.7	15,533	22.3	1,476	3,141	6,864	0
District 7	273,527	2.47	66.9	51.6	10.8	28.2	24,956	15.0	14,438	2,638	4,594	0
District 8	280,455	2.55	66.1	53.2	9.0	26.4	22,393	10.0	988	1,873	16,015	0
District 9	305,031	2.34	60.4	42.1	12.9	33.2	6,316	50.7	1,143	3,267	0	0
District 10	280,775	2.52	70.0	55.1	10.4	24.8	9,285	36.3	3,120	2,375	0	0
District 11	288,893	2.50	68.0	56.4	8.2	26.3	6,528	45.5	183	2,598	1,581	0
District 12	276,965	2.48	59.4	43.8	11.3	30.8	20,405	11.9	387	2,155	13,873	0
District 13	264,841	2.50	56.4	28.1	21.9	37.9	11,050	21.2	114	2,806	2,287	0
District 14	272,848	2.51	59.3	33.9	19.4	35.2	11,896	23.4	4,557	3,384	713	0
MINNESOTA	2,162,211	2.52	64.2	51.2	8.9	28.4	132,035	24.9	20,397	32,989	50,444	0
District 1	265,922	2.46	65.6	53.2	7.9	27.2	22,605	23.9	4,808	5,137	9,723	0
District 2	261,322	2.65	71.1	57.2	10.2	23.3	11,541	25.8	1,042	2,781	4,486	0
District 3	277,717	2.55	68.1	56.2	8.5	26.2	4,910	38.8	551	1,864	644	0
District 4	271,708	2.56	62.4	47.1	10.8	29.5	18,516	16.8	3,286	3,540	9,958	0
District 5	298,856	2.34	49.0	35.1	9.6	38.1	20,899	20.9	876	5,425	8,740	0
District 6	257,102	2.73	72.3	60.0	8.2	21.2	14,220	19.1	3,328	2,246	5,885	0
District 7	262,582	2.45	64.1	52.7	7.4	30.5	18,168	40.1	1,022	7,051	6,518	0
District 8	267,002	2.42	63.4	50.4	8.5	30.0	21,176	25.9	5,484	4,945	4,490	0
MISSISSIPPI	1,091,980	2.65	65.6	44.2	16.4	30.0	92,944	16	34,273	16,496	26,472	3,938
District 1	273,703	2.73	67.3	47.9	14.8	27.9	18,549	22.9	2,943	4,381	7,786	0
District 2	255,047	2.63	63.9	34.8	23.1	33.2	29,635	11.7	14,994	4,226	8,476	8
District 3	278,052	2.61	65.5	46.8	14.3	30.3	24,844	18.4	9,560	4,625	5,828	601
District 4	285,178	2.63	65.6	46.5	13.9	28.8	19,916	14.6	6,776	3,264	4,382	3,329
MISSOURI	2,385,135	2.49	64.0	47.7	11.7	29.5	174,867	22.7	41,956	44,866	52,869	10,217
District 1	309,334	2.30	54.3	30.8	19.2	37.6	18,789	17.6	1,344	4,741	9,050	0
District 2	308,590	2.44	67.1	55.4	8.3	27.8	11,218	55.7	2,300	7,231	1,046	0
District 3	289,118	2.67	70.8	55.8	10.0	23.7	20,754	19.1	6,107	3,662	5,666	0
District 4	288,067	2.55	64.7	50.3	9.9	28.2	35,071	13.4	6,015	5,555	11,262	10,217
District 5	317,338	2.39	56.0	37.7	13.3	36.3	13,430	31.8	1,420	5,172	2,626	0
District 6	290,251	2.56	67.5	52.7	10.0	26.4	29,357	20.5	11,433	6,573	8,326	0
District 7	303,711	2.49	66.0	50.9	10.7	27.7	19,820	22.7	2,358	4,919	9,841	0
District 8	278,726	2.55	67.3	49.9	11.8	27.0	26,428	23.9	10,979	7,013	5,052	0
MONTANA	423,091	2.41	62.1	50.4	7.7	30.4	28,803	19.2	5,338	5,200	8,332	678
At Large	423,091	2.41	62.1	50.4	7.7	30.4	28,803	19.2	5,338	5,200	8,332	678
NEBRASKA	754,490	2.48	64.3	50.9	8.9	29.2	52,015	24.4	8,084	13,519	22,073	443
District 1	253,963	2.47	64.5	51.0	8.8	27.7	19,759	19.1	3,362	4,124	10,719	443
District 2	256,532	2.55	64.5	49.2	10.5	28.9	13,560	17.6	2,325	2,632	4,750	0
District 3	243,995	2.40	63.8	52.7	7.4	31.2	18,696	35.5	2,397	6,763	6,604	0
NEVADA	1,094,613	2.70	64.0	44.9	13.0	28.1	38,240	15.2	19,891	5,005	3,336	1,022
District 1	259,459	2.74	58.4	33.3	17.0	33.0	9,823	11.3	4,771	954	1,211	0
District 2	282,126	2.51	62.7	47.2	10.1	29.2	11,981	12.8	6,685	1,334	2,125	166
District 3	297,759	2.69	65.7	49.2	11.6	26.1	2,512	58.1	352	1,044	0	0
District 4	255,269	2.90	69.0	49.1	13.9	24.4	13,924	14.2	8,083	1,673	0	856
NEW HAMPSHIRE	528,700	2.46	65.5	52.1	8.5	26.2	42,483	19.5	4,851	7,767	22,820	454
District 1	269,079	2.43	64.2	50.1	9.1	26.6	19,492	21.5	1,640	3,963	10,357	454
District 2	259,621	2.49	66.8	54.2	7.8	25.7	22,991	17.9	3,211	3,804	12,463	0
NEW JERSEY	3,218,798	2.74	69.4	51.4	13.0	25.4	183,073	23.7	44,468	45,512	55,483	1,452
District 1	273,225	2.63	67.0	46.8	15.0	27.8	9,997	33.0	2,221	3,995	2,424	0
District 2	263,366	2.62	67.7	48.4	14.7	26.4	23,612	17.9	11,704	4,360	2,376	768
District 3	279,723	2.61	70.8	54.0	11.7	23.8	14,788	26.5	6,383	4,169	0	360
District 4	273,320	2.74	69.0	55.7	9.2	26.4	7,323	50.3	1,319	4,614	1,306	254
District 5	261,262	2.80	74.3	60.9	9.3	21.4	14,105	39.2	1,041	5,005	4,364	0
District 6	254,865	2.80	70.3	53.8	11.6	24.4	28,772	12.3	2,976	3,169	15,266	70
District 7	265,255	2.80	73.8	61.3	8.8	22.4	11,298	37.9	2,789	3,543	129	0
District 8	277,396	2.77	63.2	39.3	16.9	27.7	9,471	22.0	3,043	2,492	1,409	0
District 9	268,216	2.85	70.6	47.5	16.6	25.0	5,295	26.3	1,068	1,145	468	0
District 10	272,760	2.79	64.0	35.7	21.0	31.1	19,853	11.0	7,245	2,896	6,771	0
District 11	265,797	2.68	72.8	61.1	8.4	22.8	16,008	30.3	411	5,741	9,278	0
District 12	263,613	2.79	70.4	53.5	12.2	25.6	22,551	16.9	4,268	4,383	11,692	0
NEW MEXICO	767,705	2.66	62.4	42.9	13.4	32.0	42,965	14.3	17,907	5,567	8,478	1,789
District 1	272,635	2.52	58.8	40.3	12.2	35.1	9,597	15.9	4,489	1,768	2,750	530
District 2	245,944	2.74	65.3	45.8	13.8	29.1	21,195	11.7	9,874	2,334	3,613	815

1. No spouse present.

Table E. Congressional Districts 116th Congress — Housing and Money Income

| STATE District | Housing units, 2017 | | | | | | Money income, 2017 | | |
	Total	Occupied units as a percent of all units	Owner-occupied units as a percent of occupied units	Median value[1] (dollars)	Percent valued at $500,000 or more	Median rent[2]	Per capita income (dollars)	Median income (dollars)	Percent with income of $100,000 or more
	40	41	42	43	44	45	46	47	48
MICHIGAN	4,595,274	85.5	71.3	155,700	4.5	835	30,488	54,909	23.4
District 1	450,186	63.3	79.0	139,400	5.1	665	26,968	48,416	16.2
District 2	323,146	86.6	74.8	155,000	3.4	811	27,538	56,103	20.9
District 3	300,068	92.7	72.7	166,200	3.9	846	30,190	58,999	25.0
District 4	350,440	78.1	77.5	127,000	2.5	699	26,836	49,448	18.5
District 5	331,572	85.5	71.6	101,500	1.8	711	25,344	44,383	15.3
District 6	331,060	86.6	72.4	149,900	4.6	754	29,901	53,414	21.4
District 7	306,537	89.2	76.9	157,200	3.2	775	30,106	58,899	23.4
District 8	301,687	93.0	73.6	224,900	7.0	922	36,431	71,702	35.2
District 9	323,359	94.3	68.4	156,800	5.1	928	34,559	58,742	23.7
District 10	312,743	89.8	81.4	184,000	3.2	834	32,209	63,156	28.1
District 11	304,194	95.0	75.8	244,700	10.2	1,077	43,172	82,545	40.2
District 12	297,944	93.0	64.1	154,400	5.4	931	32,260	57,034	26.1
District 13	331,681	79.8	54.0	74,400	1.3	795	20,238	35,365	11.4
District 14	330,657	82.5	55.3	125,700	5.7	911	29,737	46,500	21.5
MINNESOTA	2,437,726	88.7	71.6	224,000	7.9	939	36,156	68,388	31.6
District 1	292,250	91.0	74.3	172,200	4.2	770	31,705	61,310	25.9
District 2	272,142	96.0	75.8	263,900	8.2	1,084	39,145	81,885	40.0
District 3	290,315	95.7	75.8	294,500	17.9	1,204	48,806	89,442	45.2
District 4	284,463	95.5	64.0	248,000	8.8	1,020	36,609	68,684	32.6
District 5	314,890	94.9	53.0	235,200	10.2	1,014	37,916	63,202	29.2
District 6	273,331	94.1	81.5	235,400	5.5	896	35,341	79,826	36.9
District 7	332,597	78.9	73.8	158,300	4.7	663	29,052	55,745	21.1
District 8	377,738	70.7	77.2	174,100	4.2	746	29,506	56,055	21.9
MISSISSIPPI	1,323,754	82.5	68.5	120,200	2.8	742	23,121	43,529	15.9
District 1	333,581	82.0	73.3	122,700	2.3	725	23,901	47,681	16.8
District 2	312,799	81.5	60.7	91,900	1.8	677	19,334	35,842	11.6
District 3	334,747	83.1	72.3	125,100	4.3	765	25,285	45,475	18.1
District 4	342,627	83.2	67.2	137,900	2.6	808	23,691	45,442	16.7
MISSOURI	2,792,445	85.4	67.0	156,700	4.4	800	29,438	53,578	21.8
District 1	370,733	83.4	50.1	115,400	3.9	850	28,471	45,789	17.4
District 2	323,290	95.5	78.2	242,400	11.2	1,011	45,395	79,497	38.9
District 3	345,426	83.7	77.8	175,100	3.0	776	29,773	64,529	26.9
District 4	353,033	81.6	67.9	150,200	3.8	751	26,020	50,963	18.4
District 5	362,781	87.5	57.1	129,700	3.3	870	29,284	50,663	19.5
District 6	335,344	86.6	71.0	158,300	3.2	771	29,908	58,778	24.8
District 7	358,546	84.7	65.0	139,600	3.5	735	24,917	47,225	15.5
District 8	343,292	81.2	70.2	119,400	2.0	612	21,490	40,542	12.7
MONTANA	510,408	82.9	69.2	231,300	9.6	759	29,428	53,386	21.5
At Large	510,408	82.9	69.2	231,300	9.6	759	29,428	53,386	21.5
NEBRASKA	837,540	90.1	66.3	155,800	3.5	801	30,915	59,970	24.3
District 1	275,347	92.2	65.2	166,700	3.8	794	30,324	60,341	24.7
District 2	273,651	93.7	62.8	174,900	3.9	915	34,234	66,390	29.9
District 3	288,542	84.6	71.0	117,100	2.8	665	27,871	52,434	18.0
NEVADA	1,249,733	87.6	56.6	258,200	10.4	1,051	30,166	58,003	24.3
District 1	306,905	84.5	41.4	180,900	4.4	909	23,151	41,281	12.8
District 2	313,435	90.0	62.0	291,900	15.3	972	32,960	61,225	27.1
District 3	343,067	86.8	60.8	300,400	13.2	1,275	37,265	70,804	32.1
District 4	286,326	89.2	61.0	234,600	5.8	1,110	26,629	59,714	23.7
NEW HAMPSHIRE	634,689	83.3	69.8	263,600	9.7	1,072	38,237	73,381	35.1
District 1	322,515	83.4	67.7	276,400	11.5	1,101	39,128	73,488	35.3
District 2	312,174	83.2	72.0	250,500	7.8	1,041	37,342	73,249	34.9
NEW JERSEY	3,615,891	89.0	63.8	334,900	23.6	1,284	40,567	80,088	40.3
District 1	296,082	92.3	68.6	201,600	3.4	1,058	34,790	69,804	33.6
District 2	386,133	68.2	71.4	222,800	10.2	1,060	32,619	65,467	31.2
District 3	321,620	87.0	79.8	262,900	10.2	1,420	39,553	82,301	39.3
District 4	299,044	91.4	74.9	372,500	28.5	1,354	43,119	86,365	43.3
District 5	280,817	93.0	75.0	429,100	36.7	1,441	48,237	100,607	50.4
District 6	274,334	92.9	62.7	342,300	18.3	1,413	37,763	82,451	41.3
District 7	284,775	93.1	77.7	449,600	42.2	1,400	56,235	113,993	56.3
District 8	307,029	90.3	28.7	361,700	27.2	1,295	34,263	59,257	29.8
District 9	284,452	94.3	46.9	372,400	24.3	1,293	33,623	67,624	33.2
District 10	308,394	88.4	39.5	283,000	14.9	1,124	29,912	54,440	27.0
District 11	281,738	94.3	76.2	448,300	40.2	1,516	54,746	112,348	55.8
District 12	291,473	90.4	65.6	345,900	23.6	1,361	42,521	85,595	44.0
NEW MEXICO	937,976	81.8	67.9	171,300	6.0	813	25,311	46,744	19.2
District 1	305,319	89.3	64.2	194,700	7.1	836	28,326	50,159	21.5
District 2	314,781	78.1	68.6	133,400	2.5	727	21,945	42,507	15.9

1. Specified owner-occupied units.   2. Specified renter-occupied units.

Table E. Congressional Districts 116th Congress — Poverty, Labor Force, Employment, and Social Security

STATE District	Poverty, 2017			Civilian labor force, 2016			Civilian employment,[2] 2017				Persons under 65 years of age with no health insurance, 2017 (percent)	Social Security beneficiaries, December 2018		Supplemental Security Income recipients, December 2018
	Persons below poverty level (percent)	Families below poverty level (percent)	Percent of households receiving food stamps in past 12 months	Total	Unemployment Total	Rate[1]	Total	Management, business, science, and arts occupations	Service, sales, and office	Construction and production		Number	Rate[3]	
	49	50	51	52	53	54	55	56	57	58	59	60	61	62
MICHIGAN	14.2	9.7	13.1	4,945,632	291,020	5.9	4,654,612	36.7	39.5	23.8	6.1	2,209,084	221.7	271,833
District 1	13.1	8.3	11.3	321,570	18,507	5.8	303,063	31.1	43.9	25.0	8.2	210,905	301.7	14,793
District 2	11.8	8.1	10.5	379,013	16,664	4.4	362,349	32.3	37.7	30.0	5.1	156,967	212.9	15,551
District 3	11.7	8.2	11.0	390,252	19,134	4.9	371,118	35.8	39.4	24.8	5.7	144,489	194.3	16,757
District 4	14.5	9.0	12.4	320,092	16,877	5.3	303,215	32.6	39.9	27.5	6.6	180,479	256.7	16,308
District 5	18.6	13.3	18.9	312,600	30,282	9.7	282,318	30.5	43.9	25.6	7.4	176,898	261.0	28,947
District 6	13.4	9.3	11.7	366,728	17,476	4.8	349,252	36.2	36.4	27.4	6.7	159,978	222.7	16,930
District 7	10.8	7.1	10.0	342,437	15,787	4.6	326,650	33.0	39.2	27.8	6.5	168,061	239.5	13,516
District 8	11.1	6.5	8.6	387,583	17,703	4.6	369,880	45.0	37.9	17.1	4.0	139,168	189.0	11,624
District 9	12.4	9.8	11.4	380,388	19,964	5.2	360,424	38.5	39.5	22.0	5.9	152,011	210.9	20,503
District 10	9.6	7.1	9.4	360,088	16,499	4.6	343,589	35.0	38.5	26.5	6.0	167,589	233.5	13,002
District 11	6.0	4.0	4.6	396,972	16,247	4.1	380,725	50.3	35.7	14.0	4.0	141,411	194.3	7,953
District 12	16.4	11.1	12.5	362,259	16,574	4.6	345,685	42.2	37.5	20.3	4.2	137,777	194.6	16,472
District 13	29.6	23.3	30.6	300,999	36,851	12.2	264,148	26.4	45.5	28.1	8.5	132,849	197.1	48,844
District 14	20.9	15.1	21.7	324,651	32,455	10.0	292,196	38.5	41.6	19.9	7.3	140,502	201.8	30,633
MINNESOTA	9.5	5.8	7.8	3,070,881	110,757	3.6	2,960,124	40.8	38.4	20.8	5.1	1,032,697	185.2	93,517
District 1	11.3	6.7	7.6	365,277	11,452	3.1	353,825	36.8	36.7	26.6	5.2	138,185	204.5	9,204
District 2	5.3	4.2	5.3	402,933	15,108	3.7	387,825	41.5	38.9	19.5	3.7	114,368	162.2	7,106
District 3	5.0	3.1	4.3	403,590	12,072	3.0	391,518	48.5	37.3	14.3	4.1	123,392	172.7	7,201
District 4	11.7	8.1	10.2	393,452	15,571	4.0	377,881	44.9	39.7	15.5	5.5	117,525	164.6	17,963
District 5	14.7	9.6	11.7	429,940	18,322	4.3	411,618	48.0	37.7	14.3	6.8	97,963	135.8	22,023
District 6	5.7	3.3	5.1	405,738	12,636	3.1	393,102	36.5	38.4	25.1	3.8	115,585	161.4	7,119
District 7	11.0	6.3	7.8	339,280	9,728	2.9	329,552	33.9	37.2	28.9	6.8	155,206	234.2	10,201
District 8	11.7	6.4	9.7	330,671	15,868	4.8	314,803	33.4	41.7	24.8	5.4	170,473	255.5	12,700
MISSISSIPPI	19.8	14.9	15.3	1,319,719	92,744	7.0	1,226,975	32.5	40.3	27.2	14.2	668,877	224.1	117,083
District 1	15.9	12.2	11.9	353,081	19,729	5.6	333,352	29.4	39.8	30.8	12.4	173,299	226.6	24,132
District 2	26.2	20.8	22.0	292,076	26,065	8.9	266,011	28.6	43.7	27.7	16.3	162,433	231.6	43,470
District 3	19.6	14.3	12.8	329,171	17,086	5.2	312,085	39.1	37.0	23.9	12.8	163,989	218.9	25,352
District 4	18.0	13.0	15.0	345,391	29,864	8.6	315,527	32.8	41.1	26.1	15.3	169,156	220.0	24,129
MISSOURI	13.4	9.2	11.0	3,061,464	141,163	4.6	2,920,301	36.9	40.6	22.5	10.8	1,293,897	211.6	136,338
District 1	17.8	13.1	18.8	385,232	29,598	7.7	355,634	38.5	44.9	16.6	11.6	134,176	184.0	28,118
District 2	5.8	4.1	3.2	411,634	11,425	2.8	400,209	50.9	36.4	12.7	4.6	157,659	206.3	5,916
District 3	9.8	6.7	7.7	410,478	16,043	3.9	394,435	34.8	39.6	25.7	8.5	168,374	212.3	10,558
District 4	14.0	8.7	10.3	368,456	18,475	5.0	349,981	35.1	39.6	25.3	12.6	164,516	213.8	15,448
District 5	14.7	10.7	11.0	401,581	18,719	4.7	382,862	35.4	41.7	22.9	13.7	148,915	193.2	19,466
District 6	10.8	6.8	7.4	387,360	13,012	3.4	374,348	36.0	38.8	25.2	8.9	155,876	201.5	11,960
District 7	15.1	10.3	11.8	380,014	15,036	4.0	364,978	32.9	43.2	23.9	12.9	177,171	227.9	17,703
District 8	20.1	14.6	18.2	316,709	18,855	6.0	297,854	29.2	41.2	29.7	13.9	187,230	254.3	27,169
MONTANA	12.5	7.7	9.4	538,121	18,844	3.5	519,277	35.4	42.2	22.4	10.2	233,801	222.6	17,891
At Large	12.5	7.7	9.4	538,121	18,844	3.5	519,277	35.4	42.2	22.4	10.2	233,801	222.6	17,891
NEBRASKA	10.8	7.2	8.3	1,043,919	34,967	3.3	1,008,952	37.7	39.0	23.4	9.6	345,725	180.1	28,281
District 1	10.6	7.3	7.6	357,870	13,018	3.6	344,852	38.3	39.3	22.4	9.4	113,826	175.6	8,854
District 2	10.2	6.8	9.2	368,320	13,205	3.6	355,115	42.0	40.2	17.7	9.4	101,602	151.9	10,898
District 3	11.6	7.6	8.2	317,729	8,744	2.8	308,985	32.0	37.1	30.9	10.2	130,297	216.0	8,529
NEVADA	13.0	9.1	12.2	1,514,888	90,032	5.9	1,424,856	28.9	51.5	19.6	13.0	536,855	179.1	56,578
District 1	18.8	14.0	20.5	377,763	28,537	7.6	349,226	18.3	60.0	21.7	20.5	112,132	155.6	18,836
District 2	10.2	6.1	9.3	374,052	19,137	5.1	354,915	32.0	43.7	24.3	11.4	146,799	203.7	10,657
District 3	9.7	6.7	6.3	416,102	18,368	4.4	397,734	36.2	51.5	12.3	9.0	141,218	175.7	9,737
District 4	13.7	10.4	13.7	346,971	23,990	6.9	322,981	28.1	50.9	21.0	11.4	136,706	181.5	17,348
NEW HAMPSHIRE	7.7	4.9	7.0	756,933	28,888	3.8	728,045	41.7	38.7	19.7	6.9	305,855	227.8	18,548
District 1	8.4	5.8	7.0	388,143	15,157	3.9	372,986	42.5	39.1	18.4	7.1	151,323	224.8	9,433
District 2	7.0	4.0	6.9	368,790	13,731	3.7	355,059	40.8	38.2	21.0	6.8	154,532	230.8	9,115
NEW JERSEY	10.0	7.3	8.9	4,746,329	252,810	5.3	4,493,519	42.9	39.4	17.7	9.0	1,625,600	180.5	179,808
District 1	10.1	7.7	10.7	388,975	24,859	6.4	364,116	41.2	39.9	19.0	6.4	144,508	198.0	20,290
District 2	13.6	10.3	12.1	356,186	27,541	7.7	328,645	34.8	44.8	20.4	9.2	167,816	235.2	18,370
District 3	6.6	4.1	5.3	384,149	19,509	5.1	364,640	41.2	42.7	16.1	5.9	174,605	234.0	9,900
District 4	9.2	6.2	6.3	386,412	20,618	5.3	365,794	45.0	40.4	14.6	6.8	162,272	214.4	8,007
District 5	5.4	4.0	4.0	395,351	16,792	4.2	378,559	48.1	38.4	13.6	6.3	139,056	186.3	8,666
District 6	10.7	7.8	8.1	390,147	18,890	4.8	371,257	44.6	35.8	19.6	8.7	117,903	158.8	13,497
District 7	5.3	3.5	3.5	407,639	17,366	4.3	390,273	52.4	35.8	11.9	5.2	127,337	168.8	6,123
District 8	15.5	12.5	14.7	433,755	21,628	5.0	412,127	35.2	40.0	24.8	16.3	91,058	117.1	25,345
District 9	14.5	12.0	14.8	403,250	16,524	4.1	386,726	36.9	37.8	25.3	14.9	122,791	159.6	19,444
District 10	16.8	13.7	16.8	403,757	35,108	8.7	368,649	34.6	46.4	19.1	12.6	110,124	140.8	28,446
District 11	3.6	2.2	2.8	404,411	15,714	3.9	388,697	53.4	35.4	11.2	4.9	138,634	190.0	6,487
District 12	8.3	5.1	7.4	392,297	18,261	4.7	374,036	46.6	36.9	16.5	8.5	129,496	170.8	15,233
NEW MEXICO	19.7	15.2	17.4	931,157	61,065	6.6	870,092	37.4	43.9	18.7	10.7	436,551	209.1	62,877
District 1	15.6	11.3	15.1	338,474	17,755	5.2	320,719	41.6	43.5	14.9	8.7	139,375	200.1	18,947
District 2	21.6	17.0	21.2	289,852	21,072	7.3	268,780	30.8	45.4	23.8	10.7	147,497	212.3	22,981

1. Percent of civilian labor force.   2. Persons 16 years old and over.   3. Per 1,000 resident population estimated in the 2017 American Community Survey.

Table E. Congressional Districts 116th Congress — **Agriculture**

STATE District	Number of farms	Land in farms — Acres	Land in farms — Average size of farm (acres)	Land in farms — Harvested cropland (acres)	Value of products sold — Total ($1,000)	Value of products sold — Average per farm (dollars)	Value of products sold — Percent from crops	Value of products sold — Percent from livestock and poultry products	Government payments — Total ($1,000)	Government payments — Average per farm receiving payments (dollars)
	63	64	65	66	67	68	69	70	71	72
MICHIGAN	47,641	9,764,090	205	7,214,667	8,220,936	172,560	56.5	43.5	167,189	10,892
District 1	6,952	1,082,209	156	449,001	357,657	51,447	59.1	40.9	5,710	4,827
District 2	3,516	578,489	165	390,567	958,662	272,657	58.1	41.9	4,619	8,118
District 3	3,868	773,809	200	586,992	846,663	218,889	40.5	59.5	14,843	12,009
District 4	9,471	2,085,639	220	1,557,525	1,553,454	164,022	44.7	55.3	32,154	8,711
District 5	2,612	607,782	233	503,507	348,992	133,611	78.8	21.2	12,854	9,578
District 6	5,312	1,106,709	208	855,681	1,567,911	295,164	59.4	40.6	21,268	14,925
District 7	7,424	1,618,131	218	1,300,677	997,521	134,364	70.7	29.3	40,056	13,185
District 8	1,988	293,838	148	219,882	175,102	88,079	64.9	35.1	5,626	18,568
District 9	23	D	D	D	3,176	138,087	D	D	D	D
District 10	5,921	1,578,233	267	1,324,773	1,367,410	230,942	56.2	43.8	29,581	11,729
District 11	167	8,360	50	4,172	12,429	74,425	98.8	1.2	413	13,767
District 12	291	25,639	88	18,446	26,613	91,454	D	D	8	1,143
District 13	71	1,872	26	D	4,984	70,197	56.5	43.5	D	D
District 14	25	D	D	136	361	14,440	D	D	D	D
MINNESOTA	68,822	25,516,982	371	20,054,132	18,395,390	267,289	55.4	44.6	394,491	9,568
District 1	18,080	6,432,710	356	5,514,901	6,521,603	360,708	49.1	50.9	139,174	10,630
District 2	4,323	1,084,055	251	862,034	968,711	224,083	56.2	43.8	24,916	10,648
District 3	514	56,055	109	37,496	59,877	116,492	84.5	15.5	D	0
District 4	306	26,745	87	20,368	18,073	59,062	D	D	374	5,194
District 5	24	1,241	52	875	5,449	227,042	D	D	8,131	4,055
District 6	5,231	981,166	188	719,093	927,726	177,352	47.0	53.0	213,860	9,993
District 7	30,340	14,905,007	491	11,889,723	9,079,273	299,251	61.9	38.1	7,721	3,575
District 8	10,004	2,030,003	203	1,009,642	814,678	81,435	39.1	60.9	213,785	14,986
MISSISSIPPI	34,988	10,415,136	298	4,174,210	6,195,969	177,088	37.0	63.0	38,445	7,803
District 1	9,940	2,535,334	255	815,727	741,685	74,616	51.9	48.1	147,529	27,936
District 2	8,921	4,904,171	550	2,870,319	2,405,086	269,598	71.4	28.6	21,401	7,317
District 3	9,886	2,098,567	212	369,795	2,283,032	230,936	5.4	94.6	6,410	5,658
District 4	6,241	877,064	141	118,369	766,165	122,763	8.6	91.4	323,801	10,366
MISSOURI	95,320	27,781,883	291	13,486,275	10,525,937	110,427	52.0	48.0	78	6,000
District 1	60	4,038	67	1,734	3,917	65,283	95.5	4.5	223	5,718
District 2	232	56,434	243	15,973	19,886	85,716	95.4	4.6	16,790	5,510
District 3	11,671	2,582,240	221	1,017,877	763,114	65,385	46.9	53.1	57,041	8,620
District 4	23,209	6,321,590	272	2,819,491	2,390,061	102,980	41.6	58.4	11,009	6,817
District 5	3,599	1,113,070	309	772,182	521,467	144,892	75.8	24.2	148,718	10,355
District 6	25,268	9,149,092	362	5,265,587	3,473,872	137,481	63.0	37.0	6,746	5,324
District 7	12,945	2,313,829	179	662,898	1,412,550	109,119	9.4	90.6	83,197	19,457
District 8	18,336	6,241,590	340	2,930,533	1,941,071	105,861	71.4	28.6	284,244	27,014
MONTANA	27,048	58,122,878	2,149	9,901,226	3,520,623	130,162	45.0	55.0	284,244	27,014
At Large	27,048	58,122,878	2,149	9,901,226	3,520,623	130,162	45.0	55.0	639,975	20,745
NEBRASKA	46,332	44,986,821	971	19,460,222	21,983,429	474,476	42.4	57.6	134,195	15,708
District 1	12,307	5,386,864	438	4,463,921	5,299,528	430,611	45.6	54.4	3,892	12,761
District 2	731	177,616	243	152,180	102,706	140,501	92.6	7.4	501,888	22,812
District 3	33,294	39,422,341	1,184	14,844,121	16,581,195	498,024	41.0	59.0	5,049	16,183
NEVADA	3,423	6,128,153	1,790	573,785	665,758	194,495	41.5	58.5	D	D
District 1	16	674	42	D	394	24,625	51.5	48.5	3,915	16,313
District 2	2,440	5,359,802	2,197	464,131	456,516	187,097	43.7	56.3	D	D
District 3	72	3,477	48	D	1,501	20,847	77.7	22.3	D	D
District 4	895	764,200	854	108,581	207,348	231,674	36.3	63.7	3,494	11,344
NEW HAMPSHIRE	4,123	425,393	103	85,793	187,794	45,548	57.4	42.6	1,243	12,186
District 1	1,429	114,081	80	21,437	43,425	30,388	65.6	34.4	2,251	10,927
District 2	2,694	311,312	116	64,356	144,369	53,589	54.9	45.1	7,503	10,071
NEW JERSEY	9,883	734,084	74	411,785	1,097,951	111,095	89.7	10.3	126	6,632
District 1	323	19,769	61	12,012	50,873	157,502	97.0	3.0	3,879	12,930
District 2	2,470	242,801	98	164,407	522,859	211,684	94.6	5.4	829	12,014
District 3	950	95,629	101	45,970	98,998	104,208	92.3	7.7	431	10,512
District 4	973	46,949	48	25,493	103,382	106,251	84.7	15.3	885	8,349
District 5	1,813	109,258	60	46,313	102,405	56,484	69.5	30.5	D	D
District 6	129	6,165	48	2,383	13,972	108,310	D	D	1,076	6,482
District 7	2,409	161,144	67	89,857	130,857	54,320	85.3	14.7	D	D
District 8	3	D	D	20	D	0	D	D	D	D
District 9	10	77	8	55	0	0	D	D	D	D
District 10	4	D	D	5	60	15,000	D	D	255	6,538
District 11	287	11,013	38	3,451	17,851	62,199	95.2	4.8	D	D
District 12	512	41,235	81	21,819	54,054	105,574	85.7	14.3	63,660	18,436
NEW MEXICO	25,044	40,659,836	1,624	806,138	2,582,343	103,112	25.2	74.8	2,343	16,385
District 1	2,270	1,912,502	843	20,328	62,931	27,723	30.0	70.0	25,845	19,580
District 2	9,762	20,343,252	2,084	390,375	1,562,618	160,072	30.7	69.3		

Table E. Congressional Districts 116th Congress — Nonfarm Employment and Payroll

STATE District	Number of establishments	Total	Manufac-turing	Construc-tion	Wholesale trade	Retail trade	Health care and social assistance	Finance and Insur-ance	Real estate and rental and leas-ing	Profes-sional, sci-entific, and technical services	Information	Total (mil dol)	Average per employee (dollars)
	73	74	75	76	77	78	79	80	81	82	83	84	85
MICHIGAN	220,412	3,805,578	15.2	3.7	4.7	12.4	16.2	4.2	1.4	7.0	1.7	183,193	48,138
District 1	19,644	209,388	12.9	5.6	3.0	17.8	19.8	3.9	1.2	3.3	1.4	7,891	37,684
District 2	16,435	313,473	27.2	4.0	6.3	12.6	11.2	2.6	1.1	3.3	0.9	13,155	41,965
District 3	15,706	316,293	19.5	3.6	6.1	9.0	17.3	4.6	1.1	4.8	1.7	14,719	46,536
District 4	13,633	186,456	17.2	4.9	3.5	17.8	16.6	3.5	1.5	2.4	1.3	7,441	39,908
District 5	13,578	216,104	12.2	3.6	4.3	15.2	23.6	3.1	1.2	3.8	1.5	8,971	41,513
District 6	14,408	233,089	21.6	4.0	4.2	13.1	15.9	3.7	1.5	4.1	1.0	10,310	44,233
District 7	12,615	203,242	21.9	3.5	3.6	13.8	14.1	3.8	0.9	4.6	1.7	8,887	43,728
District 8	15,923	224,836	11.8	4.7	3.3	15.1	17.6	6.2	1.5	6.2	1.5	9,687	43,086
District 9	17,595	271,255	15.8	3.4	4.9	12.9	19.6	2.4	2.3	10.3	1.9	13,354	49,232
District 10	14,750	204,753	26.7	5.4	3.3	16.1	13.0	2.4	0.9	6.6	0.9	8,804	42,999
District 11	23,957	459,288	9.8	3.3	7.4	12.3	11.6	5.2	1.4	14.7	2.5	27,389	59,634
District 12	15,289	295,730	11.5	2.8	4.2	13.3	20.2	3.8	1.2	8.2	2.4	16,160	54,643
District 13	10,049	204,922	14.4	2.6	4.7	9.0	22.4	1.3	1.1	2.7	1.3	10,218	49,865
District 14	16,155	336,515	5.8	3.0	4.6	7.3	16.8	10.0	2.2	12.6	3.3	21,727	64,564
MINNESOTA	150,115	2,661,627	11.5	4.4	5.2	11.5	17.3	6.1	1.5	6.9	2.2	137,136	51,523
District 1	16,844	299,235	17.1	3.8	3.2	13.3	19.1	3.1	1.0	3.1	2.0	13,288	44,405
District 2	16,946	269,747	12.2	5.3	5.7	13.2	13.6	5.1	1.3	12.9	2.0	12,783	47,390
District 3	23,638	464,287	13.2	4.0	7.0	11.8	10.6	8.4	2.7	4.7	3.4	28,500	61,383
District 4	17,725	368,186	7.7	3.5	5.0	10.2	19.7	6.6	1.4	9.0	2.5	19,616	53,277
District 5	20,945	510,197	6.3	3.2	4.0	6.7	19.8	9.1	1.7	5.0	2.4	31,534	61,808
District 6	16,719	225,187	15.8	9.3	4.7	15.2	16.5	3.1	1.1	9.2	2.5	9,516	42,257
District 7	19,329	239,039	19.0	5.1	6.2	15.2	21.8	3.4	0.6	3.3	1.3	8,810	36,855
District 8	17,341	215,026	8.7	5.0	2.6	16.1	25.1	4.1	1.1	2.7	1.4	8,226	38,254
MISSISSIPPI	58,850	939,322	15.2	4.7	4.0	15.5	17.6	3.8	1.1	3.2	1.5	34,357	36,576
District 1	14,377	231,373	22.3	3.5	4.8	16.1	14.2	3.0	0.9	2.5	1.4	7,985	34,512
District 2	12,640	190,526	16.0	4.5	4.0	15.5	18.1	2.9	0.9	2.2	1.0	6,708	35,210
District 3	17,206	266,340	10.4	5.1	4.6	15.3	20.5	5.1	1.4	4.2	1.6	10,348	38,852
District 4	14,274	230,392	14.5	6.1	2.3	16.6	17.4	3.1	1.2	3.8	2.1	8,756	38,005
MISSOURI	160,912	2,494,720	10.4	4.9	5.1	13.0	16.8	5.3	1.5	6.3	1.1	112,072	44,924
District 1	24,963	420,406	10.7	4.7	6.2	7.6	15.9	4.3	1.4	5.5	2.3	22,980	54,661
District 2	25,312	449,312	4.0	4.5	4.2	12.6	16.2	7.8	1.9	9.4	2.2	23,973	53,354
District 3	17,725	235,609	14.1	7.6	4.5	16.8	14.4	3.5	1.1	4.3	3.2	9,004	38,215
District 4	16,471	206,614	12.3	5.1	3.0	17.9	20.1	5.9	1.3	3.9	1.8	7,009	33,921
District 5	21,603	396,409	7.9	5.4	6.9	11.0	16.5	6.4	1.6	10.5	1.6	20,048	50,575
District 6	16,496	221,379	17.0	4.8	4.2	16.2	16.5	4.1	1.4	3.3	3.2	8,607	38,878
District 7	19,520	304,304	12.1	3.9	5.6	14.7	17.0	3.7	1.8	4.2	1.6	11,399	37,458
District 8	18,215	206,587	15.8	4.3	4.1	17.1	24.2	3.6	1.3	2.2	2.4	6,767	32,755
MONTANA	37,626	378,463	4.8	6.6	4.4	15.7	18.6	4.5	1.5	5.4	1.3	14,543	38,426
At Large	37,626	378,463	4.8	6.6	4.4	15.7	18.6	4.5	1.5	5.4	2.2	14,543	38,426
NEBRASKA	54,265	884,450	10.4	5.2	4.7	12.7	14.7	7.1	1.3	4.6	2.2	37,715	42,642
District 1	16,883	241,684	13.7	6.1	4.1	14.4	17.2	5.7	1.2	5.4	2.5	9,548	39,505
District 2	18,147	347,534	6.4	5.7	5.1	12.4	14.9	11.2	1.9	6.2	2.9	16,978	48,853
District 3	18,881	209,352	17.6	5.4	6.5	16.7	17.3	4.7	0.7	2.5	1.5	7,356	35,136
NEVADA	64,815	1,165,298	3.7	6.2	3.1	12.6	10.4	3.2	2.6	5.1	1.5	49,208	42,228
District 1	18,466	424,742	1.2	4.3	1.8	11.5	10.2	1.9	2.6	3.8	0.9	17,285	40,696
District 2	18,592	270,369	8.6	6.6	5.0	13.2	12.2	3.0	1.9	4.9	1.8	11,995	44,365
District 3	17,693	289,072	3.3	7.7	2.9	13.2	8.9	4.8	3.6	7.4	1.6	12,384	42,840
District 4	9,587	148,057	3.6	9.0	4.2	15.8	12.6	3.2	2.2	5.4	2.1	5,881	39,719
NEW HAMPSHIRE	37,868	594,243	11.6	4.4	4.0	16.9	15.4	4.8	1.2	5.4	2.4	29,193	49,127
District 1	19,671	293,126	10.1	4.6	4.3	17.2	15.3	6.6	1.6	5.6	2.7	14,549	49,634
District 2	17,804	269,274	14.4	4.7	3.9	18.6	17.3	2.9	1.0	4.9	2.3	12,918	47,973
NEW JERSEY	231,974	3,636,293	6.0	4.3	7.3	12.8	16.1	5.5	1.6	9.0	2.4	214,758	59,060
District 1	16,024	258,122	7.6	5.4	6.3	16.0	21.0	2.4	1.4	6.9	1.8	12,103	46,890
District 2	17,169	227,916	6.9	5.7	4.5	16.4	17.7	2.5	1.5	3.6	1.1	9,074	39,815
District 3	16,727	248,515	5.3	4.3	5.2	16.6	19.7	8.6	2.0	6.6	1.8	11,954	48,102
District 4	21,476	292,275	5.2	6.6	3.7	17.1	19.2	4.1	2.3	7.8	2.7	13,628	46,628
District 5	23,129	300,398	5.0	4.4	7.7	15.9	20.7	3.7	1.3	7.2	1.7	16,918	56,319
District 6	18,825	306,117	5.6	4.6	8.9	11.1	15.2	3.3	1.7	14.9	3.0	18,716	61,139
District 7	23,352	362,809	6.6	4.7	5.7	13.5	14.7	5.5	1.3	10.8	4.4	26,928	74,221
District 8	15,496	255,223	5.2	3.4	6.1	11.2	13.3	14.8	1.4	4.3	2.2	17,263	67,640
District 9	20,991	295,993	10.1	5.1	11.9	11.8	14.2	2.8	2.4	6.4	2.6	16,606	56,102
District 10	13,495	191,406	7.0	3.3	5.4	11.0	21.2	4.8	2.3	5.8	2.1	10,704	55,921
District 11	25,520	425,500	5.5	3.5	8.5	10.9	14.1	6.9	1.7	13.9	2.2	30,861	72,530
District 12	19,016	335,689	5.6	2.7	11.8	9.8	13.3	5.9	1.1	13.4	2.5	22,656	67,492
NEW MEXICO	43,771	628,723	4.1	6.2	3.4	15.5	19.4	3.8	1.5	9.2	2.4	25,029	39,810
District 1	16,273	275,149	4.7	6.5	4.3	13.8	18.7	3.8	1.5	11.6	3.7	11,552	41,985
District 2	12,843	168,615	3.9	7.2	2.6	17.1	20.7	3.4	1.6	4.4	1.2	6,009	35,637

STATE District	Representative, 116th Congress	Land area,1 2018 (sq mi)	Total persons	Per square mile	Race alone (percent) White	Black	American Indian, Alaska Native	Asian and Pacific Islander	Some other race (percent)	Two or more races (percent)	Hispanic or Latino2 (percent)	Non-Hispanic White alone (percent)	Percent female	Percent foreign-born	Percent born in state of residence
		1	2	3	4	5	6	7	8	9	10	11	12	13	14
NEW MEXICO — Cont'd															
District 3	Ben Ray Luján (D)	44,963.7	696,690	15.5	65.2	1.5	19.1	1.4	9.0	3.8	41.1	36.2	51.0	6.7	58.3
NEW YORK		47,123.4	19,849,399	421.2	63.1	15.8	0.4	8.8	8.9	3.0	19.2	55.1	51.4	22.9	62.9
District 1	Lee M. Zeldin (R)	650.0	718,652	1,105.7	87.3	5.2	0.2	3.8	1.8	1.6	14.8	74.8	50.1	13.5	78.5
District 2	Peter T. King (R)	181.6	721,373	3,972.9	74.7	11.1	0.2	3.6	7.8	2.7	25.0	59.8	51.7	17.4	74.8
District 3	Thomas R. Souzzi (D)	254.9	725,627	2,846.4	72.8	4.3	0.2	16.5	4.2	2.1	10.6	66.7	51.2	22.9	69.4
District 4	Kathleen M. Rice (D)	110.7	728,807	6,582.8	63.9	14.7	0.4	7.1	10.1	3.9	21.3	55.6	51.6	22.9	69.5
District 5	Gregory W. Meeks (D)	51.9	798,555	15,376.0	17.4	48.1	0.4	15.3	14.8	3.9	19.5	10.5	52.6	42.2	50.5
District 6	Grace Meng (D)	29.8	761,797	25,568.8	43.3	3.7	0.4	40.7	9.1	2.8	20.4	33.1	51.8	51.6	42.6
District 7	Nydia M. Velázquez (D)	16.1	755,717	46,819.7	48.3	10.3	0.5	19.4	17.9	3.6	40.5	29.6	50.7	35.5	46.6
District 8	Hakeem S. Jeffries (D)	28.4	793,532	27,922.6	30.8	52.5	0.3	5.3	8.2	2.9	19.1	24.2	53.9	31.9	53.7
District 9	Yvette D. Clarke (D)	15.5	750,170	48,251.8	37.2	46.9	0.1	8.1	4.8	2.9	10.3	33.6	54.2	39.3	46.2
District 10	Jerrold Nadler (D)	14.0	733,275	52,201.5	68.1	4.7	0.1	18.8	5.3	3.0	12.8	61.8	51.8	30.7	45.0
District 11	Max Rose (D)	64.9	755,204	11,631.9	68.5	8.3	0.3	15.3	5.0	2.6	16.7	58.5	51.8	31.2	61.4
District 12	Carolyn B. Maloney (D)	14.8	714,279	48,288.2	72.6	5.1	0.2	14.2	5.0	2.9	14.7	63.8	51.5	25.9	42.4
District 13	Adriano Espaillat (D)	10.2	802,800	79,008.0	26.2	28.4	0.8	5.4	32.4	6.8	54.8	14.3	49.9	35.1	47.3
District 14	Alexandria Ocasio Cortez (D)	28.5	691,813	24,303.1	43.1	11.1	0.4	18.1	24.3	3.1	47.7	23.7	49.9	47.0	42.6
District 15	José E. Serrano (D)	14.5	781,143	53,808.8	17.1	36.1	0.9	1.9	40.5	3.5	66.6	2.5	52.4	37.4	50.7
District 16	Eliot L. Engel (D)	78.4	742,552	9,474.2	45.5	33.8	0.6	5.4	11.8	3.0	25.2	35.8	53.3	30.9	56.1
District 17	Nita M. Lowey (D)	382.5	746,412	1,951.2	69.5	10.5	0.3	6.0	11.1	2.7	23.0	59.0	50.8	23.6	62.3
District 18	Sean Patrick Maloney (D)	1,354.1	730,114	539.2	77.1	9.8	0.3	3.3	6.2	3.3	17.2	67.9	50.1	12.5	69.2
District 19	Antonio Delgado (D)	7,937.1	700,975	88.3	87.8	4.8	0.2	1.9	2.6	2.7	7.7	83.8	49.9	6.8	74.5
District 20	Paul Tonko (D)	1,231.4	732,130	594.5	79.2	9.7	0.2	5.4	1.9	3.6	6.5	75.7	51.3	9.7	75.0
District 21	Elise M. Stefanik (R)	15,113.9	705,669	46.7	91.6	3.5	0.7	1.0	1.1	2.1	3.5	89.9	48.7	2.9	77.8
District 22	Anthony Brindisi (D)	5,077.4	696,819	137.2	89.6	4.1	0.3	3.0	1.0	2.1	3.9	87.3	50.3	5.2	80.7
District 23	Tom Reed (R)	7,371.7	702,026	95.2	90.4	2.9	0.5	2.7	1.3	2.3	4.1	87.8	50.2	4.4	73.4
District 24	John Katko (R)	2,388.6	707,889	296.4	84.0	8.5	0.3	3.0	0.8	3.4	4.5	81.3	51.2	6.1	79.6
District 25	Joseph D. Morelle (D)	510.2	719,033	1,409.3	74.6	15.8	0.5	4.0	1.8	3.2	9.1	69.4	51.9	9.1	73.7
District 26	Brian Higgins (D)	219.1	714,521	3,260.6	70.7	18.3	0.4	4.5	2.7	3.4	6.5	68.4	51.8	8.3	78.7
District 27	Chris Collins (R)	3,973.1	718,515	180.8	93.4	2.7	0.7	0.8	0.9	1.5	2.8	91.7	50.4	3.1	84.8
NORTH CAROLINA		48,617.9	10,273,419	211.3	68.8	21.5	1.2	3.0	3.0	2.6	9.4	63.0	51.3	8.1	56.4
District 1	G. K. Butterfield (D)	5,871.1	759,049	129.3	48.5	43.7	0.8	2.3	2.4	2.3	8.1	43.2	52.5	7.4	65.7
District 2	George Holding (R)	2,698.3	835,806	309.8	71.6	19.5	0.7	1.8	3.6	2.9	9.6	65.9	51.6	7.2	53.6
District 3	Vacant	7,217.3	755,647	104.7	71.6	20.9	0.3	1.6	2.0	3.6	8.2	66.6	48.8	4.0	52.3
District 4	David E. Price (D)	732.3	856,104	1,169.0	60.7	22.2	0.2	9.3	5.1	2.4	10.8	55.3	51.1	16.5	42.7
District 5	Virginia Foxx (R)	3,969.1	758,376	191.1	79.3	14.6	0.4	1.9	1.9	1.9	9.8	72.2	51.8	6.8	64.3
District 6	Mark Walker (R)	3,910.4	768,546	196.5	71.4	20.4	0.5	2.2	3.7	1.9	10.7	65.0	51.6	7.4	64.6
District 7	David Rouzer (R)	5,944.9	800,096	134.6	74.9	18.7	0.7	1.0	2.1	2.6	9.8	67.7	51.7	6.1	60.0
District 8	Richard Hudson (R)	2,953.8	789,484	267.3	65.8	23.8	1.1	2.7	2.7	3.9	10.5	59.4	50.4	6.5	52.7
District 9	Vacant	3,873.7	788,020	203.4	66.0	18.2	7.6	3.1	2.6	2.5	8.6	60.5	51.1	7.6	56.7
District 10	Patrick T. McHenry (R)	2,590.2	760,410	293.6	81.1	12.0	0.3	1.9	2.3	2.4	6.6	76.9	52.0	5.0	64.8
District 11	Mark Meadows (R)	6,604.7	759,358	115.0	90.6	3.4	1.6	1.1	1.5	1.7	5.9	86.4	50.8	4.4	58.7
District 12	Alma S. Adams (D)	420.0	860,866	2,049.8	46.1	37.7	0.5	5.6	6.9	3.2	14.7	39.1	52.0	16.6	41.4
District 13	Ted Budd (R)	1,831.9	781,657	426.7	70.2	22.2	0.6	3.0	1.6	2.4	7.5	64.8	52.1	7.6	59.6
NORTH DAKOTA		69,000.5	755,393	10.9	86.6	3.1	5.5	1.8	1.1	2.0	3.5	84.4	48.6	4.1	62.1
At Large	Kelly Armstrong (R)	69,000.5	755,393	10.9	86.6	3.1	5.5	1.8	1.1	2.0	3.5	84.4	48.6	4.1	62.1
OHIO		40,862.5	11,658,609	285.3	81.3	12.4	0.2	2.2	0.9	2.9	3.7	78.9	51.0	4.5	74.8
District 1	Steve Chabot (R)	687.0	740,851	1,078.4	71.4	21.3	0.1	3.8	0.6	2.8	3.3	68.9	51.5	6.4	71.6
District 2	Brad R. Wenstrup (R)	3,221.6	728,153	226.0	86.5	8.9	0.3	1.6	0.4	2.4	2.0	84.8	51.2	3.1	75.1
District 3	Joyce Beatty (D)	228.0	782,878	3,433.0	53.6	34.7	0.3	4.7	2.5	4.2	7.0	50.0	51.7	11.7	66.4
District 4	Jim Jordan (R)	4,664.8	710,603	152.3	90.1	5.2	0.2	0.8	0.6	3.0	3.8	87.4	50.4	2.0	81.8
District 5	Robert E. Latta (R)	5,626.4	717,547	127.5	91.4	2.8	0.2	1.3	1.6	2.6	5.4	88.3	50.4	3.0	79.0
District 6	Bill Johnson (R)	7,214.7	696,153	96.5	95.1	2.4	0.2	0.3	0.2	1.8	1.0	94.3	49.8	0.7	83.9
District 7	Bob Gibbs (R)	3,864.8	725,665	187.8	92.4	3.8	0.2	0.7	0.3	2.5	1.9	91.1	51.1	1.7	83.9
District 8	Warren Davidson (R)	2,450.5	730,445	298.1	88.2	6.0	0.2	2.1	0.7	2.9	3.5	85.6	51.1	4.1	73.7
District 9	Marcy Kaptur (D)	464.7	720,715	1,551.0	73.5	16.3	0.4	1.7	2.9	5.3	11.4	67.1	51.1	4.8	75.0
District 10	Michael R. Turner (R)	1,130.0	721,456	638.5	76.3	16.6	0.2	2.4	1.1	3.5	2.9	74.3	51.5	4.8	68.8
District 11	Marcia L. Fudge (D)	244.5	675,475	2,762.7	39.5	53.4	0.2	2.6	1.5	2.8	4.6	37.1	53.4	6.1	73.1
District 12	Troy Balderson (R)	2,272.0	780,529	343.5	86.6	4.9	0.2	4.9	0.6	2.9	2.2	85.1	50.4	5.9	72.4
District 13	Tim Ryan (D)	894.2	715,559	800.2	82.1	11.6	0.3	1.7	0.6	3.8	3.2	80.1	51.5	3.6	76.3
District 14	David P. Joyce (R)	1,955.0	724,790	370.7	90.1	5.2	0.2	2.4	0.6	1.5	2.9	88.2	51.0	5.0	76.3
District 15	Steve Stivers (R)	4,738.8	772,776	163.1	90.8	4.0	0.1	2.2	0.6	2.3	2.4	89.2	49.8	3.6	76.3
District 16	Anthony Gonzalez (R)	1,205.3	715,014	593.2	92.9	2.0	0.1	2.3	0.3	2.3	2.4	91.2	51.0	5.1	77.7
OKLAHOMA		68,596.6	3,930,864	57.3	72.2	7.3	7.7	2.4	2.7	7.7	10.6	65.6	50.4	5.7	61.2
District 1	Kevin Hern (R)	1,631.7	803,883	492.7	71.3	8.7	6.3	3.2	3.2	7.3	11.4	63.9	51.3	7.7	58.9
District 2	Markwayne Mullin (R)	20,996.5	744,806	35.5	66.1	3.2	17.3	1.1	1.7	10.6	5.3	63.9	50.2	2.3	61.2
District 3	Frank D. Lucas (R)	34,117.2	774,066	22.7	79.3	3.6	6.1	1.6	3.4	6.1	10.1	73.9	49.3	4.6	64.6
District 4	Tom Cole (R)	9,777.3	789,947	80.8	75.4	6.7	5.4	2.5	1.9	8.0	8.8	69.9	50.3	4.5	60.6
District 5	Kendra S. Horn (D)	2,073.9	818,162	394.5	68.8	13.7	4.1	3.4	3.4	6.6	17.0	56.6	50.9	9.1	60.9
OREGON		95,986.7	4,142,776	43.2	84.4	1.9	1.2	4.8	3.0	4.8	13.1	75.6	50.4	9.9	46.0
District 1	Suzanne Bonamici (D)	3,006.5	844,175	280.8	80.0	1.8	0.7	8.3	4.1	5.1	15.1	70.4	50.3	14.2	43.9
District 2	Greg Walden (R)	69,444.4	821,129	11.8	90.0	0.6	2.2	1.2	2.5	3.4	14.0	79.3	49.9	6.4	44.1

1. Dry land or land partially or temporarily covered by water. 2. May be of any race.

Table E. Congressional Districts 116th Congress — **Age and Education**

	Population and population characteristics, 2017 (cont.)										Education, 2017		
STATE District	Age (percent)											Attainment[2] (percent)	
	Under 5 years	5 to 17 years	18 to 24 years	25 to 34 years	35 to 44 years	45 to 54 years	55 to 64 years	65 to 74 years	75 years and over	Median age	Total Enrollment[1]	High school graduate or more	Bachelor's degree or more
	15	16	17	18	19	20	21	22	23	24	25	26	27
NEW MEXICO — Cont'd													
District 3	6.1	17.6	9.4	12.3	11.9	11.6	13.6	11.0	6.5	38.4	176,038	86.6	27.0
NEW YORK	5.8	15.1	9.4	14.7	12.5	13.4	13.1	9.0	6.9	38.7	4,794,761	86.6	36.0
District 1	4.9	15.2	9.8	11.1	11.3	15.6	14.4	10.1	7.7	42.7	172,207	91.6	36.7
District 2	5.6	16.6	9.1	13.6	12.7	14.6	13.3	8.4	6.2	39.2	180,037	88.1	32.2
District 3	5.2	16.6	6.9	9.3	11.5	14.6	15.5	10.8	9.6	45.4	176,227	93.1	52.6
District 4	5.7	15.5	9.9	12.3	12.0	14.0	14.2	9.0	7.5	40.6	183,010	89.3	41.8
District 5	6.7	15.5	9.4	14.9	12.2	14.0	13.5	8.4	5.4	37.5	203,166	82.2	26.1
District 6	6.2	12.7	7.1	16.2	12.4	14.1	13.8	9.3	8.2	40.9	162,799	82.7	34.1
District 7	7.2	15.5	8.9	21.2	14.8	11.9	9.5	6.2	5.0	33.5	179,847	72.2	32.8
District 8	7.3	14.7	9.0	17.2	13.6	12.3	11.9	8.0	6.1	36.1	194,533	85.3	32.6
District 9	6.8	15.0	8.1	17.5	13.7	12.2	11.8	8.6	6.3	36.8	184,069	87.5	38.6
District 10	6.7	12.8	8.2	19.3	14.1	11.2	11.8	9.3	6.7	37.0	175,732	88.3	61.5
District 11	6.1	16.2	8.1	13.6	12.7	13.9	13.6	9.2	6.8	40.0	184,025	86.9	35.6
District 12	4.3	7.5	9.4	27.4	15.3	11.4	9.6	8.3	6.7	35.7	120,128	94.5	74.1
District 13	6.3	14.4	9.0	20.6	13.7	12.7	10.7	6.9	5.8	34.9	196,763	74.3	31.6
District 14	5.6	13.7	7.6	16.7	16.0	14.3	11.7	7.9	6.5	38.8	149,604	78.4	26.7
District 15	7.9	19.2	11.6	16.4	13.0	12.5	9.7	5.7	4.2	31.4	227,668	64.7	13.7
District 16	5.1	16.3	9.2	12.5	13.1	14.1	12.6	9.5	7.7	40.5	188,363	85.1	39.6
District 17	6.7	18.0	9.4	11.3	12.0	13.6	13.2	8.4	7.4	38.8	205,788	88.7	45.9
District 18	5.5	17.1	10.3	11.6	11.8	14.7	13.9	8.8	6.4	39.5	190,547	91.3	36.5
District 19	4.6	14.1	9.6	10.9	10.9	14.3	16.0	11.7	8.0	44.9	152,717	90.1	29.6
District 20	4.9	14.6	12.3	12.7	12.0	13.4	13.3	9.6	7.2	39.3	189,128	92.2	38.2
District 21	5.5	15.1	10.1	12.8	11.5	13.5	14.4	10.2	7.0	40.6	151,605	89.2	24.1
District 22	5.3	14.8	11.4	11.6	10.3	13.5	14.6	10.2	8.2	41.1	167,350	89.4	24.4
District 23	5.1	14.9	12.2	11.7	10.9	12.6	14.6	10.5	7.6	40.5	173,335	90.0	26.5
District 24	5.4	15.9	10.3	12.7	11.1	13.5	14.4	9.6	7.1	40.0	176,021	89.9	30.9
District 25	5.4	15.3	10.2	14.0	11.5	13.1	13.7	9.6	7.3	38.9	178,050	90.5	37.1
District 26	5.7	14.6	10.2	16.0	10.9	12.2	13.9	9.3	7.3	38.2	173,512	90.5	32.2
District 27	5.1	15.4	8.3	11.1	11.0	14.7	15.6	10.7	8.1	44.2	158,530	93.2	30.4
NORTH CAROLINA	5.9	16.5	9.5	13.2	12.7	13.5	12.8	9.6	6.2	38.8	2,521,781	87.8	31.3
District 1	5.8	15.3	11.1	14.0	11.5	12.9	13.1	9.8	6.5	38.0	193,064	83.9	28.8
District 2	6.5	19.1	7.5	12.1	13.7	14.5	12.7	9.0	4.9	38.7	222,828	90.2	35.4
District 3	6.4	15.7	12.3	13.2	11.5	11.6	12.6	10.0	6.7	37.0	179,251	88.2	24.3
District 4	5.8	15.9	11.7	16.7	14.5	13.6	10.9	6.6	4.2	34.9	239,322	92.0	54.7
District 5	5.3	15.9	10.1	11.6	12.2	13.4	13.7	10.3	7.4	40.8	180,076	85.8	27.3
District 6	5.9	16.8	8.3	11.5	12.2	14.1	13.8	10.3	7.0	41.1	183,479	85.2	24.7
District 7	5.3	15.8	9.1	11.7	12.0	13.3	13.8	11.9	7.1	41.7	180,501	87.1	26.7
District 8	6.4	17.6	10.1	14.1	12.3	13.0	11.8	8.8	5.9	36.2	204,198	89.1	27.6
District 9	6.1	18.6	8.4	11.8	13.2	14.2	13.0	9.1	5.6	39.1	206,037	88.1	34.2
District 10	5.3	15.9	8.7	12.0	12.0	14.3	13.6	10.9	7.4	41.9	165,519	86.8	24.1
District 11	4.6	14.5	7.8	10.7	11.7	13.6	14.7	13.2	9.1	45.5	154,100	86.8	26.7
District 12	6.8	17.2	9.4	18.1	15.2	13.4	10.1	6.2	3.5	34.1	219,484	89.2	41.2
District 13	5.5	16.5	9.5	12.9	12.4	13.9	12.9	9.7	6.7	39.5	193,922	88.4	28.8
NORTH DAKOTA	7.0	15.9	11.4	15.1	11.8	10.9	12.9	8.1	6.8	35.4	179,366	92.9	30.7
At Large	7.0	15.9	11.4	15.1	11.8	10.9	12.9	8.1	6.8	35.4	179,366	92.9	30.7
OHIO	6.0	16.4	9.2	13.1	11.9	13.0	13.8	9.6	7.0	39.3	2,812,859	90.3	28.0
District 1	6.6	17.8	9.8	13.6	12.0	13.0	13.2	8.1	6.0	36.8	196,792	91.0	35.1
District 2	6.1	16.2	7.5	13.7	12.3	13.3	14.2	9.8	7.0	40.1	158,802	89.0	31.2
District 3	7.4	16.6	11.5	18.2	13.0	11.6	11.1	6.5	4.3	32.6	205,895	87.9	27.4
District 4	5.6	16.7	8.8	11.9	11.9	13.4	14.1	10.1	7.4	40.8	167,322	90.6	19.1
District 5	5.8	16.8	9.9	12.1	11.5	12.5	14.4	9.8	7.2	39.5	181,231	93.0	26.9
District 6	5.2	15.4	7.8	11.5	11.6	13.4	15.3	11.3	8.5	43.5	144,772	88.5	16.0
District 7	6.0	17.1	8.4	11.3	11.4	13.3	14.1	10.6	7.8	41.2	162,013	88.4	19.5
District 8	6.2	17.2	10.3	11.8	11.6	13.0	13.6	9.4	7.0	38.7	186,791	91.3	24.8
District 9	6.1	15.9	9.4	14.2	12.0	12.9	13.7	9.2	6.6	38.0	169,909	86.6	22.1
District 10	6.0	15.9	9.9	13.4	11.3	12.6	13.6	9.8	7.6	39.0	186,541	90.1	30.3
District 11	5.8	15.4	9.7	14.3	10.9	12.3	14.8	9.2	7.5	39.0	170,320	87.3	27.2
District 12	6.2	17.6	8.2	13.2	13.5	13.9	12.7	9.0	5.8	38.3	200,554	92.9	41.3
District 13	5.1	14.7	11.0	13.0	10.8	12.9	14.3	10.2	8.0	40.6	166,366	90.9	23.1
District 14	5.5	16.4	7.3	10.9	11.4	14.2	14.9	11.3	8.2	43.7	164,938	91.9	35.3
District 15	6.1	15.8	9.7	14.6	12.8	13.2	13.2	8.5	6.1	37.7	185,826	90.8	32.2
District 16	5.5	15.8	8.0	11.4	11.3	13.3	15.0	11.3	8.4	43.3	164,787	93.7	34.2
OKLAHOMA	6.7	17.8	9.7	13.7	12.4	11.9	12.5	8.9	6.4	36.6	1,011,241	88.1	25.5
District 1	7.0	18.2	8.5	14.6	12.6	12.2	12.2	8.5	6.1	36.2	206,958	89.5	30.3
District 2	6.1	17.3	8.9	11.6	11.6	12.3	13.6	10.9	7.6	40.3	170,335	85.4	16.8
District 3	6.7	17.7	10.7	12.8	11.9	11.8	12.8	9.1	6.6	36.6	205,459	88.1	22.2
District 4	6.1	17.5	11.4	13.8	12.9	11.8	12.2	8.3	6.1	35.8	212,471	89.6	26.4
District 5	7.3	18.2	9.1	15.5	12.9	11.4	11.9	8.1	5.5	34.8	216,018	87.6	31.4
OREGON	5.6	15.5	8.9	14.0	13.3	13.3	12.5	8.9	5.5	37.8	953,051	91.0	33.7
District 1	5.9	16.5	8.2	14.9	14.4	12.5	13.2	10.4	6.7	39.3	207,602	92.5	42.4
District 2	5.7	16.0	7.8	12.0	11.7	12.3	14.2	12.5	7.8	42.3	170,567	89.4	25.0

1. All persons 3 years old and over enrolled in nursery school through college and graduate or professional school.   2. Persons 25 years old and over.

Table E. Congressional Districts 116th Congress — **Households and Group Quarters**

STATE District	Households, 2017 Number	Average household size	Family households (percent)	Married couple family (percent)	Female family house-holder[1]	One person households (percent)	Total in group quarters, 2017	Percent 65 years and over	Persons in correctional institutions	Persons in nursing facilities	Persons in college dormitories	Persons in military quarters
	28	29	30	31	32	33	34	35	36	37	38	39
NEW MEXICO — Cont'd												
District 3	249,126	2.75	63.5	43.0	14.4	31.4	12,173	17.2	3,544	1,465	2,115	444
NEW YORK	7,304,332	2.64	63.3	44.0	14.2	29.7	576,151	19.7	95,306	116,558	218,960	8,100
District 1	242,952	2.88	71.0	56.3	10.6	23.8	18,961	20.6	1,648	4,504	9,203	6
District 2	218,675	3.27	75.7	58.1	11.8	20.1	6,598	46.7	6	2,952	720	4
District 3	251,028	2.84	74.7	62.5	8.3	22.4	13,406	41.2	10	5,607	3,982	4
District 4	235,269	3.05	74.8	57.6	12.8	21.2	11,516	28.5	1,657	4,200	4,748	0
District 5	227,456	3.45	74.7	43.6	22.8	21.6	13,612	30.2	234	5,713	2,367	0
District 6	270,237	2.79	64.6	46.5	12.9	29.5	6,508	62.0	17	4,179	812	0
District 7	253,092	2.94	63.1	39.3	16.5	24.8	11,532	12.2	3,636	1,600	1,803	0
District 8	292,705	2.64	58.9	30.8	22.7	32.2	19,932	26.0	256	4,120	2,056	0
District 9	286,098	2.59	59.0	35.4	18.4	32.6	8,258	27.0	0	2,585	611	0
District 10	304,597	2.34	50.9	40.5	7.6	40.2	20,905	10.2	165	2,076	16,711	0
District 11	261,768	2.85	72.5	54.5	12.9	23.3	8,573	36.4	924	3,540	1,457	60
District 12	359,465	1.91	38.7	31.4	5.3	47.2	27,433	10.4	414	3,896	16,755	0
District 13	302,472	2.61	56.0	22.8	25.9	34.6	14,109	29.6	334	5,101	1,924	0
District 14	231,976	2.91	64.7	40.3	16.4	28.1	16,014	21.9	11,095	5,195	2,355	0
District 15	259,124	2.95	67.1	23.7	35.2	28.8	17,908	8.9	981	2,145	2,352	0
District 16	272,182	2.67	65.4	41.8	18.0	30.5	16,984	41.8	0	7,221	5,113	0
District 17	245,675	2.95	71.5	56.5	10.3	24.2	21,724	23.3	3,245	4,756	8,571	4,409
District 18	249,783	2.82	71.2	56.6	11.1	23.4	26,841	14.3	8,143	3,627	7,046	3
District 19	265,595	2.49	63.2	48.2	9.9	29.8	39,020	13.1	9,986	4,771	12,644	0
District 20	285,388	2.45	57.8	42.7	10.6	33.5	32,149	16.3	1,298	4,651	18,920	0
District 21	272,128	2.44	63.8	48.3	10.7	28.6	42,140	10.4	18,001	3,692	11,032	3,614
District 22	273,722	2.42	61.3	45.0	11.3	31.9	33,691	18.0	6,104	6,243	17,830	0
District 23	277,106	2.38	62.0	46.8	9.9	30.2	42,238	13.9	6,988	5,257	23,896	0
District 24	281,415	2.40	62.9	44.3	13.4	29.4	31,957	17.7	4,484	4,882	14,806	0
District 25	291,931	2.37	60.1	41.5	14.2	32.0	27,885	20.7	1,499	4,931	14,361	0
District 26	306,166	2.27	56.6	36.2	15.5	35.9	20,826	20.0	926	3,778	11,661	0
District 27	286,327	2.42	67.4	52.6	10.6	27.0	25,431	20.3	13,255	5,336	5,224	0
NORTH CAROLINA	3,955,069	2.53	65.5	48.2	12.7	28.6	266,771	16.6	61,680	46,638	89,795	26,326
District 1	298,934	2.43	61.7	40.1	17.6	31.3	33,195	15.6	13,922	6,285	10,496	594
District 2	298,114	2.77	76.0	60.3	11.8	20.2	9,222	21.8	1,132	3,214	1,773	5,949
District 3	288,230	2.50	67.4	50.4	12.6	26.7	36,317	6.2	6,616	2,817	8,725	19,749
District 4	331,087	2.50	60.4	45.4	11.1	29.3	29,027	7.0	5,518	2,406	22,784	0
District 5	297,784	2.46	64.8	48.8	11.3	30.4	24,541	18.3	2,268	3,598	10,492	0
District 6	300,791	2.51	67.2	48.6	13.4	28.3	14,723	23.6	2,493	3,811	6,738	0
District 7	317,831	2.46	65.3	47.5	13.2	29.4	17,485	29.2	5,511	3,495	9	33
District 8	295,832	2.59	66.8	49.8	12.4	28.7	23,567	17.1	8,325	3,469	3,449	0
District 9	282,297	2.74	70.8	52.7	13.6	24.6	14,887	45.8	50	2,736	2,155	1
District 10	304,825	2.45	63.1	46.9	11.2	30.5	14,144	30.8	2,503	4,741	4,033	0
District 11	305,022	2.44	65.3	51.1	10.4	29.8	15,930	23.1	5,915	4,622	4,965	0
District 12	329,853	2.57	58.5	39.8	13.7	33.6	13,004	10.1	4,648	3,049	13,560	0
District 13	304,469	2.50	65.9	47.2	13.3	28.0	20,729	28.6	2,779	2,395	616	0
NORTH DAKOTA	316,306	2.31	60.1	48.3	7.4	31.7	26,143	25.3	2,489	6,433	10,570	1,380
At Large	316,306	2.31	60.1	48.3	7.4	31.7	26,143	25.3	2,489	6,433	10,570	1,380
OHIO	4,667,192	2.43	63.2	45.8	12.5	30.3	317,470	25.3	76,590	83,019	106,042	571
District 1	296,321	2.43	60.2	42.0	13.5	31.7	22,225	17.7	6,431	4,486	7,060	0
District 2	297,390	2.41	65.5	48.3	12.3	29.0	10,244	55.0	880	5,887	712	0
District 3	304,414	2.50	56.0	32.4	18.2	34.0	22,998	10.7	2,353	2,793	11,851	0
District 4	280,785	2.43	65.5	49.4	11.4	29.4	28,731	17.6	15,892	5,563	5,261	0
District 5	287,898	2.43	67.3	51.5	9.8	26.7	17,928	31.9	971	6,014	8,367	0
District 6	272,868	2.47	66.2	50.8	10.5	29.0	21,966	30.8	9,881	6,354	3,595	0
District 7	281,886	2.52	68.8	52.4	11.3	26.1	15,495	35.8	795	6,223	5,129	0
District 8	276,346	2.58	67.0	51.9	10.2	26.4	17,744	24.8	1,369	4,682	8,537	0
District 9	303,638	2.33	57.5	35.5	16.3	35.0	13,963	26.5	1,894	4,930	5,512	0
District 10	299,196	2.32	61.6	43.5	13.8	32.4	28,122	21.5	1,997	5,845	12,267	547
District 11	302,266	2.16	51.5	26.0	20.4	41.5	23,620	21.5	3,906	6,243	7,446	0
District 12	293,574	2.59	68.8	55.1	9.6	25.3	18,992	19.4	6,071	3,929	6,352	0
District 13	304,871	2.28	58.3	38.5	14.4	34.5	20,522	20.6	5,134	5,394	10,204	0
District 14	287,281	2.48	66.4	52.6	9.5	28.1	11,629	40.5	2,076	5,260	1,338	24
District 15	290,515	2.55	67.1	52.1	10.1	25.8	31,727	11.1	16,670	3,476	9,591	0
District 16	287,943	2.44	66.1	54.1	8.1	28.8	11,564	51.7	270	5,940	2,820	0
OKLAHOMA	1,470,364	2.60	65.6	48.0	12.5	28.5	109,498	24.0	40,562	21,678	30,148	7,203
District 1	309,210	2.57	64.9	47.0	13.2	29.2	9,093	28.8	2,371	3,656	2,981	0
District 2	280,114	2.58	68.2	50.2	12.8	27.5	23,048	19.9	9,915	5,506	4,623	0
District 3	280,616	2.65	67.0	50.6	11.4	27.8	31,567	13.8	15,091	4,818	10,089	463
District 4	292,173	2.61	66.8	49.4	12.2	26.5	28,624	12.1	7,991	3,797	7,490	6,740
District 5	308,251	2.60	61.4	43.3	12.8	31.1	17,166	18.8	5,194	3,901	4,965	0
OREGON	1,603,635	2.53	63.0	48.7	9.9	27.7	89,553	18	22,203	11,491	23,704	178
District 1	319,240	2.60	65.1	52.0	9.0	26.2	14,319	20.7	4,641	1,964	3,338	127
District 2	325,181	2.46	65.8	50.1	10.6	27.1	21,302	19.0	8,762	2,660	1,775	13

1. No spouse present.

Table E. Congressional Districts 116th Congress — Housing and Money Income

STATE District	Housing units, 2017						Money income, 2017		
			Occupied units					Households	
			Owner-occupied			Renter-occupied			
	Total	Occupied units as a percent of all units	Owner-occupied units as a percent of occupied units	Median value¹ (dollars)	Percent valued at $500,000 or more	Median rent²	Per capita income (dollars)	Median income (dollars)	Percent with income of $100,000 or more
	40	41	42	43	44	45	46	47	48
NEW MEXICO — Cont'd									
District 3	317,876	78.4	71.3	189,500	8.3	887	25,653	47,325	19.8
NEW YORK	8,327,621	87.7	53.8	314,500	28.8	1,226	37,156	64,894	32.5
District 1	310,760	78.2	80.9	386,200	29.1	1,717	42,213	92,284	46.6
District 2	238,090	91.8	82.5	382,800	17.8	1,660	38,676	97,387	49.0
District 3	271,032	92.6	81.2	619,200	65.4	1,829	55,735	107,412	53.3
District 4	249,426	94.3	76.8	472,100	43.2	1,591	43,144	102,205	51.6
District 5	245,249	92.7	55.5	460,300	36.6	1,371	27,816	70,481	33.9
District 6	297,028	91.0	46.2	608,400	62.2	1,502	31,525	62,278	29.5
District 7	275,116	92.0	23.4	733,200	74.0	1,401	32,609	56,197	29.4
District 8	319,825	91.5	31.6	599,700	65.3	1,245	29,828	52,956	26.2
District 9	311,525	91.8	31.3	652,200	65.0	1,324	33,248	57,453	28.8
District 10	354,737	85.9	33.5	1,003,300	84.7	1,741	69,758	93,629	47.6
District 11	287,104	91.2	58.6	551,100	56.5	1,374	33,946	72,633	37.8
District 12	435,137	82.6	28.4	1,004,600	85.9	2,156	89,677	107,010	54.1
District 13	323,596	93.5	10.6	543,000	53.5	1,167	27,503	43,880	20.1
District 14	258,689	89.7	32.7	512,100	51.3	1,452	27,397	58,331	24.9
District 15	271,697	95.4	8.2	385,000	24.8	1,079	15,566	28,042	8.0
District 16	286,622	95.0	49.7	463,900	44.8	1,397	44,168	69,463	36.1
District 17	263,610	93.2	66.1	473,700	44.8	1,562	46,513	96,125	48.8
District 18	279,743	89.3	72.6	303,900	17.9	1,239	41,169	86,211	42.5
District 19	367,150	72.3	72.6	204,900	6.7	930	32,117	61,662	27.8
District 20	334,054	85.4	61.4	217,300	5.3	959	36,048	66,532	32.3
District 21	379,942	71.6	70.1	144,000	3.9	826	27,910	54,311	21.3
District 22	325,695	84.0	69.3	118,600	2.1	727	27,880	52,212	19.5
District 23	344,474	80.4	69.7	106,800	2.3	760	26,664	50,747	17.8
District 24	319,387	88.1	66.6	135,700	1.8	811	30,628	55,721	23.8
District 25	318,019	91.8	62.5	146,500	2.2	904	32,246	57,149	24.9
District 26	345,481	88.6	59.0	127,800	2.8	765	28,970	49,148	19.8
District 27	314,433	91.1	76.2	162,700	3.6	782	33,386	64,032	28.1
NORTH CAROLINA	4,622,656	85.6	65.4	171,200	7.1	861	29,560	52,752	22.4
District 1	348,032	85.9	56.7	145,600	3.6	822	25,938	43,853	18.2
District 2	326,486	91.3	74.3	214,200	8.5	923	32,986	69,552	32.9
District 3	384,575	74.9	64.4	161,800	4.6	851	26,508	50,479	18.1
District 4	359,141	92.2	58.0	264,800	14.7	1,110	37,844	70,293	34.1
District 5	365,931	81.4	68.4	150,500	4.6	713	27,682	46,513	18.2
District 6	337,512	89.1	68.9	150,800	5.3	727	27,502	49,867	19.3
District 7	395,372	80.4	69.1	160,900	6.7	821	28,216	48,345	20.1
District 8	344,073	86.0	64.6	162,200	4.5	845	27,349	51,621	20.1
District 9	311,920	90.5	71.3	195,600	11.9	830	34,478	61,369	29.9
District 10	345,300	88.3	65.9	152,800	6.0	764	26,475	47,064	17.0
District 11	402,673	75.7	73.7	169,900	6.8	739	26,207	46,337	15.9
District 12	359,236	91.8	52.7	197,900	10.1	1,073	33,011	58,787	26.3
District 13	342,405	88.9	64.2	158,400	5.2	804	28,240	50,803	19.6
NORTH DAKOTA	374,591	84.4	63.4	194,700	5.5	785	34,041	61,843	26.3
At Large	374,591	84.4	63.4	194,700	5.5	785	34,041	61,843	26.3
OHIO	5,201,701	89.7	65.8	144,200	3.4	772	30,038	54,021	22.5
District 1	327,196	90.6	60.8	162,800	5.7	774	33,425	59,719	27.5
District 2	325,777	91.3	66.9	153,700	5.7	771	32,976	57,083	25.5
District 3	339,631	89.6	45.3	134,300	2.2	864	24,531	47,123	14.8
District 4	312,495	89.9	70.1	126,400	1.9	692	27,058	52,370	18.5
District 5	312,862	92.0	71.7	140,600	2.5	712	30,693	56,835	23.7
District 6	323,767	84.3	74.9	115,000	1.8	636	25,558	47,067	15.6
District 7	307,120	91.8	72.7	142,600	1.8	694	26,871	54,045	20.2
District 8	304,947	90.6	69.4	148,200	2.1	755	28,503	58,295	23.8
District 9	354,568	85.6	57.2	102,700	2.5	718	25,392	43,182	15.5
District 10	335,780	89.1	61.4	130,100	2.3	761	29,396	51,208	21.5
District 11	363,313	83.2	47.9	93,000	4.3	756	27,390	35,954	14.5
District 12	318,136	92.3	72.5	211,300	6.7	928	37,491	71,853	35.0
District 13	340,001	89.7	64.1	102,500	1.2	721	25,896	45,177	15.0
District 14	313,205	91.7	76.5	184,800	5.0	851	37,380	67,163	31.1
District 15	318,593	91.2	69.4	172,300	4.8	907	32,266	66,694	29.4
District 16	304,310	94.6	75.3	169,600	3.1	832	35,010	66,504	29.0
OKLAHOMA	1,734,074	84.8	65.5	137,400	3.5	780	26,472	50,051	19.5
District 1	349,351	88.5	62.5	154,100	4.6	831	29,144	53,332	22.0
District 2	356,906	78.5	71.3	105,300	2.6	645	21,579	40,305	13.2
District 3	338,614	82.9	68.9	125,700	2.4	751	25,046	50,089	19.9
District 4	336,047	86.9	65.3	144,000	2.9	818	27,070	54,885	20.6
District 5	353,156	87.3	60.2	149,600	5.3	815	29,070	50,441	21.2
OREGON	1,768,582	90.7	62.8	319,200	19.6	1,079	31,950	60,212	26.3
District 1	344,672	92.6	63.6	377,900	25.7	1,300	36,864	75,585	35.7
District 2	372,943	87.2	64.9	264,800	15.7	898	27,696	51,813	18.9

1. Specified owner-occupied units.   2. Specified renter-occupied units.

Table E. Congressional Districts 116th Congress — **Poverty, Labor Force, Employment, and Social Security**

STATE District	Poverty, 2017			Civilian labor force, 2016			Civilian employment,[2] 2017				Persons under 65 years of age with no health insurance, 2017 (percent)	Social Security beneficiaries, December 2018		Supplemental Security Income recipients, December 2018
					Unemployment			Percent						
	Persons below poverty level (percent)	Families below poverty level (percent)	Percent of households receiving food stamps in past 12 months	Total	Total	Rate[1]	Total	Management, business, science, and arts occupations	Service, sales, and office	Construction and production		Number	Rate[3]	
	49	50	51	52	53	54	55	56	57	58	59	60	61	62
NEW MEXICO — Cont'd														
District 3	21.8	17.1	16.1	302,831	22,238	7.3	280,593	39.0	43.0	18.0	12.9	149,679	214.8	20,949
NEW YORK	14.1	10.4	14.8	10,194,438	560,001	5.5	9,634,437	40.9	42.7	16.4	6.6	3,627,340	182.7	628,644
District 1	6.3	4.6	5.7	370,291	13,880	3.7	356,411	41.3	40.9	17.8	5.4	152,159	211.7	9,522
District 2	7.3	4.8	7.5	390,994	15,344	3.9	375,650	36.6	44.5	18.9	5.2	135,535	187.9	9,705
District 3	5.9	3.8	4.2	361,487	12,958	3.6	348,529	51.6	37.2	11.1	5.0	148,598	204.8	7,092
District 4	6.8	5.2	5.2	385,883	13,936	3.6	371,947	43.1	41.1	15.8	6.4	138,049	189.4	9,896
District 5	11.1	8.3	17.0	410,734	29,025	7.1	381,709	30.5	49.9	19.6	7.6	112,123	140.4	28,383
District 6	12.1	10.2	9.6	394,201	14,971	3.8	379,230	36.5	46.8	16.7	11.7	119,982	157.5	19,760
District 7	23.0	19.2	25.7	385,729	24,715	6.4	361,014	39.5	45.2	15.3	9.7	87,527	115.8	32,598
District 8	21.1	15.5	24.1	389,541	25,717	6.6	363,824	38.0	46.4	15.5	6.8	113,032	142.4	50,742
District 9	15.5	11.9	21.6	390,295	28,342	7.3	361,953	45.6	42.0	12.4	8.0	103,900	138.5	31,285
District 10	16.0	11.6	11.8	395,709	17,435	4.4	378,274	58.6	32.8	8.7	5.7	105,879	144.4	21,098
District 11	13.3	11.3	13.4	363,001	18,247	5.0	344,754	42.9	40.0	17.1	5.1	132,101	174.9	28,106
District 12	10.2	6.3	5.7	460,562	15,408	3.3	445,154	68.9	26.3	4.9	4.7	108,610	152.1	14,436
District 13	25.4	22.5	31.1	430,512	38,237	8.9	392,275	36.0	49.8	14.2	8.9	110,747	138.0	55,403
District 14	13.2	11.3	15.5	371,087	19,705	5.3	351,382	29.3	49.0	21.7	11.6	97,346	140.7	18,842
District 15	36.2	33.0	48.4	346,024	46,201	13.4	299,823	17.9	63.2	18.9	9.7	96,096	123.0	70,905
District 16	10.8	8.1	12.5	384,842	21,764	5.7	363,078	42.6	43.5	13.8	7.9	127,671	171.9	21,701
District 17	10.0	6.3	7.9	385,428	19,618	5.1	365,810	46.3	40.7	12.9	6.6	129,742	173.8	10,038
District 18	8.9	5.6	7.1	371,350	16,395	4.4	354,955	40.8	41.8	17.3	5.3	136,005	186.3	11,613
District 19	12.4	8.0	10.7	345,814	17,247	5.0	328,567	37.4	41.4	21.1	6.1	168,406	240.2	15,119
District 20	11.3	6.8	11.5	391,147	22,407	5.7	368,740	45.2	40.5	14.3	3.8	152,840	208.8	19,226
District 21	13.3	9.1	13.2	328,971	16,837	5.1	312,134	35.5	41.4	23.1	6.0	172,125	243.9	18,514
District 22	14.8	9.8	15.3	336,676	18,346	5.4	318,330	35.4	42.9	21.6	5.1	167,402	240.2	21,539
District 23	15.3	9.3	13.7	334,456	17,422	5.2	317,034	35.9	40.7	23.4	6.8	167,066	238.0	19,122
District 24	14.3	9.7	14.3	353,121	20,553	5.8	332,568	38.7	42.9	18.4	4.7	156,875	221.6	20,582
District 25	14.8	10.6	16.3	380,549	21,147	5.6	359,402	43.3	40.6	16.1	4.1	156,921	218.2	25,548
District 26	18.7	13.7	19.3	369,890	20,274	5.5	349,616	37.2	45.1	17.6	4.5	157,255	220.1	28,359
District 27	8.3	6.2	9.0	366,144	13,870	3.8	352,274	37.3	41.0	21.6	3.6	173,348	241.3	9,510
NORTH CAROLINA	14.7	10.6	12.3	5,049,839	266,777	5.3	4,783,062	37.6	39.8	22.7	12.6	2,098,741	204.3	228,906
District 1	21.1	16.2	18.1	361,826	25,599	7.1	336,227	36.6	39.6	23.8	13.1	158,952	209.4	28,077
District 2	10.5	7.7	8.9	414,999	20,045	4.8	394,954	43.2	37.8	19.0	10.8	149,264	178.6	13,973
District 3	16.7	11.8	15.2	326,091	23,509	7.2	302,582	32.7	44.4	22.9	12.3	169,324	224.1	18,519
District 4	11.3	6.8	7.0	485,315	16,455	3.4	468,860	51.4	35.2	13.4	10.9	108,484	126.7	9,599
District 5	16.9	12.3	11.8	361,801	16,618	4.6	345,183	35.9	39.6	24.5	13.3	173,546	228.8	16,974
District 6	14.7	10.9	13.3	377,027	19,445	5.2	357,582	32.6	38.4	29.0	12.9	177,129	230.5	17,666
District 7	17.2	11.9	14.3	377,791	22,041	5.8	355,750	32.2	42.6	25.1	15.0	193,012	241.2	19,910
District 8	13.7	9.6	11.5	362,458	23,997	6.6	338,461	33.6	42.3	24.0	11.5	154,277	195.4	15,036
District 9	14.9	11.3	14.1	375,203	17,608	4.7	357,595	41.4	38.0	20.6	10.5	147,428	187.1	21,909
District 10	13.8	10.3	12.3	375,379	20,045	5.3	355,334	32.2	40.8	27.0	12.7	182,052	239.4	17,876
District 11	14.1	9.7	10.9	350,233	14,684	4.2	335,549	31.7	41.5	26.8	15.5	213,368	281.0	17,115
District 12	12.8	9.8	11.0	483,512	22,112	4.6	461,400	41.6	39.7	18.7	14.6	107,787	125.2	15,883
District 13	14.8	10.8	12.8	398,204	24,619	6.2	373,585	35.6	39.9	24.5	11.3	164,118	210.0	16,369
NORTH DAKOTA	10.3	6.1	6.3	419,182	12,307	2.9	406,875	37.3	39.4	23.3	8.8	133,773	177.1	8,389
At Large	10.3	6.1	6.3	419,182	12,307	2.9	406,875	37.3	39.4	23.3	8.8	133,773	177.1	8,389
OHIO	14.0	9.8	13.2	5,885,356	303,348	5.2	5,582,008	36.7	39.9	23.4	7.0	2,356,367	202.1	308,349
District 1	15.9	10.0	12.2	384,600	19,336	5.0	365,264	41.4	39.6	19.0	6.0	130,166	175.7	19,677
District 2	11.9	8.6	12.1	368,522	14,320	3.9	354,202	40.7	38.0	21.3	6.1	148,478	203.9	20,950
District 3	21.9	16.3	17.5	411,378	24,267	5.9	387,111	35.0	44.0	21.0	10.0	104,800	133.9	28,877
District 4	12.7	9.7	11.7	347,869	17,091	4.9	330,778	30.5	37.3	32.2	6.8	155,558	218.9	14,833
District 5	9.8	6.3	9.0	378,982	14,713	3.9	364,269	34.7	37.4	27.8	4.9	153,297	213.6	10,656
District 6	14.8	10.2	16.4	313,041	16,110	5.1	296,931	28.8	40.6	30.6	7.7	173,146	248.7	23,859
District 7	12.2	9.4	11.7	356,499	16,945	4.8	339,554	30.3	39.4	30.3	10.6	160,082	220.6	14,018
District 8	10.8	7.0	10.7	368,406	16,989	4.6	351,417	34.6	40.6	24.7	6.1	147,146	201.4	14,702
District 9	19.9	15.8	21.2	360,218	29,331	8.1	330,887	30.5	44.2	25.3	7.4	143,416	199.0	30,566
District 10	14.7	10.4	13.6	353,670	21,554	6.1	332,116	39.9	40.9	19.2	6.8	148,262	205.5	19,301
District 11	25.6	19.9	25.1	325,169	31,772	9.8	293,397	37.4	43.4	19.2	6.6	136,850	202.6	40,627
District 12	8.2	5.6	8.4	411,545	12,577	3.1	398,968	45.4	37.6	17.0	7.0	138,495	177.4	13,343
District 13	17.5	12.9	16.5	362,164	23,725	6.6	338,439	29.7	43.6	26.7	7.2	162,618	227.3	25,844
District 14	8.9	6.0	7.7	371,882	14,304	3.8	357,578	41.6	38.5	19.8	6.0	158,981	219.3	9,638
District 15	11.6	7.6	10.9	391,284	15,335	3.9	375,949	41.3	37.6	21.1	6.0	135,390	175.2	14,428
District 16	7.8	5.1	5.7	380,127	14,979	3.9	365,148	41.2	37.6	21.2	7.2	159,682	223.3	7,030
OKLAHOMA	15.8	11.6	13.2	1,858,021	99,619	5.4	1,758,402	35.1	40.8	24.1	16.6	789,288	200.8	96,201
District 1	14.0	10.7	12.0	405,916	23,319	5.7	382,597	38.1	40.3	21.6	15.2	151,492	188.5	17,851
District 2	19.6	14.7	17.0	307,015	20,488	6.7	286,527	29.5	40.6	30.0	22.7	185,795	249.5	26,938
District 3	15.7	10.7	11.9	360,265	16,334	4.5	343,931	33.3	39.5	27.2	15.6	155,708	201.2	14,302
District 4	13.4	9.6	11.7	381,851	18,818	4.9	363,033	36.0	41.9	22.1	13.9	153,008	193.7	16,036
District 5	16.6	12.2	13.4	402,974	20,660	5.1	382,314	37.1	41.4	21.5	16.1	143,285	175.1	21,074
OREGON	13.2	8.8	15.4	2,099,999	107,100	5.1	1,992,899	38.9	40.0	21.1	8.2	871,988	210.5	88,233
District 1	8.7	5.2	10.6	452,659	20,319	4.5	432,340	44.4	36.8	18.8	6.8	141,676	167.8	12,109
District 2	13.8	9.8	17.4	379,936	21,761	5.7	358,175	33.8	41.8	24.4	9.9	208,892	254.4	18,387

1. Percent of civilian labor force.   2. Persons 16 years old and over.   3. Per 1,000 resident population estimated in the 2017 American Community Survey.

Table E. Congressional Districts 116th Congress — **Agriculture**

STATE District	Agriculture 2017									
	Land in farms				Value of products sold				Government payments	
	Number of farms	Acres	Average size of farm (acres)	Harvested cropland (acres)	Total ($1,000)	Average per farm (dollars)	Percent from crops	Percent from livestock and poultry products	Total ($1,000)	Average per farm receiving payments (dollars)
	63	64	65	66	67	68	69	70	71	72
NEW MEXICO — Cont'd										
District 3	13,012	18,404,082	1,414	395,435	956,793	73,532	15.9	84.1	35,472	17,825
NEW YORK	33,438	6,866,171	205	3,581,095	5,369,212	160,572	39.3	60.7	59,106	9,162
District 1	466	25,862	55	16,618	199,192	427,451	90.1	9.9	76	6,333
District 2	42	432	10	120	2,985	71,071	81.0	19.0	D	D
District 3	78	4,488	58	2,845	26,075	334,295	87.7	12.3	D	D
District 4	7	207	30	22	95	13,571	100.0	0.0	X	D
District 5	X	X	X	X	X	X	X	X	X	X
District 6	3	D	D	D	58	19,333	D	D	X	X
District 7	3	D	D	3	D	D	D	D	D	X
District 8	5	6	1	6	34	6,800	100.0	0.0	D	D
District 9	11	14	1	14	6,641	603,727	D	D	D	D
District 10	3	3	1	3	14	4,667	100.0	0.0	D	D
District 11	6	D	D	D	D	D	D	D	D	D
District 12	X	X	X	X	X	X	X	X	X	X
District 13	4	8	2	4	31	7,750	100.0	0.0	D	D
District 14	X	X	X	X	X	X	X	X	D	D
District 15	X	X	X	X	X	X	X	X	X	X
District 16	4	D	D	6	122	30,500	100.0	0.0	X	X
District 17	64	3,607	56	456	5,688	88,875	88.5	11.5	D	D
District 18	834	97,545	117	41,571	101,205	121,349	76.6	23.4	472	6,841
District 19	4,978	893,753	180	386,911	453,031	91,007	47.5	52.5	4,562	5,894
District 20	1,144	153,570	134	77,467	117,643	102,835	52.4	47.6	680	4,533
District 21	5,867	1,422,164	242	667,428	987,044	168,237	20.5	79.5	6,091	6,945
District 22	4,325	857,969	198	394,978	472,075	109,150	25.6	74.4	4,719	5,157
District 23	8,113	1,647,668	203	854,912	1,065,088	131,282	35.9	64.1	15,512	9,066
District 24	2,543	572,957	225	352,684	699,584	275,102	39.9	60.1	6,333	11,349
District 25	392	69,264	177	42,514	49,178	125,454	89.2	10.8	1,757	23,427
District 26	80	12,569	157	4,774	8,567	107,088	98.9	1.1	D	D
District 27	4,466	1,104,024	247	737,743	1,174,577	263,004	42.5	57.5	18,827	14,482
NORTH CAROLINA	46,418	8,430,522	182	4,407,160	12,900,674	277,924	29.0	71.0	107,565	10,746
District 1	3,443	1,424,052	414	837,774	1,284,852	373,178	51.6	48.4	33,934	18,676
District 2	2,882	560,837	195	320,561	728,529	252,786	61.9	38.1	3,999	5,448
District 3	3,031	1,258,543	415	978,038	1,722,737	568,372	40.4	59.6	27,850	18,805
District 4	877	84,981	97	31,708	50,145	57,178	65.9	34.1	519	3,437
District 5	6,957	787,246	113	262,330	1,059,940	152,356	20.0	80.0	1,938	3,101
District 6	5,825	740,881	127	239,786	713,084	122,418	26.2	73.8	2,135	2,986
District 7	4,208	1,182,179	281	703,243	3,901,879	927,253	17.0	83.0	15,606	11,052
District 8	3,054	428,078	140	177,235	617,584	202,221	20.6	79.4	3,163	6,817
District 9	2,964	742,381	250	443,241	1,767,017	596,160	14.6	85.4	9,531	12,065
District 10	3,954	379,387	96	134,064	370,291	93,650	23.6	76.4	3,028	4,420
District 11	5,778	457,986	79	111,024	327,908	56,751	50.1	49.9	2,837	3,422
District 12	174	9,981	57	4,609	D	D	D	D	131	10,917
District 13	3,271	373,990	114	163,547	D	D	D	D	2,894	9,810
NORTH DAKOTA	26,364	39,341,591	1,492	23,976,011	8,234,102	312,324	81.1	18.9	467,034	22,770
At Large	26,364	39,341,591	1,492	23,976,011	8,234,102	312,324	81.1	18.9	467,034	22,770
OHIO	77,805	13,965,295	179	10,190,952	9,341,225	120,059	58.1	41.9	351,125	12,301
District 1	1,198	104,683	87	72,291	61,864	51,639	92.5	7.5	2,766	17,731
District 2	5,788	971,188	168	561,643	351,574	60,742	72.2	27.8	23,903	11,729
District 3	112	10,036	90	8,336	18,150	162,054	98.2	1.8	286	11,440
District 4	9,520	2,277,947	239	1,977,190	1,777,616	186,724	63.8	36.2	82,104	14,059
District 5	10,683	2,913,459	273	2,607,814	2,094,949	196,101	63.3	36.7	86,759	11,594
District 6	12,271	1,662,328	135	605,518	480,616	39,167	40.8	59.2	10,283	6,967
District 7	10,030	1,332,469	133	848,892	1,093,721	109,045	39.2	60.8	24,540	10,825
District 8	6,086	1,139,909	187	972,960	1,323,050	217,392	41.0	59.0	30,802	9,952
District 9	522	75,694	145	63,632	57,816	110,759	94.8	5.2	2,273	9,883
District 10	1,876	386,147	206	323,254	240,924	128,424	86.6	13.4	14,157	17,521
District 11	108	1,849	17	570	1,573	14,565	93.5	6.5	140	12,727
District 12	4,556	698,970	153	494,043	438,440	96,234	61.7	38.3	14,830	12,008
District 13	1,285	99,455	77	55,420	44,477	34,612	61.7	38.3	1,129	7,428
District 14	3,432	337,648	98	187,729	217,096	63,256	75.1	24.9	2,394	6,435
District 15	7,093	1,612,792	227	1,164,067	763,351	107,620	82.8	17.2	48,785	17,479
District 16	3,245	340,721	105	247,593	376,008	115,873	29.3	70.7	5,974	10,555
OKLAHOMA	78,531	34,156,290	435	7,812,594	7,465,512	95,065	20.3	79.7	232,018	11,248
District 1	3,313	588,647	178	182,107	110,733	33,424	49.2	50.8	2,543	6,218
District 2	29,177	7,890,823	270	1,392,848	2,290,737	78,512	11.2	88.8	25,153	5,613
District 3	28,506	19,928,136	699	5,158,149	4,192,913	147,089	23.7	76.3	164,878	13,484
District 4	13,511	5,008,747	371	969,680	797,804	59,048	23.8	76.2	37,282	12,272
District 5	4,024	739,937	184	109,810	73,324	18,222	30.4	69.6	2,162	4,590
OREGON	37,616	15,962,322	424	2,965,392	5,006,821	133,103	65.6	34.4	92,406	22,918
District 1	5,086	342,106	67	178,334	581,142	114,263	85.9	14.1	3,347	8,973
District 2	13,969	13,669,551	979	2,031,807	2,404,429	172,126	55.0	45.0	81,710	28,244

Table E. Congressional Districts 116th Congress — **Nonfarm Employment and Payroll**

STATE District	Private nonfarm employment and payroll, 2016											Annual payroll	
	Number of establishments	Employment										Total (mil dol)	Average per employee (dollars)
		Total	Percent by selected industries										
			Manufacturing	Construction	Wholesale trade	Retail trade	Health care and social assistance	Finance and Insurance	Real estate and rental and leasing	Professional, scientific, and technical services	Information		
	73	74	75	76	77	78	79	80	81	82	83	84	85
NEW MEXICO — Cont'd													
District 3	14,317	175,940	3.6	5.0	2.5	17.3	20.1	3.2	1.5	9.0	1.6	7,046	40,048
NEW YORK	544,073	8,178,455	5.1	4.4	4.4	11.6	18.9	6.8	2.2	7.9	3.6	521,873	63,811
District 1	23,101	240,530	7.7	8.1	5.9	17.0	20.5	3.0	1.1	6.9	1.6	12,700	52,801
District 2	20,657	248,534	11.3	9.6	8.4	14.7	15.3	2.5	1.3	5.6	2.3	11,724	47,171
District 3	29,761	385,416	3.3	4.4	7.0	10.5	22.7	7.3	2.0	9.6	2.9	24,442	63,418
District 4	24,618	269,755	3.1	6.1	3.3	14.9	22.0	5.5	1.7	7.4	1.7	12,995	48,172
District 5	11,571	159,716	1.9	5.3	2.2	12.7	18.9	1.3	1.9	2.3	0.8	6,967	43,622
District 6	18,756	167,770	2.6	7.8	3.6	14.6	33.9	3.7	2.8	4.1	1.5	6,820	40,654
District 7	22,322	227,425	4.6	6.7	6.0	10.8	22.4	4.2	2.8	5.1	2.6	9,484	41,703
District 8	11,539	136,711	3.3	3.1	3.9	15.7	29.0	3.1	2.5	2.6	1.9	5,347	39,113
District 9	12,771	125,110	0.9	2.7	1.7	12.7	44.8	1.6	3.2	3.1	2.3	4,916	39,296
District 10	40,310	810,907	1.4	2.2	3.2	6.9	12.4	13.6	2.9	12.1	8.5	74,402	91,752
District 11	16,191	154,361	1.1	7.6	2.1	16.5	33.5	2.7	1.7	3.8	1.5	6,232	40,371
District 12	70,310	1,523,839	1.3	2.7	5.0	6.6	9.0	13.3	3.4	15.2	7.3	171,221	112,362
District 13	10,098	146,859	0.3	1.5	0.5	10.1	49.8	1.4	3.6	1.9	1.4	7,862	53,535
District 14	12,251	151,251	3.3	9.9	4.6	11.5	24.2	2.1	2.4	1.9	2.0	7,175	47,440
District 15	9,235	125,450	3.9	4.6	8.3	13.6	31.1	1.4	3.8	1.9	1.4	5,416	43,169
District 16	16,283	176,729	3.5	8.6	2.6	16.6	22.4	2.3	3.6	3.4	2.2	8,026	45,416
District 17	26,445	345,251	3.9	5.6	5.3	11.6	21.8	5.8	2.1	7.2	2.5	22,442	65,001
District 18	19,320	225,181	6.3	5.1	5.1	18.2	20.2	2.8	1.5	5.8	2.3	9,900	43,963
District 19	16,879	167,396	8.2	5.6	3.4	17.3	22.5	3.5	1.2	3.2	1.6	6,245	37,305
District 20	19,043	336,634	7.0	4.3	4.1	13.0	20.1	5.8	1.4	8.5	2.7	15,952	47,386
District 21	15,532	180,068	11.1	4.8	3.0	20.2	21.5	2.5	1.1	2.7	1.9	6,690	37,153
District 22	14,267	224,510	13.5	3.2	3.6	14.8	20.6	4.9	0.9	4.3	2.1	8,630	38,440
District 23	14,500	222,997	15.3	3.5	2.7	15.0	18.4	2.5	1.1	2.9	1.5	8,294	37,193
District 24	16,415	277,393	10.3	4.4	5.6	14.2	19.3	4.4	1.6	5.8	2.0	11,941	43,048
District 25	17,182	353,784	9.7	3.4	4.1	11.6	19.0	3.7	1.8	7.2	3.0	15,829	44,743
District 26	17,567	349,800	8.6	3.4	4.9	12.0	18.9	7.5	1.6	7.7	1.8	15,392	44,003
District 27	16,241	210,491	17.4	6.1	4.8	18.9	15.0	2.6	1.2	3.2	1.3	8,520	40,475
NORTH CAROLINA	227,347	3,794,926	11.4	4.9	5.0	13.1	15.3	4.8	1.4	5.8	2.2	170,980	45,055
District 1	14,142	258,880	12.4	4.1	2.7	11.9	22.0	4.0	1.2	5.0	1.7	11,118	42,946
District 2	15,427	193,725	13.3	7.2	5.1	17.1	13.9	2.4	1.3	4.7	1.7	7,534	38,892
District 3	15,874	186,316	9.6	6.1	2.7	19.4	16.5	3.4	2.4	3.9	1.3	6,110	32,795
District 4	25,357	477,663	3.3	4.7	7.5	11.4	14.3	5.8	1.9	14.8	5.4	27,890	58,388
District 5	16,039	274,151	12.4	5.9	4.5	13.7	18.8	4.5	1.2	3.4	1.3	11,971	43,666
District 6	13,397	199,709	23.5	5.9	4.6	14.2	16.5	2.3	0.8	2.3	1.5	7,424	37,176
District 7	16,804	212,677	12.3	5.7	4.0	17.7	18.0	3.1	1.6	4.0	2.2	7,897	37,132
District 8	13,936	204,415	10.8	5.2	3.0	18.4	19.8	2.0	1.3	3.7	1.4	7,161	35,031
District 9	16,737	237,045	15.1	5.8	4.5	14.7	14.1	5.5	1.4	4.5	1.5	10,416	43,943
District 10	18,158	284,658	19.1	3.9	4.7	14.1	19.8	1.9	1.1	2.9	1.3	10,851	38,120
District 11	15,990	203,831	20.2	5.7	3.7	16.9	16.5	2.2	1.1	2.6	1.3	7,035	34,515
District 12	24,307	516,688	5.0	4.7	7.2	9.2	11.0	11.1	1.8	8.6	3.0	31,590	61,140
District 13	20,391	365,903	15.0	4.2	6.1	11.9	14.9	3.9	1.5	4.0	1.7	16,240	44,382
NORTH DAKOTA	24,601	346,947	6.9	6.7	6.6	14.6	17.7	5.1	1.6	4.6	2.1	15,817	45,588
At Large	24,601	346,947	6.9	6.7	6.6	14.6	17.7	5.1	1.6	4.6	2.1	15,817	45,588
OHIO	252,201	4,790,178	13.8	3.9	4.9	12.0	17.6	5.3	1.4	5.2	1.8	218,467	45,607
District 1	16,813	390,697	9.2	4.5	5.2	9.7	19.1	6.3	1.5	7.6	2.8	22,596	57,835
District 2	15,819	266,754	10.0	4.4	5.4	14.3	16.6	6.5	1.5	8.1	2.5	12,206	45,759
District 3	15,069	371,971	6.5	3.9	5.1	10.4	19.6	8.8	2.0	5.6	1.7	18,808	50,564
District 4	14,458	271,591	28.9	3.9	4.3	11.6	15.7	2.1	0.7	3.9	1.0	11,248	41,414
District 5	16,205	308,203	21.7	3.7	3.8	12.8	14.0	3.0	1.1	3.9	0.9	12,205	39,601
District 6	12,971	177,481	14.5	4.9	3.7	15.5	22.4	2.9	1.1	2.4	0.9	6,298	35,483
District 7	14,281	217,664	22.7	5.9	4.7	14.5	17.2	2.5	0.8	2.5	1.1	8,119	37,300
District 8	13,751	246,245	19.3	4.3	7.0	13.3	14.3	5.0	1.0	2.7	1.0	10,150	41,219
District 9	13,397	250,566	17.1	4.0	4.5	11.5	18.1	2.9	1.7	3.0	1.6	11,000	43,902
District 10	15,005	295,801	11.3	3.5	3.7	13.2	20.0	4.2	1.2	8.2	3.0	13,481	45,575
District 11	18,423	417,631	8.3	3.0	4.7	7.0	27.4	6.0	2.5	7.5	1.7	23,072	55,244
District 12	17,556	323,352	8.1	3.8	2.9	11.3	17.4	11.7	1.1	6.2	2.4	15,906	49,192
District 13	14,797	258,120	17.0	4.6	4.6	15.3	18.1	2.0	1.5	3.2	1.4	10,070	39,014
District 14	20,335	327,767	18.2	3.9	7.8	11.8	12.5	6.7	1.6	5.3	1.5	15,993	48,794
District 15	14,076	234,597	11.2	3.7	5.3	15.5	15.3	4.1	1.5	5.1	2.4	9,555	40,730
District 16	18,370	295,771	13.9	4.1	5.0	16.0	17.2	4.5	1.1	4.2	2.0	12,130	41,011
OKLAHOMA	93,232	1,360,379	9.6	5.3	4.3	13.7	16.3	4.4	1.7	5.4	2.1	57,194	42,042
District 1	21,498	377,201	11.7	5.5	4.6	12.3	15.4	4.5	2.0	6.1	2.9	17,542	46,505
District 2	13,035	162,235	14.4	4.4	3.3	16.9	23.3	3.8	0.9	2.7	1.1	5,377	33,144
District 3	17,236	187,687	12.3	6.7	4.5	16.2	14.2	3.9	1.7	3.6	1.4	7,041	37,516
District 4	16,662	207,679	8.1	5.5	2.7	17.2	18.1	4.0	1.9	4.6	1.6	7,243	34,877
District 5	24,320	381,111	5.9	4.9	5.3	12.2	15.8	5.4	1.7	6.5	2.3	17,369	45,575
OREGON	114,551	1,551,192	10.6	5.6	5.4	13.4	15.8	3.9	1.8	5.9	2.5	74,063	47,746
District 1	23,055	367,384	12.0	5.5	8.0	12.1	12.2	3.9	2.1	7.6	3.5	22,047	60,012
District 2	23,524	253,292	10.8	5.9	3.3	16.8	18.0	3.1	1.6	3.7	1.9	9,504	37,523

Table E. Congressional Districts 116th Congress — **Land Area and Population Characteristics**

STATE District	Representative, 116th Congress	Land area,[1] 2018 (sq mi)	Total persons	Per square mile	White	Black	American Indian, Alaska Native	Asian and Pacific Islander	Some other race (percent)	Two or more races (percent)	Hispanic or Latino[2] (percent)	Non-Hispanic White alone (percent)	Percent female	Percent foreign-born	Percent born in state of residence
		1	2	3	4	5	6	7	8	9	10	11	12	13	14
OREGON — Cont'd															
District 3	Earl Blumenauer (D)	1,074.5	842,158	783.8	78.5	5.2	1.1	7.9	2.4	5.0	11.3	70.5	50.6	13.3	43.7
District 4	Peter A. DeFazio (D)	17,272.3	803,611	46.5	88.3	0.7	0.8	2.7	2.3	5.1	8.0	83.6	50.7	5.2	46.4
District 5	Kurt Schrader (D)	5,189.1	831,703	160.3	85.7	1.0	1.0	3.4	3.6	5.3	16.7	74.7	50.5	9.9	52.2
PENNSYLVANIA		44,742.1	12,805,537	286.2	80.7	11.2	0.2	3.5	1.9	2.5	7.3	76.4	51.0	7.0	72.2
District 1	Brian K. Fitzpatrick (R)	78.0	728,366	9,338.1	45.6	36.7	0.3	7.4	6.7	3.2	17.8	37.0	51.2	14.6	65.5
District 2	Brendan F. Boyle (D)	74.1	726,135	9,801.4	33.8	56.6	0.2	5.1	1.7	2.5	6.2	30.6	54.3	8.8	68.2
District 3	Dwight Evans (D)	3,850.7	691,184	179.5	91.3	4.4	0.1	1.1	0.8	2.2	2.3	90.0	50.5	2.5	81.4
District 4	Madeleine Dean (D)	1,517.9	729,945	480.9	85.5	7.9	0.1	2.5	1.2	2.8	8.1	80.2	50.8	5.4	63.2
District 5	Mary Gay Scanlon (D)	10,711.4	696,063	65.0	93.3	2.7	0.2	1.9	0.3	1.5	2.1	91.9	48.8	3.4	79.7
District 6	Chrissy Houlahan (D)	860.5	728,576	846.7	84.9	5.5	0.1	5.1	2.4	2.1	6.3	81.7	50.7	8.1	71.0
District 7	Susan Wild (D)	862.5	725,762	841.5	85.7	5.7	0.1	5.2	0.8	2.5	3.0	83.6	50.8	7.4	72.8
District 8	Matt Cartwright (D)	707.0	713,998	1,009.9	87.4	4.0	0.1	5.6	1.2	1.7	5.2	83.6	50.7	9.8	66.2
District 9	Daniel Meuser (R)	5,730.1	687,620	120.0	94.2	2.9	0.1	0.6	0.4	1.8	2.3	92.5	50.8	1.8	80.4
District 10	Scott Perry (R)	8,377.6	694,398	82.9	92.7	3.6	0.2	1.1	0.7	1.7	4.4	89.5	49.9	3.4	68.2
District 11	Lloyd Smucker (R)	3,356.2	701,056	208.9	88.1	6.3	0.1	2.2	1.5	1.8	6.2	84.1	51.1	5.2	77.7
District 12	Fred Keller (R)	2,163.1	689,237	318.6	92.0	3.6	0.1	1.8	0.4	2.2	1.4	91.2	50.7	2.7	83.1
District 13	John Joyce (R)	155.2	728,475	4,694.8	64.5	17.6	0.4	10.0	5.3	2.3	14.1	56.5	52.2	18.8	65.6
District 14	Guy Reschenthaler (R)	209.3	687,028	3,282.7	71.2	20.7	0.1	3.9	0.6	3.5	2.5	69.6	52.1	5.8	76.1
District 15	Glen Thompson (R)	1,285.2	734,824	571.7	83.9	5.7	0.3	2.9	4.3	2.9	16.8	74.0	51.1	8.5	66.1
District 16	Mike Kelly (R)	997.7	731,802	733.5	82.6	7.1	0.4	2.0	3.4	4.5	19.6	71.1	51.2	8.5	68.0
District 17	Conor Lamb (D)	1,732.9	697,535	402.5	87.2	6.3	0.2	1.9	1.9	2.5	10.3	80.3	50.0	6.2	67.9
District 18	Michael F. Doyle (D)	2,072.8	713,533	344.2	92.5	2.6	0.1	2.2	0.2	2.4	1.5	91.5	51.3	3.6	80.8
RHODE ISLAND		1,034.0	1,059,639	1,024.8	81.8	6.3	0.5	3.7	4.5	3.3	15.4	72.1	51.6	13.9	55.5
District 1	David Cicilline (D)	268.6	539,250	2,007.5	77.1	8.2	0.6	3.8	6.2	4.1	18.2	66.8	51.9	17.2	49.2
District 2	James R. Langevin (D)	765.4	520,389	679.9	86.5	4.3	0.5	3.6	2.7	2.4	12.5	77.6	51.3	10.4	62.1
SOUTH CAROLINA		30,063.0	5,024,369	167.1	67.3	27.0	0.3	1.6	1.6	2.1	5.7	63.6	51.5	4.9	56.2
District 1	Joe Cunningham (D)	1,547.8	782,340	505.4	74.3	19.5	0.2	1.8	1.5	2.6	6.1	70.3	51.9	5.5	43.2
District 2	Joe Wilson (R)	3,022.4	713,488	236.1	70.2	23.8	0.3	2.0	1.7	2.0	6.0	66.0	51.4	5.5	52.6
District 3	Jeff Duncan (R)	5,268.3	687,378	130.5	76.5	18.7	0.4	0.8	1.8	1.8	5.3	73.5	50.7	3.2	64.7
District 4	William R. Timmons IV (R)	1,299.4	731,886	563.3	73.4	17.9	0.2	3.2	2.4	3.0	8.2	68.2	51.6	7.7	54.4
District 5	Ralph Norman (R)	5,505.8	718,465	130.5	68.7	26.3	0.3	1.3	1.1	2.2	4.3	66.0	51.5	3.7	56.1
District 6	James E. Clyburn (D)	8,064.1	670,725	83.2	39.0	56.7	0.2	1.2	1.3	1.5	5.4	35.4	51.5	4.1	69.1
District 7	Tom Rice (R)	5,355.1	720,087	134.5	66.6	28.6	0.4	1.1	1.6	1.8	4.3	64.0	51.8	4.1	55.3
SOUTH DAKOTA		75,809.3	869,666	11.5	84.7	2.0	8.7	1.3	0.6	2.6	3.6	82.3	49.6	3.4	64.9
At Large	Dusty Johnson (R)	75,809.3	869,666	11.5	84.7	2.0	8.7	1.3	0.6	2.6	3.6	82.3	49.6	3.4	64.9
TENNESSEE		41,234.9	6,715,984	162.9	77.7	16.7	0.2	1.9	1.3	2.1	5.4	73.9	51.3	5.2	59.7
District 1	Phil Roe (R)	4,141.9	714,912	172.6	93.8	2.9	0.2	0.8	0.8	1.5	3.7	91.2	51.0	3.1	59.7
District 2	Tim Burchett (R)	2,321.7	747,673	322.0	89.0	6.2	0.2	1.9	1.0	1.7	4.2	85.7	51.4	4.4	59.1
District 3	Chuck Fleischmann (R)	4,570.3	733,082	160.4	84.6	10.7	0.2	1.5	1.2	1.8	4.0	81.7	51.4	3.8	63.6
District 4	Scott DesJarlais (R)	5,984.8	782,024	130.7	84.7	9.5	0.2	2.0	1.2	2.4	6.7	79.5	50.8	6.0	60.5
District 5	Jim Cooper (D)	1,248.4	774,096	620.1	68.1	24.1	0.2	3.3	1.3	3.0	9.4	60.1	51.6	11.4	51.5
District 6	John W. Rose (R)	6,474.9	772,984	119.4	91.1	4.5	0.4	1.1	1.3	1.7	4.5	88.1	50.9	4.0	60.1
District 7	Mark E. Green (R)	9,160.3	778,057	84.9	84.2	9.9	0.1	2.1	0.6	3.0	4.9	80.3	50.5	3.6	51.7
District 8	David Kustoff (R)	6,848.9	716,130	104.6	74.3	19.8	0.2	2.1	1.0	2.6	3.4	72.3	51.6	3.4	66.5
District 9	Steve Cohen (D)	483.8	697,026	1,440.9	26.4	66.6	0.2	1.9	3.6	1.3	7.3	22.9	52.6	6.7	66.1
TEXAS		261,252.9	28,304,596	108.3	73.9	12.1	0.5	4.9	5.9	2.6	39.4	41.9	50.3	17.1	59.7
District 1	Louie Gohmert (R)	7,868.6	717,376	91.2	77.0	17.7	0.5	1.3	1.5	1.9	17.9	61.5	51.1	7.9	70.7
District 2	Dan Crenshaw (R)	308.7	772,262	2,501.5	67.7	12.0	0.2	8.1	8.4	3.6	32.1	45.2	49.9	21.8	49.6
District 3	Van Taylor (R)	480.8	870,763	1,811.1	68.5	9.8	0.4	15.7	2.1	3.4	15.0	56.5	50.9	22.0	42.3
District 4	John Ratcliffe (R)	10,130.5	747,188	73.8	81.3	10.2	0.9	1.2	3.9	2.6	14.4	71.3	50.9	6.7	66.9
District 5	Lance Gooden (R)	5,042.2	769,579	152.6	77.3	14.4	0.5	2.5	3.1	2.1	29.3	52.2	49.8	14.7	65.0
District 6	Ron Wright (R)	2,148.6	792,043	368.6	65.0	21.7	0.4	4.6	4.5	3.8	23.5	47.3	51.3	14.7	59.2
District 7	Lizzie Fletcher (D)	162.1	800,081	4,936.8	64.8	14.5	0.7	11.1	6.4	2.6	30.4	41.8	49.9	29.9	45.3
District 8	Kevin Brady (R)	6,055.0	863,498	142.6	82.7	9.1	0.3	3.2	2.7	2.0	22.8	63.2	49.2	12.7	58.7
District 9	Al Green (D)	165.7	789,535	4,765.8	38.9	36.7	0.2	11.7	10.3	2.2	40.8	10.1	51.7	34.8	49.3
District 10	Michael T. McCaul (R)	5,071.7	846,261	166.9	70.5	10.6	0.4	6.4	8.8	3.2	29.1	52.0	50.3	17.0	56.9
District 11	K. Michael Conaway (R)	27,832.6	759,467	27.3	84.3	3.8	0.7	1.1	8.0	2.1	39.1	55.0	50.1	9.4	70.8
District 12	Kay Granger (R)	1,441.1	806,551	559.7	78.2	8.7	0.6	3.4	5.9	3.1	23.7	61.5	50.9	10.4	60.5
District 13	Mac Thornberry (R)	38,349.5	713,480	18.6	84.3	5.4	0.8	2.0	4.1	3.5	27.2	62.9	48.8	9.8	66.3
District 14	Randy K. Weber Sr. (R)	2,446.6	765,031	312.7	70.7	20.0	0.6	3.5	2.7	2.6	26.0	49.3	49.2	11.1	65.2
District 15	Vicente Gonzalez (D)	7,804.1	790,730	101.3	83.3	1.9	0.3	1.1	11.1	2.3	82.3	14.4	50.0	22.0	65.1
District 16	Veronica Escobar (D)	710.8	742,384	1,044.4	77.0	3.6	0.5	1.5	14.7	2.7	81.0	13.1	50.9	24.3	57.8
District 17	Bill Flores (R)	7,650.6	771,567	100.9	75.2	12.9	0.5	5.0	3.9	2.5	26.2	54.1	50.4	12.5	66.3
District 18	Sheila Jackson-Lee (D)	235.3	800,402	3,402.0	50.1	34.6	0.3	4.4	8.9	1.8	44.1	16.1	49.9	23.0	60.2
District 19	Jodey C. Arrington (R)	25,835.7	734,202	28.4	83.5	6.2	0.8	1.6	5.6	2.3	36.9	53.8	49.3	8.7	71.6
District 20	Joaquin Castro (D)	199.7	806,372	4,037.9	84.2	5.1	0.6	3.0	4.3	2.8	69.7	20.9	50.8	14.7	66.0
District 21	Chip Roy (R)	5,920.9	809,322	136.7	85.5	3.9	0.5	3.7	3.2	3.3	30.3	60.5	50.8	10.5	58.2
District 22	Pete Olson (R)	1,033.5	897,080	868.0	61.2	13.2	0.2	19.2	3.3	2.7	25.5	40.2	50.7	25.6	50.0
District 23	Will Hurd (R)	58,058.2	769,276	13.3	82.1	3.5	0.7	1.3	10.1	2.3	70.3	23.2	49.1	16.4	65.4
District 24	Kenny Marchant (R)	262.8	800,103	3,044.6	64.0	12.6	0.6	14.5	5.0	3.3	24.5	45.6	50.7	24.6	45.2
District 25	Roger Williams (R)	7,622.6	789,825	103.6	83.4	6.8	0.6	3.5	2.2	3.5	18.3	68.6	50.5	7.1	56.6

1. Dry land or land partially or temporarily covered by water.   2. May be of any race.

Table E. Congressional Districts 116th Congress — Age and Education

STATE District	Population and population characteristics, 2017 (cont.) — Age (percent)										Education, 2017	Attainment[2] (percent)	
	Under 5 years	5 to 17 years	18 to 24 years	25 to 34 years	35 to 44 years	45 to 54 years	55 to 64 years	65 to 74 years	75 years and over	Median age	Total Enrollment[1]	High school graduate or more	Bachelor's degree or more
	15	16	17	18	19	20	21	22	23	24	25	26	27
OREGON — Cont'd													
District 3	5.6	13.8	8.5	17.7	16.4	12.9	11.8	8.2	5.0	37.5	191,596	92.0	41.7
District 4	4.9	14.1	11.5	12.4	11.3	11.3	14.2	12.0	8.3	41.1	187,372	91.7	27.3
District 5	5.9	17.1	8.5	12.8	12.3	12.6	13.3	10.7	6.8	39.3	195,914	89.1	31.5
PENNSYLVANIA	5.5	15.3	9.2	13.1	11.6	13.3	14.2	10.0	7.8	40.8	2,941,997	90.6	31.4
District 1	7.0	15.8	9.5	19.1	13.1	11.9	11.5	7.2	4.8	34.1	180,668	84.3	28.4
District 2	6.0	14.0	12.3	18.1	11.5	11.5	11.9	8.4	6.2	34.7	194,118	88.9	36.0
District 3	5.2	15.1	9.2	11.5	11.1	13.5	15.1	10.9	8.3	43.0	152,543	90.9	26.5
District 4	5.8	16.3	8.5	12.5	12.1	13.7	13.9	9.9	7.2	40.5	165,778	90.0	28.1
District 5	4.9	13.8	12.7	11.7	10.8	13.0	14.5	10.3	8.3	41.5	168,525	91.3	25.5
District 6	5.8	15.9	8.8	12.3	12.0	14.4	14.0	9.7	7.1	40.7	173,692	93.6	44.1
District 7	5.5	16.8	8.5	11.0	11.5	13.7	14.8	9.7	8.4	41.9	173,269	93.3	45.5
District 8	4.9	15.6	8.1	11.5	11.7	14.8	15.4	10.2	7.8	43.7	160,679	93.8	40.6
District 9	5.1	15.1	9.0	11.3	11.0	13.5	15.0	11.0	9.0	43.8	147,746	89.2	20.3
District 10	4.9	15.7	8.8	10.8	10.6	13.8	15.2	11.5	8.8	44.3	148,931	89.4	22.5
District 11	5.2	14.5	9.1	12.5	11.2	13.9	14.4	11.1	8.2	42.9	147,695	90.6	24.7
District 12	5.1	15.1	6.5	10.8	11.7	13.3	16.0	11.8	9.6	45.6	146,298	94.3	32.6
District 13	6.1	16.5	7.5	15.3	12.6	12.8	13.2	8.7	7.1	38.3	176,336	89.5	36.6
District 14	4.8	11.8	11.4	18.0	10.7	11.2	14.0	9.9	8.2	38.4	152,513	93.0	35.7
District 15	5.4	16.6	10.0	12.4	13.1	13.6	12.0	9.4	7.5	40.0	181,389	89.6	29.3
District 16	6.8	17.6	9.5	13.2	11.5	12.5	12.7	8.9	7.3	37.5	172,320	84.3	27.0
District 17	5.0	14.5	9.1	12.2	11.9	13.8	14.8	10.4	8.3	43.1	148,586	89.3	22.7
District 18	5.4	14.5	7.4	11.8	11.7	14.3	15.3	11.2	8.5	44.4	150,911	94.6	38.2
RHODE ISLAND	5.2	14.3	10.9	13.8	11.6	13.5	14.0	9.5	7.1	39.5	260,894	88.3	33.5
District 1	5.1	14.9	10.9	14.7	11.4	13.5	13.4	9.1	7.0	38.5	134,178	86.1	33.0
District 2	5.3	13.7	11.0	12.8	11.9	13.4	14.7	10.0	7.2	40.5	126,716	90.6	33.9
SOUTH CAROLINA	5.8	16.2	9.5	12.9	12.3	12.8	13.2	10.7	6.5	39.4	1,183,515	87.4	28.0
District 1	5.9	15.7	7.9	14.3	12.8	12.9	12.8	11.1	6.6	39.5	179,311	93.2	40.0
District 2	5.8	17.0	9.1	13.1	12.6	13.3	13.3	9.6	6.2	38.7	167,711	90.0	33.7
District 3	5.2	16.3	10.2	11.5	11.8	13.2	13.5	10.8	7.5	40.6	164,962	83.1	22.0
District 4	6.2	16.7	9.2	13.7	12.7	13.1	12.7	9.4	6.2	38.2	175,981	88.0	31.6
District 5	6.0	17.0	8.8	12.1	12.7	13.7	13.1	10.7	6.1	40.1	169,024	86.7	25.1
District 6	5.8	14.8	14.0	13.9	11.9	10.9	12.9	9.8	6.0	36.0	171,694	83.1	19.2
District 7	5.4	15.5	8.1	11.6	11.7	12.6	14.4	13.4	7.2	42.9	154,832	86.2	21.9
SOUTH DAKOTA	7.0	17.6	9.4	13.3	11.5	11.4	13.5	9.4	6.9	36.9	214,085	91.7	28.1
At Large	7.0	17.6	9.4	13.3	11.5	11.4	13.5	9.4	6.9	36.9	214,085	91.7	28.1
TENNESSEE	6.0	16.4	9.2	13.5	12.5	13.3	13.1	9.6	6.4	38.6	1,573,379	87.8	27.3
District 1	4.9	15.1	8.4	11.5	11.7	14.0	14.3	11.8	8.2	43.7	148,017	85.2	19.9
District 2	5.6	15.3	10.4	12.9	12.1	13.2	13.2	10.3	7.1	39.7	174,794	89.6	30.8
District 3	5.4	15.5	7.9	12.8	12.3	13.3	14.2	10.9	7.7	41.8	158,729	87.5	24.5
District 4	6.3	17.1	10.3	12.9	13.5	13.1	12.5	8.7	5.5	37.5	189,951	86.8	25.1
District 5	6.6	14.7	9.7	19.1	13.6	12.2	11.8	7.5	4.7	34.9	184,551	89.7	38.9
District 6	5.8	16.6	8.4	12.0	12.1	14.1	13.5	10.6	6.9	40.7	173,648	87.5	22.3
District 7	6.4	18.3	8.7	12.9	12.9	13.6	12.5	8.8	5.9	37.6	193,761	88.9	30.4
District 8	5.5	17.5	8.8	10.9	12.1	14.1	13.9	10.3	6.9	40.6	175,730	88.9	29.1
District 9	7.5	17.6	10.4	16.2	12.4	11.8	12.1	7.4	4.6	33.7	174,198	85.8	24.6
TEXAS	7.1	18.9	9.9	14.6	13.5	12.5	11.3	7.4	4.9	34.7	7,679,163	83.6	29.6
District 1	6.6	17.9	10.2	12.5	11.8	11.8	12.4	9.6	7.3	37.2	185,574	85.0	20.8
District 2	6.7	16.8	8.9	15.6	14.2	13.4	12.4	7.6	4.4	36.1	192,898	88.1	41.3
District 3	6.1	20.0	8.1	12.4	16.1	15.3	11.2	7.0	3.9	37.3	247,630	94.1	54.0
District 4	6.3	18.2	8.8	11.7	12.3	13.2	13.0	9.7	6.9	38.5	187,278	87.8	23.2
District 5	7.1	19.7	8.7	13.2	13.4	13.1	11.7	7.5	5.6	36.1	201,749	79.5	19.5
District 6	6.8	19.3	9.8	13.6	13.6	13.4	11.5	7.5	4.3	35.3	225,402	87.8	29.1
District 7	7.3	19.6	7.7	16.3	15.8	12.3	10.4	6.5	4.2	34.5	221,190	88.4	48.9
District 8	6.4	18.8	9.4	12.2	14.3	13.5	12.2	8.1	5.0	37.1	230,686	87.9	30.6
District 9	7.7	18.5	9.3	18.0	13.6	11.8	10.7	6.6	3.8	32.9	218,052	78.6	25.5
District 10	7.4	18.5	8.1	15.7	14.8	12.3	11.8	7.2	4.2	35.2	227,819	90.4	40.2
District 11	7.2	18.2	9.8	14.5	11.5	10.8	12.3	8.9	6.7	35.2	183,929	83.3	20.8
District 12	7.1	18.0	9.0	15.8	13.3	12.2	11.9	7.6	5.2	35.1	212,526	88.2	31.6
District 13	6.7	18.1	9.9	13.5	12.3	11.8	12.7	8.5	6.6	36.2	181,214	83.4	20.2
District 14	6.6	17.9	9.1	13.5	13.4	12.9	13.1	8.1	5.4	36.9	189,916	86.7	24.3
District 15	8.4	22.6	10.3	13.6	13.4	11.6	9.0	6.2	4.8	31.2	239,830	69.7	19.2
District 16	7.4	19.9	11.0	14.7	13.6	12.7	11.6	10.5	5.4	32.8	224,710	80.1	24.6
District 17	6.8	15.9	15.0	14.9	12.6	11.4	11.0	7.3	5.1	33.2	233,005	85.6	30.4
District 18	7.7	18.8	10.6	17.6	13.8	11.8	10.4	6.0	3.4	32.4	219,714	76.4	22.5
District 19	6.8	18.2	13.3	14.3	12.1	10.9	10.8	7.5	6.0	33.1	207,083	81.5	22.9
District 20	7.3	17.2	12.8	17.2	13.3	11.6	10.2	6.1	4.5	32.0	225,581	82.9	24.6
District 21	5.7	14.3	10.7	15.4	12.5	12.1	12.8	10.0	6.4	37.8	196,344	93.8	46.6
District 22	7.5	20.2	8.5	12.5	15.3	14.0	11.6	6.8	3.7	36.0	262,799	91.6	47.1
District 23	7.6	20.9	9.7	14.0	12.7	12.6	10.1	7.4	5.0	33.3	216,483	76.5	22.4
District 24	7.0	17.4	7.5	16.8	15.4	14.0	11.9	6.3	3.7	35.8	202,898	91.3	46.3
District 25	6.5	18.1	9.8	13.5	13.4	13.3	11.6	8.3	5.5	36.4	203,113	91.3	39.3

1. All persons 3 years old and over enrolled in nursery school through college and graduate or professional school.   2. Persons 25 years old and over.

Items 15—27

Table E. Congressional Districts 116th Congress — Households and Group Quarters

STATE District	Households, 2017						Total in group quarters, 2017	Group Quarters, 2010				
	Number	Average household size	Family households (percent)	Married couple family (percent)	Female family house-holder[1]	One person households (percent)		Percent 65 years and over	Persons in correctional institutions	Persons in nursing facilities	Persons in college dormitories	Persons in military quarters
	28	29	30	31	32	33	34	35	36	37	38	39
OREGON — Cont'd												
District 3	329,586	2.50	57.3	43.2	10.1	29.7	18,680	15.5	2,065	2,399	6,604	0
District 4	324,338	2.42	61.8	47.4	10.1	28.1	18,894	16.5	1,354	2,067	8,825	21
District 5	305,290	2.67	65.4	51.0	9.6	27.2	16,358	19.1	5,381	2,401	3,162	17
PENNSYLVANIA	5,008,751	2.47	63.4	47.5	11.4	30.4	423,488	21.0	97,820	87,775	177,332	259
District 1	270,229	2.63	54.6	28.7	18.6	37.9	17,465	9.2	10,896	2,024	7,108	14
District 2	297,368	2.32	44.2	22.8	17.5	47.8	35,529	13.8	680	4,909	23,446	0
District 3	281,083	2.36	64.4	49.1	10.5	29.2	28,129	19.5	6,328	5,188	11,315	11
District 4	282,589	2.50	67.6	52.2	11.3	25.9	22,918	20.4	6,485	3,922	7,205	37
District 5	263,199	2.47	62.2	48.7	8.6	30.7	46,230	11.4	14,533	5,088	23,276	0
District 6	277,795	2.55	67.7	54.9	8.9	25.7	20,254	24.0	3,336	4,461	7,424	0
District 7	262,015	2.67	72.2	60.6	8.4	24.0	24,950	21.2	5,890	5,118	10,160	0
District 8	270,854	2.60	69.3	57.1	8.4	25.3	10,013	46.3	1,039	4,098	1,569	0
District 9	276,921	2.40	65.5	49.8	11.1	29.2	22,526	23.8	6,117	5,134	8,771	0
District 10	259,298	2.57	67.0	53.1	9.6	28.1	27,618	15.5	11,878	4,486	10,876	0
District 11	280,380	2.40	65.1	48.6	11.7	28.6	27,496	22.1	7,333	6,231	9,991	6
District 12	289,930	2.32	65.6	52.9	8.6	29.7	15,924	32.7	4,480	4,694	3,073	6
District 13	267,730	2.68	63.9	44.3	13.8	31.3	12,093	57.8	2	6,384	1,329	121
District 14	316,620	2.08	49.0	32.3	12.7	41.7	27,821	15.0	4,663	4,194	15,905	0
District 15	278,641	2.55	67.1	50.3	11.2	25.9	23,236	21.1	1,424	5,210	13,039	63
District 16	267,130	2.67	70.0	52.6	12.5	24.0	18,111	27.5	1,132	5,327	9,156	0
District 17	274,104	2.45	64.3	46.8	12.7	29.9	24,629	25.7	7,876	6,346	7,783	1
District 18	292,865	2.37	66.1	53.6	8.7	28.9	18,546	30.3	3,728	4,961	5,906	0
RHODE ISLAND	408,748	2.49	61.6	45.5	12.1	32.3	41,924	18.5	3,783	8,420	24,687	1,385
District 1	207,523	2.49	60.6	42.4	13.8	33.5	22,702	21.3	350	4,996	13,035	1,385
District 2	201,225	2.49	62.6	48.7	10.4	31.1	19,222	15.5	3,433	3,424	11,652	0
SOUTH CAROLINA	1,905,100	2.57	65.8	47.3	14.3	28.9	136,487	13.0	41,649	19,020	46,463	19,413
District 1	294,731	2.62	65.6	52.7	10.2	28.8	9,420	15.4	531	1,662	2,560	4,436
District 2	269,788	2.57	67.9	49.8	14.2	27.2	19,609	12.8	1,458	2,391	823	11,567
District 3	260,543	2.56	68.1	48.5	14.7	26.6	20,567	14.3	7,044	3,116	9,817	0
District 4	279,956	2.55	66.4	50.0	12.4	28.1	18,126	14.5	3,776	2,832	9,668	0
District 5	275,713	2.56	67.5	48.2	13.9	28.1	12,427	20.0	5,318	2,792	3,289	611
District 6	247,452	2.54	58.3	34.8	19.6	35.5	42,564	6.5	18,400	3,087	17,383	2,799
District 7	276,917	2.55	66.1	45.8	15.9	28.8	13,774	22.4	5,122	3,140	2,923	0
SOUTH DAKOTA	344,260	2.43	62.0	48.7	8.8	31.5	33,984	21.1	6,327	7,005	10,248	597
At Large	344,260	2.43	62.0	48.7	8.8	31.5	33,984	21.1	6,327	7,005	10,248	597
TENNESSEE	2,588,655	2.53	66.0	48.5	12.8	28.3	154,724	19.8	46,957	33,041	53,136	1,544
District 1	289,787	2.41	66.7	49.3	12.3	27.8	16,993	26.7	4,577	4,466	4,176	0
District 2	298,668	2.45	64.7	49.1	10.9	28.9	16,320	19.1	1,901	3,686	10,443	0
District 3	290,781	2.45	63.5	48.8	10.9	32.0	19,984	23.8	4,913	4,071	4,884	3
District 4	289,758	2.65	71.3	53.9	11.9	22.9	15,294	21.1	3,301	3,584	6,619	0
District 5	313,397	2.40	57.9	40.7	13.2	32.0	23,238	9.0	6,769	2,588	13,660	0
District 6	292,219	2.61	71.2	54.6	11.3	24.8	11,337	36.4	2,385	3,730	2,283	0
District 7	284,158	2.68	71.3	56.5	10.7	24.3	17,772	21.2	8,311	3,918	2,350	1,250
District 8	268,254	2.60	70.5	54.0	12.5	25.5	18,253	21.3	7,494	4,158	4,748	10
District 9	261,633	2.60	56.8	28.9	22.7	37.3	15,533	14.0	7,306	2,840	3,973	281
TEXAS	9,623,874	2.88	69.6	50.7	13.7	25.0	606,511	14.9	267,405	94,278	119,834	35,260
District 1	252,240	2.73	69.5	51.8	12.4	26.2	27,582	17.3	8,132	5,093	9,123	0
District 2	281,893	2.71	66.4	51.5	10.3	27.5	9,277	18.4	2,441	1,873	2,921	0
District 3	308,230	2.82	73.3	59.4	10.0	21.5	2,933	31.9	1,061	1,326	387	0
District 4	264,157	2.76	70.0	53.9	10.7	25.7	17,730	25.8	8,850	5,078	2,237	0
District 5	258,430	2.88	71.9	52.1	13.8	23.5	25,246	14.9	17,768	3,964	938	0
District 6	264,657	2.96	74.2	55.7	13.2	21.6	8,888	32.8	689	2,419	2,137	0
District 7	292,915	2.73	66.0	51.4	11.1	27.9	1,413	58.1	3	774	5	0
District 8	287,423	2.89	74.3	58.8	10.6	21.3	31,690	8.5	23,107	2,021	2,615	0
District 9	266,248	2.95	67.9	40.9	20.0	27.0	3,031	32.7	154	1,629	1,520	0
District 10	290,104	2.87	68.3	55.1	9.7	24.2	12,591	25.7	2,453	3,156	4,344	0
District 11	266,922	2.77	68.2	52.1	11.9	27.6	19,975	18.3	9,050	3,721	3,615	1,924
District 12	290,513	2.72	67.2	50.1	12.0	27.1	15,616	20.3	5,807	3,540	3,405	202
District 13	259,603	2.60	66.5	50.1	11.5	28.8	37,444	11.8	17,511	4,208	2,479	5,487
District 14	270,799	2.70	68.4	49.4	14.3	25.9	35,196	9.5	22,748	2,861	2,869	40
District 15	230,727	3.35	78.3	53.9	18.9	18.4	17,265	14.6	8,632	2,035	1,514	0
District 16	242,341	3.00	73.0	47.3	19.6	23.6	14,162	9.8	6,076	1,482	491	5,683
District 17	283,564	2.61	63.1	44.7	13.7	28.7	32,145	11.1	8,355	3,792	14,831	0
District 18	271,657	2.86	63.7	37.6	19.7	29.5	22,547	3.8	12,624	783	5,661	0
District 19	256,456	2.70	66.4	47.8	12.7	26.8	41,598	10.0	19,845	4,073	10,748	621
District 20	254,077	3.12	67.2	43.8	16.8	25.8	12,722	11.9	4	2,081	4,846	9,322
District 21	315,100	2.51	60.1	48.1	8.4	31.6	17,077	19.9	600	4,024	7,505	3,793
District 22	285,539	3.12	80.5	66.1	11.1	15.8	6,402	21.6	4,494	1,409	4	0
District 23	229,895	3.26	76.1	55.2	16.1	20.6	19,672	7.6	16,613	1,566	193	877
District 24	308,208	2.58	64.6	49.2	11.5	29.3	3,491	65.8	53	1,913	480	0
District 25	269,625	2.80	71.0	58.0	9.7	22.3	33,861	9.6	11,967	3,274	10,926	2,822

1. No spouse present.

Table E. Congressional Districts 116th Congress — Housing and Money Income

STATE District	Housing units, 2017						Money income, 2017		
	Occupied units						Households		
			Owner-occupied			Renter-occupied			
	Total	Occupied units as a percent of all units	Owner-occupied units as a percent of occupied units	Median value[1] (dollars)	Percent valued at $500,000 or more	Median rent[2]	Per capita income (dollars)	Median income (dollars)	Percent with income of $100,000 or more
	40	41	42	43	44	45	46	47	48
OREGON — Cont'd									
District 3	352,862	93.4	58.8	386,600	28.9	1,198	34,711	64,379	30.3
District 4	355,470	91.2	62.0	246,800	10.5	921	27,788	49,666	18.7
District 5	342,635	89.1	64.9	308,100	17.8	1,064	32,389	63,710	28.1
PENNSYLVANIA	5,694,402	88.0	68.3	181,200	6.9	893	32,711	59,195	26.3
District 1	303,600	89.0	52.8	150,800	6.9	971	27,131	45,400	20.0
District 2	345,657	86.0	45.2	180,600	15.7	983	31,245	39,128	20.3
District 3	322,654	87.1	71.3	140,600	3.4	686	29,022	52,491	21.1
District 4	307,291	92.0	71.8	187,300	3.2	926	31,775	63,733	26.3
District 5	347,419	75.8	70.9	134,900	3.5	718	26,022	50,232	17.9
District 6	294,659	94.3	75.0	267,000	15.8	1,128	42,849	82,203	40.6
District 7	278,294	94.2	78.5	308,500	17.9	1,148	44,859	90,546	45.4
District 8	283,194	95.6	77.1	322,300	17.7	1,175	43,057	84,772	42.5
District 9	324,757	85.3	71.5	129,400	2.1	691	26,304	49,356	16.8
District 10	349,392	74.2	74.3	168,600	4.2	754	27,641	53,146	20.8
District 11	326,305	85.9	71.2	158,600	2.7	805	29,439	57,248	22.6
District 12	325,121	89.2	77.8	155,500	4.6	739	35,748	62,451	27.3
District 13	286,117	93.6	62.3	235,300	7.6	1,072	34,901	62,427	31.5
District 14	368,336	86.0	54.9	106,600	3.5	835	31,346	45,970	18.4
District 15	295,926	94.2	68.6	207,600	5.5	975	32,792	63,128	27.4
District 16	284,323	94.0	64.6	197,600	5.0	948	28,640	61,049	24.9
District 17	329,995	83.1	68.0	143,100	1.6	785	27,885	52,689	20.7
District 18	321,362	91.1	76.7	175,500	4.9	789	37,173	67,503	31.6
RHODE ISLAND	468,266	87.3	60.8	257,800	11.3	941	34,511	63,870	30.0
District 1	234,267	88.6	54.4	260,200	14.2	930	33,720	59,193	27.3
District 2	233,999	86.0	67.5	256,400	9.0	958	35,329	69,702	32.7
SOUTH CAROLINA	2,284,820	83.4	68.7	161,800	7.1	848	27,909	50,570	20.4
District 1	357,539	82.4	69.4	270,900	18.8	1,160	36,445	66,337	29.8
District 2	305,860	88.2	73.2	163,300	5.8	886	30,317	58,665	24.5
District 3	310,867	83.8	71.2	143,000	4.6	721	25,492	47,004	17.9
District 4	307,921	90.9	66.8	162,700	6.4	836	29,472	53,006	22.3
District 5	309,847	89.0	73.1	149,500	4.3	788	27,035	51,131	20.4
District 6	305,321	81.0	57.6	106,600	4.2	817	21,205	35,615	11.8
District 7	387,465	71.5	69.0	150,400	4.1	792	24,084	42,159	14.8
SOUTH DAKOTA	392,650	87.7	67.7	167,600	4.2	722	29,611	56,521	22.4
At Large	392,650	87.7	67.7	167,600	4.2	722	29,611	56,521	22.4
TENNESSEE	2,958,799	87.5	65.4	167,500	6.7	833	28,764	51,340	20.6
District 1	351,615	82.4	70.3	142,400	2.8	651	24,991	42,300	14.5
District 2	333,199	89.6	67.3	174,600	7.4	830	30,789	52,025	22.0
District 3	332,318	87.5	66.6	155,300	5.6	738	28,268	47,681	18.0
District 4	320,128	90.5	67.8	176,300	4.4	825	27,072	56,304	21.1
District 5	347,622	90.2	54.8	238,800	13.2	1,063	33,853	57,116	23.9
District 6	327,388	89.3	72.8	181,500	4.6	764	27,206	53,708	20.4
District 7	327,518	86.8	71.3	183,300	14.0	853	31,696	57,852	26.2
District 8	302,807	88.6	70.9	160,300	5.4	752	31,919	56,477	25.2
District 9	316,204	82.7	46.3	99,500	1.8	878	22,438	40,491	13.6
TEXAS	10,933,375	88.0	62.0	172,200	7.3	987	29,525	59,206	27.2
District 1	308,558	81.7	67.4	133,600	4.3	798	24,705	49,086	18.6
District 2	307,492	91.7	63.5	227,400	11.3	1,164	40,961	77,519	38.5
District 3	330,211	93.3	62.6	334,400	15.2	1,342	44,334	95,235	47.6
District 4	311,327	84.8	71.1	148,000	4.1	784	27,601	56,062	24.1
District 5	295,080	87.6	65.7	149,700	5.4	902	24,567	52,375	19.9
District 6	291,545	90.8	66.6	177,900	2.6	1,047	29,434	66,965	29.0
District 7	333,055	87.9	50.4	274,100	27.8	1,212	45,205	73,130	36.2
District 8	331,308	86.8	71.0	214,000	10.3	1,082	34,483	70,846	34.0
District 9	294,936	90.3	47.3	137,400	2.2	955	23,004	48,743	18.1
District 10	332,201	87.3	67.5	238,000	13.0	1,186	35,721	75,517	36.4
District 11	335,468	79.6	69.1	146,800	4.2	887	28,494	55,237	23.6
District 12	319,612	90.9	62.5	192,800	6.2	1,072	33,100	67,703	31.2
District 13	308,756	84.1	67.6	113,400	2.7	784	25,675	50,557	19.4
District 14	322,121	84.1	66.3	160,600	4.6	948	30,414	61,516	29.2
District 15	264,264	87.3	67.0	103,700	2.1	733	18,434	42,474	17.8
District 16	267,080	90.7	60.2	127,400	1.5	836	22,120	45,563	17.6
District 17	327,426	86.6	56.4	168,900	3.9	956	26,885	51,036	21.7
District 18	311,055	87.3	48.1	135,600	6.1	895	24,001	45,584	18.9
District 19	304,337	84.3	61.3	109,700	2.0	836	24,459	48,590	20.2
District 20	278,511	91.2	55.3	147,900	1.0	934	22,716	51,086	19.5
District 21	358,577	87.9	60.0	285,600	16.7	1,137	40,609	71,486	34.7
District 22	309,113	92.4	73.7	266,100	8.5	1,241	38,158	94,048	47.9
District 23	266,445	86.3	71.1	117,700	5.0	833	23,457	50,338	22.1
District 24	327,143	94.2	48.3	281,700	16.8	1,160	40,651	74,127	36.3
District 25	315,247	85.5	70.3	248,600	19.8	1,100	36,460	72,046	35.9

1. Specified owner-occupied units.   2. Specified renter-occupied units.

Table E. Congressional Districts 116th Congress — Poverty, Labor Force, Employment, and Social Security

STATE District	Poverty, 2017			Civilian labor force, 2016			Civilian employment,[2] 2017				Persons under 65 years of age with no health insurance, 2017 (percent)	Social Security beneficiaries, December 2018		Supplemental Security Income recipients, December 2018
	Persons below poverty level (percent)	Families below poverty level (percent)	Percent of households receiving food stamps in past 12 months	Total	Unemployment Total	Rate[1]	Total	Management, business, science, and arts occupations	Service, sales, and office	Construction and production		Number	Rate[3]	
	49	50	51	52	53	54	55	56	57	58	59	60	61	62
OREGON — Cont'd														
District 3	14.3	10.2	15.6	480,792	22,491	4.7	458,301	43.2	38.7	18.1	8.0	132,159	156.9	20,722
District 4	16.5	10.4	18.5	381,606	25,008	6.6	356,598	35.3	42.1	22.6	7.8	211,180	262.8	21,671
District 5	12.9	8.7	14.7	405,006	17,521	4.3	387,485	35.6	41.4	23.1	8.6	178,081	214.1	15,344
PENNSYLVANIA	12.5	8.1	12.9	6,518,369	345,226	5.3	6,173,143	38.6	39.9	21.5	6.6	2,825,178	220.6	355,814
District 1	23.9	18.2	23.2	355,180	31,448	8.9	323,732	39.7	42.5	17.8	8.3	151,432	207.9	8,234
District 2	26.0	16.1	20.3	332,849	27,645	8.3	305,204	47.2	40.9	11.8	6.2	115,445	159.0	47,406
District 3	13.2	8.9	15.7	337,858	19,198	5.7	318,660	33.2	41.2	25.7	6.2	124,686	180.4	49,742
District 4	9.9	6.2	10.5	380,229	17,626	4.6	362,603	36.4	40.2	23.4	6.9	142,893	195.8	7,383
District 5	14.9	8.7	13.3	329,899	18,426	5.6	311,473	34.7	40.1	25.2	6.0	134,158	192.7	20,980
District 6	7.2	4.6	6.2	398,174	18,412	4.6	379,762	45.9	37.5	16.6	4.7	135,139	185.5	13,229
District 7	5.1	2.8	5.1	386,277	14,855	3.8	371,422	48.0	36.0	16.1	6.4	161,213	222.1	17,601
District 8	5.9	3.3	4.9	397,557	14,667	3.7	382,890	44.3	37.9	17.8	4.7	173,635	243.2	19,635
District 9	13.4	9.2	16.7	323,690	18,168	5.6	305,522	28.8	42.3	28.9	6.9	173,611	252.5	13,251
District 10	11.3	7.2	11.9	328,426	14,392	4.4	314,034	30.8	40.5	28.7	8.6	155,716	224.2	16,446
District 11	10.4	6.9	10.5	358,878	14,968	4.2	343,910	33.0	40.7	26.3	6.5	156,653	223.5	11,259
District 12	8.9	6.1	11.1	349,851	17,265	4.9	332,586	42.6	37.8	19.6	3.4	164,259	238.3	14,498
District 13	14.3	10.2	13.8	382,832	24,022	6.3	358,810	42.6	39.6	17.8	7.8	178,842	245.5	16,493
District 14	16.7	11.4	18.2	370,720	22,082	6.0	348,638	42.4	42.2	15.4	6.0	185,015	269.3	21,157
District 15	11.1	7.8	11.1	379,994	19,784	5.2	360,210	35.9	40.5	23.6	7.3	181,566	247.1	18,336
District 16	12.4	8.4	13.3	380,972	18,158	4.8	362,814	32.8	39.7	27.5	12.1	173,295	236.8	22,626
District 17	13.1	9.6	16.3	351,817	20,323	5.8	331,494	31.3	41.4	27.3	6.0	166,203	238.3	13,356
District 18	7.6	5.1	9.0	373,166	13,787	3.7	359,379	42.2	38.4	19.3	3.5	151,417	212.2	24,182
RHODE ISLAND	11.6	7.9	15.4	570,665	32,751	5.7	537,914	38.4	43.0	18.6	5.5	225,493	212.8	32,936
District 1	13.2	9.2	17.8	286,473	16,319	5.7	270,154	36.8	43.7	19.5	6.5	110,757	205.4	18,405
District 2	10.0	6.6	13.0	284,192	16,432	5.8	267,760	40.1	42.3	17.7	4.3	114,736	220.5	14,531
SOUTH CAROLINA	15.4	11.3	12.3	2,412,222	139,747	5.8	2,272,475	34.0	42.1	24.0	13.2	1,143,297	227.6	115,194
District 1	8.8	5.1	5.9	394,785	15,866	4.0	378,919	40.9	41.3	17.9	12.0	160,511	205.2	8,853
District 2	13.0	10.0	10.0	351,984	20,347	5.8	331,637	38.3	40.7	21.0	11.8	145,315	203.7	11,797
District 3	16.7	13.3	13.1	315,552	17,171	5.4	298,381	31.3	39.6	29.2	13.2	171,673	249.8	14,936
District 4	12.9	9.1	10.6	371,380	16,866	4.5	354,514	36.6	39.3	24.0	12.5	153,720	210.0	15,307
District 5	14.9	10.9	12.2	340,390	22,125	6.5	318,265	32.0	40.3	27.7	11.4	163,268	227.2	17,559
District 6	23.8	17.0	19.4	313,350	23,210	7.4	290,140	26.3	47.4	26.3	16.1	145,970	217.6	25,644
District 7	19.2	15.1	15.8	324,781	24,162	7.4	300,619	29.5	46.9	23.6	15.7	202,840	281.7	21,098
SOUTH DAKOTA	13.0	8.4	8.9	458,678	16,208	3.5	442,470	35.0	41.4	23.6	10.7	178,999	205.8	14,642
At Large	13.0	8.4	8.9	458,678	16,208	3.5	442,470	35.0	41.4	23.6	10.7	178,999	205.8	14,642
TENNESSEE	15.0	10.9	13.5	3,292,377	162,289	4.9	3,130,088	34.9	40.8	24.3	11.2	1,452,552	216.3	176,395
District 1	16.6	12.1	15.7	328,561	18,158	5.5	310,403	30.7	43.5	25.8	12.5	202,148	282.8	22,331
District 2	14.2	9.8	11.8	378,544	16,979	4.5	361,565	38.0	42.2	19.8	9.8	171,953	230.0	18,075
District 3	14.9	11.6	14.6	341,391	16,344	4.8	325,047	33.7	39.9	26.4	11.4	178,095	242.9	21,174
District 4	13.8	10.5	11.9	396,555	16,849	4.2	379,706	31.6	38.4	29.9	11.1	161,687	206.8	17,225
District 5	14.3	10.6	10.2	443,180	17,638	4.0	425,542	41.3	39.2	19.5	13.8	117,884	152.3	16,390
District 6	12.8	9.0	11.3	373,004	15,531	4.2	357,473	32.7	40.8	26.4	9.8	184,650	238.9	16,352
District 7	11.5	7.9	11.3	356,498	17,196	4.8	339,302	36.8	39.3	24.0	9.6	157,951	203.0	15,442
District 8	13.3	10.0	13.7	334,082	15,743	4.7	318,339	38.2	40.0	21.8	8.1	160,819	224.6	17,997
District 9	24.0	19.2	21.8	340,562	27,851	8.2	312,711	28.8	44.9	26.3	14.6	117,365	168.4	31,409
TEXAS	14.7	11.3	12.0	13,918,308	716,417	5.1	13,201,891	36.4	41.0	22.6	19.4	4,224,159	149.2	649,912
District 1	18.3	12.8	14.3	318,865	19,336	6.1	299,529	31.0	41.8	27.2	20.9	153,683	214.2	21,332
District 2	10.3	7.9	5.9	421,537	17,804	4.2	403,733	44.4	37.1	18.5	16.6	99,434	128.8	13,160
District 3	6.3	4.7	2.5	475,823	17,313	3.6	458,510	54.4	35.6	9.9	11.5	98,698	113.3	7,561
District 4	13.5	9.6	12.1	350,393	17,246	4.9	333,147	33.0	40.3	26.7	17.7	158,993	212.8	19,471
District 5	13.6	11.0	12.6	356,180	16,779	4.7	339,401	29.0	42.2	28.8	22.6	129,314	168.0	16,477
District 6	10.1	7.7	7.6	411,581	16,014	3.9	395,567	36.8	42.0	21.2	17.1	113,734	143.6	12,322
District 7	13.0	9.7	7.5	417,322	21,899	5.2	395,423	48.5	36.1	15.4	16.7	87,859	109.8	10,822
District 8	10.6	7.5	7.7	408,362	20,917	5.1	387,445	39.1	39.2	21.6	16.7	135,456	156.9	12,941
District 9	17.8	15.1	18.9	403,449	27,174	6.7	376,275	29.4	45.1	25.5	25.8	91,500	115.9	26,033
District 10	7.9	5.4	7.7	446,083	19,557	4.4	426,526	44.9	37.8	17.4	14.9	117,877	139.3	12,127
District 11	12.5	9.5	9.5	357,770	15,116	4.2	342,654	31.0	40.6	28.5	21.4	143,909	189.5	15,624
District 12	9.6	6.8	8.6	416,447	19,004	4.6	397,443	39.1	40.4	20.5	16.9	124,031	153.8	13,329
District 13	14.0	11.0	11.6	339,244	14,686	4.3	324,558	28.6	42.0	29.4	20.2	131,435	184.2	13,466
District 14	13.8	10.7	14.4	353,995	18,872	5.3	335,123	34.4	39.8	25.8	17.4	129,948	169.9	18,340
District 15	25.7	21.8	25.7	340,843	20,958	6.1	319,885	28.2	48.1	23.7	28.4	108,563	137.3	29,471
District 16	20.3	16.8	18.2	336,271	21,242	6.3	315,029	32.5	47.3	20.1	21.1	117,542	158.3	26,049
District 17	18.3	12.8	12.1	386,648	17,580	4.5	369,068	38.1	40.7	21.2	14.8	116,167	150.6	16,484
District 18	22.4	19.4	21.2	387,645	27,586	7.1	360,059	29.3	43.2	27.6	25.8	95,779	119.7	27,393
District 19	17.0	11.8	13.0	349,121	17,178	4.9	331,943	32.4	43.1	24.5	18.4	124,544	169.6	16,633
District 20	17.6	14.1	13.2	403,225	22,878	5.7	380,347	33.2	45.7	21.1	18.6	115,842	143.7	21,790
District 21	10.3	6.0	4.5	434,862	14,958	3.4	419,904	46.0	40.0	14.0	13.8	146,747	181.3	11,803
District 22	8.1	6.5	6.2	452,362	26,024	5.8	426,338	52.2	33.7	14.1	11.8	104,661	116.7	11,506
District 23	17.1	15.1	16.1	338,923	17,993	5.3	320,930	29.1	43.9	26.9	21.4	130,398	169.5	22,504
District 24	7.1	5.1	4.9	464,611	17,828	3.8	446,783	46.1	38.8	15.1	15.5	91,362	114.2	7,281
District 25	10.6	6.9	6.7	376,421	16,348	4.3	360,073	45.4	34.1	20.5	11.8	133,821	169.4	10,965

1. Percent of civilian labor force.   2. Persons 16 years old and over.   3. Per 1,000 resident population estimated in the 2017 American Community Survey.

Table E. Congressional Districts 116th Congress — **Agriculture**

STATE District	Agriculture 2017									
	Land in farms				Value of products sold				Government payments	
	Number of farms	Acres	Average size of farm (acres)	Harvested cropland (acres)	Total ($1,000)	Average per farm (dollars)	Percent from crops	Percent from livestock and poultry products	Total ($1,000)	Average per farm receiving payments (dollars)
	63	64	65	66	67	68	69	70	71	72
OREGON — Cont'd										
District 3	2,807	90,555	32	31,975	239,212	85,220	88.0	12.0	146	3,650
District 4	9,064	1,280,043	141	388,197	628,301	69,318	63.0	37.0	3,910	9,799
District 5	6,690	580,067	87	335,079	1,153,738	172,457	74.2	25.8	3,294	10,073
PENNSYLVANIA	53,157	7,278,668	137	3,931,996	7,758,885	145,962	35.8	64.2	74,182	6,823
District 1	866	78,687	91	52,691	84,647	97,745	75.2	24.8	637	7,583
District 2	22	68	3	23	133	6,045	85.7	15.0	D	D
District 3	21	216	10	94	194	9,238	77.8	21.6	D	D
District 4	596	37,975	64	20,987	32,564	54,638	62.9	37.1	233	5,825
District 5	61	2,385	39	668	9,494	155,639	97.8	2.3	D	D
District 6	1,814	162,693	90	103,764	727,609	401,107	79.2	20.8	1,908	10,258
District 7	942	142,994	152	110,081	118,328	125,614	74.0	26.0	2,367	15,173
District 8	1,236	193,249	156	64,158	60,087	48,614	49.4	50.6	588	3,973
District 9	5,166	636,513	123	426,263	1,214,767	235,147	36.4	63.6	9,756	6,668
District 10	1,551	189,487	122	134,814	211,943	136,649	46.4	53.6	2,500	8,251
District 11	6,578	576,434	88	427,814	1,689,756	256,880	18.6	81.4	8,468	9,645
District 12	10,546	1,728,148	164	820,450	1,414,932	134,168	23.0	77.0	19,379	6,302
District 13	8,124	1,343,863	165	780,880	1,379,471	169,802	27.3	72.7	13,151	7,331
District 14	4,142	528,568	128	205,558	140,027	33,807	55.3	44.7	2,522	5,447
District 15	5,867	906,075	154	398,379	315,753	53,818	48.5	51.5	8,177	6,495
District 16	4,602	665,252	145	350,735	320,968	69,745	56.2	43.8	4,262	4,491
District 17	885	75,415	85	31,530	35,258	39,840	70.1	29.9	D	D
District 18	138	10,646	77	3,107	2,953	21,399	89.5	10.5	D	D
RHODE ISLAND	1,043	56,864	55	14,302	57,998	55,607	70.5	29.5	1,037	14,205
District 1	322	14,540	45	5,779	22,877	71,047	58.4	41.6	174	10,235
District 2	721	42,324	59	8,523	35,122	48,713	78.4	21.6	862	15,393
SOUTH CAROLINA	24,791	4,744,913	191	1,599,887	3,008,739	121,364	36.4	63.6	55,192	10,400
District 1	616	76,208	124	11,039	35,526	57,672	91.0	9.0	166	3,689
District 2	3,388	457,224	135	143,344	497,742	146,913	31.5	68.5	6,844	14,562
District 3	6,839	881,416	129	194,971	658,491	96,285	12.2	87.8	6,681	5,971
District 4	1,792	108,346	60	24,522	33,573	18,735	71.8	28.2	518	4,709
District 5	4,851	840,194	173	230,826	627,665	129,389	27.0	73.0	7,124	7,916
District 6	4,388	1,527,163	348	566,689	597,829	136,242	63.7	36.3	23,870	14,564
District 7	2,917	854,362	293	428,496	557,913	191,263	45.2	54.8	9,989	9,755
SOUTH DAKOTA	29,968	43,243,742	1,443	16,371,543	9,721,523	324,397	53.1	46.9	419,508	19,416
At Large	29,968	43,243,742	1,443	16,371,543	9,721,522	324,397	53.1	46.9	419,508	19,416
TENNESSEE	69,983	10,874,238	155	4,566,352	3,798,934	54,284	57.4	42.6	115,945	6,254
District 1	10,091	895,703	89	279,460	232,281	23,019	30.1	69.9	5,109	3,355
District 2	5,504	500,612	91	153,466	180,981	32,882	60.2	39.8	5,341	3,980
District 3	5,878	609,260	104	179,821	259,736	44,188	14.5	85.5	5,365	4,341
District 4	11,384	1,622,906	143	534,915	727,550	63,910	36.7	63.3	12,949	4,982
District 5	2,099	234,406	112	64,699	43,218	20,590	70.3	29.7	866	2,656
District 6	14,561	1,977,518	136	640,720	655,337	45,006	50.9	49.1	15,680	3,678
District 7	13,036	2,353,365	181	747,529	469,912	36,047	58.8	41.2	24,773	6,542
District 8	7,246	2,648,961	366	1,949,573	1,217,343	168,002	86.0	14.0	45,431	13,218
District 9	184	31,507	171	16,169	12,575	68,342	96.9	3.1	433	16,654
TEXAS	248,416	127,036,184	511	17,595,330	24,924,041	100,332	27.7	72.3	749,231	20,984
District 1	11,811	1,756,575	149	240,554	1,342,954	113,704	5.0	95.0	1,334	7,058
District 2	213	19,714	93	3,901	8,856	41,577	87.4	12.6	186	14,308
District 3	1,362	137,649	101	52,404	46,263	33,967	32.2	67.8	1,166	18,219
District 4	23,721	4,211,086	178	1,078,170	1,306,516	55,078	18.2	81.8	39,599	10,272
District 5	12,604	1,947,480	155	361,393	454,125	36,030	35.1	64.9	2,243	11,049
District 6	5,347	1,020,043	191	307,085	143,690	26,873	58.3	41.7	8,011	13,026
District 7	59	27,971	474	540	687	11,644	83.7	16.3	D	D
District 8	9,409	1,692,702	180	199,691	341,363	36,280	40.0	60.0	1,033	8,134
District 9	98	D	0	1,267	1,442	14,714	57.5	42.6	35	5,833
District 10	14,829	2,529,360	171	363,629	371,304	25,039	45.5	54.5	16,927	19,569
District 11	20,886	15,547,323	744	1,502,355	1,239,636	59,352	34.9	65.1	55,547	14,203
District 12	5,962	762,005	128	76,555	85,465	14,335	19.5	80.5	513	5,830
District 13	19,229	22,289,498	1,159	3,647,588	8,790,318	457,139	14.9	85.1	214,954	29,277
District 14	3,586	835,042	233	106,179	103,019	28,728	50.1	49.9	15,268	44,000
District 15	8,984	3,792,508	422	387,448	372,617	41,476	60.5	39.5	10,272	11,834
District 16	358	83,720	234	12,446	20,176	56,358	96.8	3.2	D	D
District 17	15,795	3,896,682	247	774,561	1,056,334	66,878	20.4	79.6	16,618	14,772
District 18	118	D	D	1,051	5,875	49,788	51.6	48.4	D	D
District 19	14,252	15,108,704	1,060	4,440,380	4,845,855	340,012	34.6	65.4	209,918	25,706
District 20	170	13,030	77	1,924	1,380	8,118	57.5	42.5	8	2,000
District 21	8,076	2,999,190	371	62,516	96,177	11,909	24.4	75.6	3,402	7,162
District 22	1,787	342,738	192	119,119	103,549	57,946	80.1	19.9	6,691	25,249
District 23	9,676	27,813,527	2,874	447,435	831,884	85,974	45.2	54.8	19,770	17,875
District 24	165	32,948	200	3,550	2,799	16,964	57.9	42.1	45	5,000
District 25	14,207	3,944,915	278	572,672	463,442	32,621	28.1	71.9	16,336	12,615

Table E. Congressional Districts 116th Congress — **Nonfarm Employment and Payroll**

STATE District	Number of establishments	Private nonfarm employment and payroll, 2016 Employment Total	Percent by selected industries Manufacturing	Construction	Wholesale trade	Retail trade	Health care and social assistance	Finance and Insurance	Real estate and rental and leasing	Professional, scientific, and technical services	Information	Annual payroll Total (mil dol)	Average per employee (dollars)
	73	74	75	76	77	78	79	80	81	82	83	84	85
OREGON — Cont'd													
District 3	26,229	398,780	7.5	5.1	5.5	10.4	15.8	5.0	2.0	7.5	2.6	20,189	50,627
District 4	19,514	243,054	12.8	5.0	3.7	15.9	19.0	3.3	1.6	3.9	2.3	9,714	39,968
District 5	21,740	270,511	11.6	6.9	5.1	15.1	16.7	3.5	1.8	4.7	1.7	11,620	42,955
PENNSYLVANIA	301,484	5,354,964	10.1	4.4	4.6	12.5	18.8	5.1	1.2	6.1	2.1	261,082	48,755
District 1	14,163	291,464	4.7	3.3	3.6	9.5	18.8	4.6	1.8	4.0	1.8	14,390	49,370
District 2	14,463	350,390	0.8	1.1	1.1	5.9	27.2	7.2	1.8	11.2	3.6	23,295	66,484
District 3	16,456	266,816	15.3	4.0	3.8	13.4	22.2	3.8	1.0	4.5	1.5	10,197	38,216
District 4	15,849	298,703	13.5	5.0	4.7	13.0	16.3	4.6	1.1	5.5	1.4	13,184	44,136
District 5	15,674	218,927	20.4	3.7	2.5	16.9	18.0	2.5	1.1	3.1	1.5	7,955	36,335
District 6	20,200	361,421	8.7	3.8	5.7	13.5	15.0	8.8	1.2	8.1	3.2	23,007	63,656
District 7	18,227	306,043	8.2	6.4	4.2	10.4	16.1	7.6	1.5	8.8	3.7	18,638	60,901
District 8	21,281	285,698	12.1	6.5	7.4	14.6	16.8	3.6	1.3	6.6	2.0	13,204	46,217
District 9	14,386	209,581	13.6	4.6	3.9	15.8	20.1	2.6	0.7	3.2	1.3	7,568	36,109
District 10	15,717	216,281	16.6	4.3	3.2	17.3	19.4	3.0	1.0	2.7	1.1	7,757	35,867
District 11	14,727	258,837	12.1	3.2	4.3	12.8	18.7	4.9	0.8	4.8	1.8	10,823	41,815
District 12	16,801	244,469	10.9	5.5	3.7	15.1	19.4	3.4	1.1	5.5	2.0	10,567	43,222
District 13	17,870	317,733	6.4	4.6	7.0	15.4	21.8	4.7	1.5	7.1	2.4	17,723	55,778
District 14	19,206	448,098	4.7	4.0	3.1	8.4	19.3	9.0	1.3	9.3	2.7	24,667	55,048
District 15	16,002	317,683	13.3	3.6	6.6	12.6	18.9	3.3	1.0	3.5	1.4	15,506	48,810
District 16	15,781	292,980	15.5	7.9	5.8	12.4	18.1	3.2	2.0	4.9	1.2	12,916	44,085
District 17	14,996	261,532	12.0	2.9	4.5	14.2	20.6	3.8	0.7	2.9	2.3	9,889	37,812
District 18	18,740	312,459	7.5	7.3	5.7	13.9	16.2	3.0	1.2	5.5	1.3	14,347	45,917
RHODE ISLAND	28,685	435,148	9.2	4.1	4.7	11.3	20.4	6.3	1.2	5.5	1.6	20,151	46,308
District 1	13,558	207,536	9.5	4.3	4.4	9.7	19.9	6.0	1.2	5.2	1.3	9,460	45,584
District 2	14,837	222,144	9.2	4.1	4.8	13.0	21.2	6.3	1.3	5.4	1.9	10,389	46,766
SOUTH CAROLINA	105,959	1,716,496	13.3	4.7	4.3	14.3	13.4	4.1	1.5	5.2	2.1	69,051	40,228
District 1	19,171	232,495	3.8	5.1	2.2	18.6	13.4	3.3	2.3	6.3	3.2	8,949	38,489
District 2	13,298	205,060	10.4	5.3	4.4	17.4	13.2	3.1	1.3	4.4	1.9	7,797	38,023
District 3	11,384	176,201	26.1	4.4	3.7	15.3	13.3	2.0	0.8	2.9	0.8	6,500	36,888
District 4	17,984	333,855	15.3	4.1	5.6	11.8	12.8	3.3	1.2	6.2	2.7	14,733	44,129
District 5	11,987	190,182	20.1	5.0	4.4	14.9	11.4	4.8	0.9	4.4	1.6	7,546	39,680
District 6	15,201	287,278	13.2	5.2	5.8	10.2	17.3	7.0	1.7	6.1	2.3	12,853	44,740
District 7	16,335	228,453	11.0	4.6	3.0	18.4	15.2	3.8	2.7	3.3	1.5	7,747	33,912
SOUTH DAKOTA	26,743	357,950	12.4	5.7	5.3	15.2	18.8	7.3	1.2	3.4	2.0	14,183	39,623
At Large	26,743	357,950	12.4	5.7	5.3	15.2	18.8	7.3	1.2	3.4	2.0	14,183	39,623
TENNESSEE	135,352	2,592,600	12.3	4.3	4.5	12.7	15.9	4.7	1.3	4.5	1.9	114,896	44,317
District 1	13,755	239,309	18.0	3.9	2.5	16.6	17.3	3.3	1.4	2.5	1.5	9,004	37,624
District 2	15,973	296,881	8.4	4.8	5.4	14.2	15.8	4.8	1.4	5.0	2.0	12,411	41,805
District 3	14,266	279,250	18.5	4.3	2.7	12.2	14.6	5.4	0.9	6.4	1.5	11,940	42,758
District 4	13,058	240,135	23.0	5.0	4.8	14.4	11.9	4.1	1.1	2.2	1.3	9,787	40,755
District 5	20,831	459,060	5.2	4.5	4.7	9.8	19.0	6.2	1.7	5.9	2.9	24,144	52,594
District 6	13,564	199,866	19.8	4.9	4.0	15.3	14.7	3.2	1.2	3.7	1.2	7,416	37,107
District 7	15,051	231,822	10.9	4.2	2.6	14.5	16.4	6.9	1.2	5.5	2.8	10,870	46,890
District 8	14,857	247,418	13.4	4.1	4.3	13.5	20.3	4.8	1.4	3.9	1.4	10,782	43,580
District 9	13,341	325,100	6.9	3.8	7.8	11.1	14.4	2.7	1.6	3.4	1.7	16,034	49,320
TEXAS	579,168	10,429,924	7.4	6.5	5.0	12.5	14.5	5.1	1.8	6.8	2.3	526,783	50,507
District 1	16,759	254,538	13.0	5.3	3.9	14.6	19.4	4.1	1.4	4.4	1.5	10,018	39,358
District 2	20,845	373,458	9.3	9.4	7.6	12.0	10.4	4.3	1.9	5.9	1.4	20,510	54,919
District 3	21,388	381,841	4.2	4.0	4.4	12.9	12.7	13.4	1.8	10.2	4.5	23,714	62,103
District 4	13,784	195,143	18.9	5.0	3.5	16.7	19.2	3.5	1.1	3.2	1.2	7,130	36,540
District 5	12,386	178,337	12.5	9.7	5.1	16.9	15.0	2.2	2.0	3.2	1.0	6,505	36,477
District 6	13,866	228,866	12.6	5.8	5.8	15.1	13.6	4.9	1.6	3.5	1.5	9,183	40,123
District 7	25,319	460,210	2.1	6.4	3.8	11.1	11.2	6.4	2.6	11.6	2.7	33,498	72,789
District 8	14,268	191,643	6.6	7.0	4.3	16.3	12.8	3.5	1.7	6.4	1.1	10,166	53,049
District 9	13,047	317,159	4.9	4.5	5.4	8.0	31.4	2.2	1.6	8.4	1.4	18,125	57,147
District 10	19,783	297,626	7.4	7.5	5.2	16.3	11.8	3.9	1.7	8.8	3.6	14,526	48,807
District 11	18,745	252,162	6.5	7.8	6.1	14.9	13.5	3.1	2.2	3.3	1.4	11,917	47,259
District 12	17,409	309,540	12.1	5.3	3.8	12.6	15.0	5.8	1.4	5.3	1.5	16,080	51,947
District 13	16,503	218,135	13.4	6.2	5.6	15.4	16.4	4.5	1.3	3.1	1.4	8,752	40,120
District 14	13,934	236,433	12.7	10.7	3.1	15.0	15.6	3.4	2.2	4.7	0.9	11,440	48,387
District 15	11,812	185,875	6.6	3.5	4.7	18.2	26.2	3.4	1.3	3.3	1.7	5,704	30,690
District 16	13,534	223,674	5.8	4.4	4.3	16.7	19.4	2.9	1.8	4.8	3.4	7,161	32,018
District 17	14,489	262,546	11.5	7.2	4.4	12.4	14.5	4.5	1.7	7.9	1.8	11,317	43,105
District 18	16,824	412,362	7.9	6.0	10.2	5.9	6.9	4.0	2.0	9.6	2.6	32,836	79,629
District 19	16,665	234,929	6.2	5.9	5.7	15.4	19.7	4.5	1.5	3.2	2.1	8,612	36,658
District 20	11,717	257,592	3.3	3.2	2.2	16.1	15.4	13.5	1.8	7.4	1.9	10,903	42,328
District 21	26,331	429,437	2.5	6.2	3.5	10.6	16.5	7.1	2.3	10.8	3.7	22,291	51,909
District 22	15,678	206,550	5.7	5.2	3.4	19.9	17.5	3.3	1.4	5.8	1.8	8,471	41,014
District 23	11,141	177,919	5.6	15.9	3.0	15.8	13.9	4.0	1.4	2.5	0.9	6,926	38,929
District 24	27,971	690,792	4.0	5.3	6.9	7.6	7.4	8.1	2.3	10.8	5.2	43,696	63,255
District 25	18087	227,290	6.1	6.1	4.3	13.7	16.7	4.3	2.5	7.9	3.6	11,604	51,052

Table E. Congressional Districts 116th Congress — **Land Area and Population Characteristics**

STATE District	Representative, 116th Congress	Land area,[1] 2018 (sq mi)	Total persons	Per square mile	Race alone (percent)				Some other race (percent)	Two or more races (percent)	Hispanic or Latino[2] (percent)	Non-Hispanic White alone (percent)	Percent female	Percent foreign-born	Percent born in state of residence
					White	Black	American Indian, Alaska Native	Asian and Pacific Islander							
		1	2	3	4	5	6	7	8	9	10	11	12	13	14
TEXAS — Cont'd															
District 26	Michael C. Burgess (R)	907.3	879,237	969.1	77.7	7.9	0.4	7.9	2.7	3.5	17.8	63.7	50.7	13.5	49.0
District 27	Michael Cloud (R)	9,120.6	740,277	81.2	85.9	5.3	0.4	1.6	5.0	1.8	53.0	39.0	50.7	8.0	75.4
District 28	Henry Cuellar (D)	9,378.9	753,502	80.3	87.2	4.7	0.2	1.6	4.4	1.9	77.3	15.7	51.2	22.1	63.5
District 29	Sylvia R. Garcia (D)	187.1	761,833	4,072.1	78.3	11.9	0.4	1.4	6.5	1.4	77.5	9.1	49.2	32.1	58.8
District 30	Eddie Bernice Johnson (D)	356.3	774,443	2,173.4	47.2	43.1	0.2	2.5	4.9	2.1	38.2	14.9	51.8	16.9	64.5
District 31	John R. Carter (R)	2,154.2	853,799	396.3	74.9	11.5	0.4	5.4	3.1	4.7	24.7	55.5	50.6	10.8	49.5
District 32	Colin Z. Allred (D)	186.1	763,452	4,102.3	68.1	14.8	0.3	8.4	5.1	3.3	25.5	48.6	50.6	22.2	50.1
District 33	Marc A. Veasey (D)	212.0	753,565	3,554.4	64.5	15.1	0.5	2.1	16.3	1.5	69.3	12.8	49.4	33.3	54.6
District 34	Filemon Vela (D)	8,190.8	727,595	88.8	91.8	1.1	0.3	0.6	4.9	1.3	85.0	13.0	50.1	18.9	70.5
District 35	Lloyd Doggett (D)	593.8	830,041	1,397.8	69.4	10.3	0.6	2.0	14.3	3.4	60.1	26.2	49.5	14.7	64.9
District 36	Brian Babin (R)	7,125.8	742,474	104.2	83.1	9.6	0.7	2.0	3.1	1.5	24.8	62.1	50.2	10.1	68.5
UTAH		82,195.3	3,101,833	37.7	85.7	1.2	1.1	3.3	5.8	3.0	14.0	78.3	49.6	8.7	61.9
District 1	Rob Bishop (R)	19,557.0	763,612	39.0	89.8	1.0	1.0	1.8	3.0	3.3	12.6	81.5	49.5	5.8	64.7
District 2	Chris Stewart (R)	40,015.0	765,809	19.1	82.3	1.2	1.0	3.8	8.6	3.0	15.7	76.3	49.6	9.5	59.3
District 3	John R. Curtis (R)	20,073.6	767,012	38.2	91.1	0.5	1.3	2.7	2.2	2.1	10.8	83.0	49.9	7.5	60.9
District 4	Ben McAdams (D)	2,549.6	805,400	315.9	79.7	2.0	0.9	4.8	9.1	3.4	16.8	72.7	49.4	11.7	62.6
VERMONT		9,217.6	623,657	67.7	94.2	1.3	0.4	1.8	0.2	2.1	1.9	92.8	50.6	4.5	51.6
At Large	Peter Welch (D)	9,217.6	623,657	67.7	94.2	1.3	0.4	1.8	0.2	2.1	1.9	92.8	50.6	4.5	51.6
VIRGINIA		39,480.6	8,470,020	214.5	67.5	19.2	0.3	6.5	2.6	3.9	9.3	61.7	50.8	12.5	49.2
District 1	Robert J. Wittman (R)	4,211.8	805,159	191.2	72.2	16.4	0.4	3.4	3.4	4.2	10.2	66.2	50.4	9.0	48.8
District 2	Elaine G. Luria (D)	1,103.8	741,514	671.8	66.9	19.6	0.3	5.8	2.3	5.2	8.3	62.3	49.6	8.5	42.8
District 3	Robert C. "Bobby" Scott (D)	625.2	739,840	1,183.4	44.8	46.3	0.4	2.4	1.8	4.3	6.5	41.3	52.0	5.4	56.2
District 4	A. Donald McEachin (D)	3,641.9	771,899	212.0	51.9	41.0	0.2	1.9	1.3	3.6	5.7	48.1	51.7	5.0	62.1
District 5	Denver Riggleman (R)	10,030.7	727,064	72.5	76.1	18.4	0.3	1.6	0.5	3.1	3.6	73.1	51.3	4.8	63.5
District 6	Ben Cline (R)	5,928.5	752,763	127.0	82.3	11.4	0.4	2.1	0.8	3.0	5.5	78.9	51.5	5.6	63.0
District 7	Abigail Davis Spanberger (D)	3,117.9	790,084	253.4	69.8	18.5	0.3	5.2	2.3	3.7	7.3	65.5	51.2	9.1	55.7
District 8	Donald S. Beyer, Jr. (D)	149.3	801,609	5,370.7	62.7	14.9	0.3	11.0	6.3	4.8	19.4	51.3	50.3	30.1	24.1
District 9	Morgan Griffith (R)	9,115.1	711,755	78.1	90.8	5.3	0.3	1.4	0.5	1.7	2.3	89.2	50.4	2.4	64.2
District 10	Jennifer Wexton (D)	1,371.2	850,118	620.0	68.4	7.6	0.3	15.9	3.3	4.5	14.3	58.7	50.1	22.6	36.3
District 11	Gerald E. Connolly (D)	185.2	778,215	4,202.6	57.7	13.2	0.4	18.5	5.5	4.7	17.4	47.2	50.8	31.9	29.1
WASHINGTON		66,452.7	7,405,743	111.4	75.4	3.7	1.3	9.2	4.6	5.9	12.7	68.6	50.1	14.3	46.9
District 1	Suzan K. DelBene (D)	6,185.3	744,868	120.4	77.3	1.4	1.3	11.9	2.9	5.4	8.8	72.4	50.1	17.5	47.8
District 2	Rick Larsen (D)	1,015.4	745,184	733.9	76.5	3.2	1.0	8.9	3.6	6.9	11.2	70.8	50.1	14.4	48.2
District 3	Jaime Herrera Beutler (R)	9,116.1	731,931	80.3	86.7	1.6	0.7	4.2	1.8	5.0	9.7	80.1	50.5	8.4	40.7
District 4	Dan Newsome (R)	19,246.4	724,053	37.6	74.9	1.0	3.2	1.9	15.4	3.7	39.2	53.5	49.5	16.3	56.2
District 5	Cathy McMorris Rodgers (R)	15,473.4	716,859	46.3	87.3	1.4	1.8	2.8	1.7	5.0	6.8	83.3	50.3	5.9	53.3
District 6	Derek Kilmer (D)	6,902.3	713,112	103.3	81.4	3.4	2.0	5.0	2.0	6.2	7.7	76.6	49.7	7.2	48.9
District 7	Pramila Jayapal (D)	144.0	768,408	5,337.6	72.9	4.2	0.4	13.1	3.2	6.3	7.7	69.1	50.6	16.7	39.6
District 8	Kim Schrier (D)	7,359.5	757,166	102.9	74.9	2.5	0.9	10.4	5.8	5.5	12.1	69.4	49.5	14.9	50.0
District 9	Adam Smith (D)	183.4	765,319	4,172.1	50.3	11.4	0.4	24.2	6.8	6.9	12.4	45.7	49.5	30.9	37.6
District 10	Denny Heck (D)	826.9	738,843	893.5	73.1	6.3	1.1	8.3	2.9	8.3	11.7	66.0	50.8	9.8	47.4
WEST VIRGINIA		24,040.9	1,815,857	75.5	92.8	4.0	0.1	0.8	0.7	1.7	1.3	92.0	50.6	1.6	70.0
District 1	David McKinley (R)	6,275.7	611,376	97.4	94.0	2.7	0.2	0.9	0.4	1.7	1.1	93.2	50.2	2.0	68.9
District 2	Alexander X. Mooney (R)	8,019.6	621,635	77.5	91.1	4.8	0.1	1.0	1.1	1.9	1.8	90.1	51.0	2.2	63.0
District 3	Carol D. Miller (R)	9,745.6	582,846	59.8	93.2	4.3	0.1	0.4	0.5	1.4	0.8	92.7	50.6	0.7	78.6
WISCONSIN		54,160.7	5,795,483	107.0	85.3	6.4	0.8	2.8	2.2	2.5	6.9	81.2	50.3	5.0	71.4
District 1	Brian Steil (R)	1,727.9	715,529	414.1	86.9	5.6	0.3	1.6	2.4	3.1	10.2	80.1	50.3	5.6	68.0
District 2	Mark Pocan (D)	4,536.8	761,806	167.9	85.5	4.5	0.4	4.6	2.0	2.9	6.7	81.3	50.3	7.5	64.8
District 3	Ron Kind (D)	11,112.0	720,944	64.9	93.4	1.2	0.5	2.3	0.8	1.8	2.7	91.7	49.7	2.6	70.9
District 4	Gwen Moore (D)	128.4	708,971	5,521.1	50.6	33.7	0.5	4.2	6.9	4.0	17.5	41.8	52.1	9.5	67.7
District 5	F. James Sensenbrenner Jr. (R)	1,891.0	730,386	386.3	90.7	2.5	0.3	3.2	1.4	2.0	5.8	86.7	50.5	5.0	76.0
District 6	Glenn Grothman (R)	4,918.7	715,060	145.4	92.2	1.8	0.4	2.5	1.2	1.9	4.6	89.1	49.6	3.6	78.4
District 7	Sean P. Duffy (R)	23,039.2	710,385	30.8	93.1	0.7	2.0	1.7	0.6	1.9	2.3	91.5	49.9	2.3	66.7
District 8	Mike Gallagher (R)	6,806.8	732,402	107.6	89.3	1.5	2.4	2.3	2.3	2.2	5.4	86.7	50.2	3.5	78.7
WYOMING		97,091.4	579,315	6.0	91.2	1.0	2.4	0.8	1.7	2.8	10.0	84.0	48.9	3.5	43.0
At Large	Liz Cheney (R)	97,091.4	579,315	6.0	91.2	1.0	2.4	0.8	1.7	2.8	10.0	84.0	48.9	3.5	43.0

1. Dry land or land partially or temporarily covered by water.   2. May be of any race.

Table E. Congressional Districts 116th Congress — **Age and Education**

STATE District	Population and population characteristics, 2017 (cont.)										Education, 2017		
	Age (percent)											Attainment[2] (percent)	
	Under 5 years	5 to 17 years	18 to 24 years	25 to 34 years	35 to 44 years	45 to 54 years	55 to 64 years	65 to 74 years	75 years and over	Median age	Total Enrollment[1]	High school graduate or more	Bachelor's degree or more
	15	16	17	18	19	20	21	22	23	24	25	26	27
TEXAS — Cont'd													
District 26	6.3	19.8	8.9	14.2	15.0	14.8	10.8	6.5	3.7	35.5	256,053	92.9	45.4
District 27	6.8	18.1	9.2	13.1	12.3	11.9	12.7	9.2	6.7	37.1	182,923	82.2	20.5
District 28	8.8	22.0	10.5	12.9	12.9	10.9	10.3	7.1	4.7	31.7	219,560	72.6	18.2
District 29	8.9	22.1	10.7	14.9	13.5	12.7	9.5	4.7	3.1	30.5	224,596	62.4	10.8
District 30	7.3	20.1	10.3	15.6	13.5	12.0	11.0	6.4	3.7	32.8	216,143	78.5	20.8
District 31	7.1	19.1	9.4	14.8	14.8	12.7	10.3	7.3	4.5	34.8	232,307	92.5	36.1
District 32	7.0	15.8	8.8	16.6	13.3	13.3	12.2	8.0	5.0	36.4	188,518	87.4	43.2
District 33	8.8	21.7	11.4	15.3	13.2	12.0	9.1	5.4	3.1	30.0	206,124	59.0	9.9
District 34	8.2	21.6	11.2	12.3	12.8	11.0	9.9	7.4	5.7	32.0	210,340	69.4	16.1
District 35	7.0	18.8	11.1	17.4	14.5	11.6	9.8	6.2	3.6	32.5	226,666	81.1	23.2
District 36	6.5	17.6	8.6	13.8	12.6	13.5	13.1	9.1	5.3	37.8	178,510	83.6	17.6
UTAH	8.2	21.7	11.3	14.6	13.7	10.2	9.6	6.5	4.3	31.0	984,783	92.1	34.6
District 1	8.1	22.5	11.3	13.5	13.7	10.1	10.2	6.5	4.1	31.0	247,132	92.3	31.5
District 2	7.7	20.0	10.3	15.5	13.3	10.4	9.8	7.7	5.2	32.7	226,459	90.3	33.1
District 3	7.7	22.1	15.0	13.3	12.2	10.1	9.3	6.2	4.1	28.4	269,220	94.6	42.2
District 4	9.1	22.0	8.6	16.0	15.4	10.3	9.1	5.7	3.8	31.5	241,972	91.7	32.4
VERMONT	4.8	14.1	10.7	11.8	11.1	13.3	15.4	11.4	7.4	42.6	144,025	92.6	38.3
At Large	4.8	14.1	10.7	11.8	11.1	13.3	15.4	11.4	7.4	42.6	144,025	92.6	38.3
VIRGINIA	5.9	16.1	9.7	13.8	13.1	13.5	12.9	9.0	6.0	38.2	2,138,155	89.7	38.7
District 1	5.9	17.9	9.0	11.6	13.1	14.4	13.0	9.4	5.6	39.1	212,754	90.8	36.9
District 2	6.1	15.1	11.5	15.9	12.1	12.2	12.7	8.4	6.0	36.1	184,717	92.7	35.0
District 3	6.5	16.3	11.2	16.0	12.3	11.9	12.4	7.9	5.6	35.0	196,550	89.5	26.6
District 4	5.9	15.4	10.0	15.4	12.5	13.1	13.2	9.0	5.5	37.5	189,199	87.5	29.8
District 5	4.9	14.7	9.9	11.6	11.1	13.1	14.7	11.7	8.2	42.6	171,593	87.3	29.1
District 6	5.7	14.5	12.3	12.2	11.6	12.3	13.3	10.3	7.9	39.5	184,922	87.5	27.3
District 7	5.6	17.6	8.1	12.7	13.0	14.0	13.4	9.5	6.1	39.7	190,170	91.6	40.3
District 8	7.0	13.9	7.4	19.6	16.7	13.2	10.7	7.0	4.5	36.1	185,396	91.2	62.2
District 9	4.6	13.8	11.4	11.1	11.4	13.6	14.2	11.6	8.4	42.9	168,168	83.7	19.9
District 10	6.4	20.2	7.6	11.4	14.7	15.7	12.4	7.2	4.4	38.0	242,442	92.4	56.1
District 11	6.2	17.3	9.1	13.8	14.6	14.3	12.3	7.6	4.6	37.4	212,244	92.0	56.8
WASHINGTON	6.1	16.1	8.9	14.9	13.2	12.8	12.9	9.2	5.9	37.7	1,750,825	91.3	35.5
District 1	6.7	16.9	6.2	14.9	14.8	13.5	13.1	8.9	5.1	38.3	174,433	94.5	43.2
District 2	5.6	14.8	10.5	14.1	13.0	12.8	13.4	9.5	6.2	38.7	178,291	92.6	32.5
District 3	5.7	17.5	7.6	12.3	12.8	13.3	13.8	10.5	6.5	39.9	171,157	91.5	27.1
District 4	7.7	21.0	9.0	13.6	12.4	11.3	11.3	8.3	5.5	34.1	199,363	79.3	20.6
District 5	5.7	15.7	11.6	13.5	11.6	11.9	13.4	10.1	6.5	37.9	184,473	93.0	29.8
District 6	5.5	14.4	8.3	13.3	12.0	12.3	14.3	12.3	7.6	41.5	146,015	92.5	30.1
District 7	5.1	10.9	9.8	20.9	14.4	13.0	11.9	8.7	5.5	36.9	163,709	95.1	60.5
District 8	6.8	18.2	8.5	12.4	14.1	13.8	13.5	7.7	5.0	37.6	189,703	91.5	34.0
District 9	5.9	15.2	8.2	18.0	14.2	13.8	11.9	7.7	5.3	36.9	169,545	89.4	43.0
District 10	6.7	16.6	9.1	15.9	12.6	12.1	12.4	9.0	5.5	36.1	174,136	91.9	28.2
WEST VIRGINIA	5.4	15.2	9.0	11.5	12.2	13.1	14.4	11.4	7.9	42.4	397,036	87.1	20.2
District 1	5.2	14.4	10.9	11.9	12.0	12.7	14.1	11.0	7.8	41.2	141,257	90.0	23.1
District 2	5.5	16.0	7.9	11.4	12.1	13.9	14.4	11.0	7.8	42.5	135,019	87.3	21.1
District 3	5.5	15.1	8.2	11.1	12.3	12.7	14.8	12.3	8.0	43.2	120,760	83.8	16.2
WISCONSIN	5.8	16.3	9.6	12.5	12.1	13.1	14.1	9.6	6.9	39.5	1,411,349	92.4	30.4
District 1	5.6	17.2	8.2	11.9	12.2	14.2	14.9	9.4	6.4	40.6	170,355	92.4	29.8
District 2	6.0	15.7	12.1	14.1	13.0	12.4	12.4	8.7	5.7	36.4	206,453	94.6	42.3
District 3	5.4	15.3	13.1	11.7	11.0	12.2	13.9	9.9	7.4	38.7	186,367	92.4	26.0
District 4	7.3	17.6	11.3	16.2	12.4	11.7	11.5	7.1	5.0	33.2	194,324	86.4	27.6
District 5	5.2	15.8	8.2	12.5	12.3	13.8	14.4	9.9	7.9	41.6	167,404	95.0	38.2
District 6	5.4	15.8	8.9	11.5	11.7	13.7	15.0	10.3	7.9	42.1	164,129	92.6	26.8
District 7	5.4	16.3	7.0	10.4	11.4	13.4	16.0	11.6	8.4	44.4	153,119	92.2	23.8
District 8	5.9	16.9	8.1	11.9	12.4	13.7	14.4	9.6	7.0	40.5	169,198	92.7	27.8
WYOMING	6.5	17.3	9.2	13.8	12.2	11.2	14.1	9.5	6.1	37.5	147,108	92.9	27.6
At Large	6.5	17.3	9.2	13.8	12.2	11.2	14.1	9.5	6.1	37.5	147,108	92.9	27.6

1. All persons 3 years old and over enrolled in nursery school through college and graduate or professional school. 2. Persons 25 years old and over.

Table E. Congressional Districts 116th Congress — **Households and Group Quarters**

STATE District	Households, 2017						Group Quarters, 2010					
	Number	Average household size	Family households (percent)	Married couple family (percent)	Female family householder[1]	One person households (percent)	Total in group quarters, 2017	Percent 65 years and over	Persons in correctional institutions	Persons in nursing facilities	Persons in college dormitories	Persons in military quarters
	28	29	30	31	32	33	34	35	36	37	38	39
TEXAS — Cont'd												
District 26	296,012	2.93	74.7	60.9	10.1	18.7	12,125	14.1	1,179	1,636	6,475	0
District 27	262,953	2.76	69.0	49.2	14.8	26.0	15,792	31.7	3,832	4,197	1,365	103
District 28	217,023	3.44	78.6	52.9	19.9	18.7	6,454	32.3	3,252	2,888	740	146
District 29	225,094	3.38	75.4	46.7	20.3	20.4	1,988	36.1	31	1,008	0	0
District 30	268,682	2.81	64.0	38.3	20.3	30.6	18,763	9.2	11,108	2,286	2,507	0
District 31	288,768	2.90	70.3	54.9	11.3	24.8	15,002	16.1	3,442	2,183	2,041	4,084
District 32	291,848	2.60	62.8	47.8	10.0	30.2	5,398	38.4	22	2,226	2,437	0
District 33	223,395	3.35	74.0	44.3	19.4	20.9	5,652	19.3	2,147	1,389	534	0
District 34	212,057	3.35	77.6	51.6	19.2	20.1	17,912	13.7	13,244	2,881	2,180	41
District 35	282,047	2.87	61.2	39.4	16.3	28.9	19,858	9.9	7,971	2,563	5,761	115
District 36	254,672	2.84	71.2	51.9	13.2	24.5	18,013	16.7	12,140	2,926	0	0
UTAH	975,448	3.13	74.1	60.7	9.0	19.6	47,561	10.4	12,666	5,854	15,666	523
District 1	240,836	3.14	75.1	61.7	8.9	18.8	8,586	10.6	1,892	1,190	3,227	488
District 2	257,113	2.92	68.6	55.7	8.6	24.4	14,508	12.1	3,459	1,763	3,443	35
District 3	229,276	3.27	78.4	66.3	8.1	15.4	16,609	7.5	441	1,279	8,960	0
District 4	248,223	3.21	75.0	59.8	10.5	19.3	7,858	12.4	6,874	1,622	36	0
VERMONT	256,629	2.33	59.9	46.7	9.2	31.0	25,053	15.0	1,592	3,588	16,895	5
At Large	256,629	2.33	59.9	46.7	9.2	31.0	25,053	15.0	1,592	3,588	16,895	5
VIRGINIA	3,120,880	2.64	67.0	50.9	11.8	26.6	242,294	12.0	1,592	30,324	84,048	37,568
District 1	277,339	2.85	75.9	61.9	9.5	19.8	16,041	13.8	4,215	2,568	6,380	3,351
District 2	276,562	2.55	68.1	50.6	12.0	25.2	35,623	11.2	1,685	2,534	7,086	7,370
District 3	281,229	2.53	64.2	40.6	18.8	29.9	27,346	5.4	6,045	3,045	11,014	24,287
District 4	281,332	2.63	61.7	41.1	16.1	31.3	31,051	10.2	19,352	2,662	2,942	316
District 5	285,558	2.44	64.6	49.0	11.3	28.8	30,080	13.8	10,972	4,052	12,206	0
District 6	291,926	2.46	63.7	48.1	11.3	29.6	34,739	12.6	4,623	4,349	19,615	1,398
District 7	286,232	2.72	71.2	55.0	11.7	23.2	11,572	19.8	4,500	2,649	3,721	0
District 8	316,395	2.51	56.7	44.0	8.7	33.7	6,713	28.6	944	2,026	1,084	846
District 9	278,407	2.44	64.1	48.6	11.4	30.1	33,568	13.1	10,091	4,288	14,085	0
District 10	277,931	3.03	78.3	66.4	8.3	16.6	7,828	18.7	1,606	907	1,068	0
District 11	267,969	2.88	70.4	56.0	10.5	23.5	7,733	13.6	1,207	1,244	4,847	0
WASHINGTON	2,840,377	2.56	64.6	49.9	9.8	26.5	142,990	18.6	31,960	22,156	35,534	12,385
District 1	276,903	2.66	70.9	59.0	8.1	22.2	8,455	23.7	2,676	1,313	620	0
District 2	290,244	2.52	62.6	49.5	8.8	26.6	14,587	20.5	1,754	2,323	3,862	2,504
District 3	275,040	2.63	67.3	52.1	9.9	24.8	7,255	35.8	1,539	1,617	0	14
District 4	245,664	2.91	70.9	51.0	13.0	23.4	9,902	25.7	4,028	2,246	382	4
District 5	283,499	2.42	62.8	47.7	10.1	28.8	29,454	11.8	5,656	2,927	13,048	513
District 6	288,384	2.41	63.7	49.6	10.1	28.5	19,424	16	8,063	3,211	1,022	5,694
District 7	348,952	2.14	48.4	38.0	6.2	37.4	20,460	13.6	1,851	2,700	10,456	362
District 8	266,990	2.81	72.5	58.7	9.2	19.8	6,279	24.8	839	1,305	2,155	0
District 9	287,462	2.62	64.3	47.6	11.4	25.5	13,336	26.9	3,031	2,422	1,348	0
District 10	277,239	2.62	67.6	49.8	12.8	25.0	13,838	17.9	2,523	2,092	2,641	3,294
WEST VIRGINIA	715,308	2.47	64.5	48.4	10.9	29.9	47,432	18.9	16,591	9,748	17,113	79
District 1	235,672	2.50	62.3	46.9	10.6	30.7	21,092	15.8	6,965	3,632	10,300	0
District 2	239,141	2.55	66.3	50.8	10.7	28.8	10,944	23.6	2,583	2,791	3,447	79
District 3	240,495	2.36	64.9	47.6	11.4	30.2	15,396	20.1	7,043	3,325	3,366	0
WISCONSIN	2,350,293	2.40	62.9	48.5	9.9	29.5	145,899	23.1	38,102	33,808	56,773	132
District 1	280,595	2.50	67.7	51.9	11.2	26.4	14,862	21.6	6,723	3,632	2,368	0
District 2	313,595	2.38	60.0	46.8	8.7	29.2	16,986	19.7	2,269	2,791	8,805	0
District 3	289,183	2.38	61.4	48.6	8.5	30.1	31,558	15.5	6,311	3,325	18,297	122
District 4	276,498	2.50	54.0	29.9	18.9	36.5	18,247	17.5	2,539	3,173	9,814	0
District 5	295,384	2.43	64.8	53.0	8.1	28.6	13,632	33.1	1,490	4,832	5,703	0
District 6	296,591	2.33	64.0	51.3	8.2	28.8	23,766	20.2	12,174	5,078	6,097	0
District 7	297,197	2.35	64.8	52.6	7.7	29.1	12,158	42.6	3,541	5,073	1,198	0
District 8	301,250	2.38	66.2	52.7	8.8	27.6	14,690	31.5	3,055	4,742	4,491	10
WYOMING	225,796	2.50	64.5	51.6	8.5	28.5	14,133	18.4	3,576	2,450	4,443	503
At Large	225,796	2.50	64.5	51.6	8.5	28.5	14,133	18.4	3,576	2,450	4,443	503

1. No spouse present.

Table E. Congressional Districts 116th Congress — **Housing and Money Income**

STATE District	Housing units, 2017						Money income, 2017		
		Occupied units					Households		
			Owner-occupied			Renter-occupied			
	Total	Occupied units as a percent of all units	Owner-occupied units as a percent of occupied units	Median value[1] (dollars)	Percent valued at $500,000 or more	Median rent[2]	Per capita income (dollars)	Median income (dollars)	Percent with income of $100,000 or more
	40	41	42	43	44	45	46	47	48
TEXAS — Cont'd									
District 26	310,402	95.4	71.5	276,500	11.6	1,225	39,666	91,650	45.1
District 27	320,099	82.1	64.0	138,800	2.9	911	27,253	52,790	23.8
District 28	246,571	88.0	69.3	121,600	1.9	818	19,825	46,777	18.6
District 29	248,694	90.5	51.7	108,000	0.9	865	17,258	42,792	13.0
District 30	293,916	91.4	49.7	134,500	2.5	967	23,804	49,972	17.5
District 31	316,673	91.2	62.9	234,700	5.6	1,089	32,064	70,346	32.4
District 32	319,208	91.4	56.7	245,800	20.6	1,151	42,846	70,640	34.9
District 33	250,352	89.2	47.2	99,000	1.5	882	16,904	42,229	10.8
District 34	261,398	81.1	66.2	84,000	1.7	699	16,575	37,977	13.1
District 35	307,335	91.8	51.8	154,000	1.8	997	23,275	48,284	17.5
District 36	307,859	82.7	72.7	137,000	2.6	892	28,492	57,908	27.6
UTAH	1,084,685	89.9	69.9	275,100	12.2	986	28,085	68,358	30.1
District 1	279,567	86.1	73.8	238,700	9.2	876	27,249	67,968	27.6
District 2	294,071	87.4	66.1	257,600	11.2	928	28,166	61,561	26.1
District 3	251,297	91.2	68.9	323,400	20.6	1,050	29,126	71,367	34.5
District 4	259,750	95.6	70.9	289,500	8.5	1,088	27,809	72,937	32.4
VERMONT	335,248	76.5	69.5	226,300	8.0	950	32,443	57,513	24.0
At Large	335,248	76.5	69.5	226,300	8.0	950	32,443	57,513	24.0
VIRGINIA	3,512,917	88.8	66.6	273,400	20.1	1,179	37,442	71,535	34.8
District 1	315,069	88.0	77.7	315,100	15.3	1,287	37,874	88,049	43.2
District 2	312,546	88.5	63.1	270,000	12.2	1,227	35,684	70,500	31.5
District 3	314,074	89.5	54.2	201,600	3.8	1,023	27,803	52,797	20.9
District 4	315,213	89.3	60.8	209,400	7.1	976	29,613	57,684	25.2
District 5	352,356	81.0	71.0	187,000	10.2	837	30,893	54,726	23.2
District 6	331,817	88.0	66.0	194,400	6.3	837	28,804	54,525	20.1
District 7	312,724	91.5	72.7	266,500	11.4	1,144	37,567	77,533	37.4
District 8	339,854	93.1	50.9	572,200	58.4	1,764	56,222	104,149	53.3
District 9	347,405	80.1	72.2	126,500	3.2	651	23,975	43,987	14.7
District 10	289,283	96.1	78.8	493,100	48.9	1,645	51,702	122,092	59.8
District 11	282,576	94.8	66.9	474,300	45.4	1,795	47,344	106,527	53.3
WASHINGTON	3,103,263	91.5	62.8	339,000	26.3	1,216	36,975	70,979	33.7
District 1	298,206	92.9	70.8	478,900	46.6	1,576	46,489	94,638	47.8
District 2	319,206	90.9	62.1	371,500	22.9	1,250	34,468	69,599	31.6
District 3	302,015	91.1	68.6	284,200	12.4	1,090	31,477	66,030	28.4
District 4	271,628	90.4	64.1	201,900	6.0	842	24,947	54,262	21.8
District 5	314,320	90.2	63.4	218,300	6.4	847	29,568	52,214	22.4
District 6	327,465	88.1	66.1	291,100	16.7	1,075	33,618	63,129	28.1
District 7	374,924	93.1	50.6	644,100	69.3	1,547	54,814	86,452	43.8
District 8	297,606	89.7	72.1	374,400	29.5	1,327	37,843	83,495	42.1
District 9	304,438	94.4	53.6	458,200	42.9	1,478	43,704	80,283	40.5
District 10	293,455	94.5	60.4	280,800	8.3	1,187	31,164	66,307	27.2
WEST VIRGINIA	892,240	80.2	72.5	119,800	2.6	690	24,478	43,469	16.0
District 1	290,632	81.1	71.5	124,400	3.4	701	26,145	47,450	17.6
District 2	300,803	79.5	74.6	141,200	2.5	732	25,711	48,426	19.1
District 3	300,805	80.0	71.5	95,900	1.8	644	21,413	36,000	11.4
WISCONSIN	2,695,303	87.2	66.6	178,900	4.8	819	31,998	59,305	24.6
District 1	307,665	91.2	69.3	198,500	5.2	884	33,601	65,381	29.2
District 2	332,770	94.2	61.8	234,100	6.8	980	35,669	68,089	30.2
District 3	327,832	88.2	68.4	158,200	3.3	749	28,472	54,704	19.9
District 4	312,687	88.4	44.3	138,300	3.7	825	24,789	42,087	15.3
District 5	312,082	94.6	69.9	233,400	7.3	911	38,207	70,709	32.6
District 6	328,104	90.4	70.8	163,500	4.9	733	32,282	59,685	23.3
District 7	423,092	70.2	76.2	159,400	3.7	700	30,490	54,355	20.7
District 8	351,071	85.8	71.0	166,200	3.4	731	32,058	61,163	24.9
WYOMING	276,733	81.6	70.8	214,300	8.9	832	30,883	60,434	25.1
At Large	276,733	81.6	70.8	214,300	8.9	832	30,883	60,434	25.1

1. Specified owner-occupied units.   2. Specified renter-occupied units.

Table E. Congressional Districts 116th Congress — **Poverty, Labor Force, Employment, and Social Security**

STATE District	Poverty, 2017			Civilian labor force, 2016			Civilian employment,[2] 2017				Persons under 65 years of age with no health insurance, 2017 (percent)	Social Security beneficiaries, December 2018		Supplemental Security Income recipients, December 2018
	Persons below poverty level (percent)	Families below poverty level (percent)	Percent of households receiving food stamps in past 12 months	Total	Unemployment		Total	Percent				Number	Rate[3]	
					Total	Rate[1]		Management, business, science, and arts occupations	Service, sales, and office	Construction and production				
	49	50	51	52	53	54	55	56	57	58	59	60	61	62
TEXAS — Cont'd														
District 26	6.6	3.8	4.3	482,720	18,847	3.9	463,873	47.7	37.7	14.6	11.0	101,276	115.2	6,338
District 27	15.6	11.3	15.9	353,396	18,454	5.2	334,942	29.1	42.0	29.0	20.8	139,821	188.9	20,568
District 28	23.6	20.2	23.1	322,507	20,841	6.5	301,666	28.1	47.3	24.6	27.9	116,318	154.4	29,446
District 29	24.1	22.0	21.2	353,694	25,823	7.3	327,871	17.7	40.9	41.3	32.6	79,051	103.8	22,019
District 30	19.3	15.5	18.5	376,028	22,530	6.0	353,498	29.0	43.6	27.4	21.6	105,842	136.7	31,878
District 31	8.9	6.5	7.6	421,800	18,936	4.5	402,864	42.9	40.4	16.7	10.9	127,367	149.2	12,304
District 32	11.2	8.1	7.4	427,756	19,922	4.7	407,834	43.2	39.1	17.7	19.1	100,844	132.1	11,433
District 33	21.2	18.0	18.3	362,750	22,635	6.2	340,115	15.7	42.5	41.8	33.5	82,794	109.9	23,425
District 34	27.8	23.1	22.4	294,912	17,209	5.8	277,703	27.8	47.1	25.1	29.6	120,637	165.8	38,672
District 35	19.5	15.2	15.0	427,821	22,119	5.2	405,702	29.9	46.8	23.3	19.3	107,472	129.5	22,221
District 36	13.9	10.6	13.1	346,941	26,811	7.7	320,130	30.3	39.3	30.5	21.1	141,440	190.5	16,724
UTAH	9.7	6.7	6.8	1,560,698	55,695	3.6	1,505,003	39.1	39.5	21.4	10.1	406,568	131.1	31,529
District 1	9.4	6.4	7.5	377,898	12,029	3.2	365,869	36.9	37.3	25.8	9.1	98,540	129.0	7,664
District 2	12.0	8.0	8.3	384,166	15,283	4.0	368,883	38.6	38.5	22.9	12.8	120,084	156.8	9,071
District 3	9.8	6.7	5.5	383,176	13,630	3.6	369,546	42.0	41.9	16.1	8.5	94,055	122.6	6,261
District 4	7.8	5.8	6.0	415,458	14,753	3.6	400,705	38.9	40.1	21.0	10.3	93,889	116.6	8,533
VERMONT	11.3	7.0	11.5	338,914	12,759	3.8	326,155	41.1	38.0	21.0	5.5	150,319	241.0	15,190
At Large	11.3	7.0	11.5	338,914	12,759	3.8	326,155	41.1	38.0	21.0	5.5	150,319	241.0	15,190
VIRGINIA	10.6	7.1	8.1	4,365,684	200,754	4.6	4,164,930	44.1	38.3	17.6	10.2	1,530,417	180.7	155,992
District 1	6.9	4.5	5.9	418,924	18,621	4.4	400,303	44.0	38.5	17.4	9.7	142,120	176.5	8,646
District 2	9.1	5.8	6.4	364,707	15,988	4.4	348,719	41.3	41.2	17.5	9.4	129,256	174.3	10,457
District 3	17.3	13.2	13.5	361,635	25,436	7.0	336,199	33.6	44.7	21.7	12.3	135,938	183.7	21,674
District 4	14.9	10.5	12.5	386,534	25,156	6.5	361,378	36.9	43.2	19.9	11.0	145,443	188.4	22,523
District 5	13.1	8.8	9.3	342,979	15,145	4.4	327,834	38.8	38.0	23.2	11.1	183,413	252.3	17,539
District 6	12.9	7.6	10.3	377,281	15,762	4.2	361,519	34.9	41.8	23.4	11.2	173,254	230.2	17,110
District 7	7.7	4.8	6.5	414,893	18,124	4.4	396,769	44.1	38.2	17.7	9.1	147,850	187.1	10,996
District 8	8.6	6.2	4.1	481,100	16,933	3.5	464,167	57.7	31.3	11.0	10.2	80,992	101.0	7,714
District 9	18.7	12.1	12.7	314,214	15,403	4.9	298,811	32.6	42.1	25.3	11.4	200,733	282.0	24,426
District 10	4.0	2.5	3.6	464,063	16,776	3.6	447,287	54.6	33.6	11.8	7.6	103,754	122.0	6,159
District 11	6.6	4.4	4.2	439,354	17,410	4.0	421,944	54.7	34.1	11.2	10.2	87,664	112.6	8,748
WASHINGTON	11.0	7.1	12.3	3,786,167	186,414	4.9	3,599,753	41.4	37.9	20.7	7.1	1,346,820	181.9	149,251
District 1	6.7	4.1	7.4	395,012	14,192	3.6	380,820	50.0	32.5	17.5	5.0	117,400	157.6	7,590
District 2	9.8	5.4	11.6	390,097	17,529	4.5	372,568	35.3	41.3	23.4	6.8	141,137	189.4	13,994
District 3	12.1	7.4	15.1	356,176	22,300	6.3	333,876	35.1	40.2	24.7	7.3	160,042	218.7	16,891
District 4	15.5	11.9	19.5	330,309	17,263	5.2	313,046	31.0	35.9	33.1	12.7	127,950	176.7	16,884
District 5	14.1	8.2	14.7	346,670	18,614	5.4	328,056	37.5	42.1	20.4	6.2	156,481	218.3	19,741
District 6	11.9	7.5	13.4	320,396	16,500	5.1	303,896	38.1	41.8	20.1	6.1	172,121	241.4	17,340
District 7	9.6	4.8	6.9	466,741	17,547	3.8	449,194	60.5	30.4	9.1	4.9	108,297	140.9	12,318
District 8	9.1	6.5	9.9	392,933	18,378	4.7	374,555	40.5	37.6	21.9	5.9	119,053	157.2	10,470
District 9	11.1	7.6	12.7	430,688	21,233	4.9	409,455	42.4	39.0	18.7	8.3	102,896	134.4	16,554
District 10	10.8	8.0	13.5	357,145	22,858	6.4	334,287	35.6	41.2	23.3	7.5	141,443	191.4	17,469
WEST VIRGINIA	19.1	14.1	16.8	777,186	51,986	6.7	725,200	33.2	42.8	24.0	7.5	475,744	262.0	72,299
District 1	17.3	10.8	13.4	280,265	17,966	6.4	262,299	34.5	41.0	24.5	7.6	149,562	244.6	19,157
District 2	16.9	13.1	15.3	282,420	19,166	6.8	263,254	34.4	42.4	23.2	6.7	156,888	252.4	19,871
District 3	23.3	18.2	21.6	214,501	14,854	6.9	199,647	30.0	45.8	24.2	8.3	169,294	290.5	33,271
WISCONSIN	11.3	7.1	10.6	3,086,662	107,459	3.5	2,979,203	36.8	38.6	24.6	6.4	1,233,379	212.8	116,810
District 1	8.5	5.7	10.9	379,767	17,968	4.7	361,799	36.1	39.5	24.4	6.4	152,552	213.2	13,711
District 2	11.7	6.0	8.2	430,263	11,483	2.7	418,780	46.3	35.8	17.9	5.3	137,596	180.6	11,331
District 3	12.3	7.0	9.9	382,412	10,958	2.9	371,454	32.7	39.9	27.4	7.1	162,565	225.5	12,235
District 4	22.5	17.6	21.8	350,124	20,001	5.7	330,123	33.5	44.2	22.3	9.1	113,893	160.6	38,963
District 5	7.4	4.6	6.1	407,378	11,905	2.9	395,473	42.3	37.9	19.7	4.2	155,763	213.3	7,628
District 6	8.8	5.4	9.5	380,119	11,236	3.0	368,883	33.5	37.9	28.6	5.6	164,944	230.7	10,188
District 7	10.6	6.5	10.8	360,250	12,876	3.6	347,374	33.7	37.3	29.0	8.0	185,081	260.5	11,553
District 8	9.0	6.4	8.2	396,349	11,032	2.8	385,317	34.4	37.1	28.5	5.4	160,985	219.8	11,201
WYOMING	11.3	7.6	6.3	297,578	15,376	5.2	282,202	34.5	37.8	27.7	14.5	112,386	194.0	6,889
At Large	11.3	7.6	6.3	297,578	15,376	5.2	282,202	34.5	37.8	27.7	14.5	112,386	194.0	6,889

1. Percent of civilian labor force.   2. Persons 16 years old and over.   3. Per 1,000 resident population estimated in the 2017 American Community Survey.

Table E. Congressional Districts 116th Congress — Agriculture

STATE District	Number of farms	Land in farms			Value of products sold				Government payments	
		Acres	Average size of farm (acres)	Harvested cropland (acres)	Total ($1,000)	Average per farm (dollars)	Percent from crops	Percent from livestock and poultry products	Total ($1,000)	Average per farm receiving payments (dollars)
	63	64	65	66	67	68	69	70	71	72
TEXAS — Cont'd										
District 26	3,405	379,288	111	109,449	135,031	39,657	26.8	73.2	1,967	9,106
District 27	12,006	4,509,855	376	1,246,336	1,211,354	100,896	56.1	43.9	54,669	28,533
District 28	7,866	4,740,139	603	201,075	266,700	33,905	28.7	71.3	7,328	14,092
District 29	118	1,957	17	176	2,006	17,000	89.2	10.8	D	D
District 30	339	30,440	90	8,664	24,115	71,136	94.4	5.6	343	14,913
District 31	4,972	1,029,430	207	316,810	191,223	38,460	54.8	45.2	10,186	14,326
District 32	268	24,824	93	6,903	4,973	18,556	47.4	52.6	149	14,326
District 33	105	3,913	37	1,382	595	5,667	86.1	13.8	D	49,667
District 34	8,728	4,198,181	481	742,909	891,631	102,158	47.6	52.4	22,756	21,488
District 35	1,119	279,641	250	55,770	50,929	45,513	76.2	23.8	1,015	11,154
District 36	6,786	987,386	146	141,443	109,757	16,174	54.5	45.5	10,717	50,552
UTAH	18,409	10,811,604	587	1,062,894	1,838,609	99,876	30.5	69.5	27,868	12,633
District 1	7,638	5,450,417	714	483,806	534,894	70,031	34.5	65.5	16,242	16,034
District 2	4,838	2,447,277	506	379,948	964,666	199,394	23.8	76.2	6,629	9,156
District 3	3,559	2,492,368	700	126,072	194,706	54,708	40.8	59.2	3,232	11,107
District 4	2,374	421,542	178	73,068	144,343	60,802	46.7	53.3	1,766	9,921
VERMONT	6,808	1,193,437	175	417,925	780,968	114,713	24.0	76.0	5,698	8,355
At Large	6,808	1,193,437	175	417,925	780,968	114,713	24.0	76.0	5,698	8,355
VIRGINIA	43,225	7,797,979	180	2,613,010	3,960,501	91,625	34.4	65.6	60,805	10,122
District 1	3,054	645,919	211	388,966	301,198	98,624	77.7	22.3	10,885	18,233
District 2	610	149,494	245	108,539	274,025	449,221	46.7	53.3	3,964	26,079
District 3	333	105,974	318	64,944	89,535	268,874	69.8	30.2	3,263	26,967
District 4	1,879	581,527	309	348,136	278,687	148,317	77.8	22.2	18,864	24,123
District 5	11,408	2,257,513	198	614,799	601,654	52,740	42.7	57.3	9,223	5,255
District 6	8,091	1,278,122	158	392,804	1,481,922	183,157	9.4	90.6	5,475	6,411
District 7	3,235	576,339	178	193,179	350,186	108,249	44.3	55.7	2,518	5,097
District 8	27	1,634	61	201	378	14,000	92.1	7.7	D	D
District 9	11,933	1,893,432	159	389,465	486,668	40,783	21.5	78.5	6,227	5,506
District 10	2,629	305,569	116	111,745	95,792	36,437	66.0	34.0	378	3,231
District 11	26	2,456	94	232	457	17,577	54.9	44.9	D	D
WASHINGTON	35,793	14,679,857	410	4,472,130	9,634,461	269,172	72.5	27.5	168,990	30,692
District 1	3,760	184,504	49	92,737	609,749	162,167	50.0	50.0	2,098	6,812
District 2	1,672	128,023	77	67,888	301,189	180,137	64.3	35.7	462	4,574
District 3	5,744	907,479	158	201,363	409,081	71,219	45.1	54.9	5,633	14,297
District 4	9,281	7,215,328	777	2,037,982	6,606,543	711,835	74.9	25.1	72,231	40,488
District 5	7,248	5,707,399	787	1,939,306	963,198	132,892	90.6	9.4	85,143	32,081
District 6	2,429	167,201	69	29,213	93,124	38,338	38.3	61.7	326	5,175
District 7	210	2,788	13	721	2,850	13,571	76.5	23.5	D	D
District 8	4,031	312,692	78	89,276	472,565	117,233	80.7	19.3	2,914	18,327
District 9	73	884	12	150	1,013	13,877	88.6	11.4	D	D
District 10	1,345	53,559	40	13,494	175,150	130,223	35.2	64.8	79	2,548
WEST VIRGINIA	23,622	3,662,178	155	736,151	754,279	31,931	20.3	79.7	9,094	4,853
District 1	9,112	1,317,106	145	271,231	155,397	17,054	21.1	78.9	D	D
District 2	8,567	1,406,851	164	298,139	437,526	51,071	16.5	83.5	3,636	4,722
District 3	5,943	938,221	158	166,781	161,355	27,150	29.8	70.2	D	D
WISCONSIN	64,793	14,318,630	221	9,234,611	11,427,423	176,368	35.6	64.4	126,583	4,609
District 1	2,798	574,614	205	472,422	470,615	168,197	D	D	13,871	10,871
District 2	9,579	2,086,402	218	1,403,770	1,652,129	172,474	39.3	60.7	30,032	5,925
District 3	18,254	4,142,195	227	2,319,178	2,783,186	152,470	40.8	59.2	31,987	3,951
District 4	39	310	8	136	3,019	77,410	D	D	D	D
District 5	3,120	647,716	208	495,739	686,285	219,963	39.0	61.0	5,237	4,007
District 6	7,975	1,753,113	220	1,333,881	1,724,547	216,244	33.4	66.6	16,772	4,706
District 7	15,205	3,428,587	225	1,960,317	2,249,708	147,958	33.3	66.7	13,222	2,949
District 8	7,823	1,685,693	215	1,249,168	1,857,935	237,496	22.2	77.8	15,462	4,217
WYOMING	11,938	29,004,884	2,430	1,544,826	1,472,113	123,313	21.6	78.4	30,218	14,410
At Large	11,938	29,004,884	2,430	1,544,826	1,472,113	123,313	21.6	78.4	30,218	14,410

Table E. Congressional Districts 116th Congress — **Nonfarm Employment and Payroll**

												Private nonfarm employment and payroll, 2016	
			Employment										Annual payroll
					Percent by selected industries								
STATE District	Number of establishments	Total	Manufac- turing	Construc- tion	Wholesale trade	Retail trade	Health care and social assistance	Finance and Insur- ance	Real estate and rental and leas- ing	Profes- sional, sci- entific, and technical services	Information	Total (mil dol)	Average per employee (dollars)
	73	74	75	76	77	78	79	80	81	82	83	84	85
TEXAS — Cont'd													
District 26	15,199	240,064	6.3	5.2	5.0	15.4	11.1	8.9	1.7	4.7	1.8	10,705	44,591
District 27	15,738	249,150	8.8	8.3	4.6	15.0	18.8	2.8	2.0	4.3	1.2	10,180	40,858
District 28	11,101	161,914	2.5	4.3	3.7	18.7	22.8	3.6	1.4	2.4	1.1	4,950	30,572
District 29	10,649	213,699	15.2	13.4	7.3	12.1	5.6	2.3	1.7	4.8	0.8	10,137	47,434
District 30	13,665	343,059	6.3	3.5	4.8	8.8	19.1	5.5	2.7	10.1	3.4	22,453	65,449
District 31	15,228	241,132	5.7	6.4	2.9	16.5	19.2	4.7	1.7	9.3	2.4	10,767	44,653
District 32	21,973	344,278	6.0	4.2	3.2	12.2	17.7	7.4	3.3	9.6	4.0	19,421	56,410
District 33	12,588	273,772	15.3	8.3	11.5	9.6	9.8	1.7	1.6	3.6	1.2	12,634	46,148
District 34	10,816	170,804	4.1	2.9	2.9	17.4	31.9	3.1	1.6	2.7	1.7	4,849	28,390
District 35	15,636	304,332	7.4	7.1	7.2	13.5	11.7	2.9	1.8	4.9	3.8	12,704	41,745
District 36	12,903	244,582	15.8	11.5	3.8	12.0	10.9	2.0	1.5	7.7	0.8	13,545	55,382
UTAH	77,504	1,239,348	9.8	6.3	4.7	12.6	11.2	5.3	1.6	7.2	3.7	54,331	43,839
District 1	17,909	231,999	17.5	6.8	3.3	15.3	12.1	4.1	2.0	6.2	1.3	8,839	38,099
District 2	21,144	373,647	10.1	5.4	5.8	10.8	11.3	5.9	1.5	7.2	3.1	17,898	47,901
District 3	19,109	261,713	5.4	5.8	3.8	13.8	12.7	4.5	2.0	7.0	5.0	10,463	39,978
District 4	18,858	303,855	9.4	9.0	5.8	14.4	11.6	6.1	1.5	8.4	5.9	14,263	46,939
VERMONT	21,174	262,705	11.4	5.3	4.5	15.2	18.6	3.6	1.3	4.9	2.7	10,828	41,219
At Large	21,174	262,705	11.4	5.3	4.5	15.2	18.6	3.6	1.3	4.9	2.7	10,828	41,219
VIRGINIA	199,548	3,254,172	7.4	5.5	3.3	13.2	13.5	4.7	1.7	14.1	2.7	170,160	52,290
District 1	17,052	214,902	5.2	9.9	5.3	18.0	12.8	4.1	1.4	9.2	1.3	8,919	41,500
District 2	16,321	229,214	4.7	5.5	2.2	15.4	12.1	5.7	3.1	10.1	1.9	8,726	38,071
District 3	16,694	334,293	14.1	4.7	3.2	13.8	18.1	3.2	1.7	7.9	2.1	15,125	45,244
District 4	15,673	273,860	9.0	6.8	4.8	11.3	16.2	5.1	1.5	7.5	1.2	13,088	47,791
District 5	16,718	207,989	12.2	6.8	2.9	15.6	17.8	3.4	1.4	5.7	1.9	8,496	40,849
District 6	18,096	308,049	14.1	5.1	3.2	14.4	15.9	4.2	1.3	4.3	1.6	11,922	38,701
District 7	18,985	291,085	3.7	5.8	4.0	15.6	14.2	10.5	1.7	8.3	2.7	14,275	49,040
District 8	20,512	360,285	1.0	4.1	1.6	10.2	9.4	2.8	2.3	26.6	3.0	24,207	67,189
District 9	14,206	208,791	20.2	3.9	4.2	16.9	16.9	2.8	1.0	3.9	1.6	7,614	36,466
District 10	22,539	338,195	5.4	7.7	3.2	11.6	10.2	2.6	1.4	21.4	3.8	19,823	58,614
District 11	22,048	431,483	0.8	2.9	2.0	10.5	10.3	6.1	1.9	30.9	6.0	33,961	78,708
WASHINGTON	186,164	2,685,355	9.9	6.5	5.0	12.5	15.2	3.7	1.8	7.5	4.9	156,915	58,434
District 1	19,264	273,387	10.2	9.5	5.1	9.1	9.3	2.2	1.5	9.1	18.2	23,558	86,171
District 2	19,869	273,601	22.8	7.4	3.0	16.2	13.4	3.7	1.5	4.4	2.3	13,847	50,609
District 3	16,100	194,262	13.0	8.6	4.4	14.7	16.8	3.5	1.7	5.6	2.2	8,965	46,152
District 4	14,187	191,422	12.6	6.2	6.4	15.9	16.8	2.3	1.6	5.8	1.2	8,244	43,066
District 5	17,033	233,124	9.1	5.6	5.6	14.4	20.6	5.3	1.8	4.5	2.0	9,964	42,743
District 6	17,157	194,723	4.8	5.8	2.5	17.0	24.2	3.4	1.7	5.3	1.5	8,173	41,972
District 7	28,807	461,573	3.9	4.4	3.6	8.9	14.4	4.7	2.4	13.0	6.3	34,422	74,575
District 8	15,426	173,457	10.0	9.7	7.2	15.1	13.5	1.8	1.4	3.6	2.9	8,417	48,527
District 9	22,852	447,136	10.2	5.0	6.9	9.1	13.9	3.6	1.9	6.2	5.1	29,862	66,786
District 10	14,837	203,713	7.0	7.9	5.0	16.3	16.0	4.2	1.9	4.4	2.1	8,560	42,022
WEST VIRGINIA	36,607	558,905	8.5	4.3	3.3	15.5	24.0	3.1	1.2	4.5	1.9	21,638	38,715
District 1	12,924	209,694	9.5	4.1	3.0	14.9	24.3	2.6	0.9	4.6	1.7	8,288	39,524
District 2	12,285	185,108	8.8	5.3	3.6	15.3	21.8	3.8	1.3	4.5	2.0	7,307	39,474
District 3	11,077	155,363	7.2	3.6	3.2	17.3	27.5	2.5	1.0	3.4	2.1	5,583	35,935
WISCONSIN	140,859	2,524,329	17.9	4.3	4.8	12.5	15.7	5.5	1.0	4.3	2.2	115,817	45,880
District 1	15,191	245,541	20.0	4.4	5.1	16.8	14.0	2.4	1.0	2.9	1.2	10,267	41,812
District 2	19,233	360,351	11.4	4.8	4.9	12.6	15.9	7.1	1.4	7.2	5.3	17,857	49,554
District 3	17,032	278,726	18.7	3.8	4.0	14.3	16.8	5.0	1.0	3.0	1.8	10,964	39,335
District 4	13,450	306,701	10.4	2.0	4.7	7.6	18.4	9.8	1.3	5.5	2.3	16,757	54,637
District 5	21,300	410,849	16.8	4.7	6.3	12.1	16.0	4.5	1.2	4.8	2.6	20,422	49,708
District 6	13,721	307,770	26.4	4.8	3.6	12.2	14.1	3.7	0.8	3.2	1.0	13,721	44,582
District 7	16,747	249,122	23.3	4.6	4.0	14.8	17.2	4.3	0.8	2.5	1.0	9,669	38,812
District 8	19,077	328,939	21.4	5.1	4.5	12.3	13.8	5.1	0.9	3.2	1.6	14,405	43,791
WYOMING	20,966	208,440	4.4	8.9	3.8	14.9	16.0	3.2	2.2	4.7	1.9	9,304	44,636
At Large	20966	208,440	4.4	8.9	3.8	14.9	16.0	3.2	2.2	4.7	1.9	9,304	44,636

APPENDIX A
GEOGRAPHIC CONCEPTS AND CODES

GEOGRAPHIC AREAS COVERED

County and City Extra presents data for states (Table A), states and counties (Table B), metropolitan areas (Table C), cities with populations of 25,000 or more in 2010 (Table D), and congressional districts (Table E).

STATES AND COUNTIES

Data are presented for each of the 50 states, the District of Columbia, and the United States as a whole. The states are arranged alphabetically and counties in Table B are arranged alphabetically within each state. Data are presented for 3,142 counties and county equivalents.

County equivalents

In Louisiana, the primary divisions of the state are known as parishes rather than counties. In Alaska, the county equivalents are the organized boroughs, together with the census areas that were developed for general statistical purposes by the state of Alaska and the U.S. Census Bureau. Four states—Maryland, Missouri, Nevada, and Virginia—have one or more incorporated places that are legally independent of any county and thus constitute primary divisions of their states. Within each state, independent cities are listed alphabetically following the list of counties. The District of Columbia is not divided into counties or county equivalents—data for the entire district are presented as a county equivalent. New York City contains five counties: Bronx, Kings, New York, Queens, and Richmond.

County changes since the 2010 census

- The independent city of Bedford, Virginia changed to town status and was added to Bedford county, effective July 1, 2013. In this book, all the data have been updated to reflect this change except the 2012 Census of Governments data in columns 171 through 193, where Bedford county does not include Bedford city.
- Wade Hampton Census Area, AK (02-270) changed its name and FIPS code to Kusilvak Census Area (02-158), effective July 1, 2015.
- Shannon County, SD (46-113) changed its name and FIPS code to Oglala Lakota County (46-102), effective May 1, 2015.
- Petersburg Borough, AK was created from part of Petersburg Census Area and part of Hoonah-Angoon Census Area. Petersburg Borough retains the FIPS code 02-195, formerly used by Petersburg Census Area, effective January 3, 2013.
- Prince of Wales-Hyder Census Area added part of the former Petersburg Census Area, effective January 3, 2013.

County changes since the 2000 census

- Broomfield County, CO, was created from parts of Adams, Boulder, Jefferson, and Weld Counties, effective November 15, 2001. The boundaries of Broomfield County reflect the boundaries of Broomfield city legally in effect on that date.
- Clifton Forge city, VA, formerly an independent city, became a town within Alleghany County, effective July 1, 2001.
- Effective June 20, 2007, the Skagway-Hoonah-Angoon Census Area in Alaska was divided into the Skagway Municipality and the Hoonah-Angoon Census Area.
- In May and June, 2008, the Wrangell-Petersburg and Prince of Wales-Outer Ketchikan Census Areas were dissolved and replaced by Wrangell City and Borough, Petersburg Census Area, and Prince of Wales Census Area. Some territory from the Prince of Wales Outer Ketchikan Census Area became part of the existing Ketchikan Gateway Borough.

METROPOLITAN AREAS

Table C presents data for 382 metropolitan statistical areas and 31 metropolitan divisions, which are located within the 11 largest metropolitan statistical areas. The metropolitan statistical areas are listed alphabetically, and the metropolitan divisions are listed alphabetically under the metropolitan statistical area of which they are components.

The U.S. Office of Management and Budget (OMB) defines metropolitan and micropolitan statistical areas according to published standards. The major purpose of defining these areas is to enable all U.S. government agencies to use the same geographic definitions in tabulating and publishing data. The general concept of a metropolitan or micropolitan statistical area is that of a core area containing a substantial population nucleus, together with adjacent communities that have a high degree of economic and social integration with the core.

New delineations of these Core Based Statistical Areas (CBSAs) based on the 2010 census were released in February 2013 and updated in July 2015. Table C in this book uses these delineations for metropolitan areas and metropolitan divisions. Micropolitan areas are not included in Table C. A few of the data items in Table C were released under the old scheme but have been aggregated from county data to the newly defined metropolitan areas. This results in a higher level of data suppression for those items. New delineations were released in August 2017, designating one new Metropolitan Area: Twin Falls, Idaho, consisting of Twin Falls county and Jerome county. It is not included in Table C because it was not a Metropolitan Area at the time of most of the data in this book. New delineations issued in 2018 included many changes but these have not yet been used in any data sources.

Appendix B lists the metropolitan areas and metropolitan divisions with their component counties and 2010 census populations. Appendix C lists the metropolitan and micropolitan areas, together with their 2010 census populations and their 2018 estimated populations.

Standard definitions of metropolitan areas were first issued in 1949 by the Bureau of the Budget (the predecessor of OMB), under the designation "standard metropolitan area" (SMA). The term was changed to "standard metropolitan statistical area" (SMSA) in 1959, and to "metropolitan statistical area" (MSA) in 1983. The term "metropolitan area" (MA) was adopted in 1990 and referred collectively to metropolitan statistical areas (MSAs), consolidated metropolitan statistical areas (CMSAs), and primary metropolitan statistical areas (PMSAs). The term "core based statistical area" (CBSA) became effective in 2000 and refers collectively to metropolitan and micropolitan statistical areas.

The 2010 standards provide that each CBSA must contain at least one urban area of 10,000 or more population. Each metropolitan statistical area must have at least one urbanized area of 50,000 or more inhabitants. Each micropolitan statistical area must have at least one urban cluster of at least 10,000 but less than 50,000 people.

Under the standards, A metro area contains a core urban area of 50,000 or more population, and a micro area contains an urban core of at least 10,000 (but less than 50,000) population. Each metro or micro area consists of one or more counties and includes the counties containing the core urban area, as well as any adjacent counties that have a high degree of social and economic integration (as measured by commuting to work) with the urban core.

If specified criteria are met, a metropolitan statistical area containing a single core with a population of 2.5 million or more may be subdivided to form smaller groupings of counties referred to as "metropolitan divisions."

As of July 15, 2015, there were 382 metropolitan statistical areas and 556 micropolitan statistical areas in the United States. Table C includes the 382 metropolitan statistical areas and the 31 metropolitan divisions. The metropolitan areas and metropolitan divisions are listed in Appendix B with their 2010 census population counts. The metropolitan areas, metropolitan divisions, and micropolitan areas are listed in Appendix C with their 2010 census populations and their 2018 estimated populations.

The largest city in each metropolitan or micropolitan statistical area is designated a "principal city." Additional cities qualify if specified requirements are met concerning population size and employment. The title of each metropolitan or micropolitan statistical area consists of the names of up to three of its principal cities and the name of each state into which the metropolitan or micropolitan statistical area extends. Titles of metropolitan divisions also typically are based on principal city names, but in certain cases consist of county names. The principal city need not be an incorporated place if it meets the requirements of population size and employment. Usually such a principal city is a census designated place in decennial census data, but it is not included in most other data sources and is not in Table D (cities) in this volume.

In view of the importance of cities and towns in New England, the 2010 standards also provide for a set of geographic areas that are defined using cities and towns in the six New England states. These New England city and town areas (NECTAs) are not included in this volume.

Appendix B lists the 382 metropolitan statistical areas, together with their component metropolitan divisions, where appropriate, the component counties of each area, and their 2010 census populations. Appendix C provides the same information for the 383 metropolitan areas delineated in August 2017 and it also includes

the 556 micropolitan statistical areas. Maps showing the metropolitan and micropolitan areas within each state can be found in Appendix D.

CITIES

Table D presents data for 1,437 cities with 2010 census populations of 25,000 or more. Corresponding data for states are also provided. The states are arranged alphabetically and the cities are ordered alphabetically within each state.

As used in this volume, the term *city* refers to places that have been incorporated as cities, boroughs, towns, or villages under the laws of their respective states. Towns in the New England states and New York are treated as minor civil divisions (MCDs) and are not included in the cities database. For Hawaii, data for the census designated places (CDPs) are included in the cities table, since the Census Bureau does not recognize any incorporated places in Hawaii. CDPs are delineated by the Census Bureau, in cooperation with states and localities, as statistical counterparts of incorporated places for purposes of the decennial census. CDPs comprise densely settled concentrations of population that are identifiable by name but are not legally incorporated as places.

Appendix E lists the 1,437 cities followed by the county where each city is located. If a city includes portions of more than one county, the population in each part is specified.

A consolidated city is an incorporated place that has combined its government functions with a county or subcounty entity but contains one or more other semi-independent incorporated places that continue to function as local governments within the consolidated government. Each consolidated city contains a core city, the area of a consolidated city not included in another separately incorporated place. The census geographic term for this core is the "balance" of the consolidated city. Thus the "balance" is essentially the core city of the consolidated government. This volume includes the consolidated city data where possible, but some data sources include numbers only for the "balance" and others do not specify which entity is represented.

Consolidated cities included in this volume are Milford, CT; Athens-Clarke County, GA; Augusta-Richmond County, GA; Indianapolis, IN; Louisville-Jefferson County, KY; Butte-Silver Bow, MT; and Nashville-Davidson, TN.

Appendix E lists these seven consolidated cities, followed by the component places and their 2010 census populations.

On January 1, 2014, Macon, Georgia consolidated with Bibb county. A small portion of Macon that was in Jones county was de-annexed. Data from years prior to 2015 represent the smaller Macon city rather than the consolidated Macon-Bibb County.

CONGRESSIONAL DISTRICTS

The congressional districts shown in this volume are the districts used for the election of the 116th Congress, which convened in January 2019. These are the districts that were established following the 2010 Census and are based on population data from that census. Data are shown for the 435 regular districts plus the District of Columbia, which has a non-voting delegate, but no representative. Corresponding data for each state also are included. States are listed alphabetically and districts numerically within each state. A map showing congressional districts for the 113th Congress is included in Appendix D.

GEOGRAPHIC CODES

Tables A, B, C, and D provide, in one or more columns at the beginning of the table, a geographic code or codes for each area.

In Table B (states and counties), a five-digit state and county code is given for each state and county. The first two digits indicate the state; the remaining three represent the county. Within each state, the counties are listed in order, beginning with 001, with even numbers usually omitted. Independent cities follow the counties and begin with the number 510. In the second column of Table B, a five-digit core based statistical area (CBSA) code is given for those counties that are within metropolitan and micropolitan areas. In Table A, a two-digit state code is provided. The state code is a sequential numbering, with some gaps, of the states and the District of Columbia in alphabetical order from Alabama (01) to Wyoming (56).

These codes have been established by the U.S. government as Federal Information Processing Standards and are often referred to as *FIPS codes*. They are used by U.S. government agencies and many other organizations for data presentation. The codes are provided in this volume for use in matching the data given here with other data sources in which counties are identified by FIPS code. The metro area codes will also enable the user to identify the metro area of which a county is a component. Table C (metropolitan areas) provides the same metro area codes for each metropolitan area, as well as metropolitan division codes where appropriate.

Table D (cities) provides, in the first column, a seven-digit state and place code. The first two digits identify the state and are the same as the FIPS codes described above. The remaining five digits are the place FIPS codes established by the U.S. government.

INDEPENDENT CITIES

The following independent cities are not included in any county; their data are presented separately in this volume.

MARYLAND
Baltimore (separate from Baltimore County)

MISSOURI
St. Louis (separate from St. Louis County)

NEVADA
Carson City

VIRGINIA

Alexandria	Manassas
Bristol	Manassas Park
Buena Vista	Martinsville
Charlottesville	Newport News
Chesapeake	Norfolk
Colonial Heights	Norton
Covington	Petersburg
Danville	Poquoson
Emporia	Portsmouth
Fairfax	Radford
Falls Church	Richmond
Franklin	Roanoke
Fredericksburg	Salem
Galax	Staunton
Hampton	Suffolk
Harrisonburg	Virginia Beach
Hopewell	Waynesboro
Lexington	Williamsburg
Lynchburg	Winchester

COUNTY TYPE

Table B (states and counties) provides, in the third column, a *county type* code that identifies each county by its metropolitan/ nonmetropolitan status and its size. These are the "rural-urban continuum codes" developed by the Economic Research Service of the U.S. Department of Agriculture.

The 2013 rural-urban continuum codes form a classification scheme that distinguishes metropolitan counties by size and nonmetropolitan counties by degree of urbanization and proximity to metro areas. The standard OMB metro and nonmetro categories have been subdivided into three metro and six nonmetro categories, resulting in a nine-part county codification. This scheme was originally developed in 1974. The codes were updated in 1983, 1993, and 2003 and slightly revised in 1988. The 1988 revision was first published in 1990. This scheme allows researchers to break county data into finer residential groups, beyond metro and nonmetro, particularly for the analysis of trends in nonmetro areas that are related to population density and metro influence. The 2013 and 2003 rural-urban continuum codes are not directly comparable with the codes from previous years because of the new methodology used in developing the 2013 metropolitan areas.

Metropolitan counties
1. Counties in metro areas of 1 million population or more.
2. Counties in metro areas of 250,000 to 1 million population.
3. Counties in metro areas of fewer than 250,000 population.

Nonmetropolitan counties
4. Urban population of 20,000 or more, adjacent to a metro area.
5. Urban population of 20,000 or more, not adjacent to a metro area.
6. Urban population of 2,500 to 19,999, adjacent to a metro area.
7. Urban population of 2,500 to 19,999, not adjacent to a metro area.
8. Completely rural or less than 2,500 urban population, adjacent to a metro area.
9. Completely rural or less than 2,500 urban population, not adjacent to a metro area.

APPENDIX B
METROPOLITAN STATISTICAL AREAS, METROPOLITAN DIVISIONS, AND COMPONENTS
(as defined July 2015)

Core based statistical area	State/ County FIPS code	Title and Geographic Components	2010 Census Population	Core based statistical area	State/ County FIPS code	Title and Geographic Components	2010 Census Population
10180		Abilene, TX	165252	11540		Appleton, WI	225666
10180	48059	Callahan County	13544	11540	55015	Calumet County	48971
10180	48253	Jones County	20202	11540	55087	Outagamie County	176695
10180	48441	Taylor County	131506				
				11700		Asheville, NC	424858
10420		Akron, OH	703200	11700	37021	Buncombe County	238318
10420	39133	Portage County	161419	11700	37087	Haywood County	59036
10420	39153	Summit County	541781	11700	37089	Henderson County	106740
				11700	37115	Madison County	20764
10500		Albany, GA	157308				
10500	13007	Baker County	3451	12020		Athens-Clarke County, GA	192541
10500	13095	Dougherty County	94565	12020	13059	Clarke County	116714
10500	13177	Lee County	28298	12020	13195	Madison County	28120
10500	13273	Terrell County	9315	12020	13219	Oconee County	32808
10500	13321	Worth County	21679	12020	13221	Oglethorpe County	14899
10540		Albany, OR	116672	12060		Atlanta-Sandy Springs-Roswell, GA	5286728
10540	41043	Linn County	116672	12060	13013	Barrow County	69367
				12060	13015	Bartow County	100157
10580		Albany-Schenectady-Troy, NY	870716	12060	13035	Butts County	23655
10580	36001	Albany County	304204	12060	13045	Carroll County	110527
10580	36083	Rensselaer County	159429	12060	13057	Cherokee County	214346
10580	36091	Saratoga County	219607	12060	13063	Clayton County	259424
10580	36093	Schenectady County	154727	12060	13067	Cobb County	688078
10580	36095	Schoharie County	32749	12060	13077	Coweta County	127317
				12060	13085	Dawson County	22330
10740		Albuquerque, NM	887077	12060	13089	DeKalb County	691893
10740	35001	Bernalillo County	662564	12060	13097	Douglas County	132403
10740	35043	Sandoval County	131561	12060	13113	Fayette County	106567
10740	35057	Torrance County	16383	12060	13117	Forsyth County	175511
10740	35061	Valencia County	76569	12060	13121	Fulton County	920581
				12060	13135	Gwinnett County	805321
10780		Alexandria, LA	153922	12060	13143	Haralson County	28780
10780	22043	Grant Parish	22309	12060	13149	Heard County	11834
10780	22079	Rapides Parish	131613	12060	13151	Henry County	203922
				12060	13159	Jasper County	13900
10900		Allentown-Bethlehem-Easton, PA-NJ	821173	12060	13171	Lamar County	18317
10900	34041	Warren County	108692	12060	13199	Meriwether County	21992
10900	42025	Carbon County	65249	12060	13211	Morgan County	17868
10900	42077	Lehigh County	349497	12060	13217	Newton County	99958
10900	42095	Northampton County	297735	12060	13223	Paulding County	142324
				12060	13227	Pickens County	29431
11020		Altoona, PA	127089	12060	13231	Pike County	17869
11020	42013	Blair County	127089	12060	13247	Rockdale County	85215
				12060	13255	Spalding County	64073
11100		Amarillo, TX	251933	12060	13297	Walton County	83768
11100	48011	Armstrong County	1901				
11100	48065	Carson County	6182	12100		Atlantic City-Hammonton, NJ	274549
11100	48359	Oldham County	2052	12100	34001	Atlantic County	274549
11100	48375	Potter County	121073				
11100	48381	Randall County	120725	12220		Auburn-Opelika, AL	140247
				12220	01081	Lee County	140247
11180		Ames, IA	89542				
11180	19169	Story County	89542	12260		Augusta-Richmond County, GA-SC	564873
				12260	13033	Burke County	23316
11260		Anchorage, AK	380821	12260	13073	Columbia County	124053
11260	02020	Anchorage Municipality	291826	12260	13181	Lincoln County	7996
11260	02170	Matanuska-Susitna Borough	88995	12260	13189	McDuffie County	21875
				12260	13245	Richmond County	200549
11460		Ann Arbor, MI	344791	12260	45003	Aiken County	160099
11460	26161	Washtenaw County	344791	12260	45037	Edgefield County	26985
11500		Anniston-Oxford-Jacksonville, AL	118572				
11500	01015	Calhoun County	118572				

Core based statistical area	State/County FIPS code	Title and Geographic Components	2010 Census Population	Core based statistical area	State/County FIPS code	Title and Geographic Components	2010 Census Population
12420		Austin-Round Rock, TX	1716289	13820		Birmingham-Hoover, AL	1128047
12420	48021	Bastrop County	74171	13820	01007	Bibb County	22915
12420	48055	Caldwell County	38066	13820	01009	Blount County	57322
12420	48209	Hays County	157107	13820	01021	Chilton County	43643
12420	48453	Travis County	1024266	13820	01073	Jefferson County	658466
12420	48491	Williamson County	422679	13820	01115	St. Clair County	83593
				13820	01117	Shelby County	195085
12540		Bakersfield, CA	839631	13820	01127	Walker County	67023
12540	06029	Kern County	839631				
				13900		Bismarck, ND	114778
12580		Baltimore-Columbia-Towson, MD	2710489	13900	38015	Burleigh County	81308
12580	24003	Anne Arundel County	537656	13900	38059	Morton County	27471
12580	24005	Baltimore County	805029	13900	38065	Oliver County	1846
12580	24013	Carroll County	167134	13900	38085	Sioux County	4153
12580	24025	Harford County	244826				
12580	24027	Howard County	287085	13980		Blacksburg-Christiansburg-Radford, VA	178237
12580	24035	Queen Anne's County	47798	13980	51063	Floyd County	15279
12580	24510	Baltimore city	620961	13980	51071	Giles County	17286
				13980	51121	Montgomery County	94392
12620		Bangor, ME	153923	13980	51155	Pulaski County	34872
12620	23019	Penobscot County	153923	13980	51750	Radford city	16408
12700		Barnstable Town, MA	215888	14010		Bloomington, IL	186133
12700	25001	Barnstable County	215888	14010	17039	De Witt County	16561
				14010	17113	McLean County	169572
12940		Baton Rouge, LA	802484				
12940	22005	Ascension Parish	107215	14020		Bloomington, IN	159549
12940	22033	East Baton Rouge Parish	440171	14020	18105	Monroe County	137974
12940	22037	East Feliciana Parish	20267	14020	18119	Owen County	21575
12940	22047	Iberville Parish	33387				
12940	22063	Livingston Parish	128026	14100		Bloomsburg-Berwick, PA	85562
12940	22077	Pointe Coupee Parish	22802	14100	42037	Columbia County	67295
12940	22091	St. Helena Parish	11203	14100	42093	Montour County	18267
12940	22121	West Baton Rouge Parish	23788				
12940	22125	West Feliciana Parish	15625	14260		Boise City, ID	616561
				14260	16001	Ada County	392365
12980		Battle Creek, MI	136146	14260	16015	Boise County	7028
12980	26025	Calhoun County	136146	14260	16027	Canyon County	188923
				14260	16045	Gem County	16719
13020		Bay City, MI	107771	14260	16073	Owyhee County	11526
13020	26017	Bay County	107771				
				14460		Boston-Cambridge-Newton, MA-NH	4552402
13140		Beaumont-Port Arthur, TX	403190	14460		Boston, MA Div 14454	1887792
13140	48199	Hardin County	54635	14460	25021	Norfolk County	670850
13140	48245	Jefferson County	252273	14460	25023	Plymouth County	494919
13140	48351	Newton County	14445	14460	25025	Suffolk County	722023
13140	48361	Orange County	81837	14460		Cambridge-Newton-Framingham, MA Div 15764	2246244
13220		Beckley, WV	124898	14460	25009	Essex County	743159
13220	54019	Fayette County	46039	14460	25017	Middlesex County	1503085
13220	54081	Raleigh County	78859	14460		Rockingham County-Strafford County, NH Div 40484	418366
13380		Bellingham, WA	201140	14460	33015	Rockingham County	295223
13380	53073	Whatcom County	201140	14460	33017	Strafford County	123143
13460		Bend-Redmond, OR	157733	14500		Boulder, CO	294567
13460	41017	Deschutes County	157733	14500	08013	Boulder County	294567
13740		Billings, MT	158934	14540		Bowling Green, KY	158599
13740	30009	Carbon County	10078	14540	21003	Allen County	19956
13740	30037	Golden Valley County	884	14540	21031	Butler County	12690
13740	30111	Yellowstone County	147972	14540	21061	Edmonson County	12161
				14540	21227	Warren County	113792
13780		Binghamton, NY	251725				
13780	36007	Broome County	200600				
13780	36107	Tioga County	51125				

METROPOLITAN STATISTICAL AREAS, METROPOLITAN DIVISIONS, AND COMPONENTS
(as defined July 2015)—*Continued*

Core based statistical area	State/ County FIPS code	Title and Geographic Components	2010 Census Population	Core based statistical area	State/ County FIPS code	Title and Geographic Components	2010 Census Population
14740		Bremerton-Silverdale, WA	251133	16620		Charleston, WV	227078
14740	53035	Kitsap County	251133	16620	54005	Boone County	24629
				16620	54015	Clay County	9386
14860		Bridgeport-Stamford-Norwalk, CT	916829	16620	54039	Kanawha County	193063
14860	09001	Fairfield County	916829				
				16700		Charleston-North Charleston, SC	664607
15180		Brownsville-Harlingen, TX	406220	16700	45015	Berkeley County	177843
15180	48061	Cameron County	406220	16700	45019	Charleston County	350209
				16700	45035	Dorchester County	136555
15260		Brunswick, GA	112370				
15260	13025	Brantley County	18411	16740		Charlotte-Concord-Gastonia, NC-SC	2217012
15260	13127	Glynn County	79626	16740	37025	Cabarrus County	178011
15260	13191	McIntosh County	14333	16740	37071	Gaston County	206086
				16740	37097	Iredell County	159437
15380		Buffalo-Cheektowaga-Niagara Falls, NY	1135509	16740	37109	Lincoln County	78265
15380	36029	Erie County	919040	16740	37119	Mecklenburg County	919628
15380	36063	Niagara County	216469	16740	37159	Rowan County	138428
				16740	37179	Union County	201292
15500		Burlington, NC	151131	16740	45023	Chester County	33140
15500	37001	Alamance County	151131	16740	45057	Lancaster County	76652
				16740	45091	York County	226073
15540		Burlington-South Burlington, VT	211261				
15540	50007	Chittenden County	156545	16820		Charlottesville, VA	218705
15540	50011	Franklin County	47746	16820	51003	Albemarle County	98970
15540	50013	Grand Isle County	6970	16820	51029	Buckingham County	17146
				16820	51065	Fluvanna County	25691
15680		California-Lexington Park, MD	105151	16820	51079	Greene County	18403
15680	24037	St. Mary's County	105151	16820	51125	Nelson County	15020
				16820	51540	Charlottesville city	43475
15940		Canton-Massillon, OH	404422				
15940	39019	Carroll County	28836	16860		Chattanooga, TN-GA	528143
15940	39151	Stark County	375586	16860	13047	Catoosa County	63942
				16860	13083	Dade County	16633
15980		Cape Coral-Fort Myers, FL	618754	16860	13295	Walker County	68756
15980	12071	Lee County	618754	16860	47065	Hamilton County	336463
				16860	47115	Marion County	28237
16020		Cape Girardeau, MO-IL	96275	16860	47153	Sequatchie County	14112
16020	17003	Alexander County	8238				
16020	29017	Bollinger County	12363	16940		Cheyenne, WY	91738
16020	29031	Cape Girardeau County	75674	16940	56021	Laramie County	91738
16060		Carbondale-Marion, IL	126575	16980		Chicago-Naperville-Elgin, IL-IN-WI	9461105
16060	17077	Jackson County	60218	16980		Chicago-Naperville-Arlington Heights, IL Div 16974	7262718
16060	17199	Williamson County	66357	16980	17031	Cook County	5194675
				16980	17043	DuPage County	916924
16180		Carson City, NV	55274	16980	17063	Grundy County	50063
16180	32510	Carson City	55274	16980	17093	Kendall County	114736
				16980	17111	McHenry County	308760
16220		Casper, WY	75450	16980	17197	Will County	677560
16220	56025	Natrona County	75450	16980		Elgin, IL Div 20994	620429
				16980	17037	DeKalb County	105160
16300		Cedar Rapids, IA	257940	16980	17089	Kane County	515269
16300	19011	Benton County	26076	16980		Gary, IN Div 23844	708070
16300	19105	Jones County	20638	16980	18073	Jasper County	33478
16300	19113	Linn County	211226	16980	18089	Lake County	496005
				16980	18111	Newton County	14244
16540		Chambersburg-Waynesboro, PA	149618	16980	18127	Porter County	164343
16540	42055	Franklin County	149618	16980		Lake County-Kenosha County, IL-WI Div 29404	869888
16580		Champaign-Urbana, IL	231891	16980	17097	Lake County	703462
16580	17019	Champaign County	201081	16980	55059	Kenosha County	166426
16580	17053	Ford County	14081				
16580	17147	Piatt County	16729				

Core based statistical area	State/County FIPS code	Title and Geographic Components	2010 Census Population	Core based statistical area	State/County FIPS code	Title and Geographic Components	2010 Census Population
17020		Chico, CA...................................	220000	18020		Columbus, IN............................	76794
17020	06007	Butte County	220000	18020	18005	Bartholomew County..................	76794
17140		Cincinnati, OH-KY-IN..................	2114580	18140		Columbus, OH...........................	1901974
17140	18029	Dearborn County........................	50047	18140	39041	Delaware County........................	174214
17140	18115	Ohio County	6128	18140	39045	Fairfield County..........................	146156
17140	18161	Union County	7516	18140	39049	Franklin County..........................	1163414
17140	21015	Boone County	118811	18140	39073	Hocking County..........................	29380
17140	21023	Bracken County	8488	18140	39089	Licking County...........................	166492
17140	21037	Campbell County	90336	18140	39097	Madison County.........................	43435
17140	21077	Gallatin County	8589	18140	39117	Morrow County...........................	34827
17140	21081	Grant County	24662	18140	39127	Perry County.............................	36058
17140	21117	Kenton County	159720	18140	39129	Pickaway County........................	55698
17140	21191	Pendleton County	14877	18140	39159	Union County.............................	52300
17140	39015	Brown County	44846				
17140	39017	Butler County	368130	18580		Corpus Christi, TX	428185
17140	39025	Clermont County	197363	18580	48007	Aransas County.........................	23158
17140	39061	Hamilton County	802374	18580	48355	Nueces County..........................	340223
17140	39165	Warren County	212693	18580	48409	San Patricio County...................	64804
17300		Clarksville, TN-KY......................	260625	18700		Corvallis, OR	85579
17300	21047	Christian County	73955	18700	41003	Benton County...........................	85579
17300	21221	Trigg County..............................	14339				
17300	47125	Montgomery County....................	172331	18880		Crestview-Fort Walton Beach-Destin, FL	235865
				18880	12091	Okaloosa County........................	180822
17420		Cleveland, TN............................	115788	18880	12131	Walton County	55043
17420	47011	Bradley County	98963				
17420	47139	Polk County................................	16825	19060		Cumberland, MD-WV	103299
				19060	24001	Allegany County.........................	75087
17460		Cleveland-Elyria, OH	2077240	19060	54057	Mineral County...........................	28212
17460	39035	Cuyahoga County	1280122				
17460	39055	Geauga County	93389	19100		Dallas-Fort Worth-Arlington, TX	6426214
17460	39085	Lake County...............................	230041	19100		Dallas-Plano-Irving, TX Div 19124...................	4230520
17460	39093	Lorain County.............................	301356	19100	48085	Collin County..............................	782341
17460	39103	Medina County	172332	19100	48113	Dallas County............................	2368139
				19100	48121	Denton County...........................	662614
17660		Coeur d'Alene, ID	138494	19100	48139	Ellis County................................	149610
17660	16055	Kootenai County	138494	19100	48231	Hunt County	86129
				19100	48257	Kaufman County.........................	103350
17780		College Station-Bryan, TX	228660	19100	48397	Rockwall County.........................	78337
17780	48041	Brazos County	194851	19100		Fort Worth-Arlington, TX Div 23104...................	2195694
17780	48051	Burleson County	17187	19100	48221	Hood County	51182
17780	48395	Robertson County.......................	16622	19100	48251	Johnson County	150934
				19100	48367	Parker County............................	116927
17820		Colorado Springs, CO	645613	19100	48425	Somervell County.......................	8490
17820	08041	El Paso County	622263	19100	48439	Tarrant County...........................	1809034
17820	08119	Teller County..............................	23350	19100	48497	Wise County...............................	59127
17860		Columbia, MO............................	162642	19140		Dalton, GA.................................	142227
17860	29019	Boone County.............................	162642	19140	13213	Murray County............................	39628
				19140	13313	Whitfield County.........................	102599
17900		Columbia, SC.............................	767598				
17900	45017	Calhoun County..........................	15175	18180		Danville, IL................................	81625
17900	45039	Fairfield County..........................	23956	18180	17183	Vermilion County........................	81625
17900	45055	Kershaw County.........................	61697				
17900	45063	Lexington County........................	262391	19300		Daphne-Fairhope-Foley, AL........	182265
17900	45079	Richland County.........................	384504	19300	01003	Baldwin County..........................	182265
17900	45081	Saluda County	19875				
				19340		Davenport-Moline-Rock Island, IA-IL..............	379690
17980		Columbus, GA-AL.......................	294865	19340	17073	Henry County	50486
17980	01113	Russell County...........................	52947	19340	17131	Mercer County............................	16434
17980	13053	Chattahoochee County	11267	19340	17161	Rock Island County.....................	147546
17980	13145	Harris County	32024	19340	19163	Scott County	165224
17980	13197	Marion County............................	8742				
17980	13215	Muscogee County.......................	189885				

Core based statistical area	State/County FIPS code	Title and Geographic Components	2010 Census Population	Core based statistical area	State/County FIPS code	Title and Geographic Components	2010 Census Population
19380		Dayton, OH	799232	20700		East Stroudsburg, PA	169842
19380	39057	Greene County	161573	20700	42089	Monroe County	169842
19380	39109	Miami County	102506				
19380	39113	Montgomery County	535153	20740		Eau Claire, WI	161151
				20740	55017	Chippewa County	62415
19460		Decatur, AL	153829	20740	55035	Eau Claire County	98736
19460	01079	Lawrence County	34339				
19460	01103	Morgan County	119490	20940		El Centro, CA	174528
				20940	06025	Imperial County	174528
19500		Decatur, IL	110768				
19500	17115	Macon County	110768	21060		Elizabethtown-Fort Knox, KY	148338
				21060	21093	Hardin County	105543
19660		Deltona-Daytona Beach-Ormond Beach, FL	590289	21060	21123	Larue County	14193
19660	12035	Flagler County	95696	21060	21163	Meade County	28602
19660	12127	Volusia County	494593				
				21140		Elkhart-Goshen, IN	197559
19740		Denver-Aurora-Lakewood, CO	2543482	21140	18039	Elkhart County	197559
19740	08001	Adams County	441603				
19740	08005	Arapahoe County	572003	21300		Elmira, NY	88830
19740	08014	Broomfield County	55889	21300	36015	Chemung County	88830
19740	08019	Clear Creek County	9088				
19740	08031	Denver County	600158	21340		El Paso, TX	804123
19740	08035	Douglas County	285465	21340	48141	El Paso County	800647
19740	08039	Elbert County	23086	21340	48229	Hudspeth County	3476
19740	08047	Gilpin County	5441				
19740	08059	Jefferson County	534543	21420		Enid, OK	60580
19740	08093	Park County	16206	21420	40047	Garfield County	60580
19780		Des Moines-West Des Moines, IA	569633	21500		Erie, PA	280566
19780	19049	Dallas County	66135	21500	42049	Erie County	280566
19780	19077	Guthrie County	10954				
19780	19121	Madison County	15679	21660		Eugene, OR	351715
19780	19153	Polk County	430640	21660	41039	Lane County	351715
19780	19181	Warren County	46225				
				21780		Evansville, IN-KY	311552
19820		Detroit-Warren-Dearborn, MI	4296250	21780	18129	Posey County	25910
19820		Detroit-Dearborn-Livonia, MI Div 19804	1820584	21780	18163	Vanderburgh County	179703
19820	26163	Wayne County	1820584	21780	18173	Warrick County	59689
19820		Warren-Troy-Farmington Hills, MI 47664	2475666	21780	21101	Henderson County	46250
19820	26087	Lapeer County	88319				
19820	26093	Livingston County	180967	21820		Fairbanks, AK	97581
19820	26099	Macomb County	840978	21820	02090	Fairbanks North Star Borough	97581
19820	26125	Oakland County	1202362				
19820	26147	St. Clair County	163040	22020		Fargo, ND-MN	208777
				22020	27027	Clay County	58999
20020		Dothan, AL	145639	22020	38017	Cass County	149778
20020	01061	Geneva County	26790				
20020	01067	Henry County	17302	22140		Farmington, NM	130044
20020	01069	Houston County	101547	22140	35045	San Juan County	130044
20100		Dover, DE	162310	22180		Fayetteville, NC	366383
20100	10001	Kent County	162310	22180	37051	Cumberland County	319431
				22180	37093	Hoke County	46952
20220		Dubuque, IA	93653				
20220	19061	Dubuque County	93653	22220		Fayetteville-Springdale-Rogers, AR-MO	463204
				22220	05007	Benton County	221339
20260		Duluth, MN-WI	279771	22220	05087	Madison County	15717
20260	27017	Carlton County	35386	22220	05143	Washington County	203065
20260	27137	St. Louis County	200226	22220	29119	McDonald County	23083
20260	55031	Douglas County	44159				
				22380		Flagstaff, AZ	134421
20500		Durham-Chapel Hill, NC	504357	22380	04005	Coconino County	134421
20500	37037	Chatham County	63505				
20500	37063	Durham County	267587	22420		Flint, MI	425790
20500	37135	Orange County	133801	22420	26049	Genesee County	425790
20500	37145	Person County	39464				

Core based statistical area	State/ County FIPS code	Title and Geographic Components	2010 Census Population	Core based statistical area	State/ County FIPS code	Title and Geographic Components	2010 Census Population
22500		Florence, SC................................	205566	24420		Grants Pass, OR	82713
22500	45031	Darlington County	68681	24420	41033	Josephine County	82713
22500	45041	Florence County	136885				
				24500		Great Falls, MT...........................	81327
22520		Florence-Muscle Shoals, AL.........	147137	24500	30013	Cascade County	81327
22520	01033	Colbert County	54428				
22520	01077	Lauderdale County.....................	92709	24540		Greeley, CO...............................	252825
				24540	08123	Weld County	252825
22540		Fond du Lac, WI	101633				
22540	55039	Fond du Lac County....................	101633	24580		Green Bay, WI	306241
				24580	55009	Brown County	248007
22660		Fort Collins, CO	299630	24580	55061	Kewaunee County......................	20574
22660	08069	Larimer County	299630	24580	55083	Oconto County	37660
22900		Fort Smith, AR-OK......................	280467	24660		Greensboro-High Point, NC..........	723801
22900	05033	Crawford County	61948	24660	37081	Guilford County..........................	488406
22900	05131	Sebastian County.......................	125744	24660	37151	Randolph County........................	141752
22900	40079	Le Flore County	50384	24660	37157	Rockingham County....................	93643
22900	40135	Sequoyah County.......................	42391				
				24780		Greenville, NC	168148
23060		Fort Wayne, IN	416257	24780	37147	Pitt County	168148
23060	18003	Allen County	355329				
23060	18179	Wells County	27636	24860		Greenville-Anderson-Mauldin, SC	824112
23060	18183	Whitley County	33292	24860	45007	Anderson County	187126
				24860	45045	Greenville County	451225
23420		Fresno, CA................................	930450	24860	45059	Laurens County.........................	66537
23420	06019	Fresno County	930450	24860	45077	Pickens County	119224
23460		Gadsden, AL..............................	104430	25060		Gulfport-Biloxi-Pascagoula, MS......	370702
23460	01055	Etowah County	104430	25060	28045	Hancock County.........................	43929
				25060	28047	Harrison County	187105
23540		Gainesville, FL	264275	25060	28059	Jackson County	139668
23540	12001	Alachua County	247336				
23540	12041	Gilchrist County	16939	25180		Hagerstown-Martinsburg, MD-WV......	251599
				25180	24043	Washington County......................	147430
23580		Gainesville, GA	179684	25180	54003	Berkeley County	104169
23580	13139	Hall County	179684				
				25220		Hammond, LA.............................	121097
23900		Gettysburg, PA...........................	101407	25220	22105	Tangipahoa Parish	121097
23900	42001	Adams County	101407				
				25260		Hanford-Corcoran, CA.................	152982
24020		Glens Falls, NY..........................	128923	25260	06031	Kings County.............................	152982
24020	36113	Warren County	65707				
24020	36115	Washington County	63216	25420		Harrisburg-Carlisle, PA................	549475
				25420	42041	Cumberland County.....................	235406
24140		Goldsboro, NC	122623	25420	42043	Dauphin County	268100
24140	37191	Wayne County	122623	25420	42099	Perry County	45969
24220		Grand Forks, ND-MN...................	98461	25500		Harrisonburg, VA........................	125228
24220	27119	Polk County	31600	25500	51165	Rockingham County....................	76314
24220	38035	Grand Forks County....................	66861	25500	51660	Harrisonburg city........................	48914
24260		Grand Island, NE	81850	25540		Hartford-West Hartford-East Hartford, CT..........	1212381
24260	31079	Hall County	58607	25540	09003	Hartford County	894014
24260	31081	Hamilton County	9124	25540	09007	Middlesex County.......................	165676
24260	31093	Howard County	6274	25540	09013	Tolland County	152691
24260	31121	Merrick County...........................	7845				
				25620		Hattiesburg, MS.........................	142842
24300		Grand Junction, CO.....................	146723	25620	28035	Forrest County	74934
24300	08077	Mesa County	146723	25620	28073	Lamar County	55658
				25620	28111	Perry County	12250
24340		Grand Rapids-Wyoming, MI	988938				
24340	26015	Barry County	59173	25860		Hickory-Lenoir-Morganton, NC......	365497
24340	26081	Kent County	602622	25860	37003	Alexander County	37198
24340	26117	Montcalm County........................	63342	25860	37023	Burke County	90912
24340	26139	Ottawa County	263801	25860	37027	Caldwell County	83029
				25860	37035	Catawba County	154358

Core based statistical area	State/ County FIPS code	Title and Geographic Components	2010 Census Population	Core based statistical area	State/ County FIPS code	Title and Geographic Components	2010 Census Population
25940		Hilton Head Island-Bluffton-Beaufort, NC............	187010	27060		Ithaca, NY..	101564
25940	45013	Beaufort County...................................	162233	27060	36109	Tompkins County	101564
25940	45053	Jasper County......................................	24777				
				27100		Jackson, MI..	160248
25980		Hinesville, GA.......................................	77917	27100	26075	Jackson County..................................	160248
25980	13179	Liberty County.....................................	63453				
25980	13183	Long County...	14464	27140		Jackson, MS..	567122
				27140	28029	Copiah County...................................	29449
26140		Homosassa Springs, FL.........................	141236	27140	28049	Hinds County.....................................	245285
26140	12017	Citrus County......................................	141236	27140	28089	Madison County.................................	95203
				27140	28121	Rankin County...................................	141617
26300		Hot Springs, AR....................................	96024	27140	28127	Simpson County.................................	27503
26300	05051	Garland County...................................	96024	27140	28163	Yazoo County....................................	28065
26380		Houma-Thibodaux, LA............................	208178	27180		Jackson, TN...	130011
26380	22057	Lafourche Parish.................................	96318	27180	47023	Chester County..................................	17131
26380	22109	Terrebonne Parish..............................	111860	27180	47033	Crockett County.................................	14586
				27180	47113	Madison County.................................	98294
26420		Houston-The Woodlands-Sugar Land, TX	5920416				
26420	48015	Austin County.....................................	28417	27260		Jacksonville, FL.....................................	1345596
26420	48039	Brazoria County.................................	313166	27260	12003	Baker County.....................................	27115
26420	48071	Chambers County...............................	35096	27260	12019	Clay County	190865
26420	48157	Fort Bend County...............................	585375	27260	12031	Duval County.....................................	864263
26420	48167	Galveston County...............................	291309	27260	12089	Nassau County..................................	73314
26420	48201	Harris County.....................................	4092459	27260	12109	St. Johns County...............................	190039
26420	48291	Liberty County....................................	75643				
26420	48339	Montgomery County............................	455746	27340		Jacksonville, NC....................................	177772
26420	48473	Waller County.....................................	43205	27340	37133	Onslow County..................................	177772
26580		Huntington-Ashland, WV-KY-OH	364908	27500		Janesville-Beloit, WI...............................	160331
26580	21019	Boyd County	49542	27500	55105	Rock County......................................	160331
26580	21089	Greenup County..................................	36910				
26580	39087	Lawrence County................................	62450	27620		Jefferson City, MO.................................	149807
26580	54011	Cabell County.....................................	96319	27620	29027	Callaway County................................	44332
26580	54043	Lincoln County....................................	21720	27620	29051	Cole County	75990
26580	54079	Putnam County...................................	55486	27620	29135	Moniteau County................................	15607
26580	54099	Wayne County....................................	42481	27620	29151	Osage County....................................	13878
26620		Huntsville, AL..	417593	27740		Johnson City, TN...................................	198716
26620	01083	Limestone County...............................	82782	27740	47019	Carter County....................................	57424
26620	01089	Madison County..................................	334811	27740	47171	Unicoi County....................................	18313
				27740	47179	Washington County............................	122979
26820		Idaho Falls, ID......................................	133265				
26820	16019	Bonneville County..............................	104234	27780		Johnstown, PA......................................	143679
26820	16023	Butte County......................................	2891	27780	42021	Cambria County.................................	143679
26820	16051	Jefferson County................................	26140				
				27860		Jonesboro, AR......................................	121026
26900		Indianapolis-Carmel-Anderson, IN	1887877	27860	05031	Craighead County..............................	96443
26900	18011	Boone County....................................	56640	27860	05111	Poinsett County.................................	24583
26900	18013	Brown County....................................	15242				
26900	18057	Hamilton County.................................	274569	27900		Joplin, MO...	175518
26900	18059	Hancock County.................................	70002	27900	29097	Jasper County...................................	117404
26900	18063	Hendricks County...............................	145448	27900	29145	Newton County..................................	58114
26900	18081	Johnson County..................................	139654				
26900	18095	Madison County..................................	131636	27980		Kahului-Wailuku-Lahaina, HI	154924
26900	18097	Marion County....................................	903393	27980	15005	Kalawao County.................................	90
26900	18109	Morgan County...................................	68894	27980	15009	Maui County......................................	154834
26900	18133	Putnam County	37963				
26900	18145	Shelby County....................................	44436	28020		Kalamazoo-Portage, MI.........................	326589
				28020	26077	Kalamazoo County.............................	250331
26980		Iowa City, IA...	152586	28020	26159	Van Buren County..............................	76258
26980	19103	Johnson County..................................	130882				
26980	19183	Washington County............................	21704	28100		Kankakee, IL..	113449
				28100	17091	Kankakee County..............................	113449

Core based statistical area	State/County FIPS code	Title and Geographic Components	2010 Census Population	Core based statistical area	State/County FIPS code	Title and Geographic Components	2010 Census Population
28140		Kansas City, MO-KS	2009342	29340		Lake Charles, LA	199607
28140	20091	Johnson County	544179	29340	22019	Calcasieu Parish	192768
28140	20103	Leavenworth County	76227	29340	22023	Cameron Parish	6839
28140	20107	Linn County	9656				
28140	20121	Miami County	32787	29420		Lake Havasu City-Kingman, AZ	200186
28140	20209	Wyandotte County	157505	29420	04015	Mohave County	200186
28140	29013	Bates County	17049				
28140	29025	Caldwell County	9424	29460		Lakeland-Winter Haven, FL	602095
28140	29037	Cass County	99478	29460	12105	Polk County	602095
28140	29047	Clay County	221939				
28140	29049	Clinton County	20743	29540		Lancaster, PA	519445
28140	29095	Jackson County	674158	29540	42071	Lancaster County	519445
28140	29107	Lafayette County	33381				
28140	29165	Platte County	89322	29620		Lansing-East Lansing, MI	464036
28140	29177	Ray County	23494	29620	26037	Clinton County	75382
				29620	26045	Eaton County	107759
28420		Kennewick-Richland, WA	253340	29620	26065	Ingham County	280895
28420	53005	Benton County	175177				
28420	53021	Franklin County	78163	29700		Laredo, TX	250304
				29700	48479	Webb County	250304
28660		Killeen-Temple, TX	405300				
28660	48027	Bell County	310235	29740		Las Cruces, NM	209233
28660	48099	Coryell County	75388	29740	35013	Dona Ana County	209233
28660	48281	Lampasas County	19677				
				29820		Las Vegas-Henderson-Paradise, NV	1951269
28700		Kingsport-Bristol-Bristol, TN-VA	309544	29820	32003	Clark County	1951269
28700	47073	Hawkins County	56833				
28700	47163	Sullivan County	156823	29940		Lawrence, KS	110826
28700	51169	Scott County	23177	29940	20045	Douglas County	110826
28700	51191	Washington County	54876				
28700	51520	Bristol city	17835	30020		Lawton, OK	130291
				30020	40031	Comanche County	124098
28740		Kingston, NY	182493	30020	40033	Cotton County	6193
28740	36111	Ulster County	182493				
				30140		Lebanon, PA	133568
28940		Knoxville, TN	837571	30140	42075	Lebanon County	133568
28940	47001	Anderson County	75129				
28940	47009	Blount County	123010	30300		Lewiston, ID-WA	60888
28940	47013	Campbell County	40716	30300	16069	Nez Perce County	39265
28940	47057	Grainger County	22657	30300	53003	Asotin County	21623
28940	47093	Knox County	432226				
28940	47105	Loudon County	48556	30340		Lewiston-Auburn, ME	107702
28940	47129	Morgan County	21987	30340	23001	Androscoggin County	107702
28940	47145	Roane County	54181				
28940	47173	Union County	19109	30460		Lexington-Fayette, KY	472099
				30460	21017	Bourbon County	19985
29020		Kokomo, IN	82752	30460	21049	Clark County	35613
29020	18067	Howard County	82752	30460	21067	Fayette County	295803
				30460	21113	Jessamine County	48586
29100		La Crosse-Onalaska, WI-MN	133665	30460	21209	Scott County	47173
29100	27055	Houston County	19027	30460	21239	Woodford County	24939
29100	55063	La Crosse County	114638				
				30620		Lima, OH	106331
29180		Lafayette, LA	466750	30620	39003	Allen County	106331
29180	22001	Acadia Parish	61773				
29180	22045	Iberia Parish	73240	30700		Lincoln, NE	302157
29180	22055	Lafayette Parish	221578	30700	31109	Lancaster County	285407
29180	22099	St. Martin Parish	52160	30700	31159	Seward County	16750
29180	22113	Vermilion Parish	57999				
29200		Lafayette-West Lafayette, IN	201789				
29200	18007	Benton County	8854				
29200	18015	Carroll County	20155				
29200	18157	Tippecanoe County	172780				

Core based statistical area	State/ County FIPS code	Title and Geographic Components	2010 Census Population	Core based statistical area	State/ County FIPS code	Title and Geographic Components	2010 Census Population
30780		Little Rock-North Little Rock-Conway, AR	699757	31540		Madison, WI...	605435
30780	05045	Faulkner County...................................	113237	31540	55021	Columbia County..................................	56833
30780	05053	Grant County.......................................	17853	31540	55025	Dane County.......................................	488073
30780	05085	Lonoke County.....................................	68356	31540	55045	Green County......................................	36842
30780	05105	Perry County.......................................	10445	31540	55049	Iowa County..	23687
30780	05119	Pulaski County.....................................	382748				
30780	05125	Saline County......................................	107118	31700		Manchester-Nashua, NH.............................	400721
				31700	33011	Hillsborough County.............................	400721
30860		Logan, UT-ID..	125442				
30860	16041	Franklin County....................................	12786	31740		Manhattan, KS...	92719
30860	49005	Cache County......................................	112656	31740	20149	Pottawatomie County...........................	21604
				31740	20161	Riley County..	71115
30980		Longview, TX..	214369				
30980	48183	Gregg County......................................	121730	31860		Mankato-North Mankato, MN	96740
30980	48401	Rusk County..	53330	31860	27013	Blue Earth County...............................	64013
30980	48459	Upshur County.....................................	39309	31860	27103	Nicollet County....................................	32727
31020		Longview, WA...	102410	31900		Mansfield, OH..	124475
31020	53015	Cowlitz County....................................	102410	31900	39139	Richland County..................................	124475
31080		Los Angeles-Long Beach-Anaheim, CA	12828837	32580		McAllen-Edinburg-Mission, TX	774769
31080		Anaheim-Santa Ana-Irvine, CA Div 11244	3010232	32580	48215	Hidalgo County....................................	774769
31080	06059	Orange County................................	3010232				
31080		Los Angeles-Long Beach-Glendale, CA Div 31084..	9818605	32780		Medford, OR..	203206
				32780	41029	Jackson County	203206
31080	06037	Los Angeles County	9818605				
				32820		Memphis, TN-MS-AR..................................	1324829
31140		Louisville/Jefferson County, KY-IN...................	1235708	32820	05035	Crittenden County...............................	50902
31140	18019	Clark County.......................................	110232	32820	28009	Benton County	8729
31140	18043	Floyd County.......................................	74578	32820	28033	DeSoto County....................................	161252
31140	18061	Harrison County...................................	39364	32820	28093	Marshall County..................................	37144
31140	18143	Scott County.......................................	24181	32820	28137	Tate County..	28886
31140	18175	Washington County..............................	28262	32820	28143	Tunica County.....................................	10778
31140	21029	Bullitt County......................................	74319	32820	47047	Fayette County....................................	38413
31140	21103	Henry County......................................	15416	32820	47157	Shelby County.....................................	927644
31140	21111	Jefferson County..................................	741096	32820	47167	Tipton County......................................	61081
31140	21185	Oldham County....................................	60316				
31140	21211	Shelby County.....................................	42074	32900		Merced, CA...	255793
31140	21215	Spencer County...................................	17061	32900	06047	Merced County....................................	255793
31140	21223	Trimble County....................................	8809				
				33100		Miami-Fort Lauderdale-West Palm Beach, FL.....	5564635
31180		Lubbock, TX	290805	33100		Fort Lauderdale-Pompano Beach-Deerfield Beach, FL Div 22744	1748066
31180	48107	Crosby County....................................	6059				
31180	48303	Lubbock County..................................	278831	33100	12011	Broward County...............................	1748066
31180	48305	Lynn County..	5915	33100		Miami-Miami Beach-Kendall, FL Div 33124.....	2496435
				33100	12086	Miami-Dade County...........................	2496435
31340		Lynchburg, VA..	252634	33100		West Palm Beach-Boca Raton-Delray Beach, FL Div 48424.....................................	1320134
31340	51009	Amherst County...................................	32353				
31340	51011	Appomattox County..............................	14973	33100	12099	Palm Beach County...........................	1320134
31340	51019	Bedford County....................................	68676				
31340	51031	Campbell County.................................	54842	33140		Michigan City-La Porte, IN..........................	111467
31340	51515	Bedford city..	6222	33140	18091	LaPorte County...................................	111467
31340	51680	Lynchburg city.....................................	75568				
				33220		Midland, MI...	83629
31420		Macon, GA...	232293	33220	26111	Midland County...................................	83629
31420	13021	Bibb County..	155547				
31420	13079	Crawford County.................................	12630	33260		Midland, TX...	141671
31420	13169	Jones County......................................	28669	33260	48317	Martin County......................................	4799
31420	13207	Monroe County....................................	26424	33260	48329	Midland County...................................	136872
31420	13289	Twiggs County.....................................	9023				
31460		Madera, CA..	150865				
31460	06039	Madera County....................................	150865				

Core based statistical area	State/County FIPS code	Title and Geographic Components	2010 Census Population	Core based statistical area	State/County FIPS code	Title and Geographic Components	2010 Census Population
33340		Milwaukee-Waukesha-West Allis, WI	1555908	34820		Myrtle Beach-Conway-North Myrtle Beach, NC-SC	376722
33340	55079	Milwaukee County............	947735				
33340	55089	Ozaukee County............	86395	34820	37019	Brunswick County............	107431
33340	55131	Washington County............	131887	34820	45051	Horry County............	269291
33340	55133	Waukesha County............	389891				
				34900		Napa, CA............	136484
33460		Minneapolis-St. Paul-Bloomington, MN............	3348859	34900	06055	Napa County............	136484
33460	27003	Anoka County............	330844				
33460	27019	Carver County............	91042	34940		Naples-Immokalee-Marco Island, FL............	321520
33460	27025	Chisago County............	53887	34940	12021	Collier County............	321520
33460	27037	Dakota County............	398552				
33460	27053	Hennepin County............	1152425	34980		Nashville-Davidson--Murfreesboro--Franklin, TN	1670890
33460	27059	Isanti County............	37816	34980	47015	Cannon County............	13801
33460	27079	Le Sueur County............	27703	34980	47021	Cheatham County............	39105
33460	27095	Mille Lacs County............	26097	34980	47037	Davidson County............	626681
33460	27123	Ramsey County............	508640	34980	47043	Dickson County............	49666
33460	27139	Scott County............	129928	34980	47081	Hickman County............	24690
33460	27141	Sherburne County............	88499	34980	47111	Macon County............	22248
33460	27143	Sibley County............	15226	34980	47119	Maury County............	80956
33460	27163	Washington County............	238136	34980	47147	Robertson County............	66283
33460	27171	Wright County............	124700	34980	47149	Rutherford County............	262604
33460	55093	Pierce County............	41019	34980	47159	Smith County............	19166
33460	55109	St. Croix County............	84345	34980	47165	Sumner County............	160543
				34980	47169	Trousdale County............	7870
33540		Missoula, MT............	109299	34980	47187	Williamson County............	183182
33540	30063	Missoula County............	109299	34980	47189	Wilson County............	113993
33660		Mobile, AL............	412992	35100		New Bern, NC............	126802
33660	01097	Mobile County............	412992	35100	37049	Craven County............	103505
				35100	37103	Jones County............	10153
33700		Modesto, CA............	514453	35100	37137	Pamlico County............	13144
33700	06099	Stanislaus County............	514453				
				35300		New Haven-Milford, CT............	862477
33740		Monroe, LA............	176441	35300	09009	New Haven County............	862477
33740	22073	Ouachita Parish............	153720				
33740	22111	Union Parish............	22721	35380		New Orleans-Metairie, LA............	1189866
				35380	22051	Jefferson Parish............	432552
33780		Monroe, MI............	152021	35380	22071	Orleans Parish............	343829
33780	26115	Monroe County............	152021	35380	22075	Plaquemines Parish............	23042
				35380	22087	St. Bernard Parish............	35897
33860		Montgomery, AL............	374536	35380	22089	St. Charles Parish............	52780
33860	01001	Autauga County............	54571	35380	22093	St. James Parish............	22102
33860	01051	Elmore County............	79303	35380	22095	St. John the Baptist Parish............	45924
33860	01085	Lowndes County............	11299	35380	22103	St. Tammany Parish............	233740
33860	01101	Montgomery County............	229363				
34060		Morgantown, WV............	129709				
34060	54061	Monongalia County............	96189				
34060	54077	Preston County............	33520				
34100		Morristown, TN............	113951				
34100	47063	Hamblen County............	62544				
34100	47089	Jefferson County............	51407				
34580		Mount Vernon-Anacortes, WA............	116901				
34580	53057	Skagit County............	116901				
34620		Muncie, IN............	117671				
34620	18035	Delaware County............	117671				
34740		Muskegon, MI............	172188				
34740	26121	Muskegon County............	172188				

Core based statistical area	State/County FIPS code	Title and Geographic Components	2010 Census Population	Core based statistical area	State/County FIPS code	Title and Geographic Components	2010 Census Population
35620		New York-Newark-Jersey City, NY-NJ-PA	19567410	36500		Olympia-Tumwater, WA.................................	252264
35620		Dutchess County-Putnam County, NY Div 20524	397198	36500	53067	Thurston County	252264
35620	36027	Dutchess County	297488	36540		Omaha-Council Bluffs, NE-IA.................................	865350
35620	36079	Putnam County	99710	36540	19085	Harrison County	14928
35620		Nassau County-Suffolk County, NY Div 35004	2832882	36540	19129	Mills County	15059
35620	36059	Nassau County	1339532	36540	19155	Pottawattamie County	93158
35620	36103	Suffolk County	1493350	36540	31025	Cass County	25241
35620		Newark, NJ-PA Div 35084.................................	2471171	36540	31055	Douglas County	517110
35620	34013	Essex County	783969	36540	31153	Sarpy County	158840
35620	34019	Hunterdon County	128349	36540	31155	Saunders County	20780
35620	34027	Morris County	492276	36540	31177	Washington County	20234
35620	34035	Somerset County	323444				
35620	34037	Sussex County	149265	36740		Orlando-Kissimmee-Sanford, FL.................................	2134411
35620	34039	Union County	536499	36740	12069	Lake County	297052
35620	42103	Pike County	57369	36740	12095	Orange County	1145956
35620		New York-Jersey City-White Plains, NY-NJ Div 35614	13866159	36740	12097	Osceola County	268685
				36740	12117	Seminole County	422718
35620	34003	Bergen County	905116				
35620	34017	Hudson County	634266	36780		Oshkosh-Neenah, WI.................................	166994
35620	34023	Middlesex County	809858	36780	55139	Winnebago County	166994
35620	34025	Monmouth County	630380				
35620	34029	Ocean County	576567	36980		Owensboro, KY.................................	114752
35620	34031	Passaic County	501226	36980	21059	Daviess County	96656
35620	36005	Bronx County	1385108	36980	21091	Hancock County	8565
35620	36047	Kings County	2504700	36980	21149	McLean County	9531
35620	36061	New York County	1585873				
35620	36071	Orange County	372813	37100		Oxnard-Thousand Oaks-Ventura, CA.................................	823318
35620	36081	Queens County	2230722	37100	06111	Ventura County	823318
35620	36085	Richmond County	468730				
35620	36087	Rockland County	311687	37340		Palm Bay-Melbourne-Titusville, FL.................................	543376
35620	36119	Westchester County	949113	37340	12009	Brevard County	543376
35660		Niles-Benton Harbor, MI	156813	37460		Panama City, FL.................................	184715
35660	26021	Berrien County	156813	37460	12005	Bay County	168852
35840		North Port-Sarasota-Bradenton, FL.................................	702281	37460	12045	Gulf County	15863
35840	12081	Manatee County	322833	37620		Parkersburg-Vienna, WV.................................	92673
35840	12115	Sarasota County	379448	37620	54105	Wirt County	5717
				37620	54107	Wood County	86956
35980		Norwich-New London, CT	274055				
35980	09011	New London County	274055	37860		Pensacola-Ferry Pass-Brent, FL	448991
				37860	12033	Escambia County	297619
36100		Ocala, FL.................................	331298	37860	12113	Santa Rosa County	151372
36100	12083	Marion County	331298				
				37900		Peoria, IL.................................	379186
36140		Ocean City, NJ.................................	97265	37900	17123	Marshall County	12640
36140	34009	Cape May County	97265	37900	17143	Peoria County	186494
				37900	17175	Stark County	5994
36220		Odessa, TX.................................	137130	37900	17179	Tazewell County	135394
36220	48135	Ector County	137130	37900	17203	Woodford County	38664
36260		Ogden-Clearfield, UT.................................	597159	37980		Philadelphia-Camden-Wilmington, PA-NJ-DE-MD	5965343
36260	49003	Box Elder County	49975				
36260	49011	Davis County	306479	37980		Camden, NJ Div 15804.................................	1250679
36260	49029	Morgan County	9469	37980	34005	Burlington County	448734
36260	49057	Weber County	231236	37980	34007	Camden County	513657
				37980	34015	Gloucester County	288288
36420		Oklahoma City, OK.................................	1252987	37980		Montgomery County-Bucks County-Chester County, PA Div 33874	1924009
36420	40017	Canadian County	115541				
36420	40027	Cleveland County	255755	37980	42017	Bucks County	625249
36420	40051	Grady County	52431	37980	42029	Chester County	498886
36420	40081	Lincoln County	34273	37980	42091	Montgomery County	799874
36420	40083	Logan County	41848	37980		Philadelphia, PA Div 37964.................................	2084985
36420	40087	McClain County	34506	37980	42045	Delaware County	558979
36420	40109	Oklahoma County	718633	37980	42101	Philadelphia County	1526006

Core based statistical area	State/ County FIPS code	Title and Geographic Components	2010 Census Population	Core based statistical area	State/ County FIPS code	Title and Geographic Components	2010 Census Population
37980		Wilmington, DE-MD-NJ Div 48864..................	705670	39460		Punta Gorda, FL..................................	159978
37980	10003	New Castle County..................................	538479	39460	12015	Charlotte County..................................	159978
37980	24015	Cecil County..	101108				
37980	34033	Salem County...	66083	39540		Racine, WI..	195408
				39540	55101	Racine County......................................	195408
38060		Phoenix-Mesa-Scottsdale, AZ...................	4192887				
38060	04013	Maricopa County....................................	3817117	39580		Raleigh, NC..	1130490
38060	04021	Pinal County...	375770	39580	37069	Franklin County....................................	60619
				39580	37101	Johnston County...................................	168878
38220		Pine Bluff, AR..	100258	39580	37183	Wake County..	900993
38220	05025	Cleveland County..................................	8689				
38220	05069	Jefferson County...................................	77435	39660		Rapid City, SD......................................	134598
38220	05079	Lincoln County......................................	14134	39660	46033	Custer County.......................................	8216
				39660	46093	Meade County.......................................	25434
38300		Pittsburgh, PA.......................................	2356285	39660	46103	Pennington County...............................	100948
38300	42003	Allegheny County..................................	1223348				
38300	42005	Armstrong County.................................	68941	39740		Reading, PA..	411442
38300	42007	Beaver County......................................	170539	39740	42011	Berks County..	411442
38300	42019	Butler County..	183862				
38300	42051	Fayette County......................................	136606	39820		Redding, CA...	177223
38300	42125	Washington County...............................	207820	39820	06089	Shasta County......................................	177223
38300	42129	Westmoreland County...........................	365169				
				39900		Reno, NV..	425417
38340		Pittsfield, MA...	131219	39900	32029	Storey County.......................................	4010
38340	25003	Berkshire County..................................	131219	39900	32031	Washoe County....................................	421407
38540		Pocatello, ID...	82839	40060		Richmond, VA.......................................	1208101
38540	16005	Bannock County....................................	82839	40060	51007	Amelia County......................................	12690
				40060	51033	Caroline County....................................	28545
38860		Portland-South Portland, ME..................	514098	40060	51036	Charles City County..............................	7256
38860	23005	Cumberland County...............................	281674	40060	51041	Chesterfield County..............................	316236
38860	23023	Sagadahoc County................................	35293	40060	51053	Dinwiddie County..................................	28001
38860	23031	York County...	197131	40060	51075	Goochland County................................	21717
				40060	51085	Hanover County....................................	99863
38900		Portland-Vancouver-Hillsboro, OR-WA.....	2226009	40060	51087	Henrico County.....................................	306935
38900	41005	Clackamas County................................	375992	40060	51101	King William County..............................	15935
38900	41009	Columbia County..................................	49351	40060	51127	New Kent County..................................	18429
38900	41051	Multnomah County................................	735334	40060	51145	Powhatan County.................................	28046
38900	41067	Washington County...............................	529710	40060	51149	Prince George County..........................	35725
38900	41071	Yamhill County.....................................	99193	40060	51183	Sussex County.....................................	12087
38900	53011	Clark County...	425363	40060	51570	Colonial Heights city............................	17411
38900	53059	Skamania County..................................	11066	40060	51670	Hopewell city.......................................	22591
				40060	51730	Petersburg city.....................................	32420
38940		Port St. Lucie, FL..................................	424107	40060	51760	Richmond city.......................................	204214
38940	12085	Martin County.......................................	146318				
38940	12111	St. Lucie County....................................	277789	40140		Riverside-San Bernardino-Ontario, CA................	4224851
				40140	06065	Riverside County..................................	2189641
39140		Prescott, AZ..	211033	40140	06071	San Bernardino County........................	2035210
39140	04025	Yavapai County....................................	211033				
				40220		Roanoke, VA...	308707
39300		Providence-Warwick, RI-MA....................	1600852	40220	51023	Botetourt County..................................	33148
39300	25005	Bristol County.......................................	548285	40220	51045	Craig County..	5190
39300	44001	Bristol County.......................................	49875	40220	51067	Franklin County....................................	56159
39300	44003	Kent County..	166158	40220	51161	Roanoke County..................................	92376
39300	44005	Newport County....................................	82888	40220	51770	Roanoke city..	97032
39300	44007	Providence County................................	626667	40220	51775	Salem city..	24802
39300	44009	Washington County...............................	126979				
				40340		Rochester, MN......................................	206877
39340		Provo-Orem, UT....................................	526810	40340	27039	Dodge County......................................	20087
39340	49023	Juab County..	10246	40340	27045	Fillmore County....................................	20866
39340	49049	Utah County..	516564	40340	27109	Olmsted County...................................	144248
				40340	27157	Wabasha County..................................	21676
39380		Pueblo, CO...	159063				
39380	08101	Pueblo County......................................	159063				

Core based statistical area	State/ County FIPS code	Title and Geographic Components	2010 Census Population	Core based statistical area	State/ County FIPS code	Title and Geographic Components	2010 Census Population
40380		Rochester, NY	1079671	41540		Salisbury, MD-DE	373802
40380	36051	Livingston County	65393	41540	10005	Sussex County	197145
40380	36055	Monroe County	744344	41540	24039	Somerset County	26470
40380	36069	Ontario County	107931	41540	24045	Wicomico County	98733
40380	36073	Orleans County	42883	41540	24047	Worcester County	51454
40380	36117	Wayne County	93772				
40380	36123	Yates County	25348	41620		Salt Lake City, UT	1087873
				41620	49035	Salt Lake County	1029655
40420		Rockford, IL	349431	41620	49045	Tooele County	58218
40420	17007	Boone County	54165				
40420	17201	Winnebago County	295266	41660		San Angelo, TX	111823
				41660	48235	Irion County	1599
40580		Rocky Mount, NC	152392	41660	48451	Tom Green County	110224
40580	37065	Edgecombe County	56552				
40580	37127	Nash County	95840	41700		San Antonio-New Braunfels, TX	2142508
				41700	48013	Atascosa County	44911
40660		Rome, GA	96317	41700	48019	Bandera County	20485
40660	13115	Floyd County	96317	41700	48029	Bexar County	1714773
				41700	48091	Comal County	108472
40900		Sacramento--Roseville--Arden-Arcade, CA	2149127	41700	48187	Guadalupe County	131533
40900	06017	El Dorado County	181058	41700	48259	Kendall County	33410
40900	06061	Placer County	348432	41700	48325	Medina County	46006
40900	06067	Sacramento County	1418788	41700	48493	Wilson County	42918
40900	06113	Yolo County	200849				
				41740		San Diego-Carlsbad, CA	3095313
40980		Saginaw, MI	200169	41740	06073	San Diego County	3095313
40980	26145	Saginaw County	200169				
				41860		San Francisco-Oakland-Hayward, CA	4335391
41060		St. Cloud, MN	189093	41860		Oakland-Hayward-Berkeley, CA Div 36084	2559296
41060	27009	Benton County	38451	41860	06001	Alameda County	1510271
41060	27145	Stearns County	150642	41860	06013	Contra Costa County	1049025
				41860		San Francisco-Redwood City-South San Francisco, CA Div 41884	1523686
41100		St. George, UT	138115				
41100	49053	Washington County	138115	41860	06075	San Francisco County	805235
				41860	06081	San Mateo County	718451
41140		St. Joseph, MO-KS	127329	41860		San Rafael, CA Div 42034	252409
41140	20043	Doniphan County	7945	41860	06041	Marin County	252409
41140	29003	Andrew County	17291				
41140	29021	Buchanan County	89201	41940		San Jose-Sunnyvale-Santa Clara, CA	1836911
41140	29063	DeKalb County	12892	41940	06069	San Benito County	55269
				41940	06085	Santa Clara County	1781642
41180		St. Louis, MO-IL	2787701				
41180	17005	Bond County	17768	42020		San Luis Obispo-Paso Robles-Arroyo Grande, CA	269637
41180	17013	Calhoun County	5089				
41180	17027	Clinton County	37762	42020	06079	San Luis Obispo County	269637
41180	17083	Jersey County	22985				
41180	17117	Macoupin County	47765	42100		Santa Cruz-Watsonville, CA	262382
41180	17119	Madison County	269282	42100	06087	Santa Cruz County	262382
41180	17133	Monroe County	32957				
41180	17163	St. Clair County	270056	42140		Santa Fe, NM	144170
41180	29071	Franklin County	101492	42140	35049	Santa Fe County	144170
41180	29099	Jefferson County	218733				
41180	29113	Lincoln County	52566	42200		Santa Maria-Santa Barbara, CA	423895
41180	29183	St. Charles County	360485	42200	06083	Santa Barbara County	423895
41180	29189	St. Louis County	998954				
41180	29219	Warren County	32513	42220		Santa Rosa, CA	483878
41180	29510	St. Louis city	319294	42220	06097	Sonoma County	483878
41420		Salem, OR	390738	42340		Savannah, GA	347611
41420	41047	Marion County	315335	42340	13029	Bryan County	30233
41420	41053	Polk County	75403	42340	13051	Chatham County	265128
				42340	13103	Effingham County	52250
41500		Salinas, CA	415057				
41500	06053	Monterey County	415057	42540		Scranton--Wilkes-Barre--Hazleton, PA	563631

Core based statistical area	State/ County FIPS code	Title and Geographic Components	2010 Census Population	Core based statistical area	State/ County FIPS code	Title and Geographic Components	2010 Census Population
42540	42069	Lackawanna County	214437	44180		Springfield, MO	436712
42540	42079	Luzerne County	320918	44180	29043	Christian County	77422
42540	42131	Wyoming County	28276	44180	29059	Dallas County	16777
				44180	29077	Greene County	275174
42660		Seattle-Tacoma-Bellevue, WA	3439809	44180	29167	Polk County	31137
42660		Seattle-Bellevue-Everett, WA Div 42644	2644584	44180	29225	Webster County	36202
42660	53033	King County	1931249				
42660	53061	Snohomish County	713335	44220		Springfield, OH	138333
42660		Tacoma-Lakewood, WA Div 45104	795225	44220	39023	Clark County	138333
42660	53053	Pierce County	795225				
				44300		State College, PA	153990
42680		Sebastian-Vero Beach, FL	138028	44300	42027	Centre County	153990
42680	12061	Indian River County	138028				
				44420		Staunton-Waynesboro, VA	118502
42700		Sebring, FL	98786	44420	51015	Augusta County	73750
42700	12055	Highlands County	98786	44420	51790	Staunton city	23746
				44420	51820	Waynesboro city	21006
43100		Sheboygan, WI	115507				
43100	55117	Sheboygan County	115507	44700		Stockton-Lodi, CA	685306
				44700	06077	San Joaquin County	685306
43300		Sherman-Denison, TX	120877				
43300	48181	Grayson County	120877	44940		Sumter, SC	107456
				44940	45085	Sumter County	107456
43340		Shreveport-Bossier City, LA	439811				
43340	22015	Bossier Parish	116979	45060		Syracuse, NY	662577
43340	22017	Caddo Parish	254969	45060	36053	Madison County	73442
43340	22031	De Soto Parish	26656	45060	36067	Onondaga County	467026
43340	22119	Webster Parish	41207	45060	36075	Oswego County	122109
43420		Sierra Vista-Douglas, AZ	131346	45220		Tallahassee, FL	367413
43420	04003	Cochise County	131346	45220	12039	Gadsden County	46389
				45220	12065	Jefferson County	14761
43580		Sioux City, IA-NE-SD	168563	45220	12073	Leon County	275487
43580	19149	Plymouth County	24986	45220	12129	Wakulla County	30776
43580	19193	Woodbury County	102172				
43580	31043	Dakota County	21006	45300		Tampa-St. Petersburg-Clearwater, FL	2783243
43580	31051	Dixon County	6000	45300	12053	Hernando County	172778
43580	46127	Union County	14399	45300	12057	Hillsborough County	1229226
				45300	12101	Pasco County	464697
43620		Sioux Falls, SD	228261	45300	12103	Pinellas County	916542
43620	46083	Lincoln County	44828				
43620	46087	McCook County	5618	45460		Terre Haute, IN	172425
43620	46099	Minnehaha County	169468	45460	18021	Clay County	26890
43620	46125	Turner County	8347	45460	18153	Sullivan County	21475
				45460	18165	Vermillion County	16212
43780		South Bend-Mishawaka, IN-MI	319224	45460	18167	Vigo County	107848
43780	18141	St. Joseph County	266931				
43780	26027	Cass County	52293	45500		Texarkana, TX-AR	149198
				45500	05081	Little River County	13171
43900		Spartanburg, SC	313268	45500	05091	Miller County	43462
43900	45083	Spartanburg County	284307	45500	48037	Bowie County	92565
43900	45087	Union County	28961				
				45540		The Villages, FL	93420
44060		Spokane-Spokane Valley, WA	527753	45540	12119	Sumter County	93420
44060	53051	Pend Oreille County	13001				
44060	53063	Spokane County	471221	45780		Toledo, OH	610001
44060	53065	Stevens County	43531	45780	39051	Fulton County	42698
				45780	39095	Lucas County	441815
44100		Springfield, IL	210170	45780	39173	Wood County	125488
44100	17129	Menard County	12705				
44100	17167	Sangamon County	197465				
44140		Springfield, MA	621570				
44140	25013	Hampden County	463490				
44140	25015	Hampshire County	158080				

Core based statistical area	State/ County FIPS code	Title and Geographic Components	2010 Census Population	Core based statistical area	State/ County FIPS code	Title and Geographic Components	2010 Census Population
45820		Topeka, KS	233870	47260		Virginia Beach-Norfolk-Newport News, VA-NC ...	1676822
45820	20085	Jackson County	13462	47260	37053	Currituck County	23547
45820	20087	Jefferson County	19126	47260	37073	Gates County	12197
45820	20139	Osage County	16295	47260	51073	Gloucester County	36858
45820	20177	Shawnee County	177934	47260	51093	Isle of Wight County	35270
45820	20197	Wabaunsee County	7053	47260	51095	James City County	67009
				47260	51115	Mathews County	8978
45940		Trenton, NJ	366513	47260	51199	York County	65464
45940	34021	Mercer County	366513	47260	51550	Chesapeake city	222209
				47260	51650	Hampton city	137436
46060		Tucson, AZ	980263	47260	51700	Newport News city	180719
46060	04019	Pima County	980263	47260	51710	Norfolk city	242803
				47260	51735	Poquoson city	12150
46140		Tulsa, OK	937478	47260	51740	Portsmouth city	95535
46140	40037	Creek County	69967	47260	51800	Suffolk city	84585
46140	40111	Okmulgee County	40069	47260	51810	Virginia Beach city	437994
46140	40113	Osage County	47472	47260	51830	Williamsburg city	14068
46140	40117	Pawnee County	16577				
46140	40131	Rogers County	86905	47300		Visalia-Porterville, CA	442179
46140	40143	Tulsa County	603403	47300	06107	Tulare County	442179
46140	40145	Wagoner County	73085				
				47380		Waco, TX	252772
46220		Tuscaloosa, AL	230162	47380	48145	Falls County	17866
46220	01065	Hale County	15760	47380	48309	McLennan County	234906
46220	01107	Pickens County	19746				
46220	01125	Tuscaloosa County	194656	47460		Walla Walla, WA	62859
				47460	53013	Columbia County	4078
46340		Tyler, TX	209714	47460	53071	Walla Walla County	58781
46340	48423	Smith County	209714				
				47580		Warner Robins, GA	179605
46520		Urban Honolulu, HI	953207	47580	13153	Houston County	139900
46520	15003	Honolulu County	953207	47580	13225	Peach County	27695
				47580	13235	Pulaski County	12010
46540		Utica-Rome, NY	299397				
46540	36043	Herkimer County	64519	47900		Washington-Arlington-Alexandria, DC-VA-MD-WV	5636232
46540	36065	Oneida County	234878	47900		Silver Spring-Frederick-Rockville, MD Div 43524	1205162
46660		Valdosta, GA	139588	47900	24021	Frederick County	233385
46660	13027	Brooks County	16243	47900	24031	Montgomery County	971777
46660	13101	Echols County	4034	47900		Washington-Arlington-Alexandria, DC-VA-MD-WV Div 47894	4431070
46660	13173	Lanier County	10078	47900	11001	District of Columbia	601723
46660	13185	Lowndes County	109233	47900	24009	Calvert County	88737
				47900	24017	Charles County	146551
46700		Vallejo-Fairfield, CA	413344	47900	24033	Prince George's County	863420
46700	06095	Solano County	413344	47900	51013	Arlington County	207627
				47900	51043	Clarke County	14034
47020		Victoria, TX	94003	47900	51047	Culpeper County	46689
47020	48175	Goliad County	7210	47900	51059	Fairfax County	1081726
47020	48469	Victoria County	86793	47900	51061	Fauquier County	65203
				47900	51107	Loudoun County	312311
47220		Vineland-Bridgeton, NJ	156898	47900	51153	Prince William County	402002
47220	34011	Cumberland County	156898	47900	51157	Rappahannock County	7373
				47900	51177	Spotsylvania County	122397
				47900	51179	Stafford County	128961
				47900	51187	Warren County	37575
				47900	51510	Alexandria city	139966
				47900	51600	Fairfax city	22565
				47900	51610	Falls Church city	12332
				47900	51630	Fredericksburg city	24286
				47900	51683	Manassas city	37821
				47900	51685	Manassas Park city	14273
				47900	54037	Jefferson County	53498

METROPOLITAN STATISTICAL AREAS, METROPOLITAN DIVISIONS, AND COMPONENTS
(as defined July 2015)—*Continued*

Core based statistical area	State/ County FIPS code	Title and Geographic Components	2010 Census Population	Core based statistical area	State/ County FIPS code	Title and Geographic Components	2010 Census Population
47940		Waterloo-Cedar Falls, IA	167819	48900		Wilmington, NC	254884
47940	19013	Black Hawk County	131090	48900	37129	New Hanover County	202667
47940	19017	Bremer County	24276	48900	37141	Pender County	52217
47940	19075	Grundy County	12453	49020		Winchester, VA-WV	128472
48060		Watertown-Fort Drum, NY	116229	49020	51069	Frederick County	78305
48060	36045	Jefferson County	116229	49020	51840	Winchester city	26203
48140		Wausau, WI	134063	49020	54027	Hampshire County	23964
48140	55073	Marathon County	134063	49180		Winston-Salem, NC	640595
48260		Weirton-Steubenville, WV-OH	124454	49180	37057	Davidson County	162878
48260	39081	Jefferson County	69709	49180	37059	Davie County	41240
48260	54009	Brooke County	24069	49180	37067	Forsyth County	350670
48260	54029	Hancock County	30676	49180	37169	Stokes County	47401
48300		Wenatchee, WA	110884	49180	37197	Yadkin County	38406
48300	53007	Chelan County	72453	49340		Worcester, MA-CT	916980
48300	53017	Douglas County	38431	49340	09015	Windham County	118428
48540		Wheeling, WV-OH	147950	49340	25027	Worcester County	798552
48540	39013	Belmont County	70400	49420		Yakima, WA	243231
48540	54051	Marshall County	33107	49420	53077	Yakima County	243231
48540	54069	Ohio County	44443	49620		York-Hanover, PA	434972
48620		Wichita, KS	630919	49620	42133	York County	434972
48620	20015	Butler County	65880	49660		Youngstown-Warren-Boardman, OH-PA	565773
48620	20079	Harvey County	34684	49660	39099	Mahoning County	238823
48620	20095	Kingman County	7858	49660	39155	Trumbull County	210312
48620	20173	Sedgwick County	498365	49660	42085	Mercer County	116638
48620	20191	Sumner County	24132	49700		Yuba City, CA	166892
48660		Wichita Falls, TX	151306	49700	06101	Sutter County	94737
48660	48009	Archer County	9054	49700	06115	Yuba County	72155
48660	48077	Clay County	10752	49740		Yuma, AZ	195751
48660	48485	Wichita County	131500	49740	04027	Yuma County	195751
48700		Williamsport, PA	116111				
48700	42081	Lycoming County	116111				

B-16

Appendix B

APPENDIX C
CORE BASED STATISTICAL AREAS
(Metropolitan and Micropolitan),
METROPOLITAN DIVISIONS, AND COMPONENTS
(as defined August, 2017)

Core based statistical area	State/ County FIPS code	Title and Geographic Components	2010 Census Population	2018 Estimated Population	Core based statistical area	State/ County FIPS code	Title and Geographic Components	2010 Census Population	2018 Estimated Population
10100		Aberdeen, SD Micro area....................	40,602	43,191	10820		Alexandria, MN Micro area..................	36,009	37,964
	46013	Brown County, SD........................	36,531	39,316		27041	Douglas County, MN........................	36,009	37,964
	46045	Edmunds County, SD......................	4,071	3,875					
					10860		Alice, TX Micro area............................	40,838	40,822
10140		Aberdeen, WA Micro area	72,797	73,901		48249	Jim Wells County, TX.......................	40,838	40,822
	53027	Grays Harbor County, WA..............	72,797	73,901					
					10900		Allentown-Bethlehem-Easton, PA-NJ Metro area........................	821,173	842,913
10180		Abilene, TX Metro area.......................	165,252	171,451					
	48059	Callahan County, TX......................	13,544	13,994		34041	Warren County, NJ........................	108,692	105,779
	48253	Jones County, TX...........................	20,202	19,817		42025	Carbon County, PA........................	65,249	64,227
	48441	Taylor County, TX..........................	131,506	137,640		42077	Lehigh County, PA.........................	349,497	368,100
						42095	Northampton County, PA.................	297,735	304,807
10220		Ada, OK Micro area...........................	37,492	38,247					
	40123	Pontotoc County, OK	37,492	38,247	10940		Alma, MI Micro area...........................	42,476	40,599
						26057	Gratiot County, MI........................	42,476	40,599
10300		Adrian, MI Micro area.........................	99,892	98,266					
	26091	Lenawee County, MI	99,892	98,266	10980		Alpena, MI Micro area........................	29,598	28,360
						26007	Alpena County, MI.........................	29,598	28,360
10420		Akron, OH Metro area	703,200	704,845					
	39133	Portage County, OH.......................	161,419	162,927	11020		Altoona, PA Metro area......................	127,089	122,492
	39153	Summit County, OH........................	541,781	541,918		42013	Blair County, PA...........................	127,089	122,492
10460		Alamogordo, NM Micro area...............	63,797	66,781	11060		Altus, OK Micro area..........................	26,446	24,949
	35035	Otero County, NM	63,797	66,781		40065	Jackson County, OK.......................	26,446	24,949
10500		Albany, GA Metro area.......................	157,308	153,009	11100		Amarillo, TX Metro area.....................	251,933	265,947
	13007	Baker County, GA	3,451	3,092		48011	Armstrong County, TX....................	1,901	1,892
	13095	Dougherty County, GA...................	94,565	91,243		48065	Carson County, TX........................	6,182	6,005
	13177	Lee County, GA.............................	28,298	29,764		48359	Oldham County, TX........................	2,052	2,131
	13273	Terrell County, GA.........................	9,315	8,611		48375	Potter County, TX..........................	121,073	119,648
	13321	Worth County, GA..........................	21,679	20,299		48381	Randall County, TX........................	120,725	136,271
10540		Albany, OR Metro area.......................	116,672	127,335	11140		Americus, GA Micro area...................	37,829	34,969
	41043	Linn County, OR............................	116,672	127,335		13249	Schley County, GA........................	5,010	5,236
						13261	Sumter County, GA........................	32,819	29,733
10580		Albany-Schenectady-Troy, NY Metro area	870,716	883,169					
					11180		Ames, IA Metro area..........................	89,542	98,105
	36001	Albany County, NY	304,204	307,117		19169	Story County, IA...........................	89,542	98,105
	36083	Rensselaer County, NY..................	159,429	159,442					
	36091	Saratoga County, NY.....................	219,607	230,163	11220		Amsterdam, NY Micro area	50,219	49,455
	36093	Schenectady County, NY................	154,727	155,350		36057	Montgomery County, NY.................	50,219	49,455
	36095	Schoharie County, NY....................	32,749	31,097					
					11260		Anchorage, AK Metro area	380,821	399,148
10620		Albemarle, NC Micro area	60,585	62,075		02020	Anchorage Municipality, AK.............	291,826	291,538
	37167	Stanly County, NC.........................	60,585	62,075		02170	Matanuska-Susitna Borough, AK.......	88,995	107,610
10660		Albert Lea, MN Micro area.................	31,255	30,444	11380		Andrews, TX Micro area.....................	14,786	18,128
	27047	Freeborn County, MN.....................	31,255	30,444		48003	Andrews County, TX......................	14,786	18,128
10700		Albertville, AL Micro area...................	93,019	96,109	11420		Angola, IN Micro area........................	34,185	34,586
	01095	Marshall County, AL......................	93,019	96,109		18151	Steuben County, IN.......................	34,185	34,586
10740		Albuquerque, NM Metro area..............	887,077	915,927	11460		Ann Arbor, MI Metro area	344,791	370,963
	35001	Bernalillo County, NM	662,564	678,701		26161	Washtenaw County, MI	344,791	370,963
	35043	Sandoval County, NM....................	131,561	145,179					
	35057	Torrance County, NM.....................	16,383	15,591	11500		Anniston-Oxford-Jacksonville, AL Metro area......................................	118,572	114,277
	35061	Valencia County, NM.....................	76,569	76,456					
						01015	Calhoun County, AL	118,572	114,277
10760		Alexander City, AL Micro Area	41,616	40,497					
	01123	Tallapoosa County, AL...................	41,616	40,497	11540		Appleton, WI Metro area.....................	225,666	237,524
						55015	Calumet County, WI........................	48,971	50,159
10780		Alexandria, LA Metro area..................	153,922	153,044		55087	Outagamie County, WI....................	176,695	187,365
	22043	Grant Parish, LA...........................	22,309	22,482					
	22079	Rapides Parish, LA........................	131,613	130,562					

Core based statistical area	State/County FIPS code	Title and Geographic Components	2010 Census Population	2018 Estimated Population	Core based statistical area	State/County FIPS code	Title and Geographic Components	2010 Census Population	2018 Estimated Population
11580		Arcadia, FL Micro area	34,862	37,489	12060		Atlanta-Sandy Springs-Roswell, GA Metro area	5,286,728	5,949,951
	12027	DeSoto County, FL	34,862	37,489		13013	Barrow County, GA	69,367	80,809
						13015	Bartow County, GA	100,157	106,408
11620		Ardmore, OK Micro area	47,557	48,177		13035	Butts County, GA	23,655	24,193
	40019	Carter County, OK	47,557	48,177		13045	Carroll County, GA	110,527	118,121
						13057	Cherokee County, GA	214,346	254,149
11660		Arkadelphia, AR Micro area	22,995	22,061		13063	Clayton County, GA	259,424	289,615
	05019	Clark County, AR	22,995	22,061		13067	Cobb County, GA	688,078	756,865
						13077	Coweta County, GA	127,317	145,864
11680		Arkansas City-Winfield, KS Micro area..	36,311	35,218		13085	Dawson County, GA	22,330	25,083
	20035	Cowley County, KS	36,311	35,218		13089	DeKalb County, GA	691,893	756,558
						13097	Douglas County, GA	132,403	145,331
11700		Asheville, NC Metro area	424,858	459,585		13113	Fayette County, GA	106,567	113,459
	37021	Buncombe County, NC	238,318	259,103		13117	Forsyth County, GA	175,511	236,612
	37087	Haywood County, NC	59,036	61,971		13121	Fulton County, GA	920,581	1,050,114
	37089	Henderson County, NC	106,740	116,748		13135	Gwinnett County, GA	805,321	927,781
	37115	Madison County, NC	20,764	21,763		13143	Haralson County, GA	28,780	29,533
						13149	Heard County, GA	11,834	11,879
11740		Ashland, OH Micro area	53,139	53,745		13151	Henry County, GA	203,922	230,220
	39005	Ashland County, OH	53,139	53,745		13159	Jasper County, GA	13,900	14,040
						13171	Lamar County, GA	18,317	19,000
11780		Ashtabula, OH Micro area	101,497	97,493		13199	Meriwether County, GA	21,992	21,068
	39007	Ashtabula County, OH	101,497	97,493		13211	Morgan County, GA	17,868	18,853
						13217	Newton County, GA	99,958	109,541
11820		Astoria, OR Micro area	37,039	39,764		13223	Paulding County, GA	142,324	164,044
	41007	Clatsop County, OR	37,039	39,764		13227	Pickens County, GA	29,431	31,980
						13231	Pike County, GA	17,869	18,634
11860		Atchison, KS Micro area	16,924	16,193		13247	Rockdale County, GA	85,215	90,594
	20005	Atchison County, KS	16,924	16,193		13255	Spalding County, GA	64,073	66,100
						13297	Walton County, GA	83,768	93,503
11900		Athens, OH Micro area	64,757	65,818					
	39009	Athens County, OH	64,757	65,818	12100		Atlantic City-Hammonton, NJ Metro area	274,549	265,429
						34001	Atlantic County, NJ	274,549	265,429
11940		Athens, TN Micro area	52,266	53,285					
	47107	McMinn County, TN	52,266	53,285	12120		Atmore, AL Micro Area	38,319	36,748
						01053	Escambia County, AL	38,319	36,748
11980		Athens, TX Micro area	78,532	82,299					
	48213	Henderson County, TX	78,532	82,299	12140		Auburn, IN Micro area	42,223	43,226
						18033	DeKalb County, IN	42,223	43,226
12020		Athens-Clarke County, GA Metro area ..	192,541	211,306					
	13059	Clarke County, GA	116,714	127,330	12180		Auburn, NY Micro area	80,026	77,145
	13195	Madison County, GA	28,120	29,650		36011	Cayuga County, NY	80,026	77,145
	13219	Oconee County, GA	32,808	39,272					
	13221	Oglethorpe County, GA	14,899	15,054	12220		Auburn-Opelika, AL Metro area	140,247	163,941
						01081	Lee County, AL	140,247	163,941
					12260		Augusta-Richmond County, GA-SC Metro area	564,873	604,167
						13033	Burke County, GA	23,316	22,423
						13073	Columbia County, GA	124,053	154,291
						13181	Lincoln County, GA	7,996	7,915
						13189	McDuffie County, GA	21,875	21,531
						13245	Richmond County, GA	200,549	201,554
						45003	Aiken County, SC	160,099	169,401
						45037	Edgefield County, SC	26,985	27,052
					12300		Augusta-Waterville, ME Micro area	122,151	122,083
						23011	Kennebec County, ME	122,151	122,083
					12380		Austin, MN Micro area	39,163	40,011
						27099	Mower County, MN	39,163	40,011

Core based statistical area	State/ County FIPS code	Title and Geographic Components	2010 Census Population	2018 Estimated Population	Core based statistical area	State/ County FIPS code	Title and Geographic Components	2010 Census Population	2018 Estimated Population
12420		Austin-Round Rock, TX Metro area......	1,716,289	2,168,316	13020		Bay City, MI Metro area	107,771	103,923
	48021	Bastrop County, TX.........................	74,171	86,976		26017	Bay County, MI..............................	107,771	103,923
	48055	Caldwell County, TX.......................	38,066	43,247					
	48209	Hays County, TX.............................	157,107	222,631	13060		Bay City, TX Micro area	36,702	36,552
	48453	Travis County, TX...........................	1,024,266	1,248,743		48321	Matagorda County, TX	36,702	36,552
	48491	Williamson County, TX....................	422,679	566,719					
					13100		Beatrice, NE Micro area	22,311	21,493
12460		Bainbridge, GA Micro area	27,842	26,575		31067	Gage County, NE Micro area	22,311	21,493
	13087	Decatur County, GA........................	27,842	26,575					
					13140		Beaumont-Port Arthur, TX Metro area ...	403,190	409,526
12540		Bakersfield, CA Metro area.................	839,631	896,764		48199	Hardin County, TX..........................	54,635	57,207
	06029	Kern County, CA	839,631	896,764		48245	Jefferson County, TX......................	252,273	255,001
						48351	Newton County, TX	14,445	13,746
12580		Baltimore-Columbia-Towson, MD Metro area	2,710,489	2,802,789		48361	Orange County, TX	81,837	83,572
	24003	Anne Arundel County, MD................	537,656	576,031	13180		Beaver Dam, WI Micro area	88,759	87,847
	24005	Baltimore County, MD	805,029	828,431		55027	Dodge County, WI..........................	88,759	87,847
	24013	Carroll County, MD.........................	167,134	168,429					
	24025	Harford County, MD........................	244,826	253,956	13220		Beckley, WV Metro area	124,898	117,272
	24027	Howard County, MD........................	287,085	323,196		54019	Fayette County, WV........................	46,039	43,018
	24035	Queen Anne's County, MD..............	47,798	50,251		54081	Raleigh County, WV	78,859	74,254
	24510	Baltimore city, MD.........................	620,961	602,495					
					13260		Bedford, IN Micro area	46,134	45,668
12620		Bangor, ME Metro area	153,923	151,096		18093	Lawrence County, IN.......................	46,134	45,668
	23019	Penobscot County, ME	153,923	151,096					
					13300		Beeville, TX Micro area	31,861	32,587
12660		Baraboo, WI Micro area......................	61,976	64,249		48025	Bee County, TX..............................	31,861	32,587
	55111	Sauk County, WI Micro area	61,976	64,249					
					13340		Bellefontaine, OH Micro area	45,858	45,358
12680		Bardstown, KY Micro area..................	43,437	45,851		39091	Logan County, OH	45,858	45,358
	21179	Nelson County, KY.........................	43,437	45,851					
					13380		Bellingham, WA Metro area	201,140	225,685
12700		Barnstable Town, MA Metro area	215,888	213,413		53073	Whatcom County, WA......................	201,140	225,685
	25001	Barnstable County, MA	215,888	213,413					
					13420		Bemidji, MN Micro area	44,442	46,847
12740		Barre, VT Micro area	59,534	58,140		27007	Beltrami County, MN.......................	44,442	46,847
	50023	Washington County, VT	59,534	58,140					
					13460		Bend-Redmond, OR Metro area............	157,733	191,996
12780		Bartlesville, OK Micro area.................	50,976	51,843		41017	Deschutes County, OR	157,733	191,996
	40147	Washington County, OK..................	50,976	51,843					
					13500		Bennettsville, SC Micro area	28,933	26,398
12820		Bastrop, LA Micro area......................	27,979	25,398		45069	Marlboro County, SC.......................	28,933	26,398
	22067	Morehouse Parish, LA.....................	27,979	25,398					
					13540		Bennington, VT Micro area..................	37,125	35,631
12860		Batavia, NY Micro area......................	60,079	57,511		50003	Bennington County, VT	37,125	35,631
	36037	Genesee County, NY	60,079	57,511					
					13620		Berlin, NH-VT Micro area	39,361	37,839
12900		Batesville, AR Micro area	36,647	37,678		33007	Coos County, NH	33,055	31,589
	05063	Independence County, AR	36,647	37,678		50009	Essex County, VT	6,306	6,250
12940		Baton Rouge, LA Metro area...............	802,484	831,310	13660		Big Rapids, MI Micro area	42,798	43,545
	22005	Ascension Parish, LA......................	107,215	124,672		26107	Mecosta County, MI........................	42,798	43,545
	22033	East Baton Rouge Parish, LA	440,171	440,956					
	22037	East Feliciana Parish, LA.................	20,267	19,305	13700		Big Spring, TX Micro area	36,238	37,847
	22047	Iberville Parish, LA.........................	33,387	32,721		48173	Glasscock County, TX.....................	1,226	1,388
	22063	Livingston Parish, LA......................	128,026	139,567		48227	Howard County, TX.........................	35,012	36,459
	22077	Pointe Coupee Parish, LA...............	22,802	21,940					
	22091	St. Helena Parish, LA......................	11,203	10,262	13720		Big Stone Gap, VA Micro area.............	61,313	56,503
	22121	West Baton Rouge Parish, LA	23,788	26,427		51051	Dickenson County, VA.....................	15,903	14,523
	22125	West Feliciana Parish, LA	15,625	15,460		51195	Wise County, VA	41,452	38,012
						51720	Norton city, VA	3,958	3,968
12980		Battle Creek, MI Metro area	136,146	134,487					
	26025	Calhoun County, MI	136,146	134,487					

Core based statistical area	State/County FIPS code	Title and Geographic Components	2010 Census Population	2018 Estimated Population	Core based statistical area	State/County FIPS code	Title and Geographic Components	2010 Census Population	2018 Estimated Population
13740		Billings, MT Metro area........................	158,934	171,677	14300		Bonham, TX Micro Area	33,915	35,286
	30009	Carbon County, MT	10,078	10,714		48147	Fannin County, TX	33,915	35,286
	30037	Golden Valley County, MT..............	884	826	14340		Boone, IA Micro area	26,306	26,346
	30111	Yellowstone County, MT..................	147,972	160,137		19015	Boone County, IA	26,306	26,346
13780		Binghamton, NY Metro area	251,725	240,219	14380		Boone, NC Micro area........................	51,079	55,945
	36007	Broome County, NY	200,600	191,659		37189	Watauga County, NC	51,079	55,945
	36107	Tioga County, NY	51,125	48,560	14420		Borger, TX Micro area	22,150	21,198
13820		Birmingham-Hoover, AL Metro area	1,128,047	1,151,801		48233	Hutchinson County, TX	22,150	21,198
	01007	Bibb County, AL	22,915	22,400	14460		Boston-Cambridge Newton, MA-NH Metro area	4,552,402	4,875,390
	01009	Blount County, AL...........................	57,322	57,840					
	01021	Chilton County, AL..........................	43,643	44,153	14460		Boston, MA Metro Div 14454.............	1,887,792	2,030,772
	01073	Jefferson County, AL.......................	658,466	659,300		25021	Norfolk County, MA........................	670,850	705,388
	01115	St. Clair County, AL........................	83,593	88,690		25023	Plymouth County, MA......................	494,919	518,132
	01117	Shelby County, AL..........................	195,085	215,707		25025	Suffolk County, MA.........................	722,023	807,252
	01127	Walker County, AL..........................	67,023	63,711	14460		Cambridge-Newton-Framingham, MA Metro Div 15764	2,246,244	2,405,352
13900		Bismarck, ND Metro area	114,778	132,678					
	38015	Burleigh County, ND	81,308	95,273		25009	Essex County, MA........................	743,159	790,638
	38059	Morton County, ND	27,471	31,095		25017	Middlesex County, MA....................	1,503,085	1,614,714
	38065	Oliver County, ND...........................	1,846	1,952	14460		Rockingham County-Strafford County-NH Metro Div 40484	418,366	439,266
	38085	Sioux County, ND...........................	4,153	4,358					
13940		Blackfoot, ID Micro area	45,607	46,236		33015	Rockingham County, NH..................	295,223	309,176
	16011	Bingham County, ID	45,607	46,236		33017	Strafford County, NH......................	123,143	130,090
13980		Blacksburg-Christiansburg-Radford, VA Metro area	178,237	184,029	14500		Boulder, CO Metro area....................	294,567	326,078
						08013	Boulder County, CO	294,567	326,078
	51063	Floyd County, VA............................	15,279	15,795	14540		Bowling Green, KY Metro area...........	158,599	177,432
	51071	Giles County, VA............................	17,286	16,844		21003	Allen County, KY	19,956	21,122
	51121	Montgomery County, VA	94,392	98,985		21031	Butler County, KY..........................	12,690	12,772
	51155	Pulaski County, VA.........................	34,872	34,066		21061	Edmonson County, KY	12,161	12,274
	51750	Radford city, VA.............................	16,408	18,339		21227	Warren County, KY	113,792	131,264
14010		Bloomington, IL Metro area	186,133	188,597	14580		Bozeman, MT Micro area	89,513	111,876
	17039	De Witt County, IL	16,561	15,769		30031	Gallatin County, MT	89,513	111,876
	17113	McLean County, IL..........................	169,572	172,828	14620		Bradford, PA Micro area	43,450	40,968
14020		Bloomington, IN Metro area.................	159,549	167,762		42083	McKean County, PA........................	43,450	40,968
	18105	Monroe County, IN	137,974	146,917	14660		Brainerd, MN Micro area	91,067	94,408
	18119	Owen County, IN	21,575	20,845		27021	Cass County, MN	28,567	29,519
14100		Bloomsburg-Berwick, PA Metro area.....	85,562	83,696		27035	Crow Wing County, MN....................	62,500	64,889
	42037	Columbia County, PA	67,295	65,456	14700		Branson, MO Micro area	83,877	87,601
	42093	Montour County, PA	18,267	18,240		29209	Stone County, MO Micro area...........	32,202	31,749
14140		Bluefield, WV-VA Micro area...............	107,342	99,986		29213	Taney County, MO Micro area	51,675	55,852
	51185	Tazewell County, VA........................	45,078	40,855	14720		Breckenridge, CO Micro area............	27,994	31,007
	54055	Mercer County, WV.........................	62,264	59,131		08117	Summit County, CO	27,994	31,007
14180		Blytheville, AR Micro area...................	46,480	41,239	14740		Bremerton-Silverdale, WA Metro area...	251,133	269,805
	05093	Mississippi County, AR.....................	46,480	41,239		53035	Kitsap County, WA	251,133	269,805
14220		Bogalusa, LA Micro area	47,168	46,582	14780		Brenham, TX Micro area	33,718	35,108
	22117	Washington Parish, LA.....................	47,168	46,582		48477	Washington County, TX	33,718	35,108
14260		Boise City, ID Metro area....................	616,561	730,426	14820		Brevard, NC Micro area	33,090	34,215
	16001	Ada County, ID	392,365	469,966		37175	Transylvania County, NC	33,090	34,215
	16015	Boise County, ID	7,028	7,634					
	16027	Canyon County, ID.........................	188,923	223,499					
	16045	Gem County, ID.............................	16,719	17,634					
	16073	Owyhee County, ID.........................	11,526	11,693					

CORE BASED STATISTICAL AREAS
(Metropolitan and Micropolitan),
METROPOLITAN DIVISIONS, AND COMPONENTS
(as defined August, 2017)—*Continued*

Core based statistical area	State/County FIPS code	Title and Geographic Components	2010 Census Population	2018 Estimated Population	Core based statistical area	State/County FIPS code	Title and Geographic Components	2010 Census Population	2018 Estimated Population
14860		Bridgeport-Stamford-Norwalk, CT Metro area	916,829	943,823	15680		California-Lexington Park, MD Metro area	105,151	112,664
	09001	Fairfield County, CT	916,829	943,823		24037	St. Mary's County, MD	105,151	112,664
15020		Brookhaven, MS Micro area	34,869	34,205	15700		Cambridge, MD Micro area	32,618	31,998
	28085	Lincoln County, MS	34,869	34,205		24019	Dorchester County, MD	32,618	31,998
15060		Brookings, OR Micro area	22,364	22,813	15740		Cambridge, OH Micro area	40,087	39,022
	41015	Curry County, OR	22,364	22,813		39059	Guernsey County, OH	40,087	39,022
15100		Brookings, SD Micro area	31,965	35,232	15780		Camden, AR Micro area	31,488	28,883
	46011	Brookings County, SD	31,965	35,232		05013	Calhoun County, AR	5,368	5,277
						05103	Ouachita County, AR	26,120	23,606
15140		Brownsville, TN Micro Area	18,787	17,335					
	47075	Haywood County, TN	18,787	17,335	15820		Campbellsville, KY Micro area	24,512	25,549
15180		Brownsville-Harlingen, TX Metro area...	406,220	423,908		21217	Taylor County, KY	24,512	25,549
	48061	Cameron County, TX	406,220	423,908	15860		Cañon City, CO Micro area	46,824	48,021
15220		Brownwood, TX Micro area	38,106	37,924		08043	Fremont County, CO	46,824	48,021
	48049	Brown County, TX	38,106	37,924	15900		Canton, IL Micro area	37,069	34,844
15260		Brunswick, GA Metro area	112,370	118,456		17057	Fulton County, IL	37,069	34,844
	13025	Brantley County, GA	18,411	18,897	15940		Canton-Massillon, OH Metro area	404,422	398,655
	13127	Glynn County, GA	79,626	85,219		39019	Carroll County, OH	28,836	27,081
	13191	McIntosh County, GA	14,333	14,340		39151	Stark County, OH	375,586	371,574
15340		Bucyrus, OH Micro area	43,784	41,550	15980		Cape Coral-Fort Myers, FL Metro area .	618,754	754,610
	39033	Crawford County, OH	43,784	41,550		12071	Lee County, FL	618,754	754,610
15380		Buffalo-Cheektowaga-Niagara Falls, NY Metro area	1,135,509	1,130,152	16020		Cape Girardeau, MO-IL Metro area..........	96,275	96,982
						17003	Alexander County, IL	8,238	6,060
	36029	Erie County, NY	919,040	919,719		29017	Bollinger County, MO	12,363	12,169
	36063	Niagara County, NY	216,469	210,433		29031	Cape Girardeau County, MO	75,674	78,753
15420		Burley, ID Micro area	43,021	44,689	16060		Carbondale-Marion, IL Metro area	126,575	124,475
	16031	Cassia County, ID	22,952	23,864		17077	Jackson County, IL	60,218	57,419
	16067	Minidoka County, ID	20,069	20,825		17199	Williamson County, IL	66,357	67,056
15460		Burlington, IA-IL Micro area	47,656	45,847	16100		Carlsbad-Artesia, NM Micro area	53,829	57,900
	17071	Henderson County, IL	7,331	6,709		35015	Eddy County, NM	53,829	57,900
	19057	Des Moines County, IA	40,325	39,138	16140		Carroll, IA Micro Area	20,816	20,154
15500		Burlington, NC Metro area	151,131	166,436		19027	Carroll County, IA	20,816	20,154
	37001	Alamance County, NC	151,131	166,436	16180		Carson City, NV Metro area	55,274	55,414
15540		Burlington-South Burlington, VT Metro area	211,261	221,083		32510	Carson City, NV Metro area	55,274	55,414
	50007	Chittenden County, VT	156,545	164,572	16220		Casper, WY Metro area	75,450	79,115
	50011	Franklin County, VT	47,746	49,421		56025	Natrona County, WY	75,450	79,115
	50013	Grand Isle County, VT	6,970	7,090	16260		Cedar City, UT Micro area	46,163	52,775
15580		Butte-Silver Bow, MT Micro area	34,200	34,993		49021	Iron County, UT	46,163	52,775
	30093	Silver Bow County, MT	34,200	34,993	16300		Cedar Rapids, IA Metro area	257,940	272,295
15620		Cadillac, MI Micro area	47,584	48,579		19011	Benton County, IA	26,076	25,642
	26113	Missaukee County, MI	14,849	15,113		19105	Jones County, IA	20,638	20,744
	26165	Wexford County, MI	32,735	33,466		19113	Linn County, IA	211,226	225,909
15660		Calhoun, GA Micro area	55,186	57,685	16340		Cedartown, GA Micro area	41,475	42,470
	13129	Gordon County, GA	55,186	57,685		13233	Polk County, GA	41,475	42,470
					16380		Celina, OH Micro area	40,814	40,959
						39107	Mercer County, OH	40,814	40,959

Core based statistical area	State/County FIPS code	Title and Geographic Components	2010 Census Population	2018 Estimated Population	Core based statistical area	State/County FIPS code	Title and Geographic Components	2010 Census Population	2018 Estimated Population
16420		Central City, KY Micro Area	31,499	30,774	16980		Chicago-Naperville-Elgin, IL-IN-WI Metro area	9,461,105	9,498,716
	21177	Muhlenberg County, KY	31,499	30,774	16980		Chicago-Naperville-Arlington Heights, IL Metro Div 16974	7,262,718	7,288,849
16460		Centralia, IL Micro area	39,437	37,620		17031	Cook County, IL	5,194,675	5,180,493
	17121	Marion County, IL	39,437	37,620		17043	DuPage County, IL	916,924	928,589
16500		Centralia, WA Micro area	75,455	79,604		17063	Grundy County, IL	50,063	50,972
	53041	Lewis County, WA	75,455	79,604		17093	Kendall County, IL	114,736	127,915
16540		Chambersburg-Waynesboro, PA Metro area	149,618	154,835		17111	McHenry County, IL	308,760	308,570
	42055	Franklin County, PA	149,618	154,835		17197	Will County, IL	677,560	692,310
16580		Champaign-Urbana, IL Metro area	231,891	239,643	16980		Elgin, IL Metro Div 20994	620,429	638,359
	17019	Champaign County, IL	201,081	209,983		17037	DeKalb County, IL	105,160	104,143
	17053	Ford County, IL	14,081	13,264		17089	Kane County, IL	515,269	534,216
	17147	Piatt County, IL	16,729	16,396	16980		Gary, IN Metro Div 23844	708,070	701,386
16620		Charleston, WV Metro area	227,078	211,037		18073	Jasper County, IN	33,478	33,370
	54005	Boone County, WV	24,629	21,951		18089	Lake County, IN	496,005	484,411
	54015	Clay County, WV	9,386	8,632		18111	Newton County, IN	14,244	14,011
	54039	Kanawha County, WV	193,063	180,454		18127	Porter County, IN	164,343	169,594
16660		Charleston-Mattoon, IL Micro area	64,921	61,693	16980		Lake County-Kenosha County, IL-WI Metro Div 29404	869,888	870,122
	17029	Coles County, IL	53,873	50,885		17097	Lake County, IL	703,462	700,832
	17035	Cumberland County, IL	11,048	10,808		55059	Kenosha County, WI	166,426	169,290
16700		Charleston-North Charleston, SC Metro area	664,607	787,643	17020		Chico, CA Metro area	220,000	231,256
	45015	Berkeley County, SC	177,843	221,091		06007	Butte County, CA	220,000	231,256
	45019	Charleston County, SC	350,209	405,905	17060		Chillicothe, OH Micro area	78,064	76,931
	45035	Dorchester County, SC	136,555	160,647		39141	Ross County, OH	78,064	76,931
16740		Charlotte-Concord-Gastonia, NC-SC Metro area	2,217,012	2,569,213	17140		Cincinnati, OH-KY-IN Metro area	2,114,580	2,190,209
	37025	Cabarrus County, NC	178,011	211,342		18029	Dearborn County, IN	50,047	49,568
	37071	Gaston County, NC	206,086	222,846		18115	Ohio County, IN	6,128	5,844
	37097	Iredell County, NC	159,437	178,435		18161	Union County, IN	7,516	7,037
	37109	Lincoln County, NC	78,265	83,770		21015	Boone County, KY	118,811	131,533
	37119	Mecklenburg County, NC	919,628	1,093,901		21023	Bracken County, KY	8,488	8,239
	37159	Rowan County, NC	138,428	141,262		21037	Campbell County, KY	90,336	93,152
	37179	Union County, NC	201,292	235,908		21077	Gallatin County, KY	8,589	8,832
	45023	Chester County, SC	33,140	32,251		21081	Grant County, KY	24,662	25,121
	45057	Lancaster County, SC	76,652	95,380		21117	Kenton County, KY	159,720	166,051
	45091	York County, SC	226,073	274,118		21191	Pendleton County, KY	14,877	14,529
16820		Charlottesville, VA Metro area	218,705	235,232		39015	Brown County, OH	44,846	43,602
	51003	Albemarle County, VA	98,970	108,718		39017	Butler County, OH	368,130	382,378
	51029	Buckingham County, VA	17,146	16,999		39025	Clermont County, OH	197,363	205,466
	51065	Fluvanna County, VA	25,691	26,783		39061	Hamilton County, OH	802,374	816,684
	51079	Greene County, VA	18,403	19,779		39165	Warren County, OH	212,693	232,173
	51125	Nelson County, VA	15,020	14,836	17200		Claremont-Lebanon, NH-VT Micro area	218,466	217,215
	51540	Charlottesville city, VA	43,475	48,117		33009	Grafton County, NH	89,118	89,786
16860		Chattanooga, TN-GA Metro area	528,143	560,793		33019	Sullivan County, NH	43,742	43,144
	13047	Catoosa County, GA	63,942	67,420		50017	Orange County, VT	28,936	28,999
	13083	Dade County, GA	16,633	16,226		50027	Windsor County, VT	56,670	55,286
	13295	Walker County, GA	68,756	69,410	17220		Clarksburg, WV Micro area	94,196	92,822
	47065	Hamilton County, TN	336,463	364,286		54017	Doddridge County, WV	8,202	8,406
	47115	Marion County, TN	28,237	28,575		54033	Harrison County, WV	69,099	67,554
	47153	Sequatchie County, TN	14,112	14,876		54091	Taylor County, WV	16,895	16,862
16940		Cheyenne, WY Metro area	91,738	98,976	17260		Clarksdale, MS Micro area	26,151	22,628
	56021	Laramie County, WY	91,738	98,976		28027	Coahoma County, MS	26,151	22,628

Core based statistical area	State/ County FIPS code	Title and Geographic Components	2010 Census Population	2018 Estimated Population	Core based statistical area	State/ County FIPS code	Title and Geographic Components	2010 Census Population	2018 Estimated Population
17300		Clarksville, TN-KY Metro area.............	260,625	292,264	17980		Columbus, GA-AL Metro area...............	294,865	305,451
	21047	Christian County, KY.........................	73,955	71,671		01113	Russell County, AL........................	52,947	57,781
	21221	Trigg County, KY............................	14,339	14,643		13053	Chattahoochee County, GA..............	11,267	10,684
	47125	Montgomery County, TN...................	172,331	205,950		13145	Harris County, GA.........................	32,024	34,475
						13197	Marion County, GA........................	8,742	8,351
17340		Clearlake, CA Micro area......................	64,665	64,382		13215	Muscogee County, GA.....................	189,885	194,160
	06033	Lake County, CA............................	64,665	64,382					
					18020		Columbus, IN Metro area	76,794	82,753
17380		Cleveland, MS Micro area	34,145	31,333		18005	Bartholomew County, IN	76,794	82,753
	28011	Bolivar County, MS	34,145	31,333					
					18060		Columbus, MS Micro area	59,779	58,930
17420		Cleveland, TN Metro area	115,788	123,625		28087	Lowndes County, MS	59,779	58,930
	47011	Bradley County, TN..........................	98,963	106,727					
	47139	Polk County, TN..............................	16,825	16,898	18100		Columbus, NE Micro area	32,237	33,363
						31141	Platte County, NE............................	32,237	33,363
17460		Cleveland-Elyria, OH Metro area..........	2,077,240	2,057,009					
	39035	Cuyahoga County, OH.......................	1,280,122	1,243,857	18140		Columbus, OH Metro area.....................	1,901,974	2,106,541
	39055	Geauga County, OH.........................	93,389	94,031		39041	Delaware County, OH	174,214	204,826
	39085	Lake County, OH.............................	230,041	230,514		39045	Fairfield County, OH........................	146,156	155,782
	39093	Lorain County, OH...........................	301,356	309,461		39049	Franklin County, OH........................	1,163,414	1,310,300
	39103	Medina County, OH..........................	172,332	179,146		39073	Hocking County, OH........................	29,380	28,385
						39089	Licking County, OH.........................	166,492	175,769
17500		Clewiston, FL Micro area......................	39,140	41,556		39097	Madison County, OH........................	43,435	44,413
	12051	Hendry County, FL...........................	39,140	41,556		39117	Morrow County, OH	34,827	35,112
						39127	Perry County, OH...........................	36,058	36,033
17540		Clinton, IA Micro area	49,116	46,518		39129	Pickaway County, OH	55,698	58,086
	19045	Clinton County, IA	49,116	46,518		39159	Union County, OH	52,300	57,835
17580		Clovis, NM Micro area	48,376	49,437	18180		Concord, NH Micro area......................	146,445	151,132
	35009	Curry County, NM	48,376	49,437		33013	Merrimack County, NH......................	146,445	151,132
17660		Coeur d'Alene, ID Metro area...............	138,494	161,505	18220		Connersville, IN Micro area	24,277	23,047
	16055	Kootenai County, ID	138,494	161,505		18041	Fayette County, IN	24,277	23,047
17700		Coffeyville, KS Micro area	35,471	32,120	18260		Cookeville, TN Micro area	106,042	112,669
	20125	Montgomery County, KS	35,471	32,120		47087	Jackson County, TN........................	11,638	11,758
						47133	Overton County, TN	22,083	22,068
17740		Coldwater, MI Micro area......................	45,248	43,622		47141	Putnam County, TN.........................	72,321	78,843
	26023	Branch County, MI	45,248	43,622					
					18300		Coos Bay, OR Micro area....................	63,043	64,389
17780		College Station-Bryan, TX Metro area...	228,660	262,431		41011	Coos County, OR...........................	63,043	64,389
	48041	Brazos County, TX..........................	194,851	226,758					
	48051	Burleson County, TX	17,187	18,389	18380		Cordele, GA Micro area......................	23,439	22,601
	48395	Robertson County, TX.......................	16,622	17,284		13081	Crisp County, GA	23,439	22,601
17820		Colorado Springs, CO Metro area.........	645,613	738,939	18420		Corinth, MS Micro area......................	37,057	36,925
	08041	El Paso County, CO.........................	622,263	713,856		28003	Alcorn County, MS	37,057	36,925
	08119	Teller County, CO...........................	23,350	25,083					
					18460		Cornelia, GA Micro area......................	43,041	45,388
17860		Columbia, MO Metro area	162,642	180,005		13137	Habersham County, GA.....................	43,041	45,388
	29019	Boone County, MO..........................	162,642	180,005					
					18500		Corning, NY Micro area......................	98,990	95,796
17900		Columbia, SC Metro area....................	767,598	832,666		36101	Steuben County, NY	98,990	95,796
	45017	Calhoun County, SC	15,175	14,520					
	45039	Fairfield County, SC........................	23,956	22,402	18580		Corpus Christi, TX Metro area............	428,185	452,950
	45055	Kershaw County, SC........................	61,697	65,592		48007	Aransas County, TX	23,158	23,792
	45063	Lexington County, SC.......................	262,391	295,032		48355	Nueces County, TX.........................	340,223	362,265
	45079	Richland County, SC........................	384,504	414,576		48409	San Patricio County, TX....................	64,804	66,893
	45081	Saluda County, SC..........................	19,875	20,544					
					18620		Corsicana, TX Micro area....................	47,735	49,565
						48349	Navarro County, TX	47,735	49,565
					18660		Cortland, NY Micro area......................	49,336	47,823
						36023	Cortland County, NY........................	49,336	47,823

CORE BASED STATISTICAL AREAS
(Metropolitan and Micropolitan),
METROPOLITAN DIVISIONS, AND COMPONENTS
(as defined August, 2017)—*Continued*

Core based statistical area	State/County FIPS code	Title and Geographic Components	2010 Census Population	2018 Estimated Population	Core based statistical area	State/County FIPS code	Title and Geographic Components	2010 Census Population	2018 Estimated Population
18700		Corvallis, OR Metro area	85,579	92,101	19260		Danville, VA Micro area	106,561	101,642
	41003	Benton County, OR	85,579	92,101		51143	Pittsylvania County, VA	63,506	60,949
18740		Coshocton, OH Micro area	36,901	36,629		51590	Danville city, VA	43,055	40,693
	39031	Coshocton County, OH	36,901	36,629	19300		Daphne-Fairhope-Foley, AL Metro area	182,265	218,022
18780		Craig, CO Micro area	13,795	13,188		01003	Baldwin County, AL	182,265	218,022
	08081	Moffat County, CO	13,795	13,188	19340		Davenport-Moline-Rock Island, IA-IL Metro area	379,690	381,451
18820		Crawfordsville, IN Micro area	38,124	38,346		17073	Henry County, IL	50,486	49,090
	18107	Montgomery County, IN	38,124	38,346		17131	Mercer County, IL	16,434	15,601
18860		Crescent City, CA Micro area	28,610	27,828		17161	Rock Island County, IL	147,546	143,477
	06015	Del Norte County, CA	28,610	27,828		19163	Scott County, IA	165,224	173,283
18880		Crestview-Fort Walton Beach-Destin, FL Metro area	235,865	278,644	19380		Dayton, OH Metro area	799,232	806,548
	12091	Okaloosa County, FL	180,822	207,269		39057	Greene County, OH	161,573	167,995
	12131	Walton County, FL	55,043	71,375		39109	Miami County, OH	102,506	106,222
18900		Crossville, TN Micro area	56,053	59,673		39113	Montgomery County, OH	535,153	532,331
	47035	Cumberland County, TN	56,053	59,673	19420		Dayton, TN Micro area	31,809	33,044
18980		Cullman, AL Micro area	80,406	83,442		47143	Rhea County, TN	31,809	33,044
	01043	Cullman County, AL	80,406	83,442	19460		Decatur, AL Metro area	153,829	152,046
19000		Cullowhee, NC Micro area	40,271	43,327		01079	Lawrence County, AL	34,339	32,957
	37099	Jackson County, NC	40,271	43,327		01103	Morgan County, AL	119,490	119,089
19060		Cumberland, MD-WV Metro area	103,299	97,915	19500		Decatur, IL Metro area	110,768	104,712
	24001	Allegany County, MD	75,087	70,975		17115	Macon County, IL	110,768	104,712
	54057	Mineral County, WV	28,212	26,940	19540		Decatur, IN Micro area	34,387	35,636
19100		Dallas-Fort Worth-Arlington, TX Metro area	6,426,214	7,539,711		18001	Adams County, IN	34,387	35,636
19100		Dallas-Plano-Irving, TX Metro Div 19124	4,230,520	5,007,190	19580		Defiance, OH Micro area	39,037	38,165
	48085	Collin County, TX	782,341	1,005,146		39039	Defiance County, OH	39,037	38,165
	48113	Dallas County, TX	2,368,139	2,637,772	19620		Del Rio, TX Micro area	48,879	49,208
	48121	Denton County, TX	662,614	859,064		48465	Val Verde County, TX	48,879	49,208
	48139	Ellis County, TX	149,610	179,436	19660		Deltona-Daytona Beach-Ormond Beach, FL Metro area	590,289	659,605
	48231	Hunt County, TX	86,129	96,493		12035	Flagler County, FL	95,696	112,067
	48257	Kaufman County, TX	103,350	128,622		12127	Volusia County, FL	494,593	547,538
	48397	Rockwall County, TX	78,337	100,657	19700		Deming, NM Micro area	25,095	23,963
19100		Fort Worth-Arlington, TX Metro Div 23104	2,195,694	2,532,521		35029	Luna County, NM	25,095	23,963
	48221	Hood County, TX	51,182	60,537	19740		Denver-Aurora-Lakewood, CO Metro area	2,543,482	2,932,415
	48251	Johnson County, TX	150,934	171,361		08001	Adams County, CO	441,603	511,868
	48367	Parker County, TX	116,927	138,371		08005	Arapahoe County, CO	572,003	651,215
	48425	Somervell County, TX	8,490	9,016		08014	Broomfield County, CO	55,889	69,267
	48439	Tarrant County, TX	1,809,034	2,084,931		08019	Clear Creek County, CO	9,088	9,605
	48497	Wise County, TX	59,127	68,305		08031	Denver County, CO	600,158	716,492
19140		Dalton, GA Metro area	142,227	143,983		08035	Douglas County, CO	285,465	342,776
	13213	Murray County, GA	39,628	39,921		08039	Elbert County, CO	23,086	26,282
	13313	Whitfield County, GA	102,599	104,062		08047	Gilpin County, CO	5,441	6,121
19180		Danville, IL Metro area	81,625	76,806		08059	Jefferson County, CO	534,543	580,233
	17183	Vermilion County, IL	81,625	76,806		08093	Park County, CO	16,206	18,556
19220		Danville, KY Micro area	53,174	54,744	19760		DeRidder, LA Micro area	35,654	37,253
	21021	Boyle County, KY	28,432	30,100		22011	Beauregard Parish, LA	35,654	37,253
	21137	Lincoln County, KY	24,742	24,644					

Core based statistical area	State/ County FIPS code	Title and Geographic Components	2010 Census Population	2018 Estimated Population	Core based statistical area	State/ County FIPS code	Title and Geographic Components	2010 Census Population	2018 Estimated Population
19780		Des Moines-West Des Moines, IA Metro area	569,633	655,409	20380		Dunn, NC Micro area	114,678	134,214
	19049	Dallas County, IA	66,135	90,180		37085	Harnett County, NC	114,678	134,214
	19077	Guthrie County, IA	10,954	10,720	20420		Durango, CO Micro area	51,334	56,310
	19121	Madison County, IA	15,679	16,249		08067	La Plata County, CO	51,334	56,310
	19153	Polk County, IA	430,640	487,204	20460		Durant, OK Micro area	42,416	47,192
	19181	Warren County, IA	46,225	51,056		40013	Bryan County, OK	42,416	47,192
19820		Detroit-Warren-Dearborn, MI Metro area	4,296,250	4,326,442	20500		Durham-Chapel Hill, NC Metro area	504,357	575,412
						37037	Chatham County, NC	63,505	73,139
19820		Detroit-Dearborn-Livonia, MI Metro Div 19804	1,820,584	1,753,893		37063	Durham County, NC	267,587	316,739
	26163	Wayne County, MI	1,820,584	1,753,893		37135	Orange County, NC	133,801	146,027
						37145	Person County, NC	39,464	39,507
19820		Warren-Troy-Farmington Hills, MI Metro Div 47664	2,475,666	2,572,549	20540		Dyersburg, TN Micro area	38,335	37,320
	26087	Lapeer County, MI	88,319	88,028		47045	Dyer County, TN	38,335	37,320
	26093	Livingston County, MI	180,967	191,224	20580		Eagle Pass, TX Micro area	54,258	58,485
	26099	Macomb County, MI	840,978	874,759		48323	Maverick County, TX	54,258	58,485
	26125	Oakland County, MI	1,202,362	1,259,201	20660		Easton, MD Micro area	37,782	36,968
	26147	St. Clair County, MI	163,040	159,337		24041	Talbot County, MD	37,782	36,968
19860		Dickinson, ND Micro area	24,199	30,997	20700		East Stroudsburg, PA Metro area	169,842	169,507
	38089	Stark County, ND	24,199	30,997		42089	Monroe County, PA	169,842	169,507
19940		Dixon, IL Micro area	36,031	34,223	20740		Eau Claire, WI Metro area	161,151	168,669
	17103	Lee County, IL	36,031	34,223		55017	Chippewa County, WI	62,415	64,135
19980		Dodge City, KS Micro area	33,848	33,888		55035	Eau Claire County, WI	98,736	104,534
	20057	Ford County, KS	33,848	33,888	20780		Edwards, CO Micro area	52,197	54,993
20020		Dothan, AL Metro area	145,639	148,245		08037	Eagle County, CO	52,197	54,993
	01061	Geneva County, AL	26,790	26,314	20820		Effingham, IL Micro area	34,242	34,208
	01067	Henry County, AL	17,302	17,209		17049	Effingham County, IL	34,242	34,208
	01069	Houston County, AL	101,547	104,722	20900		El Campo, TX Micro area	41,280	41,619
20060		Douglas, GA Micro area	42,356	43,093		48481	Wharton County, TX	41,280	41,619
	13069	Coffee County, GA	42,356	43,093	20940		El Centro, CA Metro area	174,528	181,827
20100		Dover, DE Metro area	162,310	178,550		06025	Imperial County, CA	174,528	181,827
	10001	Kent County, Delaware	162,310	178,550	20980		El Dorado, AR Micro area	41,639	39,126
20140		Dublin, GA Micro area	58,414	57,033		05139	Union County, AR	41,639	39,126
	13167	Johnson County, GA	9,980	9,708	21020		Elizabeth City, NC Micro area	64,094	63,771
	13175	Laurens County, GA	48,434	47,325		37029	Camden County, NC	9,980	10,710
20180		DuBois, PA Micro area	81,642	79,388		37139	Pasquotank County, NC	40,661	39,639
	42033	Clearfield County, PA	81,642	79,388		37143	Perquimans County, NC	13,453	13,422
20220		Dubuque, IA Metro area	93,653	96,854	21060		Elizabethtown-Fort Knox, KY Metro area	148,338	153,378
	19061	Dubuque County, IA	93,653	96,854		21093	Hardin County, KY	105,543	110,356
20260		Duluth, MN-WI Metro area	279,771	278,799		21123	Larue County, KY	14,193	14,307
	27017	Carlton County, MN	35,386	35,837		21163	Meade County, KY	28,602	28,715
	27137	St. Louis County, MN	200,226	199,754	21120		Elk City, OK Micro area	22,119	21,709
	55031	Douglas County, WI	44,159	43,208		40009	Beckham County, OK	22,119	21,709
20300		Dumas, TX Micro area	21,904	21,485	21140		Elkhart-Goshen, IN Metro area	197,559	205,560
	48341	Moore County, TX	21,904	21,485		18039	Elkhart County, IN	197,559	205,560
20340		Duncan, OK Micro area	45,048	43,265					
	40137	Stephens County, OK	45,048	43,265					

Core based statistical area	State/County FIPS code	Title and Geographic Components	2010 Census Population	2018 Estimated Population
21180	54083	Elkins, WV Micro area .... / Randolph County, WV	29,405 / 29,405	28,823 / 28,823
21220	32007 / 32011	Elko, NV Micro area........................... / Elko County, NV .... / Eureka County, NV	50,805 / 48,818 / 1,987	54,463 / 52,460 / 2,003
21260	53037	Ellensburg, WA Micro area .... / Kittitas County, WA......................	40,915 / 40,915	47,364 / 47,364
21300	36015	Elmira, NY Metro area .... / Chemung County, NY	88,830 / 88,830	84,254 / 84,254
21340	48141 / 48229	El Paso, TX Metro area .... / El Paso County, TX........................ / Hudspeth County, TX	804,123 / 800,647 / 3,476	845,553 / 840,758 / 4,795
21380	20111	Emporia, KS Micro area .... / Lyon County, KS	33,690 / 33,690	33,406 / 33,406
21420	40047	Enid, OK Metro area........................... / Garfield County, OK	60,580 / 60,580	60,913 / 60,913
21460	01031	Enterprise, AL Micro area .... / Coffee County, AL	49,948 / 49,948	51,909 / 51,909
21500	42049	Erie, PA Metro area .... / Erie County, PA...........................	280,566 / 280,566	272,061 / 272,061
21540	26041	Escanaba, MI Micro area..................... / Delta County, MI	37,069 / 37,069	35,857 / 35,857
21580	35039	Española, NM Micro area..................... / Rio Arriba County, NM	40,246 / 40,246	39,006 / 39,006
21640	01005 / 13239	Eufaula, AL-GA Micro Area.................. / Barbour County, AL..................... / Quitman County, GA	29,970 / 27,457 / 2,513	27,160 / 24,881 / 2,279
21660	41039	Eugene, OR Metro area .... / Lane County, OR	351,715 / 351,715	379,611 / 379,611
21700	06023	Eureka-Arcata-Fortuna, CA Micro area . / Humboldt County, CA......................	134,623 / 134,623	136,373 / 136,373
21740	56041	Evanston, WY Micro area..................... / Uinta County, WY	21,118 / 21,118	20,299 / 20,299
21780	18129 / 18163 / 18173 / 21101	Evansville, IN-KY Metro area .... / Posey County, IN .... / Vanderburgh County, IN .... / Warrick County, IN .... / Henderson County, KY	311,552 / 25,910 / 179,703 / 59,689 / 46,250	314,672 / 25,540 / 180,974 / 62,567 / 45,591
21820	02090	Fairbanks, AK Metro area.................... / Fairbanks North Star Borough, AK.....	97,581 / 97,581	98,971 / 98,971
21840	19101	Fairfield, IA Micro area....................... / Jefferson County, IA.....................	16,843 / 16,843	18,381 / 18,381
21860	27091	Fairmont, MN Micro Area.................... / Martin County, MN	20,840 / 20,840	19,785 / 19,785
21900	54049	Fairmont, WV Micro area..................... / Marion County, WV	56,418 / 56,418	56,097 / 56,097
21980	32001	Fallon, NV Micro area......................... / Churchill County, NV	24,877 / 24,877	24,440 / 24,440
22020	27027 / 38017	Fargo, ND-MN Metro area .... / Clay County, MN .... / Cass County, ND	208,777 / 58,999 / 149,778	245,471 / 63,955 / 181,516
22060	27131	Faribault-Northfield, MN Micro area ...... / Rice County, MN	64,142 / 64,142	66,523 / 66,523
22100	29187	Farmington, MO Micro area.................. / St. Francois County, MO................	65,359 / 65,359	66,692 / 66,692
22140	35045	Farmington, NM Metro area .... / San Juan County, NM	130,044 / 130,044	125,043 / 125,043
22180	37051 / 37093	Fayetteville, NC Metro area .... / Cumberland County, NC .... / Hoke County, NC	366,383 / 319,431 / 46,952	387,094 / 332,330 / 54,764
22220	05007 / 05087 / 05143 / 29119	Fayetteville-Springdale-Rogers, AR-MO Metro area .... / Benton County, AR......................... / Madison County, AR .... / Washington County, AR .... / McDonald County, MO..................	463,204 / 221,339 / 15,717 / 203,065 / 23,083	549,128 / 272,608 / 16,481 / 236,961 / 23,078
22260	27111	Fergus Falls, MN Micro area .... / Otter Tail County, MN	57,303 / 57,303	58,812 / 58,812
22280	32019	Fernley, NV Micro area....................... / Lyon County, NV	51,980 / 51,980	55,808 / 55,808
22300	39063	Findlay, OH Micro area....................... / Hancock County, OH	74,782 / 74,782	75,930 / 75,930
22340	13017	Fitzgerald, GA Micro area.................... / Ben Hill County, GA	17,634 / 17,634	16,787 / 16,787
22380	04005	Flagstaff, AZ Metro area .... / Coconino County, AZ	134,421 / 134,421	142,854 / 142,854
22420	26049	Flint, MI Metro area .... / Genesee County, MI	425,790 / 425,790	406,892 / 406,892
22500	45031 / 45041	Florence, SC Metro area .... / Darlington County, SC .... / Florence County, SC....................	205,566 / 68,681 / 136,885	204,961 / 66,802 / 138,159
22520	01033 / 01077	Florence-Muscle Shoals, AL Metro area / Colbert County, AL....................... / Lauderdale County, AL..................	147,137 / 54,428 / 92,709	147,149 / 54,762 / 92,387
22540	55039	Fond du Lac, WI Metro area................. / Fond du Lac County, WI	101,633 / 101,633	103,066 / 103,066
22580	37161	Forest City, NC Micro area .... / Rutherford County, NC..................	67,810 / 67,810	66,826 / 66,826
22620	05123	Forrest City, AR Micro area .... / St. Francis County, AR..................	28,258 / 28,258	25,439 / 25,439

Core based statistical area	State/County FIPS code	Title and Geographic Components	2010 Census Population	2018 Estimated Population	Core based statistical area	State/County FIPS code	Title and Geographic Components	2010 Census Population	2018 Estimated Population
22660		Fort Collins, CO Metro area	299,630	350,518	23540		Gainesville, FL Metro area	264,275	288,212
	08069	Larimer County, CO	299,630	350,518		12001	Alachua County, FL	247,336	269,956
22700		Fort Dodge, IA Micro area	38,013	36,277		12041	Gilchrist County, FL	16,939	18,256
	19187	Webster County, IA	38,013	36,277	23580		Gainesville, GA Metro area	179,684	202,148
22780		Fort Leonard Wood, MO Micro area	52,274	52,014		13139	Hall County, GA	179,684	202,148
	29169	Pulaski County, MO	52,274	52,014	23620		Gainesville, TX Micro area	38,437	40,574
22800		Fort Madison-Keokuk, IA-IL-MO Micro area	62,105	58,741		48097	Cooke County, TX	38,437	40,574
	17067	Hancock County, IL	19,104	17,844	23660		Galesburg, IL Micro area	52,919	50,112
	19111	Lee County, IA	35,862	34,055		17095	Knox County, IL	52,919	50,112
	29045	Clark County, MO	7,139	6,842	23700		Gallup, NM Micro area	71,492	72,290
22820		Fort Morgan, CO Micro area	28,159	28,558		35031	McKinley County, NM	71,492	72,290
	08087	Morgan County, CO	28,159	28,558	23780		Garden City, KS Micro area	40,753	40,554
22840		Fort Payne, AL Micro Area	71,109	71,385		20055	Finney County, KS	36,776	36,611
	01049	DeKalb County, AL	71,109	71,385		20093	Kearny County, KS	3,977	3,943
22860		Fort Polk South, LA Micro area	52,334	48,860	23820		Gardnerville Ranchos, NV Micro area	46,997	48,467
	22115	Vernon Parish, LA	52,334	48,860		32005	Douglas County, NV	46,997	48,467
22900		Fort Smith, AR-OK Metro area	280,467	282,318	23860		Georgetown, SC Micro area	60,158	62,249
	05033	Crawford County, AR	61,948	63,406		45043	Georgetown County, SC	60,158	62,249
	05131	Sebastian County, AR	125,744	127,753	23900		Gettysburg, PA Metro area	101,407	102,811
	40079	Le Flore County, OK	50,384	49,980		42001	Adams County, PA	101,407	102,811
	40135	Sequoyah County, OK	42,391	41,179	23940		Gillette, WY Micro area	46,133	46,140
23060		Fort Wayne, IN Metro area	416,257	437,631		56005	Campbell County, WY	46,133	46,140
	18003	Allen County, IN	355,329	375,351	23980		Glasgow, KY Micro area	52,272	54,206
	18179	Wells County, IN	27,636	28,206		21009	Barren County, KY	42,173	44,176
	18183	Whitley County, IN	33,292	34,074		21169	Metcalfe County, KY	10,099	10,030
23140		Frankfort, IN Micro area	33,224	32,250	24020		Glens Falls, NY Metro area	128,923	125,462
	18023	Clinton County, IN	33,224	32,250		36113	Warren County, NY	65,707	64,265
23180		Frankfort, KY Micro area	70,706	73,478		36115	Washington County, NY	63,216	61,197
	21005	Anderson County, KY	21,421	22,663	24060		Glenwood Springs, CO Micro area	73,537	77,720
	21073	Franklin County, KY	49,285	50,815		08045	Garfield County, CO	56,389	59,770
23240		Fredericksburg, TX Micro area	24,837	26,804		08097	Pitkin County, CO	17,148	17,950
	48171	Gillespie County, TX	24,837	26,804	24100		Gloversville, NY Micro area	55,531	53,591
23300		Freeport, IL Micro area	47,711	44,753		36035	Fulton County, NY	55,531	53,591
	17177	Stephenson County, IL	47,711	44,753	24140		Goldsboro, NC Metro area	122,623	123,248
23340		Fremont, NE Micro area	36,691	36,791		37191	Wayne County, NC	122,623	123,248
	31053	Dodge County, NE	36,691	36,791	24220		Grand Forks, ND-MN Metro area	98,461	102,299
23380		Fremont, OH Micro area	60,944	58,799		27119	Polk County, MN	31,600	31,529
	39143	Sandusky County, OH	60,944	58,799		38035	Grand Forks County, ND	66,861	70,770
23420		Fresno, CA Metro area	930,450	994,400	24260		Grand Island, NE Metro area	81,850	85,088
	06019	Fresno County, CA	930,450	994,400		31079	Hall County, NE	58,607	61,607
23460		Gadsden, AL Metro area	104,430	102,501		31081	Hamilton County, NE	9,124	9,280
	01055	Etowah County, AL	104,430	102,501		31093	Howard County, NE	6,274	6,468
23500		Gaffney, SC Micro area	55,342	57,078		31121	Merrick County, NE	7,845	7,733
	45021	Cherokee County, SC	55,342	57,078	24300		Grand Junction, CO Metro area	146,723	153,207
						08077	Mesa County, CO	146,723	153,207

CORE BASED STATISTICAL AREAS
(Metropolitan and Micropolitan),
METROPOLITAN DIVISIONS, AND COMPONENTS
(as defined August, 2017)—*Continued*

Core based statistical area	State/County FIPS code	Title and Geographic Components	2010 Census Population	2018 Estimated Population	Core based statistical area	State/County FIPS code	Title and Geographic Components	2010 Census Population	2018 Estimated Population
24330		Grand Rapids, MN Micro Area.............	45,058	45,108	24940		Greenwood, SC Micro area..................	95,078	95,282
	27061	Itasca County, MN......................	45,058	45,108		45001	Abbeville County, SC	25,417	24,541
						45047	Greenwood County, SC	69,661	70,741
24340		Grand Rapids-Wyoming, MI Metro area	988,938	1,069,405					
	26015	Barry County, MI	59,173	61,157	24980		Grenada, MS Micro area...................	21,906	21,055
	26081	Kent County, MI	602,622	653,786		28043	Grenada County, MS	21,906	21,055
	26117	Montcalm County, MI	63,342	63,968	25060		Gulfport-Biloxi-Pascagoula, MS Metro area	370,702	397,261
	26139	Ottawa County, MI	263,801	290,494		28045	Hancock County, MS	43,929	47,334
24380		Grants, NM Micro area...................	27,213	26,746		28047	Harrison County, MS	187,105	206,650
	35006	Cibola County, NM.......................	27,213	26,746		28059	Jackson County, MS	139,668	143,277
24420		Grants Pass, OR Metro area................	82,713	87,393	25100		Guymon, OK Micro area...................	20,640	20,455
	41033	Josephine County, OR.....................	82,713	87,393		40139	Texas County, OK	20,640	20,455
24460		Great Bend, KS Micro area	27,674	26,111	25180		Hagerstown-Martinsburg, MD-WV Metro area	251,599	268,049
	20009	Barton County, KS	27,674	26,111		24043	Washington County, MD	147,430	150,926
24500		Great Falls, MT Metro area	81,327	81,643		54003	Berkeley County, WV	104,169	117,123
	30013	Cascade County, MT	81,327	81,643	25200		Hailey, ID Micro area	27,701	29,088
24540		Greeley, CO Metro area	252,825	314,305		16013	Blaine County, ID	21,376	22,601
	08123	Weld County, CO	252,825	314,305		16025	Camas County, ID	1,117	1,127
24580		Green Bay, WI Metro area	306,241	321,591		16063	Lincoln County, ID........................	5,208	5,360
	55009	Brown County, WI	248,007	263,378	25220		Hammond, LA Metro area	121,097	133,777
	55061	Kewaunee County, WI	20,574	20,383		22105	Tangipahoa Parish, LA....................	121,097	133,777
	55083	Oconto County, WI........................	37,660	37,830	25260		Hanford-Corcoran, CA Metro area.........	152,982	151,366
24620		Greeneville, TN Micro area...............	68,831	69,087		06031	Kings County, CA	152,982	151,366
	47059	Greene County, TN	68,831	69,087	25300		Hannibal, MO Micro area.................	38,948	38,804
24640		Greenfield Town, MA Micro area	71,372	70,963		29127	Marion County, MO	28,781	28,592
	25011	Franklin County, MA......................	71,372	70,963		29173	Ralls County, MO	10,167	10,212
24660		Greensboro-High Point, NC Metro area	723,801	767,711	25420		Harrisburg-Carlisle, PA Metro area........	549,475	574,659
	37081	Guilford County, NC	488,406	533,670		42041	Cumberland County, PA..................	235,406	251,423
	37151	Randolph County, NC	141,752	143,351		42043	Dauphin County, PA......................	268,100	277,097
	37157	Rockingham County, NC..................	93,643	90,690		42099	Perry County, PA.........................	45,969	46,139
24700		Greensburg, IN Micro area................	25,740	26,794	25460		Harrison, AR Micro area	45,233	45,285
	18031	Decatur County, IN.......................	25,740	26,794		05009	Boone County, AR........................	36,903	37,480
24740		Greenville, MS Micro area................	51,137	45,063		05101	Newton County, AR.......................	8,330	7,805
	28151	Washington County, MS..................	51,137	45,063	25500		Harrisonburg, VA Metro area	125,228	135,277
24780		Greenville, NC Metro area	168,148	179,914		51165	Rockingham County, VA	76,314	81,244
	37147	Pitt County, NC...........................	168,148	179,914		51660	Harrisonburg city, VA.....................	48,914	54,033
24820		Greenville, OH Micro area	52,959	51,323	25540		Hartford-West Hartford-East Hartford, CT Metro area	1,212,381	1,206,300
	39037	Darke County, OH........................	52,959	51,323		09003	Hartford County, CT......................	894,014	892,697
24860		Greenville-Anderson-Mauldin, SC Metro area	824,112	906,626		09007	Middlesex County, CT	165,676	162,682
	45007	Anderson County, SC.....................	187,126	200,482		09013	Tolland County, CT.......................	152,691	150,921
	45045	Greenville County, SC....................	451,225	514,213	25580		Hastings, NE Micro area..................	31,364	31,511
	45059	Laurens County, SC......................	66,537	66,994		31001	Adams County, NE........................	31,364	31,511
	45077	Pickens County, SC	119,224	124,937	25620		Hattiesburg, MS Metro area	142,842	149,414
24900		Greenwood, MS Micro area...............	42,914	38,830		28035	Forrest County, MS	74,934	75,036
	28015	Carroll County, MS	10,597	9,911		28073	Lamar County, MS	55,658	62,447
	28083	Leflore County, MS	32,317	28,919		28111	Perry County, MS.........................	12,250	11,931

CORE BASED STATISTICAL AREAS
(Metropolitan and Micropolitan),
METROPOLITAN DIVISIONS, AND COMPONENTS
(as defined August, 2017)—*Continued*

Core based statistical area	State/ County FIPS code	Title and Geographic Components	2010 Census Population	2018 Estimated Population	Core based statistical area	State/ County FIPS code	Title and Geographic Components	2010 Census Population	2018 Estimated Population
25700		Hays, KS Micro area............................	28,452	28,710	26340		Houghton, MI Micro area.....................	38,784	38,332
	20051	Ellis County, KS	28,452	28,710		26061	Houghton County, MI	36,628	36,219
25720		Heber, UT Micro area	23,530	33,240		26083	Keweenaw County, MI	2,156	2,113
	49051	Wasatch County, UT	23,530	33,240	26380		Houma-Thibodaux, LA Metro area	208,178	209,136
25740		Helena, MT Micro area........................	74,801	80,797		22057	Lafourche Parish, LA......................	96,318	98,115
	30043	Jefferson County, MT	11,406	12,097		22109	Terrebonne Parish, LA	111,860	111,021
	30049	Lewis and Clark County, MT	63,395	68,700	26420		Houston-The Woodlands-Sugar Land, TX Metro area........................	5,920,416	6,997,384
25760		Helena-West Helena, AR Micro area.....	21,757	18,029		48015	Austin County, TX	28,417	29,989
	05107	Phillips County, AR.........................	21,757	18,029		48039	Brazoria County, TX.......................	313,166	370,200
25780		Henderson, NC Micro area..................	45,422	44,582		48071	Chambers County, TX	35,096	42,454
	37181	Vance County, NC...........................	45,422	44,582		48157	Fort Bend County, TX	585,375	787,858
25820		Hereford, TX Micro area.....................	19,372	18,760		48167	Galveston County, TX	291,309	337,890
	48117	Deaf Smith County, TX	19,372	18,760		48201	Harris County, TX..........................	4,092,459	4,698,619
25840		Hermiston-Pendleton, OR Micro area ...	87,062	88,888		48291	Liberty County, TX	75,643	86,323
	41049	Morrow County, OR	11,173	11,372		48339	Montgomery County, TX	455,746	590,925
	41059	Umatilla County, OR	75,889	77,516		48473	Waller County, TX	43,205	53,126
25860		Hickory-Lenoir-Morganton, NC Metro area	365,497	368,416	26460		Hudson, NY Micro area	63,096	59,916
	37003	Alexander County, NC.....................	37,198	37,353		36021	Columbia County, NY......................	63,096	59,916
	37023	Burke County, NC...........................	90,912	90,382	26500		Huntingdon, PA Micro area.................	45,913	45,168
	37027	Caldwell County, NC.......................	83,029	82,029		42061	Huntingdon County, PA....................	45,913	45,168
	37035	Catawba County, NC	154,358	158,652	26540		Huntington, IN Micro area..................	37,124	36,240
25880		Hillsdale, MI Micro area......................	46,688	45,749		18069	Huntington County, IN	37,124	36,240
	26059	Hillsdale County, MI	46,688	45,749	26580		Huntington-Ashland, WV-KY-OH Metro area	364,908	352,823
25900		Hilo, HI Micro area.............................	185,079	200,983		21019	Boyd County, KY............................	49,542	47,240
	15001	Hawaii County, HI	185,079	200,983		21089	Greenup County, KY.......................	36,910	35,268
25940		Hilton Head Island-Bluffton-Beaufort, SC Metro area	187,010	217,686		39087	Lawrence County, OH	62,450	59,866
						54011	Cabell County, WV.........................	96,319	93,224
	45013	Beaufort County, SC	162,233	188,715		54043	Lincoln County, WV........................	21,720	20,599
	45053	Jasper County, SC.........................	24,777	28,971		54079	Putnam County, WV	55,486	56,682
25980		Hinesville, GA Metro area...................	77,917	80,495		54099	Wayne County, WV	42,481	39,944
	13179	Liberty County, GA.........................	63,453	61,497	26620		Huntsville, AL Metro area	417,593	462,693
	13183	Long County, GA............................	14,464	18,998		01083	Limestone County, AL	82,782	96,174
26020		Hobbs, NM Micro area.......................	64,727	69,611		01089	Madison County, AL........................	334,811	366,519
	35025	Lea County, NM	64,727	69,611	26660		Huntsville, TX Micro area..................	82,446	87,220
26090		Holland, MI Micro area	111,408	117,327		48455	Trinity County, TX..........................	14,585	14,740
	26005	Allegan County, MI	111,408	117,327		48471	Walker County, TX	67,861	72,480
26140		Homosassa Springs, FL Metro area......	141,236	147,929	26700		Huron, SD Micro area	17,398	18,883
	12017	Citrus County, FL	141,236	147,929		46005	Beadle County, SD.........................	17,398	18,883
26220		Hood River, OR Micro area	22,346	23,428	26740		Hutchinson, KS Micro area.................	64,511	62,342
	41027	Hood River County, OR	22,346	23,428		20155	Reno County, KS	64,511	62,342
26260		Hope, AR Micro Area........................	31,606	30,067	26780		Hutchinson, MN Micro area................	36,651	35,873
	05057	Hempstead County, AR..............	22,609	21,741		27085	McLeod County, MN........................	36,651	35,873
	05099	Nevada County, AR....................	8,997	8,326	26820		Idaho Falls, ID Metro area...................	133,265	148,904
26300		Hot Springs, AR Metro area................	96,024	99,154		16019	Bonneville County, ID......................	104,234	116,854
	05051	Garland County, AR	96,024	99,154		16023	Butte County, ID............................	2,891	2,611
						16051	Jefferson County, ID	26,140	29,439
					26860		Indiana, PA Micro area	88,880	84,501
						42063	Indiana County, PA.........................	88,880	84,501

Core based statistical area	State/County FIPS code	Title and Geographic Components	2010 Census Population	2018 Estimated Population	Core based statistical area	State/County FIPS code	Title and Geographic Components	2010 Census Population	2018 Estimated Population
26900		Indianapolis-Carmel-Anderson, IN Metro area	1,887,877	2,048,703	27340		Jacksonville, NC Metro area	177,772	197,683
	18011	Boone County, IN	56,640	66,999		37133	Onslow County, NC	177,772	197,683
	18013	Brown County, IN	15,242	15,234	27380		Jacksonville, TX Micro area	50,845	52,592
	18057	Hamilton County, IN	274,569	330,086		48073	Cherokee County, TX	50,845	52,592
	18059	Hancock County, IN	70,002	76,351					
	18063	Hendricks County, IN	145,448	167,009	27420		Jamestown, ND Micro area	21,100	20,917
	18081	Johnson County, IN..........	139,654	156,225		38093	Stutsman County, ND	21,100	20,917
	18095	Madison County, IN..........	131,636	129,641					
	18097	Marion County, IN	903,393	954,670	27460		Jamestown-Dunkirk-Fredonia, NY Micro area	134,905	127,939
	18109	Morgan County, IN	68,894	70,116		36013	Chautauqua County, NY	134,905	127,939
	18133	Putnam County, IN	37,963	37,779					
	18145	Shelby County, IN	44,436	44,593	27500		Janesville-Beloit, WI Metro area..........	160,331	163,129
26940		Indianola, MS Micro area..........	29,450	25,735		55105	Rock County, WI	160,331	163,129
	28133	Sunflower County, MS	29,450	25,735					
					27540		Jasper, IN Micro area	54,734	54,975
26960		Ionia, MI Micro area..........	63,905	64,210		18037	Dubois County, IN..........	41,889	42,565
	26067	Ionia County, MI..........	63,905	64,210		18125	Pike County, IN	12,845	12,410
26980		Iowa City, IA Metro area	152,586	173,401	27600		Jefferson, GA Micro area..........	60,485	70,422
	19103	Johnson County, IA..........	130,882	151,260		13157	Jackson County, GA..........	60,485	70,422
	19183	Washington County, IA..........	21,704	22,141					
					27620		Jefferson City, MO Metro area..........	149,807	151,520
27020		Iron Mountain, MI-WI Micro area	30,591	29,704		29027	Callaway County, MO	44,332	44,889
	26043	Dickinson County, MI	26,168	25,383		29051	Cole County, MO	75,990	76,796
	55037	Florence County, WI	4,423	4,321		29135	Moniteau County, MO	15,607	16,121
						29151	Osage County, MO	13,878	13,714
27060		Ithaca, NY Metro area	101,564	102,793					
	36109	Tompkins County, NY	101,564	102,793	27660		Jennings, LA Micro Area..........	31,594	31,582
						22053	Jefferson Davis Parish, LA..........	31,594	31,582
27100		Jackson, MI Metro area	160,248	158,823					
	26075	Jackson County, MI..........	160,248	158,823	27700		Jesup, GA Micro area..........	30,099	29,808
						13305	Wayne County, GA..........	30,099	29,808
27140		Jackson, MS Metro area..........	567,122	580,166					
	28029	Copiah County, MS	29,449	28,543	27740		Johnson City, TN Metro area..........	198,716	202,719
	28049	Hinds County, MS	245,285	237,085		47019	Carter County, TN	57,424	56,351
	28089	Madison County, MS	95,203	105,630		47171	Unicoi County, TN	18,313	17,761
	28121	Rankin County, MS	141,617	153,902		47179	Washington County, TN	122,979	128,607
	28127	Simpson County, MS	27,503	26,758					
	28163	Yazoo County, MS..........	28,065	28,248	27780		Johnstown, PA Metro area..........	143,679	131,730
						42021	Cambria County, PA..........	143,679	131,730
27160		Jackson, OH Micro area..........	33,225	32,384					
	39079	Jackson County, OH	33,225	32,384	27860		Jonesboro, AR Metro area..........	121,026	132,532
						05031	Craighead County, AR	96,443	108,558
27180		Jackson, TN Metro area	130,011	129,209		05111	Poinsett County, AR..........	24,583	23,974
	47023	Chester County, TN	17,131	17,276					
	47033	Crockett County, TN..........	14,586	14,328	27900		Joplin, MO Metro area..........	175,518	178,902
	47113	Madison County, TN	98,294	97,605		29097	Jasper County, MO	117,404	120,636
						29145	Newton County, MO	58,114	58,266
27220		Jackson, WY-ID Micro area	31,464	34,721					
	16081	Teton County, ID	10,170	11,640	27920		Junction City, KS Micro area..........	34,362	32,594
	56039	Teton County, WY	21,294	23,081		20061	Geary County, KS	34,362	32,594
27260		Jacksonville, FL Metro area..........	1,345,596	1,534,701	27940		Juneau, AK Micro area	31,275	32,113
	12003	Baker County, FL	27,115	28,355		02110	Juneau City and Borough, AK..........	31,275	32,113
	12019	Clay County, FL..........	190,865	216,072					
	12031	Duval County, FL..........	864,263	950,181	27980		Kahului-Wailuku-Lahaina, HI Metro area	154,924	167,295
	12089	Nassau County, FL..........	73,314	85,832		15005	Kalawao County, HI	90	88
	12109	St. Johns County, FL..........	190,039	254,261		15009	Maui County, HI	154,834	167,207
27300		Jacksonville, IL Micro area	40,902	38,902					
	17137	Morgan County, IL..........	35,547	33,976					
	17171	Scott County, IL..........	5,355	4,926					

CORE BASED STATISTICAL AREAS
(Metropolitan and Micropolitan),
METROPOLITAN DIVISIONS, AND COMPONENTS
(as defined August, 2017)—*Continued*

Core based statistical area	State/County FIPS code	Title and Geographic Components	2010 Census Population	2018 Estimated Population	Core based statistical area	State/County FIPS code	Title and Geographic Components	2010 Census Population	2018 Estimated Population
28020		Kalamazoo-Portage, MI Metro area	326,589	340,318	28700		Kingsport-Bristol-Bristol, TN-VA Metro area	309,544	306,616
	26077	Kalamazoo County, MI..............	250,331	264,870		47073	Hawkins County, TN	56,833	56,530
	26159	Van Buren County, MI	76,258	75,448		47163	Sullivan County, TN	156,823	157,668
28060		Kalispell, MT Micro area	90,928	102,106		51169	Scott County, VA	23,177	21,534
	30029	Flathead County, MT.................	90,928	102,106		51191	Washington County, VA............	54,876	54,402
28100		Kankakee, IL Metro area	113,449	110,024		51520	Bristol city, VA	17,835	16,482
	17091	Kankakee County, IL............	113,449	110,024	28740		Kingston, NY Metro area	182,493	178,599
28140		Kansas City, MO-KS Metro area	2,009,342	2,143,651		36111	Ulster County, NY	182,493	178,599
	20091	Johnson County, KS.............	544,179	597,555	28780		Kingsville, TX Micro area	32,477	31,571
	20103	Leavenworth County, KS..........	76,227	81,352		48261	Kenedy County, TX	416	442
	20107	Linn County, KS	9,656	9,750		48273	Kleberg County, TX............	32,061	31,129
	20121	Miami County, KS	32,787	33,680	28820		Kinston, NC Micro area	59,495	55,976
	20209	Wyandotte County, KS..........	157,505	165,324		37107	Lenoir County, NC............	59,495	55,976
	29013	Bates County, MO.............	17,049	16,320	28860		Kirksville, MO Micro area............	30,038	29,938
	29025	Caldwell County, MO..........	9,424	9,108		29001	Adair County, MO............	25,607	25,339
	29037	Cass County, MO............	99,478	104,954		29197	Schuyler County, MO............	4,431	4,599
	29047	Clay County, MO.............	221,939	246,365	28900		Klamath Falls, OR Micro area	66,380	67,653
	29049	Clinton County, MO..........	20,743	20,470		41035	Klamath County, OR............	66,380	67,653
	29095	Jackson County, MO..........	674,158	700,307	28940		Knoxville, TN Metro area............	837,571	883,309
	29107	Lafayette County, MO.........	33,381	32,598		47001	Anderson County, TN............	75,129	76,482
	29165	Platte County, MO............	89,322	102,985		47009	Blount County, TN............	123,010	131,349
	29177	Ray County, MO............	23,494	22,883		47013	Campbell County, TN............	40,716	39,583
28180		Kapaa, HI Micro area....................	67,091	72,133		47057	Grainger County, TN............	22,657	23,145
	15007	Kauai County, HI.............	67,091	72,133		47093	Knox County, TN............	432,226	465,289
28260		Kearney, NE Micro area	52,591	56,159		47105	Loudon County, TN............	48,556	53,054
	31019	Buffalo County, NE............	46,102	49,615		47129	Morgan County, TN............	21,987	21,579
	31099	Kearney County, NE............	6,489	6,544		47145	Roane County, TN............	54,181	53,140
28300		Keene, NH Micro area....................	77,117	76,493		47173	Union County, TN............	19,109	19,688
	33005	Cheshire County, NH............	77,117	76,493	29020		Kokomo, IN Metro area	82,752	82,366
28340		Kendallville, IN Micro area....................	47,536	47,532		18067	Howard County, IN............	82,752	82,366
	18113	Noble County, IN............	47,536	47,532	29060		Laconia, NH Micro area............	60,088	61,022
28380		Kennett, MO Micro area	31,953	29,423		33001	Belknap County, NH............	60,088	61,022
	29069	Dunklin County, MO............	31,953	29,423	29100		La Crosse-Onalaska, WI-MN Metro area	133,665	136,808
28420		Kennewick-Richland, WA Metro area	253,340	296,224		27055	Houston County, MN............	19,027	18,578
	53005	Benton County, WA............	175,177	201,877		55063	La Crosse County, WI............	114,638	118,230
	53021	Franklin County, WA............	78,163	94,347	29180		Lafayette, LA Metro area	466,750	489,364
28500		Kerrville, TX Micro area	49,625	52,405		22001	Acadia Parish, LA............	61,773	62,190
	48265	Kerr County, TX	49,625	52,405		22045	Iberia Parish, LA............	73,240	70,941
28540		Ketchikan, AK Micro area	13,477	13,918		22055	Lafayette Parish, LA............	221,578	242,782
	02130	Ketchikan Gateway Borough, AK.......	13,477	13,918		22099	St. Martin Parish, LA............	52,160	53,621
28580		Key West, FL Micro area	73,090	75,027		22113	Vermilion Parish, LA............	57,999	59,830
	12087	Monroe County, FL............	73,090	75,027	29200		Lafayette-West Lafayette, IN Metro area	201,789	221,828
28620		Kill Devil Hills, NC Micro area...............	38,327	40,632		18007	Benton County, IN............	8,854	8,653
	37055	Dare County, NC............	33,920	36,501		18015	Carroll County, IN............	20,155	20,127
	37177	Tyrrell County, NC............	4,407	4,131		18157	Tippecanoe County, IN............	172,780	193,048
28660		Killeen-Temple, TX Metro area..............	405,300	451,679	29260		La Grande, OR Micro area	25,748	26,461
	48027	Bell County, TX	310,235	355,642		41061	Union County, OR............	25,748	26,461
	48099	Coryell County, TX............	75,388	74,808					
	48281	Lampasas County, TX............	19,677	21,229					

Core based statistical area	State/County FIPS code	Title and Geographic Components	2010 Census Population	2018 Estimated Population	Core based statistical area	State/County FIPS code	Title and Geographic Components	2010 Census Population	2018 Estimated Population
29300		LaGrange, GA Micro area......................	67,044	70,034	30140		Lebanon, PA Metro area........................	133,568	141,314
	13285	Troup County, GA...............................	67,044	70,034		42075	Lebanon County, PA	133,568	141,314
29340		Lake Charles, LA Metro area.................	199,607	210,080	30220		Levelland, TX Micro area.......................	22,935	22,980
	22019	Calcasieu Parish, LA........................	192,768	203,112		48219	Hockley County, TX	22,935	22,980
	22023	Cameron Parish, LA.........................	6,839	6,968	30260		Lewisburg, PA Micro area......................	44,947	44,785
29380		Lake City, FL Micro area......................	67,531	70,503		42119	Union County, PA	44,947	44,785
	12023	Columbia County, FL........................	67,531	70,503	30280		Lewisburg, TN Micro area	30,617	33,683
29420		Lake Havasu City-Kingman, AZ Metro area	200,186	209,550		47117	Marshall County, TN	30,617	33,683
	04015	Mohave County, AZ...........................	200,186	209,550	30300		Lewiston, ID-WA Metro area..................	60,888	63,018
29460		Lakeland-Winter Haven, FL Metro area	602,095	708,009		16069	Nez Perce County, ID	39,265	40,408
	12105	Polk County, FL.................................	602,095	708,009		53003	Asotin County, WA...........................	21,623	22,610
29500		Lamesa, TX Micro area	13,833	12,619	30340		Lewiston-Auburn, ME Metro area..........	107,702	107,679
	48115	Dawson County, TX	13,833	12,619		23001	Androscoggin County, ME.................	107,702	107,679
29540		Lancaster, PA Metro area....................	519,445	543,557	30380		Lewistown, PA Micro area	46,682	46,222
	42071	Lancaster County, PA........................	519,445	543,557		42087	Mifflin County, PA.............................	46,682	46,222
29620		Lansing-East Lansing, MI Metro area....	464,036	481,893	30420		Lexington, NE Micro area.....................	26,370	25,705
	26037	Clinton County, MI............................	75,382	79,332		31047	Dawson County, NE	24,326	23,709
	26045	Eaton County, MI	107,759	109,826		31073	Gosper County, NE	2,044	1,996
	26065	Ingham County, MI............................	280,895	292,735	30460		Lexington-Fayette, KY Metro area.........	472,099	516,697
29660		Laramie, WY Micro area......................	36,299	38,601		21017	Bourbon County, KY	19,985	20,184
	56001	Albany County, WY............................	36,299	38,601		21049	Clark County, KY	35,613	36,249
29700		Laredo, TX Metro area	250,304	275,910		21067	Fayette County, KY	295,803	323,780
	48479	Webb County, TX...............................	250,304	275,910		21113	Jessamine County, KY......................	48,586	53,920
29740		Las Cruces, NM Metro area	209,233	217,522		21209	Scott County, KY	47,173	56,031
	35013	Doña Ana County, NM	209,233	217,522		21239	Woodford County, KY.......................	24,939	26,533
29780		Las Vegas, NM Micro area	29,393	27,591	30580		Liberal, KS Micro area.........................	22,952	21,780
	35047	San Miguel County, NM	29,393	27,591		20175	Seward County, KS...........................	22,952	21,780
29820		Las Vegas-Henderson-Paradise, NV Metro area	1,951,269	2,231,647	30620		Lima, OH Metro area...........................	106,331	102,663
	32003	Clark County, NV	1,951,269	2,231,647		39003	Allen County, OH..............................	106,331	102,663
29860		Laurel, MS Micro area	84,823	84,889	30660		Lincoln, IL Micro area	30,305	28,925
	28061	Jasper County, MS............................	17,062	16,428		17107	Logan County, IL...............................	30,305	28,925
	28067	Jones County, MS.............................	67,761	68,461	30700		Lincoln, NE Metro area.........................	302,157	334,590
29900		Laurinburg, NC Micro area	36,157	34,810		31109	Lancaster County, NE	285,407	317,272
	37165	Scotland County, NC........................	36,157	34,810		31159	Seward County, NE...........................	16,750	17,318
29940		Lawrence, KS Metro area.....................	110,826	121,436	30780		Little Rock-North Little Rock-Conway, AR Metro area..................................	699,757	741,104
	20045	Douglas County, KS..........................	110,826	121,436		05045	Faulkner County, AR.........................	113,237	124,806
29980		Lawrenceburg, TN Micro area...............	41,869	43,734		05053	Grant County, AR	17,853	18,188
	47099	Lawrence County, TN	41,869	43,734		05085	Lonoke County, AR	68,356	73,657
30020		Lawton, OK Metro area	130,291	126,198		05105	Perry County, AR..............................	10,445	10,352
	40031	Comanche County, OK	124,098	120,422		05119	Pulaski County, AR	382,748	392,680
	40033	Cotton County, OK............................	6,193	5,776		05125	Saline County, AR	107,118	121,421
30060		Lebanon, MO Micro area......................	35,571	35,713	30820		Lock Haven, PA Micro area	39,238	38,684
	29105	Laclede County, MO	35,571	35,713		42035	Clinton County, PA............................	39,238	38,684
					30860		Logan, UT-ID Metro area......................	125,442	140,794
						16041	Franklin County, ID	12,786	13,726
						49005	Cache County, UT.............................	112,656	127,068

Core based statistical area	State/County FIPS code	Title and Geographic Components	2010 Census Population	2018 Estimated Population	Core based statistical area	State/County FIPS code	Title and Geographic Components	2010 Census Population	2018 Estimated Population
30880		Logan, WV Micro area	36,743	32,607	31340		Lynchburg, VA Metro area	252,634	263,353
	54045	Logan County, WV	36,743	32,607		51009	Amherst County, VA	32,353	31,666
						51011	Appomattox County, VA	14,973	15,841
30900		Logansport, IN Micro area	38,966	37,955		51019	Bedford County, VA	68,676	78,747
	18017	Cass County, IN	38,966	37,955		51031	Campbell County, VA	54,842	54,973
						51680	Lynchburg city, VA	75,568	82,126
30940		London, KY Micro area	126,369	128,215					
	21121	Knox County, KY	31,883	31,304	31380		Macomb, IL Micro area	32,612	29,955
	21125	Laurel County, KY	58,849	60,669		17109	McDonough County, IL	32,612	29,955
	21235	Whitley County, KY	35,637	36,242					
					31420		Macon, GA Metro area	232,293	229,737
30980		Longview, TX Metro area	214,369	219,417		13021	Bibb County, GA	155,547	153,095
	48183	Gregg County, TX	121,730	123,707		13079	Crawford County, GA	12,630	12,318
	48401	Rusk County, TX	53,330	54,450		13169	Jones County, GA	28,669	28,616
	48459	Upshur County, TX	39,309	41,260		13207	Monroe County, GA	26,424	27,520
						13289	Twiggs County, GA	9,023	8,188
31020		Longview, WA Metro area	102,410	108,987					
	53015	Cowlitz County, WA	102,410	108,987	31460		Madera, CA Metro area	150,865	157,672
						06039	Madera County, CA	150,865	157,672
31060		Los Alamos, NM Micro area	17,950	19,101					
	35028	Los Alamos County, NM	17,950	19,101	31500		Madison, IN Micro area	32,428	32,208
						18077	Jefferson County, IN	32,428	32,208
31080		Los Angeles-Long Beach-Anaheim, CA Metro area	12,828,837	13,291,486					
					31540		Madison, WI Metro area	605,435	660,422
31080		Anaheim-Santa Ana-Irvine, CA Metro Div 11244	3,010,232	3,185,968		55021	Columbia County, WI	56,833	57,358
						55025	Dane County, WI	488,073	542,364
	06059	Orange County, CA	3,010,232	3,185,968		55045	Green County, WI	36,842	36,929
						55049	Iowa County, WI	23,687	23,771
31080		Los Angeles-Long Beach-Glendale, CA Metro Div 31084	9,818,605	10,105,518					
					31580		Madisonville, KY Micro area	46,920	45,068
	06037	Los Angeles County, CA	9,818,605	10,105,518		21107	Hopkins County, KY	46,920	45,068
31140		Louisville/Jefferson County, KY-IN Metro area	1,235,708	1,297,301	31620		Magnolia, AR Micro area	24,552	23,537
						05027	Columbia County, AR	24,552	23,537
	18019	Clark County, IN	110,232	117,360					
	18043	Floyd County, IN	74,578	77,781	31660		Malone, NY Micro area	51,599	50,293
	18061	Harrison County, IN	39,364	40,350		36033	Franklin County, NY	51,599	50,293
	18143	Scott County, IN	24,181	23,878					
	18175	Washington County, IN	28,262	27,943	31680		Malvern, AR Micro area	32,923	33,701
	21029	Bullitt County, KY	74,319	81,069		05059	Hot Spring County, AR	32,923	33,701
	21103	Henry County, KY	15,416	16,106					
	21111	Jefferson County, KY	741,096	770,517	31700		Manchester-Nashua, NH Metro area	400,721	415,247
	21185	Oldham County, KY	60,316	66,470		33011	Hillsborough County, NH	400,721	415,247
	21211	Shelby County, KY	42,074	48,518					
	21215	Spencer County, KY	17,061	18,794	31740		Manhattan, KS Metro area	92,719	97,980
	21223	Trimble County, KY	8,809	8,515		20149	Pottawatomie County, KS	21,604	24,277
						20161	Riley County, KS	71,115	73,703
31180		Lubbock, TX Metro area	290,805	319,068					
	48107	Crosby County, TX	6,059	5,779	31820		Manitowoc, WI Micro area	81,442	79,074
	48303	Lubbock County, TX	278,831	307,412		55071	Manitowoc County, WI	81,442	79,074
	48305	Lynn County, TX	5,915	5,877					
					31860		Mankato-North Mankato, MN Metro area	96,740	101,647
31220		Ludington, MI Micro area	28,705	29,100					
	26105	Mason County, MI	28,705	29,100		27013	Blue Earth County, MN	64,013	67,427
						27103	Nicollet County, MN	32,727	34,220
31260		Lufkin, TX Micro area	86,771	87,092					
	48005	Angelina County, TX	86,771	87,092	31900		Mansfield, OH Metro area	124,475	121,099
						39139	Richland County, OH	124,475	121,099
31300		Lumberton, NC Micro area	134,168	131,831					
	37155	Robeson County, NC	134,168	131,831	31930		Marietta, OH Micro area	61,778	60,155
						39167	Washington County, OH	61,778	60,155

CORE BASED STATISTICAL AREAS
(Metropolitan and Micropolitan), METROPOLITAN DIVISIONS, AND COMPONENTS
(as defined August, 2017)—*Continued*

Core based statistical area	State/County FIPS code	Title and Geographic Components	2010 Census Population	2018 Estimated Population
31940		Marinette, WI-MI Micro area	65,778	63,417
	26109	Menominee County, MI	24,029	22,983
	55075	Marinette County, WI	41,749	40,434
31980		Marion, IN Micro area	70,061	65,936
	18053	Grant County, IN	70,061	65,936
32000		Marion, NC Micro area	44,996	45,507
	37111	McDowell County, NC	44,996	45,507
32020		Marion, OH Micro area	66,501	65,256
	39101	Marion County, OH	66,501	65,256
32100		Marquette, MI Micro area	67,077	66,516
	26103	Marquette County, MI	67,077	66,516
32140		Marshall, MN Micro area	25,857	25,629
	27083	Lyon County, MN	25,857	25,629
32180		Marshall, MO Micro area	23,370	22,895
	29195	Saline County, MO	23,370	22,895
32220		Marshall, TX Micro area	65,631	66,726
	48203	Harrison County, TX	65,631	66,726
32260		Marshalltown, IA Micro area	40,648	39,981
	19127	Marshall County, IA	40,648	39,981
32280		Martin, TN Micro area	35,021	33,415
	47183	Weakley County, TN	35,021	33,415
32300		Martinsville, VA Micro area	67,972	63,855
	51089	Henry County, VA	54,151	50,953
	51690	Martinsville city, VA	13,821	12,902
32340		Maryville, MO Micro area	23,370	22,304
	29147	Nodaway County, MO	23,370	22,304
32380		Mason City, IA Micro area	51,749	50,100
	19033	Cerro Gordo County, IA	44,151	42,647
	19195	Worth County, IA	7,598	7,453
32460		Mayfield, KY Micro area	37,121	37,317
	21083	Graves County, KY	37,121	37,317
32500		Maysville, KY Micro area	17,490	17,150
	21161	Mason County, KY	17,490	17,150
32540		McAlester, OK Micro area	45,837	43,877
	40121	Pittsburg County, OK	45,837	43,877
32580		McAllen-Edinburg-Mission, TX Metro area	774,769	865,939
	48215	Hidalgo County, TX	774,769	865,939
32620		McComb, MS Micro area	53,535	51,889
	28005	Amite County, MS	13,131	12,326
	28113	Pike County, MS	40,404	39,563
32660		McMinnville, TN Micro area	39,839	40,878
	47177	Warren County, TN	39,839	40,878
32700		McPherson, KS Micro area	29,180	28,537
	20113	McPherson County, KS	29,180	28,537
32740		Meadville, PA Micro area	88,765	85,063
	42039	Crawford County, PA	88,765	85,063
32780		Medford, OR Metro area	203,206	219,564
	41029	Jackson County, OR	203,206	219,564
32820		Memphis, TN-MS-AR Metro area	1,324,829	1,350,620
	05035	Crittenden County, AR	50,902	48,342
	28009	Benton County, MS	8,729	8,271
	28033	DeSoto County, MS	161,252	182,001
	28093	Marshall County, MS	37,144	35,451
	28137	Tate County, MS	28,886	28,759
	28143	Tunica County, MS	10,778	9,944
	47047	Fayette County, TN	38,413	40,507
	47157	Shelby County, TN	927,644	935,764
	47167	Tipton County, TN	61,081	61,581
32860		Menomonie, WI Micro area	43,857	45,131
	55033	Dunn County, WI	43,857	45,131
32900		Merced, CA Metro area	255,793	274,765
	06047	Merced County, CA	255,793	274,765
32940		Meridian, MS Micro area	107,449	100,948
	28023	Clarke County, MS	16,732	15,604
	28069	Kemper County, MS	10,456	10,027
	28075	Lauderdale County, MS	80,261	75,317
32980		Merrill, WI Micro area	28,743	27,689
	55069	Lincoln County, WI	28,743	27,689
33020		Mexico, MO Micro area	25,529	25,473
	29007	Audrain County, MO	25,529	25,473
33060		Miami, OK Micro area	31,848	31,175
	40115	Ottawa County, OK	31,848	31,175
33100		Miami-Fort Lauderdale-West Palm Beach, FL Metro area	5,564,635	6,198,782
33100		Fort Lauderdale-Pompano Beach-Deerfield Beach, FL Metro Div 22744	1,748,066	1,951,260
	12011	Broward County, FL	1,748,066	1,951,260
33100		Miami-Miami Beach-Kendall, FL Metro Div 33124	2,496,435	2,761,581
	12086	Miami-Dade County, FL	2,496,435	2,761,581
33100		West Palm Beach-Boca Raton-Delray Beach, FL Metro Div 48424	1,320,134	1,485,941
	12099	Palm Beach County, FL	1,320,134	1,485,941
33140		Michigan City-La Porte, IN Metro area	111,467	110,007
	18091	LaPorte County, IN	111,467	110,007
33180		Middlesborough, KY Micro area	28,691	26,569
	21013	Bell County, KY	28,691	26,569
33220		Midland, MI Metro area	83,629	83,209
	26111	Midland County, MI	83,629	83,209
33260		Midland, TX Metro area	141,671	178,331
	48317	Martin County, TX	4,799	5,753
	48329	Midland County, TX	136,872	172,578

CORE BASED STATISTICAL AREAS
(Metropolitan and Micropolitan),
METROPOLITAN DIVISIONS, AND COMPONENTS
(as defined August, 2017)—*Continued*

Core based statistical area	State/ County FIPS code	Title and Geographic Components	2010 Census Population	2018 Estimated Population	Core based statistical area	State/ County FIPS code	Title and Geographic Components	2010 Census Population	2018 Estimated Population
33300		Milledgeville, GA Micro area	55,149	53,171	33860		Montgomery, AL Metro area	374,536	373,225
	13009	Baldwin County, GA	45,720	44,823		01001	Autauga County, AL	54,571	55,601
	13141	Hancock County, GA	9,429	8,348		01051	Elmore County, AL	79,303	81,887
33340		Milwaukee-Waukesha-West Allis, WI Metro area	1,555,908	1,576,113		01085	Lowndes County, AL	11,299	9,974
						01101	Montgomery County, AL	229,363	225,763
	55079	Milwaukee County, WI	947,735	948,201					
	55089	Ozaukee County, WI	86,395	89,147	33940		Montrose, CO Micro area	41,276	42,214
	55131	Washington County, WI	131,887	135,693		08085	Montrose County, CO	41,276	42,214
	55133	Waukesha County, WI	389,891	403,072	33980		Morehead City, NC Micro area	66,469	69,524
33420		Mineral Wells, TX Micro area	28,111	28,875		37031	Carteret County, NC	66,469	69,524
	48363	Palo Pinto County, TX	28,111	28,875	34020		Morgan City, LA Micro area	54,650	49,774
33460		Minneapolis-St. Paul-Bloomington, MN Metro area	3,348,859	3,629,190		22101	St. Mary Parish, LA	54,650	49,774
	27003	Anoka County, MN	330,844	353,813	34060		Morgantown, WV Metro area	129,709	140,259
	27019	Carver County, MN	91,042	103,551		54061	Monongalia County, WV	96,189	106,420
	27025	Chisago County, MN	53,887	55,922		54077	Preston County, WV	33,520	33,839
	27037	Dakota County, MN	398,552	425,423	34100		Morristown, TN Metro area	113,951	118,581
	27053	Hennepin County, MN	1,152,425	1,259,428		47063	Hamblen County, TN	62,544	64,569
	27059	Isanti County, MN	37,816	39,966		47089	Jefferson County, TN	51,407	54,012
	27079	Le Sueur County, MN	27,703	28,494					
	27095	Mille Lacs County, MN	26,097	26,139	34140		Moscow, ID Micro area	37,244	40,134
	27123	Ramsey County, MN	508,640	550,210		16057	Latah County, ID	37,244	40,134
	27139	Scott County, MN	129,928	147,381					
	27141	Sherburne County, MN	88,499	96,036	34180		Moses Lake, WA Micro area	89,120	97,331
	27143	Sibley County, MN	15,226	15,028		53025	Grant County, WA	89,120	97,331
	27163	Washington County, MN	238,136	259,201	34220		Moultrie, GA Micro area	45,498	45,592
	27171	Wright County, MN	124,700	136,349		13071	Colquitt County, GA	45,498	45,592
	55093	Pierce County, WI	41,019	42,555	34260		Mountain Home, AR Micro area	41,513	41,619
	55109	St. Croix County, WI	84,345	89,694		05005	Baxter County, AR	41,513	41,619
33500		Minot, ND Micro area	69,540	75,934	34300		Mountain Home, ID Micro area	27,038	27,259
	38049	McHenry County, ND	5,395	5,816		16039	Elmore County, ID	27,038	27,259
	38075	Renville County, ND	2,470	2,374					
	38101	Ward County, ND	61,675	67,744	34340		Mount Airy, NC Micro area	73,673	71,948
33540		Missoula, MT Metro area	109,299	118,791		37171	Surry County, NC	73,673	71,948
	30063	Missoula County, MT	109,299	118,791	34380		Mount Pleasant, MI Micro area	70,311	70,562
33580		Mitchell, SD Micro area	22,835	23,166		26073	Isabella County, MI	70,311	70,562
	46035	Davison County, SD	19,504	19,790					
	46061	Hanson County, SD	3,331	3,376	34420		Mount Pleasant, TX Micro area	32,334	33,033
33620		Moberly, MO Micro area	25,414	24,763		48449	Titus County, TX	32,334	33,033
	29175	Randolph County, MO	25,414	24,763	34460		Mount Sterling, KY Micro area	44,396	47,037
33660		Mobile, AL Metro area	412,992	413,757		21011	Bath County, KY	11,591	12,383
	01097	Mobile County, AL	412,992	413,757		21165	Menifee County, KY	6,306	6,451
33700		Modesto, CA Metro area	514,453	549,815		21173	Montgomery County, KY	26,499	28,203
	06099	Stanislaus County, CA	514,453	549,815	34500		Mount Vernon, IL Micro area	38,827	37,820
33740		Monroe, LA Metro area	176,441	176,805		17081	Jefferson County, IL	38,827	37,820
	22073	Ouachita Parish, LA	153,720	154,475	34540		Mount Vernon, OH Micro area	60,921	61,893
	22111	Union Parish, LA	22,721	22,330		39083	Knox County, OH	60,921	61,893
33780		Monroe, MI Metro area	152,021	150,439	34580		Mount Vernon-Anacortes, WA Metro area	116,901	128,206
	26115	Monroe County, MI	152,021	150,439		53057	Skagit County, WA	116,901	128,206
					34620		Muncie, IN Metro area	117,671	114,772
						18035	Delaware County, IN	117,671	114,772

Core based statistical area	State/ County FIPS code	Title and Geographic Components	2010 Census Population	2018 Estimated Population	Core based statistical area	State/ County FIPS code	Title and Geographic Components	2010 Census Population	2018 Estimated Population
34660		Murray, KY Micro area	37,191	39,135	35300		New Haven-Milford, CT Metro area	862,477	857,620
	21035	Calloway County, KY	37,191	39,135		09009	New Haven County, CT	862,477	857,620
34700		Muscatine, IA Micro area	42,745	42,929	35380		New Orleans-Metairie, LA Metro area	1,189,866	1,270,399
	19139	Muscatine County, IA	42,745	42,929		22051	Jefferson Parish, LA	432,552	434,051
						22071	Orleans Parish, LA	343,829	391,006
34740		Muskegon, MI Metro area	172,188	173,588		22075	Plaquemines Parish, LA	23,042	23,410
	26121	Muskegon County, MI	172,188	173,588		22087	St. Bernard Parish, LA	35,897	46,721
						22089	St. Charles Parish, LA	52,780	52,879
34780		Muskogee, OK Micro area	70,990	68,362		22093	St. James Parish, LA	22,102	21,037
	40101	Muskogee County, OK	70,990	68,362		22095	St. John the Baptist Parish, LA	45,924	43,184
						22103	St. Tammany Parish, LA	233,740	258,111
34820		Myrtle Beach-Conway-North Myrtle Beach, NC-SC Metro area	376,722	480,891	35420		New Philadelphia-Dover, OH Micro area	92,582	92,176
	37019	Brunswick County, NC	107,431	136,744		39157	Tuscarawas County, OH	92,582	92,176
	45051	Horry County, SC	269,291	344,147					
34860		Nacogdoches, TX Micro area	64,524	65,711	35440		Newport, OR Micro area	46,034	49,388
	48347	Nacogdoches County, TX	64,524	65,711		41041	Lincoln County, OR	46,034	49,388
34900		Napa, CA Metro area	136,484	139,417	35460		Newport, TN Micro area	35,662	35,774
	06055	Napa County, CA	136,484	139,417		47029	Cocke County, TN	35,662	35,774
34940		Naples-Immokalee-Marco Island, FL Metro area	321,520	378,488	35500		Newton, IA Micro area	36,842	37,147
	12021	Collier County, FL	321,520	378,488		19099	Jasper County, IA	36,842	37,147
34980		Nashville-Davidson--Murfreesboro--Franklin, TN Metro area	1,670,890	1,930,961	35580		New Ulm, MN Micro area	25,893	25,111
						27015	Brown County, MN	25,893	25,111
	47015	Cannon County, TN	13,801	14,462	35620		New York-Newark-Jersey City, NY-NJ-PA Metro area	19,567,410	19,979,477
	47021	Cheatham County, TN	39,105	40,439					
	47037	Davidson County, TN	626,681	692,587	35620		Dutchess County-Putnam County, NY Metro Div 20524	397,198	392,610
	47043	Dickson County, TN	49,666	53,446					
	47081	Hickman County, TN	24,690	25,063		36027	Dutchess County, NY	297,488	293,718
	47111	Macon County, TN	22,248	24,265		36079	Putnam County, NY	99,710	98,892
	47119	Maury County, TN	80,956	94,340					
	47147	Robertson County, TN	66,283	71,012	35620		Nassau County-Suffolk County, NY Metro Div 35004	2,832,882	2,839,436
	47149	Rutherford County, TN	262,604	324,890					
	47159	Smith County, TN	19,166	19,942		36059	Nassau County, NY	1,339,532	1,358,343
	47165	Sumner County, TN	160,645	187,149		36103	Suffolk County, NY	1,493,350	1,481,093
	47169	Trousdale County, TN	7,870	11,012					
	47187	Williamson County, TN	183,182	231,729	35620		Newark, NJ-PA Metro Div 35084	2,471,171	2,504,672
	47189	Wilson County, TN	113,993	140,625		34013	Essex County, NJ	783,969	799,767
35020		Natchez, MS-LA Micro area	53,119	50,764		34019	Hunterdon County, NJ	128,349	124,714
	22029	Concordia Parish, LA	20,822	19,572		34027	Morris County, NJ	492,276	494,228
	28001	Adams County, MS	32,297	31,192		34035	Somerset County, NJ	323,444	331,164
						34037	Sussex County, NJ	149,265	140,799
35060		Natchitoches, LA Micro area	39,566	38,659		34039	Union County, NJ	536,499	558,067
	22069	Natchitoches Parish, LA	39,566	38,659		42103	Pike County, PA	57,369	55,933
35100		New Bern, NC Metro area	126,802	125,219					
	37049	Craven County, NC	103,505	102,912					
	37103	Jones County, NC	10,153	9,637					
	37137	Pamlico County, NC	13,144	12,670					
35140		Newberry, SC Micro area	37,508	38,520					
	45071	Newberry County, SC	37,508	38,520					
35220		New Castle, IN Micro area	49,462	48,271					
	18065	Henry County, IN	49,462	48,271					
35260		New Castle, PA Micro area	91,108	86,184					
	42073	Lawrence County, PA	91,108	86,184					

CORE BASED STATISTICAL AREAS
(Metropolitan and Micropolitan),
METROPOLITAN DIVISIONS, AND COMPONENTS
(as defined August, 2017)—*Continued*

Core based statis- tical area	State/ County FIPS code	Title and Geographic Components	2010 Census Population	2018 Estimated Population	Core based statis- tical area	State/ County FIPS code	Title and Geographic Components	2010 Census Population	2018 Estimated Population
35620		New York-Jersey City-White Plains, NY-NJ Metro Div 35614	13,866,159	14,242,759	36260		Ogden-Clearfield, UT Metro area	597,159	675,067
	34003	Bergen County, NJ	905,116	936,692		49003	Box Elder County, UT	49,975	54,950
	34017	Hudson County, NJ	634,266	676,061		49011	Davis County, UT	306,479	351,713
	34023	Middlesex County, NJ	809,858	829,685		49029	Morgan County, UT	9,469	12,045
	34025	Monmouth County, NJ	630,380	621,354		49057	Weber County, UT	231,236	256,359
	34029	Ocean County, NJ	576,567	601,651	36300		Ogdensburg-Massena, NY Micro area	111,944	108,047
	34031	Passaic County, NJ	501,226	503,310		36089	St. Lawrence County, NY	111,944	108,047
	36005	Bronx County, NY	1,385,108	1,432,132					
	36047	Kings County, NY	2,504,700	2,582,830	36340		Oil City, PA Micro area	54,984	51,266
	36061	New York County, NY	1,585,873	1,628,701		42121	Venango County, PA	54,984	51,266
	36071	Orange County, NY	372,813	381,951					
	36081	Queens County, NY	2,230,722	2,278,906	36380		Okeechobee, FL Micro area	39,996	41,537
	36085	Richmond County, NY	468,730	476,179		12093	Okeechobee County, FL	39,996	41,537
	36087	Rockland County, NY	311,687	325,695					
	36119	Westchester County, NY	949,113	967,612	36420		Oklahoma City, OK Metro area	1,252,987	1,396,445
						40017	Canadian County, OK	115,541	144,447
35660		Niles-Benton Harbor, MI Metro area	156,813	154,141		40027	Cleveland County, OK	255,755	281,669
	26021	Berrien County, MI	156,813	154,141		40051	Grady County, OK	52,431	55,551
						40081	Lincoln County, OK	34,273	34,920
35700		Nogales, AZ Micro area	47,420	46,511		40083	Logan County, OK	41,848	47,291
	04023	Santa Cruz County, AZ	47,420	46,511		40087	McClain County, OK	34,506	39,985
						40109	Oklahoma County, OK	718,633	792,582
35740		Norfolk, NE Micro area	48,271	48,504					
	31119	Madison County, NE	34,876	35,392	36460		Olean, NY Micro area	80,317	76,840
	31139	Pierce County, NE	7,266	7,142		36009	Cattaraugus County, NY	80,317	76,840
	31167	Stanton County, NE	6,129	5,970					
					36500		Olympia-Tumwater, WA Metro area	252,264	286,419
35820		North Platte, NE Micro area	37,590	36,426		53067	Thurston County, WA	252,264	286,419
	31111	Lincoln County, NE	36,288	35,185					
	31113	Logan County, NE	763	749	36540		Omaha-Council Bluffs, NE-IA Metro area	865,350	942,198
	31117	McPherson County, NE	539	492		19085	Harrison County, IA	14,928	14,134
						19129	Mills County, IA	15,059	15,063
35840		North Port-Sarasota-Bradenton, FL Metro area	702,281	821,573		19155	Pottawattamie County, IA	93,158	93,533
	12081	Manatee County, FL	322,833	394,855		31025	Cass County, NE	25,241	26,159
	12115	Sarasota County, FL	379,448	426,718		31055	Douglas County, NE	517,110	566,880
						31153	Sarpy County, NE	158,840	184,459
35860		North Vernon, IN Micro area	28,525	27,611		31155	Saunders County, NE	20,780	21,303
	18079	Jennings County, IN	28,525	27,611		31177	Washington County, NE	20,234	20,667
35900		North Wilkesboro, NC Micro area	69,340	68,557	36580		Oneonta, NY Micro area	62,259	59,749
	37193	Wilkes County, NC	69,340	68,557		36077	Otsego County, NY	62,259	59,749
35940		Norwalk, OH Micro area	59,626	58,504	36620		Ontario, OR-ID Micro area	53,936	54,276
	39077	Huron County, OH	59,626	58,504		16075	Payette County, ID	22,623	23,551
						41045	Malheur County, OR	31,313	30,725
35980		Norwich-New London, CT Metro area	274,055	266,784					
	09011	New London County, CT	274,055	266,784	36660		Opelousas, LA Micro area	83,384	82,764
						22097	St. Landry Parish, LA	83,384	82,764
36020		Oak Harbor, WA Micro area	78,506	84,460					
	53029	Island County, WA	78,506	84,460	36700		Orangeburg, SC Micro area	92,501	86,934
						45075	Orangeburg County, SC	92,501	86,934
36100		Ocala, FL Metro area	331,298	359,977					
	12083	Marion County, FL	331,298	359,977	36740		Orlando-Kissimmee-Sanford, FL Metro	2,134,411	2,572,962
						12069	Lake County, FL	297,052	356,495
36140		Ocean City, NJ Metro area	97,265	92,560		12095	Orange County, FL	1,145,956	1,380,645
	34009	Cape May County, NJ	97,265	92,560		12097	Osceola County, FL	268,685	367,990
						12117	Seminole County, FL	422,718	467,832
36220		Odessa, TX Metro area	137,130	162,124					
	48135	Ector County, TX	137,130	162,124	36780		Oshkosh-Neenah, WI Metro area	166,994	171,020
						55139	Winnebago County, WI	166,994	171,020

CORE BASED STATISTICAL AREAS
(Metropolitan and Micropolitan),
METROPOLITAN DIVISIONS, AND COMPONENTS
(as defined August, 2017)—*Continued*

Core based statistical area	State/ County FIPS code	Title and Geographic Components	2010 Census Population	2018 Estimated Population	Core based statistical area	State/ County FIPS code	Title and Geographic Components	2010 Census Population	2018 Estimated Population
36820		Oskaloosa, IA Micro area	22,381	22,000	37460		Panama City, FL Metro area	184,715	201,451
	19123	Mahaska County, IA	22,381	22,000		12005	Bay County, FL	168,852	185,287
						12045	Gulf County, FL	15,863	16,164
36830		Othello, WA Micro area	18,728	19,759					
	53001	Adams County, WA	18,728	19,759	37500		Paragould, AR Micro area	42,090	45,325
						05055	Greene County, AR	42,090	45,325
36840		Ottawa, KS Micro area	25,992	25,631					
	20059	Franklin County, KS	25,992	25,631	37540		Paris, TN Micro area	32,330	32,358
						47079	Henry County, TN	32,330	32,358
36860		Ottawa-Peru, IL Micro area	154,908	148,163					
	17011	Bureau County, IL	34,978	32,993	37580		Paris, TX Micro area	49,793	49,728
	17099	LaSalle County, IL	113,924	109,430		48277	Lamar County, TX	49,793	49,728
	17155	Putnam County, IL	6,006	5,740					
					37620		Parkersburg-Vienna, WV Metro area	92,673	90,033
36900		Ottumwa, IA Micro area	44,378	44,222		54105	Wirt County, WV	5,717	5,830
	19051	Davis County, IA	8,753	9,017		54107	Wood County, WV	86,956	84,203
	19179	Wapello County, IA	35,625	35,205					
					37660		Parsons, KS Micro area	21,607	19,964
36940		Owatonna, MN Micro area	36,576	36,803		20099	Labette County, KS	21,607	19,964
	27147	Steele County, MN	36,576	36,803					
					37740		Payson, AZ Micro area	53,597	53,889
36980		Owensboro, KY Metro area	114,752	119,114		04007	Gila County, AZ	53,597	53,889
	21059	Daviess County, KY	96,656	101,104					
	21091	Hancock County, KY	8,565	8,758	37780		Pecos, TX Micro area	13,783	15,695
	21149	McLean County, KY	9,531	9,252		48389	Reeves County, TX	13,783	15,695
37020		Owosso, MI Micro area	70,648	68,192	37800		Pella, IA Micro Area	33,309	33,407
	26155	Shiawassee County, MI	70,648	68,192		19125	Marion County, IA	33,309	33,407
37060		Oxford, MS Micro area	47,351	54,793	37860		Pensacola-Ferry Pass-Brent, FL Metro area	448,991	494,883
	28071	Lafayette County, MS	47,351	54,793		12033	Escambia County, FL	297,619	315,534
						12113	Santa Rosa County, FL	151,372	179,349
37080		Oxford, NC Micro area	59,916	60,115					
	37077	Granville County, NC	59,916	60,115	37900		Peoria, IL Metro area	379,186	368,373
						17123	Marshall County, IL	12,640	11,534
37100		Oxnard-Thousand Oaks-Ventura, CA Metro area	823,318	850,967		17143	Peoria County, IL	186,494	180,621
						17175	Stark County, IL	5,994	5,427
	06111	Ventura County, CA	823,318	850,967		17179	Tazewell County, IL	135,394	132,328
						17203	Woodford County, IL	38,664	38,463
37120		Ozark, AL Micro area	50,251	48,956					
	01045	Dale County, AL	50,251	48,956	37940		Peru, IN Micro area	36,903	35,567
						18103	Miami County, IN	36,903	35,567
37140		Paducah, KY-IL Micro area	98,762	96,647					
	17127	Massac County, IL	15,429	14,080	37980		Philadelphia-Camden-Wilmington, PA-NJ-DE-MD Metro area	5,965,343	6,096,372
	21007	Ballard County, KY	8,249	7,979					
	21139	Livingston County, KY	9,519	9,242	37980		Camden, NJ Metro Div 15804	1,250,679	1,243,870
	21145	McCracken County, KY	65,565	65,346		34005	Burlington County, NJ	448,734	445,384
						34007	Camden County, NJ	513,657	507,078
37220		Pahrump, NV Micro area	43,946	45,346		34015	Gloucester County, NJ	288,288	291,408
	32023	Nye County, NV	43,946	45,346					
					37980		Montgomery County-Bucks County-Chester County, PA Metro Div 33874	1,924,009	1,978,845
37260		Palatka, FL Micro area	74,364	74,163					
	12107	Putnam County, FL	74,364	74,163		42017	Bucks County, PA	625,249	628,195
						42029	Chester County, PA	498,886	522,046
37300		Palestine, TX Micro area	58,458	58,057		42091	Montgomery County, PA	799,874	828,604
	48001	Anderson County, TX	58,458	58,057					
					37980		Philadelphia, PA Metro Div 37964	2,084,985	2,148,889
37340		Palm Bay-Melbourne-Titusville, FL Metro area	543,376	596,849		42045	Delaware County, PA	558,979	564,751
	12009	Brevard County, FL	543,376	596,849		42101	Philadelphia County, PA	1,526,006	1,584,138
37420		Pampa, TX Micro area	22,535	21,895					
	48179	Gray County, TX	22,535	21,895					

CORE BASED STATISTICAL AREAS
(Metropolitan and Micropolitan),
METROPOLITAN DIVISIONS, AND COMPONENTS
(as defined August, 2017)—*Continued*

Core based statistical area	State/County FIPS code	Title and Geographic Components	2010 Census Population	2018 Estimated Population	Core based statistical area	State/County FIPS code	Title and Geographic Components	2010 Census Population	2018 Estimated Population
37980		Wilmington, DE-MD-NJ Metro Div 48864	705,670	724,768	38700		Pontiac, IL Micro area	38,950	35,761
	10003	New Castle County, Delaware	538,479	559,335		17105	Livingston County, IL	38,950	35,761
	24015	Cecil County, MD	101,108	102,826	38740		Poplar Bluff, MO Micro area	42,794	42,639
	34033	Salem County, NJ	66,083	62,607		29023	Butler County, MO	42,794	42,639
38060		Phoenix-Mesa-Scottsdale, AZ Metro area	4,192,887	4,857,962	38780		Portales, NM Micro area	19,846	18,743
	04013	Maricopa County, AZ	3,817,117	4,410,824		35041	Roosevelt County, NM	19,846	18,743
	04021	Pinal County, AZ	375,770	447,138	38820		Port Angeles, WA Micro area	71,404	76,737
38100		Picayune, MS Micro area	55,834	55,387		53009	Clallam County, WA	71,404	76,737
	28109	Pearl River County, MS	55,834	55,387	38840		Port Clinton, OH Micro area	41,428	40,769
38180		Pierre, SD Micro area	21,361	22,064		39123	Ottawa County, OH	41,428	40,769
	46065	Hughes County, SD	17,022	17,650	38860		Portland-South Portland, ME Metro area	514,098	535,420
	46117	Stanley County, SD	2,966	3,022		23005	Cumberland County, ME	281,674	293,557
	46119	Sully County, SD	1,373	1,392		23023	Sagadahoc County, ME	35,293	35,634
38220		Pine Bluff, AR Metro area	100,258	89,515		23031	York County, ME	197,131	206,229
	05025	Cleveland County, AR	8,689	8,018	38900		Portland-Vancouver-Hillsboro, OR-WA Metro area	2,226,009	2,478,810
	05069	Jefferson County, AR	77,435	68,114		41005	Clackamas County, OR	375,992	416,075
	05079	Lincoln County, AR	14,134	13,383		41009	Columbia County, OR	49,351	52,377
38240		Pinehurst-Southern Pines, NC Micro area	88,247	98,682		41051	Multnomah County, OR	735,334	811,880
	37125	Moore County, NC	88,247	98,682		41067	Washington County, OR	529,710	597,695
38260		Pittsburg, KS Micro area	39,134	39,019		41071	Yamhill County, OR	99,193	107,002
	20037	Crawford County, KS	39,134	39,019		53011	Clark County, WA	425,363	481,857
38300		Pittsburgh, PA Metro area	2,356,285	2,324,743		53059	Skamania County, WA	11,066	11,924
	42003	Allegheny County, PA	1,223,348	1,218,452	38920		Port Lavaca, TX Micro area	21,381	21,561
	42005	Armstrong County, PA	68,941	65,263		48057	Calhoun County, TX	21,381	21,561
	42007	Beaver County, PA	170,539	164,742	38940		Port St. Lucie, FL Metro area	424,107	482,040
	42019	Butler County, PA	183,862	187,888		12085	Martin County, FL	146,318	160,912
	42051	Fayette County, PA	136,606	130,441		12111	St. Lucie County, FL	277,789	321,128
	42125	Washington County, PA	207,820	207,346	39020		Portsmouth, OH Micro area	79,499	75,502
	42129	Westmoreland County, PA	365,169	350,611		39145	Scioto County, OH	79,499	75,502
38340		Pittsfield, MA Metro area	131,219	126,348	39060		Pottsville, PA Micro area	148,289	142,067
	25003	Berkshire County, MA	131,219	126,348		42107	Schuylkill County, PA	148,289	142,067
38380		Plainview, TX Micro area	36,273	33,830	39140		Prescott, AZ Metro area	211,033	231,993
	48189	Hale County, TX	36,273	33,830		04025	Yavapai County, AZ	211,033	231,993
38420		Platteville, WI Micro area	51,208	51,554	39220		Price, UT Micro area	21,403	20,269
	55043	Grant County, WI	51,208	51,554		49007	Carbon County, UT	21,403	20,269
38460		Plattsburgh, NY Micro area	82,128	80,695	39260		Prineville, OR Micro area	20,978	23,867
	36019	Clinton County, NY	82,128	80,695		41013	Crook County, OR	20,978	23,867
38500		Plymouth, IN Micro area	47,051	46,248	39300		Providence-Warwick, RI-MA Metro area	1,600,852	1,621,337
	18099	Marshall County, IN	47,051	46,248		25005	Bristol County, MA	548,285	564,022
38540		Pocatello, ID Metro area	82,839	87,138		44001	Bristol County, RI	49,875	48,649
	16005	Bannock County, ID	82,839	87,138		44003	Kent County, RI	166,158	163,861
38580		Point Pleasant, WV-OH Micro area	58,258	56,697		44005	Newport County, RI	82,888	82,542
	39053	Gallia County, OH	30,934	29,979		44007	Providence County, RI	626,667	636,084
	54053	Mason County, WV	27,324	26,718		44009	Washington County, RI	126,979	126,179
38620		Ponca City, OK Micro area	46,562	44,161	39340		Provo-Orem, UT Metro area	526,810	633,768
	40071	Kay County, OK	46,562	44,161		49023	Juab County, UT	10,246	11,555
						49049	Utah County, UT	516,564	622,213

Appendix C

CORE BASED STATISTICAL AREAS
(Metropolitan and Micropolitan),
METROPOLITAN DIVISIONS, AND COMPONENTS
(as defined August, 2017)—*Continued*

Core based statistical area	State/County FIPS code	Title and Geographic Components	2010 Census Population	2018 Estimated Population	Core based statistical area	State/County FIPS code	Title and Geographic Components	2010 Census Population	2018 Estimated Population
39380		Pueblo, CO Metro area	159,063	167,529	40060		Richmond, VA Metro area	1,208,101	1,306,172
	08101	Pueblo County, CO	159,063	167,529		51007	Amelia County, VA	12,690	13,013
						51033	Caroline County, VA	28,545	30,772
39420		Pullman, WA Micro area	44,776	49,791		51036	Charles City County, VA	7,256	6,941
	53075	Whitman County, WA	44,776	49,791		51041	Chesterfield County, VA	316,236	348,556
						51053	Dinwiddie County, VA	28,001	28,529
39460		Punta Gorda, FL Metro area	159,978	184,998		51075	Goochland County, VA	21,717	23,244
	12015	Charlotte County, FL	159,978	184,998		51085	Hanover County, VA	99,863	107,239
						51087	Henrico County, VA	306,935	329,261
39500		Quincy, IL-MO Micro area	77,314	75,546		51101	King William County, VA	15,935	16,939
	17001	Adams County, IL	67,103	65,691		51127	New Kent County, VA	18,429	22,391
	29111	Lewis County, MO	10,211	9,855		51145	Powhatan County, VA	28,046	29,189
						51149	Prince George County, VA	35,725	38,082
39540		Racine, WI Metro area	195,408	196,584		51183	Sussex County, VA	12,087	11,237
	55101	Racine County, WI	195,408	196,584		51570	Colonial Heights city, VA	17,411	17,833
						51670	Hopewell city, VA	22,591	22,596
39580		Raleigh, NC Metro area	1,130,490	1,362,540		51730	Petersburg city, VA	32,420	31,567
	37069	Franklin County, NC	60,619	67,560		51760	Richmond city, VA	204,214	228,783
	37101	Johnston County, NC	168,878	202,675					
	37183	Wake County, NC	900,993	1,092,305	40080		Richmond-Berea, KY Micro area	99,972	109,118
						21151	Madison County, KY	82,916	92,368
39660		Rapid City, SD Metro area	134,598	148,749		21203	Rockcastle County, KY	17,056	16,750
	46033	Custer County, SD	8,216	8,726					
	46093	Meade County, SD	25,434	28,294	40100		Rio Grande City, TX Micro area	60,968	64,525
	46103	Pennington County, SD	100,948	111,729		48427	Starr County, TX	60,968	64,525
39700		Raymondville, TX Micro area	22,134	21,515	40140		Riverside-San Bernardino-Ontario, CA.	4,224,851	4,622,361
	48489	Willacy County, TX	22,134	21,515		06065	Riverside County, CA	2,189,641	2,450,758
						06071	San Bernardino County, CA	2,035,210	2,171,603
39740		Reading, PA Metro area	411,442	420,152					
	42011	Berks County, PA	411,442	420,152	40180		Riverton, WY Micro area	40,123	39,531
						56013	Fremont County, WY	40,123	39,531
39780		Red Bluff, CA Micro area	63,463	63,916					
	06103	Tehama County, CA	63,463	63,916	40220		Roanoke, VA Metro area	308,707	314,172
						51023	Botetourt County, VA	33,148	33,277
39820		Redding, CA Metro area	177,223	180,040		51045	Craig County, VA	5,190	5,064
	06089	Shasta County, CA	177,223	180,040		51067	Franklin County, VA	56,159	56,195
						51161	Roanoke County, VA	92,376	94,073
39860		Red Wing, MN Micro area	46,183	46,403		51770	Roanoke city, VA	97,032	99,920
	27049	Goodhue County, MN	46,183	46,403		51775	Salem city, VA	24,802	25,643
39900		Reno, NV Metro area	425,417	469,764	40260		Roanoke Rapids, NC Micro area	76,790	70,250
	32029	Storey County, NV	4,010	4,029		37083	Halifax County, NC	54,691	50,574
	32031	Washoe County, NV	421,407	465,735		37131	Northampton County, NC	22,099	19,676
39940		Rexburg, ID Micro area	50,778	52,472	40300		Rochelle, IL Micro area	53,497	50,923
	16043	Fremont County, ID	13,242	13,168		17141	Ogle County, IL	53,497	50,923
	16065	Madison County, ID	37,536	39,304					
					40340		Rochester, MN Metro area	206,877	219,802
39980		Richmond, IN Micro area	68,917	65,936		27039	Dodge County, MN	20,087	20,822
	18177	Wayne County, IN	68,917	65,936		27045	Fillmore County, MN	20,866	21,058
						27109	Olmsted County, MN	144,248	156,277
						27157	Wabasha County, MN	21,676	21,645
					40380		Rochester, NY Metro area	1,079,671	1,071,082
						36051	Livingston County, NY	65,393	63,227
						36055	Monroe County, NY	744,344	742,474
						36069	Ontario County, NY	107,931	109,864
						36073	Orleans County, NY	42,883	40,612
						36117	Wayne County, NY	93,772	90,064
						36123	Yates County, NY	25,348	24,841

CORE BASED STATISTICAL AREAS
(Metropolitan and Micropolitan),
METROPOLITAN DIVISIONS, AND COMPONENTS
(as defined August, 2017)—*Continued*

Core based statistical area	State/County FIPS code	Title and Geographic Components	2010 Census Population	2018 Estimated Population	Core based statistical area	State/County FIPS code	Title and Geographic Components	2010 Census Population	2018 Estimated Population
40420		Rockford, IL Metro area........................	349,431	337,658	41180		St. Louis, MO-IL Metro area	2,787,701	2,805,465
	17007	Boone County, IL...........................	54,165	53,577		17005	Bond County, IL................................	17,768	16,630
	17201	Winnebago County, IL.....................	295,266	284,081		17013	Calhoun County, IL...........................	5,089	4,802
40460		Rockingham, NC Micro area	46,639	44,887		17027	Clinton County, IL.............................	37,762	37,639
	37153	Richmond County, NC	46,639	44,887		17083	Jersey County, IL	22,985	21,847
						17117	Macoupin County, IL	47,765	45,313
40540		Rock Springs, WY Micro area	43,806	43,051		17119	Madison County, IL	269,282	264,461
	56037	Sweetwater County, WY	43,806	43,051		17133	Monroe County, IL	32,957	34,335
40580		Rocky Mount, NC Metro area..............	152,392	146,021		17163	St. Clair County, IL	270,056	261,059
	37065	Edgecombe County, NC	56,552	52,005		29071	Franklin County, MO	101,492	103,670
	37127	Nash County, NC	95,840	94,016		29099	Jefferson County, MO	218,733	224,347
						29113	Lincoln County, MO...........................	52,566	57,686
40620		Rolla, MO Micro area.........................	45,156	44,732		29183	St. Charles County, MO	360,485	399,182
	29161	Phelps County, MO	45,156	44,732		29189	St. Louis County, MO	998,954	996,945
						29219	Warren County, MO	32,513	34,711
40660		Rome, GA Metro area........................	96,317	97,927		29510	St. Louis city, MO	319,294	302,838
	13115	Floyd County, GA...........................	96,317	97,927	41220		St. Marys, GA Micro area	50,513	53,677
40700		Roseburg, OR Micro area....................	107,667	110,283		13039	Camden County, GA	50,513	53,677
	41019	Douglas County, OR	107,667	110,283	41260		St. Marys, PA Micro Area....................	31,946	30,169
40740		Roswell, NM Micro area	65,645	64,689		42047	Elk County, PA	31,946	30,169
	35005	Chaves County, NM	65,645	64,689	41400		Salem, OH Micro area........................	107,841	102,665
40760		Ruidoso, NM Micro Area....................	20,497	19,556		39029	Columbiana County, OH	107,841	102,665
	35027	Lincoln County, NM.........................	20,497	19,556	41420		Salem, OR Metro area........................	390,738	432,102
40780		Russellville, AR Micro area.................	83,939	85,535		41047	Marion County, OR	315,335	346,868
	05115	Pope County, AR.............................	61,754	64,000		41053	Polk County, OR	75,403	85,234
	05149	Yell County, AR	22,185	21,535	41460		Salina, KS Micro area........................	61,697	60,203
40820		Ruston, LA Micro area........................	46,735	47,196		20143	Ottawa County, KS...........................	6,091	5,802
	22061	Lincoln Parish, LA	46,735	47,196		20169	Saline County, KS............................	55,606	54,401
40860		Rutland, VT Micro area.......................	61,642	58,672	41500		Salinas, CA Metro area......................	415,057	435,594
	50021	Rutland County, VT	61,642	58,672		06053	Monterey County, CA	415,057	435,594
40900		Sacramento--Roseville--Arden-Arcade, CA Metro area.................	2,149,127	2,345,210	41540		Salisbury, MD-DE Metro area.............	373,802	409,979
						10005	Sussex County, DE	197,145	229,286
	06017	El Dorado County, CA	181,058	190,678		24039	Somerset County, MD	26,470	25,675
	06061	Placer County, CA...........................	348,432	393,149		24045	Wicomico County, MD.......................	98,733	103,195
	06067	Sacramento County, CA....................	1,418,788	1,540,975		24047	Worcester County, MD......................	51,454	51,823
	06113	Yolo County, CA	200,849	220,408	41620		Salt Lake City, UT Metro area	1,087,873	1,222,540
40940		Safford, AZ Micro area.......................	37,220	38,072		49035	Salt Lake County, UT........................	1,029,655	1,152,633
	04009	Graham County, AZ	37,220	38,072		49045	Tooele County, UT............................	58,218	69,907
40980		Saginaw, MI Metro area......................	200,169	190,800	41660		San Angelo, TX Metro area	111,823	119,711
	26145	Saginaw County, MI	200,169	190,800		48235	Irion County, TX	1,599	1,522
41060		St. Cloud, MN Metro area...................	189,093	199,801		48451	Tom Green County, TX......................	110,224	118,189
	27009	Benton County, MN	38,451	40,545	41700		San Antonio-New Braunfels, TX Metro..	2,142,508	2,518,036
	27145	Stearns County, MN.........................	150,642	159,256		48013	Atascosa County, TX.........................	44,911	50,310
41100		St. George, UT Metro area..................	138,115	171,700		48019	Bandera County, TX	20,485	22,824
	49053	Washington County, UT	138,115	171,700		48029	Bexar County, TX.............................	1,714,773	1,986,049
41140		St. Joseph, MO-KS Metro area	127,329	126,490		48091	Comal County, TX	108,472	148,373
	20043	Doniphan County, KS........................	7,945	7,682		48187	Guadalupe County, TX	131,533	163,694
	29003	Andrew County, MO	17,291	17,607		48259	Kendall County, TX	33,410	45,641
	29021	Buchanan County, MO	89,201	88,571		48325	Medina County, TX	46,006	50,921
	29063	DeKalb County, MO	12,892	12,630		48493	Wilson County, TX	42,918	50,224
					41740		San Diego-Carlsbad, CA Metro area.....	3,095,313	3,343,364
						06073	San Diego County, CA.......................	3,095,313	3,343,364

CORE BASED STATISTICAL AREAS
(Metropolitan and Micropolitan),
METROPOLITAN DIVISIONS, AND COMPONENTS
(as defined August, 2017)—*Continued*

Core based statistical area	State/County FIPS code	Title and Geographic Components	2010 Census Population	2018 Estimated Population	Core based statistical area	State/County FIPS code	Title and Geographic Components	2010 Census Population	2018 Estimated Population
41760		Sandpoint, ID Micro area	40,877	44,727	42540		Scranton--Wilkes-Barre--Hazleton, PA Metro area	563,631	555,485
	16017	Bonner County, ID	40,877	44,727		42069	Lackawanna County, PA	214,437	210,793
41780		Sandusky, OH Micro area	77,079	74,615		42079	Luzerne County, PA	320,918	317,646
	39043	Erie County, OH	77,079	74,615		42131	Wyoming County, PA	28,276	27,046
41820		Sanford, NC Micro area	57,866	61,452	42620		Searcy, AR Micro area	77,076	78,727
	37105	Lee County, NC	57,866	61,452		05145	White County, AR	77,076	78,727
41860		San Francisco-Oakland-Hayward, CA Metro area	4,335,391	4,729,484	42660		Seattle-Tacoma-Bellevue, WA Metro area	3,439,809	3,939,363
41860		Oakland-Hayward-Berkeley, CA Metro Div 36084	2,559,296	2,816,968	42660		Seattle-Bellevue-Everett, WA Metro Div 42644	2,644,584	3,048,064
	06001	Alameda County, CA	1,510,271	1,666,753		53033	King County, WA	1,931,249	2,233,163
	06013	Contra Costa County, CA	1,049,025	1,150,215		53061	Snohomish County, WA	713,335	814,901
41860		San Francisco-Redwood City-South San Francisco, CA Metro Div 41884	1,523,686	1,652,850	42660		Tacoma-Lakewood, WA Metro Div 45104	795,225	891,299
	06075	San Francisco County, CA	805,235	883,305		53053	Pierce County, WA	795,225	891,299
	06081	San Mateo County, CA	718,451	769,545	42680		Sebastian-Vero Beach, FL Metro area	138,028	157,413
41860		San Rafael, CA Metropolitan Div 42034	252,409	259,666		12061	Indian River County, FL	138,028	157,413
	06041	Marin County, CA	252,409	259,666	42700		Sebring, FL Metro area	98,786	105,424
41940		San Jose-Sunnyvale-Santa Clara, CA Metro area	1,836,911	1,999,107		12055	Highlands County, FL	98,786	105,424
	06069	San Benito County, CA	55,269	61,537	42740		Sedalia, MO Micro area	42,201	42,542
	06085	Santa Clara County, CA	1,781,642	1,937,570		29159	Pettis County, MO	42,201	42,542
42020		San Luis Obispo-Paso Robles-Arroyo Grande, CA Metro area	269,637	284,010	42780		Selinsgrove, PA Micro area	39,702	40,540
	06079	San Luis Obispo County, CA	269,637	284,010		42109	Snyder County, PA	39,702	40,540
42100		Santa Cruz-Watsonville, CA Metro area	262,382	274,255	42820		Selma, AL Micro area	43,820	38,310
	06087	Santa Cruz County, CA	262,382	274,255		01047	Dallas County, AL	43,820	38,310
42140		Santa Fe, NM Metro area	144,170	150,056	42860		Seneca, SC Micro area	74,273	78,374
	35049	Santa Fe County, NM	144,170	150,056		45073	Oconee County, SC	74,273	78,374
42200		Santa Maria-Santa Barbara, CA Metro	423,895	446,527	42900		Seneca Falls, NY Micro area	35,251	34,300
	06083	Santa Barbara County, CA	423,895	446,527		36099	Seneca County, NY	35,251	34,300
42220		Santa Rosa, CA Metro area	483,878	499,942	42940		Sevierville, TN Micro area	89,889	97,892
	06097	Sonoma County, CA	483,878	499,942		47155	Sevier County, TN	89,889	97,892
42300		Sault Ste. Marie, MI Micro area	38,520	37,517	42980		Seymour, IN Micro area	42,376	44,111
	26033	Chippewa County, MI	38,520	37,517		18071	Jackson County, IN	42,376	44,111
42340		Savannah, GA Metro area	347,611	389,494	43020		Shawano, WI Micro area	46,181	45,454
	13029	Bryan County, GA	30,233	38,109		55078	Menominee County, WI	4,232	4,658
	13051	Chatham County, GA	265,128	289,195		55115	Shawano County, WI	41,949	40,796
	13103	Effingham County, GA	52,250	62,190	43060		Shawnee, OK Micro area	69,442	72,679
42380		Sayre, PA Micro area	62,622	60,833		40125	Pottawatomie County, OK	69,442	72,679
	42015	Bradford County, PA	62,622	60,833	43100		Sheboygan, WI Metro area	115,507	115,456
42420		Scottsbluff, NE Micro area	38,971	37,906		55117	Sheboygan County, WI	115,507	115,456
	31007	Banner County, NE	690	730	43140		Shelby, NC Micro area	98,078	97,645
	31157	Scotts Bluff County, NE	36,970	35,989		37045	Cleveland County, NC	98,078	97,645
	31165	Sioux County, NE	1,311	1,187	43180		Shelbyville, TN Micro area	45,058	49,038
42460		Scottsboro, AL Micro area	53,227	51,736		47003	Bedford County, TN	45,058	49,038
	01071	Jackson County, AL	53,227	51,736					

CORE BASED STATISTICAL AREAS
(Metropolitan and Micropolitan),
METROPOLITAN DIVISIONS, AND COMPONENTS
(as defined August, 2017)—*Continued*

Core based statistical area	State/ County FIPS code	Title and Geographic Components	2010 Census Population	2018 Estimated Population	Core based statistical area	State/ County FIPS code	Title and Geographic Components	2010 Census Population	2018 Estimated Population
43220		Shelton, WA Micro area	60,699	65,507	43940		Spearfish, SD Micro area	24,097	25,741
	53045	Mason County, WA	60,699	65,507		46081	Lawrence County, SD	24,097	25,741
43260		Sheridan, WY Micro area	29,116	30,233	43980		Spencer, IA Micro area	16,667	16,134
	56033	Sheridan County, WY	29,116	30,233		19041	Clay County, IA	16,667	16,134
43300		Sherman-Denison, TX Metro area	120,877	133,991	44020		Spirit Lake, IA Micro area	16,667	17,153
	48181	Grayson County, TX	120,877	133,991		19059	Dickinson County, IA	16,667	17,153
43320		Show Low, AZ Micro area	107,449	110,445	44060		Spokane-Spokane Valley, WA Metro area	527,753	573,493
	04017	Navajo County, AZ	107,449	110,445		53051	Pend Oreille County, WA	13,001	13,602
43340		Shreveport-Bossier City, LA Metro area	439,811	436,341		53063	Spokane County, WA	471,221	514,631
	22015	Bossier Parish, LA	116,979	127,185		53065	Stevens County, WA	43,531	45,260
	22017	Caddo Parish, LA	254,969	242,922	44100		Springfield, IL Metro area	210,170	207,636
	22031	De Soto Parish, LA	26,656	27,436		17129	Menard County, IL	12,705	12,288
	22119	Webster Parish, LA	41,207	38,798		17167	Sangamon County, IL	197,465	195,348
43380		Sidney, OH Micro area	49,423	48,627	44140		Springfield, MA Metro area	621,570	631,761
	39149	Shelby County, OH	49,423	48,627		25013	Hampden County, MA	463,490	470,406
43420		Sierra Vista-Douglas, AZ Metro area	131,346	126,770		25015	Hampshire County, MA	158,080	161,355
	04003	Cochise County, AZ	131,346	126,770	44180		Springfield, MO Metro area	436,712	466,978
43460		Sikeston, MO Micro area	39,191	38,458		29043	Christian County, MO	77,422	86,983
	29201	Scott County, MO	39,191	38,458		29059	Dallas County, MO	16,777	16,762
43500		Silver City, NM Micro area	29,514	27,346		29077	Greene County, MO	275,174	291,923
	35017	Grant County, NM	29,514	27,346		29167	Polk County, MO	31,137	32,201
43580		Sioux City, IA-NE-SD Metro area	168,563	169,045		29225	Webster County, MO	36,202	39,109
	19149	Plymouth County, IA	24,986	25,095	44220		Springfield, OH Metro area	138,333	134,585
	19193	Woodbury County, IA	102,172	102,539		39023	Clark County, OH	138,333	134,585
	31043	Dakota County, NE	21,006	20,083	44260		Starkville, MS Micro area	47,671	49,599
	31051	Dixon County, NE	6,000	5,709		28105	Oktibbeha County, MS	47,671	49,599
	46127	Union County, SD	14,399	15,619	44300		State College, PA Metro area	153,990	162,805
43620		Sioux Falls, SD Metro area	228,261	265,653		42027	Centre County, PA	153,990	162,805
	46083	Lincoln County, SD	44,828	58,807	44340		Statesboro, GA Micro area	70,217	77,296
	46087	McCook County, SD	5,618	5,546		13031	Bulloch County, GA	70,217	77,296
	46099	Minnehaha County, SD	169,468	192,876	44420		Staunton-Waynesboro, VA Metro area	118,502	123,007
	46125	Turner County, SD	8,347	8,424		51015	Augusta County, VA	73,750	75,457
43660		Snyder, TX Micro area	16,921	16,866		51790	Staunton city, VA	23,746	24,922
	48415	Scurry County, TX	16,921	16,866		51820	Waynesboro city, VA	21,006	22,628
43700		Somerset, KY Micro area	63,063	64,623	44460		Steamboat Springs, CO Micro area	23,509	25,733
	21199	Pulaski County, KY	63,063	64,623		08107	Routt County, CO	23,509	25,733
43740		Somerset, PA Micro area	77,742	73,952	44500		Stephenville, TX Micro area	37,890	42,446
	42111	Somerset County, PA	77,742	73,952		48143	Erath County, TX	37,890	42,446
43760		Sonora, CA Micro area	55,365	54,539	44540		Sterling, CO Micro area	22,709	21,528
	06109	Tuolumne County, CA	55,365	54,539		08075	Logan County, CO	22,709	21,528
43780		South Bend-Mishawaka, IN-MI Metro area	319,224	322,424	44580		Sterling, IL Micro area	58,498	55,626
	18141	St. Joseph County, IN	266,931	270,771		17195	Whiteside County, IL	58,498	55,626
	26027	Cass County, MI	52,293	51,653	44620		Stevens Point, WI Micro area	70,019	70,942
43900		Spartanburg, SC Metro area	313,268	341,298		55097	Portage County, WI	70,019	70,942
	45083	Spartanburg County, SC	284,307	313,888					
	45087	Union County, SC	28,961	27,410					

CORE BASED STATISTICAL AREAS
(Metropolitan and Micropolitan),
METROPOLITAN DIVISIONS, AND COMPONENTS
(as defined August, 2017)—*Continued*

Core based statistical area	State/ County FIPS code	Title and Geographic Components	2010 Census Population	2018 Estimated Population	Core based statistical area	State/ County FIPS code	Title and Geographic Components	2010 Census Population	2018 Estimated Population
44660		Stillwater, OK Micro area..................	77,350	82,040	45460		Terre Haute, IN Metro area..................	172,425	169,725
	40119	Payne County, OK	77,350	82,040		18021	Clay County, IN	26,890	26,170
44700		Stockton-Lodi, CA Metro area	685,306	752,660		18153	Sullivan County, IN........................	21,475	20,690
	06077	San Joaquin County, CA..................	685,306	752,660		18165	Vermillion County, IN.....................	16,212	15,479
						18167	Vigo County, IN	107,848	107,386
44740		Storm Lake, IA Micro area..................	20,260	19,874	45500		Texarkana, TX-AR Metro area..............	149,198	150,242
	19021	Buena Vista County, IA	20,260	19,874		05081	Little River County, AR....................	13,171	12,326
44780		Sturgis, MI Micro area	61,295	61,043		05091	Miller County, AR	43,462	43,592
	26149	St. Joseph County, MI.....................	61,295	61,043		48037	Bowie County, TX	92,565	94,324
44860		Sulphur Springs, TX Micro area	35,161	36,810	45520		The Dalles, OR Micro area..................	25,213	26,505
	48223	Hopkins County, TX	35,161	36,810		41065	Wasco County, OR........................	25,213	26,505
44900		Summerville, GA Micro area..............	26,015	24,790	45540		The Villages, FL Metro area	93,420	128,754
	13055	Chattooga County, GA....................	26,015	24,790		12119	Sumter County, FL.........................	93,420	128,754
44920		Summit Park, UT Micro area	36,324	41,933	45580		Thomaston, GA Micro area.................	27,153	26,215
	49043	Summit County, UT.........................	36,324	41,933		13293	Upson County, GA	27,153	26,215
44940		Sumter, SC Metro area....................	107,456	106,512	45620		Thomasville, GA Micro area	44,720	44,448
	45085	Sumter County, SC	107,456	106,512		13275	Thomas County, GA.......................	44,720	44,448
44980		Sunbury, PA Micro area	94,528	91,083	45660		Tiffin, OH Micro area.......................	56,745	55,207
	42097	Northumberland County, PA..............	94,528	91,083		39147	Seneca County, OH	56,745	55,207
45000		Susanville, CA Micro area	34,895	30,802	45700		Tifton, GA Micro area.......................	40,118	40,571
	06035	Lassen County, CA	34,895	30,802		13277	Tift County, GA.............................	40,118	40,571
45020		Sweetwater, TX Micro area	15,216	14,751	45740		Toccoa, GA Micro area.....................	26,175	26,035
	48353	Nolan County, TX..........................	15,216	14,751		13257	Stephens County, GA......................	26,175	26,035
45060		Syracuse, NY Metro area	662,577	650,502	45780		Toledo, OH Metro area.....................	610,001	602,871
	36053	Madison County, NY	73,442	70,795		39051	Fulton County, OH	42,698	42,276
	36067	Onondaga County, NY.....................	467,026	461,809		39095	Lucas County, OH	441,815	429,899
	36075	Oswego County, NY	122,109	117,898		39173	Wood County, OH	125,488	130,696
45140		Tahlequah, OK Micro area..................	46,987	48,675	45820		Topeka, KS Metro area.....................	233,870	232,594
	40021	Cherokee County, OK	46,987	48,675		20085	Jackson County, KS	13,462	13,280
45180		Talladega-Sylacauga, AL Micro area	93,830	90,543		20087	Jefferson County, KS	19,126	18,975
	01037	Coosa County, AL..........................	11,539	10,715		20139	Osage County, KS	16,295	15,941
	01121	Talladega County, AL	82,291	79,828		20177	Shawnee County, KS	177,934	177,499
45220		Tallahassee, FL Metro area...............	367,413	385,145		20197	Wabaunsee County, KS...................	7,053	6,899
	12039	Gadsden County, FL.......................	46,389	45,894	45860		Torrington, CT Micro area..................	189,927	181,111
	12065	Jefferson County, FL......................	14,761	14,288		09005	Litchfield County, CT......................	189,927	181,111
	12073	Leon County, FL............................	275,487	292,502	45900		Traverse City, MI Micro area..............	143,372	149,914
	12129	Wakulla County, FL........................	30,776	32,461		26019	Benzie County, MI.........................	17,525	17,753
45300		Tampa-St. Petersburg-Clearwater, FL Metro area...............................	2,783,243	3,142,663		26055	Grand Traverse County, MI..............	86,986	92,573
						26079	Kalkaska County, MI	17,153	17,824
	12053	Hernando County, FL.......................	172,778	190,865		26089	Leelanau County, MI	21,708	21,764
	12057	Hillsborough County, FL..................	1,229,226	1,436,888	45940		Trenton, NJ Metro area	366,513	369,811
	12101	Pasco County, FL..........................	464,697	539,630		34021	Mercer County, NJ	366,513	369,811
	12103	Pinellas County, FL........................	916,542	975,280	45980		Troy, AL Micro area........................	32,899	33,338
45340		Taos, NM Micro area	32,937	32,835		01109	Pike County, AL............................	32,899	33,338
	35055	Taos County, NM...........................	32,937	32,835	46020		Truckee-Grass Valley, CA Micro area....	98,764	99,696
45380		Taylorville, IL Micro area...................	34,800	32,661		06057	Nevada County, CA........................	98,764	99,696
	17021	Christian County, IL........................	34,800	32,661	46060		Tucson, AZ Metro area	980,263	1,039,073
						04019	Pima County, AZ	980,263	1,039,073

Core based statistical area	State/County FIPS code	Title and Geographic Components	2010 Census Population	2018 Estimated Population	Core based statistical area	State/County FIPS code	Title and Geographic Components	2010 Census Population	2018 Estimated Population
46100		Tullahoma-Manchester, TN Micro area .	100,210	104,001		39161	Van Wert County, OH......	28,744	28,281
	47031	Coffee County, TN..........	52,796	55,700					
	47051	Franklin County, TN........	41,052	41,890	46820		Vermillion, SD Micro area..................	13,864	14,041
	47127	Moore County, TN...........	6,362	6,411		46027	Clay County, SD...........	13,864	14,041
46140		Tulsa, OK Metro area	937,478	993,797	46860		Vernal, UT Micro area..................	32,588	35,438
	40037	Creek County, OK..........	69,967	71,604		49047	Uintah County, UT.........	32,588	35,438
	40111	Okmulgee County, OK......	40,069	38,335					
	40113	Osage County, OK..........	47,472	47,014	46900		Vernon, TX Micro area..................	13,535	12,820
	40117	Pawnee County, OK........	16,577	16,390		48487	Wilbarger County, TX.........	13,535	12,820
	40131	Rogers County, OK.........	86,905	91,984					
	40143	Tulsa County, OK..........	603,403	648,360	46980		Vicksburg, MS Micro area	58,377	55,178
	40145	Wagoner County, OK.......	73,085	80,110		28021	Claiborne County, MS........	9,604	9,002
46180		Tupelo, MS Micro area	136,268	140,552		28149	Warren County, MS........	48,773	46,176
	28057	Itawamba County, MS......	23,401	23,517	47020		Victoria, TX Metro area..................	94,003	99,619
	28081	Lee County, MS...........	82,910	85,202		48175	Goliad County, TX........	7,210	7,584
	28115	Pontotoc County, MS.......	29,957	31,833		48469	Victoria County, TX........	86,793	92,035
46220		Tuscaloosa, AL Metro area..................	230,162	243,575	47080		Vidalia, GA Micro area..................	36,346	36,080
	01065	Hale County, AL	15,760	14,726		13209	Montgomery County, GA........	9,123	9,193
	01107	Pickens County, AL	19,746	19,938		13279	Toombs County, GA	27,223	26,887
	01125	Tuscaloosa County, AL.....	194,656	208,911	47180		Vincennes, IN Micro area	38,440	36,895
46300		Twin Falls, ID Metro area..................	99,604	110,096		18083	Knox County, IN..........	38,440	36,895
	16053	Jerome County, ID	22,374	24,015					
	16083	Twin Falls County, ID......	77,230	86,081	47220		Vineland-Bridgeton, NJ Metro area	156,898	150,972
46340		Tyler, TX Metro area..................	209,714	230,221		34011	Cumberland County, NJ........	156,898	150,972
	48423	Smith County, TX...........	209,714	230,221	47240		Vineyard Haven, MA Micro area............	16,535	17,352
46380		Ukiah, CA Micro area..................	87,841	87,606		25007	Dukes County, MA	16,535	17,352
	06045	Mendocino County, CA.....	87,841	87,606	47260		Virginia Beach-Norfolk-Newport News, VA-NC Metro area.....	1,676,822	1,728,733
46460		Union City, TN-KY Micro area..............	38,620	36,387		37053	Currituck County, NC.......	23,547	27,072
	21075	Fulton County, KY	6,813	6,120		37073	Gates County, NC.........	12,197	11,573
	47131	Obion County, TN..........	31,807	30,267		51073	Gloucester County, VA.......	36,858	37,349
46500		Urbana, OH Micro area	40,097	38,754		51093	Isle of Wight County, VA.....	35,270	36,953
	39021	Champaign County, OH.....	40,097	38,754		51095	James City County, VA......	67,009	76,397
46520		Urban Honolulu, HI Metro area............	953,207	980,080		51115	Mathews County, VA........	8,978	8,802
	15003	Honolulu County, HI	953,207	980,080		51199	York County, VA..........	65,464	67,846
46540		Utica-Rome, NY Metro area	299,397	291,410		51550	Chesapeake city, VA.......	222,209	242,634
	36043	Herkimer County, NY.......	64,519	61,833		51650	Hampton city, VA..........	137,436	134,313
	36065	Oneida County, NY.........	234,878	229,577		51700	Newport News city, VA......	180,719	178,626
46620		Uvalde, TX Micro area..................	26,405	26,846		51710	Norfolk city, VA..........	242,803	244,076
	48463	Uvalde County, TX...........	26,405	26,846		51735	Poquoson city, VA.........	12,150	12,190
46660		Valdosta, GA Metro area..................	139,588	146,174		51740	Portsmouth city, VA........	95,535	94,632
	13027	Brooks County, GA..........	16,243	15,513		51800	Suffolk city, VA...........	84,585	91,185
	13101	Echols County, GA..........	4,034	4,000		51810	Virginia Beach city, VA......	437,994	450,189
	13173	Lanier County, GA..........	10,078	10,340		51830	Williamsburg city, VA.......	14,068	14,896
	13185	Lowndes County, GA........	109,233	116,321	47300		Visalia-Porterville, CA Metro area.........	442,179	465,861
46700		Vallejo-Fairfield, CA Metro area............	413,344	446,610		06107	Tulare County, CA.......	442,179	465,861
	06095	Solano County, CA..........	413,344	446,610	47340		Wabash, IN Micro area..................	32,888	31,280
46740		Valley, AL Micro area	34,215	33,615		18169	Wabash County, IN	32,888	31,280
	01017	Chambers County, AL	34,215	33,615	47380		Waco, TX Metro area..................	252,772	271,942
						48145	Falls County, TX........	17,866	17,335
						48309	McLennan County, TX	234,906	254,607
					47420		Wahpeton, ND-MN Micro area	22,897	22,493
						27167	Wilkin County, MN............	6,576	6,254
46780		Van Wert, OH Micro area	28,744	28,281		38077	Richland County, ND........	16,321	16,239

Core based statistical area	State/County FIPS code	Title and Geographic Components	2010 Census Population	2018 Estimated Population	Core based statistical area	State/County FIPS code	Title and Geographic Components	2010 Census Population	2018 Estimated Population
47460		Walla Walla, WA Metro area..................	62,859	64,981	47940		Waterloo-Cedar Falls, IA Metro area.....	167,819	169,659
	53013	Columbia County, WA..................	4,078	4,059		19013	Black Hawk County, IA.....................	131,090	132,408
	53071	Walla Walla County, WA..................	58,781	60,922		19017	Bremer County, IA.....................	24,276	24,947
						19075	Grundy County, IA.....................	12,453	12,304
47540		Wapakoneta, OH Micro area.................	45,949	45,804					
	39011	Auglaize County, OH..................	45,949	45,804	47980		Watertown, SD Micro area	27,227	28,015
						46029	Codington County, SD.....................	27,227	28,015
47580		Warner Robins, GA Metro area	179,605	193,835	48020		Watertown-Fort Atkinson, WI Micro area	83,686	85,129
	13153	Houston County, GA..................	139,900	155,469					
	13225	Peach County, GA..................	27,695	27,297		55055	Jefferson County, WI.....................	83,686	85,129
	13235	Pulaski County, GA..................	12,010	11,069					
47620		Warren, PA Micro area.........................	41,815	39,498	48060		Watertown-Fort Drum, NY Metro area...	116,229	111,755
	42123	Warren County, PA..................	41,815	39,498		36045	Jefferson County, NY	116,229	111,755
47660		Warrensburg, MO Micro area	52,595	53,652	48100		Wauchula, FL Micro area.....................	27,731	27,245
	29101	Johnson County, MO	52,595	53,652		12049	Hardee County, FL.....................	27,731	27,245
47700		Warsaw, IN Micro area	77,358	79,344	48140		Wausau, WI Metro area.....................	134,063	135,428
	18085	Kosciusko County, IN........................	77,358	79,344		55073	Marathon County, WI	134,063	135,428
47780		Washington, IN Micro area	31,648	33,147	48180		Waycross, GA Micro area.....................	55,070	55,069
	18027	Daviess County, IN	31,648	33,147		13229	Pierce County, GA.....................	18,758	19,389
						13299	Ware County, GA.....................	36,312	35,680
47820		Washington, NC Micro area	47,759	47,079					
	37013	Beaufort County, NC	47,759	47,079	48220		Weatherford, OK Micro area.....................	27,469	29,036
						40039	Custer County, OK.....................	27,469	29,036
47900		Washington-Arlington-Alexandria, DC-VA-MD-WV Metro area.........................	5,636,232	6,249,950	48260		Weirton-Steubenville, WV-OH Metro area	124,454	117,064
47900		Silver Spring-Frederick-Rockville, MD Metro Div 43524	1,205,162	1,308,215		39081	Jefferson County, OH.....................	69,709	65,767
						54009	Brooke County, WV.....................	24,069	22,203
	24021	Frederick County, MD	233,385	255,648		54029	Hancock County, WV	30,676	29,094
	24031	Montgomery County, MD	971,777	1,052,567	48300		Wenatchee, WA Metro area.....................	110,884	119,943
47900		Washington-Arlington-Alexandria, DC-VA-MD-WV Metro Div 47894................	4,431,070	4,941,735		53007	Chelan County, WA.....................	72,453	77,036
						53017	Douglas County, WA.....................	38,431	42,907
	11001	District of Columbia, DC..................	601,723	702,455					
	24009	Calvert County, MD..................	88,737	92,003	48460		West Plains, MO Micro area.....................	40,400	40,076
	24017	Charles County, MD..................	146,551	161,503		29091	Howell County, MO	40,400	40,076
	24033	Prince George's County, MD	863,420	909,308					
	51013	Arlington County, VA	207,627	237,521	48500		West Point, MS Micro Area.....................	20,634	19,386
	51043	Clarke County, VA..................	14,034	14,523		28025	Clay County, MS	20,634	19,386
	51047	Culpeper County, VA..................	46,689	51,859					
	51059	Fairfax County, VA..................	1,081,726	1,150,795	48540		Wheeling, WV-OH Metro area...............	147,950	140,045
	51061	Fauquier County, VA..................	65,203	70,675		39013	Belmont County, OH	70,400	67,505
	51107	Loudoun County, VA..................	312,311	406,850		54051	Marshall County, WV.....................	33,107	30,785
	51153	Prince William County, VA..................	402,002	468,011		54069	Ohio County, WV	44,443	41,755
	51157	Rappahannock County, VA...............	7,373	7,252					
	51177	Spotsylvania County, VA..................	122,397	134,238	48580		Whitewater-Elkhorn, WI Micro area.......	102,228	103,718
	51179	Stafford County, VA..................	128,961	149,960		55127	Walworth County, WI.....................	102,228	103,718
	51187	Warren County, VA..................	37,575	40,003					
	51510	Alexandria city, VA..................	139,966	160,530	48620		Wichita, KS Metro area.....................	630,919	644,888
	51600	Fairfax city, VA..................	22,565	24,574		20015	Butler County, KS.....................	65,880	66,765
	51610	Falls Church city, VA..................	12,332	14,772		20079	Harvey County, KS.....................	34,684	34,210
	51630	Fredericksburg city, VA	24,286	29,144		20095	Kingman County, KS.....................	7,858	7,310
	51683	Manassas city, VA..................	37,821	41,641		20173	Sedgwick County, KS.....................	498,365	513,607
	51685	Manassas Park city, VA..................	14,273	17,307		20191	Sumner County, KS	24,132	22,996
	54037	Jefferson County, WV..................	53,498	56,811	48660		Wichita Falls, TX Metro area	151,306	151,306
						48009	Archer County, TX.....................	9,054	8,786
47920		Washington Court House, OH Micro area	29,030	28,666		48077	Clay County, TX.....................	10,752	10,456
	39047	Fayette County, OH	29,030	28,666		48485	Wichita County, TX	131,500	132,064

CORE BASED STATISTICAL AREAS
(Metropolitan and Micropolitan),
METROPOLITAN DIVISIONS, AND COMPONENTS
(as defined August, 2017)—*Continued*

Core based statistical area	State/County FIPS code	Title and Geographic Components	2010 Census Population	2018 Estimated Population	Core based statistical area	State/County FIPS code	Title and Geographic Components	2010 Census Population	2018 Estimated Population
48700		Williamsport, PA Metro area	116,111	113,664	49260		Woodward, OK Micro area	20,081	20,222
	42081	Lycoming County, PA	116,111	113,664		40153	Woodward County, OK	20,081	20,222
48780		Williston, ND Micro area	22,398	35,350	49300		Wooster, OH Micro area	114,520	115,967
	38105	Williams County, ND	22,398	35,350		39169	Wayne County, OH	114,520	115,967
48820		Willmar, MN Micro area	42,239	42,855	49340		Worcester, MA-CT Metro area	916,980	947,866
	27067	Kandiyohi County, MN	42,239	42,855		09015	Windham County, CT	118,428	117,027
48900		Wilmington, NC Metro area	254,884	294,436		25027	Worcester County, MA	798,552	830,839
	37129	New Hanover County, NC	202,667	232,274	49380		Worthington, MN Micro area	21,378	21,924
	37141	Pender County, NC	52,217	62,162		27105	Nobles County, MN	21,378	21,924
48940		Wilmington, OH Micro area	42,040	42,057	49420		Yakima, WA Metro area	243,231	251,446
	39027	Clinton County, OH	42,040	42,057		53077	Yakima County, WA	243,231	251,446
48980		Wilson, NC Micro area	81,234	81,455	49460		Yankton, SD Micro area	22,438	22,869
	37195	Wilson County, NC	81,234	81,455		46135	Yankton County, SD	22,438	22,869
49020		Winchester, VA-WV Metro area	128,472	139,810	49620		York-Hanover, PA Metro area	434,972	448,273
	51069	Frederick County, VA	78,305	88,355		42133	York County, PA	434,972	448,273
	51840	Winchester city, VA	26,203	28,108	49660		Youngstown-Warren-Boardman, OH-PA Metro area	565,773	538,952
	54027	Hampshire County, WV	23,964	23,347		39099	Mahoning County, OH	238,823	229,642
49080		Winnemucca, NV Micro area	16,528	16,786		39155	Trumbull County, OH	210,312	198,627
	32013	Humboldt County, NV	16,528	16,786		42085	Mercer County, PA	116,638	110,683
49100		Winona, MN Micro area	51,461	50,825	49700		Yuba City, CA Metro area	166,892	174,848
	27169	Winona County, MN	51,461	50,825		06101	Sutter County, CA	94,737	96,807
49180		Winston-Salem, NC Metro area	640,595	671,456		06115	Yuba County, CA	72,155	78,041
	37057	Davidson County, NC	162,878	166,614	49740		Yuma, AZ Metro area	195,751	212,128
	37059	Davie County, NC	41,240	42,733		04027	Yuma County, AZ	195,751	212,128
	37067	Forsyth County, NC	350,670	379,099	49780		Zanesville, OH Micro area	86,074	86,183
	37169	Stokes County, NC	47,401	45,467		39119	Muskingum County, OH	86,074	86,183
	37197	Yadkin County, NC	38,406	37,543	49820		Zapata, TX Micro area	14,018	14,190
49220		Wisconsin Rapids-Marshfield, WI Micro area	74,749	73,055		48505	Zapata County, TX	14,018	14,190
	55141	Wood County, WI	74,749	73,055					

Appendix C

APPENDIX D
MAPS OF CONGRESSIONAL DISTRICTS AND STATES

Page		Page	
D-2 & 3	United States	D-29	Missouri
D-4	Alabama	D-30	Montana
D-5	Alaska	D-31	Nebraska
D-6	Arizona	D-32	Nevada
D-7	Arkansas	D-33	New Hampshire
D-8	California	D-34	New Jersey
D-9	Colorado	D-35	New Mexico
D-10	Connecticut	D-36	New York
D-11	Delaware	D-37	North Carolina
D-12	District of Columbia	D-38	North Dakota
D-13	Florida	D-39	Ohio
D-14	Georgia	D-40	Oklahoma
D-15	Hawaii	D-41	Oregon
D-16	Idaho	D-42	Pennsylvania
D-17	Illinois	D-43	Rhode Island
D-18	Indiana	D-44	South Carolina
D-19	Iowa	D-45	South Dakota
D-20	Kansas	D-46	Tennessee
D-21	Kentucky	D-47	Texas
D-22	Louisiana	D-48	Utah
D-23	Maine	D-49	Vermont
D-24	Maryland	D-50	Virginia
D-25	Massachusetts	D-51	Washington
D-26	Michigan	D-52	West Virginia
D-27	Minnesota	D-53	Wisconsin
D-28	Mississippi	D-54	Wyoming

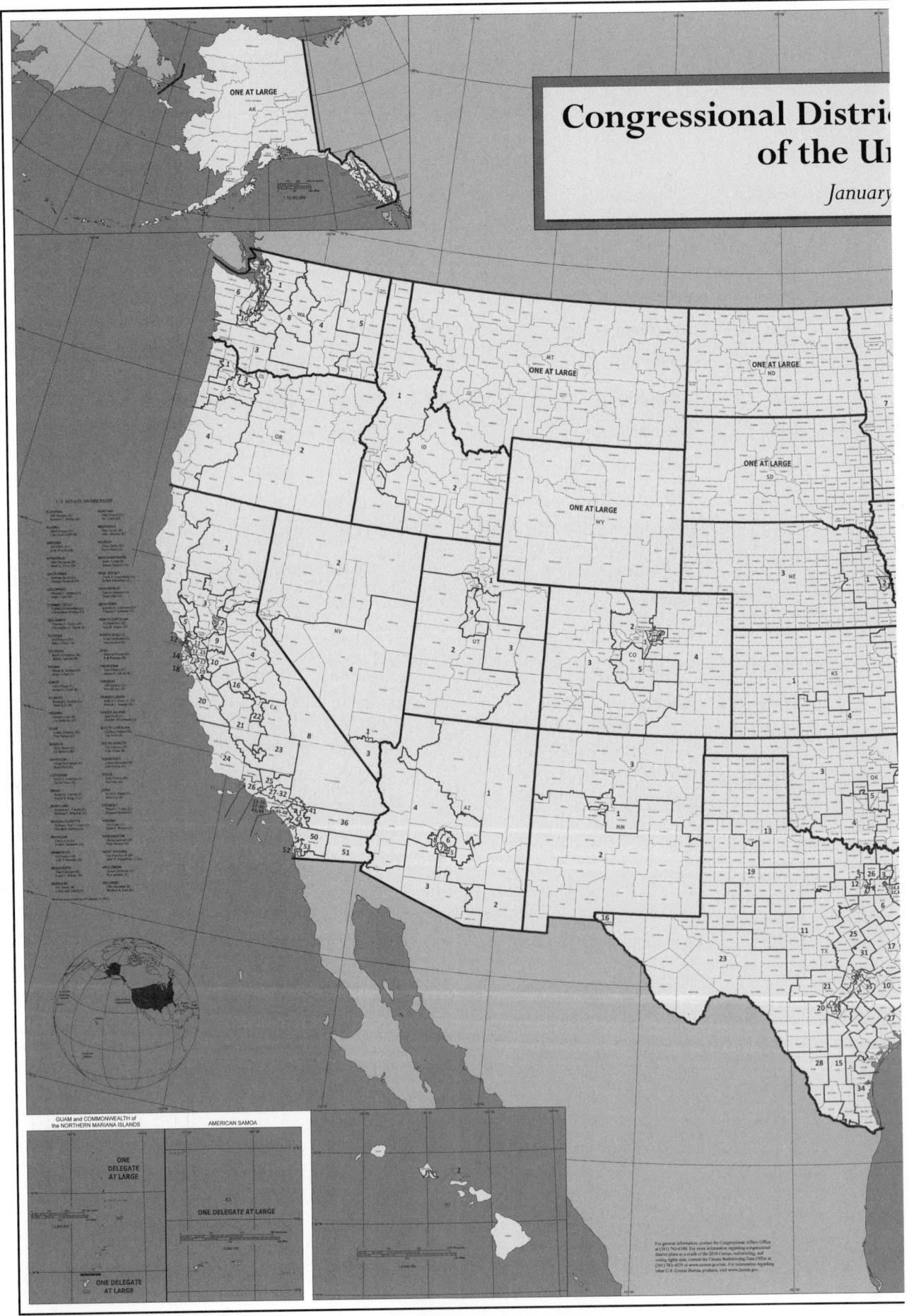

Congressional Distri...
of the U...
January...

ONE AT LARGE
AK

U.S. DEPARTMENT OF COMMERCE Economics and Statistics Administration U.S. Census Bureau
Prepared by the Geography Division

GUAM and COMMONWEALTH of
the NORTHERN MARIANA ISLANDS

ONE
DELEGATE
AT LARGE
MP

ONE DELEGATE
AT LARGE
GU

AMERICAN SAMOA

ONE DELEGATE AT LARGE

Congressional Districts of the 113th Congress of the United States
2013-2015

CONGRESSIONAL DISTRICTS OF THE 113TH CONGRESS OF THE UNITED STATES (JANUARY 2013 TO 2015)

ALABAMA - Core Based Statistical Areas (CBSAs) and Counties

N

0 10 20 30 40 Kilometers
0 10 20 30 40 Miles

TENNESSEE

Chattanooga-Cleveland-Dalton

Huntsville-Decatur-Albertville

NORTH CAROLINA

FLORENCE-MUSCLE SHOALS
Lauderdale

HUNTSVILLE
Limestone

Madison

Scottsboro
Jackson

Colbert

Franklin

DECATUR
Lawrence

Morgan

Albertville
Marshall

DeKalb

Marion

Winston

Cullman
Cullman

Cherokee

GADSDEN
Etowah

ANNISTON-OXFORD-JACKSONVILLE

MISSISSIPPI

Lamar

Fayette

Walker

Blount

BIRMINGHAM-HOOVER
Jefferson

St. Clair

Calhoun

Cleburne

GEORGIA

Birmingham-Hoover-Talladega

Talladega

Pickens

TUSCALOOSA
Tuscaloosa

Shelby

Clay

Randolph

Greene

Bibb

Chilton

Talladega-Sylacauga
Coosa

Tallapoosa

Valley
Chambers

COLUMBUS
Harris

Columbus-Auburn-Opelika

Hale

Perry

Elmore

AUBURN-OPELIKA
Lee

Muscogee

Sumter

MONTGOMERY
Autauga

Macon

Russell

Chatta-hoochee

Marion

Selma
Dallas

Montgomery

Marengo

Lowndes

Bullock

Choctaw

Wilcox

Troy
Pike

Barbour

Clarke

Butler

Crenshaw

Ozark
Dale

Henry

Dothan-Enterprise-Ozark

Monroe

Enterprise
Coffee

Washington

Conecuh

Covington

DOTHAN
Houston

Escambia

Geneva

FLORIDA

LEGEND

MOBILE
Mobile

Mobile-Daphne-Fairhope

DAPHNE-FAIRHOPE-FOLEY

Baldwin

Gulf of Mexico

Dothan-Enterprise-Ozark — Combined Statistical Area

MOBILE — Metropolitan Statistical Area

Troy — Micropolitan Statistical Area

FLORIDA — State or Statistical Equivalent

Autauga — County or Statistical Equivalent

Gulf of Mexico — Coastline

CBSA boundaries and names are as of February 2013. All other boundaries and names are as of January 1, 2012.

U.S. DEPARTMENT OF COMMERCE Economics and Statistics Administration U.S. Census Bureau

ALASKA - Core Based Statistical Areas (CBSAs) and Counties

LEGEND

FAIRBANKS — Metropolitan Statistical Area

Juneau — Micropolitan Statistical Area

CANADA — International

Bethel — County or Statistical Equivalent

Arctic Ocean — Coastline

CBSA boundaries and names are as of February 2013. All other boundaries and names are as of January 1, 2012.

CANADA

RUSSIA

Arctic Ocean

Pacific Ocean

Prince of Wales-Hyder (pt)
Wrangell
Juneau
Skagway
Haines
Yakutat
Hoonah-Angoon
Sitka
Petersburg
Prince of Wales-Hyder (pt)
Ketchikan
Ketchikan Gateway

Southeast Fairbanks
Valdez-Cordova
Anchorage
FAIRBANKS
Denali
Fairbanks North Star
ANCHORAGE
Matanuska-Susitna
Kenai Peninsula
Yukon-Koyukuk
North Slope
Northwest Arctic
Nome (pt)
Nome (pt)
Wade Hampton
Bethel
Dillingham
Bristol Bay
Lake and Peninsula
Kodiak Island
Aleutians East
Aleutians West (pt)
Aleutians West (pt)

0 75 150 225 300 Miles
0 75 150 225 300 Kilometers

LEGEND

Tucson-Nogales	Combined Statistical Area
YUMA	Metropolitan Statistical Area
Payson	Micropolitan Statistical Area
M E X I C O	International
UTAH	State or Statistical Equivalent
Apache	County or Statistical Equivalent
Pacific Ocean	Coastline

CBSA boundaries and names are as of February 2013. All other boundaries and names are as of January 1, 2012.

COLORADO

NEVADA

UTAH

Las Vegas-Henderson

FLAGSTAFF

Coconino

Show Low

Apache

NEW MEXICO

LAKE HAVASU CITY-KINGMAN

Mohave

PRESCOTT

Yavapai

N

0 20 40 60 80 Kilometers

0 20 40 60 80 Miles

CALIFORNIA

Payson

Gila

La Paz

PHOENIX-MESA-SCOTTSDALE

Maricopa

Pinal

Greenlee

Safford

Graham

YUMA

Yuma

Tucson-Nogales

TUCSON

Pima

SIERRA VISTA-DOUGLAS

Cochise

Pacific Ocean

Nogales

Santa Cruz

M E X I C O

Gulf of California

ARKANSAS - Core Based Statistical Areas (CBSAs) and Counties

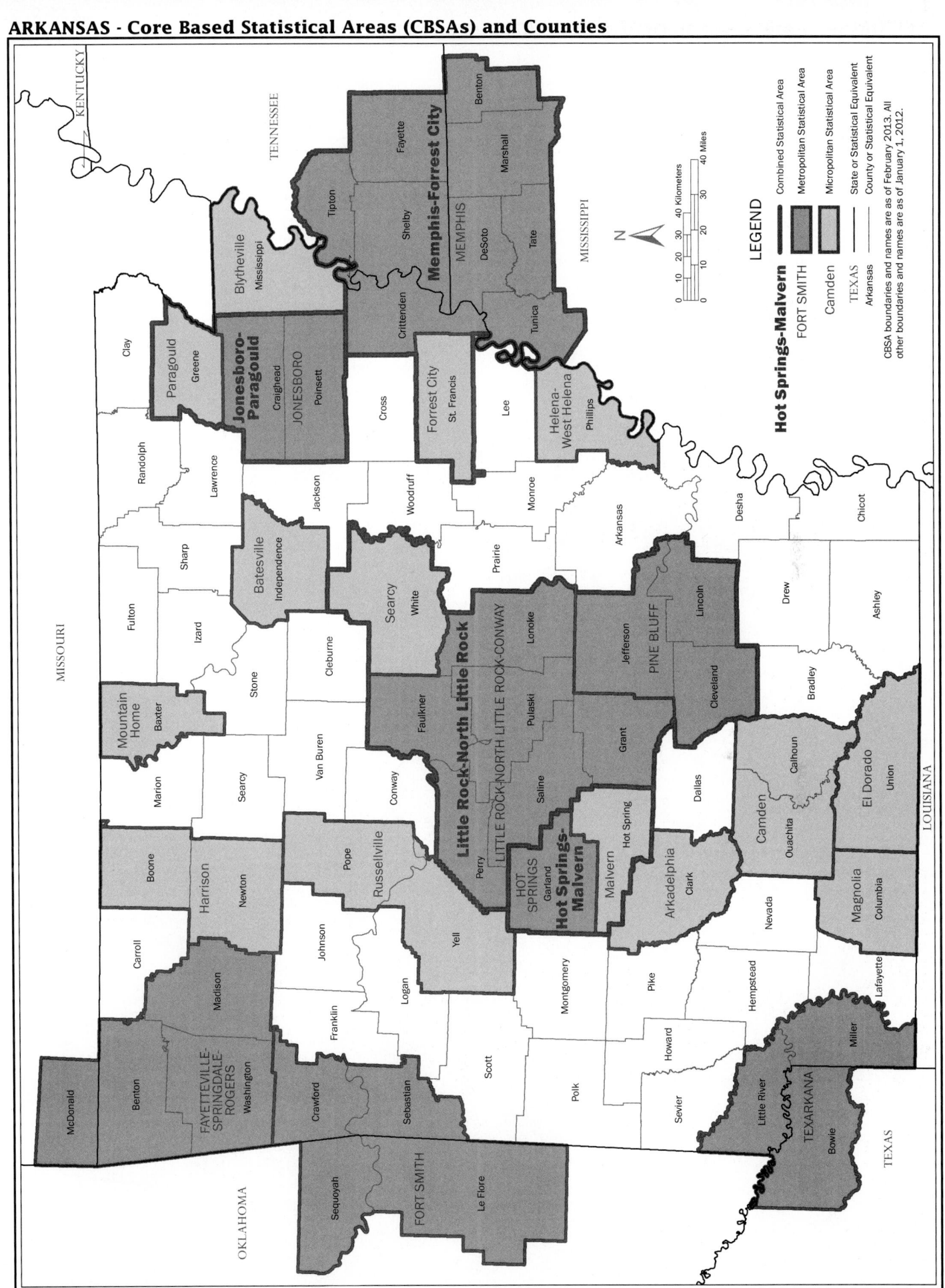

CALIFORNIA - Core Based Statistical Areas (CBSAs) and Counties

OREGON

IDAHO

Del Norte
Crescent City
Siskiyou
Modoc

Eureka-Arcata-Fortuna
Humboldt
Trinity

REDDING
Shasta
Redding-Red Bluff

Susanville
Lassen

Red Bluff
Tehama

Plumas

CHICO
Glenn
Butte
Sierra

Ukiah
Mendocino

Clearlake
Lake
Colusa
Sutter
Yuba
YUBA CITY
Nevada

LEGEND

Fresno-Madera — Combined Statistical Area
NAPA — Metropolitan Statistical Area
Ukiah — Micropolitan Statistical Area
San Rafael •••••• Metropolitan Division
MEXICO — International
NEVADA — State or Statistical Equivalent
Alameda — County or Statistical Equivalent
Pacific Ocean — Coastline

CBSA boundaries and names are as of February 2013. All other boundaries and names are as of January 1, 2012.

Truckee-Grass Valley
Sacramento-Roseville
SACRAMENTO–ROSEVILLE–ARDEN-ARCADE

Placer

El Dorado

SANTA ROSA
Sonoma
NAPA
Napa
Yolo
Sacra-mento
Alpine

1

San Rafael
Solano
San Francisco-Oakland-Hayward
Marin
Contra Costa
San Joaquin
STOCKTON-LODI
Calaveras
Amador
SONORA
Tuolumne

NEVADA

N

0 20 40 60 80 Kilometers
0 20 40 60 80 Miles

San Francisco
San Francisco-Redwood City-South San Francisco
Alameda
2
MODESTO
Stanislaus
Mariposa

Mono

San Jose-San Francisco-Oakland
Santa Clara
3
Merced
Modesto-Merced
MERCED
Madera

San Mateo
SANTA CRUZ-WATSONVILLE
Santa Cruz
MADERA
Fresno
Fresno-Madera

San Benito
SALINAS
FRESNO
Fresno
VISALIA-PORTERVILLE
Tulare
Visalia-Porterville-Hanford

Inyo

KEY
1 VALLEJO-FAIRFIELD
2 Oakland-Hayward-Berkeley
3 SAN JOSE-SUNNYVALE-SANTA CLARA

Monterey
Kings
HANFORD-CORCORAN

SAN LUIS OBISPO-PASO ROBLES-ARROYO GRANDE

San Luis Obispo
BAKERSFIELD
Kern

ARIZONA

Los Angeles-Long Beach
RIVERSIDE-SAN BERNARDINO-ONTARIO
San Bernardino

Pacific Ocean

Santa Barbara

SANTA MARIA-SANTA BARBARA

Ventura
Los Angeles-Long Beach-Glendale
LOS ANGELES-LONG BEACH-ANAHEIM

OXNARD-THOUSAND OAKS-VENTURA
Los Angeles
Orange
Anaheim-Santa Ana-Irvine
Riverside

SAN DIEGO-CARLSBAD
San Diego
EL CENTRO
Imperial

MEXICO

COLORADO - Core Based Statistical Areas (CBSAs) and Counties

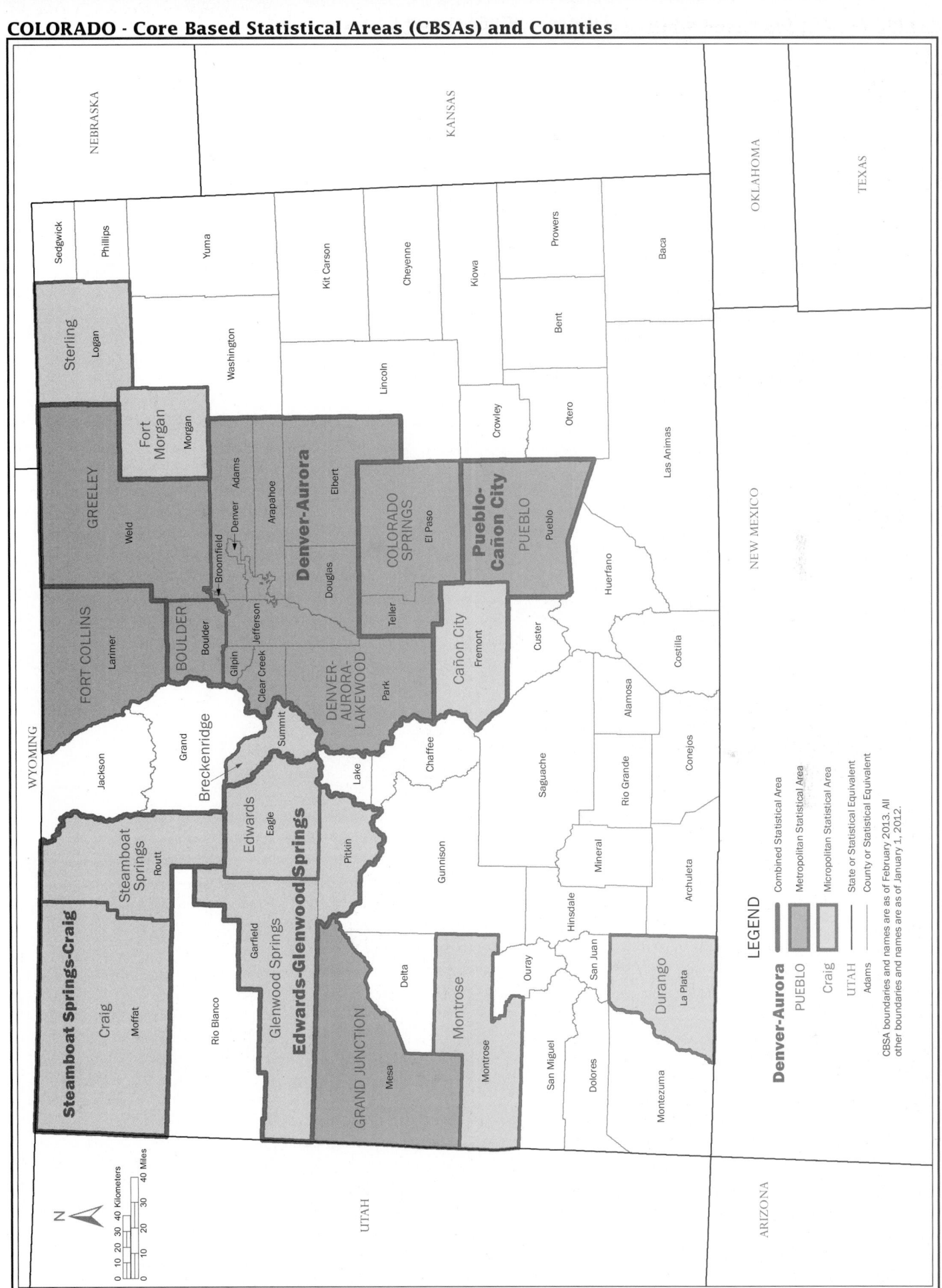

LEGEND

Denver-Aurora Combined Statistical Area

PUEBLO Metropolitan Statistical Area

Craig Micropolitan Statistical Area

UTAH State or Statistical Equivalent

Adams County or Statistical Equivalent

CBSA boundaries and names are as of February 2013. All other boundaries and names are as of January 1, 2012.

CONNECTICUT - Core Based Statistical Areas (CBSAs) and Counties

RHODE ISLAND

Worcester

Boston-Worcester-Providence (pt)

WORCESTER (pt)

Windham

NORWICH-NEW LONDON

New London

MASSACHUSETTS

Tolland

Hartford-West Hartford

HARTFORD-WEST HARTFORD-EAST HARTFORD

Hartford

Middlesex

NEW HAVEN-MILFORD

New Haven

Long Island Sound

Torrington
Litchfield

New York-Newark (pt)

BRIDGEPORT-STAMFORD-NORWALK

Fairfield

NEW YORK

NEW YORK

LEGEND

Combined Statistical Area
Metropolitan Statistical Area
Micropolitan Statistical Area

Hartford-West Hartford
NEW HAVEN-MILFORD
Torrington

State or Statistical Equivalent
NEW YORK   County or Statistical Equivalent
Fairfield
Long Island Sound   Coastline

CBSA boundaries and names are as of February 2013. All other boundaries and names are as of January 1, 2012.

N

0   3   6   9   12 Miles
0   3   6   9   12 Kilometers

Chester

PHILADELPHIA-
CAMDEN-
WILMINGTON
(pt)

Delaware

Philadelphia

Camden

Burlington

PENNSYLVANIA

Philadelphia-Reading-Camden (pt)

Wilmington

Gloucester

Cecil

New
Castle

Salem

NEW JERSEY

MARYLAND

DOVER

Kent

Delaware Bay

N

Atlantic Ocean

0 3 6 9 12 Kilometers
0 3 6 9 12 Miles

Sussex

SALISBURY

Wicomico

Worcester

Somerset

Philadelphia-Reading-Camden

Chesapeake
Bay

VIRGINIA

LEGEND

Philadelphia-Reading-Camden	Combined Statistical Area
DOVER	Metropolitan Statistical Area
Wilmington •••••	Metropolitan Division
MARYLAND	State or Statistical Equivalent
Kent	County or Statistical Equivalent
Atlantic Ocean	Coastline

CBSA boundaries and names are as of February 2013. All
other boundaries and names are as of January 1, 2012.

U.S. DEPARTMENT OF COMMERCE Economics and Statistics Administration U.S. Census Bureau

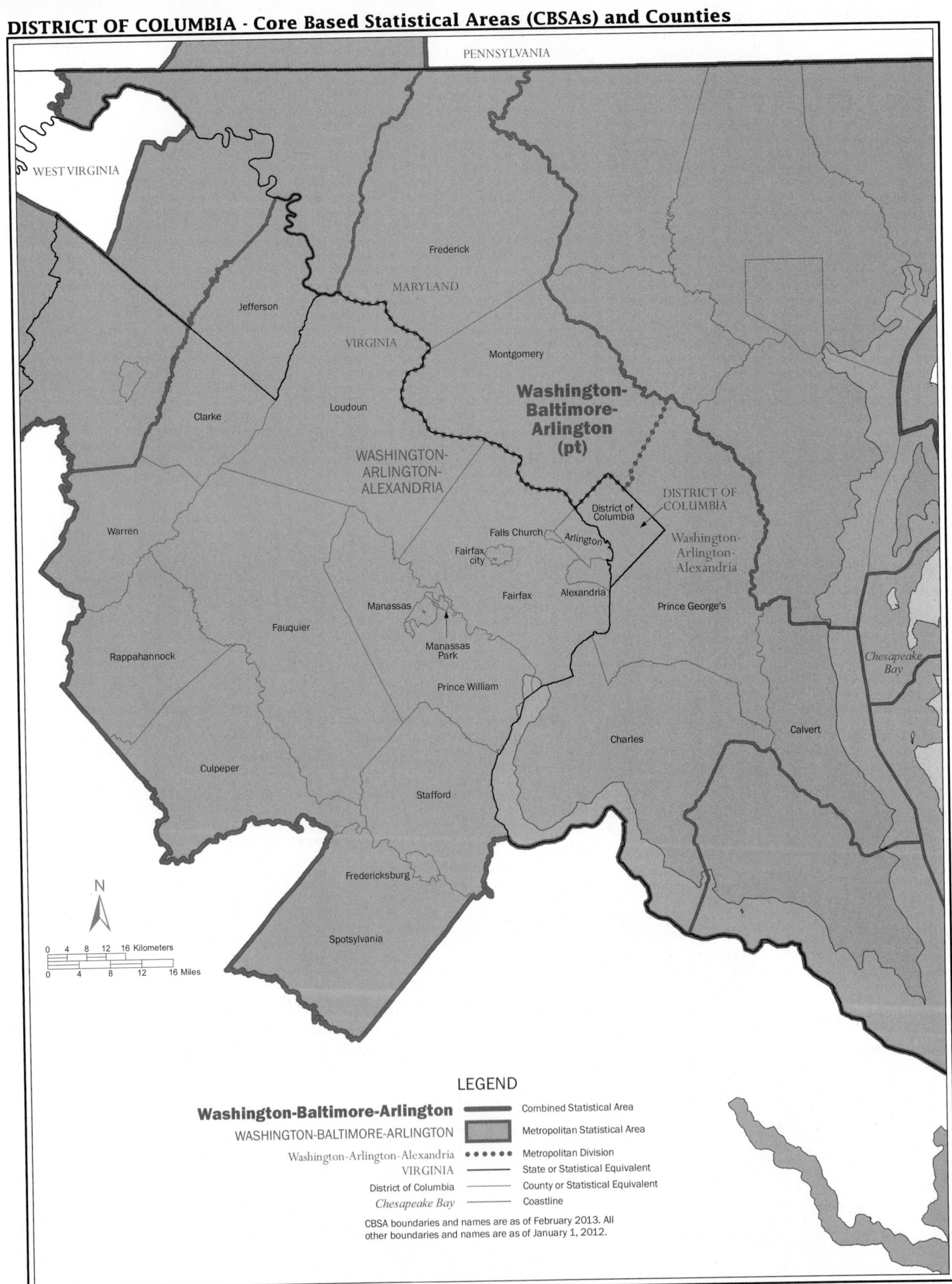

PENNSYLVANIA

WEST VIRGINIA

Frederick

MARYLAND

Jefferson

VIRGINIA

Montgomery

Clarke

Loudoun

Washington-Baltimore-Arlington (pt)

WASHINGTON-ARLINGTON-ALEXANDRIA

DISTRICT OF COLUMBIA

Warren

District of Columbia

Falls Church

Arlington

Washington-Arlington-Alexandria

Fairfax city

Manassas

Fairfax

Alexandria

Fauquier

Manassas Park

Prince George's

Rappahannock

Prince William

Chesapeake Bay

Charles

Calvert

Culpeper

Stafford

N

0 4 8 12 16 Kilometers

0 4 8 12 16 Miles

Fredericksburg

Spotsylvania

LEGEND

Washington-Baltimore-Arlington   Combined Statistical Area

WASHINGTON-BALTIMORE-ARLINGTON   Metropolitan Statistical Area

Washington-Arlington-Alexandria   ••••• Metropolitan Division

VIRGINIA   State or Statistical Equivalent

District of Columbia   County or Statistical Equivalent

Chesapeake Bay   Coastline

CBSA boundaries and names are as of February 2013. All
other boundaries and names are as of January 1, 2012.

FLORIDA - Core Based Statistical Areas (CBSAs) and Counties

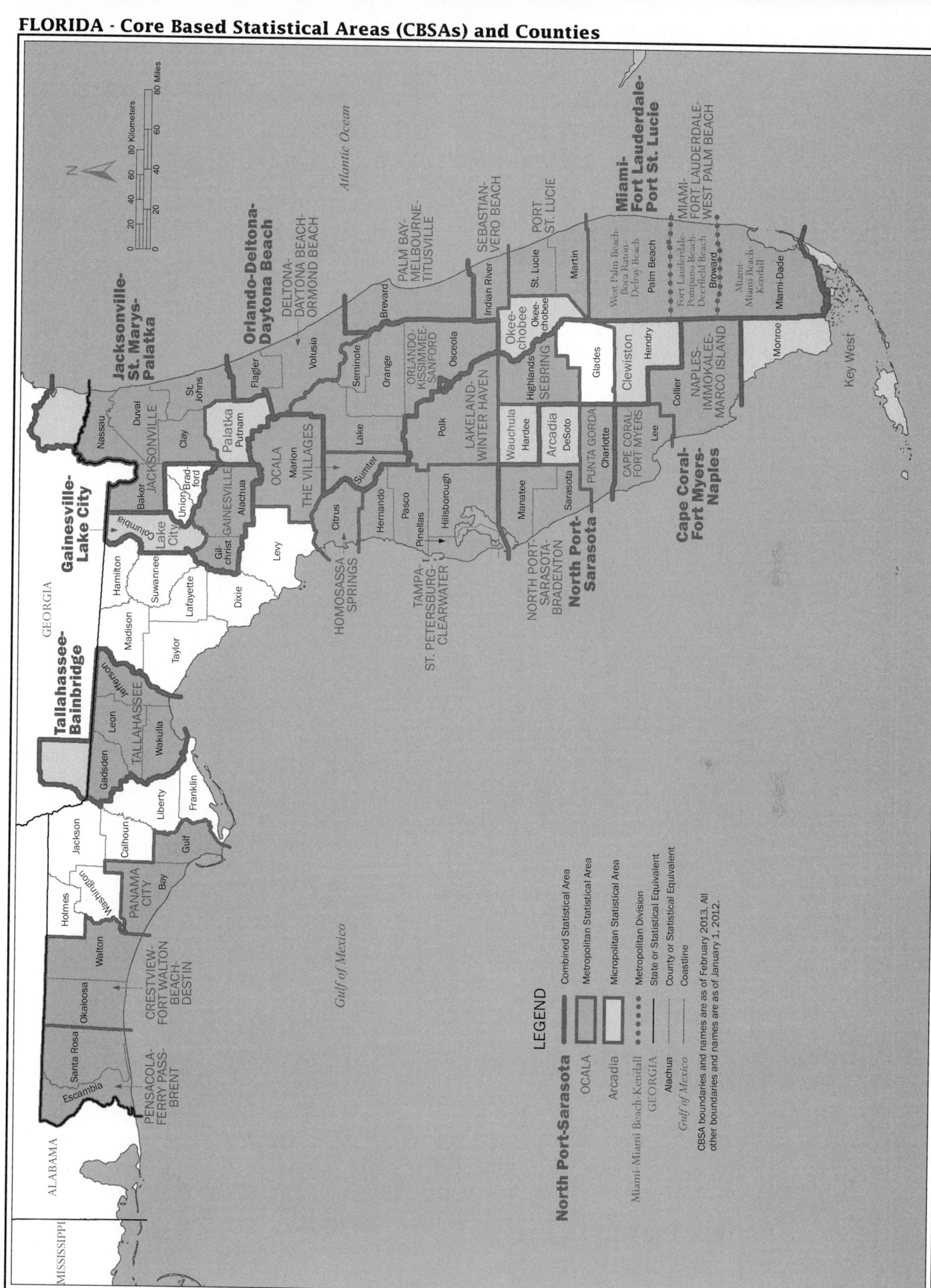

GEORGIA - Core Based Statistical Areas (CBSAs) and Counties

TENNESSEE

Chattanooga-Cleveland-Dalton (pt)

NORTH CAROLINA

LEGEND

Rome-Summerville — Combined Statistical Area

ROME — Metropolitan Statistical Area

Jesup — Micropolitan Statistical Area

ALABAMA — State or Statistical Equivalent

Harris — County or Statistical Equivalent

Atlantic Ocean — Coastline

CBSA boundaries and names are as of February 2013. All other boundaries and names are as of January 1, 2012.

Sequatchie
Hamilton
CHATTANOOGA
Marion

Dade
Catoosa
DALTON
Murray
Whitfield
Walker
Summerville
Chattooga
ROME
Floyd
Cedartown
Polk
Haralson
ATLANTA-SANDY SPRINGS-ROSWELL
ALABAMA
Carroll
Heard
LaGrange
Troup
Harris
COLUMBUS
Russell
Muscogee
Chattahoochee

Fannin
Towns
Rabun
Union
Gilmer
White
Lumpkin
Calhoun
Gordon
Pickens
Dawson
Rome-Summerville
Cherokee
Forsyth
Bartow
Atlanta--Athens-Clarke County--Sandy Springs
Paulding
Cobb
Gwinnett
Douglas
Fulton
DeKalb
Clayton
Rockdale
Walton
Coweta
Fayette
Henry
Newton
Morgan
Spalding
Butts
Jasper
Meriwether
Pike
Lamar
Monroe
Jones
Thomaston
Upson
Macon-Warner Robins
MACON
Talbot
Crawford
Bibb
Taylor
Peach
Marion
WARNER ROBINS
Houston
Twiggs
Schley
Macon

Cornelia
Habersham
TOCCOA
Stephens
GAINESVILLE
Banks
Franklin
Hart
Hall
Jefferson
Jackson
Madison
Elbert
Barrow
Clarke
ATHENS-CLARKE COUNTY
Oconee
Oglethorpe
Wilkes
Lincoln
Greene
Taliaferro
Warren
Putnam
Milledgeville
Hancock
Glascock
Jefferson
Baldwin
Washington
Wilkinson
Johnson

SOUTH CAROLINA

Edgefield
Aiken
Columbia
AUGUSTA-RICHMOND COUNTY
McDuffie
Richmond
Burke

Savannah-Hinesville-Statesboro

Jenkins
Screven
Emanuel
Candler
Statesboro
Bulloch
Effingham

Stewart
Webster
Sumter
Americus
Cordele
Crisp
Dooly
Wilcox
Dodge
Dublin
Laurens
Treutlen
Montgomery
Wheeler
Vidalia
Toombs
Tattnall
Evans
Bryan
SAVANNAH
Chatham
Liberty
HINESVILLE
Long

Columbus-Auburn-Opelika

Quitman
Randolph
Clay
Calhoun
Terrell
Lee
ALBANY
Turner
Ben Hill
Fitzgerald
Telfair
Jeff Davis
Appling
Bacon
Jesup
Wayne
McIntosh
Early
Baker
Dougherty
Worth
Tift
Irwin
Douglas
Coffee
Pierce
BRUNSWICK
Glynn
Miller
Mitchell
Moultrie
Colquitt
Berrien
Atkinson
Waycross
Ware
Brantley
Seminole
Bainbridge
Decatur
Grady
Thomasville
Thomas
Brooks
Cook
Lanier
VALDOSTA
Lowndes
Clinch
Charlton
St. Marys
Camden
Echols

Atlantic Ocean

Jacksonville-St. Marys-Palatka (pt)

Tallahassee-Bainbridge (pt)

FLORIDA

N

0 10 20 30 40 Kilometers
0 10 20 30 40 Miles

Hilo
Hawaii

Kalawao
Maui

KAHULUI-
WAILUKU-
LAHAINA

Honolulu
(pt)

URBAN
HONOLULU
(pt)

Kauai
Kapaa

URBAN HONOLULU
(pt)

Honolulu
(pt)

Pacific Ocean

N

0 40 80 120 160 Kilometers
0 40 80 120 160 Miles

LEGEND

URBAN HONOLULU	Metropolitan Statistical Area
Hilo	Micropolitan Statistical Area
Maui	State or Statistical Equivalent
	County or Statistical Equivalent
	Coastline
Pacific Ocean	

CBSA boundaries and names are as of February 2013. All
other boundaries and names are as of January 1, 2012.

URBAN
HONOLULU
(pt)

Honolulu
(pt)

MIDWAY
ISLANDS
(U.S.
Unincorporated
Territory)

U.S. DEPARTMENT OF COMMERCE Economics and Statistics Administration U.S. Census Bureau

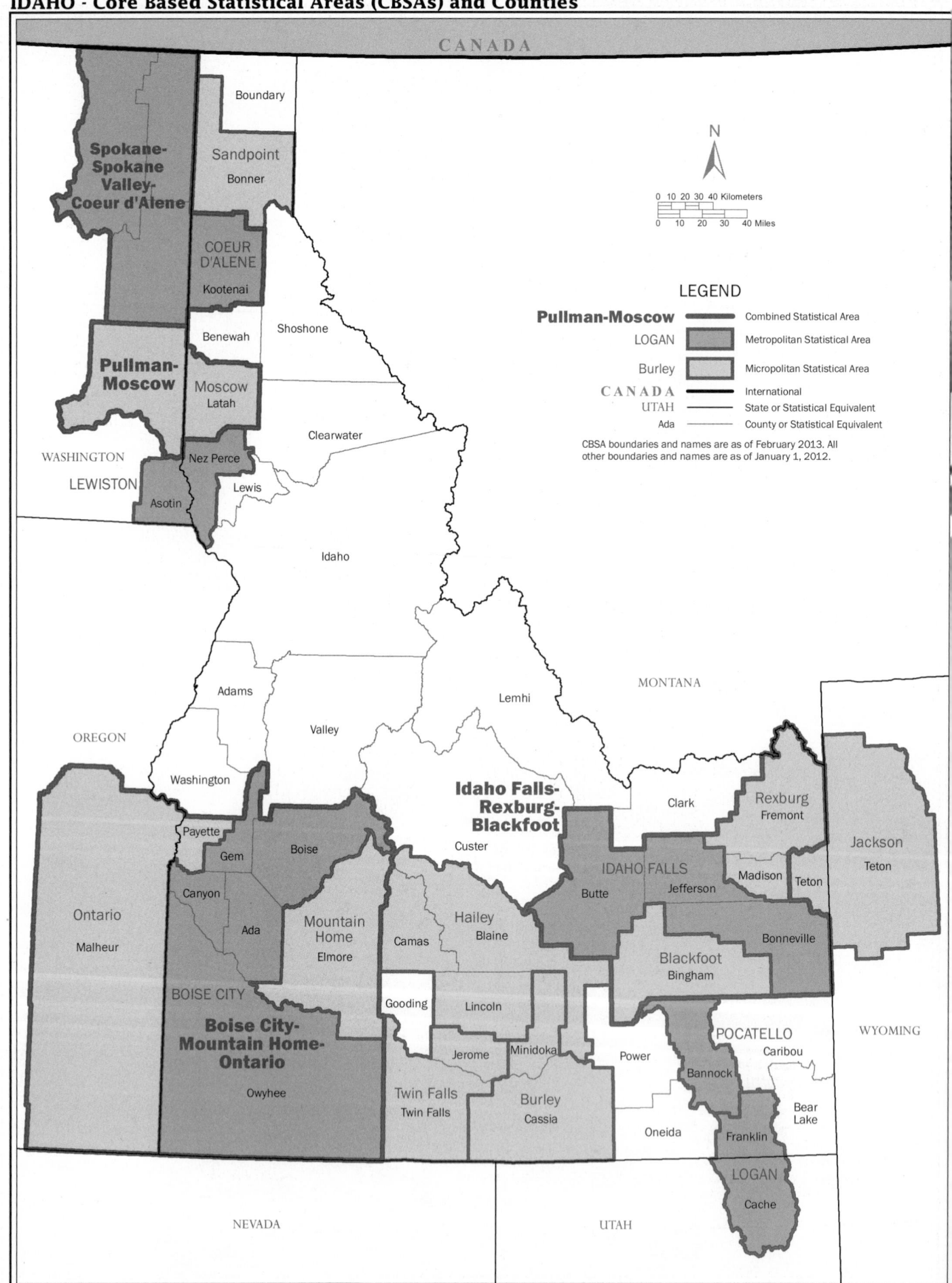

ILLINOIS - Core Based Statistical Areas (CBSAs) and Counties

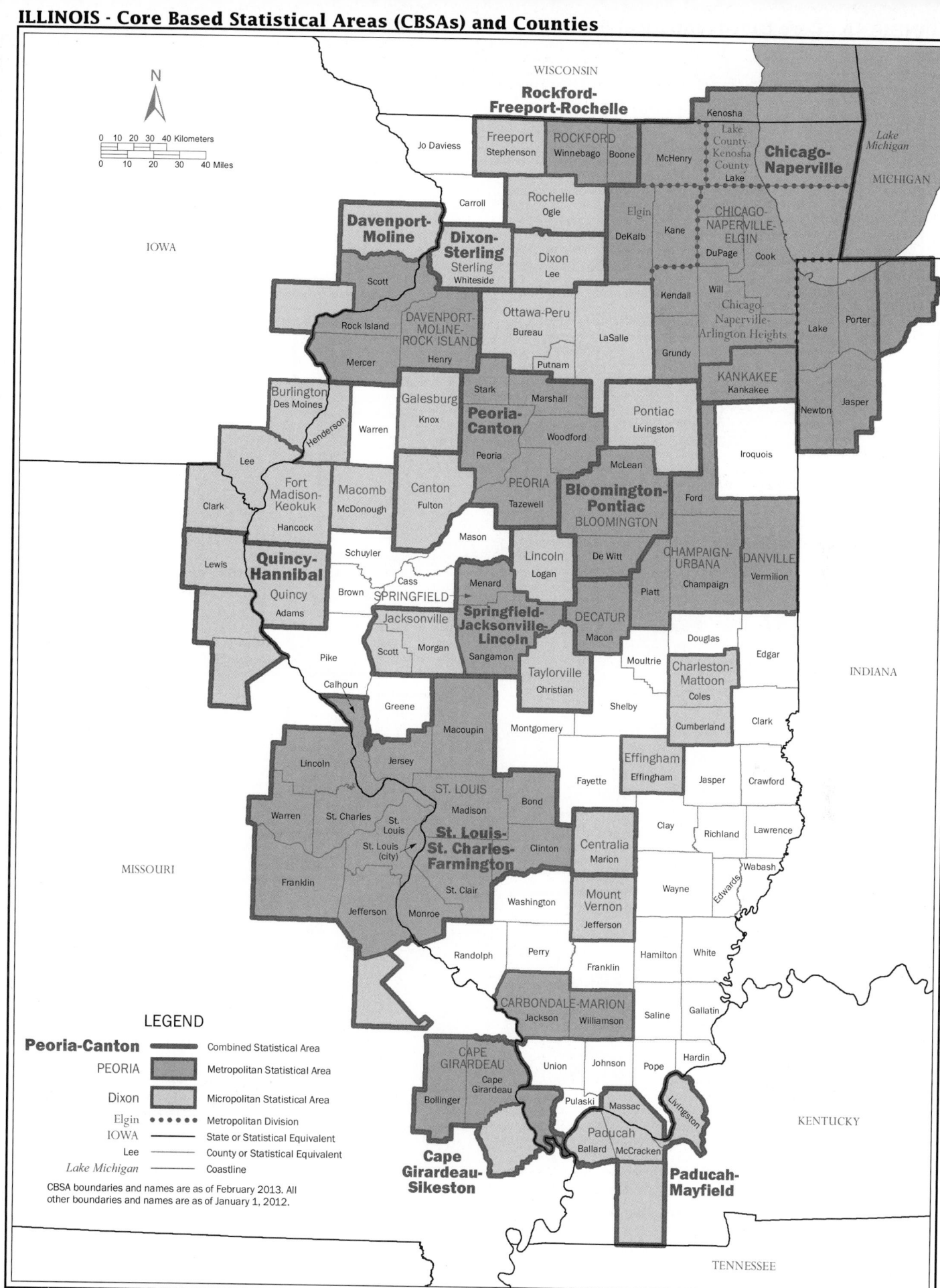

LEGEND

Peoria-Canton ━━━ Combined Statistical Area

PEORIA ▓▓▓ Metropolitan Statistical Area

Dixon ░░░ Micropolitan Statistical Area

Elgin • • • Metropolitan Division

IOWA ─── State or Statistical Equivalent

Lee ─── County or Statistical Equivalent

Lake Michigan ─── Coastline

CBSA boundaries and names are as of February 2013. All other boundaries and names are as of January 1, 2012.

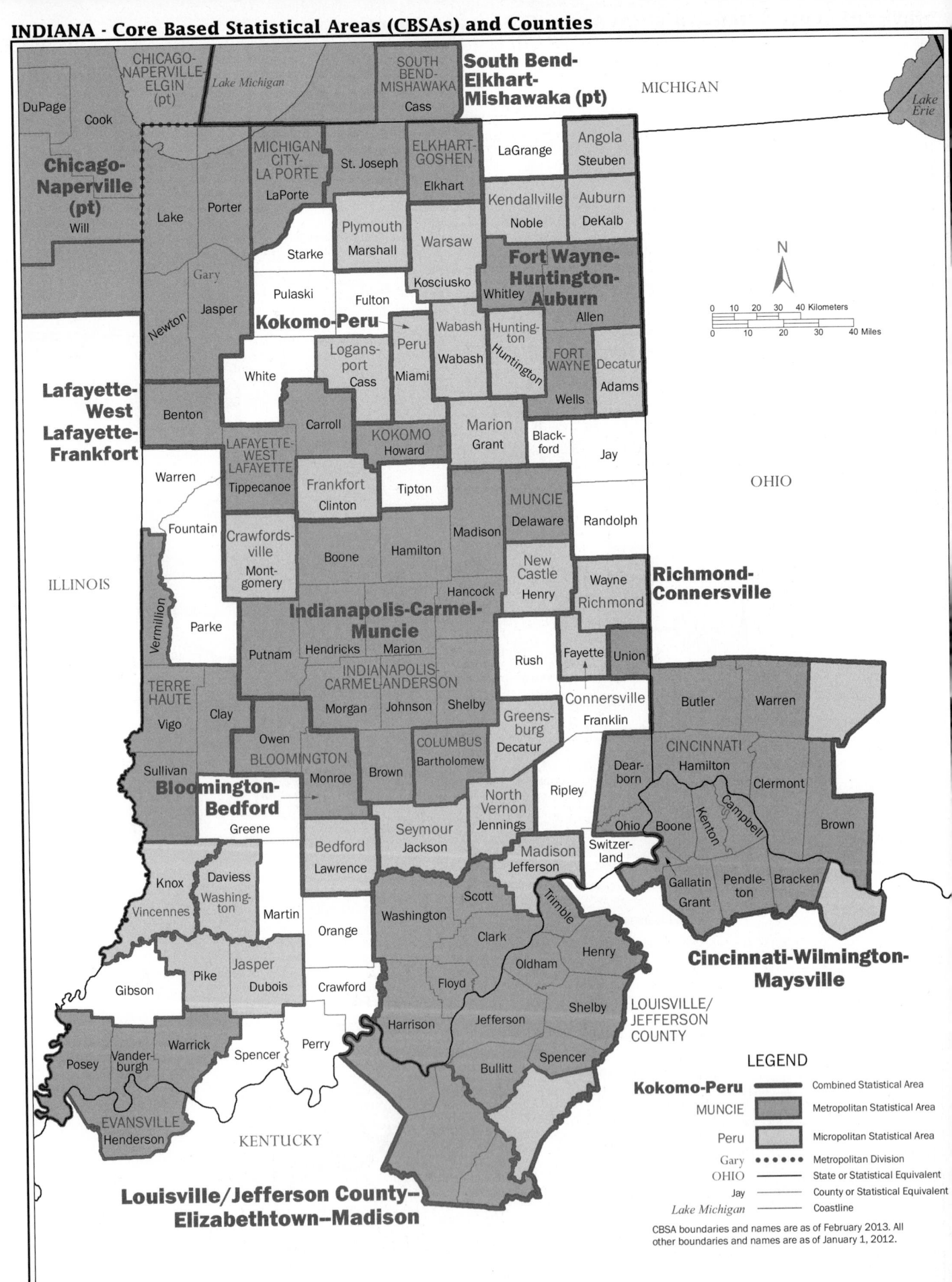

LEGEND

Kokomo-Peru	Combined Statistical Area
MUNCIE	Metropolitan Statistical Area
Peru	Micropolitan Statistical Area
Gary	Metropolitan Division
OHIO	State or Statistical Equivalent
Jay	County or Statistical Equivalent
Lake Michigan	Coastline

CBSA boundaries and names are as of February 2013. All other boundaries and names are as of January 1, 2012.

IOWA - Core Based Statistical Areas (CBSAs) and Counties

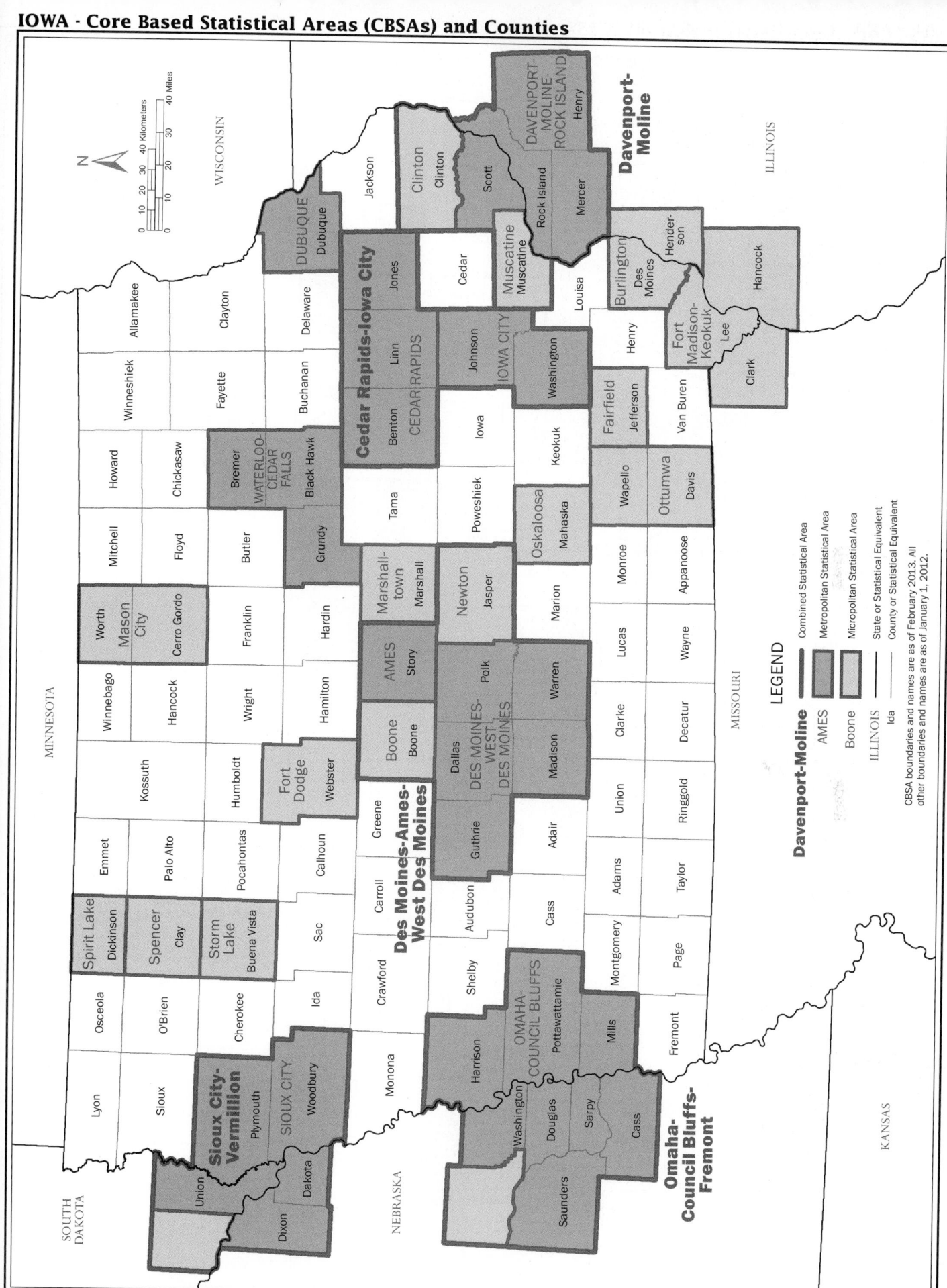

KANSAS - Core Based Statistical Areas (CBSAs) and Counties

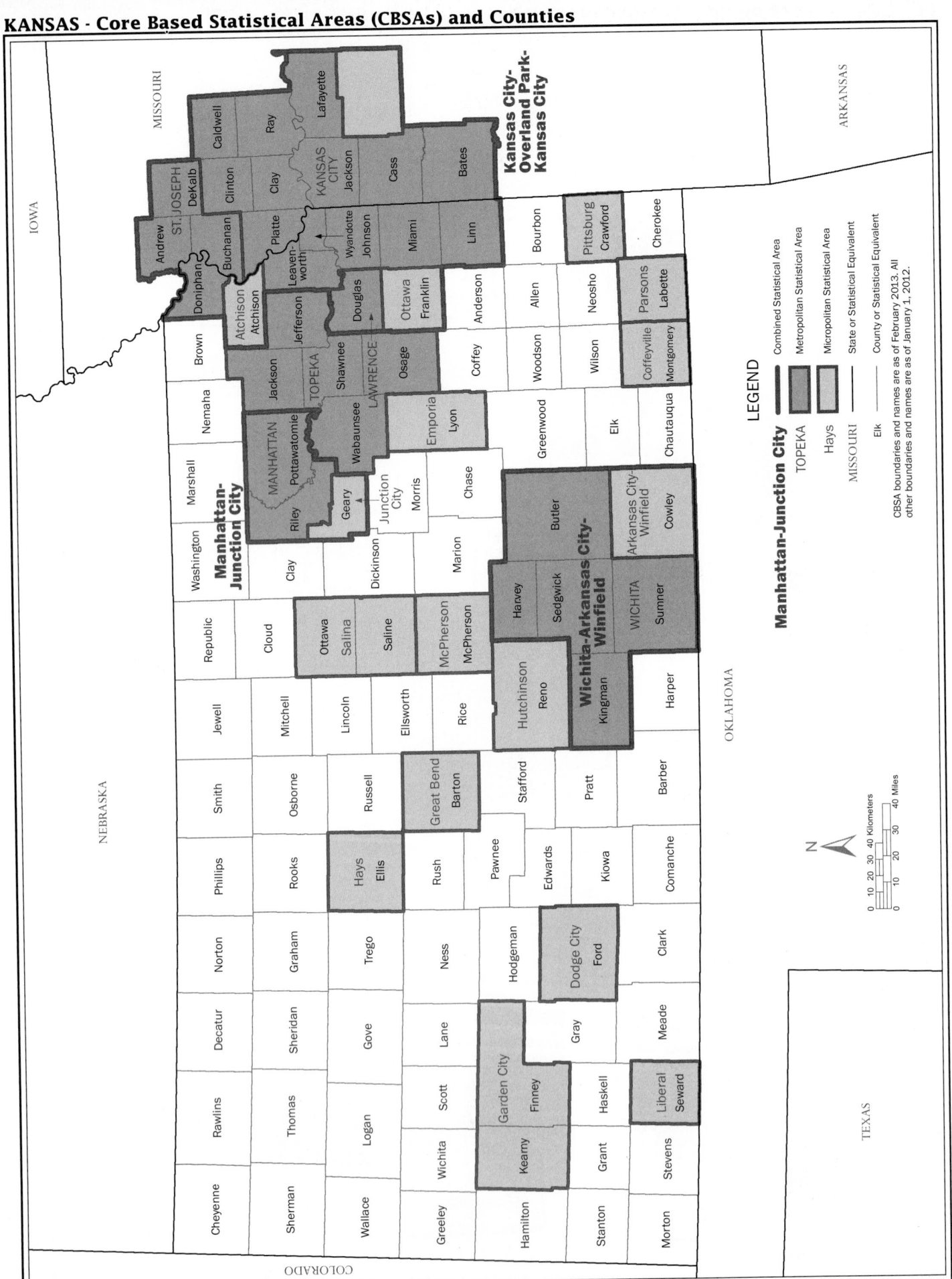

LEGEND

Manhattan-Junction City — Combined Statistical Area

TOPEKA — Metropolitan Statistical Area

Hays — Micropolitan Statistical Area

MISSOURI — State or Statistical Equivalent

Elk — County or Statistical Equivalent

CBSA boundaries and names are as of February 2013. All other boundaries and names are as of January 1, 2012.

0 10 20 30 40 Kilometers
0 10 20 30 40 Miles

KENTUCKY - Core Based Statistical Areas (CBSAs) and Counties

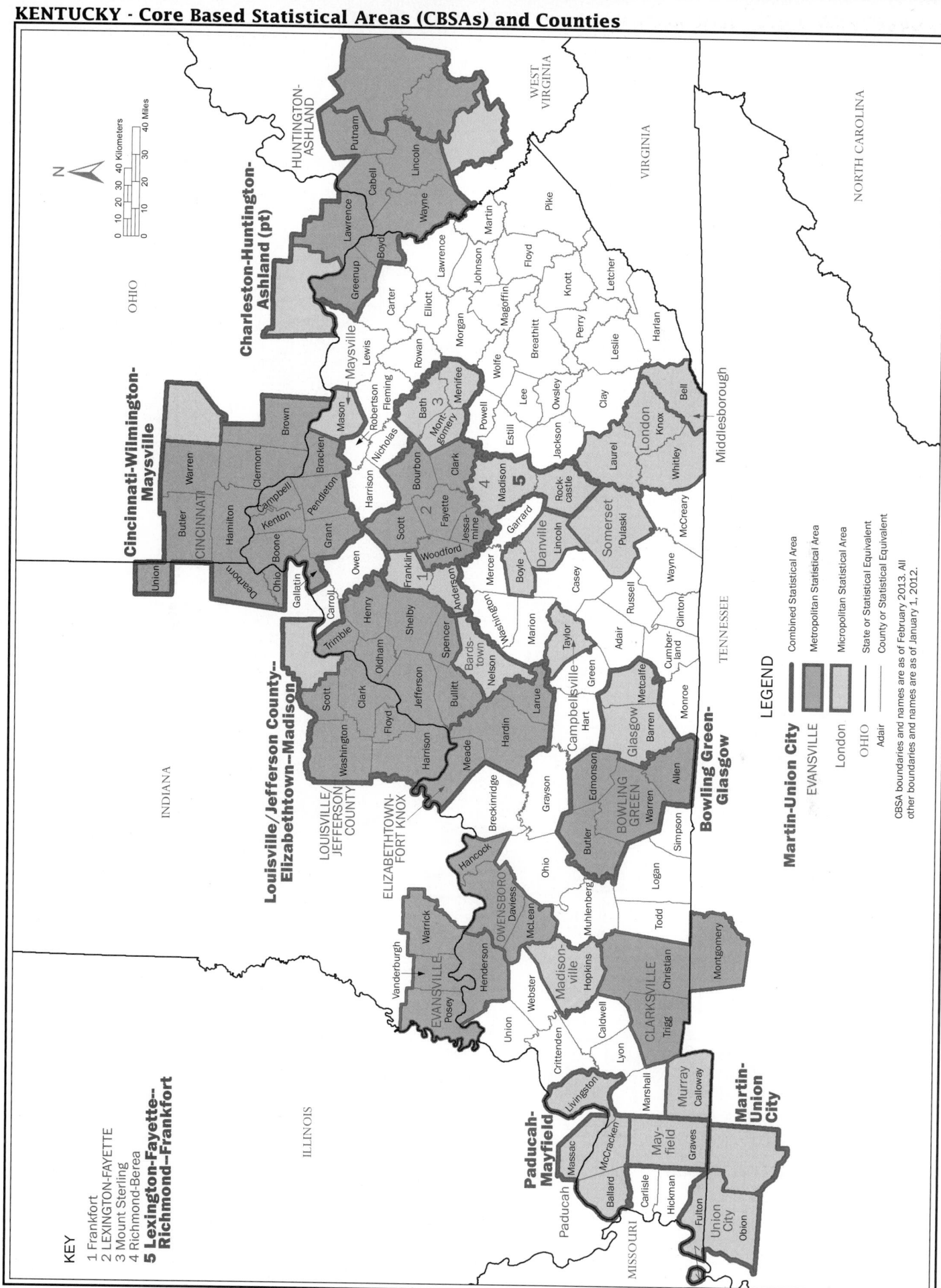

LOUISIANA - Core Based Statistical Areas (CBSAs) and Counties

ALABAMA

Gulf of Mexico

MISSISSIPPI

LEGEND

Monroe-Ruston-Bastrop

Combined Statistical Area

MONROE — Metropolitan Statistical Area

Ruston — Micropolitan Statistical Area

TEXAS — State or Statistical Equivalent

Winn — County or Statistical Equivalent

Gulf of Mexico — Coastline

CBSA boundaries and names are as of February 2013. All other boundaries and names are as of January 1, 2012.

N

0 10 20 30 40 Miles
0 10 20 30 40 Kilometers

New Orleans-Metairie-Hammond

HAMMOND

Bogalusa
Washington
St. Tammany
Orleans
Jefferson
Tangipahoa
St. Helena
Livingston
St. John the Baptist
St. Charles
St. Bernard
Plaquemines
NEW ORLEANS-METAIRIE
Lafourche
HOUMA-THIBODAUX
Terrebonne
BATON ROUGE
East Feliciana
East Baton Rouge
Ascension
St. James
Assumption
West Feliciana
West Baton Rouge
Pointe Coupee
Iberville
Morgan City
St. Mary
Adams
Natchez
Concordia
Avoyelles
Opelousas
St. Landry
St. Martin
Iberia
Lafayette
LAFAYETTE
Vermilion
Lafayette-Opelousas-Morgan City
Gulf of Mexico

East Carroll
Madison
Tensas
West Carroll
Morehouse
Bastrop
Richland
Franklin
Catahoula
LaSalle
Monroe-Ruston-Bastrop
Union
MONROE
Ouachita
Ruston
Lincoln
Jackson
Caldwell
Winn
Grant
ALEXANDRIA
Rapides
Evangeline
Allen
Acadia
Jefferson Davis
Claiborne
Bienville
Webster
Natchitoches
SHREVEPORT-BOSSIER CITY
Bossier
Caddo
Red River
De Soto
Sabine
Natchitoches
DeRidder-Fort Polk South
Fort Polk South
Vernon
DeRidder
Beauregard
Calcasieu
LAKE CHARLES
Cameron

ARKANSAS

TEXAS

U.S. DEPARTMENT OF COMMERCE Economics and Statistics Administration U.S. Census Bureau

D-22

Appendix D

MAINE - Core Based Statistical Areas (CBSAs) and Counties

N

| 0 | 10 | 20 | 30 | 40 Kilometers |
| 0 | 10 | 20 | 30 | 40 Miles |

CANADA

Aroostook

Piscataquis

Somerset

BANGOR

Penobscot

Franklin

Washington

Oxford

Augusta-Waterville

Kennebec

Waldo

Hancock

NEW HAMPSHIRE

Andro-scoggin

LEWISTON-AUBURN

Knox

Lincoln

Atlantic Ocean

Sagadahoc

Cumberland

PORTLAND-SOUTH PORTLAND

York

Portland-Lewiston-South Portland

LEGEND

Portland-Lewiston-South Portland ——— Combined Statistical Area

BANGOR ⬜ Metropolitan Statistical Area

Augusta-Waterville ⬜ Micropolitan Statistical Area

CANADA ——— International

NEW HAMPSHIRE ——— State or Statistical Equivalent

Knox ——— County or Statistical Equivalent

Atlantic Ocean ——— Coastline

CBSA boundaries and names are as of February 2013. All other boundaries and names are as of January 1, 2012.

U.S. DEPARTMENT OF COMMERCE Economics and Statistics Administration U.S. Census Bureau

MARYLAND - Core Based Statistical Areas (CBSAs) and Counties

Burlington

Camden

Gloucester

Salem

NEW JERSEY

DELAWARE

Delaware

Wilmington

New Castle

Chester

PHILADELPHIA-CAMDEN-WILMINGTON (pt)

Cecil

Philadelphia-Reading-Camden (pt)

Sussex

Atlantic Ocean

SALISBURY

Worcester

Wicomico

Somerset

Caroline

Kent

Queen Anne's

Easton

Talbot

Cambridge

Dorchester

Chesapeake Bay

Harford

BALTIMORE-COLUMBIA-TOWSON

Baltimore

Baltimore (city)

Anne Arundel

PENNSYLVANIA

Carroll

Howard

Prince George's

Calvert

CALIFORNIA-LEXINGTON PARK

St. Mary's

Frederick

Silver Spring-Frederick-Rockville

Montgomery

District of Columbia

Washington-Arlington-Alexandria

Charles

VIRGINIA

HAGERSTOWN-MARTINSBURG

Washington

Loudoun

Arlington

Falls Church

Fairfax (city)

Alexandria

Fairfax

Manassas Park

Stafford

Berkeley

Jefferson

Clarke

WASHINGTON-ARLINGTON-ALEXANDRIA

Prince William

Manassas

Fredericksburg

Spotsylvania

Washington-Baltimore-Arlington (pt)

CUMBERLAND

Allegany

Mineral

Warren

Fauquier

Rappahannock

Culpeper

VIRGINIA

Garrett

WEST VIRGINIA

N

0 10 20 30 40 Miles

0 10 20 30 40 Kilometers

LEGEND

Washington-Baltimore-Arlington

SALISBURY — Metropolitan Statistical Area

Easton — Micropolitan Statistical Area

Combined Statistical Area

Silver Spring-Frederick-Rockville ···· Metropolitan Division

VIRGINIA — State or Statistical Equivalent

Kent — County or Statistical Equivalent

Atlantic Ocean — Coastline

CBSA boundaries and names are as of February 2013. All other boundaries and names are as of January 1, 2012.

U.S. DEPARTMENT OF COMMERCE Economics and Statistics Administration U.S. Census Bureau

D-24

Appendix D

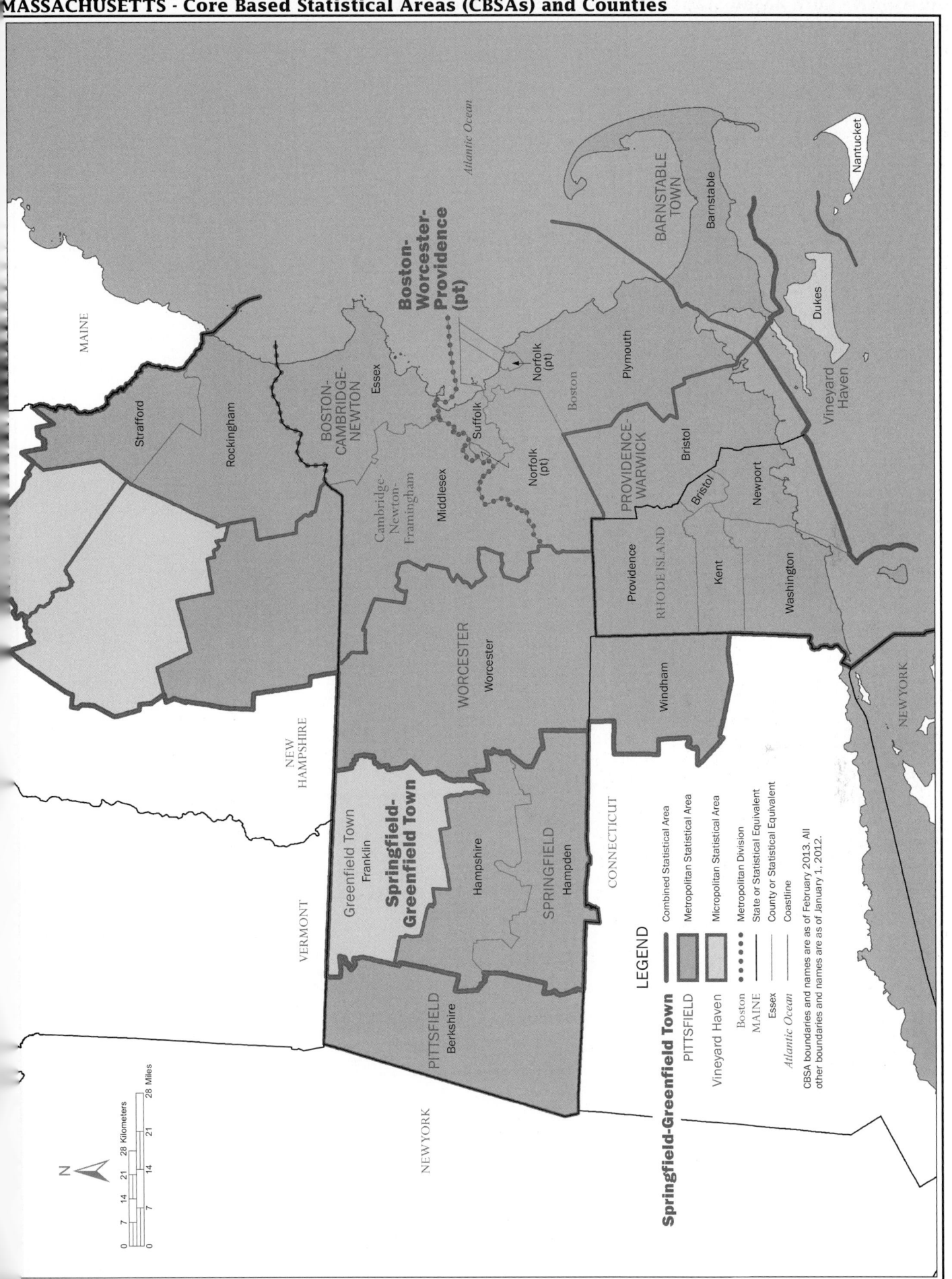

MICHIGAN - Core Based Statistical Areas (CBSAs) and Counties

U.S. DEPARTMENT OF COMMERCE Economics and Statistics Administration U.S. Census Bureau

MINNESOTA - Core Based Statistical Areas (CBSAs) and Counties

N

0 10 20 30 40 Kilometers
0 10 20 30 40 Miles

LEGEND

Rochester-Austin	Combined Statistical Area
DULUTH	Metropolitan Statistical Area
Austin	Micropolitan Statistical Area
CANADA	International
IOWA	State or Statistical Equivalent
Cook	County or Statistical Equivalent
Lake Superior	Coastline

CBSA boundaries and names are as of February 2013. All
other boundaries and names are as of January 1, 2012.

CANADA

Kittson
Roseau
Lake of the Woods

NORTH DAKOTA

Marshall

Koochiching

Cook

Pennington
GRAND FORKS
Red Lake

Grand Forks
GRAND FORKS

Bemidji
Beltrami

Lake

Polk

Clearwater

St. Louis

Lake Superior

Norman
Mahnomen

Itasca

DULUTH

Fargo-Wahpeton
FARGO
Cass

Clay

Hubbard

Brainerd
Cass

MICHIGAN

Becker

Wadena

Aitkin

Carlton

Wilkin

Crow Wing

Douglas

Wahpeton
Richland

Fergus Falls
Otter Tail

Todd

Mille Lacs

Pine

Kanabec

Grant

Alexandria
Douglas

Morrison

Traverse

Stevens

Pope

ST. CLOUD
Stearns

Benton

Isanti

Chisago

Minneapolis-St. Paul

WISCONSIN

Big Stone

Swift

Sherburne

Anoka
Ramsey

Washington

MINNEAPOLIS-ST. PAUL-BLOOMINGTON

Willmar
Kandiyohi

Meeker

Wright

St. Croix

Lac qui Parle

Chippewa

Hutchinson

Hennepin

Pierce

Yellow Medicine

Renville

McLeod

Carver

Scott

Dakota

SOUTH DAKOTA

Lincoln

Marshall
Lyon

Redwood

Sibley

Le Sueur

Faribault-Northfield
Rice

Red Wing
Goodhue

Nicollet

Wabasha

Brown
New Ulm

Pipe-stone

MANKATO-NORTH MANKATO
Murray   Cottonwood Watonwan

Blue Earth

Waseca

Owatonna
Steele

Rochester-Austin

Winona
Winona

La Crosse

Rock

Worthington
Nobles

Jackson

Martin

Faribault

Albert Lea
Freeborn

Austin
Mower

ROCHESTER
Fillmore

Houston

LA CROSSE-ONALASKA

Mankato-New Ulm-North Mankato

IOWA

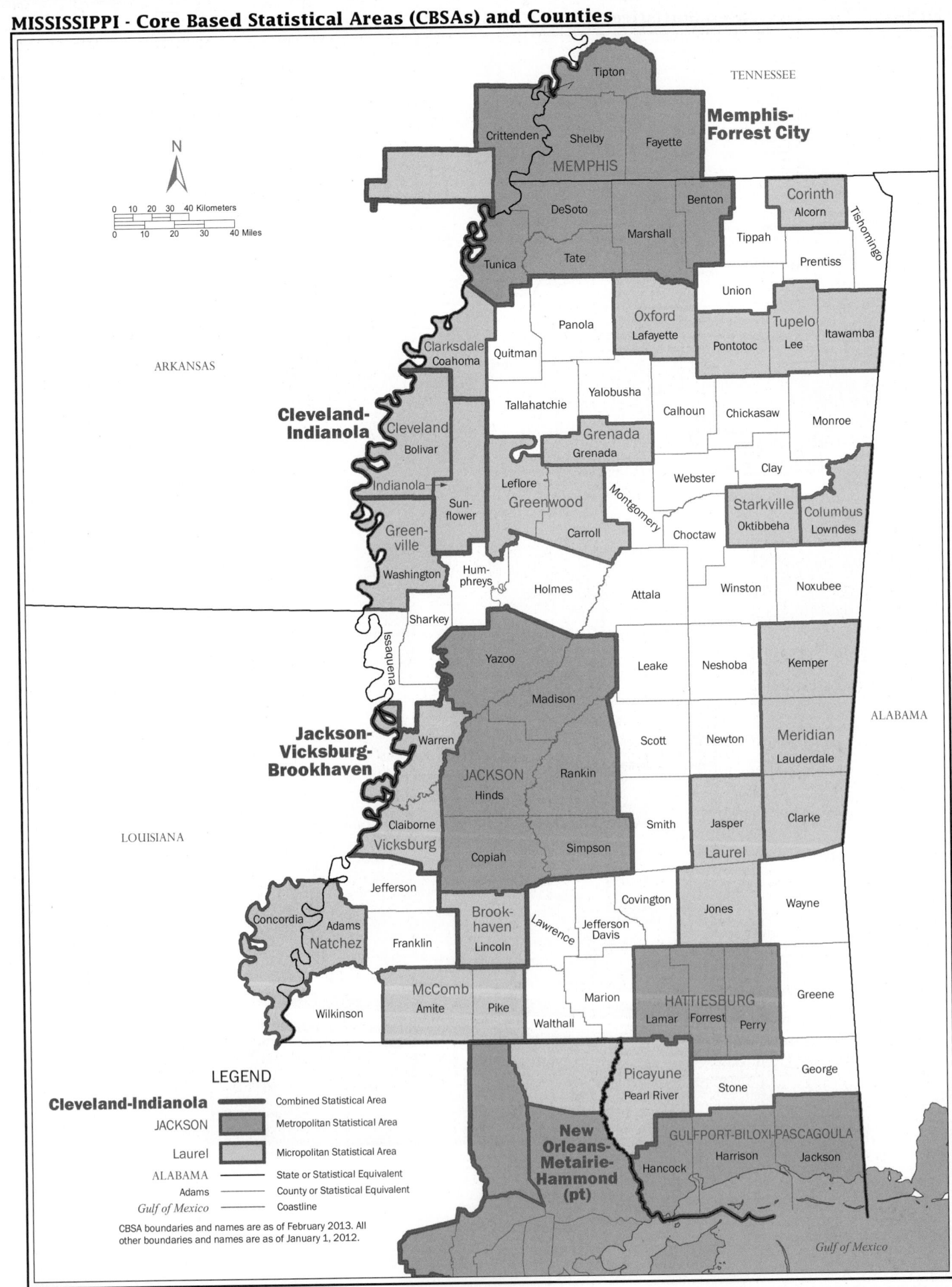

N

0 10 20 30 40 Kilometers
0 10 20 30 40 Miles

TENNESSEE

Tipton

Memphis-Forrest City

Crittenden
Shelby
Fayette

MEMPHIS

DeSoto
Benton

Marshall

Corinth
Alcorn

Tippah

Tishomingo

Prentiss

ARKANSAS

Tunica
Tate

Union

Panola

Oxford
Lafayette

Tupelo

Clarksdale
Coahoma

Quitman

Pontotoc

Lee

Itawamba

Cleveland-Indianola

Cleveland

Tallahatchie

Yalobusha

Calhoun

Chickasaw

Monroe

Bolivar

Indianola

Grenada
Grenada

Sunflower

Leflore

Webster

Clay

Starkville
Oktibbeha

Columbus
Lowndes

Green-ville

Greenwood

Montgomery

Choctaw

Washington

Carroll

Hum-phreys

Holmes

Attala

Winston

Noxubee

Sharkey

Yazoo

Leake

Neshoba

Kemper

Issaquena

Madison

ALABAMA

Jackson-Vicksburg-Brookhaven

Warren

Scott

Newton

Meridian
Lauderdale

JACKSON

Rankin

Hinds

LOUISIANA

Claiborne

Smith

Jasper

Clarke

Vicksburg

Copiah

Simpson

Laurel

Jefferson

Covington

Jones

Wayne

Concordia

Adams

Brook-haven

Lawrence

Jefferson
Davis

Natchez

Franklin

Lincoln

Wilkinson

McComb
Amite

Pike

Walthall

Marion

HATTIESBURG

Lamar Forrest

Perry

Greene

Picayune
Pearl River

Stone

George

New Orleans-Metairie-Hammond (pt)

GULFPORT-BILOXI-PASCAGOULA

Hancock

Harrison

Jackson

Gulf of Mexico

LEGEND

Cleveland-Indianola ——— Combined Statistical Area

JACKSON ▨ Metropolitan Statistical Area

Laurel ▨ Micropolitan Statistical Area

ALABAMA ——— State or Statistical Equivalent

Adams ——— County or Statistical Equivalent

Gulf of Mexico ——— Coastline

CBSA boundaries and names are as of February 2013. All
other boundaries and names are as of January 1, 2012.

MISSOURI - Core Based Statistical Areas (CBSAs) and Counties

LEGEND

Joplin-Miami Combined Statistical Area

JOPLIN Metropolitan Statistical Area

Maryville Micropolitan Statistical Area

IOWA State or Statistical Equivalent

Adair County or Statistical Equivalent

CBSA boundaries and names are as of February 2013. All other boundaries and names are as of January 1, 2012.

ILLINOIS

KENTUCKY

TENNESSEE

ARKANSAS

OKLAHOMA

KANSAS

NEBRASKA

IOWA

Mississippi

St. Louis-St. Charles-Farmington

Cape Girardeau-Sikeston

Quincy-Hannibal

Columbia-Moberly-Mexico

Kansas City-Overland Park-Kansas City

Springfield-Branson

Joplin-Miami

FAYETTEVILLE-SPRINGDALE-ROGERS

Fort Madison-Keokuk

ST. JOSEPH

KANSAS CITY

JEFFERSON CITY

COLUMBIA

SPRINGFIELD

JOPLIN

CAPE GIRARDEAU

Poplar Bluff

West Plains

Rolla

Fort Leonard Wood

Lebanon

Sedalia

Marshall

Warrensburg

Kirksville

Hannibal

Quincy

Sikeston

Branson

Counties (labels)

Bond, Clinton, Macoupin, Madison, ST. LOUIS, St. Clair, Monroe, Jersey, St. Louis (city), St. Louis, Jefferson, St. Charles, Warren, Franklin, Lincoln, Calhoun, Pike, Montgomery, Gasconade, Crawford, Washington, Farmington, Iron, Reynolds, Carter, Ripley, Shannon, Oregon, Dent, Texas, Howell, Ozark, Douglas, Wright, Laclede, Maries, Phelps, Pulaski, Cole, Osage, Callaway, Boone, Audrain, Mexico, Monroe, Randolph, Moberly, Shelby, Knox, Marion, Lewis, Clark, Hancock, Adams, Lee, Scotland, Schuyler, Adair, Macon, Chariton, Howard, Cooper, Moniteau, Miller, Morgan, Camden, Benton, Hickory, Dallas, Polk, Greene, Webster, Christian, Stone, Taney, Newton, McDonald, Barry, Lawrence, Dade, Cedar, St. Clair, Vernon, Barton, Jasper, Benton, Washington, Madison, Putnam, Sullivan, Linn, Livingston, Mercer, Grundy, Harrison, Daviess, Caldwell, Ray, Lafayette, Saline, Pettis, Johnson, Henry, Worth, Gentry, DeKalb, Clinton, Clay, Jackson, Cass, Johnson, Bates, Linn, Miami, Wyandotte, Leavenworth, Platte, Buchanan, Andrew, Nodaway, Maryville, Holt, Doniphan, Atchison, Perry, Ste. Genevieve, St. Francois, Bollinger, Cape Girardeau, Scott, Stoddard, Wayne, New Madrid, Pemiscot, Dunklin, Kennett, Butler

N

0 10 20 30 40 Kilometers
0 10 20 30 40 Miles

U.S. DEPARTMENT OF COMMERCE Economics and Statistics Administration U.S. Census Bureau

Appendix D

MONTANA - Core Based Statistical Areas (CBSAs) and Counties

NORTH DAKOTA

SOUTH DAKOTA

Sheridan

Richland

Wibaux

Fallon

Carter

Roosevelt

Dawson

Daniels

McCone

Prairie

Custer

Powder River

Valley

Garfield

Rosebud

Phillips

Petroleum

Musselshell

Treasure

Big Horn

Yellowstone

BILLINGS

Blaine

Fergus

Golden Valley

Stillwater

Carbon

Hill

Chouteau

Judith Basin

Wheatland

Sweet Grass

Meagher

Park

Liberty

GREAT FALLS

Cascade

Broadwater

BOZEMAN

Gallatin

Toole

Helena

Jefferson

Madison

Teton

Lewis and Clark

Silver Bow

Pondera

Powell

Deer Lodge

Butte-Silver Bow

Beaverhead

Glacier

Granite

Kalispell

Flathead

Lake

MISSOULA

Missoula

Ravalli

Lincoln

Sanders

Mineral

CANADA

WYOMING

IDAHO

80 Miles
80 Kilometers

NEBRASKA - Core Based Statistical Areas (CBSAs) and Counties

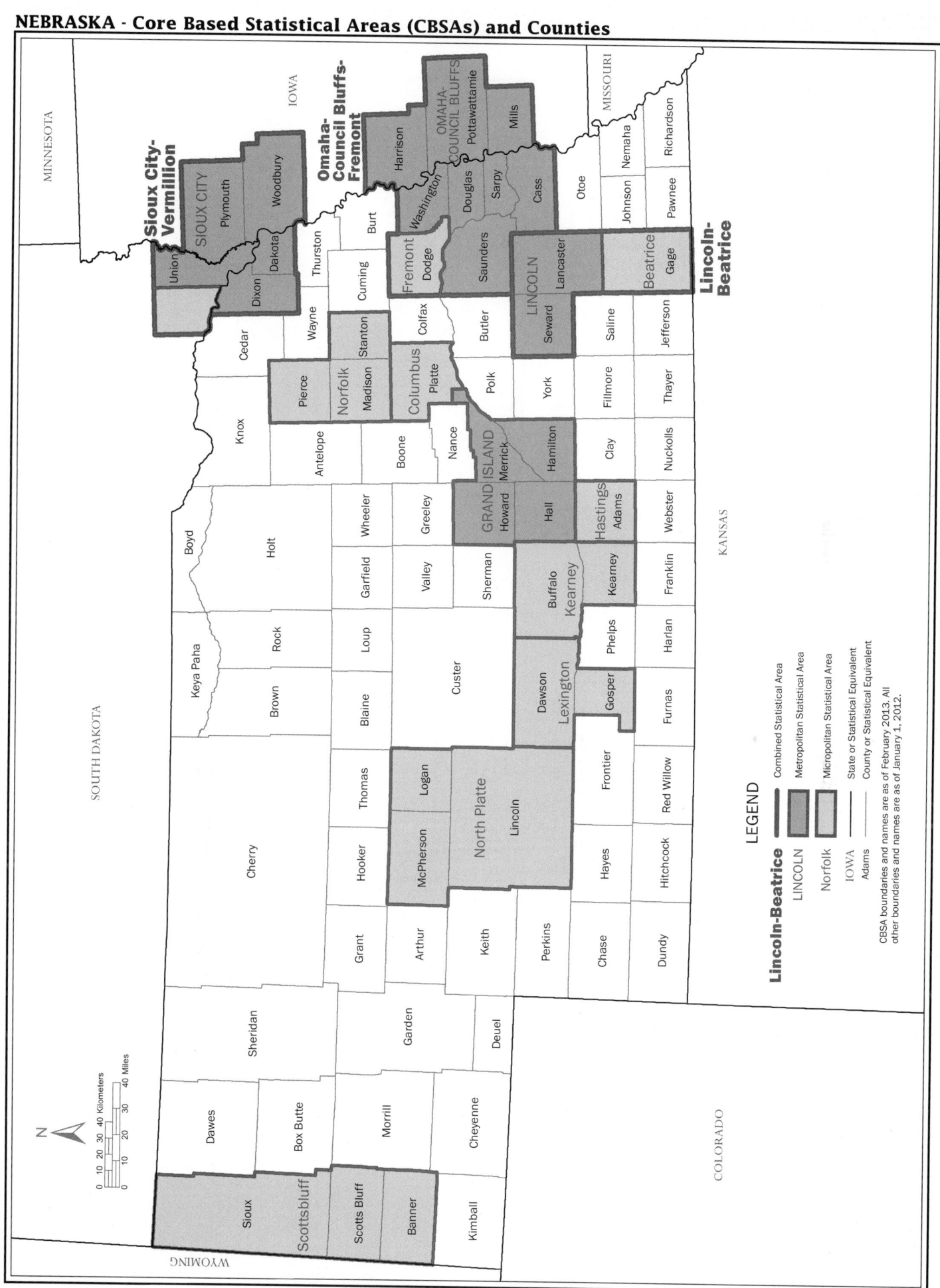

LEGEND

Lincoln-Beatrice

Combined Statistical Area

LINCOLN   Metropolitan Statistical Area

Norfolk   Micropolitan Statistical Area

IOWA   State or Statistical Equivalent

Adams   County or Statistical Equivalent

CBSA boundaries and names are as of February 2013. All other boundaries and names are as of January 1, 2012.

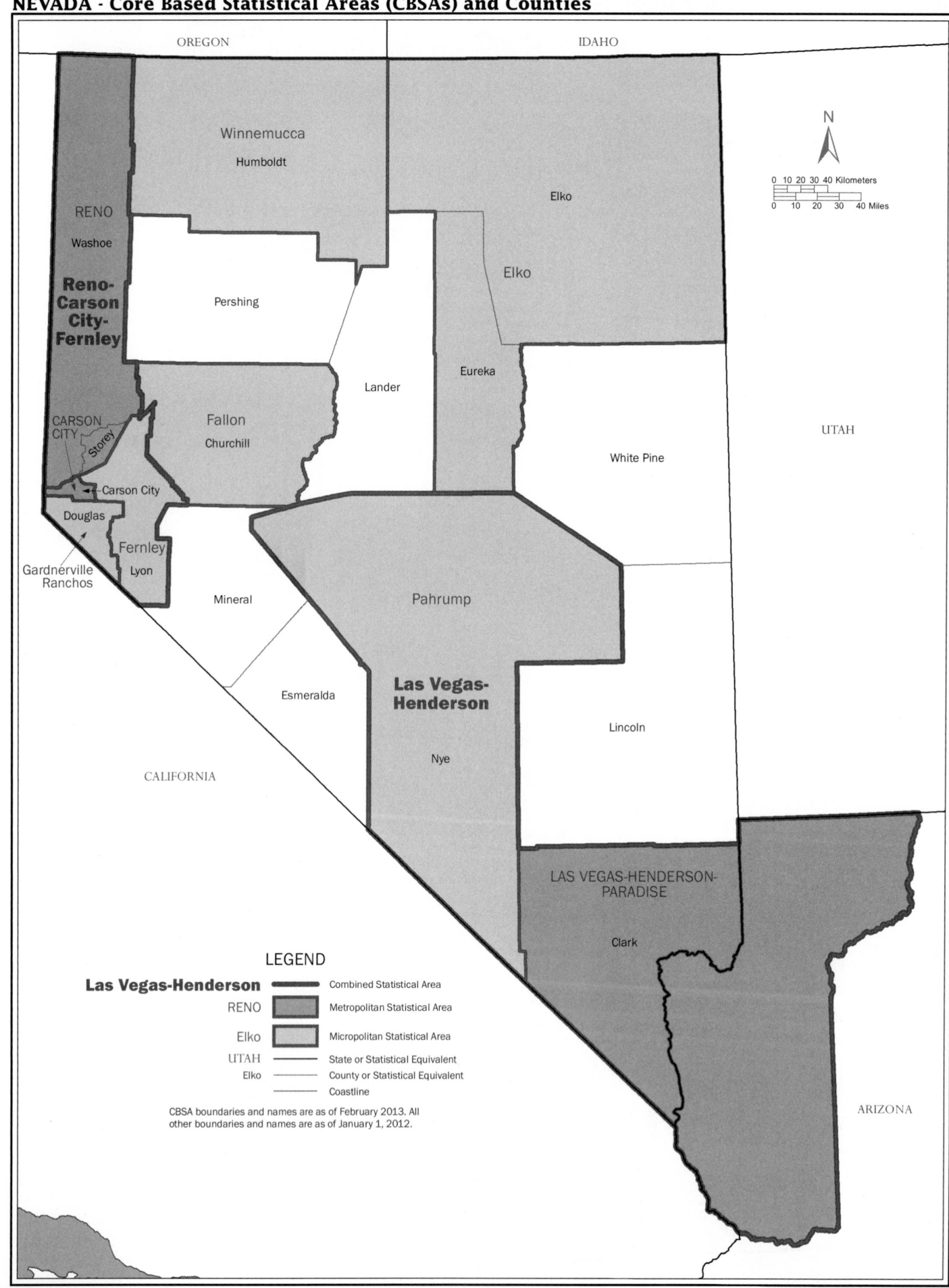

OREGON

IDAHO

N

0 10 20 30 40 Kilometers
0 10 20 30 40 Miles

Winnemucca

Humboldt

Elko

RENO

Washoe

Elko

**Reno-
Carson
City-
Fernley**

Pershing

CARSON
CITY

Storey

Lander

Eureka

Fallon

Churchill

White Pine

UTAH

Carson City

Douglas

Fernley

Gardnerville
Ranchos

Lyon

Mineral

Pahrump

**Las Vegas-
Henderson**

Esmeralda

Lincoln

CALIFORNIA

Nye

LAS VEGAS-HENDERSON-
PARADISE

Clark

ARIZONA

LEGEND

Las Vegas-Henderson	Combined Statistical Area
RENO	Metropolitan Statistical Area
Elko	Micropolitan Statistical Area
UTAH	State or Statistical Equivalent
Elko	County or Statistical Equivalent
	Coastline

CBSA boundaries and names are as of February 2013. All
other boundaries and names are as of January 1, 2012.

NEW HAMPSHIRE - Core Based Statistical Areas (CBSAs) and Counties

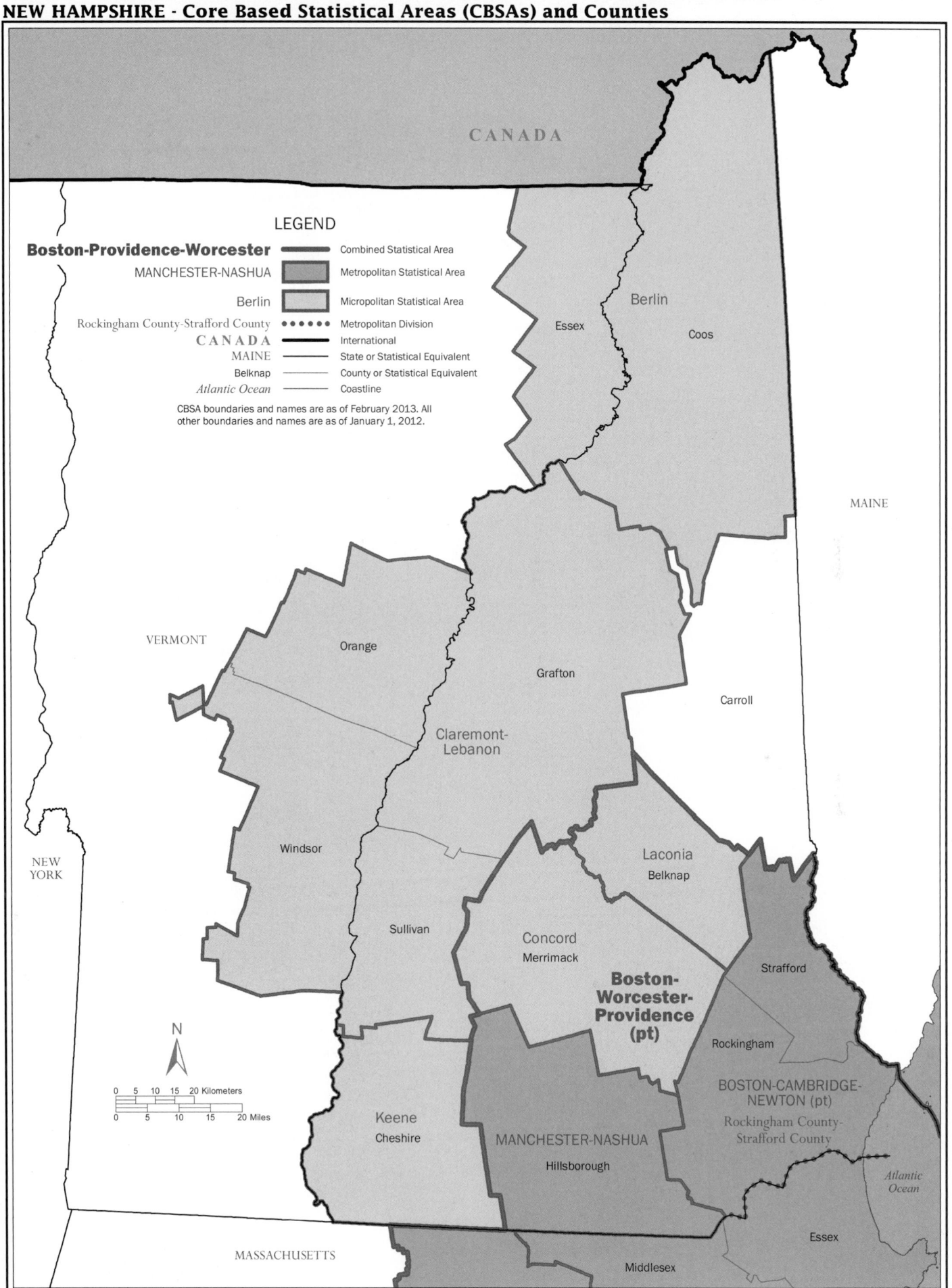

LEGEND

Boston-Providence-Worcester	Combined Statistical Area
MANCHESTER-NASHUA	Metropolitan Statistical Area
Berlin	Micropolitan Statistical Area
Rockingham County-Strafford County	Metropolitan Division
C A N A D A	International
MAINE	State or Statistical Equivalent
Belknap	County or Statistical Equivalent
Atlantic Ocean	Coastline

CBSA boundaries and names are as of February 2013. All other boundaries and names are as of January 1, 2012.

U.S. DEPARTMENT OF COMMERCE Economics and Statistics Administration U.S. Census Bureau

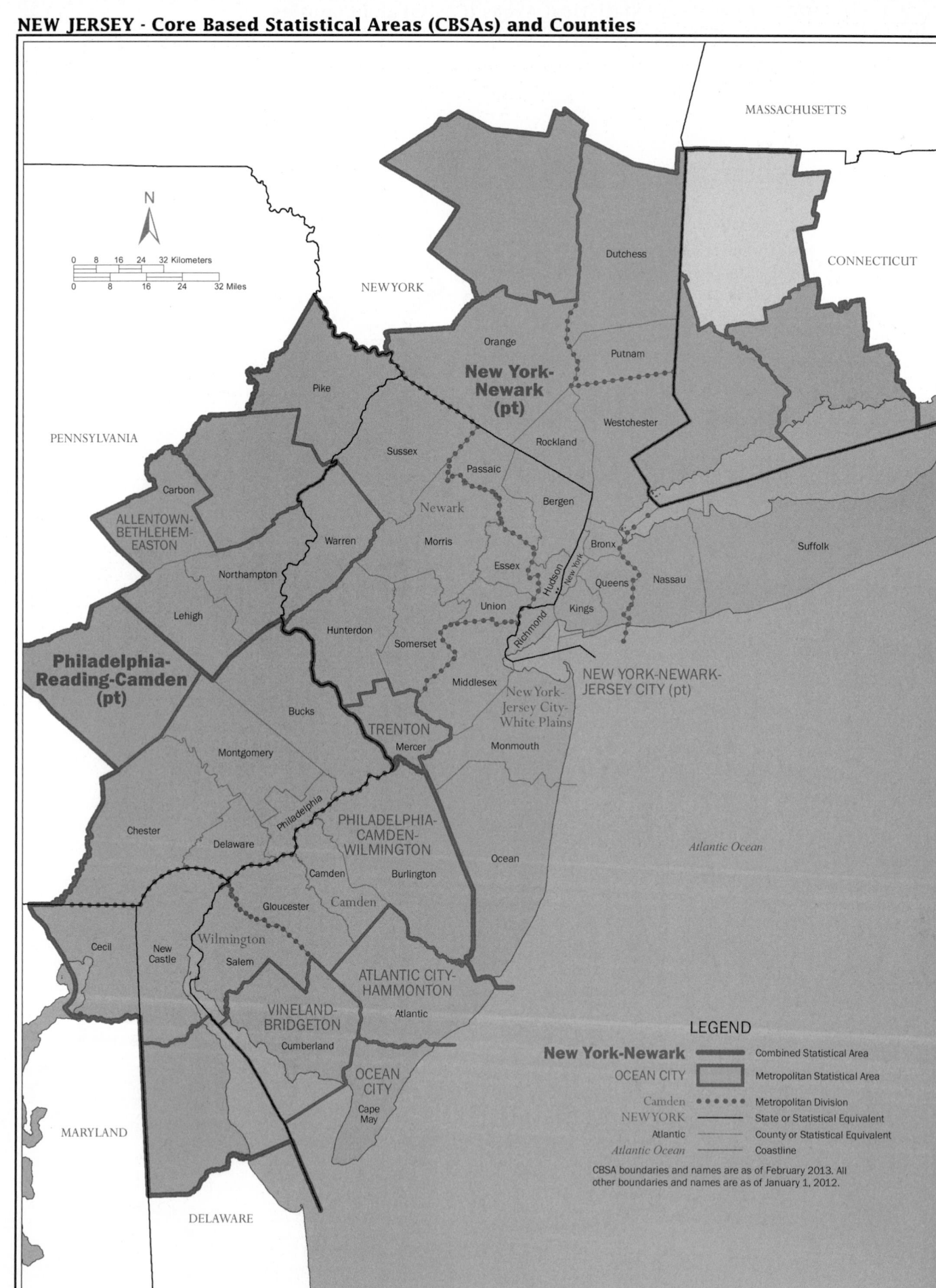

LEGEND

New York-Newark — Combined Statistical Area
OCEAN CITY ☐ Metropolitan Statistical Area
Camden •••••• Metropolitan Division
NEW YORK — State or Statistical Equivalent
Atlantic — County or Statistical Equivalent
Atlantic Ocean — Coastline

CBSA boundaries and names are as of February 2013. All other boundaries and names are as of January 1, 2012.

NEW MEXICO - Core Based Statistical Areas (CBSAs) and Counties

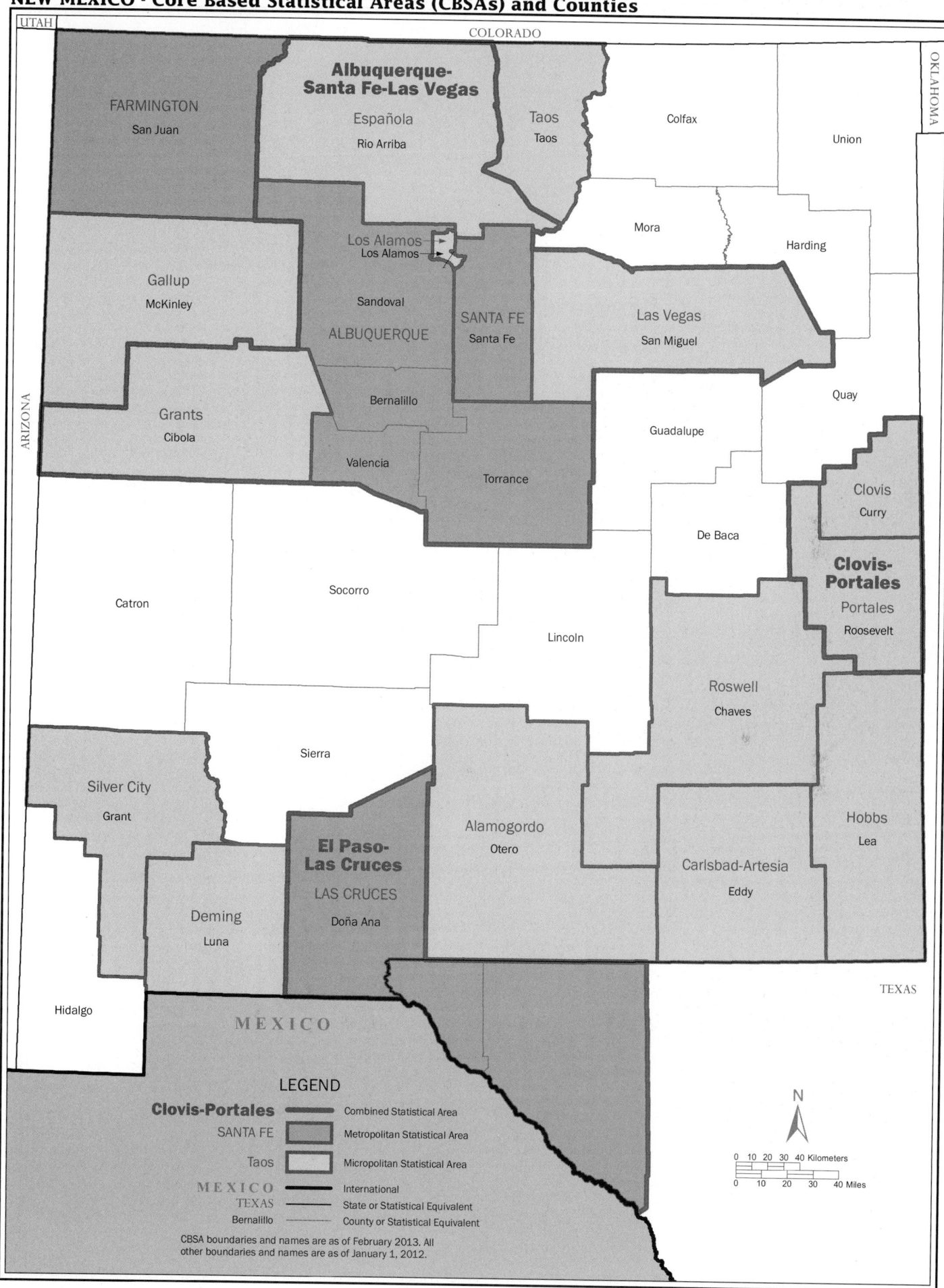

UTAH

COLORADO

OKLAHOMA

FARMINGTON
San Juan

Albuquerque-Santa Fe-Las Vegas

Española
Rio Arriba

Taos
Taos

Colfax

Union

Gallup
McKinley

Los Alamos
Los Alamos

Sandoval

ALBUQUERQUE

SANTA FE
Santa Fe

Las Vegas
San Miguel

Mora

Harding

ARIZONA

Grants
Cibola

Bernalillo

Valencia

Torrance

Guadalupe

Quay

Clovis
Curry

De Baca

Clovis-Portales

Catron

Socorro

Lincoln

Portales
Roosevelt

Roswell
Chaves

Silver City
Grant

Sierra

Alamogordo
Otero

Hobbs
Lea

El Paso-Las Cruces

LAS CRUCES

Deming
Luna

Doña Ana

Carlsbad-Artesia
Eddy

Hidalgo

MEXICO

TEXAS

LEGEND

Clovis-Portales —— Combined Statistical Area

SANTA FE ▢ Metropolitan Statistical Area

Taos ▢ Micropolitan Statistical Area

MEXICO —— International

TEXAS —— State or Statistical Equivalent

Bernalillo ---- County or Statistical Equivalent

CBSA boundaries and names are as of February 2013. All
other boundaries and names are as of January 1, 2012.

N

0 10 20 30 40 Kilometers

0 10 20 30 40 Miles

U.S. DEPARTMENT OF COMMERCE Economics and Statistics Administration U.S. Census Bureau

Appendix D

D-35

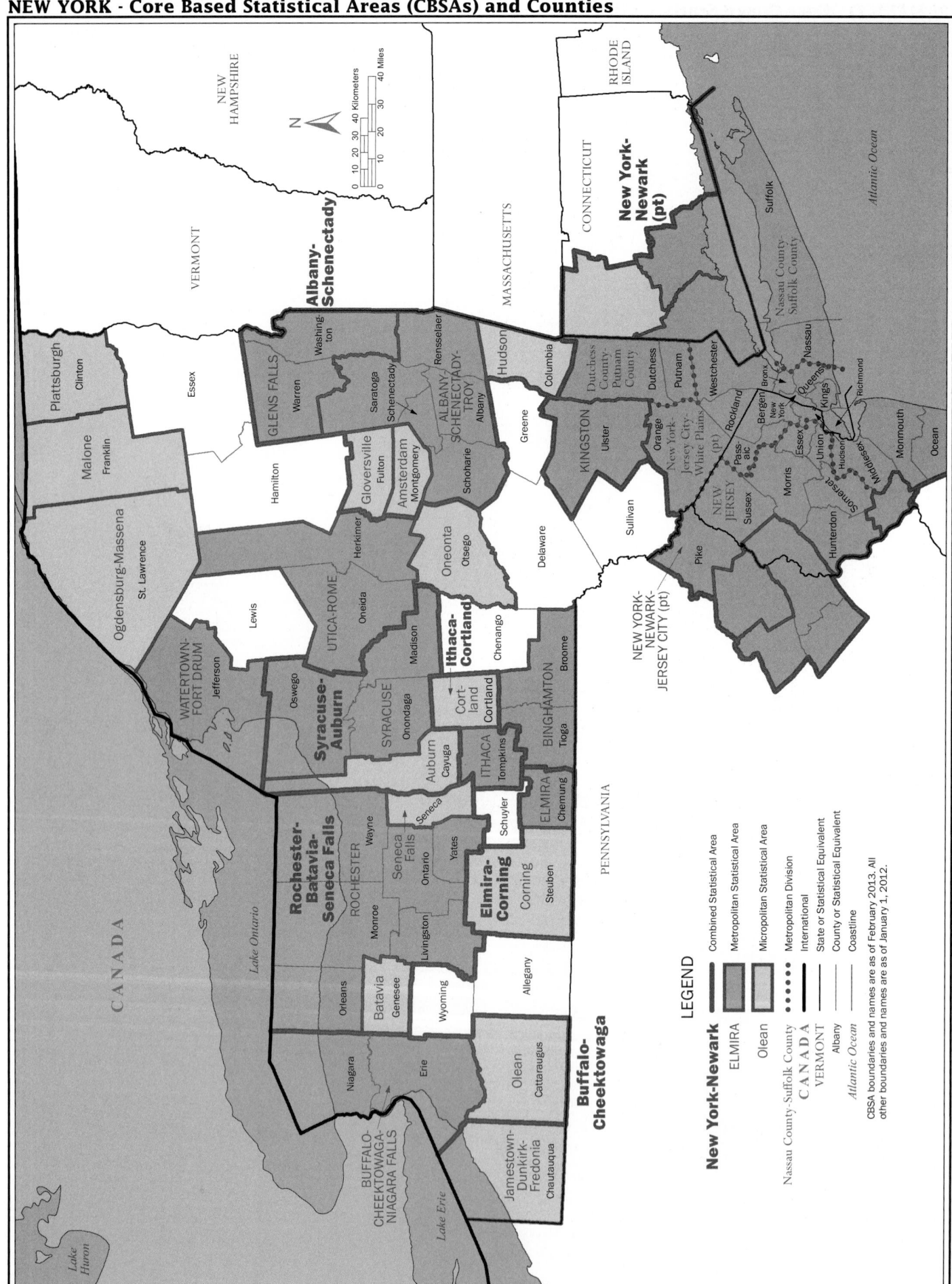

NORTH CAROLINA - Core Based Statistical Areas (CBSAs) and Counties

Virginia Beach-Norfolk

VIRGINIA BEACH-NORFOLK-NEWPORT NEWS

Chesapeake Bay

Mathews
Gloucester
York
Poquoson
Hampton
Newport News
James City
Williamsburg
Isle of Wight
Portsmouth
Suffolk
Norfolk
Virginia Beach
Chesapeake

Currituck
Camden
Pasquotank
Perquimans
Gates
Chowan
Elizabeth City
Kill Devil Hills
Dare
Tyrrell
Washington

Greenville-Washington

Hyde

New Bern-Morehead City

Morehead City
Carteret

Atlantic Ocean

Rocky Mount-Wilson-Roanoke Rapids

Northampton
Hertford
Bertie
Martin
Washington
Beaufort
Pamlico
Craven
NEW BERN
Jones
Onslow
JACKSON-VILLE

Halifax
Roanoke Rapids
GREEN-VILLE
Pitt
Greene
Kinston
Lenoir

Warren
Hender-son
Franklin
ROCKY MOUNT
Nash
Edgecombe
WILSON
Wilson
Wayne
GOLDS-BORO

Raleigh-Durham-Chapel Hill

Vance
Oxford
Granville
Wake
RALEIGH
Johnston
Durham
DURHAM-CHAPEL HILL
Dunn
Harnett

Person
Orange
Chatham
Lee
FAYETTE-VILLE
Cumberland

Duplin
Sampson
Pender
WILMINGTON
New Hanover
Brunswick

Myrtle Beach-Conway

Horry

Caswell
Alamance
BURLINGTON
Moore
Pinehurst-Southern Pines
Sanford
Hoke
Scot-land
Richmond

Bladen
Columbus

Fayetteville-Lumberton-Laurinburg

Lumberton
Robeson
Laurinburg

MYRTLE BEACH-CONWAY-NORTH MYRTLE BEACH

Greensboro-Winston-Salem-High Point

GREENSBORO-HIGH POINT

Rockingham
Guilford
Randolph
Stokes
Forsyth
WINSTON-SALEM
Davidson
Mont-gomery
Stanly
Anson
Rockingham

Mount Airy
Surry
Yadkin
Davie
Rowan
Albemarle
Cabarrus
Union
Lancaster

SOUTH CAROLINA

Alleghany
North Wilkesboro
Wilkes
Alexander
Iredell
Catawba
Lincoln
Gaston
Mecklen-burg
York
CHARLOTTE-CONCORD
GASTONIA
Chester

Charlotte-Concord

Ashe
Boone
Watauga
Caldwell
Burke
Shelby
Cleveland
Rutherford
Forest City

Avery
Mitchell
Yancey
Marion
McDowell
Polk

Asheville-Brevard

Madison
ASHEVILLE
Buncombe
Henderson
Transyl-vania
Brevard
Haywood
Jackson

Cullowhee
Swain
Graham
Cherokee
Macon
Clay

WEST VIRGINIA
VIRGINIA
TENNESSEE
KENTUCKY
GEORGIA

LEGEND

Charlotte-Concord	Combined Statistical Area
ASHEVILLE	Metropolitan Statistical Area
Boone	Micropolitan Statistical Area
VIRGINIA	State or Statistical Equivalent
Ashe	County or Statistical Equivalent
Atlantic Ocean	Coastline

CBSA boundaries and names are as of February 2013. All other boundaries and names are as of January 1, 2012.

NORTH DAKOTA - Core Based Statistical Areas (CBSAs) and Counties

CANADA

MINNESOTA

MONTANA

SOUTH DAKOTA

Polk

GRAND FORKS

Clay

Wilkin

Fargo-Wahpeton

FARGO

Wahpeton

Richland

Pembina

Walsh

Grand Forks

Trail

Cass

Ransom

Sargent

Cavalier

Nelson

Steele

Barnes

Ramsey

Griggs

LaMoure

Dickey

Towner

Eddy

Foster

Jamestown

Stutsman

Benson

Wells

Logan

McIntosh

Rolette

Pierce

Kidder

Sheridan

Emmons

Bottineau

McHenry

Burleigh

Sioux

Renville

Minot

Ward

McLean

Oliver

BISMARCK

Morton

Grant

Burke

Mountrail

Mercer

Divide

Williston

Williams

McKenzie

Dunn

Dickinson

Stark

Hettinger

Adams

Billings

Golden Valley

Slope

Bowman

LEGEND

Fargo-Wahpeton

	Combined Statistical Area
FARGO	Metropolitan Statistical Area
Minot	Micropolitan Statistical Area
	International
CANADA / MONTANA	State or Statistical Equivalent
Adams	County or Statistical Equivalent

CBSA boundaries and names are as of February 2013. All other boundaries and names are as of January 1, 2012.

40 Miles / 40 Kilometers

N

OHIO - Core Based Statistical Areas (CBSAs) and Counties

CANADA

MICHIGAN

Lake Erie

PENNSYLVANIA

Toledo-Port Clinton

Cleveland-Akron-Canton

Williams

Fulton

Lucas

Ottawa
Port Clinton

Lake

Ashtabula
Ashtabula

Defiance
Defiance

Henry

TOLEDO
Wood

Fremont
Sandusky

Erie
Sandusky

Lorain

CLEVELAND-ELYRIA

Geauga

Cuyahoga

Youngstown-Warren

YOUNGSTOWN-WARREN-BOARDMAN

Mercer

Paulding

Putnam

Findlay-Tiffin

Findlay
Hancock

Tiffin
Seneca

Norwalk
Huron

Mansfield-Ashland-Bucyrus

Medina

AKRON
Summit

Portage

Trumbull

Mahoning

Lima-Van Wert-Celina

Van Wert
Van Wert

LIMA
Allen

Wyandot

Bucyrus
Crawford

MANS-FIELD
Richland

Ash-land
Ashland

Wooster
Wayne

CANTON-MASSILLON
Stark

Salem
Columbiana

Pittsburgh-New Castle-Weirton (pt)

Hancock
Brooke

INDIANA

Celina
Mercer

Wapakoneta
Auglaize

Hardin

Marion
Marion

Morrow

Mount Vernon
Knox

Holmes

Tuscarawas
New Philadelphia-Dover

Carroll

Jefferson

WEIRTON-STEUBENVILLE

Greenville
Darke

Sidney
Shelby

Bellefontaine
Logan

Union

Delaware

Columbus-Marion-Zanesville

Licking

Coshocton
Coshocton

Harrison

Cambridge
Guernsey

WHEELING
Belmont

Ohio

DAYTON
Miami

Urbana
Champaign

SPRINGFIELD
Clark

Madison

COLUMBUS
Franklin

Zanesville
Muskingum

Marshall

Preble

Dayton-Springfield-Sidney

Greene

Washington Court House
Fayette

Pickaway

Fairfield

Perry

Noble

Monroe

Union

Cincinnati-Wilmington-Maysville

Wilmington
Clinton

Hocking

Morgan

Marietta
Washington

Parkersburg-Marietta-Vienna

Butler

Warren

CINCINNATI

Highland

Chillicothe
Ross

Vinton

Athens
Athens

Meigs

Dearborn

Hamilton

Clermont

Pike

Jackson
Jackson

Point Pleasant

Ohio

Boone

Kenton

Campbell

Brown

Adams

Portsmouth
Scioto

Gallia

Mason

WEST VIRGINIA

Gallatin

Grant

Pendleton

Bracken

Greenup

Lawrence

Boyd

Cabell

Putnam

Charleston-Huntington-Ashland

KENTUCKY

HUNTINGTON-ASHLAND

Wayne

Lincoln

LEGEND

Symbol	Description
Findlay-Tiffin	Combined Statistical Area
AKRON	Metropolitan Statistical Area
Athens	Micropolitan Statistical Area
CANADA	International
INDIANA	State or Statistical Equivalent
Adams	County or Statistical Equivalent
Lake Erie	Coastline

N

0 10 20 30 40 Kilometers
0 10 20 30 40 Miles

CBSA boundaries and names are as of February 2013. All other boundaries and names are as of January 1, 2012.

VIRGINIA

OKLAHOMA - Core Based Statistical Areas (CBSAs) and Counties

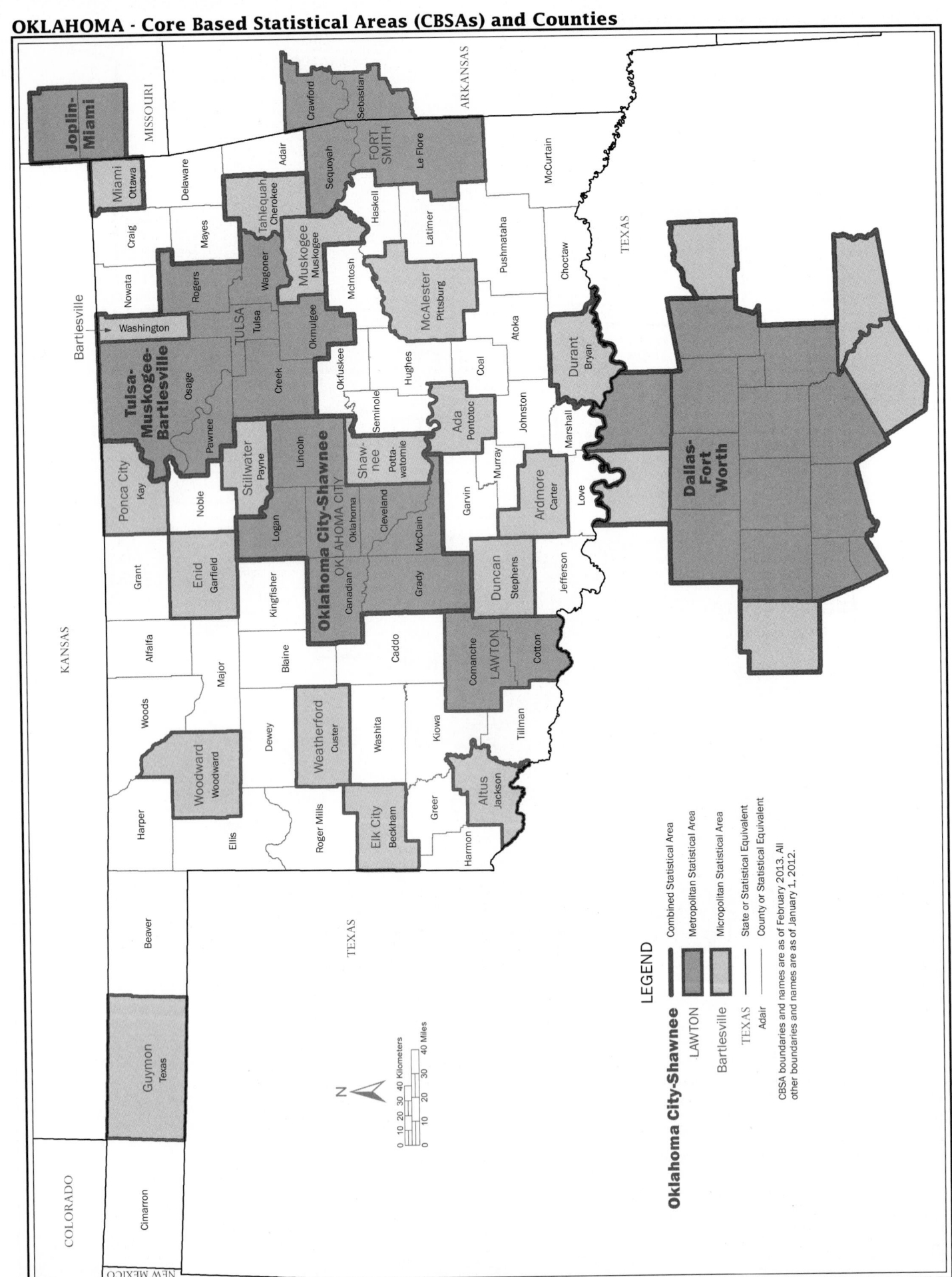

LEGEND

Oklahoma City-Shawnee
LAWTON
Bartlesville
TEXAS
Adair

Combined Statistical Area
Metropolitan Statistical Area
Micropolitan Statistical Area
State or Statistical Equivalent
County or Statistical Equivalent

CBSA boundaries and names are as of February 2013. All other boundaries and names are as of January 1, 2012.

0 10 20 30 40 Kilometers
0   10   20   30   40 Miles

U.S. DEPARTMENT OF COMMERCE Economics and Statistics Administration U.S. Census Bureau

OREGON - Core Based Statistical Areas (CBSAs) and Counties

N

0 10 20 30 40 Kilometers
0 10 20 30 40 Miles

IDAHO

WASHINGTON

NEVADA

CALIFORNIA

Wallowa

Baker

La Grande
Union

Hermiston-Pendleton
Umatilla

Morrow

Grant

Payette

Boise City-
Mountain Home-
Ontario

Ontario
Malheur

Harney

Wheeler

Gilliam

Sherman

The Dalles
Wasco

Jefferson

Bend-Redmond-
Prineville

Prineville
Crook

Lake

Hood
River
Hood
River

PORTLAND-
VANCOUVER-
HILLSBORO

Skamania

Clark

Multnomah

Columbia

Washington

Yamhill

Astoria
Clatsop

Tillamook

Polk

Portland-
Vancouver-
Salem

Clackamas

Marion

SALEM

ALBANY
Linn

Benton

Newport
Lincoln

CORVALLIS

EUGENE
Lane

BEND-
REDMOND
Deschutes

Klamath Falls
Klamath

Roseburg
Douglas

Coos Bay
Coos

Medford-
Grants Pass

GRANTS
PASS
Josephine

MEDFORD
Jackson

Brookings
Curry

Pacific Ocean

LEGEND

Medford-Grants Pass

Combined Statistical Area

ALBANY   Metropolitan Statistical Area

Brookings   Micropolitan Statistical Area

NEVADA   State or Statistical Equivalent

Baker   County or Statistical Equivalent

Pacific Ocean Coastline

CBSA boundaries and names are as of February 2013. All
other boundaries and names are as of January 1, 2012.

PENNSYLVANIA - Core Based Statistical Areas (CBSAs) and Counties

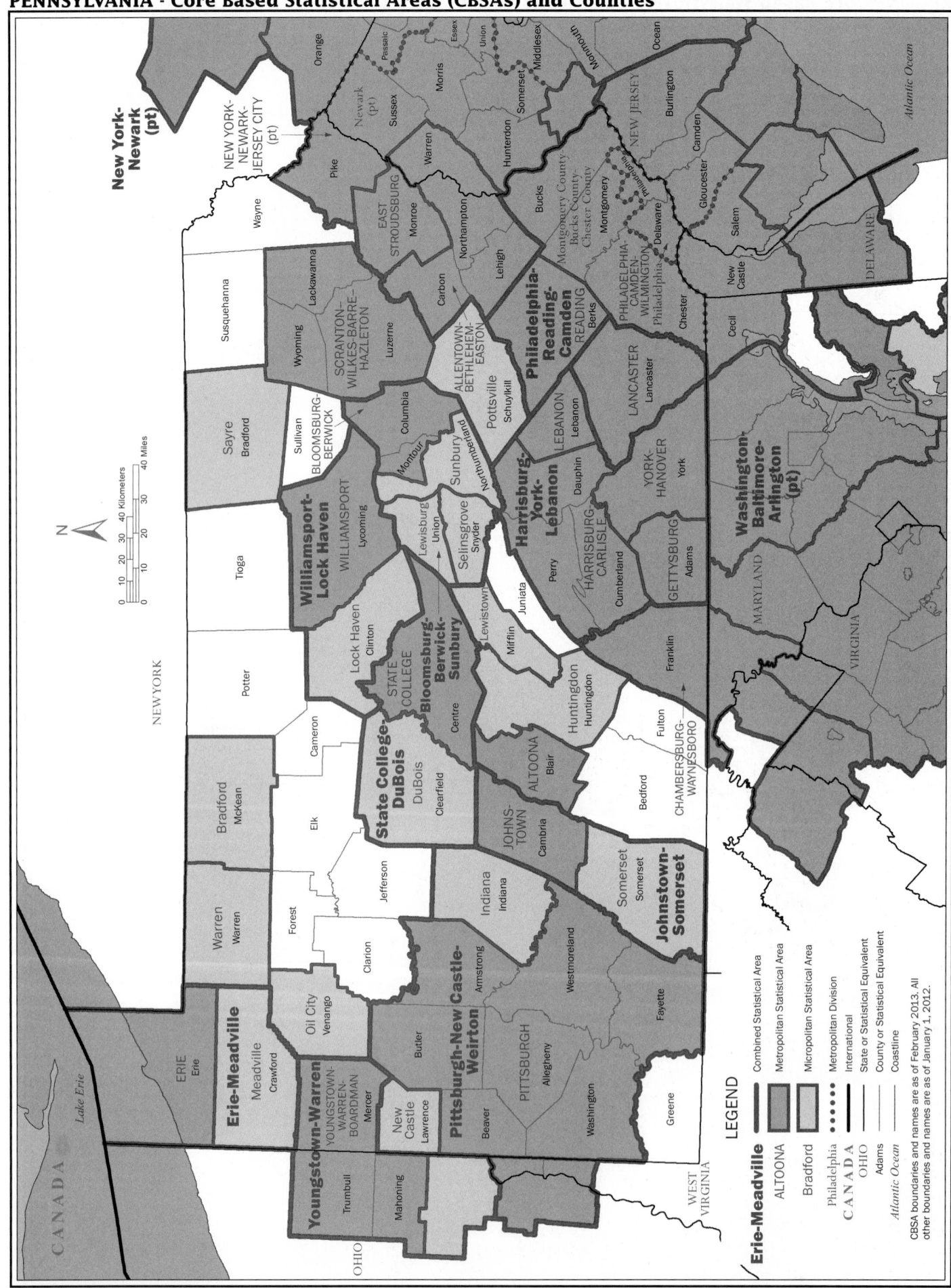

MASSACHUSETTS

Boston-Worcester-Providence (pt)

PROVIDENCE-WARWICK

Providence

Bristol

Kent

Bristol

MASSACHUSETTS

CONNECTICUT

Newport

Washington

N

0 2 4 6 8 Kilometers

0 2 4 6 8 Miles

LEGEND

Boston-Worcester-Providence ▬▬▬	Combined Statistical Area
PROVIDENCE-WARWICK ☐	Metropolitan Statistical Area
MASSACHUSETTS ────	State or Statistical Equivalent
Bristol ────	County or Statistical Equivalent
Atlantic Ocean ────	Coastline

CBSA boundaries and names are as of February 2013. All other boundaries and names are as of January 1, 2012.

Atlantic Ocean

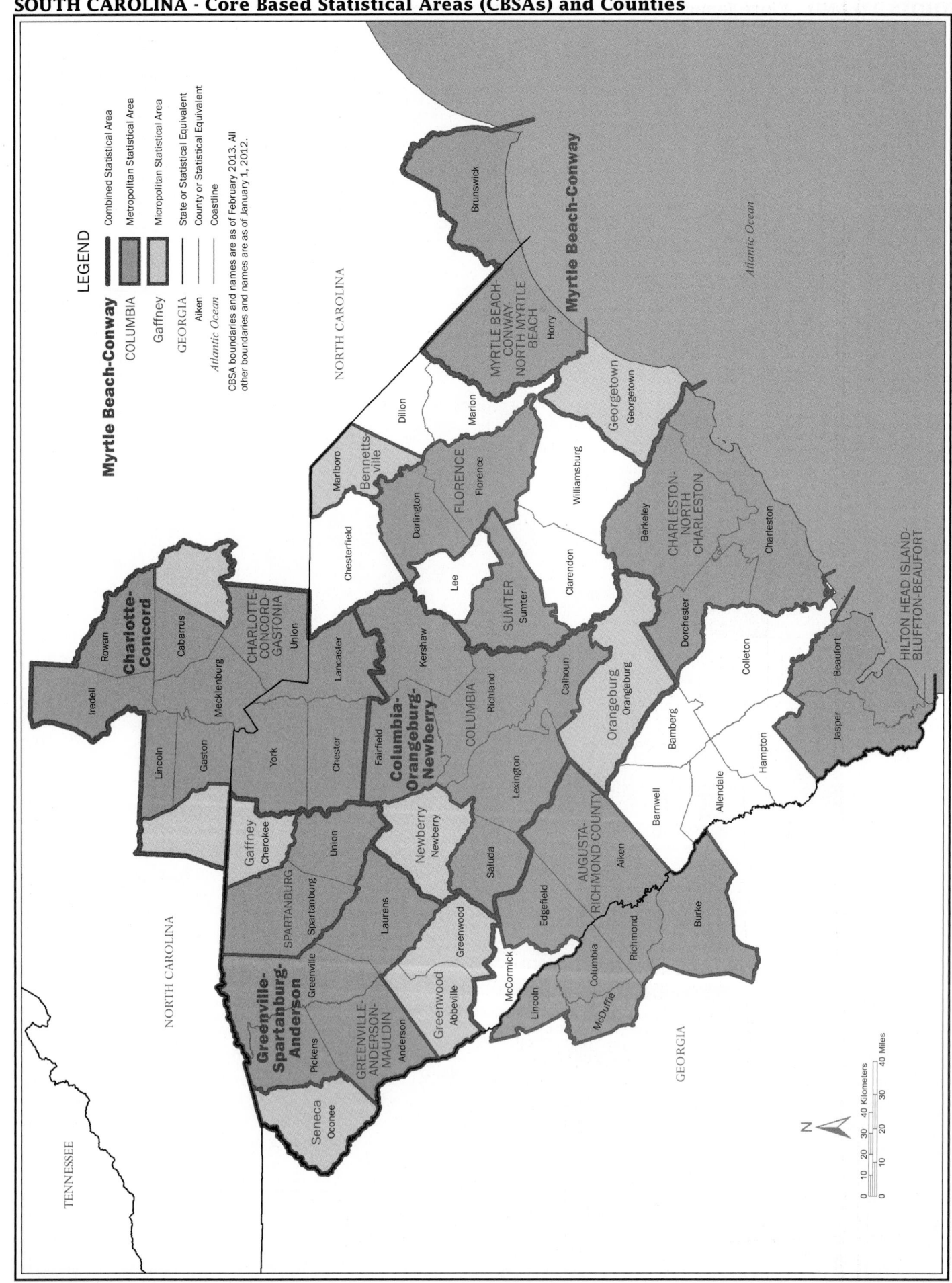

LEGEND

Myrtle Beach-Conway

Combined Statistical Area

COLUMBIA Metropolitan Statistical Area

Gaffney Micropolitan Statistical Area

GEORGIA State or Statistical Equivalent

Aiken County or Statistical Equivalent

Atlantic Ocean Coastline

CBSA boundaries and names are as of February 2013. All other boundaries and names are as of January 1, 2012.

SOUTH DAKOTA - Core Based Statistical Areas (CBSAs) and Counties

MONTANA

MINNESOTA

40 Miles

40 Kilometers

N

IOWA

NORTH DAKOTA

NEBRASKA

Roberts

Grant

Deuel

Brookings
Brookings

Moody

Minnehaha

SIOUX FALLS
Lincoln

Union

Plymouth

SIOUX CITY
Woodbury

Marshall

Day

Watertown
Codington

Hamlin

Lake

Turner

Vermillion
Clay

Dixon

Dakota

Sioux City-
Vermillion

McCook

Yankton
Yankton

McPherson

Brown

Spink

Clark

Kingsbury

Miner

Sanborn

Hutchinson

Bon
Homme

Aberdeen
Edmunds

Hanson

Mitchell
Davison

Douglas

Campbell

Walworth

Faulk

Hand

Jerauld

Aurora

Charles Mix

Potter

Hyde

Huron
Beade

Corson

Dewey

Sully

Pierre

Hughes

Lyman

Brule

Gregory

Stanley

Jones

Mellette

Todd

Ziebach

Haakon

Jackson

Bennett

Rapid City-Spearfish

RAPID CITY

Perkins

Meade

RAPID CITY

Rapid City-Spearfish

Pennington

Shannon

LEGEND

Harding

Butte

Spearfish
Lawrence

Custer

Fall River

Combined Statistical Area

Metropolitan Statistical Area

Micropolitan Statistical Area

State or Statistical Equivalent

County or Statistical Equivalent

CBSA boundaries and names are as of February 2013. All other boundaries and names are as of January 1, 2012.

MONTANA

WYOMING

LEGEND

Combined Statistical Area

Metropolitan Statistical Area

Micropolitan Statistical Area

State or Statistical Equivalent

County or Statistical Equivalent

Martin-Union City

MEMPHIS

Cookeville

GEORGIA

Bedford

CBSA boundaries and names are as of February 2013. All other boundaries and names are as of January 1, 2012.

TEXAS - Core Based Statistical Areas (CBSAs) and Counties

KEY
1 DALLAS-FORT WORTH-ARLINGTON
2 Tyler-Jacksonville
3 Jacksonville
4 Nacogdoches

LEGEND

Dallas-Fort Worth — Combined Statistical Area
WACO — Metropolitan Statistical Area
Alice — Micropolitan Statistical Area
Fort Worth-Arlington — Metropolitan Division
MEXICO — International
OKLAHOMA — State or Statistical Equivalent
Harris — County or Statistical Equivalent
Gulf of Mexico — Coastline

CBSA boundaries and names are as of February 2013. All other boundaries and names are as of January 1, 2012.

N

0 30 60 90 120 Miles
0 30 60 90 120 Kilometers

ARKANSAS · LOUISIANA · OKLAHOMA · NEW MEXICO · MEXICO

Gulf of Mexico

Longview-Marshall · Houston-The Woodlands · Victoria-Port Lavaca · Corpus Christi-Kingsville-Alice · Brownsville-Harlingen-Raymondville · McAllen-Edinburg · El Paso-Las Cruces · Dallas-Fort Worth · Wichita Falls · Lubbock-Levelland · Amarillo-Borger · Midland-Odessa · Tyler

UTAH - Core Based Statistical Areas (CBSAs) and Counties

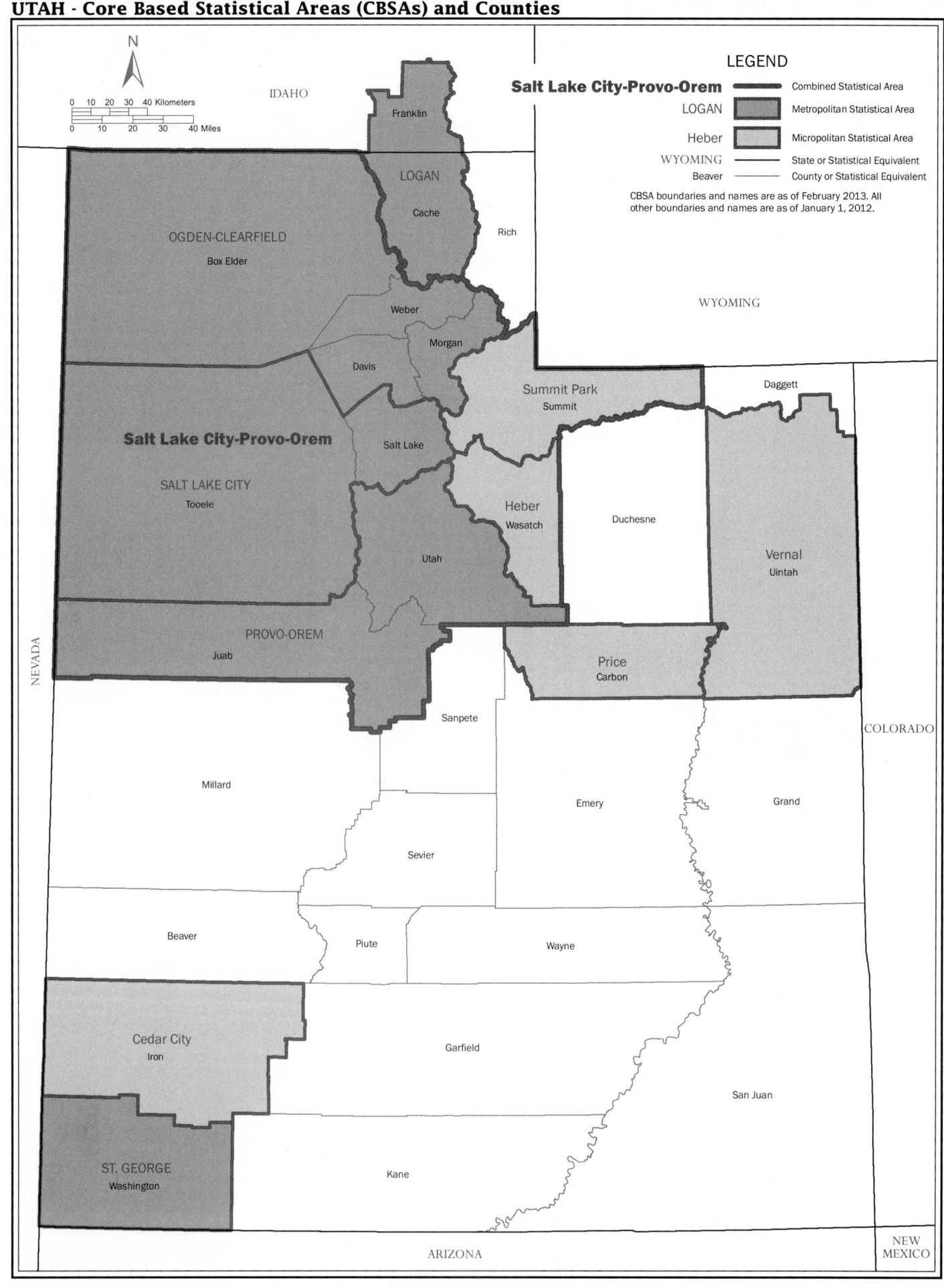

N

IDAHO

0 10 20 30 40 Kilometers
0 10 20 30 40 Miles

LEGEND

Salt Lake City-Provo-Orem Combined Statistical Area

LOGAN Metropolitan Statistical Area

Heber Micropolitan Statistical Area

WYOMING State or Statistical Equivalent

Beaver County or Statistical Equivalent

CBSA boundaries and names are as of February 2013. All
other boundaries and names are as of January 1, 2012.

Franklin

LOGAN

Cache

Rich

WYOMING

OGDEN-CLEARFIELD

Box Elder

Weber

Morgan

Davis

Daggett

Summit Park
Summit

Salt Lake City-Provo-Orem

Salt Lake

SALT LAKE CITY

Tooele

Heber
Wasatch

Duchesne

Vernal
Uintah

Utah

PROVO-OREM

Juab

Price
Carbon

NEVADA

Sanpete

COLORADO

Millard

Emery

Grand

Sevier

Beaver

Piute

Wayne

Cedar City
Iron

Garfield

San Juan

ST. GEORGE
Washington

Kane

NEW
MEXICO

ARIZONA

U.S. DEPARTMENT OF COMMERCE Economics and Statistics Administration U.S. Census Bureau

Appendix D

VERMONT - Core Based Statistical Areas (CBSAs) and Counties

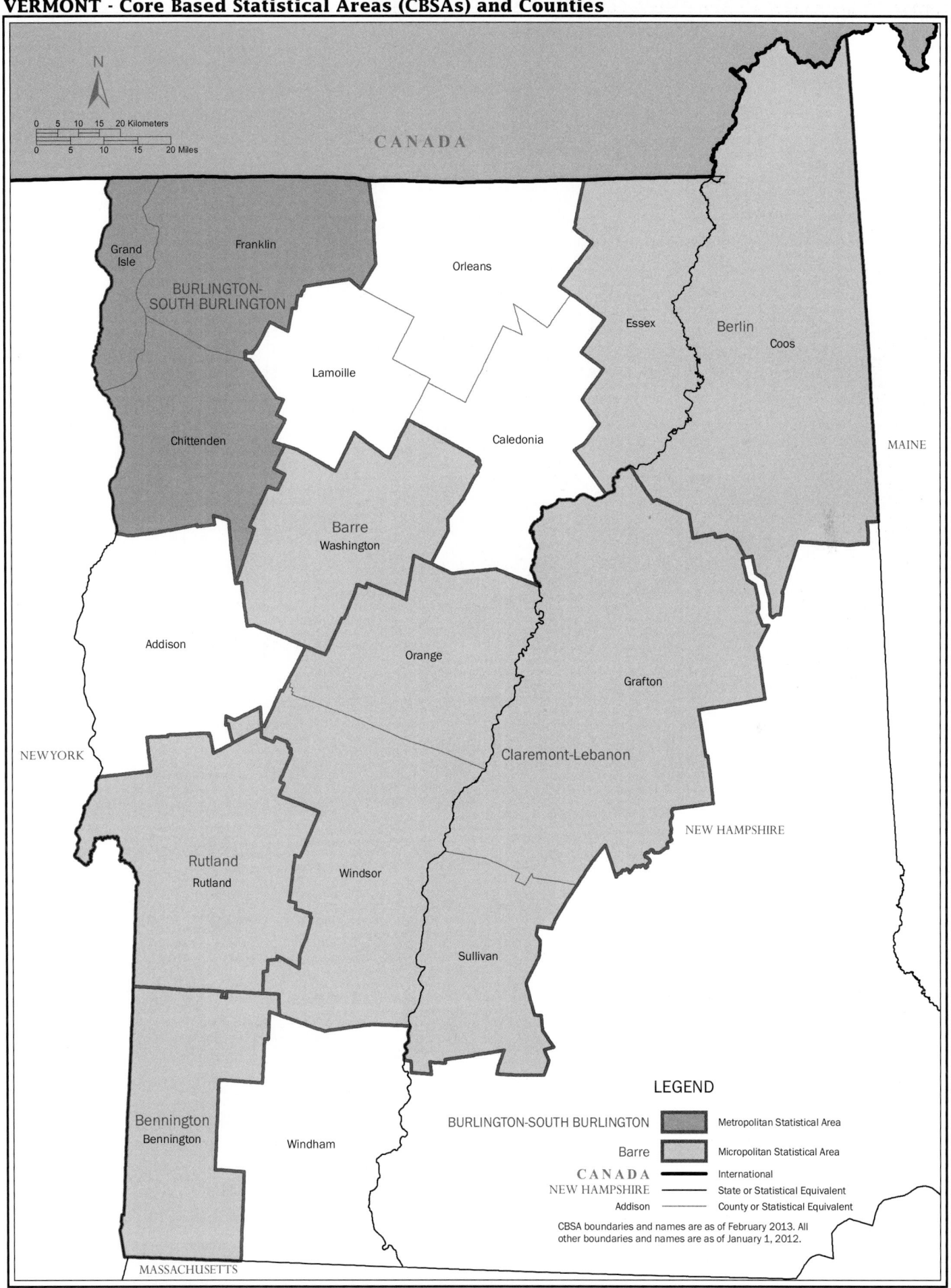

N

0 5 10 15 20 Kilometers
0 5 10 15 20 Miles

CANADA

Grand Isle

Franklin

Orleans

BURLINGTON-SOUTH BURLINGTON

Essex

Berlin

Coos

Lamoille

Chittenden

Caledonia

MAINE

Barre
Washington

Addison

Orange

Grafton

NEW YORK

Claremont-Lebanon

Rutland
Rutland

Windsor

NEW HAMPSHIRE

Sullivan

Bennington
Bennington

Windham

LEGEND

BURLINGTON-SOUTH BURLINGTON	Metropolitan Statistical Area
Barre	Micropolitan Statistical Area
CANADA	International
NEW HAMPSHIRE	State or Statistical Equivalent
Addison	County or Statistical Equivalent

CBSA boundaries and names are as of February 2013. All other boundaries and names are as of January 1, 2012.

MASSACHUSETTS

VIRGINIA - Core Based Statistical Areas (CBSAs) and Counties

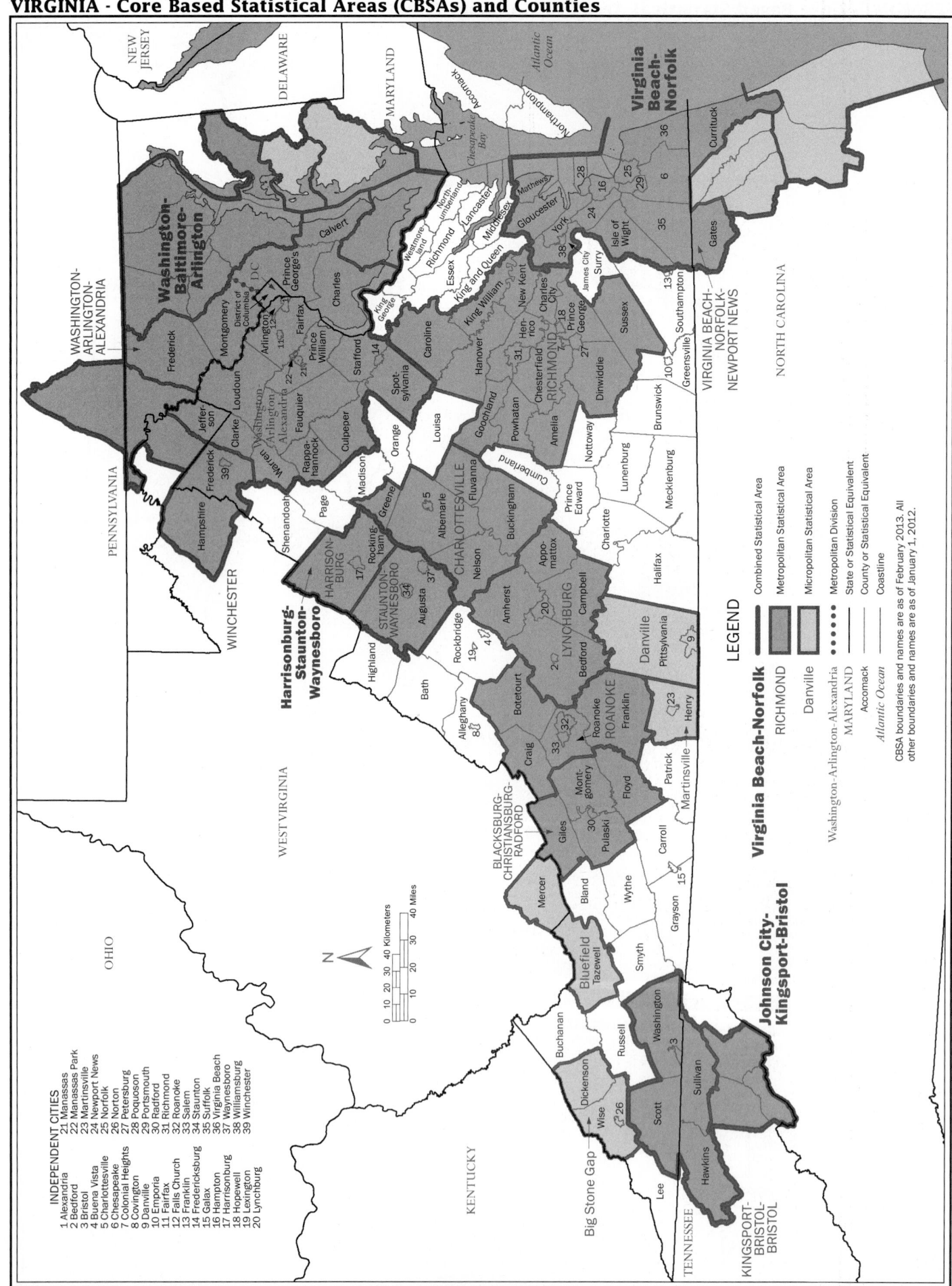

LEGEND

- Combined Statistical Area
- Metropolitan Statistical Area
- Micropolitan Statistical Area
- Metropolitan Division
- State or Statistical Equivalent
- County or Statistical Equivalent
- Coastline

CBSA boundaries and names are as of February 2013. All other boundaries and names are as of January 1, 2012.

Virginia Beach-Norfolk
- RICHMOND
- Danville

Washington-Arlington-Alexandria
- MARYLAND
- Accomack
- Atlantic Ocean

Johnson City-Kingsport-Bristol
- KINGSPORT-BRISTOL-BRISTOL

INDEPENDENT CITIES

1 Alexandria
2 Bedford
3 Bristol
4 Buena Vista
5 Charlottesville
6 Chesapeake
7 Colonial Heights
8 Covington
9 Danville
10 Emporia
11 Fairfax
12 Falls Church
13 Franklin
14 Fredericksburg
15 Galax
16 Hampton
17 Harrisonburg
18 Hopewell
19 Lexington
20 Lynchburg
21 Manassas
22 Manassas Park
23 Martinsville
24 Newport News
25 Norfolk
26 Norton
27 Petersburg
28 Poquoson
29 Portsmouth
30 Radford
31 Richmond
32 Roanoke
33 Salem
34 Staunton
35 Suffolk
36 Virginia Beach
37 Waynesboro
38 Williamsburg
39 Winchester

WASHINGTON - Core Based Statistical Areas (CBSAs) and Counties

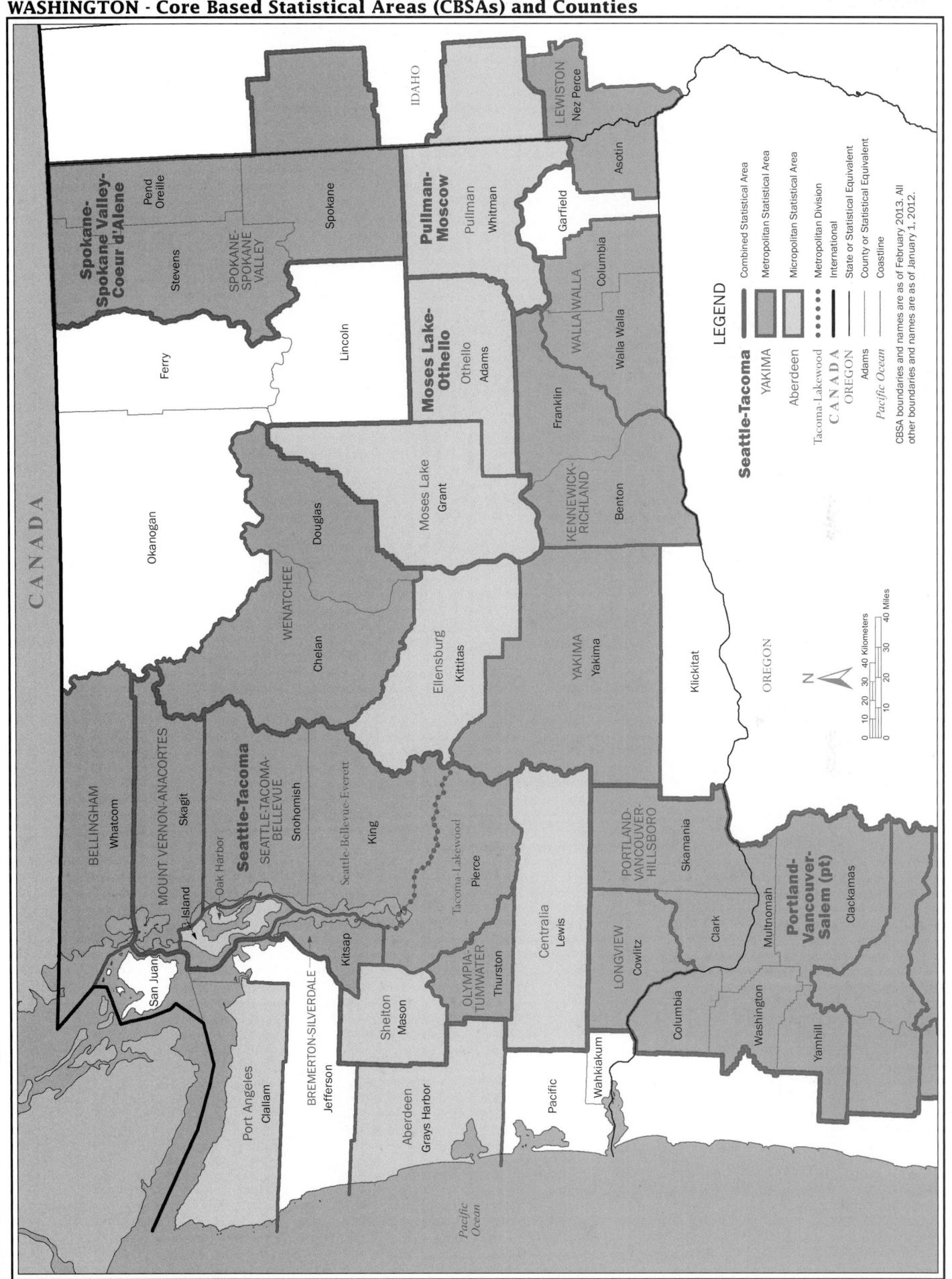

LEGEND

Seattle-Tacoma — Combined Statistical Area

YAKIMA — Metropolitan Statistical Area

Aberdeen — Micropolitan Statistical Area

Tacoma-Lakewood — Metropolitan Division

CANADA — International

OREGON — State or Statistical Equivalent

Adams — County or Statistical Equivalent

Pacific Ocean — Coastline

CBSA boundaries and names are as of February 2013. All other boundaries and names are as of January 1, 2012.

CANADA

IDAHO

OREGON

Pacific Ocean

Spokane-Spokane Valley-Coeur d'Alene
- Pend Oreille
- Stevens
- Ferry
- Spokane
- SPOKANE-SPOKANE VALLEY

- Lincoln

Pullman-Moscow
- Pullman
- Whitman

LEWISTON — Nez Perce

Asotin

Garfield

Columbia

WALLA WALLA — Walla Walla

Moses Lake-Othello
- Othello
- Adams

- Franklin

- Moses Lake — Grant

KENNEWICK-RICHLAND
- Benton

- Okanogan

WENATCHEE
- Douglas
- Chelan

Ellensburg — Kittitas

YAKIMA — Yakima

- Klickitat

BELLINGHAM — Whatcom

MOUNT VERNON-ANACORTES — Skagit

San Juan

Island

Oak Harbor

Seattle-Tacoma
- **SEATTLE-TACOMA-BELLEVUE**
- Snohomish
- Seattle-Bellevue-Everett
- King
- Tacoma-Lakewood
- Pierce
- Kitsap

BREMERTON-SILVERDALE — Jefferson

Port Angeles — Clallam

Shelton — Mason

OLYMPIA-TUMWATER — Thurston

Centralia — Lewis

Aberdeen — Grays Harbor

Pacific

Wahkiakum

LONGVIEW — Cowlitz

Columbia

PORTLAND-VANCOUVER-HILLSBORO
- Skamania
- Clark

- Multnomah

Washington

Portland-Vancouver-Salem (pt)
- Clackamas
- Yamhill

Pacific Ocean

N

0 10 20 30 40 Kilometers
0 10 20 30 40 Miles

WEST VIRGINIA - Core Based Statistical Areas (CBSAs) and Counties

LEGEND

Combined Statistical Area

Metropolitan Statistical Area

Micropolitan Statistical Area

- Metropolitan Division
- State or Statistical Equivalent
- County or Statistical Equivalent
- Coastline

Morgantown-Fairmont

WHEELING

Elkins

Washington-Arlington-Alexandria

VIRGINIA

Barbour

CBSA boundaries and names are as of February 2013. All other boundaries and names are as of January 1, 2012.

WISCONSIN - Core Based Statistical Areas (CBSAs) and Counties

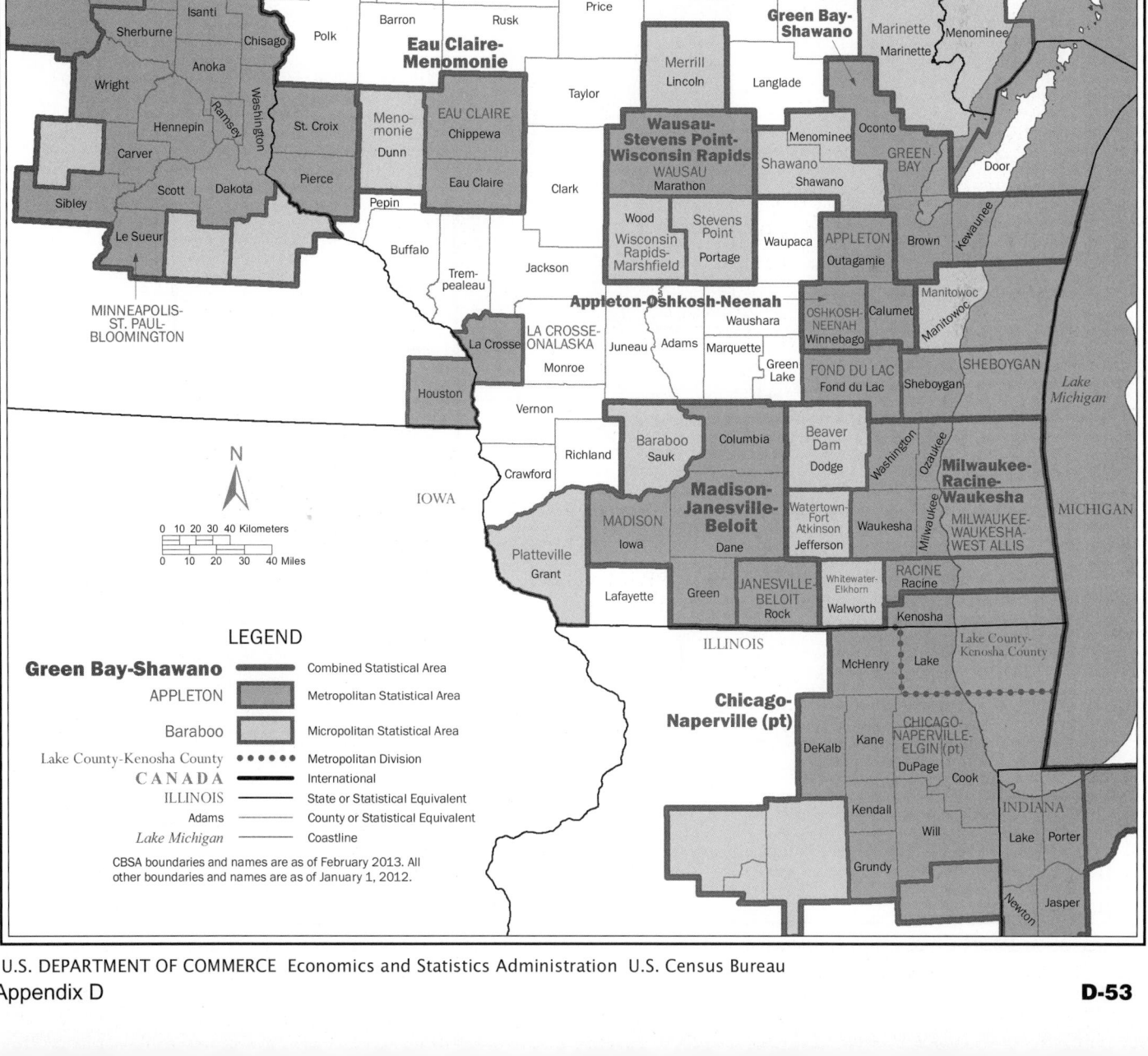

CANADA

Lake Superior

MICHIGAN

DULUTH
St. Louis

Carlton

Douglas

Bayfield

Ashland | Iron

Vilas

Iron
Mountain
Dickinson

Minneapolis-
St. Paul (pt)

Mille
Lacs

Burnett | Washburn | Sawyer

Price

Oneida

Forest

Florence

Marinette
Marinette

Menominee

Isanti

Sherburne

Chisago

Polk | Barron | Rusk

Taylor

Merrill
Lincoln

Langlade

Green Bay-
Shawano

Wright

Anoka

Eau Claire-
Menomonie

St. Croix

Meno-
monie
Dunn

EAU CLAIRE
Chippewa

Wausau-
Stevens Point-
Wisconsin Rapids
WAUSAU
Marathon

Menominee

Shawano
Shawano

Oconto

GREEN
BAY

Door

Hennepin

Ramsey

Washington

Clark

Carver

Pierce

Eau Claire

Wood

Wisconsin
Rapids-
Marshfield

Stevens
Point
Portage

Waupaca

APPLETON
Outagamie

Brown

Kewaunee

Scott | Dakota

Pepin

Sibley

Le Sueur

Buffalo

Trem-
pealeau

Jackson

Appleton-Oshkosh-Neenah

Waushara

OSHKOSH-
NEENAH
Winnebago

Calumet

Manitowoc
Manitowoc

MINNEAPOLIS-
ST. PAUL-
BLOOMINGTON

La Crosse

LA CROSSE-
ONALASKA
Monroe

Juneau | Adams

Marquette

Green
Lake

FOND DU LAC
Fond du Lac

Sheboygan

SHEBOYGAN

Houston

Vernon

Richland

Baraboo
Sauk

Columbia

Beaver
Dam
Dodge

Washington

Ozaukee

Lake
Michigan

Milwaukee-
Racine-
Waukesha

IOWA

Crawford

Madison-
Janesville-
Beloit
MADISON
Iowa

Dane

Watertown-
Fort
Atkinson
Jefferson

Waukesha

Milwaukee

MILWAUKEE-
WAUKESHA-
WEST ALLIS

MICHIGAN

0 10 20 30 40 Kilometers
0 10 20 30 40 Miles

Platteville
Grant

Lafayette

Green

JANESVILLE-
BELOIT
Rock

Whitewater-
Elkhorn
Walworth

RACINE
Racine

Kenosha

Lake County-
Kenosha County

ILLINOIS

McHenry

Lake

Chicago-
Naperville (pt)

DeKalb

Kane

CHICAGO-
NAPERVILLE-
ELGIN (pt)
DuPage

Cook

INDIANA

Kendall

Will

Lake | Porter

Grundy

Newton | Jasper

LEGEND

Green Bay-Shawano ━━━━━ Combined Statistical Area

APPLETON ▨ Metropolitan Statistical Area

Baraboo ▨ Micropolitan Statistical Area

Lake County-Kenosha County ••••• Metropolitan Division

CANADA ━━━━ International

ILLINOIS ──── State or Statistical Equivalent

Adams ──── County or Statistical Equivalent

Lake Michigan ──── Coastline

CBSA boundaries and names are as of February 2013. All
other boundaries and names are as of January 1, 2012.

U.S. DEPARTMENT OF COMMERCE Economics and Statistics Administration U.S. Census Bureau

WYOMING - Core Based Statistical Areas (CBSAs) and Counties

SOUTH DAKOTA

NEBRASKA

MONTANA

IDAHO

UTAH

COLORADO

Crook

Weston

Niobrara

Goshen

Platte

CHEYENNE
Laramie

Gillette
Campbell

Converse

Laramie
Albany

Sheridan
Sheridan

Johnson

CASPER
Natrona

Carbon

Big Horn

Washakie

Hot Springs

Riverton
Fremont

Park

Rock Springs
Sweetwater

Sublette

Jackson
Teton

Teton

Lincoln

Evanston
Uinta

LEGEND

Metropolitan Statistical Area

Micropolitan Statistical Area

State or Statistical Equivalent

County or Statistical Equivalent

Park

CHEYENNE

Jackson

MONTANA

CBSA boundaries and names are as of February 2013. All other boundaries and names are as of January 1, 2012.

N

0 10 20 30 40 Kilometers
0   10   20   30   40 Miles

APPENDIX E
CITIES BY COUNTY

The following table is arranged alphabetically by state. Under each state heading are listed all cities with a 2010 census population over 25,000 along with their component counties and the population in each component.

State Code	Place Code	County Code	Geographic Area Name	2010 Census Population	State Code	Place Code	County Code	Geographic Area Name	2010 Census Population
01			**ALABAMA**	4 779 736	01	78552		Vestavia Hills city	34 033
01	00820		Alabaster city	30 352	01	78552	073	Jefferson County	34 019
01	00820	117	Shelby County	30 352	01	78552	117	Shelby County	14
01	03076		Auburn city	53 380	02			**ALASKA**	710 231
01	03076	081	Lee County	53 380	02	03000		Anchorage municipality	291 826
					02	03000	020	Anchorage Municipality	291 826
01	05980		Bessemer city	27 456					
01	05980	073	Jefferson County	27 456	02	24230		Fairbanks city	31 535
					02	24230	090	Fairbanks North Star Borough	31 535
01	07000		Birmingham city	212 237					
01	07000	073	Jefferson County	210 609	02	36400		Juneau city and borough	31 275
01	07000	117	Shelby County	1 628	02	36400	110	Juneau City and Borough	31 275
01	20104		Decatur city	55 683	04			**ARIZONA**	6 392 017
01	20104	083	Limestone County	84	04	02830		Apache Junction city	35 840
01	20104	103	Morgan County	55 599	04	02830	013	Maricopa County	294
					04	02830	021	Pinal County	35 546
01	21184		Dothan city	65 496					
01	21184	045	Dale County	887	04	04720		Avondale city	76 238
01	21184	067	Henry County	5	04	04720	013	Maricopa County	76 238
01	21184	069	Houston County	64 604					
					04	07940		Buckeye town	50 876
01	24184		Enterprise city	26 562	04	07940	013	Maricopa County	50 876
01	24184	031	Coffee County	26 139					
01	24184	045	Dale County	423	04	08220		Bullhead City city	39 540
					04	08220	015	Mohave County	39 540
01	26896		Florence city	39 319					
01	26896	077	Lauderdale County	39 319	04	10530		Casa Grande city	48 571
					04	10530	021	Pinal County	48 571
01	28696		Gadsden city	36 856					
01	28696	055	Etowah County	36 856	04	12000		Chandler city	236 123
					04	12000	013	Maricopa County	236 123
01	35800		Homewood city	25 167					
01	35800	073	Jefferson County	25 167	04	22220		El Mirage city	31 797
					04	22220	013	Maricopa County	31 797
01	35896		Hoover city	81 619					
01	35896	073	Jefferson County	58 582	04	23620		Flagstaff city	65 870
01	35896	117	Shelby County	23 037	04	23620	005	Coconino County	65 870
01	37000		Huntsville city	180 105	04	23760		Florence town	25 536
01	37000	083	Limestone County	1 521	04	23760	021	Pinal County	25 536
01	37000	089	Madison County	178 584					
					04	27400		Gilbert town	208 453
01	45784		Madison city	42 938	04	27400	013	Maricopa County	208 453
01	45784	083	Limestone County	3 453					
01	45784	089	Madison County	39 485	04	27820		Glendale city	226 721
					04	27820	013	Maricopa County	226 721
01	50000		Mobile city	195 111					
01	50000	097	Mobile County	195 111	04	28380		Goodyear city	65 275
					04	28380	013	Maricopa County	65 275
01	51000		Montgomery city	205 764					
01	51000	101	Montgomery County	205 764	04	37620		Kingman city	28 068
					04	37620	015	Mohave County	28 068
01	57048		Opelika city	26 477					
01	57048	081	Lee County	26 477	04	39370		Lake Havasu City city	52 527
					04	39370	015	Mohave County	52 527
01	59472		Phenix City city	32 822					
01	59472	081	Lee County	4 153	04	44270		Marana town	34 961
01	59472	113	Russell County	28 669	04	44270	019	Pima County	34 961
					04	44270	021	Pinal County	0
01	62328		Prattville city	33 960					
01	62328	001	Autauga County	32 168	04	44410		Maricopa city	43 482
01	62328	051	Elmore County	1 792	04	44410	021	Pinal County	43 482
01	77256		Tuscaloosa city	90 468	04	46000		Mesa city	439 041
01	77256	125	Tuscaloosa County	90 468	04	46000	013	Maricopa County	439 041

Cities by County–*Continued*

State Code	Place Code	County Code	Geographic Area Name	2010 Census Population	State Code	Place Code	County Code	Geographic Area Name	2010 Census Population
04	51600		Oro Valley town	41 011	05	41000		Little Rock city	193 524
04	51600	019	Pima County	41 011	05	41000	119	Pulaski County	193 524
04	54050		Peoria city	154 065	05	50450		North Little Rock city	62 304
04	54050	013	Maricopa County	154 058	05	50450	119	Pulaski County	62 304
04	54050	025	Yavapai County	7					
					05	53390		Paragould city	26 113
04	55000		Phoenix city	1 445 632	05	53390	055	Greene County	26 113
04	55000	013	Maricopa County	1 445 632					
					05	55310		Pine Bluff city	49 083
04	57380		Prescott city	39 843	05	55310	069	Jefferson County	49 083
04	57380	025	Yavapai County	39 843					
					05	60410		Rogers city	55 964
04	57450		Prescott Valley town	38 822	05	60410	007	Benton County	55 964
04	57450	025	Yavapai County	38 822					
					05	61670		Russellville city	27 920
04	58150		Queen Creek town	26 361	05	61670	115	Pope County	27 920
04	58150	013	Maricopa County	25 912					
04	58150	021	Pinal County	449	05	63800		Sherwood city	29 523
					05	63800	119	Pulaski County	29 523
04	62140		Sahuarita town	25 259					
04	62140	019	Pima County	25 259	05	66080		Springdale city	69 797
					05	66080	007	Benton County	6 054
04	63470		San Luis city	25 505	05	66080	143	Washington County	63 743
04	63470	027	Yuma County	25 505					
					05	68810		Texarkana city	29 919
04	65000		Scottsdale city	217 385	05	68810	091	Miller County	29 919
04	65000	013	Maricopa County	217 385					
					05	74540		West Memphis city	26 245
04	66820		Sierra Vista city	43 888	05	74540	035	Crittenden County	26 245
04	66820	003	Cochise County	43 888					
					06			**CALIFORNIA**	37 253 956
04	71510		Surprise city	117 517	06	00296		Adelanto city	31 765
04	71510	013	Maricopa County	117 517	06	00296	071	San Bernardino County	31 765
04	73000		Tempe city	161 719	06	00562		Alameda city	73 812
04	73000	013	Maricopa County	161 719	06	00562	001	Alameda County	73 812
04	77000		Tucson city	520 116	06	00884		Alhambra city	83 089
04	77000	019	Pima County	520 116	06	00884	037	Los Angeles County	83 089
04	85540		Yuma city	93 064	06	00947		Aliso Viejo city	47 823
04	85540	027	Yuma County	93 064	06	00947	059	Orange County	47 823
05			**ARKANSAS**	2 915 918	06	02000		Anaheim city	336 265
05	04840		Bella Vista town	26 461	06	02000	059	Orange County	336 265
05	04840	007	Benton County	26 461					
					06	02252		Antioch city	102 372
05	05290		Benton city	30 681	06	02252	013	Contra Costa County	102 372
05	05290	125	Saline County	30 681					
					06	02364		Apple Valley town	69 135
05	05320		Bentonville city	35 301	06	02364	071	San Bernardino County	69 135
05	05320	007	Benton County	35 301					
					06	02462		Arcadia city	56 364
05	15190		Conway city	58 908	06	02462	037	Los Angeles County	56 364
05	15190	045	Faulkner County	58 908					
					06	03064		Atascadero city	28 310
05	23290		Fayetteville city	73 580	06	03064	079	San Luis Obispo County	28 310
05	23290	143	Washington County	73 580					
					06	03162		Atwater city	28 168
05	24550		Fort Smith city	86 209	06	03162	047	Merced County	28 168
05	24550	131	Sebastian County	86 209					
					06	03386		Azusa city	46 361
05	33400		Hot Springs city	35 193	06	03386	037	Los Angeles County	46 361
05	33400	051	Garland County	35 193					
					06	03526		Bakersfield city	347 483
05	34750		Jacksonville city	28 364	06	03526	029	Kern County	347 483
05	34750	119	Pulaski County	28 364					
					06	03666		Baldwin Park city	75 390
05	35710		Jonesboro city	67 263	06	03666	037	Los Angeles County	75 390
05	35710	031	Craighead County	67 263					

Cities by County–*Continued*

State Code	Place Code	County Code	Geographic Area Name	2010 Census Population	State Code	Place Code	County Code	Geographic Area Name	2010 Census Population
06	03820		Banning city	29 603	06	13214		Chino Hills city	74 799
06	03820	065	Riverside County	29 603	06	13214	071	San Bernardino County	74 799
06	04758		Beaumont city	36 877	06	13392		Chula Vista city	243 916
06	04758	065	Riverside County	36 877	06	13392	073	San Diego County	243 916
06	04870		Bell city	35 477	06	13588		Citrus Heights city	83 301
06	04870	037	Los Angeles County	35 477	06	13588	067	Sacramento County	83 301
06	04982		Bellflower city	76 616	06	13756		Claremont city	34 926
06	04982	037	Los Angeles County	76 616	06	13756	037	Los Angeles County	34 926
06	04996		Bell Gardens city	42 072	06	14218		Clovis city	95 631
06	04996	037	Los Angeles County	42 072	06	14218	019	Fresno County	95 631
06	05108		Belmont city	25 835	06	14260		Coachella city	40 704
06	05108	081	San Mateo County	25 835	06	14260	065	Riverside County	40 704
06	05290		Benicia city	26 997	06	14890		Colton city	52 154
06	05290	095	Solano County	26 997	06	14890	071	San Bernardino County	52 154
06	06000		Berkeley city	112 580	06	15044		Compton city	96 455
06	06000	001	Alameda County	112 580	06	15044	037	Los Angeles County	96 455
06	06308		Beverly Hills city	34 109	06	16000		Concord city	122 067
06	06308	037	Los Angeles County	34 109	06	16000	013	Contra Costa County	122 067
06	08100		Brea city	39 282	06	16350		Corona city	152 374
06	08100	059	Orange County	39 282	06	16350	065	Riverside County	152 374
06	08142		Brentwood city	51 481	06	16532		Costa Mesa city	109 960
06	08142	013	Contra Costa County	51 481	06	16532	059	Orange County	109 960
06	08786		Buena Park city	80 530	06	16742		Covina city	47 796
06	08786	059	Orange County	80 530	06	16742	037	Los Angeles County	47 796
06	08954		Burbank city	103 340	06	17568		Culver City city	38 883
06	08954	037	Los Angeles County	103 340	06	17568	037	Los Angeles County	38 883
06	09066		Burlingame city	28 806	06	17610		Cupertino city	58 302
06	09066	081	San Mateo County	28 806	06	17610	085	Santa Clara County	58 302
06	09710		Calexico city	38 572	06	17750		Cypress city	47 802
06	09710	025	Imperial County	38 572	06	17750	059	Orange County	47 802
06	10046		Camarillo city	65 201	06	17918		Daly City city	101 123
06	10046	111	Ventura County	65 201	06	17918	081	San Mateo County	101 123
06	10345		Campbell city	39 349	06	17946		Dana Point city	33 351
06	10345	085	Santa Clara County	39 349	06	17946	059	Orange County	33 351
06	11194		Carlsbad city	105 328	06	17988		Danville town	42 039
06	11194	073	San Diego County	105 328	06	17988	013	Contra Costa County	42 039
06	11530		Carson city	91 714	06	18100		Davis city	65 622
06	11530	037	Los Angeles County	91 714	06	18100	113	Yolo County	65 622
06	12048		Cathedral City city	51 200	06	18394		Delano city	53 041
06	12048	065	Riverside County	51 200	06	18394	029	Kern County	53 041
06	12524		Ceres city	45 417	06	18996		Desert Hot Springs city	25 938
06	12524	099	Stanislaus County	45 417	06	18996	065	Riverside County	25 938
06	12552		Cerritos city	49 041	06	19192		Diamond Bar city	55 544
06	12552	037	Los Angeles County	49 041	06	19192	037	Los Angeles County	55 544
06	13014		Chico city	86 187	06	19766		Downey city	111 772
06	13014	007	Butte County	86 187	06	19766	037	Los Angeles County	111 772
06	13210		Chino city	77 983	06	20018		Dublin city	46 036
06	13210	071	San Bernardino County	77 983	06	20018	001	Alameda County	46 036

State Code	Place Code	County Code	Geographic Area Name	2010 Census Population	State Code	Place Code	County Code	Geographic Area Name	2010 Census Population
06	20956		East Palo Alto city	28 155	06	32548		Hawthorne city	84 293
06	20956	081	San Mateo County	28 155	06	32548	037	Los Angeles County	84 293
06	21712		El Cajon city	99 478	06	33000		Hayward city	144 186
06	21712	073	San Diego County	99 478	06	33000	001	Alameda County	144 186
06	21782		El Centro city	42 598	06	33182		Hemet city	78 657
06	21782	025	Imperial County	42 598	06	33182	065	Riverside County	78 657
06	22020		Elk Grove city	153 015	06	33434		Hesperia city	90 173
06	22020	067	Sacramento County	153 015	06	33434	071	San Bernardino County	90 173
06	22230		El Monte city	113 475	06	33588		Highland city	53 104
06	22230	037	Los Angeles County	113 475	06	33588	071	San Bernardino County	53 104
06	22300		El Paso de Robles (Paso Robles)	29 793	06	34120		Hollister city	34 928
06	22300	079	San Luis Obispo County	29 793	06	34120	069	San Benito County	34 928
06	22678		Encinitas city	59 518	06	36000		Huntington Beach city	189 992
06	22678	073	San Diego County	59 518	06	36000	059	Orange County	189 992
06	22804		Escondido city	143 911	06	36056		Huntington Park city	58 114
06	22804	073	San Diego County	143 911	06	36056	037	Los Angeles County	58 114
06	23042		Eureka city	27 191	06	36294		Imperial Beach city	26 324
06	23042	023	Humboldt County	27 191	06	36294	073	San Diego County	26 324
06	23182		Fairfield city	105 321	06	36448		Indio city	76 036
06	23182	095	Solano County	105 321	06	36448	065	Riverside County	76 036
06	24638		Folsom city	72 203	06	36546		Inglewood city	109 673
06	24638	067	Sacramento County	72 203	06	36546	037	Los Angeles County	109 673
06	24680		Fontana city	196 069	06	36770		Irvine city	212 375
06	24680	071	San Bernardino County	196 069	06	36770	059	Orange County	212 375
06	25338		Foster City city	30 567	06	39220		Laguna Hills city	30 344
06	25338	081	San Mateo County	30 567	06	39220	059	Orange County	30 344
06	25380		Fountain Valley city	55 313	06	39248		Laguna Niguel city	62 979
06	25380	059	Orange County	55 313	06	39248	059	Orange County	62 979
06	26000		Fremont city	214 089	06	39290		La Habra city	60 239
06	26000	001	Alameda County	214 089	06	39290	059	Orange County	60 239
06	27000		Fresno city	494 665	06	39486		Lake Elsinore city	51 821
06	27000	019	Fresno County	494 665	06	39486	065	Riverside County	51 821
06	28000		Fullerton city	135 161	06	39496		Lake Forest city	77 264
06	28000	059	Orange County	135 161	06	39496	059	Orange County	77 264
06	28168		Gardena city	58 829	06	39892		Lakewood city	80 048
06	28168	037	Los Angeles County	58 829	06	39892	037	Los Angeles County	80 048
06	29000		Garden Grove city	170 883	06	40004		La Mesa city	57 065
06	29000	059	Orange County	170 883	06	40004	073	San Diego County	57 065
06	29504		Gilroy city	48 821	06	40032		La Mirada city	48 527
06	29504	085	Santa Clara County	48 821	06	40032	037	Los Angeles County	48 527
06	30000		Glendale city	191 719	06	40130		Lancaster city	156 633
06	30000	037	Los Angeles County	191 719	06	40130	037	Los Angeles County	156 633
06	30014		Glendora city	50 073	06	40340		La Puente city	39 816
06	30014	037	Los Angeles County	50 073	06	40340	037	Los Angeles County	39 816
06	30378		Goleta city	29 888	06	40354		La Quinta city	37 467
06	30378	083	Santa Barbara County	29 888	06	40354	065	Riverside County	37 467
06	31960		Hanford city	53 967	06	40830		La Verne city	31 063
06	31960	031	Kings County	53 967	06	40830	037	Los Angeles County	31 063

Cities by County–*Continued*

State Code	Place Code	County Code	Geographic Area Name	2010 Census Population	State Code	Place Code	County Code	Geographic Area Name	2010 Census Population
06	40886		Lawndale city	32 769	06	48788		Montclair city	36 664
06	40886	037	Los Angeles County	32 769	06	48788	071	San Bernardino County	36 664
06	41124		Lemon Grove city	25 320	06	48816		Montebello city	62 500
06	41124	073	San Diego County	25 320	06	48816	037	Los Angeles County	62 500
06	41474		Lincoln city	42 819	06	48872		Monterey city	27 810
06	41474	061	Placer County	42 819	06	48872	053	Monterey County	27 810
06	41992		Livermore city	80 968	06	48914		Monterey Park city	60 269
06	41992	001	Alameda County	80 968	06	48914	037	Los Angeles County	60 269
06	42202		Lodi city	62 134	06	49138		Moorpark city	34 421
06	42202	077	San Joaquin County	62 134	06	49138	111	Ventura County	34 421
06	42524		Lompoc city	42 434	06	49270		Moreno Valley city	193 365
06	42524	083	Santa Barbara County	42 434	06	49270	065	Riverside County	193 365
06	43000		Long Beach city	462 257	06	49278		Morgan Hill city	37 882
06	43000	037	Los Angeles County	462 257	06	49278	085	Santa Clara County	37 882
06	43280		Los Altos city	28 976	06	49670		Mountain View city	74 066
06	43280	085	Santa Clara County	28 976	06	49670	085	Santa Clara County	74 066
06	44000		Los Angeles city	3 792 621	06	50076		Murrieta city	103 466
06	44000	037	Los Angeles County	3 792 621	06	50076	065	Riverside County	103 466
06	44028		Los Banos city	35 972	06	50258		Napa city	76 915
06	44028	047	Merced County	35 972	06	50258	055	Napa County	76 915
06	44112		Los Gatos town	29 413	06	50398		National City city	58 582
06	44112	085	Santa Clara County	29 413	06	50398	073	San Diego County	58 582
06	44574		Lynwood city	69 772	06	50916		Newark city	42 573
06	44574	037	Los Angeles County	69 772	06	50916	001	Alameda County	42 573
06	45022		Madera city	61 416	06	51182		Newport Beach city	85 186
06	45022	039	Madera County	61 416	06	51182	059	Orange County	85 186
06	45400		Manhattan Beach city	35 135	06	51560		Norco city	27 063
06	45400	037	Los Angeles County	35 135	06	51560	065	Riverside County	27 063
06	45484		Manteca city	67 096	06	52526		Norwalk city	105 549
06	45484	077	San Joaquin County	67 096	06	52526	037	Los Angeles County	105 549
06	46114		Martinez city	35 824	06	52582		Novato city	51 904
06	46114	013	Contra Costa County	35 824	06	52582	041	Marin County	51 904
06	46492		Maywood city	27 395	06	53000		Oakland city	390 724
06	46492	037	Los Angeles County	27 395	06	53000	001	Alameda County	390 724
06	46842		Menifee city	77 519	06	53070		Oakley city	35 432
06	46842	065	Riverside County	77 519	06	53070	013	Contra Costa County	35 432
06	46870		Menlo Park city	32 026	06	53322		Oceanside city	167 086
06	46870	081	San Mateo County	32 026	06	53322	073	San Diego County	167 086
06	46898		Merced city	78 958	06	53896		Ontario city	163 924
06	46898	047	Merced County	78 958	06	53896	071	San Bernardino County	163 924
06	47766		Milpitas city	66 790	06	53980		Orange city	136 416
06	47766	085	Santa Clara County	66 790	06	53980	059	Orange County	136 416
06	48256		Mission Viejo city	93 305	06	54652		Oxnard city	197 899
06	48256	059	Orange County	93 305	06	54652	111	Ventura County	197 899
06	48354		Modesto city	201 165	06	54806		Pacifica city	37 234
06	48354	099	Stanislaus County	201 165	06	54806	081	San Mateo County	37 234
06	48648		Monrovia city	36 590	06	55156		Palmdale city	152 750
06	48648	037	Los Angeles County	36 590	06	55156	037	Los Angeles County	152 750

Cities by County–*Continued*

State Code	Place Code	County Code	Geographic Area Name	2010 Census Population	State Code	Place Code	County Code	Geographic Area Name	2010 Census Population
06	55184		Palm Desert city	48 445	06	60466		Rialto city	99 171
06	55184	065	Riverside County	48 445	06	60466	071	San Bernardino County	99 171
06	55254		Palm Springs city	44 552	06	60620		Richmond city	103 701
06	55254	065	Riverside County	44 552	06	60620	013	Contra Costa County	103 701
06	55282		Palo Alto city	64 403	06	60704		Ridgecrest city	27 616
06	55282	085	Santa Clara County	64 403	06	60704	029	Kern County	27 616
06	55520		Paradise town	26 218	06	62000		Riverside city	303 871
06	55520	007	Butte County	26 218	06	62000	065	Riverside County	303 871
06	55618		Paramount city	54 098	06	62364		Rocklin city	56 974
06	55618	037	Los Angeles County	54 098	06	62364	061	Placer County	56 974
06	56000		Pasadena city	137 122	06	62546		Rohnert Park city	40 971
06	56000	037	Los Angeles County	137 122	06	62546	097	Sonoma County	40 971
06	56700		Perris city	68 386	06	62896		Rosemead city	53 764
06	56700	065	Riverside County	68 386	06	62896	037	Los Angeles County	53 764
06	56784		Petaluma city	57 941	06	62938		Roseville city	118 788
06	56784	097	Sonoma County	57 941	06	62938	061	Placer County	118 788
06	56924		Pico Rivera city	62 942	06	64000		Sacramento city	466 488
06	56924	037	Los Angeles County	62 942	06	64000	067	Sacramento County	466 488
06	57456		Pittsburg city	63 264	06	64224		Salinas city	150 441
06	57456	013	Contra Costa County	63 264	06	64224	053	Monterey County	150 441
06	57526		Placentia city	50 533	06	65000		San Bernardino city	209 924
06	57526	059	Orange County	50 533	06	65000	071	San Bernardino County	209 924
06	57764		Pleasant Hill city	33 152	06	65028		San Bruno city	41 114
06	57764	013	Contra Costa County	33 152	06	65028	081	San Mateo County	41 114
06	57792		Pleasanton city	70 285	06	65042		San Buenaventura (Ventura)	106 433
06	57792	001	Alameda County	70 285	06	65042	111	Ventura County	106 433
06	58072		Pomona city	149 058	06	65070		San Carlos city	28 406
06	58072	037	Los Angeles County	149 058	06	65070	081	San Mateo County	28 406
06	58240		Porterville city	54 165	06	65084		San Clemente city	63 522
06	58240	107	Tulare County	54 165	06	65084	059	Orange County	63 522
06	58520		Poway city	47 811	06	66000		San Diego city	1 307 402
06	58520	073	San Diego County	47 811	06	66000	073	San Diego County	1 307 402
06	59444		Rancho Cordova city	64 776	06	66070		San Dimas city	33 371
06	59444	067	Sacramento County	64 776	06	66070	037	Los Angeles County	33 371
06	59451		Rancho Cucamonga city	165 269	06	67000		San Francisco city	805 235
06	59451	071	San Bernardino County	165 269	06	67000	075	San Francisco County	805 235
06	59514		Rancho Palos Verdes city	41 643	06	67042		San Gabriel city	39 718
06	59514	037	Los Angeles County	41 643	06	67042	037	Los Angeles County	39 718
06	59587		Rancho Santa Margarita city	47 853	06	67112		San Jacinto city	44 199
06	59587	059	Orange County	47 853	06	67112	065	Riverside County	44 199
06	59920		Redding city	89 861	06	68000		San Jose city	945 942
06	59920	089	Shasta County	89 861	06	68000	085	Santa Clara County	945 942
06	59962		Redlands city	68 747	06	68028		San Juan Capistrano city	34 593
06	59962	071	San Bernardino County	68 747	06	68028	059	Orange County	34 593
06	60018		Redondo Beach city	66 748	06	68084		San Leandro city	84 950
06	60018	037	Los Angeles County	66 748	06	68084	001	Alameda County	84 950
06	60102		Redwood City city	76 815	06	68154		San Luis Obispo city	45 119
06	60102	081	San Mateo County	76 815	06	68154	079	San Luis Obispo County	45 119

Cities by County–*Continued*

State Code	Place Code	County Code	Geographic Area Name	2010 Census Population	State Code	Place Code	County Code	Geographic Area Name	2010 Census Population
06	68196		San Marcos city	83 781	06	75630		Suisun City city	28 111
06	68196	073	San Diego County	83 781	06	75630	095	Solano County	28 111
06	68252		San Mateo city	97 207	06	77000		Sunnyvale city	140 081
06	68252	081	San Mateo County	97 207	06	77000	085	Santa Clara County	140 081
06	68294		San Pablo city	29 139	06	78120		Temecula city	100 097
06	68294	013	Contra Costa County	29 139	06	78120	065	Riverside County	100 097
06	68364		San Rafael city	57 713	06	78148		Temple City city	35 558
06	68364	041	Marin County	57 713	06	78148	037	Los Angeles County	35 558
06	68378		San Ramon city	72 148	06	78582		Thousand Oaks city	126 683
06	68378	013	Contra Costa County	72 148	06	78582	111	Ventura County	126 683
06	69000		Santa Ana city	324 528	06	80000		Torrance city	145 438
06	69000	059	Orange County	324 528	06	80000	037	Los Angeles County	145 438
06	69070		Santa Barbara city	88 410	06	80238		Tracy city	82 922
06	69070	083	Santa Barbara County	88 410	06	80238	077	San Joaquin County	82 922
06	69084		Santa Clara city	116 468	06	80644		Tulare city	59 278
06	69084	085	Santa Clara County	116 468	06	80644	107	Tulare County	59 278
06	69088		Santa Clarita city	176 320	06	80812		Turlock city	68 549
06	69088	037	Los Angeles County	176 320	06	80812	099	Stanislaus County	68 549
06	69112		Santa Cruz city	59 946	06	80854		Tustin city	75 540
06	69112	087	Santa Cruz County	59 946	06	80854	059	Orange County	75 540
06	69196		Santa Maria city	99 553	06	80994		Twentynine Palms city	25 048
06	69196	083	Santa Barbara County	99 553	06	80994	071	San Bernardino County	25 048
06	70000		Santa Monica city	89 736	06	81204		Union City city	69 516
06	70000	037	Los Angeles County	89 736	06	81204	001	Alameda County	69 516
06	70042		Santa Paula city	29 321	06	81344		Upland city	73 732
06	70042	111	Ventura County	29 321	06	81344	071	San Bernardino County	73 732
06	70098		Santa Rosa city	167 815	06	81554		Vacaville city	92 428
06	70098	097	Sonoma County	167 815	06	81554	095	Solano County	92 428
06	70224		Santee city	53 413	06	81666		Vallejo city	115 942
06	70224	073	San Diego County	53 413	06	81666	095	Solano County	115 942
06	70280		Saratoga city	29 926	06	82590		Victorville city	115 903
06	70280	085	Santa Clara County	29 926	06	82590	071	San Bernardino County	115 903
06	70742		Seaside city	33 025	06	82954		Visalia city	124 442
06	70742	053	Monterey County	33 025	06	82954	107	Tulare County	124 442
06	72016		Simi Valley city	124 237	06	82996		Vista city	93 834
06	72016	111	Ventura County	124 237	06	82996	073	San Diego County	93 834
06	72520		Soledad city	25 738	06	83332		Walnut city	29 172
06	72520	053	Monterey County	25 738	06	83332	037	Los Angeles County	29 172
06	73080		South Gate city	94 396	06	83346		Walnut Creek city	64 173
06	73080	037	Los Angeles County	94 396	06	83346	013	Contra Costa County	64 173
06	73220		South Pasadena city	25 619	06	83542		Wasco city	25 545
06	73220	037	Los Angeles County	25 619	06	83542	029	Kern County	25 545
06	73262		South San Francisco city	63 632	06	83668		Watsonville city	51 199
06	73262	081	San Mateo County	63 632	06	83668	087	Santa Cruz County	51 199
06	73962		Stanton city	38 186	06	84200		West Covina city	106 098
06	73962	059	Orange County	38 186	06	84200	037	Los Angeles County	106 098
06	75000		Stockton city	291 707	06	84410		West Hollywood city	34 399
06	75000	077	San Joaquin County	291 707	06	84410	037	Los Angeles County	34 399

Cities by County–*Continued*

State Code	Place Code	County Code	Geographic Area Name	2010 Census Population	State Code	Place Code	County Code	Geographic Area Name	2010 Census Population
06	84550		Westminster city	89 701	08	31660		Grand Junction city	58 566
06	84550	059	Orange County	89 701	08	31660	077	Mesa County	58 566
06	84816		West Sacramento city	48 744	08	32155		Greeley city	92 889
06	84816	113	Yolo County	48 744	08	32155	123	Weld County	92 889
06	85292		Whittier city	85 331	08	43000		Lakewood city	142 980
06	85292	037	Los Angeles County	85 331	08	43000	059	Jefferson County	142 980
06	85446		Wildomar city	32 176	08	45255		Littleton city	41 737
06	85446	065	Riverside County	32 176	08	45255	005	Arapahoe County	39 328
					08	45255	035	Douglas County	28
06	85922		Windsor town	26 801	08	45255	059	Jefferson County	2 381
06	85922	097	Sonoma County	26 801					
					08	45970		Longmont city	86 270
06	86328		Woodland city	55 468	08	45970	013	Boulder County	86 240
06	86328	113	Yolo County	55 468	08	45970	123	Weld County	30
06	86832		Yorba Linda city	64 234	08	46465		Loveland city	66 859
06	86832	059	Orange County	64 234	08	46465	069	Larimer County	66 859
06	86972		Yuba City city	64 925	08	54330		Northglenn city	35 789
06	86972	101	Sutter County	64 925	08	54330	001	Adams County	35 777
					08		123	Weld County	12
06	87042		Yucaipa city	51 367					
06	87042	071	San Bernardino County	51 367	08	57630		Parker town	45 297
					08	57630	035	Douglas County	45 297
08			**COLORADO**	5 029 196					
08	03455		Arvada city	106 433	08	62000		Pueblo city	106 595
08	03455	001	Adams County	2 849	08	62000	101	Pueblo County	106 595
08	03455	059	Jefferson County	103 584					
					08	77290		Thornton city	118 772
08	04000		Aurora city	325 078	08	77290	001	Adams County	118 772
08	04000	001	Adams County	39 871	08	77290	123	Weld County	0
08	04000	005	Arapahoe County	285 090					
08	04000	035	Douglas County	117	08	83835		Westminster city	106 114
					08	83835	001	Adams County	63 696
08	07850		Boulder city	97 385	08	83835	059	Jefferson County	42 418
08	07850	013	Boulder County	97 385					
					08	84440		Wheat Ridge city	30 166
08	08675		Brighton city	33 352	08	84440	059	Jefferson County	30 166
08	08675	001	Adams County	33 009					
08	08675	123	Weld County	343	09			**CONNECTICUT**	3 574 097
					09	08000		Bridgeport city	144 229
08	09280		Broomfield city	55 889	09	08000	001	Fairfield County	144 229
08	09280	014	Broomfield County	55 889					
					09	08420		Bristol city	60 477
08	12415		Castle Rock town	48 231	09	08420	003	Hartford County	60 477
08	12415	035	Douglas County	48 231					
					09	18430		Danbury city	80 893
08	12815		Centennial city	100 377	09	18430	001	Fairfield County	80 893
08	12815	005	Arapahoe County	100 377					
					09	37000		Hartford city	124 775
08	16000		Colorado Springs city	416 427	09	37000	003	Hartford County	124 775
08	16000	041	El Paso County	416 427					
					09	46450		Meriden city	60 868
08	16495		Commerce City city	45 913	09	46450	009	New Haven County	60 868
08	16495	001	Adams County	45 913					
					09	47290		Middletown city	47 648
08	20000		Denver city	600 158	09	47290	007	Middlesex County	47 648
08	20000	031	Denver County	600 158					
					09	49880		Naugatuck borough	31 862
08	24785		Englewood city	30 255	09	49880	009	New Haven County	31 862
08	24785	005	Arapahoe County	30 255					
					09	50370		New Britain city	73 206
08	27425		Fort Collins city	143 986	09	50370	003	Hartford County	73 206
08	27425	069	Larimer County	143 986					
					09	52000		New Haven city	129 779
08	27865		Fountain city	25 846	09	52000	009	New Haven County	129 779
08	27865	041	El Paso County	25 846					
					09	52280		New London city	27 620
					09	52280	011	New London County	27 620

Cities by County–*Continued*

State Code	Place Code	County Code	Geographic Area Name	2010 Census Population	State Code	Place Code	County Code	Geographic Area Name	2010 Census Population
09	55990		Norwalk city	85 603	12	14125		Cooper City city	28 547
09	55990	001	Fairfield County	85 603	12	14125	011	Broward County	28 547
09	56200		Norwich city	40 493	12	14250		Coral Gables city	46 780
09	56200	011	New London County	40 493	12	14250	086	Miami-Dade County	46 780
09	68100		Shelton city	39 559	12	14400		Coral Springs city	121 096
09	68100	001	Fairfield County	39 559	12	14400	011	Broward County	121 096
09	73000		Stamford city	122 643	12	15968		Cutler Bay town	40 286
09	73000	001	Fairfield County	122 643	12	15968	086	Miami-Dade County	40 286
09	76500		Torrington city	36 383	12	16335		Dania Beach city	29 639
09	76500	005	Litchfield County	36 383	12	16335	011	Broward County	29 639
09	80000		Waterbury city	110 366	12	16475		Davie town	91 992
09	80000	009	New Haven County	110 366	12	16475	011	Broward County	91 992
09	82800		West Haven city	55 564	12	16525		Daytona Beach city	61 005
09	82800	009	New Haven County	55 564	12	16525	127	Volusia County	61 005
10			**DELAWARE**	897 934	12	16725		Deerfield Beach city	75 018
10	21200		Dover city	36 047	12	16725	011	Broward County	75 018
10	21200	001	Kent County	36 047					
					12	16875		DeLand city	27 031
10	50670		Newark city	31 454	12	16875	127	Volusia County	27 031
10	50670	003	New Castle County	31 454					
					12	17100		Delray Beach city	60 522
10	77580		Wilmington city	70 851	12	17100	099	Palm Beach County	60 522
10	77580	003	New Castle County	70 851					
					12	17200		Deltona city	85 182
11			**DISTRICT OF COLUMBIA**	601 723	12	17200	127	Volusia County	85 182
11	50000		Washington city	601 723					
11	50000	001	District of Columbia	601 723	12	17935		Doral city	45 704
					12	17935	086	Miami-Dade County	45 704
12			**FLORIDA**	18 801 310					
12	00950		Altamonte Springs city	41 496	12	18575		Dunedin city	35 321
12	00950	117	Seminole County	41 496	12	18575	103	Pinellas County	35 321
12	01700		Apopka city	41 542	12	24000		Fort Lauderdale city	165 521
12	01700	095	Orange County	41 542	12	24000	011	Broward County	165 521
12	02681		Aventura city	35 762	12	24125		Fort Myers city	62 298
12	02681	086	Miami-Dade County	35 762	12	24125	071	Lee County	62 298
12	07300		Boca Raton city	84 392	12	24300		Fort Pierce city	41 590
12	07300	099	Palm Beach County	84 392	12	24300	111	St. Lucie County	41 590
12	07525		Bonita Springs city	43 914	12	25175		Gainesville city	124 354
12	07525	071	Lee County	43 914	12	25175	001	Alachua County	124 354
12	07875		Boynton Beach city	68 217	12	27322		Greenacres city	37 573
12	07875	099	Palm Beach County	68 217	12	27322	099	Palm Beach County	37 573
12	07950		Bradenton city	49 546	12	28452		Hallandale Beach city	37 113
12	07950	081	Manatee County	49 546	12	28452	011	Broward County	37 113
12	10275		Cape Coral city	154 305	12	30000		Hialeah city	224 669
12	10275	071	Lee County	154 305	12	30000	086	Miami-Dade County	224 669
12	11050		Casselberry city	26 241	12	32000		Hollywood city	140 768
12	11050	117	Seminole County	26 241	12	32000	011	Broward County	140 768
12	12875		Clearwater city	107 685	12	32275		Homestead city	60 512
12	12875	103	Pinellas County	107 685	12	32275	086	Miami-Dade County	60 512
12	12925		Clermont city	28 742	12	35000		Jacksonville city	821 784
12	12925	069	Lake County	28 742	12	35000	031	Duval County	821 784
12	13275		Coconut Creek city	52 909	12	35875		Jupiter town	55 156
12	13275	011	Broward County	52 909	12	35875	099	Palm Beach County	55 156

State Code	Place Code	County Code	Geographic Area Name	2010 Census Population	State Code	Place Code	County Code	Geographic Area Name	2010 Census Population
12	36950		Kissimmee city	59 682	12	54075		Palm Beach Gardens city	48 452
12	36950	097	Osceola County	59 682	12	54075	099	Palm Beach County	48 452
12	38250		Lakeland city	97 422	12	54200		Palm Coast city	75 180
12	38250	105	Polk County	97 422	12	54200	035	Flagler County	75 180
12	39075		Lake Worth city	34 910	12	54700		Panama City city	36 484
12	39075	099	Palm Beach County	34 910	12	54700	005	Bay County	36 484
12	39425		Largo city	77 648	12	55775		Pembroke Pines city	154 750
12	39425	103	Pinellas County	77 648	12	55775	011	Broward County	154 750
12	39525		Lauderdale Lakes city	32 593	12	55925		Pensacola city	51 923
12	39525	011	Broward County	32 593	12	55925	033	Escambia County	51 923
12	39550		Lauderhill city	66 887	12	56975		Pinellas Park city	49 079
12	39550	011	Broward County	66 887	12	56975	103	Pinellas County	49 079
12	43125		Margate city	53 284	12	57425		Plantation city	84 955
12	43125	011	Broward County	53 284	12	57425	011	Broward County	84 955
12	43975		Melbourne city	76 068	12	57550		Plant City city	34 721
12	43975	009	Brevard County	76 068	12	57550	057	Hillsborough County	34 721
12	45000		Miami city	399 457	12	58050		Pompano Beach city	99 845
12	45000	086	Miami-Dade County	399 457	12	58050	011	Broward County	99 845
12	45025		Miami Beach city	87 779	12	58575		Port Orange city	56 048
12	45025	086	Miami-Dade County	87 779	12	58575	127	Volusia County	56 048
12	45060		Miami Gardens city	107 167	12	58715		Port St. Lucie city	164 603
12	45060	086	Miami-Dade County	107 167	12	58715	111	St. Lucie County	164 603
12	45100		Miami Lakes town	29 361	12	60975		Riviera Beach city	32 488
12	45100	086	Miami-Dade County	29 361	12	60975	099	Palm Beach County	32 488
12	45975		Miramar city	122 041	12	62100		Royal Palm Beach village	34 140
12	45975	011	Broward County	122 041	12	62100	099	Palm Beach County	34 140
12	49425		North Lauderdale city	41 023	12	62625		St. Cloud city	35 183
12	49425	011	Broward County	41 023	12	62625	097	Osceola County	35 183
12	49450		North Miami city	58 786	12	63000		St. Petersburg city	244 769
12	49450	086	Miami-Dade County	58 786	12	63000	103	Pinellas County	244 769
12	49475		North Miami Beach city	41 523	12	63650		Sanford city	53 570
12	49475	086	Miami-Dade County	41 523	12	63650	117	Seminole County	53 570
12	49675		North Port city	57 357	12	64175		Sarasota city	51 917
12	49675	115	Sarasota County	57 357	12	64175	115	Sarasota County	51 917
12	50575		Oakland Park city	41 363	12	69700		Sunrise city	84 439
12	50575	011	Broward County	41 363	12	69700	011	Broward County	84 439
12	50750		Ocala city	56 315	12	70600		Tallahassee city	181 376
12	50750	083	Marion County	56 315	12	70600	073	Leon County	181 376
12	51075		Ocoee city	35 579	12	70675		Tamarac city	60 427
12	51075	095	Orange County	35 579	12	70675	011	Broward County	60 427
12	53000		Orlando city	238 300	12	71000		Tampa city	335 709
12	53000	095	Orange County	238 300	12	71000	057	Hillsborough County	335 709
12	53150		Ormond Beach city	38 137	12	71900		Titusville city	43 761
12	53150	127	Volusia County	38 137	12	71900	009	Brevard County	43 761
12	53575		Oviedo city	33 342	12	75812		Wellington village	56 508
12	53575	117	Seminole County	33 342	12	75812	099	Palm Beach County	56 508
12	54000		Palm Bay city	103 190	12	76582		Weston city	65 333
12	54000	009	Brevard County	103 190	12	76582	011	Broward County	65 333

Cities by County–*Continued*

State Code	Place Code	County Code	Geographic Area Name	2010 Census Population	State Code	Place Code	County Code	Geographic Area Name	2010 Census Population
12	76600		West Palm Beach city	99 919	13	55020		Newnan city	33 039
12	76600	099	Palm Beach County	99 919	13	55020	077	Coweta County	33 039
12	78250		Winter Garden city	34 568	13	59724		Peachtree City city	34 364
12	78250	095	Orange County	34 568	13	59724	113	Fayette County	34 364
12	78275		Winter Haven city	33 874	13	66668		Rome city	36 303
12	78275	105	Polk County	33 874	13	66668	115	Floyd County	36 303
12	78300		Winter Park city	27 852	13	67284		Roswell city	88 346
12	78300	095	Orange County	27 852	13	67284	121	Fulton County	88 346
12	78325		Winter Springs city	33 282	13	68516		Sandy Springs city	93 853
12	78325	117	Seminole County	33 282	13	68516	121	Fulton County	93 853
13			**GEORGIA**	9 687 653	13	69000		Savannah city	136 286
13	01052		Albany city	77 434	13	69000	051	Chatham County	136 286
13	01052	095	Dougherty County	77 434	13	71492		Smyrna city	51 271
13	01696		Alpharetta city	57 551	13	71492	067	Cobb County	51 271
13	01696	121	Fulton County	57 551	13	73256		Statesboro city	28 422
					13	73256	031	Bulloch County	28 422
13	04000		Atlanta city	420 003	13	73704		Stockbridge city	25 636
13	04000	089	DeKalb County	28 292	13	73704	151	Henry County	25 636
13	04000	121	Fulton County	391 711	13	78800		Valdosta city	54 518
13	19000		Columbus city	189 885	13	78800	185	Lowndes County	54 518
13	19000	215	Muscogee County	189 885	13	80508		Warner Robins city	66 588
13	21380		Dalton city	33 128	13	80508	153	Houston County	66 224
13	21380	313	Whitfield County	33 128	13	80508	225	Peach County	364
13	23900		Douglasville city	30 961	15			**HAWAII**	1 360 301
13	23900	097	Douglas County	30 961	15	06290		East Honolulu CDP	49 914
13	24600		Duluth city	26 600	15	06290	003	Honolulu County	49 914
13	24600	135	Gwinnett County	26 600	15	14650		Hilo CDP	43 263
13	24768		Dunwoody city	46 267	15	14650	001	Hawaii County	43 263
13	24768	089	DeKalb County	46 267	15	22700		Kahului CDP	26 337
13	25720		East Point city	33 712	15	22700	009	Maui County	26 337
13	25720	121	Fulton County	33 712	15	23150		Kailua CDP	38 635
13	31908		Gainesville city	33 804	15	23150	003	Honolulu County	38 635
13	31908	139	Hall County	33 804	15	28250		Kaneohe CDP	34 597
13	38964		Hinesville city	33 437	15	28250	003	Honolulu County	34 597
13	38964	179	Liberty County	33 437	15	51050		Mililani Town CDP	27 629
13	42425		Johns Creek city	76 728	15	51050	003	Honolulu County	27 629
13	42425	121	Fulton County	76 728	15	62600		Pearl City CDP	47 698
13	43192		Kennesaw city	29 783	15	62600	003	Honolulu County	47 698
13	43192	067	Cobb County	29 783	15	71550		Urban Honolulu CDP	337 256
13	44340		LaGrange city	29 588	15	71550	003	Honolulu County	337 256
13	44340	285	Troup County	29 588	15	79700		Waipahu CDP	38 216
13	45488		Lawrenceville city	28 546	15	79700	003	Honolulu County	38 216
13	45488	135	Gwinnett County	28 546	16			**IDAHO**	1 567 582
13	49000		Macon city	91 351	16	08830		Boise City city	205 671
13	49000	021	Bibb County	90 885	16	08830	001	Ada County	205 671
13	49000	169	Jones County	466	16	12250		Caldwell city	46 237
13	49756		Marietta city	56 579	16	12250	027	Canyon County	46 237
13	49756	067	Cobb County	56 579	16	16750		Coeur d'Alene city	44 137
13	51670		Milton city	32 661	16	16750	055	Kootenai County	44 137
13	51670	121	Fulton County	32 661					

Appendix E

E-11

Cities by County–*Continued*

State Code	Place Code	County Code	Geographic Area Name	2010 Census Population	State Code	Place Code	County Code	Geographic Area Name	2010 Census Population
16	39700		Idaho Falls city	56 813	17	09447		Buffalo Grove village	41 496
16	39700	019	Bonneville County	56 813	17	09447	031	Cook County	13 644
					17	09447	097	Lake County	27 852
16	46540		Lewiston city	31 894					
16	46540	069	Nez Perce County	31 894	17	09642		Burbank city	28 925
					17	09642	031	Cook County	28 925
16	52120		Meridian city	75 092					
16	52120	001	Ada County	75 092	17	10487		Calumet City city	37 042
					17	10487	031	Cook County	37 042
16	56260		Nampa city	81 557					
16	56260	027	Canyon County	81 557	17	11163		Carbondale city	25 902
					17	11163	077	Jackson County	25 902
16	64090		Pocatello city	54 255	17	11163	199	Williamson County	0
16	64090	005	Bannock County	54 239					
16	64090	077	Power County	16	17	11332		Carol Stream village	39 711
					17	11332	043	DuPage County	39 711
16	64810		Post Falls city	27 574					
16	64810	055	Kootenai County	27 574	17	11358		Carpentersville village	37 691
					17	11358	089	Kane County	37 691
16	67420		Rexburg city	25 484					
16	67420	065	Madison County	25 484	17	12385		Champaign city	81 055
					17	12385	019	Champaign County	81 055
16	82810		Twin Falls city	44 125					
16	82810	083	Twin Falls County	44 125	17	14000		Chicago city	2 695 598
					17	14000	031	Cook County	2 695 598
17			**ILLINOIS**	12 830 632	17	14000	043	DuPage County	0
17	00243		Addison village	36 942					
17	00243	043	DuPage County	36 942	17	14026		Chicago Heights city	30 276
					17	14026	031	Cook County	30 276
17	00685		Algonquin village	30 046					
17	00685	089	Kane County	8 433	17	14351		Cicero town	83 891
17	00685	111	McHenry County	21 613	17	14351	031	Cook County	83 891
17	01114		Alton city	27 865	17	15599		Collinsville city	25 579
17	01114	119	Madison County	27 865	17	15599	119	Madison County	22 573
					17	15599	163	St. Clair County	3 006
17	02154		Arlington Heights village	75 101					
17	02154	031	Cook County	75 101	17	17887		Crystal Lake city	40 743
17	02154	097	Lake County	0	17	17887	111	McHenry County	40 743
17	03012		Aurora city	197 899	17	18563		Danville city	33 027
17	03012	043	DuPage County	49 433	17	18563	183	Vermilion County	33 027
17	03012	089	Kane County	130 976					
17	03012	093	Kendall County	6 019	17	18823		Decatur city	76 122
17	03012	197	Will County	11 471	17	18823	115	Macon County	76 122
17	04013		Bartlett village	41 208	17	19161		DeKalb city	43 862
17	04013	031	Cook County	16 797	17	19161	037	DeKalb County	43 862
17	04013	043	DuPage County	24 411					
17	04013	089	Kane County	0	17	19642		Des Plaines city	58 364
					17	19642	031	Cook County	58 364
17	04078		Batavia city	26 045					
17	04078	043	DuPage County	0	17	20591		Downers Grove village	47 833
17	04078	089	Kane County	26 045	17	20591	043	DuPage County	47 833
17	04845		Belleville city	44 478	17	22255		East St. Louis city	27 006
17	04845	163	St. Clair County	44 478	17	22255	163	St. Clair County	27 006
17	05092		Belvidere city	25 585	17	23074		Elgin city	108 188
17	05092	007	Boone County	25 585	17	23074	031	Cook County	24 032
					17	23074	089	Kane County	84 156
17	05573		Berwyn city	56 657					
17	05573	031	Cook County	56 657	17	23256		Elk Grove Village village	33 127
					17	23256	031	Cook County	33 127
17	06613		Bloomington city	76 610	17	23256	043	DuPage County	0
17	06613	113	McLean County	76 610					
					17	23620		Elmhurst city	44 121
17	07133		Bolingbrook village	73 366	17	23620	031	Cook County	0
17	07133	043	DuPage County	1 571	17	23620	043	DuPage County	44 121
17	07133	197	Will County	71 795					
					17	24582		Evanston city	74 486
					17	24582	031	Cook County	74 486

State Code	Place Code	County Code	Geographic Area Name	2010 Census Population	State Code	Place Code	County Code	Geographic Area Name	2010 Census Population
17	27884		Freeport city	25 638	17	53234		Normal town	52 497
17	27884	177	Stephenson County	25 638	17	53234	113	McLean County	52 497
17	28326		Galesburg city	32 195	17	53481		Northbrook village	33 170
17	28326	095	Knox County	32 195	17	53481	031	Cook County	33 170
17	29730		Glendale Heights village	34 208	17	53559		North Chicago city	32 574
17	29730	043	DuPage County	34 208	17	53559	097	Lake County	32 574
17	29756		Glen Ellyn village	27 450	17	54638		Oak Forest city	27 962
17	29756	043	DuPage County	27 450	17	54638	031	Cook County	27 962
17	29938		Glenview village	44 692	17	54820		Oak Lawn village	56 690
17	29938	031	Cook County	44 692	17	54820	031	Cook County	56 690
17	30926		Granite City city	29 849	17	54885		Oak Park village	51 878
17	30926	119	Madison County	29 849	17	54885	031	Cook County	51 878
17	32018		Gurnee village	31 295	17	55249		O'Fallon city	28 281
17	32018	097	Lake County	31 295	17	55249	163	St. Clair County	28 281
17	32746		Hanover Park village	37 973	17	56640		Orland Park village	56 767
17	32746	031	Cook County	20 636	17	56640	031	Cook County	56 583
17	32746	043	DuPage County	17 337	17	56640	197	Will County	184
17	33383		Harvey city	25 282	17	56887		Oswego village	30 355
17	33383	031	Cook County	25 282	17	56887	093	Kendall County	30 355
17	34722		Highland Park city	29 763	17	57225		Palatine village	68 557
17	34722	097	Lake County	29 763	17	57225	031	Cook County	68 557
					17	57225	097	Lake County	0
17	35411		Hoffman Estates village	51 895					
17	35411	031	Cook County	51 895	17	57875		Park Ridge city	37 480
17	35411	089	Kane County	0	17	57875	031	Cook County	37 480
17	38570		Joliet city	147 433	17	58447		Pekin city	34 094
17	38570	093	Kendall County	9 749	17	58447	143	Peoria County	0
17	38570	197	Will County	137 684	17	58447	179	Tazewell County	34 094
17	38934		Kankakee city	27 537	17	59000		Peoria city	115 007
17	38934	091	Kankakee County	27 537	17	59000	143	Peoria County	115 007
17	41183		Lake in the Hills village	28 965	17	60287		Plainfield village	39 581
17	41183	111	McHenry County	28 965	17	60287	093	Kendall County	2 079
					17	60287	197	Will County	37 502
17	42028		Lansing village	28 331					
17	42028	031	Cook County	28 331	17	62367		Quincy city	40 633
					17	62367	001	Adams County	40 633
17	44407		Lombard village	43 165					
17	44407	043	DuPage County	43 165	17	65000		Rockford city	152 871
					17	65000	201	Winnebago County	152 871
17	45694		McHenry city	26 992					
17	45694	111	McHenry County	26 992	17	65078		Rock Island city	39 018
					17	65078	161	Rock Island County	39 018
17	48242		Melrose Park village	25 411					
17	48242	031	Cook County	25 411	17	65442		Romeoville village	39 680
					17	65442	197	Will County	39 680
17	49867		Moline city	43 483					
17	49867	161	Rock Island County	43 483	17	66040		Round Lake Beach village	28 175
					17	66040	097	Lake County	28 175
17	51089		Mount Prospect village	54 167					
17	51089	031	Cook County	54 167	17	66703		St. Charles city	32 974
					17	66703	043	DuPage County	543
17	51349		Mundelein village	31 064	17	66703	089	Kane County	32 431
17	51349	097	Lake County	31 064					
					17	68003		Schaumburg village	74 227
17	51622		Naperville city	141 853	17	68003	031	Cook County	74 227
17	51622	043	DuPage County	94 533	17	68003	043	DuPage County	0
17	51622	197	Will County	47 320					
					17	70122		Skokie village	64 784
17	53000		Niles village	29 803	17	70122	031	Cook County	64 784
17	53000	031	Cook County	29 803					

Cities by County–*Continued*

State Code	Place Code	County Code	Geographic Area Name	2010 Census Population	State Code	Place Code	County Code	Geographic Area Name	2010 Census Population
17	72000		Springfield city	116 250	18	28386		Goshen city	31 719
17	72000	167	Sangamon County	116 250	18	28386	039	Elkhart County	31 719
17	73157		Streamwood village	39 858	18	29898		Greenwood city	49 791
17	73157	031	Cook County	39 858	18	29898	081	Johnson County	49 791
17	75484		Tinley Park village	56 703	18	31000		Hammond city	80 830
17	75484	031	Cook County	49 236	18	31000	089	Lake County	80 830
17	75484	197	Will County	7 467	18	34114		Hobart city	29 059
17	77005		Urbana city	41 250	18	34114	089	Lake County	29 059
17	77005	019	Champaign County	41 250	18	38358		Jeffersonville city	44 953
17	77694		Vernon Hills village	25 113	18	38358	019	Clark County	44 953
17	77694	097	Lake County	25 113	18	40392		Kokomo city	45 468
17	79293		Waukegan city	89 078	18	40392	067	Howard County	45 468
17	79293	097	Lake County	89 078	18	40788		Lafayette city	67 140
17	80060		West Chicago city	27 086	18	40788	157	Tippecanoe County	67 140
17	80060	043	DuPage County	27 086	18	42426		Lawrence city	46 001
17	81048		Wheaton city	52 894	18	42426	097	Marion County	46 001
17	81048	043	DuPage County	52 894	18	46908		Marion city	29 948
17	81087		Wheeling village	37 648	18	46908	053	Grant County	29 948
17	81087	031	Cook County	37 642	18	48528		Merrillville town	35 246
17	81087	097	Lake County	6	18	48528	089	Lake County	35 246
17	82075		Wilmette village	27 087	18	48798		Michigan City city	31 479
17	82075	031	Cook County	27 087	18	48798	091	LaPorte County	31 479
17	83245		Woodridge village	32 971	18	49932		Mishawaka city	48 252
17	83245	031	Cook County	0	18	49932	141	St. Joseph County	48 252
17	83245	043	DuPage County	32 949	18	51876		Muncie city	70 085
17	83245	197	Will County	22	18	51876	035	Delaware County	70 085
18			**INDIANA**	6 483 802	18	52326		New Albany city	36 372
18	01468		Anderson city	56 129	18	52326	043	Floyd County	36 372
18	01468	095	Madison County	56 129	18	54180		Noblesville city	51 969
18	05860		Bloomington city	80 405	18	54180	057	Hamilton County	51 969
18	05860	105	Monroe County	80 405	18	60246		Plainfield town	27 631
18	10342		Carmel city	79 191	18	60246	063	Hendricks County	27 631
18	10342	057	Hamilton County	79 191	18	61092		Portage city	36 828
18	14734		Columbus city	44 061	18	61092	127	Porter County	36 828
18	14734	005	Bartholomew County	44 061	18	64260		Richmond city	36 812
18	16138		Crown Point city	27 317	18	64260	177	Wayne County	36 812
18	16138	089	Lake County	27 317	18	68220		Schererville town	29 243
18	19486		East Chicago city	29 698	18	68220	089	Lake County	29 243
18	19486	089	Lake County	29 698	18	71000		South Bend city	101 168
18	20728		Elkhart city	50 949	18	71000	141	St. Joseph County	101 168
18	20728	039	Elkhart County	50 949	18	75428		Terre Haute city	60 785
18	22000		Evansville city	117 429	18	75428	167	Vigo County	60 785
18	22000	163	Vanderburgh County	117 429	18	78326		Valparaiso city	31 730
18	23278		Fishers town	76 794	18	78326	127	Porter County	31 730
18	23278	057	Hamilton County	76 794	18	82700		Westfield town	30 068
18	25000		Fort Wayne city	253 691	18	82700	057	Hamilton County	30 068
18	25000	003	Allen County	253 691	18	82862		West Lafayette city	29 596
18	27000		Gary city	80 294	18	82862	157	Tippecanoe County	29 596
18	27000	089	Lake County	80 294					

Cities by County–*Continued*

State Code	Place Code	County Code	Geographic Area Name	2010 Census Population	State Code	Place Code	County Code	Geographic Area Name	2010 Census Population
19			**IOWA**	3 046 355	20	25325		Garden City city	26 658
19	01855		Ames city	58 965	20	25325	055	Finney County	26 658
19	01855	169	Story County	58 965					
					20	33625		Hutchinson city	42 080
19	02305		Ankeny city	45 582	20	33625	155	Reno County	42 080
19	02305	153	Polk County	45 582					
					20	36000		Kansas City city	145 786
19	06355		Bettendorf city	33 217	20	36000	209	Wyandotte County	145 786
19	06355	163	Scott County	33 217					
					20	38900		Lawrence city	87 643
19	09550		Burlington city	25 663	20	38900	045	Douglas County	87 643
19	09550	057	Des Moines County	25 663					
					20	39000		Leavenworth city	35 251
19	11755		Cedar Falls city	39 260	20	39000	103	Leavenworth County	35 251
19	11755	013	Black Hawk County	39 260					
					20	39075		Leawood city	31 867
19	12000		Cedar Rapids city	126 326	20	39075	091	Johnson County	31 867
19	12000	113	Linn County	126 326					
					20	39350		Lenexa city	48 190
19	14430		Clinton city	26 885	20	39350	091	Johnson County	48 190
19	14430	045	Clinton County	26 885					
					20	44250		Manhattan city	52 281
19	16860		Council Bluffs city	62 230	20	44250	149	Pottawatomie County	146
19	16860	155	Pottawattamie County	62 230	20	44250	161	Riley County	52 135
19	19000		Davenport city	99 685	20	52575		Olathe city	125 872
19	19000	163	Scott County	99 685	20	52575	091	Johnson County	125 872
19	21000		Des Moines city	203 433	20	53775		Overland Park city	173 372
19	21000	153	Polk County	203 419	20	53775	091	Johnson County	173 372
19	21000	181	Warren County	14					
					20	62700		Salina city	47 707
19	22395		Dubuque city	57 637	20	62700	169	Saline County	47 707
19	22395	061	Dubuque County	57 637					
					20	64500		Shawnee city	62 209
19	28515		Fort Dodge city	25 206	20	64500	091	Johnson County	62 209
19	28515	187	Webster County	25 206					
					20	71000		Topeka city	127 473
19	38595		Iowa City city	67 862	20	71000	177	Shawnee County	127 473
19	38595	103	Johnson County	67 862					
					20	79000		Wichita city	382 368
19	49485		Marion city	34 768	20	79000	173	Sedgwick County	382 368
19	49485	113	Linn County	34 768					
					21			**KENTUCKY**	4 339 367
19	49755		Marshalltown city	27 552	21	08902		Bowling Green city	58 067
19	49755	127	Marshall County	27 552	21	08902	227	Warren County	58 067
19	50160		Mason City city	28 079	21	17848		Covington city	40 640
19	50160	033	Cerro Gordo County	28 079	21	17848	117	Kenton County	40 640
19	60465		Ottumwa city	25 023	21	24274		Elizabethtown city	28 531
19	60465	179	Wapello County	25 023	21	24274	093	Hardin County	28 531
19	73335		Sioux City city	82 684	21	27982		Florence city	29 951
19	73335	149	Plymouth County	6	21	27982	015	Boone County	29 951
19	73335	193	Woodbury County	82 678					
					21	28900		Frankfort city	25 527
19	79950		Urbandale city	39 463	21	28900	073	Franklin County	25 527
19	79950	049	Dallas County	6 337					
19	79950	153	Polk County	33 126	21	30700		Georgetown city	29 098
					21	30700	209	Scott County	29 098
19	82425		Waterloo city	68 406					
19	82425	013	Black Hawk County	68 406	21	35866		Henderson city	28 757
					21	35866	101	Henderson County	28 757
19	83910		West Des Moines city	56 609					
19	83910	049	Dallas County	11 569	21	37918		Hopkinsville city	31 577
19	83910	153	Polk County	44 999	21	37918	047	Christian County	31 577
19	83910	181	Warren County	41					
					21	40222		Jeffersontown city	26 595
20			**KANSAS**	2 853 118	21	40222	111	Jefferson County	26 595
20	18250		Dodge City city	27 340					
20	18250	057	Ford County	27 340					

State Code	Place Code	County Code	Geographic Area Name	2010 Census Population	State Code	Place Code	County Code	Geographic Area Name	2010 Census Population
21	46027		Lexington-Fayette urban county	295 803	24	04000		Baltimore city	620 961
21	46027	067	Fayette County	295 803	24	04000	510	Baltimore city	620 961
21	56136		Nicholasville city	28 015	24	08775		Bowie city	54 727
21	56136	113	Jessamine County	28 015	24	08775	033	Prince George's County	54 727
21	58620		Owensboro city	57 265	24	18750		College Park city	30 413
21	58620	059	Daviess County	57 265	24	18750	033	Prince George's County	30 413
21	58836		Paducah city	25 024	24	30325		Frederick city	65 239
21	58836	145	McCracken County	25 024	24	30325	021	Frederick County	65 239
21	65226		Richmond city	31 364	24	31175		Gaithersburg city	59 933
21	65226	151	Madison County	31 364	24	31175	031	Montgomery County	59 933
22			**LOUISIANA**	4 533 372	24	36075		Hagerstown city	39 662
22	00975		Alexandria city	47 723	24	36075	043	Washington County	39 662
22	00975	079	Rapides Parish	47 723	24	45900		Laurel city	25 115
22	05000		Baton Rouge city	229 493	24	45900	033	Prince George's County	25 115
22	05000	033	East Baton Rouge Parish	229 493	24	67675		Rockville city	61 209
22	08920		Bossier City city	61 315	24	67675	031	Montgomery County	61 209
22	08920	015	Bossier Parish	61 315	24	69925		Salisbury city	30 343
22	13960		Central city	26 864	24	69925	045	Wicomico County	30 343
22	13960	033	East Baton Rouge Parish	26 864	25			**MASSACHUSETTS**	6 547 629
22	36255		Houma city	33 727	25	00840		Agawam Town city	28 438
22	36255	109	Terrebonne Parish	33 727	25	00840	013	Hampden County	28 438
22	39475		Kenner city	66 702	25	02690		Attleboro city	43 593
22	39475	051	Jefferson Parish	66 702	25	02690	005	Bristol County	43 593
22	40735		Lafayette city	120 623	25	03690		Barnstable Town city	45 193
22	40735	055	Lafayette Parish	120 623	25	03690	001	Barnstable County	45 193
22	41155		Lake Charles city	71 993	25	05595		Beverly city	39 502
22	41155	019	Calcasieu Parish	71 993	25	05595	009	Essex County	39 502
22	51410		Monroe city	48 815	25	07000		Boston city	617 594
22	51410	073	Ouachita Parish	48 815	25	07000	025	Suffolk County	617 594
22	54035		New Iberia city	30 617	25	07740		Braintree Town city	35 744
22	54035	045	Iberia Parish	30 617	25	07740	021	Norfolk County	35 744
22	55000		New Orleans city	343 829	25	09000		Brockton city	93 810
22	55000	071	Orleans Parish	343 829	25	09000	023	Plymouth County	93 810
22	70000		Shreveport city	199 311	25	11000		Cambridge city	105 162
22	70000	015	Bossier Parish	2 702	25	11000	017	Middlesex County	105 162
22	70000	017	Caddo Parish	196 609	25	13205		Chelsea city	35 177
22	70805		Slidell city	27 068	25	13205	025	Suffolk County	35 177
22	70805	103	St. Tammany Parish	27 068	25	13660		Chicopee city	55 298
23			**MAINE**	1 328 361	25	13660	013	Hampden County	55 298
23	02795		Bangor city	33 039	25	21990		Everett city	41 667
23	02795	019	Penobscot County	33 039	25	21990	017	Middlesex County	41 667
23	38740		Lewiston city	36 592	25	23000		Fall River city	88 857
23	38740	001	Androscoggin County	36 592	25	23000	005	Bristol County	88 857
23	60545		Portland city	66 194	25	23875		Fitchburg city	40 318
23	60545	005	Cumberland County	66 194	25	23875	027	Worcester County	40 318
23	71990		South Portland city	25 002	25	25172		Franklin Town city	31 635
23	71990	005	Cumberland County	25 002	25	25172	021	Norfolk County	31 635
24			**MARYLAND**	5 773 552	25	26150		Gloucester city	28 789
24	01600		Annapolis city	38 394	25	26150	009	Essex County	28 789
24	01600	003	Anne Arundel County	38 394					

Cities by County–*Continued*

State Code	Place Code	County Code	Geographic Area Name	2010 Census Population	State Code	Place Code	County Code	Geographic Area Name	2010 Census Population
25	29405		Haverhill city	60 879	25	76030		Westfield city	41 094
25	29405	009	Essex County	60 879	25	76030	013	Hampden County	41 094
25	30840		Holyoke city	39 880	25	77890		West Springfield Town city	28 391
25	30840	013	Hampden County	39 880	25	77890	013	Hampden County	28 391
25	34550		Lawrence city	76 377	25	78972		Weymouth Town city	53 743
25	34550	009	Essex County	76 377	25	78972	021	Norfolk County	53 743
25	35075		Leominster city	40 759	25	81035		Woburn city	38 120
25	35075	027	Worcester County	40 759	25	81035	017	Middlesex County	38 120
25	37000		Lowell city	106 519	25	82000		Worcester city	181 045
25	37000	017	Middlesex County	106 519	25	82000	027	Worcester County	181 045
25	37490		Lynn city	90 329	26			**MICHIGAN**	9 883 640
25	37490	009	Essex County	90 329	26	01380		Allen Park city	28 210
					26	01380	163	Wayne County	28 210
25	37875		Malden city	59 450					
25	37875	017	Middlesex County	59 450	26	03000		Ann Arbor city	113 934
					26	03000	161	Washtenaw County	113 934
25	38715		Marlborough city	38 499					
25	38715	017	Middlesex County	38 499	26	05920		Battle Creek city	52 347
					26	05920	025	Calhoun County	52 347
25	39835		Medford city	56 173					
25	39835	017	Middlesex County	56 173	26	06020		Bay City city	34 932
					26	06020	017	Bay County	34 932
25	40115		Melrose city	26 983					
25	40115	017	Middlesex County	26 983	26	12060		Burton city	29 999
					26	12060	049	Genesee County	29 999
25	40710		Methuen Town city	47 255					
25	40710	009	Essex County	47 255	26	21000		Dearborn city	98 153
					26	21000	163	Wayne County	98 153
25	45000		New Bedford city	95 072					
25	45000	005	Bristol County	95 072	26	21020		Dearborn Heights city	57 774
					26	21020	163	Wayne County	57 774
25	45560		Newton city	85 146					
25	45560	017	Middlesex County	85 146	26	22000		Detroit city	713 777
					26	22000	163	Wayne County	713 777
25	46330		Northampton city	28 549					
25	46330	015	Hampshire County	28 549	26	24120		East Lansing city	48 579
					26	24120	037	Clinton County	1 969
25	52490		Peabody city	51 251	26	24120	065	Ingham County	46 610
25	52490	009	Essex County	51 251					
					26	24290		Eastpointe city	32 442
25	53960		Pittsfield city	44 737	26	24290	099	Macomb County	32 442
25	53960	003	Berkshire County	44 737					
					26	27440		Farmington Hills city	79 740
25	55745		Quincy city	92 271	26	27440	125	Oakland County	79 740
25	55745	021	Norfolk County	92 271					
					26	29000		Flint city	102 434
25	56585		Revere city	51 755	26	29000	049	Genesee County	102 434
25	56585	025	Suffolk County	51 755					
					26	31420		Garden City city	27 692
25	59105		Salem city	41 340	26	31420	163	Wayne County	27 692
25	59105	009	Essex County	41 340					
					26	34000		Grand Rapids city	188 040
25	62535		Somerville city	75 754	26	34000	081	Kent County	188 040
25	62535	017	Middlesex County	75 754					
					26	38640		Holland city	33 051
25	67000		Springfield city	153 060	26	38640	005	Allegan County	7 016
25	67000	013	Hampden County	153 060	26	38640	139	Ottawa County	26 035
25	69170		Taunton city	55 874	26	40680		Inkster city	25 369
25	69170	005	Bristol County	55 874	26	40680	163	Wayne County	25 369
25	72600		Waltham city	60 632	26	41420		Jackson city	33 534
25	72600	017	Middlesex County	60 632	26	41420	075	Jackson County	33 534
25	73440		Watertown Town city	31 915	26	42160		Kalamazoo city	74 262
25	73440	017	Middlesex County	31 915	26	42160	077	Kalamazoo County	74 262

Cities by County–*Continued*

State Code	Place Code	County Code	Geographic Area Name	2010 Census Population	State Code	Place Code	County Code	Geographic Area Name	2010 Census Population
26	42820		Kentwood city	48 707	26	84000		Warren city	134 056
26	42820	081	Kent County	48 707	26	84000	099	Macomb County	134 056
26	46000		Lansing city	114 297	26	86000		Westland city	84 094
26	46000	045	Eaton County	4 734	26	86000	163	Wayne County	84 094
26	46000	065	Ingham County	109 563					
					26	88900		Wyandotte city	25 883
26	47800		Lincoln Park city	38 144	26	88900	163	Wayne County	25 883
26	47800	163	Wayne County	38 144					
					26	88940		Wyoming city	72 125
26	49000		Livonia city	96 942	26	88940	081	Kent County	72 125
26	49000	163	Wayne County	96 942					
					27			**MINNESOTA**	5 303 925
26	50560		Madison Heights city	29 694	27	01486		Andover city	30 598
26	50560	125	Oakland County	29 694	27	01486	003	Anoka County	30 598
26	53780		Midland city	41 863	27	01900		Apple Valley city	49 084
26	53780	017	Bay County	157	27	01900	037	Dakota County	49 084
26	53780	111	Midland County	41 706					
					27	06382		Blaine city	57 186
26	56020		Mount Pleasant city	26 016	27	06382	003	Anoka County	57 186
26	56020	073	Isabella County	26 016	27	06382	123	Ramsey County	0
26	56320		Muskegon city	38 401	27	06616		Bloomington city	82 893
26	56320	121	Muskegon County	38 401	27	06616	053	Hennepin County	82 893
26	59440		Novi city	55 224	27	07948		Brooklyn Center city	30 104
26	59440	125	Oakland County	55 224	27	07948	053	Hennepin County	30 104
26	59920		Oak Park city	29 319	27	07966		Brooklyn Park city	75 781
26	59920	125	Oakland County	29 319	27	07966	053	Hennepin County	75 781
26	65440		Pontiac city	59 515	27	08794		Burnsville city	60 306
26	65440	125	Oakland County	59 515	27	08794	037	Dakota County	60 306
26	65560		Portage city	46 292	27	13114		Coon Rapids city	61 476
26	65560	077	Kalamazoo County	46 292	27	13114	003	Anoka County	61 476
26	65820		Port Huron city	30 184	27	13456		Cottage Grove city	34 589
26	65820	147	St. Clair County	30 184	27	13456	163	Washington County	34 589
26	69035		Rochester Hills city	70 995	27	17000		Duluth city	86 265
26	69035	125	Oakland County	70 995	27	17000	137	St. Louis County	86 265
26	69800		Roseville city	47 299	27	17288		Eagan city	64 206
26	69800	099	Macomb County	47 299	27	17288	037	Dakota County	64 206
26	70040		Royal Oak city	57 236	27	18116		Eden Prairie city	60 797
26	70040	125	Oakland County	57 236	27	18116	053	Hennepin County	60 797
26	70520		Saginaw city	51 508	27	18188		Edina city	47 941
26	70520	145	Saginaw County	51 508	27	18188	053	Hennepin County	47 941
26	70760		St. Clair Shores city	59 715	27	22814		Fridley city	27 208
26	70760	099	Macomb County	59 715	27	22814	003	Anoka County	27 208
26	74900		Southfield city	71 739	27	31076		Inver Grove Heights city	33 880
26	74900	125	Oakland County	71 739	27	31076	037	Dakota County	33 880
26	74960		Southgate city	30 047	27	35180		Lakeville city	55 954
26	74960	163	Wayne County	30 047	27	35180	037	Dakota County	55 954
26	76460		Sterling Heights city	129 699	27	39878		Mankato city	39 309
26	76460	099	Macomb County	129 699	27	39878	013	Blue Earth County	39 305
					27	39878	079	Le Sueur County	4
26	79000		Taylor city	63 131	27	39878	103	Nicollet County	0
26	79000	163	Wayne County	63 131					
					27	40166		Maple Grove city	61 567
26	80700		Troy city	80 980	27	40166	053	Hennepin County	61 567
26	80700	125	Oakland County	80 980					
					27	40382		Maplewood city	38 018
					27	40382	123	Ramsey County	38 018

Cities by County—*Continued*

State Code	Place Code	County Code	Geographic Area Name	2010 Census Population	State Code	Place Code	County Code	Geographic Area Name	2010 Census Population
27	43000		Minneapolis city	382 578	28	36000		Jackson city	173 514
27	43000	053	Hennepin County	382 578	28	36000	049	Hinds County	172 891
					28	36000	089	Madison County	622
27	43252		Minnetonka city	49 734	28	36000	121	Rankin County	1
27	43252	053	Hennepin County	49 734					
					28	46640		Meridian city	41 148
27	43864		Moorhead city	38 065	28	46640	075	Lauderdale County	41 148
27	43864	027	Clay County	38 065					
					28	54040		Olive Branch city	33 484
27	47680		Oakdale city	27 378	28	54040	033	DeSoto County	33 484
27	47680	163	Washington County	27 378					
					28	55760		Pearl city	25 092
27	49300		Owatonna city	25 599	28	55760	121	Rankin County	25 092
27	49300	147	Steele County	25 599					
					28	69280		Southaven city	48 982
27	51730		Plymouth city	70 576	28	69280	033	DeSoto County	48 982
27	51730	053	Hennepin County	70 576					
					28	74840		Tupelo city	34 546
27	54214		Richfield city	35 228	28	74840	081	Lee County	34 546
27	54214	053	Hennepin County	35 228					
					29			**MISSOURI**	5 988 927
27	54880		Rochester city	106 769	29	03160		Ballwin city	30 404
27	54880	109	Olmsted County	106 769	29	03160	189	St. Louis County	30 404
27	55852		Roseville city	33 660	29	06652		Blue Springs city	52 575
27	55852	123	Ramsey County	33 660	29	06652	095	Jackson County	52 575
27	56896		St. Cloud city	65 842	29	11242		Cape Girardeau city	37 941
27	56896	009	Benton County	6 396	29	11242	031	Cape Girardeau County	37 941
27	56896	141	Sherburne County	6 785	29	11242	201	Scott County	0
27	56896	145	Stearns County	52 661					
					29	13600		Chesterfield city	47 484
27	57220		St. Louis Park city	45 250	29	13600	189	St. Louis County	47 484
27	57220	053	Hennepin County	45 250					
					29	15670		Columbia city	108 500
27	58000		St. Paul city	285 068	29	15670	019	Boone County	108 500
27	58000	123	Ramsey County	285 068					
					29	24778		Florissant city	52 158
27	58738		Savage city	26 911	29	24778	189	St. Louis County	52 158
27	58738	139	Scott County	26 911					
					29	27190		Gladstone city	25 410
27	59350		Shakopee city	37 076	29	27190	047	Clay County	25 410
27	59350	139	Scott County	37 076					
					29	31276		Hazelwood city	25 703
27	59998		Shoreview city	25 043	29	31276	189	St. Louis County	25 703
27	59998	123	Ramsey County	25 043					
					29	35000		Independence city	116 830
27	71032		Winona city	27 592	29	35000	047	Clay County	0
27	71032	169	Winona County	27 592	29	35000	095	Jackson County	116 830
27	71428		Woodbury city	61 961	29	37000		Jefferson City city	43 079
27	71428	163	Washington County	61 961	29	37000	027	Callaway County	22
					29	37000	051	Cole County	43 057
28			**MISSISSIPPI**	2 967 297					
28	06220		Biloxi city	44 054	29	37592		Joplin city	50 150
28	06220	047	Harrison County	44 054	29	37592	097	Jasper County	43 955
					29	37592	145	Newton County	6 195
28	14420		Clinton city	25 216					
28	14420	049	Hinds County	25 216	29	38000		Kansas City city	459 787
					29	38000	037	Cass County	197
28	29180		Greenville city	34 400	29	38000	047	Clay County	113 415
28	29180	151	Washington County	34 400	29	38000	095	Jackson County	302 499
					29	38000	165	Platte County	43 676
28	29700		Gulfport city	67 793					
28	29700	047	Harrison County	67 793	29	39044		Kirkwood city	27 540
					29	39044	189	St. Louis County	27 540
28	31020		Hattiesburg city	45 989					
28	31020	035	Forrest County	41 000	29	41348		Lee's Summit city	91 364
28	31020	073	Lamar County	4 989	29	41348	037	Cass County	1 917
					29	41348	095	Jackson County	89 447
28	33700		Horn Lake city	26 066					
28	33700	033	DeSoto County	26 066					

Cities by County–*Continued*

State Code	Place Code	County Code	Geographic Area Name	2010 Census Population	State Code	Place Code	County Code	Geographic Area Name	2010 Census Population
29	42032		Liberty city	29 149	32			**NEVADA**	2 700 551
29	42032	047	Clay County	29 149	32	09700		Carson City	55 274
					32	09700	510	Carson City	55 274
29	46586		Maryland Heights city	27 472					
29	46586	189	St. Louis County	27 472	32	31900		Henderson city	257 729
					32	31900	003	Clark County	257 729
29	54074		O'Fallon city	79 329					
29	54074	183	St. Charles County	79 329	32	40000		Las Vegas city	583 756
					32	40000	003	Clark County	583 756
29	60788		Raytown city	29 526					
29	60788	095	Jackson County	29 526	32	51800		North Las Vegas city	216 961
					32	51800	003	Clark County	216 961
29	64082		St. Charles city	65 794					
29	64082	183	St. Charles County	65 794	32	60600		Reno city	225 221
					32	60600	031	Washoe County	225 221
29	64550		St. Joseph city	76 780					
29	64550	021	Buchanan County	76 780	32	68400		Sparks city	90 264
					32	68400	031	Washoe County	90 264
29	65000		St. Louis city	319 294					
29	65000	510	St. Louis city	319 294	33			**NEW HAMPSHIRE**	1 316 470
					33	14200		Concord city	42 695
29	65126		St. Peters city	52 575	33	14200	013	Merrimack County	42 695
29	65126	183	St. Charles County	52 575					
					33	18820		Dover city	29 987
29	70000		Springfield city	159 498	33	18820	017	Strafford County	29 987
29	70000	043	Christian County	2					
29	70000	077	Greene County	159 496	33	45140		Manchester city	109 565
					33	45140	011	Hillsborough County	109 565
29	75220		University City city	35 371					
29	75220	189	St. Louis County	35 371	33	50260		Nashua city	86 494
					33	50260	011	Hillsborough County	86 494
29	78442		Wentzville city	29 070					
29	78442	183	St. Charles County	29 070	33	65140		Rochester city	29 752
					33	65140	017	Strafford County	29 752
29	79820		Wildwood city	35 517					
29	79820	189	St. Louis County	35 517	34			**NEW JERSEY**	8 791 894
					34	02080		Atlantic City city	39 558
30			**MONTANA**	989 415	34	02080	001	Atlantic County	39 558
30	06550		Billings city	104 170					
30	06550	111	Yellowstone County	104 170	34	03580		Bayonne city	63 024
					34	03580	017	Hudson County	63 024
30	08950		Bozeman city	37 280					
30	08950	031	Gallatin County	37 280	34	05170		Bergenfield borough	26 764
					34	05170	003	Bergen County	26 764
30	32800		Great Falls city	58 505					
30	32800	013	Cascade County	58 505	34	07600		Bridgeton city	25 349
					34	07600	011	Cumberland County	25 349
30	35600		Helena city	28 190					
30	35600	049	Lewis and Clark County	28 190	34	10000		Camden city	77 344
					34	10000	007	Camden County	77 344
30	50200		Missoula city	66 788					
30	50200	063	Missoula County	66 788	34	13690		Clifton city	84 136
					34	13690	031	Passaic County	84 136
31			**NEBRASKA**	1 826 341					
31	03950		Bellevue city	50 137	34	19390		East Orange city	64 270
31	03950	153	Sarpy County	50 137	34	19390	013	Essex County	64 270
31	17670		Fremont city	26 397	34	21000		Elizabeth city	124 969
31	17670	053	Dodge County	26 397	34	21000	039	Union County	124 969
31	19595		Grand Island city	48 520	34	21480		Englewood city	27 147
31	19595	079	Hall County	48 520	34	21480	003	Bergen County	27 147
31	25055		Kearney city	30 787	34	22470		Fair Lawn borough	32 457
31	25055	019	Buffalo County	30 787	34	22470	003	Bergen County	32 457
31	28000		Lincoln city	258 379	34	24420		Fort Lee borough	35 345
31	28000	109	Lancaster County	258 379	34	24420	003	Bergen County	35 345
31	37000		Omaha city	408 958	34	25770		Garfield city	30 487
31	37000	055	Douglas County	408 958	34	25770	003	Bergen County	30 487

Cities by County–*Continued*

State Code	Place Code	County Code	Geographic Area Name	2010 Census Population	State Code	Place Code	County Code	Geographic Area Name	2010 Census Population
34	28680		Hackensack city	43 010	35	16420		Clovis city	37 775
34	28680	003	Bergen County	43 010	35	16420	009	Curry County	37 775
34	32250		Hoboken city	50 005	35	25800		Farmington city	45 877
34	32250	017	Hudson County	50 005	35	25800	045	San Juan County	45 877
34	36000		Jersey City city	247 597	35	32520		Hobbs city	34 122
34	36000	017	Hudson County	247 597	35	32520	025	Lea County	34 122
34	36510		Kearny town	40 684	35	39380		Las Cruces city	97 618
34	36510	017	Hudson County	40 684	35	39380	013	Doña Ana County	97 618
34	40350		Linden city	40 499	35	63460		Rio Rancho city	87 521
34	40350	039	Union County	40 499	35	63460	001	Bernalillo County	130
					35	63460	043	Sandoval County	87 391
34	41310		Long Branch city	30 719					
34	41310	025	Monmouth County	30 719	35	64930		Roswell city	48 366
					35	64930	005	Chaves County	48 366
34	46680		Millville city	28 400					
34	46680	011	Cumberland County	28 400	35	70500		Santa Fe city	67 947
					35	70500	049	Santa Fe County	67 947
34	51000		Newark city	277 140					
34	51000	013	Essex County	277 140	36			**NEW YORK**	19 378 102
					36	01000		Albany city	97 856
34	51210		New Brunswick city	55 181	36	01000	001	Albany County	97 856
34	51210	023	Middlesex County	55 181					
					36	03078		Auburn city	27 687
34	55950		Paramus borough	26 342	36	03078	011	Cayuga County	27 687
34	55950	003	Bergen County	26 342					
					36	06607		Binghamton city	47 376
34	56550		Passaic city	69 781	36	06607	007	Broome County	47 376
34	56550	031	Passaic County	69 781					
					36	11000		Buffalo city	261 310
34	57000		Paterson city	146 199	36	11000	029	Erie County	261 310
34	57000	031	Passaic County	146 199					
					36	24229		Elmira city	29 200
34	58200		Perth Amboy city	50 814	36	24229	015	Chemung County	29 200
34	58200	023	Middlesex County	50 814					
					36	27485		Freeport village	42 860
34	59190		Plainfield city	49 808	36	27485	059	Nassau County	42 860
34	59190	039	Union County	49 808					
					36	29113		Glen Cove city	26 964
34	61530		Rahway city	27 346	36	29113	059	Nassau County	26 964
34	61530	039	Union County	27 346					
					36	32402		Harrison village	27 472
34	65790		Sayreville borough	42 704	36	32402	119	Westchester County	27 472
34	65790	023	Middlesex County	42 704					
					36	33139		Hempstead village	53 891
34	74000		Trenton city	84 913	36	33139	059	Nassau County	53 891
34	74000	021	Mercer County	84 913					
					36	38077		Ithaca city	30 014
34	74630		Union City city	66 455	36	38077	109	Tompkins County	30 014
34	74630	017	Hudson County	66 455					
					36	38264		Jamestown city	31 146
34	76070		Vineland city	60 724	36	38264	013	Chautauqua County	31 146
34	76070	011	Cumberland County	60 724					
					36	42554		Lindenhurst village	27 253
34	79040		Westfield town	30 316	36	42554	103	Suffolk County	27 253
34	79040	039	Union County	30 316					
					36	43335		Long Beach city	33 275
34	79610		West New York town	49 708	36	43335	059	Nassau County	33 275
34	79610	017	Hudson County	49 708					
					36	47042		Middletown city	28 086
35			**NEW MEXICO**	2 059 179	36	47042	071	Orange County	28 086
35	01780		Alamogordo city	30 403					
35	01780	035	Otero County	30 403	36	49121		Mount Vernon city	67 292
					36	49121	119	Westchester County	67 292
35	02000		Albuquerque city	545 852					
35	02000	001	Bernalillo County	545 852	36	50034		Newburgh city	28 866
					36	50034	071	Orange County	28 866
35	12150		Carlsbad city	26 138					
35	12150	015	Eddy County	26 138					

State Code	Place Code	County Code	Geographic Area Name	2010 Census Population	State Code	Place Code	County Code	Geographic Area Name	2010 Census Population
36	50617		New Rochelle city	77 062	37	10740		Cary town	135 234
36	50617	119	Westchester County	77 062	37	10740	037	Chatham County	1 422
					37	10740	183	Wake County	133 812
36	51000		New York city	8 175 133					
36	51000	005	Bronx County	1 385 108	37	11800		Chapel Hill town	57 233
36	51000	047	Kings County	2 504 700	37	11800	063	Durham County	2 836
36	51000	061	New York County	1 585 873	37	11800	135	Orange County	54 397
36	51000	081	Queens County	2 230 722					
36	51000	085	Richmond County	468 730	37	12000		Charlotte city	731 424
					37	12000	119	Mecklenburg County	731 424
36	51055		Niagara Falls city	50 193					
36	51055	063	Niagara County	50 193	37	14100		Concord city	79 066
					37	14100	025	Cabarrus County	79 066
36	53682		North Tonawanda city	31 568					
36	53682	063	Niagara County	31 568	37	19000		Durham city	228 330
					37	19000	063	Durham County	228 300
36	55530		Ossining village	25 060	37	19000	135	Orange County	30
36	55530	119	Westchester County	25 060	37	19000	183	Wake County	0
36	59223		Port Chester village	28 967	37	22920		Fayetteville city	200 564
36	59223	119	Westchester County	28 967	37	22920	051	Cumberland County	200 564
36	59641		Poughkeepsie city	32 736	37	25480		Garner town	25 745
36	59641	027	Dutchess County	32 736	37	25480	183	Wake County	25 745
36	63000		Rochester city	210 565	37	25580		Gastonia city	71 741
36	63000	055	Monroe County	210 565	37	25580	071	Gaston County	71 741
36	63418		Rome city	33 725	37	26880		Goldsboro city	36 437
36	63418	065	Oneida County	33 725	37	26880	191	Wayne County	36 437
36	65255		Saratoga Springs city	26 586	37	28000		Greensboro city	269 666
36	65255	091	Saratoga County	26 586	37	28000	081	Guilford County	269 666
36	65508		Schenectady city	66 135	37	28080		Greenville city	84 554
36	65508	093	Schenectady County	66 135	37	28080	147	Pitt County	84 554
36	70420		Spring Valley village	31 347	37	31060		Hickory city	40 010
36	70420	087	Rockland County	31 347	37	31060	023	Burke County	66
					37	31060	027	Caldwell County	18
36	73000		Syracuse city	145 170	37	31060	035	Catawba County	39 926
36	73000	067	Onondaga County	145 170					
					37	31400		High Point city	104 371
36	75484		Troy city	50 129	37	31400	057	Davidson County	5 310
36	75484	083	Rensselaer County	50 129	37	31400	067	Forsyth County	8
					37	31400	081	Guilford County	99 042
36	76540		Utica city	62 235	37	31400	151	Randolph County	11
36	76540	065	Oneida County	62 235					
					37	33120		Huntersville town	46 773
36	76705		Valley Stream village	37 511	37	33120	119	Mecklenburg County	46 773
36	76705	059	Nassau County	37 511					
					37	33560		Indian Trail town	33 518
36	78608		Watertown city	27 023	37	33560	179	Union County	33 518
36	78608	045	Jefferson County	27 023					
					37	34200		Jacksonville city	70 145
36	81677		White Plains city	56 853	37	34200	133	Onslow County	70 145
36	81677	119	Westchester County	56 853					
					37	35200		Kannapolis city	42 625
37			**NORTH CAROLINA**	9 535 483	37	35200	025	Cabarrus County	33 194
37	01520		Apex town	37 476	37	35200	159	Rowan County	9 431
37	01520	183	Wake County	37 476					
					37	41960		Matthews town	27 198
37	02080		Asheboro city	25 012	37	41960	119	Mecklenburg County	27 198
37	02080	151	Randolph County	25 012					
					37	43920		Monroe city	32 797
37	02140		Asheville city	83 393	37	43920	179	Union County	32 797
37	02140	021	Buncombe County	83 393					
					37	44220		Mooresville town	32 711
37	09060		Burlington city	49 963	37	44220	097	Iredell County	32 711
37	09060	001	Alamance County	49 308					
37	09060	081	Guilford County	655	37	46340		New Bern city	29 524
					37	46340	049	Craven County	29 524

Cities by County–*Continued*

State Code	Place Code	County Code	Geographic Area Name	2010 Census Population	State Code	Place Code	County Code	Geographic Area Name	2010 Census Population
37	55000		Raleigh city	403 892	39	16014		Cleveland Heights city	46 121
37	55000	063	Durham County	1 067	39	16014	035	Cuyahoga County	46 121
37	55000	183	Wake County	402 825	39	18000		Columbus city	787 033
37	57500		Rocky Mount city	57 477	39	18000	041	Delaware County	7 245
37	57500	065	Edgecombe County	17 524	39	18000	045	Fairfield County	9 666
37	57500	127	Nash County	39 953	39	18000	049	Franklin County	770 122
37	58860		Salisbury city	33 662	39	19778		Cuyahoga Falls city	49 652
37	58860	159	Rowan County	33 662	39	19778	153	Summit County	49 652
37	59280		Sanford city	28 094	39	21000		Dayton city	141 527
37	59280	105	Lee County	28 094	39	21000	113	Montgomery County	141 527
37	67420		Thomasville city	26 757	39	21434		Delaware city	34 753
37	67420	057	Davidson County	26 493	39	21434	041	Delaware County	34 753
37	67420	151	Randolph County	264	39	22694		Dublin city	41 751
37	70540		Wake Forest town	30 117	39	22694	041	Delaware County	4 018
37	70540	069	Franklin County	899	39	22694	049	Franklin County	35 367
37	70540	183	Wake County	29 218	39	22694	159	Union County	2 366
37	74440		Wilmington city	106 476	39	25256		Elyria city	54 533
37	74440	129	New Hanover County	106 476	39	25256	093	Lorain County	54 533
37	74540		Wilson city	49 167	39	25704		Euclid city	48 920
37	74540	195	Wilson County	49 167	39	25704	035	Cuyahoga County	48 920
37	75000		Winston-Salem city	229 617	39	25914		Fairborn city	32 352
37	75000	067	Forsyth County	229 617	39	25914	057	Greene County	32 352
38			**NORTH DAKOTA**	672 591	39	25970		Fairfield city	42 510
38	07200		Bismarck city	61 272	39	25970	017	Butler County	42 510
38	07200	015	Burleigh County	61 272	39	25970	061	Hamilton County	0
38	25700		Fargo city	105 549	39	27048		Findlay city	41 202
38	25700	017	Cass County	105 549	39	27048	063	Hancock County	41 202
38	32060		Grand Forks city	52 838	39	29106		Gahanna city	33 248
38	32060	035	Grand Forks County	52 838	39	29106	049	Franklin County	33 248
38	53380		Minot city	40 888	39	29428		Garfield Heights city	28 849
38	53380	101	Ward County	40 888	39	29428	035	Cuyahoga County	28 849
38	84780		West Fargo city	25 830	39	31860		Green city	25 699
38	84780	017	Cass County	25 830	39	31860	153	Summit County	25 699
39			**OHIO**	11 536 504	39	32592		Grove City city	35 575
39	01000		Akron city	199 110	39	32592	049	Franklin County	35 575
39	01000	153	Summit County	199 110	39	33012		Hamilton city	62 477
39	03828		Barberton city	26 550	39	33012	017	Butler County	62 477
39	03828	153	Summit County	26 550	39	35476		Hilliard city	28 435
39	04720		Beavercreek city	45 193	39	35476	049	Franklin County	28 435
39	04720	057	Greene County	45 193	39	36610		Huber Heights city	38 101
39	07972		Bowling Green city	30 028	39	36610	057	Greene County	0
39	07972	173	Wood County	30 028	39	36610	109	Miami County	959
39	09680		Brunswick city	34 255	39	36610	113	Montgomery County	37 142
39	09680	103	Medina County	34 255	39	39872		Kent city	28 904
39	12000		Canton city	73 007	39	39872	133	Portage County	28 904
39	12000	151	Stark County	73 007	39	40040		Kettering city	56 163
39	15000		Cincinnati city	296 943	39	40040	057	Greene County	467
39	15000	061	Hamilton County	296 943	39	40040	113	Montgomery County	55 696
39	16000		Cleveland city	396 815	39	41664		Lakewood city	52 131
39	16000	035	Cuyahoga County	396 815	39	41664	035	Cuyahoga County	52 131

State Code	Place Code	County Code	Geographic Area Name	2010 Census Population	State Code	Place Code	County Code	Geographic Area Name	2010 Census Population
39	41720		Lancaster city	38 780	39	77588		Troy city	25 058
39	41720	045	Fairfield County	38 780	39	77588	109	Miami County	25 058
39	43554		Lima city	38 771	39	79002		Upper Arlington city	33 771
39	43554	003	Allen County	38 771	39	79002	049	Franklin County	33 771
39	44856		Lorain city	64 097	39	80892		Warren city	41 557
39	44856	093	Lorain County	64 097	39	80892	155	Trumbull County	41 557
39	47138		Mansfield city	47 821	39	83342		Westerville city	36 120
39	47138	139	Richland County	47 821	39	83342	041	Delaware County	7 792
					39	83342	049	Franklin County	28 328
39	47754		Marion city	36 837					
39	47754	101	Marion County	36 837	39	83622		Westlake city	32 729
39	48188		Mason city	30 712	39	83622	035	Cuyahoga County	32 729
39	48188	165	Warren County	30 712	39	86548		Wooster city	26 119
39	48244		Massillon city	32 149	39	86548	169	Wayne County	26 119
39	48244	151	Stark County	32 149	39	86772		Xenia city	25 719
39	48790		Medina city	26 678	39	86772	057	Greene County	25 719
39	48790	103	Medina County	26 678	39	88000		Youngstown city	66 982
39	49056		Mentor city	47 159	39	88000	099	Mahoning County	66 971
39	49056	085	Lake County	47 159	39	88000	155	Trumbull County	11
39	49840		Middletown city	48 694	39	88084		Zanesville city	25 487
39	49840	017	Butler County	45 994	39	88084	119	Muskingum County	25 487
39	49840	165	Warren County	2 700	40			**OKLAHOMA**	3 751 351
					40	04450		Bartlesville city	35 750
39	54040		Newark city	47 573	40	04450	113	Osage County	3
39	54040	089	Licking County	47 573	40	04450	147	Washington County	35 747
39	56882		North Olmsted city	32 718	40	09050		Broken Arrow city	98 850
39	56882	035	Cuyahoga County	32 718	40	09050	143	Tulsa County	80 634
					40	09050	145	Wagoner County	18 216
39	56966		North Ridgeville city	29 465					
39	56966	093	Lorain County	29 465	40	23200		Edmond city	81 405
					40	23200	109	Oklahoma County	81 405
39	57008		North Royalton city	30 444					
39	57008	035	Cuyahoga County	30 444	40	23950		Enid city	49 379
					40	23950	047	Garfield County	49 379
39	61000		Parma city	81 601					
39	61000	035	Cuyahoga County	81 601	40	41850		Lawton city	96 867
					40	41850	031	Comanche County	96 867
39	66390		Reynoldsburg city	35 893					
39	66390	045	Fairfield County	910	40	48350		Midwest City city	54 371
39	66390	049	Franklin County	26 157	40	48350	109	Oklahoma County	54 371
39	66390	089	Licking County	8 826	40	49200		Moore city	55 081
39	67468		Riverside city	25 201	40	49200	027	Cleveland County	55 081
39	67468	113	Montgomery County	25 201					
					40	50050		Muskogee city	39 223
39	70380		Sandusky city	25 793	40	50050	101	Muskogee County	39 223
39	70380	043	Erie County	25 793					
					40	52500		Norman city	110 925
39	71682		Shaker Heights city	28 448	40	52500	027	Cleveland County	110 925
39	71682	035	Cuyahoga County	28 448					
					40	55000		Oklahoma City city	579 999
39	74118		Springfield city	60 608	40	55000	017	Canadian County	44 541
39	74118	023	Clark County	60 608	40	55000	027	Cleveland County	63 723
					40	55000	109	Oklahoma County	471 671
39	74944		Stow city	34 837	40	55000	125	Pottawatomie County	64
39	74944	153	Summit County	34 837					
					40	56650		Owasso city	28 915
39	75098		Strongsville city	44 750	40	56650	131	Rogers County	2 614
39	75098	035	Cuyahoga County	44 750	40	56650	143	Tulsa County	26 301
39	77000		Toledo city	287 208	40	59850		Ponca City city	25 387
39	77000	095	Lucas County	287 208	40	59850	071	Kay County	25 387

Cities by County–*Continued*

State Code	Place Code	County Code	Geographic Area Name	2010 Census Population	State Code	Place Code	County Code	Geographic Area Name	2010 Census Population
40	66800		Shawnee city	29 857	41	74950		Tualatin city	26 054
40	66800	125	Pottawatomie County	29 857	41	74950	005	Clackamas County	2 862
					41	74950	067	Washington County	23 192
40	70300		Stillwater city	45 688					
40	70300	119	Payne County	45 688	41	80150		West Linn city	25 109
					41	80150	005	Clackamas County	25 109
40	75000		Tulsa city	391 906					
40	75000	113	Osage County	6 136	42			**PENNSYLVANIA**	12 702 379
40	75000	131	Rogers County	0	42	02000		Allentown city	118 032
40	75000	143	Tulsa County	385 613	42	02000	077	Lehigh County	118 032
40	75000	145	Wagoner County	157					
					42	02184		Altoona city	46 320
41			**OREGON**	3 831 074	42	02184	013	Blair County	46 320
41	01000		Albany city	50 158					
41	01000	003	Benton County	6 463	42	06064		Bethel Park municipality	32 313
41	01000	043	Linn County	43 695	42	06064	003	Allegheny County	32 313
41	05350		Beaverton city	89 803	42	06088		Bethlehem city	74 982
41	05350	067	Washington County	89 803	42	06088	077	Lehigh County	19 343
					42	06088	095	Northampton County	55 639
41	05800		Bend city	76 639					
41	05800	017	Deschutes County	76 639	42	13208		Chester city	33 972
					42	13208	045	Delaware County	33 972
41	15800		Corvallis city	54 462					
41	15800	003	Benton County	54 462	42	21648		Easton city	26 800
					42	21648	095	Northampton County	26 800
41	23850		Eugene city	156 185					
41	23850	039	Lane County	156 185	42	24000		Erie city	101 786
					42	24000	049	Erie County	101 786
41	30550		Grants Pass city	34 533					
41	30550	033	Josephine County	34 533	42	32800		Harrisburg city	49 528
					42	32800	043	Dauphin County	49 528
41	31250		Gresham city	105 594					
41	31250	051	Multnomah County	105 594	42	33408		Hazleton city	25 340
					42	33408	079	Luzerne County	25 340
41	34100		Hillsboro city	91 611					
41	34100	067	Washington County	91 611	42	41216		Lancaster city	59 322
					42	41216	071	Lancaster County	59 322
41	38500		Keizer city	36 478					
41	38500	047	Marion County	36 478	42	42168		Lebanon city	25 477
					42	42168	075	Lebanon County	25 477
41	40550		Lake Oswego city	36 619					
41	40550	005	Clackamas County	34 066	42	50528		Monroeville municipality	28 386
41	40550	051	Multnomah County	2 544	42	50528	003	Allegheny County	28 386
41	40550	067	Washington County	9					
					42	54656		Norristown borough	34 324
41	45000		McMinnville city	32 187	42	54656	091	Montgomery County	34 324
41	45000	071	Yamhill County	32 187					
					42	60000		Philadelphia city	1 526 006
41	47000		Medford city	74 907	42	60000	101	Philadelphia County	1 526 006
41	47000	029	Jackson County	74 907					
					42	61000		Pittsburgh city	305 704
41	55200		Oregon City city	31 859	42	61000	003	Allegheny County	305 704
41	55200	005	Clackamas County	31 859					
					42	61536		Plum borough	27 126
41	59000		Portland city	583 776	42	61536	003	Allegheny County	27 126
41	59000	005	Clackamas County	744					
41	59000	051	Multnomah County	581 485	42	63624		Reading city	88 082
41	59000	067	Washington County	1 547	42	63624	011	Berks County	88 082
41	61200		Redmond city	26 215	42	69000		Scranton city	76 089
41	61200	017	Deschutes County	26 215	42	69000	069	Lackawanna County	76 089
41	64900		Salem city	154 637	42	73808		State College borough	42 034
41	64900	047	Marion County	130 398	42	73808	027	Centre County	42 034
41	64900	053	Polk County	24 239					
					42	85152		Wilkes-Barre city	41 498
41	69600		Springfield city	59 403	42	85152	079	Luzerne County	41 498
41	69600	039	Lane County	59 403					
					42	85312		Williamsport city	29 381
41	73650		Tigard city	48 035	42	85312	081	Lycoming County	29 381
41	73650	067	Washington County	48 035					

Cities by County–*Continued*

State Code	Place Code	County Code	Geographic Area Name	2010 Census Population	State Code	Place Code	County Code	Geographic Area Name	2010 Census Population
42	87048		York city	43 718	45	70270		Summerville town	43 392
42	87048	133	York County	43 718	45	70270	015	Berkeley County	3 643
					45	70270	019	Charleston County	1 010
44			**RHODE ISLAND**	1 052 567	45	70270	035	Dorchester County	38 739
44	19180		Cranston city	80 387					
44	19180	007	Providence County	80 387	45	70405		Sumter city	40 524
					45	70405	085	Sumter County	40 524
44	22960		East Providence city	47 037					
44	22960	007	Providence County	47 037	46			**SOUTH DAKOTA**	814 180
					46	00100		Aberdeen city	26 091
44	54640		Pawtucket city	71 148	46	00100	013	Brown County	26 091
44	54640	007	Providence County	71 148					
					46	52980		Rapid City city	67 956
44	59000		Providence city	178 042	46	52980	103	Pennington County	67 956
44	59000	007	Providence County	178 042					
					46	59020		Sioux Falls city	153 888
44	74300		Warwick city	82 672	46	59020	083	Lincoln County	21 095
44	74300	003	Kent County	82 672	46	59020	099	Minnehaha County	132 793
44	80780		Woonsocket city	41 186	47			**TENNESSEE**	6 346 105
44	80780	007	Providence County	41 186	47	03440		Bartlett city	54 613
					47	03440	157	Shelby County	54 613
45			**SOUTH CAROLINA**	4 625 364					
45	00550		Aiken city	29 524	47	08280		Brentwood city	37 060
45	00550	003	Aiken County	29 524	47	08280	187	Williamson County	37 060
45	01360		Anderson city	26 686	47	08540		Bristol city	26 702
45	01360	007	Anderson County	26 686	47	08540	163	Sullivan County	26 702
45	13330		Charleston city	120 083	47	14000		Chattanooga city	167 674
45	13330	015	Berkeley County	8 095	47	14000	065	Hamilton County	167 674
45	13330	019	Charleston County	111 988					
					47	15160		Clarksville city	132 929
45	16000		Columbia city	129 272	47	15160	125	Montgomery County	132 929
45	16000	063	Lexington County	559					
45	16000	079	Richland County	128 713	47	15400		Cleveland city	41 285
					47	15400	011	Bradley County	41 285
45	25810		Florence city	37 056					
45	25810	041	Florence County	37 056	47	16420		Collierville town	43 965
					47	16420	047	Fayette County	0
45	29815		Goose Creek city	35 938	47	16420	157	Shelby County	43 965
45	29815	015	Berkeley County	35 933					
45	29815	019	Charleston County	5	47	16540		Columbia city	34 681
					47	16540	119	Maury County	34 681
45	30850		Greenville city	58 409					
45	30850	045	Greenville County	58 409	47	16920		Cookeville city	30 435
					47	16920	141	Putnam County	30 435
45	30985		Greer city	25 515					
45	30985	045	Greenville County	18 635	47	27740		Franklin city	62 487
45	30985	083	Spartanburg County	6 880	47	27740	187	Williamson County	62 487
45	34045		Hilton Head Island town	37 099	47	28540		Gallatin city	30 278
45	34045	013	Beaufort County	37 099	47	28540	165	Sumner County	30 278
45	48535		Mount Pleasant town	67 843	47	28960		Germantown city	38 844
45	48535	019	Charleston County	67 843	47	28960	157	Shelby County	38 844
45	49075		Myrtle Beach city	27 109	47	33280		Hendersonville city	51 372
45	49075	051	Horry County	27 109	47	33280	165	Sumner County	51 372
45	50875		North Charleston city	97 471	47	37640		Jackson city	65 211
45	50875	015	Berkeley County	0	47	37640	113	Madison County	65 211
45	50875	019	Charleston County	78 393					
45	50875	035	Dorchester County	19 078	47	38320		Johnson City city	63 152
					47	38320	019	Carter County	1 252
45	61405		Rock Hill city	66 154	47	38320	163	Sullivan County	367
45	61405	091	York County	66 154	47	38320	179	Washington County	61 533
45	68290		Spartanburg city	37 013	47	39560		Kingsport city	48 205
45	68290	083	Spartanburg County	37 013	47	39560	073	Hawkins County	2 854
					47	39560	163	Sullivan County	45 351

State Code	Place Code	County Code	Geographic Area Name	2010 Census Population	State Code	Place Code	County Code	Geographic Area Name	2010 Census Population
47	40000		Knoxville city	178 874	48	11428		Burleson city	36 690
47	40000	093	Knox County	178 874	48	11428	251	Johnson County	29 111
					48	11428	439	Tarrant County	7 579
47	41200		La Vergne city	32 588					
47	41200	149	Rutherford County	32 588	48	13024		Carrollton city	119 097
					48	13024	085	Collin County	2
47	41520		Lebanon city	26 190	48	13024	113	Dallas County	49 352
47	41520	189	Wilson County	26 190	48	13024	121	Denton County	69 743
47	46380		Maryville city	27 465	48	13492		Cedar Hill city	45 028
47	46380	009	Blount County	27 465	48	13492	113	Dallas County	44 477
					48	13492	139	Ellis County	551
47	48000		Memphis city	646 889					
47	48000	157	Shelby County	646 889	48	13552		Cedar Park city	48 937
					48	13552	453	Travis County	489
47	50280		Morristown city	29 137	48	13552	491	Williamson County	48 448
47	50280	063	Hamblen County	29 131					
47	50280	089	Jefferson County	6	48	15364		Cleburne city	29 337
					48	15364	251	Johnson County	29 337
47	51560		Murfreesboro city	108 755					
47	51560	149	Rutherford County	108 755	48	15976		College Station city	93 857
					48	15976	041	Brazos County	93 857
47	55120		Oak Ridge city	29 330					
47	55120	001	Anderson County	26 271	48	16432		Conroe city	56 207
47	55120	145	Roane County	3 059	48	16432	339	Montgomery County	56 207
47	69420		Smyrna town	39 974	48	16612		Coppell city	38 659
47	69420	149	Rutherford County	39 974	48	16612	113	Dallas County	37 905
					48	16612	121	Denton County	754
47	70580		Spring Hill city	29 036					
47	70580	119	Maury County	7 023	48	16624		Copperas Cove city	32 032
47	70580	187	Williamson County	22 013	48	16624	027	Bell County	0
					48	16624	099	Coryell County	31 457
48			**TEXAS**	25 145 561	48	16624	281	Lampasas County	575
48	01000		Abilene city	117 063					
48	01000	253	Jones County	5 145	48	17000		Corpus Christi city	305 215
48	01000	441	Taylor County	111 918	48	17000	007	Aransas County	0
					48	17000	273	Kleberg County	0
48	01924		Allen city	84 246	48	17000	355	Nueces County	305 215
48	01924	085	Collin County	84 246	48	17000	409	San Patricio County	0
48	03000		Amarillo city	190 695	48	19000		Dallas city	1 197 816
48	03000	375	Potter County	105 486	48	19000	085	Collin County	46 885
48	03000	381	Randall County	85 209	48	19000	113	Dallas County	1 124 296
					48	19000	121	Denton County	26 579
48	04000		Arlington city	365 438	48	19000	257	Kaufman County	0
48	04000	439	Tarrant County	365 438	48	19000	397	Rockwall County	56
48	05000		Austin city	790 390	48	19624		Deer Park city	32 010
48	05000	209	Hays County	2	48	19624	201	Harris County	32 010
48	05000	453	Travis County	754 691					
48	05000	491	Williamson County	35 697	48	19792		Del Rio city	35 591
					48	19792	465	Val Verde County	35 591
48	06128		Baytown city	71 802					
48	06128	071	Chambers County	4 116	48	19972		Denton city	113 383
48	06128	201	Harris County	67 686	48	19972	121	Denton County	113 383
48	07000		Beaumont city	118 296	48	20092		DeSoto city	49 047
48	07000	245	Jefferson County	118 296	48	20092	113	Dallas County	49 047
48	07132		Bedford city	46 979	48	21628		Duncanville city	38 524
48	07132	439	Tarrant County	46 979	48	21628	113	Dallas County	38 524
48	08236		Big Spring city	27 282	48	21892		Eagle Pass city	26 248
48	08236	227	Howard County	27 282	48	21892	323	Maverick County	26 248
48	10768		Brownsville city	175 023	48	22660		Edinburg city	77 100
48	10768	061	Cameron County	175 023	48	22660	215	Hidalgo County	77 100
48	10912		Bryan city	76 201	48	24000		El Paso city	649 121
48	10912	041	Brazos County	76 201	48	24000	141	El Paso County	649 121

Cities by County–*Continued*

State Code	Place Code	County Code	Geographic Area Name	2010 Census Population	State Code	Place Code	County Code	Geographic Area Name	2010 Census Population
48	24768		Euless city	51 277	48	38632		Keller city	39 627
48	24768	439	Tarrant County	51 277	48	38632	439	Tarrant County	39 627
48	25452		Farmers Branch city	28 616	48	39148		Killeen city	127 921
48	25452	113	Dallas County	28 616	48	39148	027	Bell County	127 921
48	26232		Flower Mound town	64 669	48	39352		Kingsville city	26 213
48	26232	121	Denton County	64 457	48	39352	273	Kleberg County	26 213
48	26232	439	Tarrant County	212					
					48	39952		Kyle city	28 016
48	27000		Fort Worth city	741 206	48	39952	209	Hays County	28 016
48	27000	121	Denton County	7 813					
48	27000	367	Parker County	7	48	40588		Lake Jackson city	26 849
48	27000	439	Tarrant County	733 386	48	40588	039	Brazoria County	26 849
48	27000	497	Wise County	0					
48	27648		Friendswood city	35 805	48	41212		Lancaster city	36 361
48	27648	167	Galveston County	25 510	48	41212	113	Dallas County	36 361
48	27648	201	Harris County	10 295					
					48	41440		La Porte city	33 800
48	27684		Frisco city	116 989	48	41440	201	Harris County	33 800
48	27684	085	Collin County	72 489					
48	27684	121	Denton County	44 500	48	41464		Laredo city	236 091
					48	41464	479	Webb County	236 091
48	28068		Galveston city	47 743					
48	28068	167	Galveston County	47 743	48	41980		League City city	83 560
					48	41980	167	Galveston County	81 998
48	29000		Garland city	226 876	48	41980	201	Harris County	1 562
48	29000	085	Collin County	266					
48	29000	113	Dallas County	226 608	48	42016		Leander city	26 521
48	29000	397	Rockwall County	2	48	42016	453	Travis County	1 077
					48	42016	491	Williamson County	25 444
48	29336		Georgetown city	47 400					
48	29336	491	Williamson County	47 400	48	42508		Lewisville city	95 290
					48	42508	113	Dallas County	841
48	30464		Grand Prairie city	175 396	48	42508	121	Denton County	94 449
48	30464	113	Dallas County	123 487					
48	30464	139	Ellis County	45	48	43012		Little Elm city	25 898
48	30464	439	Tarrant County	51 864	48	43012	121	Denton County	25 898
					48	43888		Longview city	80 455
48	30644		Grapevine city	46 334	48	43888	183	Gregg County	78 585
48	30644	113	Dallas County	0	48	43888	203	Harrison County	1 870
48	30644	121	Denton County	0					
48	30644	439	Tarrant County	46 334	48	45000		Lubbock city	229 573
					48	45000	303	Lubbock County	229 573
48	30920		Greenville city	25 557					
48	30920	231	Hunt County	25 557	48	45072		Lufkin city	35 067
					48	45072	005	Angelina County	35 067
48	31928		Haltom City city	42 409					
48	31928	439	Tarrant County	42 409	48	45384		McAllen city	129 877
					48	45384	215	Hidalgo County	129 877
48	32312		Harker Heights city	26 700					
48	32312	027	Bell County	26 700	48	45744		McKinney city	131 117
					48	45744	085	Collin County	131 117
48	32372		Harlingen city	64 849					
48	32372	061	Cameron County	64 849	48	46452		Mansfield city	56 368
					48	46452	139	Ellis County	95
48	35000		Houston city	2 099 451	48	46452	251	Johnson County	1 652
48	35000	157	Fort Bend County	38 124	48	46452	439	Tarrant County	54 621
48	35000	201	Harris County	2 057 280					
48	35000	339	Montgomery County	4 047	48	47892		Mesquite city	139 824
					48	47892	113	Dallas County	139 731
48	35528		Huntsville city	38 548	48	47892	257	Kaufman County	93
48	35528	471	Walker County	38 548					
					48	48072		Midland city	111 147
48	35576		Hurst city	37 337	48	48072	317	Martin County	0
48	35576	439	Tarrant County	37 337	48	48072	329	Midland County	111 147
48	37000		Irving city	216 290	48	48768		Mission city	77 058
48	37000	113	Dallas County	216 290	48	48768	215	Hidalgo County	77 058

Cities by County–*Continued*

State Code	Place Code	County Code	Geographic Area Name	2010 Census Population	State Code	Place Code	County Code	Geographic Area Name	2010 Census Population
48	48804		Missouri City city	67 358	48	65600		San Marcos city	44 894
48	48804	157	Fort Bend County	61 755	48	65600	055	Caldwell County	3
48	48804	201	Harris County	5 603	48	65600	187	Guadalupe County	0
					48	65600	209	Hays County	44 891
48	50256		Nacogdoches city	32 996					
48	50256	347	Nacogdoches County	32 996	48	66128		Schertz city	31 465
					48	66128	029	Bexar County	1 157
48	50820		New Braunfels city	57 740	48	66128	091	Comal County	845
48	50820	091	Comal County	47 586	48	66128	187	Guadalupe County	29 463
48	50820	187	Guadalupe County	10 154					
					48	66644		Seguin city	25 175
48	52356		North Richland Hills city	63 343	48	66644	187	Guadalupe County	25 175
48	52356	439	Tarrant County	63 343					
					48	67496		Sherman city	38 521
48	53388		Odessa city	99 940	48	67496	181	Grayson County	38 521
48	53388	135	Ector County	98 270					
48	53388	329	Midland County	1 670	48	68636		Socorro city	32 013
					48	68636	141	El Paso County	32 013
48	55080		Paris city	25 171					
48	55080	277	Lamar County	25 171	48	69032		Southlake city	26 575
					48	69032	121	Denton County	773
48	56000		Pasadena city	149 043	48	69032	439	Tarrant County	25 802
48	56000	201	Harris County	149 043					
					48	70808		Sugar Land city	78 817
48	56348		Pearland city	91 252	48	70808	157	Fort Bend County	78 817
48	56348	039	Brazoria County	86 706					
48	56348	157	Fort Bend County	721	48	72176		Temple city	66 102
48	56348	201	Harris County	3 825	48	72176	027	Bell County	66 102
48	57176		Pflugerville city	46 936	48	72368		Texarkana city	36 411
48	57176	453	Travis County	46 636	48	72368	037	Bowie County	36 411
48	57176	491	Williamson County	300					
					48	72392		Texas City city	45 099
48	57200		Pharr city	70 400	48	72392	071	Chambers County	0
48	57200	215	Hidalgo County	70 400	48	72392	167	Galveston County	45 099
48	58016		Plano city	259 841	48	72530		The Colony city	36 328
48	58016	085	Collin County	254 525	48	72530	121	Denton County	36 328
48	58016	121	Denton County	5 316					
					48	74144		Tyler city	96 900
48	58820		Port Arthur city	53 818	48	74144	423	Smith County	96 900
48	58820	245	Jefferson County	53 814					
48	58820	361	Orange County	4	48	75428		Victoria city	62 592
					48	75428	469	Victoria County	62 592
48	61796		Richardson city	99 223					
48	61796	085	Collin County	28 569	48	76000		Waco city	124 805
48	61796	113	Dallas County	70 654	48	76000	309	McLennan County	124 805
48	62828		Rockwall city	37 490	48	76816		Waxahachie city	29 621
48	62828	397	Rockwall County	37 490	48	76816	139	Ellis County	29 621
48	63284		Rosenberg city	30 618	48	76864		Weatherford city	25 250
48	63284	157	Fort Bend County	30 618	48	76864	367	Parker County	25 250
48	63500		Round Rock city	99 887	48	77272		Weslaco city	35 670
48	63500	453	Travis County	1 362	48	77272	215	Hidalgo County	35 670
48	63500	491	Williamson County	98 525					
					48	79000		Wichita Falls city	104 553
48	63572		Rowlett city	56 199	48	79000	485	Wichita County	104 553
48	63572	113	Dallas County	49 188					
48	63572	397	Rockwall County	7 011	48	80356		Wylie city	41 427
					48	80356	085	Collin County	39 957
48	64472		San Angelo city	93 200	48	80356	113	Dallas County	415
48	64472	451	Tom Green County	93 200	48	80356	397	Rockwall County	1 055
48	65000		San Antonio city	1 327 407	49			**UTAH**	2 763 885
48	65000	029	Bexar County	1 327 381	49	01310		American Fork city	26 263
48	65000	091	Comal County	0	49	01310	049	Utah County	26 263
48	65000	325	Medina County	26					
					49	07690		Bountiful city	42 552
48	65516		San Juan city	33 856	49	07690	011	Davis County	42 552
48	65516	215	Hidalgo County	33 856					

Cities by County–*Continued*

State Code	Place Code	County Code	Geographic Area Name	2010 Census Population	State Code	Place Code	County Code	Geographic Area Name	2010 Census Population
49	11320		Cedar City city	28 857	49	76680		Tooele city	31 605
49	11320	021	Iron County	28 857	49	76680	045	Tooele County	31 605
49	13850		Clearfield city	30 112	49	82950		West Jordan city	103 712
49	13850	011	Davis County	30 112	49	82950	035	Salt Lake County	103 712
49	16270		Cottonwood Heights city	33 433	49	83470		West Valley City city	129 480
49	16270	035	Salt Lake County	33 433	49	83470	035	Salt Lake County	129 480
49	20120		Draper city	42 274	50			**VERMONT**	625 741
49	20120	035	Salt Lake County	40 532	50	10675		Burlington city	42 417
49	20120	049	Utah County	1 742	50	10675	007	Chittenden County	42 417
49	36070		Holladay city	26 472	51			**VIRGINIA**	8 001 024
49	36070	035	Salt Lake County	26 472	51	01000		Alexandria city	139 966
					51	01000	510	Alexandria city	139 966
49	40360		Kaysville city	27 300					
49	40360	011	Davis County	27 300	51	07784		Blacksburg town	42 620
					51	07784	121	Montgomery County	42 620
49	43660		Layton city	67 311					
49	43660	011	Davis County	67 311	51	14968		Charlottesville city	43 475
					51	14968	540	Charlottesville city	43 475
49	44320		Lehi city	47 407					
49	44320	049	Utah County	47 407	51	16000		Chesapeake city	222 209
					51	16000	550	Chesapeake city	222 209
49	45860		Logan city	48 174					
49	45860	005	Cache County	48 174	51	21344		Danville city	43 055
					51	21344	590	Danville city	43 055
49	49710		Midvale city	27 964					
49	49710	035	Salt Lake County	27 964	51	35000		Hampton city	137 436
					51	35000	650	Hampton city	137 436
49	53230		Murray city	46 746					
49	53230	035	Salt Lake County	46 746	51	35624		Harrisonburg city	48 914
					51	35624	660	Harrisonburg city	48 914
49	55980		Ogden city	82 825					
49	55980	057	Weber County	82 825	51	44984		Leesburg town	42 616
					51	44984	107	Loudoun County	42 616
49	57300		Orem city	88 328					
49	57300	049	Utah County	88 328	51	47672		Lynchburg city	75 568
					51	47672	680	Lynchburg city	75 568
49	60930		Pleasant Grove city	33 509					
49	60930	049	Utah County	33 509	51	48952		Manassas city	37 821
					51	48952	683	Manassas city	37 821
49	62470		Provo city	112 488					
49	62470	049	Utah County	112 488	51	56000		Newport News city	180 719
					51	56000	700	Newport News city	180 719
49	64340		Riverton city	38 753					
49	64340	035	Salt Lake County	38 753	51	57000		Norfolk city	242 803
					51	57000	710	Norfolk city	242 803
49	65110		Roy city	36 884					
49	65110	057	Weber County	36 884	51	61832		Petersburg city	32 420
					51	61832	730	Petersburg city	32 420
49	65330		St. George city	72 897					
49	65330	053	Washington County	72 897	51	64000		Portsmouth city	95 535
					51	64000	740	Portsmouth city	95 535
49	67000		Salt Lake City city	186 440					
49	67000	035	Salt Lake County	186 440	51	67000		Richmond city	204 214
					51	67000	760	Richmond city	204 214
49	67440		Sandy city	87 461					
49	67440	035	Salt Lake County	87 461	51	68000		Roanoke city	97 032
					51	68000	770	Roanoke city	97 032
49	70850		South Jordan city	50 418					
49	70850	035	Salt Lake County	50 418	51	76432		Suffolk city	84 585
					51	76432	800	Suffolk city	84 585
49	71290		Spanish Fork city	34 691					
49	71290	049	Utah County	34 691	51	82000		Virginia Beach city	437 994
					51	82000	810	Virginia Beach city	437 994
49	72280		Springville city	29 466					
49	72280	049	Utah County	29 466	51	86720		Winchester city	26 203
					51	86720	840	Winchester city	26 203
49	75360		Taylorsville city	58 652					
49	75360	035	Salt Lake County	58 652					

Cities by County–*Continued*

State Code	Place Code	County Code	Geographic Area Name	2010 Census Population	State Code	Place Code	County Code	Geographic Area Name	2010 Census Population
53			**WASHINGTON**	6 724 540	53	56625		Pullman city	29 799
53	03180		Auburn city	70 180	53	56625	075	Whitman County	29 799
53	03180	033	King County	62 761					
53	03180	053	Pierce County	7 419	53	56695		Puyallup city	37 022
					53	56695	053	Pierce County	37 022
53	05210		Bellevue city	122 363					
53	05210	033	King County	122 363	53	57535		Redmond city	54 144
					53	57535	033	King County	54 144
53	05280		Bellingham city	80 885					
53	05280	073	Whatcom County	80 885	53	57745		Renton city	90 927
					53	57745	033	King County	90 927
53	07380		Bothell city	33 505					
53	07380	033	King County	17 090	53	58235		Richland city	48 058
53	07380	061	Snohomish County	16 415	53	58235	005	Benton County	48 058
53	07695		Bremerton city	37 729	53	61115		Sammamish city	45 780
53	07695	035	Kitsap County	37 729	53	61115	033	King County	45 780
53	08850		Burien city	33 313	53	62288		SeaTac city	26 909
53	08850	033	King County	33 313	53	62288	033	King County	26 909
53	17635		Des Moines city	29 673	53	63000		Seattle city	608 660
53	17635	033	King County	29 673	53	63000	033	King County	608 660
53	20750		Edmonds city	39 709	53	63960		Shoreline city	53 007
53	20750	061	Snohomish County	39 709	53	63960	033	King County	53 007
53	22640		Everett city	103 019	53	67000		Spokane city	208 916
53	22640	061	Snohomish County	103 019	53	67000	063	Spokane County	208 916
53	23515		Federal Way city	89 306	53	67167		Spokane Valley city	89 755
53	23515	033	King County	89 306	53	67167	063	Spokane County	89 755
53	33805		Issaquah city	30 434	53	70000		Tacoma city	198 397
53	33805	033	King County	30 434	53	70000	053	Pierce County	198 397
53	35275		Kennewick city	73 917	53	73465		University Place city	31 144
53	35275	005	Benton County	73 917	53	73465	053	Pierce County	31 144
53	35415		Kent city	92 411	53	74060		Vancouver city	161 791
53	35415	033	King County	92 411	53	74060	011	Clark County	161 791
53	35940		Kirkland city	48 787	53	75775		Walla Walla city	31 731
53	35940	033	King County	48 787	53	75775	071	Walla Walla County	31 731
53	36745		Lacey city	42 393	53	77105		Wenatchee city	31 925
53	36745	067	Thurston County	42 393	53	77105	007	Chelan County	31 925
53	37900		Lake Stevens city	28 069	53	80010		Yakima city	91 067
53	37900	061	Snohomish County	28 069	53	80010	077	Yakima County	91 067
53	38038		Lakewood city	58 163	54			**WEST VIRGINIA**	1 852 994
53	38038	053	Pierce County	58 163	54	14600		Charleston city	51 400
					54	14600	039	Kanawha County	51 400
53	40245		Longview city	36 648					
53	40245	015	Cowlitz County	36 648	54	39460		Huntington city	49 138
					54	39460	011	Cabell County	45 214
53	40840		Lynnwood city	35 836	54	39460	099	Wayne County	3 924
53	40840	061	Snohomish County	35 836					
					54	55756		Morgantown city	29 660
53	43955		Marysville city	60 020	54	55756	061	Monongalia County	29 660
53	43955	061	Snohomish County	60 020					
					54	62140		Parkersburg city	31 492
53	47560		Mount Vernon city	31 743	54	62140	107	Wood County	31 492
53	47560	057	Skagit County	31 743					
					54	86452		Wheeling city	28 486
53	51300		Olympia city	46 478	54	86452	051	Marshall County	276
53	51300	067	Thurston County	46 478	54	86452	069	Ohio County	28 210
53	53545		Pasco city	59 781					
53	53545	021	Franklin County	59 781					

Cities by County–*Continued*

State Code	Place Code	County Code	Geographic Area Name	2010 Census Population	State Code	Place Code	County Code	Geographic Area Name	2010 Census Population
55			**WISCONSIN**	5 686 986	55	72975		Sheboygan city	49 288
55	02375		Appleton city	72 623	55	72975	117	Sheboygan County	49 288
55	02375	015	Calumet County	11 088					
55	02375	087	Outagamie County	60 045	55	77200		Stevens Point city	26 717
55	02375	139	Winnebago County	1 490	55	77200	097	Portage County	26 717
55	06500		Beloit city	36 966	55	78600		Sun Prairie city	29 364
55	06500	105	Rock County	36 966	55	78600	025	Dane County	29 364
55	10025		Brookfield city	37 920	55	78650		Superior city	27 244
55	10025	133	Waukesha County	37 920	55	78650	031	Douglas County	27 244
55	22300		Eau Claire city	65 883	55	84250		Waukesha city	70 718
55	22300	017	Chippewa County	1 981	55	84250	133	Waukesha County	70 718
55	22300	035	Eau Claire County	63 902	55	84475		Wausau city	39 106
					55	84475	073	Marathon County	39 106
55	25950		Fitchburg city	25 260					
55	25950	025	Dane County	25 260	55	84675		Wauwatosa city	46 396
					55	84675	079	Milwaukee County	46 396
55	26275		Fond du Lac city	43 021					
55	26275	039	Fond du Lac County	43 021	55	85300		West Allis city	60 411
					55	85300	079	Milwaukee County	60 411
55	27300		Franklin city	35 451					
55	27300	079	Milwaukee County	35 451	55	85350		West Bend city	31 078
					55	85350	131	Washington County	31 078
55	31000		Green Bay city	104 057					
55	31000	009	Brown County	104 057	56			**WYOMING**	563 626
					56	13150		Casper city	55 316
55	31175		Greenfield city	36 720	56	13150	025	Natrona County	55 316
55	31175	079	Milwaukee County	36 720					
					56	13900		Cheyenne city	59 466
55	37825		Janesville city	63 575	56	13900	021	Laramie County	59 466
55	37825	105	Rock County	63 575					
					56	31855		Gillette city	29 087
55	39225		Kenosha city	99 218	56	31855	005	Campbell County	29 087
55	39225	059	Kenosha County	99 218					
					56	45050		Laramie city	30 816
55	40775		La Crosse city	51 320	56	45050	001	Albany County	30 816
55	40775	063	La Crosse County	51 320					
55	48000		Madison city	233 209					
55	48000	025	Dane County	233 209					
55	48500		Manitowoc city	33 736					
55	48500	071	Manitowoc County	33 736					
55	51000		Menomonee Falls village	35 626					
55	51000	133	Waukesha County	35 626					
55	53000		Milwaukee city	594 833					
55	53000	079	Milwaukee County	594 833					
55	53000	131	Washington County	0					
55	53000	133	Waukesha County	0					
55	54875		Mount Pleasant village	26 197					
55	54875	101	Racine County	26 197					
55	55750		Neenah city	25 501					
55	55750	139	Winnebago County	25 501					
55	56375		New Berlin city	39 584					
55	56375	133	Waukesha County	39 584					
55	58800		Oak Creek city	34 451					
55	58800	079	Milwaukee County	34 451					
55	60500		Oshkosh city	66 083					
55	60500	139	Winnebago County	66 083					
55	66000		Racine city	78 860					
55	66000	101	Racine County	78 860					

APPENDIX F
SOURCE NOTES AND EXPLANATIONS

The following documentation is provided in the order in which items appear in the tables. Internet addresses are provided for the sources of the data. Some of the links refer to the specific data tables. Others provide information about the general data source.

TABLE A—STATES

Table A presents 355 items for the United States as a whole, for each individual state, and for the District of Columbia. The states are presented in alphabetical order.

LAND AREA, Items 1 and 4
Source: U.S. Census Bureau—2018 U.S. Gazetteer Files,
https://www.census.gov/geographies/reference-files/time-series/geo/gazetteer-files.html

Land area measurements are shown to the nearest square mile. Land area includes dry land and land temporarily or partially covered by water, such as marshlands, swamps, and river floodplains. The 2018 land areas have been aggregated from the counties as listed in the 2018 Gazetteer files.

POPULATION AND COMPONENTS OF CHANGE, Items 2–4, 31–41
Source: U.S. Census Bureau—Decennial Censuses and Population Estimates
https://www.census.gov/programs-surveys/popest.html
https://www.census.gov/programs-surveys/decennial-census/data/datasets.2010.html

The population data for 2018 are Census Bureau estimates of the resident population as of July 1, 2018.

The population data for 1990, 2000, and 2010 are from the decennial censuses and represent the resident population as of April 1 of those years.

The change in population between 2010 and 2018 is made up of (a) natural increase—births minus deaths, and (b) net migration—the difference between the number of persons moving into a particular state and the number of persons moving out of the state. Net migration is composed of internal and international migration.

POPULATION AND POPULATION CHARACTERISTICS, Items 5–23 and 45–63
Source: U.S. Census Bureau—Population Estimates and 2017 American Community Survey

https://www.census.gov/programs-surveys/popest.html
http://www.census.gov/acs/www/

Data on age, sex, race, and Hispanic origin are from the Population Estimates program. Data on place of birth are from the 2017 American Community Survey, a nationwide continuous survey designed to replace the long form questionnaire used in previous censuses.

The concept "race alone or in combination" includes people who reported a single race alone (e.g., Asian) and people who reported that race in combination with one or more of the other major race groups (e.g., White, Black or African American, American Indian and Alaska Native, Native Hawaiian and Other Pacific Islander, and Some Other Race). The "race alone or in combination" concept, therefore, represents the maximum number of people who reported as that race group, either alone, or in combination with another race(s).

The sum of the four individual race alone or in combination categories in this book may add to more than the total population because people who reported more than one race were tallied in each race category. In this book, the Asian group has been combined with the Native Hawaiian and Other Pacific Islander group, causing double-counting of persons who identify with both groups. This is especially pronounced in Hawaii.

Data on race were derived from answers to the question on race that was asked of all persons. The concept of race, as used by the Census Bureau, reflects self-identification by respondents according to the race or races with which they most closely identify. These categories are sociopolitical constructs and should not be interpreted as being scientific or anthropological in nature. Furthermore, the race categories include both racial and national origin groups.

The **White** population is defined as persons who indicated their race as White, as well as persons who did not classify themselves in one of the specific race categories listed on the questionnaire but entered a nationality such as Irish, German, Italian, Lebanese, Near Easterner, Arab, or Polish.

The **Black** population includes persons who indicated their race as "Black or African American" as well as persons who did not classify themselves in one of the specific race categories but reported entries such as African American, Afro American, Kenyan, Nigerian, or Haitian.

The **American Indian or Alaska Native** population includes persons who indicated their race as American Indian or Alaska Native, as well as persons who did not classify themselves in one of the specific race categories but reported entries such as Canadian Indian, French-American Indian, Spanish-American Indian, Eskimo, Aleut, Alaska Indian, or any of the American Indian or Alaska Native tribes.

The **Asian and Pacific Islander** population combines two census groupings: **Asian** and **Native Hawaiian or Other Pacific Islander**. The **Asian** population includes persons who indicated their race as Asian Indian, Chinese, Filipino, Japanese, Korean, Vietnamese, or "Other Asian," as well as persons who provided write-in entries of such groups as Cambodian, Laotian, Hmong, Pakistani, or Taiwanese. The **Native Hawaiian or Other Pacific Islander** population includes persons who indicated their race as "Native Hawaiian," "Guamanian or Chamorro," "Samoan," or "Other Pacific Islander," as well as persons who reported entries such as Part Hawaiian, American Samoan, Fijian, Melanesian, or Tahitian.

The **Hispanic population** is based on a question that asked respondents "Is this person Spanish/Hispanic/Latino?" Persons marking any one of the four Hispanic categories (i.e., Mexican, Puerto Rican, Cuban, or other Spanish) are collectively referred to as Hispanic.

Age is defined as age at last birthday (number of completed years since birth), as of April 1 of the census year.

The **median age** is the age that divides the population into two equal-size groups. Half of the population is older than the median age and half is younger. Median age is based on a standard distribution of the population by single years of age and is shown to the nearest tenth of a year.

The **female** population is shown as a percentage of total population.

The **foreign-born** population includes all persons who were not U.S. citizens at birth. Foreign-born persons are those who indicated they were either a U.S. citizen by naturalization or were not a citizen of the United States. Neither the census nor the American Community Survey asked about immigration status. The population surveyed included all persons who indicated that the United States was their usual place of residence. The foreign-born population consists of immigrants (legal permanent residents), temporary migrants (students), humanitarian migrants (refugees), and unauthorized migrants (persons illegally residing in the United States).

Percent born in state of residence is shown as a percentage of total population.

IMMIGRANTS, Item 24
Source: Department of Homeland Security, U.S. Citizenship and Immigration Services
http://www.dhs.gov/yearbook-immigration-statistics

The number of immigrants by state of intended residence is summarized from the administrative records of the Citizenship and Immigration Services. This information is compiled from immigrant visas and forms granting legal permanent resident status.

An **immigrant** is an alien admitted to the United States as a lawful permanent resident. Immigrants are those persons lawfully accorded the privilege of residing permanently in the United States (i.e., immigrants who receive a "green card".) They may be newly arrived individuals who were issued immigrant visas by the Department of State overseas, or they may be U.S. residents who were admitted to permanent resident status in 2017 by the U.S. Citizenship and Immigration Services.

HOUSEHOLDS, Items 25–30 and 64–68
Source: U.S. Census Bureau—2017 American Community Survey
http://www.census.gov/acs/www/

A **household** includes all of the persons who occupy a housing unit. Persons not living in households are classified as living in group quarters. A housing unit is a house, an apartment, a mobile home, a group of rooms, or a single room occupied (or, if vacant, intended for occupancy) as separate living quarters. Separate living quarters are those in which the occupants live separately from any other persons in the building and have direct access from the outside of the building or through a common hall. The occupants may be a single family, one person living alone, two or more families living together, or any other group of related or unrelated persons who share living quarters. The number of households is the same as the number of year-round occupied housing units.

The measure of **persons per household** is obtained by dividing the number of persons in households by the number of households or householders. One person in each household is designated as the householder. In most cases, this is the person, (or one of the persons) in whose name the house is owned, being bought, or rented. If there is no such person in the household, any adult household member 15 years old and over can be designated as the householder.

A **family** includes a householder and one or more other persons living in the same household who are related to the householder by birth, marriage, or adoption. All persons in a household who are related to the householder are regarded as members of his or her family. A **family household** may contain persons not related to the householder; thus, family households may include more members than families do. A household can contain only one family for the purposes of census tabulations. Not all households contain families, as a household may comprise a group of unrelated persons or one person living alone. Families are classified by type as either a "married couple family" or "other family" according to the presence of a spouse.

The category **female family householder** includes only female-headed family households with no spouse present.

POPULATION PROJECTIONS, Items 42–44
Source: U.S. Census Bureau—Population Projections Branch
https://census.gov/programs-surveys/popproj/guidance.html

Projections are estimates of the population for future dates. They illustrate plausible courses of future population change based on assumptions about future births, deaths, international migration, and domestic migration. Projected numbers are based on an estimated population consistent with the most recent decennial census as enumerated. The Census Bureau does not have a current set of state population projections and currently has no plans to produce them. This volume includes projections released in 2005, based on the 2000 census. The Census Bureau notes that these projections should be used with caution because population trends may have changed substantially since their release.

HOUSING, Items 69–92

Source: U.S. Census Bureau—2010 and 2017 American Community Survey
http://www.census.gov/acs/www/

Housing data for 2010 and 2017 are from the American Community Survey, a nationwide continuous survey designed to replace the long form questionnaire used in previous censuses. A sample of households is surveyed to provide estimates.

A **housing unit** is a house, apartment, mobile home or trailer, group of rooms, or single room occupied or, if vacant, intended for occupancy as separate living quarters. Separate living quarters are those in which the occupants do not live and eat with any other person in the structure and which have direct access from the outside of the building or through a common hall. For vacant units, the criteria of separateness and direct access are applied to the intended occupants whenever possible. If that information cannot be obtained, the criteria are applied to the previous occupants.

The occupants of a housing unit may be a single family, one person living alone, two or more families living together, or any other group of related or unrelated persons who share living arrangements. Both occupied and vacant housing units are included in the housing inventory, although recreational vehicles, tents, caves, boats, railroad cars, and the like are included only if they are occupied as a person's usual place of residence.

A housing unit is classified as **occupied** if it is the usual place of residence of the person or group of persons living in it at the time of enumeration, or if the occupants are only temporarily absent (away on vacation). A household consists of all persons who occupy a housing unit as their usual place of residence.

Housing cost, as a percentage of income, is shown separately for owners with mortgages, owners without mortgages, and renters. Also shown is the percentage of mortgaged owners and renters who pay 30 percent or more of household income on selected monthly costs. Rent as a percent of income is a computed ratio of gross rent and monthly household income (total household income divided by 12). Selected owner costs include utilities and fuels, mortgage payments, insurance, taxes, etc. In each case, the ratio of housing cost to income is computed separately for each housing unit. The housing cost ratios for half of all units are above the median shown in this book, and half are below the median. Median monthly housing costs divides the monthly housing costs distribution into two equal parts, one-half of the cases falling below the median monthly housing costs and one-half above the median.

Median value is the dollar amount that divides the distribution of specified owner-occupied housing units into two equal parts, with half of all units below the median value and half above the median value. Value is defined as the respondent's estimate of what the house would sell for if it were for sale. Data are presented for single-family units on fewer than 10 acres of land that have no business or medical office on the property.

Median rent divides the distribution of renter-occupied housing units into two equal parts. The rent concept used in this volume is gross rent, which includes the amount of cash rent a renter pays (contract rent) plus the estimated average cost of utilities and fuels, if these are paid by the renter. The rent is the amount of rent only for living quarters and excludes any business or other space occupied. Single-family houses on lots of 10 or more acres of land are excluded.

Substandard units are occupied units that are overcrowded or lack complete plumbing facilities. For the purposes of this item, "overcrowded" is defined as having 1.01 persons or more per room. Complete plumbing facilities include hot and cold piped water, a flush toilet, and a bathtub or shower. These facilities must be located inside the housing unit, but do not have to be in the same room.

Different house includes all people 1 year old and over who, a year earlier, lived in a different house or apartment from the one they occupied at the time of interview.

BUILDING PERMITS, Items 93–95

Source: U.S. Census Bureau—Building Permits Survey
http://www.census.gov/construction/bps/

These figures represent private residential construction authorized by building permits in approximately 20,000 places in the United States. Valuation represents the expected cost of construction as recorded on the building permit. This figure usually excludes the cost of on-site and off-site development and improvements, as well as the cost of heating, plumbing, electrical, and elevator installations.

National, state, and county totals were obtained by adding the data for permit-issuing places within each jurisdiction. These totals thus are limited to permits issued in the 20,000 place universe covered by the Census Bureau and may not include all permits issued within a state. Current surveys indicate that construction is undertaken for all but a very small percentage of housing units authorized by building permits.

Residential building permits include buildings with any number of housing units. Housing units exclude group quarters (such as dormitories and rooming houses), transient accommodations (such as transient hotels, motels, and tourist courts), "HUD-code" manufactured (mobile) homes, moved or relocated units, and housing units created in an existing residential or nonresidential structure.

MANUFACTURED HOUSING UNITS, Item 96

Source: U.S. Census Bureau—Manufactured Housing Survey
https://www.census.gov/data/tables/time-series/econ/mhs/shipments.html

The Manufactured Housing Survey (MHS) is conducted by the U.S. Census Bureau and sponsored by the Department of Housing and Urban Development (HUD). MHS produces monthly regional estimates of the average sales price of new manufactured homes and more detailed annual estimates including selected characteristics of new manufactured homes. In addition, MHS produces monthly estimates of homes shipped to each state.

A manufactured home is defined as a movable dwelling, 8 feet or more wide and 40 feet or more long, designed to be towed on its own chassis, with transportation gear integral to the unit when it leaves the factory, and without need of a permanent foundation. These manufactured homes include multi-wides and expandable manufactured homes. Excluded are travel trailers, motor homes, and modular housing.

BIRTHS AND DEATHS, Items 97–103

Source: U.S. Centers for Disease Control and Prevention, National Center for Health Statistics
https://www.cdc.gov/nchs/data/nvsr/nvsr67/nvsr67_08-508.pdf
https://www.cdc.gov/nchs/data/nvsr/nvsr68/nvsr68_09-508.pdf

The registration of births, deaths, and other vital events in the United States is primarily a state and local function. The civil laws of every state provide for continuous and permanent birth and death registration systems. Through the National Vital Statistics System, the National Center for Health Statistics (NCHS) obtains data on births and deaths from the registration offices of each state, New York City, and the District of Columbia.

Birth and death statistics are limited to events occurring during the year. The data are by place of residence and exclude events for nonresidents of the United States. Births or deaths occurring outside the United States are excluded.

Birth and death rates represent the number of births and deaths per 1,000 resident population enumerated as of April 1 for decennial census years and estimated as of July 1 for other years.

Figures for infant deaths include deaths of children under 1 year of age but exclude fetal deaths. The infant death rate is per 1,000 live births.

The rates of almost all causes of disease, injury, and death vary by age. Age adjustment is a technique for "removing" the effects of age from crude rates, in order to allow meaningful comparisons across populations with different underlying age structures. For example, comparing the crude death rate in Florida to that of California is misleading, since the relatively older population in Florida will lead to a higher crude death rate. For such a comparison, age-adjusted death rates are preferable.

The population estimates were developed by the Census Bureau's Population Division using a traditional cohort component method. Starting with a basic population from the 2000 census, each component of population change—births, deaths, domestic migration, and international migration—is estimated separately for each birth cohort by sex, race, and Hispanic or Latino origin.

Age-adjusted rates are calculated by applying the age-specific rates of various populations to a single standard population. In this volume, the standard population is 2000. Beginning in 2003, The Centers for Disease Control and Prevention switched to the year 2000, after many years of using the year 1940 as the standard population for age-adjusted death rates.

PERSONS LACKING HEALTH INSURANCE, Items 104–105

Source: U.S. Census Bureau—American Community Survey
https://www.census.gov/library/publications/2018/demo/p60-264.html

These estimates are from the American Community Survey, an ongoing nationwide survey that is conducted throughout the year. About 250,000 addresses per month receive the ACS. Respondents are asked whether each household member is currently covered (by specific types of health coverage) at the time of interview. The 2013 estimates were the first to use the ACS. Prior year estimates were based on the Annual Social and Economic Supplement (ASEC) of the Current Population Survey (CPS).

Those lacking coverage are the percentage of the population of each state who were not covered by private health plans purchased directly or provided by an employer, Medicaid, Medicare, or military health care.

MEDICARE BENEFICIARIES, Item 106

Source: U.S. Department of Health and Human Services, Centers for Medicare and Medicaid Services
https://www.cms.gov/Research-Statistics-Data-and-Systems/Statistics-Trends-and-Reports/CMSProgramStatistics/Dashboard.html

The Centers for Medicare and Medicaid Services (CMS) administers Medicare, which provides health insurance to persons 65 years old and over, persons with permanent kidney failure, and certain persons with disabilities. Original Medicare has two parts: Hospital Insurance and Supplemental Medical Insurance. In recent years, Medicare has been expanded to include two new programs: Medicare Advantage plans and prescription drug coverage. Medicare Advantage Plans are health plan options that are approved by Medicare but run by private companies. Medicare prescription drug plans can be part of Medicare Advantage plans or stand-alone drug plans.

Persons who are eligible for Medicare can enroll in Part A (Hospital Insurance) at no charge, and can choose to pay a monthly premium to enroll in Part B. Most eligible persons are enrolled in Part A, and most enrollees in Part A are also enrolled in Part B (Supplemental Medical Insurance.) This table includes persons who were enrolled in both Part A and Part B during 2017.

Part B beneficiaries can choose to enroll in **Original Medicare**, a fee-for-service plan administered by the Centers for Medicare and Medicaid Services, or in a **Medicare Advantage** plan. Medicare Advantage plans include private fee-for-service plans, preferred provider organizations, health maintenance organizations, medical savings account plans, demonstration plans, and programs for all-inclusive care for the elderly.

The annual Medicare enrollment counts are determined using a person-year methodology. For each calendar year, total person-year counts are determined by summing the total number of months that each beneficiary is enrolled during the year and dividing by 12. Using this methodology, a beneficiary's partial-year enrollment may be counted in more than one category (i.e., both Original Medicare and Medicare Advantage).

CRIME, Items 107–110

Source: U.S. Federal Bureau of Investigation—Uniform Crime Reports
https://ucr.fbi.gov/crime-in-the-u.s/2016/crime-in-the-u.s.-2016

Crime data are as reported to the Federal Bureau of Investigation (FBI) by law enforcement agencies and have not been adjusted for underreporting. This may affect comparability between geographic areas or over time.

Through the voluntary contribution of crime statistics by law enforcement agencies across the United States, the Uniform Crime Reporting (UCR) Program provides periodic assessments of crime in the nation as measured by offenses that have come to the attention of the law enforcement community. The Committee on Uniform Crime Records of the International Association of Chiefs of Police initiated this voluntary national data-collection effort in 1930. The UCR Program contributors compile and submit their crime data either directly to the FBI or through state-level UCR Programs.

Seven offenses, because of their severity, frequency of occurrence, and likelihood of being reported to police, were initially selected to serve as an index for evaluating fluctuations in the volume of crime. These serious crimes were murder and nonnegligent manslaughter, forcible rape, robbery, aggravated assault, burglary, larceny-theft, and motor vehicle theft. By congressional mandate, arson was added as the eighth index offense in 1979. The totals shown in this volume do not include arson.

In 2004, the FBI discontinued the use of the Crime Index in the UCR Program and its publications, stating that the Crime Index was driven upward by the offense with the highest number of cases (in this case, larceny-theft) creating a bias against jurisdictions with a high number of larceny-thefts but a low number of other serious crimes, such as murder and forcible rape. The FBI is currently publishing a violent crime total and a property crime total until a more viable index is developed.

In 2013, the FBI adopted a new definition of rape. Rape is now defined as, "Penetration, no matter how slight, of the vagina or anus with any body part or object, or oral penetration by a sex organ of another person, without the consent of the victim." The new definition updated the 80-year-old historical definition of rape which was "carnal knowledge of a female forcibly and against her will." Effectively, the revised definition expands rape to include both male and female victims and offenders, and reflects the various forms of sexual penetration understood to be rape, especially non-consenting acts of sodomy, and sexual assaults with objects. **Violent crimes** include four categories of offenses: (1) Murder and non-negligent manslaughter, as defined in the UCR Program, is the willful (non-negligent) killing of one human being by another. This offense excludes deaths caused by negligence, suicide, or accident; justifiable homicides; and attempts to murder or assaults to murder. (2) Rape is the penetration, no matter how slight, of the vagina or anus with any body part or object, or oral penetration by a sex organ of another person, without the consent of the victim. Assaults or attempts to commit rape by force or threat of force are also included; however, statutory rape (without force) and other sex offenses are excluded. (3) Robbery is the taking or attempting to take anything of value from the care, custody, or control of a person or persons by force or threat of force or violence and/or by putting the victim in fear. (4) Aggravated assault is an unlawful attack by one person upon another for the purpose of inflicting severe or aggravated bodily injury. This type of assault is usually accompanied by the use of a weapon or by other means likely to produce death or great bodily harm. Attempts are included, since injury does not necessarily have to result when a gun, knife, or other weapon is used, as these incidents could and probably would result in a serious personal injury if the crime were successfully completed.

Property crimes include three categories: (1) Burglary, or breaking and entering, is the unlawful entry of a structure to commit a felony or theft, even though no force was used to gain entrance. (2) Larceny-theft is the unauthorized taking of the personal property of another, without the use of force. (3) Motor vehicle theft is the unauthorized taking of any motor vehicle.

Rates are based on population estimates provided by the FBI. For some states, reporting is not sufficiently complete to be representative of the state as a whole. The FBI has estimated state totals for those states.

ELEMENTARY AND SECONDARY SCHOOL ENROLLMENT, Items 111 and 112

Source: U.S. Department of Education, National Center for Education Statistics—Common Core of Data
http://nces.ed.gov/ccd/elsi/

Data on public school enrollment is from the Common Core of Data 2016-2017 survey. Public school enrollment includes pre-kindergarten through grade 12 and ungraded students. The student/teacher ratio is calculated by dividing the number of students in all schools by the number of full-time equivalent teachers employed by all schools and agencies.

EDUCATIONAL ATTAINMENT, Items 113–116

Source: U.S. Census Bureau—2010 and 2016 American Community Survey
http://www.census.gov/acs/www/

Data on **educational attainment** are tabulated for the population 25 years old and over. The data were derived from a question that asked respondents for the highest level of school completed or the highest degree received. Persons who had passed a high school equivalency examination were considered high school graduates. Schooling received in foreign schools was to be reported as the equivalent grade or years in the regular American school system. Vocational and technical training, such as barber school training; business, trade, technical, and vocational schools; or other training for a specific trade are specifically excluded.

High school graduate or more. This category includes persons whose highest degree was a high school diploma or its equivalent, and those who reported any level higher than a high school diploma.

Bachelor's degree or more. This category includes persons who have received bachelor's degrees, master's degrees, professional school degrees (such as law school or medical school degrees), and doctoral degrees.

LOCAL GOVERNMENT EDUCATION EXPENDITURES, Items 117 and 118

Source: U.S. Department of Education, National Center for Education Statistics—Common Core of Data http://nces.ed.gov/ccd/

Total expenditure for education includes provision or support of schools and facilities for elementary and secondary education. It encompasses instructional, support, and auxiliary services (school lunch, student activities, and community service) offered by public school systems. Retirement benefits paid to former education employees and interest payments are not included. Current expenditure includes all components of total expenditure except capital outlay. Expenditure data are obtained by the Census Bureau through its annual survey of government finances and are supplied to the National Center for Education Statistics (NCES). Current expenditure per student is current expenditure divided by the number of students enrolled. The number of students enrolled is based on an annual "membership" count of students on or about October 1.

NCES uses the Common Core of Data (CCD) Survey system to acquire and maintain statistical data from each of the 50 states, the District of Columbia, and the outlying areas. State education agencies compile and submit data for approximately 94,000 schools and 17,000 local school districts. Typically, this results in varying interpretation of NCES definitions and different record keeping systems, leading to large amounts of missing data for several states; this absence is reflected in the data in this publication. The numbers in Table A reflect imputations and adjustments as published in *Revenues and Expenditures for Public Elementary and Secondary Education: School Year 2015-2016 (Fiscal Year 2016)*.

EXPORTS, Items 119–121

Source: U.S. Department of Commerce, International Trade Administration http://www.census.gov/foreign-trade/statistics/state/ origin_movement/index.html

The data on exports of goods by state of origin are based on the location of the exporter (the principal party responsible for exportation from the United States). Exporters are often intermediaries, so the data do not necessarily represent the states in which the goods were actually produced. The total includes re-exports of foreign goods.

INCOME AND POVERTY, Items 122–133

Source: U.S. Census Bureau—2017 American Community Survey http://www.census.gov/acs/www/

The data on income were derived from answers to questions which were asked of the population 15 years old and over. **Total income** is the sum of the amounts reported separately for wage or salary income; net self-employment income; interest, dividends, or net rental or royalty income or income from estates and trusts; Social Security or railroad retirement income; Supplemental Security Income (SSI); public assistance or welfare payments; retirement, survivor, or disability pensions; and all other income. Receipts from the following sources are not included as income: capital gains; money received from the sale of property (unless the recipient was engaged in the business of selling such property); the value of income "in kind" from food stamps, public housing subsidies, medical care, employer contributions for individuals, etc.; withdrawal of bank deposits; money borrowed; tax refunds; exchange of money between relatives living in the same household; and gifts and lump-sum inheritances, insurance payments, and other types of lump-sum receipts.

Per capita income is the mean income computed for every man, woman, and child in a particular group. It is derived by dividing the aggregate income of a particular group by the total population in that group. Per capita income is rounded to the nearest whole dollar.

Household income includes the income of the householder and all other individuals 15 years old and over in the household, whether or not they are related to the householder. Since many households consist of only one person, average household income is usually less than average family income. Although the household income statistics cover the past 12 months, the characteristics of individuals and the composition of households refer to the time of enumeration. Thus, the income of the household does not include amounts received by individuals who were members of the household during all or part of the past 12 months if these individuals no longer resided in the household at the time of interview. Similarly, income amounts reported by individuals who did not reside in the household during the past 12 months but who were members of the household at the time of interview are included. However, the composition of most households was the same during the past 12 months as at the time of interview.

Median income divides the income distribution into two equal parts, with half of all cases below the median income level and half of all cases above the median income level. For households and families, the median income is based on the distribution of the total number of households and families, including those with no income. Median income for households is computed on the basis of a standard distribution with a minimum value of less than $2,500 and a maximum value of $200,000 or more and is rounded to the nearest whole dollar.

For **family income**, the incomes of all household members 15 years old and over related to the householder are summed and treated as a single amount. Although the family income statistics cover the past 12 months, the characteristics of individuals and the composition of families refer to the time of interview. Thus, the income of the family does not include amounts received by individuals who were members of the family during all of part of the past 12 months if these individuals no longer resided with the family at the time of interview. Similarly, income amounts reported by individuals who did not reside with the family during the past 12 months but who were members of the family at

Poverty Thresholds for 2017 by Size of Family and Number of Related Children Under 18 Years

Size of family unit	Weighted average thresholds	Related children under 18 years								
		None	One	Two	Three	Four	Five	Six	Seven	Eight or more
One person (unrelated individual):	12,488									
Under age 65	12,752	12,752								
Aged 65 and older	11,756	11,756								
Two people:	15,877									
Householder under age 65	16,493	16,414	16,895							
Householder aged 65 and older	14,828	14,816	16,831							
Three people	19,515	19,173	19,730	19,749						
Four people	25,094	25,283	25,696	24,858	24,944					
Five people	29,714	30,490	30,933	29,986	29,253	28,805				
Six people	33,618	35,069	35,208	34,482	33,787	32,753	32,140			
Seven people	38,173	40,351	40,603	39,734	39,129	38,001	36,685	35,242		
Eight people	42,684	45,129	45,528	44,708	43,990	42,971	41,678	40,332	39,990	
Nine people or more	50,681	54,287	54,550	53,825	53,216	52,216	50,840	49,595	49,287	47,389

Source: U.S. Census Bureau.

the time of interview are included. However, the composition of most families was the same during the past 12 months as at the time of interview.

The **poverty status** data were derived from data collected on the number of persons in the household, each person's relationship to the householder, and the income data. The Social Security Administration (SSA) developed the original poverty definition in 1964, which federal interagency committees subsequently revised in 1969 and 1980. The Office of Management and Budget's (OMB) *Directive 14* prescribes the SSA's definition as the official poverty measure for federal agencies to use in their statistical work. Poverty statistics presented in American Community Survey products adhere to the standards defined by OMB in *Directive 14*.

The poverty thresholds vary depending on three criteria: size of family, number of children, and, for one- and two-person families, age of householder. In determining the poverty status of families and unrelated individuals, the Census Bureau uses thresholds (income cutoffs) arranged in a two-dimensional matrix. The matrix consists of family size (from one person to nine or more persons), cross-classified by presence and number of family members under 18 years old (from no children present to eight or more children present). Unrelated individuals and two-person families are further differentiated by age of reference person (under 65 years old and 65 years old and over). To determine a person's poverty status, the person's total family income in the last 12 months is compared to the poverty threshold appropriate for that person's family size and composition. If the total income of that person's family is less than the threshold appropriate for that family, then the person is considered poor or "below the poverty level," together with every member of his or her family. If a person is not living with anyone related by birth, marriage, or adoption, then the person's own income is compared with his or her poverty threshold. The total number of persons below the

poverty level is the sum of persons in families and the number of unrelated individuals with incomes below the poverty level in the last 12 months. The average poverty threshold for a four-person family was $25,094 in 2017.

The data on **poverty status of households** were derived from answers to the income questions. Since poverty is defined at the family level and not the household level, the poverty status of the household is determined by the poverty status of the householder. Households are classified as poor when the total income of the householder's family in the previous 12 months is below the appropriate poverty threshold. (For nonfamily householders, the person's income is compared with the appropriate threshold.) The income of persons living in the household who are unrelated to the householder is not considered when determining the poverty status of a household, nor does their presence affect the family size in determining the appropriate threshold. The poverty thresholds vary depending upon three criteria: size of family, number of children, and, for one- and two-person families, age of the householder.

Poverty status of children by **family type** is the percentage of children living in that particular type of family that has a family income below the poverty threshold based on family size and composition.

PERSONAL INCOME AND EARNINGS, Items 134–158

Source: U.S. Bureau of Economic Analysis, Regional Economic Accounts
http://www.bea.gov/regional/index.htm#state

Total personal income is the current income received by residents of an area from all sources. It is measured before deductions of income and other personal taxes but after deductions of personal contributions for Social Security, government retirement, and other social insurance programs. It consists of **wage and salary disbursements** (covering all employee earnings, including executive salaries, bonuses, commissions, payments-in-kind, incentive payments, and tips); various types of supplementary earnings, such as employers' contributions to pension funds (termed "other labor income" or "supplements to wages and salaries"); proprietors' income; rental income of persons; dividends; personal interest income; and government and business transfer payments.

Proprietors' income is the monetary income and income-in-kind of proprietorships and partnerships (including the independent professions), and the income of tax-exempt cooperatives. **Dividends** are cash payments by corporations to stockholders who are U.S. residents. **Interest** is the monetary and imputed interest income of persons from all sources. **Rent** is the monetary income of persons from the rental of real property, except the income of persons primarily engaged in the real estate business; the imputed net rental income of owner-occupants of nonfarm dwellings; and the royalties received by persons.

Transfer payments are income for which services are not currently rendered. They consist of both government and business transfer payments. Government transfer payments include payments under the following programs: Federal Old-Age, Survivors, and Disability Insurance ("Social Security"); Medicare and medical vendor payments; unemployment insurance; railroad and government retirement; federal- and state-government-insured workers' compensation; veterans' benefits, including veterans' life insurance; food stamps; black lung payments; Supplemental Security Income; and Temporary Assistance for Needy Families. Government payments to nonprofit institutions, other than for work under research and development contracts, are also included. Business transfer payments consist primarily of liability payments for personal injury and of corporate gifts to nonprofit institutions.

Per capita personal income is based on resident population estimated as of July 1 of the year shown.

Personal tax payments include taxes paid by individuals to federal, state, and local governments. Personal taxes include individual income taxes, estate and gift taxes, motor vehicle license taxes, and personal property taxes. Personal contributions to social insurance ("Social Security taxes") are not included, nor are sales taxes.

Disposable personal income equals personal income less personal tax payments. It is a measure of the income available to persons for spending or saving.

Earnings cover wage and salary disbursements, other labor income, and proprietors' income.

The data for earnings obtained from the Bureau of Economic Analysis (BEA) are based on place of work. In computing personal income, BEA makes an "adjustment for residence" to earnings based on commuting patterns; thus, personal income is presented on a place-of-residence basis.

Farm earnings include the income of farm workers (wages and salaries and other labor income) and farm proprietors. Farm proprietors' income includes only the income of sole proprietorships and partnerships.

Farm earnings estimates are benchmarked to data collected in the Census of Agriculture and the revised Department of Agriculture state totals of income and expense items.

Goods-related industries include mining, construction, and manufacturing. **Service-related** and other industries includes private-sector earnings in forestry, related activities, and other; utilities; transportation and warehousing; information; wholesale trade; retail trade; finance and insurance; real estate and rental and leasing; and services, which includes professional, scientific, and technical services; management of companies and enterprises; administrative and waste services; educational services; health care and social assistance; arts, entertainment, and recreation; accommodation and food services; and other services, except public administration. Government earnings include all levels of government. Industries are categorized under the North American Industry Classification System (NAICS), and are not directly comparable to years prior to 2002.

GROSS STATE PRODUCT, Item 159
Source: U.S. Bureau of Economic Analysis, Regional Economic Accounts
http://www.bea.gov/regional/index.htm#state

Gross state product (GSP) for a state is derived as the sum of gross state product originating in all industries in the state. In concept, an industry's GSP, referred to as its "value added," is equivalent to its gross output (sales or receipts and other operating income, commodity taxes, and inventory changes) minus its intermediate inputs (consumption of goods and services purchased from other industries or imported from other countries). As such, it is often referred to as the state counterpart to the nation's gross domestic product (GDP). In practice, GSP estimates are measured as the sum of distributions by industry of the components of gross domestic income—that is, the sum of the costs incurred (such as compensation of employees, net interest, and indirect business taxes) and the profits earned in production.

SOCIAL SECURITY AND SUPPLEMENTAL SECURITY INCOME, Items 160–162
Source: U.S. Social Security Administration
http://www.ssa.gov/policy/docs/statcomps/oasdi_sc/
http://www.ssa.gov/policy/docs/statcomps/ssi_sc/

Social Security beneficiaries are persons receiving benefits under the Old-Age, Survivors, and Disability Insurance Program. These include retired or disabled workers covered by the program, their spouses and dependent children, and the surviving spouses and dependent children of deceased workers.

Supplemental Security Income (SSI) recipients are persons receiving SSI payments. The SSI program is a cash assistance program that provides monthly benefits to low-income aged, blind, or disabled persons.

Data are as of December of the year shown.

CIVILIAN EMPLOYMENT, Items 163–166

Source: U.S. Census Bureau—2016 American Community Survey
http://www.census.gov/acs/www/
http://www2.census.gov/programs-surveys/acs/tech_docs/code_lists/2017_ACS_Code_Lists.pdf

The data on occupation were derived from answers to questions that were asked of all persons 15 years old and over who had worked in the past 5 years. **Occupation** describes the kind of work the person does on the job. For employed persons, the data refer to the person's job during the previous week. For those who worked two or more jobs, the data refer to the job at which the person worked the greatest number of hours. For unemployed persons, the data refer to their last job. The American Community Survey uses the occupational classification system that was developed for the 2000 census and modified in 2002 and again in 2010. This system consists of 539 specific occupational categories for employed persons arranged into 23 major occupational groups. This classification was developed based on the *Standard Occupational Classification (SOC) Manual: 2010*, published by the Executive Office of the President, Office of Management and Budget.

CIVILIAN LABOR FORCE AND UNEMPLOYMENT, Items 167–171

Source: U.S. Bureau of Labor Statistics—Local Areas Unemployment Statistics
http://www.bls.gov/lau/#tables

Data for the civilian labor force are the product of a federal-state cooperative program in which state employment security agencies prepare labor force and unemployment estimates under concepts, definitions, and technical procedures established by the Bureau of Labor Statistics (BLS). The **civilian labor force** consists of all civilians 16 years old and over who are either employed or unemployed.

Unemployment includes all persons who did not work during the survey week, made specific efforts to find a job during the prior four weeks, and were available for work during the survey week (except for temporary illness). Persons waiting to be called back to a job from which they had been laid off and those waiting to report to a new job within the next 30 days are included in unemployment figures.

PRIVATE NONFARM EMPLOYMENT AND EARNINGS, Items 172–183

Source: U.S. Bureau of Labor Statistics—Current Employment Survey
http://www.bls.gov/ces/#tables

Data for private nonfarm employment and earnings are compiled from payroll information reported monthly on a voluntary basis to the BLS and its cooperating state agencies. More than 350,000 establishments represent all industries except agriculture.

Employment is the annual average of monthly totals of persons who received pay for any part of the pay period including the 12th day of the month. Included are all full-time and part-time workers in nonfarm establishments. Not covered are government employees, proprietors, the self-employed, unpaid volunteers or family workers, farm workers, and domestic workers in households. The data by industry conform to the definitions established in the North American Industry Classification System (NAICS).

Earnings of **production workers** in **manufacturing** industries are derived from reports of gross payrolls and corresponding paid hours. Payroll is reported before deductions of any kinds. Total hours during the pay period include all hours worked (including overtime hours) and hours paid for holidays, vacations, and sick leave.

AGRICULTURE, ITEMS 184–202

Source: U.S. Department of Agriculture, National Agricultural Statistics Service—2017 Census of Agriculture
https://www.nass.usda.gov/Publications/AgCensus/2017/index.php

The Census Bureau took a census of agriculture every 10 years from 1840 to 1920; since 1925, this census has been taken roughly once every 5 years. The 1997 Census of Agriculture was the first one conducted by the National Agricultural Statistics Service of the U.S. Department of Agriculture. Over time, the definition of a farm has varied. For recent censuses (including the 2017 census), a farm has been defined as any place from which $1,000 or more of agricultural products were produced and sold or normally would have been sold during the census year. Dollar figures are expressed in current dollars and have not been adjusted for inflation or deflation.

The term **producer** designates a person who is involved in making decisions for the farm operation. Decisions may include decisions about such things as planting, harvesting, livestock management, and marketing. The producer may be the owner, a member of the owner's household, a hired manager, a tenant, a renter, or a sharecropper. If a person rents land to others or has land worked on shares by others, he/she is considered the producer only of the land which is retained for his/her own operation. The census collected information on the total number of male producers, the total number of female producers, and demographic information for up to four producers per farm.

Government payments consists of direct payments as defined by the 2002 Farm Bill; payments from Conservation Reserve Program (CRP), Wetlands reserve Program (WRP), Farmable Wetlands Program (FWP), and Conservation Reserve Enhancement Program (CREP); loan deficiency payments; disaster payments; other conservation programs; and all other federal farm programs under which payments were made directly to farm producers, including those specified in the 2014 Agricultural Act (Farm Bill), including Agriculture Risk Coverage (ARC) and Price

Loss Coverage (PLC).. Commodity Credit Corporation (CCC) proceeds, amounts from state and local government agricultural program payments, and federal crop insurance payments were not included in this category.

The acreage designated as **land in farms** consists primarily of agricultural land used for crops, pasture, or grazing. It also includes woodland and wasteland not actually under cultivation or used for pasture or grazing, provided that this land was part of the farm operator's total operation.

Land in farms is an operating-unit concept and includes all land owned and operated, as well as all land rented from others. Land used rent-free is classified as land rented from others. All grazing land, except land used under government permits on a per-head basis, was included as "land in farms" provided it was part of a farm or ranch. Land under the exclusive use of a grazing association was reported by the grazing association and included as land in farms. All land in Indian reservations used for growing crops or grazing livestock is classified as land in farms.

Irrigated land includes all land watered by any artificial or controlled means, such as sprinklers, flooding, furrows or ditches, sub-irrigation, and spreader dikes. Included are supplemental, partial, and preplant irrigation. Each acre was counted only once regardless of the number of times it was irrigated or harvested. Livestock lagoon waste water distributed by sprinkler or flood systems was also included.

Total cropland includes cropland harvested, cropland used only for pasture or grazing, cropland on which all crops failed or were abandoned, cropland in cultivated summer fallow, and cropland idle or used for cover crops or soil improvement but not harvested and not pastured or grazed.

Respondents were asked to report their estimate of the current market **value of land and buildings** owned, rented, or leased from others and rented and leased to others. Market value refers to the respondent's estimate of what the land and buildings would sell for under current market conditions.

The **value of machinery and equipment** was estimated by the respondent as the current market value of all cars, trucks, tractors, combines, balers, irrigation equipment, etc., used on the farm. This value is an estimate of what the machinery and equipment would sell for in its present condition and not the replacement of depreciated value. Share interests are reported at full value at the farm where the equipment and machinery are usually kept. Only equipment that was physically located at the farm on December 31, 2017, is included.

Market **value of agricultural products sold** by farms represents the gross market value before taxes and the production expenses of all agricultural products sold or removed from the place in 2017, regardless of who received the payment. It is equivalent to total sales and it includes sales by producers as well as the value of any share received by partners, landlords, contractors, and others associated with the operation. It includes value of organic sales, direct sales and the value of commodities placed in the Commodity Credit Corporation (CCC) loan program. Market value of agricultural products sold does not include payments received for participation in other federal farm programs. Also, it does not include income from farm-related sources such as customwork and other agricultural services, or income from nonfarm sources.

The value of crops sold in 2017 does not necessarily represent the sales from crops harvested in 2017. Data may include sales from crops produced in earlier years and may exclude some crops produced in 2017 but held in storage and not sold. For commodities such as sugarbeets and wool sold through a co-op that made payments in several installments, respondents were requested to report the total value received in 2017.

Organic farms are those that had organic production according to USDA's National Organic Program (NOP). Respondents reported whether their organic production was certified or exempt from certification and the sales from NOP produced commodities. Not included are farms that had acres transitioning into NOP production.

Farms with **internet access** are those that reported using personal computers, laptops, or mobile devices (e.g., cell phones or tablets) to access the internet. This can be done using services such as dial-up, DSL, cable modem, fiber-optic, mobile internet service for a cell phone or other device (tablet), satellite, or other methods. In 2017 respondents were also able to report connecting with an unknown service type, labeled as "Don't know" in the publication tables.

LAND USE, ITEMS 203 to 205
Source: U.S. Department of Agriculture, Natural Resources Conservation Service—2015 National Resources Inventory
http://www.nrcs.usda.gov/technical/NRI/

The National Resources Inventory (NRI) was conducted every five years between 1982 and 1997. Since 2000, NRI data have been gathered annually, using a more complex sampling design of core and rotational subsamples. It provides updated information on the status, condition, and trends of land, soil, water, and related resources on the Nation's non-federal lands. Non-federal lands include privately owned lands, tribal and trust lands, and lands controlled by State and local governments.

The 2015 NRI is based on a sample of about 800,000 locations throughout the United States (excluding Alaska and the District of Columbia). Acreages for federal land and total surface area are established through geospatial processes and administrative records. Total surface area of the contiguous United States is 1,944 million acres.

Federally-owned lands include military bases, national forests, wildlife refuges, parks, grassland game preserves, scenic waterways, wilderness areas, monuments, lakeshore, parkways, battlefields, Bureau of Land Management lands, and other federal lands.

The NRI **developed land** category includes (a) large tracts of urban and built-up land; (b) small tracts of built-up land of less than 10 acres; and (c) land outside of these built-up areas that is in a rural transportation corridor (roads, railroads, and associated rights-of-way). Urban and built-up areas consist of residential, industrial, commercial, and institutional land; construction sites; public administrative sites; railroad yards; cemeteries; airports; golf courses; sanitary landfills; sewage treatment plants; water control structures and spillways; other land used for such purposes; small parks (less than 10 acres) within urban and built-up areas; and highways, *railroads*, and other transportation facilities if they are surrounded by urban areas. Also included are tracts of less than 10 acres that do not meet the above definition but are completely surrounded by Urban and built-up land. Two size categories are recognized in the NRI: areas of 0.25 acre to 10 acres, and areas of at least 10 acres.

Rural land consists of four primary rural land types: forest, rangeland, cropland, and pasture.

Forest land is at least 10 percent stocked by single-stemmed woody species of any size that will be at least 4 meters (13 feet) tall at maturity. Also included is land bearing evidence of natural regeneration of tree cover (cut over forest or abandoned farmland) and not currently developed for non-forest use. Ten percent stocked, when viewed from a vertical direction, equates to an areal canopy cover of leaves and branches of 25 percent or greater. The minimum area for classification as forest land is 1 acre, and the area must be at least 100 feet wide.

Rangeland is composed principally of native grasses, grasslike plants, forbs or shrubs suitable for grazing and browsing, and introduced forage species that are managed like rangeland. This would include areas where introduced hardy and persistent grasses, such as crested wheatgrass, are planted and such practices as deferred grazing, burning, chaining, and rotational grazing are used, with little or no chemicals or fertilizer being applied. Grasslands, savannas, many wetlands, some deserts, and tundra are considered to be rangeland. Certain communities of low forbs and shrubs, such as mesquite, chaparral, mountain shrub, and pinyon-juniper, are also included as rangeland.

Cropland includes areas used for the production of adapted crops for harvest. Two subcategories of cropland are recognized: cultivated and non-cultivated. Cultivated land comprises land in row crops or close-grown crops, as well as other cultivated cropland; for example, hayland or pastureland that is in a rotation with row or close-grown crops. Non-cultivated cropland includes permanent hayland and horticultural cropland.

Patureland is land managed primarily for the production of introduced forage plants for livestock grazing. Pastureland cover may consist of a single species in a pure stand, a grass mixture, or a grass-legume mixture. Management usually consists of cultural treatments: fertilization, weed control, reseeding, renovation, and control of grazing. For the NRI, this includes land that has a vegetative cover of grasses, legumes, and/or forbs, regardless of whether or not it is being grazed by livestock.

Other rural land includes farmsteads and other farm structures, field windbreaks, barren land, and marshland.

WATER CONSUMPTION, Item 206

Source: U.S. Geological Survey, National Water Use Information Program—2015 Water Use Data
http://water.usgs.gov/watuse/

Every five years, the U.S. Geological Survey compiles national water-use estimates. This volume includes the total fresh and saline water withdrawals for public water supplies expressed as million gallons per day. Estimate of withdrawals of ground and surface water are given for the following categories of use:

public water supplies, domestic, commercial, irrigation, livestock, industrial, mining, and thermoelectric power. Only public water supply is included in this volume. Public supply refers to water withdrawn from ground and surface sources by public and private water systems for use by cities, towns, rural water districts, mobile-home parks, Native American Indian reservations, and military bases. Public-supply facilities provide water to at least 25 persons or have a minimum of 15 service connections. Water withdrawn by public suppliers may be delivered to users for domestic, commercial, industrial, and thermoelectric-power purposes, as well as to other public-water suppliers. Public-supply water is also used for public services (public uses)—such as pools, parks, and public buildings—and may have unaccounted uses (losses) because of system leaks or such non-metered services as firefighting, flushing of water lines, or backwashing at treatment plants. Some public-supply water may be used in the processes of water and wastewater treatment. Some public suppliers treat saline water before distributing the water. The definition of saline water for public supply refers to water that requires treatment to reduce the concentration of dissolved solids through the process of desalination or dilution.

MANUFACTURES, Items 207–216

Source: U.S. Census Bureau— 2016 Annual Survey of Manufactures
https://www.census.gov/programs-surveys/asm.html

The Annual Survey of Manufactures (ASM) has been conducted annually every year since 1949, except for years ending in "2" and "7," at which time ASM data are included in the manufacturing sector of the Economic Census. The ASM provides statistics on employment, payroll, worker hours, payroll supplements, cost of materials, value added by manufacturing, capital expenditures, inventories, and energy consumption. It also provides estimates of value of shipments for over 1,400 classes of manufactured products. The Annual Survey of Manufactures includes approximately 50,000 establishments selected from the census universe of 350,000 manufacturing establishments.

The **all employees** number is the average number of production workers for the payroll periods including the 12th of March, May, August, and November plus the number of other employees in mid-March. Included are all persons on paid sick leave, paid holidays, and paid vacations during the pay period. Officers of corporations are included as employees, while proprietors and partners of unincorporated firms are excluded.

Payroll figures include the gross annual earnings of all employees on the payroll of operating manufacturing establishments. The definition, which is the same as the one used for calculating the federal withholding tax, includes all forms of compensation, such as salaries, wages, commissions, dismissal pay, bonuses, vacation and sick leave pay, and compensation-in-kind, prior to such deductions as employees' Social Security contributions, withholding taxes, group insurance, union dues, and savings bonds. The total includes salaries of officers of corporations; it excludes payments to proprietors or partners of unincorporated concerns. Also excluded are payments to members of armed forces and to pensioners carried on the active payrolls of manufacturing establishments.

Production workers include workers (up through the line-supervisor level) engaged in fabricating, processing, assembling, inspecting, receiving, storing, handling, packing, warehousing, shipping (but not delivering), maintenance, repair, janitorial and guard services, product development, auxiliary production for the plant's own use (for example, power plant), record keeping, and other services closely associated with these production operations at the establishment covered by the report. Employees above the working-supervisor level are excluded.

The number of production workers is the average for the payroll periods including the 12th of March, May, August, and November. Not included in this classification are all other employees, defined as non-production employees, including those engaged in factory supervision above the line-supervisor level.

Production worker hours cover hours worked or paid for at the manufacturing plant, including actual overtime hours (not straight-time equivalent hours). The data exclude hours paid for vacations, holidays, or sick leave when the employee is not at the establishment. Production wages represent all compensation paid to production workers.

Value added by manufacture is derived by subtracting the cost of materials, supplies, containers, fuel, purchased electricity, and contract work from the value of shipments (products manufactured plus receipts for services rendered). The result of this calculation is adjusted by the addition of value added by merchandising operations (the difference between the sales value and the cost of merchandise sold without further manufacture, processing, or assembly) plus the net change in finished goods and work-in-process between the beginning- and end-of-year inventories.

Value of shipments covers the received or receivable net selling values; free on board plant (excluding of freight and taxes), of all products shipped, both primary and secondary; and all miscellaneous receipts, such as receipts for contract work performed for others, installation and repair, sales of scrap, and sales of products bought and sold without further processing. Included are all items made by or for the establishments from material owned by it, whether sold, transferred to other plants of the same company, or shipped on consignment. The net selling value of products made in one plant on a contract basis from materials owned by another was reported by the plant providing the materials.

In the case of multi-unit companies, the manufacturer was asked to report the value of products transferred to other establishments of the same company at full economic or commercial value, including both the direct cost of production and a reasonable proportion of "all other costs" (including company overhead) and profit (interplant transfers).

The aggregate of the value of shipments figure for industry groups and for all manufacturing industries includes large amounts of duplications, as the products of some industries are used as materials by others. Estimates as to the overall extent of this duplication indicate that the value of manufactured products exclusive of such duplication (the value of finished manufactures) tends to approximate two-thirds of the total value of products reported in the census of manufactures.

Total cost of materials refers to direct charges actually paid or payable for items consumed or put into production during the year, including freight charges and other direct charges incurred by the establishment in acquiring these materials. It includes the cost of materials or fuel consumed, whether purchased by the individual establishment from other companies, transferred to it from other establishments of the same company, or withdrawn from inventory during the year. Included in this item are cost of parts, components, containers, etc.; cost of products bought and sold in the same condition; cost of fuels consumed for heat and power; cost of purchased electricity; and cost of contract work. Aggregate of total cost of materials and total value of shipments includes extensive duplication, since products of some industries are used as materials of others.

2012 ECONOMIC CENSUS: OVERVIEW, Items 217–308

Source: U.S. Census Bureau
https://www.census.gov/programs-surveys/economic-census/library/publications.html

The Economic Census provides a detailed portrait of the nation's economy, from the national to the local level, once every five years. The 2012 Economic Census covers nearly all of the U.S. economy in its basic collection of establishment statistics. The 1997 Economic Census was the first major data source to use the North American Industry Classification System (NAICS); therefore, data are not comparable to economic data from prior years, which were based on the Standard Industrial Classification (SIC) system.

NAICS, developed in cooperation with Canada and Mexico, classifies North America's economic activities at two-, three-, four-, and five-digit levels of detail; the U.S. version of NAICS further defines industries to a sixth digit. The Economic Census takes advantage of this hierarchy to publish data at these successive levels of detail: sector (two-digit); subsector (three-digit); industry group (four-digit); industry (five-digit); and U.S. industry (six-digit). Information in Table A is at the two-digit level, with a few three- and four-digit items.

Several key statistics are tabulated for all industries included in this volume: number of establishments (or companies); number of employees; payroll; and a measure of output (sales, receipts, revenue, value of shipments, or value of construction work done).

Number of establishments. An establishment is a single physical location at which business is conducted. It is not necessarily identical with a company or enterprise, which may consist of one establishment or more. Economic Census figures represent a summary of reports for individual establishments rather than companies. For cases in which a census report was received, separate information was obtained for each location where business was conducted. When administrative records of other federal agencies were used instead of a census report, no information was available on the number of locations operated. Each Economic Census establishment was tabulated according to the physical location at which the business was conducted. The count of establishments represents those in business at any time during 2012.

When two activities or more were carried on at a single location under a single ownership, all activities were generally grouped together as a single establishment. The entire establishment was classified on the basis of its major activity and all of its data were included in that classification. However, when distinct and separate economic activities (for which different industry classification codes were appropriate) were conducted at a single location under a single ownership, separate establishment reports for each of the different activities were obtained in the census.

Number of employees. Paid employees consist of the full-time and part-time employees, including salaried officers and executives of corporations. Included are employees on paid sick leave, paid holidays, and paid vacations; not included are proprietors and partners of unincorporated businesses. The definition of paid employees is the same as that used by the Internal Revenue Service (IRS) on form 941.

For some industries, the Economic Census gives codes representing the number of employees as a range of numbers (for example, "100 to 249 employees" or "1,000 to 2,499" employees). In this volume, those codes have been replaced by the standard suppression code "D".

Payroll. Payroll includes all forms of compensation, such as salaries, wages, commissions, dismissal pay, bonuses, vacation allowances, sick-leave pay, and employee contributions to qualified pension plans paid during the year to all employees. For corporations, payroll includes amounts paid to officers and executives; for unincorporated businesses, it does not include profit or other compensation of proprietors or partners. Payroll is reported before deductions for Social Security, income tax, insurance, union dues, etc. This definition of payroll is the same as that used on IRS form 941.

Sales, shipments, receipts, revenue, or business done. This measure includes the total sales, shipments, receipts, revenue, or business done by establishments within the scope of the Economic Census. The definition of each of these items is specific to the economic sector measured.

CONSTRUCTION, Items 217–221
Source: U.S. Census Bureau—2012 Economic Census
(See Overview of 2012 Economic Census prior to Item 217)

The Construction sector (sector 23) comprises establishments primarily engaged in the construction of buildings and other structures, heavy construction (except buildings), additions, alterations, reconstruction, installation, and maintenance and repairs. Establishments engaged in the demolition or wrecking of buildings and other structures, the clearing of building sites, and the sale of materials from demolished structures are also included. This sector also contains those establishments engaged in blasting, test drilling, landfill, leveling, earthmoving, excavating, land drainage, and other land preparation. The industries within this sector have been defined on the basis of their unique production processes. As with all industries, the production processes are distinguished by their use of specialized human resources and specialized physical capital. Construction activities are generally administered or managed at a relatively fixed place of business, but the actual construction work can be performed at one or more different project

sites. This sector is divided into three subsectors of construction activities: (1) building construction and land subdivision and land development; (2) heavy construction (except buildings), such as highways, power plants, and pipelines; and (3) construction activity by special trade contractors.

WHOLESALE TRADE, Items 222–226
Source: U.S. Census Bureau—2012 Economic Census
(See Overview of 2012 Economic Census prior to Item 217)

The Wholesale Trade sector (sector 42) comprises establishments engaged in wholesaling merchandise, generally without transformation, and rendering services incidental to the sale of merchandise. The wholesaling process is an intermediate step in the distribution of merchandise. Wholesalers are organized to sell or arrange the purchase or sale of (1) goods for resale (i.e., goods sold to other wholesalers or retailers), (2) capital or durable non-consumer goods, and (3) raw and intermediate materials and supplies used in production.

Wholesalers sell merchandise to other businesses and normally operate from a warehouse or office. These warehouses and offices are characterized by having little or no display of merchandise. In addition, neither the design nor the location of the premises is intended to solicit walk-in traffic. Wholesalers do not normally use advertising directed to the general public. Customers are generally first reached via telephone, in-person marketing, or by specialized advertising that may include internet and other electronic means. Follow-up orders are either vendor-initiated or client-initiated, are usually based on previous sales, and typically exhibit strong ties between sellers and buyers. In fact, transactions are often conducted between wholesalers and clients that have long-standing business relationships.

This sector is made up of two main types of wholesalers: those that sell goods on their own account and those that arrange sales and purchases for others for a commission or fee.

(1) Establishments that sell goods on their own account are known as wholesale merchants, distributors, jobbers, drop shippers, import/export merchants, and sales branches. These establishments typically maintain their own warehouse, where they receive and handle goods for their customers. Goods are generally sold without transformation, but may include integral functions, such as sorting, packaging, labeling, and other marketing services.

(2) Establishments arranging for the purchase or sale of goods owned by others or purchasing goods on a commission basis are known as agents and brokers, commission merchants, import/export agents and brokers, auction companies, and manufacturers' representatives. These establishments operate from offices and generally do not own or handle the goods they sell.

Some wholesale establishments may be connected with a single manufacturer and/or promote and sell that particular manufacturer's products to a wide range of other wholesalers or retailers. Other wholesalers may be connected to a retail chain or a limited number of retail chains and only provide a variety of products needed by that particular retail operation(s). These wholesalers may obtain the products from a wide range of manufacturers. Still other wholesalers may not take title to the goods but act as agents and brokers for a commission.

Although, in general, wholesaling normally denotes sales in large volumes, durable nonconsumer goods may be sold in single units. Sales of capital or durable nonconsumer goods used in the production of goods and services, such as farm machinery, medium- and heavy-duty trucks, and industrial machinery, are always included in Wholesale Trade.

RETAIL TRADE, Items 227–235
Source: U.S. Census Bureau—2012 Economic Census
(See Overview of 2012 Economic Census prior to Item 217)

The Retail Trade sector (44–45) is made up of establishments engaged in retailing merchandise, generally without transformation, and rendering services incidental to the sale of merchandise.

The retailing process is the final step in the distribution of merchandise; retailers are, therefore, organized to sell merchandise in small quantities to the general public. This sector comprises two main types of retailers: store and nonstore retailers.

Store retailers operate fixed point-of-sale locations, located and designed to attract a high volume of walk-in customers. In general, retail stores have extensive displays of merchandise and use mass-media advertising to attract customers. They typically sell merchandise to the general public for personal or household consumption; some also serve business and institutional clients. These include establishments, such as office supply stores, computer and software stores, building materials dealers, plumbing supply stores, and electrical supply stores. Catalog showrooms, gasoline service stations, automotive dealers, and mobile home dealers are treated as store retailers.

In addition to retailing merchandise, some types of store retailers are also engaged in the provision of after-sales services, such as repair and installation. For example, new automobile dealers, electronic and appliance stores, and musical instrument and supply stores often provide repair services. As a general rule, establishments engaged in retailing merchandise and providing after-sales services are classified in this sector.

Nonstore retailers, like store retailers, are organized to serve the general public, although their retailing methods differ. The establishments of this subsector reach customers and market merchandise with methods, such as the broadcasting of "infomercials," the broadcasting and publishing of direct-response advertising, the publishing of paper and electronic catalogs, door-to-door solicitation, in-home demonstration, selling from portable stalls (street vendors, except food), and distribution through vending machines. Establishments engaged in the direct sale (nonstore) of products, such as home heating oil dealers and home-delivery newspaper routes are included in this sector.

The buying of goods for resale is a characteristic of retail trade establishments that distinguishes them from establishments in the Agriculture, Manufacturing, and Construction sectors. For example, farms that sell their products at or from the point of production are classified in Agriculture instead of in Retail Trade. Similarly, establishments that both manufacture and sell their products to the general public are classified in Manufacturing instead of Retail Trade. However, establishments that engage in processing activities incidental to retailing are classified in retail.

Industries in the **Motor Vehicle and Parts Dealers** subsector (441) retail motor vehicle and parts merchandise from fixed point-of-sale locations. Establishments in this subsector typically operate from a showroom and/or an open lot where the vehicles are on display. The display of vehicles and the related parts require little by way of display equipment. Personnel generally include both sales and sales support staff familiar with the requirements for registering and financing a vehicle as well as a staff of parts experts and mechanics trained to provide vehicle repair and maintenance services. Specific industries have been included in this subsector to identify the type of vehicle being retailed. Sales of capital or durable nonconsumer goods, such as medium and heavy-duty trucks, are always included in the Wholesale Trade sector. These goods are virtually never sold through retail methods.

Industries in the **Food and Beverage Stores** subsector (445) usually retail food and beverage merchandise from fixed point-of-sale locations. Establishments in this subsector have special equipment (e.g., freezers, refrigerated display cases, and refrigerators) for displaying food and beverage goods. They have staff trained in the processing of food products to guarantee the proper storage and sanitary conditions, as mandated by regulatory authority.

Industries in the **Clothing and Clothing Accessories Stores** subsector (448) retail new clothing and clothing accessories merchandise from fixed point-of-sale locations. Establishments in this subsector have similar types of display equipment, as well as employees who are knowledgeable regarding fashion trends and who can match styles, colors, and combinations of clothing and accessories to the characteristics and tastes of the customer.

Industries in the **General Merchandise Stores** subsector (452) retail new general merchandise from fixed point-of-sale locations. Establishments in this subsector are unique in that they have the equipment and staff capable of retailing a large variety of goods from a single location. This includes a variety of display equipment and staff trained to provide information on many lines of products.

INFORMATION, Items 236–246
Source: U.S. Census Bureau—2012 Economic Census
(See Overview of 2012 Economic Census prior to Item 217)

The Information sector (51) comprises establishments engaged in the following processes: (1) producing and distributing information and cultural products, (2) providing the means to transmit or distribute these products as well as data or communications, and (3) processing data.

The main components of this sector are the publishing industries, including software publishing; the motion picture and sound recording industries; the broadcasting and telecommunications industries; and the information services and data processing industries.

For the purpose of NAICS, the transformation of information into a commodity that is produced and distributed by a number of growing industries is at issue. The Information sector groups three types of establishments: (1) those engaged in producing and distributing information and cultural products; (2) those that provide the means to transmit or distribute these products as well as data or communications; and (3) those that process data. Cultural products are those that directly express attitudes, opinions, ideas, values, and artistic creativity; provide entertainment; or offer information and analysis concerning the past and present. Included in this definition are popular, mass-produced products, as well as cultural products that normally have a more limited audience, such as poetry books, literary magazines, or classical records. These activities were formerly classified throughout the existing national classifications. Traditional publishing was in manufacturing; broadcasting in communications; software production in business services; film production in amusement services; and so forth.

Industries in the **Publishing Industries, Except Internet** subsector (511) include establishments engaged in the publishing of newspapers, magazines, other periodicals, and books, as well as database and software publishing. In general, these establishments, which are known as publishers, issue copies of works for which they usually possess copyright. Works may be in one or more formats, including traditional print format, CD-ROM format, or proprietary electronic networks. Publishers may publish works originally created by others for which they have obtained the rights and/or works that they have created in-house. Software publishing is included here because the activity (creation of a copyrighted product and bringing it to market) is equivalent to the creation process for other types of intellectual products.

In NAICS, publishing—the reporting, writing, editing, and other processes that are required to create an edition of a book or a newspaper—is treated as a major economic activity in its own right, rather than as a subsidiary activity to printing, which is a manufacturing activity. Thus, publishing is classified in the Information sector, while printing remains in the NAICS Manufacturing sector. In part, the NAICS classification reflects the fact that publishing increasingly takes place in establishments that are physically separate from the associated printing establishments. More crucially, the NAICS classification of book and newspaper publishing is intended to portray their roles in a modern economy—roles that do not resemble manufacturing activities.

Music publishers are not included in the Publishing Industries subsector, but can be found in the Motion Picture and Sound Recording Industries subsector. Reproduction of prepackaged software is treated in NAICS as a manufacturing activity; online distribution of software products is in the Information sector, and custom design of software to client specifications is included in the Professional, Scientific, and Technical Services sector. These distinctions arise because of the different ways that software is created, reproduced, and distributed.

The Information sector does not include products, such as manifold business forms. Information is not the essential component of these items. Establishments producing these items are included in subsector 323, Printing and Related Support Activities.

Industries in the **Motion Picture and Sound Recording Industries** subsector (512) group establishments involved in the production and distribution of motion pictures and sound recordings. While producers and distributors of motion pictures and sound recordings issue works for sale as traditional publishers do, the processes are different enough to warrant placing the establishments engaged in these activities in separate subsectors.

Production is typically a complex process that involves several distinct types of establishments engaged in activities, such as contracting with performers, creating the film or sound content, and providing technical postproduction services. Film distribution is often to exhibitors, such as theaters and broadcasters, rather than to a wholesale or retail distribution chain. When the product is in a mass-produced form, NAICS treats production and distribution as the major economic activity, rather than as a subsidiary activity to the manufacture of such products.

This subsector does not include establishments primarily engaged in the wholesale distribution of video cassettes and sound recordings, such as compact discs and audio tapes; these establishments are included in the Wholesale Trade sector. Reproduction of video cassettes and sound recordings that is carried out separately from establishments engaged in production and distribution is treated in NAICS as a manufacturing activity.

Industries in the **Broadcasting, except Internet** subsector (515) include establishments that create content or acquire the right to distribute and subsequently broadcast content. The industry groups (Radio and Television Broadcasting and Cable and Other Subscription Programming) are based on differences in the methods of communication and the nature of services provided. The Radio and Television Broadcasting industry group includes establishments that operate broadcasting studios and facilities for over-the-air or satellite delivery of radio and television programs, including entertainment, news, and talk programs. These establishments are often engaged in production and purchase of programs and generating revenues from the sale of air time to advertisers, as well as from donations, subsidies, and/or the sale of programs. The Cable and Other Subscription Programming industry group includes establishments that operate studios and facilities for the broadcasting of limited-format programs (such as news, sports, educational, and youth-oriented programs) that are typically narrowly-focused in nature; these programs are usually available on a subscription or fee basis. The distribution of cable and other subscription programming is included in subsector 517, Telecommunications.

Industries in the **Internet Publishing and Broadcasting and Web search portals** subsector (51913) consist of establishments primarily engaged in 1) publishing and/or broadcasting content on the Internet exclusively or 2) operating Web sites that use a search engine to generate and maintain extensive databases of Internet addresses and content in an easily searchable format (and known as Web search portals). The publishing and broadcasting establishments in this industry do not provide traditional (non-Internet) versions of the content that they publish or broadcast. They provide textual, audio, and/or video content of general or specific interest on the Internet exclusively. Establishments known as Web search portals often provide additional Internet services, such as e-mail, connections to other web sites, auctions, news, and other limited content, and serve as a home base for Internet users.

Establishments that are *not* in this group include those primarily engaged in--

- Providing wired broadband Internet access using own operated telecommunications infrastructure—these are classified in Wired Telecommunications Carriers;

- Providing both Internet publishing and other print or electronic (e.g., CD-ROM, diskette) editions in the same establishment or using proprietary networks to distribute content—these are classified in Publishing Industries (except Internet) based on the materials produced;
- Providing Internet access via client-supplied telecommunications connections—these are classified in All Other Telecommunications;
- Providing streaming services on content owned by others— these are classified in Data Processing, Hosting, and Related Services;
- Wholesaling goods on the Internet—these are classified in Wholesale Trade;
- Retailing goods on the Internet—these are classified in Retail Trade;
- Operating stock brokerages, travel reservation systems, purchasing services, and similar activities using the Internet rather than traditional methods—these are classified with the more traditioal establishments providing these services.

Industries in the **Telecommunications** subsector (517) include establishments that provide telecommunications and services related to that activity (e.g., telephony, including Voice over Internet Protocol (VoIP); cable and satellite television distribution services; Internet access; telecommunications reselling services). The Telecommunications subsector is primarily engaged in operating, maintaining, and/or providing access to facilities for the transmission of voice, data, text, sound, and video. A transmission facility may be based on a single technology or a combination of technologies. Establishments primarily engaged as independent contractors in the maintenance and installation of broadcasting and telecommunications systems are classified in sector 23, Construction.

Industries in the **Data processing, hosting, and related services** subsector (518) are establishments primarily engaged in providing infrastructure for hosting or data processing services. These establishments may provide specialized hosting activities, such as web hosting, streaming services or application hosting; provide application service provisioning; or may provide general time-share mainframe facilities to clients. Data processing establishments provide complete processing and specialized reports from data supplied by clients or provide automated data processing and data entry services.

UTILITIES, Items 247–252

Source: U.S. Census Bureau—2012 Economic Census (See Overview of 2012 Economic Census prior to Item 217)

The Utilities sector (22) comprises establishments engaged in the provision of the following utility services: electric power, natural gas, steam supply, water supply, and sewage removal. Within this sector, the specific activities associated with the utility services provided vary by utility: electric power includes generation, transmission, and distribution; natural gas includes distribution; steam supply includes provision and/or distribution; water supply includes treatment and distribution; and sewage removal includes

collection, treatment, and disposal of waste through sewer systems and sewage treatment facilities.

Excluded from this sector are establishments primarily engaged in waste management. These services are classified in subsector 562, Waste Management and Remediation Services, which also collect, treat, and dispose of waste materials; however, establishments in this subsector do not use sewer systems or sewage treatment facilities.

TRANSPORTATION AND WAREHOUSING, Items 252–256

Source: U.S. Census Bureau—2012 Economic Census (See Overview of 2012 Economic Census prior to Item 217)

The Transportation and Warehousing sector (48–49) includes industries that provide transportation of passengers and cargo, warehousing and storage for goods, scenic and sightseeing transportation, and support activities related to modes of transportation. Establishments in these industries use transportation equipment or transportation related facilities as a productive asset. The type of equipment depends on the mode of transportation, which includes air, rail, water, road, and pipeline.

The transportation and warehousing sector distinguishes three basic types of activities: subsectors for each mode of transportation, a subsector for warehousing and storage, and a subsector for establishments providing support activities for transportation. In addition, there are subsectors for establishments that provide passenger transportation for scenic and sightseeing purposes, postal services, and courier services.

FINANCE AND INSURANCE, Items 257–261

Source: U.S. Census Bureau—2012 Economic Census (See Overview of 2012 Economic Census prior to Item 217)

The Finance and Insurance sector (52) comprises establishments primarily engaged in financial transactions (transactions involving the creation, liquidation, or change in ownership of financial assets) and/or in facilitating financial transactions. Three principal types of activities are identified:

(1) Raising funds by taking deposits and/or issuing securities and, in the process, incurring liabilities. Establishments engaged in this activity use raised funds to acquire financial assets by making loans and/or purchasing securities. Putting themselves at risk, they channel funds from lenders to borrowers and transform or repackage the funds with respect to maturity, scale and risk. This activity is known as financial intermediation.

(2) Pooling of risk by underwriting insurance and annuities. Establishments engaged in this activity collect fees, insurance premiums, or annuity considerations; build up reserves; invest those reserves; and make contractual payments. Fees are based on the expected incidence of the insured risk and the expected return on investment.

(3) Providing specialized services facilitating or supporting financial intermediation, insurance, and employee benefit programs.

In addition, monetary authorities charged with monetary control are included in this sector.

REAL ESTATE AND RENTAL AND LEASING, Items 262–266

Source: U.S. Census Bureau—2012 Economic Census (See Overview of 2012 Economic Census prior to Item 217)

The Real Estate and Rental and Leasing sector (53) comprises establishments primarily engaged in renting, leasing, or otherwise allowing the use of tangible or intangible assets, and establishments providing related services. The major portion of this sector comprises establishments that rent, lease, or otherwise allow the use of their own assets by others. The assets may be tangible, such as real estate and equipment, or intangible, such as patents and trademarks.

This sector also includes establishments primarily engaged in managing real estate for others, selling, renting, and/or buying real estate for others, and appraising real estate. These activities are closely related to this sector's main activity. In addition, a substantial proportion of property management is self-performed by lessors.

The main components of this sector are the real estate lessors industries; equipment lessors industries (including motor vehicles, computers, and consumer goods); and lessors of nonfinancial intangible assets (except copyrighted works).

PROFESSIONAL, SCIENTIFIC, AND TECHNICAL SERVICES, Items 267–275

Source: U.S. Census Bureau—2012 Economic Census (See Overview of 2012 Economic Census prior to Item 217)

The Professional, Scientific, and Technical Services sector (54) is made up of establishments that specialize in performing professional, scientific, and technical activities for others. These activities require a high degree of expertise and training. The establishments in this sector specialize according to expertise and provide services to clients in a variety of industries (and, in some cases, to households). Activities performed include legal advice and representation; accounting, bookkeeping, and payroll services; architectural, engineering, and specialized design services; computer services; consulting services; research services; advertising services; photographic services; translation and interpretation services; veterinary services; and other professional, scientific, and technical services.

This sector excludes establishments primarily engaged in providing a range of day-to-day office administrative services, such as financial planning, billing and record keeping, personnel services, and physical distribution and logistics services. These establishments are classified in sector 56, Administrative and Support and Waste Management and Remediation Services.

Legal Services comprises establishments primarily engaged in offering legal services such as offices of lawyers, notaries, title abstract and settlement offices, and all other legal services such as patent agent services, paralegal services, and process serving services.

Accounting, Tax Preparation, Bookkeeping, and Payroll Services comprises establishments primarily engaged in providing services, such as auditing of accounting records, designing accounting systems, preparing financial statements, developing budgets, preparing tax returns, processing payrolls, bookkeeping, and billing.

Architectural, Engineering, and Related Services comprises establishments primarily engaged in offering (1) architectural services for residential, institutional, leisure, commercial, and industrial buildings and structures as well as for landscape purposes; (2) offering engineering services, including drafting services or building inspection services; (3) offering geophysical surveying and mapping services; (4) surveying and mapping services, except geophysical; and (5) offering testing laboratory services except medical and veterinary (the testing can occur in a laboratory or on-site).

Computer Systems Design and Related Services consists of establishments primarily engaged in providing expertise in the field of information technologies through one or more of the following activities: (1) writing, modifying, testing, and supporting software to meet the needs of a particular customer; (2) planning and designing computer systems that integrate computer hardware, software, and communication technologies; (3) on-site management and operation of clients' computer systems and/or data processing facilities; and (4) other professional and technical computer-related advice and services.

HEALTH CARE AND SOCIAL ASSISTANCE, Items 276–289

Source: U.S. Census Bureau—2012 Economic Census (See Overview of 2012 Economic Census prior to Item 217)

The Health Care and Social Assistance sector (62) consists of establishments that provide health care and social assistance services to individuals. The sector includes both health care and social assistance, because it is sometimes difficult to distinguish between the boundaries of these two activities. The industries in this sector are arranged on a continuum starting with those that provide medical care exclusively, continuing with those that provide health care and social assistance, and finishing with those that provide only social assistance. The services provided by establishments in this sector are delivered by trained professionals. All industries in the sector share this commonality of process—namely, labor inputs of health practitioners or social workers with the requisite expertise. Many of the industries in the sector are defined based on the educational degree held by the practitioners included in the industry.

In this volume, taxable and tax-exempt establishments are presented separately.

Excluded from this sector are aerobic classes, which can be found in subsector 713, Amusement, Gambling and Recreation Industries; and nonmedical diet and weight-reducing centers, which can be found in subsector 812, Personal and Laundry Services. Although these can be viewed as health services, they are not typically delivered by health practitioners.

Industries in the **Ambulatory Health Care Services** subsector (621) provide health care services directly or indirectly to ambulatory patients and do not typically provide inpatient services. Health practitioners in this subsector provide outpatient services, and facilities and equipment do not usually play the most significant part in this sector's production process.

Industries in the **Hospitals** subsector (622) provide medical, diagnostic, and treatment services, including physician, nursing, specialized accommodation, and other health services, to inpatients. Hospitals may provide outpatient services as a secondary activity. Many of the services provided by establishments in the Hospitals subsector require the use of specialized facilities and equipment, both of which form a significant and integral part of the production process.

ARTS, ENTERTAINMENT, AND RECREATION, Items 290–294

Source: U.S. Census Bureau—2012 Economic Census (See Overview of 2012 Economic Census prior to Item 217)

The Arts, Entertainment, and Recreation sector (71) includes a wide range of establishments that operate facilities or provide services that meet the diverse cultural, entertainment, and recreational interests of their patrons. This sector is made up of: (1) establishments that are involved in producing, promoting, or participating in live performances, events, or exhibits intended for public viewing; (2) establishments that preserve and exhibit objects and sites of historical, cultural, or educational interest; and (3) establishments that operate facilities or provide services that enable patrons to participate in recreational activities or pursue amusement, hobby, and leisure time interests.

Some establishments that provide cultural, entertainment, or recreational facilities and services are classified in other sectors. Excluded from this sector are: (1) establishments that provide both accommodations and recreational facilities—such as hunting and fishing camps and resort and casino hotels—are classified in subsector 721, Accommodation; (2) restaurants and night clubs that provide live entertainment in addition to the sale of food and beverages are classified in subsector 722, Food Services and Drinking Places; (3) motion picture theaters, libraries and archives, and publishers of newspapers, magazines, books, periodicals, and computer software are classified in sector 51, Information; and (4) establishments that use transportation equipment to provide recreational and entertainment services, such as those operating sightseeing buses, dinner cruises, or helicopter rides, are classified in subsector 487, Scenic and Sightseeing Transportation.

ACCOMMODATION AND FOOD SERVICES, Items 295–300

Source: U.S. Census Bureau—2012 Economic Census (See Overview of 2012 Economic Census prior to Item 217)

The Accommodation and Food Services sector (72) consists of establishments that provide customers with lodging and/or meals, snacks, and beverages for immediate consumption. The sector includes both accommodation and food services establishments because the two activities are often combined at the same establishment. Excluded from this sector are civic and social organizations, amusement and recreation parks, theaters, and other recreation or entertainment facilities providing food and beverage services.

Industries in the **Food Services and Drinking Places** subsector (722) prepare meals, snacks, and beverages to customer order for immediate on-premises and off-premises consumption. There is a wide range of establishments in these industries. Some provide food and drink only; while others provide various combinations of seating space, waiter/waitress services and incidental amenities, such as limited entertainment. The industries in the subsector are grouped based on the type and level of services provided. The industry groups are full-service restaurants; limited-service eating places; special food services, such as food service contractors, caterers, and mobile food services, and drinking places. Food services and drink activities at hotels and motels; amusement parks, theaters, casinos, country clubs, and similar recreational facilities; and civic and social organizations are included in this subsector only if these services are provided by a separate establishment primarily engaged in providing food and beverage services. Excluded from this subsector are establishments operating dinner cruises. These establishments are classified in subsector 487, Scenic and Sightseeing Transportation, because they utilize transportation equipment to provide scenic recreational entertainment.

OTHER SERVICES, EXCEPT PUBLIC ADMINISTRATION Items 301–308

Source: U.S. Census Bureau—2012 Economic Census (See Overview of 2012 Economic Census prior to Item 217)

The Other Services, Except Public Administration sector (81) comprises establishments engaged in providing services not specifically categorized elsewhere in the classification system. Establishments in this sector are primarily engaged in activities such as equipment and machinery repairing, promoting or administering religious activities, grant making, and advocacy; this sector also includes establishments that provide dry-cleaning and laundry services, personal care services, death care services, pet care services, photofinishing services, temporary parking services, and dating services.

Private households that employ workers on or about the premises in activities primarily concerned with the operation of the household are included in this sector.

Excluded from this sector are establishments primarily engaged in retailing new equipment and performing repairs and general maintenance on equipment. These establishments are classified in sector 44–45, Retail Trade.

Industries in the **Repair and Maintenance** subsector (811) restore machinery, equipment, and other products to working order. These establishments also typically provide general or routine maintenance (i.e., servicing) on such products to ensure they work efficiently; this maintenance also helps prevent breakdowns and make certain repairs unnecessary.

The NAICS structure for this subsector brings together most types of repair and maintenance establishments and categorizes them based on production processes (i.e., on the type of repair and maintenance activity performed, and the necessary skills, expertise, and processes required for different repair and maintenance establishments). This NAICS classification does not delineate between repair services provided to businesses versus those provided to households. Although some industries primarily serve either businesses or households, separation by class of customer is limited by the fact that many establishments serve both types. Establishments that repair computers and consumer electronics products are examples of such overlap.

The Repair and Maintenance subsector does not include all establishments engaged in repair and maintenance. For example, a substantial amount of repair is done by establishments that also manufacture machinery, equipment, and other goods. These establishments are included in the Manufacturing sector in NAICS. In addition, the repairing of transportation equipment is often provided by or based at transportation facilities, such as airports and seaports; these activities are included in the Transportation and Warehousing sector.

A particularly unique situation exists with repair of buildings. Plumbing, electrical installation and repair, painting and decorating, and other construction-related establishments are often involved in performing installation or other work on new construction, while also providing repair services on existing structures. Although some establishments do specialize in repair, it is difficult to distinguish between these two types. Thus, all such establishments are included in the Construction sector.

Excluded from this subsector are establishments primarily engaged in rebuilding or remanufacturing machinery and equipment. These are classified in sector 31–33, Manufacturing. Also excluded are retail establishments that provide after-sale services and repair. These are classified in sector 44–45, Retail Trade.

Industries in the **Personal and Laundry Services** subsector (812) include establishments that provide personal and laundry services to individuals, households, and businesses. Services performed include personal care services, death care services, laundry and dry-cleaning services, and a wide range of other personal services, such as pet care (except veterinary) services, photofinishing services, temporary parking services, and dating services.

The Personal and Laundry Services subsector is by no means all-inclusive of the activities that could be termed personal services (i.e., those provided to individuals rather than businesses). There are many other sectors and subsectors that provide services to persons. Establishments providing legal, accounting, tax preparation, architectural, portrait photography, and similar professional services are classified in sector 54, Professional, Scientific,

and Technical Services; those providing job placement, travel arrangement, home security, interior and exterior house cleaning, exterminating, lawn and garden care, and similar support services are classified in sector 56, Administrative and Support and Waste Management and Remediation Services; those providing health and social services are classified in sector 62, Health Care and Social Assistance; those providing amusement and recreation services are classified in sector 71, Arts, Entertainment and Recreation; those providing educational instruction are classified in sector 61, Educational Services; those providing repair services are classified in subsector 811, Repair and Maintenance; and those providing spiritual, civic, and advocacy services are classified in subsector 813, Religious, Grantmaking, Civic, Professional, and Similar Organizations.

Industries in the **Religious, Grantmaking, Civic, Professional, and Similar Organizations** subsector (813) include establishments that organize and promote religious activities, support various causes through grant making, advocate various social and political causes, and promote and defend the interests of their members. This category includes only tax-exempt establishments.

The industry groups within the subsector are defined in terms of their activities, separately grouping establishments that provide funding for specific causes or for a variety of charitable causes, establishments that advocate and actively promote causes and beliefs for the public good, and establishments that have an active membership structure to promote causes and represent the interests of their members. Establishments in this subsector may publish newsletters, books, and periodicals for distribution to their membership.

GOVERNMENT EMPLOYMENT, Items 309–311
Source: U.S. Bureau of Economic Analysis—Regional Economic Accounts
http://www.bea.gov/regional/index.htm#state

Employment is measured as the average annual sum of full-time and part-time jobs. The estimates are on a place-of-work basis. Data for federal civilian employment include civilian employees of the Department of Defense. Military employment includes all persons on active duty status.

STATE GOVERNMENT EMPLOYMENT AND PAYROLL, Items 312–330
Source: U.S. Census Bureau—Annual Survey of Government Employment and Payroll
https://www.census.gov/programs-surveys/apes.html

The annual Survey of Government Employment and Payroll measures the number of federal, state, and local civilian government employees and their gross monthly payroll for March of the survey year for state and local governments and for the Federal Government.

The survey provides state and local government data on full-time and part-time employment, part-time hours worked, full-time equivalent employment, and payroll statistics by governmental function (i.e., elementary and secondary education, higher education, police protection, fire protection, financial administration, central staff services, judicial and legal, highways, public welfare, solid waste management, sewerage, parks and recreation, health, hospitals, water supply, electric power, gas supply, transit, natural resources, correction, libraries, air transportation, water transport and terminals, other education, state liquor stores, social insurance administration, and housing and community development).

Data have been collected annually since 1957. A census is conducted every five years (years ending in '2' and '7'). A sample of state and local governments is used to collect data in the intervening years. A new sample is selected every five years (years ending in '4' and '9').

State government employees include all persons paid for personal services performed, including persons paid from federally funded programs, paid elected or appointed officials, persons in a paid leave status, and persons paid on a per meeting, annual, semiannual, or quarterly basis. Unpaid officials, pensioners, persons whose work is performed on a fee basis, and contractors and their employees are excluded from the count of employees. **Full-time employees** are persons employed during the pay period to work the number of hours per week that represents regular full-time employment. Included are full-time temporary or seasonal employees who are working the number of hours that represent full-time employment. **Part-time employees** are persons paid on a part-time basis during the designated pay period. Included are those daily or hourly employees usually engaged for less than the regular full-time workweek, as well as any part-time paid officials. **Full-Time Equivalent employees** is a computed statistic representing the number of full-time employees that could have been employed if the reported number of hours worked by part-time employees had been worked by full-time employees. This statistic is calculated separately for each function of a government by dividing the "part-time hours paid" by the standard number of hours for full-time employees in the particular government and then adding the resulting quotient to the number of full-time employees.

Full-time payroll represents gross payroll amounts for the one-month period of March for full-time employees. **Part-time pay** represents gross payroll amounts for the one-month period of March for part-time employees. Gross payroll includes all salaries, wages, fees, commissions, and overtime paid to employees **before** withholdings for taxes, insurance, etc. It also includes incentive payments that are paid at regular pay intervals. It excludes employer share of fringe benefits like retirement, Social Security, health and life insurance, lump sum payments, and so forth.

Administration combines **Financial administration** and **Other government administration**. **Financial administration** includes activities concerned with tax assessment and collection, custody and disbursement of funds, debt management, administration of trust funds, budgeting, and other government-wide financial management activities. This function is not applied to school district or special district governments. **Other government administration** applies to the legislative and government-wide administrative agencies of governments. Included here are overall planning and zoning activities, and central personnel and administrative activities. This function is not applied to school district or special district governments.

Judicial and legal includes all court and court related activities (except probation and parole activities that are included at the "Correction" function), court activities of sheriff's offices, prosecuting attorneys' and public defenders' offices, legal departments, and attorneys providing government-wide legal service.

Police includes all activities concerned, with the enforcement of law and order, including coroner's offices, police training academies, investigation bureaus, and local jails, "lockups", or other detention facilities not intended to serve as correctional facilities.

Corrections includes activities pertaining to the confinement and correction of adults and minors convicted of criminal offenses. Pardon, probation, and parole activities are also included here.

Highways and transportation includes activities associated with the maintenance and operation of streets, roads, sidewalks, bridges, tunnels, toll roads, and ferries. Snow and ice removal, street lighting, and highway and traffic engineering activities are also included here. Also included are the operation, maintenance, and construction of public mass transit systems, including subways, surface rails, and buses, and the provision, construction, operation, maintenance; support of public waterways, harbors, docks, wharves, and related marine terminal facilities; and activities associated with the operation and support of publicly operated airport facilities.

Public welfare includes the administration of various public assistance programs for the needy, veteran services, operation of nursing homes, indigent care institutions, and programs that provide payments for medical care, handicap transportation, and other services for the needy.

Health includes administration of public health programs, community and visiting nurse services, immunization programs, drug abuse rehabilitation programs, health and food inspection activities, operation of outpatient clinics, and environmental pollution control activities.

Hospitals includes only government operated medical care facilities that provide inpatient care. Employees and payrolls of private corporations that lease and operate government-owned hospital facilities are excluded.

Social insurance administration includes the administration of unemployment compensation systems, public employment services, and the Federal Social Security, Medicare, and Railroad Retirement trusts.

Natural resources and Parks includes activities primarily concerned with the conservation and development of natural resources (soil, water, energy, minerals, etc.) and the regulation of industries that develop, utilize, or affect natural resources, as well as the operation and maintenance of parks, playgrounds, swimming pools, public beaches, auditoriums, public golf courses, museums, marinas, botanical gardens, and zoological parks.

Utilities, sewerage, and waste management includes operation, maintenance, and construction of public water supply systems, including production, acquisition, and distribution of water to general public or to other public or private utilities, for residential, commercial, and industrial use; activities associated with the production or acquisition and distribution of electric power; provision, maintenance, and operation of sanitary and storm sewer systems and sewage disposal and treatment facilities; and refuse collection and disposal, operation of sanitary landfills, and street cleaning activities.

Elementary and secondary education and libraries includes activities associated with the operation of public elementary and secondary schools and locally operated vocational-technical schools. Special education programs operated by elementary and secondary school systems are also included as are all ancillary services associated with the operation of schools, such as pupil transportation and food service. Also included are the establishment and provision of libraries for use by the general public and the technical support of privately operated libraries. This category includes classroom teachers, principals, supervisors of instruction, librarians, teacher aides, library aides, and guidance and psychological personnel as well as school superintendents and other administrative personnel, clerical and secretarial staffs, plant operation and maintenance personnel, health and recreation employees, transportation and food service personnel, and any student employees.

· **Higher education** includes state government degree granting institutions that provide academic training above grade 12. This includes persons engaged in teaching and related academic research as well as administrative, clerical, custodial, cafeteria, health personnel, noninstructional employees engaged in organized research, law enforcement personnel, and paid student employees.

STATE GOVERNMENT FINANCES, Items 331–350

Source: U.S. Census Bureau—State Government Finances
http://www.census.gov/govs/state/

Data are from an annual survey conducted by the Census Bureau and pertain to state government fiscal years ending on June 30, except for four states with other ending dates: Alabama and Michigan (September 30), New York (March 31), and Texas (August 31).

The state government finance data presented in this publication may differ from data published by state governments because the Census Bureau may be using a different definition of which organizations are covered under the term, "state government."

For the purpose of Census Bureau statistics, the term "state government" refers not only to the executive, legislative, and judicial branches of a given state, but it also includes agencies, institutions, commissions, and public authorities that operate separately or somewhat autonomously from the central state government but where the state government maintains administrative or fiscal control over their activities as defined by the Census Bureau.

Total **general revenue** includes all revenue except utility, liquor stores, and insurance trust revenue. All tax revenue and intergovernmental revenue, even if designated for employee-retirement or local utility purpose, are classified as general revenue.

Intergovernmental revenue covers amounts received from the federal government as fiscal aid, reimbursements for performance of general government functions and specific services

for the paying government, or in lieu of taxes. It excludes any amounts received from other governments from the sale of property, commodities, and utility services.

Taxes consist of compulsory contributions exacted by governments for public purposes. However, this category excludes employer and employee payments for retirement and social insurance purposes, which are classified as insurance trust revenue; it also excludes special assessments, which are classified as non-tax general revenue. Sales and gross receipts taxes do not include dealer discounts, or "commissions" allowed to merchants for collection of taxes from consumers. General sales taxes and selected taxes on sales of motor fuels, tobacco products, and other particular commodities and services are included.

General government expenditure includes capital outlay, a major portion of which is commonly financed by borrowing. Government revenue does not include receipts from borrowing. Among other things, this distorts the relationship between totals of revenue and expenditure figures that are presented and renders it useless as a direct measure of the degree of budgetary "balance" (as that term is generally applied).

Direct general expenditure comprises all expenditures of the state governments, excluding utility, liquor stores, insurance trust expenditures, and any intergovernmental payments.

State government expenditure for **education** is mainly for the provision and general support of schools and other educational facilities and services, including those for educational institutions beyond high school. They cover such related services as student transportation; school lunch and other cafeteria operations; school health, recreation, and library services; and dormitories, dining halls, and bookstores operated by public institutions of higher education.

Health and hospitals expenditure includes health research; clinics; nursing; immunization; other categorical, environmental, and general health services provided by health agencies; establishment and operation of hospital facilities; provision of hospital care; and support of other public and private hospitals.

Highways expenditure is for the provision and maintenance of highway facilities, including toll turnpikes, bridges, tunnels, and ferries, as well as regular roads, highways, and streets. Also included are expenditures for street lighting and for snow and ice removal. Not included are highway policing and traffic control, which are considered part of police protection

Public safety expenditure includes police and correctional institution expenditures.

Public welfare expenditure covers support of and assistance to needy persons; this aid is contingent upon the person's needs. Included are cash assistance paid directly to needy persons under categorical (Old Age Assistance, Temporary Assistance for Needy Families, Aid to the Blind, and Aid to the Disabled) and other welfare programs; vendor payments made directly to private purveyors for medical care, burials, and other commodities and services provided under welfare programs; welfare institutions; and any intergovernmental or other direct expenditure for welfare purposes. Pensions to former employees and other benefits not contingent on need are excluded.

Natural resources, parks, and recreation includes expenditures for conservation, promotion, and development of natural resources (soil, water, energy, minerals, etc.) and the regulation of industries which develop, utilize, or affect natural resources. It also includes the provision and support of recreational and cul-tural-scientific facilities, such as golf courses, playgrounds, tennis courts, public beaches, swimming pools, play fields, parks, camping areas, recreational piers and marinas, galleries, museums, zoos, botanical gardens, auditoriums, stadiums, recreational centers, convention centers, exhibition halls, community music, drama, and celebrations.

Debt outstanding includes all long-term debt obligations of the government and its agencies (exclusive of utility debt) and all interest-bearing, short-term (repayable within one year) debt obligations remaining unpaid at the close of the fiscal year. It includes judgments, mortgages, and revenue bonds, as well as general obligation bonds, notes, and interest-bearing warrants. This category consists of non-interest-bearing, short-term obligations; inter-fund obligations; amounts owed in a trust or agency capacity; advances and contingent loans from other governments; and rights of individuals to benefit from government-administered employee-retirement funds.

VOTING AND REGISTRATION, Items 351 and 352

Source: U.S. Census Bureau—Current Population Survey
http://www.census.gov/topics/public-sector/voting.html

These estimates are based on the November 2016 Voting and Registration Supplement to the Current Population Survey (CPS).

Voting rates are calculated using the voting-age population, which includes both citizens and noncitizens. The percentages in columns 351 and 352 are based on the citizen population. Statistics from surveys are subject to sampling and nonsampling error. The CPS estimate of overall turnout differs from the "official" turnout reported by the Clerk of the House of Representatives.

ELECTION STATISTICS, Items 353–355

Source: U.S. House of Representatives, Statistics of the Presidential and Congressional Election of November 8, 2016
http://history.house.gov/Institution/Election-Statistics/2016election/

Election results show the percentage of the total vote cast for the Democratic and Republican candidates, as well as the combined percentage for all other candidates in the 2012 presidential election. This information was compiled by the Office of the Clerk, U.S. House of Representatives and published on February 22, 2017.

TABLE B—STATES AND COUNTIES

Table B presents 199 items for the United States as a whole, each individual state, and the District of Columbia; and every county, county equivalent, and independent city. The counties are presented in alphabetical order within each state, and the states are also presented in alphabetical order. Independent cities, which are found in Maryland, Missouri, Nevada, and Virginia, are placed in alphabetical order at the end of the list of counties for those states. The District of Columbia is included in Table B as both a county and a state. It is also included as a city in Table D.

LAND AREA, Items 1 and 4

Source: U.S. Census Bureau—2018 U.S. Gazetteer Files,
https://www.census.gov/geographies/reference-files/time-series/geo/gazetteer-files.html

Land area measurements are shown to the nearest square mile. Land area is an area measurement providing the size, in square miles, of the land portions of each county.

POPULATION, Items 2–4

Source: U.S. Census Bureau—Population Estimates
https://www.census.gov/programs-surveys/popest.html

The population data are Census Bureau estimates of the resident population as of July 1 of the year shown. The ranks are shown for counties (including independent cities and the District of Columbia).

POPULATION AND POPULATION CHARACTERISTICS, Items 5–19

Source: U.S. Census Bureau—Population Estimates
https://www.census.gov/programs-surveys/popest.html

The concept of race, as used by the Census Bureau, reflects self-identification by persons according to the race or races with which they most closely identify. These categories are sociopolitical constructs and should not be interpreted as being scientific or anthropological in nature. Furthermore, race categories include both racial and national origin groups.

Beginning with the 2000 census, respondents were offered the option of selecting one or more races. This option was not available in prior censuses; thus, comparisons between censuses should be made with caution. In Table B, Columns 5 through 8 refer to individuals who identified with each racial category, either alone or in combination with other races. The estimates exclude persons of Hispanic or Latino origin from all race groups.

The sum of the four individual race alone or in combination categories in this book will often add to more than the total population because people who reported more than one race were tallied in each race category. In this book, the Asian group has been combined with the Native Hawaiian and Other Pacific Islander group, causing double-counting of persons who identify with both groups. This is especially pronounced in Hawaii.

The **White** population is defined as persons who indicated their race as White, as well as persons who did not classify themselves in one of the specific race categories listed on the questionnaire but entered a nationality such as Irish, German, Italian, Lebanese, Near Easterner, Arab, or Polish.

The **Black** population includes persons who indicated their race as "Black or African American" as well as persons who did not classify themselves in one of the specific race categories but reported entries such as African American, Afro American, Kenyan, Nigerian, or Haitian.

The **American Indian or Alaska Native** population includes persons who indicated their race as American Indian or Alaska Native, as well as persons who did not classify themselves in one of the specific race categories but reported entries such as Canadian Indian, French-American Indian, Spanish-American Indian, Eskimo, Aleut, Alaska Indian, or any of the American Indian or Alaska Native tribes.

The **Asian and Pacific Islander** population combines two census groupings: **Asian** and **Native Hawaiian or Other Pacific Islander**. The **Asian** population includes persons who indicated their race as Asian Indian, Chinese, Filipino, Japanese, Korean, Vietnamese, or "Other Asian," as well as persons who provided write-in entries of such groups as Cambodian, Laotian, Hmong, Pakistani, or Taiwanese. The **Native Hawaiian or Other Pacific Islander** population includes persons who indicated their race as "Native Hawaiian," "Guamanian or Chamorro," "Samoan," or "Other Pacific Islander," as well as persons who reported entries such as Part Hawaiian, American Samoan, Fijian, Melanesian, or Tahitian.

The **Hispanic population** is based on a question that asked respondents "Is this person Spanish/Hispanic/Latino?" Persons marking any one of the four Hispanic categories (i.e., Mexican, Puerto Rican, Cuban, or other Spanish) are collectively referred to as Hispanic.

Age is defined as age at last birthday (number of completed years since birth), as of April 1 of the census year.

The **female** population is shown as a percentage of total population.

POPULATION AND COMPONENTS OF CHANGE, Items 20–26

Source: U.S. Census Bureau—Decennial Censuses and Population Estimates
http://www.census.gov/main/www/cen2000.html
https://www.census.gov/programs-surveys/popest.html
http://www.census.gov/2010census/data/

The population data for 2000 and 2010 are from the decennial censuses and represent the resident population as of April 1 of those years. The 2010 estimates are based on the 2010 Census and reflect changes to the April 1, 2010 population due to the Count Question Resolution program and geographic program revisions. The components of change are based on Census Bureau estimates of the resident population as of July 1, 2018. The change in population between 2010 and 2018 is made up of (a) natural increase—births minus deaths, and (b) net migration—the difference between the number of persons moving into a particular area and the number of persons moving out of the area. Net migration is composed of internal and international migration.

Because the 2018 population estimates are based on a model that begins with a national population estimate, the county components of change do not always exactly add up to the difference between the 2010 census population and the 2018 estimates.

HOUSEHOLDS, Items 27–31

Source: U.S. Census Bureau—American Community Survey, 2017 5-year Estimates
http://www.census.gov/acs/www/

A **household** includes all of the persons who occupy a housing unit. (Persons not living in households are classified as living in group quarters.) A housing unit is a house, an apartment, a mobile home, a group of rooms, or a single room occupied (or, if vacant, intended for occupancy) as separate living quarters. Separate living quarters are those in which the occupants live separately from any other persons in the building and have direct access from the outside of the building or through a common hall. The occupants may be a single family, one person living alone, two or more families living together, or any other group of related or unrelated persons who share living quarters. The number of households is the same as the number of year-round occupied housing units.

A **family** includes a householder and one or more other persons living in the same household who are related to the householder by birth, marriage, or adoption. All persons in a household who are related to the householder are regarded as members of his or her family. A **family household** may contain persons not related to the householder; thus, family households may include more members than families do. A household can contain only one family for the purposes of census tabulations. Not all households contain families, as a household may comprise a group of unrelated persons or of one person living alone. Families are classified by type as either a "married-couple family" or "other family," according to the presence or absence of a spouse.

The measure of **persons per household** is obtained by dividing the number of persons in households by the number of households or householders. One person in each household is designated as the householder. In most cases, this is the person (or one of the persons) in whose name the house is owned, being bought, or rented. If there is no such person in the household, any adult household member 15 years old and over can be designated as the householder.

The category **female family householder** includes only female-headed family households with no spouse present.

A nonfamily household consists of a householder living alone or with nonrelatives only. Column 31 shows one-person households as a percentage of all households.

GROUP QUARTERS, Item 32

Source:
Source: U.S. Census Bureau—Population Estimates
https://www.census.gov/programs-surveys/popest.html

The Census Bureau classifies all persons not living in households as living in group quarters; this category includes both the institutional and noninstitutional populations. The institutionalized population includes persons under formally authorized, supervised care or custody in institutions, such as correctional institutions, nursing homes, mental (psychiatric) hospitals, and juvenile institutions. The noninstitutionalized population includes persons who live in group quarters other than institutions, such as college dormitories, military quarters, and group homes. This volume includes the total number of persons in group quarters.

DAYTIME POPULATION, Items 33 and 34

Source: U.S. Census Bureau—American Community Survey, 2017 5-year Estimates
http://www.census.gov/acs/www/

Daytime population refers to the number of persons who are present in an area or place during normal business hours, including workers. This can be contrasted with the "resident" population, which is present during the evening and nighttime hours. The daytime population estimate is calculated by adding the total resident population and the total workers working in the area/place, and then subtracting the total workers living in the area/place from that result. Information on the expansion or contraction experienced by different communities between their nighttime and daytime populations is important for many planning purposes, especially those concerning transportation, disaster, and relief operations.

The employment/residence ratio is a measure of the total number of workers working in an area or place, relative to the total number of workers living in the area or place. It is often used as a rough indication of the jobs-workers balance in an area/place, although it does not take into account whether the resident workers possess the skills needed for the jobs available in their particular area/place. The employment/residence ratio is calculated by dividing the number of total workers working in an area/place by the number of total workers residing in the area/place.

BIRTHS AND DEATHS, Items 35–38

Source: U.S. Census Bureau—Population Estimates
https://www.census.gov/programs-surveys/popest.html

The numbers of births and deaths are from the Census Bureau's Population Estimates Program. They represent the total number of live births and deaths occurring to residents of an area as estimated using reports from the National Center for Health Statistics (NCHS) and the Federal-State Cooperative for Population Estimates (FSCPE). The rates measure births and deaths during the specified time period as a proportion of an area's population. Rates are expressed per 1,000 population estimated as of July 1. These numbers and rates do not represent the calendar year, but rather the year-long period ending on July 1.

PERSONS UNDER 65 WITH NO HEALTH INSURANCE, Items 39 and 40

Source: U.S. Census Bureau—Small Area Health Insurance Estimates
https://www.census.gov/programs-surveys/sahie.html

The Small Area Health Insurance Estimates (SAHIE) program develops model-based estimates of health insurance coverage for counties and states. This developmental program builds on the work of the Small Area Income and Poverty Estimates (SAIPE) program. The SAHIE program models health insurance coverage by combining survey data with population estimates and administrative records. These estimates combine data from administrative records, postcensal population estimates, and the decennial census with direct estimates from the American Community Survey to provide consistent and reliable single-year estimates. These model-based single-year estimates are more reflective of current conditions than multi-year survey estimates.

MEDICARE ENROLLMENT, Items 41–43

Source: U.S. Department of Health and Human Services, Centers for Medicare and Medicaid Services
https://www.cms.gov/Research-Statistics-Data-and-Systems/Statistics-Trends-and-Reports/CMSProgramStatistics/Dashboard.html

The Centers for Medicare and Medicaid Services (CMS) administers Medicare, which provides health insurance to persons 65 years old and over, persons with permanent kidney failure, and certain persons with disabilities. Original Medicare has two parts: Hospital Insurance and Supplemental Medical Insurance. In recent years, Medicare has been expanded to include two new programs: Medicare Advantage plans and prescription drug coverage. Medicare Advantage Plans are health plan options that are approved by Medicare but run by private companies. Medicare prescription drug plans can be part of Medicare Advantage plans or stand-alone drug plans.

Persons who are eligible for Medicare can enroll in Part A (Hospital Insurance) at no charge, and can choose to pay a monthly premium to enroll in Part B. Most eligible persons are enrolled in Part A, and most enrollees in Part A are also enrolled in Part B (Supplemental Medical Insurance.) This table includes persons who were enrolled in both Part A and Part B during 2017.

Part B beneficiaries can choose to enroll in **Original Medicare**, a fee-for-service plan administered by the Centers for Medicare and Medicaid Services, or in a **Medicare Advantage** plan. Medicare Advantage plans include private fee-for-service plans, preferred provider organizations, health maintenance organizations, medical savings account plans, demonstration plans, and programs for all-inclusive care for the elderly.

The annual Medicare enrollment counts are determined using a person-year methodology. For each calendar year, total person-year counts are determined by summing the total number of months that each beneficiary is enrolled during the year and dividing by 12. Using this methodology, a beneficiary's partial-year enrollment may be counted in more than one category (i.e., both Original Medicare and Medicare Advantage).

CRIME, Items 44–47

Source: U.S. Federal Bureau of Investigation—Uniform Crime Reports https://ucr.fbi.gov/crime-in-the-u.s/2016/crime-in-the-u.s.-2016

Crime data are as reported to the Federal Bureau of Investigation (FBI) by law enforcement agencies and have not been adjusted for underreporting or overreporting. This may affect comparability between geographic areas or over time.

Through the voluntary contribution of crime statistics by law enforcement agencies across the United States, the Uniform Crime Reporting (UCR) Program provides periodic assessments of crime in the nation as measured by offenses that have come to the attention of the law enforcement community. The Committee on Uniform Crime Records of the International Association of Chiefs of Police initiated this voluntary national data collection effort in 1930. The UCR Program contributors compile and submit their crime data either directly to the FBI or through state-level UCR Programs.

Seven offenses, because of their severity, frequency of occurrence, and likelihood of being reported to police, were initially selected to serve as an index for evaluating fluctuations in the volume of crime. These serious crimes were murder and nonnegligent manslaughter, forcible rape, robbery, aggravated assault, burglary, larceny-theft, and motor vehicle theft. By congressional mandate, arson was added as the eighth index offense in 1979. The totals shown in this volume do not include arson.

In 2004, the FBI discontinued the use of the Crime Index in the UCR Program and its publications, stating that the Crime Index was driven upward by the offense with the highest number of cases (in this case, larceny-theft), creating a bias against jurisdictions with a high number of larceny-thefts but a low number of other serious crimes, such as murder and rape. The FBI is currently publishing a violent crime total and property crime total until a more viable index is developed. This book includes the crime total, as well as violent crime and property crime rates.

In 2013, the FBI adopted a new definition of rape. Rape is now defined as, "Penetration, no matter how slight, of the vagina or anus with any body part or object, or oral penetration by a sex organ of another person, without the consent of the victim." The new definition updated the 80-year-old historical definition of rape which was "carnal knowledge of a female forcibly and against her will." Effectively, the revised definition expands rape to include both male and female victims and offenders, and reflects the various forms of sexual penetration understood to be rape, especially nonconsenting acts of sodomy, and sexual assaults with objects.

Violent crimes include four categories of offenses: (1) Murder and nonnegligent manslaughter, as defined in the UCR Program, is the willful (nonnegligent) killing of one human being by another. This offense excludes deaths caused by negligence, suicide, or accident; justifiable homicides; and attempts to murder or assaults to murder. (2) Rape is the penetration, no matter how slight, of the vagina or anus with any body part or object, or oral penetration by a sex organ of another person, without the consent of the victim. Assaults or attempts to commit rape by force or threat of force are also included; however, statutory rape (without force) and other sex offenses are excluded. (3) Robbery is the taking or attempting to take anything of value from the care, custody, or control of a person or persons by force or threat of force or violence and/or by putting the victim in fear. (4) Aggravated assault is an unlawful attack by one person upon another for the purpose of inflicting severe or aggravated bodily injury. This type of assault is usually accompanied by the use of a weapon or by other means likely to produce death or great bodily harm. Attempts are included, since injury does not necessarily have to result when a gun, knife, or other weapon is used, as these incidents could and probably would result in a serious personal injury if the crime were successfully completed.

Property crimes include three categories: (1) Burglary, or breaking and entering, is the unlawful entry of a structure to commit a felony or theft, even though no force was used to gain entrance. (2) Larceny-theft is the unauthorized taking of the personal property of another, without the use of force. (3) Motor vehicle theft is the unauthorized taking of any motor vehicle.

Rates are based on population estimates provided by the FBI. The county totals published in this volume were obtained by aggregating individual reporting units within each county. If the population total for the units aggregated was less than 75 percent of the county's population (as estimated by the Census Bureau), the total was not considered representative of the county as a whole and was not published. State and U.S. totals include FBI estimates for those areas, adjusted to include areas that did not report and to correct for underreporting and overreporting, as published in the FBI's *Crime in the United States*.

EDUCATION—SCHOOL ENROLLMENT AND EDUCATIONAL ATTAINMENT, Items 48–51

Source: U.S. Census Bureau—American Community Survey, 2017 5-year Estimates http://www.census.gov/acs/www/

Data on **school enrollment** are tabulated for the population 3 years old and over. Persons were classified as enrolled in school if they reported attending a "regular" public or private school (or college) during the three months preceding the interview. The instructions were to include only nursery school, kindergarten, elementary school, and schooling which would lead to a high school diploma or a college degree as regular school. The Census Bureau defines a public school as "any school or college controlled and supported by a local, county, state, or federal government." Schools primarily supported and controlled by religious organizations or other private groups are defined as private schools.

Data on **educational attainment** are tabulated for the population 25 years old and over. The data were derived from a question that asked respondents for the highest level of school completed or the highest degree received. Persons who had passed a high school equivalency examination were considered high school graduates. Schooling received in foreign schools was to be reported as the equivalent grade or years in the regular American school system.

Vocational and technical training, such as barber school training; business, trade, technical, and vocational schools; or other training for a specific trade are specifically excluded.

High school graduate or less. This category includes persons whose highest degree was a high school diploma or its equivalent, and those who reported any level lower than a high school diploma.

Bachelor's degree or more. This category includes persons who have received bachelor's degrees, master's degrees, professional school degrees (such as law school or medical school degrees), and doctoral degrees.

LOCAL GOVERNMENT EDUCATION EXPENDITURES, Items 52 and 53

Source: U.S. Department of Education, National Center for Education Statistics, Common Core of Data (CCD), "Local Education Agency (School District) Universe Survey Directory Data", 2014-15 v.1a; "Local Education Agency (School District) Universe Survey Geographic Data (EDGE)", 2014-15 v.1a; "School District Finance Survey (F-33)", 2014-15 (FY 2015) v.1a.
https://nces.ed.gov/ccd/

Expenditures are for elementary and secondary Education which includes prekindergarten
through twelfth grade regular, special, and vocational education, as well as cocurricular, community service, and adult education programs provided by a public school system. The financial activities of these systems for all instruction, support service, and noninstructional activities are included

Current spending comprises current operation expenditure, payments made by the state government on behalf of school systems, and transfers made by school systems into their own retirement funds. Current operation expenditures include direct expenditure for salaries, employee benefits, purchased professional and technical services, purchased property and other services, and supplies. It includes gross school system expenditure for instruction, support services, and noninstructional functions. It excludes expenditure for debt service, capital outlay, and reimbursement to other governments (including other school systems).

Current expenditure per student is current expenditure divided by the number of students enrolled. The number of students enrolled is based on an annual "membership" count of students on or about October 1, collected by the National Center for Education Statistics on the Common Core of Data (CCD) agency universe file—"Local Education Agency (School District) Universe Survey."

MONEY INCOME, Items 54–57
Source: U.S. Census Bureau—American Community Survey, 2017 5-year Estimates
http://www.census.gov/acs/www/

Total money income is the sum of the amounts reported separately for wage or salary income; net self-employment income; interest, dividends, or net rental or royalty income or income from estates and trusts; Social Security or railroad retirement income; Supplemental Security Income (SSI); public assistance or welfare payments; retirement, survivor, or disability pensions; and all other income. Receipts from the following sources are not included as income: capital gains; money received from the sale of property (unless the recipient was engaged in the business of selling such property); the value of income "in kind" from food stamps, public housing subsidies, medical care, employer contributions for individuals, etc.; withdrawal of bank deposits; money borrowed; tax refunds; exchange of money between relatives living in the same household; and gifts, lump-sum inheritances, insurance payments, and other types of lump-sum receipts.

Money income differs in definition from personal income (item 62). For example, money income does not include the pension rights, employer provided health insurance, food stamps, or Medicare payments that are included in personal income.

Per capita income is the mean income computed for every man, woman, and child in a particular group. It is derived by dividing the aggregate income of a particular group by the resident population in that group as estimated in the American Community Survey. Per capita income is rounded to the nearest whole dollar.

Household income includes the income of the householder and all other individuals 15 years old and over in the household, whether or not they are related to the householder. Since many households consist of only one person, median household income is usually less than median family income. Although the household income statistics cover the 12 months preceding the interview, the characteristics of individuals and the composition of households refer to the date of interview. Thus, the income of the household does not include amounts received by individuals who were no longer residing in the household at the time of interview. Similarly, income amounts reported by individuals who did not reside in the household during all of the past 12 months but who were members of the household at the time of interview are included. However, the composition of most households was the same during those 12 months as it was at the time of interview.

Median income divides the income distribution into two equal parts, with half of all cases below the median income level and half of all cases above the median income level. For households, the median income is based on the distribution of the total number of households, including those with no income. Median income for households is computed on the basis of a standard distribution with a minimum value of less than $2,500 and a maximum value of $200,000 or more and is rounded to the nearest whole dollar. Median income figures are calculated using linear interpolation if the width of the interval containing the estimate is $2,500 or less. If the width of the interval containing the estimate is greater than $2,500, Pareto interpolation is used.

Poverty Thresholds for 2017 by Size of Family and Number of Related Children Under 18 Years

Size of family unit	Weighted average thresholds	Related children under 18 years								
		None	One	Two	Three	Four	Five	Six	Seven	Eight or more
One person (unrelated individual):	12,488									
Under age 65	12,752	12,752								
Aged 65 and older	11,756	11,756								
Two people:	15,877									
Householder under age 65........	16,493	16,414	16,895							
Householder aged 65 and older	14,828	14,816	16,831							
Three people	19,515	19,173	19,730	19,749						
Four people	25,094	25,283	25,696	24,858	24,944					
Five people	29,714	30,490	30,933	29,986	29,253	28,805				
Six people	33,618	35,069	35,208	34,482	33,787	32,753	32,140			
Seven people	38,173	40,351	40,603	39,734	39,129	38,001	36,685	35,242		
Eight people	42,684	45,129	45,528	44,708	43,990	42,971	41,678	40,332	39,990	
Nine people or more	50,681	54,287	54,550	53,825	53,216	52,216	50,840	49,595	49,287	47,389

Source: U.S. Census Bureau.

Income amounts have been adjusted for inflation to represent the final year of multi-year estimates, in this case 2013-2017 estimates. The constant-dollar figures are based on an annual average Consumer Price Index from the Bureau of Labor Statistics. Constant-dollar figures are estimates representing an effort to remove the effects of price changes from statistical series reported in dollar terms. However, the estimates do not reflect the price and cost-of-living differences that may exist between areas.

INCOME AND POVERTY, Items 58–61
Source: U.S. Census Bureau—Small Area Income and Poverty Estimates Program
https://www.census.gov/programs-surveys/saipe.html

The annual income and poverty estimates by county are constructed from statistical models that relate income and poverty to indicators based on summary data from federal income tax returns, data about participation in the Food Stamp program, and the previous census. A regression model predicts the number of people in poverty using county-level observations from the current year's American Community Survey (ACS) and administrative records and census data as the predictors. The 2005 estimates were the first to use the ACS. Prior year models were based on the Annual Social and Economic Supplement (ASEC) of the Current Population Survey (CPS). The ACS is a much larger survey than the ASEC, permitting income and poverty estimates based on a single year for many counties, Because of the differences between the two surveys, caution should be used when comparing these estimates with those from earlier years.

The **poverty status** data were derived from data collected on the number of persons in a household, each person's relationship to the householder, and income data. The Social Security Administration (SSA) developed the original poverty definition in 1964, which federal interagency committees subsequently revised in 1969 and 1980. The Office of Management and Budget's (OMB) *Directive 14* prescribes the SSA's definition as the official poverty measure for federal agencies to use in their statistical work. Poverty statistics presented in American Community Survey products adhere to the standards defined by OMB in *Directive 14*.

Poverty thresholds vary depending on three criteria: size of family, number of children, and, for one- and two-person families, age of householder. In determining the poverty status of families and unrelated individuals, the Census Bureau uses thresholds (income cutoffs) arranged in a two-dimensional matrix. The matrix consists of family size (from one person to nine or more persons), cross-classified by presence and number of family members under 18 years old (from no children present to eight or more children present). Unrelated individuals and two-person families are further differentiated by age of reference person (under 65 years old and 65 years old and over). To determine a person's poverty status, the person's total family income over the previous 12 months is compared with the poverty threshold appropriate for that person's family size and composition. If the total income of that person's family is less than the threshold appropriate for that family, then the person is considered poor or "below the poverty level," together with every member of his or her family. If a person is not living with anyone related by birth, marriage, or adoption, then the person's own income is compared with his or her poverty threshold. The total number of persons below the poverty level is the sum of persons in families and the number of unrelated individuals with incomes below the poverty level over the previous 12 months.

PERSONAL INCOME AND EARNINGS, Items 62–83

Source: U.S. Bureau of Economic Analysis, Regional Economic Accounts
http://www.bea.gov/regional/index.htm#state
http://www.bea.gov/data/income-saving/
personal-income-county-metro-and-other-areas

Total personal income is the current income received by residents of an area from all sources. It is measured before deductions of income and other personal taxes, but after deductions of personal contributions for Social Security, government retirement, and other social insurance programs. It consists of **wage and salary disbursements** (covering all employee earnings, including executive salaries, bonuses, commissions, payments-in-kind, incentive payments, and tips); various types of supplementary earnings, such as employers' contributions to pension funds (termed "other labor income" or "supplements to wages and salaries"); proprietors' income; rental income of persons; dividends; personal interest income; and government and business transfer payments.

Per capita personal income is based on the resident population estimated as of July 1 of the year shown.

Proprietors' income is the monetary income and income-in-kind of proprietorships and partnerships (including the independent professions) and the income of tax-exempt cooperatives.

Dividends are cash payments by corporations to stockholders who are U.S. residents. **Interest** is the monetary and imputed interest income of persons from all sources. **Rent** is the monetary income of persons from the rental of real property, except the income of persons primarily engaged in the real estate business; the imputed net rental income of owner-occupants of nonfarm dwellings; and the royalties received by persons.

Transfer payments are income for which services are not currently rendered. They consist of both government and business transfer payments. Government transfer payments include payments under the following programs: Federal Old-Age, Survivors, and Disability Insurance ("Social Security"); Medicare and medical vendor payments; unemployment insurance; railroad and government retirement; federal- and state-government-insured workers' compensation; veterans' benefits, including veterans' life insurance; SNAP (Supplemental Nutrition Assistance Program, or food stamps); black lung payments; Supplemental Security Income; and Temporary Assistance for Needy Families. Government payments to nonprofit institutions, other than for work under research and development contracts, are also included. Business transfer payments consist primarily of liability payments for personal injury and of corporate gifts to nonprofit institutions.

Personal income differs in definition from money income (items 54–57). For example, personal income includes pension rights, employer-provided health insurance, food stamps, and Medicare. These are not included in the definition of money income.

Earnings cover wage and salary disbursements, other labor income, and proprietors' income.

The data for earnings obtained from the Bureau of Economic Analysis (BEA) are based on place of work. In computing personal income, BEA makes an "adjustment for residence" to earnings, based on commuting patterns; personal income is thus presented on a place-of-residence basis.

Farm earnings include the income of farm workers (wages and salaries and other labor income) and farm proprietors. Farm proprietors' income includes only the income of sole proprietorships and partnerships. Farm earnings estimates are benchmarked to data collected in the Census of Agriculture and the revised Department of Agriculture statistical totals of income and expense items.

Goods-related industries include mining, construction, and manufacturing.

Mining, Quarrying, and Extracting comprises establishments that extract naturally occurring mineral solids, such as coal and ores; liquid minerals, such as crude petroleum; and gases, such as natural gas. The term mining is used in the broad sense to include quarrying, well operations, beneficiating (e.g., crushing, screening, washing, and flotation), and other preparation customarily performed at the mine site, or as a part of mining activity.

The **Construction** sector comprises establishments primarily engaged in the construction of buildings or engineering projects (e.g., highways and utility systems). Establishments primarily engaged in the preparation of sites for new construction and establishments primarily engaged in subdividing land for sale as building sites also are included in this sector.

Manufacturing comprises establishments engaged in the mechanical, physical, or chemical transformation of materials, substances, or components into new products. The assembling of component parts of manufactured products is considered manufacturing, except in cases where the activity is appropriately classified in **Construction**.

Service-related and other industries include private-sector earnings in agricultural services, forestry, and fisheries; transportation and public utilities; wholesale trade; retail trade; finance, insurance, and real estate; and services. Government earnings include all levels of government.

The **Information** sector comprises establishments engaged in the following processes: (a) producing and distributing information and cultural products, (b) providing the means to transmit or distribute these products as well as data or communications, and (c) processing data.

Professional, Scientific, and Technical Services comprises establishments that specialize in performing professional, scientific, and technical activities for others. These activities require a high degree of expertise and training. The establishments in this sector specialize according to expertise and provide these services to clients in a variety of industries and, in some cases, to households. Activities performed include: legal advice and representation; accounting, bookkeeping, and payroll services; architectural, engineering, and specialized design services; computer services; consulting services; research services; advertising services; photographic services; translation and interpretation services; veterinary services; and other professional, scientific, and technical services.

The **Retail Trade** sector comprises establishments engaged in retailing merchandise, generally without transformation, and rendering services incidental to the sale of merchandise.

The retailing process is the final step in the distribution of merchandise; retailers are, therefore, organized to sell merchandise in small quantities to the general public. This sector comprises two main types of retailers: store and nonstore retailers.

Store retailers operate fixed point-of-sale locations, located and designed to attract a high volume of walk-in customers. In general, retail stores have extensive displays of merchandise and use mass-media advertising to attract customers. In addition to retailing merchandise, some types of store retailers are also engaged in the provision of after-sales services, such as repair and installation.

Nonstore retailers, like store retailers, are organized to serve the general public, but their retailing methods differ. The establishments of this subsector reach customers and market merchandise with methods, such as the broadcasting of "infomercials," the broadcasting and publishing of direct-response advertising, the publishing of paper and electronic catalogs, door-to-door solicitation, in-home demonstration, selling from portable stalls (street vendors, except food), and distribution through vending machines. Establishments engaged in the direct sale (nonstore) of products, such as home heating oil dealers and home delivery newspaper routes are included here.

Finance and Insurance comprises establishments primarily engaged in financial transactions (transactions involving the creation, liquidation, or change in ownership of financial assets) and/or in facilitating financial transactions. Three principal types of activities are identified: raising funds by taking deposits and/or issuing securities and, in the process, incurring liabilities; pooling of risk by underwriting insurance and annuities; and providing specialized services facilitating or supporting financial intermediation, insurance, and employee benefit programs.

The **Real Estate and Rental and Leasing** sector comprises establishments primarily engaged in renting, leasing, or otherwise allowing the use of tangible or intangible assets, and establishments providing related services. The major portion of this sector comprises establishments that rent, lease, or otherwise allow the use of their own assets by others. The assets may be tangible, as is the case of real estate and equipment, or intangible, as is the case with patents and trademarks. This sector also includes establishments primarily engaged in managing real estate for others, selling, renting and/or buying real estate for others, and appraising real estate.

Health Care and Social Assistance comprises establishments providing health care and social assistance for individuals. The sector includes both health care and social assistance because it is sometimes difficult to distinguish between the boundaries of these two activities. The industries in this sector are arranged on a continuum starting with those establishments providing medical care exclusively, continuing with those providing health care and social assistance, and finally finishing with those providing only social assistance. The services provided by establishments in this sector are delivered by trained professionals. All industries in the sector share this commonality of process, namely, labor inputs of health practitioners or social workers with the requisite expertise. Many of the industries in the sector are defined based on the educational degree held by the practitioners included in the industry.

Government includes the executive, legislative, judicial, administrative and regulatory activities of Federal, state, local, and international governments. Also included are Government enterprises: government agencies that cover a substantial portion of their operating costs by selling goods and services to the public and that maintain separate accounts.

Industries are categorized under the North American Industry Classification System (NAICS), and are not comparable to years prior to 2002.

SOCIAL SECURITY AND SUPPLEMENTAL SECURITY INCOME, Items 84–86

Source: U.S. Social Security Administration
http://www.ssa.gov/policy/docs/statcomps/oasdi_sc/
http://www.ssa.gov/policy/docs/statcomps/ssi_sc/

Social Security beneficiaries are persons receiving benefits under the Old-Age, Survivors, and Disability Insurance Program. These include retired or disabled workers covered by the program, their spouses and dependent children, and the surviving spouses and dependent children of deceased workers.

Supplemental Security Income (SSI) recipients are persons receiving SSI payments. The SSI program is a cash assistance program that provides monthly benefits to low-income aged, blind, or disabled persons.

Data are as of December of the year shown.

HOUSING, Items 87–96

Source: U.S. Census Bureau—Population Estimates Program
http://www.census.gov/popest/
Source: U.S. Census Bureau—American Community Survey, 2017 5-year Estimates
http://www.census.gov/acs/www/

Housing data for 2018 are from the Population Estimates Program. Housing unit characteristics for 2013-2017 are from the American Community Survey.

A **housing unit** is a house, apartment, mobile home or trailer, group of rooms, or single room occupied or, if vacant, intended for occupancy as separate living quarters. Separate living quarters are those in which the occupants do not live and eat with any other person in the structure and which have direct access from the outside of the building or through a common hall.

The occupants of a housing unit may be a single family, one person living alone, two or more families living together, or any other group of related or unrelated persons who share living quarters. Both occupied and vacant housing units are included in the housing inventory, although recreational vehicles, tents, caves, boats, railroad cars, and the like are included only if they are occupied as a person's usual place of residence.

A housing unit is classified as occupied if it is the usual place of residence of the person or group of persons living in it at the time of enumeration, or if the occupants are only temporarily absent (away on vacation). A household consists of all persons who occupy a housing unit as their usual place of residence. Vacant units for sale or rent include units rented or sold but not occupied and any other units held off the market.

Median value is the dollar amount that divides the distribution of specified owner-occupied housing units into two equal parts, with half of all units below the median value and half of all units above the median value. Value is defined as the respondent's estimate of what the house would sell for if it were for sale. Data are presented for single-family units on fewer than 10 acres of land that have no business or medical offices on the property.

Median rent divides the distribution of renter-occupied housing units into two equal parts. The rent concept used in this volume is gross rent, which includes the amount of cash rent a renter pays (contract rent) plus the estimated average cost of utilities and fuels, if these are paid by the renter. The rent is the amount of rent only for living quarters and excludes amounts paid for any business or other space occupied. Single-family houses on lots of 10 or more acres of land are also excluded.

Housing cost as a percentage of income is shown separately for owners with mortgages, owners without mortgages, and renters. Rent as a percentage of income is a computed ratio of gross rent and monthly household income (total household income divided by 12). Selected owner costs include utilities and fuels, mortgage payments, insurance, taxes, etc. In each case, the ratio of housing cost to income is computed separately for each housing unit. The housing cost ratios for half of all units are above the median shown in this book, and half are below the median shown in the book.

Substandard units are occupied units that are overcrowded or lack complete plumbing facilities. For the purposes of this item, "overcrowded" is defined as having 1.01 persons or more per room. Complete plumbing facilities include hot and cold piped water, a flush toilet, and a bathtub or shower. These facilities must be located inside the housing unit, but do not have to be in the same room.

CIVILIAN LABOR FORCE AND UNEMPLOYMENT, Items 97–100

Source: U.S. Bureau of Labor Statistics—Local Area Unemployment Statistics
http://www.bls.gov/lau/#tables

Data for the civilian labor force are the product of a federal-state cooperative program in which state employment security agencies prepare labor force and unemployment estimates under concepts, definitions, and technical procedures established by the Bureau of Labor Statistics (BLS). The civilian labor force consists of all civilians 16 years old and over who are either employed or unemployed.

Unemployment includes all persons who did not work during the survey week, made specific efforts to find a job during the previous four weeks, and were available for work during the survey week (except for temporary illness). Persons waiting to be called back to a job from which they had been laid off and those waiting to report to a new job within the next 30 days are included in unemployment figures.

Table B includes annual average data for the year shown. The Local Area Unemployment Statistics data are periodically updated to reflect revised inputs, reestimation, and controlling to new statewide totals.

CIVILIAN EMPLOYMENT, Items 101–103

Source: U.S. Census Bureau—American Community Survey, 2017 5-year Estimates
http://www.census.gov/acs/www/

Total employment includes all civilians 16 years old and over who were either (1) "at work"—those who did any work at all during the reference week as paid employees, worked in either their own business or profession, worked on their own farm, or worked 15 hours or more as unpaid workers in a family farm or business; or were (2) "with a job, but not at work" —those who had a job but were not at work that week due to illness, weather, industrial dispute, vacation, or other personal reasons.

The **occupational categories** are based on the occupational classification system that was developed for the 2000 census and revised in 2002 and 2010. This system consists of 539 specific occupational categories for employed persons arranged into 23 major occupational groups. This classification was developed based on the *Standard Occupational Classification (SOC) Manual: 2000*, published by the Executive Office of the President, Office of Management and Budget.

Column 102 includes the Management, business, science, and arts occupations category while Column 103 combines the Natural resources, construction, and maintenance occupations and the Production, transportation, and material moving occupations.

PRIVATE NONFARM EMPLOYMENT AND EARNINGS, Items 104–112

Source: U.S. Census Bureau—County Business Patterns
https://www.census.gov/programs-surveys/cbp.html

Data for private nonfarm employment and earnings are compiled from the payroll information reported monthly in the Census Bureau publication *County Business Patterns*. The estimates are based on surveys conducted by the Census Bureau and administrative records from the Internal Revenue Service (IRS).

The following types of employment are excluded from the tables: government employment, self-employed persons, farm workers, and domestic service workers. Railroad employment jointly covered by Social Security and railroad retirement programs, employment on oceanborne vessels, and employment in foreign countries are also excluded.

Annual payroll is the combined amount of wages paid, tips reported, and other compensation (including salaries, vacation allowances, bonuses, commissions, sick-leave pay, and the value of payments-in-kind such as free meals and lodging) paid to employees before deductions for Social Security, income tax, insurance, union dues, etc. All forms of compensation are included, regardless of whether they are subject to income tax or the Federal Insurance Contributions Act tax, with the exception of annuities, third-party sick pay, and supplemental unemployment compensation benefits (even if income tax was withheld). For corporations, total annual payroll includes compensation paid to officers and executives; for unincorporated businesses, it excludes profit or other compensation of proprietors or partners.

AGRICULTURE, ITEMS 113–132

Source: U.S. Department of Agriculture, National Agricultural Statistics Service—2017 Census of Agriculture
https://www.nass.usda.gov/Publications/AgCensus/2017/index.php

Data for the 2017 Census of Agriculture were collected in 2018, but pertain to the year 2017.

The Census Bureau took a census of agriculture every 10 years from 1840 to 1920; since 1925, this census has been taken roughly once every 5 years. The 1997 Census of Agriculture was the first one conducted by the National Agricultural Statistics Service of the U.S. Department of Agriculture. Over time, the definition of a farm has varied. For recent censuses (including the 2017 census), a farm has been defined as any place from which $1,000 or more of agricultural products were produced and sold or normally would have been sold during the census year. Dollar figures are expressed in current dollars and have not been adjusted for inflation or deflation.

The term **producer** designates a person who is involved in making decisions for the farm operation. Decisions may include decisions about such things as planting, harvesting, livestock management, and marketing. The producer may be the owner, a member of the owner's household, a hired manager, a tenant, a renter, or a sharecropper. If a person rents land to others or has land worked on shares by others, he/she is considered the producer only of the land which is retained for his/her own operation. The census collected information on the total number of male producers, the total number of female producers, and demographic information for up to four producers per farm.

The acreage designated as **land in farms** consists primarily of agricultural land used for crops, pasture, or grazing. It also includes woodland and wasteland not actually under cultivation or used for pasture or grazing, provided that this land was part of the farm operator's total operation. Land in farms is an operating-unit concept and includes all land owned and operated, as well as all land rented from others. Land used rent-free is classified as land rented from others. All grazing land, except land used under government permits on a per-head basis, was included as "land in farms" provided it was part of a farm or ranch. Land under the exclusive use of a grazing association was reported by the grazing association and included as land in farms. All land in Indian reservations used for growing crops or grazing livestock is classified as land in farms.

Irrigated land includes all land watered by any artificial or controlled means, such as sprinklers, flooding, furrows or ditches, sub-irrigation, and spreader dikes. Included are supplemental, partial, and preplant irrigation. Each acre was counted only once regardless of the number of times it was irrigated or harvested. Livestock lagoon waste water distributed by sprinkler or flood systems was also included.

Total cropland includes cropland harvested, cropland used only for pasture or grazing, cropland on which all crops failed or were abandoned, cropland in cultivated summer fallow, and cropland idle or used for cover crops or soil improvement but not harvested and not pastured or grazed.

Respondents were asked to report their estimate of the current market **value of land and buildings** owned, rented, or leased from others, and rented and leased to others. Market value refers to the respondent's estimate of what the land and buildings would sell for under current market conditions. If the value of land and buildings was not reported, it was estimated during processing by using the average value of land and buildings from similar farms in the same geographic area.

The **value of machinery and equipment** was estimated by the respondent as the current market value of all cars, trucks, tractors, combines, balers, irrigation equipment, etc., used on the farm. This value is an estimate of what the machinery and equipment would sell for in its present condition and not the replacement or depreciated value. Share interests are reported at full value at the farm where the equipment and machinery are usually kept. Only equipment that was physically located at the farm on December 31, 2017, is included.

Market value of agricultural products sold by farms represents the gross market value before taxes and the production expenses of all agricultural products sold or removed from the place in 2017, regardless of who received the payment. It is equivalent to total sales and it includes sales by producers as well as the value of any share received by partners, landlords, contractors, and others associated with the operation. It includes value of organic sales, direct sales and the value of commodities placed in the Commodity Credit Corporation (CCC) loan program. Market value of agricultural products sold does not include payments received for participation in other federal farm programs. Also, it does not include income from farm-related sources such as customwork and other agricultural services, or income from nonfarm sources.

Organic farms are those that had organic production according to USDA's National Organic Program (NOP). Respondents reported whether their organic production was certified or exempt from certification and the sales from NOP produced commodities. Not included are farms that had acres transitioning into NOP production.

Farms with **internet access** are those that reported using personal computers, laptops, or mobile devices (e.g., cell phones or tablets) to access the internet. This can be done using services such as dial-up, DSL, cable modem, fiber-optic, mobile internet service for a cell phone or other device (tablet), satellite, or other methods. In 2017 respondents were also able to report connecting with an unknown service type, labeled as "Don't know" in the publication tables.

Government payments consist of direct payments as defined by the 2002 Farm Bill; payments from Conservation Reserve Program (CRP), Wetlands Reserve Program (WRP), Farmable Wetlands Program (FWP), and Conservation Reserve Enhancement Program (CREP); loan deficiency payments; disaster payments; other conservation programs; and all other federal farm programs under which payments were made directly to farm producers, including those specified in the 2014 Agricultural Act (Farm Bill), including Agriculture Risk Coverage (ARC) and Price Loss Coverage (PLC). Commodity Credit Corporation (CCC) proceeds, amount from State and local government agricultural program payments, and federal crop insurance payments were not included in this category.

WATER CONSUMPTION, Items 133–134

Source: U.S. Geological Survey, National Water-Use Information Program, Estimated Use of Water in the United States County-Level Data for 2015, version 1.0 http://water.usgs.gov/watuse/

Every five years, the U.S. Geological Survey compiles county-level water-use estimates. This volume includes the total fresh and saline withdrawals for public water supplies in 2015, expressed as million gallons per day. Estimate of withdrawals of ground and surface water are given for the following categories of use: public water supplies, domestic, commercial, irrigation, livestock, industrial, mining, and thermoelectric power. Only public water supply is included in this volume because the other categories had not been published in time for this book. The number of gallons withdrawn per person is based on the county population in 2015. Public supply refers to water withdrawn from ground and surface sources by public and private water systems for use by cities, towns, rural water districts, mobile-home parks, Native American Indian reservations, and military bases. Public-supply facilities provide water to at least 25 persons or have a minimum of 15 service connections. Water withdrawn by public suppliers may be delivered to users for domestic, commercial, industrial, and thermoelectric-power purposes, as well as to other public-water suppliers. Public-supply water is also used for public services (public uses)—such as pools, parks, and public buildings—and may have unaccounted uses (losses) because of system leaks or such non-metered services as firefighting, flushing of water lines, or backwashing at treatment plants. Some public-supply water may be used in the processes of water and wastewater treatment. Some public suppliers treat saline water before distributing the water. The definition of saline water for public supply refers to water that requires treatment to reduce the concentration of dissolved solids through the process of desalination or dilution.

2012 ECONOMIC CENSUS: OVERVIEW, Items 135–166

Source: U.S. Census Bureau https://www.census.gov/programs-surveys/economic-census/library/publications.html

The Economic Census provides a detailed portrait of the nation's economy, from the national to the local level, once every five years. The 2012 Economic Census covers nearly all of the U.S. economy in its basic collection of establishment statistics. The 1997 Economic Census was the first major data source to use the new North American Industry Classification System (NAICS); therefore, data from this census are not comparable to economic data from prior years, which were based on the Standard Industrial Classification (SIC) system.

NAICS, developed in cooperation with Canada and Mexico, classifies North America's economic activities at two-, three-, four-, and five-digit levels of detail; the U.S. version of NAICS further defines industries to a sixth digit. The Economic Census takes advantage of this hierarchy to publish data at these successive levels of detail: sector (two-digit), subsector (three-digit), industry group (four-digit), industry (five-digit), and U.S. industry (six-digit). Information in Table A is at the two-digit level, with a few three- and four-digit items. The data in Table B are at the two-digit level.

Several key statistics are tabulated for all industries in this volume, including number of establishments (or companies), number of employees, payroll, and certain measures of output (sales, receipts, revenue, value of shipments, or value of construction work done).

Number of establishments. An establishment is a single physical location at which business is conducted. It is not necessarily identical with a company or enterprise, which may consist of one establishment or more. Economic Census figures represent a summary of reports for individual establishments rather than companies. For cases in which a census report was received, separate information was obtained for each location where business was conducted. When administrative records of other federal agencies were used instead of a census report, no information was available on the number of locations operated. Each Economic Census establishment was tabulated according to the physical location at which the business was conducted. The count of establishments represents those in business at any time during 2012.

When two activities or more were carried on at a single location under a single ownership, all activities were generally grouped together as a single establishment. The entire establishment was classified on the basis of its major activity and all of its data were included in that classification. However, when distinct and separate economic activities (for which different industry classification codes were appropriate) were conducted at a single location under a single ownership, separate establishment reports for each of the different activities were obtained in the census.

Number of employees. Paid employees consist of the full-time and part-time employees, including salaried officers and executives of corporations. Included are employees on paid sick leave, paid holidays, and paid vacations; not included are proprietors and partners of unincorporated businesses. The definition of paid employees is the same as that used by the Internal Revenue Service (IRS) on form 941.

For some industries, the Economic Census gives codes representing the number of employees as a range of numbers (for example, "100 to 249 employees" or "1,000 to 2,499" employees). In this volume, those codes have been replaced by the standard suppression code "D".

Payroll. Payroll includes all forms of compensation, such as salaries, wages, commissions, dismissal pay, bonuses, vacation allowances, sick-leave pay, and employee contributions to qualified pension plans paid during the year to all employees. For corporations, payroll includes amounts paid to officers and executives; for unincorporated businesses, it does not include profit or other compensation of proprietors or partners. Payroll is reported before deductions for Social Security, income tax, insurance, union dues, etc. This definition of payroll is the same as that used by on IRS form 941.

Sales, shipments, receipts, revenue, or business done. This measure includes the total sales, shipments, receipts, revenue, or business done by establishments within the scope of the Economic Census. The definition of each of these items is specific to the economic sector measured.

WHOLESALE TRADE, Items 135–138

Source: U.S. Census Bureau—2012 Economic Census (See Overview of 2012 Economic Census prior to Item 135)

The Wholesale Trade sector (sector 42) comprises establishments engaged in wholesaling merchandise, generally without transformation, and rendering services incidental to the sale of merchandise. The wholesaling process is an intermediate step in the distribution of merchandise.

Wholesalers are organized to sell or arrange the purchase or sale of (1) goods for resale (i.e., goods sold to other wholesalers or retailers), (2) capital or durable nonconsumer goods, and (3) raw and intermediate materials and supplies used in production.

Wholesalers sell merchandise to other businesses and normally operate from a warehouse or office. These warehouses and offices are characterized by having little or no display of merchandise. In addition, neither the design nor the location of the premises is intended to solicit walk-in traffic. Wholesalers do not normally use advertising directed to the general public. In general, customers are initially reached via telephone, in-person marketing, or specialized advertising, which may include the internet and other electronic means. Follow-up orders are either vendor-initiated or client-initiated, are usually based on previous sales, and typically exhibit strong ties between sellers and buyers. In fact, transactions are often conducted between wholesalers and clients that have long-standing business relationships.

This sector is made up of two main types of wholesalers: those that sell goods on their own account and those that arrange sales and purchases for others for a commission or fee.

(1) Establishments that sell goods on their own account are known as wholesale merchants, distributors, jobbers, drop shippers, import/export merchants, and sales branches. These establishments typically maintain their own warehouse, where they receive and handle goods for their customers. Goods are generally sold without transformation, but may include integral functions, such as sorting, packaging, labeling, and other marketing services.

(2) Establishments arranging for the purchase or sale of goods owned by others or purchasing goods on a commission basis are known as agents and brokers, commission merchants, import/export agents and brokers, auction companies, and manufacturers' representatives. These establishments operate from offices and generally do not own or handle the goods they sell.

Some wholesale establishments may be connected with a single manufacturer and promote and sell that particular manufacturer's products to a wide range of other wholesalers or retailers. Other wholesalers may be connected to a retail chain or a limited number of retail chains and only provide the products needed by the particular retail operation(s). These wholesalers may obtain the products from a wide range of manufacturers. Still other wholesalers may not take title to the goods, but act instead as agents and brokers for a commission.

Although wholesaling normally denotes sales in large volumes, durable nonconsumer goods may be sold in single units. Sales of capital or durable nonconsumer goods used in the production of goods and services, such as farm machinery, medium- and heavy-duty trucks, and industrial machinery, are always included in Wholesale Trade.

The county table includes only **Merchant wholesalers, except manufacturers' sales branches and offices**, establishments primarily engaged in buying and selling merchandise on their own account. Included here are such types of establishments as wholesale distributors and jobbers, importers, exporters, own-brand importers/marketers, terminal and country grain elevators, and farm products assemblers.

RETAIL TRADE, Items 139–142

Source: U.S. Census Bureau—2012 Economic Census (See Overview of 2012 Economic Census prior to Item 135)

The Retail Trade sector (44–45) is made up of establishments engaged in retailing merchandise, generally without transformation, and rendering services incidental to the sale of merchandise.

The retailing process is the final step in the distribution of merchandise; retailers are therefore organized to sell merchandise in small quantities to the general public. This sector comprises two main types of retailers: store and nonstore retailers.

Store retailers operate fixed point-of-sale locations, located and designed to attract a high volume of walk-in customers. In general, retail stores have extensive displays of merchandise and use mass-media advertising to attract customers. They typically sell merchandise to the general public for personal or household consumption; some also serve business and institutional clients. These include establishments such as office supply stores, computer and software stores, building materials dealers, plumbing supply stores, and electrical supply stores. Catalog showrooms, gasoline service stations, automotive dealers, and mobile home dealers are treated as store retailers.

In addition to retailing merchandise, some types of store retailers are also engaged in the provision of after-sales services, such as repair and installation. For example, new automobile dealers, electronic and appliance stores, and musical instrument and supply stores often provide repair services. As a general rule, establishments engaged in retailing merchandise and providing after-sales services are classified in this sector.

Nonstore retailers, like store retailers, are organized to serve the general public, although their retailing methods differ. The establishments of this subsector reach customers and market merchandise with methods including the broadcasting of "infomercials," the broadcasting and publishing of direct-response advertising, the publishing of paper and electronic catalogs, door-to-door solicitation, in-home demonstration, selling from portable stalls (street vendors, except food), and distribution through vending machines. Establishments engaged in the direct sale (nonstore) of products, such as home heating oil dealers and home-delivery newspaper routes are included in this sector.

The buying of goods for resale is a characteristic of retail trade establishments that distinguishes them from establishments in the Agriculture, Manufacturing, and Construction sectors. For example, farms that sell their products at or from the point of production are classified in Agriculture instead of in Retail Trade. Similarly, establishments that both manufacture and sell their products to the general public are classified in Manufacturing instead of Retail Trade. However, establishments that engage in processing activities incidental to retailing are classified in Retail Trade.

REAL ESTATE AND RENTAL AND LEASING, Items 143–146

Source: U.S. Census Bureau—2012 Economic Census (See Overview of 2012 Economic Census prior to Item 135)

The Real Estate and Rental and Leasing sector (53) comprises establishments primarily engaged in renting, leasing, or otherwise allowing the use of tangible or intangible assets, and establishments providing related services. The major portion of this sector is made up of establishments that rent, lease, or otherwise allow the use of their own assets by others. The assets may be tangible, such as real estate and equipment, or intangible, such as patents and trademarks.

This sector also includes establishments primarily engaged in managing real estate for others, selling, renting, and/or buying real estate for others, and appraising real estate. These activities are closely related to this sector's main activity. In addition, a substantial proportion of property management is self-performed by lessors.

The main components of this sector are the real estate lessors industries; equipment lessors industries (including motor vehicles, computers, and consumer goods); and lessors of nonfinancial intangible assets (except copyrighted works).

PROFESSIONAL, SCIENTIFIC, AND TECHNICAL SERVICES, Items 147–150

Source: U.S. Census Bureau—2012 Economic Census (See Overview of 2012 Economic Census prior to Item 135)

The Professional, Scientific, and Technical Services sector (54) is made up of establishments that specialize in performing professional, scientific, and technical activities for others. These activities require a high degree of expertise and training.

The establishments in this sector specialize in one or more areas and provide services to clients in a variety of industries (and, in some cases, to households). Activities performed include legal advice and representation; accounting, bookkeeping, and payroll services; architectural, engineering, and specialized design services; computer services; consulting services; research services; advertising services; photographic services; translation and interpretation services; veterinary services; and other professional, scientific, and technical services.

This sector excludes establishments primarily engaged in providing a range of day-to-day office administrative services, such as financial planning, billing and record keeping, personnel services, and physical distribution and logistics services. These establishments are classified in sector 56, Administrative and Support and Waste Management and Remediation Services.

MANUFACTURING, Items 151–154

Source: U.S. Census Bureau—2012 Economic Census (See Overview of 2012 Economic Census prior to Item 135)

The Manufacturing sector (31–33) is made up of establishments engaged in the mechanical, physical, or chemical transformation of materials, substances, or components into new products. The assembling of component parts of manufactured products is considered manufacturing, except in cases in which the activity is appropriately classified in the Construction sector. Establishments in the Manufacturing sector are often described as plants, factories, or mills, and characteristically use power-driven machines and materials-handling equipment. However, establishments that transform materials or substances into new products by hand or in the worker's home, and establishments engaged in selling to the general public products made on the same premises from which they are sold (such as bakeries, candy stores, and custom tailors) may also be included in this sector. Manufacturing establishments may process materials or contract with other establishments to process their materials for them. Both types of establishments are included in the Manufacturing sector.

The materials, substances, or components transformed by manufacturing establishments are raw materials that are products of agriculture, forestry, fishing, mining, or quarrying, or are products of other manufacturing establishments. The materials used may be purchased directly from producers, obtained through customary trade channels, or secured without recourse to the market by transferring the product from one establishment to another, under the same ownership. The new product of a manufacturing establishment may be finished (in the sense that it is ready for utilization or consumption), or it may be semifinished to become an input for an establishment engaged in further manufacturing. For example, the product of the alumina refinery is the input used in the primary production of aluminum; primary aluminum is the input used in an aluminum wire drawing plant; and aluminum wire is the input used in a fabricated wire product manufacturing establishment.

Data are included for counties with 500 or more employees in the Manufacturing sector.

ACCOMMODATION AND FOOD SERVICES, Items 155–158

Source: U.S. Census Bureau—2012 Economic Census (See Overview of 2012 Economic Census prior to Item 135)

The Accommodation and Food Services sector (72) consists of establishments that provide customers with lodging and/or meals, snacks, and beverages for immediate consumption. This sector includes both accommodation and food services establishments because the two activities are often combined at the same establishment.

Excluded from this sector are civic and social organizations, amusement and recreation parks, theaters, and other recreation or entertainment facilities providing food and beverage services.

HEALTH CARE AND SOCIAL ASSISTANCE, Items 159–162

Source: U.S. Census Bureau—2012 Economic Census (See Overview of 2012 Economic Census prior to Item 135)

The Health Care and Social Assistance sector (62) consists of establishments that provide health care and social assistance services to individuals. The sector includes both health care and social assistance because it is sometimes difficult to distinguish between the boundaries of these two activities. The industries in this sector are arranged on a continuum, starting with establishments that provide medical care exclusively, continuing with those that provide health care and social assistance, and finishing with those that provide only social assistance. The services provided by establishments in this sector are delivered by trained professionals. All industries in the sector share this commonality of process—namely, labor inputs of health practitioners or social workers with the requisite expertise. Many of the industries in the sector are defined based on the educational degree held by the practitioners included in the industry.

Excluded from this sector are aerobic classes, which can be found in subsector 713, Amusement, Gambling, and Recreation Industries; and nonmedical diet and weight-reducing centers, which can be found in subsector 812, Personal and Laundry Services. Although these can be viewed as health services, they are not typically delivered by health practitioners.

OTHER SERVICES, EXCEPT PUBLIC ADMINISTRATION Items 163–166

Source: U.S. Census Bureau—2012 Economic Census (See Overview of 2012 Economic Census prior to Item 135)

The Other Services, Except Public Administration sector (81) comprises establishments engaged in providing services not specifically categorized elsewhere in the classification system. Establishments in this sector are primarily engaged in activities such as equipment and machinery repairing, promoting or administering religious activities, grant making, and advocacy; this sector also includes establishments that provide dry-cleaning and laundry services, personal care services, death care services, pet care services, photofinishing services, temporary parking services, and dating services.

Private households that employ workers on or about the premises in activities primarily concerned with the operation of the household are included in this sector.

Excluded from this sector are establishments primarily engaged in retailing new equipment and performing repairs and general maintenance on equipment. These establishments are classified in sector 44–45, Retail Trade.

NONEMPLOYER BUSINESSES, Items 167 and 168

Source: U.S. Census Bureau—Nonemployer Statistics https://www.census.gov/programs-surveys/nonemployer-statistics.html

Nonemployer Statistics is an annual series that provides subnational economic data for businesses that have no paid employees and are subject to federal income tax. The data consist of the number of businesses and total receipts by industry. Most nonemployers are self-employed individuals operating unincorporated businesses (known as sole proprietorships), which may or may not be the owner's principal source of income.

The majority of all business establishments in the United States are nonemployers, yet these firms average less than 4 percent of all sales and receipts nationally. Due to their small economic impact, these firms are excluded from most other Census Bureau business statistics (the primary exception being the Survey of Business Owners). The Nonemployers Statistics series is the primary resource available to study the scope and activities of nonemployers at a detailed geographic level.

BUILDING PERMITS, Items 169 and 170

Source: U.S. Census Bureau—Building Permits Survey http://www.census.gov/construction/bps/

These figures represent private residential construction authorized by building permits in approximately 20,000 places in the United States. Valuation represents the expected cost of construction as recorded on the building permit. This figure usually excludes the cost of on-site and off-site development and improvements, as well as the cost of heating, plumbing, electrical, and elevator installations.

National, state, and county totals were obtained by adding the data for permit-issuing places within each jurisdiction. Not all areas of the country require a building or zoning permit. The statistics only represent those areas that do require a permit. These totals thus are limited to permits issued in the 20,000 place universe covered by the Census Bureau and may not include all permits issued within a state. Current surveys indicate that construction is undertaken for all but a very small percentage of housing units authorized by building permits.

Residential building permits include buildings with any number of housing units. Housing units exclude group quarters (such as dormitories and rooming houses), transient accommodations (such as transient hotels, motels, and tourist courts), "HUD-code" manufactured (mobile) homes, moved or relocated units, and housing units created in an existing residential or nonresidential structure.

COUNTY AREA LOCAL GOVERNMENT EMPLOYMENT AND PAYROLL, Items 171-179

Source: U.S. Census Bureau—2012 Census of Governments
https://www.census.gov/programs-surveys/cog.html

These items include data for all local governments (i.e., counties, municipalities, townships, special districts, and school districts) located within the county. The Census of Governments identifies the scope and nature of the nation's state and local government sector; provides authoritative benchmark figures of public finance and public employment; classifies local government organizations, powers, and activities; and measures federal, state, and local fiscal relationships. The Employment component was mailed **March 2012** to collect information on the number of state and local government civilian employees and their payrolls.

Government employees include all persons paid for personal services performed, including persons paid from federally funded programs, paid elected or appointed officials, persons in a paid leave status, and persons paid on a per meeting, annual, semi-annual, or quarterly basis. Unpaid officials, pensioners, persons whose work is performed on a fee basis, and contractors and their employees are excluded from the count of employees. **Full-Time Equivalent employees** is a computed statistic representing the number of full-time employees that could have been employed if the reported number of hours worked by part-time employees had been worked by full-time employees. This statistic is calculated separately for each function of a government by dividing the "part-time hours paid" by the standard number of hours for full-time employees in the particular government and then adding the resulting quotient to the number of full-time employees.

March payroll represents gross payroll amounts for the one-month period of March for full-time and part-time employees. Gross payroll includes all salaries, wages, fees, commissions, and overtime paid to employees **before** withholdings for taxes, insurance, etc. It also includes incentive payments that are paid at regular pay intervals. It excludes employer share of fringe benefits like retirement, Social Security, health and life insurance, lump sum payments, and so forth.

Administration and Judicial and Legal combines **Financial administration, Other government administration, and Judicial and Legal** activities. **Financial administration includes** activities concerned with tax assessment and collection, custody and disbursement of funds, debt management, administration of trust funds, budgeting, and other government-wide financial management activities. This function is not applied to school district or special district governments. **Other government administration** applies to the legislative and government-wide administrative agencies of governments. Included here are overall planning and zoning activities, and central personnel and administrative activities. This function is not applied to school district or special district governments. **Judicial and legal** includes all court and court related activities (except probation and parole activities that are included at the "Correction" function), court activities of sheriff's offices, prosecuting attorneys' and public defenders' offices, legal departments, and attorneys providing government-wide legal service.

Police and Corrections includes all activities concerned, with the enforcement of law and order, including coroner's offices, police training academies, investigation bureaus, and local jails, "lockups", or other detention facilities not intended to serve as correctional facilities. **Corrections** includes activities pertaining to the confinement and correction of adults and minors convicted of criminal offenses. Pardon, probation, and parole activities are also included here.

Fire protection includes local government fire protection and prevention activities plus any ambulance, rescue, or other auxiliary services provided by a fire protection agency. Volunteer firefighters, if remunerated for their services on a "per fire" or some other basis, are included as part-time employees.

Highways and transportation includes activities associated with the maintenance and operation of streets, roads, sidewalks, bridges, tunnels, toll roads, and ferries. Snow and ice removal, street lighting, and highway and traffic engineering activities are also included here. Also included are the operation, maintenance, and construction of public mass transit systems, including subways, surface rails, and buses, and the provision, construction, operation, maintenance; support of public waterways, harbors, docks, wharves, and related marine terminal facilities; and activities associated with the operation and support of publicly operated airport facilities.

Health and Welfare includes **Health, Hospitals, and Public welfare.** **Health** includes administration of public health programs, community and visiting nurse services, immunization programs, drug abuse rehabilitation programs, health and food inspection activities, operation of outpatient clinics, and environmental pollution control activities. **Hospitals** includes only government operated medical care facilities that provide inpatient care. Employees and payrolls of private corporations that lease and operate government-owned hospital facilities are excluded.

Public Welfare includes the administration of various public assistance programs for the needy, veteran services, operation of nursing homes, indigent care institutions, and programs that provide payments for medical care, handicap transportation, and other services for the needy.

Natural resources and Utilities includes activities primarily concerned with the conservation and development of natural resources (soil, water, energy, minerals, etc.) and the regulation of industries that develop, utilize, or affect natural resources, as well as the operation and maintenance of **parks**, playgrounds, swimming pools, public beaches, auditoriums, public golf courses, museums, marinas, botanical gardens, and zoological parks. **Utilities, sewerage, and waste management** includes operation, maintenance, and construction of public water supply systems, including production, acquisition, and distribution of water to general public or to other public or private utilities, for residential, commercial, and industrial use; activities associated with the production or acquisition and distribution of electric power; provision, maintenance, and operation of sanitary and storm sewer systems and sewage disposal and treatment facilities; and refuse collection and disposal, operation of sanitary landfills, and street cleaning activities.

Education and libraries includes activities associated with the operation of public elementary and secondary schools and locally operated vocational-technical schools. Special education programs operated by elementary and secondary school systems are also included as are all ancillary services associated with the operation of schools, such as pupil transportation and food service. Also included are the establishment and provision of libraries for use by the general public and the technical support of privately operated libraries. This category includes classroom teachers, principals, supervisors of instruction, librarians, teacher aides, library aides, and guidance and psychological personnel as well as school superintendents and other administrative personnel, clerical and secretarial staffs, plant operation and maintenance personnel, health and recreation employees, transportation and food service personnel, and any student employees. Also included are any degree granting institutions that provide academic training above grade 12.

LOCAL GOVERNMENT FINANCES, Items 180–193

Source: U.S. Census Bureau—2012 Census of Governments
https://www.census.gov/programs-surveys/cog.html

Data on local government finances are based on result of the 2012 Census of Governments. For each county area, the financial data comprise amounts for all local governments—not only the county government, but also any municipalities, townships, school districts, and special districts within the county. Statistics from governmental units located in two or more county areas are assigned to the county area containing the administrative office.

Revenue and expenditure items include all amounts of money received and paid out, respectively, by a government and its agencies (net of correcting transactions such as recoveries of refunds), with the exception of amounts for debt issuance and retirement and for loan and investment, agency, and private transactions.

Payments among the various funds and agencies of a particular government are excluded from revenue and expenditure items as representing internal transfers. Therefore, a government's contribution to a retirement fund that it administers is not counted as expenditure, nor is the receipt of this contribution by the retirement fund counted as revenue.

Total **general revenue** includes all revenue except utility, liquor stores, and insurance trust revenue. All tax revenue and intergovernmental revenue, even if designated for employee-retirement or local utility purpose, are classified as general revenue.

Intergovernmental revenue covers amounts received from the federal government as fiscal aid, reimbursements for performance of general government functions and specific services for the paying government, or in lieu of taxes. It excludes any amounts received from other governments from the sale of property, commodities, and utility services.

Taxes consist of compulsory contributions exacted by governments for public purposes. However, this category excludes employer and employee payments for retirement and social insurance purposes, which are classified as insurance trust revenue; it also excludes special assessments, which are classified as non-tax general revenue. Property taxes are taxes conditioned on ownership of property and assessed by its value. Sales and gross receipts taxes do not include dealer discounts, or "commissions" allowed to merchants for collection of taxes from consumers. General sales taxes and selected taxes on sales of motor fuels, tobacco products, and other particular commodities and services are included.

General government expenditure includes capital outlay, a major portion of which is commonly financed by borrowing. Government revenue does not include receipts from borrowing. Among other things, this distorts the relationship between totals of revenue and expenditure figures that are presented and renders it useless as a direct measure of the degree of budgetary "balance" (as that term is generally applied).

Direct general expenditure comprises all expenditures of the local governments, excluding utility, liquor stores, insurance trust expenditures, and any intergovernmental payments.

Local government expenditure for **education** is mainly for the provision and general support of schools and other educational facilities and services, including those for educational institutions beyond high school. They cover such related services as student transportation; school lunch and other cafeteria operations; school health, recreation, and library services; and dormitories, dining halls, and bookstores operated by public institutions of higher education.

Health and hospital expenditure includes health research; clinics; nursing; immunization; other categorical, environmental, and general health services provided by health agencies; establishment and operation of hospital facilities; provision of hospital care; and support of other public and private hospitals.

Police protection expenditure includes police activities such as patrols, communications, custody of persons awaiting trial, and vehicular inspection.

Public welfare expenditure covers support of and assistance to needy persons; this aid is contingent upon the person's needs. Included are cash assistance paid directly to needy persons under categorical (Old Age Assistance, Temporary Assistance for Needy Families, Aid to the Blind, and Aid to the Disabled) and other welfare programs; vendor payments made directly to private purveyors for medical care, burials, and other commodities and services provided under welfare programs; welfare institutions; and any intergovernmental or other direct expenditure for welfare purposes. Pensions to former employees and other benefits not contingent on need are excluded.

Highway expenditure is for the provision and maintenance of highway facilities, including toll turnpikes, bridges, tunnels, and ferries, as well as regular roads, highways, and streets. Also included are expenditures for street lighting and for snow and ice removal. Not included are highway policing and traffic control, which are considered part of police protection

Debt outstanding includes all long-term debt obligations of the government and its agencies (exclusive of utility debt) and all interest-bearing, short-term (repayable within one year) debt obligations remaining unpaid at the close of the fiscal year. It includes judgments, mortgages, and revenue bonds, as well as general obligation bonds, notes, and interest-bearing warrants. This category consists of non-interest-bearing, short-term obligations; inter-fund obligations; amounts owed in a trust or agency capacity; advances and contingent loans from other governments; and rights of individuals to benefit from government-administered employee-retirement funds.

GOVERNMENT EMPLOYMENT, Items 194–196

Source: U.S. Bureau of Economic Analysis—Regional Economic Accounts
http://www.bea.gov/regional/index.htm#state

Employment is measured as the average annual sum of full-time and part-time jobs. The estimates are on a place-of-work basis. State and local government employment includes person employed in all state and local government agencies and enterprises. Data for federal civilian employment include civilian employees of the federal government, including civilian employees of the Department of Defense. Military employment includes all persons on active duty status.

INDIVIDUAL INCOME TAX RETURNS, Items 197–199

Source: U.S. Internal Revenue Servicw, Statistics of Income Program
https://www.irs.gov/uac/soi-tax-stats-county-data-2016

The Revenue Act of 1916 mandated the annual publication of statistics related to "the operations of the internal revenue laws" as they affect individuals, all forms of businesses, estates. nonprofit organizations, trusts, and investments abroad and foreign investments in the United States. The Statistics of Income (SOI) division fulfills this function by collecting and processing data so that they become informative and by sharing information about how the tax system works with other government agencies and the general public. Publication types include traditional print sources, Internet files, CD-ROMs, and files sent via e-mail. SOI has an information office, Statistical Information Services, to facilitate the dissemination of SOI data.

SOI bases its county data on administrative records of individual income tax returns (Forms 1040) from the Internal Revenue Service (IRS) Individual Master File (IMF) system. Included in these data are returns filed during the 12-month period, January 1, 2017 to December 31, 2017. While the bulk of returns filed during the 12-month period are primarily for Tax Year 2016, the IRS received a limited number of returns for tax years before 2016 and these have been included within the county data.

Data do not represent the full U.S. population because many individuals are not required to file an individual income tax return. The address shown on the tax return may differ from the taxpayer's actual residence. State and county codes were based on the ZIP code shown on the return. Excluded were tax returns filed without a ZIP code and returns filed with a ZIP code that did not match the State code shown on the return.

SOI did not attempt to correct any ZIP codes on the returns; however, it did take the following precautions to avoid disclosing information about specific taxpayers: Excluded from the data are items with less than 20 returns within a county. Also excluded are tax returns representing a specified percentage of the total of any particular cell. For example, if one return represented 75 percent of the value of a given cell, the return was suppressed from the county detail. The actual threshold percentage used cannot be released.

Column 197 show the number of returns. Column 198 shows the mean Adjusted Gross Income for the county and column 199 shows the mean income tax (line 56 on Form 1040). for the county.

TABLE C—METROPOLITAN AREAS

Table C presents 199 items for the 382 metropolitan statistical areas (MSAs) and 31 metropolitan divisions in the United States. The metropolitan areas are presented in alphabetical order, and the metropolitan divisions are presented in alphabetical order within the appropriate metropolitan area. For some data items, the metropolitan area data have been aggregated from county data sources.

LAND AREA, Items 1 and 4

Source: U.S. Census Bureau—2018 U.S. Gazetteer Files,
http://www.census.gov/geo/maps-data/data/gazetteer2018.html

Land area measurements are shown to the nearest square mile. Land area is an area measurement providing the size, in square miles, of the land portions of each county.

POPULATION, Items 2–4

Source: U.S. Census Bureau—Population Estimates
https://www.census.gov/programs-surveys/popest.html

The population data are Census Bureau estimates of the resident population as of July 1 of the year shown. The ranks are shown for metropolitan statistical areas, but exclude metropolitan divisions.

POPULATION AND POPULATION CHARACTERISTICS, Items 5–19

Source: U.S. Census Bureau—Population Estimates
https://www.census.gov/programs-surveys/popest.html

The concept of race, as used by the Census Bureau, reflects self-identification by persons according to the race or races with which they most closely identify. These categories are sociopolitical constructs and should not be interpreted as being scientific or anthropological in nature. Furthermore, race categories include both racial and national origin groups.

Beginning with the 2000 census, respondents were offered the option of selecting one or more races. This option was not available in prior censuses; thus, comparisons between censuses should be made with caution. In Table C, Columns 5 through 8 refer to individuals who identified with each racial category, either alone or in combination with other races. The estimates exclude persons of Hispanic or Latino origin from all race groups. Because respondents could include as many categories as they wished, and because the columns refer to the percentage of the population, the total will often exceed 100 percent.

The **White** population is defined as persons who indicated their race as White, as well as persons who did not classify themselves in one of the specific race categories listed on the questionnaire but entered a nationality such as Irish, German, Italian, Lebanese, Near Easterner, Arab, or Polish.

The **Black** population includes persons who indicated their race as "Black or African American" as well as persons who did not classify themselves in one of the specific race categories but reported entries such as African American, Afro American, Kenyan, Nigerian, or Haitian.

The **American Indian or Alaska Native** population includes persons who indicated their race as American Indian or Alaska Native, as well as persons who did not classify themselves in one of the specific race categories but reported entries such as Canadian Indian, French-American Indian, Spanish-American Indian, Eskimo, Aleut, Alaska Indian, or any of the American Indian or Alaska Native tribes.

The **Asian and Pacific Islander** population combines two census groupings: **Asian** and **Native Hawaiian or Other Pacific Islander**. The **Asian** population includes persons who indicated their race as Asian Indian, Chinese, Filipino, Japanese, Korean, Vietnamese, or "Other Asian," as well as persons who provided write-in entries of such groups as Cambodian, Laotian, Hmong, Pakistani, or Taiwanese. The **Native Hawaiian or Other Pacific Islander** population includes persons who indicated their race as "Native Hawaiian," "Guamanian or Chamorro," "Samoan," or "Other Pacific Islander," as well as persons who reported entries such as Part Hawaiian, American Samoan, Fijian, Melanesian, or Tahitian.

The sum of the four individual race alone or in combination categories in this book will often add to more than the total population because people who reported more than one race were tallied in each race category. In this book, the Asian group has been combined with the Native Hawaiian and Other Pacific Islander group, causing double-counting of persons who identify with both groups. This is especially pronounced in Hawaii.

The **Hispanic population** is based on a complete-count question that asked respondents "Is this person Spanish/Hispanic/Latino?" Persons marking any one of the four Hispanic categories (i.e., Mexican, Puerto Rican, Cuban, or other Spanish) are collectively referred to as Hispanic.

Age is defined as age at last birthday (number of completed years since birth), as of April 1 of the census year.

The **female** population is shown as a percentage of total population.

POPULATION AND COMPONENTS OF CHANGE, Items 20–26
Source: U.S. Census Bureau—Decennial Censuses and Population Estimates
http://www.census.gov/main/www/cen2000.html
https://www.census.gov/programs-surveys/popest.html
http://www.census.gov/2010census/data/

The population data for 2000 and 2010 are from the decennial censuses and represent the resident population as of April 1 of those years. The components of change are based on Census Bureau estimates of the resident population as of July 1 of 2016. The change in population between 2010 and 2016 is made up of (a) natural increase—births minus deaths, and (b) net migration—the difference between the number of persons moving into a particular area and the number of persons moving out of the area. Net migration is composed of internal and international migration.

Because the 2018 population estimates are based on a model that begins with a national population estimate, the county and metropolitan area components of change do not always exactly add up to the difference between the 2010 census population and the 2017 estimates.

HOUSEHOLDS, Items 27–31
Source: U.S. Census Bureau—American Community Survey, 2017 1-year Estimates
http://www.census.gov/acs/www/

A **household** includes all of the persons who occupy a housing unit. (Persons not living in households are classified as living in group quarters.) A housing unit is a house, an apartment, a mobile home, a group of rooms, or a single room occupied (or, if vacant, intended for occupancy) as separate living quarters. Separate living quarters are those in which the occupants live separately from any other persons in the building and have direct access from the outside of the building or through a common hall. The occupants may be a single family, one person living alone, two or more families living together, or any other group of related or unrelated persons who share living quarters. The number of households is the same as the number of year-round occupied housing units.

A **family** includes a householder and one or more other persons living in the same household who are related to the householder by birth, marriage, or adoption. All persons in a household who are related to the householder are regarded as members of his or her family. A **family household** may contain persons not related to the householder; thus, family households may include more members than families do. A household can contain only one family for the purposes of census tabulations. Not all households contain families, as a household may comprise a group of unrelated persons or of one person living alone. Families are classified by type as either a "husband-wife family" or "other family," according to the presence or absence of a spouse.

The measure of **persons per household** is obtained by dividing the number of persons in households by the number of households or householders. One person in each household is designated as the householder. In most cases, this is the person (or one of the persons) in whose name the house is owned, being bought, or rented. If there is no such person in the household, any adult household member 15 years old and over can be designated as the householder.

The category **female family householder** includes only female-headed family households with no spouse present.

GROUP QUARTERS, Item 32

Source: U.S. Census Bureau—Population Estimates
https://www.census.gov/programs-surveys/popest.html

The Census Bureau classifies all persons not living in households as living in group quarters; this category includes both the institutional and noninstitutional populations. The institutionalized population includes persons under formally authorized, supervised care or custody in institutions, such as correctional institutions, nursing homes, mental (psychiatric) hospitals, and juvenile institutions. The noninstitutionalized population includes persons who live in group quarters other than institutions, such as college dormitories, military quarters, and group homes. This volume includes the total number of persons in group quarters.

DAYTIME POPULATION, Items 33 and 34

Source: U.S. Census Bureau—American Community Survey, 2017 1-year Estimates
http://www.census.gov/acs/www/

Daytime population refers to the number of persons who are present in an area or place during normal business hours, including workers. This can be contrasted with the "resident" population, which is present during the evening and nighttime hours. The daytime population estimate is calculated by adding the total resident population and the total workers working in the area/place, and then subtracting the total workers living in the area/place from that result. Information on the expansion or contraction experienced by different communities between their nighttime and daytime populations is important for many planning purposes, especially those concerning transportation, disaster, and relief operations.

The employment/residence ratio is a measure of the total number of workers working in an area or place, relative to the total number of workers living in the area or place. It is often used as a rough indication of the jobs-workers balance in an area/place, although it does not take into account whether the resident workers possess the skills needed for the jobs available in their particular area/place. The employment/residence ratio is calculated by dividing the number of total workers working in an area/place by the number of total workers residing in the area/place.

BIRTHS AND DEATHS, Items 35–38

Source: U.S. Census Bureau—Population Estimates
https://www.census.gov/programs-surveys/popest.html

The numbers of births and deaths are from the Census Bureau's Population Estimates Program. They represent the total number of live births and deaths occurring to residents of an area as estimated using reports from the National Center for Health Statistics (NCHS) and the Federal-State Cooperative for Population Estimates (FSCPE). The rates measure births and deaths during the specified time period as a proportion of an area's population. Rates are expressed per 1,000 population estimated as of July 1. These numbers and rates do not represent the calendar year, but rather the year-long period ending on July 1.

PERSONS UNDER 65 WITH NO HEALTH INSURANCE, Items 39 and 40

Source: U.S. Census Bureau—Small Area Health Insurance Estimates
https://www.census.gov/programs-surveys/sahie.html

The Small Area Health Insurance Estimates (SAHIE) program develops model-based estimates of health insurance coverage for counties and states. This developmental program builds on the work of the Small Area Income and Poverty Estimates (SAIPE) program. The SAHIE program models health insurance coverage by combining survey data with population estimates and administrative records. These estimates combine data from administrative records, postcensal population estimates, and the decennial census with direct estimates from the American Community Survey to provide consistent and reliable single-year estimates. These model-based single-year estimates are more reflective of current conditions than multi-year survey estimates. The metropolitan area estimates have been aggregated from the county estimates.

MEDICARE ENROLLMENT, Items 41–43

Source: U.S. Department of Health and Human Services, Centers for Medicare and Medicaid Services
https://www.cms.gov/Research-Statistics-Data-and-Systems/Statistics-Trends-and-Reports/CMSProgramStatistics/Dashboard.html

The Centers for Medicare and Medicaid Services (CMS) administers Medicare, which provides health insurance to persons 65 years old and over, persons with permanent kidney failure, and certain persons with disabilities. Original Medicare has two parts: Hospital Insurance and Supplemental Medical Insurance. In recent years, Medicare has been expanded to include two new programs: Medicare Advantage plans and prescription drug coverage. Medicare Advantage Plans are health plan options that are approved by Medicare but run by private companies. Medicare prescription drug plans can be part of Medicare Advantage plans or stand-alone drug plans.

Persons who are eligible for Medicare can enroll in Part A (Hospital Insurance) at no charge, and can choose to pay a monthly premium to enroll in Part B. Most eligible persons are enrolled in Part A, and most enrollees in Part A are also enrolled in Part B (Supplemental Medical Insurance.) This table includes persons who were enrolled in both Part A and Part B during 2014.

Part B beneficiaries can choose to enroll in **Original Medicare**, a fee-for-service plan administered by the Centers for Medicare and Medicaid Services, or in a **Medicare Advantage** plan.

Medicare Advantage plans include private fee-for-service plans, preferred provider organizations, health maintenance organizations, medical savings account plans, demonstration plans, and programs for all-inclusive care for the elderly.

The annual Medicare enrollment counts are determined using a person-year methodology. For each calendar year, total person-year counts are determined by summing the total number of months that each beneficiary is enrolled during the year and dividing by 12. Using this methodology, a beneficiary's partial-year enrollment may be counted in more than one category (i.e., both Original Medicare and Medicare Advantage).

CRIME, Items 44–47
Source: U.S. Federal Bureau of Investigation—Uniform Crime Reports
https://ucr.fbi.gov/crime-in-the.u.s/2016/crime-in-the-u.s.-2016

Crime data are as reported to the Federal Bureau of Investigation (FBI) by law enforcement agencies. The Metropolitan Area numbers in this volume are from *Crime in the United States* and have been adjusted by the FBI to include estimates of areas that did not report. Where the FBI analysts determined that the numbers reflected underreporting or overreporting or other factors that made them unreliable, the numbers have not been included.

Through the voluntary contribution of crime statistics by law enforcement agencies across the United States, the Uniform Crime Reporting (UCR) Program provides periodic assessments of crime in the nation as measured by offenses that have come to the attention of the law enforcement community. The Committee on Uniform Crime Records of the International Association of Chiefs of Police initiated this voluntary national data collection effort in 1930. The UCR Program contributors compile and submit their crime data either directly to the FBI or through state-level UCR Programs.

Seven offenses, because of their severity, frequency of occurrence, and likelihood of being reported to police, were initially selected to serve as an index for evaluating fluctuations in the volume of crime. These serious crimes were murder and nonnegligent manslaughter, forcible rape, robbery, aggravated assault, burglary, larceny-theft, and motor vehicle theft. By congressional mandate, arson was added as the eighth index offense in 1979. The totals shown in this volume do not include arson.

In 2004, the FBI discontinued the use of the Crime Index in the UCR Program and its publications, stating that the Crime Index was driven upward by the offense with the highest number of cases (in this case, larceny-theft), creating a bias against jurisdictions with a high number of larceny-thefts but a low number of other serious crimes, such as murder and forcible rape. The FBI is currently publishing a violent crime total and property crime total until a more viable index is developed. This book includes the crime total, as well as violent crime and property crime rates.

In 2013, the FBI adopted a new definition of rape. Rape is now defined as, "Penetration, no matter how slight, of the vagina or anus with any body part or object, or oral penetration by a sex organ of another person, without the consent of the victim." The new definition updated the 80-year-old historical definition of rape which was "carnal knowledge of a female forcibly and against her will." Effectively, the revised definition expands rape to include both male and female victims and offenders, and reflects the various forms of sexual penetration understood to be rape, especially nonconsenting acts of sodomy, and sexual assaults with objects.

Violent crimes include four categories of offenses: (1) Murder and nonnegligent manslaughter, as defined in the UCR Program, is the willful (nonnegligent) killing of one human being by another. This offense excludes deaths caused by negligence, suicide, or accident; justifiable homicides; and attempts to murder or assaults to murder. (2) Rape is the penetration, no matter how slight, of the vagina or anus with any body part or object, or oral penetration by a sex organ of another person, without the consent of the victim. Assaults or attempts to commit rape by force or threat of force are also included; however, statutory rape (without force) and other sex offenses are excluded. (3) Robbery is the taking or attempting to take anything of value from the care, custody, or control of a person or persons by force or threat of force or violence and/or by putting the victim in fear. (4) Aggravated assault is an unlawful attack by one person upon another for the purpose of inflicting severe or aggravated bodily injury. This type of assault is usually accompanied by the use of a weapon or by other means likely to produce death or great bodily harm. Attempts are included, since injury does not necessarily have to result when a gun, knife, or other weapon is used, as these incidents could and probably would result in a serious personal injury if the crime were successfully completed.

Property crimes include three categories: (1) Burglary, or breaking and entering, is the unlawful entry of a structure to commit a felony or theft, even though no force was used to gain entrance. (2) Larceny-theft is the unauthorized taking of the personal property of another, without the use of force. (3) Motor vehicle theft is the unauthorized taking of any motor vehicle.

Rates are based on population estimates provided by the FBI. If the population total for the metropolitan area was less than 75 percent of the area's population (as estimated by the Census Bureau), the total was not considered representative of the metropolitan area as a whole and was not published. For many of the metropolitan areas, the FBI has estimated violent and property crimes, adjusted to include areas that did not report and to correct for underreporting and overreporting, as published in the FBI's *Crime in the United States*. If a metropolitan area was not included in *Crime in the United States,* it is not included in Table C in this volume.

EDUCATION—SCHOOL ENROLLMENT AND EDUCATIONAL ATTAINMENT, Items 48–51

Source: U.S. Census Bureau—American Community Survey, 2017 1-year Estimates
http://www.census.gov/acs/www/

Data on **school enrollment** and educational attainment were derived from a sample of the population. Persons were classified as enrolled in school if they reported attending a "regular" public or private school (or college) during the three months prior to the survey. The instructions were to "include only nursery school, kindergarten, elementary school, and schooling which would lead to a high school diploma or a college degree" as regular school. The Census Bureau defines a public school as "any school or college controlled and supported by a local, county, state, or federal government." Schools primarily supported and controlled by religious organizations or other private groups are defined as private schools.

Data on **educational attainment** are tabulated for the population 25 years old and over. The data were derived from a question that asked respondents for the highest level of school completed or the highest degree received. Persons who had passed a high school equivalency examination were considered high school graduates. Schooling received in foreign schools was to be reported as the equivalent grade or years in the regular American school system.

Vocational and technical training, such as barber school training; business, trade, technical, and vocational schools; or other training for a specific trade are specifically excluded.

High school graduate or less. This category includes persons whose highest degree was a high school diploma or its equivalent, and those who reported any level lower than a high school diploma.

Bachelor's degree or more. This category includes persons who have received bachelor's degrees, master's degrees, professional school degrees (such as law school or medical school degrees), and doctoral degrees.

LOCAL GOVERNMENT EDUCATION EXPENDITURES, Items 52 and 53

U.S. Department of Education, National Center for Education Statistics, Common Core of Data (CCD), "Local Education Agency (School District) Universe Survey Directory Data", 2014-15 v.1a; "Local Education Agency (School District) Universe Survey Geographic Data (EDGE)", 2014-15 v.1a; "School District Finance Survey (F-33)", 2014-15 (FY 2015) v.1a.

https://nces.ed.gov/ccd/

Expenditures are for elementary and secondary Education which includes prekindergarten through twelfth grade regular, special, and vocational education, as well as cocurricular, community service, and adult education programs provided by a public school system. The financial activities of these systems for all instruction, support service, and noninstructional activities are included

Current Spending comprises current operation expenditure, payments made by the state government on behalf of school systems, and transfers made by school systems into their own retirement funds. Current operation expenditures include direct expenditure for salaries, employee benefits, purchased professional and technical services, purchased property and other services, and supplies. It includes gross school system expenditure for instruction, support services, and noninstructional functions. It excludes expenditure for debt service, capital outlay, and reimbursement to other governments (including other school systems).

Current expenditure per student is current expenditure divided by the number of students enrolled. The number of students enrolled is based on an annual "membership" count of students on or about October 1.

INCOME AND POVERTY Items 54–61

Source: U.S. Census Bureau—American Community Survey, 2017 1-year Estimates
http://www.census.gov/acs/www/

The data on income were derived from responses of a sample of persons 15 years old and over. **Total money income** is the sum of the amounts reported separately for wage or salary income; net self-employment income; interest, dividends, or net rental or royalty income or income from estates and trusts; Social Security or railroad retirement income; Supplemental Security Income (SSI); public assistance or welfare payments; retirement, survivor, or disability pensions; and all other income. Receipts from the following sources are not included as income: capital gains; money received from the sale of property (unless the recipient was engaged in the business of selling such property); the value of income "in kind" from food stamps, public housing subsidies, medical care, employer contributions for individuals, etc.; withdrawal of bank deposits; money borrowed; tax refunds; exchange of money between relatives living in the same household; and gifts, lump-sum inheritances, insurance payments, and other types of lump-sum receipts.

Money income differs in definition from personal income (item 62). For example, money income does not include the pension rights, employer provided health insurance, food stamps, or Medicare payments that are included in personal income.

Per capita income is the mean income computed for every man, woman, and child in a particular group. It is derived by dividing the aggregate income of a particular group by the resident population in that group in the survey year. Per capita income is rounded to the nearest whole dollar.

Household income includes the income of the householder and all other individuals 15 years old and over in the household, whether or not they are related to the householder. Since many households consist of only one person, median household income is usually less than median family income. Although the household income statistics cover the year preceding the survey, the characteristics of individuals and the composition of households refer to the date of the survey. Thus, the income of the household does not include amounts received by individuals who were members of the household during the year if these individuals were no longer residing in the household at the time of the survey. Similarly, income amounts reported by individuals who did not reside in the household during the year but who were members of the household at the time of the survey are included. However, the

Poverty Thresholds for 2017 by Size of Family and Number of Related Children Under 18 Years

Size of family unit	Weighted average thresholds	Related children under 18 years								
		None	One	Two	Three	Four	Five	Six	Seven	Eight or more
One person (unrelated individual):	12,488									
Under age 65	12,752	12,752								
Aged 65 and older.....................	11,756	11,756								
Two people:	15,877									
Householder under age 65........	16,493	16,414	16,895							
Householder aged 65 and older	14,828	14,816	16,831							
Three people................................	19,515	19,173	19,730	19,749						
Four people..................................	25,094	25,283	25,696	24,858	24,944					
Five people	29,714	30,490	30,933	29,986	29,253	28,805				
Six people	33,618	35,069	35,208	34,482	33,787	32,753	32,140			
Seven people................................	38,173	40,351	40,603	39,734	39,129	38,001	36,685	35,242		
Eight people..................................	42,684	45,129	45,528	44,708	43,990	42,971	41,678	40,332	39,990	
Nine people or more	50,681	54,287	54,550	53,825	53,216	52,216	50,840	49,595	49,287	47,389

Source: U.S. Census Bureau.

composition of most households was the same during the year as it was at the time of the survey.

Mean household income is the amount obtained by dividing the aggregate income of all households by the total number of households. The mean is based on the distribution of the total number of households including those with no income. Mean income is rounded to the nearest whole dollar. Care should be exercised in using and interpreting mean income values for small subgroups of the population. Because the mean is influenced strongly by extreme values in the distribution, it is especially susceptible to the effects of sampling variability, misreporting, and processing errors. The median, which is not affected by extreme values, is, therefore, a better measure than the mean when the population base is small.

Median income divides the income distribution into two equal parts, with half of all cases below the median income level and half of all cases above the median income level. For households, the median income is based on the distribution of the total number of households, including those with no income. Median income for households is computed on the basis of a standard distribution with a minimum value of less than $2,500 and a maximum value of $200,000 or more and is rounded to the nearest whole dollar. Median income figures are calculated using linear interpolation if the width of the interval containing the estimate is $2,500 or less. If the width of the interval containing the estimate is greater than $2,500, Pareto interpolation is used.

Income components were reported for the 12 months preceding the interview month. Monthly Consumer Price Indices (CPI) factors were used to inflation-adjust these components to a reference calendar year (January through December). For example, a household interviewed in March 2012 reports their income for March 2011 through February 2012. Their income is adjusted to the 2012 reference calendar year by multiplying their reported income by 2012 average annual CPI (January-December 2008) and then dividing by the average CPI for March 2011–February 2012. However, the estimates do not reflect the price and cost-of-living differences that may exist between areas.

The **poverty status** data were derived from data collected on the number of persons in a household, each person's relationship to the householder, and income data. The Social Security Administration (SSA) developed the original poverty definition in 1964, which federal interagency committees subsequently revised in 1969 and 1980. The Office of Management and Budget's (OMB) *Directive 14* prescribes the SSA's definition as the official poverty measure for federal agencies to use in their statistical work. Poverty statistics presented in American Community Survey products adhere to the standards defined by OMB in *Directive 14*.

Poverty thresholds vary depending on three criteria: size of family, number of children, and, for one- and two-person families, age of householder. In determining the poverty status of families and unrelated individuals, the Census Bureau uses thresholds (income cutoffs) arranged in a two-dimensional matrix. The matrix consists of family size (from one person to nine or more persons), cross-classified by presence and number of family members under 18 years old (from no children present to eight or more children present). Unrelated individuals and two-person families are further differentiated by age of reference person (under 65 years old and 65 years old and over). To determine a person's poverty status, the person's total family income over the previous 12 months is compared with the poverty threshold appropriate for that person's family size and composition. If the total income of that person's family is less than the threshold appropriate for that family, then the person is considered poor or "below the poverty level," together with every member of his or her family. If a person is not living with anyone related by birth, marriage, or adoption, then the person's own income is compared with his or her poverty threshold. The total number of persons below the poverty level is the sum of persons in families and the number of unrelated individuals with incomes below the poverty level over the previous 12 months.

[INSERT 2017 POVERTY THRESHOLD TABLE – SEE ATTACHED PAGE]

PERSONAL INCOME AND EARNINGS, Items 62–83

Source: U.S. Bureau of Economic Analysis, Regional Economic Accounts
http://www.bea.gov/regional/index.htm#state

Total personal income is the current income received by residents of an area from all sources. It is measured before deductions of income and other personal taxes, but after deductions of personal contributions for Social Security, government retirement, and other social insurance programs. It consists of **wage and salary disbursements** (covering all employee earnings, including executive salaries, bonuses, commissions, payments-in-kind, incentive payments, and tips); various types of supplementary earnings, such as employers' contributions to pension funds (termed "other labor income" or "supplements to wages and salaries"); proprietors' income; rental income of persons; dividends; personal interest income; and government and business transfer payments.

Per capita personal income is based on the resident population estimated as of July 1 of the year shown.

Proprietors' income is the monetary income and income-in-kind of proprietorships and partnerships (including the independent professions) and the income of tax-exempt cooperatives. Dividends are cash payments by corporations to stockholders who are U.S. residents. **Interest** is the monetary and imputed interest income of persons from all sources. **Rent** is the monetary income of persons from the rental of real property, except the income of persons primarily engaged in the real estate business; the imputed net rental income of owner-occupants of nonfarm dwellings; and the royalties received by persons.

Transfer payments are income for which services are not currently rendered. They consist of both government and business transfer payments. Government transfer payments include payments under the following programs: Federal Old-Age, Survivors, and Disability Insurance ("Social Security"); Medicare and medical vendor payments; unemployment insurance; railroad and government retirement; federal- and state-government-insured workers' compensation; veterans' benefits, including veterans' life insurance; food stamps; black lung payments; Supplemental Security Income; and Temporary Assistance for Needy Families. Government payments to nonprofit institutions, other than for work under research and development contracts, are also included. Business transfer payments consist primarily of liability payments for personal injury and of corporate gifts to nonprofit institutions.

Personal income differs in definition from money income (items 54–57). For example, personal income includes pension rights, employer-provided health insurance, food stamps, and Medicare. These are not included in the definition of money income.

Earnings cover wage and salary disbursements, other labor income, and proprietors' income.

The data for earnings obtained from the Bureau of Economic Analysis (BEA) are based on place of work. In computing personal income, BEA makes an "adjustment for residence" to earnings, based on commuting patterns; personal income is thus presented on a place-of-residence basis.

Farm earnings include the income of farm workers (wages and salaries and other labor income) and farm proprietors. Farm proprietors' income includes only the income of sole proprietorships and partnerships. Farm earnings estimates are benchmarked to data collected in the Census of Agriculture and the revised Department of Agriculture statistical totals of income and expense items.

Goods-related industries include mining, construction, and manufacturing. **Service-related** and other industries include private-sector earnings in agricultural services, forestry, and fisheries; transportation and public utilities; wholesale trade; retail trade; finance, insurance, and real estate; and services. Government earnings include all levels of government. Industries are categorized under the North American Industry Classification System (NAICS), and are not comparable to years prior to 2002.

SOCIAL SECURITY AND SUPPLEMENTAL SECURITY INCOME, Items 84–86

Source: U.S. Social Security Administration
http://www.ssa.gov/policy/docs/statcomps/oasdi_sc/
http://www.ssa.gov/policy/docs/statcomps/ssi_sc/

Social Security beneficiaries are persons receiving benefits under the Old-Age, Survivors, and Disability Insurance Program. These include retired or disabled workers covered by the program, their spouses and dependent children, and the surviving spouses and dependent children of deceased workers.

Supplemental Security Income (SSI) recipients are persons receiving SSI payments. The SSI program is a cash assistance program that provides monthly benefits to low-income aged, blind, or disabled persons.

Data are as of December of the year shown.

HOUSING, Items 87–96

Source: U.S. Census Bureau—Population Estimates Program
https://www.census.gov/programs-surveys/popest.html
Source: U.S. Census Bureau—American Community Survey. 2017 1-year Estimates
http://www.census.gov/acs/www/

Housing data for 2018 are from the Population Estimates Program. Housing unit characteristics for 2017 are from the American Community Survey.

A **housing unit** is a house, apartment, mobile home or trailer, group of rooms, or single room occupied or, if vacant, intended for occupancy as separate living quarters. Separate living quarters are those in which the occupants do not live and eat with any other person in the structure and which have direct access from the outside of the building through a common hall.

The occupants of a housing unit may be a single family, one person living alone, two or more families living together, or any other group of related or unrelated persons who share living quarters. Both occupied and vacant housing units are included in the housing inventory, although recreational vehicles, tents, caves, boats, railroad cars, and the like are included only if they are occupied as a person's usual place of residence.

A housing unit is classified as occupied if it is the usual place of residence of the person or group of persons living in it at the time of enumeration, or if the occupants are only temporarily absent (away on vacation). A household consists of all persons who occupy a housing unit as their usual place of residence. Vacant units for sale or rent include units rented or sold but not occupied and any other units held off the market.

Median value is the dollar amount that divides the distribution of specified owner-occupied housing units into two equal parts, with half of all units below the median value and half of all units above the median value. Value is defined as the respondent's estimate of what the house would sell for if it were for sale. Data are presented for single-family units on fewer than 10 acres of land that have no business or medical offices on the property.

Median rent divides the distribution of renter-occupied housing units into two equal parts. The rent concept used in this volume is gross rent, which includes the amount of cash rent a renter pays (contract rent) plus the estimated average cost of utilities and fuels, if these are paid by the renter. The rent is the amount of rent only for living quarters and excludes amounts paid for any business or other space occupied. Single-family houses on lots of 10 or more acres of land are also excluded.

Housing cost as a percentage of income is shown separately for owners with mortgages, owners without mortgages, and renters. Rent as a percentage of income is a computed ratio of gross rent and monthly household income (total household income in the past 12 months divided by 12). Selected owner costs include utilities and fuels, mortgage payments, insurance, taxes, etc. In each case, the ratio of housing cost to income is computed separately for each housing unit. The housing cost ratios for half of all units are above the median shown in this book, and half are below the median shown in the book.

The proportion of **Households that have Internet Access** includes households with internet subscriptions through broadband (cable, fiber optic, or DSL), satellite, cellular data plans, or dial-up, as well as persons who have internet access without a subscription (access provided by a town or university.)

CIVILIAN LABOR FORCE AND UNEMPLOYMENT, Items 97–100
Source: U.S. Bureau of Labor Statistics—Local Area Unemployment Statistics
http://www.bls.gov/lau/#tables

Data for the civilian labor force are the product of a federal-state cooperative program in which state employment security agencies prepare labor force and unemployment estimates under concepts, definitions, and technical procedures established by the Bureau of Labor Statistics (BLS). The civilian labor force consists of all civilians 16 years old and over who are either employed or unemployed.

Unemployment includes all persons who did not work during the survey week, made specific efforts to find a job during the previous four weeks, and were available for work during the survey week (except for temporary illness). Persons waiting to be called back to a job from which they had been laid off and those waiting to report to a new job within the next 30 days are included in unemployment figures.

Table C includes annual average data for the year shown. The Local Area Unemployment Statistics data are periodically updated to reflect revised inputs, reestimation, and controlling to new statewide totals.

CIVILIAN EMPLOYMENT, Items 101–103
Source: U.S. Census Bureau—American Community Survey. 2017 1-year Estimates
http://www.census.gov/acs/www/

Total employment includes all civilians 16 years old and over who were either (1) "at work"—those who did any work at all during the reference week as paid employees, worked in either their own business or profession, worked on their own farm, or worked 15 hours or more as unpaid workers in a family farm or business; or were (2) "with a job, but not at work" —those who had a job but were not at work that week due to illness, weather, industrial dispute, vacation, or other personal reasons.

The **occupational categories** are based on the occupational classification system that was developed for the 2000 census. This system consists of 509 specific occupational categories for employed persons arranged into 23 major occupational groups. This classification was developed based on the *Standard Occupational Classification (SOC) Manual: 2000*, published by the Executive Office of the President, Office of Management and Budget.

Column 102 includes the Management, business, science, and arts occupations category while Column 103 combines the Natural resources, construction, and maintenance occupations and the Production, transportation, and material moving occupations.

PRIVATE NONFARM EMPLOYMENT AND EARNINGS, Items 104–112
Source: U.S. Census Bureau—County Business Patterns
http://www.census.gov/econ/cbp/index.html

Data for private nonfarm employment and earnings are compiled from the payroll information reported monthly in the Census Bureau publication *County Business Patterns*. The estimates are based on surveys conducted by the Census Bureau and administrative records from the Internal Revenue Service (IRS).

The following types of employment are excluded from the tables: government employment, self-employed persons, farm workers, and domestic service workers. Railroad employment jointly covered by Social Security and railroad retirement programs, employment on oceanborne vessels, and employment in foreign countries are also excluded.

Annual payroll is the combined amount of wages paid, tips reported, and other compensation (including salaries, vacation allowances, bonuses, commissions, sick-leave pay, and the value of payments-in-kind such as free meals and lodging) paid to employees before deductions for Social Security, income tax, insurance, union dues, etc. All forms of compensation are included, regardless of whether they are subject to income tax or the Federal Insurance Contributions Act tax, with the exception of annuities, third-party sick pay, and supplemental unemployment compensation benefits (even if income tax was withheld). For corporations, total annual payroll includes compensation paid to officers and executives; for unincorporated businesses, it excludes profit or other compensation of proprietors or partners.

AGRICULTURE, ITEMS 113–132

Source: U.S. Department of Agriculture, National Agricultural Statistics Service—2017 Census of Agriculture
https://www.nass.usda.gov/Publications/AgCensus/2017/index.php

Data for the 2017 Census of Agriculture were collected in 2018, but pertain to the year 2017.

The Census Bureau took a census of agriculture every 10 years from 1840 to 1920; since 1925, this census has been taken roughly once every 5 years. The 1997 Census of Agriculture was the first one conducted by the National Agricultural Statistics Service of the U.S. Department of Agriculture. Over time, the definition of a farm has varied. For recent censuses (including the 2017 census), a farm has been defined as any place from which $1,000 or more of agricultural products were produced and sold or normally would have been sold during the census year. Dollar figures are expressed in current dollars and have not been adjusted for inflation or deflation.

The term **producer** designates a person who is involved in making decisions for the farm operation. Decisions may include decisions about such things as planting, harvesting, livestock management, and marketing. The producer may be the owner, a member of the owner's household, a hired manager, a tenant, a renter, or a sharecropper. If a person rents land to others or has land worked on shares by others, he/she is considered the producer only of the land which is retained for his/her own operation. The census collected information on the total number of male producers, the total number of female producers, and demographic information for up to four producers per farm.

The acreage designated as **land in farms** consists primarily of agricultural land used for crops, pasture, or grazing. It also includes woodland and wasteland not actually under cultivation or used for pasture or grazing, provided that this land was part of the farm operator's total operation. Land in farms is an operating-unit concept and includes all land owned and operated, as well as all land rented from others. Land used rent-free is classified as land rented from others. All grazing land, except land used under

government permits on a per-head basis, was included as "land in farms" provided it was part of a farm or ranch. Land under the exclusive use of a grazing association was reported by the grazing association and included as land in farms. All land in Indian reservations used for growing crops or grazing livestock is classified as land in farms.

Irrigated land includes all land watered by any artificial or controlled means, such as sprinklers, flooding, furrows or ditches, sub-irrigation, and spreader dikes. Included are supplemental, partial, and preplant irrigation. Each acre was counted only once regardless of the number of times it was irrigated or harvested. Livestock lagoon waste water distributed by sprinkler or flood systems was also included.

Total cropland includes cropland harvested, cropland used only for pasture or grazing, cropland on which all crops failed or were abandoned, cropland in cultivated summer fallow, and cropland idle or used for cover crops or soil improvement but not harvested and not pastured or grazed.

Respondents were asked to report their estimate of the current market **value of land and buildings** owned, rented, or leased from others, and rented and leased to others. Market value refers to the respondent's estimate of what the land and buildings would sell for under current market conditions. If the value of land and buildings was not reported, it was estimated during processing by using the average value of land and buildings from similar farms in the same geographic area.

The **value of machinery and equipment** was estimated by the respondent as the current market value of all cars, trucks, tractors, combines, balers, irrigation equipment, etc., used on the farm. This value is an estimate of what the machinery and equipment would sell for in its present condition and not the replacement or depreciated value. Share interests are reported at full value at the farm where the equipment and machinery are usually kept. Only equipment that was physically located at the farm on December 31, 2017, is included.

Market value of agricultural products sold by farms represents the gross market value before taxes and the production expenses of all agricultural products sold or removed from the place in 2017, regardless of who received the payment. It is equivalent to total sales and it includes sales by producers as well as the value of any share received by partners, landlords, contractors, and others associated with the operation. It includes value of organic sales, direct sales and the value of commodities placed in the Commodity Credit Corporation (CCC) loan program. Market value of agricultural products sold does not include payments received for participation in other federal farm programs. Also, it does not include income from farm-related sources such as customwork and other agricultural services, or income from nonfarm sources.

Organic farms are those that had organic production according to USDA's National Organic Program (NOP). Respondents reported whether their organic production was certified or exempt from certification and the sales from NOP produced commodities. Not included are farms that had acres transitioning into NOP production.

Farms with **internet access** are those that reported using personal computers, laptops, or mobile devices (e.g., cell phones or tablets) to access the internet. This can be done using services such as dial-up, DSL, cable modem, fiber-optic, mobile internet service for a cell phone or other device (tablet), satellite, or other methods. In 2017 respondents were also able to report connecting with an unknown service type, labeled as "Don't know" in the publication tables.

Government payments consist of direct payments as defined by the 2002 Farm Bill; payments from Conservation Reserve Program (CRP), Wetlands Reserve Program (WRP), Farmable Wetlands Program (FWP), and Conservation Reserve Enhancement Program (CREP); loan deficiency payments; disaster payments; other conservation programs; and all other federal farm programs under which payments were made directly to farm producers, including those specified in the 2014 Agricultural Act (Farm Bill), including Agriculture Risk Coverage (ARC) and Price Loss Coverage (PLC). Commodity Credit Corporation (CCC) proceeds, amount from State and local government agricultural program payments, and federal crop insurance payments were not included in this category.

WATER CONSUMPTION, Items 133–134

Source: U.S. Geological Survey, National Water-Use Information Program, Estimated Use of Water in the United States County-Level Data for 2015, version 1.0 http://water.usgs.gov/watuse/

Every five years, the U.S. Geological Survey compiles county-level water-use estimates. This volume includes the total fresh and saline withdrawals for public water supplies in 2015, expressed as million gallons per day. Estimate of withdrawals of ground and surface water are given for the following categories of use: public water supplies, domestic, commercial, irrigation, livestock, industrial, mining, and thermoelectric power. Only public water supply is included in this volume because the other categories had not been published in time for this book. The number of gallons withdrawn per person is based on the metropolitan area population in 2015 but the water is not necessarily used locally, providing an indicator of metropolitan areas that serve as major water sources.

Public supply refers to water withdrawn from ground and surface sources by public and private water systems for use by cities, towns, rural water districts, mobile-home parks, Native American Indian reservations, and military bases. Public-supply facilities provide water to at least 25 persons or have a minimum of 15 service connections. Water withdrawn by public suppliers may be delivered to users for domestic, commercial, industrial, and thermoelectric-power purposes, as well as to other public-water suppliers. Public-supply water is also used for public services (public uses)—such as pools, parks, and public buildings—and may have unaccounted uses (losses) because of system leaks or such non-metered services as firefighting, flushing of water lines, or backwashing at treatment plants. Some public-supply water may be used in the processes of water and wastewater treatment. Some public suppliers treat saline water before distributing the water. The definition of saline water for public supply refers to water that requires treatment to reduce the concentration of dissolved solids through the process of desalination or dilution.

2012 Economic CENSUS: OVERVIEW, Items 135–166

Source: U.S. Census Bureau https://www.census.gov/programs-surveys/economic-census/library/publications.html

The Economic Census provides a detailed portrait of the nation's economy, from the national to the local level, once every five years. The 2012 Economic Census covers nearly all of the U.S. economy in its basic collection of establishment statistics. The 1997 Economic Census was the first major data source to use the new North American Industry Classification System (NAICS); therefore, data from this census are not comparable to economic data from prior years, which were based on the Standard Industrial Classification (SIC) system.

NAICS, developed in cooperation with Canada and Mexico, classifies North America's economic activities at two-, three-, four-, and five-digit levels of detail; the U.S. version of NAICS further defines industries to a sixth digit. The Economic Census takes advantage of this hierarchy to publish data at these successive levels of detail: sector (two-digit), subsector (three-digit), industry group (four-digit), industry (five-digit), and U.S. industry (six-digit). Information in Table A is at the two-digit level, with a few three- and four-digit items. The data in Tables B and C are at the two-digit level.

Several key statistics are tabulated for all industries in this volume, including number of establishments (or companies), number of employees, payroll, and certain measures of output (sales, receipts, revenue, value of shipments, or value of construction work done).

Number of establishments. An establishment is a single physical location at which business is conducted. It is not necessarily identical with a company or enterprise, which may consist of one establishment or more. Economic Census figures represent a summary of reports for individual establishments rather than companies. For cases in which a census report was received, separate information was obtained for each location where business was conducted. When administrative records of other federal agencies were used instead of a census report, no information was available on the number of locations operated. Each Economic Census establishment was tabulated according to the physical location at which the business was conducted. The count of establishments represents those in business at any time during 2002.

When two activities or more were carried on at a single location under a single ownership, all activities were generally grouped together as a single establishment. The entire establishment was classified on the basis of its major activity and all of its data were included in that classification. However, when distinct and separate economic activities (for which different industry classification codes were appropriate) were conducted at a single location under a single ownership, separate establishment reports for each of the different activities were obtained in the census.

Number of employees. Paid employees consist of the full-time and part-time employees, including salaried officers and executives of corporations. Included are employees on paid sick leave, paid holidays, and paid vacations; not included are proprietors and partners of unincorporated businesses. The definition of paid employees is the same as that used by the Internal Revenue Service (IRS) on form 941.

For some industries, the Economic Census gives codes representing the number of employees as a range of numbers (for example, "100 to 249 employees" or "1,000 to 2,499" employees). In this volume, those codes have been replaced by the standard suppression code "D".

Payroll. Payroll includes all forms of compensation, such as salaries, wages, commissions, dismissal pay, bonuses, vacation allowances, sick-leave pay, and employee contributions to qualified pension plans paid during the year to all employees. For corporations, payroll includes amounts paid to officers and executives; for unincorporated businesses, it does not include profit or other compensation of proprietors or partners. Payroll is reported before deductions for Social Security, income tax, insurance, union dues, etc. This definition of payroll is the same as that used by on IRS form 941.

Sales, shipments, receipts, revenue, or business done. This measure includes the total sales, shipments, receipts, revenue, or business done by establishments within the scope of the Economic Census. The definition of each of these items is specific to the economic sector measured.

WHOLESALE TRADE, Items 135–138
Source: U.S. Census Bureau—2012 Economic Census (See Overview of 2012 Economic Census prior to Item 135)

The Wholesale Trade sector (sector 42) comprises establishments engaged in wholesaling merchandise, generally without transformation, and rendering services incidental to the sale of merchandise. The wholesaling process is an intermediate step in the distribution of merchandise.

Wholesalers are organized to sell or arrange the purchase or sale of (1) goods for resale (i.e., goods sold to other wholesalers or retailers), (2) capital or durable nonconsumer goods, and (3) raw and intermediate materials and supplies used in production.

Wholesalers sell merchandise to other businesses and normally operate from a warehouse or office. These warehouses and offices are characterized by having little or no display of merchandise. In addition, neither the design nor the location of the premises is intended to solicit walk-in traffic. Wholesalers do not normally use advertising directed to the general public. In general, customers are initially reached via telephone, in-person marketing, or specialized advertising, which may include the internet and other electronic means. Follow-up orders are either vendor-initiated or client-initiated, are usually based on previous sales, and typically exhibit strong ties between sellers and buyers. In fact, transactions are often conducted between wholesalers and clients that have long-standing business relationships.

This sector is made up of two main types of wholesalers: those that sell goods on their own account and those that arrange sales and purchases for others for a commission or fee.

(1) Establishments that sell goods on their own account are known as wholesale merchants, distributors, jobbers, drop shippers, import/export merchants, and sales branches. These establishments typically maintain their own warehouse, where they receive and handle goods for their customers. Goods are generally sold without transformation, but may include integral functions, such as sorting, packaging, labeling, and other marketing services.

(2) Establishments arranging for the purchase or sale of goods owned by others or purchasing goods on a commission basis are known as agents and brokers, commission merchants, import/export agents and brokers, auction companies, and manufacturers' representatives. These establishments operate from offices and generally do not own or handle the goods they sell.

Some wholesale establishments may be connected with a single manufacturer and promote and sell that particular manufacturer's products to a wide range of other wholesalers or retailers. Other wholesalers may be connected to a retail chain or a limited number of retail chains and only provide the products needed by the particular retail operation(s). These wholesalers may obtain the products from a wide range of manufacturers. Still other wholesalers may not take title to the goods, but act instead as agents and brokers for a commission.

Although wholesaling normally denotes sales in large volumes, durable nonconsumer goods may be sold in single units. Sales of capital or durable nonconsumer goods used in the production of goods and services, such as farm machinery, medium- and heavy-duty trucks, and industrial machinery, are always included in Wholesale Trade.

The metropolitan area table includes only **Merchant wholesalers, except manufacturers' sales branches and offices**, establishments primarily engaged in buying and selling merchandise on their own account. Included here are such types of establishments as wholesale distributors and jobbers, importers, exporters, own-brand importers/marketers, terminal and country grain elevators, and farm products assemblers.

RETAIL TRADE, Items 139–142
Source: U.S. Census Bureau—2012 Economic Census (See Overview of 2012 Economic Census prior to Item 135)

The Retail Trade sector (44–45) is made up of establishments engaged in retailing merchandise, generally without transformation, and rendering services incidental to the sale of merchandise.

The retailing process is the final step in the distribution of merchandise; retailers are therefore organized to sell merchandise in small quantities to the general public. This sector comprises two main types of retailers: store and nonstore retailers.

Store retailers operate fixed point-of-sale locations, located and designed to attract a high volume of walk-in customers. In general, retail stores have extensive displays of merchandise and use mass-media advertising to attract customers. They typically sell merchandise to the general public for personal or household consumption; some also serve business and institutional clients. These include establishments such as office supply stores, computer and software stores, building materials dealers, plumbing supply stores, and electrical supply stores. Catalog showrooms, gasoline service stations, automotive dealers, and mobile home dealers are treated as store retailers.

In addition to retailing merchandise, some types of store retailers are also engaged in the provision of after-sales services, such as repair and installation. For example, new automobile dealers, electronic and appliance stores, and musical instrument and supply stores often provide repair services. As a general rule, establishments engaged in retailing merchandise and providing after-sales services are classified in this sector.

Nonstore retailers, like store retailers, are organized to serve the general public, although their retailing methods differ. The establishments of this subsector reach customers and market merchandise with methods including the broadcasting of "infomercials," the broadcasting and publishing of direct-response advertising, the publishing of paper and electronic catalogs, door-to-door solicitation, in-home demonstration, selling from portable stalls (street vendors, except food), and distribution through vending machines. Establishments engaged in the direct sale (nonstore) of products, such as home heating oil dealers and home-delivery newspaper routes are included in this sector.

The buying of goods for resale is a characteristic of retail trade establishments that distinguishes them from establishments in the Agriculture, Manufacturing, and Construction sectors. For example, farms that sell their products at or from the point of production are classified in Agriculture instead of in Retail Trade. Similarly, establishments that both manufacture and sell their products to the general public are classified in Manufacturing instead of Retail Trade. However, establishments that engage in processing activities incidental to retailing are classified in Retail Trade.

REAL ESTATE AND RENTAL AND LEASING, Items 143–146

Source: U.S. Census Bureau—2012 Economic Census (See Overview of 2012 Economic Census prior to Item 135)

The Real Estate and Rental and Leasing sector (53) comprises establishments primarily engaged in renting, leasing, or otherwise allowing the use of tangible or intangible assets, and establishments providing related services. The major portion of this sector is made up of establishments that rent, lease, or otherwise allow the use of their own assets by others. The assets may be tangible, such as real estate and equipment, or intangible, such as patents and trademarks.

This sector also includes establishments primarily engaged in managing real estate for others, selling, renting, and/or buying real estate for others, and appraising real estate. These activities are closely related to this sector's main activity. In addition, a substantial proportion of property management is self-performed by lessors.

The main components of this sector are the real estate lessors industries; equipment lessors industries (including motor vehicles, computers, and consumer goods); and lessors of nonfinancial intangible assets (except copyrighted works).

PROFESSIONAL, SCIENTIFIC, AND TECHNICAL SERVICES, Items 147–150

Source: U.S. Census Bureau—2012 Economic Census (See Overview of 2012 Economic Census prior to Item 135)

The Professional, Scientific, and Technical Services sector (54) is made up of establishments that specialize in performing professional, scientific, and technical activities for others. These activities require a high degree of expertise and training. The establishments in this sector specialize in one or more areas and provide services to clients in a variety of industries (and, in some cases, to households). Activities performed include legal advice and representation; accounting, bookkeeping, and payroll services; architectural, engineering, and specialized design services; computer services; consulting services; research services; advertising services; photographic services; translation and interpretation services; veterinary services; and other professional, scientific, and technical services.

This sector excludes establishments primarily engaged in providing a range of day-to-day office administrative services, such as financial planning, billing and record keeping, personnel services, and physical distribution and logistics services. These establishments are classified in sector 56, Administrative and Support and Waste Management and Remediation Services.

MANUFACTURING, Items 151–154

Source: U.S. Census Bureau—2012 Economic Census (See Overview of 2012 Economic Census prior to Item 135)

The Manufacturing sector (31–33) is made up of establishments engaged in the mechanical, physical, or chemical transformation of materials, substances, or components into new products. The assembling of component parts of manufactured products is considered manufacturing, except in cases in which the activity is appropriately classified in the Construction sector. Establishments in the Manufacturing sector are often described as plants, factories, or mills, and characteristically use power-driven machines and materials-handling equipment. However, establishments that transform materials or substances into new products by hand or in the worker's home, and establishments engaged in selling to the general public products made on the same premises from which they are sold (such as bakeries, candy stores, and custom tailors) may also be included in this sector. Manufacturing establishments may process materials or contract with other establishments to process their materials for them. Both types of establishments are included in the Manufacturing sector.

The materials, substances, or components transformed by manufacturing establishments are raw materials that are products of agriculture, forestry, fishing, mining, or quarrying, or are products of other manufacturing establishments. The materials used may be purchased directly from producers, obtained through customary trade channels, or secured without recourse to the market by transferring the product from one establishment to another, under the same ownership. The new product of a manufacturing establishment may be finished (in the sense that it is ready for utilization or consumption), or it may be semifinished to become an input for an establishment engaged in further manufacturing. For example, the product of the alumina refinery is the input used in the primary production of aluminum; primary aluminum is the input used in an aluminum wire drawing plant; and aluminum wire is the input used in a fabricated wire product manufacturing establishment.

Data are included for counties with 500 or more employees in the Manufacturing sector.

ACCOMMODATION AND FOOD SERVICES, Items 155–158

Source: U.S. Census Bureau—2012 Economic Census (See Overview of 2012 Economic Census prior to Item 135)

The Accommodation and Food Services sector (72) consists of establishments that provide customers with lodging and/or meals, snacks, and beverages for immediate consumption. This sector includes both accommodation and food services establishments because the two activities are often combined at the same establishment.

Excluded from this sector are civic and social organizations, amusement and recreation parks, theaters, and other recreation or entertainment facilities providing food and beverage services.

HEALTH CARE AND SOCIAL ASSISTANCE, Items 159–162

Source: U.S. Census Bureau—2012 Economic Census (See Overview of 2012 Economic Census prior to Item 135)

The Health Care and Social Assistance sector (62) consists of establishments that provide health care and social assistance services to individuals. The sector includes both health care and social assistance because it is sometimes difficult to distinguish between the boundaries of these two activities. The industries in this sector are arranged on a continuum, starting with establishments that provide medical care exclusively, continuing with those that provide health care and social assistance, and finishing with those that provide only social assistance. The services provided by establishments in this sector are delivered by trained professionals. All industries in the sector share this commonality of process—namely, labor inputs of health practitioners or social workers with the requisite expertise. Many of the industries in the sector are defined based on the educational degree held by the practitioners included in the industry.

Excluded from this sector are aerobic classes, which can be found in subsector 713, Amusement, Gambling, and Recreation Industries; and nonmedical diet and weight-reducing centers, which can be found in subsector 812, Personal and Laundry Services. Although these can be viewed as health services, they are not typically delivered by health practitioners.

OTHER SERVICES, EXCEPT PUBLIC ADMINISTRATION Items 163–166

Source: U.S. Census Bureau—2012 Economic Census (See Overview of 2012 Economic Census prior to Item 135)

The Other Services, Except Public Administration sector (81) comprises establishments engaged in providing services not specifically categorized elsewhere in the classification system. Establishments in this sector are primarily engaged in activities such as equipment and machinery repairing, promoting or administering religious activities, grant making, and advocacy; this sector also includes establishments that provide dry-cleaning and laundry services, personal care services, death care services, pet care services, photofinishing services, temporary parking services, and dating services.

Private households that employ workers on or about the premises in activities primarily concerned with the operation of the household are included in this sector.

Excluded from this sector are establishments primarily engaged in retailing new equipment and performing repairs and general maintenance on equipment. These establishments are classified in sector 44–45, Retail Trade.

NONEMPLOYER BUSINESSES, Items 167 and 168

Source: U.S. Census Bureau—Nonemployer Statistics https://www.census.gov/programs-surveys/nonemployer-statistics.html

Nonemployer Statistics is an annual series that provides subnational economic data for businesses that have no paid employees and are subject to federal income tax. The data consist of the number of businesses and total receipts by industry. Most nonemployers are self-employed individuals operating unincorporated businesses (known as sole proprietorships), which may or may not be the owner's principal source of income.

The majority of all business establishments in the United States are nonemployers, yet these firms average less than 4 percent of all sales and receipts nationally. Due to their small economic impact, these firms are excluded from most other Census Bureau business statistics (the primary exception being the Survey of Business Owners). The Nonemployers Statistics series is the primary resource available to study the scope and activities of nonemployers at a detailed geographic level.

BUILDING PERMITS, Items 169 and 170

Source: U.S. Census Bureau—Building Permits Survey http://www.census.gov/construction/bps/

These figures represent private residential construction authorized by building permits in approximately 20,000 places in the United States. Valuation represents the expected cost of construction as recorded on the building permit. This figure usually excludes the cost of on-site and off-site development and improvements, as well as the cost of heating, plumbing, electrical, and elevator installations.

National, state, and county totals were obtained by adding the data for permit-issuing places within each jurisdiction. Not all areas of the country require a building or zoning permit. The statistics only represent those areas that do require a permit. These totals thus are limited to permits issued in the 20,000 place universe covered by the Census Bureau and may not include all permits issued within a state. Current surveys indicate that construction is undertaken for all but a very small percentage of housing units authorized by building permits.

Residential building permits include buildings with any number of housing units. Housing units exclude group quarters (such as dormitories and rooming houses), transient accommodations (such as transient hotels, motels, and tourist courts), "HUD-code" manufactured (mobile) homes, moved or relocated units, and housing units created in an existing residential or nonresidential structure.

METROPOLITAN AREA LOCAL GOVERN-MENT EMPLOYMENT AND PAYROLL, Items 171-179

Source: U.S. Census Bureau—2012 Census of Governments
https://www.census.gov/programs-surveys/cog.html

These items include data for all local governments (i.e., counties, municipalities, townships, special districts, and school districts) located within the metropolitan area. The Census of Governments identifies the scope and nature of the nation's state and local government sector; provides authoritative benchmark figures of public finance and public employment; classifies local government organizations, powers, and activities; and measures federal, state, and local fiscal relationships. The Employment component was mailed **March 2012** to collect information on the number of state and local government civilian employees and their payrolls.

Government employees include all persons paid for personal services performed, including persons paid from federally funded programs, paid elected or appointed officials, persons in a paid leave status, and persons paid on a per meeting, annual, semiannual, or quarterly basis. Unpaid officials, pensioners, persons whose work is performed on a fee basis, and contractors and their employees are excluded from the count of employees. **Full-Time Equivalent employees** is a computed statistic representing the number of full-time employees that could have been employed if the reported number of hours worked by part-time employees had been worked by full-time employees. This statistic is calculated separately for each function of a government by dividing the "part-time hours paid" by the standard number of hours for full-time employees in the particular government and then adding the resulting quotient to the number of full-time employees.

March payroll represents gross payroll amounts for the one-month period of March for full-time and part-time employees. Gross payroll includes all salaries, wages, fees, commissions, and overtime paid to employees **before** withholdings for taxes, insurance, etc. It also includes incentive payments that are paid at regular pay intervals. It excludes employer share of fringe benefits like retirement, Social Security, health and life insurance, lump sum payments, and so forth.

Administration and Judicial and Legal combines **Financial administration, Other government administration, and Judicial and Legal** activities. **Financial administration includes** activities concerned with tax assessment and collection, custody and disbursement of funds, debt management, administration of trust funds, budgeting, and other government-wide financial management activities. This function is not applied to school district or special district governments. **Other government administration** applies to the legislative and government-wide administrative agencies of governments. Included here are overall planning and zoning activities, and central personnel and administrative activities. This function is not applied to school district or special district governments. **Judicial and legal** includes all court and court related activities (except probation and parole activities that are included at the "Correction" function), court activities of sheriff's offices, prosecuting attorneys' and public defenders' offices, legal departments, and attorneys providing government-wide legal service.

Police and Corrections includes all activities concerned, with the enforcement of law and order, including coroner's offices, police training academies, investigation bureaus, and local jails, "lockups", or other detention facilities not intended to serve as correctional facilities. **Corrections** includes activities pertaining to the confinement and correction of adults and minors convicted of criminal offenses. Pardon, probation, and parole activities are also included here.

Fire protection includes local government fire protection and prevention activities plus any ambulance, rescue, or other auxiliary services provided by a fire protection agency. Volunteer firefighters, if remunerated for their services on a "per fire" or some other basis, are included as part-time employees.

Highways and transportation includes activities associated with the maintenance and operation of streets, roads, sidewalks, bridges, tunnels, toll roads, and ferries. Snow and ice removal, street lighting, and highway and traffic engineering activities are also included here. Also included are the operation, maintenance, and construction of public mass transit systems, including subways, surface rails, and buses, and the provision, construction, operation, maintenance; support of public waterways, harbors, docks, wharves, and related marine terminal facilities; and activities associated with the operation and support of publicly operated airport facilities.

Health and Welfare includes Health, Hospitals, and Public welfare. **Health** includes administration of public health programs, community and visiting nurse services, immunization programs, drug abuse rehabilitation programs, health and food inspection activities, operation of outpatient clinics, and environmental pollution control activities. **Hospitals** includes only government operated medical care facilities that provide inpatient care. Employees and payrolls of private corporations that lease and operate government-owned hospital facilities are excluded.

Public Welfare includes the administration of various public assistance programs for the needy, veteran services, operation of nursing homes, indigent care institutions, and programs that provide payments for medical care, handicap transportation, and other services for the needy.

Natural resources and Utilities includes activities primarily concerned with the conservation and development of natural resources (soil, water, energy, minerals, etc.) and the regulation of industries that develop, utilize, or affect natural resources, as well as the operation and maintenance of **parks**, playgrounds, swimming pools, public beaches, auditoriums, public golf courses, museums, marinas, botanical gardens, and zoological parks. **Utilities, sewerage, and waste management** includes operation, maintenance, and construction of public water supply systems, including production, acquisition, and distribution of water to general public or to other public or private utilities, for residential, commercial, and industrial use; activities associated with the production or acquisition and distribution of electric power; provision, maintenance, and operation of sanitary and storm sewer systems and sewage disposal and treatment facilities; and refuse collection and disposal, operation of sanitary landfills, and street cleaning activities.

Education and libraries includes activities associated with the operation of public elementary and secondary schools and locally operated vocational-technical schools. Special education programs operated by elementary and secondary school systems are also included as are all ancillary services associated with the operation of schools, such as pupil transportation and food service. **Also included are the e**stablishment and provision of libraries for use by the general public and the technical support of privately operated libraries. This category includes classroom teachers, principals, supervisors of instruction, librarians, teacher aides, library aides, and guidance and psychological personnel as well as school superintendents and other administrative personnel, clerical and secretarial staffs, plant operation and maintenance personnel, health and recreation employees, transportation and food service personnel, and any student employees. Also included are any degree granting institutions that provide academic training above grade 12.

LOCAL GOVERNMENT FINANCES, Items 180–193

Source: U.S. Census Bureau—2012 Census of Governments
https://www.census.gov/programs-surveys/cog.html

Data on local government finances are based on result of the 2012 Census of Governments. For each metropolitan area, the data are aggregated from its component counties, and the financial data comprise amounts for all local governments—not only the county governments, but also any municipalities, townships, school districts, and special districts within the county. Statistics from governmental units located in two or more county areas are assigned to the county area containing the administrative office.

Revenue and expenditure items include all amounts of money received and paid out, respectively, by a government and its agencies (net of correcting transactions such as recoveries of refunds), with the exception of amounts for debt issuance and retirement and for loan and investment, agency, and private transactions.

Payments among the various funds and agencies of a particular government are excluded from revenue and expenditure items as representing internal transfers. Therefore, a government's contribution to a retirement fund that it administers is not counted as expenditure, nor is the receipt of this contribution by the retirement fund counted as revenue.

Total **general revenue** includes all revenue except utility, liquor stores, and insurance trust revenue. All tax revenue and intergovernmental revenue, even if designated for employee-retirement or local utility purpose, are classified as general revenue.

Intergovernmental revenue covers amounts received from the federal government as fiscal aid, reimbursements for performance of general government functions and specific services for the paying government, or in lieu of taxes. It excludes any amounts received from other governments from the sale of property, commodities, and utility services.

Taxes consist of compulsory contributions exacted by governments for public purposes. However, this category excludes employer and employee payments for retirement and social insurance purposes, which are classified as insurance trust revenue; it also excludes special assessments, which are classified as non-tax general revenue. Property taxes are taxes conditioned on ownership of property and assessed by its value. Sales and gross receipts taxes do not include dealer discounts, or "commissions" allowed to merchants for collection of taxes from consumers. General sales taxes and selected taxes on sales of motor fuels, tobacco products, and other particular commodities and services are included.

General government expenditure includes capital outlay, a major portion of which is commonly financed by borrowing. Government revenue does not include receipts from borrowing. Among other things, this distorts the relationship between totals of revenue and expenditure figures that are presented and renders it useless as a direct measure of the degree of budgetary "balance" (as that term is generally applied).

Direct general expenditure comprises all expenditures of the local governments, excluding utility, liquor stores, insurance trust expenditures, and any intergovernmental payments.

Local government expenditure for **education** is mainly for the provision and general support of schools and other educational facilities and services, including those for educational institutions beyond high school. They cover such related services as student transportation; school lunch and other cafeteria operations; school health, recreation, and library services; and dormitories, dining halls, and bookstores operated by public institutions of higher education.

Health and hospital expenditure includes health research; clinics; nursing; immunization; other categorical, environmental, and general health services provided by health agencies; establishment and operation of hospital facilities; provision of hospital care; and support of other public and private hospitals.

Police protection expenditure includes police activities such as patrols, communications, custody of persons awaiting trial, and vehicular inspection.

Public welfare expenditure covers support of and assistance to needy persons; this aid is contingent upon the person's needs. Included are cash assistance paid directly to needy persons under categorical (Old Age Assistance, Temporary Assistance for Needy

Families, Aid to the Blind, and Aid to the Disabled) and other welfare programs; vendor payments made directly to private purveyors for medical care, burials, and other commodities and services provided under welfare programs; welfare institutions; and any intergovernmental or other direct expenditure for welfare purposes. Pensions to former employees and other benefits not contingent on need are excluded.

Highway expenditure is for the provision and maintenance of highway facilities, including toll turnpikes, bridges, tunnels, and ferries, as well as regular roads, highways, and streets. Also included are expenditures for street lighting and for snow and ice removal. Not included are highway policing and traffic control, which are considered part of police protection

Debt outstanding includes all long-term debt obligations of the government and its agencies (exclusive of utility debt) and all interest-bearing, short-term (repayable within one year) debt obligations remaining unpaid at the close of the fiscal year. It includes judgments, mortgages, and revenue bonds, as well as general obligation bonds, notes, and interest-bearing warrants. This category consists of non-interest-bearing, short-term obligations; inter-fund obligations; amounts owed in a trust or agency capacity; advances and contingent loans from other governments; and rights of individuals to benefit from government-administered employee-retirement funds.

GOVERNMENT EMPLOYMENT, Items 194–196

Source: U.S. Bureau of Economic Analysis—Regional Economic Accounts
http://www.bea.gov/regional/index.htm#state

Employment is measured as the average annual sum of full-time and part-time jobs. The estimates are on a place-of-work basis. The estimates are on a place-of-work basis. State and local government employment includes person employed in all state and local government agencies and enterprises. Data for federal civilian employment include civilian employees of the federal government, including civilian employees of the Department of Defense. Military employment includes all persons on active duty status.

INDIVIDUAL INCOME TAX RETURNS, Items 197–199

Source: U.S. Internal Revenue Servicw, Statistics of Income Program
https://www.irs.gov/uac/soi-tax-stats-county-data-2016

The Revenue Act of 1916 mandated the annual publication of statistics related to "the operations of the internal revenue laws" as they affect individuals, all forms of businesses, estates. non-profit organizations, trusts, and investments abroad and foreign investments in the United States. The Statistics of Income (SOI) division fulfills this function by collecting and processing data so that they become informative and by sharing information about how the tax system works with other government agencies and

the general public. Publication types include traditional print sources, Internet files, CD-ROMs, and files sent via e-mail. SOI has an information office, Statistical Information Services, to facilitate the dissemination of SOI data.

SOI bases its county data on administrative records of individual income tax returns (Forms 1040) from the Internal Revenue Service (IRS) Individual Master File (IMF) system. Included in these data are returns filed during the 12-month period, January 1, 2017 to December 31, 2017. While the bulk of returns filed during the 12-month period are primarily for Tax Year 2016, the IRS received a limited number of returns for tax years before 2016 and these have been included within the county data.

Data do not represent the full U.S. population because many individuals are not required to file an individual income tax return. The address shown on the tax return may differ from the taxpayer's actual residence. State and county codes were based on the ZIP code shown on the return. Excluded were tax returns filed without a ZIP code and returns filed with a ZIP code that did not match the State code shown on the return.

SOI did not attempt to correct any ZIP codes on the returns; however, it did take the following precautions to avoid disclosing information about specific taxpayers: Excluded from the data are items with less than 20 returns within a county. Also excluded are tax returns representing a specified percentage of the total of any particular cell. For example, if one return represented 75 percent of the value of a given cell, the return was suppressed from the county detail. The actual threshold percentage used cannot be released.

Column 197 show the number of returns. Column 198 shows the mean Adjusted Gross Income for the metropolitan area and column 199 shows the mean income tax (line 56 on Form 1040). for the county.

TABLE D—CITIES

Table D present 146 items of data for cities with populations of 25,000 or more at the time of the 2010 census.

LAND AREA, Items 1 and 4

Source: U.S. Census Bureau—2018 U.S. Gazetteer Files,
http://www.census.gov/geo/maps-data/data/gazetteer2018.html

Land area measurements are shown to the nearest square mile. Land area is an area measurement providing the size, in square miles, of the land portions of each county.

POPULATION, Items 2-4

Source: U.S. Census Bureau—Population Estimates
https://www.census.gov/programs-surveys/popest.html

The population data are Census Bureau estimates of the resident population as of July 1 of the year shown.

POPULATION CHARACTERISTICS, Items 5–22

Source: U.S. Census Bureau—American Community Survey 2017 1-year Supplemental Estimates
http://www.census.gov/acs/www/

Data on age, sex, race, Hispanic origin, and place of birth are from the 2017 American Community Survey, a nationwide continuous survey designed to replace the long form questionnaire used in previous censuses.

Data on race were derived from answers to the question on race that was asked of all persons. The concept of race, as used by the Census Bureau, reflects self-identification by respondents according to the race or races with which they most closely identify. These categories are sociopolitical constructs and should not be interpreted as being scientific or anthropological in nature. Furthermore, the race categories include both racial and national origin groups.

On the American Community Survey, respondents were offered the option of selecting one or more races. This option was not available prior to the 2000 census; thus, comparisons between censuses should be made with caution. In this table, Columns 5 through 10 refer to individuals who identified with one specific racial category, while Column 11 includes those who selected more than one race.

The **White** population is defined as persons who indicated their race as White, as well as persons who did not classify themselves in one of the specific race categories listed on the questionnaire but entered a nationality such as Irish, German, Italian, Lebanese, Near Easterner, Arab, or Polish.

The **Black** population includes persons who indicated their race as "Black or AfricanAmerican" as well as persons who did not classify themselves in one of the specific race categories but reported entries such as African American, Afro American, Kenyan, Nigerian, or Haitian.

The **American Indian or Alaska Native** population includes persons who indicated their race as American Indian or Alaska Native, as well as persons who did not classify themselves in one of the specific race categories but reported entries such as Canadian Indian, French-American Indian, Spanish-American Indian, Eskimo, Aleut, Alaska Indian, or any of the American Indian or Alaska Native tribes.

The **Asian** population includes persons who indicated their race as Asian Indian, Chinese, Filipino, Japanese, Korean, Vietnamese, or "Other Asian," as well as persons who provided write-in entries of such groups as Cambodian, Laotian, Hmong, Pakistani, or Taiwanese.

The **Native Hawaiian or Other Pacific Islander** population includes persons who indicated their race as "Native Hawaiian," "Guamanian or Chamorro," "Samoan," or "Other Pacific Islander," as well as persons who reported entries such as Part Hawaiian, American Samoan, Fijian, Melanesian, or Tahitian.

Some Other Race includes all other responses not included in the "White," "Black or African American," "American Indian or Alaska Native," "Asian," and "Native Hawaiian or Other Pacific Islander" race categories described above. Respondents reporting entries such as multiracial, mixed, interracial, or a Hispanic, Latino, or Spanish group (for example, Mexican, Puerto Rican, Cuban, or Spanish) in response to the race question are included in this category.

Two or More Races. People may choose to provide two or more races either by checking two or more race response check boxes, by providing multiple responses, or by some combination of check boxes and other responses. The race response categories shown on the questionnaire are collapsed into the five minimum race groups identified by OMB, and the Census Bureau's "Some Other Race" category.

The **Hispanic population** is based on a separate question that asked respondents "Is this person Spanish/Hispanic/Latino?" Persons marking any one of the four Hispanic categories (i.e., Mexican, Puerto Rican, Cuban, or other Spanish) are collectively referred to as Hispanic.

The Hispanic origin question was placed before the race question and specific instructions indicated that both questions should be answered.

The **foreign-born** population includes all persons who were not U.S. citizens at birth. Foreign-born persons are those who indicated they were either a U.S. citizen by naturalization or were not a citizen of the United States. The foreign-born population consists of immigrants (legal permanent residents), temporary migrants (students), humanitarian migrants (refugees), and unauthorized migrants (persons illegally residing in the United States).

Age is defined as age at last birthday (number of completed years since birth), at the time of the interview. The American Community Survey also asked for the specific date of birth of the respondent. Both age and date of birth are used in combination to calculate the most accurate age at the time of the interview.

The **female** population is shown as a percentage of total population.

POPULATION CHANGE, Items 23–26

Source: U.S. Census Bureau—Decennial Censuses
U.S. Census Bureau—Population Estimates
http://www.census.gov/main/www/cen2000.html
https://www.census.gov/programs-surveys/decennial-census/data/datasets.2010.html
https://www.census.gov/programs-surveys/popest.html

The population data for 2000 and 2010 are from the decennial censuses and represent the resident population as of April 1 of those years. The data for 2018 are from the Census Bureau's Population Estimates Program and represent the estimated resident population as of July 1.

The change in population from 2000 to 2010 and from 2010 to 2018 is calculated from census data based on city boundaries as they existed in 2000 and 2010, respectively. No attempt was made to adjust the data to reflect boundary changes.

HOUSEHOLDS, Items 27–34

Source: U.S. Census Bureau—American Community Survey, 2017 1-year Supplemental Estimates
http://www.census.gov/acs/www/

A **household** includes all of the persons who occupy a housing unit. (Persons not living in households are classified as living in group quarters.) A housing unit is a house, an apartment, a mobile home, a group of rooms, or a single room occupied (or, if vacant, intended for occupancy) as separate living quarters. Separate living quarters are those in which the occupants live separately from any other persons in the building and have direct access from the outside of the building or through a common hall. The occupants may be a single family, one person living alone, two or more families living together, or any other group of related or unrelated persons who share living quarters. The number of households is the same as the number of year-round occupied housing units.

A **family** includes a householder and one or more other persons living in the same household who are related to the householder by birth, marriage, or adoption. All persons in a household who are related to the householder are regarded as members of his or her family. A **family household** may contain persons not related to the householder; thus, family households may include more members than families do. A household can contain only one family for the purposes of census tabulations. Not all households contain families, as a household may comprise a group of unrelated persons or of one person living alone. Families are classified by type as either a "married couple family" or "other family," according to the presence or absence of a spouse.

A **Married-Couple Family** is a family in which the householder and his or her spouse are listed as members of the same household. The category **female family householder** includes only female-headed family households with no spouse present.

A **Nonfamily Household** includes a householder living alone or with nonrelatives only. Unmarried couples households, whether opposite-sex or same-sex, with no relatives of the householder present are tabulated in nonfamily households.

The measure of **persons per household** is obtained by dividing the number of persons in households by the number of households or householders. One person in each household is designated as the householder. In most cases, this is the person (or one of the persons) in whose name the house is owned, being bought, or rented. If there is no such person in the household, any adult household member 15 years old and over can be designated as the householder.

CRIME, Items 35–38

Source: U.S. Federal Bureau of Investigation—Uniform Crime Reports
https://ucr.fbi.gov/crime-in-the-u.s/2016/
crime-in-the-u.s.-2016

Crime data are as reported to the Federal Bureau of Investigation (FBI) by law enforcement agencies and have not been adjusted for underreporting. This may affect comparability between geographic areas or over time.

Through the voluntary contribution of crime statistics by law enforcement agencies across the United States, the Uniform Crime Reporting (UCR) Program provides periodic assessments of crime in the nation as measured by offenses that have come to the attention of the law enforcement community. The Committee

on Uniform Crime Records of the International Association of Chiefs of Police initiated this voluntary national data collection effort in 1930. The UCR Program contributors compile and submit their crime data either directly to the FBI or through state-level UCR Programs.

Seven offenses, because of their severity, frequency of occurrence, and likelihood of being reported to police, were initially selected to serve as an index for evaluating fluctuations in the volume of crime. These serious crimes were murder and nonnegligent manslaughter, forcible rape, robbery, aggravated assault, burglary, larceny-theft, and motor vehicle theft. By congressional mandate, arson was added as the eighth index offense in 1979. The totals shown in this volume do not include arson.

In 2004, the FBI discontinued the use of the Crime Index in the UCR Program and its publications, stating that the Crime Index was driven upward by the offense with the highest number of cases (in this case, larceny-theft), creating a bias against jurisdictions with a high number of larceny-thefts but a low number of other serious crimes, such as murder and forcible rape. The FBI is currently publishing a violent crime total and property crime total until a more viable index is developed. This book includes the total Crime Index, as well as violent crime and property crime rates.

In 2013, the FBI adopted a new definition of rape. Rape is now defined as, "Penetration, no matter how slight, of the vagina or anus with any body part or object, or oral penetration by a sex organ of another person, without the consent of the victim." The new definition updated the 80-year-old historical definition of rape which was "carnal knowledge of a female forcibly and against her will." Effectively, the revised definition expands rape to include both male and female victims and offenders, and reflects the various forms of sexual penetration understood to be rape, especially nonconsenting acts of sodomy, and sexual assaults with objects.

Violent crimes include four categories of offenses: (1) Murder and nonnegligent manslaughter, as defined in the UCR Program, is the willful (nonnegligent) killing of one human being by another. This offense excludes deaths caused by negligence, suicide, or accident; justifiable homicides; and attempts to murder or assaults to murder. (2)) Rape is the penetration, no matter how slight, of the vagina or anus with any body part or object, or oral penetration by a sex organ of another person, without the consent of the victim Assaults or attempts to commit rape by force or threat of force are also included; however, statutory rape (without force) and other sex offenses are excluded. (3) Robbery is the taking or attempting to take anything of value from the care, custody, or control of a person or persons by force or threat of force or violence and/or by putting the victim in fear. (4) Aggravated assault is an unlawful attack by one person upon another for the purpose of inflicting severe or aggravated bodily injury. This type of assault is usually accompanied by the use of a weapon or by other means likely to produce death or great bodily harm. Attempts are included, since injury does not necessarily have to result when a gun, knife, or other weapon is used, as these incidents could and probably would result in a serious personal injury if the crime were successfully completed.

Property crimes include three categories: (1) Burglary, or breaking and entering, is the unlawful entry of a structure to commit a felony or theft, even though no force was used to gain entrance. (2) Larceny-theft is the unauthorized taking of the personal property of another, without the use of force. (3) Motor vehicle theft is the unauthorized taking of any motor vehicle.

Rates are based on population estimates provided by the FBI. If a city is not in the UCR database, or if the population total for the units aggregated was less than 75 percent of the city's population (as estimated by the Census Bureau), the total was not considered representative of the city as a whole and was not published. State and U.S. totals include FBI estimates for those areas.

EDUCATIONAL ATTAINMENT, Items 39–41

Source: U.S. Census Bureau—American Community Survey, 2017 1-year Supplemental Estimates
http://www.census.gov/acs/www/

Data on **educational attainment** are tabulated for the population 25 years old and over. The data were derived from a question that asked respondents for the highest level of school completed or the highest degree received. Persons who had passed a high school equivalency examination were considered high school graduates. Schooling received in foreign schools was to be reported as the equivalent grade or years in the regular American school system.

Vocational and technical training, such as barber school training; business, trade, technical, and vocational schools; or other training for a specific trade are specifically excluded.

High school graduate or less. This category includes persons whose highest degree was a high school diploma or its equivalent, and those who reported any level lower than a high school diploma.

Bachelor's degree or more. This category includes persons who have received bachelor's degrees, master's degrees, professional school degrees (such as law school or medical school degrees), and doctoral degrees.

INCOME, Items 42–49

Source: U.S. Census Bureau—American Community Survey, 2017 1-year Supplemental Estimates
http://www.census.gov/acs/www/

Total money income is the sum of the amounts reported separately for wage or salary income; net self-employment income; interest, dividends, or net rental or royalty income or income from estates and trusts; Social Security or railroad retirement income; Supplemental Security Income (SSI); public assistance or welfare payments; retirement, survivor, or disability pensions; and all other income. Receipts from the following sources are not included as income: capital gains; money received from the sale of property (unless the recipient was engaged in the business of selling such property); the value of income "in kind" from food stamps, public housing subsidies, medical care, employer contributions for individuals, etc.; withdrawal of bank deposits; money borrowed; tax refunds; exchange of money between relatives living in the same household; and gifts, lump-sum inheritances, insurance payments, and other types of lump-sum receipts.

Household income includes the income of the householder and all other individuals 15 years old and over in the household, whether or not they are related to the householder. Since many households consist of only one person, median household income is usually less than median family income. Although the household income statistics cover the twelve months prior to the survey, the characteristics of individuals and the composition of households refer to the date of the interview. Thus, the income of the household does not include amounts received by individuals who were members of the household during all or part of the year if these individuals were no longer residing in the household at the time of the interview. Similarly, income amounts reported by individuals who did not reside in the household during full year but who were members of the household at the time of the interview are included. However, the composition of most households was the same during the year as it was at the time of the interview.

Income of Families – In compiling statistics on family income, the incomes of all members 15 years old and over related to the householder are summed and treated as a single amount.

Median income divides the income distribution into two equal parts, with half of all cases below the median income level and half of all cases above the median income level. For households, the median income is based on the distribution of the total number of households, including those with no income. Median income for households and families is computed on the basis of a standard distribution with a minimum value of less than $2,500 and a maximum value of $200,000 or more and is rounded to the nearest whole dollar. Median income figures are calculated using linear interpolation if the width of the interval containing the estimate is $2,500 or less. If the width of the interval containing the estimate is greater than $2,500, Pareto interpolation is used.

Income components were reported for the 12 months preceding the interview month. Monthly Consumer Price Index (CPI) factors were used to inflation-adjust these components to a reference calendar year (January through December). For example, a household interviewed in March 2017 reports their income for March 2016 through February 2017. Their income is adjusted to the 2017 reference calendar year by multiplying their reported income by 2017 average annual CPI (January-December 2017) and then dividing by the average CPI for March 2016-February 2017. In addition, the 3-year estimates are inflation-adjusted to the final year. However, the estimates do not reflect the price and cost-of-living differences that may exist between areas.

Earnings – Earnings are defined as the sum of wage or salary income and net income from self-employment. "Earnings" represent the amount of income received regularly for people 16 years old and over before deductions for personal income taxes, Social Security, bond purchases, union dues, Medicare deductions, etc. An individual with earnings is one who has either wage/salary income or self-employment income, or both. Respondents who "break even" in self-employment income and therefore have zero self-employment earnings also are considered "individuals with earnings."

HOUSING, Items 50–54

Source: U.S. Census Bureau--American Community Survey, 2017 1-year Supplemental Estimates
http://www.census.gov/acs/www/

The characteristics of occupied housing units are from the 2017 American Community Survey.

A **housing unit** is a house, apartment, mobile home or trailer, group of rooms, or single room occupied or, if vacant, intended for occupancy as separate living quarters. Separate living quarters are those in which the occupants do not live and eat with any other person in the structure and which have direct access from the outside of the building through a common hall. For vacant units, the criteria of separateness and direct access are applied to the intended occupants whenever possible. If that information cannot be obtained, the criteria are applied to the previous occupants.

The occupants of a housing unit may be a single family, one person living alone, two or more families living together, or any other group of related or unrelated persons who share living quarters. Both occupied and vacant housing units are included in the housing inventory, although recreational vehicles, tents, caves, boats, railroad cars, and the like are included only if they are occupied as a person's usual place of residence.

A housing unit is classified as occupied if it is the usual place of residence of the person or group of persons living in it at the time of enumeration, or if the occupants are only temporarily absent (away on vacation). A household consists of all persons who occupy a housing unit as their usual place of residence. Vacant units for sale or rent include units rented or sold but not occupied and any other units held off the market.

A housing unit is **owner occupied** if the owner or co-owner lives in the unit, even if it is mortgaged or not fully paid for. The owner or co-owner must live in the unit and is usually the first person listed on the census or ACS questionnaire.

All occupied housing units that are not owner occupied, whether they are rented for cash rent or occupied without payment of cash rent, are classified as **renter occupied**.

Median value is the dollar amount that divides the distribution of specified owner-occupied housing units into two equal parts, with half of all units below the median value and half of all units above the median value. Value is defined as the respondent's estimate of what the house would sell for if it were for sale. Data are presented for single-family units on fewer than 10 acres of land that have no business or medical offices on the property.

Median rent divides the distribution of renter-occupied housing units into two equal parts. The rent concept used in this volume is gross rent, which includes the amount of cash rent a renter pays (contract rent) plus the estimated average cost of utilities and fuels, if these are paid by the renter. The rent is the amount of rent only for living quarters and excludes amounts paid for any business or other space occupied. Single-family houses on lots of 10 or more acres of land are also excluded.

COMMUTING, Items 55 and 56

Source: U.S. Census Bureau—American Community Survey, 2017 1-year Supplemental Estimates
http://www.census.gov/acs/www/

Means of transportation to work refers to the principal mode of travel or type of conveyance that a worker usually used to get from home to work during the reference week. This question was asked of people who indicated that they worked at some time during the reference week. People who used different means of transportation on different days of the week were asked to specify the one they used most often, that is, the greatest number of days. People who used more than one means of transportation to get to work each day were asked to report the one used for the longest distance during the work trip. The category, "Car, truck, or van," includes workers using a car (including company cars but excluding taxicabs), a truck of one-ton capacity or less, or a van. The category, **"Drove alone,"** includes people who usually drove alone to work as well as people who were driven to work by someone who then drove back home or to a non-work destination.

The question on **travel time to work** was asked of people who indicated that they worked at some time during the reference week, and who reported that they worked outside their home. Travel time to work refers to the total number of minutes that it usually took the worker to get from home to work during the reference week. The elapsed time includes time spent waiting for public transportation, picking up passengers in carpools, and time spent in other activities related to getting to work.

COMPUTER AND INTERNET USE, Items 57 and 58

Source: U.S. Census Bureau—American Community Survey, 2017 1-year Supplemental Estimates
http://www.census.gov/acs/www/

The **computer use** question asked if anyone in the household owned or used a computer and included three response categories for a desktop/laptop, a handheld computer, or some other type of computer. Respondents could select all categories that applied.

Another question asked if any member of the household accesses the **internet**. "Access" refers to whether or not someone in the household uses or connects to the Internet, regardless of whether or not they pay for the service. Respondents were to select only ONE of the following choices:

- Yes, with a subscription to an Internet service –This category includes housing units where someone pays to access the Internet through a service such as a data plan for a mobile phone, a cable modem, DSL or other type of service. This will normally refer to a service that someone is billed for directly for Internet alone or sometimes as part of a bundle.
- Yes, without a subscription to an Internet service–Some respondents may live in a city or town that provides free Internet services for their residents. In addition, some colleges or universities provide Internet services. These are examples of cases where respondents may be able to access the Internet without a subscription.
- No Internet access at this house, apartment, or mobile home- This category includes housing units where no one connects to or uses the Internet using a paid service or any free services.

MIGRATION, Items 59 and 60

Source: U.S. Census Bureau—American Community Survey, 2017 1-year Supplemental Estimates
http://www.census.gov/acs/www/

Residence one year ago is used in conjunction with location of current residence to determine the extent of residential mobility of the population and the resulting redistribution of the population across the various states, metropolitan areas, and regions of the country. Same house includes all people 1 year old and over who, a year before the survey date, lived in the same house or apartment that they occupied at the time of interview.

The percent who lived outside current county includes all persons who did not live in their current county 1 year before the interview. However, they may have lived outside their current city but still in the same county.

CIVILIAN LABOR FORCE AND UNEMPLOY-MENT, Items 61–64

Source: U.S. Bureau of Labor Statistics—Local Areas Unemployment Statistics
http://www.bls.gov/lau/#tables

Data for the civilian labor force are the product of a federal-state cooperative program in which state employment security agencies prepare labor force and unemployment estimates under concepts, definitions, and technical procedures established by the Bureau of Labor Statistics (BLS). The civilian labor force consists of all civilians 16 years old and over who are either employed or unemployed.

Unemployment includes all persons who did not work during the survey week, made specific efforts to find a job during the previous four weeks, and were available for work during the survey week (except for temporary illness). Persons waiting to be called back to a job from which they had been laid off and those waiting to report to a new job within the next 30 days are included in unemployment figures.

Table D includes annual average data for the year shown. The Local Area Unemployment Statistics data are periodically updated to reflect revised inputs, reestimation, and controlling to new statewide totals.

EMPLOYMENT, Items 65–68

Source: U.S. Census Bureau—American Community Survey, 2017 1-year Supplemental Estimates
http://www.census.gov/acs/www/

The **labor force** includes all persons 16 years old and over who were either (1) "at work"—those who did any work at all during the reference week as paid employees, worked in either their own business or profession, worked on their own farm, or worked 15 hours or more as unpaid workers in a family farm or business; or were (2) "with a job, but not at work" —those who had a job but were not at work that week due to illness, weather, industrial dispute, vacation, or other personal reasons.

Full-year, Full-Time Workers includes people 16 to 64 years old who usually worked 35 hours or more per week for 50 to 52 weeks in the past 12 months.

BUILDING PERMITS, Items 69–71

Source: U.S. Census Bureau—Building Permits Survey
http://www.census.gov/construction/bps/

These figures represent private residential construction authorized by building permits in approximately 20,000 places in the United States. Valuation represents the expected cost of construction as recorded on the building permit. This figure usually excludes the cost of on-site and off-site development and improvements, as well as the cost of heating, plumbing, electrical, and elevator installations.

National, state, and county totals were obtained by adding the data for permit-issuing places within each jurisdiction. These totals thus are limited to permits issued in the 20,000 place universe covered by the Census Bureau and may not include all permits issued within a state. Current surveys indicate that construction is undertaken for all but a very small percentage of housing units authorized by building permits.

Residential building permits include buildings with any number of housing units. Housing units exclude group quarters (such as dormitories and rooming houses), transient accommodations (such as transient hotels, motels, and tourist courts), "HUD-code" manufactured (mobile) homes, moved or relocated units, and housing units created in an existing residential or nonresidential structure.

2012 Economic CENSUS: OVERVIEW, Items 72–107

Source: U.S. Census Bureau
https://www.census.gov/programs-surveys/economic-census/library/publications.html

The Economic Census provides a detailed portrait of the nation's economy, from the national to the local level, once every five years. The 2012 Economic Census covers nearly all of the U.S. economy in its basic collection of establishment statistics. The 1997 Economic Census was the first major data source to use the new North American Industry Classification System (NAICS); therefore, data from this census are not comparable to economic data from prior years, which were based on the Standard Industrial Classification (SIC) system.

NAICS, developed in cooperation with Canada and Mexico, classifies North America's economic activities at two-, three-, four-, and five-digit levels of detail; the U.S. version of NAICS further defines industries to a sixth digit. The Economic Census takes advantage of this hierarchy to publish data at these successive levels of detail: sector (two-digit), subsector (three-digit), industry group (four-digit), industry (five-digit), and U.S. industry (six-digit). Information in Table A is at the two-digit level, with a few three- and four-digit items. The data in Table D are at the two-digit level.

Several key statistics are tabulated for all industries in this volume, including number of establishments (or companies), number of employees, payroll, and certain measures of output (sales, receipts, revenue, value of shipments, or value of construction work done).

Number of establishments. An establishment is a single physical location at which business is conducted. It is not necessarily identical with a company or enterprise, which may consist of one establishment or more. Economic Census figures represent a summary of reports for individual establishments rather than companies. For cases in which a census report was received, separate information was obtained for each location where business was conducted. When administrative records of other federal agencies were used instead of a census report, no information was available on the number of locations operated. Each Economic Census establishment was tabulated according to the physical location at which the business was conducted. The count of establishments represents those in business at any time during 2002.

When two activities or more were carried on at a single location under a single ownership, all activities were generally grouped together as a single establishment. The entire establishment was classified on the basis of its major activity and all of its data were included in that classification. However, when distinct and separate economic activities (for which different industry classification codes were appropriate) were conducted at a single location under a single ownership, separate establishment reports for each of the different activities were obtained in the census.

Number of employees. Paid employees consist of the full-time and part-time employees, including salaried officers and executives of corporations. Included are employees on paid sick leave, paid holidays, and paid vacations; not included are proprietors and partners of unincorporated businesses. The definition of paid employees is the same as that used by the Internal Revenue Service (IRS) on form 941. For some industries, the Economic Census gives codes representing the number of employees as a range of numbers (for example, "100 to 249 employees" or "1,000 to 2,499" employees). In this volume, those codes have been replaced by the standard suppression code "D".

Payroll. Payroll includes all forms of compensation, such as salaries, wages, commissions, dismissal pay, bonuses, vacation allowances, sick-leave pay, and employee contributions to qualified pension plans paid during the year to all employees. For corporations, payroll includes amounts paid to officers and executives; for unincorporated businesses, it does not include profit or other compensation of proprietors or partners. Payroll is reported before deductions for Social Security, income tax, insurance, union dues, etc. This definition of payroll is the same as that used by on IRS form 941.

Sales, shipments, receipts, revenue, or business done. This measure includes the total sales, shipments, receipts, revenue, or business done by establishments within the scope of the Economic Census. The definition of each of these items is specific to the economic sector measured.

WHOLESALE TRADE, Items 72–75

Source: U.S. Census Bureau—2012 Economic Census (See Overview of 2012 Economic Census prior to Item 72)

The Wholesale Trade sector (sector 42) comprises establishments engaged in wholesaling merchandise, generally without transformation, and rendering services incidental to the sale of merchandise. The wholesaling process is an intermediate step in the distribution of merchandise.

Wholesalers are organized to sell or arrange the purchase or sale of (1) goods for resale (i.e., goods sold to other wholesalers or retailers), (2) capital or durable nonconsumer goods, and (3) raw and intermediate materials and supplies used in production.

Wholesalers sell merchandise to other businesses and normally operate from a warehouse or office. These warehouses and offices are characterized by having little or no display of merchandise. In addition, neither the design nor the location of the premises is intended to solicit walk-in traffic. Wholesalers do not normally use advertising directed to the general public. In general, customers are initially reached via telephone, in-person marketing, or specialized advertising, which may include the internet and other electronic means. Follow-up orders are either vendor-initiated or client-initiated, are usually based on previous sales, and typically exhibit strong ties between sellers and buyers. In fact, transactions are often conducted between wholesalers and clients that have long-standing business relationships.

This sector is made up of two main types of wholesalers: those that sell goods on their own account and those that arrange sales and purchases for others for a commission or fee.

(1) Establishments that sell goods on their own account are known as wholesale merchants, distributors, jobbers, drop shippers, import/export merchants, and sales branches. These establishments typically maintain their own warehouse, where they receive and handle goods for their customers. Goods are generally sold without transformation, but may include integral functions, such as sorting, packaging, labeling, and other marketing services.

(2) Establishments arranging for the purchase or sale of goods owned by others or purchasing goods on a commission basis are known as agents and brokers, commission merchants, import/export agents and brokers, auction companies, and manufacturers' representatives. These establishments operate from offices and generally do not own or handle the goods they sell.

Some wholesale establishments may be connected with a single manufacturer and promote and sell that particular manufacturer's products to a wide range of other wholesalers or retailers. Other wholesalers may be connected to a retail chain or a limited number of retail chains and only provide the products needed by the particular retail operation(s). These wholesalers may obtain the products from a wide range of manufacturers. Still other wholesalers may not take title to the goods, but act instead as agents and brokers for a commission.

Although wholesaling normally denotes sales in large volumes, durable nonconsumer goods may be sold in single units. Sales of capital or durable nonconsumer goods used in the production of goods and services, such as farm machinery, medium- and heavy-duty trucks, and industrial machinery, are always included in Wholesale Trade.

The city table includes only **Merchant wholesalers, except manufacturers' sales branches and offices**, establishments primarily engaged in buying and selling merchandise on their own account. Included here are such types of establishments as whole-sale distributors and jobbers, importers, exporters, own-brand importers/marketers, terminal and country grain elevators, and farm products assemblers.

RETAIL TRADE, Items 76–79

Source: U.S. Census Bureau—2012 Economic Census (See Overview of 2012 Economic Census prior to Item 72)

The Retail Trade sector (44–45) is made up of establishments engaged in retailing merchandise, generally without transformation, and rendering services incidental to the sale of merchandise.

The retailing process is the final step in the distribution of merchandise; retailers are therefore organized to sell merchandise in small quantities to the general public. This sector comprises two main types of retailers: store and nonstore retailers.

Store retailers operate fixed point-of-sale locations, located and designed to attract a high volume of walk-in customers. In general, retail stores have extensive displays of merchandise and use mass-media advertising to attract customers. They typically sell merchandise to the general public for personal or household consumption; some also serve business and institutional clients. These include establishments such as office supply stores, computer and software stores, building materials dealers, plumbing supply stores, and electrical supply stores. Catalog showrooms, gasoline service stations, automotive dealers, and mobile home dealers are treated as store retailers.

In addition to retailing merchandise, some types of store retailers are also engaged in the provision of after-sales services, such as repair and installation. For example, new automobile dealers, electronic and appliance stores, and musical instrument and supply stores often provide repair services. As a general rule, establishments engaged in retailing merchandise and providing after-sales services are classified in this sector.

Nonstore retailers, like store retailers, are organized to serve the general public, although their retailing methods differ. The establishments of this subsector reach customers and market merchandise with methods including the broadcasting of "infomercials," the broadcasting and publishing of direct-response advertising, the publishing of paper and electronic catalogs, door-to-door solicitation, in-home demonstration, selling from portable stalls (street vendors, except food), and distribution through vending machines. Establishments engaged in the direct sale (nonstore) of products, such as home heating oil dealers and home-delivery newspaper routes are included in this sector.

The buying of goods for resale is a characteristic of retail trade establishments that distinguishes them from establishments in the Agriculture, Manufacturing, and Construction sectors. For example, farms that sell their products at or from the point of production are classified in Agriculture instead of in Retail Trade. Similarly, establishments that both manufacture and sell their products to the general public are classified in Manufacturing instead of Retail Trade. However, establishments that engage in processing activities incidental to retailing are classified in Retail Trade.

REAL ESTATE AND RENTAL AND LEASING, Items 80–83

Source: U.S. Census Bureau—2012 Economic Census (See Overview of 2012 Economic Census prior to Item 72)

The Real Estate and Rental and Leasing sector (53) comprises establishments primarily engaged in renting, leasing, or otherwise allowing the use of tangible or intangible assets, and establishments providing related services. The major portion of this sector is made up of establishments that rent, lease, or otherwise allow the use of their own assets by others. The assets may be tangible, such as real estate and equipment, or intangible, such as patents and trademarks.

This sector also includes establishments primarily engaged in managing real estate for others, selling, renting, and/or buying real estate for others, and appraising real estate. These activities are closely related to this sector's main activity. In addition, a substantial proportion of property management is self-performed by lessors.

The main components of this sector are the real estate lessors industries; equipment lessors industries (including motor vehicles, computers, and consumer goods); and lessors of nonfinancial intangible assets (except copyrighted works).

PROFESSIONAL, SCIENTIFIC, AND TECHNICAL SERVICES, Items 84–87

Source: U.S. Census Bureau—2012 Economic Census (See Overview of 2012 Economic Census prior to Item 72)

The Professional, Scientific, and Technical Services sector (54) is made up of establishments that specialize in performing professional, scientific, and technical activities for others. These activities require a high degree of expertise and training. The establishments in this sector specialize in one or more areas and provide services to clients in a variety of industries (and, in some cases, to households). Activities performed include legal advice and representation; accounting, bookkeeping, and payroll services; architectural, engineering, and specialized design services; computer services; consulting services; research services; advertising services; photographic services; translation and interpretation services; veterinary services; and other professional, scientific, and technical services.

Table D includes only those establishments subject to federal income tax.

This sector excludes establishments primarily engaged in providing a range of day-to-day office administrative services, such as financial planning, billing and record keeping, personnel services, and physical distribution and logistics services. These establishments are classified in sector 56, Administrative and Support and Waste Management and Remediation Services.

MANUFACTURING, Items 88–91

Source: U.S. Census Bureau—2012 Economic Census (See Overview of 2012 Economic Census prior to Item 72)

The Manufacturing sector (31–33) is made up of establishments engaged in the mechanical, physical, or chemical transformation of materials, substances, or components into new products. The assembling of component parts of manufactured products is considered manufacturing, except in cases in which the activity is appropriately classified in the Construction sector. Establishments in the Manufacturing sector are often described as plants, factories, or mills, and characteristically use power-driven machines and materials-handling equipment. However, establishments that transform materials or substances into new products by hand or in the worker's home, and establishments engaged in selling to the general public products made on the same premises from which they are sold (such as bakeries, candy stores, and custom tailors) may also be included in this sector. Manufacturing establishments may process materials or contract with other establishments to process their materials for them. Both types of establishments are included in the Manufacturing sector.

The materials, substances, or components transformed by manufacturing establishments are raw materials that are products of agriculture, forestry, fishing, mining, or quarrying, or are products of other manufacturing establishments. The materials used may be purchased directly from producers, obtained through customary trade channels, or secured without recourse to the market by transferring the product from one establishment to another, under the same ownership. The new product of a manufacturing establishment may be finished (in the sense that it is ready for utilization or consumption), or it may be semifinished to become an input for an establishment engaged in further manufacturing. For example, the product of the alumina refinery is the input used in the primary production of aluminum; primary aluminum is the input used in an aluminum wire drawing plant; and aluminum wire is the input used in a fabricated wire product manufacturing establishment.

Data are included for cities with 500 or more employees in the Manufacturing sector.

ACCOMMODATION AND FOOD SERVICES, Items 92–95

Source: U.S. Census Bureau—2012 Economic Census (See Overview of 2012 Economic Census prior to Item 72)

The Accommodation and Food Services sector (72) consists of establishments that provide customers with lodging and/or meals, snacks, and beverages for immediate consumption. This sector includes both accommodation and food services establishments because the two activities are often combined at the same establishment.

Excluded from this sector are civic and social organizations, amusement and recreation parks, theaters, and other recreation or entertainment facilities providing food and beverage services.

ARTS, ENTERTAINMENT, AND RECREATION, Items 96–99

Source: U.S. Census Bureau—2012 Economic Census

(See Overview of 2012 Economic Census prior to Item 72)

The Arts, Entertainment, and Recreation sector (71) includes a wide range of establishments that operate facilities or provide services that meet the diverse cultural, entertainment, and recreational interests of their patrons. This sector is made up of: (1) establishments that are involved in producing, promoting, or participating in live performances, events, or exhibits intended for public viewing; (2) establishments that preserve and exhibit objects and sites of historical, cultural, or educational interest; and (3) establishments that operate facilities or provide services that enable patrons to participate in recreational activities or pursue amusement, hobby, and leisure time interests.

Some establishments that provide cultural, entertainment, or recreational facilities and services are classified in other sectors. Excluded from this sector are: (1) establishments that provide both accommodations and recreational facilities—such as hunting and fishing camps and resort and casino hotels—are classified in subsector 721, Accommodation; (2) restaurants and night clubs that provide live entertainment in addition to the sale of food and beverages are classified in subsector 722, Food Services and Drinking Places; (3) motion picture theaters, libraries and archives, and publishers of newspapers, magazines, books, periodicals, and computer software are classified in sector 51, Information; and (4) establishmentsthat use transportation equipment to provide recreational and entertainment services, such as those operating sightseeing buses, dinner cruises, or helicopter rides, are classified in subsector 487, Scenic and Sightseeing Transportation.

Table D includes only those establishments subject to federal tax.

HEALTH CARE AND SOCIAL ASSISTANCE, Items 100–103

Source: U.S. Census Bureau—2012 Economic Census (See Overview of 2012 Economic Census prior to Item 72)

The Health Care and Social Assistance sector (62) consists of establishments that provide health care and social assistance services to individuals. The sector includes both health care and social assistance because it is sometimes difficult to distinguish between the boundaries of these two activities. The industries in this sector are arranged on a continuum, starting with establishments that provide medical care exclusively, continuing with those that provide health care and social assistance, and finishing with those that provide only social assistance. The services provided by establishments in this sector are delivered by trained professionals. All industries in the sector share this commonality of process—namely, labor inputs of health practitioners or social workers with the requisite expertise. Many of the industries in the sector are defined based on the educational degree held by the practitioners included in the industry.

Excluded from this sector are aerobic classes, which can be found in subsector 713, Amusement, Gambling, and Recreation

Industries; and nonmedical diet and weight-reducing centers, which can be found in subsector 812, Personal and Laundry Services. Although these can be viewed as health services, they are not typically delivered by health practitioners.

Table D includes only those establishments subject to federal tax.

OTHER SERVICES, EXCEPT PUBLIC ADMINISTRATION Items 104–107

Source: U.S. Census Bureau—2012 Economic Census (See Overview of 2012 Economic Census prior to Item 72)

The Other Services, Except Public Administration sector (81) comprises establishments engaged in providing services not specifically categorized elsewhere in the classification system. Establishments in this sector are primarily engaged in activities such as equipment and machinery repairing, promoting or administering religious activities, grant making, and advocacy; this sector also includes establishments that provide dry-cleaning and laundry services, personal care services, death care services, pet care services, photofinishing services, temporary parking services, and dating services.

Private households that employ workers on or about the premises in activities primarily concerned with the operation of the household are included in this sector.

In Table D, only firms subject to federal tax are included.

Excluded from this sector are establishments primarily engaged in retailing new equipment and performing repairs and general maintenance on equipment. These establishments are classified in sector 44–45, Retail Trade.

CITY GOVERNMENT EMPLOYMENT AND PAYROLL, Items 171-179

Source: U.S. Census Bureau—2012 Census of Governments
https://www.census.gov/programs-surveys/cog.html

These items include data for municipal governments only. They do not include any special district government entities within the city. The Census of Governments identifies the scope and nature of the nation's state and local government sector; provides authoritative benchmark figures of public finance and public employment; classifies local government organizations, powers, and activities; and measures federal, state, and local fiscal relationships. The Employment component was mailed **March 2012** to collect information on the number of state and local government civilian employees and their payrolls.

Government employees include all persons paid for personal services performed, including persons paid from federally funded programs, paid elected or appointed officials, persons in a paid leave status, and persons paid on a per meeting, annual, semi-annual, or quarterly basis. Unpaid officials, pensioners, persons whose work is performed on a fee basis, and contractors and their employees are excluded from the count of employees. **Full-Time Equivalent employees** is a computed statistic representing the

number of full-time employees that could have been employed if the reported number of hours worked by part-time employees had been worked by full-time employees. This statistic is calculated separately for each function of a government by dividing the "part-time hours paid" by the standard number of hours for full-time employees in the particular government and then adding the resulting quotient to the number of full-time employees.

March payroll represents gross payroll amounts for the one-month period of March for full-time and part-time employees. Gross payroll includes all salaries, wages, fees, commissions, and overtime paid to employees **before** withholdings for taxes, insurance, etc. It also includes incentive payments that are paid at regular pay intervals. It excludes employer share of fringe benefits like retirement, Social Security, health and life insurance, lump sum payments, and so forth.

Administration and Judicial and Legal combines **Financial administration**, **Other government administration, and Judicial and Legal** activities. **Financial administration includes** activities concerned with tax assessment and collection, custody and disbursement of funds, debt management, administration of trust funds, budgeting, and other government-wide financial management activities. This function is not applied to school district or special district governments. **Other government administration** applies to the legislative and government-wide administrative agencies of governments. Included here are overall planning and zoning activities, and central personnel and administrative activities. This function is not applied to school district or special district governments. **Judicial and legal** includes all court and court related activities (except probation and parole activities that are included at the "Correction" function), court activities of sheriff's offices, prosecuting attorneys' and public defenders' offices, legal departments, and attorneys providing government-wide legal service.

Police and Corrections includes all activities concerned, with the enforcement of law and order, including coroner's offices, police training academies, investigation bureaus, and local jails, "lockups", or other detention facilities not intended to serve as correctional facilities. **Corrections** includes activities pertaining to the confinement and correction of adults and minors convicted of criminal offenses. Pardon, probation, and parole activities are also included here.

Fire protection includes local government fire protection and prevention activities plus any ambulance, rescue, or other auxiliary services provided by a fire protection agency. Volunteer firefighters, if remunerated for their services on a "per fire" or some other basis, are included as part-time employees.

Highways and transportation includes activities associated with the maintenance and operation of streets, roads, sidewalks, bridges, tunnels, toll roads, and ferries. Snow and ice removal, street lighting, and highway and traffic engineering activities are also included here. Also included are the operation, maintenance, and construction of public mass transit systems, including subways, surface rails, and buses, and the provision, construction, operation, maintenance; support of public waterways, harbors, docks, wharves, and related marine terminal facilities; and activities associated with the operation and support of publicly operated airport facilities.

Health and Welfare includes Health, Hospitals, and Public welfare. Health includes administration of public health programs, community and visiting nurse services, immunization programs, drug abuse rehabilitation programs, health and food inspection activities, operation of outpatient clinics, and environmental pollution control activities. **Hospitals** includes only government operated medical care facilities that provide inpatient care. Employees and payrolls of private corporations that lease and operate government-owned hospital facilities are excluded.

Public Welfare includes the administration of various public assistance programs for the needy, veteran services, operation of nursing homes, indigent care institutions, and programs that provide payments for medical care, handicap transportation, and other services for the needy.

Natural resources and Utilities includes activities primarily concerned with the conservation and development of natural resources (soil, water, energy, minerals, etc.) and the regulation of industries that develop, utilize, or affect natural resources, as well as the operation and maintenance of **parks**, playgrounds, swimming pools, public beaches, auditoriums, public golf courses, museums, marinas, botanical gardens, and zoological parks. **Utilities, sewerage, and waste management** includes operation, maintenance, and construction of public water supply systems, including production, acquisition, and distribution of water to general public or to other public or private utilities, for residential, commercial, and industrial use; activities associated with the production or acquisition and distribution of electric power; provision, maintenance, and operation of sanitary and storm sewer systems and sewage disposal and treatment facilities; and refuse collection and disposal, operation of sanitary landfills, and street cleaning activities.

Education and libraries includes activities associated with the operation of public elementary and secondary schools and locally operated vocational-technical schools. Special education programs operated by elementary and secondary school systems are also included as are all ancillary services associated with the operation of schools, such as pupil transportation and food service. **Also included are the e**stablishment and provision of libraries for use by the general public and the technical support of privately operated libraries. This category includes classroom teachers, principals, supervisors of instruction, librarians, teacher aides, library aides, and guidance and psychological personnel as well as school superintendents and other administrative personnel, clerical and secretarial staffs, plant operation and maintenance personnel, health and recreation employees, transportation and food service personnel, and any student employees. Also included are any degree granting institutions that provide academic training above grade 12.

CITY GOVERNMENT FINANCES, Items 117–139

Source: U.S. Census Bureau—2012 Census of Governments
https://www.census.gov/programs-surveys/cog.html

Revenue and expenditure data are included in Table D for municipal governments only. The data do not include funds of any special district governments located in the city. For example, if a city's school district is a separate governmental unit, it is not included.

Total **general revenue** includes all revenue except utility, liquor stores, and insurance trust revenue. All tax revenue and intergovernmental revenue, even if designated for employee-retirement or local utility purpose, are classified as general revenue.

Intergovernmental revenue covers amounts received from other governments as fiscal aid in the form of shared revenues and grants-in-aid, as reimbursements for the performance of general government functions and specific services for the paying government (for example, care of prisoners or contractual research), or in lieu of taxes. It excludes any amounts received from other governments from the sale of property, commodities, and utility services. All intergovernmental revenue is classified as general revenue. Intergovernmental revenue from the state governments includes amounts originally from the federal government but channeled through the state.

Taxes consist of compulsory contributions exacted by governments for public purposes. However, this category excludes employer and employee payments for retirement and social insurance purposes, which are classified as insurance trust revenue. All tax revenue is classified as general revenue and comprises amounts received (including interest and penalties, but excluding protested amounts and refunds) from all taxes imposed by a government. Note that local government tax revenue excludes any amounts from shares of state-imposed and collected taxes, which are classified as intergovernmental revenue.

Property taxes are based on ownership of property and measured by its value. They include general property taxes related to property as a whole—real and personal, tangible or intangible—whether taxed at a single rate or at classified rates. Also included are taxes on selected types of property, such as motor vehicles or certain or all intangibles.

Sales and gross receipts taxes include "licenses" at more than nominal rates, based on volume or value of transfers of goods or services; taxes upon gross receipts or upon gross income; and related taxes based upon the use, storage, production (other than the severance of natural resources), importation, or consumption of goods. Dealer discounts "commissions," which are allowed to merchants for the collection of taxes from consumers, are excluded.

Total **general expenditure** includes all city expenditure other than specifically enumerated kinds of expenditure, including utility, liquor store, and employee-retirement and other insurance trust expenditures.

Capital outlays are direct expenditures for contract of force account construction or buildings, roads, and other improvements, and for purchases of equipment, land, and existing structures. They include amounts for additions, replacements, and major alterations to fixed work and structures. Expenditures for repair to such works and structures, however, is classified as current operation expenditure.

A major portion of capital outlay is commonly financed by borrowing, while governmental revenue does not include receipts from borrowing. Among other things, this distorts the relationship between the totals presented for revenue and expenditure and renders this relationship useless as a direct measure of the degree of budgetary "balance" (as that term is generally applied).

Public welfare expenditure covers support of and assistance to needy persons; this aid is contingent upon the person's needs. Included are cash assistance paid directly to needy persons; vendor payments made directly to private purveyors for medical care, burials, and other commodities and services provided under welfare programs; welfare institutions; and any intergovernmental or other direct expenditure for welfare purposes. Pensions to former employees and other benefits not contingent on need are excluded.

Highway expenditure is for the provision and maintenance of highway facilities, including toll turnpikes, bridges, tunnels, and ferries, as well as regular roads, highways, and streets. Also included are expenditures for street lighting and for snow and ice removal. Not included are highway policing and traffic control, which are considered part of police protection

Parking facilities include the construction, purchase, maintenance, and operation of public-use parking lots, garages, parking meters, and other distinctive parking facilities on a commercial basis.

Education is mainly for the provision and general support of schools and other educational facilities and services, including those for educational institutions beyond high school. Elementary and secondary education includes the provision of public kindergarten through high school education by local governments. It encompasses instructional, support, and auxiliary services (school lunch, student activities, and community services) offered by public school systems. Higher education consists of all local institutions of higher education.

Health expenditures include outpatient health services other than hospital care, such as public health administration; research and education; categorical health programs; treatment and immunization clinics; nursing; environmental health activities, such as air and water pollution control; ambulance service if provided separately from fire protection services; and other general public health activities, such as mosquito abatement. School health services provided by health agencies (rather than school agencies) are included here. Not included are sewage treatment operations, which are classified as part of sewerage and sanitation. **Hospital expenditures** include financing, construction, acquisition, maintenance and operation of hospital facilities, provision of hospital care, and support of public or private hospitals.

Police protection encompasses expenditures for the preservation of law and order, as well as for traffic safety. It includes police patrols and communications, crime prevention activities, detention and custody of persons awaiting trial, traffic safety, and vehicular inspection.

Sewerage and recreation include sanitary and storm sewers, sewage disposal facilities and services, and other government activities for such purposes. Street cleaning and the collection and disposal of garbage and other waste are also included.

Parks and recreation includes cultural and scientific activities, such as museums and art galleries; organized recreation, including playgrounds and playing fields, swimming pools, and bathing beaches; and municipal parks and special recreation facilities, such as auditoriums, stadiums, auto camps, recreation piers, and boat harbors.

Housing and community development includes city housing and redevelopment projects and the regulation, promotion, and support of private housing and redevelopment activities. Data from Arizona, Kentucky, Michigan, New Mexico, New York, and Virginia generally include municipal housing authorities. Housing authorities for other cities are usually classified as independent governments, and data from them are not included.

Interest on debt is the amount paid for the use of borrowed money.

Total **debt outstanding** is the total of debt obligations remaining unpaid on the date specified. **Debt issued during the year** is the amount of the outstanding debt that was recently borrowed.

CLIMATE, Items 140–146

Source: National Oceanic and Atmospheric Administration
https://www.ncdc.noaa.gov/data-access/
land-based-station-data/land-based-datasets/
climate-normals

All climate data are average values for the 30-year period from 1971 to 2000.

Mean temperatures for January and July were determined by adding the average daily maximum temperatures and the average daily minimum temperatures and dividing by two.

Temperature limits represent average daily minimum for January and average daily maximum for July.

Annual precipitation values are the average annual water equivalent of all precipitation for the 30-year period.

Heating and cooling degree days are used as relative measures of the energy required for heating and cooling buildings. One heating degree day is accumulated for each whole degree that the mean daily temperature is below 65 degrees Fahrenheit (a mean daily temperature of 62 degrees Fahrenheit will produce three heating degree days). Cooling degree days are accumulated in similar fashion for deviations of the mean daily temperature above 65 degrees Fahrenheit.

TABLE E—CONGRESSIONAL DISTRICTS OF THE 116TH CONGRESS

Members of the House of Representatives are for the 116th Congress.

LAND AREA, Items 1 and 3

Source: U.S. Census Bureau—2018 U.S. Gazetteer Files,
https://www.census.gov/geographies/reference-files/
time-series/geo/gazetteer-files.html

Land area measurements are shown to the nearest square mile. Land area includes dry land and land temporarily or partially covered by water, such as marshlands, swamps, and river floodplains.

POPULATION, Items 2–3

Source: U.S. Census Bureau—American Community Survey
http://www.census.gov/acs/www/

The population data are estimates from the American Community Survey.

POPULATION AND POPULATION CHARACTERISTICS, Items 4–24

Source: U.S. Census Bureau—American Community Survey
http://www.census.gov/acs/www/

Data on age, sex, race, Hispanic origin foreign-born residents, and percent born in state of residence are from the 2016 American Community Survey.

Data on race were derived from answers to the question on race that was asked of all respondents. The concept of race, as used by the Census Bureau, reflects self-identification by people according to the race or races with which they most closely identify. These categories are sociopolitical constructs and should not be interpreted as being scientific or anthropological in nature. Furthermore, the race categories include both racial and national origin groups.

In Table E, Columns 4 through 8 refer to individuals who identified with each racial category alone, while column 9 includes persons who identified with two or more races.

The **White** population is defined as persons who indicated their race as White, as well as persons who did not classify themselves in one of the specific race categories listed on the questionnaire but entered a nationality such as Irish, German, Italian, Lebanese, Near Easterner, Arab, or Polish.

The **Black** population includes persons who indicated their race as "Black or African American" as well as persons who did not classify themselves in one of the specific race categories but reported entries such as African American, Afro American, Kenyan, Nigerian, or Haitian.

The **American Indian or Alaska Native** population includes persons who indicated their race as American Indian or Alaska Native, as well as persons who did not classify themselves in one of the specific race categories but reported entries such as Canadian Indian, French-American Indian, Spanish-American Indian, Eskimo, Aleut, Alaska Indian, or any of the American Indian or Alaska Native tribes.

The **Asian and Pacific Islander** population combines two census groupings: **Asian** and **Native Hawaiian or Other Pacific Islander**. The **Asian** population includes persons who indicated their race as Asian Indian, Chinese, Filipino, Japanese, Korean, Vietnamese, or "Other Asian," as well as persons who provided write-in entries of such groups as Cambodian, Laotian, Hmong, Pakistani, or Taiwanese. The **Native Hawaiian or Other Pacific Islander** population includes persons who indicated their race as "Native Hawaiian," "Guamanian or Chamorro," "Samoan," or "Other Pacific Islander," as well as persons who reported entries such as Part Hawaiian, American Samoan, Fijian, Melanesian, or Tahitian.

The **Hispanic population** is based on a question that asked respondents "Is this person Spanish/Hispanic/Latino?" Persons marking any one of the four Hispanic categories (i.e., Mexican, Puerto Rican, Cuban, or other Spanish) are collectively referred to as Hispanic.

The **Non-Hispanic White alone** number in Column 11 includes only those persons who were not Hispanic and whose race was "White only."

The **female** population is shown as a percentage of total population.

The **foreign-born** population includes all persons who were not U.S. citizens at birth. Foreign-born persons are those who indicated they were either a U.S. citizen by naturalization or were not a citizen of the United States. The foreign-born population consists of immigrants (legal permanent residents), temporary migrants (students), humanitarian migrants (refugees), and unauthorized migrants (persons illegally residing in the United States).

Percent born in state of residence is shown as a percentage of total population.

Age is defined as age at last birthday (number of completed years since birth).

EDUCATION—SCHOOL ENROLLMENT AND EDUCATIONAL ATTAINMENT, Items 25–27

Source: U.S. Census Bureau—American Community Survey
http://www.census.gov/acs/www/

Data on school enrollment and educational attainment were derived from a sample of the population. Persons were classified as enrolled in school if they reported attending a "regular" public or private school (or college) during the year. The instructions were to "include only nursery school, kindergarten, elementary school, and schooling which would lead to a high school diploma or a college degree" as regular school. The Census Bureau defines a public school as "any school or college controlled and supported by a local, county, state, or federal government." Schools primarily supported and controlled by religious organizations or other private groups are defined as private schools.

Data on **educational attainment** are tabulated for the population 25 years old and over. The data were derived from a question that asked respondents for the highest level of school completed or the highest degree received. Persons who had passed a high school equivalency examination were considered high school graduates. Schooling received in foreign schools was to be reported as the equivalent grade or years in the regular American school system.

Vocational and technical training, such as barber school training; business, trade, technical, and vocational schools; or other training for a specific trade are specifically excluded.

High school graduate or more. This category includes persons who have received a high school diploma or its equivalent, and those who reported any level higher than a high school diploma.

Bachelor's degree or more. This category includes persons who have received bachelor's degrees, master's degrees, professional school degrees (such as law school or medical school degrees), and doctoral degrees.

HOUSEHOLDS, Items 28–33

Source: U.S. Census Bureau—American Community Survey
http://www.census.gov/acs/www/

A **household** includes all persons who occupy a housing unit. (Persons not living in households are classified as living in group quarters.) A housing unit is a house, an apartment, a mobile home, a group of rooms, or a single room occupied (or, if vacant, intended for occupancy) as separate living quarters. Separate living quarters are those in which the occupants live separately from any other persons in the building and have direct access from the outside of the building or through a common hall. The occupants may be a single family, one person living alone, two or more families living together, or any other group of related or unrelated persons who share living quarters. The number of households is the same as the number of year-round occupied housing units.

A **family** includes a householder and one or more other persons living in the same household who are related to the householder by birth, marriage, or adoption. All persons in a household who are related to the householder are regarded as members of his or her family. A **family household** may contain persons not related to the householder; thus, family households may include more members than families do. A household can contain only one family for the purposes of census tabulations. Not all households contain families, as a household may comprise a group of unrelated persons or of one person living alone. Families are classified by type as either a "husband-wife family" or "other family," according to the presence or absence of a spouse.

The measure of **persons per household** is obtained by dividing the number of persons in households by the number of households or householders. One person in each household is designated as the householder. In most cases, this is the person (or one of the persons) in whose name the house is owned, being bought, or rented. If there is no such person in the household, any adult household member 15 years old and over can be designated as the householder.

The category **female family householder** includes only female-headed family households with no spouse present.

GROUP QUARTERS, Items 34–39

Source: U.S. Census Bureau—American Community Survey and 2010 Census
http://www.census.gov/acs/www/
https://www.census.gov/programs-surveys/decennial-census/data/datasets.2010.html

The Census Bureau classifies all people not living in households as living in **group quarters**. There are two types of group quarters: institutional, including **correctional facilities**, **nursing homes**, and mental hospitals; and non-institutional, including **college dormitories**, **military quarters**, group homes, missions, and shelters.

HOUSING, Items 40—45

Source: U.S. Census Bureau—American Community Survey
http://www.census.gov/acs/www/

A **housing unit** is a house, apartment, mobile home or trailer, group of rooms, or single room occupied or, if vacant, intended for occupancy as separate living quarters. Separate living quarters are those in which the occupants do not live and eat with any other person in the structure and which have direct access from the outside of the building or through a common hall. For vacant units, the criteria of separateness and direct access are applied to the intended occupants whenever possible. If that information cannot be obtained, the criteria are applied to the previous occupants.

The occupants of a housing unit may be a single family, one person living alone, two or more families living together, or any other group of related or unrelated persons who share living quarters. Both occupied and vacant housing units are included in the housing inventory, although recreational vehicles, tents, caves, boats, railroad cars, and the like are included only if they are occupied as a person's usual place of residence.

A housing unit is classified as **occupied** if it is the usual place of residence of the person or group of persons living in it at the time of interview, or if the occupants are only temporarily absent (away on vacation). A household consists of all persons who occupy a housing unit as their usual place of residence. Vacant units for sale or rent include units rented or sold but not occupied and any other units held off the market.

A housing unit is owner **occupied** if the owner or co-owner lives in the unit, even if it is mortgaged or not fully paid for. The owner or co-owner must live in the unit and is usually the first person listed on the census questionnaire

All occupied housing units that are not owner occupied, whether they are rented for cash rent or occupied without payment of cash rent, are classified as renter occupied.

Median value is the dollar amount that divides the distribution of specified owner-occupied housing units into two equal parts, with half of all units below the median value and half of all units above the median value. Value is defined as the respondent's estimate of what the house would sell for if it was for sale. Data are presented for single-family units on fewer than 10 acres of land that have no business or medical offices on the property.

Median rent divides the distribution of renter-occupied housing units into two equal parts. The rent concept used in this volume is gross rent, which includes the amount of cash rent a renter pays (contract rent) plus the estimated average cost of utilities and fuels, if these are paid by the renter. The rent is the amount of rent only for living quarters and excludes amounts paid for any business or other space occupied. Single-family houses on lots of 10 or more acres of land are also excluded.

Housing cost as a percentage of income is shown separately for owners with mortgages, owners without mortgages, and renters. Rent as a percentage of income is a computed ratio of gross rent and monthly household income (total household income the past 12 months divided by 12). Selected owner costs include utilities and fuels, mortgage payments, insurance, taxes, etc. In each case, the ratio of housing cost to income is computed separately for each housing unit. The housing cost ratios for half of all units are above the median shown in this book, and half are below the median shown in the book.

Substandard units are occupied units that are overcrowded or lack complete plumbing facilities. For the purposes of this item, "overcrowded" is defined as having 1.01 persons or more per room. Complete plumbing facilities include hot and cold piped water, a flush toilet, and a bathtub or shower. These facilities must be located inside the housing unit, but do not have to be in the same room.

INCOME AND POVERTY, Items 46–51

Source: U.S. Census Bureau—American Community Survey
http://www.census.gov/acs/www/

The data on income were derived from responses of a sample of persons 15 years old and over. Total money income is the sum of the amounts reported separately for wage or salary income; net self-employment income; interest, dividends, or net rental or royalty income or income from estates and trusts; Social Security or railroad retirement income; Supplemental Security Income (SSI); public assistance or welfare payments; retirement, survivor, or disability pensions; and all other income. Receipts from the following sources are not included as income: capital gains; money received from the sale of property (unless the recipient was engaged in the business of selling such property); the value of income "in kind" from food stamps, public housing subsidies, medical care, employer contributions for individuals, etc.; withdrawal of bank deposits; money borrowed; tax refunds; exchange of money between relatives living in the same household; and

gifts, lump-sum inheritances, insurance payments, and other types of lump-sum receipts.

Per capita income is the mean income computed for every man, woman, and child in a particular group. It is derived by dividing the aggregate income of a particular group by the resident population in that group. Per capita income is rounded to the nearest whole dollar.

Household income includes the income of the householder and all other individuals 15 years old and over in the household, whether or not they are related to the householder. Since many households consist of only one person, median household income is usually less than median family income.

The **poverty status** data were derived from data collected on the number of persons in a household, from questionnaire item 3, which provided data on each person's relationship to the householder, and questionnaire items 41 and 42, which were also used to derive the income data. The Social Security Administration (SSA) developed the original poverty definition in 1964, which federal interagency committees subsequently revised in 1969 and 1980. The Office of Management and Budget's (OMB) *Directive 14* prescribes the SSA's definition as the official poverty measure for federal agencies to use in their statistical work. Poverty statistics presented in American Community Survey products adhere to the standards defined by OMB in *Directive 14*.

Poverty thresholds vary depending on three criteria: size of family, number of children, and, for one- and two-person families, age of householder. In determining the poverty status of families and unrelated individuals, the Census Bureau uses thresholds (income cutoffs) arranged in a two-dimensional matrix. The matrix consists of family size (from one person to nine or more persons), cross-classified by presence and number of family members under 18 years old (from no children present to eight or more children present). Unrelated individuals and two-person families are further differentiated by age of reference person (under 65 years old and 65 years old and over). To determine

Poverty Thresholds for 2017 by Size of Family and Number of Related Children Under 18 Years

Size of family unit	Weighted average thresholds	Related children under 18 years								
		None	One	Two	Three	Four	Five	Six	Seven	Eight or more
One person (unrelated individual):	12,488									
Under age 65	12,752	12,752								
Aged 65 and older	11,756	11,756								
Two people:	15,877									
Householder under age 65	16,493	16,414	16,895							
Householder aged 65 and older	14,828	14,816	16,831							
Three people	19,515	19,173	19,730	19,749						
Four people	25,094	25,283	25,696	24,858	24,944					
Five people	29,714	30,490	30,933	29,986	29,253	28,805				
Six people	33,618	35,069	35,208	34,482	33,787	32,753	32,140			
Seven people	38,173	40,351	40,603	39,734	39,129	38,001	36,685	35,242		
Eight people	42,684	45,129	45,528	44,708	43,990	42,971	41,678	40,332	39,990	
Nine people or more	50,681	54,287	54,550	53,825	53,216	52,216	50,840	49,595	49,287	47,389

Source: U.S. Census Bureau.

a person's poverty status, the person's total family income over the previous 12 months is compared with the poverty threshold appropriate for that person's family size and composition. If the total income of that person's family is less than the threshold appropriate for that family, then the person is considered poor or "below the poverty level," together with every member of his or her family. If a person is not living with anyone related by birth, marriage, or adoption, then the person's own income is compared with his or her poverty threshold. The total number of persons below the poverty level is the sum of persons in families and the number of unrelated individuals with incomes below the poverty level over the previous 12 months. The average poverty threshold for a four-person family was $24,230 in 2014.

The data on participation in the Food Stamp Program are designed to identify households in which one or more of the current members received food stamps during the past 12 months. Once a food stamp household was identified, a question was asked about the total value of all food stamps received by the household during that 12-month period. The Food Stamp Act of 1977 defines this federally funded program as one intended to "permit low-income households to obtain a more nutritious diet." (From title XIII of P.L. 95-113, The Food Stamp Act of 1977, declaration of policy.) Providing eligible households with coupons that can be used to purchase food increases food purchasing power. The Food and Nutrition Service (FNS) of the U.S. Department of Agriculture (USDA) administers the Food Stamp program through state and local welfare offices. The Food Stamp program is the major national income support program to which all low-income and low-resource households, regardless of household characteristics, are eligible.

CIVILIAN LABOR FORCE, UNEMPLOYMENT, AND EMPLOYMENT, Items 52–58

Source: U.S. Census Bureau—American Community Survey
http://www.census.gov/acs/www/

The **civilian labor force** consists of all civilians 16 years old and over who are either employed or unemployed.

Unemployment includes all persons who did not work during the survey week, made specific efforts to find a job during the previous four weeks, and were available for work during the survey week (except for temporary illness). Persons waiting to be called back to a job from which they had been laid off and those waiting to report to a new job within the next 30 days are included in unemployment figures.

Total employment includes all civilians 16 years old and over who were either (1) "at work"—those who did any work at all during the reference week as paid employees, worked in either their own business or profession, worked on their own farm, or worked 15 hours or more as unpaid workers in a family farm or business; or were (2) "with a job, but not at work"—those who had a job but were not at work that week due to illness, weather, industrial dispute, vacation, or other personal reasons.

The **occupational categories** are based on the occupational classification system that was developed for the 2000 census. This system consists of 539 specific occupational categories for employed persons arranged into 23 major occupational groups. This classification was developed based on the *Standard Occupational Classification (SOC) Manual: 2010*, published by the Executive Office of the President, Office of Management and Budget.

PERSONS WITH NO HEALTH INSURANCE, Item 59

Source: U.S. Census Bureau—American Community Survey
http://www.census.gov/acs/www/

The percentage of persons under age 65 with no **health insurance** shows the percentage of the population of each congressional district who were not covered by private health plans purchased directly or provided by an employer, Medicaid, Medicare, or military health care.

SOCIAL SECURITY AND SUPPLEMENTAL SECURITY INCOME, Items 60–62

Source: U.S. Social Security Administration
http://www.ssa.gov/policy/docs/factsheets/cong_stats/

Social Security beneficiaries are persons receiving benefits under the Old-Age, Survivors, and Disability Insurance Program. These include retired or disabled workers covered by the program, their spouses and dependent children, and the surviving spouses and dependent children of deceased workers.

Supplemental Security Income (SSI) recipients are persons receiving SSI payments. The SSI program is a cash assistance program that provides monthly benefits to low-income aged, blind, or disabled persons.

Data are as of December of the year shown.

AGRICULTURE, ITEMS 63–72

Source: U.S. Department of Agriculture, National Agricultural Statistics Service—2017 Census of Agriculture
https://www.nass.usda.gov/Publications/AgCensus/2017/index.php

Data for the 2017 Census of Agriculture were collected in 2018, but pertain to the year 2017.

The Census Bureau took a census of agriculture every 10 years from 1840 to 1920; since 1925, this census has been taken roughly once every 5 years. The 1997 Census of Agriculture was the first one conducted by the National Agricultural Statistics Service of the U.S. Department of Agriculture. Over time, the definition of a farm has varied. For recent censuses (including the 2017 census), a farm has been defined as any place from which $1,000 or more of agricultural products were produced and sold or normally would have been sold during the census year. Dollar figures are expressed in current dollars and have not been adjusted for inflation or deflation.

The acreage designated as **land in farms** consists primarily of agricultural land used for crops, pasture, or grazing. It also includes woodland and wasteland not actually under cultivation or used for pasture or grazing, provided that this land was part of the farm operator's total operation. Land in farms is an operating-unit concept and includes all land owned and operated, as well as all land rented from others. Land used rent-free is classified as land rented from others. All grazing land, except land used under government permits on a per-head basis, was included as "land in farms" provided it was part of a farm or ranch. Land under the exclusive use of a grazing association was reported by the grazing association and included as land in farms. All land in Indian reservations used for growing crops or grazing livestock is classified as land in farms.

Harvested cropland includes land from which crops were harvested and hay was cut, land used to grow short rotation woody crops, Christmas trees, and land in orchards, groves, vineyards, berries, nurseries, and greenhouses. Land from which two or more crops were harvested was counted only once. Land in tapped maple trees was included in woodland not pastured.

Market value of agricultural products sold by farms represents the gross market value before taxes and the production expenses of all agricultural products sold or removed from the place in 2017, regardless of who received the payment. It is equivalent to total sales and it includes sales by producers as well as the value of any share received by partners, landlords, contractors, and others associated with the operation. It includes value of organic sales, direct sales and the value of commodities placed in the Commodity Credit Corporation (CCC) loan program. Market value of agricultural products sold does not include payments received for participation in other federal farm programs. Also, it does not include income from farm-related sources such as customwork and other agricultural services, or income from nonfarm sources.

Government payments consist of direct payments as defined by the 2002 Farm Bill; payments from Conservation Reserve Program (CRP), Wetlands Reserve Program (WRP), Farmable Wetlands Program (FWP), and Conservation Reserve Enhancement Program (CREP); loan deficiency payments; disaster payments; other conservation programs; and all other federal farm programs under which payments were made directly to farm producers, including those specified in the 2014 Agricultural Act (Farm Bill), including Agriculture Risk Coverage (ARC) and Price Loss Coverage (PLC). Commodity Credit Corporation (CCC) proceeds, amount from State and local government agricultural program payments, and federal crop insurance payments were not included in this category.

PRIVATE NONFARM EMPLOYMENT AND EARNINGS, Items 73-85
Source: U.S. Census Bureau—County Business Patterns
http://www.census.gov/econ/cbp/index.html

Data for private nonfarm employment and earnings are compiled from the payroll information reported monthly in the Census Bureau publication *County Business Patterns*. The estimates are based on surveys conducted by the Census Bureau and administrative records from the Internal Revenue Service (IRS).

The following types of employment are excluded from the tables: government employment, self-employed persons, farm workers, and domestic service workers. Railroad employment jointly covered by Social Security and railroad retirement programs, employment on oceanborne vessels, and employment in foreign countries are also excluded.

Annual payroll is the combined amount of wages paid, tips reported, and other compensation (including salaries, vacation allowances, bonuses, commissions, sick-leave pay, and the value of payments-in-kind such as free meals and lodging) paid to employees before deductions for Social Security, income tax, insurance, union dues, etc. All forms of compensation are included, regardless of whether they are subject to income tax or the Federal Insurance Contributions Act tax, with the exception of annuities, third-party sick pay, and supplemental unemployment compensation benefits (even if income tax was withheld). For corporations, total annual payroll includes compensation paid to officers and executives; for unincorporated businesses, it excludes profit or other compensation of proprietors or partners.